Santa Clara County Free Library

REFERENCE

 5816

Who's Who in California

**Biographical Reference Works
Published by
The Who's Who Historical Society**

Who's Who In California

Who's Who In California Business and Finance

Who's Who Dining and Lodging on the North American Continent

Who's Who In Los Angeles County

Who's Who Executives in California

Who's Who in California

The
Sixteenth Edition
1986

Published by
THE WHO'S WHO HISTORICAL SOCIETY

SIXTEENTH EDITION
Sarah Vitale, Editor

Library of Congress Catalog Card Number 56-1715

International Standard Book Number 0-9603166-5-5

International Standard Serial Number 0511-8948

PRINTED IN THE UNITED STATES OF AMERICA

Contents

Dedication

There is properly no History;
only Biography.

— Ralph Waldo Emerson
(1803-1882)

Biography is by nature the most
universally profitable, universally
pleasant of all things: especially
biography of distinguished
individuals.

— Thomas Carlyle
(1795-1881)

Honorary Board of Directors

Guide To Biographies

The biographical profiles in **WHO'S WHO IN CALIFORNIA** are arranged alphabetically according to the surname of the biographee. Where identical surnames occur, the first given name is used. If both surname and first given name are identical, the second given name is used to arrange the names alphabetically.

In the case of compound hyphenated surnames, profiles are arranged according to the first member of the compound.

Some biographees delete part of their full name in ordinary usage. In those instances parentheses are used to indicate that portion of the name which is deleted. For example, SMITH, J(OHN) indicates that the usual form of the name is J. Smith.

Each biographical profile is uniformly composed of the following data, hereby offered in chronological order as a convenient guide:

1. Name
2. Occupation
3 Birthdate and Place
4. Parents
5. Education
6. Marriage
7. Children
8. Career
9. Career-Related Activities

10. Awards and Honors
11. Memberships
12. Creative Works
13. Military Record
14. Political Affiliation
15. Religious Affiliation
16. Hobbies/Recreation
17. Residence Address
18. Office Address

Abbreviations

A.A. Associate in Arts
AAAS American Association for the Advancement of Science
A. and M. Agricultural and Mechanical
AAU Amateur Athletic Union
AAUP American Association of University Professors
AAUW American Association of University Women
A.B. Arts, Bachelor of
AB Alberta
ABC American Broadcasting Company
AC Air Corps
acad. academy
ACLU American Civil Liberties Union
A.C.P. American College of Physicians
A.C.S. American College of Surgeons.
ADA American Dental Association
adj. adjunct, adjutant
adj. gen. adjutant general
adm. admiral
adminstr. administrator
adminstrn. administration
adminstrv. administrative
adv. advocate
advt. advertising
AEC Atomic Energy Commission
aero. aeronautical, aeronautic
AFB Air Force Base
AFL-CIO American Federation of Labor and Congress of Industrial Organizations
AFTRA American Federation TV and Radio Artists
agri. agricultural, agriculture
AIA American Institute of Architects
AIEE American Institute of Electrical Engineers
AIM American Institute of Management
AK Alaska
AL Alabama
ALA American Library Association
Ala. Alabama
A.M. Arts, Master of
Am. American, America
AMA American Medical Association
A.M.E. African Methodist Episcopal
Amer., America, American
Amtrak National Railroad Passenger Corporation
anat. anatomical, anatomy
ANTA American National Theatre and Academy
anthrop. anthropological
AP Associated Press
APO Army Post Office
apptd. appointed
AR Arkansas
ARC American Red Cross
archeol. archeological
archtl. architectural
Ariz. Arizona
Ark. Arkansas
Arts D. Arts, Doctor of
arty. artillery
ASCAP American Society of Composers, Authors and Publishers
ASCE American Society of Civil Engineers
ASME American Society of Mechanical Engineers
assn. association

assoc., associate, associated
asst. assistant
ASTM American Society for Testing and Materials
astron. astronomical
ATSC Air Technical Service Command
AT&T American Telephone & Telegraph Company
atty. attorney
AUS Army of the United States
aux. Auxiliary
Ave. Avenue
AVMA American Veterinary Medical Association
AZ Arizona

B. Bachelor
b. born
B.A. Bachelor of Arts
B. Agr. Bachelor of Agriculture
Bapt. Baptist
B.Arch. Bachelor of Architecture
B.S.A. Bachelor of Agricultural Science
B.B.A. Bachelor of Business Administration
BBC British Broadcasting Corporation
B.C., British Columbia
B.C.E. Bachelor of Civil Engineering
B.Chir., Bachelor of Surgery
B.C.L. Bachelor of Civil Law
B.C.S. Bachelor of Commercial Science
B.D. Bachelor of Divinity
bd. board
B.E. Bachelor of Education
B.E.E. Bachelor of Electrical Engineering
B.F.A. Bachelor of Fine Arts
bibl. biblical
bibliog. bibliographical
biog. biographical
biol. biological
B.J. Bachelor of Journalism
B.L. Bachelor of Letters
bldg. building
B.L.S. Bachelor of Library Science
Blvd. Boulevard
bn. battalion
bot. botanical
B.P.E. Bachelor of Physical Education
br. branch
B.R.E. Bachelor of Religious Education
brig. gen. brigadier general
Brit. British, Britannica
Bro. Brother
B.S. Bachelor of Science
B.S.A. Bachelor of Agricultural Science
BSA Boy Scouts of America
B.S.D. Bachelor of Didactic Science
B.S.T. Bachelor of Sacred Theology
B.Th. Bachelor of Theology
bur. bureau
bus. business

CA California
CAA Civil Aeronautics Administration
CAB Civil Aeronautics Board
Calif. California
Cal Tech, California Institute of Technology

Can. Canada
CAP Civil Air Patrol
capt. captain
Cath. Catholic
cav. cavalry
CBC Canadian Broadcasting System
CBI China, Burma, India Theatre of Operations
CBS Columbia Broadcasting System
CCC Commodity Credit Corporation
CD Civil Defense
C.E. Corps of Engineers
CEO Chief Executive Officer
ch. church
Ch.D. Doctor of Chemistry
chem. chemical
Chem. E. Chemical Engineer
Chgo. Chicago
chmn. chairman
chpt. chapter
CIA Central Intelligence Agency
CIC Counter Intelligence Corps
clin. clinical
clk. clerk
C.L.U. Chartered Life Underwriter
C.M. Master in Surgery
CO Colorado
CMA, California Medical Association
Co., Company, County
C. of C. Chamber of Commerce
col. colonel
coll. college
Colo. Colorado
com. committee
comd. commanded
comdg. commanding
comdr. commander
commd. commissioned
comml. commercial
commn. commission
commr. commissioner
Conf. Conference
Conn. Connecticut
cons. consultant, consulting
consol. consolidated
constl. constitutional
constn. constitution
constrn. construction
contbd. contributed
contbg. contributing
contbr. contributor
Conv. Convention
coop., co-op. cooperative
CORE Congress of Racial Equality
corp. corporation
corr. correspondent, corresponding
C.P.A. Certified Public Accountant
C.P.H. Certificate of Public Health
cpl. corporal
CSC Civil Service Commission
ct. court
C.Z. Canal Zone

d. daughter
D. Doctor
D.Agr. Doctor of Agriculture
D.A.R. Daughters of the American Revolution
dau. daughter
DAV Disabled American Veterans
D.C., DC District of Columbia
D.C.L. Doctor of Civil Law
D.C.S. Doctor of Commercial Science
D.D. Doctor of Divinity
D.D.S. Doctor of Dental Surgery
DE Delaware
dec. deceased
def. defense

Del. Delaware
del. delegate, delegation
Dem. Democrat., Democratic
D.Eng. Doctor of Engineering
dep. deputy
dept. department
desc. descendant
devel. development
D.F.A. Doctor of Fine Arts
D.F.C. Distinguished Flying Cross
D.H.L. Doctor of Hebrew Literature
dir. director
dist. district
distbg. distributing
distbn. distribution
distbr. distributor
div. division, divinity, divorce
D.Litt. Doctor of Literature
D.M.D. Doctor of Medical Dentistry
D.M.S. Doctor of Medical Science
D.O. Doctor of Osteopathy
Dr. Drive
D.R.E. Doctor of Religious Education
D.S.C. Distinguished Service Cross
D.Sc. Doctor of Science
D.S.M. Distinguished Service Medal
D.S.T. Doctor of Sacred Theology
D.V.M. Doctor of Veterinary Medicine
D.V.S. Doctor of Veterinary Surgery

E. East
Eccles. Ecclesiastical
ecol. ecological
econ., economic, economy
E.D. Doctor of Engineering
ed., educated, editor
Ed.B. Bachelor of Education
Ed.D. Doctor of Education
edit. edition
Ed.M. Master of Education
edn. education
ednl. educational
EDP electronic data processing
E.E. Electrical Engineer
elec. electrical
ency. encyclopedia
Eng. England, English
engr. engineer
engring. engineering
environ. environmental
EPA Environmental Protection Agency
Episc. Episcopalian.
ERDA Energy Research and Development
    Administration
ETO European Theatre of Operations
Evang. Evangelical
exam. examination, examining
exec. executive
exhib., exhibit, exhibition
expt. experiment
exptl. experimental

F.A. Field Artillery
FAA Federal Aviation Administration
FBI Federal Bureau of Investigation
FCA Farm Credit Administration
FCC Federal Communication Commission
FDA Food and Drug Administration
FDIA Federal Deposit Insurance Administration
FDIC Federal Deposit Insurance Corporation
F.E. Forest Engineer
fed. federal
fedn. federation
fgn. foreign
FHA Federal Housing Administration
fin. financial, finance

FL Florida
Fla. Florida
FMC Federal Maritime Commission
found. foundation
FPC Federal Power Commission
FPO Fleet Post Office
frat., fraternity, fraternal
FRS Federal Reserve System
Ft. Fort
FTC Federal Trade Commission, Federal Tariff
    Commission

Ga., GA Georgia
GAO General Accounting Office
gastroent. gastroenterological
gen. general
geneal. genealogical
geod. geodetic
geog. geographic, geographical
geol. geological
geophys. geophysical
gerontol. gerontological
gov. governor
govt. government
govtl. governmental
grad. graduate
GSA General Services Administration
Gt. Great
GU Guam
gynecol. gynecological

hdqrs. headquarters
HEW Department of Health, Education and Welfare
H.H.D. Doctor of Humanities
HHFA Housing and Home Finance Agency
HI Hawaii
hist. historical, historic
H.M. Master of Humanics
hon. honorary, honorable
Ho. of Dels. House of Delegates
Ho. of Reps. House of Representatives
hort. horticultural
hosp. hospital
HUD Department of Housing and Urban Development
Hwy. Highway
H.S., High School

IA Iowa
IAEA International Atomic Energy Agency
IBM International Business Machines Corporation
ICC Interstate Commerce Commission
ID Idaho
IEEE Institute of Electrical and Electronics Engineers
IGY International Geophysical Year
IL Illinois
Ill. Illinois
ILO International Labor Organization
IMF International Monetary Fund
IN Indiana
Inc. Incorporated
incl. include, including
ind. independent
Ind. Indiana
indsl. industrial
inf. infantry
info. information
ins. insurance
insp. inspector
inst. institute
instr. instructor
Internatl. international
intro. introduction
I.R.E. Institute of Radio Engineers
IRS Internal Revenue Service
ITT International Telephone & Telegraph Corporation
J.D. Doctor of Jurisprudence

j.g. junior grade
jour. journal.
jr. junior

Kans. Kansas
K.C. Knights of Columbus
KS Kansas
K.T. Knight Templar
Ky., KY Kentucky

L.A. Los Angeles
lab. laboratory
L.A.C.C. Los Angeles City College
lang. language
LB Long Beach
lectr. lecturer
L.D.S. Latter-Day Saints
L.H.D. Doctor of Humane Letters
L.I. Long Island
lit. literary, literature
Litt.B. Bachelor of Letters
Litt.D. Doctor of Letters
LL.B. Bachelor of Laws
LL.D. Doctor of Laws
LL.M. Master of Laws
Ln. Lane
L.S. Library Science (in degree)
lt. lieutenant
Ltd. Limited
Luth. Lutheran

m. married
M. Master
M.A. Master of Arts
MA Massachusetts
mag. magazine
M.Agr. Master of Agriculture
maj. major
M.Arch. Master in Architecture
Mass. Massachusetts
math. mathematical
MATS Military Air Transport Service
M.B. Bachelor of Medicine
M.B.A. Master of Business Administration
MBS Mutual Broadcasting System
M.C. Medical Corps
M.C.E. Master of Civil Engineering
mcht. merchant
M.D. Doctor of Medicine
Md., MD Maryland
mdse. merchandise
M.D.V. Doctor of Veterinary Medicine
M.E. Mechanical Engineer
ME Maine
M.E. Ch. Methodist Episcopal Church
mech. mechanical
M.Ed. Master of Education
med. medical
M.E.E. Master of Electrical Engineering
mem. member, memorial
met. metropolitan
metall. metallurgical
meteorol. meteorological
Meth. Methodist
Mex. Mexico
M.F. Master of Forestry
M.F.A. Master of Fine Arts
mfg. manufacturing
mfr. manufacturer
mgmt. management
mgr. manager
M.I. Military Intelligence
MI Michigan
Mich. Michigan
mil. military

Minn. Minnesota
Miss. Mississippi
M.I.T. Massachusetts Institute of Technology
mktg. marketing
M.L. Master of Laws
M.Litt. Master of Literature
M.L.S. Master of Library Science
M.M.E. Master of Mechanical Engineering
MN Minnesota
mng. managing
Mo., MO Missouri

Mont. Montana
M.P. Member of Parliament
M.P.E. Master of Physical Education
M.P.H. Master of Public Health
M.P.L. Master of Patent Law
M.R.E. Master of Religious Education
M.S. Master of Science
MS Mississippi
M.Sc. Master of Science
M.S.F. Master of Science of Forestry
M.S.T. Master of Sacred Theology
M.S.W. Master of Social Work
MT Montana
Mt. Mount
mus. museum, musical
Mus.B. Bachelor of Music
Mus.D. Doctor of Music
Mus.M. Master of Music

N. North
NAACP National Association for the Advancement of
    Colored People
N.Am. North America
NAM National Association of Manufacturers
NASA National Aeronautics and Space Administration
natl. national
NATO North Atlantic Treaty Organization
nav. navigation
NBC National Boradcasting Company
N.C., NC North Carolina
NCCJ National Conference of Christians and Jews
N.D., ND North Dakota
NE Nebraska
N.E. Northeast
NEA National Education Association
Nebr. Nebraska
neurol. neurological
Nev. Nevada
N.G. National Guard
N.H., NH New Hampshire
NIH National Institutes of Health
NIMH National Institute of Mental Health
N.J., NJ New Jersey
NLRB National Labor Relations Board
NM New Mexico
N.Mex. New Mexico
No. Northern
NORAD North American Air Defense
NOW National Organization for Women
NSC National Security Council
NSF National Science Foundation
NT Northwest Territories
numis. numismatic
NV Nevada
NW Northwest
N.Y., NY New York
N.Y.C. New York City
N.Z. New Zealand

OAS Organization of American States
obs. observatory
O.D. Doctor of Optometry
OEO Office of Economic Opportunity
O.E.S. Order of Eastern Star
ofcl. official

ofcr. officer
OH Ohio
OK Oklahoma
Okla. Oklahoma
ophthal. ophthalmological
ops. operations
OR Oregon
orch. orchestra
Oreg. Oregon
OSS Office of Strategic Services

Pa., PA Pennsylvania
P.C. Professional Corporation
Pasa., Pasadena
P.E.I. Prince Edward Island
PEN Poets, Playwrights, Editors, Essayists and Novelists
    (international association)
P.E.O. women's organization
pfc. private first class
PHA Public Housing Administration
pharm. Pharmaceutical
Pharm.D. Doctor of Pharmacy
Pharm.M. Master of Pharmacy
Ph.B. Bachelor of Philosophy
Ph.D. Doctor of Philosophy
Phila. Philadelphia
philos. philosophical
photog. photographic, photography
phys. physical
Pitts. Pittsburgh
Pl. Place
P.O. Post Office
P.O.B. Post Office Box
polit. political, politics
poly. polytechnic
prep. preparatory
pres. president
Presbyn. Presbyterian
prin. principal
proc. proceedings
prod. produced, producer
prof. professor
profl. professional
propr. proprietor
pro tem pro tempore
psychiat. psychiatric
psychol. psychological
PTA Parent-Teachers Association
pub. publisher, publishing, public
publ. publication
pvt. private

RCA Radio Corporation of America
rec. recreation
recd. received
ref. reference
rehab. rehabilitation
Rel., Religion, Rels.,
Rels., Relations
rep. representative
Repub. Republican
Res. residence
ret. retired
rev. review, revised
Rom. Cath., Roman Catholic
R.I., RI Rhode Island
R.N. Registered Nurse
ROTC Reserve Officers Training Corps
R.R. Railroad
Ry. Railway

s. son
S. South
SAC Strategic Air Command
S.A.G. Screen Actors Guild
SALT Strategic Arms Limitation Talks

S.Am. South America
san. sanitary
SAR Sons of the American Revolution
savs. savings
S.B. Bachelor of Science, Santa Barbara
SBA Small Business Administration
S.C., SC South Carolina
Sc.B. Bachelor of Science
Sc.D. Doctor of Science
sch. school
sci. science, scientific
S.D., San Diego
Sacto., Sacramento
SE Southeast
SEATO Southeast Asia Treaty Organization
secty. secretary
SEC Securities and Exchange Commission
sect. section
S.F. San Francisco
sem. seminary
Sen. Senator
sgt. sergeant
sis. Sister
S.J. Society of Jesus (Jesuit)
S.M. Master of Science
So. Southern
soc. society
sociol. sociological
sor. sorority
spec. special, specialist
splty. specialty
Sq. Square
sr. senior
S.R. Sons of the Revolution
S.S. Steamship
St. Saint, street
sta. station
S.T.B. Bachelor of Sacred Theology
S.T.D. Doctor of Sacred Theology
subs. subsidiary
supr. supervisor
supt. superintendent
surg. surgical, surgery, surgeon
SW Southwest
sym. symphony
syn. syndicate

tchr. teacher
tech. technical, technology
Tel. Telephone
temp. temporary
Tenn. Tennessee
Ter. Territory
Terr. Terrace
Tex. Texas
Th.D., Doctor of Theology
theol. theological, theology
Th.M. Master of Theology
TN Tennessee
tng. training
trans. transaction, transferred
transl. translation, translated
transp. transportation
treas. treasurer
TV television
TVA Tennessee Valley Authority
twp. township
TX Texas

U. University
UAW United Auto Workers
UCI University of California at Irvine
UCLA University of California at Los Angeles
UCSB University of California at Santa Barbara
UCSD University of California at San Diego

U.K. United Kingdom
UN United Nations
UNESCO United Nations Educational, Scientific and
    Cultural Organization
UNICEF United Nations International Children's
    Emergency Fund
univ. University
UPI United Press International
U.S. United States
U.S.A. United States of America
USAAF United States Army Air Force
USAF United States Air Force
USAFR United States Air Force Reserve
USAR United States Army Reserve
USC University of Southern California
USCG United States Coast Guard
USCGR United States Coast Guard Reserve
USIA United States Information Agency
USMC United States Marine Corps
USMCR United States Marine Corps Reserve
USN United States Navy
USNR United States Naval Reserve
USO United Service Organizations
USPHS United States Public Health Service
U.S.S. United States Ship
USSR Union of the Soviet Socialist Republics
UT Utah

VA Veterans Administration
Va., VA Virginia
vet. veteran
VFW Veterans of Foreign Wars
vice pres. vice president
vis. visiting
VISTA Volunteers in Service to America
vocat. vocational
vol. volunteer
v.p. vice president
vs versus
Vt., VT Vermont

W. West
WA Washington
WAC Women's Army Corps
Wash. Washington
WAVES Women's Reserve, U.S. Naval Reserve
WHO World Health Organization
WI Wisconsin
Wis. Wisconsin
WV West Virginia
W. Va. West Virginia
WY Wyoming
Wyo. Wyoming

YMCA Young Men's Christian Association
YMHA Young Men's Hebrew Association
YM & YWHA Young Men's and Young Women's
    Hebrew Association
Y.T., YT Yukon Territory
YWCA Young Women's Christian Association
yr. year

zool. zoological

---, to date

Who's Who in California

AAROE, GALE ROBERT, quality assurance executive; b. June 19, 1947, Eureka, Kans.; s. Murrel R. and Inez L. (Meadows) A.; m. Sonia, Dec. 29, 1983; 1 dau. Candice b. 1973; edn: BS physics, astronomy, Washburn Univ. 1969; MBA mgmt., Rochester Inst. of Tech. 1978. Career: planetarium director Washburn Univ. 1967-69; section supr. Eastman Kodak, Rochester, N.Y. 1969-73, quality assurance engr. 1973-77, Kodacolor product cons. 1977-78, photofinishing quality cons. So. Am. Region, 1978-80, tech. assoc. Gudadalajara, Mex. 1980-83, information system project mgr. Rochester, N.Y. 1983-84, dir. Video Quality Assur., San Diego 1985 – ; honors: Sigma Pi Sigma (1969); Prot.; rec: amateur astronomy, sailing. Ofc: Eastman Kodak 3099 Science Park Road San Diego 92121

AARONS, BERNICE RUTH, dietitian; b. Aug. 4, 1922, Bridgeport, Conn.; d. Herman Charles and Marie Shirley (Fonrow) Aarons; edn: BS, UC Los Angeles 1956; Reg. Dietitian (RD), Am. Diet. Assn. (1959). Career: staff dietitian Cedars of Lebanon Hosp. L.A. 1956-61; dir. of dietary svc. San Gabriel Valley Hosp., San Gabriel 1961-68; cons. dietitian Dietary Splsts. of Calif., Canoga Park 1968-70; dir. of dietary svc. Midvalley Comm. Hosp., Van Nuys 1970-72, Van Nuys Comm. Hosp., Van Nuys 1972 –, also sponsor/dir. Masters Pgm. students; mem: Am. Dietetic Assn., Calif. Diet. Assn. (Outstanding Mem. Award 1979; pres. CDA 1974-75, pres. Dist. Council CDA 1976-77, chair Calif. Dietitians w. Mgmt. Responsibilities 1984-85), Los Angeles Dist. CDA (pres. 1970-71, chair awards com. 1982-86), S.G.V. Dist. CDA; civic: City of Hope (life), Hadassah, ORT; Democrat; Jewish; rec: cooking, music. Res: 9007 E Callita St San Gabriel 91775 Ofc: Van Nuys Comm. Hospital 14433 Emelita St Van Nuys 91401

AARONS, GREGORY PIERRE, newspaper advertising co-op coordinator; b. Dec. 24, 1961, Pensacola, Fla.; s. Charles Samuel and Regina (Reeves) A.; m. Deborah, Sept. 14, 1985; 1 son, Gregory, Jr. b. 1986; edn: bus. adminstrn., CSU San Bernardino 1979-86. Career: founder, pres. The Greek Club San Bernardino 1983-85; advt. exec. San Bernardino Sun Newspaper 1985 – ; mem: Phi Beta Sigma (pres. 1984-85, v.p. 1985-86), Toastmasters Internat., Kappa Alpha Psi; publ: The Greek Guide To Life (1986); mil: E-5 USAF 1984 –, Armed Svcs. Aircraft Loadmaster; Democrat; Baptist; rec: flying, computers. Res: 2011 Arden Ave Apt 201 Highland 92346 Ofc: San Bernardino Sun Co. 399 N D St San Bernardino 92401

ABADIR, MAHER NASHED, physician; b. Dec. 17, 1941, Cairo, Egypt, nat. 1971; s. Nashed and Emtithal Sammy (Roufail) A.; m. Nabila, April 24, 1971; children: Michael, b. 1974, Mark, b. 1977; edn: PNS, Ain Shams Univ. 1959; MD, Ain Shams Sch. of Med., Cairo 1965; Bd. Cert. Anesthesiologist, Am. Bd. of Anesthesiology 1977. Career: intern Ain Shams Univ. Hosps., Cairo, Egypt. 1965; intern, res. in anesthesia UC Davis, Sacramento 1969-73; chmn. anethesia dept. Modesto City Hosp., Modesto 1973-84; pres. Stanislaus Surgery Ctr., Modesto 1984 – ; practicing anesthesiologist, Modesto 1984 – ; nat. and internat. cons. in ambulatory surgery; honors: Modesto Banking Co. 1983; mem: Am. and Calif. Socs. of Anesthesiologists, CMA (alternate del.), Am. Union of Physicians and Dentists, Am. Soc. of Freestanding Surgery Ctrs., Modesto Racquet Club; author: How to Plan and Establish a Freestanding Ambulatory Surgery Center; Republican; Coptic Orthodox; rec: tennis, swimming, travel. Res: 3113 Wycliffe Dr., Modesto 95355 Anesthesiologists, 19800 Coffee Rd. E 30, Modesto 95355

ABDEL-AAL, YEHIA A.I., biochemical toxicologist; b. Dec. 28, 1944, Minia, Egypt; s. Abdel-Hamid Ibrahim and Zineb A. (Ahmed).; m. Fadia Bashir, Sept. 9, 1969; children: Dalia b. 1973, Ghada b. 1976, Doniez b. 1978; edn: BS in agri., Assiut Univ. 1966, MS, 1970, PhD, 1975. Career: tchg. asst., asst. lectr., asst./assoc./full prof. Assiut Univ., Egypt 1966-82; research scientist Dept. Entomol. UC Davis 1982 –, co-instr. sev. grad. courses 1984 –; awards: Assiut Univ. Prize (1978), Nat. Acad. of Sci. and Technol. (Egypt, 1979); publs: 50+ research papers in nat. and internat. sci. jours. (1975-); Moslem; rec: soccer. Res: 750 B Street Davis 95616 Ofc: University of Calif. Dept. Entomology Davis 95616

ABEL, TIMOTHY, lawyer; b. Dec. 30, 1929, Williams; s. Allen Raymond and Consuelo (Benham) A.; m. Louise, June 14, 1953; children: Elizabeth Allen b. 1958, John Allen b. 1961, Robert William b. 1962; edn: AA, UC Berkeley 1953; JD, UC Hastings Coll. of Law 1957; lic. Real Estate Broker, Calif. Career: law practice, Hayward 29 yrs.; currently, senior ptr. law firm Abel & Abel, Hayward; pres. Hayward Properties; pres. West Calif. Properties; mem: So. Alameda Co. Bar Assn. (pres.), Alameda Co. Bar Assn. (dir.); mil: sgt. UMSC 1950-52; (2) Pres. Unit Citation, (4) Battle Stars, Korean Campaign; Republican; Methodist; rec: skiing, tennis, golf. Res: 300 Sheridan Ave. Piedmont 94611 Ofc: Abel & Abel, 22300 Foothill Blvd. Ste. 501 Hayward 94541

ABELAR, INA MAE, equipment technician; b. July 18, 1926, Jay Em, Who.; d. Merritt Lyle and Leeta Mae (Worthen) Cameron; m. Michael Sandoval Abelar, Nov. 17, 1951 (div. 1966); children: Debora Jean, Michelle Elaine,

Randolph Lee; edn: BA, Cal. Poly. Pomona 1978. Career: lumber estimator Keith Brown Bldg. Supply Salem, Ore. 1946-48, Whiting-Mead Bldg. Supply Vernon, Calif. 1949-51; lumber estimator, bookkeeper Trojan Lumber Co. Burbank 1952-55; bookkeeper Jerry Kalior Bkpg. Systems No. Hollywood 1959-66; chem. stock clerk to supv. instrl. support tech. II Physics Dept. Cal. Poly. Pomona 1967 –, staff council 1970-87, chmn. 1977-78, exec. bd. 1971-83; honors: Outstanding Staff Employee (1983-84), Service Award (SPS Physics Club); mem: Mu Phi Epsilon (profl. music frat., coll. advisor Gammi Chi chpt. 1980-82, treas. Claremont Alumni chpt. 1980-82, pres. 1983-86); Democrat; Protestant; rec: wood carving, rebuilding pianos, hunting, swimming, hiking, travel. Res: 1833 Benedict Way Pomona 91767 Ofc: Calif. State Polytechnic Univ. 3801 W Temple 8-238 Pomona 91767

ABELIN, RAYMOND FERRIS, motion picture and television director/producer; b. Jan. 25, 1955, Los Angeles; s. Archeck and Adele Marie (Morris) A.; edn: BA, magna cum laude, UCLA 1978; MA in prodn., cinema, USC 1983; desig: Director, Director's Guild of Am., 1985. Career: prod., writer-dir. Trans-Global Prodns. & Distrbn., Beverly Hills 1983 –; honors: The Gold Fourragere, UCLA 1978; mem: Dir. Guild of Am. Inc.; USC Cinema Curculus; United States All President's Day Soc. (prod. of prgmmg.). Address: 132 ½ So. Roxbury Dr., Beverly Hills 90212

ABERNETHY, JOHN LEO, professor of chemistry; b. Mar. 6, 1916, San Jose, CA; s. Elmer R. and Margaret May (Scott) Abernethy; BA, UCLA, 1936; MS, 1938 and PhD, 1940, Northwestern Univ.; res. assoc., Med. Ctr. UCLA. Career: asst. prof. Univ. of Texas, 1940-45; res. State Univ. System, 1950-78; vis. assoc. prof. of chem. Claremont Men's Coll., 1961-61; Fulbright Fellow, San Marcos Univ., Lima, Peru 2962-63; res. assoc. UC Davis, 1963-64; taught Navy V-12 students, Univ. of Texas, 1942-45. Editorial bd. Journ of Chem. Education, 1956-85; proceedings editor Calif Assn of Chem. Teachers; author: resrch papers on stereochemistry, enzyme catalysis, papain, Jour Chromatography; edn. papers, Journ. Chem. Edn.,1940-; text: Principles of Organic Chem.; CACT Proceedings Editor, Calif. Assn. of Chem. Teachers, 1966-. Research grants: NSF, Sigma Xi, Research Corp., Radiation Research, Lab. Nuclear Med., UCLA. Mem: pres. Sigma Xi Club, 1970-71; Alpha Chi Sigma, 1935; Phi Lambda Upsilon, 1938; Republican; Presbyterian; rec: recent publications and bio-organic chem. Res: La Venne Manor, 2555 Sixth St, La Verne 91750 Ofc: Chem. Dept., Calif State Polytechnic Univ., Pomona 91768

ABERNETHY, ROBERT GORDON, news correspondent; b. Nov. 5, 1927, Geneva, Switz.; s. Robet William and Lois May (Jones) A.; m. Jean Clarke Montgomery, Apr. 30, 1955 (dec. Apr. 1980); dau. Jane Montgomery, b. 1957; m. Marie Cheremeteff Grove, 1984; dau. Elizabeth Cheremeteff, b. 1985; edn: AB, Princeton Univ., 1950, MPA, 1952; Woodrow Wilson Sch. of Public and Internat. Affairs. Career: editor NBC News, Wash DC 1952-55; NBC correspondent London, Eng. 1955-58, Wash. 1956-58, Los Angeles 1966-77; anchorman KNBC's Sixth Hour News, 1966-70; Wash. corr. Today Show, 1977-80; wrote and narrated NBC weekly TV report Update, 1961-63; author: Introduction To Tomorrow (Harcourt, Brace & World, 1966); A Primer on Communism, Many Shades of Black, TV documentaries; trustee Princeton Univ. 1974-77; awards: Thomas Alva Edison Mass Media Award, best American history for youth (1966); honorary mayor Pacific Palisades (1971); mil: US Army 1946-48; United Ch. of Christ. Ofc: 4001 Nebraska Ave. NW, Wash DC 20016

ABERNETHY, ROBERT JOHN, real estate developer; b. Feb. 28, 1940, Indpls.; s. George Lawrence and Helen Sarah (McLandress) A.; edn: BS, Johns Hopkins Univ. 1962, MBA, Harvard Univ. 1963; certs. in real estate fin., constrn., UCLA; DPMA, Cert. Data Processor, 1968. Career: adminstv. asst. to nat. deputy campaign mgr. Humphrey for Pres. Campaign, 1968; asst. to the chief scientist Phoenix Missile Pgm., Hughes Aircraft Co., 1968-9, asst. pgm. mgr. Iroquois Night Fighter and Night Tracker Pgm. 1969-71, asst. to the controller of Space and Communications Gp. 1971, controller Technology Div. 1972-74; pres. American Standard Devel. Co., Los Angeles 1974 –. Dir.: Century Thrift and Loan 1982 -, Self Storage Mgmt. Co. 19;76-, Marathon Nat. Bank 1982-, Storage Equities 1980-, Los Angeles Bancorp 1982-, Self-Service Storage Assn. (National: dir. 1980-3, v.p. 82-83; Region 2: dir. 1977-83, v.p. 82-83). Mem: YMCA (treas. 1982-3), Harvard Bus. School Scholarship Trust (dir. 1973-), Town Hall, L.A. World Affairs Council; clubs: Calif. Yacht, St. Francis Yacht, Jonathan, Harvard Bachelors, Stanford Bachelors; mil: lt. USN 1962-66; Democrat; Presbyterian; rec: sailing, skiing; Res: 5800 W. Century Bl. Los Angeles 90009 Ofc: Am. Standard Devel. Co., 5221 102nd St. Los Angeles 90045

ABERNETHY, RODNEY ELMER, ophthalmologist; b. Aug. 6, 1921, Spokane, Wash.; s. Elmer Robert and Margaret May (Scott) A.; m. Elizabeth Naftzger, Apr. 21, 1945; children: Robert b. 1946, David b. 1949, Pamela b. 1951, Janet b. 1959; edn: AB, UC Berkeley 1944; MD, UC Sch. of Med. San

Francisco 1946; Harvard Univ. Sch. of Med. 1948-49; certified Am. Bd. of Ophthalmol. 1953. Career: intern Franklin Hosp. S.F. 1947; resident Ft. Miley Vet. Hosp. 1949-51; res. USN Hosp. Oakland 1951; pvt. practice ophthalmol. San Mateo 1953-86; asst. clin. prof. Stanford Univ. Sch. of Med.; honors: Extraordinary Service Award (Rotary 1986); mem: fellow Am. Acad. Ophthalmol., fellow Am. Coll. Surg., Calif. Assn. of Ophthalmol. (bd. dirs.), Senior Focus (bd. dirs.); works: Amigos de las Americas 1984-; mil: lt. j.g. USN 1951-53. Ofc: Rodney E. Abernethy MD, Inc. 215 N San Mateo Dr San Mateo 94401

ABKIN, MICHAEL HOWARD, systems analyst; b. June 16, 1943, Los Angeles; s. Nathan and Faye (Alpern) A.; m. Graciela Peschard, Dec. 21, 1968; 1 dau. Unmi b. 1969; edn: BA, UC Los Angeles 1966; MS, Mich. State Univ. 1970, PhD 1972. Career: research asst., 1969-71, asst. prof. Dept. Agric. Econs. and Dept. Electrical Engring. and Systems Sci., Mich. State Univ., 1971-81; consulting splst. in socioecon. analysis and simulation modeling, owner System Solutions, 1981-85; senior ops. analyst ATAC, Mt. View 1984-; honors: NASA traineeship awarded as a grad. student; mem. IEEE Systems, Man and Cybernetics Soc., Soc. for Computer Simulation; publs: 60+ jour. articles, book chpts., conf. and tech. papers; civic: Los Gatos Comm. Hosp. (Aux. vol. 1982-85), Los Gatos Comm. Services Commn. (commnr. 1984-, chmn. 1986), Rinconada Hills Assn. (dir. 1985-86); works: project mgr. in devel. policy simulation models of U.S. agric. linked to a global food trade model; wrote guidelines for info. systems approach to monitor rural devel. for UN Food and Agric. Orgn. (FAO); devel./installed policy analysis model for Govt. Venezuela; task leader on air traffic control adv. automation anal. project for IBM and the FAA (ATAC); rec: community svc., theater, bridge, travel. Ofc: ATAC 1200 Villa St Mountain View 94041

ABPLANALP, DELLOY ORVAL, holistic health co. owner; b. Nov. 28, 1931, Salt Lake City; s. Orval Ross and Elva Bernice (Hatch) A.; m. Kathleen Thurman, 1959; children: Denise, b. 1960, David, b. 1962, Matthew, b. 1969; grandchildren: Elena, b. 1978, Elizabeth, b. 1980, Daniel, b. 1982, James b. 1984; edn: BS, Brigham Young Univ. 1959; elem., sec. teaching cred. Career: church mission svc., Ch. of Jesus Christ of L.D.S., 1951-53; school tchr. 1959-61; acctg. & payroll, L.A. City Fire Dept. and Dept. Water & Power, 1961-74; tchg. holistic health, 1974-; sales mgr. Los Angeles Herald Examiner 1983-; mgr./dir. five herb cos.; awards: Million Dollar Club, Amtec Ind. (4); sales, leadershp, Natures Sunshine Prods., Nature's Laboratories and Unimont Corp. 1979; mem: Delta Phi 1955-9, Nat. Health Fedn. 1970-, L.D.S. Sociables 1965-70; publs: Holistic Health Bklet (1977), Dial An Herb Wheel (1976); mil: pfc Army Sig. Corps; Democrat (co. chmn. 1959); L.D.S. Ch. (elder, tchr.); rec: AYSO coach, referee, Little League coach. Ofc: Holistic Hlth Integ., 4917 N. Baldwin Ave. Temple City 91780

ABRAMS, DONALD IRA, physician; b. June 1, 1950, NY, NY; s. Sidney and Rosalie Vita (Brokaw) A.; edn: AB, Brown Univ. 1972; MD, Stanford Univ. Sch. of Med. 1977. Career: resident internal medicine, Kaiser Found. Hosp. San Francisco 1977-80; fellow hematology-oncology, Cancer Research Inst., UC San Francisco 1980-83; (current) asst. dir. AIDS Activities, San Francisco Gen. Hosp. 1983-, asst. clin. prof. Cancer Research Inst., Dept. of Medicine UCSF 1983-; lectr. internat. on AIDS; awards: Am. Cancer Soc. Career Devel. Award (1986-88); mem. Dir. Public Health S.F. AIDS advis. com.; mem. Am. Coll. of Physicians, Am. Soc. of Hematology, Am. Soc. of Clin. Oncology; publs: num. med. articles on AIDS and AIDS-related conditions in sci. literature; rec: travel, photog. Ofc: AIDS/Oncology Clinic, Ward 84, 995 Potrero Ave San Francisco 94110

ABUL-HAJ, SULEIMAN K., physician; b. Apr. 20, 1925, Palestine, nat. USA 1955; s. Sheikh Khalil M. and S. Butheina (Oda) Abul-Haj; m. Elizabeth Abood, Feb. 11, 1948; children: Charles b. 1948, Alan b. 1957, Cary b. 1958; edn: BS, UC Berkeley 1949; MS, UC San Francisco 1951, MD, 1955. Career: research assoc. Univ. Calif. Sch. of Medicine, San Francisco 1950-54; fellow National Am. Inst. 1955-56; surgical pathologist Brooke Army Gen. Hosp. 1957-59; chief Clinical & Surgical Pathology, Walter Reed Army Hosp. 1959-62; senior surgical pathologist USC-LA Co. Med. Center, 1962; pathologist-in-chief Community Meml. Hosp., Ventura 1964-80, and General Hosp. Ventura County 1964-74; assoc. clin. prof. USC 1963-; dir. Pathology Service Medical Group, 1970-; cons. Armed Forces Inst. of Pathology (1960-), Camarillo State Hosp. (1965-70), Tripler Army-Navy Hosp. (1964-68); awards: Borden's Award for Disting. Research (1955), Army Certificate of Achievement (1962); mem: AMA, Calif. Med. Assn., Coll. of Am. Pathologists, Am. Soc. of Clin. Pathologists, Internat. Coll. of Surgeons, NY Acad. of Scis., Internat. Platform Assn., AAAS, Am. Cancer Soc., Tricounties Blood Bank, Jonathan Club; num. publs. in fields of cancer, heart diseases, kidney diseases, skin diseases and pediatric diseases; mil: major US Army Med. Corps; Republican; rec: fine arts, antiques. Res: 105 Encinal Way Ventura 93001

ACKER, JOHN CHRISTIAN, JR., car rental agency executive; b. July 23, 1948, Jacksonville, Fla.; s. John Christian and Frances H. (Ahl) A.; m. Cathy M. Vanasco, June 28, 1983; edn: BSBA, Univ. Fla. 1970. Career: asst. mgr. Nat. Car Rental Sarasota, Fla. 1971-75, city mgr. Ft. Meyers, Fla. 1976-77, Pittsburgh, Pa. 1978-81, S.F. Airport 1982-83, zone mgr. S.F. 1984-; mem: Calif. CATRALA (car renting & leasing assn., bd. dirs.), Delta Sigma Pi (pres. 1969-70), Sunset Optimist Club (Fla., pres. 1977), Lions Club; Republican; rec: golf. Ofc: Nat. Car Rental 3 Waters Park Dr Ste 201 San Mateo 94403

ACUNA, DEANNE ROBERTA, private investigator; b. Mar. 17, 1939, Long Beach; d. Dean Robert and Roberta Lillian (Ross) Gardner; children: David b.

1960, Kimberly b. 1965; edn: AA, Long Beach City Coll. 1972. Career: paralegal investigator law firm Perona-Langer, Long Beach 1970-76; owner Reality Realty Co., Long Beach 1976-79; pvt. investigator law firm Perona-Langer LaTorraca, Beck, 1979-; real estate developer and cons. 1984-; awards: acad. scholarships 1970-72; mem. Women in Constrn., Long Beach Com. 300; civic: Betty Clooney Found. for Brain Injured Young Adults (patron), Long Beach Civic Light Opera Womens Guild; Democrat; rec: tchg. holistic health concepts. Res: 2462 Monogram Ave Long Beach 90815 Ofc: Perona, Langer, LaTorraca and Beck 300 San Antonio Dr Long Beach 90807

ADAM, STEPHEN FERENC, consultant; b. Feb. 28, 1929, Budapest, Hungary, nat. US cit. 1962; s. Istvan I. and Gizella (Mihaly) A.; m. Edie, Sept. 11, 1965; edn: BSME, Tech. Univ. of Budapest 1951, MSEE, MSME, 1952, PhDEE, 1955; tchg. credl. Calif. Career: research engr. Research Inst. of Telecom. Budapest, Hungary 1952-56; r&d engr., proj. mgr., engr. sec. mgr., chief microwave engr., prin. engr. Hewlett Packard Co. Palo Alto 1957-84; pres. Adam Microwave Cons. Inc. Los Altos 1984-; honors: Meritorious Svc. (1985), Disting. Microwave Lectr. (1984), IEEE Centennial Medal; fellow IEEE (pres. 1980, num. coms.); mem: Microwave Theory & Techniques Soc., Internat. Electrotechnical Commn. (US del.), Instrumentation & Measurement Soc. (awards chmn.), Hungarian Am. Profls. and Businessmen Assn. (pres. 1981-); 3 patents, others pending; author: Microwave Theory and Applications (Prentice Hall 1969), num. tech. articles; Republican; Catholic; rec: building house, gardening, music. Address: 1413 Brookmill Rd Los Altos 94022-5805

ADAMS, AUDREY LEE, physician; b. Mar. 27, 1952, Sioux Falls, S.Dak.; d. James R., Sr. and Louise (Lewis) Adams; m. Edward Schumann, Dec. 9, 1983; edn: BS medicine, Univ. S.Dak. 1975; MD, Northwestern Univ. 1976. Career: asst. prof. anesthesiology Univ. of Chgo. 1981-82; chief Surgical Intensive Care, and asst. prof. anesthesiol., Univ. of Calif., Irvine 1982-85; staff anesthesiol. Circle City Hosp. Corona 1985-; vol. faculty UC Irvine 1985-; awards: Univ. of Chgo. Med. Housestaff tchg. award (1982), listed Who's Who in Am. Women (1984); mem: Am. Med. Women's Assn., Soc. of Critical Care Medicine, Am. Soc. of Anesthesiology, Internat. Anesthesia Research Soc.; publs: num. research articles; rec: backpacking, skiing, sewing. Address: Huntington Beach 92646

ADAMS, CARY M., lawyer; b. Sept. 5, 1948, Memphis, Tenn.; s. Thomas M. and Granville M. (Meredith) A.; m. Carol, June 7, 1969; children: Allison, b. 1971, Healy, b. 1984; edn: BA, Univ. of Virginia 1970; JD, Univ. of Maryland 1976; admitted to Dist. of Columbia Bar 1977, Calif. Bar 1982. Career: law clerk Judge Frank A. Kaufman US Dist. Ct., Baltimore, MD 1976-77; assoc. Arnold & Porter, Wash. DC 1977-81; assoc. Memel, Jacobs, Pierno, Gersh & Ellsworth, Sacramento 1982-83, ptr. 1984-; honors: ed. in chief Maryland Law Review 1975-76; Order of the Coif, Maryland chpt. 1976; Rogel Howell Award, Univ. of MD 1976; mem: Am., Calif. and Sacramento Co. (health law sect.) Bar Assns., Nat. Health Lawyers Assn., Calif. Soc. for Healthcare Attys., Calif. Consortium of Child Abuse Councils (bd. dirs. 1983-), St. Michael's Episcopal Ch. & Day Sch. (chancellror 1983-, vestry 1983-85, sr. warden 1985); publs: Medicare Disproportionate Share Cases Proliferate, Health Law Vigil, 1985; Medicare & Medicaid Anti-Fraud & Abuse Laws: The Need for Legislative Change, Healthspan, 1985; Confronting HCFA's Prospective Payment System: A Guide For Hospitals That Are Mad As Heck and Aren't Going to Take It Anymore, Hosp. Law Newsletter, 1984; Preferred Provider Organizations, Calif. Health Law News, 1982-83; Federal Courts-Three Judges or One? A Problem Of Overlapping Power In The District Courts, Md. Law Review, 1975; recent decision, Garner v. United States, Md. Law Review, 1975; mil: E-4, US Army 1971-73; Democrat; Episcopal. Res: 830 Laverstock Way, Sacramento 95864 Ofc: Memel, Jacobs, Pierno, Gersh & Ellsworth, 555 Capitol Mall Ste. 1555, Sacramento 95814

ADAMS, GUY WILKERSON, investment advisor; b. Apr. 22, 1951, Baton Rouge, La.; s. William Porter, Sr. and Mildred Margarite (Painter) A.; m. Nancy McDonald, Jan. 27, 1979; children: Kathryn b. 1974, Laurie b. 1977, Austin b. 1981; edn: BS in petroleum engring., La. State Univ. 1974; MBA, Harvard Bus. Sch. 1984. Career: div. engr. Offshore Exploration Drilling -Internat. Div., Sonat Offshore Drilling Co., Houston, Tx. 1975-78, div. mgr. (set up overseas Exploration Divs. in Egypt, Brazil, Ivory Coast, W. Africa, Trinidad, Spain, Portugal, and Italy) 1978-82, Ops. Area mgr. (in chg. 3 divs.- Far East, Mid-East, and Europe) 1982; pres. Tooby Farms (entrepreneurial co.), Pasadena 1984-86; pres. GWA Investments, Inc., Pasadena 1986-; mem: Soc. of Pet. Engrs., Am. Assn. of Indep. Investors, Nat. Assn. of Security Dealers, Calif. Indep. Producers Assn.; civic: Arcadia PTA, Harvard Alumni (So. Calif.), Sigma Chi Alumni (Life), LSU Alumni Club of Calif.; Presbyterian; rec: skiing, jogging, tennis, karate. Res: 353 W Camino Real Arcadia 91006 Ofc: GWA Investments POB 70160 Pasadena 91107

ADAMS, NEIL RONALD, electronic engineer; b. Nov. 29, 1955, Liverpool, England; s. Ronald George and Edith Olive (Painter) A.; edn: BS in physics, electronics, honors, Manchester Univ., England 1977. Career: design engr. Marconi Radar Systems, 1977-81; current: mem. tech. staff Networking Div., Advanced Micro Devices, Sunnyvale; 6 US Patent Appls. filed (1983-86); Democrat; rec: music. Address: Sunnyvale 94086

ADAMS, ROGER RALPH, photographer, educator; b. May 12, 1936, Cherokee, Okla.; s. Ralph Hubert and Nina Maude (Morgan) A.; m. Bernadyne, June 5, 1960; children: Jeffrey b. 1967, Gregory b. 1973; edn: BA, CSU Long Beach 1971. Career: profl. photog./owner Adams Photo, Santa Ana 1962-72; current owner The House of Portraits, Hemet; photo instr. Mt. San Jacinto

Coll.; mem. Profl. Photogs. of Am., Wedding Photogs. Internat., United Methodist Men (pres. 1980); mil: sgt. US Army Reserve 1958-64; Republican; rec: travel, 3-D photog. Res: 41633 Lori Ln Hemet 92344

ADAMS, WILLIAM FRANCIS, real estate broker; b. Feb. 15, 1939, San Jose; s. Frank Wm. and Kathryn Mary Adams; m. Mary Anne Ring, Sept. 11, 1959; 1 dau., Laura Anne, b. 1967; edn: Bellarmine Coll. Prep. 1957; AA, San Jose City Coll. 1961; lic. R.E. Broker, Calif. Career: stockclk., head warehousemn., store mgr. Blue Chip Stamp Co., 1959-63, dist. mgr. No. Calif., Ore., Nev., 1963-75; realtor assoc. Century 21, 1975; realtor/co-owner Internat. R.E. Network, Adams & Miller Realtors, 1975-82, realtor/owner Silicon Valley Properties, 1982–; cons. var. lawyers real estate appraisals; mem. San Jose R.E. Board, Calif., Nat. Assn. of Realtors, Tri-County Apt. Assn.; mem. Elks, Almaden Golf & Country Club, Almaden Homeowners Assn., Bellarmine Alumni Assn.; Democrat; Catholic; rec: golf, bowling, skiing. Res: 1168 Carla Dr. San Jose 95120 Ofc: Silicon Valley Properties, 6472 Camden Ave, Ste. 102, San Jose 95120

ADAMSON, GEOFFREY DAVID, reproductive endocrinologist and surgeon; b. Sept. 16, 1946, Ottawa, Ontario, Canada; s. Geoffrey Peter and Anne Marian (Allan) A.; m. Rosemary Oddie, Apr. 28, 1973; children: Stephanie b. 1976, Rebecca b. 1978, Eric b. 1984; edn: BS honors, Trinity Coll. Univ. Toronto 1969; MD, Univ. Toronto 1973; MD Calif. 1975. Career: resident Toronto Gen. Hosp. 1974-77, fellow 1977-78; fellow reproductive endocrinol. Stanford Univ. 1978-80; pvt. practice Los Gatos 1980-83, Palo Alto 1984–; clin. asst. prof. Stanford Univ. Sch. of Med. ob-gyn dept. 1980–; honors: Ortho Award (Soc. Ob-Gyn. Canada 1977), Ontario Ministry of Health Fellow (1977-78), Hon. Life Mem., Disting. Svc. (Canadian Assn. Interns & Res. 1980); mem: AMA, Am. Coll. Ob-Gyn, Royal Coll. Surgeons (Can.), Am. Coll. Surg., Soc. Reproductive Endocrinols., Soc. Reproductive Surg., NY Acad. Scis., AAAS, Am. Fertility Soc., Pacific Coast Fertility Soc., Gynecol. Laser Soc., Am. Assn. Gynecol. Laparoscopists, Shufelt Gyn. Soc. of Santa Clara Valley, Peninsula Gyn. Soc., Santa Clara County Med. Assn., No. Calif. Resolve (bd.); publs: num. articles in med. jours.; Episcopal; rec: computers, hiking. Ofc: G. David Adamson MD APC 540 University Ave Ste 200 Palo Alto 94301

ADDINGTON, CARL WENDEL, SR., production plant executive; b. June 3, 1933, Ada, Okla.; s. Wade and Edith (Kissee) A.; m. Doris Laverne Tognoli, Mar. 31, 1957; children: Troy b. 1961, Carl, Jr. b. 1964; edn: AA, City Coll. San Francisco 1958. Career: senior dispersion tech., prodn. coord. W.P. Fuller Paint Co. So. San Francisco 1955-69; prodn. mgr. Morwear Paint Co. Oakland 1969-74; plant mgr. D.J. Simpson Paint Co. S.F. 1974-76; plant mgr. Kelly Moore Paint Co. San Carlos 1976-78; prodn. mgr. Boysen Paint Co. Oakland 1978-79; plant mgr. Universe Paint Co. Marysville 1979-81; prodn. mgr. Std.-T-Chem. Co. (div. of Montgomery Ward) San Leandro 1981–; mem: Golden Gate Paint Soc., Am. Legion, Moose Lodge, Nat. Rifle Assn.; mil: AA USN 1951-53, pfc US Army 1953-55, Occupation, Good Conduct; Democrat; Methodist; rec: flying, music, reading, singing. Res: 2442 Fiji Way San Leandro 94577 Ofc: 3016 Alvarado St San Leandro 94577

ADDIS, THOMAS H., III, golf professional/executive; b. Nov. 30, 1945, San Diego; s. Thomas H. and Martha J. (Edwards) A.; m. Susan, June 13, 1966; children: Thomas H., IV b. 1967, Bryan Michael b. 1972; ed. James Logan H.S. 1963; desig: PGA Golf Profl. Class A, PGA of Am. (1986). Career: (current) dir. of golf ops. Singing Hills Golf Club, El Cajon; owner Golf Consulting and Design; cons. Nat. Golf Found.; Dir: Southern California PGA, San Diego PGA, PGA of America (1986-88), Calif. State Open, West coast PGA Mdse. Show, San Diego County Open, San Diego Jr. Golf Assn.; awards: PGA Nat. Horton Smith Award 1978, So. Calif. PGA Golf Professional of the Year (1979), So. Cal Resort Merchandiser of Year (1978, 83), Golf Industry Mag. Retailer Award (1985); mem: Profl. Golfers' Assn. of Am. (PGA) (pres. San Diego PGA 1978-79; pres. So. Calif. PGA 1980-81-82; pres. Calif. State PGA Com. 1980-84), Golf Collectors Soc., Rotary; publs: articles in golfing mags.; Episcopal; rec: skiing, reading. Res: 1942 Vereda Ct El Cajon 92021 Ofc: Singing Hills Golf Club 3007 Dehesa Rd El Cajon 92021

ADELMANN, EUGENIA RUTH PENICK, civic volunteer; b. Nov. 23, 1920, Spokane, Wash.; d. Walter Lee and Ruth (Mac Innis) Penick; m. Carl Richard Adelmann, Jr., Aug. 7, 1943; children: Jacqueline A. (Mrs. G. S. Nolte, Jr.), C. Richard III; edn: BA in French, Univ. Idaho 1942; Tchg. cert. (H.S. French) 1942. Fundraiser, social events planner, decorator, designer fashions, needlepoint, floral; winner 2d prize Vogue Mag. competition, Univ. Idaho (1941); civic: Palo Alto Med. Research Found. Aux. (co-founder 1960-), Stanford Convalescent Home (vol. 1952-), Los Altos Hills Club (bd. 1975-), Childrens Hosp. at Stanford, Friends of Filoli; mem. Pan Hellenic 1958-60, Pi Beta Phi Frat., Los Altos Golf & Country Club; Republican; Episcopal; rec: golf, bridge, antiques, equestrian. Res: 1514 Country Club Dr Los Altos 94022

ADLAI, S. RICHARD, author, corp. executive; b. Feb. 10, 1942; s. A. Amir and Hadia (Salvatori) A.; chil: Tarick S., b. 1963, Tarisa L., b. 1970, Willie De Mille, b. 1972; edn: bus., mktg., Am. Coll. of Bus. 1962; BS, NY Univ. 1980, MBA, honors, Pepperdine Univ. 1982. Career: writer Paramount Studios, 1960-63; founder, bd. chmn. Hollywood Cinema Center Inc.; pres. Hilton Commercial Group, Inc., 1978–; author novel: King Tarick (Am. Pub., NY 1965), play: Hassan & Hanna (1966), 100 Short Stories, autobio. book: Ibn Saud; cons. re third world countries; honored for his contribns. to hwy. safety and for pioneering imports of alcohol free wines from France, Italy and Germany at White House ceremony, Dec. 11, 1984, Wash DC; elected Pepper-

dine Univ. Assocs., devel. outstanding proj. for PKE Pgm., Pepperdine 1982; chmn. Toluca Lake Photo Expo. Mem: Rotarian (T.L. pres. 1983), CofC, World Affairs Council; Republican; Episcopal; rec: photog., fishing, golf, anthropol. Ofc: Hilton Commercial Gp. Inc, Ste.10 Hilton Center, POB 2026 Toluca Lake 91602

ADLER, ALLAN WILBUR, silversmith; b. May 8, 1916, Mazula, Mont.; s. August M. and Daisey B. (Fox) A.; m. Rebecca Blanchard, Mar. 24, 1938; children: Linda Diane (Mrs. Wm. Hughes), b. 1942; Cindy Alice (Mrs. Scott Larson), b. 1952. Career: pres. Allan Adler, Inc. 1940–, bd. chmn. 1981–; designed and made the pins worn by the first seven Am. Astronauts; designed the silver flatware and holloware for the Calif. Gov.'s Mansion for Gov. Edmund Brown; designed the American Film Inst. Award (1972); designed the Famous Stevenshoe shoe campaign button; designed original Pres. Eisenhower Golf Trophy for Bob Hope Desert Classic tournament.; awards: Calif. Living Treasure (1984), Good Design Award, Mus. of Modern Art (1956), Scissors Award for Design, Calif. Fashion Grp. (1949); honored by The Smithsonian Instn. (1982) documenting 40 years of Am. Silversmithing and Allan Adler's Contbn. to Design; mem. Los Angeles County Mus. of Art, Newport Harbor Yacht Club; Presbyterian; rec: yachting, fishing. Res: 3263 Oakdell Rd Studio City 91604 Ofc: Allan Adler, Inc. 13080 Montague St Pacoima 91331

ADLER, ERWIN ELLERY, lawyer; b. July 22, 1944, Flint, Mich.; s. Ben and Helen M. (Schwartz) A.; m. Stephanie Ruskin, June 8, 1967; children: Lauren M. b. 1974, Michael B. b. 1977, Jonathan S. b. 1981; edn: BA, Univ. of Mich., 1963, JD, Harvard Law Sch., 1966, LL.M, Univ. of Mich. Law Sch., 1967. Career: assoc. Pillsbury Madison & Sutro law firm, 1967-73; assoc., partner law firm Lawler, Felix & Hall, 1973-82; ptnr. law firm Rogers & Wells, 1982-84; ptnr. law firm Richards, Watson, Dreyfuss & Gershon, Los Angeles 1985–; bd. dirs. Hollywood Opera Assocs. 1975-76; bd. dirs. Childrens Scholarships Inc. 1978-79; v.chmn. Appellate Advocacy Com. American Bar Assn.; honors: Phi Beta Kappa, Phi Kappa Phi; mem. Am. Bar Assn. 1967-, Calif. Bar Assn. 1967-, LA Athletic Club; Jewish; rec: photog., jogging. Res: 872 Norman Pl Los Angeles 90049 Ofc: Richards, Watson, Dreyfuss & Gershon, 333 So Hope St, 38th Flr Los Angeles 90071

ADLER, MEG, system sales representative; b. Apr. 5, 1957, Phila.; d. John P. and Betty (Moore) Gillane; m. Steven W. Adler, Jan. 31, 1982; 1 son, Joshua b. 1983; edn: BSBA, Univ. So. Calif. 1981; M.Indsl.Engrg. (in progress). Career: credit analyst Crocker Comml. Svcs. L.A. 1980-81; acct. exec. Comml. Credit L.A. 1981-82; sales rep. Specialized Bus. Systems Glendale 1984, designs and sells storage and retrieval systems for small parts material handling to aerospace industry; honors: Cert. of Merit (SBA Cons. Pgm. USC 1979); mem: Profl. Women's Breakfast Group (treas. 1984-85), Women's Interaction Network (steering om. 1985-); rec: ice skating, golf. Res: 5735 Woodman Apt 203 Van Nuys 91401 Ofc: 321 El Bonito Glendale 91204

ADRIANSE, HOMER RAYMOND, ocean engineering programs executive; b. Jan. 28, 1923, Grand Rapids, Mich.; s. Raymond Homer and Anna N. (Heering) A.; m. Suzanne Ward, April 4, 1945; children: William b. 1946, Joan b. 1949 (dec.), Charles b. 1950; edn: Grand Rapids Jr. Coll. 1940-41; BS, US Naval Acad. 1944; Naval Engr., Mich. Inst. of Tech. 1951. Career: contracts and materials ofcr., Polaris inspection ofcr., supvr. of shipbldg., Groton, Conn. 1957-60; Polaris project ofcr., asst. submarine type desk, Bureau of Ships, Wash. DC 1960-64; asst. repair supt., design ofcr. Bremerton Naval Shipyard 1964-67; prodn. ofcr. Mare Island Naval Shipyard 1967-70; pgm. engr. Westinghouse Oceanic Div. 1970-73, ocean engring. pgms. mgr. 1973–; mem: SNAME, ASNE, Sigma Xi, US Naval Inst., Navy League, TROA, Ondulando Club, Saticoy Golf & Country Club; mil: capt. USN; Republican, Baptist; rec: fishing, hunting, diving. Res: 171 Nob Hill Ln. Ventura 93003

AGHAMOHAMfADI, ALI M., otolaryngologist; b. Mar. 25, 1944, Natanz, Iran; s. Mohamad Hossein and Batool (Mazaheri) A.; m. Fatemeh Aghighi, Feb. 28, 1946; children: Neema b. 1973, Mazda b. 1977, Sara b. 1982; edn: premed, Pahlavi Univ., Iran 1962-64; MD, Pahlavi Med. Sch. 1970. Career: asst. prof. otolaryngol. Nat. Univ. Iran, pvt. practice Tehran Clin. & Hosp. 1980-83; pvt. practice otolaryngol. New Haven, Ct. 1983-84; Bakersfield 1984–; attg. otolaryngol. Kern Med. Ctr. Bakersfield; mem: AMA, CMA, Am. Acad. Facial Plastic Surg., Iranian Soc. Otolaryngol. (secty. gen.); mil: 2nd lt. Royal Army of Iran 1970-72; rec: chess, backgammon, fishing. Ofc: 2330 Truxton Ave Bakersfield 93301

AGUILAR, JOHN RAYMOND, financial planner; b. Nov. 1, 1950, Los Angeles; s. Edward and Gloria G. Aguilar; m. Sara, June 14, 1975; children: Alfonso b. 1979, Keith b. 1982; edn: BA, CSU Fullerton 1972. Career: ins. agt., finl. plnng., Thorkelson & Assocs., 1975-, senior cons. Creative Analysis (reg. finl. advsy. co.), Santa Ana 1980–; awards: Orange Co. General Agents Assn.-New Agent of Year, Mass. Mutual (1975), Agent of Year, Guardian Life (1984-85); MDRT (1976-77); civic: Costa Mesa CofC; publs: article in Insurance Selling (1979), reg. songwriter; rec: ski, golf, write/perform music. Res: 49 Lindberg Irvine 92714 Ofc: Creative Analysis 1072 S.E. Bristol Ste 105 Santa Ana 92707

AGUIRRE, JESUS DIAZ, JR., research and planning consultant; b. July 27, 1956, Los Angeles; s. Jose de Jesus Aguayo and Ascension (Diaz) A.; m. Laura Ann, Sept. 25, 1982; children: Jesus b. 1984, Jason b. 1986; edn: AA, East Los Angeles Coll. 1976; BBA, Loyola Marymount Univ. 1979; MBA, Calif. Polytechnic Univ. Pomona 1985. Career: project dir. J.D. Power & Assoc. Research

& Plnng. Cons., Westlake Village 1979-80; v.p., dir. of mktg. Carranza Associates, Los Angeles 1980-82; dir. of research Lotus Communications, Hollywood 1982-86; pres., owner United States Research, Beverly Hills 1984—; dir. TV syndication research Warner Bros. Burbank 1986—; instr. CSU Los Angeles p.t. 1981-82; adv. council Inst. of Retail Mgmt. Sch. of Bus. 1981-82; honors: Award for consulting svc. to small bus., SBA and Loyola Marymount Univ. 1979; Profl. Appreciation Plaque, USC 1980; mem: Inst. of Retail Mgmt. (Adv. Council), CSU Los Angeles Sch. of Bus.; works: Calif. Racial Ethnic Report 1940-1990 A Census Perspective, 1984; Hispanic Population Characteristics in Ventura/ Santa Barbara Counties, 1984; The Los Angeles Latino Market Report, 1981; Latin American Govt. Role in the International Debt Crisis, 1984; Democrat; Catholic; rec: boxing. Res: 3731 Lowell Ave. Los Angeles 90032 Ofc: U.S. Research, 270 No. Canon Dr. Ste. 1051 Beverly Hills 90210

AHRENS, CAROL J., psychotherapist; b. Dec. 26, 1945, Wash. DC; d. Theodore and Hazel L. (Mayfield) Fillo; m. Donald E. Ahrens, Apr. 10, 1065; children: Heather b. 1971, Jonathan b. 1976; edn: BA, Capital Univ. 1969; MSW, magna cum laude, Melodyland Sch. of Theol. 1980; MA, Calif. Christian Inst. 1982; PhD clin. psychol., Internat. Coll. 1984; lic. Marriage, Family & Child Therapist Calif. 1985. Career: created, developed children's music ministry Melodyland Christian Ctr. Anaheim, Calif. 1974-81; sch. counselor, therapist Catholic Soc. Svcs. Santa Ana 1981; Dept. of Public Soc. Svcs., Child Protective Svcs., Riverside Co. 1982—; marriage, family & child counselor & psychol. asst. No. Orange Co. Psychol. Svcs. Orange 1982—; cons. 4 Orange Co. Christian Schs. 1983—; ancillary staff Brea Neuropsychiatric Hosp. Brea, Calif. 1985—; cons./therapist Hotline Help Ctr. Anaheim 1984—; dir. children's music Buena Park Comm. Ch. 1982—; mem. Calif. Assn. Marriage & Family Therapists; Christian; rec: music, reading. Res: 120 Jerrilee Ln Anaheim 92807 Ofc: No. Orange Co. Psychol. Svcs. 746 E Chapman Orange 92666

AIKEN, EDWIN HERBERT, electrical engineer; b. Feb. 16, 1899, Pawhuska, Okla.; s. Herbert and Luvena Bell (Cunningham) A.; m. Mary Quarrier Brookfield, June 25, 1927; children: Mary Virginia (Doty) b. 1929, Edwin Herbert b. 1934; edn: BSEE, Wash. State Univ. 1922; Reg. Profl. Engr. (E.E.) Calif. Career: engr. several silver mines in W. Colo., then with The Magma Copper Co., Superior, Ariz. -1928; design and constrn. engr. var. power cos. incl. Puerto Rico Railway Light & Power Co., San Juan, P.R., and Texas Power & Light Co., Dallas, Tex. 1928-37; designer, project engr. Brawley Diesel Plant, Imperial Irrigation Dist., El Centro 1937, systemwide ops. engr. (All Am. Canal, substations, etc.) 1938, chief elec. engr. 1938-45; with General Electric Co., Los Angeles 1945-53, first as shop engr./supt. then num. assignments incl. field engr. assigned to Kaiser Steel Co. (Fontana), Pittsburg Steel Co. (Pittsburg, Calif.), Columbia Steel Mill (Provo, Utah), steel mills in Zenica, Yugoslavia and Jamshedpur, India, hydro-elec. plant (Ketchikan, Ala.), San Manuel (Ariz.) Copper Co.; engr. North Am. Aviation Co. 1953-67, projects incl. Navajo Missile, Reins Bomb Nav. Sys., other govt. mil. projects; pvt. research in earthquakes and volcanism, 1967-, author, publisher: Why the Earth Quakes; life mem. IEEE; mil: pfc Students Army Tng. Corps, 1918; Republican; rec: study of earthquakes, horticulture. Res: 432 Garden St Arroyo Grande 93420

AIKEN, ROY FRANKLIN, space systems co. executive, ret.; b. Jan. 16, 1931, Watkinsville, Ga.; s. George Henry and Lillian Alle (McCarty) Akin; m. Kathleen Gibson Wys, Oct. 23, 1976; children: Theodore b. 1953, Victoria b. 1954, Terrence b. 1961, Timothy b. 1963; edn: spl. courses in electronics, Navy Airborne Sch., Memphis Tn. 960 hrs), Naval Radar Opr., North Is., San Diego (480 hrs), Warner Robins, Ga. (960 hrs), adv. electronics and computer (2880 hrs), mgmt. (240 hrs), Hughes Aircraft Co. Career: owner/opr. TV Repair Shop, Athens, Ga. 1953-54; electronic techn., supr./instr. Warner Robins AFB, Ga. 1954-61; supr. Prodn. Test, Hughes Aircraft Co., Long Beach 1961-78, gen. supr. Test & Assembly, 1978-80, supt. Mfg., 1980-84, mgr. Mfg. SSD, 1984-86, ret.; mem. HAC Mgmt. Club; civic: VFW Post 2075, Junior Achievers (cons.), Lakewood City Children's League (football, baseball coach), Boy Scouts Am. (scoutmaster); mil: airman US Navy Air Force; Republican; Baptist; rec: photog., computer systems. Res: HCR No.2 Box 594 Springville 93265

AINLAY, FORREST CALEY, sales executive; b. Apr. 23, 1915, Farnam, Nebr.; s. Thomas Watson and Louise Pearle (Caley) A.; m. Helen Buck, Feb. 14, 1974; edn: BS, Univ. of Denver 1936. Career: controller, office mgr. Crest Labs., Burbank and succeeding cos. (acquired by Stuart Co., then Atlas Chem., then ICI), 1951-, indsl. rels. mgr. Stuart Co. Div. ICI America, Pasadena, 1960-75; v.p./mgr. group sales Bronson Pharm., La Canada 1976—; dir. Janco Inc., Burbank (1975-85); mem. Am. Soc. of Personnel Adminstrs., Personnel and Indsl. Relations Assn. (dir. 1966-70), Alpha Kappa Psi frat. (life 1932-); mil: cpl. US Army 1945-46; Republican; Prot.; rec: fishing, golf. Res: 2545 Janet Lee Dr La Crescenta 91214 Ofc: Bronson Pharmaceuticals 4526 Rinetti Ln La Canada 91011

AINSLIE, RICHARD G., life insurance executive; b. Apr. 4, 1916, Los Angeles; s. Edgar and Elizabeth (Chesney) A.; desc. of Mr. Chesney, design & drafting plans of Suez Canal 1958; desc. John Knox, 1505-72, Scottish reformer and founder of Presbyterianism; div.; 2 children: Paul Richard b. 1947, Susan Cynthia b. 1950; edn: BS, Purdue Univ. 1939, MS, 1940, postgrad. work, USC 1943-44; RHU, Reg. Health Underwriter (1979). Career: tchr. and coaching, Purdue 1939-40; tchr., head football/basketball coach Whitman Coll., Wash. 1940-42; safety engr. Consol. Steel, Calif. 1942-44; recreation dir. AirService Command, Ohio 1944-46; head football coach Wittenberg Coll., Ohio 1946; basketball, baseball coach Creighton Univ., 1947-48; agent Minn. Mutual Life

Ins. Co., Los Angeles 1948-58, general agent, 1958—, also field council 1961, 63, 75-76; European Ins. Conf., 1961; awards: Million Dollar Round Table (Honor Roll 23 years; Life & Qual. mem. 1952-81), Outstanding Profl. Salesman in Am. (1967-68), Leading Producers Round Table (Health & Life Qual.), Nat. Quality Award (25 years); mem: Internat. Assn. Health Underwriters 1969-81, MDRT 1952-81, Nat. Football Found. & Hall of Fame, Los Angeles Life Undw. Assn. Inc., Purdue Alumni Assn. (life), Life Ins. & Trust Council of L.A., Nat. Assn. of Health Undw. (RHU); clubs: Los Angeles Athletic, Oakmont Country (Glendale), The Mariner Club; publs: Military, Naval & Tropical Hygiene (USC 1943), Pitching Efficiency of Am. League Pitchers (Purdue 1940), Tips from the Table (Profl. Life Undw. 1968); rec: golf, snooker, music. Res: 3000 Country Club Dr Glendale 91208 Ofc: Richard G. Ainslie Agency, Minnesota Mutual Life Insurance Co. 3108 Los Feliz Blvd Los Angeles 90039

AINSWORTH, ELIZABETH PARRISH, educator, ret.; b. Sept. 6, 1916, Elizabeth, N.J.; d. George H. and Violet I. (Shepperd) Parrish; m. Jarvis D. Dean, 1940; m. 2d John Leroy Ainsworth, 1969; children: Mary Ann (Smith) b. 1942, Judith D. (Bradshaw) b. 1944; edn: BS, Univ. Mich. 1939; secondary edn. cred., UC Los Angeles 1959, sec. spl. edn., CSU Los Angeles 1960; Calif. Secondary Tchg. Cred., 1960. Career: tchr. Widney High Sch., Los Angeles 1959-69, subst. tchr. San Marino High Sch., San Marino 1980-85, ret.; pres./pgm. chair Pasadena Found. for Medical Research (1970-75); civic: Alliance Francaise de Pasadena (1975-, pres.), Pasadena Symphony Orch. (Women's Com., publicity chair 1980), Vieilles Maisons; Republican (vol.); Presbyterian; rec: music, French, travel. Address: San Marino 91108

AKMAL, MOHAMMAD, physician; b. Sept. 14, 1942, Tanda, Pakistan; d. Murad Khan and Badr-Um (Nisa) Swati; m. Sarwar S. Akmal, July 11, 1973; children: Aamir b. 1974, Yasir b. 1976, Nasir b. 1981; edn: pre-med. Islamia Coll. Univ. Peshawar, Pakistan 1962; MD, Khyber Med. Sch. 1967; lic. phys. in England, Calif., Ohio. Career: intern in gen. medicine Khyber Tchg. Hosp., Peshawar, Pakistan 1967-68; resident internal med., gen. surgery, orthopedics in var. hosps. England, res. in gen. medicine, neurol., nephrology in Derby, England 1970-73; medical registrar in gen. internal medicine Southend Group of Hosps., Southend-on-Sea, Essex, Eng. 1973-75; renal fellowship The Christ Hosp. Univ. Cinti., Ohio 1975-77; adv. fellowship in nephrology LA Co.-USC Med. Center, Los Angeles 1977-78, instr. in medicine 1978-81, physician splst. LAC-USC Med. Center 1981—; asst./assoc. prof. of med. USC 1981—, dir. of Renal Clinics, and dir. of Renal Research Labs.; recipient AMA Physician Recogn. Award (1978, 82); mem: Kidney Internat. Assn., Kidney Found. of So. Calif., Am. Heart Assn., AAAS; contbr. 20 publs. in med. jours., 16 abstracts and 5 book chpts.; rec: travel, sports, museums, swimming. Mail: 12834 Queensborough Dr Cerritos 90701 Ofc: Rm 4250 Unit 1 LAC-USC Medical Center Los Angeles 90033

ALANIZ, MIGUEL JOSE CASTANEDA, city librarian; b. Oct. 21, 1944, Los Angeles; s. Francisco Martinez and Amalia (Castaneda) A.; m. Mercedes, June 7, 1980; edn: AA edn., Chabot Coll. 1972; BA child/human devel., CSU Hayward 1974; MLS, CSU Fullerton 1975; MPA (in progress), CSU San Bernardino; Calif. Comm. Coll. Tchg. credential. Career: Spanish Services librarian, Alameda County 1975-77; branch lib. mgr. San Jose Public Library 1977-78, Santa Ana Public Library 1978-79; coord. Young Adult/ Outreach Svcs., San Bernardino County Library 1979-82, div. chief of tech. processing, 1982-84; city librarian City of Azusa 1984—; awards: grad. research fellow in library sci., CSUF 1974-75; mem: Am. Library Assn., Calif. Library Assn., Reforma (Nat. Assn. Hispanic Librarians), cofounder Bibliotecas Para La Gente (orgn. providing lib. svcs. in Spanish lang.); mil: E5 US Army 1965-71; rec: collect exotic autos, rare books, unusual pets. Ofc: City of Azusa Library 729 N Dalton Ave Azusa 91702

ALBERS, HARRY FRANCIS, dentist/educator; b. Sept. 2, 1950, Oss, Netherlands; s. Hans J. and Helen J. (Kurvers) Albers; edn: Bach. BioChem., UC Berkeley, 1973; DDS, UCLA 1977; gen. practice residency VA Hosp.SF 1978. Career: pvt. dental practice, Santa Rosa 1978—; instr. UCSF Dental Sch., 1978-80, Univ. of the Pacific/SF, 1980—; lectr. on dentistry internationally; author textbook: Tooth Colored Restoratives (7th ed., 1985); honors: Phi Beta Kappa 1973, mem: Am. Dental Assn., Calif. Dental Assn.; rec: photog., writing, gardening. Res: 8676 Nina Ct., Cotati 94928 Ofc: 95 Montgomery Dr. Ste. 106, Santa Rosa 95404

ALBERS, WALTER JOHN, business owner; b. Feb. 19, 1953, Oakland; s. Lawrence and Evelyn (Kayl) A.; m. Patricia Pisciotto, Apr. 19, 1975; edn: tech. service tng. certs. Apple Computer, 1982, Corvus Systems, 1983; authorized dealer, Novell, 1985; warranty svc. tng., IBM, 1984. Career: grocery clk. Alpha Beta Corp., San Leandro 1969-73; hd. groc. clk. Albertson's Corp., Fremont 1973-75; senior sales rep. Putnam Buick, Burlingame 1975-81; senior sales rep. Microland, Newark 1981-83; owner/pres. Micro Computer Svcs., Hayward 1982—; instr. Alameda and Contra Costa Cos. Tchr. Edn. Ctr. (1981-85); honors: West Coast Top Salesman Award, Auto. Dealers Assn. (1981); mem. Hayward CofC, Bur. Electronic and Appliance Repair, Calif. State Electronics Assn., Electronic Service Dealers of No. Calif; co-founder Macintosh User's Group; co-founder/v.p. Soc. for the Prev. of Cruelty to Apples (ed./pub. SPCapple Newsletter); Republican; Catholic; rec: travel, computers. Ofc: Micro Computer Services 23000 Connecticut St Ste 6 Hayward 94545

ALBERT, ALAN ALEX, sculptor; b. Aug. 2, 1927, Many, La.; s. Alex A. and Clara (Marcieca) A.; edn: San Francisco Art Inst. 1948-49, stu. w/Richard Diebenkorn, David Parks, Elmer Bischoff. Career: sculptor, owner Alan Albert Designs; pioneered devel. of sculptural techniques using fiberglass, polyester resins, and other contemporary mediums, 1950s–, gained nat. recogn. with series of one-man shows incl. Cellini Art Gal., Richmond Art Ctr., Crocker Art Galleries, in 1960s; work on permanent display: UC Berkeley, Harrahs, the Golden Nugget (Las Vegas, Atlantic City), Bank of Am. and var. public buildings nat.; represented in design showrooms in S.F.; commnd. major art works: Univ. of Calif., Am. Chem. Soc., Saks Fifth Avenue, Bank of Am., Donald Trump, Steve Wynn; honors: commnd. Am. Chem. Soc., Commemorative tapestry Dr. Joel Hildebrand 100th birthday (1981); S.F. Mayors Cup, San Francisco Art Fest. (1968); mem. Am. Amateur Athletic Union 1952-65, East Bay Garden Soc. 1968-79; mil: US Navy 1945-48, 1950-52; avoc: body building (winner 40 physique trophies 1953-65 incl. Mr. S.F., Mr. No. Calif.), gardening, contemporary furniture design (publ. in Designers West 1985). Address: Alan Albert Designs 624 Humboldt Richmond 94805

ALBERT, WARD WIAN, lawyer; b. Mar. 19, 1950, Glendale; s. Ward N. and Francis (Gladwin) A.; 1 dau., Wendy Amber b. 1983; edn: BS, Western State Univ. 1975, JD, 1977; admitted Calif. State Bar 1977. Career: atty. sole practice, San Diego 1977-79; ptnr. Hulting & Albert, Temecula 1979-81; sole practitioner, Temecula 1981–; instr. bus. law, Mt. San Jacinto Jr. Coll.; mem: Calif. Young Lawyers Assoc. (treas.), Public Service Law Corp. (pres.), Southwest Riverside County Bar Assn. (pres.), Temecula Valley CofC (pres.); mil: E5 USCG; Republican; Protestant. Ofc: 27403 Ynez Road Ste 203 Temecula 92390

ALBERTONI, MARC DOMINIC, certified public accountant; b. Jan. 9, 1955, Santa Maria; s. Ottorino and Felicita (Invernizzi) A.; edn: AA, Allan Hancock Coll. 1975; BS, Calif. State Polytechnic Univ., S.L.O. 1977; lic. CPA, Calif. 1984. Career: acct. Asmussen, Leighton & Carter CPAs, San Rafael 1977-79; asst. audit mgr. So. Pacific Transportation Co., San Francisco 1979-84; asst. controller Western Communications Inc., Walnut Creek 1984–; mem: AICPA, Calif. Soc. CPAs; Catholic; rec: motorcycling, auto mechanics. Res: 2738 Oak Rd. #134 Walnut Creek 94596 Ofc: Western Communications Inc., 2855 Mitchell Dr. Ste. 210 Walnut Creek 94598

ALBRIGHTH, HEATHER AUN, business counselor; b. Jan. 5, 1939, Auburn; d. John Author (Jackson A. Hall) and Lilly Irene (Terry) Hall; m. Gene Elliot, June 5, 1954; children: Deleanna b. 1955, Janie b. 1957, Catrinia b. 1960, Rochelle b. 1961, GiGi b. 1963, Joe b. 1964, Corrine b. 1964; edn: American River Coll. 1976; BS, Sierra Coll. 1977; AA, Yuba Coll. 1983; desig: creative analyst, M. Lee (1980). Career: nurse aide 1953-76; apts. rental clerk 1979-81; employee State Bd. of Edn. 1981-82; physic counselor, owner, mgr. Idea's Unlimited, Clearlake 1982–; awards: State Merit Award, State Bd. of Edn. 1982; mem: State Woman's Club (1st v.p. 1981-82), Calif. Bus. Woman's Club, Clearlake Grange, Optimists, Boy and Girl Scouts of Am. (Girl Scout leader 1976, Cub Scout leader 1975, Brownie leader 1974); works: Portable Camper Steps, 1985; Don't Cry Now, Cry Tomorrow, 1982; Don't Make Me Grow Up, 1983; You Too Can Use Healing Hands, 1985; Democrat; Baptist; rec: reading cards, flying, sewing. Address: Clear Lake 95422

ALDERMAN, ROBERT FRANK, civil engineer; b. Aug. 1, 1932, Los Angeles; s. Frank Edward and Frances Louise (Adams) A.; m. Eunice Alderman, Sept. 11, 1953; children: Jeffrey b. 1955, Karen b. 1957; edn: BSCE, Stanford Univ. 1954; Reg. Profl. Civil Engr., Calif. 1958. Career: engring. aide Calif. Div. of Highways, Los Angeles 1950-53; laborer Renz Constrn., Sant Clara 1954; design engr. Alderman & Swift, So. Pasadena 1955-58; asst. water supt. City of Alhambra, Alhambra 1958-64; project engr. Toups Engineering, Santa Ana 1964-66; v.p. Willdan Associates, Anaheim 1966-79; dir. of engring. San Luis Engring. Inc., Arroyo Grande 1979–; instr. math and hydraulics Santa Ana Coll. 1970-79; instr. water and waste water treatment Allen Hancock Coll. Santa Maria 1980-83; honors: Award of Merit, Inst. of Transportation Engrs. 1978; mem: Am. Soc. of Civil Engrs. (br. pres. 1983-85), Am. Public Works Assn., Pub. Rels. Com., Inst. of Transportation Engrs, Am. Water Works Assn., Temple City Toastmasters (past pres. 1962); Republican; Nazarene; rec: golf, travel, photog. Res: 6080 Joan Pl. San Luis Obispo 93401 Ofc: San Luis Engineering Inc., P.O. Box 1127 Arroyo Grande 93420

ALDERSON, GERALD ROBERT, energy co. president; b. Aug. 28, 1946, San Jose; s. Raymond Charles and Phyllis Laverne (Boston) A.; m. Gail Bradbury, Aug. 24, 1970; children: Alison b. 1974, Anne b. 1976, Katie b. 1978, Kory b. 1981; edn: BS, Occidental Coll. 1968; MBA, Harvard Bus. Sch. 1970. Career: staff acct. Arthur Andersen & Co., San Francisco 1970-71; dir. acctg. Itel Corp., S.F. 1972-74; controller 1974-75, v.p./controller 1975-76, v.p. Planning and Control 1976-78, pres. Lease Fin. Div. Itel 1978-80; pres./CEO U.S. Windpower, Inc. 1981–; dir: World Airways (1985-), Genstar Container Corp. (1981-), RMR Corp. (1981-), U.S. Windpower Inc., Energy Fin. Corp. (1981-), KSTS-TV (1984-); mem. Finl. Execs. Inst., Harvard Bus. Sch. Alumni Assn., Phi Gamma Delta frat., Bankers Club; Republican. Res: 152 Valley Hill Moraga 94556 Ofc: U.S. Windpower Inc. 500 Sansome St Ste 600 San Francisco 94111

ALDRICH, DAVID LAWRENCE, public relations executive; b. Feb. 21, 1948, Lakehurst N.A.S., NJ; s. Clarence Edward and Sarah Stiles (Andrews) A., Jr., LCDR, USN (ret.); m. Benita Massler, Mar. 17, 1974; edn: Ocean Co. Coll., NJ 1967-8, Sophia Univ., Tokyo 1970-1, CSU Dominguez Hills 1976. Career: reporter/columnist Ocean Co. Daily Observer, NJ 1967-68; asst. public information, City of Commerce, Ca. 1974-77; pub. rels. mgr./adminstv. asst. Calif. Federal Svgs, Los Angeles 1977-78; v.p./group supr. Hill & Knowlton, L.A. 1978-81; v.p./mgr. W. Div., Ayer Public Relations, N. W. Ayer, L.A. 1981-84;

pres. Aldrich & Assocs., Public Relations Counsel, 1984–; mem. L.A. Athletic Club. Mil: s/sgt USAF 1968-72. Democrat. rec: travel, drum & bugle corps competitions, fresh water fishing. Res: 666 E Ocean Blvd Penthouse A Long Beach 90802 Ofc: Aldrich & Assocs., 110 Pine Ave Ste 510 Long Beach 90802

ALEKSICH, STEVEN, engineer; b. Apr. 7, 1920, Peoria, Ill.; s. Zivan and Matilda (Boda) A.; edn: BSME, Bradley Univ. 1955; Reg. Profl. Engr., Calif. Career: airframe design engr./ standards engr., North Am. Aviation Inc., Downey 1955-60; mem. tech. staff Apollo/Saturn, Rockwell Corp. 1960-68; components engr. Lockheed Aircraft, Burbank 1968-70; components engr. Litton Systems, Inc. Van Nuys/ Woodland Hills 1970-73; mem. tech. staff, project engr. Space Shuttle, Rockwell Internat., Downey 1974-75; standards engr. Kirk Mayer Inc. (job shop) TRW, Redondo Beach 1975-76; senior prodn. design engr. Northrop Corp., Hawthorne 1976–; mem. US Marine Raider Assn. Inc. (v.p. bd. dirs.); mil: USMC 1942-45; Eastern Orthodox; rec: design, make and play tamburas (stringed musical instruments of Serbian origin similar to mandolins and guitars). Res: 8227 Arrington Ave Pico Rivera 90660 Ofc: Northrop Corp. One Northrop Ave Hawthorne 90250

ALEXANDER, BRUCE B., contractor; b. Feb. 28, 1949, Jacksonville, Fla.; s. Richard Hillard and Helen Severance (Space) A.; m. Stephania Sue Evans, Sept. 2, 1972; children: Mary Elizbeth b. 1979, Erin Leigh b. 1981; edn: BA in mktg., Georgia St. Univ. 1974; Calif. lic. contr. Career: ops., First Nta. Bank Atlanta 1968-72; regl. mgr. Nt. Service Corp. 1972-78; gen. mgr. AAA Approved Plumbing & Heating 1978-81; owner/pres. Neighborhood Services Inc. 1981–; dir. Whittier Village Childrens Ctr. 1982-; mem. Nat. Assn. of Plbg., Htg. & Air Condtg. Contrs.; works: designed a computer system (to be marketed to contrs. within his industry nat.); gives seminars in field at nat. convs.; subject of articles in Contractor Mag., Plumbing & Mechanical Mag.; blt. co. into largest service contr. in Calif. for home plbg., htg. and air condtg. (1981-); mil: USNR-R 1968-74; Republican; Methodist (edn., fin. coms.); rec: skiing, sailing, bridge. Res: 172 Reposado Dr La Habra Heights 90631 Ofc: 17420 S Broadway Ave Gardena 90631

ALEXANDER, JOHN DAVID, college president; b. Oct. 18, 1932, Springfield, Tenn.; m. Catharine Coleman, 1956; children: Kitty, John, Julia; edn: BS, Southwestern at Memphis, 1953; postgrad., Louisville Presbyterian Theol. Sem. 1953-54; PhD, Oxford Univ. 1957; LLD (hon.), USC 1970, Occidental Coll. 1970, Centre Coll. of Kentucky 1971. Career: instr., asst. prof., assoc. prof. Old Testament, San Francisco Theol. Sem. 1957-65; pres. Southwestern at Memphis 1965-69; pres. Pomona Coll., Claremont 1969–; Am. Sec. Rhodes Scholarship Trust 1981-; bd. dirs., Am. Council on Edn. 1981-; Nat. Commn. on Acad. Tenure 1971-72, Panel of Gen. Profl. Edn. of the Physician, Assn. Am. Med. Colls. 1982-; trustee, Tchrs. Ins. and Annuity Assn. 1970-; Woodrow Wilson Nat. Fellowship Found. 1978-, Webb Sch., Claremont 1970-72; dir. Great Western Fin. Corp. 1973-, British Inst. 1979-, Community Supported TV So. Calif., KCET, Inc. 1979-; bd. dirs., Louisville Presbyterian Theol. Sem. 1966-69; honors: Rhodes Scholar, Christ Ch. Coll., Oxford Univ. 1954; mem: Assn. Am. Colls. (commn. on liberal lng. 1967-69, chmn. commn. on instl. affairs 1970-73); So. Assn. Colls. and Schs. (exec. council of commn. on colls. 1969); Am. Council on Edn. (dir. 1981-); Am. Oriental Soc.; Soc. Bible Lit.; Soc. for Religion in Higher Edn.; Los Angeles CofC (dir. 1972-73); Phi Beta Kappa; Phi Beta Kappa Alumni So. Calif. (pres. Alpha Assn. 1974-76); Omicron Delta Kappa; Bohemian (San Francisco); Century Assn., NYC; Zamorano. Ofc: Pomona College, 333 College Way, Claremont 91711

ALEXANDER, ROBERT EUGENE, investment co. president; b. June 25, 1922, Indianapolis, Ind.; s. Claude Phillip and Helen Nova (Cory) A.; m. Virginia, Feb. 7, 1943; children: Michael Eugene, Rebecca Rae; edn: PhD in nutrition, Drs. Univ. 1983; desig: gen. security rep., NASD 1970. Career: auto svc., Bobs Service, Rialto 1945; state mgr. Sterling Life/Ozark Nat., 1968-78; stockbroker Fin. Service Corp. div. ICH, 1970-78; (current): founder/bd. chmn. Robert E. Alexander & Assocs. (ins., finl. investment plnng.), Alexander Financial Services Corp. (pensions, inv. svcs.), 1979–, Drs. Univ. Preventive Health Clinics Internat. Inc., 1981–, All American Investments, Inc.; seminar speaker; cons. 700 Club (CBN-TV network); dir. AFS Corp., Clinic 21, All Am. Inv. Corp.; advisor Bicentennial Constn. of USA 1986-87; civic: CBMC (secty.), Lions Club, Pearl Harbor Survivor Assn., Disabled Am. Vets, San Bernardino CofC, VFW, Amputees Are Able Inc., Gideons, Elks, 700 Club, PTL Club; publs: Alexander Fin. Services Newsletter, Multi-Level Mktg. Tapes, tchr. Investment Diamonds - Sales & Resales (1979-); mil: quartermaster US Navy 1940-45, Pearl Harbor survivor; Republican (Ronald Reagan team); Assembly of God; rec: classic autors, golf, track, charitable fundraising. Ofc: All American Inv. Corp. 2015 North D St San Bernardino 92405

ALEXANDER, ROBERT JOHN, insurance agcy. president; b. June 30, 1945, Pittsfield, Mass.; s. Robert Fischer and Eleanor R. (Behan) A.; 1 son: Robert F. III, b. 1974; edn: BA, Regis Coll., Denver 1968. Career: National Adjusters, Inc. 1970; with Conneticut Gen. Life Ins. Co. 1970-80; nat. acct. sys. 1970-72; brokerage acct. exec. 1972-80; pres. RJA & Assocs., Inc., Beverly Hills 1980–; mem: Bldg. Ind. Assn.; Los Angeles Life Underwriters Assn.; Million Dollar Round Table; Beverly Hills Estate Plng. Council; mil: E-5, US Army, M.P. 1968-70; rec: skiing, running, golf. Res: 529 Rodeo Dr Beverly Hills 90212 Ofc: RJA & Assocs., 9465 Wilshire Blvd, Ste 511, Beverly Hills 90212

ALEXANDER, THOMAS LEY, university executive, teacher, writer; b. Oct. 20, 1908, Plant City, Fla.; s. Thomas Ferdinand and Mamie Estelle (Ley) A.; m. Laura Lenora Thrower ; children: Laura b. 1936, Joan b. 1938, Penny b. 1945; edn: AB, Univ. of Florida 1931; Columbia Univ. 1932; MA, Duke Univ. 1935; Princeton Univ. 1942; Stanford Univ. 1943; PhD, American Univ. 1965; Univ. Tchg. Cert., Calif. Career: sch. supt., Fla. 1933-42; Fgn. Service US State Dept. Australia, Egypt, Germany 1950-60; ICS research dir. State Dept., Wash. DC 1960-65; dir. public affairs Cape Cod Coll., evaluator Spl. County Pgms., fed. funding for univ. pgms., Boston and Hyannis, Mass. 1965-72; instr. politics Saddleback Community Coll. 1972–; past pres. Laguna Greenbelt 1978-83; chair City of Laguna Beach Economic Com. 1979-82; honor: Certs. of Svc., Orange Co. Bar Assn. (1977), Innerwheel of Orange Co. (1986); contbr. articles and photography, Nature Mag., Life, 1940-60; mil: comdr. USNR 1941-62, WWII; Democrat; Protestant; rec: writing, music, photog. Res: 2285 Temple Hill Dr. Laguna Beach 92651

ALF, EDWARD ALFRED, engineer, consultant, entrepreneur; b. Oct. 17, 1930, Great Falls, Mont.; s. Alfred I. and Ruth J. (Walker) A.; m. Marianne R., May 6, 1961; 1 dau. Lee Joanne b. 1962; edn: Montana Sch. of Mines 1948-49; Montana St. Univ. 1952-55. Career: section chief Air Resources Lab., Las Vegas 1960-69; staff engr., div. mgr. Holmes & Narver Inc., Las Vegas 1969072; chief engr. Bureau of Communications, City of Portland, Ore. 1972-76; cons. prin. 1976-77; engr./ cons. Fluor Engrs. Inc. 1977–; honors: Mt. Alf named in his honor (1961, approved US Bd. on Geographic Names); mem. Radio Club of Am, Internat. Platform Assn.; mil: s/sgt. US Air Force 1951-52; Republican; Episcopal; rec: woodworking, fishing; Res: 400 S Flower, No. 84, Orange 92668 Ofc: Fluor Engineers Inc. 3333 Michelson Dr Irvine 92730

ALI, MIR MURTUZA, physician; b. Nov. 16, 1944, Hyderabad, India, nat. US cit. 1983; s. Mir Hafiz and Shah Jahan (Begum) A.; m. Fouzia, Mar. 29, 1974; children: Wasif b. 1975, Shazia b. 1980, Rubina b. 1983; edn: Pre Univ. Course, Sci. Coll. Saifabad Osmania Univ. 1961; MBBS, Kakatiya Med. Coll. Osmania Univ. India 1968. Career: rotating intern Osmania Gen. Hosp. 1968-69; pediat. resident Inst. Child Health Hyderabad, India 1969, internal med. Osmania Gen. Hosp. 1969-70, internal med., geriatrics Bury Gen. Hosp. England 1970-71, int. med. 1971-72, int. med. chest diseases 1972-77; staff phys. psychiatry Moose Lake (Minn.) State Hosp. 1977-78; phys. int. med. VA Med. Ctr. Dayton, Ohio 1978-81, chief res. 1981; pvt. practice int. med. Bucyrus, Ohio 1981-84, Anaheim, Calif. 1984–; faculty Wright State Univ. Dayton 1978-81; honors: Distinction (IMBBS exam); mem: Am. Coll. Phys., Ohio Med. Assn., Crawford County Med. Soc., Islamic Med. Assn., Islamic Soc. of No. Am.; publs: tech. articles in med. jours.; Islam; rec: photog. Ofc: Anaheim Family Practice Assocs. 201 E Palais Rd Anaheim 92805

ALIYAR, V.P., cardiologist; b. Jan. 3, 1950, Erattupetta, Kerala, India; d. V.K. and M.K. (Haleema) Pareed; m. Anu Aliyar, Nov. 25, 1973; children: Anju b. 1975; Alina b. 1980; edn: PDC, St. Georges Coll., Univ. of Kerala 1967; MBBS, Kottayam Med. Coll., Univ. of Kerala 1972; Diplomate Am. Board of Internal Medicine, Diplomate ABIM Cardiovascular Diseases. Career: practiced medicine in India 1972-76; 1-yr internship, 3-yr residency, 2-yr cardiology fellowship tng. in Univ. Mich. affiliated hosps.; internist and cardiologist, West Covina currently, att. Queen of the Valley Hosp., InterCommunity Hosp.; Fellow Am. Coll. of Cardiology; mil: capt. Med. Corps USAR; rec: photog., travel. Res: 2700 Allman Covina 91724 Ofc: 906 S Sunset West Covina 91790

ALKHASEH, LADIMER, engineer; b. May 1, 1958, Hamedan, Iran; s. Luther and Margreat (Ebrahimzaya) A.; edn: BS civ. engrg., Calif. State Polytechnic Univ. Pomona 1980, Masters Engrg., 1981, candidate MBA, 1980-; registered civil engr. Calif., Ariz. 1983. Career: design & prof. engr. Cygna Consulting Engineers Marina del Rey 1980-83; pres. Gershfeld/Alkhaseh Engineers 1983–; staff Calif. State Polytechnic Univ. civil engrg. dept.; honors: National Dean's List 1980, Phi Kappa Phi 1979, Chi Epsilon 1980, Tau Beta Pi 1978; mem: Structural Engrg. Assn. So. Calif., Internat. Conf. of Building Officials, People & Govt. Org.; Christian; rec: tennis, swimming, waterskiing. Res: 2457 Santa Rosa Ct Upland 91786 Ofc: Gershfeld/Alkhaseh Engineers 320 West G St, Ste 104, Ontario 91762

ALLAHYARI, ALBERT FARIBORZ, real estate broker; b. Mar. 27, 1936, Kashan, Iran, nat. US cit. 1969; s. Amonallah and Malektaje F. (Sheibani) A.; m. Carol, Jan. 11, 1966; children: Shireen Elise b. 1968, Jenine Malek b. 1970, Amon Albert b. 1974; edn: Fresno City Coll. 1960-62, bus. admin. Lincoln Univ. 1965, Anthony Sch. of Real Estate 1978; Calif. lic. real estate broker 1978. Career: teller Golden Gate Nat. Bank; real estate agt. Sins & Goodwin R.E. Co.; owner/pres. Allahyari & Assocs., real estate brokerage, 1978–; civic: Masons, Lions Club, Big Brothers (Yolo Co. advis. bd.); Republican; Catholic; rec: golf, chess, hiking. Res: Rt 1 Box 340 Esparto 95627 Ofc: Allahyari & Assocs. 828 Esparto Ave Esparto 95627

ALLARA, DARRYL WAYNE RODGERS, theatrical consultant/ administrator; b. Apr. 1, 1946, Plainfield, N.J.; s. John and Beatrice A.; edn: BA cum laude US Internat. Sch. of Perf. Arts 1973; M.Arts, Univ. Ariz. 1974. Career: box office mgr. San Diego Civic Theatre, San Diego 1974-75; box office mgr./ house coord. US Army Bicentennial Project at the John F. Kennedy Center, Wash DC 1976; box office/company mgr. Lindy Opera House, Los Angeles 1977; bus. rep. Am. Guild of Variety Artists 1977; theatre adminstr. Actors' Equity Assn. 1977-80; cofounder/v.p. adminstrn. First Impressions Theatrical Services Co., Los Angeles 1979–; employment cons. Am. Theatre Assn.; resume & mktg. splst. to entertainment industry; honors: past Nat. Student Rep. to Army Theatre Arts Assn., distinguished achieve. award Am. Theatre Assn./ Army Theatre Arts Div., Melvin R. White Scholarship, nominee Forbes Pub. Co. Business in the Arts Awards (twice); mem: Am. Theatre Assn., Army Theatre Arts Assn., Hollywood CofC; coauthor mystery play "A Medal for Murder" (1981), musical mystery about the late Sarah Winchester "Sarah" (1986), publ: You May Never Get A Second Chance to Make a First Impression (1980); mil: sp5 US Army 1967-69, Army Commendn. (2), Good Conduct, Award of Merit, Merit. Unit Cit., Vietnam Service medals; rec: build Stained Glass Windows. Ofc: 6607 Sunset Blvd West Wing Hollywood 90028

ALLARD, EDWARD TIERNAN, III, quality control/productivity, management/marketing consultant and fundraising; b. Aug. 3, 1945, Moulton, Ala.; s. Edward T., Jr. and Mary Elizabeth (Terry) A.; m. Lucille Roybal, Apr. 4, 1981; children: Lisa b. 1967, Ricardo b. 1969, Angelia b. 1970, Guy-Mark b. 1976; edn: MBA, Univ. of Miami. Career: served pvt. to capt. US Marine Corps, 1963-73, decorated Navy Commendn. with Battle Valor, Vietnam, USMC Section, electronics engrg. analog/ digital computers, air traffic control ofcr., air strike control ofcr., H&HS tng. ofcr.; emcee local weekly TV show WQAD-TV 3 yrs.; intern, sr. cons., dir. of mktg. United Way of Am., 1973-83; v.p. mktg./member rels., Los Angeles Area CofC, 1984-85; pres., Professional Consultant Group and Consultant Services of America, Pasadena 1985–; v.p. Deming Method Consulting Group, N. Miami Beach, Fla. 1986–, cons. on productivity & quality improvement; cons. govt. agcys. and pvt. orgns. on mgmt., mktg., quality, 1970s-; honors: mem. USMC Generals Honor Roll and mem. USMC Shooting Team; mem. Am. Mgmt. Assn., Am. Mktg. Assn., Sales & Mktg. Execs. Assn.; civic: Hospice of Pasadena (bd. dirs.); Baptist; rec: learning/improvement. Address: Pasadena 91107

ALLEN, ELAINE HANDSMAN, public relations executive; b. July 28, 1939, Bklyn.; d. Philip Lerner and Beatrice (Goodman) Handsman; m. Robert Milton John Allen (lcdr USN, ret.), May 6, 1967; children: Erica Wendy b. 1968, Meredith Julie b. 1969, Price Philip b. 1973, Seth Andrew b. 1973; edn: AB in Am. studies/journ., Syracuse Univ. 1960; MSW, Adelphi Grad. Sch. Social Work 1964; USN Woman's Ofcr. Sch., Newport R.I. 1965; US Naval War Coll. certs: Def. Econs. & Decision Making 1985/6, Strategy and Tactics 1986/7; cert. social wkr. NY (1964). Career: public rels. Gal Friday, NYC 1960; intake casewkr. Dept. Child Welfare, Co. of Westchester 1964-65; served ensign to ltjg US Navy 1965-67: public info. ofcr. (1st woman to hold pos. in San Diego) Naval Tng. Center, San Diego, pub. info. ofcr. and instr. in counter-insurgency/socio-political subjects Naval Amphibious Sch., Coronado; discharged USN 1967, decorated Navy Achieve., Nat. Def. medals; lcdr. US Naval Reserve 1975–, pub. affairs ofcr. Naval Reserve Center, S.D. 1977-81, adminstrv. ofcr. Naval Reserve Audiovisual Command 0194 1982-84, pub. affairs ofcr./asst. adminstrv. ofcr. Naval Reserve Anti-Submarine Warfare Wing, Pacific 0194, Naval Air Reserve, S.D. 1984-86, adminstrv. ofcr. Naval Reserve Ofc. of Info., Det. 310, Houston 8/86; civilian career: pres. Big Red Bow Inc. (gift shops chain) 1979-82; v.p./dir. Gifts & Things Inc. (11 gift shops chain) 1982-85; currently pres. Pomp & Circumstance (PR and ceremony cons.); pres./dir. Velvet Hammer Inc. 1973–; honors: selected USN Chief of Information Merit Award Judge (10/85), Junior Ofcr. of Year, S.D. Chpt. Naval Reserve Assn. and So. Calif. Dist. nominee for Nat. Jr. Ofcr. of Year award (1986), Navy League Woman of Mil. Achievement Award (1977); mem: Naval Reserve Assn. (NRA Nat. Advis. Com. 1979-; Dist. life mem. 1976, chpt. v.p. 1986-87, pub. affairs ofcr. 1977, 86), S.D. Woman's Council Navy League (exec. bd., reserve and recruiting chair 1975-79), Navy League/S.D. Council (exec. bd.), The Naval Order of the U.S. (life 1986-), AAUW, Syracuse Univ. Alumni Assn.; civic: Southwest Jazz Ballet/Houston (1986-), Fort Fisher Sea Cadet Corps (escort and protocol ofcr. 1977-79), Neighborhood Assn. Brown's Valley, Napa (founding pres.), Coronado Schs. Found. (Supt.'s Club), Girl Scouts Am. (1949-), Coronado H.S. Parents Aquatics Booster Club (Pub. Affairs 1985); works: dissertation 'Battered Child Syndrome Rev.' used as source material for PBS spl. (1964), num. news stories and photographs pub. in nat. and regl. civilian and mil. news media, scriptwriter/prod. var. Navy stories for So. Calif. TV, contbg. photojournalist Coronado Journal; rec: finl. mgmt. 12 accts. Res: 543 A Ave Coronado 92118

ALLEN, HOWARD NORMAN, cardiologist; b. Nov. 19, 1936, Chgo.; s. Herman and Ida Gertrude (Weinstein) A.; children: Michael b. 1971, Jeffrey b. 1974; edn: BS, Univ. Ill. Coll. of Med. 1958, MD, 1960; Diplomate Am. Bd. Int. Med. 1968, Cardiovascular Disease 1974. Career: intern L.A. Co. Gen. Hosp. 1960-61; resident int. med. VA Ctr. Wadsworth Gen. Hosp. L.A. 1961, 1964-66; fellow cardiol. Cedars-Sinai Med. Ctr. L.A. 1966-67, St. Georges Hosp. London 1967-68; dir. cardiac care unit Cedars of Lebanon Hosp. div. Cedars-Sinai Med. Ctr. 1968-74, dir. pacemaker eval. ctr. Cedars-Sinai Med. Ctr. 1968–; attg. phys. cardiol. Sepulveda VA Hosp. 1972–; dir. Cardiac Noninvasive Lab. Cedars-Sinai Med. Ctr. 1972–; cons. Sutherland Learning Assoc. Inc. 1970-75; prof. med. UCLA; honors: Alpha Omega Alpha 1959; mem: fellow Am. Coll. Phys., fellow Am. Coll. Cardiol., Am. Heart Assn. (fellow Council Clin. Cardiol., greater L.A. bd. dirs. 1979-, chmn. pgm. com. 1981-83, secy. 1984-85, med. v.p. 1985-86, pres.-elect 1986-); publ: book chaps. and arts. in field of cardiol.; mil: capt. US Army (MC) 1962-63. Ofc: Cedars-Sinai Med. Ctr. 8700 Beverly Blvd Los Angeles 90048

ALLEN, HOWARD PFEIFFER, utilities company chairman and CEO; b. Oct. 7, 1925, Upland, Calif; s. Howard Clinton and Emma Maude (Pfeiffer) A.; edn: BA cum laude, Pomona Coll. 1948; JD, Stanford Univ. Law Sch. 1951; m. Dixie Mae Illa, May 14, 1948; chil: Alisa Cary, b. 1957. Career: asst. dean Law Sch/ asst. prof. law, Stanford Univ. 1951-54; with So Calif Edison Co. 1954–: spl rep. 1954, asst. to v.p. 1955, spl. counsel 1959, v.p. 1962, v.p. and asst. to pres.

1969, sr. v.p. 1971, exec. v.p. 1973-80, pres.1980-84, bd. chmn. and chief exec. ofcr., 1984–; bd. Edison Electric Institute; dir: Southern Calif. Edison, Cal Fed Inc. & Calif Fed Svgs & Loan, Northrop Corp., Kaiser Steel Corp., ICN Pharmaceuticals Inc., PSA Inc. & Pacific Southwest Airlines, Computer Sciences Corp., MCA Inc.; awards: Whitney M. Young, Jr. award, L.A. Urban League; Award of Merit, L.A. Junior CofC, 1982; Resolutions of recognition from State of Calif., County of Los Angeles, City of Los Angeles; mem. The Business Council; bd. Calif. CofC; mem. Pres.'s Panel, Dun's Business Month; mem. Bretton Wood Com.; bd. LA World Affairs Council; v.chmn., founding bd. mem. L.A. Olympic Organizing Com., 1984 Olympics; mem. Mayor's Select Com. for 1984 summer Olympics; dir. LA County Fair Assn.; dir. Calif. Economic Devel. Corp.; bd. trustees Com. for Econ. Devel.; Nat. Protestant co-chmn. and bd. mem. NCCJ; mem. Soc. of Founders, NCCJ; trustee, exec. com. mem. L.A. County Mus. of Art; mem: US Supreme Ct. Bar, Calif. State Bar, Am., Calif., L.A. Co., S.F. Bar Assns., Stanford Law Assn., Am. Judicature Soc.; clubs: California (LA), Jonathan Club, (LA), Los Angeles CC, Bohemian (SF), Pacific Union (SF), O'Donnell Golf (Palm Springs), La Quinta Hotel Golf; Ofc: 2244 Walnut Grove Ave. Rosemead 91770

ALLEN, JEFFREY M., lawyer; b. Dec. 13, 1948, Chgo.; s. Albert A. and Miriam F. (Feldman) Allen; m. Anne Marie, Aug. 9, 1945; children: Jason M., b. 1978, Sara M., b. 1980; edn: AB, UC Berkeley 1970, JD, Boalt Hall Law Sch. 1973; lic. Calif. real estate broker 1977. Career: partner law firm Graves, Allen, Cornelius & Celestre, Oakland 1973–, legal practice spec. in real estate; lectr. in real estate St. Mary's Coll.; pres. M.C. Technologies; dir. num. real estate, investment cos.; mem: Am. Bar Assn. (vice chmn. gen. practice sect. real property com., co-chmn. subcom. on use of computers in real estate transactions), Calif. State Bar Assn., Alameda Co. Bar; Phi Beta Kappa, Oakland Athletic Club, Commonwealth Club, Rotary Internat., PTA; contbr. law revs.; Democrat; rec: computers, photog., skiing. Ofc: Graves, Allen, Cornelius & Celestre, 2101 Webster St Ste 1500 Oakland 94612

ALLEN, JOSEPH CAROTHERS, mining & metallurgical engineer, ret.; b. May 4, 1904, Grand Forks, N.D.; s. Charles and Sara Margaretta (Carothers) A.; m. Clara Stoltze, Oct. 11, 1931 (dec.); m. 2d. Maria Frugone, June 30, 1956; children: Robert b. 1932, Elaine b. 1933, Gloria b. 1958; edn: BS mining engring., Univ. N.D. 1929; Reg. Profl. Engr. (Mining, Metalurg.). Career: exec., Camp dir., Boy Scouts Am., 1922-29; jr. engr. Andes Copper Mining Co., Potrerillos, Chile 1929-32; instr. metallurg./supvr. Denbeigh Gold Investigation, Univ. of N.Dak. 1932-35; mine shift foreman Cerro de Pasco (Peru) Copper Corp. 1935-38; gen. foreman Andes Copper Mining Co., Chile 1938-43; prin. mining engr./div. mgr. (Strategic Minerals Pgm., Board of Econ. Welfare FEA, US Embassy, Rio de Janeiro) Raul Soares, Brazil 1943-45; metallurg. engr., gen. supt., asst. gen. mgr., mgr. Chile Exploration Co. (Anaconda) Chuquicamata, Chile 1945-67, ret.; pvt. consulting, USA and Latin Am., 1967-80; honors: Orden al Merito Bernardo O'Higgins, Govt. of Chile (1965), hon. Dr. of Engring., Univ. of N.Dak. (1967), Legion of Honor, Am. Mining & Metallurg. Engrs. (1978) in recogn. of 50 yrs. service to mining industry; mem: Am. Inst. of Mining, Metallurg. & Petroleum Engrs., Alpha Tau Omega, Masons, Boy Scouts Am. (scoutmaster); sev. publs. in field; Republican; Presbyterian; rec: Boy Scout work, camping, golf. Res: 2873 Chamise Way Hemet 92343

ALLEN, MELANIE, clinical psychologist, educator, writer, consultant; b. Dec. 8, 1939, Mnpls.; d. Samuel David and Francis Marilyn (Fagen) Finkelstein; edn: Univ. of Minn. 1956-58; BA cinema, w/honors, UCLA, 1961; The Sorbonne-Paris, 1963-64; BA psych., CSU Northridge, 1969; PhD psych., USC, 1974. Career: prodn. asst. Ency. Britannica Films 1961-62; Fulbright Fellowship to Inst. de Filmologie, The Sorbonne, 1963-64 and appt. to Bd. of Editors, Rives (Revue des echanges univs.); property dept. hd. and film writer for prod. Norman Lear, Tandem Prodns., Columbia Pictures 1965-67; grad. tchg. fellowship USC 1969-72; NIMH fellowship/intern in clin. pxych. 1972-73, HEW Maternal and Child Care postdoc. fellowship 1973-74, consulting psychologist 1974-79, Children's Hosp. of L.A.; instr. psych. and humanities divs. Art Center Coll. of Design 1973-77; guest lectr. Calif. Inst. of the Arts 1975-76; prof. psych. Antioch Coll./West 1973-79; pvt. practice Clin. Psychology spec. Family Systems, Pediatric Psychol., Sherman Oaks 1974–; asst. prof. CSUN 1974–; tech., creative cons. to film industry; lectr. various univs., hosps., schools, public agencies; mem. bd. of eds. Jour. of Humanistic Psychol. 1980-; dir. grad. tng. pgm in psychol. Ryokan Coll. 1983-. Num. guest appearances on radio and TV; author: Primary: An Intro. to Humanistic Psychology (w/Charlotte Buhler) 1972, Make em Laugh (w/Wm. Fry) 1975; 100+ short stories, poems, arts. Awards: Chimes (acad. hon.), Tau Beta Sigma, Sigma Alpha Iota (music), Psi Chi (psych. frat); Delmar Ickes Awd., CSUN 1969; recognition for theoretical achievements in psychol.; invited to Intl. Invitational Cong. on Humanistic Psychol., Amsterdam 1970, Wurzburg, Ger. 1971, Nat. Endowment for Humanities Conf., Tucson 1975, 1st Internat. Cong. on Humour and Laughter, Wales 1976; rec: music, photog., travel. Res: Sherman Oaks 91403

ALLEN, NANCY LEE (STUCHELL), accountant, financial executive; b. Aug. 8, 1934, McKeesport, Penn.; d. Ernest Melvin and Helen Margaret (Kughn) Stuchell; m. Harold Allen Jr., April 6, 1956; children: Michael b. 1959, Denise b. 1960, Debbie b. 1963, Diane b. 1965; edn: BSBA, CSU Long Beach 1977; MS in taxation, CSU Fullerton 1986; CPA, Cert. Cost Analyst, Cert. Profl. Estimator, Cert. Real Property Appraiser. Career: auditor Defense Contracts Audit Agency, Orange Co. Assessor's Ofc.; v.p. finance WEGA, Placentia; controller Pella Products, Santa Ana; currently, v.p. finance Authentic Wood Windows & Doors, Irvine; bd. dir. WEGA; mem: Am. Inst. CPAs, Assn. of Govt. Accts., Beta Alpha Psi; Republican; Protestant; rec: golf. Ofc: WEGA, 355C West Crowther Placentia 92670

ALLEN, ROBERT CHARLES, transportation/warehousing executive; b. Aug. 26, 1940, Houston, Tx.; s. James Arthur and Myrtle L. (Fisher) A.; m. Vickie, Oct. 21, 1979; children: Dennis b. 1960, James b. 1962, Renda b. 1965, (step) Joshua b. 1977; edn: Chabot Coll. 1966-67. Career: v.p. Jenmar Internat., Los Angeles 1978-82; dispatcher, ops. mgr., gen. mgr. The Myers Group Inc., 1983, dir. 1984, v.p./mgr. Myers Express Forwarding 1985; mng. dir., cons. Warehouse Technology, Commerce 1986–; pres. Pacific Seaboard Dist. Long Beach; mem. Long Beach Police Ofcrs. Assn., Masons; mil: pfc US Army, Good Conduct; Republican; Prot.; rec: numismatics, golf, tennis, treasure hunter. Res: 4722 Phelan Ave Baldwin Park 91706 Ofc: Pacific Seaboard Dist. POB 2649 Long Beach 90802

ALLEN, WILLIAM ELMER, funeral director; b. Nov. 6, 1922, Sherwood, Ore.; s. William E. and Minnie Lou (Walker) A.; m. Irene, June 15, 1944; 1 son, Gary; edn: mortuary sci., Coll. of Mortuary Science 1946. Career: owner, opr. Morticians Embalming Svc., Los Angeles 1946-52; owner, opr. Allen Mortuary, Turlock 1952–; honors: Silver Beaver, Boy Scouts of Am. 1956; Proclamotion, State of Calif. Chmn. of Calif. Vets. Bd.; Proclamation, Correctional Inds. Commn. Chmn.; mem: Am. Red Cross (pres.), Stanislaus Co. Boy Scouts of Am. (pres. 1961, Yosemite Council 1964-66), Calif. Veterans Bd., Correctional Industries Commn., Masons, American Legion, Century Club, Stanislaus State Univ., Stanislaus Co. Red Cross (past pres.), Foreman Stanislaus Co. Grand Jury; political appointee of Calif. Govs. Reagan, Brown, Deukmejian; mil: sgt. US Army Air Corps 1942-45; Democrat; Methodist; rec: politics. Ofc: Allen Mortuary, 237 No. Broadway Turlock 95380

ALLEN, WILLIAM VINCENT, JR., consultant; b. Sept. 27, 1938, Boston, Mass.; s. William Vincent and Isabel Genevive (Perry) A.; children: William b. 1964, Jeanne b. 1965, Joanne b. 1967, Nancy b. 1969; edn: BS, Boston Coll. 1965; CPA, Mass. (1969), Fla. (1973), Calif. (1985). Career: audit senior Peat, Marwick, Mitchell, Boston, Mass. 1965-69; treas. Sterling Inst., Boston, Mass. 1969; audit supvr. Touche Ross, NY, NY 1970-73; audit supvr. Peat, Marwick, Mitchell, Miami, Fla. 1973-74; audit mgr. Spear, Safer, Miami, Fla. 1974-76; pres. Allen & Associates, Irvine 1976–; pres. Mariposa Womens Ctr. 1986-87; lectr. Am. Inst. CPAs 1983-86; audit prof. Univ. of Miami and Fla. Internat. Univ.; spkr. var. convs. and meetings; mem: Am. and Fla. Inst. CPAs, Mass. and Calif. Soc. CPAs, Nat. Assn. Accts., Boston Coll. Club of Fla. (past pres.), Boston Coll. Club of Los Angeles; autor: Guide to Preparation of Financial Statements, 1983; mil: cpl. USMC 1957-61; rec: racquetball, basketball. Res: 35 Bearpaw Apt. 39C Irvine 92714 Ofc: Allen & Associates, P.O. Box 16187 Irvine 2713

ALLER, THOMAS ARTHUR, optometrist, research & development co. president; b. Sept. 16, 1957, East Lansing, Mich.; s. Curtis C. (PhD) and Mary G. (Alldridge) Aller; m. Virginia Low, Pharm.D., Sept. 5, 1982; edn: BA in zool., honors, UC Berkeley 1979, BS in physiological optics, honors, 1981; OD, UCB Sch. Optometry, 1983; lic. OD, Calif. State Bd. Opt. 1983. Career: optometrist in pvt. practice, Concord 1984–; pres./founder Computer-eyes-ed Software Innovations; clin. investigator, Precision Cosmet Co. Inc., 1984; awards: Harold Cohn Mem. Award, Am. Opt. Found. (1983), nominee Nuemueller Award (1983); editor The Eye Opener, Alameda-Contra Costa Counties Opt. Socs. (1984-86), contbg. editor The Optometry Edition (1985-86); Phi Beta Kappa; mem: Am. Opt. Assn., Calif. Opt. Assn., BVI, LVCNC, Rotary, Concord CofC (Diplomats, Edn. coms.); publs: Exerceyes (a software product), and related software in devel.; rec: inventions, classic car restoration, golf. Res: 3720 Boxwood Ct Concord 94519 Ofc: 4180 Treat Blvd Ste B Concord 94518

ALLINGTON, ROGER WALTER, engineering executive; b. July 12, 1933, French Camp, Calif.; s. Walter Morrill and Elsie Irene (Coleman) A.; m. Ruth Ilene Howell, Nov. 10, 1967; children: Laura, Ronald, Katherine, Edie, stepchildren: Brady, Randel, Richard, Terrie Winniford; edn: CSU Fresno 1951-52; Chapman Coll. 1952-53; Fresno City Coll. 1954-64; reg. Profl. Engr. Alaska, Wash., Ore., Calif. Career: rd. div. engr. Ventura County Dept. Pub. Works 1966-69; state traffic engr. Alaska Dept. of Hwys. Juneau 1969-73; land & engrg. ofcr. Sealaska Corp. Juneau 1973-78; chief engr. Alaska Grp. Kramer, Chin & Mays Juneau 1978-81; gen. mgr., c.e.o. Shaan- Seet Inc. Craig, Ak. 1981-82; design stds. engr. Alaska Dept. Transp. Juneau 1982-85; dep. dir. transp. City of Beverly Hills 1985–; assemblyman City and Borough of Juneau 1976-79; co-chair Alaska Coastal Policy Council 1977-79; mem: Am. Soc. Civil Engrs., Nat. Soc. Profl. Engrs., Inst. Transp. Engrs., Illuminating Engrs. Soc., Internat. Right of Way Assn., Am. Pub. Works Assn., Beverly Hills Lions; publ: Alaska Traffic Manual, Alaska Hwy. Preconstrn. Manual - Chpt. 13 Design; Republican; Presbyterian; rec: choral singing, swimming. Res: 330 E Cordova St #205 Pasadena 91101 Ofc: City of Beverly Hills 450 N Crescent Dr Beverly Hills 90210

ALLISON, JOHN THOMAS, management consultant; b. Mar. 11, 1946, Concord, Ca.; s. John Pershing and Mary M. (Reese) A.; m. Sally Rittenhouse, Apr. 4, 1981; children: Anne Marie b. 1968, Joseph b. 1976, Elizabeth b. 1984; edn: BA, UC Berkeley 1976; MA, Antioch Univ. 1976; PhD, The Wright Inst. Grad. Sch of Psych. 1983; PhD, Columbia Pac. Univ. 1983; MFCC, Marriage, Family & Child Counselor, Bd. of Behavioral Sci. Examiners 1982. Career: exec. dir. Petaluma People Services Center, 1976-78; exec. dir. NCCW, Inc. 1978-82; pres. The Firm, Inc. Social Sci. Consultants, 1982-84; Pacific Gas & Elec. Co. 1984–; director, co-founder Swords to Plowshares (Veterans Rights orgn.); faculty CSU Sacramento, Antioch Univ., Columbia Pac. Univ., Golden Gate Univ.; bd. mem. various regional non-profit social svc. orgns.; honors: merit certs., Nev. Co. Bd. of Suprs., 1982, Nev. Co. Community Svcs. Council, 1981. Mem: Assn. of Labor/Mgmt. and Consultants on Alcoholism (AL-MACA), Calif. Assn. of Marriage, Family Therapists, Calif. Assn. of Rehabilitation Facilities; mem. Big Brothers/Big Sisters of Nev. Co., Nev. Co. Arts Council; profl. papers, publs.; mil: capt. USMC 1965-70; Democrat; rec: distance running, gardening. Res: 1692 Oak Way Chico 95926 Ofc: PG&E 350 Salem St Chico 95926

ALLISON, LAIRD BURL, professor emeritus of management; b. Nov. 7, 1917, Saint Marys, W. Va.; s. Joseph Alexander and Opal Marie (Robinson) A.; m. Katherine Hunt, Nov. 25, 1943; 1 son, William, b. 1945; m. 2d. Genevieve Elmore, Feb. 1, 1957; edn: BS in personnel and indsl. rels., magna cum laude, USC 1956; MBA, UCLA 1958. Career: lectr., asst./assoc./ prof. of mgmt., CSU Los Angeles 1956-83, asst. dean undergrad. studies, Sch. of Business and Econ. 1971-73, and assoc. dean ops., 1973-83; prof. emeritus of mgmt., CSULA; vis. asst. prof. of mgmt. CSU, Fullerton (summer 1970). Honors: Phi Kappa Phi, Beta Gamma Sigma, Omicron Delta Epsilon, Phi Eta Sigma hon. socs.; Ford Found. Faculty Fellowship Awd. 1960. Mem: Acad. of Mgmt.; Alpha Kappa Psi Profl. Bus. Frat.; Am. Assn. of Individual Investors; The Inst. of Mgmt. Scis. (TIMS); Western Econ. Assn. Internat.; World Future Soc.; orgns: Faculty Emeriti Assn., CSULA; Ret. Public Employees Assn. of Calif.; USS Astoria Assn. Collaborated in devel. new BSc degree program in Mgmt. Sci. (1963), CSULA. Mil: chief interior communications electrician, USN, 1936-51, medals: Am. Def., Am. Theatre Campaign., Asia-Pac. Theatre Cmpgn., WWII Victory, GCM; battles: Coral Sea, Midway, Guadalcanal, Savo.; survivor of sinking of USS Astoria (CA 34) in Battle of Savo. Rec: history, travel, photog., hiking. Res: 1615 So El Molino St Alhambra 91801

ALLISON, MARVIN LAWRENCE, journalist; b. Aug. 8, 1934, Phoenix, Ariz.; s. George Lewis and Dorothy A. (Kinsella) A.; m. Patricia Ann Kiley, Apr. 2, 1954; 1 son, Marvin L., b. 1955; edn: Neiman fellow, Harvard Univ. 1968-69; Sorbonne, Paris 1952-53; stu. Long Beach St. Coll. 1953-54. Career: reporter Downey (Calif.) Live Wire, 1955-57; copy editor Long Beach Independent, also Press-Telegram, 1957-62; reporter 1963-66; copy editor Stars & Stripes newspaper, Darmstadt, Germany 1962; city editor Ind. Press-Telegram, Long Beach, 1966-68, mng. editor, 1969-76; asst. to pub. Lexington (Ky.) Herald-Leader, 1976-77; assoc. editor Detroit (Mich.) Free Press 1977-78; senior vice pres./editor Long Beach (Calif.) Ind. Press-Telegram, 1978 – ; mem: AP Mng. Editors Assn. (dir.), Am. Soc. of Newspaper Editors (com. chmn.); mem. Sigma Delta Chi Club- Harvard (L.A.). Res: POB 201, Surfside 90743 Ofc: Long Beach Press-Telegram, 604 Pine Ave Long Beach 90844

ALLISON-HATCH, TIMOTHY WHITING, secondary school administrator, educator; b. July 22, 1948, Minneapolis; s. Francis W. and Augustine Pardee (Shaw) Butler; m. Susan Allison, July 10, 1981; edn: BA, Occidental Coll. 1971; MA in tchg., Northwestern Univ. 1978; M.Ed., UC Los Angeles 1984; Calif. Sec. School Administrative Credential (1984). Career: tchr. (chair hist. dept.) Kabala Sec. Sch., Sierra Leone, W. Africa 1974-77; tchr. (soc. studies dept. chair) Mayfield Senior Sch., Pasadena 1978-83; academic dean (acting) San Domenico Sch., San Anselmo 1984-85, dean of faculty 1985 – ; awards: Coe Fellow, Inst. of Am. Studies, Oyster Bay, NY (1980), United Presbyn. Ch. Junior Year Abroad Scholar, Univ. of Ghana (1969-70); mem. Western Assn. of Schools and Colls. (school accreditation teams 1985-86), Calif. Assn. of Independent Schs. (acad. services com. 1980-82), Nat. Council for the Social Studies (1978-83), Marin Cyclists; Democrat; Mennonite; rec: bicycling, reading. Res: 47 A Fair Oaks St San Francisco 94110 Ofc: San Domenico Sch 1500 Butterfield Rd San Anselmo 94960

ALLMETT, JOHN RAYMOND, business owner; b. Aug. 25, 1942, Los Angeles; s. Raymond Daniel and Gladys DeEtte (Walker) A.; m. Caroline Geiger, Apr. 25, 1981; edn: grad. So. Lake Tahoe H.S. 1960; voc. tchg. credentials, Nev. State. Career: patrolman to undersheriff Douglas County (Nev.) Sheriff's Dept., 1965-75, ret. (disabled by Multiple Sclerosis); worked p.t. Nevada State Crime Commn.; taught photog. and fingerprints to police agencies throughout Nevada; founder/owner (with wife also disabled by MS disease) Allmett's Fine Jewelry, Gardena 1982 – ; mem. nat. Jewelry Bd. of Trade, Gardena Valley CofC, Moose Lodge; Republican; Roman Catholic; rec: people, photog., jewelry. Res: 15115 S Vermont Gardena 90247 Ofc: Allmett's Fine Jewelry POB 3126 Gardena 90247

ALPETER, V. RAY, human resource management consultant; b. Apr. 8, 1932, Dover, Ohio; s. Franklin Burnett and Clara (Harding) A.; edn: BS in bus. adm., Univ. Ore. 1953. Career: data adminstrn. TWA, Los Angeles 1953-55; personnel adminstrn. McDonnell Douglas 1955-69; indep. consultant 1969-77; owner/pres. R & A Consulting Services, Ltd. 1977 – ; instr. Mich. State Univ. (1983-85), Am. Mgmt. Assn. (1974-85); advisor Am. Payroll Assn. (1981-), mem. US Senate Advisory Council (1981-); honors: Silver Snoopy Award, NASA (1969), Photographer's Award (1981), Aviation Hall of Fame (hon. mem.), National Geographic (hon. mem.); mem. Am. Mgmt. Assn., Profl. Consultants of Am.; clubs: Windjammers Yacht, U.S. Yacht Racing Union, Single Sailors of Am.; author 2 books: Developing a Human Resource Mgmt. Information System; The Payroll Administor; articles in profl. jours.; num. pub. photos; rec: sailing, photog. Address: Los Angeles 90066

ALTES, OTTO GEORGE, realtor; b. May 31, 1902, Mingo, Iowa; s. George and Henrietta (Schreiner) A.; m. Arletta Craig. June 6, 1933; children: Wesley Craig b. 1935, Robert George b. 1937. Career: farmer; owner Gamble Store

Chatfield, Minn. 1936-47; real estate sales Santa Rosa 1948, life, fire ins. sales 1949, broker 1950 – ; honors: Director Award of Appreciation (Sonoma County Multiple Listing Svc. 1968); mem: Sonoma Co. Bd. Realtors, Sonoma Co. Multiple Listing Svc. 1951-, Knights of Pithias, The Dukes; Republican; Methodist; rec: gardening, church activities. Address: 1943 Montgomery Dr Santa Rosa 95405

ALTMAN, MARTIN M., lawyer; b. Feb. 28, 1926, Chgo., Ill.; s. William K. and Celia (Wogman) A.; 1 son, Daniel P. b. 1959; edn: BS in bus. adm., USC 1952; JD, honors, Univ. San Fernando 1973; cert. govt. contract mgmt., UCLA; postgrad. work in psych., Los Angeles Univ.; admitted Calif. State Bar, US Dist. Ct. (1974). Career: atty./assoc. Hindin, McKay, Levine & Glick, Beverly Hills 1974, Fishman & George, 1975, George Fracasse, 1976, Samuel De Lugg, 1977, Joseph L. Drociak 1978; govt. contract mgmt., Lockheed and McDonnell Douglas; atty. pvt. practice, Marina Del Rey current; arbitrator: L.A. Superior Ct., Santa Monica Municipal Ct., Am. Arb. Assn.; judge pro tem Santa Monica Muni. Ct.; honors: Dean's List, Law Rev. (1973); mem: Am. Bar Assn., Calif. State Bar, Santa Monica Bar Assn., Calif. Trial Lawyers Assn., LA County Bar Assn., S.W. Bar Assn., Lawyers Club; civic: Nat. Contract Mgmt. Assn., VFW, Ida M. Cummings Aux.- Home for the Aged, US Nat. Champion- Helms Hall of Fame, Van Nuys CofC, Masons; mil: US Air Force 1944-47; Democrat; rec: sail, scuba, tennis. Ofc: Martin M. Altman, Esq. 13226 Admiral Ave Ste C Marina Del Rey 90292

ALTMAN, ROBERT T., judge; b. Aug. 2, 1939, Bklyn.; s. Leon S. and Lillian (Tiktin) A.; m. Caroline, Aug. 22, 1965; children: Catherine b. 1972, Susan b. 1977; edn: AB, UC Los Angeles 1961; JD, Harvard Law Sch. 1964; admitted Calif. State Bar 1964. Career: atty. law firm Loeb & Loeb, 1964-69; deputy dist. atty. Los Angeles County, 1969-80; apptd. judge Superior Court, L.A. County 1980 – ; tchg. Calif. Judicial Coll., Pepperdine Law Sch.; lectr. to num. profl. orgns.; honors: Phi Beta Kappa; mem. Calif. Judges Assn., City of Hope; rec: tennis, golf, jogging. Ofc: Los Angeles Superior Court 111 North Hill St Los Angeles 90012

ALVAREZ, JOHN, real estate broker; b. Dec. 24, 1921, Mexico; s. Jose and Eulalia (Mendoza) A.; m. Carmen Garcia (dec. 1980), June 14, 1953; children: Elza b. 1954, David b. 1956, Sylvia b. 1958, Elizabeth b. 1965. Career: pres: Monterey Realty Co., Monterey Constrn. Co., Eastern Group Publications Inc.; dir. Pan Am. Bank of Los Angeles; pres. Carmen Alvarez Cancer Fund, Inc.; mem: 3rd v.chmn. E. L.A. Multiple Listing Svc.; 2nd v.p. Montebello Realty Bd.; Community Brokers Svc.; Gr. L.A. CofC; Internat. Assn. R.E. Counselors, Inc.; Mutual Selling Svc. of Montebello; Monterey Park chpt. City of Hope (life); L.A. Police Band Assoc., Inc.; L.A. Olympic Citizens Adv. Com.; Democrat; Catholic; rec: golf. Res: 1036 Crest Vista Dr Monterey Park 91754 Ofc: Monterey Realty Co., 5833 E Beverly Blvd Los Angeles 90002

ALVAREZ, JOSE E., elected city official, real estate broker, educator; b. Jan. 3, 1924, Aguacate, Havana, Cuba, nat. US cit. 1967; s. Jose Emilio and Luisa Maria (Clara) A.; m. Rosie Jones, June 14, 1959; edn: A. Bible Lit., Baptist Bible Inst., Graceville, Fla. 1957; BA, Calif. Baptist Coll. Riverside 1959; B.Div., M.Div., Golden Gate Sem. Mill Valley 1962, 72 ; MA, Stanford Univ. 1967; Calif. gen. secondary and stud. tchg. credentials (life), 1967, 69. Career: student missionary, pastor Spanish mission, Home Mission Bd. of So. Baptist Convention in Calif. 1958-62; clerk YMCA Berkeley 1962-64; tchr. Del Norte County High Sch. 1964-82, ret.; real estate broker 1982 – ; elected city council, 4-year term, 1984; mem: Nat. Edn. Assn., Calif. State Teachers Assn., local, Calif. and Nat. Bd. Realtors, Elks, Moose, Odd Fellows, CofC; Republican; Methodist. Address: 705 F St Crescent City 95531

ALVAREZ-SANDOVAL, EMANUEL, educator, realty co. owner; b. Dec. 25, 1935, Santander del Cauca, Colombia; nat. US Cit. 1971; s. Anastacio and Martina (Sandoval0Catacoli) Alvarez-Gomez; m. Olga Linda Flores, June 19, 1972; children: Barbara b. 1975, Marta Emerald b. 1979; edn: AA, East L.A. Coll. 1970; BA, CSU Los Angeles 1972; MA, Am. Baptist Sem. of the West 1973; std. secondary credl. CSULA 1974-75; JD, Valley Univ. Sch. of Law 1978; PhD, Walden Univ. 1984. Career: pastor Baptist Ch. San Cristobal, Venezuela 1957-63, Los Angeles 1964-67; ins. rep. Certified Life Ins. of Calif. 1966-67; income tax preparer self-employed 1968-78; real estate agent Gold Key Realty Monterey Park 1978-79, Herbert Hawkins West Covina 1979-80; real estate broker, owner Emanuel's Realty Co. West Covina 1980 – ; instr. East L.A. Comm. Coll. Dist. 1975 – , Citrus Comm. Coll. Dist. 1986; tchr. Birmingham H.S., L.A. Sch. Dist. 1976 – ; pvt. sch. tchr. 1957-58; acct. 1955-57; bookstore owner 1959-62; honors: Presdl. Spl. Award (Repub. Nat. Com. 1982), Pres. Award (Certified Life Ins. Co. of Calif. 1967); mem: Nu Beta Epsilon nat. law frat., Am. Baptist Alumni Assn., CSULA Alumni Assn., Am. Baptist Cred. Union, AFT Coll. Guild, CTA, NEA, UTLA; pres., founder West Covina Christian Ctr. 1981; publs: num. articles in religious, legal, philos. fields; author: Basic Spanish/ A New Approach (for pub. 1988), The Buddha or Christ?, Should There Be Popes?; Republican; Assembly of God; rec: piano, travel, writing, poetry. Res: 556 N Lyall Ave WEst Covina 91790 Ofc: Emanuel's Realty Co. 556 N Lyall Ave Ste A West Covina 91790

ALYANAK, KURKEN, real estate developer, architect; b. May 11, 1951, Istanbul, Turkey; s. Leon and Sona (Mardirosyan) A.; m. Talin Bohcali, July 9, 1985; edn: M. Arch., Istanbul Technical 1979; M.Arch., UC Los Angeles 1983. Career: pres. Alyanak Constrn. Co. 1975-80; arch. staff Kamnitzer Cotton Vreeland, 1980-82; v.p. Thomas Safran and Assocs. 1982-85; pres. Alyanak Constrn. Co., 1985 – ; civic: Ararat Home of Los Angeles Inc.; Address: Marina Del Rey 90292

AMACKER, JEFFERSON Z., JR., manufacturing co. president; b. Dec. 14, 1935, Kentwood, La.; s. Jefferson Z. and Ruth Jeanette (Smith) A.; m. Loretta Schwartz, Aug. 6, 1960; children: Jeff III, b. 1961, Marla b. 1962, Carl b. 1970; edn: BS, mil. sci., US Mil. Acad. 1957; BS, astronautics, USAF Inst. of Tech. 1963; MBA (in prog.), Pepperdine Univ. Career: engring. mgr., 747 Pgm. Mgr., dir. Avionics, American Airlines, Tulsa, Okla. 1967-71; pgm. dir. Singer Co., Little Falls, NJ 1971-77; v.p. mktg. Simmonds Precision, Vergennes, Vt. 1977-80; gen. mgr. Systron Donner, Inertial Div., Concord 1980-83; dir./pres./CEO Leach Corp., Buena Park 1983–; bd. dir. LRE Electromedical 1984-, Astral Medical 1984-, Hayden Scientific 1985-; guest lectr. MIT, 1975, USAF Test Pilot Sch., Edward AFB 1967; cons. USAF Scientific Adv. Bd. 1973; Singer Co. rep. to Poland & Russia 1973-74; mem: Inst. of Navigation; West Point Soc. of Orange Co.; Aircraft Owners & Pilots Assn.; Corona del Mar Touchdown Club; Balboa Bay Club; 11 pub. tech. papers; mil: capt. USAF Fighter Pilot 1957-67, Commdn. Medal; Republican; racquetball. Res: 7 Montpelier Dr Newport Beach 92660 Ofc: Leach Corp., 6900 Orangethorpe Ave Buena Park 92620

AMADOR, GILBERT E., U.S. customhouse broker; b. June 6, 1933, Tracy; s. Epigmenio and Andrea (Solis) Amador; m. Eunice E. Nevarez, Dec. 2, 1966; children: David, b. 1965; Daniel, B. 1968; Darin, b. 1972; edn: AA, Stockton Coll.; U.S. customhouse broker, U.S. Treasury, 1967; Internat. Freight Forwarder, Fed. Maritime Commn., 1968; Internat. Air Freight Consolidators, IATA, 1970. Career: messenger H.H. Elder & Co., U.S. customhouse brokers, 1959-62; with Bruce Duncan Co., customhouse brokers 1962-65; founding ptr. Reg. W. Winter, customhouse broker 1965-67; founding broker, pres. G. Amador Corp., 1967–; chmn. bd., Cali-America Line, Ltd.; mem: Foreign Trade Assn.; The L.A. Customs & Freight Brokers Assn.; L.A. CofC; The Mexican CofC; Orange Co. CofC; mil: cpl., US Army, Korean War; Republican; Baptist; rec: oil painting. Res: 2137 Indian Creek Rd., Diamond Bar, CA 91765 Ofc: G. Amador Corp., 121 West Hazel St., Inglewood 90302

AMBLER, READ, judge; b. July 23, 1939, Hinsdale, Ill.; s. Harold and Marion Ermina (Read) A.; m. Cheryl Kathryn Ashenbrenner, Nov. 2, 1974; children: Harold b. 1965, Heather b. 1971, Christian (stepson) b. 1971, David b. 1982, Brady b. 1983; edn: BA, Dartmouth Coll. 1961; LLB, Stanford Law Sch. 1968; admitted to Calif. Bar, US Ct. of Appeals (9th Cir.), US Dist. Ct. (No. Dist.), 1969. Career: deputy public defender Santa Clara County, 1970-73; pvt. practice atty., assoc. Morgan, Beauzay & Hammer, San Jose 1969-70, shareholder MacLeod, Fuller, Muir & Godwin, Los Altos 1973-75, ptnr. Nichols & Ambler, Palo Alto 1975-80; judge Santa Clara County Superior Court, apptd. by Gov. Brown Jr. 1980-, elected 1982–; mem. gov. com. Ctr. for Judicial Edn. & Research 1984-86, Calif. Judicial Council Advis. Com. on Legal Forms 1983; Stanford Law Sch. bd. vis. 1969-71; honors: Volunteers in Parole Founders Award (1983), Stanford Law Sch./ Santa Clara County Bar Assn. outstanding law student award (1968); mem: Calif. Judges Assn., Volunteers in Parole (bd. dirs. 1984-), Santa Clara Bar Assn. 1969-80 (pres. 1977; chmn. 1979 del. to State Bar Conf. of Dels.), Barrister's Club (pres. 1973); civic: trustee Good Samaritan Hosp., Los Gatos (1976-78), Santa Clara County Law Related Edn. Com. (chmn. 1983-), Child Advocacy Council (Adv. bd. 1983-85); mil: lt.jg US Navy 1961-65; Democrat; Protestant; rec: running. Res: Los Altos 94022 Ofc: Santa Clara County Superior Court 191 N First St San Jose 95113

AMELIO, GILBERT NEIL, independent film producer, artist, consultant; b. Dec. 14, 1929, N.Y.C.; s. Frank Gilbert and Frances (Sarno) A.; m. Beverly O., Dec. 30, 1950; children: Frank, Susan, Glorina, Marisa; edn: BFA, USC 1948; BA, Loyola Univ. 1951; LLB, Univ. Detroit 1965. Career: served to lt. col. US Air Force 1951-53, 57-73, chief of protocol and public relations USAF Academy, Colo.; pres. GAA (Gil Amelio Associates, Inc.), Costa Mesa 1973-80, exec. dir. RSML Ltd., Sydney, Australia 1976-79; TV prod. for CBN-TV, Virginia Beach, 1980; current: entrepreneur in motion pictures (independent prod., packager), independent television prod. 1979–; num. performing and speaking engagements, TV appearances; cons. Scherer Assocs., Inc. (clients incl. Rockwell Int'l., Los Alamos Lab., var. engring. corps.); pres. The Legacy Group, Inc. 1985-; awards: Emmy nominee for "The Face of Christ" (multimedia- sculpture, drama, music), CBS-TV Los Angeles (1969-70), and RIM Award for same performance (1977), Internat. Film, TV Awards of New York (1969), Columbus Film Festival Award (1969-70), John M. Costello Loyalty Award (Loyola Univ.); mem: Fellow Australian Advtsg. Inst. of Sydney, NATPE (assoc.), The Athenaeum (La Jolla, 1983), Lions Internat. (Sydney, Australia), Phi Beta Gamma (nat. art frat.); art works incl. oil paintings, bronzes (current), book on Byzantine Art in progress; mil: num. Air Force decorations; Republican; Christian; rec: classical music, sculpting, painting. Address: Irvine 92714

AMERINE, ROBERT EUGENE, health care co. executive; b. Dec. 30, 1951, McMinnville, Ore.; s. Frances Marion and Helen Mable (Jahn) A.; m. Catherine, Nov. 3, 1973; children: Annette b. 1979, Jared b. 1983; edn: BA bus. admin., magna cum laude, Azusa Pacific Univ. 1977; CPA Calif. 1983. Career: dept. mgr. Montgomery Ward & Co. Eagle Rock, Calif. 1973-74; acct. Archer, Bulmahn & Co. Pasadena 1976-80; mgr. Booth & Booth CPAs Pasadena 1980-83; asst. controller Monrovia Nursery Co. Azusa 1983; v.p. fin. Treatment Ctrs. of Am. 1983–; honors: Cert. of Merit for Outstanding Scholastic Achievement (Azusa Pacific Univ. 1976), Alpha Chi 1977; mem: Calif. Soc. CPAs 1983-, Am. Inst. CPAs 1985-; treas. Bresee Ave. Ch. of the Nazarene 1977-; audit com. chmn. Pasadena 1st Nazarene Ch. 1983-84; mil: sgt. USMC 1971-73; Republican; Protestant; rec: physical fitness, outdoor activities. Ofc: Treatment Centers of America 150 N Santa Anita Ste 410 Arcadia 91006

AMICK, LELITA FRANCEE, automotive trade magazine publisher; b. March 4, 1949, Hot Springs, So. Dak.; d. Mervin Martin and Ramona Carolina (Smith) A.; children: Troy b. 1966, Tania b. 1968, Alexandria b. 1975. Career: auto body repair bus., 1973-78; pub. first, then 2d. Autobody Newsletter for N. San Diego County Chpt. of Calif. Autobody Assn. (CAA), 1978; pub. Voice mag. for State CAA, 1978; writer/pub. spl. project publication "X-Body Repair" with General Motors Service Research, Warren Mich. (1979) for first Internat. Autobody Exposition, NY; freelance writer var. trade mags. 1979-83, owner/pub. Management, Advertising & Publications, Inc., Oceanside 1983–, pub. Autobody News (monthly trade mag. distbd. Calif., Ariz., Nev. & Hawaii, 1983-), Western Wrench (mechanical newsletter distbd. So. Calif., Ariz., Nev., 1984-); pub. 1985 ed. Collision Repair Digest for Soc. of Collision Repair Splsts. (w/members in US, Canada & Australia); mem: Am. Mgmt. Assn., Nat. Assn. for Female Execs., Automotive Parts and Accessories Assn., Auto Internat. Assn., Book Publicists of San Diego, L.A. Press Club; publicity chair Calif. I-Car (Inter- Industry Conf. on Auto Collision Repair); Republican; rec: bicycling. Ofc: Management, Advertising & Publications Inc. 1743 So Hill St Oceanside 92054

AMIRVAND, BAGHER, biomedical engineering co. president; b. Mar. 22, 1951, Iran; s. Mohammad Ali and Parvin D. (Momenzadeh) A.; m. Afsaneh Khatibloo, July 21, 1978; edn: BS, Univ. of Wash. 1973; MS in computer sci., Univ. of Minn. 1975, PhD in biomed. engring., 1979. Career: scientist/grad. asst. Honeywell Co., 1975; pres. Amir Enterprises, Inc. 1979; pres. Finetex Co., Inc., Irvine 1980–; tchg. asst. Univ. Minn. 1974-75, postdoctoral research 1979-80; corporate mgmt. of sev. large real estate devel. projects; mem. IEEE, Computer Soc.; research: Analysis and Quantification of Asynchronous Myocardia Contraction of Heart; Moslem; rec: volleyball. Res: 1238 Polaris Dr Newport Beach 92660 Ofc: Finetex Company Inc. 18552 MacArthur Blvd Irvine 92715

AMOAH, JOHN SYLVESTER, marketing co. executive; b. Sept. 23, 1948, Agoma, Ghana; s. Joseph Kwasi and Nana Abema (Akyaa) A.; 1 child, Nana Akyaa b. 1983; edn: BS, econ., UC Berkeley 1971, MS econ. 1973, PhD (abd) 1975; adv. cert. (physics, chem., biol.) Univ. of Sci. and Tech., Kumasi, Ghana 1969. Career: systems analyst Electronic Data Systems, San Francisco 1975-76; dir. cost mgmt. Northrop Corp., Los Angeles 1976-79; pres./dir. Etron Inc. (electronic products mktg.), Accra, Ghana 1979-83; pres. Elsafe Inc., El Segundo, Calif. 1983–; bd. chmn. Regency Car Rental Co., L.A. honors: Dean Ryerson Award for Achievement, UCB (1971); pres. African Students Assn. of No. Am. (1970-72); publs: US Worker Productivity - The Japanese Challenge, Fortune Mag. (8/79); Catholic; rec: music, theatre. Ofc: Elsafe Inc. 360 N Sepulveda Blvd Ste 2010 El Segundo 90245

AMOROSO, FRANK, communications systems engineer; b. July 31, 1935, Providence, R.I.; s. Michele and Angela Maria Barbara (D'Uva) A.; edn: BS, MSEE, Mass. Inst. Tech. 1958; Purdue Univ. 1958-60; Univ. Turin, Italy 1964-66; Reg. Elec. Engr. Calif. 1971. Career: instr. E.E., Purdue Univ. 1958-59; research engr. Melpar Inc., Roxbury, Mass. 1959, MIT Instrumentation Lab., Cambridge, Mass. 1960, Litton Systems Advanced Devel. Lab., Waltham, Mass. 1960-61; engr. Melpar Applied Sci. Div., Watertown, Mass. 1961; mem. tech. staff RCA Labs. David Sarnoff Research Center, Princeton, N.J. 1962-64, Mitre Corp., Bedford, Mass., 1966-67; sr. applied mathematician Collins Radio Co., Newport Beach 1967-68; communication systems engr. No. Am. Rockwell Corp., El Segundo 1968-71, Northrop Electronics Div., Palos Verdes Peninsula 1971-72; commun. systems engr., senior staff engr. Hughes Aircraft Co., Fullerton 1972–; instr. Continuing Engring. Edn. pgm. George Washington Univ., Wash. DC; reviewer for IEEE journal: Transactions on Communications; awards: RCA Labs. Award (Princeton) for research leading to Advanced Digital Magnetic Recording (1964), Italian Govt. scholarship for grad. study in math. Univ. of Turin (1964-66), patent awards at Hughes Aircraft (1984, 85); senior mem. IEEE; exec. gov. World Plan Exec. Council (transcendental meditation); publs: contbr. 18 papers in profl. journals (1965-), sold 19 non-fiction features (all with by-line) in var. mags. (1969-); mil: 1st lt. US Army 1961-62; rec; scuba diver, journalist. Res: 271-D West Alton St Santa Ana 92707 Ofc: Hughes Aircraft Co POB 3310 Fullerton 92634

AMOROSO, RICHARD LOUIS, roboticist; b. Apr. 24, 1946, Medford, Mass.; s. Louis Raymond and Marjorie Lou (McCathie) A.; m. Juliette Sherer, Jan. 10, 1981; 1 dau. Juliette b. 1983; edn: BS psychol., Univ. Mass. Amherst 1972; spl. student psychol., Stanford Univ. 1972-73; postgrad. courses, Harvard Univ. 1980-81; New England Sch. of Acupuncture 1981-82. Career: dir. Amoroso Inst. of Psychol. Palo Alto 1972-76; oper. Harvard Smithsonian Astrophysical Observatory Cambridge, Mass. 1981-82; acupuncturist Cambridge 1982-83; owner Noetics (Oriental Med. Supply) Cambridge 1982-83; ptnr. Copies Plus Cambridge 1982; owner CJ Graphics Berkeley 1983-84; pres. Amoroso Robotics Inc. Winchester, Mass. 1982-84; pres. Amarobot Inc., owner Robotoy Co. Berkeley 1983–; honors: 2nd Place (Mass. State Science Fair for Linear Particle Accelerator 1964); mem: AAAS 1982-83, Robotic Soc. of Am. (bd. 1984-85, chpt. head 1985), Homebrew Robotics Club 1983-, Nat. Personal Robot Assn. 1985-; inventor: Hydrobot- programmable ednl. robot powered totally by hot & cold water; publ: The Robot Coloring Book, Robotic Fun Paddue, the Kidnap of Roboddy Android (all Noetic Press 1986), in progress: 50 Robots You Can Build, Whydaya Wanna Robot For (joke book); Republican; L.D.S.; rec: scuba, flying, running. Res: 3600 Lakeshore Ave Oakland 94610 Ofc: Amarobot Inc. 906 Bancrofy Way Berkeley 94710; Robotox Co. 2913 Ohio St Richmond 94804

AMORY, THOMAS CARHART, management consultant; b. Oct. 29, 1933, NY, NY; s. George Sullivan and Marion Renee (Carhart) A.; m. Elisabeth Jackson, June 21,1956; children: Renee b. 1957, Caroline b. 1959, Gillian b. 1968; m. 2d Carolyn Pesnell, May 10, 1969; edn: AB, Harvard 1956. Career: comml. mgr. NY Telephone Co. 1957-60; sales mgr. Royce Chemical Co. E. Rutherford, NJ 1960-62; asst. to chmn. Seatrain Lines Inc. Edgewater, NJ 1963-65; mgmt. cons. Booz, Allen & Hamilton NYC 1966-67; ptnr. Wm. H. Clark Assocs. Inc. NYC 1967-75, pres. 1976-83; pres. Carre Orban & Ptnrs. NYC 1984-85; vice chmn. Wm. H. Clark Assocs. Chgo. 1985–; dir: Seatrain Lines 1961-65, Assn. of Exec. Recruiting Cons. 1978-82; mem: Mus. of City of NY (trustee 1971-), Venture Fund, Episcopal Diocese of NY (trustee 1980-86), Brook, River, Clove Valley Rod & Gun, Tuxedo (NY), Yeamans Hall (Charleston, SC), Sankaty Head, Nantucket Yacht, Birnam Wood (Santa Barbara); Republican; Episcopal; rec: tennis, golf, shooting, fishing. Res: 749 Fuera Ln Montecito 93108 Ofc: Wm. H. Clark Assocs. Inc. 200 E Randolph Ste 7912 Chicago IL 60601

ANANEH-FIREMPONG, OWUSU, physician, internist; b. Feb. 18, 1951, Agogo, Ghana; s. Benjamin R.D. and Margaret A. (Appeah) Ananeh-Firempong; m. Sheila, June 1978; children: Owusu II b. 1979, Adoma b. 1981, Nana Frema b. 1983; edn: BA biol., Brandeis Univ. 1975; MD (honors Orthopaedic Surgery), Univ. So. Calif. Sch. of Med. 1979; Diplomate Nat. Bd. Med. Examiners (1980), Internal Medicine Bd. eligible (1982). Career: admitting physician Lancaster Community Hosp., Lancaster 1978-83; p.t. physician East LA Kidney Center, Los Angeles 1980-82; pvt. practice internal medicine, rhumatology, rehabilitation in Lancaster 1982–; chief exec. Reident; att. phys. Antelope Valley Hosp. (Lancaster), and Palmdale Gen. Hosp.; honors: L. Wein Internat. Scholar and Dean's Honor List, Brandeis Univ. (1972-75); mem. assoc. Am. Coll. of Physicians; multilingual: English, five African langs., French, Spanish; Conservative; Christian; rec: soccer, travel, poetry, music. Ofc: 907 W Lancaster Blvd Ste 101 Lancaster 93534

ANARGYROS, NEDRA F. HARRISON, cytologist; b. Dec. 3, 1915, NY, NY; d. Leverette Roland and Florence Martha (Pickard) Harrison; grandmother Florence Willingham Pickard, author, painter; m. Spero Drosos Anargyros, Oct. 21, 1940 (div. 1969); edn: Emerson Coll. Boston 1934-36; UC San Francisco 1957. Career: Power's model 1938; original model for The Dragon Lady of Milton Caniff's Terry & the Pirates 1939; rode the Quadrille on horseback first yr. of NY World's Fair in Wild West & Rodeo; small part in Albert Johnson's The American Jubilee 1939-40; student pilot's license Tifton, Ga. 1941; pilot tng. pgm. Avenger Field, Sweetwater, Tex. 1942; head cytology lab UCSF; mem: Am. Soc. Clin. Pathols. (affil.), Am. Soc. Cytotechnol. (affil.), Women Flyers of Am.. DAR (1st vice regent 1970), Colonial Dames of Am., Huguenot Soc. of Calif., UDC, Phi Mu Gamma, Pres.'s Club of Mercer Univ. (Macon, Ga.); Republican; Christian Science; rec: travel, scuba (cert. 1972). Res: 2503 Clay San Francisco 94115 Ofc: Univ. Calif. Svc. SF Gen. Hosp. Bldg 3 Rm 121 San Francisco 94110

ANAWATI, JOSEPH SOLIMAN, pharmacist; b. Dec. 25, 1941, Alexandria, Egypt, nat. US cit. 1985; s. Soliman Y. and Rosine N. (Anawati) A.; m. Malak Sabbagh, Oct. 5, 1969; children: Kevin b. 1971, Caroline b. 1973; edn: B.PH and PH.CH, Alexandria Univ. Sch. of Pharmacy 1966, M.Pharm. 1968; MBA in bus. adm., City Executive Coll. 1985. Career: medical rep. Eli Lilly Co., Cairo and Libya , 1966-71; supvr. sales & mktg. Upjohn Co. 1971-73, dist. mgr. (Cairo) 1973-75, area mgr. (all Middle East) 1975-79; group area mgr. (Middle East, Africa) Allergan Pharmaceutical, Irvine 1979-82; prodn. & plant mgr., dir. of export MD Pharmaceutical, Santa Ana 1982–; internat. cons. pharmaceutical bus. overseas; recipient mgmt. awards, Mayor Tom Bradley and City of Los Angeles; mem. Board of Pharmacy, Egypt; club: Los Caballeros (Orange Co.); Greek Orthodox; rec: basketball, volleyball. Res: POB 8871 Fountain Valley 92728 Ofc: MD Pharmaceutical 3501 W Garry Santa Ana 92704

ANDAL, CESAR DIMAANDAL, physician, general surgeon; b. Feb. 20, 1947, Batangas, Philippines, nat. 1977; s. Rafael Alvarez and Sofia Marasigan (Dimaandal) A.; m. Luzviminda Manag, Nov. 3, 1975; children: Andrea Lucille b. 1977, Ian Plaridel b. 1981; edn: Univ. Santo Tomas Coll. of Science, Philippines 1964-68; MD, Univ. Santo Tomas Coll. of Med. 1972; admitted to practice, Calif. 1977, Philippines 1973. Career: surgical res. Homer G. Phillips/ Wash. Univ. St. Louis, Mo. 1977, McKeesport Hosp., McKeesport, Penn., Children's Hosp. Pittsburgh, Cleveland Clinic Thoracic and Cardiovasc. Surg. Cleveland, Ohio 1980-83; med. and surgical staff, St. Luke's Hosp., Seton Med. Ctr., Ralph K. Davis Med. Ctr.; honors: hon. mention, Pa. Am. Coll. of Surgeons 1981; award, Alpha Phi Omega 1983; mem: Alpha Phi Omega Internat. Philippines Inc. Alumni Assn. of No. Calif. (found. pres. 1983, chmn. bd. 1986), Grace United Methodist Ch. (v.chmn. Stewardship com. 1985, parish- pastor rel. com. 1985), Philippine Med. Soc. of No. Calif., Filipino Businessmen & Profls. Assn., Soc. of Phillippine Surgeons in Am., Batangas Assn. of Calif., Univ. of Philippines Alumni (hon.); works: Jejunal and Ileal Diverticular Disease and its Significance- a 5 year study, pub. Am. Coll. of Surgeon PA chpt., Pitts., Penn. 1981; Democrat; Christian; rec: jogging, camping, baseball. Res: 801 Lisbon St., San Francisco 94112

ANDECK, ANDREW, real estate broker, communications co. executive; b. Nov. 9, 1918, Des Moines, Iowa; s. Casper and Beulah Andeck; m. Virginia Randolph Atkinson, Aug. 1946; 1 son, Andrew Atkinson, B. 1948; edn: BA summa cum laude, Univ. of Tex. 1942. Career: pres. Andrew Andeck Co., Palm Desert; vice pres. River Communication Co. (T.V.); fmr. pres. AREA Research Co., MAP Investment Co.; fmr. planning commnr. City of Indian Wells ;

elected four-yr. term Indian Wells City Council; past pres. and orgnzr. La Jolla Town Council 1964-65; past pres. La Jolla Real Estate Brokers Assn. 1963; clubs: Rotary of Indian Wells (pres.), Balboa Bay Desert (dir.), Monterey Country, Lakes Country; mil: maj. USMC 1942-46, Phil. Liberation (2 stars), Pacific (6 stars) medals; Presbyterian (trustee); rec: tennis, swim, church. Address: POB 1196, Palm Desert 92261

ANDERSEN, JACK A., manufacturing co. executive; b. Sept. 13, 1938, Santa Monica, Calif.; s. Chester B. and Myrtle M. (Soderlind) A.; m. Jutta, July 21, 1973; children: Jack Bradley b. 1968, Jason Jurgen b. 1975; edn: BS, UC Los Angeles 1962. Career: br. mgr. IBM Corp. Armonk, NY 1963-79; v.p. mktg. Nat. Advanced Sys. Santa Clara 1979; v.p. sales & mktg. Nat. Computer Sales Irvine 1980; v.p. mktg. Fujitsu Sys. of Am. L.A. 1980-83; v.p. mktg. Media Sys. Technol. Irvine 1983-84; senior v.p. Printronix Inc. Irvine 1984–; bd. govs. Infomart Dallas 1985-, Techmart San Jose 1986; mem. Am. Electronics Assn.; mil: E-6 USAR 1963-69; Republican; Protestant; rec: tennis, exotic cars, skiing. Ofc: Printronix Inc. 17500 Cartwright Rd Irvine 92713

ANDERSON, BARBARA LOUISE, library director; b. Jan. 5, 1933, San Diego; d. Lorenzo and Louise (Morgan) A.; 1 son, Sean Allen; edn: BS, San Diego State Univ. 1954; MLS, Kans. State Tchrs. Coll. 1955. Career: branch librarian Los Angeles Pub. Library 1956-59; reference, young adult librarian San Diego Pub. Library 1959-64; librarin U.S. Army, Europe 1964-69; coordinator Serra Reference Proj., Serra Regl. Lib. System, San Diego 1969-71; head readers svcs. Riverside City and County Pub. Library 1972-74; county librarian San Bernardino County Library 1974–; bd. dirs: Inland Empire Symphony 1982-; Riverside Mental Health Assn. 1975-79; mem: ALA; Calif. Library Assn.; Black Caucus of Calif. Library Assn.; Congress of Pub. Library Systems (pres. 1983); Calif. Co. Librarian Assns; Calif. Soc. Librarians (pres. 1974-75); AAUW (pres., Riverside 1976-77); NAACP; Bus. and Profl. Women San Bernardino; publs: contbr. arts. to publs. in field. Ofc: 104 W. 4th St., San Bernardino 92415

ANDERSON, BRADFORD SCOTT, communications co. president; Sept. 11, 1949, Lincoln, Nebr.; s. Harold Bernard and Phyllis Alene (Yenne) A.; m. Pamela Jo Promack, April 7, 1972; children: Laura Michele b. 1978; Brian Christopher, b. 1981; edn: BSEE, CSU Long Beach 1975; MBA, Pepperdine Univ. 1985; lic. commn. contractor, Calif. Contractors State Lic. Bd. 1984. Career: pres./ CEO Network Cable Systems, Inc.; pres. Wideband Data Corp.; mgr. broadband commn. TRW Systems, Redondo Beach; author var. arts. in tech. journs.; tchr. tech. classes; mem: Soc. of Cable Television Engrs.; Nat. Cable Television Assn. (apptd. to eng. comm. 1982-84); IEEE; YMCA; Boy Scouts of Am.; Ofc: Network Cable Systems, Inc., 4106 Michelle Dr., Torrance 90503

ANDERSON, CHARLES HOWARD, computer executive; b. April 5, 1947, Los Angeles; s. Nathan H. and Drusilla Julia Mae (Howard) A.; edn: AA, El Camino Jr. Coll. 1971; BS, USC 1973, MBA, 1974. Career: sales rep. IBM Data Processing Div., Los Angeles 1973, distbn. industry splst. 1974-75; senior sales rep., OEM mgr. Digital Equipment Corp., Los Angeles 1975-78; mktg. mgr. Control Data, Los Angeles 1978-81, nat. svc. mgr. 1981-83, Calif. Central Dist. mgr. 1984-85; regrl. mgr. Kurzweil Applied Intelligence 1985–; cons. adv. bus. plnng. to minority businesses 1974-76; honors: IBM 100 Percent Club 1974; Digital Equipment Corp. 100 Percent Clubs, 1975, 1976, 1977; Control Data 100 Percent Club 1979, 1981, 1982, 1983; Cert. in Food Mktg. Mgmt., USC 1972; mem: Am. Mktg. Assn., Ebonics, Ladera Heights Neighboroood Orgn.; publs: The Southern California Chain Store Shopper, 1973; Western Consumer Attitudes Toward the Food Industry, 1972; mil: sgt. USAF 1966-69; Democrats, Methodist; rec: flying, tennis, dog training. Res: 6290 Mosley Ave. Los Angeles 90056 Ofc: Kurzweil AI, 2049 Century Park East Ste. 1100 Los Angeles 90067

ANDERSON, CHARLES MICHAEL, paint co. executive, information resources; b. July 15, 1944, Londonderry, No. Ireland; s. Albert and Elizabeth (McDaid) A.; m. Terri Good, Oct. 9, 1981; 1 son, Sean Michael b. 1983; edn: BS, No. Ill. Univ. 1966; MBA, Univ. So. Calif. 1970; CPA Calif. 1970. Career: staff acct. Price Waterhouse Co. Chgo. 1966-69, mgmt. cons. L.A. 1970-72; mgmt. cons. pvt. practice Manhattan Beach 1972-73; mgr. corp. budget Great Southwest Corp. L.A. 1973-76; dir. internal audit Standard Brands Paint Co. Torrance 1976-85, inventory control systems 1985–; assoc. prof. acctg. CSU Long Beach 1979–; pres. Calif. Mus. of Sci. and Industry adv. bd. 1978-, chmn. bd. 1980-81; mem: Am. Inst. CPAs (Who's Who in Soc. 1986), EDP Auditors Assn., Catholic Big Brothers 1973-84, WEst End Tennis & Racquet Club 1978-, Joie De Vive Homeowners Assn. (pres. 1981-84, treas. 1986); mil: cpl. USMCR 1967-73; Democrat; Catholic; rec: all sports, travel, photog. Res: 1155 11th St Unit 1 Manhattan Beach 90266 Ofc: Standard Brands Paint Co. 4300 W 190th St Torrance 90509

ANDERSON, EDWARD MASIAH, JR., contract administrator, management consultant, entrepreneur; b. Sept. 18, 1959, Los Angeles; s. Edward M. and Inez (Vaughn) A.; edn: BA, UC Los Angeles 1981; JD, Hastings Coll. of Law 1984. Career: law clk. Nat. Labor Relations Bd., Div. of Judges, San Francisco 1983; judicial law clk. U.S. Bankruptcy Ct., Los Angeles 1984; mgmt. cons. Anderson Management Group, Los Angeles 1984–; contract negotiator Jet Propulsion Lab./Caltech (NASA), Pasadena 1985–; contract administrator Candle Corp. legal svcs. dept. 1986–; honors: dean's list, Univ. of Md. (1977) and CSU Northridge (1978); artistic achieve. award (Festival in Black), City of Los Angeles Mayor (1976); mem. Masons, Angel City Lodge (1986); Democrat; Catholic; rec: tennis, jazz/ classical piano. Res: 1815 Wellington Rd Los Angeles 90019

ANDERSON, EDWARD WESLEY, physician; b. Nov. 21, 1929, Spokane, Wash.; s. Gunnar Herman and Albertina Sophia (Lund) A.; m. Christine, Aug. 22, 1985; 1 son, Eric b. 1985; edn: Chem. Engr., Gonzaga Univ. 1953; MD, USC 1963. Career: refinery equipt. design and sales 1955-59; intern Deaconess Hosp., Spokane, Wash. 1963-64; physician, senior mem. Fullerton Family Practice, Fullerton 1964—; bd. mem. (chief of staff 1985) Fullerton Comm. Hosp., Anaheim Meml. Hosp.; mem. Orange County Health Planning Commn.; mem: Fellow Am. Acad. Family Practice (1979), AMA, Calif. Med. Assn., Orange County Med. Assn.; club: Sunny Hills Racquet; mil: 1st lt. US Army Ordnance Corps 1953-55; Republican; rec: sports. Ofc: Fullerton Family Practice 2720 N Harbor Blvd Ste 100 Fullerton 92635

ANDERSON, GERALD VERNE, metallurgical engineer; b. Oct. 25, 1931, Long Beach; s. Gordon Valentine and Aletha Marian (Parkins) Anderson; edn: BS, UC Berkeley, 1958, AA, Long Bch City Coll. 1952; m. Helen Jean Harman, May; 7, 1954; children: Lori Jean (Fronk), b. 1957, Gregory Verne, b. 1958, David Harman, b. 1959, Lynn Elaine (Lee), b. 1961, Brian Earl, b. 1970, Michael Gordon, b. 1973. Career: research analyst North. American Aviation (Downey) 1953-55, sr. resrch engr. (Los Angeles) 1958-62, project leader (Palmdale) 1962-64; sr. metallurgist Autonetics, Anaheim 1964-65; R&D splst. Douglas Aircraft, Santa Monica 1965-66, Gp. leader 1966-68; tech. splst. McDonnell Douglas Astronautics, Huntington Bch 1968-84, section chief 1984—; mem. Corp. Metals Joining Panel, No Am. Aviation 1965; inst. Am. Soc. for Metals, L.A. 1965-69; cons. Japanese Space Pgm. Nagoya, Japan, 1972-73; cons. European Spacelab Pgm, Turin, Italy, 1976-77; instr. Seminary, L.D.S. Church, Westminster 1970-77; Profl. Metallurgical Engr., Calif. 1965-; listed: Leading Men in Am., Who's Who in Orange Co.; mem: Am. Soc. for Metals; Internat. Platform Assn.; Citizen's Adv. Com. Huntington Bch 1972; Westminster Human Resources pilot planning com., 1974, Bicent. Com., 1976; Patentee: electron beam welding, portable electron beam welding; mil: m/sgt. Nat.Guard 1951-8, GCM; Republican; LDS Ch., Bishop; rec: ski, family camping, photog. Res: 13401 Lee Dr. Westminster 92683 Ofc: McDonnell Douglas Astronautics, 5301 Bolsa Ave. Huntington Bch 92647

ANDERSON, GRANT SHERMAN, financial planner; b. Nov. 15, 1906, Chgo.; s. George Morris and Mary (Grant) A.; widower; 1 dau. Terre-le b. 1947, three grandchildren; edn: BS in E.E., Univ. New Mex. 1930; MA, USC 1938; Reg. Profl. Engr. (civil and electrical) Calif. 1947. Career: tchr. physics, chem. Pacific Military Acad., Culver City 1930-31; bus. owner, Los Angeles 1931-33; capt. US Army Reserve in chg. Civilian Conservation Corps Camps, camp cmdr. in chg. Calif. 1933-34, Ida. 1934-36, Wash. State 1936-37; bus. owner 1937-38; civil engr. US Govt. 1938-43, active duty AUS Corps of Engrs. in Calif., Mont., Idaho, 1943-46, civil engr. US Govt. 1957; asst., chief engr. City of Los Angeles Dept. of Airports 1947-76, in chg. design and constrn. for Dept. at LA Internat. Airport, Ontario Internat. Airport, and Van Nuys Airport; ret.; personal investments and finl. planner; mem: Retired Officers Assn. (1947-), Mil. Order of World Wars (1969-), Optimists Club (bd. govs. LAX 1970-); works: reconstrn. of main runway at Ontario Airport without taking the single runway (accommodating one million+ annual passengers) out of service; mil: lt. col. US Army Corps Engrs. 1943-46; Republican; rec: finl. planning, travel, 3 grandchildren. Address: 5845 Doverwood Dr Apt 202 Culver City 90230

ANDERSON, IRIS ANITA, educator; b. Aug. 18, 1930, Forks, Wash.; d. James Augustus and Alma Elizabeth (Haase) Gilbreath; m. Donald Rene Anderson; children: Karen C. b. 1952, Susan A. b. 1953, Gayle L. b. 1957, Brian D. b. 1959; edn: BA teaching, Univ. Wash. 1969; MA Eng., Seattle Univ. 1972; tchg. cred. English lang. K-12 (1977), Adminstrn. (1978), Comm. Colls. (1978). Career: tchr. Issaquah (Wash.) Sr. High Sch. 1969-77; tchr. Los Angeles Sr. High Sch. 1977-79 (also dist. curriculum council chmn., middle sch. plan, edn. assn. curriculum chmn., planned programmed budget proj. chmn., edn. assn. instructional planning chmn. trimester system, accreditation evaluation, advisor Nat. Honor Soc., YMCA-YWCA v.p.); nutrition vol. Santa Monica Hosp.; honors: W-Key Activities Scholarship Hon. (Univ. Wash.); mem: Wash. Speech Assn., Nat. Edn. Assn., CRTA, Sigma Kappa, Am. Assn. Univ. Women, League Women Voters, Nat. Thespians, Santa Monica Hosp. Aux. Volunteers; Desert Beautiful, Palm Springs Panhellenic, Desert Four Republican Women, Palm Desert Women's Club, CPA Wives Club, Bob Hope Cultural Ctr., others; publ: Conservationist's Dilemma (Sea Pen, Marine Sci. Soc. of the Northwest 1975); Republican; Protestant. Res: POB 6000 Palm Desert 92261

ANDERSON, JAMES WALLACE, SR., research chemist, assayor; b. Dec. 16, 1926, Salt Lake City, Utah; s. James Louis and Ruby Jacoba (Neelemen) A.; m. Betty Jane, Nov. 19, 1976; children: James Jr. b. 1959, Judy Lynn b. 1956, Bonnie Lou b. 1953; edn: AA, Coll. of the Pacific, Stockton Coll.; analytical chemistry, International Schs.; Tech. Trade Tchrs. Cred., Mt. San Antonio Coll. 1973. Career: portable lab truck driver Q Fever Lab., US Govt. Lab Tech., Riohondo Research Ctr. 1947; BOD COD Inhoff Settlement Sewer Plant test E-Coli & Straph tests Calif. State Dept. of Public Health, Berkeley 1948; research chemist, product devel., water treatment cons. Los Angeles Chemical, So. Gate 1951, currently, chemist, sales; water treatment formulations Aquatronics 5 Inc. 1959-79, pres. 1979—; chief chemist Los Angeles Chemical Co. 1981-83; chief chemist Aquatronics Inc. 1969-; sales Los Angeles Chemical Co. 1983-86; mem: Am. Chemical Soc., INACT, Masons, Scottish Rite, Shriners; mil: US Army Infanthry 1945; rec: assaying, lost wax creations, black light

ndetications. Res: 706 Bagnall St. Azusa 91702 Ofc: Aquatronics Inc., 706 Bagnall St. Azusa 91702

ANDERSON, JOHN JESSE, research engineer; b. Sept. 21, 1958, El Paso, Tex.; s. Wm. Jesse, III and Sue (Francis) A.; m. Leslie Ann, Dec. 27, 1980; edn: BSME, San Diego State Univ. 1980, post grad. 1980-83; engrg. mgmt., UC San Diego 1984-; Reg. Profl. Mech. Engr. Calif. 1983. Career: student co-op San Diego State Univ./ research lab Solar Turbines Inc. 1979-80; assoc. engr. Solar Turbines 1980-82, research engr. 1982-83, devel. engr. 1983-84, senior research engr. 1984—; honors: Most Outstanding Engrg. Design Student (SDSU 1980); mem: ASME, Machine Vision Assn./ Soc. of Mfg. Engrs. (charter), SDSU Alumni and Assoc., Greater San Diego Science Fair Judge 1981-; num. research reports in field of advanced mfg. process; Republican; Catholic; rec: sailing, sports, home renovation. Res: 5597 Mt Acara Dr San Diego 92111 Ofc: Solar Turbines Inc. 2200 Pacific Coast Hwy San Diego 92111

ANDERSON, KURT BRADFORD, architect; b. Oct. 22, 1952, Bakersfield; s. Hal G. and Dorothy Jean (Harrison) A.; m. Cathy, May 15, 1982; edn: AA arch., Bakersfield Coll. 1972; BS arch., Calif. State Polytech. Univ. 1974; BA pub. rels., CSU San Jose 1977. Reg. Architect, Calif. 1984. Career: worked as lifeguard and diving instr., waiter, World Airways flight attendant, -1978; pub. rels. dir. Sunset Mag. Western Home Awards, 1975; chief designer Creative Design Co. 1976-79; design and agcy. coord., Speed Fab-Crete/ Raisch Builders, Design-Build Constrn. Co., 1979-82; regl. dir. CDA Engineers 1982-83; ptnr. The Schieron-Anderson Orgn., 1983; architect/prin. Andarch Assocs., 1984—; mem. Am. Inst. of Architects; works: designer 100+ structures (1976-); Republican; Episcopal; rec: skiing, fitness, baseball, biking. Ofc: Andarch Associates 300 Orchard City Dr Ste 137 Campbell 95008

ANDERSON, LEO ELLIS, lawyer; b. Feb. 20, 1902, Gettysburg, So. Dakota; s. Laurits Martin and Leonora (Ellis) A.; m. Hollis Norris, Nov. 1, 1931, dec., m. 2d. Pauline Murray, Feb. 12, 1961; children: Denise, b. 1933, David, b. 1936; edn: BS, USC 1924, LLB, 1927; Consul of Republic of Latvia 1932. Career: Meserve Mumper & Hughes 1927, ptr. 1938-75; semi-ret., of counsel 1975—; dir. Lennox Ind. Internat. 1959-; pres. Forest Lawn Meml. Parks 1978-; past pres. Midler Ave. Realty; mem: Masons (past Grand Master Calif. & Hawaii), Al Malaikah Temple of Shrine (past potentate 1968), San Gabriel Country Club (pres. 1952-53), Jonathan Club, University Club of Los Angeles; Republican (chmn. L.A. Co. Rep. Central Com. 1936-40, chmn. Calif. Rep. Central Com. 1946-48); Protestant; rec: golf. Ofc: Los Angeles

ANDERSON, MARION RUTH, bacteriologist, real estate broker; b. 1898, Sturgeon Bay, Wisc.; d. Wm. Tait and Louisa Jane (Bagley) Anderson; edn: BA, Univ. of Wisc., Madison 1920. Career: bacteriologist, Serologist Lab., St. Lukes, Chgo. 1920-22; sole opr. State Hygienic Lab., Beloit, Wisc. 1922-25, Lab. Childrens Hosp., Chgo. 1926-27, Los Angeles Co. Health Dept., 1928-29, Childrens Hosp., Los Angeles 1929-32; currently owner/realtor, L.B. Anderson Co., Los Angeles; hon. life mem. Calif. Assn. of Realtors; mem. Univ. of Wisc. Alumni Club, Good Samaritan Hosp. Aux., Melrose Neighborhood Assn.; Republican; Episcopal; rec: int. painting & furniture, walking. Address: L.B.Anderson Co., 800 N. June St Los Angeles 90038

ANDERSON, MARK ROY, real estate developer, taxation lawyer; b. June 12, 1954, Vancouver, Wash.; s. Royal John and Marie Josephine (Fitzwater) A.; m. Janus, July 2, 1983; 1 dau. Elizabeth b. 1984; edn: BS, Univ. of Nev. 1976; JD/ MBA, Univ. of Pacivic 1980; admitted bar: Nev., U.S. Tax Ct. Career: tax atty. Arthur Anderson & Co., San Francisco 1979-82, pvt. practice, Anderson & Edwards, Beverly Hills 1982-85; pres. Marlin Industries (real estate devel. co.), Beverly Hills 1983 ; nat. featured speaker to securities dealers, tax profls., accts. and finl. planners; addressed US House of Reps. Ways and Means Com., chaired by Mr. Rosetnkowsky, on effect of proposed tax law changes upon R.E. inv. community (1985), and appeared (one of 5) before the IRS hearing on inv. tax credit; mem: Am. Trial Lawyers Assn., Am. Bar Assn. (Sect. on Taxation, Internat. Law Sect. on Taxation), San Francisco Bar Assn. (Bus. Law Sect.), Nevada Bar Assn. (Sect. on Tax.); publs: ed. Taxation & Syndication Report (1983), Certified Historic Restorations (1984); Republican; Catholic. Ofc: Marlin Industries 8601 Wilshire Blvd Ste 1100 Beverly Hills 90211

ANDERSON, MEL, college president; b. Sept. 28, 1928, Oakland; s. Edwin Albert and Lillian Frances (Redmond) A.; edn: BA, St. Mary's Coll. 1952, hon. D.Litt., St. Albert's Coll., Oakland, hon. D.H.L., Lewis Univ.,Ill.; Career: instr. Sacred Heart High Sch, San Francisco 1952-56; v.prin. La Salle H.S., Pasadena 1956-62; prin. San Joaquin Meml. H.S., Fresno 1962-64; prin. St. Mary's H. Sch., Berkeley 1964-69; pres. St. Mary's Coll. of Calif., Moraga 1969—; exec. com. Assn. Independent Calif. Colls. & Univs., 1980-; bd. dirs. Ind. Colls. of No. Calif.; chmn. Regional Assn. East Bay Colls. & Univ. 1979-81; mem. Commonwealth Club of Calif. Democrat. Roman Catholic. Address: Bro. Mel Anderson, F.S.C., St. Mary's Coll. Moraga 94575

ANDERSON, MELVIN EDWIN, manufacturing co. president; b. June 19, 1943, Oakland; s. Melvin Palmer and Frances Marion (Erceg) A.; m. Susan, Sept. 10, 1966; children: Jill b. 1970, Scott b. 1974; edn: AA, San Jose City Coll. 1963; BA, CSU San Jose 1965. Career: sales and mktg. mgr. U.S. Divers Corp., Santa Ana 1972-81; v.p. sales & mktg. L.M. Gerson Co., Middleboro, Mass. 1982; pres. M. Anderson Assoc., Santa Ana 1982-83; founder, bd. chmn., pres. Respiratory Systems, Inc. (life support mfg. co.), Irvine 1984—; recipient num. sales and marketing awards; mem: Safety Equip. Distbg. Assn., Nat. Fire Protection Assn., Orange County CofC, U.S. Tennis Assn.; works:

co-designer Emergency Breathing Systems; rec: tennis, football. Res: Mission Viejo Ofc: Respiratory Systems Inc. 18102 Skypark South, Ste J&K, Irvine 92714

ANDERSON, MICHAEL ROBERT, sales executive; b. Nov. 3, 1953, Mnpls., Minn.; s. Arthur Robert and Patricia Carlson Anderson; m. Rebecca Pierce, June 6, 1981; edn: BSEE, Univ. of Minn. Inst. Tech. 1976; MSSM, USC 1981. Career: LSI designer Hughes Aircraft Co., Fullerton 1977; sales rep. Hewlett Packard, Fullerton 1977; sales rep. Group III Electronics, Irvine 1981, regional sales mgr. 1983; sales rep. Lisp Machines Inc., Los Angeles 1985 − ; Kappa Eta Kappa Beta Chpt. Alumnus; rec: sports, computers, travel. Res: 28152 Bedford Laguna Niguel 92677 Ofc: Lisp Machines Inc., 6033 Century Blvd Ste 900 Los Angeles 90045

ANDERSON, NOLAN JON, b. Aug. 25, 1944, Howard, S.D.; s. Norman Arvid and Lulu E. (Zimmerman) A.; children: Stacy, b. 1966, Christine, b. 1971, Sarah, b. 1979; edn: BS in pharm., S.D. State Univ. 1967; BS medicine, Univ. of S.D. 1972; MD, Texas Tech. Univ. Sch. of Med. 1974; Fellow Am. Coll. of Surgeons 1981. Career: intern, Southwestern Sch. of Medicine, 1975; res. in surgery Kern Med. Center, 1978; group practice of surgery, Delano, Ca. 1978 − ; chief of staff Delano Regional Med. Center 1981-82, chief of surgery 1983-84; awards: Upjohn Achievement Award 1974, Resident of the Year award 1976-7, 77-8; mem. AMA, CMA, Kern County Med. Soc., Kiwanis; publs: contbr. med. journals; Republican; Methodist; rec: flying, running. Ofc: 1205 Garces Hwy, Ste 303, Delano 93216

ANDERSON, RAYMOND HARTWELL, JR., engineer; b. Feb. 25, 1932, Staunton, Va.; s. Raymond Hartwell and Virginia Boatwright (Moseley) A.; m. Dana Wilson, Sept. 5, 1959; children: Kathryn, b. 1960, Margaret, b.1962, Susan, b. 1963; edn: BS, ceramic eng.,Va. Polytech. Inst. 1957, BS, metallurg. eng. 1958, MS, metallurg. eng. 1959. Career: metallurgical engr. Gen.Dynamics, Ft. Worth, Tex. 1959-61; sr. metallurg. engr. Babcock & Wilcox Co., Lynchburg, Va. 1961-65; Douglas Aircraft Co., Santa Monica, Ca. 1965-67; materials R&D splst. McDonnell Douglas, Santa Monica 1967-71; sr. technical splst. McDonnell Douglas, Huntington Bch. 1971 − ; asst. prof. metallurgy, Va. Poly. Inst. 1958-59; Am. Soc. for Metals teaching staff 1966-69; cons. engr., metallurgy, 1967-68. Honors: Tau Beta Pi (earth sci.), Alpha Sigma Mu (metals), Omicron Delta Kappa (leadership), Sigma Gamma Epsilon, Scabbard & Blade (mil.). Mem: Corrosion Soc. 1957-70, Am. Ceramic Soc. 1957-70, Am. Nuclear Soc. 1961-65, De Molay 1952-; BSA Merit Badge Com. 1970. Patentee (2); publs: contbr. sci. jours. Mil: lst lt. US Army Ord. 1954-56, Nat. Svc. ribbon. Republican. Prot. rec: sports cars, philately, gardening, stereo music systems. Res: 1672 Kenneth Dr. Santa Ana 92705 Ofc: McDonnell Douglas, 5301 Bolsa Ave Huntington Bch 92647

ANDERSON, RICHARD IVAN, educational psychologist; b. Sept. 14, 1952, Akron, Iowa; s. Ivan Wilfred and Marianne (Kerr) A.; m. Jean Johnson, Aug. 11, 1973; edn: BS, Iowa State Univ. 1974; MS, Univ. of Ill. 1977, PhD cand. 1986. Career: computer pgmmr./analyst Standard Oil Co. (Indiana), Chgo. 1974-75; research/tchg. asst. Dept. Comp. Sci., Univ. of Ill., 1975-76, research asst. Ctr. for the Study of Reading, 1976-78, tchg. asst. Dept. Ednl. Psychol. 1978-80, 83, research asst. Aviation Research Lab., 1980-83; cons. Training Div., Pacific Bell, San Ramon 1983 − ; honors: Phi Beta Kappa (1974), Phi Kappa Phi (1974), Pi Mu Epsilon (1974), Phi Delta Kappa (1977), Kappa Delta Pi (1977); mem. Assn. for the Devel. of Computer-Based Instrnl. Systems, Am. Ednl. Research Assn., Assn. for Ednl. Data Systems; publs: num. conf. and tech. papers, articles in profl. jours.; rec: ski, tennis, hiking. Res: 6550 Ascot Dr Oakland 94611

ANDERSON, ROBERT ALEXANDER, manufacturing co. executive; b. June 17, 1943, San Francisco; s. Hugh and Patricia Inez (Hollett) A.; m. Mary Louise, Apr. 11, 1980; children: Melissa b. 1966, Scot b. 1971, Justin b. 1972; edn: BA zool., San Jose State Univ. 1971; Lincoln Univ. Law Sch. 1972-73. Career: deputy sheriff L.A. Co. Sherrif's Dept. 1974-83; pres. Defense Moulding Ent. Inc. Carson 1982 − ; curator of reptiles Mus. of Vertebrate Zool., San Jose State Univ. 1968-71; Modern Plastics Mgmt. Advisory Panel 1986-87; honors: commendation for outstanding performance in the line of duty, L.A. Co. Bd. of Supvrs. (1981), Silver Star for Bravery, Am. Police Hall of Fame (2/26/86); patent: improved cartridge magazine 1983; Republican; Catholic; rec: hunting, fishing, jogging, reading. Res: 19009 Laurel Park Rd Apt 481 Dominguez Hills 90220 Ofc: Defense Moulding Enterprises Inc. POB 4328 Carson 90745

ANDERSON, ROBERT WHITNEY, investment counselor, ret.; b. Aug. 8, 1916, Springfield, Ill.; s. Alban Jennings and Marguerite (Sell) A.; m. Dorothy Ann Maar, Aug. 7, 1943; 1 son, Stuart Tyler (MD, asst. prof. anesth. UCI) b. 1950; edn: BS cum laude, UC Berkeley 1943; MBA, Stanford Univ. 1948. Career: chief of survey Pacific Gas & Elec. Co., Pit River Dam Project 1942-43; chief of survey Swinerton & Walberg, San Francisco 1946; economic engring. staff Standard Oil of Calif. 1946-47; senior v.p. Scudder, Stevens & Clark, Los Angeles 1948-75, ret.; lectr. USC Grad. Sch. of Bus. 1963-65; honors: Tau Beta Pi (1942), Sigma Xi (1943), Chi Epsilon (1943), Interfrat. Scholastic Honor Soc. (pres. 1942-43); civic: City of Rolling Hills Estates (founder 1957, councilman 1957-74, mayor 1959-60), Rolling Hills Intermediate Basketball League (vol. coach 1963-78), Phi Delta Theta frat.; mil: capt. US Army Corps of Engrs. Active Duty 1943-46, maj. Army Mil. Intel. Reserves 1949-57; Republican; Episcopal; rec: tennis, bridge (Nat. Master Rating). Res: 71 Cypress Way Rolling Hills Estates 90274

ANDERSON, SCOTT WILSHIRE, hotel executive; b. Sept. 24, 1950, San Diego; s. Albert L. and Jean (Wilshire) A.; m. Maggie Maaskant, June 18, 1971; children: Paul, b. 1980, Lauren, b. 1982; edn: BA, Wash. State Univ. 1972. Career: positions with Western Internat. Hotels: Continental Plaza, Chgo. 1972-75, South Coast Plaza, Irvine, Ca. 1975-77, Ariz. Biltmore, Phx. 1977-79; Hotel del Coronado: vice pres./ res. mgr. 1979-80, senior v.p./mgr. (1980-83), pres./gen. mgr. 1983 − ; also pres. del Coronado Travel; dir. Hotel/ Motel Adv. Com. for San Diego Comm. Colls.; recipient Outstanding Young Citizen, San Diego Jaycees 1981, 82; mem: Coronado CofC (dir.), Coronado Hotel/Motel Assn. (chmn.), Calif. Hotel/Motel Assn. (dir.), S.D. Hotel/Motel Assn. (pres.), S.D. Conv. and Vis. Bur. (dir.); trustee Childrens Hosp. and Health Ctr. Address: Del Coronado Hotel, 1500 Orange Ave Coronado 92118

ANDERSON, WARREN E., company president; b. May 22, 1951, Pittsburgh, Pa.; s. Warren E. and Mary Kay (Fletcher) A.; edn: BSME, Univ. Cincinnati 1974; MBA, Santa Clara Univ. 1982; Calif. Comm. Coll. Tchg. Credl. 1978; IBM Sys. Sci. Inst. 1980; Certified Data Processor 1981. Career: computer programmer Mitre Corp. Boston 1974-75; mgr. sales & mktg. sys., senior sys,. analyst Intel Corp. Santa Clara 1975-80; database adminstr. Capital Preservation Fund Palo Alto 1980-82; pres., chmn. Anderson Soft-Teach San Jose 1982 − ; honors: Herman Schneider Scholar (1973), Cooper-Bessemer Scholar (1969), Admission w/ Distinction (Univ. Cincinnati 1969), Football Scholar (1969); mem: Inst. for Certification of Computer Profls., Kiwanis Key Club (pres. 1968-69), Sophos Hon. Soc. (1970-71), Delta Tau Delta (asst. treas. 1971-72); publ: Life Insurance as an Investment (Coop Engrg. Mag. 1969). Res: 2161 Blossom Valley Dr San Jose 95124 Ofc: Anderson Soft-Teach 2680 N First St San Jose 95134

ANDOW, ANGEL, construction executive, electrical engineer; b. May 21, 1928, El Paso, Texas; s. Charles and Glafira V. Andow; m. Ruperta Bejarano, July 31, 1955; children: Andrew James b. 1964, Richard Franklin b. 1965; edn: BS in EE, Texas Western Coll., Univ. Tex. 1954; UCLA 1961, 63, Univ. Ill. 1969; Reg. Profl. Engr. (Electrical) Calif. 1971. Career: engr., estimator, v.p. Barr Electric Corp., 1968-70; engr. and estimator L.K. Comstock, Inc. 1970-72; project mgr. Fischbach and Moore, Inc. (Titan I missile launch facility), 1961; pres., bd. chmn., mgr. Alpha Electrical Corp., San Jose 1972 − ; mem. American Legion (v-cmdr. 1972); works: The Korean Woman, 1950-51 (Copyright 1983); Letters to Big Jim Regarding Narrul Purigo, Cashinum Iman (in prog.); mil: sgt. USMCR -1951, commendation and award from Gen. Lemuel Shepherd, Jr., USMC Commandant, citation ribbon with Combat V, Maj. Gen. G.C. Thomas; Republican; Roman Catholic; rec: music, salt water fishing, golf. Ofc: Alpha Electrical Corp. 2128 D North First St San Jose 95131

ANDREINI, ELIZABETH BRAUN, educator; b. Aug. 7, 1949, Pittsburgh, Pa.; d. Louis Ernest and Alice Waterman (McCoy) Braun; m. Alan Andreini, Apr. 20, 1975, div. 1981; 1 son, Alan, Jr. b. 1979; edn: AA, Centenary Coll. for Women 1969; BS, Youngstown State Univ. 1972; NASD Reg. Representative, New York Inst. of Finance 1975. Career: asst. youth dir. YWCA, Portland, Me. 1972-74; adminstrv. asst. Oppenheimer & Co. Inc., N.Y. 1974-76; ofc. mgr. Paine Webber Jackson & Curtis, N.Y. 1976-77; instnl. office coord. Oppenheimer & Co. Inc., San Francisco 1982-84; teacher's aide Reed School, Tiburon 1985 − ; comml. modeling p.t. with 3 San Francisco agencies; honors: Bonnie Benn Jesser Award for all-around excellence, Centenary Coll. (1968); mem. Colonial Dames XVII Century, DAR, Junior League of S.F.; Republican; Episcopal; rec: modeling, dancing, acting. Res: 59 Idlewood Rd Kentfield 94904

ANDRESS, THOMAS PRESTON, JR., engineer, marketing executive; b. Mar. 22, 1935, Wiggins, Miss.; s. Thomas Preston, Sr. and Thelma Mae (Moody) A.; m. Bobbie S. Hutchinson, Jan. 25, 1964; children: Courtney Ann b. 1968, Thomas Christian b. 1977; edn: BSEE, Miss. State Univ. 1957. Career: mem. tech. staff, field engr. Hughes Aircraft Co. (at many air bases wordwide) 1957-73, MTS group head L.A. 1974-75, asst. mktg. mgr. Wash. DC 1976-77, mgr. China Lake Dist. 1977 − ; honors: Nat. Honor Soc. (1953), Man of the Year, Bus. & Profl. Women's Club (1986); mem: Navy League (pres. 2 terms, exec. v.p., v.p. 1977-86), Assn. of Old Crows, Assn. for Retarded Citizens (pres. 3 terms, secty.), Selective Svc. Sys. (bd.), Kiwanis (past pres.), Ridgecrest CofC (secty., v.p.), Ridgecrest Comm. Hosp. Found., Fire Mtn. Found.; Republican; So. Baptist; rec: music (vocal & trumpet), gardening, reading. Res: 709 Sydnor Ridgecrest 93555 Ofc: Hughes Aircraft Co. POB 1077 Ridgecrest 93555

ANDREWS, VERN L., executive; b. Dec. 3, 1946, Trona, Calif.; s. Robert V. and Alice Rose (Diezel) A.; m. Marie Anderson, Aug. 6, 1977; children: Vonda b. 1964, Bobby b. 1968, Paul b. 1971, Velvet b. 1972, Joshua b. 1982; edn: Ariz. Dept. of Public Safety Acad. 1968, Ariz. Western Coll. 1970, No. Ariz. Univ. 1974. Career: supv. criminal investigations unit Ariz. Dept. of Public Safety, Phoenix 1964-81; v.p./gen. mgr. Edward H. Bohlin Co., Hollywood 1981-85; dir. western apparel & accessories, Republic Pictures Corp., Los Angeles 1985 − ; honors: named Member of Year (1980); mem. Burbank CofC, Frat. Order of Police (past pres., life mem.), Houston Livestock Show & Rodeo (life); civic: fund raising for L.A. Blind Children/L.A.P.D., Nat. Easter Seals, Casa De Los Ninos (battered children's home); author ms., Walking On The Edge; Republican; rec: golf, boating, fishing. Res: 20155 Keswick St #211 Canoga Park 91306 Ofc: Republic Pictures Corp. 12636 Beattrice Los Angeles 90066

ANDRIANO-MOORE, RICHARD NORVEL, naval officer, ret.; b. May 25, 1932, Petaluma; s. Norvel Moore and Thelma Elizabeth (Cook) Koch-Andriano; m. Janice Hironaka, Jan. 10, 1976; children: Erika b. 1976, Stephen b. 1978; edn: BA, CSU San Jose 1956; grad. work UC Irvine; MBA, Pepperdine Univ. 1977; cert. Naval War Coll., Newport, R.I. 1980-81, 1981-82; desig: Surface Warfare Ofcr., USN (1972). Career: commnd. ensign USN 1957-, 1st lt./gunnery ofcr. USS Jefferson County (LST 1068) 1957-60; tchr. (7th, 8th gr.) Oasis Sch., Thermal, Calif. 1960-63; Navy duty: personnel & legal ofcr. USS Maury (AGS-16) 1963-65, CO Naval & Marine Corps Reserve Tng. Ctr., Pt. Arthur, Tx. 1965-68, dept. hd./ops. ofcr. USS Muliphen (LKA-61) 1968-69, asst. Surface & ASW Pgm. ofcr., 1970-72, Surface Pgm. ofcr. 11th Naval Dist. 1972-74, CO Hunters Pt. Naval Reserve Ctr., San Francisco 1974-75, CO Navy and Marine Corps Reserve Ctr., San Bruno 1975-79, dir. adminstrn. Nat. Com. for Employer Support of the Guard and Reserve, Office of Secty. Def., Wash DC 1979-82, comdr. recruiting coord. Region 1, Alameda 1982-84, chief of staff Naval Reserve Readiness Command Region 20, Treasure Is., S.F. 1984-85, ret.; decorated Def. Merit. Service (1982), Navy Commendn. (1973, 85), authorized by SecDef to wear the Office of the Secty. of Def. I.D. Badge (1980), Command Ashore Insignia (1974), Surface Warfare Insignia (1978), USN Recruiting Badge w/2 gold wreaths (1983, 84), Expt. Pistol Shot (1978); honors: War Service Medal (1974), Silver Good Citizenship Medal (1978), Patriot Medal (1985), SAR; hon. dir. Navy League of U.S./San Mateo Co. Council (1975-79); 2d deg. Brown Belt, Kodakan Judo Assn., Tokyo; mem: Sigma Nu Frat. (chpt. pres. 1955), Nat. Soc. SAR (pres. S.F. chpt. 1976-77, chmn. Nat. DAR Cmte 1979-81, v.p. No. Calif. Soc. SAR 1984-86, pres. Calif. Soc. SAR 1986-), Mil. Order of Loyal Legion of U.S., Calif. Commandery (Recorder 1976-78, v.comdr. 1978-82, comdr. 1986-), The Augustan Soc., Gen. Soc. of Mayflower Desc., Gen. Soc. of the War of 1812, Hospitaller Order of St. John of Jerusalem (Knight Hospitaler 1983), Naval Order of U.S.; civic: Liberty Sch. PTA, Konocti Girl Scout Council, Ret. Ofcrs. Assn.; publs: chief ed. Calif. Compatriot (1986-); Republican; Prot.; rec: travel, Civil War relics, genealogy. Res: 197 Upland Dr Petaluma 94952

ANDROSEVIC, SNJEZANA NIVES, aerospace financial analyst; b. Nov. 6, 1959, Zagreb, Yugoslavia, nat. US cit. 1980; d. Slobodan Danny and Bozica Vlasta (Kropek) Androsevic; edn: BBA, Loyola Marymount Univ. 1982; MBA pgm., Pepperdine Univ. current; Calif. real estate lic. (1979). Career: asst. controller F&I Investment Co., Beverly Hills 1978-84; finl. analyst Rockwell Internat., El Segundo 1984-85, Northrop Electronics 1985-; inv. and finl. cons. to SDA Mgmt. Co. 1984-; awards: Jesuit Merit Award (1978), LMU Honors Pgm. (1978-82), Alpha Sigma Nu (1981-); mem. Nat. Assn. of Female Execs., Sigma Sigma Sigma sor.; Republican; rec: languages (Serbo/Croatian, French, German, Spanish), philately, skiing, theatre. Res: 7348 W 89th St Los Angeles 90045 Ofc: 2301 West 120th St Hawthorne 90250

ANGEL, BARBARA JEAN, school psychologist; b. Aug. 30, 1930, South Gate; d. George William and Juanita Pearl (Llewellyn) Newell; m. Donald L. Angel, Nov. 28, 1953; children: Amy, b. 1957; Suzanne, b. 1960; edn: AA, Mt. San Antonio Coll. 1951; BA, UC Santa Barbara 1953; MA, Claremont Grad. Sch. 1970; sch. psychologist cred., CSU, Fullerton 1972; Sch. Psychologist, Calif. 1972; lic. Ednl. Psychologist, Calif. 1981. Career: psychometrist/ tchr. Devereux Schs., Goleta 1954-56; psychometrist, Morovia Unified Sch. Dist., 1965-67, Claremont Unified Sch. Dist., 1967-70; psychologist Chino Unified Sch. Dist., Chino 1970-; dist. rep. to devel. master plan for spl. edn.; devel. original proposal for gifted pgm. in Chino Sch. Dist.; coms. (chmpsn.) Spl. Edn. Region, and mem. panel on psychologist role in educ. wrkshp., Cal Poly; rep. Calif. St. Dept. of Edn. spl. edn. pgm. reviews; mem: Chino Assn. Mgmt. Personnel (secty.); Calif. Assn. of Sch. Psychologists & Psychometrists; Calif. Assn. for the Gifted; Pi Lambda Theta; Pomona Valley Geneol. Soc.; First place awards for needlework, L.A. County Fair 1974, 75; Republican; Congregational; rec: Calif. hist., Am. Indian hist., sewing. Res: 111 East Kirkwood Ave Claremont 91711 Ofc: Chino Unified School Dist., 5130 Riverside Dr Chino 91710

ANGELOTTI, ROBERT HENRY, marketing executive; b. Mar. 26, 1958, Erie, Pa.; s. Henry Richard and Ann Florence (Di Placido) A.; m. Maren C., June 20, 1981; children: Christopher Anthony b. 1983, Jaclyn Ann b. 1984; edn: BA commun./theol., Loyola Marymount Univ. 1980. Career: gen. mgr. KXLU-AM/FM Radio, Los Angeles 1980; account exec. Joy Prodns.,/ The Joy Agency Inc., L.A. 1980-81, dir. Media Relations 1981-83, v.p. Media Rels. Joy Prodns/ The Joy Agency 1983; dir. publicity/promotions & spl. mkts. The Sparrow Corp., L.A. 1983-; cons. Paulist Communs., Youth Outreach Unlimited, Pacific Constrn. Mgmt. Group, The Crystal Cathedral, Mercy Corps Internat., Catholic Communs. Network, Compassion Internat., Fr. Michael Manning Inc.; honors: Alpha Sigma Nu, nat. Jesuit Hon. Soc. (1980), presdtl. cit. for scholarship, Loyola Marymount (1980); mem: Gospel Music Assn., Christian Press Assn., Loyola Marymount Univ. Alumni Assn.; publs: 100+ articles for entertainment, trade and consumer periodicals (1981-); Republican; Roman Catholic; rec: collect rare books, water sports, stu. theology and history. Ofc: 9255 Deering Ave Chatsworth 91311

ANGUIANO, LUPE, b. Mar. 12, 1929, La Junta, Colo.; d. Jose and Rosario (Gonzales) A.; edn: MA in adminstrn. and edn., Antioch Univ. 1978. Career: religious tchr. Our Lady of Victory Missionary Sister, 1949-65; supr. teenage leadership pgm. (15 Teen-Post projects) Los Angeles Fedn. of Neighborhood Ctrs., 1965-66; helped write Bilingual-Bicultural Edn. Act., US Ofc. of Edn., 1967-68; S.W. regl. dir. NAACP Legal Def. and Edn. Fund, 1969; HEW pgm. chief Women's Action, Calif. Region, 1970-73; regl. dir. (S.W. region) for the Spanish Speaking, Nat. Council of Catholic Bishops, 1973-77; founder, pres., CEO Nat. Women's Employment and Edn. Inc. (NWEE), 1977-, founder/

adminstr. of Women's Employment and Edn. Model Pgm. (WEEMP) 1973, also designed a Model Child Care Tng. Pgm., devel. funding for WEE affil. pgms. in San Antonio, Dallas and El Paso, Tx.; Phoenix, Ariz.; Ventura, Calif.; Tacoma, Wash.; Denver, Colo. (1980-82); pres./CEO Lupe Anguiano and Assocs., 1982-; honors: featured in CBS-TV "An American Portrait" and in Poster series commemorating Statue of Liberty Centennial (2/85), CBS-TV "60 Minutes segment "Getting Off Welfare" (11/80), A Gallery of Women traveling nat. exhib. by Adolph Coors Co. (1985-87), Fedn. of Republican Women, Wash DC (1985), Geo. Wash. Medal, Freedom Found. (1985), listed in 100 US Influential Hispanics for the 1980's, Hispanic Bus. Mag. (1983), 1983 Brindis Award, Nat. Women's Pol. Caucus, 1983 Pres.'s Volunteer Action Award, Wonder Woman Award, Warner Communs. (1982), Vista Award (1980), Woman of the 80s, Ms. Mag. (1980), citation, Texas State House of Reps. (1978); mem. Guadalupe Cultural Arts Ctr./San Antonio, Am. Mgmt. Assn., Am. Soc. of Profl. and Exec. Women, Nat. Assn. Female Execs., Nat. Womens Pol. Caucus (adv. council), Women in Communs., San Antonio Mexican CofC; Democrat; Catholic. Res: 1205 Redwood St Oxnard CA 93030 Ofc: National Women's Employment and Education Inc. (NWEE) 650 South Spring St Ste 625 Los Angeles 90014

ANNAU, MARSHALL EUGENE, real estate broker; b. June 22, 1930, Great Falls, Mont.; s. Joseph Victor and Madeline Pauline A.; edn: BA, Univ. Montana Missoula 1952; finance, Coll. of Marin 1961; real estate, L.A. Valley Coll. 1972. Career: exec. svc. mgmt. Litton Inds. Royfax div., AM Corp. Bruning div., Xerox Corp. 1960-70; real estate speculator 1970-77; real estate sales 1977-81, corp. broker 1982-; r.e. dept. v.p. First Transtate Financial Group and subsids. Encino; mem. San Fernando Valley Bd. Realtors; rec: woodworking, motorcycling. Ofc: First Transtate Financial Group 16000 Ventura Blvd Ste 1201 Encino 91436

ANNOTICO, RICHARD ANTHONY, investor; b. Sept. 17, 1930, Cleveland, Ohio; s. Tony and Grace (Kovarik) A.; edn: BA, honors, Ohio Univ. 1953, grad. work, UCLA 1956-8, LLB, JD, Southwestern Law Sch., 1963. Career: dir. internat. sales Liberty Records, Los Angeles 1958-62, vice pres. 1962-64; investment counselor, 1964-68; investor, 1969-; mem. Los Angeles City Bd. of Human Relations Commnrs. 1977-84, pres. 1983-4; mem. L.A. City Transportation Commn. 1984-; bd.govs., Calif. State Bar Assn., 1983-; exec. com. Small Bus. Adv. Bd., Calif. State Senate; past bd. dirs. John Rossi Found.; past mem. L.A. City-Co. Adv. Com. on Consolidation. Awards: Cavaliere Ufficiale (Knight Ofcr.); Order of Merit, Repub. of Italy. Mem. Beta Theta Pi (Beta Kappa chpt.), Phi Delta Phi (Pound Inn); mil: 1st lt. USAF 1955-56. Rec: tennis, nautilus. Address: 1870 Veteran Ave. Los Angeles 90025

ANSLOW, ROBERT EDWARD, electronics co. executive; b. June 12, 1932, Detroit; s. Robert Elmer and Dorothy (Davies) A.; m. Carolyn C. Simpkinson, Apr. 6, 1957; children: Robert b. 1959, Elizabeth b. 1962; edn: BSChE, Mass. Inst. Technol. 1954; MBA, Harvard Grad. Sch. of Bus. Admin. 1956. Career: var. positions in mktg., product plnng., acquisitions Raytheon Co. Lexington, Mass. 1956-65; controller, v.p., pres. Roanwell Corp. NYC 1965-73; dir. worldwide sales Semiconductor Div. Rockwell Internat. Anaheim, Newport Beach 1973-85; v.p., gen. mgr. Plessey Semiconductors USA Irvine 1985-; lectr. West Coast Univ. 1984-85; honors: Tau Beta Pi, Sigma Xi; mem: Inst. Elec. Electron. Engrs. (senior), Semiconductor Industry Assn. (coop. technol. com., public policy com. 1983-85), Defense Electronics Mag. Advisory Com. 1985-; mil: capt. USAR 1956-64; Republican; Episcopal; rec: travel, antique cars. Res: 1833 Santiago Dr Nerport Beach 92660 Ofc: Plessey Semiconductors 3 Whatney Irvine 92718-2806

ANSTEDT, THEODORE ROOSEVELT, JR., sales motivation and training co. president; b. Sept. 28, 1944, St. Louis, Mo.; s. Theodore R. and Anna Louise (Freund) A.; m. Suzanne Jane Oldfield, June 7, 1980; edn: BA, honors in humanities, summa cum laude, Stanford Univ. 1967, MA, 1969. Career: v.p./ sales tng. dir. Bank of Am., San Francisco 1970-73; v.p. mkt. support U.S. Leasing, S.F. 1973-77; dir. tng. Tratu/McGraw Hill, Los Angeles 1977-79; exec. v.p. mktg. Spectrum Tng. Corp., Boston 1979-81; pres. Merit Tng. Corp., S.F. 1981-; dir. A16 Investments (1970-); honors: Phi Beta Kappa; mem. Assn. of Tng. & Devel., Nat. Speakers Assn., Stanford Alumni Club, S.F. Symph. Assn., S.F. Ballet Assn., S.F. Opera Assn., S.F. Mus. Assn.; publs: series of works on mktg., sales mgmt., sales, motivation, mng. customer service; mil: Marines OCS; Republican; Prot.; rec: swim, ski, travel, writing. Res: 105 Roblar Ave Hillsborough 94010 Ofc: Merit Training Corp. Ste 200 2121 S El Camino Real San Mateo 94403

ANTHONY, JACK RALPH, investigator; b. MAr. 28, 1928, Compton, Calif.; s. Theodore Ralph and Anita Claire (Mayo) A.; m. Irene, July 4, 1982; edn: AA cum laude, E. L.A. Coll. 1968; BA, CSU Los Angeles 1972; lic. pvt. investigator; advanced P.O.S.T. cert. Calif. Career: sgt. organized crime bureau L.A. County Sheriff's Dept. 1957-79 (ret.); senior investigator Lockheed Cal. Co. 1979-82, Northrop Advanced Sys. Div. 1982-; instr. East L.A. Coll. 1970-72; mem: Profl. Peace Ofcrs. Assn., Nat. Rifle Assn., Audubon Soc., Sheriff's Relief Assn., Moose, Eagles; mil: t/sgt. USAF; Republican; Protestant; rec: pistol shooting, skeet, trap, benchrest rifle. Res: 238 Hawk Lane Palmdale 93550 Ofc: Northrup Advanced Systems Div. 8900 E Washington Blvd Pico Rivera

ANTHONY, MARY CARMEL, county law librarian; b. June 3, 1925, Visalia; d. Francisco Cardoso and Virginia (Cotto) Jacques; m. Jack Gerard Anthony, Nov. 27, 1976; edn: stu., Coll. of Sequoias 1944-46; cert. 4C's Coll., Fresno

1967. Career: operator Pacific pTelephone Co., Visalia 1944-46; sec. State Bd. Equalization, Visalia 1946-47; clerk typist County Farm Advisors, Visalia 1947-49; clerk typist Dept. Motor Vehicles, Visalia 1968-69; clerk typist II, Juvenile Probatian Dept., Visalia 1969-70; dep. clerk Jury Commrs. Office, Visalia 1971-73; county law librarian Tulare County, Visalia 1973–; mem: Public Employees Assn. Tulare Co.; Am. Assn. Law Libraries; San Joaquin Valley Library System; Assoc. Bus. Girls Calif.; Kaweah Delta Dist. Hosp. Guild; V.F.W.; Catholic. Res: Visalia 93291 Ofc: County Civic Center, Room 1 , Visalia 93291

ANTONOVICH, MICHAEL D., supervisor, Los Angeles County; b. Aug. 12, 1939, Los Angeles; s. Michael A.; single; edn: BA, CSU Los Angeles 1963, MA, 1967; grad. Pasadena Police Acad., Reserve Officer Sch. 1967; Rio Hondo Reserve Ofcr. Advanced Tng. Sch. 1978; Intercollegiate Studies Inst., Hoover Instn., Stanford Univ. 1968, 69, 70; prog. for senior execs. in state and local govt., JFK Sch. of Govt., Harvard 1984; Air War Coll., Nat. Security Forum, Maxwell AFB 1984. Career: govt.-hist. instr. L.A. Unified Sch. Dist. 1966-72; bd. trustees L.A. Comm. Coll. Dist. 1969-73; elected to Calif. State Assem. (Repub. Whip 1976-78) 1972-78; v.p. and project dir. J. Phil Johnson Corp., 1979-80; Atlantic Treaty Assn. del. to Iceland, 1977; elected Fifth Dist. Supvr., County of Los Angeles 1980-84, re-elected 1984-88; chmn. L.A. Co. Economic Devel. Corp. Trade Delegation Japan, Taiwan 1983; bd. dirs. George Miller Constrn. Co., 1975-, Pacific Data Mgmt. Corp. 1984-; instr. CSU Los Angeles 1979, 85, Pepperdine Univ. 1979; bd. regents Christ Lutheran Coll. 1978-86; pres. So. Calif. Regl. Assn. of County Supvrs. 1984-85; apptd. by Pres. Reagan to US/Japan Advis. Commn. 1984; Commn. of White House Fellowships 1982-85; honors: Outstanding Legislator of Year, Calif. Repub. Assem. 1973-4, 74-5, 76-7; Statesman of Year award, Calif. Pro-Life Council 1976; Am. Conf. of Young Political Leaders del. to Japan 1974; Alumni of Year 1977, CSULA; Alumni Award of Merit, CSULA Alumni Assn. 1983; Legislator of Year Award, L.A. Co. Federated Repub. Women 1976; Man of Year, So. Calif. Repub. Heritage Groups Council 1977; mem. Republican State Central Com. Calif. 1964-, v. chmn. Calif. Repub. Party 1982-84, chmn. 1985; hon. chmn. Pres. Reagan 1980 Pres. Campaign, steering com. Reagan-Bush 1984; mem. Glendale Sym. Orch. Assn. (bd. govs. 1973-), CSULA Alumni Assn. (bd. dirs. 1970-74), Glendale CofC (1975-), Elks, Good Shepherd Lutheran Home for Retarded Children, Am. Red Cross, Native Sons of Golden West, L.A. Zoo Assn., So. Pasa. Police Reserves, The Philadelphia Soc., Sigma Nu Frat. Res: Glendale Ofc: Hall of Administration, Room 869, 500 W Temple St Los Angeles 90012

APPLE, JAN, insurance agency executive; b. Minden, Nebr.; d. Harold E. and R. Gladyce (Modine) Jorgensen; m. Philip R. Apple, Jan. 5, 1952; children: Victoria b. 1952, Sandra b. 1954, Rick b. 1955. Career: exec. secty. Calif. Dump Truck Owners Assn., 1964-79, Credit Union mgr., gen. mgr., editor monthly publ. Dump Truck News; pres. Apple Ins. Services, Inc., Laguna Beach 1979– ; mem. ins. coms. in Calif. Dump Truck Ops. Assn. and other trucking assns. Ofc: Apple Ins. Services 1745 S Coast Hwy Laguna Beach 92651

APPLEGATE, D. RONALD, lawyer; b. May 4, 1942, Sand Springs, Okla.; s. Roy G. and Opal Dorothy (McCray) A.; m. Sandra Ann Beltracchi, Aug. 20, 1972; children: Wade, b. 1975; Brooke, b. 1978; Blake, b. 1980; edn: BA, Anderson Coll., Anderson, Ind. 1966; JD, Whittier Coll. of Law 1975; admitted to Calif. State Bar 1975. Career: city police ofcr., Anderson, Ind. 1964-66; pub. sch. tchr., Anderson, Ind. 1965-66; US Army 1966-68; soc. wkr., Los Angeles Co. 1969-73; welfare fraud investigator, Glendale 1973-75; corp. counsel Forest Lawn Co., Glendale 1976-81; gen. practice criminal defense & civil litigation 1981–; judge pro tem.: Los Angeles Municipal Ct.; Compton Municipal Ct.; instr.: Los Angeles City Coll.; Glendale City Coll.; Pro bono counsel, Vietnam Vet Leadership pgm.; mem: L.A. Co. Bar Assn. (Com. on Alcohol Abuse); State Bar of Calif. (Com. on Alcohol Abuse); Am. Bar Assn.; Am. Cancer Soc. (instr. Stop Smoking Clinics); mil: Spec. 5/c, US Army 1966-68; Democrat; rec: current events, reading novels, family outings. Res: 1339 Virginia Ave Glendale 91202 Ofc: 619 S Westlake Ave, 1st Flr, Los Angeles 90057

APPLEMAN, WAYNE DOUGLAS, human resources development executive; b. July 8, 1937, Wausau, Wis.; s. Wilbur Ross and Alberta Marie (Kohlenbach) A.; m. Penny Ann Sears, Dec. 21, 1959; children: Todd Douglas, Scott Douglas; edn: BA psych., Ohio Wesleyan Univ. 1959; bus. & law, Ohio St. Univ. 1960-61. Career: tng. mgr. var. cos. in midwest, 1961-71; mgr. Mgmt. Devel. Svcs., State of Calif., Sacto. 1971-75, mgr. Instrn. Design 1975-78, asst. chief Personnel Devel. Div. 1978-81, mgr. Quality of Work Life 1981-83, chief Mgmt. & Staff Devel. 1983-85; chief Staff & Orgn. Devel. Calif. State Lottery, Sacto. 1985–; pres. Appleman & Assocs. 1982–; guest lectr. CSU Sacto. (1981-84), UC Davis (1984-86); recipient Torch Award, ASTD (1978); mem: Am. Soc. Tng. Devel. (chpt. pres. 1975, asst. regl. v.p. ASTD 1977-78, 81-82, nat. com. chair 1982-83), Internat. Assn. of Quality Circles (chpt. charter pres. 1981); civic: United Way (chmn. 1975-76), adv. com. Mgmt. & Supvn. Dept. Sierra Coll. (chair 1977-80); contbg. author book: Going Public- Quality Circles in the Public Sector (1984); Republican; Presbyterian (elder); rec: choral music, tennis, investing. Ofc: Calif. State Lottery 600 N Tenth St Sacramento 95814

APPLETON, JAMES R., university administrator; b. Jan. 20, 1937, North Tonawanda, NY; s. Robert Martin and Emma I. (Mollnow) A.; m. Carol Koelsch, 1959; children: Steven b. 1960, Jon b. 1963, Jennifer b. 1966; edn: AB, soc. scis., Wheaton Coll. 1958; MA, and PhD in higher edn. adm. & soc. psych., Mich. State Univ., 1965. Career: assoc. dir. Residence Hall Programs, Mich. State Univ. 1963-65; assoc. dean of students Oakland Univ., 1965-68, dean for student life 1968-69, assoc. prof. Behavioral Scis., 1969-72, v.p. 1969-72; v.p. for student affairs Univ. of So. Calif., Los Angeles 1972-82, v.p. for development, 1982–; vis. lectr. Mich. St. Univ. Coll. of Edn., 1969, 72; mgmt. cons. to business and indus.; frequent lectr. neighboring instns., community events, alumni meetings and profl. confs.; honors: Alpha Tau Omega (1980), Phi Kappa Phi (1981), nominated by "Change" one of 100 emerging young leaders of the Acad. (1978), Fred Turner Award, NASPA (1980); mem: Nat. Assn. of Student Personnel Adminstrs. (nat. pres. 1974-75, nat. exec. com. 1969-76), bd. dirs. (chmn. 1975-76) NASPA Inst. of Resrch & Devel. 1975-80, The Council for the Advancement of Small Colls., Am. Assn. Univ. Profs., Council for Advance. and Support of Edn.; author (with C.M. Briggs, J.J. Rhatigan): Pieces of Eight: The Rites, Roles, and Styles of the Dean (NIRAD 1978); articles in profl. and scholarly journals, guest ed. NASPA J. (4/71); mil: ofcr. US Army 1958-60; Presbyterian; rec: vocal music, golf, jogging. Res: 29370 Quailwood Dr Rancho Palos Verdes 90274 Ofc: USC, University Park ADM 104, Los Angeles 900788-2017

ARAMBULA, RUDY HINOJOS, co. president, engineer; b. Apr. 15, 1932, San Angelo, Tex.; s. Natividad Rocha and Paula Villa (Hinojos) A.; m. Bertha Morin, Dec. 3, 1949; children: Rudy Jr. b. 1950, Steve M. b. 1951, Cynthia M. b. 1957; edn: Bakersfield Coll. eve. sch. 1951-60. Career: mechanic Transocean Air Lines, Minner Field, Calif. 1950-52/ assembly line mech., leadman (Super Constellation, U-2) Lockheed, Bakersfield 1952-57; mech./gen. mgr. Sunland Service Sta., Bakersfield 1957-59; mech./gen. foreman Bakersfield Hydraulic Jack Co., 1959-67; owner/pres. Air Draulics Sales & Service, 1967–; awards: FAA Pilot & Proficiency Award, Phase I, II, III (1978, 80, 82), Father of the Year, San Clemente Mission (1970); mem: K.C. (Grand Knight 1969), Aircraft Owners Assn. (chpt. pres. 1972), Nat. Rifle Assn., Admiral Callahan Gen. Assembly (Faithful Navigator 1971-72), Kiwanis (pres. 1982), San Clemente Mission Aux. (pres. 1969-75), Houchim Blood Bank (4 gal.), Frat. Order of Eagles, Civil Air Patrol (1975-, 2d lt. Search & Rescue Team 1983), Boy Scouts Am. (leader 1963-65), Bakersfield Police Reserve (1954-58); works: hydraulic & pneumatic Power Drive Units; Democrat; Catholic; rec: hunting, deep sea fishing, flying. Res: 2320 Elton Ave Bakersfield 93306 Ofc: AirDraulics Sales & Service 2914 Union Ave Bakersfield 93305

ARBUCKLE, PAMELA SUSAN, dentist; b. Mar. 12, 1955, Oakland; d. Ruby Mims Arbuckle; edn: AS, Laney Coll. 1975, AB, UC Berkeley 1977; BS, DDS, UC San Francisco 1982; MPP, UC Berkeley 1984. Career: policy analyst Congl. Research Svc. Wash. DC summer 1983; staff dentist San Francisco Gen. Hosp., Central Health Ctr. Oakland, lead dentist Alameda North County Jail; staff dentist Alameda County Health Care Services Agency; bd. mem. Alameda County Bd. of Supvs. subcom. on Dental Health 1983-; honors: Outstanding Young Women of Am. 1984, Community Service Award (UCSF 1982); mem: Nat. Dental Soc. of Bay Area (chpt. v.p. 1985, secty. 1983-84), Am. Assn. Public Health Dentists 1986; Berkeley Maternal, Child and Adolescent Health Bd. (vice-chair), Head Start Health Advisory Bd., UC Berkeley Alumni Assn. Gov. Council 1984-87; Democrat; Catholic; rec: photog. Res: 1262 Ocean Ave Emeryville 94608 Ofc: Alameda County Health Care Services Agency 470 27th St Oakland 94612

ARDALAN, SIAVOSH, marketing consultant; b. June 4, 1959, Teheran, Iran; s. Soltan Hamid and Haydeh (Saghri) A.; m. Samila Sadri, Sept. 28, 1982; edn: BA in pub. affairs, USC 1981, MA in urban studies 1983. Career: student coord., supvr. fundraising, USC 1981-83; gen. mgr. B.M.A., Culver City 1983-84; gen. mgr. Prremium Promotions Inc., Marina Del Rey 1984-85; mktg. cons./pres. U.S. Business Owners Assn., Sherman Oaks 1985–; awards: Dean's List (1980-81), Planning Dept. scholarship (1982), USC; mem. Am. Planning Assn. 1982-83, Am. Entrepreneur Assn. 1982-; vol. Salvation Army, Am. Red Cross; Republican; rec: music (keyboard), photog. Address: Sherman Oaks 91413

ARELLANO, LEONARDO AUSTRIA, dentist; b. Mar. 8, 1956, San Diego; s. Rafael Nuarin and Josefina M. (Austria) A.; edn: undergrad. UC Los Angeles 1974-77; BS in dental hygiene UC San Francisco 1979, DDS, 1984. Career: coordinator, instr. UCSF Sch. of Dentistry Summer Orientation Pgm., 1978; dental hygienist for Charles B. Darke, DDS, San Francisco 1980-82, Philip Hordiner, DDS, San Francisco 1980–; dentist owner gen. pvt. practice, San Francisco 1984–; awards: Wives of Navy Doctors Club scholarship, USN (1978), Calif. State Scholar (1974-78), life mem. Calif. State Scholarship Fedn. (1974); mem: Am. Dental Assn., UCSF Dental Alumni Assn. (chmn. 1979 South of Market Health Fair; asst. regl. corresp. 1978-79 Pacific Regl. meeting of Am. Assn. of Dental Schs.), Am. Dental Hygienists Assn., Calif. Dental Assn.; works: 3d Place, photography, 1973 Ventura County Fair; Black Belt in Filipino martial art of Kali (1984); rec: martial arts, photog., music. Ofc: Leo Arellano, DDS, 5300 Geary Blvd Ste 315 San Francisco 94121

ARFA, CARL, interior construction co. executive; b. Sept. 5, 1924, NY, NY; s. Meyer and Lillian (Paley) A.; m. Judith Barbara, June 27, 1973; children: Barbara b. 1948, Barry b. 1951, Lawrence b. 1952, Sheryl b. 1955, Alan b. 1959; edn: AA, City Coll. New York 1944, AA Pace Coll. 1947; lic. Gen. Contractor, Calif. (1984), Hawaii, Nev., Utah. Career: v.p., pres. Arfa Decorators, NY 1948-72; pres. Dwoskin Decorating Co., Atlanta, Ga. 1972-76; pres./CEO Arfa Interior Services Co. Inc. 1976–; exec. dir. Viscount Hotel, Las Vegas, Nev. 1985-; v.p. Tybee Prodns., Hollywood; pres./CEO Interstate Interior Contrs., S.F.; honors: Man of the Year Monticello Hosp. (1966), chmn. Sullivan Co. Commun. Coll. Advis. Com. 1964; Republican Party Man of the Year (1981); mem. Am. Soc. of Int. Designers, Nat. Assn. of Gen. Contrs., Painters & Decoraters of Am. (chmn. (1972); mem. Kiwanis, Knights of Pythias, VFW (cmdr.), Jewish War Vets. (cmdr.), Am. Legion, Sullivan County Park Commn. (chmn.); mil: US Army 1943-46, ETO; Republican (v.chmn., Pres. Task Force charter mem.); Jewish; rec: music, performing arts, golf. Ofc: 1177 California St Ste H San Francisco 94108

ARFMAN, HAROLD THOMAS, utility co. executive; b. Mar. 12, 1922, Del Rio, Texas; s. Harry and Lizetta (Schweers) A.; m. Marilyn Brenner, Apr. 21, 1945; children: Susan (Crabtree) b. 1948, Craig b. 1950; edn: undergrad. Schreiner Mil. Inst. 1940, Univ. N.C. 1943; BBA, So. Methodist Univ. 1944, BSME, 1949; Calif. Reg. Profl. Engr. (Mech.). Career: dir. Material Mgmt., San Diego Gas & Electric, San Diego currently; held var. mgmt. positions in power plant engring., electric system planning, power plant ops., govtl. affairs, inter-utility (power) contracting and material mgmt. for over 30 yrs.; mem. governing bodies for Electric Utility Plnng. and Engring. Coms. (Calif. Power Pool and Western Energy Supply and Transmission Assocs.); past chief negotiator for SDG&E in devel. of first elec. interconnection agreement between a USA utility and the Mexican nat. utility, Comision Federal de Electricidad; Registered lobbyist State of Calif., 1976, 77; instr. steam and nuclear power courses in US Navy Reserve Ofcrs. Sch., San Diego; honors: Sigma Tau, Lambda Chi Alpha; mem: Edison Electric Inst. (Prime Movers, Interconnection Arrangements, Purch. & Stores coms.), Pacific Coast Elec. Assn., Pacific Coast Gas Assn., Nat. Assn. of Purch. Mgmt., San Diego CofC; clubs: San Diego Yacht, University (S.D.), Coronado Golf, S.D. Council of Diving Clubs; publs: tech. articles on steam power plant design and op., elec. utility system interconnections and mats. mgmt. in Power Mag., Electric Light and Power, Utility Purch. and Stores Mag.; mil: lt. cmdr., shipboard duty WWII, USNR; Republican; Protestant; rec: golf, skin diving, wind surfing. Res: 609 Rosecrans St San Diego 92106 Ofc: San Diego Gas & Electric Co. 101 Ash St (POB 1831) San Diego 92112

ARGUE, JOHN C., lawyer; b. Jan. 25, 1932, Glendale; s. J. Clifford and Catherine Emily (Clemments) A.; m. Leah Eliabeth Moore, June 29, 1963; children: Eliabeth Anne b. 1967, John Michael b. 1968; edn: AB in commerce, fin., Occidental Coll. 1953; LLB, USC Law Sch. 1956; admitted Calif. State Bar 1957. Career: atty., ptnr. Argue & Argue, Los Angeles 1958-59, Flint & MacKay, 1960-72, senior ptnr. Argue Freston Pearson Harbison & Myers, 1973—; dir: Cal Fed Inc., Calif. Federal Savings & Loan, Trust Services of Am., LAACO, Inc.; advis. dir. Auto Club of So. Calif.; trustee USC, Pomona Coll.; nat. trustee Washington Opera; dir. Nat. Club Assn.; dir. Central City Assn.; dir. L.A. Area CofC; honors: Sports Headliner of Year, L.A. Press Club (1978), Sparkplug Award as The Man Most Responsible for Bringing the 1984 Olympics to L.A., LA Area CofC (1979), William May Garland award, So. Calif. Com. for the Olympic Games (1979), Spirit of Los Angeles award, L.A. Hdqtrs. City Assn. (1979), Centennial award (1980) and Hall of Fame (1984), LA Athletic Club, Track Hall of Fame, Occidental Coll. (1980), disting. service, Am. Heart Assn. LA (1982), Merit award, USC Gen. Alumni Assn. (1984), Disting. Eagle Scout Award, BSA (1984), Outstanding Citizen PRISMS award, Pub. Rels. Soc. Am. (1985), Calif. Ptnrship Award (1985), The Emmett Award, 100 Club (1985), Salerni Collegian (hon.), Scapa Praetor (hon.); mem: Town Hall (pres. 1985), Chancery Club (pres. 1985), SCCOG (pres. 1972-), LAOOC (founding chmn.), So. Calif. Golf Assn. (pres. 1980), Republican Assocs., Am. Heart Assn. (dir.), Central City Assn., LA Council of Internat. Visitors, World Affairs Council, LA Hdqtrs. City Assn.; clubs: California (pres. 1983-84), Oakmont Country (pres. 1972), Flint. Cyn. Tennis, Riviera CC, LA Athletic, LA Country, Rotary (LA), Men's Garden (LA), The Newcomen Soc., 100 Club of LA, Lincoln, Twilight; mil: staff, Comdr.-in-Chief, US Army Europe, Heidelberg, Ger. 1957-58; Republican; Protestant; rec: golf, tennis, skiing. Res: 1314 Descanso Dr La Canada 91011 Ofc: Argue Freston Pearson, 801 South Flower St Los Angeles 90017

ARKON, D., lawyer, corporate director; b. Aug. 30, 1958, NYC; s. R.J. and S.L. (Smith) A.; edn: BS biol., Yale Univ. 1977; JD, Harvard Law Sch. 1980. Career: pvt. law practice, 1981-84; currently ptnr. law firm Pennoyer, Smith, & Arkon; dir. SDA Assn. (bus. cons./mktg. co.); honors: No. Calif. Young Lawyer of Year (1984); mem: Am. Bar Assn., Trial Lawyers Assn., Plaintiff's Counsel League, Yale Alumni Assn.; publ: The unknown 'Letters of Marque and Reprisal' Clause, Calif. Law Rev. (Fall 1982); rec: chess, soccer, softball, travel. Res: Box 72 Capitola 95010

ARMOUR, GORDON CHARLES, manufacturing co. emerging technology specialist; b. June 1, 1929, Denver, Colo.; s. Gordon Thomas and Doris Hilda (Stoker) Armour; m. Margaret C. Graney, Sept. 22, 1951; children: Doris C. b. 1956, Thomas S. b. 1961; edn: Long Beach City Coll. 1948-51; BS bus. administrn., UC Los Angeles 1953, MBA, 1957, PhD, 1961; Reg. Profl. Engr. Calif. 1978. Career: senior indsl. engr. Johns-Manville Prod. Corp. Long Beach 1957-59; asst. prof. Grad. Sch. of Bus. Indiana Univ. Bloomington 1961-64; mgmt. sys. splst. No. Am. Aviation Anaheim 1964-68; chief mgmt. sys. and planning No. Am. Rockwell Anaheim 1968-69, exec. advisor ops. 1969-73; indsl. planning splst. computers Rockwell Internat. Anaheim 1973-79, exec. advisor computers 1979-81, mgr. telecommunications 1981-82, mgr. computer technol. 1982-83, emerging technol. splst. 1983—; cons. General Water Heater 1956, City of Anaheim Data Proc. Sys. & D.P. Dir., Selection Rev. Panel 1980; vis. prof. UCLA Grad. Sch. of Bus. 1963; honors: Calif. Schol. Fedn. (1947), Beta Gamma Sigma (1959), J.O. Downing Scholar (1953), Ford Found Postdoc. Fellowships (1959, 60, 61, 63, 64), Research Fellowship (Indiana Univ. 1962); mem: Am. Inst. Indsl. Engrs. (senior), Nat. Mgmt. Assn., CASA/ASME, Soc. Mfg. Engrs. (mfg. mgmt. council), Tilsmen frat. (pres. exec. council 1950); publs: articles in Management Science (1963),

Harvard Bus. Rev. (1964), L' E'tude du Travail (1965), profl. jours.; mil: cpl. USMCR 1953-56; lt. j.g. USNR 1957-67; Republican; Protestant; rec: scuba, tennis. Res: 12812 Bubbling Well Rd Santa Ana 92705 Ofc: Rockwell Internat. 3370 Miraloma Ave AC41 Anaheim 92803

ARMSTRONG, ALICE CATT, editor, author; b. Feb. 7, Kansas; d. Charles Harmon and Florence Iles (Pakenham) C.; edn: Art Inst. Jr. Coll., Kansas; num. special courses; pvt. sch., dramatic arts; hon. degrees: Dr. Humane Letters, St. Olav's Acad., Sweden 1969; LLD, No. Pontifical Acad., France 1969; Litt.D., St. Andrew's Univ. of England 1969; D.Litt., St. Paul's Coll. and Sem., Rome 1970; PhD, Colo. State 1972; Dr. Cultural Arts, Bodkin Bible Inst., Va. 1973; PhD, Gr. China Arts Coll., Hong Kong 1974; LLD, Lagos Coll., Nigeria 1976. Career: actress Pasadena Playhouse, Artists Exchange; tchr. dramatic arts, H.S., adult groups, own studio, Hollywood 1947-49; founder, pres. Who's Who Hist. Soc., 1954-78; pub./ed. Who's Who in L.A. Co. 1949, Who's Who Execs. in Calif. 1963, Who's Who Dining and Lodging on the No. Am. Continent 1958, Who's Who in Calif. 1954-78; founder, dir. Exec. Dinner Club, Beverly Hills 1958; internat. chair Sibelious Centennial Concert, Hollywood Bowl 1965; recipient approx. 40 awards incl. Ky. Col. 1976, Woman of Achiev., Calif. Women of the Golden West 1951, Career Girl of Hollywood 1951, Nat. Travel Guide Award, Nat. Writers Club 1958, Wisdom Mag. Award of Honor 1965, Am. Edn. League Award 1966; mem: Profl. Writers Guild of L.A., Nat. Writers Club, Nat. Soc. Children's Book Writers, Celebrity Books and Authors, Freedoms Found. at Valley Forge (awards com. Women's div.), Magna Charter Dames (life), Sovereign Colonial Soc. of Americans of Royal Descent, Bel-Air Fed. Repub. Women's Club (pres. 1980), So. Calif. Women's Press Club; Christian (ordained minister). Res: 1331 Cordell Pl Los Angeles 90069

ARMSTRONG, JUANITA MAE, bank officer; b. Mar. 21, 1934, Iola, Ill.; d. Glen and Nancy Isabel (Pruett) Patrick; children: Glenda b. 1958, Timothy b. 1962. Career: credit checker to asst. br. mgr. Security pacific Bank 1967-77; asst. br. mgr., asst. v.p./ asst. mgr. Fullerton Br., asst. v.p./ br. mgr. Fountain Valley Br. Barclays Bank 1977—; honors: Cert. of Merit (Orange County Supvs. 1982, 83); mem. Girls & Boys Club of Fountain Valley/ Hunt. Beach (bd. 1967-, secty., pres., treas.); Republican; Methodist; rec: reading, dancing, walking the beach. Ofc: Barclays Bank of Calif. 18085 Brookhurst Fountain Valley 92708

ARMSTRONG, ORVILLE A., lawyer; b. Jan. 21, 1929, Austin, Tx.; s. Orville Alexander and Velma Lucille (Reed) A.; m. Mary Dean Macfarlane, Nov. 15, 1949; children: Anna b. 1951, John b. 1953, Paul b. 1943; edn: BBA, Univ. of Texas, Austin 1953; LLB, USC 1956; admitted to bar: Calif. 1957, US Ct. of Appeals (9th Cir.) 1958, US Supreme Ct. 1980. Career: atty., ptnr. Gray Binkley Pfaelzer & Robertson 1956-61, ptnr. Pfaelzer, Robertson, Armstrong & Woodard 1961-66, ptnr. Armstrong & Lloyd 1966-75, ptnr. Macdonald, Halsted & Laybourne 1975—; pres. ORV-1, Inc.; honors: Beta Gamma Sigma (1953), Fellow Am. Coll. of Trial Lawyers (1983-); mem. State Bar of Calif. (bd. govs. 1983-, v.p./treas. 1986, pres. 1986-87), LA County Bar Assn. (trustee 1971-72), Chancery Club (pres. 1981), Am. Bar Assn., Am. Judicature Soc., Assn. of Business Trial Lawyers, Am. Arbitration Assn., LA World Affairs Council; club: California (LA); mil: sgt. USAF 1946-49; Democrat; Baptist; rec: golf, gardening. Res: 2385 Coniston Pl San Marino 91108 Ofc: Macdonald, Halsted & Laybourne, Citicorp Plaza, 36th floor, 725 S Figueroa St Los Angeles 90017

ARNESON, PAMELA KAREN, real estate broker; b. Sept. 16, 1944, Mpls., Minn.; d. Guy and Jeannette Georgine Owen (Eddings) Moore; children: John b. 1960, Julie b. 1962; edn: real estate lic., Anthony Schools 1975-76, broker's lic., 1978; num. personal growth splty. courses; Dale Carnegie Human Relations 1986; investment courses. Career: med. asst. Joseph C. DeFrancisco MD Alhambra 1971-77; real estate sales Baldwin Realty Arcadia 1976-78, broker assoc. 1978—; honors: Million Dollar Club (1979, secty. 1982-83), Multi-Million Dollar Club (1980, v.p. 1982-83), Top Listor (1981), other sales awards (1979-); mem: Calif. Assn. Realtors 1976-, Arcadia Tournament of Roses, Arcadia CofC; Republican; Protestant; rec: horseback riding, dogs & cats, golf. Res: 33 Eastern Ave Apt 6 Pasadena 91107 Ofc: Baldwin Realty 909 S Santa Anita Ave Arcadia 91006

ARNOLD, DANA IAN, co. president; b. Aug. 9, 1948, Los Angeles; s. Robert Z. and Shirley Jacobson A.; m. Randee, Jan. 24, 1971; children: Rachael b. 1978, Jason b. 1980, Shayna b. 1982; edn: BA, UC Los Angeles 1970; MBA, honors, Pepperdine Univ. 1985. Career: v.p. Photo Engring. Corp. 1975; founder, senior exec. v.p. ops., dir. Hasco Internat. 1983; pres. Coemptor Corp. 1984; bd. chmn./CEO E.S.P.I. -Electronic Space Products Internat., 1985—; senior mgmt. cons. T.L. Ents.; honors: past pres. UCLA Alumni Band (1975), gen. dir. Cota Symphony Assn. (1971); Democrat; Jewish; rec: pvt. pilot. Ofc: E.S.P.I. 31194 La Baya Dr Ste 100 Westlake Village 91362

ARNOLD, R. STEVEN, lawyer, professional athletes representative, co. president; b. Mar. 15, 1938, N.Y.C.; s. Arnold H. and Matilda (Ostrow) A.; edn: AB, Brown Univ. 1959; LLD, Columbia Univ. 1962; admitted N.Y. bar. Career: legal counsel to Ency. Brittanica, Grey Advt., Doyle, Dane, Bernbach; founder/chmn. bd. Pro Sports, Inc. 1964—; past mem. bd. dirs./dir. of player personnel Am. Basketball Assn., formulated the "hardship rule," which led to merger with the NBA; past mem. bd. dirs. World Hockey Assn., later merged with NHL; past dir. of player personnel World Team Tennis; pres. World Sports Ltd. S.A., and organizer of the Internat. Basketball Assn. (1st profl. European basketball league to play internat.) 1973; co-founder World Football League and sole owner Houston Texans Franchise, 1974; current: pres./co-founder Nat. Womens Volleyball League; bd. chmn. World Telemedia, Inc. (tv prodn. & distbn. co.). Res: 4386 Paradise Dr Tiburon 94920

ARNOLD, T. BEN, chemical engineer; b. Jan. 27, 1916, Hunter, Ark.; s. Ben and Emma (DuBaun) A.; m. Joe Ann R. (dec.), Dec. 29, 1941; children: Sandra b. 1945, Thomas b. 1946, Linda Jo b. 1948, James b. 1949, Robert b. 1954, Donald b. 1956; edn: BS chem. engring., Louisiana State Univ. 1940, MS, 1942; Reg. Profl. Engr. (chem., mech.) Calif. Career: mgr. refinery, Vickers Petroleum Co., Wichita, Kans. 1953-58; engring. design adminstr. Ralph Parsons Co., L.A. 1958-69; mgr. shale oil devel. project Atlantic Richfield Co., Grand Junction, Colo. 1969-70, mgr. gen. engring. dept. ARCO, Dallas 1970-73, mgr. Prudhoe Bay Project ARCO, L.A. 1973-75, ret.; mem: Am. Chem. Soc., NY Acad. of Sci., Am. Inst. Chem. Engrs.; publs: misc. articles on refining (1948-56), 2 patents on oil prodn. equip.; Republican; Methodist; rec: oil painting, gardening.

ARNOLDSEN, RONALD PHARO, dentist; b. Feb. 24, 1949, Kimberly, Nev.; s. Jay Pharo and Venus (Jackman) A.; edn: BS, Univ. of Nevada Los Vegas 1975; DDS, USC 1980. Career: criminalistic lab techn. Metropolitan Police Dept., Las Vegas 1 1/2 yrs.; practice gen. and family dentistry, Grover City 1981–; mem: USC Dental Alumni Assn., Rotary (bd. dirs.), Grover City CofC, Arroyo Grande; mil: Yn3 USNR; Republican; Latter Day Saints; rec: woodworking, golf, basketball. Res: 1692 Brighton Ave. Grover City 93433 Ofc: 176 No. 9th St. Grover City 93433

ARON, ANTHONY MAX, lawyer; b. Sept. 12, 1951, Los Angeles; s. Max and Eileen (Toney) A.; m. Carole Deets, Sept. 28, 1979; edn: BA, summa cum laude, UC Los Angeles 1973; JD, UCLA Sch. of Law 1976; admitted Calif. State Bar 1976. Career: atty. prin. solo practice, Marina Del Rey 1976-77, Westchester 1977-79, Panorama City 1979-81, Huntington Beach 1981–; trial atty. in med. malpractice and gen. personal injury law; of counsel to Law Offices of Al Schallau (LA) 1977-80, Gordon Stemple (Century City) 1979-81, Kenneth L. Knapp, ALC (Costa Mesa and Newport Beach) 1981-; atty. arbitrator Orange County Superior Ct. Arbitration, 1985; tchg. asst. in legal resrch. and writing UCLA Sch. of Law, 1976; cons. in Automotive Products Liability to Greene, O'Reilly, & Broillet Law Corp., L.A. 1977-79; honors: Phi Beta Kappa (1973), Moot Ct. Honors Pgm. UCLA (1975-76), Ni Que Degree in Kendo (Samurai Sword Fencing), Internat. Kendo Fedn. (1973), Autocross Driver of Year, Volvo Sports America/P1800 Register (1981), Bank of Am. Award in music (1969); mem: Orange County Trial Lawyers Assn., Orange County Bar Assn., Los Angeles Trial Lawyers Assn. 1977-80, Los Angeles County Bar Assn. 1978-80; contbr. Advocate Newsletter, L.A. Trial Lawyers Assn. (11/81); rec: racing car mechanics, autocross/slalom racing.

ARON, DAVID MICHAEL, physician; b. Nov. 14, 1950, NY, NY; s. George and Rita (Dashefsky) A.; m. Barbara Barlow, July 11, 1981; 1 dau., Allison b. 1984; edn: BA in biol. (summa cum laude, deptl. honors, valedictorian) NY Univ. 1973; MD, Univ. of Penna. 1978. Career: intern, resident Montefiore Hosp., Bronx, NY 1978-81; physician in pvt. practice, Whittier, Calif. 1981–, founder, pres. Heights Med. Center multispecialty grp. 1982–; emerg. phys. (Chief of Medicine 1984-85) Whittier Hosp.; cons. phys. CSU Fullerton; honors: 1978 Young Scientist Award of Sigma Xi; 1978 Eleanor Mactavis Award (for research); 1978 Founder's Day Award; Phi Beta Kappa 1977, Caducean Soc. 1970, Sigma Xi 1971; youngest on record to be elected chief of med. Whittier Hosp.; mem: Fellow Am. Coll. of Med., Whittier CofC, Better Bus. Bureau, Rotary, Kiwanis; med. research on Acetylcholine release in rats; Jewish; rec: tennis, boating. Ofc: David M. Aron, MD 2514 S Hacienda Blvd Hacienda Hts 91745

ARONOFF, CAROL ARMSTRONG, city librarian; b. Dec. 3, 1945, Denver; d. William F. and Barbara J. (Strong) Armstrong; m. Richard N. Aronoff, Apr. 29, 1978; edn: BA, UCLA 1967, MLS, 1968. Career: reference librarian Santa Monica Pub. Library 1968-72, head borrowers' svcs. 1972-74, city librarian 1974–; gen. adv. bd. Santa Monica Coll. 1975-; elder Bel Air Presbyterian Ch. 1979-81, deacon 1983-84; adv. council UCLA Library Sch. 1981-; chmn. Met. Co-op. Library System 1979; mem: ALA; Calif. Library Assn. (pres. 1982, chmn. forum coord. com. 1976-77); Congress Calif. Pub. Library Systems (chmn. 1980); League Calif. Cities (revenue and taxation policy com. 1983-); Freedom to Read Found.; Republican; Ofc: Santa Monica Public Library, 1343 6th St., Santa Monica 90401

ARONSOHN, PAUL LEWIS, physician - oncologist; b. Nov. 18, 1942, Bklyn., NY; s. Charles M. and Hortense L. (Moss) A.; m. Kristine R., May 14, 1977; edn: BA, Univ. of Mich. 1964; MD magna cum laude, Univ. of Bologna 1970; splty. board cert. 1978, Diplomate Am. Coll. Physicians 1978. Career: med. internship, residency Providence Hosp., Southfield, Mich. 1971-75, fellowship in hematology and oncology, 1975-76, med. dir. Intensive Care, 1976-77; pvt. practice in Mich., 1977-81, Fountain Valley, Ca. 1981–; med. dir. Southeast Mich. Hospice 1978-80, Mich. Hospice Found. 1977-80, Town & Country Hospice, Garden Grove, Ca. 1982-84; advis. bd. Norman Davidson Cancer Center, Mission Viejo 1985-; named Teacher of the Year Providence Hosp. Southfield, Mich. 1980; mem: AMA, Am. Soc. of Int. Med. 1976-80, Internat. Soc. of Chemotherapy, Am. Coll. of Physicians, Sherlock Holmes Soc. of Los Angeles; works: dir. To Your Health seminars, 1985; clin. investigator Southwest Oncology Group (Kansas City) 1978-81; Univ. of So. Calif. Cancer Network 1982-; Republican; Jewish. Res: 49 Montecito, Corona del Mar 92625 Ofc: The Hematology-Oncology Group of So. Calif. 11160 Warner, Ste 313, Fountain Valley 92708

ARRAS (YUHAS), DEANNA MARIE, county govt. administrative assistant; b. July 9, 1937, New Britain, Conn.; d. Damiano Francis and Angelina Catherine (Reina) Arras; div.; children (nee Yuhas): John b. 1960, Maryann b. 1962; edn: BFA, Syracuse Univ. 1957, BA, Ryder Coll. 1959; lic. real estate broker 1986. Career: media center dir./librarian Chino Unified Sch. Dist. 1973-80; realtor/ptnr. ERA American Diversified Realtor, Chino 1980–; adminstrv. asst. to bd. chmn. San Bernardino County Board of Supvrs., 1983-85, to 4th Dist. Supvr. 1985–, chair S.B. Co. Day Creek Project 1984-85, S.B. Co. chair Gov.'s com. Neighborhood Watch 1985; mem. West S.B. Co. Board of Realtors (legis. com. 1980-, co-chair comm. rels. com. 1980-), Chino CofC (bd. 1983-); civic: Soroptimist Internat. of Chino, Chino Comm. Hosp. (Citizens bd. dirs.), Chino Family YMCA (pres. bd. mgrs.), Chino Hist. Soc., LA Co. Mus. of Art (patron), Prado Tiro Found. (hon. bd.); Democrat; Catholic; rec: golf, travel. Res: 778 Via Montevideo Claremont 91711 Ofc: San Bernardino County Government Ctr 385 N Arrowhead Ave San Bernardino 92415-0110

ARRIAS, FRANK, auto valutaion co. president; b. June 9, 1945, Aruba, Netherland Antillies; s. Joseph W. and Ercila A. (Lique) A.; children: Peter b. 1966, Daniel b. 1967. Career: var. pos. sales, mgmt., ownership in automotive indus., 1966-, founder/bd. chmn. Compucar Inc., Agoura Hills 1984–; created and wrote Automotive Total Loss Valuation System used by major ins. carriers in finding fair market value on automobile for total loss purposes; Presbyterian. Ofc: Compucar Inc. 28720 Canwood Ste 201 Agoura Hills 91301

ARRINGTON, CLIFF R., manufacturing and materiel executive; b. April 28, 1935, Walnut Springs, Texas; s. Albert C. and Amye (Boyd) A.; m. Carole, Oct. 9, 1960; children: Eddie b. 1952, Velecia b. 1954, Rhonda b. 1955, Chris b. 1959, Carole b. 1961; edn: Arlington State Coll. 1954-57; BSME, Drexel Inst. of Tech. 1959; MSOM, UCLA Grad. Sch. of Mgmt. 1982; Cert., Stanford Grad. Sch. of Mgmt. 1984. Career: var. pos. LTV Bell, Ft. Worth, Texas 1954-56; supvr. insp., quality control Menasco Mfg., Ft. Worth, Texas 1956-65; mgr. quality control Boeing Vertol Div., Phila. 1965-70; dir. materiel and quality conrol VPC (Volkswagen) SVB, Volkswagen, Ft. Worth, Texas 1970-77; dir. mats. & ops. Hughes Aircraft, El Segundo 1977-80; v.p. mfg. & mats. HR Textron Inc., Valencia 1980–; mem: Fellow Am. Soc. of Quality Control, Fellow Nat. Assn. of Purchasing Mgrs., Soc. of Mfg. Engrs. (senior); civic: mem. indsl. adv. councils of Cal Poly Pomona and CSU Northridge, Vista Ridge Homeowners Assn. (pres. Valencia); publs: article, Quality in the First Person, 1969; mil: lt. USN 1950-54; Republican; Catholic; rec: golf, flying, woodworking. Ofc: HR Textron Inc. 25200 W. Rye Canyon Rd. Valencia 91355

ARRITOLA, DONALD LOUIS, mechanical engineer; b. June 14, 1946, Boise, Ida.; s. John Carlos and Florence (Greiner) A.; m. Carol, Jan. 25, 1969; children: Michelle b. 1970, Todd b. 1972; edn: Univ. Ore. 1964-66; BS, Mech. Univ. of Ariz. 1970; CSU Long Beach 1971-72; Reg. Profl. Mech. Engr. Calif. 1974. Career: student engr. Hughes Aircraft Tuscon, Ariz. 1969; design engr. No. Am. Rockwell (B-1 bomber) 1970-72; supv. mech. engr. Bechtel Power Corp. (design of several nuclear power plants) 1973-79; owner, v.p. engrg. ESI Engrg. Svcs. Inc. cons. firm 1980–, dir. 1981–; honors: Nat. Defense Edn. Grant (Univ. Ariz. 1968-69), Elliot-Ulman Meml. Scholarship (Univ. Ariz. 1967-69); mem: Am. Soc. Mech. Engrs., Proj. Mgmt. Inst., Elks; Republican; Catholic; rec: golf, jogging, swimming. Ofc: ESI Engineering Services Inc. 10 Douglas Dr Ste 100 Martinez 94553

ARROL, JOHN, corporate executive; b. Aug. 6, 1923, Cambuslang, Scotland; nat. 1934; s. William and Isabella (Gordon) A.; edn: BSBA, Xavier Univ. (Cincinnati) 1953, MA, Vanderbilt Univ. (Nashville) 1964; m. Jane Trice, June 18, 1949; children: Robert, b. 1950, Nancy Ann, b. 1952, David, b. 1961, William, b. 1964. Career: cost analyst Ford Motor Co., Mich. and Ohio, 1949-57; finl. analyst Curtiss Wright Corp., N.J. 1957-58; asst. controller Avco Corp., Oh., Tenn., Ind., 1958-64; v.p., controller Globe-Union Inc., Milw., Wisc. 1964-70, v.p., chief finl. ofcr. 1971-73; sr. v.p. finance The Rucker Co., Oakland, Ca. 1973-77; sr. v.p. finance NL Petroleum Svgs., Houston 1977-78; v.p., chief finl. ofcr. Gardner-Denver, Dallas 1978-79; exec. v.p. Systron-Donner Corp., Concord 1980-81, chmn. 1982–; Dir.: bd. chmn., Hughes Electronic Devices (1981-84), Paragon Technology Co. (Pleasant Hill, 1983-85), Lightgate, Inc. (Berkeley, 1983-84), Pantle Mining Co. (Grass Valley, 1981-85), Roconex Corp. (Milpitas, 1979-84), Universal Semiconductor Inc. (San Jose, 1983-), bd. chmn. San Jose Capital Corp. (S.J.). Mem. adv. council Sch of Bus. Univ of San Francisco; adv. bd. Mt.Diablo Council BSA; bd. trustees Calif. Found. for the Retarded (1985-); publs: art., Budgeting for Direct Material Inventories, NAA Bull. 2/62; mil: US Maritime Svc, USNR 1942-45; rec: china trade paintings. Res: 2427 Alamo Glen Dr. Danville 94526 Ofc: Systron-Donner Corp. 2720 Systron Dr. Concord 94518

ARROW, KENNETH J., economist; b. Aug. 23, 1921, NY, NY; s. Harry I. and Lillian (Greenberg) A.; m. Selma Schweitzer, Aug. 31, 1947; children: David, b. 1962; Andrew, b. 1965; edn: B.Sc. in soc. sci., The City Coll. 1940; MA, Columbia Univ. 1941; PhD, 1951. Career: research assoc. Cowles Commn. for Research in Economics, Chgo., Ill. 1947-49; asst. prof. economics Univ. of Chgo. 1948-49; acting asst., assoc. and prof. of economics, statistics and ops. research, Stanford Univ., Stanford, CA 1959-68; prof. economics, James Bryan Conant Univ. prof., Harvard Univ., Cambridge, Ma 1968-79; Jean Kenney prof. of economics, prof. of ops. research, Stanford Univ., Stanford, CA 1979–; pres. Internat. Economic Assn. 1983-86; pres. Internat. Soc. for Inventory Research 1983-; bd. dirs. Varian Assocs., Inc., Abt Assocs., Inc., Fireman's Fund Ins. Co.; honors: John Bates Clark Medal, Am. Economic Assn. 1957; Nobel Meml. PRize in Economic Sci. 1972; Order of the Rising Sun, second class, Japan; mem: Econometric Soc. (fellow, pres. 1958); Am. Econ. Assn.

(distng. fellow, pres. 1972); Inst. of Mgmt. Scis. (pres. 1962); Nat. Acad. of Scis.; Am. Philosophical Soc.; Am. Acad. of Arts and Scis.; Finnish Acad. of Scis.; British Acad.; author: Socil Choice and Individual Values, 1951, 1963; Essays in the Theory of Risk-Bearing, 1971; Limits of Organization, 1974; co-author: Studies in the Mathematical Theory of Inventory and Production, 1958; mil: capt. U.S. Army Air Corps 1942-46; Democrat; Jewish; rec: bicycling, music. Res: 580 Constanzo St., Stanford 94305 Ofc: Department of Economics, Stanford University, Stanford 94305

ARTHAUD, ROBERT PAUL, insurance broker; b. June 18, 1925, Aberdeen, Wash.; s. Edward Paul and Gertrude Bertha (Sather) A.; edn: Univ. of Wash., Seattle 1941-43; desig: Certified Ins. Counselor (1978), LUTC Personal and Business Grad. (1977, 78), Life Underwriter, Series Six, Fire and Casualty Agt./Broker, Life and Health Broker, Estate Planner. Career: juvenile lead and star (profl. name, Robert Arthur) of 38 motion pictures and over 100 TV dramas, including The Lone Ranger, Sky King, 1944-59; current: owner insurance brokerage, Encino; honors: Valley Business Alliance Humanitarian of the Year (1983), Hollywood Appreciation Soc. (1985), So. Calif. Motion Picture Council- Super Star Actor (1985); civic: founder The Community Guild, Project Rainbow; mem. Municipal Elections Com. of Los Angeles; Republican (State and Nat. Repub. Party; founder Log Cabin Repub. Club); author (novel) His Other Half; mil: US Navy V-12 Pgm. 1944; Community Ch. Res: 5420 Lindley Ave Townhouse 23 Encino 91316 Ofc: Robert Arthur Ins. Agency Inc. 18075 Ventura Blvd Ste 227 Encino 91316

ARTZ, KENNETH DUDLEY, commercial artist; b. Apr. 4, 1910, Eldon, Mo.; s. Carl Anthone and Rosa Lee (Madole) A.; m. Mildred Wood, June 20, 1933 (div.); 1 dau. Anne b. 1934; m. 2d Twyla Hill, Mar. 19, 1960 (div.). Career: spent several years traveling the country painting signs on assignment, came to South Gate, Calif. in 1947, self-employed painting signs, pictorials, logos, murals; mem. Elks for many years; Democrat; Protestant; rec: gardening, reading, sports. Address: 9640 Atlantic Ave South Gate 90280

ASHER, HOWARD RALPH, company president; b. Sept. 29, 1947, Long Beach; s. Ralph Eugene and Joyce Colleen (Johnson) A.; m. Carol Yokota, Mar. 28, 1965; children: Stacey, b. 1966, Randy, b. 1969; edn: BA in bus.adm., UCLA 1969; cont. edn. in orthopaedic surg. and products, jt. reconstrn., fractured hip, hip and knee replacement, orthopaedic nursing, Univ. Calif., various hosps. and med. schs., USA and abroad, 1969-. Career: sales rep. Howmedica, Inc., Rutherford, N.J. 1970-72; eastern area sales mgr. Am. Hosp. Supply/V. Mueller, Innomed Orthopedics, Chgo. 1972-75; mktg. mgr. Cutter Biomedical, San Diego 1972-78; sales & mktg. dir. Hexcel Medical, Dublin 1978-79; pres. Asher, Buckman & Assocs., Walnut Creek 1979-81; pres. Advanced Biosearch Associates, Danville 1981–, opened East Coast ofc. in Atlanta, Ga. 1983-, Wash. DC ofc. 1984-, estab. subsidiary corp., ABA Internat., Ltd., Danville; mem: Regulatory Affairs Profl.Soc., The Food & Drug Law Inst., AAAS, Med. Mktg. Assn.; publs: papers presented AAOS Nursing Course on Orthopedic Nursing, Atlanta, 1975; VII Ann. Northlake Surg. Seminar, Chgo. 1977; 5th Ann. Cong. Orthopedic Nurses Assn., New Orleans 1978, and 6th Ann. Cong., Anaheim 1979; 52nd Ann. Sci. Meeting, Am. Soc. of Plastic and Reconstructive Surgeons, Inc., Dallas 1983; audio-visuals: Surg. Techniques for Internal Fixation (1974), Care and Hndlg. Internal Fixation Appliances (1975), Basic Skills Employing Swiss Technique to Internal Fixation (1977); works: assists developing nations in improving their health care delivery systems; Republican. Christian. rec: swim, tennis, woodwrkg. Res: 30 Hidden Oak Ct., Danville 94526 Ofc: Advanced Biosearch Assocs., 3880 Blackhawk Rd Danville 94526

ASHLEY-FARRAND, MARGALO, lawyer; b. July 26, 1944, NY, NY; d. Joel Thomas and Margalo Francis (Wilson) Ashley; m. Thomas Ashley-Farrand, Dec. 11, 1981; children: Marc Bennet b. 1965, Alisa Bennet b. 1968; edn: UCLA 1962-63, Univ. of Pittsburgh 1972-74; BA, NYU 1978; JD, Southwestern Univ. Sch. of Law 1980. Career: asst. to mgr. of editorials WCBS-TV, 1977-78; paralegal/office mgr. (FCC law), Fly, Shuebruck, Blume, Gaguine, Boros and Shulkind law firm, 1976; legal asst. to Sylvia Roberts, Atty. 1973-74; secretary 1974-80; solo law practice, Wash DC 1981-82, ptnr. law firm Ashley-Farrand & Smith, Glendale, Calif. 1983–; honors: Themis Soc. Scholarship (1980), Outstanding Young Women of Am. (1980); mem: Los Angeles County Bar Assn., San Fernando Valley Bar Assn., Glendale Bar Assn., Women Lawyers Assn. of Los Angeles; civic: La Leche League 1967-71; NOW (East Hills chpt. convenor, pres. treas. 1972-74; Penn. State bd. 1972-74; Hollywood chpt. pres. 1974-75; NYC Chpt. bd. 1975-78), ACLU, Los Angeles Women's Coalition for Better Bdcstg. (convenor, coord. 1974-75); Democrat. Ofc: Ashley-Farrand & Smith, 225 W Broadway Ste 500 Glendale 91204

ASHWORTH, MARK SHEPHERD, trial lawyer; b. Apr. 20, 1951, Provo, Utah; s. Dell Shepherd and Bette Jean (Brailsford) A.; m. Debra, June 6, 1976; children: Carissa Anne, b. 1977, Andrew Karleus-Shepherd, b. 1981, Justin Parrish, b. 1983, Michael Christopher, b. 1984; edn: BS, Brigham Young Univ. 1972; JD, Western State Univ. 1978; admitted to Calif. State Bar 1978, US Dist. Cts. (Central, No. Dists. Calif.), US 9th Circuit Ct. of Appeals. Career: trial atty. civil litigation, Law Offices of Mark A. Smith, APC, El Toro 1978–; Calif. counsel to sev. publicly held corporations; pres. Mark S. Ashworth, APC; mem. ABA (Litigation Sect.), Orange County Bar Assn., Calif. Trial Lawyers Assn.; Eagle Scout, active in BSA, Kiwanis, var. youth groups; Democrat; Ch. of Jesus Christ of L.D.S. Ofc: Mark A. Smith APC, 22956 El Toro Rd., El Toro 92630

ASKEW, GEORGE VANCE, aerospace co. executive; b. Sept. 16, 1925, Chgo.; s. George Lafayette and Isabel (Brown) A.; m. Norma Jean Zediker, Nov. 1947; children: Chris (Geo. V. Jr.) b. 1948, M. Shannon b. 1952, Scot b. 1953; edn: Stanford Univ. 1949-50, US Naval Line & Post Grad. Sch. 1950-51; AB mgmt., Geo. Wash. Univ. 1965; Nuclear Safety Engr. Career: US Navy 1943-65, naval aviator, test pilot, pgm. mgr., final tour Wash. DC Bur. of Naval Weapons; asst. pgm. mgr. flight simulators Hughes Aircraft Co. 1965–; mgmt. cons.; career counselor 1978-81; honors: grad. w/ distinction (US Naval Schs. Treasure Island); mem: Stanford Alumni Assn. (life), GWU Alumni, Friends of KCET, SPEBSQSA, Assn. Naval Aviation, US Naval Inst.; publs: num. tech. papers on automatic flight control and missile guidance sys.; mil: cmdr. USN 1943-65; Republican; Baptist; rec: golf, tennis, horses, sailing. Res: 77 San Roque Ave Ventura 93003 Ofc: Hughes Aircraft Co. Los Angeles

ASLAN, MUZAFFER, physician, internist; b. Feb. 28, 1923, Civril, Turkey; s. Ali Galip and Huriye (Ince) A.; m. Rosa Maria Gonzalez, Nov. 14, 1953; children: Aliskender b. 1957, Alp b. 1962; edn: BS, Istanbul Univ. Sch. of Sci. 1942;; MD, Istanbul Univ. Med. Sch. 1947. Career: resident infectious diseases Willard Parker Hosp. N.Y.C. 1952-53; res. int. med. St. Mary's Hosp. Brooklyn 1954-55, Jewish Chronic Disease Hosp. 1955-56; senior med. res. Kaiser Found. Hosp. Oakland 1959-60; staff Santa Monica Hosp. 1981–, Antelope Valley Hosp. Lancaster 1963-81, Lancaster Comm. Hosp. (founding member) 1965-81; pvt. practice int. med. L.A. 1981–; instr. int. med. EGE Univ. Med. Sch. Izmir, Turkey 1957-59; Ross-Loos Med. Grp.; staff Queen of Angels Hosp. L.A. 1960-63; mem: CMA, LACMA, Am. Coll. Phys., Turkish Am. Club So. Calif.; publ: articles in med. jours.; Republican; rec: music, travel. Res: 1356 Stradella Rd Los Angeles 90077 Ofc: 11600 Wilshire Blvd, Ste 8, Los Angeles 90025

ASMUS, JULIA RUSS, association executive, ret.; community volunteer; b. Sept. 25, 1919, Hastings, Colo.; d. John and Mary (Marolt) Russ; m. B.A. Wilcox, 1935 (annulled 1944); 1 son, Bruce Allen Wilcox b. 1936, m. 2d Roy V. Asmus, Mar. 9, 1947; children: Mary Ann Asmus (dec.) b. 1953, (adopted) Lisa Kris Asmus b. 1961, Lorn Kurt Asmus (dec.) b. 1961; edn: grad. Montebello H.S. Career: documents clk. Ration Board, Bell, Calif. during WWII; copper tube insp., later cafeteria mgr. Phelps Dodge Copper Prods., Commerce 1940s; secty./asst. Dr. Carl Ross O.D. (1939-40), Dr. Henry Rubin O.D. 1941-42, Dr. Phillip Glasser O.D. 1942-47, all in Maywood; licensed day care, infants, 15 yrs.; mgr. Bell Gardens Chamber of Commerce, 8 yrs, ret. 1981; num. honors incl: Resolutions from Assemblyman Art Torres, Sen. Alex Garcia, and also Sen. Art Torres; hon. service awards local sch. PTA, Montebello Tchrs. Assn., Nat. PTA; Outstanding Older American (City of Bell Gardens 1986); civic: past pres. Live Oak Primary PTA, Bell Gardens Intermediate PTA, Bell Gardens H.Sch. PTA, Montebello Council PTA (1st v.p. 1986); Soroptomist Internat. of Bell Gardens (secty., chair Sch. Improvement Com.); Central City Redevelopment City of Bell Gardens (v. chair); Youth Service Bur. (advis. com.); Bell Gardens- Pocahontas, TaLaHa Council #277; Senior Citizens Young at Heart; AARP; Buckle-Up- Montebello Child Passenger Safety Seat loan pgm. (secty.); St. Gertrude Altar Soc. (pres.); Regional Library Council (apptd. by Bell Gardens City Council 1984)Democrat; Catholic; rec: youth work, poetry. Res: 6828 Marlow Ave Bell Gardens 90201

ASPIS, LESLIE JANE, dentist; b. Mar. 16, 1954, NYC; d. Jack Isaac and Sydelle (Berkowitz) Aspis; m. Stephen Brunton, July 4, 1986; edn: BA in biol., Univ. Rochester 1974; DMD, Fairleigh Dickinson Sch. of Dentistry 1978. Career: paralegal Hockert, Pressman & Flamm, NY, NY 1977; TV actress, prodn. asst., video editor KVC Video, NY, NY 1978; general dental practice, NYC 1978-80; v.p. Plexus Communications (nat. media seminars) 1980-81; group dental practice, Century City, Calif. 1981-82, Bakersfield, 1982; solo family practice dentist, Point Reyes Station, 1983–; honors: student research fellowships 1972, 74, 75, 76, 77, 81; mem: Nat. Dental Council, Am. Assn. of Hosp. Dentists, Am. Soc. for Geriatric Dentistry, Gerontol. Soc. of Am., Am. Fedn. of Aging Research, First Dist. Dental Soc.-NY, Calif. Dental Assn., Am. Dental Assn., Acad. of Gen. Dentistry (fellowship cand.), Marin County Dental Soc. (chair Health Edn. and Community Awareness coms.); civic: Healthfair 85 (dental chpsn. for Marin County), Marin Arts Council, ACLU, Physicians for Social Responsibility; works: produced and presented 4-hour seminar and 90-min. cassette: Media in Hospitals (1981). Address: 116 Third St Seal Beach 90746

ASTROLIO, PHIL DON, insurance executive; b. June 10, 1934, Phoenix, Ariz.; parents: Phillip and Susie (Lechuga) A.; children: Tina Louise b. 1958, Melody Marie b. 1960; edn: cert., Los Angeles City Coll. 1958-60. Career: sales rep. Certified Life Ins. Co. 1970-76; sales rep. Mutual of Omaha 1976-79, asst. mgr. 1979-82, general mgr. 1982–; honors: AMTC Graduate; mem. San Jose Life Underwriters Assn.; club: Schoebers Athletic; mil: USN, Good Conduct, P.U.C.; Democrat; Catholic; rec: tennis, wt.lift. Res: 3036 Shadow Springs Pl San Jose 95121 Ofc: P.D. Astrolio Div. Off., Mutual of Omaha, 6840 Via Del Oro Ste 230 San Jose 95119

ATKINSON, SHERIDAN EARLE, lawyer, financial analyst; b. Feb. 14, 1945, Oakland, Calif.; s. Arthur Sheridan and Esther Louise (Johnson) A.; m. Marjorie, Aug. 13, 1966; 1 son: Ian b. 1972; edn: BS, Univ. Calif. 1966; JD, Univ. San Francisco 1969; MBA, Univ. Calif. 1971; postgrad. study, Univ. So. Calif., CSUH, Humboldt State Coll.; admitted Calif. State Bar 1970. Career: prin. Atkinson & Assoc. fin. and mgmt. cons. corp. and bus. valuations San Francisco 1968–; assoc. Charles O. Morgan, Jr., S.F. 1972-76; sole practice S.F., Kensington and Roseville 1976–; mem: Am., Calif. bar assns.; mil: USAR 1970-76; Republican. Res: 1045 Key Route Blvd Albany 94706

ATTIYEH, ROBERT S., management consultant; b. June 10, 1934, Oak Park, Ill.; s. Semeer and Dorothy L. (Krentz) A.; m. Linda Harden, July 20, 1963;

children: Robert b. 1964, Jenny b. 1965; edn: BSEE, Cornell Univ. 1956; MBA, Harvard Univ. 1961. Career: bus. unit mgr. TRW Inc., Los Angeles 1961-67; assoc./prin. McKinsey & Co. Inc., Los Angeles 1967-74, dir. 1979-; mng. dir. McKinsey & Co. Inc., Scandinavia, Copenhagen, Denmark 1974-79; writer num. articles for the business press on export strategy, mergers/acquisitions, bus. strategy; civic: L.A. Natural Hist. Mus. (bd. trustees 1982-, bd. pres. 1984-), House Ear Inst., L.A. (bd. dirs. 1982-, v.chmn. 1985-), Family Service of L.A. (bd. 1970-74); clubs: California, Flintridge Riding, Riviera Tennis; mil: lt. US Navy 1956-60; rec: cattle ranching, Paso Robles. Res: 210 S Canyon View Dr Los Angeles 90049 Ofc: McKinsey & Co. Inc. 400 S Hope St Ste 800 Los Angeles 90071

AUDETT, THEOPHILUS BERNARD, lawyer; b. Feb. 12, 1905, Giltedge, Mont.; s. Joseph Abraham and Katherine Amanda (Johnson) A.; m. Corinne Lowery, Sept. 21, 1939; 1 dau. Katherine b. 1947; edn: JD, Univ. Wash. 1926. Career: var. positions US Customs Svc. 1930-51, asst. deputy commr. Hdqs. USCS Wash DC 1951-63, customs expert US delegation GATT Geneva 1959, 60, chmn. interdepartmental com. for study of antidumping legislation Wash DC 1962; of counsel firm of Stein, Shostak, Shostak & O'Hara L.A. 1965–; honors: Exceptional Svc. (US Treas. Dept. 1963), listed Who's Who Am. Law, Who's Who in the World; mem: Phi Sigma Kappa, Am. Bar Assn. (customs law com. 1967-68), Calif. State Bar Assn., Assn. Customs Bar, Les Amis du Vin; mil: capt. US Army 1943-45; Republican. Res: 348 S Orange Grove Blvd Pasadena 91105 Ofc: Stein, Shostak, Shostak & O'Hara 3580 Wilshire Blvd Los Angeles 90010

AUERBACH, ARTHUR MICHAEL, orthopedic surgeon; b. Feb. 19, 1937, N.Y.C.; s. Samuel and Gertrude (Steinberg) A.; m. Odette Rauch, June 23, 1985; children: Adam b. 1967, Amy b. 1968, Stefan b. 1971; edn: BA, Cornell Univ. 1957; MD, Univ. Chgo. 1961. Diplomate Am. Board Orthopedic Surgery. Career: gen. surgical intern and resident Cornell Univ. N.Y. Hosp. 1961-63; phys. USN 1964-65, ship's surgeon USS Hornet (aircraft carrier) 1 yr., phys. Orthopedic Dept. Naval Hosp. Camp Le Jeune, N.C. 1 yr.; orthopedic residency Mayo Clinic 1965-68; pvt. practice gen. orthopedic surg., Oakland 1968–; chief of surgery (1986), past pres. (1978) Oakland Hosp.; cons. orthopedic surgeon Rehab. Unit, Fairmont Hosp. and Amputation Clinic, San Leandro; pres. Arthur M. Auerbach Properties, gen. ptnr. Redwood Athletic Club (Oakland), bd. dirs./exec. bd. Trans Pacific Nat. Bank (S.F.); honors: Alpha Epsilon Delta (1957), Phi Beta Kappa (1957), Alpha Omega Alpha (1961); Fellow Am. Acad. Orthoped. Surgeons, Fellow Am. Coll. of Surgeons, Fellow Internat. Coll. of Surgeons; mem. Western Orthoped. Assn., Am. Coll. of Sports Medicine, Am. Occupational Med. Assn., Royal Soc. of Medicine (London), Bay Area Knee Soc., Am. Running and Fitness Assn.; mil: lt. cmdr. USNRR, Active Duty 1963-65; Republican. Ofc: Oakland Orthopaedic Medical Group Inc. 3300 Webster St Ste 803 Oakland 94609

AUERBACH, LEONARD B., consulting co. president, educator; b. Sept. 19, 1946, N.Y.C.; s. Herschel and Ruth Raisa (Vodnoy) A.; m. Carol Turquexa, June 20, 1982; children: Alexander b. 1984, Benjamin b. 1984. Career: BA, honors, Univ. of Wisc., Madison 1967; grad. work Univ. of Chgo. 1967-68; PhD, UC Berkeley 1973. Career: co-founder/v.p. Puka Jewelry Mfg. Co., Honolulu 1974-75; founder/pres. Royal N Corp. (import/export), Berkeley 1977-80, dir. 1977-; pres./bd. chmn. Auerbach Assocs. Inc. (mgmt. cons.), Berkeley 1977–; co-founder/dir. Intraview Systems Corp. (interactive video co.) 1984-; v.p. Merit Securities Inc., Tiburon 1984-85; founding faculty mem. St. Mary's Coll. Executive MBA Pgm., Moraga 1975–, prof. St. Mary's Coll. 1982-; lectr., vis. prof. UC Berkeley (1975-), USC Inst. for Systems Mgmt. Pacific Region, Honolulu (winters 1977-83), Central Mich. Univ., Honolulu (1984), UCB Ext., Chaiang Mai, Thailand (1983); cons. to Longs Drug Stores, Walnut Creek (1979-), Del Monte Corp., S.F. (1975-78), Delta Calif. Indus., S.F./Oakland (1976-79), Ryder/P.I.E., Walnut Creek (1981-82), Kaiser Aluminum and Chem. Corp., Oakland (1985-6), others; honors: Flood Fellow, Univ. Calif. (1973), Commencement address, St. Mary's Coll. Grad. Sch. of Bus. (1978); mem. Am. Fedn. of Tchrs./UCB local (1973-76), People's Lobby, Alameda Co. (chmn. 1972-74); publs: (text) Thinking for Decisions (S.R.A. 1975), var. profl. papers in field; Jewish; rec: surfing. Address: Auerbach Assocs. Inc. 952 Euclid Ave Berkeley 94708 Ofc: St. Mary's College POB M Moraga 94575

AULD, ROBERT HENRY, JR., biomedical engineer; b. Sept. 19, 1942, Akron, Ohio; s. Robert Henry and Elsie Mae (Rollans) A.; m. Carla Moore, 1961; children: Shiela Kay b. 1969, Jason Craig b. 1970; edn: BS, Univ. San Francisco 1978; Reg. Profl. Engr. Calif 1978; certified clin. engr. 1976, internat. cert. 1984. Career: reg. svc. mgr. Scientific Prods. Div. Am. Hosp. Supply Corp. Menlo Park, Calif. 1963-67; gen. mgr., owner Laboratory Instrument Service Campbell, Calif. 1967-77; nat. mgr. Lab. Mktg. Devel. Honeywell Inc. Biomedical Svcs. Denver, Colo.; cons. biomed. engr. Robert Auld Ent.; dir. research & devel., instr. Foothill Coll. Los Altos; maintenance seminar & workshop dir. ASMT Phoenix 1978, Keene Coll. Union, NJ 1978, CAMLT-Calif. Monterey, Santa Clara, S.F., Marin chpts. 1977-79; workshops Stanford Sch. of Med. 1980; mem: Assn. for Advancement of Medical Instrumentation, IEEE, ISA, Am. Soc. Med. Technol., Calif. Assn. Med. Lab. Technol., NY Acad. of Sciences, Masons; publ: 30+ articles in med. trade jours.; invented device for measurement of oxygen exchange in blood; devel. Single Source Service of health care facilities and "parts banks"; mil: ET2 USN 1959-63; Republican; Protestant; rec: restoration of antique instruments & telephone equipt. Address: 3604 Julio Ave San Jose 95124-3126

AUSMAN, ALLAN DUANE, executive/ consultant; b. Sept. 15, 1944, Eau Claire, Wisc.; s. Irving Milton and Helen Lucille (Feldman) A.; m. Nancy Kasson, Aug. 5, 1973; 1 son: Andrew, b. 1977; edn: BBA indsl. mgmt., Univ. of Wisc. 1966; MBA, USC 1967. Career: asst. to v.p. of ops., ops. mgr., MIS mgr., asst. gen. mgr. ops. Bullocks 1967-73; lead cons. Mc Sweeney & Assocs. 1973-75; lead cons./ ptr. Newport Group 1975-77; dir. fin. analysis, dir. pgm. mgmt., dir. ops. plnng. & support Sperry Univac Minicomputer Operations 1977-82; pres. Minicomp., Inc. 1982-84; pres. & gen. mgr. Western Medical Systems Inc. 1984–; mem: Jaycees (loc. pres., state dir.); Univ. of Wisc. Alumni (loc. v.p.); Republican; Methodist; rec: skiing, racquetball. Res: 26151 Paseo Marbella, San Juan Capistrano 92675 Ofc: Western Medical Systems

AVERBOOK, BERYL DAVID, vascular surgeon; b. Aug. 17, 1920, Superior, Wis.; s. Abraham B. and Clara (Ziechig) A.; m. Gloria Sloane, Apr. 2, 1955; children: Bruce Jeffery b. 1956, Allen Wayne b. 1960; edn: Superior State Teachers Coll. 1938-39; BS, Univ. Wis. 1942, MD, 1945; postgrad. tng. Univ. of Colo. 1948-50. Career: intern Akron (Ohio) City Hosp. 1945-46; surgical resident Fort Logan VA Hosp., Denver, Colo. 1948-50; Rochester (NY) Gen. Hosp. 1950-51; Wadsworth VA Hosp., Los Angeles 1951-54; chief of surgical services Harbor Gen. Hosp., L.A. 1954-61; estab. pvt. med. practice spec. in general and vascular surgery, Torrance 1961–; instr. in surgery Univ. Calif. Med. Ctr., Los Angeles 1954-58, asst. prof. of surgery 1958-61, clin. asst. prof. surgery 1961-65; mem: AMA, Calif. Med. Assn., NY Acad. of Sci., Long Beach Surgical Soc., Los Angeles Acad. of Medicine, Am. Geriatric Soc., Soc. of Head & Neck Surgeons, Am. Men of Medicine, Soc. for Clin. Vascular Surgery, L.A. County Med. Assn., UCLA Harbor Collegium (bd. dirs.); mil: lt. capt. Med. Corps US Army. Res: 6519 Springpark Ave Los Angeles 90056 Ofc: Beryl D. Averbook, M.D. 3640 Lomita Blvd Ste 202 Torrance 90505

AUSTIN, GENE KENT, electrical contractor; b. Sept. 11, 1952, Sacramento; s. Merle Eugene and Violet Alvina (Cherryholmes) A.; m. Trinette Marie, Aug. 13, 1983; 1 son, Andrew b. 1985; grad. Rio Americano H.S. 1970. Career: electrician Austin Electric 1970-76; electrical foreman Mountaineer Electric 1977-80; supt. Integral Constrn.; owner/pres. Gene Austin Electric Inc., Sacto. 1981–; Republican; rec: ski, fish. Ofc: Gene Austin Electric Inc. 2753 Crosby Way Sacramento 95815

AUSTIN, REX L., transportation co. owner; b. Jan. 10, 1949, Kermit, Tex.; s. Rector H. and Dorothy F. (Hill) Austin; m. Deborah Sue Harden, July 2, 1983; edn: ground tng., pilot, Accelerated, Inc. 1980. Career: owner/opr. Boat Transit Inc., Newport Beach, subhauler, 1970-71; attendant Cavanaugh Chevron Service, Encinitas, 1971-72; driver Skylark Mobile Home Sales, Vista 1972-73, Bickford Mobile Home Movers, Escondido 1973-74; owner Rex Transport, Encinitas 1974–, mobile, modular, trailer, transport, Calif., Ariz. and Nev.; owner Rex Pilot Car Service, 1975–; owner Rex Mobile Home Setups, 1975–. honors: Plaque from men of E Troop, First Cavalry. mem: Highway Carriers Assn. Calif. (elected mem. bd. dirs. 1983-86); V.F.W. 1972-; Am. Legion 1973-; Riverside Pilots Inc. 1979-; Am. Sand Racing Assn. 1980-; So. Coast Surfing Assn. 1966-7; Nat. Riflemen's Assn. 1961; patentee: mobile home dolly (1975). Cartoonist, H.S. newspaper 1967; unpubl. songs; mil: sgt. E5, US Army 1968-70, GCM, Commendation. Republican (Repub. Nat. Com. 1980-, Presdtl. Task Force); Christian; rec: motorcycle, jeep racing, flying. Res: 596 Transit, Riverside 92507. Ofc: Rex Transport, 598 Hermes, Encinitas 92024

AUSTIN, ROBERT, export co. president; b. June 21, 1960, NYC; s. George and Virginia (Epps) A.; m. Lavern, Sept. 18, 1982; 1 dau. Candice b. 1985; edn: BS bus. mgmt., Univ. Md. 1983; Dipl., Aviation Maint. Adminstrn. Sch. (1978), Aviation Data Analysis Sch. (1979). Career: data analysis technician USMC Presidential Helicopter Squadron, Quantico, Va. 1978-82; data techn. Xon Tech Inc., Van Nuys 1983-86; pres. Excaliber Import-Export Co. Ltd., Canoga Park 1985–; tchg. asst. (English as 2d language to Japanese assocs.); honors: Dulles Internat. Airport, Preparation 81', Metropolitan Washington Airports (1981); mem. Valley Internat. Trade Assn., Export Mgrs. Assn. of Calif.; mil: cpl. US Marine Corps 1978-82, GCM, Presidential Service; Republican; Sunni Muslim; rec: outdoor photog. Ofc: Excaliber Import-Export Co. 19908 Roscoe Blvd Ste 6 Canoga Park 91306

AUTRY, ORVON GENE, singer, actor, broadcasting executive; b. Sept. 29, 1907, Tioga, Tex.; s. Delbert and Elnora (Ozment) A.; m. Ina Mae Spivey, Apr. 1, 1932 (dec. 1980); m. 2d. Jacqueline Ellam, July 1981; edn: grad., Tioga High Sch. 1925. Career: railroad telegraph operator, Sapulpa, Okla. 1925; first phonograph record of cowboy songs 1929; radio artist Station WLS, Chicago 1930-34; motion picture actor 1934–; starred in 88 musical Western feature pictures, 95 half-hour TV pictures; pres., chmn. bd. Calif. Angels; radio stations: KMPC, Hollywood, KSFO, San Francisco, KVI-AM and KPLZ-FM, Seattle, WCXI and WCXI-FM, Detroit; mem: Internat. Footprinters; Masons (33 deg.); Shriners; Elks; composer 250+ songs incl. That Silver-Haired Daddy of Mine, 1931, You're the Only Star in My Blue Heaven, 1938, Dust, 1938, Tears On My Pillow, 1941, Be Honest With Me, 1941, Tweedle O'Twill, 1942; Here Comes Santa Claus, 1948; mil: USAAF, 1942-45. Address: c/o Golden West Broadcasters, 5858 W. Sunset Blvd., Hollywood 90078

AVAKOFF, JOSEPH CARNEGIE, plastic surgeon; b. July 15, 1936, Fairbanks, Alaska; s. Harry B. and Margaret (Adams) A.; m. Theodora Law, May 7, 1966; children: Caroline b. 1968, Joseph b. 1969, John b. 1972; edn: AA, UC Berkeley 1956, AB, 1957; MD, UC San Francisco Sch. of Med. 1961; JD, Univ. Santa Clara Sch. of Law 1985; bd. certified surgeon 1967, plastic surgeon 1973; real estate broker Calif. 1980. Career: physicist USN Radiol. Defense Lab. S.F. 1955-57; clin. instr. surgery UC Davis Sch. Med. 1967-70; pvt. practice surg. Sacramento 1966-70, plastic surgery San Jose 1972–; honors: Phi Eta Sigma (UCB 1955), Phi Beta Kappa (UCB 1957); mem: AMA, CMA, Am. Soc. Plastic & Reconstrv. Surg., Santa Clara County Med. Soc., Union Am. Phys. &

Dentists, Advis. Commn. on Health to City of San Jose, So. Valley YMCA (bd. mgrs. 1977-80); author: The Curse of Dr. Zymogen (unpubl.); num. articles in profl. jours., presentations for profl. socs.; Republican; Presbyterian; rec: music, photog., computer programming. Ofc: 15899 Los Gatos-Almaden Rd Ste 9 Los Gatos 95030

AVERY, JAMES HARRISON, bank organization consultant, economist; b. Apr. 18, 1943, Los Angeles; s. Robert Alfred and Vivian (Harker) A.; m. Lynn Hylton, Jan. 22, 1972; children: Emily b. 1973, James M. b. 1974, Peter b. 1976, Juliaette b. 1979, John b. 1983; edn: BS, Brigham Young Univ. 1966. Career: sales adminstr. Eldon Inds. 1966-67; v.p. research/ advtg. Far West Financial Corp. 1967-72; owner, pres. Marketing, Economic Research & Counsel San Luis Obispo 1972—; dir. Co Bank Financial Corp. 1984-, Commerce Bank of S.L.O. 1984-, Heritage Oaks Bank 1982-83; mem: S.L.O. Edn. Found. (dir., organizer), Rotary 1984-, Boy Scouts of Am. 1972- (scoutmaster, asst. scoutmaster, var. coms.), S.L.O. Youth Soccer (coach 1984-85); mil: sgt. USMCR 1967-73; Republican; L.D.S.; rec: sailing, skiing. Ofc: MERC POB 3009 San Luis Obispo 93403

AVERY, LILLIAN MARKOS, personnel research consultant; b. Aug. 17, 1918, LaCrosse, Wisc.; d. Nicholas and Ida Mary (Haddad) Markos; m. Edward John Avery, Aug. 1, 1943; 1 son, Mark Joseph b. 1960; edn: AA, Coll. of Commerce LaCrosse (now Western Wisc. Tech. Inst.) 1939; CSU Los Angeles 1962-72; UCLA Extn., 1962-66. Career: 43 years in public employment svc. work including positions with US Employment Svc., Calif. State Atty. General's Ofc., Calif. Employment Devel. Dept., assignments in unemployment ins., employment svc., placement, farm labor pgms., counselor, occupational analyst; test devel. analyst; Los Angeles Area Occupational Analyst, 1961-70; dir. Calif. Test Devel. Field Center L.A. (one of 4 geographic Dept. of Labor field ctrs.) 1970-85, ret.; personnel research cons. Cooperative Personnel Svcs. Inglewood 1985—; guest lectr. on job analysis, test development, testing; honors: recogn. award for devel. of USES Interest Inventory, Nat. Employment Counselors Assn. (1984), recog. award for Public Svc. Occupations Curriculum Proj. (1974), Outstanding mem. Personnel Testing Council of So. Calif. (1984, 85), nom. Stephen E. Bemis Meml. Award (1986), mem: Personnel Testing Council of So. Calif. (v.p. pgms. & conf. coord. 1982-84), Internat. Assn. Personnel in Employment Security, Calif. Adult Edn. Assn.; works: directed development, constrn., standardization of USES Interest Inventory (1981), USES Interest Check List (1979), Spanish Lang. edition of Gen. Aptitude Test Battery (1977), Spanish editions of Interest Inventory and Interest Check List (1984); contbr. Guide for Occupational Exploration (1979, 2d ed. 1984); Catholic; rec: writing, travel, church activities. Ofc: Cooperative Personnel Svcs. Inglewood 90301

AVERY, MARVIN LYNN, petroleum co. executive; b. Apr. 6, 1950, Houston, Tex.; s. Russell Woodrow and Mary Genelle (Hines) A.; m. Marcia, Oct. 25, 1969; children: Steven b. 1972, Kevin b. 1975; edn. (p-t night student): math, Univ. Houston 1968-77; BS math., CSU Bakersfield 1979, MBA finance, 1983. Career: programmer, analyst Occidental Petroleum Corp. Houston 1973-76, pgmmg. mgr. 1976-78, supv. sys. & pgmmg. Occidental Exploration & Prodn. Co. Bakersfield 1978-79, planning & control splst. 1979-80, sys. splst. 1980-81, senior bus. sys. analyst 1981-82, financial coord. 1982-84, senior financial analyst Occidental Petroleum Corp. L.A. 1984-86; mem: Strategic Mgmt. Soc. 1983-, CSU Bakersfield Bus. Alumni 1983-; publ: term paper selected for presentation Strategic Mgmt. Conf. in Paris 1983; Republican; So. Baptist (deacon); rec: tennis, church activities. Res: 27465 N Garza Dr Saugus 91350

AWENDER, JOSEPH ERNEST, chiropractor; b. Mar. 20, 1938, New England, N.D.; s. Anton and Mary (Haas) A.; children: Virginia b. 1963, Joe Jr. b. 1965, Charisse b. 1966, Jeffrey b. 1976; edn: DC, Palmer Chiropractic Coll. 1960. Career: chiropractor pvt. practice, So. San Francisco 1960—; named Doctor of Year, S.F. Chiropractic Soc. (1972); mem: Calif. Chiro. Assn. (past dir.), Chiropractic Knights of Round Table (charter), Elks, South S.F. CofC (past dir.); Republican; Catholic; rec: pvt. pilot, hunting, equestrian. Res: 1061 High Rd Woodside 94062 Ofc: 1115 Mission Road South San Francisco 94080

AWTRY, JOHN HIX, lawyer, insurance executive, military officer; b. July 29, 1897, Quitman, Texas; s. Emmett and Elizabeth (Willims) A.; m. Nell Catherine Jacoby, April 24, 1922; 1 dau, Nell Catherine (dec.); edn: LLB, Univ. of Texas 1921, JD, 1969; admitted to practice, US Supreme Ct. Bar, Texas Bar, Us Ct. Mil. Appeals, US Ct. Claims. Career: Fed. Bank of Dallas 1917-19; Govt. Savings Div. Treasury Dept. 1919-20; ins. on intra and interstate motorbuses and trucks, 17 yrs.; participant drafting Motor Carrier Act 1935; pres. First Reins Co., Hartford, Conn. 1936-41; pres. John H. Awtry & Co. Inc., NYC, owner, Dallas; honors: selected Lesure Worlder, Roosmoor Leisure World; name inscribed in Ct. of Honor, Washington; Shriner of Year, Leisure World Shrine Club, 1985; mem: Am. Automobile Assn. (asst. in formation Nat. Motor Bus. Div., nat. bd.), NY So. Soc., 12th Army Group Assn. (life), Judge Advocs. Assn. (life), NY State CofC Fedn. (life), Am., Texas (Fedn. Grand Jury Assn.) and Dallas Bar Assns. (life), NY Mil. Order World Wars, Am. Legion (life),' Washington Texas Soc., Univ. of Texas Ex-Students Assn. (life), Ret. Ofcrs. Assn. (life), Am. Assn. Ret. Persons (past pres. Leisure World chpt.), Patriotic Letterwriters Club, Orange Co. Rt. Ofcrs. Club, El Toro-Santa Ana Marine Corp Air Sta. Ofcrs. Club, Disabled Ofcrs. Assn., Assn. US Army, Nat. Sojourners (life), Lambda Chi Alpha, Scottish Rite, Shriners, Scarsdale Golf Club, Dallas Athletic Club (life), Dallas Exchange (pres., life), Nat. Exchange (nat. pres., 2 terms), Army and Navy; mil: col. US Army, ret., staff Gen. Omar Bradley 1944, Gen Staff War Dept. 1946-49, chief contracts & procurement br. Judge Advoc. Div., Euro. Cmmdn. 1949-50, Army Panel, Armed Svcs. Bd. of Contract Appeals, Ofc. Asst. Secty. Army., Wash., Bronze Star, Legion of Merity, US Atty. Gen. Commdn.; Republican; Baptist. Res: P.O. Box 2833, 3337-2A Punta Alta Rossmoor, Leisure World, Laguna Hills 92653

AXE, JOEL HARVEY, electronics industry administrator; b. Sept. 9, 1911, Hollywood, Calif.; s. Harry Delvin and Mae Jean (Mauldin) A.; m. Deborah Cooper, Sept. 27, 1934; children: Sharon b. 1937, Susan b. 1942, Diane b. 1944, Doreen b. 1948; edn: bus. adminstrn., Alexander Hamilton Inst.; spl. courses Calif. Inst. Technol., Sears; Reg. Profl. Engr. (Elec.) Calif. Career: engr. to chief engr. Breting Radio Mfg. Co., Gilfillan Bros. Inc.; acting communications engr. Los Angeles Police Dept. (w/ complete responsibility for op. of police radio system, later on spl. assignment w./ the Criminal Investigation Lab.); asst. intercept ofcr., as liaison between mil. & civilian ops., FCC; proj. engr. (8 yrs.), dir. of quality control (1 yr.), Hoffman Labs. (prod. mil. electronics for USN, USAF, US Army, AEC); asst. to pres. Pacific Mercury Electronics; mem. senior staff Ramo Woolridge Div. TRW; proj. mgr. engrg. sect. Hydro Air div. Crane Co.; engr., designer Teledyne Water Pik; instr. Edison Technical Inst.; mem: AFCEA (chpt. treas. 1957), Pac. Mercury Mgmt. Club (pres. 1957), Future Engrs. Show (vice chmn. 1958, chmn. 1960), WESCON; mem. credit com. RWE Credit Union 1961, 62; inventor latest relation to solid state biasing (1978); 3 patents; Republican; Protestant; rec: amateur radio, model constrn. Address: POB 1851 Canyon Country 91351; 11415 Morgan Rd Agua Dulce

AXON, DONALD CARLTON, architect, consultant; b. Feb. 27, 1931, Haddonfield, NJ; s. William Russell, Sr. and Gertrude (Ellis) A.; m. Janice, Mar. 16, 1968; children: Donald b. 1953, James b. 1955, Marianne b. 1957, Darren b. 1958, William b. 1961; stepchildren: Jonathan b. 1948, Elise b. 1956; edn: B.Arch., Pratt Inst. 1954; MS arch., Columbia Univ. 1966; arch. NY 1959, Calif. 1971, Pa. 1963. Career: ptnr. Bailey & Axon AIA Assocs. Long Beach 1960-66; pgmmr.. proj. mgr. CRS Houston 1966-69; pgmmr., planner Kaiser Permanente Med. Care Group Los Angeles 1969-75; pgmmr., med. dir. DMJM L.A. 1975-79; proj. mgr. Lyon Assocs. L.A. 1979-80; pres. DCA/AIA Inc. L.A. 1980—; instr. USC Bldg. Sci. Pgm. 1978-82; instr., team leader AHA-UCLA sponsored planning & programming seminar 1975; guest lectr. UCLA Sch. of Arch. 1976, 77, Texas A&M Grad. Sch. Arch. 1977; liaison Kaiser Found. Hosps., UCLA Sch. of Arch. and Urban Planning Hosp. Pgm. 1973; profl. advisor Univ. Texas Dept. Arch. 1968-69; advisor to chmn. Rice Univ. Sch. of Arch. Masters Pgm. in Hosps. 1968-69; profl. dir. Future Archs. of Am. 1965-66; honors: Honor Award (Progressive Architecture Design Awards Pgm. 1955), First Prize (student team proj. 1953), Full Tuition Scholarship (Columbia Univ.), L.A. Beautiful Award (for KFH Norwalk Hosp.), Excellence in Design (Orange Co. chpt. AIA); mem: AIA (nat. com. on Architecture for Health chmn. 1980, chpt. dir. 1983-84, v.p., 1985, pres. 1986), Calif. Council AIA, Archtl. Found. of L.A. (founding mem., v.p. 1985), Internat. Conf. Bldg. Officials, Am. Assn. Hosp. Planners (dir. 1982-, chmn. regl. pgm. com.), Am. Hosp. Assn., Assn. Western Hosps., Internat. Health Orgn., Fellow Royal Soc. Health, Archtl. Guild (USC), Crestwood Hills Assn. (bd. 1971-83, pres. 1973-75), Brentwood Community Fedn. (bd. 1973-75, 1st v.p. 1974-75); apptd. by gov. to Bldg. Safety Bd., Ofc. of Statewide Health Planning & Devel.; Calif. Seismic Safety Commn. Hosp. Act Task Force 1976-77, Hosp. Act Legislation Task Force 1980. Ofc: Donald C. Axon AIA 823 Hanley Ave Los Angeles 90049

AYAD, NABIL, industrial distribution co. president; b. Feb. 5, 1951, Cairo, Egypt, nat. 1976; s. Ezzat A. and Lamia S. (Abuljebain) A.; m. Jakki Monroe, June 4, 1973; children: Talia, b. 1979; Danielle, b. 1980; edn: HSD, German Evangelic Sch. 1969; AA, Coll. of Marin 1973; BBA, S.F. State Univ. 1976. Career: ofc. clerk Dayco Export Import, Cairo, Egypt 1969-70; territory sales mgr. E.D. Bullard Co., Sacto., CA 1976-84; pres. Orion Sales Assocs. Inc., Petaluma, CA 1985—; grad., Dale Carnegie Sales Course; honors: salesman of the yr., E.D. Bullard Co. 1981; mem: Countrywood Homeowners Assn. (bd. dirs.); Republican; rec: photog., skeetshooting, tennis. Res: 113 Miller Ct., Petaluma 94952 Ofc: Orion Sales Associates Inc., 921 Transport Way, Petaluma 94952

AYALA, RUBEN SAMUEL, state senator; b. Mar. 6, 1922, Chino; s. Mauricio R. and Erminia (Martinez) A.; m. Irene Morales, July 22, 1945; children: Buddy, Maurice Edward, Gary; edn: stu., Pomona Jr. Coll. 1941-42; grad., Nat. Electronics Sch., Los Angeles 1948. Career: city councilman City of Chino 1962-64, mayor 1964-66, bd. supvrs. 1966-73; chmn. San Bernardino Co. Bd. Supvrs. 1968-72; mem. Calif. State Senate 1974— (chmn. agricultural and water resources com. 1976-; mem. revenue and taxtation com. 1973-; mem. Transp. com. 1981t); Chino Sch. Bd. 1955-62; chmn. San Bernardino Co. Health Com. 1968-72; Chino Police Commn. 1964-66; Chino Parks and Recreation Commn. 1962-64; mem. Nat. Alliance of Businessmen Com., Washington 1970; chmn. W. Valley Planning Agency 1968-72; steering com. Co. Hwy. Safety Orgn. 1968-72; bd. dirs. Pomona Freeway Assn. 1968; honors: Calif. Legislator of the Year, 1980; mem: Chino Valley CofC (Citizen of Year 1980); Assn. Calif. Water Agencies; Assn. Calif. Engrs.; Am. Legion; Native Sons of Golden West; Kiwanis. Ofc: 353 W. 6th St. Ste. 103, San Bernardino 92401

AYANOGLU, ESER, research scientist; b. Aug. 22, 1948, Yozgat, Turkey; s. Ahmet and Sabahat (Allioglu) A.; m. Gulesi Aydin, July 7, 1975; edn: BA, Ankara Univ. 1970; PhD, Istanbul Univ. 1975; postdoc., Stanford Univ. 1976-78. Career:asst. prof. Istanbul Univ. 1975-76, 1978-80; research scholar Stanford Univ. Chem. Dept. 1976-78, 1980—, currently supv. Djerassi Group; mem: AAAS, Sierra Club; research: discoverer or co-discoverer 50+ novel organic molecules isolated from plants or invertebrates; author 20+ sci. publs.; co-author book series Cultures in Common w. Suzanne Rocca-Butler

1985-; mil: reserve lt. Turkey 1976; rec: internat. dance tchr., computer generated music and imaging, writing. Res: 2062 Yale St Palo Alto 94306 Ofc: Stanford Univ. Chem. Dept. Stanford 94305

AYCOCK, FELIX ALFRED, lawyer; b. June 14, 1933, San Antonio, Texas; s. Felix Alfred and Ellen Antoinette (Dimeline) A.; m. Linnea Marie Nunn, Sept. 1, 1970; children: Lindy b. 1955, Daniel b. 1957, Susan b. 1959; edn: AA, Fresno Jr. Coll. 1957; BS CSU Fresno 1959; LLB, San Francisco Law Sch. 1963; admitted Calif. State Bar 1964. Career: ptnr. Hanna, Brophy, MacLean, McAleer & Jensen, Fresno; lectr. and writer on legal aspects of labor law, employment and workers compensation; honors: Phi Kappa Phi; mem. ABA, Calif. and Iowa bar assns.; mil: p.o. 2/c USN; rec: sailing. Ofc: 2310 Tulare St Fresno 93721

AYER, FREDERICK LATHAM, military officer; b. Jan. 15, 1940, Keokuk, Iowa; s. Frank McDill and Doris Belle (Arnold) A.; m. Theresa Sekan, June 5, 1963; edn: BS in chem. engring., Ariz. State Univ. 1963; MS in mgmt., Rensselaer Polytech. Inst. 1967. Career: chemical engr. E.I. DuPont de Nemours, Wilmington, Del. 1963; chem. engr. Air Force Aeropropulsion Lab., Wright Patterson AFB, Oh. 1964-67; project mgr. Minuteman System Pgm. Ofc., Norton AFB, San Bernardino, Calif. 1967-71; asst. prof. Aerospace Studies, Univ. of Minn., 1971-74; deputy dir. of projects A-10 System Program Ofc., Wright-Patterson AFB, Oh. 1974-78; chief Joint Service Activities Ofc., HQ Air Force Systems Command, Andrews AFB, Wash DC 1978-83; deputy for Acquisition Logistics, AF Ballistic Missile Ofc., Norton AFB, San Bernardino 1984-; apptd. Secretariat, Joint Logistics Commanders 1981-83; faculty advisor Univ. of Minn. Arnold Air Soc. 1971-74; mem. Am. Mgmt. Assn. (1968-73), Air Force Assn. (1963-), Porsche Club of Am.; publs: var. tech. papers; mil: col. US Air Force, Meritorious Service Medal w/o.l.c. (1978, 83), AF Commendn. Medal w/o.l.c. (1971, 74), Joint Logistics Cmdrs. Merit Cert. (1983); Presbyterian; rec: sports cars, antiques. Res: 1245 Mills Ave Redlands 92373 Ofc: Ballistic Missile Office/AL, Norton AFB, San Bernardino 92409

AYOUB, KENNETH LOUIS, company president; b. Dec. 13, 1941, Montreal, Canada, nat. US cit. 1977; s. George D. and Sophie A.; m. Dale, May 16, 1965; children: Mark b. 1970, Darlene b. 1967; edn: BA, McGill Univ. 1963; courses fin./admin., Concordia 1963-65. Career: mgr./op. RCA Corp., Montreal, Canada 1966-71; independent finl. advisor var. corporations in US and Canada, 1971-77; current: pres. Swiss Corp. of America (USA) Inc. (corporate financing to Fortune 500 cos.); honors: Advtsg. & Mktg. Club (top award for sales) RCA (1968); Statue of Liberty, Ellis Island Centennial Commn. (1985); apptd. Knight for St. Ignatious of Antioch (High Ch., 1985); mem. Am. Mktg. & Sales Club; rec: boating, golf, equestrian. Ofc: Swiss Corp. of America (USA) Inc 7361 Topanga Canyon Canoga Park 91303

AZAFRANI, GILBERT S., lawyer; b. June 5, 1949, Casablanca, French Morocco, nat. 1971; s. Simon and Marie (Benisti) A.; edn: BA, magna cum laude, Pace Univ., NYC 1972; MA, w/ distn., Fordham Univ. 1974; PhD, w/ distn., 1978; JD, Pace Univ. Sch. of Law 1980. Career: law clerk Securities & Exch. Comn., NY Regl. Counsel's Ofc., 1979-80; staff atty. US Treas. Dept., Dist. Counsel Ofc., IRS, Los Angeles 1980-81; pvt. practice Miller & Daar, Beverly Hills 1981-; Municipal Ct. Judge (Pro Tem) 1983-; honors: tchg. fellow, Fordham Univ. 1972-78; tchg. asst. Law Review, Pace Univ. Sch. of Law 1979-80; Phi Sigma Iota; Delta Theta Phi; mem: Central, Northern, Southern & Eastern US Dist., US Ninth Circuit Ct. of Appeals, US Tax Ct.; Calif. Trial Lawyers Assn., Lawyers Club of L.A.; Beverly Hills, Am. (Tax Sect.), & Calif. Bar Assns.; ASCAP, L.A. Songwriters Showcase; Democrat; rec: swimming, sailing, poetry. Res: 1725 Promenade, Apt 329, Santa Monica 90401 OFc: Miller & Daar, 9100 Wilshire Blvd, Ste 720, Beverly Hills 90212

BAABA, YOUEL A., engineering-construction co. executive; b. July 23, 1930, Baghdad, Iraq; s. Abraham and Mariam (Agakhan) B.; m. Alice R. Michael, Dec. 21, 1957; children: Raman b. 1958, Sargina b. 1960; edn: BS, CSU San Jose 1957; MBA, Golden Gate Univ. 1972. Career: came to USA in 1952; geologist, oil & gas exploration in western states 1957-64; engr., project engr., project engring. mgr., project mgr. (petroleum refineries, petrochem. plants, shale oil, etc.) Bechtel Corp. 1964-86, project assignments in USA, Japan, Australia, UK and Middle-East, ret. 1986; pres./CFO Jay Cook Transport Corp. (trucking co.), 1986-, also real estate devel., almond farming; mem. Assyrian Found. of Am. (pres. 1965-72); Republican; Christian (Assyrian Ch. of the East). Res: 50 Dias Ct Elsobrante 94803 Ofc: Jay Cook Transport Corp 2536 Patterson Rd Riverbank 95367

BACANI, NICANOR GUGLIELMO VILA, civil engineer, builder; b. Jan. 10, 1947, Dagupan City, Philippines; s. Jose Montero and Felisa Lomibao (Vila) B.; m. Julieta San Antonio Carlos, June 24, 1972; children: Julinor b. 1973, Jazmin b. 1976, Joymita b. 1978, Normina b. 1980, Nicanor, Jr. b. 1982; edn: BS civil engring., Univ. of the Phil. 1968, ME (civil), 1973; Reg. Profl. Civil Engr., Calif. (1970). Career: structural designer Tecphil Consultants, Quezon City, Phil. 1969; struct. engr. Fr Estuar, PhD & Assocs. 1970-72; civil struct. engr. Bestphil Cons., Dagupan City 1972-73; engring. mgr. Supreme Struct. Prods. Inc. (post-tension), Manila 1973; chief engr. Techphil Cons., Quezon City 1974-76; v.p. Erectors Inc., Makati 1977-81; pres. NGV Bacani, MCE & Assocs. Internat., New Jersey, Los Angeles, and Manila 1981-; cons. MMC OCPlanning, Manila (1980-), Geo. J. Fosdyke Assocs., L.A. (1985-); lectr. and guest speaker var. univs., Phil. (1982-); recipient (10+) awards from var. organizations and govt. agcs. for sharing knowledge in earthquake engring., pre-stressed concrete, str. steel, constrn. mgmt., others; mem. Internat. Assn. for Bridge & Struct. Engrs., Switz. (1985-), Am. Mgmt. Assn., Pre-Stressed

Concrete Inst., ACI, Assn. Struct. Engrs. of Phils. (dir. 4 terms), PICE, UP Alumni Engrs. Assn. (life); publs: Assn. Struct. Engrs. of Phils.(ASEP) Manual for Detailing Earthquake Resistant Design for Buildings (1983); chief stress designer of 5-star 700-rm multi-story Phil. Plaza Hotel (1976); rec: guitarist, jogging, swimming. Ofc: NGV Bacani, MCE & Assocs. POB 875255 Los Angeles 90087

BACH, CATHERINE ANDREWS, lawyer; b. Apr. 18, 1951, Pasadena, Calif.; d. Robert Wallace and Patty Jean (Calloway) Andrews; m. Bruce Allen Bach, Mar. 31, 1979; edn: BA, Stanford Univ. 1973; JD, Northwestern Univ. Sch. of Law 1978; Harvard Law Sch. 1977-78; admitted Mo. State Bar 1980, Calif. 1981. Career: atty. Brobeck, Phleger & Harrison S.F. 1978-79, Lasky, Haas, Cohler, & Munter, P.C., S.F., gen. corp. law spec. in intellectual property (biotechnol. and computer) law 1979-; dir. Customized Programming Svcs. Inc. (L.A. based computer software co.), Internat. Resources Trading Corp. (Los Altos based timber co.); mem: Am. Bar Assn. 1980-, Am. Judicature Soc. 1979-, Calif. Acad. of Sci., S.F. Ballet Assn., Yuppie Cotillion Corp. (v.p. and c.f.o.); Republican; Episcopal; rec: ballet, opera, aerobics, singing, jazz dance. Ofc: Lasky, Haas et al. 505 Sansome St, Ste 1200, San Francisco 94111

BACHMAN, ADELIA A., college president; b. Nov. 1, 1936, Hutchinson, Kans.; d. Harold P. and Mildred A. Guizlo; m. Dr. V. Charles Bachman, Feb. 14, 1979 (dec. 1985); children (nee Goodwin): Sandra A. b. 1960, Douglas K. b. 1963; edn: BA, MA, PhD, Berean Christian Coll.; accred. counselor, United Christian Counseling Assocs.; accred. hosp. chaplain, BHCCI Assoc.; ordained minister, Berean Ch. of the Scriptures. Career: illustrator, graphic arts supvr. MRC Dept. Wichita State Univ., Wichita, Kansas 1975-80; founder/ pres. Studio Dee, Long Beach 1980-; pres. Berean Christian Coll., Long Beach 1985; honors: Woman of the Yr. 1983; Christian. Res: 6801 Millmark Ave Long Beach 90805 Ofc: Studio Dee, 2234 E Broadway Long Beach 90803; Berean Christian College Adminstrative Office, 2238 Broadway Long Beach 90803

BACHMANN, CHARLES JOHN, civil engineer; b. Dec. 18, 1953, Rochester, N.Y.; s. Edward John and Rita Ann (Albright) B.; edn: BS in C.E., cum laude, Coll. of Environmental Sci. & Forestry, Syracuse, N.Y. 1976; MSCE, USC, 1978; Reg. Profl. Engr. (Civil) Calif. 1979. Career: chief Surveyor Party, Edwards & Kelcey Inc., Syracuse, N.Y. 1976-77; design engr. Boyle Engring. Corp., Newport Beach 1978-79; project engr./ project mgr. Lowry & Assoc., Irvine 1979-83; project mgr./vice pres. McGoldrick Engineers Inc., Temecula 1984-; mem. Water Pollution Control Fedn.; rec: computer pgmmg. for small bus. applications. Res: 4583 Cove Dr Carlsbad 92008 Ofc: McGoldrick Engineers Inc. 27780 Front St Ste G Temecula 92390

BACHRACH, RONALD GEORGE, lawyer, tax and investment consultant; b. Feb. 14, 1957, NY, NY; s. Ernest A. and Eve (Steinberg) B.; edn: BA high honors, State Univ. NY, Binghamton 1979; JD, Golden Gate Univ. Sch. of Law 1982; desig: (ChFC) Chartered Finl. Cons. (in progress). Career: research asst. to Prof. Mort Cohen, Golden Gate Univ. Sch. of Law, summer 1980; law clerk Garay & Foreman, San Francisco summer 1981; legal asst. Consol. Capital Cos. Inc., Emeryville 1981-82; legal asst. law ofc. Gregory Hartwell, S.F. 1982; atty. law ofc. Ronald D. Foreman, S.F. 1983; assoc. dir. advanced underwriting The Equitable, Larkspur 1984-, cons. and tng. for sixteen western states in areas of pension, employee benefits, retirement inv. accts., tax advantaged life and finl. products, bus. ins., estate plng., and computers; instr. Contg. Edn. Seminars for CPAs; mem. ABA, State Bar of Calif., Barristers Club, Bar Assn. of San Francisco; civic: Am., Calif., Marin County Red Cross, Disabled Am. Vets, Marin Co. Senior Citizens, Kevin Collins Found. for Missing Children, SPCA; pro bono community legal services; Democrat; Jewish; rec: Tae Kwon Do, softball, basketball league, bowling, skiing. Res: 1550 Bay St Apt 261 San Francisco 94123 Ofc: The Equitable 700 Larkspur Landing Circle Ste 200 Larkspur 94939

BACIGALUPI, ISABELLE PINA, health care consultant; b. Nov. 16, 1926, Yountville; d. John Mena and Maria (Pavon) Pina; m. Louis B. Bacigalupi, May 20, 1949; children: Barton b. 1950, Mark b. 1953, Jorjan b. 1955, Jay b. 1956, Tammy b. 1963; edn: B.Nsg., St. Mary's Coll. of Nursing, S.F. 1947; tchg. credential, UC Santa Cruz 1974; BA, Univ. Redlands 1978, MA mgmt., 1982; desig: RN, Calif. (1948), Public Health Nurse (1978), State Tchg. Credential (1974). Career: 1965-74: RN, Student Health Ctr., San Francisco State Univ.; cons. stroke pgm. Stanford Univ.; farm labor nse. Pub. Health Dept., Santa Cruz and dir. of nurses, Santa Cruz; 1974-82: Health Facilities RN for State of Calif., San Jose (evaluations of health facilities to ensure compliance with state regs.; speaker pub. & pvt. groups); 1982-: pres. ISALOU, Ent. (consultants): conduct time mgmt. seminars, cons. to health facilities, instr. Santa Cruz County Regl. Occupational Pgms.; chair Public Health Commn., Santa Cruz County 1984-85, 85-86; apptd. mem. Calif. Dept. Health Services Women's Advis. Commn. 1980-82; mem: Calif. Assn. Health Career Educators, Calif. Assn. Health Facilities, Peninsula Skilled Nurses Assn. (bd. dirs. 1983, 85), Am. Red Cross (bd. dirs. Santa Cruz Chpt. 1985-86), Pet Enhancement Therapy Soc. (bd. dirs. 1985-86), Univ. of Redlands Alumni Assn., Quota Club of Santa Cruz (pres. 1985-86), Santa Cruz CofC (Ambassador), Sister Cities Commn., League of Women Voters, UCSC Affils. (Friends of Library), Toastmasters; Republican (secty. Rep. Central Com. 1985-86); rec: RVing, white water rafting, pub. speaking. Res: 401 Ocean View Ave Santa Cruz 95062 Ofc: Isalou, Ent., 401 Ocean View Ave Santa Cruz 95062

BADER, W. REECE, lawyer; b. Oct. 31, 1941, Portland, Ore.; s. Wm. Lange and Phyllis Harriet (Cole) B.; m. Jean McCarty, Aug. 3, 1963; children: Lawson b. 1966, Cole b. 1969; edn: BA, Williams Coll. 1963; LLB, Duke Univ.

1966; admitted all Calif. Cts., US Supreme Ct., US Ct. of Appeals (D.C., 9th, 3d, Fed. Cir.), US Dist. Cts. in D.C. and Calif., US Claims Ct. Career: law clk. Hon. Warren E. Burger, US Ct. of Appeals, D.C. Circuit 1966-68; atty. assoc. Orrick, Herrington & Sutcliffe, San Francisco 1968–, ptnr. 1974-, chmn. Litigation Dept. 1982-85; mem. legal adv. bd. Hastings Law Center Found., 1981-; mem. US Judicial Conf. adv. com. Fed. Rules of Civil Procedure, 1982-; lectr. Calif. Continuing Edn. of the Bar (1979-), Calif. Bus. Law Inst. (1980-82), Practicing Law Inst. (1979, 84), Securities Indus. Assn. seminars (1980-); arbitrator Am. Arb. Assn. (1979-), NASD, Inc. (1979-), S.F. Superior Ct. (1981-); mem: Am. Bar Assn. (Litigation Sect.), Calif. State Bar (chair pretrial subcom. Litigation Section 1984-), Bar Assn. of S.F., Lawyers Club of S.F., Calif. Trial Lawyers Assn, Am. Judicature Soc., US Supreme Ct. Hist. Soc., D.C. Bar Assn. (inactive), Christian Legal Soc.; bd. trustees North Park Coll. & Sem., Chgo. (1984-), adv. bd. Mt. Hermon Assn., Inc. (1979-82, 84-), pres. Bay Area Christian Conciliation Service, Inc. (1984-); Democrat; Evangelical Covenant Ch.; rec: model trains, squash, softball. Ofc: Orrick, Herrington & Sutcliffe, 600 Montgomery St San Francisco 94111

BADHAM, ROBERT EDWARD, congressman; b. June 9, 1929, Los Angeles; s. Byron Jack and Bess (Kissinger)B., m. Anne Carroll; children: Sharon, Robert, William, Phyllis, Jennifer; edn: AB, Arch., Stanford Univ. 1951. Career: mem. Calif. Assembly 1962-76; mem. 95th-99th Congresses form 40th Calif. Dist.; chmn. Republican study com., Rep. research task force nat. def.; mem. Rep. policy com.; armed services com.; house adminstrn. com.; v.chmn. congl. travel and tourism caucus; exec. com. Nat. Rep. Congl. Com. Active Boy Scouts; mem: Am. Legion; Phi Gamma Delta; mil: lt. (j.g.) USNR 1951-54; Republican; Lutheran, Ofc: 180 Newport Ctr. Dr. Ste. 240, Newport Beach 92660; 2438 Rayburn House Office Bldg., Wash. DC 20515

BADHAM, VIRGINIA EVELYN DABNEY, pianist, singer, poet; b. July 20, 1907, Portland, Ore.; dau. (Ore. pioneer) Richard Temple and Martha Amanda (Renshaw) Dabney; m. Edward Dick Badham, May 21, 1929, div. 1953; four daus: Beverly, b. 1931, Marilyn, b. 1932, Patricia, b. 1937, Cheryl, b. 1948; 15 grandchildren: edn: grad. Marlborough Sch.1927, stu. USC 1927-28; stu. piano (11 yrs.) with Calbreath Studios of Portland, Ore. and Olga Steeb Studios, Los Angeles; vocal stu. (15+ yrs.) with Elizabeth Green Happ, Ingenuus Bentzar and Florence Russell Studios; stu. ballet, Norman Gould Studios 1923, ballroom dancing, Ernest Ryan Studios 1923-26. Career: piano debut at age 13 in Portland, Ore.; piano tchr., Los Angeles and Newport Bch; singers' accompanist; concert singer, Women's Lyric Club, L.A. (Wilshire Ebell and Biltmore Theatres, etc.). Works: num. music compositions; poetry, 550+, 2 pub. in Todays Greatest Poems (1983), Am. Poetry Anthology (1983); lyricist; jewelry designer; bldg. designer; mem: Pi Beta Phi (USC) Alumnae, Coronets of Nat. Charity League, chrtr mem. Lido Isle Players; orgnzr. Mothers of Am. postcard campaign during Korean War; author many religious writings on healing; Christian Sci.; rec: geneal. resrch, design, singing, study of extraterrestrial life and space travel. Res: 204 Collins Ave. Balboa Is. 92662

BAHARVAR, JAMSHID JIM, physician, internist; b. June 15, 1946, Teheran, Iran; s. Morad and Azize (Haroonian) B.; m. Oct. 1985; edn: grad., Am. Coll. Teheran 1962; Pahlavi Univ. Med. Sch. 1971 ; lic. phys. NY, Calif. 1979. Career: intern Jewish Meml. Hosp. NY 1975-76; resident Long Island Jewish Med. Ctr. NY 1976-77; fellowship geriatric med. Jewish Inst. for Geriatric Care 1976-77; fellowship nuclear med. L.I. Jewish Hosp.1977-78; phys. pvt. practice Santa Monica 1978–; instr., cons. var. hosps.; on staff 10 hosps. in L.A. area; mem: World Med. Assn., Am. Geriatric Soc., Am. Coll. Phys., Am. Soc. Internal Med.; publs; articles in med. jours.; mil: med. ofcr. Iran Army 1972-73; Jewish; rec: sports, music, piano, dancing, sailing. Ofc: 2021 Santa Monica Blvd Ste 535 Santa Monica 90404

BAHME, RICHARD BEALE, agricultural consultant, forensic agronomist; b. Dec. 23, 1918, Los Angeles; s. John William and Jessie Irene (Beale) B.; m. Anna McQueen Hanlin, Aug. 31, 1946; children: Robert Hanlin b. 1951, John Beale b. 1953; edn: BS, UC Berkeley 1940, MS, 1947, Ph.D., 1949; certified profl. agron., profl. soil scientist, profl. crop scientist, reg. profl. forester. Career: research agronomist E.I. DuPont Co. Wilmington, Del., Sacto. 1949-54; chief agronomist Pacific Guano Co. Berkeley 1954-58; western reg. agron. Nat. Plant Food Inst. S.F. 1958-64; v.p. agric. devel. Uniconsult Inc. LaFayette 1964-67; agric. cons., pres. AgriDevelopment Co. Orinda 1967–; pres. Agbiochem Inc. Orinda 1976–; owner/mgr. Agridevelopment Research Orchards Los Molinos; honors: Sigma Xi; mem: Am. Soc. Farm Mgrs. and Rural Appraisers, Am. Soc. Agronomy (bd. dirs. Calif. sect.), Crop Sci. Soc. of Am., Calif. Fertilizer Assn. (soil improvement com.), Am. Soc. Range Mgmt., Am. Chemical Soc., United Nations Industrial Devel. Org. (fertilizer cons.); clubs: Orinda Country, Lake Almanor Country, Berkeley Lions, S.F. Press and Union League, Big C Soc.-Bear Backers, Calif. Alumni Assn., Sigma Chi; publ: num. tech. papers on soil fertility and irrigation; patent on process for making fertilizer from waste pickling liquor 1966; mil: capt. US Army Anti-Aircraft Arty. 1941-46; Republican; Episcopal; rec: orchids, fishing, hunting, tennis, stamp collecting. Address: Orinda 94563

BAILEY, GEORGE M., library director; b. Feb. 13, 1924, Millers, Md.; married, two children; edn: BA, Franklin and Marshall Coll. 1946; MA hist., Univ. Pa. 1947; MALS, Univ. Wisc. 1953; cert. mgt., Claremont Grad. Sch.; lib. automation insts.: Univ. Ill., Am. Lib. Assn., IBM. Career: instr. hist. Franklin and Marshall Coll., Heidelberg Coll. (Tiffin, Oh.), Univ. Wisc., 1947-51; intern in lib. adminstrn. UC Berkeley, 1953-54; librn. Soc. Sclis. Ref. Svcs, 1954-55; librn. UC Davis 1955-59, hd Ref.Dept. 1958-9; chief Ref. & Spl. Services, Northwestern Univ., 1959-63, and asst. planner of new lib. bldg.; exec.secty. Assn. of Coll. and Resrch Libs., div. Am. Lib. Assn., Chgo 1963-68; acad. librarian cons.; frequent spkr. lib. assns.; chief librarian/prof. York Coll., City Univ. of NY, 1968-71 (planned new lib. facility; devel. staff and collection for new college lib.); assoc. dir. Libraries, The Claremont Colls.,Claremont 1971–, acting dir. of libs. 1973-4. cons. US Office of Edn.; accreditation vis. Western Assn of Schs and Colls, 1973-, Am. Lib. Assn 1978-; mem: ALA, Calif. Lib Assn., Beta Phi Mu, Phi Alpha Theta, Archons (NY), Zamorano Club (L.A.). Res: 2129 Villa Maria Rd. Claremont 91711 Ofc: The Assoc. Dir. of Libraries, The Claremont Colleges, Claremont

BAILEY, JAMES PAUL, producer/writer/financial executive; b. May 2, 1949, Columbus, Oh.; s. Paul Shannon and Loretta Mary (Criado) B.; edn: BA music, Nat. Conservatory of Music 1976; MBA, Franklin Univ. 1979; Calif. Real Estate Broker lic., 1979. Career: pub. rels./prodn. crew WLW-C TV (Columbus, Oh.) Dance-O-Rama Series, 1963-67; real estate sales Roberts Realty, 1976, asst. mgr. Doheny Realty, 1978-79, R.E. broker 1979-; estab. 2 cos. writing & producing audio/visual: founder/pres. James Bailey Prodns. 1979–, Inc. 1982-, also founder/pres. Entertainment Directions Unlmtd., 1983–; delinquency counselor; spkr. for The Olympic Experience pgm. for disadvantaged youths (founder Olympic Gold Medalist Bill Toomey); speaker bus. seminars; sales awards: Million Dollar Club, Roberts Realty 1977-78), Champions Unlmtd. pres.'s award Sasco Cosmetics No. 1 Recruiter Nat. (1980); civic: USABF boxing coach/patron 1984 Olympic Team; coach/sponsor AYSO Soccer, Del Obispo Boys Baseball, Regl. All Star Boys Baseball (1977, 78), The Olympic Exp.; mem. Calif. Assn. Realtors, Nat. Assn. Realtors, Dana Pt. CofC; subject interviews var. periodicals (1981-); mil: E3 USMC 1967-69, VietNam Svc., VietNam Cpgn. medals, Pres. Unit Cit.; Christian; rec: running, handball, music. Res: 33864 Pequito Dr Dana Point 92629 Ofc: James Bailey Productions Inc. 34184 Coast Hwy Ste 205 Dana Point 92629

BAKER, CAMERON, lawyer; b. Dec. 24, 1937, Chgo.; s. David Cameron and Marion Ruth (Fitzpatrick) B.; m. Katharine Solari, Sept. 2, 1961; children: Cameron b. 1963, Ann b. 1964, John b. 1967; edn: Univ. of Notre Dame 1954-57; AB, Stanford Univ. 1958; LLB, UC Berkeley 1961. Career: atty., assoc. Adams, Duque and Hazeltine, Los Angeles 1961-62; Pettit & Martin, San Francisco 1962–, exec. com. 1971-82, 1984-, mng. ptnr. 1972-81, 1984-; dir. (mem. Audit Com.) Leslie Salt Co., S.F. 1971-78; del. Union Internationale des Avocats (1983-); mem. Am. Bar Assn. (Fin. com., coms. on Law Firms, Small Bus., Law & Acctg., Internat. Bus. Law, Ptnrship and Unincorp. Bus. Orgns.), Boalt Hall Alumni Assn. (dir. 1982-84), Phi Delta Phi (pres. 1961), Beta Theta Pi; civic: French-Am. CofC; elected City Council, Belvedere (1976-80), mayor (1978-79); clubs: Bohemian, Belvedere Tennis, Tiburon Peninsula. Res: 38 Alcatraz Ave Belvedere 94920 Ofc: Pettit & Martin 101 California St 35th Flr San Francisco 94111

BAKER, D. KENNETH, college president; b. Oct. 2, 1923, Glasgow, Scotland, nat. 1956; s. David Thomas and Edith Rose (Horner) B.; m. Vivian Christian Perry, Sept. 13, 1947; 1 son, Richard R., b. 955; edn: BSc, McMaster Univ. (Hamilton, Can .) 1946; PhD, Univ. of Penna. 1953. Career: asst., assoc., prof. of physics, Union College, Schenectady, NY 1953-65; mgr. profl. personnel and univ. relations General Electric Resrch. and Devel. Ctr., Schenectady, NY 1965-67; acting pres. St. Lawrence Univ., Canton, NY 1969 (Feb.-Sept.), v.p. and dean, 1967-76; pres. Harvey Mudd Coll., Claremont, Calif. 1976–; cons.: Alco Products, Schenectady, NY 1954-55; Gen. Elec. Co., Schenectady 1956-57; Nat. Sci. Found., Wash DC 1954-64; Agcy. for Internat. Devel., Wash DC 1962; Ronald Press Co., NYC 1964; advis. Advisory Council, Los Angeles Council of Engrs. and Scientists, 1976-78; mem. (chmn. 1982, 83) Advisory Com. Inst. for the Advance. of Engring. 1978-; mem: American Inst. of Physics, Rotary (Claremont), California Club (LA), Newcomen Sunset, Sunset (Pasa.), University Club (Claremont); co-author w/A.T. Goble: Elements of Modern Physics. Res: 495 East Twelfth St Claremont 91711 Ofc: Harvey Mudd College, Kingston Hall, Claremont 91711

BAKER, HARRY DE GARMO, construction co. president; b. Mar. 1, 1935, Los Angeles; s. Harry D. and Mabel Alison (Braasch) B.; m. Joyce Ione Quick, Nov. 21, 1976; 1 dau. Cherie Ann, b. 1963; edn: AA, Santa Monica CC, 1960, UCLA 1961; Calif. Lic. State Contractor 1983. Career: police ofcr. city of Santa Monica, 1958-65; computer opr. Hughes Aircraft, Culver City 1965-67; examiner Nat. American Ins. Co., L.A. 1967-71; v.p. Oakshire Corp., L.A. 1971-72; mgr. Clark Porche Constrn. Co., San Bernardino 1972-83; pres. Baker/Ginger Construction, Inc. Glendora 1983–; awards: 3d pl. USMC District Pistol Championships, 1964; mem: Footprinters Intl., Retired Police Officers of Santa Monica, San Bernardino/ Riverside Adjusters Assn., Masons; mil: sgt. USMC 1953-58, GCM, Pres. Unit. Cit., Nat. Def. medal, Exp. Rifleman/Pistol; Republican; Prot.; rec: fishing, travel. Res: 535 E. Whitcomb Ave Glendora 91740 Ofc: Baker/Ginger Constrn. Inc. 510 S. Vermont Glendora 91740

BAKER, ROBERT HALEM, automobile dealer; b. Oct. 1, 1931, Los Angeles; s. Halem and Dortis (Peterson) B.; m. Sherrill, May 1, 1954; children: Michael Vincent b. 1955, Elizabeth Diane b. 1958, Theresa Suzanne b. 1961, Mary Janeen b. 1962, Christopher Robert b. 1963; edn: Woodbury Sch. of Bus., spl. courses and tng. seminars. Career: auto sales, sales mgr. Fleetline Mgmt. Svcs., Chevrolet dealerships in Lakewood, Los Angeles, San Diego, and El Paso, Tx., 1954-65; pres./dealer opr. Bob Baker Chevrolet Inc., Indpls. 1966-79, bd. chmn./finl. ptnr. dealerships in Elwood, Ind. 1971-77; Valleywood Chevrolet, Napa, Calif. 1973-79, Ron Baker Chevrolet, Los Gatos 1974-80, British Leyland Franchise, Anaheim 1978-79, current pres. Rekab Ents. Inc. (holding co. 8 auto franchises): University Ford, San Diego 1979-, Bob Baker Volkswagen/Chrysler-Plymouth, Carlsbad 1981-, Santa Maria

Ford, Santa Maria 1984-, and Santa Maria AMC/Jeep/Renault 1985-, Bob Baker Chevrolet and Bob Baker Isuzu, National City 1985-; dir: Westwood Life Ins. Co., Nat. Ins. Co.; awards: Chevrolet Service Supremacy 1974-79, Chrysler 5 Star Award 1982, Chrysler Pacesetter Award 1985, Ford Vice Pres.'s Club 1980-83, Ford Disting. Achievemt. 1979-85; mem: Chevrolet Regional Dealer Council 1972-75, Chevrolet Nat. Dealer Council 1975-76, Chrysler Dealer Council 1980-81, Ford Dealer Council 1980-81, San Diego Co. Chrysler/Plymouth Dealers Advt. Assn. (pres. 1983-84, dir. 1983-85), Motor Car Dealers Assn. of So. Calif. (dir. 1982-84, treas. 1985-86), Ford Dealers Advt. Assn. of So. Calif. (chmn. 1982, dir. 1980-86), Motor Car Dealer Assn. of San Diego Co. (pres. 1984-85, dir. 1981-86); civic: St. Vincent De Paul (adv. bd.), Catholic Comm. Svcs. (dir.), USD Pres.'s Club, Rotary, Am. Diabetes Assn., Boys Club Am.; clubs: Lomas Santa Fe CC, Rancho Santa Fe CC, Ironwood CC; Republican (Pres. Task Force); Catholic. Ofc: Rekab Enterprises Inc 730 Camino Del Rio N San Diego 92108

BAKER, ROBERT M.L., JR., university president; b. Sept. 1, 1930, Los Angeles; s. Robert M.L. and Martha (Harlan) B.; m. Bonnie Vold, Nov. 14, 1964; children: Robert Randall b. 1959, Robert M.L. b. 1965, Robin b. 1968; edn: BA, physics, math., UCLA 1954, MA, physics, 1956, PhD, astronomy, engring., 1958. Career: cons. Douglas Aircraft Co.; senior scientist Aeronutronic 1957-60; proj. ofcr. Space Sys. Div. of USAF 1960-61; hd. astrodynamic research ctr. Lockheed 1961-64; assoc. mgr., mathematical analysis Computer Science Corp. 1964-80; pres. West Coast Univ. 1980-, prof. engring. West Coast Univ.; honors: UCLA physics prize; Outstanding Young Man of Yr. 1965, Dirk Brouwer Award 1976, Phi Beta Kappa, Sigma Xi, Sigma Pi Sigma (pres., UCLA 1954); mem: Fellow Am. Astronautical Soc., British Interplanetary Soc., British Astronomical Soc., AAAS and Meteoritical Soc., Am. Physical Soc. of Am. Astronomical Soc., Los Angeles Mens Garden Club, Univ. YMCA (UCLA pres. 1954-56), publs: An Introduction to Astrodynamics, 1960, rev. 1967; Astrodynamics- Advanced and Applied Topics, 1967; ed. Journ. of Astronautical Sciences 1966-; joint ed. Proceedings of the 1961 Internat. Astronautics Fedn.; rec: tennis, computer programming. Res: 8123 Tuscany Ave., Playa del Rey 90293 Ofc: West Coast University, 440 Shatto Pl., Los Angeles 90020

BAKER, RONALD EUGENE, auto dealer; b. Mar. 30, 1945, Topeka, Kans.; s. Harry M. and Catherine L. (Woody) Baker; m. Judy, Aug. 24, 1963; 1 son Raymond, b. 1965; career: president, three corps.; mem. Elks; Baptist; address: 5515 N. Blackstone Ave. Fresno 92710

BAKER, SUSAN MARION, life underwriter, financial executive; b. Dec. 28, 1942, Norfolk, Va.; s. Anthony Jr. and Marion Hazel (Harwood) B.; children: Jeannette b. 1962, Michael b. 1963, Leslie b. 1964, Jonathan b. 1969, Anthony b. 1970; edn: real estate, Chaffey Coll. 1972-74; CLU cand., Am. Coll. (1982-), Registered Rep., fin'l. services. Career: real estate agent Forest E. Olson/Coldwell Banker, Corona 1973; real estate broker Susan M. Baker Co. Real Property Investments, Carlsbad 1978; life underwriter Primary Co. New York Life Ins. Co. 1982, currently, ins. agent and broker, San Diego; honors: Top Ten, Million Dollar Club Forest E. Olson (1974-77), Exec. Council, New York Life Ins. Co. 1983-86; mem. Nat., Calif. and No. San Diego Co. (pres. elect 1986) Life Underwriters Assns., Life Underwrs. PAC; civic: Toastmasters (pres. 1982-83), Profl. Referral Orgn. Inc. (pres. 1982-83), Carlsbad CofC, Ramona CofC, Ramona Pioneer Hist. Soc. (v.p. 1985-87), Guy B. Woodward Mus.; works: packaging/ mktg. promotion of spl. events and fund raisers; Catholic; rec: public service, community involvement. Res: P.O. Box 1218 Ramona 92065 Ofc: New York Life Insurance Co., P.O. Box 1166 San Diego 92112

BAKER, TERRY RONALD, physician; b. Aug. 29, 1940, Pittsburg, Pa.; s. Leonard and Frances (Piatt) B.; m. Lynne Dickson, Aug. 21, 1983; 1 son: Jonathan b. 1970; edn: BA, Cornell Univ. 1962; MD, Univ of Rochester 1966; bd. certified ophthalmologist Am. Bd. of Ophthalmology 1975. Career: pvt. practice of ophthalmology in San Francisco; assoc. prof. ophthalmology Univ. Calif. San Francisco; mem. Am. Acad. Ophthalmology, Am. Coll. Surgeons, Cordes Soc.; mil: lcdr. USPHS 1968-70; rec: skiing, tennis, painting. Res: 17 Longwood Dr San Rafael 94901 Ofc: Terry R. Baker MD 490 Post St, Ste 1505, San Francisco 94102

BAKSHI, KRISHNA G., controller; b. Nov. 22, 1933, India, nat. US cit. 1976; s. Brij Lal and Kaushalya (Bali) B.; m. Anu Radha, June 26, 1958; children: Nisha b. 1959, Sanjay b. 1963, Shikha b. 1966; edn: LLB, Delhi Univ. 1960; MBA, Pepperdine Univ. 1978. Career: acct. Am. Embassy New Delhi, India 1956-71; controller Delta Boats Redwood City, Calif. 1971-72, acct. Levy Zentner S San Francisco 1972-74; controller Amfac Elec. Supply Inc. 1974-80, Independent Elec. Supply Inc. San Carlos 1980-; honors: Meritorious Award (US Embassy New Delhi); mem. Elks 1982-; Hindu; rec: reading. Res: 602 Bainbridge St Foster City 94404 Ofc: Independent Elec. Supply Inc. 1370 Bayport Ave POB 1263 San Carlos 94070

BAKST, ABRAHAM ALFRED, engineer, real estate executive, investor; b. Jan. 12, 1922, Palmer, Mass.; s. Isadore and Minnie (Kaplan) B.; a Bklyn. synogogue built @ 1890 is named after his gr.gr.gr.grandfather Aaron David (orthodox rabbi in Russia); m. Pauline Day (Dep. Atty-Gen., Hawaii 1948-9) July 10, 1948, div. 1959; 1 dau. Katherine (hd. tchr. Child Care Devel. Ctr., UCI & CSULB, 1973-6) b. 1949; son-in-law, Richard Thornley (Dep. Atty-Gen., Nev. 1977-81); edn: Bklyn. Coll. 1938-42, U. of Hawaii 46-7, Cal Poly 49-50; AA in real estate, Long Bch C.C. 1961; Orange Coast Coll. 78-9; mil. certs., Bellevue/Naval Resrch Lab. 43-4. Career: radar insp. War Dept., N.J. 1942; petty ofcr. USNR (radio, radar supr. P.T. Boat Squad.), So.Pac. 1942-5; teletype

opr. War Dept., Hawaii 1946-7; electronic engr. all Naval and Marine Corps Air Stations, 14th Naval Dist. (H.I.), Pearl Harbor 1947-9, pioneered first VHF radio teletype and terminal network in Navy 1947, asst. proj. engr. VLF radio propagation characteristic test, Pac. area 1948; electronic sci./staff Navy Dept., Inyokern 1950; electronic engr.: Douglas Aircraft, Rockwell Internat., Hughes Aircraft, Hoffman Radio, Varec Indus., 1951-8; supr. Nebeker Realty, Calif. 1958-61; owner/ broker/ investor Bakst Realty Enterprises, Anaheim 1961-; founder/ pub./ed. News Forecasting Newsletter (1958); advisor on news foresight, seven US Presidents, Congress, 1953-. Honors: capt. (champion) Bklyn. Coll. chess team, H.S. champion chess team, listed in World Almanac-1942 for chess play in coll. tourn. (1941), later was Calif. Chess Champion; listed in P.T.Boats Knights of the Sea (1982). Jewish; rec: news analysis, chess. Address: 210 N. Brookhurst St. Anaheim 92801

BALCER, EUNICE MARY, tax auditor; b. Jan. 13, 1927, Phila.; d. Romey George Harrison and Mildred Bertha (Hood) Sowell; m. Raymond John Balcer, May 11, 1946; children: Cheryl Ruth b. 1947, Donna Marie b. 1953, Lisa June b. 1957; grad. Upper Darby Senior H.S. 1945. Career: tax examiner, taxpayer service splst., auditor, coordinator, Internal Revenue Service, 1967-; recipient IRS spl. award, 2 Adopted Suggestions; mem. DAR, Rebekah; Republican; Presbyterian; rec: quilting, needlework. Address: Laguna Niguel 92677

BALCH, GLENN MCCLAIN, JR., clergyman; b. Nov. 1, 1937, Shattuck, Okla.; s. Glenn McClain and Marjorie (Daily) B.; m. Diana Gale Seeley, Oct. 15, 1970; children: Bryan, Gayle, Wesley, Johnny; edn: stu., Panhandle State Univ. 1958-60, So. Methodist Univ. 1962-64; BA, S.W. State Univ. Okla. 1962; BD, Phillips Univ. 1965; MA, Chapman Coll. 1973, MA in Edn. 1975, MA in Psych. 1975; PhD, U.S. Internat. Univ. 1978; postgrad., Claremont Grad. Sch. 1968-70, Univ. Okla. 1965-66. Career: ordained to ministry Methodist Ch. 1962; sr. minister First Meth. Ch., Eakly, Okla. 1960-63, First Meth. Ch., Calumet, Okla. 1963-65, Goodrich Meml. Ch., Norman, Okla. 1965-66, First Meth. Ch., Barstow 1966-70; asst. dean Chapmann Coll., Orange 1970-76; v.p. Pacific Christian Coll., Fullerton 1976-79; pres. Newport Univ., Newport Beach 1979-82; sr. minister Brea United Meth. Ch. 1978-; edn. cons. USAF 1974-75; mental health cons. U.S. Army 1969; cons. Hanford Police Dept. 1983-; Comm. Adv. Bd. Minority Problems 1975; Mayor's rep. to County Dependency Prevention Commn. 1968-69; mem. bd. dirs. For Kid's Sake, Orange Co. Human Service Advis. Bd., O.C. Child Abuse Services Advis. Commn., Brea Econ. Devel. Com.; honors: recipient Eastern Star Religion Training Award 1963, 1964; Broadhurst fellow 1963-65; mem: Calif. Marriage Therapists Assn.; Rotary; Masons; Shriners; Elks. Res: 1016 Steele Dr., Brea 92621 Ofc: 480 No. State College, Brea 92621

BALDWIN, ALAN CHARLES, electronics co. executive; b. June 7, 1952, London, England; s. Charles Alfred and Rose (Nelson) B.; edn: BS, London Univ. 1973; PhD, Univ. of Leicester 1976. Career: research scientist, Stanford Research Inst., Menlo Park 1976-81; research and devel. mgr. Branson/IPC, Hayward 1981-84; dept. mgr. Technol. Devel. Intel Corp., Santa Clara 1984-; exec. bd. Semiconductor Research Corp. (1984-); honors: mem. City and Guilds of London (1974); mem. AAAS, Nat. Geographic Soc., Sierra Club; publs: 30+ tech. papers, 2 book chpts.; rec: ski, sail, photog. Res: 122 Walter Hays Dr Palo Alto 94303 Ofc: Intel Corp. 3065 Bowers Ave Santa Clara 95051

BALDWIN, ALLEN PETERS, housing agency executive; b. July 7, 1940, Oak Park, Ill.; s. B. George and Dorothy B. (Orr) B.; m. Linda, Sept. 9, 1967; children: Tiffani b. 1968, Jami b. 1970, Deborah b. 1971, Peter b. 1975; edn: Bradley Univ. 1961-63. Career: contracts adminstr. Cosmodyne Corp. 1966-69; real estate dir. Sterling Savings & Loan 1969-73; proj. mgr. Watt Inds. Inc. 1973-77; proj. mgr. Country Club Homes 1977-78; exec. dir. Orange County Community Housing Corp. 1978-; Gov. appointee to Bd. of Calif. Housing Finance Agency; bd. Aliso Viejo Housing Opportunities Corp.; councilmember City of Lake Elsinore 1978-82; chmn. So. Calif. Assn. of Govts. Community Devel. Com. 1981-82; mem. League of Calif. Cities Community Devel. Com. 1978-82; chmn. Riverside County Conf. of Mayors and Councilmembers 1980-81; dir. Elsinore Valley Mun. Water Dist. 1984-85; dir. Lake Elsinore Valley CofC 1983; treas. Lake Elsinore Valley Soccer Club 1983-84; mil: E4 USN 1957-61; Republican; Episcopal; rec: youth, community affairs. Res: 16496 Lash St Lake Elsinore 92330 Ofc: Orange Co. Community Housing Corp. 1833 E 17th St Ste 207 Santa Ana 92701

BALDWIN, BARRETT STONE, farm co. president; b. Apr. 23, 1897, Delano, Calif.; s. Morice Henry and Sarah (Timmons) B.; m. Lena Fontain, Sept. 2, 1918; children: June b. 1919, Lawrence b. 1920, Barrett Jr. b. 1921, Jeraldine b. 1922, Barbara b. 1926; m. 2d Louise Chiuppi, June 8, 1962. Career: laborer 1918-40; oper. dairy 1940-76, farmed up to 4000 acres, owned 3200 of these acres, set 5 children up in farming in 1950; pres. B.S. Baldwin Farms Inc.; county campaign mgr. for Richard Nixon in Calif. Gov. race; mem: Kern County Farm Bureau Orgn., Kern Co. Milk Producers Orgn., Masonic Lodge; support Masonic Homes, Salvation Army.; Republican. Res: 2908 McCall St Bakersfield 93304 Ofc: 2942 Engel Rd Bakersfield 93309

BALESTRERI, THEODORE JEROME, restaurateur/developer; b. June 30, 1940, Bklyn.; s. Vincent Jerome and Viola Georganne (Crispo) B.; m. Velma, May 16, 1971; children: Theodore, II b. 1972; Vincent Frank b. 1977; edn: Monterey Penin. Coll., 1959, and Lewis Hotel Management Sch., Wash DC. Career: ptnr/owner, founder Sardine Factory restaurant in Cannery Row area of Monterey, 1968- (respons. for redevel. of Cannery Row hist. area; corp. owns 70%), later acquired The Rogue restaurant (on Wharf #2), San Simeon Restaurant (nr Hearst Castle) San Simeon, The Gold Fork in Carmel (fmrly The

Butcher Shop); current bd. chmn./pres. (parent co.) Restaurants Central/ Foursome Development; also active in comml. real estate, farming, and opr. franchise for Wendy's Internat. (3-county area, N.Calif.); guest lectr. var. state and nat. conventions, univs., bus. and finl. instns., restaurant/ hotel seminars and convs.; apptd. by Gov. Deukmejian to Tourism Commn.; honors: Gold Plate Award, Am. Acad. of Achievement (1982), Silver & Gold Plate Awards, Internat. Foodservice Mfrs. Assn. (1984), Hon. Doctorate of Foodservice, NAFEM (1985), Escoffier Soc. Award Medallion, num. civic awards; feature cover article w/wife Velma, Money Mag. (11/81); restaurant awards for The Sardine Factory incl. The Ivy Award (Travel/ Holiday Mag., 1971-), Nation's Rest. News Hall of Fame, Mobil Travel Guide Award, The Armstrong Gourmet Guide as one of Calif.'s Top 10 Restaurants, one of 50 rests. in USA to serve at Pres. Reagan's Inauguration (1981, 1985); mem. Nat. Rest. Assn. (pres. 1985-86), Calif. Rest. Assn. (pres. 1983-84), Nat. Inst. for Foodservice Industry (bd. trustees), The Culinary Inst. of Am. (corp. mem.), Monterey Penin. Hotel and Rest. Assn. (past pres.), No. Calif. Rest. Assn. (past pres. & founder), Confrerie de la Chaine des Rotisseurs (past chpt. pres.); mem. Monterey Co. Sheriff's Advis. Council; mil: US Army; Catholic; rec: tennis, racketball. Res: POB 655 Pebble Beach 93935 Ofc: Restaurants Central/ Foursome Development 765 Wave St Monterey 93940

BALLARD, J. THEODORE, plumbing, heating and air conditioning co. owner; b. May 2, 1928; s. Joseph Otho and Mary Pearl (Taylor) B.; children: Jodie b. 1950, Melanie b. 1959; Calif. lic. Plmbg., Htg., Air Condtg. and Solar Contr. Career: owner Ballard's Plumbing, Heating and Air Conditioning Co., Anaheim 1965 — ; real estate owner/ptnr., Huntington Beach, Anaheim Hills, Anaheim; awards: Hon. Kentucky Colonel; mem: Plmbg., Htg., Air Condtg. Assn. of Calif., Model T Club of Am., Order of Moose; mil: served to col. US Army; Republican; rec: pvt. pilot (single engine, land), hunting, fishing. Res: 17982 Via Ranchero Yorba Linda 92686 Ofc: Ballard's Plumbing, Heating and Air Conditioning Co., 1509 No. Kraemer Unit G Anaheim 92806

BALLOU, RICHARD ALFRED, construction co. executive; b. June 10, 1941, Seattle, Wash.; s. Roger A. and Ella Jane (Kelsey) B.; m. Linda C., May 19, 1979; children (adopted): Debbie b. 1961, Jack b. 1963, Kathy b. 1964, Jimmy b. 1967, Troy b. 1969; edn: Syracuse Univ. 1958-60; BSBA, Queens Coll. 1964; Career: surveyor, field engr., supt., pchsg. agent, dist. mgr., constrn. mgr., proj. mgr., v.p., gen. mgr. George A. Fuller Co. NY, NY 1961-81; constrn. mgr. Turner Constrn. Co. Los Angeles 1981-83; senior proj. mgr. Swinerton & Walberg Co. L.A. 1983 — ; cons. CPM/ Scheduling to Women in Constrn. 1972-75; mem. Am. Concrete Inst. 1977; mil: 1st lt. NY Air Nat. Guard 1962-68; Republican; Protestant; rec: tennis, golf, boating, travel, reading. Res: 2215 Fortuna Newport Beach 92660 Ofc: Swinerton & Walberg 680 Wilshire Pl Los Angeles 90005

BALLUFF, JOHN EDWARD, lawyer; b. Dec. 23, 1938, Chgo.; s. John J. and Minette L. (LeClerg) B.; m. Julibeth, Mar. 21, 1964; children: Kevin b. 1971, Suzanne b. 1976; edn: AB, UC Berkeley 1960; LLB, UC Berkeley Boalt Hall 1963; admitted Calif. State Bar 1963. Career: atty. Sullivan, Roche & Johnson Santa Barbara 1964-68; chief counsel Calif. Senate Judiciary Com. Sacramento 1969-70; senior atty. Calif. Judicial Council Sacto. 1971-73; pvt. practice Landels, Ripley & Diamond Sacto. 1973-77; v.p. and counsel state govt. relations Wells Fargo & Co. 1977 — ; advisory bd. McGeorge Law Sch. Law Review 1969-73; mem: Calif. State Bar (admin. of justice com. 1976-78), Am. Bar Assn., Sacto. Co. Bar Assn., Boalt Hall Alumni Assn., Univ. Calif. Alumni Assn., St. Francis Yacht Club, Sacto. Symphony Assn., Crocker Art Museum Assoc., Koloa Broiler Yacht Club, Elks; Republican; Episcopal; rec: sailing, skiing. Res: 3600 W Lincoln Ave Sacramento 95818

BALSAMO, ROBERT JOSEPH, realtor, investor; b. June 5, 1938, Oyster Bay, NY; s. Robert J., Sr. and Ann E. (Juliano) B.; 1 dau. Catherine Anne; edn: BS, CSU Long Beach 1962, MBA, 1968. Career: engr., planner No. Am. Aviation Downey 1962-65; pgm. control adminstr. TRW Sys. Group Redondo Beach 1965-68; pgm. adminstr. Xerox Electro Optical Sys. Pasadena 1968-70; ops. analyst Aerojet Electro Systems Co. Azusa 1970-72; master pgm. planner Northrop Corp. Hawthorne 1972-73; broker Real Estate Shoppe La Palma 1973-78; pres. Real Estate Execs. La Palma 1978-84; broker Century 21 Castle La Palma 1984 — ; honors: Realtor of the Year (Buena Park- Cypress- La Palma Bd. Realtors 1982); mem: Buena Park- Cypress- La Palma Bd. Realtors (pres. 1985, v.p. 1984, dir. 1983, 86), Calif. Assn. Realtors (state dir. 1985-86); mil: US Army 1956-59; Republican. Res: POB 435 Cypress 90630 Ofc: Century 21- Castle 5410 La Palma Ave La Palma 90623

BALTZ, ROBERT FRANCIS, air force officer; b. Dec. 13, 1946, New Rochelle, N.Y.; s. Joseph Martin and Mary Elizabeth (O'Brien) B.; m. Charlotte Escobosa, July 27, 1985; edn: BS bus. adm., Villanova Univ. 1969; MA adm., Univ. of Central Mich. 1983. Career: served to major US Air Force 1970 — : chief adminstrv. security 1839th Electronics Installation Gp, Keesler AFB Miss. 1970-72; deputy missile combat crew comdr. 571st Strategic Missile Sq., Davis-Monthan AFB Ariz. 1972-75; missile combat crew comdr. 571 SMS 1975-77; ops. ofcr. Detach. 3 14th Missile Warning Sq., Mill Valley AFS Calif. 1977-80; chief Standardization and Evaluation Div. 12th Missile Warning Gp, Thule AB Greenland 1980-81; ops. ofcr. Detach. 3, 1st Space Wing, Maui, Hawaii 1981-84; chief op. location AW Air Force Opnl. Test and Eval. Ctr., Sunnyvale AFS Calif. 1984 — ; awards incl: 15th AF Excellence (1976), Combined Fed. Campaign Achievement (1979), Outstanding Achieve. (1974) and Best Titan Wing (1974), SAC Missile Combat Competition; decorated Good Combat Medal (1972), Combat Readiness (1977, 81), AF Commendn. (1980,

81, 84); Republican; Roman Catholic; rec: Am. Contract Bridge League (Qualified dir.). Ofc: AFOTEC/OL-AW POB 3430 Sunnyvale 94088

BANCROFT, RICHARD ANDERSON, superior court judge; b. Aug. 30, 1918, Albany, NY; s. Wm. E. and Anna B. (Anderson) B.; m. Barbara, July 28, 1967; children: Richard, Jr. b. 1942, William b. 1943, David b. 1957; edn: BA, Howard Univ. 1942, JD 1951; LLM, UC Berkeley Boalt Sch. of Law 1952. Career: law practice in San Francisco Bay area, 1952-76; apptd. Superior Court Judge 1976 — ; mem. Commn. on Judicial Performance; faculty Center for Judicial Edn. & Research; trustee Alameda County Law Library; mem. Calif. Judges Assn.; publs: artices in 1952 Calif. Law Review, chap. in 1963 Workmen's Compensation book, sev. pub. opinions of Calif. Dist. Ct. of Appeal 1983; mil: sgt. USMC WWII; rec: reading, fishing. Res: Berkeley Ofc: Alameda Superior Court, 2115 Oak Dept. 21, Oakland 94612

BANGASSER, RONALD P., physician; b. Jan. 25, 1950, Freeport, Ill.; s. Paul Francis and Florence (Ihm) B.; m. Susan, June 19, 1971; children: Debra b. 1978, Sandra b. 1981; edn: BA, Northwestern Univ. 1971; MD, Chgo Medical, 1975. Career: hyperbaric oxygen research St. Lukes Presbyn. Hosp. Milwaukee, 1975; navy diving medical officers tng. (through Undersea Med. Soc.), Wash DC 1977; family practice residency, UC Los Angeles 1978; pvt. practice phys. Valley Family Medical Group, Yucaipa 1977 — ; pres. Scuba Dive Shop, Inc. 1978 — ; bd. dirs. San Bernardino County Med. Center, 1977-78, 1980-; bd. dirs. Found. for Med. Care (chmn. Hosp. Util. Rev. Com.) 1984-85; med. staff Redlands Community Hosp. (chmn. Family Practice Dept. 1983-84, chmn. Quality Assur. Com. 1985, exec. com. 1981-85); team physician San Bernardino Valley Coll. 1977-85, diving med. safety ofcr. CSU Long Beach 1982-85, instr. nurse practitioner UC San Diego 1980-82, Family Practice staff instr. UC Los Angeles 1979; awards: Tiny Campora Award (1984), Sir Turtle Award, Cayman, tourism (1984); mem: AMA, CMA, CALPAC; NAUI (Nat. Assn. Underwater Instrs.) Diving Instr. 1975-, Regional Mgr. 1977-, Crossover Dir. 1977-78, spkr. Internat. Conf. on Underwater Edn. (1978, 79, 82, 83, 85), conf. dir. So. Calif. Conf. on Underwater Edn. 1980-81, conf. dir. NAUI Dives Cayman 1984; ; instr. in underwater photog.; Catholic; rec: scuba diving. Res: 12724 Valley View Redlands 92373 Ofc: Valley Family Medical Group 11985 Fourth St Ste 100 Yucaipa 92399

BANSAL, RAHUL, manufacturing co. executive; b. Mar. 12, 1957, Jabalpur, India; d. Ramesh Chandra and Mohini (Thawani) Jain; m. Sangita Bansal, May 4, 1985; 1 child, Yash b. 1977; edn: B. Commerce, Univ. of Delhi 1976; MBA mktg., H.P. Univ. 1978; MBA fin., UC Riverside 1981. Career: controller Air Transport Mfg., Glendale 1982 — ; ptnr. Indo-American Consultants, L.A. 1984 — ; cons. Inter-America Productions, L.A. 1982-; honors: Merit Scholar UC Riverside (1980); mem. Am. Mgmt. Assn.; mem. Plaza de La Raza (L.A.), Iskcon (internat. soc. for Krishna consciousness); rec: reading, travel. Res: 400 E California Blvd Apt 9 Pasadena 91106 Ofc: Air Transport Mfg. Co. 1100 Grand Central Ave Glendale 91201

BARATTA, MARIO ANTHONY, civil engineer; b. Oct. 17, 1942, San Salvador, El Salvador; nat. US cit. 1961; s. Mario Augusto and Maria (Rivera) B.; m. Barbara Smith, June 13, 1964; children: Anthony Paul b. 1966, Lisa Marie b. 1969; edn: BCE, Santa Clara Univ. 1964, MBA 1983; MSCE (structures) Stanford Univ. 1971; cert. Nat. Security Mgmt., Indsl. Coll. Armed Forces 1975; Reg. Civil Engr. Calif., Hawaii, Canal Zone. Career: mil. civil engr./ cdr. US Navy 1961-84: officer in chg. of constrn., Yokosuka, Japan 1964-67, Canal Zone 1967-69; pub. works ops. ofcr., Vietnam 1969-70; asst. dir. pub. works dept. Marine Corps Air Station, El Toro, Calif. 1971-73; nuclear weapons effects ofcr. Offutt AFB, Nebr. 1973-76; ofcr. in chg. of constrn. Naval Shipyard, Pearl Harbor, Hawaii 1976-78; asst. acquisition ofcr. Pacific Div. Naval Facilities Engring. Cmd. 1978-80; pub. works/ ofcr. in chg. constrn. Moffett Field Naval Air Sta. 1980-83; dir. Facilities Systems Office, Port Hueneme 1983-84, ret.; dir. constrn. services County of Santa Clara, 1984 — ; recipient num. appreciation awards for coaching soccer teams; mem: Tau Beta Pi, ASCE, SAME, NSPE, APWA, AIA, CSPE, Toastmasters Internat. (pres. Pearl Harbor Club 1978), Engineer's Club San Jose, past pres. soccer clubs in Hawaii (1976-80) and Nebr. (1975-76); mil. awards: Energy Conservation Award, Pearl Harbor Naval Shipyard (1978), Commendn., Cmdr. Naval Forces Southern Cmd. (1969), decorated Bronze Star w/Combat V, Jt. Service, Nat. Def. Service, Vietnam Service w/4 Stars, Rep. Vietnam Meritorious Unit Cit. and Gallentry Cross w/Palm; publs: article in Military Engineer (1974); rec: jogging, bowling, computers. Res: 1617 Garvey Pl San Jose 95132 Ofc: County of Santa Clara 911 Bern Ct Ste 100 San Jose 95112

BARAZONE, MOUNQUE, manufacturing & distributing co. executive, inventor; b. Dec. 9, 1948, Cleveland, Ohio; s. Abraham and Helen (Leverstein) B.; edn: Cleveland State Univ. 1967-68. Career: mgr. Chagrin Valley "66", Moreland Hills, Ohio 1969-73; v.p. Data Information Services Corp., Chgo. 1973-78; adminstrv. asst. to the pres., W.J. Lazynski Inc. Contractors, Milwaukee 1978-80; founder/ pres./ bd. chmn. Earth Fabrics, Inc. (Geosynthetics and mfr. of equip.) and Geotextile Apparatus Co. Div. (exclusive distbr. in Calif., Nev. and Hawaii for Crown Zellerbach, Exxon Chemicals, non-exclusive distbr. for Amoco Fabrics, Hoescht Fibers, and Burcan Mfg. Inc.), co. is now the biggest independent distbr. of geosynthetics in the western USA; past dir. Data Information Service Corp., dir. Lake Calif. POA; lectr. Stanford Univ. (1985), ASCE/Fresno State chpt. (1985), U.S. Forest Service (1984, 85, 86); awards: Crown Zellerbach Leading Sales Distbr. (1982, 83, 84, 85), Exxon Chemicals Americas Marketing Excellence (1985); Nat. Fedn. of the Blind Pres.'s Club (1985-86); mem. Assoc. Gen. Contractors of Am. (Disaster

Assistance Com.), Indsl. Fabrics Assn. Internat., Soc. of Am. Mil. Engrs.; mem. Nat. Fedn. of the Blind./Pres.'s Club, Internat. Kempo Karate Assn.; works: devel. and patented machinery used to install paving fabrics on hwys., U.S. patent #4555073 (11/26/85), w/ 4 related patents pending (US and fgn.); other patents pending for material handling equipment: a fabric roll puller, braking mechanism for rotatable core support for a fabric roll, multi-shafted adjustable roll mover; Copyrights for a Construction Bid Mgmt. computer system; Jewish, Rel. Sci.; rec: wind surf, snorkel, Karate, flower gardening. Res: 22141 Buckeye Pl Lake California 96022 Ofc: Earth Fabrics Inc PO Box 5217 Cottonwood 96022

BARBA MARTIN HARPER, VERA ELIZABETH, real estate broker; b. Dec. 21, 1923, King City, Calif.; d. Peter and Anita Louise (Cevallos) Barba; m. Leland Harper, Nov. 6, 1982; children: George Winje b. 1941, Louise Miller b. 1944; edn: stu. fashion design, Nat. Corresp. Sch. 1939-40, art stu. w/ Roy Keister 2 yrs., real estate courses UC Ext.; Calif. lic. real estate broker. Career: seamstress (design, alterations) Ford Cleaners, 1940-46, self-empl. 1946-54; real estate assoc. John Realty, El Cerrito 1954-56, owner/broker Winje Realty 1956-64, owner/broker Martin Realty, San Jose 1964-86; prop. second hand store, Campbell 1978-, incorporated 1986, pres. Tickled Pink Inc. (antiques and collectables, 2 retail stores), Campbell 1986–; honors: 1st prize costume design Ludina Edgecum Sch. of Dance, Napa; mem. West Contra Costa Bd. Realtors (1956-64, Top Lister award), San Jose Bd. Realtors (1964-86), UC Alumni Assn., El Cerrito CofC (1960-64); works: portrait artist and landscapes; Democrat; rec: art, raising birds, sewing. Address: San Jose 95128

BARBERS, RICHARD GEORGE, physician, educator; b. Jan. 12, 1949, Philippines, nat. US cit. 1975; s. Jesus Victor and Mary (Fernandez) B.; edn: BS, Loyola Coll. 1971, MD, Georgetown Univ. 1975; Board certified in Internal Medicine, Pulmonary Disease, Allegy & Immunology. Career: intern internal medicine, USC-Los Angeles County Medical Ctr., 1975-76; resident, int. medicine, UCLA-Cedars Sinai Medical Ctr. 1976-78, postdoc. fellowship UCLA Medical Ctr. in clinical immunology & allergy, 1979-81, in pulmonary disease, 1981-82; assoc. med. dir. of SCU, Valley Medical Ctr., 1978-79; asst. prof. of medicine UCLA Sch. of Medicine, 1982–, assoc. dir. UCLA Asthma and Immunologic Lung Disease Ctr.; honors: Tri Beta nat. honor soc.; mem: Am. Coll. of Physicians, Am. Thoracic Soc., Am. Acad. of Allergy & Immunol., Am. Coll. of Chest Physicians, Am. Fedn. of Clin. Research; contbr. num. research papers and articles in med. journals; Ind. Democrat; Roman Catholic; rec: sailing, bridge, marathon runner. Ofc: UCLA School of Medicine CHS Rm 37-131 Los Angeles 90024

BARCA, GEORGE GINO, financial and wine executive; b. Jan. 28, 1937, Roseville, Calif.; s. Joseph and Annie (Muschetto) B.; m. Maria Solafani, Nov. 19, 1960; children: Anna Maria b. 1961, Joseph b. 1963, Gina b. 1967, Nina b. 1967; edn: AA, Grant Tec. Jr. Coll. 1957; LLB, Lasalle Univ. 1961. Career: pres., gen. mgr. Barca Wine Cellars of Calif. (and parent corp., Barcamerica Corp.); previously with United Vintners Inc. (Italian Swiss Colony, Inglenook, Lejon-Petri) prior to sale of co. 1969; dir. Calif. Vintners Inc., Calif. Wine Cellars Inc., Am. Vintners Inc., Am. Wine Cellars Inc., Calif. Grape Growers; mem: Calif. Farm Bureau, Metropolitan CofC, Nat. Fedn. Independent Bus., Better Bus. Bureau, Dun & Bradstreet; Catholic; rec: travel. Res: 5750 B.P.F.E. Rd Roseville 95678

BARDELLA, CLAIRE MITCHELL PETERSEN, scholarship administrator; b. Sept. 22, 1914, Oakland; d. Roland C. Stuart-Mitchell and Ethel Petry Mitchell St. John; stepfather Pierce Louis St. John, concert violinist; m. Chris R. Petersen II (law prof., v.p. Lincoln Univ., San Francisco), Oct. 17, 1937, dec. 1961; m. Darrell Bardella (pilot), Dec. 15, 1962; edn: BA, magna cum laude, Stanford Univ. 1935. Career: child prodigy singer (one of Stanford Univ. Prof. Terman's gifted children), San Jose Normal Sch., performer in sev. operettas at San Jose State Univ.; pres. Calif. Scholarship Fedn., Palo Alto H.Sch., editor Literary Mag., awarded Yearbk. scholarship to Stanford Univ., 1931; profl. singer various churches, Palo Alto, NBC radio with Hans Leshke, 1932-34; soloist S.F. Municipal Chorus, 1933; poetry/music pub. by Stanford Press, 1934; lead singing role in Stanford Gaities, 4 yrs.; secty. to v.p. Bank of Am. subs. California Banks, Inc., 1936; cons. to American delegation of UN Peace Conf. under Dean Virginia Gildersleeve, 1945; honors: Phi Beta Kappa (1934); pres. Delta Delta Delta Sor. 1934; pres. German Hon. Soc. 1933-4; Deans List 1934; mem: Internat. Platform Assn., Stanford Womens Club, S.F. (dir. 6 yrs.); AAUW (pres. SF branch 1943-45, honored by Gr. Brit. for contbn. to Brit. War Relief; orgnzr. Hospitality Pgm. for Service Women in S.F.; orgnzr. luncheon honoring 60 famous internat. women 1945; Past Presidents Council); pres. Phi Beta Nat. Profl. Orgn. of Music Dance and Drama; Scholarship chmn. Phi Beta Kappa, S.F.; judge, Bank of Am. Coll. Awards, 1981. Publs: travel arts. in Stanford Mag., Tri Delta Mo., 1975-82, contbr. Famous Alumni Cookbook (Stanford Press). Soloist, artist mem. Woodside Sym. Guild. Rec: tennis, entertaining, travel. Res: 1895 Pacific Ave. San Francisco 94109

BARDEN, MARY MARGARET, architect, ret.; b. Sept. 28, 1900, Aspen, Colo.; d. Dennis and Mary Frances (Woods) Sullivan; m. John Barden, July 14, 1926; children: John Jerome b. 1931, Joan Marie b. 1936, James Dennis b. 1942; edn: Sacramento Jr. Coll. 1919-20; reg. architect, Calif. 1952. Career: co-owner Barden Constrn. Co. 1934-80; cons./ designer on several redeveloped historical bldgs. in Old Sacramento; works: Holy Family Ch. and Sch., Citrus Heights (exterior mosaic of Holy Family); Cenacle Retreat, Sacramento; Cormelite Monasteries, Sacramento and Georgetown; Catholic Herald Bldg.; over 6,000 Sacramento homes, specializing in French Normandy, Tudor, Calif. Ranch Style; others; works featured in Better Homes & Gardens and other publs.; Republican; Catholic; rec: music, art. Res: 1151 Bell St Apt A Sacramento 95825

BARHAM, RODNEY J., controller; b. June 5, 1957, Arlington, Va.; s. Hugh Flannery and Julia Mae (Swain) B.; m. Jeanette Dickerson, Aug. 10, 1979; children: Sean b. 1982, Eileen b. 1984; edn: AA applied sci./ bus. adminstrn., Columbus Coll. 1979, BBA, 1979; MBA, Nat. Univ. 1983. Career: asst. controller HDS Concessions Inc. Solana Beach 1979-80; financial analyst Foodmaker Inc. San Diego 1980-82, info. center cons. 1982-83; dir. financial ops. HDS Concessions 1983-85; controller Compucable Corp. San Marcos 1985–; bd. dirs. HDS Concessions; mem: Nat. Guard Assn. of US 1979-, Nat. Guard Assn. of Calif. 1979-; Nat. Eagle Scouts of Am. Assn., Delta Chi Frat. 1979-; mil: capt. US Army, Calif. Nat. Guard; Republican; Catholic. Ofc: Compucable Corp. 180 Vallecitos de Oro San Marcos 92069

BARKER, CHARLES MORSE, III, real estate developer; b. June 1, 1956, Oakland; s. Charles, Jr. and Leona Ann (Elsken) M.; m. Theresa Christine Kent, Apr. 27, 1980; children: Diana b. 1984, Alexandra b. 1986; edn: stu. UCB 1974-75, Merritt Coll. 1976-77, 80-85, CSU San Diego 1978; Calif. lic. real estate broker. Career: broker assoc. C.A. Clark Realtors, Castro Valley 1979-81; gen. ptnr. Merritt Equities Group (investment co.), Oakland 1981-, in chg. real estate devel. and acquisitions, 1982–; mem. Oakland Board of Realtors; works: rehabilitation of 98-unit Turn of the Century bldg., Madison Park Apts., placed on Nat. Register of Historic Places; Republican; Catholic; rec: sailing, military miniature collection, tennis. Res: 990 Grosvenor Pl Oakland 94610 Ofc: Merritt Equities Group 1547 Sixth Ave Oakland 94606

BARKER, KAREN JEAN TILLISON, real estate broker; b. July 8, 1938, Boggstown, Ind.; d. James Russell and Gladys Mae (Lancaster) Tillison; 1 dau: Toni, b. 1961; edn: Fresno City Coll. 1968-85; BA, Western States Univ., MBA, 1985; R.E. courses, Anthony Schs., Fresno 1974, 77; Calif. R.E. sales lic., 1974, R.E. broker lic., 1977; GRI, Calif. Assn. Realtors 1982; Internat. Certified Appraiser 1984; Manufactured Home Appraiser 1985; lic. EMT, Emergency Med. Techn., Co. of Fresno 1976; Notary Public, Calif. 1981. Career: oper. Indiana Bell Tel. 1954-56; clerk, clerk-typist 1956-60; tchr. Patricia Stevens Modeling Sch. 1957-60; water acctg. City of Fresno 1960-61; sr. acct. clerk Fed. Mktg. Order, Grape Crush Admin., Fresno 1963; clk., Calif. Hwy. Patrol, Fresno 1963-67; radio dispatcher/ law enforcement Calif. Dept. of Fish & Game, Fresno 1967-71; real estate agent Chalet Realty, SKA, Realtors, Lodge Pole Realty, Shaver Lake 1974-79; broker/ owner Karen Barker, Realtors, Shaver Lake 1979–; co-founder East Ponderosa Ranches, a land devel. co. 1981; active in land devel., timber ops., road constrn., subdiv.; real estate sales, r.e. appraising; mem: Nat. Assn. of Realtors; Calif. Assn. Realtors; Fresno Bd. Realtors; senior mem. Internat. Orgn. of Real Estate Appraisers; Democrat; Presbyterian; rec: photog., High Sierra Wilderness Area pack trips, x-c skiing. Res: 41617 Tollhouse Rd Shaver Lake 93664 Ofc: Karen Barker, Realtors, Hwy 168/ Dinkey Creek Rd POB 313 Shaver Lake 93664

BARKER, ROBERT J., financial executive; b. Feb. 22, 1946, Glendale, Calif.; s. Albert and Margaret E. (Windle) B.; edn: BSEE, UC Los Angeles 1968, MBA, 1970; Cert. in Mgmt. Acctg. 1983. Career: bus. instr. Foothill Coll. 1975; cost analyst Lockheed 1976-78; cost acctg. supv. Monolithic Memories Inc. 1978-80, cost acctg./ budget mgr. 1980-84, financial sys. mgr. 1984; currently dir. finance WaferScale Integration Inc.; dir: MMI Fed. Credit Union 1977-84, Veterans Task Force 1980-; mem: Nat. Assn. Accts., Toastmasters (pres. 1986, ednl. v.p. 1985), MMI Scholarship Com. 1981-84; mil: capt. USAF 1970-74; Republican; Methodist; rec: jogging, sports. Res: 911 Yorkshire Dr Los Altos 94022 Ofc: Waferscale Integration Inc. 47280 Kato Rd Fremont 94538

BARKLEY, MICHAEL TAYLOR, certified public accountant, auditor; b. Oct. 29, 1955, Great Falls, Mont.; s. Victor Braswell and Iris (Wyss) B.; m. Karen, Aug. 15, 1981; 1 dau. Amanda b. 1985; edn: BS, Brigham Young Univ. 1982; CPA lic. Calif. 1985. Career: asst. mgr. Skaggs Drug Store, Auburn, Wash. 1976-77; Mormon missionary to Fukuoka, Japan 1977-79; senior audit staff acct. Price Waterhouse, Los Angeles 1982–; mem: Am. Inst. CPAs, Calif. Soc. CPAs, Am. Acctg. Assn.; Republican; Ch. of Jesus Christ of L.D.S.; rec: racquetball, bicycling, backpacking. Address: Los Angeles

BARLETTA, JOSEPH F., newspaper executive, lawyer; b. Oct. 1, 1936, Punxsutawney, Pa.; s. Michael A. and Vandolyn R. (Raffetto) Barletta; m. Marilyn Minetti, Feb. 23, 1969; edn: AB, Marietta Coll. 1959, JD, Duquesne Univ. 1963. Career: partner Barletta & Barletta, Ellwood, Pa. 1963-66; labor rels. mgr. The Wall Street Journal, Princeton, N.J. 1966-70; v.p. dir. employee rels./ v.p. dir. ops. Chicago Tribune, 1970-76; v.p. dir. employee rels./ v.p. dir. adminstrn./exec.v.p./gen. mgr. New York Daily News, 1976-81; partner Seyfarth, Shaw, Fairweather and Geraldson, NYC 1981; pres. San Francisco Newspaper Agcy., 1982–; commr. Public Utilities City & County of San Francisco; Dir. Lebhar-Friedman, Inc.; bd. advisors Jour. of Inst. of Socioeconomic Studies; trustee Marietta Coll.; trustee Univ. of San Francisco; bd. govs. S.F. Sym.; bd. dirs. S.F. Conv. and Visitors Bur.; bd. dir. Midsummer Mozart Festival; mem. Community Bd. St. Mary's Hosp.; mem. Mayor's Fiscal Advisory Com.; mem: Am. Bar Assn., Am. Newspaper Publishers Assn. (chmn. Human Resources Com.), Lotos Club, Friars Club (NY), Bankers Club (SF), The Family (SF), University Club (SF), Knights of Malta; mil: served in Ohio Nat. Guard. Res: 2222 Hyde St. San Francisco 94109 Ofc: San Francisco Newspaper Agency, 925 Mission St., San Francisco 94103

BARNA, LILLIAN CARATTINI, superintendent of schools; b. Jan. 18, 1929, NYC; d. Juan and Dolores Elsie Nieves (Alicea) Carattini; m. Eugene Andrew Barna, July 1, 1951; children: Craig Andrew, Keith Andrew; edn: AB, Hunter Coll. 1950; MA, San Jose State Univ. 1970. Career: tchr. NYC Sch. Dist. 1950-52, Whittier Sch. Dist. 1952-54; tchr. high sch. 1954-56; tchr. presch. Long Beach and Los Gatos 1958-67; supvr. early childhood edn. San Jose Unif. Sch. Dist. 1967-72, sch. adminstr. 1972-80, supt. sch. 1980—; cons. in field; honors: Western Reg. Puertorican Council Achiev. award 1980; Assn. Puertorican Profls. Achiev. award 1981; Outstanding Achiev. in Edn., CSU 1982; Woman of Achiev., Santa Clara Co. Commn. on Status of Women; Distng. Alumni, San Jose Mercury News, San Jose State Univ.; mem: Nat. Assn. Edn. Young Children; Tchrs. English to Spkrs. of Other Langs.; Women Leaders in Edn.; Calif. Reading Assn.; Calif. Assn. Women Adminstrs.; Assn. Calif. Sch. Adminstrs.; Phi Kappa Phi; Delta Zeta. Ofc: 1605 Park Ave., San Jose 95126

BARNARD, DAVID KEITH, SR., farmer, rancher; b. Nov. 20, 1919, Ovalo, Tex.; s. John Harvey and Letha Eudora (Strickland) B.; m. Mary, Jan. 10, 1948; children: David Jr. b. 1950, Danny b. 1953, Donald b. 1954. Career: farmer, owner 4500 acres w/ 3 sons Bakersfield, 500 head cattle; pres. So. Valley Gin 1976-86, dir. Wheeler Ridge, Maricopa Water Storage Dist. 1981-86; mem. Better Bus. Bureau; mil: staff sgt. US Army 1942-45, Bronze Star; Democrat; Baptist; rec: fishing, horseback riding, hunting, safari. Address: Rt 3 Box 1061 Bakersfield 93309

BARNARD, DOUGLAS T., interior designer; b. May 27, 1943, Hawthorne; s. Ralph Russel and Gladys Lydia (Bouch) B.; m. Mary Walshe, May 21, 1977; edn: BA cum laude, Woodbury Univ. 1969. Career: senior designer, estimator Barnard Bros. Painting and Decorating, San Fernando 1962-67; design asst. with John Patton, ASID, Los Angeles 1967; senior designer Carole Mitchell Interiors, L.A. 1968; senior designer Arthur Elrod Assocs. Int. Design and Raiser/ Elrod Int. Design (respons. for design projects nat.) 1969-75; v.p./ design dir. Douglas Barnard, Inc. (DBI) (internat. residential and comml. design), 1975—, completed projects in 10 states and 9 countries incl. residences, offices, aircraft, ocean - going yachts, medical facilities and hotels; DBI design projects featured in 3 books and 12 + mag. articles; guest lectr. Woodbury Univ. 1981, 82; panelist Am. Inst. of Int. Design Nat. Conf. (1968); mem: Brooks Coll. Curriculum Advis. Council, Am. Soc. of Int. Design (past bd. dirs. LA Chpt.), Am. Inst. of Int. Design, Nat. Soc. of Int. Designers (past pres. LA Student Chpt.), Santa Monica Area CofC, Main Street Assn., Santa Monica Heritage Museum Soc.; mil: sgt. E5 US Army 1961; Democrat; Prot.; rec: skiing, bodybuilding, tennis. Ofc: Douglas Barnard Inc 2219 Main St Santa Monica 90405

BARNARD, JO ELLEN, surgeon; b. Dec. 24, 1941, Los Angeles; d. Marion Cecil and Cleo Pauline (Fenderson) B.; m. Lewis Richard Walton, Dec. 19, 1971; 1 son: Lewis Richard, Jr. b. 1981; edn: BA, La Sierra Coll. 1962; MD, Loma Linda Univ. 1966; bd. cert. Am. Bd. of Surgery. Career: surgical res. Loma Linda Univ. White Meml. Hosp. 1972; intern Riverside Gen. Hosp. 1967. Career: surgeon Niles Surgical and Medical Group, Bakersfield 1973—; staff San Joaquin Community Hosp. (exec. com. 1985-); honors: Personalities of the West & Mid West, Outstanding Young Women of Am.; mem: AMA, Calif. Med. Assn., Kern Co. Med. Assn., Loma Linda Univ. Womens Auxiliary (pres. 1974-75), Bakersfield Adventist Acad. School Board (chair 1985-86); author: How To Live Six Extra Years (Woodbridge, 1981); Seventh Day Adventist; rec: Arabian horses, music, swimming, health lectures. Res: 2701 Rio Vista Bakersfield 93306 Ofc: Niles Surgical and Medical Group 2121 Nile St Bakersfield 93305

BARNARD, RUSSELL PAUL, design and development co. executive; b. Mar. 13, 1946, Hawthorne; s. Ralph Russel and Gladys Lydia (Bouch) B.; edn: BA, CSU Northridge 1969, MA, Stanford Univ. 1973. Career: City desk reporter Sacramento Bee 1967, ed. Northridge-Reseda Post 1968, wine writer Pittsburgh Post-Gazette 1968-69; owner R and R Offset Prodns., San Fernando and Bakersfield, 1969-72; instr. Dept. Communs., Stanford Univ. 1972-73, asst. prof. journ., CSU Northridge 1973-75; cons. to internat. corp./ dir. feasibility study (on viability of an English lang. daily newspaper in Middle East), Kuwait 1976; pres./dir. ops. Douglas Barnard, Inc. (DBI) interior design firm doing bus. internat., 1975—; pres. Barnard Mgmt. Services (BMS), personal mgmt. entertainment industry clients, 1978—; gen. ptnr., mng. ptnr. var. real estate devels., 1979—; honors: Nat. Newspaper Fund Award for work on Sacto. Bee (1967), Publicity Club of L.A. scholarship (1967), Sigma Delta Chi (nat., chpt. awards), CSU Northridge hon. life mem. Assoc. Student Body (1968), Outstanding grad., Journalism (1968), Chilton R. Bush- Copley News Fund Award (1972); profl. awards: DBI included in Interior Design Mag. survey of "100 Interior Design Giants" (1980), design projects featured in 3 books and 12 + mag. arts.; civic: NCCJ/ Santa Monica Chpt. (bd.), Santa Monica Conv. and Vis. Bureau (bd.), S.M. Heritage Sq. Museum Soc. (charter mem.), S.M. Bldg. & Safety Commn., S.M. CofC (bd.), S.M. City Council Task Force on Comml. & Indsl. Devel., Main St. Assn. (chmn.), Ocean Park Comm. Orgn., S.M. City Coll. (advis. com.); Indep.; Prot.; rec: reading/writing fiction. Ofc: DBI 2219 Main St Santa Monica 90405

BARNES, GAIL B., dental technician lab owner; b. June 20, 1950, Modesto; d. Stewart Wells and Betty Jean (Bumgardner) Bradley; m. Randy Barnes, March 24, 1973; 1 dau, Melissa b. 1978; edn: AA, Modesto Jr. Coll. 1971; CSU Stanislaus 1971-73. Career: Custom Craft Dental Lab 1973-79; founder, owner, opr. Denture's Plus 1979—; First Woman mem., 2nd lt., Alameda Co. Sheriff's Mounted Posse 1979—; rec: equestrian. Address: 321 Scott St. Livermore 94550

BARNES, JAMES FRANKLIN, import company president, ret.; b. Dec. 1, 1923, Witchata Falls, Tex.; s. Thomas Edwin and Opal Oma (Bass) B.; m. Kathleen Elene Bagwell, Nov. 30, 1959; edn: Colorado Coll., Inst. of Contemporary Arts. Career: profl. musician 1942-50; monastic member of Ramakrishna Order, 1952-59; gen. mgr. radio station KBMS, 1960-62; pres. K. & J. Imports, Inc., 1963-85; awards: Roy Harris Scholar in musical composition, Colo. Coll. (1948-50); works: num. choral musical compositions; Vedanta (Hindu); rec: music, photog. Res: 3165-A Alta Vista Laguna Hills 92653

BARNES, ROGER LEE, heating plant engineer, ret.; b. Dec. 17, 1932, Rocky Ridge, Ohio; s. Frank Addison and Elma Sofie (Scheaffer) B.; m. Nancy Margaret Siddons; children: Perry Jay, Kathy Ann, Sabina Marie, Glen Addison; edn: eng., CSU Long Beach 1955; Lic. Heating Plant Engr., City of Los Angeles 1956. Career: justice of the peace Mayfield Tap, Penington Co., Minn. 1965; Mayor City of Blaine, Minn. 1970; currently, pres. Orange Co. Assn. for Retarded Citizens; REA Bd., Minn. 1965-67; honors: Mayor Bradley, Los Angeles 1983; Lt. Gov.'s Award, OCARC 1983; mem: Blind Veterans of Am., VFW, Am. Legion, OCARC, Lions Club; mil: s/sgt. USAF 1950 53, Korean Svc., GCM, Commendation; Lutheran; rec: painting. Res: 16702 Dale Vista Ln. Huntington Beach 92647 Ofc: 2010 W. Chestnut St. Santa Ana 92703

BARNES, WILLIE R., lawyer; b. Dec. 9, 1931, Dallas, Tex.; s. Jasper M. and Mary L.(Roberts) B.; m. Barbara B. Plummer, Aug. 17, 1985; children: Michael, b. 1954, Sandra, b. 1957; edn: BA, UCLA 1953, JD, UCLA Law Sch 1959; Splst. in Real Estate Securities (SRS). Career: with Dept. of Corporations, Los Angeles 1960-79 (various atty. positions 1960-68, suprv. Corporations Counsel 1968-70, asst. commnr. 1970-75, commnr. 1975-79); partner firm of Manatt, Phelps, Rothenberg & Tunney, Century City 1979—. Pres., Midwest Securities Commnrs. Assn. 1978-79; lst v.p. North Am. Securities Adminstrs. Assn. 1978-79; v.p., dir. UCLA Law Alumni Assn. 1973. Awards: UCLA Law Sch. Alumnus of the Year 1976, President's awd., Black Businessmen Assn of L.A. 1977, 78. Mem: State Bar of Calif. (Bus. Law Sect. Exec. Com., Com. on Corps., Com. on Corp. Governance & Takeovers), L.A. County Bar Assn. (Exec. Com., Bus. & Corp. Sect.), Beverly Hills Bar Assn. (Exec. Com., exec. com. Corps &: Comml. Sect.), Century City Bar Assn. (bd. govs.), Am. Bar Assn. (Corp., Banking & Bus. Law, Fed. Regulation of Securities, Franchise, Commodities & State Reg. Securities), Inst. Certified Financial Planners (chmn. Leveraged Real Estate Task Force 1985-86); chmn. Knox Keene Health Care Svc. Plan Com. 1976-79; gen. counsel/dir. UCLA Alumni Assn.; co-mng. ed. California Bus. Law Reporter; mil: pfc US Army 1954-56; rec: sports, photog. Ofc: Manatt, Phelps, et al 11355 W. Olympic Blvd. Los Angeles 90064

BARNETT, I. DAVID, chiropractor; b. June 14, 1956, Hamilton, Ontario, Can.; s. Percy and Toby (Organ) B.; edn: sr. honors matriculation, Hillfield-Strathallen Coll. 1974; BA, York Univ. Toronto 1978; DC, Texas Chiropractic Coll. 1982; lic. chiropractor, Calif., NY, Fla., Prov. Ontario. Career: postgrad. in chiro-cybernetics Roberds Chiropractic Clinic, Nashville, Tenn.; assoc., head of roentgenology, head of sports treatment pgm. Tahoe Chiropractic Clinic; dir. P. Barnett Constrn., Hamilton, Ont., Can.; honors: Merit, Texas Chiropractic Coll. 1981-82; mem: Diplomate Nat. Bd. of Chiropractic Examiners, Diplomate Canadian Chiropractic Examining Bd.; research: sports injuries treatment pgm. spec. snow skiing injuries; rec: snow skiing, cycling, photog. Ofc: Tahoe Chiropractic Clinic, 3121 Harrison Ave. So. Lake Tahoe 95702

BARNEY, RICHARD VIRT, financial advisor; b. Mar 16, 1944, Martinez; s. Gordon Virt and Doreen (Hipwell) B.; m. Holly, June 6, 1968; children: David b. 1969, Derek b. 1973, Sean b. 1978, Kristi b. 1979; edn: undergrad. Univ. Calif., 1962-63; BA, Brigham Young Univ. 1967, MS 1969; MBA, Pepperdine Univ. 1983; Cert. Finl. Plnnr. (CFP) Coll. for Finl. Plnng. 1981. Career: loan ofcr. Bank of Am., San Francisco 1971-72; Mason McDuffie Investment Corp., Walnut Creek 1973-74; v.p. Unison Assocs., Walnut Creek 1975-77; pres. Corvest Finl. Group, 1977-82; v.p. J.P. King Finl. Advisors, 1983; pres. Barney & Co., 1984—; honors: pres.'s cabinet Great Am. Life Ins. Co. (1977, 78), listed 1st ed. Who's Who in Finl. Plnng. (1985); mem: Internat. Assn. for Finl. Plnng. (East Bay chpt. dir. 1981-82), Inst. of CFP (1980-), BYU Mgmt. Soc.; civic: Boy Scouts Am. (commnr. 1980-), Walnut Creek Little League, Diablo Valley Fly Fishermen; research publ. (1983); Republican; Ch. of Jesus Christ of Latter-day Saints; rec: fly fishing, family. Res: 619 Nantucket Ct Walnut Creek 94598 Ofc: Barney & Co 2855 Mitchell Dr Ste 245 Walnut Creek 94598

BARNUM (DAMMEYER), PATRICIA KATHLEEN, public relations advertising agency owner; b. Feb. 20, 1947, Bakersfield, Calif.; d. Bernard F. and Barbara J. (Nabers) Brown; m. Theodore Dammeyer, May 1, 1982; children: Christopher Scott b. 1969, Piper Lynn b. 1972; edn: BA, Univ. Colo. 1970; Calif. Comm. Coll. Tchg. Credl. (provsl.). Career: asst. mktg. dir. Rancho Calif.; owner interior design co. Kathy Barnum & Assocs., mng. Design Ctr. for Sagewood Homes Newport Beach; organizer, promoter, roller skating instr. Outerskate Skating Sch. Mission Viejo; staff cons., writer Surfer Publs., wrote monthly Tips column for Roller Skating mag.; judge NBC SportsWorld; asst. to producers, v.p. Newport Presentations Ltd. multimedia indsl. shows, mtgs., convs.; mtg. planner, conv. producer Meeting Masters Newport Beach; currently owner Barnum, O'Donnell & Assocs. Laguna Niguel; listed: Who's Who Profl. & Exec. Women; mem: Soc. of Roller Skating Tchrs. of Am., Sch. Site Council- Capistrano Unif. Sch. Dist., Meeting Planners Internat., Capo. Bch. Homeowners Assn., Capo Bch. CofC (bd. dirs.), Orange County Woumen's

Found., Women in Communications; Republican; Catholic; rec: skiing, skating. Res: 34640 Camino Capistrano Capistrano Beach 92624 Ofc: Barnum, O'Donnell & Assocs. 27324 Camino Capistrano Ste 221 Laguna Niguel 92677

BARON, ALLEN A., finance executive, accountant; b. Feb. 21, 1941, Bklyn., s. Irving and Rose (Leviton) B.; children: Neil b. 1964, Marci b. 1967; edn: BS, CSU Los Angeles 1962; Certified Public Acct., Calif. 1966. Career: tax mgr. Price Waterhouse, Los Angeles 1962-69; tax mgr. Republic Corp., L.A. 1969-70; ptnr. Baron & Weiss An Acctncy. Corp., Beverly Hills 1970-80; finl. v.p. and dir. Martin Lawrence Limited Editions, Inc., Van Nuys 1980–; honors: Eagle Scout, Boy Scouts Am. 1956; mem: Calif. Soc. CPAs, Am. Inst. CPAs, So. Calif. Balloon Assn.; Republican; Jewish; rec: hot air balloonist. Ofc: Martin Lawrence Limited Editions, Inc. 16250 Stagg St Van Nuys 91406

BARON, NORMAN ARTHUR, physician, internist, rheumatologist; b. Nov. 16, 1946, NY, NY; s. Sidney and Frieda (Wirth) B.; m. Sonia-Paz Soto-Aguilar, Oct. 23, 1976; children: Pascale Emily b. 1978, Jason Allan b. 1981, Michelle Amy b. 1985; edn: BA, Boston Univ. 1968; MD, Univ. Bologna 1974. Career: intern French and Policlinic Hosp. NYC 1974-75; resident internal med. Hosp. for Joint Diseases and Med. Ctr. 1975-77; fellow clin. rheumatol. Rutgers Univ. 1977-79; splst. rheumatic diseases and internal med. Santa Maria, Calif. 1977–; chmn. Dept. Med. Valley Comm. Hosp. Santa Maria 1980-81, interim chmn. 1979; mem: Santa BArbara County Med. Soc. (bd. 1980-82), Am. Rheumatism Assn., Arthritis Found. (med. edn. com.), Am. Soc. Internal Med., Calif. Soc. Internal Med.; research: causes of biologic false positive serologic test for syphilis; rec: antique furniture restoration. Ofc: Arthritis Clin. of Santa Maria Inc. Norman Baron MD 504 E Plaza Dr Ste 1 Santa Maria 93454

BARRETT, ANTHONY JAMES, lawyer; b. July 9, 1926, Lawrence, Nebr.; s. Edmund J. and Elenora M. (Gilsdorf) B.; m. Leah, March 10, 1961; children: William, Leisa, Michael, Linda, Sheila, Jennifer; edn: LLB, McGeorge Coll. of Law 1960; Univ. of Santa Clara; San Jose State Coll. Career: pvt. practice 1961-; senior ptnr. Barrett, Marvin, Good & Newlan; pres. Barrett Newlan & Matheny; pres. Barett, Penney & Byrd, Sacramento 1978–; pres. No. Calif. Defense Counsel Assn.; dir. Calif. Defense Counsel; treas. Am. Bd. of Trial Advocates, Sacramento chpt.; mem: Calif. & Sacramento Co. Bar Assns., Defense Research Inst., Internat. Assn. of Ins. Counsel; Dixon Fire Dist. (commnr.), Dixon Booster Club (past ofcr., dir.), No. Calif. Sight Assn. (past ofcr., dir.), Eye Found. (past dir.); mil: yeoman 1/c USN, WWII, Korean War; Catholic. Ofc: Barrett, Penney & Byrd, P.O. Box 13160 Sacramento 95813

BARRETT, JAMES MORGAN, stockbroker; b. Nov. 30, 1937, Chgo., Ill.; s. Maurice John and Isabel Agnes (Gorman) B.; m. Eleanor Anderson, Sept. 19, 1981; children: Gina, b. 1960; Lisa, b. 1966; Darby, b. 1968; Anna, b. 1973; edn: BBA, Cal- Western Univ. 1963; mem. Selective Svc. Draft Bd., San Diego. Career: profl. football player, NY Jets safety 1963-64; vice pres. investments Prudential-Bache, Rancho Bernardo, San Diego; lectr. on investments, San Diego Co.; mem. US Airborne Assn., Kiwanis Club; past pres. Continental Little League Baseball; vol. high sch. football coach; Assn.; mil: Sgt. E5, US Paratrooper Ranger, Spl. Forces 1955-57, spl. forces Vietnam 1965; Republican; Catholic. Res: 12042 Fairhope Rd San Diego 92128 Ofc: Prudential Bache, 16536 Bernardo Center Dr San Diego 92128

BARRETT, KIM BERNADETTE, business consultant; b. Oct. 10, 1950, San Jose; d. Bernard and Lorraine (Thibert) B.; edn: AA, int. design, West Valley Coll. 1970, AS in model bldg. tech., 1981; BBA in gen. bus., cum laude, Nat. Univ. 1984, MBA in human rels., 1986. Career: tchg. asst., Model Bldg., West Valley Comm. Coll., 1973-75; model builder (Piping, Aircraft wind tunnel) Dynamic Engring., Va. 1975-77; mock-up mech. (developmental aircraft) Hughes Helicopters, Calif. 197-79; model builder (indsl. and test aircraft) Magee-Bralla, 1979-83, mktg. (scale models) 1983-84; current: indep. contr. (scale models) Nissan Design, US Navy, Allison Engring., Ham. Standard; owner KB Barrett & Assocs. (communication skills cons.), Carlsbad; profl. speaker for assns. and corps., 1983-; instr. Communication Skills Workshops for Access Learning and Mira Costa Coll., 1984; honors: Outstanding achieve., West Valley Coll. (1975), appreciation, GROW (Giving & Receiving Orgn. for Women) (1984); mem. Am. Soc. Tng. & Devel., Nat. Speakers Assn., Am. Engring. Model Soc. (1973-, chair Edn. 1974-6, Scholarship 1975-6, Mktg. 1985-6); civic: Grow (1982-84) Carlsbad CofC (Edn. com. 1985-6), Oceanside Police Assn., Serenity House half-way house for women alcoholics (vol.); publs: sev. profl. papers (1977-); rec: metal and woodworking, mechanics, ink drawings. Ofc: 6992 El Camino Real Ste 104-450 Carlsbad 92008-9990

BARRETT, WILLIAM RUSSELL, JR., commercial banker; b. Oct. 11, 1945, Holyoke, Mass.; s. William Russell and Mary Arline (Turlotte) B.; m. Barbara I., Sept. 20, 1969; children: Christopher b. 1972, William b. 1975, Scott b. 1983; edn: BA, Brown Univ. 1967; MBA, Univ. of Chicago Grad. Sch. of Bus. 1975. Career: asst. mgr. Chemical Bank, NY 1975-78; v.p. First Nat. Bank of Louisville 1978-80; senior v.p. National Westminster Bank 1980–; chmn. organizing com., Los Angeles Trade & Investment Misson to U.K.; mem: Los Angeles Area CofC, British Am. CofC, Central City Assn., City of Hope, Los Angeles Athletic Club; mil: capt. USAF 1968-73; Episcopal; rec: outdoor activities. Res: 243 Surfview Dr. Pacific Palisades 90272 Ofc: National Westminster Bank, 400 So. Hope St. Ste. 1000 Los Angeles 90071-7891

BARRIENTOS, SOL GELENA, nursing home administrator; b. Dec. 30, 1946, Naujan, Oriental Mindoro, Philippines, nat. US cit. 1986; d. Apolonio Ramos and Emeliana (De Castro) Gelena; m. Fidelino D. Barrientos, Dec. 26, 1981; edn: BS elem. edn., Manuel L. Quezon Univ. 1966, MA edn., 1968, PhD edn., 1976, postgrad. psychol., sociol., spl. edn., 1976-80. Career: ESL instr. Maryridge Sch. Tagaytay, Phil. 1967-70, St. Joseph Coll. Bankok, Thailand 1970-74; grad. prof. Ottanez Univ. Quezon City, Phil. 1975-77; thesis advisor, grad. prof. Araneta Univ. Manila 1974-78; dean acad. affairs Meycauayan Coll. Phil. 1978-81; thesis advisor, grad. prof. Manuel L. Quezon Univ. 1976-81; activity dir. Alden Terrace Convales. Hosp. Los Angeles 1982; asst. adminstr. Bird Haven Christian Convales. Hosp. Paramount, activity dir. Norwalk 1982-83, adminstr. Paramount 1983-84, adminstr. 2 convales. hosps. and 2 bd. & care 1984, Rancho Los Padres Norwalk 1984-85; regl. adminstr. 5 skilled nsg. homes 1985–; honors: Golden Eagle Award- Outstanding Educator of the Philippines 1982; mem: Phil. Assn. Colls. & Univs. 1975-81, Young Christian Orgn.; first reserve WAC in univ. 1966, 1 star; Catholic; rec: travel. Res: 3423 Crooked Creek Dr Diamond Bar 91765 Ofc: Everhealth Found. 8000 S Painter Ave Whittier 90602

BARRINGER, JOSEPH A., real estate broker, syndicator; b. Aug. 3, 1932, Salisbury, N.C.; s. Benjamin A. and Lorena (Arndt) B.; edn: BS in aero eng., N.C. State Univ. 1956. Career: systems design engr. Martin Co., Denver 1959-62; project mgr. United Technology Ctr., Sunnyvale 1962-64; sales agt. Calif. Land Sales, Beverly Hills 1964-66; mgmt. cons. to Lockheed Missiles & Space Co., Sunnyvale 1966-68; self-empl. in real estate, 1968–, owner BB&A Props. (R.E. syndication); US patent holder; mil: capt. US Air Force 1956-59; Republican (Pres. Task Force); Lutheran. Res: 525 E Maude St Sunnyvale 94086 Ofc: BB&A Properties 420 Florence St Palo Alto 94301

BARSAN, RICHARD EMIL, oral & maxillofacial surgeon; b. Dec. 18, 1945, Selma, Ala.; s. Emil O. and Letitia (Dobrin) B.; m. Sandra Sherrick, June 22, 1974; children: Kelly Lynn b. 1982, Robert Scott b. 1984; edn: BSChE, Univ. Cincinnati 1968; DDS, Ohio State Univ. 1979; oral & maxillofacial surg., La. State Univ. 1984. Career: chem. engr. Tex., NY, Ill., Calif. 1968-76; gen. dental practice residency VA Hosp. Sepulveda, Calif. 1979-80; oral & maxillofacial sug. res. New Orleans 1980-84; pvt. practice oral & maxillofacial surg. La Jolla, Calif. 1984–; att. staff L.A. Co.-USC Med. Ctr. 1986; honors: Omicron Kappa Upsilon 1979, Chrysler Scholarship Grant 1964, dental class pres., student council (OSU 1978-79); mem: Am. Dental Assn. Calif. Dental Assn., San Diego Co. Dental Assn., Am. Assn. Oral & Maxillofacial Surg. (clinician annual mtg. 1983), Am. Bd. Oral Surg. (bd. elig.), So. Calif. Soc. Oral & Maxillofacial Surg. (provsl.), Toastmasters, Paul Revere Study Club (treas. 1986); publ: tech. article in dental jour.; clin. presentation First Internat. Congress on Preprosthetic Surg. 1985; mil: USAR 1969-76; Republican; rec: computers, diving, running. Ofc: 470 Nautilus St Ste 212 La Jolla 92037

BARTKOWSKI, HENRY M., pediatric neurosurgeon; b. March 14, 1948, Buffalo, N.Y.; s. Henry B. and Eleanor M. (Jarzebinski) B.; m. Ladonna Urbanski, Apr. 8, 1978; chil: Christopher, b. 1980, Rebecca, b. 1982; edn: BA, Canisius Coll. 1970; MD, SUNY at Buffalo Sch of Med. 1976; PhD anatomical sci., SUNY at Buffalo Grad. Sch. 1977. Career: surg. intern UC Med Ctr, San Francisco 1976-77; neurosurg. res. NY Univ. Med. Ctr 1977-81; asst. prof. Neurological Surgery, UCSF 1981–; acting chief Neurosurgery Service, SF Gen Hosp., 1981–. awards for acad. excellence, SUNY at Buffalo Grad. Sch 1974, 75, 76; mem: AMA, AAAS, AANS, Calif. Assn. of Neurol. Surgeons, Calif. Med. Assn., Cong. of Neurol. Surgeons, Electron Microscopy Soc. of Am., Internat. Soc. of Cerebral Blood Flow and Metabolism, NY Acad. of Scis., San Francisco Med. Soc., SF Neurol. Soc., Soc. for Neurosci., Internat. Microsurg. Soc., Soc. of Magnetic Resonance in Medicine, Phi Chi med. frat., US Squash Racquets Assn., Harding Pk. Golf Club, No. Calif. Golf Assn., US Chess Fedn., S. Elizabeth's Mens Club.; contbr. arts. med. jours.; Republican; Catholic; rec: squash, golf, chess. Res: 481 Yale St. San Francisco 94134 Ofc: Univ. Calif. Med. Ctr. Parnassus Ave. 787-M, San Francisco 94143

BARTLESON, MAVIS ELLIOTT, real estate developer, shopping center owner; b. May 4, 1925, Perth, Western Australia; came to USA in 1946 (warbride, Army transp. USS Fred C. Ainsworth); d. Thomas Hughan and Rose Mitchell (Elliott) Gibson; m. 2d. Stuart Bartleson, Aug. 1, 1963; children: Sandra b. 1947, William b. 1948, Petrea Anne b. 1953; edn: bus., Univ. of Western Australia 1943; Calif. lic. Real Estate Broker 1953. Career: owner/builder Bartleson Co., devel. resort in Baja, Mexico, builder/devel. statewide in Calif.; owner (leasing dir.) shopping center, travel agency, bowling center; mem. research council Scripps Inst.; mem: Children's Home Soc., Santa Maria Country Club, Santa Maria Arts Council, Santa Maria Symphony, Lincoln Club; mil: "Wran" (decoder & cypher) Women's Royal Australian Naval Svc., WWII 1943-46; Republican; Episcopal; rec: pvt. pilot, travel, boating. Res: 2280 Crystal Dr. Santa Maria 93455 Ofc: Bartleson Company, 1110 E. Clark Ave. Ste. N Santa Maria 93455

BARTLETT, JOHN P., company executive; b. Dec. 6, 1944, Pittfield, Mass.; s. Walter W. and Catherine P. (McCasland) B.; m. Susan Lea, Sept. 9, 1984; children: Timothy Andrew b. 1966, Andrea Lynn b. 1971; edn: AA, Diablo Valley Coll. 1974; BS, Univ. Md. 1968. Career: dir. fleet svcs. San Francisco Leasing; mem: Red River Valley Fighter Pilots Assn. (River Rats), Travis AFB Hist. Soc. (charter), Kiwanis (past pres.), Nat. Assn. Fleet Adminstrs.; mil: USAF, Silver Star; Republican; Lutheran; rec: flying, aircraft memorabilia. Ofc: San Francisco Leasing 1000 Van Ness Ave San Francisco 94109

BARTZ, ALAN, lawyer; b. Oct. 25, 1946, Chicago, Ill.; s. Arthur E. and Irene (Laudonio) B.; m. Lonnie Morgan, Feb. 3, 1968; children: Morgan b. 1968, Aaron b. 1970, Lindsay b. 1985; edn: BA, Bowling Green State Univ. 1968; JD, Western State Univ. 1976; admitted to Calif. Bar 1977. Career: junior high sch. instr. 1968-76; atty. prin., Newport Beach 1977–; judge pro tem Orange

County Superior Ct. 1985-86; honors: Dean's award, Bowling Green St. Univ. (1968), founder/pres. Bowling Green Law Soc. (1966); Am. Jurisprudence Award, Constn., (1976); mem: ABA (Gen., Litigation Sects.), Orange County Bar Assn. (Pro Bono Publico Service Award 1980); Community Assn. Irvine (pres. 1979); Theta Chi Frat. (ofcr. 1965-67); Republican (pres. Young Repubs. McHenry Co., Ill. 1973); Methodist; rec: tennis, skiing, swimming. Res: 1 Flintridge Irvine 92715 Ofc: Alan Bartz APLC, 3 Corporate Plaza Ste 201 Newport Beach 92660

BARZA, ALLAN BERNE, psychiatrist; b. Mar. 19, 1945, Ottawa, Can., nat. 1963; s. John and Jeannette Gladys (Berman) B.; edn: 1962 National Merit Scholar; BA, North Park Coll. 1970, MD, Abraham Lincoln Sch of Med., Univ. of Ill. Coll. of Med., 1974. Career: pvt. practice psychiatry, Walnut Creek 1978–; att. phys. Walnut Creek Hosp., 1978-, v.p. med. staff 1982, acting med. director 1983, chief of staff 1984; clin. supr./tchr. Walnut Creek Hosp. Soc. Svc. Pgm., 1978-; cons. for skilled nursing psychiatric facility, 1978-79; att. psychiatrist Concord Group Home, 1978-; staff psychiatrist Contra Costa Co. Hosp., Martinez 1977-79; cons. psychiatrist Vocat. Rehab., Contra Costa Co., 1979; participating psychiatrist UCSF Postgrad. Seminars. Diplomate Am. Bd. of Psychiatry & Neurology 1980. Mem: Calif. Med. Assn., ACCMA, East Bay Psychiatry Soc. Mil: splst.4 US Army 1965-67, Vietnam Campaign, Commend. from Gen. Peers.; Jewish; rec: tennis, hiking, skiing. Res: 369 Hampton Rd. Piedmont 94611. Ofc: 2121 Ygnacio Valley Rd. D-4 Walnut Creek 94598

BASHAM, WILLIAM HARRISON, engineering co. executive; b. May 25, 1941, Daylight, Tenn.; s. Flavil L. and Ella Florine (Mitchell) B.; m. Marifrances Renfro, Aug. 4, 1973; children: Barbara b. 1964, Gregory b. 1966, Marty b. 1970; edn: Cal. Poly. Univ. Pomona 1961-63; UC Riverside 1959-61; BBA summa cum laude, Nat. Univ. 1984, MBA finance, 1985; lic. profl. civil engr. Calif., Nev., Ariz., Colo. Career: proj. job leader hwy. design sec. for Caltrans San Bernardino 1963-72; proj. planner W.R. Showalter & Assocs. S.B. 1977-78; v.p., prin. engr. land devel. CM Engrg. Assocs. S.B. & Vista 1979–, regl. mgr. Vista Ofc. 1981–; mem: Calif. Soc. Profl. Engrs. (chpt. 1st v.p. 1980-81, treas. 1979-80), Am. Soc. Civil Engrs., Nat. Soc. Profl. Engrs., Am. Pub. Works Assn., S.B. Historical Soc., Calif. Council Civil Engrs. & Land Surveyors, BSA (cubmaster, com. chmn.), Santa Margarita YMCA (bd. mgmt. 1985-), Rotary (bd. 1984-, pres.-elect 1987-88); Republican; Am. Baptist (trustee Judson Baptist Ch. 1974-75); rec: early Am. antiques, bottle collecting, baseball, golf, fishing. Res: 1268 Eucalyptus Ave Vista 92803 Ofc: CM Engrg. Assocs. 550 W Vista Way Ste 308 Vista 92803

BASHEIN, BARBARA JUNE, professional services firm partner; b. June 3, 1944, Lakewood, NJ; d. Hyman and Ann Mary (Kulen) Bashein; 1 dau, Robin Vereeke b. 1971; edn: BS, Carnegie- Mellon Univ. 1965; MS, USC 1969. Career: h.s. math tchr. Los Angeles City Schs., Los Angeles 1965-67; mathematician The Rand Corp., Santa Monica 1967-69; pgmmr./ analyst Quotron Systems Inc., Los Angeles 1969-72; project mgrl. Citicorp- Transaction Technology Inc., Los Angeles 1972-76; mgr. software devel. Lexar Corp., Los Angeles 1976-81; ptr. mgmt. info. cons. div. Arthur Andersen & Co., Los Angeles 1981–; freq. spkr. on trends in telecommunications and ofc. sys. incl. Financial Execs. Inst., Assn. of Retail MIS Dirs., Los Angeles Area CofC; honors: apptd. by Mayor Bradley, Blue Ribbon "Save the Books" Com. for Los Angeles Central Lib.; mem: Assn. of Telecommunication Cons., Orgn. of Women Execs. (Membership Com.), Santa Monica PTA; Republican; rec: swimming, bicycling. Ofc: Arthur Andersen & Co., 911 Wilshire Blvd. Los Angeles 90017

BASILIO, GREG GOMEZ, accountant; b. Nov. 13, 1934, Tacloban City, Philippines, nat. US cit. 1974; s. Domingo Engracial, Sr. and Aurelia (Gomez) B.; m. Teresita Ramos, Oct. 8, 1964; children: Ralph b. 1965, Joseph b. 1968; edn: BS in bus. adm., with honors, Divine Word Univ. 1957; spl. courses Mt. San Antonio Coll., Rio Hondo Coll.; desig: Certified Public Acct., Calif. 1982; Career: chief acct. Philippine Match Co., Cebu 1960-68; staff auditor Harry L. Nourse Audit Co., Santa Monica 1969-74; cost acct. Royal Crown Beverage Co., Los Angeles 1974-75, chief acct. 1975-79, asst. controller 1979-85; finl. analyst Lever Brothers Co., Inc., L.A. 1985–; ptnr. Ramos, Basilio & Assocs., CPAs; mem. Filipino Accts. of So. Calif., Calif. Soc. CPAs, Leyte-Samar Assn. (Los Angeles), Engkantada-U.S.A. (Los Angeles), Filipino Catholic Assn. (L.A.); works: installed acctg. system for a logging and lumber milling co. (1957); mil: ROTC grad., Phil. 1955; Republican; Catholic; rec: racquetball, bowling, fishing. Res: 1716 S Ardcale Ave Rowland Hts 91748 Ofc: Lever Brothers Co. 6300 E Sheila St Los Angeles 90040

BASSETT, RUSSELL DALE, JR., farmer; b. June 9, 1957, Sanger; s. Russell Dale and Dorothy Grace (Phillips) B.; m. Marta Cortez, Nov. 8, 1980; children: Russell, III b. 1982, Matthew b. 1985; edn: AA, Coll. of the Sequoias 1977; BS, agri. mgmt., Calif. State Polytech. Univ. SLO 1979. Career: asst. family bus., Dales Sporting Goods & Basset's Cricket Ranch, Visalia 1969-79; var. pos. as forklift opr., machine shop mech. 1975-79, loan ofcr. Visalia Prodn. Credit Assn. 1981-84; mgr., prin. Bassett's Cricket Ranch, 1984–; honors: State Proficiency Award, Calif. Future Farmers Am. (1975), Am. Farmer degree, Nat. FFA (1976), Outstanding voc. stu. Coll. of the Sequoia (1978), Alpha Zeta (agri. hon.), Calif. Agri. Leadership Pgm. (1985); mem. Tulare County Farm Bureau, Redwood FFA Boosters, Lions, Ducks Unlimited, Alpha Epsilon Pi frat.; Republican; Baptist; rec: softball, ski. Res: 365 S Mariposa Visalia 93277 Ofc: 535 North Lovers Ln Visalia 93291

BASSO, JOSEPH, advertising agency principal; b. Oct. 21, 1938, Chgo.; s. Sylvan T. and Agnes M. (MacMahon) B.; m. Jeannette, 1977; children: Cory b.

1961, Randall b. 1963, Ashley b. 1981; edn: bus. courses Northwestern Univ. 1961. Career: sales, mktg. dept. Admiral Corp. 1961-63; Babcock Corp. 1963-69; account supr. Durel Advt. 1969-72; pres./CEO Basso & Assocs. Inc., Newport Beach 1972–; mem. Orange County Advt. Fedn., Orange Coast Venture Group (charter), Pepperdine Assocs., Golden West Coll. Adv. Board, Christian Outreach Mission (bd.); clubs: Balboa Bay, John Wayne Tennis, Newport Beach Tennis, Lahaina Yacht; mil: USAF 1956-59; Republican; Christian; rec: tennis. Res: 5 Belmont Newport Beach 92660 Ofc: Basso & Associates Inc POB 8030 Newport Beach 92660

BATCHELOR, ELIZABETH, acupuncturist; b. July 5, 1950, New Britain, Conn.; d. Wm. Loring and Beatrice Bette (Porter) Batchelor; gr.grandfather, John Bidwell, scout for John Sutter (1849); edn: BS, Boston Univ. 1972; grad. Am. Coll. for Traditional Chinese Medicine 1984; certified Acupuncturist, Calif. 1984. Career: tchr. elementary sch. 1972-75; currently pvt. practice acupuncturist, psychic healer, herbologist Traditional Medicine, Woodacre 1984–; mem. Acupuncture Alliance Assn.; psychochemical research, electromagnetic energy fields in the human body; Zen Buddhist; rec: ballet, jazz dance, swim, equestrian. Ofc: Traditional Medicine 74 Carson Rd Woodacre 94973

BATEMAN, L. RUSSELL, investor; b. Oct. 4, 1940, Elizabeth City, N.C.; s. Claude and Alma M. Bateman; m. Sandra M., Sept. 4, 1978; children: Loyd Russell Jr. b. 1963, Angela M. b. 1961, (step) John N. Wagnon b. 1970, Jennifer N. Wagnon b. 1976; desig: finl. planner/stockbroker NASD (1969). Career: account exec. Mutual Fund Assoc., Lancaster 1969-74, Putnam Finl. Svcs. 1974-78, University Securities 1978-82; acct. exec./ dist. mgr. sales br. office, Finl. Network Investors Corp. 1982–; instr. Adult Edn. in Investments, Antelope Valley Coll.; speaker nat. co. conventions, Palmdale Bd. Realtors, Retired Fed. Emp., Retired Tchrs., var. service clubs; honors: Golden Scale Council-Putnam, FNIC Top Prods. Award, Western Traveler's Life-Top (3 consec. years), Mutual Fund Assoc., Century Club; mem. Internat. Assn. Finl. Plnnrs./L.A. chpt., Lancaster CofC, Board of Trade (dir.), Elks; mil: t/sgt. US Air Force 1958-78; AVPAC (dir.); rec: econs., travel, success stories. Res: 44805 Kingtree Lancaster 93534 Ofc: Financial Network Investors Corp. 858 W Jackman Ste 209 Lancaster 93534

BATESOLE, DALE F., clergyman, TV host; b. Oct. 1911, Ferguson, Iowa; s. John Floyd and Elsie Rebecca (Campbell) B.; m. Genell GRundhoefer, Aug. 12, 1974; edn: Grad. Safety Engr., Kansas Univ. Ext. 1943; Ordained Minister, Unity Sch. of Christianity 1959. Career: br. mgr. Western Grocer Co., Marshalltown, Iowa 1930-48; sales rep. Schultz Burch Biscuit Co. 1948-56; minister Unity Christ Ch., St. Louis, Mo. 1958-64; co-founder Forsyth Sch., St. Louis, Mo. 1961; faculty Unity Sch. of Christianity 1960-61; founder, 1st exec. dir. Charles and Myrtle Fillmore Found., Lee's Summit, Mo. 1964-67; sch. bd. trustee Maricopa Co. Sch. Dist. 1970-71; cons. to psychiat. svc. VA Hosp., Phoenix, Ariz. 1971-76; founder Unity Ch. of Sedona, Ariz. 1973; orginator, presenter Psycho- Cybernetics Sems. nationwide 1973; instr. Psycho- Cybernetics, No. Ariz. Univ. Coll. of Bus. Admin. 1975-77; minister Unity of the Desert, Palm Springs 1977-79; prod., dir., host, daily TV pgm. There Is A Way (fmrly. The Unity Way) 1979–; pres. Unity Student Minister's Assn.; counselor, tchr., lectr. A.A. 1960–; mem. Assn. of Unity Churches; publs: newspaper articles, columns for Red Rock News, Sedona, Ariz. 1973, 1974, Carefree Enterprise, Carefree, Ariz. 1970-72; Republican; rec. tennis, music, jogging. Res: 909 Sandpiper Palm Desert 92260 Ofc: There Is A Way, P.O. Box 2721 Palm Springs 92263-2721

BATTAGLIA, JOSEPH CHARLES, numismatist, publisher; b. Feb. 8, 1941, Buffalo, N.Y.; s. Joseph Nick and Patricia T. (Dubreville) B.; children: Jason b. 1970, Chris b. 1973; edn: BA, USC 1962; JD, Loyola Law Sch. 1965; admitted Calif. State Bar 1966. Career: active practice of law, 1966-80; bd. chmn. Gold & Silver Emporium, and editor/pub. Gold & Silver Forecaster News, 1980–, ed. The Coin Street Journal; honors: Western Regl. Moot Court Champion, past pres. Century City Bar Assn., past v.p. Italian/Am. Lawyers of Calif., 1985 Coin Dealer Man of the Year; mem: Calif. State Bar Assn., Am. Numismatic Assn., Calif. Profl. Numismatist Assn., Industry Council on Tangible Assets, Calif. Coin Dealers (exec. bd., chmn. PAC); contbr. num. articles in LA Times, Coin World, Numismatic News, the Numismatist, others; Roman Catholic; rec: mem. Rodeo Cowboys Assn./ team roping events, fish, hunt, ski. Ofc: Gold & Silver Emporium 16764 Ventura Blvd Encino 91436

BATZEL, ROGER ELWOOD, director Lawrence Livermore Laboratory; b. Dec. 1, 1921, Weiser, Ida.; s. Walter G. and Inez R. (Klinefelter) B.; m. Edwina Lorraine Grindstaff, Aug. 18, 1946; children: Stella Lyne, b. 1953, Roger Edward, b. 1955, Stacy Lorraine, b. 1960; edn: BS, Univ. of Ida., Moscow 1947; PhD, UC Berkeley 1951. Career: Lawrence Livermore Lab., Univ. of Calif., 1953–, associate dir., 1961-71, director, 1971–; mil: USAF 1943-45; rec: outdoor sports. Res: 315 Bonanza Way, Danville 94526 Ofc: POB 808, Livermore 94550

BAUCCIO, FEDELE ROBERT, food service co. executive; b. Aug. 21, 1942, Bklyn.; s. Salvatore Fedele and Michelena Vicenza (Suppa) B.; m. Suzanne, Aug. 7, 1965; children: Scott b. 1966, Eric b. 1968, Kurt b. 1972; edn: BA econs., Univ. Portland 1964, MA bus. adm., 1966; AMP grad. Harvard Univ. Sch. of Bus. 1985. Career: with Saga Corp., 1960–: student worker Univ. Portland 1960, full-time mgr. 1963, foodservice dir. 1964, dist. mgr. 1969, regl. ops. dir./personnel dir. 1972, regl. v.p. 1973, v.p. ops. 1980, pres. bus. & indus. div. 1981, pres. Black Angus Restaurant Div. (chain of 117 restaurants in 17 states and Canada), 1985–; honors: Pacific Metro Award nominee for outstanding contbn. Contract/Indsl. Foodservice Industry; mem. Harvard Bus. Sch. Assn./N. Calif.; mem. bd. St. Joseph's Sch. of Cupertino (bd. pres. 1980-83); Republican; Roman Catholic; rec: golf, ski. Ofc: Stuart Anderson's Black Angus Restaurants 4410 El Camino Real Ste 201 Los Altos 94022

BAUER, DENNIS KEITH, co. executive; b. July 8, 1947, Inglewood; s. William Melvin and Emma Ruth (Fernsler) B.; div.; children: Eric b. 1973, Wendy b. 1975; edn: BS, UCLA 1971, MPH, 1972. Career: Los Angeles Co. Health Svcs. Dept. 1972-83; admin. asst. 1974-77, dir. ambulatory care Coastal reg., Long Beach 1977-80, asst. dir. audit div. 1980-82, dir. 1983; CFO The Penguin Corp. 1984, CEO 1985–; past dir. Harbor Credit Union; cons. Calif. Dept. of Health 1975-78; mem: Am. Public Health Assn., Nat. Mgmt. Assn.; mil: splst. 5/c US Army 1968-69; Republican; rec: water sports, skiing. Ofc: The Penguin Corp. 19738 Beach Blvd. Huntington Beach 92648

BAUER, JEROME LEO, JR., chemical engineer; b. Oct. 12, 1938, Pittsburgh, Pa.; s. Jerome L., Sr. and Anna Mae (Tucker) B.; children: Lori b. 1964, Trish b. 1965, Jeff b. 1967; edn: BS in chem. eng., Univ. of Dayton 1960; MSChE, Penn State Univ. 1963; postgrad. Ohio State Univ. 1969; Reg. Profl. Engr. Ohio. Career: asst. prof. Univ. of Dayton 1963-67; mgr. Adv. Composites Dept., Ferro Corp., Cleveland 1967-72; Lockheed Missiles & Space Co. Inc., Sunnyvale 1972-74; project devel. engr. Convair Div. Gen. Dynamics, 1974-77; dir. research Furane Div. M&T Chemicals Inc., 1980-82; mem. tech. staff, splst. adv. composite mats. Jet Propulsion Lab., 1977-80, 82–, provided mats. support on deep space exploration pgms., conducted reliability survey of all NASA ctrs.; recipient SAMPE award of merit (1983); mem. Am. Inst. of Chem. Engrs. (founding chmn. Dayton Sect. 1964-66), Soc. for Adv. of Mat. and Process Engring. (mem. chmn. No. Calif. Sect. 1973-74, chmn. San Diego sect. 1976-77, chmn. L.A. chpt. 1977-78, internat. treas. 1978-82, gen. chmn. 31st Internat. Symposium/ exhibition 1986); publs: ed. Material Scis. for the Future (SAMPE 1986), 25+ tech. papers in chem. kinetics, thermodynamics, rheology, adv. composite mats.; Republican; Episcopal; rec: carpentry, photog., camping. Res: 1935 Alpha #205 Glendale 91208 Ofc: Jet Propulsion Lab 4800 Oak Grove Dr (157 507) Pasadena 91109

BAUM, KENT TAYLOR, stockbroker; b. Dec. 1, 1953, Coos Bay, Ore.; s. Herman William and Elizabeth Elaine (Taylor) B.; edn: BA econs., magna cum laude, UC Santa Barbara 1975; BA econs., Univ. Bath, England 1976; MBA finance, w/ honors, UC Los Angeles 1978. Career: assoc. Goldman, Sachs & Co. 1978-83; ptnr. Woodman, Kirkpatrick & Gilbreath 1983-84; Hambrecht & Quist 1984-85; assoc. Alex. Brown & Sons Inc. 1985–; trustee Martin Luther Tower 1980-86; mem: UCLA Grad. Sch. Mgmt. Alumni Assn. (area v.p., dir. 1978-81), Phi Sigma Kappa Alumni Assn, Commonwealth Club, Olympic Club, St. Francis Yacht Club; Republican; Lutheran (finance chmn. St. Mark's Luth. Ch. 1979-83); rec: piano, tennis, swimming, basketball. Res: 240 Mallorca Way San Francisco 94123 Ofc: Alex. Brown & Sons Inc. 350 California St Ste 810 San Francisco 94104

BAUMAN, JAMES JOHN, real estate broker; b. Dec. 2, 1928, Ponca, Neb.; s. James Alvin and Helen Lorraine (Beller) B.; m. D. Jeanne Lute, May 15, 1949; 1 dau. Helen b. 1952; edn: AA acctg., bus. law, CSU San Diego 1953; realtor Calif. 1965. Career: sales mgr. Sears Glendale, Calif. 1952-64; real estate sales 1965-67, broker Redding 1967–. owner, pres. Bauman Realty Inc.; honors: Million Dollar Club (1977-78), Multi-Million Dollar Club (1984-85), Realtor of the Year (1977); mem: Shasta County Bd. Realtors (pres. 1977), Calif. Assn. Realtors (dir. 1976-77), Nat. Assn. Review Appraisers (senior); Calif. Real Estate Political Action Com., Fed. 99 Club, Century Club, Gideons Internat. (treas.); mil: cpl. USMC 1946-49; Republican; Lutheran (elder 1981-, ch. pres. 1980); rec: flying. Res: 950 Royal Oak Dr Redding 96001 Ofc: Bauman Realty Inc. 1155 Hilltop Dr Redding 96003

BAX, RONALD FRANK, electronics manufacturing co. executive; b. Oct. 30, 1941, Niagara Falls, NY; s. Frank Lou and Margaret Violet (Hallenbeck) B.; m. Gail Barber, Aug. 26, 1961; children: Keith Robert, Bronwyn Lee; edn: BA, George Mason Univ. 1977; Johns Hopkins Univ. 1979. Career: sr. engr. Scope Electronics, Fairfax, Va. 1966-69; sr. engr. Recognition Equipment, Rockville, Md. 1969-72; eng. mgr. Acuity Systems, Reston, Va. 1972-75; cons., chief engr. Three Square, Alexandria, Va. 1972-76; prin. engr./ mgr. R&D Pfizer Medical Systems, Columbia, Md. 1975-82; cons./ engring. mgr. Diasonics M.R.I. (Magnetic Resonance Imaging), So. San Francisco 1982–; cons. C.T. Scanners & M.R.I. 1981-84; v.p. Ear Three Systems 1982–; listed, Who's Who in the East 1979-84; mem: Boy Scouts of Am. (Unit Commnr. 1976-79); patents: Jogging Computer 1974, Laser Lensmeter 1977, Scanning Apparatus 1980, Electro Cardiographic Storage 1982, Dark Current Compensation 1982; method for controlling x-ray tube emissions 1982, Gradient Power Supply 1984; mil: E4 USAF 1960-64; Republican; Catholic; rec: antique cars, electronics. Res: 554 Forest Ave Palo Alto 94301 Ofc: Diasonics M.R.I., 533 Cabot Rd, So. San Francisco 94080

BAXTER, LEE JOSEPH, sales engineer, executive; b. July 11, 1932, NY, NY; s. Leo Jerome and Anne Barbara (Abromoski) B.; m. Fredericka Farmer, June 5, 1953; children: Charles Lee b. 1959, Martha Jo (Miguel) b. 1961; edn: AA, Pasadena City Coll. 1954; desig: senior engr. mfg., Am. Soc. Tool & Mfg. Engrs. Career: sales engr. Meyer Sheet Metal Mach. Co., Los Angeles -1954; regl. sales mgr. Pullmax Co., Chgo. -1966; sales engr. Burgmaster Co., Los Angeles -1968; sales engr. Machinery Sales Co., L.A. -1971; sales engr. Oliver Mach. Co., Grand Rapids, Mich. -1979; current: design & sell complete furniture plants and cabinet shops/dist. mgr. Stiles Machinery, Grand Rapids; vocational advisor L.A. County Schs./ advsy. bd. L.A. Trade & Tech. Coll.,

Cerritos Coll., Don Bosco Tech. Coll.; mem. Assn. of Western Furniture Suppliers (dir., chmn. Western Woodworking & Furniture Supply Fair), Am. Soc. Mfg. Engrs. (senior), Soc. of Plastics Engrs., Numerical Control Soc. (pres. 1969); civic: Pasadena PFC Club (v.p. 1968), VICA (state judge), Masons, Shriners, Scottish Rite; contbr. short arts. in nat. trade periodicals; mil: s/sgt USAF; Catholic; Conservative; rec: working with sch. dists. to devel. vocational pgms. Res: 618 W Longden Ave Arcadia 91006 Ofc: Stiles Machinery 1315 John Reed Ct Industry 91744

BEAL, MICHELE CHRISTINE, lawyer; b. Mar. 7, 1959, Los Angeles; d. M. Meredith and Rohelia (Burrell) Beal; edn: AB, Stanford Univ. 1980; JD, UC Boalt Hall 1983; admitted Calif. State Bar 1984. Career: atty. assoc. Richards, Watson, Dreyfuss & Gershon, Los Angeles 1983–; mem: Calif. Bar Assn., Los Angeles County Bar Assn., Women Lawyers of Los Angeles, Black Women Lawyers Assn.; bd. dirs. Los Angeles Urban League; chair arts council Calif. Afro-Am. Museum; Democrat; Ch. of God in Christ; rec: travel, tennis, skiing. Ofc: Richards, Watson, Dreyfuss & Gershon 333 S Hope St 38th Fl Los Angeles 90071

BEAN, GERALD ALAN, newspaper executive; b. Mar. 17, 1943, Peoria, Ill.; s. Harold Franklin and Shirley Jane (Dreiman) Bean; m. Brenda M. Carlson, May 28, 1967; children: Scott b. 1972, Eric b. 1976; edn: BS in journ., Univ. Ill., Urbana 1966. Career: with Rockford (Ill.) Register Star, 1966-81, general mgr. 1978-79, pres./pub., 1979-81; gen. mgr. Gannett Satellite Information Network, Wash. DC, 1981-82; gen. mgr. USA Today, Wash. DC, 1982-83; vice pres. of Gannett West newspaper group and pres./pub. The Sun, San Bernardino 1983–; mem. bd. dirs. San Bernardino Hosp. Corp.; mem. Am. Newspaper Pubs. Assn., Calif. Newspaper Pubs. Assn.; mem. bd. dirs. Inland Action Inc., Inland Empire Cultural Found., St. Bernardine Hosp. Found., San Bernardino Co. Museum Found., CSU San Bernardino (bd. of councillors). Ofc: The Sun, 399 North D St., San Bernardino 92401

BEAN, ROBERT NELSON, aerospace co. executive, reliability engineer, ret.; b. Jan. 24, 1920, Wash. DC; s. Cecil Nelson and Velma Jane (Martin) B.; m. Doris Eileen Fitch, Aug. 22, 1943; 1 son, Robert Michael b. 1946; edn: BSEE, Duke Univ. 1943; Statistical Quality Control, Case 1947; Transistor Circuit Analysis, Santa Clara Univ. Grad. Sch. 1962; Profl. Quality Engr., Calif.; Profl. Elec. Engr., Texas. Career: prodn. engr. Brush Development Co., Cleveland, Ohio 1947-49; instrumentation engr. Convair Navy Ordnance Aerophysics Lab., Daingerfield, Texas 1949-59; group lead engr. reliability engring. Lockheed Missiles & Space Co. 1959-82; ret.; splst. in support Maintenance Engring. and Logistics; honors: v.p. Lockheed Mgmt. Assn., Awards 1969, 1970, Community Activities 1971-72; mem: Instrument Soc. of Am. (ArkLaTex sect., secty. treas. 1953-54), IEEE (senior), Soc. of Logistics Engrs., Demolay, Master Mason, Scottish Rite, Shrine, Elks, White Shrine of Jerusalem, Eastern Star, Ameranth, Toastmasters, Reserve Ofcrs. Assn., San Jose Civic Light Opera Aux., Silicon valley Computer Soc., Silicon Valley Color Computer Club; works: computer programs for logisitics and life cycle costing; mil: commdr. USNR 1943–, ret.; Republican; Presbyterian; rec: computer programming, boating, fishing. Res: 1574 Poppy Way Cupertino 95014 and 69 Rio Vista Ln. Red Bluff 96080

BEATON, ROY HOWARD, manufacturing co. executive, ret.; b. Sept. 1, 1916, Boston; s. Howard John and Mary Eva (La Voie) B.; m. Margaret Marchant July 22, 1939 (dec. 1978), m. 2nd Leora Schier, June 26, 1982; children: Constance b. 1944, Roy H., Jr. b. 1949; edn: BSCE, Northeastern Univ. 1939; D.Eng. (C.E.), Yale Univ. 1942; Reg. Profl. Engr. Wash 1948, Wisc. 1961, Calif. 1977. Career: E.I. Du Pont Manhattan Proj. Chgo., Oak Ridge, Hanford 1943-46; chief. engr., mgr. design, gen. mgr. constrn. engrg. Hanford Works General Electric Co. Richland, Wash. 1946-57, gen. mgr. neutron devices G.E. Milwaukee 1957-63, gen. mgr. Apollo Pgm. Daytona Beach 1963-67, v.p., gen. mgr. electron. syst. div. Syracuse, N.Y. 1968-74, senior v.p., group exec. nuclear energy San Jose 1975-81; honors: hon. D.Sc. (Northeastern Univ. 1967), NASA Public Service Award (Apollo Pgm. 1969); elected Nat. Acad. Engrg. 1977; mem: Am. Inst. Chem. Engrs., Nat. Soc. Profl. Engrs., Inst. Elec. & Electron. Engrs., Am. Astro. Soc., Am. Inst. Aero. & Astro., Am. Nuclear Soc., N.Y. Acad. of Sci.; past mem., bd. dirs: Santa Clara Co. Manufacturers Group (1977-81), United Way (1977-82), San Jose CofC (1978-83); approx. 10 classified patents on separation of plutonium from uranium and fission products (Manhattan Proj. 1943-44), Republican; Episcopal; rec: hiking, jogging, swimming, touring, photog. Res: POB 1018 Saratoga 95071

BEAULIEU, ROGER NORMAND, operations budget administrator; b. Feb. 28, 1943, Van Buren, Me.; s. Martin E. and Gertrude (Beaupre) B.; m. Aldonna Shields, Nov. 29, 1969; children: Andrea b. 1970, Roger b. 1972; edn: AA, Los Angeles Pierce Coll. 1973; BS, CSU Northridge 1975. Career: budget adminstr. Litton Systems, Woodland Hills; recipient commendn. for community service, Ventura Co. Bd. of Supvrs. (1977), Moorpark City Council (1984); civic: Moorpark Community Exec. Bd. (chmn. formation com. 1976), 1st Moorpark Unified Sch. Dist. Bd. (mem. 1980-83), 1st Moorpark City Council (1983-84); mil: sp5 US Army 1962-65; Catholic; rec: camping, photog. Res: 14792 E Stanford St Moorpark 93021 Ofc: Litton Guidance & Control Systems 5500 Canoga Ave MS 55 Woodland Hills 91367-6698

BECHTEL, JAMES HARVEY, physicist; b. March 25, 1945, Bellefontaine, Ohio; s. Pearl Conrad and Laura Crystal (Wearly) B.; m. Jean O'Neil, Aug. 20, 1983; edn: BS, Miami Univ. 1967; MS, Univ. of Mich. 1968, PhD, 1973. Career: research asst. Univ. of Mich., Ann Arbor, Mich. 1971-73; research fellow

Harvard Univ., Cambridge, Mass. 1973-76; senior research scientist, General Motors Research Labs, Warren, Mich. 1976-79, staff research scientist 1979-82, group leader, chemical and optical physics 1983; v.p. TACAN Aero Space Corp., Carlsbad 1983-85; mng. ptr. BBO Enterprises, La Jolla 1985–; vis. scientist Mass. Inst. of Tech. 1982; honors: Phi Beta Kappa, Sigma Xi; Fellow, Optical Soc. of Am. 1981; mem: Am. Physical Soc., Optical Soc. of Am. (pres. Detroit sect. 1981), Am. Assn. for Adv. of Science, New York Acad. of Sciences, Am. Chemical Soc., Friendship Force of San Diego Co., UC San Diego Endowment Com., Mensa, Intertel; num. profl. publs. Ofc: BBO Enterprises, 7910 Ivanhoe Ave. Ste. 502 La Jolla 92037

BECHTEL, STEPHEN D., JR., industrialist; b. May 10, 1925, Oakland; s. Stephen D. and Laura (Peart) Bechtel; m. Elizabeth Mead Hogan, 1946; 2 sons, 3 daughters; edn: civil engr. stu. Univ. of Colo. 1943-44; BS, Purdue Univ. 1946; MBA, Stanford Univ. 1948; Hon. Dr. Engrg., Purdue Univ. 1972; Hon. Dr. of Sci., Univ. of Colo. 1981. Career: employed by Bechtel 1941–, held broad variety of jobs and responsibilities both in the field and San Francisco Home Office; Director, 1951-; vice pres.,1952-55; sr. vice pres., 195-57; exec. vice pres., 1957-60; pres., 1960-73; chairman, 1973–. Chmn. Boards & Exec. Com., Bechtel Group, Inc., 1973-; chmn. Sequoia Ventures, Inc., 1980-; chmn. Bechtel Canada Ltd., 1972-. Dir.: Internat. Bus.Machines; chmn. National Acad. of Engineering; mem. (fmr. v.chmn.) The Business Council; councillor (life; fmr.chmn.) Conference Bd.; mem. Policy Com., The Business Roundtable; mem. Labor-Mgmt. Group; honors: Officer, French Legion of Honor, Engrg. News Record's Construction Man of the Year 1974, Moles' Award for Outstanding Achievement in Constrn. 1974, ASCE Civil Engrg. Mgmt. Award 1979, ASME 1980 Centennial Award, AAES 1982 Chairman's Award, 1980 Herbert Hoover Medal, 1985 Washington Award. Mem: The Beavers, Commonwealth Club of Calif. (SF); clubs: Augusta Nat. Golf, Bankers (SF), The Blind Brook Club Inc. (NYC), The Mount Royal (Montreal), Pac. Union (SF), Ramada (Houston), SF Golf, SF Tennis, Thunderbird CC (Palm Springs), Vancouver (B.C.), Villa Taverna (SF), The York (Toronto). Publs: num. profl. articles incl. New Edisons and New Technologies (1979); Calif.'s Contbn. to the Multiplier Effect (1979); The Climate for Innovation (1979); Technology: Foundation for America's Future Well Being (1980); mil: USMCR 1943-48; Protestant; rec: golf, tennis, hiking, photog. Res: POB 3809, San Francisco 94119. Ofc: 50 Beale St. San Francisco 94105

BECK, WALTER HENRY, real estate investor; b. Sept. 3, 1929, Belvedere, Ill.; s. Adolph and Esther (Kolinsky) B.; m. Sylvia Walden, Sept. 16, 1950; 1 child, Shira b. 1972; edn: BA econs., high honors, Calif. State Coll. 1961, grad. stu. UCLA 1961-62. Career: hd. of mkt. research- Los Angeles, Sunkist Growers, 1962-63; dir. mktg. (Chgo.) Midas Muffler Co., 1965-67; So. Calif. Area dir. Arby's Internat., 1967-71; indep. investor in restaurants (spec. Arby's, Denny's) and real estate, pres. FSM and Sylmar Ents.; honors: Sigma Tau Sigma (1958); mem. Junior CofC 1961; rec: biking, aerobics. Res: 9524 Dalegrove Dr Beverly Hills 90210 Ofc: FSM 17941 Ventura Blvd Encino 91316

BECKEL, CARL LEE, lawyer; b. Aug. 27, 1948, Ventura; s. Carl Clifford and Dorothy Esther B.; m. Debra, Aug. 11, 1984; 1 dau: Monica, b. 1976; edn: AA, Ventura Coll. 1968; BA,summa cum laude, CSU Fresno 1974; JD, Ventura Coll. of Law 1979; admitted to Calif. Bar 1979. Career: sales Electrolux 1974; route sales Pepsi Cola Bottling 1979; former ptr. Beckel & Howard 1982; currently, atty. pvt. practice, Ventura; recipient Non-Commissioned Ofcr.'s Leadership Sch. Speech Award; mem: Phi Kappa Phi; Am., Calif. and Ventura Co. Bar Assn.; mil: staff sgt. USAF, Air Force Commdn., GCM, Marksmanship; Democrat; rec: bodybuilding, travel. Ofc: Law Ofcs. Carl L. Beckel, 3585 Maple St. Ste. 256, Ventura 93003

BECKER, JOSEPHINE MOORE (Madge), librarian/consultant; b. Sept. 1, 1928, Portland, Ore.; d.JesseW. and Madge J. (Guthrie) Moore; m. Henry C.Becker, Jr., Lt. Col. AUS (Ret.), Jan. 30, 1970; edn: AB, Western Coll for Women (Oxford, Ohio) 1949; MLS, Univ. Ill. Sch. Lib. Sci. (Urbana) 1952. Career: br. supr./ adminstrv. asst. Yakima Valley (Wash.) Regional Lib., 1954-59; field librn. US Army Spl Serv., Ger. 1959-61; county librn. Plumas Co., Quincy, Calif. 1961-64; city librn. Longview, Wash. 1964-70; city librn. Vallejo, Calif. 1970-74; acting co. librn. Solano Co., Fairfield 1973-74 and county librarian, 1974-83; partner C&J Enterprises, lib. mgmt. consultants, 1982–; secty. Solano Co. Lib. Authority, 1975-83; chmn. North Bay Coop. Lib. System, 1974-75; secty. Calif. Inst. of Libraries, 1976-78; pres. Pub. Lib. Execs. of Central Calif., 1977; v.p., pres. elect. Wash. Lib. Assn. 1969-70; Recipient Bess Sawhill Robertson Award for excellence in English, Western Coll. 1949; mem: Soroptimist (pres.1965-7,77-8); Beta Phi Mu; rec: collect books, travel, photog. Address: c/o MCCA Box 2870 Estes Park, CO 80517

BECKLEY, TODD ALLAN, mortuary/cemetery executive; b. Oct. 2, 1946, Downey; s. Willard Fencil and Lucille Clara (Rausch) B.; m. Kim Berry, Oct. 5, 1968; children: Sarah b. 1976, Ross b. 1979, Timothy b. 1981; edn: Cerritos Coll. 1966; grad. Calif. Coll. Mort. Sci. 1968; Calif. lic. funeral dir., embalmer 1968. Career: apprentice Utter-McKinley Mortuaries 1965-68; mgmt. Utter-McKinley Mortuaries in Compton, East Los Angeles and Downey, 12 years; asst. to the pres. & gen. mgr. in design and constrn. of Memory Garden Mort. & Chapel, Brea 1977-, vice pres. 1982, pres./gen. mgr. 1982–; honors: City of Brea Man of the Year (1985), Kiwanian of Year (1982, 84, 85), appreciation, For Kids Sake; mem. Orange County Funeral Directors Assn. (pres. 1986; industry spokesman to num. groups); civic: Brea CofC (bd.), Brea Community Emergency Council (pres.), Brea Kiwanis Club (pres. 1982-83), Brea Country Fair (chmn.), Brea-Olinda H.S. Key Club (advisor),; Republican; Catholic; rec: photog., water ski. Ofc: Memory Garden 455 W Central Ave Brea 92621

BEDFORD, JOHN DAVID, co. president; b. Jan. 18, 1925, Glendale; s. Wm. Hugh and Besse (Simpson) B.; m. 3d Lorelei Button, June 25, 1959; children: Darlene b. 1943, Susan b. 1947, Toni Rae (dec.) b. 1953, John b. 1955; grad. Alhambra High Sch. 1942. Career: auto dismantling, 1950; trucking bus., 1952-70; pres. Bedlo, Inc. (auto dismantling/ salvage bus.), 1968–, in San Gabriel Valley area 1968-70, San Luis Obispo 1970-, and in Santa Maria 1975-, and Lompoc 1976-; pres. Bedford Ents. Inc. (refuse bus.), Santa Maria 1980–, opened branch (boat bus.) in Bradley 1986-; indep. consultant in industry 1970-; honored annually (1974-) by S.L.O. City Fire Dept. and Santa Maria City Fire Dept. for activities using Jaws of Life Vehicle extricating equip.; mem. So. Calif. Auto Dismantlers Assn.; mem. Masons, Elks; works: swimming instr. Water Safety and Lifesaving (1940-43, 46-48), won 1st Pl. award, Boy Scouts Am. Swim Meet, KIVA (1939), 1st Pl. Alhambra Parks Dept./ LA County Metropolitan Swim Meet (1940); mil: cpt. US Army Air Force 1943-45, Asiatic Pacific Campaign medal, Phil. Liberation Ribbon, Good Conduct, Victory, Air medals; Indep.; Prot.; rec: water sports. Res: 3111 East Beach Circle (Oak Shores) Bradley 93426 Ofc: Bedlo Inc./ Bedford Ent. Inc. 1498 Black Rd Santa Maria 93454

BEDORTHA, MICHAEL WILLIAM, insulation contractor; b. Nov. 23, 1949, Tillamook, Ore.; s. Kenneth and Betty Anne (Reichers) B.; m. Cristal, Mar. 23, 1974; children: Joseph b. 1974, Melanie b. 1977; edn: Mt. Hood Comm. Coll. 1969-70, Ore. State Univ. 1970-73. Career: owner/mgr. Trout Creek Game Preserve, Ashwood, Ore. 1970-73; owner Bedortha Reforestation, Eugene 1973-76, founder/tchr. Bedortha School of Reforesters 1975-76; game mgr. Kah-Nee-ta Resort, Warm Springs, Ore. 1976-77; mgmt. Fred Meyer Stores, Portland 1977-80; rental remodeling bus., Reno, Nev. 1980-82; sales mgr. All Weather Insulation, Reno 1982-83; contr. prin. Bedortha Insulation, Thousand Oaks, Calif. 1983–; owner Bedortha Brothers Cattle Co., 1985–; honors: var. collegiate athletic (track) awards; mem. Insulation Contractors Assn. (Retrofit Com.), Jaycees (pres. Fairbanks 1979, v.p. Corvallis 1980), Elks; works: devel. line of BGR (Big Game Repellent) spray equipt. (1975); Republican (Pres. Task Force 1983-), Ch. of Jesus Christ of Latter Day Saints; rec: hunting, fishing. Ofc: Bedortha Insulation POB 3518 Chatsworth 91313

BEE, BOB, advertising agency president; b. May 18, 1946, Los Angeles; s. Anthony Vallejo and Edith (Tabb) Benites; m. Leslie, Aug. 3, 1985; edn: NY Inst. of Photog. 1967-68; AA, El Camino Jr. Coll. 1970. Career: photog. Cagle Studios, Inglewood 1968-69; salesman Century Chevrolet, Inglewood 1969-70; ins. agt. Washington Nat. Insurance, Carson 1970-71; domestic sales Rover-Internat. Playtex Corp. USA 1971-74; owner Bob Bee's Profl. Photography 1974-78; pres. Bee-Dawn Ents., Sacto. 1978-80; ptnr. Pacific States Advt., Sacto. 1980-81; author/pub. The Positive Image, Buena Park 1982-84; pres. Positive Images Ink., Anaheim 1984–; guest speaker on motivation, modeling, advt., var. civic groups and high schs.; mem. Anaheim CofC (dir., chmn. Small Bus. Com., Ambassadors, Rediscover Anaheim); mil: US Navy 1964-68, Purple Heart, Bronze Star, Vietnam Svc.; Republican; Prot.; rec: sports. Res: 333 Rob Way Anaheim 92801 Ofc: Positive Images Ink. 2275 W Lincoln Ave Ste U Anaheim 92801

BEECHKO, ANDREW JOHN, medical equipment product manager; b. Aug. 16, 1956, Danville, Pa.; s. Nicholas and Olga (Gierman) B.; edn: BA biol., St. Michael's Coll. Winooski, Vt. 1978; MBA mktg., CSU San Bernardino 1980. Career: product splst. assoc. Bear Medical Systems Inc. 1980-82, prod. splst. 1982-84, prod. mgr. 1984–; honors: var. company awards; mem. CSU San Bernardino Alumni Assn.; works: training & instrn. manuals, product accessory inventions, research ventilation techniques; Republican; Catholic; rec: racquetball, skiing, running, tennis. Res: 600 Central Ave Apt 58 Riverside 92507 Ofc: Bear Medical Systems Inc. 2085 Rustin Ave Riverside 92507

BEEKMAN, JANET LAURA, educator; b. July 24, 1939, Gustine; d. Salvadore and Mary E. (Totten) DeAngeles; m. Robert Beekman, Feb. 11, 1962; children: Tyrone b. 1965, DeAna b. 1967; edn: BA, Univ. of Pacific 1961; MEd, CSU San Francisco 1967; adminstrv. credential, Univ. San Francisco 1984. Career: elem. sch. tchr. Stockton Unified Sch. Dist. 1961, Wurzburg, Germany 1962, Turlock Unified 1963, Jefferson Elem. (Daly City) 1963-69, San Mateo County Schs., Juvenile Hall 1968, Hillsborough City Sch. Dist. 1969-78, Hughson Union Sch. Dist. 1978-82, Sylvan Union Sch. Dist. and Empire Elem. 1983, Ceres Unified Sch. Dist. 1984–, prin. Caswell Elem. Sch. 1985–; Workshop facilitator, Conf. Speaker (1967-); demonstration tchg., devel. mentor tchg. plan, gifted pgm.; honors: Thespians Award (1957), Bank of Am. Fine Arts achieve. award (1957), Project Discovery, Bell and Howell recogn. (1965), AFS Service Award (1983); mem: Assn. of Calif. Sch. Adminstrs., Stanislaus Reading Council, Calif. Reading Assn., Internat. Reading Assn., Phi Delta Kappa, Calif. Tchrs. Assn., Nat. Edn. Assn., AFS (Internat./ Intercultural Exchange Pgms., Modesto Chapts.), Ceres Western Art Steering Com.; publs: The Reading Teacher, CRA Qtrly J. (1983); The Literature Ladder for Literacy Lovers (1982); contbr. arts. in Stanislaus Chpt. Adminstrs. Newsletter SCAN (1981), The Instructor (1968), Elementary English (1968); Republican; Presbyterian; rec: music, cooking, travel. Res: 3312 Birmingham Dr Modesto 95355 Ofc: Caswell Elementary School (POB 307) 1801 N Central Ave Ceres 95307

BEESON, MONTEL EILEEN, gerontologist, administrator; b. Dec. 22, 1939, El Dorado, Ark.; d. Waymon Willett and Myrtle May (Roach) B.; edn: BS, CSU Hayward 1963; MA, Holy Names Coll. 1979; nursing home adminstr., Calif. 1984; community coll. instr. cred., Calif. 1979. Career: dist. exec. Arizona Catus-Pine Girl Scout Council, Pheonix, Ariz. 1963-66; dist. exec. San Francisco Bay Girl Scout Council, Brisbane 1966-68, bus. mgr., Oakland 1968-71; exec. dir. Shabonee Girl Scout Council, Moline, Ill. 1971-73; exec. dir. Tongas-Alaska Girl Scout Council, Ketchikan, Ala. 1973-74; exec. dir. Muir Trial Girl Scout Council, Modesto 1974-78; asst. admistr. Beulah Home Inc., Oakland 1980 – ; rehab. cons. Career Advancement Ctrs. 1979-80; honors: Preceptor, Nursing Home Adminstrs., BENHA 1985; Outstanding Young Women of Am. 1972; mem: Am. Coll. of Health Care Adminstrs., Calif. Assn. of Homes for the Aging, Am. Soc. on Aging, Nat. Fedn. of Bus. & Profl. Women, Soroptomist Internat., Girl Scouts of the USA; Republican; Methodist; rec: cross-country skiing, history, travel. Res: 3393 Kiwanis St. Oakland 94602 Ofc: Beulah Home, Inc.,4690 Tompkins Ave. Oakland 94619

BEESON, PHILLIP ALAN, welding engineering executive; b. Jan. 6, 1926, Payette, Ida.; s. Joseph Greene and Emma Virginia (Clemensen) B.; m. Peggy Caldwell; children: Karen b. 1948, Lindsay b. 1951, Cynthia b. 1954, Heidi b. 1963; edn: AS, Idaho State Coll. 1945; BS, metallurg. engring., Univ. Idaho 1950; Reg. Profl. Engr. (Met. 1291) Calif. 1966. Career: metallurgist Bradley Mining Co., Stibnite, Ida. 1950-52; supt. Am. Smelting & Refining, Chihuahua, Mex. 1952-56; welding engr. North Am. Aviation, El Segundo 1958, supv. welding lab. 1958-64; senior splst. Rockwell Internat., Canoga Park and El Segundo, 1964-77; mgr. welding engring. The Marquardt Co., Van Nuys 1977 – ; awards: Lambda Chi Alpha (chpt. ofcr. 1949), Rockwell Internat. recognition incentive (1962, 64), cost reduction award (1968), PTA hon. service award (1977); mem: Am. Welding Soc. (sect. chmn. 1984-), Am. Inst. Mining & Metallurg. Engrs. (chpt. pres. 1949), Robotics Internat. of SME, American Legion (v.comdr. 1957), Am. Soc. Metals; holder three patents in metal fabrication (1964, 66, 69); NASA Innovation (1980); num. tech. papers, 1960-; mil: seaman 1/c USNR 1944-46, Pacific Area, Good Conduct, Victory medals; Republican (Ventura Co. Central Com. 1976-80, ex. com., co. chmn. Paul Gann); Protestant; rec: golf, bridge. Res: 637 W San Doval Pl Thousand Oaks 91360 Ofc: The Marquardt Co 16555 Saticoy St Van Nuys 91409

BEGELMAN, MARK DAVID, retail co. executive; b. July 9, 1947, Newport, R.I.; s. Maurice and Aida B.; m. Pamela, Nov. 9, 1980; 1 son, Matthew b. 1984; edn: AA, Sullivan Comm. Coll. 1967; BA, Dowling Coll. 1971. Career: buyer Abraham & Straus, Bklyn., N.Y. 1969-76; divisional merch. mgr. Jordan Marsh, Miami, Fla. 1976-81; senior v.p./gen. mgr. John Breuner Co., San Ramon, Calif. 1981-86; pres./chief exec. The Office Club, Concord 1986 – ; honors: State Finalist Deca. (1965); mem. Furniture Rental Assn. of Am. (pres. 1982-86); civic: Commack Vol. Ambulance Corps (v.p.); mil: Army Nat. Guard 1970-72; Republican; Jewish; rec: fitness, guitar. Res: 31 Abington Ln Alamo 94583 Ofc: The Office Club 1355 Willow Way Ste 110 Concord 94520

BEHNKE, CARL WILLAM, sales & marketing executive; b. July 27, 1960, Kingston, NY; s. Walter William and Alice Marie (West) B.; edn: BS, Trenton State Coll. 1983. Career: communications rep. Western Union Santa Ana 1984; sales, mktg. exec. WCT Inc. Santa Ana 1984 – ; mem: Nat. Acad. Songwriters, Trenton State Coll. Alumni; writer 57 songs (unpublished); rec: songwriting, philosophy, tennis, golf. Res: 1030 W MacArthur Blvd Apt 85 Santa Ana 92707 Ofc: WCT Inc. 2901 Warner Ave Santa Ana 92704

BEHRENDT, JOHN THOMAS, lawyer; b. Oct. 26, 1945, Syracuse, Kans.; s. Thomas Franklin and Anna Iola (Carrithers) B.; m. Theresa Elmore, Oct. 27, 1985; children: Todd b. 1970, Gretchen b. 1973; edn: BA, Sterling Coll. 1967; JD cum laude, Univ. Minn. 1970. Career: atty., assoc. and ptnr. Gibson, Dunn & Crutcher, Los Angeles and New York 1970 – ; honors: Order of the Coif, Univ. of Minn. Law Review; mem: Am. Bar Assn. (Internat. Law Com., Law and Acctg. Com.); clubs: Jonathan (LA), Union League (NYC); mil: capt. US Army 1971-74; Republican; Presbyterian; rec: fly fishing, skiing, hunting. Res: 101 Ocean Ave, L6, Santa Monica 90402 Ofc: Gibson Dunn & Crutcher 2029 Century Park East, Los Angeles 90067, 9 W 57th St New York NY 10019

BEHZAD-ASSIRI, FERIEDOON (Fred Assiri), engineer; b. Apr. 25, 1941, Shiraz, Iran; s. Ahmad and Zibandeh (Eatezadi) B.-A.; m. Farima Abbassi, Sept. 4, 1968, div. 1978; 1 son, Homan, b. 1970; edn: BS in gen. engring., Abadan Inst. of Tech. 1965; MS in civil engring., USC 1973; postgrad. wk. in plate and shell, USC 1974; cert. in earthquake engring. and adv. concrete design, UCLA Ext. 1975, 76; Reg. Profl. Engr. (Civil) in Calif. (1975), Colo., Minn., N.D., Kans., Tex. Career: structural engr. National Iranian Oil Co., Abadan, Iran 1965-67, project engr. 1967-70, senior struc. engr. 1970-71; design engr. Ralph M. Parsons Co., Pasadena, Torrance, Calif. 1972-73; struc. engr. 1973-74, senior struc. engr. 1974, prin. struc. engr. 1974-77, chief structural engr. Western Precipitation Div., Joy Mfg. Co., Los Angeles 1977 – , respons. for all co. structural wk. in area of environmental pollution control equip. (spec. in Dry Flue Gas Desulphurization and particulate removal systems for major utilities; self-empl. cons./designer comml. bldgs., schools and hotels, Abadan-Khoramshar, Iran 1967-71; awards: gold medal for cost improvements, 5 consecutive yrs., Joy Mfg. Co.; mem. Struc. Engrs. Assn. of So. Calif.; past bd. mem. Iranian Soc. of Engrs. (1970), past pres. Student Council Abadan Inst. of Tech. (1964-5); publs: profl. paper, ASME meeting, NY 1979; mil: lt. Iranian Army; Moslem; rec: skiing. Res: 13969 Marquesas #319B Marina del Rey 90292-6039 Ofc: Joy Mfg Co. 4565 Colorado Blvd Los Angeles 90039

BEIER, STEVEN MARK, health care corporate executive; b. Feb. 12, 1947, New Rochelle, N.Y.; s. Herbert Donald and Lillian (Elson) B.; 1 child, Colin b. 1977; edn: BA, Rutgers Coll. 1969; MCP, Harvard Univ. 1975; PhD (abd), Univ. Pa. 1976; desig: Am. Inst. of Certified Planners (AICP). Career: project plnnr. Tippetts Abbitt McCarthy Stratton (TAMS), NY, Va., Mass., 1969-72; plnng. ofcr. Boston Redevel. Authority, also prof. Boston Architl. Center Sch. of Arch., 1972-73; grad. faculty/PhD (abd) Univ. Pa. 1975-76; div. chief/chief plnnr. Dept. Devel., City of Newport News, Va. 1976-81, also adj. prof. Coll. of Wm. and Mary, Golden Gate Univ.; pres. dp/m assocs. inc., Hampton, Va. 1980-83; asst. v.p. Corp. Devel. (Health Care- mergers & acquisitions), Am. Medical Internat., Beverly Hills 1983 – ; awards: 1907 Foundation research fellow Fels Ctr. of Govt., Univ. of Pa. (1976), Disting. Planning award Am. Plnng. Assn./Va. (1980); mem: Am. Inst. Certified Plnnrs., Am. Plnng. Assn., The Soc. for Hosp. Plnng. (AHA), Va. Hosp. Assn., Am. Soc. Public Adminstrn.; works: Urban Design Research: Built Environments' impact on individual Psycho-Social Behavior (1974-76), Productivity, Efficiency and Levels of Service of Urban Transp. Systems (1978); Indep.; rec: classical music, sail, mtn. climbing. Res: 142 Hart Ave Santa Monica 90405 Ofc: American Medical Internat. 414 N Camden Dr Beverly Hills 90210

BEIERLE, ROBERT THOMAS, scientist, electronics engineer; b. Nov. 3, 1945, Long Beach; s. William Frank and Dolores (Mounce) B.; m. Sally Jane Benson, Nov. 18, 1982; AS, Mt. San Antonio Coll. 1972; BSEE, Calif. St. Polytech. Univ. 1975, grad. stu. 1984. Career: design engr. General Dynamics, Pomona 1975-79; principal designer Hughes Aircraft GEADGE pgm. (German Air-Ground Environ. Def. Sys.), Fullerton 1979-82; sr. mem. tech. staff/ hd. guidance control design gp. ADCAP pgm. Hughes Aircraft 1982 – ; currently, senior staff engr., tech. supv.; tchg. asst., radar sys. & signal processing, Cal Poly, Pomona 1976-77; awards: academic scholarship, CalPoly 1975; Academic Outstanding Scholarship awd., IEEE Student chpt. 1975; Hughes Aircraft Zero Defects Awd. 1984; mem: IEEE; Nat. Mgmt. Assn.; co- designed guidance & control sys. Cal Poly Rose Parade Float (Princess Awd.) 1974; mil: Sgt., USAF 1963-67, Vietnam, Nat. Defense Svc. Medal; GCM; Catholic; landscape design, sailing, inventing. Res: 20980 E. Gold Run Dr Diamond Bar 91765 Ofc: Hughes Aircraft, Ground Systems Group, Malvern & Gilbert, Fullerton 92634

BEKEY, GEORGE ALBERT, computer science and robotics institute executive; b. June 19, 1928, Bratislava, Czech.; s. Andrew and Elizabeth (Magyar) B.; m. Shirley White, June 10, 1951; children: Ronald Steven; Michelle Elaine; edn: BSEE, UC Berkeley 1950; MS, UCLA 1952; PhD, 1962; Reg. Elec. Engr. & Control Sys. Engr., CA. Career: tchg. asst., research engr. UCLA Sch. of Eng. 1950-54; US Army Signal Corps. 1954-56; mgr. computer ctr. Beckman Instruments, L.A. 1956-58; group ldr., section hd., senior staff engr. TRW Systems, L.A. 1958-62; asst. prof. Dept. Elec. Engring. USC 1962-64, assoc. prof. 1964-68, prof. Dept. Elec. Engring., Biomedical Engring. and Computer Sci., USC 1968 – , co-dir. Sys. Simulation Lab. 1962-66, chmn. Elec. Engring.-Sys. Dept. 1970-72, 1978-82, dir. Biomed. Engring. Inst. 1972-75; dir. USC Robotics Inst. 1983 – , chmn. USC Computer Science Dept. 1984 – ; ed. IEEE Journ. of Robotics and Automation; assoc. ed. Mathematical Biosciences, Mathematics and Computers in Simulation, and Transactions of the Soc. for Computer Simulation; gen. chmn. 7th Internat. Symposium on System Identification and Process Parameter Estimation, Wash. DC 1982; honors: Sigma Xi Nat. Lectr. (1976-77), distng. faculty award USC Sch. of Engring. (1976); mem: Soc. of Computer Simulation, AAAS, Fellow IEEE (1972), World Affairs Council; publs: co-author Hybrid Computation (1968), ed. Proceedings of Conf. on Mathematical Models of Public Systems (1971), co-editor Hospital Information Systems (1972), num. book chpts. and tech. papers; mil: U.S. Army 1954-56. Res: 4654 Encino Ave., Encino 91316 Ofc: University of So. California, EE-Systems, Los Angeles 90089-0272

BELEY, GENE RICHARD, writer, robotics co. president; b. Dec. 27, 1939, Livingston, Mont.; s. Frank R. and Beulah May (Fuhs) B.; m. Jill Muir, June 24, 1986; children: Scott b. 1965, Shaun b. 1967, Melisa b. 1972; edn: BA pub. rels., San Jose State Univ. 1963; MS in journ., UC Los Angeles 1967. Career: newspaper jobs Yellowstone News, Billings Gazette; TV copywriter, Sta. KOOK-TV, Billings, Mont.; video tape coord. and asst. to mgr. of Elections Unit, NBC-TV, Burbank 1966-67; fulltime reporter/photog. Ventura (Calif.) Star Free Press, 3 yrs.; freelance writer num. articles in nat. magazines incl. Parents', TWA Airlines mag., Modern Bride; West Coast Communs. rep. for Atlantic Richfield, 2 yrs.; also began small bus. with coin op. machines, 1969, and pioneered electronic game rooms in Los Angeles bowling ctrs., 1970s (obtained 1st arcade permit after 30 yr ban; helped rewrite legislation affecting coin-op bus. in sev. cities; began pioneering show robots 1977, founder/pres. Android Amusement Corp., now Android Industries, Inc., 1977 – , designed six generations of show robots (customers incl. Hugh Hefner/ The Playboy Mansion West; CBS-TV's The Price is Right; The Frontier Hotel, Las Vegas; others worldwide), DC-1 early robot selected for 3 yr travelling exh. of Am. Craft Museum; current show robot, Mr. (T) Telebot; author biography of Ray Bradbury: The Idea Beast of Beverly Hills (1986); mem. Robotics Industries of Am.; mil: pfc Army Nat. Guard; rec: boating, photog. Ofc: Android Industries Inc POB 1240 Morgan Hill 95037

BELL, ERNEST L., JR., motel owner; b. Nov. 9, 1942, Franklin, N.H.; s. Ernest Leo Sr. and Nina Elizbeth (Martel) B.; m. Brenda Pauline; children: Lisa b. 1963, Mike b. 1965, heidi b. 1974; edn: AA, El Camino Jr. Coll. 1976. Career: mechanic Continental Airlines, LAX 1966-77; owner, real estate broker Realty Masters, Torrance 1977-80; owner, 49er Motel, Weaverville 1980 – ; mem: Am. Hotel Assn., Masons, Lions, Elks; mil: s/sgt. USAF 1962-66, num. unit citations; Republican; rec: rats, music, sports. Ofc: 49er Motel, 718 Main Weaverville 96093

BELL, GARY RAY, optometrist; b. July 15, 1947, Tulsa, Okla.; s. Joseph Henry and Hazel Lee (Adams) K.; m. Janice, Dec. 30, 1978; children: Jacquelyn b. 1981, Stephanie b. 1982; edn: BS, UC Berkeley 1970, OD, 1972; MS, CSU Fullerton 1984; Reg. Optometrist, Calif. 1973. Career: optometrist pvt. practice 1974–; instr. So. Calif. Coll. of Optometry 1879-81; cons. Lions Club Sight Conservation Pgm. 1977-; honors: Scabbard & Blade, ROTC 1968; Distng. Mil. Grad., ROTC 1970; Cert. of Achiev., US Army 1974; Dean's Council, UC Berkeley 1977; Gold Shovel Award, Corona CofC 1984; mem: Am. Optometric Assn., Calif. Optometric Assn. Congress (del. 1984-85), Corona Host Lions Club (past pres., sight conservation chmn.), Navy League, Corona CofC; research: myopia, late '70s; publs: A Review of the Sclera and Its Role in Myopia, Journ. of Am. Optometric Assn. 1978; The Coleman Theroy of Accomedation and It's Relevance to Myopia, Journ. of Am. Optometric Assn. 1974; mil: 1st lt. US Army 1972-74; Evangelical; rec: running, singing. Res: 405 E. Monterey Rd. Corona 91719 Ofc: Dr. Gary R. Bell, 807 W. Grand Ave. Ste. A Corona 91720

BELL, MARY ALICE, publisher, writer, auto leasing agent; b. July 23, 1922, Warren, Ohio; d. Anthony and Angela Marie (DeSanti) Marcella; m. Arley James Bailes, Nov. 19, 1941 (div. 1974); children: Roger James b. 1942, Faith Orpha Ann b. 1950; 2 grandchildren, 1 great grandson; m. 2d Jack H. Bell, May 10, 1986; edn: CSU Long Beach 1963; Orange Coast Jr. Coll. 1968; Palomar Jr. Coll. 1971; Cuesta Jr. Coll. 1977; pre-std. cert., other courses, Am. Inst. Banking 1956-68. Career: direct sales Watkins Prods. Warren, Ohio 1940; owner, oper. refreshment concession Lake Milton, Ohio 1941; real estate sales Gordon Ball, Warren, Ohio 1952-53; sampler Trumbull Co.- Coca Cola Co. Warren, Ohio 1953-54; teller, escrow ofcr. Bank of Am., var. So. Calif. branches 1956-68; automobile sales Sam Priestly Lincoln Mercury Dealership Oceanside 1968; escrow ofcr. Escondido Nat. Bank Poway 1969-71, US Nat. Bank LaVerne 1972-74, (first br. mgr.) Marina Fed. Savings & Loan Avalon 1974-76, Crocker Nat. Bank Paso Robles 1976-78, Indian Wells 1978-80 (opened 5 new escrow ofcs. for above banks); owner, publr. Marcella Press Palm Desert 1980–; correspondent writer Daily News, Palm Desert Post, contbr. Carlsbad Journal 1980–; auto leasing rep. Golden Bear Leasing Del Mar 1982–; lic. life ins. sales rep.; honors: Eistedford Contest Winner (1939), Nat. Honor Soc., speech contest winner (Crocker Nat. Bank 1974); mem: Norwalk Bus. & Profl. Women's Club (treas. 1960), Chiche's, Bank of Am. Women's Speech Club, Desertair Toastmasters (charter mem., pres. 1979-82), No. County Toastmasters 1982-, Desert Beautiful (Palm Desert 1979-), Desert Four Repub. Women Federated (1st v.p. 1981-82), La Quinta Historical Soc. (founder, 1st pres. 1984-87); past mem: Bd. of Realtors, Calif. Escrow Assn., Avalon CofC, Quota Club (Paso Robles, corr. secty. 1978), Dateland Toastmistress Club (historian 1979); author: book of poetry Ryme and Thought; song: Color Fills the World; rec: golf, travel, sewing. Address: 2510 Regency Cir Fullerton 92633

BELL-BROWN, BRENDA JOYCE, airline executive; b. June 20, 1947, San Pedro, Calif.; d. Luther and Louise (Cullen) White; m. Jimmy Brown, Jan. 10, 1986; 1 son, Robert David Bell b. 1971; edn: AA, Los Angeles Harbor Coll. 1970; BA, CSU Los Angeles 1973. Career: reservations sales agent Am. Airlines L.A. 1974-76, customer svc. rep. 1976-78, instr./ qual. control analyst 1978-79, supv. reservation sales 1979–; Am. Airlines Western reservations ofc. coord. 1984 Olympics, Statue of Liberty Campaign 1984-; mgmt. rep. to Quality of Worklife Pgm. 1985-; devel. quality awareness workshop 1984-85; co-owner Jolo Baked Goods/ Gifts 1983–; honors: Svc. Award (AA 1975), Mother of the Year (Nettles Acad. 1981); mem: Am. Airlines Mgmt. Club 1978 (bd. of control 1979), Black Americans Political Assn. of Calif. 1982-83, Women's Support Group (chair), Black Women's Forum 1983, PTA Nettles Acad. (pres. 1982), Markham Med. Magnet 1982-83, King-Drew Med. Magnet 1983-84 (secty. 1983), Calif. Afro-Am. Museum L.A. (secty. 1983-); publ: poetry in Nat. Anthology of High School Students 1959; Democrat; Baptist; rec: writing poetry/ short stories, cooking. Ofc: American Airlines Los Angeles 90048

BELLAIRE, MARC, fine artist; b. July 30, 1925, Toledo, Ohio; s. Fredrick Francis and Edna Octavia (Bellaire) Fleischman; christened Donald Edmund Fleischman; edn: pvt. study w/ Ernest Spring (Am. water-colorist) 1940-43, w/ Alexander Zlatoff-Mirsky (painter, tchr., fmr. curator Hans Teichert Collection of NYC), Chgo. 1948-50; art stu. Wayne Univ., Detroit, 1946, Am. Acad. of Art, Chgo., 1947-48, Immaculate Heart Coll., Los Angeles Art Inst. Career: artist at large, paintings, sculpture, ceramics, 1940–; designer Libby Glass Co., LaSalle & Koch Co. (display), Toledo, O.; Textiles and Wallpapers, Chgo.; Sascha Brastoff Co., Santa Monica; estab. art studio, Bellaire, Inc, Culver City, Calif. 1950-56, turned bus. over to mgmt. in 1956; created num. wax and fiberglass sculptures w/Katherine Stubergh (now Mrs. Tom Keller of Hawaii), spl. effects for Hollywood films, Disneyland and Las Vegas showplaces during early 1950s; personal appearances at major dept. stores and lectr./tchr. design seminars throughout US and Canada on series of tours, art museums, univs., recreation depts. and pvt. ceramic studios, 1956-82; staff writer Ceramics Monthly Mag. (Profl. Publs., Columbus, O. 1956-), contbg. writer Popular Ceramics Mag., Los Angeles (1982-); author 5 books; num. One-man shows and group exhibs.; frequent judge nat. and internat. ceramic guilds; mem. Palm Springs Desert Mus., Desert Art Assn., Civic Arts Assn.; mil: Pharm. mate 3c US Navy, Victory rib., Asia Pac.; rec: sailing, cycling. Ofc: Marc Bellaire Studio 33-669 Date Palm Dr Cathedral City 92234

BELLIS, DAVID J., educator; b. May 1, 1944, Nashville, Tenn.; s. Carroll J. and Helen Louise (Jett) B.; m. Ann Seagreaves, Dec. 23, 1972; 1 son: James Carroll b. 1984; edn: BA, UC Los Angeles 1966; MA, Univ. So. Calif. 1969, Ph.D., 1977. Career: profl. musician 1959-65; asst. exec. housekeeper Hotel Sahara Las Vegas 1966-67; intake counselor Narcotics Prevention Proj., Los Angeles 1970-72; instr. Long Beach City Coll. 1970-78; dir. West End Drug Abuse Control Coord. Council 1972-75; cons. Project HEAVY L.A. 1975-78; dir. econ. planning East L.A. Community Union 1978-80; lectr. USC 1978-85; asst. dir. Youth Gang Svcs. L.A. 1981-82; lectr. CSU San Bernardino; city councilman Signal Hill, Calif. 1980–, mayor 1982-83; honors: Outstanding Lecturer (USC 1982); author: Heroin and Politicians (Greenwood Press 1981), Political Corruption as Organized Crime (Lexington Books 1984); Democrat; Jewish; rec: music, flying. Res: 2058 Terrace Dr Signal Hill 90806 Ofc: CSU San Bernardino 5500 University Pkwy San Bernardino

BELLOWS, R. G., SR., lawyer; b. Feb. 8, 1945, Middletown, Ohio; s. John Cecil and Geraldine B.; m. Kathleen Krug, July 26, 1963; children: Rick, Jr. b. 1964, Billie-Sue b. 1965, Wendy b. 1967, Heather b. 1975, Geraldine b. 1976, Joshua b. 1978, Amanda b. 1979; edn: AA, York Coll. of Penna. 1974; BS, Western State Univ. 1977, JD, 1980; admitted Calif. State Bar 1981. Career: design engr. in building constrn. industries 1963-69; advanced marine technology div. Litton Indus. 1970-75; v.p. engring. Frigitemp Marine 1976-80; atty. prin. Pitkin & Bellows, San Diego 1980–; recipient appreciation cert. as pres. of Lions Optometric Vision Clinic; mem. Assn. of Trial Lawyers of Am., Calif. Trial Lawyers Assn., Fellow Acad. of Malt Scotch Whisky, Lions Club (host S.D.); founder Lions Deaf Recreation Ctr. of San Diego; Republican; Latter Day Saints; rec: model railroading. Ofc: Pitkin & Bellows 110 West C St Ste 1014 San Diego 92101

BELZ, BOB, lawyer; b. Mar. 6, 1936, Chgo.; s. Frank Lyle and Cleo Clara (Swisher) Belz; m. Mary Orr, Aug. 20, 1960; chil: Tanya L., b. 1962, Carey L., b. 1965; edn: AA, Lamar Jr.Coll. 1960, BA, Univ. Okla. 1963, JD, Humphrey's Sch of Law, 1972. Career: district scout exec. BSA, 1963-67; claims rep. Farmers Ins. Gp. 1968-73; pvt. practice law, 1973–; bd.dirs. Auto Club of Am. 1975-; judge pro tem, Manteca Ct. 1980; mem. San Joaquin Co. Adv. Bd. on Alcohol Problems 1981-; listed: Who's Who In Am. Law, Internat. Men of Distinction, Men of Achievement, Internat. Who's Who of Contemporary Achievement; awarded Atty of Experience in Dissolution, Trial, Personal Injury by Calif. Trial Lawyers Assn.; mem: Rotary Club (dir. Internat. Svc 1963-5), Toastmasters Club 1963-5, 1971-3, Nu Beta Epsilon law frat. 1971-; Calif. Trial Lawyers Assn. (chpt pres. 1975) 1968-; Am. Bar Assn. 1973-; mil: sgt. USMC 1955-59; Republican; Catholic; rec: runner 1980- (Quicksilver Running Club pres. 1983-4), ski, golf. Res: 455 Curtwood Ct. Manteca 95336 Ofc: Bob Belz, Inc. APLC, Stockton 95202

BELZ, HELENE FULTON, psychologist, educator, administrator; b. Nov. 15, 1916, Melones, Calif.; d. John Allen and Anita (Bertheau) Fulton; m. John Francis Belz MD, Mar. 9, 1940; children: Virginia b. 1942, Caroline b. 1944, Katherine b. 1945; edn: BS, Univ. Nev. Reno 1938; RN, Stanford Univ. 1939, MA guidance, 1963, PhD ed. psychol., 1972. Career: senior op. rm. nurse Stanford Univ. Hosp. 1940-42; asst. husband, rural pediatrician cons. Oregon State Bd. Health 1942-44; exec. secty. Citizen's Sch. Survey Com. Yuba City 1945-59; homemaker, community svc., planning commn. 1950-59; research asst. clin. psychol. and vocational rehab. Stanford 1960-62; coord. gifted pgms. East Side Union H.S. Dist. 1962–, dist. psychol. 1966–, adminstr. psychol. svcs. 1972–; presentations to profl. groups; adj. research on learning and devel. of adolescents, assessment of handicapped youths; honors: Pi Lambda Theta; mem: AERA, NorCal Gifted Assn., CASP, Pi Beta Pi, Stanford Alumni; former mem: Earthwatch, Red Cross, Audubon Soc., Sierra Club, Stanford Med. Wives & Mothers Club, PTA; publ: article in AERA jour. 1984; Episcopal; rec: travel, grandchildren, archeology, birds, outdoors, home & garden. Ofc: East Side Union H.S. District 830 N Capitol Ave San Jose 95133

BENDER, BILL, western artist; b. Jan. 5, 1920, El Segundo; s. Joseph Edward and Pauline (Beck) Bender; m. Helen, Dec. 22, 1957; grad. El Segundo H.S. 1937. Career: broke and sold broncos, 1932-37; rode and worked on location in western movies, 1936-37; cowboyed, 1938- until stopped by injury; began painting scenes from own life; profl. western artist 1950s–; painted for US Air Force in S.E. Asia, and the Cadet Tng. pgm for USN in Pensacola, Fla.; currently: gallery painting; illustrator books, greeting cards, prints and calendars for Leanin' Tree Pub. Co., Boulder, Colo.; honors: hon. lifetime dir. Death Valley 49ers, hon. life mem. Mountain Oyster Club (Tucson), hon. life mem. Living Desert Assn. (Palm Desert), hon. Tailhook Airedale, USS Lexington; mem: Fellow Am. Inst. of Fine Arts (L.A.), Fellow Am. Artists Profl. League (NY), life mem. Cowboy Hall of Fame (Okla.City), mem. The Westerners (L.A.), The Westerners (S.D.), advis. bd. San Dimas Festival of Western Arts; Republican; Prot.; avocation: writing. Address: Star Rte. Box 154, Oro Grande 92368

BENDER, DWAIN FRANK, insurance co. sales executive; b. July 23, 1941, Dishman, Wash.; s. Frank Walter and Dorris (Dunham) B.; m. Victoria Hill, July 3, 1963; children: Bradley b. 1964, Wesley b. 1970; edn: BS, Northrop Inst. of Tech. 1970. Career: fire pprotection engr. Factory Mutual Engring. Assn., Los Angeles 1970-74, senior adjustor 1974-79; acct. exec. Allendale Mutual Ins., 1979-82, dist. sales mgr. (Orange) 1982-85, reg. v.p./mgr. comml. prop. ops., 1985–; awards: Northrop Inst. of Tech. pres.'s undergrad. award (1970), Allendale Mutual Ins. outstanding sales achieve. (1980); past mem. Nat. Fire Prevention Assn., So. Calif. Soc. of Fire Protection Engrs.; civic: Burbank Red Cross (past dir.), mem. Burbank Public Service Dept. Advis. Bd. (1986); mil: s/sgt. Washington Air Nat. Guard 1965; Republican; Prot.; rec: hist., outdoors. Res: Burbank Ofc: Allendale Mutual Insurance Co 6301 Owensmouth Ave Ste 200 Woodland Hills 91367

BENDICK, WALTER HARRY, health care administrator; b. Nov. 11, 1947, Cleveland, Oh.; s. Walter Herman and Delilah Evelyn (Rhodes) Bendick; edn: RN, US Army, 1976; BS, Chapman Coll., 1984; 1 son, Robert, b. 1970. Career: nursing supr., Johnson & Johnson, Los Angeles 1975-78; Pheresis Unit supr., West Hills Med. Center, Canoga Park 1979-81; branch office dir. National In-Home Health Svcs., Los Angeles 1981-85; qual. assurance dir. Nat. Med. Homecare L.A. 1985–; mem: C.A.H.S.A.H. (co. mem.) 1981-, Veterans Care L.A. (v.p.); mil: E5, US Army 1968-73, decorated Vietnam. rec: travel, theater. Res: 14838 Lassen St. Mission Hills 91345 Ofc: Nat. Med. Homecare 10780 Santa Monica Blvd Ste 330 Los Angeles 90048

BENDISZ, KAZIMIERZ, mechanical engineer; b. Feb. 11, 1914, Warsaw, Poland, nat. US cit. 1973; s. Ryszard and Janina (Orlowska) B.; m. Maria Tomczak, April 16, 1950, div. 1961; children: Anna b. 1951, Zofia b. 1953; edn: 2nd lt. Military Coll. of Artillery, Torun, Poland 1933-35; BS, Univ. of Warsaw, Poland 1939; MS, Univ. of Munich, Ger. 1947; Profl. Mech. Engr., Calif. 1970. Career: supvr. Power Press Design Ofc., Warsaw 1948-53; cons. engr., Warsaw 1954-63; senior asst. Machine Design Dept., Univ. Warsaw 1963-65; research engr. Inst. for Chem. Engring., Stuttgart, W.Ger. 1965-68; design engr. Anchor Valve Co., Hayward 1968-69; design engr. Pacific Gas & Electric Co., San Francisco 1970-79; mech. engr., author 1980–; instr. machine design, mechanisms Heald Engring. Coll., San Francisco 1970-79; mem: Am. Soc. of Mech. Engrs., Mechanics Inst. of San Francisco; author: article, Separation of Liquids of Low Viscosity from Substances of High Viscosity, Polish, Przemysl chemiczny, 1953; book, Pipe Loops and Bends, Design for Flexibility Tables, 1984; research, rotary shaft seals, Inst. for Chem. Engring., Stuttgart, W.Ger. 1965-68; mil: 1st lt. Polish Army Artillery 1933-39; rec: chess. Address: 390 Clementina #605 San Francisco 94103

BENECH, GRANT FRANCIS, real estate co. executive; b. Aug. 21, 1957, San Jose; s. Wallace Edmond and Flora Mae (Infante) B.; edn: AA, Modesto Jr. Coll. 1977; BS, UC Berkeley 1979, MBA (cum laude), 1981; Calif. lic. R.E. Broker (1984). Career: chief finl. ofcr., treas., secty. California Capital Exports, Inc., Oakland 1981-84; splst./cons. Bank of Am. Mortgage Banking, Menlo Park 1984-85; pres. Realequity Assocs., Inc., Oakland 1985–; mem. Calif. Assn. of Residential Lenders, World Trade Assn., Commonwealth Club of Calif.; publs: An Analysis of Alternative Mortgage Instruments (BofA 3/81); Republican; Catholic; rec: sports car/racing enthusiast, tennis. Res: 2521 Regent St, 8, Berkeley 94704

BENGE, ALICE JEAN, private investigator; b. Set. 21, 1948, San Bernardino; d. George W. and Elva M. Davis; m. Charles L., Sept. 20, 1968; children: David Alan b. 1969, Jason William b. 1971. Career: matron San Bernardino Co. Sheriffs Dept. 1972-78; deputy San Bernardino Co. Marshals Ofc. 1978-80; founder, pvt. investigator, corp. pres. A.B.I. Attorney Svc., Redlands 1980–; Democrat; Protestant; Res: 1762 E. Citrus Redlands 92373 Ofc: A.B.I. Attorney Service, 511 Brookside Redlands 92373

BENJAMIN, ALFRED, photographer; b. Aug. 14, 1916, Hamburg, Germany, nat. US cit. 1954; s. Martin Edmund and Roberta (Goldtree) B.; m. Selma, Mar. 19, 1940; children: Roberta b. 1944, Wendy b. 1946; edn: photog., Reimann Sch. & Studios London 1938, sci. photog., 1939; adult edn. tchg. credl. Calif. 1959; Reg. Biological Photog. 1964. Career: photog. Henry Hirsch Cancer Inst. Hamburg, Germany 1934-36; chief med. photog. Queen Mary's Hosp. Roehampton nr. London, Eng. 1943-48; freelance med. & sci. photog. Los Angeles 1948-55; med. photog. Rancho Los Amigos Hosp. Downey 1955-61; dir. audio-visual dept. Orthopaedic Hosp. L.A. 1961-85, senior research photog. 1985–; photog. tchr. Hollywood Community Adult Sch. L.A. 1959–; assoc. Royal Photog. Soc. (Eng.) 1939–; fellow Biological Photog. Assn. 1980- (chpt. pres. 1965, v.p. 1964, 1966-69); mem: Soc. photographic Scientists and Engrs., Nat. Photog. Instrs. Assn., Am. Thermographic Soc.; works: devel. techniques for assisting medical diagnosis by means of photography utilizing infrared, thermography and electrophoretic photography; publs: num. tech. articles in med. and profl. jours.; Democrat; Jewish; rec: painting, acting, counseling. Res: 1213 Pacific St Santa Monica 90405 Ofc: Orthopaedic Hosp. 2400 S Flower St Los Angeles 90007

BENKE, PATRICIA DARLENE, judge; b. Apr. 15, 1949, New Castle, Pa.; d. Joseph Elias and Bess (Namey) Jacobs; m. Donald Benke, June 26, 1971; children: Michael, b. 1982, Peter, b. 1983; edn: AA, Pasadena Jr. Coll. 1969; BA, CSU San Diego, highest honors, 1971; JD, Univ. of S.D. Sch. of Law 1974. Career: law clk. two San Diego law firms: Gray, Cary, Ames & Frye and Holt, Rhoades and Hollywood, 1973-74; deputy atty. gen., criminal div., Calif. State Atty. Gen., 1974-83; gov. apptd. judge San Diego Municipal Ct., 1983-85, judge Superior Court, 1985–; Atty. Gen.'s rep. State Conf. on the Judiciary, Task Force on Probation and Parole (1977), to Dist. Attys. Regional Cons. (1978, 80); honors: Phi Kappa Phi, Mortar Board (1971), recognition awards, Nat. Awards Pgm. (1978), San Diego Career Womens Assn. (1983); mem: Assn. of Calif. Deputies Atty. Gen. 1975-83 (State Pres. 1978, S.D. Chpt. Pres. 1977); first chpsn. Women in Public Law, S.D. 1980; Calif. Bar Assn. 1974-83, S.D. County Bar Assn. 1974-83 (first chpsn. Appellate Com. 1980), Lawyers Club of S.D. (bd. dirs. 1980-82), Calif. Women Lawyers 1980-83; past vol. for KPBS-TV (pub. tv); past mem. S.D. Co. Child Abuse Coord. Council, Mission Trails Rev. Bd., S.D. Park and Recreation Bd. (1979-83); publs: co-compiled Peace Officer's Penal Code (1978, Bancroft-Whitney); contbr. law jours., newspaper editorial pages; rec: writing. Res: 4703 Constance Dr San Diego 92115 Ofc: S.D. Superior Ct. 220 W. Broadway, San Diego 92101

BENNETT, ARTHUR DAVID, insurance agent; b. Feb. 15, 1939, Inwood Park, Long Island, NY; s. Yezekiel and Leona Mildred (Muzzillo) B.; m. Melanie Hinton, Apr. 8, 1967; 1 son: Brian, b. 1970. Career: sales rep. Mutual of Omaha Ins. Co. 1976-80; sales rep. Sentry Ins. Co. 1980-83; employer services rep. Calif. Human Devel. Corp. 1983-84; agent Allstate Ins Co. 1984–; bd. dirs. USS Arizona Meml. Mus. Found. 1972-74; chmn. Hawaii St. Veterans Day Com. 1973; awards: Shore Sailor of the Yr., US Naval Communications Station, Wahiawa, Hawaii 1973; Pres.'s Club, Mutual Omaha 1978; mem: Fleet Reserve Assn. (pres. Kenitra, Morocco Br. 189, 1969; pres. Pearl Harbor, Hawaii Br. 46, 1972-74; v.p. Northwest Reg. 1974-75); Am. Legion (fin. ofcr. Wahiawa, Hawaii Post 22, 1973, 74); B.P.O. Elks; mil: E7, USN 1956-76; GCM (5); Nat. Defense Medal; Navy Unit Commdn.; Meritorious Unit Commdn.; Naval Security Gp. Merit. Svc. Awd.; Republican; Lutheran; rec: bowling, photog. Res: 617 Crane Dr Suisun City 94585 Ofc: Allstate Ins. Co. 1549 Gateway Blvd Fairfield 94585

BENNETT, BILL CHARLES, company executive; b. Aug. 2, 1934, Dardanelle, Ark.; s. Charley and Velma Irene (Jones) B.; m. Wilma Henley, Dec. 20, 1954; children: Deborah, b. 1956; Rodney, b. 1959; Jerry, b. 1962; Calif. Cert. Pest Control Advisor/Opr. Career: with Wilbur Ellis Co., 1958–, currently mgr. San Joaquin Branch; worked with his sons and father to engr. & build world's first multi-row 30-inch cotton picker; Democrat; Protestant. Res: 25317 Scaggs Street Tranquillity 93668 Ofc: Wilbur Ellis Co., El Dorado & Colorado Ave San Joaquin 93660

BENNETT, GUY RUSSEL, accountant; b. Jan. 31, 1952, Bellingham, Wash.; s. Ralph D. and Peggy L. (Straus) B.; m. Catherine Galvin, Jan. 9, 1982; children: Ashley b. 1982, Lauren b. 1984; edn: BA, Western State Coll. of Colo. 1977; Certified Public Acct., Calif. Career: jr. acct. Rudnick & Abbot, Gunnison, Colo. 1976-78; controller Ptarmigan Mountain Properties 1978-79; senior acct./mgr. Bundsen & Wallace, Los Altos 1980-82; prin. ptnr. Guy R. Bennett, CPA, Redwood City 1982-84; pres., mng. ptnr. Bennett & Collins Acctncy. Corp., Redwood City 1984–; dir. Geographics Corp.; apptd. Port Commnr., Port of Redwood City (1985-); mem: Am. Inst. of CPAs, Calif. Soc. of CPAs; civic: Redwood City- San Mateo County CofC (bd. dirs.), Redwood Shores Rotary Club (treas.), Churchill Club; Republican; rec: skiing, stamps & coins. Ofc: Bennett & Collins, 483 Seaport Ct Ste 102 Redwood City 94063

BENNETT, JAMES PETER, lawyer; b. Oct. 4, 1954, Urbana, Ill.; s. Walter Alonzo and Eleanor (Ander) B.; m. Lindsay Morse, Nov. 28, 1981; 1 dau. Brynn, b. 1985; edn: BA, Univ. Ariz. 1976; JD, Peppedine Univ. 1979; Dip. in Internat. Law, Univ. Salzburg/ McGeorge Univ., 1984; admitted Calif. State Bar 1979, US Supreme Ct. Bar. Career: atty. Travelers Ins. Co., Los Angeles 1980-82; atty. Union Oil Co. of Calif. 1982-84; vice pres., gen. counsel, mem. bd. dirs., Petrocal Energy Corp., San Marino 1985–; honors: Phi Eta Sigma (scholastic hon.); mem. Am., Calif. bar assns., Phi Gamma Delta (pres. Upsilon Alpha chpt. 1976); rec: sports, literature. Ofc: Petrocal Energy Corp. 2485 Huntington Dr, Ste 5, San Marino 91108

BENNETT, JOAN CAROL, government lawyer; b. Oct. 6, 1949, Los Angeles; d. Marvin Thomas and Gloria Natalie (Rinaldi) Bennett; div.; 1 dau. Anne Bernal b. 1976; edn: BA (Fulbright Scholar), Ripon Coll. 1971, grad. wk. Univ. de Toulouse, France 1972; JD, Univ. of La Verne 1977; admitted Calif. State Bar. Career: trial atty.; Felony Trial Team, Contra Costa County Dist. Atty. Office, 1981-83; civil and criminal defense cases, law firm Gorelick and Gorelick, 1983; asst. dist. atty. supvr. Municipal Ct. Dept. and felony Preliminary Hearing Dept., San Francisco Dist. Atty. Office, 1984–; guest prof. Golden Gate Univ. 1983-85; mem. Hayward Unified Sch. Dist. PTA; mil: sgt. US Army 1975-81, commnd. lt. USNR 1981-; cargo expert, decorated rifle expert, Army Letter of Appreciation, Navy Letter of Commendation; Democrat; Ch. of Rel. Sci. (bd. dirs. Contra Costa); rec: piano, horticulture. Ofc: S.F. District Atty. 880 Bryant St San Francisco 94103

BENNETT, MARGARET PATER, artist; b. Jan. 27, 1939, Hackensack, N.J.; d. John and Helen Cay (Voorhees) Pater; edn: grad. Mary A. Burnham Prep. Sch., Mass. 1957; grad. Inst. de Phonetique, Paris, France 1960, and art stu. Sorbonne, Acad. Julian, 1959-60; BS in design, tchg. cert., Univ. of Mich. 1962. Career: tchg. fellow Sch. Arch. & Design Univ. Mich. 1961; secty. So. Regl. Council, Atlanta, Ga. 1962-63; art tchr. in elem. and secondary schs., 1964-68; supvsg. tchr. Sch. of Edn., Univ. Mich. 1964-66, adminstr. arts pgm. 1966-68; dir. The Print Shop (graphic arts gallery), Ann Arbor, Mich. 1968-70; tchr. Sch. of Holography, San Francisco 1970-71; alternative edn. tchr./counselor (live in exptl. pgm.) Orinda Pub. Schs., 1972-74; indep. artist showing in theme event regl. and nat. art festivals, contbg. artist num. galleries and catalogs, and prop. small wholesale gift bus., 1974–; adminstr. devel. & rental of comml. property S.F. 1978-80; commemorative designer Mercedes-Benz Centennial 1986; honors: outstanding tchr., Ann Arbor (1966), design awards: Gift and Decorative Accessories Mag. (1979), Harvest Fest. (1983), Am. Fest. of Arts, Crafts & Music, Amsterdam, Holland (1985), Culinary Arts 1984, Del Mano Gal., Los Angeles (1985); mem. Am. Assn. of Tchrs. 1964-68, Ann Arbor Art Guild 1969-71, San Pablo Potter's Studio Guild 1972, Berkeley Arts 1973-85, Marin Exhib. Guild 1986-, S.F. Street Artists 1975-77, Nat. Assn. of Unknown Players 1986; civic: Nat. Wildlife Fedn., Sierra Club, Defenders of Wildlife, Humane Soc., Wilderness Soc., Nat. Heart Assn., Salesian, Brotherhood for the Blind; works: mag. cover "On Holography" (1971), contbg. artist to "Space Atlas" (1972), created original table service of multiple pieces on 16th century hist. theme (1974-86); Presbyterian; rec: gardening, writing, music (clarinet, guitar). Studio: 5607 Sobrante Ave El Sobrante 94803

BENNINGHOVEN, HAZEL F., civic worker; b. June 10, 1904, San Jose; d. Rev. James and Emma (Stephens) Falconer; granddau. of L.D. Stephens (Calif. Gold Rush 49er, and author memoirs: Life Sketches of a Jayhawker of 49); m. Benninghoven, Aug. 8, 1927; children: Jim b. 1929, Don b. 1931, Ann b. 1939; edn: AB, UC Berkeley 1925, Grad. Sch. of Social Work 1926, Secondary Tchr. credential, UCB 1926. Career: head Dependent Children's Dept., Associated Charities of San Francisco and tchr. night school Oakland High Sch. (while husband completed med. sch.); volunteer wkr. in social services ever since: served as mem. (pres. approx. 2 dozen bds.) 42 bds. of dirs. (nat., state, San Mateo County, and Bay Area boards) incl. first woman to be named chair of allocations United Way of the Bay Area (w/ 250 vols. and $24 million to allocate to 240 agencies); currently mem. six boards; mem. (chmn. 10 yrs.) Koshland awards com. (com. selects the most outstanding adminstr. and the most outstanding social worker in state for cash awards); honors: award for involvement in humanitarian causes, The Peninsula Community Found.; current mem: Phi Mu Frat. (nat. pres), AAUW (pres. San Mateo County), Am. Med. Assn. Medical Aux. (Western rep.), pres. San Mateo Co. chpt.), Family Service Agency (bd. pres.), Assistance League of San Mateo Co. (a founder), United Way of the Bay Area (Social Plng. Council); Republican; Congregational. Res. 125 Robin Rd Hillsborough 94010

BENNION, ADAM SCOTT, oral and maxillofacial surgeon; b. June 15, 1948, Salt Lake City, Utah; s. Richard Young and Lucile (Jensen) B.; m. Jeanne Bridwell, Aug. 31, 1971; 1 dau., Julia Sharp b. 1982; edn: BS, Univ. of Utah 1970; DDS, Univ. of Pacific 1974; MD, Vanderbilt Univ. 1981; Diplomate Nat. Bd. of Med. Exams. 1982, Am. Bd. of Oral & Maxillofacial Surgery 1982. Career: oral surgery resident (3-yr.) Vanderbilt Univ., chief res. in oral surgery Harvard Sch. of Dental Med., gen. surgery res. (2-yr) Mass. Gen. Hosp.; instr. in oral & maxillofacial surgery in both Harvard Medical Sch. and Harvard Sch. of Dental Medicine, 1981-82; pvt. practice oral & maxillofacial surgery in Thousand Oaks, Calif. and Simi Valley, Calif., 1983—; instr. (dental asstg.) Simi Valley Adult Sch.; chief Westlake Comm. Hosp. Dental Dept.; named Most Promising Oral Surgeon, Class of 1974 Univ. of Pacific Dental Sch.; mem. Am. Dental Assn., AMA, Am. Assn. of Oral & Maxillofacial Surgeons, Nat. Dental Council (bd. dirs.), Calif. Dental Assn., So. Calif. Soc. of Oral & Maxillofacial Surgeons, Assn. of Western Oral & Maxillofacial Surgeons, Santa Barbara/Ventura County Dental Soc., Conejo Valley Dental Study Club, Simi Valley Dental Study Club (v.p.); works: artist, opaque watercolors and pastels, exhib. two one-man shows, Mass. Gen. Hosp. (1981, 82); mil: sgt. Air Nat. Guard 1967-73; Independent; Theist; rec: art, tennis. Res: 4231 Beaucroft Ct Westlake Village 91361 Ofcs: 1987 Royal Ave Simi Valley 93065; 179 Auburn Ct Thousand Oaks 91363

BENSON, DOUGLAS ARTHUR, airline computer analyst; b. March 4, 1956, Hillsboro, Ore.; s. Roy Arthur and Betty Ione (Hirschy) B.; edn: BS, Univ. of Oregon 1979; Cert. Data Processing, Inst. for Cert. of Computer Profls. 1985. Career: pgmmr., analyst Genasys Corp., Rockville, Md. 1979-81; pgmmr., analyst Airline Tariff Publishing Co., Dulles Internat. Airport, Wash. DC 1981-82; pgmmr., analyst Nat. Automobile Dealers Assn., McLean, Va. 1982-84; computer splst. Western Airlines Mktg. Applications, Los Angeles 1984—; mem. Sigma Nu.; Democrat; Methodist; rec: ski, travel. Res: 207 Kelp St. Manhattan Beach 90266 Ofc: Western Airlines, 6171 West Century Blvd. Los Angeles 90045

BENSON, JAMES BERNARD, JR., clinical hypnotherapist; b. May 8, 1930, Phila.; s. James B., Sr. and Elizabeth Sloan (Smeaton) B.; m. Hiroko, Apr. 14, 1955; edn: BA, police sci., Pacific Coll. 1976; Certified Clin. Hypnotherapist, Psycho-Neurol. Found. (1985). Career: chief criminal investigator US Marine Corps, 1947-66; corporate ofcr. Bank of America, So. Calif. 1966-85, ret.; clinical hypnotherapist in pvt. practice, Anaheim 1985—; honors: hon. LLD, Nat. Law Enforcement Acad. (1968), hon. D.D., Ch. of the Gospel Ministry (1975), num. military and law enforcement awards (1947-66); mem: Am. Assn. of Profl. Hypnotherapists, Am. Hypnotherapy Assn., Assn. for Past Life Research and Therapy, Am. Counselors Soc., The Nat. Soc. of Hypnotherapists, Orange County Mental Health Assn.; author 2 books of poetry: Devotion in Blue, Lawmans Lament; mil: s/sgt. USMC 1947-66; Republican; Prot.; rec: photog. Res: 1400 S Sunkist St #199 92806 Ofc: James Benson R.H. 935 S Gilbert Ste 13 Anaheim 92804

BENSON, LENNARD BERT, childrens services worker III; b. Mar. 12, 1954, Seattle, Wash.; s. Lennard Bert (dec.) and Bernice F. (Ferm) B.; m. Monika B., Aug. 2, 1981; 1 son: David, b. 1983; edn: AA, Valley Coll. 1975; BA, CSU Northridge 1976; MA, Pepperdine Univ. 1980; PhD cand., Calif. Grad. Inst. 1981-; Calif. Comm. Counselor Credential, Instr. Cred. Psych., Comm. Coll. Student Personnel Wkr. 1980. Career: mental health unit asst. Olive View Health Ctr., Los Angeles 1975; counselor ex-offender college students, Northridge 1976; pres. Drannel Game Co., L.A. 1977-80; substitute tchr. L.A. Co. Schs. 1978-81; GS1, County Probation Dept., L.A. 1976-77; deputy probation ofcr., Los Angeles 1977-80; CSW III, L.A. Co. Dept. of Children's Svcs. 1980—; Calif. Inst. Juvenile Recreation Research, L.A. dir. 1977-80; mem: Calif. Assn. of Marriage & Family Therapists; works: Probation Simulation board game 1977; Democrat; rec: boating. Res: 13770 Terra Bella St Arleta 91331 Ofc: L.A. County Dept. of Children's Svcs., 5026 Santa Monica Blvd Los Angeles 90029

BENZ, RONALD THOMAS, otolaryngologist; b. April 17, 1942, Milwaukee, Wisc.; s. Herman S. and Beatrice M. (Quinn) B.; m. Rita Kautza, Nov. 27, 1971; children: Michael, b. 1976, Jennifer, b. 1978, Nicholas, b. 1980; edn: BS, Carroll Coll. 1964; MD, Marquette 1968. Career: intern LAC/ USC Med. Ctr. 1968-69, res. otolaryngology 1971-75; otolaryngologist pvt. practice 1976—; asst. clin. prof. surgery UC San Diego Med. Sch.; pres. elec. San Diego Acad. Otolaryngology; chief of staff, Coronado Hosp. 1983; v.chief otolaryngology Childrens & Mercy Hosp.; mem: AMA, CMA, San Diego Med. Soc., Fellow Am. Acad. Otolaryngology, Head & Neck Soc., Cottilian Club; mil: lt. USNR (MC) 1969-71; Catholic; rec: sports, travel. Ofc: 2001 4th Ave., San Diego 92101

BERA, JOHN EMIL, artist, designer, craftsman; b. Mar. 30, 1928, Chgo.; s. John Stanley and Helen (Wiszowaty) B.; m. Madeleine Laisne, Sept. 26, 1960; children: Nathalie b. 1965, Stephan b. 1970; edn: Chgo. Acad. Fine Art 1949-52, Am. Acad. Art/Chgo. 1952-56, stu. art hist. Chgo. Art Inst., stu. drafting Ill. Inst. of Tech.; stu. w/ Louis Grell, church muralist, Chgo., evenings 10 yrs. Career: artist/designer Karl Hackert Studios, Chgo. 1956-58, Michaudel Studio of Stained Glass 1959, Drehobl Bros. Art Glass Studio 1960-61; artist designer of stained glass, self-empl. 1961—; 1 year study tour of Europe, Scandinavia, Brit. Isles vis. cathedrals, museums, stained glass studios and glass factories; instr. stained glass, Oakton (Ill.) Comm. Coll., 5 yrs.; awards: Apprentice Artist Competition, Stained Glass Assn. Am. (1957), relig. art award Holy Name Cathedral, Chgo.; mem: Stained Glass Assn. Am. (bd. dirs., accredited tchr./mem. edn. com. involved with testing candidates for tchg. stained glass), Stained Glass Guild of North Co./S.D. (pres. 1986), Rotary Internat. (designed and fabricated Stained Glass Window for internat. hdqtrs. in Evanston, Ill., window appeared on cover of Rotarian Internat. mag. 10/84); works: design and execution of stained, leaded & faceted Dalle glass windows for approx. 100 churches in USA, also num. pvt. commns.; num. publs. in stained glass trade jours.; mil: s/sgt./air traffic controller US Air Force 1946-49; Catholic; rec: photog., watercolor and oil painting, figure drawing, travel. Res: 17877 Corazon Pl San Diego 92127 Ofc: John Bera Studios 774 N Twin Oaks Valley Rd San Marcos 92069

BERETZ, PAUL B., manufacturing co. financial executive; b. Oc.t 15, 1938, Wash. DC; s. O. Paul and Marthe E. (Szabo) B.; m. Jane M., Nov. 9, 1963; children: Charles b. 1965, Melissa b. 1966, John Paul b. 1968, Michele b. 1971, Claudine b. 1973; edn: BBA, Univ. of Notre Dame 1960; MBA, Golden Gate Univ. 1974. Career: mgr. central credit Union Carbide Corp. 1961-81; gen. mgr. Bayox/ Almac Inc., Oakland 1981-83; dir. of credit Crown Zellerbach Corp., San Francisco 1983, asst. treas. 1983—; faculty Golden Gate Univ. Grad. Sch., San Francisco 78-79; faculty St. Mary's Coll. Bus. Sch., Moraga 1977-79; honors: Exec. Award, Stanford Univ. Grad. Sch. of Credit & Fin. Mgmt. 1972-74; mem: Credit Research Found. (bd. trustees, NYC 1984-), Nat. Assn. of Credit Mgmt. (v.p., No. and Central Calif. 1977-79), Nat. Alumni Assn. Univ. of Notre Dame (bd. dirs. 1983-86); author: Managing Commercial Credit, Am. Mgmt. Assn. 1982; sev. mag. articles on finance; mil: US Army 1961-64; Catholic; rec: tennis, jogging, gardening. Res: 21 Sara Ln. Walnut Creek 94595 Ofc: Crown Zellerbach Corp., One Bush St. San Francisco 94104

BERGAN, JOHN DEAN, real estate broker; b. July 23, 1942, Tucson, Ariz.; s. Irvan James and La Veta Noreen (Pierson) B.; m. La Vonne, April 22, 1961; childen: Lynda b. 1970, Crissy b. 1978; Calif. lic. Real Estate Broker (1983). Career: owner, dealer Western Auto Store, Vista 1968-72; ptnr., dealer European Motors, Pasadena 1972-73; real estate agt. Red Carpet Realtors, Westminster 1974-77, comml./indsl. real estate, American-Pacific Realty, Santa Ana 1978-83; corp. broker/pres./CEO U.S. Realty, Santa Ana 1983—, also corp. broker/v.p. U.S. Mortgage Corp. and Integrity Financial, 1985—; mil: sgt. US Army, Ger. 1961-64; Republican; Christian; rec: golf, jogging, swimming. Ofc: U.S. Realty, 1913 E. 17th St. Ste. 213 Santa Ana 92701

BERGEN, ROBERT LEE, lawyer; b. Dec. 1, 1925, Los Angeles; s. Walter Goza (dec. 1926) and Marjorie Marie Bergen; div.; children: Darcy, b. 1957, Dennis, b. 1962, Darla, b. 1963, David, b. 1966, Darrin, b. 1969, Damon, b. 1971; edn: BBA, Woodbury Coll. 1949; LLB, LaSalle Univ. 1957. Career: investigator Dun & Bradstreet, San Diego 1948-55; title examiner Union Title & Trust Co., S.D. 1955-57; chief deputy city atty. City of San Diego, 1958-65; trial atty. Mathews, Bergen, Potash & Grier, S.D. 1965—; secty., San Diego City Planning Commn., 1958-65. Honors: US National Bicycle Racing Champion 1982 (Trextertown, Pa.). Mem. State Bar of Calif. 1958-, S.D. County Bar Assn. 1958-, admitted to US Supreme Ct. 1971; mem: Am. Numismatic Assn., 20-30 International, BSA, Am. Youth Hostels (life), cert. ofcl. US Cycling Fedn. Publs: num. law arts. Mil: USN, WWII, participant invasion of Iwo Jima 2/19/45. Republican. rec: bicycle racing, collect Indian artifacts, coins, seashells. Res: 10050 Cristobal Dr. Spring Valley 92077. Ofc: Mathews, Bergen, Potash & Grier, 121 Broadway Ste. 652, San Diego 92101

BERGER, STEVEN BARRY, teacher; b. Dec. 29, 1946, NY, NY; s. Bernard I. and Sylvia B. (Reff) B.; edn: BS, MIT 1967, PhD, 1973. Career: tech. staff ITEK Corp., Optical Systems Div., Lexington, Mass. 1976-77; American Journ. of Physics, MIT, Cambridge, Mass. 1975-78; senior project engr. TRW Defense & Space Sys. Group, Wash. Ops., McLean, Va. 1978-80; research physicist Naval Research Laboratory, Wash. DC 1981-82; project mgr. Analytical Systems Engrng. Corp., Arlington, Va. 1982; sys. engr., scientist TRW Space & Technology Group, Redondo Beach 1983-85; mathematics faculty Chadwick Sch., Palos Verdes 1986—; honors: Nat. Defense Edn. Act Russian Language Fellow, 1965; Nat. Science Found. Grad. Fellowship, 1972; Post-doctoral Fellowship, Fight- For-Sight Inc. 1974; Sloan Found. Grad. Fellowship 1973; mem: Sigma Xi, Am. Physical Soc., IEEE, Toastmasters, Smithsonian Assoc., Sierra Club; publs: in archival profl. journs.; Jewish; rec: classical piano. Ofc: 19009 Laurel Park Rd. Ste. 174 Compton 90220-6037

BERGER-HAZZARD, CAROLYN EMMA, psychotherapist; b. Dec. 26, 1944, Springfield, Mass.; d. Henry R. and Olivine V. (Richards) Berger; m. Gary C. Hazzard, Sept. 17, 1983; edn: BA, psych., Univ. Mass. 1966; MA, marriage & family counseling, US Internat. Univ., San Diego 1979, PhD psychology, 1984. Reg. Psychological Asst., Calif. BMQA 1984. Career: elementary sch. counselor, 1977; vocational rehabilitation counselor VA Regl. Guidance Ctr., 1978-80; patient care vol. Hospice of the North Coast 1983-84; counselor in substance abuse outpatient clinic, San Diego 1984–; pvt. practice therapist p.t. 1985-; instr. p-t USIU Sch. of Bus. & Mgmt. 1978-84; computer cons. San Diego St. Univ. 1981-83; mem: Soc. of Psychologists in Addictive Behaviors, Calif. Womens Commn. on Alcoholism; Democrat; Self-Realization Fellowship; rec: dancing, health, exercise. Ofc: Pathways, 4312 Cass St San Diego 92109; 2775 Via De La Valle Ste 205 Del Mar 92014

BERGFALK, BETTY RUTH, school counselor; b. July 20, 1934, Los Angeles; d. Bruno and Clementine Emelia (Slawski) Nowacki; m. Vernon C. Bergfalk, May 1, 1983; children (nee Rush): Geoffrey Thomas b. 1957, Gary Troy b. 1961, Stephen L. b. 1965, Stephanie L. b. 1965; edn: BA, San Diego State Univ. 1959; MS, Univ. La Verne 1982; life credl. elem. edn. Calif. 1959; pupil personnel svcs. credl. Calif. 1981. Career: savings bookkeeper Chula Vista Bank of Am. 1952-53; asst. rec. dir. Chula Vista 1959; tchr. Poway Union Sch. Dist. 1959-60, Ector Sch. Dist. Odessa, Tex. 1960-61, Corona- Norco Unif. Sch. Dist. 1962-85; elem. sch. counselor Victor Schs. Victorville 1985–; parent effectiveness workshop leader 1986; resource person San Bernardino County Child Abuse Task Force 1986; adv. bd. CSU San Bernardino Rehab. Counseling Pgm. 1986; US Olympic volunteer (protocol, fencing) 1984; mem: Riverside Mother of Twins Club (1st v.p. 1969, treas. 1968), Parents Without Partners (chpt. v.p. edn. 1981-82), Christian Political Action Com. (founder, co-chmn. 1984-); publs: High School Anthology (prose & poetry 1952), research papers on counseling (1982, 85); Republican; Protestant; rec: sewing, gardening, singing, travel. Res: 771 S Sycamore Ave Rialto 92376 Ofc: Victor School District Spl. Svcs. 16821 A St Victorville 92392

BERGFALK, VERNON C., quality assurance executive; b. Nov. 27, 1936, St. Paul, Minn.; s. Carl A. and Lucille S. (Swanson) B.; m. Betty, May 1, 1983; children: Mark b. 1962, Connie b. 1964, Jodi b 1970, David b. 1975; edn: San Bernardino Valley Coll. 1979; New England Aeronautical Inst. 1973; Embry-Riddle Aeronautical Univ. 1975; Citrus Belt Law Sch. 1982. Career: quality assurance rep. Defense Contract Admin. 1977–; mem. fencing team, Summer Olympics 1984; chmn. Scholarship Com., SAMPE 1983; mem: Soc. for Adv. of Material & Processing Engring., Am. Soc. for Quality Control, Air Force Assn.; works: paper, The Effects of Quality on Marking 1983; mil: t/sgt. USAF 1954-75, Air Force Commdn., Vietnam Svc.; Republican; Protestant; rec: camping, fishing, photog. Ofc: DCAS- Management Area Office, 1800 Highland Duarte 91010

BERGIN, BONITA M., educator, association executive; b. Jan. 22, 1945, Port Angeles, Wash.; d. George A. and Elaine P. (Myhr) Bratsberg; m. James A. Bergin, Mar. 19, 1967; edn: BA, Sonoma St. Univ. 1970, MA 1980; doctoral cand. Nova Univ.; Calif. tchg. cred. (elementary, secondary, vocational, comm. coll.). Career: instr. Shepparton Girls High Sch., Shepparton, Victoria, Australia 1971-73; instr. Konya Maarif Kolleji, Konya, Turkey 1973-74; instr. Lewis Adult Edn. Ctr., Santa Rosa 1976-82; instr. Santa Rosa Junior Coll., Santa Rosa 1980–; founder/exec. dir. Canine Companions for Independence; conceived, pioneered and developed concept and methodology for tng. dogs to help people with physical disabilities other than blindness, dogs now placed throughout the USA, Canada, Israel and Holland; honors: Internat. Delta Soc.'s Model Program Award (1984), City of Santa Rosa Merit Award (1983); founder Friends of Refugees; founder Calif. Assn. of Substitute Tchrs.; mem. SSU Alumni Assn.; author Dynamic Relationships in Practice (Latham Found.); rec: horseback riding. Res: 4945 Grange Road Santa Rosa 95404 Ofc: CCI, 1215 Sebastopol Rd Santa Rosa 95407

BERGLAS, CHRISTIAN CHARLES, publisher; b. Apr. 3, 1955, Anderlecht, Belgium, US res. 1982; s. Braekman Pierre Louis and Suzanne Jeanne Coppens; edn: pol. sci., Univ. Libre de Bruxelles 1973-77. Career: with Dofina Internat., Brussels; gen. mgr. Coppens S.A., Brussells; ptnr. Private Collections Inc., Los Angeles; currently ptnr./pres. The Authentic Journal Inc.; mem. Am. Newspapers Collectors Soc.; served in Belgian Navy 1972-73; Catholic; rec: antique maps collector (splst. 17th C.). Res: 600 W 9th St Los Angeles 90015 Ofc: The Authentic Journal Inc 3120 Via Mondo Rancho Dominguez 90221

BERKES, LESLIE JOHN, consulting psychologist; b. Aug. 18, 1946, Simbach, Ger., nat. 1956; s. Leslie Michael and Maria Piroska (Villanyi) B.; m. Cheryl Kaye Stelter, Dec. 28, 1968; children: Adrienne b. 1976, Andrew b. 1978, Katy b. 1980; edn: BS, USC 1968; MS, Naval Postgrad. Sch. 1969; PhD, UC Irvine 1976; clin. psychology respecialization cert., Wright State Univ. 1982; lic. psychologist Calif. (1984), Ohio (1980). Career: mgmt. auditor US General Acctg. Ofc. 1972-74; research specialist, assoc. dir. Public Policy Research Orgn., UC Irvine 1974-76; asst. prof. organizational behavior Ohio State Univ. 1976-82; clin. assoc. prof. psychology Wright State Univ. 1982-83; cons. psychologist Management Health & Devel. Corp., Malibu 1983-85; pvt. practice psychology, Santa Monica 1984–; v.p. Netmap Internat. S.F.; adj. faculty UC Irvine Grad. Sch. of Mgmt. 1985; tchr. Monterey Inst. Foreign Studies 1969, San Diego State Univ. 1980; cons. Orange. Co. Bd. Supvrs. 1974, Univ. of Calif. 1976, Ohio No. Univ. 1978, Ohio Civil Svc. Employees Assn. 1977, Ohio Dept. Natural Resources 1979, Columubus Police Dept. 1979, Am. Chem. Soc. 1981, Bd. Coop. Ednl. Svcs., NY 1982, Wright State Univ. Sch. Profl. Psychology 1982; mem: Beta Gamma Sigma; Acad. of Mgmt. (spkr., reviewer, publs.), Am. Psychological Assn., Am. Inst. Decision Scis., Am. Soc. for Pub. Admin., Am. Civil Liberties Union, Com. on Police Support, Acad. of Mgmt., Am. Med. Joggers Assn., Internat. Assn. Applied Psychology, Soc. for Indsl. and Orgnl. Psychology, Soc. for Psychological Study of Social Issues; num. arts. in profl. journs.; mil: lt. USN 1968-72, USNR 1980-, Med. Svcs. Corps, Vietnam Svc.; Democrat; Catholic; rec: classical music, theater, carpentry. Res: 7513 Flight Ave. Los Angeles 90045 Ofc: Netmap Internat. San Francisco 94111

BERKLAND, JAMES OMER, government geologist; b. July 31, 1930, Glendale; s. Joseph Omer and Gertrude Madelyn (Thompson) B.; m. Janice Lark Keirstead, Dec. 19, 1966; children: Krista Lynn b. 1969, Jay Olin b. 1974; edn: AA, Santa Rosa Jr. Coll. 1951; AB, UC Berkeley 1958; MS, San Jose State Univ. 1964; PhD, cand., UC Davis 1972; Cert. Engring. Geologist, Calif. Career: physical sci. techn. US Geological Survey, Menlo Park 1958-64; engring. geologist US Bur. Reclamation, Sacto. 1964-69; cons. geologist, Davis 1969-72; asst. prof. of geology Appalachian State Univ., Boone, NC 1972-73; engring. geology instr. CSU San Jose 1974-75, adj. prof. of geology 1975-76; county geologist Santa Clara Co., San Jose 1973–; Geotechn. Advisory Com., San Jose 1973-75; West Valley Legis. Com. 1980-; Calf. Conv. Coordg. Com., AEG 1978; spkr. Deposit Receipt Annual Seminar, San Jose Bd. of Realtors 1979-85; Bay Area Reviewing Geologists 1981-; The Mining Lamp 1982-; honors; Dedicatee, Proceedings Vol. 2nd Annual Conf. Quaternary History of SE United States (1977), sole recipient, SABER Soc. Award (1979), plaque Stanford Univ. 1985; mem: Fellow Geological Soc. of Am. (Abstract Review Com. 1977-78), Peninsula Geological Soc. (treas. 1978-79), Assn. of Engring. Geologists (v.chmn. 1977-78), Seismol. Soc. of Am., Saber Soc. (co-founder 1973, pres. 1976-77), AAAS, Chaparral Poets, San Jose Hist. Museum Assoc., Sierra Club, EERI, King of Clubs Lions (charter, San Jose), Sons of Norway, Creekside-Park Place Homeowners Assn. (v.p. 1980-81), West Coast Aquatics (pub. rels. ofcr. 1980-85); publs: lead author, What is Franciscan?, AAPG Bulletin 1972; 50+ publs. in Science, Geological Soc. of Am. Bulletin, Calif. Geology, Internat. Geology Cong., Montreal 1972, Open Earth, others; originator, Seismic Window Theory for Earthquake prediction (1974), HF Separation of Radiolaria (1964); Democrat; Protestant; rec: earthquake history, seismic precursors, fish, jog. Res: 14927 E. Hills Dr. San Jose 95127 Ofc: Santa Clara County, 70 W. Hedding St. 7th Flr. San Jose 95110

BERKMAN, JACK MARTIN, marketing communications co. president; b. Oct. 13, 1946, San Francisco; s. Sidney Allen and Bella (Dworkin) B.; edn: BA, CSU Northridge 1969. Career: public relations staff General Motors, Detroit 1969-71; account supr. Herbert H. Rozoff Assocs., Public Relations Counsel, Chgo. 1971-73; nat. dir. of public rels./dir. of sales and mktg., American Housing Guild, San Diego 1973-75; v.p. and dir. of mktg. Rancho La Costa Properties, La Costa 1975-76; pres. Berkman & Daniels, San Diego 1976–; guest lectr. in pub. rels. var. univs., Pub. Rels. Soc. of Am. (PRSA) Seminar in PR practices 1981; awards: San Diego's most outstanding citizens, S.D. Jaycees (1980), merit cert. Senior Citizens Comm. Medical Clinic and the Leukemia Soc. of Am. Inc., profl. awards for excellence from S.D. Bldg. Contrs. Assn., Sales and Mktg. Council, the Bldg. Industry Assn. of So. Calif., S.D. Ad Club, S.D. Communicating Arts Group, 'SAM' awards for best brochure devel. and best PR campaign, Sales and Mktg. Council (1982), his firm voted first of the five top PR firms in San Diego, The Communicator Mag. (1982); mem: PRSA (1973-), S.D. Bldg. Contrs. Assn., Sales and Mktg. Council (exec. bd.), S.D. Press Club (1st v.p.), Nat. Assn. of Real Estate Editors, Soc. of Profl. Journalists, Sigma Delta Chi; civic: S.D. Repertory Theatre (bd.), San Diegans, Inc., Combined Arts and Edn. Council of S.D. (past chmn. PR com.), S.D. Symphony Assn., Anti-Defamation League of B'nai B'rith, Cancer Soc., Boys' Clubs, Nice Guys, Gas Lamp Quarter Dist. Assn.; pub. nat. newsletter BDI Report (semi-annually, 1980-), mem. advis. bd. S.D. Business Jour.; rec: golf, tennis, racquetball. Res: 2842 Dove St San Diego 92103 Ofc: Berkman & Daniels 1717 Kettner Blvd Ste 100 San Diego 92103

BERKSON, DEVAKI, chiropractor, author, lecturer; b. Dec. 24, 1948, Chicago; s. Abraham R. and Elynor Roz B.; edn: BA, Univ. Mich. 1969; MA, Goddard Coll. 1973; DC, Western States Chiro. Coll. 1979. Career: lectr. in field 1983–, for Context Inst. Stanford 1985; dir., founder Berkson Health Clinic Los Altos 1984–; cons. Sierra Vitamin Co. 1985; founder, instr. Nutri Guidance 1986; honors: Bottherman Most Disting. Service Award 1983, Most Disting. (Santa Clara Chiro. Soc. 1983); mem: Am., Calif. Chiro. Assns., Am. Internat. Med. Soc., Orthomolecular Med. Soc., Pottenger Orgn., Nat. Fedn. of Nutrition; author: Foot Book (1977), Body, Mind & Spirit (1981); rec: tennis, aerobics, poetry. Ofc: Berkson Clinic 4600 El Camino Real Ste 213 Los Altos 94022

BERLIN, JAN, clinical psychologist; b. Sept. 25, 1950, Wash. DC; s. Robert B. and Sarah (Miller) B.; m. Peggy Henning, July 22, 1978; children: Geoffrey Ross b. 1982, Lara Nicole b. 1985; edn: BA, Univ. of Maryland 1972; MA, UCLA 1974; PhD, UCLA 1980. Career: reg. psychological asst. Newton Ctr. for Clinical Hypnosis, Los Angeles 1978-81; co-founder PRISM Ctr., Pacific Palisades 1980-83; lic. clin. psychologist, Los Angeles 1981–, San Diego 1984–; dir. Inst. for Consciousness Research, Los Angeeles 1982; vis. faculty UCLA 1983-84; pres., founder MAXXIS Inc., Solana Beach 1983–; cons. fed. agencies, hosps. and pvt. corp.; motivational spkr.; performance enhancement splst.; honors: Phi Beta Kappa 1973; NIMH Fellow, 1972, 1973, 1975; Nat. Student Register 1972, 1973; mem: Am. Psychological Assn., Assn. of Humanistic Psychology, Internat. Imagery Assn., Encinitas CofC; publs: Embrace the Challenge, The Premature Labor Handbook, (Robertson & Berlin; Doubleday

1986); founder, Stress Utilization concept. 1985; Meeting the Challenge of Excellence, 1985; num. articles and presentations on the use of visualization techniques for performance enhancement and psychotherapeutic growth; rec: t'ai chi, swim, meditation, aerobic dance. Ofc: MAXXIS Inc., 228-A S Cedros Solana Beach 92075

BERMAN, NORMAN SCOTT, neurologist; b. Nov. 28, 1951, Chgo.; s. Lewis Leonard and Selma (Katz) B.; m. Judy, May 8, 1982; edn: BS, No. Ill. Univ. 1974; MD, Chgo. Med. Sch. 1977. Career: intern Hines VA Hosp. 1977-78; resident Loyola Med. Ctr. 1978-81; fellow evoked potentials Columbus Hosp. 1981-82; instr. Chgo. Med. Sch. 1981-82; pvt. practice 1981—; affil. Cook County Hosp. 1981-82, Columbus- Cuneo- Cabrini Med. Ctr. 1981, Grossmont Dist. Hosp., Alvarado Comm. Hosp., El Cajon Valley Hosp. 1983—; honors: Omicron Delta Kappa, Phi Sigma; mem: AMA, Am. Acad. Neurology, Chgo. Neurol. Soc., Central Neurol. & Psychiatric Assn., San Diego Med. Soc., S.D. Neurol. Soc., Rotary, Optimists; worked to obtain first magnetic scanner in San Diego; Jewish; rec: music. Ofc: 8760 Cuyamaca Ste 201 Santee 92071

BERMAN, SAUL J., management consultant; b. Jan. 1, 1946, Phila.; s. Sherwood S. and Leona (Habelson) B.; m. Jann Gillen, June 6, 1980; 1 child, Ashley Scott b. 1984; edn: BS econ., Univ. of Penn. 1967; MBA, Columbia Univ. 1969, PhD 1973. Career: asst. prof. USC Sch. of Bus. 1972-7; divisional v.p. The Broadway 1977-82; case leader Boston Consulting Group,1982-86; Practice dir. Strategic Mgmt. Consulting, Price Waterhouse, Century City 1986—; advocate Calif. Coastal Commn. (1976-82), apptd. L.A. County Beach Commn. (1977-79); mem. Town Hall of Calif., Wharton Sch. Club, Univ. of Penn. Alumni Club (dir.), Marina City Club; rec: tennis, running. Res: 7511 W 81st St Playa del Rey 90293 Ofc: Price Waterhouse 1880 Century Park East Los Angeles 90067

BERNAT, JOSEPH D., stockbroker, investment counselor, ret.; b. June 10, 1913, Detroit, Mich.; s. Joseph and Appolonia (Chodnicka) B.; m. Gertrude Zajaczkowski Sept. 3, 1934; m. 2d Marjorie Jenkinson, Sept. 25, 1954; children: Arlene Steele b. 1940, J. Alan b. 1946, David b. 1955, Cynthia Amerson b. 1960; edn: BS, Detroit Inst. Tech. 1939; Wayne Univ. 1940-41, Columbia Univ. 1945-46, CSU San Francisco 1960-62, NY Inst. of Fin. 1966. Career: tire builder (night shift while att. coll.) Uniroyal, Detroit 1934-39, test supvr. 1939-42, test coordinator, report writer 1946-48; project engr. Testing & Devel., Uniroyal, Western States 1948-62 (conservation of rubber projects, dam projects, mining ops. and large logging ops.); supply/salvage ops. (Mangla Dam project in Pakistan and Kashmir) Guy F. Atkinson, Pakistan 1962-65; stockbroker Meyerson & Co., San Francisco 1966-72, ret.; v.p. bd. dirs. Mason Auto Supply, S.F. 1958-66; panelist Univ. of Wash. Transp. Conf. (3 yrs); participant var. transp. confs.; honors: recogn. awards Rohnert Park Unif. Sch. Dist. (1983), Sonoma County Office of Edn. (1985), Optimist Club of San Rafael (1978), High Twelve Club of S.F (1971); mem. Nat. Assn. of Security Dealers 1967-71; civic: S.F. Business League (bd.), United Taxpayers of Marin (cofounder, 3000 mems.), Marin United Taxpayers (bd. 4 yrs), Marin Vocational-Edn. Com. (Citizen Adviser), Coalition against Peripheral Canal (steering com.), 9th Assem. Dist. Citizens Action Panel; active in Cub Scouting, cubmaster/ founder Internat. Cub Scout group; Sea Scouts (donor boat); publs: approx. 250 letters pub. in var. newspapers (1973-85); mil: lt. US Navy 1942-45, Res. (Intel.) 1948-58; Ind. Democrat; Prot.; rec: travel (61 countries), gardening, golf. Res: 501 Dennett Ct Rohnert Park 94928

BERNIE, BARBARA SYLVIA, acupuncturist-consultant, foundation president; b. July 3, 1918, N.Y.C.; d. Harry Aaron and Frances (Taub) Orshansky; m. Norman Bernie, Dec. 9, 1944; children: Clifford Arthur b. 1948, Jonathan David b. 1953; edn: aviation courses, Rutgers Univ. 1939-41; MA equiv., N.Y. Sch. Interior Design; No. Am. Coll. of Chinese Acupuncture, Canada 1971; Coll. of Chinese Acup., U.K. 1972-74; adv. clinical tng. under Miriam Lee, C.A. (Calif.), Master An Tai Liu, C.A. (Taiwan), Dr. Yoshio Manaka, M.D. (Japan); Shanghai Coll. of Traditional Chinese Medicine 1977; Chinese lang., Stanford Univ. 1977-78; tchg. lic., N.Y. (1942); Certified Acupuncturist, Calif. (1975). Career: registrar NY Sch. of Interior Design 1942-55, head of Color Dept., splst. in color research, cons. to home furnishing indus., architects & bldrs.; acupuncture apprenticeship 1972-75, lobbied for state certification of acupuncturists, developed workshops and contg. ednl. pgms. in acupuncture; cons. to Calif. State Acupuncture Examining Com. following legalization of acup. 1975, examining commnr. 1976-80; pvt. acup. practice, Burlingame 1976-80; founder/pres. Am. Found. of Traditional Chinese Medicine, San Francisco 1982—, developing ednl. research and jt. venture pgms. with PRC, Korea and Japan; developed TV Satellite med. exchange pgm. between PRC and USA 1983-84; successfully lobbied for passage of AB3806 (permitting tchg. of acupuncture techniques in Calif. by splsts. with out-of-state or internat. licenses), 1982-83; honors: the first to take a group of American acupuncturists to China (1979), first Am. woman acupuncturist invited to observe practice of oriental medicine in Korea, Cert. of Appreciation (Calif. Acupuncture Alliance 1986); mem: Center for Chinese Medicine, Calif. Certified Acupuncturists Assn., Acup. Assn. of Am. (founding pres.), Traditional Acup. Found., Nat. Commn. for the Certification of Acup., S.F.-Shanghai Friendship Com., League of Women Voters, Stanford Univ. Womens Club; publs: booklet, Psychology of Color - Research and Applications; Democrat; rec: music, art, Qi Gong & dance, Chinese language. Ofc: American Foundation of Traditional Chinese Medicine 2390A Powell St San Francisco 94133

BERNSTEIN, LAWRENCE ALLEN, architect/industrial designer; b. Aug. 28, 1932, York, Pa.; s. Phillip Gordon and Evelyn (Greenfield) B.; m. Johanna Navarro, Feb. 10, 1979; 1 dau. Brenda b. 1959; edn: indsl. engring. and arch.

M.I.T. 1951-58; Reg. Architect, Calif., Va., Wash DC. Career: Tallesin fellow with Frank Lloyd Wright 1958; prin. L.A. Bernstein & Assos., Carmel 1959-67; pres. Concepts LAB Inc. N.Y.C. 1968; chief arch., dir. design center new town Linganore, Md., Fredrick, Md. 1971-73; pres., bd. chmn., dir. architecture and design prin. The Advanced Design Ctr., San Antonio and Los Angeles, 1973-76; dir. design Diker-Moe Assocs., Los Angeles 1976-77; prin. Bernstein Assocs., L.A. 1977-80, bd. chmn., pres. Lawrence Allen Bernstein Assocs., Inc. 1981—; dir. new product devel. Dart Advanced Design Ctr., N.Y.C. and L.A., 1967-71; recipient num. awards incl. 1st award for engring. excellence Cons. Engrs. Council/USA for Lake Linganore Dam and Dams on Twin Lakes Anita (1972), spl. recogn. award Nat. Assn. Home Builders (1973), 1st award for excellence Environ. Monthly Mag. (1974), 1st Honor award Monterey Bay chpt. AIA for Mira Obs. (1983); mem. AIA, Soc. Plastics Engrs., Rotary; Judao/Christian; rec: astronomy, skiing, model making. Address: 6456 Surfside Way Malibu 90265

BERNSTEIN, RALPH L., lawyer; b. July 27, 1914, NY, NY; s. Sol H. and Fannie (Zimbler) B. (aka Burns); m. Zelda G., Feb. 25, 1980; children: Linda B. b. 1942, Joel J. b. 1947; edn: City Coll. NY 1931-35; LLB, Fordham Univ. Sch. of Law 1938; admitted NY State Bar 1939, Wash DC 1963, Fla. 1963, Calif. 1966, US Supreme Ct. 1957, US Ct. Appeals (2nd Cir. 1957, 5th Cir. 1963, 9th Cir. 1975, DC 1963), US Dist. Ct. (east NY 1944, so. NY 1944, so. Fla. 1963, mid. Fla. 1963, cent. Calif. 1967), US Tax Ct. 1946, Bd. Immigration & Naturalization Svc. 1944, Treas. Dept. 1944. Career: assoc. atty. & solo practice NYC 1939-50; senior ptnr. Bernstein & Margolin and successor firms NY 1950-61, practice included S.E.C., trial counsel, appellate practice, adminstrv. law, local & national, comml., real estate and corp.; ptnr. Bernstein & Sherr and suc. firms Sarasota, Fla., practice included trial & appellate practice, civil and criminal law, comml. law, bankruptcy, real property, corp. law, probate & negligence, taxation; Calif. practice bankruptcy, trial & corp. counsel, probate; acting police justice Village of New Hyde Park NY 1954; counsel Union Free Sch. Dist. NY 1951-54, 1954-57; former dir. New Hwy Waterworks Inc., All State Properties Inc., Certified Industries Inc., First Lumber Corp., Wenwood Orgn. Inc., Lawyers Mortgage & Title Co., Mini Mart Corp.; lectr.Fla. Bar Contg. Edn.; honors: State of Israel Shalom Award (1972); mem: ABA, Fed. Bar Assn., Comml. Law league of Am., Sarasota County Bar Assn., Fla. Criminal Defense Attys. Assn., Acad. Fla. Trial Lawyers, Knights of Pythias (past chancellor), BSA (past asst. dist. commr.), New Hyde Park CofC (past exec. secty.), NY Assn. School Attys. (past exec. secty.), Hebrew Mutual Benevolent Soc. (past secty.), Kiwanis Club of New Hyde Park NY (past pres., founder), Sister Kenny Found. Fund Drive- NY (past chmn.), B'nai B'rith, Nassau County Magistrates Assn., Am. Soc. Legal History; Republican; Jewish; rec: sculpture, painting, carpentry. Address: Rancho Mirage 92270

BERQUIST, RICHARD J., physician; b. Apr. 17, 1951, Phila., Pa.; s. James R. and Elaine D. (Sajna) B.; m. Anna Fong, June 10, 1979; children: Eric b. 1982, Lisa b. 1984; edn: BA, UC Los Angeles 1973; MPH, UCLA Sch of Pub. Health 1975; MS, UC Berkeley 1977; MD, UC San Francisco Sch. of Med. 1979; bd. certified family phys. Am. Bd. Family Physicians 1982. Career: intern, res. fam. med. Valley Med. Ctr. Fresno 1979-82, advanced tng. psychosomatic med. 1982-83; staff emerg. phys. Fresno Comm. Hosp. 1982-85; pvt. practice Fresno 1983—; clin. instr. and prof. UCSF Sch. of Med.; cons. Samaritan Counseling Ctr.; honors: Outstanding Young Men of Am. 1984; mem: Fresno Assn. Interns & Res. (pres. 1981-83), Fresno Med. Soc.; publ: research papers 1971,75; Democrat; Relig. Sci.; rec: skiing, jogging, camping, classical guitar. Res: 1069 W Sierra Fresno 93711 Ofc: 5305 N Fresno St, Ste 103, Fresno 93710

BERRY, BENJAMIN HAWKINS, JR., company executive; b. Sept. 24, 1948, San Juan, Puerto Rico; s. Benjamin Hawkins and Eleanor (Stone) B.; m. Susan Betker, Oct. 12, 1974; children: Katie b. 1977, Jonathan b. 1981; edn: AA, Southwestern J.C. 1968, BS, San Diego State Univ. 1972. Career: Batch Input mgr., Cable Data, Sacramento 1977-79; ops. mgr. Gill Management Services, San Jose 1979-83, designer/constrn. supr. of 16,000 sq. ft. Computer Center; senior acct. mgr. Paradyne, San Mateo 1983—; mem. Coyote Creeks Homeowner Assn.; mil: USMC O.C.S. grad. 1970; Republican; Methodist; rec: golf. Res: 4942 Scarlett Way San Jose 95111 Ofc: Paradyne, 1710 So Amphlett, Ste 116, San Mateo 94402

BERRY, RUSSELL WILCOX, property management co. executive; b. Feb. 4, 1951, N.Y., N.Y.; s. Thomas Eugene and Bette (Mills) B.; m. Carol Ann, Sept. 1, 1973; 1 dau. Kate b. 1980; edn: BA, Marietta Coll. 1973; grad. work Univ. Md., 1974-75; Cert. Property Mgr. (CPM) 1980. Career: resident mgr. Walnut Grove Apartments, Rockville, Md. 1973-76; prop. mgr./ exec. v.p. Woodmont Managements Inc., Belmont, Calif. 1976—; instr., real estate courses, Coll. of San Mateo; mem. Inst. of Real Estate Mgmt.; Republican; Catholic; rec: tennis, running, ski. Ofc: Woodmont Managements, Inc. 1050 Ralston Ave Belmont 94002

BERTELSEN, MARK SKOV, merchant; b. Nov. 27, 1935, Vandborg, Denmark, nat. US 1967; children: Kristianna b. 1970, Flemming b. 1973, Juliana 1977; edn: bookkepping, Norre Nissum, Denmark 1954; mgmt., Hasleu Framingschool 1957. Career: mgr. Danish demonstration farm, Skorelund and Karlby, Denmark 1958-60; exch. student, Weasenham Farms, Feltwell, Eng. 1960-61; exch. student Chattham, Ontario, Can. 1961-62; num. pos. incl. laborer to mgr. in farming to 12 yrs. in constrn., USA 1962-75; currently, importer and retailer Fantasia, Ventura 1975—; mem: Danish Lodge of Santa Barbara (pres. 1975, 1976); mil: Danish C-F, Herning, Denmark 1955-56; Republican; Lutheran; rec: piano, skiing. Res: 762 Mission Park Dr. Santa Barbara 93105 Ofc: Fantasia, 454 E. Main St. Ventura 93001

BERZINS, LAIMONIS ILGVARS, company executive; b. Oct. 26, 1927, Valka, Latvia, nat. US cit. 1954; s. Janis and Pauline (Drubins) B.; m. Lija Ozols, Jan. 31, 1952; children: Raymond b. 1952, Peter b. 1962; edn: Univ. Augsburg Germany 1946-49; UCLA 1949; Cert. Mfg. Engr. 1972. Career: plant mgr. Western Die Casting 1955-75; gen. mgr. Kolsters Tool & Die 1975-76; v.p. Golden Gate Die Casting 1976−; mem: Soc. Die Casting Engrs. 1967- (chmn. 1975-77), Soc. Mfg. Engrs., DeMolay (advisor 1968-76); co-publr. SME Monthly Bulletin; mil: 1st sgt. US Army MP 1949-55; Democrat; Lutheran; rec: bowling, golf, track & field, fishing. Res: 1239 Bay St Alameda 94501 Ofc: Golden Gate Die Casting 10201 Pearmain St Oakland 94603

BESS, LUDMILA BORIS, obstetrician-gynecologist, b. Mar. 11, 1939, Odessa, USSR, nat. USA 1983; d. Boris Mark and Olga Khaim (Shaichet) Ratiner; m. Fred Bess, Aug. 16, 1960; 1 son, Oleg b. 1961; edn: MD, Odessa USSR Med. Sch. 1962; MD/Ob-Gyn., Tulane Sch. of Med. 1984; junior fellow Am. Bd. of Obstets. & Gyn., 1981; lic. USSR 1962, Louisiana 1983, Calif. 1983. Career: staff physician, 1964-70, in chg. Labor and Delivery Unit, 1970-76, Women's Hosp., Odessa, USSR; emergency room physician South Louisiana Med. Ctr., Houma, La. 1978-80; intern, resident Tulane Univ. Sch. of Med., chief obstets. & gynecol. svcs. Charity Hosp. of New Orleans 1983-84; physician in pvt. practice Ob-Gyn, Los Angeles 1984−; mem. So. Med. Assn., Los Angeles Co. Med. Assn. (Ins. Com.), Russian Am. Republican Club; Jewish; rec: Renaissance art, philately. Ofc: 6360 Wilshire Blvd Ste 305 Los Angeles 90048

BETTS, BARBARA LANG, lawyer, rancher; b. Apr. 26, 1926, Anaheim; d. W. Harold and Helen (Thompson) Lang; m. Bert A. Betts (fmr. Calif. state treas.), July 11, 1962; children: J. Chauncey Hayes, IV, b. 1953; Frederick Prescott Hayes, b. 1955; Roby F. Hayes b. 1957; Bruce Harold Betts, b. 1966; edn: BA, magna cum laude, Stanford Univ. 1948; LLB, Calif. Western Univ. (fmr Balboa U.), 1951; admitted to Calif. State Bar 1952, US Dist. Ct., S. and N. Dists. Calif. 1952, US Ct. of Appeals, 9th Circuit 1952, US Supreme Ct. 1978. Career: ptnr. law firm Barbara Lang Hayes & Roby F. Hayes, 1952-60; city atty. City of Carlsbad, 1959-63; pvt. law practice, Oceanside 1952-60, San Diego 1960−, Sacto. 1962−; rancher, 1948-58, 1967−; v.p. W.H. Lang Corp., 1964-70; secty. Internat. Prod. Assn., 1967-; v.p. Isle & Oceans Marinas Inc., 1970-80; secty. Margaret M. McCabe, M.D., Inc. 1976-; commnr. Carlsbad Planning Commn. 1959, v.p. San Diego County Plnng. Congress, secty. Pub. Affairs for San Diego and Imperial Co. 1954, pres. of Pres.'s Council S.D. and Imperial Co. 1958-59; dir. N. San Diego Co. chpt. for retarded children 1957-57; honors: Phi Beta Kappa 1948, Calif. Scholarship Fedn. (life); mem: Am., San Diego County, Calif. Trial Lawyers bar assns., Am. Judicature Soc., Nat. Inst. of Municipal Officers (1959-63), US Supreme Ct. Hist. Soc., CofC (Oceanside, San Diego), N. San Diego County Assn., Traveler's Aid (chmn. 1952-54), AAUW, Bus. & Profl. Womens Club 1953-63, Soroptimist Internat. (pres. Mexico Soroptimist Internat. 1958-59), S.D. Hist. Soc., Fullerton Jr. Asst. League 1956-66, DAR 1956-64; Democrat (State Central Com. 1954-62, co-ch. 28th Cong. Dist. 1960-62, del. Dem. Nat. Conv. 1960); Protestant; rec: fishing, hunting. Res: Betts Ranch, Elverta 95626 Ofc: 8701 E Levee Rd Elverta; 3119 Howard Ave San Diego 92104

BETTS, BERT A., former State of California treasurer; b. Aug. 16, 1923, San Diego; s. Bert A., Sr., and Alma (Jorgenson) B.; m. Barbara Lang; children: Terry Lou, Linda Sue, Sara Ellen, Bert Alan, Randy Wayne, John Chauncey, Frederick Prescot, LeAnn, Roby F., Bruce Harold; edn: BA, Calif. Western Univ. 1950; CPA, 1950; grad. Internat. Acctg. Soc. Career: ptnr. CPA firm, 1950, prin. 1951-59; college tchr., acct.-tax., 1950-58; elected State Treas. of Calif., 1958, re-elected 1962-67 (youngest ever elected to a State Constnl. office; also 1st state-level executive ofcr. from S.D. County in this century); prop. Betts Finl., Real Estate and Mgmt. Cons. firm, 1967-77; treas., chief exec. Internat. Prodn. Assocs. 1968-72; trustee Fidelity Mortgage Investors, 1970-78; dir. Lifetime Communities Inc., 1978-; past mem. State Soc. Govtl. Accts. Commn., Nat. Assn. of State Auditors, Comptrollers and Treas., Municipal Forum of NY; past pres. bd. trustees Lemon Grove Sch. Dist.; past fin. com. Girl Scouts (S.D.); active in BSA (Sacto.); citizens adv. coms. to govt. agencies; past treas. S.D. Cerebral Palsy Found.; pres. Sacto. Co. Am. Cancer Soc. 1967-68; mem: Calif. Municipal Treasurers Assn. (hon.), Am. Inst. of CPAs, Nat. Assn. of Accts., Am. Accts. Assn., Calif. Soc. of CPAs (past v.p. S.D. chpt.), AF Assn. (past v-comdr.), VFW, Am. Legion, Intl. Order of Foresters, past pres. Lemon Grove Mens Club, Lions Club, Masons, Beta Alpha Psi, Alpha Kappa Psi; Democrat (S.D. Co. Central Com.); Presbyterian. Res: Betts' Ranch, E Levee Rd, Elverta 95626 Ofc: 441 Sandburg Dr Sacramento 95819

BEUMER, DELBERT HARRY, stockbroker; b. Jan. 6, 1931, Holland, Indiana; s. Frank Emil and Lydia Clara (Linstrot) B.; m. Marlene Hill, Feb. 27, 1957; children: Judi, 1958; Jeff, b. 1959; Jeanine, b. 1960; Kimberly, b. 1963; edn: Evansville Coll. 1949-51; BBA, mktg., Univ. of Miss. 1953; MBA, corp. fin., Univ. of Wash. 1955; Cert. Fin. Plnr. 1978. Career: data processing, supply & plng., USN 1955-60; spl. asst. to comndr., defense fuel supply ctr., USNR, Cameron Station, Va. 1981−; assoc. v.p./ asst. mgr. Dean Witter Reynolds, Palo Alto 1960−; mem: Peninsula Stock & Bond Club (pres. 1970-71); Naval Reserve Assn.; Grace Lutheran Ch. (pres. 1976); Los Altos Lutheran Ch. (chmn. Bd. of Deacons 1981); mil: Rear Admiral, USNR, 1982-, Joint Svc. Commdn. Medal; Republican; Lutheran; rec: flying, building, gardening. Res: 452 University Ave Los Altos 94022 Ofc: Dean Witter Reynolds, 555 University Ave Palo Alto 94301

BEVERETT, ANDREW JACKSON, real estate broker; b. Feb. 21, 1917, Midland City, Ala.; s. Andrew J. and Ella L. (Adams) B.; m. Martha Sophia Landgrebe, May 26,1 951; children: Andrew J. III, James Edmund, Faye A.; edn: BS, Samford Univ. 1940; MBA, Harvard Univ. 1942. Career: exec. pos. in corp. plnng. and mgmt. United Air Lines, Chicago, Ill. 1946-66; senior mktg. & economic cons. Mgmt. & Economics Research Inc., Palo Alto 1966-71; senior economist Stanford Research Inst., Menlo Park 1971-72; pres. Edy's on the Peninsula Shores, Palo Alto 1972-78; real estate broker and tax counselor, Saratoga 1979−; mem: Phi Kappa Phi, Nat. Assn. of Enrolled Agents, Am. Assn. of Realtors; mil: lt. USNR 1942-46. Res: 19597 Via Monte Dr. Saratoga 95070 Ofc: 12175 Saratoga- Sunnyvale Rd. Ste. A Saratoga 95070

BEVERLY, ROBERT G., state senator, lawyer; b. July 1, 1925, Belmont, Mass.; s. William James and Helen (Graham) B.; m. Elizabeth Louise Weisel, 1946; children: William J., Barbara L., Robert Graham, Brian C.; edn: Univ. Pitts. 1943, UCLA 1946-48; LLB, Loyola Univ., Los Angeles 1951; admitted to Calif. State Bar 1952. Career: practicing atty., 1952−; elected mem. Calif. State Assem., 46th Dist., 1967-76, minority floor leader, 1973-76; elected mem. Calif. State Senate, 1979−; mayor, city councilman Manhattan Beach, 1958-67; mem. Republican State Central Com., del. Rep. Nat. Conv. 1972, 80, 84, alt. del. 1976; mem. YMCA, Am. Legion; mil: cpl. USMC 1943-46. Res: 1611 S. Pacific Coast Hwy Suite 102 Redondo Beach 90277 Ofc: California State Senate, Sacramento 95814

BEYER, PATRICIA ANN, telecommunication executive, lawyer; b. Nov. 22, 1953, San Diego; d. Thomas Emmanuel and Esther May (Turner) B.; m. Richard Herzog, June 13, 1980; edn: BA, San Diego State Univ. 1977; JD, Univ. San Diego 1982. Career: bookkeeper/head teller Kearny Mesa Fed. Credit Union San Diego 1975-78; client svc. rep. Citicorp Info. Resources Inc 1978-80, telecommunications mgr. (3-state area) 1980-84, western reg. telecom. mgr. 1984−; chair western reg. Citicorp Telecom. Users Group 1985; S.D. State Univ. Advis. Com. for Telecom 1985; honors: Appreciation Award (S.D. State Univ. Coll. of Extended Studies 1984-85); mem: Am., S.D. Co. bar assns.; Democrat; Catholic. Ofc: Citicorp Information Resources Inc 7847 Convoy Ct, Ste 101, San Diego 92111

BHARDWAJ, PREM KUMAR, engineer; b. July 19, 1956, New Delhi, India; s. Rameshwar Chander and Bhagwati Devi B.; edn: BSEE, Univ. Mysore (India) 1978; MSEE, Univ. Dublin (Ireland) 1982. Career: senior applications engr. Unitron India 1978-80; lectr. NIHE Dublin, Ireland 1980-82; mktg. mgr. Encon Inc. 1982-84; field applications engr. Signetics Corp. 1984−; cons. MA Sys. 1984-85, Compuguys 1984-85; Hindu; rec: computers. Res: 1024 Cedar Gables Dr San Jose 95118 Ofc: Signetics Corp. 811 E Arques Ave MS 47 Sunnyvale 94086

BHATIA, ZENUDDIN SARAFALI, geotechnical engineer; b. Nov. 22, 1942, Dohad, Gujarat, India, nat. US cit. 1985; s. Sarafali D. and Kjatija S. B.; m. Fizza Zen, Feb. 25, 1968; children: Saida b. 1969, Sabbir b. 1973, Zahira b. 1978; edn: B.Engr. (civil engrg.), M.S. Univ. of Baroda, India 1965; diploma Fortran IV computer pgm.; Reg. Profl. Engr. Calif. 1983. Career: exec. engr. Bombay Port Transit India 1966-80; ops. mgr. Leighton & Assoc. Inc. Palm Desert, Calif. 1980-85; engrg. op./ofc. mgr. Aako Geotech. Engrg. Inc. Riverside 1985−; cons. soil engr.; several awards in India and US; mem: Profl. Engrg. Assn., Am. Soc. Civil Engrs., AMIE India; arranged first celebration of Indian Independence Day in Indio, Calif. 1984; Islam; rec: cricket, travel, social works. Res: 2615 S Plum Pl Ontario 91761 Ofc: 1465 Spruce St, Ste H, Riverside 92507

BHATNAGAR, ASHOK KUMAR, civil engineer; b. Aug. 11, 1944, Ajmer, India; s. Jagdish Sarup and Sarla B.; m. Juhi, June 5, 1972; children: Samir b. 1973, Avichal b. 1977; edn: BS civil engring., Thapar Engg. Coll., Patiala 1964; Civil Engr., Punjab Univ. 1964. Career: exec. engr. Govt. of Rajasthan, India 1964-83, (time out) on spl. assignment as civil engring. expert with Repub. of Iraq, 1974-77; civil (transportation) engr., Transportation Agcy., State of Calif., 1984−, in charge of a dam project; mem. Instn. of Engrs. India (1968-; coord. var. engring. seminars 1966-80), Am. Soc. Civil Engrs. (assoc. 1983-); publs. on economic use of water in "GEAR" (1978). Res: 2241 Santa Clara #N Alameda 94501

BICKEL, JOHN HAROLD, lawyer; b. Sept. 24, 1931, Evansville, Ind.; s. Harold L. and Sallie Love (Banks) B.; m. Lurline Sampson, Sept. 20, 1958; children: Harold Sampson b. 1961, Courtney Jean b. 1964; edn: AB, Stanford Univ. 1952, LLB, 1960; admitted Calif. State Bar 1961. Career: atty. assoc. Landels, Ripley & Diamond, San Francisco 1960-, ptnr. 1967−; mem. San Francisco Boys & Girls Club (pres. 1985-), The Guardsmen (v.p. 1968-71); clubs: Olympic, Bohemian; mil: lt. USNR 1952-56; Republican; Protestant; rec: squash. Res: 3220 Jackson St San Francisco 94118 Ofc: Landels, Ripley &: Diamond, 450 Pacific Ave San Francisco 94133

BIENATI, LAWRENCE MARIO, retail drug chain personnel executive, author, lecturer; b. March 15, 1956, Oakland; s. Frank Sam and Frances Bienati; m. Catherine Coffman, Dec. 6, 1980; children: Christina Maria, Amanda Catherine; edn: BS (I.R.P.A.), CSU Hayward, 1979, MBA, 1980. Career: food clerk, Safeway Stores, Inc. 1974-80, employment rep. 1980-81, director, Training, 1981-83, supvr. Employee Relations, 1983-85; mgr. Employee Relations, Longs Drug Stores, 1985−; honors: Speaker of the Year, CSUH, 1980; Winner of 10 major awards intercollegiate speech and debate competition; exceptional achievement award, Safeway Stores Inc. 1984; mem: Toastmasters Internat.,

Nat. Speakers Assn., Am. Mgmt. Assn., Am. Soc. for Tng. and Devel., Am. Soc. of Personnel Adminstrs., Boy Scouts Am., Colombo Club; author: pamphlet: Get That Job (Rotary Clubs Intl.; book: How can I get the experience if you won't let me have the job: the secrets of getting your first job; rec: backpacking, public speaking, rafting. Res: 110 Persimmon Dr. Vallejo 94589 Ofc: Longs Drug Stores California, Inc., 141 N Civic Dr Walnut Creek 94596

BIGGERS, JOHN ALVIN, automotive and industrial co. president; b. Oct. 27, 1926, Durham; s. Alvin C. and Bessie I. (Green) B.; m. Esther L. Debler, April 20, 1946; children: Curt G.; Merlene A. and Marlene J. (twins); Calvin B.; ed. public schs., Chico and Sacto. Career: with Globe Auto Supply Co. 1941-44; with Biggers Industrial Gerlinger (formerly Gerlinger Motor Parts Co., renamed 1/1/86) Sacramento 1944–, gen. mgr. 1950–, v.p. 1959-68, pres. 1968– : Biggers Indsl. Div. originated 1903 and part of corporate structure; gen. ptnr. Auto Quip Leasing 1973-83; pres. Standard Motor Parts 1974-78; chief exec. Johnny Biggers Video Prodns. (tv. sports news and video custom prodns.) 1982–; bd. dirs. Eskaton; chmn. Calif. Tax Liability Tax Force (sec.treas. 1982-, pres. 1985); mem. Crime Alert Bd. Sacto. Police Dept./CofC 1981-; automotive industry resource person on legislative matters, chmn. automotive sect. United Crusade 1957-62; dist. finance com. Boy Scouts Am. 1959-62 (del. Gen. Assembly Internat. Portland, 1964, Kansas City, 1968, 1980, Miami Bch., 1972, Dallas, 1972, alt. del. Anaheim, 1985); dir. Sact. Safety Council (pres. Safetyville 200 Club); adv. council Sacto. City Coll., Cosumnes Jr. Coll. Dist., adv. bd. Los Rios Jr. Coll. Dist.; pres. Sacto. Metro Industry Edn. Council 1978-82, pres. emeritus 1983-; chmn. bus. & career div. Sacto. County Schs.; past adv. council Preston Sch. Industries; past dir. Fairhaven Home for Unwed Mothers, 4 yrs.; hon. Dep. Sheriff (1967), assoc. mem. Internat. Chiefs of Police (1965), charter mem. Calif. State Sheriffs Assn. (1985); mem: Sacto. Parts Jobbers Assn. (pres. 3 terms), Automotive Wholesalers Assn. (chmn. Calif. Assn. of Wholesalers & Distbrs. 1985), CofC, Sacto. Camelia Soc., (past) Young Execs. Forum of Asia, Rotary, Internat. Platform Assn.; works: contractor/ builder/ asst. design engr. of Rail Power Car (first blt.) for 1984 Los Angeles Olympics, for Rose Parade and Super Bowl; design engr./ contr. var. aerospace agencies; design engr. sev. food processing plants; guest num. talk shows; frequent lectr.; Republican (nat. senatl. com., congl. com., charter Reagan Presdtl. Task Force); Nazarene Ch. (Dist. Adv. Bd.); rec: music, videography, 4-wheeling. Res: 5372 Monalee Ave Sacramento 95819 Ofc: 2020 Kay St Sacramento 95814; Biggers Industrial Gerlinger, 555 Sequoia Pacific Blvd. Sacramento 95814

BIKHAZI, LEYLA ABU-HAYDAR, psychotherapist- consultant; b. May 31, 1938, Hammana, Lebanon, nat. 1961; parents: Isaac S. Abu-Haydar (honored for lifetime svc. as chief acct., British Govt. in Anglo- Egyptian Sudan) and Saada N. Abu-Haydar; First Cousin: Dr. Nagib Abu-Haydar, physician and ex-prime minister of Edn., presently mayor in Lebanon; First Cousin: Munir Abu-Haydar and Nicholar Haddad, Army physicians & surgeons, British Govt., Anglo- Egyptian Sudan; sev. medals of hon.; div.; children: Nadim B., b. 1967; Paul H., b. 1969; edn: MSW, USC 1960. Career: U.S. Info. Svc. Am. Embassy, Beirut, Lebanon 1956-58; instr. psychiatric & med. soc. wrk. Am. Univ., Beirut 1962-64; Dept. of A.F. Okinawa, Ryukyu Islands, sr. psych. soc. wkr. cons. staff, Whittier Hosp. 1979; staff Charter Baywood Hosp.; fellow, Soc. for Clinical Soc. Wrk. 1977; Am. Assn. of Sex Educators Counselors & Therapists 1979; Internat. Platform Assn. 1982; Town Hall of Calif. 1982; Who's Who of Calif. Exec. Women 1983; Republican. Res: 7760 S Vale Dr Whittier 90602

BILECKI, RONALD ALLAN, financial planner; b. July 15, 1942, Cincinnati, Ohio; s. Allan Frederick and Ruth Hilda (Parker) B.; m. Judy, Jan. 25, 1964; children: Sherry b. 1967, Sean b. 1970; edn: chem. major, CSU Los Angeles 1968; Cert. Finl. Planner, Coll. for Finl. Planning (1982), Reg. Investment Adviser, SEC (1985), Calif. Dept. Corps. (1986). Career: insurance agt. New York Life Ins., Covina 1973-75, asst. mgr. Los Angeles office 1975-79; indep. finl. plnnr., Rosemead 1979-81; pres. Financial Designs Corp., San Gabriel 1981–; finl. plnng. cons. So. Calif. Edison Co.; finl. plnng. seminars for So. Calif. Edison, City of Los Angeles and LA Dept. Water & Power employees; mem. Internat. Assn. for Finl. Plnng. Inc.; Republican; Christian; rec: chess, jogging, hiking. Ofc: Financial Designs Corp. 7220 Rosemead Blvd Ste 206 San Gabriel 91775

BILHEIMER, STEPHEN C., business executive, civic leader; b. Arkadelphia, Ark.; s. Charles Wm. and Edna (Carpenter) B.; m. Jeanne Summerfield, May 5, 1928; children: Mary Flave, b. 1935, Peter, b. 1937; edn: BS, Ore. State Coll. 1927; USC; Dr. Bus. Adm., Woodbury Coll. Career: partner, dir. Phelps-Terkel, Inc., Los Angeles 1925-54; pres. Silverwoods Stores, 21 stores, 1964-67, chmn. bd. 1967–; dir. Calif. Federal S&L Assn. 1945-; bd. dirs. Good Samaritan Medical Ctr.; past pres. LA Airport Commn.; bd. dirs. Calif. Mus. Sci & Indus.; pres. Calif. Mus. Found.; past pres. LA Stock Exchange, So. Calif. Visitors Council, Central City Assn.; dir. Downtown Businessmen's Assn. 1954; dir. Better Bus. Bur. 1954-; dir. Bel-Air Bay Club 1954-; pres. LA CofC 1962-63, dir. 1963-; pres. All-Year Club So. Calif. 1966-67; past pres. LA Rotary Club No. 5; honors: outstanding alumnus, USC Sch. of Bus. Adm., 1963, General Alumni Assn. Award for outstanding serv., 1968; Man of Year, Los Angeles Realty Bd., 1969; Humanitarian of Year, Aid-United Givers, 1972; Brotherhood Award, NCCJ, 1972; Bishop's Award of Merit, Episcopal Diocese of L.A., 1972; hon. trustee Republican Assocs.; mem. Masons, Los Angeles Country Club; Episcopal; rec: hunting, fishing, golf. Res: 142 S Rockingham Ave, West Los Angeles Ofc: 558 S Broadway Los Angeles 90012

BILLIG, PAUL MARK, manufacturing co. executive; b. Nov. 22, 1941, NY, NY; s. Saul Cyrus and Mildred (Sher) B.; children: Eric b. 1968, Brett b. 1971; edn: BS, textiles sci., Phila. Coll. 1963. Career: vice pres. sales West Coast, Croscill Home Furnishings; honors: Volunteer of Year, Parks & Rec. Dept. City of Los Angeles (1977); mem. Banington Center Services Assn. (pres.); mil: pfc USMC 1963-64, Res.; democrat; Jewish; rec: youth coaching all sports. Ofc: Croscill Home Furnishings 2412 Wilshire Blvd Santa Monica 90403

BILLINGS, LOIS BRAND, insurance co. executive; b. Feb. 20, 1943, Los Angeles; d. Leslie and Angeline (DeLucia) Brand; children: Bradley John, b. 1967, Jennifer Joanne, b. 1968, Cynthia Maureen, b. 1970; edn: BA in English, CSU Los Angeles. Career: pres. Professional Food Development, 1977-81; v.p. Huntington-Brand Corp., 1977-83; broker Prudential Ins. Co., 1979-83, with Transamerica Occidental Life, Los Angeles Branch, 1984–; awards: 1980 rookie of year, sev. nat. sales awards 1980-83; mem. Tournament of Roses Assn., Bus. & Profl. Women's Club (Arcadia), CofC, Nat. Assn. of Life Underwriters; founding bd. mem. Calif. Republican Assem. (Bev. Hills, Holmby Hills, Bel-Aire chapters); publs: bus. arts., El Monte Herald, poetry pub. No. Calif. Review; Catholic; rec: gourmet cooking, writing. Res: 331 Cambridge Dr Arcadia 91006 Ofc: Transamerica Occidental Life, Los Angeles

BILOWITZ, LOUIS I., pension plan consultant; b. April 22, 1947, NY, NY; s. Herman and Arline (Ochs) B.; m. M. Carol Lingo; children: Kyle, b. 1976, Shane b. 1985. Career: pres. Corporate Pensions Insurance Services, Inc., Los Angeles 1983–; partner Pension Architects, Inc., L.A. 1983–; partner Insurance Architects, Insurance Agency. Inc., L.A. 1983–; guest lectr. on Pension Planning. Awards: Top of the Table, 1983; leading pension prod. in Am., 1982, 83, 84, 85 and leading overall prod. in Am., 1983, General American Life. Mem: Am. Youth Soccer Assn. coach; UCLA Sustaining Donor; junior varsity soccer coach La Canada H.S.; publs: art. in life ins. selling, 1982; Republican; rec: athletics, music. Res: 5000 Palm Dr. La Canada 91011. Ofc: Corp. Pensions Ins. Svcs Inc. 716 S. Olive St., 2nd flr. Los Angeles 90014

BINARD, HELEN ANN, real estate broker, investor; b. May 9, 1913, Cedar Rapids, Nebr.; d. Joseph Bernard and Gertrude Elizabeth (Welding) Lickhus; m. Donatus Ezsbon Binard, 1938, dec. 1972; children: William b. 1939, David b. 1940, Michael b. 1950; edn: bus. St. Charles Acad., Stratton, Colo. 1931-32, AA, UCLA, 1938, spl. courses Pasadena City Coll. Career: semi-profl. singer var. choirs, modeling p.t., 1936-38; escrow ofcr. Pasadena Escrow Co., Pasa. 1938-42; real estate broker/prin., Altadena 1953 –; mem. UCLA Alumni Assn. (life), Phrateres Council UCLA (Bannister chpt. pres. 1937), Theta Phi Alpha sor. (pres. elect 1937), L.A. Blue Book (1976-); publs: article, Better Homes & Gardens (1952); Republican; Catholic; rec: singing, dancing. Res: 1848 E Loma Alta Dr Altadena 91001 Ofc: Helen A. Binard 2509 N Lake Ave Altadena 91001

BINKLEY, ROBERT LYNN, research & development, computers; b. Apr. 23, 1940, Bloomington, Ind.; s. Lynn Ransom and Lucille (Rhodes) B.; children: Jennifer b. 1963, Eric b. 1966; edn: corresp., I.C.S. 1960, Indiana Univ. 1962. Career: computer ops., Sage Syst., USAF 1959-63; with N.C.R. Corp. 1963-80: service rep. (cash registers, accting. mach.) 1963, computer tech. Indianapolis 1966, computer traveling maint. Dayton, Oh. 1969, N.C.R. Operating System Support (VRX), Los Angeles 1976, instr. System Integration, 1980; freelance micro computer cons., I.S.G. Inc. (operating syst., firmware, syst. integ.), 1981–; devel. C.A.E. System for comp. design currently; mil: airman 2/c USAF 1959-63; Republican; Methodist; rec: computers, stamps, photog. Ofc: I.S.G. Inc. 920 E Broadway Glendale 91205

BINSTOCK, JEFFREY H., dermatologic surgeon; b. Jan. 18, 1950, Pittsburgh; s. Mervin L. and Doris D. B.; m. Randee Burstein, Jan. 30, 1972; edn: BA w/ distn., Univ. Wisc. 1971; MD, Univ. Pittsburgh 1975; bd. certified Am. Acad. Dermatol.; Diplomate Am. Bd. Dermatol. 1979, Nat. Bd. Med. Examiners 1976. Career: intern, Hartford Hosp. 1975-76; resident dermatol. Albany Med. Ctr. 1976-79; fellow dermatol. surg. UC San Francisco 1979-80, assoc. clin. prof. dermatol. 1980–; cons. dermatol. surg. Vets. Hosp. Martinez; attg. phys. Pacific Med. Ctr. S.F.; honors: Sutnick Award (Am. Coll. Chemosurg. 1979), Scholarship (Am. Soc. Dermatol. Surg. 1977), Research Fellowship (Univ. Pitts. Sch. of Med. 1971); mem: Am. Coll. Chemosurgery, Am. Acad. Facial Plastic & Reconstrv. Surg., Am. Soc. Dermatol. Surg., Am. Acad. Cosmetic Surg., Am. Soc. Lipo-Suction Surg., Internat. Soc. Dermatol. Surg., Am. Acad. Dermatol., Pacific Dermatol. Soc., S.F. Dermatol. Soc., S.F. Med. Soc.; num. presentations to profl. socs. and univs., publs. in med. jours. Ofc: Dermatologic Surgery Ctr. A Med. Group Inc. 450 Sutter St Ste 826 San Francisco 94108

BIRD, KENNETH DEAN, physician; b. Mar. 20, 1952, Oklahoma City, Okla.; s. Earl Alford and Nancy Louise (Jessup) B.; m. Nettie, July 24, 1980; children: Celeste b. 1978, Kenny b. 1982; edn: BS in biol., highest honors, Univ. Texas (Arlington) 1975, MD, honors, Univ. Texas (Galveston) 1979. Career: pediatric residency, Univ. Texas Med. Branch 1980; stu. US Naval Aerospace Med. Inst. 1981, USN flight surgeon NAS Lemoore, Calif. 1981-84; pvt. gen. practice medicine, Lemoore 1984–; honors: Alpha Chi; mem. Lemoore Union Elem. School Bd.; mem. Kings County Sub Area Health Systems Adv. Com.; mem. Calif. Med. Assn., Kings County Med. Soc.; mil: lcdr. USNR, Navy Achievement, Navy Expedit., Humanitarian medals; rec: wt. lifting, backpacking. Res: 1515 Mulberry Ln Lemoore 93245 Ofc: Family Medical Group, 810 East D St Lemoore 93245

BIRD, ROSE ELIZABETH, chief justice Calif. Supreme Ct.; b. Nov. 2, 1936, Tucson, Ariz.; edn: bA, magna cum laude, Long Is. Univ. 1958; JD, UC Berkeley 1965; admitted State Bar of Calif. 1966. Career: clerk to chief justice Nev. Supreme Ct. 1965-66; deputy public defender (first woman to hold pos. in Santa Clara County), senior trial dep., chief apellate div. Santa Clara Co. Pub. Defender's Ofc. 1966-74; faculty mem. Stanford Univ. Law Sch. 1972-74; secty. Calif. Agri. and Services Agency (gov.'s cabinet) 1975-77 (first woman to serve as a Cabinet Sec. in Calif.); chief justice Calif. Supreme Ct. 1977—; chmn. Calif. Jud. Council (first woman apptd. to Calif. Supreme Ct.); mem. bd. vis. Univ. of Santa Clara Sch. of Law, and Stanford Law Sch.; pres. bd. dirs. UC Hastings Coll. of Law; bd. councilors USC Law Ctr.; honors: fellow Ford Found. 1960; awarded Third Year Honors Competition Prize, Boalt Hall Sch. of Law 1965; num. articles in law revs.; Democrat. Address: Supreme Court, Calif. State Bldg., 350 McAllister St., San Francisco 94102

BIRDSALL, LUCY ELLEN, geologist; b. Oct. 20, 1914, Mansfield, Conn.; d. Rollin L. and Lucy Ellen (Storrs) B.; edn: Bay Path Bus. Inst.; BS, Univ. of Conn. 195C; George Washington Univ. 1950-52; UCLA Ext. Sch. 1954; geologist, Calif. 1970. Career: geophysical technician US Geological Survey, Geophysicas Br., Wash. DC 1950-53, Information Specialist 1953—; honors: hon. mem. Pacific Sect. Am. Assn. Petroleum Geologists 1979; Meritorious Svc. Award, US Geological Survey 1984; Distng. Alumni, Univ. of Conn. (Storrs) 1985; hon. mem., So. Coast Geological Soc. 1985, Geological Soc. of Am., 25 year mem.; mem: Branner Geological Soc. (treas.-secty. 25 yrs., pres. 1979-80), Los Angeles Basin Geological Soc. (pres. 1980), Nat. Am. Assn. Petroleum Geologists, Assoc. Eng. Geologists, Los Angeles Minerals Soc., Pacific Minerals Soc., Women's Overseas Svc. League (pres. 1972-73, 1975-76); author: chpts. on geologic information in Assn. of Eng. Geologists (L.A. chpt.), So. Coast Geological Soc., and Pacific Sect. of Am. Assn. Petroleum Geologists; mil: sgt. WAC 1943-46, Southwest Pacific; Republican; Methodist; rec: photog. Ofc: U.S. Geological Survey, Public Inquiries Office, Rm. 7638 Federal Bldg., 300 No. Los Angeles St. Los Angeles 90012

BISGAARD, EDWARD LAWRENCE, investment co. executive/CPA; b. July 26, 1946, El Centro; s. Edward Lawrence, Sr. and Gail (Chambers) B.; edn: BS, Calif. State Polytechnic Univ., Pomona 1971. Career: senior acct. Arthur Young & Co., Los Angeles 1971-74; controller King Internat. Corp., Beverly Hills 1975-78; asst. treas. of twelve mutual funds managed by Capital Research & Mgmt. Co., Los Angeles 1979—, vice pres. Business Mgmt. Div., Capital Research &: Mgmt. Co., L.A. 1982—. mem: AICPA, Calif. CPA Soc., Toastmasters; Republican. Res: 4139 Via Marina No. 905 Marina Del Rey 90292. Ofc: Capital Research & Mgmt. Co., 333 S Hope St. Los Angeles 90071

BISHOP, KENDALL ROGER, lawyer; b. Mar. 3, 1939, Los Angeles; s. Leo R. and Edith Brody B.; m. Diane, Feb. 5, 1967; children: Randall L. b. 1968, Lauren M. b. 1970, Allison b. 1973; edn: BA, with distinction, Stanford Univ. 1961; JD, Univ. Calif. 1964. Career: assoc. atty. O'Melveny & Myers 1965-73; ptnr. head Paris Ofc. 1974-77; ptnr. 1973—; lectr. Calif. Ctg. Edn. Bar; honors: Ford Found. Fellow (Univ. Rome 1964-65); mem: Am., Calif. (corp. com. 1980-82), L.A., Internat. bar assns.; Bev. Hills Bd. Edn. (com. for balanced budget, chmn. revenue enhancement com.); Democrat; Jewish; rec: tennis, photog., travel. Ofc: O'Melveny & Myers 1800 Century Park E Los Angeles 90067

BJORNSON, WALLACE ERWIN, foundation president; b. May 31, 1917, Lakota, N.Dak.; s. Adelstein S. and Dora (Jones) B.; m. Betty Mayfield, July 19, 1948; children: Lawrence E. b. 1950, Bruce N. b. 1954; edn: BS elec. engring., N.D. State Univ. 1939; grad. Air Command & Staff Sch. 1946; MSEE, Johns Hopkins Univ. 1951; grad. Armed Forces Staff Coll. 1959. Career: radio engr. Crosley Radio, 1939-41; served to lt. col. US Air Force 1941-61; mgr. Ford Motor Co., Aeronutronic Div. 1961-62; dir. Internat. Elec. Div., Internat. Tel. & Tel. 1962-64; supvr. Rockwell Internat. 1964-75; current: pres., bd. chmn. Golden Rain Found. (gov. body, Leisure World); honors: Commendn. Medal (2) USAF, Scabbard & Blade mil. frat.; mem. Kiwanis/ Saddleback (pres. elect 1986), Tau Beta Pi, Elks, Travel Club (1100 mem.; pres. elect 1986); Presbyterian; rec: chess, golf, travel. Address: Laguna Hills 92653

BLACK, CAREN LEA, musical theatre director; b. Jan. 11, 1948, Sterling, Ill.; d. Leslie L. and Cathryn M. (Heller) B.; m. Russell Stemple, Nov. 7, 1982; edn: B.Music, Northwestern Univ. 1970; MA theatre, 1972; music cert., Paris Am. Acad. 1968; dance cert., Paris Am. Acad. 1969. Career: founder/ dir. Creative Arts Workshop, Danville 1975-77; founder/ dir. Contra Costa Children's Repertory Co., Inc., Danville active, 1975-80, sabbatical status, 1980—, currently working to reopen; advr. Calif. Youth Teatre, Los Angeles 1980-84; currently, exec. asst. Decade Prodns., Los Angeles; mem: Contra Costa Nat. Orgn. for Women; works: Cherubim, a new musical, 1978; Cherubim VS Seraphim, a new musical, 1979; 16 pub. songs; 2 books in progress; Democrat; rec: parapsychology. Res: 9340 Hwy 9 Ben Lomond Ofc: POB 3026 Ben Lomond 95005

BLACK, HUBERT PERRY, college president; b. Aug. 10, 1926, Birmingham AL; s. W.L. and Vera (Brannon) B.; m. Ulna Burell, May 13, 1945; children: Hubert Jr., b. 1947; David, b. 1949; edn: Lee Coll. 1949-50; BS, Jacksonville St. 1953; M.Edn., Univ. of Chattanooga 1956; Ed.D., Univ. of Tenn. 1965. Career: dean of students/ prof. of edn. Lee Coll., Cleveland, Tenn. 1954-68; dean of students Chesapeake Comm. Coll., Wye Mills, Md. 1968-69; dean of edn. Lee Coll., Cleveland, Tenn. 1969-75; dir./ chief exec. Troy State Univ., Bay Minette, Ala. x975-80; pres. West Coast Christian Coll., Fresno 1980—; conv. spkr., profl. and denominational groups; awards: Lifetime PTA; mem: Assn. of Tchr. Educators; Ala. ATE (pres. 1974-75); NEA; AAHE; Optimist;

Rotary; works: Religious and Philosophical Fds. of Education, 1967; Philosophy, the Quest for Meaning, 1970; mil: US Army Paratroopers 1944-46, Pacific Theatre; Democrat; Ch. of God; rec: golf, spectator sports, walking. Res: 6387 N 10th, Fresno 93710 Ofc: West Coast Christian Coll., 6901 N Maple Fresno 93710

BLACK, WILLIAM ALFRED, physician; b. June 22, 1900, Dayton, Wash.; s. Charles Crittendon and Martha Luretta (Dillas) B.; edn: AB, UC Berkeley 1923, Cert. of Completion in Edn. 1924, MA, 1934; MD, Washington Univ., St. Louis 1942; Lic. Physician and Surgeon, Mo. (1942), Calif. (1943), Alaska (1955). Career: secondary sch. tchr., Pleasanton 1924-25, Los Angeles 1925-30, San Jose 1935-36, San Francisco 1936-40; currently, pvt. medical practice; med. dir. Morrison-Knudsen, Aramco 1947-49; Afghanistan 1952-54; honors: Sigma Xi, UNiv. of Calif. 1935; mem: Sacto. Chpt. AAFP (secty.- treas., v.p.), AAFP, Am. and Calif. Med. Assns., Sacramento- El Dorado Co. Med. Soc., Los Angeles Co. Med. Soc. (past), Alameda Co. Med. Soc. (past), Lions Club, Air Force Assn., Sacramento Valley Pilots Assn., Ben Ali Shrine; publs. in physiology and ulta violet radiation; mil: maj. US Army Air Corps; US Army Med. Corps 1943-46; Republican; Methodist; rec: flying, photog. Res: 11005 Fair Oaks Blvd. Fair Oaks 95628 Ofc: Fair Oaks Clinic, 7949 California Ave. Fair Oaks 95628

BLACKBURN, JIM D., real estate broker; b. Feb. 20, 1951, Knox City, Tex.; s. Jim Bill and JoAnn (Harper) B.; m. Edith M., Sept. 23, 1972; 1 dau. Diane M. b. 1976; edn: undergrad. Pacific Univ.; AA, cert. in real estate, Diablo Valley Coll. 1982; JD, John F. Kennedy Univ. Sch. of Law 1986; Calif. R.E. lic. 1982. Career: sales mgr. Napa Project, Ferguson & Wollman Consulting Engrs., Security Owners Corp., Martinez; honors: MAME Sales Awards (1983, 84, 85); mem. Nat. Assn. Realtors, Calif. Assn. Realtors, C.C.C. Bd. Realtors, S.M.C.; mil: air controlman 2/c USNR; rec: ski. Res: 943 Snow Dr Martinez 94553 Ofc: c/o Security Owners Corp. 555 Escobar St Martinez 94553

BLACKSTOCK, WILLARD EDGAR, III, regional distribution executive; b. Oct. 17, 1946, Bklyn., NY; s. Willard, Jr. and Florence Lillian (Mahany) B.; edn: AA, Fullerton Coll. 1973; CSU Fullerton 1974-77, CSU LB 1986. Career: shop mgr. Hall's Auto Parts Inc., Norwalk 1973-79; prop. Bud's Marine Service, Sunset Beach 1980-83; dist. sales mgr. (So. Calif., Az., Nev.), now regional distbn. mgr. SKF Automative Products Inc., Commerce 1979-80, 1983—; recipient Sales Performer award (1981); civic: Cypress Volleyball Assn. (mgr., dir.); Republican; rec: tennis, volleyball, bowling. Res: 7157 Fillmore Dr Buena Park 90620 Ofc: SKF Automotive 6413 Bandini Blvd Commerce 90040

BLAKE, GARY BOMAN, advertising agency executive; b. Apr. 1, 1947, San Diego; s. Ross Clifford and Cecily Anne (Boman) B.; m. m. Lynette Holland, Sept. 7, 1985; children; Ashley Lauren b. 1983; edn: Univ. of Copenhagen 1969-71; BA, Whittier Coll. 1969. Career: asst. to creative dir. J. Walter Thompson, Copenhagen, Denmark 1970-72; mktg. & merchandising cons. Warner Bros. Records 1975-77; creative dir. Lamber & Blake 1977-80; principal The Blake Agency, Inc. 1981—; awards: CLIO radio advtg. 1980, S.F. Art Dirs. Club, radio advtg. 1984; mem: Rotary Internat.; San Francisco Art Dirs. Club (pres. 1982); No. Calif. Assn. of Advtg. Agencies; Sons of the Am. Revolution; Republican; Methodist; rec: tennis, skiing. Res: 2812 Russell Berkeley 94705 Ofc: 1045 Sansome, Ste 304, San Francisco 94111

BLAKE, KEVIN E., airline marketing executive; b. Dec. 23, 1956, Mnpls., Minn.; s. Ewald E. and Marjorie I. (Van Dusen) B.; m. Joan Wedgewood, Apr. 12, 1980; edn: mortuary sci., Univ. of Minn. 1976-79. Career: with Ozark Airlines 1979—; station agent, Sioux City, Iowa 1979-80; sales rep., Peoria, Ill. 1980-82; dist. mktg. mgr., San Diego 1982—; Subscribers of Sabre Club; mem: Skal Club, San Diego; Sales & Mktg. Execs. of San Diego; ASTA (S.D. chpt.); Transp. Club of S.D.; CON/VIS Airline Com.; Big Brothers of Am.; rec: sports (tennis), coin collecting. Res: 2852 Cazadero Dr La Costa 92008 Ofc: Ozark Air Lines, 2667 Camino Del Rio S, Ste 246, San Diego 92108

BLAKELY, EDWARD JAMES, educator, regional planning consultant; b. Apr. 21, 1938, San Bernardino, Calif.; s. Edward and Josephine (Carter) B.; m. Maaike Cornelia, July 2, 1971; children: Pieta Cobi b. 1974, Brette Dyrek b. 1981; edn: AA, San Bernardino Valley Coll. 1958; BA, UC Riverside 1960; MA, UC Berkeley 1963; PhD, UC Los Angeles 1970. Career: mgr. Pacific Tel. & Tel. 1960-63; tng. dir. Western Community Action Tng. 1965-68; asst. to Asst. Secty. of State Wash. DC 1968-71; asst. chancellor Univ. Pittsburgh 1971-74; assoc. dean Coll. of Ag. UC Davis 1974-77; asst. v.p. Univ. Calif. System 1977-85, chmn. dept. city & regl. planning 1986—; cons. to internat. agencies and several nations on economic devel.; honors: German Academic Scholar (1984), Vis. Fellow (Australian Inst. Urban Studies 1985), Fulbright Fellow (1985); mem: Am. Planning Assn., Community Devel. Soc. (bd. 1982-84), Am. Sociol. Assn., Rural Sociol. Assn., Pvt. Industry Council City of Oakland, Calif. Ag. Policy Ctr. (bd.); publs: articles in field; mil: 1st lt. USAF 1961-63, Outstanding Ofcr. Candidate; rec: running, football, tennis. Res: 2709 Alida St Oakland 94602

BLANCHARD, ELIZABETH YIP LEE, psychologist; b. Feb. 5, 1929, Hong Kong, China, nat. Am. citizen; d. Frank and Mary (Chin) Yip; m. Joseph L. Blanchard, Mar. 23, 1972; children: Richard L. Lee, b. 1950; Lester L. Lee, b. 1952; Vanetta Lee Wihlidal, b. 1953; edn: BA, Coll. of the Pacific 1958; MA, 1962; EDD, 1972; ednl. psychologist, State of Calif. 1962. Career: tchr./ counselor Stockton Unif. Sch. Dist. 1957-64; counselor, adminstr. San Joaquin Delta Coll. 1964-70; lectr. UC Davis Ext. 1970-71; testing ofcr. Univ. of Pacific

1970-72; clin. co-therapist Catholic Social Svcs. 1969-71, Transaction Anlysis Inst. 1960-70; seminar staff Esalen Inst., Monterey, Gestalt Psychotherapy Inst., Lake Tahoe, CA 1970-71; psychologist pvt. practice 1972-85; lectr. Cal-Lutheran Coll. 1973-76; staff psychologist Alta Calif. Regl. Ctr., 1973-74, Foster Grandparents pgm., Stockton State Hosp. 1974-75, San Joaquin Co. Hosp. Mental Health 1974; dir. BA., MA and Doctoral Pgms. in Bilingual Edn. UOP Sch. of Edn., 1976-78; psychologist San Joaquin Delta Coll. 1978–; awards: Scholarship, S.F. State Coll. 1962, San Jose State Coll. 1960, U. of Hawaii 1965, Fellow UOP 1971; regl. scholar 1969, state scholar 1970, Delta Kappa Gamma; Delta Coll. Staff Devel. Awd. 1979; mem: AAUW, Calif. Tchrs Assn., Phi Delta Kappa (1st woman pres. U.O.P. Chpt. 1980-81), Western Assn. of Schs. and Colls. (Accredit. Team), W. Psychological Assn., Phi Kappa Phi, Fellow Am. Psychol. Assn., Delta Kappa Gamma, Nat. Educators Assn., Stockton Tchrs. Assn., CofC; Soroptimist (pres. Stockton 1979-80; edn. chair all clubs in US, Japan, Carribean Is., Mex., S.A. 1984-6, gov. Sierra Pacific region 1988-90); v.ch. San Joaquin County Grand Jury 1981-82; Naval Ofcrs. Wives Club; bd. Regional Agcy for the Aged 1980-6; scholarship judge Bank of Am. (1977-8), Gemco (1973-86); Rotary Anns, Stockton Women Club (pres. 1964-5), PTA pres. 1963-4, United Way Crusade, ARC swim instr.; Republican; Catholic; rec: writing. Res: 3684 Wood Duck Circle Stockton 95207 Ofc: Delta College, 5151 Pacific Ave Stockton 95207

BLANCHARD, LON, general contractor; b. July 8, 1952, Los Angeles; s. Lester L. and Darcia S. (Saperstein) B.; m. Carol, Mar. 31, 1979; children: Leon b. 1980, Lance b. 1982; edn: BA pol. sci., CSU Long Beach 1975. Career: constrn. supt./contr., building apartment complexes and waterfront homes, 1977, restaurants 1978; founder/owner Construction 'R' Us, Inc., Corona 1983-, sold in 1985, now dir. of constrn., 1985–; mem. Nat. Assn. of Home Building Industry Assn., Home Builders Council, Sales & Marketing Council, Commercial & Industrial Council; Democrat; Jewish. Ofc: Construction 'R' Us, Inc. 129 Maple St Ste A Corona 91720

BLANCHETTE, JAMES EDWARD, psychiatrist; b. Aug. 28, 1924, Syracuse, NY; s. Joseph Marcel and Margaret Catherine (Vincent) Blanchette; m. Shirley Ruth Brisco, Sept. 1, 1948 (dec. May 4, 1981); edn: BA, Syracuse Univ., NY, 1950; MD, SUNY, Syracuse Coll of Med., 1953. Career: intern St. Vincent's Hosp., NYC 1953-54; res. Patton State Hosp., Calif. 1954-55; Met. State Hosp., Norwalk 1957-59; pvt. practice psychiatry, Redlands 1959–; chief profl. edn. Patton State Hosp., 1960-64; tchg. cons., 1964-; asst. clin. profl. psychiatry Loma Linda Med. Sch.; mem. staffs Loma Linda Med.Center, San Bernardino Comm. Hosp., St. Bernadine Hosp.; cons. in psychiatry Redland Comm. Hosp.; USAAF Band, Wash DC, 1945-47; USAAF M.C., 1953-55. Diplomate Am. Bd. Med. Examiners; Dip. Am. Bd. Psychiatry and Neurology; Fellow Am Psychiat. Assn;, Bd. Psychiatry and Neurology; mem: AMA, CMA, Pan-Am.Med. Assn., San Bernardino Med. Soc., So. Calif. Psychiat. Soc. (pres. Inland chpt. 1963-4, 1983-4), Royal Soc. Health, Am. Med. Soc., AAAS, Internat. Platform Assn., Phi Mu Alpha, Arrowhead Allied Arts Council, San Bernardino (past pres.), Elks, US Power Squadron, Dist. 13, P/D/C; USCG Aux.; clubs: Shark Is. Yacht, Hollywood Yacht; musician (string bass) fmrly with AF Band (Wash DC), Syracuse Sym., Univ. of Redlands Sym., Loma Linda Univ. Sym., Riverside Sym.; rec: boating. Res: 972 W. Marshall Blvd., San Bernardino 92405 Ofc: 236 Cajon St., Redlands 92373

BLANK, LAWRENCE FRANCIS, independent computer consultant; b. Oct. 4, 1932, Detroit, Mich.; s. Frank Alphonse and Marcella Alice (Pieper) B.; m. Carol Mann, Oct. 12, 1963; children: Ann b. 1965, Steven b. 1966, Susan b. 1968, Lori b. 1969; edn: BS, Xavier Univ. 1954. Career: asst. engr. General Electric Co., Evendale, Ohio 1956-60; research engr. General Dynamics Astronautics, San Diego 1960-62; tech. staff Computer Sciences Corp., El Segundo 1962-64; pgmmng. mgr. IBM Fed. Systems Div., Los Angeles 1964-69; pgmmng. mgr. Xerox Data Systems, El Segundo 1969-74; ind. computer cons. 1974–; mem: Assn. for Computing Machinery, Independent Computer Cons. Assn.; Republican; Catholic. Res: 608 Epping Rd. Palos Verdes Estates 90274 Ofc: 3838 Carson St. Ste. 328 Torrance 90503

BLANTON, JOHN ARTHUR, architect; b. Jan. 1, 1928, Houston; s. Arthur Alva and CarolineArnold (Jeter) Blanton; m. Marietta Newton, Apr. 10,1954 (dec. Apr. 3, 1976); chil: Jill Lewis b. 1958, Lynette Rowe b. 1961, Elena Blanton b. 1965; edn: BS, arch., Rice Univ. 1949. Career: assoc., Richard J. Neutra, F.A.I.A., Los Angeles 1950-64; architect pvt. practice, Manhattan Beach 1964–; instr. UCLA ext. 1967-75; instr. Harbor Coll. 1970-72; contbr. book revs. AIA Journal, 1972-75; awards: Red Cedar Shingle, Nat. AIA, 1979; CofC awards 1969, 70, 71, 74, 75, 82. Mem: AIA, Soc. Architl. Historians, Rotary Intl. Works: his bldgs. appear in Architecture in Los Angeles: A Compleat Guide (5); Sunset Mag., L.A. Times Home mag., Bicentennial Ed. AIA Journal; mil: US Signal Corps 1951-53; Ofc: John Blanton, AIA, 2100 Sepulveda, Ste 14, Manhattan Bch 90266

BLASIAR, KENT MICHEL, communications service co. executive; b. Oct. 31, 1952, Los Angeles; s. Clarence Joseph and Evelyn Marie Blasiar; m. Andrea, Sept. 11, 1982; 1 son, Bradley b. 1983; edn: bus. admin., USC 1977. Career: salesman, Alert Communications Co., 1966-69, bookkeeper 1969-70, data proc. mgr. 1970-76, office mgr. var. offices 1976-79, area mgr. 5 offices 1979-85, exec. v.p. in charge all telephone answering service ops. and all computer ops., 1985–; mem. Telephone Answering Services of Calif. (pres., dir.), ATAE nat. assn. (dir.), Am. Mgmt. Assn.; Republican; Catholic; rec: skiing (water, snow), baseball, basketball. Ofc: Alert Communications Co. 5515 York Blvd Los Angeles 90042-2499

BLASIOLA, GEORGE CHARLES, II, aquatic research biologist; b. June 16, 1949, Camden, N.J.; s. George C. and Wanda Dolores (Dziedzic) B.; edn: BS, Univ. of Miami 1972; MA in marine biol., CSU San Francisco 1980; postgrad. wk. CSU Hayward 1982. Career: aquatic biologist/supr. water analysis and pathology lab., Calif. Acad. of Scis., San Francisco 1973-79; pathobiologist/exec. mgr. AquaVet Div., Novalek Inc., Hayward; pres./bd. chmn. Profl. Assn. of Pet Industries (nat. non-profit ednl. assn.), Concord 1984–; adj. prof. CSU Hayward; cons. and contbg. ed. Fish Health Pet Age Mag. (1981-), review bd. J. of Aquariculture & Aquatic Scis. (1980-), contbg. ed. Fish biology, Freshwater & Marine Aquarium Mag.(1979-), contbg. ed. Marine Aquarist Publs. (1976-79); awards: appreciation, Zen Nippon Airinkai Koi Soc./Hayward (1983), PAPI bd. dirs. (1985); mem: Am. Fisheries Soc., No. Calif. Assn. Parasitologists, Calif. Acad. Scis., Aquatic Research Inst., Internat. Assn. of Aquatic Animal Medicine; contbr. num. research articles and presentations in field; Republican; Catholic; rec: skin diving, racquetball, weightlifting. Res: 2000 Crystal Springs Rd San Bruno 94066 Ofc: Novalek (Aquavet Div) 2242 Davis Hayward 94545

BLATTNER, RICHARD JOSEPH, physicist/ financial executive; b. May 8, 1944, St. Louis, Mo.; s. Eugene John and Marie Catherine (Pratte) B.; m. Ronna Brockmeier, Mar. 21, 1969; children: Richelle b. 1970, Russell b. 1974; edn: BS in physics, So. Ill. Univ. 1969, MS 1971. Career: physical sci. technician Fed. Bur. of Investigation Lab., Wash DC 1971; research asst., chem., Indiana Univ., Bloomington 1972; research chemist Materials Research Lab., Univ. of Ill., Urbana- Champaign, 1973-79; cofounder, exec. v.p., chief finl. ofcr. Charles Evans and Assocs., Redwood City, Calif. 1979–; vis. lectr. in applied physics & elec. engring. CalTech. 1978; invited lectr. NASA Lewis Res. Ctr. 1985; honors: Bohemishe Physicalische Soc. (1985), apptd. alternate del. to White House Conf. on Small Business by Cong. Tom Lantos (1986); mem. Am. Physical Soc., Am. Vacuum Soc., Am. Soc. for Metals, Am. Soc. for Metallurg. Engrs.; contbr. num. articles in sci. jours.; mil: pfc US Army 1966-67; Christian Ch.; rec: golf. Res: 1279 W 31st Ave San Mateo 94403 Ofc: Charles Evans & Associates 301 Chesapeake Redwood City 94063

BLAYLOCK, BRANDON ALLEN, bank executive; b. Apr. 22, 1957, San Diego; s. Albert John and Margaret Cleo (Stevens) B.; m. Elizabeth Jones, July 24, 1982; edn: BSCE, Univ. So. Calif. 1979, MS petrol. engrg., 1983; MBA, UC Los Angeles (1987); Reg. Profl. Civil Engr. Calif. 1982, petroleum engr. 1984. Career: senior proj. engr. (on loan to Arco Oil and Gas Co.) Exxon Co. Century City, Pasadena and Thousand Oaks 1979-84; asst. v.p., petroleum engr. Crocker Nat. Bank L.A. 1984–; honors: Chi Epsilon 1978, Pi Epsilon Tau 1983; mem: Am. Soc. Civil Engrs. (pres. undergrad. chap. 1978), Soc. Petroleum Engrs., Sigma Phi Epsilon (USC, former bd. dirs.); Republican; Episcopal; rec: golf, skiing. Res: 1633 Banning Way San Marino 91108 Ofc: Crocker Bank 333 S Grand Ave, 53rd floor, Los Angeles 90071

BLEEKER, RALPH CORWIN, company president; b. Mar. 4, 1924, Hamlin County, S.Dak.; s. Neil and Minnie (Meyer) B.; m. Jacqueline Ries, Nov. 24, 1949; children: Linda Jeanne b. 1951, Neil Corwin b. 1953, James Ray b. 1957, Michelle Jan b. 1958, Mark Alan b. 1960; edn: diesel repair with USN, var. automotive mechanics schs., num. bus. and service mgmt. seminars. Career: driver, equip. opr. Lance, Lance and England Constrn. Co. (constrn. of AFB), Watertown, S.D.; motor machinist, USN 1943-46; line mechanic Severin Motors Inc. (auto dealership), Long Beach 1946-53; service mgr. Bellflower Branch, 1953-70; owner/opr. Midway Auto Service, Midway City 1970-77; prin./ sec.treas./ asst. mgr. Standard Motor Parts (machine shop, parts house), Long Beach 1977-82, consultant 1982 – ; owner/opr. Automotive International Service, San Juan Capistrano 1982–; pres. Corwin Industries Corp.; awards: Silver Arrow, Wood Badge and Scoutmaster Award, BSA; mem: CofC, Am. Motor Parts and Service Mgrs. Club (pres. 1958-63), Boy Scouts of Am. (Cub Master, Scout Master); mil: USN 1943-46; Republican; rec: woodworking, horticulture. Res:13678 McNally Rd Valley Center 92082 Ofc: Automotive International, 26362 Via De Anza San Juan Capistrano 92675

BLENKINSOP, RICHARD W., manufacturing co. president; b. Jan. 15, 1931, McMinnville, Ore.; s. Richard E. and Emma M. (Schreiber) B.; m. Jeanne, Mar. 21, 1964; children: Brian b. 1966, Robert b. 1968, Gregory b. 1970; edn: Linfield Coll. 1948-50; BS bus. adm., Univ. of Ore. 1952; MS retailing, New York Univ. 1953. Career: dist. sales mgr. U.S. Gypsum Co. 1958-71; v.p. sales Western Metal Lath Co. (Div. Triton Group Ltd.), La Mirada 1971-84, pres. 1984–; mil: enlisted US Navy 1953-55. Ofc: Western Metal Lath Co. 15220 Canary Ave La Mirada 90638

BLESH, CHARLES HENRY, educator; b. Feb. 7, 1931, Smithwick, So. Dak.; s. Newton Arlington and Gertrude Sophia (Hook) B.; m. Lorene Tedford, Aug. 10, 1980; edn: B.Vocational Edn., CSC Los Angeles 1970; MA, CSU Los Angeles 1972. Career: supv. welding, certified welder/ fabricator Los Angeles area 1956-67; vocational welding instr. Dept. Social Svcs. L.A. Unified Sch. Dist. 1967-68; instr. vocational welding Compton Unif. Sch. Dist. 1968-72; instr. indsl. arts Orange Unified Sch. Dist. 1972-75, dept. chmn. 1975-76; instr. weld technol. Orange Coast Coll. 1976-78, asst. div. chmn. technol./ prof. 1978 –, mem. curruculum council, acad. senate, futurism com., weld advis. com.; leader seminars on weld testing and inspection for Chiyoda Corp. of Yokohama, Japan 1984, 85, 86; conductor seminars, nat. welding instr., supv. nat. weld inspector's exam for Am. Welding Soc.; listed Who's Who in Comm. Colls. 1986; mem: Calif. Edn. Assn., Nat. Edn. Assn., Calif. Indsl. Educators Assn., Phi Delta Kappa, Mason (32 degree), Am. Welding Soc. (chmn.

1982-83, secty. 1979-80, edn. chmn. 1978-79); Republican; Protestant; rec: camping, motor biking, travel. Res: 405 N Shasta St Anaheim 92807 Ofc: Orange Coast Coll. 2701 Fairview Rd Costa Mesa 92626

BLINN, ROBERT MURRAY, manufacturing co. executive; b. Sept. 15, 1926, Pasadena; s. Robert M. and Billie (Akin) B.; children: Robert III, David, James, Katie; edn: Pasadena City Coll. 1946-48. Career: v.p./owner Acromil Corp., 1960-64; owner/pres. Acro-Trace Corp., Huntington Beach 1962—; mem. Huntington Beach CofC; mil: boatswain mate 2c US Navy 1943-46, Asiatic Pac., Am. Def., WWII, Victory, Japanese Occup. medals; Republican; Prot.; rec: boating, fishing, golf. Ofc: Acro Trace Corp. 17582 Gothard St Huntington Beach 92647

BLISS, MARSHALL SIDNEY, lawn equipment co. president; b. Dec. 27, 1910, Oakland; s. George Sidney and Minnie Evelyn (Brown) B.; m. Vesta Blyther, June 29, 1972; children: George b. 1937, Nancy (Barclay) b. 1938, Walter b. 1949. Career: owner Bliss Texaco, Oakland 1940-45, Bliss Auto Service, Lake Tahoe 1946-50, Bliss Shell Service, Sacramento 1950-55, owner/ pres./ bd. chmn. Bliss Power Lawn Equipment Co. Inc., Sacto. 1956—; mem. Republican Clubs, Exchange, Masons; Presbyterian. Res: 192 Southgate Rd Sacramento 95815 Ofc: Bliss Power Lawn Equipment Co. Inc. 101 Commerce Sacramento 95815

BLOCK, ALAN ROBERT, lawyer; b. Oct. 5, 1946, Los Angeles; s. Harold Louis and Jeanette Sylvia (Manick) B.; m. Jan K. Mussinger, Aug. 8, 1976; 1 son, Justin, b. 1978; edn: BA, USC 1969; JD, Univ. of San Diego Sch of Law 1972; admitted to Calif. State Bar 1972. Career: deputy atty. general State of Calif. Dept. of Justice, Los Angeles 1972-78; pres. Law Offices of Alan Robert Block, Inc. 1979—; judge pro tem L.A. Superior Ct. 1984-85; advis. bd. Calif. Senate Select Com. on Small Bus. Ents. 1984-85; honors: Nat. Order of the Barristers 1972; Phi Delta Phi Graduate of the Year, Univ. of S.D. Sch. of Law, 1972, Law Rev. 1972, Honor Court Justice, 1972, Moot Ct. Bd. mem. 1972; mem. Los Angeles County, Beverly Hills, and Century City bar assns., Bev. Hills CofC, B.H. National Little League bd. dirs. (1985), Amie Karen Cancer Fund bd. dirs. (1985); rec: baseball, tennis. Law Offices of Alan Robert Block Inc. 9911 W Pico Blvd, Ste 590, Los Angeles 90035

BLOOM, EDWARD JOHN, international financial consultant; b. July 27, 1908, Camp Joseman Ilo, Ilo, Philippine Islands (US Army Post); s. Lt. Edward John and Pauline (Suing) B.; m. Helen M. Peterson, Feb. 11, 1939; children: Jacqueline (Rogers) b. 1941, Felice (Crowell Cavallera) b. 1939; edn: LLB, Gonzaga Univ., Spokane 1929; Grad. Sch. of Engring., Univ. of Wash. 1930; Princeton Univ. Grad. Sch. 1931-32; admitted to State Bar of Idaho (1929), Wash. State Bar (1930), Calif. State Bar (1932). Career: designed and built three (then largest) Bucket Line gold dredges, two in Calif., one in Mont., 1933-39; AS & R to 1942; pres. Idaho Smelting Inc. (secondary aluminum smelters in NW, Tx. and Hawaii) 1946-53; internat. fin. cons., lawyer 1953— overseas work Suez Canal Authority 1963-80, Lebanon 1963; general counsel Universal Metal Exploitations Inc., Nev. 1970-85, pres. 1985—; pres. Idaho Smelting (Philippines) 1946-53; mem. Am. Inst. of Mining, Metallurg. and Petroleum Engrs. (50 Year Mbrship Award 1984), Soc. of Explosives Engrs. (gen. counsel 1970-), Lions Club (1946-); mil: lt. AVS, US Naval Air Corps 1942-46; Republican; Roman Catholic; rec: research into earth and rock movements. Res: 2611-C Linden Way Palm Springs 92264 Ofc: Universal Metal, 708 Eastview Las Vegas Nevada 89107

BLOOMFIELD, HAROLD H., psychiatrist, author; b. Oct. 8, 1944, NY, NY; s. Max and Fridl (Waldman) B.; m. Sirah Vettese, Feb. 21, 1982; 1 child, Shazara Maxine b. 1983; edn: BS, Univ. Pittsburgh 1965; MD, State Univ. NY, Downstate Med. Center 1969; internship Kaiser Hosp., San Francisco 1970; psychiatry residency, Yale Univ. Sch. of Med. 1973; MD, Psychiatrist lic. Calif. 1970. Career: dir. of psychiatry Inst. of Psychophysiological Medicine, San Diego 1974-78; dir. psychiatry North County Holistic Health Center, Del Mar 1978—; prof. of psychology Univ. of Humanistic Studies, San Diego 1980—; speaker and seminar leader for univs., major corporations and gen. public, nat. and worldwide; 7 internat. lecture and seminar tours, 1975-83; frequent appearances on nat. t.v. shows incl. Phil Donahue, Hour Magazine, and Merv Griffin; author: TM: Discovering Inner Energy and Overcoming Stress (Delacorte Press, NY 1975), How To Survive the Loss of a Love (Simon and Schuster/Lion Press, NY 1976), Happiness: The TM Program, Psychiatry, and Enlightenment (Simon and Schuster/Dawn Press, NY 1976), The Holistic Way to Health & Happiness (Simon and Schuster, NY 1978), How to Enjoy the Love of Your Life (Doubleday, NY 1979), Inner Joy: New Strategies for More Pleasure and Satisfactions in Your Life (Harper & Row, NY 1980), Making Peace With Your Parents (Random House, NY 1983); The Achilles Syndrome (Random House, NY 1985); Making Peace With Yourself (Ballantine, NY 1986); num. book chapters and profl. articles; honors: Excellence award, Brandeis Univ. 1984, Golden Apple Award, the Learning Scene 1983, Award for Excellence, Assn. for Holistic Health 1985; mem: Am. Psychiatric Assn., San Diego Psychiatric Soc., Assn. for Holistic Health (founder), Am. Holistic Med. Assn., Physicians for Social Responsibility, Internat. Physicians for Social Responsibility; Democrat; Jewish; rec: jogging, family. Ofc: 1011 Camino Del Mar Ste 234 Del Mar 92014

BLUEMLE, PAUL EDWARD, college administrator; b. Sept. 9, 1926, Springfield, Ohio; s. Carl Henry and Mary Ann (Wolbert) B.; m. Helen Jean Smith, Sept. 13, 1958; children: Joy b. 1959, Christine b. 1960, Jude b. 1962, Laura b. 1964, Peter b. 1966; edn: BS magna cum laude, Xavier Univ. Ohio 1951; MA, Univ. Ore. 1953; Mich. State Univ. 1957-63. Career: reporter News & Sun

Springfield, Ohio 1943-51; grad. asst. Univ. Ore. 1951-53; exec. secty. YCS Nat. Hdqs. Chgo. 1953-54; dir. pub. rels. Thomas More Coll. Covington, Ky. 1954-55; bus. mgr. Today Mag. Chgo. 1955-56; instr. Mich. State Univ. 1956-59; ed. univ. pubs. Bowling Green State Univ. 1959-60; asst. dean, assoc. prof. Wayne State Univ. Detroit 1960-76; admissions dir., asst. dean, asst. acad. v.p. Univ. Detroit 1976-80; city clerk Pleasant Ridge, Mich. 1980-81; asst. to acad. v.p. Northwood Inst. Midland, Mich 1982-83; admissions dir. Holy Name Coll. Oakland 1983—; dir. Chgo. Research Group Inc. 1956-73; cons. Northwood Inst. 1983-84, The Coll. Bd. San Jose 1986; honors: Fulbright Scholar alternate (1951), T. Neil Taylor Award (Univ. Ore. 1953), Outstanding Faculty Award (Wayne State Univ. 1975); mem: Soc. Profl. Journalists (chpt. dir. 1957-58), Am. Assn. Univ. Profs. (chpt. secty. 1972-74), Nat. Assn. Coll. Admission Counselors 1976-; publs: Mass Media (Change 1969), Pleasant Ridge, Then and Now: A History (1981); mil: tech. sgt. US Army 1945-46, Army Commdn.; Christian. Res: 2235 Lincoln Apt 207 Lincoln House Apts Alameda 94501 Ofc: 3500 Mountain Blvd Oakland 94619

BLUMENFELD, ELI, lawyer; b. May 17, 1933, NY, NY; s. Wm. E. and Bessie (Rappaport) B.; m. Nancy Sue Greenberg, Dec. 2, 1973; children: Beth C. b. 1958, Robert K. b. 1963, Jennifer P. b. 1968, Whitney S. b. 1978, Kevin J. b. 1983; edn: BS with honors, 1958; JD, UC Los Angeles 1963. Career: acct., bus. mgr. Charles Goldring, Esq., Los Angeles 1962-64; dist. counsel IRS in Portland, Ore. and Los Angeles, 1964-69; atty. mem. law firm Mitchell, Silberger & Knupp, Los Angeles 1969; atty. solo practice Los Angeles 1969—; mem. ABA, Calif. Bar Assn., LA County Bar Assn., Beverly Hills Bar Assn., Vista Del Mar Presidents (chmn. fundraising 1979-, vp 1981-, chmn. bd. 1985-); clubs: Hillcrest Country, Lake Arrowhead Country; publs: tax articles; mil: US Navy 1951-55; rec: golf, tennis. Ofc: 1900 Ave of the Stars, 2440, Los Angeles 90067

BLYTHE, STEPHEN PHILIP, investment banker, small business consultant; b. Apr. 18, 1958, Bury Lane., England; s. Philip Arthur and Evelyn Barbara (Park) B.; m. Eliza Bethe Gail, Dec. 22, 1979; children: Jonathan b. 1982, Khrista b. 1984; edn: BS acctg., Ohio State Univ. 1980; CPA, Calif. 1981; State lic. insurance rep. 1985; Reg. Securities Rep., Securities Prin., and Finl. Prin., NASD, 1985. Career: CPA with Price Waterhouse & Co., 1979-81, Ernst & Whinney, 1981-84; CPA prin./ systems cons. to small bus. Blytheco., El Toro 1979—; exec. v.p./ chief finl. ofcr. Pacific Capital Ltd.; dir. PCL; honors: Beta Alpha Psi, Beta Gamma Sigma, Phi Sigma; mem. Calif. Soc. of CPAs (EDP com.); co-founder, dir. The Orange Apple Computer Club (900+ members) 1981-; author/pub. 10 computer pgms. (utilities and games); rec: personal computers, skiing, boating, golf. Ofc: Pacific Capital Ltd. 2323 N Broadway Ste 450 Santa Ana 92706

BOAM, KEITH CARLYLE, country club manager; b. Nov. 16, 1936, Idaho Falls, Idaho; s. Wayne and Nora (Fredinburg) B.; m. Martha, Aug. 6, 1955; children: David Gerard b. 1959, Douglas Keith b. 1962, Dera Lu b. 1969; edn: BS, Univ. of Idaho 1957. Career: salesman Stokeley-Van Camp, Oakland 1958-62; salesman K & C Food Sales, Los Angeles 1862-64; asst. sales mgr. Lamb Weston, Portland, Ore. 1965-66; v.p., gen. mgr. Continental Processors, Lafayette 1967-77, pres. 1977-79; exec. vp Continental Holding Co., Lafayette 1979-81; owner Rainbow Mktg., Lafayette 1981—; owner Pleasant Hill Country CLub, Pleasant Hill 1983—; mem: Am. Mgmt. Assn., President's Assn., Pleasant Hill CofC, Foodsters Inc., Lafayette CofC; Democrat; rec: golf, hunting. Res: 10 Joplin Ct. Lafayette 94549 Ofc: Pleasant Hill Country Club, 1093 Grayson Rd. Pleasant Hill 94523

BOAS, ROGER, city and county official; b. Aug. 21, 1921, San Francisco; s. Benjamin and Larie (Klien) B.; m. Nancy Lee Magid, July 6, 1958; children: John Roger, Christopher, Anthony, Lucy Anne; edn: AB, Stanford Univ. 1942; vis. fellow Nuffield Coll., Oxford (Eng.) Univ. 1982. Career: pres. Boas Internat. Motors, San Francisco 1946-76; chief adminstrv. officer City and County of San Francisco, 1977—; mem. Bd. Supervisors City and County of San Francisco, 1962-73; chmn. Calif. Democratic Central Com. 1968-71; prod./moderator weekly ednl. TV program World Press, 1960-76; mil: 1st lt. US Army 1942-45, ETO, decorated Silver Star, Bronze Star. Ofc: City Hall Room 289, San Francisco 94102

BOESEL, JO ANN MAE, business consultant; b. Sept. 20, 1932, Madison, Wisc.; d. Mandt and Julia Kathleen (Card) Homme; m. J. Philip Boesel, Jr., June 11, 1955 (div. 1981); children: John III b. 1956, Robert Mandt b. 1957, Julie Ann b. 1958; edn: Benton Harbor (Mich.) Comm. Coll. 1962-64; Des Moines Area Comm. Coll. 1979-80; Dale Carnegie Sales Course 1981; Mesa Coll. San Diego 1982-83. Career: secty., model 1950-54; stewardess Am. Airlines Chgo. 1954-55; ofc. mgr. Oakley for Lt. Gov. campaign Des Moines 1977; Republican del. to county, dist. and state convs., Iowa 1977-80; ofc. mgr., volunteer coord. Connally for Pres. campaign Des Moines 1979; group coord. Travel & Promotions 1980; exec. dir. Republican Assocs. of San Diego County 1982; bus. cons. Enterprising Concepts 1983—; adminstrv. asst. World Affairs Council of San Diego 1984; sales assoc. Am. Airlines 1984—; bd. dirs. Pacific Bluffs Corp. I and IV; mem. San Diego Writers/ Editors Guild 1984 (assoc.), Am. Airlines Kiwi Club; Republican; Protestant; rec: writing, art. Res: 4046 Mt. Acadia Blvd San Diego 92111

BOEX, HAROLD ARTHUR, real estate broker/developer; b. Dec. 17, 1933, Chgo., Ill.; s. Harold Anthony and Agnes Virginia (Hood) B.; m. Mary Helen Schuette, Dec. 5, 1958; children: Shirley Ann b. 1960, Anthony Robert b. 1961, Laura Frances, b. 1962; lic. Calif. R.E. Broker, lic. B-1 Gen. Contractor. Career: v.p. real estate, Systech Fin. Corp., Walnut Creek 1965-73; v.p./dir.

Pacific Northwest Fin. Corp. 1980-84; dir. Solano Fed. S&L, 1980-84; pres./ dir./ prin., H & B Developers (real estate devel. co.), Walnut Creek 1973–; ptnr. Sterling Finl., Lafayette 1982-; cons. govt. redevel. agencies; mem: Building Indus. Assn. (past pres. E. Div.; chmn. bd./dir. No. Calif. Reg.); Pacific Coast Bldrs. Conv. (past pres.); Calif. Bldg. Indus. Assn. (dir.-treas.); Nat. Assn. of Home Bldrs. (dir.); trustee Bldg. Indus. PAC; mem. Vallejo CofC, Vallejo Yacht Club, Elks; mil: USN; Republican; Catholic; rec: boating, fishing, travel. Res: 15 Lily Court, Walnut Creek 94595 Ofc: H & B Developers, 1825 Sonoma Blvd Vallejo 94590

BOGAN (HARVEY), HAZEL FAY, lawyer, manufacturing co. executive, ret.; b. Nov. 9, 1894, near Shingle Springs, Calif.; d. George Washington and Willamet Barbara (Heusner) Harvey; (gr. grandfather Henry Chandler Harvey of Vt. came to Sacramento in 1840s, Sacto. civic leader, councilman; m. Charles Francis Bogan, Sept. 9, 1917; edn: Metro. Bus. Coll. S.F. 1911; LLB highest honors, San Francisco Law Sch. 1927, JD, 1936; admitted to practice Calif. Cts. 1927, US Supreme Ct. 1937. Career: with W.P. Fuller & Co. San Francisco 1911-54, stenographer credit dept. 1911-14, secty. 1914-17, secty. to pres. 1917-26, asst. to pres., pension plan coord. 1926, interviewing singly over 3000 employees in 12 western states 1928-33, var. mgmt. assignments 1934-36, pchsg. agent 1937-54 (ret.); volunteer social and legal work 1954-; invited spkr. Mills Coll. num. times; subject of articles and testimonials (e.g. Allen P. Allensworth Market News Svc. 1954, Hardware World 1938) for outstanding achievement for woman in bus. world; served OPA for price controls during WWI; mem. Eastern Star; Republican; Presbyterian; rec: outdoor sports. Res: 1137 Stanley Dollar Dr Manor 3 Walnut Creek 94595

BOGEBERG, JOEL ROBERT, psychotherapist; b. Nov. 18, 1948, Flushing Meadows, NY; s. Gotfred and Edith (Bowe) B.; m. Suzanne, Aug. 30, 1981; edn: AA in food tech., St. Univ. NY 1968; BA in spl. edn., Goddard Coll., Plainfield, Vt. 1971; MA in counseling & guidance, CSU Northridge 1977. Calif. lic. Marriage, Family & Child Therapist; Elementary Sch. cert., Vermont. Career: career counselor and remedial edn. instr. Neighborhood Youth Core, Pawtucket, R.I.; counselor, instr. of learning/emotionally disabled, Mountain Road Sch. group home, Jeffersonville, Vt.; dir. of high sch. pgm./ ednl. therapist Beverly Ctr., Los Angeles; asst. dir./psychotherapist Academic Therapy and Counseling Ctr., Encino; sch. psychologist Mountain View Acad., Calabasas; psychotherapist in pvt. practice, Encino currently; consulting and tng. seminars for var. public and pvt. orgns.; instr. CSU Northridge, Glendale Comm. Coll.; mem: Calif. Assn. of Marriage & Family Therapists (bd. mem., pub. rels. chair), Calif. Assn. of Ednl. Therapists, Toastmasters Internat. (bd. mem., pub. rels. chmn.), Speakers Bur. of Gr. Los Angeles, Encino CofC, Assn. of Indsl. Recreation Council, Woodman 36 Homeowners Assn. (pres. 2 consec. terms); works: devel. innovative multi-media presentation to improve parent-child relationships; Christian; rec: profl. photog. (awards on state and nat. level); tennis, watersports. Res: 1194 Calle Pinata Thousand Oaks 91360 Ofc: 15720 Ventura Blvd Ste 602 Encino 91436

BOGEVOLD, TRYGVE, printing co. executive, ret.; b. Apr. 15, 1912, Waco, Tex.; s. Johannes Enderson and Sophia (Olsen) B.; m. Eve Moriarty, July 6, 1940; 1 dau. Sue Ann b. 1943; edn: BS, Tex. A&M Univ. 1933; Indsl. Coll. of the Armed Forces 1956. Career: div. engr. Shell Oil Co. Sacramento 1940; owner, pres. Bofors Inc. printing co. San Mateo 1946-78, chmn. bd. 1978-86 (ret.); pres., owner Bofors San Jose Inc. 1960-66; pres., owner Trybo Ents. Inc. (holding co.) 1960-74; pres. Children's Health Home for Mentally Retarded Children & Adults San Mateo County 1961; honors: Outstanding Support (Children's Health Home 1962); mem: Peninsula Golf & CC (v.p. 1962), Silverado Condominiums (chmn. bd. govs. 1969), No. Calif. Golf Assn. (pres. 1971), US Golf Assn. 1971- (dir. Good Shepherd Fund found. for handicapped 1973-), clubs: Silverado Country, Spyglass Hill Golf, Royal Kannapali Golf; works: created the computer-assisted handicap system used by golfers in Calif. since 1972; currently mem. USGA Handicap Research Team; mil: col. US Army Corps of Engrs. 1940-46, USAR 1946-72, Am. Defense, Euro. Afr. Middle Eastern Campaign, Am. Campaign, WWII Victory, Army Commdn.; Republican; Lutheran; rec: golf. Res: 301 Ascot Rd Hillsborough 94010

BOGUE, DONALD JOSEPH, educator; b. Sept. 11, 1930, Raymond, Wash.; s. Joseph A. and Esther (Peterson) B.; m. Marian Ann, Aug. 29, 1952; children: Stephen b. 1953, Debra b. 1959; edn: ThB, theology, Central Bible Coll. 1951; PhD, philosophy, Union Univ. 1976; MA, curriculum, Pacific Western Univ. 1976, EdD, adminstrn., 1977; Ordained minister Assemblies of God (1953). Career: pres./founder Andor Colleges, Inc., San Jose 1970-84, Stockton and Modesto, 1985–; pres. Bogue Investment Fund, Bogue Ents., B&B Adv. & Mktg., Andon Ednl. System; accreditation cons. to 40+ colls. and univs., cons. Health Care Ministries, Internat. 1975–; conv. speaker, clergyman 1970–; pastor Modesto, Milpitas, Gilroy, Fresno, 1958-68; project dir. Del E. Webb Constrn. Co., Cedar Rapids, Iowa 1955-57; Honors: Outstanding Young Man of Year, Jaycees (1956), Spl. Honor, Bayamon, Puerto Rico (1985), No. Calif. Flood Relief chmn. (1965); mem. Nat. Assn. of Health Career Schools (bd. 1976-84), Calif. Assn. of Paramedical Schools (ofcr., bd.), Accrediting Bureau of Health Edn. Schs., Elkhart, Ind. (v.chmn., commnr., 1975-84), Calif. State Post-Secondary Advisory Commn.; author: How To Teach Teachers to Teach Allied Health (1982), National Allied Health College Cost Survey (1980, 82, 84), Maintaining Student Retention (1978); Ind.; Assemblies of God; rec: sports. Ofc: Bogue Enterprises 2155 West March Ln Ste 1-E Stockton 95207

BOHN, BETH MARIE, training and sales management executive; b. Dec. 9, 1954, Berlin, Wisc.; s. Bernold Martin and Joan Elizabeth (Jewell) B.; m. Gary Macheel, June 26, 1982; edn: BS, Univ. of Wisc. 1979. Career: staff nurse LaCrosse Lutheran, LaCrosse, Wisc. 1979-80; dir. telephone sales Maryland Cup Corp., Los 1980-81, territory mgr. 1981-82; dist. mgr. Avon Products Inc., Los Angeles 1983-84, sales tng. mgr. 1984–; mem: Nat. Assn. of Profl. Saleswomen, Nat. Assn. for Female Execs. Inc.; art exhibs: The Cotton Exchange, Los Angeles (1984), Los Angeles Contemporary Exhib., Art Gallery; Republican; Lutheran; rec: art, baseball, football. Res: 2420 Lakeview Ave Los Angeles 90039 Ofc: Avon Products, 2940 E Foothill Blvd Pasadena 91121

BOHN, ROBERT HERBERT, lawyer; b. Sept. 2, 1935, Austin, Texas; s. Herbert and Alice (Heinen) B.; m. Gay, June 4, 1957; children: Rebecca b. 1958, Katherine b. 1965, Robert, Jr. b. 1968; edn: BBA, Univ. Texas 1957; LLB, 1963; admitted Calif. State Bar 1964, US Supreme Ct. Career: tax law editor Commerce Clearing House, Inc. San Francisco 1964-65; assoc. atty. Boccardo, Blum, Lull, Niland, Teerlink & Bell, San Jose 1965-81; ptnr. The Boccardo Law Firm, San Jose 1981–, exec. com. mem.; judge pro tem Santa Clara Co. Superior Ct.; arbitrator Am. Arb. Assn.; lectr. Calif. Continuing Edn. of Bar; listed Who's Who in Am. Law; mem: Calif. State Bar Assn., Santa Clara County Bar Assn., Calif. Trial Lawyers Assn., Am. Trial Lawyers Assn.; mem. Phi Gamma Delta frat., Texas Cowboys, Internat. Platform Assn.; mil: capt. USAF 1958-61; Republican (Pres. Task Force, US Senatl. Club, sustaining mem. Rep. Nat. Com.); Christian (Los Gatos Christian Ch.); rec: skiing, boating, photog., music. Res: 20056 Karn Cir Saratoga 95070 Ofc: The Boccardo Law firm, 111 West St John St San Jose 95113

BOLAM, MILDRED LA VONNE, realtor; b. July 14, 1941, Norfolk, Neb.; d. Earl and LaVonne Gertrude Young (Belmer) Mumm; m. Ronald Eugene Bolam, May 27, 1967; children: Deborah Adora b. 1961, Leslie Leon b. 1960; edn: Cert. of Convenience, Dept. of Ins. Calif. 1977; real estate sales, Dept. Real Estate Calif. 1985; notary public 1985. Career: policy typist, title secty., trust adminstrv. secty. Ticor 1969-72, mgr., asst. ins. agent, ofc. mgr. 1972-78; owner Mil e' B Artistry, iinc. into Pic n Slide; realtor Century 21; ofc. mgr. Pic n Slide Upland; art instr. Jonmar Enterprises, Montclair, Pomona Art Gallery; honors: VIP (C-21), Dist. Award of Merit (BSA 1974); mem. BSA (Dist. Tng. Chmn. 1973-75, council tng. chmn. 1976); Republican; Baptist; rec: art, oil painting, golf, helping others. Res: 1625 East G St Ontario 91764 Ofc: Century 21 Gold Post 2527 S Euclid Ontario 91672

BOLDING, GENEVIEVE T., governmental services executive; b. Oct. 30, 1929, Minersville, Pa.; d. Matthew and Katheryn (Richardson) Trenosky; m. Fred A. Bolding, Nov. 27, 1954; children: Patricia Ann (Bleckley), b. 1955; Sallie Mae (Sutter), b. 1957; Allan F., b. 1959; Alice Marie, b. 1961; edn: BA in bus. adm., with great distinction, San Jose State Coll. 1952. Career: secty. FBI, San Francisco 1952-55; district mgr. Marinwood Community Services Dist. since formation of dist., 1960–. Honors: Key Club, Phi Beta Kappa; mem. various charitable orgns. Catholic. rec: cooking, sewing. Address: Marinwood Comm. Svcs Dist. 536 Miller Creek Rd. San Rafael 94903

BOLIA, NORMAN EARL, university health and safety executive; b. Nov. 9, 1930, Ellingburg, NY; s. Earl William and Elsie Rose (Miller) B.; m. Dolores J., Nov. 5, 1950; children: Norman Jr. b. 1951, Patricia J. b. 1953, Beverly S. b. 1958; edn: BS engrg., Denver Univ. 1961; MS indsl. rels., UC Los Angeles 1973; Reg. Profl. Engr. Calif. 1975. Career: safety ofcr. UC Riverside 1970-73; assoc. dir. health & safety UC Irvine 1973–; State Bd. Profl. Engrg. testing 1978–; honors: NACUBO Award of Honor (1982), Cert. of Appreciation (City of Irvine 1984); mem: Am. Soc. Safety Engrs., System Safety Soc., World Safety Orgn., Irvine City Council 1983-84; mil: USAF 1948-70, safety ofcr., lt. col. USAFR 1970–; Republican; Southern Baptist; rec: travel. Res: 7938 La Casa Way Buena Park 90620 Ofc: UC Irvine 92717

BOLLINGER, JOHN, architect, planner, developer; b. April 12, 1943, London, Eng., nat. US cit. 1956; s. Luzer and Sarah Rosalie (Mayer) B.; m. Paula J. carter, Aug. 10, 1975; 1 dau, Lara Renee b. 1980; edn: B.Arch., USC 1966, M.Arch. 1968, DBS, 1971; Cert. Pub. Admin., CSU Long Beach 1978; Lic. Architec. (1976) and Gen. Contracto (1982), Calif. Career: designer Richard Neutra Assoc., Glendale 1962; project mgr. Larwin Groups Inc., Beverly Hills 1970-72; project coord. Bank of America Premises, Los Angeles 1972-75; assoc. planner City of Long Beach 1975-80, senior planner 19-84; world trade ctr. project mgr. Port of Long Beach 1979-84; prin. Joan Bollinger Architect, Fullerton 1976–; developer Bldg. Resources Interface, Fullerton 1982–; pres. The Mentor Group, Los Angeles 1984–; dir. Jewish Bus. & Profl. Network Orange Co. 1985-; lectr. Somata USC Ext. 1970-; tchg. asst. USC Arch. 1968-71; honors: Archetictural Guild Fellowship; Weyerhauser Found. Research Grant; Clayton Baldwin Meml. Award; Am. Inst. of Architects Fellowship Award; Calif. State Fellowship; mem: Am. Inst. of Architects; AIP, AEP, Architectural Guild, Orange Co. World Trade Assn., Internat. Bus. Assn., JBPN, Inland Internat. Trade Assn., Long Beach CofC, Internat. Mktg. Assn. of Orange Co., Pomona World Trade Assn., FCEE, CSI, BIA, IHC, ASTM, NAHB, Assn. of Arch. in Govt., USC Alumni Assn., Downtown Long Beach Lions Club, Town Hall; works: creativity lecture series, 1970; research, The Mother of Invention, Arts & Architecture, 1967; The Work of Konrad Wachsmann, AIA Journ. 1972; Kinematics of Building System Assembly, Univ. Pub. 1970; European Ind. Bldrs., L.A. Times 1972; Master Plan, Port of Long Beach 1978; Risk Mgmt. Plan, Port of Long Beach 1979; World Tarde Ctr. Research Study, Port of Long Beach 1981; Pomona City WTC Study 1985; Fresno Agritrade Ctr. Study 1986; Democrat; Jewish; rec: computers, philately, painting. Res: 717 No. Carhart Ave. Apt. 64 Fullerton 92633 Ofc: The Mentor Group, 9200 Sunset Blvd. Ste. 601 Los Angeles 90069

BOLMAN, ROBERT HILL, management consultant; b. Jan. 13, 1906, Lawton, Okla.; s. Robert Oliver and Sylvia (Hill) B.; m. Nevada Hayward (dec.), Apr. 7, 1930; m. 2d Edith Bain, Jan. 23, 1937; children: Gay (Stern) b. 1931, Sylvia (Williard) b. 1942; edn: Ba, Stanford Univ. 1927. Career: asst. secty. Bishop Trust Co. Ltd., Honolulu 1927-36; asst. v.p. Union Bank, Los Angeles 1936-44; exec. v.p., dir. Pasadena 1st National, also pres., dir. Bank of Beaumont, 1944-47; v.p., dir. Oakland Bank of Commerce, 1947-54; exec. v.p., dir. Bank of California Internat., also senior v.p. The Bank of Calif., 1954-69; management cons., 1970-; resident advisor Dow Banking Corp., Zurich 1971-73; dir: Products Research and Chemical (1972-74), Computer Sci. Corp. (1973-86); past dir: Mercantile Printing Co., Bergstrom Music Co. (Honolulu), Western Die Casting, Home Found. Svgs. & Loan; trustee emeritus Calif. Coll. of Arts & Crafts; dir. Arthritis Found./ East Bay Chpt., Oakland; dir. Merritt-Peralta Found., Oakland; past active mem: Honolulu Jr. CofC (dir), LA CofC (govt. affairs com. 1939), US Treasury War Fin. Com. (1941-45), Russian War Relief (So. Calif. dir./treas. 1942), United War Relief (dir. So. Calif. 1943), Pasa. Art Inst. (trustee 1945), Calif. Bankers Assn., Indep. Bankers Assn. (pres. So. Calif. 1943, pres. No. Calif. 1953), Crippled Children's Soc. (dir. Alameda Co. 1950), Alameda County United Fund (pres. 1958), United Bay Area Crusade (dir. 1957), SF CofC, US CofC, Monterey Inst. of Fgn. Studies (trustee 1972-73), Monterey County Supervisor (1974), Japan Soc. of S.F., World Affairs Council (dir. Palm Springs 197778), Am. Security Council (nat. advis. bd.); clubs: Claremont Country, Bohemian, Pacific Union.; Republican; Episcopal. Address: 5295 Broadway Terr Oakland 94618

BOLT, LAURI L., chiropractor; b. Sept. 30, 1951, Fresno, Calif.; d. Donald Ben and Esther R. (Rangel) B.; edn: Fresno City Coll. 1974-75; Foothill Coll. 1978-79; AA, Santa Barbara City Coll. 1980; BS, Cleveland Chiro. Coll. 1982, DC, 1984; Dental Asst. Cert., Galen Coll. 1971. Career: Sahara Tahoe 1975-77; doctor of chiropractic, nutrition cons. State St. Chiro. Ofcs. Santa Barbara 1985-86, Chiropractic Fitness Center Carpinteria 1986-; honors: Delta Tau Alpha (Cleveland Chiro. 1980-84); mem: Internat., Am., Calif. Chiro. Assns.; CofC, Young Democrats, Santa Barbara Ski Club; Democrat; Christian; rec: portrait drawing, skiing, juggling. Res: 1755 Grand Ave Santa Barbara 93103 Ofc: Chiropractic Fitness Center, Shepards Place, 1015 Casitas Pass Rd Carpinteria 93013

BOLTON, ROD H., electronic manufacturing co. president; b. Aug. 7, 1944, Los Angeles; s. Roger L. and Marion J. (Warnack) B.; m. Sonya Leah Stroud, June 27, 1970; children: Lecia b. 1973, Brent b. 1978, Blake b. 1982; edn: BA, CSU Fullerton 1966, MBA, 1967. Career: mgr. ops. ATO div. Beckman Instruments 1967-72; dir. sales & svc. adminstrn. Gen. Automation 1972-75; regl. gen. mgr. Anthony Industries 1975-80; v.p., gen. mgr. Elpac Electronics 1980-84; pres. Electronic Solutions/ Scanbe (div. of Zero Corp.) 1984-; conductor mgmt. tng. seminars; honors: Most Outstanding Grad. Student (1967), Alumni of the Year (1973); mem: Christian Exec. Ofcrs. of San Diego, Am. Electronics Assn. (mem. com.), Scripps Ranch Little League; Baptist; rec: tennis. avoc: personal improvement, motivation research. Res: 10489 Avenida Magnifica San Diego 92131 Ofc: Electronic Solutions 6790 Flanders Dr San Diego 92121

BONDOC, NICHOLAS ROMMEL, JR., lawyer; b. June 23, 1938, Pomona; s. Nicholas Rommel and Gladys Sue (Buckner) B.; m. Alberta Young, Dec. 13, 1967; children: Daphne, b. 1961, Patience, b. 1970, Margaret, b. 1972, Nicholas, b. 1976; edn: BA, Stanford Univ. 1960, JD, 1963; admitted to practice 1964. Career: assoc. Melvin Belli, San Francisco 1964-66; assoc. Vincent Hallinan, San Francisco 1966-69; sole practitioner, San Francisco 1969-; spec. criminal law 1973-; mem: Phi Beta Kappa; No. Calif. Criminal Trial Lawyers Assn. (pres. 1978-79); San Francisco Bar Assn. (Judiciary Com. 1982-85); singer: Sally Stanford's Valhalla Inn, Sausalito 1977-82; Democrat; Wesleyan. Res: 509 Canyon Rd., Novato 94947 Ofc: 899 Ellis, San Francisco 94109

BONHAM, TERRENCE JAMES, lawyer; b. June 8, 1938, Richmond; s. Harry L. and Helen (Gately) Bonham; m. Joyce E. Trout, July 28, 1968; 1 dau. Teresa Jeannette; edn: BA, St. Mary's Coll. of Calif. 1960, JD, UC Hastings Coll. of the Law 1963. Career: attorney firm of Halde, Battin, Barrymore & Stevens in Santa Barbara 1968-73; partner Barrymore, Stevens & Bonham, 1973-74; Reilly, Holzhauer, Denver & McLain in Ventura 1974-80; partner firm Lawler & Ellis, Ventura 1980-; arbitrator Civil Panel Ventura; Hearing Ofcr. Co. of Santa Barbara Retirement Bd. & Civil Svc. Commn.; Judge pro tem Co. of Ventura, Co. of Santa Barbara; lectr. Bridging the Gap, CTLA, Arbitration Gps. and Assns. Mem. Ventura Co. Bar Assn. (fmr. exec. com., atty. client chmn.), Am. Bd. of Trial Advocates (pres. 1985 SB-VTA-SLO), State Bar Calif., Am. Bar Assn., Ventura Bar Assn., So. Calif. Defense Counsel. Listed Who's Who in Am. Law, 3d ed. Mem. Knights of Columbus, 4th Deg. (Faithful Navigator), Elks, Trade Club of Ventura. Mil: capt. Judge Adv. Gen. Corps, US Army 1964-68, Bronze Star, Vietnam Campgn. Medal. Republican (Presdtl. Task Force, Repub. Senatl. Com., US Supreme Ct.). Catholic. rec: painting (oils). Res: 2348 Kudu Pl. Ventura 93003. Ofc: Lawler & Ellis, 2151 Alessandro Dr. Ste. 220, Ventura 93001

BONINI, JEAN FRANCES, lawyer; b. June 7, 1948, NY, NY; s. Ulysses J. and Margaret M. (Dillon) B.; edn: BBA, St. John's Univ. 1969; MBA, USC 1974; JD, Univ. of San Diego Sch. of Law 1980; admitted Calif. Bar 1980. Career: personnel asst. Am. Photographic Corp., NYC 1968-69; High Sch. Recruitment Program coord., Bankers Trust Co., NYC 1969-70; pers. analyst Orange County (Calif.) Medical Ctr., 1970-73; labor relations analyst Orange County Personnel Dept., Santa Ana 1973-75; personnel mgr. Orange County Environ-

mental Mgmt. Agcy., 1975-76; personnel analyst City of San Diego, 1976-78; pers. mgr. Kaiser-Permanente Medical Care Pgm., San Diego 1978-80; atty. law firm Jackson, Lewis, Schnitzler & Krupman, Los Angeles 1980-81, law firm Schachter, Kristoff, Ross, Sprague & Curiale, San Francisco 1982-83; atty. Labor Relations & Legal Affairs, Am. Bdcstg. Co., Los Angeles 1983-; atty. vol. L.A. Free Clinic 1984-; mgmt. instr. Santa Ana Community Coll. 1975-76; mem. Charter Review Com., County of San Diego 1979-80; mem. Am., Calif., Los Angeles County bar assns.; Ind.; Ofc: American Bdcstg. Co. 4151 Prospect Ave Hollywood 90027

BONNEY, GEORGE WILLIAM, judge; b. Aug. 22, 1923, Midwest, Wyo.; s. George William and Bertha Anne (Ormsby) B.; m. Kerminette Schweers, Aug. 27, 1949; children: Susan Mary, George William III, Michael Kermit; edn: AB, Univ. Wis. 1950, LL.B 1952; admitted to Calif. State Bar 1952. Career: law practice in San Jose 1952-; ptnr. Rankin, Oneal, Luckhardt, Center, Ingram, Bonney, Marlais & Lund, 1967-; judge Santa Clara Municipal Ct. 1972-80, Santa Clara Co. Superior Ct., 1980-; Dist. chmn. Santa Clara Co. chpt. BSA, 1967-, mem. exec. bd. 1967-; mem. Saratoga Parks and Recreation Commn. 1970-; mem. Conf. Calif. Judges, Am., Calif. (conf. dels.), Wis., Santa Clara Co. bar assn., Univ. Wis. Alumni Assn., Santa Clara Co. Trial Lawyers Assn. (pres. 1971), Santa Clara Co. Conf. Municipal Judges (pres. 1977), Sigma Phi Epsilon, Rotary. Res: 12740 Carniel Ave. Saratoga 95070 Ofc: 191 N 1st St San Jose 95113

BONSACK, ROLF H., business owner; b. Jan. 23, 1937, Salz-Gitter Bad, W. Ger.; nat. 1961; s. Elli Bonsack; m. Sharon Browning, Feb. 13, 1960; chil: Robert, Kevin, Vivian, Thomas, David; edn: stu. mining-iron, trade sch., Ger. Career: immigrated to San Francisco in 1954, worked as a baker for St. Mary's Hosp., S.F. 1954-59, Stemple's Bakery in S.F. and San Jose, 1959-77; owner Rolf's Wash & Dry's (now in 4 locations) Coin Washer & Dryer Service, 1970-. Mem: Coin Laundry Assn., No. Calif. Laundromat Assn., San Jose CofC, Better Bus. Bur.; Democrat. Christian. Address: Coin Washer & Dryer Service, 4415 Samson Way, San Jose 95124

BOOKER, HERBERT WESLEY, lawyer; b. June 1, 1949, Dayton Ohio; s. Richard Johnson and Mary Mildred (Chambers) B.; m. Wrise, Aug. 19, 1972; edn: BA, Denison Univ. 1971; JD, Univ. Mich. Law Sch. 1973; admitted Calif., Mich. State Bars, US Dist. Cts. Mich., central dist. Calif. Career: mediator Univ. Mich. Mediation Svc. Ann Arbor, Mich. 1973-74; asst. US atty. US Atty's Ofc. Central Dist. Calif. 1978-; instr. bus. law Allan Hancock Coll. 1976-78; rotating instr. Dept. of Justice Advocacy Inst. 1975, 86; honors: Director's Award for Equal Employment Opportunity (Dept. of Justice 1984); mil: capt. USAF (JAGC) 1974-78; rec: painting, music, art. Ofc: US Attorney's Office 312 N Spring St Ste 1154 Los Angeles 90012

BOONE, JARRETT SMITH, clinical psychologist; b. Feb. 7, 1939, Memphis, Tenn.; s. Stephen and Myrtle Bernice (Gray) B.; children: Jamila b. 1968, Kamilah b. 1974, Jarrett b. 1980; edn: BS, Univ. Wash. 1968, PhD, 1972. Career: intern Langley-Porter Neuropsychiatric Inst., 1970-71; psychotherapist Center for Psychol. Services and Research, 1970-72, Highline Comm. Mental Health Ctr., 1971-72, Central City Comm. Mental Health Ctr., 1972-73; staff psychologist VA Medical Ctr. San Francisco, Mental Health Hygiene Clinic 1977-79, Alcohol Outpatient Clinic 1979-80; cons. psychologist Bayside Adolescent Residential Treatment Ctr., 1982-84; pvt. practice, San Francisco 1984-; consulting psychologist var. agencies, group homes (S.F.); staff psychologist Center for Spl. Problems A Forensic Outpatient Facility, 1981-; clin. assoc. prof. Fuller Theol. Sem., Grad. Sch. of Psychology; asst. prof. CSU Los Angeles 1972-77, guest lectr. Windsor Univ. (LA), UCLA, Univ. S.F.; mem: Am. Psychol. Assn., Assn. of Black Psychologists/So.Calif., Western Psychol. Assn., Nat. Assn. Black Social Wkrs., Union of Coll. and Univ. Profs. (Rep. at large), Nat. Council for Community Mental Health Ctrs., Am. Assn. of Sex Educators, Counselors and Therapists, Rap Cities diversionary pgm. (bd. dirs.), Internat. Diversified Developers (bd. dirs.), Assn. of Black Coll. Faculty, Forensic Mental Health Assn.; num. research and profl. papers, workshops, TV and radio appearances; mil: sgt. US Army 1960-62; Catholic; rec: chess. Res: 111-B Chester Ave Fairfax 94930 Ofc: 2166 Hayes St Ste 302 San Francisco 94117

BORCHERT, IRVIN EMMETT, realtor; b. Mar. 26, 1916, Cherry Creek, Nev.; s. Harry C. and Josephine (Burke) B.; m. Jessie McClure, May 26, 1940; children: Douglas b. 1942, Mark b. 1945, Stephen b. 1948; Career: early jobs incl. sheep herding, svc. stn. oper., comml. pilot, flight instr. WWII, crop duster; oil distbr. (Shell) Borchert & Smith Nampa, Ida. 1946-50; comml. rep. Richfield Oil Co. Sacramento area 1950-55; salesman to gen. sales mgr. Moss & Moss Realtors Sacto. 1955-78; pres. Greenhaven Realtors, Gallery of Homes 1978-; instr. Grad. Realtors Inst. 1975-76; honors: Million Dollar Club (charter mem.), Salesman/ Citizen of the Yr. (1970-71), Best Dressed of Calif. (1970); mem: Sacto. Bd. of Realtors (pres. 1978), Calif. Assn. Realtors (regl. v.p. 1980), Nor-Cal Investment Multiple Listing Svc. (pres. 1975), Sacto. Area Commerce & Trade Orgn. (bd. 1978-), Calif. Real Estate Cred. Union (bd.), ARC (bd. trustees), Sacto. Metro CofC; publ: autobiography, I'm One of Those Bastards (1976); Democrat; Catholic; rec: flying. Res: 1337 Gagle Way Sacramento 95831 Ofc: Greenhaven Realtors 6355 Riverside Blvd Sacramento 95831

BORDE, MADHUSUDAN, cardiologist; b. Jan. 4, 1948, Bhainsa Dist., India; s. Ambadasrao and Mainabai B.; m. Usha Joshi, Feb. 10, 1972; children: Madhuri b. 1977, Manish b. 1979; edn: P.U.C., New Science Coll. Hyderabad, India 1963; MBBS, Osmania Univ. 1972; Diplomate Am. Bd. Internal Med. &

Cardiol. Career: physician Price Georges Gen. Hosp. & Med. Ctr. 1974-77; phys. (fellowship) Northwestern Univ. Med. Sch. Chgo. 1977-79; cardiol. David Grant Med. Ctr. Travis AFB Calif. 1979-81; pvt. practice Vallejo, Calif. 1981 –; instr. med. Northwestern Univ. Med. Sch., David Grant USAF Med,. Ctr.; mem: Am. Coll. Phys., Am. Coll. Cardiol. (affil.); mil: major USAF 1980-81; rec: reading, travel. Res: 512 Blue Ridge Ct Vacaville 95688 Ofc: 1460 N Camino Alto Ste 106 Vallejo 94590

BORENS, KERBY KENT, manufacturing company executive; b. March 17, 1950, Pomona; s. Kerby Frank and Melba (Ross) B.; m. Sharon Rose, Jan. 30, 1970; children: Jason b. 1971, Shannon b. 1976, Amber b. 1980, Rebecca b. 1984; edn: BS, Calif. Polytechnic Univ. Pomona 1972; CSU Los Angeles 1968-69. Career: sales rep. Sweetheart Cup Corp., Los Angeles 1973-75; sales rep. Sealed Air Corp., Commerce 1975-79, regl. sales mgr. 1979-81, nat. sales mgr. 1981-83; div. mgr. Cooley Inc., Anaheim 1983 –; mem: Soc. of Pkg. & Handling Engrs. (corp., profl.), City of Commerce Jaycees (founding mem.); Republican; Catholic; rec: stained glass, tennis. Ofc: Cooley Inc., 3845 E. Miraloma Ave. Anaheim 92806

BORGHI, DOUGLAS STEFEN, motion picture writer/producer/director; b. May 9, 1950, Bronx, N.Y.; s. Ercole Stefen and Edith Bernedette (Brac) B.; ed. Iona Prep. Sch., 1968. Career: pres. Revenge Pictures, Los Angeles 1972 –, writer, prod., dir. num. commercials, ednl. films, spl. effects. tests, spl. effects sequences for motion pictures, computer animation for Sesame Street, also writer on major motion pictures; motion pictures include: On Dangerous Ground, Master Blaster, The Sacrifice, Silverwings; founder/pres. Americana Soc. (dedicated to accurate presentation of Am. heritage in film indus.) 1986-; mem. L.A. County Museum 1975-; Emersonian; Catholic; rec: breeding Am. Staffordshire Terriers. Ofc: Revenge Pictures POB 24295 Los Angeles 90024

BORJAL, ARMANDO C., veterinarian; b. Feb. 1939, Philippines, nat. 1978; s. Jose B. and Aurea C. (Carilo) Borjal; m. Mabel Dioneda, Feb. 6, 1966; children: Madeleine b. 1966, Sarah b. 1968, Michelle b. 1970, Jerome b. 1972, Armando, Jr. b. 1980, Adelle b. 1984; edn: DVM, Univ. of the Phil. 1964; MPA, CentroEscolar Univ., 1971. Career: Meat & Food Insp., Calif. Dept. of Food & Agri., Sacramento 1973-74, veterinary med. ofcr. I, II, 1974-76; animal tech. III (lab. animals), Calif. Dept. of Health Svcs., Berkeley 1976-79; pvt. practitioner (small animal) vet. 1979 –; vet. Addison St. Pet Hosp., Berkeley 1979-80, cons. 1980-; mgr./vet. Bay Cities Spay & Neuter Clinic, Milpitas 1980; currently owner, mng. vet. A.B. and C. Vet. Clinic, Union City; awards: letterman, Univ. of Phil. varsity volleyball (team capt. 1963)1960-63, varsity track & field 1960-63, winner 1st campus marathon. mem: Calif. Filipino Veterinary Practitioner, No. Calif. Assn. of Filipino Vets., Fgn. Graduates Vet. Assn. in USA 1976, Phil. Vet. Med. Assn., Calif. Vet. Med. Assn., Am. Vet. Dental Soc., Smithsonian Instn.; mem: Examining panel Filipino Bilingual Pgm. 1978; mem. Excelsior Neighborhood Assn. (SF) 1980; charter mem. Venerable Knight Vets. frat.; pub. sci. papers; Democrat; Catholic; rec: jog, swim, volleyball, basketball. Res: 231 Athens San Francisco 94112 Ofc: A.B. and C. Vet. Clinic, 4235 Horner St Union City 94587

BORLAND, JOHN OGAWA, electronic material scientist; b. June 29, 1958, Brooklyn, NY; s. John Henry and Masako (Ogawa) B.; m. Laura Piper, Aug. 24, 1985; 1 son: Jonathan Michael b. 1986; edn: BS, Mass. Inst. of Tech. 1980, MS, 1981. Career: vis. material scientist NASA Marshall Space Flight Ctr., Huntsville, Ala. 1978; student engr. III Hughes Aircraft Malibu Research Lab., Malibu 1979 –; vis. material scientist NTT Masashino Electrical Communications Lab., Tokyo, Japan 1980; electronic material scientist National Semiconductor Corp., Santa Clara 1981-83; senior staff engr. Applied Materials Inc., Sant Clara 1983 –, guest lectr. Stanford Univ.; mem: Electrochemical Soc.; Materials Research Soc., Am. Assn. for Crystal Growth, IEEE, Am. Assn. for Adv. of Sci.; research: CMOS technology, Latch-up, Advanced Silicon Material and Epi technol.; author: 20+ tech. papers; rec: running. Res: 3923 Sophist Dr. San Jose 95132 Ofc: Applied Materials Inc., 3050 Bowers Ave. M/S 0115 Santa Clara 95054

BORMES, DAVID MICHAEL, real estate financial executive; b. May 16, 1956, Milwaukee; s. Robert E. and Patricia A. (Mullen) B.; m. Kathleen, Aug. 2, 1974; children: Victoria b. 1975, Stephanie b. 1977; edn: Creighton Univ. 1974-76; BS, Northern St. Coll. 1977. Career: branch mgr. Gen. Elec. Credit Corp., Chgo. 1977-80, area mgr. 1980-82, region ops. analyst, Cinti., O. 1982-83, region bus. devel. mgr. 1983, constrn. loan analyst, Portland, Ore. 1983-84, investment mgr., Walnut Creek, Calif. 1984 –; awards: GECC Winners Circle (1985), GECC Pinnacle Club (1985); mem. GECC Bay Area Mktg. Council, K.C.; Democrat; Catholic; rec: golf, hunting, sailing. Res: 878 Dover Circle Benicia 94510 Ofc: General Electric Credit Corp. 1320 Willow Pass Rd Ste 560 Concord 94520

BORNMANN, LEWIS JOSEPH, systems engineer; b. Oct. 12, 1936, Atlantic City, NJ; s. Lewis Joseph and Sue (Berish) B.; m. Barbara Nelle Long, Feb. 14, 1974; children: Siobhan, b. 1967; Lewis, b. 1967; Christopher, b. 1970; edn: BS, Indiana Inst. of Tech. 1965; MS, Univ. of Wisc. 1969. Career: project asst. Ind. Inst. of Tech., Fort Wayne, Ind. 1964-5; analyst/pgmmr. The Boeing Co., Renton, Wash. 1965-6; proj. ldr. Computer Ctr. Univ. of Wisc., Madison, Wis. 1966-9; proj. ldr. Control Data Corp. 1969-72; tech. staff Calma Co., Sunnyvale, Calif. 1972-3; proj. mgr. Control Data Corp., Sunnyvale 1973-5; senior analyst Stanford Univ. 1975-6; section mgr. EG&G Idaho, Idaho Falls, Ida. 1976-8; mgr. information proc., STD Research Corp., Arcadia, Calif. 1978-80; instr. cybernetic systems, San Jose State Univ. 1981; sys. engr. Gen. Elec. Co., Space Sys. Div., Sunnyvale 1980 –; mem. ACM 1965- (Assn. Stds. Com.,

Com. on Chpts., past ACM Council Pacific Reg. Rep., ch. Eastern Idaho Chp., ch. San Gabriel Chp.), IEEE; mil: USAF 1958-61; rec: jog, ski, ham radio. Res: 1326 Chewpon Ave Milpitas 95035 Ofc: General Electric, 4041 North First St San Jose 95134

BOROUMAND, FERIDOON, civil engineer; b. Oct. 3, 1941, Isfahan, Iran; s. Ismail and Kobra (Khaef) B.; m. Cecilia, Dec. 22, 1972; chidren: Gitta b. 1967, Ramin b. 1977; edn: AA, Hartnell Coll. 1966; BSCE, San Jose State Univ. 1969; reg. profl. civil engr., Calif. Career: proj. ngr. Shuirman Rogoway & Assoc., Los Angeles 1969-72; hd. civil dept. Farman Farmayan & Asoc., Tehran, Iran 1972-76; gen. mgr. Armed-Tessa Constrn. Co., Tehran, Iran 1976-79; proj. engr. Rogoway. Borkovetz, Los Angeles 1979-81; principal civil engr., designer, Alhambra 1981-83; proj. mgr. Pace Eng. Co., Encino 1983 –; honors: Medal of Honor for excellence in civil eng. svc., Govt. of Iran 1975; mem: Am. Soc. Civil Engrs., U.S. Soccer Fedn. (cert. referee), NCAA (cert. soccer referee); rec: sports, soccer referee. Res: 5900 Ostrom Ave. Encino 91316 Ofc: Pace Engineering Inc., 5435 Balboa Blvd. Ste. 101 Encinco 91316

BORRELL, GEORGE R., physician; b. April 21, 1920, Paris, France, nat. US cit. 1956; s. Luis Rivero and Maria (Hermosillo) B.; 1 dau, Leonore Aliza b. 1961; edn: B. Biol. Scis., German Sch., Mexico City 1937; MD, Medical Military Sch., Mex. City 1945. Career: physician, chief of staff Bella Vista Hosp. 1964-65; med. dir. Evaluation Ctr. Med. Group 1966-74, Allergy Control Med. Group, Canoga Park 1975 –; lectr. in clin. immunology and allergy Internat. Immunology Inst.; past pres. Council of Mexican American affairs 1963-65; founder, past pres. Mexican Am. Opportunity Found. 1965; awards: Am. Cancer Soc. Spkr.'s Award, 1956; Bella Vista Comm. Hosp. Merit Award, 1965; Pepsi Cola Co. Merit Award 1964; mem: Am. Med. Assn., Am. Acad. of Environmental Med., Royal Soc. of Health, Am. Coll. of Allergists; publs: Immunotolerance- A Re-Discovered Treatment of Allergies; mil: maj. Mexican Army Med. Corps 1950; Democrat; Catholic; rec: sailing, writing. Res: 14013 Old Harbor Lane Apt. 315 Marina del Rey 90291 Ofc: Allergy Control Medical Group, 22030 Sherman Way Ste. 305 Canoga Park 91303

BORUM, WILLIAM DONALD, construction executive; b. Dec. 26, 1932, St. Louis, Mo.; s. William Doris and Lura Mae (Jackson) Borum; m. Mary Bullard, Nov. 29, 1952; children: Mary, b. 1953, Patricia, b. 1958, Kimberly, b. 1962; edn: BA,bus., Univ. Nebr. 1967; MA, internat. rels., USC 1971; diploma, US Army Engr. Sch., Ft. Belvoir, Va. 1960, Command and Gen. Staff Coll., 1968, NATO Def. Coll., Rome, Italy 1976. Career: commnd. 2d lt. US Army Corps of Engrs. 1954, co. comdr./platoon leader in USA, 1954-56, in Germany, 1956-60; 1st lt., 1956; served in Lebanon, 1958; capt., 1960; engr. advisor to Imperial Iranian Army, 1962-65; maj., assigned to Pentagon, 1966; served in 65thEngineers,25th Inf. Div., Vietnam, 1966-67; lt. col., assigned to Pentagon, 1968; served in Brit. Def. Staff, Ministry of Def., London, 1969-71; comdg. ofcr., 35th Engr. Batt., 1972; assigned to Ofc of the Chief of Engrs., Wash DC 1973-75; Ofc of the Deputy Chief of Staff, Ops., Dept. of Army, Pentagon; full colonel Hdqtrs. NATO Allied Forces Central Europe 1976-79; deputy comdr. So. Pac. Div., Corps of Engrs., 1979-84, responsible for mil. constrn. involving 3000 govt. employees and over 9000 contractor personnel (projects incl. Space Transport Sys. and the MX Missile facilities); constrn. exec. w. Williams and Burrows Inc., bldg. new air terminal S.F. Internat. Airport 1984 –; instr. US Army Engr. Sch., Ft. Belvoir 1961-62; mil. awards (20) incl. Def. Superior Svc, Legion of Merit, Bronze Star, Air Medal w/two Oak Leaf Clusters, Purple Heart, Cross of Gallantry w/Palm, Vietnam Svc w/5 battle stars, Sr. Parachutist; mem: Am. Acad. Polit. and Social Sci., Soc. of Am. Mil. Engrs., Commonwealth Club of Calif., Am. Mgmt. Assn., Acad. of Polit. Sci. (NY), US Parachute Assn., Assn. of US Army, The Fusion Found., Smithsonian Assocs. (nat.); Republican; Episcopal (lay reader, chalice bearer); rec: skydiving, internat. rels., classical music. Res: 1805 Alderwood Ct San Mateo 94402 Ofc: Williams & Burrows 500 Harbor Blvd Belmont 94002

BOSCACCI, EDWARD WILLIAM, JR., water resources engineer; b. nov. 7, 1956, San Francisco; s. Edward Wm. and Barbara Ann (Atkinson) B.; edn: BS, UC Berkeley 1979, MS, 1980; Reg. Profl. Engr. (Civil), Calif. Career: student engr. United Technologies Co./ Chemical Systems Div., Sunnyvale 1977-78, Calif. Water Quality Control Board, Region 2, Oakland 1978-80; tchg. asst. UCB 1979-80; engr. Leedshill-Herkenhoff, Inc., San Francisco 1980 –; honors: Chi Epsilon; mem. Am. Soc. of Civil Engrs.; civic: Commonwealth Club of Calif., Sierra Club, Nature Friends of Calif.; Democrat; Catholic; rec: guitar, bicycling, skiing. Res: 507 Del Valle Circle El Sobrante 94803 Ofc: Leedshill-Herkenhoff Inc. 1275 Market St Ste 1500 San Francisco 94103

BOSCH, GEORGE HUMBERTO, private investigator; b. Dec. 25, 1928, Ecuador, nat. US cit. 1968; s. Cesar A. and Carmela (Merizalde) B.; m. Wilma, Aug. 10, 1956; children: George H., Jr. b. 1957, Carlos Fernando b. 1959, Lizeth b. 1960; edn: Medical Central Univ. Quito, Ecuador 1960; Glendale Coll. 1968-70; DD, Universal Life Coll. 1978; USA lic. Pvt. Investigator, lic. Pvt. Pilot. Career: plant supv. corrugation div. Container Corp., Cali Valle, Colombia 1948-52; hospital aide Medical Prevention Ctr. Ecuador 1953-63; lab chemist/ mgr. Quality Control Lab., Drewry, and Kodak, 1963-77; pvt. investigator Paas Ctr. Glendale, Calif. 1978 –; cons. var. attys. (criminal & civil); Democrat; Catholic; rec: football. Res: 3301 Park Vista Dr. Glendale 91214 Ofc: Paas Ctr. 1145 E Broadway Glendale 91205

BOSSELOO, FERNANDO, electrical engineer; b. Dec. 24, 1956, Mexico City, Mex., nat. 1983; s. Eduardo and Maria- Dolores C. B.; reg. profl. engr., Calif. 1984. Career: Bechtel Power Corp. 1981-85; control sys. engr. Susquehanna Nuclear Power Plant, San Francisco 1981-82; instrumentation and control sys.

engr. Diablo Canyon Power Plant, San Francisco 1982-83; res. instrumentation and control sys. engr. Diablo Canyon Nuclear Power Plant, San Luis Obispo 1983-85; res. instrumentation and control sys. engr. Diablo Canyon, Pacific Gas and Electric Co., San Luis Obispo 1985—; mem: Tau Beta Pi, Eta Kappa Nu, Instrument Soc. of Am., Profl. Assn. of Diving Instrs. Internat., Northwind Aviation Inc.; rec: pvt. pilot, scuba, photog., language (speak, read and write English, French and Spanish). Res: 241 Ocean View Ave. #Q Pismo Beach 93449 Ofc: Pacific Gas and Electric Co., P.O. BOx 117, Avila Beach 93424

BOTHWELL, CHUNG T. N., financial planner; b. Nov. 19, 1949, Saigon, Vietnam; d. Tang Van and Nghi Thi (Tran) Nguyen; m. Anthony Peirson Xavier Bothwell, Dec. 22, 1973; children: Anthony Peirson Xavier II, Thomas Theodore; edn: BBA, Univ. Miami (Fla.) 1974, MBA, 1980. Career: budget analyst Fla. Power & Light Co. Miami 1973-78; asst. to dean grad. pgm. sch. of nursing Univ. Wisc. Madison 1978-79; mgr. budget & cost Central Life Assurance Co. Madison 1980-83; senior budget analyst Lawrence Livermore Nat. Lab. Livermore, Calif. 1983-84, prin. acct. 1984-85, asst. to ops. mgr. laser isotope separation 1985—; commr. Alameda County Human Relations Commn. 1985-; Madison City Human Svcs. Commn. 1982-83; honors: Internat. Student Scholar (Univ. Miami 1973); mem: Nat. Assn. Accts. (chpt. dir. comm. responsibility 1986-87, assoc. dir. hospitality 1985-86, dir. & ed. newsletter 1984-85, assoc. dir. manuscripts 1983-84), Am. Assn. Univ. Women (chpt. v.p. 1985-86, Acad. Mgmt. 1978-, Livermore Social Concerns Com. 1984- (chair 1985-86), Am. Red Cross (proj. chair 1978-79); publ: How to Improve Financial Planning with a Budget Manual (Mgmt. Acctg. J. 1985); Republican; Catholic. Res: 1823 Paseo Laguna Seco Livermore 94550-1678 Ofc: Lawrence Livermore Nat. Lab. 7000 East Ave Livermore 94550

BOTTS, PAT LUCILLE, real estate broker; b. Oct. 2, 1925, Los Angeles; d. Greenie "Jack" L. and Oma Belle (Bodle) Trotter; m. Albert F. Botts, Sr. Dec. 29, 1949; children: Patricia, b. 1941, Albert, b. 1950; edn: real estate courses, Napa Coll., num. profl. R.E. courses; Calif. Real Estate Lic. 1963. Career: real estate broker/owner Botts Realty & Land Co., Napa; past owner/opr. var. retail businesses, Lazy-B Kennel (boarding, tng., breeding purebred dogs), comml. fishing vessel SAVO (fishing tuna and salmon); first female motorcycle police ofcr. in Calif.; welder in Kaiser Shipyard on Liberty Ships Richmond, Calif. 1942-44; polit. activist local, state, nat. (both Calif. Senators submitted bills for public causes in her behalf); spkr./activist in successful campaign to restore usage of Lake Berryessa to public recreation, 1963-85; listed Who's Who Am. Women; mem. Napa Co. Bd. of Realtors, Calif. Assn. of Realtors, Nat. Assn. of Realtors, Lake Berryessa CofC (past pres.); dir. Napa Co. Devel. Council; dir. Environmental Ctr., Napa; dir. Consumer Awareness Office, Napa; coordinator Safe Nuclear Energy Iniative; dir. Citizens Council for Napans Tomorrow; columnist, Lake Berryessa News; Democrat; Prot.; Res: Mecca Ranch 7001 Hwy 128 Napa 94558 Ofc: Botts Realty & Land Co. 3377 Solano Ave, Ste. 420, Napa 94558

BOURBAN, ROGER ARSENE, (aka Le Garcon Rapide), restaurateur, athlete, actor, lecturer; b. May 10, 1948, Sion, Switz., nat. 1980; s. Marcel and Jeanne (Schmelzbach) Bourban; edn: apprentice cook, restaurant/hotel touring, Sion, Switz. 1964-6; Ecole Hoteliere, De La Societe Suisse Des Hoteliers, Lausanne, Switz. 1967-9; Nelson Sch., London, Eng. 1970; stu. Lee Strasberg Theatre Inst., Actors and Dirs. Lab. Career: waiter Gitana Grill Rm., Geneva, Switz. 1968; maitre D' Hotel De La Tete Noire, Rolle, Switz. 1970; sommelier Surfer's Paradise, Australia 1971; mgr. New & Old El Camino Real Restaurant, Sydney, Austral. 1972; (with noted chef, mentor Jean Bertranou 1972-5) as chef La Chaumiere, Beverly Hills 1972-4, captain L'Ermitage, Los Angeles 1974-5; captain Le Restaurant, L.A. 1975-7; asst. dir./Habitation Leclerc Hotel, Port Au Prince, Haiti 1978; captain Ma Maison, L.A. 1979-80; prop. Cafe Monet Bistro, L.A. 1980-82; lim. ptnr. Nicky Blair's Restaurant L.A.; currently restaurant cons., freelance restaurateur & sports personality/athlete, worldwide personal appearances giving cooking & baking demonstrations, lectr. on health, exercise, nutrition, home entertaining. Actor in films, on TV & TV commercials; featured personality num. TV shows. Athlete: mem. Swiss Snow Ski Team 1965-6; mem. Swiss Nat. Judo team 1966-8, participant/instr. judo events 1963-, 2d deg. Black Belt Nidan, winner num. nat. events incl. Judo Championship, Sydney, Aust. Running awards: 5 World Records, Guinness Bk. of World Records, 1981-; World's Fastest Running Waiter 1976-, winner 170+ Waiters' Races internat.; 1981 Waiter's Hall of Fame; runner NY Marathon (4), London (2), N.Z., Hawaii, Korea, Rio De Janeiro marathons; other sports incl: snow & water skiing, tennis, swimming, golf, horseback riding, car racing. Mem: SAG, AFTRA; vol. Calif. Spec. Olympics, United Cerebral Palsy/ Spastic Chil. Found., Am. Diabetes Assn. Ind.; Catholic; Address: Bourban Internat. 320 N. LaPeer Dr. #103, POB 2992, Beverly Hills 90213

BOUSQUET, JOHN FREDERICK, locksmith; b. Nov. 19, 1948, Wash. DC; s. Kenneth Joseph, Sr. and Margaret Isabel (Sherrin) B.; edn: BS, Lehigh Univ. 1971; hold 32 certs. in locksmithing courses, Assoc. Locksmiths of Am., Calif. Locksmith Assn., var. lock mfr. service courses; Master Kleidologist, Lockmaster, Keying Engr., lic. C61 Contractor. Career: mobile lock shop owner 1971-85, prin. Smith Engineering & Contract Services, Ames Research Center, Nat. Aeronautics and Space Adminstrn., Moffett Field 1985—; instr. masterkeying, Calif. Locksmith Assn.; authored an amendment to the penal code restricting and registering sale of lock picks and car openers which became a city ordinance (S.F.) and is to become state law (1984); cons. nationally on masterkeying; honors: Mem. of the Year 1982, Calif. Locksmith Assn. San Francisco Bay Chpt.; mem. Assoc. Locksmith of Am., C.L.A. (secty. 1983); publs: tech. art., Locksmiths Ledger. Res: 112 Eucalyptus Ave. South San Francisco 94080 Ofc: Smith Engring. & Contract Services, Ames Research Center, NASA, Moffett Field 94035

BOUTTE, ANTHONY MICHAEL, architectural technology consultant, educator; b. May 31, 1949, Oakland, Calif.; s. Frank K. Perry and Ruthye L. Perry-Boutte; m. Sheryl J. Bize, Apr. 3, 1971; 1 dau. Angela M. b. 1977; edn: AS soc. & behav. sci., Merritt Coll. 1971, AS math, 1979; BS HROB, Univ. San Francisco 1980. Career: designer UC Berkeley Lawrence Lab. 1974-79; proj. designer Jordan Assocs. S.F. 1979-80; senior archtl. designer Bechtel Petroleum Inc. San Francisco 1980-83; owner, prin. A B Plans Berkeley 1983—; arch./ engrg. technol. instr. Engrg. Socs. Com. for Manpower Tng./ CETA S.F. 1980-81, Peralta Colls. Oakland 1981-83; math. tutor 1982; math. instr. Montgomery H.S. Santa Rosa 1983; lectr. productivity strategies Calif. Employees Assn. Fresno 1978, East Bay Skills Ctr. Oakland 1983, 85; cons. affirm. action/ EEO compliance US Dept. Labor 1980-81; honwrs: Union Steward of the Month (Calif. State Employees Assn. 1978), Second Place (Police Pistol Competition Chabot Gun Club 1983), Appreciation (Bay Area Community Svcs. 1983); mem: Am. Inst. Archs., Nat. Orgn. Minority Architects, No. Calif. Council Black Profl. Engrs., Chabot Gun Club, Knowland Park Highlands Homeowners Assn., Nat. Trust for Historical Preservation; Democrat; Catholic; rec: handgun collecting, competition shooting. Res: 4743 Stacy St Oakland 94605 Ofc: A B Plans POB 444 Berkeley 94704-0444

BOVIS, PIERRE GERARD, art dealer; b. Feb. 3, 1943, Nice, France, nat. US cit. 1969; s. Marcel Marius and Marie Louise (Fournaise) B.; m. Shirley Anne, Dec. 28, 1984; children: Natalie, Amy; edn: Beaux Arts Nice, Paris; anthropol., archeol., UC Berkeley 1963-64. Career: owner Bovis Bead Co., Bovis Primitive Arts San Diego 1964—, appraiser, dealer fine American Indian arts, primitive arts from Africa, Oceania, Nepal, Tibet; former founder 1965-, owner Winona Trading Post Santa Fe, New Mex.; honors: many national cups and ribbons, 1st prizes at national shows; listed Who's Who in Art and Antiques, vol. II, Cambridge, Eng.; mem: Appraisers Assn. of Am. (senior 1966-), Antique Appraisers Assn. of Am. (senior 1968-), Internat. Turquoise Assn., Indian Arts & Crafts Assn., Southwest Assn. on Indian Affairs, Genuine Relics Soc., Am. Assn. Museums; co-author: (w/ C. Miles) Am. Indian & Eskimo Basketry- A Key to Identification (1969), Pine Ridge 1890- An Eye Witness Account of the Events Surrounding the Wounded Knee Massacre (1971), Trade Beads of the World- Identification and Pricing (1983); mil: sgt. French Fgn. Legion; Republican; Catholic; also collect Napoleonic arms and armor. Res: POB 12626 San Diego 92112 Ofc: Bovis Bead Co. 652 Fifth Ave San Diego 92101

BOWE, LEONARD NICHOLAS, insurance agency owner; b. Feb. 1, 1940; Chippewa Falls, Wisc.; s. Alfred Jacob and Florence Sylvia B.; children: Nikki b. 1965, Michael b. 1966, Tanya b. 1967; edn: BSBA, Marquette Univ. 1962; MBA, Golden Gate Univ. 1969; std. designated subjects tchg. credl., Cerritos Coll. 1970; lic. life, fire, casualty ins. agent Calif. 1979. Career: personnel mgr. S&W Fine Foods Redwood City, Calif. 1967-69; supv. Ford Motor Co. L.A. 1969-70; area sales mgr. H.J. Heinz Co. L.A. 1970-73; dist. sales mgr. Heublein Inc. L.A. 1973; asst. mgr. grocery sales planning H.J. Heinz Pittsburgh 1973-76; SW regl. sales mgr. Peter Paul Inc. Dallas 1976-77; western regl. sales mgr. Lifesavers INC Walnut Creek, Calif. 1977-79; owner State Farm Ins. Agcy. Dublin, Calif. 1979—; honors: Eagle Scout (1954), Ambassador of the Yr. (Dublin CofC 1982); mem: Dublin CofC, Soc. for Advancement of Mgmt. (past. dir.), Amador Valley Athletic Club, Knights of Columbus, Dublin Tennis Club; mil: capt. USAF 1962-67; Republican; Catholic; rec: piano, golf, tennis, boating, camping. Res: 6820 Eden Dr Dublin 94568 Ofc: State Farm Ins. 7465 Village Pkwy Dublin 94568

BOWEN, RICHARD DUANE, architect, corporate executive; b. Jan. 22, 1932, Albia, Iowa; s. Joe and Rose Ruth (Angel) B.; m. Mavis Louise, June 16, 1956; children: Stephen Duane b. 1960, Marc David b. 1964; edn: Iowa State Univ. Sch. Arch. 1955-57, USC Sch. Arch. 1957-58,Irvine Law Sch. 1982, Am. Coll. of Law 1983; BBA, National Univ. 1985, MBA Candidate 1986; Calif. lic: Architect; Reg. Building Designer; Gen. Contr.; also lic. contr. in solar, insulation, accoustical, concrete, drywall, earthwork, paving, flooring, glazing, masonry, painting, decorating, sheet metal. Career: (past): chief ops. officer for major builders; gen. contr., builder/devel. Dinnes, Bowen & Frey architectural firm; exec. v.p. State Wide Investors, Inc. (R.E. devel.), Cypress 1972; current sole owner architecture and devel. corp. of large (over 200 units) real estate projects; arbitrator Am. Arbitration Assn.; planning commnr. City of Lynwood; chmn. Southeast Area Planning Council, L.A. Air Pollution Control; mem. City of Long Beach coms: (housing elements, zoning); mem. Long Beach Police Assn., So. Calif. Builders Assn., Disabled Vets., Amvets, Nat. Univ. Alumni Assn. (life), Rotary, PTA, CofC, Elks, Vietnam Freedom Memorial (designer), Coordinating Council, Jaycees (bd.), Optimists (pres.), Lions (pres.), Lynwood Redevel. Found. (pres.), Sports Booster Club, Youth Employment Bureau (bd.); awards: one of 10 Outstanding Young Men of Am. (1968), recognition and medals: Cities of Lynwood, Long Beach, Los Angeles, County of Los Angeles, Optimist Internat., Lions Internat., Valley Forge Found., Long Beach Police Ofcrs. Assn.; mil: served in USN; Republican; Protestant; rec: art, fishing, golf. Address: Los Alamitos 90720

BOWERS, GORDON ALLAN, police administrator, management consultant; b. Dec. 3, 1945, Portsmouth, Va.; s. J. Dexter, Jr. and Annette Ruth (Parker) B.; m. Donna L. Gobble, Jan. 30, 1971; children: Michael b. 1975, Matthew b. 1980; edn: BA, USC 1972; MA, Chapman Coll. 1982; grad. FBI Nat. Acad. 1984. Career: salesman McGraw-Hill Information Systems; police ofcr. Arcadia P.D. 1971-73, served through ranks to lt. Burbank Police Dept., 1973–, currently comdr. of Personnel and Tng. Bureau, city coord. for supvsy. tng., facilitator for "Investment in Excellence," comdr. Police Reserves; mgmt. and planning cons. (Future Flow); p-t faculty Glendale Community Coll.; honors: Mayor's commendation, Profl. Esteem award (3), num. citizen's commendns.; mem: Nat. Mgmt. Assn. (dir., v.p.), Forum 2000, FBI Nat. Acad. Assocs., Burbank Police Assn., Calif. Peace Ofcrs. Assn., Internat. Police Assn.; civic: Rotary of Burbank (dir. 1985-), Calvary Bible Ch., Mensa, Theta Xi frat. (USC chpt. pres. 1968-69), Boy Scouts Am. (past Cubmaster and Explorer advisor); publs: var. P.D. mgmt. articles and reports; editor Lookout (bi-monthly crime prev. newsletter, circ. 2,500); originated the "Unusual Occurrence Manual," "Mobilization Directory" and Planning Unit for research projects; Republican; Baptist; rec: photog., racquetball, micro-computers. Ofc: c/o Future Flow POB 791 Burbank 91503; Burbank Police Dept. 272 E Olive Ave Burbank 91502

BOWERS, ROBERT GLENNE, lawyer; b. Jan. 23, 1939, Ventura, Calif.; s. Glenne C. and Lillian F. (Kennedy) B.; m. Susan L., Apr. 9, 1961; 1 child: Shayne L. b. 1963; edn: AA, Imperial Valley Coll. 1965; BA, CSU San Diego 1971; JD, Cabrillo Pacific Nat. Univ. 1977; admitted Calif. State Bar 1979. Career: aircraft assembler Rhr Aircraft San Diego 1959-62; mechanic ARCO Svc. Stn. S.D. 1962-63; police ofcr. El Centro Police Dept. 1963-66, San Diego Police Dept. 1966-79; atty. pvt. practice El Cajon 1979–; police instr. 1963-66, 1966-76; Commn. on Police Ofcr. Stds. and Tng. 1963, 66, 72, 74; honors: City Mgr. Cert. of Achievement 1970, Cert. of Merit (Grossmont Coll. 1980-82), Am. Jurisprudence Awards (Cabrillo Pacific Nat. Univ. 1975-76); mem: Am., Calif, Foothill bar assns.; San Diego Trial Lawyers Assn.; mil: USN 1957-59; Republican; Presbyterian; rec: water sports, deep sea fishing. Ofc: 343 E Lexington Ave, Ste 109, El Cajon 92020

BOWERY, JAMES ALAN, computer network architect; b. Jan. 30, 1954, Des Moines, Iowa; s. Robert Wright and Rose Evelyn (Frazier) B. Career: computer conferencing system programmer Nat. Sci. Found. Univ. Ill. 1974; pgmmr./ analyst Plato Corrections Proj. Univ. Ill. 1976-77; system pgmmr./ architect for Plato Proj. Control Data Corp. Mpls. 1977-81; mgr. interactive architectures Viewdata Corp. of Am. Miami 1981-83; pres. telecomputing Assocs. San Diego 1983–; cons. Sci. Applications Internat. Corp. La Jolla 1984; mem: Independent Computer Cons. Assn. 1983-, Sierra Club, L5 Soc. (pres. 1986), Space Studies Inst. (senior assoc. 1981-). Res: 5425 Waverly Ave La Jolla 92037 Ofc: Telecomputing Assoc. Box 1981 La Jolla 92038

BOWLES, JAMES KEVIN, risk management broker; b. Feb. 7, 1954, Ridgecrest; s. Wm. James and Joy Etta (Dolan) B.; m. Carol Ann, Oct. 29, 1985; edn: BA in journ., E. Wash. State Coll. 1978; RMA, Risk Mgmt. Broker/ Assoc., Piver Sch. of Ins. 1973; lic. fire & cas. ins. broker, Wash. (1973), Calif. (1981). Career: founder/co-ptnr. with father, Spokane branch office Bill Bowles & Assocs. Ins. Agcy., 1973-74; ins. agcy. comml. risk mgmt. account mgr. in Calif. 1978-, currently mng. gen. ptnr./risk mgmt. broker Bill Bowles & Assocs. (comml. risk mgmt. brokerage), Ridgecrest; elected chief finl. ofcr. CISA, Inc. (Calif. non-profit public benefit, ednl. assn. to promote safety and risk mgmt. within var. pvt. indus.) 1983-; honors: Outstanding achieve. award, Safeco Cos. Agent's Sch., Seattle (1973); mem. Ins. Info. Inst., Independent Ins. Agts. & Brokers Assn., Western Assn. of Ins. Brokers, Chartered Prop. & Cas. Underws. Soc. (applicant); publ: art., Am. Agent & Broker (11/83); mil: sgt. US Air Force 1974-76, USAF Top Secret Sec. Clearance, Good Conduct, Vietnam Cpgn.; Republican; rec: sport hunting/fishing, firearms collector. Res: 612 Sylvia Dr Ridgecrest 93555

BOWLES, JOHN EDWARD, investment executive; b. July 28, 1932, Hollywood; s. Dr. Dwight Frederick and Elizabeth C. (Thompson) B.; m. Carol Everson, June 5, 1982; children: Denise b. 1963, John b. 1965, Nancy b. 1970; edn: BBA, Univ. of Ore. 1956; MBA, USC 1959; desig: Charter Finl. Analyst, Finl. Analyst Soc. (1965). Career: securities analysts Farmers Insurance Group, Los Angeles 1957-, asst. investment dir. 1960-68; v.p. Lehman Brothers, Inc. N.Y. 1968-75, v.p./regional mgr. 1975-84, currently senior v.p. Shearson Lehman, Los Angeles 1984–; instr. in security analysis UC Los Angeles; mem: Los Angeles Bond Club (pres., bd.), L.A. Soc. of Finl. Analysts (bd.), Calif. Securities Industry Assn. (bd.), Jonathan Club, L.A. Tennis Club; mil: 1st lt. US Army 1955-57; Republican; Presbyterian; rec: golf, tennis. Res: 130 North Windsor Blvd Los Angeles 90004 Ofc: Shearson Lehman 515 South Figueroa Ste 1400 Los Angeles 90071

BOWLING, BRUCE DOUGLAS, dentist; b. Aug. 18, 1948, San Jose; s. Richard Story and Drucilla (Howe) B.; m. Alicia, Nov. 26, 1969; children: Sharon b. 1971, Douglas b. 1973, Richard b. 1975, David b. 1978, Anne b. 1980, Robert b. 1982; edn: Brigham Young Univ. 1966-67, 1970-71; DDS, UCLA 1975. Career: pres. pvt. gen. practice dentistry, Bruce D. Bowling, DDS, Inc., APC, Gridley 1977–; honors: Den Leaders Award, Scouters Key, Dist. Award of Merit (Boy Scouts of Am.); mem: Butte-Sierra Dental Soc., Manzanita Sch. Dist. Bd. Trustees, Boy Scouts of Am. (v.p. tng. Buttes Area Council); mil: capt. US Army 1975-77, Army Commdn.; Republican; Ch. Jesus Christ LDS, rec: flying, scuba, fishing. Res: 1139 Gridley Ave. Gridley 95948 Ofc: Bruce D. Bowling, DDS, Inc., 1080 Sycamore St. Gridley 95948

BOWMAN, CRAIG EUGENE, industrial service co. president; b. Aug. 26, 1941, Ponca City, Okla.; s. Clarence Eugene and Helen Louise (Bleakley) B.; children: Charles b. 1960, Paula b. 1962. Career: v.p./gen. mgr. Chemical Waste Systems, Browning Ferris Industries; western regl. mgr. Serv Rigs, Inc.; gen. mgr. Universal Engineering Inc.; current: pres./chmn. Internat. Catalyst Inc., Los Angeles; Republican; Baptist; rec: flying, hunting, fishing, golf. Res:

6420 Green Valley Cir Culver City 90230 Ofc: International Catalyst 12833 S Broadway Los Angeles 90061

BOWMAN, JACQUELINE BONNIE, educator; b. Dec. 28, 1936, Los Angeles; d. John and Margaret E. (Hagen) Glatz; m. Robert Bowman; edn: BA, sociol. (elem. tchg. cred.), La Verne Univ. 1957; ednl. psych., CSCLA and USC, 1963-66; MA, sec. tchr. cred., Pasadena Coll. 1967; ednl. psych. (gen. admin. cred.) UC Riverside 1968-70; PhD, USC 1974; Profl. Cert., Consortium for Adv. Leadership, ACSA 1981-83; lic: State Marriage, Family Child Counseling; Ednl. Psychologist; Psychologist. Career: Charter Oak Unified Sch. Dist., Covina 1958-: tchr. Gr. 3, 1958-63; psychometrist 1963-66; sch. psychologist 1966-69; coordinator of spl. edn. 1969-71; dir. Pupil Personnel Services and Spl. Edn. 1971–, also dir. Staff Devel. 1982; asst. supt. support svcs.1985; past instr. La Verne Univ., UCLA; psychologist Whittier Guidance Ctr., 1966-69; mem: Nat., Calif. (chpsn.) Assn. of Sch. Psychologists; Calif. (pres.), Charter Oak Chpt. Assn. of Sch. Adminstrs.; Assoc. Calif. Sch. Adminstrs. (pres. reg. XV 1981-82, bd. dirs. 1983-86); Nat. Spkrs. Assn.; Assn. for Supvsn. and Curriculum Devel.; Council for Exceptional Children; AAUW; Calif. Assn. for Neurol. Handicapped Children; Calif. Assn. for the Gifted (chpsn.); E. San Gabriel Valley Cooperative Edn. Pgms. (chpsn.); Phi Lambda Theta; mem. Toastmistress, Assistance League, Native Daus. of Golden West, PTA, v.p./bd. dirs. Edgewood Family Counseling Agcy. Res: 938 Arrow Hwy San Dimas 91773 Ofc: Charter Oak Unif. Sch. Dist., POB 9, Covina 91723

BOYD, CULLEN DICKSON, retail business owner/contractor; b. Aug. 30, 1911, Cleburne, Tx.; s. Samuel Edgar and Lula Maye (Dickson) B.; m. Margurite Lee Dickson, Mar. 17, 1945; edn: grad. Army Air Corps tng. schs. in Airplane & Engine Mechs., 1945. Career: sales clk., installer floor coverings, bookkeeping, Stuckert-Ownes Lumber Co. and O.J. Johnston Co., Fort Worth, Tx. 1935-39; roofing contr. and supplier assoc. Moncrief-Lenor Mfg. Co., Dallas 1939-42; with Van Buren Lino & Shade, Anaheim 1945-48; owner/contr. Boyd's (floor and window coverings), Oceanside 1948–; civic: Lions Internat. (life. mem. 1986, Perfect Att. Award 1951-86, Old Monarch 1951-61, 100 Percent pres.'s award 1971-72; Carlsbad Club pres. 1954-55; Oceanside Host Club pres. 1971-72; Zone chmn. Dist. 4L6 1974-75; Internat. Conv. del. Las Vegas 1971-72, Dallas 1986-86); mil: sgt. QM Supply Tech. Army Air Corps 1942-45, 4 Overseas Bars, Good Conduct Medal; Democrat; Prot.; rec: photog., miniature trains, story telling. Address: Boyd's 1101 S Hill St Oceanside 92054

BOYD, GARY LYNN, data communications analyst; b. May 24, 1947, Kansas City, Kans.; s. Kenneth Robert and Audrey Mae (Norsworthy) B.; m. Khanh, Apr. 23, 1973; children: Gary, Jr. b. 1968, William b. 1971, David b. 1973, James b. 1978; edn: commun. tech. courses, USAF, jr. colls. Career: radio techn. US Air Force, 1966-75; supr. Jerrold Electronics, Kansas City, Mo. 1975-76; techn. Honeywell Corp., Inglewood, Ca. 1977-79; computer field engr. NCR/ Comten Corp., Los Angeles 1979-81; sr. tech. support analyst voice/data integration TRW /ISD Corp., Anaheim 1981–; invention: Closed Cycle Engine using ambient heat as energy source (disclosed 1974); fmr. mem. Mensa; mil: s/sgt. USAF 1966-75, Expt. Marksman, Bronze Star; L.D.S. Ch.; rec: orthomolecular medicine. Res: 514 East Fir Brea 92621 Ofc: TRW/ISD 1761 W Katella Ave Anaheim 92804

BOYD, ROBERT EARL, industrial forklift dealer; b. July 27, 1928, Omaha, Nebr.; s. Clarence Earl and Mildred Estelle (Gantz) B.; m. Hazel, Nov. 28, 1952; children: Pamela Jean b. 1958, Terrence Bormann b. 1961; edn: BS, Univ. Kans. 1950; MBA, Northwestern Univ. 1951. Career: sales Automatic Transportation Co. (div. Yale & Towne) 1953-, market research mgr. 1956-, advtsg. & sales promotion mgr. Automatic Lift Truck (div. Eaton Yale & Towne) 1963-, dist. sales mgr. Automatic & Yale Divs., Eaton Corp. 1968-; pres./owner Golden West Equip. Co., Richmond 1972–; mem: Richmond Shimada Commn. (bd. dirs.), Richmond CofC (bd. dirs.), Rotary; mil: pvt. E2 US Army 1951-53, CIC; Republican; Christian Sci.; rec: photog. Res: 3708 Hidden Springs Ct El Sobrante 94803 Ofc: Golden West Equipment Co. 194 23rd St Richmond 94804

BOYD, ROBERT SPROTT, lawyer; b. Dec. 27, 1941, San Francisco; s. R. Mitchell S. and Mary (Mitchell) B.; m. Mary Ellen, Oct. 4, 1974; children: Zachary b. 1975, Alexander b. 1980, Halina b. 1985; edn: BS, UC Berkeley 1965; JD, Hastings Coll. of Law 1971. Career: atty. Hancock, Rothert & Bunshoft San Francisco 1972-75, Bronson, Bronson & McKinnon S.F. 1975-77; pres. and atty. Boyd and Murray Santa Rosa; tchr. Empire Law Sch. 1978-80; honors: Hastings Coll. Law Journ. 1970-72; mem: Calif., Sonoma Co. bar assns.; Sebastopol Planning Commn. (chmn.); publ: Hastings Law Journ. 1972; mil: lt. USNR ordnance disposal, underwater demolition 1965-69. Res: 1350 Watertrough Rd Sebastopol 95472 Ofc: Boyd & Murray 827 Third St Santa Rosa 95404

BOYLES, J. EDWIN, chiropractor; b. July 4, 1942, Chicago, Ill.; s. Ralph Edwin and Carolle Marie (McCandless) B.; m. Karen Hohenstein, June 20, 1981; edn: BS, Baker Univ. 1974; DC, Life Chiropractic Coll. 1984. Career: prodn. supvr. A.G. Becker Securities, Chicago, Ill. 1974; dist. mgr. Chrysler Corp., Chicago, Ill. 1976; adminstrv. asst. to chmn. bd. Comdisco, Chicago, Ill. 1978; acct. exec. Hallmark Cards, Chicago, Ill. 1979-80; owner Boyles & Assoc. Chiropractic Life Ctr., West Los Angeles 1980–; mem. Brent-Air Lions; Republican; Protestant. Res: 15325 Magnolia Blvd. Apt. 201 Sherman Oaks 91403 Ofc Boyles & Assoc., 11518 W. Pico Blvd., West Los Angeles 90064

BOYLLS, JOHN CHARLES, engineering executive; b. Sept. 16, 1942, Memphis, Tenn.; s. Stanley Smith and Kathryn Ann (Anderson) B.; m. Virginia Wright, July 15, 1967; desig: FAA flight instr. (1976). Career: devel. engr. Scripps Instn. of Oceanography, La Jolla 1970-82; oceanographic instrumentation design cons. Sea Systems, Encinitas 1976–; advanced flt. tng. splst. Executive Aviation Services, Carlsbad 1976–; engring. mgr. Access Research Corp., Encinitas 1983–; FAA Accident Prevention Counselor; honors: Gold Seal Flight Instr., FAA (1980); mem. IEEE, Assn. of Old Crows, AAAS, Nat. Assn. of Flight Instrs., Am. Mgmt. Assn.; publs: contbr. tech. articles in Marine Geol. J. (1977), IEEE Oceans Conf. Proceedings (1979, 85); mil: E5 US Navy 1964-68, Naval Unit Cit., 2 Commendns., Am. Spirit Honor Medal; 1st lt. Calif. State Mil. Reserve 1982–; Republican; United Methodist; rec: electronics. Address: Encinitas 92024

BOYNTON, WILLIAM LEWIS, manufacturing co. official; b. May 31, 1928, Kalamazoo, Mich.; s. James Woodbury and Cyretta (Gunther) Boynton; m. Kei Ouchi, Oct. 8, 1953; edn: various mil., tech. insts., seminars. Career: served in US Army; 1948-74, ret. non-commnd. ofcr.; asst. mgr. Speigel J&R, Kalamazoo 1947-48; faculty mem. Western Mich. Univ., 1955-58; Rockwell/ Collins Divs.: materiel coordinator 1974-78, supr. 1978-81, coordinator 1981–; mem. Nat. Mgmt. Assn.; advisor to Bus./Economic Devel. Com., Calif. State Legislature 1979–; bd.trustees Orange Co. Vector Control Dist. 1980–; mem: Smithsonian Inst., Nat. Geographic Soc., Non-Commnd. Ofcrs. Assn. (life), Assn. of the US Army, AF Assn., Am. Security Council, Japanese-Am. Citizen League; mil: decorated Bronze Star, 1970, Merit. Svc. Awd. 1974, Army Commendations 1967, 69, 72, Presdtl. Unit Cit. 1970, Presdtl. Cit., Korea, 1952, GCM 1951-74, num. letters of commendation; listed in Who's Who in Fin. and Indus., Who's Who in the World, Who's Who in the West; Republican; Catholic; rec: oriental hist., woodcraft. Res: 5314 W. Lucky Way, Santa Ana 92704Ofc: Rockwell Int.-CCSD, 3731 W. Warner Ave, POB 11963, Santa Ana 92711

BRACKEN, HAROLD AUSTIN, manufacturing co. executive; b. Dec. 2, 1928, Hollywood; s. Chester A. and Sadie A. Bracken; m. Dolores Whitley, June 30, 1950; children: Gary, b. 1952; Jeffrey, b. 1954; Laura, b. 1955; edn: BA, UCLA 1950. Career: var. field & gen. ofc. assignments, Ford Div., Ford Motor Co. –1971; v.p. Gulf States Toyota 1971-73; regl. mgr. Toyota Motor Sales, San Francisco 1973-75; div. mgr. 1975-76; nat. sales mgr. 1976-80; v.p./ nat. sales mgr. 1980-82; v.p. sales & distribution 1982-83; gp. v.p. Toyota Motor Sales, Torrance 1983–; honors: Phi Kappa Psi, frat.; mem: Virginia Country Club; Monterey Country Club; Long Beach Police Ofcrs. Assn.; mil: capt. USAF 1951-53; Republican; Methodist; rec: Republican; Methodist; rec: golf, tennis, jogging. Res: 4265 Virginia Vista Long Beach 90807 Ofc: Toyota Motor Sales, USA, Inc., 19001 S Western Torrance 90509

BRADFORD, ROBERT KENT, mortgage banking co. executive; b. Aug. 19, 1944, Salt Lake City; s. Donald Hamilton and Helen (Farnworth) B.; m. Jo Ann, Mar. 14, 1968; children: Julie b. 1969, Sara b. 1973, Bob b. 1974, Lisa b. 1976; edn: BS sociol., Univ. Utah 1968, MBA, 1970; real estate broker Calif. 1982. Career: staff acct. Peat, Marwick, Mitchell & Co. CPAs San Jose 1970-71; v.p., treas. Medallion Mortgage Co. Santa Clara 1971-77; v.p. Suburban Coastal Corp. Newport Beach 1977-79; v.p., treas. Yashik Mortgage Co. Charleston, SC 1979-80; v.p., CFO Capital Pacific Mortgage Co. Modesto 1980–; dir: Capital Pacific Mortgage Co. 1980–, Central State Title 1981-83; mem. Boy Scouts of Am.; Republican; L.D.S.; rec: reading, basketball, gardening, woodworking, swimming. Res: 2445 Edgebrook Dr Modesto 95354 Ofc: Capital Pacific Mortgage Co. 2813 Coffee Rd Ste C Modesto 95355

BRADLEY, THOMAS, city official; b. Dec. 29, 1917, Calvert, Tex.; s. Lee and Crenner (Hawkins) B.; m. Ethel Arnold, May 4, 1941; children: Lorraine, Phyllis; edn: stu., UCLA 1937-40, Loyola Univ. 1954; LLB, Southwestern Univ. 1956; admitted State Bar of Calif. 1956. Career:with Los Angeles Police Dept., 1940-61, lt. 1959-61; ind. law practice, Los Angeles 1961-63; mem. Los Angeles City Council 1963-73; mayor, Los Angeles 1973–; founder Bank of Finance, Los Angeles; v.p. Friendship Day Camp; chmn. Western reg. adv. council Joint Ctr. Polit. Studies; USC Med. Ctr. Aux. Adv. bd. Cal. Tomorrow (men's adv. com. L.A. Co.), McCobb Homes for Boys, Salesian H.S.; adv. bd. dirs. So. Calif. Conf. Commun. Rels.; bd. dirs. Gr. Los Angeles Urban Coalition, Housing Assistance Council Inc.; Indian Culture and Edn.; South-Central Improvement Action Council; honors: Hon. PhD, Humanity Research Ctr. of Bev. Hills 1976, Hon LLD, Brandeis U., Oral Roberts U, Pepperdine U., Loyola Marymount U., Wilberford U., 1974, Whittier Coll. (1976), Yale, USC, Princeton, Busan Nat. U. Korea, 1979, Southwestern U. Sch. of Law, 1980, Antioch U., N.Caro. Central U., 1983, Howard U., 1985; Award League Calif. Cities 1968-69; achiev. Kappa Alpha Psi 1969; Los Angeles Brotherhood Crusade 1970-71; svc. award Neighborhood Adult Participation 1971; mem: Nat. League Cities (pres. 1973; League Calif. Cities (pres. L.A. Co. div 1968-69); Nat. Assn. Regl. Councils (pres. 1969-71); So. Calif. Assns. Govts. (pres. 1968-69); Am., Calif. and L.A. Co. (legislation com.) Bar Assns.; Langston Law Club; NAACP; Urban League (dir.); UN Assn. U.S.A. (local dir.); Loyola Human Rels. Alumni; Assn. for Profl. Law Enforcement; Nat. Conf. Mayors; Soc. Order Blue Shield; Kappa Alpha Psi (nat. pres. 1964-67); Methodist. Ofc: Office of the Mayor, City Hall, Los Angeles 90012

BRADLEY, VINCENT DE PAUL, physician; b. Oct. 16, 1944, Phila.; children: Katie b. 1962, Brad b. 1971, Scott b. 1974, Nicole b. 1977, Sean b. 1981; edn: BA, St. Joseph's Coll. 1966; MD, Hahnemann Med. Coll. 1970; Diplomate Nat. Bd. Med. Examiners 1974, Am. Bd. Internal Med. 1974, ABIM subsplty. gastroenterol. 1975. Career: intern Naval Regional Med. Ctr. San Diego 1970-71, resident internal med. 1971-73, fellow gastroenterol. 1973-75 staff internist, gastroenterol. Camp Pendleton 1975-78, dir. internal med. clin. 1975-78; pvt. practice internal med., gastroenterol. Encinitas 1978–; staff Tri-City Hosp. Oceanside, Scripps Encinitas Hosp., Scripps La Jolla Hosp. 1978–; chmn. med. dept. Scripps Encinitas Hosp. 1981-83; honors: Alpha Omega Alpha; fellow Am. Coll. Gastroenterol. mem: Am. Coll. Phys., Am. Soc. Gastrointestinal Endoscopy, San Diego County Med. Soc.; publs: articles in med. jours. Ofc: 317 El Camino Real Ste 30 Encinitas 92024

BRADSHAW, CYNTHIA ANN, chiropractor; b. April 18, 1957, Watsonville; d. Alvin Perry and Joyce Marie (Perkins) B.; div.; 1 son: Graham b. 1980; edn: AA, American River Coll. 1980; DC, Life Chiropractic Coll. West 1983; stu., Chico State Univ. Career: v.p., assoc. Chiropractice Care Ctr., Paradise 1984-85, pres., owner 1986–; scoliosis screening, local schs.; mem: Am. and Calif. Chiropractic (treas. 1985) Assns., Internat. Network of Women Chiropractors, CofC; rec: skiing, bicycling, travel. Res: 5359 Harrison Rd. Paradise 95969 Ofc: Chiropractice Care Center, 795 Birch Paradise 95969

BRAHMA, CHANDRA SEKHAR, professor of civil engineering; b. Oct. 5, 1941, Calcutta, India, nat. US cit. 1981; s. Nalini Kanta and Uma Rani (Bose) B.; m. Purnima, Feb. 18, 1972; children: Charanjit b. 1973, Barunashish b. 1974; edn: B.E. civil engrg., Calcutta Univ. 1963; MSCE, Mich. State Univ. 1965; PhDCE, Ohio State Univ. 1969; Reg. Profl. Engr. Calif. 1983, NH 1980, Wisc. 1980, Utah 1980, Tex. 1982. Career: asst. engr. Govt. of West Bengal Calcutta, India 1962-63; research asst. Mich. State Univ. 1963-65; instr. research assoc. Ohio State Univ. 1965-69; proj. geotech. engr. Frank H. Lehr Assocs. E. Orange NJ 1969-70, John G. Ruetter Assocs. Camden, NJ 1970-72; asst. prof. Worcester Poly. Inst. 1972-73; senior, prin. engr. Daniel, Mann, Johnson & Mendenhall Baltimore 1973-79; proj. mgr., senior engr. Sverdrup & Parcel & Assoc. Inc. St. Louis 1979-80; prof. civil engrg. CSU Fresno 1980–; cons. law ofcs. of Maderosian & Swanson Fresno 1985-, Sverdrup & Parcel & Assocs. 1980-, Expert Resourses Inc. Peoria Hts., Ill. 1981-, The Twinning Labs. Fresno 1982-, Progressive Subsurface Surveys India 1972-; assoc. Soil Analysis & Found. Engrg. Co. Phila. 1972-74; vis. prof. Universidad de la Republica Montevideo, Uruguay 1984; mem. num. coms. CSU Fresno; honors: Fulbright Lectrg. Award (Council for Internat. Exchange of Scholars 1984), Outstanding Leadership (Am. Soc. Civil Engrs. 1985), Tau Beta Pi (1984), Outstanding Civil Engr. (ASCE 1985), Fulbright Cert. (Bd. Fgn. Scholars 1984), Outstanding Prof. (student chpt. ASCE CSU Fresno 1985), NSF grantee (1981), Chi Epsilon, Sigma Xi; mem: Am. Soc. Civil Engrs. (sec. dir. 1985-86, br. pres. 1984-85, v.p., pgm. chmn. 1983-84, secty. 1981-83, mem. nat. coms.), Am. Soc. Testing & Materials (mem. nat. coms.), Internat. Soc. Rock Mechanics, Internat. Soc. Soil Mechanics and Found. Engrg., Nat. Soc. Profl. Engrs., Calif. Soc. Profl. Engrs., Jr. CofC (hon. internat. mem.); invited guest Rotary Internat., Exchange Club; Publs: num. articles in profl. jours.; Democrat; Hindu; rec: music, chess, bridge, table tennis. Res: 1365 Shirley Ave Clovis 93612 Ofc: CSU Maple & Shaw Ave Fresno 93740

BRAINARD, MICHAEL FORSYTHE, contracts management and corporate officer; b. Aug. 1, 1952, Cleveland, Ohio; s. John Sidney and Chris B.; edn: BA, U.S. Internat. Univ. 1974; JD, Calif. Western Sch. of Law 1978; admitted Calif. Bar 1979. Career: adminstrv. hearing participant, San Diego 1975; legis. analyst Science Applications Internat. Corp., La Jolla 1977-78, contracts rep. SAIC, La Jolla 1978-82, group contracts mgr. SAIC, Palo Alto 1982-83, McLean, Va. 1983-85, asst. v.p./group contracts mgr. SAIC, La Jolla 1985–; instr. Aquisition Mgmt. grad. pgm. West Coast Univ., San Diego 1985-86; honors: assoc. ed. Calif. Western. Internat. Law Journ.; mem: Am. and Calif. Bar Assns., Nat. Contract Mgmt. Assn., Phi Delta Phi, Smithsonian Inst., Centurion Club, Ultimate Players Assn.; co-author, Evaluationof Laws and Regulations Impacting Land Use of Dredged Material Containment Areas, tech. rep. D-78-55, US Army Corps of Engrs. 1978; Republican; Episcopal; rec: tennis, theater, water sports. Ofc: Science Applications Internat. Corp., 1200 Prospect St. La Jolla 92037

BRALYE, GEORGE CHRISTIAN, construction consultant; b. Sept. 16, 1911, San Francisco; s. William and Catherine Marie (Christiansen) B.; m. Edna Henriques, Sept. 25, 1941; children: Christine Anne b. 1954, Nicole Jean b. 1948, Lynette Marie b. 1950, William Anthony b. 1954; edn: BS, Univ. of Pacific 1938. Career: sr. cons. constrn. Jacobs Assoc. S.F.; mgr. constrn. controls Bechtel Co. Saudi Arabia; constrn. mgr. Van Houton Co Iran, Utah Internat. Australia; mgr. ops. engrg. Utah Constrn & Mining S.F.; Constrn. Arbitration Bd.; mem: Am. Soc. Civil Engrs. (life), US Com. on Large Dams, Engrs. Club of S.F., Calif. Profl. Engrg. Assn.; co-author: Handbook of Heavy Constrn. (McGraw-Hill 1970); mil: lt. US Army Combat Engrs.; Republican; Catholic; rec: golf, sports spectator. Res: 18200 Robin Ave Sonoma 95476 Ofc: Jacobs Assoc. 500 Sansome St Ste 700 San Francisco 94111

BRAMHAM, DAVID LE ROY, sand & rock, excavating co. president; b. July 18, 1938, Sebastopol; s. Norman Wm. and Marjorie Irene (Layton) B.; m. Grace Anderson (Joyal), Nov. 30, 1969; children: Norma b. 1970, Michael b. 1972; edn: BA in bus. adm., Pacific Union Coll. 1961. Career: asst. mgr. N.W. Bramham Co. (family bus.), Sebastopol 1961-66; owner/opr. Dave Bramham Trucking Co., Santa Rosa 1966-76, and Dry Creek Sand & Gravel, Healdsburg 1970-76 (sold both cos. 1976); purch. Blue Rock Co., Forestville 1975-78 (sold 1978), dir./ secty. treas. Don Wesner Inc., Blue Rock Co. 1978-; honors: Am. Legion (acad.) award (1957); mem. Nat. Fedn. of Indep. Bus., Calif. CofC; civic: Seventh-day Adventist Parochial Sch. Board 12 yrs. (fin. com. chmn., and lay advis. mem. No. Calif. Conf. edn. com.); former mem. and treas. Redwood Chordsmen barbershop singers (Santa Rosa) and barbershop quartet, sing solos for talent pgms., ch. services, funerals and weddings, throughout Calif.; former mem. Horseless Carriage Club of Am.; former secty./treas. & pres. elect Redwood Region Youth Assn.; former church youth dir. and church treas.; Republican; Seventh-day Adventist; rec: gospel singing, baseball fan. Ofc: Don Wesner Inc. 7888 Hwy 116 Forestville 95436

BRANCA, JOHN GREGORY, lawyer; b. Dec. 11, 1950, Bronxville, NY; s. John Ralph and Barbara (Werle) B.; edn: AB, cum laude, Occidental Coll., 1972, JD, UCLA Law Sch., 1975. Career: songwriter, recording artist, Original Sound Records, 1968-70; lawyerfirm of Kindel &: Anderson, 1975-77, Barovick Konecky Braun Schwartz kay & Schiff, 1977-81, partner Ziffren, Brittenham & Gullen, 1981—; Dir. L.A. Sound, Inc. (Beach Boys), Michael Jackson Prodns, Inc. Honors: chief ed., UCLA-Alaska Law Rev. 1974-5, Am. Jurisprudence Award; mem: Am. Bar Assn., Calif. Bar Assn., Bev. Hills Bar Assn., Phi Alpha Delta law frat, Wm. Stewart Young Soc.(Occidental Coll.), UCLA Chancellor's Assocs. Num. publs. incl. Attorney Fee Schedules and Legal Advertising: The Implications of Goldfarb, 24 UCLA Law Rev. 475-522, 1977; rec: travel (Caribbean), basketball, music. Ofc: Ziffren, Brittenham & Gullen, 2049 Century Park East, #2350, Los Angeles 90067

BRANCH, JACQUELINE ALICE GIBSON, city parks and recreation executive; b. Tacoma, Wash.; d. Ray and Madeline Zoe (Roberts) Gibson; 1 son, Ron b. 1959; edn: BA, Univ. Puget Sound. Career: Metropolitan Park Dist. Tacoma, Wash.; S.F. Housing Authority; parks & rec. cons. Marin & S.F. Counties; YWCA San Rafael; parks & rec. dir. Corte Madera 1970—; cons. Marin Assn. for Retarded Citizens; bd. Marin Senior Coord. Council, CofC, Volunteer Bureau of Marin, YMCA Metropolitan, United Way Marin, Youth Soccer Assn.; cons. HEW Head Start Pgm.; conf. spkr. Hawaii Parks & Rec. Assn.; honors: Outstanding Profl. (Calif. Parks & Rec. Soc. 1984), Citizen of the Yr. (CofC 1985), Outstanding Svc. (YMCA 1985); mem: Calif. Parks & Rec. Soc. (state bd., dist. pres., secty./ treas.), YMCA (bd), Easter Seal Soc., Fourth of July Com., Marin County Black Leadership Forum, Italian Athletic Club; publs: articles in profl. and local mags. and newspapers; rec: travel photog. Res: 487 Montecito Dr Corte Madera 94925 Ofc: 498 Tamalpais Dr Corte Madera 94925

BRANDIS, MURRAY, trading co. president; b. Jan. 4, 1919, N.Y.C.; s. Frank and Sadie (Kligman) B.; m. Gertrude, Aug. 27, 1939; children: Linda b. 1943, Larry b. 1947; grad. Amarillo Sr. H.S. 1935. Career: pres. General Trading Corp., 1940—, started bus. purchasing salvage mdse. with $8.00 (sales now $3 million+); cons. appraiser various types of mdse.; invited guest of Pres. Carter to attend function for Premier Deng Chou Peng of China (1979); mem. Non Foods Merchandisers West; Shriners (charter El Bekal Shrine), Eastern Star, Masons; mil: m/sgt. Air Corps Supply 1942-45, Australia, New Guinea, Philippines svc.; rec: antique meissen ceramics, ivories. Res: 1125 Tehachapi Dr Long Beach 90807 Ofc: General Trading Corp 757 E 9th St Los Angeles 90021

BRANDON, JOHN GUNN, research scientist; b. May 19, 1946, Indianapolis, Ind.; s. John J. and Barbara Mary (Burgar) B.; m. Dorothy Ann Dreyfus, Dec. 17, 1971; children: John Robert, b. 1976; Patrick David, b. 1979; edn: BA, UC Davis 1969, PhD, 1982; pvt. pilot, SEL, FAA 1972; amateur radio lic., gen. class, FCC. Career: water quality lab tech. Norton Simon Industries 1971-73; supvr. 1973-82; supvr. Esmark Corp. 1983; founder, owner Bio Acoustics Research Laboratories 1983—; founder, co-owner Philanthis Software 1984—; supvr. Beatrice Foods, Inc. 1984—; honors: Chancellors Patent Award, 1971; Sigma Xi, assoc. 1981, mem. 1983; mem: Entomological Soc. of Am., Am. Radio Relay League, Yolo Amateur Radio Club; publs: PhD dissertation, UC Davis - Brain Research, 1982; Proc. Ninth Congress of the Internat. Union for Study of Social Insects, 1982; Episcopal; rec: sailing, fishing, amateur radio. Res: 1410 Monarch Lane, Davis 95616

BRANDON, MICHAEL WAYNE, system design consultant; b. Apr. 5, 1943, Indpls.; s. Samuel Cheatham and Dorothy Lucy (Shelby) B.; m. Gail Pearson, Aug. 29, 1982; 1 child, Miliano b. 1978; edn: BSME, Purdue Univ. 1966; MBA, Univ. Wisc. 1972; Reg. Profl. Engr. (EIT) Indiana (1966). Career:field service mgr., Xerox, 1972-78; acct. exec. Illinois Bell, 1978-81; product mgr. Control Data, 1981-82; sales engr. General Motors, 1983-84; system design cons. Pacific Bell, Los Angeles 1984—; real estate sales agt. Tarbell Realtors, 1986-; honors: Nat. Honor Soc. of Secondary Schs., Mensa Soc.; mem. Nat. Assn. of MBAs (corresp. secty.), Kappa Alpha Psi, PTA, Dem. Club of Culver City; contbr. article in By Design (Pac. Bell tech. publ.); mil: ROTC; Democrat; Baptist; rec: chess, tennis. Res: 4901-100 Indian Wood Rd Culver City 90230 Ofc: Pacific Bell 1010 Wilshire Blvd Ste 925 Los Angeles 90017

BRANDT, GEORGE EDGAR, JR., travel co. executive; b. Sept. 23, 1919, Wash DC; s. George E. Brandt and Dorothy Lyman Coventry; m. Aileen Allen, Apr. 24, 1948; 1 son, George III b. 1949; edn: BS, US Naval Acad. 1941; Certified Travel Counselor (CTC), Inst. of Cert. Travel Counselors (1979). Career: served to capt. US Navy 1941-70, awarded Legion of Merit, Bronze Star with V, Joint Services Commendn. Medal; pres. Greenbrae Travel Inc., 1971—, dba Greenbrae Travel, Mill Valley Travel, Terra Linda Travel, San Marin Travel; mem: Am. Soc. of Travel Agts., Pacific Area Travel Assn., Retired Ofcrs. Assn. (life), US Naval Acad. Assn. (life); clubs: Royal Bangkok Sports, Army Navy (Wash DC), Marvelous Marin Breakfast, Virginia Beach (Va.) Civic League; rec: photog. Ofc: Greenbrae Travel Inc. 332 Bon Air Center Greenbrae 94904

BRANKOVICH, MARK J., restaurateur; b. Mar. 4, 1922, Rijeka, Yugoslavia, nat. 1956; s. Joseph M. and Rose (Haydin) B.; m. Marilyn Severin, Jan. 4, 1956; chlidren: Mark, b. 1957; Laura, b. 1966; edn: BA in philosophy; stu. Univ. of Zurich 1943-44, Univ. of Geneva 1944-45, Univ. of Padua, Italy 1946. Career: born into a hotel family on the Adriatic Coast; arrived in USA 1951; owner/founder The Golden Deer (Bistro type restaurant), Chgo. 1953; club mgr. Gaslight Club, NY 1956; opened/mgr. The New New York Club 1957; gen. mgr. of four clubs 1958, and exec. v.p. 1959-; acquired Italian Deli.- Market in Burbank 1969, expanded into a wholesale bakery, wholesaler of Italian splties.: Monte Carlo- Italia Foods, Inc., Burbank 1969—; opened 3 restaurants named Pinocchio, in Burbank, Santa Monica, Westwood Village; Republican; Serbian Orthodox. Res: 1250 N Hilldale Ave Los Angeles 90069 ofc: Monte Carlo-Italia Foods, Inc., 3103 W Magnolia Blvd Burbank 91505

BRANNAN, WILLIAM WAYLAND, real estate broker; b. July 13, 1923, San Francisco; s. Wm. Smith and Ramona Cora (Hoag) B.; m. Marian Gimby, Mar. 26, 1951; children: Carol b. 1954, John b. 1955, Ann b. 1957, Thomas b. 1959, James b. 1962, Paul b. 1965, Kathleen b. 1969; edn: AB, Stanford Univ. 1952. Career: life ins. salesman Guardian Life, 1951-55; real estate salesman Timmer Realty, 1955-71, Fox & Carskadon, 1971-76, Frank Howard Allen, 1977-82; self-empl. realtor and appraiser, San Rafael 1982—; condr. workshops on telephone techniques throughout No. Calif., 1978-82; honors: Realtor Assoc. of the Year 1980, Marin Co.; dir. St. Vincent's Sch. for Boys; dir. Marin County Bd. of Realtors; mem. Kiwanis Club, Serra Club, Knights of Columbus; chmn. 1st Annual Town Picnic Parade, San Rafael 1980; author book and cassette tapes on tel. techniques (1981), art. in Calif. Real Estate Assn. Mag. (1980); mil: company scout, pfc, 517th Parachute Inf. Regt. 1943-45, Purple Heart, Pres. Cit.; Republican; Catholic; rec: handwriting analyst, golf. Res: 108 Coleman Dr San Rafael 94901 Ofc: William Brannan, Realtor, POB 881, San Rafael 94901

BRANSON, HARLEY KENNETH, manufacturing co. legal executive; b. June 10, 1942, Ukiah; s. Harley Edward and Clara Lucile (Slocum) B.; m. Carole Ann, Aug. 25, 1963; 1 son, Erik b. 1968; edn: AA, liberal arts, San Francisco City Coll. 1963; BS acctg., fin., San Jose State Univ. 1966; JD, Santa Clara Univ. 1968; admitted Calif. State Bar 1969. Career: law clk. to Judge James M. Carter, US Ct. of Appeals (9th Circuit) 1968-69; atty./ptnr. Klitgaard & Branson Inc., Attys. at Law, San Diego 1969-72; atty., Jennings, Engstrand & Henrikson, APLC, 1972-78, ptnr. 1976-78; div. legal counsel Ralston Purina Co., Van Camp Seafood Div., San Diego 1978-83; v.p./ gen. counsel Castle & Cooke Inc., Bumble Bee Seafoods Div., San Diego 1983-85; corporate secty., exec. v.p., gen. counsel, Bumble Bee Seafoods, Inc. 1986—; honors: Div. of Business Honor Roll SJSU, James R. Emery Scholar (1966-68), Farmers Ins. Group Scholar (1966-68), articles ed. Santa Clara Lawyer (1967-68); mem: Am. Corp. Council Assn., Am. Soc. of Corp. Sectys., Nat. Food Processors Assn. (lawyers com., claims com.), Am. Bar Assn. (Internat. Law, and Corp., Banking & Bus. Law sects.), Calif. Bar Assn. (Bus. Law sect.), Internat. Bar Assn., S.D. Co. Bar Assn. (chmn. CEB 1976); civic: Rotary, World Affairs Council, Mission Valley Council Inc. (bd. dirs. 1977-78), S.D. CofC, YMCA (soccer coach); contbr. law journals; Republican; rec: racquetball, cycling. Ofc: Bumble Bee Seafoods Inc 5775 Roscoe Ct San Diego 92123

BRAUN, JEROME IRWIN, lawyer; b. Dec. 16, 1929, St. Joseph, Mo.; s. Martin H. and Bess (Donsker) B.; children: Aaron Hugh, b. 1959, Susan Lori, b. 1963, Daniel Victor, b. 1967; edn: AB, Stanford Univ., 1951, LL.B, Stanford Law Sch. 1953. Career: lst lt. Judge Advocate Gen. Corps. US Army, 1953-57; assoc. atty. Long & Levit, San Francisco 1957-58, Law offces Jefferson Peyser, 1958-62; founding partner Elke, Farella & Braun, now Farella, Braun & Martel, San Francisco 1962—; instr., law, S.F. Law Sch., 1958-69; mem: Calif. Acad. of Appellate Lawyers (past pres.), Am. Judicature Soc., Am. Coll. of Trial Lawyers, Calif. State Bar Assn. (chmn. Adminstrn of Justice Com. 1977, chmn. Lawyer Reps. to 9th Circuit Judicial Conf. 1982, frequent moderator Cont. Edn. of the Bar pgms.); speaker various State Bar convs. in Calif., Ill., Nev., Mont.; mem. Am. Bar Assn., Bar Assn. of S.F., Jewish Welfare Fedn. of S.F., Marin Co. and the Penin. (past pres.), S.F. United Jewish Comm. Ctrs. (past pres.). Awards: Lloyd W. Dinkelspiel Outstanding Young Leader, Jewish Welfare Fedn., 1967; honoree, Mex.-Am. Legal Defense Fund, 1979.mil: pvt. US Army 1953-4; lst lt. Judge Adv. Gen. Corps, 1954-7. Ofc: Farella, Braun & Martel, 235 Montgomery St. 30th Fl. San Francisco 94104

BRAUN, STANLEY, insurance co. executive; b. July 2, 1937, NY, NY; s. Herman and Gussie B.; m. Madeline Littman, Dec. 25, 1959; children: Cindy Karen b. 1962, Dina Jill b. 1965, Suzanne Alyse b. 1969; m. 2d Ardis Knoppel, May 11, 1985; edn: BS banking & finance, NY Univ. 1959. Career: v.p. CNA Ins. NY, Chgo., L.A. 1959-74; senior v.p. Harbor Ins. Co. L.A. 1974-76; pres. Mission Ins. Co. L.A. 1976-84; exec. v.p. Fairmont Ins. Co., Fairmont Financial Inc. 1984-86; pres., CEO Fairmont Ins. Burbank 1986—; founder Raritan Valley Civic Assn. Hazlet, NJ 1965; mem: L.A. Athletic Club, Calabasas Golf & CC, Burbank CofC; Republican; Jewish; rec: hiking, camping, tennis, golf, travel, reading. OFc: Fairmont Ins. Co. 4111 W Alameda Ave Burbank 91505

BRAUTBAR, NACHMAN, physician, educator; b. Oct. 22, 1943, Haifa, Israel, nat. 1980; s. Pinhas and Sabina (Lohite) B.; m. Ronit, Mar. 25, 1969; children: Sigalit, b. 1969, Shirley, b.1972, Jaques, b. 1979; edn: MD, Hebrew Univ. Sch. of Medicine 1968; Fellow in Nephrology, UC Los Angeles Med. Sch. 1977. Career: fmr. asst. prof. med. UCLA and dir. of Home Dialysis; assoc. prof. med., pharmacology and nutrition, USC Med. Sch. 1980—; resrch. in metabolism (magnesium, phosphorus, calcium) and interaction with vitamin D and chronic renal failure, internat. authority in muscle metabolism; recipient acad. awards 1969, 76, awards for excellence, Am. Heart Assn. 1980, 2d Intl. Cong. on Bioenergetics, L.A. 1984; mem. Nat. Kidney Found. of S. Calif. (chmn. resrch. com.); Am. Heart Assn. (L.A. afil. study sect.); Soc. for Bioenergetics; Jewish Fedn.; cons. to Hollywood Presbyn. Med. Ctr.; spkr. for the Israeli Consulate; author 150 publs. and book chapters; cons. to editl. bds. of 15 sci. journals; Republican; Jewish; rec: classical music, stamps, sports. Res: 10808 Ashton Ave Los Angeles 90024 Ofc: USC, Dept. of Med. Div. Nephrology, Unit 1, 2025 Zonal Ave, Los Angeles 90033

BRAWLEY, JOHN HARRIS, mosquito control executive, ret.; b. March 12, 1920, Preshing, Okla.; s. William Lee and Evelyn Jane (Chisum) B.; children: Carolyn b. 1949, Carl b. 1954, Kevin b. 1961; edn: grad. law, LaSalle Ext. Univ. 1966; certs: Pub. Health Vector control, USPHS, 1972; Pub. Admin., CSU Hayward 1973; Mosquito Control Technician, Calif. State Health Dept. 1974; Pub. Employee Rels., Univ. of San Francisco 1975. Career: bus. mgr. Delta Mosquito Abatement Dist., Visalia 1948-50; mgr. Kings Mosquito Abatement Dist., Hanford 1950-61; mgr. Butte Co. Mosquito Abatement Dist., Oroville 1961-66; mgr. Contra Costa Mosquito Abatement Dist., Concord 1966-76, ret. 1976; bd. dirs. Am. Mosquito Control Assn. 1971-73; honors: Meritorious Svc. Award (1973-74) and Emeritus mem. (1977), Am. Mosquito Control Bd.; mem: Calif. Mosquito Control Assn. (pres. 1962, Legis. Advoc. 1970-76, hon.), Am. Mosquito Control Assn., Civitan Club, Hanford, Toastmasters Club, Hanford, Rotary Club, Gridley, Calif. Trial Lawyers Assn., Am. Legion, Pleasant Hill (post cmmdr. 1970-), Nat. Rifle Assn. (life); publs: papers on mosquito resistance to pesticides, the need for tng. and certification of mosquito control workers, detrimental effects of labor unions on mosquito control; instrumental in securing certification for mosquito control workers in Calif.; mil: m/sgt. USAF 1941-45, Euro. Air Offensive w/ 6 Battle Stars; Republican; Baptist; rec: camping, hunting, fishing. Res: 12327 Road 36 ½ Madera 93637

BRAY, ABSALOM FRANCIS, JR., lawyer; b. Nov. 24, 1918, San Francisco; s. A.F., Sr. (presiding Justice, Ct. of Appeal) and Leila (Veale) B.; grandson of Sheriff R.R. Veale, Contra Costa Co., 1895-1935; m. Lorraine Paule, June 25, 1959; children: Oliver Whitney, b. 1954, Brian Keith, b. 1955, Margot Elizabeth, b. 1957; edn: AB, Stanford Univ. 1940; JD, USC Sch of Law 1949. Career: legal dept. Iowa Ord. Plant, Burlington 1940-42; pvt. practice law, 1949–, pres. Bray, Baldwin, Egan & Breitwieser, APC, attys. at law; adv. bd. Bank of Am. 1953-65; mil: lt. USNR 1942-46, WWII, Navy Commendn., Navy Unit Citation; mem: Vets. of Fgn. Wars (cmdr.), Am. Legion (cmdr.), Contra Costa Co. Devel. Assn. (pres. 1959-60), Contra Costa Council (pres.), Navy League US (pres. Contra Costa council 1981-83), State Bar of Calif., Contra Costa Co. BAr Assn. (past pres.), Contra Costa Co. Tuberculosis and Pub. Health Assn. (past pres.), Contra Costa Co. Hist. Soc., E. Clampus Vitus, Martinez Historical Soc. (pres. 1984), Soc. of Calif. Pioneers; chmn. nat. bd. dirs. Camp Fire Girls 1959-61, 1969-71 and past chmn. Region V, CA, NV, UT, AZ, HI; chmn. John Muir Dist., BSA, 1968; Salvation Army (com.); life mem. Martinez PTA; Rotarian (past pres.); Masons; Elks; Republican; Episcopal (Vestry); rec: photog., ship models, hiking. Res: 600 Flora St Martinea Ofc: Bray, Baldwin, Egan & Breitwieser, APC, Ward and Ferry Sts., Martinez 94553

BRAY, GEORGE A., physician, educator; b. July 25, 1931, Evanston, Ill.; s. George A. and Mary (Hamilton) B.; m. Marilyn, Dec. 31, 1983; children: George, b. 1961, Thomas, b. 1963, Susan, b. 1965, Nancy, b. 1967; edn: AB summa cum laude, Brown Univ. 1953; MD magna cum laude, Harvard Univ. 1957. Career: intern Johns Hopkins Hosp. 1957-58; research assoc. Nat. Heart Inst. 1958-60; research fellow Nat. Inst. for Med. Research, Mill Hill England 1960-62; fellow, then asst. prof. of medicine, Tufts-New England Med. Center, 1962-70; assoc. prof., then prof. and dir. of Clin. Research Center, Harbor-UCLA Medical Ctr., 1970-81; nutrition coordinator, Dept. HEW, 1978-79; prof. of medicine physiology and biophysics USC, 1981–; bd. dirs. Am. Diabetes Assn. So. Calif. Affil. 1984-87; bd. dirs. Prader-Willi Found. of Calif. 1978-83; honors: Phi Beta Kappa 1952, Alpha Omega Alpha 1957, Book Prize, Am. Medical Writers Assn. 1976, Sam E. Roberts Award in Nutrition 1977, Wellcome Visiting Prof. 1978, Willendorf Award 1980, Wolffe Meml. Lectr. 1982, W.L. Asher Lectr. 1984; mem. Am. Soc. for Clin. Nutrition (Councillor 1982-84, pres. elect 1985-86), AAAS (Council Del. for Medical Scis. 1985-89), The Endocrine Soc., The Am. Physiological Soc., Am. Inst. of Nutrition, Fellow Am. Coll. of Physicians, Am. Soc. for Clin. Investigation, Assn. of Am. Physicians, Am. Diabetes Assn., No. Am. Assn. for the Study of Obesity (pres. 1982-84); author: The Obese Patient (Phila., W.B. Saunders, 1976), 550 other publs. incl. papers, chapters, books and abstracts; mil: sr. asst. surgeon USPHS; Congregational; rec: history of medicine. Ofc: University of Southern Califiornia /Diabetes, 2025 Zonal Ave., Los Angeles 90033

BRAZIL, ELIZABETH ANNE, social worker, music educator/consultant, business owner; b. Feb. 5, 1941, Visalia; d. Byron William, Jr. and Mary Wallace (Fisher) Jennings; single parent, 1 son (adopted) Robert Dale b. 1979; edn: AA, Coll. of Sequoias 1960; AB, San Jose St. Coll. 1963; tchg. creds: Spec. Sec. (Music) and. Gen. Elem. 1963; MSW, CSU Fresno 1979; Pupil Personnel Cred., UC Berkeley 1980; Comm. Coll. Counselor and Tchr. Credls. Career: classroom tchr. Earlimart Sch. Dist. 1963-64; vocal music tchr. 1964-65; classroom music tchr. Dept. of Def. Overseas Dependent Schs., Naha, Okinawa 1965-67, Wiesbaden, W. Ger. 1967-69; instru. & classrm. music tchr. Visalia Unified Sch. Dist. 1969– (on leave); pvt. music tchr. 1957–; prof. music edn. Pacific Coll., Fresno 1982-; cons. music edn., var. sch. dists., Tulare Co. 1982-; clin. soc. wkr., Visalia 1979–; tchr. women of the Jail, Visalia Adult Sch. 1981-; owner/ originator Better Scents by Anne (cosmetics for body & bath), Visalia 1981-; owner/ mgr. investment real estate, Visalia, Fresno, Porterville & Chico 1970-; presenter Tulare Co. Curriculum Conf. 1981, 83; prod./ dir. (sch. musicals), Hansel and Gretel (1968), Tom Sawyer (1969), Let George Do It (1982), num. talent shows, holiday pgms., other sch. prodns. 1963-; listed Who's Who in Exec. Women; mem: Visalia Toastmistress Club (charter); Consciousness Raising Womens Gps.; Drug Diversion Meetings; Visalia Players Comm. Theatre; Nat. Edn Assn.; Calif. Tchrs. Assn.; Visalia Unified Tchrs. Assn.; Overseas Edn. Assn.; Music Educators Nat. Conf.; Tulare- Kings Music Educators Assn.; NASW; Clin. Soc. Wkrs. Assn.; author: Self Esteem Through Music (K-3) and (4-6) and Holiday Songs, cassette tapes and guides for music in the classroom, 1981; Band Starter Method, 1973; Live From Farmersville, It's Monday Morning!, a play on therapy, 1979; coauthor: Comprehensive Evaluation Instrument and Awards for Beginning Band Students, 1974; designer: sev. bd. games for profl. tchg. purposes, multimedia presentations; Democrat; Prot.; rec: arts & crafts, Koi carp, parakeets, basset hounds, travel, computers. Res: 1708 S Linwood Ave Visalia Ofc: Visalia Unified Sch. Dist., 315 E Acequia St Visalia 93277

BREAKEY, LISA KATHERINE, speech-language pathologist; b. Oct. 21, 1945, Los Angeles; d. Melvin Harvey and Inez (Rey) Smith; edn: BA, UC Santa Barbara 1967; MA, CSU San Jose 1975; Calif. State Lic. 1975; Cert. Clin. Competence, Am. Sp. Hearing Assn. (1976), Calif. Comm. Coll. tchg. credential (spl. edn.) 1977. Career: staff speech pathologist Manitoba (Canada) Rehab. Hosp. 1968-69, Kingston (Ont., Can.) Health Unit 1969-70, dir. Speech Therapy Unit, Kingston Health Unit 1970-73; pvt. practice, San Jose 1975–; cons. Atari, Inc. 1977-79, Evergreen Valley Comm. Coll. 1977-80, Livermore VA Med. Ctr. 1979-83; honors: Phi Kappa Phi, Outstanding Achievement Award (CSHA 1986), appreciation awards ASHA (1982, 83, 84); mem: Am. Speech- Language and Hearing Assn. (legislative councilor Calif. 1986-88), Calif. Speech- Language- Hearing Assn., Calif. Sp. Pathols. and Audiologists in Pvt. Practice (pres. 1983-85), Profl. Group for Adult Communication Disorders (1st pres. 1977), Bay Area Group for the Non-Oral; former mem., Bay Area Pvt. Practitioners in Sp. Pathol. (pres. 1977), Bay Area Neurolinguistic Group, Ednl. Consortium for the Aging (rep. 1978-80); num. profl. presentations, workshops (1975-). Address: 2444 Moorpark Ave Ste 300 San Jose 95128

BREESE, THOMAS JAMES, physician, b. Jan. 13, 1943, Peoria, Ill.; s. Richard Orville and Helen Margaret (Conroy) B.; m. Dale; children: Heather b. 1973, Jeb b. 1974; edn: St. Ambrose Coll. 1964; MD, Loyola Univ. 1968; Diplomate Am. Board of Pediatrics 1976. Career: intern Kaiser Found. Hosp., Oakland 1968-69; battalion surgeon, USAR Med. Corps, Vietnam 1970-72; pediatric resident Kaiser Found. Hosp., Oakland 1972-73; pediatric pulmonary fellowship UC San Francisco 1974; cons. pediatric pulmonary medicine No. Calif. Region, KGH/TPM6, asst. chief Pediatric Dept., Kaiser Hosp. Oakland, 1976–; asst. prof. of pediatrics and attending physician UC Medical Center, San Francisco 1981-; mem. Am. Thoracic Soc.; contbr. sci. articles med. jours.; mil: major US Army Med. Corps 1970-72, Bronze Star, Combat Medics badge; rec: classic motorcycle restoration. Ofc: Kaiser Foundation Hospital 280 West MacArthur Blvd Oakland 94611

BREIER, SHELDON IRA, clergyman, lawyer, C.P.A, writer; b. Oct. 20, 1942, Los Angeles; s. Maurice Benjamin and Helen Rose (Epstein) B.; m. Penny Livermore-Packard, Feb. 14, 1983; 1 dau. Teri b. 1964; edn: JD, Southwestern Univ. Sch. of Law 1972; lic. CPA, Calif. 1969; clergyman Movement of Spiritual Inner Awareness, 1982; admitted to Calif. State Bar 1973, US Dist. Ct. and US Cts. of Appeal 1973. Career: musical arranger and singer: The Safaris, "Image of a Girl," 1960 (rock and roll gold record); CPA practice, Los Angeles 1962-72; student intern with Federal Public Defender (co-founder Southwestern Univ. chap. Law Students Civil Rights Research Council and also the Nat. Lawyers Guild/ Southwestern - Loyola Law Sch. chap. Legal Aid Soc.); asst. dist. atty. Los Angeles County Dist. Atty. Office, 1973-77; asst. public defender LA County Pub. Defender Office, 1978-81; pvt. practice criminal trial law, 1981–; past bd. dirs. Heartlight Sch. (Calabassas), Southwest Coll. of Life Science (Santa Fe, N.M.); founder Young Professionals for Robert Kennedy (1968 LA campaign for Presidency), Calif. Campaign to Reduce Voting Age to 18 (1969), LA County Farm Workers Grape boycott in Los Angeles (1969), Bradley for Mayor (1969) and for Governor (1982) campaigns; mem. Los Angeles City/County Task Force on the Homeless, Heartfelt Project John-Roger Found., Insight Transformational Seminars, Ministerial Services in Action (past bd. mem.); publs: four arts. on the Homeless in LA Daily Journal, Santa Monica Evening Outlook, Movement News and (editorial) KBIG Radio, 1985; Democrat; rec: community service. Ofc: 12021 Wilshire Blvd, Ste 277, West Los Angeles 90025

BREIMER, STEPHEN FABIAN, entertainment attorney, motion picture producer/ writer; b. Dec. 6, 1951, NYC; s. Charles William and Anne (Cyril) B.; edn: BA, Stanford Univ. 1972; JD, UCLA Sch. of Law 1985. Career: agent trainee William Morris Agency 1972-73; prodn. asst., story ed. Bruce Cohn Curtis, Hal Landers and Bobby Roberts Producers; asst. prod. "Chatterbox" and "Joyride", Am. Internat. Pictures 1974-77; prodn. assoc., story ed. Philip Barry Jr.; asst. prod. "Down Home", "Arthur Among the Animals" (tv pilots), "First You Cry" (NBC movie of the wk.); assoc. prod.: "Happily Ever After" (CBS movie of the wk.), "Friendly Fire" (Emmy award winning ABC movie of wk.) 1978-79; dir. creative affairs, Royal American Pictures 1980-81; prod., co-screenwriter "Night Warning" (theatrical motion picture, Comword 1983, Showtime 1984); legal asst. to chmn. Federal Communications Commn. 1984; Pollock, Blomm & Dekom law firm 1985–; awards: Golden Scroll Award 1982 and Best Low-Budget Feature 1982, "Night Warning", Acad. of Sci. Fiction, Fantasy and Horror Films; author: The Financial Interest and Syndication Rules: An Analysis of the FCC's Controversial Proposal for Repeal, Entertainment Publg. 1984; The Arts Handbook, Clark Boardman Co. Ltd., 1984, 1986; Copyrighting Literary and Visual Charaters: A Picture is Worth a Thousand Words, Entertainment Publg. 1986; mem: Stanford Alumni Assn., Am., Los Angeles Co. and Beverly Hills Bar Assns. Ofc: Pollock, Bloom & Dekom, 9255 Sunset Blvd. 10th Flr. Los Angeles 90069

BREITHAUPT, RICHARD HOAG, JR., real estate developer, investor; b. Feb. 15, 1953, Yeadon, Pa.; s. Richard H. and Florence Elizabeth (Budd) B., Sr.; edn: BS in bus. ad./mgmt., CSU Northridge 1976, MBA in fin., CSULA 1977. Career: finl. and mktg. analystAseptic Thermo Indicator Co., Inc., No. Hollywood 1972-76; dir. real estate acquisitions Western Consulting Group, Inc., Beverly Hills 1976-78; pres./CEO, Walika, Inc. (real estate investment and devel. co.; developing & investing in comml. office complexes, hotels, apts., condominiums, etc.), Northridge 1978—. Awards: Silver Beaver (1982), Great Western Council District Award of Merit (1979), Silver Shark and Silver Arrow, Order of the Arrow (1971), Silver Thunderbird (1974), Boys Scouts of Am.; mem: Boy Scouts of Am. (Great Western Council v.p. 1982, W. L.A. County Council exec. v.p. 1984-, Regional v.p. 1985-, nat. exec. bd. 1984-, Regional Com. exec. bd. 1982-, Nat. Com. 1982-3, Nat. Properties Com., Nat. Scouting Com.), Assn. MBA Execs. 1977-, Classic Thunderbirds of Am. Car Club 1972-; author: A History of Scouting Through Insignia (1976), A History of the Order of the Arrow (1979); num. arts. and BSA publs.; Republican; Episcopal; rec: camping, stamps & coin collector, classic cars. Res: 17201 Parthenia St. Northridge 91325Ofc: Walika, Inc. 15233 Ventura Blvd Ste 608 Sherman Oaks 91402

BREKKE, TED ALLEN, educator; b. Aug. 9, 1937, Maywood, Calif.; s. Spencer Alan and Elsie Marie (Millington) B.; m. Gail Newell, Dec. 27, 1969; 1 dau. Kristin b.1973; edn: AA, Long Beach City Coll. 1958; Geo. Williams Coll.Chgo. 1959-60; BA, CSU Long Beach 1961; MS, CSU Hayward 1975.Career: tchr. Seal Beach Sch. Dist. 1963-65, Mt. Diablo Unif.Sch. Dist. 1965-86; vice prin. Pacheco Elem. Sch. 1980-81, Holbrook Elem. Sch. Concord 1981-84; instr. Kidnet Acid Rain Proj. in conj. w/ Dickinson Coll. and Harvard Univ. 1985-86; Parks, Rec. & Open Space Commn. City of Walnut Creek 1981-85; rep. Calif. State Dept. of Edn. for consol. application pgm.reviews 1982; mem. Calif. State Instructional Materials Eval.Panel, Math 1981; adv. bd. Mt. Diablo Gifted & Talented 1980-81; Calif. Dept. Health Svcs. Dental Health Advis. Com. 1985-86; instr. Chapman Coll. extn. 1986-; mem: Calif. Tchrs. Assn. (urban area salary com. 1968), Calif. Math Council (presider Asilomar 1980-81), Assn. of Calif. Sch. Adminstrs. (newsletter), Diablo Mgmt. Assn. (bd. 1981-83, ethics com., newsletter), Mt. Diablo Tchrs. Assn. (pres. 1969-70), Calif. Assn. for Gifted Students (presenter 1979), Phi Delta Kappa (v.p. membership 1982-83), Nat.Edn. Assn., East Bay Council of Tchrs. of Social Studies, Calif.Assn. Tchrs. of Eng., Diablo Educators Group (pres. 1972), BSA (cubmaster 1967), Mt. Diablo Comm. Advis. Com. 1984-85, Calif.Assn. Park & Rec. Commrs. & Bd. Mems., Internat. Platform (Wash.DC 1981-82), Oak Grove Swim & Tennis Club; publs: 2 curriculum guides, contbr. Nature Study J. (1975); lang. arts presentation TV Channel 6 (1975); mil: USNAF 1961-63; Republican; Lutheran; rec: sailing, backpacking, gardening. Res: 2957 Filbert Dr Walnut Creek 94598 Ofc: Mt. Diablo School District

BRENNAN, CLINTON C. C., corporate executive; b. Apr. 26, 1927, Norwood, Mo.; s. FrankV Cooney and Pearl Elizabeth Brennan; m. Margaret Emily Zilla, Aug. 3, 1951; children: Brett, b. 1955; Brenda, b. 1960; edn: BS, Univ. of Houston 1949; CmfgE, Soc. of Mfg. Engrs., Robitics Internat. Career: So. regl. sales mgr. Control Data Corp., Houston, Tex. 1969; v.p. sales Brevet Internat., Palos Verdes 1972; v.p. Grubic Assocs., Mt. View 1975; sr. staff cons. MacDonnel Douglas Corp., Monrovia 1977; currently, CIM cons. & lectr.; council mem./chmn. legal & fin. com. Mayor Pro-Tem, Hilshire Village, Tex. 1967-69; mem: Tex. League of Cities; Admiral, Tex. Navy 1969; Numerical Control Soc. (past pres. L.A. Co. chpt.); Soc. Mfg. Engrs. (past pres. Orange Coast chpt.); mil: BM 1/c, USN 1944-46, Unit Citation w/ Stars; rec: antique auto restoration, geology, earth sci. Res: 504 W Huntington Dr Arcadia 91006

BRENNAN, JAMES FRANCIS JOSEPH, ESQ., business owner; b. Nov. 27, 1948, Rochester, NY; s. Francis James and Josephine Ann (Messina) B.; edn: regents scholar, St. Thomas Aquinas Inst. 1963-67, spl. courses Monroe Comm. Coll., La Mesa Jr. Coll. Career: mgr. Endicott-Johnson, Brockport, NY 1968; missionary Catholic Orders, Salesians and Oblates of the Immaculate Heart of Mary; founder/pres. Lampstand Co. Inc. Express, 1970—, Lampstand Intertec Internat., Lampstand Inc., 50/50 Inc., Campstand Internat. (camp for patients at Patton State Hosp.); tch. individuals how to start-up in bus.; honors: Group Fishing Champion, Gr. No. Lakes Lake Paper Co. (1965); mem. Am. Mgmt. Assn., The Pres.'s Assn. (Carter 1976), Internat. Platform Assn. (bd.), Blue Army- Salesian Missions, Legion of Mary, Disabled Am. Vets; inventor Bladder Tank (1974); mil: cpl. USMC, 26 decorations incl. Vietnam Cits., Nat. Def., Combat Award; Democrat; Catholic. Ofc: Lampstand Co. Inc. Express 3102 E Highland Ave Ste N22 Patton 92369

BRENNER, LEON CHARLES, marketing executive; b. June 9, 1946, Detroit, Mich.; s. Sol and Nettie (Goldstein) B.; m. Lana Tu, Aug. 19, 1983; edn: BS, Mich. State Univ. 1969, MA, 1971. Career: owner Velocipede Peddler, E. Lansing, Mich. 1972-75; internat. trade assoc. Consulting Associates, San Francisco 1975-78; mng. dir. Yulsan American, San Francisco 1978-80; v.p. Coastal Dynamics Corp., NYC, NY 1980-82; mktg. dir. Nady Systems Inc., Oakland 1982—; hon. bus. guest P.R.C. 1979; mem: Am. Mgmt. Assn., Am. Mktg. Assn., Commonwealth Club, Calif. Council for Internat. Trade; works: Guide to American Diversified, 1985; rec: mosaics, impressionistic art. Res:

490 9th Ave. San Francisco 94118 Ofc: Nady Systems Inc., 1145 65th St. Oakland 94608

BRENT, ALLAN ARTHUR, securities brokerage executive; b. Aug. 10, 1931, London, England; s. Lawrence Arthur and Emily (Bugg) B.; div.; children: Kirsten b. 1964, James b. 1965, Gavin b. 1967, Jonathan b. 1969; edn: matriculation, Woodhouse/Cambridge Univ., U.K. 1948, Higher Sch. cert., 1949; Fellow, Inst. of Chartered Sectys. & Adminstrs., City of London Coll., 1955, Fellow, Chartered Inst. of Arbitrators, 1970; Fellow, Inst. of Taxation, London Sch. of Econs., 1960; desig: FCIS (1955), FCI Arb. (1970), FTII (1960), Profl. Inst., U.K. Career: mng. dir. Grendon Trust Ltd., 1971-73; senior cons. Alpha Beta Consultants Ltd., 1973-77, 1978-81; chief exec. Projects, Interncontinental Fuels Ltd., 1977-78; v.chmn., pres. Beare Bros. & Co. Inc. (NYSE), 1981-83; pres. Dania Securities Inc. (NASD, SIPC), Newport Beach 1983—; magistrate, gen. commnr. of taxation; honors: mem. Council (nat. pres. 1969-70) Inst. of Taxation 1963-80; mem. Council, Chartered Inst. Sectys. & Adminstrs. 1972-79; mem. Internat. Fiscal Assn.; Knight (governor) Royal Soc. of St. George; clubs: Athenaeum (London), City Livery (London); publs. on moncy mgmt., mil. capt. Brit. Army RAOC Paratroops 1949-51, 1956 (Suez); Ch. of England; rec: tennis, sailing, travel, wildlife. Ofc: Dania Securities Inc. 5031 Birch St Ste C Newport Beach 92660

BRET, GEORGES G., science co. executive; b. July 4, 1935, Lyon, France; s. Ferdinand and Paulette (Aubert) B.; m. Marie Therese Le Gall, July 4, 1959; children: Eric b. 1960, Pierre Michel b. 1964; edn: ingenieur, Ecole Sup Electricite Paris 1959; MS physics, Case Western Reserve 1961; PhD physics, Paris Univ. 1967. Career: research engr. Thomson CSF France 1963-67; charge' de recherche CNRS France 1967-68; prof. physics Paris Univ. 1968-71; founder, chmn., pres. Quantel France 1971—, Quantel Calif. 1976—; chmn. AFIMES French import corp.; chmn., pres. The Bay Global Group internat. mktg. and technol. assessment San Jose; honors: Officier de l'Ordre du Merite (France); publ: 30 in sci. jours.; 10 patents; mil: capt. French Army (ret.); rec: travel. Res: 2580 Homestead Rd Santa Clara 95051 Ofc: Quantel 390 Reed St Santa Clara 95050

BREWERTON, RHODA PARAMORE, real estate broker; b. June 24, 1924, N.Y.; d. Bert and Sadie (Morrison) Brown; m. 2d. Lyndon Brewerton, Aug.21, 1962; 1 dau. Patricia Susan Paramore b. 1946; edn: grad. Metropolitan Bus. Sch., 1941-44; Calif. lic. real estate broker (1966), grad. Real Estate Inst. (1976). Career: realtor, West Hollywood 1966—; mem: Nat. Assn. Realtors, Calif. Assn. Realtors (dir. 1970-76, 81-85, 20th Dist. regional v.p. 1975, dir. at large 1977-78, state conv. chmn. 1985, Interboard Arbitrator 1981-86), West Hollywood Bd. Realtors (dir.1970-72, pres. 1973-74, Realtor of Year 1974-75), Beverly Hills Bd.Realtors (Salesman of Year 1973, Spl. Service Award 1976, mem. Profl.Stds. 1981-), West Hollywood CofC (1st woman pres. 1982-83). Res: 1532 W Hayworth Ave Los Angeles 90046

BRICKELL, JOHN TILTON, internal auditor; b. Dec. 23, 1933, Washington, N.C.; s. Abner Tilton and Inez Ernestine (Wedding) B.; m. Natividad Castro, Apr. 25, 1957; children: John, Jr. b. 1958, Timothy b. 1960, Janice b. 1964; edn: acctg., Kings Coll. 1959; Cert. Internat. Auditor, ITA (1974). Career: regional internal audit mgr. First Charter Finl. Corp. (Am. Svgs.), San Jose 1962-76; chief internal auditor San Francisco Fed. Svgs & Loan, S.F. 1976—; mem. Inst. Internal Auditors 1964-; mil: storekeeper 2/c US Navy 1953-57, Nat. Def., Korean Svc., Good Conduct; Democrat; Catholic; rec: garden, woodwork. Res: 2716 Wakefield Dr Belmont 94002 Ofc: San Francisco Federal S&L 39138 Fremont Blvd Ste 201 Fremont 94538

BRIDGES, ROBERT LYSLE, lawyer; b. May 12, 1909, Altus, Ark.; s. Joseph Manning and Jeffa Alice (Morrison) B.; m. Alice Marian Rodenberger, June 10, 1930; children: David Manning, James Robert, Linda Lee; edn: AB, Univ. Calif. 1930, LLB, 1933; admitted Calif. State Bar 1933, U.S. Supreme Ct. 1938. Career: atty. assoc. law firm Thelen & Marrin, San Francisco 1933-39, ptnr. firm 1939—, firm name Thelen, Marrin, Johnson & Bridges, 1941-; bd. trustees (chmn. 1985-) Univ. Calif., Berkeley Found.; pres. permanent Class of 1930, Univ. Calif.; trustee, exec. com. John Muir Memorial Hosp.; mem. Am., Calif., San Francisco bar assns., World Affairs Council (trustee, exec. com.); Republican; clubs: Links (NYC), Commonwealth of Calif., World Trade, Pacific Union, Stock Exchange (SF), Claremont Country (Oakland), California (LA). Res: 3972 Happy Valley Rd Lafayette 94549 Ofc: 2 Embarcadero Center San Francisco 94111

BRIDGES-OLIVIER, LINDA MAUREEN, doctor of oriental medicine, acupuncturist, herbalist; b. May 9, 1938, Los Angeles; d. James Alonzo and Agnes (Zenobia) Bridges; m. Stanley Olivier, Nov. 25, 1961, div. 1976; children: Lydia b. 1962, Karana Dharma b. 1964, Michael b. 1966, David b. 1968; edn: AA, East Los Angeles Comm. Coll. 1974; Dip. Nsg., LAC/USC Sch. of Nsg., 1976; BS, S.A.M.R.A. Univ. of Oriental Healing Arts, 1982, OMD/PhD, 1985; desigs: RN; Certified Acupuncturist Calif. BMQA (1976), Std. Tchg. Credential, adult edn. (1976). Career: choreographer, dir. Daenia Dance Workshop, Los Angeles 1958-61; dance instr. YWCA, Compton 1961-64; psycho-motor therapist Al Manar Sch. for Psychologically Impaired, US Peace Corps, Rabat, Morocco 1970-72; dance therapist Stevely Board & Care for Chronic Psychiatric, 1972-73; staff nurse, dance therapist Rancho Los Amigos Hosp., Downey 1976-78; staff nse. Thalians Mental Health Comm. Ctr. L.A. 1978-82; founder/dir. Rhythmic Living, L.A., 1978—, Glendale, 1983—, acupuncturist, herbalist, doctor of oriental medicine, psycho-motor therapist, transpersonal counselor; internat. cons.; health editor Forte Ents., 1982-84; recipient service awards: L.A. City Schs. (1970), Kiwanis Club of Angeles Mesa (1980, 82),

UCLA Pre-Med. Program (1985); mem: Assn. of Holistic Health 1977-81, So. Calif. Assn. of Black Psychologists 1980-83, Am. Public Health Assn. 1984-85, Assn. of Humanistic Psychology 1977-79, Am. Assn. of Dance Therapists 1972-84, num. community groups; works: Colour Me Love, An Anthology of Poetry, 1979; Rhythm as an Ednl. Teaching Tool, 1978; dance performance by students, Moroccan Public T.V., 1972; annual nat. workshop presentation, Assn. of Black Psychologists, 1980-; Democrat; Universalist; rec: art, modern dance, swimming. Ofc: Arizona Health Care Clinic Ste 102 Glendale 91204; 1054 S Hauser Los Angeles 90019

BRIERTON, CHERYL WOOTTON BLACK, lawyer; b. Nov. 11, 1947, Hartford, Conn.; d. Charles Greenwood and Elizabeth (Grechko) Wootton; m. John Thomas Brierton, Sept. 6, 1982; 1 son John G. b. 1983; edn: BA, Wellesley Coll. 1969, JD, Univ. San Diego Sch. of Law 1982; admitted Calif. State Bar 1983, US Dist. Ct. (so. dist. Calif.) 1983. Career: tchr., librarian Anglican H.S. Grenada, West Indies 1972-74; property adminstr. The Crab Hole Bequia St. Vincent Grenadines, West Indies 1974; deputy dir. Transalpino Internat. Student Travel Paris 1975-76; asst. dir. adminstrn. YMCA Proj. Oz San Diego 1976-78; juvenile justice staffperson The Community Congress 1978-81, proj. dir. community anti-crime proj. 1978-80, asst. coord. policy planning & advocacy 1979-81; field dir. Calif. Child, Youth & Family Coalition 1981-83; asst. exec. dir. Community Congress of San Diego 1984-85, exec. dir. Calif. Child, Youth & Family Coalition 1985-86; atty. U.S. Defense Dept. 1986–; honors: Am. Jurisprudence Award- Constnl. Law (1980), Gilman Meml. Scholarship, Univ. San Diego (1979); mem: San Diego County Bar Assn., NAACP, Mensa; Protestant; rec: sailing. Res: 1329 Bancroft St San Diego Ofc: Defense Logistics Agency, Defense Depot Tracy, Tracy 95376

BRIGGS, JOHN WILLIAM ("BILL"), co. president; b. Feb. 26, 1944, Altoona, Pa.; s. Ralph and Hazel Elizabeth (Gibson) B.; m. Mary S., Nov. 28, 1975; children: Sean b. 1978, Kevin b. 1980; edn: BS, Penn State Univ. 1966. Career: tool design engr. Lockheed Missile and Space Co., Sunnyvale 1966-70; customer service engr. National Can Corp., Santa Clara 1971-73; chief engr. Golden State Runway Corp., Campbell 1973-78; pres./chmn. bd./CEO, Pioneer Conveyors, Inc. 1978–; recipient profl. achievement awards: Zero Defects Design award (1968), Security Check out Procedure (1969), Lockheed Missiles and Space Co.; mem./soccer coach Youth Teams, Christian Athletic Assn. and YMCA; works: New Overhead Conveyor Design Profile, Golden State Runway (1976); mil: E4 USNR 1960-64; Republican; Lutheran. Ofc: Pioneer Conveyors, Inc. 437 Queens Ln San Jose 95112

BRIGHT, WILLIAM EDWARD, management consultant; b. May 5, 1914, Scranton, Pa.; s. William Edward and George May (Cure) B.; m. Anne Safford, July 17, 1937; children: William 1941-1948, Susan b. 1945, Megan b. 1953; edn: AB, Brown Univ. 1936; MS indsl. rels., Loyola Univ., Chgo. 1967. Career: var. pos. in mktg. and corporate personnel, then mgr. Employee Rels., Pure Oil Co., 1943-65; staff Corp. Indsl. Rels., mgr. Manpower Planning & Devel., Unocal Corp., 1966-77, ret.; mgmt. cons. var. major corps. 1977-; Internat. Exec. Service Corps, Venezuela 1982; vis. prof. Northwestern Univ. (1956, 57), instr. continuing edn. programs Univ. of Chgo., CalTech; speaker Diebold Internat. Conf., Stockholm, Sweden (1978); recipient Outstanding Publication award, Los Angeles Tng. & Devel. Soc. (1977); mem: Human Resource Planning Soc. (founding bd., 1977-82), The Conference Board (council mem. 1957-77), Am. Soc. for Tng. & Devel. (1951-77), Kiwanis (1940-48), Sons in Retirement (1980-); publs: art., Harvard Bus. Review (Jan. Feb. 1976), contbr. var. bus. & profl. jours.; book of poetry "Avocations" (Plainview Press, 1984); var. forecasting computer models; Republican; Presbyterian; rec: reading, writing, bridge, golf. Res: 345 Pythian Rd Santa Rosa 95405

BRIGMAN, BETTIE JEAN, senior clinical dietition; b. Dec. 19, 1935, Linden, Tx.; d. Felton and Zettie Mae (Lockett) Epps; m. Arnold A. Brigman, Apr. 21, 1960; children: Arnold, Jr. b. 1961, Michael b. 1963, Vincent b. 1965; edn: BS, Prairie View A&M Univ., 1958; postgrad. studies CSU San Jose 1985; Reg. Dietitian, Am. Dietetic Assn. 1959. Career: asst. dir. food svcs. Kentucky State Coll., Frankfort, Ky. 1959-60; subst. tchr. Wiesbaden, W.Germany Elem. Sch. 1962; staff therapeutic dietitian El Camino Hosp. Mt. View, Calif. 1964-65, 67-68, senior clin. dietitian 1978–; instr. Nutrition seminars for student nses., Heart Assn.; instr. seminars on public health nutrition for welfare recipients; participated in food fairs, var. hosp. and Girl Scout orgs.; awards: Mary Gibbs Jones Scholar, Prairie View Univ. (1956), Employee safety commendation award (1971), appreciation, Am. Heart Assn. (1977), El Camino Hosp. (1973), Woman of Year, San Jose Mercury News (1973); mem: Am. Dietetic Assn., Calif. Diet. Assn., Peninsula Diet. Assn. (Quality Assur. Com. 1979-86), Nat. Kidney Found. (1978-80), Am. Heart Assn. (Nutrition Com. 1976-83), Ky. Tchrs. Assn. (1959-60); civic: PTA (1967-80), Fremont H.S. Athletic Booster Club and Acad. and Student Pop. Task Force (1980-84), UOP Athletic Booster Club (1983-86); publs: El Camino Hosp. Diet Manual 1974 (revised yearly 1975-84); contbg. ed. El Camino Hosp. Cardiac Rehab Tchg. Manual (1974), Physician Nutrition Diet Therapy Handbook (1985), Nutrition Newsletter (ongoing); contbg. ed. San Jose Dietetic Assn. Quality Assurance Manual (1986); Democrat; Baptist; rec: tourism, bowling, board games. Res: 1212 Sargent Dr Sunnyvale 94087 Ofc: El Camino Hospital 2500 Grant Rd Mt View 94042

BRILL, ROBERT DENSMORE, government contract negotiator; b. Apr. 7, 1941, Los Angeles; s. William Martin and Claire Josephine (Lee) B.; 1 dau. Denise Jacqueline b. 1965; edn: BA Eng., UC Davis 1973; MA Eng., CSU Sacramento 1982; JD, Univ. No. Calif. Law Sch. 1985; AAS flight engrg., Comm. Coll. of Air Force 1986; pvt. investigator Calif. 1976. Career: state prison guard Calif. Men's Colony East, San Luis Obispo 1965; police ofcr. City of Sacramento 1966-75; pvt. investigator The Brill Agcy. 1976–; subs. tchr. San Juan Unified Sch. Dist. 1978; contract negotiator Dept. of Defense 1982–; volunteer lobbyist parental-child kidnapping; ed. Am. Para-Legal Reporter; honors: Am. Spirit Honor Medal (Nat. Com. for the Army, Navy, AF, Marines); mem: alumni assns., Am. Taekwondo Assn. (red belt); mil: s/a USNR 1958-60, USAF 1960-63, tsgt. USAFR 1964-; Republican; rec: jogging, fitness, Taekwondo, reading, writing poetry, politics, swimming. Res: POB 1715 N Highlands 95660-1715

BRINDEL, FRANKLIN DYSON, engineer; b. May 23, 1915, Pittsburg, Pa.; s. Harold Franklin and Helen (Meeds) B.; m. Gwendolyn Marie Forster, May 7, 1938; children: Barbara Joan b. 1939, Warren Franklin b. 1943, Edward Allen b. 1947; edn: BS, univ. Tulsa 1936; postgrad. math., Northwestern Univ. 1936-37; Naval Electronic Sch., Bowdoin Coll. 1943; Naval Radar Sch., M.I.T. 1943; Naval Aircraft Radar Sch., NAS Corpus Christi, Tex. 1943; Reg. Control Sys. Engr. Calif. Career: instrumentation sales engrg. & mgmt. 1948-70; Ehrhart & Assocs. Engrg. Co. 1964-69; Bechtel Corp. 1969-70; mgr. control engrg. Davy McKee 1970-81; supv. engr. Brown & Caldwell 1981–; honors: Nat. Honor Soc. (Okla. Mil. Acad.); mem: Instrument Soc. of Am. 1947-, Am. Assn. Retired Persons, Mt. Diablo Hosp. Cardiac Volunteers; publ: children's stories, George the Fly; mil: lcdr. USNR 1942-46, ATO, PTO w/ 2 Battle Stars; Republican; Ch. of Christ (elder); rec: fishing, elec. organ, music, reading, writing. Res: 514 Baylor Ct Benicia 94510 Ofc: Brown & Caldwell 3480 Buskirk Pleasant Hill 94523

BRINEGAR, KIMBERLY PARK, speech pathologist; b. Jan. 30, 1952, Akron, Ohio; d. William Earl Jr. and Anna Mary (Evans) Park; m. William Brinegar, June 23, 1973; children: Kerianne Elizabeth b. 1977; John William b. 1980; edn: BS, La Verne Coll. 1974, MS, 1976; D.Edn., Univ. of La Verne 1987; Speech Pathologist, Am. Speech Lang. Hearing Assn. 1982; Lic. Speech Pathologist, Calif. 1982. Career: speech patologist Chino Unif. Sch. Dist. 1974-75 speech pathologist and pgm. asst. to severe lang. disorders/ aphasia pgm. and dist. mgmt. trainee Claremont Unif. Sch. Dist. 1975–; dist. staff devel. com. chprsn. 1984, lang. speech hearing chprsn. 1981-83, co-chprsn. East San Gabriel Valley Community Adv. Com. 1984-85; honors: dept. hons. in speech pathology, LaVerne Coll. 1974; cert. of clin. competency, Am. Speech Lang. & Hearing Assn. 1982; listed Who's Who in Colls. and Univs. 1974; mem: Am. and Calif. Speech Lang. Hearing Assns.; Republican; Presbyterian; rec: needlepoint. Res: 1585 Wedgewood Way Upland 91786 Ofc: Claremont Unified School Dist., 2080 No. Mountain Ave. Claremont 91711

BRINKER, CONNIE JUGE, graphoanalyst; b. July 15, 1928, New Orleans, La.; d. Edward Joseph and Faustine Madeline (Aleman) Juge; m. Robert Brinker, Jan. 4, 1948; children: Richard b. 1948, Susan b. 1952, John b. 1957, Craig b. 1958, Randy b. 1964; edn: cosmetology, N.O. Beauty Coll. 1963; Fullerton Coll. 1975-6; Lifetime tchg. credentials, Cosmetology, Graphoanalysis, State of Calif. 1974; Certified graphoanalyst 1972, Questioned Document examiner 1974, Master Cert. graphoanlyst, The Internat. Graphoanalysis Soc. 1978. Career: owner Brinker and Associates, Fullerton 1979–, opened beauty salon 1979-, estab. bus. in Graphoanalysis and Questioned Documents 1980-; instr. No Orange Co. Comm. College Dist. 1974-84; currently teaching privately; honors: Sharon Topper Humanitarian Award, Fullerton Coll. 1976; Graphoanalyst of the Year-So Calif. 1977, Cooperator of the Year 1977, Excellence of Perf. 1980, (IGAS) Internat. Graphoanalysis Soc.; Pres. Emeritus Honor 1980, So Calif. Chpt. Graduation spkr. 1982, IGAS Chgo. Mem: IGAS (life), World Assn. of Document Examiners (So. Calif. chpt. pres. 1978-9, Proficiancy Recogn. Award 1984); mem. Citrus chpt. Nat. Psoriasis Found. 1969-83; Cub Scout Den Mother (11 yrs), Girl Scouts (6 yrs); publs: arts. in Jour. of Graphoanalysis, World Assn. of Document Examiners Exchg., Research Project IGAS 1984; paper presented on History of the Writing Instrument at World Assn. of Document Examiners Annual Seminar in Chgo. 1985; Democrat; Catholic; rec: antique clock repair, jewelry design, nutrition, study of herbs. Res: 2129 West Houston Ave Fullerton 92633 Ofc: Brinker and Associates 107 North Woods Ave Fullerton 92632

BRISCOE, PEARL KNAPP, psychologist; b. Jan. 7, 1901, Ripley, Ohio; d. James Luther and Jessie Maud (Wood) Gilliland; m. Robert Talbot Knapp (dec. 1957), June 14, 1925; m. 2d Charles Frederick Briscoe May 5, 1969; edn: RN, Huntington Meml. Sch. Nsg. 1925; BA, UC Los Angeles 1928, MA, 1938, PhD, 1949; lic. clin. psychol. Calif.; certified marriage, family, child counselor Calif. Career: worked with L.A. Juvenile Hall, Child Guidance Clinic L.A., Central Clinic L.A. Pub. Schs.; tchg. fellow UCLA 1936-37; psychol. L.A. Psychiatric Svc. tng. doctoral candidates 1942-57; chief psychol. Cedar's of Lebanon Hosp., Cedars-Sinai Med. Svc. L.A. 1957-69 (ret.); mem. num. coms., attended seminars, APA conventions; honors: Sigma Xi, Psi Chi, Diplomate ABPP; mem: L.A. Co. Mus. of Art, Nat. Trust for Historical Preservation, South West Mus., Women's Club Calif. Inst. Technol., Scripps Coll. Fine Arts Found., Friends of Beckman Auditorium (Caltech), L.A. World Affairs Council, East Pasadena Republican Club, Friends of Huntington Library, League of Women Voters; Republican; Protestant; rec: travel, hiking, sculpting, collecting Indian artifacts. Res: 1801 N Country Lane Pasadena 91107

BRITTELL, LOIS ELAINE, clinical psychologist; b. Mar. 26, 1936, Saskatoon, Can.; d. Abram Shelley and Martha Evelyn (Heide) Ediger; m. Ralph Brittell, June 23, 1959; edn: BA magna cum laude, CSU Bakersfield 1976; MA, Rosemead Grad. Sch. of Profl. Psychol. 1978; PhD, Rosemead Sch. of Psychol. Biola Univ. 1986. Career: NCR machine oper. Bank of Am. 1955-64; acctg. clerk Griswold & Wight Modesto 1966-68, Prudential Ins. Modesto 1969-71, City of Bakersfield 1971-73; therapist Fullerton Psychological Svcs. 1979-82, No. Orange County Psychol. Svcs. 1982, Covina Psychol. Svcs. 1982-86;

psychol. intern The Psychol. Ctr. Pasadena 1981-82; tchg. asst. Biola Univ. 1980-81, Fuller Grad. Sch. OF Psychol. 1981-82; honors: Vocational Arts Award (Bank of Am. 1954), Citation, Excellence of Svc. (City of Bakersfield 1972), listed Who's Who Am. Univs. & Colls. 1980, Psi Chi (1981); mem: Calif. State Psychol. Assn., Christian Assn. for Psychol. Studies, Rosemead Grad. Student Assn. (pres., chmn. exec. com., student rep. acad. council); papers presented: Western Psychol. Conf. (Santa Clara Univ. 1975), Am. Psychol. Assn. Annual Conv. (Toronto 1978, Wash. DC 1986), Western Gerontol. Soc. Annual Conf. (San Diego 1982); Republican; Christian; rec: writing, gardening. Res: 2113 Jeffrey Cir Placentia 92670 Ofc: Lois Brittell Clinical Psychol. 3333 Brea Canyon Rd Diamond Bar 91765

BROADBENT, AMALIA SAYO CASTILLO, graphic artist, designer; b. May 28, 1956, Manila, Phil., nat. US cit. 1986; d. Conrado Camilo and Eugenia De Guzman (Sayo) Castillo; m. Barrie Noel Broadbent, Mar. 14, 1981; children: Charles b. 1983, Chandra b. 1985; edn: Maryknoll Coll. 1972-73; Karilagan Finishing Sch. 1973; BFA, advt., Univ. of Santo Tomas 1978; French language, Alliance Francaise, Manila, San Francisco, 1979-82. Career: graphic artist-designer/prin. A.C. Broadbent Graphics, S.F.; freelance art dir. Ogilvy & Mather Direct; freelance prodn. artist Grey Advt.; honors: Dean's List (1977), 3d pl. bronze medal, drawing contest (1974), Univ. of Santo Tomas; mem: Nat. Assn. of Female Execs., Makati Dance Troupe, YMCA, Alliance Francaise; works: freehand drawing 'Daing Na Isda' (1974); Roman Catholic; Ofc: A.C. Broadbent Graphics 805 Leavenworth Ste 506 San Francisco 94109

BROCHEY, ROBERT O., microfilm co. president; b. May 27, 1949, Dubois, Pa.; s. Russell Harrison and Marsha Jane (Brochey) Hoffman; m. Michelle Lafaye, Mar. 8, 1974; children: Damian b. 1974, Julia b. 1978; edn: San Diego City Coll. 1973-74, tchg. cred. 1980. Career: switchman US Steel Corp., Gary, Ind. 1967-68; asst. microfilm camera technician Westinghouse Elec. Corp. 1974-78, Micro-Service, San Diego 1978-79; ops. mgr. Micrographics Resources Center, La Mesa 1979-80; owner/pres. Aztec Micrographics, El Cajon 1980−; instr., micrographics, San Diego Comm. Coll. 1980-; advsry. com. San Diego Comm. Coll. Dist.; mem: Nat. Micrographics Assn. (bd. dirs. S.D. chpt. and editor The Borderline quarterly pub.); civic: S.D. Childrens Theatre (1982-), S.D. Zool. Soc. (1982-); works: devel. Micro Nav Chart System, used as a navigational aid in the Voyager Aircraft for world record flight; research in microfilm mgmt. systems and law firm case retrieval systems; mil: signalman, p.o.3/c, US Navy 1968-72, Vietnam Campaign, Good Conduct, Korean, Vietnam Combat medals; Democrat; rec: flying light aircraft. Res: 1431 Woodrow Ave San Diego 92114 Ofc: Aztec Micrographics 1935 N Marshall Ste 1 El Cajon 92020

BRODERICK, LOUISE ANTOINETTE, educator, nursing home administrator, ret.; b. Mar. 29, 1916, Calexico; d. Edward Nicholas and Viola (Sick) Drum; m. Charles M. Broderick, June 6, 1937; 1 son, Charles Edward b. 1944; ed. pub. schs.; nse. tng. San Diego Jr. Coll., 1948; courses, CSU San Diego and UCSD Ext.; Calif. lic. Nursing Home Adminstr., Std. Tchg. Credential. Career: dist. supr. 5 offices, Pacific Tel. Co., 1937-44; prin., adminstr. Broadway Home, 1946-61, v.p. and treas. Broadway Home, Inc. 1961-80, Char-Lou Manor 1972-81; adminstr. The Broderick, Inc. 1966-67, pres. and treas. 1962-76; tchg. Small Bus. Adminstrn., Residential Care Homes Adult Edn., San Diego 1972-73; honors: co-founder (1963), Fellow Emeritus Am. Coll. of Nsg. Home Adminstrs. (1981), Woman of Achievement, Bus. and Profl. Women of San Diego Co. (1966); cons. Calif. Dept. Pub. Health Hosp. Advis. Council. 1961-64, mem. (chmn. 1964, 68) Advis. Council On Residential Care Homes, State Dept. Social Welfare 1957-73; del. White House Conf. on Aging 1961, Surgeon Gen.;s Conf. on Prev. of Crippling Arthritis 1965; mem: Am. Nsg. Home Assn. 1957 74, Calif. Assn. of Nsg. Homes, (pres. 1962 64), Sanitarium and Rest Home Assn. of San Diego (orgnzr. 1947, pres. 1956-57), (CARCH) Calif. Assn. of Residential Care Homes, Gerontol. Soc.; civic: Eastern Star, Scottish Rite Women's Club, Zonta Internat.; writer monthly column, Community Care, CARCH News (1974-); profl. jour. articles (62, 63, 64); Christian Ch.; rec: china painting, swimming. Address: 4342 West Point Loma Blvd Apt E San Diego 92107

BROEKEMA, DIRK, JR., mortgage banking co. president; b. Feb. 5, 1936, Chgo.; s. Dirk and Sophie (Kummer) B.; m. Michele; children: Dirk, III b. 1962, Detje b. 1965, Shaun Melby b. 1966; edn: courses in fin., Univ. Ariz. 1960. Career: senior v.p. Union Bank, Tucson, Az. 1963-68; regl. v.p. Union Bank, Los Angeles and San Jose offices 1968-73; pres. U.S. Financial Mortgage Co., San Diego 1973-75; pres./CEO Commercial Standard Title Ins. Co., S.D. 1975-77; pres. First California Title Co., S.D. 1977-78; pres. Bowest Corp., La Jolla 1978−; dir. La Jolla Pacific Savings & Loan; civic: bd. dirs.: Scripps Clinic and Research Found., UCSD Found., Nat. M.S. Soc., Greater San Diego Sports Assn., Holiday Bowl (pres. 1985-86), La Jolla CofC, San Diego hall of Champions, mem. Civic Round Table; clubs: La Jolla Country, Fairbanks Ranch Country; mil: capt. US Army Transp. Corps 1961-63; Republican; Episcopal; rec: golf, tennis. Res: 16781 Via Los Rosales Rancho Santa Fe 92067 Ofc: Bowest Corp. 3300 North Torrey Pines Ct La Jolla 92037

BROKL, DAVID JAMES, communication co. executive; b. Mar. 4, 1943, Palo Alto; s. Arnold Stanley and Annette C. (Chidlaw) B.; m. Dorene, Oct. 23, 1982; children: Scott b. 1965, Yvonne b. 1968, Debra b. 1970, Barbara b. 1972; edn: USAF Air Univ. 1963-64, Chaffey Coll. 1967, Occidental Coll. 1969, Univ. So. Calif. 1986, Duke Univ. 1986. Career: with GTE, 1965−; craft employee, Claremont 1965, supr., San Bernardino 1967, tech. writer, Santa Monica 1968, instr. Electronic Systems, Downey 1970, systems analyst, Long Beach 1972, engr. Electronic Sys., Santa Monica 1976, engring. supr. 1977, project engr. 1978, adminstr., mgr. Switching 1981-82, gen. mgr. project mgmt. 1984, gen.

mgr. project mgmt./project plnng., GTE, Thousand Oaks 1985−; mgmt. cons. self-empl. 1981−; recipient profl. awards: Project Mgmt. Inst. (2 in 1985), Who's Who in Proj. Mgmt. (P.M.I. 1986), North Elec. Co. (1975), innovation in industry Sony Corp. of Am. (1970); Colonel -Aide-De-Camp, Gov. State of N.M. (1964); mem: Internat. Project Mgmt. Assn. (bd. dirs. Project Mgmt. Inst. both nat. and Calif. chpt.), Am. Mgmt. Assn., Indep. Telephone Pioneers Assn.; civic: Equestrian Trails Inc./ Manna, Conejo Valley Food Bank (vol.), Youth Employment Service (vol.); author: CCTV & You (1970), Communications as Modern As Tomorrow (1972), contbr. feature articles in nat. publ. Tel. Engring. & Mgmt. (1971, 75, 79), prod. nat. distbd. video The PMI Story (1985); mil: sgt. USAF 1961-65; Republican; Christian; rec: off-road vehicle adventuring, antique vehicle restoration, equestrian. Res: 2231 Goldsmith Ave Thousand Oaks 91360 Ofc: GTE One GTE Place Ste 3573A Thousand Oaks 91362

BRONK, TERESA MAE, accountant; b. Feb. 1, 1957, Sacramento; d. Paul Joseph and Rosemarie (Jereczek) B.; edn: AA, American River Coll. 1976; BS, CSU Sacramento 1979; MBA, Loyola Marymount Univ. 1984; Certified Public Acct., Calif. Career: acct. Arthur Young CPAs, Anchorage ofc. 1979, Los Angeles ofc. 1980-83, San Jose ofc. 1983-84, mgr. Palo Alto ofc. 1984−, splst. in high tech. mfg. and high tech. related cos.; adj. prof. MBA night sch. pgm. Santa Clara Univ. 1984; mem: Am. Inst. CPAs, Calif. Soc. CPAs, Resource Center for Women; publs: Two Asian Management Styles: China and Japan (12/83), This is Me (poetry collection, 1983); Republican; Catholic; rec: cooking, poetry writing, int. decor. Res: 2511 Betlo Ave Mt. View 94043 Ofc: Arthur Young 660 Hansen Way Palo Alto 94306

BROOKE, CHARLES THOMAS, consulting electrical engineer; b. April 29, 1911, Cincinnati, Ohio; s. Clarence Martin and Stella Louella B.; m. Annabel Hoem, Aug. 9, 1952, dec. 1979; children: Michael Thomas b. 1943, Charles Dean b. 1954, Cherilyn Dianne b. 1956; edn: BSEE, Univ. of Cincinnati 1935; Reg. Profl. Elec. Engr., Calif. 1949. Career: design engr. Auto Lite 1934-37; Underwriters Laboratory Inc.: inspector, Cincinnati and Cleveland 1937-41, project engr., Chicago 1946-47, supvsg. inspector, Los Angeles 1947-54, assoc. field engr., Santa Clara 1954-76; currently, p.t. cons. engr. to computer cos. in the Bay area; cons. engr. computer design and safety, Ramtek 1978-85, Ford Aerospace 1977-78, National Semiconductor 1984−, By Video 1984−, RAMCO 1983-84, Elsenhower Tunnel (Denver) 1982-83; honors: Highest Award, IBM 1985; Magicians Order of Merlin, Ex Calibur; mem: Internat. Brotherhood of Magicians 1936−, Hollister Elks, Masons, Islam Shrine; publs: Switchboard Handbook, 1974; Fixture Handbook, 1973; How to Speak In Public, 1972; Elec Fuse Table, 1970; mil: capt. US Army CAC, active 1941-46, 6 yrs. Reserve; ROTC 1929-35; Democrat; Protestant; rec: profl. magician, lapidarist, golf, wood carving. Res: 460 Donald Dr. Hollister 95023

BROOKES, CRITTENDEN EDWARDS, psychiatrist; b. May 8, 1931, Oakland; s. Arthur Blayne and Ruth (Crittenden) B.; m. Mauna Berkov; children: Lisa b. 1968, Aaron b. 1971, Jedidiah b. 1977, Jesse b. 1981; edn: BA, CSU Chico 1952; MA, Stanford Univ. 1953, PhD, 1956, MD, 1960; Cert. Jungian Analyst, Soc. Jungian Analysts 1967. Career: clin. instr. Dept. Psychiatry UC Med. Ctr. 1964-67, asst. clin. prof. 1967-75, assoc. clin. prof. 1975−; asst. Dept. Psychiatry Mt. Zion Med. Ctr. 1964-67, adj. 1967-76, asst. chief 1976−; pvt. practice 1964−; awards: Stanford Univ. Honor Scholarship 1953; Henry J. Kaiser Family Scholarship in Med. 1957-58; USPHS Student Fellowship in Pharmacology 1957; Stanford Univ. Sch. of Med. 1959-60; Spec. Fellowship in Psychiatry, Stanford Univ. Sch. of Med. 1959; mem: Jungian Analysts of No. Calif., C.G. Jung Inst. (Curriculum Com., San Francisco), APA, Am. Med. Assn., NCPA, Fellow No. Calif. Psychiatric Assn., Am. Acad. of Psychoanalysis; author: A Jungian View of Transpersonal Psychotherapy, Seymour Boorstein's Interpersonal Psychotherapy, Sci. & Behavior Books, Palo Alto 1980; The Group As Corrective for Failure in Analysis, Gerhard Adler's Success and Failure in Analysis, G.P. Putnam's Sons, NY 1974; mil: senior surgeon US Public Health Svc. 1960-64. Ofc: 407 Locust St. San Francisco 94118

BROOKES, MONA E., artist, educator; b. May 9, 1937, Los Angeles; d. John A. and Mary E. (Baker) Brookes; 1 son, Mrk Evan Hall b. 1965; edn: Chouinard Art Inst. 1957; BA in art/psych., Pepperdine Coll. 1958; grad. work in graphic arts, CSU Northridge 1973, 78. Career: probation ofcr. County instns. for delinquent youth 1958-64; employment counselor State pgms. for parolees and probationers 1964-72, adminstr. State Employment pgms. 1973-77; artist in residence, Calif. Arts Council 1978-80, devel. Monart Drawing Method (1979); owner/founder Monart School of the Arts (drawing schs. for children), Santa Monica 1981−; art cons., speaker, lectr., conduct tchr. tng. workshops in pub. & pvt. sch. systems nat.; mem. bd. dirs. West L.A. Childrens Museum; bd. advisors Performing Trees; mem./cons. Free Arts Clinic; works: devel. Monart Drawing Method (1979), childrens art work shown in museums, TV shows, schs. and community ctrs. nationwide; author: Drawing With Children, A Method Designed for Children That Works for Adults Too (Tarcher Press 1986); rec: dancing. Address: Monart School of the Arts 2223 Cloverfield Santa Monica 90405

BROOKS, EDWARD FRANCIS, engineer; b. July 18, 1946, Dayton, Ohio; s. Forrest Leon and Dorothy Jane (Kellhofer) B.; m. Nancy, Jan. 17, 1981; children: Shannon b. 1972, Diana b. 1974; edn: B.Aero. & Astro. Engrg., Ohio State Univ. 1969, MS, 1970. Career: test engr. TRWRedondo Beach 1970-78, section head engrg. scis. lab. 1978-80, dept. staff 1980-81, chief devel. engr. 1981-86, senior sys. engr. proposal ops. 1986−; pvt. cons. Dieterich Std. Corp. Boulder, Colo. 1975-80; honors: Tau Beta Pi, Sigma Gamma Tau, Texnikoi (Ohio State Univ.); mem: Am. Inst. Aero. & Astro., Am. Mgmt. Assn., TRW Golf Club (pres. 1986, newsletter ed. 1984, 85, club champion 1984), TRW Ski

Club, TRW Volleyball Club, (former mem. TRW tennis, softball, chess clubs); patents: 4, 3 pending; publs: tech. articles in profl. jours.; Democrat; Catholic; rec: sports, music (guitar and vocals, writing), coach and mentor for daughter Shannon's track career. Res: 925 24th St Hermosa Beach 90254 Ofc: TRW Electronics & Defense One Space Park 01/2040 Redondo Beach 90254

BROOKS, SAM HERMAN, insurance brokerage firm president; b. March 3, 1935, Windsor, Ont., Can.; nat. 1965; s. Jacob Issac and Rachel (Wainger) B.; m. Faye Barret, Dec. 27, 1964 (dec. 1985); children: Deborah b. 1955, Robert b. 1957,Judi b. 1959; edn: grad. Calif. Sch. of Insurance (Pasadena) 1958; Life Underwriters Tng. Council 1960; num. underwriting courses; RHU, Nat. Assn. of Hlth. Underwriters, 1979; Life Underws. Tng. Council Fellow 1985. Career: agent/staff mgr. Prudential Ins. Co., Whittier 1956-63; estab. own ins. firm, Samuel H. Brooks & Assocs., Beverly Hills 1964-71, moved bus. to Rowland Hgts. 1971, incorporated in 1973; chmn. bd. Amalgamated Ins. Brokers Corp., Rowland Hgts. 1973–; apptd. to Calif. senate Adv. Commn. on Real Property Ins. 1984; ins. adv. com. to Assemblyman Frank Hill; Nat. Assn. of Life Underwriters awards: Nat. Quality awards 1980, 84, Million Dollar Round Table (11 times, life mem. 1985), Five Million Dollar Forum (1975,6), Nat. Sales Achievement awards (6), others. Mem: Nat. Assn. of Life Underwriters, Nat. Assn. of Health Underwriters, Ind. Ins. Agents & Brokers Assn., Nat. Assn. of Notaries, Western Assn. Ins. Brokers, Walnut Valley CofC, Better Bus. Bur.; 32nd Deg. Mason, Shriner, Acad. of Magical Arts. Publs: contbr. Occidental Life Ins. Co. mag. (1964); Republican; Hebrew Christian; rec: music, travel, autos. Res: 18103 E. Galatina St. Rowland Hts 91748 Ofc: Amalgamated Ins. Brokers Corp. 1750 Sierra Leone Ave Rowland Heights 91748

BROPHY, DONALD RICHARD, III, chiropractor; b. Aug. 4, 1955, Fresno; s. Donald Richard, Jr. and Yvonne Lee (Adams) B.; m. Sheryl Lynn, July 9, 1979; 1 son: Donald Richard, IV b. 1981; edn: BA, CSU Hayward 1979; DC, Palmer West 1983, resident radiology 1983-84. Career: currently, group practitioner Oak Bay Chiropractic Clinic; Cert. Disability Evaluator; CCA Certified Independent Med. Examiner; inst. med. mgmt., chiropractic mgmt. Fireman's Fund Ins. Co.; lectr. ICA/DVICA; ICA Edn. Subcom.; letr. Calif. Applicants Atty. Assn.; mem: Alameda CCA (v.p), IHBA; publs: paper, Chiropractic vs. Medical Manangement of Low Back Injuries; Republican; Lutheran; rec: flying, drag boat racing. Ofc: Oak Bay Chiropractic, 494 Hawthorne Blvd. Oakland 94609

BROSNAN, FAYE LEE, school psychologist; b. Nov. 10, 1930, Calexico; d. Eddie E. and Jennie (Chan) Lee; m. Leonard Alan Brosnan, July 25, 1958, div. 1972; 1 dau. Sandra Lee b. 1960; edn: AB, UC Los Angeles 1954; ME, Loyola Univ. 1973; MA, Loyola Marymount Univ. 1981; PhD, Claremont Grad. Sch. 1984. Career: tchr., English and literature, Manual Arts High Sch., 1960-65, trained student tchrs from UCLA at Univ. H.S. 1965-72; counselor 1972-81, drug abuse counselor Hollywood H.S. 1972-74, ecology pgm. evaluator 1974-75, devel.Opportunity Room pgm. Sun Valley Jr. H.S. 1976-77, counselor/tchr.Tri-C pgm. for expelled students 1977-80, ESL counselor Verdugo Hills H.S. 1980-81; sch.psychologist, Severely Handicapped Sch., Los Angeles Unified Sch.Dist., (schs. in Gardena, Carson, Central L.A., South Central L.A., San Fernando Valley) 1981–; mem. L.A. School Psychologists Assn.; rec: travel, sci. & humanities seminars. Res: 484 E California Blvd Unit 28 Pasadena 91106 Ofc: L.A. Unified School Dist. 450 N Grand Ave Rm H-120 Los Angeles 90012

BROWN, ALONZO HAROLD, wholesale distributor, real estate broker; b. Nov. 7, 1908, Chickasha, Okla.; s. John Wesley and Mry Emma (Whiteside) B.; m. Cletice Settle, R.N., July 6, 1929; children: Robert Gholson b. 1933, Peter J. (adopted); edn: Hill's Bus. Coll., Okla. City 1928. Career: hosp. bus. mgr. 1930-34; v.p./sales mgr. Beck Oil Co., 1940-46; warehouse distbr. oils, greases and automotive batteries, 1947-63; real estate broker 1958-73, ret.; full time vol. service Am. Heart Assn. 1973–, mem. Speakers Bureau, tchr. CPR, trainer CPR instrs.; vol. speaker Downey Comm. Hosp., active in installing Life Line systems in homes of invalids; gave home & care to sev. children so they could continue their edn.; honors: selected by KABC-TV to represent midwesterners who helped make Los Angeles Area a great place to live, shown nat. during the LA Olympics; Am. Heart volunteer of year (1983), recipient service awards Downey Rotary Intl. (1984), Am. Cancer Soc.(1945), L.A.County citation (WWII); civic: Rotary (Paul Harris Fellow), SPEBSQSA barbershop singing (charter pres., club earned 2d Pl. in internat. competition 1960), Happy 29ers Club (founder couples gp. 1979); Republican; Prot. (Maywood Baptist Ch. 20 yrs., Downey First Baptist Ch. 30 yrs., choir mem. 30 yrs.); rec: hunt, fish, singing. Res: 7655 Noren St Downey 90240

BROWN, BARBARA FLETCHER, lawyer; b. Oct. 20, 1937, Hartford, Conn.; d. Irving A. and Francis (Kostin) Fletcher; m. John W. Brown, June 7, 1959; children: Alison Hilary b. 1962, Meredith Leslie b. 1965; edn: Wells Coll. Aurora, NY 1955-57; BA w/ distn., St. Joseph Coll. W. Hartford, Conn. 1959; Univ. Conn. Sch. of Law 1973-74; JD, Univ. San Diego Sch. of Law 1976; admitted Calif. State Bar 1977; certified legal splst. family law. Career: asst. US atty. So. Dist. Calif. 1977-79; assoc. atty. Brennan & LaRocque 1979-81; ptnr. LaRocque, Brown & Campbell 1981-83; sole practitioner 1984–; lectr. var. community orgns. on family law; Cable TV appearances; radio series You and the Law (KOWN); judge pro tem 1983-84; judge Univ. San Diego Moot Ct. Competition 1977-81, F. Lee Bailey Nat. Moot Ct. Comp. 1982-84; panelist Lawyers Club Seminar on Family Law 1985; mem: San Diego County Bar Assn. (del. to State Bar Conf. 1981, judicial evaluation and family law splsts. coms.), Calif. State Bar (com. on fed. cts.), San Diego Trial Lawyers Assn., Calif. Women Lawyers (bd., exec. com., chair appts. com.), Lawyer's Club of San Diego (pres., chair judicial eval. and appt. com.), San Diegans for Independent Judiciary, Legal Aid Soc. (bd.), Am. Assn. Univ. Women., Anxiety Treatment Ctr. (bd.), City Club of San Diego; rec: travel, painting. Res: 8505 Prestwick Dr La Jolla 92037 Ofc: 11717 Bernardo Plaza Ct Ste 220 San Diego 92128

BROWN, CAROL N.S., financial planner; b. Dec. 2, 1943, Atlanta, Ga.; d. Homer Bates and Eulalia (Napier) Sutton; m. W. Hilory Brown, June 11, 1977; stepchildren: James b. 1969, Kathleen b. 1973; edn: BA, Agnes Scott Coll. 1965; grad. work Peabody Coll. 1966-67; tchg. cert. Univ. of Chattanooga 1967; MBA pgm., Golden Gate Univ. 1982-; Cert. Finl. Planner (CFP) 1982; Reg. Finl. Plnng. Practitioners (1984). Career: sales agt. Lincoln Nat. Life Ins., San Francisco, Atlanta, 1975-77; No. Calif. pension rep. Crown Life Ins. Co., San Francisco 1977-79; group health and pension rep. Mutual of N.Y., San Francisco 1979-80; reg. rep. Judith Briles & Co., Palo Alto 1980-81; reg. prin. Pvt. Ledger Fin. Serv. Inc., Los Altos 1981–; pres. Financial Resource Team, Inc., Los Altos 1981–; community coll. instr: Foothill, San Jose State, Redwood City Comm. Center, San Mateo Comm. Colls., Los Altos Recreation Dept.; media guest appearances on var. finl. pgms., KCBS radio (1985, 86), "Ask the Expert" KGO TV (1985), Finl. News Network, Ch. 60 (1986); mem. Internat. Assn. for Finl. Plnng. (pres. elect Santa Clara Co. chpt. 1986-87), Finl. Plnng. Forum, Western Pension Conf., Peninsula Life Underws., Inst. CFPs, Peninsula Profl. Womens Network, AAUW; contbr. news articles in San Jose Mercury News (1983, 85), Country Almanac (1986); Republican; Methodist; rec: music, cooking. Res: 2323 Sharon Rd, 137, Menlo Park 94025 Ofc: Financial Resource Team Inc. 199 First St Ste 300 Los Altos 94022

BROWN, DAVID EDWARD, manufacturing co. executive; b. July 11, 1937, Boston, Mass.; s. Eugene and Dora (Williams) B.; edn: BA, Syracuse Univ., 1959. Career: area sales rep. in Mich. and Ohio, then mgr. Los Angeles Office/ So. Calif. area, Vanity Fair Mills, NYC 1961-73; sales mgr. Royal Robes, NYC 1974; pres. David Brown Calif. & David Brown Boutique (Div. Wior Corp.), Los Angeles 1974–; honors: exchange student in W. Berlin, Germany in 1st American Field Service student exchange pgm. (1954); civic: nat. patron Metropolitan Opera, NYC; Republican; rec: duplicate bridge, opera buff. Res: 6732 Hillpark Dr Apt 505 Los Angeles 90058 Ofc: David Brown Calif. 2761 Fruitland Ave Los Angeles 90058

BROWN, DOLORES HICKS, federal government worker; b. Nov. 14, 1936, Waco, Tx.; d. Henry, Jr. and Evelyn Harkey; m. Elder Barney Hicks, Jr., 1957; children: Victoria Franchon b. 1959, Teri Lynn b. 1961, David Lawrence b. 1963; m. 2d James C. Brown, 1977; edn: AA, Los Angeles City Coll. 1956; Cerritos Jr. Coll. 1973. Career: dental asst., then secty., 1956-72; insp. US Food & Drug Adminstrn. 1972-74, investigator 1974-85, supvsry. investigator/ consumer safety ofcr. FDA, Los Angeles 1985–; awards: Federal Womens' Program Mgr. of the Year (1975), L.A. Volunteer merit award Los Angeles City Human Rels. Commn. (1976); mem: Federally Employed Women (W. reg. rep. 1985-86), Assn. of Food & Drug Ofcls., Toastmasters Club; civic: Museum Service Council, Calif. Afro-American Museum (pres. 1985-86); Project Adv. Council, Central Bus. Dist., L.A. Community Redevel. Agcy. (1984-86); Order of Eastern Star (Worthy Matron, Rachel Chpt. 1984-86); Democrat; Baptist; rec: photog., gardening. Res: 1558 W 48th St Los Angeles 90062 Ofc: US Food & Drug Administration 1521 W Pico Blvd Los Angeles 90015

BROWN, ELIZABETH LILLIAN, physician; b. Aug. 12, 1916, NY, NY; d. Joseph and Dora (Engel) B.; edn: MD, Albany NY Med. Coll. 1943; Cert. A.B. Pediatrics, Sub Pediat. Al. Career: intern pediat. Fordham Hosp. 1944; resident pediat. Flower & Fifth Ave. Hosp. 1944, Greenpoint Hosp. Brooklyn 1949-50; staff West Hills Med. Ctr. Canoga Park, Calif., West Park Hosp, Canoga Park Hosp.; fellow Am. Acad. Pediats.; mem: Nat. Soc. Asthma Care Phys. (treas.), L.A. Allergy Soc., L.A. Pediat. Soc., Am. Allergy Assn; author: Yearbook of Pediatrics, Eczema Vaccinatum, Report of a Recovery; Jewish; rec: fishing, ranching. Address: 23300 Erwin St Woodland Hills 91367

BROWN, GEORGE MILTON, manufacturing co. executive; b. Feb. 23, 1911, Oregon City, Ore.; s. Ernest Rennen and Elvia Mabel (Smith) B.; m. Corinne G. Furman, July 28, 1934 (dec. 1975); children: Joyce (Lanphere) b. 1935, Kenneth b. 1938; m. 2d Phyllis M. Furman, June 26, 1976; edn: BA in chem., UC Los Angeles 1933. Career: analytical chemist Monolith Portland Cement Co., 1933-42; mgr. Hornkohl Lab. 1942-44; drilling fluid supvr. Haliburton Co. 1944-48; founder/pres. Brown Mud Co., 1958-69; asst. mgr. Western Reg., Dresser Industries 1963-69, controller W. area Petroleum Div. 1969-72, ret.; current: owner Brown Furniture (custom made furniture), Hermosa Beach; mem. Alpha Chi Sigma (1933-70), Am. Chem. Soc. (1933-70), Am. Petro. Inst. (1944-72); works: Research on oil based drilling fluids 1942-56, Patent (1956); Research on soil sealants for water conservation 1958-65, Patent (1965); Christian; rec: wood-working, rose and camellia horticulture, photog., travel. Address: POB 457, 1538 Prospect Ave Hermosa Beach 90254

BROWN, IAN STEVEN, cosmetic surgeon; b. Aug. 17, 1948, NYC; s. R. Aaron and Lana (Levin) B.; m. Judith Summers, 1979; edn: AB, psych., Bucknell Univ. 1970; MD, Buffalo Med. Sch. 1974; bd. certified plastic surgeon. Career: surgical residency Kaiser Hosp., Los Angeles 1974-76, ENT-Facial Plastic residency White Memorial Hosp., Loma Linda Univ., L.A. 1976-79; founder Beverly Hills Cosmetic Surgery Medical Group; fellow Internat. Coll. of Surgeons; mem: Am. Med. Assn., Calif. Med. Assn., Los Angeles Co. Med. Assn., Am. Soc. Cosmetic Surgeons, Am. Rhinologic Soc., Am. Soc. Liposuction Surgeons, Internat. Soc. Aesthetic Surg., Am. Soc.

Cosmetic Breast Surg., Internat. Acad. Cosmetic Surg., L.A. Soc. of Otolaryngology, Head & Neck Surg.,Calif. Soc. of Specialty Plastic Surgeons, Am. Acad. Facial Plastic & Reconstructive Surgery; rec: scuba. Res: 929 19th St., 2, Santa Monida 90403 Ofc: Beverly Hills Cosmetic Surgery Medical Group, 465 N. Roxbury Dr, Ste. 1007, Beverly Hills 90210

BROWN, JAY WHITNEY, art dealer; b. Jan. 28, 1958, Gadsden, Ala.; s. William E.W. and Constance Nell A. (McDonald) B.; edn: Amherst Coll. 1978-82; Emory Univ. 1976-78. Career: membership assoc. Guggenheim Mus., NYC 1978; registrar's assoc. Tate Gallery, London 1978; appraiser's assoc. Sotheby's, Wash. DC and Palm Beach, Fla. 1979-81; writer's staff ABC News, Wash. DC 1981, 1982-83; bus. mgr. Frederick Brisson Prodns. Inc., NYC 1983; dir. Bernard Jacobson Gallery, Los Angeles 1984-85; owner, dir. Jay Whitney Brown Fine Art, Los Angeles 1985 – ; lectr., seminars to academic and profl. groups; cons. var. corps.; mem: Los Angeles Co. Mus. (Modern & Contemp. Arts Council), Children's Mus. of Los Angeles, Soc. of the Four Arts (Palm Beach, Fla.), The Princess Grace Found. (Los Angeles coord.), West Hollywood CofC, Griffith Park Polo, Palm Beach Polo, Municipal Arts Soc. (NYC), Found. for Children With Learning Disabilities; publs: Gallery publishes num. catalogues for academic record, essays by Jay Whitney Brown and others; Republican; Episcopal; rec: horses, polo, soccer. Ofc: Jay Whitney Brown Fine Art, 1444 N Laurel Ave Los Angeles 90046

BROWN, JOHN ALLEN, aerospace electronics co. executive; b. June 27, 1949, Columbus, Ind.; s. John F. and Florance M. (Blanford) Green; edn: AAS in electronics, Indiana Voc. Coll. 1979; desig: field engring. splst. Career: technician Bendix Field Engring. Corp., Ascension Island 1979-, then with Buckhorn, Edwards AFB, Calif.; current: network controller Jet Propulsion Lab.; bd. chmn. A.S.T.R.A.L., Lancaster; mil: US Navy 1969-73, Indiana Nat. Guard; Roman Catholic; rec: camping, old movies, computers. Address: A.S.T.R.A.S. 4563 W Avenue (M-4 #10) Lancaster 93536

BROWN, JOHN MACKENZIE, audio-visual show producer; b. Aug. 21, 1951, Los Angeles; s. Gordon M. and Evelyn (Collins) B.; m. Velma, Dec. 17, 1983; 1 dau. Megan Mackenzie; edn: AA, Saddleback Coll. 1971; BA theatre arts, CSU Fullerton 1974, MA cand. Career: Kawasaki Audio-Visual Svcs. 1976-78; pres., sole owner The Showpros Tustin 1978 – ; have designed programs for Kawasaki, Kodak, Del Taco, Am. McGaw, Abby Medical; cons. Greyhound Creative Svcs.; honors: Most Outstanding (Saddleback Fine Arts Dept. 1971); mem: Assn. for Multi-Image, Boy Scouts of Am.; Republican; Episcopal; rec: camping, swimming. Res: 21 Fulton Irvine 92620 Ofc: The Showpros 14662 Franklin Ste H Tustin 92680

BROWN, JOSHUA, air transport co. president; b. Jan. 27, 1948, Poplar Bluff, Mo.; s. Charles Bryon and Ellen Jane (Sisco) B.; m. Cathie, Dec. 29, 1984; children: Noah b. 1970, Deva b. 1979. Career: asst. supv., supv. Pharmaseal Labs., Irwindale 1968-70; sales rep., sales mgr. Airland Air Freight, Los Angeles Airport (LAX) 1970-71, San Francisco Airport 1972-73; sales rep. Jet Air Freight, LAX 1973-74; dist. sales mgr. Right-O-Way Air Freight, 1974, nat. sales mgr. 1975-76, v.p. sales 1977-79, exec. v.p. 1979-83, pres./ chmn. bd./ CEO and sole stockholder (bought back all stock) 1983 – ; Dir: JCB Trucking, Ocean Transport Internat., America's Carrier's, Row Produce; mem. Los Angeles Airport Transp. Orgn. (TEC Group/ co. chief execs.); mem. ATO, alumni assns. Murray (Ky.) State Coll. and Univ. of Mo., Quarter Horse Assn. of Am.; Republican; Nazarene Ch.; rec: skiing, scuba, horse breeding. Res: 9881 Deerhaven Dr Santa Ana 92705 Ofc: Right-O-Way 180 S Prospect Tustin 92680

BROWN, LAWRENCE, lawyer; b. July 30, 1945, Bronx, N.Y.; s. Harold and Doris (Malach) B.; m. Judith, Oct. 28, 1972; children: Darin Adams b. 1976, Melissa Lynn b. 1978; edn: JD, Univ. of Pacific McGeorge Sch. of Law 1971; admitted Calif. State Bar 1971. Career: atty. sole practice 1971-72; ptnr. Chern & Brown 1972-76, Brown & Nazarian 1976-77; sole practice, Encino 1977 – ; prof. of law Mid-Valley Coll. of Law 1974-80; judge pro tem Los Angeles County Municipal Ct. 1977-; mem. Calif. State, Los Angeles County, San Fernando Valley bar assns., City of Hope (pres. We Hope Chpt. 1983-5); Ofc: Lawrence Brown, Atty. 16633 Ventura Blvd, Ste 940, Encino 91436

BROWN, LESTER LOVELAND, engineer; b. Oct. 16, 1917, Cleveland, Ohio; s. Burton Neamiah and Grace Eola (Loveland) B.; m. Roberta Parnham, July 1, 1940; children: Richard b. 1941, Ronald b. 1948; edn: BS, UCLA 1955. Career: served apprentice seaman to warrant ofcr., radio electrician US Navy, 1936-45; v.p. American TV Labs., Hollywood 1946-50; instr. Hollywood Radio & TV correspondence sch. for students in India and South Africa, 1950-55; senior engr. Kay Lab (now Cohu Electronics), San Diego 1955-57; senior engr. Sandia Labs., Albuquerque, NM 1957-59, Litton Systems, Beverly Hills 1959-61, Teledyne Labs., Hawthorne 1961-65; electrical engr. Calif. State Dept. of Water Resources, 1965-79; cons. for hydroelectric opr. tng. and plant startup for Madera Irrigation Dist., 1984-85; recipient 3 awards: first to use high speed computers in solution of problems concerning high voltage underground transmission systems; with DWR, edited final report (elec. sects.) $2 billion state water project; patentee (UCLA best senior project); DWR service awards for work on Devil Canyon Power Plant, Edmonston Pumping Plant, devel. original operating procedures; publs: Historical Atlas, Vols. I to 6, utilizing microcomputer plotter for map generation, 1984-85; Republican; Protestant; rec: bicycling, hist. buff. Res: 2348 Hooke Way Sacramento 95822

BROWN, LULA MAE, mortgage broker; b. June 30, 1950, Swift-town, Miss.; d. Robert B. and Mary Ann Brown; 1 dau: Latanya, b. 1979; edn: AA, Laney Jr.

Coll. 1970; BS, CSU Hayward 1972; MS 1973; Calif. Comm. Coll. Instr. & Counselor Cred. 1975. Career: counselor Calif. St. Univ., Stanislaus1973-75; intake counselor Alameda Co. Proj. Intercept 1976-77; R.E. salesprsn. Sarkis Realty 1976-80; fin. aid counselor UC Berkeley 1977-78; loan ofcr. Granite Home Loans, Ltd. 1980-81; owner/ mgr. First L.B. Financial Resources Inc. 1981 – ; mem: Alameda Co. Bd. Realtors; US CofC; Exec. Female Orgn.; Democrat; Baptist; rec: entertaining, bowling, travel. Res: First L.B. Financial Resources Inc., 3640 Grand Ave, Ste 214, Oakland 94610

BROWN, MARLENE ANN, sales executive; b. Jan. 25, 1953, Eureka; d. Stanley Eugene and Florence Lee (Roberts) Clayton; m. Mark Bruce Brown, Sept. 18, 1982; edn: Hartnell Jr. Coll. 1971-3. Career: salespsn. Sears Roebuck & Co., Salinas 1971-73, personnel interviewer, 1973-75; medical asst. Dr. Theodore Bradley, Monterey 1975-76; accts. payable P.E. O'Hair & Co. (wholesale plumbing) Salinas 1976-78, asst. purchaser 1979-83, purchasing agt. 1979-83, sales mgr. 1983 – ; honors: Past Worthy Advisor Internat. Order of Rainbow for Girls, 1970. Democrat; Presbyterian. Res: 7660 Sundown Lane Salinas 93907 Ofc: P.E. O'Hair & Co. 1355 Burton Ave Salinas 93901

BROWN, MICHAEL STEPHEN, advertising & public relations agency owner; b. Nov. 4, 1937, Champaign, Ill.; s. Vernon Mathew and Ruth Ann (Warwick) B.; m. Leah, Aug. 27, 1966; children: Cynthia b. 1971, Laura b. 1974; edn: BS, So. Ill. Univ. 1961. Career: acct. supv. J. Walter Thompson S.F. 1965-71, Hal Lawrence 1971-74; part owner Lawrence & Lierle Palo Alto 1974-75; v.p.Bozelle & Jacobs Palo Alto 1975; owner Mike Brown Advtg. and Pub.Rels. San Mateo 1977 – ; honors: several creative awards for ads; mem: Peninsula Press Club (v.p. 1986), Sierra Club, SIU Alumni Assn.; mil: lt. USN 1961-64; Democrat; rec: hiking, gardening, carpentry. Res: 3720 Fernwood St San Mateo 94403 Ofc: Mike Brown Advt. & Public Rels. 161 W 25th Ave Ste 208 San Mateo 94403

BROWN, PAUL VERNON, physician; b. Mar. 20, 1922, Pocatello, Ida.; s. Fred William and Ida Belva (Wakely) B.; children: Paul b. 1948, Susan b. 1949, Kathy b. 1971; edn: BS pharm., Idaho State Univ. 1944; MD, Northwestern Univ. 1947; qualified Am. Bd. Internal Med. 1954. Career: rotating intern Wesley Meml. Hosp. Chgo. 1947-48; resident Virginia Mason Hosp. & Clin. Seattle 1948-49, Colo. State Hosp. Pueblo 1949-50; senior med. resident Fresno County Hosp. 1950-51l chest resident Tulare Kings Co. Hosp. Springville 1951-52l pulm. fellow UC San Francisco 1979; 1st internist internal med. & chest diseases, cons. Stockton State Hosp. 1952 – ; mem. staff St. Joseph's Hosp. and Dameron Hosp. Stockton 1952-77, courtesy staff 1977 – ; cons. Bret Harte Hosp. (Murphy's) 1952-55, San Joaquin Co. Hosp. 1956-86, courtesy staff 1986 – ; cons. Calif. Dept. Vocational Rehab. 1956 – ; advis. to Selective Svc. for phys. in San Joaquin Co. during 1960s; v.p. Easy Software Co. Salt Lake City 1985-; fellow Am. Coll. Chest Phys. 1962; mem: AMA, San Joaquin Co. Med. Soc., Calif. Med. Soc., Calif., Am. Thoracic Socs., Calif. Soc. Internal Med.; mil: US Army 1944-46, USAR 1946-59, C.O. 1st train rail ambulance 1957-59, major Calif. Nat. Guard 1959-61, acting lt. col. as 49th div. arty. surg. 1960-61; Republican; L.D.S.; rec: stamps, astronomy. Res: 9406 Trenton Way Stockton 95212 Ofc: Paul Brown MD 1617 N California Ste IE Stockton 95204

BROWN, ROBERT EDWARD, computer systems co. financial executive; b. Mar. 8, 1953, Santa Monica, Calif.; s. Charles Thomas and Muriel Anna (Hopwood) B.; m. Barbara Jurist, Apr. 8, 1979; edn: BS computer sci., UC Los Angeles 1975, MBA, 1977; CPA Calif. 1986; cert. in Mgmt. Acctg., Nat. Assn. Accts. 1980. Career: audit asst. Peat, Marwick, Mitchell & Co. L.A. 1977-78; financial analyst System Devel. Corp. Santa Monica 1978-81, mgr. financial analysis 1981-83, div. controller Camarillo 1984 – ; mem: Phi Eta Sigma, Beta Gamma Sigma, Boy Scouts of Am. (council exec. bd.); rec: skiing, hiking. Ofc: System Development Corp. 5151 Camino Ruiz Ste B254 Camarillo 93010

BROWN, ROBERT JAMES EDWARD, police/security training specialist; b. July 21, 1933, Indianapolis; s. James E. and Anna Louise (Watkins) B.; m. Wilma, Apr. 24, 1977; children: Aubrey Warren b. 1955, Wanda b. 1956; edn: police sci. stu. Merritt, Contra Costa Co., Alameda jr. colls. 1968-70, Univ. of Heidelberg 1951, UCB ext. 1981; tchg. credential, Calif. (1979). Career: dep. Dade County Sheriff's Dept., Miami, Fla. 1953; police sgt. Manhattan Div., NY, also investigator, store detective Mills Investigating Svc.; security ofcr. Peralta Sch. Dist., Oakland 1966; patrolman for AEC, UCLRL, Livermore; security supr. ASUC, Berkeley Campus 1980 – ; police/security tng. splst., D.O.D. (major), deputy chief of police, prop. R&B Security Training Acad., Oakland 1979 – ; honors: meritorious svc. cits., NYC Police Dept (1964, 66), Nat. Police Hall of Fame (1965), svc. assistance award BART (1978), community svc., Menelik Shrine Temple (1981); mem: Calif. Peace Ofcrs. Assn., Am. Soc. for Indsl. Security, Am. Legion, Masons, Shriners, NAACP, Spl. Police Ofcrs. Assn. (grand lectr.), Burbank Neighborhood Assn., Citizens for Law and Order; mil: US Army 1950-53, ETO; Democrat; Bahai; rec: fishing, firearms. Address: R/B Security Training Academy 5920 Laird Ave Oakland 94605

BROWN, RONALD ALLEN, lawyer; b. Sept. 20, 1946, New Haven, Conn.; s. Allen Lincoln and Helen Catherine (Radcliffe) B.; edn: AB, Dartmouth Coll. 1968; MPA, Harvard Univ. JFK Sch. of Govt. 1974; JD, Harvard Law Sch. 1973. admitted DC Bar 1975, Calif. 1979. Career: staff atty. bd. govs. Fed. Reserve System (legal div.) Wash DC 1974-77; v.p., corp. counsel Syndicated Communications Inc. Wash DC 1977-78; senior counsel Bank of Am. S.F. 1978-84, Hong Kong Legal Office 1984 – ; honors: Cert. of Merit (Bay Area Urban Bankers Assn. 1982), Dean's List 1967-68; mem: Calif. State Bar, Wash.

DC Bar, S.F. Bar Assn., Am. CofC-Hong Kong, Am. Club (Hong Kong), Bay Area Urban Bankers Assn. (secy. 1980-82); co-author: (w. Dr. Suzanne Stafford, 1984) Carrier Opportunities under the Export Trading Co. Act; mil: splst. 4/C US Army Infantry 1969-70, Vietnam Campaign, Commendation, Combat Infantry, Good Conduct, Air Medal w. OLC, Army Comdn. w. OLC; Democrat; Catholic; rec: reading, tennis, skiing, swimming, chess. Res: 1101 B Tregunter Tower 14 Tregunter Path Hong Kong Ofc: Bank of America 12 Harcourt Rd, Ste 21/F, Hong Kong

BROWN, STEVEN EUGENE, credit union executive; b. Apr. 18, 1959, San Luis Obispo; s. Wm. Paul and Helen Elizabeth (Miller) B.; m. Carrie, Mar. 1, 1986; edn: BA, CSU Stanislaus 1983; spl. courses var. profl. schs.; cert. credit union mgmt. Western Reg. CUNA Sch. 1986; lic. Life and Disability Insurance Agt. Career: summer teller and collector, var. credit unions, p.t. 1977-80; teller and collector San Joaquin County Grange Credit Union, full-time 1980-83; gen. mgr. Food Processors Credit Union, Modesto 1983–; co-founder/chief exec. Hewitt West (Ore. based mutual fund orgn.); pres. bd. dirs. W.P. Rail Systems FCU, Sacto. 1980-85; awards: profl. sch. scholarship, Calif. Credit Union League chpt. (1984); mem: Credit Union Executive Soc. (1985-), Calif. Credit Union League (1977-); civic: Big Valley Grace Comm. Ch. (staff H.S. Varsity Fellowship), mem. var. traveling softball teams; publs: The Impact of Mergers on the Bottom Line (1984); seminar leader, Personal Computers- Impact on Credit Unions (1986); Am. Baptist; rec: softball, sports trivia, Walt Disney trivia, Bible study. Ofc: Food Processors Credit Union 2801 Finch Rd Modesto 95353

BROWN, STEVEN LEWIS, oral and maxillofacial surgeon; b. Sept. 25, 1951, Santa Monica; s. Guy E. and Mary Carolyn (Hilliard) B.; m. Patti A. Yost, May 20, 1978; 1 son, Jordan, b. 1983; edn: BA, UCLA 1973; DDS, UC San Francisco Med. Ctr. Sch. of Dentistry 1977; residency, splst. oral & max. surg., (chief res. 1981) UCSF Med. Ctr., San Francisco Gen. Hosp., VA Hosp., S.F., 1978-81. Career: oral & Maxillofacial surgeon in pvt. practice, Citrus Hts.; staff Roseville Comm. Hosp., Mercy San Juan Hosp.; cons. to Kaiser Permanente Hosps.; panel mem. Calif. Childrens' Svc., and The Cleft Panel Sutter Meml. Hosp.; honors: Am. Dental Soc. of Anesthesiol. award 1977; Mosby Pub. Co. awd. 1977; TMJ Resrch. Found. awd. for outstanding thesis in temporomandibular joint resrch. 1981; Delta Sigma Delta (life). Mem: Am., Calif. dental assns.; Sacto. Dist. Dental Soc.; Fellow Am. Assn. of Oral & Maxillofacial Surgeons; Western Soc., No. Calif. Soc. Oral & Maxillo. Surgeons; cert. Basic and Adv. Cardiac Life Support, and CPR; publs: arts. in med. jours.; co-prod. teaching film for dental students (1978); Republican; Prot.; rec: portrait artist. Res: 1509 Pine Valley Cir. Roseville 95678 Ofc: Steven L. Brown, DDS, Inc. 8035 Madison Ave, G-1, Citrus Hts 95610

BROWN, THOMAS OWEN, transportation executive; b. Sept. 23, 1913, St. Louis, Mo.; s. Wm. Young and Florence Mary (Francis) B.; m. Arlene Darling, Mar. 16, 1946; edn: Washington Univ., St. Louis, Mo. 1930-31; Univ. of Tex. 1931-33; reg. transp. exec., Interstate Commerce Commn. 1936. Career: entered transportation indus. (4th gen. of family to work in railroading), 1933-, indsl. traffic mgr. for A.P. Green Co., 1934-43; dist. traffic and sales mgr. Western Air Lines, San Francisco 1946-49; founder/pres. and chmn. bd. Coast Counties Express, Inc. Los Angeles 1953-80, ret.; taught num. classes in transp. and practice before the I.C.C.; mem: Citizens Legal Defense Alliance (dir), Am. Trucking Assn. 1946-80, Munitions Carriers Conf. 1950-80, var. Traffic Clubs, Transp. Orgns. and profl. fraternal orgns.; civic: L.A. CofC, Fellow Huntington Library, San Marino (vol. mem. Manuscripts Dept.), contbg. mem. var. hist. socs.; clubs: L.A. Athletic, L.A. Turf; author biography of John Colter of the Lewis & Clark Expedition; mil: capt. US Army 1943-46, 1950-52; Republican; rec: hist. research. Res: 1502 Royal Blvd Glendale 91207

BROWN, VIVIAN HOPE, business owner; b. April 21, 1926, Whittier; d. Clyde Thomas and Ruth Lee (Johnson) Frampton; m. Monte William Brown, July 4, 1965 (dec.); children: Marcia, b. 1946; Susan, b. 1950; Steven, b. 1957; edn: Fullerton Jr. Coll. 1945; Santa Ana Bus. Coll. 1945. Career: prop. of lodge, Old Station, Calif.; opr. plumbing and sheet metal shop, Alturas; one of first women contractors, Redding 1967; fmr. owner/ opr. Capri Shoppe, Anderson; property mgmt. 1985-; awards: trip to Catalina Island for dramatics, 1940; mem: Soroptomists Internat.; PTA; Costa Mesa Hist. Soc.; Anderson CofC; Lady of the Elks; Dr. Hawes Girls Choir; Emblem Club #515 (Redding); Girls League modeling 1943; Protestant; rec: travel, reading. Address: P.O. Box 1630 Redding 96099

BROWN, WILLIAM HERBERT, lawyer; b. Apr. 18, 1940, Los Angeles; s. Herbert Wm. and Gwendolyn (McCuistion) B.; m. Mary Beth Young, July 23, 1965; children: Mary Lynne b. 1966, Kimberly b. 1968, Michael b. 1970, Meghan b. 1973, Steven b. 1974, James b. 1977, Rebecca b. 1979, Kristina b. 1980; edn: BA, Brigham Young Univ. 1964; JD, UC Los Angeles 1967; admitted Calif. State Bar 1968; C.P.A., Calif. 1970. Career: prin. Haskins & Sells, CPAs, Los Angeles and New York City, 1966-74; mgr. Xerox Corp., Stamford, Conn. 1974-79; dir. Itel Corp., San Francisco 1979-80; partner Alexander Grant & Co., CPAs 1980-81; atty. at law, Morgan Hill 1981–; elected city councilman, City of Morgan Hill 1982-; chmn. Santa Clara County Transp. Commn. 1984-85; mem: Internat. Fiscal Assn. 1980-83, Calif. Bar Assn. 1968-, Calif. Soc. of CPAs 1970-; Rotarian; Republican; Ch. of Jesus Christ of Latter-Day Saints. Res: 16465 Jackson Oaks Dr., Morgan Hill 95037 Ofc: William H. Brown, 17705-I Hale Ave, Morgan Hill 95037

BROWN, WILLIE LEWIS, JR., state assemblyman, lawyer; b. Mar. 20, 1934, Mineola, Tx.; s. Willie Lewis and Minnie (Collins) B.; m. Blanche Vitero, 1957; children: Susan Elizabeth, Robin Elaine, Michael Elliott; edn: AB, San Francisco State Coll. 1955; JD, UC Berkeley 1958. Career: elected mem. Calif. State Assembly, 1965–, house speaker, 1980–; mem. County Democratic Com., 1960-62, Dem. State Central Com., del. Dem. Nat. Conv. 1968, del., chmn. Calif. delegation, 1972, del. 1976, co-chmn. Calif. delegation 1980, del. Dem. Nat. Mid-Term Conf. 1974; awards: fellow Crown Coll. UC Santa Cruz; mem. Black Am. Polit. Assn. Calif. (founder, past chmn.), Phi Alpha Delta, Alpha Phi Alpha; mil: served with USNG. Res: 540 Van Ness Ave San Francisco 94102 Ofc: Office of the Speaker, State Capitol Sacramento 95814

BROWNING, JAMES ROBERT, federal judge; b. Oct. 1, 1918, Great Falls, Mont.; s. Nicholas Henry and Minnie Sally (Foley) B.; m. Marie Rose Chapell; edn: LLB with honors, Mont. State Univ. 1941, (Hon.) LLD, Univ. Mont. 1978; admitted to Mont. State Bar 1941, Wash DC Bar, 1952. Career: with antitrust div. US Justice Dept., 1941-51, chief N.W. Regional Antitrust Office, 1948-51, 1st asst. civil div., 1951-52, exec. asst. to atty. gen. of US, 1952-53, chief Exec. Office for US Attys., 1953; ptnr. Perlman, Baldridge, Lyons & Browning, Wash DC 1953-58; clk. Supreme Ct. of US, 1958-61; judge US Court of Appeals, Ninth Circuit, San Francisco, 1961–, now chief judge; lectr. fed. antitrust law NY Univ Sch. Law, 1953, Georgetown Univ. Law Ctr. 1958; mem. Am. Law Inst., Am., Fed. (nat. bd. govs. 1952-61) bar assns., Am. Judicature Soc., Inst. Jud. Adminstrn., Am. Soc. Legal Hist.; mil: US Army 1943-46, decorated Bronze Star. Ofc:P.O. Box 547, San Francisco 94101

BRUCKER, WALTER TULEY, architect; b. Feb. 14, 1937, Louisville, Ky.; s. Wm. Tuley and Katherine Boggess B.; m. Meredith Lindley, May 13, 1965; 1 child, Carson Lindley b. 1969; edn: BS, Univ. Louisville 1959; M.Profl. Arts, Art Center Coll. of Design 1962; AIA, Am. Inst. of Arch. (1970). Career: designer Wm. L. Pereira & Assocs. 1962-68; project dir. Albert C. Martin & Assocs. 1968-73; dir. interior design Charles Luckman & Assocs. 1973-75; dir. facilities planning Reel/Grobman Assocs. 1975-80; pres. TAG - The Automotive Group, 1980-83; pres. Studio 5 - Design Corp., 1983-85; chief exec. Pasadena Design Studio, 1985–; guest lectr. Art Center, USC, UCLA, UC Irvine, UC San Diego, 1975-; awards: Ford Co. indsl. arts awards (2), H.U.D. 1st place furniture design, U.S. Steel design award; Hon. Order of Kentucky Cols. (1968); mem. Am. Inst. of Arch., Indsl. Designers Soc. of Am.; co-chairman City of Hope fundraising (1984); Jonathan Club (1964-74); mil: E6 40th Armored Div. Adj. Gen. Staff US Army; Republican; Episcopal; rec: restoration antique autos. Res: 548 S Berkeley Ave San Marino 91108 Ofc: Pasadena Design Studio 1041 E Green St Pasadena 91106

BRUEGGEMANN, RONALD MAURICE, physician; b. Jan. 15, 1950, Enid, Okla.; s. Arthur Wm. and Elpha Ireta (Berry-Hudson) B.; edn: BS biomed. engring., Northwestern Univ. The Technological Inst. 1972; Hahnemann Med. Coll. 1972-74; MD, UC Irvine Coll. of Med. 1977. Career: sup. phys. primary care Medicenter Mission Viejo, Calif. 1984; dir. phys. primary care Family Health Med. Grp. El Cajon, Calif. 1984; assoc. The Los Gatos Medic, Los Gatos, Calif. 1985–; primary care phys. Camp Pendleton Naval Hosp. Oceanside 1984–; clin. volunteer phys. UCSF Evening Clin., Haight-Ashbury Med. Clin. 1982-84; mem: AMA; Internal Med. Soc. of San Diego; S.D. Co. Med. Soc.; Assn. of Mil. Surg. of the U.S.; Am. Coll. Phys.; Phi Delta Epsilon med. frat. alumnus; Reserve Ofcrs. Assn.; Assn. of Naval Aviators; Delta Kappa Epsilon alumnus; publ: In Defense of the Engineer (Northwestern Engineer Fall 1971); mil: capt. USAR (MC) 1978-82, Pres. Unit Citation, lt. cmdr. USNR (MC) 1982-, Nat. Defense Svc. Medal; Republican; Episcopal; rec: water sports, travel, flying. Res: 655 Corbett Ct, Ste. 606, San Francisco 94114-2207 Ofc: 655 Corbett Ct San Francisco 94114

BRUGGEMAN, LEWIS LE ROY, physician; b. Sept. 9, 1941, NY, NY; s. Louis LeRoy and Edwina Jane (Mickel) B.; m. Ann, May 27, 1965; children: Gretchen b. 1970, Kurt b. 1973; edn: AB, Dartmouth Coll. 1963; BMS, Dartmouth Med. Sch. 1965; MD, Harvard Med. Sch. 1968; bd. cert. diagnostic radiol. Am. Coll. of Radiol. 1973. Career: res. diag. radiol. Columbia Presbyterian Med. Ctr. N.Y.C. 1968-71; chief radiol. Bremerton Reg. Med. Ctr. Wash. 1971-73; pvt. practice diag. radiol. So. Coast Med. Ctr., So. Laguna, Calif. and Saddleback Comm. Hosp., Laguna Hills 1974–; dir. dept. of radiol. S.C.M.C. 1973-, bd. trustees 1985-; mem. Am. Coll. Radiol., Radiol. Soc. of No. Am., Calif. Radiol. Soc., AMA, CMA, Harvard Club of So. Calif.; publ: 2 tech. arts. for med. journs.; mil: lt. cdr. USN (MC) 1972-73; REpublican; rec: tennis, skiing. Ofc: So. Coast Radiol. Med. Grp. Inc. 28 Monarch Bay Plaza, Suite J., S Laguna 92677

BRUNO, DAVID ALLEN, electrical contractor, real estate broker; b. Jan. 3, 1945, Morgantown, W.Va.; s. Edward and Emma Bruno; m. Peggy Crosby, May 13, 1975; children: Dennis, b. 1966, Tina, b. 1972, Kristy, b. 1974, Dustin, b. 1978; edn: AA, Fresno City Coll. 1969. Career: electrician 1967-, elec. constrn. supr./service mgr. Bruno Electric Inc., Fresno; real estate broker/ owner Tradewinds Real Estate and Inv. Co.; currently owner D.A. Bruno Ents.; mem. Nat. Electrical Contrs. Assn.; mil: E4 USAF 1963-67, Vietnam Cpgn., Pres. Unit. Cit. Res: 6025 N. Montana Clovis 93612 Ofc: Bruno Electric Inc. 4363 N. Valentine Fresno 93612

BRUST, DAVID, physicist; b. Aug. 24, 1935, Chgo.; s. Clifford and Ruth (Klapman) B.; edn: BS, Cal Tech 1957, MS, Univ. Chgo. 1958, PhD 1964. Career: resrch. assoc. Purdue Univ. 1963-64; resrch. assoc/asst. prof. Northwestern Univ. 1964-68; theoretical resrch. physicist Lawrence Radiation Lab., Livermore 1968-74; pres. Material System Analysts, Oakland 1973–; cons. Bell Tel. Labs, Murray Hill, NJ 1966. Mem: Am. Physical Soc., Am. Assn. Coll. Profs., Internat. Solar Energy Soc., Pacific Assn. of AAU, Sierra Club,

Sigma Xi; works: devel. first successful theory to explain optical absorption of light and photoelectric emission in semiconductors 1963-75; 25 publs. in field; rec: music, sailing, nature, language. Address: PO Box 13130 Oakland 94661

BRUTON, ALPHEAS C., resort hospitality executive; b. Sept. 30, 1946, Atlanta, Ga.; s. Alpheas C. and Johanna H. (Schoaten) B.; m. Margorie Gayle, April 11, 19796; children: Johanna b. 1977, Alpheas b. 1979; Jenea b. 1981; edn: BBA, San Angelo State Univ. 1972. Career: num. pos. var. independents 1961-72; var. exec. & staff pos. Hilton Hotels 1972-74, Continental Hotels 1974-77; gen. mgr., exec. asst. Village Green Corp.1977-79; gen. mgr. Furnace Creek Inn & Ranch Resort, Death Valley 1979—; mem: Lions, Kiwanis, Alpha Kappa Lambda, Native Sons; Republican; Protestant; rec: history. Ofc: Furnace Creek Inn & Ranch Resort, Death Valley 92328

BRUYERE, DENNIS PAUL, real estate broker, entrepreneur; b. Apr. 7, 1947, Ogdensburg, N.Y.; s. Joseph Paul and Audrey L. (Paulsen) B.; div.; children: Garey b. 1967, Paula b. 1970; edn: AA, Compton Jr. Coll. 1968; CSU Los Angeles, UCLA Ext., 1969-72, Pepperdine Univ., 1973; desig: Grad. Realtors Inst. (GRI) Calif. Assn. Realtors 1976, Cert. Residential Splst. (CRS) Nat Assn. Realtors 1978, Gold Card Exchangor, Nat. Exch. Counselors 1978; var. Century 21 certs. (CIS inv. splst., CRS res. splst., VIP 301 referral broker). Career: sales mgr. Hallmark Realty 1970, LCOA Investment & Realty Inc. 1971, Verpet Devel. 1972, Viren Realty 1973-75; broker/owner and gen. sales mgr. Century 21 Granada Realty (50+ lic. sales agts. in 2 branch offices), Bellflower 1975—, also owner Granada Mgmt. & Maint., and an escrow co.; real estate investor; tchr. seminars 1977-80; mem. Calif. Assn. Realtors (CAR), Rancho Los Cerritos Bd. Realtors (dir. 3 terms, co-chmn. MLS), Long Beach Bd. Realtors, Norwalk-La Mirada Bd. Realtors; contbg. author "Residential Real Estate Financing" (CAR, 1978); Republican; rec: surf, swim, travel. Res: 8420 Fairton St Paramount 90723 Ofc: Century 21 Granada Realty Bellflower 90706

BRYAN, JAMES BEVAN, mechanical engineer; b. May 6, 1926, Alameda, Calif.; s. James Matthew and Miriam (Bevan) B.; m. Edith, Dec. 16, 1950; children: Susan b. 1952, Bill b. 1955; edn: BS, UC Berkeley 1951; Reg. Mech. Engr. Calif. 1954. Career: mfg. engr. Westinghouse Elec. 1951-55; Lawrence Livermore Nat. Lab. 1955—, devel. of higher accuracy measuring machines and machine tools, currently metrology group leader; cons. precision engrg. to 15 Am. companies; advis. panel Nat. Research Council to Nat. Bureau of Stds. metrology div.; honors: SME Internat. Research Medal (1977), Archimedes Engrg. Award (Calif. Soc. Profl. Engrs. 1979); mem: fellow Soc. Mfg. Engrs. (seminar chmn.), Internat. Inst. for Prodn. Engrg. Research (secty., v.p., pres. metrology working group, finance com.), Am. Nat. Stds. Inst. (charter, com. chmn.); patent: for method of testing measuring machines; research: thermal errors in high precision machines and solutions to the problem; works: num. tech. reports, author significant ANSI stds.; mil: 2nd lt. US Maritime Svc. 1944-50; rec: sailing, scuba, travel. Res: 5196 Golden Rd Pleasanton 94566 Ofc: Lawrence Livermore Nat. Lab. L-332 Livermore 94550

BRYANT, FRED WILLIAM, public accountant/investment manager; b. Apr. 17, 1914, McKinneysburg, Ky. (birthplace named after gr.grandfather James Franklin McKinney); s. Jonah and Samantha Helena (King) B.; m. Paulina DeLaney (b. Dunkirk, NY) Sept. 3, 1939; children: William K. b. 1940, Richard E. b. 1942, James G. b. 1945, Elizabeth Helena b. 1948; edn: grad. Metropolitan Business H.S., Los Angeles 1939, UCLA Night Sch., 1943; lic. Bus. Acct. (1940), Public Acct. (1943), State of Calif. Career: shipping clk. Drucker & Co., Cincinnati 1929-30, var. work in cafes, mines, farms, ranches Canada and US middle-west 8 years, bicycled (dr. advised bicycle riding as remedy for burned ankle, Idaho mine accident) to Los Angeles; messenger telegraph co., transferred to audit dept., L.A., then personnel clk., San Francisco; file clk. NBC, Hollywood; acctg. for Lockheed Corp., No. Am. Aviation, Baash-Ross Tool Co., San Pedro Pipe & Steel, Calif. Shipbuilding, Haskins & Sells, Basic Magnesium; prin. own public acctg. practice, Los Angeles 1944—, investment mgmt. reg. as Bonanza Holding Co. in Calif. and Ore., 1949—, full time inv. mgmt. 1977-; mem. Polar Bear Club (Treasure Is., Laguna Beach); rec: swimming. Address: 208-D Ave Majorca Laguna Hills 92653

BRYANT, HARVEY LEE, company executive; b. Oct. 9, 1929, Enid; s. William Harvey and Pearl (Dixon) K.; m. Joanne C., April 2, 1958; children: Leslie b. 1960, William b. 1962, Jane b. 1964; edn: BS, Univ. of Okla. 1952; Reg. Profl. Engr., Okla. Career: var. supvy.& mgmt. pos. Exxon, worldwide 1954-72; v.p., gen. mgr. internat. Ashland Exploration Co. 1972; v.p., gen. mgr. intrnat. Amerada Hess Corp. 1973-79; v.p. ops. Mesa Pet co. 1979; exec. v.p., dir. Petro Lewis Corp. 1980-81; pres., CEO, founder Align Energy Corp. 1982-83; pres., CEO, dir. Berry Pet Co. 1983—; dir. Berry Industries 1983-; dir. Sawyer of Napa; pres. Berry Holding Co., Berry & Ewing Co., Berry Oil Co., Ethel D Co.; mem: Am. Inst. Mec. Engrs., SPWLA, AAPG, Boy Scouts of Am. (Sierra Council); Needs; works: 19 patents in USA, Canada, Venezuela, Peru, others; mil: lt. j.g. USN 1952-54, Letters of Commdn. for Korean War; Republican; Presbyterian; rec: hunting, jogging, swimming. Res: 829 Philippine Taft 93268 Ofc: Berry Petroleum Co., P.O. Bin X Taft 93268

BRYDGES, J. GAIL, quality-of-life advocate; b. Jan. 27, 1950, El Centro; d. Robert Lawrence and Janet Ruth (Thompson) Graham; m. Richard Ross Brydges, Jan. 2, 1982; children: Brooks b. 1969, Kelly b. 1972, Megan b. 1982; edn: BA, USC 1972; MPA, National Univ. 1986. Career: travel coord. Holmes & Narver Engring., Orange 1976-78; ofc. mgr. TSV Inc., Solana Beach 1978-79; ind. cons., contractor, clients incl: J.G. Lloyd Ent. Inc., Calabasas

1980-82; City of Coronado 1983-84; Dept. of Defense, San Diego 1984-85, City of Coronado 1986; currently, adminstrv. intern to the city mgr., Coronado; CEO J.G. Lloyd Ent. 1980-82; dir. Navy Family Job Resource Ctr. 1984-85; workshop presenter, Women's Opportunities Week, San Diego; adimnstrv. intern to the city mgr., Coronado 1986; mem: Municipal Mgmt. Assts. of So. Calif., Assn. of Part Time Profls., Naval Ofcr.'s Wives Club Bd., Navy Mil. Family Assn., Women's Opportunities Week, Navy Family Svc. Ctr., OEC Command Ombudsman; research: Navy Spouses: Demographic Survey, 1985; publs: Spouse Employment Assistance Program Policy & Procedures Manual, Dept. of Defense; Compensation Corporation: A Model Organization, Edgington & Asoc. 1985; rec: gardening, music. Res: 105 Rendova Circle, Coronado 92118 Ofc: Office of the City Manager, City of Coronado, 1825 Strand Way Coronado 92118

BUCHANAN, DONALD RAYMOND, lawyer; b. Oct. 7, 1949, North Long Beach, Calif.; s. Leonard Irl and Marjorie Lucille (Lizotte) B.; edn: BA, honors, Calif. State Univ. Fullerton 1979; JD, Western State Univ. 1983; admitted to Calif. State Bar 1983. Career: lawyer, supervising atty. for Orange Co. Welfare Coalition; honors: Phi Kappa Phi, CSU Honor Society Scholarship Award (1979); Democrat; rec: bridge. Res: 9772 Santiago Villa Park 92667 Ofc: 143 Yorba St Tustin 92680

BUCHWALTER, RALPH MC KNIGHT, business executive; b. Dec. 29, 1933, San Bernardino; s. Ralph Nelson and Sybil C. (McKnight) B.; m. Sandra Kay Bradley, June 22, 1975; children: Ralph P., b. 1961, Douglas M., b. 1964, Jennifer C., b. 1965, (stepsons) Robert W. Beecham, b. 1962, Steven Todd Beecham, b. 1963; edn: BA, Stanford Univ. 1955; Chouinard Art Inst. 1956; MA, Claremont Grad. Univ. 1964. Career: sales mgr., No. Calif., for S.K.Smith Co. of Los Angeles and Chgo. (mfrs. of custom books and binder covers, sales and art design), San Francisco 1956-60; joined family bus. (estab. by parents 1931) as gen. ptnr./sales mgr. R.N. Buchwalter Co. (vending co. of customer convenience products, coffee, candy, etc. serving San Bernardino & Riverside Cos.) 1960-, prin. Gen. Ptnr. 1979—; v.p./gen. mgr. Federal Alarm (family bus. acquired in 1953, now one of largest ind. security cos. in state), 1962-, pres./gen. mgr. 1979—, with four offices in Orange, San Berdo. & Riverside Cos.; pres./gen. mgr. Inland Desert Security & Communications, Inc. (fmr. Palm Desert Answering Svc.) Rialto 1972—, (acquired McKee Communications 1975), now largest chain of profl. answering svcs. serving Orange, Rvsd., San Berdo. Cos.; honors: 1st Place, Best Business Idea of Year 1982, Nat. Fire & Burglar Alarm Assn.; awards US Jaycees 1965, 1982, San Bernardino YMCA 1978, 79, 80, 81, hon. mem. Colton Jaycees. Mem: Nat. Indsl. Advt. Assn., Am. Soc. for Indsl. Security, Riverside Art Assn., Rialto Jaycees (past pres.), Rotary, YMCA (past pres.; bd. dirs.), Elks, Masons; Republican (alternate State Central Com.); Methodist; rec: artist (exhibs.), camping, boating. Ofc: Federal Alarm, 300 S. Sycamore Rialto 92376

BUCK, LESLIE S., investment banker; b. Dec. 17, 1946, Montclair, N.J.; s. Junior C. and Florence (Simpson) B.; edn: AB, Princeton Univ. 1968; MBA, Harvard Bus. Sch. 1973. Career: Sea Pines Co., 1973-76; v.p. fin. R.L. Burns Corp. 1977-79; ptnr. Buck, Dine & Ryan, Investment Bankers, San Diego 1980—; dir: Lockhart Industries, Consol. Computer Services Inc.; mem. UCSD Chancellors Associates, N.W. YMCA, La Jolla Beach & Tennis Club; mil: lt. US Navy, Pres. Unit Cit., Navy Commendn., 5 Combat Air Medals, Vietnamese Service; rec: tennis, scuba. Ofc: Buck, Dine & Ryan 1420 Kettner Blvd Ste 500 San Diego 92101

BUCKELEW, (HELEN) JEAN, real estate broker; b. June 13, 1931, Ada, Okla.; d. Lark F. and Leva (Turner) Jackson; m. Clyde Buckelew, Aug. 21, 1949; children: Deborah, b. 1951, Larry, b. 1953; cert. Exec. Broker Devel. Series, USC, 1981; Calif. lic. real estate broker 1982. Career: real estate agt. Day Realty, Pomona 1969, Heckmer Realty, Pomona 1969, Herbert Hawkins Co., Altadena 1976; broker assoc. Herbert Hawkins Co., Glendora 1982-84; owner Jean Buckelew Realtor, Glendora 1984—; sales awards: Hawkins Million Dollar Club 1976-78, 80-83; Azusa-Glendora Bd. of Realtors highest dollar volume and highest number of closed sale escrows through multiple listing svc., 7/82; Top earner Hawkins E. Div. 9/82; 2nd place Azusa-Glendora Bd. of Realtors highest dollar volume 1-85; mem: Nat., Calif. Assn. of Realtors, Azusa-Glendora Bd. of Realtors (grievance com. 1985, multiple listing svc. com. 1985), Soroptimist Club 1978-80; rec: oil painting, swimming. Res: 111 Oak Forest Cir Glendora 91740 Ofc: Jean Buckelew Realtor Glendora

BUCKLEY, CHARLTON HENRY, company executive; b. May 21, 1937, San Francisco; s. Henry M. and Anita M. (Nolan) B.; m. Susan L. Cranmer, 1968; children: Sarah b. 1969, Sean b. 1972; edn: BS, UC Berkeley 1960. Career: pres./CEO Robt. F. Smith Co. (roofing contr.), San Francisco 1960—; pres./ CEO C.H. Buckley Inc. (resort, bdcstg., contracting), S.F. 1971—. Ofc: Henry Broadcasting 2277 Jerrold Ave San Francisco 94124

BUCKLEY, JAMES WHITNEY, public library administrator; b. Aug. 16, 1933, Los Angeles; s. George W. and Alta L. (Hale) B.; m. Margaret Wall, Aug. 7, 1965; children: Kathleen Ann, b. 1966, James W., b. 1972, John W., b. 1979; edn: AA, LA Harbor Coll. 1953; BA, CSU Long Beach 1960; MLS, USC 1961, MPA, 1974. Career: branch librarian Los Angeles County Public Library, 1961-68; regional librn. Orange County Public Lib., 1968, director of public services, 1969-74; county librn. San Mateo County Public Lib. 1974-77, Marin County Public Lib. 1978; city librn. Torrance Public Lib. 1978—; mem. advisory bd. Friends of Calif. Libraries, 1974-; pres. Calif. County Librarians 1977, founding pres. Calif. Council of City Librarians, 1984; exec. dir. Calif. Nat. Library Week, 1970; mem. Am. Library Assn., Calif. Library Assn., Am.

Soc. for Public Adminstrn.; Rotarian; mil: sp3 US Army Med. Corps 1955-57; rec: sports, walking, music. Res: 25002 Paseo Arboleda, El Toro 92630 Ofc: Torrance Public Library, 3301 Torrance Blvd Torrance 90503

BUCKLEY, TIMOTHY STEVEN, superior court judge; b. Sept. 26, 1945, Hanford; s. Frank G. and Helen M. (Broderick) B.; m. Constance J. Muffley, July 20, 1968; children: Alison b. 1971, Steven b. 1976; edn: BA, UC Santa Barbara 1967; JD, Univ. of Santa Clara 1973. Career: atty., ptnr. Dunn, Timm, Mayo & Buckley in Hanford 1973-74, Atkinson & Buckley in Lemoore 1974-75, Sharp, Maroot, Behrens & Buckley in Lemoore 1975-76; instr. West Hills Coll., 1975-76; justice Hanford Justice Ct., 1978-85; judge Kings County Superior Ct., Hanford 1985–; mem. Legislative Com., Calif. Judicial Council 1980; honors: Univ. of Santa Clara Law Review; mem. Calif. Judges Assn.; civic: Rotary, Kiwanis, YMCA (bd. trustees); mil: E5 US Army 1968-70; Republican; Catholic; rec: baseball. Res: 2935 13th Ave Hanford 93230 Ofc: Kings County Government Center 1400 West Lacey Blvd Hanford 93230

BUCKOWSKI, KENNETH ALLEN, video communications co. president; b. Sept. 9, 1948, Detroit, Mich.; s. Theodore and Elizabeth Rose (Safian) B.; m. Maria Christina Cazares, June 29, 1974; children: John b. 1977, Michelle b. 1979, Jennifer b. 1983; edn: BA, Sacred Heart Sem. 1970; MBA, Pepperdine Univ. 1982; Sony Tech. Tng. Sch. 1985-86. Career: radio/TV dir. Catholic Archdiocese of Detroit, Mich. 1967-70; founder/dir. Our House Drug Crisis Center, Plymouth, Mich. 1970-71; writer/ Creative Audio dir. Franciscan Communications Center, Los Angeles 1971-73; sales mgr. Production Systems Inc., Hollywood 1973-76; founder/pres. Studio Spectrum Inc. (fmr. Studio Service Center) video dealership, Burbank 1976–; communications cons. Xerox Corp. (1986-), Synod of So. Calif. (1984-), media advisor Burbank/ Glendale Sch. Dists. (1985-), media splst. Activities for Retarded Children (1984-); honors: Nat. Honor Soc. (1966), Man of the Year Plymouth City Council (1971), Supplier of Year 20th Century Fox (1982), Disting. Dealer Sony Corp. (1986); mem. Soc. of Motion Picture and TV Engring.; civic: Cubmaster BSA Pack 131, Glendale; Activities for Retarded Children, N. Hollywood; publs: The Applications and Entrepreneurial Implications of Video Communications in non-media related corporations (1982), The Video Communications Handbook (1986); films and videos: "Serendipity", "What Sound are You?", "Season of Struggle", "Doors", "It's Eleven PM", "Canticle of the Earth"; Democrat; Roman Catholic; rec: mountain climbing, photog., public speaking. Res: 1450 Imperial Dr Glendale 91207 Ofc: Studio Spectrum Inc. 1056 N Lake St Burbank 91502

BUECHNER, FREDERICK WILLIAM, financial consultant; b. June 3, 1905, N.Y.C.; s. Charles Cornelius and Evelyna Marie (Barton) B.; m. Kay Stafford, Jan. 2, 1928; children: Joan b. 1928, Barbara b. 1936 edn: BS in econs., City Coll. N.Y. 1926; desig: NYSE reg. rep., Cert. Finl. Planner (CFP). Career: stockbroker Dyer Hudson, N.Y. and Weingarten & Co., N.Y.C., 1930-40; finl. cons./v.p. Shearson Lehman Bros. Inc. and predecessor cos., members NYSE, 1945–; freelance journalist, investigator on assignment basis for the Spadea Syndicate and No. Am. Newspaper Alliance (UPI), Travel Mag., others 1954-68; lectr., writer, seminar condr.; honors: Silver Cross for conspicuous svc., Gov. Thomas E. Dewey, N.Y. (1958), merit cert. for service on Army Advis. Com. (1949-60), gold medal for promoting friendship between the Chinese and Am. peoples, Gen. Chiang Kai-shek (1958), Pulitzer Prize journ. nominee for story on the U-2 incident; civic: San Jose Stock & Bond Club (charter pres.), San Jose Host Lions Club (past pres.), S.J. Round Table (past pres.), Calvary Youth Center (past pres.), Mzuri Safari Club (past pres.), Phi Sigma Kappa, Commonwealth Club (general club speaker 3t), Scottish Rite; mil: Ofcrs. Reserve Corps 1926-40, col. US Army WWII 1940-45 (staff of Gen. Omar Bradley, Ft. Benning and Gen. J. Lawton Collins during Normandy Invasion; later, spl. security ofcr. for Eisenhower and Churchill), 2 bronze stars, 2 purple hearts, 2 commendns. from Gen. Eisenhower; Republican; Episcopal; rec: hunting, painting, writing, geopolitics. Res: 19915 Bella Vista Saratoga 95070 Ofc: Shearson Lehman Bros. 10080 N Wolfe Rd Cupertino 95014

BUENTIPO, MARILOU MARCOS, physician; b. Apr. 2, 1946, Manila, Philippines, nat. US cit. 1984; d. Julio Miguel and Florecita Manglapuz (Leal) Marcos; children: Susan M. b. 1966, Sandy M. b. 1970; edn: BS, Univ. Santo Tomas 1965, MD, 1972. Career: rotating intern Univ. Santo Tomas 1971-72; phys. Maternity and Children's Hosp. Manila 1972-73, Malcanang Clin. 1972-73; phys. asst. Central Med. Group L.A. 1973-74; phys. asst., asst. hosp. adminstr. Pacific Glen Hosp. Glendale 1974-76; intern ob-gyn Detroit Meml. Hosp., So. Macomb Hosp. Detroit 1979-80; gen. surg. res. I Martin Luther King Jr. Gen. Hosp. L.A. 1980-81, res. II ob-gyn 1981-82, res. III ob-gyn 1982-83; gen. med. practice and med. dir. methadone pgm. Inglewood Med. & Mental Health Svcs. 1983-84; gen. med. practice Beverly West Med. Ctr. L.A. 1983; solo practice L.A. 1984–; med. dir. Sacred Heart Convales. Hosp. Pasadena 1985; Award: Fgn. Med. Graduates Dialogue (Assn. Phil. Practicing Phys. of Am. 1976); mem: Assn. Fgn. Med. Grads. (pres. 1984-), Univ. Santo Tomas Alumni Assn. of So. Calif. (co-founder, advisor), Fil-Am. Community of L.A. (bd.), Phil. Med. Soc. of So. Calif., AMA, Am. Soc. Bariatric Physicians; Catholic; rec: music, organ, piano, guitar. Ofc: Marilou M. Buentipo MD Inc. 4149 W Pico Blvd Los Angeles 90019

BUGGS, CHARLES WESLEY, educator; b. Aug. 6, 1906, Brunswick, Ga.; s. John Wesley and Leonora Vane (Clark) B.; m. Maggie Lee Bennett, Dec. 27, 1927; 1 dau. Margaret Leonora b. 1947; edn: AB, Morehouse Coll. 1928; MS, Univ. Minn. 1932, PhD, 1934. Career: instr. biol. State Coll. for Colored Students Dover, Del. 1928-29; prof. chem. Bishop Coll. Marshall, Tex.

1934-35; prof. biol., chmn. nat. scis. div. Dillard Univ. New Orleans 1935-43, 1949-56, chmn. acad. adminstrn. com. 1951-52, dir. Sch. Health Summer Inst. 1953; instr., asst. prof., assoc. prof. bacteriol. & clin. pathol. Wayne Univ. Sch. of Med. Detroit 1943-49; prof., chmn. microbiol. dept. Howard Univ. Sch. of Med. Wash. DC 1956-71, prof. emeritus 1972–; pgm. dir., edn. splst. Calif. Reg. Med. Pgms. Area IX, Charles R. Drew Postgrad. Med. Sch. L.A. 1969-72, dean faculty of allied health scis. 1972; vis. prof. microbiol. USC Sch. of Med. 1969-76, UCLA 1969-72; prof., lectr. CSU Long Beach 1973-83; cons. Abbott Labs 1948-49, Upjohn Co. 1948-49, US Ofc. of Edn. 1948, Phelps-Stokes Fund Conf. 1954; del. to first 3 Buck Hill Falls confs. on prep. for med. edn. in liberal arts colls. 1950, 52, 58; NSF del. Bryn Mawr Conf. on biol. research in lib. arts colls. 1954; mem. Jt. Bd. on Sci. Edn. Wash. DC 1969; Awards: Rosenwald Scholar (1931-34), Sigma Xi (1932), Shevlin Fellow in Med. (1933), Rosenwald Fellow (1942), 20 Famous Black Am. Scientists (Nabisco poster 1980), research grants (Sigma Xi, Rockefeller Found.), recogn: Howard Unv. ooll. of Med. (1971), Watts-Willowbrook Regl. Health Com. (1972), Nat. Med. Assn. Found. (1972), Nat. Med. Assn. (1985), Nat. Soc. Allied Health (1985), Mayor Tom Bradley, L.A. City Council, State Sen. Diane Watson, US Cong. Julian C. Dixon; inducted Educators Hall of Fame (Mid-Cities Alliance of Black Sch. Educators 1985), Man of the Yr. (Elsinore NAACP 1984-85); fellow: Wash. Acad. Scis., Am. Acad. Microbiol., AAAS; mem: Am. Assn. Dental Schs., Am. Pub. Health Assn., Am. Soc. Microbiol., NY Acad. Scis., Arthritis Found. (1971-73), State Alcoholism Adv. Council 1972-73, Comprehensive Health Planning Assn. of L.A. Co. (bd. 1972-73); publs: num. articles in med., scholarly and sci. jours. Address: 5600 Verdun Ave Los Angeles 90043

BUI, DUC M., otolaryngologist; b. June 29, 1934, Phanrang, Vietnam, nat. 1981; s. Thong Xuan and Le Thi (Truong) Bui; m. Thai Tran, Apr. 26, 1959; children: Tam b. 1959, Ailien b. 1961, Hana b. 1962, Khanh b. 1964, Thao b. 1966, Khang b. 1968, An b. 1970; edn: MD (with honors), Saigon Med. Sch. 1962; residency in otolaryngology, Louisville (Ky.) Univ. 1981. Career: asst. prof. Hue Med. Sch., Saigon 1970; ear nose throat asst. Wurzburg Univ., W. Ger. 1972; chmn. ENT Dept. Hue Univ., Vietnam 1973-75, asst. dean med. sch. 1974; instr. in surgery Univ. Louisville, Ky. 1975-77, residency in ENT, 1977-81, chief res. 1980-81; pvt. practice, pres. Duc M. Bui, MD, Inc. Westminster Ca. 1982–; pres. Vietnamese Physicians Assn. in Calif. 1983-84; awards: Saigon Med. School Scholarship 1954-60; Fellow Am. Acad. of Otolaryn. 1982; mem. German Otolaryn. Soc. Soc. 1972; v.p. Vietnam Otolaryn. Soc. 1973; sec.-gen. Vietnamese Students Assn. 1954-55; pres. Viet. Vol. Youth Svc. 1958-60; mil: surgeon chief 1st div. Army Repub. Vietnam 1962-63; Buddist; rec: photog., antiques. Res: 3491 Eboe St Irvine 92714 Ofc: Duc M. Bui MD, Inc. 9131 Bolsa Ave, Ste. 201, Westminster 92683

BUI, HANH QUANG, architect, real estate broker; b. July 7, 1913, Sadec, S. Vietnam; s. Anh Quang and Kiem Thi (Phan) B.; m. Thya Nguyen, May 1970 (dec. 1976); legal guardian of Theresa b. 1971; edn: Baccalaureat II, Univ. of Paris, France 1935; Urbaniste, Inst. d'Urbanisme, Paris 1946; architect D.P.L.G., Ecole Nat. Superieure des Beaux-Arts 1942; Reg. Architect, Calif. (1981), AIA, Am. Inst. of Arch. (1985); Calif. lic. real estate broker (1981). Career: architect Ministry for Reconstrn. & Planning in Paris, mem. Architects Order (Paris), 1945-49; architect in pvt. practice and prof. Faculty of Architecture, Univ. of Saigon, Viet Nam 1955-75; architect pvt. practice, Calif. 1981–, realtor assoc. Century 21 O.J. Creel, Oceanside 1981–; honors: 1st class medal Nat. Order for Culture & Edn., Republic of Viet Nam; mem. AIA/ San Diego, Oceanside Bd. of Realtors, Vietnamese Am. Architl. Friendship Assn. (pres.); works: architect of the Nat. Library of Saigon (pictured in 2 postage of Viet Nam); mil: 2d lt. French Army 1939-40; Buddhism; wood working. Res: 629 San Luis Rey Dr Oceanside 92054

BUI, HUM DAC, physician; b., June 30, 1943, Tayninh, Vietnam; s. Chieu Van and Nghiem Thi (Nguyen) B.; m. Hong Dang, June 10, 1968; children: Hoan b. 1969, Hao b. 1971, Cam-Han b. 1972, Hiep b. 1973; edn: PCB, Saigon Faculty of Scis. 1962; MD, Saigon Med. Sch. 1968; cert. Am. Bd. Surg. 1985. Career: chief of surg. Tayninh Mil. Hosp. Vietnam 1968-74; county counselor Tayninh 1974-75; chief resident gen. surg. Martin Luther King Jr. Hosp. L.A. 1980-81; chief of surg. Lanterman Devel. Ctr. 1983; surg. staff Pomona Valley Comm. Hosp. 1984; chief med. staff, chief surg. Lanterman Devel. Ctr. Pomona 1985–; mem: Vietnamese Medico Surg. Assn., Vietnamese Med. Council, County Counselor Assn., cand. group Am. Coll. Surg., AMA, CMA, World Med. Assn.; publs: med. reports, US and Vietnam; mil: capt. Vietnamese Army Mil. Med. Bloc 1968-74, num. decorations; Republican; Buddhist; rec: tennis, ping pong, fishing, gardening. Res: 1608 Smiley Heights Dr Redlands 92373 Ofc: Lanterman Devel. Ctr. Pomona 91768

BUI, TAM DUY, physician-surgeon; b. Sept. 8, 1934, Hanoi, Vietnam; s. Tinh Van and Dinh Thi (Nguyen) Bui; m. VietHuong Do, July 17, 1955; children: VietHa, b. 1957, Linh, b. 1958, Thien, b. 1961, VietHong, b. 1968; edn: MS (physiol.) Univ. of Saigon Faculty of Scis. 1958; MD, Univ. of Saigon Faculty of Med. 1960; PhD (biochem.) UC Med. Ctr. S.F., 1964; OMD (Dr. Oriental Med.), S.F. Coll. of Acupuncture & Oriental Med. 1983; Calif. lic. physician and surgeon, 1983. Career: prof./chmn. dept. biochem. Univ. of Saigon Faculty of Med. 1966-79; resrch. dir. clin. chem. lab. Pasteur Inst. of Saigon, 1965-75; dean Sch. of Med. Univ. of Hue (Vietnam) 1968-71; dean Sch. of Med. Minh Duc Univ., Saigon 1971-75; v.chmn. Fund of Reconciliation and Reconstrn. in Indochina, World Council of Chs. 1972-75; prof. of acupuncture and hd. Dept. of Western Med., San Francisco Coll. of Acupuncture, S.F., Ca. 1980–; staff phys. Neumiller Meml. Hosp., Marine City 1983-; honors: first prize in math. Nat. Inter-Coll. Tournament V.N. 1952; medal of merit in med. edn. (1968), and medal of merit in youth and culture (1970), Pres. Govt. of V.N.; pres. Founder's Com. of Protestant Univ. in V.N. 1974; mem: AMA 1985-, V.N. Med. Assn. 1960-75; Korean (hon.) Med. Assn. 1967; founder/pres. Gio Khoi Assn. 1966-75; v.p. V.N. Underwater Exploration and Hunting Assn. 1960-75; hon. pres. V.N. Oriental Med. Assn. 1970-75; hon. pres. V.N. Table Tennis Nat. League 1970-75; hon. adv. Nat. Conserv. of Music in Saigon 1973-75; works: 46 med. resrch. publs.; spons. 36 M.D. Candidates in conducting their med. & surgical theses; presented Biochem., Acupuncture and Medico-surg. Resrch. to profl. confs. internat. 1962-75; Prot.; rec: synthesis of West-East cultures. Res: 1496 36th Ave San Francisco 94122 Ofc: Sixth-Clement Med.-Dental Clin., 307 6th Ave San Francisco 94118

BUIE, ROBERT FRANK, real estate development co. president; b. May 29, 1942, Washington DC; s. Paul Douglas and Mary Margaret (Bullock) B.; m. Pamela Nosler, Jan. 2, 1984; children: Tatia b. 1969, Garrett b. 1975; edn: BS civil engring., Virginia Tech. 1964; MBA, Harvard Univ. 1971. Career: naval flight ofcr. USN, S.E. Asia 1964-69; var. positions Avco Community Developers 1971-75, v.p. gen. mgr. San Diego Div. Avco 1975-78, exec. v.p. Avco Community Developers 1978-83; pres. The Buie Corp., real estate devel. in San Diego and Orange Counties, 1983 –; mem. Building Industry Assn. (bd. dirs.), Presidents Council, Palomar Hosp. Advis. Board, Marbella Assn. (pres.); clubs: San Diego Yacht, The Centre; mil: lcdr. USN-R, active duty 1964-69; Republican; Methodist; rec: skiing, boating. Res: 13013 Olmeda Ct San Diego 92128 Ofc: The Buie Corporation 16536 Bernardo Center Dr San Diego 92128

BUKRY, JOHN DAVID, geologist; b. May 17, 1941, Baltimore; s. Howard Leroy and Irene Evelyn (Davis) Snyder; edn: undergrad., Colo. Sch. of Mines 1959-60; BA, The Johns Hopkins Univ. 1963; Univ. Ill. 1965-66; MA, PhD, Princeton Univ. 1965, 1967. Career: geologist US Army Corps of Engrs., Baltimore 1963; research asst. Mobil Oil Co., Dallas 1965; geologist US Geological Survey, La Jolla 1967-75, geologist in charge 1975-84; geologist US Minerals Mgmt. Service, La Jolla 1984 –; research assoc. Geol. Research Div. UC San Diego 1970-; cons. Deep Sea Drilling Project, La Jolla 1967-; guest lectr. 3d Internat. Planktonic Conf., Germany (1974); shipboard micropaleontologist on D/V Glomar Challenger (5 DSDP Cruises 1968-78); mem. NSF-JOIDES Stratigraphic Correlations Panel 1976-79; ed. Marine Micropaleontology (1976-83), editl. bd. Micropaleontology (1985-); awards: fellowships at Princeton Univ., Mobil Oil Co. (1965-67), Am. Chem. Soc. (1966-67); elected fellow AAAS (1981), Explorers Club (1979), Geol. Soc. of Am. (1975); mem. Am. Assn. of Petroleum Geologists, Paleontol. Research Instn., Sigma Xi; civic: S.D. Shell Club, S.D. Soc. Natural Hist., Hawaiian Malacological Soc., The Nature Conservancy, Zool. Soc. of S.D.; author two sci. books in field; contbr. identification and definitions for 300 new species of fossil marine phytoplankton used to give geological ages for ocean bottom sediments pub. in sci. jours.; rec: basketball, photog., shell collector. Ofc: USMMS (A-015), Scripps Institution of Oceanography La Jolla 92093

BUMGARNER, STEPHEN LEE, pediatric dentist; b. June 26, 1950, Kansas City, Mo.; s. Fred Olin, Jr. and Patricia B.; edn: BA, St. Louis Univ. 1972; DDS, Univ. Mo. 1979. Career: pediat. dental resident Chindren's Hosp. Med. Ctr. of No. Calif. 1981-83; postdoc. pgm. in pediat. dentistry UC Sch. of Dentistry 1983. Career: clin. assoc. Washington Univ. Sch. of Dental Med. 1979-81; dental resident Children's Hosp. of No. Calif. 1981-83; pediat. dentist pvt. practice San Francisco 1983 –; attg. dentist Children's Hosp. Oakland; mem. Bay Area Pedodontic Study Club; honors: Senior Award (Am. Acad. Dental Radiol. 1979), scholarship and fellowship (St. Louis Univ. 1972), Oriflame (Men's Svc. Orgn. of St. Louis Univ. 1970-72), Eta Sigma Phi (chpt. secty., nat. chmn. 1971), Beta Beta Beta (1970), Nat. Honor Soc. (1968); mem: Am. Dental Assn., Am. Soc. Dentistry for Children, Am. Acad. Pedodontics (bd. elig.), Am. Acad. Dental Radiol., Calif. Soc. Pediatric Dentists, The Museum Soc., Big Brothers/ Big Sisters, Century Club (SLU), UCSF Alumni Assn., SLU Alumni Assn., UMKC Sch. of Dentistry Alumni Assn.; research: mouth-held appliances for quadriplegics; Republican; Catholic; rec: running, cycling. Ofc: 450 Sutter Ste 2116 San Francisco 94108

BUNN, MAURICE HENRY, research co. executive, corporate pilot; b. Oct. 13, 1940, Oneonta, NY; s. Kenneth Arnold and Elizabeth Theresa (Schneider) B.; div.; children: Christopher b. 1968, Anthony b. 1970; edn: BSE (aero option), summa cum laude, Ariz. State Univ. 1968; MSE (aero-astro), Stanford Univ. 1969; MBA, CSU Dominguez Hills 1978; lic. real estate broker 1980; FAA lic. comml./instrument pilot (1982). Career: served to capt. US Air Force 1958-78, radar tech. 1958-64, electronics instr. Avionics Sch. 1965, exchange scientist West Germany 1972-74, engr. General Research Corp. 1978-83, dir. Los Angeles Operations 1983 –; awards: Nat. Olde Guard Prize, ASME (1968), Air Force Scientific Achieve. Award (1970); honors: Phi Kappa Phi, Tau Beta Pi, Pi Tau Sigma; mem. ASME, AIAA; civic: Planning commns. (Redondo Beach, El Segundo, Manhattan Beach), Homeowners assns. (Hawthorne, Manhattan Beach); contbr. tech. papers Cong. of Internat. Astro. Fedn. (Baku, Russia 1974, Prague, Czech. 1978); mil. decorations: AFCM, SAEMR, GCMOL (Army), AFGCM, AFOUA; publs: tech papers, Internat. Astro. Fedn. Congresses (1974, 78); rec: aviation, skiing, woodworking. Res: 3 Catalina Ct Manhattan Beach 90266 Ofc: General Research Corp. 240 N Nash St El Segundo 90245

BUNZEL, JOHN H., Hoover Instn. senior research fellow; b. Apr. 15,1924, NYC; s. Ernest Everett and Hariett (Harvey) Bunzel; m. 2d Barbara Bovyer, May 11, 1963; children: Cameron, Reed; edn: AB, pol.sci., magna cum laude, Princeton Univ. 1948; MA, sociol., Columbia Univ. 1949; PhD, pol. sci., UC Berkeley 1954; LL.D.(hon.), Univ. Santa Clara 1976. Career: tchr. CSC San

Francisco, 1953-56, Mich. State Univ. 1956-57; pres. CSU San Jose, 1970-78; sr. resrch fellow, Hoover Instn., Stanford Univ., 1978 – . Author: The American Small Businessman (Knopf 1962), Issues of American Public Policy (Prentice-Hall 1964, 2d ed. 1968), Anti-Politics in America (Knopf 1967), New Force On the Left: Tom Hayden And The Campaign Against Corporate America (Hoover 1983); Challenge To American Schools (Oxford, 1985); coauthor monograph: The Calif. Democratic Delegation of 1960; columnist (biwkly) San Jose Mercury-News; contbr. NY Times, Wall St. Jour., scholarly and polit. jours.; conducted wkly TV pgm. (KPIX-S.F.) 1964. Recipient Presidential Award, No. Calif. Polit. Sci. Assn. (1969), cert. of honor, S.F. Bd. of Suprs. (1974); research grantee: Ford Found. (Fund for the Republic) 1958-60, (Com. on resrch in pub. affairs, Stanford Univ.) 1960-61, (vis. scholar Ctr. for Adv. Study in Behavioural Scis) 1969-70; Rabinowitz Found. 1961-62; Rockefeller Found.1965-66.Dir., No. Calif. Citizenship Clearing House, 1959-61; mem: Am., No. Calif.(pres, 1962-3) Polit. Sci. Assn. Democrat (del. nat. conv.1968). Res: 1519 Escondido Way Belmont 94002. Ofc: Hoover Instn. Stanford Univ. Stanford 94305

BUONOMO, LOUIS JAY, physician, surgeon; b. Mar. 13, 1909, Ashtabula, Ohio; s. Anthony and Rosina (Scardino) B.; m. Juanita Cockrum, Sept. 5, 1939; children: Juana Lou b. 1940, Louis, Jr. b. 1943, Diana Lee b. 1946; edn: Western Reserve Univ. 1927-30; BA, Ohio Univ. 1934; NY Med. Coll. 1937; DO, L.A. Coll. of Osteopathic Phys. & Surgeons 1946; MD, Calif. Coll. Med. UC Irvine 1962; L.A. County Civil Svc. Commn. Position No. 1, Final Ave. Grade 96.40% (1946).Career: intern L.A. County Osteo. Unit. 1946-47; gen. practice and surgery Colusa, Calif. 1949-77; med. staff Glendale Comm. Hosp. 1946-49, Colusa Meml. Hosp., Colusa Eskaton Hosp., Colusa Comm. Hosp. 1949-86; Colusa County Med. Health Ofcr. 1982 –; past chief of staff Colusa Meml. Hosp.; pres. part-owner Williams (Calif.) Valley West Convales. Hosp. 1966-84, corp. pres. 1980 –; Colusa County Emergency Med. Svcs. ofcr., mem. Maternal, Child & Adolescent Health of Calif. 1982 –; mem: AMA, CMA, Yuba- Sutter- Colusa County Med. Soc., Calif. Conf. Local Health Ofcrs., Health Ofcrs. Assn. of Calif., Rotary, Colusa Golf & CC; Republican; Methodist; rec: golf, fishing, travel. Res: 918 Sioc Colusa 95932 Ofc: Colusa County Health Dept. 251 E Webster St Colusa 95932

BURCH, GERRITSON HILBERT, computer co. president; b. Jan. 4, 1942, Woodbury, NJ; s. Harris M. and Marion L. (Hilbert) B.; m. Jane Ellen Rogers, Oct. 17, 1982; children: Eddie, b. 1970; Christopher, b. 1975; edn: Monmouth, 1959-60; AS, Coll. of Canyon 1979; CSU Northridge 1980-. Career: served to Chief E7, US Navy 1960-1980, ret. (Nat. Defense, Pistol Exp., 5 GCM); classified wk. Lockheed Co., 1980-82; pres. Computer Systems Ctr., Newhall 1982 –; pres. GHB/ Ross, Inc.; cons. GHB/ Ross, Inc. 1981-; cons. TGA Video 1981-82; mem: Boy Scouts of AM.; YMCA Indian Guides; Masons; Nat. Rifle Assn.; AYSO; Hart Baseball; Republican; Protestant; rec: show cars, computer games, guns. Res: 23817 Daisetta Dr Newhall 91321 Ofc: Computer Systems Center, 23422 Lyons Ave Newhall 91321

BURCHARD, THOMAS KIRK, psychiatrist; b. Feb. 16, 1948, Boston, Mass.; s. Charles Henry and Helen (Schwab) B.; m. Diane Margolese, Nov. 14, 1980; edn: BS, Antioch Coll. 1970; MD, Univ. Va. 1972; bd. certified adult psychiatry (1980), child psychiatry (1981), Am. Bd. Psychiatry & Neurology; physician & surgeon Calif. Bd. Med. Qual. Assur. Career: intern, pediatrics, Cinti. Childrens Hosp. 1974-75; resident, adult psychiatry, Sepulveda VA Hosp. 1975-77; fellowship, child psychiatry, UCLA-NPI, 1977-79; dir. child and family pgms. Community Hosp. of Monterey Peninsula Mental Health Ctr. 1979 –; asst. prof. psychiat. UCLA; mem. No. Calif. Psychiatric Soc. (pres. Central Coast Counties Chpt.) Ofc: Community Hosp. Monterey Peninsula, POB HH, Monterey 93940

BURCHELL, LINDA NICHOLE, clinical psychologist; b. June 9, 1946, Wichita, Kans.; d. Thomas Willis and Bette Mae Dunlap; 1 child, Kennyon b. 1978; edn: BA, CSU Hayward 1969; MA, Pepperdine Univ., L.A. 1973; PhD, The Union Graduate Sch., 1977; lic. psychologist, State Bd. 1983. Career: psychotherapist Philanthropon House, Wash. DC 1973-75; exec. dir. Tanana Chiefs Health Authority, Fairbanks, Alaska 1975-77; pvt. practice cons. var. health agencies, Fairbanks 1977-78, Long Beach, Calif. 1978-80; psych. asst. Jerry Cunninghan, PhD, Granada Hills 1980-81; clin. dir. New Horizons Counseling and Mental Hlth. Svcs. Inc., Clinton, Okla. 1980-81; clin. psychologist prin. in pvt. practice, Orange 1983 –; mem: Psi Chi (pres. 1973), Assn. of Humanistic Psychol., Am. Assn. Marriage & Family Therapists, Orange CofC; publs: Native American Healing in Psychotherapy; Republican; Jewish; rec: scuba, calligraphy, dancing. Ofc: Burchell Psychological Services Orange 92667

BURCKLE, ALTON GEORGE, lawyer; b. Aug. 22, 1923, Louisville, Ky.; s. Alton George and Muriel (Wynn) B.; m. Mary Lewis, May 25, 1951; children: Edwynne b. 1952, George b. 1955, Carrie b. 1957, James b. 1958, John b. 1960; edn: Tenn. Poly. Univ. 1943-44; JD, Univ. Louisville 1948; MBA, Univ. Dayton 1964. Career: mem. law firm Fears, McCrocklin & Burckle 1948-50; mem. Judge Advocate Gen. Dept. USAF 1950-68, Asst. Chief Trial Counsel of the USAF, counsel to McDonnell Douglas Corp., pvt. practice spec. in corp. matters 1968 –; bd. dirs. Shur-Lok Corp. 1970-; mem: Am., Calif., Ky., Orange Co. Bar Assns., Orange County Health Planning Council (bd. 1979-81), Navy Yacht Club, Dana Pt. Yacht Club, Mesa Verde CC; mil: served 1943-45; col. USAF 1951-67, Air Medal, Commdn.; Catholic; rec: golf, sailing. Res: 28635 Vista Ladera Laguna Niguel 92677 Ofc: 511 E First St Tustin 92680

BURDETT, JOSEPH WILLIAM, lawyer; b. Oct. 23, 1936, Peoria, Ill.; s. Joseph L. and Elizabeth (Williams) B.; m. Mary Jean Pasco, June 15, 1958; children: Eric William b. 1970, Jennifer Lynn b. 1973; edn: BS, Bradley Univ. 1957; MS, Univ. Utah 1962; JD, Stanford Univ. Sch. of Law 1965. Career: certified public acct., Price Waterhouse & Co., Ill. 1957-59; ptnr. Kindel & Anderson, Los Angeles 1965–; bd. dirs. Sunset Post, Inc. (1981-), Sunset Teleproduction Center (1984-); frequent lectr. on tax topics; author num. tax articles; mem: ABA, Am. Inst. CPAs, Calif. Soc. CPAs, Stanford Alumni Assn.; past bd. dirs. Easter Seal Soc., Nat. Assn. for People with Disabilities; club: Jonathan, Los Angeles (pres. 1981-82, bd. dirs. 1979-82); mil: ofcr. USAF 1959-62; rec: tennis, skiing, theater. Ofc: Kindel & Anderson, 555 S Flower St Ste 2600 Los Angeles 90071

BURDSALL, DEAN LEROY, accountant; b. June 4, 1935, Indianapolis, Ind.; s. Ralph K. and Florence G. (Duncan) B.; m. Georgia Vent, June 1, 1957; children: Kevin b. 1960, Craig b. 1962, Scott b. 1968, Jeffrey b. 1970; edn: BA, Pasadena Coll. 1957; CPA, Calif. 1968. Career: staff acct. Peat, Marwick, Mitchell & Co., San Jose 1960-68; corp. controller GRT Corp., Sunnyvale 1968-71; staff acct. brooks, Stednitz & Rhodes Accty. Corp., San Jose 1971-74, prin. 1974–; mem: Am. Inst. CPAs, Calif. Soc. CPAs, Rotary (pres. West Valley San Jose 1984-85, past secty., treas.), San Jose CofC (audit com.), Youth for Christ (bd. dirs. Santa Clara Co.); mil: spec. 4 US Army 1958-60; Republican; Protestant; rec: tennis, boating, fishing. Res: 6531 Gillis Dr. San Jose 95120 Ofc: Brooks, Stednitz & Rhodes, 1600 Willow St. Ste. 200 San Jose 95125

BURFORD, JAMES SCOTT, investment executive, stock broker; b. July 22, 1962, Salem, Ore.; s. Maurice James and Edwina Ray (Ballard) B.; m. Hannah, June 29, 1985; edn: BS, Univ. of Oregon 1984. Career: investment exec., stockbroker Wedbush, Noble, Cooke Inc., Los Angeles 1984–; recipient Hard Charger Award, Republican Party 1978; Republican; rec: skiing, scuba diving. Res: 1943 Rodney Dr. Apt. 218 Los Angeles 90027 Ofc: Wedbush, Noble, Cooke, Inc., 615 So. Flower Ste. 405 Los Angeles 90017

BURGOS, LUIS ANTONIO, psychologist; b. Oct. 23, 1950, Colombia, S.A.; s. Francisco and Clara (Navarrete) B.; edn: BA, Univ. Ark. 1975; MEd, Univ. Mo. 1976; PhD Clin. Psych., US Internat. Univ. 1984. Career: Internat. Exchange student counselor, Hqtrs. YFU Ann Arbor, Mich.; community and clin. psychology intern Mercy Hosp. & Med. Ctr., San Diego 1979-80; cons. Raleigh Hills Hosp., Nat. City Mental Health, Linda Vista Health Care Center, 1981–; pvt. practice HMO Advanced Health Care, 1982–; vis. prof. Univ. Andes, Atlantic Univ., Colombia S.A. (1983-); honors: Psi Chi; mem. Am. Psychological Assn., San Diego Acad. of Psychologists, Interam. Soc. of Psychol.; civic: YMCA, Salvation Army, Masons; publs: On Depression (1983), On Alcohol Abuse & Dependency (1985); unpub. poetry; Democrat; rec: boating, handicrafts. Res: 2380 Cardinal Dr Apt 28 San Diego 92123 Ofc: Advanced Health Care 2423 Camino del Rio South, Ste 111, San Diego 92108

BURKE, MONICA ANNETTE, registered nurse; b. May 6, 1957, Lowell, Mass.; d. Lothar Ulrich and Annette (Kronshnabel) Fuchs; m.Donald Burke, Sept. 18, 1983; edn: BS biol., Univ. Lowell 1979; BS nursing, Southwestern Mass. Univ. 1981; Reg. Nurse 1981; ASPO Certified Childbirth Educator 1983. Career: reg. nurse Ob-Gyn Cedars- Sinai Med. Ctr. L.A. 1981-82, maternal/ child health Simi Valley Adventist Hosp. 1982-86, perinatal svcs. Kaiser Permanente Med. Ctr. Woodland Hills 1986–; certified childbirth educator; certified lactation educator, cons.; honors: Dr. Henry Sills Kiwanis Scholarship (1975), New England Dist. Kiwanis Internat.Award (1975); mem: Am. Soc. Psychoprophylaxis in Obstetrics (area rep. 1985-), La Leche League Internat., Nurses Assn. of Am. Coll.Ob-Gyn, Cesareans/ Support Edn. & Concern; Republican; Protestant; rec: travel, photog., cooking, needlework. Address: 2848 N. Woodrow Ave Simi Valley 93065

BURKE, THEODORE ELLIOTT, restaurateur; b. Oct. 10, 1946, Phila.; s. Joseph Elliott and Gloria Ann (Theodore) B.; m. Carole, Aug. 16, 1973; children: Joslyn b. 1977, Natalie b. 1981, Kelly b. 1983, Elliott b. 1985; edn: BS, Santa Clara Univ. 1972; student Univ. of the Americas 1968, Inst. Fgn. Studies 1972. Career: waiter, bartender Shadowbrook Restaurant Capitola, Calif. 1972, asst. mgr. 1973-78, co-owner Shadowbrook and Crow's Nest Restaurant in Santa Cruz 1978–; pres. Culinary Enterprises (dba Shadowbrook); v.p. Harbour Svcs. (dba Crow's Nest); mem. advis. panel Restaurant Business 1979; honors: Businessman of the Year (Santa Cruz Indsl. Edn. Council 1984, Capitola CofC 1986), Award of Excellence (Santa Cruz Co. Visitors Bureau 1985), Resolution of Appreciation (Capitola City Council 1982), Acknowledgement (Calif. State Assembly 1985); mem: Calif. Restaurant Assn. (dir. 1980-), Long Marine Lab. (dir. 1982-, treas. 1986), Capitola CofC (dir. 1984-), Santa Cruz CofC (dir. 1982), Pasatiampo Inc. Golf Club (pres. 1985-86), Santa Cruz Co. Conv. & Vis. Bureau (pres. 1982), Assocs. of Good Govt., PEOPLE of Santa Cruz Co. (chmn.); co-devel. payroll software for restaurant applications. mil: US Army 1968-70; rec: golf, winemaking. Ofc: Shadowbrook Restaurant POB 65 Capitola 95010

BURNAM, JACK LEONARD, lawyer; b. Sept. 19, 1924, St. Joseph, Mo.; s. Clark A. and Flossie B. B.; m. Eleanor Jackson, 1947; children: Jack II b. 1953, Joanne Leslie b. 1956; m. 2d Marilyn Kopmann, 1982; edn: AA, San Francisco City Coll. 1944; BA, Univ. Calif. 1947; LLB, UC Hastings Coll. of Law 1951; LLM, JD, Univ. Lincoln 1952. Career: secty., law clerk to US Judge Michael Roche 1953-55; pvt. law practice spec. in personal injury, criminal, probate and family law S.F. 1955–; judge pro tem municipal ct. S.F. 1985–; mem: ABA, S.F. Bar Assn., Calif. Trial Lawyers Assn., Am. Trial Lawyers Assn., Elks, PTA (pres. 1971), BSA (ofcr. 1975); publs: book chpts. concerning legal activities for prisoners in Alcatraz 1963 (Doubleday), num. jour. articles; Democrat; Protestant. Rec: swimming, golf. Res: 434 Montecito Blvd Napa 94558 Ofc: One Hallidie Plaza Ste 805 San Francisco 94102

BURNETT, CAROL STEVENS, real estate co. executive; b. Feb. 15, 1939, Portland, Ore.; d. Ellis John and Rachael (Williams) Stevens; m. G. Keith Burnett, Sept. 8, 1962; children: Keith, Jr. b. 1967, Michael b. 1970; edn: BS, Ore. State Univ. 1961; Calif. lic. Real Estate Broker (1978). Career: secty., asst. The Draper Cos., San Francisco 1962-64; adminstrv. asst. Dohemann & Co., San Rafael 1964-67; real estate sales Parker Assocs., Saratoga 1974-76, Saratoga Foothills 1976-78; sales asso. Cornish & Carey Realtors 1978-86, senior v.p./mgr. Saratoga Office, 1986–; recipient corp. sales achieve. awards (1983, 84); mem: Nat. Assn. Realtors, Calif. Assn. Realtors, San Jose Bd. of Realtors, Los Gatos/Saratoga Bd. of Realtors (dir. 1983, 84; chair Grievance 1985, chair Bd. Orientation & Tng. 1986); civic: Junior League of San Jose (1974-), S.J./Cleveland Ballet Council (1986), Saratoga Ednl. Found. (1982-84); club: Brookside Swim & Racket (pres. 1984-86); Republican; Episcopal; rec: tennis, travel. Ofc: Cornish & Carey Realtors 12175 Saratoga/ Sunnyvale Rd Saratoga 95070

BURNETT, JAMES ROBERTS, manufacturing co. executive; b. May 3, 1926, Goshen, N.Y.; s. James Roberts and Anna May (Mowbray) B.; m. Marion Deubler, June 19, 1948; children: Terry Lynn, James M.; edn: BME, Rensselaer Polytechnic Inst. 1949; Alma (Mich.) Coll. 1943-44; midshipman tng., ensign USNR, Columbia Univ. 1945. Career: var. suvpvsy. pos. in plant engring., prodn., maint., 1949-63; gen. supt. Parish Div. Dana Corp., Reading, Pa. 1963-65, plant mgr. Parish Div. Dana Corp., Trenton, Mich. 1965-67; staff mem. chg. of new mfg. processes Dana Corp. 1967-76; asst. v.p. of subsidiaries Budd Co. 1969-71, plant mgr. Budd Automotive of Canada 1971-74, gen. mgr. Automotive Frame Div. 1974-76; pres. Peerless Div. Lear Siegler Corp. 1976-80; v.p. mfg. Farr Co., El Segundo 1980–; dir: Budd Automotive Canada (1974-76), Peerless Canada Div. Lear Siegler (1976-80); civic: chmn. bd. supvrs. Lower Alsace Township, Pa. 1959-65; bd. YMCA Wyandotte, Mich. 1966; mem. Elks, Pi Kappa Alpha frat.; mil: lt. sg US Navy 1943-46, Reserve 1946-51; Republican; Presbyterian; rec: golf. Res: 3402 Seaglen Dr Rancho Palos Verdes 90274 Ofc: Farr Co 2301 Rosecrans El Segundo 90245

BURNETT, LYNN BARKLEY, educator; b. Oct. 20, 1948, Reedley; parents: Charles Erbin and Ruth Clarice (Erickson) B.; edn: BS, Columbia Pacific Univ., MSc,; candidate: Dip. in Nat. Security Mgmt., Nat. Defense Univ. of the US; Ed.D, Nova Univ. Ctr. for Higher Edn. Career: assoc. dir. Central Valley Emergency Med. Svcs. System Devel. Pgm., Fresno 1974-75; course dir. Pre-Hosp. Advanced Life Support Tng. Pgm. for Emerg. Paramedics, Valley Med. Ctr. of Fresno 1975; health sci. prof. CSU Fresno 1977–, dir. Center for Cont. Edn. in the Health Professions, Sch. of Hlth. and Social Wk., CSU, 1981–; afil. faculty Advanced Cardiac Life Support, Am. Heart Assn. 1973-; med. adv. Fresno Co. Sheriff's Dept. 1979-; cons. in health, human behav., emerg. med. 1975–; expert witness on med. issues; estab./dir. inaugural Paramedic Tng. Pgm. Co. of Fresno, 1974-75; mem. examining bd. State Mil. Reserve, 1981-; honors: cert. of appreciation for public service, Fresno Police Dept. 1969; Am. Heart Assn. bronze medal 1974; Award of Appreciation, Am. Cancer Soc. 1985; mem:. The Chemical People (steering & adv. com., chmn. 1983-85), Citizens League to Expose Abuse and Negligence (chmn. 1976-), Am. Soc. of Law and Medicine, Am. Coll. Sports Med., AAAS, NY Acad. of Scis., Am. Assn. Suicidiology, Am. Fedn. for Clin. Research, Am. Trauma Soc., The Hastings Ctr. Inst. of Soc., Ethics and the Life Scis., Am. Cancer Soc. (Fresno County Unit pub. edn. chmn. 1984-, orgn. v.p. 1985-), AM. Heart Assn., Fresno County Safety Council (secty. 1984-85, pres. 1985-), Fresno County Adv. Bd. on Drug Abuse (chmn. 1985-), Emerg. Med. Care Com. of Fresno County (v-chmn. 1984-85), Am. Assn. of Univ. Profs., Nat. Edn. Assn., Am. Acaed. Forensic Scis., Assn. Mil. Surgeons of US, Soc. of Prospective Med., Am. Pub. Health Assn., Assn. of Indsl. Coll. of Armed Forces, Am. Nat. Red Cross, Fellowship of Christian Peace Ofcrs., Fellowship of Christian Athletes, Evangelicals for Social Action^lif. Regional Med. Pgms., state and county subcoms.; publs: cons./contbr. Calif. State Plan for Emerg. Med. Services (1975); mil: maj. Med. Reserv. Calif. State Mil. Reserve and Air Nat. Guard 1970-, CA Svc. Medal; Democrat; Baptist; rec: music, athletics. Res: POB 4512 Fresno 93744 Ofc: CSUF Fresno 93740

BURNEY, CHARLES FRANKLIN, JR., research and development executive; b. Sept. 24, 1927, Dallas, Tex.; s. Charles Franklin and Martha Ann (Juhan) B.; m. Lillian Longarini, June 18, 1955; children: Charles b. 1956, Laura b. 1957, James b. 1959; edn: Univ. Ga. 1951-53; BA, Calif. State Univ. 1970, MA, 1971; Ed.D, Univ. Tulsa 1973; Reg. Profl. Engr. Mass.Career: field engr. Philco Corp. Phila. 1953-56; pgm. mgr., proj. mgr. for major AF and Navy security systems Boston, Mtn. View, Calif. 1956-71; asst. prof. physics Univ. Tulsa 1971-73; dir. solid state prods. div. Addington Labs. Sunnyvale 1974-78; v.p. research & devel. ARA Inc. 1978–; mem: IEEE, PGRQC; patents: 18 in fields of electronics and mechanics; mil: arm 3/c USNR 1944-46, active 1946-50; Republican; Christian; rec: flying, boating, amateur radio. Res: 319 Tuve Orland 95963 Ofc: Franklin Research & Devel. 518 Monterey Orland 95963

BURNEY, VICTORIA KALGAARD, chief executive officer; b. Apr. 12, 1943, Los Angeles; d. Oscar Albert and Dorothy Elizabeth (Peterson) K.; children: Kim Elizabeth, J. Hewett; edn: BA honors, Univ. Montana 1965; MA, Univ. No. Colo. 1980; postgrad., Webster Univ. 1983-84. Career: exec. dir. Hill County Community Action Havre, Montana 1966-67; community orgn. splst. ACCESS Escondido, Calif. 1967-68; pgm. devel. and comm. orgn. splst. Community

Action Pgms. Pensacola, Fla. 1968-69; cons. Escambia County Sch. Bd. Pensacola 1969-71; pres. Kal Kreations Kailua, Hawaii 1974-77; instr., dir. Ofc. of Human Resources Devel. Palomar Coll. San Marcos, Calif. 1978-81; pres., CEO IDET Corp. San Marcos 1981 − ; cons. County of Riverside 1983; mem: Calif. Assn. Local Econ. Devel., Oceanside Econ. Devel. Council (bd. 1982-), O'side CofC, San Marcos CofC (bd. 1982-), Carlsbad CofC (indsl. council 1982-), Escondido CofC (indsl. comml. devel. com. 1982-), Vista CofC (vice chair econ. devel. com. 1983-84), Vista Econ. Devel. Assn., Nat. Job Tng. Partnership, Job Tng. Assn. of San Diego, Am. Mgmt. Assn., Nat. Mgmt. Assn., San Diego Econ. Devel. Corp. Pgm. Planning Com., O'side Republican Women's Club Fed., Calif. Employment & Tng. Adv. Council, Social Svcs. Coord. Council (exec. com. 1982-83), San Diego County Public Welfare Adv. Bd. (chmn. 1981), Casa de Amparo (bd.), S.D. Com. on Handicapped, No. County Community Action Pgm. (bd. 1978), S.D. County Golden Eagle Club, YMCA; publs: articles NASPA News (1980), J. of Nat. Edn. Assn. (1971); Republican (elected official S.D. County Central Com., assoc. mem. Calif. Central Com.). Ofc: IDET Corp. 1125 Linda Vista Dr Ste 101 San Marcos 92069

BURNS, ROBERT DOUGLASS, company executive; b. Mar. 11, 1939, San Diego; s. Robert Vincent and Helen Patricia (McNamara) B.; m. Shirlie, Nov. 12, 1977; children: James b. 1963, John b. 1964. Career: home building constrn. trades in San Marin Co. 1960-63; dispatcher Quarry Products, Richmond 1963-70; traffic mgr. No. California Trucking, Concord 1970-72; owner Grand Lake Sew & Vac Center, Oakland 1972-85; pres. Vacuum Services Inc., 1985 − ; mem. Vacuum Assn. Cooperative Services, Inc. (charter bd. dirs. 1980-, pres. 1981-83), Grand Avenue Merchants Assn./Oakland; club: Bridge Marina Yacht (House com.); mil: airman 3c US Air Force 1956-60; Republican; Presbyterian; rec: boating. Ofc: Vacuum Services Inc. 3250 Grand Avenue Oakland 94610

BURNS, TERENCE NEILON, financial consultant; b. Apr. 8, Duluth, Minn.; s. Stanley J. and Mary E. (Moore) B.; children: Kevin b. 1966, Margaret b. 1970; edn: BA, Coll. of St. Thomas 1959; MBA, Univ. of Minn. 1962. Career: nat. sales mgr. Hyland Lanbs, 1963-70; product mgr. Abbott Labs., 1970-73; ptnr. The Newport Group, 1973-84, mng. ptnr. 1984 − ; mil: sgt. US Army 1960-62; rec: racquetball, spectator sports. REs: 20 Odyssey Court Newport Beach 92660 Ofc: The Newport Group 12961 Cowan Irvine 92714

BURPEE, ANDREW NELSON, chiropractor, health club owner; b. Dec. 29, 1940, Newport, R.I.; s. Walter and Esther Phyllis (Baker) B.; edn: undergrad. Univ. of Buffalo 1956-57, Canadian Meml. Chiropractic Coll. 1958; DC, Los Angeles Coll. of Chiro. 1963; postgrad. Parker Chiro. Research Found. Career: chiropractor assoc. Lowell Cripe, DC, Mar Vista 1966-67; owner/ dir./ dr. of chiropractic Headache, Neck & Back Pain Cliics in Santa Ana, Fullerton, Orange, and Cypress, 1968 − ; owner/dir. Fit for Life Health Club, Cypress 1980 − ; honors: Mr. High School, City Competition (1952, 53), Teen-Age Weight Lifting (1958), winner num. Power Lifting, Odd Lifting and Endurance Contests in Venice Beach (1964, Mr. Muscle Beach (1966), Mr. Western America (166), San Diego Open Contest Chin and Dip Competition (accomplished 49 Chins and 65 Parallel Bar Dips), Holder Venice Beach Record of Strict Curl with Head Back and Butt against the Post (1968), Senior Olympics Power Lifting Champion (1980), Mr. America Over 40 Years (1981); mem: Internat. Chiro. Assn., ICA of Calif., Profl. Chiro. Soc. of Am., Am. Chiro. Assn. (ACA Council on Sports Injuries, ACA Council on Athletics and Phys. Fitness); preceptor faculty L.A. Coll. of Chiro., Parker Chiro. Research Found.; mem Sigma Chi Psi frat. works: physical fitness expert recognized for therapeutic innovations in treatment of skeletal/muscle disorders, and embodies health benefits as an active competitor for over 22 years; rec: bodybuilding, water sports. Address:Headache, Neck & Back Pain Clinics, 1104 West 17th St Santa Ana 92706

BURRHUS, RICHARD WILLIAM, chiropractor; b. May 22, 1949, Los Angeles; s. Victor Eugene (lt. col. US Army, ret.) and Elizabeth (Struve) B.; m. Georgine Wells, Oct. 20, 1973; edn: undergrad. Cerritos Coll. 1968-70, Loma Linda Univ. 1971-72, CSU Fullerton 1972-73; BS, Los Angeles Coll. of Chiropractic 1976, DC, 1977; Calif. lic., Diplomate Nat. Board Chiropractic Examiners. Career: intern, assoc. 1977-80; chiropractor prin. in pvt. practice, Dana Point 1980 − ; cons. Eden Health Found.; honors: Dana Point Civic Assn. award for architectural excellence and landscape design (1986), named Citizen of the Day, Sun-Post News of San Clemente (1985); mem. Am. Chiro. Assn., Calif. Chiro. Assn.; civic: Dana Point CofC (bd. dirs., Ambassador), Rotary, US Lighthouse Soc. (charter); publ: article on spinal function, Windsurf Mag. (1985); mil: E5 US Naval Air Reserve 1968-74. Res: 34095 Crystal Lantern Dana Point 92629 Ofc: Richard W. Burrhus DC Inc. 24721 La Plaza Dana Point 92629

BURRILL, G. STEVEN, accounting firm executive; b. Sept. 15, 1944, Madison, Wis.; s. George T. and Frances L. (Gump) B.; m. Kelli Fitzpatrick, Aug. 28, 1984; children: Jeffrey b. 1969, Peter b. 1971, Thomas b. 1971; edn: stu. Univ. Ariz., Tucson 1962-64; BBA, Univ. Wis., Madison 1966; New College- Berkeley 1984-86; CPA, Calif. Career: staff acct. Arthur Young & Co., San Francisco 1966-70, mgr. 1970-74, prin. 1974-77, ptnr. 1977 − ; lectr. on internat. business, acctg., fin.; seminar leader ednl. pgms. for mgmt. personnel; instr. of graduate pgms. Golden Gate Univ.; chmn. AY's Nat. High Technol. Grp., 1983-; frequent author, lectr., internat. speaker on mgmt./fin. of high tech. cos.; mem: Am. Inst. CPAs, Calif. Soc. CPAs, Am. Electronics Assn., Pan Am. Soc. of S.F.; civic: The Exploratorium (bd.), No.Calif. Rehab. Found. (bd. pres.), Am. Social Health Assn. (pres., dir.); Republican; Pres-

byterian; rec: running, golf, tennis, gardening. Res: 41 Rico Way San Francisco 94123 Ofc: Arthur Young One Sansome St Ste 3500 San Francisco 94104

BURSON, HERCHEL WILLIS, business executive; b. Nov. 29, 1920, Los Angeles; s. Howard Marquis and Audrey (Hayes) B.; m. Martha Almy, Jan. 8, 1944; children: Cathy b. 1945, David b. 1946, Diane b. 1949, Robert b. 1954, Mary Louise b. 1956; edn: BS, UC Los Angeles 1949, Cert. 1971. Career: dist. salesman Union Hardware Metal Co. L.A. 1958-60; regl. salesman Am. Chain & Cable L.A. 1960-63; nat. sales mgr. Sonic Aviation Inglewood 1963-64; dir. mktg. Proto Tool Co. L.A. 1964-71; nat. sales mgr. Thorsen Tool Co. Emeryville 1971-75; pres. HWB Co. Danville 1975 − ; pres. Mr. Sales Assocs. Danville 1982 − ; cons. Bar's Leaks Western 1983 − ; mem: The Westerners Club (pres. 1978), Automotive Boosters Club (pres. 1982), Automotive Affiliated Representatives (pres. 1985), UCLA Alumni (life), Masons (past master), Navy League, Shrine, Greenbrook Townhouse Assn. (pres. 1977-78), Western League Order DeMolay (advisor) 1967-68), Cub Scouts of Am. (sec./treas. W. L.A. 1959-61); mil: cdr. USNR 1942-69, Pacific Theatre; Republican; Protestant; rec: golf. Address: 114 Summerside Cir Danville 94526

BURSTEEN, DAVID BRUCE, marketing executive; b. Sept. 16, 1957, Highland Park, Ill.; s. Jack D. and Annette Vivian (Turen) B.; m. Donna Marie Grider, Jan. 15, 1978; 1 dau: Amanda, b. 1983; edn: AA, L.A. Valley Coll. 1977. Career: past dir. of advtg. Malibu Grand Prix Corp.; v.p. mktg. Phone-In-Drive Thru Markets, Inc., W. Los Angeles; currently v.p. sales Essex Video, Inc., Northridge 1985 − ; cons: Laff Stop 1979-80, Video Vision 1981-82, Infobase 1983-84, USC Food Ind. Pgm. 1983; sem. spkr: Pierce Coll., Students in Advtg. 1981, Promise and Pitfalls of Electronic Shopping 1983; honors: Player of the Year, M.G.P. 1980; honorary citizenship, Louisville, Ky. 1980; mem: L.A. CofC; Chatsworth CofC; Bnai Brith; Gateway Hospital; L.A. Ad Club; rec: skiing, cars, high tech. Res: 22244-5 James Alan Cir., Chatsworth 91311 Ofc: Essex Video, Inc., POB 1055, Northridge 91324

BURSTEIN, SARA LEE, corporate treasurer; b. June 26, 1929, Detroit, Mich.; d. Ben and Rose Elaine (Staman) Cohn; m. King Burstein, June 18, 1961; children: Michael, b. 1962, David, b. 1964. career: court clerk Santa Monica Municipal Ct., 1950-58; exec. secty. Rohm & Haas, Los Angeles 1958-62; treas. Amber Leather Co., Inc., Santa Ana 1965 − ; mem: Silver Circle of Orange Co. (fin. secty.), Orange Co. for Cystic Fibrosis Found., Am. Jewish Com. (Orange County exec. bd.), World Affairs Council, Guild for the Ctr for Perf. Arts (Sound of Music chpt.), Braille Inst. Aux., Las Socias of Orange Co., Friends of the Library Found. (adv. bd. 1986-), Freedoms Found. of Am., Century Investment Club (past pres., corres. sec., finl. sec.), South Coast Repertory Golden Circle Support Gp., PBHA (1st woman elected to bd. dirs.), Balboa Bay Club; Newport Beach Hadassah (past bd. mem.), Temple Bat Yahm, Newport Bch (past v.p.; v.p.Sisterhood 1982); Newport Harbor Republican Women, Bev. Hills Repub. Club, Badham Boosters. Jewish. rec: swim, gourmet food.Res: 651 Bayside Dr Newport Beach 92660 Ofc: Amber Leather Co.Inc. 2850 S Harbor Blvd Santa Ana 92704

BURT, GORDON LANSING, civil engineer; b. July 2, 1913, Minneapolis, Minn.; s. Alva Lawrence and Hattie Theresa (Westburg) B.; m. Winifred Virginia Hall, June 6, 1942; children: Lawrence b. 1946, Allen b. 1952; edn: BSCE, honors, Rose-Hulman Inst. of Tech. 1935; postgrad., Univ. of Wisc. and UC Berkeley; Reg. Civil Engr., Calif. 1948; past registration, Ind., Ore. and Wash. Career: railroad civil engr. 3 yrs.; civil engr. spec. water and waste water; City Mgr., Hayward 1948-49; and City Engr., Portland, Ore.; public health engr., Riverside Co. Health Dept., 1972-83, ret.; instr. civil engr. Rose Hulman Inst. of Tech. 1943-44; honors: Pres. Oregon Technical Council 1959; Founder, Izaak walton League chpt., Seattle, Wash. 1964; mem: Fellow Am. Soc. of Civil Engrs. (life, pres. Ore. sect. 1955), Am. Water Works Assn. (life), Water Pollution Control Fedn. (life, chmn. Safety Com. 1965-70), Diplomate Am. Soc. Environmental Engrs., Riverside High 12 Club, Scottish Rite, Victoria Palms Lodge and Evergreen Lodge (F&AM), York Rite Masonic Bodies, Alpha Tau Omega, Blue Key, Tau Beta Pi; publs: 2 articles on sewage works safety 1968, 1970; mil: capt. US Army MOS- sanitary engr. 1944-47; Episcopal; rec: home movies, carpentry, gardening. Res: 4167 Kingsburg Pl. Riverside 92503

BURTNETT, STEVEN CHARLES, judge; b. July 29, 1942, Hollywood; s. Joseph Mark and Mildred (Walker) B.; m. Judith Jean Lambert, June 29, 1968; 1 son, Steven Christian; edn: BS, Iowa State Univ. 1964, JD, UC Hastings Coll. of the Law 1967; grad. Calif. Center Ind. Edn. and Research, Berkeley 1975; admitted to Calif. State Bar 1967. Career: intern in pub. affairs Coro Found., 1967-68; dep. dist. atty. Los Angeles County, also dep. in chg. juvenile branch Norwalk Superior Ct. 1968-74; commnr., judge pro tem Los Cerritos Municipal Ct., Bellflower 1974 − ; instr. CSU Long Beach, 1972-; field dep. Joe Blatchford for Cong. campaign 1968; mem. steering com. Mike Donaldson for Cong. campaign 1970; chmn. bd. mgrs. Los Cerritos YMCA 1979-82; mem. Speakers Bur., Calif. State Gov. Campaign 1982; mem. Am., Calif., Los Angeles County, S.E. Dist. bar assns., Nat. Dist. Attys. Assn. (LA County del. to nat. conv. 1971), Am. Judicature Soc., Calif. Court Commnrs. Assn., SAR, Sons Union Vets of Civil War, Hastings Alumni Assn. (pres. bd. govs.), Sigma Alpha Epsilon, Phi Delta Phi, Rotary, Commonwealth Club; honors: chief editor Voir Dire, Hastings Coll. Law 1967-8; Republican; Methodist. Res: 16911 Coral Cay Huntington Beach 92649 Ofc:10025 E. Flower St. Bellflower 90706

BURTON, MARY BIGELOW, photographer, tax consultant, electric firm executive; b. Perry, NY; d. Albert E. and Rebecca Ann (Miller) Davis; m.

Richard Harned Bates, 1940 (div. 1947), m. 2d Floyd Burget Bigelow, 1948 (div. 1952); 1 dau. Judith Lynne; m. 3d Rudy Gray Burton, Nov. 17, 1962; edn: Rochester Bus. Inst., Am. Inst. Banking 1938; Woodbury Coll. 1944; UC Los Angeles 1945. Career: var. banking pos. 1936-41; advt., oil bus. 1944-50; secty./ treas. Emerald Bay Community Assn. Laguna Beach 1950-52, Tel-I-Clear Sys. Inc. Laguna Beach 1952-54; owner, oper. Bigelow Bus. Svcs. Laguna Beach 1954–; owner Meri-Bee Originals, co-owner, mgr. Burton Electric Laguna Beach 1963–; staff fin. ofcr. USCG Aux. Div. II; asst. bd. dirs. Three Arch Bay Dist. So. Laguna 1957-73; honors: num. civic awards, Leading Lady in Bus. (Laguna News-Post 1971); mem: Nat. Soc. Public Accts., Inland Soc. Tax Cons. Inc., Soc. Calif. Accts., Dana Point Power Squadron, Girls Club (bd.), World Affairs Council, Laguna Beach CofC, Mermaids (info chmn. Festival of Arts 1966, 67, 68), Cousteau Soc., Nat. League of Am. Penwomen, Lyric Opera and Opera League (Laguna Beach), UC Irvine, Laguna Beach Friends of Library, Joe Thurston Found. (bd. 1957-64), First Nighters; clubs: Altrusa Internat., West Coast Yacht, Dana Pt. Yacht, Riviera, Anchorettes; rec: sailing, power boating, photog., dancing, writing. Address: 697 Catalina St Laguna Beach 92651

BUSBY, LEON RICHARD, airline pilot; b. July 8, 1936, Poplar Bluff, Mo.; s. Lowrie Thathcher and Nondes Dio (Pitman) B.; m. Elaine Palmer, June 14, 1960; children: Ronald b. 1962, Russell b. 1963, Barbara b. 1972; edn: BA, Washington Univ., St. Louis 1958. Career: commnd. ofcr./pilot US Air Force 1960-69, aircraft comdr. B-52, over 100 combat missions SE Asia, safety ofcr.; lt. col. USAF Reserve 1969-, flt. comdr. C-141 1969-76, liaison ofcr. and area athletic coord. for USAF Acad. 1976-; pilot Western Airlines, Los Angeles 1969–; served on two Congl. Review Coms. for selecting candidates for West Point, Annapolis and the AF Academy; mem. CSU Long Beach panel for military studies (1985-); counsel students in 10 local high schs. on ROTC, AF Academy, and flying as a vocation (organized annual presentation by engrs. working in US Space pgms. for H.S. finalists for AFROTC engring. scholarships); honors: Outstanding USAF Reserve Ofcr. in Western US (1985); mil. decorations: Air Medal w/ 4 oakleafs, AF Commendn. w/ oakleaf, AF Achieve. Medal; mem. Airline Pilot Assn. (pres. 1958), Sigma Alpha Epsilon Frat.; civic: Palos Verdes Senior Div. Baseball (bd. mem., v.p. 1976-77), Soccer (commnr. 1985); Republican; Methodist (ch. bd.); rec: skiing, golf, science. Res: 30712 Rue de la Pierre Rancho Palos Verdes 90274

BUSBY, MARVIN L., engineering consultant; b. Aug. 18, 1915, Los Angeles; s. Chester A. and Mollie (Lehman) B.; m. Elizabeth Krug, Jan. 13, 1939; children: Michael b. 1939, Susan b. 1942, Steven b. 1949; edn: BS chem. engring., USC 1937. Career: chem. engr., plant foreman, dist. supt. Union Oil Co., var. locations Calif. 1936-48; self-empl. cons., independent oil opr., 1948-57; design engr./div. mgr. Rheem Mfg. Co., var. locations Calif., 1957-63; chem. engr., mgr. of engring., dir. of engring. Swedlow, Inc. Garden Grove 1964-78, ret.; engring. cons. prin., Anaheim 1978–; v.p./dir. Vacuum-Press Internat. 1983-85; faculty USC 1940-42; honors: Tau Beta Pi (1947), Orange County Plant Engineer of the Year (1974-75), "Mr. Industry" nat. award (1973); mem: Am. Inst. Plant Engrs. (Orange Co. pres. 1971-73), Am. Inst. Chem. Engrs. (O.C. senior counselor 1985); civic: coached Little League Baseball (7 yr) and Pop Warner Football (5 yr), mem. Anaheim CofC, Trojan Football Alumni Club, Hon. Order Kentucky Colonels; works: 2 US patents: Deep Well Casing Pump (1945), Gear Oil Filtration System (1950); Republican; rec: golf. Res: 320 W Brookdale Pl Fullerton 92632 Ofc: Busby Engineering Consultants 408 S Beach Blvd Ste 208 Anaheim 92804

BUSCH, ERNEST LELAND, insurance agent; b. Nov. 26, 1922, Sacramento; s. Henry and Martha (Kamamerer) B.; m. Jeane Davis, April 15, 1945; children: Larre' b. 1946, Jeffrey b. 1953; edn: Univ. of San Francisco 1942; Coll. of the Pacific 1943; BA, USC 1948, MS, 1949; adv. agency mgmt., Stanford Univ. 1958. Career: center, USC Football 1946-47; football coach Merced H.S. 1948-51, Chico State 1952-53; ins. mgr. Artz- Cook, Sacramento 1954-62; currently, chmn. bd. Ernie Busch Ins. Associates; honors: Coach of the Year, Merced H.S. 1949-1950; Coach of the Year, Chico State 1953; Distng. Award, US Jr. CofC 1950; mem: Western Assn. of Ins. Brokers; publs: Policies Holders Right to Know, Underwriters Ins. Report; mil: 1st lt. USMC 1943-46; Republican; rec: golf, hunting. Res: 3104 Calle Verde Ct. Sacramento 95821 Ofc: EBIA, 865 Howe Ave. Ste. 310 Sacramento 95825

BUSCH, PETER JONATHAN, lawyer; b. June 24, 1952, Evanston, Ill.; s. Albert Eliot and Vera (Ellman) B.; m. Catharine S. Barnes, June 6, 1982; 1 son, Frank b. 1983; edn: BA magna cum laude, Yale Coll. 1974; JD, Univ. Va. 1977; admitted to Calif. State Bar (1981), US Ct. of Appeals (9th Cir.), US Dist. Ct. (No. Dist. Calif.). Career: law clk. to Chief Judge Frank M. Coffin, US Ct. of Appeals for the First Circuit, 1977-79; law clk. to Justice William J. Brennan, US Supreme Ct., 1979-80; atty., dir. Howard, Rice, Nemerovski, Canady, Robertson & Falk, APC, San Francisco 1980–; mem. Bar Assn. of San Francisco, Calif. Bar Assn., Am. Bar Assn. (Sects. of Litigation and Urban, State & Local Govt. Law). Ofc: Howard, Rice, Nemerovski, Canady, Robertson & Falk, APC, Three Embarcadero Ctr 7th Flr San Francisco 94111

BUSH, ELMER W., corporate president; b. Nov. 26, 1923, Sacramento; s. Charles J. and Alice Ellen (Pitiman) B.; m. Felomena T. Cimaroli, Nov. 26, 1973; 1 son: Michael M. b. 1959; edn: Master Engr. Aircraft, Dallas Aircraft Engring. Coll. 1943; Mastr Engr. Internal Combustion Engines, Chevrolet Motor Div. 1943; Technical Splst. Turbo Superchargers, Honeywell 1944; Splst. Aircraft Hydraulics, Army Air Force Sch. of Hydraulics 1944; Splst. Hydramatic Props. & Controls, Hamilton Standards Propeller Div. 1944; Master Mech. Engr., US Army Air Force 1944. Career: welding inspector Kaiser Shipbldrs., Richmond 1940-42; master air craft engr. US Army Air Force; founder, pres., chief chemist Pal-Pen Chemical Corp. 1950–; pres., exec. engr. Condensator Inc. 1975–; inventor: dry cleaning chemicals; patent, Pal-Gun, for spotting garments; patent, condensator supplementary carburetor; farm machinery; mil: m/sgt. US Army Air Force 1943-46, (2) Pres. Unit Citations, 9 Battle Stars, European Theatre, WWII; Catholic; rec: boating, water skiing, skin diving. Address: 2010 Trimble Way Sacramento 95825

BUSH, JOHN ANDREW, computer service conglomerate executive; b. Aug. 26, 1956, Dayton, Ohio; s. George Archer and Ruth Lillah (Sturdevant) B.; edn: AA, Long Beach City Coll. 1980; AS cand., Mt. San Antonio Coll. Career: supvr. customer svc., lead electronics techn. PerSci Inc., Los Angeles 1981-82; field engr. (computer based office automation equip.) C.P.T. Corp., 1981; founder/owner/CEO P.P.S. (statewide computer svc. co.) 1981–, Peripheral Labs, and MCM Systems, hdqtrs. Diamond Bar 1981–, clients incl. Beckman Instruments, USN, Johns Hopkins Hosp., and TRW; tech. cons. MCM Ents. (Palo Alto), CTC (Bev. Hills), Powerine Oil Co. (Santa Fe Springs); mem. Internat. Assn. of Cromemco Users (1981-), Cromemcohorts (1982-); works: conceptual design, mktg., and mfr. sev. computer support products incl. "PCPU" multi-processor and "Frame Analyzer" system analyzer testing equip.; mil: p.o. 2/c US Navy, splst. in Top Secret cryptographic electronics support, 1974-80; Republican (Local precinct election ofcl.; trustee Repub. Pres. Task Force); Lutheran; rec: ski, recreational shooting, camping. Res: 547 S Great Bend Dr Diamond Bar 91765

BUSHMAN, JANINE MARIE, accountant; b. Jan. 20, 1954, Santa Monica; s. Garry Jr. and Janice Marie (Gregory) B.; edn: BS, CSU Northridge 1975; MBA, Loyola Marymount Univ. 1983; CPA, Calif. 1977. Career: acct., senior acct. Laventhol & Horwath CPAs 1975-79; asst. mgr. internal audit Monogram Industries 1979-80, senior financial analyst 1980-81; mgr. financial reporting Xerox Computer Svcs. 1981-83, mgr. of acctg. 1983-84, mgr. financial plnng. 1984–; mem: Am. Inst. CPAs, Calif. Soc. CPAs; Republican; Protestant; rec: travel. Ofc: Xerox Computer Services, 5310 Beethoven St. Los Angeles 90066

BUSTEED, BEATRICE, financial planner, trust administrator; b. Jan. 8, 1938, Los Angeles; d. Ignacio Peter and Clemencia (Armijo) Val Verde; m. Donald J. Busteed, Jan. 23, 1982; edn: AA, Trade Tech. Jr. Coll. 1957; BA, English, CSU Los Angeles 1974; MBA bus. adm., Pepperdine Univ. 1983; desig: CFP (in progress). Career: secty. Pacific Fin. (Transam.), Los Angeles 1957-61, Western Precipitation (Joy Mfg.), L.A. 1961-62, E.S. Dulin individual 1962-71, Neil Petree individual 1968-73, John O'Melveny individual 1974-84; probate paralegal O'Melveny & Myers law firm, L.A. 1973-86; bus. mgr. Alice O'Melveny individual 1980-, reg. rep. Financial Network Invest. Corp., L.A. 1984-, trust adminstr. John O'Melveny Trust 1986-; indep. bus. mgr. and trust adminstr., 1986–; honors: Rockwell Internat. Graduate Fellow, Pepperdine Univ. (1982), Phi Kappa Phi (1974); mem. Internat. Assn. for Finl. Plnng., Town Hall of Calif., Mensa (bd. Greater L.A. Area 1975-78); Republican; Catholic. Res: 5530 Thornburn St #204 Los Angeles 90045 Ofc: 3701 Wilshire Blvd Ste 700 Los Angeles 90010

BUTLER, JOHN CARLETON, lawyer, broadcaster; b. April 24, 1954, Woodland; s. Thomas Adney and Janet Carolyn (Anderson) B.; edn: BA, Loyola Univ. Los Angeles 1975; JD, Loyola Law Sch. 1980; admitted to Calif. Bar 1980. Career: news correspondent KHJ Radio, Los Angeles 1976-78; news correspondent KIIS Radio, Los Angeles 1979; news and public affairs dir. KROY Radio, Sacramento 1980; correspondent and morning anchor ABC Radio News, NY 1981–; recipient, Ohio State Univ. Journalism Award for ABC news series, Crime in America, 1984; mem: Am. and Calif. Bar Assns., No. Calif. Radio- Television News Dirs. Assn., Calif. Associated Press TV-Radio Assn. (dir. 1980); Episcopal. Res: P.O. Box 356 Robbins 95676 and 267 Mountain Rd Pleasantville, NY 10570 Ofc: ABC News/ Radio, 125 West End Ave., New York, NY 10023

BUTLER, MORSE RODNEY, public accountant; b. June 7, 1914, Salt Lake City; s. George H. and Catherine (Johnson) B.; m. Miriam, Dec. 24, 1938; children: Beverly James b. 1940, Kay Gabbert b. 1942; edn: BS, Univ. of Calif. 1936, General Sec. Tchg. Credential 1937. Career: tchr. San Luis Obispo Jr. High Sch. 1937-41; hd. Business Dept., San Luis Obispo Jr. Coll. 1941-44; ptnr. Hall & Butler, Tax Consultants 1948-50; owner Morse R. Butler Public Acct. 1951-69; ptnr. Butler & Bourdon, Public Accts. 1969-80; public acct./pres. Morse R. Butler Inc. 1981–; honors: Luther Gulich Award, Campfire Girls; mem: Soc. of Calif. Accts. (past state pres.), Nat. Soc. of Public Accts., Nat./ Calif. Soc. of Enrolled Agents; clubs: Rotary (past pres. S.L.O.), Shrine (treas. S.L.O.), Masons (past master King David's Lodge); Republican; Presbyterian; rec: travel. Res: 1394 Andrews St San Luis Obispo 93401

BUTTERWORTH, RICHARD SYDNEY, real estate co. executive; b. Apr. 4 1943, Pasadena, Calif.; s. Frederick Sydney and Helen (Bettcher) B.; m. Melinda Waring, May 10, 1980; children: David Richard b. 1981; BS, Univ. Wyoming 1969. Career: sales mgr. Rockwell Internat. computer div. Anaheim 1972-77; investment, retail & ofc. mktg. splst. Grubb & Ellis Comml. Brokerage Co. Newport Beach 1977-81; v.p. acquisitions, dispositions and investment advisory svcs. Landauer Assocs. Inc. Santa Ana 1981-82; owner First Nat. Properties Irvine 1982-83; real estate cons. 1983-85; owner Industrial. Comml. Consultants 1985–; honors: Broker of the Year (Rancho California 1985); mem: Toastmasters, Econ. Devel. Council; mil: USAR tng. 1963; Republican; non-denominational; rec: golf, tennis, skiing, swimming. Res: 1312 Joy Rd Fallbrook 92028 Ofc: Industrial/Commercial Consultants 27393 Ynez Ste 252 Rancho California 92390

BUTTS, EDMUND STANLEY, physician; b. Mar. 30, 1936, NY, NY; s. Edward S. and Ruby E. (Phipps) B.; m. Diana J., Sept. 21, 1963; children: Edmund b. 1964, Melanie b. 1967, Kyle b. 1971; edn: BS, City Coll. of NY 1957; MD, Meharry Med. Coll. 1961. Career: residency tng. Internal Med., Hematology and Nephrology, SUNY 1961-66; cons. Kidney Branch USPHS, chief Dialysis Section Kidney Disease Control Pgm. 1966-68; dir. Regional Hemodialysis Center Kaiser Permanente, L.A. 1968-85, asst. area medical director 1984-85, chief Dept. Internal Medicine So. Calif. Permanente Med. Group, L.A. Medical Center 1985—; honors: Outstanding Board mem. Crenshaw YMCA 1981; v.p. Network Coordinating Council Area IV; cons. Medical Devices Panel, FDA; club: 100 Black Men; mil: lt.cmdr. USPHS; rec: photog., golf, tennis, travel. Res: Los Angeles Ofc: Kaiser-Permanente Med. Group 4950 Sunset Blvd Los Angeles 90027

BUU, HIEP, civil engineer; b. Oct. 23, 1926, Hue, Viet Nam; s. Hao and Luu Thi (Nguyen) Ung; m. Dong Thi Doan, July 27, 1954; children: Doan Huan b. 1955, Doan Nhan b. 1957, Ngoc Ha b. 1959, Han Doan b. 1959, Doan Tan b. 1962, Doan An b. 1962; edn: BS, Saigon Univ. 1954; profl. engr. (civil) 1978. Career: chief of public works, var. provinces, Central and South Viet Nam 1954-66; dir. Saigon City Public Works 1967-71; dep. mayor tech. br., Saigon 1972-75; civil engr., Sacramento Co. Dept. of Public Works 1975-85; currently proj. engr.; chmn. devel. com. Saigon 9th Dist. coop., Lyons Assocs. Co. 1970-72; chmn. reconstrn. com. Saigon City Streets coop., R.M.K. and USAID 1971-73; adv. bd. Saigon Water Direction 1968-75; adv. bd. Saigon Electricity Direction 1970-75; honors: 9 medals, Public Works, Soc. Works, Edn., Reconstrn., and Heroic medals, Govt. of Viet Nam 1954-75; Medal of Honor, Pres. of Repub. of Viet Nam 1971; Medal of Honor, Pres. of Repub. of Korea 1972; honors, State Dept. of Transportation of Indiana, Fla. 1959, La., Ala., Ark. 1973; mem: Am. Mil. Engrs.; Profl. Engrs. Assn.; Profl. Engrs. Assn. of Sacramento Co.; Vietnamese Community Assn. of Sacramento (adv. bd.); works: City Street maintenance 1967; Manpower in underdeveloped countries in Public Works projects 1968; Republican; Buddhist; rec: tennis, music, photog. Res: 3350 Routier Rd. Sacramento 95827 Ofc: Sacramento County, 827 7th St. Sacramento 95814

BYKOWSKI, RONALD FRANCES, real estate franchise executive; b. oct. 3, 1943, Burwyn, Ill.; s. Andrew Alexander and Cahterine Anne (Sovidzal) B.; m. Linda, Feb. 6, 1982; children: Kenneth b. 1967, Christopher b. 1970, Janie b. 1971, Sean b. 1975; edn: BS in aero. engring., CSU San Jose 1966, MS cybernetic systems, 1971; LLB, La Salle Univ. Ext. 1974; desig: Calif. R.E. Broker lic., Ins. lic.; NASD reg. rep., Calif., Nev.; Calif. Comm. Coll. Life tchg. creds. 1976. Career: engr./ asst. pgm. mgr. Sentinel Missile Pgm., Philco-Ford, Palo Alto 1968-69; product mgr. System Engring., SCM Corp., Palo Alto 1969-71; communication and info. systems cons. Public Systems, Inc., Sunnyvale 1971-72; exec. dir. Calif. Council on Criminal Justice, Region M., Monterey 1972-77; real estate assoc., gen. sales mgr. Century 21 Loomis and Powers Realtors Inc., Salinas 1977-79; sales and mgmt. devel. tng. Century 21, 1980-83, dir. inv. svcs. Century 21 Real Estate, Insurance and Securities pgm. 1983-84; exec. dir. Century 21 Real Estate of No. Calif., Inc., Walnut Creek 1984—, dir. franchise sales, ins., ofc. automation, and securities sales; awards, Century 21: Million Dollar Prod. (1977), Achievement in R.E. Mgmt. (1978), Franchise Sales (1985); mem. Contra Costa Co. Board Realtors, Nat. Assn. Securities Dealers, Calif. Real Estate Flyers (vice air marshal), Aircraft Owners and Pilots Assn.; civic: Monterey Co. Unified Sch. Dist. (chmn. bd. dirs. 1975); author textbook: A Decision Assisting Mgmt. Information System for the Evaluation of Alternatives (Stanford Univ. Press 1971); Criminal Justice Planning: A Practical Approach (Justice Systems Devel. Inc. 1976); mil: 1st lt. US Army Signal Corps; Republican; Catholic; rec: pvt. pilot, tennis. Res: 1157 Fair Weather Circle Concord 94518 Ofc: Century 21 Real Estate of No Calif. Inc. 1777 N California Blvd Ste 300 Walnut Creek 94596

BYLAND, SAMUEL SMALLWOOD, ophthalmologist; b. Mar. 30, 1934, St. Louis, Mo.; s. Samuel James and Dorcas Elizabeth (Gallaher) B.; m. Maria Meisering, Jan. 30, 1965 (div. 1984), m. 2nd Barbara Garland-Frazier, Dec. 15, 1985; children: Samuel Henry b. 1965, Robert James b. 1968; edn: BA (drama major), Washington Univ. St. Louis 1956; MD, Univ. of Mo. Columbia 1960; Diplomate Am. Bd. of Ophthalmology 1968; Fellow Am. Acad. of Ophthalmology 1969. Career: pvt. practice ophthalmology, 1967—; mem: AMA, CMA, Alameda-Contra Costa Med. Assn., No. Calif. Soc. To Prevent Blindness (bd. dirs. 1973-), East Bay Ophthalmologist Soc. (secty. 1978-80), Veterans of Fgn. Wars; mil: capt. US Army 1965-67, Vietnam Service; rec: scuba, skiing, river rafting, travel, comparative philosophy, music, songwriting. Res: 815 Juanita Dr Walnut Creek 94595 Ofc: 1808 San Miguel Dr Walnut Creek 94596

BYRNE, NOEL THOMAS, sociologist, educator; b. May 11, 1943, San Francisco; s. Joseph Joshua and Naomi Pearl (Denison) B.; 1 dau. Ginger Melyn b. 1966; edn: BA in sociol., CSU Sonoma 1971; MA in sociol., Rutgers Univ. 1975, PhD cand. 1986. Career: instr. sociol., Douglass Coll., Rutgers Univ., 1974-76, Hartnell Coll. 1977-78; lectr. sociol. and mgmt., CSU Sonoma Sch. Bus. and Econs., 1978—; review ed. Symbolic Interaction (1980-83), research dir. CSUS Mgmt. Grad. Survey Projects (1983-86); awards: Dell Publishing Award, grad. sociol., Rutgers Univ. (1976-77), Louis Bevier Fellow (1977-78); mem. Am. Sociol. Assn., Soc. for the Study of Social Problems, Soc. for the Study of Symbolic Interaction, AAAS, Pacific Sociol. Assn.; contbr. num. articles and reviews in profl. jours., presentations profl. confs.; Democrat; rec: photog., collector sequential art (splst. Carl Barks). Res: 330 W Sierra Ave Cotati 94928 Ofc: Mgt Dept School of Business & Economics Sonoma State Univ. Rohnert Park 94928

BYRNE, THOMAS FREDERICK, lawyer; b. May 28, 1946, Faribault, Minn.; s. Vincent Joseph and Evelyn Cecelia (Zimmerman) B.; m. Susane, June 20, 1969; children: Kevin b. 1972, Ryan b. 1978; edn: BA, Coll. of St. Thomas 1968; JD, Univ. of the Pacific 1976; admitted to state bars of Minn. 1976, Calif. 1978 and Florida 1978. Career: pilot US Air Force, Wurtsmith AFB, Mich. 1969-73; assoc. atty. Doherty, Rumble & Butler, St. Paul, Minn. 1976-78; division counsel Honeywell, Inc. Avionics Div., St. Petersburg, Fla. 1978-80; assoc. atty. Spridgen, Barrett, Achor, Luckhardt, Anderson, James & Ziegler, Santa Rosa, Calif. 1980-82; ptnr. Babin, Seeger & Byrne, Santa Rosa 1983—; Air Force Acad. (USAFR) liaison officer for Sonoma County; mem: ABA, Calif., Minn. & Fla. State Bar Assns., Assn. of No. Calif. Defense Counsel; civic: Annadel Soccer Club (B Team coach), Boy Scouts Am. (cub scoutmaster), YMCA (campaign com. 1985); mil: major USAF, active duty 1968-73, two Air Medals with OLCs; Republican; Catholic; rec: tri-athalon competition (USTS 1985), comml. pilot lic. Res: 430 Yulupa Ave Santa Rosa 95405 Ofc: Babin, Seeger & Byrne 209 8th St Santa Rosa 95405

BYRNE-HERNANDEZ, MARY PATRICIA, real estate broker-appraiser; b. Feb. 24, 1952, Toronto, Can., nat. US cit. 1957; d. George Christopher and Josephine B. (Thompson) Byrne; m. Charles Hernandez, Feb. 28, 1981; 1 son, Charles George b. 1983; edn: AA, honors Foothill Coll. 1972; BA in econs., honors, UC Santa Cruz 1974; MBA in finl. plnng., Golden Gate Univ. 1986; desig: AACA, cert. appraiser (1983). Career:dept. mgr. Sears Roebuck & Co., 1970-78; dir./v.p. relocation svcs. Van Vleck Realtors, 1978-83; owner/broker/ indep. fee appraiser MBH Properties and Appraisal, Fremont 1983—; bd. dirs. San Jose Day Nursery (1982-83); awards: Dale Carnegie Award (1980), Million Dollar Award (1979, 83, 84); mem. Employee Relocation Council (speaker ERC Spring Confs. 1982, 85, 86), AAUW, Assn. of Leading Ladies; publ: Intro. to Relocation Manual on devel. a relocation real estate dept., ERC; Republican; Roman Catholic; rec: cooking, gardening. Ofc: MBH Properties 60 Espada Ct Fremont 94539

BYRON, RALPH LOUIS, cancer surgeon; b. Feb. 22, 1914, Los Angeles; s. Ralph Louis and Semone Pearl (Ruch) B.; m. Dorothy A. DeMott, Jan. 3, 1941; children: Joanne (Northrup) b. 1943, Roderick b. 1947, Jonathan b. 1953, Richard b. 1958; edn: BA in chem. UC Los Angeles 1935; MD, UC San Francisco Medical Sch. 1940. Career: resident in surgery UC Med. Sch. 1941-48; surgical unit with US Marines in Pacific 1944-46; asst. dir. Cancer Research Inst. Univ. Calif. 1948-52; pvt. practice surgery, San Francisco 1952-55; chief of surg. City of Hope Medical Center 1955-79; chief of cancer surgery City of Faith 1981-83; surgeon Arcadia Surgical Group, 1985—; clin. prof. surgery UC Irvine, Loma Linda Med. Sch., Oral Roberts Med. Sch.; honors: Mathematics, Chemistry, Medicine; mem. AMA, Am. Coll. of Surgeons; author: Surgeon of Hope; contbr. monthly article Power mag.; 77 sci. publs.; mil: lt. USNR; Republican; Protestant; avo: tch. Bible classes. Res: 1147 San Marino Ave San Marino 91108 Ofc: Arcadia Surgical Gp 65 N First Ave Arcadia 91006

CAESAR, HUGO VICTOR, orthopaedic surgeon; b. May 24, 1939, Trinidad; m. Donna; children: Camille, Carmia, Claire, Michael, Gregory, Kristin; edn: BS, Howard Univ. 1964, MD, 1968; UC Los Angeles; intern Maimonides Hosp., 1968-69; resident Howard Univ. 1969-73; diplomate Am. Bd. of Orthopaedic Surgery 1974. Career: pvt. practice orthopaedic surgery, Inglewood, Calif. 1974—; mem., supporter Howard, UCLA alumni. Ofc: Hugo V. Caesar, MD Inc. 336 E Hillcrest Blvd, Ste 510, Inglewood 90301

CAESAR, VANCE ROY, newspaper executive; b. Dec. 22, 1944, New Kensington, Pa.; s. Jack and Norma N. (Wiles) C.; m. Carol Ann, Apr. 22, 1967; 1 son, Eric Caesar b. 1971; edn: BS, The Citadel; MBA, Fla. Atlantic Univ.; grad. Stanford Exec. Pgm. Career: (past) assoc. ed. Detroit Free Press; dir. consumer mktg., dir. prodn., and adminstrn., asst. to exec. v.p. Detroit Free Press; (current) senior v.p./gen. mgr. Press-Telegram, Long Beach 1978—; mem. Am. Newspaper Publishers Assn. (chmn. Readership and Circulation Task Force); mem. The Executive Com.; civic: United Way (bd. Region III), Long Beach CofC (pres. Marketing Council), Memorial Medical Ctr. (trustee), Am. Cancer Soc. (L.B.), Long Beach City Coll. Found., CSU Business Round Table (past chmn.), Corporate Council of the Arts, Rotary; mil: AF Reserves; Republican; rec: mountaineering, skiing, gardening. Res: 4357 Dogwood Ave Seal Beach 90740 Ofc: Press-Telegram 604 Pine Ave Long Beach 90844

CAILLOUETTE, JAMES C., physician; b. June 2, 1927, Los Angeles; m. Joanne Thompson, Dec. 17, 1950; children: Laure b. 1955, James b. 1957, Anne b. 1959; edn: AB, Coll. of Puget Sound 1950; MD, Univ. Wash. Sch. of Med. 1954; Diplomate Am. Bd. Ob-Gyn 1962. Career: intern Los Angeles Co. Gen. Hosp. 1954-56, resident ob-gyn 1956-59, attg. staff 1959—; provisional staff Huntington Meml. Hosp. Pasadena 1959-61, assoc. 1961-67, active 1967—; courtesy staff St. Luke's Hosp. Pasadena 1959, gyn. surg. privileges 1959, assoc. 1961-69; instr. USC Sch. of Med. 1959-64, asst. clin. prof. 1964-69, assoc. clin. prof. 1969-78, cl prof. ob-gyn 1978—; dir. Aquatain Co.; ptnr. Cotton Med. Ctr. Ltd., Silverbow Farm Partnership; bd. dirs. CalTech 1983-; trustee Polytechnic Sch. Pasadena 1969-79; honors: Phi Sigma, Alpha Omega Alpha, Norman W. Clein Award and Thesis Honors (UW Sch. of Med. 1954); fellow: Am. Coll. Obstets. & Gynecol. 1962, Am. Coll. Surg. 1971; mem: AMA, CMA (asst. secty. ob-gyn sect. 1968-69, secty 1969-70, chmn. 1970-71), NY Acad. Scis., Assn. Profs. of Gyn. & Obstets., Pacific Coast Ob-Gyn Soc. (pgm. chmn. 1969, asst. secty. historian 1979-81, ed. transactions 1979-82), Pasadena Med. Soc., LACMA, Pasadena Physicians United Crusade (chmn. bd. 1961-63), Salerni Collegium (USC Sch. of Med.), L.A. Ob-Gyn

Soc. (sr. counselor 1972-74, secty./treas. 1975-76, v.p. 1976-77, pres. 1977-78), March of Dimes, Oak Knoll Property owners Assn. (v.p. 1965-75), Scripps Home (bd.), Music Ctr. for Performing Arts (founder), Soc. of Fellows of Huntington Library, Sigma Chi, Nu Sigma Nu; clubs: Univ. (Pasadena), Valley Hunt (bd. 1980-86, v.p. 1983-84, pres. 1984-85), Calif., The Athenaeum (Caltech); publs: 20+ articles in med. jours.; 3 patents granted; major areas of research: septic shock, clotting defects (pregnancy), obstet. anesthesia, human behavior, hypo-immune state in pregnancy; mil: active duty USNR 1945-46. Address: 50 Bellefontaine St Pasadena 91105

CAIN, PATRICIA JEAN, certified public accountant; b. Sept. 28, 1931, Decatur, Ill.; d. Paul George and Jean Margaret (Horne) Jacka; m. Dan L. Cain, July 12, 1952; children: Mary Ann, b. 1963; Timothy, b. 1965; Paul, b. 1967; edn: Univ. of Mich. 1949-52; Pasadena City Coll. 1975-76; BS, CSU Los Angeles 1977; MBA, 1978; CPA, Calif. 1981. Career: CPA/tax supr. Stonefield & Josephson Accty. Corp., Los Angeles 1979—; part time lecr. CSU, Los Angeles 1983; honors: Thanks Badge, Highland Rim Girl Scout Council, Oakridge, Tenn. 1959; Thanks Badge, Sierra Madres Girl Scout Council, Pasadena; Nat. Delegate, Girl Scouts 1975; mem: AICPA; Calif. Soc. CPAs (Calif. State Profl. Conduct Com., Taxation Com., Microcomputers Users Discussion Gp.); AWSCPA; Beta Alpha Psi; Girl Scouts of USA; Million Belles Investment Club; Wrightwood CofC; Democrat; Episcopal; rec: fishing, skiing, rug making. Res: 3715 Fairmeade Rd Pasadena 91107 Ofc: Stonefield & Josephson, 3731 Wilshire Blvd, Ste 800, Los Angeles 90010

CAIN, RICHARD WILSON, clergyman, professor; b. Feb. 26, 1926, Mailon, Okla.; s. Lloyd D., Jr. and Zelma Mae (Leddy) C.; edn: AB, USC 1949; STB, Boston Univ. 1952, STM, 1953; DD, Univ. of Pacific 1963; ordained United Methodist Ch. 1952. Career: minister Silverado United Methodist Ch. 1954-58, Monterey Park UMC 1958-62, dist. supt.-Los Angeles 1962-68, minister First UMC of Phoenix 1968-77; pres. Sch. of Theology at Claremont, 1977—; mem. University Club; mil: US Air Force; Republican. Res: 970 West 22nd Upland 91786 Ofc: School of Theology 1325 N College Ave Claremont 91711

CALAFIURA, MARIE BERNADETTE, certified public accountant; b. Feb. 20, 1946, Cleveland, Ohio; d. Basilio Charles and Josephine S. (Ingrassia) Calafiura; edn: BS in edn., Bowling Green State Univ., 1968; grad. work, CSU Fullerton 1976-78, Golden Gate Univ. 1981, Salisbury State Coll. 1986. Career: basic business education tchr. Bedford (Ohio) City Schs. 1968-70; bookkeeper, tax verification, Diehl Evans & Co., Santa Ana, Calif. 1970-73; bkkpr., staff acct. Simonis, Moreland Accountants Inc., Newport Beach 1973-80; staff acct. C.L. Young CPA, Costa Mesa 1980; audit/acctg. cons. Lok Products Co., Fullerton 1981, asst. to V.P. to Finance, Internal Control auditor, tax adminstrn., 1982; controller Gen. Flex Corp., Fresno 1983-84; controller Grumman Energy Systems Co., Corcoran 1984-85, dir. of fin. Electronics System Div. Grumman Corp., Salisbury, Md. Site, Salisbury, Md. 1985—; honors: Phi Beta Lambda, 1968; mem: Calif. Soc. of CPAs 1981-, Nat. Accts. Assn. 1981-, Fresno CofC 1983-85 (Small Bus. Affairs Com.), Calif. Small Business Conf. 1984-85; past mem. var. teacher assns.; Aida Chpt. Orange County Music Center (steering com. 1980-1, recording secty. 1981-2); Beta Sigma Phi 1975- (Council pres. 1982-3); Republican; Catholic; rec: reading, community events, crocheting, theater. Res: Starbridge Dr. (POB 2076) Salisbury Md. 21801

CALDWELL, WILLIAM MACKAY, IV, international manufacturing executive; b. July 23, 1947, Boston, Mass.; s. William Mackay III and Mary Louise (Edwards) C.; m. Kathleen Fogwell, Mar. 19, 1977; children: William Mackay V, b. 1979; Blake Harrison, b. 1982; Tyler Robert, b. 1984; edn: BA, USC 1969; grad. study, Christ Coll., Cambridge, Eng. 1970; MBA, Wharton Sch. 1973; Multi National Enterprise Fellow, Wharton Sch. 1972. Career: mktg. admstr. Sepulveda Properties, Inc., Standard Oil of Calif.; sr. assoc. Booz, Allen & Hamilton; v.p. mktg. Flying Tiger Line; sr. v.p. fin. & admin. Van Vorst Industries 1980-83, pres. 1983—; also CEO, Union Jack Gp., Inc.; dir: Southern Cross Inds., KYCO, Inc., Englander Co.; mem: Newcomen Soc., Town Hall, Foreign Trade Assn., Calif. Club, Bel Air Club, Jonathan Club; Presbyterian. Res: Marina del Rey Ofc: Van Vorst Industries, P.O. Box 927, Pasadena 91102

CALHOUN, ROBERT MILTON, real estate developer; b. Nov. 25, 1918, Bakersfield; s. David and Miriam (Kamp) C.; m. Elaine Dupont, Nov. 20, 1971; children: Heather b. 1973, Colleen b. 1961; edn: Bach., UCMA 1950; PhD, hon., Los Angeles Univ. Arts & Scis. Career: real estate developer and investor, Beverly Hills 1946—; prin. Calhoun Properties, Beverly Hills; mem: Am. Soc. of Profl. Cons., Nat. Assn. of Fin. Cons., Beverly Hills Tennis Club, The Cellar Club, Beverly Hills Health Club, Rotary; author: The Power Profane, Fawcett Publs. 1979; mil: USN 1942-45; Republican; Protestant; rec: tennis, swimming. Res: 818 No. Doheny Dr. Los Angeles 90069 Ofc: Calhoun Properties, 9701 Wilshire Blvd. Beverly Hills 90212

CAMANGA, LYDIA URGENA, physician; b. Mar. 27, 1927, Majayjay, Laguna, Philippines; d. Adriano Ganjoco Urgena and Teofila Macula Brioso; m. Perfecto Camanga, May 2, 1955; children: Marissa b. 1956, Necitas b. 1960, Perfecto, Jr. b. 1961, Rumela b. 1963, Tristan b. 1967; edn: AA, Centro Escolar Univ. 1947; MD, Univ. Santo Tomas 1952. Career: intern Pangasinan Prov. Hosp. Dagupan City, Phil. 1952-53; resident Zambales Prov. Hosp. Iba, Zambales, Phil. 1953-55; sch. phys. St. Joseph Inst. Candon, Ilocos, Sur, Phil. 1956; pvt. practice Candon, San Mateo Isabella, Quezon City, Phil. 1956-62; res. phys. Bulacan Prov. Hosp. Malolos, Bulacan, Phil. 1962-69, phys. in charge 1969-70; res. phys. San Pablo City Hosp. Phil. 1970-73; g.p. res. phys. Grant Hosp. of Chgo. 1976-78; housestaff phys. Martha Washington Hosp. Chgo. 1978-81; med. dir. Porterville Family Health Ctr., Calif. 1981-84, Family Walk-

In Med. Ctr. Fresno 1985—; gen. sci. instr. Dasol Acad. 1950, biol. instr. Bay View H.S. 1951; mem: several Philippine med. socs. and assns., Am. Coll. Gen. Prac., Am. Med. Women's Assn., Tulare Med. Soc., Calif. Med. Soc., AMA, Fresno-Madera Med. Soc., Legion of Mary, Filipino-Am. Assn. of Fresno & vicin., Holy Family Guild; Catholic; rec: reading, piano, music, movies. Res: 113 W Wrenwood Fresno 93704 Ofc: Family Walk-In Med. Ctr. 4440 N First, Ste 111, Fresno 93726 and 2770 W Shaw Fresno 93711

CAMORONGAN, MARIO CARIDA, engineer; b. Mar. 2, 1956, Pangasinan, Philippines; s. Marciano Calimlim and Genoveva Siguin (Carida) C.; m. Severina Dimalanta, Mar. 26, 1978; children: Melissa b. 1978, Marlene b. 1982; edn: BSCE, Univ. Pagasinan 1976; Reg. Civil Engr. Calif. 1983, Philippines 1977, Wash. 1984. Career: constrn. engr. Nat. Irrigation Adminstrn. Philippines 1976-80; design engr. TDK and Assoc. Concord, Calif. 1980-81; proj. engr. Santina & Thompson engrs. Concord 1981-84, James R. Stedman & Assoc. Walnut Creek 1984—; mem: Am. Soc. Civil Engrs. 1982-, Filipino-Am. Soc. of Archs. & Engrs., Diablo Valley Filipino Am. League; rec: fishing, bowling. Res: 2933 Honeysuckle Ct Antioch 94509 Ofc: J.R. Stedman & Assoc. 365 Lennon Ln, Ste 100, Walnut Creek 94598

CAMPAGNA, EDWARD THOMAS, physician; b. Oct. 1, 1944, Buffalo, NY; s. Vincent Joseph and Mary Antonetta (D'Agostino) C.; m. Margaret, Sept. 6, 1969; children: Mark b. 1972, Laura b. 1976, John b. 1981; edn: BS, Canisius Coll. 1966; MD, Creighton Univ. Sch. of Med. 1970; intern, Millard Fillmore Hosp., Buffalo 1971; res., internal med., 1974; Diplomate, Am. Bd. of Internal Med. 1976. Career: pvt. practice Gen. Intern Med., Placentia 1976—; chief of dept. of med. Placentia Linda Comm. Hosp. 1978-82, v. chief of staff 1983-84, chief of staff 1985-86; awards: Dexter S. Levy Awd., for excellence in bedside med., Millard Fillmore Hosp 1974; mem: AMA, CMA OCMA, ASIM, CSIM, ACP; mil: maj. US Army 1974-76, Nat. Defense 1975, Korean Svc. 1976; Republican; Catholic; rec: golf, tennis. Res: 19282 Stonecrest Ln Yorba Linda 92686 Ofc: The Internal Medical Gp., 1041 E Yorba Linda Blvd Ste 5 Placentia 92670

CAMPBELL, DALMAR JOHN, publisher; b. Nov. 29, 1939, Merced; s. Dale Keegan and Marguerite Grace (Dexter) C.; m. Charlotte Ruth Burney, Apr. 1, 1978; children: Mark, b. 1964; Lori, b. 1965; Tami, b. 1968; step-children: Greg, b. 1959; Jeff, b. 1962; Laura, b. 1964; edn: AA, Fresno City Coll. 1968; BA, CSU Fresno 1974; 5th yr. tchg. cred., 1976; fine arts tchr. K-14; indsl. arts tchr. 7-12. Career: parts salesman; plywood salesman; comml. artist; typographer/printer; advt. salesman; currently publisher Mariposa Gazette; instr. courses Fresno City Coll. 1976-78; honors: recognition, Soc. of Profl. Journalists, VFW Citation; mem: CNPA; CPA; Sigma Delta Chi; Masons; Moose Lodge; Rotary; Hosp. Found.; Arts Council; CofC; exhib. oil paintings, San Joaquin Art Annual (1975), var. other shows; metal sculptor; owner ceramics bus.; mil: sp4/c US Army 1956-64; Democrat; Prot. Res: 4576 Yaqui Gulch Rd Mariposa 95338 Ofc: Mariposa Gazette, POB 38, 9th & Jones, Mariposa 95338

CAMPBELL, DEBRA ANN, convalescent hospital administrator; b. Apr. 21, 1953, Modesto; d. Jack Benjamin Cushenberry and Shirley Ann (Paradee) Conover; m. Kenneth Campbell, Jr., Dec. 17, 1982; edn: Modesto Jr. Coll.; Nursing Home Administr. lic., Calif. 1980. Career: asst. bkkpr. Yosemite Convalescent Hosp., Modesto 1975-76, personnel dir. 1976-80, acting adminstr. 1980-86, patient care coord. 1986—; mem: Calif. Assn. of Health Facilities Progress Valley, No. Calif. Council of Activity Coordinators, Medical Records Assn.; civic: Gray Panthers (1981-84), Ombudsman (1982-84), Mental Health Advisory Bd. (Exec. Bd. 1984-); Democrat; Assemblies of God; rec: cycling, swimming, wt. lifting. Res: 1040 Springfield Way Modesto 95355 Ofc: Yosemite Convalescent Hospital 159 East Orangeburg Ave Modesto 95350

CAMPBELL, DONALD OTIS, physician; b. March 3, 1936, Loma Linda; s. Otis W. and Delia E. (Nasser) C.; m. Elizabeth Short, June 22, 1963; children: Catherine D. b. 1964, Julie S. b. 1967; edn: Stanford Univ. 1954-57; MD, USC 1961; intern, surgical res. Santa Fe Coat Lines Hosp., Los Angeles 1961-63; post grad., UCLA 1984, Harvard 1984; Fellow Am. Acad. of Family Physicians (1981). Career: house physician Santa Fe Hosp., Los Angeles 1965-66; individual pvt. practice of medicine, family and gen. practice, 1966—; med. dir. South Bay Independent Physicians Individual Practice Assn.; exec. com. (chief Dept. Family Practice 1983, 1986-) Torrance Meml. Hosp. Medical Ctr., Torrance 1983-; mem: AMA, Calif. Med. Assn., LA Co. Med. Assn., Salerni Collegium, Phi Chi Med. Frat.; Palos Verdes Penin. CofC 1968-78 (dir. 74-76) Kiwanis 1966-80; mil: capt. Med. Corps USAF 1963-65; rec: gardening, woodwork, photog., plate collector. Ofc: 927 Deep Valley Dr Rolling Hills Estates 90274

CAMPBELL, EVERETT OLIVER, physician; b. Nov. 15, 1934, Chgo.; s. Everett Wayne and Rose (Brazile) C.; children: Paul b. 1959, Jill b. 1963, Everett b. 1965, Allyson b. 1967, Melvin b. 1970, Oliver b. 1972; edn: MD, Univ. Mich. 1958; Diplomate Am. Board of Obstets.-Gynecol. Career: mil. physician, chief Dept. of Ob-Gyn, US Army Hosp. Fort Chaffee, Ark. 1962-64; pvt. practice obstetrics-gynecology in Gardena, currently; asst. clin. prof. Dept. Ob-Gyn, UC Los Angeles; mem: Am. Coll. of Ob-Gyn, Calif. Med. Soc., Los Angeles County Med. Soc., Assn. for Holistic Health (pres. 1985), Planetary Soc., Calif. Perinatal Soc. (past pres.-elect); publs: Cancer, A Preventable Disease; mil: capt. Med. Corps US Army 1962-64. Res: 27336 Sunnridge Rd Rolling Hills 90274 Ofc: 1141 W Redondo Beach Blvd Ste 200 Gardena 90247

CAMPBELL, HARRY MEIKLE, consulting civil engineer; b. Feb. 4, 1922, Los Angeles; S. Harry, Sr. and Grace (Alward) M.; m. Karen E. Hose, Apr. 3, 1964; children: Tyrra Jo b. 1948, Nancy June b. 1950, Martin James b. 1960; edn: BSCE, UC Berkeley 1943; BS in bus., UC Los Angeles 1964; tchg. credential, El Camino Coll. 1966; Reg. Profl. Civil Engr., Calif. Career: engring. ofcr., capt. US Marine Corps 1942-46; resident engr. and project engr. Am. Bridge Co., 1946-50; structural designer Fluor Corp. 1950-54; transp. engr. Div. of Hwys, State of Calif. 1955-73; pres. Harry M. Campbell Engring. Corp., Los Angeles 1973–; condr. seminars, hwy. engring. fundamentals and civil engring. registration, Calif. State Div. of Hwys. 1958-73; chmn. Nat. Com. for Integration of Engring. Edn. and Practice, 1974-78; mem. ASCE (chmn. Engr. Edn. Com.), Am. Soc. of Engring. Edn.; civic: 25 yr club for CalTrans, First Aid instr. Am. Red Cross, Doves Pgm. for L.A. Unified Sch. Dist., Marines Meml. Club (S.F.), VFW Post 3261, Disabled Am. Vets #101; publs: T6 (Thoughtful training tends toward tremendous transactions) 1976, composer of music, 1940-42; Republican; Baptist; rec: music, fishing, gardening. Res: 15912 Chanera Ave Gardena 90249 Ofc: Campbell Engineering Co. 1052 West 6th St Ste 418 Los Angeles 90017

CAMPBELL, JOSEPH LOUIS, manufacturing co. executive; b. Sept. 15, 1932, Tampa, Fla.; s. Edwin Louis and Grace Olympia (LoRe) C.; m. Rachel Ray Russell, Sept. 22, 1951; children: Michael b. 1953, Dennis b. 1958; edn: BSChE, Univ. Fla. 1957; ops. mgmt. UC Los Angeles, 1974; Reg. Profl. Engr., Calif. Career: lab. tech. US Phosphoric Products, Tampa 1952-53; test engr., engr.-in-charge Rocket Engine Test Center, senior research engr. No. Am. Aviation Inc., Los Angeles 1957-61; exec. asst., indsl. planning splst. No. Am. Rockwell, Los Angeles 1962-70; Rockwell Internat. project engr., program rep., Los Angeles, material mgr. and asst. site dir., Phila., and Alabama, 1971-82, project mgr. Plant Machining Modernization, 1983–, ACT tng. instr., 1976; mgmt. cons./owner CAM Ents. 1979–; awards: community service, Canoga Park (1965), outstanding achievement - Saturn Pgm., Rockwell Internat.; mem: Am. Inst. Chem. Engrs., Am. Inst. Indsl. Engrs. (treas. 1968-70), Nat. Mgmt. Assn. (treas. 1972), Soc. of Mfg. Engrs., Fellow Inst. for Advancement of Engring.; civic: scoutmaster BSA (1964-66), pres. Agoura Sport Booster Club (1969-70), Mullwood Home Owners Assn. (v.p. 1967); mil: USAF Reserves 1951-53, Electronics instr.; Democrat; Protestant; rec: sports, fishing, airplane modeling. Address: Canoga Park 91364

CAMPBELL, NETTIE JEANNE TAY, sculptor, painter; b. Apr. 13, 1929, San Francisco; d. Virgil Clarence and Alma Francis Medina (Stone) Tays; m. Alan L. Campbell, Jan. 16, 1949; children: Steven b. 1951, Leslie b. 1953; edn: grad. Sequoia H.S. 1947, stu. Foothill, De Anza Colls.; pvt. studies in Japanese brush w/ T. Mikami 1956-60, portraiture w/ Thomas Leighton 1959-73, sculpture w/ Ruth Cravath 1973-76. Career: clk. doctor's office, Redwood City 1947-48, civil svc. flt. maint. test aircraft NACA Ames Lab, Moffett Field, Mt. View 1948-50; artist: paints in oils, pastels, and watercolors; carves in marble, wood and works in clay and wax for bronze castings; dir. Tays Art Studio, Mt. View 1960s–; pvt. tchg.painting, sculpture Art Center California, San Jose 1979-82; awards: Mikami Award (1960), num. invitational shows, juried awards in oils, pastel, watercolor, and sculpture- local, state and nat. exhibs.; spl. exhib. Rosicrucian Mus. Gallery (Oct.-Nov. 86); mem. Artist Equity, Soc. of Western Artist, Nat. Watercolor Soc., Santa Clara Valley Watercolor Soc., Nat. League of Am. Pen Women Inc. (pres. Santa Clara Co. chpt. 1978-80, pres. Nor-Cal 1980-82, nat. 3d v.p. 1982-84); civic: Santa Clara County Art Council (exec. bd.), CofC, Business Women of Los Altos, Mex./Amer. Mus., De Young Mus./ S.F., Tritan Mus./S.C., Nat. Mus. Women Art/Wash DC; Republican; Prot.; rec: writing. Studio: Los Altos 94022

CAMPBELL, RICHARD GEORGE, plastics co. president; b. Nov. 14, 1932, Detroit; s. Richard George and Eva Naomi (Johnson) C.; m. Marie, Feb. 2, 1961; children: Richard b. 1955, Jay b. 1956, Steven b. 1961; edn: BSME, CSU Los Angeles 1967; MMS, West Coast Univ. 1972; MBA, Univ. Chgo. 1979. Career: chief engr. Falcon Plastics Oxnard 1966-69, plant mgr. 1969-72; equip. and facilities mgr. Johnson & Johnson New Brunswick, NJ 1973-76, plant mgr., Chgo. 1976-81; dir. mfg. Abbott Laboratories No. Chgo. 1981-85; pres. Venture Plastics Santa Ana 1985–; me4m: Soc. Plastic Inds., Soc. Plastic Engrg.; Modular IV patent applied Abbott Laboratories 1981; Methodist; rec: flying, swimming. Res: 23861 Voyager St Laguna Niguel Ofc: Venture Plastics 2420 W 3rd St Santa Ana 92703

CAMPBELL, RICHARD WALLACE, consulting civil and structural engineer; b. July 26, 1925, Los Angeles; s. Max Wilbert and Lillian Emma (Hansen) C.; 1 dau, Candis Goeller b. 1959; edn: BECE, USC 1950; Civil Engr. (1953) and Structural Engr. (1956), Calif. Career: cons. structl. engrs., Los Angeles; cons. architects- engrs., Japan and Greece; cons. civil and structural engring., spec. rehab., restoration and reclamation in Los Angeles Basin 1957–; active on tech. coms., Structural Engrs. Assn.; honors: Fellow Am. Soc. of Civil Engrs.; past pres. CSES; Tau Beta Pi, Chi Epsilon, Sigma Zi; mem: CEAC, SEAOSC, Fellow Am. Soc. of Civil Engrs., Chi Epsilon, ICBO, ACI, PCI, PTI, Mensa; works: structural design of bldgs. of every class and material incl. 36-level parking structure, structl. design of environmtl. structures incl. bridges, small dams, wastewater treatment facilities, pipelines; value engrg. studies; mil: SK 3/G US Navy Seabees 1943-46, North Africa; Protestant; rec: skiing, bridge, boating. Ofc: 766 1/2 Waterman Ave. No., San Bernardino 92410

CAMPBELL, ROBERT DONALD, chiropractor; b. Nov. 10, 1952, Lansing, Mich.; s. Charles L. and Jean Ellen (McCulloch) C.; edn: AA, Napa Valley Coll. 1980; Life Chiropractic Coll. West 1980-82; DC, Palmer Coll. of Chiropractic, Davenport, Iowa 1984; Cert. of Proficiency, Adv. Sacro-Occipital Technique, Palmer Coll. of Chiropractic 1983-84. Career: currently, chiropractor Burlingame Chiropractic Clinic, Burlingame; dir. pub. rels., chiropractic cons. Prime Time Athletic Club, Burlingame and Family Fitness Athletic Club, Foster City; asst. Dr. Monte Greenawalt DC (founder Foot Levelers Inc.)-Orthopaedic Advr. 1983-84; recipient, Outstanding Young Men of Am., 1985; mem: Am., Calif. and San Mateo Co. Chiropractic Assns., Burlingam CofC, Sacro-Occipital Technique Club (advr., Palmer Coll. of Chiro. 1982-84), Prime Time Athletic Club; rec: physical fitness. Res: 46 West 4th Ave. #215 San Mateo 94402 Ofc: Burlingame Chiropractic Clinic, 100 El Camino Real Burlingame 94010

CAMPBELL, RONALD LEROY, psychologist; b. Oct. 1, 1934, Butler, Pa.; s. Albert Edwin and Min Aleta (Larimore) C.; m. Carmen Martinez, 1971; edn: AA in bus., San Francisco City Coll. 1957; BA & MA, anthropology, CSU San Francisco, 1962-77; MPA pub. adm., cnsortium of CSUs, 1975-78, MA, clin. psychol., Antioch Univ. 1980; PhD, integral psychol., Calif. Inst. of Integral Studies. Career: owner, mgr. Watkins Prods. (sales orgn.) 1961; supr., partner Annette's Bakery 1962; exec. dir. Ctr. for the Holistic Scis., Menlo Park 1974-81; counseling/psychology,Counselors and Consultants, Inc., Menlo Park, San Jose 1982–; instr. UCB ext., Univ. of S.F., Goldengate Univ., Chapman Colls., 1968-81; mem. bd. govs. Calif. Inst. of Integral Studies, 1982; pres. Integral Science Inst., 1983-; editor Phoenix Jour.of Transpersonal Anthropology, 1977-; contbg. ed. Bay Area Anthropol. News 1974-79; res. in Am.-Mex. comm. devel. proj. in rural village, Mex. 1966, in Indian village, Mex. 1977; awards: Darsansagar Dipl. 1970; cultural integration fellowship for resrch in Asian and integral studies; appreciation, Local 101 AFL-CIO, 1978; mem: Assn. for Transpersonal Anthropol. Internat. (bd.trustees 1983-87, v.p. 1981-87), Calif. Inst. of Integral Studies Alumni Assn. (pres. 1982), AAAS, Am. Soc. for Pub. Adminstrn., Assn. for Transpersonal Psychology, Am. Anthropol. Assn., Soc. for the Anthropol. of Visual Communication. Author: Anthropological Field Tng. in Hweyapon, Mexico: A Critique with Brief Ethnography; The Concept of Man in Integral Psychology; Extinction Perio; The Photo Symbolistic Technique; Alicia: A Woman's Journey into Conscious Living. Contbr. num. arts., books, film revs., scholarly jours. Mil: airman 2d cl. US Army, USAR, Air Nat. Guard, 1953-60. Democrat; Unitarian; rec: homing pigeons, martial arts, travel. Res: 6 Big Tree Rd. Woodside 94062. Ofc: 845 Oak Grove Ave. Menlo Park 94025

CAMPBELL, W. GLENN, director Hoover Instn. on War, Revolution and Peace; b. Apr. 29, 1924, Komoka, Ont., Can.; nat. 1953; s. Alfred Edwin and Delia (O'Brien) C.; m. Rita Ricardo, Sept. 15, 1946; chil: Barbara Lee (Bizewski), b. 1954, Diane Rita (Porter), b. 1956, Nancy Elizabeth, b. 1960; edn: BA, Univ. W. Ont. 1944, MA, Harvard Univ. 1946, PhD, 1948. Career: instr. in econ. Harvard Univ. 1948-51; resrch econ. US CofC, Wash DC 1951-54; resrch dir. Am. Enterprise Inst. for Public Policy Resrch, Wash DC 1954-60, program adviser 1960-; dir. Hoover Instn. on War, Revolution and Peace, Stanford 1960–; chmn., bd. trustees Ronald Reagan Presdl. Found. 1985-; chmn. Pres's Intell. Oversight Bd., 1981-; mem. Pres's Fgn. Intell. Advis. Bd., 1981-; chmn. Am. Panel of the Jt. Com. on Japan-US Cultural and Ednl. Coop., 1983-; chmn. Japan-US Friendship Commn. 1983-; mem. Bd. of Regents, Univ. Calif. 1968- (chmn. 1982); mem. Nat. Sci. Bd., Nat. Sci. Found., 1972-78; mem. Pres's Com. on Sci. and Tech. 1976; mem. Pres's Commn. on White House Fellow 1969-74; chmn. Reagan-Bush Task Force on Edn. 1980; mem. Reagan-Bush Task Force on Fgn. Policy (1980) and Task Force on Inflation Policy (1980); mem. Personnel Advis. Com. to Pres. Reagan 1980-81; bd. dirs. Com. on the Present Danger, 1976-; bd. dirs. Mont Pelerin Soc. 1980-; mem. Adv. Bd. Ctr. for Strategic and Internat. Studies, Georgetown Univ. 1980-; mem. bd.vis. Bernice P. Bishop Mus., Honolulu 1979-; trustee Herbert Hoover Presidential Lib. Assn. 1964- ; mil: Canadian Navy 1943-44. Res: 26915 Alejandro Dr. Los Altos Hills 94022. Ofc: Hoover Instn. Stanford 94305

CAMPBELL, WALLACE DONALD, physician; b. May 4, 1910, Carrington, No. Dak.; s. Charles Sherman and Wilhelmina (Merkel) C.; m. Veta, Nov. 17, 1948; children: Cheryl b. 1951, Richard b. 1952; edn: BS, Walla Walla Coll. 1942; MD, Loma Linda Univ. 1944. Career: physician pvt. practice, Los Angeles 1946-74; medical consultant Dept. Disability, State of Calif. 1974–; mem: AMA, Calif. Med. Assn., Fresno-Madera Co. Med. Soc., Am. Soc. Abdominal Surgeons; mil: capt. Med. Corps US Army 1944-46, PTO; Republican; Protestant; rec: golf, travel, viticulture. Res: 6696 N Malsbary Fresno 93711 Ofc: Calif. DSS, 1625 E Shaw Ave Fresno 93726

CAMPBELL, WILLIAM M., III, real estate development and construction co. president; b. March 7, 1944, Durham, No. Carolina; s. William M. Jr. andmary Julia (Miller) C.; m. Margaret Ose, Dec. 27, 1969; children: Christopher b. 1971, Elizabeth b. 1980; edn: BS, honors, CSU Sacramento; MBA, CSU Sacramento 1968. Career: controller John Hancock Mutual Life Ins. Co.; pres. The Camray Companies, Sacramento 1971–; adv. bd. River City Bank, Sacramento 1978-; bd. dirs. Sacramento Co. Day Sch. 1976-82; honors: Blue Key, Calif. CPA Exam.; mem: Sacramento Co. Day Sch., Sacramento YMCA (pres.); mil: USAR; Presbyterian; rec: tennis, skiing, backpacking. Ofc: Camray Development & Constrn. Co., 7919 Folsom Blvd. Sacramento 95826

CAMPBELL, WILLIAM RICHARD, publishing executive; b. Oct. 18, 1939, Omaha, Nebr.; s. Myron Torbert and Margaret Louise (Swisher) C.; children: Wendy b. 1964, Timothy b. 1966, Tod b. 1966; edn: BS, Bradley Univ. 1961. Career: salesman/mgr. Scott Paper Co., 1961-64; sales mgr./dir. mktg. American Hosp. Assn., 1964-70; dir. sales & mktg. Healthcom Pub. Co., 1970-72; owner Fox Ad West, 1972-82; co-owner Mediacor, Inc. (publishing firm),

Oakland 1982–; mem. US Congressional Adv. Bd. to Nat. Security Council; listed Who's Who in Advt.; mem: Medical Mktg. & Media, Bradley Alumni Club, Sigma Chi Alumni Club (secty); publs: arts in Medical Mktg. & Media, Am. Surgical Dealer; mil: cpl. USM.R 1961-67; Republican; Lutheran; rec: sports, antique autos. Res: 2126 Greencrest Dr El Cajon 92020 Ofc: Mediacor, Inc. 2204 Lakeshore Ave, Ste 9, Oakland 94606

CAN, SUMER, electronics engineer; b. Dec. 24, 1947, Koyulhisar, Sivas, Turkey; s. Mahmut Celalettin and Bedriye (Erzurumlu) C.; m. Aysel Pala, Oct. 6, 1972; children: Argun b. 1975, Tankut b. 1985; edn: MSc. Technical Univ. of Istanbul 1972; M. Applied Sci., Univ. Toronto 1977; postgrad. wk. Univ. Santa Clara 1981-83; desig: Profl. Engr. (P.E.) Assn. of Profl. Engrs. of Ontario (APEO) 1979. Career: lectr./scientist Tech. Univ. of Istanbul, Turkey 1972-74; research and tchg. asst. Univ. Toronto, Can. 1974-78; elec. engr. Litton Systems Ltd., Can. 1978-80; senior elec. engr. Nat. Semiconductor Corp., Santa Clara 1980-81; prin. engr./scientist Sperry Corp. and Control Data Corp., Santa Clara 1981-84; senior design engr. Signetics Corp., 1984–; mem: Assn. of Profl. Engrs., Turkey (1972-), IEEE (1975-), Assn. of Profl. Engrs. of Ontario, Canada (1979-), Smithsonian Inst.; publs: five invention disclosures, nine tech. papers in Electronics and Systems Theory, num. sci. journal articles; rec: drawing, biological and sociological systems. Res: 1575 Tenaka Pl Sunnyvale 94087 Ofc: Signetics Corp. 811 E Arques Ave Sunnyvale 94086

CANALE, MARY LOUISE, computer services executive; b. Aug. 18, 1944, Omaha, Neb.; d. George Henry and Philomena (Van Den Eynde) C.; edn: BA poli. sci., cum laude, Golden Gate Univ. 1975, MPA, 1976; BS equiv., IBM & DOD courses, profl. tng. in computer scis. Career: civil svc. with DoD, DHEW, DHHS 1962-81; mgr. spl. proj. & planning/ mkt. research Computer Sciences Corp. 1982–; nat. chair DHHS/ HCFA Pvt. Sector Group 1983-84; honors: num. employment related awards; mem. Californians for Nuclear Safeguards 1976-81; rec: swimming, gardening, camping, hiking. Res: 2670 Park Hills Dr Sacramento 95821 Ofc: Computer Sciences Corp. 2000 Evergreen Sacramento 95821

CANNON, WILLIAM SHELTON, lawyer; b. Feb. 13, 1946, Hollywood; s. Wm. Joseph, Jr. and Martha Ruth (Shelton) C.; m. Sara Pettit, Aug. 25, 1968; children: Marnee b. 1974, Christopher b. 1980; edn: BA, Calif. Western Univ. 1967, JD, 1973; admitted Calif. State Bar 1973. Career: tchr. La Mesa-Spring Valley Sch. Dist. 1968-69; atty. assoc. Fredrick, Brandt & Cannon 1973-74, Stickney, Orlieb, Moats & Byrne 1974-80, Mason & Cannon 1980-81; ptnr. Atherton, Allen, Mason, Cannon & Geerdes, Chula Vista 1981–; honors: Calif. Western Law Review 1968-69, Phi Alpha Delta law frat.; mem. ABA, San Diego County Bar Assn., South Bay Bar Assn. (pres. 1985), Kiwanis Club of Bonita (pres. 1981); civic: mem. (chmn. 1985) Chula Vista Planning Commn. 1983-; chmn. Sweetwater Comm. Planning Group 1974-78; mem: (pres. 1978-80) Sweetwater Valley Civic Assn. 1973-83; Republican; rec: bicycling. Res: 4080 Bermuda Dunes Pl Bonita 92002 ofc: Atherton, Allen, Mason, Cannon & Geerdes 345 F Street Ste 200 Chula Vista 92010

CANTOS, EARL JAMES, JR., lawyer; b. June 12, 1956, San Diego; s. Judge Earl James and Irene Rita (Trifiatis) C.; m. Carolina; edn: BS in bus. mgt., San Diego State Univ. 1978, JD, Univ. of San Diego 1981. Career: real estate broker, v.p., secty. Cantos Realty, a Calif. Corp., 1974–; assoc. law offices of Glen R. Roberts, 1981-82; prop. law offices of Earl J. Cantos, Jr., San Diego 1982-84; senior policy cons. Calif. State Assembly 1984–; awards: Laurels for Leaders, 1974. mem: Battered Women's Svcs-YWCA (adv. bd. mem. 1980-82); Am. Bar Assn.; San Diego Co. Bar Assn. (Immigration Com. 1982-84, liaison between S.D. and Tijuana, Mex. 1982-84, Internat. Law Sect. 1982-84); S.D. Trial Lawyers Assn.; Barristers; Phi Alpha Delta legal frat. (v.p. 1980-1); Nat., Calif. Assn. of Realtors, 1974-; S.D. Bd. of Realtors, 1974-; Christian Legal Soc.; Saints Constantine and Helen Greek Orth. Ch. Parish Council (Young Adult League adv. 1979-84, choir); Opa Greek Folk Dance Troupe; Sigma Chi frat.; Life Loyal Sig.; Toastmasters Internat.; World Trade Assn. inventor: patented wind percussion instrument (1979); background singer for Light of Heaven (prod. Erini Prodns. label) by Rita Cantos Cartwright; contbg. ed. En Banc, law jour. Univ. of S.D. 1980-1. Republican (Calif. State Central Com.1981-; Repub. Assocs.; Young Repubs.; Repub. Bus. & Profl. Club). Greek Orth. rec: Greek folk dancing, singing, ski. Res: 5249 Marlborough Dr San Diego 92116 Ofc: 1100 J St Rm 315 Sacramento 95814

CAO, TUYET ANH, real estate broker; b. Sept. 16, 1943, Saigon, Vietnam, nat. US cit. 1986; d. Co Hon and Sau Aka Hanh Thi (Ho) C.; m. Lam Nguyen, Dec. 25, 1969; children: Son Nguyen b. 1971, Minh Nguyen b. 1973; edn: BA edn., Univ. Saigon 1967; cosmetology license, Lakewood Beauty Sch. 1982; real estate broker 1984. Career: tchr. Eng. var. high schools Vietnam 1967-75; hairdresser, manicurist Rowland Heights 1982; real estate agent Coldwell Banker Buena Park 1983, UBI Garden Grove 1984, Pacific Land Investment Westminster 1984–, in chg. of leasing large shopping center, Westminster and Magnolia, Westminster (1st Vietnamese woman broker in chg.); honors: Best Student (1956-63), Ist Rate Winner (H.S. Grad. Exam. 1963), Best Tchr. (Eng., Social Activities 1969), Agent w/ Most Leads in Orange County (Coldwell Banker 1983); publs: How To Study English, How To Teach English Grammar, How To Do English Test in High School Graduation Exam. (1968-70); Buddhist; rec: swimming, tennis, ping pong, flower arrangement, music. Res: 5710 Dairy Ave Long Beach 90805 Ofc: Pacific Land Investment 9561 Bolsa Ave Westminster 92683

CAPLAN, ALAN MAYER, lawyer; b. June 29, 1944, Pittsburgh, Pa.; s. Larry and Ida (Cabin) C.; edn: BS, honors, Univ. of Wisc. 1966; JD, Georgetown Univ. 1969; admitted Calif. State Bar 1971, DC Bar 1969. Career: Vista volunteer in Cleveland, O. 1969-70; legal counselor CSU Hayward, 1970-71; pvt. law practice, ptnr. Bushnell, Caplan & Fielding, San Francisco 1971–; judge pro tem San Francisco Municipal Ct.; mem. Calif. State Bar Assn., San Francisco Bar Assn., Lawyers Club of S.F., Nat. Lawyers Guild, Calif. Attys. for Criminal Justice (Amicus Com.), No. Calif. Criminal Trial Lawyers Assn. (treas.), Bay Area Lawyers for the Arts. Res:434 B Union St., San Francisco 94109 Law Ofc: Bushnell, Caplan & Fielding, 680 Beach St, Ste 372, San Francisco 94109

CAPPELLO, A. BARRY, lawyer; b. Feb. 21, 1942, Flushing, N.Y.; s. Gus and Ann (Klukoff) C.; m. Mary Ann Peterson, Aug. 31, 1970; children: Blythe b. 1973, Brent b. 1978, Eric Rheinschild b. 1961; edn: AB, UC Los Angeles 1962, JD, 1965.Career: deputy atty. general State of Calif. 1965-68, chief trial deputy 1968-70; asst. dist. atty. Santa Barbara County 1970-71; city atty., Santa Barbara 1971-77; current: ptnr. Cappello & Foley, Santa Barbara; bd. trustees Las Positas Park Found.; honors: Phi Delta Phi, Lambda Chi Alpha; mem. ABA (Litigation Sect., chmn. Urban Environment Com. 1980-82), State Bar of Calif., Santa Barbara County Bar Assn.; publs: "Santa Barbara Oil: Production & Pollution" (pub. City of S.B. 1974); past mem. Republican County Central Com.; rec: running, tennis. Res: 4225 Mariposa Dr Santa Barbara 93110 Ofc: Cappello & Foley, 831 State St Santa Barbara 83101

CAPPS, ANTHONY T. (CAPOZZOLO), international public relations executive; b. April 19, Pueblo, Colo.; s. Nicolo and Ann (Salomone) Capozzolo; m. Theresa Cecelia Harmon, Nov. 12, 1919. Career: dance dir., choreographer, prod. mot. pic. TV and radio; feat. Profl. Dance Team, Biltmore Bowl, Cocoanut Grove, L.A.; St. Catherine Hotel, Catalina 1939-42; dance dir., prod.NBC, ABC, KCOP-TV, Columbia Pictures, 20th Century Fox and Calif.studios 1940-60; govt. tours, Puerto Rico, Cuba, Jamaica, Dominican Repub., Haiti 1954; prod. "Latin Holiday", t.v. series of Latin Am.; exec.dir. Lockheed and Vega Aircraft Co.activities, Burbank, L.A., Glendale, Pomona, Pasadena, Bakersfield, and Taft plants; internat.pub. rels. dir: Howard Manor, Palm Springs Key Club, Country Club Hotel, Palm Springs Ranch Club; owner, Desert Sun Newspapers, KDES Radio, Palm Springs, Cameron Ctr. and Cameron Enterprises and Oil Co., Burbank radio sta., Murietta Hot Springs Hotel, Health and Beuaty Spa, Palm Springs- Coachella Valley; founder, pres., dir. Tony Capps Enterprises; num. t.v. interviews on Relig. and Polit.Hist.of Ballet and Opera of last 500 yrs.; chmn., exec. dir.golf and tennis tournaments, benefit dinners for civic leaders, govs., senators, congressmen, United Fund for City of Hope (3 times), Nat.Cystic Fibrosis Fund, Palm Springs (Bob Hope) Golf Classic; created adv. gimmick for Colgate and Cugat, Coca Cola; estab. Anthony Capps Art Gallery Med. Ctr.; Nat. Football Found.and Hall of Fame (founder, pres. Tri-County chpt.; founder, co-chmn. Annual Golf Classic), Nat. Artists and Art Patrons Soc.of City of Hope (founder, pres.), Eisenhower Meml. Hosp. Aux.(charter), Opera Guild of the Desert, Palm Springs Pathfinders, Desert Art Ctr. of Coachella Valley, Palm Springs Desert Mus., AFTRA, Smithsonian Inst., Am.Security Council (Wash. DC), L.A.Co. Mus. of Arts (Patron), The Cousteau Soc. Internat., Nat.Trust for Hist. Preservation (Wash.DC), Balboa Bay Club; columnist, The Am. Film Inst. Wash. DC, The Reporter 1962-63, Desert Sun Palm Springs, L.A. Daily News; Catholic.rec: charities. Res: 2715 Junipero Ave. Palm Springs

CARA, THOMAS EDWARD, culinary reporter; b. April 22, 1910, San Francisco; s. Humbert and Felicita (Scaglia) C.; m. Mary Valvano, Jan. 3, 1942; children: John b. 1943, Christopher b. 1948; edn: BA, St. Mary's Coll. 1933. Career: estab. Thomas Cara Ltd. Culinary Importers, San Francisco 1947–; first. comml. importer on Pacific Coast of Caffe Espresso Machines for home and bus. 1948; first. to conduct gourmet cooking classes in conjuction w/ importing bus., chefs incl. M. Ghioud of Ernies, Paul Mayer and M. Wolfe of Mark Hopkins Hotel; first to conduct all-male cooking classes; mem: Am. Legion Salesian Post (co-founder Post 599, San Francisco, commdr. 1949-50), Commonwealth Club, Knights of Columbus; mil: col. US Army, ret., C.O. CWCD (G-2) Presidio 1958-65; Democrat; Catholic. Res: 451 Lombard St. San Francisco 94133 Ofc: 517 Pacific St. San Francisco 94133

CARBREY, CRAIG JOSEPH, real estate developer; b. July 11, 1948, Colusa; s. Glenn Joseph and Inez Marie (Allgire) C.; m. Joan R., Aug. 23, 1969; children: Ryan b. 1971, Cameron b. 1975; edn: BSBA, San Jose 1971. Career: property mgr. William Kenny Property Mgmt., Saratoga 1971; real estate appraiser Sequoia Mortgage Co., San Jose 1971-72; senior real estate appraiser Union Bank, Oakland 1972-73; loan ofcr. Norris, Beggs & Simpson, Sacramento 1974-78; regl. mgr. Barry S. Slatt Mortgage Co., Sacramento 1978-83; pres. CaminoWest Projects, Sacramento 1984-86; pres. RYCAM Inc., Sacramento 1986–; bd. dir. Resource Magazine; bd. dirs. Allied Savings Bank; honors: Charles A. Suffied Award; Outstanding Real Estate Student, San Jose State; mem: Nat. Assn. of Indsl. and Ofc. Parks, Folsom Youth Soccer League, Folsom Swim Team; Republican; Catholic; rec: snow and water skiing. Res: 120 Redrock Ct. Folsom 95630 Ofc: RYCAM Inc., 1435 River Park Dr. Ste. 405 Sacramento 95815

CARD, JOSEFINA JAYME, social psychologist; b. Apr. 27, 1946, Manila, Philippines; d. Fortunato Rabadilla and Josefina (Bulatao) Jayme; m. Stuart K. Card, Jan. 26, 1972; children: Gwyneth b. 1978, Tiffany b. 1982; edn: AB math., summa cum laude, Maryknoll Coll. 1966; MA psych., Carnegie-Mellon Univ. 1969, PhD psych. 1971. Career: asst. prof. Dept. Psych. Ateneo Univ., Manila; research psychologist Suicide Prevention Ctr., Pittsburgh, Pa. 1972-73; senior research assoc., then prin. research scientist American Insts. for Research, Palo Alto; currently pres./prin. scientist Sociometrics Corp.,

Palo Alto; cons. Nat. Insts. of Health; editl. bd. Psychosocial Stress; honors: Asian Student Leader award, US Dept. of State (1966); mem: Am. Psychol. Assn. (secty. Div. 34), Population Assn. of Am., Am. Sociol. Assn., Am. Public Health Assn.; author: Lives After Vietnam (Lexington Books, 1983), Data Archive on Adolescent Pregnancy and Pregnancy Prevention (1982-87); rec: family. Res: 3191 Cowper St Palo Alto 94306 Ofc: Sociometrics Corp. 685 High Ste 2E Palo Alto 94301

CAREY, FRANK ROBERT, financial-tax planning executive; b. Aug. 12, 1939, Troy, NY; s. Frank J. and mary T. (Egan) C.; m. Virginia D. Klischer, July 6, 1980; children: Kathleen, b. 1960, David, b. 1963, Jeanne, b. 1965, Patrick, b. 1968, Daniel, b. 1977, Heather, b. 1981; edn: BS, West Coast Univ. 1964; MS, 1966; tchg. cred. (adult edn.) Calif. 1978; enrolled agent, Dept. of the Treas. 1981; reg. rep., NASD 1970, reg. prin. 1984; life and disability ins. lic., Calif. 1970. Career: admin. asst. Librascope, Glendale 1959-63; eng. adminstr. Electronic Specialty Co., Glendale 1963-64; staff adminstr. Litton Inds., Woodland Hills 1964-65; eng. adminstrn. supvr. Hycon Co., Monrovia 1965-68; v.p. Probabilistic Software Inc., Montrose 1968-70; self- empl., tax plnng., ins. sales, Covina Valley 1968 –; securities sales, var. broker dealers ending with Titan Capital Corp 1970 –; gen. agent Carey Agcy., San Dimas 1975 –; br. mgr.- reg. principle Titan Capital Corp., San Dimas 1984 –; tchr. Hacienda- La Puente Unified Sch. Dist. Adult Edn. 1977-; honors: Million in Force and Quality Awards, Sunset Life Ins. Co.; mem: Puddingston Tiberon Homeowners Assn. (bd. dirs.); works: linear pgmmg. tech. paper presented to 10th Annual West Coast Reliability Symposium of Am. Soc. for Quality Control; Republican; Catholic; rec: tennis, hunting, chess. Res: 798 Pinewood Ln., San Dimas 91773 Ofc: Carey Tax Planning and Agency, 458A West Arrow Hwy., San Dimas 91773

CAREY, MICHAEL RAYMOND, sales executive; b.· Sept. 11, 1952, San Bernardino; s. Raymond Spencer and Ione Cecilia (Davis) C.; edn: BS, UC Berkeley 1975; Chartered Life Underwriter (CLU) cand. 1986. Career: agt., dist. sales mgr. Equitable Finl. Services Corp., San Francisco 1975 –; awards: job performance rated in top 5 percent of co.'s 900 mgrs. nat. (1985), Nat. Qualify and Nat. Sales Achievement awards (8 years), Bradford King Award nominee Calif. Alumni Assn. (1986); mem: Nat. Assn. of Life Underw., San Francisco Life Underw. Assn. (bd.), Million Dollar Round Table, Gen. Agents and Mgrs. Assn. (bd.), Am. Soc. CLU (stu. mem.), Kappa Sigma frat. (bd. Beta XI); civic: UC Alumni Assn. (Bear Backers Waldorf Club, Young Alumni Assn., The Sprowl Assocs.), S.F. Museum Soc., March of Dimes, Irwin Meml. Blood Bank, Medic Alert Found. Internat.; works: design computer applications for Equitable sales force throughout U.S.; Republican; Roman Catholic; rec: bodysurf, softball, ski, sailing. Res: 3 Captain Dr #202 Emeryville 94608 Ofc: Equitable Financial Services 524 Golden Gate Ave 2nd Flr San Francisco 94102

CARL, ROBERT EUGENE, audiologist; b. May 3, 1932, Catawissa, Pa.; s. Fredrick Russell and Edna Rose (Kreischer) C.; m. Dolly Mack, Jan. 26, 1952; children: Joyce Ann b. 1953, Barbara Ellen b. 1959; edn: BA speech path., CSU Los Angeles 1980, MA audiology, 1985. Career: asst. health physicist US Radium Corp., Bloomsburg, Pa. 1955-70; clin. audiologist pvt. practice, owner Carl's Hearing Instruments, Glendale, Calif. 1970 –; staff audiologist Glendale Adventist Medical Ctr.; recipient pres.'s achievement awards, MAICO Hearing Instruments (1972, 73, 74, 75, 76); fmr. mem. Los Angeles Hosp. Assn.; past instr. for licensing examinees Calif. hearing aid dispensers; mem: Nat. Hearing Aid Soc., Nat. Board for Certification in Hearing Instrument Scis., Am. Speech Hearing-Language Assn., Hearing Aid Assn. of Calif.; civic: Glendale CofC, Kiwanis, Masons, Scottish Rites, Shriners, Republican Buck & Ballot Brigade; publs: article, What To Do If You Think You Need a Hearing Aid (1985); mil: sgt. US Marine Corps 1951-55, decorated Korean Svc. w/battle star; Republican (Calif. St. Central Com.); Prot.; rec: music, mem. Al Malaikah Shrine Band (pres. 1985), leader Dixieland Jazz Band. Res: 1401-109 Valley View RdGlendale 91202 Ofc: Carl's Hearing Instruments 236 N Glendale Ave Glendale 91206

CARLIN, JEAN EFFAL, psychiatrist; b. July 24, 1930, Hibbing, Minn.; s. Effal O. (Anderson) C.; edn: BA, Univ. of Minn. 1950, BS, 1952, MA, 1953, MD, 1954, PhD, 1959. Career: intern 1954-55, resident in psychiatry Univ. of Minn. 1955-56; faculty, chief of Student Health Svc. North Park Coll., Chicago 1956-58, Long Beach VA Hosp. and CSU Long Beach 1958-60; pvt. gen. med. practice, Long Beach 1961-67; resident in psychiatry 1967-69; vol. physician to Viet Nam 1969, 1971; staff psychiatrist UC Irvine Med. Sch. 1969-71; assoc. dean UC Irvine Coll. of Med. 1974-78; chief of profl. edn. Fairview State Hosp. 1978-80; dir. Residency Edn. in Psychiatry, Drew Med. Sch. 1980-82; assoc. prof., dir. Residency Edn. in Psychiatry, Univ. of Okla. Meml. Hosp., Oklahoma City, Okla. 1982-85; cons. Indian Health Svc. 1984-86; fellow in psychiatry and law USC/ LAC Med. Ctr., Los Angeles 1986 –; cons. Dept. of Prisons 1986 –; mem: Am. and Calif. Med. Assns., Am. Psychiatric Assn.; mil: col. Army Nat. Guard, 143rd Evac. Hosp.; Covenant Ch. of Am. Res: 616 Island View Dr. Seal Beach 90740

CARLISLE, ARTHUR LAVORN, chiropractor; b. Nov. 13, 1956, Marion, Ala.; s. Arthur Lee and Eula Mae (King) C.; m. Harriet Johnson, Mar. 22, 1981; edn: BS in human biol., Pasadena Coll. of Chiro. 1982, DC, 1984; Certified Nutritional Cons., Donsbach Univ. 1985; Cert. X-ray Supvr. and Opr. (1985), lic. Chiropractor (1985), Calif. State Board. Career: lab. asst. and clinician Ecology Health Center, Pasadena 1982-85; chiropractor/owner Carlisle Chiropractic Clinic, Monterey Park 1985 –; lectr. local civic orgns. and youth groups; subject of feature articles in The Tuskegee News (6/84), The

Pasadena Gazette (8/84), The News Digest (1985), The Monterey Park Progress (7/85); awards: Southwestern Pres.'s Club award (1977), student body pres. PCOC (1983), Dean's List (1984), PCOC outstanding proficiency in clin. practice (1984), nom. Outstanding New DC of the Year (Calif. Chiro. Assn. 1986); mem: Calif. Chiro. Assn./San Gabriel Chpt. (treas. 1986), Monterey Park CofC (Ambassador, nom. bd. dirs. 1986-89), Flying Samaritans Inc., Lion's Club, MERCI Journal Com.; civic: Monterey Park Rotary, Hemophilia Found. of So. Calif., East Los Angeles Skills Center Advis. Council, LACCS Speaker's Bureau, Miss Monterey Park Pageant, MPK Civic Clubs Coordinating Council, MPK Eye and Ear Screening Com.; contbr. research article in J. of Mammalogy (1982); Worldwide Ch. of God; rec: tennis, Scrabble, flying, skiing. Ofc: Carlisle Chiropractic 1901 S Atlantic Blvd Ste G Monterey Park 91754

CARLSGAARD, ROWENA ANNE, speech pathologist; b. Feb. 17, 1953, Merced; d. Norman Stephen and Dolores Mae (Wilson) Mazzei; m. Frederick Carlsgaard, July 4, 1981; children: Emma b. 1982, Hannah b. 1985; edn: AA, Merced Comm. Coll. 1973; BA, CSC Stanislaus 1975, MA, 1977, Speech & Hearing Svcs. Credential, 1977; Cert. of Clin. Competence, ASHA 1979; lic. speech path. Calif. BMQA. Career: speech/language pathologist Livingston Union Sch. Dist., Livingston 1978-85; pvt. practice Speech, Language Hearing Clinic, Atwater 1985 –; Ofc. of Merced County Supt. of Schools 1986 –; Master tchr. CSC Stanislaus 1979-85, supr. for sp./lang. pathologists in state licensing and nat. certification pgm.; mem: Am. Sp. Lang. Hearing Assn., Calif. Sp. Lang. Hearing Assn., Public School Caucus, Merced Catholic Comm. League of Am. Wheelmen; Catholic; rec: sewing, bicycling. Res: 812 West 23rd St Merced 95340 Ofc: Speech, Language Hearing Clinic Heights Ave Atwater 95301

CARLSON, EDWIN THEODORE, computer co. executive; b. Mar. 6, 1936, Berwyn, Ill.; s. Theodore Wm. and Edwina (Warner) C.; m. Janice Lynn, Apr. 28, 1983; children: Christian Alexandra b. 1983; edn: BS engring., US Naval Academy 1961. Career: nat. mktg. mgr. Xerox Corp., El Segundo 1969-78; v.p. sales Computer Scis. Corp., El Segundo 1978-81; information sys. & service mgr. Control Data Corp., Dallas, Tx. 1981-84; gen. mgr. Businessland Inc., Orange 1984 –; mem. Am. Mgmt. Assn., US Naval Academy Alumni Assn.; publs: contbr. articles to computer jours. & mags.; mil: 2d lt. USAF 1961-63; Republican; Lutheran; rec: water skiing, golf, tennis, racquetball. Res: 947 Clear Creek Canyon Diamond Bar 91765 Ofc: Businessland 302 West Katella Orange 92667

CARLSON, JAMES LOWEN, insurance broker; b. Aug. 30, 1942, NY, NY; s. Charles Elon and Lucille Gertrude (Lowen) C.; m. Rosanne Gordon, Apr. 30, 1983; 1 son, Tyler Louis b. 1984; edn: BA, The Ohio State Univ. 1964; Assoc. Risk Mgmt., Ins. Ed. Assn. 1977. Career: agent, dist. sales mgr. Allstate Ins. Co. 1968-73; comml. acct. exec. Johnson & Higgins 1973-80; v.p., comml. account mgr. Frank B. Hall & Co. 1980-83; bus. agent mgr. Nationwide Ins. 1983-86; v.p. C.A. McClin & Co. Tustin 1986 –; honors: Phi Beta Rho (1960), Toastmaster of the Year (1979), num. sales achievement awards, photog. contest achievement awards 1968-80; mem: Western Assn. Ins. Brokers 1980-83, Toastmasters Internat.; mil: USMC 1964-68, Navy Commdn., Pres. Unit. Citn., Vietnam Defense, Vietnam Campaign; Republican; Catholic; rec: golf, running, photog. Res: 8 Nuevo Irvine 92715 Ofc: C.A. McClin & Co. 17731 Irvine Blvd Ste 205 Tustin 92680

CARLSON, JAMES QUENTIN, company president; b. Jan. 5, 1943, Tekamah, Nebr.; s. Clair Abram and Gayle Geraldine (Garner) C.; m. Louis LaNelle Tordoff, April 20, 1968; children: Dwaine Hollis b. 1972, Jaime Louella b. 1975, Wendy Lynn h. 1967, Troy Jon b. 1965, Dawn Christine b. 1963; edn: spl. tng., Los Angeles Trade Sch. 1966, Nissan Motor Corp., Nat. Inst. for Automotive Excellence (Wash. DC), Automotive Inst.; exec. tng., Rotary Internat. 1982; Grad. Pilot Cert., FAA 1971; Master of Psycho-Cybernetics, Am. Isnt. of Motivational Sci.; Career: svc. mgr. Garner Service Ctr., Chino 1962; upholsterer Charlotte Furniture Co., Anaheim 1963; mgr.- foreman O.F. Parsons Excavating & Grading, Garden Grove 1964; owner Survey Stake Co., Garden Grove 1965; gen. ptr. Enco Svc., Riverside 1966-67; tchn. svc. mgr. Econo Datsun Inc., Riverside 1968-69; owner: Lilac Beauty and Wig Salon, Bloomington 1970; Blomington Shell Svc. 1970; Enno's Pups Kennels, Fontana 1972; LaNelles Coiffures, Bloomington 1973; Jimmy on the Sport "Mobile Auto Repair", Bloomington 1972, San Diego 1976 –; honors: Hon. Mem., Boys Town USA, Omaha, Nebr. 1970; Club Svc. (1981), Community Svc. (1981), Dist. Gov. Svc. Above Self Award (1981-82), Paul Harris Fellow (1984) No. San Diego Rotary; mem: United Fedn. of Small Bus., No. San Diego Rotary (Pres. 1983-84); Republican; Methodist; rec: pvt. pilot, boating, camping. Res: 5936 Charing San Diego 92417 Ofc: Jimmy on the Spot, The Lincoln Blvd. Ste. 211, 7380 Clairemont Mesa Blvd. San Diego 92111

CARLSON, RICHARD WARNER, journalist, film producer; b. Feb. 10, 1941, Boston, Mass.; s. W.E. and Ruth Carlson; m. Patricia Caroline Swanson, Feb. 17, 1979; children: Tucker McNear b. 1969, Buckley Peck b. 1971. Career: journalist Los Angeles Times 1962-63; United Press Internat. 1963-65; ABC-TV, San Francisco and Los Angeles 1966-75; freelance writer, stringer Time Magazine, Look, others 1966-70; dir., prod. documentaries NBC-TV, Burbank 1975; anchorman CBS-TV, San Diego 1975-76; senior v.p., v.p. fin. Great American Fed. Savings Bank 1976-84; dir: Delmar News Press 1976, Calif. Gen. Mortgage Inc. 1978, San Diego CofC; awards: recipient, num. profl. awards incl. six Assoc. Press TV and Radio awards for investigative reporting, news analysis and commentary; (4) Golden Mike awards; (3) Emmy awards, (2) San Diego Press Club awards; (3) Foster Peabody awards for Excellence,

Investigative Reporting; L.A. Press Club Grand Award; Nat. Headliners Award; apptd. by Pres. Reagan to President's Council on Peace Corps 1982; mem: Jr. League of San Diego (Fin. Advy. Bd.), La Jolla Soccer League (sponsor), Muscular Dystrophy Assn. (dir. San Diego), Citizens for Open Space, Actors & Others (pres. L.A. 1972-76), A.J. Liebling Soc. of L.A. (co-founder), San Diego Coalition, Calif. CofC, Sigma Delta Chi, La Jolla Beach Club, Mid Ocean Club; mil: col. Calif. National Guard; Republican (v.p. Bus. & Profl. Club 1978, Senate advy. Commn. 1978); Episcopal. Res: 7956 Ave. Alamar La Jolla 92037 Summer: Crockett Island, Lake Christopher, Woodstock, ME 04219 Ofc: 9191 Towne Centre Dr. Ste. 410 San Diego 92122

CARMIEN, J. ALLEN, manufacturing co. executive; b. June 16, 1919, Seattle, Wash.; s. Roy Parry and Winifred (Jenott) C.; m. Kelly Sullivan, Oct. 11, 1974; children: Craig Allen b. 1951, Kathie Leigh b. 1954; edn: M.E., USC 1942; MBA, UC Los Angeles 1964; Reg. Profl. Engr., Calif. Career: engr., chief engr., sales mgr., vice pres. sales, pres., then owner New Plastic Corp., 1939-, name chg. to Nupla Corp. 1968–, acquired Hart Systems Corp. 1985, currently chief exec. ofcr. and bd. chmn. Nupla Corp. and Hart Systems Corp.; mem: Soc. Plastic Ind. (pres.), Soc. Plastic Engrs. (pres.), Hand Tool Inst. (pres.), Hardware Inst. (pres.), AFTA; Al Malika Shrine; clubs: Jonathan, Marina Yacht, Jonathan Yacht, 4th July Yacht (commodore); Republican; rec: boating. Res: 525 N Maple Dr Beverly Hills 90210 Ofc: Nupla/Hart 11912 Sheldon Sun Valley 91352

CARNAHAN, THOMAS WILLIAM, real estate broker; b. Sept. 17, 1954, Hollywood; s. Joseph Baines and Mary Ella (Bennett) C.; m. Nancy Morr, June 5, 1976; 1 child, Kinsley b. 1982; edn: BS, Univ. Colo., Boulder 1976. Career: real estate sales, Boulder, Colo. 1975-76; sales mgr. P.W.C. Realtors, Woodland Hills 1976-80; v.p./sales mgr. New Homes, Merrill Lynch Realty, 1981-85; owner/pres. Carnahan & Assocs., A Real Estate Corp., Woodland Hills 1985–; honors: Realtor Asso. of Year (1981) San Fernando Valley Bd. Realtors (SFVBR); mem. Nat. Assn. Realtors (Calif. dir. 1984-86, MLS com.), Calif. Assn. Realtors (Dist. 18 dir. 1978-, MLS com., chmn. Jurisdiction com. 1986), SFVBR (dir. 1979-, speakers bur., chmn. MLS com. 1981, exec. com. 1982-, video MLS Task Force 1986); civic: Variety Club of So. Calif. (charity), CofC; Republican; Presbyterian; rec: tennis, photog., ski. Ofc: Carnahan & Assoc. 20121 Ventura Blvd Ste 100 Woodland Hills 91364

CARNEY, CALLIE IRENE, non-profit govt. agency executive director; b. July 12, 1934, Camden, Ala.; d. Richard and Rosa B. (Kennedy) Bryant; m. James Carney, Feb. 17, 1951; children: Carolyn b. 1952, James Jr. b. 1954, Joseph b. 1955, Mary b. 1956, Richard b. 1957, David b. 1958, Shrielle b. 1960, Kimberly b. 1965. Career: expert examiner State of Calif., 1966-; past pos. as personnel splst. Calif. State Personnel Board, Community Services coord. for housing, regl. tng. dir. 14 states/chair WACTI, Nat. Office Economic Opportunity, cons. to Sacto. Police Dept., Calif. Homemakers Assn., Dept. of Edn., Calif. Dept. of Corrections and Calif. Youth Authority; apptd. exec. dir. Women's Civic Improvement Center (anti-poverty agcy.), Sacramento 1982–; works: first black woman to serve on Sacramento City Council; City record for most exp. in rehabitation of low income housing units and social service to residents, involved in 4 major projects totalling 1-½ to 2 million dollars each; Democrat; Prot.; rec: music. Res: 3288 9th Ave Sacramento 95817 Ofc: Women's Civic Improvement Club Inc. 3555 3rd Ave Sacramento 95817

CARNEY, PATRICK JAY, architect; b. July 24, 1955, Branson, Mo.; s. Leslie Jay and Edith Lenore (Condit) C.; edn: B.Arch., Calif. State Polytechnic Univ. S.L.O. 1977; M.Arch., UC Berkeley 1980; D.I.S., Royal Acad. of Arch., Univ. of Denmark, Copenhagen 1976-77; Internat. Lab. of Arch. and Urban Design, Urbino, Italy 1980; Reg. Architect, Calif. (1984). Career: staff architect, designer, project mgr., William L. Pereira Assocs., Los Angeles 1977-78, Kamnitzer Cotten Vreeland, Los Angeles 1980-81, Bull Field Volkman Stockwell, San Francisco 1981-82, Rod Freebairn - Smith Assocs., S.F. 1982-83, Hearst & Chen Architects, S.F. 1983–; also head architl. & interiors consulting firm, Patrick J. Carney Architect, San Francisco; awards: John K. Branner Traveling Fellowship, UCB (1980), Eisner Prize in Arch. (mention) UCB (1980), scholarship award to Internat. Lab. of Arch. and Urban Design, UCB (1980); mem: Am. Inst. of Architects, Nat. Trust for Historic Preservation; Democrat; rec: skiing (snow, water), politics, architl. hist. research, photog. Ofc: Patrick J. Carney Architect, 1745 Page St Ste 1 San Francisco 94117

CARPENTER, DONALD BLODGETT, real estate appraiser; b. Aug. 20, 1916, New Haven, Conn.; s. Prof. Fred Donald and Gwendolen (Blodgett) C.; m. Barbara Adams, June 28, 1941 (dec. 1978); m. 2d Lee Burker McGough, Dec. 28, 1980; chil: Edward G. (b.1952), John D. (b.1957), William V. (b.1959), Andrew J. (b.1960), Dorothy J. (b.1962), James J. (b.1964) McGough; edn: Ph.B., Univ. VT 1938; Sonoma St. Univ. 1968-9, Mendocino Comm. Coll. 1977, Coll. of the Redwoods 1984-85; certifications: Cert. Review Appraiser, 1980, Sr. Cert. Valuer, 1981; Int. Cert. Appraiser, 1984; Manufactured Housing Cert. Appraiser, 1983. Career: reporter, Burlington Daily News, VT, 1938-39; guide chair opr. Am. Express Co., NY World's Fair, 1939; underwriter Gen. Exchange Ins. Corp., Newark, NJ 1939-40; sales correspondent J. Dixon Crucible Co., Jersey City, NJ 1940-42; sales rep., San Francisco 1946-52; field supr. The Travelers Ins. Co., S.F. 1952-58; gen. agent, Gen. Am. Life Ins. Co., S.F., 1958-59; Western supr. Provident Life & Accident Ins. Co., S.F. 1959-60; brokerage supr. Aetna Life Ins. Co., S.F. 1960-61; maintenance cons. J.I. Holcomb Mfg. Co., Mill Valley 1961-68; ednl. serv. rep. Marquis-Who's Who, Inc., Mill Valley 1963-68; tchr./coach Mendocino Jr.-Sr. H.Sch., 1968; real prop. appraiser Co. of Mendocino, 1968-81, ind. real estate appraiser, 1982–; tchr. Coll. of the Redwoods 1985–; mem. Assn. of Govt. Appraisers, 1974-; Nat. Retired Tchrs Assn.; MHCA, 1983; Calif. Assn. of Realtors, afil., 1982-; Relocation Information Svc. Inc. 1982-; awards: scholarship-leadership awd., Kappa Sigma Internat. Frat. 1937-8; Comm. Sportsman of the Year, Booster Club, 1971; Paul Harris Fellow, 1979, Rotary Intl. Dist. Gov. awds. 1974, 76; mem: Am. Legion 1945-(Post Comdr. 1972-3, Past Comdrs. of Calif. 1973-); Kappa Sigma Intl. Frat. (life); Am. Diabetes Assn. 1973-; Mendocino Cardinal Boosters 1968-(charter, life; pres. 1971); Mendocino Co.Employees Assn., 1968-81; Reserve Ofcrs Assn. of the US (life; chpt. pres. 1954, 56; state v.p. 1958-61); Rotary Internat. 1969-(club pres. 1975-6, dist. gov. area rep. 1977-8); Univ. of VT. N.Calif. Alumni Assn. (founding pres. 1964); Mendocino Art Center 1965-; Mendocino Hist. Resrch, Inc. (Docent, 1982-); Univ. Newspaper, ed. in chief, 1937-8; Int. Frat. Chptr. alumni publ., ed. 1937-8; Univ. Frosh Handbook ed. 1937-8; ed. Rotary Club Membership Directory, 1971-; mil: Lcdr. USNR, ret. 1968; C.O. USNR Unit 1967-8, Secty. Navy Commend. 1946, Comdt. Naval Dist. Commend. 1968; Republican; Congregational; rec: historian, genealogy, philately, tennis. Res: Box 87, Mendocino 95460 Ofc: Appraisal Services, 10801 Gurley Ln Mendocino 95460

CARPENTER, ROBERT HUDSON, manufacturing co. executive; b. July 16, 1930, Los Angeles; s. Earl Raymond and Elsa (Munster) C.; m. Janice Ogden Vest, Oct. 12, 1984; son, Michael Edward Vest b. 1968; edn: Webb Sch. 1944-48; AB, Stanford Univ. 1952, Stanford Grad. Sch. of Internat. Relations 1952. Career: mktg. rep. Time Inc., New York and San Francisco, 1956-59; account exec. J. Walter Thompson Co., N.Y. 1959-63; v.p. Marsteller Inc., Los Angeles 1963-73; pres. Robert H. Carpenter Inc., L.A. 1973-83; pres. Commercial Guardian Inc. subs. Baskin-Robbins Ice Cream Co. 1983–; clubs: California (LA), Regency (LA), Beach (Santa Monica), University (SF); mil: lt.jg USNR 1953-56; Republican; Episcopal. Res: 164 S Las Palmas Ave Los Angeles 90004 Ofc: Commercial Guardian Inc. 1920 Corporate Way Anaheim 92801

CARR, JERI DARLENE, public relations executive; b. June 26, 1952, Los Angeles; d. Sam H. and Evelyn Jeanette (Jolin) Caraeff; m. Marvin Benson, Apr. 20, 1985; edn: AA, Valley Jr. Coll. 1972; BA, CSU Northridge 1975; BA, UC Los Angeles 1978. Career: asst. Budget Dress Buyer, Kline Kinsler buying office, Los Angeles 1971-73; assoc. Dress Buyer, AMC buying office, Los Angeles 1973-75; mgr./merchandiser Gladys Fowler clothing store, Century City 1975-77; senior acct. exec. Irwin Zucker Promotions in Motion, Hollywood 1977-81; v.p. (non music) New Image Public Relations, Hollywood 1981-83; pub. rels. prin./ pres. Jeri Carr Public Relations, Inc., Sherman Oaks 1983–; honors: winner CSUN Forensics and Debate Tournament (1973); mem: Publicity Club of Los Angeles (chair mem. activities 1985-), Nat. Assn. of Female Execs., Public Relations Roundtable/ San Fernando Valley Br.; civic: bd. govs. Save-A-Life Inc., L.A. (charity); num. profl. publs. for clients; rec: tennis, cooking, int. decor. Ofc: Jeri Carr Public Relations, Inc. 13437 Ventura Blvd Ste 217 Sherman Oaks 91423

CARR, KENNETH GERALD, aerospace co. executive; b. May 30, 1937, Iowa Falls, Iowa; s. Gerald and DeLoris Arlene (Stone) C.; m. Joan, Nov. 8, 1978; children: Kurt Kenneth b. 1958, Canda Joy b. 1961, Kevin Dean b. 1965, Christa Jean b. 1967; edn: Carlsbad Jr. Coll.1957-58; Santa Ana Jr. Coll. 1962-63; Golden West Coll. 1968; cert. bus. mgmt., Orange Coast Coll. 1968; cert. indsl. rels. UC Los Angeles 1971; cert. bus. mgmt., UC Irvine 1976; BS bus.mgmt., Pacific Western Univ. 1979. Career: section supv. Ford Aerospace & Communications Corp. Newport Beach 1962-76, pgm. mfg.mgr. 1976-77, mgr. prodn. control dept. 1977-83, mgr. prodn.dept. 1983–; honors: Community Svc. Citation (Ford Motor Co.1974, 78); mem: Soc. Mfg. Engrs., Newport Beach CC, Hoag Meml.Hosp. 552 Club; mil: USMC 1956-58; Republican; Lutheran; rec: restoring classic cars. Res: 1038 Sea Lane Corona Del Mar 92625 Ofc: Ford Aerospace & Communs. Corp. Ford Rd Newport Beach 92660

CARREY, NEIL, lawyer; b. Nov. 19, 1942, Bronx, NY; s. David L. and Betty (Kurtzberg) C.; m. Karen K., Apr. 9, 1980; children: Scott b. 1967, Douglas b. 1972, Dana b. 1973, Jana b. 1981, Christopher b. 1984; edn: BS in acctg. Wharton Sch. Univ. of Penn. 1964; JD, Stanford Law Sch. 1967; admitted to Calif. State Bar 1968. Career: assoc. atty. firm of De Castro, West, Chodorow & Burns, Inc. 1967-, ptnr. 1969-, vice pres. 1979–; lectr. USC Sch. of Paralegal Profls. 1977-; honors: General Alumni Soc. Award, Univ. of Penn. 1976; Who's Who in Am. Law (1979); mem. The Group (orgn. of splst. of closely held bus.), Am. Bar Assn., Western Pension Conf.; ofcr. Vista Del Mar Child Care Center 1968-; bd. dirs. Univ. of Penn. Alumni Soc. of So. Calif. (pres. 1971-79); bd. dirs. Nat. Little League, Santa Monica Little League (treas. 1984-85, pres. 1985-); parent rep. sec. sch. curriculum com. Santa Monica Sch. Dist. 1981-82; club: Mountaindate Tennis; Republican; Jewish; rec: tennis, painting. Res: 616 23rd St Santa Monica Ofc: De Castro, West, Chodorow & Burns, Inc. 10960 Wilshire Blvd, Ste. 1800, Los Angeles 90024

CARRITHERS, WALLACE MAXWELL, manufacturing co. executive, ret.; b. Aug. 26, 1911, Pittsburg, Kans.; s. Harry Wallace and Henrietta (Hassell) C.; m. Dorcas Williams, Apr. 15, 1937; children: Edith C. b. 1942, Judith H. b. 1943, Davis W.M. b. 1943; edn: CPA, Univ. Ill. 1943; BS commerce, Central YMCA Coll. 1946. Career: clerical, ofc. mgmt. and public acctg. staff positions, 1931-43; systems mgr., asst. controller, controller/asst. treas. A.B. Dick Co., 1943-69; program ofcr./instr. Univ. of Kentucky Coll. of Bus. & Econs., 1970-76; founder/pres. Carden, Inc. 1977–; adult edn. and guest lectr. Univ. of Chgo., Northwestern Univ., Univ. of Ill., and DePaul (Chgo. 1946-57); coauthor textbook: Business Information & Accounting Systems (1967); Management Handbook (Assn. Ed. Am. Mgmt. Assn. 1971); honors: Boy Scouts Am. Silver Beaver Award (1968), Kentucky Colonel (1972), Am. Inst. of CPAs

40-year membership award (1984); mem: Finl. Execs. Inst. (1952-67), Theosophical Soc. in Am. (1977-), Nat. Retired Tchrs. Assn. (1977-); civic: Help of Ojai Inc., Field Mus. of Natural Hist., The Smithsonian Assocs.; club: Ojai Valley Racquet; Republican Nat. Com.; rec: gardening, painting, stamps & coins, golf. Res: 14 Taormina Ln Ojai 93023

CARROLL, DAVID WILLIAM, computer writer/consultant, b. May 16, 1949, Portland, Ore.; s. Cecil Thomas and Florence Emily (Grant) C.; m. Carol Lynn (Cantando) Sylvain, Nov. 17, 1984; step children: Theresa Marie, b. 1969, Georgia Bahia, b. 1972, Nicholas Joshua, b. 1975; edn: Univ. of Wash., Portland State Univ., Pomona Coll. 1967-68; lic. pvt. pilot, instr., FAA; 3rd class radiotele. lic., telecomm. installation supvr., FCC; cert. locksmith. Career: engr. Arcata Communications 1971-73; owner Carroll Telecom 1973-75; mgr. Key Technology Co. 1975-77; engr. Calif. Microwave, 1977-79; tech. mgr. Vector Communications 1979-80; cons. on mil. projs. Lockheed Missiles and Space Corp. 1980; sales mgr. Fulcrum Computer Sys. 1980-81; senior programmer Videosoft Corp. 1982; current owner Amador Computer Service, Pine Grove and cons. in computer/electronics systems num. firms; dir. World Videovend Corp.; mem: Mensa, Audio Eng. Soc., IEEE, ACM, Am Inst. of Indsl. Engrs., Am. Mgmt. Assn., Civil Air Patrol; 4H Leader; author: Telecommunications with the IBM PCjr (1984), MultiPlan for the Commodore 64 (1984), The Information Professional's Guide to Online Database Services (Scott, Foresman & Co., 1985); The Handbook of Business Data Communications for the IBM PC (Dow Jones- Irwin, 1985); Programming with Turbo Pascal(Micro Text/ McGraw Hill, 1985); num. arts. and tech. papers; Democrat; Protestant; rec: photog., stagecraft, horses. Res: 23522 A Shake Ridge Rd., Volcano 95689; Amador Computer, P.O. Box 699, Pine Grove 95665

CARSON, THOMAS CLAUDE, real estate investment broker; b. Jan. 21, 1949, Annapolis, Md.; s. Albert Cunningham and Olivia Katherine (Brown) C.; m. Louella Marie, July 4, 1985; edn: BA, UC Berkeley 1972, MBA, 1977; Calif. lic: R.E. Broker (1976), Variable Contract Ins. (1985), Life & Disability Ins. (1985); Reg. Prin. (Securities), NASD (1985); Cert. Finl. Planner (CFP), Coll. for Finl. Plnng. (1986). Career: real estate appraiser Security Pacific Nat. Bank, San Francisco 1973-75; broker/owner Carson Props. aka Vestron, Berkeley 1976–; guest lectr. Laney Coll.; mem. Nat. Assn. Realtors, Calif. Assn. Realtors, Berkeley Bd. Realtors (dir.); civic: Lions Club of Berkeley (v.p.), Lions Eye Found, Elks, Berkeley CofC, Berkeley Breakfast Club; publs: Multiple Regression Analysis of Rents in Berkeley vs. Parameters Assoc. with Housing Needs; served in US Coast Guard Civilian Svc.; rec: pvt. pilot, bridge, sailing, scuba. Ofc: Carson Properties aka Vestron 1913 Addison St Berkeley 94704

CARTER, BRIAN ROBERT, judge; b. Nov. 10, 1925, Paris, France; s. David and Jeanne (Richmond) C.; parents Am. citizens; m. Margaret Helen Schwarz, Feb. 14, 1958; children: Brian Robert, Scott David; edn: BS in EE, Univ. Iowa 1950, postgrad. work Univ. Kansas City 1958; JD, Pepperdine Univ. 1969; admitted to Calif. State Bar 1970. Career: staff adviser Westinghouse Electric Corp., Pitts. 1952-54, promotion mgr. Kansas City, Mo. 1954-58, program mgr., Baltimore 1958-62; dir. licensing electronics North Am. Rockwell Corp., 1964-74; practice law Newport Beach, Santa Ana and San Diego, 1970-82; judge Municipal Ct., Newport Beach, 1982–; judge pro tem Orange County Ct. System, 1976-78; mem. Calif. State Bar, Orange County Bar, Iowa Alumni Assn. (named to Order Golden Hawk 1967), Beta Kappa Lambda, Masons, Bahia Corinthian Yacht Club (commodore 1972-3); publs: articles on yachting in var. mags.; mil: served with USNR, USMCR, 1943-45, decorated Purple Heart; Episcopal. Res: 4732 Cortland Dr Corona del Mar 92625 Ofc: Carter and Hobart, 601 N Parkcenter Dr Santa Clara 92705

CARTER, FANYA, psychologist; b. July 23, 1933, Los Angeles; d. Victor and Adrea Carter; children: Sheri b. 1955, Leigh b. 1957, Robin b. 1960; edn: AA, Pierce Coll. 1962, BA, Peppedine Univ. 1972, MA 1973; PhD, Calif. Grad. Inst. 1981; Calif. lic. Marriage & Family Counselor (1974), Psychologist (1982). Career: actress in films, TV and radio shows, 1965-70; psychiatric asst. 1970-73; pvt. practice marriage family counselor/prin. 1974-81, clin. psychologist/prin. 1981–; honors: The Voice for Armed Forces Radio (1965); mem. APA, CSPA, Los Angeles County Psych. Assn.; civic: Social Services Commn. LA County, Hollywood Bowl Mus. (advis. bd.); publs: L.A. Times syndicated articles: Preparing Your Child for First Day of School (9/15/85), How to Motivate Your Child to Study (8/25/85); Democrat; Jewish; rec: dance, yoga, nutrition, art, philosophy. Res: 515 Ocean Ave, 608N, Santa Monica 90402 Ofc: 12301 Wilshire Blvd Ste 515 Los Angeles 90025

CARTER, MARSHA ANN, financial planning & information systems executive; b. Aug. 8, 1944, New Orleans, La.; d. Charles and Florence Mary (Calvey) C.; 1 son: David R. Dade, b. 1972; edn: BS, UCLA Grad. Sch. of Bus. 1972. Career: The Rand Corp., Santa Monica 1967-76; research assoc.; assoc. mathematician; planning analyst; deputy dir.; pgm. mgr.; sr. planning anlyst, The Eaton Corp., Cleveland, Ohio 1976-77; Hughes Aircraft Co., El Segundo, Calif. 1977–; computing splst., senior splst., sect. head, dir. fin. planning & info. systems; corp. data processing coord., Hughes Aircraft 1983-; chmn. DOD Flexible Progress Payment, Hughes 1980-83; awards: Hyland Awd., Performance Inprovement Awd.; Cost Improvement Awd.; All- Star Basketball Player; YWCA Cert. of Achiev.; mem: Am. Mgmt. Assn.; Aerospace Inds. Assn. of AM., Inc.; Nat. Contract Mgmt. Assn.; Manhattan Beach Country Club; YMCA; Hughes Woman's Forum; num. publs. in ind. journs.; Democrat; Catholic; rec: swimming, hiking, skating. Res: 2704 Curtis Ave Redondo Beach 90278 Ofc: Hughes Aircraft Co., 200 N Sepulveda, Bldg C2 M/S A153, POB 1042, El Segundo 90245

CARTER, STEPHEN DARNEL, micro computer analyst; b. Dec. 29, 1954, Bakersfield, Calif.; s. Eddie Lee and Claria Mae (Robinson) C.; edn: Cal. Poly. S.L.O. 1973-75; BA, UC San Diego 1978; MA, Univ. Iowa 1980, MS, 1981; planner, Am. Planning Assn. Career: outreach counselor, research analyst UC San Diego 1975-78; grad. asst. Univ. Iowa 1978-80; planner I East Central Iowa Council of Govt. Iowa City 1979-81; proj. adminstr. supv. Bechtel Power Corp. Downey, Calif. 1981-83, lead field adminstr. Phoenix 1981-84, budget/ planning adminstr. Norwalk 1984–, micro computer instr./ cons. 1986–; honors: Outstanding Coll. Grad. - Civic Improvement (1978); mem: Internat. City Mgmt. Assn., Am. Planning Assn., Alpha Phi Alpha, Am. Soc. Plastic Engrs., L.A. Urban League, United Way; inventions: Automated Task Completion System (1982), Energy Utilization/ Consumation Computerized Model (1980), Computerized Overhead Budget Control System (1985); Independent, Christian; rec: photog., sports. Ofc: Bechtel Power Corp. 12440 E Imperial Hwy Ste 37 Norwalk 90652

CASASSA, CHARLES STEPHEN, S.J., university chancellor emeritus; b. Sept. 23, 1910, San Francisco; s. Charles S. and Margaret G. (Power) C.; edn: BS, Univ. of Santa Clara, Santa Clara, CA 1934, MA, 1935; STL, Alma Coll., Los Gatos, 1939; PhD, Univ. of Toronto and Pont. Inst. of Mediaeval Studies, Toronto, Can. 1936; Hon. Degrees: DD, Univ. of Judaism, 1964; STD, USC, 1965; LHD, Calif. Coll. of Med., 1965; LL.D, St. Mary's Coll., 1967; LHD, Hebrew Union Coll., Jewish Inst. of Religion, 1967; LL.D, Univ. of S.F., 1969; DHL, Marymount Coll., 1969; LHD, Univ. of Santa Clara, 1973; LHD, Loyola Marymount Univ., 1981. Career: ordained priest, 1938; instr. Loyola Univ., 1939-41; asst. prof. Santa Clara Coll. 1946-49, dean of art, 1948-49; pres. Loyola Univ. of Los Angeles 1949-69, chancellor 1969-84, chancellor emeritus 1984–; trustee: Gonzaga Univ. (1972-77, trustee emeritus 1977-), Univ. of S.F., Loyola Marymount Univ., Independent Edn. Council of Calif.; dir. Knudsen Found.; mem: Independent Colls. of So. Calif., Inc. (pres. 1956-58); Los Angeles CofC (bd. dirs. 1966-67), LA World Affairs Council (bd. dirs.), Friendship Day Camp Inc. (pres.), Knights of Columbus; Rotarian (hon. mem. L.A. Rotary 1977); adv. bd. Junior League of L.A. 1978-81; Roman Catholic; rec: reading mystery stories. Address: Loyola Marymount University, Los Angeles 90045

CASE, JOHN MC KENNA, building products co. president; b. Aug. 19, 1946, San Francisco; s. John R. and Jean (McKenna) C.; m. Andrea Wilcox, Mar. 15, 1975; children: Andrew b. 1982, Catherine b. 1984; edn: BA, CSU San Diego 1968. Career: pres./CEO The Case Cos. (family owned wholesale bldg. mats. bus.; father dec. 1968), 1968–, divs. include Case Products Co., Pella Windows & Doors Inc., and Case Lighting Resources Div. (founded 1969; he devel. custom technique for framing light to fit the exact contours of the lighted object i.e. sculpture, painting, piano keyboard, landscape feature, etc.); dir. Sun Savings 1981-85; honors: Who's Who in Am. Colls. and Univs. (1968), Lambda Chi Alpha frat. Nat. Achievement Award (1968), Outstanding Young Citizen of San Diego, S.D. Jaycees (1977), one of five Outstanding Young Cit. of California, Calif. Jaycees (1981), AIA award for remodel of La Jolla villa (1985), listed in "America's Finest" Interior Designers Diary (1986, 87); civic: Young Friends of San Diego Symphony (co-founder 1973, bd. 1973-75), Combined Arts and Edn. Council (trustee 1973-76), La Jolla Mus. of Contemp. Art (trustee 1975-86, v.p. 1977), S.D. Young Execs. Club (pres. 1975), S.D. CofC (dir. 1976-77), La Jolla Playhouse (dir. 1983); Republican; Catholic. Res: 7342 Country Club Dr La Jolla 92037 Ofc: The Case Companies 969 Buenos Ave San Diego 92110

CASELLI, JACLYN RUTH, library coordinator; b. Mar. 28, 1921, Boston; d. Jacob Bates and Eleanor Ruth (Jackson) Abbott; m. Reginald Louis Caselli, Aug. 18, 1945; children: Pamela Anne, Patrick Bates, Kevin Wade, Reginald Louis, Michele Susan, Suzette Marie; edn: stu. Penna. State Univ. 1938-40, AA, San Jose City Coll. 1970; BA with distinction, San Jose State Univ. 1976, MLS, 1979. Career: with Yankee Mag., Dublin, N.H. 1940-42; with Eric Clearinghouse in Information Resources, Sch. Edn., Stanford Univ., 1979–, dir. acquisitions 1970-77, library coordinator Research Libraries Info. Network, 1976–, library user services coordinator Research Libraries Group, 1977–; honors: 2 Gold medals, 1 Silver medal Internat. Senior Olympics (1979); mem: Am., Calif. Special library assns., Nat. Wildlife Soc., Audubon Soc., Amateur Athletic Union, Athletic Conf., Sierra Club, Phi Kappa Phi; mil: WAVES, 1942-45. Res: 1528 Carmel Dr. San Jose 95125 Ofc: RLIN Stanford Univ. Stanford 94305

CASELLINI, RENZO CARLO, dental technologist; b. Aug. 8, 1945, Chur, Switz.; s. Mauro M. and Mathilda (Meier) C.; m. Irene, Feb. 22, 1973; 1 dau. Ilona Cornelia, b. 1982; edn: Certified Dental Techn. (CDT), honors, Dental Tech. Coll., St. Gallen, Switz. 1965; CDT, cert. Nat. Bd. USA, 1976. Career: mgr. supvr. in father's dental studio (3d generation lab. dental techn.), Chur, Switz. 1966-72; supvr. ceramist Van Nuys, Calif. 1973, 1974–; owner/pres. Swiss Quality Dental Ceramics Inc., Los Angeles 1977–; cons./rep. Hadax Co. (Switz.) 1984-; founder RCC's Dental Products (devel. RCC Color Liquid, porcelain build-up chemical), 1985-; bd. dirs. Am. Tooth Industries, Oxnard (1985-); holds num. table clinics for Calif. Dental Assn. and West Dental Soc. (1976-); guest speaker nat. and abroad dental socs.; mem: Calif. Dental Lab. Assn., So. Calif. Dental Assn., Asklipion Oral Implants Study Group (lectr. on implants 1977-); clubs: Touch Inc. (Bev. Hills), Century West (L.A.), Tennis Club (Chur, Switz.), Swiss Ski Assn., High Mile Club (LA); mil: Swiss Army 1964; Catholic; rec: ski (downhill, x-c), tennis, race car driving. Res: 2527 La Condesa Los Angeles 90049 Ofc: Swiss Quality Dental Ceramics Inc 1100 Glendon Ave Ste 832 Los Angeles 90024

CASEY, THOMAS FRANCIS, computer co. president; b. Jan. 3, 1952, Waterbury, Conn.; s. Thomas F. and Ellen A. (Henry) C.; edn: BA, Univ. of Conn. 1973. Career: product mktg. mgr. Am. Hosp. Supply Corp., div. McGaw Labs., Irvine 1974-78; co-founder/v.p. Home Health Care of Am., Newport Beach 1978-80; v.p. Ren U.S.A., div. Kema Nobel Sweden 1980-82; bd. chmn./pres./CEO AUDRE, Inc., San Diego 1983–; dir. Lundell Laboratories, Phoenix, Az.; honors: Who's Who in Am. Junior Colls. (1971); mem. So. Calif. Technology Execs. Network, Internat. Motor Sports Assn. Inc.; co-founder 1st high-tech. home medical supply co.; bus. developer of the leading Artificial Intel. Based Automatic Digitizing and Recognition Computer System; Republican; rec: automobile racing, scuba. Ofc: AUDRE, Inc. 10915 Technology Pl San Diego 92127

CASEY-LEE, PATRICIA A., civil engineering firm executive; b. May 14, 1947, Oakland; d. Chester Clarence and Helen Louise (Baker) Spearing; m. Stanley P. Lee, Dec. 7, 1985; 1 son, Brian D. b. 1966; edn: AA, Modesto Jr. Coll. 1983; bus. adminstrn., CSU Stanislaus. Career: accts. receivable clerk Montgomery Ward, Modesto 1965-66; secty. new accts., loan processor Central Bank, Waterford 1969-72; adminstrv. asst. Mid-Valley Engrg., Inc., Modesto 1972–, Notary 1974-, small claims rep. 1980-; honors: Scholarship (Modesto Bd. of Realtors 1965), Outstanding Credit Personality (Modesto Credit Bur. 1972), Assoc. of the Yr. (Bldg. Industry Assn. 1985), Leadership Awd. (Modesto CofC 1985-86), winner essay contest Modesto J.C. (1967); mem: Native Daus. of the Golden West 1974-81 (outside sentinel 1976), Women in Constrn. Industry 1979-, Exec. Club of Modesto (coord. 1981-82), Phi Epsilon Phi sor. (past pres., council v.p. 1982, nat. 3rd v.p. 1985, 1st. v.p. 1986), Bldg. Industry Assn. Aux. (treas. 1982, pres. 1985), Nat. Assn. Exec. Sectys., Modesto CofC (ambassador 1984-); co-chpsn. Citizens for Diversified Energy 1982, co-chpsn. Am. Cancer Soc. Cook-Off 1982; vol. Crisis Ctr. of Stanislaus Co.; Republican; Episcopal; rec: skiing, tennis, golf, bowling. Res: 1433 Seneca Ct Modesto 95351 Ofc: Mid-Valley Engineering Inc., 900 H St Ste G Modesto 95354

CASH, PEG ELIZABETH, real estate broker/executive; b. Jan. 24, 1923, Mineola, Long Is., N.Y.; d. John and Cordelia (St. Hilaire) Shea; m. Thomas Tarasovich (dec. 1966), 1944; m. 2d Frank H. Cash, Dec. 16, 1967; edn: spl. courses Booth & Baylis Coll., Bridgeport, Conn. 1940-41, Ft. Lauderdale Univ. 1975, Coll. of the Desert 1978; Calif. lic. real estate sales (1971), real estate broker (1978). Career: secty. to purch. agt. Chance Vought Aircraft, Stratford, Conn. 1944-46; came to Calif. 1946; secty., City of Los Angeles Bldg. and Safety Dept., 1946-60, exec. secty. to L.A. City Council adminstrv. secty. to late Councilman Harold A. Henry, Wilshire Area, 1961-66; real estate agt. Holiday Realty, Palm Springs 1971, real estate broker 1978–; v.p. Mercury Property Mgmt. Inc. and v.p./broker Mercury Real Estate Services, Palm Desert; profl. awards: Million Dollar Sales Club (1972-74), Reno Sch. of Exchanging Gold Card; mem. Palm Desert Board of Realtors (chmn. publicity 1979-81, secty. Local Govt. Rels. Com. 1982-), Calif. Assn. of Realtors, Nat. Assn. of Realtors, Civic Center Womens Council (L.A.), P.S. Desert Circus; Republican; rec: painting, knitting, bingo. Res: Bermuda Dunes. Ofc: Mercury Real Estate Services 73 260 El Paseo, Ste 3-A Palm Desert 92260

CASHMAN, ROBERT LYNN, envelope co. president; b. Jan. 25, 1932, Hartley, Iowa; s. Chester Floyd and Kathern May (Fuller) C.; m. Georgia E. McClintock, Mar. 22, 1956; children: Karen Jean (Roscoe) b. 1956, Lynn Marie b. 1959, Kim Christine (Standley) b. 1961; edn: BSBA, UC Los Angeles 1956. Career: mgmt. trainee Aetna Casualty 1956-59; broker/prin. Cashman Ins. Counselors 1959-72, sold brokerage to ITT, 1972, employeed by ITT, 1972-75; acquired Nat. Envelope Co. 1972, acquired 3 other small ep. cos., merged & formed Pacific Ep. Co., bd. chmn./pres./sole owner, 1976–; pres. Hallmark Litho Inc.; bd. chmn. Crown Technology Inc.; awards: INC. mag. 'Inc. 500' list of 500 fastest growing cos. in US (1962, 63, 64, 65, 66) and Usual Suspects Award for contbns. to Inc. articles on mgmt./ strategy, Bus. to Bus. Mag. list of Top 100 cos. in Orange Co., and Santa Ana Register list of O.C. top 50 cos. (1985), spl. awards for vol. work, L.A. Olympic Organizing Com. and L.A. Organizing Com. XV World Games for the Deaf, others; mem. Young Pres. Orgn. (1959-74), Quiet Birdmen, Quarter Century Wireless Assn., NRA (CRPA); civic: Anaheim YMCA (pres., dir. Camp Osceola), Anaheim CofC, Anaheim Mus., Mayor's Advsy. Bd., Planetary Soc., CHOC Padrinos; mil: 2d lt. US Army Nat. Guard 1951-53; Republican; Methodist; rec: amateur radio (K6DQK), flying, astronomy, photog., shooting. Res: 18482 Park Villa Pl Villa Park 92667 Ofc: Pacific Envelope Co. 1600 E Winston Rd Anaheim 92805

CASILLAS, JOSEPH H., manufacturing engineer; b. Dec. 28, 1931, Gallup, N.M.; s. Fernando M. and Catalina (Hernandez) C.; m. Julia Melendez May 1, 1954 (decd. 1981); m. 2nd Teresa Robles, July 30, 1983; children: Joyce Anne b. 1959, Joseph L. b. 1961, Jeffrey Mark b. 1964; edn: Orange Coast Coll. 1958; mgmt., CSU Long Beach 1974; indsl. tech., Long Beach City Coll. 1976; indsl. tech. CSU Long Beach 1984; Reg. Profl. Engr. Calif. 1978. Career: strl. assembly McDonnell Douglas 1952-56, machinest-duplicating 1956-64, shop-mid. mgmt.-fabrication 1964-77, mgr. fabrication 1977-80, senior tool engr. 1980-81, br. mgr. methods engrg. 1981-85, fabrication expert MD-80 MDC-China (PRC) co-prodn. pgm. 1985–; honors: Recruiter of the Year (VFW 1972); mem: Full Gospel Businessmen's Fellowship Internat., V.F.W. (post cmdr. 1960-61, 1961-62, 1971-72), Am. Legion; publ: staff Mfg. Methods Engrg. Newsletter 1985; mil: sgt. 1/c US Army 1950-52, Commdn. ribbon w/ medal pendant, Combat Infantryman's Badge, UN & Korean Svc.; Democrat; Christian; rec: bowling, golf. Res: 11606 Candytuft Cr Fountain Valley 92708 Ofc: McDonnell Douglas Corp. 3855 Lakewood Blvd Long Beach 90846

CASILLAS, JUAN FLORES, veterinarian; b. April 18, 1944, Corpus Christi, Texas; s. Arthuro Flores and Maria Refugio (Flores) C.; m. Debra, Aug. 2, 1982; children: Consuelo b. 1968, Isabella b. 1970, Juan b. 1973, Esiquio b. 1974, Alexis b. 1983, Vanessa b. 1984; edn: BS, Tuskegee Inst. 1967, DVM, 1969. Career: veterinarian Animwal Med. Ctr., Compton 1969; equine practice, San Fernando Valley 1970-71; owner Montebello Veterinary Hosp., Montebello 1971–; owner Huntington Park Dog and Cat Hosp., Huntington Park 1974–; owner East Los Angeles Dog and Cat Hosp., E. Los Angeles 1976–; owner Lynwood Dog and Cat Hosp., Lynwood 1984–; owner Maywood Dog and Cat Hosp., Maywood 1985–; currently, exec dir. Casillas Veterinary Hosps. Inc.; pres. Calif. State Bd. of Veterinary Med. Examiners 1976-81; bd. dirs. Calif. Student Loan Finance Corp. 1980-; honors: Civic Svc. Award, City of Commerce 1982; Cert. of Merit, Calif. State Bd. of Veterinary Med. Examiners 1981; mem: Calif. and Golden State Veterinary Med. Assns., Rotary, Masons, Senior Citizens Assn. (bd. dirs. E. Los Angeles- Montebello area); Democrat; Catholic; rec: archery, fishing, reading. Ofc: Casillas Veterinary Hospitals Inc., 2437 W. Whittier Blvd. Montebello 90640

CASSELL, MARION ALEXANDER, investor; b. Sept. 27, 1909, Gary, West Va.; s. James Gibony and Mary Lee (Phillippi) C.; m. Hazel Moreland, July 1, 1955; edn: BA, Ohio State Univ. 1934, grad. work in hist., pol. sci., 1935-36, Ohio State Law Sch. 1937-38; naval indoctrination Princeton Univ. 1942-43. Career: var. pos. in constrn. industry (in 14 states) 1934-42, including Hoover Dam and Maxon Constrn. Co. on US Naval Arsenal, Burns City, Ind.; comdr. US Navy 1942-46, WWII, cmdg. ofcr. USS LST 126 (survived Westlock explosions in Pearl Harbor; evacuated survivors from 5 ships sunk in the Philippine Sea Battle with Japanese, and then weathered typhoon that sank 2 more destroyers; his LST 126 arrived Island of Leyte for Return to Phil., 2 days before Gen. MacArthur); co-owner/v.p. American Constrn. Equipment Inc., Los Angeles 1947-50; co-owner tract housing constrn. co., Kentwood Homes, Norwalk; purch. dir. Pacific Cast Iron Pipe & Fitting Co., South Gae 1951-58; contract price analyst US Dept. of Def. 1958-72, at TRW Inc., Redondo Beach 1966-72; negotiated multimillion dollar contracts for govt. mil. and space programs, incl. the Moon, Apollo and Neptune Programs; investments, 1972-86; asst. to hd. of Adult Eve. Sch. Ohio State Univ. 1935-36; mil. honors: USN Commendn., 7 combat stars, Rated in top ten percent of Cmdg. Ofcrs.; mem: Delta Sigma Phi frat. (Life), The Adventurers Club, Hobos of Am., Masons, Blue Lodge, Scottish Rite, Shriners, Retired Ofcrs. Assn., Navy League; Republican; United Methodist; hobby: adventure- crossed US 83 times, hoboed over Western US, world traveler. Address: 18 Via Majorca Rolling Hills Estates 90274

CASSELLE, DAWNE ASTRIDE, advertising counselor, entrepreneur; b. Apr. 16, 1943, Phila., Pa.; d. Jack T. and Bernice Constance (Smith) C.; div.; 1 son, Todd Anthony Poindexter, b. 1961; edn: AA in bus., LA City Coll., Pierce Jr. Coll., 1973; BA, UCLA 1975; JD, UCLA Sch. of Law 1980; contg. edn. wkshops, seminars. Career: owner Casselle & Associates (pub. rels., advt., promotions, mktg. resrch.), Los Angeles; profl. public spkr.; honors: Phi Alpha Delta, Moot Ct. Hons. Pgm., staff ed. UCLA Black Law Journal; mem: Women's Referral Service, Nat. Fed. Bus. & Profl. Women, NAFE, Wilshire CofC, Am. Entrepreneurs Assn., UCLA Alumni Assn.; contbg. writer var. newspapers and mags.; mem. Republican Predtl. Task Force; Baptist/Sci. of Mind. Address: Caselle & Assoc. 3333 W 2nd St, 53-204, Los Angeles 90004

CASTLE, RICHARD EDWIN, real estate syndicator; b. Jan. 5, 1943, N.Y.C.; s. Eli N. and Mildred (Meyerson) C.; children: Pamela A. b. 1966, James N. b. 1968; edn: BS acctg. CSU Hayward 1969; att. Drake Univ., Univ. of Ariz., John F. Kennedy Law Sch.; Advanced Post Cert. in law enforcement, State of Calif. (1969); Calif. lic.real estate agt. Career: patrolman Oakland Police Dept.1964-, apptd. sgt.of police 1969-84, ret.; currently active as Police Reserve in Contra Costa Co. Sheriff's Ofc. Marine Patrol; pvt.real estate investments 1975–, owner/gen. ptnr. apt. complexes; co-owner Dublin Travel Agcy.; past tchg. in police acads., guest instr. in auto theft (comml.) CSU San Jose, frequent guest speaker var. service clubs and civic orgns.; honors: Blue Star and Medal of Valor as Sgt.of Police; sports awards on P.D. teams- softball, football, basketball, bowling; mem.Oakland Police Ofcrs. Assn., Sigma Phi Epsilon frat. (treas. Tucson chpt.1963-64), Western States Auto Theft Investigators, Antioch CofC, Incline Village CofC; civic: police ofcr. off duty vol. work with underprivileged youth groups, Pop Warner Football (coach 5 yrs), Little League (coach 2 yrs); works: unique style of property rehabilitation & mgmt.generating comfortable and affordable housing as well as community improvement; mil: hon. disch. USMCR (6 yrs) and USAR (2 yrs); rec: racquetball, fishing, boating, bridge. Res: 1645 Taylor Blvd Lafayette 94549

CASTRO, JOSEPH RONALD, physician, oncologist, cancer researcher; b. Apr. 9, 1934, Chgo.; s. Dr. Cosimo and Agnes C. (Lenhart) C.; m. Barbara Ann, Oct. 12, 1957; children: Joseph, Margaret, Anne, Eileen, Michael, Kathleen; edn: BS Nat. Sci., Loyola Univ. Chgo. 1956, MD, 1958; Fellow Am. Coll. Radiology. Career: radiation oncology and cancer research Univ. of Texas 1967-71, Univ. of Calif. 1971–; dir. Particle Radiation Oncology, UC Berkeley Lawrence Lab., 10 yrs.; pioneered use of Californium neutron therapy and clin. research in heavy charged particles; current prof. and v.chmn. Radiation Oncology UC San Francisco and dir. Radiotherapy, Lawrence Berkeley Lab.; fmr. chmn., bd. trustees No. Calif. Cancer Pgm.; awards: hon. mem. Rocky Mountain Radiological Soc., Special award, Univ. of Tokyo 1982; mem. var. profl. radiation and oncology socs.; club: Il Cenacolo; mil: US Navy 1956-66; rec: sailing, horses. Res: 24 Lochness Ln San Rafael 94901 Ofc: Lawrence Berkeley Laboratory, Bldg 55, Berkeley 94720

CASTRO, REMEDIOS RAMOS, import-export consultant; b. Oct. 1, 1953, Manila, Phil.; s. Manuel N. and Florencia M. (Ramos) C.; edn: BA, Manuel L. Quezon Univ. 1974, LLB, 1978; Reg. Representative NASD (1986). Career: asst. legal ofcr. Rizal Technol. Colls., Pasig, Manila, Phil. 1979-80; insurance agt. Sun Life of Canada, Los Angeles 1980-84; ins. agt., CIGNA, 1984–; exec. cons. dba The Manila Connection, L.A. 1986–; mem. Phil. Bar Assn. (1978-); Democrat; Catholic; rec: hist. and lang. of the Philippines. Ofc: The Manila Connection 6565 Sunset Blvd Ste 200 Los Angeles 90028

CASTRO, RODOLFO HADER, county government executive; b. May 31, 1942, Riverside; s. Doroteo G. and Lillian Lucero (Diaz) C.; edn: AA (honors), Riverside City Coll. 1967; BS (honors), Calif.State Poly. Coll. 1970; MBA, Harvard Univ. 1973; stu. city govt., mgmt., & politics, Oxford Univ. (Eng.) 1980; advanced mgmt. studies, Yale Univ. 1986. Career: dep. dir. Econ. Opportunity Bd., 1971; asst. dir. LULAC Nat. Edn. Svc Ctrs, 1973-75; exec. dir. L.N.E.S.C., 1975; exec. dir. Community Svc Dept., San Bernardino Co., 1976–; pres. Rodolfo H. Castro and Assocs., Inc.; apptd. by Gov. Deukmejian to Calif. State Social Svcs. Advsry. Bd. 1985; apptd. Children's Policy Council for San Bernardino County 1986; honors: Energy Conserv. Award. DOE (1980), Calif. Legis. Resolution 305(5/15/81), recogn.US Congl. Record (5/5/81), CalPoly Sch of Bus.Alumni of Year (1981), Nat. Assn. of Counties Achieve. Award (1984) life mem. Alpha Gamma Sigma (1967); listed Who's Who in Am. Colls. and Univs. (1971); mem: Mex.-Am. Commn. of San Bernardino (dir.), Am. Soc. for Pub. Adminstrn., Harvard Bus. Sch. Alumni Assn. (life), Oxford Preservation Trust (life); mil: sgt.E-5, US Army, State Commend. Ribbon, GCM. Republican: cand. US Congl. 37th Dist. Calif. 1982 (sustaining Calif. RP, Repub. Nat. Com., Calif. Repub.Hispanic Council, Mex.-Am. Polit Assn.). Catholic.Res: 250 N.Phillips, Banning 92220Ofc: Community Svc Dept. San Bernardino Co., 686 E. Mill St. San Bernardino 92415

CATANIA, PATRICK NICHOLAS, pharmacy educator; b. July 17, 1944, Meadville, Pa.; s. Salvatore Ralph and Petrina Virginia (Consiglio) C.; m. Harriet Frances Riggar, Aug. 22, 1970; edn: prepharm., CSU Fresno 1962-64; BS, Sch. of Pharm. Univ. of Pacific 1968; MS, Univ. Pac. Grad Sch. 1970, PhD, 1973; Reg. Pharmacist Calif. 1968, Nev. 1968. Career: community pharmacist central Calif. 1968-70; pharm. faculty Univ. Pacific Sch. of Pharm. 1970–, sect. head clin. Experience Pgms. 1981-83, currently prof., chmn. Clin. Pharm. Dept. and Pharm. Adminstrn. 1983–; cons. Interferon and antivirals, Creative Strategies Internat. San Jose 1982; cons. pharm. Hillhaven Conv. Hosp. Stockton 1977-84; cons. Frost & Sullivan Inc. NY 1982-85; ed. adv. bd. US Pharmacist 1984-86; honors: Outstanding Young Men of Am. 1978, Rho Chi, Phi Kappa Phi; mem: Am. Pharm. Assn., Calif. Pharm. Assn., Am. Soc. Hosp. Pharm., Calif. Soc. Hosp. Pharm., Am. Soc. Consultant Pharms., Am. Heart Assn. (chmn. emerg. cardiac care com. 1984-), Kappa Psi (regl. supv. 1973-82), Sundance Running Club (past secty.); publ: 50+ papers and presentations on pharm. and health care research (1971); patent holder for wound dressings in USA, Eng. France, Canada; mil: sp5 Calif. Army Nat. Guard 1969-75; Republican; Catholic; rec: running, x-c and downhill skiing, bowling, reading, travel. Res: 5303 Wood Duck Ct Stockton 95207 Ofc: School of Pharmacy Univ. of Pacific Stockton 95211

CATTELL, MICHAEL JAMES, optometrist; b. April 8, 1955, Seattle, Wash.; s. Bryon Neville and Lois Lorraine (Hodgson) C.; edn: Univ. of Wash. 1973-75; BS, Pacific Univ. 1978, OD, 1979. Career: longshoreman Columbia Wards Fisheries, Dillingham, Alaska 1976-78; optometrist R.G. Fellman, Portland, Ore. 1979-81; optometrist David Shultz, Northridge 1981-84; optometrist, self-empl., North Hollywood 1984–; honors: Bausch & Lomb Science Award, 1973; McCurdy Meml. Academic Scolarship, Univ. of Wash. 1974-75; Most Valuable Runner, Cross- Country & Track 1972 73; mem. Student Optometric Assn. (rep.), Pacific Univ. Coll. of Optometry, Calif. Optometric Assn., San Fernando Valley Track Club; Republican; Christian; rec: running, basketball, hunting. Res: 11124 Camarillo St., No. Hollywood 91602 Ofc: Michael J. Cattell, OD, 11311 Camarillo St. Ste. 215, No. Hollywood 91602

CATTELL, NANCY GOSSARD, lawyer, educator; b. Jan. 6, 1921, Lima, Ohio; d. Oliver P. and Dorothy (Boesel) Gossard; m. David T. Cattell, Sept. 17, 1948, div. 1969; children: Jody Ann b. 1953, Herbert Daniel b. 1954; edn: BS, Univ. Mich. 1941; MA, Columbia Univ. 1949; JD, Loyola Univ. L.A. 1971; M.Phil., Columbia Univ. 1973. Career: served pvt. to major US Army 1942-47, chief mil. personnel Mil. Govt. in Germany; Continuing Edn. splst. UC Los Angeles Extension 1972-76, devel. paralegal tng. programs; counselor/ prof. word processing, Santa Monica Coll., 1960–, tchg. political sci., bus. law, adminstrn. of justice, and computers; dir. ETA Travel Assocs., Inc.; awards: Am. Assn. of University Women Fellowship (1953); mem: Calif. State Bar, Los Angeles County Bar Assn., Santa Monica Coll. Faculty Assn. (pres. 1976-78), Attorney Gen.'s Volunteer Advis. Council; author: College and Career (Appleton-Century-Crofts, 1970), Inquiry or Inquisition (Nat. Assn. of Legal Assistants); mil: maj. Women's Army Corps 1942-47, decorated Am. Campaign, Eur.-Afr.-Middle Eastern Campaign, WWII Victory, WAAC Service, Army of Occup. medals; Democrat; rec: photog., travel, archaeology, pvt. pilot. Res: 2611 Eleventh St, 4, Santa Monica 90405 Ofc: Santa Monica College 1900 Pico Blvd Santa Monica 90405

CAUDRON, JOHN ARMAND, safety engineer/expert witness, b. Sept. 26, 1944, Compton; s. Armand Robert and Evelyn Emma (Hoyt) C.; m. Marilyn Fairfield, Mar. 16, 1968; children: Melita b. 1973, Rochelle b. 1976; edn: AA, Ventura Coll. 1965; BA, CSU Fullerton 1967; civil engring, Univ. Nevada, Reno 1975-78; MSS, USC 1980. Career: mgr. Snyder Research Labs-Reno, Reno, Nev. 1976-78; v.p. Snyder Research Labs, Inc. Pico Rivera, Calif. 1978-83, pres. El Monte 1983-85; tech. evaluation cons./ pres. Fire & Accident Reconstruction, Rowland Hgts 1985–; mem: Firearms Research & Identification Assn. (pres.), ASCE, Am. Soc. Safety Engrs., Am. Soc. Metals, Geol. Soc. Am. (Geotech.), Nat. Fire Protection Assn., Nat. Safety Council; civic: PTA (safety chmn.), Boy Scouts Am. (counselor), Fort Tejon Hist. Assn.; publish newsletter re: tech. aspects of accidents - product failure, property damage, personal injury; mil: Republican; Christian; rec: mil. hist., firearms, photog., exploring. Res: 18638 Alderbury Dr Rowland Hgts 91748 Ofc: 1608 Nogales St Ste 360 Rowland Hgts 91748

CAVAYERO, STEPHEN BRUCE, electronics manufacturing co. president; b. Dec. 24, 1957, Bronx, NY; s. Morris and Rita (Berg) C.; m. Amy, May 16, 1982; edn: State Univ. of NY Binghamton 1977-78; BA, UCLA 1980. Career: regl. sales mgr. A & M Mktg. Cons. Inc., Canoga Park 1980-81; trade rels. mgr. Pepsi Cola Bottling Group, Los Angeles 1981-83; pres., owner Cavaco Internat., Tarzana 1983–; cons. Univolt Corp. of Am., Canoga Park 1983; cons. sales and mktg. Van Slyke Inc., San Bernardino 1983-; cons. importing, mfg. and purchasing in the orient 1983-; honors: NCAA Div. 3 Champion Wrestling, State Univ. of NY 1977, 1978; Athlete of th Year, State Univ. of NY 1977, 1978; NCAA Div. I, Freshman 1st Team All American, Wrestling 1977; NCAA All American Wrestling 1977, 1978; mem: SUNY Binghamton Wrestling Team (capt.), Pre-Law Soc. (UCLA), UCLA Wrestling Team, UCLA Alumni Assn., Statue of Liberty (charter contbr.); works: created and devoloped associated internat. br. ofcs., Cavaco Internat., Taipe, Taiwan, Hong Kong, Tokyo, Seoul and Pusan, So. Korea; rec: boating, music, theater. Res: 18214 Burbank Blvd. Apt. 122 Tarzana 91356 Ofc: 18653 Ventura Blvd. Ste. 293 Tarzana 91356

CAVENDER, HOWARD MARION, insurance and equities sales executive; b. Nov. 25, 1924, Manila, Phil.; s. Howard M. and Dorothy Mae (Grey) C.; m. Betsy Skinner, Feb. 4, 1950; children: Kieran b. 1952, Virginia b. 1953, James b. 1959; edn: MS in finl. svcs., The American Coll. 1984; desig: CLU, Chartered Life Underw. (1974), ChFC, Chartered Finl. Cons. (1984). Career: asst. v.p. Robert Dollar Co., Manila 1947-63; mgr./treas. Globe Wireless Ltd., Manila 1947-63; pres. L.M. Hausman & Co., Manila 1955-59; atty. in fact, Ayala y Cia, Manila 1959-63; agent, branch mgr. Sun Life of Canada, Calif. 1964-77; ins. splst. Merrill Lynch, Calif. 1977-82; assoc. brokerage mgr. Transam. Occidental Life, 1982-84; salesman Transam. Ins. & Finl. Services, 1985–; recipient profl. awards, Sun Life of Canada (1966), Transam. Occidental Life/ Merrill Lynch (1981); civic award, Manila Lions Club (1952); mem: Nat. Assn. of Life Undw. (chpt. dir. 1976), Am. Soc. of CLU (chpt. pres. 1980; nat. liaison team mem.), Internat. Assn. of Finl. Planners, S.F. Estate Plng. Council, CofC; mem. Masons, Elks (past grand exalted ruler), Sharon Hts Golf & Country Club; mil: cpl US Army Air Force 1943-45 PTO decorations; Republican; Episcopal; rec: photog., big band music. Ofc: Transamerica Insurance Services 200 Pringle Ave Ste 250 Walnut Creek 94596

CECCHETTI, ROY EMILIO, wine industry marketing executive; b. Feb. 13, 1957, San Francisco; s. Guido and Albina (Scannavino) C.; m. Rachael Nivens, June 27, 1981; edn: internat. bus., Loyola Univ. of Chgo. at Rome, Italy 1977-78; BSC fin., Univ. of Santa Clara 1979; Exec. Mgmt. Tng. Prog. 1980. Career: acctg. supvr. Bechtel Group Inc., San Francisco 1979-82; controller Bertolli USA, Inc. South San Francisco 1983; asst. to controller Optical Coating Lab. Inc., Santa Rosa 1984; acctg. mgr. Chas. Schwab & Co. Inc., S.F. 1985; winemaker prin. Cecchetti Sebastiani Cellar, Inc. Sonoma 1985–; finl. cons. wine industry mktg.; mem. Am. Mgmt. Assn., Wine Inst.; clubs: Olympic (SF), Assoc. Lucchesi Nel Mondo (SF); active Citizens United for Assem. Don Sebastiani, Sonoma; Republican; Roman Catholic; rec: basketball, baseball, golf, music, spectator sports. Res: 19450 Franquelin Pl Sonoma 95476 Ofc: Cecchetti Sebastiani Cellar Inc. 710 W Napa St Ste 4 Sonoma 95476

CEDAR, PAUL ARNOLD, clergyman; b. Nov. 4, 1938, Mnpls.; s. Carl Benjamin and Bernice Myrtle (Peterson) C.; m. Jean Lier, Aug. 25, 1959; children: Daniel b. 1961, Mark b. 1963, Deborah b. 1967; edn: BS, No. State Coll. 1960; M.Div., No. Baptist Theol. Sem. 1968; D.Min., Am. Baptist Sem. of the West 1973; grad. work Trinity Divinity Sch., Univ. Iowa, Wheaton Grad Sch., CSU Fullerton. Career: youth minister in Cedar Rapids, Iowa 1960-63; crusade assoc. Billy Graham Evangelistic Assn. 1963-65; senior pastor Naperville, Ill. 1965-67; crusade dir. Billy Gram Evang. Assn. 1967-69; senior pastor Yorba Linda, Calif. 1969-73; exec./evangelistic pastor First Presbyn. Ch., Hollywood 1975-80; senior pastor Lake Ave. Congregational Ch., Pasadena 1981–; founder, pres. Dynamic Communs. Inc., 1973–; adj. prof. Fuller Theol. Sem., Talbot Tehol. Sem.; vis. prof. Trinity Divinity Sch.; advsry. bd. Am. Inst. of Family Relations; awards: life mem./nat. Pi Kappa Delta award (1960), Am. Bible Soc. outstanding Bible Reading (1967); mem: Hollywood Ministerial Assn. (1979-80), Rotary/Hollywood (1978-80), Hollywood Coord. Council (chaplain 1980), Christian Assn. for Psychol. Studies (1977-); seminar leader Nat. Convocation of Christian Leaders (1979-80), del. Consultation on World Evangelization, Pattaya, Thailand (1980); author: Seven Keys to Maximum Communication (Tyndale House 1980), Becoming a Lover! (Tyndale House 1978), Sharing the Good Life! (1980); Congregational; rec: athletics, music, writing, carpentry. Res: 1771 E Orange Grove Pasadena Ofc: Lake Ave Congregational Church 383 N Lake Ave Pasadena 91101

CEDERGREN, HARRY ROLAND, civil engineer; b. Jan. 2, 1911, Seattle, Wash.; s. Robert and Ellen (Lind) C.; m. Evelyn, Jan. 1, 1939; 1 dau., Berneal b. 1941; edn: BSCE, Univ. of Wash. 1938; MS, Harvard Univ. 1939. Career:

civil engr. US Corps of Engrs., Portland, Ore. 1938-48; asst. city engr., Stockton 1948-51; senior materials & research engr. Calif. Div. of Hwys., Sacramento 1951-63; senior engr., supvrsn. dam safety State of Calif., Sacramento 1963-67; cons. civil engr., Sacramento 1967–; psl. lectr. Univ. of Calif. Ext. Dept. 1962, 1968; honors: Tau Beta Pi; Sigma Ki; mem: Fellow Am. Soc. Civil Engrs. (life), U.S. Com. of Large Dams, Highway Transportation Bd.; works: invented num. methods for analyzing seepage in dams and other engring. works; books publd. by John Wiley & Sons 1967, 1974, 1977; chpts. in num. engring. ref. book; num. tech. arcticles in engring. journ. 1940-85; Presbyterian; rec: genealogy, photog. Res: Sacramento

CEDILLOS, RON, aerospace testing co. president; b. July 31, 1950, Los Angeles; s. Art and Anna Gloria (Romo) C.; children: Michelle b. 1976, Ronnie b. 1977; edn: El Camino Coll. 1970-72. Career: profl. athlete, Karate; motion picture actor; bd. chmn./CEO, Cedillos Testing Co., Inc., Downey; lectr. USC; honors: Hon. Doctorate, LAAC/Pepperdine Univ.; mem: Am. Soc. of Non-Destructive Testing; Who's Who in Aero Space; exec. bd. Los Angeles Area Council BSA; mil: paratrooper, US Army 1967-70; Republican; Christian; rec: sailing, tennis. Ofc: Cedillos Testing Co. Inc. 12309 S Woodruff Ave Downey 90241

CELMER, DAVID ALVIN, consulting construction engineer, contractor; b. Jan. 31, 1958, Kingston, Pa.; s. Alvin Ronald and Irene C.; m. Miriam J. Weigel, Aug. 2, 1983; 1 dau. Jennifer Ashley b. 1984; edn: B. Arch. Engrg., Penn. State Univ. 1980; cert. engrg. mgmt. for constrn., UC Los Angeles 1984; MBA pgm., USC 1985-; Reg. Profl. Engr. Calif. (1983), Calif. lic. Mechanical Contr., Electrical Contr. Career: field engr. US Army Corps of Engrs. 1977-78; lead mech. engr. Honeywell Inc. L.A. 1981-83; mech. engr., proj. mgr. United Technols., Carrier- L.A. 1983-84; constrn. engr. Tishman Constrn. Corp. L.A. 1984-85, Dinwiddie Constrn. Corp. L.A. 1985–; pres. EquitySpec Cons. Engrs. Inc., EquitySpec Capital Sourcing Group Inc., EquitySpec Land Devel. Corp., The EquitySpec Group Inc., owner EquitySpec Devel. Co.; honors: Profl. Technical Excellence Award (Honeywell 1982), Nat. Commendation (US Dept. of Army 1978); mem: Nat. Soc. Architectural Engrs. (founding 1986), Constrn. Specs. Inst. (profl.), Mensa, Sierra Club, Penn. State Engrg. Alumni Orgn.; expert witness; publ: num. tech. papers 1983-; rec: family field trips, sailing, computers, German automobiles. Ofc: EquitySpec 5901 Warner Ste 492 Huntington Beach 92649

CERADSKY, VICKIE MARIE, real estate appraiser/broker; b. Jan. 5, 1939, Wichita, Kans.; d. Clarence H. and Oloween G. (Winkleman) Clark; m. Kenneth W. Ceradsky, Apr. 30, 1980; children: Keith b. 1957, Scott b. 1960, Linda b. 1967, Nancy b. 1962, Matthew b. 1958; edn: MS, Wichita Univ. 1973; AA in real estate; Calif. lic. R.E. Broker (1978), Appraiser (1980), Notary (1982); cert. Am. Assn. Certified Appraisers Inc. Career: asso. realtor cos: Has Hall, and Wm. L. Dieterte, Riverside; Dick Felber, Edgemont, 1969-72; project mgr. Volwood Realty and Devel. Corp., No. Hollywood; tract sales mgr. Kaufman and Broad, and Citation Homes; owner AAA Appraisal Service, Vallejo currently; mem. Vallejo CofC (econ. devel. com.); Democrat; rec: Japanese Bunka, building doll houses, gardening. Address: AAA Appraisal Service 175 Bluebird Ct Vallejo 94591

CERDA, J(OSE) LUIS, educator; b. Nov. 25, 1949, Lockney, Tex.; s. Cruz, Sr. and Patricia (Jimenez) C.; edn: BA in fine arts, Stanford Univ. 1973, MA in edn., 1975; Calif. Std. Sec. Tchg. Cred. (1986). Career: staff asst. Woodward-Clyde Cons., San Francisco 1976-80; graphic artist freelance, Palo Alto, S.F., 1980-81; staff photog. Cable Car Clothiers, S.F. 1981-83; tchr. (art, English, photog.) Pittsburg Unified Sch. Dist., 1985–; tchr. Butte Co. Pgm. for edn. of migrant children; adv. La Raza Club, Pittsburgh H.S.; honors: life mem. Calif. Scholarship Fedn. (1969), Bank Am. award in fine arts (1969), recogn. and edn. award, Calif.State Assembly (1985), edn. award United Council of Spanish Speaking Orgns. (1985); mem. Calif. Tchrs. Assn., Nat. Edn. Assn., United Council of Spanish Speaking Orgns. (bd. 1986), Hispanic Roundtable of Contra Costa Co., Stanford Alumni Assn.; Democrat; Catholic; rec: drawing, calligraphy, study of hist., music. Res: 274 Bay Crest Dr Pittsurg 94565 Ofc: Pittsburgh High School 250 School St Pittsburg 94565

CERRITO, ORATIO A., financial advisor; b. Mar. 10, 1911, Cleveland, Ohio; s. Carl and Lillian (Di Vita) C.; m. Rita McCue, Oct. 2, 1931 (div. 1947); children: Lillian b. 1932, Rita-Diane b. 1939; m. 2d. Maria Capri, Dec. 18, 1947; children: Miriam b. 1948, Linda b. 1952, Claudia b. 1960; edn: John Carroll Univ. 1934-36; LLB, Cleveland Law sch. 1940; admitted Ohio State Bar 1941. Career: foreman Chase Brass & Copper Co., Euclid, O. 1931-41; atty. assoc. Sindell & Sindell, Cleveland 1941-42; law violations investigator US Dept. of Labor, Cleveland 1942-44; civilian splst./head of price office (fixed prices for occupied Italy), Allied Mil. Govt., Rome1944-45; Hq. distbn. ofcr. UN Relief & Rehab. Assn., Athens, Greece 1945-46; pres./gen. mgr. U.S. Store Fixture Co., Cleveland 1946-52; acct. exec. Research Inst. of Am., Cleveland 1952-54, Los Angeles 1954-60; regl. mgr. Marlin Indsl. Div., So. Calif. 1960-81; finl. advisor/mgr. O.A. Cerrito Family Trust, 1981-. Address: 18173 Santa Cecilia Cr. Fountain Valley 92708

CHA, JONG WHAN, plant ecologist; b. June 19, 1935, Seoul, Korea, nat. US cit. 1970; s. Du Su and Ul Soon (Han) C.; m. Soon, Apr. 25, 1965; children: John b. 1966, Sarah b. 1967, Robert b. 1970; edn: BS, Seoul National Univ. 1958, MS 1960; PhD, Dong Kuk Univ. 1966; postdoctoral, UC Los Angeles 1977. Career: dean Bateson Sch. of Horticulture, Paramount, Calif. 1971-72; vis. prof. UC Los Angeles, 1971-74; prof. Dong Kuk Univ., Seoul, Korea 1966-76; postdoc. UCLA 1975-77, mem. research staff UCLA 1977–; owner Na Sung Department Stores, Los Angeles 1976–; honors: appreciation, Seoul Nat. Univ. Alumni Assn. (1986), Testimonial award, Korean Olympic Com. (1984); mem: Internat. Soil Sci. (1974-), Am. Horticultural Soc. (1975-), Am.-Korean Assn. of Edn. (pres. 1984-86), Korean Benefit Assn. (v.p.), Korean-Am. Scholarship Fund Assn. (pres.); publs: 162 research papers and 32 books; Mormon. Ofc: 3072 West Olympic Blvd Los Angeles 90006

CHACON, JILL SUZANNE, restaurateur; b. Mar. 23, 1945, Chgo.; d. Benjamin Arthur and Marianne Margaret (Boetticher) Lindauer; widow, Sergio F. Chacon; children: Brett b. 1963, Christopher b. 1974, Sean b. 1983; grad. Hollywood H.S. 1962. Career: waitress 1962-65, 1966-72; bank teller 1965-66; restaurant owner Puerta del Sol, North Hollywood 1972–; mem. Glendale CofC (1977-83), No. Hollywood CofC (1972-), Glendale AYSO youth soccer (coach); Republican; rec: swim, cooking, water skiing. Res: 1304 Oberlin Dr Glendale 91205 Ofc: Puerta del Sol 11669 Sherman Way No Hollywood 91605

CHAFIN, SAMUEL LEROY, clinical chemist; b. Jan. 26, 1928, Richmond, Va.; s. William L. and Anna (Ware) C.; m. Emma DeShay, Aug. 12, 1955; children: Sheryl b. 1956, Samuel II b. 1957, Dawn b. 1959; edn: BS, Tenn. State Univ. 1972; MS, Loma Linda Univ. 1978. Career: med. technologist Riverside Hosp., Nashville, Tenn. 1965-70, Madison Hosp., Madison, Tenn. 1970-74; staff med. technologists, senior technologists, supvr. Immunology sect., chief med. technologists Chemistry sect., Loma Linda Univ. Med. Ctr., Loma Linda 1974–; asst. prof. Med. Tech. Sch. of Allied Health Professionsl, Loma Linda Univ.; awards: Alpha Mu Gamma Award; Ambassador of the Month, Madison Hosp. 1974; Grad. Sch. Alumni Treas. 1978-82; pres. Calif. Soc. for Med. Technologists Inland Chpt. 1982, Loma Linda Univ. Admissions Com. Sch. of Med. Tech. (Cont. Edn. Exec. Com.), Am. Soc. of Clin. Pathologists, Am. Soc. for Med. Technology, Am. Assn. of Clin. Chemists, Am. Soc. of Microbiology, Nat. Registry of Clin. Chemists, Nat. Certification Agency for Med. Technologists, Calif. Soc. for Med. Technologists (pres. 1986-87); mil: machinists mate 3/c P.O. USN 1946-50, European, WWII; Democrat; Seventh Day Adventist; rec: alpine and water skiing, racquetball, chess. Res: 11595 Poplar St. Loma Linda 92354 Ofc. Loma Linda Univ. Med. Ctr., 11234 Anderson St. Loma Linda 92354

CHALMERS, R. SCOTT, property management executive; b. Mar. 27, 1947, Ross; s. William and Eleanor May (Schwerin) C.; m. Cynthia L. Gaddy, Aug. 21, 1971; children: Christa b. 1975, Cara b. 1978; edn: A, Napa Jr. Coll. 1970; BA, CSU Chico 1972; MBA, 1974. Career: mobile home ind. (4 yrs.); controller real estate devel. & const. corp. (3 yrs.); founder/ pres. RSC Associates, Inc. 1981–; mem: Calif. Apart. Assn. (Budget Com.); No. Valley Propety Owners Assn.; Rotary; Butte Special Olympics (pres. 1982-84); Greater Chico CofC (bd. dirs.) mil: E-4 US Army 967-69; rec: softball, swimming, golf. Res: 1675 Hooker Oak Ave Chico 95926 Ofc: RSC Associates, Inc., 676 E First Ave Ste 14 Chico 95926

CHALMERS, ROBERT BRUCE, civil engineer; b. Jan. 2, 1957, Costa Mesa; s. John Traile and Genevieve Margaret (Mack) C.; m. Karen, Sept. 25, 1982; 1 dau. Laura b. 1985; edn: BS, UC Los Angeles 1980; Reg. Profl. Engr. (Civil) Calif. Career: draftsman/ designer P.R.C. Toups Engring., Orange 1979; lab. asst. UCLA 1979-80; jr. civil engr./ designer Woodside/Kubota & Assocs., Inc. 1980-83, project engr./ project mgr., 1983–; honors: Eagle Scout, BSA (1972); mem. Orange County Water Assn. (1985-); mem. Alpha Gamma Omega Frat., Orange Park Acres Homeowners Assn.; Republican; Protestant; rec: skiing, camping, woodworking. Res: 20212 Frank St Orange 92669

CHAMBERLAIN, JOHN PAUL, lawyer; b. June 11, 1943, Brooklyn, NY; s. Leslie John and Helen (Chesne) C.; children: Keith Andrew, b. 1974; Jason Randolph, b. 1976; edn: BA, honors, Brooklyn Coll. (CUNY) 1965; JD, Univ. of Colo. 1968; admitted to practice, Colo. 1968, Wash. DC 1972, NY 1973, Calif. 1980. Career: asst. treas. Chase Manhattan Bank, NYC 1968-74; Judge Advocate, USAF 1969-72; asst. v.p. Nat. Bank of No. Am. 1974-78; asst. v.p. Security Pacific Nat. Bank, Los Angeles 1979-80; pvt. practice, law, Santa Ana 1980–; staff instr. Calif. Comm. Colls.; chmn. bd. Gluten Intolerance Soc. of Calif. 1983; honors: Mil. Judge, USAF 1970; Outstanding Young Men of Am., Jaycees 1970; Man of Achiev., UK 1976; Chmn. Rockland Co. New York Heart Assn. 1977-78; mem: Am. Bar Assn. Subcom. on Aerospace law Insts.); NY, Calif. & Wash. DC Bar Assns.; Gluten Intolerance Soc. of Calif.; Am. Heart Assn.; publs: sev. arts. on law, var. legal & profl. journs. 1970-; mil: capt. USAF 19969-72; rec: sailing, astronomy, pvt. aviation. Res: 295 Topeka Irvine 92714 Ofc: 401 Civic Center Dr W, Ste 1000, Santa Ana 92701

CHAMBERLIN, EUGENE KEITH, historian, educator; b. Feb. 15, 1916, Gustine; s. Charles Eugene and Anina Marguerite (Williams) C.; m. Margaret Rae Jackson, Sept. 1, 1940; children: Linda (Davies) b. 1941, Thomas Wayne b. 1944, Rebecca (Washburn) b. 1948, Adrienne Colleen (1950-1981), Eric Carl (dec. 1963); edn: BA in hist., UC Berkeley 1939, MA in Mexican hist. 1940, PhD in Latin Am. hist. 1949; seminar and field work CSU San Diego and Peru (Fulbright Hays grantee) 1982. Career: reader UC Berkeley in Mex. hist., 1938-40, in Calif. hist., 1945-46; misc. work 1940-41; tchr. Spanish and Latin, Lassen Union High Sch. and Jr. Coll., Susanville 1941-43; tchr. hist., Elk Grove Jt.Union H.S. 1943-45; tchg. asst. UCB 1946-48, instr. 1948-51; asst.prof. hist., Mont. State Univ., Missoula 1948-54, summer tchg. in Bozeman, 1953; prof. hist. & govt., San Diego City Coll. 1954-78; vis. lectr. Latin Am. hist., S.D. State Coll. 1965-67, UCLA Ext.1964-66, UCSD Ext. 1966-67; lectr. Mexican and S.W. hist. & recent world hist., S.D. Comm. Colls. T.V. 1969-77; prof. hist., Miramar Coll., S.D. 1978-83; prof. Calif. and Latin Am. hist., S.D. Mesa Coll. 1983–; awards: Rockefeller-Huntington Library grantee (1952), outstanding educator S.D. City Coll. (1970), merit award S.D. Cong. of Hist. (1978), Fulbright-Hays grantee, Peru (1982), Phi Alpha Theta hist. hon. (1946); mem: Phi Alpha Theta/Montana State Univ. (founder, faculty adv. 1949-54), AAUP (1949-, secty. Mont. St. Univ. chpt. 1953-54, pres. S.D. City Coll. chpt. 1956-57, mem. nat. coms., mem. Nat. Council 1967-70, pres. Calif. Conf. 1968-70, acting exec. secty., Calif. 1970-72), Am. Hist. Assn. (1948-, Beveridge-Dunning Com. chmn. 1984), S.D. Co. Cong. of Hist. (pres. 1976-77, newsletter ed. 1977-78), Pac. Coast Council on Latin Am. Studies (1955-), Cultural Assn. of the Californias (1964-), E Clampus Vitus (mem., chpt. offcs. 1962-, historian 1970-, bd. proctors 1983-), Transierra Roisterous Alliance of Senior Humbugs (1975-, bd. dirs. 1980-, pres. 1982-83), Mont. Acad. Scis. (1949-54); publs: approx. 40 arts. and num. book revs. in profl. jours. and separate pamphlets mostly on N.W. Mex., US Southwest, Calif. hist., ch. hist., comparison of Mex. and Peruvian hists. (1951-); Calif. Democrat; Ch. of the Brethren (nat. conf. del. 1986); rec: hist., gardening. Res: 3033 Dale St San Diego 92104

CHAMBERLIN, ROBERT JOSEPH, marketing executive; b. Sept. 8, 1929, Weatherford, Tex.; s. Tracy W. and Dorothy P. (O'Hare) C.; m. Ilene Krepps, Sept. 17, 1978; children: Robin, b. 1962, Russell, b. 1950; edn: BA mktg./BS psych. (Top 10% of class) Duke Univ. 1951. Career: salesman and broker, reg. rep. NASD, 1951-62, dir. of sales and respons. for taking public cos. (Ins. Co. of Texas, Am. Atlas Ins. Co., Am. Gen. Life Ins. Co., Am. Trust Life Ins., Lanark Corp., Lone Star Boat Co., ARA); v.p./dir. of sales Hawaii Clay Prods. Inc. 1963-68; auto sales and leasing mgmt. dealerships (Town and Country Ford, Holiday Ford, Oasis Ford, Gateway Ford, and Downtown L.A. Motors) 1969-80; founder/pres./CEO, Modern Methods of Mdsg. Inc. and affils., Am. Nat. Energy Programs Corp., All Am. Distbrs. Inc., 1981-85; current pres./ CEO, American Atlas Sales & Leasing Inc., and All American Finl. Services Inc.; past owner/opr. supper clubs in Hawaii, and prod. nightclub, radio & tv shows featuring jazz artists (incl. Herb Jeffries, Anita O'Day, Ray McKinley & Glen Miller Orch., Buddy Rich, Joe Williams, Billy Daniels); honors: Lambda Chi Alpha, pres. Shoe N' Slipper Club (Duke 49-51), USMC Heavyweight Champion Boxing (1948); mem: Granada Hills CofC, Better Bus. Bur., Jaycees (TX, HI); mil: gunnery sgt., mem. Pres. Truman's staff, US Marine Corps, decorated Silver Star, Bronze Star, Purple Heart, Pres. Unit Cit.; Democrat; Baptist; rec: reading, travel. Res: 15455 Glenoaks Blvd, 9 Sir Henry, Sylmar 91342 Ofc: Modern Methods Mdsg. Inc. 17050 Chatsworth, 106-115, Granada Hills 91344

CHAMBERS, JACQUES MARTIN, health insurance broker; b. May 5, 1940, Okla. City, Okla.; s. Guy Curtis and Jayme (Ledgerwood) C.; edn: BA, Okla. State Univ. 1963; Univ. Okla. 1963-66; Chartered Life Underwriter 1976. Career: group underwriting trainee Employers Ins. of Wausau 1966, group health underw. L.A. 1967-69, mgr./ group underw. 1970-73, mgr. employee benefits mktg. 1974-82; independent health ins. broker Burbank 1982-85; co-founder Triad Ins. Group L.A. 1985, v.p. health ops. 1985–; bd. dirs. Los Padres Health Plan S.L.O. 1979-81; various panels and seminars on health ins. in Calif.; seminars United Way on health ins. for non-profit groups; mem: Sunset Junction Neighborhood Alliance (bd. 1981-), Echo Park Comm. Coord. Council (pres. 1984-), Central City Action Com. (pres., bd. 1985-), Comm. Edn. Network, Queen of Angels Med. Clin. Adv. Council, Belmont H.S. Accred. Com., Virgil Jr. H.S. 75th Anniversary Com., Friends of Hollyhock House (docent); adv. council: El Centro del Pueblo, Echo Park/ Silverlake Child Care Ctr., Hollywood Sunset Community Clinic; mil: Okla. Nat. Guard 1958-63; Democrat; rec: theatre, music. Ofc: Triad Ins. Group 3540 Wilshire Blvd Ste 600 Los Angeles 90010

CHAMBERS, MARK JAMES, employee benefit specialist/sales executive; b. Jan. 2, 1953, Lompoc; s. Donald James and Carol Ann (Fair) C.; m. Debra Kingston, Mar. 28, 1976; children: Nathaniel James b. 1979, Elizabeth Ann b. 1982; edn: BS, Lewis and Clark Coll. 1975; Certified Employee Benefit Splst., Wharton Sch. Univ. Penna./ Internat. Found. Employee Benefit Plans (1985). Career: Vista vol., Portland, Ore. 1973-74; youth advocate and job devel. splst., City of Portland 1975-76; branch ops. ofcr. First State Bank of Ore. 1976-77; group rep. Standard Ins. Co., Portland and Orange County, Calif. 1977-81, group and pension rep., Orange County 1981-83; mgr. San Jose Group Office, Standard Ins. Co., 1983–; instr. Ins. Edn. Assn.; cons. advisor to independent ins. brokerage firms; honors: Nat. Presbyterian Scholar (1971-75), finalist Disting. Alumni Award, Lewis and Clark Coll. (1983); mem. Nat. Assn. of Life Undw., Calif., San Jose affils.; civic: Am. Field Service (adminstr. exchange pgm. 1981-83), Ballistic United Youth Soccer Assn. (Pleasanton), San Jose CofC (Young Leaders Pgm 1984-85), Bay Area Friends of Lewis and Clark (com. chair); Republican; Presbyterian; rec: soccer player and youth coach, golf, antique autos. Ofc: Standard Ins. Co. 1570 The Alameda Ste 328 San Jose 95128

CHAMPE, CYNTHIA S., banking executive; b. Sept. 6, 1949, Albuquerque, NM; d. Thomas A. and Cynthia A. (Trinkle) Whelan; m. Charles R. Champe, June 6, 1970; ed. Univ. New Mexico, Wright State Univ., Leeward Coll., UC San Diego. Career: adminstrv. asst. to treas. New Mexico Svgs. & Loan Assn., Albuquerque 1969; supvr. Loan Serv. Dept., Fidelity Fed. Svgs. & Loan Assn., Glendale, Calif. 1974; adminstrv. asst. mortgage banking dept. Home S&L Assn., Los Angeles 1977, loan packaging supvr. 1978; adminstrn. ofcr. residential real estate dept. Lloyds Bank Calif., L.A. 1980; secondary market loan ofcr. Carlsberg Mortgage Corp., Santa Monica 1981, regional prodn. control mgr. Chase Home Mortgage Corp., Houston, TX 1982; mgr. Citicorp Securities Markets, Inc., Houston 1984;v.p. Security Pacific Capital Markets Group, L.A. 1985–; honors: Nat. Honor Soc. 1966, acad. scholarship 1967; Review Mortgage Underwriter, 1983. Registered Rep/NASD - Series 7, 1984, Series 63, 1984, Outstanding Young Women of Am., 1984; mem: LA Assn. of Profl. Mortgage Women, Nat. Assn. of Rev. Appraisers & Mortgage Underwriters; publs: Encounter: An Anthology of Modern Poetry, 1967; rec: writing, equestrian, sailing. Ofc: Security Pacific Capital Markets Group, 300 S Grand Ave, 21st Floor, Los Angeles 90071

CHAMPLIN, PHILIP ALDEN, superior court judge; b. Sept. 1, 1939, Annapolis, Md.; s. Jackson S. (R.Adm. USN ret.) and Betty (Trotter) C.; m. Lynne Barbara, Nov. 3, 1966; children: Christopher b. 1970, Catherine b. 1973; edn: BA, Yale Univ. 1961, JD, UC Boalt Hall 1964; admitted Calif. State Bar 1965, US Supreme Ct. 1971, Ct. Appeals (9th Cir.) 1965, US Dist. Ct. (No. Dist. Calif.) 1965. Career: assoc. atty. Coombs & Dunlap, Napa 1965-67, ptnr. Coombs, Dunlap, Dunlap & Champlin 1967-77; city atty. Yountville 1967-77, and dep. city atty. Napa 1966-77; apptd. judge Municipal Ct. Napa County 1977-79; appointed judge Superior Ct. Napa County 1979, elected 1980–; chmn. Napa Co. Criminal Justice Planning Com. 1978-; awards: Silver Beaver, Silverado Council BSA, Paul Harris Fellow, Rotary Intl.; mem. Calif. Judges Assn. (chair Juvenile Law Com. 1985), Cow County Judges Assn. (pres. 1985-86), Napa Co. Bar Assn. (pres. 1970), Napa Rotary (pres. 1983-84), Silverado Council BSA (pres. 1983-84, tng. staff Woodbadge course 1985). Res: 595 Montecito Bl Napa 94558 Ofc: Napa Superior Court, 825 Brown St Napa 94558

CHAN, ALFRED, JR., dentist; b. Mar. 7, 1940, Colon, Rep. of Panama, nat. US cit. 1977; s. Alfred and Edith Victoria (Low) C.; edn: BA, Whittier Coll. 1962; PhD, Univ. of Ill. 1968; DDS, UC Los Angeles 1978. Career: research scientist Bio Science, Van Nuys 1969-70; dir. research & devel., Reference Labs., N.H. 1970-71; dentist assoc. George Mizushima, DDS, Los Angeles 1984-85, Gregory Robins, DDS, Montebello 1985–; asst. clin. prof. USC Sch. of Dentistry 1983-85; mem. Am. Dental Assn., Calif. Dental Assn., L.A. Dental Soc., So. Bay Chinese Am. Assn. (pres. 1985); Republican; Methodist; rec: computer, classical guitar. Res: 741 S Garfield Ave Apt H Monterey Park 91754 Ofc: Gregory Robins Family Dentistry 1400 W Whittier Blvd Montebello 90640

CHAN, BRIAN Y., engineer/scientist; b. Sept. 10, 1956, China, nat. US cit. 1981; s. Tung W. and Siu M. (Lee) C.; m. Jeanie Cheng, July 15, 1982; edn: BSEE, UC Berkeley 1979; MS computer sci., Univ. of Santa Clara 1984; postgrad. work Stanford Univ. 1984-; Reg. Profl. Engr., Calif. (1983), Cert. in Data Processing (C.D.P.), Inst. of Certification of Computer Profls. (1984). Career: jr. engr./scientist IBM Corp., San Jose 1980-, assoc. engr. 1981-82, senior assoc. engr. 1983-84, staff engr./scientist 1985–; awards: Datherina Desharton Scholar, UCB (1977), Gen. Dwight F. Johns Award, Soc. of Am. Mil. Engrs. (1983), Eta Kappa Nu (1978); mem. Am. Mensa; Christian; rec: music, exercise, exploration. Ofc: IBM, 5600 Cottle Road San Jose 95193

CHAN, CHUEN-RONG, research analyst/statistician; b. Feb. 11, 1954, Singapore; s. Peng-Yuan and Soo-Moi (Chew) C.; m. Poh-Heng Ho, July 17, 1983; edn: indsl. technol. cert. City & Guilds, London 1977; BS, and MS (sec. edn., math), Univ. of Bridgeport, Conn. 1981, 82; PhD (research methods & evaluation), UC Los Angeles 1986; tchg. creds. in math. (Conn.), and indsl. arts (Singapore). Career: tchr./edn. ofcr. Tanglin Tech./Henderson Sec. Sch., Singapore 1975-80; tutor (refugees), dir. of summer sch., Blackrock (Conn.) Congregational Ch. 1980-82; tchr. Fairfield Woods Jr. H.S., Unquowa Sch., Conn. 1981-82; staff research assoc. UCLA Center for Study of Evaluation, 1982-84, tchg. assoc. Grad. Sch. of Edn. 1983-85; research analyst/ statistician Chancellor's Ofc., Calif. Community Colls., Sacramento 1986–; independent cons. 1983-85, awards: Univ. Calif. Tuition Scholarship, edn. (1984-5, 85-86), Profl./ Scholarly Conf. Travel Grant (3/85); mem: Am. Ednl. Research Assn., Am. Stat. Assn., Nat. Council on Measurement in Edn., Calif. Comm. Coll. Student Finl. Aid Adminstrs. Assn., Nat. Assn. of Student Finl. Aid Adminstrs., Am. Psychol. Assn.; publs: sev. research papers; Republican; Christian; rec: stamps & coins. Res: 2237 Hurky Way No.82 Sacramento 95825 Ofc: Access to Education 1107 Ninth St Sacramento 95814

CHAN, DAVID RONALD, certified public accountant, lawyer; b. Aug. 3, 1948, Los Angeles; s. David Yew and Anna May (Wong) C.; m. Mary Anne, June 21, 1980; children: Eric David, b. 1981, Christina Mary, b. 1982; edn: AB, econ., UCLA 1969; MS, bus. adm., UCLA 1970; JD, UCLA Sch. of Law, 1973. Admitted to Calif. State Bar, US Ct. of Appeals (9th Cir.), US Claims Ct., US Tax Ct. Career: staff accountant Touche Ross & Co., Los Angeles 1970; acct. Oxnard Celery Distbrs. Inc., L.A. 1971-73; tax. dept. Kenneth Leventhal & Co., L.A. 1973–, presently mgr. National Tax Dept.; gen. ptnr. DRC Saticoy Enterprises, 1980–; real estate broker; co-dir. KL Tax Hall of Fame, 1980–; awards: John Forbes Gold Medal, Calif. Soc. of CPAs, 1970; Elijah Watt Sells Certificate, Am. Inst. of CPAs, 1970; Newton Becker Award, 1970; Resolution of Appreciation, Chinese Hist. Soc. of Am., 1975; Phi Beta Kappa, Beta Gamma Sigma, Beta Alpha Psi, num. other hons.; mem. Chinese Hist. Soc. of So. Calif. (founding mem., past bd. dir.); Orgn. of Chinese Americans, Chinese for Affirmative Action; Hawaii Chinese Hist. Center; Chinese Cultural Found. of San Francisco; Chinese Hist. Soc. of Am.; L.A. County Bar Assn.; So. Calif. Chinese Lawyers Assn.; Am. Assn. of Atty-CPAs; Am. Inst. of CPAs; Calif. Soc. of CPAs; co-founder Legends of Tax (tax profl. social orgn.); UCLA Alumni Assn. (life); UCLA Bruin Bench; UCLA Coll. of Letters and Scisc. Dean's Council organizing com.; L.A. Bicentennial 200 Speakers Bur.; Am. First Day Cover Soc.; L.A. Bd. of Realtors M.L.S.; Internat. Orgn. of Real Estate Appraisers (Certified Residential Appraiser); publs: num. articles on taxation, philately, and Chinese-Am. studies incl: The Five Chinatowns of Los

Angeles, A Postcard View of Chinatown, The Tragedy and Trauma of the Chinese Exclusion Laws, Chinese-American Heritage: Historical and Contemporary Perspectives, Structuring the Real Estate Syndicate, Pre-Combination First Day Covers, Sale of Property Developed on Leased Land; contbr. restaurant review, East West Chinese Am. Jour.; frequent spkr. on Chinese role and history in the US; Republican (Nat. Com.); rec: philately, photog., post cards, sports memorabilia. Res: 4127 Don Diablo Dr Los Angeles 90008 Ofc: 2049 Century Park East, Ste. 1700, Los Angeles 90067

CHAN, DIANA GONG, accountant; b. Sept. 23, 1954, Clarksdale, Miss.; d. Sing Gong, Jr. (dec.) and Magen Gong Jensen; m. Douglas M.Q. Chan, July 23, 1979; edn: BBA, Univ. of Miss. 1976; MBA program, Golden Gate Univ., 1983 candidate; Certified Public Acct., Calif. (1982). Career: owner, artistic dir. Diana's School of Dance, 1974-76; auditor Deloitte, Haskins & Sells, CPAs 1976-77; finl. acct. Chevron USA Inc. 1977-79; tax mgr. Peat Marwick & Mitchell CPAs 1978-83; current: ptnr. C & C Properties; v.p. fin. Peninsula Valley Development; owner Diana Gong Chan, CPA; controller Peninsula Auto Stores; prof. Foothill Comm. Coll. 1982—; honors: Miss Chinatown of the Mid Peninsula (1977), Miss Hong Kong San Francisco (1978), Miss Future Business Executive (1975), Miss Mississippi Teenager Finalist (1972), Miss Voice of Democracy for Am. Legion Aux. (1972), General Foods Inc., Betty Homemaker Award (1972), Nat. Assn. Dancer of the Year (1973), Beta Alpha Psi (acctg. hon.), Phi Beta Lambda (pres. 1974-75), Univ. Dancers (pres. 1974-75), Phi Gamma Nu (pres. 1975-76), Univ. Miss. Flag Corps 1975-76, Outstanding Young Women of Am. (1985), Quill and Scroll (1972), Miss. Pub. Affairs TV commentator for the Univ. of Miss. 1975-76; mem: Calif. Soc. of Public Accts., Nat. Assn. Accts., Am. Soc. of Women Accts., Asian Business League, Am. Inst. CPAs; civic: city commnr. Germantown Personnel Com. (1976-78); mayor's Youth Advis. Bd. (1975-76), United Way (comm. chmn. for Peat, Marwick, Mitchell 1983), Chinese Community Ctr. (secty. 1978), Fgn. Student Advis. Bd. (1974-76); guest lectr. Univ. of Santa Clara (1981); choreographer for Little Miss Clarksdale Pageant; Republican; Baptist; rec: skiing, aerobics, cooking, speaking. Address: Diana Gong Chan, CPA, 206 Forrester Rd Los Gatos 95030

CHAN, ESTHER MAN-KWAI, real estate broker, medical corporation executive; b. Aug. 25, 1946, Kwangsi, China; nat. 1978; d. William and Doris (Young) Tsai; m. Samuel Chan, MD (past pres. Chinese Physicians of So.Calif.), Dec. 27, 1969; children: Kenneth b. 1972, Gary b. 1975, Kevin b. 1977, Kinman b. 1979; edn: Chinese Univ. of Hong Kong 1964-66, Biola Coll. 1966-67; BA, sociol., CSU Los Angeles 1969; grad. stu. Tufts Univ. 1969; real estate sales lic., Anthony Sch. 1975; lic. real estate broker 1976. Career: founder Chinese Svc Ctr of Los Angeles, 1969; statistician State of Tenn. Dept. of Pub. Hlth Stat. Div.1969-74; real estate sales agent First Am. Realty, Torrance 1974-75; R.E. broker/pres. Chancellor Realty Inc., Rolling Hills Estates 1977—; dir. Samuel C. Chan, M.D. Inc.; apt. owner/bldg. contr. 1980-, condo conversion 1982-; investment R.E. Broker; dealer Chinese antiques; prin. J.E.S. Trading Co.; co-ordinator hlth care elderly; awards: scholarships: Chinese Univ. of Hong Kong 1964-7, Tufts Univ. Grad. Sch of Sociol. 1969; spl. commendations, Gov. of Tenn. 1970, LA Mayor Tom Bradley, 1982; mem: Chinese Physician Soc., Rolling Hills, Torrance Bds. of Realtors, CofC. Democrat; Prot.; rec: tennis, fish,riding. Res: 25421 Gallup Circle Laguna Hills 92653 Ofc: Chancellor Realty Inc. 916 Silver Spur Rd Ste 203 Rolling Hills Estates; Samuel C. Chan MD, 2777 Pacific Ave Ste N Long Beach 90806

CHAN, FLORENCE MAY HARN, librarian; b. Victoria, B.C., Canada; d. Jack Nam and Eva (Lowe) Yipp; chil: Jonathan Hoyt, b. 1960, Barry Alan, b. 1963; edn: BA, Univ. of Brit. Columbia 1953; MLS, UC Berkeley 1956; MA, CSU San Jose 1976. Career: circulation/ref. asst. Victoria (B.C.) Pub. Lib., 1953-54; cataloger Golden Gate Coll., San Francisco 1956-57; catalog/ref. libn. Coll. of San Mateo, 1957-60; catalog/ref. libn. Canada Coll., Redwood City 1968-75, coord. lib. svcs., 1975—, curator Center for the American Musical, Canada Coll.; publs: (worktext) Using Library Resources (1976); art., College and Research Libraries News, Dec. 1984; pres. Asian American Comm. Council of San Mateo Co.; mem: ALA, Calif. Lib. Assn., Community Coll. Media Assn., San Mateo Co. Hist. Assn., Phi Kappa Phi hon. soc.; Episcopal. Ofc: Canada Coll. 4200 Farm Hill Blvd. Redwood City 94061

CHAN, GODFREY RONALD, hotel and restaurant executive; b. May 28, 1928, Port of Spain, Trinidad, West Indies; s. Joseph and Laura Eva (Chan) C.; m. Ena Young, Dec. 10, 1950; children: Margarita b. 1951, Diana b. 1953, Jane b. 1964. Career: owner, opr. Kapok Restaurant, Port of Spain, Trinidad 1962—, bd. chmn., mng. dir. Kapok Hotel and Restaurants Ltd., 1970—; bd. chmn., mng. dir. Caribbean Trinity Co. Ltd. 1975—; mem. Chinese Fedn. of Trinidad and Tobago (pres. 1975-77); rec: badminton, table tennis, travel. Res: 195 Merced Ave San Francisco 94127 Ofc: Kapok Hotel 18-20 Cotton Hill Port of Spain Trinidad West Indies

CHAN, JOHN IN-SANG, civil engineer, contractor; b. Aug. 24, 1954, Canton, China, nat. US cit. 1980; s. Kwok C. and Helen S. (Mei) C.; m. Grace Lai-Man, Oct. 4, 1980; edn: BSCE, USC 1980; Calif. Reg. Profl. Engr. (Civil) 1983, lic. Gen. Engring. and Building Contr. 1983. Career: jr. civil engr. Calif. Dept. of Transp. 1980-83; pres. Titan Constrn. Co. Inc., So. Pasadena 1984—; v.p. Technites Architectural & Engring. Co., So. Pasadena 1983—; Christian; rec: track & field, drama, singing. Ofc: 1499 Huntington Dr Ste 401 South Pasadena 91030

CHAN, JOSEPH TIM-YAU, physical therapist, acupuncturist; b. March 15, 1954, Hong Kong; s. Gordon Kwok-Tok and Jannine So-Har (Wong) C.; m.

Stella Yeung, Mar. 8, 1981; 1 son, Dominic R. b. 1984; edn: BA in biol., East Carolina Univ., N.C. 1976, BS in phys. therapy, 1980; BS in acupuncture, S.A.M.R.A. Univ. of Oriental Medicine 1983, postgrad. OMD Pgm., 1983-. Career: staff physical therapist, Centinela Hosp. Medical Center (CHMC), 1980-, senior physical therapist 1983-, clin. splst. (PT) physical therapy 1984—, asst. in devel. of Pain Mgmt. Pgm., coord. of PT aspect of Pain Mgmt. Pgm., 1981-, originated Post Surgical Transcutaneous Electrical Nerve Stimulation Pgm. for orthopedic related surgical patients 1982-, clin. instr. and preceptor for P.T. students 1982-, worked with Peoples Repub. of China physicians in orthopedic & sport medicine technol. exchange 1983, devel. hosp. acupuncture pgm. 1984, coord. of Lateral Electrical Surface Stimulation pgm. for scoliosis patients 1985-; presentations: acupuncture, Everywhere Show KNBC TV (1981), electroacupuncture, Am. P.T. Assn./ Fla. Chpt. (1985), Putting Pain Out of Business, CHMC (1985), exercise for Scoliosis patient (1984), fitness for children, CHMC (1985), Prevention and Treatment for Back Injury, CHMC (1985); honors: Who's Who Among Students in Am. Univs. & Colls. (1976), Mary Helms Scholar (outstanding senior Biol. Scis.) East Carolina Univ. (1976), Undergrad. Research Award, N.C. Collegiate Acad. of Sci. (1976), Sigma Xi (1976), Honor Roll, ECU (1973-76), Phi Sigma Pi nat. scholar (1975-76), Chi Beta Phi (chapt. v.p. 1975-76); mem: Am. P.T. Assn. (Orthopedic & Clin. Electrophysiol. Sect.), No. Caro. P.T. Assn., Calif. P.T. Assn., Center for Chinese Medicine, Acupuncture PAC, Toastmaster Internat. (charter mem. 1985); research: Auricular Acupuncture: A new treatment for smoking (1980); Catholic; rec: photog, travel, music. Ofc: P.T. Dept. Centinela Hospital 555 E Hardy St Inglewood 90301

CHAN, KWOK-FONG, acupuncturist; b. Aug. 6, 1934, Canton, China, nat. US cit. 1975; s. Henry M. and Wai-Har (Chu) C.; m. Mee-Yung Liu, June 27, 1969; children: Alice b. 1970, Lisa b. 1971, David b. 1972; edn: BA, Canton Coll. 1959; acupuncture, Cheung Chung Kang Chinese Medicine Inst. 1962. Career: acupuncturist, Hong Kong 1962; Acupuncture Ctr. of Washington, Wash. DC 1973; Acupuncture Research Ctr. Inc., Tenn. 1976; Oriental Acupuncture Ctr., Los Angeles 1977—; mem. United Acupuncturists of Calif.; Taoism; rec: meditation, Tay Jyi Chyung (Kung Fu). Res: 4042 Maxson Rd. #B El Monte 91732 Ofc: Oriental Acupuncture Center, 3201 No. Figueroa St. Los Angeles 90065

CHAN, LARRY M., hotelier, developer; b. Hong Kong; s. Chak Fu and Esther Chi (Wong) C.; m. Lillian, Dec. 1, 1976; children: Josephine, Joyce, Dennis; edn: dip. Leysin American Sch. 1972; BSBA, Univ. Denver 1976, MBA, 1977. Career: finl. analyst, resident mgr. Hotel Plaza; gen. mgr./dir. Park Lane Hotel; chief ops. U.S. Hotelier Assn.; current: pres. C&L Finl. Inc., Pacific Renaissance Assocs. (devel. 1.5 million sq. ft. mix use project in East Bay with office & residential towers, a hotel and retail mall), Ramada Renaissance Hotel (S.F.), Coco Palm Resort Hotel (Hawaii); bd. dir. 20+ cos., var. real estate syndications; internat. bd. of govs. JFK Univ.; honors: Keys to the City (San Francisco, Oakland); civic: Hillsborough Sch. Found. (bd.), Bay Area Asian Business League (exec. adv. com.); Catholic; rec: tennis, var. sports. Address: San Francisco 94102

CHAN, LELAND LEO, lawyer, corporate financial executive; b. Feb. 15, 1950, San Francisco; s. Louis Hong Yow and Jane (Yim) C.; m. Victoria Owyang, July 20, 1975; children: Cheryl b. 1981, Amanda b. 1985; edn: AA, City Coll. of San Francisco 1970; BS, UC Berkeley 1972; MBA, USC 1973; JD, Santa Clara Univ. 1983; admitted Calif. State Bar 1983. Career: proposal pricing analyst Ford Aerospace & Communications Corp., Palo Alto 1973-75, contract finl. analyst 1975-76, senior ops. finl. analyst 1976-77, supvr. of contract finl. analysis 1978-82, supvr. contracts adminstrn. and fin., 1982—; atty. pvt. law practice, 1983—; gen. counsel to CAL-5 Corp., 1985-; Real Estate Sales, 1979-83; founding mem. Asian Business Assn. UCB (1973) awards: Calif. State Scholar (1970-72), Doreen B. and Calvin K. Townsend Scholar (1971); mem: Am. Bar Assn., State Bar of Calif., Asian Am. Bar Assn. of the Greater Bay Area, Univ. Calif. Alumni Assn. (Chinese Chpt.), USC Alumni Assn.; civic: Chinese Am. Citizens League of Santa Clara County (v.p. 1978, Scholarship Selection Com. 1978), Fremont Unif. Sch. Dist. Science Fair Judge (1984), active in local political campaigns 1976-; publs: num. profl. papers incl. The Law of Privacy and the Use of Polygraphs in Employment (1983); rec: karate, tennis. Address: Fremont 94536

CHAN, PATRICK YING, company president; b. Apr. 8, 1966, Hong Kong, nat. US cit. 1972; s. James Leung and Helen Yun (Fan) C.; edn: BS, San Francisco St. Univ. 1984. Career: dir. public rels. Student World Trade Assn., San Francisco 1985, senior v.p. 1985; acct. exec. SFSU Sch. of Bus. Journal 1985-; mgmt. cons. VIP Printing, S.F. 1985—; senior v.p. Asian Business Assn. 1985—; pres. Ambience Prodns. Pacifica; mem: Commonwealth Club of Calif., Am. Mktg. Assn. (stu. affil.), Internat. Trade Council (stu. affil.); civic: Boy Scouts Am. (asst. scoutmaster), Am. Red Cross (CPR instr.), SFSU Alumni Assn., US Tennis Assn., Alpha Phi Omega, Club Asean (activities coord.); publs: editor/ pub. Interprise (newsletter of internat. trade), and Connection (newsletter of Asian Am. bus.); Democrat (Nat. Com. mem.); Christian; rec: golf, tennis, sailing, piano. Ofc: Ambience Prodns. POB 1314 Pacifica 94044

CHAN, PAUL MING, engineer; b. Dec. 12, 1954, nat. US cit. 1978; s. Hui and Yingtao (Lee) C.; m. Helen, Jan. 19, 1959; 1 dau. Jessica b. 1983; edn: BS, UC Berkeley 1979; Reg. Profl. Engr., Calif.; lic. real estate agt. (1980-). Career: nuclear engr. Dept. of Navy, 1979; project engr. Bechtel Corp. 1982; utilities engr. Calif. Public Utilities Commn., 1983—; pres. PC Trading Co. (import-export), 1984-; cons. VIP Bus. Consultants, San Francisco; honors: appreciation, The Salvation Army; mem. Profl. Engrs. in Calif. Govt. (1983-); research: in utility regulations; Democrat; Salvation Army (Sun. Sch. gchr., Corps Council). Res: 2822 Moraga St San Francisco 94122 Ofc: Calif. Public Utilities Commission 505 Van Ness Ave San Francisco 94102

CHAN, RAYMOND K., dentist; b. Dec. 18, 1952, San Francisco; s. Thomas Wo and Jeannie Chan; m. Mary Ho, Sept. 6, 1980; edn: AB, honors, UC Berkeley 1975; DDS, Northwestern Univ. Dental Sch. 1979. Career: research asst. Am. Dental Assn., Chgo. 1977-79; clinical instr. Northwestern Univ. Dental Sch., Chgo. 1979-80; assoc. dentist Northwestern Univ. Med. Assocs. 1979-80; owner/ gen. dentist, San Lorenzo 1981–, (inc. 1982); ADA Research Asst. 1977-79; clinical instr. Northwestern Univ. Dental Sch. 1979-80; ed. Northwestern Univ. Dental Sch. Newsletter 1977-79; awards: Sci. Awd., Air Force ROTC; Academic Awd., Air Force ROTC; mem: Am., Calif. & Ill. Dental Assns.; Chgo. & S. Alameda Co. (bd. dirs.) Dental Socs.; Acad. of Gen. Dentistry; bd. dirs. Chinese Christian Schs.; publs: Follow- up Guide for new Christians, 9/82; Northwestern Univ. Dental Sch. Newsletter (2 yrs.); mil: USAF ROTC; Republican; Christian. Res: 748 Crocus Dr San Leandro 94578 Ofc: Raymond K. Chan, DDS, Inc., 15522 Hesperian Blvd San Lorenzo 94580

CHAN, RAYMOND YUEN-FONG, ophthalmologist; b. Nov. 2, 1948, Shanghai, China, nat. 1979; s. Joy Ka-on and So-Ying (Cheung) C.; m. Helen Chang, Feb. 25, 1982; children: Stephen b. 1983, Christine b. 1984; edn: BS, aero. eng., BS, mech. eng., Cal Poly 1971; MS, Cal Tech 1972; PhD, 1975; MD, Univ. of Miami Sch. of Med. 1977; fellow, Am. Acad. Ophthalm.; diplomate, Am. Bd. Ophthalm. Career: clinical instr. Baylor Coll. of Med., Houston, Tex. 1977-81; staff ophthalmologist Scripps Clinic & Research Found., La Jolla 1981–; clinical instr. UC San Diego 1983–; spkr. Eighth Biennial Cataract Surgical Congress, Houston, Tex. 1982; spkr. Am. Acad. of Ophthalm. Annual Meeting 1982; awards: Everett L. Goar Research Awd. in Ophthalm., Baylor Coll. of Med. 1979, 80; 1st pl. research paper awd., Tex. Ophthalm. Assn. 1980; fellow Am. Coll. Surgeons; mem: Phi Kappa Phi; Tau Beta Pi; Sigma Xi; Assn. of Research in Vision & Ophthalm.; Am. Acad. Ophthalm.; Baylor Ophthalm. Alumni Assn.; San Diego Eye Bank, Research to Prevent Blindness, Inc.; num. pub. writings.; rec: bridge, chess, tennis. Res: 12986 Polvera Ave San Diego 92128 Ofc: Scripps Clinic, 10666 N Torrey Pines Rd La Jolla 92037

CHAN, RICHARD ALLAYE, physician; b. Hong Kong; s. Nasingue Allaye and Rosa (Lee); m. Ann, May 2, 1964; children: Denise b. 1966, Richard b. 1968, Laura b. 1969, Michelle b. 1971; edn: MD, Royal Coll. Surgeons, Dublin, Ireland 1956; desig: MRCP, Royal Coll. of Physicians, U.K. (1963), FACP, Am. Coll. of Physicians (1972). Career: med. residency and fellowship, England 1958-63; cons. physician practice, Hong Kong 1963-67; fellowship UC Davis 1969-71; att. med. staff Roseville Comm. Hosp. (exec. com. 1975-77), Mercy San Juan Hosp., Mercy Gen. Hosp., and American River Hosp.; pres. Chan, Zietlin & Klug Med. Corp., Roseville; asst. clin. prof. of medicine UC Davis; trustee Medical Care Found. of Sacto. (1985-); mem: Placer-Nevada Co. Med. Soc. (bd. dirs. 1976), Found. Health Plan-Sacto. (utilization rev. com. 1984-), Calif. Med. Assn., AMA, Am. Soc. of Internal Medicine; contbr. article in Annals of Internal Medicine (1971); Roman Catholic; rec: skiing, golf. Res: 4150 Buchanan Dr Fair Oaks 95628 Ofc: Chan, Zietlin & Klug Med. Corp. 406 Sunrise Blvd Roseville 95678

CHAN, SAMUEL CHEUNG-FAI, physician; b. Feb. 22, 1947, Hong Kong, nat. 1978; s. Tim and King Wan (Ng) C.; m. Esther Tsai, Dec. 27, 1969; children: Kenneth b. 1972, Gary b. 1975, Kevin b. 1977, Kinman b. 1979; edn: BS, CSU Los Angeles, 1968, MD, Vanderbilt Univ. Med. Sch., 1973; Diplomate Am. Bd. of Family Practice (1977, 84). Career: res. physician in surgery Vanderbilt Univ. Hosp. 1973-74; mem. Family Practice Dept. Kaiser Hosp., Harbor City, 1974-75; physician in pvt. practice, 1975–, med. dir./pres. Advanced Multispecialty Med. Group Inc., Long Beach, faculty UCLA-Harbor Div. Dept. of Family Medicine 1979-; awards: recogn. for work with senior citizens, L.A. Mayor Bradley (1982), most outstanding student research award Vanderbilt Med. Sch. (1973); mem: Chinese Physician Soc. of So. Calif. (pres. 1980, advisor 81-), Am. Acad. of Family Practice, Calif. Med. Assn., Los Angeles Co. Med. Assn.; coauthor book chpt. in Sugars in Nutrition The Nutrition Found. (ed. Horace L. Sipple), Acad. Press Inc.; Democrat; Christian; rec: tennis, ski, fish, guitar. Res: 25421 Gallup Cir Laguna Hills 92653 Ofc: Advanced Multisplty. Med. Group Inc., 4301 Atlantic Ave Ste 8 Long Beach 90807

CHAN, STEVEN S., semiconductor co. engineering executive; b. Oct. 6, 1949, Hong Kong, nat. US cit. 1977; s. Yit-Ming and Cheong-Yuen (Lee) C.; m. Rosa Cho; children: James b. 1972, Janey b. 1976; edn: BSEE, Worcester Polytech. Inst. 1971, MSEE, 1980. Career: engr. Adams-Smith Inc., Hudson, Mass. 1972-74, dir. engring. 1975-76, v.p. 1977-79; staff engr. Ampex Corp., Redwood City, Calif. 1980-81; group leader LSI Logic Corp., Milpitas 1982-83, mgr./dir. ASIC Design & Devel., 1984–; honors: Tau Beta Pi, Eta Kappa Nu, Pi Mu Epsilon; mem. IEEE; works: 5 patents awarded in field of Audio Video Systems, 2 patents pending in field of semicondr. logic design; num. tech. papers presented at profl. confs.; rec: tennis, skiing. Res: 4100 Lark Ct Fremont 94536 Ofc: LSI Logic Corp. 1551 McCarthy Blvd Milpitas 95035

CHAN, WILLIAM CHOP, oral and maxillofacial surgeon; b. Mar. 8, 1948, Canton, China, nat. US cit. 1968; s. Wan Nam and How Yit (Tse) C.; m. Gayle Cheung, July 21, 1973; children: Michael b. 1974, Stephanie b. 1976; edn: AA, City Coll. S.F. 1969; BS in E.E., UC Berkeley 1970, MSEE, 1971; DDS, UC San Francisco 1976; Certif. in Oral & Maxillofacial Surg., UCSF 1979. Diplomate Am. Board of Oral & Maxillofacial Surgeons (1981). Career: staff engr. Hughes Aircraft, 1971; asst. clin. prof., oral & maxillofacial surg., UC San Francisco 1979–; chief of oral & maxillofacial surg. Mt. Zion Hosp. and Medical Ctr., S.F. 1981–; pvt. practice of oral & maxillofacial surg., S.F. 1979–; awards: 4 scholarships, UC Berkeley (1969, 70), Eta Kappa Nu (1970), Tau Beta Pi (1970), Phi Beta Kappa (1970), Willard Fleming Award in Oral Surgery, UCSF (1976); mem: fellow Am. Assn. of Oral & Maxillofacial Surgeons, Am. Dental Assn., UCSF Oral & Maxillofacial Surg. Alumni Assn. (bd. dirs. 1982-83); civic: Chinatown Community Children Ctr. (bd. dirs. 1980-83), CPR instr. for S.F. Dental Soc. (1979-); publs: num. research studies (1970-), contbr. med. and dental jours.; num. lectures, profl. presentations; Democrat; rec: music, camping, family. Res: 1998 8th Ave San Francisco 94116 Ofc: 2001 Van Ness Ave Ste 401 San Francisco 94109

CHAN-ONG, BETTY Q.B., dietitian, food services executive; b. Jan. 9, 1957, Singapore; d. Buck Seng and Ai Ngim (Lim) Chan; m. Iwan Ong, Nov. 20, 1983; edn: dip. St. Andrew Coll. 1977; AS, Union Coll. 1979; BS, Loma Linda Univ. 1981; Reg. Dietitian, Am. Dietetic Assn. (1981). Career: dietitian in clin. practice Loma Linda Univ. Med. Center 1981-82; dir. of dietetics Needles Desert Comm. Hosp. 1982-86; dir. of foodservices, CPC Santa Ana Psychiatric Hosp. 1986–; group tchg. 1973-; honors: 2d pl. in speech contest (1973), participant Welkaton Award, Nat. Dean's List (1979); mem: Am. Dietetics Assn. (1980-, hd. hostess for conv.), Health Care Delivery Systems (profl. mgmt. mem.); Seventh-Day Adventist (gen. supt. Loma Linda Chinese SDA Ch. 1982/3, 1986/7; dir. of campmeeting 1985/6; dir. of food prodn. 1981-3); rec: badminton, ice-skating, pub. speaking. Address: Santa Ana 92705

CHANDLER, DOROTHY, dance consultant; b. April 6, 1909, Berkeley; d. Elbert Milam and Winifred (Goodrich) C.; m. Donald Ballard, 1930; children: Paul, b. 1935, Bernard b. 1938, Baptiste b. 1948; edn: Central Wash. Tchrs. Coll. 1928; Univ. of Wash. 1934; UC Berkley and San Francisco 1944. Career: former ballerina; currently, owner/ sole instr. Ecole de la Danse Ballet Sch. of Thousand Oaks; regl. dir. to Calif. State supvr., Chicago Nat. Assn. of Dance Masters (CNADM) 1955-; vol. tchg. USO, Girl Scouts, Parks; instr. ballet class 1st Cong. Ch. of Los Angeles; mem. Dance Congress of NY; charter assoc. Folk Dance Fedn.; Republican; Congregational. Studio: Dorothy Chandler Ecole de la Danse, 96 No. Erbes Rd. Thousand Oaks 91362

CHANDLER, JOHN HERRICK, college president; b. Aug. 7, 1928, San Francisco; s. Ralph William and Gwen Thornton (Herrick) C.; m. Nancy Gordon Phillips, Dec. 10, 1955; children: John, Seth, Will; edn: AB, UCLA 1952; BD (Danforth fellow), Univ. Chgo. 1958, PhD (fellow), 1963. Ordained to ministry Episcopal Ch. 1960. Career: instr. English Dartmouth Coll., 1961-63; asst. prof. UCLA, 1963-64; assoc. prof., dean spl. programs Ohio Univ., 1964-67; v.p. Danforth Found., St. Louis, 1967-71; pres. Salem Coll. and Acad., Winston-Salem, N.C. 1971-76; pres. Scripps Coll., 1976–; trustee Newton Coll. Sacred Heart, 1970-75, Thacher Sch., 1977-; dir. Clayton (Mo.) Bd. Edn. 1970-71; mem. University Club (LA), Twilight Club. Ofc: Scripps College, Balch Hall, Claremont 91711

CHANDLER, OTIS, communications co. executive; b. Nov. 23, 1927, Los Angeles; s. Norman and Dorothy (Buffum) C.; m. Bettina Whitaker, Aug. 15, 1981; chil: (prev. m.): Norman Brant, b. 1952, Harry Brant, b. 1953, Cathleen, b. 1955, Michael Otis, b. 1958, Carolyn, b. 1963; edn: The Cate Sch., Phillips Acad.; BA, Stanford Univ. 1950. Career: various positions, Times Mirror, 1953–: trainee in mech., editorial, circ., advt. depts. 1953-57; asst. to pres., 1957-58; mktg. mgr. Los Angeles Times, 1959-60, publisher 1960-80; vice pres. Newspaper Div. Times Mirror, 1961-65, dir. 1962-; pres. Newspaper and Forest Products, 1965-66; Exec. Com., bd. dirs. 1966-, bd. chmn. and Editor-in-Chief, 1981–. Dir: F.X. Pfaffinger Found., Times Mirror Found., Chandis Securities Co., Chandler Sherman Corp., dir. Pres.'s Council on Physical Fitness and Sports; dir. World Wildlife Fund-US; honors: Delta Kappa Epsilon (pres. 1950), 4-Yr. Letterman, capt. Track Team 1950 (Stanford Univ.); co-capt. USAF Track Team 1952; hon. LL.D., Colby Coll. 1966; hon. LL.D., Claremont Grad. Sch. 1978; num. journalism awards: USC (1962), Lovejoy (1966), Columbia Univ. (1967), Univ. Mo. Honor Medal (1969), Ohio Univ. Sch of Journ. Carr Van Anda (1973), Univ. of Ks. Allen White (1975), CORO (1978), Nat. Collegiate Athletic Assn. Theo. Roosevelt (1979), Gallagher Report (1980), Univ. Tex. Coll. Comm. DeWitt Carter Reddick (1982).Mem: Am. Newspaper Pubs. Assn. (dir. 1968-77; Found. trustee 1969-78), Am. Soc. Newspaper Editors, Calif. Newspaper Pubs. Assn., Calif. Press Assn., Inter-Am. Press Assn., Soc. Profl. Journalists, Sigma Delta Chi; clubs: California, Regency, So. Calif. Safari; mil: Navy midshipman 1946-48; 1st lt. USAF 1951-53; rec: classic & sports cars, surfing, hunting, weightlifting, track & field. Ofc: Times Mirror, Times Mirror Sq. Los Angeles 90053

CHANDRARATNA, PREMINDRA ANTHONY NIRMAL, b. July 27, 1941, Kandy, Ceylon; US cit.; m. Roanne; children: Nirmal and Previn; edn: MB, BS, Univ. of Ceylon 1964; (MRCP) Royal Coll. of Physicians, London 1967; MD (distinction in medicine, obstets. & gyn.), Univ. of Ceylon 1968; Diplomate Am. Bd. Internal Medicine (1974), Dip. subsplty. cardiovascular disease (1976); phys. lic. Fla. (1973), Va. (1973), Okla. (1975), Calif. (1976).Career: medical intern Gen. Hosp., Colombo, Ceylon 1964; pediatric surg. intern Lady Ridgeway Hosp., 1964-65; sr. house med. ofcr.Wembly (Eng.) Hosp. 1965-66; house phys. cardiology, Hammersmith Hosp., London 1967; registrar Edgware Hosp., Middlesex, Eng. 1967-69, London Chest Hosp. 1969-70; research fellow and instr. cardiol. Univ.of Rochester Med. Center, Rochester, NY 1971-73; staff cardiologist Mount Sinai Med. Ctr., Miami Beach, Fla. 1972-75; Cardiographics Lab. Univ. Okla. Health Scis. Ctr. & VA Hosp. 1975-77; VA Hosp., Long Beach 1977-80; staff cardiologist/ dir. Echocardiography and Graphics, LA Co.-USC Med. Ctr. 1981–; tchg: Univ. Miami (1973-75), Univ.

Okla. (1975-77), UC Irvine and VA Hosp. Long Beach (1977-80), vis. prof. Univ. of Ariz. (1983), prof. of med. USC Sch. Med. (1981-); awards: 10 research grants, NIH, Warner-Lambert Inc., Biomed. Research Support, others; mem: L.A. Soc. Echocardiography (dir. 1981-83, v.p. 1983), L.A. Cardiology Soc., Am. Heart Assn. (Fellow Council of Clin.Cardiol.), AHA/ G. L.A. affil. (50th Ann. Fall Symp. com. 1982, judge Young Investigators Forum), Am. Soc. Echocardiography, Fellow Am.Coll. Cardiol., Fellow Am. Coll. Physicians, W. Soc. for Clin. Investigation, AAAS, NY Acad. Scis.; publs: contbr. num. arts. in med. jours., abstract in Year Book of Medicine (1975), num. presentations internat. med. confs. (1976-). Res: 30932 Marne Dr Rancho Palos Verdes 90274 Ofc: USC Section of Cardiology 2025 Zonal Ave Los Angeles 90033

CHANG, DAVID TSUNG-TANG, pharmacist; b. June 7, 1952, Taipei, Taiwan, nat. US cit. 1970; s. Kuang Yu and Anna Cheng-Ying (Chiang) C.; m. Gloria Lowe, July 22, 1978; children: Lianna b. 1983, Davis b. 1986; edn: UC Berkeley 1970-72; D.Pharm., UC San Francisco 1976; Reg. Pharm., Calif. 1976. Career: staff pharmacist UCLA Hosp., 1978-79, Brotman Hosp., Culver City 1979; dir. pharm. San Fernando Comm. Hosp., 1979-83; clin. pharm. coord. Northridge Hosp., 1983; dir. pharm. Clinishare Home I.V. Therapy, Northridge 1983—; honors: Regents Scholar, UCSF (1973), Rho Chi Pharm. Soc. (1974), Employee of the Year, San Fernando Comm. Hosp. (1982); mem. Am. Soc. Hosp. Pharmacist 1976-85, Calif. Pharmacists Assn. 1986-; coauthor research paper, J. Am. Pharm. Assn.; rec: travel. Res: 17548 Doric St Granada Hills 91344 Ofc: 18300 Roscoe Blvd Northridge 91328

CHANG, DUK SU, physician; b. Aug. 1, 1923, Seoul, Korea, nat. US cit. 1979; s. Suk Chul and Dal Ye (Lee) C.; m. Ok Hui Chung, Feb. 3, 1956; children: Ke Suk b. 1949, Ke Man b. 1951, Ke Sun b. 1954, Ke Hun b. 1956, Ke Hyon b. 1963; edn: MD, Yonsei Univ. Sch. of Medicine 1948; DPHJ, Singapore Univ. Postgraduate Sch. of Public Health 1961; OMD, San Francisco Coll. of Acupuncture and Oriental Medicine 1984; ECFMG (Ednl. Council for Fgn. Med. Grads.), Am. Med. Assn. (1971); Calif. lic. Acupuncturist (1976). Career: research mem. The Korea Oriental Med. Acad., Seoul 1954-58; chief physician The Seung Sim Won Oriental Med. Hosp., Seoul 1958-70; jr. physician Central State Hosp., Petersburg, Va., USA 1973-74; lectr. oriental medicine The Instn. of New York Academic Soc. of Acupuncture, N.Y., The Farang Acupuncture Inst., San Francisco, UC Davis Sch. of Medicine Extension course, 1974-76; pvt. practice acupuncture & herbal, Pleasant Hill 1976—; asst. prof. microbiol., Yonsei Univ. 1966-68; prof. oriental medicine, San Francisco Coll. of Acupuncture 1983-84; awards: appreciation, Korea Oriental Med. Acad., ACCS Step Stone, Sacramento (1984), San Francisco Coll. of Acupuncture (1983), merit award, Acupuncture Research Lab. (1974); mem. World Academic Soc. of Acupuncture (chief US Branch 1975-), Internat. Acup. Research Soc.; publs: Evolution of Principles of Oriental Medicine (1968), Evaluation of Yin Yang Five Elementary Theory based on Malignant Metastases (1973); mil: maj., surgeon Republic Korean Army 1950-54; Zen Buddhist; rec: painting, gardening, soccer. Res: 6289 Girvin Dr Oakland 94611 Ofc: Dr. Chang's Acupuncture and Herb Ctr 401 Gregory Lane 12 Pleasant Hill 94523

CHANG, GARY KAI, structural engineer; b. Dec. 17, 1935, Anhui, China, nat. US cit. 1972; s. Lawrence L. and Lily Y. (Ting) C.; m. Betty Sheau-pyne, Dec. 21, 1963; children: Lawrence Lichung b. 1964, Winston Liming b. 1967; edn: BS, Taiwan Univ. 1958; MS, USC 1962, E.C.E., USC 1969; Reg. Profl. Engr. (structural 1968, civil 1965), Calif.; Comm. Coll. tchr. credential (life) 1975. Career: senior structural engr. Albert C. Martin and Assocs., Los Angeles 1965-68; v.p. Mackintosh & Mackintosh, Inc., Los Angeles 1968-73; prin. Century Engineering Co., Torrance 1973—; senior lectr. USC 1969-, instr. Pasadena City Coll. 1975; mem: ASCE, Structural Engrs. Assn. of So. Calif.; research: Behavior of steel connections under cyclic loadings; rec: skiing, basketball, dancing. Res: 1476 Via Coronel Palos Verdes Estates 90274 Ofc: Century Engineering Co. 24719 Narbonne Ave Lomita 90717

CHANG, JEFFRY S.C., real estate broker, investor; b. June 17, 1954, Taipei, Taiwan, nat. US cit. 1978; s. Philip H. and Shirley H. (Hsu) C.; edn: BS engring., UC Berkeley 1978; Calif. lic. Real Estate Broker (1984). Career: assembly and pkg. engr., then sr. devel. engr. Fairchild Semiconductor Bipolar Div., Mt. View; devel. engr. Hewlett Packard (CICO), Cupertino; mfg. engring. mgr. Gould Electronics Microwave Div., San Jose; current: partner Philip Chang & Sons Assocs., Novato 1973—; owner JSC Assocs., Mt. View; pres./ dir./ CEO Executive Inn Inc. (dba Sunnyvale Holiday Inn), Sunnyvale 1984— and Horizon Properties Inc. Mt. View 1985—; mem. Am. Chinese Engr. Soc., Calif. Hotel & Motel Assn., San Jose Bd. Realtors and MLS, (fmr): MEPE (Electronic Plastic Pkg.), Internat. Soc. Hybrid Mfg., Semiconductor Equip. & Mat.; Buddhist; rec: stamps, swim, travel. Ofc: Executive Inn, Inc. 1217 Wildwood Ave Sunnyvale 94086

CHANG, JOHN HU-SEN, high technology corporation executive; b. July 3, 1938, Kweiyang, China, nat. US cit. 1967; s. Hung Chun and Yu-Chen C.; m. Katherine Shen, Aug. 8, 1964; children: John b. 1965, Derek b. 1969, Leslie b. 1971, Lauren b. 1972; edn: BSME, Princeton Univ. 1960; MS applied physics, Harvard Univ. 1961; PhD, Princeton Univ. 1967; MBA, UC Los Angeles 1984. Career: tchg. fellow Harvard Univ. 1960-61; research scientist Allis Chalmers Co. 1961-62; research asst. Princeton Univ. 1962-66; senior research scientist Avco Exerett Research Lab. 1966-69, TRW 1969-84, section head 1969-73, dept. mgr. 1973-81, asst. lab. mgr., bus. area mgr. 1981-84; dir., exec. v.p., chief ops. Helionetics Inc. 1984-86; dir., pres. HLX Laser Inc. 1986—; dir. Pacific Analysis Corp. 1984-85; honors: Outstanding Contbn. to Fluid Mechanics (Harvard Univ. 1961), Fellowship (Princeton 1962), Bonthion Meml.

Trophy (Princeton 1960); mem: Am. Inst. Aero. & Astro., Am. Meteriol. Soc., Naval Submarine League, Eckert Meml. Scholarship Com., Princeton Schools Com. (area chmn.), AYSO (coach 16 yrs.); publs: 25+ articles in field of fluid mechanics and applied physics; Democrat; Catholic; rec: sports. Res: 26609 Menominee Pl Rancho Palos Verdes 91274 Ofc: HLX Lasers 5452 Oberlin Dr San Diego 92121

CHANG, MING-LIANG, real estate developer, bank director; b. June 29, 1941, Shanghai, China, nat. US cit. 1973; s. Yung-Ching and Yu-hsiang (Shih) C.; m. Rosa Fu, Dec. 31, 1969; children: Lora b. 1972, Lori b. 1977; edn: BS, Cheng-Kung Univ. 1964; MS, City Univ. of N.Y. 1967. Career: civil engr. Tibbetts-Abbetts-McCarthy-Straton 1966-68; asst. project engr. State of Calif. Dept. of Transp. 1969-75; pres. C & R Constrn. Co. 1975-81; pres. O'shuming Ents. Inc., Alhambra 1980—; dir. United National Bank; mem. ASCE, Alhambra CofC; rec: sports, bridge, travel. Res: 1872 S Oakgate St Monterey Park 91754 Ofc: O'shuming Enterprises Inc. 215 W Pomona Blvd Ste 202 Monterey Park 91754

CHANG, PAUL PENG-CHENG, engineer; b. Aug. 19, 1931, Kiangsu, China, nat. 1973; s. Su-An and Hwei-Lin (Lou) C.; m. Kristina H., Aug. 19, 1968; children: Conway, b. 1969; Tina, b. 1971; edn: BS, Taiwan Chen-Kung Univ. 1956; ME, Okla. Univ. 1966; civil engr., Calif. 1970; structural engr., Ill. 1970; engr., Nebr. 1976; structural engr, Nevada 1978; structural engr., Utah 1981; engr., Ohio 1984. Career: engr. Taiwan Power Co. 1958-64; engr. Sargent & Lundy Engrs., Inc. 1966-68; supvg. engr. Bechtel Power Corp. 1968-74; principal engr. Kaiser Engrs. Power Corp. 1974-80; chief engr. Gibbs & Hill, Inc. 1980—; pres./ owner PPC Consulting Engrs. 1970—; designed more than a thousand modern skylights & greenhouses; mil: Taiwan, China; rec: music, sports. Address: 44577 Parkmeadow Dr Fremont 94538

CHANG, SEBASTIAN TSUN, international development co. executive; b. July 28, 1912, Shanghai, China, nat. 1964; s. Che-Shon and Ming Kuon (Yu) C.; m. Foong Tsze Chung, Aug. 15, 1941; chil: Alie, b. 1943; Jason, b. 1944; Lilee, b. 1948; Willy, b. 1952; edn: BS, Kiangsi Provincial Engring. Coll., 1934; MS, Sheffield Bennett Engring. Coll. 1937; EOAC, US Army Engr. Sch. 1953-4; NS&E, Indsl Coll. of Armed Forces USA 1961; cons. engr. in mil. & civil def., Ministry of Econ. R.O.C., 1944. Career: dir./secty. general, Resrch & Devel. of nat. defense, Ministry of Def., Taiwan and prof. of nuclear warfare & logistics, War College; tech. advisor Land Bank of Taiwan; v.p. Internat. Devel. Co. Taiwan; currently: dir./cons. engr. Pac Pacific Inc. USA; dir. Internat. Assn. of Real Estate. Awards: Medal of Victory 1946; Medal of Royalty 1948; recognition for estab. the Civil Def. Shelter Design & Constrn. System, Taiwan. Mem: Am. Soc. of Mil. Engrs. (v.p. & acting pres. Taiwan chpt. 1954-77); Internat. Auto Club (dir. Taiwan chpt. 1962-5). Author text: Shelter Design in Nuclear Age; Republican; Catholic; rec: travel, auto-test. Res: 5222 Noble Ave Van Nuys 91411 Ofc: PAC Pacific Inc. 9552 Frankirst Ave Sepulveda 91343-1911

CHANG, SHIRLEY (ZHANG, XIAO YI), acupuncturist/ Chinese medical doctor; b. Apr. 25, 1948, Fuzhou, Fujian, PRC; d. Mai Lin and Min (Lee) Zhang; m. James Chee Yee, June 17, 1981; edn: apprenticeship w/ traditional Chinese M.D., 1965—; BA, Canton Western Med. Inst. 1978; BA, Canton Chinese Med. Inst. 1980; Certified Acupuncturist, Calif. 1981. Career: practice Chinese medicine, PRC 1968-80, also hosp. lab. tech., 1976-79; prin. Chinese Acupuncture & Herbal Clinic, Santa Cruz, Calif. 1983—; rec: music, writing. Res: 270 Alturas Way Soquel 95073 Ofc: Chinese Acupuncture & Herbal Clinic, 707 N Branciforte Ave Santa Cruz 95062

CHAO, ALEXANDER WU, physicist; b. July 2, 1949, Taipei, Taiwan, China; s. Tu Hong and Roung (Chiang) C.; m. Patricia, May 30, 1973; children: Clifford b. 1979, Laura b. 1982; edn: BS, Tsin-Hwa Univ. Taiwan 1970; PhD, State Univ. NY Stony Brook 1974. Career: postdoc. Stanford Linear Accelerator Ctr. 1974-76, staff 1976-82, beam dynamics group leader 1982-84, head accelerator physics div. Superconducting Super Collider Central Design Group 1984—; mem. Am. Physical Soc. Ofc: SSC/CDG c/o Lawrence Berkeley Lab. 1 Cyclotron Rd Berkeley 94720

CHAPIN, JOHN KEITH, lawyer, author, editor; b. Nov. 15, 1946, Goodland, Kans.; s. Orville Edward and Florence Ada (Updike) C.; m. Carolyn O'Neal, Aug. 20, 1970; edn: BA, Univ. Colo., Boulder 1968; JD, Univ. Texas Sch. of Law 1971; admitted to state bars: Texas (1971), Colo. (1972), Calif. (1973). Career: atty. advisor US Gen. Services Adminstrn. reg. office, San Francisco 1972-78; dep. county counsel Sonoma County 1979-80, Solano County 1980-85; editor Construction Litigation Reporter 1981-83; govt. editor California Tort Reporter 1983-85; assoc. editor Federal Litigator 1985-, legal editor Univ. of Calif. Continuing Edn. of the Bar 1985—; dir., secty. New Gate Theatre Co., SF 1976; dir., secty. San Francisco Poverty Theatre Co., SF 1974-76; recipient Presidential Citation (Pres. Jimmy Carter) for outstanding achievement (1978); author: Tort Claims Against Public Entities and Employees, Div. VII Calif. Torts (Matthew Bender & Co., 1985); mil: USAR, JAGC, 1968-74; Democrat; Methodist; rec: fiction and poetry writing; drama (acting, writing). Res: 2423 Prospect Street Berkeley 94704 Ofc: Continuing Education of the Bar, 2300 Shattuck Ave Berkeley 94704

CHAPMAN, CHARLES LOTHROP, wine marketing consultant; b. Jan. 20, 1926, San Francisco; s. George Eric and Blanche Teresa (Lothrop) C.; m. Ann, Nov. 23, 1970; children: Linda b. 1951, Laurie b. 1952, Eric b. 1953; edn: 3-yr. Tech. Cert., CSU San Luis Obispo 1949; BA, CSU Fresno 1950; Life tchg. cred., Calif. Comm. Colls. (1981). Career: theatre mgr. Fox West Coast Theatres, 1950; mdse. controller Sears 1953; owner/pres. The Wine Cave 1965;

gen. mgr. Wine & Liquor Discount Mart 1985; bus. and mktg. cons., 1985—; instr. mktg. Calif. Community Colls.; mem. Soc. of Wine Educators (bd., chmn. 1981 Internat. Conf.); civic: Rotary Internat. (Paul Harris Fellow), Boy Scouts Am. (exec. bd. Sonoma Mendocino County Council), Easter Seals/Clear Water Ranch for Children (bd.); mil: pfc US Army Inf. WWII, Patton's 3rd Army, decorated Combat Inf., Expt. Marksman, ETO, Good Conduct, Purple Heart; rec: golf, photog., fishing. Res: 1112 Sunnyslope Dr Santa Rosa 95404

CHAPMAN, ROBERT EATON, insurance executive; b. July 9, 1927, Stockton, Calif.; s. Laurence Heilman and Dorothy (Fletcher) C.; m. Valeria Janzen, Sept. 16, 1951; children: Dorothy b. 1955, Mark b. 1957, Karen b. 1963; edn: BS, UC Berkeley 1952. Career: claims examiner to field ofc. mgr. State Disability Ins. Pgm. Calif. Employment Devel. Dept. 1957—; mem. Toastmasters Internat. 1973-76 (past. chpt. pres.); mil: hosp. corpsman USN 1945-46; Democrat; Protestant; rec: golf, hiking, reading. Res: 55 Bahia Way Apt 8 San Rafael 94901 Ofc: Employment Devel. Dept. 745 Franklin St Rm 202 San Francisco 94914

CHAPPELL, ARTHUR BENJAMIN, JR., recreational facilities developer; b. Mar. 22, 1950, Sacramento; s. Arthur B., Sr. and Judy Ruth (Golden) C.; edn: CSU San Diego 1975-77, spl. courses Dale Carnegie (1984-), Sacto. Valley Mktg. Assn. (1983-). Career: var. pos. to dist. mgr. sales Frito Lay Inc., 1974-78; devel. recreational facilities, 1981-, founder/owner Racquetball Fitness & Swim Center, Auburn 1981—; awards: AARA Jr. Nationals (1983), recogn. for community service: Assn. of Retarded Citizens of Placer County (1986), Mother Lode Spl. Olympics and Sierra Coll. (1986), local Hospice program, Optimist Club, Auburn Rec. Park; mem. Recreational Mgmt. Assn. (pres. 1984), Auburn CofC, Rotary, Sacto. Valley Mktg. Assn., Oakcreek Homeowners Assn. (pres. 1984); works: recording artist, record with Capital Records, Hollywood (1974); rec: racquetball, ski, scuba. Ofc: Old Auburn Court House 11558 F Ave Auburn 95603

CHAPPELL, JOANNE C., art publisher, corporate art consultant; b. Dec. 15, 1937, Hammond, Ind.; d. Arnold and Bertha (Taussig) Loeffler; m. Robert Chappell, June 15, 1958; div.; children: Marc b. 1959, Barry b. 1961, Anne b. 1966; edn: AB, Indiana Univ. 1960, Acad. of Fine Arts Chgo. 1961. Career: artist, one person exhibs. include Indpls. Mus., Evansville Mus.; buyer and seller of fine art, Europe, and exclusive importer/pub. of print editions by sev. European artists (also domestic publ. of 200+ print and poster images); founder Editions Limited Art Gallery, Indpls. 1969—, founder/dir. Editions Limited West, San Francisco 1978—; mem. Am. Bus. Womens Assn./S.F. chpt.; rec: ski. Ofc: Editions Limited 333 Fifth St Studio B San Francisco 94107; Editions Limited West 1 Market Plaza San Francisco 94105

CHAPPELL, JOHN F., telecommunications executive; radio/ television broadcasting instructor; b. July 10, 1948, Oakdale; s. George F. and Helen M. (Wormington) C.; edn: AA, Modesto Jr.Coll. 1968; tchg. cred., UC Berkeley 1979. Career: announcer KSRT-FM stereo, Tracy, Calif. 1966-68; announcer, engr. KCEY Radio, Turlock 1968-70; radioman USN, Vietnam 1969-71; pgm. dir. KFIV Radio, Modesto 1971-74; announcer, performer Early Dawn Enterprises (restaurant chain), Modesto, Fresno 1979-80; announcer, engr., pgrmmr. KBEE/KBEE-FM, McClatchy Broadcasting, Modesto 1974-79; telecommunications ops. supr. Modesto Jr. Coll., 1974—, instr. radio/tv broadcasting 1983—; cons. Western States Tech. Assistance Resource, Univ. Wash., Seattle; mem. Stanislaus Amateur Radio Assn. 1977-, Internat. Brotherhood Elect. Workers, Radio/TV Engrs. Union 1974-78, Calif. Sch. Employees Assn. 1981-, US Hang Gliding Assn. 1980-, Nat. Experimental Aircraft Assn. (v.p. Chpt. 90), Continental Luscombe Assn. 1980-; built & fly a Quicksilver Ultralight Aircraft, currently constructing/testing a Q-2 exptl. fiberglass airplane 1980-; mil: PO3 USN 1969-71. Methodist. rec: flying exptl.aircraft, motorcycling, tv photog. Res: 3708 Carlisle Ct. Modesto 95356Ofc: Modesto Jr. Coll. College Ave Modesto

CHARCHOL, JACK RICHARD, civil engineer; b. Feb. 23, 1938, Bowling Green, Ohio; s. John Joseph and Mary Maxine (Smith) C.; m. Peggy Elizabeth Field, Feb. 18, 1978; children: Jackie Lynn b. 1960, Daniel Joseph b. 1962, Julie Pauline b. 1967, Jeffrey Brandon b. 1982; edn: Univ. of Toledo 1956-61; Reg. Profl. Engr., Ohio (1965), Ind. (1968), Reg. Civil Engr., Mich. (1968), S.C. (1972), Calif. (1973); Reg. Land Surveyor, Ohio (1972). Career: project engr. Lucas County Engrs. Office, Toledo, O. 1959-65; ptnr. Finch/Charchol & Assocs., Toledo 1965-74; office mgr. Williamson & Schmid, Irvine 1974-76; ptnr. Stanley C. Morse Consulting Engrs., Anaheim 1976-82; owner J.R. Charchol & Assocs., Laguna Hills 1982-85, ptnr. Charchol/Hartman & Assocs., 1985—; mem: ASCE, Am. Council of Civil Engrs. and Land Surveyors; civic: founder Orange County Performing Arts Ctr., Nat. CofC (Wash DC); Democrat; Protestant; rec: woodworking, skiing, fishing, bowling. Res: 33092 Elisa Dr Dana Point 92629 Ofc: Charchol/Hartman & Assoc., 25201 Paseo de Alicia Ste 100 Laguna Hills 92653

CHARITAN, ARNOLD, business executive; b. Apr. 10, 1927, Yonkers, NY; s. Jack and Alys (Katz) C.; m. Gladys Korn, Aug. 2, 1947; chil: Jeffrey Alan, b. 1949, Janeen Lisa, b. 1952; edn: BS, Ariz. State Univ. 1951, MA, Azusa-Pac. Coll. 1974; exec. pgm. cert. UCLA Grad. Sch of Mgmt. 1976. Career: cost analyst Douglas Aircraft, El Segundo 1951-59; adminstr. Northrop Corp., Hawthorne 1959-64; prin. Charitan Mtge. & Ins.,Torrance 1964-66; district mgr. Auto Club of So. Calif., Century City 1966—; instr. bus. mgmt. L.A. Harbor Coll. 1974-; lic. Real Estate Broker, Calif.; apptd. by Sen. pro tem David Roberti to Task Force, Auto & Truck Ins. 1982; mem: UCLA Exec. Pgm.

Assocs. (bd. dirs., pres. 1981), Town Hall West Adv. Bd., Zionist Orgn of Am. (bd. dirs.), L.A./Lusaka Sister City Com. (past bd.dirs.), Jewish War Vets (bd.dirs.), Century City CofC (bd. dirs.), B'nai B'rith, Beverly Hills Bus & Profl. Men's Assn., Calif. Tax Reduction Movement, LA World Affairs Council, Westside Forum (chmn.), publs: pamphlet on real estate investments (1982). Mil: USN 1945-46. Republican; Jewish; rec: racquetball, tennis. Res: 1477 Glendon Ave. Los Angeles 90024. Ofc: Auto Club of So. Calif. 1950 Century Park East Los Angeles 90067

CHARLES, MICHAEL FELTON, orthopedic surgeon; b. Dec. 22, 1949, San Francisco; s. Felton and Iris Josephine (Pete) C.; m. Beverly Roberts, June 12, 1977; edn: BS, Simon Fraser Univ. 1972; MMS, Rutger's Med. Sch., Piscataway 1975, MD, 1977. Career: resident Martin Luther King Jr. Hosp., Los Angeles 1978-81, chief res. 1981-82, also orthopedic splst. cons. MLK Jr. Sickle Cell Center (1980-82), King-Drew Med. Sch. Admissions Com. (1979-82), South Central Health Found. (1981-82); currently orthopedic practice in Berkeley; honors: nat.conf.presenter Am. Orthopedic Residents Assn. 17th Annual Conf., Wash DC (1982), intern of year MLK Hosp./Drew Med. Ctr. (1978); publs: Metrizamide Computer Tomography in the Post Operative Spine (1982); rec: photog., biking, creative writing. Ofc: 2500 Milvia St Ste 114 Berkeley 94704

CHARLES, REGINA, real estate broker; b. May 5, Woburn, Mass.; d. Thomas and Agnes Lyons; m. Heinrich Charles, Sept. 19, 1959; children: Maria b. 1960, Kevin b. 1961, Peter b. 1963, Patrick b. 1968; edn: AA, Kathleen Dell Sch. 1949; Boston Univ. 1950-51; desig: GRI, Grad. Realtor Inst. (1977). Career: airline stewardess United Air Lines 1952-59; office mgr. Harrington Oaks Realtors, Thousand Oaks 1976-80, owner/broker 1980—; mem. Conejo Valley Bd. Realtors (chair Profl. Stds. com. 1982, 86), Equitable Realty Network, Conejo Women in Bus. (charter); Republican; Catholic. Res: 1091 La Cresta Thousand Oaks 91360 Ofc: Harrington Oaks Realtors 554 N Moorpark Thousand Oaks 91360

CHASE, EMMETT, physician; b. July 25, 1952, Hoopa, Calif.; s. Leon Ernest and Geraldine (Spencer) C.; m. Lynne Ammon, June 17, 1970; div.; children: Maybeline b. 1973, Emmett Jr. b. 1976, Joel b. 1979; edn: BS, UC Davis 1978; MD, Stanford Univ. 1982. Career: medical resident So. Colo. Family Medicine, Pueblo, Colo. 1982-83; program dir. Consolidated Tribal Health, Ukiah, Calif. 1983-84, medical dir., 1985—; medical dir. Lake County Tribal Health, Lakeport 1985—; Physician Asst. supvr. and preceptor, also Medical Student preceptor, CTH, 1985; honors: Indian Professional award, Indian Health Service/ CA Prog. Ofc., 1985 the First Hupa tribal member to become a doctor, the First California Indian to graduate from Stanford Medical Sch., the First Calif. Indian to become a practicing physician in Calif.; mem. Am. Assn. of Indian Physicians (secty. bd. dirs. 1985-86); works: video for Mendocino County Edn. Dept. encouraging Indian students to stay in sch. (1985); polit: Hupa Tribal mem.; avocation: encouraging Indian children. Res: 27111 Oriole Dr., Willits 95490 Ofc: Consolidated Tribal Health, 564 South Dora, Ste D, Ukiah 95482

CHATZKEL, SHERRIE LYNN, physician, radiologist; b. Aug. 1, 1949, Phila.; d. Benjamen and Doris (Presser) Chatzkel; m. Robert Harwell, Jan. 5, 1986; edn: BA, Temple Univ. 1971; MS, Medical Coll. of Pa. 1976; MD, Temple Univ. 1976; Board certified Diagnostic Radiology (1980). Career: intern in internal medicine Univ. of South Fla. 1976-77, resident in radiol., UC Los Angeles 1977-80, fellowship in ultrasound-CT Jefferson Univ., Phila. 1980-81; asst. prof. Hahnemann Medical Coll., Phila. 1981-82; staff radiologist Long Beach (Calif.) Meml. Hosp. 1982-83; staff radiologist Valley Hosp. 1983-85; staff phys., interim acting chief Long Beach VA Hosp 1985-; mem. Radiol. Soc. of No. Am., Am. Inst. of Ultrasound in Medicine, L.A. C. Radiol. Soc. Ultrasound Div.; coauthor 4 research articles in med. jours.; Jewish; rec: astronomy, art. Res: 10669 Kinnard St Apt 4 West Los Angeles 90024

CHAVEZ, CESAR, union official; b. Mar. 31, 1927, Yuma, Ariz.; married; 8 children. Career: mem. staff Community Service Orgn., Calif. 1952-58, gen. director 1958-62; organized Nat. Farm Workers Assn. 1962, merged with Agricultural Workers Organizing Com., AFL-CIO, 1966, to form United Farm Workers Organizing Com., Delano, Calif., pres. United Farm Workers of Am., AFL-CIO, 1972—; mil: USNR 1944-45; Roman Catholic. Address: United Farm Workers of America, P.O. Box 62, Keene 93531

CHAVEZ, JUANITA G., lawyer; b. Mar. 6, 1935, Coffeyville, Kans.; d. Howard H., Sr. and Ollie E. (McLaughlin) Glenn; m. Marston J. Chavez, Jan. 26, 1974; children (by prior marriage): Deborah b. 1954, Max, III b. 1956, Jacolyn C. (Fellin) b. 1958; edn: BA, St. Univ. Iowa 1961, MA, CSU Long Beach 1965, JD summa cum laude, Northrop Univ. 1981; admitted Calif. State Bar 1981. Career: tchr., administr. Los Angeles City Schs., 21 years; atty. sole practice, San Pedro 1982—, spec. in probate, family law, corporations, and unlawful temination of employment; honors: Alpha Delta Kappa, Woman of the Year (1985); mem. ABA, Calif. Bar Assn., L.A. County Bar Assn., Harbor Bar Assn., Harbor Found. for the Retarded (bd. dirs.), AAUW (past pres.), Alpha Delta Kappa, San Pedro Peninsula CofC (dir.), YWCA (dir.), Legal Aid of Long Beach (vol.), Rainbow Services for Battered Women (vol.); Democrat; Catholic; rec: reading. Ofc: 590 West 7th St San Pedro 90731

CHAVEZ, LONNIE SAMUEL, clergyman, educator, retired military engineer; b. May 22, 1929, Gunnison, Colo.; s. Alonzo Samuel and Irene Araminta (Fernandez) C.; m. Evelyn Wright, Oct. 11, 1948; children: Teresa b. 1949, Christine b. 1953, Laura b. 1957; edn: undergrad., Grossmont Coll. 1976-77; BS, cum laude, Christian Heritage Coll. 1978; grad. USMC Combat Engr.

Ofcrs. Sch. 1960, Utilities Ofcrs. Sch. 1965; ordained Baptist minister (1977). Career: prodn. crew Ralston Purina Co. (Oakland) 1949-50, prodn. leadman (Spokane, Wash.) 1953-56; pvt. US Marine Corps 1946-48; sgt. USMC 1950-52; major USMC 1956-75, decorated Navy Commendn. Medal; pastor First Spanish Baptist Ch., El Cajon 1975-78; missionary Home Mission Board, So. Baptist Convention, Calif. 1978-80, currently dir. Language Missions SBGCC, and Seminar instr., 1980–; v.p. So. Baptist New Work Fellowship, 1985-86; recipient appreciation certifs., Fgn. Mission Board, and Baptist World Alliance; mem. Christian Heritage Coll. Alumni, V.F.W.; publs: booklet and workbook: A Winning Strategy for Ethnic Ministries (1982, 1984); Republican; Baptist; rec: fishing, carpentry. Res: 4034 North Briarwood Fresno 93705 Ofc: Southern Baptist Convention of California 678 East Shaw Ave Fresno 93710

CHAVEZ, MICHAEL ANDREW, building supply co. president; b. Nov. 17, 1945, Albuquerque, N.M.; s. Alfred Duran and Virginia Laura (Baca) C.; m. Jane Lynn, Nov. 19, 1978; children: Tammy b. 1964, Michael b. 1981, Juanita b. 1985; Calif. lic. real estate broker (1981-). Career: mktg. dir. Tyrrell Inc., San Diego 1967-73; pres. Universal Video 1973-75; mktg. dir. Guardian Brokers 1976-82; pres. All American Bldg. Supply, Pine Valley 1982–, and pres. Tropical Tan Tanning Salons, San Diego; awards: Salesman of Year, Tyrrell (1971), Million Dollar Round Table, Guardian Finl. (1977-82); author: The Success Guide for Today's Woman (1977). Res: 29072 Rocky Pass Rd Pine Valley 92062 Ofc: Tropical Tan 11269 Camino Ruiz San Diego 92126

CHEEVES, LYNDELL DUANE, financial co. executive; b. Jan. 7, 1932, Oklahoma City, Okla.; s. James L. and Clarice Jewell (Lambert) C.; m. Dorothy Anne Machenheimer, July 20, 1952; children: Susan b. 1953, Larry b. 1954, Donna b. 1957; edn: BA, Pepperdine Univ. 1953; MA, Univ. of La Verne 1966; EdD, UC Los Angeles 1971. Career: prof. La Verne Coll., 1964-68; asst. dean and prof. Coll. of the Desert, Palm Desert 1968-74; assoc. dean Pepperdine Univ., Malibu 1956-61, 74-76; dean Cochise Coll., Douglas, Ariz. 1976-78; pres. Feather River Coll, Quincy, Calif. 1978-80; pres. Advanced Financial Planning, Orange 1981–; prof. of mgmt. Pacific Christian Coll., Fullerton (1981-85); ednl. cons.to many colls.; mem. Internat. Assn. of Finl. Planners, Inst. Certified Finl. Planners, Pi Kappa Delta nat. speech frat., Rotary; Republican; Ch. of Christ (ordained minister); rec: travel, bowling, baseball, basketball. Ofc: Advanced Financial Planning 1224 E Katella Ste 206 Orange 92667

CHEHOCK, DONALD P., lawyer; b. Sept. 21, 1907, Anita, Iowa; s. Henry Walter and Beulah (Bryan) C.; m. Margaret McHugh (dau. of Mayor and Mrs. C.N. McHugh of Cedar Falls, Iowa), June 30, 1938; children: Bryan b. 1939, Robert b. 1941, Donald, Jr. b. 1942; edn: Coe Coll. 1925-27; BA, Univ. of Iowa 1929, JD, 1931; admitted to State Bar of Iowa 1931, State Bar of Calif. 1953; Certified Tax Splst. 1973. Career: general law practice at Osage, iowa 1931-44, apptd. City Atty. of Osage, 1935-38; elected County Atty., three terms 1939-44, also local counsel for Rural Electrification Adminstrn., 1938-44; govt. svc. in Tax Court Litigation Div., Office of Chief Counsel, IRS, 1944-76, in Dallas (1944-51) and Los Angeles (1951-76) Offices in trial and supvsry. posts; most of his trials involved taxpayers controverted income tax cases in US Tax Ct., involving precedent-making type issues; cases he tried or their appeals have now been cited over 1,000 times as case authority by var. federal cts.; part time pvt. practice, San Marino, Ca. 1976-; honors: award, Secty. of the US Treasury Wash. DC (1971); Order of the Coif (1931); Award of Merit, Coe Coll. (1977); Big Ten Club awd. as outstanding Univ. Iowa Alumnus (1983); mem: Calif., Iowa, and Federal Bars; past pres. Univ. Iowa Alumni Assn. of So. Ca.; past pres. Iowa (state) Assn. of So. Calif.; Big Ten Club of So. Calif. (pres. 1979; ed. Newsletter 1981-); City Club of San Marino; Kappa Sigma Frat.; Prot.; rec: sports. Address: 1358 San Marino Ave San Marino 91108

CHELLAPPA, RAMALINGAM, university educator; b. April 8, 1953, Tanjore, Madras, India; d. Muthukrishnan and Kamakshi (Rajagopalan) Ramalingam; m. Vishnu P. Chellappa, June 16, 1983; edn BE, honors, Madras Univ. 1975; ME, distn. Indian Inst. of Sci. 1977; MSEE, Purdue Univ. 1978, PhD, 1981. Career: grad. research asst., instr. Purdue Univ., W. Lafayette, Ind. 1977-81; grad. research asst., faculty research asst. Univ. of Maryland, College Park, Md. 1979-81; asst. prof. USC 1981-85,assoc. prof. 1985–; honors: Presidential Young Investigator Award 1985; IBM Faculty Devel. Award 1985; Jawaharlal Nehru Meml. Award 1975; mem: IEEE (senior), Am. Assn. for Artificial Intelligence, Eta Kappa Nu, Tau Beta Pi; works: author or co-author 2 collected works, 4 book chpts. and 50+ journ. and conf. papers; rec: tennis, music. Res: 3601 Jasmine Ave. Apt. 6 Los Angeles 90034 Ofc: Univ. of Southern Calif., Los Angeles 90089-0272

CHEN, DANIEL KWEE-SU, acupuncturist, herbalist; b. Sept. 12, 1940, Pyapon, Burma; s. Nyunt Min and Ah Su (Kwon) C.; m. Alice Ai-Sain L., May 26, 1968; children: Alina b. 1969, Aileen b. 1970, John b. 1972, James b. 1974; edn: BA, Rangoon Univ. 1963; Dipl., Present Day Chinese Acupuncture and Medicine, Hong Kong 1970; Certified Acupuncturist, Calif. State Bd. 1984; Diplomate in Acup., (NCCA) Nat. Commn. for Cert. of Acupuncturists 1985. Career: practise Chinese acupuncture, moxibustion and herbs in Burma, 1962-81; prin. Chinese Acupuncture Inst. 1971-81; acupuncturist, herbalist prin. Chen's Clinic, Daly City 1984–; honors: Shwedagon Pagoda (1975-78), Hitaythe Assn. (1978); mem: Calif. Certified Acup. Assn. (CCAA), Burma Chinese Physicians Assn. (secty. 1967-71), Lions Club of Rangoon (past pres.), Masons (past master Burma Lodge, current mem. S.F. Lodge); Buddhist; rec: swimming, badminton, travel. Address: Chen's Clinic, 68 Woodland Ave Daly City 94015

CHEN, JEFF, hotel investment and management executive; b. Aug. 24, 1937, Tainan, Taiwan, ROC, nat. US cit. 1972; s. Chang-Pei and Chue-Yen (Won) C.; m. Julie Hsu, July 10, 1965; children: Jack J. b. 1966, Jenny J. b. 1967; edn: MS, Univ. of Texas, Austin 1966. Career: chmn., CEO, pres. Master Hotel Systems Inc., Los Angeles; dir. American Internat. Bank, Los Angeles; recipient, high achiev. award of mgmt.; mem. Am. and Calif. Hotel and Motel Assn. Res: 7854 Calmcrest Dr. Downey 90240 Ofc: Master Hotel Sytems Inc., 1455 Monterey Pass Rd. Ste. 202 Los Angeles 91754

CHEN, JERRY CHIH-LI, physicist, company executive; b. Sept. 18, 1936, Fuchow, Fukien, China; s. Bei-ping and Ru-liang (Lin) C.; m. Shirley Wang, Jan. 25, 1969; children: Guang-min b. 1973, Guang-qun b. 1975; edn: BS, Tunghai Univ., Taiwan 1961; MS, Worcester Polytechnic Inst. 1965, PhD, 1969. Career: asst. prof. physics Pan American Coll., Edinburg, Texas 1969-70; electronics engr., owner Friendship TV & Electronics Svcs., Oakland 1972-78; computer engr., ptr. Suntek Associates, San Jose 1978-81; pres., dir. Kentex International Inc., Palo Alto 1979–; dir., secty. Eastwind Books & Arts Inc. 1979-80; honors: Sigma Xi 1970; mem: IEEE, Am. Chemical Soc. (Rubber Div.), Tech. Assn of the Pulp & Paper Industry, Soc. of Photo- Optical Instrumentation Engrs., Combustion Inst.; publs: Eastwind Mag. 1971-75; mil: 2nd lt. Chinese Army 1961-62; Christian; rec: bridge, swimming. Res: 2154 St. Francis Dr. Palo Alto 94303 Ofc: Kentex International Inc., 1718 Broadway Redwood City 94063

CHEN, KUO-CHING, acupuncturist; b. Oct. 17, 1924, Hsiaoshan, Chekiang, China; s. Wen-Jui and Shih (Kung) C.; m. Yuan-Yuan, Mar. 4, 1967; children: Ju-Ching b. 1969, Chi-Yu b. 1972; edn: Chinese Literature & Art Coll., China 1942-45; Chih-Chiang Univ., China 1946-47; one-yr. advance course acupuncture Taipei, Taiwan 1960; PhD in oriental medicine, Asian Am. Acupuncture Med. Univ., USA 1984; Cert. Acupuncturist, Calif.State Board (1978). Career: acupuncturist prin., Kuo-Ching Chen Acupuncture Clinic, Taipei, Taiwan 1949-83, acupuncture master of 15 apprentices 1964-85; Chen's, K.C. Acupuncture, South Pasadena 1983–, splst. in clin. treatment of neck pain, back pain and infertility; clinic supvr. Acupuncture Coll. Los Angeles Univ.1985-; honors: first doctor in Republic of China to treat Pres.M. Hubert Maga, Rep. of Dahomey with(1963), plaque inscribed "The Doctor that Performs Wonders" from Fernando Sanchez R., Amb. of Costa Rica (1982), Medal Plaque from Chinese Acupuncture Soc. (1980); mem.Taipei Acupuncture Assn. (gen. adminstr. 1961-67), Chinese Acupuncture Assn. 1960- (chmn. edition & paperselection com. 1966-68, chmn.promotion com. 1969), Nat. Commn. for Certification of Acupuncturists (1984-85), Acupuncture Assn. of So. Calif. (dir. 1985-); dissertation: Introduction of Chinese Acupuncture 1983-84; research: clin. diagnosis using reflex points on hands, extra points, Chinese massage and acupuncture techniques 1962-; Buddhist; rec. gardening, Chinese brush painting. Ofc: Chen's, K.C. Acupuncture 2130 Huntington Dr Ste 216 South Pasadena 91030

CHEN, LAWRENCE LIEREN, structural engineer; b. Aug. 2, 1949, Tainan, Taiwan, nat. US cit. 1982; s. Yie Chin and Sue Shar (Hsieh) C.; m. Eleanor, Dec. 1977; 1 son, Richard b. 1978; edn: BS, Nat. Taiwan Univ. 1971; MS, UC Berkeley 1974; Reg. Structural Engr. Ill. 1978, Reg. Profl. Engr. Calif. 1984. Career: structural engr. Klein & Hoffman Inc. Chgo. 1975-78; str. engr. splst. Sargent & Lundy Engrs. Chgo. 1979-81; str. engr. group leader Peter F. Loftus Corp. Chgo. 1979-81; senior engr. Procan Internat. Inc. Des Plaines, Ill. 1981-83, Ralph M. Parsons Co. Pasadena 1984–; mem: Profl. Engrs. of Calif., Str. Engrs. of Ill., Am. Formasan Club; mil: 2nd lt. AF Rep. of China; Buddhist; rec: gardening, hiking, music. Res: 821 N Stoneman Ave, Ste A, Alhambra 91801 Ofc: Ralph M. Parsons Co. 100 W Walnut St Pasadena 91124

CHEN, LIWEI, national marketing & sales executive; b. Sept. 2, 1950, Taiwan, China; s. Aken Hsu-Ching and Jeh Jung (Tsai) Chen; m. Suzie S.M. Yang, May 1979; sons: Raymond Eric, b. 1981, (twins) Allen Thomas and Victor Brian, b. 1983; edn: BSME, nt. Taiwan Univ., Taipei 1972; MSME, Northwestern Univ. (Ill.), 1976; MBA, Univ. of So. Calif. 1979; lic: Reg. Profl. Engr. State of Calif. (ME 18581), State of Wash. (ME 18117). Career: analytical engr. Borg-Warner Corp., Van Nuys, 1976-77, design engr. 1977, project engr. 1977-78, sr. proj. engr. 1978-79, sr. mech. engr. Nuclear Products, Masoneilan Div. McGraw-Edison Co. Montebello, 1979, Nuclear Engrg. Section Mgr. 1979-80, mktg. & contract adm. mgr. 1981-82, mktg. & sales adminstrn. mgr. U.S. Operations 1982-84, mktg., sales & distrbn. mgr. 1984; mgr. sales distbn. and warehouses Masoneilan No. Am. Ops., Dresser Valve & Controls Div., Dresser Inds., Inc. 1985–; also cons. Righton Ind. & Engrg. Co., L.A. 1979-83; cons. Tsong-Tai Enterprises (USA) Co. L.A. 1979-83; cons. Innomatic Systems, Inc. Garland, TX 1980–; cons. Numertek, Inc. Taiwan 1981–; cons. M.J.R. Component, Inc. Chatsworth, CA 1984–; awards: res. assistantship, Northwestern Univ. 1974-76; mem: Amer. Mktg. Assn., Amer. Soc. Mech. Engrs. (assoc), Nat. Soc. of Profl. Engrs., Amer. Soc. for Quality Control, Beta Gamma Sigma scholar; rec: music, bridge, tennis, fishing. Res: 402 S Carole Ln Orange 92669 Ofc: 1040 S. Vail Ave Montebello 90640

CHEN, PO-JEN, accountant, real estate broker; b. Jan. 31, 1956, Tainan, Taiwan; s. Ming-Tsong and Shiu-Ching (Lee) C.; edn: B. Commerce, Nat. Chung Hsing Univ. Taiwan 1978; MBA, Univ. Wisc. Madison 1979; CPA Calif. 1983, Colo. 1982; Cert. Mgmt. Acct. 1983; Real Estate Broker Calif. 1985. Career: auditor ARA Services Inc. Los Angeles 1979-81; CPA Kunz & Smigiel CPAs Culver City 1981-82; auditor McCulloch Corp. Los Angeles 1982-83; sole proprietor Po-Jen Chen Certified Public Accountant & Real Estate Broker Pasadena 1983–; finance & tax columnist Chinese Daily News, Internat. Daily News and Centre Daily News 1983–; honors: Legislative Scholar (Univ. Wisc.

Oshkosh 1978); mem: Am. Inst. CPAs, Nat. Assn. Accts., Nat. Assn. Realtors, Calif. Assn. Realtors, Pasadena Bd. of Realtors; rec: reading, travel. Res: 8876 E Camino Real Ave San Gabriel 91755 Ofc: Po-Jen Chen CPA & Real Estate Broker 35 N Lake Ave, 7th floor, Pasadena 91101

CHEN, YUNG-CHENG JOSEPH, physician; b. June 10, 1951, Taipei, Taiwan; s. Mao-Sung and Mei (Ro) C.; m. Ruth, Feb. 11, 1978; 1 son, Daniel b. 1980; edn: MD, National Taiwan Univ. 1976; MPH, Harvard Sch. of Pub. Health 1983; Calif. lic. BMQA 1984. Career: cmdr. Health Platoon, Taiwan Army, Taiwan 1976-78; gen. psychiatry resident Nat. Taiwan Univ. Hosp., Taipei 1978-81, chief resident 1981-82; child psychiatry fellow UCLA Neuropsychiatric Inst., Los Angeles 1983-85; awards: two-yr scholarship at Harvard Univ. (1981); mem. AMA, Am. Psychiatry Assn., Am. Acad. of Child Psychiatry, Mass. Med. Assn., Am. Public Health Assn.; research: epidemiol. study of geriatric psychiatric patients in instn.; adolescent mental health; family function study; mil: lt. Taiwan Army Med. Corps 1976-78; Baptist; rec: travel, philately, literature. Res: 1267 37th Ave San Francisco Ofc: UC San Francisco Dept. of Psychiatry & Langley Porter Psychiatric Inst. 401 Parnassus Ave San Francisco 94143

CHENG, BEN S., real estate broker; b. Dec. 15, 1953, Taipei, Taiwan; s. Stanway and Lucy (Tai) C.; m. Peggy, Oct. 23, 1983; edn: BS, UC Berkeley 1976; tchg. cred., CSU Los Angeles 1978; lic. real estate sales Calif. 1979, broker 1983. Career: sales assoc. Herbert Hawkins Realtors, Alhambra 1979-81, East-West Realty, Monterey Park 1982-83; broker assoc./tng. dir. Cathay Realty, 1984—; profl. awards: top producer East-West Realty (1982, 83), Multi-Million Dollar Club (1979-); mem. West San Gabriel Bd. Realtors), J.B.M. Fishing Club; rec: fishing, tennis. Ofc: Calif. Real Estate Professionals POB 1391 Alhambra 91802

CHENG, PETER YU-HUNG, electronic engineer; b. Feb. 4, 1952, Hong Kong, nat. US cit. 1984; s. Yuk Kwan and Sussy Shui-Wan (Kao) C.; m. Pearl Po-Yee Li, Mar. 21, 1981; edn: BSEE summa cum laude, Wash. State Univ. 1974; MSEE, Univ. Penn. 1976; postgrad. work in engring. mgmt. and E.E. (Honors Coop. Pgm.), Stanford Univ. 1982-. Career: design engr. Texas Instruments Co., Houston 1977-78; Intel Co., Santa Clara, Calif. 1978-79; senior design Intersil Co., Cupertino 1979-80, Intel Co., Santa Clara 1980-81; devel. engr. Hewlett Packard Co., Cupertino 1981-82, project mgr. 1982—, chmn. Hewlett Packard VLSI Design Technology Conf. 1983-; awards: Fellow Univ. of Penna. (1974-76), Grad. Students Council (pres. 1975), S. Town Stephenson Scholar (1974), Internat. Exchange Award, Wash. State Univ. (1971-74), Tau Beta Pi (1972), Phi Kappa Phi (1974); mem: IEEE, AAAS, Am. Mgmt. Assn., Am. Assn. for Artificial Intel., Stanford Alumni Assn. (life); publs: tech. papers var. profl. confs. (1977-86); Republican; Christian; rec: tennis, fine arts, classical music, bridge. Res: 10229 Palo Vista Rd Cupertino 95014 Ofc: Hewlett Packard 53U-85 5301 Stevens Creek Blvd Santa Clara 95051

CHERNOFF, DAVID J., advertising executive; b. Sept. 20, 1922, NY, NY; s. Joseph and Bertha (Malkin) C.; m. Lita, Mar. 28, 1947; children: Karen b. 1951, Debra b. 1955, Beth b. 1959; edn: ASTP, Catholic Univ. 1943; BBA, City Coll. of N.Y. 1951; MBA, N.Y.U. Grad. Sch. of Mgt. 1955. Career: controller Fairchild Hiller Corp., Rosecranz 1964-69; Fansteel, Inc., Compton 1969-70; treas., controller Echo Sci. Corp., Pasadena 1970-71; dir. fin., bus. mgr. Effectiveness Tng. Inc., Solana Beach 1971-82; v.p. adminstrn. & fin./v.chmn. bd. dirs. Ashley-Wayne Advt. Inc., 1982—; adj. prof., bus. mgt., National Univ.; mem. Am. Inst. of Corp. Controllers, NYU Grad. Sch. Alumni Assn.; mil: sgt. US Army Signal Corps 1942-46, (5) Combat Stars; Republican; rec: tennis, walking. Res: 3205 Azahar Pl Carlsbad 92008 Ofc: Ashley-Wayne Adv. Inc. 6920 Miramar Rd Ste 202 San Diego 92121

CHERNOW, ELI, superior court judge; b. Nov. 24, 1939, Pittsburgh, Penna.; s. Morris and Jean (Yahr) C.; m. Arlene Canter, Aug. 17, 1968; children: Mari b. 1972, Jordana b. 1976, Ilana b. 1979; edn: BS, Calif. Inst. of Tech. 1961; JD, Harvard Law Sch. 1964, Frederick Sheldon Traveling Fellow, 1964-65; admitted to Calif. State Bar 1965. Career: law practice, ptnr. Tuttle & Taylor 1965-72; assoc. prof. of law USC Law Center 1972-74; special asst. to Gov. Edmund G. Brown, Jr. for enviornmental matters 1975-77; apptd. judge Superior Court Los Angeles 1977—; mem: L.A. County Bar Asn., AM. Judicature Soc., San Fernando Valley Bar Assn.; bd. trustees Stephen S. Wise Temple; contbr. articles in Envir. Law Quarterly (1974); Jewish. Ofc: Los Angeles Superior Court 111 N Hill St Los Angeles 90012

CHESS, STEPHEN JOHN, physician and surgeon; b. June 29, 1914, Fourstates, W. Va.; s. John and Theresa (Cernalavic) C.; m. Dorothy Haasch, Nov. 21, 1940; children: Dorothy b. 1950, Stephanie b. 1952, John b. 1953, Robert b. 1957, Thomas b. 1958; edn: BS 1936 and MS 1939, Marquette Univ.; MD, Medical Coll. of Wisc. 1942; PhD in surgery, Univ. of Ill. Sch. of Medicine, 1949; Diplomate Am. Bd. of Surgery (1950), Am. Bd. of Abdominal Surgery (1969). Career: Fellow in Surgery, Research & Ednl. Hosps., Univ. of Ill. Sch. of Medicine 1943-44; chief surgical resident Hines VA Hosp., Hines, Ill.; asst. chief surgeon, Chicago, Milwaukee & St. Paul R.R. and attending surgeon Wesley Meml. Hosp. and Northwestern Univ. Sch. of Medicine, Chgo., 1948; chief surgeon Buenaventura Med. Clinic, Inc., Ventura 1950—; attending surgeon (chief of staff 1973) Community Meml. Hosp., (chief of staff 1971-72) Ventura County General Hosp., St. John's Hosp., Oxnard and Ojai Valley Community Meml. Hosp.; cons. in surgery Camarillo State Hosp. 1955-57; mem. bd. dirs. California Medical Review, Inc. contracting with fed. govt. for medical review in the State of Calif., 1985—; Fellow Am. Coll. of Surgeons 1950; mem. Ventura Co. Med. Soc. (pres. 1975), Ventura Area Profl. Stds.

Review Orgn. (pres. 1977-78); apptd. to State Council by Secty. HEW, 1978; clubs: Exchange Club of Ventura (founding mem., bd. dirs. 1950), K.C. (3d deg. 1954), Phi Chi Med. Frat. (1939-), Kiwanis Club; contbr. num. publs. on med. research, med. subjects 1939-; mil: major M.C., US Army 1944-46, PTO, Bronze star medal for Okinawan Campaign; Roman Catholic; rec: gardening. Res: 155 Lakewood Ave Ventura 93004 Ofc: Buenaventura Medical Clinic Inc. 2705 Loma Vista Rd Ventura 93003

CHESTER, JOHN E., company executive; b. Nov. 9, 1932; NY; s. John E. and Helen (Burns) C.; m. Arden, Sept. 20, 1952; children: John III, b. 1953; Kevin, b. 1954; Stephen, b. 1959; edn: BA, Queens Coll. 1958; RN, USN 1953; ORT, Med. Corps. Sch., USN 1951; adv. mgmt. pgm., Internat. Mgmt. Inst., Columbia Univ. 1974. Career: v.p. comml. devel., internat. & R&D Edward Weck Co. 1971-74; v.p. mktg. V.Mueller Div. Am. Hosp. Supply Corp. 1974-76; dir. mktg./ sales for European, Mideastern, African, Canadian & So. Am. internat. bus. units Am. Hosp. Supply Corp. 1976-79; v.p./ gen. mgr. Searle Surgical Sys. 1979-81; v.p./ gp. exec. Bristol-Myers Corp. 1981-82; pres. Unitek Corp., Monrovia 1982-; pres./COO Thoratec Laboratories Corp. 1985 ; mem: Dental Mfrs. Assn.; Health Ind. Mfrs. Assn.; mil: USN 1950-54; Republican; Catholic; rec: golf. Res: 636 Pomello Dr Claremont 91711 Ofc: Thoratec Laboratories Corp. 2448 Sixth St Berkeley 94710

CHEVALIER, PAUL EDWARD, employee relations executive; b. Jan. 30, 1939, NYC; s. Arthur and Grace (Eaton) C.; m. Anne-Marie Leitner, May 4, 1963; 1 son: Marc, b. 1967; edn: BA, Columbia Coll. 1960; LLD, Columbia Sch. of Law 1966; MBA, Columbia Grad. Sch. of Bus. 1966; AMP, Harvard Bus. Sch. Adv. Mgmt. Pgm. 1979; admitted to practice, US Supreme Ct., Ill. Supreme Ct.; arbitrator, Am. Arbitration Assn. Career: employee rels. pgm. General Electric 1966-67; Western reg. mgr. labor rels. Montgomery Ward 1967-72; dir. labor rels. Carter Hawley Hale Stores, Inc. 1972-74; v.p. employee rels. 1974—; chmn. employee com. Am. Retail Fedn. (1979-82), employee rels. com. Business Roundtable; dir. UBA, Inc. 1976-82; dir., treas. Calif. Employment Law Council; dir. So.Calif. Center for Non-Profit Mgmt.; mem: Am. Bar Assn., Am. Retail Fedn., Calif. Retail Assn., Harvard Bus. Sch. Assn./So. Calif. (pres. 1984-85); clubs: Jonathan, L.A. Athletic; mil: lt. USN 1960-63, USNR 1963-66; Republican; Catholic; rec: bibliophile, scuba, running. Res: 2405 Glendower Ave Los Angeles 90027 Ofc: Carter Hawley Hale Stores, Inc., 550 S Flower St Los Angeles 90071

CHEW, ARLENE SALLY, real estate broker; b. Sept. 9, 1957, Alameda, Calif.; d. Leland Ralph and Sally (Chong) C.; edn: BS finance/ mktg., CSU Hayward 1980; real estate broker 1982. Career: tour guide S.F. during Coll.; transp. trainee Brae Corp. S.F. 1980-81; trade dir. Business Exchange Inc. S.F. 1981-82; real estate broker TRI Comml. Brokerage S.F. 1982-84; pres., owner Cybus Group (r.e. brokerage specializing in ofc. leasing & comml. sales) 1984—; mem: Women in Real Estate, S.F. CofC, First Thursday Club (founder, women's networking orgn.), S.F. Network Group (v.p.); publs: contbg. ed. real estate newsletter Creative Concepts in Real Estate (1981); Republican; Presbyterian; rec: fishing, squash, symphony. Ofc: Cybus Group 1 Maritime Plaza Ste 1300 San Francisco 94111

CHIANA, STEVEN JOSEPH, optometrist; b. Oct. 18, 1956, Lynwood; s. Joseph Phillip and Phyllis Marie (Ewing) C.; edn: BA biochem., CSU Fullerton 1980; BS, visual sci., Ill. Coll. Optometry 1984, OD, 1984. Career: optician, Dr. M. Stack, Anaheim, 1976-80; optometrist, ptnr. Your Eyes Only, Tucson, Ariz. 1984; optometrist prin. var. locations, Orange County; mem: Am. Optometric Assn. (Gen. and Contact Lens Sect.), Volunteer Optometric Services to Humanity, The Soc. for the Advancement of Full Scope Optometry. Res: 1244 East Third, 102, Long Beach 90802

CHIANG, GEORGE CHIHMING, educator, engineer, general contractor, real estate broker, appointed arbitrator, project management consultant; b. Sept. 12, 1931, China, nat. US cit.; s. Chien Pai and Ching S. (Chien) C.; m. Hedy Wu, Aug. 1978; children: Della b. 1960, Denise b. 1962, Nadine b. 1966; edn: BS, National Taiwan Univ. 1954, MSCE, USC 1958; MS, aero. eng., USC 1962; PhDE, Stanford Univ. 1967; Exec. Pgm., UCLA 1981; Reg. Profl. Civil Engr. (1960), Structural Engr. (1962), Lic. Gen. Contractor (1979) and Real Estate Broker (1979), Calif. Career: v.p. R.R. Bradshaw Inc., Van Nuys 1959-64; assoc. prof., chmn. civil engring. CSU Fullerton 1968-73, prof. engring. 1974—; treas. Chinese Development Corp., Los Angeles 1972-80; pres. Sincere Devel. Corp., Los Angeles 1976-80; pres. CMC Assocs., Los Angeles 1974—; ptr. Conreal Co., Alhambra 1980-85; mem: Internat. Assn. of Spatial and Shell Structures, Am. Mgmt. Assn., Am. Arbitration Assn., Dean's Council UCLA Grad. Sch. of Mgmt.; publs: var. tech. reports in engring., project devel. and mgmt.; rec: swimming, music. Res: 435 So. LaFayette Park Pl. Apt. 213 Los Angeles 90057

CHIBURIS, WILLIAM CHRISTOPHER, title insurance co. executive; b. June 18, 1931, Omaha, Nebr.; s. Christopher and Emma B. (Vodicka) C.; m. Shirley Charlene Lee Hellman, Sept. 10, 1977; children: Michael b. 1957, Kerry b. 1959, Nicholas b. 1961, William b. 1963, (step) nee Mack: Gary b. 1959, Steven b. 1961, Michael b. 1967, Julie b. 1970; edn: stu. Ariz. St. Univ. 1949-50. Career: title ofcr. Security Title Ins. Co., Modesto 1955-57; escrow/title ofcr. Stanislaus County Title Co. 1957-60; v.p. Western Title Ins. Co., 1960-63; pres./CEO Stanislaus Title Guaranty Co. 1963-77; pres. Golden Pacific Constrn., Golden Pacific Designs and Golden Pacific Finl., 1977-79; pres. Calif. Finl. Co. 1979-82; pres. Dual Arch Internat., 1982-85; asst. div. mgr. No. Calif. and No. Nev., Stewart Title Ins. Co., 1985—; mil: major USAF 1950-54, navigator combat air crew Korea, DFC, Air Medal w/2 clusters, Purple Heart,

Commendn. Medal, UN Svc., Korean Def., Good Conduct, Nat. Def. Svc., Marine Corps Reserve medals; Democrat; Seventh Day Adventist; rec: collect stamps, lead soldiers. Res: 2209 Glasgow Dr Ceres 95307 Ofc: Stewart Title of Modesto 822 Twelfth St Modesto 95354

CHIGOS, DAVID, university president; b. Mar. 29, 1933, Scranton, Pa.; s. Andrew D. and Emma (Kossmann) C.; m. Ruth Elizabeth Chamberlain, May 22, 1954; children: Catherine Mary (Bradley), Carla Jane (Sotelo), Lisa Anne, Laura Elizabeth; edn: BS in chem., W.Va. Wesleyan Coll. 1954, LLD (hon.), 1980; MA in counseling and guidance, US Internat. Univ. 1968, PhD, 1972. Career: commd. ensign US Navy 1957, advanced through grades to capt. ret. 1983; indsl. relations Convair Aerospace div. Gen. Dynamics Corp., San Diego 1967-70; faculty Univ. Calif. Extension, San Diego 1967-81, CSU San Diego Extension, 1968-71, San Diego Evening Coll., 1967-71; pres. National Univ., San Diego 1971—; cons. in field; mem. bd. dirs. COMBO, San Diego Sym., NCCJ; mem. Nat. Mgmt Assn. (Gold Knight Award 1979), Convair Nat. Mgmt. Assn. (hon. life), San Diego Safety Council (hon.), AAAS, Am. Assn. Presidents Independent Colls. and Univs., Nat. Independent Colls. and Univs., Personal Mgmt. Assn., Am. Soc. Tng. and Devel., Naval Reserve Assn. (life), Navy League US (life, Scroll of Honor 1979, nat. dir. 1980-, pres. San Diego Council 1981-82), Reserve Officers Assn. (life); clubs: San Diego Yacht, Kona Kai, Cuyamaca, University (S.D.), Army-Navy (Wash DC), Rotary (hon.). Ofc: 4141 Camino del Rio, San Diego 92108

CHILADAKIS, CHARALAMBOS I., chemical engineer; b. May 9, 1932, Chania, Crete, Greece, nat. 1962; s. John C. and Athena (Giannaris) C.; m. Georgia Stephanos, Apr. 27, 1958; children: Athena b. 1964, John b. 1965; edn: BS chem. eng., UC Berkeley 1961, MS chem. eng. 1962. Career: cryogenic engr. in chg. Low Temperature Facility of the W.F.Giauque Low Temp. Lab., UC Berkeley 1962-80; coll. engr. (respons. for engring. devel. in chem. engring. and chemistry) UCB Coll. of Chemistry 1981—; lctr. on research lab. safety, UCB 1982-86; cons: Chlorogard Corp. (1963-65), MFTF Project, Lawrence Livermore Lab. (1977), EIP Corp. of Calif. (1985); civic: Univ. Art Mus. UCB, Smithsonian Instn., Nat. Air and Space Mus.; publs: Peak Nucleate Boiling Fluxes for Liquid Oxygen at Flat Horizontal Platinum Surfaces at Buoyancies Corresp. to Accelerations Between -.03 and 1GE; Discovery of Nb Organometalic Compounds; Work with Superconductivity; design Novel 7.5 Megawatt Electromagnets; devel. num.original Cryogenic Divises incl. Liquefaction cycles; Democrat; Greek Orth.; rec: home bldg. and architl. design. Ofc: College of Chemistry Univ. Calif. Berkeley 94720

CHIMENT, RAY F., bottling co. president; b. June 16, 1925, Dunsmuir; s. Giuseppi Sebastiano and Angelina Buonvenuta (Dal Bon) C.; m. Helen Lamb, Apr. 23, 1949; children: David b. 1952, Jean b. 1954, Lynn b. 1957; edn: CSC Chico 1946, Coll. of Siskiyou 1974. Career: American Railway Express agt. 1947-48; US Postal Service 1948-52; ptnr. C&C Distbg. Co. 1952-61; owner/ pres. Pepsi Cola Bottling Co., Mt. Shasta 1961—; bd. chmn. Mt. Shasta Bottling & Distbg. Co.; mem. Knights of Columbus, Am. Legion, Disabled Am. Vets., Elks, Sons of Italy, Lions Club, Rotary Internat.; mil: 2d lt. US Army 1943-47, Silver Star, Bronze Str, Purple Heart; Catholic; rec: wine collector. Res: 309 Ida St Mt. Shasta 96067 Ofc: Pepsi Cola Bottling Co 302 Chestnut St Mt Shasta 96067

CHIN, MING WILLIAM, lawyer; b. Aug. 31, 1942, Klamath Falls, Ore.; s. Sam Wong and Suie Fong C.; m. Carol, Dec. 19, 1971; children: Jennifer, b. 1974, Jason, b. 1976; edn: BA, Univ. of S.F. 1964; JD, 1967; admitted to State Bar of Calif. 1970. Career: dep. dist. atty. Alameda Co. 1970-72; currently ptnr. Aiken, Kramer & Cummings, Inc., Oakland; mem: Calif. and Alameda Co. Bar Assn.; Univ. S.F. Alumni Assn.; St. Vincent's Day Home- Oakland; mil: capt., US Army 1967-69; Commendation Medal Vietnam 1969; Bronze Star 1969; Republican; Catholic; rec: running, skiing, tennis. Res: 173 Oyster Pond, Alameda 94501 Ofc: Aiken, Kramer & Cummings, 1 Kaiser Plaza, Ste. 550, Oakland 94612

CHIPRUT, ROBERTO O., physician; b. Jan. 4, 1948, Mexico City, Mex.; s. Menahem and Rebecca (Ovadia) C.; m. Nira Shepsales, May 16, 1971; children: Rebecca, b. 1973, Yuval, b. 1975, Daniel, b. 1982; edn: BA, Nat. Univ. of Mex. 1964, MD, 1972. (ABIM) Board Cert. in Internal Medicine, 1978, (ABGE) Board Cert. in Gastroenterology, 1979. Career: intern, Tel-Aviv Sch. of Med., Israel 1970; internist Scott and White Hosp. Baylor Sch. of Med., 1972-74; gastroenterol. fellow, 1974-76; hepathol. fellow, 1976-77, Univ. of Miami, Fla.; pvt. practice internal medicine and gastroenterol., Long Beach 1978-84, Beverly Hills 1984—, att. phys. Harbor-UCLA Med. Center, 1981-, tchg. att. phys. Cedars Sinai Med. Center, L.A. 1980-; chief gastroenterol. St. Francis Med. Center, Lynwood 1982; hon. cons. int. med. Military Med. Sch., Mex. 1979; asst. clin. prof. UCLA, 1981-; mem: Fellow Am. Coll. of Physicians, Am. Gastroenterol. Assn., Am. Soc. for Study of Liver Diseases, Am. Endoscopic Soc., Am. Soc. Int. Medicine; 35 publs. in field of gastroenterol. and hepatol.; Jewish; rec: music. Res: 15535 Aqua Verde Dr Bel Air Los Angeles 90077 Ofc: 8631 W Third St, Ste 1030E, Los Angeles 90048

CHIS, JOHN EDWARD, sales management executive; b. Aug. 15, 1956, Cleveland, Ohio; s. John Joseph and Vivian (Embrecia) C.; m. Julie Quilter, Aug. 23, 1980; children: John Joseph b. 1984, Jaime Ann b. 1986; edn: BS, Univ. of Akron 1978. Career: sales sys. support Telxon Corp., Akron, Ohio and Chicago, Ill. 1978-80, dist. salesmgr., Kansas City, Mo. 1980-82, Western reg. sales mgr., Los Angeles 1982-84, v.p. sales Western div. 1984—; honors: 1st Salesman, Telxon Corp. 1982; Man of the Year, Telxon Corp. 1983; mem. Sorin Soc. (Notre Dame); Republican; Catholic; rec: running, swimming, stock market. Res: 33472 Cockleshell Dr. Laguna Niguel 92677 Ofc: Telxon Corp., 6556 Caballero Blvd. Buena Park 90620

CHIU, VINCENT, physician, scientist; b. Sept. 23, 1949, Canton, China; s. Lan-Sang and Chee-Yin (Sum) C.; edn: BA, Univ. Wisc. 1970; PhD, Univ. Ill. 1974; MD, Univ. Autonoma de Ciudad Juarez 1981. Career: instr. chem. Univ. Ill. 1974-75; research sci. Univ. Miami 1976-79; med. staff phys. Univ. Neb. 1981-84; pvt. practice internal med. 1984—; cons. internal med.; fellow Fla. Heart Assn. 1977-78; mem. AMA; publ: num. on mechanism of muscle contraction and relaxation and membrane transport. Res: 109 S Almansor Alhambra 91801

CHIU, YU KAM, acupuncturist, Chinese herbalist; b. Feb. 16, 1930, Tai Shan, China; s. Wai Choi and Tui Yet (Chan) C.; m. Dai, Aug. 28, 1949; children: Sui Bing b. 1952, Ying Ying b. 1960, Ting Ting b. 1964, Chi Kuen b. 1966, Fai Kuen b. 1964; edn: Canton Med. Coll. 1958-63; Chuang Shan Med. Coll. 1964; Guangdong Province Hosp. (cardiovascular study) 1966-67; Guangdong Chinese Med. Coll. 1970. Career: phys. Tai Shan Co. Hosp. China 1963-70, head of med. ward 1971-74, presider of phys. 1975-79; acupuncturist, Chinese herbalist Sun Wah Clinic Hong Kong 1979-81, Chinese Med. Unite Clinic San Francisco 1984—; publ: articles in Chinese med. jours.; Christian. Res: 1370 Pine San Francisco 94109

CHMURA, MICHAEL PHILIP, accounting firm president; b. June 2, 1946, Chgo.; s. Philip Michael and Michaeline Josephine (Migon) C.; m. Gail Strickland, June 28, 1969; children: Christopher b. 1973, Devon b. 1974; edn: BBA, Loyola Univ. Chgo. 1968; CPA Calif. 1970, Ill. 1968. Career: auditor, CPA Peat, Marwick, Mitchell & Co. 1968-72; controller Carnation Co. L.A. 1972; mgr., CPA C.C. Peterson L.A. 1973; pres. Michael P. Chmura Accountancy Corp. 1973—; trustee Wu Educational Trust; honors: Beta Alpha Psi 1968; mem: Calif. Soc. CPAs (chmn. mem. com. 1971), Am. Inst. CPAs, Braemar CC, Tarzana Baseball Assn. (commr.); Catholic; rec: golf, baseball coach. Res: 4524 Deanwood Dr Woodland Hills 91364 Ofc: 23287 Ventura Blvd Woodland Hills 91364-1033

CHO, IM HYUN, life underwriter; b. June 30, 1952, Seoul, Korea, nat. US cit.; d. Kyu Tae and Chun Soo (Park) Chung; m. Yong Won Cho, July 10, 1976; 1 son, Terry b. 1977; edn: BS, Seoul Nt. Univ.. Career: life ins. agent/ corp. mgr. Equitable Life Assurance Soc.; pres. Dale Insurance Service Inc., Santa Ana; honors: Million Dollar Round Table, leading agt. GAMA of Orange Co. (1984); mem. Nat. Assn. Life Underw., MDRT, LUTC; Catholic; rec: tennis, swimming. Res: 445 S Citrus Ave Los Angeles 90036 Ofc: Equitable Life Assur. Society 1055 N Main St Ste 700 Santa Ana 92702

CHO, JONATHAN HYUN, dentist; b. Apr. 28, 1938, Seoul, Korea, nat US cit. 1985; s. Byung Hong and Mak Nae (Cho) C.; m. Christine, Sept. 23, 1967; children: Kathryne b. 1968, Claudia b. 1970, Lucy b. 1973; edn: MS, Seoul Nat. Univ. 1970, DDS, 1966; DDS, Sao Paulo Univ. Brazil 1976; Calif. lic. 1981. Career: dental surgeon Air Forces of Korea 1967-70; owner Dr. Cho's Dental Clinic Korea 1970-74, Brazil 1976-79; mng. dr. Dr. Campbell Dentistry 1981-84; owner Dr. Jonathan H. Cho DDS Reseda 1984—; mem: Am., Calif. Dental Assns., Korean Dental Assn. of USA (v.p. 1983-85); Presbyterian; rec: fishing. Ofc: 18905 Sherman Way Reseda 91335

CHO, SANG GON, tax consultant; b. Jan. 24, 1939, Korea, nat. US cit. 1975; s. Soon Young and Young Ok (Bae) C.; m. Young Ja, Sept. 6, 1964; children: Sandra b. 1970, Grace b. 1974; edn: BA law, Sung Kyun Kwan Univ. 1962; jr. acct., Oakland City Coll. 1965; BA acctg., San Francisco State Coll. 1968; MBA, San Francisco State Univ. 1974; enrolled agent IRS. Career: acct. C.D. Ericson Co. Oakland 1968-69; auditor Am. President Lines S.F. 1969-70, Calif. State Bd. of Equalization Oakland 1970-75; tax analyst Fireman's Fund Ins. Co. S.F. 1975-—; owner Lucky Realty & Investmant Santa Clara 19-—; instr. Mission Coll. Santa Clara 1986; honors: Dean's List (Oakland City Coll. 1965), winner Slogan Contest (Korea Times 1979); mem: Nat. Assn. Enrolled Agents, San Jose Real Estate Bd., Delta Sigma Pi, Am. Conservatory Theatre, Honam Friendly Assn. of No. Calif. (v.p., bd.), Korean-Am. CofC of Santa Clara County, Korean Resident Assn. of Santa Clara County; publs: newspaper articles, Tax Aspects of Real Estate, Pleasure of Jogging to be Shared; mil: Korean Army; Democrat; Catholic; rec: jogging, classical music, reading, writing. Res: 19425 Via Real Dr Saratoga 95070 Ofc: Lucky Realty & Investment 3105 El Camino Real Ste 204 Santa Clara 95051

CHOA, KONG CHAN, civil engineer; b. June 8, 1946, Rangoon, Burma; s. Keng Hong and Kim Tee (Tan) C.; m. Agnes, Aug. 11, 1977; 1 son, Paul b. 1985; edn: B.Engring., Rangoon Inst. of Tech. 1970; MSCE, CSU Los Angeles 1977; Reg. Profl. Engr. (Civil Eng.) Calif. 1975. Career: engring. aide City of Pacifica, 1972-73; civil engr. C.F. Braun & Co., Alhambra 1973-74; asst. engr. Kaiser Engrs., Oakland 1974-75; senior civil engr. C.F. Braun & Co., Alhambra 1975-78; design team supr. Lockman and Assocs., Monterey Park 1978-79; senior civil engr. Ralph M. Parsons Co., Pasadena 1979-80; prin. civil engr. Singmaster & Breyer, NY, NY 1980-81; senior civil engr. Jacobs Engring., Pasadena 1981—; mem. Am. Soc. Civil Engrs.; Buddhist; rec: sight seeing, photog., tennis. Res: 724 Topacio Dr Monterey Park 91754 Ofc: Jacobs Engineering Group, 251 S Lake Ave Pasadena 91101

CHONG, MARY DRUZILLEA, nursing executive; b. Mar. 8, 1930, Fairview, Okla.; d. Charles Dewey and Viola Haddie (Ford) Crawford; m. Nyuk Choy Chong, Aug. 24, 1952, div. 1968; children: Anthony b. 1954, Dorlinda b. 1955; edn: AA, El Camino Jr. Coll. 1950; grad. nse. L.A. County Gen. Hosp. Sch.

Nsg. 1953; BSN, PhN, CSU Los Angeles 1968. Career: staff nse. USC-L.A. County Gen. Hosp., 1957, UCLA-Harbor Gen. Hosp., Torrance 1958-69, hd. nse. Chest Medical Unit, 1969-72; instr. Voc. Nurse Program, YWCA Job Corps, L.A. 1972-74; Mobile Intensive Care nse. Victor Valley Hosp., Victorville 1974-79; dir. nsg. San Vicente Hosp., L.A. 1980-82, Upjohn Healthcare Svcs., L.A. 1982-85, Bear Valley Comm. Hosp. Home Health Agcy., Big Bear Lake 1986—; mem: Nat. Assn. for Female Execs., AAUW, Hosp. Discharge Planners Assn., CSULA Alumni Assn., Internat. Platform Assn.; Democrat; Prot.; rec: gardening, crafts. REs: POB 697 Lucerne Valley 92356 Ofc: Bear Valley Comm. Hosp. Home Health Agcy. 41870 Garstin Rd Big Bear Lake 92315

CHONG, YONG CHIN, rose grower; b. June 15, 1940, Kyungki-Do, Korea; s. Dae Hun and Jungboon Ahn C.; m. Sunok Lee, Mar. 20, 1971; children: James b. 1974, Joseph b. 1976; edn: BA, Sungkyunkwan Univ. Seoul, Korea 1967; Woodbury Univ. L.A., Calif. 1971-73. Career: instr. planting & gardening Chung Shin Girls' H.S. Seoul, Korea 1959-67; tchr. Woosok H.S. Seoul 1967-71; owner Yong's Market L.A. 1974-77, Sun Farms Ontario 1977-83; owner, oper. Eden Rose Farms Fallbrook 1983—; ed. staff New Korea Times L.A.; honors: Mayor's Award (Yoju City, Korea); mem: So. Calif. Flower & Plant Assn. 1983-, Korean Farmers Assn. of So. Calif. (dir., secty. gen. 1974-77), Korean Literary Soc. of Am. (dir.), Young Korean Acad. (dir.); publs: anthology Spring of Ontario (1980), collections of essays and articles contbd. to newspapers and mags. (1987); mil: Korean Army 1961-63; Presbyterian; rec: fishing. Address: Eden Rose Farms 9109 Huntley Rd Fallbrook 92028

CHOONTANOM, SAMAN, surgeon; b. Aug. 14, 1939, Nakornpathom, Thailand; s. Ta and Chalam (Borugsa) C.; m. Wadhana, Jan. 31, 1968; children: Priscill b. 1970, Darlene D. b. 1972; edn: MD, Chienemai Med. Sch. Thailand 1964; certified Am. Bd. Surg. 1973. Career: pvt. practice general and vascular surgery; staff San Bernardino Comm. Hosp., St. Bernardine Hosp.; fellow Internat. Coll. Surg., mem. Tri-County Surg. Soc., CMA; Republican; Buddhist. Res: 3634 Juniper Dr San Bernardino 92404

CHOU, CHIH-HWA, acupuncturist; b. Jan. 15, 1918, Sinhwa Hunan, China; s. Chu Jen and Feng Tai (Lee) C.; m. Yen-Ching Su, 1941; children: Sabrina Liu b. 1942, Tom C. b. 1944; edn: BS, National Tchrs. Coll. 1943; Cert. Acupuncturist, Calif.; Diplomate, Nat. Commn. for the Certification of Acupuncturists. Career: prof. acupuncture Grad. Sch. of Chinese Med. Sci., China Med. Coll., Taiwan 1974-78; chmn. Seminar of Acupuncture, Chinese Acupuncture Sci. Research Found. 1975-78; ed. in chief Chinese Traditional Med. Research Quarterly, Chinese Traditional Med. Research Found. 1976—; award: A Man of Extensive and Excellent Learning, Sem. of Acupuncture, Chinese Acupuncture Sci. Research Found. 1978; Hon. Advr., United Acupuncturists of Calif. 1982; author: book on Chinese theories, Acupuncture and Science, 1977; New Explanations of the Midday and Midnight Law in Acupuncture, in English with Matrix 1978; Ying-Yang, I-Ching Number System of Chinese Change Book and Genetic Code, 1978; Confucian; rec: Chinese painting and calligraphy, Taoist yoga, jogging. Res: 2062 Mori Ln. Orange 92667 Ofc: Medical Dental Center, 1500 E. Katella Ave. Ste. F Orange 92667

CHOU, LIN, real estate development co. president; b. Aug. 18, Taipei, Taiwan, nat. US cit. 1977; s. Chi Chong and Chen (Nu) C.; m. Chun Chiang, Nov. 9, 1974; 2 sons: Raymong, Johnny; edn: BS, Linfield Coll. 1964, grad. sch. Univ. of Nev. 1967; desig: CREA (cert. real estate appraiser) 1983, CRA (cert. review appraiser) 1983. Career: owner Four Seas Investment Co. 1978-81; ptnr. Safeway Ents. 1979-81; owner/pres. VIP Investments/Builders 1983—, Chou & Assocs. (finl.) 1984 ; mem. Nat. Assn. of Realtors, Nat. Assn. of R.E. Appraisers (senior), Nat. Assn. of Review Appraisers (senior), Taiwan-Am. CofC (pres.); mil. service Taiwan; Republican (Pres. Task Force); Christian; rec: photog. Ofc: 205 S San Gabriel Blvd San Gabriel 91776

CHOU, LOUIS SHENG-TSI, physicist, diplomat; b. March 18, 1944, Taipei, Taiwan, ROC; s. Chin Baye and Gin (Chang) C.; m. Maria Chang, July 26, 1968; children: Andy S. b. 1969, Paula A. b. 1974; edn: BS, Nat. Taiwan Univ. 1967; MS, Univ. of Mass. 1971; PhD, Univ. of Maine 1973. Career: research assoc. Univ. of Rhode Island 1973-74; assoc. prof. Nat. Chiao-Tung Univ., Taiwan, ROC 1974-76; vis. prof. Univ. of Rhode Island 1976-77; research assoc. UIRI, ITRI, Taiwan, ROC 1977-78; prof. and dean of studies Taiwan prov. Kaohsiung Inst. of Tech., Taiwan, ROC 1978; prof. and chmn. Nat. Chiao-Tung Univ., Taiwan, ROC 1978-80, prof. and dir. 1980-81; dir. Nat. Youth Commn. 1981-83; dir. science div., coord. Council for No. American Affair, Los Angeles ofc. 1983—; mem: Chinese Physics Soc., Chinese Optical Engring. Soc., Sigma Xi; works: 18+ publs. in liquid crystal area; prin. investigator for (5) sci. research projects; Catholic; rec: basketball, Soccer, kung-fu. Address: Los Angeles 90010

CHOU, WESLEY HSIEN-CHANG, neurologist; b. Jan. 11, 1952, Taiwan; s. Wei-Hsin and Chiung-Yin (Chang) C.; m. Christine, Dec. 14, 1982; 1 dau., Audrey b. 1983; edn: MD, National Taiwan Univ. 1978. Career: intern, resident in internal medicine Univ. of Ill. at Urbana/Champaign, 1981-83; senior resident in neurology UC Irvine 1983—; mem. Am. Acad. of Neurology, NY Acad. of Scis., AAAS; mil: Taiwan Army; Christian; rec: tennis, bridge. Res: 87 Firwood Irvine 92714 Ofc: Univ. California Irvine Medical Center, Orange 92668

CHOUDHURI, STAYENDRA NATH, administrative engineer; b. Dec. 14, 1942, Delhi, India; s. Dr. N. N. and Suprava C.; m. Sreelata, Nov. 20, 1971; children: Aditya b. 1973, Anand b. 1976, Saipriya b. 1983; edn: BSEE, Indian Inst. of Tech., India 1964; MBA, USC 1974; grad. work on 2nd MS, 1975-77; Reg. Profl. Engr., Calif. career: electrical engr. (plant engring. and expansion, new product dev.) DCM Group, India 1964-69; senior staff engr. Firestone Tire Co., 1969-78; energy mgmt. engr. (energy pgm. mgr. for the 19 campus system) Calif. State Univs., 1978—; honors: recognition by So. Calif. Edison Co. for energy conservation CSU, Long Beach campus; mem: Nat. Soc. of Profl. Engrs., Assn. of Physical Plant Adminstrs., Calif. Soc. Profl. Engrs. (past pres. Long Beach Chpt.); civic: churchgrp. social work and weekly feeding of the poor pgm.; Hindu. Res: 19711 Rumford Ln Huntington Beach 92646 Office of the Chancellor, The Calif. State Univ. 400 Golden Shore Ste 228 Long Beach 90802

CHOUNG, JOON HO, physician; b. Feb. 17, 1938, Kyunggi-do, Korea; s. Won Bock and Han Soon (Kim) C.; m. Jong, Oct. 9, 1967; children: Clara b. 1968, Rosa b. 1970, Paul b. 1978; edn: MD, Catholic Medical Coll., Seoul 1963. Career: instr. Catholic Medical Coll., Seoul 1971-73; clin. asst. prof. Hahnemann Med. Coll., Phila 1978; pvt. practice internal med., Los Angeles 1979—, attending physician Good Samaritan Hospital; mem. Am. Soc. of Internal Medicine, Los Angeles County Med. Assn., LA Cancer Soc. (bd. 1981-83); rec: tennis, golf. Ofc: LA Medical Center 3671 West Sixth St Los Angeles 90020

CHOW, STEPHEN, real estate consultant, developer; b. Jan. 15, 1948, Canton, China, nat. 1975; s. Herbert P.H. and Ngoi Chun (Lau) C.; edn: BA, San Francisco State Univ. 1974; MBA, Golden Gate Univ. 1976; R.E. Broker, Calif. 1976; Calif. Comm. Coll. Instr. Credential 1976. Career: partner Anderson, Chow & Assoc., San Francisco 1976; pres. American Investment Holding Co., S.F. 1980; v.p. Golden Gate Corp., S.F. 1982-84; v.p. Anros Properties Corp. S.F. 1984—; US investment cons. individual & corp. clients from Hong Kong, Philippines, Taiwan & Singapore; awards: Awd. for Significant Mktg. Achiev., Am. Mktg. Assn. 1978; mem: Am. Mgmt. Assn.; Am. Real Estate Exch.; Internat. Trade Council of San Francisco; S.F. Bd. Realtors; World Trade Club; Chinese CofC, S.F.; publs: var. info. packets for Far Eastern Investors as introduction to US Investment 1980-84; num. sems. in Asia- Pacific reg. on US Investment Real Estate 1980-84; cons. to sev. major US developers for China Hotel devel. projects in various cities in People's Rep. of China; Republican; rec: racquetball, skiing, photog. Res: 607 Banibridge St Foster City 94404 Ofc: Anros Properties Corp. 300 Montgomery St Ste 788 San Francisco 94104

CHRISTENSEN, DEAL, business consultant; b. Nov. 6, 1905, Spanish Fork, Utah; s. Hyrum M. and Catherine (Butler) C.; m. K. Arvilla Peterson, Aug. 29, 1926; children: Deal, Jr. b. 1928, Catherine Patrisha b. 1929; edn: NY Univ. Bus. Sch. 2 yr. corresp. sch.; Henegar's Bus. Sch. 1925; Brigham Young Univ. 1923-24. Career: sales (in top 20 sales gp. nat.) J.C. Penney Co., Watsonville 1934-36, mgr. J.C. Penney Co., Reedley 1937-45, San Rafael 1945-51; founder/owner Chrislows Dept. Store, Inc., Los Gatos 1951—, 2d store in Saratoga, 1983—; finl. planning cons.; founder/pres. Modular Homes, Inc. 1950; finl. ofcr./gen. ptnr. Guaranty Water Heater Co. 1947; honors: Man of Year, Watsonville (1935), recognition for relocating and providing for 12,000 displaced Japanese in Reedley (1942); mem. Commonwealth Club (SF), Kiwanis (past pres.), Reedley CofC (pres., dir.); works: chmn. 8th War Bond Drive, Reedley Dist. (1942; set nat. record), started Flight Club and blt. 165 acre Airport, Reedley (1943); Republican; Latter Day Saints; rec: golf, trout fishing, flying. Res: 1660 Gaton Dr Apt 8 San Jose 95125 Ofc: Chrislow's Dept. Store Inc. 201 N Santa Cruz Los Gatos 95030

CHRISTENSEN, DON REED, dentist; b. Jan. 15, 1948, Gunnison, Utah; s. Hans Reed and Rhoda May (Peterson) C.; m. Deborah Harrell, Nov. 15, 1975; children: Dale b. 1976, Dawn b. 1978, Dane b. 1981, David b. 1983; edn: AS, Snow Coll. 1968; BS, Univ. Utah 1970; DMD, Univ. Ore. Dental Sch. 1974. Career: pvt. practice of dentistry, Fresno 1974—, ptnrship. 1974, solo practice with emphasis on endodontics, reconstruction and cosmetic dentistry, 1975—; mem: Am. Dental Assn., Calif. Dental Assn., Fresno-Madera Dent. Assn., Acad. of General Dentistry, Rotary Internat., Executive Assocs. of Fresno; Republican; Latter Day Saints; rec: water and snow ski, racquetball. Res: 9143 N Maple Fresno 93710 Ofc: 5528 North Palm Ave Ste 121 Fresno 93704

CHRISTENSEN, DONN WAYNE, executive; b. Apr. 9, 1941, Atlantic City, NJ; s. Donald F. and Dorothy L. C.; children: Donn Jr. b. 1964, Lisa b. 1965; edn: BS, Univ. Santa Clara 1964. Career: West Coast div. mgr. Ford Motor Co. 1964-65; agt. Conn. Mutual Life Ins. 1965-68; founder, pres. Christensen & Jones Mgt. & Ins. Svcs. Inc. 1969—; bd. dirs. Research Devel. Systems Inc., Duarte Drug Abuse Council, Mid-Valley Mental Health Ctr., Institutl. Review Bd. White Meml. Hosp. L.A.; honors: Man of the Year (L.A. Gen. Agents and Mgrs. Assn. 1970, 72, 73, 74); mem: Nat. Life Underwriters Assn., Calif. Life Underwriters, Nat. Assn. Music Mfgs. & Merchants, Am. Soc. Pension Actuarys, Duarte Drug Abuse Council (pres. 1974-75), Foothill Comm. Concert Assn. (pres. 1970-73), Woodlyn Property Owners Assn. (pres. 1972-73), L'Ermitage Found. 1985, No. Ranch CC 1985; rec: tennis, bicycling, travel. Res: 4000 Pulido Ct Calabasas 91302 Ofc: Christensen & Jones Inc. 1015 Wilshire Blvd Los Angeles 90017

CHRISTENSEN, LESTER JAMES, regional sales executive; b. May 4, 1933, Omaha, Nebr.; s. Lester James and Hortense (Elbert) C.; m. Irene, Apr. 18; children: Scott, Lisa, David, Suzanne, Thomas; edn: BS in commerce, The Creighton Univ. 1956; MS in econs., Univ. Colo., Colo. Spgs. 1959. Career: salesman, Gen. Electric Co., Omaha, Nebr. 1960-66, area sales mgr. Kansas City 1966-67, field sales mgr. Cleveland 1968-70, dist. sales mgr. Phila.

1971-76, regl. sales mgr. 11 Western States, GE Co., Los Angeles 1977–; mem: Reserve Officers Assn., LA CofC, Assn. of US Army; mil: col. USAR, Merit. Service Medal; Republican; Catholic; rec: sky diving, flying vintage aircraft. Ofc: General Electric Co. 2747 S. Malt Ave Los Angeles 90040

CHRISTENSEN, MARK WILLIAM, land surveyor; b. April 18, 1951, Mineola, NY; s. William Cleveland and Claire (Berthe) C.; m. Olga, June 14, 1975; children: Mark b. 1977, Tamara b. 1980; edn: AAS, Paul Smith's Coll. 1971; Lic. Land Surveyor, Calif. 1983. Career: mgr. Denny's Inc., Escondido 1975-77; surveyor Won S. Yoo Engring., Temecula 1977-79; surveyor, senior designer McGoldrick Engrs. Inc., Temecula 1979–; mem: Alpha Phi Omega (nat. svc. frat.), Loyal Order of the Moose, Rancho Community Ch. (ranger Boys Brigade); mil: QM 3/c USN 1971-75, ret.; Democrat; Catholic; rec: philately, coins, camping. Res: 30930 Mira Loma Dr. Temecula 92390 Ofc: McGoldrick Engineers Inc., 27720 Jefferson St Ste. 200 Temecula 92390

CHRISTOPH, WILLIAM RICHARD, lawyer; b. Dec. 26, 1947, Oak Park, Ill.; s. G. William and Elizabeth Christine Christoph; m. Kerry, Feb. 15, 1976; children: Nicholas b. 1980, Courtney b. 1983; edn: BA, Wabash Coll. 1969; JD, Univ. of Wisc. Law Sch. 1978; criminal defense atty, admitted to practice, Wisc. Bar (state & fed.) 1978; Calif. Bar (state & fed.) 1979. Career: 2nd lt. Infantry Platoon Commdr. USMC 1969-71 (Vietnam 1970); capt. Cobra Gunship Pilot, 1972-76 (Saigon 1975); deputy city atty., City of San Diego 1979; self- empl. criminal defense atty., Vista 1980–; bus. law tchr. Palomar Coll. 1980-81; mem: Calif., Wisc. & Am. Bar Assns.; San Diego Trial Lawyers Assn.; mil: capt. USMC 1969-76, Bronze Star, Combat Action, Vietnamese Campaign, Philippine Pres. Unit Citation; Vietnamese Cross of Galantry; rec: sailing, diving. Res: 623 Hunter St Oceanside 92054 Ofc: William R. Christoph, APC, 400 S Melrose, Ste 101, Vista 92083

CHUNG, BURK HIM, trading co. president; b. Aug. 27, 1922, Canton, China; s. Kao How and Han (Chau) C.; m. Mary Lin, Nov. 8, 1952; children: Amy b. 1953, Luke b. 1956, Michael b. 1961; edn: BA, UC Berkeley 1951; grad. stu. San Francisco State Univ. 1951-52. Career: teacher Chinese language, Kin Kuo High Sch., San Francisco 1948-51; reporter, editor, ed.-in-chief, bd. dirs. The Young ChinaNews Daily, S.F. 1951-58; pres. On Ning Tong Co., S.F. 1958–; pres. Superior Trading Co., S.F. 1959–; pres. Antioch Village Apt. Complex, Antioch, Calif. 1979-; pres/CEO C.S.W., Inc., S.F. 1979–; pres., bd.chmn. United Internat. Trading Co., Hong Kong 1979-83; pres. Belmont Plaza Shopping Center property, Belmont, Calif. 1979-; founding bd. dir. United Meat Packing Co. Slaughterhouse, No. Dist., Taiwan; lst vice chmn. of bd. Sincere Fed. Svgs & Loan Assn., S.F. 1980-82; apptd. by Mayor Dianne Feinstein mem. S.F. Internat. Hotel Block Devel. Citizens Advis. Com. (1979); awards: citation for comm. crisis leadership 1967, S.F. Chinese CofC; recognition for pioneer work devel. the USA mkt. for Korean ginseng products, Korean Office of Monopoly, 1976; mem: Kong Chow Benevolent Assn. (Kong Chow Temple), USA dir., nat. & regl. secty. gen., supr. chmn. bd. of suprs. 1954-; S.F. Chinese CofC (interim pres. 1967). Republican (bd.dirs. Calif. Chinese-Am. Repub. Assn.); Roman Catholic (bd., St. Mary's Chinese Sch.); rec: reading, writing, travel. Res: 639 Teresita Blvd San Francisco 94127 Ofc: Superior Trading Co. 837 Washington St San Francisco 94108

CHUNG, DAVID KIM, development and design co. president; b. Dec. 24, 1958, Davis; s. Dr. James Insuk and Marilyn Chongsoon (Kim) C.; edn: BS, econs./comp. sci., UC Davis 1982. Career: pres. Displays Unlimited, Los Altos 1981–; project mgr. Televideo Systems, Sunnyvale 1981-85; sales mgr. Novell Inc., Mountain View 1985–; prin. Chung, Nadzam, Passarello & Rostomily Corp. (1986-); rec: triathlete, tennis, skiing, music. Res: 1871 Lakebird Dr San Jose 95124 Ofc: Novell Inc. 1804 Stierlin Rd Ste 110 Mtn View 94043

CHUNG, GILL TAIK, veterinarian; b. June 25, 1935, Seoul, Korea; s. Jai Oh and Dong Sim (Lee) C.; m. Young Ok, Dec. 27, 1964; children: James b. 1965, David b. 1969; edn: DVM, Seoul National Univ., Korea 1958, MS, 1960; postgrad. study, Univ. of Minn. 1960-61; PhD, Univ. of Queensland 1968; lic. veterinarian, Calif. (1981). Career: lectr. Seoul National Univ., Korea 1962-69, asst. prof. 1969-72, assoc. prof. 1972-78; postdoctoral research fellow UC Los Angeles, 1980-81; veterinarian small animal practice, owner Canyon Hills Animal Hosp., Chino 1981–; mem: Am. Vet. Med. Assn., So. Calif. Vet. Med. Assn.; publs: 20 research papers re veterinary microbiology and public health; Christian; rec: music. Ofc: Canyon Hills Animal Hospital 14656 Pipeline Ave Chino 91709

CHUNG, HUKUN, real estate broker; b. Oct. 19, 1936, Kyungnam, Rep. of Korea, nat. US cit. 1980; m. Connie, 2 sons: David, Kenneth; edn: BA, Dong-A Univ., Busan, Korea 1961; real estate cert., Chabot Coll. 1978; L.A.Trade Tech. Coll. 1974-75; Calif.lic. R.E.broker (1979). Career: high sch. economics tchr., Korea 1961; pres. Jinyang Co. Ltd. 1967; asst. to gen. mgr.(Mr. Howard) of Calif. 1974; realtor assoc.Century 21 Grove Way Realty 1977; realtor/ owner Bestwest Realty 1980; ruling elder Mt.Eden Ch.; cert. bus. counselor, Inst. of CBC 1981; awards: Centurion, Century 21 No. Calif. (1977), Top Selling Sales Agt.(1979) and Top Listing Sales Agt. (1979) Century 21 Grove Way; mem: Inst. of Cert.Bus. Counselors,Nat. Assn. Realtors, Calif. Assn.Realtors, East Bay Market Groupe (1981); mil: lt.Republic of Korea Army, Gold Medal Awd. 1958; Presbyterian: founder Fremont Korean Presbyn. Ch. (1978), ruling elder Mt. Eden Presbyn. Ch. (1982-84) estab. bilingual svc. (1982), com. on evangelism San Francisco Presbytery, Presbyn. Ch. USA 1986-87); rec: painting.Res: 24261 Monument St Hayward 94545 Ofc: Bestwest Realty, 759 West 'A' Street Hayward 94541

CHUNG, JOHN WEI-MING, acupuncturist; b. Dec. 28, 1932, Taiwan, China; s. Teh-Fu and Lin-Fong C.; m. Agee Kou, Feb. 1, 1957; children: Jack Wen b. 1958, Fumiko Kelly b. 1960; edn: Dr. Oriental Med., PhD, SAMRA Univ. of Health Scis. 1983; Certified Acupuncturist, Oriental Med. Instr., Calif.; Lic. Acupuncturist, 1974. Career: pvt. practice acupuncture and Chinese med.; awards: Outstanding Practitioner of Art of Oriental Healing; Cert. of Merit, Australian Ambassador Peter Barbour, 1982; author: Something That Money Cannot Buy. Address: 13441 Sylvan St. Van Nuys 91401

CHUNG, THOMAS YONGBONG, import-export co. president; b. Apr. 1, 1927, Jinyoung, Korea, nat. US cit. 1975; s. Jong Do and Myung Ree (Hwang) C.; m. Channyum, June 16, 1979; edn: BA, Kukmin Coll. 1956; grad. stu. CSU Long Beach 1960; MA, Southern Ill. Univ. 1962; postgrad. work, UC Los Angeles 1965. Career: customs insp., Koreauntil 1958; pres. K & A Industrial Co., Los Angeles 1965-73; pres. His & Her Hair Goods Co., Los Angeles 1973–; mem. Am. Economics Assn.; invention: Capless Wig (1972); Democrat; rec: scuba diving, golf. Res: 650 Pencin Dr Whittier 90601 Ofc: 5377 Wilshire Blvd Los Angeles 90036

CHUNG, WOO CHUL, engineer; b. Aug. 22, 1953, Seoul, Korea, nat. US cit. 1985; s. Joo Sung and June Hee (Han) C.; m. Jung Kim, July 7, 1980; children: Augustine b. 1982, Gina b. 1983; edn: BS, CSU Long Beach 1980; MS, USC 1985; Reg. Profl. Engr. (mech.), Calif. 1984. Career: mech. engr. City of Los Angeles Dept. of Water & Power, 1981–, air pollution engr. spec. in NOX reduction; honors: Tau Beta Pi (1979); assoc. mem. ASME; works: project ldr. in design, installation and testing of Thermal Denox System at utility boiler (first in USA); Republican; Catholic; rec: golf. Res: 221 South Lucerne Blvd Los Angeles 90004 Ofc: Los Angeles Dept. Water & Power, 111 No Hope St Ste 604 Los Angeles 90051

CHURCH, WILLIAM HOWARD, educator, management consultant; b. June 13, 1911, Boise, Idaho; s. Maxfield I. and Lillian (Kingsburg) C.; m. Winifred Davies, March 19, 1940; 1 son, Addison b. 1946; edn: BA, Whittier Coll. 1933; Calif. Secondary Tchg. Cred., USC 1939, MS, pub. admin., 1940, doctoral work, 1949-50. Career: instr. Fullerton J.C. 1939-41; inspector US Dept. of Justice, Immigration and Naturalization Svc., Los Angeles Dist. Ofc. 1941-42; asst. to Calif. Legislative Auditor 1942; pain analyst Calif. Taxpayers Assn., Calif. Sch. Costs 1941-47; pain analyst Orgn. Control Sect., Ofc. Chief Asst. Supt. Los Angeles City Schs. 1946-47; dir., ptr., prin. cons. Administrative Mgmt. Svc. 1947–; concurrently, city mgr. City of Whittier 1949-51; vis. prof. USC 1951-52; dir. Internat. Mgmt. Edn. Pgm., Univ. of Ankara 1953; cons. Calif. Legislative Analyst on Calif. Hosp. Admin. Costs Efficiency 1953; cons., trustee Santa Monica Med. and Surgical svcs. Corp. 1953-55; cons. to Presidential Commn. on Intergovtl. Rels. and spl. research advr. Task Force on Nat. Health Policies, Grant-in-Aid Pgms., Med. Edn. and Hosp. Constrn., Wash. DC 1954-55; deputy mgr. engr. Secty. of Navy 1955-6; civilian founder, academic chmn., senior prof. mgmt. Naval Postgrad. Sch., Monterey 1956–, currently, emeritus senior prof. of mgmt.; dir. AMS Mgmt. Cons.; technology rep. USN, NSF and Public Technology Inc., 4 cities 1979-81; honors: 1st Fulltime Fellow in Govt., USC 1938; Lambda chpt., Phi Sigma Alpha, USC 1950; Navy Commdn. for Navy Mgmt. Rev. and Control Pgm. CNO 1944; mem: Commonwealth Club (San Francisco, founder Monterey Bay area chpt.), Soc. for Adv. of Mgmt. (now. Am. Mgmt. Assn.), Soc. for Adv. of Pub. Admin. (founder Monterey Bay area chpt.), Del Monte Forest Homeowners Assn. (past pres.), Pebble Beach Sanitary Dist. (founder 1970-80), Monterey Co. Grand Jury, Monterey Peninsula CofC, Naval Reserve Assn. (life), Reserve Ofrs. Assn., Am. Political Sci. Assn., Western Govtl. Research Assn., Nat. Security Council, Navy League, Sunrise Rotary of Monterey; works: ed., publr. Handbook of Civilian Personnel Mgmt. for Navy and Marine Corps Ofcrs. 1969-78; mil: capt. USNR, ret., Victory, Am. Field Svc.; Republican; Protestant; rec: golf, swimming, travel. Res: 1071 Marcheta Ln. Pebble Beach 93953 Ofc: Naval Postgraduate Sch., Code 54Cy, Dept. of Admin. Scis., Monterey 93940

CHWEH, STEVEN SEOKHO, librarian; b. Jan. 15, 1944, Naju, Korea, nat. 1980; s. Chang-Kyu and Woo-Nim (Hong) C.; m. Janie Okkyoung Hahn, Sept. 25, 1979; 1 son: Daniel, b. 1982; edn: BA, Kyung Hee Univ. 1966; MS, Louisiana State Univ. 1971; PhD, Univ. of Pitts. 1976. Career: lang. instr. US Peace Corps Tng. Ctr., Hilo, Hawaii 1968-69; hd. acquisitions librarian Henderson State Univ., Arkadelphia, Ark. 1971-74; asst. prof. USC, Los Angeles 1976-81; sys. analyst/ pgmr. Computer Automation, Irvine 1981-82; pres. Computermation, Mission Viejo 1982–; tech. svc. supvr. Newport Beach Pub. Lib., Newport Beach 1983–; bd. dirs. Assn. for Korean Studies 1977-; honors: Beta Phi Mu, internat. lib. sci. hon. soc. 171; Outstanding Young Men of America, Jaycees 1979; mem: Am. Lib. Assn.; Calif. Library Assn.; Am. Soc. for Info. Sci.; Calvary Ch., Costa Mesa; publs: num. arts. in library journs.; mil: lt. Korean Army Artillery 1966-68; Christian; rec: Tae Kwon Do (black belt), Red Cross cert. water safety instr., senior life guard. Res: 21454 La Capilla Mission Viejo 92691 Ofc: Newport Beach Public Library, 856 San Clemente Dr Newport Beach 92660

CICI, ANGELO SANTO, engineering executive; b. Nov. 1, 1937, Milwaukee, Wisc.; s. Joseph Vito and Antonia (Gatti) C.; m. Arlene Johnson, Jan. 30,1 977; children: Angela b. 1958, Joseph b. 1961, Kelly b. 1963; stepchildren: Kristine Haney b. 1966, Ronald Haney b. 1968; edn: BSEE, Northrop Univ. 1963; JD, Western State Univ. 1972; Cert. Exec. Mgmt. Pgm., Pepperdine Univ. 1972. Career: sys. engr. to senior sys. engr. North American Rockwell Inc., Autonetics Div. 1963-67; supvr. to sect. mgr., then dept. mgr. Hoffman Electronics Corp., Navcom Systems div. 1967-74; engring. mgr. to dir. Litton Systems Inc., Guidance & Control Sys., Woodland Hills 1974–; mem: IEEE (senior), Nat.

Security Indsl. Assn. (Life Cycling Costing Study, Reliability Sect. 1970-71), Quality & Reliability Assurance, Hoffman Employees Fed. Credit Union, Nat. Mgmt. Assn. (pres. Hoffman Electronics Corp. chpt. 1972-73); publs: Computerized Reliability Optimization System, 1971; contbr. papers to profl. symposiums; mil: P.O. 2/c US Coast Guard 1954-58; Democrat; Catholic. Res: 29024 Tackaberry Ct. Agoura Hills 91301 Ofc: Litton Systems Inc. GCSD, 5500 Canoga Ave. Woodland Hills 91365

CIPANI, ENNIO CIRO, educator, psychologist; b. Mar. 26, 1952, Queens, N.Y.; s. Ennio Leo and Elvira (Portante) C.; m. Lucinda, June 26, 1981; children: Lorenzo b. 1982, Vanessa b. 1985; edn: BA, Fla. Tech. Univ. 1973, MS, 1975; PhD, Fla. State Univ. 1979; Calif. Lic. Psychologist (1983). Career: psychotherapist Sunland Tng. Ctr., Orlando, Fla. 1973-76, Orlando Comm. Correctional Ctr., 1975; Vocational Rehab. devel. living skills project, Tallahassee 1977-79; asst. prof. Univ. of Wisc. 1980; So. and No. Wisc. Center for the Devel. Disabled, Union Grove and Eau Claire, 1979-81; asst. prof. Dept. of Spl. Edn./Severely Handicapped Credential coord., Univ. of the Pacific Sch. of Edn., Stockton 1981–; behavioral cons. Lodi Unified Sch. Dist., Adult Devel. Ctr., Central Valley Tng. Ctr., Regl. Adolescent Treatment Pgm., Alta Calif. Regl. Ctr./Sacto. and East Bay Regl. Ctr./Oakland; mem. Council for Exceptional Children, Am. Assn. of Mental Deficiency, Assn. for Behavior Analysis; publs: num. book chapters and profl. jour. articles; devel. Videotape tng. materials on errorless learning formats for adults, computer instrn. pgm. for remedial math.; ed. Community skills tng. for handicapped children and adolescents (Haworth Press); author sev. UOP grant pgms. (1981-). Res: 8063 Richland Way Stockton 95209 Ofc: University of the Pacific Stockton 95211

CIRESE, ROBERT CHARLES, real estate investment and counseling executive; b. Feb. 25, 1938, Oak Park, Ill.; s. Ferd L. and Ruth O. Cirese; div.; children: Lesley Caren, b. 1965; Jeffrey Robert, b. 1967; edn: BS, DePaul Univ., Chgo. 1960; MS, Univ. of Ill. 1963; UC Berkeley 1964; CRE designation, Am. Soc. of R.E. Counselors 1983; lic. R.E. Broker, Calif. 1983; Calif. Coll. Tchg. Cred. 1973. Career: assoc. prof. Golden Gate Univ., San Francisco 1967-72; v.p. Larry Smith & Co., S.F. 1972-77; dir. Coopers & Lybrand, S.F. 1977-79; v.p. Rubloff Inc., S.F. 1979-85; prin. Cirese Assocs. 1985–; real estate counseling for corps., instns. & pub. agencies; expert witness; lectr.; honors: tuition scholarship UCB Grad. Sch. (1963); mem: Am. Soc.of Real Estate Counselors (ASREC), Am. Inst. or Real Estate Appraisers, Urban Land Inst.; San Francisco Plng. & Urban Research Assn., S.F. Ballet Assn., Univ.Calif. Alumni Assn. (Bear Backer), Stanford Univ. Alumni Assn. (Buck Fund); works: num. economic impact reports, mkt. & fin. feasibilty studies, real estate investment analyses; mil: Ill. Nat. Guard, 33rd Mil. Police Co. 1956-63; Unitarian; rec: running, spectator sports, ballet. Res: 54 Buckelew St Sausalito 94965 Ofc: Cirese Associates 400 Montgomery St Ste 604 San Francisco 94111

CISPER, THOMAS FRANCIS, manufacturing management consultant; b. Sept. 27, 1931, Kansas City, Mo.; s. Joseph A. and Albertine A. (Lenherr) C.; m. Naomi, June 24, 1961; children: Christopher b. 1962, Kathleen b. 1964, Paul b. 1966, Thomas b. 1967, Mark b. 1973; edn: Rockhurst Coll. 1948-50; Cert. Bus. Adminstrn., Univ. Mo. 1961; UC Los Angeles extn. 1968-70; Certified Profl. in Prodn. & Inventory Mgmt. Fellow 1977. Career: mfg. mgr. Wemco Sacramento 1971-79; proj installation mgr. mfg. sys. TRW Inc. Sunnyvale 1979-83; materials mgr. Spectra Physics Mtn. View, Calif. 1983-84; pres. T.F. Cisper Inc. 1984–; mem. Am. Prodn. and Inventory Control Soc. (chpt. pres. 1978, v.p. 1976-78, secty. 1975); mil: yeoman 2/c USN 1950-54, Good Conduct; Catholic; rec: cooking. Res: 1066 Mitchell Ct San Jose 95128 Ofc: T. F. Cisper Inc. POB 1397 Campbell 95008

CISSNA, ROBERT LEE, mortgage banker, lawyer; b. Apr. 17, 1940, Seattle, Wash.; s. Jack Raymond and Evelyn (Barker) C.; edn: AA cum laude, L.A. City Coll.; cert. history, lit. & arch., lang., Univ. of Perugia, Italy 1962-63; BA in hist., Univ. Wash. 1965; Naval Aviation Ofcrs. Sch. 1966; JD, L.A. Coll. of Law 1974; Calif. lic. real estate broker; admitted to Calif. State Bar 1980. Career: promo. Seattle World's Fair 1962; ground mgr. Santa Fair themed amusement park, Federal Way, Wash. 1958-65; Navy-Acct. & Arch. Designer 1966-68; promo. mgr. Johnson Wax Co., Montreal World's Fair 1967; acct. Walt Disney Prodns., Capitol Records and Interpace's Franciscan Dinnerware Plant; controller Tariq M. Shamma Assoc.; sec.treas. Canyon Lake (Ca.) Property Owners Assn.; bd. dirs. Lake Elsinore Park & Rec. District; mem: Am., Calif. State, Los Angeles County bar assns., Trial Lawyers of L.A., Am. Trial Lawyers, L.A. Lawyers Club, Orange County Trolley Museum, postcard clubs of So. Calif., Santa Monica, and Pasadena, YMCA, Laguna Bch Prop. Owners Assn., S.W. 8 Prop. Owners Assn. (Federal Way, Wash.); postcard publisher; amusement park planner; Republican (fiscal conservative, civil libertarian); Presbyterian; rec: antiques and sports. Address: POB 4811 Los Angeles 90051

CLABAUGH, ELMER EUGENE, JR., lawyer; b. Sept.18, 1927, Anaheim; s. Elmer Eugene and Eleanor Margaret (Heitshusen) Clabaugh; chldren: Christopher Chapman, Matthew Martinson; edn: BBA cum laude, Woodbury Coll. 1951, BA summa cum laude, Claremont McKenna Coll. 1958, JD, Stanford Law Sch.1961.Career: gen. service staff US State Dept., Jerusalem, Tel Aviv 1951-53; field staff Pub. Adminstrn. Svc., El Salvador, Ethiopia, USA 1952-57; admitted to Calif. Bar 1961; deputy dist. atty. Ventura Co., Calif.1961-62; mem. firm Hathaway, Clabaugh, Perrett & Webster in Ventura 1962-79; individual practice, 1979–; State Inheritance Tax referee, 1968-78; city atty. City of Thousand Oaks, 1964-69, City of Simi Valley, 1969-71; bd. dirs. San Antonio Water Conservation Dist.; bd. dirs. Ventura Comm. Meml. Hosp.; trustee Ojai Unified Sch. Dist. 1974-; mem. Pres's Adv. Council, Claremont Coll. 1975-; mem: Calif. Bar Assn., Am. Arbitration Assn., Phi Alpha Delta; Republican. rec: hunting, tennis. Res: 241 Highland Dr Channel Islands Harbor 93030 Ofc: 1190 S Victoria Ave Suite 305 Ventura 93003

CLAES, DANIEL JOHN, medical research director; b. Dec. 3, 1931, Glendale; s. John Vernon and Claribel (Fleming) Claes; m. Gayla Blasdel, Jan. 19, 1974; edn: AB magna cum laude, Harvard Univ. 1953; MD cum laude, Harvard Med. Sch. 1957. Career: intern UCLA, 1957-58; Boywer Found. Fellow, resident in medicine, L.A., 1958-61; pvt. practice spec. in diabetes mellitus, Los Angeles 1962–; Am. Eye Bank Found. vice pres. 1978-, dir./med. res. 1980-; awards: Boywer Found. awd. for excellence in medicine, 1958; mem: Los Angeles Co. Med. Assn., Harvard Club of So. Calif., Harvard Med. Sch. Club of So. Calif. Contbr. to profl. literature on computers in med. and on diabetes mellitus. Ofc: Daniel J. Claes, MD, Inc. 845 Via de la Paz Ste A236 Pacific Palisades 90272

CLARK, CRAIG WILLIAM, commercial real estate executive; b. Sept. 11, 1940, Shreveport, La.; s. Herman Wm. and Thelma Louise (Powell) C.; m. Brown Pickering, May 5, 1973; children: Cantrell b. 1976, C. William b. 1979; edn: Kilgore Jr. Coll. 1958-50, Univ. of Southwest L.A. 1960; BS, US Naval Acad. 1965; Calif. lic. Real Estate Broker. Career: v.p. Willis M. Allen Co., La Jolla 1970-73; bd. chmn. and pres. C. W. Clark, Inc. (comml. bldg. devel.), La Jolla 1974–; mem: Internat. Council of Shopping Centers (So. Calif. pgm. chmn. 1983, 84), Calif. Bus. Properties (advis. bd.); clubs: Bachelor Club of San Diego (pres. 1973), Golden Triangle Rotary, La Jolla (founding bd. 1986), Ducks Unlimited S.D. (chmn. 1983), Fairbanks CC, Green Head Hunting Club (bd.); mil: lcdr, SC, USNR 1965-72, Navy Commendn. (Combat V), Vietnam Service (Bronze star), Nat. Def. Service, Navy Unit Commendn., Rep. of Vietnam; Republican; Presbyterian; rec: bird hunting, fishing, golf. Res: POB 96 Rancho Santa Fe 92067 Ofc: C. W. Clark, Inc. 4180 La Jolla Village Dr Ste 300 La Jolla 92037

CLARK, DAVID C., security-energy management co. president; b. May 16, 1957, Hollywood; s. David G. and Bonnie R. (Callister); m. Wendy, Aug. 8, 1980; children: Matthew b. 1981, Rachel b. 1986; edn: BS in acctg., Brigham Young Univ. 1981. Career: acct. Summa Corp., Los Angeles 1975-76; missionary service in Ecuador 1976-78; dist. sales mgr. Eagle Systems Internat., Utah 1979-81, regional & divl. sales mgr. Eagle Systems, Hayward, Ca. 1982-84, area v.p. 1985; pres./CEO Amtech, Inc., Hayward 1986; pres./CEO Amtech Security & Energy Mgmt., Inc., 1986–; awards: acad. scholarship BYU (1978-79), profl. mgmt. awards, Eagle Systems (1980, 81, 83, 85); mem. Insulation Contrs. Assn. (pres. Gr. Bay Area 1985, dir. govtl. rels. 1986), Nat. Burglar Alarm Assn.; civic: asst. Varsity Boy Scout commnr. Mission Peak Dist. (1985, 86), Explorer Scout adult leader (1983, 84); Republican; Latter Day Saints; rec: volleyball, basketball. Res: 41121 Kathleen St Fremont 94538 Ofc: Amtech Security & Energy 26203 Production Ave Ste 12B Hayward 94545

CLARK, DAVID SIMONDS, poultry pathologist, ret.; b. Nov. 27, 1914, Sivas, Turkey; s. Charles Ernest and Ina Van Loo (Clawson) C.; m. Barbara Fitzgerald, Feb. 12, 1943; children: Susan b. 1944, David b. 1945, Leslie b. 1954; edn: DVM, Michigan State Univ. 1940. Career: small animal vet. practice Santa Ana 1940-41; livestock disease control splst. Dept. of Agriculture Hanford, Calif. 1948-51; asst. vet. patholo. Livestock and Pathol. Lab Calif. Dept. of Ag. San Gabriel 1951-58; dir. research Demler Farms Inc. Anaheim 1959-80; pvt. cons. poultry disease control 1980-82; mem: Am. Vet. Med. Assn. (life), Calif. Vet. Med. Assn., US Livestock Sanitary Assn., Am. Assn. Avian Pathol., Western Poultry Disease Workers' Conf. (pres. 1967), Alpha Gamma Rho, Alpha Psi; publ: articles for AVMA Jour. and Avian Diseases; research: chicken microbiology, developed vaccine; mil: major US Army Vet Corps 1941-45; Protestant; rec: science, philosophy, bridge, gardening. Res: 2831 Colorado Ln Orange 92667

CLARK, DEBRA JEAN, hotel chain sales executive; b. Aug. 27, 1952, Patuxent River, Md.; d. Conrad Wayburn and Helen Jean (Thompson) Lively; m. Kenyon Edwin Clark, July 21, 1985; 1 son, Kenyon Austin b. 1986; edn: BS, Temple Coll. 1974; grad. work Univ. Tenn. 1975-76, Grossmont Coll. 1977-78. Career: dir. sales & mktg., 2 San Diego hotels, Travelodge Internat., 1978-83; dir. sales & mktg. Bartell Hotels (9 hotels, 7 in San Diego), 1983–; conduct sales blitz teams in Calif. cities for Ramada; train sales support staff for 4 Bartell Hotels; mem. Hotel Sales & Mgmt. Assn., Travel & Transp. Council, Executive Club, Indsl. Recreation Council, Nat. Assn. Catering Execs.; civic: San Diego Zool. Soc., S.D. Humane Soc., Mothers Against Drunk Driving, Spl. Olympics; Baptist; rec: scuba, racquetball, tennis, golf. Res: 10580 Atrium Dr San Diego 92131 Ofc: Bartell Hotels 4875 N Harbor Dr 5th Floor San Diego 92106

CLARK, JEFFRY RUSSELL, counseling psychologist, consultant, researcher; b. Oct. 12, 1950, Wareham, Mass.; s. John Russell and Barbara Jean (Roberts) C.; children: Stephen Russell, Jeffrey John Taylor; edn: BS, Trinity Coll. 1975; M.Ed., American Univ. 1979; PhD, Stanford Univ. 1986. Career: social worker Monmouth Family Ctr., Middletown, NJ 1975-76; counselor Annandale Correctional Ctr., Annandale, NJ 1977, Temple Hills Counseling Ctr. 1977-79; adminstrv. dir. Stanford Counseling Inst. 1979-82; counselor Emergency Treatment Ctr., Palo Alto 1981–, coord. tng. 1985–; cons. Peninsula Children's Ctr.; mem: Annadale Jaycees (pres. 1978-79), Am. and Western Psychological Assns., Am. Assn. for Counseling and Devel., Assn. for Adv. Behavior Therapy; mil: USMC 1969-71; research: children of divorce, stress and insomnia. Res: 114d Escondido Village Stanford 94305

CLARK, KAREN ELIZABETH, industrial engineer; b. Feb. 28, 1955, Battle Creek, Mich.; d. Charles G. and Thelma Elizabeth (Robertson) C.; edn: BSIE, Purdue Univ. 1978; MBA, Pepperdine Univ. 1986; Reg. Profl. (Indsl.) Engr. Calif. (1985). Career: technical splst., Douglas Aircraft Co., Long Beach 1985–; fmr. project engr. with Glendale Fed. Savings, Glendale 1984-85, Northrop Corp., Electronics Div., Hawthorne 1983-84, Hill Refrigeration Corp. Div. Emhart Indus., Commerce 1983, Gen. Mills Div., Laureldale, Pa. 1982-83, Gen. Motors Assembly Div., Arlington, Tx. 1980-81; vol. cons. Women's American ORT; guest lectr. CSU Northridge; awards: full tuition scholarship to Purdue, Kellogg Co., Alpha Pi Mu, Pepperdine tuition scholarship (1985); mem: Inst. Indsl. Engrs. (chpt. bd. mem. 1984-86), Cameo Woods Homeowners Assn. (bd. dirs., treas.); Republican; Methodist. Address: P.O. Box 10339 Marina Del Rey 90295

CLARK, RICHARD HERBERT, financial consultant; b. Sept. 1, 1943, West Hartford, Conn.; s. Herbert Dewitt and Esther Alice (Sherman) C.; div.; children: Scot b. 1967, Heather b. 1970; edn: BA, Parsons Coll. 1966, grad. bus. stu. Hardin Simmon Univ. 1971; USAF navigator 1967. Career: account exec. Merrill Lynch, Santa Ana 1975, senior account exec., 1980, asst. v.p. Merrill Lynch, Orange 1984–, tax investment coord., market analysis-tech.; honors: Pres.'s Club (1981, 82, 83), MLPF&S; clubs: Ferrari Owners, Porsche Club Am.; mil: major USAFR, liason ofcr. USAF Acad./Orange Co. 1984-86, decorated Air Medal 4 o.l.c., Vietnam Svc. 1970-72; Republican; Episcopal; rec: tennis, golf. Res: 26 Southwind Irvine 92714 Ofc: Merrill Lynch 200 S Manchester Ste 110 Orange 92668

CLARK, SUE JANET, travel consultant; b. Oct. 17, 1929, Vancouver, Wash.; d. Day Walter and Dorothy Janet (White) Hilborn; children: Leslie Lora b. 1955, Kyle Scott b. 1956, Sidne Suzanne b. 1957, Brian Casey b. 1959; edn: AA, Stephens Coll. 1949; Northwestern Univ. 1949-51; BA, Univ. of Wash. 1952. Career: continuity dir. KING-TV, Seattle 1952-54; traffic mgr. KTNT-TV, Tacoma, Wa. 1954; free-lance public relations cons. 1966-70; continuity dir. KTIM, San Rafael 1966-68; coordinator of volunteer services Sunny Hills Residential Treatment Ctr. for Emotionally Disturbed Teenagers, San Anselmo 1968-73; adminstrv. asst. tech. publs., Bechtel Power Corp., San Francisco 1973; dir. univ. rels. UC San Francisco 1973-77; real estate agt. Home & Land Co., San Rafael 1977-80; pres. Lindberg-Clark, Inc., Hotel Leger, Mokelumne Hill, Calif. 1978-82; writer (1966–) SJ Clark Literary Agency, 1982–; Penn Corp. spl. supvsr. 1984-85; honors: Phi Beta (1950), Matrix Table, Seattle (1952); Certified, Am. Assn. of Vol. Services Coordinators (1972); Million Dollar Club, real estate, Marin Co. (1978); mem: Calaveras County CofC (dir. 1982-84), Vol. Bur. Marin County (bd. 1978-80), San Francisco Easter Seal Soc. (bd. 1974-77), Nat. Soc. of Fund Raisers (charter, bd. dirs. 1969-77), Pub. Relations Soc. of Am. (1975-77), Alpha Delta Pi (life); works: articles on fundraising, pub. rels. in profl. jours. (1968-73), guest speaker num. confs., workshops, seminars (1968-77); contbg. writer articles and poetry Terra Linda News, Pacific Sun, Independent Jour. (1967-73); Lyrical Treasures, Earthshine, P.S. The Universe Sings, Journeys of the Poet/Prophet (1983); Republican; Presbyterian.Res: 756A San Jose Ave San Francisco 94110 Ofc: Travel Consultants 1390 Market St San Francisco 94012

CLARK, TIMOTHY G., manufacturing co. executive; b. May 24, 1939, Pasadena; s. Benjamin C. and Margaret J. (Genereux) C.; m. Diana Martell, Oct. 27, 1962; 1 dau., Pamela b. 1966; edn: AB, USC 1961; MBA, Harvard Bus. Sch. 1965. Career: product mgr./ sales supr. General Foods Corp., White Plains, NY, Denver, Los Angeles, 1965-68; vice pres. mktg. Arrowhead Water, Los Angeles 1973-75; ptnr. Booz, Allen & Hamilton, New York 1968-73, Los Angeles 1975-81; ptnr. Coopers & Lybrand, Los Angeles 1981-85; pres./chief exec. ofcr. Delaney Sash & Door Co., Inc., Los Alamitos 1985–; chmn. bd. dirs. Center for Non-Profit Mgmt.; pres., dir. Harvard Bus. School Assn. of So. Calif.; clubs: Jonathan, Annandale Golf, Harvard (NY), Milbrook (Greenwich, Conn.), Balboa Bay; Republican; Protestant; rec: golf. Ofc: Delaney Sash & Door Co., Inc. 10850 Portal Dr Los Alamitos 90720

CLARKE, JUDY CLARE, lawyer; b. Sept. 6, 1952, Havre de Grace, Md.; d. Harry Wilson and Patsy Ruth (Munroe) Clarke; m. Thomas (Speedy) Rice, Dec. 31, 1977; edn: BA psychol., Furman Univ. 1974; JD, Univ. of S.C. 1977. Career: trial atty. Federal Defenders of San Diego, 1978-83, exec. director 1983–; faculty Hastings Coll. of Advocacy 1983, Nat. Inst. Trial Advocacy 1983–; faculty Nat. Criminal Defense Coll. 1982-, bd. of regents 1985–; mem. Calif. Attys. for Criminal Justice (bd. govs. 1984-), Criminal Defense Lawyers Club, Criminal Defense Bar Assn., Nat. Assn. Criminal Defense Lawyers 1979- (bd. dirs. 1985-); publs: Bail Reform Act of 1984, Drury Law Reporter; Federal Sentencing - Federal Defense Manual (1982-); Ind.; rec: jogging. Ofc: Federal Defenders, 101 W Broadway, Ste 440, San Diego 92101

CLARY, CARTER DE FRIEST, viticulture researcher; b. Mar. 30, 1951, Pasadena, Calif.; s. Everett Burton and Mary (DeFriest) C.; m. Susan Cuneo, Sept. 20, 1980; children: Elizabeth b. 1982, William b. 1984; edn: BS, Univ. Calif. 1975; MS, Mich. State Univ. 1977. Career: research assoc. agricultural mechanization Viticulture and Enology Research Center CSU Fresno 1977–; adj. prof. plant sci. dept. CSU Fresno; honors: Doefer Engrg. Concept of the Year (Am. Soc. Ag. Engrs. 1977); mem: Am. Soc. Ag. Engrs. 1976-, Am. Soc. Enology & Viticulture 1977-(scholarship com. 1984-85); publ: co-author chpt. in Principles and Practices for Harvesting Fruits and Nuts (Cargill Obrien Fridley AVI publ.); rec: outdoor activies, woodworking, constrn., electronics, winemaking. Ofc: VERC CSU Fresno 93740-0089

CLAWSON, RAYMOND W., petroleum company president; b. San Jose, Calif.; s. Benjamin B. and Mae (Names) C.; m. Barbara M. Robbins, 1965; children (by previous marriages): Russell Miller, Raymond Walden; edn: Montezuma Sch. (Los Gatos), Palo Alto Mil. Acad., Pasadena Mil. Acad., American Univ. (L.A.). Career: independent oil producer; vice pres. C.C. Warren & Co. Stock Brokers, Oakland 1924-27; ind. operator exploration and devel. oil properties, New Mexico 1936–; publisher Los Angeles Mirror, 1945-47; pres. Ariz. Securities Inc., L.A. 1947-49; geophysics cons. in offshore oil drilling ops. Gulf of Mexico 1963–, North Sea 1970–; chmn., CEO Clawco Petroleum Corp., Newport Beach 1979–; awards: Cert. of Merit for Distinguished Serv. in Petroleum Exploration and Devel., London, Eng. (1973); clubs: Balboa Bay (Newport Beach), Acapulco Yacht (Mex.); Protestant; rec: travel. Address: POB 2102, Newport Beach 92663

CLAYTON, BERNARD MILES, JR., insurance brokerage co. executive; b. Jan. 26, 1953, Ketchikan, Alaska; s. Bernard, Sr. and June Ester (Thompson) C.; m. Elizabeth, Mar. 12, 1982; edn: AA bus. adminstrn., cum laude, El Camino Coll. 1974; BSBA cum laude, CSU Long Beach 1976. Career: ins. underwriter Gamble Aden Life Ins. Co., 1976-77; dir. mktg. Ruland & Mattingley, 1977-83; v.p./gen. mgr. General Benefits Ins. Serv. Corp., 1983–; bd. dirs. So. Calif. Health Resources Center (1986-); mem: Orange Co. Assn. of Health Underws. (charter, bd. 1986-), Orange Co. Health Plnng. Council (Assembly del. 1985-), Orange Co. Employee Benefit council; publ: art., Ethical Issues in Health Care (1985); Republican; Christian; rec: ski, tennis, travel. Ofc: General Benefits Insurance Services Corp. 500 City Pkwy West Ste 113 Orange 92668

CLEARY, JAMES W., university president; b. Apr. 16, 1927, Milwaukee; m. 1950; edn: Ph.B, Marquette Univ. 1950, MA, 1951; PhD (univ. fellow 1954-5), Univ. Wis. 1956. Career: instr., dir. forensics high sch., Wis. 1949-51; instr. speech, head coach debate Marquette Univ., 1951-53; from instr. to asst. prof. speech, 1956-61, assoc. prof. speech, 1961-63, prof. speech Univ. Wis., 1963-66, then vice chancellor acad. affairs, 1965-69; pres. CSU Northridge, 1969–; bd. dirs. Region 1 United Way; honors: outstanding Teaching award Central States Speech Assn. 1959, Alumni award for coll. teaching Marquette Univ. 1960, Alumnus of Year award 1963; mem: Western States Speech Assn., Speech Assn. Am., Am. Inst. Parliamentarians (bd. dirs.), Am. Assn. State Colls. and Univs. (chmn. 1982-83); publs: articles in field; editor Bibliog. Rhetoric and Public Address (1964), Robert's Rules of Order Newly Revised (1970, 80), John Bulwer's Chirologia-Chironomia, 1644: A Critical Edition (1974). Adress: 18111 Nordhoff St., Northridge 91330

CLEMENTS, HERMAN, security services co. president; b. Mar. 13, 1930, Atlanta, Ga.; s. James and Irene (Campbell) C.; m. Murle, Dec. 15, 1965; children: Ricy b. 1959, Ronald b. 1965; edn: bus. adm., Blayton Business Coll. 1958; crim. justice, Compton Coll. 1972, Mich. St. Univ. 1975, CSU Los Angeles 1978; Calif. lic. Security Splst. (1980). Career: distbn. clerk US Post Office, Atlanta, Ga. 1953-60; security ofcr., County of Los Angeles, 1960-64, supvsy. security ofcr. 1965-67, head security ofcr. 1967-70, chief Park Security Services, 1970-81; owner/pres. Herman Clements Security Services, Inc., Carson 1981–; cons. security services; lectr. Mich. State Univ. on law enforcement in parks adminstrn.; honors: Individual Contbn. award, L.A. County Dept. Parks & Rec., chmn. United Way award 1978-79, recogn. for profl. achievement in Free Ent. System, Business Devel. Center of Calif. (1985); mem: Calif. Security Mgrs., Calif. Crime Prevention Ofcrs. Assn., Calif. Contract Security Guard Assn. Inc., Black Business Mens Assn., LA CofC, Community Club, Tamarind Ave Church Social; mil: s/sgt. USAF 1950-53, Korean Service, UN Service, Nat. Def. Service, Good Conduct medals; Democrat; Prot.; rec: golf, tennis, swimming. Res: 19415 Tajauta Ave Carson 90746 Ofc: Herman Clements Security Services Inc. 22035 S Main St Ste 28 Carson 90745

CLEWETT, RAYMOND WINFRED, design engineer, business executive; b. Nov. 7, 1917, Upland, Calif.; s. Howard Jasper and Pansy Gertrude (Macy) C.; m. Hazel Royer, June 11, 1938; children: Alan b. 1943, Patricia b. 1945, Charles b. 1948, Richard b. 1956, Beverly b. 1958; edn: Chaffey Jr. Coll. 1936-37. Career: exptl. mechanic, research mech., research dept. foreman, test lab. foreman, wind tunnel model builder, master machinist Douglas Aircraft Co. Santa Monica, Calif. 1937-45; shop mgr., design engr. new prod. devel. Lear Inc. L.A. 1945-51; shop mgr., design engr. The Rand Corp. Santa Monica 1951-83; owner, chief engr. Hy-Tech Engrg. & Devel. Lab. Malibu 1983–; instr. Curtis Wright Tech. (on leave from Douglas Aircraft); cons. Pacific-Sierra Research Corp. L.A., Rand Corp.; mem: Soc. Mfg. Engrs., Am. Soc. Metals, AAAS; publs: num. articles on reading aids for visually handicapped, patent held; Republican; Protestant; rec: photog., nat. history, travel, family. Ofc: Hy-Tech Engrg. & Devel. Lab. 7069 Fernhill Dr Malibu 90265

CLINE, CAROLYN JOAN, plastic surgeon; b. May 15, 1941, Wakefield, Mass.; d. Paul S. and Elizabeth (Flom) Cline; edn: BA, honors, Wellesley Coll. 1962; MA, Univ. Cincinnati 1965; PhD, Washington Univ. (St. Louis, Mo.) 1970; diploma Washington Sch. Psychiatry 1972; MD, Univ. of Miami (Fla.) 1975. Career: research asst. Harvard Dental Sch., Boston 1962-64; research asst. physiology Laser Lab., Children's Hosp. Research Found., Cin., 1964, psychology dept. Univ. Cin., 1964-65; intern in clin. psychol. St. Elizabeth's Hosp., Wash. DC 1966-67; psychologist Alexandria (Va.) Community Health Ctr. 1967-68; research fellow NIH, Wash. DC 1968-69; clin. psychologist Kingsbury Ctr. for Children, Wash. DC 1969-73; solo practice clin. psychology, Wash. DC 1970-73; asso. Nat. Acad. Scis., 1974; intern internal medicine Univ. Wis. Hosps., Ctr. for Health Sci., Madison 1975-76; resident in surgery

Stanford Univ. Med. Ctr. 1976-78; fellow microvascular surgery UC San Francisco 1978-79; resident in plastic surgery St. Francis Hosp., S.F. 1979-82; pvt. practice plastic and reconstrv. surgery, San Francisco 1982–; honors: Wellesley Coll. Scholar (1958-62), Teaching Fellowship, Psi Chi (1964-66), Univ. Fellowship Award (1965-70); mem: Calif. Med. Soc., San Francisco Med. Soc., Royal Soc. of Medicine; frequent guest on med. topics, Bay Area radio shows; lectr. on cosmetic surgery; profl. papers and med. journal articles; rec: pianist. Res: 60 Alta St San Francisco 94133 Ofc: 450 Sutter St Ste 2431 San Francisco 94108

CLINE, JOHN DENNIS, engineer; b. Feb. 25, 1949, Pittsburgh, Pa.; s. John Joseph and Eleanor Ruth (Joyce) C.; m. Karen, June 19, 1971; children: Erin b. 1977, Kevin b. 1981; edn: AS in electronics, West Hills Comm. Coll. 1975; BSEE, CSU Fresno 1980; MSEE, CSU Long Beach 1985; Reg. Profl. Engr., Calif. 1984. Career: US Navy aviation fire control technician, 1969-78, pub. affairs ofcr./ instr. integrated avionics sys. Naval Air Station Lemoore, Calif. 1975-78; senior systems engr. Hughes Aircraft Co. Radar Systems Group Engring. Div., respons. for system and circuit design of computer- based spl. test equip. for airborne radar systems, 1981–; Eta Kappa Nu; mem. Nat. Soc. of Profl. Engrs., IEEE; mil: chief p.o. US Navy 1969 78, Nat. Def. Service, Vietnam Service, Vietnam Campaign medals, Navy Unit Commendn., Merit. Unit Commendn. (RVN); Roman Catholic; rec: tennis, photog. Res: 19929 Hawthorne Blvd Torrance 90503 Ofc: Hughes Aircraft Co. POB 92426 Los Angeles 90009

CLINTON, JOHN HART, newspaper publisher; b. Apr. 3, 1905, Quincy, Mass.; s. John Francis and Catherine Veronica (Hart) Clinton; m. Helen A. Amphlett, Feb. 18, 1933 (dec. 1965); chil: Mary Jane (Clinton) Zirkel, b. 1934, Mary Ann (Clinton) Gardner, b. 1937, John H., Jr., b. 1944; m. 2d. Mathilda A. (Schoorel) van Dillen, Feb. 22, 1969; stepsons: Paul A. van Dillen, b. 1945, Erik van Dillen, b. 1951; edn: grad. Thayer Acad. 1922, AB, Boston Coll. 1926, LL.B and JD, Harvard Law Sch. 1929. Career: admitted to Calif. Bar 1930, Mass. Bar 1930; since practiced in S.F.; assoc. firm Morrison, Foerster, Holloway, Clinton & Clark and predecessor, 1939-41, partner, 1941-72; of counsel Morrison & Foerster, 1972–; pres. Leamington Hotel, Oakland 1933-47; pres. Amphlett Printing Co., San Mateo 1943–, publ. San Mateo Times, 1943–, ed. 1960–; hon. mem. Exec. Com. San Mateo Co. Council BSA; bd. dirs., pres. Bay Meadows Found.; regent emeritus Notre Dame Coll. Decorated Knight Equestrian, Order of Holy Sepulchre of Jerusalem. mem: FCC; Am., S.F., San Mateo Co. Bar Assns.; State Bar of Calif. (past chmn. Com. on Free Trial and Free Press, past co-chmn. Calif. Bench/Bar Media Com.); Am. Bar Assn.; Am. Judicature Soc.; Nat. Lawyers Club; Am. Law Inst.; San Mateo Co. Devel. Assn. (pres. 1963-5); San Mateo Co. Hist. Assn. (pres. 1960-4); Calif. Press Assn. (pres. 1970, chmn. bd.); Am. Newspaper Pub. Assn. (press/bar rels. com.; mem. Task Force); Calif. Newspaper Publs. Assn. (chmn. Legal Com.); Wine and Food Soc., S.F.; Am. Soc. Newspaper Eds.; Assn. Catholic Newsmen; Nat. Press Photogs Assn.; Intl. Platform Assn.; Newcomen Soc.; Commonwealth Club of S.F. (past pres.); S.F. Commercial Club; Bohemian Club (S.F.); San Mateo Rotary Club (past pres., chmn. Pgm. Advr. Com.); Elks; Bombay Bicycle Riding Club, Burlingame;, Sequoia Club, Redwood City. Res: 131 Sycamore Ave San Mateo 94402 Ofc: Amphlett Printing Co., 1080 S Amphlet Blvd San Mateo 94402

CLISHAM, PATRICK MICHAEL, healthcare executive; b. Feb. 25, 1944, Altantic City, NJ; s. William Francis and Margaret Stephanie (Hall) C.; m. Edelgard Gorg, April 29, 1984; children: Patrick Michael Victor b. 1969, Ryan Michael b. 1974, Charles W. Gilbert b. 1971, Trudi J. Gilbert b. 1974; edn: BA, St. Mary's Seminary & Univ. 1966; MBA, Golden Gate Univ. 1978; MA, Pepperdine 1982; Nursing Home Adminstr., Calif. 1978. Career: fifth grade tchr. Christ the King Sch., Haddonfield, NJ 1966-68; mil. intelligence ofcr., US Army, USA & Rep. of So. Vietnam 1968-73; adolescent case worker Youth Svc. Ctr., Lawton, Okla. 1974; hotel mgr. Kipling Retirement Hotel, Los Angeles 1976-77; nursing home adminstr. American Health Ctrs., Newport Beach 1978-84; v.p. plnng. & devel. Country Villa Svc. Corp., Culver City 1984–; family therapist trainee Senior Health & Peer Counseling Ctr., Santa Monica 1985-; mem: Calif. Assn. Marriage & Family Therapists, Calif. Assn. Health Facilities, Am. Legion, VFW; mil: capt. US Army Mil. Intelligence 1968-73, Bronze Star, Army Commdn., Vietnam Campaign; Democrat; Catholic; rec: radio electronics, quiz shows, current events. Res: 148 Glendora Ave Covina 91724 Ofc: Country Villa Service Corp., 11266 Washington Pl Culver City 90230

CLOSS, JOHN DAVID, lawyer; b. Sept. 19, 1928, Denver, Colo.; s. Carl H. and Vida Lucile (McGinnis) C.; m. Louise, Nov. 25, 1980; children: Michael b. 1958, Beverly b. 1960; edn: geol. engr., Colo. Sch. of Mines 1950; JD, Southwestern Univ. 1972; admitted bar: Calif. (1972), Az. (1978). Career: geologist in So. America, Africa, 1950-60, So. Calif. Gas Co., and other pos., 1960-74; lawyer in pvt. practice, Los Angeles 1974-80, Needles 1980–; mem: Fellow AAAS, AAPG, LATLA, CTLA, San Bernardino Co. Bar Assn., Mohave Co. Bar Assn.; civic: Elks, Eagles, Rotary; mil: 2d lt. US Army Engrs. 1954-55; Republican; rec: camping. Law Offices of Closs & Closs, 121 "F" St Needles 92363

CLOUGH, ELAINE BUCHHOLZ, librarian; b. July 2, 1921, Green Bay, Wis.; d. Helmuth Henry and Lenora Elizabeth (Augustine) Bucholz; m. Robert Francis Clough, June 5, 1943; children: Betty Elaine, Jeanette Marie; edn: BA, Univ. Wis. 1943, BLS, Simmons Coll., Boston 1944. Career: research librarian Turck, Hill & Co., NYC 1944-48; branch librarian Conejo Library, Thousand Oaks 1967-70; bus. research librarian Ventura County Library Services, Ven-

tura 1970–; grad. studies librarian Calif. Lutheran Coll., Thousand Oaks 1978–; trustee Pequannock Twp. Public Library, Pompton Plains, N.J. 1961-65, pres. 1963-65; Pequannock Twp. neighborhood chmn. Morris Area Council Girl Scouts USA, 1962-65; SCORE/ACE Counseling Pgm., SBA, 1974-; v.p. LWV, Pompton Plains 1959-62; mem: Special Libraries Assn., Calif. Library Assn., Am. Library Assn., AAUW, Wis. Alumni Assn., Simmons Coll. Library Sch. Alumni Assn. Res: 1324 Buckingham Dr., Thousand Oaks 91360 Ofc: PO Box 771 651 E Main St Ventura 93002

CLUNIE, ROBERT KENT, sociologist- educator; b. Nov. 12, 1929, Santa Paula; s. Robert and Myrtle Isabel (Ireland) C.; s. Robert Clunie; m. Nadine Marcia Rudo, July 6, 1976; 1 dau, Jill b. 1969; edn: MA, San Jose State Univ. 1965, MCP, UC Berkeley 1960; MA, San Jose State Univ. 1957; AA, Yuba Coll. 1953; grad. work, Brigham Young Univ. 1969-70. Career: asst. city plnnr. City of Fremont 1960-61; asst. urban plnnr. Plnng. dept. Santa Clara County, San Jose 1961-63; instr. sociology Yuba Coll., Marysville 1965-66; instr. social sci. Oakmont H.S., Roseville 1966-69; grad. asst. Brigham Young Univ., Provo, Utah 1969-70; prof. sociology De Anza Coll., Cupertino 1970–, mens varsity tennis coach 1983–; plnng. cons. Douglas Co., Nev. 1978-79; interim exec. Council of Govts. of Southeast Idaho (7 counties) 1972; adv. bd. Fairoaks Mental Health Svcs., Santa Clara Co. 1973-76; exec. bd. De Anza Coll. Faculty Senate 1980-83; cons. in formulating gen. plan Douglas Co., Nev. 1978-79; developed num. area plnng. studies, Santa Clara Co. Plnng. Dept. incl. Evergreen, Edenvale, Almaden, and Eastside 1961-63; awards: Internship and Fellowship, Idaho State Univ., Pocatello, Ind. 1972-; mem: Am. Inst. of Plnnrs., Nat. Council on Family Relations, Internat. Platform Assn., Am. Acad. of Political and Social Sci., Am. Acad. of Arts and Scis., Calif. Community Coll. Tennis Coaches Assn.; mil: seaman 1/c USN 1950-52; Democrat; Protestant; rec: tournament tennis player, spectator sports, literature. Res: 21081 Red Fir Ct. Cupertino 95014 Ofc: De Anza College, Stevens Creek Blvd. Cupertino 95014

COATE, NANCY ANN, co. president; b. Nov. 29, 1946, Piqua, Ohio; d. Dale Elliot and Virginia Isabel (Makley) C.; edn: Univ. of Wis. 1970-71, Genesee Coll. 1966-68. Career: exec. secty. Giddings & Lewis, Inc., Fond du Lac, Wis. 1969-74; coord. Community Awareness Pgm., CSU San Diego 1974-79; mgr. advt./pub. relations, Doric Scientific, San Diego 1978-82; mktg. asst. Mepco/ Electra, San Diego 1982-84; pres./CEO NAC Assocs., El Cajon 1984–; mgmt. cons., 1981-; honors: Woman of Year, Fond du Lac, Wis. (1974), annual certs. appreciation San Diego Comm. Christmas Center (1977-85), 2d pl. Wisconsin Woman of the Year (1975); civic: San Diego Better Bus. Club, S.D. Profl. Womens Club (1978-81), S.D. Comm. Christmas Ctr. (v.chair), Nat. Space Inst., Great Oaks Village residential home for devel. disabled (bd. dirs. 1985-); ed./pub. Pet Pourri; Republican; Episcopal; rec: Rockwell Plate collector, sports, animals. Ofc: NAC Associates 1704 Wind River Road Ste A El Cajon 92020

COCKRELL, FRANK BOYD, II, entrepreneur; b. May 3, 1948, Redding; s. Alfred Marion, Sr. and Blanche Delma (Webb) C.; children: Catherine b. 1972, Francis b. 1973, Ross b. 1980, Brooke b. 1983; edn: AA, Shasta Jr. Coll. 1968; BA, CSU Sacramento 1970; McGeorge Sch. of Law 1970-72; acting schs. Sherwood Oaks, Clu Gulager, 1976-79. Career: owner Cockrell's Produce Co., 1966-67; acct. trainee Safeway Stores Inc., Div. Hq., Sacto. 1968-70; chief cons. Calif. State Senate, Elections & Reapportionment Com. 1970-71; campaign mgr./staff var. political candidates for local judgeships to govs. (Reagan, Laxalt) 1966-77; asst. to Dir. of Office of Econ. Opportunity, Sacto. 1971; owner VIP Limousine Service, Sacto. 1972-79; pres./CEO Cockrell Ents., Sacto. (motels, service stns., investments, car rentals, auto repair shops) 1973-78; pres./CEO Cockrell Prodns. Inc., Los Angeles (motion pictures, oil) 1978–; fnl. cons.; film prod./actor; honors: Bank of Am. music award (1966); mem. Screen Actors Guild, AFTRA (1977); Optomist Clubs Internat. (lt. gov. 1977; pres. Sacto. Club 1976); Young Republicans (pres. Shasta Coll. Y.R. 1966-68, chmn. Shasta County Y.R. 1966-68, pres. McGeorge Law Sch. Y.R.); Republican (State Central Com. 1974-76, Assembly cand. 6th Dist. winner primary/ lost gen. election, 1974); rec: scuba, ski, equestrian. Ofc: Cockrell Productions Inc POB 1731 Studio City 90069

COCKRELL, WILLIAM JASPER, III, accountant; b. July 7, 1942, Jacksonville, Fla.; s. Wm. Jasper, Jr. and Bethel Aurora (Hughes) C.; m. Sharon Gerrie, Sept. 9, 1967; edn: BSBA, CSU Los Angeles 1968; MBT, USC 1974; MBA, Pepperdine Univ. 1978; Certified Public Acct., Calif. 1971. Career: staff acct. Orvis & Douglas, Los Angeles 1969-70, senior tax acct. Hurdman & Granstoun 1970-73; tax supr. Laventhol & Horwath 1973-74, 1975-76; prin. Palmer, Wiggs & Heston, Agana, Guam 1974-75; tax mgr. Arthur Young & Co., Beverly Hills 1977-78; tax mgr. Price Waterhouse & Co., Newport Beach 1978-79; CPA prin., Balboa Island 1979–; mem. Club of 1000, USC (futures research) 1981-; bd. dirs. MBAN V, Inc. (1978-), CCC Steel, Inc., Compton (1984-); co-trustee T.F. Haller Trust 1978-; instr. Master of Taxation pgm. Northrop Univ. 1976-77; mem: Am. Inst. of CPAs, Calif. Soc. CPAs (Ethics Com., Taxation Com.), Guam Soc. CPAs 1974-75 (chmn. Ethics Com.), Newport Beach-Irvine Estate Planning Council, Accounting Circle USC, Los Angeles Athletic Club, Phi Kappa Tau frat., USC Alumni Assn.; coauthor monthly tax and fnl. column, The Valley Entertainer, Sherman Oaks; mil: midshipman USN 1960-61; Republican; Christian; rec: scuba diving. Address: William J. Cockrell, CPA, POB 337 Balboa Island 92662

COELHO, DAVID RODRIGUES, computer software engineer, entrepreneur; b. Aug. 28, 1958, Kenewick, Wash.; s. Francis R. and Ruth A. (Freeman) C.; edn: BSEE, Stanford Univ. 1980. Career: research asst. Stanford Univ.

1977-80; cons. Hewlett-Packard 1979-80; founder, dir., and mgr. computer facilities Silicon Valley Research, Palo Alto 1979-81, co. name chg. 1981, Silvar Lisco, Menlo Park, mgr. CAD devel. 1982-84, mgr. verification devel. 1984—; founder Coelho Pyrotechnics (pyrotechnic contracting), Palo Alto 1982—; founder, dir. The Mill Valley Program (non-profit ednl.) 1977-; founder, pres. ZetaTech, Inc. 1986-; honors: violin soloist Orch. Piccola (toured to Italy and Festival of Two Worlds), scholarship stu. S.F. Conservatory of Music, Marin Music Chest scholarship (1976), Lenore Irish Scholar (1975), mem. Young Professionals Orch. (1977), concermaster of Forest Meadows Summer Fest. Orch.; mem: IEEE, Assn. for Computing Machinery, Pyrotechnics Guild Internat. Inc., Calif. Pyrotechnics Assn.; mem. Delta Kappa Epsilon frat. (ofcr. 1978), Kelp divers/ Calif., Stanford Alumni Assn. (life), Am. Assn. of Individual Investors (life); num. tech. publications and presentations profl. confs.; Democrat; rec: pyrotechnics, enology, sailing, parachuting, scuba. Ofc: ZetaTech 32773 Goshen St Union City 94587

COELHO, TONY, congressman; b. June 15, 1942, Los Banos; s. Otto and Alice C.; m. Phyllis, June 10, 1967; children: Nicole, Kristin; edn: BA, Loyola Univ. of Los Angeles 1964. Career: asst. for agriculture to Congressman B.F. Sisk, 1965-70, adminstrv. asst., 1970-78; mem. 96th-98th Congresses from 15th Dist. Calif., chmn. Democratic Congl. Campaign Com., 1981—, majority whip-at-large, 1981—, mem. Dem. Steering and Policy Com., 1981—. Ofc: 403 Cannon House Office Bldg., Wash. DC 20515

COFFILL, WILLIAM JAMES, lawyer; b. Dec. 1, 1949, Sonora; s. Wm. Charles and Marjorie Louise (Segerstrom) C.; edn: BA, Occidental Coll. 1972; JD, UOP McGeorge Sch. of Law 1976; admitted to Calif. State Bar 1976. Career: partner Coffill & Coffill, attys., Sonora 1977—; mem. Am., Calif. State, Tuolumne County (pres. 1985) bar assns.; bd. dirs. Sonora Lions Club; bd. dirs. Mother Lode Chap. Am. Red Cross; Friends Tuolumne County Library; Republican (Rep. Central Com.); Episcopal. Res: 376 E Summit Ave Sonora 95370 Ofc: Coffill & Coffill, 23 N Washington St Sonora 95370

COGERT, EDWIN, building contractor; b. Dec. 4, 1932, Brooklyn, NY; s. Jack D. and Deborah (Friedman) C.; m. Barbara Smyler, Nov. 13, 1954; children: Randi b. 1956, Barry b. 1958, Caryn b. 1963; edn: BS degree. Career: gen. mgr. Arleta Realty, San Fernando Valley 1957-59; territorial dir. Parents Magazines Cultural Inst., Hollywood 1959-65; sales mgr. Hasko Bldrs., Los Angeles 1965-67; gen. mgr. U.S. Plywood Remodeling Ctrs., Los Angeles 1967-70; gen. mgr. Transamerican Constrn., Huntington Beach 1970-73; COE Bonded Builders Inc. and owner Edwin B. Cogert Custom Bldr. 1973—; constrn. cons.; mil: sgt. USAF; Republican; Jewish; rec: sculpture. Ofc: Bonded Builders Inc. and Edwin Cogert Custom Builder, 15840 Ventura Blvd. Ste. 330 Encino 91436

COHEN, CYNTHIA MARYLYN, lawyer; b. Sept. 5, 1945, Brklyn.; d. Bernard and Evelyn (Berman) Cohen; edn: AB, Cornell Univ. 1967; JD cum laude, NY Univ. Sch. of Law 1970; mem. NY State Bar 1971-, Calif. State Bar 1980-, Federal Bar of NY 1971-, Fed. Bar of Calif. 1980-, Sup. Ct. Bar 1979-. Career: assoc. atty. Simpson Thacher & Bartlett, NY, NY 1970-76; assoc. atty. Kaye, Scholer, Fierman, Hays & Handler, NY, NY 1976-80; atty. Stutman, Treister & Glatt Profl. Corp., Los Angeles 1980—, shareholder mem. 1981-; Student-Faculty Curriculum and Clin. Program Coms., and Student Research Advisor, NYU 1968-70; honors: Order of the Coif (1970), Founder's Day Cert. (1969), John Norton Pomeroy Scholar (1968-70), Law Rev. (1968), NYU; Am. Jurisprudence Awards; Cornell Dean's Scholarship 1963-67; NY State Regents Scholarship 1963-70; mem: Am. Bar Assn. (Antitrust Sect.), Bar Assn. of City of NY (Trade Reg. Com. 1976-79), NY State Bar Assn. (ch. Class Action Com. 1979), Assn. of Bus. Trial Lawyers, L.A. County Bar Assn. (Antitrust, Comml., Bankruptcy Sects.), Calif. Bar Assn. (Antitrust, Bus. Sects.); Girl Scouts 1954-59; Delta Gamma Sor.; NY chpt. Am. Cancer Soc. (dir. 1977-80); Democrat; Jewish; rec: collector books, wine, tennis. Res: 4818 Bonvue Ave Los Angeles 90027 Ofc: Stutman, Treister & Glatt PC, 3699 Wilshire Blvd, Ste. 900, Los Angeles 90010

COHEN, EVE, administrative law judge; b. July 22, 1940, Jerusalem; d. Morris and Sara (Lubliner) Sternlight; m. Howard Ira Cohen, Sept. 10, 1960; children: Darrel Phillip, Sheri Dana, Halli Frances, Daniel Matthew; edn: BA, UCLA 1957; JD, Loyola Univ. L.A. 1964. Career: assoc. Marvin Cahn, Hollywood 1965-66; sole practice law, Hollywood 1966-71, Century City 1971-72; adminstrv. law judge Calif. Unemployment Insurance Appeals Bd., Van Nuys 1972—; instr. in field; chair Speakers Bur. San Fernando Valley, 1972; mem. Lawyers Club Los Angeles City (dir. 1975), San Fernando Valley Bus. Profl. Assn., Religion in Media; author: Diary of A Sabra - Faith in Action (1980), Your Way to Kingdom Living (1982); Republican; Jewish. Ofc: 6150 Van Nuys Blvd Van Nuys 91400

COHEN, JONATHAN ALAN, lawyer, developer; b. June 10, 1952, Los Angeles; s. Jehudah Moses and Evelyn Ayeroff (Donnerstag) C.; m. Vivien, Apr. 3, 1982; 1 dau. Jennieke Amelia b. 1983; edn: BA, San Francisco State Univ. of Major Sociol. 1974; MP, Univ. So. Calif. Sch. of Urban & Regl. Planning 1978; JD, Univ. San Francisco Kendrick Hall Law Sch. 1981; admitted Calif., Fla. State Bars 1982. Career: chief environmental planner VTN L.A.; v.p. Calif.-Real Estate Processing Svc. S.F.; pres. Land Devel. Resources S.F.; atty. Law Ofcs. Jonathan A. Cohen S.F.; ptnr. Cohen & Hsu S.F.; gen. ptnr. Live Oak Assocs. and Live Oak Assocs. II; dir. Land Devel. Resources, Habitat Devel. Corp.; mem: ABA (taxation sect.), S.F. Bar Assn., RESSI, Contra Costa Council, Sacramento CofC, Bldg. Ind. Assn. of No. Calif., Bldg. Ind. Assn. of Superior Calif.; Jewish; rec: swimming, hiking, scuba, skiing. Ofc: Cohen & Hsu, One Market Plaza, Spear St Tower, Ste 2210, San Francisco 94105

COHEN, MARK J., real estate broker; b. Nov. 19, 1942, Stockton; s. Samuel and Sadie (Tager) C.; 1 son, Eric b. 1975; desig: Calif. lic. R.E. broker (1974), GRI, Grad. Realtors Inst. (1978), CRS, Cert. Residential Splst. (1979), Cert. Real Estate Brokerage Mgr. (1986). Career: v.p. Sonoma Co. Abstract Bureau 1969-74; realtor 1974—, owner/broker Mark J. Cohen GRI, CRS, Santa Rosa; mem: Sonoma Co. Multiple Listings Svc. (dir. 1978-80), Sonoma Co. Bd. Realtors (dir. 1981-86), Calif. Cert. Residential Splsts. (pres.1983); clubs: Sonoma Co.Scrabble (pres. 1983-84), Optimists of Santa Rosa (pres. 1985-86); articles: Title News, Am. Land Title Assn.1971, 1972, Real Estate Today 1979, 1984, Games Mag. 1986; rec: cartoon art collector, magician, writer. Res: 1719 Jeffery St.Santa Rosa 95404 Ofc: Mark J. Cohen GRI CRS, 589 Mendocino Ste. 5 Santa Rosa 95401

COHEN, MISHA RUTH, acupuncturist, educator; b. Nov. 8, 1951, Tallahassee, Fla.; d. Bart Leonard and Jacqueline Margot (Freeman) Cohen; edn: Oberlin Coll. 1969-72; OMD, San Francisco Coll. of Acupuncture and Oriental Medicine, 1986, highest honors certification pgm. 1983; Lincoln De-Tox Acupuncture Sch. 1976-78; Certified Acupuncturist, Fla. (1982), Calif. (1983), Tchg. Credential, Traditional Oriental Medicine (1983). Career: offset printer in Oberlin, Ohio and NYC, 1972-76; acupuncture practitioner, NYC 1976-79; shiatsu, pvt. practice, San Francisco 1979-83, also Osento Bath House, S.F.; shiatsu and acupressure instr., San Francisco and New York, 1976-83; acupressurist College Med. Ctr., San Francisco 1981-83; clin. and didactic prof. San Francisco Coll. of Acupuncture and Oriental Medicine, 1983—; senior acupuncturist, herbalist, owner/dir. Quan Yin Acupuncture & Herb Center of San Francisco, 1984—; cons. to Certified Acupuncture Practitioners, 1983-; guest lectr. New Coll. (adj. faculty 1986), UC Berkeley, San Francisco St. Univ., Am. Coll. of Traditional Chinese Medicine, Jewish Feminist Conf., Whole Life Expo (SF), Vibrant Health Seminar, UCSF Nat. AIDS Conf.; devel. classes and exams for the State Board Examination; mem: Am. Assn. of Acupuncture and Oriental Medicine (1982-), Oriental Medicine Faculty Assn. (founding mem. 1985, chair Curriculum Devel. Task Force); civic: San Francisco Aids Alternative Healing Project (founder 1985-); Jewish Women for a Secular Middle East (founding mem. 1982-); works: devel. series of health workshops focusing on health from a socio-economic viewpoint (1980-83); health columnist, North Mission News (1984-86); interviewee in Out From Under pub. by Spinsters Ink (1983); article in Pacific J. (6/86); Jewish; rec: skiing, pottery, photog. Ofc: Quan Yin Acupuncture & Herb Center of San Francisco 513 Valencia San Francisco 94110

COHEN, STEVEN GERALD, manufacturing co. president; b. Nov. 28, 1943, Providence, R.I.; s. Norman and Emma (Grossman) C.; m. Judith, Aug. 15, 1965; children: Lisa b. 1966, Shari b. 1970, Shawn b. 1974; edn: BS in mktg., Bryant Coll. 1966. Career: sales splst. Allied Chemical, L.A. 1967-69; mktg. rep. Philip A. Hunt Chem. Co., L.A. 1969-71; Mark-Themoplastic splst. Kamco Plastics 1971-, and direct mgmt. involvement var. PMC cos., 1971—,pres. Plastic Services & Products Inc. (div. PMC Companies, Sun Valley 1977—, and pres.Technical Plastic Extruders Inc., Newark, N.J. 1982—; civic: vol. mem. Mayors Council for Youth Advancement 1980-82; Republican; Jewish; rec: white water rafting, travel. Calif. Ofc: Plastic Services & Products Inc. 12243 Branford St Sun Valley 91352

COLBERT, EARL JAY, orthodontist; b. Nov. 16, 1942, Wash. DC; s. Lawrence L. and Sylvia (Hirsch) C.; m. Sherry Graham, Oct. 18, 1969; children: Laura, b. 1973, Michele, b. 1974; edn: The American Univ. 1961-63; DDS, Georgetown Univ. Dental Sch. 1967; Cert.Orthodontics, Howard Univ. Coll. of Dentistry 1972. Career: dental ofcr., actg. dept. hd. US Navy Dental Corp., MCRD San Diego and USS Kearsarge, 1967-69; gen. dentistry, Wash. DC 1969-70; self- empl. orthodontist, Huntington Beach 1972—; recipient appreciation, Mayor of Huntington Beach; mem: Naval Reserve Assn., Reserve Ofcrs. Assn., Navy League, Am. Assn. of Orthodont., Huntington Beach CofC, Sister Cities Assn. (bd. dirs.), Rotary (bd. dirs.), Calif. Childrens Services Panel in Orthdontics for Orange, LA Counties, Nat. Fedn. of Independent Bus.; vol: Civil Defense, Multiple Sclerosis, Orange Co. Music Ctr. Guild, OC Performing Arts Guild; PTA; past pres. Boca Orthodontic Study Gp.; invention: orthodontic rotating device; mil: dental ofcr. USNR 1967-69, cmmdr. USNR 1969-, cmdg. ofcr. Navy Reserve Fleet Hospital Combat Zone Hdqtrs. Unit, 1985-; Merit. Unit Cit., Vietnam Svc.; rec: inventions, models. Res: 3696 Montego Dr., Huntington Beach 92649 Ofc: Earl J. Colbert, DDS, Inc., 5112 Warner Ave, Ste. 104, Huntington Beach 92649

COLE, DONALD FRED, co. president; b. July 26, 1942, Detroit, Mich.; s. Fredrick Arthur and Babetta Charlotte (Godlie) C.; m. Berneil Smith, Dec. 29, 1967; children: Roslyn, b. 1970; Aldon, b. 1973; Catherine, b 1981; edn: AB, Univ. of Mich. 1965. Career: CEO Interstate Mfg. Corp., Romeo, MI 1968-76; pres. Cole Industries, Inc. and subs. cos. 1976—; subs. cos: Solana Lumber, Waterstreet Wholesale Lumber, Fallbrook Lumber, Temecula Lumber, K-RAM Radio, K-ITT Radio; mem: San Diego Lumber & Wood Prods. Assn., Young Pres.' Orgn., San Diego Symphony, San Diego Opera; mil: lt. USNR 1965-68; Episcopal; rec: golf, sailing, choral & vocal music. Res: 1856 Viking Way La Jolla 92037 Ofc: Cole Industries, 1640 Tidelands Ave National City 92050

COLE, EDWIN LOUIS, clergyman; b. Sept. 10, 1922, Dallas, Tx.; s. Edwin L. and Florence (Goodrum) C.; m. Nancy Corbett, Jan. 31, 1946; children: Paul Louis b. 1950, Lois (Bivins) b. 1952, Joann Marie b. 1954; edn: BA, Union Univ. 1978, PhD, 1979. Career: pastor, churches in Sonora, San Bruno, and Chico, Ca. 1952-60; missionary - evangelism, 1960-63; pres. Men's Ministries for denomination, 1963-69; pastor, Concord, Ca. 1969-74; gen. mgr. WHCT/TV, Hartford, Ct. 1974-76; minister-at-large, CBN Network, 1976-78; pastor,

Costa Mesa, Ca. 1978-81; pres. Edwin Louis Cole Ministries Inc. dba Manhood Ministries 1981−; chmn. Com. for Internat. Goodwill; radio pgm. host, Maximized Manhood; founder Project Timothy; bd. dirs. High Adventure Ministries; dir. Voice of Hope Bdcstg.; awards: Emmy Awards (1973, 74) for TV Christmas Spls., S.F. Chpt. of TV Arts & Scis.; charter bd. mem. M-2 Prison Rehab. Pgm., Calif. 1971-73; mem. Gov. Reagan's Commn. for Children & Youth 1969-72; author: Maximized Manhood (Whitaker Press), Courage (Harrison House), Potential Principle (Whitaker Press) total 1,000,000 copies in print; mil: pharm. mate 1/c USCG 1941-45; Republican; Assemblies of God; rec: swim, tennis, sailing. Res: 1806 Port Stirling Pl Newport Beach 92660 Ofc: Box 825 Corona Del Mar; Box 610588 Dallas, TX 75261

COLE, EMORY MC LEOD, JR., school district electronic services manager; b. Nov. 28, 1946, San Francisco; s. Emory McL. and Florence Althea (Lyon) C.; m. Lynn Dee James, Apr. 4, 1967; children: Cynthia b. 1966, Tammy b. 1968, Sheila b. 1971, Emory III b. 1977; edn: AA in electronics, San Bernardino Valley Coll. 1978; desig: cert. techn. (NABER) Nat. Assn. of Bus. & Ednl. Radio, 1984. Career: foreman John's Campers Inc., San Bernardino 1969-74, nightly camper maint., 1978-79; warranty svc. mgr. Majestic Motor Homes, San Jacinto 1974-76; electronic techn. Stockwell & Binney, S.B. 1976-79; customer engr. Control Data Corp., Los Angeles 1979-80; engring. techn. Test Systems Internat., Santa Fe Springs 1980-81; asst. mgr. AV/Electronics Dept., Chino Unified Sch. Dist., 1981−; mem. Assn. of Communication Techns., Assn. Public Safety Communs. Officers, Chino Assn. of Mgmt. Personnel, Elks; designer: Remote Monitor/Alarm for Computer Uninterrupted Power Source (1985); mil: E4 US Air Force 1964-68, decorated NDSM, VSM, RVCM, SAEMR, AFGCM; Democrat; Methodist; rec: bowling, fishing, computers. Res: 25556 Gould St Loma Linda 92354 Ofc: Chino Unified School District 5130 Riverside Dr Chino 91710

COLE, JEFFERY ALLYN, insurance general agent; b. Feb. 14, 1943, Porterville; s. James A. and Magaret L. (Salisbury) Waggie; m. Gwendolyn A., Aug. 30, 1969; children: Casey b. 1975, Kelly b. 1977, Derek b. 1980; edn: AA, Porterville Coll. 1964; BS, CSU Long Beach 1969; Chartered Life Underwriter, American Coll. 1983, Chartered Financial Cons., 1984. Career: owner, opr. Cole's Store For Men, Porterville 1971-73; Whiteash Lake Realty, Whitefish, Mont. 1974-76; dept. mgr. Montgomery Ward, Great Falls, Mont. 1976-77; regl. mgr. La-Farm Ins., Sacramento 1977-85; gen. agent Franklin Financial Plnng. Group, Benicia 1985−; honors: Nat. Sales Achiev.; Nat. Quality Award; L.U.T.C.; L. Imra Mgmt. Award; mem: Rotary (dir. Porterville, Spkrs. chmn., Brentwood), Elks, Ducks Unlimited (past chmn.), Am. Soc. CLU, Mt Diablo Nat. Assn. of Life Underwriters; works: Junior Nationals, Snow Skiing, 2 yrs.; created 1st Regl. Mag., The Grapevine, Cal-Farm Ins.; Republican; Episcopal; rec: skiing, fishing, hunting. Res: 503 Nottingham Dr. Brentwood 94513 Ofc: Franklin Financial Planning Group, 1060 Grant Benicia 94510

COLE, JOSEPHINE ELIZABETH, educator, lecturer; b. Jan. 18, 1913, San Francisco; d. Joseph Aeneas and Elizabeth (Brown) Foreman; m. Audley Cole, June 18, 1941; edn: BA, UC Berkeley 1932, MA edn., 1958; gen. adminstrv. credl., San Francisco State Univ. 1968. Career: instr. social studies, French St. Vincent's H.S. San Francisco 1936-42; dir. retail selling S.F. Parochial High Schools 1939-42; tchr. Raphael Weill Sch. 1943-46, Balboa H.S. 1948-64, counselor, dir. dist. demonstration Eng. classes 1950-64; youth counselor Youth Opportunities Ctr. 1966-67; proj. head Youth Guidance Svc. Ctrs. for Dist. Supv. AA, student relations for entire dist. 1968-74 (ret.); school liaison ofcr. US Dept. of State 1974-76; area supv. Law in a Free Society, proj. of Center for Civic Edn. Calabasas; seminar leader US Postal Svc. Oakland 1984-85; workshops public speaking Internat. Studies Acad. 1985, Park & Rec. Dept. 1986; faculty workshop leader Newcomer H.S. 1984; honors: Internat. Awareness Award (Delta Kappa Gamma 1985), Spkr. of the Year (Kiwanis 1984, 85), Woman of the West (Iota Phi Lambda 1984), 2nd Place Internat. Woman of the Year (1985), Hall of Fame- edn. (Am. Biographical Inst. 1985-86), Essay prize winner (S.F. Fair 1985), Disting. Svc. (S.F. Bd. of Supvs. 1985); mem: Delta Kappa Gamma (adm. chmn., v.p.), Internat. Tng. in Communication (formerly Toastmistress, council pres. 1984-85), Sister City Assn. (Osaka, Japan 1971-), Act-So (youth pgm. of NAACP, chmn. judges 1985-), Nobirukai (Japanese newcomers assn., organizer of Eng. classes for new arrivals; devel. Curriculum for Basic Skills Centers, proj. funded by S.F. Mayor's Criminal Justice Council 1981; author: Have You Met Your Inner Self? (1986); Democrat; Rel. Science; rec: study of comparative religions, languages, psychology. Res: 1598 36th Ave San Francisco 94122

COLE, KENNETH CAREY, JR., accountant; b. July 29, 1928, Cambridge, Mass.; s. Kenneth Carey and Alice Atwood (Campbell) C.; m. Barbara Tindell, Dec. 18, 1954; children: Steven Tindell b. 1957, Elizabeth Carey b. 1959, Robert Campbell b. 1961; edn: BBA, Univ. Wash. 1951; MBA, Stanford Univ. 1956; CPA Calif. 1968; Certified Mgmt. Consultant 1980. Career: computer systems adminstr. General Elec. Co. Schenectady, NY 1956-59; acct. rep. Radio Corp. of Am. San Francisco 1959-61; mgmt. cons. Deloitte, Haskins & Sells S.F. 1961-69, ptnr. 1969-75, ptnr. in charge Regional mgmt. cons. practice 1975-84 (retired); prof. acctg. and info. systems CSU Hayward 1984−; lectr. info. systems Univ. S.F. 1983, UC Santa Cruz 1984; mem: Am. Inst. CPAs, Calif. Soc. CPAs, Inst. Mgmt. Cons., Inst. Internal Auditors, Commonwealth Club S.F., Olympic Club S.F., Los Altos Golf & CC, Soc. of Mayflower Descendants; mil: US Army Counter Intelligence Corps 1952-54; Republican; Presbyterian. Res: 906 Terrace Dr Los Altos 94022 Ofc: CSU School of Business Hayward 94542

COLE, LEE, business owner; b. Oct. 12, 1951, San Francisco; s. Maurice Buddy and Ila Mark Cole; edn: Columbia Univ. 1969-72; seamanship, Lundberg Sch. Piney Point, Md. 1972. Career: merchant seaman 1972-74; taxi driver NYC 1974-75; mgr. Skateboard City 1975, owner 1976, later evolved into Skates on Haight, San Francisco's oldest skateboard/ rollerskate store; honors: Outstanding Contributions (for Skates on Haight by Greenpeace, raised over $100,000 with 2 skate-a-thons), Skates on Haight products encapsulated in Oakland Museum in spl. exhibit until year 2000; frequent spkr. at AA and NA meetings, involved with alcohol/ drug recovery pgms.; author: I Can Swim You can Swim (Ten Speed Press 1978); hosted Smithsonian Exhibit on whales; subject of book on craftsmanship (Solzer & Hail 1981); rec: long-distance motorcycling. Ofc: Skates on Haight 1818 Haight St San Francisco 94117

COLE, LEE STEWART, consultant, criminal investigator, writer; b. Nov. 8, 1927, Winston- Salem, N.C.; s. Jesse Stewart and Anna Josephine (Hill) C.; m. Jeanne M. (dec. 1980), m. 2d Zetta M., May 2, 1984; children: Leigh Stewart b. 1953, Shawn Hawkins b. 1955; edn: LLB, Am. Sch. of Law 1950; att. Univ. N.C. 1946, UC Berkeley 1964; Calif. tchg. cred. (crim. investig.). Career: spl. agent, 1955-69, asst. div. mgr. Nat. Automobile Theft Bureau, San Francisco 1969-76; pres./CEO Lee S. Cole & Assocs. Inc., also Lee Books Co., Novato 1976−; instr. and coord. Adminstrn. of Justice Dept., San Jose St. Univ.; recipient num. recogn. awards var. law enforcement groups in Calif. and Puerto Rico; mem. Soc. Automotive Engrs., Am. Soc. for Metals, Calif. Peace Ofcrs. Assn., Internat. Assn. Arson Investigators, Internat. Assn. Vehicle Theft Investigators; author/pub. books: Vehicle Theft Investigation, Bike Theft, Vehicle Identification 1938-1986, The Investigation of Motor Vehicle Fires (1st, 2 ed.), Motorcycle Identification, Okie Mafioso (a novel); mil: sgt. US Army, MP Crim. Investig. Div. 1950-53, Good Conduct, German Occup., Korean Service medals; rec: music, research. Ofc: Lee S. Cole & Assocs. Inc. POB 906 Novato 94948

COLE, WARD MASON, dentist; b. March 10, 1953, Sacramento; s. Clyde Mason and Jean Elaine (Robinson) C.; m. Edilia Campaneria, Dec. 10, 1982; children: Alana Edilia b. 1984, Ward Jason b. 1986; edn: AA, Sacramento City Coll. 1973; BA, CSU Sacramento 1975; BS, UC San Francisco, DDS, 1981. Career: dentist, co-owner Cole Family Dental Ctr., Folsom 1984−; lectr. to civic group; participant in health fairs, oral cancer screening; mem: Am. and Calif. Dental Assns., Sacramento Dist. Dental Soc., Lions, Folsom CofC, Capital City Lodge Masons, Sacramento Scottish Rite, Ben Ali Shrine; mil: lt. USN Dental Corps 1981-84; Republican; Catholic; rec: pvt. pilot (single engine). Ofc: 6611 Folsom- Aubrun Rd. Ste. M Folsom 95630

COLEMAN, JOHN MOSLER, manufacturing co. executive; b. June 20, 1947, NY, NY; s. Martin S. and Janet I. (Mosler) C.; m. Linda Greif, Aug. 24, 1971; edn: BS, Union Coll. 1970; MBA, New York Univ. Grad. Sch. Bus. Adm., 1972. Career: asst. mgr. Franklin Nat. Bank, N.Y.C. 1971-74; asst. secty. Irving Trust Co., N.Y.C. 1974-77; v.p. admin. Harbor Universal, Inc., San Leandro 1977−, pres. Harbor Universal, Inc., Los Angeles 1977−; dir: Harbor Universal Inc. 1977-, Benedetti Corp. 1977-; mem: Los Angeles Design Alliance (dir. 1983-), Calif. Metal Trades Assn. (bd. dirs. 1980-82), PDC Contract Mfrs. Assn. (exec. com./ dir. 1981, pres. 1983-85, chmn. 1986); civic: University Synagogue (bd. dirs. 1985-), Cedars Sinai Med. Ctr. (bd. govs. 1980-), Nat. Ctr. Hyperactive Children (chmn. bd. advisors 1986-); clubs: Riviera Tennis (LA), Harmonie (NY); mil: sp5 US Army Reserves 1968-73; Jewish. Ofc: Harbor Universal Inc. 1500 S Evergreen Ave Los Angeles 90023

COLEMAN-MAXWELL, CORALIE VIER, insurance agent; b. June 23, 1947, Lodi, Calif.; d. Wesley E. and Beverly Ann Genetti (Looser) Smith; m. Howard H. Maxwell, Apr. 29, 1984; edn: BA anthropology, UC Santa Barbara 1969. Career: probation ofcr. San Joaquin County 1969-72, Shasta County 1972-77; ins. adjuster Indsl. Indemnity, Stockton 1977-80; ins. agent State Farm Ins., Stockton 1980−; awards: Millionaire Club (1982-85), Legion of Honor (1982-84), 5 Star Agent (1984), State Farm; Nat. Quality Award, NALU (1983, 85); mem. Nat. Assn. Life Underws. (Stockton chpt.), Nat. Assn. Profl. Saleswomen, Bus. & Profl. Womens Club; Planned Parenthood of San Joaquin Valley (bd. dirs. 1985-, fundraising co-chair 1986); Unitarian; rec: travel, x-c ski, golf. Ofc: 4550 N Pershing Ste 4 Stockton 95207

COLLIER, ALICE BILLMAN, commercial real estate broker; b. Apr. 3, 1951, Buffalo, N.Y.; d. Charles Robert and Maxine Mary (Dixon) Billman; m. Glenn, Apr. 17, 1982; children: Jason b. 1979, (step) Glenn, Jr. b. 1969; edn: BA, Univ. Calif. 1973, grad. work. 1974-75; Calif. lic. real estate broker 1982. Career: prop. adminstr. (512,000 sq ft prime ofc. space) Western Terrain Inc., Newport Beach and Houston, Tx., 1977-82; pres./ major shareholder MACAP Internat. Inc., Signal Hill 1982−; honors: Dean's List, Univ. Calif. (1973, 74); civic: Signal Hill CofC, Long Beach CofC, Lakewood Village Little League; Democrat; Presbyterian; rec: guitar. Ofc: MACAP International Inc. 2699 E 28th St Ste 402 Signal Hill 90806

COLLIER, CHARLES ARTHUR, JR., lawyer; b. Apr. 18, 1930, Columbus, Ohio; s. Charles Arthur and Gertrude Clara (Roe) C.; m. Linda, Aug. 5, 1961; children: Sheila b. 1963, Laura b. 1965; edn: AB magna cum laude, Harvard Coll. 1952; LLB, Harvard Law Sch. 1955. Career: law clerk US Dist. Ct. cent. dist. Calif. 1959-60; assoc. tty. Freston & Files L.A. 1960-66; assoc., ptnr. Mitchell, Silberberg & Knupp 1967-82; ptnr. Irell & Manella 1982−; lectr. Contg. edn. of Bar, var. assns. and seminars; fellow Am. Coll. Probate Counsel; mem: Calif. State Bar (Taxation sect., Estate Planning, Trust and Probate Law section chmn. 1980-81, exec. com. 1977-82), ABA (Real Property, Probate and Trust Law sect.), Internat. Acad. Estate & Trust Law, L.A. Co. Bar Assn. (Probate & Trust Law sect.), Harvard Club of So. Calif. (pres. 1971-73, dir. 1966-74), Assoc. Harvard Alumni (regl. dir. 1975-79, v.p. at large 1979-82); publs: num. articles in legal jours.; mil: USN 1955-57; Republican; Protestant; rec: travel, gardening. Res: 1075 S El Molino Ave Pasadena 91106 Ofc: 1800 Ave of the Stars Ste 900 Los Angeles 90067

COLLIGAN, RICHARD THOMAS, photographer; b. Sept. 20, 1940, Morristown, NJ; s. John Patrick and Betty Joy (Saltonstall) C.; m. Anna Robin, 1984; children: Brandie Bea b. 1985, Lori b. 1962, Linda b. 1964, Shawn b. 1966; edn: John Jay Coll. of Criminal Justice 1965-68; NYCPD Police Acad.; NYCPD Plainclothes Investigator Sch. Career: patrolman/ plain clothes investigator, NYC Police Dept. 1962-69; sales rep. Julius Schmid Pharmaceutical Co. 1969-70; automobile salesman & wholesaler 1970-76; security lt./ tng. spec./ asst.mgr. contract security police force, Los Angeles Air Force Station 1976-80; mgr. Waltgard Security 1980-82; dir. of security H.L. Yoh Co. 1983–; Los Angeles Air Force Station Tng.Splst. 1979; photog./ prop. with wife Anna, ARC Studios (comml., restoration, indsl., advt., spl. events, assignments, portfolios), Torrance 1985–; awards: NYC Police Dept. Commdn. for Excellent Police Duty (2); Police Ofcr. of Month, New York Journ. Am. 1965; mil: BMSN USN 1957-61; Republican (Pres. Task Force). Res: 502 Ave G, Apt 11, Redondo Beach 90277 Ofc: ARC Studios 800 W Carson Ste 7 Torrance 90502

COLLINS, GERALD CHESTER, savings and loan association executive; b. July 28, 1946, Los Angeles; s. Chester and Harriet (Hart) C.; m. Midge Bigham, May 31, 1968; children: Julie b. 1975, Bart b. 1977; edn: BA, CSU Northridge 1971. Career: asst. loan dept. head California Federal, head ofc. 1974-76, asst. v.p., loan dept. head, regl. loan mgr., Visalia 1979-85; regl. loan mgr. No. California, Gibraltor Savings 1985–; pres., CEO VIAH Inc.; past pres. Energy Com., City of Visalia; past pres. Cal Fed Political Action Com.; tchr. Inst. of Fin. Edn. chpt. 208; mem: West Visalia Kiwanis, Visalia United Methodist Ch. Commn. on Edn., Calif. Nevada Conf. of United Methodist Ch. (Ch. Expansion of Bd. of Conf. Life div.); works: developed and printed Money Management System used at sems. and counseling sessions statewide; mil: splst. 5 US Army 1966-69, GCM; Republican; Methodist; rec: tennis. Res: 7514 Stonedale Dr. Pleasanton 94566 Ofc: Gibraltar Savings, 5776 Stoneridge Mall Rd. Ste. 145 Pleasanton 94556

COLLINS, H. GENE, lawyer, b. Sept. 16, 1943, Stonega, Va.; s. Hiram and Edith (Mabe) C.; m. Karen Jo, June 13, 1964; children: Curtis b. 1965, Gene b. 1971; edn: AA, Fullerton Coll. 1971; JD, Western State Univ. 1976; admitted Calif. State Bar 1981. Career: law enforcement ofcr. Brea Police Dept., Orange County Sheriff, Los Angeles County Sheriff, 16 years; atty. prin. pvt. practice in Fullerton 1981–, spec. labor law- wrongful termination; honors: Who's Who Law Students (1976), Orange County Trial Lawyers Student of Year (1976); mem. Calif. Bar Assn., Orange County Bar Assn.; mil: cpl. USMC. Ofc: H. Gene Collins, Atty. 2201 East Chapman Ave Fullerton 92631

COLLINS, JOANNE ANITA, educator; b. Aug. 2, 1946, Chgo.; d. Elmer and Lucille (Dombrowski) C.; edn: BS in math. (highest honors Coll. of Phys. Sci.), Ill. Inst. of Tech. 1968, MBA, 1970; PhD, acctg. & info. sys., Northwestern Univ. 1976; desig: CPA, Ill. (1976), CMA (Cert. Mgmt. Acct.), NAA (1981), CCA (Cert.Cost Anal.), ICA (1984), CTA (Cert. Tax Acct.), Inst. for Cert. of Tax Profl. (1985). Career: EDP opr. Internat. Harvester, Chgo. 1965-70; finl. analyst Continental Can Co., Chgo. 1970-73; instr. Ill. Inst.of Tech., Chgo. 1968-70; economic analyst Sargent & Lundy, Chgo.1973; asst. prof. acctg. The Wharton Sch., Univ. of Pa., Phila.1976-82; current: prof. acctg. CSU Los Angeles; honors: Arthur Andersen and Co. Found. Doctoral Dissertation Fellow (1975-76), Ill.Inst. of Tech. Alumni Award for acad. achieve. (1968), Legion of Honor, Chapel of Four Chaplains, Phila. (1980), disting. service award, MENSA (1981), Outstanding Young Women of Am. (1981), study grantee Sch. of Bus. and Econs. (1984); mem: Am. Acctg.Assn., Am. Inst. CPAs, Nat.Assn. Accts. (winner 2 mss. awards at internat. conv. 1985; Author of Year, L.A. chpt.1983, 84, 85), Inst. of Mgmt. Acctg., Am.Women's Soc. of CPAs (L.A. chpt.charter), Calif. Soc. CPAs, Am. Soc.of Women Accts., Inst. of Cost Analysis; Democrat; Unitarian; rec: theatre, parapsychology. Res: 8329 Rush St Rosemead 91770 Ofc: Cal State Los Angeles 5151 State University Dr Los Angeles 90032

COLLINS, RICHARD MATTHEW, municipal compliance officer; b. July 27, 1954, Perth Amboy, NJ; s. John James and Jean Shirley (Bohlen) C.; 1 son, Christopher b. 1982; edn: AA, Antelope Valley Coll. 1977; BA, CSU Northridge 1979; Southwestern Univ. of Law 1982; Real Estate Cred., Calif. Career: admin. intern City of Lancaster 1979-80, plnng. intern 1980-81, code enforcement ofcr. 1981–; pres. Antelope Valley Council on Alcoholism and Drug Dependency, 1983-85; Antelope Valley Health Plnng. Council 1981-; recipient, Outstanding Young Men of Am., Jaycees, NY, NY 1983; mem: So. Calif. Assn. of Code Enforcement Officials, Municipal Mgmt. Assn., Am. Plnng. Assn.; Republican (pres. Antelope Valley Young Republicans 1980, ofcl. Calif. Repub. Party 1985, mem. Repub. Nat. Party Wash DC 1985); Episcopal; rec: art, music, water sports, basketball. Res: 1835 West Avenue K-10 Lancaster 93534 Ofc: City of Lancaster, 44933 No. Fern Ave. Lancaster 93534

COLLINS, ROBERT HILLIARD, III, natural resource co. president; b. May 5, 1935, Beverly Hills; s. Robt. H. and Nancy (Morgan) C.; m. Emily Ann Banks, Apr. 24, 1970; 1 dau., Jayne Mordell; edn: BS, mech. eng., Stanford Univ. 1957, Stanford Advanced Mgmt. Coll. Career: project engr. Pacific Gas & Electric, San Francisco 1957; asst. to v.p./project engr. Occidental Petroleum

Corp. and subsidiaries 1959-62; div. gen. mgr. Cyprus Oil Co., Houston 1961-63; asst. to chief ops. ofcr. Cyprus Mines Corp., Los Angeles 1964-67; pres. Collins Investments, L.A., 1967-74; pres. Inter-Tech Resources Inc., L.A., 1969-74; pres. Reserve Syn. Fuels, Signal Hill, Ca. 1974-80; pres. Getty Synthetic Fuels, Inc. (resource recovery: methane gas from landfills), Signal Hill 1980–; co-inventor Corrosion Control Process; mem: Am. Inst. Mech. Engrs., Soc. of Petroleum Engrs., Soc. of Mining Engrs.; Am. Inst. Chem. Engrs.; Stanford Alumni Assn.; clubs: Buck of Month and Block S. Orgn., Engrs. of So. Calif., Petroleum, Jonathan, Balboa Bay, Bel Air Country; mil: USNR 1957-59; rec: water sports, golf, tennis, bridge. Res: 2387 Kimridge Rd Beverly Hills 90210 Ofc: 2750 Signal Pkwy Signal Hill 90806

COLLINS, ROSEMARY L., company president; b. Jan. 24, 1932, Lincoln, Nebr.; d. Ernest L. and Henrietta M. (Vanderheiden) Litty; m. 2d Richard M. Collins (pres. Meadow Farms Foods), Nov. 7, 1981; chil.(by prev. marriage): Joseph T. Weidinger, III, b. 1953, Catherine Mary Weidinger, b. 1954; edn: CTC (Cert. Travel Counselor), Inst. of Cert. Trvl. Agts. Career: pub. rels. asst. to V.P., Hughes Tool Co., 1960-65; mgr. Visitor Relations, Litton Ship Systems, 1965-70, supr. Employee Services, Litton Ship Systems, spl. asst. to the pres., Parker Hannifin, 1970-71; mgr. Volt Tech. Corp., 1971-75; pres. Roses Int'l., 1975–; vice pres. Senor Foods (restaurant chain), 1984–; mem. 42 Whirley-Girls (internat. lic. women helicopter pilots), 1963-; mem. Civil Service Com. City of Hermosa Beach, 1973-77. Republican. rec: tennis,bridge, water-ski. Res: 3212 Walnut Ave. Manhattan Beach 90266. Ofc: Roses International 17264 Hawthorne Blvd. Torrance 90504

COLLIS, MICHAEL VINCENT, communications electronics co. owner; b. Jan. 31, 1959, Linwood; s. Carroll Eugene and Jeanie Elisibeth (Sullivan) C.; 1 dau. Kimberly b. 1984. Career: service mgr. AudioVideo Specialist, Downey 1979-82; engring. tech. Standard Communication Corp., Carson 1982-83; communications tech. San Bernardino Co. Communs. Dept., 1985–; prop. Collis Engring., 1984–; cons. to Catholic Diocese of San Bernardino Dept. Electronic Communs. (1985-); civic: vol. Pasa. Tournament of Roses Communs. (recipient annual appreciation awards for participation in parade t.v. communications, 1979-), Amateur T.V. Network (engr. 1983-), San Bernardino County Communs. Assn., Am. Radio Relay League; works: designed and built (then most powerful in state) amateur TV Relay Sys.; designed and mktd. TV down converter (1st GAaS FET 1200MHz); Republican; Catholic; rec: amateur radio, garden, airplanes. Address: Collis Engineering (POB 1594) 21678 Job's Peak Crestline 92325

COLOSIMO, FRANK L(OUIS), radio and t.v. broadcaster; b. Mar. 6, 1950, Pittsburgh, Pa.; s. Richard Louis and Colette Donna (Paillusson) C.; edn: BA, linguistics, Santa Clara Univ. 1972; spl. courses: Columbia Sch. of Bdcstg. 1972, Coll. of the Redwoods 1978, Sch. of Commun. Electronics S.F. 1978. Career: announcer, prod. KEST-radio, San Francisco 1975; KVXJ-FM Crescent City 1976; v.p. public radio sta. KFMI, Eureka 1976-77; comml. prod. freelance and for sta. KVIQ-TV, also booth announcer (ABC/ NBC) Eureka 1977-79; promotion dir., news ed. KMPH-TV, Visalia/ Fresno 1980; video tape ed. for CNN, L.A. Bureau, Robert Wold Communs., Hollywood 1981; current: bdcstr. ESPN and Metro-Media TV; comml. announcer for Video General, Long Beach, and Don Floyd Prodns., Redlands; editor KHJ-TV news dept., freelance announcer, and dir.; writer/prod./dir. "Hotspot" Italian T.V. show (1984); writer "Look to the Sky" for Tatum Communs. (1983); awards: Best News Reporting Div. A., Golden Mic Award for editing Radio-TV News Assn. of So. Calif. (1983); mem. TV Acad. of Arts & Scis.; rec: aeronautics, astronautics. Res: 4121 Wilshire Blvd #408 Los Angeles 90010

COLOVIC, DORIS, florist; b. May 31, 1954, Jellico, Tenn.; d. Kenneth Calvin and Hattie (Teague) Tolliver; m. Alex Colovic, May 4, 1978; edn: UCLA Ext. 1975-76. Career: assoc. Wisteria Florist, Sierra Madre 1972-73; co-owner, opr. Plantasia, Glendale 1973–; co-owner, opr. Twiggs, Glendale 1983–; instr. indoor plant care classes, Plantasia 1975-76; design cons., floral designer, interior plant design 1975-; mem: Los Angeles Internat. Fern Soc., Calif. Cactus Soc., US CofC; Democrat; Protestant; rec: birds, music, skiing. Res: 5315 La Forest Dr. La Canada 91011 Ofc: Plantasia, 2840 No. Verdugo Rd. Glendale 91208

COLVIN, LLOYD DAYTON, construction co. president; b. Apr. 24, 1915, Spokane, Wash.; s. George R. and Edna M. (Teeter) C.; m. Iris Atterbury, Aug. 11, 1939; 1 dau. Joy b. 1940; edn: BS, Univ. of Calif. 1938; grad. AUS Command and Gen. Staff Coll., Ft. Leavenworth, Ks. 1947; grad. Univ. of Heidelberg, Ger. 1955. Career: served to col. (ret.) US Army Signal Corps, 23 years; supvr. constrn. projects in Alaska, N.J., N.C., Calif. and Europe; currently pres. Drake Builders, Richmond, Calif.; coauthor (w. Iris Colvin) best selling Book of the Month book, How We Started Out Building Our Own Home In Our Spare Time and Went On To Make A Million Dollars in the Construction Business (Prentice Hall); rec: amateur radio. Address: Drake Builders, 5200 Panama Ave Richmond 94804

COMBS, RICHARD ENNIS, U.S. Magistrate, b. Nov. 3, 1903, Visalia; s. James Ennis and Maude (Brown) C.; m. Marjorie Pool, Dec. 23, 1933; children: Richard E., Jr. b. 1935, Elizabeth B. 1939, John b. 1940, Mary b. 1944; edn: AB, UC Berkeley 1926, JD, UC Hastings Law Sch 1931. Career: atty. law firm McClure & Combs, Visalia 1931-42; counsel to Pres. Calif. Senate, 1940-70; counsel to Speaker Calif. Assembly, 1939-41; counsel, Calif. Legis Com. on Counter-Subversive Activities, 1940-70; cons., US Commn. on Govt Security, Wash DC, and editor Commn's Report to Pres. Eisenhower, 1956-7; cons., L.A. City Bd. of Edn., 1967-70; author 14 reports on Subversive

Activities to Calif. Legis., 1945-70; US Commnr., Sequoia-Kings Cyn Nat. Parks, 1970-1; US Magistrate, Eastern Dist. Calif., 1971–; assoc. mem. English Magistrates Assn., London; secty. Nat. Council of US Magistrates, 1979-80; awards: appreciation, Calif. Senate, Am. Jewish League Against Communism, Am. Legion, DAR, US Commn. on Govt. Security; mem: Calif. Hist. Soc., Tulare Co. Hist. Soc., Book Club of Calif, Friends Bancroft Lib., Alpha Chi Rho, Phi Delta Phi frats. Republican; past chmn. Tulare Co. Dem. Central Com. Protestant. rec: collector press books and first editions. Res: 45063 N Fork Dr Three Rivers 93271 Ofc: US Magistrate, Ash Mtn, Three Rivers 93271

COMPEAN, RICHARD, health care educator; b. Sept. 21, 1945, Globe, Ariz.; s. Albert Joseph and Carmen (Quijada) C.; edn: AB, honors, Univ. San Francisco 1967; MA in English, UC Davis 1969, PhD 1973. Career: coll. English instr. UC Davis 1968-73; tng. asst. Calif. Dept. of Social Welfare, Sacramento 1973-74; tng. mgr. Calif. Public Utilities Commn., San Francisco 1974-76; senior tng. coordinator Tymshare Transaction Services (WSBA), San Francisco 1976-77; senior tng. and devel. splst. Crocker Nat. Bank, S.F. 1977; coordinator continuing profl. edn., Kaiser-Permanente Medical Care Pgm., Oakland 1978–; lectr. UC Davis Ext., S.F. Comm. Coll., Univ. San Francisco; cons. Crocker Nat. Bank, Bay Area Community Project, var. state and city agencies; mem: Organization Devel. Network, Am. Soc. for Health Manpower Edn. and Tng., Am. Soc. for Tng. and Devel. (v.p. Golden Gate chpt. 1979, newsletter editor 1976, 80-81); publs: Twelve Ways to Manage Stress, Growing Up Is (Sometimes) Hard To Do; Democrat; Roman Catholic; rec: music, running, biking. Res: 810 38th Ave San Francisco 94121 Ofc: Kaiser-Permanente, Regional HRD, 3505 Broadway Ste 1431 Oakland 94611

COMSTOCK, MARIE ALKIRE, psychotherapist; b. March 3, 1942, Point Pleasant, NJ; d. Nicholas and Lucille (Vitolo) Bilella; m. Robert Alkire, Jan. 10, 1983; children: Tammy Bevins, Angela Shama; edn: BA, UC Riverside 1978; M., Internat. Univ. Los Angeles 1984; Marriage Family and Child Counselor, Calif.; Psychological Asst., Calif. 1986. Career: substance abuse counselor My Family Inc., Riverside 1977-79; asst. adminstr. Children's Human Devel. Ctr., UC Riverside 1974-80; instr. Riverside City Coll. and child devel. EAP, Alcoholic Studies 1979–; woman's pgm. coord., counselor, outreach coord. Riverside County Mental Health, Drug Abuse Control Svcs., Riverside 1980-84; psychological asst., marriage family child counselor, Center for Active Psychology, Riverside 1981–; instr. San Bernardino Valley Coll., San Bernardino 1985–; bd. mem. Riverside Co. Coalition for Alternatives to Domestic Violence; honors: Riverside Co. Mental Health Recogn. Award 1980; Senior Ctr. Award, Corona 1982; mem: UC Riverside Steering & Task Force Commn., Riverside Co. Local Plnng. Commn., Norco/ Corona Emergency Counsel, UC Riverside Adv. Com. for the Psychology Ctr., Bus. & Profl. Women (pres. Riverside chpt. 1976); publs: articles in child abuse, spousal abuse and cross cultural bilingual research; Democrat; Catholic; rec: painting, meditation, yoga. Ofc: 7302 Magnolia Ave. Riverside 92504

CONDON, EUGENE CARL, company executive; b. Nov. 22, 1918, San Francisco; s. Michael Rea and Augusta (Koslausky) C.; m. Evelyn Jean Mandolsi, Jan. 4, 1947; children: Michael b. 1947, Caroline b. 1949, Janice b. 1951, Susan b. 1954, Diane b. 1955, Eugene, Jr. b. 1959, Thomas b. 1961; grad. Galileo H. Sch. 1937. Career: clk. Claymont Food Store, iceman Bay Cities Ice Co., driver Lowrie Paving Co., brewer Burgermeister Brewing Corp.; current: owner Condon & Sons Lumber Co., San Mateo; past pres. Ice Wagon Drivers Union Local No. 519 (1949-51); mem. Apostleship of the Sea; mil: sgt. US Army Corps of Engrs. 1942-45; Republican; Catholic. Res: 1501 Cypress Ave Burlingame 94010 Ofc: Condon & Sons Lumber Co. 117 East 25th Ave San Mateo

CONDON, STANLEY C., physician; b. Feb. 1, 1931, Glendale; s. Charles C. and Alma Mae (Chinn) C.; m. Vaneta, May 19, 1965; children: Lori b. 1965, Brian b. 1966, David b. 1967; edn: BA, La Sierra Coll. 1952; MD, Loma Linda Univ. Sch. of Med. 1956; certified Am. Bd. of Internal Med. 1968; certified subspecialty Gastroenterology 1977. Career: with Los Angeles County Gen. Hosp., intern 1956-57, res. general pathology 1959-61, attending staff 1963-65; res. internal med. White Meml. Med. Ctr., Los Angeles 1961-63; intr. med. Loma Linda Univ. Sch. of Med. 1963-65; head internal med. dept., dir. intern-res. tng. program, Manila Sanitarium & Hosp., Philippines 1965-71; chief res.-intern med. outpatient clinic Loma Linda Univ. Med. Ctr. 1972-74; Fellow gastroenterology, Barnes Hosp., Wash. Univ. Sch. of Med., St. Louis 1974-76; asst. prof. med. Loma Linda Univ. Sch. of Med. 1976–, med. dir. nutritional support svc. 1984–; mem: AMA, CMA, San Bernardino Co. Med. Soc., Inland Soc. of Internal Med. (pres. 1985), Am. Gastroenterological Assn., Am. Soc. for Parenteral & Enteral Nutrition; publs. in med. journs.; mil: capt. US Army Med. Corps 1957-59; Republican; Seventh Day Adventist; rec: trombone, choral singing, photog. Res: 11524 Ray Court Loma Linda 92354 Ofc: Loma Linda Univ. Medical Ctr., Gastroenterology Section, Loma Linda 92350

CONE, LAWRENCE ARTHUR, physician; b. Mar. 23, 1928, NY, NY; s. Max and Ruth (Weber) C.; m. Mary Osborne, Aug. 20, 1960; 1 son, Lionel A. Cone, MD; edn: AB, NY Univ. 1948; MD, Univ. of Berne, Switz. 1953. Career: intern Dallas Hosp., Dallas, Tex. 1954-55; resident in med. NY Med. Coll. and Metropolitan Hosps., NYC 1957-60; fellowship immunology & infectious diseases NYU Sch. of Med. 1960-62; asst. clin. prof. of medicine & microbiology, NY Med. Coll. 1962-65; assoc. prof. medicine NY Med. Coll. 1965-72, chief Dept. of Immunol. & Infectious Diseases 1962-72; chief of immunology, infectious disease & med. oncology Eisenhower Medical Center, Rancho Mirage, Calif. 1972–, chmn. Dept. Medicine 1976-82, pres. med. staff 1984-88; clin. assoc. prof. med. UCLA Sch. of Med. 1984-; awards: Career Scientist Health Research Council NY (1960-66); Fellow Am. Coll. of Physicians (1962), Fellow Royal Soc. of Med. (1963); club: Tamarisk Country (R.Mirage); over 50 publs. in medical jours., contbg. author 2 books; mil: capt. US Army Med. Corps 1955-57; Republican; rec: fishing, golf, hunting. Res: Palm Springs 92262 Ofc: L.A. Cone, MD, Eisenhower Medical Center Rancho Mirage 92270

CONKLIN, WARREN CRAIG, superior court judge; b. May 1, 1937, Oakland; s. Harold Wilbur and Marian Elinor (Rowe) C.; m. Lora Kuether, Apr. 4, 1964; children: Glenn b. 1967, April b. 1968, Robin b. 1970; edn: BS, Univ. Calif. 1960; JD, UC Boalt Hall 1964; admitted Calif. State Bar 1965, US Ct. of Appeals (9th Cir.), US Dist. Ct. (Central & So. Dists. Calif.) 1965. Career: dep. probation ofcr. San Luis Obispo Co. 1960-61; jr. counsel Calif. State Dept. Public Works (Div. Contracts and Rights of Way) 1964-65; assoc. of Lloyd E. Somogyi, public defender contract, San Luis Obispo 1965-66; pvt. practice of law, Atascadero, ptnr. Wright & Conklin, 1966-70, solo practice, 1970-75; judge Justice Ct. San Luis Obispo County, 1967-75, judge Municipal Ct. (presiding judge 1975, 77, 80) 1975-82; judge Superior Ct. (presiding judge 1984, 85), St. of Calif., Co. of San Luis Obispo 1982–; faculty mem. Center for Judicial Edn. and Research (CJER) 1984-86, and Calif. Coll. for Trial Judges 1974-79; mil: lance cpl. USMC 1956-58; Republican; Protestant; rec: golf, racquetball, bridge. Res: POB 998 Atascadero 93423 Ofc: Co. San Luis Obispo Rm 355 County Govt. Center, San Luis Obispo 93408

CONLEY-KOBY, THELMA P., family conciliation court mediator; b. April 26, 1920, Harrah, Okla.; d. William E. and Tressie (Perkins) Carpenter; m. Pierre Koby, May 10, 1978; children: Terri b. 1946, Wendi b. 1950; edn: Central State Coll. 1976. Career: social svc. worker San Bernardino Adoptions Svcs. 1963-79; social svc. practitioner, court ofcr. Dependency Unit-Childrens Svcs., Riverside 1979-81; family mediator Family Counciliation Court, Riverside Superior Ct. 1981–; also, pvt. practice mediation and family therapy; freq. spkr. on adoption, divorce and child custody/ visitation, mediation; mem: Calif. Assn. of Marriage & Family Therapist (Inland Empire chpt.), Calif. Chpt. Calif. Family & Conciliation Cts.; rec: organist, theatre, concerts. Res: 5168 Weymouth Way, Pilgrim Creek Estates, Oceanside 92056

CONLON, JACK MARTIN, real estate executive; b. Oct. 8, 1931, Parsons, Kans.; s. John Thomas and Alice M. C.; m. Kathi Bergman, Feb. 29, 1984; children: Lisa b. 1955, Catherine b. 1957, Julia b. 1958 (dec.), Casey b. 1985; edn: BS, Kans. Univ. 1957, grad. work USC 1957-58; lic. C.P.A., Calif. (1960). Career: CPA, Peat Marwick Mitchell, Los Angeles 1957-59, Kansas City 1960-63; pres. Coachella Valley Svgs & Loan, Palm Springs 1963-72; exec. v.p. Sunrise Co., L.A. 1972-76, pres. Sunrise Co., Palm Desert 1976–; instr. American S&L Inst. 1965, 66; pres. Tri-County Soc. Svgs & Loan Controllers 1966; listed Who's Who in Am.; civic: United Way (dir., treas. 1966-67), P.S. Conv. & Vis. Bureau (dir., treas. 1967-72), P.S. CofC (pres. 1971); Phi Kappa Psi frat.; mil: US Navy; Republican; rec: golf. Res: 70-263 Sonora Rd Rancho Mirage 92270 Ofc: 75-005 Country Club Dr Palm Desert 92260

CONMY, PETER THOMAS, city historian, librarian emeritus; b. July 8, 1901, San Francisco; s. Thomas Cherry and Mary Henrietta (Richter) C.; m. Emiliette Constance Storti, July 11, 1928; chil: (Mrs.) Constance Louise Prothero, b. 1929; Thomas Peter, b. 1934; edn: AB, UC Berkeley, 1924, MA, 1927, EdD, 1937; MA, Stanford Univ. 1941; MLS, UC Berkeley 1947; JD, Univ. of San Francisco 1952. Career: instr. San Francisco Public Schs. (tchr. Jr. High, Sr. High, Evening High), 1926-43; city librarian Oakland Pub. Library, 1943-69, ret. 1969, apptd. Librarian Emeritus and City Historian by Oakland City Council. Hist. writer on Native Sons of Golden West, Knights of Columbus, dir. Historical Reserve, 1937–; mem. Knights of Columbus (past Grand Knight), Elks (past Exalted Ruler), Am. Lib. Assn., Calif. Lib. Assn. (pres. 1961). Republican. Catholic. Res: 1066 Ardmore Ave Oakland 94610

CONN, ROSCOE IMRIE, real estate broker, general contractor, ret.; b. Aug. 11, 1915, Roseburg, Ore.; s. Henry Roscoe and Ethel Estella (Imrie) C.; m. Mona Elizabeth Sehl, Dec. 27, 1939; children: Michael b. 1941, Richard b. 1945, Gregory b. 1949; edn: BS, ag. engring., Ore. State Univ. 1939; honors cert. Ft. Ord Military (speech) 1944; spl. real estate courses, W. Valley Coll. 1979, R.E. Trainers Inc. 1982. Career: (current) broker/owner B&V Trailer and Barn Sales; gen. contr./owner B&V Constrn. Co., San Jose; (past) supr. Farm Security Adminstrn., Rural Rehab. Div., Ore., Wash. 1939-41; distbn. mgmt., Australia, for Am. equipment firm 1946-52; owner/mgr. two equip. cos., Calif. 1952–; owner Four Star Motel; honors: Alpha Zeta (Agri.), Alpha Delta Sigma (journalism), Scabbard & Blade (mil.); mem. Australian mem. Nat. Fgn. Trade Council of NY 1949-51; Calif. St. CofC 1954-65; San Jose CofC; Elks; BSA scoutmaster; patent: for reverse- Ford Tractors 1953; mil: capt. US Army in S.W. Pacific, 1941-46 (Papaun Medal, S.W.P.A. Medal, Exp. Rifle, spl. commendn. Maj. Gen. H.H. Fuller); Catholic; rec: golf, hunting, fishing. Res: 14795 La Rinconada Dr Los Gatos 95030 ofc: B&V Trailer and Barn Sales, B&V Construction Co., 10000 Monterey Rd San Jose 95037

CONNELL, RICHARD CURTIS, real estate broker; b. Dec. 8, 1926, St. Paul, Minn.; s. John Thomas and Hildur Linnea (Johnson) C.; m. Juno Mc Mannis, April 20, 1952 (dec. June 1978); m. 2d Judith Grady, May 31, 1980; children: Kathleen, b. 1953, Susan, b. 1956, Brian, b. 1959; edn: UC Berkeley 2 yrs. Career: sales mgr. Moore- Vieth Realtors, Santa Rosa 1971-75; owner- broker Dick Connell Realtor, Santa Rosa 1975–; honors: life mem. Million Dollar Club, Realtor of Year Sonoma Co. Bd. Realtors 1978; mem: Sonoma Co. Bd. Realtors (dir. 6 yrs., pres.); Calif. Assn. Realtors (dir. 6 yrs.); Nat. Assn. Realtors; Sonoma Co. MLS; Santa Rosa Babe Ruth Baseball (mgr., bd. dirs.);

Cardinal Newman H.S. (past pres. Men's Assn., past pres. Bd. Regents); race horse breeder; mil: sgt. US Army 1944-46; Republican; Catholic; rec: horse racing, golf, sports. Res: 382 Irwin Ln., Santa Rosa 95404 Ofc: Dick Connell Realtor, 539 E St., Santa Rosa 95404

CONNOLLY, RICHARDINE JOY, manufacturing co. executive; b. Mar. 10, 1922, Hornell, N.Y.; d. Archie Albert and Laura May (Lockwood) Pierce; m. Paul J. Connolly, Sr. (dec.), Mar. 11, 1967; children: Larry M. Burns b. 1946, Patrick L. Burns b. 1949, Shelly I. Fabian b. 1952; edn: Kentfield Coll. 1939-40; RN, Franklin Hosp. Sch. of Nsg., 1940-43. Career: staff nurse, asst. hd. nse. Franklin Hosp., San Francisco 1943-44; Veni sectionist, unit hd. nse. American Red Cross Blood Bank, Los Angeles and San Francisco, 1944-45; RN, var. hosps. and medical offices, Pasadena, Alhambra and Whittier, 1945-67; United Ad Label Co. Inc., Santa Fe Springs 1967−, corp. pres. 1982−, research and devel. line of pressure sensitive labels for the medical profession; Am. Red Cross instr. Healthcare 1949-57, ARC disaster nursing 1970-75; mem: Medical Mktg. Assn. (1975-), Presbyterian Intercommunity Hosp. Found. (bd. dirs. 1983-87), CofC (Whittier, Santa Fe Springs), Soroptomist Internat., Am. Business Womens Assn.; Republican; Catholic; rec: crafts, travel, family. Res: 15937-A Alta Vista Dr La Mirada 90638 Ofc: United Ad Label Co. Inc. 10035 S. Greenleaf Santa Fe Springs 90670

CONNOR, WESLEY NEALE, insurance broker; b. Feb. 20, 1950, Pittsburgh, Pa.;. s. W. Neale and Jacqueline Jane (Hilbert) C.; m. Sally Linda Cook, Aug. 12, 1978; edn: BS commun., Ohio Univ. 1972; MBA, Ohio State Univ. 1975; desig: Cert. Ins. Counselor (1978), LUTC (1977). Career: sales rep. Procter & Gamble Distbg. Co., Pittsburgh 1972-74; ins. agent James E. Black & Assocs., Inc., Columbus, Ohio 1975-78, v.p. Black & Connor Ins. Agcy. Inc., 1978-82; agt./broker Nationwide Ins. Co., Orange 1983-86; pres. Connor Finl. Services Inc., Garden Grove 1986−; bd. dirs. Profl. Ins. Agents Assn., Columbus, O. 1980-81; awards: Chairman's Award, Ohio Ins. Inst. (1981), Pres.'s Conf. and Circle of Excellence (1985, 86), Life Exec. Award (1986), Nationwide Ins. Co.; mem. Sigma Chi frat., Ohio Univ. Alumni Assn., Ohio State Univ. Alumni Assn.; civic: US Olympic Organizing Com. (tv & media rels. com. 1982-84); Republican; rec: golf, swim, travel. Ofc: Connor Financial Services Inc 11602 Knott St Ste 12 Garden Grove 92641

CONNORS, DONALD ROBERT, financial consultant; b. Dec. 7,1940, Steubenville, Ohio; s. Joseph and Lois Elizabeth (Still) C.; edn: BS, Muskingum Coll. 1962; MBA, Indiana Univ. 1965; postgrad., Purdue Univ. 1964, New York Univ. Grad. Sch. of Bus. 1969-71; Cert. Data Processor, Data Processing Mgmt. Assn. 1966; Cert. Fin. Analyst, Inst. of Cert. Fin. Analysis 1975. Career: tech. staff Mitre Corp., Wash. DC 1967-69; security analyst College Retirement Equities Fund, NY, NY 1969-70; securities analyst Standard & Poor's Intercapital, NY, NY 1971-72; investment ofcr. Marine Bank, Milwaukee, Wisc. 1973-77; mgr. fin. analysis Texas Instruments Watch Div., Midland, Texas 1978; senior fin. analyst U.S. Leasing, San Francisco 1979-80; pgm. control adminstr. FMC Corp., San Jose 1980-86; currently, cons. to smallbus.; honors: Signa Pi Sigma. Address: San Jose 95111

CONNORS, RAY, communications counselor, writer; b. Aug. 26, 1908, Great Barrington, Mass; s. Michael W. and Agnes (Quigley) C.; m. Jeannette Couture, 1939; children: Michele b. 1940, Andree b. 1942, Stacie b. 1958; edn: BA, Univ. Notre Dame, 1931. Career: journalist, New England, 1931-41; airline pub. relations, 1941-48; publicity mgr. Lockheed Aircraft, 1950; pub. rels. dir. Stromberger, LaVene & MacKenzie, 1958; v.p. and West Coast pub. rels. mgr. D'Arcy-MacManus & Masius, Inc., to 1973; pres. TheRayConnorsCompany, Inc., 1973−. Honors: pres. Los Angeles Public Relations Counselors; chmn. bd. advisors Mount St. Mary's Coll.; hon. life mem. and pub. rels. counselor Calif. Mortgage Bankers Assn.; guest lectr. Calif. State Colleges; Achievement Award, So. Calif. Mortgage Bankers Assn. Author, num. essays pub. in general periodicals. Republican. Catholic. Rec: travel, golf. Res: 22766 Tolana Dr. Laguna Niguel 92677

CONOVER, ROBERT WARREN, librarian; b. Oct. 6, 1937, Manhattan, Kans.; s. Robert Warren and Grace Darline (Grinstead) C.; edn: BA, Kansas State Univ. 1969; MA, Univ. Denver 1961. Career: librarian, supervising librarian County of Fresno, 1961-66; county librarian County of Yolo, Woodland 1967-68; dir. City of Fullerton Public Library, 1968-73, City of Pasadena Public Library, 1973-80; Palos Verdes Library Dist., P.V. Peninsula 1980−; mem: ALA, Orange County Library Assn. (pres. 1971), Spl. Libraries Assn., Calif. Library Assn. (pres. Yosemite chpt. 1965, mem. Council 1981), Libraria Sodalitas (dir. 1981), Santiago Library System Council (pres. 1972), Palos Verdes CofC, Rancho de los Palos Verdes Hist. Soc. (bd. dirs. 1981), University Club (Pasadena), Rotary, past pres. Fresno Jaycees (1963), Pi Kappa Alpha; Republican; Episcopal. Ofc: 650 Deep Valley Dr., Palos Verdes Peninsula 90274

CONOVER, WILLIAM GARDNER, financial executive; b. April 25, 1923, Long Branch, NJ; s. Charle Cox and Marjorie (Gardner) C.; m. Miriam McCormack, Aug. 14, 1948; children: Matthew b. 1951, Douglas b. 1953, Christine b. 1959, Laura b. 1961; edn: BSME, UC Berkeley 1950, MBA, 1951; desig: reg. Tax Preparer, Calif. lic. Real Estate Broker, reg. prin. NASD, Chartered Life Underwriter (CLU), Cert. Finl. Planner (CFP). Career: salesman to v.p. var. finl. and indsl. cos., 1951-, currently pres. Conover & Co. Inc. (fmr. Coordinated Financial Programs) spec. in finl. estate, tax and bus. planning services, Lafayette; awards: Agency Man of Year, Nat. Quality Award, 1st Place in Securities and Ins. Plnng.; mem. Estate Planning Council of the East Bay, Internat. Assn. Finl. Plnnrs., Nat. Assn. of Realtors, Am. Soc.

CLUs, Rotary; mil: US Navy, So. Pacific, D.F.C. (2), Air Medal (6); Republican; Protestant. Res: 24 Dolores Way Orinda 94563 Ofc: Conover & Co. Inc., 925 A Village Center Lafayette 94549

CONSOLACION, FRANCO HERMINIA, accountant, college professor; b. Dec. 11, 1938, Baguio City, Philippines; s. Jose de los Santos and Coleta Sanchez (Herminia) C.; m. Ma. Lourdes S. Ancheta, May 14, 1966; children: Franco, Jr. b. 1969, Rosavilla b. 1969, Garry b. 1972; edn: BBA acctg., Univ.of the East Manila, Phil. 1962; MBA acctg., Univ. Philippines 1967; LLB, Univ. of the East 1973; MBA fin. mgmt., John F. Kennedy Univ. 1977; CPA Calif., Phil.; Lifetime Coll. Tchg. Credl. Calif. Career: finance mgr. Republic Flour Mills Inc. Manila 1964-67; senior ptnr. Consolacian & Espiritu CPAs Manila 1966-73; senior bank examiner Central Bank of Phil. Manila 1967-73; senior acct. UC San Francisco 1973-81; instr. City Coll. S.F. 1978-80; profl. lectr. Grad. Sch. Bus. Golden Gate Univ. 1981-82; mgr. C&C Profl. Cons. S.F. 1981-82; pres. Consolacion & Partible CPAs Inc. S.F. 1982−; honors: 5th in Phil. CPA exam, First Place short story writing contest (1960), Public Svc. Award Phil. Consulate of S.F. (1981), Most Outstanding Filipino Acct., Supv. Carol Ruth Silver S.F. (1981), Leadership awards (Filipino Assts. Assn. 1980, 82), commendns. Calif. Bd. Accountancy (1983), Calif. Legislature (1983), Assy. Willie L. Brown Jr. (1983), Bd. Supvs. City & Co. of S.F. (1981), Top Awardee Fil-Ams. of No. Calif. (1984), appreciation Fil-Am Council of S.F. for comm. leadership (1986); mem: Am. Inst. CPAs, Soc. Calif. Accts., Filipino Accts. Assn. (founder, pres.), Fil.-Ams. of Contra Costa (auditor), Cong. of Fil.-Am. Citizens (regl. dir.), Fil.-Am. Council of S.F. (bd.), K.C., US Jaycees, Fil. Am. Democratic Club; publ: Multi-National Corps.: How They Affect the Econ., Pol. and Social Devel. of the Philippines (1977); Democrat; Catholic; rec: bowling, shooting, fishing. Res: 1835 Hoke Ct Pinole 94564 Ofc: Consolacion & Partible CPAs Inc. 833 Market St Ste 510 San Francisco 94103

CONTRERAS, ALEJANDRO, lawyer; b. Feb. 26, 1949, Mexico City, U.S. citizen 1965; s. Ildelfonso and Alicia (Salazar) C.; m. Ruth S. Contreras, Nov. 16, 1985; 1 dau: Marisol Teresa b. 1981; edn: BS, St. Mary's Coll. 1972; JD, Univ. of Santa Clara 1975; certified court interpreter, State of Calif. 1979. Career: atty. supvr. Community Legal Services, San Jose 1975-79; pres. Law Offices of Alejandro Contreras, Law Corp., San Jose 1979−; teaching asst. Council in Legal Ednl. Opportunities 1974-75; bd. dirs. Community Legal Services 1984-85, San Jose Day Nursery 1981; awards: Cesar Chavez Community Leadership Award 1971-72, Community Leadership award 1974-75; mem: Am., Calif., Santa Clara County (Personal Injury, Immigration Law sects.) bar assns., Am., Calif., Santa Clara County Trial Lawyers Assns., Nat. La Raza Lawyers Bar Assn. (chair Profl. Growth Com. 1978), San Jose Mexican-Am. CofC; past mem. La Raza Students Assn. (pres. 1973-74, editor Chicano Students Jour. 1970-71), St. Mary's Coll. Chicano Students Theatre Group; Independent; Christian; rec: theater, swimming, x-c and water ski, karate. Res: San Jose Ofc: Alejandro Contreras, Law Corp. 28 N First St, Ste 500, San Jose 95113

CONWAY, BILL E., radio show producer, business owner; b. Aug. 1, 1941, Handford, Calif.; s. Forrest and Maggie (Foyle) C.; m. Lola, Oct. 10, 1983; children: Sharon b. 1955, David b. 1963, Danwyn b. 1965; edn: B. Theol., L.I.F.E. Coll. 1964; BA, CSU Long Beach 1967. Career: founder seven businesses 1960−; currently producer Hollywood network radio talk show Great People Who Are Changing the World; pres. TPIC Corp.; profl. musician; honors: Letter of Commdn. (Pres. Jimmy Carter); publ: on business principles; mil: USN 1963; Democrat; Protestant; rec: flying, art, music, writing, sacred singing. Ofc: POB 11400 Costa Mesa 92627

COOGAN, JOHN LESLIE (JACKIE), actor; b. Oct. 26, 1914, Los Angeles; s. John Henry and Lillian Rita (Dolliver) C.; m. Dorothea Odetta Hanson, May 27, 1950; children: John Anthony, Joann Dolliver, Leslie Diane (Franklin), Christopher Fenton; edn: stu. Santa Clara Univ. 1931-32, USC, 1933-34. Career: appeared in num. motion pictures, 1916−, incl. Skinner's Baby, 1916, The Kid, 1919, The Actress, 1953, Fine Madness, 1965, Shakiest Gun In The West, 1967, Rogues Gallery, 1967, Little Sister, 1968, Marlo, 1968; appeared on num. TV shows, 1947−, incl. Playhouse 90, 1955, Studio One, 1956, Johnny Carson, 1965, Mike Douglas, 1965, Regis Philbin, 1966, Les Crane, 1966, Joey Bishop Show, 1967, U Don't Say, 1967, Truth or Consequences, 1967, Woody Woodbury, 1967, Name of the Game, 1968, 69, 70, Red Skelton, 1970, Jeanie, 1970, Julia, 1970, The Interns, 1970, Partridge Family, 1970, Stump the Stars, 1970, Barefoot in the Park, 1970, Matt Lincoln, 1970, This Is Your Life, 1977, Adams Family, 1977, Hawaii 50 and San Francisco Beat, 1970s; appeared on t.v. series Cowboy G-Men, 1951-53, McKeever and Colonel, 1960s, Addams Family, 1963-65; appeared in stage plays Blue Denim, 1969, Come Blow Your Horn, 1969; toured US and Europe with Donald O'Connor, 1950; toured US with Ted Cassidy, summer stock 1963-65; awards: Papal medal Pope Pius 10th, 1924, Order of King George (Greek Govt.) 1924, Justinian Cross, Greek Orthodox Ch., 1924; mem. Screen Actors Guild, AFTRA, Am. Guild Variety Artists, Equity, Acad. Motion Picture and TV Arts and Scis., WWII Glider Pilots Assn., 1st Air Commandos, Star of Burma Assn.; author: Jackie Coogan Child Labor Law (1937); mil: USAAF 1941-45, CBI, decorated D.F.C. Air medal. Res: Palm Springs Ofc: c/o Kitty Davis Publicist, P.O. Box 1305, Hollywood 90028

COOK, DANIEL STEVEN, dentist; b. July 16, 1944, Dallas, Texas; s. Robert Leland and Fanny Agnes (Hoot) C.; m. Cheryl L., June 9, 1967; children: Cheri Suzanne b. 1970, Steven Daniel b. 1973, David Ryan b. 1977; edn: BS biol., Abilene Christian Univ. 1967; DDS, Loma Linda Univ. 1977; lic. dentist, Calif. (1978), Texas (1978). Career: founder/owner dental pvt. practice, Solvang 1978-83, Santa Maria Dental Group, Santa Maria 1983—; honors: Danforth Found. "I Dare You" award (1962); mem: Am. Dental Assn., Calif. Dental Assn. (Cal-D-PAC chmn. 1981-82), Central Coast Dental Soc. (pres. 1983-84), Acad. of Gen. Dentistry, Am. Acad. of Implant Dentistry; civic: Noontime Kiwanis, Santa Maria CofC; mil: E5 US Army 1967-69, Vietnam, Bronze Star, Meritorious Service; Republican; Ch. of Christ; rec: photog., hiking. Res: 3818 Lisa Way Santa Maria 93455 Ofc: 725 S Broadway Santa Maria 93454

COOK, RICHARD DANA, engineering executive; b. Aug. 1, 1930, Salt Lake City, Utah; s. A. Keate and Pauline (Boucher) C.; m. Lawrene B. Cook, Nov. 3, 1950; children: Danise b. 1957, Patrice b. 1962, Elyse b. 1967; edn: BS in physics, Univ. Utah 1951, postgrad. work 1952-44. Career: senior systems analyst Mitre Corp., Burlington, Mass.; research dept. mgr. Electronics Corp. of Am., Cambridge, Mass.; prin. research scientist AVCO Everett Res. Labs., Everett, Mass.; senior engring. splst. Aerojet Electra Systems, Azusa, Calif.; senior staff to laboratory mgr. TRW, Redondo Beach; current: senior pgm. mgr. LORAL EOS, Pasadena; pres. La Zap, Inc. (laser engring. & cons.); instr. Laser Fundamentals & Laser Safety; honors: Sigma Pi Sigma physics hon. soc. (1955); mem: IEEE (computer sect.), SPIE (founding mem.), LIA, SMPTE, ISA, Optical Soc. of So. Calif.; civic: Claremont Schs. (advisory bd.); inventions: Fission product monitor (1957), Laser cutting head (1982), Laser beam diagnostic system (1983); mil: yeoman 3c US Navy 1951-53; Republican; Prot.; rec: computer scis., cabinetry. Res: 2614 N Sweetbriar Dr Claremont 91711 Ofc: LORAL 300 N Halstead St Pasadena 91109

COOK, ROBIN ELLEN, commercial and industrial real estate; b. Oct. 11, 1945, Lennox, Calif.; d. Wm. Walter Joseph and Rose (Leibovitz) Cook; edn: grad. South H.S., Torrance 1963; study year, Geo. Wash. Univ. Career: staff US Information Service, New Delhi, India, Brussels, Belgium, and Belgrade, Yugoslavia 1969-77, USIA study grantee 1975-6; ins. broker spec. in Fine Arts Ins., Los Angeles 1977-82; interior decorator Interiors by Robin, Marina Del Rey, 1983-84; Sanjo Investments 1985—; Republican. Address: Sanjo Investments 4040 Del Rey Ave Ste 1 Marina Del Rey 90292

COOK, WILLIAM ROBERT, business counsultant; b. March 4, 1925, Sacramento; s. George Barker and Albentina (Nuenke) C.; m. Jeanne, Feb. 14, 1947; children: David b. 1949, Robert b. 1953; edn: UC Berkeley 1943; Univ. of Redlands 1944-45; USMC Schs. 1945, 1950; Internat. Corres. Schs. 1951-52; Iternat.Accts. Soc. 1967; Tax Preparer, Calif. Career: asst. mgr. Gilmore Fabricators Inc. 1951-55; secty., dir. S & R Engineering Inc. 1955-60; pres., dir. Wilco Engineering Inc. 1960-67; self. empl. tax svc. 1967-69; controller, corp. secty. Lectriks Inc. 1969-76; self. empl. bus. cons. 1976—; corp. secty., dir. Miller & Jones Inc.; Design Electric, gen. ptr. C & M Enterprises and The Bridge Group; mem: Nat. Assn. of Tax Consultors, Calif. Tax Profls., Circle of Friends Children's Hosp., Nat. Acad. of Scis., Masonic Lodge, Rossmoor Golf Club; mil: 1st lt. USMCR 1943-46, 1950-51; Republican (Calif. & Nat. Com.); Presbyterian (inactive elder); rec: golf, travel. Ofc: Walnut Creek 94595

COOKE, JONATHAN EDWARD, hotel industry executive; b. June 21, 1924, Spokane, Wash.; s. Jonathan Edward and Doris DeAngeles (Aldrich) C.; m. Virginia Paul, Aug. 13, 1949 (decd.); children: Victoria Ann b. 1954, Jonathan b. 1957 (decd.); edn: psychol., Univ. Wash. 1946-50; Seattle Univ. 1948-49. Career: var. sales positions Milwaukee RR, Pacific Northern Airlines, Japan Air Lines; regl. sales dir. Sheraton Hotels Internat., Fred Harvey Hotels; nat. & internat. sales mgr. Sheraton Hotels, AMFAC Hotels; gen. mgr. 6 hotels Wash., Ore., Calif.; nat. sales Hawaii Visitors Bureau, Tucson Convention Bureau, pres., exec. dir. Bay Plaza Mgmt. Corp. Concord; instr. hotel sales S.F. Coll., Tucson Jr. Coll., lectr. sales, mgmt.; mem: Hotel Sales Mgmt. Assn. (past v.p., pres.), Internat. Brotherhood of Magicians, Soc. Am. Magicians (past pres.); publ: articles for profl. and trade assns. and clubs; mil: US Army 1943-46; Christian; rec: magic, oil painting, high country camping. Address: 1803 Manzanita Dr Concord 94519

COOKE, JOSEPHINE GLORIA, mortgage banking executive; b. May 5, 1931, Phila.; d. Harry E. and Marion Eletha (Teal) C.; 1 dau. Tracey Marion b. 1955; edn: Virginia Union Univ. 1951-53; Cheyney State Teachers Coll. 1953-55; mortgage banking, Northwestern Univ. Sch. of Mortgage Banking 1973. Career: tchr. Phila. Bd. of Edn. 1965-67; v.p. The Colwell Co. L.A. 1969-83; senior v.p. Cypress Financial Corp. Pasadena 1983—; instr. Calif. Mortgage Banking Sch. L.A. 1983-84; honors: Cert. of Achievement (Leadership Luncheon III L.A. 1983), Svc. Award (City of L.A. 1983); mem: Mortgage Bankers Assn. of Am. 1976-, Calif. Mortgage Bankers Assn. 1983-, Zonta Club of L.A. 1976-, 10th Dist. Women's Steering Com. of L.A., Mid-City CofC; Democrat; Protestant; rec: dressmaking, machine knitting, music. Ofc: Cypress Financial Corp. 94 S Los Robles Ave Ste 350 Pasadena 91101

COOKE, RALPH WILLIAM, III, graphic designer/illustrator; b. May 6, 1953, Eauclair, Wis.; s. Ralph Wm., Jr. and Margaret (Flanders) C.; m. Kay Evans, Oct. 6, 1984; edn: Monterey Penin. Coll. 2 yrs.; Illustrators and designers workshop: Paris 1980, Monterey 1981; AIGA Nat. Design conv.: MIT Boston 1985, Aspen Design Conf. 1985, Stanford Design Conf. 1986. Career: illustr., graphic artist Naval Postgraduate Sch., 1974-79; art dir. Monterey Life Mag., 1979-82; corporate art dir. Cambridge Plan Internat., 1982-83; prin./ creative dir. Cooke Graphic Arts (communication design spec. in printed mats.), 1983—; honors: 3 Maggie (nat. award for magazine design) awards, 42 awards, Monterey Bay Ad Club (11 in 1986), named Art Dir. of Year (1985), illustrations included in num. fine art collections i.e. Original in Ansel Adams Archives; founding pres. PiCA (People in Comm. Arts) non-profit design orgn. (1984-); mem. Am. Inst. of Graphic Arts, Graphic Artist Guild, STA, Monterey Bay Ad Club, Am. Advt. Assn.; civic: CofC, support var. local charities; works: illustr. children's book: What is a California Sea Otter; won Willis White Award for best designed Kite; Republican; rec: golf, travel. Address: POB 8747 NPS Monterey 93943

COOMBS, KEVIN CHASE, lawyer; b. Sept. 13, 1955, Los Angeles; s. Richard Holt and Gale (Chase) C.; m. Leslie Marie Kenyon, Mar. 30, 1984; div.; 1 son, Randal Kenyon; edn: AA, Santa Monica City Coll. 1975; AB, UC Los Angeles 1977; JD, Southwestern Univ. Sch. of Law 1980; admitted Calif. State Bar, US Ct. of Internat. Trade (1982), US Ct. of Claims (1982), US Ct. of Custom and Patent Appeals, US Ct. of Mil. Appeals. Career: law clerk Butler & Davidson, Beverly Hills 1977-78; Lipman, Saltzburg & Star, Encino 1978; Karno & Schwartz, Encino 1978-81; atty. law firm Edward J. Seltzer, Beverly Hills 1981; atty. prin. Kevin C. Coombs, Culver City 1981—; dir. Am. Certified Toner Inc. (1976-77), Sturdee Mfg. Co. Inc. (1973-81); speaker on constrn. law, 1981-; honors: 1st Pl. statewide legal debate, Santa Monica Coll. (1975), courthouse finalist Moot Ct. Southwestern Univ. Sch. of Law (1978), Phi Kappa Psi (1975), Phi Alpha Delta (1978); mem: Calif. Trial Lawyers Assn., ABA, L.A. Co. Bar Assn., Culver City Bar Assn. (v.p. 1984), L.A. Trial Lawyers Assn., Assn. of Trial Lawyers of Am., Culver City Bd. Realtors (1983), UCLA Alumni Assn. (chmn. UCLA House of Horrors 1976, 77, alumni advisor UCLA Mardi Gras 1978-), Culver City CofC, Culver City Exchange Club (1982-84), Jaycees, Elks; clubs: C.C. Brigade (1982-), Pineapple Isle Yacht; Republican; Presbyterian; rec: tennis, scuba, equestrian. Ofc: 11101 Washington Blvd Culver City 90232

COOMES, GERALDINE SAWYER, educator; b. Mar. 20, 1935, San Francisco; d. Albert Pierce and Margaret (Bird) Sawyer; m. Joseph E. Coomes, Jr., June 17, 1955, div. 1985; children: Bryan b. 1960, Harlan b. 1961; edn: AA, Santa Rosa Jr. Coll. 1954; AB with honors, Sacto. State Coll. 1960, grad. work 1965; Univ. of La Verne 1981; Calif. Tchg. Cred. (gen. K-8) 1960. Career: recreation dir. County of Sonoma, Santa Rosa 1954, playground dir. City of Berkeley 1955, clk. Registrar's ofc. UCB 1955-58; substitute tchr. Sacto. Unified Sch. Dist. 1967-69, San Juan U.S.D., Sacto. 1968-71, Elk Grove U.S.D. 1980-84, Sacto. County Office Edn. (3 dists.) 1985-86; apptd. Sacto. County Office of Voter Reg. & Elections (judge 1964-79, supr. election bd. 1980-85); awards: 3d pl./named Miss Personality, Miss Sonoma County comp. (1953); civic: mgr. singing group The Mockingbirds (vol. entertain nsg. homes), PTA (pres. Thos. Jefferson Elem. 1967-68); club: College Greens Swim & Racquet; publs: World of Poetry Anthols. (1983, 84, 85, 86), Golden Poet Award (1985, 86); Democrat; Presbyterian; rec: bowl in 3 leagues, feed wild sparrows. Res: 8322 Citadel Way Sacramento 95826

COOPER, ALLEN OWEN, administrative law judge; b. May 31, 1913, Norfolk, Nebr.; s. Charles Edwin and Mona Hazel (Owens) C.; m. Mary Badertscher, Apr. 3, 1943; children: Barbara b. 1944, Robert b. 1948, Mary b. 1951; m. 2d. Patten Parsons, Feb. 16, 1985; edn: BA, Grinnell Coll. 1935; LLB (JD), Harvard Univ. 1938 (69); admitted Calif. State Bar 1939; US Administrv. law Judge, US Dept. HEW 1973. Career: pvt. law practice in Los Angeles 1939-41; junior counsel State Dept. Employment, Sacto. 1941-42; meterologist US Army Air Corps in U.S. and India, 1942-46; referee Unemployment Ins. Appeals Bd., Sacto. 1946-49; var. legal positions with state agencies, Sacto. 1950-58, referee Workers Compensation Appeals Bd., Sacto. 1958-73; adminstrv. law judge US Govt., Sacramento, Calif. and Peoria, Ill., 1973-79, ret.; small pvt. law practice, 1979-; honors: Phi Beta Kappa (1934); mem. Calif. State Bar Assn. (1939-), Federal Adminstrv. Law Judges Conf. (1978-), Soc. of Mayflower Descendants (Calif. pres. 1983-84), United Christian Centers, Sacto. (pres. 69-70), So. Sacto. Lions Club (pres. 78-79), SAR, Harvard Club (Sacto.), Comstock Club; publs: editor The California Mayflower (1983-85); author History of Westminster Presbyterian Church 1856-1966 (1966); compiled California Public Welfare Decisions (2 vols. 1957); mil: tech. sgt. Air Corps US Army 1942-46; Republican; Presbyterian; rec: fishing, bowling. Res: 6081 Holstein Way Sacramento 95822

COOPER, JOSEPH, lawyer, realtor; b.Dec. 20, 1937, Hemingway, S.C.; s. Harmon and Mary (McCutcheon) C.; 1 son, Kenneth b. 1962; edn: JD, McGeorge Sch of Law 1969. Career: attorney at law, owner and pres. Joseph Cooper Law Corp., 1970—, corp. pres. since 1980; realtor, owner Cooper Real Estate Service, 1965—; honors: recipient Resolution of Calif. Legislature, 1971, and City of Sacramento, 1972, for community activities; mem: Calif. State Bar, Sacramento Co. Bar Assn., Calif. Trial Lawyers Assn., Nat. Bar Assn., Am. Trial Lawyers Assn.; mil: E-4 US Army 1960-62; Democrat; Methodist; rec: movies, travel, sports. Res: 23 Sail Ct Sacramento 95831. Ofc: Joe Cooper Law Corp., 901 H St Ste 403 Sacramento 95814

COOPER, JOSEPH JOHN, advertising sales representative; b. Aug. 19, 1954, Long Beach, Calif.; s. Ben Z. and Geneva Marie (Gee) C.; m. Rosemarie A., Aug. 13, 1977; children: Brian b. 1981, Andrew b. 1983; edn: BS bus. adminstrn., CSU Long Beach 1980; reg. rep. NYSE 1980. Career: acct. exec. Dean Witter Reynolds Inc. Long Beach 1980-81, Bateman Eichler, Hill Richards, Inc. 1981-86; advt. sales rep. GTE Directories Sales Corp. L.A. 1986—; honors: Beta Gamma Sigma (CSULB 1978); mem: Masons (marshal); rec: golf, jogging. Ofc: GTE Directories Sales Corp. Los Angeles 90040

COOPER, LARRY MORRIS, corporate marketing executive; b. Oct. 16, 1947, Durant, Okla.; s. Morris L. and Alice Joyce (Pearson) C.; m. Deborah Galbraith, Dec. 22, 1973; children: Christopher b. 1976, Michael b. 1978, Matthew b. 1982; edn: BBA mktg., Univ. Okla. 1969. Career: brand mgr. Austin Reed Div., Hartmarx Corp., Chgo. 1969-76; v.p. sales, mktg. Workwear

Corp., Cleveland, O. 1977-80; v.p. sales, mktg. Barco of Calif., Gardena 1980-84; sr. v.p. sales, mktg. Brookhurst Inc., Los Angeles 1985– ; mem. Nat. Assn. of Uniform Mfrs., Am. Mgmt. Assn.; civic: City of Santa Ana Personnel Board (chmn.) and Econ. Devel. Commn., Bowers Mus. (bd.), Nat. Geographic Soc., Smithsonian Soc., Little League of Am.; Democrat; Christian; rec: golf, tennis, softball. Res: 2713 N Lowell Santa Ana 92706 Ofc: Brookhurst Inc 3751 S Hill St Los Angeles 90007

COOPER, MICHELE MARIE, company president; b. Jan. 20, 1948, Muskegon, Mich.; d. Russell L., Sr. and Betty Jean (Lightfoot) Cooper; edn: cert. Healds Bus. Coll. 1971; spl. courses, communications, CSU Long Beach, CSU Fullerton. Career: freelance secretarial svc. var. aircraft cos., 1971-78, Haladay Publs., 1978-81; self-empl. owner/pres. Speedy Fingers Inc. (spec. in writing, typing & printing brochures, fliers, mailings, etc.) 1981– , and Aurora, Unlimited (consulting, pub. rels.), 1983– ; artist's rep.; advtg. cons. Metamorphoses Mag.; coauthor (w/Russ Cooper) The Family Cooper (pub. Aurora, Unltd. 1983), The One-Minute Los Angeles Ticket Guide (6/84); sev. books in progress; honors: listed in Daily Pilot (newspaper), Saluting Orange Coast's Women in Business (1983), hon. mention Secty. of the Yr., KWIZ-FM; mem: NOW; WIM; The Network; Summit; Calif. Emerging Artists; Artists Helping Artists; Cetacean Soc.; Romance Writers Assn.; Group W Cable Club (Fullerton); Hospice Ever Health In-Home Care (steering com., vol.); Battered Women (secty. 1981); World Vision; Jerry Lewis Muscular Distrophy Flashtype Telethons; mil: YN3, yeoman/Pentagon, US Navy 1967-70, Vietnam War medal; Republican; rec: writing, photog., crafts. Ofc: Fullerton Finl. Towers, 1440 N. Harbor Blvd, Ste. 800, Fullerton 92635

COOPER, SHERRIE JUNE, head injury center director; b. May 15, 1953, Olympia, Wash.; d. John Grant and Shirley Mae (Strunk) Dotson; m. Ira Cooper, April 9, 1978; 1 dau: Shifra b. 1985; edn: BS, Univ. of Oregon 1977; MS, Adelphi Univ. 1980; Speech Language Pathologist. Career: language speech pathologist Lincoln Co. Sch. Dist. 1977-78; mobile hearing, screening asst. Adelphi Univ. 1979-80; head speech language pathologist Easter Sea Soc., Eugene, Ore. 1980-83; exec. dir., co-founder, pres. Ctr. for Neuro Ednl. Therapies Inc., Eugene, Ore. 1982-84; dir. Residential Head Injury Ctr., Northridge Hosp., Northridge 1984– ; tutor learning disabled pupils; mem. T.G.I. Care, Philanthropy; honors: Outstanding Young Women of the Year, 1982; mem: Am. and Ore. Speech & Hearing Assns., Nat. and So. Calif. Head Injury Founds., Mounted Assistance Unit of State of Calif. Park Sys.; rec: flying, weaving, equestrian. Res: 15034A Varsity St. Moorpark 93021 Ofc: Northridge Medical Center, 18300 Roscoe Blvd. Northridge 91328

COOPERMAN, STEVEN G., physician, eye surgeon; b. Mar. 3, 1942, NY; s. Nathan and Pearl (Dardick) C.; m. Nancy Graef, Oct. 22, 1983; children: Jacki b. 1969, Kelly b. 1972; edn: BS, UC Berkeley 1962; MD, Northwestern Med. Sch. 1966. Career: intern, res., ophthalmology, UCLA 1966-67, 1969-72; chief res. eye surgery Jules Stein Eye Inst. 1972; Food & Drug Admin., Wash. DC 1967-69; founder Am. Intraocular Implant Soc. 1974; tchg. staff Jules Stein Eye Inst., UCLA; currently, eye surgeon, Beverly Hills; dir. Ulta Med. Devices, Inc.; cons. in lens implant field, num. cos.; honors: Fight for Sight Fellowship 1966; Los Angeles Soc. of Physicians 1983; mem: AMA; Am. Acad. of Ophthalm.; Royal Soc. of Health; works: development of intra ocular lens; Republican; rec: tennis, music, travel. Res: 12250 Richwood Dr Los Angeles 90049 Ofc: 435 N Roxbury Dr Beverly Hills 90210

COPELAND, WILLIAM JACK, physician; b. Sept. 18, 1950, Batesville, Ark.; s. Jack Dempsy and Hazel Jane (Jesson) C.; m. Teena, Aug. 13, 1972; children: Gary b. 1979, Gayle b. 1982, Mindy b. 1985; edn: BA, UCLA 1972; MD, St. Louis Univ. 1976; Diplomate Am. Board OB-Gyn 1982. Career: intern OB-Gyn, St. Louis Univ. 1976-77; resident OB-Gyn. Univ. of South Florida 1977-79, chief resident 1979-80; pvt. practice OB-Gyn in Lancaster, Calif. 1980– , treas. Antelope Valley Medical Group, Inc. 1985-; chmn. Dept. OB-Gyn, mem. exec. com. Antelope Valley Hosp.; instr. Antelope Valley Hosp. Family Practice Residency Pgm., recipient Outstanding Clin. Faculty awards (1981, 83); mem: AMA, Calif. Med. Assn., Los Angeles County Med. Assn., Am. Coll. of OB-Gyn; chair United Jewish Appeal for Antelope Valley (1984-); Ind.; Jewish; rec: sailing. Ofc: 44241 15th St West Ste 202 Lancaster 93534

COPENBARGER, LLOYD GAYLORD, lawyer; b. Feb. 25, 1941, Geary, Okla. s. Lloyd Gaylord and Audrey Mabel (Goss) C.; m. Laura, Aug. 28, 1959; children: Larry b. 1964, Gwen b. 1962; edn: BA, Univ. Okla. 1969; JD, Univ. Okla. Sch. of Law 1971. Career: ptnr. (spl. in estate planning, bus. law, non-profit corp. law) Copenbarger & Copenbarger Irvine, San Jose, Tucson, Denver and Seattle; instr. Univ. Okla. Ctng. Edn. Dept.; mem: Am., Calif., Ohio, Okla. bar assns.; bd. dirs: Canyon Acres Residential Ctr., Paradise Springs Conf. and Retreat Ctr. Valyermo, World Missionary Press New Paris, Ind.; publ: Making Sense of Wills & Trusts, What You Need to Know about Estate and Gift Tax Law; Republican; Christian; rec: flying, skin diving, skiing. Ofc: Copenbarger & Copenbarger 2171 Campus Dr, Ste 200, Irvine 92715

COPLEY, HELEN KINNEY, publisher; b. Nov. 28, Cedar Rapids, Iowa; d. Fred Everett and Margaret (Casey) Kinney; m. James S. Copley, Aug. 16, 1965 (dec. 1973); 1 son: David Casey, b. 1952. Career: chmn. of the corp./chmn. exec. com./dir. The Copley Press, Inc., La Jolla 1973– , CEO/sr. mgmt. bd., 1974– ; chmn. bd. Copley News Service, San Diego 1973– ; publisher The San Diego Union and The Tribune, S.D.; chmn. editorial bd. Union-Tribune Pub. Co., 1976-; chmn. bd., trustee James S. Copley Found., 1974-; mem. Council of Trustees, Freedoms Found. at Valley Forge; trustee, Howard Hughes Medical Inst.; v.chmn. bd. trustees, Univ. of San Diego, 1973-; trustee emeritus, Scripps Clinic and Resrch Found. Mem: La Jolla Mus. Contemporary Art; S.D. Hall of Sci.(life); Nat.Press Club, Wash DC; S.D. Press Club; San Francisco Press Club; Gr. L.A. Press Club; Wash. Crossing Found. (hon. chmn., dir.); Am. Newspaper Publ. Assn. (dir. ANPA; chmn. & pres. ANPA Found.); Am. Soc. Newspaper Editors; Am. Press Inst.; Calif. Newspaper Publ. Assn.; Calif. Press Assn.; Nat. Newspaper Assn.; San Diego CofC; La Jolla Town Council, Inc.; Scripps Mem. Hosp. Aux.; The Army and Navy Club (Wash DC); YWCA (life); ZoologicalSoc. of S.D.; Star of India Aux. (life); S.D. Soc. of Natural Hist.; (life) Patroness, Makua Auz.; Friends of Internat. Center, La Jolla; S.D. Sym. Assn.; Republican Assocs. So. Calif.; Sigma Delta Chi; Aurora (Ill.) CC; Univ. S.D. Pres.; La Jolla Beach and Tennis Club; La Jolla CC; Cuyamaca; S.D. Yacht. Roman Catholic. Res: 7007 Country Club Dr. La Jolla 92037. Ofc: 7776 Ivanhoe Ave. La Jolla 92037

CORBIN, STEVEN M., accountant; b. Apr. 20, 1953, Romney, W. Va.; s. Walter R. and W. Marie (Sneathen) C.; m. Anna Marie, May 12, 1979; 1 dau. Rachel b. 1983; edn: BS, Fairmont State 1974; MBA, W. Va. Univ. 1976; CPA Pa. 1978, Calif. 1979. Career: CPA Arthur Young & Co. Pittsburgh 1976-79, Price Waterhouse Newport Beach 1979-83; ptnr. Corbin & Wertz Newport Beach 1983– ; instr. CSU Fullerton 1982-84; lectr. var. civic, profl. groups; mem: Am. Inst. CPAs, Calif. Soc. CPAs, Pa. Inst. CPAs, Vol. Ctr. of So. Orange Co. (bd. dirs., treas. 1982-); rec: golf, reading, outdoor sports. Res: 1101 W Carriage Dr Santa Ana 92707 Ofc: Corbin & Wertz 1 Civic Plaza, Ste 275, Newport Beach 92660

CORDELL, FLORENCE MAY, civic volunteer; b. Dec. 24, 1920, Ava, Mo.; d. Hobart Jerry and Mayme Bell (LaKey) Silvey; m. Charles Cordell, May 11, 1944; children: Pamela b. 1945, Charles, Jr. b. 1951; tchg. certif. Southwest Mo. State Univ. 1939-42. Career: public sch. tchr. Douglas County, Mo. 1942-43; joined the Waves, WWII, served as SpT (link trainer) 2/c tchg. instrument flying to 1500 Naval aviation cadets (incl. husband), 1943-44; helped found the Wesley United Methodist Ch., El Cajon 1947 (Sunday Sch. tchr. 10 yrs., choir mem. 25 yrs., exec. bd. 3 yrs.; current chair Christian Personhood); vol. Mental Hygiene work 21 yrs.; mem./ chair Am. Cancer Assn. fund drives, E. San Diego 1970-; vol. COAD; vol. with medical Plastic Surgery Team in Mexico 1 yr.; recipient Spl. Mission Recogn., United Methodist Women Pacific S.W. Conf. (1982); mem. DAR/ Litisha Coxe Chpt., El Cajon Womens Club, Grossmont Hosp. Aux.; research in nutrition, preventive & holistic medicine; publ: study course for ch., Sociology of the Family (1985); Republican; rec: symphony, needlepoint, gourmet cook, oil painting. Res: 525 S Orange Ave El Cajon 92020

CORDI, MARIO MATTHEW, educator; b. Oct. 2, 1920, Springfield, Mass.; s. Antonio and Fortunada (Velardi) C.; m. Reiko Okazaki, Dec. 27. 1954; children: Angela, b. 1960, Michael, b. 1961, Bunji, b. 1963, Yoshi, b. 1964; edn: AA, San Antonio Coll. 1960; BA, St. Mary's Univ. 1962; M.Ed, Loyola Univ. 1967; Pupil Personnel Svcs. Cred., Loyola 1969; Marriage, Family and Child Counselor (MFCC), 1970. Career: sch. tchr., counselor, psychometrist 1964-83, ret.; US Merchant Marine, staff ofcr., jr. asst. purser and pharmacists mate 1947-; cons. to local sch. dist. 1983-84; dep. registrar of voters 1978-; mem: Los Angeles, and Calif. Personnel & Guidance Assns.; Calif. Counseling and Guidance Assn.; The Nat. Acad. of Counselors & Family Therapists (life mem. 1973-); Calif. Assn. of Sch. Psychometrists and Psychologists; VFW; Knights of Columbus; Confrat. of Christian Doctrine; Freedoms Found. Com., Retired Enlisted Orgn., Nat. Guard Assn. of Calif., Mental Health Assn. of L.A. Co., Nat. Ret. Tchrs. Assn., AARP, Calif. Tchrs. Assn., Nat. Edn. Assn., Am. Legion, YMCA; mil: chief pharm. mate, USN 1939-45, Reserve 1946-48; m/sgt. US Army 1948-62, Reserve 1962-; maj. Calif. State Mil. Reserve 1980-; decorated WWII Victory, Am. Defense, Nat. Defense, Asia- Pac. Theatre, GCM (USN 1, AUS 4) Korean Svc., UN Svc.; Republican; Catholic; rec: numismatics, golf, WWII history. Res: 17318 Harvest Ave, Cerritos 90701

COREN, LANCE SCOTT, auto industry consultant; b. Dec. 19, 1949, Inglewood; s. Melville and Shirley Ann (Ehrlich) C.; edn: BS in bus. adm., CSU Long Beach 1972; JD, L.A. Univ. Sch. of Law 1974; MBA, Cal-Western Univ. 1976; ins. law cert., UCLA, 1975; comparative psychology cert., Grad. Inst., 1975; desig: Internat. Automotive Cons. (first and only US resident to receive F.I.A. certification), Fedn. Internat. De L'Automobile, Paris, France (1984), Lloyd's of London Ins. Undws.; certifed expert witness, Superior Cts of Calif., Nev., Ariz., New York. Career: auto claims adjuster Gulf & Western Cos. Ins. Div., 1974-77; western region claims mgr. Lloyd's of London Underwriters, 1977-80; exec. v.p. The Corenco Corp., 1983– ; pres./CEO L.S.C. Enterprizes Group Inc., 1980– ; judge var. Concours d' Elegance events; awards: Presidential Sports Award- Skiing, Nat. Competition U.S. Cup (1973), Outstanding Young Men of Am. (1985); mem: Internat. Soc. of Automotive Appraisers (pres. 1983-84), Am. Assn. of Auto Appraisers (pres. 1984-85), Inter-Industry Conf. on Auto Collision Repair (instr. 1984-85); civic: Soroptimist Internat. (fundraiser 1983), Children's Home Soc. of Calif. (fundraiser 1985); clubs: Sports Car Club of Am., Internat. Motor Sports Assn., Ferrari Owners (1982-), Cobra Owners (1978-), Lamborghini Owners (1981-84), Mercedes-Benz Owners (1984-), Pantera Owners (1979-83); author: The International Firm: A Study of U.S. Multinational Enterprises in the World Economy (1976, 88 pp); mil: Air Force ROTC 1967; Democrat; Jewish; rec: tennis, skiing, auto racing. Ofc: 3634 Spencer St Ste 117 Torrance 90503

CORLESS, JOE DONALD, pediatrician, allergist; b. June 4, 1934, Walla Walla, Wash.; s. Donald Edward and Elizabeth (Gilmore) C.; m. Judy, Sept. 30, 1978; children: Ruth b. 1962, Phillip b. 1964, Jeffrey b. 1981; edn: Univ. Idaho; MD, Baylor Univ. Coll. of Med. 1959; bd. certified Am. Bd. Pediats. 1966.

Career: rotating intern Orange County Med. Ctr. 1962-63, pediat. resident 1962-63, Wm. Beaumont Gen. Hosp. El Paso, Tex. 1963-65, chief res. 6 mo., neurol, psych. 6 mo., allergy preceptor 12 mo.; Madigan Gen. Hosp. Tacoma, Wash. 1965-67, chief pediat. outpt. clin., pediat. allergy clin. 1966-67; pvt. practice pediat. 1967–; staff Children's Hosp. of Orange County, St. Joseph's Hosp. of Orange, Western Med. Ctr. Santa Ana, UCI Med. Ctr., Med. Ctr. of Garden Grove; instr. pediats. Univ. Wash. Med. Sch. 1966-67; assoc. clin. prof. pediats. UCI Med. Sch.; mem., chmn. num. coms. at var. hosps.; lectr. seminars and assn. mtgs.; honors: Sigma Delta Chi (1954), Phi Beta Kappa (1955), Nat. Found. Grants (Baylor 1957-58), Order of Cloud & Banner (Chinese Army 1962), Pres. Citn. (OC Med. Assn. 1977), Outstanding Tchr. Award, Vol. Faculty (UCI Med. Ctr. 1976-77, 1977-78, CHOC 1978-79); fellow Am. Acad. Pediats. 1967 (exec. com. 1978-81); mem: Orange County Pediat. Soc. (pres. 1977-78, bd. 1974-79), Southwest Pediat. Soc. 1976-, Am. Perinatal Assn. 1979-, Am. Lung Assn. of OC (pediat. com.), Am. Coll. Allergy, OC Soc. for Allergy and Immunol. (charter); publs: num. articles in med. jours.; mil: major US Army 1960-67, USAR 1967-, Army Commdn.; Protestant; rec: photog. Ofc: Joe D. Corless MD 999 Tustin Ave Ste 15 Santa Ana 92705

CORLEW, JERRY PAUL, manufacturing co. president, photographer- writer; b. May 7, 1952, West Palm Beach, Fla.; s. Corwin Elson Hinson Jr., adopted s. Arthur Clarence and Rosemond Melama (Turner) Corlew; m. Cynthia Lynn, Feb. 14, 1978; 1 son, Shawn Paul b. 1985. Career: constrn. trade 1971-76; photog.-writer, poster and artprint distbr., prop. HighLite Prodns., 1976–; fishing lure designer, mfr., distbr., pres. Anglers Pro Splties., Casmalia 1983–, conduct Bass Fishing Seminars and on-the-water tchg. (1983-); profl. bass fishing angler (sportfishing) U.S. Bass Fishing Assn. of Am. (Calif., Ariz., N.M., Nev., Utah) 1983–; guest speaker Anti-Toxic Waste Dumping issues, Loyola Univ. (Hilton Bus. Ethics Week, 1986), San Luis Obispo Lions Club (1986); awards: 4 time recipient Sports Afield Disting. Angler Award, State of Calif. (1983), Fenwick Woodstream Master Fisherman Award (1984), 1st Pl. Gold Coast Bass Tournament, Lopez Lake, Calif., Gold Coast Bass Team (1983) and 3d Pl. Gold Coast Bass Tourn., Lake Margarita, Calif. (1986), 4th Pl. Tom Mann's Fish World research angler team rally tournament, Lake Eufaula, Ala. (1983), 8th Pl. U.S. Pro Team Open, W. Bass/Riverside Resort, Ariz. (1984), Ranked 38th in W. USA, W. Bass Fishing Assn. (1984); mem: Gold Coast Bass Team (secty. 1984), Bass Anglers Sportmans Soc., Ala. (1983-), U.S. Bass Fishing Assn., Ariz. (1983-), West Coast Bass (1985-), Profl. Bass Anglers Assn. of Am. (cert. profl. mem. 1985-); publs: writer, ed., photog., pub. Gold Coast Bass Team News 1984; contbr. articles West Coast Fisherman, U.S. Bass News, BassMaster Mag.; cover photo Western Bass Mag. (1984), approx. 40 photos pub. (1976-); designer-inventor: Shake'n Dart (TM), CrawJig (TM), SoftCraw (TM), Shake'n Worm (TM), Shake'n Shad (TM), BabyCraw (TM), Cullin' Beam (TM), GliderCraw (TM), Bass Pack (TM), 1983; Democrat; rec: collector Indian relics, antique bottles, antique fishing tackle. Ofc: Anglers Pro Specialities, HighLite Productions (Box 134) 3446-B Point Sal Rd Casmalia 93429

CORMAN, MYRNA GAIL, real estate executive; b. Apr. 27, 1943, Detroit, Mich.; d. Sidney and Annabelle (Freeman) Brasler; children: Jeffrey Lloyd b. 1965, Gregory Eric b. 1969; real estate broker 1980. Career: real estate sales 1974-85; mgr. Fine Homes div. of Merril Lynch Realty No. L.A. 1985–, br. mgr. Encino Ofc.; honors: sold $1 million first year in real estate; Leading Edge Soc. (Merril Lynch); mem: San Fernando Valley Bd. Realtors, Nat. Assn. Realtors, Calif. Assn. Realtors; rec: knitting. Res: 19542 Anadale Dr Tarzana 91356 Ofc: Merrill Lynch 17047 Ventura Blvd Encino 91316

CORNETT, JEFFREY ROBERT, chemical co. president; b. Apr. 28, 1955, Santa Ana; s. Robert Carey and Willa Jean (Abplanalp) C.; edn: UCLA 1973-76. Career: sales (p.t. during coll.), then nat. sales mgr. (7 yrs) McLane Mfg., 1975-82; v.p. sales Chem. Lab Products, Ontario 1982, pres. 1983–, also exec. v.p. Cornett Jojoba Farms; mem: NSPI, Chamber of Commerce, Masons, Maserati Club Am.; co-founder High Desert Jojoba Coop.; Republican; Methodist; rec: ski, racquetball, hunting, equestrian. Res: 2288 Wilderness St (POB 1218) Running Springs 92382 Ofc: Chem Lab Products 5160 E Airport Dr Ontario 91761

CORR, WILLIAM PHILIP, physician, internist; b. Feb. 15, 1900, Horicon, Wis.; s. Rev. Wm. James and Dr. Anna (Brown) C.; m. Magdalene Huchthausen, M.D. Sept. 9, 1924; two sons: Donald John, M.D. and Wm. Philip, Jr., M.D.; m. 2d. Betty Adams McCarty, June 22, 1970; edn: BA, Lawrence Univ., 1919; AB, Univ. Wis., Madison 1921; MD, Univ. Chgo. Rush Med. Coll. 1924; postgrad. tng. Univ. Minn. Mayo Found. 1927-31; bd. certified Am. Board Internal Medicine 1937. Career: intern L.A. Gen. Hosp. 1923-24; resident Lutheran Sanitarium, Wheatridge, Colo. 1924-25; gen. practice, Juneau, Wis. 1925-27; instr. in pathology Univ. of Wis., Madison 1927-28; fellow in medicine Mayo Clinic and Found. 1928-31; co-founder (with Ray B. McCarty, MD, FACS) of Riverside Med. Clinic, Riverside, Calif. 1935, senior internist 1935-73, M.D. Emeritus 1973-; mem. UC Riverside coms. (Human Subjects Research, Biohazards, Animal Lab. Care); clin. prof. Loma Linda Univ. Sch. of Med. 1953-, prof. emeritus 1968; civilian cons. to Surgeon Gen. of the Army for the Far East 1954, civilian cons. in med. March Air Force Base Hosp. 1948-60; honors: Master Am. Coll. of Physicians (1972), Honored Prof. Loma Linda Univ. Sch. of Med. (1976), Alpha Omega Alpha faculty mem. (1968); mem: Am. Coll. of Physicians (gov. So. Calif. 1964-70, v.p. 1970-71), LA Acad. of Med. (pres. 1959-60), Calif. Soc. Internal Med. (pres. 1952-53), Riv. County Med. Assn. (pres. 1950-51), Inland Soc. Int. Med. (pres. 1958), CMA (chmn. Judicial Commn. 1970-72); co-founder Am. Geriatrics Soc. W. Div. (1971-72); mem. Calif. Bd. Med. Examiners Dist. Rev. Com. 1966-68; past pres. Riv. Co. Heart Assn. (1950-53), Riv. Co. Health and TB Assn. (1950-52); Rotarian (1947-); contbr. 18 arts. sci. jours.; mil: col. Med. Corps US Army WWI 1918, WWII 1941-46, Army Reserve 1924-; decorated Legion of Merit (1946); Republican; Methodist; rec: music, writing, family, friends. Res: 5145 Myrtle Ave Riverside 92506

CORRIN, ALLAN AYER, produce sales co president; b. Mar. 31, 1927, Long Beach; s. Wm. Roger and Chrystene (Ayer) C.; m. Charlene Wood, Jan. 27, 1951; 1 dau. Debra Kay b. 1952; edn: AA, Long Beach City Coll. 1948, stu. UCLA 1949, UC Berkeley 1950. Career: dir. internat. field ops. Theron Hooker, Los Angeles 1950-62, v.p./internat. field rep. Hooker-Corrin, Reedley 1962-71, v.p./dir. outside ops. Consol.-Hooker 1966-71, v.p./dir. outside ops. Consol.-Westgate, L.A. 1966-71; current: pres./CEO Corrin Produce Sales, Inc. 1971–, Tree & Vine Mgmt. Co. 1974–, Specialty Ag Equip. Inc. 1978–; apptd: Mt. Antonio Coll. Ag Advis. Bd. (dir. 1958-62), Fresno County Redevel. Corp. (dir. 1979-82), SBA Western Dist. (cons. 1976-80); guest lectr. Cal Poly San Damus (1960), UC Riverside (1961), CSU Fresno (1978-84), honors: Exporter of the Year, SBA (1984), Farmer of Year, Reedley CofC (1975); mem: United Fresh Fruit and Vegetable Assn. 1958- (dir. mdsg. & mgmt. div. 1968-71), Produce Mktg. Assn. 1972- (dir. foodsvc. div. 1981-85), Calif. Grape & Tree Fruit League 1960- (dir. 1966-, pres. 1974-75); civic: LA CofC (1958-64), Fresno Co. and City CofC 1965- (dir. 1978-82, v.p. ag. div. 1980-82), Reedley CofC 1971- (dir. 1984-87, v.p. 1986-87), Reedley Coll. (Ag Dept. cons. 1972-80), Kings Cyn Unif. Sch. Dist. Ag Dept. (cons. 1968-); works: devel. patented plant varieties (Black Pearl, 1982, Corrin Seedless, 1982), sev. copyrights for produce labels and art (1971-); mil: sp3 US Navy 1945-46, Victory Medal, PTO; Republican; Prot.; rec: water ski, swim, sail. Res: 6541 S Holbrook Ave Reedley 93654 Ofc: Corrin Produce Sales Inc POB 48 Reedley 93654

CORTADA, RAFAEL LEON, college president; b. Feb. 12, 1934, NYC; s. Rafael Cortada-Forgas and Yvonne Bernier-Hernandez; m. Selonie Jolissaint-Head, June 24, 1961; children: Celia, Natalia, Rafael; edn: AB, Fordham Univ. 1955; MA, Columbia Univ. 1957; PhD, Fordham Univ. 1967; cert. Inst. Ednl. Mgmt., Harvard Univ. 1974. Career: instr. New Rochelle (NY) High Sch., 1957-64, City Univ. NY, Bronx, 1958-64; asst. prof. Univ. Dayton (Ohio), 1964-66; cons. Fgn. Service Inst., US State Dept., Wash DC 1966, desk officer W.I., 1966-69; assoc. prof. history Fed. City Coll., Wash DC 1968-69, assoc. provost, prof. history, 1969-70; prof. history, dean community edn. and urban resources Medgar Evers Coll.-CUNY, Bklyn. 1970-71; prof. history, v.p. acad. affairs Hostos Community Coll., Bronx 1971-74; pres. Metropolitan Comm. Coll., Mnpls. 1974-77, Community Coll. Baltimore, 1977-82; pres., supt. El Camino Coll./ El Camino Community Coll. Dist., Torrance, Calif. 1982–; vis. assoc. prof. Caribbean hist. Howard Univ., Wash DC 1967-68; mem. adv. bd. grad. fellowship pgm. Danforth Found., 1976-81; mem. adv. com. Am. Assn. Community and Jr. Colls. Internat. Edn. Consortium, 1975-79; mem. state licensure team N.J. Dept. Edn., 1972; mem. overseas liaison com. Am. Council Edn., 1971-80; acad. adv. bd. East Harlem Exptl. and Bilingual Inst., 1971-75; mem. accreditation teams Middle States Assn. Colls. and Sec. Schs., 1970-; internat. adv. council Media Systems Corp., 1976-78; adv. com. creative pgmmg. Sta. KTCA-TV, Mnpls. 1976-77; mem. cabinet Mayor of Balt., 1978-82, Balt. Mayor's Literacy Commn. 1981, Health and Welfare Council Central Md., 1981-82; pres. N.E. region Council Black Am. Affairs, 1980-82; mem. US Nat. Commn. UNESCO, 1979-, v.chmn. 1980; community adv. bd. Pub. Bdcstg. System, Md. 1978-82; trustee Woodbourne Sch., Balt. 1979-82, chmn. 1981-82; trustee Blue Cross/ Blue Shield, 1976-77; bd. govs. Univ Guayana, 1971-; mem. African Studies Assn. (v.p. Wash. task force African Affairs 1969-), Am. Hist. Assn. (program planning com. conv. 1970); mil: 1st lt. US Army 1955-57; author: Echoes of World Civilization (2 vols., 1963), Black Studies: An Urban and Comparative Curriculum (1975); collaborator TV series: The College and Urban Problems (1970); contbr. articles to profl. jours. Ofc: 16007 Crenshaw Blvd., Torrance 90277

CORY, CAROL, financial planner; b. Sept. 5, 1948, Memphis, Tenn.; d. Charles Franklin and Mary (Liddell) Cory; m. Luis Fondevila, Dec. 14, 1980; edn: BA, honors, Ga. State Univ. 1970; Reg. Securities Principal; Certified Fin. Planner, Coll. Fin. Plnng. 1984. Career: owner Surety Investment Services, fin. planning firm (spec. in tax sheltered annuities for public sch. employees and non-profit orgns.) splst. in field 1978–; branch mgr., NASD broker/dealer, Titan Capital Corp.; honors: Alpha Lambda Delta, Crimson Key; mem: Internat. Assn. of Fin. Plnnrs., Inst. of CFPs, Am. Assn. of Univ. Women; Episcopal; rec: ballet, raising birds. Res: 2323 Canyon Dr Hollywood 90068 Ofc: Surety Investment Services, 4311 Wilshire Blvd Ste 615 Los Angeles 90010

COSGROVE, JOHN F., insurance co. executive; b. Feb. 19, 1931, Santa Barbara; s. John J. and Frances J. (Hamill) C.; m. Josephine M. Napolitan, Dec. 26, 1959; div. 1974; children: Kevin b. 1960, John b. 1964, Kathleen b. 1961; edn: AB, soc. scis., San Luis Rey Coll. 1952; 5 yrs. grad. work in theol., hist., law, Univ. San Francisco. Career: underwriting mgmt. trainee Cigna, Los Angeles 1959-61; Div. Surety rep. (San Francisco) Safeco Ins. Cos., 1961-66, nat. mgr. Tng. & Product Devel. (Seattle) 1966-71, Div. Surety mgr. (Portland, Ohio, So. Calif.) 1971-78, asst. v.p. 1978-81; asst. v.p./ops. mgr. Indsl. Indemnity Finl. Corp., S.F. 1982-85, senior v.p./contr. finl. svcs., 1985–; mem. Surety Underws. Assns. (No. Calif., Seattle, Portland), Assoc. Gen. Contrs. of Am. (nat. assoc.), The Beavers; clubs: Engrs. (SF), Mus. Soc. (SF), Commonwealth (SF), The Naturist Soc.; mil: US Army 1956-58; Republican. Ofc: Industrial Indemnity Financial Corp. Three Embarcadero Ctr. Ste 900 San Francisco 94111

COSTA, NICHOLAS, real estate broker-developer; b. April 16, 1932, NYC, NY; s. Joseph and Ann (Calgano) C.; m. Sandra McClure, Oct. 18, 1967; children: Ann b. 1959, Joseph b. 1961, Nicholas Jr. b. 1962, Michael b. 1968, Shawn b. 1971, Cassandra b. 1973, Scott b. 1974; edn: stu., Fordham Coll. and Fordham Law Sch., NYC. Career: internat. comml. real estate cons./ broker/ developer; ptr. Corporate Planners & Coordinators Development Co., Los Angeles 1970–; chmn. bd. dirs. CPC- Corp. Plnnrs. & Coords. Inc.; real estate advr. num. banks and trusts throughout US; bd. dirs., v.p., CFO Los Angeles Ballet, Los Angeles Ballet Exec. Com.; bd. trustees Craft & Folk Art Mus., Los Angeles; recipient, Exec. Award, Research Inst.; mem: The Real Estate Bd. of NY, Nat. Bd. of Real Estate Cons., Calif. Yacht Club, Balboa Bay CLub, Riviera Tennis Club, Belair Beach Club; mil: 1st lt. (pilot) USAF; Catholic; rec: author, composer, boating. Res: 129 No. Rockingham Los Angeles 90069 Ofc: Corporate Planners & Coordinators Inc., 10960 Wilshire Blvd. Los Angeles 90024

COSTOUROS, GEORGE JOHN, educator; b. Nov. 29, 1933, Amalias, Greece, nat. US cit. 1972; s. John S. and Alexandra Christos (Sougleri) C.; m. Joanna George, Aug. 16, 1970; children: John b. 1972, Nick b. 1974; edn: BA, Athens (Greece) Grad. Sch. of Bus. & Econ. 1956; BS and MS, honors, CSU San Jose 1964, 1965; MBA, honors, Univ. of Santa Clara 1968, PhD 1972. Calif. lic. real estate broker. Career: capt./ acctg. and fin. ofcr. Greek Air Force, 1956-62; acct. for sev. small firms p.t. 1962-65; staff acct. Ampex Corp., Redwood City, 1965-68; prof. of business (acctg.), Upper Div. & grad. levels, CSU San Jose, 1968–; pres., co-owner Aresco Inc. (R.E. investment co.); bus. cons. for high tech. cos.; vis. prof.; past instr. Stanford Univ., Univ. of Santa Clara; honors: Beta Alpha Psi, 1st (of 80 candidates) in State Qualifying Exams; mem. Acad. of Acctg. Historians, Am. Acctg. Assn., Am. Inst. CPAs, Am. Hellenic Ednl. Progressive Assn.; publs: monograph on acctg. hist., textbook on acctg. theory, 18 articles, var. profl. papers; Republican; Greek Orthodox; rec: travel, swimming, camping. Res: 163 Westhill Dr Los Gatos 95030 Ofc: California State University, School of Business, San Jose 95195

COTA, HAROLD MAURICE, professor of environmental engineering; b. Apr. 16, 1936, San Diego; s. Florencio Moisa and Doris Alberta (Wright) C.; m. Judith Pritchard, June 30, 1959; children: Rebecca b. 1962, Cynthia b. 1964, Michael b. 1966; edn: BS, UC Berkeley 1959; MS, Northwestern Univ. 1961; PhD, Univ. Okla. 1966. Career: student engr., San Diego Gas & Elec. Co., summers 1954-58; research engr. Lockheed Missiles & Space Co., Sunnyvale 1960-62; grad. asst. Univ. Okla. 1962-6; prof. Cal Poly San Luis Obispo, 1966–, dir. Environmental Research Found., 1979-, dir. Cal Poly's Air Pollution Areawide Tng. Ctr., 1983-; pres. APC Software; cons. in air, water and noise pollution control; mem. research screening com. Calif. Air Resources Bd. 1985-88; honors: Diplomate Am. Acad. of Environmental Engrs.; recipient Lyman A. Ripperton Award, Air Poll. Control Assn. (1984); mem: Am. Inst. Chem. Engrs., Am. Indsl. Hygiene Assn., Inst. of Noise Control Engrs., Calif. Regional Wqater Quality Control Bd. 1970-84 (chmn. 1976-77), Air Poll. Control Assn. (dir. 1978-80, chair Contg. Edn. Div. 1984-, v.chair Edn. Council, editor newsletter West Coast Sect. 1979-86); leader Boy Scouts Am. 1979-; publs: on Fuel Cells, Thermodynamics, Air Pollution, Microcomputer Appls.; Republican; Methodist; rec: swimming. Ofc: Civil/ Environmental Engineering, Cal Poly, San Luis Obispo 93407

COTCHETT, JOSEPH WINTERS, lawyer; b. Jan. 6, 1939, Chicago, Ill.; s. Joseph Winters and Jean (Renaud) C.; children: Leslie F., Charles P., Rachael E.; edn: BSE, Calif. Polytechnic Coll. 1960; LLB, UC Hastings Coll. of Law 1964; admitted to Calif. Bar 1965. Career: engr. Bechtel Corp., San Francisco 1961; law practice, San Mateo 1965–; chmn. San Mateo Co. Heart Assn. 1967-68; pres. San Mateo Boys Club 1971; mem. Commn. on Judicial Performance; honors: Research Fellow, Am. Bar Found.; mem: Am. Bd. Trial Advocs., Fellow Internat. Acad. of Trial Lawyers, Calif. Trial Lawyers Assn., State Bar of Calif., Commonwealth, Press Club (San Francisco); co-author: with R. Cartwright, California Products Liability Actions, 1970; with F. Haght, California Courtroom Evidence, 1972; with Elkind, Federal Courtroom Evidence, 1976; contbr. articles to profl. journs.; mil: US Army Intelligence Corps 1960-61, now Col. Judge Advoc. Gen's. Corps. Res: 840 Malcolm Rd. Burlingame 94010

COTE, JOSEPH TERRANCE, professional society executive; b. Sept. 27, 1943, Muskegon, Mich.; s. Raymond Ambrose and Bernice Catherine (McGarvie) C.; m. Gloria, Dec. 11, 1964; children: Thomas b. 1965, Angela b. 1968; edn: BS, Ferris State Coll. 1967; MAS, Univ. Ill. 1971; CPA Mich. 1970. Career: auditor Arthur Andersen & Co. Detroit 1967-70; instr. Ferris State Coll. Big Rapids, Mich. 1971-73; controller Lorin Inds. Muskegon, Mich. 1973-74; tech. adminstr. Am. Inst. CPAs NY 1974-78; dir. contg. profl. edn. Calif. Soc. CPAs Palo Alto 1978–; adj. prof. Columbia Univ., Pace Univ., Long Island Univ.; honors: Delta Sigma Pi Scholarship Key (1968), Highest GPA, Top Acctg. Grad. (Ferris Sch. of Bus.), Acctg. Achievement Award (Ernst & Ernst 1968), Tchg. Assistantship (Univ. Ill. 1970-71); mem: Am. Inst. CPAs, Calif. Soc. CPAs, Mich. Assn. CPAs, Am. Acctg. Assn., Am. Soc. Tng. & Devel., Middletown, NJ Jaycees (dir., treas.); Catholic; rec: running. Res: 1532 Channing Ave Palo Alto 94303 Ofc: California Society CPAs 1000 Welch Rd Palo Alto 94304

COTTAM, CALVIN, chiropractor; b. Mar. 28, 1925, Salt Lake City; s. Nephi Livesay and Edwardena (Parry) C.; edn: design & paper sculpture, Chouinard Art Inst. (now Cal Arts) 1949; MA in psychol., David Seabury Sch of Psychology, 1953; DC, Cleveland Chiro. Coll. 1965. Career: Dr. of Chiropractic, lic. in Calif., New Zealand; co-founder, instr. Foundation for Living, Problems Anon., Creative Self Research, 1953-64; co-presenter Living Today (radio pgm.), Los Angeles 1954-55; extensive travels w/parents on cranial adjusting tchg. tours in US and Can. (father, Nephi Cottam, D.C., originator of cranial adjusting, Craniopathy); tours incl. World Chiropractic Congress, Switz.(1970), Spain (1971), Greece, USSR, Turkey, Yugoslavia (1972), acupuncture and shiatsu tour, Japan, Taipei, Hong Kong, Singapore, Thailand (1972), genealogical resrch in England, Wales, Ireland, Belgium, France (1973), and Scotland, Scandinavia; instr. craniopathy in Sydney, Australia, vis. New Zealand, Fiji, Tahiti (1975), tchr. craniopathy in USA, Mex., Can. (1976-81), Egypt, Israel, China (1983), China again (1984), Europe (1984), Brazil, Argentina, Alaska (1986); participant first ofcl. chiropractic info. exchange group invited to China, 1983. Dir: Inst. for the Study of Human Resources 1985–; author: Head First for Health, House-Warven (1952), Fun, How To Take a Vacation Every Day, Living Without Strain, Don't Be Afraid of your Mind, Magic of Meditation; (w/Bert Mitchell Anderson) How To Write True To Yourself (1960); (w/Reid Rasmussen, DC) Craniopathy for You and Others (1975); Cranial/Facial Adjusting/Craniopathy Step-by-step (1985), Illustrated seminars (1986); prod. (with Reid Rasmussen, DC, brother by adoption) six one-hr video tapes showing cranial technics/craniopathy for Chiropractic Video Studies, Inc. of NY (1981); art. in Digest of Chiro. Economics 1981; presented paper, The Smithsonian 1981; mem: Nat. Writers League (nat. pres. 1958); David Seabury Sch of Psychol. Alumni Assn. (pres. 1955-6); Internat. New Thought Alliance (ch. Govt. Affairs 1957); CofC; Civil Def.; Nat. Vocational Guidance Assn., Wilshire Center, Country Club Park Info. Council (co-chair 1986-); mil: s/sgt US Army, M.C., WWII & Korean conflict. rec: comparative studies of ancient philosophies and current beliefs. Address: 1017 S. Arlington Ave. Los Angeles 90019

COUCH, MARCUS DOUGLASS, investment counselor; b. Aug. 27, 1916, Denver, Colo.; s. Maurice Douglass and Vermonte Agnes (Young) C.; m. Roberta Brunn, Aug. 31, 1940; children: Michael b. 1941, Susan b. 1951; edn: grad. Am. Inst. Banking, 1939; desig: CMB, GRI (1969), RECI (1976), Calif. Assn. Realtors; CRS (1979), Nat. Assn. of Realtors. Career: mgr. San Francisco Theatres, 1932-35; teller Bank of America, S.F. 1935-42; foreman Plate Shop, Kaiser Shipyard No.3, Richmond 1942-44; carpenter foreman Wm Gibson, Palo Alto 1946-49; owner/pres. Doug Couch General Contractors, Inc. 1949–; broker/owner, Doug Couch Realtors, Inc. 1951–; owner Doug Couch Painting Contr. 1952-55; prin. Doug Couch Ins. Broker 1953–; v.p. treas., Doug Couch Devel. Co. Inc.; lectr. Univ. Calif. Ext.; awards: Realtor of the Year, Palo Alto Bd. Realtors (1957), Spike Club, Life mem. Nat. Assn. Home Builders (1960); mem. Am. Arbitration Assn. (Panel of Arb.), Nat. Assn. of Review Appraisers & Mortgage Underwriters (CRA, Sr. Mem., RMU), Internat. Inst. of Valuers (Sr. Cert. Valuer), Internat. Orgn. of R.E. Appraisers (CMHA, Cert. Mfd. Housing Appraiser); mem: Palo Alto Bd. Realtors (past pres.), Sunnyvale Bd. Realtors, Los Altos Bd. Realtors, San Jose Real Estate Bd., Mt. View Bd. Realtors (past pres.), Calif. Assn. of Realtors (life hon. dir.), Assoc. Investment & Exchange Counselors, Nat. Assn. Realtors, Peninsular Exchangers, Nat. Assn. Home Builders (v.p.), Calif. Farm & Land Inst., Nat. Farm & Land Inst., Internat. Assn. Finl. Plnnrs., Internat. R.E. Fedn., Realtors Nat. Mktg. Inst.; civic: Foothill Comm. Coll. (R.E. advis. com.), Palo Alto Optimist Club (pres.), Kiwanis, Commonwealth Club of Calif., S.F. Press Club, British-Am. Club, Disabled Am. Vets. (life), Stanford Univ. Alumni Assn., Stanford Buck Club (life), Am. Red Cross Palo Alto Chpt. (Disaster Survey Dir.); mil: m/sgt. USAF 1944-46. Res: 67 Bay Tree Ln Los Altos 94022 Ofc: Doug Couch, Inc. 560 Oxford Ave Palo Alto 94006

COUGHLIN, SISTER MAGDALEN, college president; b. Apr. 16, 1930, Wenatchee, Wash.; d. William Joseph and Cecilia (Diffley) C.; edn: BA, The Coll. of St. Catherine 1952; MA, Mt. St. Mary's Coll. 1962; PhD, USC 1970. Career: hist. tchr. Alemany H.S., Calif. 1960-61; hist. tchr. St. Mary's Acad., Los Angeles 1961-63; asst. prof. of hist. Mt. St. Mary's Coll., L.A. 1963-70; dean for acad. devel. Mt. St. Mary's Coll., L.A. 1970-74; provincial councilor/ regl. supvr. Sisters of St. Joseph of Carondelet, L.A. 1974-76; pres. Mt. St. Mary's Coll., L.A. 1976–; bd. trustees Marianne Frostig Ctr. for Ednl. Therapy; bd. dirs. Ind. Colls. of So. Calif. 1976–, pres. of bd. 1982-83; bd. trustees Coll. of St. Catherines 1982-; bd. dirs. Assn. of Catholic Colls. & Unvs. 1979-; awards: Haynes Dissertation Fellowship 69-70; Fulbright Scholarship, Univ. of Nijmegen, The Netherlands 1952-53; Doctor of Humane Letters, honoris causa, Loyola Marymount Univ. 1983; mem: Calif. Hist. Soc.; Am. Hist. Soc.; Fulbright Alumni Assn.; Phi Alpha Theta; Phi Gamma Mu; Delta Epsilon Sigma; Kappa Gamma Pi; Lambda Iota Tau; Women in Bus.; Womens Trusteeship; works: Missionary and Smuggler: Agents of Disobedience of Civilization?, Some Calif. Catholic Reminiscences for the US Bicentennial 1976; Commercial Foundations of Political Interest in the Opening Pacific, Calif. Hist. Soc. Quarterly, Vol. XLX, 1971; Boston Smugglers on the Coast (1797-1812): An Insight Into the American Acquisition of California, Calif. Hist. Soc. Quarterly 1967; Catholic; rec: reading, sewing, walking. Address: Mount St. Mary's College, 12001 Chalon Rd Los Angeles 90049

COUTURE, PHILLIP QUINN, financial planner; b. Jan. 15, 1946, Pleasantridge, Mich.; s. Joseph B. and Arois L. (Ward) C.; children: M. Lance b. 1967, Troy b. 1970; edn: El Camino Coll., L.A. Harbor Coll. 1964-70; mktg., mgmt., tech. skills tng., 1200 hrs. 1971-83; Certified Financial Planner 1985;

Cert. Fin. Cons. 1986; Reg. Investment Advisor, SEC, Calif. 1984. Career: independent ins. agent 1971-74; v.p. M.A. James Ins. Agcy. L.A. 1974-77; pres. Couture & Assocs. Inc. Corona del Mar 1977—; instr. Sierra Univ. Huntgn. Beach 1986; honors: Outstanding Award (Ch. of Rel. Sci. 1983-84), Outstanding Financial Planning (Consol. Investment Svc. Inc. 1984, 85); mem: Inst. Cert. Financial Planners 1982-, Internat. Assn. Financial Planners 1979-, Financial Profl. Adv. Panel 1985, Certified Financial Cons. Assn. (bd.), Newport Beach Harbor CofC, Shark Island Yacht Club, John Wayne Tennis Club; publs: articles, column Celebration Tribune, Ch. of Rel. Sci. 1983-84); Republican; Ch. of Rel. Sci.; rec: yachting, skin diving, dancing. Ofc: Couture & Assocs. Inc. 1111 Bayside Dr Ste 200-D Corona del Mar 92625

COVINGTON, JAMES ROBERT, commercial recreation executive; b. Oct. 4, 1949, Redlands; s. Robert Allen and Mary Elizabeth (Anderson) C.; m. Dale, Aug. 24, 1974; children: Mary b. 1976, Ellen b. 1976, William b. 1981, Christopher b. 1984, Cathleen b. 1985; edn: BA, Univ. of La Verne 1972; Calif. St. Life Tchg. credential 1983. Career: pres. Keon Ltd., Redlands 1966-68; treas. Far West Recording Prodns. Inc., Hollywood 1968-72; tchr. Chino Unified Sch. Dist , 1972-82; finl. cons. Covington Ents., Redlands 1972 82; owner/pres./mgr. Redlands Swim & Tennis Club, 1982—; awards: 1st pl. Nat. Music Guild Soc. competitions (1959-62), Outstanding educator Chino Unif. Sch. Dist. (1974); mem: So. Calif. Tennis Club Owners Assn. (bd. dirs. 1983-), Rotary (bd.), Redlands YMCA, Redlands CofC; works: composer musical works performed at univs. and colls. (1968-74); devel. state of the art filtration systems for comml. swimming pools (1984-85); Ch. of the Brethren; rec: entrepreneurship. Ofc: Redlands Swim and Tennis Club 12626 Wabash Redlands 92373

COWAN, DEBORAH ANN, database consultant; b. June 26, 1955, Sacramento; d. Donald Raymond and Genevieve Marie Wilson; m. Robert Cowan, Apr. 15, 1978; 1 dau. Elizabeth b. 1984; edn: BS, Calif. Inst. Technol. 1977; profl. engr. Calif. 1980. Career: engr. C.F. Braun & Co. Alhambra 1977-79, Ralph M. Parsons Pasadena 1979-80; sr. engr. C.F. Braun 1980-85; prop./v.p. software Lost Voltigeur Ent. San Dimas 1985—; mem: Am. Inst. Chem. Engrs., Assn. of Women in Computing; Christian; rec: horses. Ofc: Lost Voltigeur Ent. 1148 Wagon Wheel Ct San Dimas 91773-1040

COWAN, MICHAEL GEORGE, management consultant; b. May 8, 1940, Union City, N.J.; s. Morris and Ann (Stern) C.; m. Elaine Loewentheil, Sept. 23, 1983; children: Marci b. 1963, Howard b. 1965; edn: BS, mgmt. engring., Univ. Vermont 1962; MS mgmt. sci., Steven's Inst. 1968. Career: methods engr. General Motors, N.Y. 1962-63; senior indsl. engr. Westinghouse, N.J. 1963-66; asst. indsl. engr. dept. head, General Foods, N.J. 1966-72; mgmt. cons. Touche Ross & Co., N.Y. and N.J., 1972-79; v.p./gen. mgr. Durex, Inc., N.J. 1979-81; pres. C&H Datapunch Services Inc., Calif. 1981-82; prin. CT Assocs. 1985—; pres. Michael G. Cowan Assocs. Inc. 1983—; dir. Investors Guild of Am.; adj. prof. mktg. Middlesex County Coll. 1977-78; mem: Nat. Council Physical Distbn. Mktg. (v.p., pgm. chmn.; annual conf. co-chmn. & speaker), Am. Inst. of Indsl. Engrs. (senior mem.), Indsl. Mgmt. Club of North Hudson (v.p.), Conejo Valley CofC; works: micro computer software (copyrighted, commmercially pub. 1986); patent disclosure on machine design, Gen. Foods (1972).

COWAN, WARREN J., public relations industry executive; b. Mar. 13, NY, NY; s. Rubey Joel and Grace (Andriesse) C.; children: Linda, Bonnie, Claudia; edn: BA, UC Los Angeles 1946. Career: chmn. bd. Rogers & Cowan Inc. L.A.; entertainment chmn. United Way of Am.; mem: Motion Picture Acad. Arts & Scis., TV Acad. Arts & Scis., Friars Club; mil: USAAF 1942-45; Ofc: Rogers & Cowan Inc. 10000 Santa Monica Blvd Los Angeles 90067

COWDEN, MARY CAROLYN, accountant; b. July 16, 1955, Dayton, Ohio; d. Richard Newel and Dorothy Louise (McGinnis) C.; edn: BSBA acctg., cum laude, Miami Univ. 1976; Certified Public Acct., Ohio (1978), Calif. (1985); Calif. real estate lic. (1985). Career: Touche Ross & Co., Cinti. 1976-79, Ernst & Whinney, Los Angeles 1979-82; Chryssostomides, Inc., Lancaster 1982-85; pvt. practice Lancaster 1985—, tax preparation, planning, income tax audits, acctg. services; honors: Beta Alpha Psi, Beta Gamma Sigma, Who's Who Among Am. High Schs., Buckeye Girls State (H.S.); mem: Am. Inst. CPAs, Am. Womens Soc. CPAs, Am. Soc. of Women Accts., The Ohio Soc. of CPAs, Calif. Soc. CPAs, AAUW, Lancaster CofC; Republican; Methodist; rec: antique collecting, numismatics, swimming. Res: 1104 W Ave O-4 Palmdale 92441 Ofc: Mary C. Cowden, CPA 44846 Cedar Ave Lancaster 93534

COX, FRANCES NORALLEN, educator; b. Oct. 15, 1919, Goodyear, Ariz.; d. Arthur Clinton and Florence E. (Miller) Plake; m. N. James Cox, Nov. 24, 1948; children: James b. 1950, Douglas b. 1958; edn: BA, Ariz. State Univ. 1941; stu. CSU San Francisco, Santa Clara Univ., Notre Dame Coll., UC Santa Cruz, UC Berkeley, CSU San Jose; tchg. cred. Elementary (Life Cert.), Ariz. (1941), Ore. (1950), Calif. (1954), Resource Splst. (Learning Handicapped), Calif. (1972). Career: classroom tchr. Phoenix (Ariz.) 1941-49, Fresno (Ca.) City Schs. 1949-50, Fresno County Schs. 1953-56, Portland (Ore.) City Schs. 1960-64, tchr./resource splst. Palo Alto Unified Schs., 1964—; devel. curriculum in Kdg. literature and elem. sci., Phoenix (1941-43); lead panel Assn. for Childhood Edn. Conv., Ariz. St. Univ. (1946), lead demonstr. for 2d gr. games for Fresno Co. Schs., Fresno St. Coll. (1954), lead demonstr. for social studies for Portland City Schs., Portland Tchrs. Inst. (1962), master tchr. Fresno St. Coll. (1953), Ore. St. Univ.; mem: Palo Alto Tchrs. Assn. (recipient WHO Award for outstanding svc. 1986), Remedial Reading Tchrs. (1961-73), Re-

source Splst. Orgn., Nat. Tchrs. Assn., Calif. Tchrs. Assn. (Political Action rep.), NEA, tchr. orgns. in Phoenix, Fresno, and Portland, PTA (1941-), Nat. Profl. Bus. Sor. (1941-47); mil: pilot Civil Air Patrol 1941-42, Pilot Wings (1941); Prot.; rec: travel, politics, environment, art. Res: 911 La Mesa Dr Menlo Park 94025 Ofc: Palo Alto Unified Schools 25 Churchill Ave Palo Alto 94306

COX, HOBERT HARRY, JR., religious organization executive; b. June 21, 1921, Brownsville, Pa.; s. Hobert H. and Vera (Felker) C.; m. Dorene Hinsdale, July 16, 1952; children: Rebecca b. 1953, David b. 1956, Charles b. 1966; edn: BA, Northwestern Coll. 1954; Dip. (masters level), Wisconsin Univ. 1960-63; Dip., Internat. Exchange Assoc. 1979; Cert. Internal Auditor, Inst. Int. Aud. (1973); Calif. Comm. Colls. Ltd. Service Cred. (life). Career: asst. to comptroller Northwestern Nat. Bank, Mnpls. 1955-67, auditor Sioux Falls branch 1967-69; auditor First Nat. Bank and Trust, Ontario 1969-74, Hacienda Bank, Whittier 1974-76; dir. Southwest Baptist Conf. Found. 1976-79; internat. controller Inter Aid (relief orgn.) 1979-81; assoc. minister of fin. Southwest Baptist Conf., 1981—; chmn./CEO Verdugo Home Inc., Hemet 1982-; awards: life mem. Minn. PTA (1967), Silver Key award, NABAC (Am. Inst. of Banking); mem. Inst. of Internal Auditors Inc. (pres. Inland Empire chpt. 1974-75), Christian Mgmt. Assn.; civic: Lions Intl., Ontario City Safety Council (safety commnr.), Chaffey H.S. Advis. Com.; publs: (manuals) Organizational Structuring, Trouble Shooting Distressed Not-For-Profit Organizations, Visionary; mil: US Navy 1942-45; Ind.; Prot.; rec: Bible study/tchg. Res: 1515 N Boulder Ave Ontario 91762 Ofc: Southwest Baptist Conference 925 N Sunset Ave West Covina 91790

COX, J. ELIZABETH, business owner; b. Dec. 30, 1951, Flint, Mich.; d. Michael H. and Opal L. (Sewell) Egan; m. Christopher Arthur Cox, July 4, 1978; 1 son, Sean Christopher b. 1969; Cert. Pediatric Nursing Asst. 1976. Career: owner, oper. Mrs. Elizabeth Cox: Pet Tattooer (horses, dogs, livestock) for six years; guest speaker various animal breeding clubs; provider free tattooing of seeing-eye guide dogs, dogs of the hearing-impaired, search & rescue dogs and K-9 dogs; motto: I have a warm heart for cold noses; created cartoons for Puppy Reporter news magazine 1980-81; Democrat; Catholic; rec: computers, collecting depression glass, pet (Irish Wolfhound). Address: 1610 N Millard Rialto 92376

COX, JUDITH M., healthcare administrator; b. Aug. 5, 1941, Rockford, Ill.; d. Mahlan and Dorothy (Jacobs) Vaughan; 2 children: Melinda (Bergensheim), DDS, b. 1959, John Marks b. 1963; Cert. Nurse Asst.; Calif. Lic. Nsg. Home Adminstr., BEHA (1984). Career: cert. nurses aide in newborn nursery, Grossmont Hosp. 1964-66; team leader, treatment aide, then night chg., Cloisters of the Valley, 1967-73; mem. corporate team adminstr. systems, supr. housekeeping, Ancillary Services supvr. Calif. Convalescent Hosp., La Mesa 1973-, adminstr. 1981-86, adminstr. and admission preceptor The Cloisters of La Jolla, 1986—; tng. preceptor for Adminstrs. in Tng.; mem. Calif. Assn. of Healthcare Facilities, Am. Coll. of Healthcare Adminstrs., La Mesa CofC; Christian, mem. Navajo Missions, Christian Childrens Fund; rec: crafts. Ofc: The Cloisters, 7160 Fay Ave La Jolla 92037

COYE, KEITH ALLAN, consulting firm executive; b. Oct. 30, 1947, Bath, NY; s. Harry and Esther (Packard) C.; m. Lorraine Tardif, Aug. 1, 1969; children: Cameron b. 1971, Michelle b. 1974; edn: AS, Wentworth Inst. 1967; Northeastern Univ. 1967; Saddleback Coll. 1975; BA, Boston Univ. 1978. Career: New Products supr. Digital Equip. Corp. (DEC), Mass. 1972-73, Branch Service Mgr., Calif. 1973-75, mktg. splst., Mass. 1975-76, European mktg. mgr., Mass. 1976-78, Sr. Account mgr., Calif. 1978-80; CEO, bd. dirs., Consulting Services Corp., Calif. 1980—. Exec. cons. San Mateo Regl. Computer Network, 1980-; speaker San Diego Microcomputer Conf. 1982; mem: Nat. Assn. Underwater Instrs. 1975-; Am. Modeling Assn. 1977-; Am. Platform Assn.; Nat. Spkrs. Assn.; South Bay Computer Club, Leader Assembly Lang. subgp. 1981; Piconet CPM Club (pres. 1983); Nat. Fedn. Independent Businessmen. works: devel. scholarship tracking system, 1982), Nat. Assn. of Sec. School Principals, 1978-82; designed, implemented DEC system-10 Error Analysis and Reporting System (SYSERR), 1972-80. Mil: pvt. USMC 1968, top secret clearance, Bettis Atomic Lab., 1969-73; author Micro to Mainframe Connection (Dr. Dobbs J. 2/84); Protestant. rec: computers, woodwork, chess. Address: Consulting Services Corp., 36 Railway Ave Campbell 95008

CRABTREE, JOHN EDISON, import executive; b. Mar. 19, 1939, Boise, Idaho; s. Edison M. and Helen Maxine (Blanton) C.; edn: BA, USC 61; MS, 1967; Customhouse broker lic., US Customs Svcs. 1979. Career: mgr. Container Care Corp., Wilmington 1970-71; self- empl. apt. owner/ mgmt. cons. Tustin, San Pedro 1968-74; proj. mgr. Howard Hartry Inc., Wilmington 1974-77; team supvr. Frank P. Dow Co., Inc., Los Angeles 1977-78; import mgr. Ted. L. Rausch Co., Long Beach 1978-80; owner Antique Furniture Import Bus., San Pedro 1980-82; import mgr, Harry W. Hamacher, Inc., Westcoast Div., San Pedro; mem: Yachting Olympic Games Weighmaster 1984; Cabrillo Beach Yacht Club (Protest Com. 1981-84); Olson 30 Owners Assn. (1st pres. 1979-80); pres. Small Boat Owners Racing Assn. (pres. 1980); US Yacht Racing Union, Newport, R.I.; mil: 1st lt. USMC 1961-64, Armed Forces Expeditionary Medal; Republican; Christian Sci.; rec: sailboat racing. Res: 1240 Stonewood Ct San Pedro 90732 Ofc: Harry W. Hamacher, Inc., 1300 S Beacon St, Ste 114, San Pedro 90731

CRAIN, JOHN GARLAND LYFORD, industrial real estate broker; b. April 20, 1915, Bethany, Mo.; s. Harry Isaac and Grace Anna (Meek) C.; m. Claire V.

Yegge, Dec. 30, 1939; children: Lawrence D. b. 1941, Cilfford G. b. 1944; edn: indsl. orgn., UCLA 1943; Lic. Practitioner, Interstate Commerce Commn. 1944; Lic. Real Estate Broker, Calif. 1964. Career: job swiching Remington Rand, National Freight Carloading, Douglas Aircraft 1941-44; freight bill auditor 1944-47; freight bill auditor, freight transportation cons., indsl. devel. cons. (mem. Am. Indsl. Devel. Council) Craine & Assoc. 1948-80; retd.; lic. real estate broker and ICC Practitioner; honors: Hon. Mem., Ballut Abyad Temple Shrine, Albuquerque, N.Mex.; Hon. Mem., Shrine Sudan Temple, New Bern, No. Carolina; mem: Torrance, Centinela Valley, Ventura and Conf. of Calif. Hist. Socs. (co-regl. v.p.), Good Sam's Club (charter mem. Gold Coasters chpt.), Ventura Co. Hist. Soc. (Docent Council); Republican; Protestant; rec: CCHS activities. Res: 85 Poinsetta Gardens Dr. Ventura 93004

CRAMOND, RICHARD, JR., missile facilities development executive; b. June 30, 1945, Minneapolis; s. Richard, Sr. and Emelia Hilma (Lundstrom) C.; m. Edna M. Hantzche, Dec. 21, 1973; edn: BS engring., cum laude, CSU Long Beach 1968; MSCE, Univ. N.M. 1970; PhD struc. engring., Univ. Ill. 1974; Reg. Profl. Engr. (Civil) Calif. 1975. Career: naval architect Long Beach Naval Shipyard, 1968; research asst. E.H. Wang Civil Engring. Research Facility, 1968-70, Univ. Ill., 1970-73, A.H-S Ang Consulting Engr., 1972-73; with TRW, 1973– : mem. tech. staff, 1973-75, section hd. Engring. Analysis Sect. 1975-78, asst. project mgr. (ocean thermal energy conversion proj.) 1978, senior project engineer (design and devel. M-X protective structures) 1978-80, facilities dept. mgr. (all TRW M-X facilities devel.) 1980-84, mgr. Silo Hardening Technology Dept., 1984– ; honors: Tau Beta Pi (1967), Chi Epsilon (1969), Phi Kappa Phi (1972); mem: ASCE (subcom. Dynamic and Impact Loads on Structurres), Am. Inst. of Aero. and Astro., Soc. for Exptl. Stress Analysis (bd. New Mex. Sect. 1969); publs: technical reports (5); Presbyterian; rec: hiking, fishing. Res: 36226 Ginger Tree Trail Yucaipa 92399 Ofc: TRW, POB 1310, San Bernardino 92402

CRANSTON, ALAN, US senator; b. June 19, 1914, Palo Alto, Calif.; s. William and Carol (Dixon) C.; m. Geneva McMath, Nov. 6, 1940 (div. 1977); children: Robin MacGregor b. 1947 (dec. 1980), Kim Christopher b. 1951; m. 2d Norma Weintraub, May 1978; edn: BA, Stanford Univ. 1936. Career: fgn. correspondent Internat. News Svc. Europe and Africa 1936-38; investment, property mgmt. and real estate bus. Palo Alto 1947-58; elected state controller of Calif. 1959-67; elected US Senator 1968, Democratic Whip 1977; chief Fgn. Lang. Div., Ofc. of War Information, Wash. DC 1942-44; mem: Calif. Dem. Council (pres. 1953-57), Calif. Dem. Central Com. (exec. commn. 1954-60), Overseas Press Club of Am.; author: The Killing of the Peace (1945), co-author The Big Story (play, 1940); mil: pvt. US Army 1944, sgt. 1945, WWII; Protestant; rec: sports, swimming, running. Ofc: Senate Ofc. Bldg. Wash DC 20510

CRANSTON, ROBERT WEATHERSTON, III, neurosurgeon; b. Nov. 9, 1926, Minneapolis, Minn.; s. Robert W., II and Elizabeth (Morrison) C.; div.; children: Robert W. b. 1955, Jane Alice b. 1957, Susan Lee b. 1960, Ruth Ellen b. 1962; edn: Univ. of Minn. 1942-45; MS, Univ. of Wisc. 1947, MD, 1949; certified Am. Board of Neurosurgery (1962). Career: intern Evanston Hosp., Evanston, Ill. 1949-50; physician Med. Corps US Navy 1950-52; gen. practice in No. Dak., 1952-55; resident in neurosurgery Univ. of Wis. 1955-59; neurosurgeon with the Duluth Clinic 1959-60; pvt. practicing neurosurgeon, San Diego area 1960– ; mem: AMA, San Diego Med. Soc. (alt. del. to CMA), Calif. Med. Assn., Neurosurg. Advis. Bd. to CMA, Am. Assn. of Neurological Surgeons, Congress of Neurological Surgeons, Calif. Assn. of Neurological Surgeons (founding bd. mem., bd. dirs. 3 yrs.), Western Fedn. of Neurol. Sci. (bd. dirs. 3 yrs.), San Diego Acad. of Neurosurgeons, Union of Am. Physicians and Dentists (past pres. Local 7901), Halt, Ralph B. Cloward Soc. (founding bd. mem.), La Mesa CofC (past bd. dirs.); mil: lt. USNR Med. Corps 1950-52; rec: scuba diving, comml. salmon and albacore fishing. Ofc: Robert W. Cranston MD Inc. 5565 Grossmont Center Dr La Mesa 92041

CRAWFORD, JAMES MERLIN, university administrator; b. May 27, 1930, Chico; s. James Morgan and Olive Naomi (Lynn) C.; m. Frances Lorraine Berry, Sept. 4, 1949; children: Cynthia Lee b. 1951, James Michael b. 1952; edn: DDS, Loma Linda Univ. 1960; MPH, Harvard Univ. 1969. Career: staff mem. New England Meml. Hosp., Stoneham, Mass. 1969-70; asst. prof. School of Health, Loma Linda Univ. 1970-72, acting chmn. Dept. of Health Edn. 1972-74, chmn. 1974-77, dean Sch. of Health, LLU 1977– ; dir. of Health Edn., Christian Leadership Seminars 1974; honors: Hon. Alumnus, Sch. of Health, LLU; Fellow, Internat. Coll. of Dentists; Alumnus of the Year, Sch. of Dentistry LLU; mem: Am. Dental Assn., Am. Public Health Assn., Harvard Alumni Assn., Am. Soc. of Preventive Dentistry. Ofc: School of Health, Loma Linda University, Loma Linda 92350

CRAWFORD, JOHN EDWIN, engineer; b. Jan. 29, 1943, Long Beach; s. Albert Thomas and Valera (Doxey) C.; m. Andrea, Nov. 8, 1970; edn: BS, UC Berkeley 1965, MS, 1967; Reg. Profl. Engr. (civil) Calif. 1974. Career: research structural engr. Naval Civil Engring. Lab., Port Hueneme, 1967-81; engring. splst. (simulation integrity of spacecraft and hardened structures) Aerospace Corp., El Segundo 1981– , guidance and tchg. nonlinear analysis of structures; cons. for Air Force, Dames and Moore, the Swedish govt., and others in powder metallurgy, submersible window design, airfield pavement design tools; author num. tech. reports and papers; awards: Guest scientist for ongoing Swedish govt. project to advance mfg. tech. of hardmetal products; civic: active in land use and park preservation matters, preservation of rural Topanga, mem. Sierra Club, Audubon Soc., TASC; prepared num. presentations before Coastal Commn., L.A. County Planning Commn., var. state and fed. agencies; rec: stone masonry, wood working. Ofc: Aerospace Corporation, POB 92957, Los Angeles 90009

CRAWFORD, JOHN THOMAS, consulting engineer; b. Jan. 20, 1936, Los Angeles (5th generation Californian, grandparantage from father purchased Rancho San Pasqual before Calif. was state-1950); s. James Donald and Sadie May (Abernathy) C.; m. Cecile J., Jan. 7, 1956; children: John b. 1956, James b. 1958, Joel b. 1959, Darren b. 1969. edn: Pasadena City Coll. 1953-55; UC Los Angeles extn. 1956-60; State Jt. Apprenticeship Pgm.-Surveyors 1963-65; Reg. Land Surveyor Calif. Career: v.p., dir. planning DCI Land Devel. Co. 1968-70; v.p.-ptnr. H.M. Scott & Assoc. Rosemead-Carson 1960-68; survey field supv. Nat. Engrs., Industry 1970-83; pres./ owner John T. Crawford & Assoc. Civil Engrs. & Land Surveyors, Walnut 1983– ; surveying instr. summer pgm. Cal. Poly. Pomona; cons. to chmn. bd. Dominguez Estates, Watson Land Co., THUMS (Texaco, Humble, Union, Mobil, Shell) Islands Long Beach Harbor; honors: Constrn. Project of the Year (Am. Soc. Civil Engrs. 1980), 1st Place Painting-Water Color (Nat. Art Contest), published in National Anthology of Poetry (3 poems); mem: Calif. Land Surveyors Assn., Calif. Surveyors Historical Soc., Am. Soc. Civil Engrs. and Land Surveyors, Rotary, Kiwanis, Industry Hills Tennis Club; mil: ROTC Coll.; Republican; Protestant; rec: fishing, tennis. Res: 20329 Rim Ridge Rd Walnut 91789 Ofc: John T. Crawford & Assoc. Walnut, Blythe, Bokel-Crawford Assoc. Hemet

CRAWFORD, MATTHEW E., JR., life insurance general agent; b. June 6, 1943, Prairie View, Tx.; s. Rev. Matthew E., Sr. and Cornell G. (Cleaver) C.; m. Florence Johnson, Dec. 21, 9174; 1 dau. Michele b. 1967; edn: AA, Pasadena City Coll. 1964; BA in bus. adm., Prairie View A&M Univ. 1973. Career: ops. ofcr. Bank of Am., 1964-65; letter carrier US Post Office, 1965-67; police ofcr. City of Pasadena, 1967-68; field rep. Gen. Motors Acceptance Corp., 1969-75; fin. asst. Allstate Ents., 1975-76; customer acct. rep. Ford Motor Credit Co., 1976-78; self-empl. 1978-81; field underwriter New York Life, 1981-82; life ins. gen. agt. Crawford, Matthews & Assocs., Pasadena currently; mem: So. Calif. Urban Coalition and Western Bus. Devel. Center (bd. dirs.), Foothills Life Underws. Assn. (bd.), Pasadena-San Gabriel Valley Life Underws. Assn. (bd.); civic: Am. Legion, NAACP, Urban League, Masons, Phi Beta Lambda Bus. Frat.; mil: airman US Air Force; Democrat; Baptist; rec: bowling, golf, community affairs. Res: 1208 N Michigan Ave Pasadena 91104 Ofc: Crawford, Matthews & Assocs. 1143 N Lake Ave Ste 4 Pasadena 91104

CREECH, RAY, real estate broker; b. July 9, 1917, Italy, Tex.; s. Otto Benton and Maybell (Reybolds) C.; m. Sharon Lee Hull, Oct. 21, 1971; children by previous marriage: Kenneth, b. 1940, Patricia, b. 1942, Donald, b. 1945, Gregory b. 1947, Jerry, b. 1951; edn: BA, Whitworth Coll. 1956; grad. work San Diego State Univ., UCSD. Career: tchr. Lakeside Sch. Dist. 1956-57, Jamul Sch. Dist. 1958-59, Santee Sch. Dist. 1980-86; real estate broker 1960-85, broker Ray Creech Realty 1983– ; honors: Grand Cross of Colors, Rainbow for Girls; hon. mem. Bethel 60, Jobs Daughters; Scout Master, Spokane, Wash. 1952-54; Little League Mgr., El Cajon 1956-57; mem: Masons (Master Lakeside 1977, La Mesa 1981, cmdr Imperial Valley 1984), Future Tchrs. of Am. (pres. Whitworth Coll. chpt. 1955); mem. com. Santee Tchrs. Assn.; mil: sgt. maj. USMC 1938-51; Republican; Protestant; rec: camping, hiking, swimming. Res: 6860 Maury Dr., San Diego 92119 Ofc: Ray Creech Realty, 1136 Broadway, No. 3, El Cajon 92021

CREED, DANIEL EDWARD, superior court judge; b. Aug. 16, 1941, San Francisco; s. Michael and Josephine (Murphy) C.; m. Kathy J. Lamphere, June 19, 1965; children: Jerry b. 1965, Daniel Mark b. 1969; edn: AB, Univ. of San Francisco; JD, Golden Gate Coll. 1968. Career: San Francisco Police officer 1964-68; senior adult probation ofcr. City & Co. of San Francisco 1968-71; dep. dist. atty. County of Santa Clara 1971-80; elected judge Superior Court, San Jose 1980– ; mem. State Bar of Calif., Santa Clara County Bar Assn., Elks, Rotary, St. Thomas More Soc., Santa Clara Council Boy Scouts Am.; Republican; Catholic; rec: golf, Destruction Derby. Res: 450 Royale Park Dr San Jose 95136 Ofc: 191 No First St San Jose 95113

CREIGHTON, ELMER FREEMAN, JR., service company executive; b. May 31, 1938, McCormick, So. Carolina; s. Elmer Freeman and Alma (Graves) C.; m. Jacquelyn Mills, Jan. 19, 1979; children: John b. 1966, Kathryn b. 1963, Shawn b. 1968; edn: BSChE, Clemson Univ. 1960. Career: product splst. General Electric Co., Gainsville, Fla. 1965-66, mgr. mktg., Irmo, So. Carolina 1966-68; with ARA Services Inc. 1968– ; cons. prin., Atlanta, Ga. 1968-71; div. mgr., Greenville, So. Carolina 1971-75, regl. gen. mgr. 1975-79; sales v.p., El Segundo 1979-81, area v.p. 1981– ; ARA Vending Policy Com. (1981-82); mem: So. Carolina Automatic Merchandising Assn. (pres. 1976), Soc. for Adv. of Mgmt. (pres. 1974-75), Jr. CofC, Boy Scouts of Am. (scoutmaster, Greenville chpt. 1964); mil: 1st lt. US Army 1961; Republican; Methodist; rec: tennis, golf. Res: 6802 Lawnhaven Dr. Huntington Beach 92648 Ofc: ARA Services Inc., 17116 Valley View La Mirada 90638

CRENSHAW, GEOFFREY ALLEN, private investigator; b. Oct. 31, 1953, Visalia; s. Wm. Allen and Letty Jean (Snowden) C.; edn: spl. courses Coll. of the Sequoias, CSU Fresno, UC Davis; Calif. lic. Pvt. Investigator (1979). Career: sgt./peace ofcr., Calif., 1971-79 (recipient 11 commendns., certificates from Dept. of Justice, Bahn-Fair Inst., State of Calif.); founder/dir. The Argus Co., 1979– ; ptnr. Sutter Creek Gallery (1982-85); mem. Peace Ofcrs. Research Assn. of Calif., Calif. Assn. Licensed Investigators (chmn. coms.), World Assn. of Detectives, CofC; publs: Plaintiff constrn. personal injury question guide (c. 1983), Flat fee formulae for Pvt. Investigators (c. 1985); Republican; Baptist. Ofc: The Argus Co. POB 4347 Visalia 93278

CRENSHAW, PERRY FRANKLIN, veterinarian; b. July 20, 1958, Ocala, Fla.; s. Perry Lester and Janice Mae (Stokes) C.; edn: B. Gen. Agri., Okla. State Univ. 1980, DVM, 1983. Career: veterinarian Emerg. Animal Clin. Sherman Oaks 1983–, Clark Vet. Hosp. Newhall 1983–; At Home Mobile Vet Service (self-owned house call service for animals) 1984–; honors: President's Academic Awards (OSU 1976-79), Outstanding 1st Year Vet. Med. Student 1980, 3rd Year 1982; mem: Am. Vet. Med. Assn., Okla Vet. Med. Assn., L.A. World Affairs Council, L.A. Opera League; Republican; Southern Baptist; rec: tennis, cycling, coin collecting, art appreciation. Res: 8400 Laydon Ave, Apt 11, Sepulveda 91343 Ofc: At Home Mobile Vet Svc. 5152 Sepulveda Blvd Sherman Oaks 91403

CREWS, RICHARD LAWRENCE, university president, physician; b. July 11, 1937, NYC; edn: BA magna cum laude, Phi Beta Kappa, Williams Coll. 1959; MD, Harvard Med. Sch. 1963; internship S.F. Gen. Hosp., 1963-64; res. in psychiat. Letterman Gen. Hosp., Presidio of S.F., 1965-68. Career: Medicine and Psychiatry: served to maj., US Army M.C. 1964-71, psychiat. ward ofcr. Brooke Army Med. Ctr., Ft. Sam Houston, Tex. 1964-65, chief of psychiatry and neurology, Womack Army Hosp. and chief of mental hygiene cons. service, Ft. Bragg, N.C., 1968-71; pvt. practice psychiatry, Mill Valley, Calif. 1971–; cons. Calif. State Disability Evaluation Bd., 1974–; clin. practice Homeopathy and Nutritional Counseling, 1977-80; Edn. and Adminstrn.: lectr. in psychol., US Army Edn. Ctr. 1969-70, lectr. Univ. of N.C. Grad. Sch of Social Work, 1970-71; cofounder Brookwood Gen. Hosp., Santa Rosa, Calif. 1971; pres. Brookwood Hosp. Corp., 1975-80; lectr. in psychol. Coll. of Marin, 1971-72, Dominican Coll., San Rafael 1972-75; exec./clin. director Creative Living Centers of Marin Co., 1972-75, Wholistic Health and Nutrition Inst. (bd. dirs. 1977-) 1977-79; cofounder/pres. Columbia Pacific Univ., San Rafael 1978–; cofounder No. Am. Coll. of Natural Health Scis., Mill Valley and San Rafael, 1978, faculty 1978-80; chmn. Spl. Com. on Authorization Standards, Council for Pvt. Postsec. Ednl. Instns. of Calif., 1982-; chief edtl. advisor Internat. J. of Holistic Health and Medicine, 1982-; mem: Mensa, Intertel, AMA, CMA, Sonoma Co., Marin Co. Med. Assns., Am., No. Calif. Psychiat. Assns., Health Scis. Communications Assn., Am. Holistic Med. Assn; decorated Legion of Merit, US Army (1970); num. academic, med. publs. Address: 112 Edgewood Ave Mill Valley 94941

CRISCUOLO, WENDY LAURA, lawyer; b. Dec. 17, 1949, NY, NY; d. Joseph Andrew and Betty Jane (Jackson) C.; edn: BA design, with honors, UC Berkeley 1973; JD, Univ. San Francisco 1982. admitted Calif. State Bar, Supreme Ct. 1984. Career: space planner Gen. Svcs. Adminstrn. S.F. 1973-79; senior interior designer E. Lew & Assoc. S.F. 1979-80; design dir. Beier & Gunderson Inc. Oakland 1980-81; senior interior designer Environmental Planning & Research S.F. 1981-82; interior design cons. Mill Valley 1982–; law clerk to Judge Spencer Williams US Dist. Ct. S.F. 1983-84; atty. Ciros Investments 1984–; dir. Marin Citizens for Energy Planning San Rafael 1986–; instr. legal research & writing USF 1983; honors: USF Law Review 1983, nom. for dept. citation in design (UCB 1973); mem: Calif. State Bar, Queen's Bench, Calif. Women Lawyers, Commonwealth Club, Pi Beta Phi; publ: Guide to the Laws of Charitable Giving (3rd ed. rev. 1983), Interior Design for Genstar Corp. (Corp. Design 1982), novel in progress; Republican; Episcopal; rec: creative writing. Ofc: Mill Valley

CRISELL, ROBERT WILLIAM, commercial real estate developer; b. Feb. 24, 1943, Los Angeles; s. Wm. Millard and Margaret Mary (Goodjohn) C.; m. Toni Ann Hammer, June 26, 1965; children: Robert b. 1970, Jennifer b. 1971, Gregory b. 1973; edn: BS in real estate, USC 1965; Calif. lic. real estate broker (1966). Career: sales agt., senior sales cons. Coldwell Banker Comml. Brokerage, Los Angeles and San Diego, 1965-73; v.p. Howard S. Wright Devel. Co., Seattle 1973-75; pres. Crisell Props. of Calif. Inc. (shop ctr. dev. San Diego, Orange and Riverside Counties), 1976–; chmn. bd. Family Devel. Found., Julian; honors: Coldwell Banker Top 20 Salesmen (1971); mem. Internat. Council of Shopping Ctrs.; scoutmaster Boy Scouts Am.; club: Vista Valley Country; Republican; Christian; rec: backpacking, fishing, golf. Res: 4938 San Jacinto Cir Fallbrook 92028 Ofc: Crisell Properties POB 2099 Escondido 92025

CRITCHFIELD, BURKE M., lawyer; b. June 28, 1930, Deadwood, So. Dakota; s. Harry M. and Kathryn (Gage) C.; m. Paula, Dec. 30, 1955; children: Pamela b. 1956; Bradley b. 1960; edn: AA, George Washington Univ. 1951; BA, Macalaster Coll. 1952; JD, Univ. of So. Dakota 1960. Career: assoc. Pillsbury, Madison & Sutro, 1960-61; sr. ptr. Miller, Critchfield, Eaton & Noonan 1961-79; sole practitioner 1979–; trustee Alameda Co. Law Library 1963-; donors: Man of Yr., Livermore CofC 1963; President's Award, Livermore CofC 1971; Man of Yr., Eagles Club 1980; mem: Calif. Bar Assn. (bd. govs. 1983-85, pres. 1984-85), Alameda Bar Assn. (pres. 1979), Livermore CofC (pres. 1964-66), Livermore- Amador Valley Bar Assn. (pres. 1972-73); mil: 2nd lt. US Army Intell. Corps; rec: skiing, fishing. Ofc: 1171 Murrieta Blvd. Ste. 1 Livermore 94550

CROCKER, CLAIRE DENIS, hospital administrator; b. Feb. 5, 1924, Ontario, Canada, nat. US cit. 1955; d. Philias Joseph and Gertrude (Galipeau) Denis; m. Lewis Crocker, Jan. 8, 1980; edn: BSN, summa cum laude, Seattle Univ. 1952; MSN, Catholic Univ. of Am. 1956; Reg. Nurse, 1952. Career: supr. Providence Hosp., Seattle 1960-62, 1971-74; adminstrv. asst. Providence Hosp., Anchorage, Alaska 1962-67, 1974-75; adminstr. DePaul & Mt. St. Vincent,

Seattle 1967-71; pres. Sisters of Providence Health Care Corp., Seattle 1975-79; adminstr. and senior equipt. planner Nat. Medical Ents., Calif. 1980-82; adminstr. Harbor Crest, San Pedro Peninsula Hosp., San Pedro 1982-83, Earlwood Conv. Hosp. (Summit Health Corp.), Torrance 1983-84, Extended Care Hosp. of Anaheim, 1984–; clin. instr. Seattle Univ. 1952-53, asst. prof. 1957-60; honors: Sigma Theta Tau (1955), Pi Gamma Mu (1956); mem., chmn. Alaska Board of Nsg. 1962-67; orgns: Bus. & Profl. Womens Club (secty.), Anaheim CofC, Palos Verdes Shores Womens Golf Club (pres. 1985); works: estab. Chronic Dialysis Pgm. Alaska Kidney Found., served on Alaska Methodist Univ. Nsg. Edn. Com. to plan and estab. school of nursing; Republican; Roman Catholic; rec: golf, music. Res: 2275 West 25th St Apt 168 San Pedro 90732 Ofc: Extended Care Hospital of Anaheim 501 S Beach Blvd Anaheim 90824

CROCKER, MYRON DONOVAN, judge; b. Sept. 4, 1915, Pasadena; s. Myron Wm. and Ethel (Shoemaker) C.; m. Elaine Jensen, Apr. 26, 1941; children: Glenn, Holly; edn: AB, Fresno State Coll. 1937; LLB, UC Berkeley 1940; admitted to Calif. State Bar 1940. Career: special agent FBI, 1940-46; practised law Chowchilla, 1946-48; asst. dist. atty. Madera County, 1946-51; judge Chowchilla Justice Ct., 1952-58, Superior Ct. Madera County, 1958-59; US judge Eastern Dist. Calif., Sacramento 1959–; named Outstanding Citizen Chowchilla, 1960; mem. Chowchilla CofC (secty.), Lions Club; Republican; Mem. Madera County Repub. Central Com. 1950-; Lutheran. Ofc: US District Courthouse, 1130 O St., Fresno 93721

CROLL, RICHARD CAMPBELL, investor; b. Oct. 24, 1939, Evanston, Ill.; s. Frederick W., Jr. and Florence I. (Campbell) C.; m. Carol, May 25, 1985; edn: BA, Colorado Coll. 1964; desig: Reg. Rep., NYSE. Career: past account exec. Chapman Howe, Chgo.; current self empl. investor: venture capital, real estate syndication, inv. banking; mem. Audubon Soc., World Affairs Council; clubs: Olympic, Mt. Tam Racket, University (Evanston, Ill.), Knollwood (Lake Forest, Ill.), The Priory (Kentfield, Calif.); Republican; Presbyterian; rec: bird watching, travel, ESL tutor. Address: Kentfield 94904

CRONIN, DOUGLAS PHILLIP, electronics co. president; b. Jan. 29, 1936, Seattle, Wash.; s. Robert Hawks and Irma May (Pritchard) C.; children: Lisa Gay (Kale) b. 1958, Wendy Maureen b. 1960; edn: BSME, Ore. State Coll. 1958; MBA, Pepperdine Univ. 1968; PhD, Jackson State Univ. 1975. Career: pres. Engineering Design & Devel., 1959-81; pres. ED&D Mfg. Co., 1981-84; pres./CEO ED&D Electronics, a Sunbank Co., 1985–; dir. GT Equip. Co., Quantum Internat. Prodns.; honors: DeMolay Chevalier (1958); mem. Am. Ordnance Assn., US Army Assn., Republican Assocs.; rec: ski, stained glass. Res: 10310 Riverside Dr Toluca Lake 91602 Ofc: ED&D Electronics 3110 Winona Ave Burbank 91504

CRONIN, KENNETH GARLAND, financial institution executive; b. Jan. 20, 1918, Topeka, Kansas; s. Frank Joseph and Florence May (Miller) C.; m. Marlyss, April 16, 1966; 1 son, Kenneth Jr. b. 1970; edn: indsl. mgmt., Lake Forest Coll. 1957-61. Career: Crocker Nat. Bank, San Francisco 1963-70; Santa Clara Savings, Santa Clara 1970-74; v.p., regl. mgr. Calif. Federal Savings, Los Angeles 1974–; honors: New Club Bldg. Award, Excellence-Pueblo De San Jose 1976-77; Outstanding Svc. Award, Santa Clara Kiwanis Club 1975-76; Cert. of Appreciation, Santa Clara Co. Bar Assn. 1983; mem: Palo Alto CofC (pres. 1983-84), Nat. Library of Sports, Santa Clara Kiwanis Club (pres. 1974-75); publs: articles, Santa Clara Co. Bus. Mag. 1977-82; mil: 1st sgt. US Army 1942-46; Republican; Methodist; rec: gardening, music. Res: 1022 Belford Dr. San Jose 95132 Ofc: California Federal Savings & Loan, 3755 El Camino Real Santa Clara 95051

CROSS, PETER DENNIS, co. executive; b. July 12, 1932, New London, New Hampshire; s. Harry A. and Dorothea Mary (Flanagan) C.; m. Bonnie Healey, Feb. 17, 1962; children: Peter, Jr. b. 1962, Laura b. 1963; BS in soc. sci., Fairfield Univ. 1959; MBA, Pepperdine Univ. 1984. Career: asst. regional mgr. Pinkerton's Inc., N.Y.C. 1951-69; v.p. Sanitas Service Corp., Hartland, Ct. 1970-73; pres. Andes & Cross Services Inc., Glendale, Ca. 1976–; mem: Guard Service Assn. (pres./founder), Am. Soc. for Indsl. Security, Calif. Assn. of Licensed Investigators, Calif. Contract Guard Service Assn.; Club: Verdugo; mil: US Army 1953-55; Republican; Roman Catholic. Res: 1339 N Columbus Ave Glendale 91202 Ofc: Andes & Cross Services Inc. 1110 Sonora Ave Ste 101 Glendale 91201

CROSS, REGINALD, JR., "CAPPY", public safety communications manager; b. Apr. 9, 1953, Portchester, N.Y.; s. Reginald and Jean (Davidson) C.; m. Mary Ellen, Dec. 17, 1977; 1 dau. Meghan b. 1981; edn: cert. US Army Signal Sch., 1970-71; cert. tech. Nat. Assn. Business & Edn. Radio (1984). Career: U.S. Army tech. controller, Stratcom-Europe, 1971-73; tolls maint. techn. State of Conn. D.O.T., New Haven 1974-75; product mgr. Abbott Coin Counter Co., Stamford, Conn. 1975-78; service mgr. Abbott Money Processing, Inglewood, Calif. 1978-79; techn. So. Bay Regl. Public Comm., Hawthorne 1979-80; techn. USGS Seismic Lab., CalTech 1980-81; tech. services mgr. So. Bay Regl. Comm., Hawthorne 1981–; indep. cons. comm. systems, 1984-; mem. Assoc. Public Safety Comm. Officers, Inc. 1982-; mil: sp4 US Army 1970-73; rec: sailing, motorcycling, hiking, travel, computers, tng. parrots. Res: 5208 Conant St Long Beach 90808 Ofc: South Bay Regional Public Communications Authority 12227 S Hawthorne Way Hawthorne 90250

CROSS, ROBERT MC INTOSH, educator, college dental program director; b. Aug. 23, 1920, Chgo.; s. Guy and Elsie Margaret (Isaac) C.; div.; edn: stu. UCLA 1976-78; BA in voc. edn., CSU Long Beach 1982, MA in voc. edn.,

1986; desig: Cert. Dental Techn. (1959). Career: owner/opr. Cross Dental Lab. 1951-60; dist. mgr. Universal Dent. Co. 1960-64; western mgr. Cosmos Dent. Co. 1964-70, Stern Dent. Co. 1970-76; dent. tech. instr. Southland Coll. 1976-77; dir. Dental Lab. Tech. Pgm., Cypress Coll. 1977–; mem: Nat. Denturist Assn. (bd. dirs. 1982-88, edn. chmn. 1981-86, named 10 Yr Pioneer 1976), So. Calif. State Dent. Lab. Assn. (1951-60, pres. Bay Area chpt. 1958); publs: dental arts. in Dental Lab World, Orient Express (1980), The Latin Connection (1981), An Am. in Europe (1983); mil: lt. Dental Corps USNR (ret.) 1942-69; Democrat; Catholic. Res: 5447 Twin Lakes Dr Cypress 90630 Ofc: Cypress College 9200 Valley View St Cypress 90630

CROSSLAND, PAUL NICHOLAS, accountant; b. Nov. 5, 1933, Chicago, Ill.; s. Walter Nicholas and Wilma Marie (DeFoe) C.; m. Nancy Cummings, Sept. 24, 1955; children: Jeffery b. 1956, James b. 1957, Paul b. 1959, Cynthia b. 1961; edn: BS, Univ. of Ill. 1956. Career: ptr. Alexander Grant & Co. CPAs, Chicago, Ill. and Los Angeles 1958–; mem: Am. Inst. CPAs, Calif. Soc. CPAs, Los Angeles CofC, California Club, Oakmont C.C., Los Angeles Athletic Club; mil: 1st lt. 1956-58; Republican; Protestant; rec: golf. Res: 3101 Country Club Dr. Glendale 91208 Ofc: Alexander Grant & Co., 611 W. 6th St. Ste. 3100 Los Angeles 90017

CRUISE, JAMES ROBERT, physician; b. Nov. 2, 1934, Dott, W. Va., s. Murray Ray and Mary Sue (Hill) C.; m. Carol Anne, June 5, 1962; children: Cheryl Anne b. 1963, Deanna b. 1968, James Robert, II b. 1972; edn: Ariz. State Univ. 1957-59; Mt. San Antonio Coll. and San Bernardino Valley Coll. 1961-65; BS physical therapy, Loma Linda Univ. 1961, MD, 1969. Career: agricultural laborer Mesa, Az. 1946-53; copper miner Magma Copper Mining Co., Superior, Az. 1956-59; physical therapist Pacific State Hosp., Pomona, Calif. 1961-65; med. sch. 1965-69, medical residency 1969-72, Loma Linda Univ.; pvt. practice internal medicine and nephrology, Ukiah 1972–, dir. Hemodialysis Unit Ukiah 1976-; staff Hillside Comm. Hosp. (chief of int. medicine 1974-80), Mendocino Comm. Hosp. (chief med. staff 1980); lectr. on diabetes mellitus; mem. Mendocino County Heart Assn.; mem. Nashville Songwriters Assn. Internat. (1984-); author 2 novels, 100+ poems, approx. 50 songs; mil: sgt. USMC 1953-56, 4 Ribbons, GCM; Republican; Seventh Day Adventist; rec: writer, musician (play 6 instruments), amateur magician, artist. Res: 1175 Bel Arbres St Redwood Valley 95470 Ofc: James R. Cruise MD Internal Medicine, 234-B Hospital Dr Ukiah 95482

CRUISE, KATHLEEN, utility co. president; b. Apr. 10, 1947, Wash. DC; d. Robert A. and Jessie E. (Rubini) Cruise; m. Bruce G. Mills, Apr. 11, 1970; children: Dylan b. 1973, Emily b. 1977; edn: B.Arch., Va. Polytech. Inst. and State Univ. 1970; MBA, Golden Gate Univ. 1982; Reg. Architect, Calif. (1975). Career: architl. intern Paul Conklin Quigg Assocs., Arlington, Va. 1964-69; assoc. Lardner, Lardner and Assocs., Auburn, Calif. 1971-75; architl. assoc. City and County of San Francisco, 1976-77; Golden Gate Regional architect Pacific Gas & Elec. Co., San Francisco 1979-85, regional building supt. 1985–; instr. PG&E Tng. Ctr.; lectr. Cogswell Coll. (1983), Am. Inst. of Architects, Orgn. of Women Architects; mem: A.I.A., Constrn. Specification Inst., Orgn. of Women Archs. (steering com 1976, 82); civic: Aquarius Swim Club (bd.), Town Sch. for Boys Parents Assn. (advis. com. 1985), Katherine Delmar Burkes Sch. Parents Assn., Richmond Dist. Community Assn.; rec: running, skiing, gardening. Address: San Francisco 94121

CRUMP, GERALD FRANKLIN, lawyer; b. Feb. 16, 1935, Sacramento; s. John Laurin and Ida May (Banta) C.; m. Glenda Roberts Glass, Nov. 21, 1959; children: Sara Elizabeth b. 1972, Juliane Kathryn b. 1974, Joseph Stephen b. 1977; edn: AB, UC Berkeley 1956, JD, 1959; MA, Baylor Univ. 1966. Career: judge advocate USAF 1960-63; deputy county counsel Los Angeles County 1963–, legislative rep. 1970-73, chief Public Works Div. 1973-84, senior asst. county counsel 1984-85, chief asst. county counsel 1985–; lectr. Pepperdine Univ. (1978), Univ. Calif. (1982); mem: State Bar of Calif. (del.), Am. Bar Assn., Los Angeles County Bar Assn. (chmn. Govt. Law Sect. 1983-4), Am. Judicature Soc., Am. Acad. of Polit. and Social Sci., Calif. Historical Soc., Reserve Officers Assn., Air Force Assn., Phi Alpha Delta, Delta Sigma Phi; mil: capt. USAF 1960-63, Merit. Svc., AF Commdn., (current) col. USAFR. Res: 4020 Camino de la Cumbre, Sherman Oaks 91423 Ofc: Los Angeles County Counsel, 648 Hall of Administration, Los Angeles 90012

CRUZ, LYDIA FLORO, convalescent hospital executive administrator; b. Dec. 26, 1937, Philippines, nat. US cit. 1975; d. Tiburcio Guzman and Filomena Alarilla (Cruz) Floro; m. Leonard Cruz, Sept. 27, 1967; children: Jsoeph Anthony b. 1968, Joyce Anne b. 1970; edn: BS, Univ. of St. Thomas 1957; Accredited Record Technician, Am. Med. Records Assn. 1976; Lic. Nursing Home Adminstr., Calif. 1980. Career: h.s. tchr. St. Mary's Acad., Philippines 1957-63; bank bookkeeper Philippine Nat. Bank, Manila 1963-67; med. secty. Roosevelt Hosp., NY 1967-72; med. record designee Beverly Manor, Burbank 1974, Buena Vista Manor, Duarte 1977; asst. ofcr. mgr. Monrovia Convalescent Hosp., Duarte 1978; exec. adminstr. Bird Haven Christian Conv. Hosp., Bellflower 1981-84; v.p. Bird Haven Corp. 1982; exec. adminstr. Serrano Conv. Hosp. North & South, Los Angeles 1984–; mem: Am. Medical Records Assn., Calif. Med. Record Assn., Catholic Women's League, Philippine American Assn. of Diamond Bar; rec: swimming, tennis. Res: 2635 Indian Creek Rd. Diamond Bar 91765 Ofc: Serrano Convalescent Hospital, 5401 Fountain Ave. Los Angeles 90029

CRYER, RODGER EARL, counselor, educator; b. Apr. 2, 1940, Detroit, Mich.; s. Earl Wilton and Mary Venetia (Miller) C.; m. Bellaflor, June 22, 1986; children: Joseph b. 1970, Noel b. 1978; edn: undergrad., Ohio Wesleyan Univ. 1958-60; AB, San Diego St. Univ. 1965; AM, Stanford Univ. 1974; PhD, Columbia-Pacific Univ. 1985. Career: counselor/tchr. J.W. Fair Intermediate Sch., San Jose; summer sch. tchr. The Foundry Sch. (Juvenile Ct. Sch. pgm.); counseling pvt. practice; adj. prof. CSU San Francisco and CSU San Jose; awards: summer fellow in sociol., Western Interstate Commn. for Higher Edn.; doctoral dissertation grant Colgate-Palmolive Fund, Stanford Univ.; mem: Calif. Tchrs. Assn. (State Council rep., budget com. 1983-), Parental Stress Hotline and Services of San Jose, Inc. (vol. counselor 1984-85); works: Decision-Making Heuristic; Democrat; Unitarian; rec: bicycling, x-c skiing. Res: 3975 Ambler Ct San Jose 95111 Ofc: POB 21917 San Jose 95151-1917

CSENDES, ERNEST, finance and engineering executive; b. Mar. 2, 1926, Satu-Mare, Rumania, nat. US cit. 1955; s. Edward O. and Sidonia (von Littman) C.; m. Catharine Tolnai, Feb. 11, 1953; children: Audrey Carol b. 1959, Robert A. Edward b. 1963; edn: BA, Prot. Coll., Hungary 1944; BS, Univ. of Heidelberg 1948, MS and PhD, 1951. Career: research asst. organic chem., Univ. of Heidelberg 1950-51; research assoc. biochem. Tulane Med. Sch., New Orleans 1951-52, fellow Harvard Univ. Chem. Dept. 1952-53; research chemist, Organic Chemicals Dept., E.I. Du Pont de Nemours & Co., Wilmington, Del. 1953-56, Elastomer Chems. Dept. 1956-61; dir. R&D, Armour & Co., Agric. Chem. Div., Atlanta, Ga. 1961-63; v.p. corp. devel. Occidental Petroleum Corp., L.A. 1963-64, exec. v.p. Research, Engring. & Devel. 1964-68, exec. v.p./ chief op. ofcr. Occidental Research & Engring. Corp., 1963-68; pres./ bd. chmn./ CEO TRI Group (offshore finl. cos.), Bermuda 1968–; chmn./CEO Micronic Technologies Inc., L.A. 1981-85; research in the areas of of biochemistry, dyestuffs, elastomers and plastics, fertilizers and pesticides, energy raw materials, petrochemicals, off-shore finance and Eurodollar securities; honors: Pro Mundi Beneficio gold medal, Brazilian Acad. of Humanities (1976), acclaimed for regional devel. programs related to agric. and natural resources in Europe, No. Africa, USSR, Far East and India; mem: Fellow AAAS, N.Y. Acad. of Sci., Am. Chem. Soc., Royal Soc. of Chem., Am. Inst. of Chemists, Am. Inst. Aero. & Astro., Sigma Xi, German Chem. Soc., Am. Mgmt. Assn., Am. Inst. of Mgmt., Explorers Club (NY), Global Action Economic Inst. (NY); works: 250 books, reports, articles in sci. and trade papers and patents; Republican; rec: collect 18th Century decorative art/ France, music (violin & chamber music; graduate Music Conservatory). Res: 18114 Wakecrest Dr Malibu 90265

CUKINGNAN, RAMON A., JR., cardiovascular surgeon; b. Jan. 8, 1944, San Jose, Philippines; s. Ramon, Sr. and Ines (Arellano) C.; m. Bernadette M. Calviello, Dec. 19, 1969; children: Jennifer b. 1970, Marietta b. 1973, Amanda b. 1974, Michael b. 1979, Tara b. 1980; edn: AA, Univ. of Santo Tomas 1962, MD, 1967. Career: intern and resident in general surgery New York Univ., Bellevue 1968-73, resident in cardiovascular and thoracic surgery, 1973-75; chief of thoracic and cardiovascular surgery Wadsworth VA Hosp., 1975-79; asst. prof. of surgery UC Los Angeles 1975-79, asst. clin. prof. surgery 1979–; staff phys. Little Company of Mary Hosp., Torrance Meml. Hosp.; mem: Fellow Am. Coll. of Surgeons, Fellow Am. Coll. of Cardiology, Am. Assn. for Thoracic Surgery, Soc. of Thoracic Surgeons, Western Thoracic Surg. Assn., Am. Heart Assn., AMA, Los Angeles County Med. Assn.; num. profl. presentations, abstracts and articles in med. journals; rec: horticulture, swimming. Ofc: 23451 Madison St Ste 260 Torrance 90505

CULBERT, SANDRA KAY, entrepreneur, business consultant; b. July 27, 1945, Robinson, Ill.; d. David Crockett and Alice Mae (Harmon) Carruth; m. James Richard Culbert, Dec. 29, 1976; children: Kimberlee Mae b. 1963, Jennifer Lynn b. 1963, Jami Rene b. 1979; edn: Ariz. State Univ. Tempe 2 yrs. Career: exec. secty., jr. acct. McDonald's Hamburger San Jose 1965-69; ofc. mgr. NY Lif Ins. Scottsdale, Ariz. 1970-74; realtor, relocation dir. Century 21 Real Estate Scottsdale 1974-76; owner/ oper. Badgeman Designs 1977-82, SKC Designs Mission Viejo, Calif. 1977–; adminstrv. dir./ bus. cons. Mr. Build San Diego 1983-85; p.r. cons. Localpro Svc. Corps San Diego 1985–; mem: Nat. Assn. Female Execs. 1985, Girl Scouts of Am., Easter Seal Soc., Internat. Montessori Soc., League of Women Voters, Republican Women's Club, Assn. for the Retarded, Humane Soc.; Republican; Christian; rec: skeet shooting, tennis, horseback riding, travel. Res: 1627 Citrus Hills Ln Escondido 92027 Ofc: Localpro Svc. Corps 935 Pennsylvania Ave Escondido 92027

CULVER, CHARLIE WILSON, business and management consultant; b. Dec. 6, 1924, Fort Apache, Ariz.; s. Orris Charlie and Christina Mable (Williams) C.; m. Wilma, May 18, 1945; children: Linda b. 1945, Sandra b. 1948, Margaret b. 1950, Charles b. 1953; edn: spl. courses UCLA, 1974. Career: prop. dry cleaning and laundry bus., Dubois, Wyo. 1948-60; adminstrv. mgr. Teledyne Inc., Pasadena 1960-67; ops. mgr. G and H Technol., Santa Monica 1967-76; purch. dir. Underwater Technol. (internat. diving co.), Santa Barbara 1976–; elected City councilman, Dubois, Wyo. 1948-58; dir. Montecito Sanitary Dist. (1983-), dir. Montecito Assn. (1983); clubs: Rotary (pres. elect), Channel City (S.B.), Masons; mil: tech. sgt. US Army Paratroop Sch. 1943-46; Republican; Episcopal; rec: politics, investments, gardening. Res: 128 Olive Mill Rd Montecito 93108 Ofc: Underwater Technology 116B E Yanonali St Santa Barbara 93101

CULVER, L. BYRON, real estate investments & brokerage co. president; b. July 17, 1926, Santa Ana, Calif.; s. Lord Byron and Eunice Verga (Bradley) C.; m. Sharon Einer, May 1, 1956; children: Malanie b. 1956, Suzanne b. 1959, L. Byron III b. 1961, Richard b. 1963, Elizabeth b. 1964, Kathleen b. 1965; edn: BS phys. ed., Cal. Poly. Univ. S.L.O. 1950; Gen. Secondary Tchg. Credl. Calif. 1950. Career: dir. athletics, varsity football/ baseball coach Imperial (Calif.) H.S. 1950-55; pres. Culver Farms Inc. Holtville 1955-70; pres. L. Byron

Culver & Assocs. Rancho Santa Fe 1970–; trustee Rancho Santa Fe Sch. Bd. 1964-77, pres. 5 yrs.; mem: Nat. Realtors Assn., Calif. Realtors Assn.; mil: gunners mate 2/c USN WWII 1944-46; Republican; Protestant; rec: fly fishing. Res: Sobre Los Cerros POB 876 Rancho Santa Fe 92067 Ofc: L. Byron Culver & Assocs. Culver Bldg El Tordo St Rancho Santa Fe 92067

CUMMINGS, MARILYN LOUISE, tutoring center owner; b. Sept. 20, 1932, Chgo.; d. Blaine and Ruth Louise (Niekamp) C.; div.; edn: grad. So. Sem. 1952; grad. work CSU Long Beach, 1957-61; spl. courses w/Mae Carden 1969. Career: engring. dept. Pac. Tel. Co., Compton 1953-5; music tchr. Music Center Studios, San Pedro 1955-7, founder/co-dir. Musicland Studios (main ofc., S.P.) 1957-64; music tchr./coord., Betty Thomas Music Sch., Torrance 1965-7, others; dist. mgr. Field Ent. Ednl. Corp. 1967-9; tutor/field rep. Wingrock Sch. Inc., Torrance 1969-71; area mgr. Am. Incentive to Read, L.A. 1969; founder/director Marilyn Cummings Tutoring Ctr., San Pedro 1969–; advt. rep. Christian Sci Monitor, 1971-3, 76; recipient sales award Field Ent. Ednl. Corp. 1967; mem: Accordion Fedn. of No. Am. (judge Music Contest 56-64, 78-), Sweet Adelines (bd.dirs. 1982-4), San Pedro CofC 1982- (Bus. and Edn. Com.), Bus. & Profl. Womens Club; past mem. BBB, Accordion Tchrs Guild, Toastmistress, Hermosa Harmony Singers (v.p. 1977-80); asst. coordinator for chartering of Leads Club/San Pedro 1986; devel. successful method for teaching reading to illiterate and slow learners 1969; Christian Sci. (bd. 1973-6). Res: 333 So Grand Ave San Pedro 90731 Ofc: Marilyn Cummings Tutoring Center, 312 No Gaffey St, 101-2, San Pedro 90731

CUNNINGHAM, ADELLA ANNE, physician; b. Aug. 2, 1922, Valentine, Nebr.; d. John Leonard and Grace (Heffelfinger) Cunningham; edn: undergrad. Univ. Northwestern; BA, Univ. Ill. 1953, MD, 1957; Board certified Acad. Family Practice, 1970. Career: intern and resident in obstetrics, Conn.; staff phys. in chg. Sutter County (Calif.) Hosp.; pvt. practice in Los Gatos and San Jose, currently; tchg., Stanford family practice residency, San Jose; pgm.; Cancer Soc. lectr. for indsl. firms and colls.; citizen rep. Cabrillo Comm. Coll./ Santa Cruz County; served on Calif. Med. Assn. Com. on the Environment calling attention to nuclear waste disposal issue (still unresolved); initiated first state legislation for radiation protection for women (until then women were not covered by Calif. X-Ray laws); mem. Am. Acad. of Family Practice (past pres. Santa Clara Chpt.; chaired PRSO Com. to estab. hearing procedures for peer review), first woman to serve on Santa Clara Valley Med. Soc./ Santa Clara Bar Assn. Medical-Legal Liaison Com., in that position directed attention to problems of child abuse; publs: contbr. articles in Med. World News, and Female Patient med. jours.; rec: photog., gardening, real estate. Mail: POB 1332 Los Gatos 95031 Ofc: 4155 Moorpark Ste 5 San Jose 95117

CUNNINGHAM, REBA SUE, registered nurse; b. Dec. 30, 1943, Ada, Okla.; d. Thomas John and Ruby Gertrude (Dilbeck) Arms; children: Randall b. 1963, Katherine b. 1964; edn: AA, Coll. of Sequoias 1974; Family Plng. Nse. Practitioner, UC San Francisco 1980; Maternity Nse. Practitioner, CSU San Jose 1985; BSN, Univ. of N.Y. 1986; RN, Calif. St. Bd. 1974. Career: psychiatric techn. Porterville Dev. Center, Porterville 1970-74, RN, 1975–, Health Svcs. splst. 1980-82, Family Plng. Nse. Practitioner, Family Planning of Tulare Co. 1980-84, nse. splst. Acute Pediatrics, Porterville Developmental Ctr. 1982–; speaker var. civic groups, and in-hosp. tour guide; instr. CPR, First Aid, R.N. Contg. Edn.; mem. RN/LVN Profl. Orgn. (1977-); civic: Porterville Family Health Ctr. (bd. 1981-83), Rape Crisis of Tulare Co. (1976-78); works: devel. slide illus. pgm. on acute pediatric patients (1985); Democrat; Methodist; rec: golf, reading. Ofc: Porterville Developmental Center Porterville 93257

CUNNINGHAM, RICHARD REUBEN, insurance co. executive; b. Jan. 27, 1944, Santa Ana; s. Joseph Edward and Carolyn Lois (Cline) C.; m. Sharron, Sept. 5, 1971, children: Jeffrey b. 19606, Scott b. 1967, Robert b. 1967, Richard II b. 1972, Ryan b. 1974; edn: BA, Chapman Coll. 1966; Lic. Ins. Agent, Calif. 1966. Career: letter carrier Downey Post Ofc. 1964; sales trainee Champion Ins. Inc. 1965-, lic. ins. agent sales 1966-, ptnr./v.p. 1971-, ptnr./pres. 1974-, sole prop./pres. 1976–; honors: President's Club (1977), Comml. Council (1979), Safeco Ins. Co.; mem: Indsl. Agents & Brokers Assn. of Calif., Downey Kiwanis (pres. 1976); Republican; Protestant; rec: golf, hunting, fishing. Res: 9317 Gaymont Downey 90240 Ofc: Champion Insurance Inc., 11516 Downey Ave. Downey 90241

CUPP, MARY KATHERINE HYER, psychiatric social worker; b. Jan. 17, 1932, O'Brion, W.Va.; d. Oral Otis and Icie Hyer Barsotti (McCracken) Hyer; edn: BA, W. Va. State Coll. 1967; MSW, W. Va. Univ. 1970; LCSW, Bd. of Behavioral Sci. Examiners of Calif.; Acad. of Cert. Soc. Wkrs., Nat. Assn. of Soc. Wkrs. Career: sales, collection, pub. spkr. Chesapeake Potomac Telephone Co., W.Va. 1948-67; statistician West Virginia Dept. of Welfare 1967-68; placement and case mgmt. State of Calif. Dept. of Mental Hygiene, South Gate 1970-73; adoptions wkr. Los Angeles Co. Adoptions, W. Covina 1973; psychiatric soc. wkr. Camarillo State Hosp., Camarillo 1973–; tchg. cons. Camarillo State Psychiatric Residency Pgm. 1980-; honors: commendation, Gov. George Deukmejian 1983; mem: Nat. Assn. Soc. Wkrs.; Save Our Streetlights (pres. 1979-80); Democrat; Methodist; rec: bridge, roses. Res: 1091 Dara St, Camarillo 93010 Ofc: State of California Camarillo State Hospital, Box A, Camarillo 93011

CUROTTO, RICKY JOSEPH, lawyer; b. Dec. 22, 1931, Lomita Park; s. Enrico and Nora Marie (Giusso) C.; m. Lynne Therese Ingram, Dec. 31, 1983; children: Dina b. 1960, John b. 1962, Alexis b. 1969; edn: BS cum laude, Univ. of San Francisco 1953; JD, USF Sch. of Law 1958. Career: assoc. Peart, Baraty & Hassard, San Francisco 1958-60; sr. counsel for Land Devel. Div., Utah International Inc. and v.p. of related real estate cos. 1961-82; asst. secty. Utah Internat. Inc., 1966–, senior counsel for Ops. & Bus. Devel. Div., 1983–; secty./counsel Ross Valley Homes Inc., 1965–; Dir: First Security Realty Services Corp., Simco Indsl. Mortgage Co., Garden Hotels Inv. Co., of counsel, Curotto Law Ofcs. S.F. and Sacramento 1984–; bd. trustees, Univ. of San Francisco; honors: apptd. to Nat. Panel of Arbitrators, Am. Arbitr. Assn. 1962; Bur. of Nat. Affairs award 1958; USF Alumni distinguished service award 1981; USF Athletic Hall of Fame 1985; mem: State Bar of Calif., San Francisco Bar Assn., Am. Bar Assn., Am. Corp. Counsel Assn., Commonwealth Club of Calif. (past chmn. Lawmaking Procedures Sect.), USF Alumni Assn.; mem. Calif. Assn. for act, SF Mus. Soc., Assn. of Governing Bds. of Univs. & Colls., Pi Sigma Alpha, Phi Alpha Delta; publs: art. USF Law Rev., Winter 1975; mil: 1st lt. US Army 1954-56; Republican; Catholic. Res: 86 Pelican Ln Redwood City 94065 Ofc: Utah International Inc., 550 California St, Rm. 700, San Franciso 94104

CURRIE, ALLAN BRUCE, real estate executive, lawyer; b. May 26, 1947, Ross; s. Allan Bell and Ann Regina (Finn) C.; m. Colleen, Dec. 31, 1979; edn: BSC, Univ. of Santa Clara 1969; JD, UC Hastings Coll. of Law 1972; LLM, Georgetown Law Ctr. 1975; admitted to Calif. Bar. Career: sr. v.p. asset mgmt. Security Properties Inc., Seattle, Wash. 1985-86; investor, advr. and atty. Belvedere 1983-84; sr. v.p. and gen. counsel McNeil Corp., San Mateo 1977-82; atty. Cotton, Seligman & Ray, San Francisco 1976; legal advr. to sr. commnr. Securities and Exch. Commn., Wash. DC 1972-75; honors: Hastings Law Review; Hastings Thurston Honor Soc.; mem: Calif. Bar Assn. (Partnership and Unincorp Assn. com., sect. 1982-83), chmn. No. Calif. Assn. for St. Vincent's Sch. for Handicapped Santa Barbara; Catholic. Res: 36 Andrew Tiburon 94920 Ofc: 2201 6th Ave. Ste. 1500, Seattle, Wash. 98121

CURRIE, J. DAVID, chiropractor, b. June 15, 1954, San Antonio, Texas; s. John Daniel and Dorothy J. (Johnson) C.; m. Mary, July 1, 1978; children: Cherise Lynn b. 1981, Daniel David b. 1983, Brett James b. 1986; edn: AA, Chabot Coll. 1978; DC, Palmer Coll. of Chiropractic 1981; Cert. Disability Evaluator, Calif. Chiropractic Assn. 1985. Career: assoc. doctor Thornton Chiropractic corp., Monterey 1981-82; instr. technique dept. Palmer Coll. of Chiropractic West, Sunnyvale 1982-83; pvt. practice Currie Chiropractic Corp., Fremont 1982–; pres. San Francisco Bay Gonstead Study Group 1984; honors: Diplomate, Gonstead Clinical Studies Soc. 1984; Pi Tau Delta 1981; Cert. in X-Ray Profiency, Erhardt, Davenport, Iowa 1980; mem. Parker Chiropractic Research Found. 1982; Diplomate, Nat. Bd. of Chiropractic Examiners 1981; mem: Optimist Club of Fremont (v.p. 1983-84), Lions Club, Capitola Host; mil: splst. E-4 US Army 1973-76, GCM, Nat. Defense Svc.; Republican; Baptist; rec: baseball (semi-pro. player and little league coach), fishing, golf. Res: 2464 Becket Dr. Union City 94587 Ofc: Currie Chiropractic Corp., 37982 Fremont Blvd. Fremont 94536

CURRIE, SUNYA LOUISE, antique dealer, jewelry designer; b. Oct. 7, 1927, Los Angeles; d. Jack and Sadie Ellen (Rosen) Lofsky; m. Malcolm R. Currie, June 21, 1951, div.; children: Deborah Ann, b. 1953, David Malcolm, b. 1955, Diana Michelle, b. 1962; edn: BA, UC Berkeley 1951. Career: antique dealer, Venice 1973-81, Beverly Hills 1981-84; jewelry designer Sunya Currie, Pac. Palisades 1979–; mem: Women in Bus.; Nat. Assn. of Antique Dealers; Antique Dealers of So. Calif.; Nat. Assn. of Women Bus. Owners; Nat. Assn. of Female Execs.; Who's Who Internat.; Internat. Club Elite; Patrons Arts Soc.; Republican; Jewish. Res: 1022 Maroney Ln., Pacific Palisades 90272 Ofc: Sunya Currie, 845 Via de la Paz, Ste. A-723, Pacific Palisades 90272

CURRY, F. HAYDEN, lawyer; b. Oct. 30, 1940, NY, NY; s. Edgar Hayden and Nancie (Stewart) C.; edn: BA, Yale Univ. 1963, LLB, Univ. of Virginia 1967; admitted Calif. State Bar 1970. Career: S. Fla. Legal Svcs. 1967-69; Legal Aid Soc. Alameda Co. 1969-75; atty., broker Clifford, Curry & Cherin Oakland 1975–; guest tchr. JFK Community Coll.; honors: Hypnosis Soc. of Calif. Award 1974; Fulbright Fellowship 1963; BALIF Book Award 1981; mem: BALIF; EBG/L Democratic Club; Oakland Bd. of Realtors; 5th St. Sailors; author: Legal Guide for Lesbian and Gay Couples (1980, 4th edit. 1986); Democrat; rec: sailing, skiing. Res: 4432 Piedmont Ave Oakland 94611 Ofc: Clifford, Curry & Cherin 3070 Richmond Blvd Oakland 94611

CURTIS, GLENN HOUSTON, periodontist; b. Aug. 16, 1909, Nashville, Tenn.; s. John Earnest and Lillie Mae (Lowden) C.; m. Ruth Deyo, June 24, 1941; edn: male nurse grad. Hinsdale Sanitarium & Hosp. 1930; AB, Emory Univ. 1944, DDS, 1947; MS in periodontics, Univ. Mich. 1955. Career: X-ray technician Miami-Battle Creek, Miami Springs, Fla. 1931-35; tchg. fellow Univ. Texas Dental Div., Houston, Tx. 1947-48; pvt. practice dentistry, Corpus Christi, Tx. 1948-51, San Bernardino 1962–, practice limited to periodontics specialty; assoc. prof. periodontics Loma Linda Univ. Sch. Dentistry, 1955-62; mem: Am. Soc. X-ray Technicians (life), Am. Acad. Periodontology, Am. Dental Assn., Calif. Dental Soc., Western Soc. Periodontology (past pres.), Nat. Assn. SDA Dentists (past pres.), Riverside, San Bernardino Orchid Soc.; mil: served from pvt. to s/sgt. US Army 1942-44, 1st lt. to major US Air Force 1951-53, USAF Reserves 1953-. Res: 1409 Bella Vista Crest Redlands 92373 Ofc: 2130 Arrowhead Ave San Bernardino 92405

CURTIS, JESSE WILLIAM, judge; b. Dec. 25, 1905, San Bernardino; s. Jesse Wm. and Ida L. (Seymour) C.; m. Mildred F. Mort, Aug. 24, 1930; children: Suzanne, Jesse W., III, Clyde Hamilton, Christopher Cowles; edn: AB, Univ. Redlands 1928, LL.D, 1973; JD, Harvard, 1931; admitted to Calif. State Bar, 1931. Career: pvt. practice, 1931-35; ptnr. Guthrie and Curtis, 1935-40, Curtis and Curtis, 1946-50, Curtis, Knauf, Henry and Farrell, 1950-53; judge Superior Ct. Calif., 1953-62; judge US Dist. Ct. Central Calif., 1962–; bd. dirs. YMCA (past pres.), Good Will Industries, Crippled Children's Soc., Arrowhead United Fund; chmn. San Bernardino County Heart Fund; adv. bd. Community Hosp.; mem. Am., Calif., Los Angeles County bar assns., Am. Judicature Soc., Am. Law Inst., Town Hall of Calif., LA World Affairs Council, Classic Yacht Assn., Newport Harbor Yacht Club; Phi Delta Phi; Democrat; Congregational. Res: 305 Evening Star Ln Newport Beach 92660 Ofc: U.S. Courthouse, 312 No. Spring St., Los Angeles 90012

CURTIS, ROLLIN HUGH, JR., pest control co. owner; b. Nov. 14, 1935, Russellville, Ark.; s. Rollin H., Sr. and Ethyl (Taylor) C.; m. Carol June, July 3, 1957; children: Debra b. 1958, Mike b. 1960, Laura b. 1961, Sherrie b. 1963; grad. Arvin H. S. 1954. Career: empl. Clark Pest Control 1958-67, Cox Pest Control 1967-71; owner Curtis Pest Control, Bakersfield 1972–; mem. Pest Control Oprs. of Calif. (ofcr. So. Valley Pest Control Assn.); clubs: Knights of Pythias (Chancelor Comdr.), Order of Moose, Eagles, So. Calif. Golf Assn.; mil: p.o. 2c, US Navy 1954-58; Democrat; Prot.; rec: golf. Res: 6220 Olive Dr Bakersfield 93308 Ofc: Curtis Pest Control 412 Kentucky Bakersfield 93305

CUTINO, BERT PAUL, restaurateur, entrepreneur; b. Aug. 7, 1939, Monterey; s. Paul and Rose (Aiello) C.; m. Bella, Nov. 12, 1972; children: Marc b. 1964, Michele b. 1968, Bart b. 1974; edn: AA, Monterey Peninsula Coll. 1964; desig: Certified Executive Chef, Am. Culinary Fedn. (1983). Career: co-owner Sardine Factory Restaurant, Cannery Row area of Monterey, 1968–; co-owner/dir. of food ops. Restaurants Central (includes Sardine Factory, The Rogue, The Gold Fork, and San Simeon Restaurants) 1973–; co-owner/v.p. commercial real estate co. (owns & ops. shopping centers, office bldgs., retail stores in Monterey area and var. devel. projects i.e. 70% of Cannery Row, completed new 350-rm luxury hotel) 1973–; co-owner/v.p. Wendy's Franchise for tri-county area of No. Calif., 1983–; bd. dirs. Monterey Penin. Schs. Found.; advis. bd. Mont. Penin. Coll. Culinary Pgm.; honors: Resolution for community service State of Calif., disting. alumni award Calif. Assn. of Comm. Colls. (1982), winner bronze and two gold medals in culinary show competition (1969); rest. awards (Sardine Factory) include: Ivy Award, Travel/ Holiday Mag. (1971-), Nation's Rest. News Hall of Fame, Mobil Travel Guide Award, The Wine Spectator's Grand Award, Knights of the Vine Golden Vine Award, Stanley Black Fashion Award for Pleasurable Dining, Armstrong Gourmet Guide (Calif.'s Top 10 Rest.), Town and Country (Calif.'s Top 7 Rest.), one of 50 rests. selected to serve at Pres. Reagan's Inauguration (1981, 1985); mem: Am. Culinary Fedn. (W. regl. v.p. 1985-86), Am. Acad. of Chefs (ACF hon. soc.), Les Amide Escoffier Soc. (Medal of Honor), Am. Inst. for Food and Wine, Confrerie de la Chaine des Rotisseurs, Knights of the Vine (Master Knight), Wine Investigation for Novices & Oenophiles, Wine and Food Soc., Calif. Rest. Assn., Nat. Rest. Assn., Monterey Penin. Chefs Assn. (past pres., bd. chmn.); founder/show chmn. Culinary Arts Salon, Calif. Wine Fest., Monterey (1982-); recipes pub. in Gourmet Mag., Bon Appetit, num. other mags.; mil: hosp. corpsman USNR 1961-67; Republican; Catholic; rec: tennis, movie buff. Ofc: Restaurants Central 765 Wave St Monterey 93940

CUTLER, ALBERT DAVID, weight control co. president; b. Feb. 3, 1936, Jersey City, NJ; s. Jacob and Gertrude (Winograd) C.; children: Robyn b. 1961, Dori b. 1964, Allison b. 1970; edn: Cert. of Completion, Newark Sch. of Fine & Indsl. Arts. Career: artist, sales DiFranza- Williamson Agcy. NYC; artist small agcys. NYC, freelance artist Benton & Bowles NYC; art dir. Best Foods Inc. NYC; franchise owner Chicken Delight Jersey City, NJ; co-founder, pres., dir. Weight Watchers Orgn. in Orange, San Diego, Riverside, San Bernadino counties 1967–; co-founder, dir. Skinney Haven Restaurants Inc.; mem: Metro. Mus. of Art, Mus. Modern Art L.A., L.A. County Mus., Bower's Mus., Newport Hills Mus.; mil: USAR; Jewish; rec: skiing, swimming, sports. Ofc: Weight Watchers of Orange & San Diego Counties Inc. 2041 W Main St Santa Ana 92706

CUTTEN, MERRITT EDWARD, management consultant; b. May 8, 1917, San Francisco; s. Merritt Atchinson and Madeleine Agnes (Hoey) C.; m. Pauline Wood, July 20, 1940; children: Merritt b. 1942, Merlene b. 1945, Charles b. 1948; m. 2d Betty Baruch, Aug. 3, 1957; edn: AB engrg., Stanford Univ. 1939; Reg. Profl. Engr. Mass. 1947, Calif. 1948; Certified Mgmt. Cons. 1970. Career: engrg., prodn. & mktg. positions to product-line mgr. Gen. Elec. Co. 1939-54; br. mgr. G.S. Marshall Co. 1954-63; v.p. sales Safe-T-Mike Corp. 1963-64; co-owner Craig, Cutten, Inc. cons. to mgmt. 1964-77; dir. engrg. & quality assurance Paceco Inc., subsid. of Fruehauf Corp. 1977-79; mktg. mgr. Electro Lube Devices Inc., div. of Jacksonville Shipyard Inc., Fruehauf Corp. 1979-82; senior assoc. Inst. of Mgmt. Consultants 1982–; dir., secty. Realastic Inds. 1970-75, dir., pres. G/F Inds. Inc. 1975-76; honors: Tau Beta Pi, Gamma of Calif. (1938); mem: Univ. Club (SF), THe Museum Soc. (SF), Alpine Meadows Greenbelt & Rec. Commn. (pres.), Alpine Meadows Ski Club (treas.); research: electrochemical mining process 1951-54; Republican; Unitarian; rec: skiing, tennis, investment. Address: POB 1233 No. 2 Alpine Cir Tahoe City 95730

DABNER, JACK DUANE, motion picture writer/director; b. Jan. 29, 1930, Billings, Mont.; s. Charles Duane and Violet Virginia (Prout) D.; m. Mary Louise Nelson, Sept. 8, 1950; children: Donald Duane b. 1951, Timothy Carl b. 1953, Richard Dana b. 1957, Jayne Marie b. 1961; edn: Univ. Ore. 1951-52, Mont. State Univ. 1952-53, 1964-67; ordained minister Evangelical United Brethren Ch. (1964). Career: dir. prodn. Good News Prodns., Chester Springs, Pa. 1953-56; asst. to pres. Yellowstone Boys Ranch, Billings 1958-60; pastor Evang. Ch., Bozeman and Billings, Mont., 1960-70; asst. dir. Radio-TV Campus Crusade, San Bernardino, Calif. 1970-75; pres. Seven Star Prodns., Long Beach 1975–; exec. dir. Nat. Assn. for Media Evangelism, Hollywood 1978–; mem. bd. dirs. World Gospel Crusade, 1982–, bd. chmn. 1986; mem. bd. dirs. Fellowship of Christians in the Arts, Media, and Entertainment 1977-; writer/dir. films: The Genesis Flood and Noah's Ark (1977), A Sure Foundation (Pres.'s award 1983) 1982; prod./dir. film: The Silent Scream (So. Calif. Motion Picture Council award 1985) 1984; instr. Haggai Inst., Singapore; listed Who's Who in Religion 1985-; Republican. Res: 2803 Silva St Lakewood 90712 Ofc: Seven Star Productions POB 17126 Long Beach 90807

DADERIAN, STAR ASDGHIG DIKRANOUHI, physician, surgeon; b. Nov. 29, 1949, Beirut, Lebanon, nat. 1976; d. Missak Setrak and Aznive Mariam (Guekjian) D.; edn: BS zoology, UC Los Angeles 1975; MD, Univ. Autonoma of Guadalajara 1979. Career: intern Swedish Covenant Hosp. Chgo. 1980; res. neurol. UCLA-Reed Neurol. Inst. 1982-83. Career: cancer research on Ehrlich Ascitis tumor cells, UCLA, 1972-75 research on prevention of cell clumping and agglutination, UCLA 1975-76; reg. charge nse. Santa Monica Hosp. Med. Ctr. 1972-75; postdoc. research fellow UCLA-Jules Stein Eye Inst. on ophthalmic pathology and instr. med. students and residents on eye diseases, 1982; capt. Medical Corps US Army 39th Gen. Hosp., Los Angeles 1984–; awards: UCLA Scholarship 1972-73, Mortar Board (1973), Chancellors Marshall for Coll. of Letters & Sci. UCLA 1973-74, Outstanding med. student award Univ. of Guadalajara 1979; mem. AMA, Christian MEd. Soc., Am. Armenian Missionary Assn., Haigazian Coll. Alumni Assn., Armenian Profl. Soc., Latin Am. Missionary Assn.; publs: biochemical research (UCLA Sch. of Med. 1974); Republican; Christian Armenian Orthodox; rec: piano, tennis, community svc. Res: 625 23rd St Santa Monica 90402 Ofc: 349th General Hospital 1350 San Pablo St Los Angeles 90033

DADURKA, VICKI, lawyer; b. Shamokin, Penna.; d. Edward David and Florence Marie (Pilarski) D.; edn: Santa Monica Coll. 1973-74; JD, Univ. of San Fernando Law Sch. 1979; Cert. Fin. Mgmt., NYU 1982; admitted to practice, State Bar of Calif. 1980. Career: var. legal/ exec. sectl. & adminstrv. pos., Calif. & Penna. (incl. work on Berrigan Bros. & Pentagon Papers political trials); paralegal Pratter & Young, Beverly Hills 1976-78; legal asst. Gibson, Dunn & Crutcher, Century City 1978-79; atty., sole practitioner, gen. practice law, Los Angeles 1980-84; proj. coord. Los Angeles Olympic Organizing Com. 1984–; awards: Outstanding Young Women of Am. 1978; Am. Jurisprudence Awd. 1979; Spl. Svc. Awd., Dauphin Co. Young Democrats 1971; mem: Am. & Los Angeles Co. Bar Assns.; Women Lawyers Assn.; Nat. Assn. Female Execs.; Daupin Co. Young Democrats; rec: antiques, decorating, photog. Res: 1933 Manning Ave Los Angeles 90025 Ofc: Vicki Dadurka, Esq., POB 25778, Los Angeles 90025

DAGGETT, ROBERT S., lawyer; b. Sept. 16, 1930, LaCrosse, Wisc.; s. Willard Manning and Vida Naomi (Sherman) Daggett; bro. Willard M. Daggett, Jr., M.D. (heart and vascular surgeon; Harvard Med. Sch. faculty, staff Mass. Gen. Hosp., Boston; Fellow Am. Coll. of Physiol.; lectr, writer on med. subjects); m. Helen Neal Hosler, July 19, 1976; children: Ann, b. 1962, John, b. 1964; edn: AA, Univ. Wisc. 1950; AB, (honors in polit.sci., highest honors in journalism), UC Berkeley 1952, and JD, 1955. Career: partner San Francisco law firm of Brobeck, Phleger & Harrison, 1966–; major comml. litigation esp. antitrust, intellectual prop., securities and other corp. litigation. Admitted to Calif Bar 1955, US Supreme Ct. Bar 1967, admitted in various Fed. Cts.; adj. prof. Hastings Coll. of Law and mem. Adv. Bd., Hastings Center for Trial and Appellate Advocacy; instr. Federal Ct. Practice Pgm. and apptd. mem. Teaching Com.(No.Dist. of Calif.); frequent lectr., writer on legal subjects; judge in Nat. Moot Court competition. Winner, Joffre Debate between UC and Stanford, 1952; asst. coach of debate, Univ. Calif., 1954-55. Mem: Bohemian Club (SF), State Bar of Calif., Am. Bar Assn.(Sects. on Litigation, Antitrust, Judicial Adminstrn.), Bar Assn. of S.F., Am. Judicature Soc., Phi Delta Phi legal frat., Theta Xi frat., Order of the the Golden Bear; past mem. Bd. Visitors, UC Santa Cruz: Coll. V. Coauthor Rev. of Selected Code Legislation, Cal.Cont.Edn.of Bar 1955; participant in legal pgms., seminars. Mil: lst lt. US Army JAGC, QMC 1956-60. Republican. Protestant. rec: photog., music. Ofc: Brobeck, Phleger & Harrison, No. 1 Market Plaza, San Francisco 94105

DAHLHEIMER, DONALD JOSEPH, management consultant; b. Apr. 23, 1931, St. Louis, Mo.; s. Joseph Adam and Marie Barbara (Fraum) D.; m. Adelma Mae Gresham, Jan. 29, 1954; children: Mark b. 1954, Dona b. 1955, Philip b. 1957, Craig b. 1959; edn: St. Louis Univ. 1953-4; Washington Univ. 1960-2; profl. seminars 1966, 69. Career: sales supr. Campbell Soup Co., Detroit 1953-64; gen. mktg. mgr. Pet Inc., St. Louis, Mo. 1964-69; v.p. mktg. The Borden Co., Coral Gables, Fla. 1969-71; exec. v.p. Lindsay International, San Mateo, Ca. 1971-76; pres. Dalheimer & Associates, Inc., Belmont 1976–; chmn. Trident Prods. Inc., Hayward 1985–; faculty The Princeton Research Inst.; lectr. PRI Mergers, Acquisitions & Divestitures Seminars; lectr. Univ. Calif., Wash. Univ.; apptd. Ky. Col. by Gov. Nunn, 1971; works: initiated the 1979 acquisition of Lawry's Foods Inc. by Thomas J. Lipton for $66.2 million cash; mil: sgt. USMC, 2 Battle Stars, Korea; Conservative; Catholic; rec: fine arts collector. Ofc: 2752 Waltham Cross Belmont 94002

DAIGLE, FREDERICK JOSEPH, information security specialist; b. Apr. 21, 1924, Boston, Mass.; s. Archie Joseph and Margaret Rita (Hart) Daigle; m. Sheila Clinkenbeard, June 1, 1975; children: Denise b. 1951, Tina Dotson b. 1959; edn: BS in bus. adm., Southwestern Univ. 1983; lic. real estate broker, Calif. Career: commnd. warrant ofcr. USN, worldwide svc., 1941-62, ret.; chief of classification mgmt. Lockheed Missile & Space Co., Sunnyvale 1962-80, staff information security splst., responsible for new bus. proposals and estab. security pgms. in new corp. cos., Lockheed Corp., 1980-85 (ret.);

corp. broker, v.p. OCA Inc. dba Ocean Colony Realty, Half Moon Bay 1985−; chmn. bd.dirs. Lockheed Missile & Space Co. Nat. Mgmt. Assn. (mgmt. edn. pgm.); honors: Woodbridge Award of Excellence (Nat. Classification Mgmt. Soc. 1984); mem. NCMS, Nat. Classification Mgmt. Soc. (Founders Com.; bd.dirs. 9 yrs.; nat. pres. 1974, 1979; nat. seminar chmn. 1968, 73, 80; senior mem. of the soc.; awarded six certs. of appreciation). Publs.: contbg. ed. NCMS Jour. (1964 , 66, 74) and Bull. (bi-mo., 1969-80), num. arts. Mil: decorated 8 campaign medals w/5 combat stars; Republican; Catholic; rec: youth leader, golf, real estate broker. Res: 2309 Burning Tree Rd., Half Moon Bay 94019; Ofc: Ocean Colony Realty 2000 Fairway Dr Half Moon Bay 94019

DAIGNAULT, LEATRICE, merchant; b. Feb. 6, 1926, Fairport, NY; d. Floyd and Katie (Saporito) Sorgi; m. Ray Daignault, Sept. 24, 1949; edn: Rochester Bus. Inst. Career: bus. rep. Pacific Telephone 1947-55; owner w/husband The Hat nightclub, El Monte 1953−; vocalist, entertainer; mem: Calif. Dining & Beverage Assn. (pres. 1980-84, chmn. bd. 1984-, first woman pres., chmn., first to hold ofc. of pres., chmn. 4 consec. yrs.), Women of the Moose (1st chaplain 1955-56, 1st elected senior regent 1956-57, collegian 1982-), El Monte Women's Democrat Club; chmn. Muscular Dystrophy Drive for City of El Monte 1977-; Democrat; Catholic; rec: collect miniature shoes. Res: Covina 91723 Ofc: The Hat, 12121 E Valley Blvd El Monte 91732

DAILEY, MAE HILEMAN, charitable association executive; b. Oct. 19, 1907, Mabel, Ore.; d. Richard and Martha Jane (Trotter) Hileman; m. Earl Dailey, Nov. 8, 1944; raised (orphans) Sheila Trotter b. 1949, Tom Trotter b. 1952; edn: BA, Univ. of Ore. 1929; 2 yrs. grad. study, U. of Chgo., Chgo. Theol. Seminary; Registered Social Worker. Career: teacher high sch. 5 years; asst. exec. dir. Children's Home, 5 years, exec. director, 12 yrs.; Mothers March director, March of Dimes, 13 years; ret. Honors: listed in Women of Our Valley by Bertha Rice; Women of the Year (3 times), Bees Clubs; Vol. of the Year, League of Friends. Mem. Childrens Home Bd. 3 yrs.; YWCA Bd. Bd. 16 yrs (bd. pres. 3 yrs); San Jose Appeals Bd. 5 yrs.; Sierra Club (life mem); Quota Club (pres. 1950-2; regional v.p. Quota Int.); San Jose Womens Club (2nd v.p., sect. chpsn); Congregational; rec: hiking, camping. Res: 1127 Delynn San Jose 95125

DAILEY, THOMAS ALFRED, real estate developer; b. Jan. 1, 1933, South Bend, Ind.; s. Harold Robert and Lillian Bertha (Moor) D.; m. Bonnie Yvonne Groves, July 20, 1957; children: Jill b. 1962, Connie b. 1963, Bob b. 1969, Mike b. 1971; edn: BS, Indiana Univ. 1955, MBA, 1956, LLB, 1962. Career: bldg. mgr. Murdock Devel. Co. 1962-63; gen. counsel Rolen Diversified Investors Inc. 1963-67; West Coast atty., 13 ofcs., Owens Corning Fiberglass, Santa Clara 1967-70; div. counsel indsl. div. Kaiser Aetna, Oakland 1970-74, reg. mgr. indsl. div., 1974-76; condominium bldg./ developer self-empl. 1976−; mem: Am. and Calif. Bar Assns., Asoc. Bldg. Industry, YMCA (Oakland Central), Christian Businessmen's Assn. of Walnut Creek/ Concord; mil: 1st lt. USAF 1956-59; Republican; Presbyterian (deacon). rec: jogging, tennis, coaching. Res: 411 Bolla Pl. Alamo 94507 Ofc: POB 966 Alamo 94507

DALE (PLANAMENTO), SHARON KAY, real estate broker; b. San Francisco; d. Terrill Odin and Alice Ernestine (Anthony) Glenn; div.; 1 dau. Kimberly; edn: AS, Fresno City Coll. 1982; bus. adm. major CSU Fresno 1983-; Calif. lic. R.E. Broker (1978). Career: sales assoc. Red Carpet Realtors, Fresno 1974-77; broker/owner U.S. Cities Realtors, dba Pierson & Planamento, Inc. 1977-80, dir. Div. II (No. Calif., Nev.) U.S. Cities Realtors Corp. 1978-80; broker assoc. Easterbrook Constrn., 1980-81, 83-84; exec. secty. Valley Med. Ctr., 1981−; broker assoc. Adanalian & Jackson Real Estate, Fresno 1981-83, 84−; mem. Calif. Assn. Realtors, Fresno Board of Realtors (MLS 1974-), Women's Trade Club of Fresno; civic: Saint Agnes Service Guild, Valley Med. Center Aux., Mental Health Assn., Ednl. T.V. Channel 18 (vol.); club: Sierra Sport & Racquet (charter); Republican; Prot.; rec: golf, tennis, photog., travel. Res: 366 W Warner #101 Fresno 93704 Ofc: Adanalian & Jackson Real Estate 5649 N Palm Ave Fresno 93704; Valley Medical Center 445 S Cedar Ave Fresno 93702

DALES, JEAN FRANCES MURPHY, real estate broker; b. Aug. 8, 1937, Santa Monica, Calif.; s. Frank Albert and Barbara Patricia (Wurts) Murphy; children: Laurie J. b. 1963, Bradford S. b. 1965; edn: BFA, Univ. So. Calif. 1959; real estate broker 1980; notary public 1980-84. Career: dir. art Anoakia Sch. Arcadia, Calif. 1960; news broadcaster Teleprompter Newport Beach 1975; real estate sales MacNab Irvine, Newport Beach 1976; real estate broker Newport Home Loan 1980, Jean Dales & Co. Broker Mortgage Newport Beach 1980-86; owner, pres. Laurie J- Private Collection jewelry sales, ptnr. Limited Editions Catalog N.B. 1985−; honors: Fine Arts Honor Soc. (USC 1958), Artist of the Month (Newport Beach 1970, 71); paintings shown Safari Group, Reno 1973; Republican; Protestant; rec: modeling, art, needlework. Ofc: Jean Dales & Co. 38 Vienna Newport Beach 92660

D'ALVIA, LOUIS JOSEPH, construction co. executive; b. June 2, 1948, NY, NY; s. Augustine A. and Elvira C. (Mele) D'A.; m. Linda J. Adkison, Dec. 4, 1982; children: Adam b. 1974, William b. 1978, John b. 1984; edn: BS in psychology, Loyola Marymount Univ. 1970; grad. work in bus., CSULA, 1972-76; lic. CPA, Calif. 1978; Career: audit mgr. Arthur Andersen & Co., 1976-84; splst. in constrn. and mfg., also general finl. consulting; vice pres., chief finl. ofcr. D. Harris Constrn. Co., Upland (nationwide contr. spec. in retail store remodeling) 1984−; dir. 3 privately held corps.; seminar instr. Calif. Inst. of Tech.; mem: Am. Inst. CPAs, Calif. Soc. of CPAs, Upland CofC; pres. Mountain Meadows Homeowners Assn.; treas. Pomona AYSO; Demo-

crat; Roman Catholic; rec: softball. Res: 1861 Paseo La Paz Pomona 91768 Ofc: D. Harris Construction Co. Inc. 1151 West Ninth St Upland 91786

DAM, CYRUS KING, III, lapidary; b. July 28, 1905, San Francisco; s. Francis Herbert and Inez (Shippee) Dam; m. Marjorie Lane, May 15, 1930; children: John Lane b. 1931, Carolyn Inez b. 1933; edn: BSME, Univ. of Nev., Reno 1929; cert. Hobby Gemology, Calif. Fedn. of Mineralogical Socs. 1959; certs. in mil. schs. incl. Corps of Engrs. Advanced 1957. Career: Hetch Hetchy Water Supply and S.F. Water Dept. 1929-36; battn. cdr. and ETO staff, Corps. of Engrs. 1941-46; dist. chief of engrg. div. and brigade staff Corps of Engrs. Reserves 1946-65; assoc. to senior engr. Fed. Power Commn. 1936-41, 1946-75; owner Cyrus K. Dam, Lapidary, Corte Madera 1958−; hydraulic engr., compiler and editor, River Basin Planning Reports 1946-75; exec. secty. Columbia Basin Interagency Commn. 1949-50; honors: Outstanding Performance (Fed. Power Commn. 1971), Best in Faceting Div. (Eastern Fedn. Min. and Lapid. Socs., Wash. DC 1967), 12 Blue Ribbons in faceting (1965-74), Spl. Award (Fed. Power Commn. 1964), Long Timers Award (ROA 1980), Hiram Award (Nat. Sojourners); mem: ASME, Soc. of Am. Mil. Engrs., Fed. Exec. and Profl. Assn., Reserve Ofcrs. Assn., Retired Ofcrs. Assn., Masons, Nat. Sojourners (chpt. pres. 1952), Heroes of '76 Camp Cdr. 1953, Order of Eastern Star (patron 1950), Scottish Rite, Shrine, S.F. Gem & Mineral Soc. (pres. 1956), Marin Mineral Soc. (fedn. dir.); publ: Cyrus King Dam, Jr. (1843-1907) Branch, a genealogy of the 9th through 14th generations in Am. (accepted by Lib. of Congress 1981); mil: col. Corps of Engrs. 1954, Reserves 1928-41, 1946-65, 6 svc. ribbons; Republican; Presbyterian; rec: photog., geology, travel. Address: Cyrus K. Dam 45 Buena Vista Ave Corte Madera 94925

DAMLUJI, NAMIR FAISAL, physician; b. June 15, 1952, Beirut, Lebanon, nat. US cit. 1983; s. Faisal Farouk and Mona (Baroody) D.; m. Gina Subhiyah, Dec. 18, 1978; children: Mona b. 1981, Omar b. 1984; edn: Baccalauriet, Baghdad Coll. 1968, MD honors, 1975; Diplomate Am. Bd. Psych. and Neurol. 1983. Career: intern, resident, Univ. Rochester NY 1977-79; resident, senior res. psych. Johns Hopkins Hosp. 1979-81; pvt. practice psych. 1981−; asst. clin. prof. psych. UC San Diego 1982−; med. dir. Mood Disorders Clin. San Diego 1982-83; med. dir., Project Enable - Neighborhood House Assn. 1985; chief med. edn. Alvarado Pkwy Inst. 1984−, clin. dir. mental health unit 1985−; assoc. investigator Feighner Research Inst. 1981−; mem: Am. Psych. Assn. 1978-, San Diego Psych. Soc. 1981-, World Psych. Assn. 1981-, World Fedn. Mental Health 1981-, Am. Acad. Clin. Psych. 1981-, Royal Automobile Club of Eng. 1982-; publs: num. articles in psych. jours., 1 book, num. lectures; rec: tennis, horseback riding, sailing, gardening, chess. Res: 6741 Ave Manana La Jolla 92037 Ofc: Psychiatric Centers of San Diego 9834 Genesee Ave Ste 427 La Jolla 92037

DANA, DEANE, county supervisor; b. July 9, 1926, NY, NY; s. Deane and Dorothy Bartlett (Lawson) D.; m. Doris Weiler, July 14, 1951; children: Deane III, Marguerite, Diane, Dorothy; edn: mech. engring., Stevens Inst. of Tech. 1951; Reg. Profl. Engr. (indsl.) Calif. Career: district mgr. Pacific Tel. Co. 1953-80; elected supervisor 4th District, Los Angeles County Board of Supvrs. 1980−, chmn. 1984; chmn. Coliseum Commn., v.chair LA County Transp. Commn.; honors: Hon. LLD, Pepperdine Univ. (1985); mem. Rotary Club (of L.A. and Venice-Marina), Am. Legion, Elks, Pepperdine Univ. Assocs., Santa Monica Coll. Assocs., Calif. Assn. of Compensatory Edn., L.A. Area Council Boy Scouts Am. (exec. bd.), Californians for a Strong Am., Calif. Shore and Beach Preservation (dir.), Town Hall of Calif.; mil: 1st. lt. US Air Force; Republican (Rep. Central Com. of Calif.); Episcopal; rec: golf, tennis, water skiing. Ofc: County of Los Angeles 500 West Temple St Ste 829 Los Angeles 90012

DANANDEH, SAEED, engineer; b. Aug. 21, 1952, Tehran, Iran; s. Nosrat and Ghodsieh (Ghaysar) D.; m. Oranous, July 11, 1983; edn: BSC (CNAA) w/honors, N.E.London Polytechnic 1976; M.Engr., Sheffield Univ. 1977. Career: structural eng. asst. Computer Engring., NCR Nat. Cash Register, London, UK 1972; struc. eng. asst. S.B. Tietz and Partners, U.K. 1973-76; civil engr. VTN Consol. Inc., Irvine 1978-80; struc. eng. assoc. City of Long Beach, 1980−; mem: ASTM, ASCE, Prestressed Concrete Inst., Am. Concrete Inst., Internat. Conf. of Building Ofcls., Struc. Engrs. Assn. of Calif.; research in field of concrete; Bahai World Faith; rec: sports, movies, cars, travel. Res: 104 Briarwood, Irvine 92714 Ofc: City of Long Beach, 333 W. Ocean Blvd Long Beach

DANG, CHAT VAN, physician; b. Apr. 10, 1947, Cantho, Vietnam, nat. USA 1984; s. Chieu Van and Nga Ngoc (Nguyen) D.; m. Hang, Mar. 19, 1976; children: Alexis b. 1978, Alan b. 1981; edn: MD, Saigon Med. Sch. 1972; Diplomate Am. Board of Surgery 1981. Career: intern McLaren Gen. Hosp., Flint, Mich. 1975-76; surgery resident King-Drew Med. Ctr., L.A. 1976-80; physician splst. Charles R. Drew Med. Sch., L.A. 1980-81, asst. prof. of emergency medicine, 1982-; physician splst. Los Angeles County King-Drew Med. Ctr. 1981−; instr. Advanced Trauma Life Support (1981-) and Advanced Cardiac Life Support (1981-); honors: Best Resident award, Dept. Surg. King-Drew Med. Ctr. (1980), faculty of the year awards (81-82, 82-83) Emerg. Med. Residency Pgm.; faculty Annual Trauma Seminar, Anaheim (1984, 85); mil: gen. surgeon Med. Corps Armed Forces Republic of Vietnam (1972-75); rec: photog., computer pgmmg. Ofc: King-Drew Medical Center 12021 S Wilmington Ave Los Angeles 90059

DANG, VIET VAN, ophthalmologist; b. Mar. 26, 1949, Viet Nam, nat. US cit. 1982; s. Khoi Van and Tra Thi (Do) D.; m. Thuy thu Tran, Nov. 16, 1982; 1 son, Irving Q. b. 1984; edn: MD, UC Irvine Coll. of Med. 1981; intern in internal medicine UC San Francisco, resident in ophthalmology UC Irvine. Career: (current) pvt. practice, Westminster; ophthalmologist Kaiser Hosp. Eye Clinic, Bellflower; attending surgeon UC Irvine Med. Center; recipient Outstanding student research award UCI; mem: AMA, CMA, Am. Acad. of Ophthalmology; publ: Coin Rubbing Vietnamese Attitudes Toward Health Care JAMA 9/81; rec: fishing, hunting. Ofc: Viet Van Dang, MD 9361 Bolsa St Ste 208 Westminster 92683

DANIEL, ERNO SCIPIADES, physician; b. Dec. 15, 1946, Budapest, Hungary; Derivative Citizen 1964; s. Erno and Katinka (Scipiades) D.; m. Martha Peaslee, Aug. 14, 1976; children: Kristina, b. 1977, Michael, b. 1979, Mary, b. 1980; edn: BS in chem., Calif. Inst. of Tech. 1968; MS in chem., UC San Diego 1970, PhD in phys. chem., 1971; MD, UC Los Angeles 1975; Board Cert. in Internal Medicine, 1981. Career: teaching and research asst., UC San Diego 1968-71; resident phys. Dept. of Internal Med., UCLA 1975-78; internist and geriatrician phys. Dept. of Internal Med., Santa Barbara Med. Foundation Clinic, 1978 – ; chmn. Dept. of Internal Medicine, S.B. Clinic 1984; bd. mem. Gerontology Edn. Project, S.B.; Research and Edn. Com., S.B. Med. Found. Clinic; med. adv. bd. Alzheimer's Assn. of S.B.; awards: Conger Prize, Caltech 1967, NSF Undergrad. Research Fellowship, CalTech 1968, Calif. State Grad. Fellowship 1968, Fellowship Am. Coll. of Physicians 1983, Outstanding Young Men of Am. Award 1983, travel grant Internat. Research and Exchanges Bd., NY 1985; Fellow Am. Coll. of Physicians, mem. Am. Geriatrics Soc., Calif. Inst. of Tech. Alumni (life), UCLA Alumni (life); violinist Santa Barbara Sym. orch. 1961-64; producer and co-host TV weekly series, Senior Forum, KCOX TV 3, Santa Barbara; co-founder/ co-editor sci. journal, Proceedings of the Santa Barbara Medical Foundation Clinic; publs in med. jours., sci. jours.; rec: American Indian hist. and arts. Ofc: Santa Barbara Medical Found., 215 Pesetas Ln., Santa Barbara 93102

DANIELS, GEORGE ALBERT, engineering executive; b. March 11, 1909, Somers, Conn.; s. Wm. Herbert and Blanche (Avery) D.; m. Blanche Franck (dec.), Nov. 13, 1943; edn: BS in elec. engring., UC Berkeley 1932; courses in mech. and civil engring.; Reg. Profl. Engr. (mech.) Calif. (1946-), lic. Real Estate salesman (1971-83), Reg. rep. NASD (-1983). Career: bridge engr. San Francisco/ Oakland Bay Bridge, State of Calif., 1934-36; field engr., chief insp. plant constrn., Standard Oil Co., Richmond 1937-39; field engr., project engr., senior engr. Constrn./ chief engr. Chemical Plants, Shell Chemical Co. 1939-71, ret. (spec. in plant constrn. & plant maint.; helped devel. of Shell Chemical Engring. Stds.; design splst. in compressors, reciprocating compressors, vibration free systems); mem. Ventura Engrs. Club (1955-62), Univ. of Calif. Engrs. Club; works: Heat Exchanger design, Gas Compressor design; mil: comdr. CEC USNR, 1941-45; Republican; Christian; rec: golf, stain glass, fishing. Res: 300 East H St #218 Benicia 94510

DANNEMEYER, WILLIAM EDWIN, congressman; b. Sept. 22, 1929, South Gate; s. Henry Wm. and Charlotte Ernestine (Knapp) D.; m. Evelyn Hoemann, Aug. 27, 1955; children: Bruce, Kim, Susan; edn: BA, Valparaiso Univ. 1950; JD, Univ. Calif. Hastings Law Sch., 1952; admitted to Calif. State Bar, 1952. Career: sole practice law, Fullerton 1957-79; asst. city atty., Fullerton, 1959-62; judge pro tem Municipal Ct., Fullerton, 1966-76, Superior Ct., 1966-76; elected rep. Calif. State Assembly, 1963-66, 1977-78, elected rep. to 96th, 97th US Congresses from 39th Dist. Calif., mem. Coms. on Energy and Commerce, Post Office, Civil Service; bd. dirs. Lutheran Ch., Mo. Synod, So. Calif. Dist.; bd. dirs., pres. bd. Orange County Luth. High Sch.; chmn. spl. gifts Capital Fund Drive, Boy Scouts Am., 1966-67; No. Orange County finance chmn. Billy Graham Crusade, 1969; served with CIC, US Army, Korean War; named Outstanding Young Man of Yr., Fullerton Jr. CofC, 1965; mem. Orange County Bar Assn. (past dir.); Republican. Ofc: Longworth House Office Bldg., Wash. DC 20515

DANUPATAMPA, EKACHAI, engineer; b. Oct. 4, 1942, Bangkok, Thailand; nat. Jan. 25, 1978; s. Yok-Hoo and Uy-Ty (Ung) D.; m. Voranart Tanehsakdi, May 26, 1973; 1 son, Irv b. 1980; edn: Dip. in E.E., Thonburi Inst. of Tech., 1965; BSEE with distinction, Feati Univ., 1968; MSEE, CSU Long Beach, 1974; EEE, USC, 1979. Career: senior facilities design splst. Rockwell Internat. Corp., El Segundo 1985 – ; sr. control engr. C.F. Braun & Co., Alhambra 1980-85; electrical project engr. Rodrigue & Assocs., Inc., L.A. 1979-80; E.E., Dept. of the Navy (NCEL), Port Hueneme, 1978-79; electrical project engr. Carnation Co., L.A. 1974-78; mem: IEEE, ISA, CSULB Alumni, USC Alumni; Democrat; Buddhist; rec: jog, biking, jump rope. Res: 1136 Vera Cruz St Montebello 90640 Ofc: Rockwell International Corp. 2031 E Mariposa Ave El Segundo 90245

DARDICK, KAREN LYNN, public relations counselor; b. Nov. 29, 1944, N.Y.C.; d. David and Sylvia (Better) D.; edn: BS, and MS in journ., Northwestern Univ. Medill Sch. Journ. 1967, 1968. Career: feature writer The Hollister Press, Winnetka, Ill. 1968; asst. ed. Modern Maturity Mag., Long Beach 1970; founder/ pres. Karen Dardick Public Relations, 1977 – ; mem. IWOSC, Women's Internat. Network, Alpha Chi Omega, San Fernando Valley Rose Soc.; Republican; Self-Realization Fellowship; rec: gardening. Address: 4351 Prospect Ave Los Angeles 90027

DARLING, RICHARD L., real estate developer; b. Aug. 24, 1938, Brainard, Minn.; s. Delbert E. and Gertrude Nora (Etzler) D.; children: Richard L. Jr., Robert L. (dec.); edn: BS, USC 1961, Lic. Gen. Contractor and Real Estate Broker, Calif.; Career: dir., gound. devel. and constrn. num. income producing properties; founder City Savings & Loan Assn. 1982, currently, chmn. bd.; mem: Urban Land Inst., BACC, No. Rancho Country Club, Jonathan Club;

publs: handbook on formulas for real estate investment analysis; rec: skiing, tennis, jogging. Res: 3707 Capstan Circle Westlake Village 91361 Ofc: Tandam Realty Group, 6834 Hollywood Blvd. Ste. 400 Hollywood 90028

DARLING, SCOTT EDWARD, lawyer; b. Dec. 31, 1949, Los Angeles; s. Dick and Marjorie Helen D.; m. Deborah L., Aug. 22, 1981; children: Ryan b. 1975, Jacob b. 1978; edn: BA, Univ. of Redlands 1972; JD, USC 1975; admitted to practice, Calif. State Bar. Career: travel counselor World Travel Inc., Riverside 1968-72, asst. mgr. 1972-76; campaign mgr. Grant Carner for Cong., Riv. 1976; assoc., partner law firm of Falsetti, Crafts, Pritchard & Darling of Riverside 1978-84; senior ptnr. Darling, Medof & Miller, Riverside 1984 – ; pres. Newport Harbor Devel. Co., Inc. 1983-; bd. dirs. Tel-Law, Inc. (nat. public svc. legal info. system) 1978-80; judge protem Riverside Superior Ct. 1980; mem. Calif. Assn. of Realtors atty's panel; honors: Outstanding Young Men of Am. 1979-83; Calif. Scholarship Fedn. life mem.; charter mem. High Sch. Hall of Fame; Sickle Cell Orgn. Eddie D. Smith Award 1981; mem: Am., Riverside Co. (spkrs bur.) Bar Assns.; Native Sons of Golden West; bd. dirs. ARC Riv. Co.; bd. dirs. Heart Assn. Riv. Co.; citizens com. UC Riv.; bd. dirs. Inland Area Sickle Cell Orgn.; World Affairs Council; Friends of the Mission Inn; Lions Club; bd. dirs. Hispanic CofC; Riv. Jaycees; Republican: cand. for Congress 36th Dist. 1982; asst. treas. Calif. State Repub. Party 1980-82; Harvest Christian Fellowship. Res: 5496 Fargo Rd Riverside 92506 Ofc: Darling, Medof & Miller, 7121 Magnolia Ave Riverside 92504

DATE, JUDY L., state employment program representative; b. July 12, 1941, Modesto; d. Louis James and Marybelle Bernice (Macedo) Oliver; m. Larry Date, Mar. 21, 1983; edn: AA, Modesto Jr. Coll. 1975. Career: staff clk. Pacific Tel. & Tel., Modesto 1961-67; claims asst., adjudicator, now overpayment splst. State of Calif. Employment Devel. Dept., Turlock 1975 – ; mem. Calif. State Employees Assn., Beta Sigma Phi/ Upsilon Kappa chpt. (past pres.; Chapter Sweetheart 1983, Girl of the Year 1984); Republican; Catholic. Address: Turlock 95380

DAUGHADAY, DOUGLAS ROBERT, electronics engineer; b. Mar. 13, 1954, Highland Park, NJ; s. Robert Owings and Mary (Kirkpatrick) D.; edn: BSEE, cum laude, W. Va. Inst. of Tech. 1976; MSEE, USC 1979; engr. in tng., State of W.Va. 1976. Career: tech. staff Hughes Aircraft Co., Culver City 1977-79; sr. engr. Litton Guidance and Control Systems, Woodland Hill 1979-80; lab. engr. Airesearch Mfg. Co. of Calif., Torrance 1980-84; tech. staff The Aerospace Corp., El Segundo 1984 – ; awards: Masters fellowship, Hughes Aircraft Co. 1977-9; mem: Nat. Assn. of Underwater Instrs. 1982-; IEEE stu. mem. 1973-6; USC Gen. Alumni Assn. (life); The Persona Pgmmg. Center calculator club; Democrat; Christian; rec: Scuba diving, photog. Res: 3221 Overland Ave, 5217, Los Angeles 90034 Ofc: The Aerospace Corp. 2350 East El Segundo Blvd El Segundo 90245

DAUGHERTY, ROBERT JOHN, manufacturing co. executive; b. Oct. 4, 1942, San Francisco; s. Robert Sanford and Mary (Vasquez) D.; m. Sandra Martin, Apr. 2, 1966; children: Kimberly b. 1967, Christopher b. 1969, Nicholas b. 1971; edn: N.M. Mil. Inst. 1960-62; US Naval Acad. 1962-63; BA in sociol., Univ. of Tulsa 1966. Career: profl. football player, halfback San Francisco 49ers Football Team, 1966-68; salesman Vetra Corp., Palo Alto 1968-69, Fredrickson Metal Products, San Jose 1969-70, G&M Sheet Metal, Concord 1970, Onet Sheet Metal, San Francisco 1970; founder/bd. chmn./chief exec. K.C. (Kimberly & Christopher) Metal Products (structural hardware), San Jose 1970 – ; rec: running. Ofc: K.C. Metal Products 1960 Hartoc Dr San Jose 95131

DAVES, IRA ALEXANDER, physician; b. Oct. 28, 1933, New Bern, N.C.; s. Ira Alexander and Winifred Ernestine (Turrentine) D.; m. Alice R., May 31, 1956; children: Ira A., III, b. 1958, Cathy D., b. 1959, Angela P., b. 1966, Pamela K., b. 1967; edn: BS, Howard Univ. 1954, MD, 1961. Career: med.-surgical intern Freedman's Hosp., Wash. DC 1962; gen. and thoracic surgical res. Harbor Gen. Hosp. and UCLA 1962-67; instr. surgery, UCLA 1967-68; asst. clin. prof. surgery USC 1969-74, assoc. clin. prof. surgery 1975 – ; So. Calif. Am. Coll. of Surgeons Award 1965; mem: Alpha Omega Alpha, AMA, CMA, Los Angeles Med. Assn., Los Angeles Surgical Soc., NAACP, Urban League, 100 Black Men (Los Angeles chpt.); research: gastric enzymes and gastric hormones 1963-65; mil: capt. USAF 1954-57; Republican; Protestant. Res: Beverly Hills

DAVID, DAVE E., obstetrician, gynecologist; b. Aug. 11, 1951, Queens, NY; s. Manny and Lenore (Osherowitz) D.; edn: BS zool., Univ. Fla. Gainesville 1974; MD, Univ. So. Fla. Med. Sch. 1978. Career: intern Harvard Med. Sch. 1978-79; resident ob-gyn Tufts Univ. 1978-82; phys. Laguna Hills Ob/Gyn Inc. 1982-83; pvt. practice Newport Beach 1983 – ; affil. hosps: Hoag Meml. Newport Beach, UC Irvine Med. Ctr., Mission Comm. Hosp. Mission Viejo (active staff 1982-83), Saddleback Comm. Hosp. Laguna Hills (active staff 1982-83), St. Joseph Hosp. Orange, Costa Mesa Hosp.; clin. instr. UC Irvine Med. Sch.; honors: Pres. Honor Roll., Dean's List, Premed. Honor Soc., scholarship grants, pres. Kappa Sigma (Univ. Fla.), class pres. 3 yrs., Mosby Scholastic Award, CIBA Award (Univ. So. Fla. Med. Sch.); mem: AMA, CMA, Am. Coll. Ob-Gyn, Orange County Med. Assn., Orange County Ob-Gyn Soc.; past mem: Am. Acad. Fam. Phys., Mass. Acad., Fam. Phys.; publs: article in ob-gyn jour., book reviewse in J. of AMA. Res: 1982 Port Locksleigh Pl Newport Beach 92660 Ofc: 1401 Avocado Ave Ste 709 Newport Beach 92660

DAVIDSON, LANCE SAMUEL, real estate syndicator; b. Aug. 28, 1953, San Francisco; s. Alan Mark and Barbara (Stanton) D.; m. Tamara Leigh, Aug. 24, 1986; edn: AB, Stanford Univ. 1975; JD, Vanderbilt Univ. Sch. of Law 1981;

admitted Calif. state Bar 1983, Ore. 1981; real estate broker Calif. 1984. Career: research economist The Brookings Inst. Wash. DC 1975-76; analyst (top secret clearance) Inst. Defense Analyses Arlington, Va. 1976-78; assoc. atty. Stoel, Rives, Boley, Fraser & Wyse Portland, Ore. 1981-82; atty. pvt. practice San Francisco 1983–; real estate syndicator; mem: Calif. Assn. Realtors, Nat. Assn. Realtors, Concordia- Argonaut Club, Soc. Calif. Pioneers, Soc. Mayflower Descendants, Tennessee Squires Assn.; publ: num. articles on mil. issues, law and Calif. history; Democrat; Jewish; rec: swimming, tennis, skiing, chess. Res: 6 Tartan Way Mill Valley 94941 Ofc: Law Ofcs. of Lance S. Davidson 1038 Redwood Hwy Ste 1 Mill Valley 94941

DAVIDSON, OLIVIA MAGANA, real estate broker; b. Jan. 12, 1946, Jalisco, Mexico, nat. US cit. 1980; d. Alfonso and Emma (Jimenez) Magana; 1 son, Omar Troy Roose b. 1969; edn: AA, L.A. Valley Coll. 1983; Calif. lic. Real Estate Broker (1985). Career: prop. House Cleaning Service, San Fernando Valley 1965-68; export mgr.'s asst. Price Pfister Brass dba Prico Corp., Pacoima 1970-81 real estate sales agt. Golden Rule Realty, Panorama City 1976-85; owner/broker Regal Realty, Panorama City 1985–; recipient profl. sales awards (1978, 80, 81); mem. Nat. Assn. Realtors, San Fernando Valley Board Realtors; Republican; Catholic. Res: 17471 Tuscan Dr Granada Hills 91344

DAVIDSON, WILLIAM WARD, III, computer co. sales executive; s. William Ward, Jr. and Ann Elizabeth Nancy (Wilds) D.; m. Linda Speelman, June 8, 1965; children: William b. 1968, Lisa b. 1969, Christina b. 1975; edn: BS psychol., Univ. Md. 1966; American Univ. 1967-68; Mgmt. Devel., No. Eastern Univ. 1981. Career: programmer IBM Corp. Wash. DC 1966-69, salesman Roanoke, Va. 1969-72; salesman Digital Equipment Corp. San Francisco 1972-74, group sales mgr. S.F. 1974-78, dist. sales mgr. Chgo. 1978-81, prod. line mgr. Boston 1981-84; v.p. sales & support Culler Scientific 1984–; honors: Apollo Achievement Award (NASA 1969); mil: USAF 1960-64; Republican; Presbyterian; rec: tennis, golf, scuba. Res: 2040 Plaza Bonita Santa Barbara 93103 Ofc: Culler Scientific 100 Burns Pl Santa Barbara 93117

DAVIES, WILLIAM RALPH, service co. executive; b. Aug. 17, 1955, Santa Barbara; s. Ralph Emmett and Georgann Marie (Cordingly) D.; m. Karen L. Blake, May 12, 1984; edn: AA in real estate, Am. River Coll. 1978; BS, CSU Sacto. 1980; MBA pgm. internat. bus., Golden Gate Univ. 1984; cert. Princeton Research Inst. 1985; Calif. lic. R.E. Broker 1978. Career: real estate assoc. Kiernan Realtors, Sacto. 1975-77; partner R.E. firm, 1977; real estate investment cons./prop. mgr., 1978-80; broker assoc. MBA Business Brokers, Sacto. 1980-, bought co., pres./bd. chmn. 1985–, cons. in merger & acquisition industry nat.; dir. Revanche, Inc. (1984-); cons. Gala Restaurants (1982-83); honors: Dean's list CSUS (1978); mem. Internat. Bus. Club Grad. Sch. (1984), Internat. Bus. Brokers Assn., Sacto. Board of Realtors (1976-78); civic: Sacto. CofC, World Wildlife Fund; publs: Retrospective Study - Gobal Debt Crisis (1984, to be pub. by Dr. A. Desta), Econometric Model-Internat. Technology Transfer (1982); Republican; rec: internat. hist., bridge, golf. Ofc: William R. Davies, Inc. 1325 Howe Ave Ste 105 Sacramento 95825

DAVIS, ANITA WILLIS, city finance ofcl.; b. June 1, 1954, Little Rock, Ark.; d. Welford Monroe, Jr. and Estella Louise (Holt) Willis; m. James Davis, June 3, 1978; 1 son, James, III b. 1984; edn: BA, PHilander Smith Coll. 1977; MBA, CSU Dominguez Hills 1979; Calif. lic. real estate agt, Comm. Coll. tchg. cred. Career: contract compliance adminstr. City of Los Angeles, 1977-78; adminstr., grants mgmt. splst. Community Devel. Dept., City of L.A. 1978-84, sr. loan ofcr. Small bus. lending pgm./rehab. fin. ofcr. 1984–; hold seminars for Small Bus. owners (1985-86), Assn. of Amway Distbrs.; recipient commendn. L.A. Comm. Devel. Dept. (1983), svc. award Challengers Boys Club (1982); mem. Assn. of MBA Execs., Nat. Assn. of Urban Bankers, Nat. Black MBA Assn., Nat. Assn. Realtors, Alpha Kappa Alpha Sor.; civic: March of Dimes Walk Am., United Negro Coll. Fund; publs: City of L.A. Small Business Revolving Loan Fund Guidelines (1984); Democrat; CME Ch.; rec: music, fiber artist. Res: 1633 S Cimarron St Los Angeles 90019 Ofc: City of Los Angeles Community Dev. Dept. 215 W 6th St Ste 300 Los Angeles 90014

DAVIS, CHESTER BALDWIN, real estate broker, investor, inventor; b. Jan. 18, 1912, Hammond, Okla.; s. Oscar Cary and La Vina (Wilson) D.; m. Lucille A. Brown, Sept. 24, 1943; 1 dau, Doris A. b. 1933; edn: Univ. of Calif. cont. edn.; Calif. lic. Real Estate Broker. Career: real estate agt., broker Waade Realty Co. 1960-74; real estate investor; inventor Worm Threader, owner Worm Threader Mfg. Co.; honors: Million Dollar Club; Top Salesman, Waade Realty Co.; mem: Granada Lodge, Masons; mil: chief bosuns mate USN Constrn. Batallion, Victory Medal Asiatic- Pacific Four Stars; rec: fishing. Res: 3921 Continental Way Carmichael 95608

DAVIS, DONALD EUGENE, banker; b. Sept. 1, 1930, Maquoketa, Iowa; s. J. LeRoy and Mary A. D.; children: Michael b. 1953, Patrick b. 1958; edn: MS, CSU Los Angeles 1964; BBA, Univ. of Detroit 1958. Career: v.p., mgr. Imperial Bank, Anaheim 1973-74; founding senior v.p., COO, bd. dirs. Bank of Redlands, Redlands 1974-80; founding pres., CEO, bd. dirs. Palm Desert National Bank, Palm Desert 1980–; tchg. staff San Bernardino Valley Coll., San Bernardino 1973-78; bd. dirs. Bank of Redlands 1974-80; chmn. bd. dirs. Western Hwy. Carriers Ins. Exch. 1978-81; Calif. Bankers Assn. Bd. of Dirs. Region 12; bd. dirs. Palm Desert Rotary 1984-86; founding chmn. bd. El Paseo Merchants Assn.; tchg. staff Am. Inst. of Banking 1963-70; mem: Am. and Calif. Bankers Assns., Western Independent Bankers Assn, Palm Desert Rotary, Palm Desert El Paseo Merchants Assn., Palm Valley Country Club; mil: s/sgt. USAFI 1950-55; Republican; Catholic; rec: golf, travel,

fishing. Res: 12 Santa Clara Dr. Rancho Mirage 92270 Ofc: Palm Desert National Bank, P.O. Box 1777 Palm Desert 92261

DAVIS, DONALD WOODARD, investment banker, ret.; b. Nov. 25, 1904, Chenoa, Ill.; s. Exum Woodard and Melissa (Waldron) D.; m. Florence L'Hommedieu, June 29, 1929; 1 dau., Diane b. 1932; edn: AB, Univ. of Ill. 1926; grad. work, Northwestern Univ. 1928, 1930, 1931; mem. New York Stock Exchange. Career: investment banker: dir. of research Folds Buck & Co., Chgo.; dir. of sales James R. Buck & Co., Chgo.; senior ptnr. Thompson, Davis & Phipps, Chgo.; v.p. Wagenseller & Durst, Los Angeles; senior v.p., dir. Dempsey, Tegeler & Co., Los Angeles, ret. 1970; guest lectr. Investment Bankers Assn. advanced finl. seminar, Wharton Grad. Sch. of Fin., Univ. of Penna.; mem. Los Angeles Stock Exchange Club; civic: Lake San Marcos Home Owners Assn. (bd. dirs.), Home Owners Assn. Laguna Hills (bd. dirs.), United Way/San Diego County (bd. dirs.), Kiwanis Club (pres.); publs: contbr. num. arts. to Midwest financial jours.; mil: lcdr. Supply Corps US Navy 1942-46, letter of commendn. from USN Secty. Knox; Republican; Episcopal (senior warden, chmn. fin. com.); rec: travel, photog., dancing, walking. Res: 1353 Rossmoor Tower II, Laguna Hills 92653

DAVIS, EDWARD MICHAEL, state senator; b. Nov. 15, 1916, Los Angeles; s. Michael and Christine (Hart) D.; edn: BS cum laude, USC 1961; LLD (hon.), Calif. Grad. Sch. Theology. Career: chief Los Angeles Police Dept., 1969-78; mem. Calif. State Senate, 1980–; adj. prof. USC, CSU Los Angeles; honors: Man of Year, Encino Lodge B'nai B'rith, 1974, Headliner of Year 1975, Greater L.A. Press Club, outstanding American, L.A. Philanthropic Found., 1977, hon. mayor Chatsworth CofC; mem. Am. Legion (comdr. 1957), Internat. Assn. Chiefs of Police (pres. 1976-7); author: Staff One (1978); mil: USNR, 1942-45; Episcopal. Ofc: California State Senate Sacramento 95814

DAVIS, FENELON FRANCIS, geologist; b. Jan. 15, 1905, Oakland; s. William James and Josephine (Fenelon) D.; m. Helen Ann Burke, May 1, 1943; children: Rosalie Ann, b. 1946; Elizabeth Joann, b. 1949; edn: BS, UC Berkeley 1928, grad. study UCB 1932-3; reg. geologist (No.385), Calif. 1970; lic. real estate assoc. 1977. Career: research field geologist Std. Oil Co. of Calif., So. Calif., Los Angeles Basin, West Texas, Gulf Coastal Plain, 1928-31; sales engr. Webb and French, Berkeley 1934-38; petroleum engr. Calif. State Lands, Huntington Beach 1939-40; geologist Calif. State Mines and Geology, statewide, 1941-62, sr. geologist, 1963-73; cons. geologist, self-emp., Sacramento 1974-86; mgr. Mineral Resources Pgm., State Mines and Geol. 1965-73, Safety Ofcr. 1968-73; cons. on mine pollution to Water Quality Bd., mercury and energy crises to Resources Agcy.; awards: cert. of pub. service, State Dept. of Conserv. 1964; comendation, Senate, Calif. St. Legislature, 1973; mem: Am. Assn. Petroleum Geologists 1928-32; Peninsula Geol. Soc. 1960-68; Sacramento Geol. Soc. 1968-86 (pres. 1978); Am. Inst. Mining Engrs. 1957-86 (pres. Sacto Section 1970); Calif. State Empls. Assn. 1954-86 (pres. Chap. 78, 1964-66, delegate. 1983-86); Comstock Club; Sacto. bd. of Realtors; author Mineral Resources section in Calif. Ocean Area Plan for US Dept. of Navig. & Ocean Devel. (1970); over 60 pub. reports on mineral resources in Calif. 1950-75; mil: ROTC 1924-26; SIR 1982-86; Republican; Catholic; rec: music, travel, real estate. Res: 4309 Kenston Way Sacramento 95822

DAVIS, GEORGE T., lawyer; b. May 29, 1907, St. Louis, Mo.; s. Thomas D. and Emma Kelchhauser; m. Ginger, July 12, 1974; edn: AA, Sacramento Jr. Coll. 1926; BA, UC Berkeley 1928; LLB, Boalt Hall UC Berkeley 1931; admitted Calif. State Bar 1931; Cert. splst. Criminal Law, Calif. Bd. of Legal Spec. Career: deputy dist. atty., San Francisco 1931-33; solo practitioner, splty criminal law - homicide cases (chief counsel Tom Mooney murder 1934-41); espionage investigator US Army, 1942-45; asst. dist. atty. (Pat Brown), S.F. 1945-47; solo practitioner 1948–, chief counsel Caryl Chessman (1955-60), has handled and tried 150+ First Degree Murder cases (1985: Korea - rape, Guam - murder, Germany - murder, Hawaii - income tax evasion, Spain - extradition, Los Angeles - murder); prof. Nat. Coll. of Advocacy, Golden Gate Sch. of Law; past pres. War Meml. Bd. Trustees, S.F. (apptd. by 4 different mayors); mem: Calif. Trial Lawyers Assn., Assn. of Trial Lawyers of Am., Am. Bd. of Criminal Lawyers (co-founder and past pres.), Lawyers Club of S.F., Calif. Attys. for Crim. Justice, 33 deg. Mason, Shriner; clubs: Olympic (SF), Outrigger (Honolulu), Wild Oak Saddle (Santa Rosa), Press (SF); publs: contbr. book chapter in "Verdicts Were Just," subject of biography "Due Process," by Brad Williams; frequent lectr. bar assns., profl. orgns.; mil: capt. US Army 1942-45; Democrat (N. Calif. chmn. Harry Truman campaign); Christian; rec: polo (two goal player), golf, cattle ranching. Res: 1998 Vallejo St San Francisco 94123 Law Ofcs. George T. Davis 1522 Vallejo San Francisco 94109

DAVIS, JOHN WARREN, contracting specialist; b. Feb. 14, 1946, York, Pa.; gr.grandson, W.F.Davis, founder Anchor Serum Co. and St. Joseph (Mo.) Stockyards and mem. Mo. State Legislature; gr.son, Frank A. Davis Sr., lawyer, St.Joseph, Mo.; son, Lillian M. (Billings) and Frank A. Davis Jr., real estate broker; edn: AA, San Diego City Coll. 1975; BA, Drake Univ. 1968; desig: CPCM, Nat. Contract Mgmt. Assn. (1985). Career: real estate investment, mgmt. sales, 1972-80; contract adminstr. Office of Naval Research, Stanford Univ., 1980-84, contracting ofcr. US Navy, Corona 1984-86, contract splst. Navy Space Systems Activity, Air Force Station, Los Angeles 1986–; Mem: Internat. Platform Assn, Lake Norconian Sailing Club, Apartment Rental and Owners Assn., (past) Stanford Sailing Assn.; mil: E5 US Army 1968-72, Vietnam Campaign (2/60 device) and Vietnam Svc. (2 stars) medals,

Army Commendation, medals,; Prot.; rec: sailing, swim, travel. Res: 815 Rimpau Ave No. 18, Corona 91719 Ofc: Navy Space Systems Activity POB 92960 Los Angeles 90009-2960

DAVIS, JUDITH GRACE, insurance co. executive; b. Feb. 11, 1947, San Francisco; d. Harry Benjamin and Grace Alice (Behnke) Southward; children: Deena, b. 1966; Nicol, b. 1967; John, b. 1969; edn: AA, Canada Coll. 1971; LUTC I, Personal Ins. Cert., Life Underwriting Tng. Council 1981. Career: acct. svc. rep. Wells Fargo Bank, Redwood City 1965-67; receptionist/ lab. & pathology asst. Kaiser Permanente Med. Gp., Redwood City 1965-67; bus. mgr. Canada Coll. Newspaper, Redwood City 1971; dist. rep. Certified Life Ins., Eureka 1977-82; field tng. supvr., Santa Rosa/ mgr. Eureka Ofc., Cert. Life 1982 − ; profl. awards: Pres.'s Club (1978), Quota Buster Awd. (1983), Agen of the Month (1980, 81, 82), Life Rally Trophy (1980), V.P. Awd. (1978), Certified Life Ins.; mem: Humboldt- Del Norte Life Underwriters Assn. (pres. 1984-85); Nat. & Calif. Assns. Life Underwriters; Womens Ins. of Humboldt Co.; BPW Humboldt Bay (legis. chair); Republican; rec: observing waterfowl. Res: 1458 Reasor Rd McKinleyville 95521 Ofc: Certified Life Ins., Box Y, 350 E St, Ste 301, 312, Eureka 95501

DAVIS, KEVIN ROBERT, investor; b. Jan. 9, 1945, Milwaukee, Wisc.; s. Emmett Matthew and Mary Ruth (McCarten) D.; m. Karen Susanne Veley, Nov. 9, 1963; div.; children: Christopher b. 1964, Cameron b. 1969; edn: BS, Univ. of Wisc. 1967. Career: computer salesman, IBM, Madison, Wis. 1967-69; computer pgmmr./analyst Hughes Aircraft Co., Culver City 1969-75; real estate investor, owner/pres. Davis Mgmt. Corp., Los Angeles 1975 − ; writer movie screenplays 1968 − , incl. "The Jail" (1968), "The Hoax" (1970), "The Heirhunters" (1971), "Great Adventure" (1972), "The Campus Town Rapist" (1974), "Run-Through" (1978, stage play), "Strangers in Blood" (1986); mem. Los Angeles Apt. Assn., screenwriters and actors guilds: WGA, SAG, AFTRA, AEA, Amnesty Internat., Mensa, Beverly Hills Mens Charities; Ind.; rec: skiing, fitness, folkdancing. Res: 456 S Spalding Dr Beverly Hills 90212-4104 Ofc: Davis Management Corp. 2029 Century Park East Ste 1110 Los Angeles 90067

DAVIS, LORETTA DELL, business owner; b. July 27, 1939, Cloudchief, Okla.; d. James Clyde Harold and Helen Frances (Duck) Jay; m. James Porter Davis, Feb. 13, 1960; children: Judy (Keys) b. 1960, James b. 1963; edn: AS in printing, Modesto Jr. Coll. 1986. Career: mgr. Jay's Rest Home, Modesto 1965-70; line wkr. Tri Valley Growers, Modesto 1975-79; asst. in Printshop, Modesto Jr. Coll., 1983-85; founder/prop. Patterson Prints, 1985 − ; mem. DAR (Lineage Res. nat. 1986-), Nat. Soc. Colonial Dames, Stanislaus Co. Geneal. Soc., Eastern Star; author: Ducks that Migrated West (1986); founder Jay Family Assn.-West and editor Jay News; ed. Davis Data Exchange; Democrat; Prot.; hobby: genealogy research. Res: 4406 Moffett Rd Ceres 95307 Ofc: Patterson Prints 220 N El Circulo Patterson 95363

DAVIS, MARTIN CHARLES, chiropractor; b. Nov. 6, 1957, Waterloo, Iowa; s. Frank Earl and Jeanette Crystal (Kress) D.; m. Teri, Sept. 17, 1983; edn: AS, Coll. of the Canyons 1979; BS, Cleveland Chiropractic Coll. 1981, DC, 1982; DC, Calif. 1983. Career: assoc. Dr. Lowell Birch DC, San Jose 1983; assoc. Dr. James Bourque DC, Watsonville 1983-84; assoc. Dr. Don L. Hayes DC, Salinas 1984-85; treating phys. Dr. Martin C. Davis DC, San Jose 1985 − ; honors: Diplomate, Nat. Bd. of Chiropractic Examiners 1982; Emergency med. Technician I, 1981; mem: Am. Chiropractic Assn., Delta Tau Alpha (treas. 1981); Republican; Lutheran; rec: mountain climbing. Res: 2244 So. Rodeo Gulch Rd. Santa Cruz 95062 Ofc: Martin C. Davis DC, 860 S Winchester Blvd Ste B San Jose 95128

DAVIS, PATRICIA ANN, chiropractor; b. Dec. 14, 1948, Glendale; d. Robert E. and B. Patricia Pitt; m. Terry Ackley, Apr. 17, 1982; edn: AA, Glendale Coll. 1969; BS, Los Angeles Coll. of Chiro. 1979, DC, 1979; lic. Calif., Colo., Ore. State Bd. Chiro. Examiners; Diplomate Nat. Bd. Chiro. Examiners 1979. Career: chiropractor prin. in pvt. practice, Glendale 1980; owner/v.p. Westward Travel, Inc., Redondo Beach 1981 − , and Western Stage Lines, Inc., 1983 − ; owner/dir. Riviera Village Chiropractic and Nutrition Center, Redondo Beach 1984 − , Riviera Village Wholistic Health Assocs. 1985 − ; past instr. L.A. Coll. of Chiropractic; honors: Dean's list, LACC (1979), Delta Sigma (1979), Sigma Chi Psi (1979); mem: Am. Chiro. Assn., Am. Public Health Assn. (Radiologic Health Sect.); civic Westside Community for Independent Living, Redondo Beach CofC, Torrance Jayceees; Republican; rec: swimming, skiing, scuba, travel. Ofc: 1718 S. Catalina Ave Ste B-2 Redondo Beach 90277

DAVIS, PATRICIA LOUISE, dyer-weaver; b. July 24, 1939, Wash DC; d. James B. and Delpha (Payne) D.; edn: BA, Memphis State Univ. 1962; MA, CSU San Francisco; Career: asst. instr. English Dept., San Francisco State Univ., 1967; self-employed dyer and street artist, 1970-72; currently self-empl. dyer and weaver, prop. Summer and Winter, Petaluma; train apprentices for cottage industry; guest weaver for Art Train (community orgn.); mem. Chileno Valley Spinners and Weavers Guild, World Peace Movement N.S.A.; works: tie-dyed teepee, 7' x 9' (1962), tapestry 3' x 4' (1978), num. hand dyed and woven garments; Independent; Buddhist; rec: body building, dancing. Address: Summer & Winter 1272 Berrydale Dr Petaluma 94952

DAVIS, PETER QUINCY, banker; b. Feb. 13, 1940, US Naval Base, C.Z.; s. Nathaniel Burt and Frances Foster (Dearing) D.; m. Carroll Ward, Apr. 15, 1960; children: Susan b. 1961, Jennifer b. 1965, edn: BBA, Calif. Western Univ.

1963; lic. real estate broker, Calif. 1980. Career: indsl. engr. Ryan Aeronautical Co., 1960-64; banker, various positions leading to vice pres. and mgr., Bank of Am., 1964-76, banker, Bank of Commerce Commerce, San Diego, 1976-, chief exec. ofcr./pres. 1978 − ; dir. Centre City Devel. Corp. 1977 − , pres. 1984 − ; instr. San Diego Comm. Coll.; chmn. for Cong. Jim Bates Fiscal and Monetary Adv. Bd.; chmn. Mayor's Transp. Com.; hon. dep. sheriff, S.D. County (pres. 1985-); mem: Robert Morris Assos., Am. Inst. Banking (instr.), San Diego CofC (treas.); clubs: Kiwanis, City; mil: US Army 1959-60, USAR 1960-65; Republican; Presbyterian. Res: 6112 Syracuse Ln San Diego 92122 Ofc: Bank of Commerce, 7980 Clairemont Mesa Blvd San Diego 92111

DAVIS, RICHARD ALLEN, corporate executive; b. July 15, 1929, Chgo.; s. Harold Aaron and Hilda May (Gulliver) D.; m. Betty, Mar. 25, 1950; div.; children: Holly b. 1956, Jeff b. 1957, Gary b. 1962; m. 2d Lona French, Oct. 6, 1985; edn: BSEE, Drexel Univ. 1959; MSEE, UCLA 1966; grad. stu. USC 1966-7; research in Human Info. Processing UCLA 1974-6; Cert. in Data Processing (CDP), Data Processing Mgmt. Assn. (DPMA) 1965; Cert. in Radiation Health & Safety, Calif. 1976. Career: prior (20 yrs.) mgmt./ technical/ consulting experience in systems, computers, software, telecomm.; founder/pres. R&D Management Inc., Fullerton 1969-70; mktg. mgr./pgm. mgr. Hughes Aircraft Inc., Fullerton 1971-76; mgr. Adv. Pgms., Computer Automation Inc., Irvine 1976-78; dir. adv. plnng. Bell Northern Research Inc., Palo Alto 1979-80; independent cons. (Harris Telecom Div., Compath, Intel, Fujitsu Ltd., Texas Instruments, Tymeshare, CIT-Alcatel S.A.) 1980-82; founder/ dir./ VP Ops. Softyme, Inc., San Francisco 1982-84; chmn. Software Farms Inc. 1984 − ; lectr., mgmt., JF Kennedy Univ.; lectr., comp. sci., CSU Sacto. 1982; cons., system analysis, UC Ext. 1984; awards: Pepsi Cola Natl Scholar 1947, Hughes Doctoral Fellow 1975; orgns: fmrly active in BSA (inst. repr.), YMCA (Indian Guides/Gra-Y Leader), No. Orange Co. Child Guidance Center (bd. dir.); Patents: differential-integral PCM synchronizer; five others pending; num. publs., seminars 1963-; mil: cpl. US Army Ord., Guided Missile Sch. (instr.) 1954-56; Prot., Siddha Yoga; rec: pvt. pilot, guitar, writing (fiction/non-f.), biking. Res: Berkeley Ofc: Software Farms 1404 Glendale Ave Berkeley 94708

DAVIS, RICHARD GATES, company general manager, chief executive officer; b. Oct. 27, 1920, Boston, Mass.; s. Merle Halsey and Edith Rebecca (Gates) D.; m. Elizabeth Caldwell, Sept. 10, 1950, Cynthia b. 1954, Richard Jr. b. 1957; edn: BCE, Cornell Univ. 1941; MBA, Harvard Grad. Sch. of Bus. 1948. Career: div. mgr. Pepperidge Farm Inc. Downers Grove, Ill. 1950-58, v.p. froz. foods Norwalk, Conn. 1958-63; exec. v.p. Texize Chemicals Inc. Greenville, SC 1963-66, Dart Chemical Group L.A. 1966-69; independent cons. Rolling Hills 1970-77; pres. Sea World Seafood Inc. Wilmington 1978-82; pres. Amtrad Inds. Rancho Dominguez 1982 − ; dir: Brownberry Ovens Inc. Oconomowoc, Wisc. 1964-66, Franklin Elec. Light Co. Inc. Franklin, Vt. 1973 − ; honors: Tau Beta Pi (Cornell Univ. 1941), Baker Scholar (Harvard Bus. Sch. 1948); mem: Groc. Mfrs. Sale Execs. (secty. 1956), Bakers Club of Chgo. (secty. 1957), Chgo. Foundlings Home (chmn. 1956), Lake Carmi Campers Assn. (secty. 1984-), Exec. Svcs. Corp of So. Calif. 1984-; mil: lt. col. US Army 1941-46, European Campaign; Republican; United Ch. of Christ; rec: golf, bridge, carpenter. Res: 19009 Laurel Park Rd, No 491, Rancho Dominguez 90220

DAVIS, ROBIN, restaurateur; b. Dec. 5, 1940, San Diego; d. Robert E. and Mary Porter (Baer) Riera; m. James E. Clinton, June 10, 1983; children: Lisa (Larmore) b. 1960, Joseph Riedemann b. 1964; edn: spl. courses Mesa Coll. 1972-74; Calif. R.E. lic., GRI, Grad. Realtors Inst. (1976), Cert. Bus. Counselor (1974). Career: owner/broker del Enterprises, San Diego 1976-82; owner/pres. Las Chalupas, Inc. dba Consuelo's Restaurants, San Diego 1976 − ; mem: San Diego Board of Realtors (chair bd. dirs. 1978-81), Calif. Assn. of Realtors (dir. 1978-82), Nat. Assn. Realtors (charter mem. Women's Council of Realtors 1978, pres. elect 1986), Comml. R.E. Council, Calif. Restaurant Assn., Nat. Rest. Assn.; civic: S.D. CofC (Speakers Bur. 1982-), Neighborhood Revitalization Com. (1981-82), Food Sanitation Adv. Charter Com. (1983-85), Health Dept. Adv. Com. (1983-85), Fire Dept. Sprinkler Task Force (1984-), Nice Guys (1984-85), CSUD Pres.'s Circle (1983-84), Small Bus. Assn.; publs: article in Communique (12/85 NAR); Roman Catholic. Res: 6862 Fashion Hills Blvd San Diego 92111 Ofc: Consuelo's 2263 Sunset Cliffs Blvd San Diego 92107

DAVIS, RON EDWIN, physician; b. May 25, 1949, Bridgeton, N.J.; s. Leland Eugene and Gertrude Bell (Dickinson) D.; m. Christine Pederson, Jan. 11, 1975; children: Emily b. 1977, Nathan b. 1980, Holly b. 1982; edn: BS, Salem Coll. W.Va. 1969; MD, Loma Linda Univ. Sch. of Med. 1973. Career: pvt. practice family and gen. med. Chino, Ontario, Sun City, Calif. 1974 − ; chief of staff Chino Gen. Hosp. 1979; med. staff Doctor's Hosp. Montclair, Christian Hosp. Perris; med. dir. Inland Christian Home Ontario, Suntown Convales. Hosp. Montclair; honors: Am. Legion Citizenship Award, Laudati Awards (Salem Coll. 1966-68), Alpha Omega Alpha (hon. med. soc.) 1972; mem: Am. Assn. Phys. & Surg., Chaffey Comm. Coll. Gov. Bd. 1981-85; publ: editor Civil War Diary and Letters of John Bacon Hoffman of Shiloh, New Jersey (1979); Republican; Seventh-Day Baptist; rec: Western Americana, early Calif. paintings, mining. Res: 3740 Ulla Ln Lake Elsinore 92330 Ofc: 27640 Encanto, Ste. B, Sun City 92381; 2232 S Mountain Ontario 91672

DAVIS, RONALD FRANKLIN, communications co. executive; b. June 17, 1943, Asheville, NC; s. Edgar Franklin and Geneva Snow (Kuykendall) D.; m. Karen Starleaf, Aug. 2, 1980; edn: BS, NC State Univ. 1968; MBA, Univ. So. Calif. 1985. Career: engr./ scientist splst. McDonnell Douglas Astronautics Co. Huntington Beach 1970-80; senior engr. Interstate Electronics Corp. Anaheim 1980-81; engrg. splst. Ford Aerospace & Communications Co. Newport Beach 1981-85; mgr. sys. integration Communication Mfg. Co. Long Beach 1985—; mem: Am. Inst. Aero. & Astro., Am. Mgmt. Assn. (chpt. awards chmn., newsletter ed.), Orange Coast IBM PC Users Group (treas.); author: Microkey (w/ K. Starleaf 1982), other technical publs.; rec: reading, computers. Res: 350 E 22 St Costa Mesa 92627 Ofc: Communication Mfg. Co. 3300 E Spring St Long Beach 90801

DAVIS, RONALD H., communications co. executive; b. Dec. 13, 1934, Los Angeles; s. David R. and Ruth C. (Bush) D.; children: David R. b. 1962, Todd A. b. 1965; edn: USC 1952-56. Career: v.p./dir. Welbourne, Div. of B.W.A., 1970-72; senior v.p. Cantor, Fitzgerald & Co., Inc. 1972-75; current: pres./dir. Corporate Finance Consultants; pres. Creative Art Images L.A.; bd. chmn. American Credit Card Telephone Co.; bd. dirs. Am. Cancer Soc., Calif. div.; mil: sp4 US Army. Res: 1631 Schuyler Rd Beverly Hills 90210 Ofc: 9301 Wilshire Blvd Ste 212 Beverly Hills 90210

DAVIS, WILLIAM RANDALL, manufacturing co. president; b. Oct. 31, 1946, Phila.; s. Wm. Wilson and Frances Jean (Fox) D.; edn: BS, with distinction, US Naval Acad. 1968; MS in math., US Naval Postgrad. Sch. 1969, MBA, Stanford Grad. Sch. Bus. 1977. Career: assoc. McKinsey & Co., Los Angeles Office 1977-82; cofounder/pres. Sentex Systems Inc., Glendale 1983—; honors: mem. Student Senate, Stanford GSB (1976); mem. Naval Acad. Alumni Assn., Stanford Bus. Sch. Alumnni Assn.; inventions: Tel. Entry Systems, Card Reader and Keypad Entry Systems (mfd. by Sentex); mil: nuclear submarine ofcr. USN 1969-75, awarded ASW 'A' for the outstanding weapons dept. in Pacific Submarine Force (1975); rec: ski, tennis, music. Res: 536 California Terrace Pasadena 91105 Ofc: Sentex Systems Inc. 109 E Harvard St Glendale 91205

DAWES, DAVID FORD, land and development co. president; b. July 29, 1909, Muskogee, Okla.; s. Maurice and Ethel (Ford) D.; m. Dorothy L. Snyder, Jan. 5, 1933; children: David Alan b. 1934, Stuart Edward b. 1936, Mary Lou b. 1943; edn: Okla. Univ. 1927-28; realtor 1945. Career: store mgr., salesman Safeway Stores 1931-37; milk route sales Golden Gate Creamery Long Beach 1938-39; salesman Automobile Club of So. Calif. 1939-42; personnel Northrup Aircraft Hawthorne 1942-45; realtor David Dawes Realty Torrance 1945-68; pres. Western Land & Devel. Co., Rancho Carlsbad Country Club 1969—; honors: Realtor of the Year (Gardena 1962); mem: Gardena Bd. Realtors 1956-69, Hawthorne Bd. Realtors, Torrance Bd. Realtors, Masons (32 degree, Worshipful Master 1984), Scottish Rite, Shrine, Knights Templar, Rotary, Carlsbad Boys Club); secty., v.p. commr. San Diego County Flood Control 1975-80, Carlsbad Municipal Water Dist. Spl. Citizens Com. 1973-74. Republican; Protestant; rec: swimming, golf. Res: 3428 Don Juan Dr Carlsbad 92008 Ofc: Western Land & Devel. Co. 5200 El Camino Real 92008

DAWSON, WILLIAM JAMES, orthodontist; b. May 16, 1930, San Francisco; s. Wm. James and Augusta (Rude) D.; m. Judith Riede, Aug. 11, 1962; children: William b. 1954, Wendy b. 1963, Nancy b. 1967, Sarah b. 1968, Evelyn b. 1970; edn: BA, UC Berkeley 1952; DDS, UC San Francisco 1958. Career: private practice of orthodontics, San Rafael 1958—; clin. instr. in oral histology, UC San Francisco 1958-60, mem. UC Cleft Palate Panel 1958-75, clin. instr./asst. research dentist UCSF 1960-75; councilman Town of Ross 1967-79; mem. State of Calif. Public Employees Retirement System Bd. of Adminstrn. 1969-76; mem. State Bd. of Dental Examiners 1985—; honors: Omicron Kappa Upsilon; Diplomate Am. Bd. of Orthodontics 1969; Fellow Royal Soc. of Health 1972; Paul Harris Fellow (Rotary Internat.); mem· Marin Co. Dental Soc., Am., Calif. Dental Soc., Am. Assn. of Orthodontists, Pacific Coast Soc. of Orthodontics, Fedn. Dentaire Internat., Coll. of Diplomates Am. Bd. Orthodontics; orgns: citizens adv. com. Dominican Coll. (pres. 1975-6), exec. com. Marin Property Owners Assn. (pres. 1981-2), M. Co. United Way Bd., Rotary Club of San Rafael (pres. 1978-9), bd. dirs. Terwilliger Nature Ctr., v.chmn. Lincoln Club of No. Calif., Calif. State Republican Central Com. (assoc. mem.), Sierra Club (life), Bohemian Club, Am. Rifle Assn. (life), Trout Unltd. (life); arts. in dental jours.; mil: s/sgt. USAF 1951-54; Republican; Episcopal; rec: fish, garden, tennis. Res: POB 977, Ross 94957 Ofc: ll Greenfield Ave San Rafael 94901

DAY, ALBERT JAMES, accountant; b. Jan. 29, 1937, Hollywood, Calif.; s. Albert Root and Regina Margaret (Ford) D.; edn: BS, Univ. San Francisco 1960; CPA Calif. 1963. Career: gen. ptnr. R.M. Day & Co. Burlingame 1960—; tax splst. Peat, Marwick, Mitchell & Co. CPAs S.F. 1960-66; tax ofc. mgr. Main, LaFrentz & Co. CPAs S.F. 1966-70; secty.-treas. R. Ford & Co. Burlingame 1966—; owner Albert J. Day Co. CPAs San Mateo 1970—; gen. mgr. Wahba Accts. CPAs San Jose 1982-84; pres. TE Financial Group San Jose 1984-86; trustee/ treas. Am. Found. for Homeopathy of Wash. DC and Hahnemann Med. Coll. of the Pacific S.F.; mem: Am. inst. CPAs, Calif. Soc. CPAs. World Trade Club; Republican. Ofc: Day & Co. POB 1634 Burlingame 94011-1634

DAY, LA PORTE, MERCILINE "Heidi" IMMAGDALENA, real estate broker; b. June 26, 1929, Raleigh, N.D.; d. Solamon and Irena (Ternis) Ihli; m. Dominic John, Sept. 18, 1950; children: Sean b. 1955, Joseph b. 1956, Lawrence b. 1957, Andre b. 1958, Niel b. 1960, Noreen b. 1962; edn: Coll. of Edn., Great Falls, Mont. 2 yrs.; Calif. lic. real estate broker (1968). Career: real estate assoc. Walker & Lee Co., others 1968-, owner/broker Heidi's Chateau Realty, Whittier 1975-, assoc. Realty World Charlie Corsi, Fullerton 1981, owner/broker Hi-Lo Realty, Fullerton 1982—; recipient num. Salesman of Month awards; mem. Nat., Calif. Realtors Assn., North Orange Co. Board of Realtors, Realty Investment Assn. of Calif., Fullerton CofC, Better Bus. Bur.,

Fullerton Moose; Catholic; rec: numismatics, fishing, billiards. Ofc: Hi-Lo Realty 1016 W Commonwealth Fullerton 92633

DAY, WYNNE GREGORY, lawyer; b. May 15, 1954, Corona; s. Wynne Carl and Teresa Ann (Martins) D.; m. Roanna L. Williams, Oct. 6, 1979; 1 dau. Kristiina Melissa b. 1984; edn: BA Eng. Lit., UC San Diego 1975; JD, UC Los Angeles Sch. of Law 1978; admitted State Bar of Calif. 1978. Career: certified law student Law Ofc. of Leland H. Bray 1976-78, assoc. atty. 1978; sole practitioner 1979—; Inyo County Spl. Prosecutor 1980; apptd. judge pro tem of Inyo County Justice Ct., 1980; honors: UCLA Moot Ct. honors pgm. 1976-78; mem. (pres. 1977-78) UCLA Christian Law Students Assn. 1976-78; mem: Inyo-Mono Counties Bar Assn. (pres. 1985), Christian Legal Soc., Ctr. for Law and Religious Freedom, Friends and Alumni of UCSD, Gideons Internat., Nat. Fedn. of Ind. Business; Democrat; charismatic Christian; rec: basketball, classical music, simulation war-gaming. Res: Rt. 2 Box 86 Bishop 93514 Ofc: 149 S Fowler St Ste C Bishop 93514

DAYANI, HANK H., airline catering co. controller; b. Nov. 27, 1959; s. David and Shahin (Oheb) D.; cdn: BS, West Chester St. Univ. 1981; MBA, Univ. of Phoenix 1985; Calif. Disability & Life Ins. lic. (1981); cert. in food service op., Univ. Minn./ Saga Mgmt. Devel. Ctr. (1982); Calif. Comm. Colls. instr. credential. Career: food service mgr. (op. univ. kitchen serving 11,000 meals daily) M.W. Wood Food Svc. Ents. 1977-79; mgmt. cons. Small Bus. Inst. 1979-81; Edn. Div., Saga Corp. (asst. dir. foodsvc. ops. Loyola Marymount Univ.), 1981-84; asst. v.p./controller Dobbs Internat. Svcs. (5 airline catering facilities), Los Angeles 1984—; comm. coll. instr. 1985-; mem: Am. Mgmt. Assn., Nat. Restaurant Assn., In-flight Service Assn., Nat. Assn. of Catering Execs., Les Toque Blanches (L.A. chpt. internat. chefs assn. based in Paris); research: organizational theory & behavior; food service ops.; Republican. Res: 435 N Oakhurst Dr #601 Beverly Hills 90210

DEADRICH, PAUL EDDY, lawyer-realtor; b. Jan. 30, 1925, Lakeport, Ca.; s. John A. and Grace E. (Jackson) D.; m. Irene Banks, Dec. 11, 1982; children: Marjanne Robinson b. 1947, Nancy Wolfer b. 1950, Dianne Deadrich-Rogers b. 1952, Bettianne Buck b. 1955, John F. b. 1963, David b. 1968; edn: AA, UC Berkeley 1946; JD, Hastings Coll. of the Law 1949. Career: real estate sales agt., 1947-50; self-empl. attorney, San Leandro 1950-61; atty., realtor, ins. agt. in Twain Harte, 1961-73; law practice in Loomis 1973-75, in Cameron Park 1975-78; missionary at Apostolic Alliance Mission, Gibi, Liberia 1978-82; atty., realtor in San Leandro, Ca. 1982—; judge of Justice Court, Tuolumne 1964-67; dir. Alameda Contra Costa Transit Dist. 1956-61; physical edn. instr./ coach Mother Lode Christian Sch., Tuolumne 1969-73; adminstr., coach and teacher Loomis Christian Sch. 1974-75; honors: Outstanding young man of the year San Leandro, 1955, J.Cs.; mem: So. Alameda Co. Bd. of Realtors, pres. San Leandro Breakfast Club 1985-; pres. So. San Leandro Kiwanis Club 1985-; S.L. chpt. exec. v.p. Full Gospel Men's Fellowship 1983-; past pres. Twain Harte Rotary 1966-7; past pres. Tuolumne Co. Bd. of Realtors 1973; past pres. Broadmoor Mens Club 1958; past pres. Chabot Lions Club 1956-7; past pres. Twain Harte Hi-12 Club; past pres. Family Counseling Agcy of So. Alameda Co.; past cmdr. DAV Chap. 67, San Leandro; mil: pfc 11th Armored Div. WWII in Fr., Belgium 1943-45, Bronze Star, Purple Heart, Combat Inf. Badge; Creation Missions Ch. (missionary Liberia 1978-82); rec: gardening, fishing, backpacking. Res: 1808 Pearl St Alameda 94501 Ofc: 2062 Washington Ave San Leandro 94577

DEADY, GENE MARTIN, university professor; b. May 29, 1931, Chardon, Ohio; s. Willard Martin and Eva Lucile (Blair) D.; m. Jo Ann Phelan, Sept. 11, 1954; children: David Martin b. 1959, Michael Gene b. 1963; cdn. BA, Chico State Coll. 1953, MA, 1961; PhD, UC Berkeley 1968. Career: sci. tchr. Elk Creek (Calif.) H.S. 1954-55, Marysville Union H.S. 1955-58, Piedmont H.S. 1958-60; sci. dept. chmn. Piedmont Unif. Sch. Dist. 1960-68; prof. edn. CSU Chico 1968-82, prof. emeritus 1982—; exec. panel Far West Lab. for Ednl. Research & Devel.; cons. several sch. dists. and State Bd. Edn.; honors: Disting. Svc. (Calif. State Bd. of Edn.); mem: Nat. Sci. Tchrs. Assn., Calif. Sci. Tchrs. Assn. (past pres., secty.), Nat. Assn. Research in Sci. Tchg., Phi Delta Kappa, Masons, Scottish Rite, Fly Fishing Club of Chico; publs: contbg. author Addendum to Calif. State Science Framework, Science for the 1980's (Calif. State Dept. of Edn.); Democrat; Methodist; rec: fly fishing, genealogy. Res: 4 Lakewood Way Chico 95926 Ofc: Ednl. Dept. CSU First & Normal Chico 95929

DEAN, DONALD EDWIN, consulting engineer; b. Feb. 12, 1926, Pacific Grove; s. Theodore Edwin and Gladys (Ernest) D.; children: Steven Craig b. 1958, Michelle Jeanette b. 1969; edn: AA, Hartnell Coll. 1949; BS, CSU San Jose 1952. Reg. Profl. Engr. (mech., mfg.) Calif. Career: plant mgr. Industrial Dynamics Inc., Torrance 1964-66; systems mgr. Cosmodyne Corp., Torrance 1966-67; chief engr. Indsl. Div. Republic Corp., Gardena 1967-70; owner/dir. Profit Design Consultants, San Pedro 1971—; v.p. engring./dir. Safety Technology Inc.; awards: Design & Technology award S.P.E. (1978); mem: Fluid Power Soc. (dir. 1968-70), Soc. of Plastics Engrs. (dir. 1974-78); works: energy conservation, S.P.E. (1965), 5 US Patents: metal forming machinery, thermoforming, heat welding; mil: Army Ground Forces, Korea; Republican; Prot.; rec: sailing, lead 20-piece big band. Ofc: Profit Design Consultants 565 W 5th St Ste 1 San Pedro 90731

DEAN, MAJOR JAMES, publisher/editor; b. Nov. 11, 1923, Dallas, Tex.; s. Francis Claude and Alpha Aletha (Phillips) D.; m. Vida D. Baker, July 21, 1946; children: Major J., Jr. b. 1948, David Denhan b. 1952, Victoria Lynn b. 1957;

edn: AA, Tyler (Tex.) Jr. Coll. 1947. Career: reporter Tyler, Tex. Courier Times, 1947, subsequently sports editor, city ed., mng. ed.; copy ed. Houston, Texas Chronicle, 1953-54; mng. ed. Pampa, Tex. News, 1954-56; ed. Lima, Ohio News, 1956-60; asst. city ed. Houston Chronicle, 1960-62; news ed., executive ed., editor The Register, Santa Ana, Ca. 1962-81; current: owner/pub./editor Orange County Business Line monthly newspaper, and pres. Jim Dean Orgn. Inc. pub. rels. co., Santa Ana; awards: first place writing, AP Texas Sports Writers Assn. 1950; general excellence newspaper award, Ohio Editors Assn. 1959; US Indsl. Assn. medallion for edtl. writing 1980; num. press club citations; Jim Dean journalism scholarship estab. Chapman Coll. in 1981; Sky Dunlap award, Orange Co. Press Club 1981; mem: v.p. Texas Sports Writers Assn. 1949; pres. Ohio UPI Editors Assn. 1959; pres. So. Cal. United Press Editors Assn. 1978; pres. O.C. chpt. Sigma Delta Chi; bd. mem. O.C. Press Club; bd. mem: O.C. CofC., O.C. Economic Devel. Corp., NCCJ, O.C. chpt. Alzheimers & Rel. Diseases Assn., adv. bd. CSU Gerontol. Ctr. Fund Drive; mil: s/sgt. Army Signal Corps 1942-45, Pac. Theater cpgn., GCM; Prot.; rec: writing, reading, travel, vol. svc. Address: The Jim Dean Orgn. Inc. 12800 Garden Grove Blvd Ste H Garden Grove 92643

DEAN, RICHARD MASON, educator, co. president; b. Apr. 4, 1951, Pomona; s. Louis Mason and Mary Louise (Fandre) D.; edn: BS in bus. mgt., Calif. State Polytech. Univ. 1974, BS in econs. 1978, MSBA 1980, MS econs. 1984; Calif. Life Community Coll. tchg. credential, Bus. Edn. (1978), Bus. and Indsl. Mgmt. (1979), Administr. cred. (1986), Economics, Ofc. & Related Technols., Computer & Related Technols., Profl. Edn. (life, 1985). Career: acct. Rowland Unified Sch. Dist., Rowland Hts. 1975-79; work experience coord. Chaffey Joint Union High Sch. Dist., Ontario 1979-82; lectr. Mgmt. Human Resources Dept. Cal Poly Univ., Pomona 1982-85; tchr. Arroyo High Sch., El Monte Unif. Sch. Dist. 1985—; pres. University Word Processing, Fullerton 1982—; cons. Gentek Corp., La Verne 1984; guest lectr. General Dynamics, Pomona 1984; cons. Houghton Mifflin Pub. Co., Boston 1984-; mem: Nat. Business Educators Assn., Calif. Bus. Educators Assn.; sponsor Arroyo H.S. Info. Systems Club; publs: Easy Computations Software (for appls. in mktg., fin., acctg. and stats.), How to Program in B.A.S.I.C., Easy Librarian Software, (all copyrighted 1982); Republican; Congregational; rec: golf, skiing (snow, water), stockmarkets. Ofc: University Word Processing 2733 Pine Creek Circle Fullerton 92635-2936

DEAR, LORNE ALBERT, electronic data processing executive; b. Nov. 29, 1952, Edmonton, Alberta, Can., nat. US cit. 1971; s. Wallace E. and Edith Mona (Chorley) D.; m. Terry Heil, Dec. 4, 1976; children: David b. 1979, Leanne b. 1981; edn: BA in acctg., CSU Fullerton 1974; MSBA, EDP auditing, Cal Poly, Pomona 1984; grad. dip. USAF War Coll. 1986. Career: clk., asst. mgr. (full-time during coll.) Fazio's Shopping Bag, Anaheim 1969-74; auditor, supv. auditor, regional office staff mgr. US Gen. Acctg. Office, Los Angeles Regl. Office, 1974-82; EDP Audit pgm. mgr. Information Technol., HQ USAF Audit Agcy., Norton AFB, San Bernardino 1982—; frequent speaker and writer on info. system security, spkr. 1986 AF Info. Mgmt. Conf., 1985 Nat. EDP Auditor Assn. Control and Security Conf., 1984 AF Small Computer Conf.; instr. EDP auditing AFAA, and subs. tchr. Cal Poly Pomona; ptnr. Automated Business Services 1986—; cons. Secure Memory Inc. 1985-; honors: AFAA Outstanding Project Supvr. (1985), sev. merit awards, Air Force (1983, 84, 85, 86), GAO merit awards (1979, 80); mem. EDP Auditor Assn. Inc.; civic: Yucaipa Methodist Ch. (hd. Computer Automation Proj., Admin. Bd.), San Bernardino Civic Light Opera Assn., Beta Gamma Sigma; publs: Planning for the Security of Local Area Networks (Auerbach Pub. Inc. 1986), Data Security Mgmt. Series (1986), EDP Auditors Role in Systems Development (AF Comptroller Mag. 10/86), LANS: Evaluating Security Needs (Auerbach Pub. 1986), Data Security Mgmt. Series (pending); Democrat; Methodist; rec: camping, woodwork, racquetball. Res: 35656 Teriann Ln Yucaipa 92399 Ofc: HQ USAF Audit Agency Norton AFB San Bernardino 92409-6001

DE ARMOND, BEATRICE JEANNETTE, hobby center owner/developer; b. Mar. 3, 1913, Northumberland, N.H.; d. Frank Nicklas and Bertha Rebbeca (Hapgood) Parker; m. Jay O. De Armond, Aug. 7, 1930; children: Jacquelin, b. 1934; Yvonne, b. 1943. Career: opened antique shop, expanded one shop at a time; currently, owner /designer Hobby City doll & toy museum (variety of hobby shops in 25 distinctive bldgs.), Anaheim; frequent judge, Doll Shows; mem. Anaheim, Stanton CofC; Long Beach, Anaheim Doll Collectors Clubs; Western Shores chpt. DAR; Republican (Womens Fed. Club); Methodist. Address: Hobby City, 1238 So Beach Blvd Anaheim 92804

DEAVER, DOUGLAS ROSS, distribution co. executive; b. Sept. 16, 1947, Minneapolis, Minn.; s. Harry Gilbert Jr. and Virginia (Wollman) D.; m. Diane Kather, June 15, 1985; stepchildren nee Newpher: Shana b. 1974, Sharon b. 1976; edn: BS, Purdue Univ. 1970, MS, 1971. Career: Crown Zellerbach 1972-81; customer svc. analyst 1972-73; materials analyst 1973-74; supvr. ops. sys. 1974-75; prodn. supvr. 1976-77; asst. supt. 1977-79; fin. analyst 1979-81; gen. parts mgr. Williams & Lane 1981-85; exec. v.p. Sierra Detroit Diesel Allison 1985—; honors: Distng. Student, Purdue Univ. 1970; mem: Council of Logistics Mgmt., Am. Prodn. and Inventory Control Soc.; mil: capt. USAR Field Artillery; Repubican; Presbyterian. Res: 253 Corliss Dr. Moraga 94556 Ofc: Sierra Detroit Diesel Allison, 1077 Eastshore Hwy. Berkeley 94710

DEAVERS, WILLIAM PURSER, JR., aerospace engineering executive; b. Sept. 13, 1925, Alexandria, La.; s. Wm. Purser and Elizabeth Jean (Archer) D.; m. Louise Aiken, Apr. 23, 1946; children: Wm. Franklin b. 1948, John Thomas b. 1950, Richard Lewis b. 1952, Patricia Ann b. 1954, Pamela Diane b. 1954, Ann Louise b. 1956; edn: Geo. Washington Univ. 1941-43; BSME, Univ. Md.

1951; UCLA 1955-58. Career: Rocket Fuze designer, Naval Ordnance Lab., White Oak, Md. 1951-54; mgr. Ammunition Components Br. US Naval Weapons Ctr., China Lake 1954-56, mgr. Anti-Submarine Warfare Br., 1956-59; mem. tech. staff Space Technology Labs., Redondo Beach 1960-65; mgr. Ballistic Missile Propulsion, TRW Systems, San Bernardino 1965-75, mgr. Ballistic Missile Propulsion System Project Engring. 1975—, support to Air Force Sci. Advis. Board, Spl. AF Propulsion Investigatory Panels; co-chair Joint AF-AIAA Future Systems Propulsion Panel 1985; awards: scholarship award USN, Lowell Tech. Inst. (1944), Meritorious Civilian Svc. award USN (1955); mem: ASME (1947-58), Am. Ordnance Assn. (1954-59) 1st pres. China Lake Posts Adm. Soc. for Public Admins. (1956-59), Am. Rocket Soc./AIAA (1960-); Rotarian; num. classified publs.- Rockets, Missiles, Anti-Submarine Warfare; mil: lt. jg US Navy 1943-46, Res. 1946-58; Republican; Quaker; rec: cabinet maker, fly fisherman. Res: 310 W South Ave Redlands 92373 Ofc: TRW, Ballistics Missile Div. POB 1310 San Bernardino 92402

DE BRA, DANIEL B., educator, university engineering laboratory director; b. June 1, 1930, NY, NY; m. Esther Slater Crosby; children: Corinne, Elisabeth, Heidi, David, Kathryn Ann; edn: BE mech. engring., Yale Univ. 1952; MS mech. engring., MIT, 1953; PhD, engring. mechs., Stanford Univ. 1962. Career: supr. Dynamics and Control Analysis, Guidance & Control Dept., Satellite Systems, Lockheed Missiles and Space Co., Sunnyvale 1956-64; Stanford Univ. lectr., 1964-69, prof., 1969—, currently prof. of aeronautics and astronautics, prof. of mech. engring., dir. Guidance & Control Lab., Stanford Univ.; cons. in (diamond turning) precision metrology, Lawrence Livermore Lab.; splst. in satellite control, inertial instrument devel., autopilots, and mfg. technology precision machine tools; honors: Indsl. Research Award 100, for successful flight of first drag free satellite (1973), Thurlow Award, Inst. of Navigation (1982), Life mem. US Nat. Acad. of Engring. (1981); mem: Fellow Am. Inst. Aero and Astro (v.p. edn. 1973-75), Am. Astronautical Soc., Am. Geophysical Union, Am. Soc. Mech. Engrs., CIRP, IEEE, Inst. of Navigation, Internat. Fedn. Automatic Control (chmn. Space Com. 1982-84), Soc. Automotive Engrs., Fellow Soc. Mech. Engrs.; contbr. 67 publs. in sci., tech. and profl. journals; mil: lt. col. USAF (Ret.); Republican; Protestant. Address: Stanford University Dept of Aero & Astro, Stanford 94305

DE BUS, DAVID WARING, psychologist; b. Oct. 18, 1948, Los Angeles; s. Louis Kissam and Bemi (Bemis) DeB.; m. Denyse Beaudet, PhD, Mar. 17, 1984; edn: AB English, magna cum laude, UC Los Angeles 1969; Rel. M., Sch. of Theology at Claremont 1974; PhD profl. psych., US Internat. Univ. 1979; UC San Diego 1985-. Career: coordinator Council on Healing the Whole Person, Internat. Cooperation Council L.A. 1978-80; chief psychol. Center for Creative Health San Diego 1980-81; clin. dir. Hanbleceya - a therapeutic community for schizophrenia Lemon Grove 1981-85; psychol. pvt. practice 1980—; workshops, lectures US, Canada on transpersonal psychology 1980-84; co-founder NOUMENA, a vehicle for workshops and lectures; honors: Phi Beta Kappa (UCLA), Merit Scholar (School of Theol. Claremont); mem: Phys. for Social Responsibility, Athenaeum Music and Arts Library; research: healing powers of music, music therapy for schizophrenics; publ: poetry, readings in S.D., music compositions, publ. in Internat. Assn. of Therapeutic Communities; Democrat; United Methodist; rec: music, poetry, painting. Res: 425 Bonair St, No. 2, La Jolla 92037

DECKER, MAHRIA LEMAR FALCON, artist, real estate broker, community activist; b. May 23, 1923, Hamilton, Ont., Canada, nat. US through parents 1927; d. (adopt.) Samuel and (nat.) Maria Francesca (Miele) Falcon; m. Gene Dallas Decker, July 1944 (dec. 1956); children: Gregory Dallas, architect, b. 1945, Candace Ashley (Shapiro), artist, b. 1949, Deborah Francesca (Leene), graphic artist, b. 1950; edn: dress design, Woodbury Coll. 1940-42; Chouinard Sch. of Fine Arts 1955; (on scholarship) Maria Louis French Sch. of Dress Design, L.A. 1959; bus. adminstrn. UCLA 1960-63; Calif. lic. R.E. Broker (1961), Life & Disability Ins. Agt. (1959); Cert. Interior Decorator. Career: singer/performer as singing team with husband in opera and musicals, radio and TV, throughout USA 1944-56; founder/broker Mahria Decker Real Estate & Insurance Brokerage, Westchester (L.A. Airport area) 1961-77; moved to Mendocino 1977; currently broker/prin. Sun & Sea R.E. Brokerage (bldg. homes designed by son Greg Decker), Mendocino; mem. advsry. coms. Mendocino Co.; candidate for Los Angeles City Council 6th Dist. 1970s; active var. civic orgns. and local art assns.; founder/pres. Greater Westchester Home Owners Assn. Inc. (1966) and Airport Cities Action Com. (both orgns. estab. to defend homeowners against unfair airport condemnation procedures; legal actions filed cont. through 1970s to 1982; in 1976 2d Civil Action Case #45591, Supreme Ct. Calif., City of L.A. vs. Mahria L. Decker set a legal precedent and rules in condemnation by govt. agcs.; another Supreme Ct. case estab. the Fed. Relocation Act 1979, requiring relocation grants for forced condemnation moves; GWHA Inc. devel. and proposed laws to govern flight patterns and noise pollution now in effect in Airports in Calif. and nat.); Independent; rec: fine arts oil painter, environmentalist. Ofc: Sun & Sea R.E. Brokerage POB 294 Manchester 95459

DECLARK, DENNIS GEORGE, behavior analyst; b. March 24, 1950, Redlands; s. Bernard Warren and Frances Bochran (Linabury) D.; m. Patricia, March 11, 1972; children: Katey b. 1972, Kirk b. 1978, Kory b. 1983; edn: BA, UC Irvine 1972; MBA, Calif. State Coll. San Bernardino 1975; MA, Calif. Polytechnic Univ. SLO 1975; D.Edn., Univ. of San Francisco 1985; Reg. Psychological Asst., Calif. 1985; Calif. Comm. Coll. tchg. credentials (counseling, bus. and indsl. mgmt., banking and fin., psychology and spl. edn.). Career: margin, cash accounts bookkeeper Merrill, Lynch, Pierce, Fenner & Smith, Newport Bd. 1972, acct. exec., Riverside 1972-75; behavior analyst Tri-

Counties Regl. Ctr., San Luis Obispo 1976–; instr. Chapman Coll. 1985-; profl. presentations: Individualized Behavior Programs in Natural Environments, 1979; Intensive Behavioral Intervention Program Specialist (1979), Behavioral Interventions in Naturalistic Environments (1980); research paper: The Effects of a Response-Class Relationship Between Prompts to Increase and Decrease Responding on Compliance Training with Developmentally Disabled Preschool Children (1985); Democrat; Catholic; rec: sailing, racquetball, bicycling. Ofc: Tri-Counties Regional Center, 1428 Phillips Ln. Ste. 202 San Luis Obispo 93401

DE CRISTOFARO, JOSEPH ANTHONY, association executive; b. Jan. 28, 1948, Bronx, NY; s. Francis Anthony and Flora D.C.; m. Elizabeth, Sept. 11, 1976; 1 dau, Maria b. 1980; edn: BA, Adelphi Univ. 1969; MA, State Univ. of NY 1972, MA, 1974; Cert. Life Tchg. Cred., Calif. 1975. Career: secondary tchr. State Univ. of New York, grad. div. and secondary, New York, life coll. cred. Spanish & Latin American studies 1969-77; exec. dir. United Way of North San Diego Co. 1977-80; asst. exec. v.p. COMBO, Combined Art Council of San Diego 1980-82; exec. dir. Big Brothers of San Diego 1982–; also, gen. ptr. U.S. Export & Trading Co.; asst. lectr Latin Am. Cultural Devel., State Univ. of NY; Cert. Trading Co., U.S. Export Trading Co., U.S. Dept. of Commerce, San Diego Co. 1982-; honors: Outstanding Young Citizen Award, San Diego Jaycees 1976, 1977; mem: Nat. Conv. Big Brothers/ Big Sisters of Am., Nat. Profl. Soc. of Caseworkers, Lions, Italian Catholic Fedn. (Escondido); works: designation campaigns for small non-profit orgs., Big Brothers/ Big Sisters Nat. Conv. Symp. 1983; Republican; Catholic; rec: golf, sailing, opera. Res: 1218 Rees Rd. Escondido 92026 Ofc: Big Brothers of San Diego, 8949 Complex Dr. San Diego 92123

DEDDEH, WADIE PETER, state senator; b. Sept. 6, 1920, Baghdad, Iraq; s. Peter Joseph and Hannai (Mona) D.; m. Mary-Lynn Drake, 1951; 1 son, Peter Charles; edn: AB, Univ. Baghdad 1946; MA, Univ. Detroit 1956. Career: tchr. Arabic lang. Army Language Sch., Monterey, Calif. 1949-54; tchr. Sweetwater High Sch., National City 1959-62; prof. polit. sci. Southwestern Coll., Chula Vista 1962-6; mem. Calif. State Assembly, 1967-76, chmn. pub. employees and retirement com.; mem. Calif. State Senate, 1976–; del. Democratic Nat. Conv., 1980; mem. Calif. Tchrs. Assn., NEA, Calif. Jr. Coll. Faculty Assn., GI Forum, Knights of Columbus; Catholic. Res: 368 Surrey Dr., Bonita 92002 Ofc: California State Senate, State Capitol, Sacramento 95814

DEEB, CAREN ANN, periodontist; b. May 1, 1956, Encino; d. Edward and Marion Rhoda (Nader) D.; m. Robert Kouri, Jan. 26, 1985; edn: BA, CSU Northirdge 1978; DDS, USC 1983, cert. periodontics, 1985. Career: pvt. practice periodontist in assn. with father, Toluca Lake and Newport Beach; p.t. instr. USC Sch. of Dentistry; conducting research in periodontics (bone grafting, juvenille periodontics and diabetes) USC Sch. of Dentistry; mem: Am. Assn. Periodontics, Am., Calif., Orange Co. and San Fernando Valley Dental Assns., Calif. and Western Socs. Periodontists, Newport Harbor Acad. of Dentistry, CofC; Republican; Orthodox; rec: tennis, golf. Res: 10120 Riverside Dr. Toluca Lake 91602 Ofc: 10116 Riverside Dr. Ste. 301 Toluca Lake 91602

DEEDWANIA, PRAKASH C., physician, medical administrator; b. Aug. 28, 1948, Ajmer, India; s. Gokul C. and Paras (Garg) D.; m. Catherine E.; 1 dau., Anne; edn: pre-med. Univ. of Rajasthan 1963, MD (honors in pharmacol.), 1969; Diplomate in internal med. (1975), pulmonary (1976), and cardiol. (1977), ABIM. Career: rotating intern, postgrad. res. in medicine J.L.N. Med. Coll. Hosp. Center, Ajmer, India 1970-71 med. intern Coney Is. Hosp./ Maimonides Med. Ctr., Bklyn. 1971-72; med. res. VA Med. Ctr., Bronx/Mt. Sinai Sch. of Med., N.Y. 1972-73, chief res. 1973-75; cardiol. fellow Univ. of Ill. Abraham Lincoln Sch. of Med., Chgo. 1975-76, senior research fellow in cardiol. 1976-77; supvsy. att. phys. St. Joseph's Hosp., N.Y. 1973-75, Weiss Meml. Hosp., Chgo. 1975-77; cons. in cardiol. and pulmonary Bd. of Health, Chgo. 1976-77; chief Cardiology, VA Med. Center/Univ. of Va., Salem

DEERING, WARREN HENRY, superior court judge; b. May 25, 1924, Moneta, Va.; s. Henry and Nola Blanche (Starkey) D.; edn: BS, Northwestern Univ. 1948, LLB, 1950, LLM, USC 1952; admitted Calif. State Bar 1952. Career: dep. atty. gen. State of Calif., Los Angeles 1958-69, asst. atty. gen. 1969-70, chief asst. atty. gen. 1970-72; judge Municipal Court, Los Angeles 1972-80; judge Superior Court, Los Angeles 1981–; mem. bd. trustees So. Calif. Coll. of Optometry 1969-81; dir. Western State Coll. of Law 1969-; faculty Calif. Judges Coll., Berkeley; mem. Calif. Judges Assn., Northwestern Univ. Alumni Assn. of So. Calif. (past pres.); author and co-author: two books on legal procedures (Univ. Calif. Contg. Edn. of Bar); mil: s/sgt. Air Force 1941-45, Air Medal; Republican; rec: archaeology, astrophysics. Res: 9653 Highridge Dr Beverly Hills 90210

DE FAZIO, CHARLES ANTHONY, recording studio engineer/owner; b. May 2, 1957, Summit, N.J.; s. Charles A., Sr. and Theresa Agnes (Garguilo) DeF.; edn: BBA, Univ. Notre Dame 1979; cert. Soundmaster Recording Engr. Sch. 1980. Career: internal auditor Brentwood Svgs & Loan, Long Beach 1980; staff acct. Eiki Internat. Inc., Laguna Niguel 1981; chief finl. ofcr./prin. New World Audio, Inc., San Diego 1981-85; recording engr./owner MixMasters (24 track recording studio) San Diego, 1985–; sound engr. Maranatha Chapel; honors: Dean's list (1975-79); mem. Creation Sci. Research Inst.; Republican; Christian; rec: music, sports, Bible study. Res: 4240 Menlo Ave #20 San Diego 92115 Ofc: Mixmasters 4877 Mercury St San Diego 92111

DE GUZMAN, MIGUEL TIONG, engineer; b. Dec. 19, 1938, Philippines, nat. US cit. 1978; s. Ildefonso Garcia and Corazon (Tiong) DeGuzman; m. Liwayway, June 8, 1965; children: Joseph b. 1966, Michael b. 1972; edn: BSCE, Univ. of the Pilippines 1961, grad. studies, 1966; cont. edn., UC Berkeley 1980; Reg. Profl. Civil Engr., Calif. 1970; Reg. Profl. Engr., Georgia (1974), Mass. (1977) and Conn. (1984). Career: structural engr., resident engr. Thomas J. Davis Inc., Agana, Guam 1967-69; senior structural engr. Parsons Brinckerhoff, Boston, Mass., Atlanta, Ga. and San Francisco, Calif. 1969-80; engring. supvr., structural group leader Cygna Energy Svcs., San Francisco 1980-84; sub-cons. structural engr. Barnes & Jarnis Inc., Boston, Mass. 1984; pres. Eastern Seaboard Engring. Corp., Boston, Mass. 1984-85; supvg. structural engr. Parsons Brinckerhoff, Seattle, Wash. 1985–; bd. dirs. Eastern Seaboard Engring. Corp. 1984-85; instr. in civil engring. Univ. of Pangasinan, Philippines 1964-66; honors: 3rd Pl., Philippine Civil Svc. Examinations for Civil Engrs. 1962; mem: Nat. Soc. of Profl. Engrs., Soc. of Am. Mil. Engrs.; co-author: Seismic Analysis of the 101 California Building, a 50- story steel frame bldg. in downtown San Francisco, 1984; Democrat; Catholic; rec: computers, writing, baseball. Res: 322 Ramona Ave. El Cerrito 94530

DEHLSEN, JAMES G.P., business development executive; b. Apr. 27, 1937, Guadalajara, Jalisco, Mexico; s. James A. and Frances Lee (Purnell) D.; m. Deanna C. Carlsen, Aug. 12, 1960; children: James B., b. 1968, Deanna F., b. 1970, Wren B., b. 1977; edn: BS, USC, 1962, MBA, 1963. Career: acct. exec. Dean Witter and Co., Newport Beach 1963-68; pres. Shareholders Mgmt. Internat., London, Eng. 1968-70; pres. Center Finance, London, Eng. 1970-73; consultant, Newport Beach 1973-76; founder/chmn. The Triflon Co., Newport Beach 1976-80; founder/pres./chmn. Zond Systems Inc., Tehachapi 1980–; founder and fmr. v.chmn. Kern County Wind Energy Assn., 1982; sponsor, Human Powered Speed Championship, 1978; spl. adviser re Cost and Performance of New Electric Generating Technologies, Office of Tech. and Assessment, Wash DC; mem. Danish-Am. CofC; works: copyrights: Triflon (1966), Zond (1980); patent: Aerosol Nozzle System (1977); inventions: Ball-point pen system (sold rights to Parker Pen Co., 1960); publs: Triflon - New Concept in Lubrication, pub. in Tribology (1978); mil: A/1L USAF 1954-58; Republican; Prot.; rec: art, painting, sculpting, music. Res: 21121 Carriage Lane Tehachapi 93561 Ofc: Zond Systems Inc., 112 So Curry St Tehachapi 93561

DE JARNETT, LARRY R., diversified manufacturing co. executive; b. June 7, 1940, Harrisburg, Ill.; s. Raymond Preston and Fern Berdell (Moye) D.; m. Mary Cotton, June 16, 1962; children: Steven Bradley b. 1966, Laura Elizabeth b. 1969; edn: BS, So. Ill. Univ. 1962, MS, 1963. Career: asst. coord. sys. & procedures So. Ill. Univ., Carbondale, Ill. 1963-64; sys. analyst, project leader, sys. review mgr. Ford Motor Co., corp. sys. ofc., Dearborn, Mich. 1964-70, ops. analysis mgr., automotive assembly div. 1970-72, div. ys. mgr. engine div. 1973-77, senior mgmt. svcs. assoc., internal cons. finance staff 1978-70; corp. v.p. information systems Lear Siegler Inc., Santa Monica 1979–; lectr. So. Ill. Univ. 1964; chmn., presenter var. AMA, Industry and Tech. sems. 1965-67; honors: Alumni Achiev. award for Distng. Profl. Achiev., So. Ill. Univ. 1984; Mgr. of the Year, Soc. for Adv. of Mgmt., So. Ill. Univ. 1980; mem: Soc. for Information Mgmt. (chmn. 1984-85), Assn. of Systems Mgmt. (profl.), St. Peter's by the Sea Presbyterian (ruling elder), St. John's Hosp. & Health Ctr. (bd. adv. com. 1982-84), Computers & Information Systems Assn. (UCLA), Claremont Grad. Sch. (adv. bd. 1985-), CSU Los Angeles Ctr. for Information Research Mgmt. (bd. dirs. 1982-85); Republican; Presbyterian; rec: golf, reading. Ofc: Lear Siegler Inc.- Corporate Office, P.O. Box 2158 Santa Monica 90406

DE KERNION, JEAN BAYHI, physician; b. Jan. 26, 1940, New Orleans; s. Paul Sidney and Anna Antoinette (Bayhi) deKernion; m. Mary Rourke, May 10, 1969; children: David b. 1970, Kara b. 1971, Grant b. 1976; edn: BS, Loyola Univ. 1961; MD, Louisiana State Univ. 1965; bd. certified Am. Bd. Surgery 1973, Am. Bd. Urology 1975. Career: surg. intern Univ. Hosps. of Cleveland 1965-66, jr. asst. surg. resident 1966-67; NIH clin. assoc. surg. branch Nat. Cancer Inst. 1967-69; senior res. urology and gen. surg. Univ. Hosps. of Cleveland 1969-73; chief urol. div., chief genitourinary tumor research pgm. Sepulveda (Calif.) VA Hosp. 1973-78; attg. urologist UCLA Student Health Ctr., Olive View Hosp. Sylmar, Harbor Gen. Hosp. Torrance 1973-78, USPH Hosp. New Orleans, Tulane Univ. Hosp., VA Hosp. New Orleans, Alexandria, La., Huey P. Long Meml. Hosp. Pineville, Charity Hosp. of New Orleans, Lallie Kemp Charity Hosp. Independence, La. 1978-80; head urologic oncol. UCLA Sch. of Med. 1980–, acting chief urol. div. 1984–; dir. clin. pgms., dir. genitourinary oncol. pgm. area Jonsson Comprehensive Cancer Ctr. UCLA 1980–; asst. prof. surg./urol. UCLA Sch. of Med. 1973-78; assoc. prof. urol. Tulane Univ. Sch. of Med. 1978-80; assoc. prof. surg./urol. UCLA Sch. of Med. 1980-82, prof. 1980–; mem. and chmn. num. hosp., assn. and nat. coms., Am. Bd. Urol. Exam. Com. 1974-79; cons. US Food & Drug Adminstrn. 1982-, Nat. Cancer Inst. 1985; ed. num. med. publs.; honors: Tri-Beta Nat. Honor Soc. (1961), Agramonte Premed. Hon. Soc. (1961), Nat. Hon. Med. Soc. (1965), Phi Kappa Phi (1965), Fellowship (Am. Heart Assn. 1964), Urban Maes Surg. Award (1965), Crile Surg. Research Fellow (1969-72), Clin. Fellow (Am. Cancer Soc. 1972-73), num. research grants; fellow Am. Coll. Surgeons 1980; mem: AMA, CMA, LACMA, Assn. for Acad. Surg., Am. Urol. Assn., LA Urol. Soc., UCLA Cancer Ctr., Am. Urol. Assn., Am. Assn. Clin. Urols., Am. Assn. Cancer Research, Am. Soc. Clin. Oncol., Soc. Univ. Surgeons, Pan-Pacific Surg. Assn., Bay Surg. Soc. (pgm. chmn. 1984), Pacific Coast Surg. Assn., Am. Assn. GenitoUrinary Surgeons, Soc. Urologic Oncol. (founding mem. 1984), Bel Air Bay Club, New Orleans CC; num. articles in med. jours.; mil: USPHS; Republican; Catholic; rec: running, study of French lang. Res: 360 Alma Real Pacific Palisades 90277 Ofc: UCLA Med. Ctr. 10833 LeConte Ave Rm 66-131 Los Angeles 90024

DE KLOTZ, FRED WESLEY, lawyer; b. Apr. 19, 1931, Elizabeth, NJ; s. Fred Wesley and Isabel (Brindley) De K.; children: Andrea, b. 1960; Wesley, b. 1962; Cara, b. 1966; edn: BS, UC Berkeley 1953; LLB, Univ. of Santa Clara 1959. Career: atty. assoc. Richard Lowey, Atty., Beverly Hills 1959-60, Steven Nakishima, Atty., San Jose 1960-61, solo practice San Jose 1961-62, 1965-70, partnership practice with John J. Hayes, 1962-65; DeKlotz & Baker, San Jose 1970−; mem. Calif. State Bar Assn., Santa Clara Co. Bar Assn., Sigma Alpha Epsilon frat.; clubs: Sainte Claire; mil: capt. Army Inf. 1953-55, Reserve 1955-61; Republican; Presbyterian; rec: sailing, skiing, tennis, small cattle ranch. Res: 16158 Bachman Ave, Los Gatos 95030 Ofc: 1200 Community Bank Bldg, 111 W St. John St San Jose 95113

DE LA ROSA, JAMES, electronics engineer; b. July 25, 1930, Santa Paula; s. Juan and Guadalupe Rivas (Villa) De La R.; m. Maria Luisa Figuera, July 4, 1954; children: James, Jr. b. 1957, Lizabeth b. 1962, George b. 1964, Herminia b. 1965; edn: stu. UCLA 1949-50, 85; BSEE, USC 1960. Career: electronic design engr. Radar Fire Control Sys., Hughes Aircraft Co., Culver City and El Segundo, 1954-60; lead engr. missile research Rockwell Internat., Downey 1960-64, lead engr. unmanned and manned Apollo Spacecraft 1964-69 (culminating in first man on the moon 1969), lead engr. and original designer of the Space Shuttle flight control system, 1969-73, 1976-80; self empl., owner Valley Time Clock Co., El Monte 1973-76; project engr. Inertial Upper Stage Spacecraft, The Aerospace Corp., El Segundo 1980-83; engring. cons. prin., 1983−, cons. Nord-Micro and Litef Computer Cos. of West Germany (1983), The Aerospace Corp. (1983, 84), Northrop Corp. (1984), Garrett AiResearch, Tucson, Az. (1985, 86); awards: Engr. of the Month, Rockwell Internat. (9/79), Calif. Businessman of Year, TELACU/L.A. (1974); mem. Am. Mgmt. Assn., IEEE; civic: World Hunger Orgn., World Runners Orgn., League of United Latin Am. Citizens; mil: sgt. US Air Force 1950-54; Catholic. Address: James De La Rosa Associates 16345 Denley St Hacienda Heights 91745

DELBO, LARRY GORDON, insulation contractor; b. Sept. 21, 1920, Chowchilla, Calif.; s. Frank and May (Gordon) D.; m. Margaret Wright, Sept. 19, 1941; children: Judith Ann b. 1944, Joanne Linda b. 1946, Kenneth Lawrence b. 1948; edn: Biola Coll. 1951-52. Career: ptnr. Advanced Installation Inc. 1955-59; pres. L.A. Weatherstrip Co. Inc. 1971-76; v.p., secty. Advanced Installations Inc. 1976-82; pres. L.A. Insulation Co. Inc. 1982−; dir: Fickett Towers, World Witness Evangelism; honors: Hall of Fame Award (Insulation Contrs. Assn. Calif. 1985); mem. Insulation Contrs. Assn. (3-time chpt. pres., state pres. 1984, dir., ofcr. 6 yrs.); mil: pharm. mate 1/c USN 1943-46; Republican; Christian. Res: 23708 Stagg St Canoga Park 91304 Ofc: L.A. Insulation Co. Inc. 7721 Deering Canoga Park 91304

DELINGER, JACK EMIL, physical culturist/ consultant/ manufacturer/ writer; b. June 22, 1926, Oakland; s. Wm. Jacques and Ida May (Peterson); m. Loretta Beatrice Soper, Dec. 18, 1949; 1 son, John Errol b. 1951; edn: H.S.grad. Oakland Tech. High 1944. Career: profl. athlete/ prin., performing at fairs, night clubs, TV, stage and clubs as understander of acrobatic act, 1945-49; West Coast mgr. in mail order sales for Weider Health and Fitness and feature writer Weider Publs., 1951-55; owner/pres. Delingers Figure & Physique Equipment (mfr., supplier and cons. for phys. tng. and gym & exercise equip.), Oakland 1955−; feature writer and assoc. ed. Strength & Health - Mr. America, Your Physique - Muscle Builder; featured in mags. and mag. covers internat.; judge for beauty and body building contests, and frequent guest of honor; awards: Mr. America 1949 (for best developed Athlete on the Am. Continent) AAU (1949), Mr. Universe (Worlds' Best Built Man) NABBA (1956, held at the Paladium Theater, London), selected Mr. No. California (1946), Mr. California (1947), Mr. Western America (1948); mem. Am. Guild of Variety Artists (1945-49), Nat. Sporting Goods Assn., Mount Diablo Tng. Club; holder patents for Exercise Equip., prop. trademarks, copyrights for physical tng. courses: Beauty Gym Course for Women, Jack Delinger Barbell Dumbbell Tng. Course, Universal Figure & Physique Course - Physical Transfiguration; Catholic; rec: training show dogs, making driftwood lamps, remolding. Ofc: 5255-5257 College Ave Oakland 94618

DELL'ERGO, ROBERT JAMES, lawyer; b. Mar. 2, 1918, Berkeley, Calif.; s. Cosmo and Lilian James (Rennie) D.; children: Robert, Marilee, Richard; edn: BA, UC Berkeley 1939, JD, LLB, Boalt Hall 1942. Career: atty. Brobeck, Phleger & Harrison, 1946; ptnr. Millington & Dell'Ergo, Attys. 1947-57; sole practitioner atty. 1957-71; ptnr. Dell'Ergo & Tinsley, Attys., Redwood City 1972−; mem: San Mateo County Bar Assn. (pres. 1954; chaired com. for passage of inferior ct. reorgn. legislation in Calif.; chmn. com. formed to recommend Municipal Ct. orgn. in San Mateo County re geographical dists. and no. of judges Redwood City); CofC (pres. 1958); bd. trustees (chmn. 2 years) Sequoia Union High Sch. Dist. 1951-57; mem. Redwood City Six Year Plan Com.; clubs: Palo Alto Elks, Redwood City Antlers, Native Sons of the Golden West, Am. Legion (atty.), Sons of Italy in Am. (pres. Redwood City 1948, chmn. Grand Lodge Laws Commn. 6 yrs.), Internat. Platform Assn.; mil: lt. active duty USNR 1942-46; Democrat (chmn. San Mateo Co. JFK for Pres. Campaign); Protestant; rec: photog., music, jogging, skiing. Res: 220 Palo Alto Ave, 102, Palo Alto 94301 Ofc: Dell'Ergo & Tinsley, Attys. 1900 Broadway Ste 200, Redwood City 94063

DELLAR, LINCOLN, broadcasting co. executive, rancher; b. Aug. 11, 1906, Seattle, Wash.; s. Joseph and Clara (Rein) D.; m. Sylvia Harwood, Oct. 5, 1950; children: William C. b. 1943, Toni M. b. 1944; edn: BA, UC Berkeley 1931. Career: asst. dir. station rels. CBS New York, and gen. mgr. WBT Charlotte, N.C. 1936-40; v.p. gen. mgr. Radio KSFO San Francisco 1940-42; civil svc. chief Bdcst. Bureau Ofc. of War Information, Pacific Area 1942-45; owner, opr. var. radio stations in Sacramento, Stockton, Fresno, Bakersfield, San Bernadino, Riverside, 1945-83, and co-owner stations in Seattle, Spokane, and Portland 1954-58; current: owner TV stations in Sacramento and Bakersfield; senior ptr. KPRL-KDDB, Paso Robles; rancher Coachella Valley; mem: Pioneer Broadcasters, Birnam Wood Golf Club, Coral Casing Beach Club, Desert Island Country Club, Rancheros Vista Dores; dir., Performance Arts Scholarship Fund, Santa Barbara; Republican; Presbyterian; rec: golf, equestrian, swimming. Res: 1983 Inverness Ln. Montecito 93150 Ofc: Lincoln Dellar & Co., P.O. Box 5365 Santa Barbara 93150

DELLUMS, RONALD VERNIE, congressman; b. Nov. 24, 1935, Oakland; m. Leola Roscoe Higgs; three children; edn: AA, Oakland City Coll. 1958; BA, San Francisco St. Coll. 1960; MSW, Univ. Calif. 1962. Career: psychiat. social worker Calif. Dept. Mental Hygiene, 1962-64; program dir. Bayview Community Center, San Francisco 1964-65; assoc. dir., dir. Hunters Point Youth Opportunity Center, 1965-66; planning cons. Bay Area Social Planning Council, 1966-67; dir. concentrated employment program San Francisco Econ. Opportunity Council, 1967-68; senior cons. Social Dynamics, Inc. 1968-70; elected mem. Berkeley City Council, 1967-71; elected mem. 92nd - 98th Congresses from 8th Calif. Dist.; lectr. San Francisco St. Coll., UC Berkeley; mil: USMCR, 1954-56; Democrat. Ofc: 2136 Rayburn House Office Bldg, Wash. DC 20515

DE LONG, HAL EUGENE, financial consultant; b. Sept. 14, 1933, Flint, Mich.; s. David Howard and Anna (Lichnovsky) DeLong; m. Carol Copeland, Nov. 13, 1976; children: Larry, Steven, Linda; edn: AA, San Bernardino Valley Coll. 1958; att. UCLA 1960-62; Calif. lic: real estate broker (1962), ins. agt. (1971), investment/securities broker (1979). Career: real estate investor, 1959−; founder/bd. chmn. Remco (R.E. & mgmt. co. apt. bldgs.) and Am. Inst. of Real Estate (training co. for pvt. investors in purch. of bargain R.E.), Santa Ana; tng. instr./inv. cons. Merrill Lynch and Gibralter Sav. & Loan; internat. real estate & finl. inv. trainer/speaker in US, Europe, Asia and So.Am.; honors: selected as rep. of California to Statue of Liberty ceremonies, N.Y. (July 4, 1986); guest speaker to FHA/HUD Real Estate Nat. Conv., Wash DC (7/85); mem: Nat. Assn. Housing & Devel./Wash DC, L.A. Income and Inv. Assn., L.A., Anaheim Board Realtors, Nat. Speakers Assn./Phoenix, Ariz., Nat. R.E. Syndicators and Brokers, Nat. Acad. of Authors; sponsor Calif. Dept. of R.E. ednl. course; author: Instant Profits- Acquisition of Wealth Throuth Real Estate 91986), Let's Deal in Real Estate (1985), Legal Study Guide in Finance (1984), Finl. Freedom Through Real Estate Investing (1981), Secrets to Success (1982); Republican (Young Rep.); rec: tennis, boating, fishing. Ofc: American Inst. of Real Estate 2107 N Broadway Ste 108 Santa Ana 92706

DELPHENICH, WILLIAM CARLTON, architect; b. June 22, 1951, Oak Park, Ill.; s. John Stewart and Elsie Carlton (Chapman) D.; m. Pamela Palmer, Oct. 20, 1985; edn: So. Ill. Univ. 1974-75; B.Arch., So. Calif. Inst. of Arch. 1980; Reg. Arch. Calif. Career: engrg. mgr. Electronic Enclosures El Segundo 1976-79; space planner P.Patrick Murray Inc. L.A. 1979-81; proj. mgr. Howard Lathrop & Assoc. Santa Monica 1981-83; prin. Smith/Delphenich Santa Monica 1983; proj. mgr. Olympic Butler Assoc. L.A. 1983−; mem: Am. Inst. Archs., Constrn. Specs. Inst., Mus. of Contemp. Art L.A.; mil: sgt. USAF 1970-74, SEA Campaign, Vietnam Svc., USAF Commendn.; rec: travel, photog., scuba. Res: 5951 Canterbury Dr No 3 Culver City 90230 Ofc: Olympic Butler Assoc. 11400 Olympic Blvd Los Angeles 90064

DE LUCA, ROSALIA MARIA, certified public accountant; b. Feb. 2, 1954, San Diego; d. Giuseppe Salvatore and Rosalia (Gaipa) De Luca; edn: Matura Dip. in acctg., Duca Degli Abruzzi, Italy 1974; BS acctg., Univ. San Diego 1979; CPA Calif. 1983. Career: bookkeeper, travel agent Balboa Travel Inc. San Diego 1975-76; bookkeeper Vagabond Hotels S.D. 1976-78; tutor Mildred C. Hagen Tutoring Svc. La Jolla 1977−; desk clerk, night auditor Richmar Inn SD. 1978; acctg. clerk math dept.-tchr's asst. Univ. S.D. 1978; acct. Lustig & Foley CPAs S.D. 1979; staff acct. Leaf & Cole CPAs S.D. 1979-81, Glenn Youmans & Co. CPAs Bonita 1981-82; self-employed CPA S.D. 1981−; honors: Dean's List (USD); rec: sewing, swimming, tennis, jogging, travel. Address: POB 33911 San Diego 92103

DELURGIO, ESTHER MAY, computer professional/business systems executive; b. June 12, 1944, Denver, Colo.; d. James Harry and May Lucile (Ruple) Mosher; m. Phil Delurgio, May 30, 1981; children: Cheri M. Lawton b. 1962, Ronald B. Lawton b. 1965, John E. Dwire b. 1971; edn: BBA, Wichita State Univ. 1974, MBA, 1979. Career: pgmmr. Singer Corp., Denver, Colo. 1969-70; grad. Asst. Wichita State Univ. 1974-75; account mktg. rep. IBM Corp., Wichita, Kans. and Los Angeles, 1975-83; dir. Business Systems, Mattel Toys, Hawthorne 1983−; awards: IBM- 100 Percent Clubs (5), Golden Circle (1981); civic: Los Angeles Art Museum. Res: 510 The Village Apt 403 Redondo Beach 90277 Ofc: Mattel Toys, 5150 Rosecrans Blvd Hawthorne 90250

DE MASSA, JESSIE G., librarian; edn: BS in journ., Temple Univ., Phila.; MLS, CSU San Jose, 1967; postgrad. Univ. Okla., USC, others. Career: tchr. Palo Alto Unified Sch. Dist., 1966; librarian Antelope Valley Joint Union High Sch. Dist., Lancaster 1966-68, ABC Unified Sch. Dist., Artesia 1968-72; dist. librarian Tehachapi Unified Sch. Dist., 1972-81, also media splst.; free lance writer, 1981−; Fellow Internat. Biog. Assn.; mem. Calif. Media and Library Educators Assn., Calif. Assn. Sch. Librarians (exec. council), AAUW (bull. editor, assoc. ed. state bull.); publs: articles in profl. jours. Res: 9951 Garrett Circle, Huntington Beach 92646

DE MERS, (FOY) RONALD JAMES, industrialist; b. May 20, 1954, Iron River, Mich.; s. Louis Leonard and Anne Mae (Stefanovich) D.; nephew of Charlie & Eddie Foy (of 7 Foys vaudeville fame), nephew of John King (industrialist, owner of TV, radio stations, hotels); edn: BBA, Loyola Univ. L.A. 1977; Career: prodn. accounting Charles Fries Prodns., CBS Studio City 1977-78; film distbn. (multi-nat.) Am. Cinema Svcs. (affil. Am. Distbrs. Inc.), Beverly Hills and Wometco, Miami, Fla. 1979; fin. and prodn. scheduling CBS-TV, Hollywood 1979-80; pres. Foy Ents. Inc. 1982—; ptnr./sr. v.p. fin., distbn. & mfg. Claude Videau Internat. (clothing mfr.); bd. dirs. Filmex; worked on spl. projects and publicity ICPR Public Rels., Beverly Hills; fin. assoc. on film Semi Tough; spl. projects Acad. of TV Arts & Scis.; served as pres. adv. bd. Dept. of Mental Health on Children's Programming, Wash. DC; developed commls. (Smokey Bear) Foote, Cone, Belding, L.A. and IBM, NY; bus. cons. Dunn & Bradstreet L.A.; fund raising coms.: A Salute to the President (dinner, Bev. Hills), US Olympic Organizing Com. (for US athletes), Save the Cable Cars (S.F.); mem: Calif. Republican Golden Circle, US Congl. Adv. Bd., State Bd. L.A. World Affairs Council, Acad. TV Arts & Scis., affil. Acad. of Motion Pic. Arts & Scis., Am. Film Inst.; works: archtl. design A-Frame house 1972; Republican; rec: skiing, power boat racing, scuba, Arabian horses. Ofc: 9200 Sunset Blvd Ste 825 Los Angeles Mail: POB 10665 Beverly Hills 90213

DEMLER, EDMUND NILE, commercial poultry breeder/egg producer; b. Feb. 21, 1915, Fairbury, Ill.; s. Ernest John and Emmy Axeline (Pedersen) D.; m. Agnes Walsh; children: John b. 1946, Paul b. 1947, Tom b. 1948, Kevin b. 1950, Donna b. 1953, Edmund J. b. 1957, David b. 1959; grad. Long Beach Poly H.S. 1933. Career: poultry breeder, owner/mgr. Demler Farms Inc., Anaheim and San Jacinto, 1948—, had largest volume white leghorn hatchery in world in 1970s, one of largest volume egg producers in Calif. since 1975, now have six sons in egg bus. with over 1,500,000 birds on ranches in So. Calif.; mem. Calif. Poultry Commn. (chmn. 1955-60), Calif. Hatchery Fedn. (chmn. 1960-62), Orange Prodn. Credit Assn. (dir. 1955-, chmn. 1975-84), USDA Newcastle Task Force in So. Calif. (1971-73), Inland Empire Poultry Assn. (founding chmn. 1962-65), Riverside Fly Abatement Com. (chmn. 1972-76); past advis. com. (chmn. 3 yrs) Prodn. Credit Bank, 11th Dist. Sacto. (10 yrs); Rotarian; works: devel. Demler type wire pen for poultry breeding (early 50s); birds won num. statewide egg laying contests (1950s); mil: m/sgt. USAF 1942-45; Republican; Prot.; rec: hist. buff (Civil War, Gen. Custer), rosarian, raise & exhibit fancy poultry. Res: 3502 Venture Dr Huntington Harbour Ranch: Demler Egg Ranch 21350 Warren Rd San Jacinto 92383

DEMPSEY, THOMAS GREGWER, consultant; b. Nov. 23, 1924, Dubuque, Iowa; s. John T. and Mabel (Magee) D.; m. Dorothy, May 30, 1946; children: Michael b. 1947, Terrence b. 1948, Kevin b. 1955, Timothy b. 1958, Mary b. 1964, Kathleen b. 1967; edn: spl. courses, City Coll. S.F. 1968; Calif. lic. Pvt. Investigator, lic. Pvt. Patrol, lic. Real Estate Agt. Career: police capt. San Francisco Police Dept. 1947-79, ret.; chief of police S.F. Internat. Airport, 1978-79; cons. prin. D&A Security, 1979—; chief security cons. var. functions; recipient 3 merit awards, 15 chief commendns. S.F.P.D., Police Ofcr. of the Year (S.F.P.D. 1964); civic: YMCA (bd.), Sirs (bd.), S.F.P.D. Credit Union (chmn. bd. dirs.); mil: PHM US Navy 1943-46; Democrat; Catholic; rec: sports, hist. Address: D&A Security 2066 42nd Ave San Francisco 94116

DE NATALE, THOMAS VINCENT, JR., lawyer; b. Feb. 21, 1949, Los Angeles; s. Thomas Vincent and Alpha (Policastri) DeN.; m. Susan, Oct. 14, 1978; children: Erin b. 1981, Shannon b. 1984; edn: BA psych., UC Los Angeles 1971; JD, San Fernando Valley Coll. of Law 1975; admitted Calif. State Bar 1975. Career: assoc. atty. John J. Schimmenti El Segundo 1975-77; ptnr. law firm Schimmenti, Mullins, Berberian & DeNatale 1978-80; assoc. atty. Di-Giorgio, Davis, Klein, Wegis & Duggan Bakersfield 1981-83, ptnr. Klein, Wegis & Duggan 1984-; mem: Am. L.A. Co., Kern Co. bar assns.; Calif. Trial Lawyers Assn., Italian Heritage Dante Assn. (secy. 1984-); Democrat; Catholic/Presbyterian; rec: tennis, golf, softball. Ofc: Klein, Wegis & Duggan 1111 Truxton Ave Bakersfield 93301

DE NEVE, ROBERT JACOB JOHNATHON, electro-optical test engineer; b. Feb. 13, 1960, Soesterberg, The Netherlands; s. Alexander and Christine (Hey) de Neve; m. Jennifer Lyn Byrd, Nov. 3, 1984; edn: tech. courses, (electronics) Mission Coll. 1981-84, (optics) Univ. Rochester 1985, (lasers) San Jose City Coll. 1985-. Career: electro- mech. tech., precision surveyor Stanford Linear Accelerator Center, 1978-80; electro-optical test engr. KLA Instruments Corp., Santa Clara 1980—; cons. Photonics Interface; mem. Soc. Photo-Optical Instrumentation Engrs., IEEE; Catholic. Res: 150 Serena Way Santa Clara 95051 Ofc: KLA Instruments Corp. 2051 Mission College Blvd Santa Clara 95054

DENGLER, HUGH JAMES, general contractor; b. Mar. 2, 1931, Detroit, Mich.; s. Joseph Phillip and Marie Emma (Newman) D.; m. Patricia Ann Morey, Feb. 11, 1956; children: Eric b. 1957, Guy b. 1959, Rex b. 1962, Roger b. 1964, Alan b. 1966; edn: Sch. of Real Estate Law (Orlando) 1961-62, architl. drafting, Chgo. Tech. Coll. 1958-59, bldg. constrn., Internat. Corresp. Schs. (Pa.) 1955, Accelerated Real Estate Schs. (S.F.) 1978; lic. gen. contr., 1955-; lic. pvt. pilot (1972); citizens radio sta. lic. (1969-74), radio tel. opr. (1972-) Career: carpenter, foreman Joseph A. Dengler, Builder, Detroit 1947-50, Dunkirk, N.Y. 1951-52; insp. -assembly, Trim A Seal Corp., Detroit 1950-51; insp. -Differential Dept., Ford Motor Co., Detroit 1951; ship carpenter US Navy (MSTS 3 Ships) 1952-55; gen. contr./owner Dengler Constrn. & Supply Co. (Dunkirk and Fredonia, NY, Orlando, Fla., Santa Rosa, Ca.) 1955—; ptnr. Trans-Florida Mortgage & Inv. Co. Inc. (1960-61), Trans-Florida Ins.

Corp. (1955-), Trans-Florida Real Estate Corp. (1955-); gen. contr. Sears, Roebuck & Co., Santa Rosa 1971-85; recipient Excellence Award, Sears, Roebuck & Co. (1974); mem: Fla. Assn. of Realtors (1961-63), Nat. Pilots Assn. (1972-78), Am. Legion; publs: Family newsletter (genealogy, 1984-), Labor Policy Curriculum (Buffalo Catholic Diocese 1968); mil: damage controlman wood 3/c USN 1952-55, Reserves 1955-60, Korean Svc., UN, Navy Occup. Europe, Nat. Def. Svc., Good Conduct medals; Catholic; rec: music (clarinetist), skating, flying. Address: Dengler Construction & Supply Co 1277 St Francis Rd Santa Rosa 95405

DENNEY, ALBERT (AL) BROWN, JR., designer; b. Waco, Tex.; s. Dr. Albert Brown and Mary Elizabeth (Fason) D.; m. Christine, artist; 1 son, Rick b. 1959; edn: Texas Chiropractic Coll. Career: producer, dir., owner Independent Artists Prodn., 1965—; R.E. Broker, owner Den Real Co., 1961—; designer waterfalls and complete environments, owner The Dennehy Touch (formerly Den-Ney Originals), 1973—; writer/dir. BBC award winning films: "Ghana Today," "Puberty Rites of the TWI;" writer "Operation Hillbilly," "Illegal Entry" (Cannes Award); awards: 3d Place, Dir., Cannes Film Festival (1971), two 1st Place, Underwater Photog., Underwater Photographic Soc. (1967, 69); mem: Directors Guild of Am., Internat. Photographers Local 659, Am. Film Inst., Am. TV Arts & Scis., Am. Soc. of Lighting Directors, Am. Legion, Elks, VFW; mil: cpl. USMC 1953-56; Republican; Universalist; rec: fishing, huntig, scuba diving, orchids and bromeliads. Address: 20360 Haynes St Winnetka 91306

DENNIS-STRATHMEYER, JEFFREY ALLAN, tax lawyer; b. Oct. 9, 1945, Phila.; s. Lowell F. Dennis and Nancy C. (Mills) Strathmeyer; children: Jeffrey b. 1974, Christopher b. 1977; edn: AB, Stanford Univ. 1967; JD, UC Davis 1973; admitted Calif. State Bar 1973. Career: pvt. practice of law, Salinas 1973—; legal editor Estate Planning, and California Probate Reporter; mem. Small Business & Farms subcom. Estate Planning Sect., State Bar of Calif.; frequent commentator on Calif. Law Revision Commn. proposals for Probate Code Reform; num. publs. include: "Minors Custodianships Come of Age," Calif. Lawyer (4/85); "The IRS Requires Cotenants to Consent to Section 2032A Elections: Overreaching or Confusion?" in Taxes (4/84); mil: lt. jg US Navy Supply Corps 1967-70, Mil. Assistance Command, Viet Nam Cert. Achievement; Republican (past chmn. Mont. Co. Central Com.); Episcopal; rec: religious studies. Res: Box 1581 Salinas 93902 Ofc: CEB, 2300 Shattuck Ave Berkeley 94704

DENNISON, RICHARD L., corporate president; b. Aug. 13, 1939, Portland, Ore.; s. Vernon and Georgia Pearl (Buchannan) D.; m. Kim Khuu, Aug. 12, 1966; 1 son, John b. 1967; edn: Portland State Coll. 1957-8, 1961-2. Career: copy boy the Oregonian, Ore. 1955-57; seaman US Merchant Marine Internat., 1957-58; copywriter Fred Meyer, Ore. 1958-60; sales rep. Am. Greetings, Ore., Ida. 1964-66; mng. dir. Muller & Phipps, S.E. Asia 1966-75; mng. dir. All World Entertainment, Calif., internat., 1979—; pres., sole stockholder Riden Internat. Inc. (an all entertainment distbn. co.), Calif., internat., 1976—; mem. Amvets; mil: sgt. US Army 1961-63; Republican; Prot.; rec: sports. Address: 6024 Paseo Palmilla Goleta 93117

DENSON, GAIL, certified public accountant; b. Mar. 26, 1939, Ogden, Utah; s. John McInnes and Rubye Mae (Bartholomew) D.; m. Onie Stringer, Feb. 23, 1978; children: Martin b. 1960, Michael b. 1961, Monte b. 1962, William b. 1968, Christina b. 1971; edn: AA, Los Angeles City Coll. 1961; BA, Univ. Redlands 1963; MBA, Univ. Beverly Hills 1981, PhD, 1986; CPA, Calif. Career: staff acct. Olincy & Olincy, Los Angeles 1963-66; controller The VP Co., Pasadena 1966-68; v.p. Nanodyne Inc., Pasadena 1968-69; controller American Micro Devices, San Gabriel 1969-70; staff acct. Victor J. Backus, CPA, San Gabriel 1970-72; pres. Gail Denson An Acctncy. Corp., 1972—; pres. Sierra Care, Inc.; dir. National Nurse, Inc.; mem: Am. Inst. CPAs, Calif. Soc. CPAs, Hospital Finl. Mgmt. Assn., Calif. Assn. of Health Facilities, Am. Coll. of Nsg. Home Adminstrs., Town Hall of Calif., Rotary; Republican; Latter Day Saints; rec: flying. Res: 165 W Arthur Arcadia 91006 Ofc: 9124 E Las Tunas Temple City

DEOL, SHIVINDER SINGH, physician; b. June 4, 1953, Ahmedgarh, India, nat. USA 1984; s. Col. Tej Bhan Singh and Joginder Kaur (Benepal) Deol; m. Harjit Kaur, Apr. 9, 1977; children: Randeep b. 1980, Vikramjit b. 1982; edn: Premed., DAV Coll., Chandigarh, India 1971; MBBS, Armed Forces Med. Coll., Poona, India 1975; MD, Univ. of Tenn. Center for Health Scis., Memphis 1981; Diplomate Am. Board of Family Practice; Fellow Am. Acad. of Family Physicians. Career: group practice Manor Medical Group Inc., Bakersfield 1982-83; solo med. practice, 1983—; chmn. Dept. of Family Practice, Greater Bksfld. Memorial Hosp., 1985; vice chief of staff Bksfld. Comm. Hosp., 1985; bd. dirs. Physicians Radiology Gp., Bksfld. 1985-; co-owner Mehfil (Indian cuisine); mem: Kern County Med. Soc. (Found. com.), CMA, AMA, Indian Med. Assn., Rotary (Paul Harris Fellow); works: vol. physician to inpatients, Salvation Army Rehabilitation Center; Republican; Sikh; rec: community affairs, sports. Res: 1205 Calle Extrano Bakersfield 93304 Ofc: Shivinder S. Deol MD, 1611 First St Bakersfield 93304

DE OLIVEIRA, PAOLO C., film executive/ writer; b. Sept. 2, 1953, Rio de Janiero, Brazil; s. Roberto Menezes and Millicent Frances (Schwendeman) de Oliveira; m. B.J. Miller, July 14, 1986; edn: AB, Brown Univ. 1975. Career: admission ofcr. Brown Univ. 1975-77, asst. dir. admissions 1977-79; story editor The Movie Co. L.A. 1982, v.p. creative affairs 1982-85; dir. creative affairs Internat. Cinema Corp. L.A. 1982, v.p. creative affairs 1982-85; dir. creative affairs Embassy Pictures Corp. L.A. 1985; currently writer/ producer; honors: Phi Beta Kappa

1975; assoc. producer Louisiana (HBO/ Cinemax miniseries 1983), The Bay Boy (Orion Pictures 1984), The Blood of Others (HBO miniseries 1984), The Boy in Blue (20th Century Fox 1985); co-author: Getting In! (Workman Publ. NY 1983), Getting to the Right Job (Workman Publ. 1986); related articles in Forbes, NY Times; rec: writing, skiing, racquetball. Address: Los Angeles

DE ORNELLAS, STEVE PAUL, research scientist; b. July 30, 1954, San Jose; s. Harry Joseph and Carolyn Ruth (Ames) De O.; m. Cecile, Aug. 23, 1976; children: Emily b. 1980, Stephen b. 1983; edn: BS in chem., CSU San Jose 1977, MS chem., 1979. Career: assoc. engr. Raytheon Semiconductor, 1973; research fellow Lawrence Livermore Labs, 1975-77; research scientist Ames Research Center, 1977-79; senior engr. Nat. Semiconductor Corp., 1980-81; v.p. Lam Research Corp., 1981–; tchg. assoc. SJSU 1978-79; honors: Semi Technical presentation award (1984, 85), ERDA fellowship LL Labs (1975-77); mem. AVS, ECS; works: patent pend., Multi Frequency Discharge System, Silicide Formation for Mos Application; publ: Laser Annealing for Mosfets; Republican; Christian; rec: woodworking, fishing, camping. Res: 1091 Gruwell Pl San Jose 95129 Ofc: Lam Research Corp. 47531 Warm Springs Blvd Fremont 94329

DEPOOTER, RUDY AUGUST, entrepreneur; b. June 21, 1954, Herentals, Belgium, nat. 1972; s. George Alfons and Maria Hilda (Van Looy) DePooter; m. Amber Tennant, June 28, 1975; children: Brooke b. 1980, Ashley b. 1983, Grant b. 1985; edn: BS in pub. adm., USC 1976. Career: adminstrv. analyst Los Angeles Community Coll. District, 1976-78; nat. facilities coordinator E.F. Hutton & Co., 1978-79; dir. of real estate Fortune Advertising, 1979-80; commercial leasing rep. The Irvine Co., 1980-81; founded own company, The Winchase Co., Diamond Bar 1981–, full service comml. real estate brokerage (leasing, sales, mgmt., etc.); pres. Service Master Bldg. Maintenance, full-svc. cleaning co. 1985–; mem: Bldg. Owners & Mgrs. Assn., Diamond Bar CofC; rec: running, swimming. Res: 1 Trail Ridge Circle, Phillips Ranch 91766. Ofc: The Winchase Co. 23441 Golden Springs Dr Ste 129 Diamond Bar 90765; Service Master Bldg. Maintenance 1213 E Warner Ave Santa Ana 92705

DESAI, THAKORBHAI CHHOTUBHAI, civil engineer, real estate investor; b. March 7, 1942, Palsana, Gujarat, India, nat. US cit.; s. Chhotubhai D. and Kashiben C. D.; m. Bharti, Feb. 28, 1970; children: Neilam b. 1981, Darpan b. 1983; edn: BSCE, M.S. Univ., Baroda, India 1965; MSCE, Utah State Univ. 1968; profl. civil engr., Calif. 1975. Career: civil engr. PG&E 1968-78; currently, pres. and/or bd. dirs. D.M. Investment Inc. Indiana Corp; Desai Marolia Investment, Kentucy Corp.; MDM Investment, Indiana Corp.; Newport Investment Inc., Ohio Corp.; also: gen. ptr. Desai-Patel Property Mgmt. and Calif. syndication, Washington Court Partnership, Ukiah. Res: 1418 Sonoma Ave Santa Rosa 95405

DESDIER, STEVEN ROSS, accountant; b. Oct. 11, 1952, San Diego; s. Dominic Jose Dupont Desdier Lozano and Audree LaVerne Leischner; edn: BA, summa cum laude, U.S. Internat. Univ. 1970; Cert. in Taxation, UC San Diego 1981; Enrolled Agent, IRS; Cert. Fin. Plnnr., Coll. for Fin. Plnng. Career: ast. menswear buyer Miller's West Dept. Store 1970-77; life & disability ins. agent Home Life Ins. Co. 1976-78; acct. San Francisco AIDS Found. 1985–; reg. rep. Am. Pacific Securities 1982–; v.p. Desdier Inc. dba DESCO 1977–; honors: Recogn. of Contributions, GSDBA Found. 1985; mem: Gr. San Diego Bus. Assn. (pres. 1984-85, treas. 1980-84, bd. mem. 1980-85), Golden Gate Bus. Assn. (v.p. admin. 1985-86, bd. mem.), Nat. Assn. of Bus. Councils (treas. and bd. mem. 1982-84), San Diego Co. Citizen's Scholarship Found. (treas. 1982-84, bd. mem. 1981-84), Calif. Assn. of Ind. Accts. (v.p. 1985-86), Nat. Soc. of Public Accts., Nat. Assn. of Enrolled Agents, Inland Soc. of Tax Cons.; Republican; Lutheran; rec: coins, oriental art.

DE SIO, ANTHONY WILLIAM, company executive; b. Feb. 2, 1930, NY, NY; s. Oresto and Concetta (Curci) DeSio; m. Delores Lannie, June 27, 1959; children: Douglas b. 1965, Darcy b. 1967; edn: BSEE, Univ. of Conn. 1957; Cert. of Bus. Adm., Univ. of Santa Clara 1970. Career: engring. mgr., pgm. mgr. Lockheed Missiles :& Space Co., Sunnyvale 1958-71; space asst. Exec. Ofc. of the Pres. of the U.S., Wash DC, 1971-72; mgr. Earth Resources Applications Pgm, Gen. Elec. Co., King of Prussia, Pa. 1973-75; deputy v.p. Western Union Space Comm. Inc., Upper Saddle River, NJ 1976-78; dir. of prodn. pgms. Linkabit Corp., San Diego 1979-80; cofounder/ prin./ pres./ CEO, Mail Boxes Etc. USA, Inc., Carlsbad; bd.dirs: Mail Boxes Etc. USA, Inc.; Internat. Mail & Communications, Inc.; Duraquip Equipment Leasing Co., Inc.; honors: achievement award, Pres.'s Commn. on Personnel Exchange by Pres. Nixon, 1972; mem: Pres.'s Executive Interchange Assn. 1971-; Am. Mgmt. Assn. 1960-70; Inst. ofp Radio Engrs. 1958-60; publs: art. in field, 1974; mil: petty ofcr. USN 1948-52; Republican; Catholic; rec: golf, tennis. Res: 1920 Swallow Ln Rancho La Costa 92008 Ofc: Mail Boxes Etc. USA, Inc., 7690 El Camino Real, Ste 206, Carlsbad 92008

DE SMIDT, FRANK JOSEPH, broadcasting co. president; b. Sept. 4, 1941, San Francisco; s. Paul Jerome and May Elizabeth (Ahern) D.S.; m. Deborah Kay Yoakum, Sept. 4, 1984; children: Michael b. 1985, Jonathan b. 1986; Peralta Coll. 1962-65. Career: gen. mgr. KPEN-FM radio 1978-82; pres. Los Altos Broadcasting Inc. 1978-84; pres. L.D.S. Enterprises Inc. dba Straw Hat Pizza of Milpitas 1981–; del. 2nd Calif. State Conf. on Small Bus. 1982; del. cand. White House Conf. on Small Bus., San Francisco 1986; Milpitas Commmunity Task Force 1982-83; honors: Distng. Svc. (1973, 1978), Cert. of Appreciation (1977), Pres.'s Award (1981), Milpitas CofC; mem: Milpitas CofC (pres. 1972-73, dir. 1972-, chmn. Govt. Affairs Com. 1980-), Milpitas Rotary 1985-; Democratic (State Central Com. 1983-85); Catholic; rec: music, politics, civic.

Res: 3020 Via Del Coronado San Jose 95132 Ofc: L.D.S. Enterprises Inc., 560 No. Abel St. Milpitas 95035

DE SURE, ALBERT J., financial consultant; b. May 5, 1908, Pittsburgh, Pa.; s. David and Eva (Pritzker) DeS.; m. Dorothy, Aug. 3, 1980; 1 son, Douglas; edn: Kemper Mil. Acad., Warren G. Harding Sch. of Law; Reg. rep. NASD; lic. real estate broker (Calif., Nev.). Career: stockbroker, Jack Cravin Co., N.Y., Calif. Investors, Calif.; investment banker, finl. cons. (spec. in fin., cash controls, mergers and acquisitons, banking rels.) num. US & internat. cos.; real estate broker, pres. A.J. DeSure Associates, Inc., San Diego; honors: Internat. Boxing Hall of Fame (life), San Diego Guardians (life); mem: Nat. Assn. of Fin. Consultants, Nat. Assn. of Real Estate Appraisers (fmr.). Res: 6116 Caminito Pan San Diego 92120

DETTERMAN, ROBERT L., energy co. executive; b. May 1, 1931, Norfolk, Va.; s. George Wm., Sr. and Jenneille (Watson) D.; m. Virginia Armstrong, Apr. 19, 1958; children: Janine b. 1961, Patricia b. 1964, Wm. Arthur b. 1967; edn: BS, Va. Polytechnic Inst. 1953; PhD, Oak Ridge Sch. of Reactor Technol. 1954; desig: CFP, Inst. of Cert. Finl. Planners (1986). Career: test dir. Foster Wheeler Corp. 1954-59; senior research engr. Atomics Internat. 1959-62, chief project engr. 1962-68; dir. bus. devel. Rockwell Internat. 1968-84, mgr. of internat. programs, 1985–; dir. Aerospace Safety Div., Atomic Indsl. Forum (1965-70); nuclear cons. Danish Govt. (1960); pres. Bo-Gin Inc., 1970-; honors: Tau Beta Pi, Eta Kappa Nu, Phi Kappa Phi; mem: Am. Nuclear Soc., Atomic Indsl. Forum, Inst. of Cert. Finl. Plnnrs.; mem. Morris Animal Found. (chmn.), The Magic Castle, SPVA, Arabian Horse Trust (treas.), Internat. Arabian Horse Assn.; Republican; rec: Arabian Horses, orchids. Res: 120 Colt Ln Thousand Oaks 91360 Ofc: Rockwell International 6633 Canoga Ave Canoga Park 91304

DEUKMEJIAN, GEORGE, governor of California; b. June 6, 1928, Menands, NY; s. George and Alice (Gairden) D.; m. Gloria M. Saatjian, Long Beach, Feb. 16, 1957; children: Leslie Ann, b. 1964, George Krikor, b. 1966, Andrea Diane, b. 1969; edn: BA, Siena Coll. 1949, JD, St. John's Univ. Sch. of Law 1952. Career: deputy county counsel, Los Angeles; fmr partner law firm Riedman, Dalessi, Deukmejian & Woods, Long Beach; elected Assemblyman, Calif. Legislature, 1963-67; Senator 1967-78: Senate Majority Leader 1969-71, Senate Minority Leader 1974-78; State Atty. Gen. 1978-82; Gov., 1982–; mil: US Army 1953-55. Mem: Navy League, Am. Legion, Elks Club, L.B. Episcopal. rec: golf. Ofc: Capitol, Sacramento 95814

DEUTSCH, LAURENCE VICTOR, film producer/director; b. Mar. 18, 1933, Los Angeles; s. Victor H. and Jewell M. (O'Conner) D.; m. Georgia Martin, Aug. 4, 1973; children: Brian b. 1968, Christopher b. 1979, Michael b. 1981; edn: BS, USC Sch of Architecture 1962. Career: worked with Office of Charles Eames on the IBM Pavillion, 1964 NY World's Fair; staff designer for Herb Rosenthal and Assocs. Design Director projects for the AF Mus., So. Calif. Gas Co. Energy Exhib., IBM Pavillion in Osaka, Japan, AT&T Corp. Exhib., others; design cons. Saul Bass and Assocs., Queen Mary Project, Franciscan China, Mus. of Sci. & Indus., various indsl. clients; estab. own Audio Visual firm in 1969, pres./CEO Laurence Deutsch Design, Inc., Los Angeles 1969–, designing and creating graphics, exhibits, films and audio-visual productions. Num. profl. awards include Grand Award of the Internat. Film and TV Festival of NY (only W. Coast firm so honored), 26 awards for film and audio-visual prodn. in 1982, nine awards for film he directed for Nissan Motors: A Matter of Pride. Mem: Assn. of Multi-Image (AMI), Informational Film Producers of Am. (IFPA), Soaring Soc. of Am. Mil: US Army 1952-54. rec: soaring. res/ Ofc: Laurence Deutsch Design, Inc. 751 N. Highland Ave. Los Angeles 90038

DEUTZ, MAX FRANK, judge; b. July 26, 1917, San Antonio, Tex.; s. Frank Joseph and Katherine W. (Teich) D.; m. Agnes McEvoy, Apr. 13, 1957; children: Nancy, b. 1942, Richard, b. 1945, Jean Marie, b. 1948; edn: BS in bus. adm. USC, 1939, JD, 1941; admitted Calif. Bar 1942. Career: asst. US Attorney, 1945-61, chief Civil Div., Los Angeles 1953-57, chief asst. 1957-61; pvt. practice law Pollock & Deutz 1962-67; apptd. judge Superior Court by Gov. Reagan 1967–; mem. Federal Bar Assn. (Regional v.p. 1960), Calif. Bar Assn., L.A. Bar Assn., Legion Lex USC, Am. Judicature Assn., Calif. Judges Assn., Sigma Phi Epsilon, Delta Theta Phi, Alpha Kappa Psi, Beta Gamma Sigma (nat. bus. hon.); mil: tech. sgt. US Army 1942-45, capt. USAF 1951-52, decorated Asiatic Pac. Ribbon w/4 cpgn. stars, Philippine Ribbon w/2 stars; Republican; Episcopal. Ofc: Superior Court, 111 N Hill St Los Angeles 90012

DEVEAU, NELSON JOSEPH, quality assurance manager; b. Oct. 10, 1924, Boston, Mass.; s. Frank N. and Agatha M. (Comeau) D.; m. Lucille R. Hart, July 18, 1971; children: Roberta L. b. 1946, Theresa E. b. 1954, Jennifer L. b. 1956, Matthew D. b. 1959; edn: BSQE, Columbia Pacific Univ., 1985, DBA, 1986; Reg. Profl. Engr., Calif. 1976. Career: Centaur/ Atlas space pgms. & missiles General Dynamics, San Diego 1963-64; quality assurance splst. Defense Contracts Admin. Svcs., San Bruno 1966-79; senior quality assurance engr. Watkins Johnson Co. Space Div., Palo Alto 1979-84; quality assurance mgr. Narda Microwave Western Ops., San Jose 1984–; honors: Outstanding Performance awards (2), 1972, 1974; mem: Am. Soc. of Quality Control (senior), Elks; works: study of quality control requirements for automated testing 1985; mil: master chief radarman E-9 USN 1942-63; rec: numismatics, golf, bowling. Res: 6556 Milton Ct Magalia 95954

DE VORE, RONALD EDWARD, pharmaceutical manufacturing co. executive; b. Nov. 4, 1947, Helena, Mont.; s. Edward Louis and Juanita Lena (Hagerty) DeV.; m. Cheryl Lombard, Aug. 12, 1978; children: Jeff b. 1965, Donald b. 1968; edn: BS edn., Montana State Univ. 1968, M. Spl. Edn. 1969; MBA, Seattle Univ. 1972. Career: sales rep. Ross Labs. Yakima and Seattle, Wash. 1970-74; dist. sales mgr. Ross Labs. Seattle 1974-76; area sales & mktg. mgr. McGaw Labs Houston 1976-79; dir. mktg. Cutter Med. div. Cutter Labs Berkeley 1979-83; mktg. cons. 1983-84; v.p. gen. mgr. Kabi Vitrum Inc. Alameda 1984–; preceptor St. Mary's Coll. Sch. of Bus. 1980-83; dir. NeuroMark Inc. 1983-84; cons. Univ. Oregon dept. ednl. devel. 1971-73; honors: Sales Rep. of the Year (western region Ross Labs 1972), Outstanding Young Businessman of Yr. (Bellevue CofC 1975), Indsl. Recogn. Award (Am. Soc. Enteral & Parenteral Nutrition 1981); mem: Am. Mgmt. Assn., Am. Soc. Enteral & Parenteral Nutrition, Medical Mktg. Assn., Am. Dietetic Assn. (hon. 1975), Northwest Coalition for Profl. Edn., San Ramon Valley Soccer Club; 1 patent; health publs; mil: E-2 US Army 1968 (med. discharge); Republican; Presbyterian; rec: golf, travel, tennis. Res: 9456 Thunderbird Dr San Ramon 94583 Ofc: Kabi Vitrum Inc. 1311 Harbor Bay Pkwy Alameda 94501

DE VOTO, TERENCE ALAN, radio station executive; b. Aug. 2, San Francisco; s. Albert Anthony and Virginia Louise (Kohnke) De V.; m. Christine McKannay, Jan. 24, 1976; children: Tommy b. 1977, Mark b. 1980, Julie b. 1983, Carolyn b. 1985; edn: BBA, Gonzaga Univ. 1968. Career: v.p. trading dept. Birr, Wilson & Co., 1968-74; account exec. KFOG Radio 1974-78, KSFO Radio 1978-81; local sales mgr., nat. sales mgr., gen. sales mgr., gen. mgr. KYUU Radio 1981–, current: v.p. NBC/ gen. mgr. KYUU; mem. No. Calif. Bdcstrs. Assn. (bd. dirs. 1984-), Mdsg. Execs. Club (bd. dirs. 1984-); clubs: Olympic, Guardsmen; Republican; Catholic; rec: sports, music. Res: 50 Wolfe Canyon Rd Kentfield 94904 Ofc: NBC/ KYUU Radio 530 Bush St San Francisco 94108

DEVOUS, ARNOLD SCOTT, physician; b. July 15, 1952, Astoria, Ore.; s. Homer William and Juanita Faye D.; edn: BS, high honors, Eastern Montana Coll. 1976; MD, high honors clin. evaluations, Univ. of Utah 1980. Career: intern int. med. Providence Hosp. Southfield, Mich. 1980-81; pvt. practice Wyoming 1982-83; fellowship chem. dependency Dr. David Smith Haight Ashbury Free Med. Clin. 1985; resident, phys. family practice, currently researching placebo effects and addiction processes incl. alcoholism; mem: AMA, SMA, AAFP; publ: med. jour. art. on birth control for wild horses; mil: O-2 USAR (MC) also enlisted, Good Conduct; Republican; rec: all sports, hunting, fishing, photog., literature, research. Ofc: San Francisco 94117

DEWAN, RAJ K., real estate broker, b. Apr. 1, 1946, Bahawalpur (Punjab) India, US permanent res.; d. Kuldip Singh and Suraj (Kaur) Dhaliwal; m. Sat Paul Dewan, Apr. 4, 1967; 2 sons: Asheesh b. 1969, Puneet b. 1972; edn: BS in biol., Govt. Coll. for Women, Ludhiana, India 1963; MS in chem., Univ. Allahabad, India 1966; Calif. lic. Real Estate Broker; Series 22 Licensee. Career: chemist, State Lab., Lincoln, Nebr. 1967-69; Montessori Sch. owner/ tchr., Santa Ana 1974-78; real estate sales Coldwell Banker, Santa Ana 1979-80, splst. in income props. Hanes Co., Santa Ana 1980-83 (Top Producer 1983); sales & acquisition (income and comml. props.) ReMax Realtors, Costa Mesa 1984–; cons., acquisition ofcr. R.N. Assocs., Tustin; assoc. First Am. Investment Securities, Inc., Irvine, lic. in syndications; mem. Real Estate Investment of Orange Co., Costa Mesa-Newport Beach Bd. Realtors, Nat. Assn. Sec. Dealers; rec: oil painting, ceramics. Res: 15 Rainstar Irvine 92714 Ofc: ReMax Realtors 234 E 17th St Ste 117 Costa Mesa 92627

DEWEY, DONALD WILLIAM, editor-publisher; b. Sept. 30, 1933, Honolulu; s. Donald Wm. and Theckla Jean (Engeborg) Dewey; m. Sally Ryan, Aug. 7, 1961; children: Michael b. 1962, Wendy b. 1968; edn: Pomona Coll. 1953-55. Career: sales engr. Pascoe Steel Corp., Pomona 1955-56, div. Reynolds Aluminum Co., Los Angeles 1956-58, Switzer Panel Corp., Pasadena 1958-60; sales and gen. mgr. Western Pre-Cast Concrete Corp., Ontario 1960-62; founder, editor & pub. R/C Modeler Magazine (1963-), Freshwater and Marine Aquarium Mag. (1978-); pres., bd. chmn. RC Modeler Corp., RCM Publications; v.p., co-dir. Project Alert, Inc. 1981-84; author: Radio Control From the Ground Up (1970), Flight Training course (1973), For What It's Worth (vol.1 1973, vol.2 1975); num. sci. articles. Mem: Oceanic oc., Internat. Oceanographic Found., Smithsonian Assocs., Internat. Assn. of Aquatic Animal Medicine, Fedn. of Am. Aquarium Socs., Am. Philatelic Soc., Soc. of Philatelic Americans, Am. Topical Assn., APS Writers Unit 30, Am. First Day Cover Soc., United Postal Stationery Soc., Confederate Stamp Alliance, Am. Air Mail Soc., Bureau Issues Assn., Am. Revenue Assn., Canal Zone Study Group, Pitcairn Islands Study Group, Pet Indus. Jt. Adv. Council, NY Acad. of Scis., Smithsonian Instn., Sierra Madre Hist. Soc., Friends of the Sierra Madre Lib.(life), Internat. Betta Congress, Am. Killifish Assn., Am. Catfish and Loach Assn., No. Am. Native Fishes Assn; mil: HM-3, Hosp. Corps, USNR 1951-53. Republican (US Presdtl. Trust, US Congl. Club, US Senatorial Club, The Conservative Caucus, Presdtl. Task Force, Repub. Nat. Com.) Prot. rec: writing, marine biol., stamps. Res: 410 W. Montecito Ave. Sierra Madre 91024. Ofc: R/C Modeler Corp. 144 W. Sierra Madre Blvd. Sierra Madre 91024

DEWITT, JOHN BELTON, conservation executive; b. Jan. 13, 1937, Oakland; s. Belton and Florence (Jeffery) D.; m. Krma, Sept. 17, 1960; edn: BS in wildlife conserv., UC Berkeley 1959. Career: ranger naturalist Nat. Park Service, Yosemite Nat. Park 1957-58, Mt. Rainer Nat. Park 1959, Death Valley Nat. Monument 1960; Land Law examiner, information ofcr. and land appraiser Bur. of Land Mgmt., 1960-64; asst. secty. Save-the-Redwoods League, 1964-71, exec. dir. and secty., 1971–; dir. Nature Conservancy No. Calif. Chapter (1976-77), advis. council Trust for Public Land (1975-78), dir. Tuolumne River Preserv. Trust (1981-85), advis. council Anza Borrego Desert Com. (1983-); awards: Nat. Conserv. Award, DAR (1982), Golden Bear Award, Calif. State Park & Rec. Commn. (1982), Gulf Oil Conserv. Award (1985), Calif. State Park Rangers Assn. Award (1985); mem: Sierra Club, Am. Forestry Assn., Nat. Parks Assn., Wilderness Soc., Nat. Audubon Soc.; publs: California Redwood Parks & Preserves (1982, reprinted 1985); Prot.; rec: fishing, hiking, gardening. Ofc: Save-the-Redwoods League 114 Sansome St Ste 605 San Francisco 94104

DIACONESCU, VIRGIL I., accountant; b. Mar. 23, 1923, Gaesti, Romania, nat. US cit. 1985; s. Ilie S. and Rada I. (Iordache) D.; m. Madeleine M. Cailian (math. tchr.), May 11, 1946; children: Adrian Boldur (businessman) b. 1948, Alina Lavinia (acct.) b. 1953; edn: M. Law magna cum laude, Univ. Bucharest (Romania) 1945, M. Econs., 1946; judge, Justice Dept. of Romania 1948; notary public Calif. 1981; income tax preparer Calif. 1982. Career: lawyer Romania 1945-48; judge Municipal Ct. Bucharest 1948-50; bus. math. tchr. Bucharest 1951-63; economist for var. designing orgns. Bucharest 1963-68; gen. auditor Dept. Agriculture Romania 1969-78; acct. Project Heavy San Fernando Valley 1980-83, pgm. dir. E.S.T.A.T. (Energy Svcs., Tech. Assistance & Tng.) 1983-86; pvt. practice public acctg., tax prep. and notarial svcs., 1986–; honors: Outstanding Svc. (Proj. Heavy 1986); mem: Nat. Notary Assn., Am. Assn. Retired Persons, Assn. Informed Senior Citizens; publ: articles in Romanian mags., novel in progress; Republican; Christian; rec: crossword puzzles, writing. Res: 6642 Wilkinson Ave Apt 4 N Hollywood 91606 Ofc: Project Heavy San Fernando Valley 12011 Victory Blvd Ste 200 N Hollywood 91606

DIAMOND, ARLENE, real estate brokerage and mortgage co. president; Sept. 30, 1936, Los Angeles; edn: spl. courses Pierce Coll.; Calif. lic. real estate broker, mortgage broker, fire & casualty ins. broker, life & disability ins. gen. agent. Career: pres. Retail Training Inst. (sales tng. sch.) 1970-75; owner/pres. Prestige Ins. Services Inc. 1976-80; real estate agt. Exclusive Realtors 1981-82; mortgages 1982–; pres. Unlimited Capital Resources Inc., and Real Estate Inv. Corp.; host Talk Radio show on mortgages (1985); recipient num. sales contest awards; Republican; Prot. Res: POB 1149 Reseda 91335 Ofc: Unlimited Capital Resources Inc. 7232 Canby Ave Ste 1 Reseda 91335

DIANI, A. J., construction co. executive, restaurant owner; b. Jan. 11, 1922, San Francisco; s. Lorenzo and Mary (Balzani) D.; m. Gayle, Sept. 22, 1979; children: Cecilia b. 1947, Robert b. 1949, Susan b. 1950, James b. 1951, Michael b. 1955. Career: founder/bd. chmn. A.J. Diani Constrn. Co., Inc. gen. engring. and bldg. constrn. co. operating statewide, 1949– (3 sons now assocs.); owner The Landmark Restaurant and Lounge, Santa Maria 1982–; founding bd. chmn. Bank of Santa Maria 1977-; ptnr. Alamo Transport, Alamo Rock Co., Diani & Ibsen (land inv.), Diani & Shepard (land inv.), Diani & Assocs. (land dev.), Blue Ribbon Assocs. (R.E. dev.), Indsl. Park West (comml. indsl. dev.), A.J. Diani & Sons (equip. rental), Diani & Diani Investments, Palisades Inv. Gp., Black Road Inv. Gp.; mem. Comdr's Advis. Council, Vandenberg Air Force Base (1973-), bd. trustees Santa Maria Arts Council (1979), YMCA Bldg. Com. (1978), S.M. Joint Union High Sch. bd. trustees (1965-73, chmn. 1967-73), Orcutt Union Sch. Dist. bd. trustees (1961-65); guest lectr. Orc. Inst. of Tech. 1970-; mem. 28th Annual Nat. Security Air War Coll., Maxwell AFB, Ala.; regional coord. Nat. Com. for Action; mem: Assoc. Gen. Contrs. of Am. (nat. dir. 1975-), Assoc. Gen. Contrs. of Calif. (state pres. 1976, dir. Tri-Counties Dist. 10 yrs.), Constrn. Industry Council of Calif. (state pres. 1972-73), Santa Maria Valley Developers (founding dir., pres. 1966-67), Am. Inst. of Constructors; civic: S.M. Valley CofC (pres. 1964), Santa Barbara Sheriff's Aero Squadron, Friends of Santa Barbara Co. (dir. 1973), Boys Clubs of Am. (Outstanding Public Svc. Award 1985); mil: boatswain mate USN 1942-46, So. Pac. and Asia. Ofc: A. J. Diani Construction Co Inc POB 636 Santa Maria 93456

DIBBLE, FRANCES B., educator; b. June 10, 1950, Allentown, Pa.; d. Louis J. and Arlene M. (Eroh) Bauer; m. David Van Vlack Dibble, May 3, 1984; edn: BS in edn., Kutztown State Coll., Pa. 1972; BA in hist., Holy Names Coll. 1980; MA, edn. of exceptional children, CSU San Francisco 1982; Optacon cert., Univ. Pittsburgh 1973, SAVI cert. UC Berkeley 1973; Tchg. cred. (visually impaired, orientation and mobility splst.). Career: tchr. of the visually impaired (children and adults), 1972–: Overbrook Sch. for the Blind, Phila. and Montgomery County Intermed. Unit, Norristown, Pa. 1972-75; Calif. Sch. for the Blind, Berkeley 1975-80; cons. to State Dept. of Rehab., 1980-82; tchr. Orientation and Mobility, Ho'Opono, Hawaii summer 1982; Visually Impaired Presch. Pgm., Glenview Sch., Oakland 1982–, also instr. parents of blind children in Braille, coord. YWCA swim pgm. for the blind, mem. Transition Team asstg. blind students find employment; award: Carnation Co. award for tchg. excellence (1980); mem. Council for Exceptional Children (pres. elect 1986), Calif. Assn. of Orientation and Mobility Splsts. (ed. 1982-83), Assn. for the Edn. and Rehab. of Visually Impaired and Blind, Internat. Inst. for V.I. and Blind Preschool; civic: Calif. Native Plant Soc., Calif. Hist. Soc., Oral Hist. Assn.; publs: article in J. of Visual Impairment and Blindness (10/84); Episcopal; rec: violin, gardening (Calif. natives). Res: 2806 Bellaire Pl Oakland 94601 Ofc: Glenview School 4215 LaCresta Ave Rm 2 Oakland 94602

DICKASON, RUSSELL JAMES, electronic systems engineer; b. Feb. 15, 1923, Cleveland, Ohio; s. Marcel Gimbert and Ethel Marie (Werger) D.; m. Nancy Oletta Desmond, Nov. 3, 1961; 1 son, Alan Russell b 1950; stepchildren:

Kimberly Ann b. 1952, Burt Blair b. 1958; edn: BS in E.E., Case Western Univ. 1946; postgrad. stu. UC Los Angeles Ext. 1955-65, CSU Fullerton 1962-4, San Mateo Coll. 1981-2. Career: test engring. Gen. Elec. Co., Schenectady, NY 1946-7; instr. in elec. engring. Univ. of Cincinnati, 1947-50; design engr. GE Co., Cleveland, Ohio 1951, Victoreen Instruments, Cleveland 1951-2; sr. elec. engr. Thompson Products Div., Cleveland 1953; section mgr. Cmd. & Control Systems, Hughes Aircraft Co., Fullerton, Calif. 1953-69; proj. mgr. Litton Ship systems, Pascagoula, Miss. 1970-3; pgm. mgr. (Navy contracts) Teledyne Inc., Torrance, Calif. 1974; eng. supr. Hughes Aircraft Co. 1975-80; engrg. mgr. elec. power systems Lockheed Missile & Space Co., Sunnyvale 1980−; instr. semicondr. electronics, No Orange Co. Comm. Coll.; honors: Eta Kappa Nu; mem. IEEE 1947-80; faculty adv. Illumination Engring. Soc. student br. 1948-50; Republican; Methodist; rec: duplicate bridge. Res: 1016 Continentals Way No. 307 Belmont 94002-3133 Ofc: Lockheed Missile/Space Co., Bldg 151A/Dept. 62-16, 1111 Lockheed Way Sunnyvale 94088-3504

DICKE, LOWELL MARTIN, corporate executive; b. Sept. 6, 1939, Topeka, Kans.; s. Ernest Frederick and Edna Dorothy (Larson) D.; div.; children: (stepson) Brian Hamblet b. 1964, Charlotte b. 1972; edn: BA econ., honors, Univ. Kans. 1961; MA econ., Yale Univ. 1965; JD, Yale Law Sch. 1965. Career: asst. treas. Fluor Corp. 1972-77; vice pres./gen. mgr. Bechtel Financing Services Inc. 1977-78; ptnr. Montgomery Securities, 1978-80; mktg. cons. and oil and gas cons. 1980-85; v.p., chief fin. ofcr., bd. dirs. and mgmt. com. Fayette Mfg. Corp.; awards: Arthur Boynton Scholar in Economics (1960), Who's Who in Calif. Bus. & Finance; mem. Calif. Bar Assn., Yale Club of NYC; Republican; Episcopal; rec: tennis, gardening, woodwkg. Res: 770 Garland Dr Palo Alto 94303 Ofc: Fayette Mfg. Corp. 628 Central Ave Tracy 95376

DICKERSON, WILLIAM ROY, lawyer; b. Feb. 15, 1928, Uniontown, Ky.; s. Benjamin Franklin and Honor Mae (Staples) Dickerson; edn: BA in acctg., CSU, 1952; JD, UCLA,1958. Career: admitted to practice Calif., 1959, US Supreme Ct., 1978, US Tax Ct., 1972; deputy city atty. and ex-officio city prosecutor, Glendale, 1959-62; atty., office of James Brewer, Los Angeles 1962-68, firm of LaFollette, Johnson, Schoreter & DeHaas, 1968-73; owner pvt. law practice, William R. Dickerson & Assocs., Los Angeles 1973−, splst. in defense of CPAs (defended 880+ suits), adminstr. accts.' malpractice ins. pgm. for First State Ins. Co. and New England Reins. Corp., 1979-; frequent spkr. CPA socs.; faculty Practicing Law Inst.; instr. Pepperdine Univ.; judge pro tem L.A. Municipal Ct., L.A. Traffic Ct., and West L.A. Small Claims Ct.; arbitrator Civil cases L.A. Superior Ct.; elected mem. bd. dirs. Los Feliz Improvement Assn.; mem: Soc. of Calif. Accountants (mem. Ednl. Found., Inc.), Calif. State Bar, Los Angeles Co. Bar Assn., Am. Bar Assn. (Profl. Liability Com.), Assn. of Trial Lawyers of Am., San Fernando Valley Criminal Bar Assn., Century City Bar Assn., Fed. Bar Assn., Nat. Soc. of Public Accts., Assn. of So. Calif. Defense Counsel, Am. Film Inst., Internat. Platform Assn.; mil: M.P., US Army 1946-7, Spl.Svcs. Entertainment. Res: 5006 Los Feliz Bl.Los Angeles 90027. Ofc: William R. Dickerson & Assocs., 813 N Doheny Dr Beverly Hills 90210

DICKSON, RICHARD KELLOGG, II, securities attorney; b. Mar. 23, 1946, Youngstown, Ohio; s. Richard Kellogg and Vivian Zoe (Carter) D.; edn: BS, UC Berkeley 1968, MBA, USC, 1970, JD, Univ. of the Pacific 1976; admitted to practice State Bar of Calif. 1976. Career: staff acct. Arthur Young & Co., Oakland 1971-72; corporation counsel, Calif. Commnr. of Corporations, Los Angeles 1976-79; securities atty., pvt. practice own firm, Newport Beach 1979−, corp. atty. for num. public cos. incl. Gentronix Labs. Inc., Morro Rock Resources Inc., Entertainment Telecomm. Television Inc.; honors: Traynor Soc. (1976); mem. Calif., Orange Co. Bar Assn.; mil: pvt. USAR 1968-70; rec: sports, literature. Law Ofcs. of Richard K. Dickson, II, 1100 Quail St, Ste 114, Newport Beach 92660

DIEHL, RUSSELL REED, investment banker; b. June 20, 1946, San Clemente, Calif.; s. Russell Reed and Beverly (Burress) D.; m. Diane Grace Kyle, Aug. 24, 1969; children: Russell b. 1977, Reed b. 1978; edn: BA, Lake Forest Coll. 1968; MS, Am. Grad. Sch. Internat. Mgmt. 1971. Career: internat. ofcr. Bank of NY 1973-75; v.p. internat. div. Union Bank Los Angeles 1975-78; mng. ptnr. Diehl & Co. Newport Beach; occasional lectr. USC Bus. Sch. 1978−; mem: Am. Finance Assn., Nat. Assn. Accts., Reg. Investment Advisors, Lincoln Club, Rotary Internat., 552 Club; bd. Rehab. Inst. of So. Calif., Hoag Hosp.; publ: monthly newsletter to clients; mil: USMC 1968-71; Republican; Episcopal; rec: rugby, photog. Res: 40 Westport Irvine 92714 Ofc: Diehl & Co. 1201 Dove St Newport Beach 92660

DIGILIO, CAROLYN ANNE, health care administrator; b. Oct. 12, 1942, Bridgeport, Conn.; d. Dominic Anthony and Gertrude Marie (Astegher) Digilio; edn: RN (Salutatorian), Danbury Hospital, Conn. 1963; cert. Chemical Dependency Counselor, Calif. State Univ., 1983; BA, Antioch Univ. 1985. Career: administr., dir. of nurses Centinela Park Convalescent Hosp. 1967-83; RN/intervention splst. Raleigh Hills Hosp., 1983-85; (current): cons. chem. dependency counselor Behavior Health Services; psychiatric nurse; chem. dependency nurse Cedars-Sinai Hosp.; writer, contbr. monthly column women's paper; speaker Prevention Sector, Alcoholism Ctr. for Women; rec: writing, wood sculpting. Address: Gardena

DIGIORNO, ROBERT ALLEN, dentist; b. Jan. 18, 1956, Patterson; s. John Peter and Charlene Annette (Capps) D.; Edn: BA, Univ. of the Pacific 1978; DDS, Univ. of the Pacific Dental Sch. 1981. Career: pure-pak opr. Avoset Food Corp., Gustine 1974-78; associateship in destistry 1981-82; owner solo practice gen. dentistry, Gustine 1983−; staff San Luis Conv. Hosp. and Westside Hosp.;

chmn. Stanilaus Nat. Dental Health Month; honors: Dale Mead Sportsmanship Award, Gustine Elem. Sch. 1972; mem: Am. and Calif. Dental Assns., Staislaus (chmn. Dental Health Edn.) and Yosemite Dental Socs., Am. Assn. for Functional Orthodontics, Delta Sigma Delta, Rotary (bd. dirs. 1985, advtg. co-chmn. 1985-86, pres. elect 1986-87, pes. 1987-88), Gustine CofC (bd. 1986-89), Univ. of Pacific Alumni, Univ. of Pacific Dental Sch. Alumni, Physicians & Surgeon Club Alumni, Omega Phi Alpha Alumni, Gustine HS Booster; publs: sports ed. and weekly columnist, high school paper 1974; weekly dental column, The Gustine Press and The Newman Index; Democrat; Catholic; rec: skiing, golf, softball. Res: 970 South Ave. Gustine 95322 Ofc: Robert A. DiGiorno, DDS, 680 South Ave, No. 9, Gustine 95322

DI JULIO, R(OBERT) DAVID, lawyer; b. Jan. 27, 1946, Phila., Penn.; s. Felix A. and Bula May (Westly) D.; m. Stephanie Rose Scher, May 23, 1981; children: Robin Scher, b. 1973, Jaime Scher, b. 1967; edn: BS in eng., BS in bus. admin., Drexel Univ. 1969, MS, 1970; JD, Southwestern Sch. of Law 1983; admitted to practice, Calif. 1969. Career: prin. scientist Environmental Research & Technology; dept. hd. So. Calif. Assn. of Govts.; gen. counsel, v.p. ops. Renewable Energy Ventures Inc., Encino; mem. Carter Pres. Transition Team; dir. Renewable Energy Ventures Inc.; cons. Nat. Sci. Found., Environmental Protection Agency, Nat. Transportation Research Bd.; pres. Council on Environmental Quality; honors: Washingtonian of the Year 1974; Outstanding Acheiv., Metropolitan Washington Council of Govts. 1973; Outstanding Acheiv., So. Calif. Assn. of Govts. 1984; mem: Am. and Calif. Bar Assns.; Am. and Calif. Wind Energy Assns.; Am. Air Pollution Control Assn.; works: invented and developed Metropolitan Washington Council of Govts. Air Quality Index; rec: computers, tennis, canines. Res: 3717 Effingham Pl., Los Angeles 90027 Ofc: Renewable Energy Ventures Inc., 16311 Ventura Blvd., Encino 91436

DILL, JOSEPH MORROW, dentist; b. Dec. 27, 1956, San Pablo; s. Dr. Joseph Norval and Elsie Louise (Hathaway) D.; edn: BS, Univ. of the Pacific 1979, DDS, UOP Sch. of Dentistry, 1982; lic. dentist, Calif. BDE 1982. Career: dentist with US Public Health Service, Fort Peck Indian Reservation, N.E. Montana, 1982-84; pvt. practice gen. dentistry in San Francisco Bay Area, 1984−; staff Poplar Comm. Hosp. 1982-84; dentist, cons. Poplar Conv. Hosp. 1982-84; biology instr. Fort Peck Comm. Coll. 1983; mem: Am. Dental Assn., Calif. Dental Assn., S.F.Dental Soc., ADA Continuing Edn. Registry; mil: lt. Nat. Health Service Corps; rec: skiing, tennis, golf. Res: 425 Via Royal Walnut Creek 94596 Ofc: 5230 Diamond Heights Blvd San Francisco 94131; 11 Santa Maria Way Orinda 94563

DILLARD, THADDEUS CHARLES, II, dentist; b. Nov. 8, 1952, Los Angeles; s. Thaddeus C. and Ermalene E. (Colwell) D.; m. Kolleen Maria Faxio, Sept. 29, 1985; edn: BS, Wilberforce Univ. 1974; DDS, Howard Univ. 1982; Gen. Practice Residency Cert., Nat. Inst. of Mental Health, St. Elizabeths Hosp., Wash. DC 1983. Career: dental resident National Inst. of Mental Health, St. Elizabeth Hosp., Wash. DC 1982-83; staff dentist Montgomery Co. Detention Ctr., Rockville, Md. 1984-85; pvt. practice 1982−; Consumer Health Inc., Consumer Dental Network 1985−; currently, mng. dentist; mem: Acad. of Gen. Dentistry, Am. and Calif. Dental Assns., Am. Assn. of Hosp. Dentists, Wilberforce Univ. Alumni Assn., Howard Univ. Dental Sch. Alumni Assn.; recipient, photography award, Howard Univ. 1982; rec: photog., sailing, equestrian. Ofc: 2700 Martin Luther King Blvd. Los Angeles 90037

DI MEGLIO, ANGELA, speech pathologist; b. Oct. 28, 1956, NY, NY; d. John and Jacqueline (Valdinato) DiMeglio; edn: BA, Hunter Coll. 1978; MS, Penn. State Univ. 1980; Cert. Speech- Language Pathologist, ASHA (1980). Career: speech-language pathologist Alta Bates Hosp., Albany 1981-83, senior sp.-lang. pathologist Kentfield Med. Hosp., Kentfield 1983-84; sp.-lang. pathologist prin. in pvt. practice, Kentfield 1984−; cons. Head Injury Recovery Ctr., Berkeley 1983; awards: Anne Shaeker-Schulman Scholarship Award; mem: Am. Sp./Lang./Hearing Assn., Calif. Sp. & Hearing Assn., Calif. Speech Pathologists & Audiologists in Pvt. Practice, Bay Area Group for Adult Communication Disorders; civic: Marin Conservation League, Mono Lake Com., Sierra Club, ACLU, Klanwatch Network, Nat. Orgn. for Women (pres. Marin Chpt. 1982-86), Planned Parenthood, Com. to Defend Reproductive Rights, Nat. Abortion Rights Action League, Marin Nuclear Freeze; rec: politics, skiing, reading, bicycling, hiking. Address: 21B Stadium Way Kentfield 94904

DIMMETTE, ROBERT MARVIN, physician-pathologist; b. July 13, 1921, White Oak, N.C.; s. Rev. Joel Walter and Margaret Pauline (Robertson) D.; m. Marion Wilcox, Apr. 25, 1947; children: Robert, Jr. b. 1948, Timothy b. 1950, Sally b. 1954, Pattie b. 1956; edn: AA, Brevard Coll. 1938; BA, High Point Coll. 1941; MD, Bowman Gray Sch. of Med., White Forest Univ. 1944; lic. phys. in Calif., N.C., and Md.; Diplomate Am. Coll. Pathologists. Career: intern Kings Co. Hosp. Bklyn. 1944-45, surg. res. Norfolk Gen. Hosp., Va. 1945-46, res. surg. Tilton Gen. Hosp. Ft. Dix, NJ 1946-47, res. path. US Naval Hosp. Phila. 1947-50; chief Lab. Services US Naval Hosp., Annapolis 1951-53, head pathol. research Namru, Cairo, Egypt 1953-56; head path. anat. 1955-56, head Clin. Path. US Naval Hosp. and Med. Sch. Bethesda, Md. 1956-60; chief Lab. Ser. & Clin. Research US Naval Hosp. San Diego 1960-71; dir. Labs. Villa View Hosp., San Diego 1971; (current) chief of pathology and dir. labs. Bay Hosp.. Medical Center, Chula Vista 1971−; assoc. prof. pathology UC San Diego Sch. of Med.; prof. of pathology USC, Los Angeles; advis. bd. Greater San Diego Health Plan; mem: Fellow Am. Soc. of Clin. Path., AMA, CMA, San Diego Med. Soc., San Diego Soc. of Path.; num. med. journal publs. and med. seminars; mil: capt. USN, Dist. Service Award, Meritorious Service Award; Republican; United Methodist; rec: fishing, agronomy. Res: 1051 Myrtle Way San Diego 92103 Ofc: Bay Hospital Med. Center, 435 H Street Chula Vista 92010

DI MUCCIO, MARY-JO, librarian; b. June 16, 1930, Hanford; d. Vincent and Teresa (Yovino) Di Muccio; edn: BA, Immaculate Heart Coll., L.A. 1953, MLS, 1960; PhD, US Internat. Univ., San Diego 1970. Career: tchr. parochial schs., San Francisco 1949-54, Los Angeles 1954-58; tchr. Govt. of Can., Victoria, B.C. 1959-60; asst. librarian Immaculate Heart Coll., Los Angeles 1960-62, head librarian, 1962-72; adminstrv. librarian Sunnyvale Public Library, 1972–; bd. dirs., past pres. Sunnyvale Community Services; mem. Am., Calif., Catholic (past pres. exec. bd.), Special Libraries lib. assns., Bus. and Profl. Women (pres. Peninsula Dist.), Calif. Women in Govt., Soroptomists; publs. in field of edn.; Roman Catholic; rec: tennis, travel. Ofc: 1500 Partridge Ave. Bldg. 7, Sunnyvale 94087

DINALLO, RICHARD N., JR., lawyer; b. Apr. 8, 1946, Passaic, NJ; s. Richard N. and Viola E. (Ivy) D.; edn: AB, Univ. of Notre Dame, 1967; JD, Georgetown Univ. Law Ctr. 1970, LLM, 1972; MBA, Golden Gate Univ. 1986; admitted Calif. State Bar 1971, Dist. of Columbia Bar 1971. Career: atty Carter-Hawley-Hale Stores Inc., Los Angeles 1975-76, Yellow Cab Co., San Francisco 1975-76, Dept. of Justice, S.F. 1980-81, Div. of Labor Stds. Enforcement, S.F. 1976-82; atty. prin. pvt. practice law, San Francisco 1982–; former law school prof.; Spl. Entertainment Hearing Judge; mem. State Bar Assn., Calif. Trial Lawyers Assn. of Calif.; works: largest minimum wage case ever prosecuted by State Labor Commnr.; published case opinion on criminal sentencing as dep. atty. general; mil: airman AF Nat. Guard; rec: skiing. Law Ofcs. Richard N. Dinallo, 535 Pacific Ave San Francisco 94133

DINGMAN, ROBERT W., executive search consultant; b. Aug. 23, 1926, St. Louis, Mo.; s. Rev. Briggs P. and Gladys M. (Hazelton) D.; m. Janice Meade; children: Laurie b. 1954, David b. 1956, Daniel b. 1961; edn: BA, Houghton Coll., N.Y. 1950; MS studies psychol., Boston Univ. 1951. Career: pres. Robert W. Dingman Co. Inc., Westlake Village; honors: Alumnus of Year, Houghton Coll. (1982), disting. business award Westlake Rotary, comm. svc. award Conejo Valley CofC; mem. Calif. Exec. Recruiters Assn. (dir.), Assn. Exec. Search Consultants; civic: Whitworth Coll., Spokane, Wn. (bd. trustees 10 yrs.), Pasadena Christian Sch. (bd. mem./pres. 3 yrs.), Hospice of the Conejo (bd. 6 yrs., pres. 3 yrs.); clubs: Jonathan (LA), North Ranch Country (Westlake Village); mil: enlisted US Army WWII, Purple Heart, ETO, 3 Stars; Republican; Presbyterian (elder); rec: tennis. Res: 4531 Tam O'Shanter Dr Westlake Village 91362 Ofc: Robert W. Dingman Co. Inc. 32131 W Lindero Canyon Rd Westlake Village 91361

DINNIN, LEONA (LEE) COLLINS, cartographer; b. Apr. 30, 1923, Indianapolis; d. Wm. Frederick and Mae Marie (Myers) C.; m. Wm. S. Dinnin, May 8, 1943; edn: AB in bio-chem., Franklin Coll., 1944; desig: cartographer, USGS (1966). Career: cartographic compilation aid, U.S. Geol. Survey, 1951, progressed through all cartography map positions, Western Mapping Ctr. of Nat. Mapping Div. USGS, 1951-82 (supv. map preparation for Mariana Islands, Fort Apache Indian Reserv., DMA Survival Map, and Photorevision Test; ongoing team mem. for public liason incl. tours and tng. sems.; frequently assigned to assist fgn. dignitaries and elected ofcls.; liason with other USGS Divs.; bd. dirs. and pres. of Interdivision activity group) ret. as staff cartographer, 1982; independent map cons./cartographer, 1982–; awards: USGS Suggestion Awards (1955, 57), Superior Performance Award (1976); mcm. Am. Cong. on Surveying & Mapping (charter mem., dir. No. Calif. Sect. 1980-81, secty./treas. 1982-83, vice chair 1984, chmn. 1985-86) Am. Soc. for Photogrammetry and Remote Sensing; served on primary coms. of virtually all nat. and state conv. directorates for ACSM/ASPRS functions on West Coast since 1971; civic. Los Trancos Woods Comm. Assn. (past pres. 2 terms); rec: photog., painting, writing poetry, collect owls, maps, dictionaries. Address: 1196 Los Trancos Rd Portola Valley 94025

DIRKSEN, EDWARD WILLIAM, clergyman, educator; b. July 10, 1933, Los Angeles; s. Edward and Emma Lucille (Whitnack) D.; m. Patrica, June 1, 1958; children: Wendelyn (Cox) b. 1960, Peter b. 1962, Todd b. 1964, Thom b. 1968; edn: BA, La Sierra (now Loma Linda Univ.) 1955; MA, BD, Seventh-day Adventist Theol. Sem. (Potomac Univ., Andrews Univ.) 1959, 60; BCM, and MCM in church music, The So. Baptist Theol. Sem. Sch. of Church Music 1966, 67; Ordained Minister, Elder, Seventh-day Adventist Ch. (1967). Career: church pastor Seventh-Day Adventist var. dists. in Wis. 1960-64, Ind. 1967-70; hosp. chaplain Pewee Valley (Ky.) Hosp. 1964-67, Linda Valley Conv. Hosp., Loma Linda, Calif. 1967-78; asst. prof. of Biblical Languages and Music, Antillian Coll., Mayaguez, Puerto Rico 1970-74; Bible counselor Voice of Prophecy Bible Sch., Newbury Park, Calif. 1985; tchr. ESL, El Monte Union High Sch. Dist., Adult Edn., 1979–; mem. Nat. Assn. of Professors of Hebrew, Soc. of Biblical Literature, var. ministerial assns.; works: spkr. radio ministry var. stations in Wis., Ind., Kans. (1963, 68, 69, 77); series of newspaper articles on the Christian Sabbath (1970-71); devel. spl. typewriter keyboards: Tasothat (The All Symbol Old Testament Hebrew-Aramaic), Tasskant-Gt (Septuagint Koine Attic New Testament Greek), Tort (1975); composer, Let No Man Despise Thy Youth, for male chorus (1969), hymn: Great King of Glory, Come! (1983); Republican; rec: photog., classical music. Address: 10685 Curtis St Loma Linda 92354

DISPOTO, CHARLES GERALD, JR., construction co. president; b. July 17, 1924, Bklyn.; s. Charles, Sr. and Ester Oliva; stepmother, Josephine Spinelli; m. Vincenza Anne De Masi, June 1, 1947; children: Joanne Ruth b. 1948, Charlene Sofia (Vanover) b. 1952; edn: architl. grad., I.C.S. Correspondence

Sch., Pa., 7 yrs.; Calif. State lic. Bldg. Contractor. Career: carpenter foreman indsl. projects, Terminal Constrn. Inc., 1947-48, supt. 1948-59; supt. indsl. & comml. bldgs., Muscarelle Constrn. Inc. 1960-65; bldr. hotel and casino (Las Vegas) and aeronautical coll. (San Francisco), 1965-75; founder/pres. Avid Constrn. Inc. (blt. mil. dollar cold storages), Delano 1975–; mem. advis. com. County Supvr. 1st Dist.; active in econ. devel. plnng. City of Delano and Delano Chamber of Commerce (dir., econ. devel. chmn.); mem. Italian Heritage Dante Assn. (dir.); works: sculpture: 7-ft. wine maker statue (won 2d pl. Kern County Fair), 7-ft. statue of St. Jude (Grand Sweepstake Kern County Fair), carved 9-ft Ionic Columns (for res. and office bldg.); mil: carpenter's mate 3/c US Navy 1942-45, destroyer svc.; Catholic (Eucharistic minister); rec: gardening, sculpture, dancing. Res: 707 Vassar St Delano 93215 Ofc: Avid Construction Inc. 1230 Glenwood St POB 1118 Delano 93216

DISTEFANO, PETER ANDREW, insurance agency owner; b. Nov. 26, 1939, NY, NY; s. Peter Julian D.; children: Diane b. 1963, Daniel b. 1965, Donald b. 1968; edn: City Coll. of S.F. 1965; AA, Orange Coast Coll. 1975; CEBS, Wharton Sch. of Bus. 1983; Reg. Profl. Health Underwriter. Career: agent Mutual of NY San Francisco 1971-72; regl. mgr. Hartford Ins. Group Santa Ana 1972-77; pres. Lachman & Assoc. Inc. Lafayette 1977-80; pres., owner Distefano Ins. Svcs. Inc. Benicia 1980–; tchr. small bus. owner pgm.; honors: Million Dollar Round Table (1984), Salesman of the Yr. (Am. Found. Life 1983); mem. Nat. Assn. Life Underwriters, Nat. Assn. Health Underws., Soc. Reg. Profl. Health Underws., Profl. Ins. Agents of Calif./ Nev., Acad. Producer Ins. Studies, Nat. Assn. Security Deals, Internat. Found. Employee Benefit Plans, Contra Costa- Solano Counties Easter Seal Soc., Chilpancingo Vista Corp. (bd.), Calif. State Easter Seal Soc. (bd.); mil: PO3 USN 1957-62, Good Conduct; Republican; Greek Orthodox, rec: weightlifting, conditioning. Ofc: Distefano Ins. Svcs. Inc. 835 First St POB 696 Benicia 94510

DIVELBISS, WARREN LEWIS, communications executive; b. Jan. 25, 1941, Salina, Kans.; s. Lewis George and Evelyngrace (Fox) D.; edn: Kansas Wesleyan Univ. 1959-61; BA, Mich. State Univ. 1963; grad. work Univ. Denver 1968-69; tchg. cred. CSU San Bernardino 1975-76. Career: radio announcer KIUL, Garden City, Kans. 1964-, moved to television, 1966–, var. t.v. pos. include studio supr., prod./dir./writer, facilities scheduling dir., and asst. gen. mgr.; worked with Satellite Technology Demonstrn. 2 yrs.; current: asst. gen. mgr. KVCR TV/FM, San Bernardino; founder/pres. Future Trac Assocs. (cons. on new technologies) 1981-; tchg. fellow Univ. of Denver 1968-69, evening instr. San Bernardino Valley Coll. 1975-82; recipient num. appreciation awards var. civic and charitable orgns.; mem. World Future Soc./L.A. Chpt. (pres. 1981-82); civic: Boy Scouts Am. (Explorer Scouts advisor), Lions Club Internat., San Bernardino Host (pres. 1986-87), Am. Nat. Red Cross (Service Center Advis. Bd. chair 1985-87), Riverside Operation Quake-Safe (bd.); frequent speaker var. groups; contbr. essays and book chpts. in sev. books; rec: gardening, music listening, discussing the future. Res: 3736 San Rafael Way Riverside 92504 Ofc: KVCR TV/FM 701 S Mount Vernon Ave San Bernardino 92410

DI VITA, ANTHONY J., bank executive; b. Oct. 29, 1959, National City; s. Girolamo A. and Frances J. Di V.; edn: Grossmont Colls. 1978-79. Career: sr. supr., chief supr., branch mgr. (Spring Valley, Rancho Bernardo, Del Mar) Household Bank 1979–, currently bank mgr. El Cajon branch; mem. Household Bank Employee Advis. Com.; honors: Grossmont Dist. H.S. Leaders Orgn. laurels award (1977); mem. El Cajon CofC. Ofc: Household Bank 1790 E Main St El Cajon 92021

DIXON, DEAN OWEN, marketing executive; b. July 25, 1945, Baraboo, Wis.; s. Myer Eldon and Ruby Luvera (Hupenbecker) D.; m. Gail, May 8, 1965; 1 son, Todd b. 1968; edn: Ariz. St. Univ. 1963-65, CSU Long Beach 1965-67. Career: mgr. Factory Sales/ Traffic, Varec Inc., 1967-70; asst. nat. sales mgr. Merit Abrasive Prods. Inc., 1970-78; territory mgr. Sancap Abrasives Inc., 1978-79; mktg. mgr. Jet and Western Abrasives Inc. 1979–; awards: Rotary Found. Group Study Exchange to New South Wales, Australia (1980); civic: City of Buena Park Centennial (exec. bd., 1986-87), B.P. Hist. Soc. (1974-, trustee 1978-79, v.p. 1979-84), Orange County Hist. Commn. (1980-82), O.C. Hist. Soc. (1978-), B.P. CofC (1974-80), Silverado Days Com. (1974-), B.P. Boys Club (com. 1980-), Am. Found. for Sci. of Creative Intelligence (1973-); works: coauthor GSE Report (1980), writer/prod. Cable-TV prodn. Natural History in North Orange County (1985); Republican; Methodist; rec: bibliophile. Ofc: Jet and Western Abrasives Inc 4383 Fruitland Ave Vernon 90058

DJANG, SUKHYUNG, dentist, b. Nov. 12, 1947, Seoul, Korea; s. Doohoon and Oksoo D.; m. Shihee, July 2, 1978; children: Mabel b. 1979, Robin b. 1983, Benzamin b. 1984; edn: pre-dental, Seoul Univ. Sch. Liberal Arts & Sci., 1970, DDS, Seoul Univ. Dental Sch. 1975; DDS, USC Dental Sch. 1984. Career: dental intern and resident Nat. VA Hosp. Seoul, Korea 1975-77; Army dentist in Korea, 1977-80; practicing dentist, 1984–; counselor health dept. Korean Street Journal, Los Angeles 1984-; mem. Am. Soc. for Geriatric Dentistry; contbg. columnist: Oral Hygiene, Korean Street J. (community weekly newspaper) 1984-85; mil: capt. Army Med. Corps 1977-80. Res: 3449 Montrose Ave La Crescenta 91214 Ofc: 15424 Nordhoff St Sepulveda 91343

DLUGOSZ, JOHN ANDREW, healthcare services executive; b. Oct. 18, 1938, Buffalo, N.Y.; s. John F. and Florence E. (Bouquard) Dugos; m. Norma A. Hussar, June 23, 1962; edn: BA, Canisius Coll. 1960. Career: prodn. wkr., then route svc. and sales Coyne Laundry, Buffalo, N.Y. 1956-66; supvr. Service Indsl. Laundry, Kansas City, Mo. 1966-69; prodn. supvr. Environmentals Inc.,

Los Angeles 1969-73; gen. mgr. Angelica Healthcare Svces., L.A. 1973-84, regl. mgr. 1984–; mem. Textile Rental Supply Assn.; civic: Soc. for Preservation of Variety Arts, Toastmasters, W. Covina Camping Club, Via Verde CC; mil: E4 US Army 1961-63; Democrat; Roman Catholic; rec: golf, fishing, bowling. Res: 24309 Delta Dr Diamond Bar 91765 Ofc: Angelica Healthcare Svcs 1575 Case St Orange 91766

DO, CHI MINH, dentist, acupuncturist; b. May 2, 1952, Kaoyao, Kwangtung, China; s. Quoc and Huu Kiet (Huynh) Do; m. Man Linh Trinh, Apr. 26, 1985; 1 dau. Joanna b. 1985; edn: BDS, Nat. Taiwan Univ. Sch. of Dentistry 1977; CMD, China Nat. Bd. of Med. Examiners, 1982; acupuncture course, Veterans Gen. Hosp., R.O.C. 1981-82. Career: research mem. Chinese Acupuncture Sci. Research Found., Taipei, Taiwan, ROC, 1972; dentist assoc. Ko Kin Hoa Dental Clinic, Taipei 1977-79; practitioner/owner E-Ping Dental & Acupuncture Clinic, Taipei 1979-82; acupuncturist Zhesen Acupuncture & Chinese Medicine Center, Laguna Hills currently; dentist assoc. Francis K. Wong DDS Inc., 1985; recipient citation from The Acupuncture Assn. of R.O.C. for contbns. in field (1981); mem: Taipei Dental Assn., R.O.C. Dental Assn., Taipei Acup. Assn., British Acup. Assn., Acup. Med. Assn. of So. Calif. (dir., vice chmn. of finance div.), Southeast-Asian Chinese-Am. CofC (dir. 1985); publ: Case Report of Coccyx Fracture (Sci. of Acupuncture Mag. 1986); rec: poetry writing. Res: 7162 Heil Ave Apt 3 Huntington Beach 92647 Ofc: Zhesen Acupuncture Center 25283 Cabot Rd Ste 105 Laguna Hills 92653

DOBELIS, GEORGE, manufacturing co. executive; b. July 31, 1940, Riga, Latvia, nat. US cit. 1957; s. John A. and Dorothy A. (Arins) D.; m. Dolores Ann Nagle, Dec. 2, 1972; children: Sally Ann Berg, Christian Eric Berg, Kurt Conrad Berg; edn: BA, Santa Monica Coll. 1963. Career: mfg. supv. Com Tech Inc. 1964-65; proj. engr. Elco Corp. El Segundo 1965-69, Masterite Inds. Torrance 1969-70; engrg. mgr. Elco Corp. 1970-76, new prods. mgr. 1976-78; pres. Connector Technol. Inc. Anaheim 1978–; mem. Inst. Elec. Electron. Engrs.; publ: tech. articles co-authored with other engrs.; mil: sgt. Calif. Nat. Guard 1963-69; Republican; Lutheran; rec: golf, swimming, bowling, camping. Ofc: Anaheim

DOBY, ALLEN E., parks and community services administrator; b. Oct. 26, 1934, Miss.; s. Allen and Carrie O. (Pruitt) D.; m. Lafaye Ealy, June 20, 1981; edn: AA, Compton Coll. 1958; BS, CSU Northridge 1973. Career: recreation leader County of Los Angeles, 1958, asst. rec. dir. 1959, rec. dir. 1959-62, dist. recreation director 1970-75; dir. Parks and Recreation, City of Compton 1975-80, City of Santa Ana (first Black dept. hd. apptd. in city's 112 year hist.) 1980-84, exec. dir. Recreation and Community Service Agency (incl. the Library, Museum, Rec. & Parks Dept., and Cable TV), 1984–; advsry. bd. Southwest Comm. Coll. Rec. Dept.; awards: Profl. Adminstr. of Year (1977); mem. Ethnic Minority Soc., NRPA, Salvation Army/Compton (bd. dirs.); instr. recreation adminstrn. Cerritos and Compton Community Colls.; mil: E5 US Army 1955-57, Good Conduct; rec: auto racing, sports, dancing. Res: 2003 N Baker St Santa Ana 92706 Ofc: City of Santa Ana 20 Civic Center Plaza Santa Ana 92702

DOCKSON, ROBERT RAY, savings and loan assn. executive; b. Oct. 6, 1917, Quincy, Ill.; s. Marshal R. and Letah L. (Edmundson) Dockson; m. Katheryn V. Allison, S.F., Mar. 4, 1944; 1 dau. Kathy Kimberlee, b. 1948; edn: AA, Springfield Jr.Coll. 1937, BA, Univ. Ill. 1939, MFS, USC 1940, PhD, 1946. Career: asst. prof. , dur. Bur of Econ. and Bus. Resrch, Rutgers Univ. 1946-48; economist Western Home Ofc. Prudential Ins. Co. , 1948-51; economist Bank of Am., San Francisco 1951-53; prof./ hd. Mktg. Dept. , USC Sch of Commerce, 1953-59, and dean/prof. bus. economics, USC Sch of Bus. Adminstrn., 1959-69; dir. Fed. Svgs. & Loan Assn. , 1969–, pres. 1970-, chmn. of bd./ CEO, 1973-85; chmn. bd. Cal Fed Savings, 1977–; chmn. bd. CalFed Inc. 1984–; Dir: Internat. Lease Fin. Corp., Computer Scis. Corp., Fed. Reserve Bank of S.F. - L.A. Dist., Pacific Lighting Corp., IT Corp., McKesson, Olga Company, Transam. Income Areas, Inc.; Amer. Splst for US State Dept.; trustee Orthopaedic Hosp.; bd. govs. John Randolph Haynes and Dora Haynes Found.; trustee Rose Hills; trustee Pepperdine Univ.; mem. bd. councilors, USC Grad. Sch. Bus. Adminstrn. Awards: Asa V. Call achievement awd., Star of Solidarity, Italian Govt.; Disting. Community Svc. awd., Brandeis Univ.; Housing Man of Year, Nat. Housing Conf.; Whitney M. Young Jr. awd, Urban League of L.A.; Miracle Man of the Year, Miracle Mile Lions Club; Spirit of Los Angeles Awd., LA City Hdqtrs. Assn. Mem: Gr. L.A. CofC (pres. 1975), W. Internat. Trade Assn., Newcomen Club, L.A. Rotary Club, Lincoln Silver Dollar, Commonwealth, Bohemian, Birman Wood Golf, The One Hundred Club of L.A. Mil: USN 1942-45. Ofc: California Fed. Svgs. & Loan, 5670 Wilshire Blvd. Los Angeles 90036

DOFFLEMYER, ROBERT TODD, farmer; b. Dec. 3, 1918, Exeter; s. Wm. Todd and Josephine Cameron (McIntosh) D.; m. Margaret Cutler, Feb. 15, 1947; children: John b. 1948, Virginia b. 1949, William b. 1953; edn: BA econs., Stanford Univ. 1941. Career: ptnrship farming with father, 1946-60, formed Dofflemyer Corp. 1960, pres. 1967–; pres. Antelope Heights Water Co.; mem. Am. Legion; civic: Venice Hill Prep. Sch. (founding bd. pres. 8 yrs.); estab. Dofflemyer Scholarship for Eagle Scouts at Stanford Univ.; mil: capt. US Army Field Arty. 1942-45, ETO, 4 battle stars, Pres. Unit Cit., Belgian Fourragere; Republican; Prot.; rec: sports. Res: 23351 Lomitas Dr Woodlake 93286 Ofc: Dofflemyer Corp. 20820 Ave 296 Exeter 93221

DOLAN, PATRICK MICHAEL, association executive; b. Nov. 29, 1938, Chgo.; s. Patrick Raymond and Pearl (Pulver) D.; children: Michael b. 1969, Kelley b. 1971; edn: BA in math./US hist., Univ. Kans. 1963, BS in edn., 1964;

grad. work Univ. Calif. 1965-66; Calif. Life Tchg. Cred. Career: tchr. Orange Unified Sch. Dist. 1965-66, Anaheim U.S.F. 1966-67; systems analyst IBM, 1967-69, field support mgr. 1969-72, system instr. , 1972-75, systems mgr. 1975-77; sr. systems cons. Coopers and Lybrand, 1978-79; asst. sr. v.p. Nat. Assn. of Realtors, 1979-80, div. v.p. 1980-84; exec. v.p. So. Alameda County Board of Realtors, 1984–; dir. Rapid Radial Transport, 1975-78; awards: NSF grantee (1966), IBM v.p.'s award (1975); mem: Nat. Educators Assn. 1965-67, Am. Soc. Assn. Execs. (mem. com. 1982-86), World Future Soc., CofC (Hayward, Fremont, Pleasanton); mil: pfc USMC 1956-57; Catholic; rec: scuba, ski, chess. Ofc: So. Alameda County Board of Realtors 2144 Mission Blvd Hayward 94541

DOLAN, PAUL RICHARD, real estate investor; b. Feb. 25, 1931, Hollywood; s. John A. and Irene May (Dunn) D.; m. Meri-Ellen, June 15, 1979; 1 dau., Lara b. 1983; edn: BS, UC Berkeley 1953, MBA 1955; Calif. lic. Real Estate Broker. Career: mfg. mgr. General Electric Co., 1955-58; cons. McKinsey & Co., 1958-61; pres. var. cos. 1962-75; investor/advisor, pres. Inter Investments, 1976–; vis. prof. CSU Los Angeles Graduate Sch. of Mgmt. 1966-68; recipient var. scholarships, sales awards and speaking honors, Young Pres. Orgn. (1963-67); clubs: English Speaking Union (London), Am. International Club (Geneva), var. civic orgns.; author annual publ: Outlook for U.S. Real Estate (1982-); mil: s/sgt. US Army 1953-55, Korea; Republican; Ch. of Scientology; rec: photog., writing. Res: 2525 Via Campesina Palos Verdes Estates 90274 Ofc: 405 Via Chico Ste 8 Palos Verdes Estates 90274

DOLBY, RAY MILTON, audio engineering co. chariman; b. Jan. 18, 1933, Portland; s. Earl Milton and Esther Eufemia d(Strand) Dolby; m. Dagmar Baumert, Aug. 19, 1966; chil: Thomas Eric, David Earl; edn: stu. San Jose State Coll. 1951-2, Wash. Univ., St. Louis 1953-4; BSEE, Stanford Univ. 1957; PhD, physics (Marshall scholar1957-60, Draper's studentship 1959-61, NSF fellow 1960-1), Pembroke Coll., Cambridge (Eng.) Unvi., 1961. Career: electronic tech., jr. engr., Ampex Corp., Redwood City 1949-53; engr., 1955-7, sr. engr. 1957; fellow Pembroke Coll.,res. on long wavelegnth X-rays, 1961-3; cons. U.K. Atomic Energy Authority, Chandigarh, Punjab, India 1963-5; owner/chmn. bd. Dolby Labs, Inc., S.F./London, 1965--; trustee University High School, S.F. 1978-84; bd. dirs. S.F. Opera; bd. govs., S.F. Sym.; mem. Marshall Sholarship Selection Com., Western Region 1979-85; honors: Beech-Thompson Award Stanford Univ. 1956; Emmy Awd., contbn. to first video recorder, 1957; Trendsetter Awd. Billboard 1971; top 200 Execs. Bicentenial awd, 1976; Lyre awd, Inst. High Fidelity, 1972; Emile Berliner Maker of the Microphone awd, 1972; Sci. and Engring. awd. Acad. Motion Picture Arts & Scis, 1979; fellow Audio Engring. Soc. (pres. 1980-81, bd. govs. 1972-72, 79-84), Silver dMedal Awd. 1971; fellow Brit. Kinemetograph, Sound, TV, Soc., fellow Soc. Motion Picture & TV Engrs., Samuel L. Warner awd. 1978; Poniatoff Gold Medal 1982, Progress Medal 1983; Hon. Fellow, Pembroke Coll., Cambridge 1983; mem: IEEE; Tau Beta Pi; St. Francis yacht Club. Patentee; inventions, research publs. in video tape rec., X-ray microanalysis, noise reduction and quality improvements in audio and video systems; mil: US Army 1953-4. Ofc: 100 Portrero Ave. San Francisco 94103

DOLD, WALTER A., lawyer; b. May 8, 1895 , San Fransisco; s. Peter and Wilhelmine C. (Weissemburg) D., m. Jeanette E. Harrison, Jan. , 24, 1923, children: Jean Ella Youngling b. 1926, Jeanette U. Bernhard b. 1927; edn: JD, Golden Gate Univ. 1919; admitted Calif. State Bar 1919. Career: attny. pvt. practice 1919--; Chief Deputy City Atty. San Francisco 1926-52; dir. Franklin Savings & Loan Assn.. 1982-86; mem: ABA, Calif. State Bar, Bohemian Club, Shrine (past potentate); mil: storekeeper 3/c USN 1918-19; Republican; rec: study of economics. Res: 200 Santa Clara Ave. San Francisco 94127 Ofc: 703 Market St. Ste. 510 San Francisco 94103

D'OLIVEIRA, JOSEPH G., certified public accountant; b. July 14, 1942, Georgetown, Guyana; m. Yolanda O., Jan. 5, 1974; edn: AA, E.Los Angeles Coll. 1972; BS,honors in acctg., Cal State Polytechnic Univ., Pomona 1973; grad. cert. in bus. fin., City Univ. L.A. 1984. Career: CPA, pvt. practitioner, 1975-81; partner firm D'Oliveira, Lim, Weber & Co., CPAs, Los Angeles 1981-85; ptnr. Fortune Builders 1982–; Hon. Consul, Repub. of Guyana, Feb.1976-; bus. mgr. Kedren Comm. Mental Hlth. Ctr, L.A. 1975-78; Olympic Attache, Los Angeles Olympics, 1984; trustee, City University of Los Angeles; advis. bd. Pacoima Youth Culture Center, Esquire Boys & Girls Club; awards: Public Svc. awd. 1983, Guyanese Community Council, USA; Orgn. of Caribbean Am. People's, Inc. Bicentennial awd. for outstanding contbns. made to the USA; appreciation cert., City of Los Angeles; Resolutions from Calif. State Senate, City & County of L.A., Calif. State Senate Rules Com.; Cert. of Recogn., Calif. State Assembly; Congl. Recogn., US Congress; Golden Arrow Achievement, People & Govt. of Guyana; mem: Nat. Assn. of Black Accts.; Soc. of Calif. Accts.; Am. Inst. of CPAs; Calif. Soc. of CPAs; Phi Kappa Phi Honor Soc. 1973-; Carriben Action Lobby (2d v.chmn.; treas. So. Calif. chpt.); The Eight Dist. Improvement Assn.(treas.); 100 Black Men of Los Angeles, Inc.; Guyana-Am. Social Club 1970- (pres. 1976-7); mil: E6 US Army 1966-69, decorated bronze star, Vietnamese Svc., Viet.Campaign, GCM; Catholic; rec: ice hockey, cricket, boxing, track & field. Res: 3916 Carnavon Wy Los Angeles 90027 Ofc: Fortune Builders 611 S Wilton Pl Los Angeles 90025

DOMAGAS, MARCELINO SORIANO, accountant, lawyer; b. June 2, 1923, Calasiao, Pangasinan, Philippines, nat. US cit. 1970; s. Fortunato Untalan and Asuncion Miranda (Soriano) D.; m. Segundina Mendoza, Aug. 20, 1945; dau.

Irma b. 1959; edn: BSC, Far Eastern Univ. 1949; LLB, San Sebastian Coll. 1957; CPA Philippines 1953, Calif. 1982; atty. Supreme Ct. Phil. 1961. Career: chief acct. National Dollar Stores Ltd 1970-73; staff acct. Hirose & Oto CPAs 1973-74; controller Copper Wheel Inc 1974-75; acct. Southside Community Center 1975-76, Concerted Services Project 1976-78, CCC Supt. of Schools 1978-80; cons. Concerted Services Project 1980–; practicing CPA 1982–; chmn. fin. & budget com., bd. dirs., field dir. Sandes Industries Inc.; prof. San Sebastian Coll & Malayan Colls. Philippines; honors: TPA Merit Award (Travelers Protective Assn. of Am. 1976), Trophy-Star Council Award (Knights of Columbus 1977-78), Presidential Trophy (United Pangasinanes of Am. Inc. 1984), Pres. Trophy (TPA 1984); mem: Phil. Inst. CPAs (nat. dir. 1982), Am. Inst. cpas, Calif. Soc. CPAS, United Pangasinanes of Am. (pres.), Knights of Columbus (grand knight), Travelers Protective Assn. of Am. (pres.), Oakland Diocese Vicarate (v.p.), Filipino Speaking Council (bd. dirs.); mil: cpl. AC 1941-45, USAFFE Asiatic-Pacific Campaign, Service Medal; Democrat; Catholic; rec: tennis, bowling, golf, skating, basketball. Address: 2350 Foothill Blvd Oakland 94601

DOMBROW, RICHARD LYLE, lawyer; b. Mar. 5, 1944, Flagstaff, Ariz.; s. Roman J. and Clementine C. (Casmire) D.; m. Eileen C., Apr. 4, 1976; children: Derian C. b. 1967, Kathleen b. 1984; edn: BS, San Jose St. Univ. 1966; JD, USC 1969; Cert. Family Law Splst. (CFLS) Calif. State Bar. Career: dep. dist. atty. Los Angeles Dist. Atty's Ofc. 1969, pvt. practice law, Orange 1971-75, senior ptnr. Dombrow and McKenna, Orange 1975-79, pvt. practice, Tustin 1979–; planning commnr. City of Tustin 1972-74; honors: Active 20-30 Internat. mem. of the Decade (1970s), Falstaff Mgmt. Achievement Awd. 1966; mem: Am., Calif., Orange County (Family Law Sect. pgm. chmn. 1984-85) bar assns.; clubs: Santa Ana Active 20-30 Club Internat. (pres. Santa Ana 1978; dist. gov. 1979-80), World Council of Young Mens Service Clubs (v.chmn. 1981), Rotary; Republican; Episcopal; rec: skiing, model building. Ofc: 335 Centennial Way Tustin 92680

DOMINGUEZ, JACK MANUEL, vocational rehabilitation consultant; b. June 16, 1937, Los Angeles; s. Manuel Jose and Josephine (Gomez) D.; m. Merlinda Espinoza, Sept. 30, 1978; 1 stepchild, Regina Eidarous b. 1971; edn: undergrad. Occidental Coll. 1957-60; BA and MA in hist., CSU Los Angeles 1964-76; grad. stu. public adminstrn. CSU Long Beach 1978-79; Calif. Adult Tchg. Cred. (1975); Cert. Insurance Rehab. Splst. (1985). Career: fundraiser Impact House (Drug Treatment Ctr.), Pasadena 1973-76; job developer (Mexican Am. Opportunity Found.) Susanville (Calif.) Prison, 1976-77; comm. alcoholism educator City of Pasadena Health Dept., 1977-78; vocational cons. Comprehensive Rehab. Services, Arcadia 1978-79, Vocational Rehab. Services, El Monte 1979-80, Fremont Indemnity Co., Los Angeles 1980-81; prof. health scis. dept. CSU Los Angeles 1980–; owner Del Rey Rehabilitation Consultants, Pasadena 1981–; bd. dirs. Impact House (1976-77); seminar lectr. on substance abuse, Nurses Edn. Soc., W. Covina (1985-), trainer Substance Abuse Counselor Pgm., Coldwater Canyon Hosp., N. Hollywood (1984-); awards: recognition for service, Impact House (1976), Cert. of Appreciation for Contribution to Cooperative Edn., CSU Los Angeles (1986); mem. Nat. Rehabilitation Assn., Nat. Assn. of Rehab. Professionals; mil: sp5 US Army 1960-63; Catholic; rec: stamps, fishing, current lit. on drug research. Ofc: Del Rey Rehabilitation Consultants 424 S Rosemead Blvd Pasadena 91107

DONG, RICHARD GENE, mechanical engineer; b. Mar. 16, 1935, Sacramento; s. Chester Q. and May (Wong) D.; m. Mae, May 19, 1968; children: Michael b. 1970, Catherine b. 1972; edn: PhD, UC Berkeley 1964. Career: senior staff engr. Lawrence Livermore National Laboratory, 1963–; consulting engr. pvt. practice; honors: Tau Beta Pi, Xi Epsilon, Pi Tau Sigma; founder Alternative Learning Program, San Ramon Sch. Dist.; 50+ profl. publs.; rec: painting, house design, camping, skiing. Res: 38 Hornet Court Danville 94526 Ofc: Lawrence Livermore National Laboratory POB 808 Livermore 94550

DONLON, WILLIAM CHRISTOPHER, surgeon; b. oct. 17, 1952, NY, NY; s. William Aloysius and Margaret Ann (O'Donovan) D.; m. Marianne Truta, May 28, 1983; edn: BA, Hofstra Univ. 1974, MA, 1975; DMD, Tufts Univ. 1979; Diplomate Am. Bd. Oral & Maxillofacial Surg. Career: electron microscopist/ animal surgeon The Salk Inst. La. Jolla 1975-76; resident, chief res. oral & maxillofacial surg. Mt. Sinai Med. Ctr. NYC 1979-82; pvt. practice oral & maxfl. surg. So. San Francisco 1983–; clin. asst. prof. O&M surg. Univ. Pacific 1982–; dir. Facial Pain Research Ctr. Univ. Pacific; chmn. oral surg. & dentistry section Peninsula Hosp. Burlingame 1986-88; honors: Geo. Bates Research Award (1st Prize 1978, 79); fellow: Am. Assn. O&M Surgeons, Internat. Assn. O&M Surg., Am. Dental Soc. of Anesthesiol., Am. Coll. O&M Surg.; mem: Am. Dental Assn., AMA, AAAS, Am. Cleft Palate Assn., Western Soc. O&M Surg., European Assn. Maxfl. Surg., No. Calif. Soc. O&M Surg. (bd. dirs. 1986-88); publs: articles in med. jours.; rec: popular music, computers. Ofc: 1135 Mission Rd Ste 101 S San Francisco 94080

DONOFRIO, ROBERT ALLEN, engineering executive; b. Oct. 8, 1941, San Francisco; s. Faust F. and Elizabeth L. (Puccetti) D.; m. Maxine, June 30, 1974; children: Daniel, Angela, Lisa, Gina, Michael; edn: BS, indsl. engring., CSU San Jose 1965; Reg. Profl. Engr., Calif. 1970. Career: indsl. engr. San Francisco Naval Shipyard, 1965-69; prodn. engr. Mare Island Naval Shipyard, 1970-74, supvr. ventilation engring. 1975-80, project engr. 1981–; university campus engineering recruiting, 1984-; honors: Equal Employment Opp. Award (Mare Island Naval Shipyard, 1985), Employee of the Year (M.I.N.S., 1985); mem. Inst. of Indsl. Engrs., San Jose State Univ. Alumni Assn., Lambda Chi Alpha Frat. Alumni Assn.; mem. Citizens Adv. Com. to Sonoma County Bd. Suprs. and Planning Dept.; coach Calif. Youth Soccer League, and Senior League Baseball; works: Proposal for wind power for prodn. of combustible gas, US Dept. of Energy Appropriate Energy Technology Small Grants Pgm. (1980); Democrat; Episcopal (bd. dirs. St. John's Episcopal Ch. 1984-); rec: photog., videotaping, cycling. Res: 1033 Goodwin Ave Penngrove 94951 Ofc: Mare Island Naval Shipyard Vallejo 94592

DONOVAN, DOLORES ANN, lawyer, educator; b. July 26, 1945, Dearborn, Mich.; d. John Daniel and Mary Dolores (Flajole) Donovan; edn: BA, Stanford Univ. 1967, JD, Stanford Law Sch. 1970. Career: staff atty. Lawyers Mil. Def. Com. in Saigon, South Vietnam (found.-funded free legal asst. to troops in Vietnam) 1970-71; staff atty./ asst. to Ramsey Clark in U.S. v. Ahmad (Harrisburg 7 case involving Fr. Philip Berrigan, others) 1971-72; mem. trial counsel team to Daniel Ellsberg in U.S. v. Russo & Ellsberg, 1972-73; ptnr. law firm Donovan & Ryan, San Francisco 1973-75; prof. of law (crim. law, crim. procedure, crim. practice, comparative law, family law) Univ. San Francisco Sch. of Law 1975–; cons. La Casa de las Madres (shelter for battered women) 1975-7; honors: vis. scholar Harvard Law Sch. (1981), Phi Beta Kappa (1967); mem. Calif. State Bar Assn. (com. on legal svcs. to the poor 1977-78, com. on human rights 1979-81, com. on jury instrns. 1979-80), D.C. Bar Assn., S.F. Bar Assn. (subcom. on battered women 1977-78), Calif. Women Lawyers, Soc. Am. Law Tchrs. (bd. dirs.), Assn. Am. Law Schs. (chair Sect. on Women in Legal Edn., Crim. Justice Sect.); contbr. articles in law revs.; rec: hiking, equestiran. Res: 69 Elsie St San Francisco 94110 Ofc: University of San Francisco School of Law 2130 Fulton Ave San Francisco 94117

DOODY, THOMAS EDWARD, psychiatrist; b. Jan. 8, 1921, San Francisco; s. Maurice C. and Pauline (Kenyon) D.; m. Martha Hooley, July 9, 1949; children: Jo Elizabeth b. 1950, Michael b. 1954; edn: AB, Stanford Univ. 1943; MD, Geo. Washington Univ. 1948; Diplomate Am. Board of Psychiatry & Neurology. Career: res. asst. Microbiol., Stanford Sch. of Medicine 1943-44; staff, adminstrv. psychiatrist, and chief of Aftercare Facility, Calif. State Hosp. Stockton 1949-51, 53-60, initiated (with assistance of psychologist Ned Dutton, PhD) innovative therapeutic community program for chronic schizophrenics; also initiated patient governing pgm. for alcoholics; staff psychiatrist State Mental Hygiene Clinic, Sacto. 1960-61; pvt. practice in Sacto., 1961–, psychiatric units in Sutter Meml. and American River Hosps.; tchg. first-year psychiatric residents Stockton State Hosp. 1964-65; elected mem. Am. Acad. Clin. Psychiatrists 1985; mem: Am. Psychiatric Assn. (nat. del. 1968-9), Calif. Med. Assn., Stanford Hist. Soc. (charter); mil: lt. jg. Med. Corps USN 1951-53; Republican; Episcopal; rec: running, jogging. Res: 8819 Bluff Ln Fair Oaks 95628 Ofc: 2417 Capitol Ave Sacramento 95816

DOOLITTLE, LESLIE ARNOLD, wholesale distributor, ret.; b. Jan. 12, 1916, Devon, Mont.; s. Ivan Homer and Eva Estelle (Morse) D.; m. Emma Louise Cate, June 8, 1936; children: Peggy b. 1936, Rosalie b. 1937, Carole b. 1942, Diana b. 1949; edn: grad. high sch. 1933. Career: started distbg. bus. in 1934-, sole prop./mgr. until 1975, sold bus. to Glaser Bros., asst. mgr. Glaser Bros. 1975-81, ret.; mem. Masons, Eastern Star; Ind. Republican; Methodist; rec: travel. Address: Clovis 93612

DOORNBOS, DANIEL LEE, writer, editor; b. Sept. 20, 1956, Los Angeles; s. Myron Wm. and Rama Jeanette (Mace) D.; m. Kathleen Reeder, Nov. 17, 1984; edn: AA, Fullerton Coll. 1984; BS, Univ. Phoenix 1986. Career: mssy. Ch. of Jesus Christ L.D.S. Caracas, Ven. 1980-82; investor rep. Phares Mktg. Inc. Reno 1982; field engr. Gousha/ Chek-Chart San Jose 1982–; honors: Alpha Gamma Sigma (Fullerton Coll.); mem: Soc. Automotive Engrs. 1983, Am. Soc. Agricl. engrs. 1983, Masons, Scottish Rite; publ: tech. editor Tractor Digest 1983-; mil: sgt. US Army 1976-80, Good Conduct, Army Commdn.; Republican, Ch. of Jesus Christ of L.D.S.; rec: personal finance. Res: POB 26034 San Jose 95159 Ofc: Gousha/ Chek-Chart POB 6227 San Jose 95150

DORFFELD, JOSEPH CHARLES, restaurant executive; b. Aug. 10, 1955, Corpus Christi, Tx.; s. Charles Eugene and Doris Sue (Standley) D.; m. Jerilyn Downer, Jan. 1, 1986; edn: BS psych., Ariz. State Univ. 1977. Career: mgr. Jeremiah's Restaurants, Inc., Santa Barbara 1976-82; TGI Friday's, Inc., Dallas, Tx. 1982-85; Playboy Clubs, Internat., Chgo. 1985–; awards: Gold medal "Best Appetizers" TGI Fridays, Desert Sun newspaper, Palm Desert, Calif. (1984); Paul Wallach "Best Restaurants" list, Playboy Club (1985); mem. Nat. Rest. Assn.; Catholic. Res: 209 Spencer Dr Las Vegas, NV 89101 Ofc: Tramps Restaurant 4405 W Flamingo Ave Las Vegas, NV 89103

DORIS, DON WESLEY, publishing executive; b. Aug. 6, 1929, Tulare; s. Robert Charles and Margaret Vivian (McKim) D.; m. Dorothy Gates, Dec. 18, 1950; children: Dianne b. 1951, Dan b. 1953, David b. 1955; edn: BS, CSU Fresno 1950. Career: ranch mgr. Sierra View Herefords, Clovis 1950-57; field ed. Western Livestock Journal (Crow Publs.), Los Angeles 1957-61; pub. Stockman's Weekly, Clovis 1961-66; western rep. Am. Polled Hereford Assn., Kansas City, Mo. 1972–; Calif. and Nev. field ed. Western Livestock Journal (subs. Crow Publs.), Denver, Colo. 1983–, dir. livestock advtg. 1983-, v.p. Crow Publs., 1985-; dir. Agri-Services Found. 1961-65; honored for outstanding contbn. to beef industry by Am. Polled Hereford Assn. and Calif.-Nev. Polled Hereford Assn. (1983); devel. and estab. the first Range-Ready bull sales in the beef industry in US (1965-66); founder Clovis Western Improvement Assn. (1968); Republican; Prot.; rec: boating. Res: 2706 W Ashlan No. 32 Fresno 93705 Ofc: Crow Publications 4701 Marion St Denver Colo 80216

DORNEMAN, ROBERT WAYNE, manufacturing engineer; b. Nov. 13, 1949, Oaklawn, Ill.; s. Robert John and Julia (Vorchenia) D.; m. Katrina Holland, July 30, 1977; 1 dau., Tamara b. 1984; edn: BA in biol. sci., CSU Fullerton

1974; profl. certs., Universal Instruments (1976); Calif. lic. real estate broker (1978). Career: mfg. engr. Gen. Telephone, Anaheim 1974-77; Xerox/Century Data, Anaheim 1977-80; advanced mfg. engr. MSI Data, Costa Mesa 1980-83; sr. mfg. engr. Parker Hanifin, Irvine 1983-86; sr. advanced mfg. engr. Western Digital, 1986–; splst., early pioneer in automated assembly of circuits utilizing high density components and packaging; cons. Base Two, Fullerton (1980); mem. Nat., Calif. Assn. Realtors, North Orange County Bd. of Realtors, Internat. Soc. for Hybrid Microelectronics, Tau Kappa Epsilon frat., Phillips Ranch Assn./ Pomona; rec: auto restoration, landscape arch., billiards. Res: 56 Meadow View Dr Phillips Ranch Pomona 91766 Ofc: Western Digital 2445 McCabe Way Irvine 92714

DORROH, PAUL ELTON, insurance co. executive; b. Apr. 11, 1943, Angels Camp, Calif.; s. Elton W. and Helen (Davis) D.; m. Vida Firouzbakht, May 29, 1968; 1 dau. Atissa b. 1975; edn: BA, UC Berkeley 1965, JD, Boalt Hall 1973; admitted Calif. State Bar 1973. Career: US Peace Corps 1965-67; US Fgn. Svc. Ankara, Turkey 1968-70; atty. Pillsbury, Madison & Sutro S.F. 1973-80; chmn., CEO Glenn, Nyhan & Assocs. S.F. 1980–; chmn. Empire Casualty Co.; pres. Am. Healthcare Holdings 1985–; honors: Order of the Coif 1973. Ofc: Glenn, Nyhan & Assocs. San Francisco 94105

DORSEY, JAMES ROBERT, surveyor, land & boundary consultant; b. Dec. 10, 1936, Los Angeles; s. Alvin Afton and Lucile Naomi (Widbin) D.; m. Elsie Jaramillo, Feb. 2, 1957; children: James Edward b. 1958, Thomas Eugene b. 1962; edn: L.A. City Coll. 1955-56, East L.A. Coll. 1958, UCLA 1960-61, 74, Am. River Coll. 1968-69, Moorpark Coll. 1972-74. Expt. Witness; Lic. Land Surveyor, Calif., Ariz. Career: title engr. Title Ins. & Trust Co., Los Angeles 1955-61; title ofcr./right of way engr. Cal-Trans. Dist. VII, L.A. 1961-63; title unit supr. State Dept. Water Resources, So. Dist., L.A. 1963-67; chief title ofcr. Calif. State Lands Commn., Sacto. 1967-71; asst. v.p. Safeco Title Ins. Co., Home Office, L.A. (organized Title Research Dept., in chg. of boundary underw., spl. cons. to Calif. Land Title Assocs. on wetland boundaries, held seminars on Legal Descriptions and Boundary Problems) 1971-77; prin. James Dorsey & Assocs. Land & Boundary Cons., Simi Valley 1977–; apptd. by Gov. Deukmejian to Calif. State Bd. Registration for Profl. Engrs. and Land Surveyors (1984-); mem: Internat. Right of Way Assn., Am. Cong. on Surveying & Mapping, Calif. Land Surveyors Assn. (past state pres.; founding pres. and chpt. rep. L.A.-Ventura chpt.; rep. CLSA vs. Ventura Co. Surveyor to reduce map checking prices from $850 to $100), Rotary; publs: Insuring Wetlands; num. papers on boundary matters; coauthor A Study on Swamp & Overflowed Lands in Calif. (Safeco Title Ins. Co. 1976); Republican; Lutheran; rec: sports, fishing, telling stories. Res: 6490 #-5 Twin Circle Ln Simi Valley 93063 Ofc: James Dorsey & Assocs. 4505 E Industrial St Ste 2L Simi Valley 93063

DOTY, JACK EVERETT, real estate investor, developer; b. Nov. 12, 1941, Oakland; s. Abraham Richard and Frances Edith (Bishop) D.; m. Nancy McCann, May 27,1984; children: Elizabeth Ann b. 1963, John Joseph b. 1964; edn: UC Berkeley 1959-62. Career: subofc. mgr. IBM Office Prods. Div. 1965-69; dir. real estate mgmt. Hanford Freund & Co. 1969-71; CEO Best Schumann & Doty Co. 1971-75; CEO J.E. Doty & Assoc. 1975-79; CEO, sole owner Metro Pacific Corp., San Francisco 1979–; donate exec. San Francisco Strategic Plan Housing Task Force 1981-83; chmn. San Francisco CofC Housing Com. 1979-82; San Francisco Mayor's Fiscal Adv. Com. 1969 and Indsl. Devel. Com. 1967; founder, pres. Comm. Assn. Mgmt. Inst. 1976-79; nat. spkrc. Comm. Assn. Inst. 1976-79; mem: San Francisco CofC, Soc. of Calif. Pioneers, Calif. Hist. Soc., Found. for San Francisco Archtl. Heritage, San Francisco Plnng. & Urban Renewal; Republican; Congregational (trustee). Res: 900 Bush St. San Francisco 94115 Ofc: Metro Pacific Corp., 980 Bush St. San Francisco 94109

DOTZLER, FREDERICK JOSEPH, venture capitalist; b. Oct. 31, 1945, Harlan, Iowa; s. Aloysius Joseph and Cecelia Rose (Gau) D.; m. Cassandra, Nov. 17, 1972; children: Whittney b. 1980, Cecelia b. 1982; edn: BS indsl. engring. Iowa St. Univ. 1967; M.Econs., honors, Univ. of Louvain, Belgium 1971; MBA, Univ. Chgo. 1972; spl. courses, Northwestern Univ., Roosevelt Univ. Career: computer salesman IBM, Des Moines 1967-69; acquisitions & mfg. Searle, Skokie, Ill. 1972-76, dir. mktg. 1976-79; dir. mktg. Millipore, Bedford, Mass. 1979-81; v.p. mktg. Merrimack Labs., Hudson, Mass. 1981-83; gen. ptnr. Crosspoint Venture Partners, Mountain View, Calif. 1983–; Dir: Vitaphore Corp. (1985-), BankPro Systems Inc. (1985-), Estabrooks Digital Graphics Corp. (1984-), Crosspoint Biomedical Ventures (1985-), Microfield Graphics, Inc. (1986-), NeuroCare, Inc. (1986-), founder Innovex Press (1982); honors: Chi Epsilon (1965), Tau Beta Pi (1966), Gamma Epsilon Sigma (1966), Knights of St. Patrick (1966), Cardinal Key Merit Award (1967), scholarships: Iowa State (1963-67), Univ. Chgo. (1969), Univ. Louvain (1971); mem. Western Assn. of Venture Capital, Pharmaceutical Advt. Club (1976-79); author/pub. The Marketing Idea Generator (1982), coauthor book chpt. in Guide to Venture Capital Sources (1984), contbg. writer San Jose Business Jour. (1985-); mil: pfc Army Reserves 1969-75; Republican; Catholic; rec: travel, family, writing. Res: 19686 Via Grande Saratoga 95070 Ofc: Crosspoint 1951 Landings Dr Mountain View 94043

DOUBLEDEE, DEANNA GAIL, engineer; b. July 29, 1958, Akron, Ohio; d. John Wesley and Elizabeth Catherine (Nellis) D.; m. Philip H. Simons, Jan. 1, 1986; edn: BS, Ohio State Univ. 1981. Career: engr. ocean sys. div. Gould Inc., Cleveland, Ohio 1981-82; engr. II aircraft div. Northrop corp., Hawthorne 1982-83; tech. staff TRW Inc. Defense Sys. Group, Redondo Beach 1983-85, work package mgr 1985-86, project staff engr. 1986–; math/ sci. tutor System Devel. Div., TRW Inc.; honors: Outstanding Performer for the Software Sys. Lab., TRW Inc. Defense Sys. Gp. 1985; mem: IEEE (Computer Soc.), Am. Assn. of Ind. Investors, World Tae Kwon Do Fedn., Ohio State Univ. Alumnae Assn., Ohio State Univ. Alumnae Scholarship House Assn.; Democrat; Catholic; rec: travel, water skiing, photog. Ofc: TRW Inc., One Space Park Redondo Beach 90278

DOUGHERTY, HOWARD WILLIAM, oil and gas producer; b. Jan. 5, 1915, Kansas City, Mo.; s. Frank C. and Elsie (Braecklein) D.; m. Aug. 3, 1940; children: William, Robert, Patrick, Michael, Mary, Peter; m. 2d. Violeta van Ronzelen, Sept. 15, 1984; edn: BS, Stanford Univ. 1938. Career: oil and gas producer, Pasadena 1947–; dir. Santa Anita Consol. Inc.; pres. Pioneer Kettleman Co., Book Cliffs Oil & Gas Co.; pres. Trend Oil Co.; pres. Bret Harte Realty Co.; dir. and v.p. Hollywood Turf Club 1954-80, ret.; mem: Conservation Com. Calif., Neuro Sics. Inst. (trustee), Ind. Petroleum Assn. of Am., API, IPAA, Am. Inst. Mech. Engrs. (past), Beta Theta Pi, Los Angeles Country Club, Calif. Club, Bohemian, Birnan Wood Golf Club, Valley Hunt Club, San Gabriel Valley Boy Scouts, Los Angeles Boy Scouts, Pres.'s Circle of Los Angeles Co. Mus., Founders of Los Angeles Music Ctr., So. Calif. Tennis Assn. (dir.), Youth Tennis Found. of So. Calif. (pres.), Loyola Marymount Univ. (former regent), St. Mary's Coll. (past bd. trustees), Villanova and Woodside Priory (past bd. trustees). Res: 379 W. Bellevue Dr. Pasadena 91105 Ofc: 77 No. Oak Knoll Ave. Ste. 103 Pasadena 91101

DOUGLAS, JOE ROSS, athletic coach-manager; b. Nov. 10, 1936, Clarksburg, West Va.; s. James and Mittie Eunice (Robertson) D.; edn: BS in math. and phys. ed., Texas Christian Univ. 1959; MS, Ore. State Univ. 1968. Career: coach Sterling High Sch., Sterling City (sch. won league track title by 100 pts.), Tx. 1960; coach track and cross country Westchester H.S., Los Angeles 1968-76; coach Santa Monica City Coll. 2 yrs.; founder/pres./coach Santa Monica Track Club, Santa Monica 1972–, coaching world class athletes (coach and/or mgr. to 9 Olympians: Carl Lewis, Kirk Baptiste, Johnny Gray, Carol Lewis, Mark Handelsman, Bill McChesney, Mike Durkin, Mark Enyeart and Ed Mendoza); pres. Athletics Internat. Inc., mmgr. and agent for athletes, cons. with meet dirs. worldwide 1975–; personal mgr. of Carl and Carol Lewis; chmn. So. Calif. Assn. of the Athletics Cong. (SCA-TAC), 1980-; num. press and t.v. interviews concerning coaching techniques, athletes tng.; instr. Santa Monica City Coll.; awards: Voted outstanding middle-distance coach in So. Calif. (1981, 82) and Coach of the Year (1985), SCA-TAC; competed for TCU 1956-59, participant in two and four mile relays at the Drake relays (1958); competed for Los Angeles Track Club 1961-64; set an American age group 35-year old record of 12.2 in the 100 meters in Santa Monica (8/12/72); civic: L.A. Co. Mus. of Art (patron); Republican; rec: listening to music, playing trumpet, art, backpacking. Ofc: Athletics International Inc. 1801 Ocean Park Blvd Ste 112 Santa Monica 90405

DOUGLAS-YOUNG, JOHN DERRICK, author; b. June 29, 1913, Richmond, Surrey, U.K., nat. US cit. 1961; s. George Frederick and Mabel (Davies) D.-Y.; m. Leatrice Pierce, Apr. 10, 1965; edn: MA, Christ's Coll., Cambridge 1935. Career: pilot/squadron leader Royal Air Force 1935-54, exptl. work on radar and Loran, (mentioned in Dispatches); technical writer Rockwell Internat. (participant in Minuteman II & III, Apollo, F-111 pgms.), 1961-78; self-empl. author, 1978–, books (all Prentice-Hall): Complete Guide to Reading Schematic Diagrams (3d ed. 1986), Complete Guide to Electronic Test Equip. and Troubleshooting Techniques, Practical Oscilloscope Handbook, Technician's Guide to Microelectronics, Illus. Ency. Dictionary of Electronics (2d ed. 1986), Microelectronics: A Standard Manual and Guide, Illus. Ency. Dictionary of Electronic Circuits, Discovering Electronics; senior mem. Soc. for Technical Communication (1965); Republican; Episcopal; rec: amateur rancher. Res: 32912 Ascot Way Sun City 92381

DOWBAK, GREGORY MAX, plastic surgeon; b. Nov. 26, 1947, Bklyn.; s. Max and Alexandra (Homza) D.; edn: undergrad. Ind. Univ. 1965-68; MD, State Univ. NY Downstate 1972, Diplomate Am. Bd. Plastic Surg. 1985. Career: solo practice, 1981–, in plastic and reconstrv. surgery, cosmetic surgery of breast, hand, burn and maxillo-facial surgery; pres. Gregory Dowbak, MD, Inc.; honors: cert. of distinctive service as Vascular Research Fellow (1977), AMA Physicians Recogn. Award (1983); mem. Central Calif. Plastic Surgery Soc. (v.p. 1983-85), Merced Track Club 1982-; contbr. article, Orthopaedic Review (7/83); Orthodox Ch. of Am.; rec: marathon runner (best time: 3 hrs, 14 min., 1985 SF Marathon). Res: 22 San Ramon Irvine 92715 Ofc: Gregory Dowbak MD Inc. Newport Beach

DOWNES, JOHN R., business consultant, writer; b. Nov. 6, 1938, London, Eng.; nat. US cit. 1952; s. John R. and Edna Jane (Palmer) D.; m. Susan, Aug. 25, 1961; children: Geoffrey b. 1962, Jennifer b. 1963, Scott b. 1966, Jill b. 1969, Joshua b. 1975; edn: Whitworth Coll., Spokane 1956-57, CSU Long Beach 1960-61. Career: pres. Downes Scollard & Oliver Advtg., Washington State 1967-70; pres. Dover American Corp., Spokane 1970-73; pres. National Syndications, Inc. 1973-78; pres. Lease One Corp., 1978-83; ptnr. Performance Concepts, San Luis Obispo, Calif. 1983–; cons. Manufacturers Hanover Bank, N.Y. 1981-, First Penna. Bank, Phila. 1980-82; conducts workshops, seminars, and sales tng. confs. for business & industry; producer/creator motivation pgms. and sales tng. pgms.; devel. NonConfrontation Selling sales philosophy and techniques that reduce confrontation between seller and buyer; author: How to be Irresistible Through the Power of Persuasion (1982); Non-Confrontation Selling (1984); Lease One Showroom Leasing (1980); Republican; Protestant; rec: chess, piano, golf, public speaking. Res: 3358 Barranca Ct San Luis Obispo 93401 Ofc: Performance Concepts PO Box 5160 San Luis Obispo 93403

DOYLE, GERALD WAYNE, private investigator; b. Dec. 11, 1935, Bristow, Okla.; s. Homer Phines and Glinnie May (Winnette) D.; m. Theresa, Dec. 17, 1937; children: Gregory b. 1957, Jeffrey b. 1959; edn: AA, Riverside City Coll. 1964; BVE, CSU Long Beach 1972; MPA, Univ. So. Calif. 1974; police executive;, Calif. Commn. on Peace Ofcr. Tng. and Stds. 1977. Career: dep. sheriff, lt. (comdr. Riverside Sheriff's Acad. 5 yrs., investigative lt. 4 yrs, Riverside team comdr.) Riverside County Sherriff Dept., 1960-75; chief of police City of Chino, 5 yrs.; pvt. investigator prin., currently; instr. Riverside City Coll. (1964-74), Mt. San Jacinto Comm. Coll. (1974-76), Chaffey Coll. (1976-78), Univ. of Calif. (1978-79); named Officer of the Year, Riverside County (1964), Man of the Year for Chino Valley (1980); mem: Riverside Sheriff's Assn. (pres. 1968-70), Calif. Combat Shooters Assn. (pres.), Calif. Peace Ofcr's Assn. (chmn. Crime Prev. Com. 1976-80); civic: Perris Valley Lions Club (v.p.), Mt. San Jacinto Coll. Found. (bd. dirs., area v.p.), Perris City Personnel Review Bd.; publs: contbr. to brochure on Crime victims rights as mem. of Gov's Crime Prev. Task Force (1978-80), 5 articles in Internat. Police Chiefs Assn. mag. (1976-80); mil: USAF 1954-60, Okla. Nat. Guard 1949-50; Republican; Prot.; rec: golf, biking. Res: 23330 Carlita Circle Perris 92370

DOYLE, MICHAEL CARROLL, manufacturing company executive, lawyer; b. Nov. 29, 1942, Miami, Fla.; s. Carroll and Gwendolyn (Breitenstein) D.; m. Kathelyn, June 3, 1963; children: M. Britt b. 1965; William b. 1967; edn: BBA, Univ. of Cincinnati 1964; JD, Chase Coll. of Law 1969; admitted State Bars of Ohio (1969), Georgia (1969), Wisconsin (1971), and Calif. (1975); CPA Ohio 1966. Career: CPA Alexander Grant & Co. Cincinnati 1964-69, Atlanta 1969-70, mng. ptnr. Milwaukee 1970-73, house counsel and nat. dir. Chgo. 1973-74, reg. ptnr. Los Angeles; ptnr. atty. Stone & Doyle Pasadena 1978—; chmn. and chief finl. ofcr. Econolite Control Prods. Inc. Anaheim 1978-, Calif. Chassis Inc. 1982—; mem: Am., Calif. bar assns.; Calif. Soc. of CPAs; Am. Inst. of CPAs; clubs: Jonathan, Annandale Golf, Flintridge Riding, Flint Cyn. Tennis; trustee: Episcopal Theol. Sch. Claremont, Flintridge Prep. Sch., Homemakers of Pasadena; Republican; Episcopal; rec: tennis. Res: 1055 Lagunita Rd Pasadena 91105 Ofc: Stone & Doyle 77 N Oak Knoll Ave, Ste. 114, Pasadena 91101

DOYLE, ROBERT ALAN, psychiatrist; b. June 12, 1935, Chgo.; s. Robert Morrison and Carmen Clara (Dorweiler) D.; m. Cary Tilton, May 10, 1969; children: Anne de Peyster Cary b. 1970, Brude Dickinson Stoever b. 1968, Henry von Hoff Stoever b. 1966; edn: BS, Mich. State Univ. 1957; MD, Yale Univ. 1961; MD, Duke Univ. Med. Sch. 1963; psychiatrist Am. Assn. Psychiatry 1969. Career: psychiatric residency Duke Hosp., Durham, N.C. 1963-69; staff psych. Broward Gen. Hosp. Ft. Lauderdale 1969-84; chief of staff Coral Ridge Psych. Hosp. 1969-84; assoc. med. dir. Brightside ACT Carmel 1984—; staff psych. Comm. Hosp. Monterey Peninsula 1984—; mem: Am. Psych. Assn., AMA, Carmel Valley Garden Club, Royal Horticultural Soc., Am. Hortl. Soc., Asain Art Soc.; mil; capt. USAF 1966-68; Republican; Episcopal; rec: gardening, Chinese Armorial Porcelain collector. Ofc: 3855 Via Nona Marie, Ste 109, Carmel 93922

DRABEC, TERESE A., government lawyer; b. Aug. 13, 1953, Alameda, Calif.; d. Charles and Emma (Jaegel) D.; edn: BA honors, UC Santa Barbara 1976; JD, Univ. Santa Clara Law Sch. 1982; admitted Calif. State Bar 1982; lic. river guide Calif., Idaho, Ariz. Career: river guide for ECHO, The Wilderness Co., Ariz. Raft Adventures incl. Grand Canyon Nat. Park, whitewater instr. for several river outfits and schools incl. UC extn. 1973—; park ranger Crater Lake Nat. Park 1976-77; camp dir. Youth Conservation Corps Whiskeytown Nat. Recreation Area 1978; dept. chmn. girls p.e. dept., varsity volleyball coach Head-Royce Sch. Oakland 1977-79; guide Outward Bound river expedition Rio Apurimac Peru 1980; area mgr., acting personnel dir. ECHO 1980; research asst. Prof. Sheridan Downey 1980; law clerk for chief asst. US Atty. Sanford Svetcov San Francisco 1981; research asst. 1982; law clerk Calif. Atty. Gen. Ofc. S.F. 1981-83; deputy dist. atty. Almeda County 1983—; honors: Dean's List (Univ. Santa Clara 1979-80), Emery Law School (1980-82); mem: Calif. State Bar, Calif. Dist. Attys. Assn., Student Bar Assn. (Univ. Santa Clara, v.p. 1981); rec: reading, hiking, swimming, tennis, photog., kayaking. Res: 6400 Heather Ridge Way Oakland 94611

DRAEGER, JAMES MATTHEW, lawyer; b. Sept. 21, 1953, San Francisco; s. Francis J. and Mary A. (Diepenbrock); m. Tavvia Lynn Rossiter, Feb. 28, 1981; 1 son, Tyler b. 1983; edn: BA, Univ. of Portland 1975; JD, San Francisco Law Sch. 1980; admitted Calif. State Bar 1980. Career: law clerk to City Atty. of Menlo Park, 1980-81; atty. sole prop. Menlo Park 1981-84, assoc. Chernick & Draeger, 1984—; corp. counsel and asst. sect., Draeger's Supkts., Inc.; mem. Calif., San Mateo County bar assns.; secty. Woodside Priory Sch.; alumni orgns.; Republican; Roman Catholic; rec: ski, backpack, photog. Ofc: 770 Menlo Ave, Ste 101, Menlo Park 94025

DRAKE, E. MAYLON, college president; b. Feb. 8, 1920, Nampa, Ida.; s. Austin Henry and Daisy Norma (Smith) D.; m. Lois Noble, Oct. 12, 1940; children: E. Christopher b. 1946, Cameron Lee b. 1952; edn: AA, Pasadena City Coll. 1939; BS, Univ. So. Calif. 1951, MS, 1954, EdD, 1963. Career: supt. Duarte Unified Schs. 1954-64; supt. Alhambra City Schs. 1964-70; chief deputy supt. L.A. County Schs. 1970-78; prof. ednl. adminstrn. USC 1964—; pres. Los Angeles Coll. of Chiropractic Whittier 1980—; chmn. Mgmt. & Evaluation Commn. of Calif. Dept. of Edn.; pres. Task Force for Integrated Edn.; honors: Am. Educators Medal (Freedom Found. of Valley Forge 1965), Educator of the Yr. (L.A. County Chiro. Soc. 1982); mem: Calif. Chiro. Assn., Am. Assn. Sch. Adminstrs., Calif. Assn. Ednl. Auditors (pres. 1975), Duarte Rotary (pres.

1960), Educare USC (pres. 1967), Whittier CofC, PTA (hon. life); author: No Two Alike (1960), What's Right About Education (1963), Education of the Leukemia Child (1957), The Educational Program Audit (1973); Republican; Protestant; rec: travel, fine arts, literature. Res: 517 Norumbega Rd Monrovia 91016 Ofc: L.A. Coll. of Chiro. 16200 E Amber Valley Dr Whittier 90604

DRAKE, WILLIAM ARTHUR, audio visual productions officer; b. Oct. 2, 1924, Columbus, Ohio; s. William Arthur and Helen Marie (Wheatley) D.; m. Allison, Aug. 27, 1949; children: William Arthur b. 1960, Constance Allison b. 1955; edn: BFA, MFA Ohio Univ. 1949; Reg. Biol. Photog.,Biol. Photog. Assn. 1981; Certified Profl. Photog., Profl. Photogs. of Am. 1984. Career: assoc. prof. photog. & cinema Ohio State Univ. 1949-68; film prodn. mgr. audio visual div. A.B. Dick Co. Chgo. 1968-71; v.p. Modern Audio Techniques Long Beach 1971-72; real estate, securities, ins. sales 1972-74; audio visual prodn. ofcr. Southwest Regl. Med. Edn. Ctr. VA Med. Ctr. Long Beach 1977—; audio visual cons. Interdepartmental Com. for Nutrition in National Defense NIH and DoD; honors: 4 CINE Awards, 20 nat., internat. film festival awards; assoc. Inst. Med. & Biol. Illustration, London, Eng. 1984; mem: Internat. TV Assn., Univ. Film & Video Assn. (conf. v.p 1962-68), Nat. Acad. TV Arts & Scis. (life, chpt. pres.), Profl. Photogs. Orange County (dir. 1986), Biol. Photog. Assn. (chpt. dir. 1982-84), vice chmn. 1984-86, chmn. 1986), Huntington Beach Allied Arts Bd, Elks, Optimists; works: 300+ educational motion pictures, photog. exhibitions; mil: col. US Army, staff splst Selective Service System 1942-80, Meritorious Svc., Exceptional Svc. (Sel. Svc.); Republican; United Ch. of Religious Sci.; rec: photog., travel, reading. Res: 17422 Coronado Lane Huntington Beach 92647 Ofc: VA Med. Ctr. 5901 E 7th St Long Beach 90822

DRAPER, GILBERT LAWRENCE, retail co. president; b. Mar. 8, 1929, N.Y., N.Y.; s. William and Minna (Bangel) D.; children: Anne b. 1955, Ruth b. 1958, Dean b. 1968; edn: BBA, City Coll. New York 1951. Career: exec. tng. Alexanders Dept. Store, Bronx, N.Y. 1951-52; buyer Abraham & Strauss Dept. Store, Bklyn. 1952-55; salesman, La Mode Buttons, B.Blumenthal & Co., Inc., N.Y. 1956-66; owner/pres. Drapers Music Center, Inc. Palo Alto 1967—; mem. Sierra Club (chmn. Camera Sect. 1981-84); rec: photog., tennis, golf. Res: 9 Orchard Hill Rd Woodside 94062 Ofc: Drapers Music Center 330 California Ave Palo Alto 94306

DRAPER, TIMOTHY COOK, venture capitalist; b. June 11, 1958, Highland Park, Ill.; s. Wm. Henry and Phyllis (Culbertson) D.; m. Melissa Parker, Aug. 14, 1982; 1 dau. Jessica b. 1984; edn: grad. Phillips Acad., Andover 1976; BSEE, Stanford Univ. 1980; MBA, Harvard Bus. Sch. 1984. Career: pres. Draper-Roizen Productions, Stanford 1980-82; sales devel. engr. Hewlett-Packard Co., Cupertino 1980-82; advisor to co. pres. Apollo Computer, Chelmsford, Mass. 1983; corporate fin. assoc. Alex Brown & Sons, Inc. San Francisco 1984-85; chief exec. Draper Assocs./California Partners, Menlo Park 1985—; dir. Unity Systems, PSI Star, Home Security Centers, Data Technology Corp.; clubs: Churchill Club of Santa Clara Co. (dir. 1985-86), Bay (S.F.), Decathlon (Santa Clara); creator of Stanford: The Game (1980); Republican; Presbyterian; rec: game design, computer software, tennis. Ofc: Draper Assocs./ California Partners 3000 Sand Hill Rd Ste 4-210 Menlo Park 94025

DRAPER, WILLIAM EARL, accountant; b. June 10, 1905, Sylvia, Kans.; s. Marion Alfred and Reca Ann (Stuart) D.; m. Marydell, Sept. 6, 1928; children: Dorothy Jean b. 1929, Robert Earl b. 1930, Coralea Ann b. 1938, Eloise Marydell b. 1945; edn: BA, Univ. Kans. 1924; Calif. lic. Public Acct. (1946), Real Estate Broker (1945); minister, So. Calif. Dist. Assemblies of God (1936). Career: bookkeeper Kansas Reserve State Bank, Topeka 1918-20, Merchants Nat. Bank, Lawrence, Kans. 1920-23, Bank of Italy, Fresno, Calif. 1924-25; office hd. posting dept. Foster-Kleiser Outdoor Advtg. Co., Fresno 1925-35; pastor Assembly of God Ch., Clovis 1935-39; owner Draper Home Appliance Co., Fresno 1936-38; dept. mgr. Zellerbach Paper Co., Fresno 1939-44; real estate broker prin., Fresno 1945-82, public acct. 1945-83; mem: Calif. State Board of Realtors, Fresno Bd. of Realtors, Soc. of Calif. Accts., Fresno Chpt.; active lic. Christian worker, So. Calif. Dist. Council Assemblies of God (Light for the Lost Council), Full Gospel Business Men's Fellowship Internat. (founding dir.; first secty-treas.; current treas./v.p.; first exec. v.p.; first pres. Fresno Chpt., current dir.); Christ Ambassadors youth group (v.p. 1929-30; dist. dir. No. San Joaquin Valley chpt. 1930-40); Full Gospel Tabernacle Assem. of God, Fresno (youth leader, Sun. Sch. tchr., deacon, treas., elder 1926-83); rec: golf, tennis. Address: 749 East Portals Fresno 93710

DRATWA, ROBERT EDWARD, graphic arts sales and marketing executive; b. Jan. 19, 1942, Chgo.; s. Bruno Edward and Florence Marie (DeFrank) D.; m. Jean Marie Smith, Oct. 5, 1977; edn: BS mktg., Indiana Univ. 1965; MBA mktg., Western Mich. Univ. 1966; profl. cons. 1986. Career: mktg. dir. R.H. Donneley Corp. Chgo. 1967-73, Berkley Tech. Corp. Chgo. 1973-76; mktg. cons. Chgo. 1976-80; sales mgr. D.S. America Santa Ana, Calif. 1980-84; comml. prods. mgr. Chemco PhotoProducts Co. Inc. Huntington Beach 1984-85; dir. sales & mktg. DIC America Inc., Electronic Prepress Div. 1986—; spkr. Lasers in Graphics Conf.; election judge; reserve sheriff deputy; mem: Tech. Assn. Graphic Arts (com. chmn.), Lithographers Club (secty.), Am. Assn. Profl. Cons.; publ: Automated Image Assembly: Panacea or Puffery (article 1985); mil: sgt. Air Nat. Guard 1967-73, marksman & leadership awards; Lutheran; rec: golf, target shooting, classic auto collecting. Res: 7 Rossano Ln Irvine 92720 Ofc: DIC America Inc. 119 E Star of India Ln Carson 90746

DRAZY, FLOVIA, artist, educator; b. July 30, Chgo.; d. Cephas and Jessie (Boehtler) Huet; m. Richard Douglas, Dec. 7, 1941; edn: Loyola Univ. 1937-41, Northwestern Univ. 1940-41; stu. painting Brera Inst. (Milano, Italy at age 6), Acad. of Krakow, Warsaw Sch. of Fine Art, Imperial Sch. of Fine Art (Tokyo), Ecole des Beaux Arts (Paris), Matisse Paris (Nice), and with Fernand Legar (1943), Hans Hoffman, J.E.Carlson. Career: artist, painter, exhibiting and selling since age 12 – ; one woman shows in Los Angeles, Munich and exhibs. in Berlin, Rome, Paris and Warsaw; tchr. painting classes, 30 yrs; owner gallery, Miss Dilly's House, Los Angeles 1957-75; rep. by Gallery Unlimited (Long Beach), Beverly Hills Hotel, others; work in public and pvt. collections incl. Wadsworth VA Hosp. (89 paintings), The Chapel In the Canyon, Canoga Park (two 30x40 paintings of Christ); mem. Artists Equity, AFTRA, Am. Portrait Soc., Beverly Hills Art League, Nat. Assn. Female Execs.; writer/prod. childrens radio series- Storytime (1945-47), writer/prod. film series on art- Art As You Like It (1952), prod. series of cassettes on Colour & Oil Painting, currently putting them in book form, the first completed- Landscape (1986); Republican; Christian; rec: finl. cons. Res: 6419 San Vicente Blvd Los Angeles 90048

DREHER, GLEN AUBREY, JR., petroleum engineering co. executive; b. Oct. 10, 1950, Bastrop, La.; s. Glen and Betty Joyce (Benefield) D.; m. Gail Lynette Agan, July 12, 1986; edn: BS pet. eng., Louisiana Tech. Univ. 1973. Career: petroleum engr., prodn. engr., reservoir/unitization engr., gas completion/ fracturing engr., Gulf Oil Co., Lafayette, La. and Houston, Tx., 1973-77; sr. reservoir engr. Gulf Oil Co. (Nigeria) Ltd., Lagos, Nigeria, W.Africa 1977-81, zone ops. supt. Escravos Terminal, Nigeria 1981-84; area engr. Reservoir, Gulf Exploration and Prodn. Co., Bakersfield 1984-85; mgr. engring. Cabinda Gulf Oil Co. (Chevron Corp.) Malongo, Cabinda, Rep. Popular de Angola, S.W. Africa 1985 – ; owner, pres. Nomadic Investment Corp.; honors: Pi Epsilon Tau, Outstanding Young Men of Am. (1985); mem. Soc. Petroleum Engrs. 1969- (pres. stu. chpt. 1973; mem. Nigeria chpt. 1978-84, Angola chpt. 1986-); Junior Achievement Sponsor (1976); mil: 1st lt. US Army 1971-77; Republican; Ch. of Christ; rec: back-country exploration, travel. Res: 8000 Calle Espada Bakersfield 93309 Ofc: Cabinda Gulf Oil Co. c/o Chevron Overseas Petroleum Intl 6001 Bollinger Cyn Rd San Ramon 94583-0946

DREISKE, JANE DIANE, hotel entrepreneur; b. Sept. 2, 1942, Antigo, Wisc. in a log house on parents' 80-acre milk farm; d. Wm. Daniel and Freida Violet (Helmig) Wendt; m. Donald Dreiske, Dec. 30, 1961, div. 1971; children: Daniel b. 1967, Joseph b. 1969; grad. Antigo H.S. 1960; grad. airline tech. sch. (Humbolt), Mnpls. 1961. Career: teletypist Pan Am Airways, San Francisco 1961-63; exec. secty., graphics design Dee Tozar Advtg. Agcy., Redwood City 1963-64; claims adjuster Glen Slaughter & Assocs., Oakland 1964-65; office mgr. Dr. Liechti MD, Rheem 1965-67; owner/opr. Imperial '400' Hotel, El Cajon 1967-68, El Rancho Motor Hotel, Torrance 1969-71; exec. Toyota Motor Disbtr., Torrance 1969-71, Motorola Corp., Denver, Colo. 1971; also opr. beauty shop and tel. answering svc.; owner/opr. Chalet Lodge Motor Hotel, Tarzana 1971-75, Casa Blanca Motor Hotel, Palm Springs 1975-76, Travelodge Motor Hotel, Rancho Bernardo 1977-79, Travelodge Motor Hotel, Palm Springs 1975-76, Lotus Inn & Casino, Las Vegas 1982-84, one of 112 (only 4 women) non-restricted gaming licensees, Nev. Gaming Control 1983-84; current: owner/opr. Best Western Date Tree (120 units), Indio 1976 – , Western Host Motor Hotel (72 units), Palm Springs 1983 – , founder/owner Desert Inst. of Travel (sch. for travel agts.) 1985 – , and Desert Travel Agcy. 1986 – ; mem: Calif. Lodging Ind. Assn. (dir. 1982-), Indio Hotel Assn. (chair 1986), Best Western Internat. (gov. 1980-); civic: Indio CofC (dir. 1981-86), Indio's Annual Hot-Air Balloon Fest. (founder/com. 1983-84, chair 1984-85), Annual Desert Bicycle Classic, Palm Desert (co-chair 1985-86); Republican; Prot.; rec: flying, travel, ski. Res: 73-860 Grapevine Palm Desert 92260 Ofc: 81-909 Indio Blvd Indio 92201

DREKSLER, MOSHE Y., design and manufacturing co. executive; b. Mar. 24, 1927, Tel Aviv, Israel, nat. US cit. 1962; s. Jacob and Leah (Pachter) D.; m. Jean D., Aug. 6, 1955; children: Donne, Harlan, Shoshana, Doron, Tamir; edn: techn., Mech. Inst., Tel Aviv; AA, Pasadena City Coll. 1953; BS, Calif. St. Polytech. Univ. 1956; Reg. Profl. Engr., Calif. 1979. Career: test engr. Westinghouse Corp., Staunton, Va. 1956-58; design & application engr. Frick Co., Waynesboro, Pa. 1958-60, chief engr. Design & Dev., 1960-69; v.p. engring. Dunham Bush, West Hartford, Conn. 1969-73; mfg. & design mgr. Mycom Corp., Torrance 1973-78, cons. 1978-81, v.p. sales 1981-83, v.p./mgr. GCS Div. 1983 – ; instr. seminars, tech. presentations: Cal Poly, CARSES, RETA, etc.; mem. ASHRAE, ASME, ASTM (inactive), Pacific Energy Assn., Rotary (inactive); 21 patents and disclosures: Westinghouse (6), Frick (12), Mycom (3); tech. publs. ASME (1976), Purdue Compressor Conf. (1976); mil: capt. Israeli Armed Forces, Mapping & Air Photo field commn.; Republican; Jewish; rec: chess. Ofc: Mycom Corp 19475 Gramercy Pl Torrance 90501

DRESIA, WILLIAM FREDRICK, educator, ret.; b. Nov. 2, 1904, Columbus, Kans.; s. Wm. and Anna Maria (Fehrenbach) D.; m. Evelyn Joyce Davies, Apr. 2, 1939; children: David R. b. 1941, Sara (Basque) b. 1945; edn: BS, Univ. Okla. 1927; MA, photo chem., Stanford Univ. 1929, postgrad. work, Munich Univ., Ger. 1933-34, Calif. State Tchr. cred., Stanford 1934; NSF study grant, AEC Commn. Oak Ridge, Tenn. 1955; spl. courses, Reed Coll. 1958; Calif. Gen. Secondary Tchg. and Adminstrn. certs. Career: instr. N.E. Okla. Jr. Coll. 1929-32; sci. tchr. public schs. Los Angeles County 1934-44; headmaster pvt. sch. La Loma Feliz Sch., Santa Barbara 1944-45; sci. dept. tchr./dept. hd. San Rafael (Ca.) High Sch., 1945-70, ret., new H.S. sci. building named Dresia Hall in his honor (1970); apptd. US Dept. of State rep. to Internat. Atomic Energy Agcy., Vienna Conf. 1968; spl. research chemist (radio-active tracers) Calif. Research Corp. 1956; spl. instr. (NSF funded pgm. to upgrade sci. tchg.) UC Berkeley, UC Santa Barbara, and Coll. of Marin 1956-69); honors: Alpha Chi Sigma (1926), Phi Lambda Upsilon (1929); mem: Calif. Sci. Tchrs. Assn. (pres. 1962-63), Am. Assn. of Physics Tchrs. (emeritus 1970-, v.p. Calif. Div. 1963-64), Marin County Retired Tchrs. Assn. (exec. council 1974-80), Sons in Retirement (founding charter Br. #47); civic: Commonwealth Club of Calif. (1969-), Marin Coalition (founding charter mem. 1974), West End Neighborhood Assn. of San Rafael (charter mem. 1978, pres. 1981-83); founded and endowed Science Award, San Rafael H.S. (1977); publs: sev. tech. papers and profl. journal articles, contbr. poems var. mags. and anthologies; mil. service 1925, Marksman medal; Republican; rec: photog., hiking, organ playing, classical Greek drama. Res: 107 Santa Margarita Dr San Rafael 94901

DREW, WALLACE THOMAS, stockbroker; b. Sept. 16, 1917, Wausau, Wisc.; s. Walter Stanley and Christine Elizabeth (Noren) D.; m. Katherine House, Jan. 26, 1942; chidren: Wallace T., Jr. b. 1943, Elizabeth (Carlsson) b. 1946, Katherine (Margolin) b. 1951; edn: BA, Univ. of Wisc. 1937. Career: advt. mgr. Bristol Myers Co., N.Y. 1948-54; v.p./acct. supvr. Cunningham & Walsh, N.Y. 1954-59; v.p., dir. Coty Inc., N.Y. 1959-64; v.p. Beech Nut-Lifesavers, N.Y./ pres. Lander Co., N.Y. (wholly owned subs.), 1964-68; mng. dir. Revlon Internat., London, Eng. 1968-71; stockbroker/v.p. Smith Barney Harris Upham & Co., Santa Barbara 1971 – ; honors: Disting. Citizen award, City of Santa Barbara (1984), recogn. awards ADL, B'nai B'rith; past mem. Drug Chemical & Allied Trades Assn., NYC (pres. 1968, dir. 1961-68); civic: Lobero Theatre Found., S.B. (pres. 1978), Work Inc. handicapped workshop, S.B. (pres. 1979), Boys Club of S.B. (v.p. 1982-86), S.B. Symphony Assn. (v.p. 1980-86), Tres Condados Girl Scout Council (treas. 1982-86), Nuclear Age Pac. Found., S.B. (v.p. 1983-86); mil: major US Army Corps of Engr. 1941-46, First US Army Hq., Europe and Philippines, decorated Bronze Star, 7 Battle Stars; Republican; Episcopal (sr. warden 1984); rec: sailing, collect books. Res: 142 Northridge Rd Santa Barbara 93105 Ofc: Smith Barney Harris Upham & Co. 200 E Carrillo Ste 300 Santa Barbara 93101

DREXLER, BRUCE ALAN, chiropractor; b. Feb. 23, 1956, St. Paul, Minn.; s. William Edward, Sr. and Joyce Marie (Marko) D.; edn: Los Angeles Valley Coll.; San Diego Mesa Coll. 1974-75; Univ. of Minn. 1975-76; DC, cum laude, Cleveland Coll. 1980. Career: assoc. Murphy Chiropractic, Chula Vista 1980-81; mgr. Dr. Spivey's Ofc., Lakeside 1983-84; owner Drexler Chiropractic Ofc., Lakeside 1984 – ; Recipient, 3 Outstanding Svc. Awards, Cleveland Coll., Los Angeles 1978-79; mem: Sigma Chi Psi (past pledge dir., justice and regent), Lakeside CofC (bd. dirs.); Republican; Catholic; rec: guitar (18 yrs.), volleyball. Ofc: Drexler Chiropractic, 9746 Winter Gardens Blvd. Lakeside 92040

DRISCOLL, ROBERT EARL, psychotherapist, educator; b. Nov. 21, 1945, Louisville, Ky.; s. Glen Robert and Dorothy June (Little) D.; children: Mark, b. 1973, Barbara, b. 1976, Angela, b. 1979; edn: BA, So. Calif. Coll. 1979; MA, U.S. Internat. Univ. 1980, Psy.D., 1982, PhD, 1984. Calif. lic. MFCC (marriage, family, child counselor) 1983. Career: dir. Psychological Services, Clinica Del Mar, 1980-82; pres./chmn. Alternatives, 1982 – ; univ. dean Psychol. Studies, 1983-85; clin. psychol. prof. National Univ., 1984 – ; dir. Educational Services Unlmtd. 1980 – ; personnel mgmt. cons. Counties of Los Angeles, Orange, Riverside, and San Diego, 1983-; lectr. CA Psychology Series; honors: San Diego Outstanding Citizen 1975, CofC; mem: Calif. Assn. Marriage Family Counselors, Am. Soc. for Sci. Study of Sex, Western Psychol. Assn., Am. Psychol. Assn., North Am. Adlerian Soc., Christian Assn. of Pastoral Counselors, S.D. Multiple Sclerosis Soc. (bd. dirs.), S.D. Soc. for Sex Edn. & Therapy, S.D. Mental Health Assn., Inst. of Noetic Scis., Calif. Hist. Soc., S.D. Comm. Arts Assn., S.D. Theatre Goers Soc.; publs: 14 journal arts. in psychology rel. to personality, motivation and devel.; mil: USN 1968-76, Vietnam Svc., Navy Achievement; rec: sailing, travel, theatre. Res: 4625 Florida St, 2, San Diego 92116 Ofc: 2525 Camino del Rio South, Ste 215, San Diego 92108

DROBNICK, RICHARD LEE, economist/educator; b. Feb. 12, 1945, Waukegan, Ill.; s. Joseph J. and Eleanor A. (McDermott) D.; m. Sheri A. Brown, Apr. 10, 1976; 1 son, Gregory b. 1981; edn: BS econs., Bradley Univ. 1967; MA econs., Univ. So. Calif. 1973, PhD econs., 1979. Career: peace corps volunteer Malaysia 1967-69; primary sch. tchr. Chgo. 1969-70; dir. Peace Corps Ag. Tng. Pgm. Malaysia 1971-72; staff economist Ctr. for Futures Research Univ. So. Calif. 1976-79, dir. 20-Yr. Forecast Proj. 1979-82, senior research assoc. 1982 – ; dir. Internat. Bus. Edn. and Research Pgm., Grad. Sch. Bus. Adminstrn., USC 1982 – ; cons. Nat. Sci. Found., Nat. Acad. Sci., US Dept. of Ag., US Peace Corps, num. corps.; TV and radio commentator; mem: Indonesian CofC of the West (pres. 1985-, dir. 1984-), L.A. Com. on Fgn. Relations, World future Soc., Asia Soc., Acad. Internat. Bus., East Asian Studies Ctr. (USC); co-author: Neither Feast nor Famine: Food Conditions to the Year 2000 (w/ S. Enzer & S. Alter, Lexington Books 1978); num. articles on internat. trade issues in acad. and popular mags.; rec: golf, tennis, skiing; avoc: real estate (Ill.). Res: 2634 Hollyridge Dr Los Angeles 90068 Ofc: Grad. Sch. of Bus. USC Los Angeles 90089-1421

DROST, KATHLEEN ANDERSON, speech pathologist; b. Apr. 8, 1957, Jamestown, NY; d. Robert James and Joyce Mary (Palm) Anderson; m. Russell C. Drost, June 29, 1985; edn: AA, Orange Coast Community Coll. 1978; BA, CSU Long Beach 1980; MA, CSU Fullerton 1983, grad. adminstrn. credential pgm., CSUF 1986-; Calif. lic. Speech Pathologist (1983), Clin. Rehabilitative Credential (life); Cert. of Clin. Competency, ASHA Review Bd. Career: speech/ lang. pathologist La Habra Elementary Sch. Dist., 1983, Jurupa Unified Sch. Dist., Riverside 1983−; honors: Phi Kappa Phi (1979); mem: Am. Speech Lang. Hearing Assn., Calif. Speech Lang. Hearing Assn., Calif. Tchg. Assn., Nat. Tchrs. Edn. Assn.; Democrat; Catholic. Res: 17272 Chestnut St Yorba Linda 92686 Ofc: Ina Arbuckle Elementary, 3600 Packard St Riverside 92509

DROWN, EUGENE ARDENT, government land management specialist; b. Apr. 25, 1915, Ellenburg, N.Y.; s. Frank Arthur and Jessie Kate D.; m. Florence Marian Munroe, Mar. 5, 1938; 2 daus: Linda Harriet b. 1942, Margaret Ruth b. 1946; edn: BS, Utah State Univ. 1938; grad. stu. Mont. State Univ. 1939-40; PhD in Public Adminstrn., Univ. Beverly Hills 1979; desig: Calif. Reg. Profl. Engr., Profl. Land Surveyor, Profl. Forester. Career: park ranger Nat. Park Service Yosemite Nat. Park 1940-47, forest ranger US Forest Service, Calif. Region 1948-56, forest mgr. and devel. splst. US Bur. Land Mgmt., Calif. 1956−; forest engring. cons., 1970−; research and devel. coordinator US Army at UC Davis 1961-65; mem. adv. bd. Sierra Coll. 1962-; honors: Nat. Service medal Am. Red Cross; mem = Nat. Soc. Profl. Engrs., Soc. Am. Foresters, Am. Inst. Biol. Scientists, Ecol. Soc. Am., Res. Officers Assn., US Nat. Rifle Assn., Internat. Rescue and First Aid Assn., Internat. Platform Assn , Bulldog Sentinels of Superior Calif., Masons, Shriners; civic: active Boy Scouts Am., Am. Red Cross (instr. 1954-); mil: US Army 1941-45, Bronze Star, Silver Star; Methodist (lay spkr.); rec: hunting, fishing. Res: 5624 Bonniemae Way Sacramento 94824

DROZD, GERALD DONALD, real estate accounting co. president; b. Sept. 3, 1943, Chicago, Ill.; s. Casey Frank and Frances Helen (Zakrzewski) D.; m. Clara, June 15, 1968; children: Peter b. 1972, Cynthia b. 1977; edn: BBA, Loyola Univ. 1965. Career: audit mgr. Milwaukee Road Ry., Chicago, Ill. 1966-68; controller CTC Computer Corp., Seattle, Wash. 1969-71; acctg. mgr. Rockwell Internat., Pittsburg, Penn. 1971-75; controller Encyclopedia Britannica Inc., Chicago, Ill. 1975-82; pres., owner IKON Inc., San Mateo 1983−; dir. STM Computer Corp.; dir. Financial Execs. Inst. 1975-; Catholic; rec: golf, skiing, photog. Res: 1320 Brandt Rd. Hillsborough 94010 Ofc: IKON Inc., 2855 Campus Dr. San Mateo 94403

DRUDING, FRANK, engineering executive; b. Nov. 19, 1927, Phila.; s. Charles Francis and Mabel Rebeca (Turner) D.; m. Noel Tucher, Oct. 28, 1950; children: Diane b. 1951, Gretchen b. 1952, Candace b. 1954, Christopher b. 1956, Cynthia b. 1963, Andrea b. 1964; edn: US Merchant Marine Acad. 1945-47; BME, Univ. of Santa Clara 1950; MS in engring. mechs., Stanford Univ. 1957, postgrad. work 1957-59. Career: mgr. Satellite Automatic Control Systems, Lockheed MSD, Sunnyvale 1957-61; chmn./pres. Mellonics Inc., Sunnyvale 1961-65; Div. pres. Mellonics Div. Litton Industries, Sunnyvale also corp. v.p. Litton Systems Inc., Beverly Hills 1965-71; bd. chmn./CEO IOMEC Inc., Santa Clara 1971-76; dir. Software Engring., Ford Aerospace, Palo Alto 1977-79, dir. Spl. Pgms., 1979-84, corp. dir. Engineering Technol., 1984−; fmr. bd. chmn. Spectra Electronics Inc.; fmr. dir. Golden Pacific Airlines; v.chmn. Software Productivity Consortium; chmn. AFCEA/DOD ADA Study Team; mem. AIAA, AFCEA, ASME; civic: Elks, Nat. Rifle Assn., Am. Legion, Stanford Alumni Assn., Univ. of Santa Clara (regent 1968-78); club: St. Francis Yacht; mil: 1st lt. USAF Strategic Air Command 1950-54; Republican; Roman Catholic; rec: sailing, flying, flyfishing. Ofc: Ford Aerospace 3939 Fabian Way Ste 357 (MS-H01) Palo Alto 94303

DRULIAS, DEAN JAMES, chiropractor; b. Jan. 11, 1955, Los Angeles; s. James Gus and Esther (Arapkales) D.; m. Merry A., June 27, 1985; edn: BS biology, Whittier Coll. 1977; DC, Cleveland Coll. of Chiro. 1982; Diplomate Nat. Board of Chiro. 1981. Career: rehabilitation counselor Center for Ex-Convicts, El Monte 1978; semi profl. baseball mgr./player, 1979-80; owner/ opr jewelry business, 1976 84; chiropractic practice, Torrance 1982−; mem. Ahepa (Greek org.); mgr. & sponsor Redondo Beach Softball Club; Republican; Greek Orthodox. Res: 2024 MacArthur Rancho Palos Verdes 90732 Ofc: 1408 Crenshaw Torrance 90501

DRURY, DONALD VICTOR, librarian, stained glass artist; b. Oct. 22, 1927, London; came to USA, 1957; s. Victor John and Mary Gray (Angus) D.; m. Dorothy Perry, Nov. 25, 1959; edn: BA, Univ. Cambridge, 1959, MA, 1953; MLS, UC Berkeley, 1972. Career: dir., mgr. Lowndes & Drury Ltd., London 1950-57, 69-70; designer, craftsman Cummings Studios, San Francisco 1957-59, Hogan Studios, San Jose 1959-62; owner, mgr. Donald V. Drury Stained Glass Studio,San Francisco 1962-69; dir. libraries Menlo Coll., Atherton 1972−; mem. adminstrv. council South Bay Coop. Library System, 1982-; bd. dirs. Coop. Information Network, 1978-82; mem. ALA, Calif. Library Assn.; Democrat; Episcopal. Res: Menlo College Apt. 3A, Atherton 94025 Ofc: Bowman Library, Menlo College Atherton 94025

DRURY, MARY ELLEN, real estate development executive; b. Mar. 21, 1946, Colfax, Wash.; d. Cecil Edwin and Irene Fern (Devin) Wassem; div.; edn: grad. Rubidoux H.S. 1964. Calif. lic. General Contr., Real Estate Sales. Career: secty. Sunrise Co., Palm Desert 1972-73; bus. ptnr. Fred Drury & Sons Masonry, 1973-81, corp. ofcr. 1982-83; secty. Sunrise Co./ Nat. Mortgage & Land Co., 1975-77, adminstrv. asst. 1977-79, dir. customer service 1979-83, v.p. 1983−; bus. ptnr. Chaparral Restaurant, Anza 1979-80; honors: Bank of Am. academic award (1963); civic: Soroptomist Internat. of P.D. (pres., exec. bd. House of Hope 1985-87), Riverside County Coalition for Alternatives to Domestic Violence (exec. bd.), Arch. Review Bd./ City of Palm Desert; Republican; Presbyterian; rec: crafts, flying. Res: 72750 Sage Ct Palm Desert 92260 Ofc: Sunrise Co 75-005 Country Club Dr Palm Desert 92260

DUBNICK, ARNOLD J., chiropractor; b. Jan. 14, 1932, Brooklyn, NY; s. Samuel and Frances (Shur) Dubnick; m. Shirley, Dec. 28, 1957; children: Joel b. 1952, Carrie b. 1960, David b. 1965; edn: Columbia Univ. 1949-51; DC, L.A. Coll. of Chiro. 1955; Long Island Univ. 1955-57; BS pharm., Coll. of the Pacific 1960. Career: chiro. N.Y. 1955; instr. math jr. h.s. 1956-57; chiro. 1957-58; pharmacist 1960-64; chiro. 1964-81; art photog. 1981−; chiro. 1984−; independent med. examiner Calif. State Div. of Indsl. Accidents, Workers Comp. Appeals Bd.; honors: Delta Sigma 1955, Top Purchase Award (photog., Fairfield-Susuin Art Show 1982); mem: Am., Calif., Sacto. Valley Chiro. Assns., Valley Indsl. Claims Assn., Profl. Photogs. of Am., Calif.; publs: photog. works, N.Y. Graphics Soc. Inc. (1985) and Mirage (1986); mil: USAFR, active duty 1951; Jewish; rec: photog. Ofc: Arnold J. Dubnick, DC, 701 Howe Ave, Ste C5, Sacramento 95825

DU BRIN, STANLEY, physician, director medical clinics; b. June 3, 1928, NY, NY; s. Leonard B. and Claire (Lehman) DuB.; m. Magda Arruda, Dec. 31, 1976; children: Dean b. 1952, Skipper b. 1953, Richard b. 1957, Kathleen b. 1957; edn: AB, Ohio Univ. 1944; USNR Midshipman's Sch. Columbia Univ. 1944; AB/BS, Denison Univ. 1946; MD, UC Irvine 1962. Career: developer, mem. bd. dirs. Woodland Park Community Hosp., Canoga Park 1957-62; nchief of staff Van Nuys Community Hosp., Van Nuys 1964-72; medical dir. MD Medical Clinics, 1980−; mem. Am., Calif., Orange County Med. Assns.; author: Acupuncture and Your Health, 1974 (1st American M.D. to write book on subject); mil: lt jg USNR 1942-46; Republican; Catholic. Ofc: MD Medical Clinics, 1300 N. Kraemer Blvd Anaheim 92806, 2630 S Harbor Blvd Santa Ana 92704, 7441 Garden Grove Blvd Garden Grove 92641

DUCAS, MARK ANTHONY, building code inspector; b. June 7, 1955, Fresno; s. Joseph Tony and Joyce Delores (Schafer) D.; m. Kathleen P., Jan. 15, 1983; 1 son, Dominic, b. 1976; edn: BS, Calif. State Univ. 1978; Cert. Bldg. Ofcl., Council of Am. Building Officials (1984); Internat. Conf. of Bldg. Officials certs: Bldg. Insp. (1983), Plans Examiner (1983), Spl. Insp. Reinforced Concrete, Pre-stressed Concrete, Struc. Steel & Welding (1984). Career: carpenter A-M. Builders, Fresno 1975-78; struc. engring. tech. City of Fresno, 1978-79, bldg. constrn. insp. 1979−; Building Code consultant: Ginder Devel. Corp. 1981-; honors: recogn. for voluntary school, community and youth wk., Rotary Intl. Dist. 522 (1972); life mem. Calif. Scholarship Fedn. (1973); mem: Internat. Conf. of Building Ofcls. San Joaquin Valley Chpt.; Nat. Fire Protection Assn.; CSUF Alumni Assn.; Sigma Chi Frat. Alumni Assn.; Fresno City Employee Assn.; Fresno Trades Club; St. Therese Sch. Parents Club; publs: devel. "Standard Plan" files for tract-house projects (1978), Basic Wood Engineering (new engring. tech. pamphlet, 1979); Republican; Catholic; rec: skiing, fitness, model trains. Res: 3165 W. Floradora Fresno 93711 Ofc: City of Fresno Development Dept. 2326 Fresno St. Fresno 93721

DUCATO, JOHN BUCK, banker; b. May 25, 1937, San Francisco; s. Alfred and Marie Viola (Buck) D.; m. Candace Hazard, Apr. 4, 1964; children: Caroline b. 1967, Jennifer b. 1971; edn: BA, UC Berkeley 1958. Career: v.p. First Interstate Bank of Calif., San Francisco 1959-69; 1st v.p. Blyth Eastman Dillon, N.Y.C., S.F. 1969-74; v.p. Lloyds Bank Calif., S.F. 1974-77; senior v.p. Crocker Nat. Bank, S.F. 1977-86; exec. v.p. Bank of San Francisco, 1986−; clubs: Pacific Union, Bohemian, Burlingame CC, Chicago; mil: capt. USAR; rec: horses, fishing, hunting. Res: 223 West Santa Inez Hillsborough 94010 Ofc: Bank of San Francisco 351 California St San Francisco 94104

DUCIN, JEANINE, military officer, registered nurse, b. Mar. 24, 1961, Pittsburgh, Pa.; d. John and Jean Elizabeth (Schilpp) Ducin; edn: BSN, summa cum laude, Mt. St. Mary's Coll., Los Angeles 1983; Calif. lic. Reg. Nurse (1983). Career: ofcr, USAF Nurse Corps, staff nsc. OD/GYN Unit, USAF Hosp., Vandenberg 1983−, OB/GYN Unit inservice coordinator 1985−, mem. Staff Devel. Com. (1985-), Com. to Develop Std. Nsg. Care Plans (1985-), Immediate Care Team (1985-); honors: outstanding senior nsg. student award, Mt. St. Mary's Coll. (1983), Dean's List (1979-83), Nat. Dean's List (1979-83), Nurse of the Quarter award (1985), OB/Gyn Unit Nurse of the Month award (3/86); mem. Kappa Gamma Pi (Catholic Honor Soc.), Delta Epsilon Sigma (Catholic Honor Soc.), Vandenberg AFB Officer's Club; works: presenter and certifying ofcl. Nursing InService Tng. Pgm. cert. RNs in Blood Adminstrn. (9/85); presenter "Care of the Post-Partum Patient" seminar: (11/85), "OB/Gyn Unit Equipment" seminar (4/86); mil: 1st lt. (Secret Security Clearance), USAF Nurse Corps 1983−, Basic Tng. Ribbon (1984); Republican; Catholic; rec: cooking, travel, aerobics, hist. novels. Res: POB 6271 Vandenberg AFB 93437 Ofc: USAF Hospital Vandenberg, Vandenberg AFB 93437

DUCKETT, ROY DELBERT, JR., organizational consultant; b. Oct. 16, 1938, Texarkana, Ark.; s. Roy, Sr. (gospel singer w/ Humming Bees of Texarkana) and Daisy Ora (Jackson) D.; edn: BA, Morehouse Coll. (Atlanta, Ga.) 1961; MA, Atlanta Univ. 1962; cert. London Sch. of Econ., U. of London (Eng.), 1962-3; postgrad. Wash. State Univ., 1963-4; MPH, UC Berkeley 1973; postgrad., Vista Coll. 1976-80; cert. Profl. Legal Secty. (PLS), Coll. of Alameda 1982; D.D., ordained minister Universal Life Ch., Modesto 1981; John F. Kennedy Law Sch. 1981; cert. Legal Asst. Pgm., Merritt Coll. 1982-3; med./dental asst. tng. Oakland Coll. of Med. 1983-4. Career: tchg. asst. Dept. of Sociol., Wash. State Univ., 1963-4, instr. Dept. Sociol., Texas Southern Univ., 1964-5; epidemiol. coord. Calif. Div. Am. Cancer Soc., San Francisco 1966, and asst. svc. dir. 1968-72; social wkr. Dept. of Social Svcs, S.F. 1966; asst. supt. Soc. Svcs. S.F. Redevel. Agcy. A-2 Proj., 1966-68; adminstr. No. Oakland- Emeryville Children and Youth Project, Alameda Co. Hlth Care Svcs Agcy, Oakland 1973-78; profl. pub. typist, writer, orgnzl. cons., notary public, 1978 – ; pres. Dr. Roy D. Duckett, Jr., Oakland 1978 – , pres. Dr. Roy D. Duckett, Jr. Church, Inc., 1978 – ; legal secty. Port Atty's Ofc., City of Oakland, 1981-85; adminstrv. secty. Central Health Ctr., Alameda County Health Care Svcs. Agcy., Oakland 1985 – ; process server, notary public, legal asst., med. asst., cons., Calif. lottery ticket retailer, investigator, stationery/ofc. supplies sales, gay counseling, writing; awards: scholarship Morehouse Coll. (57-8), fellowship Atlanta Univ. (61-2), Charles E. Merrill Euro. Study-Travel grant (62-3). Mem: Am. Pub. Health Assn., Calif. Assn. of Photocopiers and Process Servers, Golden Age Total Emancipation Soc., asst. commr. Internat. Reserve State Trooper, Inc.; author: Witchcraft: A Digest; Money: A Digest; The Light Skinned Negro: America's Greatest Threat; Wills; Sadism/ Masochism; How To Get Power; Pleadings and Court Cases: A Collection; journal arts. Republican (precinct capt.) rec: exercise, writing. Address: Roy D. Duckett, Jr., 1146 12th St. Oakland 94607

DUDLEY, PERRY, JR., manufacturing co. executive; b. June 5, 1928, New Haven, Conn.; s. Perry and Ella (Leach) D.; div.; children: Bruce Lawrence b. 1959, Virginia Barbara b. 1961; edn: BSEE, Purdue Univ. 1952; MBA, Univ. Santa Clara 1966. Career: sales engr. Reliance Electric, Los Angeles 1952-60; indsl. & Mil. sales engr. GTE Sylvania, Burlingame 1960-65; appls. engr./product mgr./ customer splst., Varian Associates, Palo Alto 1965-68; product mgr. Profl. Video Products Div., Ampex Corp., Redwood City 1968-70; pgm. mgr. Ednl. Delivery Systems & Cont. Edn. Pgms., Genesys Systems, Palo Alto 1972-73; comml. & indsl. real estate broker/salesman, Palo Alto 1973-80; pgm. mgr. Dalmo Victor Textron, Belmont 1980-85; instr. Dept. Mgmt. & Mktg., CSU San Francisco; cons. on cont. edn. pgms., Cornel Univ., Univ. of Bridgeport; mem: Nat. Assn. of Mgmt., Assn. of Old Crows, Assn. of Iron & Steel Mfrs. (charter), Papermakers & Assocs. of So. Calif.; orgns: Purdue Club of Los Angeles (pres.), Young Republican Club of Pasadena (pres.), Mensa; publ: article on op. of klystron tubes, Broadcast Mgmt. & Engring. mag. (1968); mil: electronic tech. 3/c US Navy 1946-48, WWII Victory Medal; Republican; Presbyterian; rec: music, sailing, cruising, photog. Address: Menlo Park 94025

DUELL, MARK LAWRENCE, SR., chiropractor; b. Dec. 24, 1951, Dhahran, Saudi Arabia; s. Kenneth Edward and Sarah (Crawford) C.; m. Patti, Oct. 22, 1977; 1 son, Mark Jr. b. 1985; edn: AA, Moorpark Coll. 1978; BS, Cleveland Chiro. Coll. 1982, DC, 1983; Diplomate, Calif. Nat. Bds. (1985). Career: sales agt. Brown Realtors, Westlake Village 1978-79; mgr. Pardee Constrn. Co., Camarillo 1979-80; assoc. dir. Hurley Chiropractic Clinic, Santa Barbara 1984; owner, dir. Duell Chiropractic Clinic, 1985 – ; cons., research dir. Activator Methods, Inc., Los Angeles 1983; honors: Sigma Chi Psi, cert. Parker Chiro. Research Found. (1982); mem: Am. Chiro. Assn. (ACA Council on Roentgenology), Calif. Chiro. Assn. (Student chpt. pres. 1983), Activator Methods Research Group, Parker Chiropractic Research Found., Rotary Internat., Goleta CofC, Santa Barbara Mens Golf Club; publs: The Force of the Activator Adjusting Instrument, Digest of Chiro. Economics (1984); mil: cpl. USMC 1970-72, Vietnam Svc., Nat. Def., Vietnam Merit. Cit., Pistol Expt., Rifle Sharpshooter; Republican; Episcopal; rec: golf, tennis, helicopters. Ofc: Duell Chiropractic Clinic, 5350 Hollister Ave Ste A3 Santa Barbara 93111

DUFF, STEPHEN ASHWORTH, chiropractor; b. May 20, 1924, Ross, Calif., 5th generation Californian; s. Alfred Wm. and Laura (Marshall) D.; m. Yvonne Burnham, Apr. 23, 1946; children: Stephen b. 1948, Laura b. 1950, Adrienne b. 1951, Bryan b. 1953, Leonard b. 1955, Andria b. 1957, Denise b. 1959, Richard b. 1962; edn: DC, Palmer Sch. of Chiropractic 1947; postgrad., San Francisco Coll. of Chiropractic 1948; Lic. DC, Calif. St. Board 1948. Career: chiropractor in pvt. practice, 1949 – ; cons., X-Ray research, Polaroid Corp. 1977; tchg. Duff Seminars at Life Coll. West and Healdsburg Chiropractic Clinic, profl. symposiums nat. and internat.; num. lectrs. Sherman Coll., Pacific States Chiro. Coll., Life Chiro. Coll., others; trustee Sherman Coll. of Straight Chiropractic 10 yrs.; honors: named Calif. Chiropractor of the Year (1959); I.C.A. research awards (1964, 66), first Calif. recipient D.D. Palmer Sci. Award for Research & Chiropractic Standards (1972); mem. Calif. Chiropractic Assn. (bd. dirs. 1951, 65, dir. at large 1960), No. Calif. Chiro. Assn. (pres. 1952-53), Fellow Internat. Chiro. Assn. (3-time pres. Disting. Fellows ICA, Calif. State Rep. 1950-82, bd. dirs., research com. 1982, chmn. Internat. Conf. on the Spine 1983); author: Chiropractic Clinical Research (Interpretation of Bilateral spinal skin temperature differentials); discoverer of Duff Points, X-Ray Film Landmarks of Measurement; mil: pvt. US Marine Corps 1941, 3 Bronze Battle Stars; Republican; Christian; rec: ranching, thorobred horses and cattle. Res: 120 Deer Park Ave San Rafael 94801 Ofc: Precision In Chiropractic Care 1104 Irwin St San Rafael 94901

DUFFY, LUCILLE MARDAGA, master graphoanalyst; b. Jan. 11, 1922, Elmhurst, Ill.; d. Wm. Henry and Ilona Emilie (Schwarz) Mardaga; m. Charles Morris Duffy, Apr. 24, 1942; children: Ilona b. 1943, Dinah b. 1946, Suzanne b. 1946, Charles, Jr. b. 1949; edn: B.Ed., San Fernando Valley St. Coll. 1959, M.Ed., CSU Northridge 1973; Tchg. credentials: Elem. - Life (1959), Reading Splst. -Life (1968), instr. Comm. Colls. -Life, Supvr. (1973), Adminstr. (1979); desig: certified graphoanalyst (1982), master graphoanalyst (1985), Internat. Soc. of G.A.; Career: elementary tchr. Los Angeles Unified Sch. Dist. 1959-76, master tchr. 1967-76, tchr. exceptional children 1961-62, reading splst. 1968-69, dir. Reading Lab. Serania Sch. 1973-75; prof. (developmental communications) L.A. Community Colls., Mission and Pierce, 1976-83; owner/ptnr. Duffy and Duffy Assocs., Handwriting Analysts; awards: Alpha Phi Alumnae scholar (1958), Dean's List (1959), SFVSC Honor Scholarship Soc., Serrania PTA hon. service award (1975); mem: ACE (pres. 1962), Internat. Reading Assn. (1968-83), UTLA (1969-75), AFT (1976-83), Calif. Ret. Tchrs. Assn. (1983-); civic: Nat. Assn. Parliamentarians (1968-), CSAP, ETA Pi, Bus.

& Profl. Women (1968-), Friends of Leonis Adobe (1973-79), Calabasas Hist. Soc. (1980-), Calif. Hist. Soc., Malibu Creek St. Pk. Docents; publs: (textbook) Reading in Review; (news article) Plummer House; (research) Career Counseling and Handwriting Analysis (1986); Illus. lectures: Portraits of the Past, Pioneer Women of San Fern. Valley, The Real Death Valley Scotty; Christian Ch.; rec: crafts, photog., travel. Res: 5367 Winnetka Ave Woodland Hills 91364

DUITCH, DENNIS GRAY, accountant; b. Sept. 29, 1944, Des Moines, Iowa; s. Paul R. and Louise (Gray) D.; m. Nancy Lynn Toran, Aug. 3, 1984; children: Daryl Lynn b. 1971, Stacey Renee b. 1974; edn: BBA, Univ. Iowa 1966; MBA finance, Northwestern Univ. 1970; CPA Ill., Calif. Career: CPA mgr. Alexander Grant & Co. Chgo., S.F., Beverly Hills 1966-75; founder, mng. ptnr. Duitch & Franklin 1975 – ; faculty Calif. CPA Found. City Coll. S.F., Pepperdine Univ.; mem: Am. Inst. CPAs, Calif. Soc. CPAs, Thalians Presidents Club, Regency Club; Republican; rec: piano, skiing. Res: 16961 Encino Hills Dr Encino 91436 Ofc: Duitch & Franklin CPAs 10920 Wilshire Blvd, 14th floor, Los Angeles 90024

DUITZ, ROBERT ALLEN, tax accountant; b. Sept. 16, 1949, Los Angeles; s. David and Phyllis D.; div.; children: Shanna b. 1978, Jamie b. 1984; edn: BA, UC Los Angeles 1971; desig: Enrolled Agent (E.A.), IRS (1976). Career: owner/prin. acctg. tax service, RD's Tax & Bookkeeping Service, Campbell 1975 – ; mem: Santa Clara County Private Industry Council (chmn.), Mission Soc. of Enrolled Agents (dir.), Calif. Soc. of E.A., Nat. Soc. of E.A.; civic: Campbell CofC (pres. elect 1986), Kiwanis, Santa Clara Co. Congl. Action Com., Accountants Advis. Com. for Assem. Ernie Konnyu, Central Com. to elect Tom Legan state sen., NFIB; lctrs. statewide on federal income taxation, num. articles on taxation. Ofc: RD's Tax & Bookkeeping Service 393 E Hamilton Ave Ste B Campbell 95008

DUKE, ELLEN KAY, marketing executive; b. June 7, 1952, Indianapolis, Ind.; d. Richard Thomas and Ruby Mae (Wright) D.; edn: World Campus Afloat, Chapman Coll. 1972; BS public affairs, Indiana Univ. 1975; grad. study, Portland State Univ. 1981. Career: news reporter KLOO Radio and Salem Statesman Corvallis, Ore. 1977-79; legis. staff Oregon State Legislature Salem 1979; public involvement coord. Metro Portland 1980; acct. mgr. Thunder & Visions Portland 1980-83; bus. devel. splst. Computerland Corp. Hayward, Calif. 1984 – ; Dale Carnegie instr.; honors: Informed Spkr. Award (Toastmasters 1981); mem: Assn. Female Execs., Library Bd. Commr. (chair), Sierra Club, ACLU, Amnesty Internat.; publ: num. news articles; Communication Skills (a training film 1975); Democrat; Unity; rec: public speaking, dancing. Ofc: Computerland 30985 Santana St Hayward 94544

DUKES, WALTER CLAUDE, dentist; b. Dec. 20, 1951, Ely, Nev.; s. George Earl and Hope Waletta (Shellenberger) D.; m. Diane Beilby, Dec. 29, 1977; children: Jonathan b. 1978, Elizabeth b. 1981, Alycia b. 1982; edn: BS microbiol., Brigham Young Univ. 1975; DDS, Creighton Univ. 1978. Career: pvt. practice general dentistry, 1978 – ; TMJ Preceptorship faculty, section Gnathology and Occlusion, UC Los Angeles Sch. of Dentistry, 1984 – ; vis. lectr. UCLA Sch. of Dentistry; awards: Mosby Scholar (1978); mem: Am. Dental Assn., UCLA TMJ Clinic Associate Study Club, LDS Bus. and Profl. Assn.; Republican; LDS; rec: pvt. pilot. Res: 406 Lincolnwood Pl Santa Barbara 93110 Ofc: 1847 Cliff Dr Santa Barbara 93109

DULUDE, WM. J., consulting engineer; b. Feb. 14, 1927, Dassel, Minn.; s. Stephen E. and Clara (Boylan) D.; m. Barbara Hewitt, Sept. 18, 1954; children: Evert Michael b. 1958, William Douglas b. 1960; edn: BSEE, CalPoly Univ. 1952; Reg. Profl. Eng. in Ariz., Calif., Mont. Career: thirty-two years profl. experience as corporate ofcr., project and engring. mgmt., constrn. mgmt., and engring. design of utility and indsl. facilities; currently: senior v.p./dir. SAI Engineers, Inc. 1976 – ; v.p./dir. SAI Geothermal, Inc.; pres./dir SAI Constructors, Inc. 1983 – ; mem: IEEE, Constrn. Specification Inst., Engrs. Club of San Francisco; mil: seaman USN 1944-46; Republican; rec: cooking, fishing, woodworking. Res: 8211 Claret Ct San Jose 95135 Ofc: SAI Engineers, Inc. 3030 Patrick Henry Dr Santa Clara 95135

DUMKE, GLENN S., university chancellor, educator; b. May 5, 1917, Green Bay, Wis.; edn: AB, hist., Occidental Coll. 1938, AM 1939, LL.D 1960; PhD, UCLA 1942; H.L.D., Univ. Redlands 1962, LL.D, Univ. of Bridgeport (1963) Transylvania Coll. (1968), Pepperdine Coll. (1969), Hebrew Union Coll. (1968), Windham Coll. (1969), Our Lady of the Lake Univ. (1977), Dickinson State Coll. (1978). Career: teaching asst. UCLA 1940-1; instr. history Occidental Coll. 1940-43, asst. prof. 1943-46, assoc. prof. 1947-50, prof. history 1950, Norman Bridge prof. Hispanic Am. hist. 1954, dean faculty 1950-57; pres. San Francisco State Coll. 1957-61; vice chancellor, Calif. State Colls., L.A. 1961-62, chancellor Calif. State Univs. and Colls., 1962-82; pres. Inst. for Contemporary Studies, 1982 – . Dir: Barclay Bank of Calif., The Olga Co.; trustee Nat. Exec. Service Corps. fmr. chmn. exec. com. Western Interstate Commn. for Higher Edn.; founding bd. Civilian/Mil. Inst., USAF Acad. Found.; chmn. fin. com. Council on Postsec. Accreditation; exec. com. Calif. Council for Humanities in Pub. Policy 1974-77; chmn. Calif. Selection Com. for Rhodes Scholarships, 1966; mem. Am. Assn. State Colls. and Univs. com. on State Rels.; bd. vis. USAF Air Univ.; fmr. bd. vis. USAF Acad.; bd. commnrs., Nat. Commn. on Accrediting 1959-65, 70-74; bd. mem. Am. Council Edn. 1967-8; trustee Calif. Industry-Edn. Council; resrch fellow Huntington Lib. 1943-5; Haynes Found. grantee, 1943. Mem: Am. Mgmt. Assn. (bd.dirs. 1970-3, 74-77, 80-83); Univ. Club S.F.; Calif. CofC (bd.dirs.); Inst. internat. Edn. (So. Calif. advis. bd.1972-); Los Angeles Club; Bohemian; Commonwealth; Town Hall; Regency; past mem. bd. dirs: L.A. Area CofC,

L.A. World Affairs Council, Am., Calif. Hist. Soc., Am. Pacific Coast Com. on Humanities (1st chmn. 1968-), council for econ. edn. Assn. Higher Edn., Jt. Council Econ. Edn., Western Coll. Assn. (past chmn. mbrship & standards com.). Author: The Boom of the Eighties in So. Calif. (1944), Mexican Gold Trail (1945), A Hist. of the Pacific Area in Modern Times (1949, coauthor: Dr. Osgood Hardy), The Tyrant of Bagdad (1955, nom de plume Glenn Pierce); coauthor, ed.: From Wilderness to Empire: A History of Calif. (1959); contbr. arts. profl. and popular publs. Methodist. Address: 16332 Meadow Ridge Rd. Encino 91436

DUMMIT, MARC CHARLES, physician; b. Feb. 10, 1953, Springfield, Mo.; s. Charles Allen and Audrey (Brown) D.; edn: BA cum laude, Yale Univ. 1976; MD, UCLA Sch. of Medicine 1982; postgrad. residency internal med., Presbyterian/St. Luke's Hosp. 1983. Career: staff physician Public Health Service, Kernville; med. dir. Kern Valley Hospice Pgm.; current: medical dir. Emergency Room and dir. Home Health Pgm., Kern Valley Hosp., Lake Isabella; chmn. quality assurance com. Kern Valley Hosp.; mem: AMA, Calif. Med. Assn.; has initiated an active house call pgm. for housebound elderly and terminally ill; mil: staff phys. Nat. Health Service Corps 1983-85; Democrat; Protestant; rec: mountaineering, kayaking, musician. Res: POB 808 Kernville 93238 Ofc: Kern Valley Hospital 5312 Laurel Ave (Rt 1, Box 152) Lake Isabella 93240

DUNCAN, DORIS GOTTSCHALK, information systems educator; b. Nov. 19, 1944, Seattle Wash.; d. Ray R. and Marian (Onstad) D.; edn: BA, Univ. of Wash. Seattle 1967, MBA, 1968; PhD, Golden Gate Univ. 1978; Certified in Data Processing (CDP) 1980, and Cert. Systems Profl. (CSP) 1985, Inst. for Cert. of Computer Profls.; Cert. Data Educator (CDE) 1984, Data Edn. Cert. Council. Career: communications cons. Pacific NW Bell Telephone Co., Seattle 1968-71; mktg. supr. AT&T, San Francisco 1971-73; senior cons. project leader Quantum Sci. Corp., Palo Alto 1973-75; dir. analysis program Input Inc., Palo Alto 1975-76; dir. information scis. dept. Golden Gate Univ., San Francisco 1982-83, mem. info. systems adv. bd., 1983–; prof. acctg. and info. systems CSU Hayward, 1976–; cons. pvt. cos., 1975-; lectr. San Jose State Univ. 1973-4, Univ. of Puget 1970-71; Loaned exec. United Good Neighbors, Seattle 1969; nat. committeewoman, bd. dirs. Young Republicans, Wash. 1970-71; advisor Junior Achievement, San Francisco 1971-72, Junior Club of Seattle 1969-71; awards: nat. grantee, DPMA, to devel. model curriculum in Graduate Computer Info. Systems, 1984; mem: Data Processing Mgmt. Assn. (pres. S.F. Chpt. 1986; bd. dirs. DPMA Internat. Interest Group in Edn. 1985-86, recipient service award 1982, individual performance award 1984), Assn. Computing Machinery; author: Computers and Remote Computing Services (1983); num. publs. in profl. journals and conf. proceedings; current work: curriculum devel., profl. certification, industry standards, design of data bases and data banks; rec: sailing, skiing, photog. Address: CSU Hayward, Hayward 94542

DUNFEE, GORDON EARL, real estate executive; b. Nov. 9, 1950, Plainfield, N.J.; s. Gordon M. and Merciee J. (Franke) Dunfee; m. Linda; children: Saige, Taylor, Derek, Shannon; edn: BS, Univ. Vermont 1972; JD, Univ. San Diego 1979; admitted Calif. State Bar & Fed. Practice 1979. Career: sales mgr. 3M Co., San Diego; sales assoc. Coldwell Banker; v.p. The Lusk Co., S.D. currently; honors: San Diego Law Rev. (1978); mem. Mira Mesa Bus. Park Assn. (dir., pres.), NADIP (dir.); Republican; Christian; rec: ski, surf, swim. Ofc: The Lusk Co 5897 Oberlin Dr Ste 204 San Diego 92106

DUNHAM, JEFFREY ALAN, investment counseling co. president; b. Sept. 12, 1961, Loveland, Colo.; s. Richard L. and Delene K. Dunham; edn: Grossmont Coll. 1980; bus. adm., finl. svcs. major CSU San Diego 1979-83, MBA cand. 1983-; desig: CFP cand., Col. for Finl. Planning. Career: active in real estate 1977- (investor since age 15); founding ptnr. investment banking firm McKewon & Timmons (affil. of venture capital co. Enterprise Mgmt. Co.); founder/pres. Dunham & Greer, San Diego currently; dir. Internat. Heritage Co.; honors: outstanding Intern of Year (1982-83), CSU San Diego; mem. IAAFP, Am. Assn. of Individual Investors, San Diego Stock & Bond Club, SDSU Bus. Alumni; Republican; rec: flying, tennis, waterskiing. Res: 5626 Baja Dr San Diego 92115 Ofc: Dunham & Greer Inc. 5075 Shoreham Pl Ste 240 San Diego 92122

DUNIWAY, BENJAMIN CUSHING, U.S. judge; b. Nov. 21, 1907, Stanford, Calif.; s. Clyde A. and Caroline M. (Cushing) D.; m. Ruth Mason, Oct. 28, 1933; children: Anne (Barker), Carolyn (Hoffman), John M.; edn: BA, Carleton Coll. 1928, hon. LLD, 1981; LLB, Stanford Univ. 1931; BA (Rhodes Scholar), Oxford Univ. 1933, MA, 1964; admitted to Calif. State Bar 1931. Career: law practice, San Francisco 1933-42, 47-59, partner firm Cushing, Cullinan, Duniway & Gorrill, 1947-59; regional atty. OPA, San Francisco 1942-45, regional adminstr. 1945-47, asst. to adminstr., Wash DC 1945; justice Dist. Ct. Appeals, 1st Appellate Dist. Calif., S.F. 1959-61; US circuit judge 9th Circuit Ct. Appeals, 1961-76, senior judge, 1976–; judge Temp. Emergency Ct. Appeals US, 1979–; mem. com. trial practice and techniques Jud. Conf. US, 1969-74, mem. com. jud. stats., 1970-76; dir. Schlage Lock Co., 1951-59; chmn. Gov's Commn. Met. Area Problems, 1958-59; pres. Community Chest, S.F. 1956-57, Calif. Conf. Social Work, 1950, Family Service Agcy., S.F. 1950-51, Urban League S.F., 1952; trustee Carleton Coll. 1958-71, Stanford Univ. 1962-72; trustee James D. Phelan Found. 1957-71, pres. 1969-71; trustee Rosenberg Found. 1960-75, pres. 1964, 68-70; bd. dirs. Legal Aid Soc., S.F. 1955-70, Family and Childrens Agcy. S.F., 1948-51; life gov. Mill Hill Sch., Eng. 1933-; honors: Presidential Cert. of Merit, 1947, Order of Coif, Phi Beta Kappa, Delta Smiga Rho; mem. ABA, Am.Judicature Soc., Am. Law Inst., Conf. Calif. Judges, S.F. Bar Assn., Soc. Calif. Pioneers, World Affairs Council S.F.; clubs: Chit Chat, Commercial (S.F.); author (with C.J. Vernier) American Family Laws, Vol. II, 1932. Office: P.O. Box 547, San Francisco 94101

DUNLAP, SUSAN CLAIRE, artist/designer; b. Jan. 15, 1948, Santa Rosa; d. Edwin Veghte and Marilyn Lucille (Keeler) D.; edn: int. design stu., CSU San Jose 1970, 74, 77, Foothill Comm. Coll. 1973, 77; grad. (MA in prog.), Fuller Theol. Sem. Career: badminton instr. Men's P.E. Dept. San Jose St. Univ., 1970; general artist Goodwill Indus., Santa Clara 1968-70; interior designer K.B.M. Office Furniture, San Jose 1970-73; dir. Int. Design Dept. H.S. Crocker Co., Inc. Santa Clara 1973-78; partner Dunlap Marconi Design Co. (int. design firm), Palo Alto 1978-81; currently free lance artist/designer, Menlo Park; lectr: Owner-Builder Center 81-2, AAUW 82, Ch. Fellowship Gp. 83, Design Symp. Canada Coll. 83; cons. State Dept. of Alcohol & Drugs 1982; awards: service, City of Menlo Park 1984; Calif. State Scholarship 1968-70; mem: Mendocino Art Center 1979-82; Orgn. of Women Architects & Design Profls. (founding bd. 1974-6); El Gatito Coop. Gallery 1972; chmn. Environ. Beautification Commn. Menlo Park 1982-3; Menlo/Atherton AAUW (bd. 1982-3); works: Evening Good Trail & Great Spirit Path (commnd. City of Menlo Park), sculptural word-rock poems inspired by Indian pictographs, 500 tons of stone, 1800 foot path in city park, 1981-84; various soft sculpture commns. (jute, leather): Viking Freight System 1978, Syva/Syntex Corp. 1980; watercolor commn., Young Amb. Mag. 1983; media coverage KNTV 1980, 83; Democrat; Presbyterian (Singles Outreach Bd., nat. mission & evangelism coms.); rec: writing (book), composing music, gardening. Address: Susan Dunlap Design Co. 220 Chester St Menlo Park 94025

DUNN, JOHN MICHAEL, hotel executive; b. Oct. 29, Escondido; s. John Delano and Edna (Newell) D.; m. Yvonne D. Dunn; children: John Michael, Jr. b. 1964, Patrick b. 1966, John G. b. 1967, Jeff b. 1967, Eric b. 1970; edn: AA, (Hilton Outstanding Grad., Hotel & Rest. Dept.) City Coll. of S.F., 1966; BA, S.F. State, 1968; cert: prof., Hotel & Rest. Mgmt. Career: cook, bartender, hotel night clerk, -1967; conv. & sales, Hilton Hotels, S.F. 1967-68; restaurant mgr/supr. Lyons Restaurants Inc., Burlingame 1968-70; gen. mgr./v.p. Hunters Inn, Santa Maria 1970-72; mng. gen. partner Topper Motor Hotel & Rest., Taft 1973–; mem: Nat., Calif. Restaurant Assns., Calif. Hotel Assn., Taft CofC, Kern Co. Bd. of Trade, Taft Petroleum Club, Chefs de Cuisine of Greater Bakersfield; cons. to Kern Co. Supr. Trice Harvey; mil: USCG 1958-62; Democrat; Catholic; rec: golf, cooking, photog. Res: 501 A St., Taft 93268 Ofc: Topper Hotel, 101 E. Kern Ste 29, Taft 93268

DUNN, MICHAEL DAVID, health care co. executive; b. Oct. 28, 1944, Chgo.; s. Philip Samual and Joan Mamie (Osten) D.; m. Ronna Kravitz, June 14, 1964; children: Brian b. 1966, Rhoda b. 1969, Jennifer b. 1973; edn: BS, Ill. Inst. of Tech. 1964; grad. certifs. Marquette Univ. 1965, Univ. of Wisc.-Milwaukee 1964-65. Career: corporate mfg. staff Allis Chalmers, 1964-65; plant supt. Essex Wire, 1965-66; mfg. mgr. Sunbeam 1966-67; project mgr. Gauger & Diehl, CPA 1967-68; pres. Advanced Health Systems Inc. 1969-82; bd. chmn. Westworld Community Healthcare Inc., 1982-; dir: PharmaKinetics Labs. (1985-), Inst. of Health Mgmt. (1976-), First Western Health (1985-); honors: Who's Who in Am. Colls. & Univs. (1963); mem: Hosp. Information Systems Sharing Group (v.p. & dir. 1972-77), Center for Alcohol Studies, Rutgers Univ. (1979-); publs: num. tech. and research publs. incl. Criteria for Evaluating and Choosing a Computer System (Hospital Progress 1974); Republican; Jewish. Res: 32221 Cook Ln San Juan Capistrano 92675 Ofc: Westworld Community Healthcare Inc. 23832 Rockfield Rd Lake Forest 92630

DUNN, PHILIP HOWARD, lawyer; b. May 11, 1947, Billericky, Chelmsford, Eng.; s. Dr. Richard C. and Irene I. (Snelson) D.; edn: AA, Santa Monica City Coll. 1968; BS in bus., CSU Long Beach 1-0; JD, Whittier Coll. Sch of Law 1977; admitted to practice US Supreme Ct., Calif. Supreme Ct. Career: 2 years law clerk to Command Judge Advocate, Fort Ord, Calif.; 2 years law clerk to three judges, L.A. Municipal Ct.; law clerk Pub. Defenders Office; pvt. law practice/ pres. Dunn & Roth, Santa Monica 1977–; rep. plaintiffs in case of Harrison vs. Yong (LASC 355875), after 5 week jury trial received largest verdict (1.3 mil. dollars) in the country ever in a habitability case; mem: Santa Monica Bar Assn., L.A. Trial Lawyers Assn.; mil: sp4 US Army 1971, decorated Good Conduct Medal; rec: ski, sail, surf, soaring, karate, chess. Ofc: Dunn & Roth, PC, 2953 Lincoln Blvd Santa Monica 90405

DUONG, TIEN HONG, mechanical engineer; b. Dec. 20, 1951, Nam Dinh, Vietnam, nat. US cit. 1981; s. Ham Dang and Ngan Thi (Vu) D.; m. Minh-Trang Thi Dao, Sept. 1, 1979; 1 son, Timothy Minh-Tuan b. 1983; edn: BSME, Univ. Utah 1976, BS indsl. engrg., 1977, MSME, 1986; Reg. Profl. Engr. Calif. 1984. Career: stress analyst Rockwell Internat. Canoga Park 1978-81; piping stress analyst C.F. Braun Co. Alhambra 1981-82; staff engr. Hughes Aircraft Canoga Park 1982–; instr. basic and fortran programming Rockwell co.-sponsored pgm.; mem: Am. Soc. Mech. Engrs., Vietnamese Student Assn. (writing staff member, Univ. of Utah); Republican; Catholic; rec: painting (oils, acrylic), reading, stocks, photog. Res: 20446 Hemmingway St Canoga Park 91306

DUPON, NORMAN RICHARD, financial planner; b. Apr. 25, 1939, Chgo.; s. Hilaire and Helene D.; m. Johanna C., Dec. 15, 1965; children: Matthew b. 1973, Caroline b. 1977; edn: BS, Univ. Ill. 1962; M.Ed, Univ. Ariz. 1963; desig: Chartered Life Underw. (CLU), 1972, Cert. Finl. Planner (CFP) 1985, SEC lic. stockbroker Series 7, 1984. Career: asst. prof. Univ. Alaska 1963-64; ins. agt. Penn Mutual Life Ins. Co., 1964-70, Home Life of New York, 1970-80; finl. planner, prin. Dupon Finl. Services, San Gabriel 1980–; mil: pfc US Army; Prot.; rec: swim. Res: 865 Chester San Marino 91108 Ofc: Dupon Financial Services 7220 Rosemead Ste 208 San Gabriel 91775

DURBROW, ROBERT TERRILL, water agencies association executive, ret.; b. Apr. 3, 1908, Oroville; s. Wm. and Blanche (Terrill) D.; m. Geraldine Elmgren (dec.); m. 2d. Shirley Stoecker, July 28, 1951; children: Robert Jr. b. 1939, Philip b. 1940, Linda b. 1946 (adopted), Douglas b. 1954; edn: BS, UC Berkeley and UC Davis, 1932; Calif. State Secondary Sch. Tchg. credential, 1933. Career: mgr. 1500-acre ranch (rice, dairy, hogs, poultry) in Glenn County 1927-30; Smith-Hughes agric. instr., Dept. hd. Liberty Union High Sch., Brentwood 1934-37; asst. USDA Farm Advisor, Merced County 1937-41; exec. dir., mgr., treas. Assn. of Calif. Water Agencies, San Francisco and Sacto. (hon. life mem.), 1945-73, cons. and mem. bd. dirs., 1973-; secty. treas. Calif. Reclamation Assn. (1945-73); mem. Univ. of Calif. Water Resources Center Advis. Council (1967-); mem: Am. Water Works Assn. (1946-73, hon. life mem.), Nat. Water Resources Assn. (1946-73, hon. life mem.), Commonwealth Club of Calif., State CofC (Water Resources Com. 1968-), Sons in Retirement (past br. pres. 1969), Lions Club; publs: coauthor/hist. research coord. ACWA's 75-Year History (304 pp.); mil: lt. col. US Army Reserve (ret.), active duty 1941-45; Republican; Prot.; rec: photog., poetry. Res: 5277 Glancy Dr Carmichael 95608 Ofc: ACWA 910 K St Ste 250 Sacramento 95814

DURRANT, DEAN OBORN, podiatrist; b. Dec. 1, 1929, Tooela, Utah; s. Randell Porter and Emily Jorgensen (Oborn) D.; m. Dian Overson, Apr. 10, 1953; children: Kathrine b. 1954, Calleen b. 1959, Russell b. 1961, Joyce b. 1963, Suzanne b. 1967, Ronda b. 1971, LaDean b. 1972; edn: AA, City Coll. of San Francisco, 1955; BS, DPM, Calif. Coll. of Podiatric Med. 1960. Career: pvt. practice podiatry, Vallejo; trustee Calif. Coll. of Podiatric Med., 1974; secty. Solano Co. Comprehensive Health Planning Council, 1974-75; chief Podiatry Staff, Broadway Hosp., Vallejo 1978-81; mem: Am. Podiatry Assn. (commnr. Region 12, Rev. Com.), Calif. Podiatry Assn. (pres. 1974-75); civic: Boy Scouts Am., Vallejo (counselor1963-64), Valljo Symp. Assn. (dir. 1968-72), Toastmasters 956 (pres. 1972), Naval Lodge 78, Elks, Masons, Shriners; mil: communs. tech. 1/c US Navy 1953-55; Democrat; Latter-Day Saints (elder, Sunday sch. tchr.). Res: 1325 Hestla Way Napa 94558 Ofc: Dean O. Durrant DPM, APC, 609 Georgia St Vallejo 94590

DURVASULA, SRINIVASA RAVI KUMAR, engineer; b. Nov. 2, 1955, Guntur, Andhra Pradesh, India, nat. US cit. June 3, 1986; s. Venkata Reddi Pantulu and Varahalamma (Prabhala) D.; m. Viswa Bharathi, Oct. 15, 1984; edn: BSME, M.S. Ramaiah Coll. of Engring., Bangalore 1979; MS engring. mechs., Penn State Univ. 1983. Career: mech. engr. (design of magnetic disk drives for computers) Tandon Corp., Chatsworth 1983-84; devel. engr. (cardiac pacemakers) Pacesetter Systems Inc., Sylmar 1985-; instr. engring. Penn State Univ. 1980-82; awards: Prize for project on Hand Pump Repair Tooling, Karnataka State Council for Sci. and Tech., Bangalore, India (1978); mem. Archimedes Circle USC Sch. of Engring. (1983-85); publs: Hand Pump Repair Tooling (1979), research on Strength of Porous Metals (1982); Hindu; rec: painting, Kantian philosophy, physics. Address: Sylmar 91342

DURYEA, JAMES JOHN, JR., lawyer; b. Jan. 9, 1950, San Francisco; s. James John and Dorothy Marie (Dean) D.; m. Sara Hornstein, Sept. 20, 1975; children: James John III b. 1978, Kathryn Jo b. 1982; edn: AB history, Georgetown Univ. 1972; JD, UC Hastings Coll. of Law 1975; admitted Calif. State Bar 1975, U.S. Supreme Ct. 1981, U.S. Ct. of Appeals (9th Circuit) 1975, U.S. Dist. Cts. (No. Dist. 1975, E. Dist. 1980, Cent. Dist. 1976). Career: assoc. Law Offices of James J. Duryea, PC 1975-79; ptnr. Kieth & Duryea 1979-81; principal Law Offices of James Duryea, Jr. 1981-; panelist antitrust seminars for industry groups 1982-; mem: ABA (antitrust sect. 1976-); S.F. Bar Assn. 1975- (judiciary com. 1983-); Barristers Club of S.F. (chair antitrust sect. 1979-84); 9th Circuit Model Jury Instruction Com. 1983; S.F. Bar delegate to State Bar Conference of Delegates (1979-83); Bohemian Club; Olympic Club; Guardsmen; dir. Family Svcs. Agcy.; Democrat; Catholic; rec: modern Am. history, philosophy, tennis, swimming, golf. Res: 3363 Washington St San Francisco 94118

DUSHANE, STEVEN DAVID, manufacturing/marketing co. executive; b. Nov. 1, 1957, Los Angeles; s. Sidney M. and Lillian (Epstien) D.; edn: Taft Coll. 1976-78, BS, Univ. Utah 1979. Career: founding prin./ exec. v.p. respons. for engring. design, product devel. and mdsg., Janeil Corp., Reseda 1980-, designed satellite equip. line ($80,000,000+ in sales); frequent lectr. on tech. aspects of satellite t.v.; mem. Aircraft Owners and Pilots Assn.; Democrat; Jewish; rec: flying, skiing. Ofc: Janeil Corp. 6850 Canby Ave Ste 106 Reseda 91335

DUTCHER, CRAIG EUGENE, manufacturing co. executive; b. Dec. 1, 1953, Portland, Ore.; s. Donald Eugene and Marilyn Elizabeth (Moore) D.; m. Kelley Cimmiyotti, Aug. 22, 1978; children: Patrick b. 1979, Tierney b. 1980, John b. 1984; edn: BA, St. Mary's, 1978. Career: foreman U.S. Steel Corp., Pittsburg, Calif. 1976, asst. gen. foreman 1978, gen. foreman 1980, process mgr. 1983, supt. Tin Products, USS/Posco, 1986-; mem. Assn. of Iron & Steel Engrs.; civic: Little League Baseball, youth swimming pgms.; Democrat; Catholic; rec: sports. Res: 7 London Ct Clayton 94517 Ofc: USS/Posco POB 471 Pittsburg 94565

DUTTON, DONALD STEVEN, information systems executive; b. Mar. 10, 1947, Kalispell, Mont.; s. Donald Zedoc and Roberta Estella (Lewis) D.; edn: Grays Harbor JC 1965-6; BBA, National Univ. 1977, MBA 1980; cert. computer sci., Coleman Coll. 1973; cert. data processing, Inst. for the Cert. of Computer Profls. 1982. Career: asst. date processing supr. Allied Administrators, San Diego 1972-3; computer ops. Rohr Ind., Inc., Chula Vista 1973-7; comp. pgmmr. analyst 1977-9; sr. pgmmr./analyst Foodmaker Inc., S.D.

1979-80, system project leader 1980-1, software apps. mgr. 1981-4; mgr. Systems, Denny's Inc., La Mirada 1984-; adj. faculty National Univ. 1980-3, UCSD 1983-4; information systems cons. City of Carlsbad 1983-4; profl. seminars, S.D. Regl. Tng. Ctr. 1983-4; mem: D.P. Mgmt. Assn. (bd. dirs. S.D. chpt. 1981-3, com. chmn.), Toastmasters (past pres.), S.D. Blood Bank; mil: E4 US Navy 1966-70; Christian. Res: 24852 Via Del Rio El Toro 92630 Ofc: Denny's Inc. 16700 Valley View Ave La Mirada 90637

DWAN, LOIS SMITH, journalist; b. Dec. 27; d. Allan A. and Mable Anne (Garret) Smith; m. Robert Dwan, Aug. 7, 1940; children: Judy b. 1941, Robert b. 1942, Alan b. 1943, Hugh James b. 1954, Katherine b. 1955; edn: BA, Dominican Coll. 1935; grad. work, Stanford Univ. 1939. Career: Society columnist Baker (Ore.) Democrat-Herald, 1935-36; publicity, advtg., Portland, Ore. 1936-38; freelance writer Los Angeles Mag., 1964-65, staff writer, restaurant columnist, 1965-66; restaurant columnist Los Angeles Times, 1966-84; awards: Editorial award L.A. Times (1978), Lois Dwan scholarship estab. by L.A. restaurants (1984); mem: Am. Inst. of Wine & Food (bd.), Soc. of Bacchus, Restaurant Writers Assn. (founder, pres.); publs: "Guide to L.A. Restaurants" (1970, 72, 77, 80, 82, 84), L.A. Section Mariani "Coast to Coast Dining" (1986), copy for "California Cooking" (1986); Democrat; Catholic; rec: gardening, cooking. Address: Santa Monica 90402

DWORSKY, DANIEL LEONARD, architect; b. Oct. 4, 1927, Mpls.; s. Lewis and Ida Claire (Fineberg) D.; m. Sylvia Taylor, Aug. 10, 1957; children: Doug b. 1959, Laurie b. 1961, Nancy b. 1965. edn: B.Arch., Univ. Mich. 1950. Career: design critic; instr. arch. Univ. So. Calif. 1968, 83, 84; honors: Fellowship Am. Inst. Arch. 1953, Merit Awards (So. Calif. chap. AIA 1957, 66, 69, 80, 82, 85), Governor's Design Award (Calif. 1966), L.A. Grand Prix (So. Calif. AIA 1967, Honor (So. Calif. AIA 1963, 66, 69, 73, 74, 77, 80, 83), AIA Nat. Honor 1974, Calif. Council AIA Firm Award 1985; Calif. Council AIA Honor Awards 1963, 66, 69, 74, 80, 83, 84; mem. Lambda Alpha. Res: 9225 Nightingale Dr Los Angeles 90069 Ofc: Dworsky Assoc. 2029 Century Park East, Ste 350, Los Angeles 90067

DYE, ROSS WINTON, clergyman; b. Jan. 9, 1925, Spencer, W.Va.; s. R.N. and Olive E. (Elliott) D.; m. Norma Prescott, July 21, 1945; children: Gregory b. 1951, Celeste b. 1962, Suzanne b. 1964; edn: BS, West Virginia Univ. 1948; Oklahoma City Univ. 1952. Career: minister Church of Christ, Bowie, Texas 1948-52, Midwest City, Okla. 1952-54, Jackson, Miss. 1954-58, San Antonia, Texas 1958-66, Wash. DC 1966-78, Anaheim 1978-; bd. trustees Ohio Valley Coll., Parkersburg, W.Va. 1968-72; mem. Disciples of Christ Historical Soc.; spkr., 33 states and 12 foreign countries; honers: literary award, Christian Woman Mag. 1962; mem: Disciples of Christ Historical Soc., Rotary (past chaplain 1964-66); publs: staff writer, 20th Century Christian; num. articles in Gospel Advocate; author: Words of Comfort, 1962; The Other Sheep, 1963; mil: s/sgt. US Army Air Corps 1943-45, Air Medal w/ 3 Oak Leaf Cluster; Republican; Ch. of Christ; rec: gardening. Res: 1040 Downing St. Anaheim 92805

DYER, ALAN GORDON, university educator, consultant; b. Mar. 30, 1941, San Diego; s. Robert B. and Velma A. (Griffith) D.; m. Beverly, May 27, 1961; children: Dale b. 1961, Donna b. 1962; edn: BA sociol., CSU San Bernardino 1968; MA edn., Pepperdine Univ. 1975. Career: child social worker Corona, Calif. 1968-69; adult sch. educator Rialto/ San Bernardino 1974-; univ. instr. extended day pgm. CSU San Bernardino, upward bound instr. 1977-81; dir., cons. Fon-Ri Edn. Svcs. 1975-; honors: Phi Delta Kappa, Alpha Kappa Delta; mem: Assn. of Calif. School Adminstrs., Calif. Council Adult Edn., Rialto Jaycees, Kiwanis; mil: E-5 USNR 1959-69, Calif. Air Nat. Guard, Good Conduct, Meritorious Commdn., Vietnam Svc., Armed Forces Reserve, Naval Reserve, Nat. Defense; Democrat; L.D.S.; rec: music (guitar instr.), travel. Address: 19256 Arbeth Rialto 92376

DYER, ANDREW ROY, corporate planner; b. Apr. 30, 1951, Nashville, Tenn.; s. Andrew Johnson and Gladys Marie (Kelly) D.; edn: BS, math., Univ. Tenn. 1973; BE in EE, Vanderbilt Univ. 1974; MBA, fin., Univ. of Tenn. 1975. Career: prin. systems analyst Teledyne Brown Engring., Huntsville, Ala. 1976-78; ops. auditor Data-Design Labs., Cucamonga 1978-80; sr. acctg. systems analyst Calif. Fed. Svgs., Los Angeles 1980-81; sr. mem. tech. staff Teledyne Systems Co., Northridge 1981-; awards: Best Economic Forecaster for 1979, So. Calif. Corp. Planners Assn.; Outstanding Young Men in Am. 1981; Who's Who in the West 1986; recognition, Planning Execs. Inst. 1980, 81; Sturges Mem. Scholarship, Univ. of Tenn.; mem: Planning Execs. Inst. (vp LA chpt. 1981-2); So. Calif. Corp. Planners Assn. (treas. 1980-81); World Future Soc. (pres. LA chpt. 1979-80); fellow Brit. Interplanetary Soc.; IEEE; Am. Inst. of Aero. and Astro.; Am. Mktg. Assn.; Assn. of MBA Execs.; Assn. of Old Crows; Assn. for Corp. Growth; Acad. of Sci. Fiction, Fantasy and Horror Films; ACLU, NOW, Sierra Club, Orgn. for Adv. of Space Inds. and Settlement, LA Sci. Fantasy Soc., Mensa, Intertel, L.A. Astronomical Soc., Planetary Soc.; rec: astronomy. Res: 22446 Burbank Blvd Woodland Hills 91367 Ofc: Teledyne Systems Co. 19601 Nordhoff St Northridge 91367

DYSON, ARTHUR THOMAS, architect; b. Feb. 24, 1940, Hawthorne, Calif.; s. Homer Harry and Thyra Grace (Moe) D.; m. Juanita M. Juers, Nov. 23, 1961; children: Katrina Deanna b. 1962, Tianna Thyra b. 1963; m. 2d Audrey Marie Roberts, Sept. 9, 1970; son, Marc Aaron b. 1972; edn: Univ. Wisc. 1958, Univ. Okla. 1961. Career: architectural apprenticeship w. Frank Lloyd Wright, Architect, Taliesin, Spring Green, Wisc., Taliesin West, Scottsdale, Ariz. 1958-59, w. Bruce Goff, Arch., Bartlesville, Okla. 1959-61, w. William Gray Purcell, Arch., Pasadena, Calif. 1961-62; ptnr. Gage, Dyson & Assocs., Arch.

& Engrg., Fresno 1967-71; pvt. practice, Arthur Dyson & Assoc., Environmtl. Design, Fresno 1971— (best known for creating unorthodox archtl. forms and a leading exponent of inventive arch. in USA); lectr. on innovative arch. throughout US; instr. advanced archtl. design Univ. of No. Carolina, Charlotte 1986; chmn. Fresno Comm. Devel. Commn. 1975-77; chmn. Fresno Urban Plnng. Task Force 1974-77; chmn. Environmtl. Devel. Orgn. 1969-73; co-chmn. Urban Workshop 1974; publs: num. articles on creative arch. and the environment; personal archtl. works publ. nationally, internationally incl. Japan, France & Eng.; exhibitions incl. Royal Inst. of Brit. Archs. Mus., Auraria Higher Edn. Ctr., Univ. Colo., Univ. NC Charlotte, Frank Lloyd Wright Sch. of Arch., Univ. Okla., Calif. State Univs. Res: 3239 E Bellaire Way Fresno 93726 Ofc: Arthur Dyson & Assoc. 754 P St Fresno 93721

EAKLE, A. KEMPER, III, insurance co. executive; b. Nov. 3, 1942, Staunton, Va.; s. Avis K. Jr. and Marie T. (Thurber) E.; m. Donna, Aug. 10, 1961; children: Jeffrey b. 1964, Michele b. 1966, Andrea b. 1968, Robert b. 1972, Matthew b. 1975; edn: BA, San Francisco State Univ. 1964, MA, 1971; MBA, Pepperdine 1978. Career: mgr. JC Penny 1964-66; field supvr. Travelers Ins. Co. 1966-68; Home Office mgr. Royal Ins. Co. 1968-74, Home Office mgr. indsl. indemnity 1974-79; dir. of mktg. Great American Ins. Co., 1979—, currently, vice pres., San Jose; instr. City Univ. 1986; honors: Coll. of Ins. Exec. Pgm., 1981; Calif. Community Coll. Instr. Cred., 1972; mem: Mgmt. Ptrs.- Pepperdine Univ., San Francisco State Alumni Assn. (life), San Francisco Conservatory of Music; Republican; Episcopal; rec: tennis, golf, racquetball. Res: 6723 Elwood Rd. San Jose 95120 Ofc: Great American-West, 1735 N First St San Jose 95112

EASON, FRANCIS JOSEPH, physician; b. Feb. 13, 1938, Mnpls., Minn.; s. Donald Audrey and Loretta Josephine (Morello) E.; edn: BA cum laude, Univ. of Minn. 1960, BS, MD, 1964; certifed Am. Board of Surgery 1972. Career: intern Orange County (CA) Med. Center 1964-65; gen. surgery residency Long Beach VA Hosp., 1965-68, Graduate Hosp., Phila. 1968-69, US Naval Hosp., San Diego 1969-71; Camp Pendleton (CA) Naval Hosp., 1971-73; pvt. solo practice of gen. surgery, Poway 1973—; med. staff (first pres., 1977) Pomerado Hosp., Poway; awards: AMA and CMA Recognition Awards 1969-; mem: Fellow Am. Coll. of Surgeons 1976, AMA, CMA, San Diego Soc. of Gen. Surgeons, Nat. Wildlife Fedn., Nat. Geographic Soc., Nat. Humane Soc.; club: Tennis-Escondido; mil: cdr. USN Med. Corps 1969-73; Roman Catholic; rec: tennis. Res: 1230 W 13th Ave Escondido 92025 Ofc: 15644 Pomerado Rd, D-So, Poway 92064

EATON, LEWIS SWIFT, financial executive; b. Aug. 10, 1919, San Francisco; s. Edwin Morrow and Gertrude Thayer (Swift) E.; m. Virginia Stammer, Apr. 21, 1950; children: William b. 1951, Joan b. 1953, John b. 1956; edn: BS, Stanford Univ. 1942. Career: financial exec. Guarantee Savings & Loan Assn. 1946-, pres. 1956—; chmn. bd. Guarantee Financial Corp. 1972—; honors: Foundation Award (Fresno State Univ.), Bus. Sch. Award (CSUF 1978), Leon S. Peters Award (1984); mem: Calif. Savings & Loan League (pres. 1960-61), US S&L League (pres. 1971), Stanford Univ. Alumni Assn. (pres. 1975-76), Fresno CofC (pres. 1967), Fresno Metro. Mus. (pres. 1978-), Fresno Zool. Soc. (pres. 1958); pres. Bd. of Edn. Fresno Unified Sch. Dist. 1958-66; mil: capt. US Army Transp. Corps 1942-46, Army Commdn.; Republican; Episcopal; rec: photog., golf, tennis, skiing. Res: 4115 N Van Ness Blvd Fresno 93704 Ofc: Guarantee Financial Corp. 1177 Fulton Mall Fresno 93721

EBERSOLE, GEORGE DAVID, manufacturing co. executive; b. July 11, 1936, Plattsmouth, Nebr.; s. George Benjamin and Wilma (Shepard) E.; m. Beverly Sullivan, Nov. 28, 1957; children: Karen b. 1961, Kent b. 1963, Kyle b. 1972; edn: BSME, Milwaukee Sch. of Engring. 1961; MSME, Univ. of Wisc., Madison 1963; PhD engring., Univ. of Tulsa 1971; Reg. Profl. Engr., Oklahoma. Career: independent consultant 1963; senior group leader R&D Dept., Phillips Petroleum Co., Bartlesville, Ok. 1963-73; asst. to v.p. R&D Frito-Lay Inc., Irving, Tx. 1973-74; gen. division mgr. Metal Products Group, Hoover Universal, Ann Arbor, Mich. 1974-80; pres. Energy Absorption Systems, and pres. Spin Cast Plastics (wholly owned subs. Quixote Corp.), Chgo. 1980—; mem. ASME; contbr. var. profl. publs., sev. patents; Presbyterian. Res: 7831 Forest Hill Ln Palos Hts Ill 60463 Ofc: Energy Absorption Systems One East Walker Dr Chicago 60601

EBINER, ROBERT MAURICE, lawyer, b. Sept. 2, 1927, Los Angeles; m. Paula H. Van Sluyters, 1951; children: John, Lawrence, Marie, Michael, Christopher, Joseph, Francis, Matthew, Therese, Kathleen, Eileen, Brian, Patricia, Elizabeth, Ann; edn: undergrad., Loyola Univ., L.A. 1949, JD, Loyola Univ. Sch of Law 1953. Career: general, civil and trial law practice, W. Covina 1954—; judge pro tem Los Angeles Superior Ct., Citrus Municipal Ct.; arbitrator Am. Arbitration Assn. 1965- and L.A. Superior Ct. 1979-; instr. of law Alhambra H.S. eve. 1955-58; Disciplinary Hearing Panel, Calif. State Bar; mem. Fed. Court Central Dist. of Calif. Mem. Am., Calif., L.A. Co., Eastern (pres.1965-6) and Citrus (arts., Citrus Bar Bull. 1962-3) Bar Assns.; founder Queen of Valley Hosp. 1959; mem. Hosp. Men's Club 1971- (bd. dirs. 1973-6); trustee Queen of the Valley Found. 1983-; organizer and meet dir. La Puente Spl. Olympics 1985; meet dir. Bishop Amat Relays (h.s. track & field) 1980-; mem. Catholic Welfare Bur. (bd. dirs. 1978-), Archdiocese of LA, Catholic Welfare Bureau (San Gabriel Valley pres. 1956-60, budget chmn. 56-69); mem. Catholic Social Services, San Gabriel Valley (pres. 1969-72, bd. 69-74); charter bd. dirs. Am. Cancer Soc. N.E. Los Angeles Co. Unit 1973-78 (chmn. By-laws com.); bd. dirs. W. Covina United Fund 1958-61 (chmn. Budget Com. 60-61); orgnzr. Jt. United Funds of E.San Gabriel Valley (bd.dirs. 1961-8); charter bd.dirs. United Way, L.A. Co. Area V, 1962-70 (Budget Panel chmn.

1980); mem: West Covina CofC (pres. 1960); Knights of Columbus (3rd deg.1955-, Advocate So. Calif. chpt. 1973-4); Knights of Columbus (4th deg. 1955-), Bishop Amat H.Sch. Booster Club (pres. 1978-80, bd.dir. 1973-); charter, Kiwanis Club of W. Covina 1958- (pres. 1976-7, bd.dirs. 72-, Inter.Club chmn. Div. 35, 1977-8, Amb. for CA-NV-HA Found. 1978-9, Lt. Gov. Kiwanis Div. 35, 1980-1, Kiwanian of the Year 1978 & 1983). Recipient Disting. Service Award 1978, LA Co. Human Rels. Commn.; mem. LA Co. Dist. Atty. Adv. Council, 1974-82. Democrat (cmpgn. mgr. Cong. Ronald B. Cameron 1964, State Central Com. 1963-8). rec: fishing, collector hist. memorabilia. Res: 2734 Sunset Hill Dr. W. Covina Ofc: 1502 W. Covina Pky. West Covina 91790

ECHEAGARAY, MARK KAY, manufacturing co. engineering director; b. Sept. 20, 1957, Detroit, Mich.; s. Manuel and Dorthy Ann (McDermit) E.; m. Denise Caroline Hathaway, June 15, 1981; children: Anthony b. 1982, Jessica Anne b. 1983; edn: AS electro mech., Chabot Coll. 1977; BSEE, Cal. Poly. Univ. 1980; MSEE, Stanford Univ. 1984; Reg. Profl. Engr. Calif. 1982. Career: service engr. ABC Communications Hayward 1974-77; field sys, investigator Digital Sound Research Sunnyvale 1978-79, tiger team engr. 1980-81, senior engr. San Lorenzo 1981-83, dir. 1983-86, engrg. dir. intelligent sys. group 1986—; instr. Foothill Coll.; trade show seminars; honors: Engr. of the Year (D.S.R. 1983, 84, 85), Second Place Civil Air Patrol Ground Search & Rescue Crew (1984); mem: IEEE 1975-, Audio Engrg. Soc. 1977-, Civil Air Patrol Search & Rescue, Amateur Radio Emerg. Repeater Svc.; inventions: ultra high speed digital laser audio storage disc (1981), NCD speech recognition processor (1983); Republican; Catholic; rec: bicycling, automotive, mountain climbing, photog. Ofc: Digital Sound Research 1716 Bockman Rd Lab 12 San Lorenzo 94580

ECKERSLEY, NORMAN C., bank president; b. June 18, 1924, Leith, Britain; s. James N. and Beatrice (Chadwick) E.; 1 dau. Catherine Anne (Robins) b. 1951; edn: Manchester Univ., U.K.; LLD, Univ. of Strathclyde, Scotland. Career: acct. The Chartered Bank, in Bombay 1948-52, Singapore 1952-54, Sarawak 1954-56, Pakistan 1956-58, Hong Kong 1958-60, mgr., Hamburg, Ger. 1960-62, area mgr., India 1962-67, Thailand 1967-69; pres. The Chartered Bank of London, 1969-74, bd. chmn. 1974-79; bd. chmn. Standard Chartered Bancorp. (USA) 1978-81; deputy chmn. Union Bank, Los Angeles 1979-80; chmn./chief exec. The Pacific Bank, San Francisco 1983—; honors: Commander, Order of British Empire (CBE); mem: Overseas Bankers Assn. (Calif. chmn. 1972-74), Calif. Council of Internat. Trade (dir.), San Francisco CofC, World Trade Assn., Bay Area Council (dir.), Scottish/Am. Inv. Com. (chmn.), commnr. S.F. Art Commn.; clubs: Royal & Ancient Golf (Scotland), Royal Troon Golf (Scotland), San Francisco Golf, World Trade (SF), Stock Exchange (SF), Pacific Union (SF); mil: Royal Air Force 1940-46, D.F.C.; Ch. of Scotland; rec: golf, art, travel. Ofc: The Pacific Bank 101 California St Ste 3390 San Francisco 94111

ECKHAUS, LEONARD I., company president; b. Sept. 18, 1942, NYC; s. Sidney A. and Hortense E.; m. Linda Rosenthal, July 11, 1962; children: Lee, b. 1966, Jill, b. 1969; edn: Newburgh Free Acad. 1957-60, Orange Co. Comm. Coll. 1960-62. Career: senior computer opr. IBM Corp., Poughkeepsie, NY 1967-70; mgr. Eastern Region Data Centers, TRW Inc., NYC 1970-71; network control mgr. TRW Inc., Anaheim, Calif. 1971-73, mgr. operational planning 1973-74; asst. dir. data processing ops. Los Angeles County Supt. of Schools, Downey 1974-81; pres. Data Center Management Services, Anaheim 1981—; recognized by D.P. indus. as the leader in the computer ops. field; mem: Assn. for Computer Ops. Mgrs. (founding pres. 1980), Internat. Congress of Jewish Marriage Encounters (pres. 1980-81), Jewish Marriage Encounters of So. Calif. (bd. dirs. 1979-81); publs: num. tech. and mgmt. arts. in The Computer Operations Mag., media coverage in Computerworld, Govt. Computing News, Computerworld Canada, Wall St. Journal's Employment Daily; Jewish; rec: woodwork, bowling, music. Res: 4729 Bond Ave Orange 92669 Ofc: Data Center Mgmt Services, 11501 Brookhurst, Ste 201, Garden Grove 92640

EDELL, NORMAN, lawyer b. Sept. 26, 1925, Chicago, Ill.; s. Louis J. and Mary (Primack) E.; m. Gloria, Dec. 20, 1980; 1 dau: Marsha b. 1950; edn: BS, Woodbury 1949; JD, Southwestern 1966. Career: assoc. Seymour Fagan 1967-70; ptnr. Fagan, Klugman, Monroe & Edell 1970-72, sole practitioner 1973-80; pres. Norman Edell, APC dba Karen & Edell, Beverly Hills 1980—; Judge Pro Tem; Am. Arbitration Assn. Arbitration Panels; mem: Calif., Los Angeles and San Fernando Valley Bar Assns., Supreme Ct. of US, Am. Arbitration Assn., Los Angeles Trial Lawyers Assn., Themis Soc., Internat. Footprint Assn. (past pres.), Friars Club of Calif. (commiteeman), Variety Clubs Internat.; mil: capt. USAF 1943-73, navigator; rec: philately, sports, charities. Ofc: Karen & Edell, 8665 Wilshire Blvd. Pent. Beverly Hills 90211

EDELSTEIN, PAULA, entertainment co. executive; b. Oct. 10, 1950, Houston, Tx.; d. Dr. Moritz V. and Judith B. Craven; m. Ronald Steven Edelstein, Dec. 27, 1981; edn: BA, Univ. Ill. 1974. Career: exec. asst. Paramount Pictures, Los Angeles 1983-85; pres. Adesta Prodns., Glendale 1984—; exec. asst. to v.p. Walt Disney Co., Burbank 1984-85; exec. asst. to pres. Motown Prodns., L.A. 1985—; honors: Phi Theta Kappa (1970), Who's Who Am. Women (1986); mem: Am. Mgmt. Assn., Nat. Assn. of Female Execs., Hollywood Radio & T.V. Soc., Women in Film; Democrat; rec: equestrian. Address: Glendale

EDEN, HARRY DANIEL, aerospace co. executive; b. Jan. 16, 1930, Cincinnati, Oh.; s. Louis Ehoodin and Ida (Ruthrozen) E.; m. Nina Schuler, June 25, 1955, (dec.); children: Miriam L., b. 1957, educator; Deborah, b. 1960, engr.;

Richard A., b. 1962, Dr. Vet. Med.; edn: BS in E.E., Univ. of Idaho 1955; MS, aerospace systems mgmt., USC 1969; Reg. Profl. Nuclear Engr., Calif. 1977. Career: senior design engr. Raytheon Corp., Oxnard 1958-62; contract mgr. and Electronics Research Lab. mgr. Northrop Corp., Thousand Oaks 1962-67; project mgr. High Technology Space Systems and Solar Systems Pgms. (for USAF Space Div., US Dept. Energy, US Customs Service, others) The Aerospace Corp., El Segundo 1967 – ; owner/ ptr. Camarillo Medical Lab.; guest lectr. on space technology and project mgmt.; awards: Outstanding Achiev., IEEE; Superior Achiev., USN; Cert. of Achiev., USAF Ballistic Missile Sys.; senior mem. Am. Inst. of Elect. & Electronic Engrs.; mem. AAAS; num. publs. in field; mil: elec. tech. USN 1948-1950; rec: singing, camping. Res: 15515 Sunset Blvd., No.121, Pacific Palisades 90272 Ofc: The Aerospace Corp., El Segundo 90009

EDEN, RAYMOND L., association executive; b. July 19, 1925, Lee, Ill.; s. Bennie and Hannah E.; m. Ellen Mercer, Aug. 17, 1945; 1 son, Steven M., b. 1958; edn: BS, high honors, No. Ill. Univ.; grad. work Northwestern Univ. 1950, NY Univ. 1955, Univ. Chgo. 1961. Career: executive secty. Crippled Children's Center, Peoria, Ill. 1953-59; exec. dir. Illinois Heart Assn., 1962-66, California Heart Assn., 1966-69; adminstr. San Mateo Medical Clinic, 1969-70; exec. vice pres. American Heart Assn., Los Angeles 1970 – ; lectr. UCLA; faculty Center for Non-Profit Mgmt.; pres. Council on Volunteer Health Agencies, L.A.; pres. Los Angeles CPR Consortium; mem. Claremont Grad. Sch. Exec. Pgm. Advisory Council 1979-80; mem. State of Calif. Cardiac Care Com.; adv. com. UCLA Professional Designation Pgm. for Voluntary Agency Execs.; honors: Earl Beagle Award (nat.) for outstanding leadership; Fellowship and pres. 1981-2, Soc. of Heart Assn. Profl. Staff; Senior Men's Hon. Soc.; Fellowship Award, Alpha Gamma Delta; mem: Nat. Assn. of Social Workers, Acad. of Certified Social Workers, So. Calif. Assn. of Execs., Los Angeles Area CofC (Clean Air Com.), Rotary Internat., Shriners, California Club; mil: US Army 1944-46, ETO, battle ribbon/2 stars, purple heart, bronze star; Republican; Neighborhood Ch. bd. trustees 1975; rec: tennis, jogging, travel. Res: 30317 Via Cambron R. Palos Verdes Estates 90274 Ofc: American Heart Assn., Gr. LA Affil., 2405 West 8th St Los Angeles 90057

EDGAR, CAROL FRANCES-REGINA, art club president; b. Aug. 14, 1924, New Britain, Conn.; d. Sam and Phyllis Catherine (Rockett) Genovese; m. Henry Edgar, Feb. 23, 1946; children: Kathryn b. 1947, Linda b. 1949, Richard b. 1955. Honors: hon. mention in nationwide art contest late 30's; mem: Ruskin Art Club (pres. 1980-82, 1985-86, treas. 1986-87), Women's Internat. Club (pres. 1977-79, scholarship chmn. 1979-81), Societe de Charite des Dames Francaise (treas. 1979-83, 1979-87, 2nd v.p. 1978-79), Women's Club of Hollywood (art chmn. 1985-87); creative works: glass etching, early '60s; glass etcher w. St. Catherine's Guild, St. Mark's Episcopal Ch. 1963-66; Republican; Methodist; rec: collector of art objects, glass etching. Res: 2900 Canada Blvd Glendale 91208

EDGAR, JAMES MACMILLAN, JR., certified public accountant; b. Nov. 7, 1936, NY, NY; s. James Macmillan and Lilyan Dolores (McCann) E.; m. Judith Storey; children: Suzanne b. 1960, James III b. 1961, Gordon b. 1967; edn: B.ChE, Cornell Univ. 1959, MBA w/ distinction, 1960; CPA; Cert. Mgmt. Cons. Career: new product rep. E.I. duPont de Nemours, Wilmington, Del. 1960-63; mktg. svcs. rep. 1963-4; with Touche Ross & Co., 1964-78, Detroit cons. 1964-6, mgr. 1966-8, partner 1968-71, San Francisco partner-in-chg. mgmt. services opns. for No. Calif./Hawaii 1971-8; founding partner Edgar, Dunn & Co., Inc., S.F. 1978 – . mem. S.F. Mayor's finl. advis. commn. 1976-, exec. com. 1978-; chmn. Revenue Subcom. 1981-83; mem: Assn. for Corp. Growth (pres. S.F. chpt. 1982-3, dir. Nat. Bd. 1983-), Am. Inst. of CPAs, Calif. Soc. of CPAs, Inst. of Mgmt. Cons. (regl. v.p. 1973-80, dir. 75-77, v.p. bd. dirs. 77-80), Am. Mktg. Assn., S.F. CofC (chmn. City Budget Commn. 1976-8), University Club, Commonwealth Club, Cornell Univ. Council 1970-3, Tau Beta Pi; awards: for contbns. to profl. mgmt., Cornell Univ Grad. Sch. of Bus. Pub. Adminstrn. 1978; appreciation for pub. service, City & Co. S.F. 1978; patentee: non-woven fabrics. rec: fishing, hunting. Res: 10 Buckeye Way, Kentfield 94904. Ofc: Edgar, Dunn & Co. Inc. 847 Sansome St San Francisco 94111

EDGERLY, CHARLES ESTES, veterinarian; b. Nov. 12, 1940, s. Alvin Crowell and Maurine (Estes) E.; m. Lee Groves, June 15, 1963; children: Linda b. 1966, Debra b. 1969; edn: BS, Univ. Calif. 1962, DVM, 1964; Calif. lic. DVM (1964). Career: owner/dir. Reedley Veterinary Hosp., Reedley 1967 – ; secty. bd. dirs. Tulare-Kings Veterinary Emergency Service, Inc. 1983-; honors: life mem. Phi Kappa Phi and Phi Zeta, 1964; Approved mem. hosp. (1976-), Certified mem. hosp. (1980-), Am. Animal Hosp. Assn.; mem: Tulare Kings Vet. Med. Assn. (pres. 1972, secty. 1985-), Calif. Vet. Med. Assn. (ad hoc com. small animal practice stds. 1986), Am. Vet. Med. Assn.; civic: Dinuba Rotary (1966-), Fresno Bonsai Soc. (mem. 1969-, pres. 1981-83, treas. 1984-), Reedley H.Sch. Band Boosters (v.p. 1985); rec: gardening, Bonsai, computers. Res; 695 Ann Drive Reedley 93654 Ofc: Reedley Veterinary Hospital 21311 E Dinuba Ave Reedley 93654

EDMONDSON, JERRY MAC, energy equipment designer; b. Mar. 20, 1933, Dallas, Tx.; s. Dalton C. and Mae Orene (Caywood) E.; m. Diane Palacios, July 28, 1985; children: Sheri Lynn b. 1953, Gregory Lee b. 1956, James Paul b. 1981, Summer Cay b. 1986; edn: BSME, ICS, 1956. Career: chief engr. Sauder Industries, 1956-63; mgr. oil & gas prods. Panhandle Steel, 1963-66; mng. dir. Northsea-Alaska Co., 1966-69; mgr. bids & contracts Trico Superior Inc., 1969-80; founder/ pres. Heavy Oil Treating Co., Buena Park 1980 – ; honors: Hon. Dr. of Sci., London Inst. of Applied Research (1972), Who's Who in Technol. (1981); mem. Soc. of Petroleum Engrs., AIME; patents: improved method of treating heavy crude oil, geothermal actuated method for producing fresh water and elec. power, and improved wellhead gas prodn. unit; Republican; Prot.; rec: golf, water activities. Res: 238 62nd St Newport Beach 92663 Ofc: HOTCO 6970-8 Aragon Circle Buena Park 90620

EDWARDS, DON, congressman; b. Jan. 6, 1915, San Jose; children: Leonard Perry II, Thomas Charles, Samuel Dyer, Bruce Haven, William Don; edn: grad. Stanford Univ. 1936, Stanford Law Sch. 1938; admitted to Calif. State Bar. Career: special agent FBI, 1940-41; elected mem. 88th-99th congresses from 10th Dist. Calif.; mil: USN 1942-45; Democrat. Ofc: House Office Bldg., Wash. DC 20515

EFFRON, JOEL ARTHUR, company president; b. Feb. 11, 1944, Detroit, Mich.; s. Samuel David and Harriet Marshall (Nadelweiss) E.; m. JoAnn Rodgers, Aug. 6, 1972; 1 dau. Amanda b. 1980; edn: BSIE (indsl. eng.), UC Berkeley, 1965, MSIE, 1967. Career: mgr. cust. svc. quality assurance, TWA, NY, NY 1968-70, mgr. cus. svcs. industrial engineering, 1970-72, director reservations svcs., 1972-74; pres./dir. ComPath, Oakland, Ca. 1974-80; owner J. Effron & Associates, 1980 – ; pres. Codart, Novato 1982-82; pres. Zendex Corp., Dublin, Ca. 1982-85; dir: Metacom (Oakland) 1978, Zendex Corp. 1981-; bd. advisors Bay Alarm Co. 1984-; cons. Arthur D. Little Inc., S.F. 1981-82; mem: NATA (dir.) 1975-80; Calif. Interconnect Assn. (dir.) 1975-80; Rotarian; author: Data Communications Techniques and Technologies, 1984; rec: skiing, swim. Ofc: J. Effron & Assocs. Inc., POB 10456 Oakland 94610-0456

EGAN, EDWARD JOSEPH, JR., adhesives and roof coatings manufacturing co. president; b. Oct. 4, 1943, NY, NY; s. Edward Joseph, Sr. and Ann (Coakley) E.; m. Elizabeth Schwartz, Jan. 17, 1964; children: Elisabeth b. 1964, Edward, III b. 1966, Kevin b. 1970, Daniel b. 1977; edn: BA, Notre Dame Univ. 1965; MBA, USC 1969. Career: nat. mktg. mgr. American Can Co., Greenwich, Conn. 1970-73, regl. mgr. 1973-76, dir. mktg. & sales 1976-77; pres. General Can Co., Los Angeles 1977-82; pres./CEO Henry Holding Co., Los Angeles 1982 – ; mem: Can Mfrs. Inst. (bd. dirs., exec. com.), Carpet & Rug Inst., Adhesives & Sealants Council, Packaging Club, Packaging Inst., Nat. Paint & Coatins Assn., Co. Calif. Paint & Coatings Assn.; civic: Intra-Sci. Research Found. (chmn. & pres. 1982-), La Canada Little League (coach 1977-), Am. Heart Assn., Nat. Kidney Found., Am. Cancer Research Found.; advis. bd. Sacred Heart High Sch. (1978-83), St. Francis H.S. (1979-), St. Bede Grammar Sch. (treas. 1976-); clubs: Jonathan, Annandale Golf, La Canada-Flintridge Golf, L.A. Athletic, Winged Foot Golf, The Apawamis; Republican (pres. La Canada Young Rep. 1968); Roman Catholic; rec: golf, swim, tennis, theatre arts. Res: 1090 E Rubio St Altadena 91001 Ofc: Henry Holding Co. 5608 Soto St Huntington Park 90255

EGAN, WILLIAM JOSEPH, III, lawyer; b. Aug. 15, 1947, New Orleans, La.; s. William Joseph, Jr. and Margaret H. (Harrison) E.; m. Renee, Oct. 16, 1982; 1 son: Jason, b. 1983; edn: BS, Louisiana State Univ. 1970; JD, Tulane Univ. 1975; admitted to the bars of Louisiana State 1975, Calif. 1976, Texas 1977, U.S. Patent 1977. Career: assoc. Deutsch, Kerrigan & Stiles, New Orlean, La. 1975-76; patent atty. Exxon Prod. Research Co., Houston, Tex. 1976-77; patent atty. Chevron Research Co., San Francisco 1977-80; ptr. Flehr, Hohbach, Test, Albritton & Herbert, San Francisco 1980 – ; honors: Tau Beta Pi, Eta Kappa Nu, Tulane Moot Ct. Bd., Phi Delta Phi; mem. Am., La., Tex., Calif. and San Francisco Bar Assns., Patent Law Assn. of San Francisco, Barristers Club; Democrat; Catholic; rec: physical training. Ofc: Flehr, Hohbach, Test et al, 4 Embarcadero Ste. 3400, San Francisco 94111

EGGLESTON, ADELBERT JAMES, chiropractor; b. Sept. 28, 1959, Stockton, Calif.; s. James Russell and Elaine Holt (Schnautz) E.; m. Karen Edwards, Oct. 15, 1983; children: Candace Marie b. 1984, Amanda Elaine b. 1985; edn: AA, San Joaquin Delta Jr. Coll. 1980; DC, Life Chiro. Coll.-West 1983. Career: senior and radiol. intern dir. Life Chiro. Coll. W. Clinic Hayward 1982-83; assoc. Fink Chiro. Stockton 1983-84; owner Pershing Oaks Chiro. Stockton 1984 – ; instr. Adjustive Seminar Life Chiro. Coll. W. 1981-83; tchr. Commodore Stockton Skills Sch. 1983 – ; mktg. lectr. San Joaquin Delta Jr. Coll. 1984; tchr. John R. Williams 1985, Head Start Pgm. 1985; Career Day Gifted Children Madison Sch. 1985; tchr., football trainer St. Mary's H.S. 1985-86; honors: Clin. Excellence Award (Life Chiro. Coll.-W. CLin. 1981-83), Presidential Award of Honor (Jaycees 1983), Young Achiever of the Month (Stockton Valley Life Mag. 1985); mem: Gonstead Clin. Studies Soc. 1981-, Internat. Chiro. Assn. 1982-, ICA Calif., San Joaquin Co. Chiro. Found. 1983-, Calif. Chiro. Assn. 1984-, Stockton Bus. Referral Club (pres.), Rotary Internat. (fellowship chmn.), CofC, San Joaquin Co. Council on Wellness and Physical Fitness (pres.), Leadership Stockton, YMCA (bd. mem.), United Cerebral Palsy Assn., Masons, CofC Blue Blazers; publ: articles written for Port-O-Call 1985, Tune Uptimes 1985-6; Republican; Catholic; rec: water and snow skiing, sailing, racquetball, golf. Res: 3517 Chatsworth Ct Stockton 95209 Ofc: Pershing Oaks Chiropractic 7819 N Pershing Ave Stockton 95207

EHLING, LELAND REX, county health officer, b. Oct. 27, 1930, Abbyville, Kans.; s. A. W. and Flora M. (Dunn) E.; m. Marta Borbon, June 19, 1965; children: Leonor b. 1966, Dominic b. 1967, Andre b. 1969; edn: BA, Univ. Kans. 1952, MD 1955; MPH, UC Berkeley 1968. Diplomate Am. Board of Pediatrics (1963), bd. eligible Am. Board of Preventive Medicine and Pub. Health. Career: instr. in pediatrics Univ. of Colo. 1960-62; dir. Maternal and Child Health (MCH), Pima Co. Health Dept., Tucson, Az. 1962-64; pvt. practice pediatrics, Tucson 1964-67; Pub. Health Med. Ofcr., Alameda Co. Hlth Dept, Oakland 1967; regional med. dir., MCH, HSMHA, DHEW, Region

V, 1968-71, deputy dir. Div. Hlth Services, MCH, HSMH, DHEW, 1971-73; acting asst. bur. dir. Community Health Svcs., DHEW, 1973-74; health ofcr./ dir. Merced Co., 1974-77; asst. dir. Family Hlth Svcs. Az. Dept. of Hlth Svcs, Tempe 1977-78; dir. Personal Health Svcs., Human Svcs. Agency, PHMS, County of Orange, Santa Ana 1978-79; health ofcr. and dir. of public health, County of Orange, Health Care Agcy. 1979 –; adj. prof. CSU San Diego Sch. of Pub. Health; recipient recognition awards, Pima Co. (Az.) Board of Health (1966), Merced Co. Board of Supvrs. (1976), County of Orange Alcohol Board (1983); mem: Am. Pub. Health Assn., Orange Co. Med. Assn., Health Ofcrs. Assn. of Calif., Calif. Conf. of Local Health Ofcrs. (Regulations coord., chair Personal Health Svcs. 1984-85, pres. 1986-87); Rotary; contbr. num. articles in med. jours. and bulletins; mil: med. ofcr. US Air Force 1956-58; Democrat; Catholic; rec: gardening, travel. Res: 14851 Yucca Ave Irvine 92714 Ofc: County of Orange, Health Care Agency, Public Health, 515 N Sycamore St Santa Ana 92701

EHRBAR, ROBETTE GAYLE, financial executive; b. Nov. 23, 1956, Hollywood; d. Robert George and Lucia Colette (Coy) Ehrbar Sr.; edn: Calif. Polytech. Univ. Pomona, 1973-5; reg. Series 7, SEC, 1980. Career: teller Hacienda Div. of Mitsubishi Bank, West Covina 1976; accts. receivable Soundesign Western, City of Industry 1977; municipal ops. mgr. Western Rgn., Loeb Rhoades Hornblower-L.A. 1977; asst. v.p. Paine Webber, L.A. 1978; 2nd v.p. Smith Barney, L.A. 1981; vice pres./municipal bond trader & dept. mgr., Lehman Bros, L.A. 1983 –. Mem. L.A. Municipal Bond Club; Collie Club of Am., Smooth Collie Assn. of Am., San Gabriel Valley Collie Club; Republican; Presbyterian; rec: show, breed, profly. handle dogs. Res: 1512 Sekio Ave. Rowland Hts. 91748 Ofc: Lehman Brothers Kuhn Loeb, 515 So. Figueroa 14th Flr, Los Angeles 90071

EHRLICH, EMLEN HALL, lawyer, real estate broker; b. May 12, 1942, NYC; d. Andrew Douglass and LeMoyne (Noyes) Hall; m. 2d Paul R. Ehrlich, Oct. 10, 1985; children (by previous marriage): Andrew Guggenhime b. 1968, Lisa Guggenhime b. 1970, Mia Guggenhime b. 1973; edn: BA, Wellesley, 1964, JD, UC Boalt Hall 1968; admitted Calif. State Bar 1968; lic. real estate broker 1979. Career: atty. in private practice, 1968-79; independent real estate broker, 1979-85; real estate agent Sotheby's Internat. Realty, San Francisco 1985 –; honors: Phi Beta Kappa (1964), Order of Coif (1968); mem. Calif. State Bar Assn., San Francisco Board of Realtors; Republican; Episcopal; rec: golf (ten-time Olympic Club Golf Champion), tennis. Res: 26 Presidio Terrace San Francisco 94118 Ofc: Sotheby's International Realty, 3667 Sacramento St San Francisco 94118

EHRMAN, ELAINE WERTHEIMER, psychologist; b. July 28, 1926, Cleveland, Ohio; d. Joseph and Theresa (Schemnite) Wertheimer; m. Donald Ehrman, Dec. 12, 1963; children: Cynthian Graham b. 1947, David Graham b. 1950, Leslie Fried b. 1957, Richard Erhman b. 1965; edn: B. Music Edn., Northwestern Univ. 1951; MA, Stanford Univ. 1964; MS, Pacific Grad. Sch. of Psychology 1978, PhD, 1979. Career: pvt. practice, Menlo Park 1970 –; currently, dir. Menlo Psychiatry & Psychotherapy Ctr.; clin. faculty Stanford Univ. Dept. of Psychiatry; cons. for group therapy Belmont Hills Psychiatric Hosp.; mem: Am., Calif. and San Mateo Co. Psychological Assns., No. Calif. Group Psychotherapy Soc., A.K. Rice Inst., Am. Assn. of Sex Educators Counselors & Therapists, San Francisco Acad. of Hypnosis, No. Calif. Soc. of Hypnosis, Assn. of Family & Conciliation Cts.; dissertation: A Comparative Investigation of Identification and Expectancy Theories as Related to Marriage (1978); rec: tennis, bridge. Res: 1250 San Mateo Dr. Menlo Park 94025 Ofc: Elaine W. Ehrman PhD, 1187 University Dr. Ste. 4 Menlo Park 94025

EHRMAN, MICHAEL ALAN, accountant, consultant; b. March 26, 1953, Pittsburgh, Penn., s. Richard Hunter and Florence Thelma (Fine) E.; m. Debbie, June 18, 1977; children: Michael Jr. b. 1978, Brian b. 1984; edn: BS, USAF Inst. 1974; BAS law, Guilford Coll. 1976; MBA, Moody 1977; Lic. Public and Mfrs. Acct., No. Carolina 1977. Career: CFO MAES Co., High Point, NC 1974-83; pres., owner Special Co., High Point, NC 1975-78; CFO Joseph Henry Associates, San Dimas 1983-85; pres., owner Michael Ehrman & Assoc., High Point, NC and Pomona 1978 –; corp. acct., cons. Assured & Storage Management Corps. 1985 –; CFO, v.p. fin. Joseph Henry Assoc./ Stak Pak 1983-85; mem: Jaycees (pres. 1980-81), Toastmasters (pres. 1981), High Point CofC, Order of De Molay, Officer's club, Saber Club, City of Jamestwon (Fire Lt.); works: mgmt. paper on organization & ops. of metropolitan police dept.; mil: 1st lt. USAF-R 1973-74, 1985-, Pres. and Unit Citations, USAF Rifle & Pistol Team, GCM, Nat. Defense, Expert w/ Bronze Star; Republican; Christian. Ofc: Michael Ehrman & Assocs. 1265 B W. Fernleaf Ave. Pomona 91766

EHRSAM, ELDON EDWARD, operations research analyst; b. July 8, 1936, Bern, Kans.; s. Loyd and Elma Elizabeth (Bauman) E.; m. Clara Louise Schwartz, Nov. 20, 1939; children: Elizabeth Sue b. 1959, Jeffrey b. 1961, John b. 1968, Brian b. 1969; edn: BS, Washburn Univ. 1962; MS, USC 1969; cert. (MS equiv.) UC Santa Barbara 1973; Calif. lic. real estate broker. Career: physicist Naval Ordnance Lab, Corona, Ca. 1962-65; electronic engr. AF Western Test Range, Vandenberg AFB, 1965-68, project engr. Space & Missile Test Center, VAFB 1968-73, telemetry systems mgr. 1973-76, ops. research analyst 1976 –; real estate broker, Real Property Investments, Solvang 1976 –; securities rep. Vestcap Sec. Corp., Solvang 1982 –; honors: BSA District Award 1979, Who's Who in West (16, 17, 18, 19th eds.), Jane's Who's Who in Aviation & Aerospace (1983); mem: AIAA, Vandenberg Chpt. councilmem. 1980-81, Internat. Platform Assn., Nat. Assn. of Realtors, Nat. Assn. of Sec. Dealers, Real Estate Securities and Syndication Inst., Sigma Pi Sigma,

Masons, Elks; coauthor four tech. papers, presented Internat. Telemetry Confs. 1969-75; Democrat; United Methodist; rec: racquetball, jogging, camping. Res: 3087 Fairlea Rd Santa Ynez 93460 Ofc: Air Force Western Space & Missile Center, Code XRT, Vandenberg AFB 93437

EICHOLZ, JON T., real estate co. development/ construction co. executive; b. Aug. 3, 1938, Evanston, Ill.; s. George H. and Virginia E. (Trusdale) E.; m. Linda Bauer, Nov. 10, 1984; edn: BS arch. engrg., Univ. Kans. 1961; real estate lic. Calif.; constrn. lic. Hawaii. Career: pres. Pacific Constrn. Co. Ltd. Honolulu 1972-78; v.p. Pankow Devel. Corp. Altadena, Calif. 1978-85; pres. JTE Devel. Corp. Pasadena 1985-86; regl. ptnr., exec. v.p. Oxford Devel. Enterprises Inc. L.A. 1986 –; mem: Assoc. Gen. Contractors Assn. (pres./ dir.), Constrn. Industry Legislative Assn. Honolulu (1#pres., dir. 1974-77, Young Presidents Orgn. (1973-78), Urban Land Inst. (1975-77), Elks, Rotary, CofC. Res: 1753 Oak Grove San Marino 91108 Ofc: Oxford Devel. Enterprises Inc. 16133 Ventura Blvd Ste 1270 Encino 91436

EIN, MICHAEL ELLIOT, physician; b. July 28, 1947, Newark, NJ; s. Harry Norman and Jacqueline (Lax) E.; m. Pamela, June 30, 1974; children: Harry, b. 1978, Ashley, b. 1982; edn: BSc, Union Coll., Schenectady, NY 1969; MD, CM, McGill Univ. 1973; Diplomate Am. Bd. of Internal Medicine in both internal med. and infectious diseases. Career: med. intern Kaiser Found. Hosp., San Francisco 1974, med. resident UC Davis, 1975-77; clin. and research fellow in infectious diseases Baylor Coll. of Med., 1977-79; pvt. practice of infectious diseases 1979 –; cons. in infectious diseases VA Hosp., Martinez 1979 –; asst. clin. prof. of med. UC Davis Sch. of Med. 1979-1985; assoc. clin. prof. of med. UC Davis Sch. of Med. 1985 –; chmn. instnl. review bd. 1982-84, vice chmn. dept. of med. 1984-86, Mt. Diablo Hosp. Med. Center, Concord; honors: outstanding research award, Baylor Coll. of Med. 1978; mem: Fellow Am. Coll. of Physicians, elected mem. Infectious Disease Soc. of Am., Am. Soc. for Microbiology; Union of Am. Physicians and Dentists; publs: contbr. med. jours., sci. confs.; rec: ski, numismatics. Ofc: Michael E. Ein MD, Inc. 2485 High School Ave, Ste 303 Concord 94520

EISWALD, FRED B., real estate broker; b. Sept. 7, 1930, Longview, Wash.; s. Adolph John and Annabelle (Donahe) E.; m. Elizabeth Brink, Feb. 23, 1952; children: Gregg, b. 1955, Karen (Klebba), b. 1957; Calif. lic. real estate sales 1978, R.E. broker 1982. Career: lineman Conn. Light and Power Co., Willimantic, Conn. 1952-53; auto mech. Leonard Motors, Willimantic 1953-56, P&M Auto, Burbank, Ca. 1956-58, Herb Hull Chevron, Pasadena 1958-60; owner Fred's Auto Service, Thousand Oaks 1960-70; service advisor Parkwood Lincoln-Merc., Woodland Hills 1970-77, Kemp Ford, Thousand Oaks 1977-79; realtor/mgr. Century 21 America, Thousand Oaks 1979-82, Cen.21 Davies, Thousand Oaks 1982 –, desig. broker 1984 –; adv. bd. City Savings & Loan Westlake Village 1984 –; owner Olde Gentle Presents Antiques, Westlake 1983 –; awards: CofC Service Award, Million Dollar Club, Multi-Million Dollar Club, Y's Man of Year; mem: Conejo Valley Bd. of Realtors 1979- (dir. 1986-), YMCA, Rotary, Glass of the Past, Adventure Unlmtd. Youth Group, Thousand Oaks Booster Club, PTA, Republican Club; works: award winning restoration of 1930 Model-A auto (1961), and 1932 Duesenberg (1969); mil: elect. tech. 3cl. USN 1948-52, GCM, Honorman's Award; Republican; Prot.; rec: antiques, numismatics, restorations. Res: 1643 Valley High Ave Thousand Oaks 91362 Ofc: Century 21 Davies, 223 Thousand Oaks Blvd Ste 100, Thousand Oaks 91360

EKELUND, JOHN JOSEPH, college president; b. Jan. 19, 1928, Washington; s. Kenneth Oscar and Marjorie (Buscher) E.; m. Lynn Marie Schumacher, May 3, 1952; children: John Joseph, Christopher P., Terri L., Peter L., Tracy A., Patricia M., C. Kent; edn: BS, US Naval Acad. 1949; MS in systems analysis, Univ. Rochester 1969. Career: commnd. ensign USN, 1949, advanced through grades to rear adm., 1976; service in Korea and Vietnam; chief staff Naval Forces, Vietnam, 1972-73; comdr. guided missile cruiser USS Albany, 1973-75; dean Naval War Coll., 1975-76; dep. dir. naval edn. and tng. Office Chief Naval Ops., Wash DC 1976-77; nat. intelligence officer CIA, 1977-78; comdr. US South Atlantic Force, 1978-80; supt. Naval Postgrad. Sch., Monterey, Calif. 1980-83, ret. 1983; pres. Calif. Maritime Acad., Vallejo, 1983 –; decorated Legion of Merit, Meritorious Service medal, Joint Commendation medal; mem. US Naval Acad. Alumni Assn., US Naval Inst.; devel. math. treatment of modern submarine torpedo fire control, 1956. Ofc: California Maritime Academy, P.O. Box 1392, Vallejo 94590

ELEGADO, D. G., real estate broker; b. July 4, 1937, Philippines, nat. US cit. 1969; s. Anselmo E. and Consuelo F. E.; m. Estrella E., July 19, 1963; children: Eric b. 1964, Aileen b. 1965, Roy b. 1971, Lani b. 1973; edn: BS in agri. engring., Central Luzon Agri. Univ., Phil. 1960; Reg. Profl. Engr. (agri.) Phil. (1960), Calif. lic. R.E. Broker (1984). Career: agricultural engr. Agri. Credit & Coop. Financing Adminstrn., aManila 1960; math. instr. Pampanga Nat. Agri. Coll., Phil. 1961; quality control engr. Firestone Tire & Rubber Co., Salinas, Calif. 1964; spl. agent Prudential Ins. Co. of Am., San Diego 1969-80; assoc. ERA Real Estate, San Diego 1980-84; broker/owner Elegado Realty, S.D. 1984 –; hoors: Nat. Quality & Sales Achieve. award NALU, Filipino-Am. Assn. of S.D. community service award (1982-85); mem: Nat. Assn. Life Underws. (1968-80), San Diego Bd. Realtors (1980-); civic: Lions, Filipino-Am. Assn. S.D. (v.p. 1986); columnist, R.E. Sect., Philippine Free Press/L.A. (1985), Star-News, Sentinel Publ., S.D. (1986-); mil: 2d lt. Corps of Engrs. Armed Forces of Phil. 1962; Democrat; Christian; rec: tennis. Res: 8032 Montara Ave San Diego 92126 Ofc: Elegado Realty 10717 Camino Ruiz #119 San Diego 92126

ELIAN, GILBERT JEFFREY, surgeon, ophthalmologist; b. Oct. 22, 1943, Bklyn.; s. Arthur Isidore and Ruth (Schnitzer) E.; m. Sylvia Moroyoqui, Oct. 5, 1985; edn: BA, Queens Coll. 1964; M:D, Upstate Med. Center 1968. Career: residency tng. in ophth. North Shore University Hosp., Manhasset, NY 1971-74; pvt. practice surgery, ophthalmology 1974—; founder, pres. San Jose Eye Center; mem. Calif. Assn. of Ophthalmology (bd. dirs.), Santa Clara County Council on Aging (advis. mem.), AMA, Calif. Med. Assn., Santa Clara County Med. Soc. (Medical Expert Panel); mil: lt. US Navy 1969-71; Ind.; Jewish; rec: art collector, ski, tennis, photog. Res: 140 Tillman Ave San Jose 95126

EL KEBIR, MAHMOUD A., healthcare executive; b. Oct. 2, 1935, Egypt; nat. US cit. 1976; s. Abdelhamid A. and Ihsan (Mustafa) El Kebir; m. Laila M., Jan. 12, 1968; children: Hatem b. 1969, Mona b. 1972, Amal b. 1974, Hanaa b. 1977; edn: B.Com., Cairo Univ., Egypt 1964; MBA, CSU Northridge 1975. Career: staff acct. Cedars-Sinai Medical Center, Los Angeles 1974-77, senior acct. 1974-77, mgr. Gen. Acctg. 1977-79, dep. assoc. dir. of fin., 1979—; mem. Health Financial Mgmt. Assn., Cash Mgmt. Assn. of So. Calif.; rec: swim, painting. Res: 5595 Valinda Ave Alta Loma 91701 Ofc: Cedars-Sinai Medical Center 8700 Beverly Blvd Los Angeles 90048

ELLENSHAW, (PETER), artist; b. May 24, 1913, London, England; s. William and Adeline (Eyles) E.; m. Bobbie, June 1, 1942, Atlanta, Ga.; children: Harrison b. 1945, Lynda b. 1958; edn: Chevening Sch., Kent, Eng.; understudy, W. Percy Day O.B.E. Career: asst. to W. Percy Day O.B.E. 1934-40; pilot instr. Royal Air Force 1940-45; matte artist, spl. effects London Film Prod. 1945-46; matte artist MGM Studios, London 1946-47; artist, spl. effects Walt Disney, London 1947-53; artist, prodn. designer, spl. visual effects dir. Walt Disney, Burbank 1953-79; artist Fine Arts, Santa Barbara; art show judge; honors: nom. for Academy Awards, art direction, Bed Knobs & Broomsticks, 1971, Island at the Top of the World, 1974, and The Black Hole, 1979; Academy Oscar, 20 Thousand Leagues Under the Sea 1954, and spl. effects, Mary Poppins, 1964; Retrospective, Dept. of Film, Mus. of Modern Art, 1979; mem: Birnam Wood Country Club, La Cumbre Country Club; mil: flying ofcr. Royal Air Force 1941-45; rec: painting.

ELLICKSON, DEANE LOUIS, insurance brokerage executive; b. Sept. 16, 1934, Chgo.; s. Ray and Madeline G. (Morris) E.; m. Lorraine, May 31, 1955; children: Suzanne b. 1958, Sherri b. 1961, Debra b. 1964, Lorne b. 1968, Deanna b. 1971; edn: stu. law LaSalle Univ. 1958-61, spl. courses, U.S. Internat. Univ., Golden Gate Univ., comm. colls.; Calif. lic. Ins. Broker, life & disab. agent (1960). Career: ins. investigator supr. Retail Credit Co., Santa Monica 1958-60; spl. agt. Bankers Life Co. of Iowa, L.A. 1960-62; group ins. rep. Occidental Life Ins. of Calif., L.A. 1962-65; profl. staff cons. Calif. Tchrs. Assn., Burlingame 1965-79, dept. supr. 1967-75; staff cons. and agcy. coord. Ednl. Community Ins. Services Inc., San Mateo 1979—; prop. Rancho Pistachio Co. (pistachio orchard devel. co.), Temecula 1981—; dir. First Finl. Credit Union, Glendale (1985-); recipient suggestion award Retail Credit Co. (1958), achievement award, Occidental Life (1962, 64), service awards: City of Huntington Beach, H.B. Rotary, H.B. Neighborhood Watch (1978), Liberty Bell Award, Orange Co. Bar Assn. (1978), La Cresta Prop. Owners Assn. golden telephone award (1984); civic: Arevalos Elem. Sch. Site Council (1968-79), Fountain Valley Dist. Supt.'s Spl. Advis. Com. (1974-77), H.B. Neighborhood Watch (founding com., bd., pres., 1975-78; secured O.C. grant funds for orgn. 1977), cons. var. Neighborhood Watch groups in So. Calif. (1975-84), H.B. Police Dept. and Civil Def. Aux. (spl. communs. team 1976-78), LaCresta Prop. Owners Assn. (pres. 1982-83); life mem. Calif. Rifle and Pistol Assn., Nat. Rifle Assn.; publs: Fgn. Dinner Menu & Cookbook (1986); mil: sgt.-major US Army Corps of Engrs., Pres. Unit Cit., Korean War, Good Conduct, 1957; Democrat; rec: shooting, avocado grower, woodworking. Res: 4009 Paseo Chaparro Murrieta 92362 Ofc: Ed Comm, Inc. 15403 Grand Ave Ste C Lake Elsinore 92330

ELLINWOOD, STEVEN LEE, building materials wholesaler; b. Aug. 25, 1943, Saginaw, Mich.; s. Royal Arthur and Winifred Virginia (Kiefer) E.; m. Annah, Aug. 29, 1964; 1 son, Jeffery Troy b. 1967; edn: BS in bus. adm., Central Mich. Univ. 1965. Career: var. mgmt. tng. pos. Wickes Lumber Co., Saginaw, Mich. 1968-72, dir. Finl. Plnng. & Research, 1972-74, controller 1974-77, v.p. fin. & adminstrn. 1977-79, v.p. western area ops., Sacramento, Calif. 1979-81; v.p. retail ops. Erb Lumber, Birmingham, Mich. 1981-82; pres./ CEO Building Material Distbrs. Inc., Galt 1982—; dir: Sterling Pacific Bldg. Matl. (1984-), Nat. Bldg. Matl. Assn. (1984-); mil: capt. US Army Arty. 1965-68, Bronze Star, Air Medal w/3 Cluster; rec: racquetball, golf. Ofc: Building Material Distributors Inc. 225 Elm Ave Galt 95632

ELLIOTT, DON EUGENE, international cost valuer, investment banker; b. May 25, 1932, Topeka, Kans.; s. Claude Earl and Dorothy (Grace) E.; 1 son, Brian Alexander b. 1962; edn: bus. mgmt., San Bernardion Valley Coll. 1956-58; civil, mech. engring., I.C.S., 1961-65; desig: Cert. Review Appraiser, N.R.A.M.A. (1984), Senior Cert. Valuer, Internat. Inst. (1984). Career: switchman Santa Fe R.R. and var. pos. in constrn. to maint., 1955-60; sales engr., tractors, Case Co., South Gate 1960-64; tradesman var. constrn. pos., 1964-82; also indep. bus. & trading cons. prin. Universal Trade Market; pres./chmn. bd. Elliott Internat. Devel.-Investment Co.; pres./chmn. bd. Express Tabsclean / Europe; mfr. Final Shine Glove; mem. Nat. Assn. Review Appraisers & Mortgage Underws., Am. Legion, Investors Internat., Private Placement Club; works: originated idea to consol. 9 State of Calif. depts. into one agency- Cal-Trans (1962); mil: US Navy 1951-55, Korean combat, Japanese occup., commendn. on recon missions; Republican (Task Force); Christian;

rec: fishing, philately, counseling young adults. Ofc: Elliott International 19000 MacArthur Blvd Ste 1159 Irvine 92715

ELLIOTT, JOHN MICHAEL, product design executive; b. March 9, 1950, Santa Barbara; s. John Wesley III and Francis Jean (La Barge) E.; m. Laura Hendershot, Dec. 20, 1980. Career: profl. musician turing U.S. 1973-75; studio engr. KTYD AM/FM, Santa Barbara 1975-77; product devel. mgr. Infinity Systems Inc., Canoga Park 1977-79; prodn. mgr. HBI, Santa Barbara 1979-81; cos. General Audio of No. Am. 1981-82; pres., chief designer Counterpoint Electronic Systems Inc., San Diego 1982—; prop. General Audio of No. Am.; honors: Coty Award for 3 products in Japan, Counterpoint; Golden Sound Award, Japan; mem: Audio Engring. Soc., Summit Workshops Inc.; works: winner, Design & Engring. Award 1984; winner, Internat. Audio Review Class 1A Rating; rec: music, backpacking, camping. Ofc: Counterpoint, 10635 Roselle St. San Diego 92121

ELLIOTT, MYRTLE EVELYN KEENER, educator; b. Apr. 11, 1898, Annawan, Ill.; d. John William and Mary Elizabeth (Baldwin) Keener; m. Dr. L. Louis Elliott, Aug. 10, 1935; 1 dau. Mary Ellen; 3 stepchildren: Winona, Joan, James; edn: AB, Cornell Coll. 1921, MA, Columbia Univ. 1926, postgrad. Ohio State Univ., Univ. Chgo., San Francisco State Coll. Career: teacher (Latin, Eng.) Guthrie Co. H.S., Panora, Ia. 1921-23, (Latin, Soc. Sci.) H.S., Dewitt, Ia.. 1923-25; head Eng. Dept./Dean of Girls, H.S., Kemmerer, Wyo. 1926-29; girls' adviser US Indian Svc. 1931-35; teacher (Eng., Latin) Cut Bank, Mont. 1944-46; spl. teacher, Educable Mentally retarded, Kern Co. Supt. of Schools Office, Bakersfield 1949-68, ret. 1968; cont. tchg. pvt. students in reading, 1968—; honors: Internat. Reading Assn. 1981; Phi Beta Kappa 1924; life mem. Calif. Teachers Assn.; publs: contbr. Understanding the Child (1950, 2), The Instructor (1953, 56); Republican; Catholic. Res: 2709 Fourth St. Bakersfield 93304

ELLIS, ERLEAN MARY, chemical marketing co. president; b. Jan. 10, 1953, Cornwall, N.Y.; d. Wm. Thomas and Ann (Dyshuk) Ellis; edn: BA, Univ. South Fla. 1974; Calif. real estate lic. Career: 1st woman sales trainee, Union Oil Chem. Div., 1975, worked in Charlotte area, Atlanta regl., Chgo. div. offices 1975-77, sales rep. Los Angeles area, 1977-78; sales for var. chemical distbrs. 1978-83; founder/pres. Orbital Chemical Corp. 1983—, customers incl. Continental Airlines, Alcoa, NASA Ames Research; mem: Chem. Mktg. Assn., Am. Electroplaters Soc. (dir. 1984), Internat. Food Technologists, AAUW (pgm. chmn. and speaker nat. math-sci. conf. 1983); rec: play piano/sing, swim, tennis. Ofc: Orbital Chemical Corp. 3532 Katella Ave Ste 213 Los Alamitos 90720

ELLIS, JOHN WILSON, lawyer, b. Oct. 27, 1931, Beaumont, Tex.; s. Lacoste George and Bobbie Mae (Lee) E.; father, L.G. Ellis, retired head Geophysical Dept. Sun Oil Co., holder num. patents in field of geophysics; m. Marilyn White, Sept. 2, 1960; children: Scott b. 1961, Holly b. 1963; edn: BA, Univ. of Tex. 1954, JD, 1958. Career: practiced law in Texas 1958-62; Shearson, Hammill & Co., 1962-64; Bank of Am. Trust Officer, 1966-72; asst. prof. (contracts, wills, personal prop., ins., creditors' rights), So. Texas Coll. of Law 1965-66; practice of law in Calif. 1972—; past mem. bd. govs. and instr. comml. law, Am. Inst. of Banking; instr. bus. law, Santa Barbara City Coll.; instr. wills & trusts Santa Barbara Coll. of Law and Ventura Coll. of Law 1984-85; served as trustee, Endowment Fund Trust and dir. Santa Barbara Sym. Orch. Assn.; fmr. commnr. Santa Barbara Golf Course Commn.; mem: Bar Assns. of Calif., Tex., Santa Barbara County; Estate Planning Council of Santa Barbara; Profl. Golfers Assn. Hole-In-One Club; Republican; rec: golf, hiking, backpacking. Res: 577 No Hope Ave Santa Barbara 93110 Ofc: Atty. at Law, 233 E. Carillo St Santa Barbara 93101

ELLIS, JOSEPH ALDEN, III, non-profit organization executive; b. Nov. 4, 1947, Montclaire, N.J.; s. Joseph A., II and Dorothy Aileen (Boyd) E.; m. Laurel, Aug. 22, 1970; children: Angela b. 1974, Hollie b. 1979, Joseph IV b. 1983; edn: grad. Moody Bible Inst. 1970; BA, Columbia Coll. 1971. Career: staff mem. Campus Crusade for Christ, 1970—, currently internal devel. cons. spec. in internat. sector; honors: Outstanding Young Men of Am. (1973); mem. Christian Businessmens Com.; works: graphic designs, logos, service marks; Republican; Prot.; rec: design, woodworking. Res: POB 6014 San Bernardino 92412 Ofc: Campus Crusade for Christ Arrowhead Springs San Bernardino 92414

ELLIS, MICHAEL ANDREW, systems consultant; b. May 16, 1958, Los Angeles; s. James Harris and Gudrun Mathie (Stange); m. Johanna Diane Elliott, Aug. 23, 1980; 1 son, Andrew James b. 1984; edn: BA, CSU Long Beach 1980. Career: systems designer Sperry Corp., Irvine 1980-82; pres. Prism Computer Corp., Costa Mesa 1982—; cons. in system design methodology govt. agencies and large corporations; works: developed design methodology for application of 4th generation computer-based systems; Republican; Lutheran; rec: philosophical studies, natural scis., teaching. Ofc: Prism Computer Corp. 575 Anton Blvd 3rd Floor Costa Mesa 92626

ELLIS, RONALD DAVID, lawyer; b. Aug. 7, 1948, Santa Monica; s. James Stephen, Jr. and Jeanne LaVere (MacEachern) E.; m. Eva Rodriguez, May 19, 1984; edn: AB, cum laude, UCLA 1970; JD, Duke Univ. Sch. of Law 1973; admitted to Calif. Bar 1975. Career: tax sr. Coopers & Lybrand, Los Angeles 1973-75; tax mgr. Information Magnetics Corp., Santa Barbara 1975-77; tax counsel Penn Life Co., Santa Monica 1977-78; tax counsel Rockwell Internat., El Segundo 1978-81; dir. of taxes Rohr Industries Inc., Chula Vista 1981—; pres., dir. Rohr Foreign Sales Corp.; mem: Tax Execs. Inst., Community Med. Ctr. (dir. 1984-85); mil: capt. usar 1973-79, Cert. of Achiev.; Republican;

Presbyterian; rec: flying, photog. Res: 2348 Santa Fe Ave., Torrance 90501 Ofc: Rohr Industries, Inc., Foot of H Street, Chula Vista 92012

ELLIS, STEPHEN BRIAN, finance co. executive; b. Mar. 30, 1932, NY, NY; s. Emil K. and Thelma K. Ellis; div.; 1 son, Craig Steven, b. 1959; edn: BA, Long Island Univ. 1952; CSU Northridge 1963-4; LLB, Blackstone Law Sch. 1966. Career: pres. Key Industries (real estate finance) 1963-74; pres. Dream Inn Hotel, Santa Cruz 1974-75; pres. Los Angeles Helicopter Airlines, 1975-76; vice pres./partner ICS Financial Services, Inc., 1976−; dir. Hotel Consultants of Am. 1974-5; dir. Pacific Seaboard Airlines 1975-7; honors: 11-year mem. Mayor Sam Yorty's Community Adv. Com. (LA); mem: founder, The Magic Castle (Hollywood); San Francisco Mus. Soc.; bd. dirs. Salvation Army; POPAS (Patrons of the Perf. Arts); bd. dirs. Am. Repertoire Theatre from Europe; publs: newspaper column, Los Angeles Daily News 1963-65, num. mag. articles; mil: psychol. warfare splst. US Army 1953-55; Republican; Jewish; rec: magician. Res: 1200 Chickory Lane Brentwood 90049 Ofc: Stephen Brian Ellis & Assocs. 12077 Wilshire Blvd Los Angeles 90049

ELLISON, DIANE MARIE, writer, investor; b. June 18, 1941, Aberdeen, Wash.; d. Russell Mathis and Syster Constance (Anderson) Ellison; children (nee Rowe): Dawn b. 1964, Robert b. 1967; edn: BA in sociol., cum laude, Univ. Wash. 1964; Std. tchg. cred., UC Irvine 1970; MS in human resource mgmt., Chapman Coll. 1984. Career: profl. athlete, World Champion Log Roller 1960-70, featured ABC Wide World of Sports (1966, 68), promotion and publicity work: Seattle Worlds Fair 1962, Weyerhauser Co. lumber convs. 1967, GE Co. , Warner Buck Sports Shows Ents. 1961-69, Knotts Berry Farm Log Ride 1966-70, Woman to Woman nat. t.v. 1983; youth counselor, 1963-, tchr., 1971-, tennis coach, 1977-; sales rep. N.Y. designer womens apparel, Doncaster line 1980-81; owner Ellison Timber & Properties, Aberdeen, Wash.; author: Reach for the Shy (1986); mem. Alpha Ci Omega, Univ. Wash. and Chapman Coll. alumni assns.; civic: Junior Achievement Advisor, Zonta Internat., vol. var. youth groups; Republican; Presbyterian. Address: 2202 Pavillion Dr Santa Ana 92705

ELLSWORTH, FRANK L., college president; b. May 20, 1943, Wooster, Ohio; s. Clayton S. and Frances (Fuller) E.; 1 dau., Kirstin Lynne; edn: AB, cum laude, Case Western Reserve Univ. 1965; M.Ed., Penna. State Univ. 1967; MA in Am. lit., Columbia Univ. 1969; PhD, Univ. Chgo. 1976. Career: asst. dir. devel. Columbia Law Sch., 1968-70; dir. spl. projects/ prof. lit. Sarah Lawrence Coll., 1971; asst. dean Law Sch., Univ. Chgo., 1971-79, instr. social sci. collegiate div., 1975-79; pres. Pitzer College, Claremont, Calif. 1979−, also prof. polit. studies, 1979-. Mem. vis. coms. Case Western Res. Coll.; bd. dirs. Independent Colls. So. Calif., exec. com. 1983-, pres. 1985-; bd. dirs. Southwestern Univ. Sch. of Law, exec. com. 1985-; bd. fellows Claremont Univ. Center; honors: first recipient, Distinguished Young Alumnus, Western Res. Coll., Case W. Res. Univ., 1981; hon. chpsn. Salute to Minority Edn., The Golden State Minority Found. 1980-; mem: Am. Hist. Assn., Council for the Adv. of Sec. Edn., Friends of Huntington Lib., Hist. of Edn. Soc., Young Presidents Orgn.; clubs: Arts Club of Chgo., LA World Affairs Council, Town Hall of Calif., Univ. Clubs of Claremont, LA, Zamorano Club of LA; frequent public spkr., lectr.; articles in profl. jours. Office of the Pres., Pitzer College, 1050 No Mills Ave Claremont 91711

ELTERMAN, HAROLD LESTER, insurance agent; b. Jan. 16, 1926, Boston, Mass.; s. Morris and Irene E.; m. Muriel, Dec. 8, 1946; children: Shirley b. 1952, Marlene b. 1952, Michael b. 1948; edn: grad. Brookline H.S. 1942. Career: div. mgr. Sears, 1956-63; owner H.L. Elterman & Assocs. Inc. (ins. brokerage), La Mirada 1963−; honors: City of La Mirada Outstanding Citizen (1970), Boy Scouts Am. Dist. Award of Merit, Silver Beaver Award, Jaycees disting. service award (1960, 61); mem. Whittier Indep. Ins. Agents Assn. (past v.p.); civic: City of La Mirada Public Safety Commn. (18 yrs), Los Angeles County (Commnr. 1974-; Sheriffs Reserve Ofcr. 1972-; past mem. Dist. Attys. advis. bd.), Norwalk/La Mirada Unified Sch. Dist. Bd. of Edn. (pres. 1980-81), Long Beach Girl Scouts Council (5 yrs), United Way (bd. 1967-68), Boy Scouts Am. (dist. chmn. 1968), La Mirada Hosp. (past bd. dirs.)., City of Hope (chpt. pres. 1964-65), Am. Heart Assn. (chpt. pres. 1986), La Mirada CofC (pres. 1967, 68, 83), Exchange Club (past pres.), Kiwanis (bd.), VFW; mil: cpl. USMC 1943-46, unit cits.; Democrat; Jewish; rec: tennis, police activities. Address: La Mirada 90638

ELTON, CAROL B., real estate broker; b. Feb. 11, 1918, Lakewood, Ohio; d. J. H. "Brad" and Elsie M. (Jackson) Bradfute; m. T.C. "Charlie" Elton, Nov. 20, 1937; edn: art stu. Carnegie Inst. Tech. 1935-37, Chaffey Coll., Ontario 1952-57; spl. courses Chaffey Coll., Alta Loma, Coll. of the Siskiyous, var. schs., 1963-; desig: Lifetime Tchg. Cred., Calif. (R.E.) 1979; RECI (Real Estate Cert. Inst.); GRI (Grad. Realtors Inst.) Calif. Realtors Assn. 1973; CRS (Cert. Residential Splst.) and RNMI (Realtor Nat. Mktg. Inst.) Nat. Assn. Realtors 1979; Sr. MHA (Mfg. Home Appraiser) and ICA (Internat. Cert. Appraiser) IREA 1982. Career: sales agt. Betty McNay, Realtor, Upland, with var. other R.E. offices; sales/mgr. P. Smith, Ontario; clk. Am. Red Cross, office mgr. Girl Scouts, legal sec. Archie Mitchell, Atty.; sales/mgr. Reinhard Realty, Ontario; assoc. broker Associated Realty Exchange, Upland; broker prin. dba Carol B. Elton, Realtor; owner/broker Home Realty, Ontario and Scott Valley; also mgr. Gibralter Mines; mem: Nat., Calif. Assn. Realtors, Siskiyou County Bd. Realtors; civic: Scott Valley Dalmations, CofC, AARP, Siskiyou Co. Hist. Soc. (life), Ft. Jones Womens Club, Internat. Apple Corps, tax aide pgm. vol. Yreka (1974-75); num. art awards for oil and water color paintings; Methodist; rec: vintage home restoration and decorating, nature. Res: 10206 Quartz Valley Rd Mugginsville 96037 Home Realty POB 60 Greenview 96037

ELY, LEONARD WHEELER, business owner; b. Oct. 2, 1923, Palo Alto, Calif.; s. Leonard Wheeler and Jessica Foster (Wilbur) E.; m. Shirley Rose, Aug. 30, 1947; children: Leonard b. 1950, Margaret b. 1953; edn: AB, Stanford Univ. 1948, MBA, 1950. Career: buyer J.C. Penney Co. S.F.; salesman David Rose Packard IH Trucks Richmond 1950-53; western sales mgr. Hiller Engrg. Redwood City 1953-54; owner Ely Motor Co. Redwood City 1954-70, Leonard Ely Co. Menlo Park 1961-85, Atherton Lease Palo Alto, Menlo Park 1962−; honors: Tall Tree Tribute (1982), Stanford Assocs. Award (1982) & Gold Spike (1986); mem: Penninsula Auto Dlrs. Assn., No. Calif. Motor Car Dlrs. Assn. (bd. dirs.), Chrysler Dlrs. Council (nat. chmn.), Comm. Found. of Santa Clara (pres.), Elizabeth F. Gamble Fedn. (pres.), Palo Alto Research Inst. (chmn. advis. bd.), Filoli (bd. dirs.), Children's Hosp. at Stanford, Palo Alto Med. Found. Lytton Gardens, Stanford Centennial Commn., Miramonte Mental Health (past pres.), Univ. Club of Palo Alto, Castilleja Sch. Found. (past chmn.); mil: 1st lt. USAF 1942-45, Air Medal; Republican; Episcopal; rec: fishing. Res: 2161 Bryant St Palo Alto 94301 Ofc: Atherton Lease Corp. 300 El Camino Real Menlo Park 94025

EMERSON, JOHN BONNELL, lawyer; b. Jan. 11, 1954, Chgo., Ill.; s. James G. and Margaret (Bonnell) E.; not married; edn: BA, Hamilton Coll. 1975; JD, Univ. of Chgo. Law Sch. 1978; admitted to Calif. State Bar 1978. Career: assoc. atty. Manatt, Phelps, Rothenberg, Tunney & Phillips in Los Angeles 1978-83, partner 1983−; mem: Calif. Law Revision Commn. 1982-85; editl. bd. Calif. State Senate Select Com. for Long Range Policy Planning 1985−; Democratic Nat. Com. 1985−; chmn. Calif. Democrats for New Leadership 1985−; co-chmn. The DNC Lexington Group 1981-; Calif. chmn. Americans with Hart 1983-4; Democrat; Presbyterian. Res: 3280 Mountain View Ave Los Angeles 90066 Ofc: Manatt, Phelps et al, 11355 W Olympic Blvd Los Angeles 90064

EMLEY, CHRISTOPHER FIELDING, lawyer; b. Dec. 15, 1943, NYC; s. Don Pomeroy and Theresa (Willman) E.; children: Cassandra b. 1970, Don b. 1974; edn: BA, pol. sci., UC Berkeley 1964; JD, UC Hastings Sch of Law 1967; admitted Calif. State Bar 1967. Career: staff atty. Legal Aid Soc. of San Francisco, 1967-71; partner Jenkins and Emley, 1971-73; sole practitioner, 1973-78; sole practice with assocs., San Francisco 1978−; instr. Family Law for Paralegals, S.F. State Univ. 1982-; pres. bd. Legal Services for Children 1979-81; pres. bd. Legal Assistance to the Elderly 1983-; vice pres. Child Abuse Council of San Francisco 1974-75; honors: Award of Merit Bar Assn. of S.F. 1977, State Bar bd. govs. Pro Bono Service award 1983; mem: Calif. State Bar (chair Juvenile Justice Com. 1981-2, del. Conf. of Dels. 1977-), Bar Assn. of San Francisco (bd. dirs. 1979-81; chair Juvenile Justice Sect. 1975-79, chair Lawyer Referral Service Com. 1978-79, chair Voluntary Legal Services Program Bd. 1980-, chair Custody & Visitation Subsect., Family Law Sect. 1979-81), Gov.'s Task Force on Child Abuse Treatment and Prevention 1973, Am. Acad. of Pediatrics Child Abuse Com. 1976-80; publs: articles for S.F. Attorney (The Split, 1982), ABA Guide to Solo Practice (1984), Moebius (The Family Contract Project, 1984). Ofc: 801 Lincoln Way Ste. A, San Francisco 94122

EMMOTT, R. CAMERON, urologic surgeon; b. Oct. 14, 1947, Prairie Grove, Ark.; s. Ralph Cameron and Isabel Graeme (Wright) E.; m. Carol Burgess, May 23, 1969; 1 son: Parker b. 1982; edn: BA, Southern Meth. Univ. 1969; MD, Okla. Univ. 1973. Career: resident surg. UC San Francisco (incl. fellowship guest worker Nat. Cancer Inst.) 1978; pvt. practice urol. San Mateo, Burlingame 1980−; clin. instr. U.S.F. Med. Ctr.; honors: All-America Swim Team UCSF 1967, 68, 69; Alpha Omega Alpha; mem: Mills Hosp. Found. (bd. gov.), San Mateo Co. Med. Found. (bd. dirs.), St. Francis Yacht Club; publ: num. scientific; Republican; Episcopal; rec: yachting. Ofc: 1750 El Camino Real, Ste 307, Burlingame 94010

ENDERUD, KAREN LYNN, data processing executive; b. July 20, 1952, Los Angeles; d. James Wm. and Anna Lucille (Deese) Price; m. W.D. Enderud, Jr., Nov. 6, 1982; edn: Cerritos Jr. Coll. 1971-72. Career: pgmmr. analyst, project leader, project mgr., current dept. mgr. First Interstate Services Co., Diamond Bar 1981−; mem. Am. Mgmt. Assn., Nat. Assn. Female Execs.; Democrat; Catholic; rec: equestrian, golf, garden. Address: Diamond Bar 91765

ENDO, JAMES KOICHI, wholesale nursery co. president; b. June 7, 1960, Calif.; s. Fukutaro "Frank" and Sachiko "Betty" E.; edn: AA in bus. acctg., L.A. Pierce Coll. 1981; acctg., USC 1981-82. Career: bookkeeper Summer House Restaurant, Woodland Hills 1980; records clk. DataProds. Corp., 1980-81; bkkpr. Exec. Fin. Corp., Tarzana 1981; acctg. clk. Mgmt. Assistance Group Inc., 8/82; pres. The Northern Plant Co., Inc. Morgan Hill 1983−; honors: Alpha Gamma Sigma (chpt. v.p. 1980-81), Phi Beta Lambda (chpt. pres. 1979-81), L.A Pierce Coll. Faculty Assn. Scholar and Dean's List Book Scholar (1981), Outstanding Young Men Am. (1983); mem: Calif. Assn. of Nurserymen (dir. Peninsula Chpt. 1983-), Calif. Landscape Contrs. Assn./S.F., Bedding Plants Inc., Nat. Fedn. Indep. Bus./Calif., US CofC, USC Acctg. Soc.; civic: San Jose Inst. of Contemp. Art (vol. 1985-86), San Fernando Valley Japanese Comm. Ctr. (1967-74), West Valley YMCA (1974-75), USC Stu. Govt. (Audit Bd. 1981) Asian Pac. Stu. Outreach (1981-82); Democrat; Agnostic; rec: ski, tennis, golf. Address: The Northern Plant Co Inc POB 387 Morgan Hill 95037

ENEA, SANTO, dental technician; b. June 2, 1954, Pittsburg, Calif.; s. Joseph Paul and Rosa (Geraci) E.; edn: AA, Diablo Valley Coll. 1974; stu. Los Medanos Jr. Coll. 1978-80; desig: Dental Techn. Career: dental techn., lab. mgr. Yosemite Dent. Lab., Pittsburg, 1975-77; owner 1977-81; dental techn./

owner Enea Dent. Lab., Pittsburg 1982–; mem. Nat. Assn. Dental Labs. 1978-84; civic: Pittsburg CofC (named Citizen of Year 1985), Sons of Italy, Pittsburg Bus. & Profl. Assn., Nat. Fedn. of Indep. Businessmen, Pittsburg Hist. Soc.; works: Italian-Am. Fishing Boat Monument (1984), Pittsburg Columbus Day Fest./Parade (84, 85, 86), Delta Fest. Fun Run (82, 83, 84, 85, 86); Democrat; Roman Catholic; rec: genealogy. Res: 218 Mariposa Dr Pittsburg 94565 Ofc: Enea Dental Lab 224 East 10th St Pittsburg 94565

ENGEL, JEROME SHELDON, certified public accountant; b. Nov. 24, 1946, Phila, Pa.; s. David Morton and Ethel (Berman) E.; m. Shirley R. Fischer, July 1, 1979; children: Benjamin b. 1981, Jesse b. 1983; edn: BS acctg. Penn. State Univ. 1968; MS acctg., Wharton Sch. 1970; CPA lic. Pa., Calif., N.Y. (1972). Career: CPA/ dir. Entrepreneurial Services Gp., Arthur Young & Co., San Francisco, ptnr. 1982–; mem. Am. Inst. CPA, Calif. Soc. CPA, Nat. Assn. Accts., N.Y. Soc. CPA, Penna. Soc. CPA; Rotary Club; contbg. author: Start-Up Companies (Law Journal Seminars Press), Financing for Growth (Wiley). Ofc: Arthur Young & Co. One Sansome St San Francisco 94104

ENGEL, RICHARD GARDNER, maintenance engineering co. president; b. March 12, 1944, Phila.; s. USAF Col.(ret.) Gardner W. and Marian A. (Coll) Engel; 1 dau., Kimberly Jean, b. 1967; edn: BSME, Okla. State Univ. 1967; JD, Western State Univ. 1974; admitted Calif. State Bar 1975. Career: mech. engr. NASA; assoc. engr. Lear Jet Co.; field engr. Elliott Co.; field and sales engr. Solar Div.; project engr. C.E. Miller Corp.; mech. engr. Bechtel Corp., Internat. Power, engring. field changes for fgn.constrn. of nuclear power plants; pres. Pacific Coast Indsl. (providing gen. power plant maint., overhaul); currently, CEO/pres. Powerplant Specialists, Inc. (overhaul, repair, maint. of large boilers and turbines for utility cos. domestic and internat., overhaul and turnarounds of refineries: SCE, LADWP, PG&E, SDG&E, Chevron, Texaco, Union Oil, Korea Electric, VEACO, Kerr-McGee). Mem. ASME, Pacific Energy Assn., Energy Club of Los Angeles, LA CofC; Republican; Episcopal; clubs: Ferrari Owners, El Toro Flying. Res: 11 Beacon Bay Newport Bch 92660 Ofc: Powerplant Specialists, Inc. 666 W Baker Ste 413 Costa Mesa 92626

ENGELHARDT, JONATHAN ALAN, manufacturing co. executive; b. March 12, 1961, Sasebo, Japan; s. James Henry and Rita Barbara E.; edn: AA, Panama Canal Coll. 1981; AA, Mesa Coll. 1983. Career: defense maps Inter-American Geographic Soc., Panama 1979; asst. mgr. Mad Jack's Stereo, San Diego 1981-83; corp. accts. Audio Engineering Svcs., San Diego 1983-84; corp. promotion/ advtg. Advanced Cellular Phone Co., San Diego 1984; corp. promotions mgr. Elegant Eel, San Diego 1985; currently pres./CEO Photogram Inc., San Diego; cons. Film Express, San Diego; sems., Starting your own Greeting Card Company, 1986; honors: featured in San Diego Union Entrepreneurs (1985), finalist San Diego Co. Speech teams (1979); mem: Internat. Photo Mktg. Assn. (Charter), Internat. Mini-Lab Assn., Junior Execs. Inc., Polaroid Instant Club, Pacific Beach Town Council, Save the Coaster Com., Inventors Club; works: ivention, Photo Fun-Letters, Photogram Inc. (pat. pend. 1984), Photo Fun-Notes (pat. pend. 1986); Republican; Catholic; rec: athletics, philanthropy, photog. Ofc: Photogram Inc. P.O. Box 90361 San Diego 92109

ENGELS, CHERYL ELAINE, communications co. executive; b. Oct. 22, 1943, Napa; d. Lawrence Philip and Elaine Helen (Giauque) Harris; m. John Peralta Engels, May 3, 1970; children: Ceseley b. 1972, Jason b. 1976; edn: BA, Univ. of the Pacific 1965. Career: with Pacific Tel., Santa Rosa 1965-82: asst./ traffic operating mgr., 1965-7, traffic op. mgr. 1967-9, 1971-77, asst. traffic supt. 1969-71; Operator Svcs. staff mgr. (S.F.) 1977-79, force mgr. (Santa Rosa) 1979-83; mgr. Opr. Svcs. AT&T Communications, Santa Rosa 1984–; guest lectr. CSU Sonoma 1982; adviser (1965-8), bd. dirs. (1970-2) Jr. Achievement; treas. Santa Rosa Central Soccer Club 1981-2. Awards: Outstanding Junior Woman Delta Delta Delta 1964; art awards Napa County Fair 1964, 65; exhib. Jack London Art Show 1965. Mem: Order of Eastern Star (majority mem. Jobs Daus., Rainbow for Girls), Telephone Pioneers of Am.; Democrat; Prot.; rec: painting, golf, tennis. Res: 2054 Rolling Hill Dr Santa Rosa 95404 Ofc: AT&T Comm. 520 Third St, Rm 431, Santa Rosa 95401

ENGH, DOUGLAS MARSHALL, physician; b. Oct. 6, 1949, Hollywood, Calif.; s. Robert Paul and Christine (White) E.; m. Teri, Sept. 16, 1978; 1 dau. Heather Lea b. 1982; edn: BA, UC Los Angeles 1976, MD, 1982; Diplomate Nat. Bd. Med. Examiners 1983. Career: lifeguard Los Angeles City Aquatics 1969-77; paramedic L.A. City Fire Dept. 1978; intern internal med. UCLA San Fernando Valley pgm. 1982-83; resident ophthalmol. UC Irvine 1983-86; emerg. room phys. La Palma Intercommunity Hosp., Van Nuys Comm. Hosp., Buena Park Comm. Hosp., Midwood Comm. Hosp. Stanton 1983-86; ophthalmol. Long Beach and Orange County 1986–; CPR instr. 1977; emerg. med. tech. instr. 1981; honors: Recogn. (AMA 1985), Cert. of Appreciation (Am. Nat. Red Cross 1975-77); mem: AMA 1978-, Am. Acad. Ophth. 1984-, Calif. Assn. Ophth. 1984-, Internat. Assn. Ocular Surgeons, Christian Med. Soc. (UCLA) 1978-82; bd. mem., bible tchr. Huntington Harbor Comm. Ch.; counselor LifeLine, Hollywood Pres. Ch. 1975; research Jules Stein Eye Inst. 1981; mil: airman 2/c US Air Nat. Guard 1969-71, Commdn. for Meritorious Svc.; Republican; Protestant; rec: swimming and water polo (varsity 1973-74), rowing (varsity crew UCLA 1974-76), golf, football (semipro 1970), scuba. Ofc: Serra Med. Clinic, Sun Valley 91352

ENRIGHT, STEPHANIE V., financial consultant; b. Mar. 24, 1929, Los Angeles; d. Stephen P. and Violet G. (Guthrie) Veselich; m. Robert J. Engriht, Nov. 26, 1949, (dec.); children: Craig, b. 1954; Brent, b. 1958; Erin, b. 1961; Kyle, b. 1968; edn: AB, USC 1949; MS, 1975; Cert. Financial Plnnr. 1981. Career: cons. Co. of Orange 1976-79; fin. counselor and plnnr. SEC Gp.; dir. Pacific Home Bldrs. 1960–; pres. Enright Financial Consultants, Torrance 1981–; profl. adj. faculty UCLA, USC 1981-; freq. lectr. to civic and social gps.; honors: Fin. Plnnr. of the Month, I.A.F.P.; mem: I.A.F.P. (dir. 1982-83); Inst. of CFPs; Torrance CofC; Centurion Club; YMCA; Pan Asian Soc.; publs: radio, The Mis. Biz, Miz Prodns., KCME; arts. in Geoscience, Women in Film, Senior Life, and Confidential Planning Services; Republican; Catholic; rec: travel. Res: 35 Chuckwagon Rd., Rollings Hills 90274 Ofc: Enright Financial Consultants, Union Bank Tower, 21515 Hawthorne Blvd., Ste. 210, Torrance 90503

ENRIGHT, WILLIAM BENNER, judge; b. July 12, 1925, New York City; s. Arthur Joseph and Anna Beatrice (Plante) E.; m. Bette Lou Card, Apr. 13, 1951; children: Kevin A., Kimberly A., Kerry K.; edn: AB, Dartmouth Coll., 1947; LLB, Loyola Univ., Los Angeles, 1950; admitted to Calif. State Bar 1951. Career: dep. dist. atty. San Diego County, 1951-54; ptnr. law firm Enright, Levitt, Knutson & Tobin, San Diego, 1954-72; judge US Dist. Ct. So. Dist. Calif., San Diego 1972–; mem. adv. bd. Joint Legislative Com. for Revision of Penal Code, 1970-72, Calif. Bd. Legal Specialization, 1970-72; mem. Judicial Council 1972; bd. dirs. Defenders Inc., 1965-72 (pres. 1972); Diplomate Am. Bd. Trial Advocates, Fellow Am. Coll. Trial Lawyers, Am. Bar Found., mem. Am., San Diego County (dir. 1963-64, pres. 1965) bar assns., State Bar Calif. (gov. 1967-70, v.p. 1970, exec. com. law in a free soc. 1970-), Dartmouth Club San Diego, Rotary; Am. Judicature Soc., Alpha Sigma Nu, Phi Delta Phi; mil: sensign USNR, 1943-46. Ofc: 940 Front St., San Diego 92101

ENSWORTH, HEATHER MAY, clinical psychologist; b. Aug. 16, 1955, Pasadena, Calif.; d. George, Jr. and Faith Naomi (Rudy) E.; edn: BA cultural anthro., sociol., summa cum laude, Middlebury Coll. 1977; MA theol., Fuller Theol. Sem. 1982, PhD clin. psychol., 1983; lic. psychol. Calif. BMQA 1985. Career: tchg. asst. Fuller Theol. Sem. Grad. Sch. of Psych. Pasadena 1979-83; grad. psychol. clerk USC Med. Ctr. 1980-81; clin. psychol. intern St. John's Hosp. Santa Monica 1981-82; postdoc intern USC Med. Ctr. 1983-84; psychol. asst. Assoc. Psychol. Svcs. Pasadena 1982-85, clin. psychol. 1985–; adj. faculty Fuller Theol. Sem. 1983–; community cons., instr. workshops; honors: Phi Beta Kappa, Herbert H. Lehman Fellow (1977), Clare Headington Meml. Scholar (1980), Gene Wesley Pfrimmer Meml. Scholar (1980), Travis Award (1982), John P. Davis Jr. Meml. Scholar (1983); mem. Am. Psychol. Assn.; Democrat; Episcopal. Ofc: Assoc. Psychol. Svcs. 2 N Lake Ste 610 Pasadena 91101

ENTIN, BRUCE LANCE, investor relations, public relations executive; b. Feb. 7, 1951, NY, NY; s. Hannah (Goodman) E.; m. Pesia, May 20, 1972; children: Aviva b. 1978, Ari b. 1980; edn: BA, magna cum laude, City Coll. of NY 1973. Career: bus. staff writer Los Angeles Herald Examiner, Los Angeles 1973-76; ed. California Apparel News, Wall St., Los Angeles 1978-80; bus. columnist, writer San Jose Mercury News, San Jose 1980-82; v.p. Atari Inc., Sunnyvale 1982-84; v.p. investor rels., corp. communs. LSI Logic Corp. 1984–; cons. National Semiconductor Corp. 1984–; honors: Created Bits & Bytes Electronics Column, San Jose Mercury News 1981; Journalism Intern Award, 1973; Gr. Los Angeles Press Club Journalism Awards 1980; Atrium award for Outstanding Reporting, Univ. of Georgia Sch. of Journalism; mem: Sigma Delta Chi, San Jose Mus. of Art. (bd. dirs.), Mayor's Olympic Torch Com., San Jose Film Festival (contbr. 1984); Jewish; rec: long distance bicycling, jogging. res: 2635 Malaga Dr. San Jose 95125 Ofc: LSI Logic Corporation, 790 Sycamore Dr. Milpitas 95035

ENTRIKEN, ROBERT KERSEY, university professor; b. Jan. 15, 1913, McPherson, Kans.; s. Fred Kersey and Opal (Birch) E.; m. Jean Finch, June 5, 1954; children: Birch b. 1956, (by previous marriage): Robert, Jr. b. 1941, Edward b. 1943, Richard b. 1947; edn: AB, Univ. Ks. 1934; MBA, Golden Gate Univ. 1961; postgrad. The City Univ. Grad. Business Sch., London 1971-73; desig: Chartered Property Casualty Underwriter (CPCU) 1953. Career: insurance broker in Houston, Tx. and McPherson, Kans., 1935-39; asst. mgr. Cravens, Dargan & Co., Houston, Tx. 1939-42; branch mgr. Nat. Surety Corp., Memphis, Tn. and San Franciso, 1942-54; v.p. Fireman's Fund Ins. Co., San Francisco 1954-73; adj. prof. Golden Gate Univ., 1953-73, prof. of mgmt., 1974–; underwriting mem. Lloyd's of London; bd. dirs. Northstar Prop. Owners Assn.; mem: Surety Underws. Assn. (past pres.), No. Calif. Chpt. CPCU (past pres.; named Ins. Profl. of Year 1981), Ins. Forum of San Francisco (trustee, past pres.), Chartered Ins. Inst. (UK), Ins. Inst. of London, Risk and Ins. Mgmt. Soc., Musicians Union Local No. 6 (life), Acad. of Political Sci., Assn. of Naval Aviation, Am. Risk and Ins. Assn., University Club (SF), Commonwealth Club of Calif., Marines' Meml. Club, World Affairs Council, The English-Speaking Union, Brit.-Am. Club of No. Calif., Naval Order of the U.S., US Naval Inst., Phi Delta Theta frat.; frequent contbr. to trade and profl. jours.; mil: capt. USNR 1944-73; Republican; Episcopal; rec: music, ski, travel. Ofc: Golden Gate University 536 Mission St San Francisco 94105

EPSTEIN, BERNICE DIENER, real estate broker; b. July 1, 1929, NY, NY; d. Joseph and Regina (Feldman) Diener; div. 1965; children: Sara, b. 1958, Marvin, b. 1962; edn: BA, Univ. of Ariz. 1951; MA, CSU Long Beach 1978; Cert. Personnel, Columbia Univ. 1952-3; desig: Calif. Sec. Teach. Cred., 1974, Calif. S.D.S. Teach. Cred., 1976. Career: research, Columbia Univ. 1951-52; personnel adminstr. Times Facsimile, NYC 1952-55; personnel dir. A.J. Siris, NYC 1955-57; employment & claims asst. Employment Devel. Dept., State of Calif., 1973-74; tchr. Reg. Occupnl. Programs (retail), 1974-79; real estate agt. West World Prop., Herbert Hawkins, Palm Springs 1979-83; owner/broker B.E. Realty Investments, Palm Springs 1983–; tchr. Palm Springs Unified Sch.

Dist., DECA chmn.; mem. Mayor's Com. P.S. General Plan and Palm Hills Gen. Plan; mem. Energy Commn., P.S.; mem. Suicide & Crisis Intervention Center, Desert Mental Hlth.; mem. Calif. Tchrs. Assn. 1974-79; mem: Palm Springs Bd. of Realtors (comm. rels.), CAR, NAR; P.S. League of Women Voters (pub. dir., pres.); P.S. CofC (Retail Trades com.); Gold Card; Exchange Club; Coachella Valley Tennis Assn.; Democrat; Jewish; rec: poetry writing, hiking, travel. Res: 210 N. Farrell Dr Palm Springs Ofc: B.E. Realty Investments, Palm Springs 92262

EPSTEIN, KARL ELLIOT, orthopedic surgeon; b. Baltimore, Md.; s. Joseph and Josephine (Zierler) E.; m. Valerie, Aug. 17, 1985; children: Jesse, Olivia; edn: BA, Univ. Md. 1975; residency gen. surg. Albert Einstein Affil. Hosp. 1975-76, res. orthopedic surg. 1976-79; Diplomate Am. Bd. Orthopedic Surgery. Career: orthopedist Kaiser Hosp. 1979-81; pvt. practice ortho. surg., sub splty. hand surg. and sportsmedicine 1981–; fellow Am. Bd. Orthoped. surg.; mem. LA Co. Med. Assn.; rec: weight lifting, karate, skiing. Address: 5400 Balboa Blvd, Ste 222, Encino 91316

ERBURU, ROBERT F., communications co. executive; b. Sept. 27, 1930, Ventura; s. Michael Peter and Kathryn (Sarzotti) Erburu; m. Lois Stone, July 31, 1954; daus.: Susan Kit (Mrs. George D. Reardon) b. 1956, Lisa Ann (Mrs. Mark Williams Cocalis) b. 1960; edn: BA, USC 1952, JD, Harvard Law Sch. 1955. Career: atty. firm of Gibson, Dunn & Crutcher, Los Angeles 1955-61; elected gen. counsel and secty. Times Mirror Co., L.A. 1961, vice pres. 1965-69, sr. v.p. 1969, pres. 1975-, COO 1980, CEO 1981–, bd. dirs. 1968-; dir./v.p. The Times Mirror Found.; dir. The Tejon Ranch Co. 1975-; dir. Metro. Los Angeles YMCA 1973-, v.chmn. 1976-; dir. Ind. Colls. of So. Calif. 1973-, chmn. 1976-7; bd. trustees Marlborough Sch. 1974-, pres. 1979-81; bd. visitors UCLA Grad. Sch of Mgmt. 1974-; bd. trustees Huntington Lib. 1981-, bd. overseers 1976-81; bd. trustees The William and Flora Hewlett Found. 1980-; bd. trustees Pfaffinger Found.; Com. to Visit the Harvard Law Sch. 1978-; Council of Fgn. Rels. 1980-; bd. dirs. Carrie Estelle Doheny Found. 1981-, Fletcher Jones Found. 1982-. Awards: Am. Jewish Com. Human Rels. Award; NCCJ So. Calif. Region Brotherhood awd. 1979. mem: Am. Bar Assn., State Bar of Calif., Soc. of Profl. Journalists, Sigma Delta Chi. Ofc: The Times Mirror Co. Times Mirror Sq. Los Angeles 90053

ERICKSON, NEAL FRANKLIN, engineering contractor; b. May 28, 1942, Sacramento; s. Franklin E. and Helen A. (Stewart) E.; m. Cheryl Nagel, Jan. 21, 1967; 1 son, Christopher b. 1970. Career: v.p. Erickson Co./ Arden Sand & Gravel 1963-74; secty./ treas. Arden Sand & Gravel 1970-74; v.p. Erickson Co. (comml. real estate & mortgage co.) 1975-86; ptnr. Erickson-Arden Co. 1980-85; pres. Sacramento Aggregates Inc. (formerly Erickson-Arden) 1985–; mem: Rotary, Sacto. County 4-H (leader), Sacto. Horsemen's Assn.; mil: ss USAFR 1963-69; Republican; Lutheran; rec: golf, art, hunting, horses. Ofc: Sacramento Aggregates Inc. 5411 Mayhew Rd 95826

ERIKSEN, KNUT, offshore structures engineer; b. Dec. 2, 1950, Eidsvoll, Norway; s. Erik and Eva (Pedersen) E.; m. Teresa E. Earhart, May 21, 1983; edn: sivilingenior, Norwegian Inst. of Technol. 1975; MSCE, Wash. State Univ. 1979; M. Internat. Mgmt., Am. Grad. Sch. of Internat. Mgmt. 1981; Reg. Civil Engr. Calif. 1983. Career: asst. proj. mgr./ strl. design engr. Ing. F. Selmer A/S, Oslo, Norway 1976-80; strl. design engr. Morrison-Knudsen Co. Inc. San Francisco 1981-84; senior strl. engr. Earl & Wright Cons. Engrs. S.F. 1984–; award for design of a Norwegian agricultural bldg. 1977; mem: Norweg. Soc. of Chartered Engrs. 1976, Am. Soc. Civil Engrs. 1982, Norweg.-Am. CofC 1984; mil: corp. Infantry Royal Norwegian Army 1970-71; rec: x-c skiing (competitor), orienteering (competitor). Ofc: San Francisco

ERNSTER, JOHN HARRY, manufacturing co. executive; b. Sept. 26, 1921, Chgo.; s. Harry Albert and Eleanor (Moody) E.; m. Joan Kelm, Nov. 27, 1969; children: John b. 1947, Peter b. 1949, joan Paige b. 1952, Michael b. 1955; edn: BS, Univ. Ill. 1946. Career: pres. Ideal Creamery Springfield, Ill. 1950-58; v.p. Consolidated Creameries Chgo. 1958-60; v.p. Dry Milks Inc. Chgo. 1960-61; mgr. Instawhip Inc. Detroit 1961-62; v.p. Instawhip Inc. L.A. 1962-69; c.e.o.l Exelpro Inc. L.A. 1969–; bd. dirs. Luxembourg Cheese Factories; mem: Inst. Food Technologists, Vernon CofC; num. inventions, patents re seafood processing, brewing by-products, meat products, pet food prods., dairy prods.; mil: ensign USNR 1942-46; Republican. Ofc: Exelpro Inc. 3760 E 26th St Los Angeles 90023

ERONEN, ERIC T., yacht importer; b. Oct. 17, 1919, Helsinki, Finland; s. Antti T. and Martta A. (Salonen) E.; m. Sirke Lausala, Aug. 4, 1946; 1 dau. Arja-Leena b. 1949; edn: BS in mktg., Helsinki Univ. Grad. Sch. of Bus. 1945; MS in mktg. (Fulbright Scholar) Columbia Univ. Grad. Sch. of Bus. 1952; stu. Stockholm Univ. 1945, London Sch. of Bus. & Pol. Sci. 1947. Career: export sales mgr. in Finnish Forest & Paper Industries, with study trips to Sweden and England, 1945-50; prop. Finnware Trading Corp. (copperware), NYC 1952-57 and Finlander Boats Inc., N.J. 1956-61; distbr. and reg. sales mgr. (E. & W. Coasts) Crestliner Div. Bigelow-Sanford Corp. 1961-66; owner Recr. Eqpt. Co. (boat distbr.) 1966-76; owner Nord Yachts (yacht imports), Newport Beach 1976–; cons. to W.Coast Marine Div. Chrysler Corp. 1975; mem. Finn.-Am. CofC (charter, past dir. NYC and LA chpts. 1955-), So. Calif. Marine Assn. (1961-); fmr. mem. Lions Intl. Host Club NYC (1955-61), Finnish Male Choir of N.Y. (2d tenor 1955-61); unpub. translations of Finnish folklore; mil: capt. in Finnish Army 1939-44, decorated; Ev. Lutheran; rec: classical music, hist. Res: 4800 Sunnybrook Ave Buena Park 90621 Ofc: Nord Yachts 3400 Via Oporto Ste 3 Newport Beach 92663

ERRICKSON, MARVIN ORION, syndicator-real estate, oil, gas and minerals; b. Mar. 17, 1943, Denver, Colo.; s. Milton Orion and Martha Elizabeth (Fedde) E.; children: Julie Joy b. 1969, Dana Kristen b. 1973; edn: geophys. engr. Colo. Sch. of Mines 1965; JD, Univ. Colo. Sch. of Law 1968; Reg. Profl. Engr. (1965), admitted bar: Colo. (1968), Calif. (1974). Career: geophysical engr. Mobil Oil Co. 1964-65; atty. and real estate broker, investor, syndicator of real estate, oil, gas and mineral groups 1973–; mil: capt., dep. staff judge advocate US Army, JAG, 1969-73; Republican; Prot.; rec: ski, marathon runner. Ofc: 7910 Ivanhoe Ave Ste 315 La Jolla 92037

ERVIN, PATRICIA CONNELLY, association executive; b. Dec. 23, 1924, Owatonna, Minn.; d. James B. and Mavilda D. (Scoville) Connelly; edn: BA, USC 1950, MA, 1954, UCLA Law Sch. 1958. Career: tchr. public schools 1954-58; founder and current leader Holistic Healing Group 1972–; founding mem. Assn. for Holistic Health 1976-; vice pres. Philosophical Research Soc. (PRS), Los Angeles; lectr. on holistic healing and philosphy PRS 1979–; pres. United Nations Assn. of Los Angeles; advis. bd. WAND; bd. dirs. Valley Mayors Fund for The Homeless; honors: UN Peace Award, UN Assn. of U.S., So. Calif. Div. (1978); Independent; Christian. Ofc: Philosophical Research Society 3910 Los Feliz Blvd Los Angeles 90027

ESGUERRA, LARRY SABARILLO, IV, bank executive; b. May 7, 1949, Manila, Philippines; s. Hilario Gonzales and Josefina Soriano (Sabarillo) E.; edn: BSBA, Univ. Phil. 1969. Career: cert. pub. acct. J. L. Maranan & Assocs., CPAs, Manila 1969-71; res. auditor Citibank, N.A., Philippine Branches, 1971-75, insp. Citibank Internat. Insp. Team for Asia/Pacific/Europe region 1975; mgr. Controllership Div., Filcapital Devel. Corp., Manila 1976; lectr. ASEAN Center for Finl. Tech., Ateneo de Manila Grad. Sch. of Bus., 1978; practicing CPA, Manila 1970-79; asst. v.p. Assoc. Citizens Bank, Manila 1976-79; fin. ofcr. JRK Devel. Corp., Manila 1976-84; v.p. and cashier/comptroller Pacific Union Bank & Trust, Menlo Park 1979-84; v.p. Fin., Golden Bay Credit Union, 1984–; dir. Corporate Resource Consultants, Manila 1978-79; mem: Inst. of Internal Auditors/SF, Am. Mgmt. Assn., Philippine Inst. of CPAs, Bank Adminstrn. Inst./Phil. chpt.; fmr. mem. Asian Tax Assn., Assn. of CPAs in Commerce & Indus., Manila; coauthor: Comml. Banking Ops. in the Philippines (1979), Katha Publs., Phil., ofcl. fin. textbook Univ. of the East, Phil.; prin. author: Ops. Policy & Procedure Manual, Assoc. Citizens Bank; Catholic; rec: photog. Res: 500 W Middlefield Rd, 145, Mountain View 94043 Ofc: Golden Bay Credit Union, POB 127, NAS Moffett Field 94035

ESHAGIAN, JOSEPH, ophthalmologist; b. Mar. 15, 1951, Tehran, Iran, nat. US cit. 1982; s. Ebrahim and Touran (Monasebian) E.; edn: BS w/distinction, Univ. Mich. 1971; MD, SUNY Upstate Med. Ctr. 1975; bd. certified, Am. Board of Ophthalmology 1980. Career: intern in internal medicine & neurol., Univ. of Mich. Hosp., Ann Arbor 1975-76; res. ophthal., Univ. of Iowa Hosps. & Clinics, Iowa City 1976-79; owner/pres. Dr. Joseph's Eye Medical Clinic, Inc. Los Angeles; tch. ophthalmology residents at Hollywood Presbyn. and White Meml. Hosps.; presentations at nat. profl. meetings (1978-), lectr. univ. seminars (1971-); mem: Nat. Honor Soc. (1968-), Am. Acad. of Neurology, Assn. for Resrch in Vision and Ophth., Nat. Assn. of Residents and Interns, Iowa Med. Soc. (1977-79), Am. Assn. Ophth., Johnson Co. Med. Soc. (1977-79), Contact Lens Assn. of Ophthalmologists Inc., Med. Eye Svcs. of Calif. Inc., Am. Acad. Ophth., AMA, CMA, L.A. County Med. Assn., Am. Soc. Contemporary Ophth., Internat. Glaucoma Cong.; clubs: Kiwanis, Lions (v.p.); rec: philately, movies, videos. Ofc: 1200 N Vermont Ave Los Angeles 90029

ESKIND, SIR NORMAN JO ANDREW (The Lord Manchester), co. president, consulting statistical analyst; b. Aug. 11, 1955, NY, NY; s. Sigmund Harold and Jean Grace (Hepner) E.; edn: BA arts, McGill Univ., Montreal, Can. 1980; M.Internat. Econ. and M. Internat. Rela., Univ. of Paris, France 1982. Career: statistician Anders, Aktiebolaget, Stockholm, Sweden 1980-83; estate appraiser Scandphil Assocs., San Jose, Calif. 1983-84, v.p. 1985–; chief investment ofcr. Norman-James Assocs., San Jose 1985; Buyout of Anders, AB of Sweden 1985, named pres./CEO Norman-Anders Inc., Mountain View, Calif. 1985–; civic: American Red Cross, Canadian Cultural Orgn., McGill Grads. Soc. of No. Calif., Royal Philatelic Soc. of Can. (life), Soc. of Israel Philatelists (life.); author: Anzac Participation in World War I; The European Economic Community and Member Nations' Stockmarkets: Winners and Losers in International Trading, 1973-83; rec: pvt. pilot, philatelist, painting, photog. Address: Norman-Anders Inc 3412 Churin Dr Mountain View 94040-4533

ESOIMEME, JAMES EBHODAGHE, artist; b. July 21, 1950, Ibore-Ishan, Bendel, Nigeria; s. Jackson Yamaboh and Asabi E.; m. Victoria, Feb. 26, 1981; children: Iguehi b. 1981, Ehireimen b. 1983, Ebhodaghe b. 1985; edn: Diploma Govt. Technical Coll., Sapele, Nigeria 1970; AA, Coll. of Alameda 1979; BA and BFA, San Francisco State Univ., 1984; cert. mech. engr., City & Guilds of London. Career: sr. mechanical techn. Asbestos Co., Lagos, Nigeria; supvr. maint. Guiness Bottling Co., Lagos; supvr. Zim's Food Chain Inc., San Francisco; vol. physical fitness instr. Shoreline Hosp., Alameda; current: graphic designer, cons.; roller skating cons.; band member Rim and the Believers S.F.; awards: Art scholarship (1984), 1st Place, Sculpture, Gold Award (1984), hon. mention painting (1983) San Mateo County Fair; Roller skating awards, Presidential Sports Award, Wash DC (1980, 82), novelty award St Patrick's Day Parade, Oakland (1984), gold trophy, Cowboy Parade, Oakland (1984), 1st Place (Black Cowboy Parade Oakland 1985), 2nd Place Independence Day Torchlight Parade Benecia City 1985); mem. Org. of Concerned Nigerians Abroad Inc. (bd. dirs., provost); Catholic; rec: dancing, swimming. Res: 1601 Market St, 301, Oakland 94607 Mail: Graphic Art, POB 773, Oakland 94604

ESPINOZA, RODRIGO HONORIO, computer consultant; b. Jan. 13, 1963, Sewell, Chile; s. Eduardo Honorio and Rose-Marie Barbara (Gibbons) E.; m. Jill Hodgson, Oct. 16, 1982. Career: ptnr./ops. mgr. Americana Travel, South Gate 1982–; cons. (mfg. cos.), pres. RHE Systems, 1984–; tng. cons., instr. AT&T; recipient achievement cert. for Unix and "C", AT&T (1985); mem. South Gate CofC, Unix Users Gp.; works: devel. computer software- Prodn. Scheduling System; Republican; rec: software, electronics. Res: 900 N Story Pl Alhambra 91801 Ofc: RHE Systems 3338 Tweedy Blvd South Gate 90280

ESSALAT, FARROKH, architect; b. Jan. 25, 1945, Teheran, Iran; s. Nasrollah and Akhtar (Abedini) E.; m. Sonia Mirhosseini-Vakili, June 1976; 1 child, Kamran b. 1978; edn: BS in arch., Univ. College, London Univ. 1965, MS in arch., 1967; Reg. Architect, Royal Inst. of British Architects, 1969, Architects Registration Council of U.K. Career: faculty mem. Faculty of Fine Arts, Teheran Univ. 1969–, asst. prof. 1969-74, Dir. of Studies and Research 1971-74, assoc. prof. arch. 1974-78, and chmn. of Sch. of Architecture, mem. var. coms. and dir. Faculty Publications Bd.; currently architect, pres. Aratta Collaborative Architects Teheran/San Francisco 1974–; works: Master Plan Tehran Univ., Research Ctr. Aryamehr Univ., Tehran, Master Plan and design Sadough Univ., indsl. complexes in Tehran and the Caspian, var. residential and comml. projects; contbr. The Archtl. Review (London) and var. publs. of Univ. of Teheran; translated into Persian two books: The Pioneers of Modern Design by Nikolaus Pevsner (1977), New Movement in Cities by Brian Richards (1978); rec: painting, piano. Res: 35 Aster Hillsborough 94010 Ofc: Aratta Collaborative 24 East Third Ave 1st Fl San Mateo 94401

ESTABROOK, WILLIAM CHARLES, professional engineer, ret.; b. Dec. 27, 1920, Odessa, NY; s. Harold Charles and Edith Alleine (Smith) E.; edn: BSEE, Purdue Univ. 1949; Control System Engr. Calif. 1977. Career: field svc. engr. Am. Locomotive Co. Schenectady, NY 1949-55; test engr. Lockheed- Calif. Co. 1955-74; senior design engr. Lockheed Missiles & Space Co. Sunnyvale 1974; power sys. study leader, design splst. Lockheed Aircraft Svc. Co., Jet Propulsion Lab. 1974-77; prin. engr. Boeing Aerospace Co., Jet Propulsion Lab. 1977-83 (ret.); mem: Disabled Am. Vets. (life), Masons 1942-, Caterpillar Club 1944, Am. Legion 1945-68 (vice cmdr.), VFW 1945-54, La Canada CofC and Community Assn. 1955-82, WEstern Collaborate Heart Study Group 1960-; deacon, trustee Montrose Community Ch. 1964-; mil: 1st lt. USAAC 1942-45, ETO, Purple Heart (POW Germany 5/44-5/45), Air Medal; publs: author or co-author 20+ tech. reports. Res: 1730 Bonita Vista Dr La Canada 91011

ESTANCIO, DIOSCORO PASAYAN, veterinarian; b. Apr. 16, 1942, Laguna, Philippines, nat. 1980; s. Vitaliano Borja and Simona Canicosa (Pasayan) E.; m. Aleli, Dec. 22, 1966; children: John Edward b. 1967, Maria Aleni b. 1969, Eileen Francis b. 1970, Donna Marie b. 1977, Lilani Ann b. 1982; edn: DVM, Univ. of Philippines 1964; int. med. vet., UC Santa Cruz 1974; gen. surg. vet., UC Irvine 1974-75, vet. cardiol., 1977. Career: surg. urol. research Hosp. for Sick Children Toronto, Can. 1966-68; microbiol. tech. TB div. Ontario Dept. of Health Toronto 1968-70; veterinarian S.F. SPCA Hosp. 1970-74; chief vet. Valley Vet Hosp. San Gabriel 1974-76, All Pet Vet. Clin. N. Hollywood 1976-78; hosp. dir. Animal Med. Hosp. Pasadena; vet. cons. Aerojet Inc. 1974-75; honors: Top Ten Vets. of Philippines 1965; mem: Calif. Assn. of Filipino Vet. Practitioners (pres. 1984-), Optimist Club of Rose Bowl Pasadena, Worshipful Master-Nilad Lodge; publ: tech. art. in canine jour.; Republican; Catholic; rec: golf, tennis, bowling, marksmanship. Res: 1991 New York Dr Altadena 91101 Ofc: Animal Medical Hosp. 2116 E Colorado Blvd Pasadena 91107

ESTES, EDWIN WILSON, JR., lawyer, real estate broker; b. Sept. 6, 1958, San Diego; s. Edwin W., Sr. and Lavonne Vida (Zinniker) E.; edn: BA, USC 1980; JD, Pepperdine Univ. Sch. of Law 1983; desig: Realtor (1984). Career: pres. Dale E. Wood Realty, Inc.; gen. counsel Land Equities, Inc., Reliable Funding, Inc., West Coast Detail, Inc.; honors: Olympic Torch Runner 1984, Boy's Club bd. dirs. Rookie of Year, 1984; mem: ABA, San Diego County Bar Assn., Vista Board of Realtors (treas. 1985); Boy's Club of Vista (v.p., bd. dirs., pres.-elect); mem. Rotary, USC Gen. Alumni Assn., Conservative Order of Good Guys; Republican; Protestant; rec: water sports. Res: 933 Vale Terrace Vista 92083 Ofc: Dale E. Wood Realty Inc. 902 S Santa Fe Vista 92083

ESTES, FLOSSIE WRIGHT, realtor (ret.); b. May 14, 1903, Porterville, Okla. (then Indian Terr.); d. William Rodrick and Elba Missouri (Milburn) Wright; m. Clarence C. Estes, Apr. 13, 1923; children: Jack Clifton b. 1924, Charles Glynn b. 1925, Benjamin Curtis b. 1933; edn: num. coll. courses, Hills Bus. Coll., San Bernardino Jr. Coll., Coll. of the Desert. Career: secty, bkpr., oper. Telephone Private Exchange 1918-23, Santa Fe RR, Los Angeles 1943; real estate broker Rialto, br. ofcs. in Fontana 1947-61; served on Arbitration Bd. Rialto late 1950's; recipient with husband, Benjamin Franklin award 1979 and Johnson Valley Hon. Plaque 1980 for humanitarian svcs.; mem: Calif. Real Estate Bd., World Orgn. of China Painters, VFW Aux., WWI Vets. Aux., Royal Neighbors of Am., Order of Eastern Star, Ameranth, White Shrine, Daus. of Nile of Jerusalem; Republican; Ind. Fundamental Ch. of Am.; rec: panting, needlework. Res: 55580 29 Palms Hwy, Sp 14, Yucca Valley 92284

ESTRIN, ROBERT L., motion picture film editor; b. Mar. 3, 1942, Lakewood, N.J.; s. Herman and Rachel Leah (London) E.; m. Mary Lloyd, July 4, 1975; children: Zoe Lloyd b. 1979, Jesse London b. 1983, Eliot Musser b. 1983; edn: BA, Goddard Coll. 1968; MFA, San Francisco Art Inst. 1970; desig: A.C.E., Am. Cinema Editors (1985). Career: pres. New American Cinema 1975–, indep. prod. Boots of Spanish Leather (1-hr documentary, 1983), The Boss' Son (winner Best Feature Film, Miami Film Fest. 1978); resource ed. Sundance Inst. 1985–; founder American Cinematheque (1985); motion picture film editor feature films: Desert Hearts (Samuel Goldwyn Co., 1986), What Happened to Kerouac (New Yorker Films, 1986), Breathless (Orion 1983), Badlands (Warner Bros. 1974, winner Ten Best Lists- Esquire, NY: Times, Time, NBC), The Candidate (Warner Bros. 1972, winner Acad. Award 1972), Pipe Dreams (Avco- Embassy), Mirrors; ed. T.V. films: Maricela (1 hr. Wonderworks, PBS 1/86), Creation of the Universe (90 min. sci. spl. PBS 11/85), Help Wanted (CBS spl. 3/82, Emmy nom.), Almos' A Man (PBS Am. Short Story series 4/77), It Couldn't Be Done The Unexplained (two 1-hr. spls. for Ency. Brit. and Bell Tel., NBC, 4/70), ed. sev. documentary films for USIA, PBS, Whitney Mus. incl. Brazil (1971), Imogene Cunningham (1970), The Numbers Start With the River (nom. Acad. Award, Best Doc. Short Subject, 1972); honors: Am. Cinema Editors Eddie Award nom. for outstanding achievement in film editing "Creation of the Universe" (1986); active mem. Acad. of Motion Picture Arts & Scis 1986-; mem. IATSE Local 776, Am. Cinema Editors, Gen. Service Found. (dir. 1980-); mil: cpl US Marine Corps 1960-63. Address: Santa Monica 90401

ESTVANDER, DALE ZOLTON, real estate broker; b. Aug. 10, 1944, Detroit, mich.; s. Steven Paul and Helen T. (Sasfy) E.; m. Rena Mae Hefley, July 30, 1967; children: Brent Arthur, b. 1971; (stepson) James Paul Long, b. 1963; edn: AA, San Bernardino Valley Coll. 1977; spl. courses Chaffey Coll., Valley Coll.; Calif. Lic. Real Estate Broker. Career: supr. Kaiser Steel Corp., Fontana 1965-83; broker/owner Century 21 Ability Realty, 1982–; tng. instr., OSHA, Kaiser Steel 1980-2; Notary Public, Calif. 1973-; honors: Million Dollar Club Cen. 21; mem: Nat., Calif. Assn. of Realtors; San Bernardino Valley Bd. of Realtors 1972-; Realty Safety Assn.; Nat. Notary Assn.; Nat. Fedn. of Independent Business; Assn. of Iron and Steel Engrs. 1968-; Rialto CofC (dir. 1983-5, pres-elect 1985-86); Jaycees (pres. Rialto 1976; Dist. 23 vp 1978), J.C.I. Senators of Calif., Calif. Tigers, Am. Legion, B.P.O.Elks 1985-; Frat. Order of Eagles, Nat. Hot Rod Assn., 82nd Sport Parachute Club 1963-4; mil: E4 US Army 1961-64; Democrat; Catholic; rec: sky-diving, auto racing. Res: 2389 N. Sycamore Ave Rialto 92376 Ofc: Century 21 Ability Realty, 1154 N. Riverside Ave Rialto 92376

ETHANS, ALEXANDER ARTHUR, quality assurance engineer; b. Aug. 19, 1929, Highland Park, Mich.; s. Arthur Constantine and Sofia (Ma) E.; m. Mavis, May 14, 1977; children: Thomas Arthur b. 1955, Karen Ann b. 1957; edn: BBA, Univ. Detroit 1962; Reg. Profl. Engr. (Quality, Indsl.), Calif. 1967. Career: indsl. engr., branch mgr. McDonnell Douglas (MDC) 1967-70, field service indsl. engr. Apollo/Skylab (MDC) Fla. 1971-73; senior staff cons. Case & Co. Internat. Consultants 1973-74, WOFAC Internat. Cons. 1974-75; facilities mgr. Fenwick Products 1975-77; section mgr. qual. assur. (MDC) St. Charles, Mo. 1977-80, splst. quality audits (MDC) Huntington Beach 1980-84, senior splst. quality (MDC) Saudi Arabia 1981-85, mgr. quality audit (MDC) Douglas Aircraft Long Beach, Calif. 1985–; lectr. var. colls. on quality assur., indsl. engring.; mem. Delta Sigma Pi (internat. bus. frat.), Am. Soc. of Quality Control; past mem. Council (Orange Empire) Boy Scouts Am.; mil: fireman 1/c US Navy 1948-51, sgt. US Air Force 1950-52; Democrat; Greek Orthodox; rec: model making, electric trains. Res: 10471 Oakhaven Dr Stanton 90680 Ofc: Douglas Aircraft Co. 3855 Lakewood Blvd Ste 7-39, Long Beach 90846

ETHERIDGE, KEVIN MICHAEL, termite control co. president; b. Feb. 1, 1956, Detroit, Mich.; s. Harold and Anne Louise (Read) E.; 1 dau. Karalee Brooke b. 1982; edn: Cypress Coll. 1974-76. Career: shop labor Best Way Termite Control and The Way Co., La Habra 1972-, became vice pres./mgr. Best Way Termite Control 1978-82; ind. dealer Snap On Tools, Alhambra 1983; founder/pres. Contractors Termite Control Inc., Brea 1983–, and Contractors Fumigation Inc., 1984–; honors: Special Olympics Pgm. (1985), Adopt a House Pgm., No. Orange Co. Board of Realtors; mem: Orange Co. Dist. Pest Control Oprs. of Calif. (v.chmn.), No. Orange Co. Board of Realtors (affil.); Roman Catholic; rec: water skiing, boating. Ofc: Contractors Termite Control Inc. 855 West Lambert Rd Brea 92621

ETZEN, STANLEY BERNARD, printing co. executive; b. Apr. 25, 1930, Davenport, Iowa; s. Bernard Clemens and Inez Cora (Legg) E.; m. Martha, Dec. 13, 1984; children: David b. 1955, Mark b. 1958; edn: BSME, Univ. Iowa 1953; MBA mktg., Univ. Chgo. 1959; real estate broker Calif. Career: engrg., exec. sales R.R. Donnelley Chgo. 1956-68; mktg. mgr. Times Mirror PRESS L.A. 1968-73; pres., CEO Day Printing Corp. Pomona 1973-84, Dayco Graphics Inc. Pomona 1984–; Disting. Vis. Lectr. Cal. Poly. Univ. 1978-83; mem: Printing Industry Assn. (bd. 1978-80), Pomona CofC (v.p. 1978-80); mil: lt. USN Civil Engr. Corps. 1953-56; Republican; Lutheran (ch. pres. 1973-74, 82-83). Res: 2359 Alamo Heights Diamond Bar 91765 Ofc: Dayco Graphics Inc. POB 2647 Pomona 91769

EU, MARCH FONG, California Secretary of State; b. Mar. 19, 1927, Oakdale; d. Yuen and Shin (Shee) Kong; children: Matthew Kipling, Marchesa Suyin; edn: BS, UC Berkeley, M.Ed, Mills Coll., EdD, Stanford Univ., postgrad. work Columbia Univ., CSC Hayward; Calif. State Teaching Creds., Jr. Coll. Adm.- Supr. Career: div. chmn. Univ. California Medical Ctr., San Francisco; dental hygienist Oakland Public Schs.; div. supr. Alameda County Schs.; lectr. Mills College; mem. (pres. 1961-62) Alameda County Bd. of Edn. 1956-66, pres. Alameda County Sch. Bds. Assn. 1965; spl. cons. Calif. State Dept. Edn.; education, legislative cons. Santa Clara County Office of Edn., Sausalito Public Schs., others 1962-66; elected rep. to Calif. State Legislature 15th Assem. Dist., 1966-68, 70-72; elected Calif. Secty. of State 1974, 2d term 1979-83, 3d term 1983-87; apptd. Calif. Chief of Protocol, 1975-83; chair Calif. State World

Trade Commn., 1983–; honors: Eastbay Intercultural Fellowship (1959), Phoebe E. Hearst Bay Area Woman of Year (1968), Calif. Retain Liquor Dealers Inst. Woman of Year (1969), VFW Loyalty Day Award (1970), Calif. Assn. of Adult Edn. Adminstr. merit cit. (1970), hon. LLD, Western State Univ. (1975), Annual Humanitarian Award, Women's Center Coll. of Marin (1978), 'Asian American on the Move' award for politics, LA City Employees Asian Am. Assn. (1975), Disting. Comm. Coll. Alumni Award, Calif. Comm. Colls. and Jr. Colls. Assn. (1976), hon. LLD, Univ. of San Diego Sch. of Law (1977), annual award Nat. Notary Assn. (1979), Outstanding Woman Award, Nat. Women's Pol. Caucus (1980), Person of Year, Miracle Mile Lions Club (1980), Milton Shoong Hall of Fame Humanitarian Award (1981), Citizen of Year, Council for Civic Unity of the SF Bay Area (1982), leadership award Ventura Co. Young Democrats (1983), Democrat of Year, San Mateo Dem. Com. (1983), Woman of Achievement, LA chpt. Hadassah (1983), hon. mem. Calif. Agric. Aircraft Assn. (1974), bd. dir. New Voter Ednl. Research Found. (1975), hon. mem. Women in Mgmt. (1976), mem. bd. councillors USC Sch. of Dentistry (1976), hon. mem. Calif. Landscape Contrs. Assn. (1976), Calif. Women for Agric. (1980), Folsom Hist. Soc. (1982), Phi Alpha Delta Law Frat. Internat. (1982), mem. Nat. Commn. on the Observance of Internat. Women's Year (1977), life mem. Navy League; mem: Oakland Econ. Devel. Council (v. chmn. adv. com. Youth Student Centers, Ford Found. project 1962-63), Council of Social Planning, judge Mayor's Com. on Excellence of Youth 1964, Oakland YWCA bd. dirs. 1965; hon. mem. So. Calif. Dental Assn.; charter pres. Chinese Young Ladies Soc. of Oakland; mem. CTA, Elm PTA (hon., life, charter, pres.), Hadassah (life), AAUW, Delta Kappa Gamma; Democrat (del. Nat. Conv. 1968, exec. com. Calif. Dem. Central Com.). Ofc: 1230 J Street Sacramento 95814

EVANS, BRYN BENNETT, JR., insurance co. executive; b. June 7, 1943, Long Beach; s. Bryn Bennett and Lynn Rose (Petticord) E.; m. Billie Ann, Feb. 14, 1966; children: Bryn III b. 1968, Doug b. 1970, Jenny b. 1973; edn: BA, Whittier Coll. 1967. Career: with Allstate Insurance Co. 1967–; svcs. supvr., Santa Ana 1967-69, svcs. div. supvr. 1969-71, tng. & telecomm. mgr. 1971-75; Western zone telecomm. mgr., Menlo Park 1975-78, Western zone claim ops. mgr. 1979-80; dist. claim mgr., Stockton 1980-84; senior dist. claim mgr., San Ramon 1984–; mem: Elk Horn Country Club, Roundhill Country Club; mil: E-6 National Guard 1964-70; Republican; Presbyterian; rec: golf, softball. Res: 47 Hagen Oaks Ct. Alamo 94507 Ofc: Allstate Insurance Co., 2323 Crow Canyon Rd. San Ramon 94583

EVANS, FLORA JEANETTE TAYLOR, funeral director, educator; b. Nov. 10, 1922, Dallas, Tx.; d. Sham and Ruth Lillian (Webster) Taylor; div.; children: Cheryl Faye, Billie Sue, Keith R. and Ricardo M. Evans; edn: AA, Merritt Jr. Coll. 1967; BA, CSU Hayward 1969, MA 1972; PhD, Nova Univ., Ft. Lauderdale, Fla. 1979; Calif. lic. Life Ins. Agent (1946), Beautician (1947), Notary Public (1952). Career: Civil Service, 10 years; controller Hudston Funeral Home and Jackson Funeral Home, 10 years; dir./owner Saints Christian Funeral Chapel, Oakland 1965–; founder/dir. Midtown Rehab. Center, Inc. (CETA tng. pgm.) 1975-80; tchr. bus. courses and bus. math., Emery High Sch. 1981-82; instr. Peralta Comm. Coll. 1970-, Merritt Campus, Laney Outreach Campus; currently substitute tchg. Oakland Unified Sch. Dist.; awards: Community Service Award (1984), appreciation Comm. Agencies, City of Oakland, Alameda County Pgms., Bus. & Profl. Woman of Year (1980), Alameda Co. Chapt. I. Foster Parents Assn. cert. of appreciation 10 years svc. (1984), Dr. Barbara R. Harris comm. svc. award, Outstanding Business Woman, Iota Phi Lambda Sor. Inc. Beta Mu Chpt./Oakland (1985), Outstanding Tchr., PTA Devel. Center for Handicapped Children (1985); mem: R.R. Retirement Womens Aux., Nat. Council of Negro Women, Bus. & Profl. Women; civic: lic. Foster Mother, Alameda Co. (15 years); missionary worker for the needy; publs: "Spiritual Poems" set to music by Bettys Music Makers of St. Petersburg, Fla. (1986) and Media Promotions, Nashville, Tenn. (1986); Ch. of God in Christ. Address: Saints Christian Funeral Chapel 936 W MacArthur Blvd Oakland 94608

EVANS, GLENN KENNETH, mechanical engineer; b. Mar. 9, 1943, Hyannis, Nebr.; s. Harvey Willis and Ida Eva (Connally) E.; edn: BSME, South Dak. Sch. of Mines & Technology 1972. Career: sales engr. Anning-Johnson, Burlington 1973-75, G.M. Cooke Assocs., Berkeley 1976-78; test cell engr. NARF (Naval Air Rework Facility) Alameda, Alameda 1978-80; systems engr. Bechtel Corp., San Francisco 1980-83, Saudi Arabian Bechtel Co., Dhahran, Saudi Arabia 1983-84, Bechtel Corp., S.F. 1984-85, project engr. Bechtel, Bakersfield 1985–; honors: Pi Mu Epsilon (1972), Spl. Achievement Award ($1000) for work done at NARF Alameda (1980); mem. Am. Soc. of Mech. Engrs., Instrument Soc. of Am.; mil: capt. US Marine Corps 1966-69; Republican; Congregational; rec: flying, reading. Res: 510 Real Rd Apt 21 Bakersfield 93309 Ofc: Bechtel, 5100 California Ave Ste 107, Bakersfield 93309

EVANS, I. J., educator/business executive; b. July 26, 1917, Davidson, Okla.; s. Isaac J. and Doscia May (Duncan) E.; m. Fern Wallace (Outstanding Elem. Tchrs. of Am. 1975), June 20, 1949; edn: BS, Okla. State Univ. 1940, MS 1946, EdD 1949. Career: principal Potter Valley High Sch., Ukiah Union H.S.Dist. 1949-54; dist. supt. Owens Valley Unified Sch. Dist. 1954-57; founder/pres./CEO, Evans Enterprises, pvt. real estate and investment firm, 1958-82, ret. 1982; awards: medal of merit by Pres. Ronald Reagan, 1982; mem: US Senatorial Club 1982-85; Grad. Club, Okla. State Univ. (pres. 1946); Nat. Edn. Assn. 1949-57; Nat., and Calif. Assn. of Sec. Sch. Adminstrs. (v.p. No. Coast Sect. 1950), 1949-57; pres. North Hills Democratic Club 1958; Internat. Platform Assn. 1984-85; Town Hall of Calif 1984-85; mil: USAAF, WWII, 1942-45, served in S.W. and Western Pacific, decorated Phil. Lib., GCM, Battle stars for New Guinea, Biak, Leyte and Luzon (Phil.), Okinawa; Republican (Presdtl. Task Force 1982-85); Protestant; rec: golf, hiking, photog., travel, writing. Res: 16741 Armstead St. Granada Hills 91344

EVANS, LOUISE, clinical psychologist; b. San Antonio, Tex.; d. Henry Daniel and Adela (Pariser) Evans; m. Tom R. Gambrell, MD, Feb. 23, 1960; edn: BS, Northwestern Univ. 1949; MSc in psychol., Purdue Univ. 1952, PhD in clin. psychol., 1955; Diplomate in Clin. Psychol., Am. Bd. of Examiners in Profl. Psychol., 1966. Career: tchg. asst. Purdue Univ. 1950-51; intern Menninger Found., Topeka State Hosp., 1952-53; staff psychol. Kanakee State Hosp., 1954-55; post-doc. fellow in child clin. psychol., USPH Menninger Found., 1955-56; staff psychol. Kings Co. Hosp., Bklyn. 1957-78; dir. of psychol. clin. and instr. Barnes Hosp., Washington Univ. Sch. of Med., St. Louis, Mo. 1959; pvt. practice, Fullerton, Calif. 1960–; psychol. cons. Fullerton Community Hosp., 1961-81, staff cons. Martin Luther Hosp., Anaheim 1963-70; fellowships: Internat. Council of Psychologists Inc., Royal Soc. of Health, AAAS, Am. Orthopsych. Assn., Am. Psychol. Assn.; honors: 1st Citizenship award, Purdue Alumni Assn. 1975; service award, Yuma, Ariz. Headstart Pgm. 1972; 1st PTA scholarship, Evansville, Ind. 1945; scholarship, Northwestern Univ. 1945; keynote speaker num. civic, ednl., collegiate programs 1950-; del. US and Calif. Traffic Safety Confs. 1964; mem: Calif., Orange County, L.A. County psychol. assns., L.A. Soc. of Clin. Psychol., Am. Acad. of Political and Social Sci., Am. Judicature Soc., alumni assns., Pi Sigma Pi frat., Center for the Study of the Presidency, fellow World Wide Acad. of Scholars; rec: antiques. Ofc: 905-907 W Wilshire Ave, Fullerton 92632

EVANS, THOMAS J., III, savings and loan executive; b. Oct. 1, 1951, Glendale; s. Thomas J., Jr. and Patricia G. (Corbosiero/Guarinio) E.; div.; two sons: Tommy, b. 1976, Darrell, b. 1979. Career: asst. mgr. loan svcs. Empire Savings and Loan Assn. 1971-72; asst. v.p./mgr. loan svcs. ops. Great Western Svgs. & Loan Assn. 1972-78; v.p./ corp. secty./ dir. Oceanside Insurance Agcy., 1981-82; senior v.p./chief loan ofcr. First Federal Savings Bank of Calif., 1978-82; founder and bd. chmn./ pres./ chief exec. Unified Savings Bank, Northridge 1982-1984; consultant var. finl. instns. and real estate devel. projects, 1984; chief lending ofcr. Concord-Liberty Savings & Loan, 1985–; pres./ chief exec. Windtree Mortgage Co., 1984–; mem: Calif. League of Savings Instns. (dir. Los Angeles Home Loan Counseling Center 3 terms, speaker six confs.), Nat. Assn. of Review Appraisers and Mortgage Underwriters, Los Angeles Escrow Assn., Inst. of Trustee Sale Ofcrs., Los Angeles Loan Service Mgrs. Assn., Inst. of Finl. Edn., Santa Monica Land Use Com. (chmn.), Inglewood Neighborhood Housing Svc. Res: 4429-7 Saugus Ave Sherman Oaks 90403 Ofc: Windtree Mortgage Co., 15300 Ventura Blvd., Suite 522, Sherman Oaks 91403

EVERS, ALFRED CLARK, JR., chiropractor; b. Oct. 13, 1945, Kingman, Ariz.; s. Alfred Clark and Lois Fay (Finch) E.; m. Elaine Fitzgerald, Feb. 10, 1973; children: Amy b. 1974, Joanna b. 1976, Adam b. 1981; edn: AA, San Bernardino Valley Coll. 1979; DC, Palmer Coll. of Chiro. 1982, Diplomate Nat. Bd. Chiro. Exmrs. Career: combat medic, x-ray tech. US Army Vietnam, Japan 1967-70; x-ray tech. French Hosp. L.A. 1970-71; emissions tech. Automotive Envir. Systems Inc. Westminster 1972; elegibility worker II San Bernadino Co. Dept. of Public Soc. Svcs. 1973-79; chiropractor, dir. Evers Chiro. Ctr. Redlands 1982–; Calif. Chiro Assn., Rotary Internat., Rancho Mirage, Redlands CofCs; mil: sp/4 US Army 1967-70, Combat Medic Badge, Vietnam Campaign, Purple Heart; Catholic; rec: artist, photog. Res: 1006 White Mtn Rd POB 64 Big Bear City 92314 Ofc: Evers Chiropractic Ctr. 802 W Colton Ave Ste F Redlands 92373

EWELL, A. B., JR., lawyer, agri-businessman; b. Sept. 10, 1941, Elyria, Ohio, s. Austin Bert and Mary Rebecca (Thompson) E., Sr.; desc. John Ewell, b. 1734, Scotland, settled in Plymouth Co., Mass. 1975; m. Kristine Ballantyne, Feb. 14, 1976; children: Austin B., III b. 1978, Brice B. b. 1982; edn: BA, Miami Univ. 1963; LLB, JD, UC Hastings Coll. of Law 1966; admitted Calif. State Bar (1966), US Dist. Ct., E. Dist. Calif. (1967), US 9th Circuit Ct. Appeals (1967). Career: atty., assoc. law firm Parichan, Krebs & Levy, Fresno 1966-70, law firm McCormick, Barstow, Sheppard, Coyle & Wayte, Fresno 1970-84; pres. A.B. Ewell, Jr., APC, 1984–; gen. counsel Kings River Water Assn. 1979-, Dudley Ridge Water Dist. 1980-, Friant Water Users Authority 1984-, Mid Valley Water Dist.; mem. Task Force on Prosecution, Cts. and Law Reform of Calif. Council on Criminal Justice (1971-74); mem. Am. Bar Assn. (Sect. on Natural Resources, Water Resources Com., Sect. on Real Prop., Probate and Trust Law), Fresno Co. Bar Assn., Barristers Club of Fresno Co. (1972-76), Phi Alpha Delta Alumni Assn., Hastings Coll. of Law 1066 Club, Alumni Assn., The Water Found. (1978-), Western Water Edn. Found. (1980-), Fresno Co. Water Advsy. Com., San Joaquin River Flood Control Assn. (chmn.), Nat. Farm Water Alliance; affil. Assn. of Calif. Water Agencies, San Joaquin Valley Agri. Water Com. (1979-); civic: Commonwealth Club of Calif. (Sect. of Agri. and Water), Fresno East Community Ctr. (dir. 1971-73), Fresno Comm. Council (1972-73), Fresno City, Co. Hist. Soc., CSU Fresno Pres.'s Club and Bulldog Found., Rotary, Firelands Hist. Soc., Spirit of '76 Mus. and Hist. Soc., Fresno Metro. Ministry (sustaining mem.), Fresno Metro. Mus. of Art, Hist. & Sci. (trustee, sustaining mem.), St. Agnes Med. Ctr. Found. (advis. council), US Small Bus. Assn. Nat. Advis. Council, Sigma Nu Alumni Assn., Prodn. Credit Assn. (1964-), Friends of Latin Am. (organizing dir. 1980); research project: 'The Sufferers Lands' (hist. and settlement of Huron and Erie Cos., OH); Republican, mem. Calif. State Central Com. (1974-), Exec. Fin. Com. (1978-), Fresno Co. Central Com. treas./exec. com. (1971-72), past v.p. Calif. Repub. Assy. of Fresno, chmn. The Lt. Gov.'s Club, Fresno Co. (1980-), campaign chmn.; Congregational; rec: hist. research, antique books, guitar, tennis. Ofc: A.B. Ewell, Jr., APC, 83 E Shaw Ave Ste 203 Fresno 93710

EWING (PRICE), JEANNINE ALLEENICA, management consultant; b. Oct. 29, 1947, Cleveland Cuyahoga, Ohio; d. Alfred M. and Annabelle (Wilson) Ewing; m. Thurman R. Price, Sept. 2, 1976; edn: BS, Case Western Reserve, 1969; MA, Vanderbilt Univ. 1974; AS, Mission Coll. 1982; MBA Stanford Univ. 1985; stu. Univ. of Phoenix Sch of Bus. 1982-. Career: coordinator of health services National Health Profile System, Nashville, tenn. 1970-74; mgmt. cons. First So. Devel. Co., Memphis, Tenn. 1974-77; mgmt. cons. (Employee Assistance pgms.), Awareness Concept, San Jose 1977-80, exec. v.p. 1981-; counselor Nat. Semiconductor, Santa Clara 1980-81; awards: community svc., Houston, Tex. 1975; scholastic, Mission Coll. 1980, 82; mem. Am. Business Women's Assn., Redwood City; author: The Girl I Never Knew, An Act of Love, The Dreamer (unpub. novel); Democrat; Catholic; rec: writing. Address: San Jose

EWING, BARBARA WATERS, real estate broker, notary; b. June 23, 1918, Santa Ana; d. Charles Vest and Bertha Rosemary (Conner) Davis; m. Robert A. Waters, Jr. (decd.); children: Robert A. III b. 1942 (dec.), Teresa A. b. 1943, Charles T. b. 1944, James J. b. 1945, Sharon W. b. 1949, Patricia L. b. 1951, Joellen W. b. 1954, Barbara W. b. 1956; m. 2d Donald Dean Ewing, July 12, 1973; edn: BA, UC Berkeley 1939; tchg. degree, UC Santa Barbara 1940; real estate sales, Anthony R.E. Sch. 1971, r.e. broker, 1980; r.e. broker Calif. 1984. Career: 15 yrs. real estate, broker, notary; active in volunteer and community affairs; advis. bd. mem. Tri-Valley Haven for Women; 13 yrs. million-dollar sales; mem. So. Alameda County Bd. Realtors (multiple listing com., nominating com., membership com., vice chmn. ethics & profl. conduct com.), Alpha Delta Pi (past secty., council mem., dir. pledges), Assistance League of San Mateo County (charter mem., sustaining mem., past v.p., treas.), St. Matthew's Mothers Club (v.p.), St. Bartholomew's Women's Group (pres.), Altar Soc. (pres.), Calif. Golf Club (pub. rels. chmn.), Boy Scouts (den mother), Girl Scouts (leader), Catholic Social Svc. San Mateo County (bd.), Am. Red Cross (volunteer); writer monthly real estate newsletters, brochures; Republican; Catholic; rec: oil painting, flower arranging, gardening, formerly raised, trained, and showed St. Bernards. Res: 1230 Marina Cir Byron 94514 Ofc: Stocking Realty 392 S Livermore Ave Livermore 94550

EYER, CLARENDON BENNETT, JR., chemical engineer; b. Mar. 6, 1898, Evanston, Ill.; s. Clarendon Bennett and Cora Alive (Knowlton) E.; gr.-uncle, Marcus Perrin Knowlton, Chief Justice Supreme Ct. Mass.; desc. Col. Thomas Knowlton, Revolutionary War; m. Joyce Taylor, Feb. 15, 1969; stepchildren: William Joseph Allen, Jr. b. 1953, Emily Allen Erickson b. 1947; edn: Harvard Sch., L.A. 1969, Stanford Univ. 1921. Career: chem. engr. Am. Trona Corp., 1922-23; chem. engr., treas. Smith-Emery Co., 1923-34; chem. dept. Calif. Inst. of Tech., 1949-50; research chemist 1950-, Inorganic Chem. Research and Process Devel.; honors: Alpha Chi Sigma, Phi Lambda Upsilon; foreman Federal Grand Jury, Los Angeles 1960-61; mem. Phi Gamma Delta, Athenaeum, Valley Hunt Club; mil: ofcrs. tng. US Army WWI; Republican; Presbyterian; rec: sailing. Res: 986 Kewen Dr San Marino 91108

EYHERABIDE, STEPHEN PETER, lawyer; b. Apr. 21, 1919, Maricopa; s. Pascal and Grace (Iroulgui) E.; m. Dora, July 1945; children: Michelle b. 1947, Pascal b. 1949, Stephen b. 1952, Germaine b. 1955, Bernadette b. 1960; edn: AB, Stanford Univ. 1948; LLB, Univ. of S.F. 1951. Career: lawyer assoc., Mack & Bianco, Bakersfield, 1951, partner of Mack, Bianco, King & Eyherabide, 1954, partner law firm of King & Eyherabide, 1965, sr. partner law firm Eyherabide, Pearl, Beckman & Eyherabide, Bksfld. 1982-; mem: State Bar of Calif., Am. Bar Assn., Kern County Bar Assn. (pres. 1967-8); mil: capt. US Army Inf., Purple Heart, Silver Star; Republican; Catholic; rec: flower gardening. Res: 4281 Country Club Dr Bakersfield 93306 Ofc: Eyherabide, Pearl, Beckman & Eyherabide, 1400 Chester Ave, Ste N, Bakersfield 93301

EYTH, EDWARD CARL, industrial designer; b. June 30, 1955, Pittsburgh, Pa.; s. Edward Joseph and Elizabeth Regina (Braun) E.; edn: AA visual communs., Art Inst. of Pittsburgh 1975; BS w/distinc., Art Center Coll. of Design 1985. Career: senior designer Steve Sherer Inc., Rancho Mirage 1978-81; art dir. The Jones Agency, Palm Springs 1981-83; design cons. Industrial Design Affiliates, Beverly Hills 1985; pres./senior designer The Design Firm of Ed Eyth, La Canada 1985-; instr. Art Center Coll. of Design, Pasadena; design cons. var. TV and film prodn. studios; indsl. design cons. var. cos.; awards: Gen. Motors Scholar (1984), G.E. Engring. Plastics Design Competition- 1st Pl. Award for hosp. equip. design (1984); mem. Soc. of Plastics Engrs., Soc. of Automotive Engrs., Mensa, World Wildlife Fund; works: Product design: co-designer of voice-activated, hands-free telephone (1983); rec: sculpture, tennis. Address: 4640 Ocean View Blvd La Canada 91011-1423

EZAKI, RAMSEY ALAN, dentist, dental consultant; b. Aug. 29, 1952, Los Angeles; s. Floyd Yogi and Nami (Nakagawa) E.; m. Janine Yokochi, July 5, 1975; 1 son, Brandon b. 1980; edn: BA in bus. adm., and BA in music theory, perf., Whittier Coll. 1974; DDS, USC 1980. Career: dental practise in Walnut, and Whittier; clin. instr. USC Sch. of Dentistry 1980; dental practice mgmt. consultant; dental cons. Unified Sch. Dists. of Montebello, Walnut Valley; cons. dental assisting program Rio Hondo Comm. Coll. 1981-; faculty Los Angeles Music and Met Sch. 1970-73; cons. Am. Heart Assn.; cons. Gr. LA Comm. Cancer Control Ctr.; honors: City of Montebello Jr. Citizen of the Month 1970; mem. Am., Calif., Hawaii, San Gabriel Valley Dental Assns., Fellow Acad. of Internat. Dental Studies, Acad. of Gen. Dentistry; mem. Whittier Coll. Alumni

Assn. (bd. dirs. 1985), Whittier Coll. Lancer Soc., USC Century Club; musician: Burbank Sym. Orch., Rio Hondo Sym., Montebello Civic Light Opera, church pianist (11 yrs.) Beverly Presbyn. Ch.; Presbyterian. Res: 15628 Condesa Dr Whittier 90603 Ofc: Ramsey A. Ezaki, DDS Inc. and Assocs.: Valley Professional Center, 20709 Colima Rd, Ste. 206, Walnut 91789; The Village, 6517 Greenleaf Ave Whittier 90601

EZELL, JAMES TERRELL, telephone co. president; b. Aug. 21, 1939, Ovett, Miss.; s. Cecil Earl and Maejewl (Byrd) E.; m. Jolean, Nov. 21, 1959; children: James, Jr. b. 1960, Brenda b. 1962, Jon b. 1964, Michelle b. 1966, Gordon b. 1971, Christopher b. 1975. Career: served to chief petty ofcr. (ICC) US Navy, 1957-67; bench tech. RCA Service Co., Lansing, Mich. 1967-69; comml. accts. TV Telephone RCA Service Co., San Diego 1969-71; sales & svc. rep. Universal Comms. Systems Inc., Pacific N.W. 1970-72; svc. mgr. Gen. Comms. Engring., 1972-77; owner/pres. James Ezell's Telephone Co. E-Z Tel, Inc., Livermore 1977-; mem. Press Club of S.F., Livermore CofC; Baptist; rec: family, camping, fishing, equestrian. Res: 318 Lloyd St Livermore 94550 Ofc: E-Z Tel Inc 2271 S Vasco Livermore 94550

FABIONAR, VICTOR ROBERT, architect; b. Oct. 31, 1946, Reedley; s. Irenio Javar and Cecilia (Moreno) F.; children: Sabina b. 1984, Vera b. 1984; edn: AA, Coll. of Sequoias 1966; Reg. Architect, Calif. 1982. Career: draftsman, job captain Walter Vogel Arch. 1970-74; project arch. Mathis Assocs., Arch. & Engr., 1975-82; prin. Victor R. Fabionar Architect, Fresno 1982-; designer 20 outpatient health care facilities (1975-); mil: E4 USMCR 1967-73; Democrat; Catholic; rec: handball, gardening. Address: Victor R. Fabionar, Arch. 921 E Hampton Fresno 93704

FACHIN, GARY MICHAEL, lawyer; b. June 29, 1948, Bakersfield, Calif.; s. John and Lucille Barbara (Bauer) F.; m. Karen, Aug. 6, 1977; children: Cara b. 1978, Ryan b. 1981; edn: BA physics, UC Santa Barbara 1970; JD, Univ. San Francisco 1975; admitted Calif. State Bar 1975. Career: assoc. atty. Wagy, Bunker, Hislop & Lewis 1975-79; sole practitioner 1979-81; ptnr. Fachin & McCartney 1981-83, Fachin, McCartney & Twisselman 1983-; dir. Greater Bakersfield Local Devel. Corp. 1981-83; honors: Outstanding Student in Phys. Sci. (Bakersfield Coll. 1968), Phi Beta Kappa (UCSB 1970); mem: Calif. State Bar (bus. law, tax, probate & astate plng. sects.), Am. Bar Assn. (real property, probate and trust sect.), Bakersfield East Rotary; Republican; Catholic; rec: reading, gardening. Res: Rt 10 Box 596 Bakersfield 93313 Ofc: Fachin, McCartney & Twisselman 1830 Truxtun Ste 212 Bakersfield 93301

FACKLER, MARTIN L., military surgeon, wound ballistics research director; b. Apr. 8, 1933, York, Pa.; s. Martin Luther and Naomi Dorcas (Gibbs) F.; m. Nancy Aleen Gray, Sept. 29, 1964; edn: AB, magna cum laude, Gettysburg Coll. 1951-55; MD, Yale Univ. Sch. of Med. 1955-59; Diplomate Am. Bd. Surg. Career: staff surg. NSA Hosp. DaNang RVN 1967-68, USN Hosp. Yokosuka, Japan 1969-71; chief dept. of surg. USN Hosp. Memphis, Tenn. 1972-74, 2nd Gen. Hosp. Landstuhl, Germany 1977-80, Army Hosp. Ft. Carson, Colo. 1980-81; dir. Wound Ballistics Lab Letterman Army Inst. of Research, Presidio of S.F. 1981-; cons. w/ local, state and nat. law enforcement groups and criminalistics labs on gunshot effects on the body, expert witness; honors: Phi Beta Kappa (Gettysburg Coll.); fellow Am. Coll. Surg.; mem. Commonwealth Club, S.F. publs: 38 articles in med. lit. (1972-86), 60 exhibits and presentations (1980-), patent awarded for surgical retractor retaining device (1984), devised process of measuring wounding effects using tissue simulant; mil: US Navy 1960-75, col. US Army 1975-, Army Commdn.; rec: foreign lang. study, gunsmithing, welding, tennis, scuba, flying. Res: 1809 Wyman Ave Presidio San Francisco 94129 Ofc: Letterman Army Inst. of Research Presidio San Francisco 94129

FACTOR, MAX, III, lawyer; b. Sept. 25, 1945, Los Angeles; s. Sidney Bernard and Dorothy (Levinson) F.; m. Susan Gail Barg, June 19, 1966; 1 dau., Jennifer Lee b. 1969; edn: BA magna cum laude, Harvard Coll. 1966; JD, Yale Law Sch. 1969. Career: law clerk US Ct. of Appeals 6th Cir. Cleveland, Ohio 1970-72; mng. atty. Calif. Law Ctr. L.A. 1972-74, Consumer Protection Sect. L.A. 1974-78; pvt. attorney (real estate/business litigation) Beverly Hills 1978-; bd. mem. (past pres.) Beverly Hills Unified Sch. Dist.; honors: Disting. Svc., Pub. Edn. Award (BH Bd. of Edn.), Max Factor III Day (Bev. Hills); mem: Bd. of Councilors USC, Jewish Comm. Found. (trustee), BH Edn. Found. (bd., past pres.), Bev. Hills CofC (bd., pres. elect); publ: Report of Hearing Examiner in Los Angeles City Nursing Homes, How To Choose a Nursing Home, How To Choose an Attorney, What To Do If You've Been Taken by an Auto Mechanic (1974-78); Jewish; rec: golf. Ofc: Kehr, DeMeter, Factor & Herman 1975 Century Park East Ste 1760 Los Angeles 90067

FAETH, WILLIAM HOWARD, neurosurgeon; b. June 30, 1925, Waterbury, Conn.; s. William H. and Rose E. (Withey) F.; m. Christine Donovan, Dec. 29, 1982; children: William, b. 1951, David, b. 1953, Penelope, b. 1955, Shawn, b. 1957; edn: MD, Tufts Univ. 1949. Career: pres. Valley Neurological Medical Group, Burbank; dir. Western Security Bank; chmn. bd. St. Joseph Med. Ctr. Found.; trustee St. Joseph Med. Ctr. Adv. Bd.; mem: St. Joseph Med. Ctr. Profl. Staff (pres. and chief of staff 1974, 1975); Lakeside Golf Club (pres. 1985); mil: capt. USAF (MC) 1950-51; rec: big game hunting. Ofc: 2701 W. Alameda Ste. 606, Burbank 91505

FAHN, ALEX, corporate executive, farmer; b. Dec. 15, 1923, Germany; s. Joseph and Charlotte (Hoffman) F.; m. Shirley, Mar. 9, 1946; children: Hillard b. 1947, Lorene b. 1948, Roberta b. 1952; edn: Sacramento City Coll. 1941-42,

Univ. Ariz. 1942-43. Career: sales dept. Sacramento Bag Mfg. Co., 1945-55, vice pres. 1955-74, pres. 1974—; ptnr. Belli & Fahn Farms, 1958—; ptnr./gen. mgr. F & S Farms, 1974—; mem: Calif. Farm Bureau, Calif. Sugar Beet Growers Assn., Calif. Tomato Growers Assn., Textile Bag Mfg. Assn., Textile Bag Processors Assn.; civic: Am. Israel Public Affairs Com. (nat. exec. com.), Sacto. Jewish Fedn. (pres. Sacto.), Council of Jewish Fedns. (nat. exec. com.), Harry Truman Dem. Club; mil: cpl. US Air Force 1943-45, Presdtl. Unit Cit.; Democrat; Jewish (cong. pres.); rec: music, community service. Ofc: Sacramento Bag Mfg. Co. POB 1563 Sacramento 95807

FAIN, WILLIAM HART, JR., architect; b. July 14, 1944, Los Angeles; s. Wm. H. and Jesslyn (Kaye) F.; m. Jennifer Nelson, May 29, 1977; children: Elizabeth Nelson b. 1980, Margaret Minton b. 1984; edn: B.Arch., Univ. Calif. 1968; Certificate Town Planning, Univ. of Manchester, Eng. 1970; M.Arch. in urban design, Harvard Univ. 1975; Reg. Architect, Calif. 1973. Career: urban planner Office of the Mayor, N.Y.C. 1970-72; urban designer Boston Redevel. Authority 1973-75; development advisor City of Richmond, Va. 1976; spl. asst. HUD, Wash DC 1977-80; exec. vice pres. William L. Pereira Assocs., Los Angeles 1980—; awards: fellow Nat. Endowment for the Humanities (1972), fellow Nat. Endowment for the Arts (1978), profl. recognition award, Progressive Architecture Mag. (1976); mem. Am. Inst. of Architects; civic: trustee Los Angeles Library Assn., dir. Arch. & Design Council, Mus. of Contemporary Art (LA); club: Los Angeles Tennis. Ofc: William L. Pereira Associates 5657 Wilshire Blvd Los Angeles 90036

FAIR, SHIRLEY HELEN, interior designer; b. Mar. 22, 1936, Bridgeport, Mich.; d. Carl Paul and Agnes (Henny) Kaufeld; m. Dick Edgerton Fair, Mar. 27, 1947, div. 1976; children: Kima Lee b. 1956, Miesa Lynn b. 1960; edn: grad. Chgo. Sch. of Design, 1966; bus. lic. City of La Habra. Career: interior designer, prin. Interiors by Shirley Fair, La Habra 1966—; columnist on interior design: The Hacienda Highlander, Hacienda Hts. (1967-72), Las Vegas Sun (1970-72), Saginaw (Mich.) News, 2 yrs., San Gabriel Valley Tribune (1967-68), Whittier Daily News (1972-83), Orange County Register (1971-); lectr. on design, Crystal Cathedral, Christian Womens Clubs, num. groups; honors: one of selected designers for Whittier Design House (1985); mem. Interior Design Soc., CofC (mbrshp. com. 1983-84), Sunset Womens Club, Hacienda Hts. (pres. 1964-66); Republican; Lutheran; rec: creative sewing, reading, writing. Address: Interiors by Shirley Fair, 1321 Brookdale Ave La Habra 90631

FAIRBAIRN, ROBERT WALTER, electrical contractor; b. Dec. 25, 1921, Los Angeles; s. Walter Pardo and Dorothy Gladys (Brydone-Jack) F.; m. Betty Louise Danielson, March 18, 1944; chilren: Christine Lee, b. 1946, Robert Daniel, b. 1948; edn: Univ. of Wash. 1939-42; lic. elec./bldg. contractor, Calif. 1965. Career: assoc. traffic engr. City of Seattle (Wn.) Engring. Dept. 1945-50; elec. estimator Donald W. Close Co., Seattle 1950-53; chief elec. estimator Rosendin Elec. Inc., San Jose, Ca. 1953-55; gen. mgr. Hill Bros. Elec., Sunnyvale 1955-67; pres./owner Hill Electrical Contractors, Sunnyvale 1967-85; pres./owner Pardo Co. 1985—; mem: Nat. Electrical Contractors Assn. 1968- (bd. dirs. 1970-, past v.p., pres., gov.); Elec. Contractors of Cal-Nev-Hawaii (v.p. 1981-85); chmn. Bay Area Council-NECA Contractors 1976; San Jose, Sunnyvale CofC; clubs: Coyote Pt. Yacht Club, Yacht Racing Assn., Palo Alto Elks, De Anza Racket Club, Los Altos Tennis Club; mil: capt. USAAF, 6th AF, 43rd Fighter Sq. 1942-45; polit: state legis. chmn. Elec. Contractors of Calif.; rec: sailing, tennis, ski; Res: 24700 Voorhees Dr. Los Altos Hills 94022 Ofc: Pardo Co. 24700 Voorhees Dr Los Altos Hills 94022

FALL, CHARLES RICHARD, utility co. executive; b. July 28, 1946, Hanford, Calif., s. Cloyd E. and Mary F. (Browning) F.; m. Valerie, May 30, 1980; children: Cathy b. 1968, Jennifer b. 1970, Stephanie b. 1984; edn: AA, West Hills Coll. 1966; BS, CSU Fresno 1972. Career: prodn. coord. Southwest Forest Inds. Sanger 1973-74; engr. Pacific Gas & Elec. Co. Fresno 1974-78, comml. rep. Woodland 1978-80, mgt. Lemoore 1980-84, Mariposa 1984—; pres. Foothill Financial Inc. 1985-86; dir. Mainland Investments 1984-86; honors: Disting. Svc. (City of Lemoore 1980), Outstanding Ednl. Achievement (Pacific Svc. Employees Assn. 1978); mem: Pacific Coast Elec. Assn., Am. Planning Assn., Pacific Svc. Employees Assn., Lions Club (pres. 1986), Rotary, Mariposa CofC (v.p. 1984), Mariposa County Planning Commn. (vice chmn. 1986), Mariposa County Assessment Appeals Bd. 1986, Lemoore Planning Commn. 1980; Republican; rec: civic svc., handiwork. Res: 5706 Harris Cutoff Rd Mariposa 95338 Ofc: Pacific Gas & Elec. Co. POB 158 Mariposa 95338

FALLER, JOEL ANTHONY, civil engineer; b. May 4, 1956, Oil City, Pa.; s. Gerald Michael and Helen Agnes (Herrmann) F.; m. Bonnie, June 23, 1979; children: Ryan b. 1980, Garrett b. 1984; edn: BSCE, Univ. Nev., Reno 1979; candidate MBA mgmt. pgm., UC Berkeley; Reg. Profl. Civil Engr., Calif. 1982. Career: project engr. on sev. EPA funded environmental projects, 1979-82, project engr. responsible for design of an aqua-culture farm for processing algae used as protein food supplement, 1983, project engr. during design and constrn. of hazardous waste clean-up project and treatment facilities, 1984; resident engr. during constrn. of EPA funded environmental project on San Francisco Bay, Sausalito; (current) resident engr. Kennedy/ Jenks/ Chilton Engrs., San Francisco; awards: Scholar-Athlete Award (1974), Who's Who in Am. Among High Sch. Students (1974), Calif. State Scholar (1974), Four yr athletic scholarship (1975-78), High Sch. Football All-American; mem: ASCE, Water Pollution Control Fedn., Am. Water Works Assn.; contbg. writer article in Engineering News Record re project to help clean-up San

Francisco Bay; Roman Catholic; rec: tennis, skiing, golf, family. Ofc: Kennedy/ Jenks/ Chilton Engineers 657 Howard St San Francisco 94105

FALOTICO, S(ALVATORE) JOHN, chemistry teacher; b. Jan. 1, 1922, NYC, NY; s. Rocco F. and Maria Giovanna (Di Dio) F.; m. Anne Marie Lynch, April 24, 1954; children: Francis b. 1955, John b. 1956, Margaret and Michael b. 1957; edn: BA, UCLA 1949; MA, CSU Northridge 1960. Career: h.s. chemistry tchr., San Fermando and Monroe H.S., San Frenando Valley 1950—; Italien Greyhound dog breeder, ed. and writer on dogs and the genetic patterns of breeding 1958—; owner, Treasures Old and New, Hidden Hills; mil: corpsman V12 Ofcs. Pgm. US Navy. Res 5431 Jed Smith Rd. Hidden Hills 91302

FAN, CHEN YU, mechanical engineer; b. Feb. 1, 1959, Palembang, Indonesia; s. Koei Siu and Sie Moy (Fan) Lie; edn: BS in engring., Univ. of Alberta 1981, MSE, 1983; Calif. lic. Gen. Building Contr., Real Estate Broker. Career: research asst. Dept. Mgmt. Sci. & Op. Research, Univ. of Alberta 1979-81; grad. research asst. Dept. Mech. Engring. & Alberta Oil Sands Technol. Research Authority, Edmonton, Canada 1981-83; real estate brokcr/projcct supr. Via Pacifica Realty Inc., 1984; mech. project engr. Wilson F. So and Assocs., Apple Valley, Calif. 1985; real estate broker/v.p. L.Y.W. Finl. and Mortgage Inc. and gen. mgr. L.Y.W. Devel. Inc., Los Angeles 1986—, proj. mgr. for all constrn. and devel. projects; pres. Fan Constrn. Co., Gen. Bldg. Contr., Monterey Park; mem. ASME, Am. Indsl. Inst. of Engrs., ASHRAE, Assn. Profl. Engrs. and Geologists and Geophysicists of Alberta, U.S. Badminton Assn., Nat. Assn. Gen. Contrs.; publ: A Model for Jet Piercing of Oil Sands, ASME J. (1984); Catholic; rec: ski, badminton, racquetball, tennis. Res: 603 N Moore Ave Apt B Monterey Park 91754 Ofc: L.Y.W. Development Inc. 808 No Spring St Ste 808 Los Angeles 90012

FANN, ALBERT LOUIS, clergyman/actor/theatrical ensemble director; b. Feb. 21, 1925, Cleveland, Oh.; s. Albert Louis and Beulah Fann; m. Barbara Bowman, Sept. 17, 1963; children: Shelley, b. 1957, Tracy, b. 1961, Melanie, b. 1963, Albert, b. 1969; edn: Cleveland Inst. of Music 1959; D.D., Living Ministries Internat. Coll. 1981. Career: actor on Broadway in The Wiz (the Lion), in Rickety Rocket (voice-over lead, Rickety), in Live & Times of Eddie (Col. Flanders); TV: The Jeffersons, Happy Days, Good Times; ensemble: "Songs in the Key of Life" (Stevie Wonder), "Sounder" album; film actor in The French Connection, Sophisticated Gents (NBC Mini-series), Parasite (3-D movie); film commercials for Santa Barbara Svgs., Wesson Oil, Wheaties, AT&T Yellow Pages, McDonalds, Nyquil, etc.; exec. dir. The Al Fann Theatrical Ensemble, NY and Calif., 1965—; artistic dir. Haryou Anti-Poverty Pgm., NYC 1964-70; asst. dir. Cotton Comes To Harlem (Warner Bros. film) 1969; assoc. prod. Come Back Charleston Blue (Warner Bros. film) 1973; dir. NY Bd. of Edn. 1960-69; instr. Hunter Coll. 1972; mental scientist/exec. dir. Al Fann Ministries for Higher Mind Devel.; founder: Mind Recording Co., Miracles in Mind Pub. Co., Olympic Sugar Babies Internat.; formed pop. singing group, The Higher Minds; ofcl. spokesman/chief fundraiser for The Derrick Gordon Heart Fund (heart transplant recipient 1983); writer/prod. The Ballad of Derrick Gordon (hit song). Awards: Andy Awd., excellence in TV commls. 1969; Audelco Awd., Advt. Club of NY, 1973; Calif. Comml. Actor of Month (46 commls.); 14 awds. for "King Heroin" (CATV, 1971), Nat. Cable TV Assn.; recognition, Who's Who in Amer., Ebony Mag. vol. Blk. Hist., LA Times View Sect. (82). Mem: SAG, AFTRA, Concerned Black Artists for Action (v.p.), NAACP (life hon. mem.). Author: Devel. of the Under-Privileged Mind (1978), Drama Book Splst.; (play) King Heroin, presented to White House staff; served in US Army. Res: 19649 Citronia St Northridge 91324 Ofc: Dr. Albert L. Fann, The Al Fann Theatrical Ensemble, 6043 Hollywood Blvd Hwd. 90028

FANTOZZI, RICHARD DONALD, surgeon; b. June 8, 1951, Chgo. Ill.; s. William and Veronica (Furth) F.; m. Janet Salih, May 2, 1981; edn: BA, Northwestern Univ. 1972; MD, Univ. of Ill. 1976. Career: res. surg. UC San Francisco; surgeon Scripps Clinic La Jolla; assoc. prof. UC San Diego; honors: Beta Beta Beta; Phi Eta Sigma; mem: fellow Am. Coll. Surg., fellow Am. Acad. Head/Neck Surg., Mrs. Richards Inc. (pres.); publ: num. arts. in med. journs.; rec: sailing. Res: POB 2621 Rancho Santa Fe Ofc: Scripps Clinic and Research Foundation 10666 N Torrey Pines Rd La Jolla 92037

FARHA, JIMMIE LEROY, commercial real estate broker; b. Feb. 12, 1932, Alva, Okla.; s. Henry S. and Saada Elizabeth (Zakoura) F.; m. Patricia A. Connor, Sept. 14, 1957; children: Jimmie, Jr., b. 1958; Catherine, b. 1961; edn: BA, Wichita Univ. 1954; MA, Webster Coll. 1974. Carcer: comptroller Travis AFB 1975-7; mgr. Ashwill- Burke, Vacaville 1978-82; mgr./broker Bishop-Hawk, Vacaville 1982—; mem: No. Solano Co. Bd. of Realtors, Bay Area Brokers Assn., Council of Military Orgns. (chmn. 1982-3), Masons, Shriners, Air Force Assn. (Comm. Leader of Yr. 1982); civic: Pvt. Indus. Council (chmn. Solano Co. 1985-86), Vacaville CofC (dir. 1983-, chmn. Indsl. Comml. Com. 1982-4, chmn. Mil. Affairs Com. 1984-85), Center for Employment Training (indsl. rels. adv. bd. 1982-4); awards: spl. svc. Calif. Human Devel. Gp. 1983, Rotary (dir. 1982-3; mil: col. USAF 1954-77, Distg. Svc., D.F.C, 8 air medals, 2 USAF Commend., Vietnam Svc.; rec: walking, swimming. Res: 560 Ridgewood Dr Vacaville 95688 Ofc: Bishop-Hawk, 419 Mason St, Ste 208, Vacaville 95688

FARIA, LISA MARIE, government lawyer; b. June 22, 1953, San Jose, Calif.; d. Joseph Ralph and Emily Maxine (Mesquite) F.; m. Thomas Wanschura, Oct. 22, 1983; edn: BA, Univ. Santa Clara 1975, JD, 1978; admitted Calif. State Bar 1979. Career: law clerk Bell, Sheppard & Faria APC Fremont, Calif. 1977-79,

Alameda Co. Dist. Atty. Oakland 1979; dep. dist. atty. misdemeanor jury trial staff Oakland Municipal Ct. 1979-80, preliminary exams. Fremont Mun. Ct. 1980-82, felony trial staff atty. Oakland Superior Ct. 1982-83, felony calendar mgr. 1983, felony team leader Fremont Mun. Ct. 1983 –; lectr. Fremont Unified Sch. Dist. 1980-; tchr. tactics Explorer Scouts 1980-; Delegate-At-Large Boy Scouts of Am.; public mem. Atty. Gen. Oral Boards 1984; commr. Alameda Co. Consumer Affairs Commn. 1983-85; mem: Calif. State Bar, Alameda Co. Bar Assn., Calif. Dist. Attys. Assn.; Democrat; Catholic; rec: physical fitness, farming, cooking, furniture refinishing. Ofc: Alameda Co. District Atty. 1225 Fallon, Ste 900, Oakland 94612

FARMER, GENE AVON, private investigator; b. Oct. 11, 1920, Greenwood, Ind.; s. George and Lucile Farmer; m. Geraldine L. Stein, Dec. 14, 1941; div. 1958; children: Trudy Lynn (Kearney) b. 1943, Jo Laine (Gross) b. 1946; edn: BS, Bradley Univ. 1950; BS in electronic engring., West Coast Univ. 1962; commn. Army Inst. for Profl. Devel. 1985. Calif. lic. pvt. investigator (AQ6293), cert. locksmith, FAA lic. jet and prop. pilot. Career: tool & die maker, engr. Caterpiller Tractor Co., Peoria, Ill. 1941-45; engr. Hiram Walker & Son, 1945-50; mech. engr. Compton (Calif.) Tool & Die Co. 1950-55, Falco Machine & Tool, Gardena 1955-58, No. Am. Aviation, Downey 1958-61; electronics, engr. and project adminstr. Rockwell Corp., Anaheim 1961-71, ret. 1975; pvt. investigator for Atty. Michael J. Quigley, Orange 1971-73; agency owner/mgr. Farmers Investigations, 1975 –; honors: appreciation, Am. Police Acad. (1983), Calif. Nat. Guard Commendn. Medal (2) and Proficiency Ribbon; mem: Internat. Police (Spl. Agt.), Calif. Assn. of Licensed Investigators, Reserve Ofcrs. Assn. (lt. col. ARNG 1984), Calif. State Mil. Reserve Ofcrs. Assn. (pres. Inland Empire), Hemet CofC, VFW (life), Nat. Rifle Assn., Am. Police Assn., Masons (past master, Scottish Rite, York Rite, Shriners); mil: lt. col. Calif. State Mil. Reserve (exec. ofcr. 403rd Batt. 4th Brigade, Calif. 1983-86), US Army Coast Arty. Fort Amador, Panama Canal, decorated Am. Def., Fgn. Svc., Army Commendn.; Republican (Pres. Achiev. Award 1982); Baptist; rec: flying. Address: 36770 W Florida Ave Sp31 Hemet 92343

FARMER, ROBERT, lawyer, insurance underwriter, stockbroker; b. Apr. 5, 1936, Detroit, Mich.; s. Frank Robert and Gladys Evelyn (Parry) F.; m. Mary Marshall, Apr. 16, 1955; children: Michael b. 1956, Renee b. 1957, Patrick b. 1959, Brian b. 1960, Suzanne b. 1961, Michele b. 1963; edn: B.L.S., Univ. Okla. 1966; LLB, LaSalle Ext. Univ. 1971; M. Marine Affairs, Univ. R.I. 1973; grad. Naval War Coll. 1973. Career: served to capt. (O-6) US Coast Guard 1954-80, Qualified Comdr. at sea and ashore; last at sea command, Polar Icebreaker Burton Island; consulting atty./owner Visa and Immigration Advisory Service, 1980 –; field underwriter NY Life, 1980 –, registered rep. NY Life Securities Corp. 1984 –; Notary Public 1980-; exec. distbr. TMT, Marin Co. 1982-83; mem: Am. Bar Assn., Barristers Club of S.F., Am. Immigration Lawyers Assn., Marin Co. Bar Assn., Calif. State Bar Assn., Sons in Retirement, Order of the Moose, Toastmasters (past pres. Duluth, Minn.), Cornhuskers of Marin Square Dance Club (pres. 1982-83), Armed Forces Benefit & Aid Assn. (dist. mgr. 1984-), Hamilton Ball & Chain Bowling League (pres. 1985-86), Marin Co. Special Olympics (vol. coach 1981-), ULC Inc. Novato (pastor); publs: Disaster Recovery Manual (New Orleans 1972, Cleveland 1962, San Francisco 1980); mil. awards: Am. Def., CG Achieve., Antarctic Service, Artic Service, CG Commendn. medals, Exp. Pistol, Rifle Marksman, Merit Commendns.; rec: bowling. Address: 639 Midway Blvd Novato 94947

FARMER, SUE BLANTON CARPENTER, educational computer software co. executive; b. Apr. 16, Brookneal, Va.; d. Dr. George Robert (Col. ret.) and Clara Eason (Elliott) Carpenter; m. Paul R. Farmer, Apr. 29, 1961; children: Laura Eason b. 1964, Christopher Blanton b. 1969; edn: Cours Racine, Le Visnet, France 1949, L'ecole des Beaux Arts, Fountainebleau, Fr. 1950, Washington-Lee H.Sch. 1953, The Corcoran Art Sch. 1954; BA, Mary Washington Coll., Univ. of Va. 1957. Career: exec. asst. to the chmn. bd. McCann-Erickson, Inc. (advtsg.), NYC 1958-61; exec. asst. to to vice pres. MGM, Inc., NYC 1961-64; dir. The Ridgwood (N.J.) YMCA, 1975-81; adminstr., pub. rels., The Brokaw Co., Los Angeles 1983-84; vice pres. Compass Software Corp., Encino 1984 –; cons. lectr. Weight Watchers Internat., Inc. 1981-; Water Safety instr. 1976-81; N.S.W.G.A. Rated Horseback Riding instr. 1953-56; honors: Zeta Phi Eta speech frat., Alpha Psi Omega dramatics frat., Who's Who in Am. Colls. & Univs., 1956, 57; mem. Actors Equity Assn. (1957-58), Ridgewood Art Assn. (1980-81), Aquacons (profl. synchronized swimming club, 1978-81), New Jersey Masters Swim Team (1976-81); works: profl. artist, num. paintings & sculpture (1961-); founder/prod./dir. Gov.'s Is. Community Theatre (1957-60); Prot.; rec: swimming, equestrian, duplicate bridge. Res: 17171 Roscoe Blvd Apt 126 Northridge 91325 Ofc: Compass Software Corp. 17000 Ventura Blvd Ste 220 Encino 91316

FARNSWORTH, DIANA VEIT, plastic surgeon; b. Nov. 28, 1934, Brooklyn, NY; s. Walter Lionel and Jenny Wilhelmina (Sulby) Veit; m. Edward Farnsworth, June 29, 1962; children: Matthew Dean b. 1964, Gwendolyn Jane b. 1966, Valerie Laura b. 1973, Andrew VanTrent b. 1975; edn: AB, Cornell Univ. 1955; MD, Harvard Univ. 1960; lic. med. Mass. 1963, NY 1967, Calif. 1976; certified Am. Bd. Plastic Surgeons 1975. Career: intern surg. Cleveland Metropolitan Gen. Hosp. 1960-61; resident neurol. Lemuel Shattuck Hosp. Boston 1961-62; res. gen. surg. Beth Israel Hosp. Boston 1962-64, Meml. Hosp. Worcester 1965-67; res. plastic surg. NY Hosp. Cornell Med. Ctr. 1967-68; fellow plastic surg. Lenox Hill Hosp. NY 1968-69; res. plastic surg. Mt. Sinai Hosp. NY 1969-72; attg. surg. Long Island Jewish Hillside Med. Ctr. New Hyde Park, NY 1972-76; pvt. practice Port Washington, NY 1972-76, Beverly Hills, Calif. 1976-80, L.A. 1980-84, Beverly Hills 1984 –; affil. Cedars Sinai Med. Ctr., St. John's Hosp., Beverly Hills Med. Ctr., Westside Hosp., Hol-

lywood Presbyterian Med. Ctr.; instr. plastic surg. Mt. Sinai Sch. of Med. Univ. NY 1971-72; mem: Am. Soc. Plastic & Reconstrv. Surg., LA Soc. Plastic Surg., LA County Med. Women's Assn. (pres.), NY Regl. Soc. Plastic & Reconstrv. Surg., Am. Med. Women's Assn., Hollywood Acad. Med., LA County Med. Assn.; rec: sailing, photog., sculpture, skiing. Ofc: 9001 Wilshire Blvd Ste 202 Beverly Hills 90211

FARRELL, DAVID LAWRENCE, accountant; b. Dec. 12, 1956, Torrance; s. James and Carla F.; m. Anne Williamson, May 10, 1985; edn: BA, UC Santa Barbara 1978; MBT, USC 1985; CPA, Calif. 1981. Career: senior acct. Peat, Marwick, Mitchell & Co., Los Angeles 1978-80; ptr. Parks, Palmer, Turner & Yemenidjian, Los Angeles 1980 –; mem: Am. Inst. CPAs, Calif. Soc. CPAs, Accounting Circle- USC; rec: skiing, golf, tennis. Ofc: Parks, Palmer, Turner & Yemenidjian, 8075 W. Third St. Los Angeles 90048

FARSAKIAN, LARRY ROUPEN, dentist; b. June 19, 1956, Visalia; s. Souren Sam and Betty Louise (Simonian) P.; m. Wendy Koshgarian, July 2, 1983; edn: Coll. of the Sequoias 1974-76; BA, CSU Fresno 1978; DDS, Loyola Univ. Sch. of Dentistry 1984. Career: dental lab techn. 1980-81, resident in dentistry Loyola Univ. Med. Ctr., Foster McGraw Hosp. 1984-85; currently, dentist pvt. practice, Visalia; honors: Am. Assn. of Endodontics Award 1984; Loyola Dental Sch. Block Drug Essay Award 1984; mem: Am. Dental Assn., Chicago Dental Soc., Delta Sigma Delta, Alpha Sigma Nu, Acad. of Gen. Dentistry, Am. Assn. of Hosp. Dentists, St. Mary Armenian Apostolic Ch. of Yettem (Armenian Ch. Youth Orgn. 1970-85, treas. 1978-79, chmn. 1979-80), Knigts of Vartan; Apostolic; rec: sports. Res: 3016 W. Vassar Dr. Visalia 93277 Ofc: 102 No. Stevenson Visalia 93291

FASANARO, TOMMY STEPHEN, dentist; b. May 3, 1946, Berkeley, Calif.; s. Thomas Salvadore and Adele Charlotte (Myhre) F.; m. Judith Almeida, Oct. 25, 1980; 1 dau. Anne Marie b. 1981; edn: Univ. San Francisco 1964-67; DDS, Univ. of the Pacific 1971. Career: assoc. dentist to Dr. Robert Van Galder Pleasant Hill 1971-72; solo practice 1973 –; seminar on cosmetic bonding given to dentist at Calif. and Am. Dental Assns. 1985; honors: CSF life member 1964, Tau Kappa Omega (dental honor soc. 1971), Merit Award (Am. Fund for Dental Health 1984); mem: Am., Calif. Dental Assn., Contra Costa Dental Soc. (trustee, chmn. dental health edn. com. 1985-86), Acad. of Reconstrv. and Cosmetic Dentistry 1981, Acad. of Cosmetic and Adhesive Dentistry (v.p., pres. elect 1985-86), Am. Assn. for Dental Research 1986, Pleasant Hill CofC; publ: article in dental jour. Res: 149 Pioneer Ave Walnut Creek 94596 Ofc: 70 Doray Dr Pleasant Hill 94523

FATTAL, GEORGE CHARLES, business owner; b. May 17, 1941, Cairo, Egypt, nat. US cit. 1959; s. Andre and Olga (Baccash) F.; m. Odette, Aug. 22, 1964; children: Lisa b. 1965, Denise b. 1968; edn: BA, UC Santa Barbara 1963; MS, USC 1966; Calif. Std. Life. Elem. Tchg. Cred. & Elem. Adminstrn. Cred. (1966). Career: instr. UC Santa Barbara 1969; educator, sch. adminstr., pioneer in Early Childhood Edn. field, 21 years, supt. of schs. Hickman, Calif. 1970-83; owner Fattal AM/PM Mini Market, Modesto 1983 –; mem. Calif. Sch. Administrs. Assn. (charter mem., bd. dirs. 1970s), Kiwanis of Modesto (1972-75), Executive Club of Modesto; publs: How to Organize a Summer Sch. (USC, 1966); Republican; Catholic; rec: organist, boating, racketball. Ofc: Fattal AM/PM Mini Market 2924 McHenry Ave Modesto 95350

FAULKNER, THOMAS LEE, chiropractor; b. Feb. 14, 1943, Dayton, Ohio; s. Don and Frances Arlene (Hohman) Mitchell; m. Linda Faulkner, Feb. 12, 1977; children: Diana Lee b. 1961, Tony Lee b. 1964; edn: Univ. Miss. 1962-66; DC magna cum laude, Cleveland, Ohio 1976. Career: chiropractor pvt. practice Campbell, Calif. 1977 –; research cons. World Health Orgn., UN, Geneva, Life Chiro. Coll. West, Spinal Column Stress Research Soc.; faculty instr. Palmer Chiro. Coll. 1982; strl. cons. med. and chiro. clins., Bankers Life Ins., Great Western Ins., Aetna Ins., Blue Cross, Phoenix Mutual Ins., and others; mem: Internat. Coll. Spinal Column Stressology (v.p. 1982-83, pres. 1984-85), Internat. Chiro. Assn., Spinal Stress Research Soc., Elks, Optimists, Nat. Street Rod Assn., Internat. Show Car Assn., Sigma Pi; publs: article in med. jour., book: The Anatomical Systems of the Human Body; Republican; Protestant; rec: antique auto restoration. Res: 1177 Fairfield ave Santa Clara Ofc: 72 W Cambbell Ave Campbell 95008

FAWCETT, J. SCOTT, real estate developer; b. Nov. 5, 1937, Pittsburg, Pa.; s. William Hagen and Mary Jane (Wise) F., Jr.; m. Anne Mitchell, Dec. 30, 1960; children: Holly b. 1961, John (1965-1983); edn: BS, Ohio State Univ. 1959. Career: dist. dealer rep. Shell Oil Co., San Diego 1962-66; dist. real estate rep. Shell Oil, San Francisco 1970-71; head office land investments rep. Shell Oil, Houston 1972-75; pres./CEO Marinita Devel. Co., Newport Beach 1976 –; lectr. in land devel. related fields; mem: Internat. Council of Shopping Centers (ICSC), Inst. of Business Appraisers, Nat. Assn. of Review Appraisers and Mortgage Underwriters, Calif. Lic. Contractors Assn., Building Indus. Assn., Internat. Right of Way Assn., Internat. Inst. of Valuers, Am. Assn. of Certified Appraisers, Urban Land Inst., Nat. Assn. Real Estate Execs. (pres. L.A. chpt. 1975), US CofC, Town Hall of Calif., Internat. Platform Assn., Toastmasters (pres. Scottsdale, Ariz. Club 1968, pres. Hospitality T. Club, San Diego 1964), Univ. Athletic Club, Ohio State Univ. Alumni Assn., Phi Kappa Tau Alumni Assn.; mil: M.P., US Army, Mil. Dist. of Wash. 1960-61; Republican; Catholic; rec: gardening, tennis, ski. Res: 8739 Hudson River Circle Fountain Valley 92708 Ofc: Marinita Development Co. 3835 Birch St Newport Beach 92660

FAXON, LINDA JOYCE, pharmacist; b. Sept. 29, 1942, Los Angeles; d. William Edward and Janis (Blackman) Kafton; m. Ed Faxon, June 20, 1964; 1

dau. Melanie b. 1972; edn: BS pharm., Oregon State Univ. 1965. Career: pharmacist Bakers Profl. Pharm., Eugene, Ore. 1965-68, Corner Pharmacy, Ponca City, Okla. 1968-69; staff pharm. Bass Meml. Baptist Hosp., Enid, Okla. 1969-72; dir. of pharm. Circle City Hosp., Corona, Calif. 1972—; inservice tchg. to nursing staff of hosp.; honors: Lambda Kappa Sigma (women's pharm. honor soc. 1964), Rho Chi (pharm. hon. 1965); mem: Am., Calif., Inland Socs. of Hosp. Pharms. 1972-, Citrus Label Soc. 1981-; pianist United Methodist Ch. of Corona 1978-; chmn. Worship Commn. 1979-81; Democrat; rec: collecting So. Calif. citrus labels, mortars & pestles. Res: 2098 Wren Ave Corona 91719 Ofc: Circle City Hosp. 730 Magnolia Ave Corona 91719

FEARHELLER, DAVID GALE, investment banker; b. Apr. 3, 1944, Columbia, Mo.; s. Vern and Jewell Kay (Marlow) F.; m. Gail, Apr. 15, 1978; children: Jaclyn b. 1979, (stepson) Matthew Romain b. 1972; edn: BBA, So. Methodist Univ. 1966; MBA, Univ. Wis. 1968; CPA lic. Texas (1967), Ill. (1969). Career: mgr. consulting svcs. Ernst & Whinney, Chgo. 1966-71; v.p. John Nuveen & Co., Chgo. 1972-83; mng. dir. and nat. mgr. Healthcare Banking, Dean Witter Reynolds Inc., San Francisco 1983—; mem. Am. Inst. CPA, Calif. Soc. CPAs, Am. Hospital Assn. (Council for Finance 1979-81); clubs: S.F. Tennis, L.A. Athletic; publs: series of articles in Modern Healthcare Mag., paper on Tax-Exempt fin. for hosps., AHA 74th Convention; mil: sp5 USAR; Republican (Precinct Wkr., Chgo.); Jewish; rec: tennis, wine collector. Res: 20 Orange Ct Hillsborough 94010 Ofc: Dean Witter Reynolds 101 California 2nd Floor San Francisco 94111

FECHHEIMER, DAVID BURGESS, investigator; b. Apr. 30, 1942, Cincinnati, Ohio; s. Karl Bissinger and Juliet (Esselborn); children: Zachary b. 1982, Sam b. 1983; edn: BA, San Francisco State Univ. 1966. Career: v.p. Lipset Svc. San Francisco 1967-76; owner David B. Fechheimer S.F. 1976—; mem: Calif. Assn. Legal Investigators, Nat. Assn. Legal Investigators, World Assn. of Detectives, Fla. Assn. of Pvt. Investigators, S.F. Tennis Club, Mechanics Inst.; publs: articles relating to Dashiell Hammett, film "Hammett", editor, contbr. City Magazine of S.F., Hammett issue. Address: 2319 Hyde St San Francisco 94109

FEE, NANCY HOPWOOD, fund raiser; b. March 9, 1961, Palo Alto; d. Joseph Milton and Elizabeth (Crawford) F.; edn: BA, honors, Mills Coll. Career: patron asst. Metropolitan Opera 1984-85; devel. assoc. San Francisco Opera 1985—; mem. Katherine Delmar Burke Sch. Alumnae Assn. (bd. dirs.). Ofc: San Francisco Opera, 301 Van Ness Ave San Francisco 94102

FEIN, WILLIAM, ophthamologist/educator; b. Nov. 27, 1933, NY, NY; s. Samuel and Beatrice (Lipschitz) F.; m. Bonnie Fern Aaronson, Dec. 15, 1963; children: Stephanie Paula b. 1968, Adam Irving b. 1969, Gregory Andrew b. 1972; edn: BS, Coll. of the City of N.Y. 1954; MD, UC Irvine Med. Sch. 1962; diplomate, Am. Bd. of Ophthamology 1969. Career: resident ophthalmol., L.A. County Gen. Hosp. 1963-66; post res. tng. in ophthalmic plastic surgery, Manhattan Eye and Ear Hosp. 1966-7; instr. ophthalmol. UCI Med. Sch. 1966-9, instr./assoc. clin. prof. ophthalmol. USC Med. Sch. 1969—; chmn. Dept. Ophthalm. Midway Hosp. 1975-9; v.p. California Eye Med. Clinic, Inc. 1969-83; chief of Ophthalm. Clinic Svcs., Cedars Sinai Med. Ctr. 1979-81, chmn. Div. of Ophthalm., 1981—; chmn. Ellis Eye Ctr. 1984—; lectr. new techniques in ophthalm. plastic surgery, num. hosps., conventions; mem: Am. Soc. of Ophthalm. Plastic and Reconstrv. Surgery; Am. Acad. Ophthalmol.; Los Angeles Soc. of Ophthalmol.; AMA; Calif. Med. Assn.; LA Med. Assn.; publs: num. arts. in med. literature describing new ophthalmic surgeries; Jewish. Res: 718 No. Camden Dr Beverly Hills 90210 Ofc: 415 No Crescent Dr Beverly Hills 90210

FEINER, JERZY-GEORGE LEOPOLD, architect, artist, painter; b. Feb. 20, Lwow-Leopolis, Poland; s. Edward and Maria F.; m. Anna Kaczorowska, Jan. 26, 1961; children: Paul b. 1961, Peter b. 1963, Kate b. 1966; edn: master artist, Acad. of Fine Art, Cracow, Poland; postgrad. stu. Oslo, Norway 1960; PhD Polytech. Univ., Cracow 1966, and Doctor Habiliteted, 1975. Career: pres. Art Studio & Design; prof. arch., researcher Interreflection Light Theory (grantee Nat. Endowment for the Arts 1984), cons. Art Dept. UCLA; lectr., cons. Illumination Lab., Penn State Univ. 1978, lectr. internat.; muralist and painter (comml. and residential), 1969—, murals include Mercyhurst Coll. Pa.; City Hall Capranica, Viterbo, Italy; Palazzo, La Trinita, Italy; group exhibs. include Royal Gal. of Portrait Painters in London, G.B. 91968), Polish Contemp. Art, Copenhagen (1974), Poland (1976), Galerie am Rabensteig, Vienna (1978), Gal. of Painting, Goeteborg, Sweden (1978), Novi Sad, Yugoslavia (1978), Festival in Edinburgh (1981), Victoria Keri, London (1981), Gal. Dei Polacchi, Rome (1982), Gannon Univ., Erie, Pa. (1983), Beverly Hills (Ca.) Art League (1983, 84), Pacific Art Guild's annual juried Spring Art Show, L.A. (1984); awards: for restoration of hist. frescoes, Capranica, Italy (1983), hon. PhD for humanitarian achievements Euro-Africana Academia, Rome (1982), research grantee King Fasal Univ., Saudi Arabia (1980), Gold Cross of Merit, Counsel of State, Poland (1978) num. prizes and medals for architl. works; mem. The Polish Inst. of Arts and Sci. of Am. Inc., Com. Internat. Eclairage, Com. T.C.; num. architl. publs. (Poland 1963-; internat. 1979); Daily Light Refractor (Polish Patent Ofc., 1975); rec: philately. Ofc: Pegasus 5235 Laurel Cyn Blvd, N Hollywood 91607

FEINGOLD, KEITH HOWARD, marketing and sales executive; b. Feb. 28, 1958, Greensberg, Pa.; s. William J. and Sandra L. (Hurwood) F.; m. Caryn, Dec. 1, 1984; edn: BS bus. adminstrn., Univ. Ariz. 1980. Career: founder, cons. Spektra Mgmt. Cons. Tucson, Ariz. 1979—; senior analyst Advanced Micro Devices Sunnyvale, Calif. 1981-83; acct. mgr. Comshare Inc. Chgo. 1983-84;

senior mktg. sales rep., acct. mgr. Cincom Systems S.F. 1984—; honors: Outstanding Sales Achievement (Kinney Co. 1979, 80), Delta Tau Delta, Class V.P. (Univ. Ariz. 1977), Top Salesman Western Reg. (Cincom 1984, 85, 86); mem: Am. Mgmt. Assn., Data Proc. Mgmt. Assn., Am. Prodn. & Inventory Control Soc., Sunnyvale CofC, S.F. CofC, S.F. Bay Club, Bay Area Indsl. Sports League, Univ. Ariz. Alumni Assn.; Republican; Jewish; rec: computers, basketball, skiing, cycling, scuba. Ofc: Cincom Systems 100 Spear St Ste 820 San Francisco 94123

FEINSTEIN, DIANNE, mayor; b. June 22, 1933, San Francisco; d. Leon and Betty (Rosenburg) Goldman; m. Bertram Feinstein, Nov. 11, 1962; 1 dau: Katherine Anne. Career: inern, pub. afflair, Coro Found., San Francisco 1955-56; asst. to Calif. Indsl. Welfare Commn., Los Angeles and San Francisco 1956-57; v.chmn. Calif. Women's Bd. Terms and Parole, Los Angeles and San Francisco 1962-66; chmn. San Francnisco City and co. Adv. Com. for Adult Detention, San Francisco 1967-69; supr. City and County of San Francisco 1969-79; mayor, San Francisco 1979—; pres. San Francisco City and Co. Bd. Supvrs. 1970-72, 1974-76; mem. Mayor's Com. on Crime 1967-69; chmn. Environ. Mgmt. Task Force Assn. Bay Govts. 1976-; exec. com., del. gen assembly, Assn. Bay Area Govts. 1970-; Bay Conservation & Devel. Commn. 1973-; chmn. bd. regents, Lone Mountain Coll. 1972-75; honors: Women of Achiev., Bus. and Profl. Women's Clubs of San Francisco 1970; Distng. Woman, San Francisco Examiner 1970; mem: Multi-Culture Inst. (dir.); Calif. Tommorow; Bay Area Urban League; Plnng. and Conservation League; Friends of Earth; Chinese Culture Found.; No. Central Coast Regl. Commn.; Sierra Club; Propeller; Commonwealth. Ofc: 200 City Hall, San Francisco 94102

FELANDO, GERALD NICHOLAS, state assemblyman; b. Dec. 29, 1934, San Pedro, Calif.; s. Nicholas and Winifred (Stanovich) F.; m. Joyce, May 25, 1985; children: Cynthia b. 1954, Nicholas b. 1956; edn: AA, Los Angeles Harbor Coll. 1960; DDS, Univ. So. Calif. 1964. Career: pvt. dental practice 1964-78; assemblyman Calif. State Assembly (51st Dist.) 1978—, committees: Gov's. Advisory Task Force on Long Term Care, Employment of Handicapped, Aging (chmn.), Pacific Marine Fisheries Commn., Pac. Fisheries Leg. Task Force, Commn. of the Californias, Jt. Leg. Audit Com., Jt. Com. on Fisheries & Aquaculture, Select Com. on Child Abuse, Govtl. Orgn. Com., Judiciary Com., Utilities & Commerce Com. (vice chmn.), Republican Caucus Whip 1984, Rep. Caucus Chmn. 1985-86; honors: Legislator of the Year (Calif. Assn. Phys. Handicapped 1984, United Cerebral Palsy Assn. 1985, L.A. chpt. Nat. Soc. for Children and Adults with Autism 1983, Calif. Gov's. Com. for Employment of the Handicapped 1983), Medal of Commdn. (VFW 1984), num. other awards of appreciation from various agencies and societies; mem: Am. Dental Assn., Western Dental Soc., Calif. Dental Assn., Rotary, Masons, Scottish Rite, Shrine, Elks, several CofCs, Yugoslav-Am. Club of San Pedro, Nat. Exchange Club, Assn. for Retarded Citizens SW, Rancho de los Palos Verdes Hist. Soc., Palos Verdes Community Arts Assn., Friends of the Library, Catalina Conservancy; publ: Unusual Three-Dimensional Bite Mark Evidence in a Homicide Case (Jour. of Forensic Sci., vol.2 no.3), Political Awareness is Part of the Practice (CDA Jour. Aug. 1985); Republican; Catholic; rec: jogging, tennis, golf, spectator football, track & field. Ofc: State Capitol Rm 2114 Sacramento 95814

FELD, LEONARD JACK, dental surgeon; b. Sept. 17, 1941, Pittsburgh, Pa.; s. Henry and Gerda (Kanarienvogel) F.; m. Claudia, Dec. 13, 1975; children: Yascha b. 1971, Abraham b. 1977, Sara b. 1981; edn: BS, CSU Hayward 1969; DDS, Univ. So. Calif. 1975. Career: dentist San Gabriel Valley Dental Group; senior ptnr. Southeast Dental Group; honors: Am. Assn. Endodontists (1975); mem: Alpha Omega (pres.), Rotary (pres.); works: developer periodontal maintenance pgm.; publ: Quintessence Internat., US (1984), Greece (1985), Germany (1985), Japan (1985), Italy; mil: sp4 US Army 1962-65, Sharpshooter-Expert, Spl. Forces; Jewish; rec: golf, swimming. Ofc: Southeast Dental Group 4332 E Slauson Maywood 90270

FELDMAN, HENRY, hotel executive; b. July 15, 1945, Manchester, England, nat. US cit. 1980; s. Dr. Harold M. and Vera (Oppenheim) F.; m. Betty M. Martin, Apr. 8, 1982; 1 dau. Leah b. 1983. Career: gen. mgr. Resort Hotels, 1967-82, senior v.p. Hotel Ops. 1977-82; v.p./ mng. dir. Claremont Resort Hotel, Oakland 1982—; mem. Oakland Conv. & Visitors Bureau (bd. dirs.); Republican; Jewish; rec: golf, tennis. Res: 22 Alvarado Pl Berkeley 94705 Ofc: Claremont Resort Hotel, Ashby & Domingo Aves., Oakland 94623

FELDSTEIN, MARVIN, accountant; b. March 10, 1924, Los Angeles; s. Ben and Fannie (Klein) F.; m. Ann, Jan. 3, 1953; 1 son: Barry b. 1959; edn: BSBA, UCLA 1948; Public Acct., Calif. 1952. Career: Internal Revenue Svc., Los Angeles 1950-54; Harry G.L. Hankin CPA, Beverly Hills 1955-57; Morris Korman & Co., Los Angeles 1958-63; public accountant self-empl. 1965—; mem: Soc. of Calif. Accts.; mil: pfc US Army 1942-45, Bronze Medal, European Theatre; Republican; Jewish; rec: tennis (USTA ranked senior brackets, intercollegiate player UCLA). addres: Marvin Feldstein Public Accountant, 4343 Mentone Ave. Culver City 90230

FELICITA, JAMES THOMAS, aerospace co. executive; b. May 21, 1947, Syracuse, NY; s. Anthony Nicholas and Ada (Beech) F.; edn: Syracuse Univ. 1965-66; AB, Cornell Univ. 1969; Harvard Univ. 1969; Univ. So. Calif. 1970; Govt. Contract Mgmt., UC Los Angeles 1974-77. Career: motion picture editor/ producer Jacques Descent Prodns. Hollywood 1970-71; social welfare examiner Onondaga County Dept. of Social Svcs. Syracuse, NY 1972-73; underwriter Transamerica Corp. L.A. 1974; contract negotiator US Naval Regional Contracting Ofc., Long Beach 1974-80; contract negotiator Hughes

Aircraft Co. El Segundo 1980-81, head NASA contracts 1981-83, mgr. major pgm. contracts 1983 –; organized aerospace wing of Calif. Mus. of Sci. & Industry L.A. 1983; honors: NY State Regents Scholar (1965-69), Syracuse Univ. Trustee Scholar (1965-66), Cost Savings Commdn. (Pres. Gerald Ford 1976); Sustained Superior Performance Award (USN 3 yrs.); mem: Nat. Space Club, Planetary Soc., Hughes Mgmt. Club, Cornell Alumni Assn. of So. Calif., Nat. Contract Mgmt. Assn.; Republican; Protestant; rec: military & space models, rare books, modern art. Res: 8541 Kelso Dr Huntington Beach 92646 Ofc: 999 N Sepulveda Ste 711 El Segundo 90245

FELKER, DAVID R., manufacturing/sales co. executive; b. Sept. 4, 1957, Torrance; s. Roy L. and Colleen M. (Rowland) F.; m. Joanne, Jan. 1982; edn: econs. major UCLA 1975-78. Career: store mgr. Stero Plus, Los Angeles 1978-79; mgr. Bel-Air Audio, L.A. 1977-78, 79-80; nat. mktg. mgr. Leland Energy Corp., L.A. 1980-83; pres./CEO Bi-Pro Industries, Inc. Culver City 1983 –; instr. num. sales and motivation seminars, 1981-; honors: Who's Who Am. High Sch. Students, life mem. Calif. Scholarship Fedn., recipient appreciation award Torrance CofC; mem. Mensa Soc., Collie Club of Am. (chpt. v.p.); patent: trapping method for insects (1983); Democrat; Catholic; rec: skiing, water sports, Collie breeding and showing. Ofc: Bi-Pro Industries Inc 212 N Eucalyptus Dr El Segundo 90245

FELLOWS, RALPH M., engineer/underwriter; b. Nov. 17, 1932, Denver, Co.; s. Matthew A. and Gertrude M. (Wynkoop) F.; m. Violet C. Valenti, June 29, 1985; edn: AA, Okla. State Univ. 1957; Calif. Reg. Profl. Engr. Career: grad., USNR Mobile Fire Tng. Sch., mem. Navel Air Base Fire Dept. Crash Crew 1950-5; ins. appraisal and engring. staff mem., General Ins. Co. of Am., Los Angeles area 1957-65; engring. supvr. L.A. Ofc., Oil Insurance Assn. 1966-77; internat. protection consultant 1972-82, broker rep. petroleum accounts. M & M Protection Consultants, L.A. 1978-82; engr./ underwriter Starr Technical Risks Agency, Inc., 1983 –; profl. work conducted in approx. 30 US states and 14 fgn. countries; guest spkr.: Long Beach Petroleum Club, Gov.'s Safety Conf., Oil and Petrochem. Div., Wash.; mem: Soc. of Fire Protection Engrs.; L.A. Fire Forum; Am. Petroleum Inst.; Nat. Fire Protection Assn.; Masons (inspector Grand Lodge F&AM); Shrine; Scottish Rite; mil: fireman USNR 1953; Republican; Protestant; rec: photog. Res: 3039 Cardinal St Anaheim 92806 Ofc: Starr Technical Risks Agency 3699 Wilshire Blvd Los Angeles 90010

FEND, EILEEN, personnel service executive; b. Oct. 29, 1927, Salt Lake City, Utah; d. Mark L. and Louise B. (Irvine) Warburton; m. Helmut Fend, June 21, 1975; children: Pamela Greene b. 1945, Teri Gervais b. 1952, Mark Hartman b. 1963; edn: stu. Utah St. Univ., El Camino Coll.; cert. profl. mgmt., USC 1985. Career: purch. agent Futurecraft (aerospace co.), Industry, 5 yrs.; dir. Vivian Woodard Cosmetics, Panorama City, 11 yrs.; owner/pres. On Call Personnel (temp. help personnel agcy.), Manhattan Beach 1978 –; bd. chmn. Hour Gang Personnel, Orange County 1982 –; mem: Internat. Assn. of Personnel Women (coord. Duologue Vendor Com.; hostess Nat. Mid-Winter Board meetings), Calif. Assn. of Personnel Cons. (Temp. Svcs. Sect.), Personnel and Indsl. Rels. Assn. Inc., Business Mgmt. Assn. (bd.), Women in Mgmt. (bd.), Leads Club, South Bay Mktg. Network, CofC (Manhattan Bch, Redondo Bch, Torrance), Nat. Assn. of Women Bus. Owners (Pub. Affairs Com.); mem. scholarship bds. of Bank of Am./ Redondo Bch. and El Segundo Rotary Club; participant CSU Dominguez Hills South Bay Business Roundtable; rec: competition skier. Address: On Call Personnel 505 N Sepulveda Blvd Manhattan Beach 90266

FENTON, DONALD MASON, chemist; b. May 23, 1929, Los Angeles; s. Charles Youdan and Dorothy (Mason) F.; m. Margaret, Apr. 24, 1953; children: James Michael b. 1957, Douglas Charles b. 1959; edn: BS, UC Los Angeles 1952, PhD, 1958. Career: chemist Rohm & Haas Co. 1958-61; senior research chemist Union Oil Co. Brea 1962-67, research assoc. 1967-72, senior research assoc. 1972-82, mgr. planning & devel. 1982 –; cons. AMSCO div., Union Oil 1967-73; chmn. Petroleum Environmental Research Forum; chmn. Gordon Research Conf. on Hydrocarbon Chemistry 1975; mem: Am. Chem. Soc. (Petroleum Research Fund Adv. Bd. 1980-), Toastmasters (chpt. pres. 1973), Alpha Chi Sigma (chpt. pres. 1953), Sigma Xi; publs: 90 US patents; 10 papers; 1 book chpt.; mil: US Army 1953-55. Res: 2861 Alden Pl Anaheim 92806 Ofc: Unocal 3765 Valencia Brea 92621

FENTON, JOHN VINCENT, health care executive; b. Oct. 24, 1945, NY, NY; s. Robert and Catherine (O'Dwyer) F.; m. Stella C., Jan. 2, 1980; children: John, Jennifer, Kimberly; edn: BS in pre-med., biol., Manhattan Coll. 1968; phys. therapy, Columbia Univ. 1969; MBA in health sci. mgmt., Century Univ., Beverly Hills 1981; Cert. Nursing Home Extended Care Facilities Adminstrn. 1973; lic. Phys. Therapist, Calif., N.Y., Mich., N.J. Career: med., recreational asst. in Cardiac hosp. St. Frances Hosp., Roslyn, NY 1962-64; emergency med. technician St. Vincent's Hosp. NYC 1964-69; dir. ctr. services Cerebral Palsy Treatment Ctr., Albany, NY 1964-69; asst. adminstr. Menorah Home and Hosp., Bklyn. 1971-73; exec. adminstr. N.Y. Med. Coll., Mental Retardation Inst., 1973-76; adminstr. Jewish Bd. of Guardians, NYC 1977-78; adminstrv. asst. North Detroit Gen. Hosp. 1978; senior phys. therapist Brotman Meml. Hosp., Culver City, Calif. 1978-79; cons. rehab. services, dir. AMI/ Westside Hosp., Los Angeles 1979-82; dir. rehab. medicine, Brotman Medical Ctr., Culver City 1982 –; exec. dir. profl. services, cons., corp. ofcr. Creative Escapes, Beverly Hills 1980 –; instr. Russell Sage Coll. Sch. Phys. Therapy 1969-71, Albany Med. Coll. Sch. Nsg. 1969-74, N.Y. Med. Coll. 1973-76; fmr. mem. Pleasantville (NY) Sch. Bd. 1977, W. Howbrook (NY) review panel Fed. Govt., 1976; mem: Am. Phys. Therapy Assn., Am. Assn. Mental Deficiency, Am. Hosp. Assn., Am. Coll. Sports Medicine, Am. Coll. Nsg. Home Ad-

minstrs., Assn. Adminstrs. Mental Health and Retardation Facilities; Democrat; Roman Catholic. Res: 2247 20th St Apt 4 Santa Monica 90405 Ofc: Brotman Medical Center 3828 Delmas Terrace Culver City 90230

FERGUSON, GLENN CHARLES, geologist; b. Jan. 23, 1906, Grenola, Kans.; s. Charles and Carrie (Dozer) F.; m. Pauline Orrick, Aug. 25, 1974; children: Gail Alice b. 1931, Lee Ann b. 1940; edn: AB, Univ. So. Calif. 1929, MA, 1932; Reg. Geologist Calif. 1933. Career: jr. paleontologist Pacific Western Oil Co. 1929-30; div. paleontol. stratigrapher Union Oil Co. 1933-44; ptnr. Ferguson & Bosworth (oil exploration/production) 1944 –; pres. Laymac Corp. Bakersfield; chmn. bd. F&B Energy Inc. Kingwood, Tex.; past bd. dirs. Cal-Pure Oil Co.; mem: Independent Petroleum Assn. of Am. (past reg. v.p.), San Joaquin Valley Oil Producers Assn. (past pres.), Independent Oil & Gas Producers of Calif. (past pres.), Calif. Independent Producers Assn. (past. chmn. bd.), Bakersfield CC (past pres.), Bakersfield CofC (past bd. dirs.); publ. bulletin Div. of Mines, Dept. Nat. Resources Calif. 1943; Republican; Presbyterian; rec: golf. Address: Bakersfield

FERGUSSON, OLATUNGIE CLARENCE, chiropractor; b. Apr. 10, 1949, Freetown, Sierra Leone; s. Eugene Clarence and Marquis Gertrude (Solomon) F.; edn: BS, honors, St. Augustine's Coll. 1976; DC, Pasadena Coll. of Chiro. 1983. Career: asst. production mgr. Burlington Ind. Chem. Div. Greensboro, N.C. 1976-78; design engr. Chevron USA El Segundo, Calif. 1978-80; owner chiropractic clinic L.A. 1984 –; honors: Who's Who Students in Am. Univ. & Coll. 1975-76, Most Outstanding Student - Biology (St. Augustine's Coll. 1975), Beta Kappa Chi (nat. sci. hon. soc., v.p. 1975); mem: Calif. Chiro. Assn., Am. Black Chiro. Assn.; Christian; rec: tennis, soccer, ping-pong, movies, travel. Ofc: O.C. Fergusson, D.C. 3756 Santa Rosalia Dr, Ste 208, Los Angeles 90008

FERNANDES, WAYNE JOSEPH, financial executive; b. Aug. 14, 1955, Fall River, Mass.; s. John Souza and Eleanor Irene (DeMoura) F.; edn: AS, Massasoit Comm. Coll. 1975; BS acctg., Bryant Coll. 1978. Career: mgmt. acct. State Street Bank & Trust Co., Boston 1978-79; asst. controller Allianz Underwriters, Inc., Los Angeles 1979-83; asst. v.p./controller Westwood Nat. Corp., Mission Viejo 1983-85; exec. v.p./CFO Westech Ins. Network Inc., Mission Viejo 1986 –; cons. prin. WJF Finl. Svcs.; mem. Ins. Acctg. ans Systems Assn.; civic: Smithsonian Instn., Calif. Spl. Olympics, Animal Protection Inst., Mothers Against Drunk Driving, Japan Karate Assn. Internat., Am. JKA Karate Registry; rec: Karate, racquetball. Ofc: WJF Financial Services 25108 Marguerite Pkwy Ste B-11 Mission Viejo 92692

FERNANDEZ, ALFRED PETER, college district administrator; b. July 26, 1935, San Diego; s. Alfonso R. and Pola (Pickering) F.; m. Dolores Russell, May 1, 1952; children: Christina, Virginia, Pamela, Steven; edn: BA, UCLA, 1957, MA, 1959; PhD, USC, 1976. Career: assoc. engring. geologist Calif. Div. Hwys., Los Angeles 1960-62; assoc. prof. geology Chaffey Coll., Alta Loma 1962-69; admission ofcr. CSU Los Angeles, 1969-71; assoc. dean continuing edn. Santa Monica Coll., 1971-74; dean instruction Ventura Coll., 1974-80; pres. Los Angeles Mission Coll., San Fernando 1980-82; chancellor Ventura County Community Coll. Dist., 1982 –; mem. Chancellor's Adv. Com. on Gen. Edn., 1982-; mem. council Ventura County Ednl. Tng. Adminstrn., 1975-78; trustee Neighborhood Youth Assn.; div. vice. chmn. United Way; mem. Assn. Calif. Community Coll. Adminstrs., So. Calif. Community Coll. Chief Exec. Officers Assn., Assn. Mexican-Am. Educators, Calif. Tchrs. Assn., Assn. Engring Geologists, Calif. Coll. and Univ. Faculty Assn., Indsl. Assn. San Fernando Valley, Mexican-Am. Polit. Assn. Pomona (chmn.), UCLA Alumni Assn., San Fernando CofC, Sylmar CofC; Democrat; Roman Catholic. Res: 981 Scenic Way Dr., Ventura 93003 Ofc: 71 Day Rd Ventura 93003

FERNANDEZ, CARLOS PEDRO, dental surgeon; b. Nov. 26, 1925, Havana, Cuba, nat. US cit. 1971; s. Antonio Fernandez and Ana (Ponce) F.; m. Lourdes C. Gonzalez, Nov. 25, 1983; children: Maria de Lourdes b. 1959, Rodolfo b. 1963; edn: DDS, Univ. Havana 1954; DDS, Univ. So. Calif. 1969. Career: gen. practitioner pvt. practice Havana, Cuba 1954-61; dir. of dentistry La Esperanza Hosp. Havana 1954-61; dentist Guggenheim Dental Clinic NYC 1961-62; pvt. practice L.A. 1969 –; operative clin. instr. Univ. So. Calif. 1973-80; expert examiner Calif. Bd. Dental Examiners Sacramento 1980-84; honors: Instr. of the Year (USC Dental Sch. 1974); mem: Dental Soc. Havana (treas. 1955-61), Latin Am. Dental Soc. (pres. 1978), Foreign Dental Assn. L.A. (pres. 1979), Am. Dental Assn., L.A. Dental Soc. Cuban CofC (pres. 1973), Century Club (USC); rec: hunting, fishing. Ofc: Glendale

FERNANDO, DAYANTHA MANILAL, accountant; b. Oct. 23, 1951, Panadura, Sri Lanka, nat. US cit. 1979; s. Titus Peter Joseph and Chitranganie Lolita (Dias) F.; m. Cherene, April 26, 1972; children: Dayantha II b. 1976, Thilan b. 1979, Krishani b. 1981; edn: AA, Rio Hondo Coll. 1975; BSBA, CSU Long Beach 1977; CPA, Calif. 1980. Career: staff acct. Harold J. Zivetz Accty. Corp., LosAngeles 1977; audit mgr. Touche Rosse & Co., Los Angeles 1978 –; mem: Am. Inst. CPAs, Calif. Soc. CPAs, Sri Lanka America Assn. of So. Calif. (past pres.), Los Angeles World Affairs Council. Res: 18520 Clydepark Ave. Cerritos 90701 Ofc: Touche Ross & Co., 3700 Wilshire Blvd. Los Angeles 90701

FERRARI, PIERINO JOHN, personnel training executive, ret.; b. June 15, 1922, Fornaci Di Barga, Italy, nat. US cit. 1943; s. Giulio and Celeste (Biagiotti) F.; m. Geraldine, Sept. 30, 1946; children: Frederic b. 1948, Peter b. 1950; edn: grad. Arms Acad., Shelburne Falls, Mass. Career: in business with father in Mass. 1945-53; serviceman, So. Calif. Gas Co., 1953-, transf. into tng.

dept. to produce Audio-Visual material, 1957-, dir. of tng. material/prod. co. orientation and tng. videos, -1983, ret.; mem. Acad. of TV Arts & Scis.; Am. Film Inst.; mil: sgt. US Army Signal Corps 1945; Independent; Catholic; rec: photog., electronics. Res: 1961 Old Canyon Dr Hacienda Heights 91745

FERRELL, WALTER EUGENE, resources co. president; b. Aug. 3, 1919, Milford Center, Oh.; s. LeRoy and Elizabeth (Stillings) F.; m. Ursula, Mar. 3, 1973; children (by previous marriage): Mara, b. 1949, Michael, b. 1952; stepchildren (nee Aubrey): Brian b. 1955, Mark b. 1957, Susan b. 1959; edn: BSBA, Ohio State Univ. 1942; UCLA 1956-57; Enrolled Agent, U.S. Treas. 1963. Career: sys. analyst Ford Motor Co., Dearborn, Mich. 1947-48; factory acct. factory acctg. supvr. Norris- Thermador Corp., Los Angeles 1948-60; tax cons., self- empl., Whittier 1960-65; founder, chmn., pres. Unitax Inc., Anaheim 1965-76; mgmt. advr. Tymshare- Unitax Inc., Anaheim 1976-79; co-founder, pres., dir. True North Inc., Mission Viejo 1981; co-founder, pres., dir. Nevada North Resources Inc., Vancouver, B.C., Can. 1983—; dir. Barr Engineering Inc., Santa Fe Springs 1973-; v.p., pres. Nat. Assn. of Computerized Tax Processors, Wash. DC 1974-76; mem: Soc. of Calif. Acctnts. (assoc.), Citrus chpt.; mil: 1st lt., co. cmmdr., U.S. Army Ordnance 1942-46; Republican; Protestant; rec: motor homing, reading. Res: 26011 Montanoso Dr., Mission Viejo 92691

FEUER, MARK JEFFREY, agricultural production co. executive; b. Aug. 18, 1946, Los Angeles; s. Siegmund H. and Katy (Mane) F.; edn: BA in psychol., CSU Northridge 1974; JD, Univ. San Fernando Valley Coll. of Law 1978; Calif. lic. Real Estate Broker 1976; admitted Calif. State Bar. Career: real estate broker Century 21, Van Nuys 1976-80; supr. Calif. Casualty Mgmt. Co., Los Angeles 1980-83; atty. pvt. practice in Tarzana and Porterville, 1983-84; pres./dir. Galloway Farms, Inc. 1984—, v.p./dir. M.L. Galloway Internatl. (Calif. Corp.) dba Galloway Farms Internat.; v.p./dir. M.L. Galloway Farms Internat. (public Utah Corp.); public speaker var. service clubs and orgns.; mem. Los Angeles County Bar Assn.; mil: E5 US Navy, Vietnam Service; rec: writer; fishing, collecting nautical antiques, sailing. Address: Porterville

FEUSTEL, HELMUT ERICH, research engineer; b. Mar. 16, 1947, Berlin, W. Germany; s. Walter Julius and Margarete (Krempel) F.; m. Verena Rosenkranz, Nov. 21, 1984; edn: BS in eng., Technische Fachhochschule Berlin 1971; MS eng., Technische Univ. Berlin 1977, PhD eng., 1983. Career: design engr. Farbwerke Hoechst AG, Frankfurt 1971-73; staff scientist Spl. Research Field for Hosps., Berlin 1977-80; staff scientist/lectr. Technical Univ. Berlin, 1980-83, also tech. cons. for energy savings in hosps., Klima System Technik, 1982-83; staff scientist Lawrence Berkeley Lab., Berkeley, Calif. 1983—; freelance writer, Clima Commerce Internat., 1980-; cons. software implementation, IBM-PC, AVAL GmbH, Berlin, 1982-83; mem. Zweiter Vorsitzender (v.p. 1985) Assn. of Archs. and HVAC Engrs.; book in progress (Mit Volldampf durch die Rocky Mts.), sev. publs. on energy conservation; rec: trains, model R.R., sailing. Ofc: Lawrence Berkeley Lab (Bldg 90 Rm 3074) Berkeley 94720

FIELDS, EUGENE EMANUEL, salon owner; b. Oct. 27, 1950, Bklyn.; s. Irving and Naomi F.; m. Marsha; edn: Nassau Comm. Coll.; desig: master stylist, Vidal Sassoon, England 1977. Career: tng. instr. Peter's Place, Great Neck, NY; mens style dir. Nu-Best & Co., Manhatten, NY; stylist Nardi, Manhatten; current: salon owner/opr. Eugene Champs Hair Design, Thousand Oaks, Calif.; mem. Rotary Intl., Chamber of Commerce; Democrat; Jewish; rec: computers, dogs. Res: 28818 Conejo View Dr Agoura 91301 Ofc: Eugene Champs 2251 Thousand Oaks Blvd Thousand Oaks 91362

FIELDS, S., printing co. president; b. Feb. 8, 1954, Savannah, Ga.; s. Wm. and Frances (McMakin) F.; grad. Berkeley Prep. H.S. Career: began in mailroom, current pres. City Printers, San Francisco; recipient Good Fellow award, Chamber of Commerce/City of San Francisco; mem. Theatre Guild, Actors Equity, Am. Mgmt. Assn.; Rotarian; avocation: playwright, dancer/ mime, musician (1975-); rec: sports, dancing, Marilyn Monroe fan. Res: 945 Larkin #24 San Francisco 94109

FIFE, THOMAS EVAN, stockbroker; b. Jan. 25, 1949, Van Nuys; s. Thomas Elwood and Elsie Francis (Amsubury) F.; m. Michele, Sept. 30, 1979; children: Kim b. 1968, Kenny b. 1968; edn: Fresno City Coll. 1970-72; tng., Nat. Restaurant Exec. Devel. 1973, Nat. Assn. Secs. Dealers 1985; desig: stockbroker, tax shelter splst., finl. plnng. coordinator (SEC, Calif. St. Securities Commn., Chgo. Bd. Trade, NYSE, Calif. Ins. Commn.). Career: head chef Stanley's of Fresno, 1970-76; owner Packing House Restaurant, 1976-79; sales mgr. Select Business Systems, Visalia 1979-83; cons. B.R.S. Ents., Fresno 1983-84; stockbroker, finl. plnng. coord. E.F. Hutton & Co., Visalia 1984—; mem. advis. com. (occup. edn.) State Center Comm. Coll.; orgns: Visalia Tennis Club, Beyond War, Visalia Raquet Club, Calif. Food & Wine Soc.; publs: Selling for the 80's (1983), The Consulting Approach (1984), Future Funding (1986); mil: sgt. USAF 1967-70 Intel.; Republican; Presbyterian; rec: skiing, tennis. Res: 2137 E Howard St Visalia 93277 Ofc: E.F. Hutton 801 W Main St Visalia 93291

FIGGINS, DONALD PAUL, real estate broker; b. July 18, 1906, Jewell Co., Kansas; s. Orian G. and Blanche Mary (Lowe) F.; m. Grace H. Cary (dec.), May 26, 1927; children: Norene b. 1928, Donald Dennis b. 1932; edn: grad. Chaffee H.S. 1925, Calif. lic. real estate broker. Career: telegraphy opr. Santa Fe R.R.; wholesale poultry buyer and rancher 1947; realtor 1947—, now semi-ret.; mem: Future Farmers of Am. (hon. mem.), Redlands Bd. of Realtors (hon. mem.), Calif. Assn. Realtors (hon. mem.), Nat. Assn. Realtors; inven-

tion: easy rest back rest; rec: fishing, hunting, billiards. Res: 11050 Bryan St. Space 18 Yucaipa 92399 Ofc: Figgins Realtors Inc., 408 E. State St. Redlands 92373

FIKES, JAY COURTNEY, professor of anthropology; b. June 14, 1951, San Luis Obispo; s. J C and Virginia Lee (Roberts) F.; m. Lebriz Tosuner, Apr. 17, 1979; edn: BA cum laude, UC Irvine 1973; M.Ed in bilingual edn., honors, Univ. San Diego 1974; MA in anthropol., Univ. Mich., Ann Arbor, 1977; PhD, anthropol., 1984. Career: tutor, bilingual chemistry, Pala Indian Reservation, summer 1974; instr. anthropol./archaeol., Allan Hancock Community Coll., Santa Maria 1975-76; teaching fellow in anthropol. Univ. Mich., Ann Arbor 1976-79; anthropological fieldwork among the Huichol Indians of Jalisco, Mex. 1979-81; housing cons. to Navajo Indian Nation, 1983; owner Cuatro Esquinas Traders (splst., wholesaler quality American Indian art) 1979—. Recipient two scholarships, Univ. Mich.; orgnzr. Carlsbad Fiesta Patria and served on Carlsbad Bicentennial Com., 1975; mem: NY Acad. of Scis., AAAS, Anthropological Assn., Rotary Internat., Internat. Platform Assn.; author: Huichol Indian Identity and Adaptation; arts., Mich. Discussions in Anthropology (1978), Dialectical Anthropology (1983), El Palacio (1983). rec: hike, camp, gardening. Res: 2421 Buena Vista Cir. Carlsbad 92008

FILES, GORDON LOUIS, appellate court presiding justice, ret.; b. Mar. 5, 1912; s. James Ray and Anna (Louis) F.; m. Kathryn Thrift, Nov. 24, 1982; children: Kathryn A. b. 1944, James G. b. 1948; edn: AB, UC Los Angeles 1934; LLB, Yale 1937; admitted Calif. State Bar 1937. Career: law clerk 8th Circuit Ct. of Appeal 1937-38; atty. law firm Freston & Files, Los Angeles 1938-59; judge Superior Ct. Los Angeles 1959-62; presiding justice Ct. of Appeal, Calif. 2d div. 1962-72, administrating presiding justice 2d dist. 1969-72; Judicial Council of Calif. 1964-71 1973-77; Governing Com., Ctr. for Judicial Edn. and Research; honors: Phi Beta Kappa, Order of the Coif; mem: Bd of Trustees Los Angeles Co. Bar 1952-6; Bd. of Govs., State Bar of California 1957-8, Am. Bar Assn., fellow (lifetime) Am. Bar Found., Am. Judicature Soc., Inst. of Judicial Admin., Calif. Judges Assm., Chancery Club (L.A.), Am. Legion, Phi Delta Phi, Bd of Editors, Yale Law Sch. 1936-7, lecturer, Univ. of So. Calif. Law Sch. 1959-64; mil: lt., US Naval Reserve 1942-46; Democrat. Res: 154 S Arroyo Blvd Pasadena 91105

FILLET, ROBERT EARL, investment banker; b. Nov. 29, 1921, NY, NY; s. Maxwell Edward and Frances (Palley) F.; children: Mitchell b. 1948, Andrea b. 1951; edn: BBA cum laude, Nat. Univ.; Met.D., honors, Fathers of St. Thomas, Imperial Beach; MA and PhD, Univ. for Humanistic Studies, San Diego. Career: finl./mgmt. cons. for 33 orgns. since 1948, and in partnership w. Gen. Sandy Pitofsky cons. to another 15 corporations and 3 govts. (including Pepsicola Corp., Western Union, Builders Credit Corp., Kroeger Inc. Detroit Div., Fotochrome Inc., Sunkist Beverages, Nat. Distillers, Faberge Inc., Republic of Haiti, Rep. of Korea, Govt. of Pakistan); founder/pres. U.S./China Chamber of Commerce, Wash DC (and cons. to US Congress re China comml. and econ. relations) 1972-76; current: pres. Fillet Capital Corp., Los Angeles; also cons. in govt. assisted financing in real estate devel., 1980-; prof. Univ. for Humanistic Studies; instr. CSU San Diego Ext.; academic advis. bd. Nat. Univ.; mem. Am. Mgmt. Inst., Am. Legion (Silver Star cit.); civic: Kiwanis (past pres. S.D. Old Town Club), Boy Scouts Am. (com. Tarrytown, NY), NY State Ofc. of Civil Def. (dir. aviation), Mental Health Assn. (chmn. Speakers Bur., S.D.); mil: lt. col. USAF ret., combat duty China, India, D.F.C., Air Medal (4), Purple Heart (4); Rel. Sci.; rec: flying, tennis. Ofc: Fillet Capital Corp. 1815 Butler Ave Ste 114 Los Angeles 90025

FINA, JOHN JAY, architect, engineer; b. July 24, 1921, Cleveland, Ohio; s. Joe and Virginia (Giovenco) F.; div.; children. Larry b. 1948, Leslie b. 1950, Peggy b. 1953; edn: undergrad. Oberlin Coll. 1943-45, Case Western Reserve Univ. 1946-47; BS in architl. engring., Univ. Ill. 1949; grad. work Northwestern Univ. 1956-57; Reg. Architect, Calif. (1972), Nat. Council of Architl. Bds. (1976), Reg. Profl. Engr., Calif. (1978). Career: designer and draftsman New York Central R.R., Dept. of Bridges & Buildings, 1949-51, redesigned NY Central Passenger Station; designer A.J. Boynton and Co., Archs. and Engrs., Chgo. 1951-53; mgr. Struc. Design Div., Delta-Star Electric Div., H.K. Porter, Chgo. 1953-59; staff engr. Argonne Nat. Lab. Argonne, Ill. 1959-62; proj. engr. Holmes & Narver, Inc., Los Angeles 1962; senior faculty engr. Jet Propulsion Lab., Pasadena 1962-68; staff engr. Agbabian-Jacobsen Assocs., Los Angeles 1968; project constrn. mgr. Lockheed-Calif. Co., Burbank 1968-70; architl. designer, field and office coord., Litton Systems, 1970-72; project constrn. mgr. K mart Corp., Covina 1972-86, ret.; AEC 'Q' Clearance (1959, 62), DOD 'Secret' Clearance (1959, 62, 69); honors: Ohio State Champion Gymnast (1940), Big Ten Collegiate Gymnastic Champion (1948), capt. Univ. of Ill. gymnastic team (1949), "I" Men's Soc.; mil: US Navy 1942-46; mem. Lambda Chi Alpha, Nat. Com. to Preserve Social Sec. and Medicare; mil: S1/c US Navy 1942-46, Am. Theater, Pacific Theater (3 Stars), Victory Medal, Good Conduct Medal; Republican; Catholic; rec: painting, gardening. Res: 2712 Marina Blvd, 19, San Leandro 94577

FINDLEY, REGINALD SCOTT, accountant; b. July 24, 1956, Fresno; s. Wallace Gordon and Winifred Willideen (Jantz) F.; edn: AABA, Reedley Coll. 1976; BSBA, cum laude, CSU Fresno 1978; CPA, Calif. 1981. Career: staff acct. Louis Milakovich PA, Dinuba 1978-83; staff acct. Forest A. McQuenn CPA, Dinuba 1983-85; CPA Reginald S. Findley CPA, Dinuba 1985—; honors: Beta Alpha Psi, Sigma Iota Epsilon, Beta Gamma Sigma; Bank of Am. Community Coll. Award; mem: Am. Inst. of CPAs, Calif. Soc. of CPAs, Dinuba Rotary, Dinuba CofC; rec: golf. Ofc: Reginald S. Findley CPA, 1224 E. El Monte Way Dinuba 93618

FINE, DONALD JACK, retail store owner; b. Apr. 12, 1932, N.Y.C.; s. Jack and Irma F.; div.; children: Betsy b. 1964, Ivy b. 1967, Nevada b. 1974; edn: BA, New York Univ. 1956. Career: co-owner Cuzzens Mens Store, Fountainbleau Hotel in Miami Beach, Fla. 1958-64, opened 12 additional shops in major US cities; currently owner/pres. D. Fine, Inc. (retail mens clothing), San Francisco; mem. Post Street Bus. Assn., SF Conv. Bureau; clubs: Habor Point Racket (Mill Valley), Bigwood Golf, Cross Country Ski, Sun Valley Idaho Golf; works: participant on radio pgms. on style and fashion in Fla. and Milano, Rome (1980-), designer exclusive menswear; mil: capt. USAF, 1956-57; rec: tennis, golf, biking, x-c skiing. Res: 1060 Stirrup Ln (POB 3006) Ketchum ID 83340 Ofc: D. Fine Inc. 300 Post St San Francisco 94108

FINE, RANDALL EDGAR, lawyer; b. Dec. 11, 1951, Downey; s. Delbert Elton and Martha Ann (Smith) F.; stepfather: Robert Earl Parish; m. Marie, Aug. 20, 1983; stepchildren: David Bohm, Joshua Bohm, Gabriel Bohm; edn: AA, Cerritos Coll. 1976; CSU Long Beach; BS, Western State Univ. 1979, JD, 1980; admitted to bars of Supreme Ct. of calif. 1983, US Fed. Dist. Ct. 1985. Career: senior atty. Randall E. Fine & Assoc., Huntington Beach; counsel, dir. sev. client corps.; mem: Fed. (Central Dist. of Calif.), Calif. and Orange Co. Bar Assns., Internat. Law Soc., Los Angeles Trial Lawyers Assn., Delta Theta Phi; Christian; rec: skiing, creative machining, sport fishing. Ofc: Randall E. Fine & Associates, P.O. Box 3083 Huntington Beach 92605

FINERMAN, MATTHEW LAWRENCE, physician; b. July 4, 1951, Los Angeles; s. Wilmore Bernart and Muriel Ruth (Weinstein) F.; edn: BA, honors, UCLA 1973; MD, Loyola- Stritch 1976. Career: resident otolaryngology head and neck surgery 1978-81, pvt. practice 1981−; assoc. clin. prof. head and neck surgery UCLA; hoors: Tchg. Award in Head & Neck Surgery, UCLA 1983-84; Chancellor's Marshall, UCLA; staff: UCLA, Cedars-Sinai, Calif. Med. Ctr., Midway Med. Ctr. of the Good Samaritan, St. Vincent Med. Ctr., Midway Med. Ctr.; mem: Fellow Am. Acad. of Otolaryngology Head and Neck Surgery; co-author: article on laryngeal changes in rheumatoid arthritis 1983; Jewish; rec: piano, travel. Res: 605 N Treton Dr Beverly Hills 90210 Ofc: 727 W 7th St Ste 945 Los Angeles 90017

FINK, HOWARD JOEL, insurance company executive; b. Aug. 4, 1944, Los Angeles; s. Irving Isadore and Ruth (Alexander) F.; m. Hanne Bruberg, May 21, 1966; children: Pauline, b. 1966; Lisa, b. 1969; Vikki, b. 1971; edn: bus. acctg. courses, L.A. Valley Coll. 1962-66; CLU Am. Coll. 1981; Chartered Financial Cons. 1985. Career: dist. sales mgr. (13) stores Firstone Tire and Rubber Co., 1966-72; Insurance industry, 1973−; pres. PFP Financial & Insurance Svcs., Inc., 1977−; sales mgr. Los Angeles Madvin Agency of Pacific Mutual, vice pres. Finl. Mgmt. Services, Inc. 1983, moderator Life Underwriters Tng. Council, 1982. Awards: sales mgr. of the year, 1979, Pacific Mutual; mem: Million Dollar Round Table, San Fernando Valley Life Underwriters (bd. dirs.), Amer. Assn. of Chartered Life Underwriters, Internat. Assn. Fin. Planners, Knights of the MDRT; mem. Chancellor's Honor Roll at UCLA., Beverly Hills Estate Counselor's Forum; rec: tennis. Res: 7608 Rudnick St Canoga Park 91304; Ofc: Financial Management Services, Inc. 15760 Ventura Blvd, No. 1732, Encino 91436

FINK, JAMES WILLIAM, international business development executive, consultant; b. Sept. 11, 1939, Los Angeles; s. Frederick G. and Alma Irene (Eslick) F.; m. Linda Reavis, Apr. 22, 1967; children: Christi, Kevin, Andrew; edn: BA, Azusa Pacific Univ. 1961; postgrad., CSU Los Angeles, CSU Fullerton 1962-63. Career: var. mfg. and operational positions 1962-76; dir. internat. materials control Revell, Inc., Venice, Calif. 1976-78, v.p. corp. materials mgmt. and qual. assurance 1978-79, v.p. engrg. 1979-83, gen. mgr. Revell, Hong Kong 1980-83, corp. sec. 1982-83; pres., dir. Jalack Enterprises, Garden Grove 1984−; lectr. MBA pgm. Azusa Pacific Univ.; mem: Am. Prodn. & Inventory Control Soc., Nat. Assn. Purchasing Mgmt., Internat. Material Mgmt. Soc., Am. Soc. Quality Control, Fgn. Trade Assn. So. Calif.; Republican. Ofc: 12181 Le Ann Dr Garden Grove 92640

FINK, MILDRED ROSE, educator; b. Jan. 1, 1918, Lindsay; d. Laurence Eugene and Martha (Milhous) Gibbons; m. John Fink, May 18, 1940; children: Laurence b. 1942, John b. 1945, Martha b. 1947; edn: AA, Porterville Jr. Coll. 1937, Santa Barbara St. Univ. 1938; B.Ed. CSU Fresno 1957; M.Ed. Whittier Coll. 1970. Career: tchr. (Gr.3) Strathmore Elementary Sch., 32 yrs.; her class presented annual operetta (adapted from musicals incl. Winnie-the-Pooh, Pinocchio, Mary Poppins, Snow White, Wizard of Oz, Let Freedom Ring) 1970-85; honors: Eighth Grade Graduation dedicated to her (1985), "Mascot Mom" to school band; mem: Calif. Tchrs. Assn., Stathmore Elem. Tchrs. Assn. (pres. 2 terms); civic: S.E. Tulare County Republican Women, Lindsay Comm. Theater League (secty), Lindsay Hosp. Guild, AAUW, Tulare County Hist. Soc.; Republican (Tulare Co. Central Com. 10 yrs); Presbyterian (deacon, 2 terms). Res: 721 B Lafayette Lindsay 93247

FINKELSTEIN, JAMES ARTHUR, management consultant; b. Dec. 6, 1952, NYC; s. Harold Nathan and Lilyan Crystal F.; m. Lynn Gould, Mar. 24, 1984; 1 son, Matthew James b. 1985; edn: BA, Trinity Coll. 1974; MBA, Wharton Sch., Univ. of Penna. 1976. Career: cons. firm of Towers, Perrin, Forster & Crosby, Inc., Boston 1976-78; mgr. compensation Pepsi-Cola Co., Purchase, NY 1978-80; mgr. business analysis Emery Worldwide, Wilton, Ct. 1980-81; vice pres. Meidinger Inc., Rowayton, Ct. 1981-83; prin. The Wyatt Co., San Diego 1983−; mem. Camp Com., State YMCA of Mass. and R.I., 1976-; bd. dirs. Pro Arte Chamber Singers of Conn. 1981-2; instr. UCSD Ext. Pgm. 1984-85. Honors: Morris Prize for excellence in music 1974; Pi Gamma Mu 1974; Outstanding Young Men of Am. 1981, US Jaycees; mem: Am. Compensation

Assn., Am. Soc. for Personnel Adminstrn., Am. Camping Assn.; Big Brothers/Big Sisters of Am. (bd. dirs., Fairfield Co. 1980-82); Nat. Alumni Assn. of Trinity Coll. (exec. com.); Lomas Santa Fe CC; publs: arts., Jour. of Big Brothers Practices (10/76), Personnel Jour. (11/78). Musical theatre lead roles Troupers Light Opera Co. (Stamford, Ct.), 1980-2; frequent soloist various churches. Democrat; Unitarian; rec: sports, music, camping. Ofc: The Wyatt Co 9339 Genesee Ave Ste 300 San Diego 92121

FINKEN, MARJORIE MORISSE, columnist-editor; b. June 29, 1918, St. Louis, Mo.; d. William J. and Alice (Seidler) Morisse (O'Hern); gr.granddau. of Ferdinand Diehm, 1842-1916, Imperial and Royal Consul of Austria-Hungary in St. Louis, Mo. 1882-1915; grandniece of Albert Diehm, apptd. food admr. two Ill. counties by Pres. Hoover, 1914-18; bro. Richard Diehm Morisse (dec. 1968), aud. of USC, 20 years; m. John W. Finken, Apr. 26, 1940, div. 1957; 1 son Richard Dale, b. 1943; edn: grad. Los Angeles H.S. 1936; stu. dress design Chouinard Inst. of Art 1937-38; art maj., L.A. City Coll. 1938-40. Career: profl. photographer; freelance photog. and rep. South Bay Daily Breeze, 1956, restaurant editor 1956−, columnist: Munchin with Marge, and Marge to Midnight, 1956−; apptd. Calif. Rec. Commnr., Manhattan City Sch. Adminstr. 1954-60; awards: first Rose & Scroll, Manhattan Bch CofC, 1954; mem: Phi Epsilon Phi (secty-treas L.A. chpt. 1942-3,44-5); So. Bay Sym. Assn. (pub. chmn. 1954-5); So. Bay Comm. Arts Assn. (pub. chmn. 1954-6); Women of Moose Lodge No.323 (secty.,pub.ch.,corr. secty. 1957-9); South Bay Hosp. Aux. (charter secty., dir. 1959-61); Greater L.A. Press Club; Calif. Press Women (bd., L.A. chpt.); Restaurant Writers Assn. (secty. L.A. Co. 1967-70); L.A. Restaurant Writers Assn. (pres. 1977-79); Los Angeles Mus of Art; Altrusa Internat. Inc. (pres. Redondo Beach chpt. 1983-85); rec: theater, concerts, art. Res: 223 Ave F, Redondo Beach 90277 Ofc: Daily Breeze, 5215 Torrance Blvd. Torrance 90509

FINLEY, EUGENE NORMAN, filmmaker, b. Mar. 17, 1944, Alexandria, Va.; s. John W. and Marguerite B. Finley; edn: BA, C.W.Post Coll. 1966; MA, Univ. of Ariz. 1967. Career: sound editor motion picture films: Semi-Tough, Almost Perfect Affair, The Island; music editor: More American Grafiti, Making of Raiders of the Lost Ark; created sound effects for: Star Trek II, 48 Hours; director documentaries, Finley-Hill Co., current project documentary on: Golden Gate Bridge; prod./dir./editor television spl.: Mr. Adler and the Opera, awarded Cine Golden Eagle for film, 1982; invented Finley-Hill Sound Mixer for motion picture post prodn. (pat. 1984); rec: rowing, motorcycles. Address: Finley-Hill Co. 346 Corte Madera Ave Corte Madera 94925

FINN, SARA SHIELS, public relations executive; b. July 12, Cincinnati, Ohio; d. Paul Vincent and Freda K. (Kohstall) Shiels; m. Thomas Finn, Nov. 11, 1952; children: Shawn, Paula, Anne-Marie, Sara Louise; edn: BA Eng., Maryville Coll. 1950. Career: advtg. & pub. rels. rep. San Diego Magazine 1964-71; dir. pub. rels. Univ. San Diego 1971−; honors: Internat. Papal Soc., Equestrian Order of the Holy Sepulchre of Jesus (Pope John Paul II 1982, elevated to Lady Comdr. 1985); mem: San Diego Press Club, Pub. Rels. Club of San Diego (dir.), Pub. Rels. Soc. of Am. (dir.), Pub. Rels. Soc. of Am. (S.D. chpt. bd.), Internat. Affairs Bd. of City of San Diego, Partners for Livable Places (dir.), San Diego CofC, Council for Advancement & Support of Edn., Alumnae of the Sacred Heart (pres. 1979-81), San Diego Mus. of Art; Catholic; rec: travel. Res: 2179 Caminito Tiburon La Jolla 92037 Ofc: Univ. San Diego Alcala Park San Diego 92110

FINNIN, MICHAEL TIMOTHY, corporate president/management consultant; b. Dec. 13, 1946, Akron, Ohio; s. William Leo and Helen Ruth (McKinney) F.; edn: stu. Univ. of Mich. 1970, West Coast Univ. 1974, UCI 1976, Calif. Coast Univ. 1979−; Cert. Computer Tech. 1972, Data Comm. Engr. 1974, Control Data Ins.; Cert. Vocational Edn. Instr., Calif. Career: specs. writer Ford Motor Co. Engring. and Research, Dearborn, Mich. 1966-68; owner MTF Enterprises, Detroit 1969-72; instr. Burroughs Corp., Industry, Ca. 1972-73; sr. instr Control Data Inst., Anaheim 1973-76; mgr. Publications Svcs., Gen. Automation Inc., Anaheim 1974-77; founder/owner MTF Associates (cons. high-tech. publs.), Norco 1977−; co-founder/vice chmn. of bd. Communique Telecommunications, Inc. (resrch, devel., mfg. of computerized telephone switching equip.), Ontario, 1983−; co-founder/pres. Internat. Wire And Cable, Inc. (mfr. comm. & telephone connectorized cable), Ontario, 1983−; cons. high-tech. cos. in tng. and documentation; mem: Soc. for Tech. Comms., Am. Mgmt. Assn., Am. Legion, Disabled Am. Vets, Loyal Order of Moose; publs: over 40 tech. publs, many tng. courses, various sales collaterals, 1975-; mil: Disabled Vet. US Army 1968. rec: photog., autos, motorcycling, horseback riding. Res: 2830 Valley View Ave Norco 91760 Ofc: POB 968 Norco 91760

FINROW, THOMAS M., lawyer; b. Sept. 13, 1950, Portland, Me.; s. Douglas W. and Mary Virginia (Ford) F.; m. Coleman Cheryl, Feb. 1972; children: Christina b. 1977, Casondra b. 1981; edn: Seattle Pac. Univ. 1968-72, BS Law, Western State Univ. 1978, JD, 1980; admitted Calif. State Bar 1981, US Claims Ct. 1985. Career: atty. pvt. sole practice, 1982−, splst. in govt. contract claims and litigation, esp. constrn. contrs., subcontrs. and suppliers; worked for govt. contractors 1970-82; awards: Am. Jurisprudence Award (Property) 1977; mem. Am. Bar Assn., Am. Soc. of Safety Engrs., San Diego County Bar Assn.; publisher: Navy Construction Law Newsletter (1985); Republican; Baptist; rec: skiing, fishing, model airplanes. Ofc: 2067 First Ave San Diego 92101

FIPPS, MICHAEL WAYNE, corporate treasurer, certified public accountant; b. Aug. 24, 1942, Tabor City, N.C.; s. David Earl and Ina (Etheridge) F.; m. Angelique, July 15, 1972; children: Sean b. 1973, Brandon b. 1978; edn: BA,

Univ. N.C. 1968; CPA Calif. 1978. Career: acct. Platt, Warren & Swinson CPAs Wilmington, N.C. 1966-68, Baxter Labs. Morton Grove, Ill. 1968-70; auditor Allstate Ins. Co. Hdqs. Skokie, Ill. 1970-71, Flying Tiger L.A. 1971-73; auditor, subcontroller, etc. Bergen Brunswig Corp. L.A. 1973 –, treas. 1985; mem: Financial Execs. Inst., Calif. Soc. CPAs, Am. Inst. CPAs; Republican; rec: sailing, running, reading. Ofc: Orange

FIREHAMMER, RICHARD A., JR., international business and tax consultant; b. July 15, 1957, Rockford, Ill.; s. Richard A. Sr. and Shirley A. (Rustlie) F.; m. Bonnie J. Rice, May 25, 1985; edn: BS, Indiana Univ. 1979; JD, Whittier Coll. Sch. of Law 1987; CPA, Calif. 1983. Career: staff acct. Whipple & Co. CPAs, Indianapolis, Ind. 1979-82; staff internal auditor Host Internat. Inc., Santa Monica 1982-83; senior internal auditor Marriott/ Host, Santa Monica 1983, mgr. of spl. projects 1984, lease compliance and rental mgr. 1984-86; internat. bus. and tax cons. Finley, Kumble, Wagner, Heine, Underberg, Manley, Myerson & Casey Beverly Hills 1986 –; honors: ed. in chief Whittier Law Review 1986-87; mem: Am. Inst. CPAs, Calif. Soc. CPAs, Am. Bar Assn. (Stu. Div.), Nat. Assn. of Accts. (dir. Ednl. Projects 1979-80); publs: Whittier Law Review, Mergers and Acquisitions- Federal Income Tax; Continuing Proprietary Interest Now Has Little to Do With Equity, 1985; Republican; Catholic; rec: skiing, tennis, puzzles. Res: 821 18th St. Hermosa Beach 90254 Ofc: Finley, Kumble et al. 9100 Wilshire Blvd Beverly Hills 90212

FIRESTONE, ANTHONY BROOKS, vintner; b. June 18, 1936, Akron, Ohio; s. Leonard K. and Polly (Curtis) F.; m. Catherine Boulton, Guildford, Eng., 1958; edn: BA, Columbia Coll. Career: with Firestone Tire & Rubber Co., 1960-72; vintner, pres. The Firestone Vineyard, Los Olivos 1972 –; dir: Firestone Tyre & Rubber Co. (G.B.), Growth Realty Cos., Tejon Ranch, Bank of Montecito; mil: enlisted corpsman US Army 1957-59; clubs: California, Cypress Point, Rancheros Visitadores; Episcopal (lay reader); rec: horses. Res: POB 36, Los Olivos 93441 Ofc: POB 244, Los Olivos 93441

FIREY, WARREN WILLIAM, SR., sales company ownwer; b. Sept. 23, 1923, Litchfield, Ill.; s. Jesse Northcutt and Elsie (Matthews) F.; m. Barbara Hunnicutt, Dec. 17, 1943; children: Warren Jr. b. 1944, Cynthia b. 1950; Denise b. 1959; edn: Long Beach State Coll. 1945-49; Univ. of Calif. Ext. 1950-62. Career: nat. sales mgr. Wesson Oil & Snowdrift Inc., New Orleans, La. 1951-62; nat. sales mgr. Festival Foods, Los Angeles 1962-67; mktg. dir. Calo Pet Foods Div., Borden Corp., Columbus, Ohio 1967-75; owner, mgr. Firey Sales, Sacramento 1975 –; mem: 20/30 Club, Toastmasters, Am. Legion, Boy Scouts of Am., Jr. Achievement (advr.), Western World Pet Supply Assn.; mil: s/sgt. US Army 1941-44; Democrat (pres. Huntington Beach Young Democrats 1948); Protestant; rec: philately, waterskiing, fishing. Res: 4924 Marlborough Way Carmichael 95608 Ofc: Firey Sales, 8179 Belvedere Ave. Sacramento 95826

FISCHER, ANNE KATRINE, lawyer; b. Nov. 20, 1951, Stamford, Conn.; d. Steen Christian and Maryanne (Bruun) F.; m. A. Lawrence Suther, Feb. 20, 1982; edn: BA, Univ. of Redlands 1973, MSEd, USC, 1975; JD cum laude, Western States Univ. 1982; admitted Calif. State Bar 1983. Career: community worker Los Angeles County Supt. of Schs., Cerritos 1974-76; tchr. Tracy Contn. High Sch. Cerritos 1976-83; atty. solo practice, 1983-84; atty. Fischer & DiFabbio, Ventura 1985 –; prof. Ventura Coll. of Law; honors: Am. Jurisprudence Awards (contracts II, criminal law, family law, corporations, wills, uniform comml. code), Law Review; mem: Calif., Ventura County bar assns., Ventura County Profl. Women's Network, Coalition Against Household Violence (bd.), CofC, Ventura County Taxpayers Assn., Friends of the Ventura Co. Commn. for Women (treas.); Republican. Ofc: Fischer & DiFabbio 5725 Ralson Ste 218 Ventura 93003

FISCHER, AUGUST ANTONIUS, executive; b. Feb. 7, 1939, Zurich, Switz.; s. August and Elisabetha (Zanola) F.; m. Gillian Streete, May 27, 1961; children: Natalie b. 1965, Russel b. 1968; edn: BS in printing tech./bus. adm., KGS Zurich, 1960. Career: mgmt. pos. E.I. Du Pont De Nemours Co. in Geneva, Frankfurt, London, Paris, Chgo. and Wilmington, Del., 1962-78; mng. dir. NAPP Systems (Europe) Ltd., England 1978-81, pres. NAPP Systems (USA) Inc., San Marcos, Ca. 1981 –; mem: The Pres.'s Assn.; Roman Catholic; rec: travel, golf. Ofc: NAPP Systems (USA) Inc. 360 S Pacific St San Marcos 92069

FISCHER, EDWARD PRESTON, surgical oncologist; b. June 3, 1939, Lima, Ohio; s. Edward B. and Evelyn Evangelina (Fiester) F.; m. Martha Hoeper, May 2, 1981; children: Tahlia b. 1983, Margeaux b. 1985; edn: BS, Wheaton Coll. 1961; MD, Baylor Coll. of Med. 1965; lic. med. Texas 1965, Calif. 1972; bd. certified Am. Coll. Surgeons 1978. Career: intern USAF Scott AFB, Ill. 1965-66; pediatrics 3rd AF Hq. London 1966-68; ob-gyn 7520 AF Hosp. London 1968-70; resident Baylor Coll. of Med. Houston 1970-72, res. I, research asst. 1970-71, asst. surg. 1971-72; res. gen. surg. II, III, IV (chief) Kern County Gen. Hosp. Bakersfield 1972-75; Am. Cancer Soc. fellow Univ. Texas System Cancer Ctr. Houston 1975-76; active staff Mercy Hosp., San Joaquin Comm. Hosp., Greater Bakersfield Meml. Hosp., Kern Med. Ctr. 1976 –, Lindsay Dist. Hosp., Univ. Hosp. UC San Diego 1978 –; cons. surg. Delano Comm. Hosp. 1978 –, John C. Fremont Hosp. Mariposa 1979 –; v.p. Kern Med. Ctr. 1983-84, chief of staff 1984 –; mem: U.T. M.D. Anderson Assocs. 1984 –; chmn. & mem. num. coms. at var. hosps.; clin. assoc. prof. of nsg. CSU Bakersfield 1981 –; ed. Kern County Med. Soc. Bulletin; abstract ed. Surgery, Gynecol. & Obstetrics 1976 –; liaison assoc. Commn. on Cancer, Am. Coll. Surg. 1977-; honors: Intern of the Year (USAF Hosp. 1966), Physicians Achievement Award (AMA 1972, CMA 1975-76, 1976-78) fellow: Am. Coll. Surg. 1978, AM. Coll. Angiology 1978, Internat. Coll. Surg. 1983; mem: Am.

Cancer Soc. (div. rep. 1979-81, chpt. pres. 1983-84), Kern County Gen. Hosp. Intern & Residents Assn. (v.p. 1973-74, pres. 1974-75), Am. Trauma Soc. (founding mem. 1974), Kern County Med. Soc., Michael E. DeBakey Internat. Cardiovascular Soc., Aircraft Owners & Pilots Assn., Rotary Internat. (bd.); mil: USAF (MC) 1965-70. Res: 4300 Flintridge Bakersfield 93306 Ofc: Edward P. Fischer M.D. 4001 Union Ave Bakersfield 93305

FISCHER, JEANETTE LUCILLE, occupational therapist; b. Nov. 13, 1937, Albert Lea, Minn.; d. Stewart Joseph and Bessie Lucille Stockett; m. Richard Allen Fischer, Oct. 22, 1960; children: Richard Arnold b. 1962, Robert Andrew b. 1966; edn: BS occ. therapy, Washington Univ. St. Louis 1960; MA health facility mgmt., Webster Coll. St. Louis 1981. Career: occupational therapy dept. aide St. Louis State Hosp. 1958-59; dir. psych. occup. therapy Alexian Bros. Hosp. St. Louis 1960-61; dir. occup. therapy Americana Healthcare Ctr. Florissant, Mo. 1975-79; mgmt. cons. Occup. Therapy Cons. St. Louis 1978-81; chief occup. therapist Physical Medicine & Rehab. Dept. St. Mary's Health Ctr. St. Louis 1979-81; dir. occup. therapy Fullerton (Calif.) Care Convales. Hosp. 1981-84; Orange region coord. Intermountain Health Care Rehab. Svcs., occup. therapy div, Orange 1984 –; guest spkr. hosps. and assns.; mem: Am. Occup. Therapy Assn., Occup. therapy Assn. of Calif. chpt. v.p. 1983-84), L.A. Occup. Therapy Dirs. Forum, Mo. Occup. Therapy Assn. (ed. newsletter 1960-62, treas. 1963-65, pub. rels. coord. 1966, pgm. chmn. 1978-79, pres. 1980-82), World Fedn. of Occup. Therapy, Midland Valley Estates Improvement Assn.; author: Productivity Measurement, Management Techniques for Physical and Occupational Therapists (Ed. Carroll English, English Pub. Co. 1984), research reports. Res: 4217 Elder Ave Seal Beach 90740 Ofc: Intermountain Health Care Rehab. Svcs. 1915 W Orangewood Ave Ste 221 Orange 92668

FISCHER, JUDD STUART, investment banker; b. Sept. 14, 1952, NY, NY; s. Mortimer Alexander and Lucille Edna (Lehman) F.; m. Martha Overby, Apr. 5, 1980; stepdau. Erin Rhoades b. 1969; edn: BA cum laude, Tufts Univ. 1974; econs. major, UC San Francisco 1978-80. Career: splst. setting up securities subsidiaries; mgr. Nat. Advanced Systems, Mt. View 1979-81; v.p. fin. Fiscal Funding Co., Inc., San Francisco 1981-84; exec. v.p. Grigsby & Assocs., S.F. 1983-84; v.p. public fin., Birr, Wilson & Co., Inc. 1984 –; mem. BENS, NASD (Assn. Municipal Leasing, speaker at nat. conf.); civic: Jewish Comm. Center, Smithsonian, Metropolitan Mus.; rec: creative writing, golf, tennis. Res: 330 Freitas Ct Danville 94526 Ofc: Birr, Wilson & Co. Inc. 155 Sansome St 4th Flr San Francisco 94104

FISCHL, PETER L., inventor, company president; b. July 19, 1930, Budapest, Hungary, nat. 1962; s. Tibor and Edith (Neubauer) F.; m. 2d. Catherine Csemy; children: Tibor (by previous m.); Catherine Victoria, b. 1975; edn: AS, Los Angeles Trade Tech., 1974. Career: with family owned bus. (of 75 years) in Budapest; preparation mgr., California Homes Publ.; cameraman, Walt Disney Studios, Burbank; currently pres., The Mini "T" Electric Motor Car Co., Inc., Glendale (dealers in Palm Springs, sold 2 cars to Prince Abdulaziz of Saudi Arabia); inventions: spl. meat cooker/warmer (1946), Fischl Tournament Chess Set (1974), Mini "T" Car Wonder (1982); co. will produce first gasoline model auto (20 mph) in 1984 (will appear in sev. motion pics., TV shows); rec: chess (rated 1680 by Am. Chess Fedn.), piano, magic. Address: 1140 Highland Ave Glendale 91202

FISHER, DELBERT ARTHUR, academic physician; b. Aug. 12, 1928, Placerville; s. Arthur Lloyd and Thelma (Johnson) F.; m. Beverly Carne, Jan. 1951; children: David b. 1956, Mary b. 1958, Thomas b. 1958; edn: BA, UC Berkeley 1950, MD, UC San Francisco 1953; Diplomate Am. Bd. of Pediatrics 1959. Career: pediatric resident UC San Francisco 1953-55; pediatric endocrinology fellow Univ. Oregon Med. Sch. 1957-60; asst. prof., assoc. prof., prof. of pediatrics Univ. Arkansas Med. Sch. 1960-68; prof. of pediatrics UCLA Sch. Med. 1968 –, chief Pediatric Endocrinology, Harbor-UCLA Med. Ctr., Torrance 1968-75, research prof. developmental & perinatal biology 1975-85, assoc. chmn. Pediatrics, Harbor-UCLA Med. Ctr. 1974-85, prof./chmn. Dept. Pediatrics, 1985 –; chief editor J. Clin. Endocrinol. Metab. (1978-83), Pediatric Research (1984-89); subspecialty com. Pediatric Endocrinology, Am. Acad. Ped. 1976-79, Written Exam com. 1977-80; author over 300 sci. articles, 80 book chapters, 5 books; research related to developmental biology and endocrinology and to clin. endocrinology; most recent book: (w/ F. DeLange, P. Malvaux) Pediatric Thyroidology (Karger AG, Basel, 1985); awards: Phi Beta Kappa (1964), Alpha Omega Alpha (1985), NIH Research career devel. award (1964-68), Am. Acad. of Ped. Research Award (1982); mem: W. Soc. for Ped. Research (pres. 1982-83), The Endocrine Soc. (pres. 1983-84), Am. acad. Ped. (1960), Soc. Pediatric Research (v.p. 1973-74), Am. Ped. Soc., Am. Throid Assn., Am. Soc. Clin. Invest., Lawson Wilkins Ped. Endo. Soc. (pres. 1982-83); mil: capt. USAF Med. Corps 1955-57; Democrat; Protestant; rec: sailing, swimming, jogging. Res: 4 Pear Tree Ln Rolling Hills Estates 90274 Ofc: Dept. Pediatrics, Harbor-UCLA Medical Center 1000 W Carson St Torrance 90509

FISHER, EARL WEBSTER, JR., stock brokerage president; b. Aug. 18, 1935, Hollywood; s. Earl W. and Sofia (Brockman) F.; m. Carol R., Aug. 22, 1959; 1 dau., Audrey E. b. 1967; edn: BA, Pomona Coll. 1957; Fulbright Scholar to Germany in music, 1961. Career: opera singer in Germany 1961-68, sang in Coburg, Heidelberg and Muenster on full year contracts; stock broker, 1968 –, founder (with 3 ptnrs.), pres. Stern Fisher Atkinson Inc, Los Angeles 1978 –; mem. bd. Idyllwild Sch. of Music and the Arts, bd. Catholic Big Brothers; works: perform regularly with the Palisades Sym. and Isomata, also Lieder recitals in Davis and Santa Monica; mil: 6 mos. Army; Democrat; Roman Catholic; rec: photog., singing, racquetball. Ofc: Stern Fisher Atkinson Inc 623 West 6th St Ste 716 Los Angeles 90014

FISHER, ROBERT LEWIS, education and training consultant; b. July 3, 1929, Berlin, Pa.; s. Lewis Milton and Erma Grace (Stevanus) F.; children: Jane b. 1952, Susan b. 1958; edn: BS, Univ. Md. 1957, M.Ed., 1970. Career: tech. writer Sandia Corp. Albuquerque, NM 1957-59; tng. group supv. Vitro Labs Silver Spring, Md. 1959-63; mgr. eastern div. Data Design Labs Arlington, Va. 1963-73; v.p. Aero- Science Corp. Rockville, Md. 1973-74; pgm. mgr. Data Design Labs Arlington, Va. 1974-76; mgr. eastern ops. TRIGA Arlington, Va. 1976-79; tng. mgr. western region ARINC Research Corp. San Diego 1979 –; mem: Nat. Soc. Performance and Instruction, Armed Forces Soc. for Communication and Electronics, Soc. Logistics Engrs., Nat. Security Indsl. Assn. (space com.); publ: var. tech. reports and mgmt. plans devel. under govt. contracts; mil: tech. sgt. USAF 1948-52; Democrat; Protestant; rec: gardening, woodwork. Res: 5616 Michael St San Diego 92105 Ofc: ARINC Research Corp. 4055 Hancock St San Diego 92110

FISHLER, THOMAS GEORGE, educator, counselor; b. Sept. 7, 1923, McClave, Colo.; s. Alex and Goldie Blanche (Johnson) F.; m. Nadine L. Nichols, June 12, 1947; m. 2d Kris I. Dishneau, Feb. 19, 1960; children: Stephen b. 1950, Deborah b. 1954, Kimberly b. 1958, Thomas C. b. 1981; edn: BA, deaf edn., Gallaudet Coll., Wash DC 1942-47; postgrad. Colo. Coll. 1956-60; grad. work UC Riverside 1967-69, CSU Los Angeles 1963-66. Career: tchr., counselor Sch. for Deaf, Morgantown, N.C. 1947-48; editor/pub. Ketchikan (Alaska) Daily News 1949-52; tchr., counselor Sch. for Deaf & Blind, Colo. Springs, Colo. 1952-60, Sch. for Deaf, Riverside, Calif. 1960 –; spl. edn. curriculum coord./instr. Riverside City Coll. (1969-75), spl. edn. cons. CSU Northridge (1961-63), CSU San Diego (1973-75); insurance/ securities broker; founder/ pres. Raincross Lions Club for Deaf (1975-76); conv. chmn. of Tri-Group dedicated to eliminating communication barriers for the deaf (1965); honors: comm. svc. award, Ketchikan (1952), disting. svc. award CSUN; mem. Colo. Assn. of Deaf (pres. 1958-59), Calif. Assn. Deaf (v.p. 1964-73), Calif. Assn. Tchrs. of Hearing Impaired (pres., ed. 1964-68), Nat. Assn. of Deaf, Nat. Com. to Preserve Soc. Sec. & Medicare, Cousteau Soc., Nat. Platform Assn., Raincross Lions Club, Smithsonian Soc., Gallaudet and Colo. Coll. Alumni Assns.; publs: contbns. to profl. jours. in edn. of the deaf; Democrat; Baptist; rec: outdoors, tennis. Ofc: School for Deaf 3044 Horace St Riverside 92507

FISHMAN, JOEL LAWRENCE, public relations co. president; b. Oct. 12, 1947, Los Angeles; s. Herman Jerome and Dorothy (Feld) F.; m. Catherine Doubleday, June 23, 1974; edn: BA, UC Berkeley 1969; JD, USC Law Center 1976; admitted Calif. State Bar 1977, Dist. Columbia Bar. Career: adminstrv. asst. US Cong. Thomas Rees 1970-73; corporate and entertainment lawyer 1976-83; dir. Cross-Country Olympic Torch Relay Project, LA Olympic Organizing Com. 1983-84; pres. Joel L. Fishman & Assocs. (Public Relations, marketing, fundraising), 1984 –; honors: Phi Beta Kappa 1969, Key to City of Indianapolis 1984; mem. Calif., D.C. bar assns., Public Relations Soc. of Am.; chmn. Calif. Lexington Group bus., profl., polit. orgn.; exec. com. UCLA Govtl. Rels. Prog.; Los Angeles Conservancy; Coro Found.; works: planned and organized the 1984 x-c Olympic Torch Relay and related multi-million dollar youth sports fundraiser (1983-84); publ: article in Special Events Report (4/85); Democrat; Jewish; rec: sailing, tennis, music (percussionist). Ofc: Joel L. Fishman & Associates 450 No Roxbury Dr Ste 602 Beverly Hills 90210

FITZGIBBONS, JO ANN, college professor, writer, lecturer; b. Feb. 18, 1934, Blakely, Ga.; d. Robert Lee and Ruth Marie (Glass) Jordan; m. Robert Fitzgibbons, De4c. 22, 1956; children: Kathy b. 1957, Nancy b. 1959, Eleanor b. 1960; edn: So. Business Univ. Atlanta, Ga. 1951-53; Ga. State Univ. 1953-54; tchg. credl., UC Los Angeles 1973. Career: secty. West Co. Atlanta, Ga. 1953-56; fashion model Atlanta, Memphis 1952-69; Phil-A-Halle Maid of Catlon Contest 1968-69; instr. Dress for Success for employees of various corps. 1974-76; instr. flight attendants; instr. fashion Saddleback Coll. 1981-84, fashion seminars UC Irvine; owner, designer Fitzgibbons Color & Fashion Ctr. Upland; instr. Chaffey Comm. Coll.; producer fashion shows; honors: Outstanding Young Women of Am. (1966), Recogn. Award, Excellence in the Arts (West End Republican; Women 1976); mem: Nat. Charity League, Upland Assistance League, Republican Women, San Antonio Comm. Hosp. Soc., Republican; Nat. Com., Repub. Pres. Task Force, Upland CofC Golden Circle; book: Truth in Living Color (1986); Christian; rec: swimming. Res: 1080 W Buffington Upland 91786 Ofc: Fitzgibbons Color & Fashion Ctr. 1655 N Mountain Ave Ste 105 Upland 91786

FITZSIMMONS, LARRY ALLEN, electronics engineer, computer scientist; b. Sept. 3, 1946, Kimberly, W.Va.; s. Jerome James and Lillian Mae (Belcher) F.; edn: BSEE, summa cum laude, Univ. New Haven 1975; MSCS, UCLA 1982. Career: electronics design engr. Philips Medical Sys., Shelton, Conn. 1974-79; electronics design engr. Consolidated Controls, Bethel, Conn. 1979-80; senior tech. staff Hughes El Segundo 1980 –; research: next generation computer architectures and technologies for data and signal processing, fault tolerant computing systems; honors: UNH Acad. Scholar 1972, CRC Chemistry Award 1972, EE Honor Soc. 1975-76, Hughes Fellowship 1980-82; mem: UNH Alumni Assn., UCLA Alumni Assn.; mil: Sp5, US Army 1965-68, NCSM, MRM w.MSL BAR, Letters of Commdn., USAR 1968-71; Catholic. Res: 4475 Pacific Coast Hwy, J206, Torrance 90505 Ofc: Hughes, Box 902, El Segundo

FJELSTAD, MICHAEL MAURICE, lawyer; b. May 23, 1947, Rapid City, So. Dak.; s. John Erwin and Marjorie Elizabeth (Wintrode) F.; edn: BS, San Jose State Univ. 1969; MBA, UCLA 1971; JD, Univ. of Santa Clara 1977; admitted to Calif. Bar 1978; CPA, Calif. 1977; Real Estate Broker, Calif. 1974; Calif. Jr. Coll. Tchg. Cred. Career: auditor Kenneth Leventhal & Co CPA, Los Angeles and San Francisco 1971-72; revenue agent IRS 1972-76; atty., CPA, broker self-empl. 1976 –; instr. De Anza Coll. 1978-79; honors: Kenneth Leventhal Fellowship Award, 1971; mem: Am. Bar Assn., Am. Inst. CPAs, Calif. Soc. CPAs, Calif. Assn. of Realtors; rec: writing, weightlifting, swimming. Res: 414 Rio Del Mar Blvd Aptos 95003 Ofc: Michael M. Fjelstad, 1790 Winchester Blvd. Ste. 1 Campbell 95008

FLACCO, SIDONIE MARIANNE, medical center executive; b. Dec. 1, 1930, Phila., PA; d. Paul and Marie Margaret (Spaeth) Alemann; m. Richard Flacco (dec. 1964), Feb. 5, 1949; children: Paul b. 1950, Richard b. 1955, Renee b. 1955; edn: BA, Univ. of La Verne 1970; M.Ed. 1971. Career: data reduction Aerojet, Azusa 1963-8; instr. in German/ coord. of German Dept. Univ. of LaVerne 1971-2; asst. to Dean of Contin. Edn. 1972-4; chief therapist St. Luke Hosp., Pasadena 1974-5; marriage & family counselor, pvt. practice, LaVerne 1975-83; asst. dir./ clinical supvr. Memorial Med. Ctr. of Long Beach Adolescent Chemical Dependency Unit 1983-84; pvt. practice Claremont 1984 –; organizer/ consultant, Court Diversion Pgm.; instr. Grad. Counseling, supvr. counselors and students; honors: Calif. rep. at 1959 Cured Cancer Congress, Wash. DC; Am. Cancer Soc. 1960 Poster Family; featured on Ralph Edwards TV show, This Is Your Life; mem: nat. Alliance of Family Life; Calif. Assn. of Marriage & Family Therapists; Nat. Assn. of Alcoholism Counselors; Calif. Assn. of Alcoholism Counselors; publs: contbr. theories and assistance for book: Pendulum of Choice by Johanna Alemann; subject of biographic article, Redbook Mag. 1958; author: Adolescent Chemical Dependency Unit program at Memorial Med. Ctr. of Long Beach; Democrat; Protestant; rec: poetry, philosophy, study groups. Address: 605 Colby Cr Dr, No. 6, Claremont 91711

FLACHMANN, MICHAEL CHARLES, college English professor; b. Nov. 3, 1942, St. Louis, Mo.; s. Charles Randall and Charlotte Marie (Widen) F.; m. Kim Marschel, Aug. 30, 1969; children: Christopher Michael b. 1982, Laura Marschel b. 1986; edn: BA, Univ. of the South 1964; MA, Univ. of Virginia 1965; PhD, Univ. of Chicago 1972. Career: instr. English Southern Ill. Univ., Edwardsville, Ill. 1965-68; grad. student in English lit. Univ. Chgo. 1969-72; asst. prof. English Dept. CSC Bakersfield 1972-76, assoc. prof. 1976-81, prof. 1981 –; dir. ednl. pgms. and damaturge Calif. Shakespearean Fest. and La Jolla Playhouse 1979-84; dramaturge Utah Shakespeare Fest.; honors: Phi Beta Kappa, DuPont Fellow Univ. Va., Harper Fellow Univ. Chgo., Distng. Prof., Calif. State Coll. Bakersfield; mem: Modern Language Assn., Shakespeare Assn. of Am., Early English Text Soc., Renaissance Soc. of Am.; publs: co-author, Shakespeare's Lovers, and, Shakespeare's Women, So. Ill. Univ. Pres.; co-ed., Beware the Cat, Huntington Lib. Press.; co-autohr, The Prose Reader: Essay for College Writers, Prentice Hall Pub.; articles in Shakespeare Quarterly, Studies in English Literature, Medieval and Renaissance Drama in England, The Renaissance Soc. of So. Calif. Newsletter; rec: tennis, judo (3rd degree black belt). Res: 1236 Fairway Dr. Bakersfield 93309 Ofc: Calif. State Coll., 9001 Stockdale Hwy., Bakersfield 93309

FLAKS, HOWARD ERROL, physician/weight reduction specialist; b. Dec. 15, 1952, Johannesburg, S. Africa; s. Jack, MD, and Audrey F.; edn: BA, Univ. of the Witwatersrand, S.A. 1973, honors degree in psych. 1974, MD, 1980; MA in psych., cum laude, Univ. of S. Africa 1975; lic. MD, Calif., S. Africa; Qual. Clin. Psychologist. Career: intern in surg. and internal med., J.G. Strijdom Hosp., S. Africa; res. int. med., Cedars Sinai Med. Ctr., Los Angeles; currently: full time wt. reduction practice, Beverly Hills; cons., communicable diseases, LA County; instr. USC (Central Health Dist., L.A.); one of official physician 1984 Olympic Games; mem: Bev. Hills CofC, AMA, CMA, LA Co. Med. Assn., Am. Soc. of Bariatric Physicians (pub. rels. chmn.), Am. Soc. of STD, So. African Med. Assn., So. African Psychol. Assn., Am. Coll. of Nutrition; Advis. Council BSA, Youth Leadership Soc., Univ. of Witwatersrand Alumni Soc.; frequent spkr. on med. and psych. aspects of obesity; num. publs. in field; num. TV interviews on subject of obesity; contbg. ed. Muscle & Fitness Mag.; Jewish; rec: talent scout for a model agcy. Ofc: Howard Flaks MD, 9400 Brighton Way, 202, Beverly Hills 90210

FLANAGAN, ROBERT JAMES, JR., health care executive; b. May 10, 1945, Youngstown, Ohio; s. Robert, Sr. and Lucile Alexis (Donnet) F.; m. Sally Anne Leahy; children: Robert b. 1967, Jennifer b. 1971, Lawrence b. 1975; edn: AB, acctg., Grove City Coll. 1967; MS in acctg., Ariz. State Univ. 1968, PhD in acctg., 1971; Certified Public Acct., Ill. and Md. Career: audit mgr. Coopers & Lybrand, Chgo. 1970-74; v.p. fin. Maryland Hosp. Assn., Lutherville, Md. 1974-76; ptnr. C.W. Amos & Co., Baltimore 1976-78; group v.p./corp. treas. Am. Hosp. Assn., Chgo. 1978-82; exec. v.p. Pacific Health Resources, Los Angeles 1982-, currently pres. and chief exec. ofcr.; bd. dirs: Pacific Health Resources; chmn. bd. Convenience Care Centers, Inc.; chmn. bd. PHR Capital Corp.; chmn. bd. PHR Employee Leasing Corp.; past dir. Green Road Mgmt. Co., Am. Hosp. Assoc. Services, Inc.; awards: Nat. Edn. Act doctoral fellow 1967-70; mem. Am. Inst. CPAs; clubs: Elks, Great Lakes Cruising, Los Angeles Athletic; coauthor: Hospital Computer Systems Planning (1981), finl. jour. article (1978); Roman Catholic; rec: photog., sailing, tennis. Res: 3224 Griffith Park Blvd Los Angeles 90027 Ofc: Pacific Health Resources 1423 South Grand Ave Los Angeles 90015

FLATLEY, DANIEL K., investment banker; b. Aug. 5, 1953, Milwaukee, Wisc.; s. James Michael and Suzanne Nell (Futch) F.; edn: AB, honors, Univ. of Notre Dame 1975; JD, Georgetown Univ. Law Ctr. 1978; MBA, The Wharton Sch. Univ. of Penn. 1982; admitted to Fla. Bar (1978). Career: law clerk to

Chief US Dist. Ct. Judge William Stafford 1978-80; atty. Johnson, Blakely, Pope, Bokor & Ruppel 1982-84; mng. dir. Madsen & Co. Inc., Los Angeles 1985−; honors: Law Review, Georgetown Univ.; mem: Florida Bar Assn., Bars of U.S. Dist. Cts. for No. and Middle Dists. of Fla. and Fifth and Eleventh US Circuit Cts. of Appeal, The Wharton Club of Los Angeles, The Notre Dame Club of Los Angeles (dir. Manger 2); Democrat; Catholic. Ofc: Madsen & Co., 624 So. Grand Ave. Ste. 2900 Los Angeles 90017

FLEISCHER, WAYNE NEAL, financial planning co. president; b. Jan. 9, 1945, Pittsburgh, Penn.; s. Benjamin and Edna Leatrice (Krauss) F.; m. Rosemarie, Sept. 2, 1979; children: Jennifer b. 1980, Jonathan b. 1982; edn: MSM (mgt.) and MSFS (finl. svcs.) pgms., American Coll., Bryn Mawr, Pa. current; Calif. lic. Life and Disability Analyst, Reg. Tax Interviewer; reg. prin. NASD; commodity trading advisor CFTC; desig: Cert. Finl. Plnnr. (CFP), Chartered Finl. Cons. (CFS), Chartered Life Underwriter (CLU). Career: finl. plnnr., pres., IFP Advisors Ltd., Ventura 1981−; tchg. finl. plnng. practitioner, IAFP, LUTC; honors: Top Ventura Finl. Plnng.; mem: IAFP, VALU, ICFP, Nat. Soc. of Public Accts., Nat. EA Soc., MDRT, Registry of Finl. Plnng. Practitioners; author: articles for industry; Republican; rec: flying. Ofc: IFP Advisors Ltd., 1767 Goodyear Ave. Ste. 14 Ventura 93003

FLEISCHMANN, ERNEST MARTIN, music administrator; b. Dec. 7, 1924, Frankfurt, Germany; s. Gustav and Antonia (Koch) F.; m. Elsa Leviseur, Sept. 22, 1953; div.; children: Stephanie b. 1962, Martin b. 1963, Jessica b. 1965; edn: B.Commerce, Univ. of Cape Town, 1950, B.Music, 1954; postgrad. studies, South African Coll. of Music 1954-56. Career: conductor Johannesburg Symphony Orch., 1942; asst. condr. South African Nat. Opera, 1948-51, and Cape Town University Opera, 1950-54; condr. South African Coll. of Music Choir, 1950-52, and Labia Grand Opera Company, 1953-55; music organizer Van Riebeeck Festival, Cape Town 1952; dir. of Music and Drama, Johannesburg Festival, 1956; gen. secty. London Symphony Orch., 1959-67; dir. for Europe, CBS Records, 1967-69; exec. dir. Los Angeles Philharmonic and general dir. Hollywood Bowl, 1969−; awards: John Steinway Award for disting. service to music (1979), Pres.'s Special Award, Assn. of Calif. Symphony Orchestras (1980), Award of Merit, Los Angeles Junior CofC (1985); mem: Am. Symphony Orchestra League (v.chmn. bd. dirs.), Calif. Confedn. of the Arts (bd. dirs.). Ofc: Los Angeles Philharmonic, 135 North Grand Ave Los Angeles 90012

FLEMING, ROBERT EDWARD, advertising co. executive; b. Apr. 29, 1950; s. Robert and Rhana June (Lyle) F.; edn: Northeastern Univ. 1969-70; Harvard Univ. 1970-71; MBA, Hamilton Univ. 1974. Career: pres. Fleming Corp. Boston 1973-76; v.p. Pacific Advtg. L.A. 1976-80; advtg. dir. Sohio 1980-81; pres. Aptech Inc. 1981-83; dir. corp. communications Optical Radiation Corp. 1984-86; dir. Adlab Corp.; cons. Castle & Cook & Sonoma Vineyards 1984; honors: Art Directors Award (ADC 1980), Gold Award (Ad. Mgmt. Assn. 1977), Mktg. Gold Award (US Mktg. Assn. 1981), Communs. Silver Award (ACC 1982); mem: Am. Mgmt. Assn. 1984-, US CofC 1982-, Advtg. Club of L.A., Ad Club of Boston 1976, Calif. Photog. Club; publ: article In House Agencies (Ad Week 1983); 1st high-quality co-op advtg. pgm. 1983; Republican; Catholic; rec: photog. Res: 18653 Ventura Blvd Apt 342 Tarzana 91356 Ofc: Optical Radiation Corp. 1300 Optical Dr Azusa 91702

FLEMING, THOMAS JAMES, real estate consultant; b. June 8, 1899, Chgo.; s. Cornelius James and Catherine (Murphy) F.; m. Theodora Lynch, Dec. 19, 1931, Dec. 1963; children: Thomas J., Jr. b. 1921, William Campbell b. 1923; Career: real estate w/ Potter Palmer Estate, Chgo. 1916-19; Ross, Browne & Fleming, Chgo. 1919-, ret. mng. partner 1950−; moved to Palm Springs, Calif. 1951, moved to La Jolla 1955; past pres., treas., dir. of 919 Corp., Chgo.; active in devel. of North Mich. Ave. (Magnificent Mile), Chgo. 1916-50; Chgo. Real Estate Bd. (pres. 1941, chmn. of renting & mgmt. div. 1931-4-5; dir. 1936-8, 1942-3); past mem. Ill. Assn. of Real Estate Bds., Am. Chpt. of Internat. R.E. Fedn., Citizens Bd. of Loyola Univ. of Chgo.; past dir.: Coachella Valley SVLCC (P.S.), La Jolla Trust & Svgs Bank; donor, UCSD Cancer Ctr.; past bd. mem. San Diego Mus. of Art; mem: La Jolla Mus. Art (life), Scripps Clinic & Resrch Found. Assocs., S.D. Opera Guild (past dir.), S.D. Sym. Orch. Assn. (past dir.), Univ. S.D. Pres. Club; UCSD Sch. of Med. Assocs. (charter), Opera Guild of the Desert (fmr); Republican. Address: 5329 La Jolla Hermosa Ave La Jolla 92037

FLETCHER, LOIS LORETTA, real estate broker; b. Sept. 13, 1926, Leflore Co., Okla.; d. Alec L. and Ruth (Cox) Burnett; m. Eugene Fletcher, Nov. 18, 1959; edn: San Diego State 1942-44, Mesa Coll. 1970-72, UC San Diego 1972, City Coll. 1973; desig: GRI, CRS, CRB, CE, Senior Appraiser, Cert. Counselor. Career: asst. librarian National City Public Library 1942, 43; bookkeeper, asst. prop. mgr. Burnett & Horning, National City 1944-55; real estate sales agt., broker, 1955−, broker/owner Fletcher Realty, Smyrna, Ga. 1955-70, San Diego 1970−; real estate exchange splst., wrote Beginning Exchange Course for R.E. (1977), taught exchange courses; recipient 15 plaques for Exchanging, 52 certs. of Merit and Outstanding Service, Exchangor of the Year; named Woman of Achievement, Pres.'s Council of Womens Service, Bus. & Profl. Clubs of San Diego (1980); mem: NAR (life mem. RAP-Realtors Active in Politics), Calif. Assn. Realtors (dir. 10 yrs), San Diego Bd. Realtors (dir. 10 yrs, v.p. 1984, 1986), Calif. Womens Council of Realtors (gov. 1983), 99 Club (pres. So. Calif. chpt. 1986), FLI, NCE, WCR, NIREC, NIREA, University Ave Bus. Assn.; Republican (Pres. Task Force); Catholic; rec: oil painting, gourmet cooking, fishing, piano. Ofc: Fletcher Realty 3583 University Ave San Diego 92104

FLETCHER, RUFUS BURTON, JR., lawyer, educator; b. Dec. 25, 1950, Ocala, Fla.; s. Rufus Burton, Sr. and Emma Callie (Hunter) F.; edn: AA, Lake City Comm. Coll. 1970; BS, Univ. West Fla. 1975, MBA, 1976; JD, Western State Univ., 1980; Calif. Tchg. Credl., Law, Mgmt., Mktg.; admitted Ga. State Bar 1980, Calif. 1981. Career: atty., owner Fletcher & Assocs., Torrance 1981−; prof. El Camino Coll. 1980−; assoc. atty. Mix & Hodges, Redondo Beach 1981-82; honors: Corpus Juris Secundum awd., Honors Moot Ct. dir. 1979-80, advocate 2d place team 1978, Law Review edtl. bd. 1979-80; listed Who's Who Among Students in Am. Univs. & Colls. (1974-75), Outstanding Young Men of Am. (1973); mem: Toastmasters (Judges Night pgm. chmn. 1979), Internat. Law Soc. 1979-80, Phi Alpha Delta 1978-80, Sigma Alpha Epsilon (pres. 1974-76); mil: cpl. MP, USMC 1970-73; Republican; Advent Christian; rec: skiing, jogging. Res: 17009 Ainsworth Ave Torrance 90504 Ofc: Fletcher & Assocs., 18436 Hawthorne Blvd Ste 101 Torrance 90504

FLICK, JOHN EDMOND, corporate executive; b. Mar. 14, 1922, Franklin, Pa.; s. E. L. and Mary M. Flick; m. Lois A. Lange, Apr. 20, 1946; children: Gregory A., b. 1947; Scott E., b. 1952, Lynn E., b. 1956; Ann E., b. 1960; edn: stu. Univ. of Penn., Northwestern Univ., 1941-44, 45; LL.B., 1948; grad. Legal Judge Advocate General's Sch., Univ. of Va. 1960-61; admitted to State Bar of Calif., Ill., Fed. Dist. and Appeals Cts., US Supreme Ct. Career: atty. at law and faculty mem. Calif. Western Univ. Law Sch., 1949-50; faculty US Mil. Acad., West Point 1954-57; counsel-dir. contracts Litton Industries, Ind. 1963-67; senior v.p., gen. counsel, secty., dir. Bangor Punta Corp., 1967-70; bd. dirs. Piper Aircraft Corp., 1969; senior v.p., gen. counsel Times Mirror Co., 1970−; dir. Tejon Ranch Co. 1975−; author: State Tax Liability of Servicemen and Their Dependents, Wash. and Lee Law Rev. (1964); honors: acad. awards, Lawyers Cooperative Co., Judge Adv. Assn., Am. Bar Assn., 1961, Army Commendation Medal; mem: Am., Calif., Los Angeles County bar assns., Judge Adv. Alumni Assn., Bd. of Visitors Northwestern Univ. Law Sch., Am. Soc. of Corp. Sectys., Jonathan Club; chmn. Los Angeles Advis. Bd. of the Salvation Army; mil: ofcr. Judge Adv. Gen.'s Corps 1950-63, lt. col. USAR (ret.). Ofc: Times-Mirror Square, Los Angeles 90053

FLOOD, J(OHN) PATRICK, detective, instructor; b. Oct. 10, 1946, Omaha, Neb.; s. Charles B. and Mary C. (Swotek) F.; m. Carolyn, June 28, 1969; children: Ryan b. 1976, Kelley b. 1979; edn: AA, American River Coll. 1971; BA, St. Mary's Coll. 1978; MA, Chapman Coll. 1981; lifetime jr. coll. tchg. credl. Career: salesman Sears Roebuck 1969-72; detective Sacramento County Sheriff's Dept. 1972−; instr. Law Enforcement Acad., No. Calif. Law Enforcement Tng. Ctr.; spkr. seminars UC Davis; cons. Calif. Youth Authority, several No. Calif. municipal agencies, school dists., social/ medical/ psychological svcs.; mem: Calif. Juvenile Ofcrs. Assn., Calif. Sexual Assaults Investigators Assn., Boy Scouts of Am., USC Delinquency Control Alumni; publs: articles in field, Chief of Police (1983); mil: E-4 USNR 1967-69, Vietnam Svc., Vietnam Disting. Svc.; Republican; Episcopal (jr. warden); rec: investments, real estate, boy scouts. Ofc: Sacramento County Sheriff POB 988 Sacramento 95805

FLOR, LOY LORENZ, chemist, corrosion engineer, consultant; b. Apr. 25, 1919, Luther, Okla.; s. Alfred Charles and Nellie Margurette (Wilkerson) F.; m. Virginia L. Pace, Oct. 1, 1946; children: Charles b. 1950, Scott b. 1952, Gerald b. 1954, Donna Jeanne b. 1959, Cynthia Gail b. 1960; edn: BA in chem., San Diego State Coll. 1941; Reg. Profl. Engr., Calif. Career: Helix Water Dist., La Mesa 1947-84, supr. corrosion control 1956-84, chief chemist and supr. of water quality 1963-84; independent cons., 1984−; mem: Am. Chem. Soc. (chmn. San Diego Sect. 1965), Am. Water Works Assn. (chmn. Water Quality Div., Calif. Sect. 1965), Nat. Assn. of Corrosion Engrs. (chmn. W. Region 1970), Masons; mil: 1st lt. USAAF 1941-45; Republican; Presbyterian; rec: travel/camping, hiking, swim. Ofc: 11315 Manzanita Rd Lakeside 92040

FLORA, JAMES HOWARD, utility co. executive; b. Feb. 25, 1926, Burbank; s. Marshall John and Myrtle Johanna (Anderson) F.; m. Patricia, Aug. 20, 1948; children: Susan b. 1955, Debra b. 1957; edn: BA, Univ. Redlands 1950; Calif. lic. Real Estate Broker (1984). Career: lighting cons. So. Calif. Edison Co., 1951-54, power cons. 1954-60, area devel. cons. 1960-69, exec. asst. 1970-73, area mgr. 1973−; apptd. City of La Habra Planning Commn. (1968-81, chmn. 1969, 75, 81), elected La Habra City Council (1984-88), chmn. Redevel. Agency (1985-86), mayor pro tem (1986-87), chmn. Indsl. Devel. Authority (1985-86), mem. Orange County League of Cities; apptd. Santa Fe Springs Public Improvement Corp. (v.p. 1979-); mem: Downey CofC (pres. 1975-76), Santa Fe Springs CofC (pres. 1977-79), La Habra CofC, La Habra Tennis Club (pres. 1979-80); patron Childrens Hosp. of Orange Co.; mil: radioman 2/c US Navy 1944-46, Pres. Cit.- Okinawa, So. Pacific battle stars; Republican; Presbyterian; rec: golf, tennis. Address: La Habra 90631

FLORA, ROBERT EUGENE, corporate security executive; b. Feb. 5, 1931, Watertown, NY; s. Frank Vona and Alfonsina (Beronidinelli) F.; m. Wanda E. Ashcroft, Oct. 31, 1952; children: Roberta b. 1953, Therese b. 1954, Mark b. 1956, Michael b. 1957, Marcia b. 1959, Patrick b. 1960; edn: BS aero. engrg., AF Inst. of Technol. 1959; MBA, Univ. So. Calif. 1965. Career: commr. parks & rec. Torrance 1969-73, Saratoga 1975-80; pgm. mgr. ESL Inc. Sunnyvale 1974−; honors: Beta Gamma Sigma (USC 1965); mem: ASIS, AFA, Rotary Internat., USC Alumni, Retired Ofcrs. Assn., Bay Area Trojan Club, United Way (trustee); mil: lt. col. USAF 1952-74, 7 Air Medals, Vietnam Cross, Disting. Svc.; Republican; Catholic; rec: handball. Res: 19560 Ardmore Ct Saratoga 95070 Ofc: ESL Inc. 495 Java Dr Sunnyvale 94088-3510

FLORENCE, KENNETH JAMES, lawyer; b. July 31, 1943, Hanford; s. Ivy Owen and Louella (Dobson) F.; m. Verena Demuth, 1967; edn: BA cum laude, Whittier Coll, 1965; JD, UC Hastings Coll of Law 1974. Career: dist. plant mgr. Pacific Tel. & Tel. Co., San Francisco Bay Area, 1969-71; attorney, firm of Parker, Milliken, Clark & O'Hara, Los Angeles 1974-77; partner, firm of Dern, Mason, Swerdlow & Floum, Los Angeles 1978-84; founding ptnr. firm of Swerdlow & Florence, Beverly Hills 1984—; honors: Boswell Scholarship 1961, Pi Sigma Alpha, Phi Alpha Theta; past pres., Westside Legal Services, Inc.; mem: Am. Bar Assn., NOW, Sierra Club. Mil: lt. USNR 1966-69, Eur., S.E.Asia; decorated bronze star, Navy Commend.; Democrat; Prot.; rec: running, sports. Res: 1063 Stradella Rd Los Angeles 90077 Ofc: Swerdlow & Florence 9401 Wilshire Blvd Ste 828 Beverly Hills 90212

FLORENCE, TESSIE LIM, travel consultant; b. Sept. 19, 1943, La Libertad, Negros Oriental, Philippines; d. Pacita A. Lim; m. Louis L. Florence (dec. 1985), Mar. 10, 1980; edn: BS in elem. edn., Silliman Univ. 1965, MA in sci. tchg., 1975, tchr. credential in spl. sci., 1975. Career: grade sch. tchr. BPS, La Libertad, Neg. Or., Philippines 1965-72; supvsg. instr. Silliman Univ. Elem. Sch., Dumaguete City, Phil. 1972-74; spl. sci. tchr. Dole Internat. Sch.-Polomolok, South Cotabato, Phil. 1974-76; book advisor Timelife, Philippines, Makati, Phil. 1976-77; asst. mktg. dir. Bancom, Makati 1977-78; subscription mgr. Casalinda, Makati 1978-79; pres./owner American Asian Worldwide Services, Orcutt, Calif. 1980—; travel overseas sales cons. Santa Maria Travel, 1982-; honors: Girl Scout of the Philippines (1971), Nat. Sci. Devel. Board (1975); mem. Silliman Univ. Alumni Assn. of So. Calif. (pres. 1985); civic: Philippines election Quick Return Coord. (non-partisan) (1965-70), Southpoint Estates Homeowners Assn. (1982-); publs: Marriage, Visa and Travel Guidebook to Malaysia and to the Philippines based on the Immigration and Naturalization Laws of Canada and United States (1980, 82, 84, 85); Catholic; rec: travel, swimming, snorkling, golf. Ofc: American Asian Worldwide Services POB 2777 Orcutt 93455

FLORES, CARLO J., management consultant executive; b. Sept. 27, 1925, Hermosa Beach; s. Joseph N. and Alice Frida (Elsener) F.; m. Ruth Marie Smith, Sept. 18, 1924; children: Susan b. 1954, Audrey b. 1956, Gary b. 1960, Yvonne b. 1966; edn: dipl. Swiss Sch. of Commerce, Zurich, Switzerland 1944; BA high honors, San Francisco State Univ. 1954; grad. wk. SFSU Sch. of World Business, 1954-55. Career: apprentice WITAG, Internat. Freight Forwarders, Zurich, Switz. 1941-44; export mgr. Soule Steel Co., San Francisco 1954-59; gen. mgr./pres. General Contractors, Comml. Building Sales, Inc., Honolulu 1959-62; constrn. coord. Torres Concrete Constrn. Co., Mt. View 1962-67; entrepreneur World Business Inc., Menlo Park 1967-75; exec. analyst, dir. tng., chief exec. survey service George S. May Internat. Co., S.F. 1975—, current mng. dir. Western American Div.; honors: GSMIC Million Dollar Club (1977); mem. Internat. Rels. & Econs. Club/ S.F. (1952-54), Junior World Trade Assn./ S.F. (1954-57), Export Mgr. Club/ S.F. (1956-59), Gen. Contrs. Assn./ Honolulu (1959-62), Redwood City CofC (1967-), Toastmasters Intl./ Redwood City (1972-75), Am. Mgmt. Assn./ NYC (1976-),; mil: USAF 1945-48, US Army 1950-52; Republican; Lutheran; rec: hiking, skiing, tennis, photog., technical writing, gardening. Res: 1026 Connecticut Dr Redwood City 94061 Ofc: George S May Intl. Co., Western American Div., 230 Twin Dolphin Dr Ste A Redwood City 94065

FLORES, JULIO C., children's home executive; b. July 27, 1940, Aguas Buenas, Puerto Rico; s. Felipe and Florita (Rivera) F.; m. Lillian, July 24, 1965; children: Mel b. 1971, Michelle b. 1973; edn: BS sociol., Calif. State Univ. 1970; MSW (social work), UC Los Angeles 1975. Career: licensing supv. L.A. County Dept. of Adoptions; exec. dir. Children's Baptist Home of So. Calif.; cons., tchr., pvt. counseling; honors: Dean's List (1969); mem. UCLA Alumni Assn.; research project on drug prevention; mil: airman basic USAF 1965; Republican; Baptist (asst. pastor); rec: singing. Res: 3330 Stonybrook Dr Anaheim 92804 Ofc: Children's Baptist Home 7715 S Victoria Inglewood 90305

FLORES, NORA VALEZA, dietician; b. Oct. 5, 1944, Philippines, nat. US cit. 1976; d. Vivencio T. and Eugenia T. (Lumbao) Valeza; m. Rodolfo Flores, Jr., Nov. 8, 1968; children: Lily V. b. 1970, John V. b. 1976; edn: BS foods & nutrition, Univ. St. Tomas 1965; grad. study, CSU Los Angeles 1973; Reg. Dietician 1980. Career: dietetic intern Veterans Meml. Hosp. 1965-66; chief dietician Singian Meml. Hosp. Manila, Phil. 1967-69; assoc. dietician Ontario Comm. Hosp. 1976-78, Doctor's Hosp. Montclair 1978-80, food svc. dir. 1980-82, clin. nutrition dir. 1982—; cons. dietician Valley Hosp., Ontario Comm. Hosp., United Home Health Care Svcs.; honors: 7th Place Dietician's Bd. Exams (Manila 1967); mem: Am. Dietetic Assn., Calif. Dietetic Assn., Inland Dietetic Assn., Am. Heart Assn., Montclair Meals on Wheels (bd.), site volunteer Montclair Health Fair Expo 1983-86; publs: nutrition articles for local newspaper, developed/ moderated nutrition edn. pgms. on weight control, hypertension, and diabetes; appeared on KNBC special "Premiere- Health Fair '85" to promote Health Fair sites throughout So. Calif.; rec: music, reading, gardening, jogging, hiking. Res: 1119 W Francis Ontario 91762 Ofc: Doctor's Hosp. of Montclair 5000 San Bernardino Montclair 91763

FLORIAN, VICTOR RAUL, finance & marketing executive; b. Feb. 22, 1946, Lima, Peru, nat. US cit. (in process); s. Jose and Angela Manuela (Vergara) F.; m. Monica Predazzi, Jan. 10, 1976; 1 son, Brandon P. b. 1980; edn: AA, Moorpark Coll. 1972; BSBA, CSU Northridge 1975; MA internat. mgmt., Am. Grad. Sch. of Internat. Mgmt. 1976. Career: branch rep., asst. mgr. Public Fin. Corp., Van Nuys, 1977-78; internat. finl. analyst Security Pacific Nat. Bank, Los Angeles 1978-79, asst. controller 1979-81, senior finl. analyst 1981-84; tax

cons., corp. finl. & mktg. adviser VRF Finl. Group, 1984—; honors: appreciation, Peruvian CofC of Calif. (1984), Van Nuys CofC (1986); mem. Peruvian Found. for the Sci., Technol. and the Arts (dir. fin. 1985-), Van Nuys CovC (Vanguard Com.), Peruvian CofC of Calif. (newsletter ed./pub.; dir. spl. pgms., chmn. seminar 'Peruvian-L.A. Expo. 1986); publs: ed./pub. Servicios Profesionales Latinos, quarterly newsletter for L.A. area Latin community; Independent; Catholic; ski, tennis, collect biographies of world leaders. Ofc: VRF Financial Group 14748 Victory Blvd Van Nuys 91411

FLUEGEL, DONALD RAYMOND, chiropractor; b. Mar. 21, 1955, Wilkes-Barre, Pa.; s. Donald Raymond and Jane (Warnecke) F.; edn: AS, Broome Comm. Coll. 1975; BS chem., State Univ. of NY Buffalo 1979; BS, Nat. Coll. 1981; DC, Nat. Coll. Chiro. 1982; Chiro. Calif. 1984. Career: athletic trainer while attending school; Wagner Chiro. Ctr. after graduation; currently own practice in Los Angeles 1985—; mem: Calif. Chiro. Assn., Am. Chiro. Assn., L.A.-Metro Chiro. Soc. (pres.), Am. Back Soc. (founding fellow), Beverly Hills CofC; rec: skiing, weightlifting, swimming, tennis. Res: 124 Edgemont Apt 1 Los Angeles 90004 Ofc: Chiropractic Assoc. of Beverly Hills 6317 Wilshire Blvd Ste 401 Los Angeles 90048

FLUHARTY, JESSE ERNEST, lawyer, retired jurist; b. July 25, 1916, San Antonio, Tex.; s. Jesse Ernest and Gwendolyn (Elder) F.; m. Ernestine Gertrude Corlies, Oct. 25, 1945; 1 son, Stephen; edn: stu. San Diego St. Univ. 1935-36; JD w/ distinction, Univ. of Pacific, 1951; cert. in adminstrv.law (1976), court mgmt. (1978), court adminstrn. (1979), National Judicial Coll. Career: admitted to Calif. Bar 1951; individual practice law, Sacramento 1951-60; presiding workers' compensation judge, Stockton 1960-67, Los Angeles 1967-81, Long Beach 1981-83; law ofc. Stephen Fluharty 1983—; instr. Paralegal Studies, Pasadena City Coll. Honors: Judge of the Year 1983, Lawyers Club of L.A. Co. Past pres. Family Service Agcy., Sacto. 1958-9; Comm. Council, Stockton and San Joaquin Co., 1965; Service Club Council, L.A. 1973-4; Glendale Hills Coord. Council, 1976-8; Chevy Chase Est. Assn. 1971-7; chmn. San Joaquin Co. Rec. & Park Commn. 1963-7; mem: Calif. State Bar, L.A. Co. Bar Assn., Glendale Bar Assn., Am. Judicature Soc., Lions (pres. L.A. chpt. 1971-2), Lawyers Club of L.A. (past pres.), Masons, Shriners, Chevy Chase CC; Verdugo Club; publs: arts. in law revs., ednl. manuals. Mil: US Army, 1943-45, Bronze Star, Merit Cit., Phil. Liberation Medal; Republican (formerly Democrat, Sacto. Central Com. v.chmn. 1959-60, nom. 3d Assem. Dist. 1953); Congregational (trustee). Res: 3330 Emerald Isle Dr. Glendale 91206 Ofc: 50 N Central Ave Glendale 91203·

FLYNN, JOHN ALLEN, lawyer; b. Jan. 12, 1945, Riverside, Ill.; s. Wm. and Marian Rae (Gustafson) F.; m. Kathey Walker, June 18, 1966; children: Judson b. 1972, Erin b. 1972; edn: AB, Stanford Univ. 1966; JD, UC Hastings Coll. of Law 1969; admitted to State Bar of Calif. 1970, US Dist. Cts., US Ct. of Appeals Ninth Cir. 1970, US Sup. Ct. 1975. Career: partner Graham & James, Attys., San Francisco 1969—; guest spkr., Practicing Law Inst., 'Maritime Personal Injury,' Los Angeles 1980, San Francisco 1982; guest spkr. Lloyd's of London Press, 'Maritime Claims,' S.F. 1984; recipient Am. Jurisprudence Awd. in Community Property 1969; mem: Am Bar Assn.; Maritime Law Assn. (Practice and Proceedure com. 1983-); San Francisco Bar Assn. (chmn. Admiralty Com. 1978-); Catholic; rec: skiing, swimming. Res: 60 Idlewood Rd Kentfield 94904 Ofc: Graham & James, One Maritime Plaza, Ste 300, San Francisco 94111

FLYNN, MICHAEL MATTHEW, insurance and financial services executive; b. May 24, 1935, Duluth, Minn.; s. Thomas Francis, Jr. and Lucille Beatrice (Zellman) F.; m. Lynne McCracken, Mar. 15, 1963; children: Matthew b. 1965, Ryan b. 1973; edn: BA, UC Los Angeles 1957; Chartered Life Underwriter, Am. Coll. 1974. Career: gen. agent Banker's Life, Neb. 1961-68; v.p. Shadur, LaVine & Assoc. 1968-75; currently pres. Flynn Assocs. Insurance Mkt., Inc., chmn. Flynn Financial Assocs., Inc., NASD Reg. Prin.; spkr. estate planning councils and ins. orgns. throughout the US; mem: Calif. Assn. Life Underws. (pres. 1975-76, trustee pol. action com. 1980-83), San Fernando Valley Life Underws. Assn. (pres. 1969-70), 65 Roses Club (charter), Cystic Fibrosis Found 1982, Am. Soc. CLUs (chpt. pres. 1985-86, Nat. Assn. Ind. Life Brokerage Agencies (chmn. 1985-86), Internat. Assn. Fin. Planners, Nat. Assn. Health Underws.; publs: num. articles in ins. jours.; mil: USAR 1958-64; Republican; rec: tennis. Res: 5118 Genesta Ave Encino 91316 OFc: Borden Flynn Assocs. 16130 Ventura Ste 400 Encino 91356

FOCH, NINA, actress, educator; b. Apr. 20, 1924, Leyden, Netherlands, nat. 1932; d. Dirk (composer-condr., founder NYC Sym.) and Consuelo (Flowerton) Foch; m. James Lipton, June 6, 1954; m. 2d Dennis R. Brite, Nov. 27, 1959; 1 son, Schuyler Dirk; m. 3d Michael Dewell (founder, pres. Nat. Repertory Theatre Found.), Oct. 31, 1967; edn: Miss Hewitt's Classes, NYC; grad. Lincoln Sch., Columbia Univ. 1939; stu. painting, Parsons Sch. of Design, stu. acting w/ Stella Adler. Career: film actress, 1944—: with Warner Bros., then Columbia Pictures (18 feature films), 20 feature films var. other studios; Broadway stage debut in John Loves Mary, 1947-48, followed by num. stage roles, fundraising tour for Am. Shakespeare Festival, 1967; founder w/ John Housman, The L.A. Theatre Group, now at LA Music Center; sang Anna in The Seven Deadly Sins, S.F. Ballet and Opera, 1966; spl. guest Seattle Repertory Theatre in west coast premiere of Albee's All Over, 1973; lead roles in num. TV dramas, 1947—, appearances on all major talk shows; co-host 3 seasons, CBS News series with Walter Cronkite; guest star num. TV series incl. Lou Grant Show (1980 Emmy nom.); currently starring in ABC's Shadowchasers, 1985—; assoc. film dir. The Diary of Anne Frank, 1959; adj. prof. of drama Univ. of So. Calif. 1966-8, 78-80; artist-in-res. Univ. of N.C., 1966,

Univ. Ohio, Columbus, 1967, CalTech, 1969-70; sr. faculty Am. Film Inst. Ctr. for Advanced Film Studies, 1974-77; founder/tchr. Nina Foch Studio, Hywd 1973−; mem: Acad. Motion Picture Arts & Scis. (exec. com. Fgn. Film Award), Am. Cancer Soc. (hon. Crusade chmn. L.A. 1970), Hollywood Acad. of TV Arts & Scis. (gov. 1976-7); rec: cooking, needlework. Address: Nina Foch Studio, POB 1884 Beverly Hills 90210

FOGARTY, THOMAS JAMES, cardiovascular surgeon; b. Feb. 25, 1934, Cincinnati; s. Wm. Henry and Anna Isabella (Ruthemeyer) F.; m. Rosalee Brennan, Aug. 28, 1965; children: Thomas b. 1967, Heather b. 1969, Patrick b. 1972, Jonathan b. 1975; edn: BS in biol., Xavier Univ. 1956; MD, Univ. of Cinti. Coll. of Medicine 1960. Diplomate Am. Bds. of Surgery (1970), Thoracic Surgery (1974). Career: intern and resident Univ. of Ore. Med. Sch., Portland 1960-65, instr. in surgery 1967-68; chief resident and instr. in surgery Div. Cardiovascular Surg., Stanford Univ. Med. Center 1969-70, asst. clin. prof. of surg. 1971-73; pvt. practice cardiovascular surg. Stanford Univ. Med. Center, Stanford 1973-78, pres. med. staff 1977-79; pvt. practice cardiovascular surgery Sequoia Hosp., Redwood City 1978−, dir. cardiac surg. 1980−; founder, devel., mgr. of 6 cos. (all 6 ventures colminated in successful mergers); bd. dirs. Santa Clara Found. for Med. Care, Satellite Dialysis Centers (both nonprofit corps. to reduce costs of quality health care); guest speaker nat. cardiovascular socs.; awards: fellowships (1961-62, 65-67, 68-69), grantee: Am. Heart Assn., NIH, Inventor of the Year, S.F. Patent & Trademark Assn. (1980), Disting. Sci. Presentation, Am. Coll. of Surgeons (1971, 73, 75, 81), Astrolobe Award-Most Disting. high sch. grad. (1974); mem: AMA, Calif., Santa Clara Co. Med. Socs., Samson Thoracic Surg. Soc., The Soc. for Thoracic Surgeons, Am. Coll. of Surgeons, The Internat. Cardiovascular Soc., The Soc. for Vascular Surgery, S.F. Surg. Soc., Am. Heart Assn., Am. Coll. of Cardiology, Pac. Coast Surg. Assn., Bay Area Vascular Soc., Soc. for Clin. Vascular Surg., Pan Pac. Surg. Assn., Andrew G. Morrow Soc.; mem. Calif. Wildlife Assn., Ducks Unlimited, Calif. Vintners Assn., medical Friends of Wine, Rapley Trail Improvement Assn.; publs: 62 sci. articles and textbook chpts. on gen. and cardiovascular surgery; inventor, 40+ patents in surgical instrumentation; Republican; Roman Catholic; rec: fishing, hunting. Ofc: 770 Welch Rd Ste 201 Palo Alto 94304

FOGEL, NORMAN I., synagogue administrator; b. Dec. 23, 1939, Los Angeles; s. Edward G. and Frieda (Moder) F.; m. Kathleen, May 8, 1971; children: Melissa b. 1972, Stephanie b. 1974, Jeremy b. 1976; edn: BA, UC Los Angeles 1962; desig: Fellow in Temple Adminstrn. (FTA), Board of Certifications, Union of Am. Hebrew Congregations. Career: asst. dir. Temple Emanuel, Beverly Hills 1962-65; exec. dir. Temple Solael, Woodland Hills 1965-66, Temple Beth Israel, San Diego 1966-71; adminstrv. v.p. Brandeis Inst., Simi Valley 1971-78; exec. dir. Temple Israel, Boston, Mass. 1978-83; exec. dir. Stephen S. Wise Temple (largest synagogue in the world), Bel Air 1983−; mem. nat. MUM Com., UAHC; honors: Commendations, County of Ventura, City of Simi Valley; mem. Nat. Assn. of Temple Adminstrs. (exec. bd., treas.); civic: past mem. (chmn.) Simi Valley Plnng. Commn., Ventura County Human Rels. Commn.; mil: US Army Reserve 1957-65; Republican; Jewish; rec: tennis, racquetball. Ofc: Stephen S. Wise Temple, 15500 Stephen Wise Dr Los Angeles 90077

FOGG, VERA VIRGINIA, lawyer; b. Nov. 4, 1908, Caddo Co., Okla; d. Charles Robert and Susie Ann (Huddleston) F.; edn: private study; admitted Calif., Texas state bars. Career: secty. State Dept. of Education, Austin, Tx. 1930-34; assoc. atty. law firm Mann & Mann, Laredo 1935-37, E.G. Aycock, atty., Fort Worth 1938-40; county atty. Hardeman Co., Quanah 1942-48; pvt. law practice, in Fort Worth 1949-52; worked in legal offices, Calif. 1952-57; pvt. law practice, San Fernando Valley 1957-67, 1970; office dir. 1966-67, deputy exec. dir. San Fernando Valley Neighborhood Legal Services, 1968; atty. pvt. practice 1970−; honors: recognition for more than 50 years service rendered to Community, State and Nation, State Bar of Texas (1982), named Tarzana CofC Woman of the Year (1986), listed Who's Who of Am. Women, World Who's Who of Women (3d ed.); mem: Texas, Calif., Los Angeles County bar assns., Tarzana CofC (bd. dirs. 1971-76), L.A. Dist. Assembly of Delphian Chapters (past parliamentarian), Adela Rogers St. John's Round Table West; former mem: Soroptimist Club (past pres., W.Valley), Internat. Women Lawyers, Quanah CofC (past pres.), Bus. & Profl. Womens Club (past dist. dir. Texas B&PW); Republican; Prot.; rec: music, literature, gardening. Address: 5317 Mecca Ave Tarzana 91356

FOLEY, JAMES EDWARD, III, real estate services co. executive; b. Feb. 24, 1952, Bangor, Maine; s. J. Edward, II and Beatrice Mary (Michaud) F.; m. Jennifer Seymour, May 16, 1986; edn: grad. Higgins Classical Inst. 1970; Univ. of Maine 1975. Career: asst. J. Edward Foley Estate, Bangor, Me. 1975-77; investment advisor Jones Lang Wootton, N.Y.C. 1977-78, mgr. investment dept., Los Angeles 1978-79, ptnr., N.Y.C. 1979-81, senior ptnr., Houston, Tx. 1982-84, senior ptnr. Jones Lang Wootton, San Francisco 1985−; guest lectr. Univ. of St. Thomas; mem: Urban Land Inst. (Exec. Council), Real Estate Board of New York 1977−, Nat. Trust for Hist. Preservation; club: Castine Yacht; Republican; Episcopal; rec: skiing, sailing, bird hunting. Res: 1000 Mason St San Francisco 94108 Ofc: Jones Lang Wootton 710 One Embarcadero Ctr San Francisco 94111

FOLLICK, EDWIN DUANE, educator, administrator, chiropractic physician; b. Feb. 4, 1935, Glendale; s. Edwin Fulfford and Esther Agnes (Catherwood) Follick; edn: BA, CSU Los Angeles 1956, MA, 1961; MA, Pepperdine Univ. 1957; MPA, 1977; PhD and D.Theol., St. Andrews Theol. Coll., Free Prot.

Epis. Sem. (London) 1958; MS in LS, USC 1963; M.Ed. 1964; Adv. M.Edn. 1969; LL.B, Blackstone Law Sch. 1966, JD 1967; DC, Cleveland Chiro. Coll., L.A. 1972; PhD, Acad. Theatina, Pescara 1978. Career: teacher/lib. adminstr. Los Angeles City Schs. 1957-68; law librarian Glendale Univ. Coll of Law, 1968-9; coll. librarian Cleveland Chiro. Coll., L.A. 1969-74, dir. Edn. and Admissions 1974-85, and dean Student Affairs 1976-86; prof. Jurisprudence, 1975−; chaplain of the coll. and ednl. cons. 1986−; extern prof. St. Andrews (London) 1961; assoc. prof. Grad. Sch. Pub. & Bus. Adminstrn., Newport Univ. 1982−; dir. West Valley Chiro. Health Center, 1972−; honors: Cavaliere Intl. Order Legion of Honor of Immaculata (Italy); Knight of Malta, Order St. John of Jerusalem; Ritter, Der Intl. Legion Friedrich II von Schwaben Teutonische Miliz; Comdr. Chevalier, Byzantine Imperial Order of Constantine the Great; Comdr. Ritter, Order of St. Geron; Chevalier, Order of St. Lazarus; mem: Am. Chiro. Assn., Internat. Chiro. Assn., ALA, NEA, Am. Assn. Sch. Librarians, Assn. Coll. and Resrch. Librarians, Am. Assn. Law Librarians, Nat. Geographic Soc., Phi Delta Kappa, Sigma Chi Psi, Delta Tau Alpha. mil: chaplain's asst. US Army Air Def. Command 1958-60; Democrat; Episcopal. Res: 7022 Owensmouth Ave Canoga Pk 91303 Ofc: 590 N Vermont Av Los Angeles 90004

FOLTZ, RONALD E., ophthalmologist; b. Oct. 30, 1942, Sterling, Ill.; s. Robert E. and Belva L. (Magill) F.; m. Marcia Richert, July 3, 1971; children: Kirsten b. 1975, Gretchen b. 1979, Ryan b. 1981, Amanda b. 1983; edn: BS, Wheaton Coll. 1964; MD, Univ. of Ill. Coll. of Medicine 1968; diplomate Am. Board of Ophthalmology 1979. Career: ophthalmology resident Deaconess Hosp. Buffalo, NY 1971-74; pvt. practice ophthalmology in Placerville, 1975−; staff physician Marshall Hosp.; research: Intraocular lenses; mem: Am. Acad. of Ophth., Christian Medical Soc. (pres. Univ. Ill. Chpt. 1968), Calif. Assn. of Ophth. (Speakers Bureau 1984), AMA, Calif. Med. Assn., Sacto. El Dorado Med. soc. (bd. dirs. 1986), Internat. Soc. Refractive Keratoplasty; mil: lt. USNR 1969-71, Bethesda Naval Hosp., Vietnam Svc.; Ind.; Baptist; rec: economic philosophy, music, travel. Ofc: Ronald E. Foltz MD Inc. 1000 Fowler Way Placerville 95667

FONG, FILBERT T., health physicist; b. Feb. 19, 1934, San Francisco; s. Joe Y. and Fong (Poy) F.; m. Mildred Lum, Feb. 1960; children: Glenda Joyce b. 1961, Wendi Rae b. 1965; edn: BA, San Francisco State Univ. 1957; lic. Safety Engr. Calif. Career: health physicist Naval Radiological Defense Lab. 1957-68, Naval Ordnance Lab. 1968-69, Mare Island Naval Shipyard 1969-70, Calif. Dept. of Health 1970-76, NRC Reg. V. 1976-80, US Dept. of Energy, Oakland 1980−; radiological emergency coord. US Dept. of Energy Reg. 7, hazardous waste pgms. mgr.; mem: Health Physics Soc., Hong On Tong Soc. (bd.). Res: 1401 Whitecliff Way Walnut Creek 94596 Ofc: US Dept of Energy 1333 Broadway Oakland 94612

FONG, HENRY HUNG, engineer; b. June 10, 1942, Chungking, China, nat. US cit. 1963; s. Tsung-Sen and Dr. Suen-Hsi (Yang) F.; m. Alice C.P. Ting, Jan. 9, 1977; children: Tyrone b. 1970, Sylvia b. 1972, Shana b. 1981; edn: BSCE, UC Berkeley 1964, MSCE, 1966; postgrad. work, structures, UCLA 1968-72. Career: stress engr. General Dynamics/Convair Div. 1966-68; struc. engr. McDonnell Douglas Astronautics Co., 1968-78; senior staff engr. Hughes Aircraft Co., 1978-80; engring. assoc. PDA Engring., Santa Ana 1980-86, supr. Tech. Publs., PATRAN Div., mgr. tech. communs. MARC Analysis Research Corp., 1986−; (engring. projects include: Atlas-Centaur rocket, missiles, spacecraft, Space Shuttle, Skylab, heliostats for Solar One facility in Barstow, LNG carriers, weapons, oil pipelines in frozen soil); honors: Chi Epsilon (1964), invited speaker to spl. engring. conf. in Taipei, Taiwan (11/79), var. academic research insts. in Shanghai and Beijing, China (1982); mem. ASME (1984-); mem. Calif. Chinese Club; publs: contbr. 30+ tech. articles and book chpts. in computer-aided engring., finite element appls., interactive graphics (1981-86), two ASME "cover" articles, co-author one book, tech. reviewer for 3 internat. engring. jours.; Democrat; rec: bridge, philately. Res: 1016 Powell St San Francisco 94108 Ofc: MARC Analysis Research Corp., 260 Sheridan Ave Ste 200 Palo Alto 94306

FONG, RONNIE LEE, civil engineer; b. Jan. 17, 1955, San Francisco; s. Jack Lee and Dorothy (Der) F.; m. Joan Chen, Nov. 10, 1984; edn: BS civil engring., UC Berkeley 1978; Reg. Profl. Engr. (Civil) Calif. Career: asst. transp. engr. TJKM, Walnut Creek 1978-79; jr., asst. civil engr. (design section of airport engring.) Port of Oakland, 1979-81, civil engr./project mgr., 1981−, project mgr. Terminal II 1981-85 (completed $40 million constrn. project on time and within budget); assoc. mem. Nat. Soc. Profl. Engrs., Calif. Soc. Profl. Engrs., Am. Soc. Civil Engrs.; dir. Engring. Alumni Soc. UCB; Branch Council mem. S.F. Chinatown YMCA; past chmn. Missions Com., Cumberland Presbyn. Ch., S.F.; Student Speaker, UCB Engineering Coll. Commencement Ceremonies (1978), panel spkr. ASCE Conv., S.F. (1984), seminar spkr. InterVarsity Christian Fellowship SF'83 Urban Conf.; Christian. Res: 6292 Lido Ct Newark 94560-1202 Ofc: Port of Oakland 66 Jack London Sq Oakland 94607-3798

FORD, ELIZABETH BLOOMER (MRS. GERALD R. FORD), wife of 38th U.S. President; b. Apr. 8, 1918, Chgo.; d. Wm. Stephenson and Hortence (Heahr) Bloomer; m. William Warren, 1942, div. 1947; m. 2d Gerald R. Ford, Oct. 15, 1948; children: Michael Gerald, John Gardner, Steven Meigs, Susan Elizabeth; ed. Bennington Sch. Dance, 1936-38; LLD (hon.), Univ. Mich. 1976. Career: dancer Martha Graham Concert Group, NYC 1939-41; model John Powers Agcy., NYC 1939-51; fashion dir. Herpolsheimer's Dept. Store, Grand Rapids, Mich. 1943-48; dance instr. Grand Rapids, 1932-48; mem. Nat. Commn. on Observance of Internat. Women's Year, 1977; trustee Eisenhower

Med. Center, Palm Desert; adv. bd. Rosalind Russell Med. REsearch Fund; hon. chair Palm Springs Desert Mus.; hon. bd. dirs. The Lambs Inc. (Libertyville, Ill.); co-ch. Betty Ford Center Com.; hon. mem. Golden Circle of Patrons, Center Theatre of Performing Arts; (past) active in Cub Scouts Am., Cancer Fund (Alexandria, Va.); honors: Distinguished Woman of Year 1975, Nat. Art Assn.; Silver Anniversary Humanitarian award Phila. Assn. Retarded Children, 1975; Rita V. Tishman Human Relations award Womens Div. Anti-Defamation League, 1975; Silver Spirit of Life award L.A. City of Hope Nat. Med. Center, 1976; Centennial award McCall's mag. 1976; Media award Phila., 1976; Parson's award N.Y. Parson's Sch. Design, 1976; Woman of Year 1976, Ladies Home Jour.; Alfred P. Sloan Jr. Meml. award, 1977; USO Woman of Year 1977. Author: The Times of My Life (1979). Address: PO Box 927 Rancho Mirage 92770

FORD, GERALD RUDOLPH, JR., 38th President of the United States, b. July 14, 1913, Omaha; s. Gerald R. and Dorothy (Gardner) F.; m. Elizabeth Bloomer, Oct. 15, 1945; children: Michael Gerald, John G., Steven M., Susan Elizabeth; edn: AB, Univ. Mich. 1935; LLB, Yale Univ. 1941; LLD (hon) Mich. State Univ., Aquinas Coll., Spring Arbor Coll., Albion Coll., Grand Valley State Coll., Belmont Abby Coll., Western Mich. Univ.; admitted to Mich. State Bar, 1941. Career: law practice in Grand Rapids, Mich. 1941-49; assoc. firm Butterfield, Amberg, Law & Buchen, 1946-51, partner Amberg, Law, Buchen & Fallon, 1951-59, Buchen & Ford, after 1960; elected mem. 81st to 93d congresses from 5th Mich. Dist., mem. Appropriations Com., minority leader, 1954-73; apptd. vice president United States of Am., 1973-74, elected US President, 1974-77; bd. dirs: Santa Fe Internat., GK Techs., Shearson Loeb Rhoades, Pebble Beach Corp., Tiger Internat., Amax Inc.; honors: distinguished service award, Grand Rapids Jr. CofC, 1948, one of ten outstanding young men in US, US Jr. CofC, 1950, Sports Illus. Silver Anniversary All-American 1959, Congl. distinguished service, Am. Polit. Sci. Assn. 1961, George Washington award, Am. Good Govt. Soc. 1966, Gold Medal award Nat. Football Found. 1972; mem. Am., Mich., Grand Rapids bar assns., Delta Kappa Epsilon, Phi Delta Phi, Masons, University Club, Peninsular (Kent County) Club; author: A Time To Heal: The Autobiography of Gerald R. Ford (1979), Global Stability (1982); coauthor: Portrait of the Assassin; mil: served to lt. comdr. USN 1942-46; Republican; Episcopal. Address: P.O. Box 927, Rancho Mirage 92270

FORD, HATTIE MARIE, real estate broker; b. Dec. 19, 1943, Monroe, La.; d. James Edward and Lurry Ellen (Wright) Williams; m. James Everett Ford, Jan. 25, 1970; 1 child, Marques b. 1977; edn: spl. courses, Am. Trade Sch. 1962, Lumbleau Sch. of R.E. 1973; Calif. lic. Real Estate Broker (1977), Ins. Agent (1978); lic. evangelist Fellowship Temple (1976). Career: sales/mgr. Century 21 King Realty, Los Angeles, ERA Dodd Real Estate, L.A.; broker/adminstr. Golden Eagle Real Estate, Fairfield; currently broker/owner H.M. Ford Realty & Investments, Fairfield; honors: Vocalist of Year (1977-78); mem. Nat. Assn. Realtors, L.A. Bd. Realtors (1970-83), Solano Bd. Realtors (1983-); Democrat; Baptist; rec: music, camping. Address: H.M. Ford Realty 2712 Vista Serena Fairfield 94533

FORD, JOHN JOSEPH, transportation executive; b. Feb. 10, 1937, Moline, Ill.; s. Robert Alvin and Mary L. (Chapman) F.; m. Carole L. Wink, 1958; 3 sons: Edwin, Jeffrey, Gregg; edn: BA, FSU, 1958; MBA, USC, 1972. Career: past indsl. mktg. mgr. Xerox Corp., Torrance; past branch mgr. A.B. Dick Co., Los Angeles; currently pres./chief exec., Dave Systems, Inc., Santa Ana, and Community Transit Services, Inc., Anaheim; dir.: Dave Consulting Inc., Dave Systems Inc., Dave Systems Northwest Inc., Community Transit Svcs. Inc., Positive Image Inc., Community Svcs. Inc. Transmax Inc., Ameride Inc., Norcal Trans. Inc. Awards: Jaycee Spoke and Outstanding Young Man awds.; Pacemaker, A.B.Dick Co.; Par Club, Xerox Corp.; mem: Am. Mgmt. Assn., Presidents Assn., Nat. Assn. Corporation Directors, Orange Co. CofC, Lions Club; publs: transp. research, spl. transit services, Dial-A-Ride publs.; mil: A/1c USAF, two Unit Awds.; Republican; Prot. Res: 2382 Bayfarm Pl Santa Ana Hts 92707. Ofc: Dave Systems Inc. 1450 East 17th St Ste 100 Santa Ana 92701

FORD, LARRY CREED, medical scientist; b. Sept. 29, 1950, Provo, Utah; s. Creed D. and Gladys Mae (Garlick) F.; m. Diane Lewis, June 5, 1970; children: Larry, Jr. b. 1975, Scott David b. 1978, Kerilyn b. 1980; edn: BS, magna cum laude, Brigham Young Univ. 1971; MD, honors, UCLA Sch of Med. 1975; Dip. Nat. Bd. of Med. Examiners 1975. Career: intern int. med., VA Wadsworth Medical Ctr., Los Angeles, 1975-6; res. obstets-gyn., UCLA Sch. of Med., 1976-9, chief res. 1979-80, fellowship in biol. chem., 1977-80; asst. prof. UCLA Sch. of Med., 1980-, dir. research Ctr. for Ovarian Cancer, 1981-; founding mem./scientist Sexually Transmitted Disease Resrch Council, 1981-; mem: Am. Soc. for Microbiol., Phi Eta Sigma Hon. Frat., NY Acad. of Sci., AAAS; awards: 1st Place 18th Internat. Sci. Fair and AUS, AF, AEC Awards (1966); publs: medical jour. articles, med. book chapters; Republican; Ch. of Jesus Christ of LDS; rec: hunt, shoot, geneal. Ofc: Dr. Larry C. Ford, UCLA Los Angeles 90021

FOREE, ROBERT LYNN, educator, import co. president; b. June 18, 1938, Oakland; s. Stewart James and Dorothy Anne (Palmer) F.; m. Jane, July 29, 1978; children: Kevin Lynn b. 1979, Brian James b. 1980; edn: AA, Oakland City Coll. 1958; BA, San Francisco State Univ. 1960; MED, Mississippi Coll. 1970; PhD, Walden Univ. 1973; Calif. Life Tchg. Cred. (Edn. & Adminstn.). Career: educator Palo Alto Unified Sch. Dist. 26 years, final 10 yrs. head tchr./counselor Stanford Univ. Escondido Sch. (incl. non-English speaking children from many countries); bd. chmn./pres. Foree Ents. Inc. (coin laundries import

broker), 1983-, opened office in Austria 1985; honors: hon. mem. Calif. Peace Ofcrs. Assn., Phi Delta Kappa (1967); mem: Calif. Coin Laundry Assn. (v.chmn. bd. dirs.); mem. Huguenot Soc. (pres. State Branch; 3d. v.p. nat. 1982-83), Elks, Moose; publs: short articles; Republican; Presbyterian; rec: fishing, hunting. Res: 1510 Fordham Way Mountain View 94040-3033

FOREMAN, JACK PRESTON, film studio executive; b. Apr. 3, 1924, Los Angeles; s. John and Lillian Mae (Young) F.; m. Barbara Jones, Oct. 17, 1964; children: Christin b. 1959, Glenn b. 1957; edn: BA, USC 1950. Career: director of film prodn. ops. CBS TV, Los Angeles 1950-60; CEO Samuel Goldwyn Prodns., L.A. 1960-80 (acquired & renamed 1980), v.p./gen. mgr. Warner Hollywood Studios, 1980-; honors: DKE (hon. cinema frat.) at USC; mem: Acad. of Motion Picture Arts & Scis. 1965- (sci., tech. awds. com. 1966-); pres. Hollywood CofC 1978; pres. Permanent Charities Com. of Motion Picture and TV Indus. 1984; bd. trustees, Motion Picture & TV Fund 1965-80; mil: Sgt. 5th AF Photo Recon. Sqd. 1943-6, presdtl. unit cit.; Republican; rec: boating. Res: 151 No. Bristol Los Angeles 90049 Ofc: Warner Hollywood Studios, 1041 No Formosa Ave Los Angeles 90046

FORGNONE, ROBERT, lawyer; b. Dec. 4, 1936, Paterson, N.J.; s. Samuel and Caroline (Calcagno) F.; m. Betty Jean, Aug. 18,1 962; 1 son, Charles Robert b. 1972; edn: AA, Los Angeles City Coll.; BS, CSU Long Beach 1967; JD, Loyola Univ. (L.A.) Sch. of Law 1970; admitted Calif. State Bar 1971, US Supreme Ct., US Ct. of Appeals (9th Cir.), and all Fed. and State Cts. in Calif. Career: atty. assoc. law firm Gibson, Dunn & Crutcher, 1970-78, partner 1978-; mem: ABA, Calif. State Bar, Los Angeles County Bar Assn. (exec. com. Trial Lawyers Sect.), Lawyer Pilots Bar Assn., Supreme Ct. Hist. Soc.; regent Loyola Marymount Univ.; mem. Loyola Law Sch. Alumni Assocs.; advis. com. Horesemans Benevolent and Protective Assocs.; bd. trustees David Bernard Meml. Found.; mil: A/1c USAF 1957-61; Republican; Catholic; rec: pvt. pilot, breeding and racing thoroughbred race horses. Res: 14819 Mar Vista St Whittier 90605 Ofc: Gibson Dunn & Crutcher 333 South Grand Ave Los Angeles 90071

FORSBERG, KEVIN JOHN, consulting co. executive; b. July 20, 1934, Oakland; s. Ted Otto and Gladys (Reid) F.; m. Cindy Jane Beason, Jan. 1, 1981; children: Ian b. 1957, Chenoa b. 1963; edn: BSCE, M.I.T. 1956; MS engrg. mechanics, Stanford Univ. 1958, PhD, 1961, cert. Stanford Exec. Pgm., 1979. Career: tech. staff Lockheed Missiles & Space Co. Sunnyvale 1956-61; mgr. solid mechanics Lockheed Palo Alto Research Labs. 1963-71, asst. dir. 1971-73; pgm. mgr. Lockheed Missiles & Space Co. Sunnyvale 1973-84; v.p. Consulting Resources Inc. Santa Clara 1984-; grad. sch. lectr. Santa Clara Univ. 1984-; UC Santa Cruz 1985-; honors: Public Svc. Award (NASA 1981); fellow Am. Soc. Mech. Engrs. (chmn. num. coms. 1968-; mem. Am. Inst. Aero. & Astro 1961-; chmn. Citizen's Com. on High School Edn. Redwood City 1969-70; author: 21 articles in profl. jours.; co-author: handbook Project Management & Project Leadership (1985); mil: capt. US Army Corps of Engrs. 1961-63; rec: photog. Res: 1225 Vienna Dr Apt 584 Sunnyvale 94089 Ofc: Consulting Resources Inc 5333 Betsy Ross Dr Santa Clara 95052

FORSTON, ROBERT F., temporary personnel co. president; b. Oct. 17, 1940, St. Paul, Minn.; s. Gerald Wayne and Marguerite Mary (Bliesath) F.; m. Anne Zobrist, Aug. 2, 1962; children: Melanie, Scott, Jenny, Jason, David; edn: BA, Univ. Minn. 1963, MA 1966, PhD 1968; Drake Univ. Law Sch. 1975-76. Career: assoc. prof. speech commun. (dept. chmn. 1971-76), Drake Univ. 1968-77, assoc. prof. of law 1976-77; pres./CEO Its Personnel, Inc. dba Active Temps, 1977-; commnr. Iowa Supreme Ct. Contg. Edn. 1975-77, Am. Acad. of Judicial Edn. 1974-75; cons. Nat. Coll. of State Judiciary, Reno (1974), Federal Reserve Bank of Chgo., Catholic Ch., IRS; awards: research grantee, Margaret & James Kelly Found. for the Decision-Making Process in the Am. Civil Jury (1968); mem. Indep. Temporary Service Assn. (regl. v.p. 1984-), Speech Commun. Assn. (1965-77), Central States Speech Assn. (1966-77), Internat. Commun. Assn. (1968-77), Burbank CoC; publs: Public Speaking as Dialogue (Kendall/Hunt 1970), articles in law revs. and profl. jours. Ofc: Its Personnel Inc 361 E Magnolia Ste A Burbank 91502

FORSYTH, DAVID STEWART, V, pharmacist; b. Oct. 14, 1903, Phila.; s. David Stewart and Anna Elizabeth (Jones) F.; m. Ardys Stevens, June 30, 1935; children: David b. 1939, Norma b. 1945 (dec.); edn: Pharm.D., Univ. So. Calif. 1925, bus. adminstrn. classes USC, contg. Career: owner Fourth Ave. Pharmacy 1927-32; group mgr. engrg. Douglas Aircraft (WWII); owner Lennox Pharm. 1959-; honors: Kappa Psi frat. key, Rho Chi hon. soc., Grand Cross of Color (1955), Rainbow Svc. Award (Rainbow Girls 1981), Svc. Award (Lions Club 1982), York Cross of Honor (L.A. Priory 1974); mem: Rotary, Elks, Masons (Grand Historian Cryptic Masons 1981, Illustrious Master Harbor Council 1967, Master Hermosa Lodge 1953, High Priest 1963, 70, 71), Knights Templar (comdr. 1965), Hist. Soc. of Centinela Valley (charter mem., dir.), past. mem. Manhattan Beach and Lennox CofCs, West Coast Yacht Club (founder 1934), So. Calif. Yachting Assn. (staff commodore, past vice commodore and rear commodore); publ: articles on model railroading in newspapers; Republican; Christian; rec: model railroading, stamps, photog., printing. Res: 1137 Ronda Dr Manhattan Beach 90266 Ofc: Lennox Pharmacy 10800 Hawthorne Blvd Lennox 90304

FORTIER, JOHN J., physician-internist, b. Oct. 22, 1928, Hull Que Canada, nat. US Cit. 1959; s. Jacques L. and Laurette F.; m. Linda M. Mastro, Aug. 7, 1971; children: Gregory b. 1956, Julie b. 1957, Laurie b. 1974, Amy b. 1978, James F. (1960-1984); edn: senior matriculation 1946, MD, Univ. of Ottawa 1951; Splst. in Internal Medicine, subsplty. Pulmonary Diseases and Cardiology. Career: postgrad. tng. in internal medicine, cardiology, hematology Mt. Carmel Mercy Hosp. and Wayne County Hosp., Detroit, 1951-53; chief resident int. med. Colo. State Hosp. 1953-54; chief resident pulmonary diseases, Springville, Ca. 1954-56; physician Dept. of Med. Fitzsimmons Army Hosp. 1956-58; pvt. practice, 1958–, staff (past chief Dept. Medicine) San Gabriel Valley Medical Center; var. real estate interests; mem: Calif. Med. Assn., Los Angeles County Med. Assn. (past pres. Dist. 12; past Legis. Com.), Am. Coll. Physicians, Calif. Soc. of Internal Medicine; mil: capt. US Army Med. Corps 1956-58; Republican; Catholic; rec: ski, jog, travel. Ofc: 1001 East Main St Alhambra 91801

FOSS, KIMBERLY LINNEA, financial consultant; b. Feb. 18, 1962, Auburn; d. George Harry and Gloria Edna (Wilcox) Foss; edn: Sierra Comm. Coll. 1980-81, BS bus. adm., CSU Chico 1984. Career: var. jobs thru coll., drug store clk., cosmetic cons., health club instr./sales; acct. exec. asst. Birr, Wilson Co. Inc., Paradise 1983-84; finl. cons., corporate svcs. coord. Merrill Lynch Pierce, Fenner & Smith Inc., San Ramon 1984–; honors: Masonic Scholarship (1982), Dean's list (1980, 81); mem. Soroptomist Intl., Phi Chi Theta Alumni (dir. Contra Costa Co.); publs: mktg. & demographics research report; Republican; Presbyterian; rec: triathelete, travel, bike touring. Res: 9085 Alcosta Blvd #384 San Ramon 94583 Ofc: Merrill Lynch 3130 Crow Canyon Pl San Ramon 94583

FOSTER, BETTY IRENE, insurance agent, broker; b. Aug. 15, 1927, Amarillo, Tex.; d. Ira Oliver and Susan Rankin (Corkle) Scott; m. Leonard Foster, July 19, 1947; 1 dau. Susan Ann b. 1955; ins. agent, broker Calif. Career: ins. secty. Wadleigh Ins. Inc. Long Beach 1964-81; fire & cas. ins. agent/ broker Shellrose Ins. Agency Huntington Beach 1981–. Ofc: Shellrose Ins. Agcy. Huntington Beach 92647

FOSTER, CLYDE THURSTON, gold mine owner-operator; b. Apr. 30, 1911, Ukiah (his birth cert. is No. 59 in Mendocino Co.); s. Raymond Osborne and Grace Lorain (Thurston) F.; married and widowed twice; edn: Santa Rosa Jr. Coll. 1928-29, Macky Sch. of Mines, Univ. of Nev. 1930-31, Stanford Univ. 1943. Career: first underground mining for father at Twin Sisters Mine in Nevada County, 1927, and Sweetwater Mine (acquired 1933); miner (and owner) Sleeping Beauty Mine 1931-52, and Sweetwater Mine, 1931–; also worked as micropaleontologist (w/micro fossils from Artic Slope) USGS, Fairbanks, Alaska 1946; computer US Corps of Engrs., Anchorage 1948; survey party chief AEC, Atomic Test Site Nev. and hydro elec. projects (Merced River, Tuolumne River, American River, Yuba River, Rancho Seco Nuclear Generating Plant), 1951-73; owner/opr. Sweetwater Mine, Mariposa (mining with the machinery, methods & language of the 1930s), 1952–; instr. Stamp Mill Sch. (the only sch. of its kind) Mariposa Hist. Soc.; mil: tech. sgt. US Army WWII & Korea, 6 yrs Active Duty, 9 decorations. Address: Sweetwater Mine POB 382 Mariposa 95338

FOSTER, DUDLEY EDWARDS, JR., educator; b. Oct. 5, 1935, Orange, N.J.; s. Dudley Edwards and Margaret (DePoy) F.; edn: Occidental Coll. 1953-56; AB, UC Los Angeles 1957, MA, 1958; doctoral study, USC 1961-70; Fellow, Trinity Coll. of London (FTCL), Trinity Coll. of Music, Univ. of London, 1960. Career: lectr. in music Immaculate Heart Coll., L.A. 1960-62; dir. of music Holy Faith Episcopal Ch., Inglewood 1963-66; lectr. in music CSU Los Angeles 1968-71; dir. of music First Lutheran Ch. of L.A. 1968-72, St. Paul's Episcopal Ch., Tustin 1973-74; prof. of music L.A. Mission Coll. 1975–; frequent appearances as organ recitalist/conductor; awards: tchg. fellow UCLA (1958-60), USC (1961), Disting. v.p. Los Angeles Coll. Tchrs. Assn. (1981-); mem: Calif. Tchrs. Assn., Nat. Edn. Assn., Am. Guild of Organists, Town Hall of Calif., Internat. Platform Assn., Medieval Acad. of Am.; musical compositions. String Quartet (1960), Passacaglia for Brass Instruments (1969), Toccata for Brass Ensemble (1970), O Scarum Convivium, for trumpet & organ (1972), Introduction, Arioso, and Fugue, for cello & piano (1974); Republican; Episcopal; rec: Persian cats. Res: 2020 DuFour Ave Redondo Beach 90278 Ofc: Los Angeles Mission College 1212 San Fernando Rd San Fernando 91340

FOSTER-VARGAS, CHRISTIE DALEE, lawyer; b. Dec. 25, 1951, New Haven, Conn.; d. H. Oliver and Janice DaLee Foster; m. David Vargas, Jan. 13, 1980; 1 son: David b. 1983; edn: Western Mich. Univ. 1970-71; BA, magna cum laude, Eastern Mich. Univ. 1975; JD, cum laude, Univ. of San Diego 1978; admitted to Calif. Bar 1978. Career: buyer Solar Turbines, 1978; contract adminstr., senior contract adminstr. Sundstrand Turbomach, San Diego 1980–; mem: Nat. Contract Mgmt. Assn., San Diego County Bar Assn., Calif. Bar Assn. Ofc: Sundstrand Turbomach Contracts Dept. 4400 Ruffin Road San Diego 92123

FOUDRAY, SAMUEL HOUSTON, real estate appraiser-consultant; b. Sept. 14, 1935, Long Beach; s. Charles William and Norma Aldine (Cook) Foudray; m. Martha Siggson, Apr. 26, 1959; children: Robin, b. 1954, Linda, b. 1957; edn: AA, honors, Compton Coll. 1956; RM, Am. Inst. R.E. Appraisers, 1980; SRA, Soc. of R.E. Appraisers 1981; CRA, Nat. Assn. of Review Appraisers 1977. Career: real estate agt/appraiser, 1964-73; self-emp. real estate appraiser, 1973-80; pres. Samartha Corp., Paramount 1980–; instr./owner Real Estate Procedures (a R.E. Seminar co.); past: profl. musician; instr. Anthony Schs. (1974-5), Century 21 (1976), Realty World (1976); mem: Soc. of Real Estate Appraisers (pres. Long Bch./So Bay chpt. 1981-2); Paramount CofC (pres. 1977-8); Paramount Lions Club (pres. 1977-8); dir. Rancho Los Cerritos Realty Bd., 1976-78; Town Hall of Calif. Author: Competitive Market Analysis Techniques (text for R.E. seminars); creator and host cable TV pgm.

This Is Real Estate; Republican; Lutheran; rec: travel, sports. Res: 9856 Hoback St. Bellflower 90706 Ofc: Samartha Corp. 15726 Paramount Blvd. Paramount 90723

FOULDS, DONALD DUANE, corporate executive; b. Feb. 4, 1925, Saginaw, Mich.; s. Joseph William and Florence Francis (Blumenthal) F.; m. Doris Roberts, Mar. 4, 1949; children: Michael, b. 1955, Scott, b. 1958, Nancy, b. 1960; edn: BS, US Naval Acad. 1948; BSEE, USN Postgrad. Sch., Monterey 1955; MSIE, Purdue Univ. 1956; Naval War Coll., Newport, RI 1961. Career: served ensign through the ranks to comdr. US Navy, 1948-67: after command of USS Desoto Co., apptd. section hd. Prodn. and Quality Control and branch hd. Missile Branch, Polaris/Poseidon Ballistic Missile Pgm., 1963-67, ret 1967; var. mgmt. pos. Northrop Corp. Electro-Mech. Div., 1967–, dir. procurement 1968, exec.v.p. Olson Labs (subs. Northrop) 1971, dir. mktg. 1974, asst. to corp. v.p.-planning 1976, exec. asst. to pres. and chief operating ofcr. 1977, v.p. Countertrade 1983-; also pres./bd.chmn. Kingsbury Aviation, Inc. 1977-81; mem. aero. advy. com. North Orange Co. Comm. Coll. (1982-), trustee So. Calif. Hist. Aviation Soc. (1981-); honors: Tau Beta Pi, Naval Acad. Crew Squad capt. (1948); mem. IEEE (1950-65), Assn. of US Army (secty. Gr. L.A. Chpt., treas. 7th Region 1983-86); Republican; Episcopal; rec: comml. and instrument rated pilot. Res: 4849 Blackhorse Rd Rancho Palos Verdes 90274 Ofc: Northrop Corp. 1840 Century Park E. Los Angeles 90067

FOULKES, JOHN DAVID, non-profit organization executive; b. Feb. 24, 1929, Altadena; s. Frank James and Helen Virginia (Stahley) F.; m. Betty J. Cochran, June 18, 1954; children: Deborah b. 1956, Susan b. 1958; edn: BA, Antioch Univ. 1980. Career: v.p., mgr., Dist. Trust ofc., Glendale Security Pacific National Bank 1953-77; v.p. exec. search firm Ott & Associates, Pasadena 1977-81; ast. to pres. World Vision, Monrovia 1981–; mem: Rotary, San Marino City Club, Town Hall of Los Angeles; mil: cpl. US Army 1949-53, Occupation Forces Ger.; Republican; Protestant (active layman Lake Ave. Congl. Ch., Pasadena); rec: friends, travel. Res: 1385 Belhaven Rd. San Marino 91108 Ofc: World Vision, 919 W. Huntington Dr. Monrovia 91016

FOUTZ, REYNOLD LYAL, dentist, educator; b. Apr. 14, 1907, Los Angeles; s. Chester L. and Goda (Clotfelter) F.; m. M. Vivian Gers, Oct. 17, 1931; edn: DDS, USC Sch. of Dentistry. Career: dentist self-empl. pvt. practice, ret.; asst. tchr. postgrad. classes in prosthetics USC Sch. of Dentistry 1977-78; honors: Alpha Tau Epsilon, class pres. USC Grad. Class of 1929, elected permanent pres. 1938; life mem: Am. Dent. Assn., Calif. Dent. Assn., Los Angeles Dent. Soc., Beverly Hills Acad. of Dentistry (pres. 1957-58), Xi Psi Phi Dent. Frat.; clubs: Los Angeles Country, Los Feliz Kiwanis (charter), Beverly Hills Kiwanis (ret.); mil: capt. USN(R) Ret., 42 yrs. svc., Pacific Area w/Battle star, Letter of commendn.; Republican; Protestant; rec: golf. Res: 4246 Beeman Ave Studio City 91604

FOX, DANIEL NORMAN, lawyer; b. Aug. 28, 1929, Los Angeles; s. Jack and Rae (Epstein) F.; m. Roberta Lynn, Dec. 10, 1966; children: Paul b. 1954, Anne b. 1957, Martin b. 1969, Sheila b. 1971; edn: BA, Univ. Chgo. 1950, JD, 1955; admitted Calif. State Bar. Career: pvt. practice of law, civil and criminal since 1958, law offices in Pomona, 1960–; critical writer on law and civil liberties; author Calif. Contg. Edn. of the Bar text on Dividing Community Property, the article "Problems of Divorcing Spouses Who Together Operate an Unincorporated Business," other arts. on criminal, civil and family law; profl. musician, performer oriental violin; past adj. prof. Music, CalPoly Univ. Pomona; judge pro tem Municipal Ct. Pomona; arbitrator Am. Arbitration Assn. 1964-; honors: rep. Univ. Chgo. (alma mater) var. academic functions; mem. Calif., Los Angeles County bar assns., ACLU, Local 47 Am. Fedn. of Musicians; mil: pvt. US ARmy 1955-57. Ofc: Daniel N. Fox, Atty. 477 S Main St Pomona 91/66

FOX, FRANCIS THOMAS, SR., management consultant; b. Mar. 11, 1920, Worcester, Mass.; s. Thomas Francis and Elizabeth Florence (Prendergast) F.; m. Patricia Farrell, Oct. 18, 1951; children: Francis, Jr. b. 1952, Patricia b. 1954, Brigit b. 1955, Colleen b. 1956, Susan b. 1958; edn: BS in bus. adm., Holy Cross Coll. 1941; Accredited Airport Exec., Am. Assn. of Airport Execs. (1947). Career: airport mgr. Worcester, Mass. 1946-53; asst. dir. of aviation, Phila., Pa. 1953-54; pres. Fox Travel Service, Worcester, Mass. 1955-58; gen. mgr. Los Angeles Dept. of Airports 1958-68; dir. of aviation Hughes Tool Co., Las Vegas, Nv. 1968-73; pres. F.T. Fox Internat. Inc., L.A. 1973-79; city mgr. City of San Diego, 1979-84; pres. Francis T. Fox & Assocs., San Jose 1984–; dir: Host Internat. (1969-79), Northrop Univ. (1973-79), McCulloch Internat. Airline (1975-79), Sabins Indus. (1975-); honors: apptd. by Pres. Kennedy to Pres.'s Commn. on Aviation Goals (1961-63), Aviation Man of the Year (1967); mem. Am. Assn. of Airport Execs (pres. 1966-67), Airport Oprs. Council Internat. (v.p. 1968); clubs: Rotary, Aero Club of No. Calif., La Rinconada Country; publs: book of verse: The Airport Man (1966); mil: major, aviator USMC 1942-46; Indep.; Roman Catholic; rec: golf, flying, writing. Res: 1058 S Winchester Blvd San Jose 95128 Ofc: F.T. Fox & Associates 1754 Technology Dr Ste 128 San Jose 95110

FOX, GARY MICHAEL, physician; b. Aug. 29, 1950, St. Louis, Mo.; s. Jerome Gilbert and Sylvia Ruth (Brimer) F.; m. Robin, May 19, 1979; 1 dau. Lindsay b. 1984; edn: BS, Univ. Miami 1972, MD, 1976; resident OB-Gyn, Jackson Meml. Hosp. 1976-80; certified Am. Board OB-Gyn. 1983. Career: residency in obstets.-gyn. Jackson Meml. Hosp., Miami, Fla.; physician, co-dir High Risk Obstetrics Clinic, Kaiser Found. Hosp. South Sacramento, 1980–, chief Dept. of OB-Gyn 1983–; mem. No. Calif. OB-Gyn Soc., Fellow Am. Coll. of Obstetrics-Gynecology; Democrat; Jewish; rec: reading, racquetball. Ofc: Kaiser Foundation Hospital 6600 Bruceville Rd Sacramento 95823

FOX, JOHN DANIEL, financial analyst; b. Nov. 23, 1961, Fullerton; s. Robert C. and Beverly Jane (Rawlings) F.; m. Barbara Slocum, Feb. 14, 1987; edn: BS in fin., USC 1983. Career: loan agt. Salvason-Bush & Co., 1983-84; loan agt. Income Property Funding Inc., Santa Ana 1984, then v.p., ptnr., bd. dirs. 1984-, pres. 1985—; ptnr. C.F. Devel., 1985-; assoc. C.M. Properties Inc., 1985-; mem. USC Young Alumni of O.C. (dir.), USC Commerce Assocs., Sigma Chi, Newport Harbor Costa Mesa CofC (Commerce Indsl. Com.); clubs: Balboa Bay, Sunny Hills Racquet, Univ. Athletic; Republican (Calif. Young Repubs., Ed. Zschau for US Senate com.); Catholic; rec: tennis, ski, basketball, philately. Res: 308 Sapphire Ave Balboa Is 92662 Ofc: C.M.P. Inc. POB 501 Santa Ana 90702

FOX, KAREN SUE, real estate developer, b. Mar. 31, 1946, Pittsburgh, Pa.; d. Jacob M. and Leona R. (Hartstein) Kline; m. Louis J. Fox, July 12, 1970; children: Ariel b. 1975, Cole b. 1984; edn: undergrad. USC 1964-66; BA, CSU San Jose 1968; MFA, UC Davis 1970; Calif. lic. real estate agt. (1978), broker (1986). Career: art instr. and artist, 1968-73; interior designer/prin. Concept Interior Designs Inc., 1970-75; real estate developer, dir. Sweetwater Devel. Inc. (real estate syndicator), 1975—; broker Sweetwater Land Co. Inc. 1986—; art instr. UCD, UCD Ext. (1969-73), Davis Art Ctr. (1970-71), Sacto. City Coll., Am. River Coll. (1971, 72); awards: All Univ. Art Fest., UCB (1969); 6th Nat. Sculpture Conf., Lawrence, Kans. (1970); City of Davis: Visual Improvement Award (1976), art conf. grants (1977, 78), Resolution of appreciation for service to affordable housing (1984); mem: Davis Area CofC, Davis Small Bus. Network, Econ. Devel. Council of Davis, Internat. Council of Shopping Ctr., Yolo County Board of Realtors, Pence Gal. (Davis), Davis Art Ctr., Crocker Art Mus. (Sacto.), Nat. Crafts Council, Smithsonian Instn., Planned Parenthood; active in Davis civic and cultural affairs (1974-); works: developed first passive solar apt. complex with HUD insured loan; devel. first limited equity housing co-op without any govt. subsidies; publs: num. feature stories in home and real estate sects. Sacto. Union, Sacto. Bee, Multi-Housing News, 1984-; guest var. local radio and TV pgms., 1986; Democrat; Jewish; rec: skiing, art. Res: 1120 Road 103 Davis 95616 Ofc: Sweetwater Development 423 E St Davis 95616

FOY, JOSEPH OWEN, pharmacist; b. Dec. 29, 1923, Glendo, Wyo.; s. Ed Sr. and Rose B. (Ferguson) F.; edn: BS, Creighton Univ. 1951; Lic. Pharmacist, Calif. 1954. Career: pharmacist Immanuel Deaconess Hosp., Omaha, Nebr. 1951-54; pharmacist Vossbrink Pharmacy, San Rafael 1954-58; pharcist South Shore Drugs, San Pedro 1958-60, CEO 1960—; mem: Calif. Pharmacists Assn. (academy mem. 1965), Knights of Columbus, Nat. Assn. of Retail Druggists, Elks, Am. and So. Bay Pharmaceutical Assns., Calif. Pharmacist Political Action Com.; mil: USN 1942-46; Democrat; Catholic; rec: travel, swimming. Ofc: South Shore Drug, 1625 W. 25th St. San Pedro 90732

FOY, LAURETTA BEATY, helicopter pilot/heliport consultant; b. May 30, 1912, Oklahoma City, Okla.; d. Fredrick Ernest and Kathryn Graham (Keffer) Beaty; m. 2d Robert W. Foy (dec.), May 16, 1945; children: James b. 1934, Ernest b. 1936, Shawn b. 1949; edn: Occidental Coll. 1929-32; pilot US Army Air Corps, 318th AAF FTD, Sweetwater, Tx. 1942; AUS 1st OTU (Instrument Sch.), St. Joseph, Mo. 1943; AUS 4th OTU (Pursuit Sch.), Brownsville, Tx. 1943; AAF SAT (Sch. Applied Tactics) 1944; FAA lic. Comml. Pilot (Single Engine Land & Sea, Instrument, Multi Engine Land, Rotorcraft-Helicopter), Instr. (1940-). Career: Busby Berkeley dancer, photog. & stunt double, Warner Bros. Pictures, 1932-41; demonstration pilot, test pilot Piper Aircraft Corp., Lock Haven, Pa. 1941-42; test pilot, No. Am. Aviation Inc. 1946-68; independent flight instr. 1952-62; chief helicopter instr. Belmont Aviation Co., Long Beach 1962-64; Helicabs (Rooftop Taxi Svc.) Los Angeles, 1964; chief helicopter pilot Pacific Airmotive Corp., Burbank 1965-68; chief pilot Southland Helicopters div. Hughes Tool Co., Long Beach 1968-74; helicopter & heliport cons. Bell Helicopter Co., Van Nuys 1974-79; pres. Heliport Consultants, Malibu 1979-84; semi-ret.; flt. instr. Peninsula Aviation (Alexair, Inc.) Torrance; apptd. mem. (chair 1970) FAA Women's Advis. Com. on Aviation (1967-70), Presidential Aviation Advis. Commn., Wash DC (1970-73), Calif. Gov.'s Aerospace Aviation Task Force, Sacto. (1969-79); honors: 1st Pl. winner All-Women Transcontinental Air Race (1949), Silver Medal Award, FAA (1970), Max Schumacher Award for advance. of use of helicopters, HAA (1975), Raise Your Sites (Heliports) Award, HAI (1984); mem: Screen Actors Guild (1935-), Musicians Union, Loc. 47 (1950-70), Whirly-Girls (internat. pres. 1976-77), Fifinella (WASP), Am. Helicopter Soc., 99s, Profl. Helicopter Pilots Assn. (pres. 1978-79); publs: editor Flight Safety Found.: Helicopter Safety Bull.; mil: WASP pilot, US Army Air Corps, Air Transport Command, Ferrying Div. 1943-44, decorated 3 campaign ribbons, Am., WWI, Victory, Hon. Svc.; capt. Air Force Reserv. 1950-58; Republican; Christian Sci.; rec: piano, pipe organ, swimming. Res: 100 Mildas Dr Malibu 90265

FRAILICH, STEPHEN MICHAEL, lawyer; b. Dec. 16, 1952, Mnpls.; s. Irving and Harriet F. (Mondshane) F.; edn: BA, Univ. of Minn. 1975; JD, Univ. of San Fernando Valley Coll. of Law 1979. Career: treas. Unique Jewelers Inc., Bev. Hills 1980; vice pres. D & R Jewelers Inc., Encino 1981; pres. Law Ofcs. of Stephen M. Frailich & Assocs. APLC, Van Nuys 1982—, spec. in personal injury practice; acting judge Municipal Ct.; mem: Calif. State Bar, San Fernando Valley Bar Assn., L.A. Trial Lawyers Assn., L.A. County Bar Assn., Am. Bar Assn., Am. Jewish Congress, NAACP; works: 1st yr of law practise won a $100,000 pers. inj. settlement, 2nd yr became law corp. with 2 offices, 9 employees; Democrat (mem. Bobbie Fiedler election com.); Jewish; rec: tennis, trombonist, dunebuggies, write poetry. Res: 10860 Paso Robles Granada Hills 91344 Ofc: Law Offices of Stephen M. Frailich & Assocs. APLC, 14328 Victory Blvd Suites 207-9, Van Nuys 91401

FRAIZER, CLIFF(ORD) LEWIS, general aviation consultant; b. May 20, 1909, Seattle, Wash.; s. Clifford and Grace Adelaide (Kidd) F.; m. Lillian Taskinen (dec. 1981), Sept. 1, 1936; edn: completed 8th gr. Durant Grammer Sch., Oakland 1926, Santa Ana Evening H. Sch. 1956; AA, Orange Coast Coll. 1959; FAA lic. Gen. Aviation Cons., Fixed Base Opr. Career: served in US Marine Corps Reserve 1932-35, active duty USMC 1935-57: aircraft and engine mechanic North Island NAS, San Diego 1935-42; engring. chief, South Pacific (incl. Guadalcanal) 1942-, engring. chief Norfolk, Va. and El Toro Calif. 1944, aboard carriers USS Point Cruze (VMTB 464) and USS Rendova (VMF 214) 1945; stu. aviation maint. USMC tech. sch., then taught Fundamentals of Reciprocating Engines, NCOIC; aviation engring. ofcr. in jet fighters (VMF 115, VMFN 513), Korea 1956; instr. aviation tech. adminstrn., El Toro MCAS 1957; civilian career: aircraft inspr. Long Beach Airomotive 1957; owner, flight instr., instrument flt. instr., gen. aviation cons. Cliff Frazier's A & E Inspection Service, Orange Co. Airport, 1957—; honors: Resolution Commendn. for 50 years of safe flying, Orange County Bd. Supvrs.; mil. decorations incl. Good Conduct w/4 stars, Am. Def. Service, Am. Campaign, Asiatic-Pac. Campaign w/4 stars, WWII Victory, Korean Svc. w/2 Stars, UN Svc. medals, Merit. Decoration from Admiral W.F. Halsey for Action on Guadalcanal; mem: Aircraft Owners & Pilots Assn. (1957-), Toastmasters Intl. (1960-70), O.C. Taxpayer's Assn. (1965-68), Citizens Advis. Com. General Plan Pgm./ Santa Ana (1965) and Charter Rev. Com. (1966); Republican (del. 1964-68; cand. Orange Co. Supvr. 1st Dist. 1964, 68); Prot.; rec: stu. of hist., constnl. govt. Res: 2049 S Halladay St Santa Ana 92707

FRANCAVILLA, ROBERT JOHN, lawyer; b. May 4, 1957, Los Angeles; s. Ernest J. and Pauline E. (Gravlin) F.; edn: BBA, Univ. San Diego Law Sch. 1980, JD, 1983; admitted Calif State Bar 1983, US Dist. Ct. (so. dist. Calif.). Career: law clerk San Diego City Dist. Atty's. Ofc. 1983; judicial extern Hon. Gordon Cologne 4th Dist. Ct. of Appeal 1983; assoc. atty. Shifflet, Sharp & Walters 1983-85, Casey, Gerry, Casey, Westbrook, Reed & Hughes 1985—; mem; ABA, San Diego County Bar Assn.; rec: running, fitness, surfing, golf, karate, tennis, cooking. Res: 7924 Camino Tranquilo San Diego 92122 Ofc: Casey, Gerry et al. 110 Laurel St San Diego 92101-1486

FRANCIS, TIMOTHY DUANE, chiropractor; b. Mar. 1, 1956, Chgo.; s. Joseph Duane and Barbara Jane (Sigwalt) F.; edn: BS biol., Los Angeles Coll. of Chiropractic 1982, DC (magna cum laude), 1984; MS in nutrition/biol., Univ. of Bridgeport 1986; bd. qual. as team physician, LACC Postgrad. Sch. 1984-85. Career: pvt. practice chiropractic, 1984—; faculty Univ. of Nev., Reno 1976-80, L.A. Coll. of Chiropractic 1983-85; honors: Phi Kappa Phi (1978; Scholar of Year award 1980), Charles F. Cutts Scholar (1980), Delta Sigma (1982), Nat. Dean's List (1981-84); Republican; Catholic; rec: karate, bodybuilding, shooting. Res: POB 43455 Las Vegas NV 89116 Ofc: L.V. Chiro. Center 1111 Las Vegas Blvd N. Ste A Las Vegas NV 89104

FRANDRUP, CHARLES FRANCIS, electrical engineer; b. Nov. 1, 1947, Marysville, Calif.; s. Walter Henry and Marian Frances (Streit) F.; m. Jeane, June 5, 1976; children: Karen Kraft, Scott Kraft, Heidi Frandrup, Erich Frandrup; edn: BS in E.E., Calif. State Polytech. Coll. S.L.O. 1970; MBA, St. Mary's Coll. of Calif. 1986; Reg. Profl. Engr. (E.E.) Calif. (1976). Career: elec. engr. Fed. Power Commn., San Francisco 1970-72; elec. engr. Pacific Gas & Elec. Co., 1972—; mem. IEEE, Pacific Coast Elec. Assn.; Republican; Prot.; rec: sports. Res: 3404 Del Monte San Mateo 94403 Ofc: PG&E Electric T&D Dept. Room 3031, 77 Beale San Francisco 94106

FRANK, ROBERT WALLACE, lawyer; b. Oct. 23, 1955, Yerrington, Nev.; s. Wallace C. and Evelyn Mary (Larrimore) F.; edn: AB, San Diego State Univ. 1977; LLB, UC Hastings Coll. of Law 1980; admitted Calif. State Bar 1980, U.S. Ct. of Appeal 9th circ. 1985. Career: assoc. atty. Rhoades, Hollywood & Neil Law Firm San Diego 1980—; honors: Phi Beta Kappa 1977, Kappa Sigma (pres. 1976-77); mem: S.D. Co. Bar Assn., S.D. Co. Barristers (bd. dirs. 1982-84), Assn. So. Calif. Defense Counsel 1981-; author: Magnuson-Moss Warranty Legislation Analysis; Catholic; rec: fishing, hunting, sports, antique car collection. Res: 1138 Agate St San Diego 92109 Ofc: Rhoades, Hollywood & Neil 1010 2nd Ave, Ste 1712, San Diego 92101

FRANKIEL, STEVEN MARKS, accountant; b. Apr. 21, 1958, Oakland; s. Harry and Mary Ellen (Marks) F.; m. Marlene Beth, Jan. 6, 1985; edn: BA bus. econs., with honors, 1979; CPA Calif. 1984. Career: sales and use tax auditor State Bd. of Equalization 1979-81; senior acct. London & Heisman Acctg. Corp. 1982—; treas. Westwood Kehilla (religious congregation); mem: Calif. Soc. CPAs, Am. Inst. CPAs, Sierra Club, Nature Conservancy; artistic works: portfolio of nature photographs; rec: bicycling, hiking, photog. Ofc: London & Heisman 11661 San Vicente Blvd, Ste 900, Los Angeles 90049

FRANKLIN, BRUCE RENALDO, computer co. executive; b. July 17, 1954, Pleasanton, Calif.; s. Reuben Clyde and Agatha Alfrieda (Jones) F.; m. Suzanne Lydston, Feb. 7, 1976, div. 1982; m 2d Lynette Goltry, Nov. 1984; children: Chris Goltry, Heather Goltry; edn: Am. River Jr. Coll. 1972; US Naval Acad., Annapolis 1972-74; Air Technical Tng. Ctr., 1976; Riverside Comm. Coll. 1978; desig. Electronic Computer Systems Repairman, USAF 1976. Career: life & disability agt. John Hancock Mutual Life Ins. Co., Sacto. 1974; mgr. Taco Bell, Sacto. 1975; USAF comp. repairman, March AFB, 1975-79; field engr. No. Telecom Systems Corp., 1979-80, Philips Medical Systems, 1980, Datapoint Corp., Brea 1981-82; supr. field engring., World Computer Corp., Torrance 1982-84, Digital Equip. Corp. 1984-85; instr. Squadron, AF, 1975-6; honors: Airman of the Month (2), 1978; mem: US Naval Acad. Alumni Assn. (bd. dirs. 1985, class rep. 1976), Non-commnd. Officers Assn. 1975-79,

Trendsetters of Sacto. 1972; mil: midn. USN 1972-4, sgt. USAF 1975-9, USNR 1984-; Republican; Christian; rec: golf, weight tng., music. Res: 1649 Carbon Cyn Rd Chino Hills 91710-2310

FRANKLIN, JAN F., telephone co. executive; b. Feb. 3, 1945, Richmond, CA; d. Godfrey and Catharine Bishop; m. Marlin R. Franklin, Apr. 6, 1968; edn: Oakland City Coll. 1963-5; Sacramento State Coll. 1965; Contra Costa Coll. 1965-7, 1969; Univ. of Hawaii 1970. Career: with Pacific Bell 1963–; order writer, Oakland 1963-5; svc. rep., Richmond & Sacto. 1965; bus. ofc. supvr. Oakland & Richmond 1966; bus. ofc. mgr., Pittsburg 1971; traffic op. mgr., San Francisco 1974; personnel mgr. S.F.; currently dist. mgr. Info Sys. Devel., San Ramon; awards: Woman of Yr., Richmond Bus. & Profl. Women 1973; Key Contract Mgr. to the Richmond City Council, Pac. Bell 1970-80; judge Bank of Am. Achievement Pgm.; listed: Outstanding Young Women of Am. 1975; mem: Bus. & Profl. Women's Club 1967 (past pres.), P.E.O., Nat. Assn. of Exec. Females 1983, Am. Soc. of Tng. Devel. 1983, Am. Mgmt. Assn.; apptd. mem. Richmond Police/ Comm. Rels. Task Force 1971; elected to Richmond Comm. Devel. Commn. 1975; Republican; Lutheran; rec: public speaking. Res: 5733 Amend Rd Richmond 94803 Ofc: Pacific Bell 2600 Camino Ramon Rm 4E103 San Ramon 95883

FRANTZ, JOHN CORYDON, librarian; b. Aug. 25, 1926, Seneca Falls, NY; s. John Clark and Cora May (Gilbert) F.; m. Vivien May Rowan, Dec. 31, 1947; children: Sheila, Keith, Jay; edn: AB, Syracuse Univ. 1950, BS, 1951, MS, 1952. Career: cons. Wis. State Library, 1954-58; dir. Green Bay (Wis.) Public Library, 1958-61; dir. pub. library grants US Office of Edn., 1961-67; dir. Brooklyn Public Library, 1967-70; dir. Nat. Book Com., 1970-75; exec. chmn. Pahlavi Nat. Library, Tehran, Iran 1974-77; librarian San Francisco Pub. Library, 1977–; bd. dirs. REading is Fundamental, Bookmobile Services Trust, Am. Reading Council, Metro Research Libraries Council; mem. Am., NY State, Calif. library assns.; club: Coffee House (NYC); mil: US Army 1945-47. Res: 1390 Market St San Francisco 94102 Ofc: Public Library Civic Center San Francisco 94102

FRASCINO, ROBERT JAMES, physician; b. June 12, 1952, Rochester, N.Y.; s. Angelo Joseph and Jennie (Giancola) F.; edn: BA biol, cum laude, Oberlin Coll. 1974; MD, Univ. of Cinncinnati Coll. of Med. 1978; Diplomate Nat. Bd. of Med. Examiners 1979, bd. certified Am. Bd. of Pediat. 1983, Am. Bd. of Allergy and Clin. Immunol. 1983. Career: research extern. drug studies VA Hosp. Sleep and Dream Ctr. Cincinnati; intern, res. in pediat. Childrens Hosp. Med. Ctr. of No. Calif. 1978-80; fellow allergy and clin. immunol. UC San Francisco 1980-82; chief res. allergy/clin. immunol. S.F. Gen. Hosp. 1981-82; cons. allergy/immunol. VA Med. Ctr. Palo Alto 1983-84; pvt. grp. med. practice allergy/immunol. Sunnyvale Med. Clin. 1983–; asst. clin. prof. med. Stanford Univ. Med. Ctr. 1983–; honors: Sigma Xi 1974, Howard Hanson Award (piano, Eastman Sch. of Music) 1970, Travel Grant Award (Park-Davis/ Am. Coll. of Allergy) 1980; mem: Am. Acad. Allergy and Clin. Immunol., Am. Coll. Allergy, Am. Acad. Pediat., AMA, CMA, Allergy Assn. of No. Calif., Western Soc. of Allergy/Immunol., Calif. Soc. Allergy/Clin. Immunol., Am. Assn. Immunol. and Allergy, Joint Council Allergy and Immunol., Journal Club-Allergy; publ: Audio Digest vol. 4, no. 4 1981; num. classical piano concerts in Am. and Europe, orig. piano solo compositions; Democrat; Catholic. Res: 248 Walker Dr, No. 17, Mountain View 94043 Ofc: Sunnyvale Med. Clin. Inc. 596 Carroll St Sunnyvale 94086

FRASER, JAMES MICHAEL, lawyer; b. Nov. 16, 1954, Victoria, B.C., Can.; nat. USA 1985; s. Jack McGuinness and Rose Rita (Zomar) F.; m. Deborah, Mar. 15, 1980; edn: BA, UC Los Angeles 1976; JD, Western State Univ. 1980; admitted Calif. State Bar 1981. Career: law clerk Paul, Hastings, Janofsky & Walker, Los Angeles 1976-77; law clk. Orange County Public Defender, Santa Ana 1978-80; lawyer, sole practitioner, Santa Ana 1981–; lectr. College Legal Community (C.L.C.), Fullerton 1981-; tutor law students, Western St. Univ.; awards: appreciation for volunteer services, State Bar of Calif. 1983, 84; mem: Am., Calif., Orange County (OC Bar/Med. Assn. liason com.) bar assns., Orange County Legal Aid Soc., College Legal Community (volunteer), Sierra Club; Roman Catholic; rec: fishing, skiing, backpacking, travel. Res: 8116 E. Carnation Way, Anaheim 92806 Ofc: James Fraser, 401 Civic Center Dr, Ste 1000, Santa Ana 92701

FRATIANNE, ROBERT DEWEY, superior court judge; b. Nov. 12, 1929, Cleveland, Ohio; s. Carmen John and Angela Rachel (Gallucci) F.; m. Peggy MacDonald, Feb. 14, 1981; children: Mary Beth b. 1956, Nicholas John b. 1957, Linda Sue b. 1960, Angela Claire b. 1963, Robert Joseph b. 1967; edn: BS bus. admin., Miami Univ. Ohio 1951; LLB, Southwestern Univ. L.A. 1960; admitted to practice Supreme Ct. Calif., U.S. Dist. Ct. so. dist. Calif., U.S. Ct. of Appeals 9th circ. 1962; U.S. Supreme Ct. 1975. Career: claims examiner Allstate Ins. L.A. 1956-60; atty. pvt. practice L.A. 1960-78; judge L.A. Municipal Ct. 1978-81; justice pro tem Calif. Appellate Ct. 1981; judge L.A. Superior Ct. 1981–; Supervising Judge 1986; Oral Review Bd. L.A. Police Dept. 1973-75; Dist. Atty. Advisory Com. 1976-77; tchr. judge in camp Constl. Rights Found. 1980-85; Resolutions: no. 90 Calif. Senate 1976, Co. of Los Angeles 1975; mem: Calif., San Fernando Valley (del. state bar 1975, crim. law chmn. 1976, resolutions com. 1976), S.F. Valley Crim. (pres. 1975, 1st v.p. 1974) bar assns.; Calif. Judges Assn., Italian-Am. Lawyers of Calif. (1st v.p. 1977, pres.-elect 1978), L.A. Co. Probation Com., Our Lady of Lourdes Men's Club (past pres.), Kiwanis, Encino CofC, YMCA (trustee), Sigma Nu, Delta Theta Phi; mil: yeoman 3/c USCG 1951-54; Democrat; Catholic; rec: golf, painting. Ofc: The Superior Court 900 Third St San Fernando 91340

FRAZER, CLOYCE CLEMON, educator (ret.); b. Jan. 2, 1919, Warren, Ark.; s. Charles Columbus and Maude Mae (Jones) F.; m. Beverley Mundorff, Apr. 10, 1942; edn: dip. USAF Flt. Tng., 1944; BA, San Jose State Coll. 1952; MA CSU Sacto. 1961. Career: aircraft mech. Matson Air Transp. Div., Oakland 1946-48; flight instr. Moreau Flying Serv., Oakland 1948-49; instr. aircraft mechanics, Aero Industries Tech. Inst., Oakland 1949-50; indsl. arts tchr. Folsom (Ca.) Unified Sch. Dist., 1953-54; indsl. arts tchr. Sacto. City Unif. Sch. Dist. 1954-63; indsl. arts tchr., dept. head, San Mateo Union High Sch. Dist., 1963-83; also pres. Crestmoor H.S. Faculty Assn. 1965-6, mem. planning coms. for new H.S. and writing curriculum materials; awards: hon. mentions for two metal sculptures, 1967, San Mateo Co. Fair and Floral Fiesta; mem: Epsilon Pi Tau, Caterpillar Club, Nat. Edn. Assn., Calif. Tchrs. Assn., Calif. Ret. Tchrs. Assn.; Calif. Aerospace Edn. Assn. (treas. 1983-, pres. Northern Sect. 1978-9); Calif. Indsl. Edn. Assn.; Vocational Edn. Assn.; Aircraft Owners and Pilots Assn.; Exptl. Aircraft Assn. (Outstanding Individual Achievement Award 1982); Am. Craft Council; publs: articles in ednl. jours., various curriculum mats.; mil: served to Maj., USAF, Reserve, 1941-79, WWII Victory, Asia-Pac. Svc., Am. Theater Svc. medals; Democrat; Prot.; rec: fishing, flying. Res: Belmont 94002

FRAZER, GREGORY JAMES, audiologist; b. Sept. 28, 1952, Sacramento, Calif.; s. Wilbur Robert and Miriam Dorthy (Quinn) F.; edn: BA speech pathol. and audiol., CSU Sacramento 1974; MS audiol. & counseling deaf/ hearing impaired, Univ. Utah Salt Lake City 1976; PhD audiol., Wayne State Univ. Detroit 1981. Career: intern, resident Univ. Utah Med. Ctr. Salt Lake City 1974-76, Detroit Med. Ctr. 1976-78, Henry Ford Hosp. Detroit 1978-81; dir. audiol. Midwest Health Ctr. Dearborn, Mich. 1981, Pulec Ear Clin. Los Angeles 1982, Auditory-Vestibular Ctr. Panorama City 1982–, Olive View Med. Ctr. Van Nuys 1984–; clin. prof. dept. head & neck surg. UCLA 1986–; honors: Calif. State Scholar (1970-71), Rehab. Svcs. Grant (1974-76), Phi Kappa Phi (1976), Grad. Profl. Scholar (Wayne State Univ. 1979-80), Dean's Honor List (1970-74); mem: Am., Calif. Speech Lang. Hearing Assns., Internat. Electric Response Audiometry Study Group, Am. Tinnitis Assn., Am. Auditory Soc., Centurions of the Deafness Research Found., Assn. for Research in Otolaryngol., Calif. Speech Pathols. & Audiols. in Pvt. Practice, Am. Acad. Otolaryngol., jay. Hearing Conservation Assn., Nat. Assn. for Hearing & Speech Action, Calif. Hearing Aid Assn., Nat. Hearing Aid Soc., Acad. of Dispensing Audiols., San Fernando Valley Speech Pathol. & Audiol. Assn. (exec. council), Better Hearing Inst. Adv. Bd. 1986-, Sigma Alpha Epsilon, Tri-Network Ski Club; Republican; Catholic; rec: snow and water skiing, golf, tennis, backpacking, jogging. Ofc: Auditory- Vestibular Ctr. 14427 Chase St Panorama City 91402

FREEHILL, KENNETH PAUL, theatrical services co. president; b. Aug. 18, 1950, Urbana, Ill.; s. Louis Anthony and Crescentia Amelia (Rock) F.; edn: BFA, Univ. Ariz. 1973. Career: tchr. Ariz. public schs., 1974; performer and group leader Childrens Theatre Midwestern Tour, 1975; founder/pres. Pentangle Theatre, Chgo. 1976-79; co-founder First Impressions Theatrical Svcs. Co., Los Angeles 1979–; mktg. and promotions cons. Am. Theatre Assn., Army Theatre Arts Assn.; awards: univ. scholarship, Univ. Ariz., Business in the Arts Awards (2), Forbes Pub. Co., disting. achieve. award Am. Theatre Assn./ Army Theatre Arts Div., first ofcl. "King" of Hollywood Movie Trivia (1982); mem. Am. Theatre Assn., Army Theatre Arts Assn., Hollywood CofC; coauthor: You May Never Get A Second Chance to Make a First Impression (1980, Hollywood), A Medal for Murder (mystery play, 1981), Sarah (musical mystery about the late Sarah Winchester, 1986); rec: motion picture hist. Ofc: 6607 Sunset Blvd, West Wing, Hollywood 90028

FREELAND, EUGENE LINCOLN, lawyer; b. Nov. 21, 1925, San Diego; s. Eugene Louis and Vera (Good) L.; m. Carol Hart Freelend, Dec. 30, 1978; children: Ann Woodhouse b. 1954; Bently Freeland b. 1956; Jessica Berger b. 1972; edn: Pomona Coll. 1943-44; BA UC Los Angeles 1948; JD, Hastings Coll. of Law 1951; admitted to Calif. State Bar 1952. Career: atty., Gray, Cary, Ames & Frye 1954-59, partner 1959–; mem: Univ. Club San Diego (pres. 1962-63); Am. Bd. Trial Adv. (nat. mem. chmn. 1959-65); Nat. Assn. Railroad Trial Counsel (v.p. Pac. region 1965-67); Hastings Coll. of Law Alumni Assn. (pres. 1969-70); Hastings Coll. of Law 1066 Found. (pres. 1984-); Rancho Santa Fe Golf Club; mil: USAAC aviation cadet 1943-45; Republican; Nonsectarian; rec: bird hunting, golf, cooking. Res: P.O. Box 732 Rancho Santa Fe 92067 Ofc: Gray, Cary et al, 1700 First Interstate Plaza San Diego 92101

FREELAND, ROBERT FREDERICK, librarian; b. Dec. 20, 1919, Flint, Mich.; s. Ralph V. and Susan Barbara (Goetz) F.; m. June Voshel, June 18, 1948; children: Susan Beth (Mrs. Kenneth S. Visser), Kent Richard; edn: BS, Eastern Mich. Univ., 1942; MS, USC, 1948, postgrad. 1949; postgrad. UCLA 1960, Univ. Mich. 1950-52, Calif. State Univ. 1956-58; Litt.D (hon.), Linda Vista Bible Coll., 1973. Career: music supr. Consol. Schs. Warren (Mich.), 1946-47; music dir. Carson City (Mich.) Pub. Schs., 1948-49; librarian, audio-visual coordinator Ford Found., Edison Inst., Greenfield Village, Dearborn, Mich. 1950-52; librarian, audio-visual coord. Helix High Sch. Library, 1952-76; librarian San Diego City Coll., 1953-54, San Diego County Library 1955-56, San Diego Public Library, 1968–; librarian, prof. library sci. Linda Vista Bible Coll., El Cajon 1976–; guest prof. CSU San Diego 1963-66, UC San Diego 1969-71, Linda Vista Bible Coll. 1970-72; lectr. San Diego City Coll. 1954-65, Grossmont Coll., El Cajon 1966-68; awards: Freedoms Found., Falley Forge, Pa. scholar 1976-80, leadership award Grossmont Union High Sch. Dist., La Mesa 1970, 71, 72; mem: NEA (life), ALA, Assn. for Ednl. Communication and Tech., Western Ednl. Soc. for Telecomms., CTA, Muslic Library Assn. So. Calif. (adv. exec. bd.), Calif. Library Assn. (pres. Palomar chpt. 1972-73), Sch.

Library Assn. Calif. (rtreas. 1956-58), Calif. Media and Library Educators (charter), Am. Legion, Ret. Officers Assn., S.D. Aerospace Mus., S.D. Mus. Art; Christian Reform. Res: 4800 Williamsburg Lane Apt 223 La Mesa 92041 Ofc: 7323 University Ave., La Mesa 92041

FREEMAN, KENNETH DONALD, public accountant; b. Dec. 8, 1912, Oakland; s. Herbert Reid and Florence (Carr) F.; m. Amelia Anna Tyler, Dec. 8, 1936; children: Kenneth M. b. 1938, Donald T. b. 1943, Lionel W. b. 1944, Shirley A. b. 1948; edn: Merrit Bus. Sch. 1931-35; Lincoln Law Sch. 1942-45; US Treas. Dept. Tng. courses 1942-49. Career: orchestra leader Ken Freeman's Californians 1931-36; clerical US Dept. of Agriculture 1936-42; deputy collector IRS 1942-51; public acctg. svc. 1952−; mem: Calif. State Bd. of Accountancy 1979− (v.p. 1981), Calif. Tax Reform Assn. (bd. dirs. 1980-), Gov.'s Advis. Commn. of Children & Youth 1964-65, Alameda County Institutions Commn. 1966-70, Alameda County Tax Assessment Appeals Bd. 1970-74; Alameda County for Prevention of Juvenile Delinquency 1970-74, Oakland NAACP Credit Union (past chmn. supr. com.), Area Council of Social Planning (past treas.), fmr. Diocese Social Justice Commn., Hanna Boys Ctr., Sonoma 1972-78 (past asst. treas., bd. dirs.), Soc. Calif. Accts., Knights of Columbus, Holy Name Soc. St. Bernard's Ch. (pres. 1952-53), St. Vincent De Paul Soc. Alameda County (bd. dirs. 1945-51); publs: music editor & sports writer Calif. Voice 1934-41; Democrat (State Central Com. exec. bd. 1964-70); Catholic; rec: golf, fishing. Res: 3426 Pierson St Oakland 94619 Ofc: 1452 70th Ave Oakland 94621

FREEMAN, PAUL M., JR., consultant; b. Dec. 16, 1952, Shreveport, La.; s. Paul M. and June A. (Sisman) F.; m. Teresa, June 11, 1952; 1 son, Travis b. 1978; edn: AA, Cypress Jr. Coll. 1973; UC Irvine 1973-75; UC Los Angeles 1977. Career: owner The Gallery Audio Video Lab, La Habra 1972-74; owner Overland Recording Studio, Costa Mesa 1975-80; v.p. Internat. Automated Media, Irvine 1980-82; indep. recording engr./prod., 1982−; ptnr. Renaissance Software, Santa Ana 1984−; prod. "The California Project" first pop Compact Disc recording (DDD), Telarc Records 1984; engineered Disneyland Main Street Electrical Parade, and world's largest laser show, Epcot Center Florida (Disney); recipient Indsl. Arts Award, Ford Aeronautics Div. (1975). Address: Renaissance Software 1171 Appian Way Santa Ana 92705

FREEMAN, RICHARD DEAN, consulting co. executive; b. Nov. 27, 1928, Rushville, Ind.; s. Verne Crawford and Mary Phyllis (Dean) F.; m. Mary Jane Barkman, Aug. 21, 1950; children: Debra b. 1952, Phyllis b. 1954, Richard b. 1955, Tom b. 1959; edn: BS, Aeronautical Engring., Purdue Univ. 1950, BS, Naval Sci. & Tactics, 1950; MS, Krannert Sch.- Purdue 1954. Career: supvr., indsl. engr. General Motors Corp., Warren, Ohio 1954-58; prodn. mgr. TRW, Ramo-Wooldridge Div., Denver, Colo. 1958-61; sales mgr. Curtiss-Wright Corp., Albuquerque, N.Mex. 1961-62; mgr. missile pgms. Hughes Aircraft Corp., Los Angeles 1962-68; v.p. LTV Electrosystems (now, E-Systems), Dallas, Texas 1968-72; v.p. Rockwell Internat., Autonetics Div., Los Angeles 1972-74; pres. Internat. Pacific Co., Newport Beach 1974−; senior lectr. West Coast Univ., Los Angeles 1974-78; secty. Proteus Corp., Newport Beac; chmn. Technology Assoc. Corp., Newport Beach 1984-85; honors: Distng. Engring. Alumnus, Purdue Univ. 1973; Man of the Year, Sgima Alpha Tau 1971; mem: Mil. Order of World Wars, Kappa Sigma, Masons, Consistory (32nd degree), Nat. Eagle Scout Assn., Purdue Alumni Assn., Boy Scouts of Am. (dist. chmn., scoutmaster, cubmaster); works: documentary film, Zeros of the Pacific, Nippon TV 1979; feature film/ book, Equator, 1984; mil: capt USMC 1946-58, Pres. Unit Citation, Naval Commdn., WWII Victory, Am. Defense, Korean Campaign w/ 3 Battle Stars, UN Ribbon, Korean Pre. Unit Citation; Republican; Protestant; rec: search & exploration for Amelia Erhart's Aircraft, Marshall Is. Res: 3910 Topside Ln. Corona Del Mar 92625 Ofc: 240 Newport Center Dr. Newport Beach 92660

FREID, ALLAN NATHAN, optometrist; b. Sept. 27, 1928, Memphis, Tenn.; s. Fred Robert and Mae (Shainberg) F.; div.; children: Mark b. 1961, Lenore b. 1963, Carrie b. 1964; edn: AA, UC Los Angeles 1949; BS, UC Berkeley 1951, M.Opt., 1952. Career: served to 1st Lt. US Army Med. Service Corps 1954-57; optometrist pvt. practice, 1957-85; clin. prof. UC Berkeley Sch. of Optometry 1950-85; vice pres. So. Calif. Coll. of Optometry, Fullerton 1985−; honors: Optometrist of Year, Santa Clara Co. Opt. Soc. (1961, 68, 84), Alumnus of Year, UCB Sch. of Opt. Alumni Assn. (1980), Award for excellence in low vision Retinitis Pigmentosa Internat. (1985); mem: Santa Clara Co. Opt. Soc. 1958-85 (pres. 1967, 68), Calif. Opt. Assn. (pres. 1983-84), Orange Co. Opt. Soc., Am. Optom. Assn., Am. Acad. of Optom. (chmn. Section on Low Vision 1977, 78); club: Saratoga Lions 1954-85 (pres. 1962-63); num. articles in profl. and medical jours.; Republican; Jewish; rec: walking. Ofc: Southern California College of Optometry 2575 Yorba Linda Blvd Fullerton 92631

FREINHAR, JACK P., psychiatrist; b. July 3, 1957, NY, NY; s. Herman William and Ida Gertrude F.; edn: BS biochem., BA psychol., State Univ. NY Binghamton 1979; MD, Univ. Miami Sch. of Med. 1983. Career: extern USC Adolescent Locked Psychiatric Unit 1982; intern UC Irvine Med. Ctr. 1983-84, resident 1984−; therapist Clin. for Learning Disabilities SUNY Bonghamton 1976, therapist alcohol clin. 1978; asst. ward chief locked inpatient unit VA Med. Ctr. Long Beach 1984, acting ward chief 1984, founder, lectr. psychopharmacology & DSM III Res./ Med. Student Lecture Series 1984; cons. HEW Com. on Delusions of Parisitosis 1984; editor Internat. J. of Psychosomatics 1985−; honors: Phi Beta Kappa (1978); mem: Am. Acad. Family Phys. 1980-, Am. Psychiatric Assn. 1983-, Internat. Psychosomatics Inst. 1985−; publs: contbr. 20+ articles in med. jours., presentations Long Beach VA Med. Ctr. 1983-; rec: weightlifting. Ofc: UCI Med. Ctr. Orange 92668

FREITAS, FRANK LOUIS, county official; b. June 5, 1943, Bristol, R.I.; s. Frank T. and Mary Gertrude (Perry) F.; m. Connie Coggeshall, Oct. 5, 1963; chil: Christina Marie, b. 1969, Kenneth Walter, b. 1970; edn: AA, Cuesta Coll. 1968; BS, Calif. State Polytechnic Univ. 1969; CPA, Calif. 1972. Career: staff acct. Arthur Andersen & Co., Los Angeles 1969-71; staff acct. Diehl, Evans & Co., Arroyo Grande, 1971-72; prin. CPA, Arroyo Grande 1972-73; deputy co. auditor-controller San Luis Obispo 1973-77, co. treas. (asst. 1974-77), tax collector, pub. adminstr., 1974−; trustee Co. Pension Plan; mem. Empl. Suggestion Awd. Com.; mem: Calif. Assn. of Co. Treas. and Tax Collectors (past pres.); State Assn. of Co. Pub. Adminstrs. of CA; Calif. Soc. of CPAs; Internat. Found. of Empl. Benefit Plans; clubs: Lions Internat. (past pres. Arroyo Grande); Toastmasters Intl. (past pres., Spkr of Yr 1978, Club 83); PTA (past pres.); So. S.L.O. Co. Hist. Soc.; Republican; rec: chess, public spkg., camping, computer pgmmg. Res: 602 Cerro Vista Arroyo Grande 93420 Ofc: San Luis Obispo County, POB 1149, San Luis Obispo 93406

FRELICH, ROBERT MILTON, JR., transportation co. executive; b. Jan. 31, 1946, Austin, Tx.; s. Robert M. and Doris (Simmons) F.; m. Jan, Apr. 1980; children: Rob b. 1970, Krissy b. 1972; edn: BSME, Univ. Texas, Austin 1969; MBA, Univ. of Houston 1972. Career: maint. eng. Dow Chem., Freeport, Tx. 1969-71; budget supr. Southern Pacific Transp. Co., var. locations 1971-81, mgr. of budgets, San Francisco 1981−; mem. ASME, AMA, Boeing Computer Services EIS Users Group (bd. 1984-85), Univ. of Tex. Alumni Assn.; Republican; Methodist; rec: photog., golf. Address: San Francisco 94947

FRELIGH, ROBERT JOHN, audio visual center senior photographer; b. Nov. 9, 1936, Rochester, Minn.; s. Wilfred Protacio and Irene Viola (Comstock) F.; edn: AA photog., Santa Monica City Coll. 1961; Calif. vocational trade cert. in photog., Santa Monica City Coll. Voc. Div. 1961. Career: pres. photog. firm. spl. in comml. advtg. L.A. 1961-66; photog. audiovisual ctr. CSU Long Beach 1966-83, senior photog. 1983−, staff devel. supv. photog. trainees 1982−; honors: Best of Show (Internat. Film Producers of Am. Cindy Award 1981), Silver Awards (Internat. Film & TV Festival NY 1979, 85), Cert. of Merit (Photo. Exhibition L.A. County Mus. of Nat. History 1967); mem: Profl. Photogs. of Am., Profl. Photogs. of Calif., Santa Monica CofC 1961-66, Marina del Rey CofC 1963-66, West L.A. CofC 1964-66, YMCA 1961-66 (spl. advisor bd.), Internat. Y's Men's Club, Fountain Valley Amateur Radio Club 1985-; works: photog. for sci. and technical publs., cover photographs Science Mag. (1969), Ednl. & Indsl. Television (1977), Quality Progress (1979), photo. illustrations for textbook on sports injury, Modern Principles of Athletic Training (1981), The Clumsy Child (2d ed.); Republican; Christian; rec: ham radio operator, camping, fishing, hiking, church youth group outreach coord. Ofc: Audio Visual Ctr. CSU 1250 Bellflower Blvd. Long Beach 90840

FRENCH, PRESLEY BURDETTE, life insurance sales executive; b. May 10, 1921, Central City, Nebr.; s. Crawford Hunter and Ida Maurine (Dughman) F.; m. Violetta Hill, Mar. 27, 1943; children: Linda, b. 1944; Brian, b. 1946; Patricia, b. 1950; Bette Jean, b. 1955; edn: UC Berkeley 1946-7; BSc, cum laude, Armstrong Univ. 1950; Life Ins. Mktg. Inst., Purdue Univ. 1957; Life Ins. Agcy. mgmt. courses, 1961; Adv. Sch. Ins. Mktg., So. Methodist Univ. 1961. Career: agent New York Life 1946; agt. Western Life Ins. Co. 1947-68; exec. agcy. asst. Home Ofc. 1950-4, General Agent (co's leading agcy.) 1954-9, supt. of agencies for No. Calif. & Hawaii 1959-68, mng. Gen. Agent Western Life & AMEV Investors 1968-81; Sr. Agcy. Consultant Western/ St. Paul Life Cos. 1981-3, ret.; charter mem. Western Agcy. Officers Conf.; charter mem. Western/ St. Paul Cos. Communique Panel; exec. v.p. Twin Rivers Lodge Assn.; awards: Ins. Exec. of 1955, Armstrong Univ. Alumnus Assn.; Pres. Trophy 1964; Western Life Million Dollar Round Table; mem: NALU: Nat. CofC; DAV; NRA (life); 4th Marine Div. Assn. (life); Navy League; Masons 32 degrees Islam Temple Shrine; mil: CPhM USN Fleet Marine Force: sev. personal cits., commends., Purple Heart, Pres. Unit Cit., Navy- Marine Corps. Medal, Navy Unit Commendn.; Republican; Presbyterian; rec: hunt, fish, target shooting. Res: 28 Eastwood Dr San Mateo 94403

FREY, PAUL E., waterfowl and conservation theory expert; b. Nov. 10, 1953, Berkeley, Calif.; s. Ken and Vi Frey; edn: AS, Long Beach City Coll.; BA, Univ. So. Calif.; MS, CSU Long Beach, UC Los Angeles; ScD ecol. mgmt., Inst. of Sci. Acad., Univ. of M. Career: v.p. Ken Frey Enterprises, pres. P. Frey Cons. Firm; cons. var. conservation orgns. and govtl. advis. bds.; apptd. Pres. Reagan's Task Force on Waterfowl Survival (POWDR); apptd. by ratification to review US's involvement in world conservation; honors: Henry Followorth Conservation Award of Merit; mem. 27 svc. orgns. (bd. mem. of 3); publ. research on two environmental projects and two papers on man's physical fitness relating to elements and stress factors; past athlete- baseball. Ofc: K.E.F. Enterprises POB 2734 Seal Beach 90740

FREY, STEPHEN LOUIS, distribution management executive; b. Oct. 28, 1939, Paterson, NJ; s. Stephen F. and Caroline (Cacay) F.; m. Maria Del Carmen Asquerino-La Cave, July 15, 1960, San Lucar de Bda, Spain; children: Stephen, b. 1961; Daniel, b. 1963; Anthony, b. 1967; Robert, b. 1969; edn: BA, honors, Univ. of Maryland 1972; MS, USC 1973; cert. MTM Practioner, Methods Time Measurement Inst. 1979; cert. profl. mats. handling engr., S.P.H.E. 1975. Career: warehouse mgr. Navy Exchange, Rota, Spain, distbn. mgr. Navy Exch. Complex, Wash. DC; sr. systems engr. Navy Resale Svc. & Support Ofc., NY, then distbn. div. mgr., San Diego, mgr. distbn. ops. NRSSO 1964-84; currently pres. Warehouse Distbn. Consulting Group, San Diego; instr. Miramar Comm. Coll. 1981; cons. for L.A. Olympic Com. Distbn. Ctr. 1984; mem: Nat. Council of Physical Distbn. Mgmt.; Inst. of Indsl. Engrs.; Phi Kappa Phi honor soc.; author: Warehouse Operations: A Hand Book (1983,

Dilithium Press); Mgt.'s Guide to Cost Efficient Warehousing (1982, Dartnell); Warehouse Time Calculator (1983); mag. articles 1981-4; mil: petty ofcr. 2/c USN 1957-62, GCM, Nat. Def.; Catholic; rec: author/lectr. Address: Warehouse Distribution Consulting Group, 5750 Guincho Road San Diego 92124

FREY, WILLIAM CHARLES, engineering executive, real estate broker; b. May 20, 1935, Syracuse, N.Y.; s. Wm. Charles and Doris Mary (Schaub) F.; div.; edn: BSEE, Purdue Univ. 1958; Calif. lic. R.E. Broker. Career: staff engr. (NASA) Jet Propulsion Lab., Pasadena 1960-69, NASA group supr. 1969-76, NASA section mgr. 1976-83, system mgr. software devel., Spl. Dept. of Def. Projects 1983–; instr. Univ. of Taiwan (1982), Cal Tech (1980), Pasadena City Coll. (1978-80); honors: Eta Kappa Nu (1958), NASA Exceptional Service Medal (1982); mem. Caltech Mgmt. Club, Calif. Avocado Growers Assn. (treas.), Calif. Apartment Owners Assn., Town Hall of Calif.; club: Bel Air Bay; var. patent disclosures in software devel. engring.; Catholic; rec: ski, tennis, sailing, model trains. Res: 11408 Burnham St Los Angeles 90049 Ofc: Jet Propulsion Lab 4800 Oak Grove Dr Pasadena

FRICKER, JOHN ARTHUR, pediatrician, professor of pediatrics; b. Nov. 11, 1931, Detroit, Mich.; s. Franklin and Elizabeth Jane (Cossitt) F.; m. Patricia Bedford, Sept. 10, 1955, children: Elizabeth b. 1964, Karen b. 1966; edn: Wesleyan Univ. 1949-51; BA, Wayne State Univ. 1956; MD, Case Western Reserve Univ. 1961; Diplomate Am. Bd. Pediatrics 1966. Career: intern pediat. Grace-New Haven Hosp. 1961-62, asst. resident 1962-64, res. 1964-65; pediatn. So. Calif. Permanente Med. Grp. 1965-68, ptnr. 1968–; phys. in charge The Woodland Hills Clin. 1977-83; instr. pediat. Yale Univ. 1964-65; clin. instr. pediat. 1968-72 UC Los Angeles, asst. clin. prof. 1972-80, assoc. clin. prof. 1980–; honors: Clinical Tchg. Award (UCLA Dept. of Pediat. 1974, 78, 83, 84, 85); mem: fellow Am. Acad. Pediat., L.A. Pediat. Soc.; Diocesan Council (1976-84), Standing Com. (1980-84) Episcopal Diocese of L.A.; deputy to Gen. Convention of the Episcopal Church 1982, 85; dir. Anna Jeffries Trust; mil: hosp. corpsman 3rd class USNR 1951-53; Episcopal; rec: stained glass. Ofc: So. Calif. Permanente Med. Grp. 20940 Burbank Blvd Woodland Hills 91367

FRIEDL, RICK, college president; b. Aug. 31, 1947, Berwyn, Ill.; s. Raymond J. and Ione L. (Anderson) F.; m. Diane Marie Guillies, Sept. 2, 1977; chidlren: Richard, Angela, Ryan; edn: BA, CSU Northridge 1969; MA (Calif. State Grad. fellow 1970-72), UCLA 1976; MA, USC 1979; PhD, Univ. Central Calif. 1982. Career: dept. mgr. Calif. Dept. Indsl. Relations, 1973-78; mem. faculty dept. political sci. USC, 1978-80; pres. Pacific Coll. of Law, 1981–; bd. dirs. Calif. State Univ. Northridge 1979; mem. Am. Polit. Sci. Assn., Latin Am. Studies Assn., Acad. Polit. Sci., Pacific Coast Council Latin Am. Studies; author: The Political Economy of Cuban Dependency (1981). Res: P.O. Box 449, Beverly Hills 90213

FRIEDMAN, LOUIS J., dentist; b. Sept. 7, 1916, Brooklyn, NY; s. Adolph and Fannie F.; m. Seena Ruth Shevitz; m. 2nd Charlotte F. Shack, June 14, 1975; children: (from 1st marriage) Beth, Matt, (step) Richard, Herb, Sally Tarr, Adrian Solovy; edn: Univ. of Ala. 1936-39; DDS, Univ. So. Calif. 1942. Career: staff Cedars of Lebanon Hosp. Hollywood, presently Kennedy Hosp.; prosthodontist, practice limited to full and partial dentures and bonded porcelain veneers; instr. Continuous Dental Education; mem: Am. Fedn. Dentaire Internat., Am. Dental Soc. (life), other civic orgs. and clubs; publ: art. on full denture prosthetics; mil: capt. US Army dental surg. 50th combat engrs. regt., Am. Theater, Asiatic-Pacific Theatre, WWII Victory; Democrat; rec: magic (for Retarded Children of the Desert and Battered Children of Banning, Calif.), sculpture, oil painting, writing short stories. Res: 39360 Peterson Rd, No 63, Rancho Mirage 92270 Ofc: Cathedral Medical Plaza 68-860 Perez Rd Ste S Cathedral City 92234

FRIEDMAN, MILTON, economist, author; s. Jeno Saul and Sarah Ethel (Landau)F.; m. Rose Director, June 25, 1938; children: Janet, David; edn: AB, Rutgers Univ. 1932, LLD, 1968; AM, Univ. Chgo. 1933; PhD, Columbia Univ. 1946; LLD, St. Paul's (Rikkyo) Univ. 1963, Kalamazoo Coll. 1968, Lehigh Univ. 1969, Loyola Univ. 1971, Univ. N.H. 1975, Harvard Univ. 1979, Brigham Young Univ. 1980, Dartmouth Univ. 1980, Gonzaga Univ. 1981, ScD, Rochester Univ. 1971, LHD, Rockford Coll. 1969, Roosevelt Univ. 1975, Hebrew Union Coll. (L.A.) 1981, LittD, Bethany Coll. 1971, PhD (hon.), Hebrew Univ. (Jerusalem) 1977. Career: assoc. economist Nat. Resources Com., Washington, 1935-37; mem. research staff Nat. Bur. Econ. Research, NY, 1937-45, 48-81; vis. prof. econs. Univ. Wis., 1940-41; prin. econ. economist, tax research div. US Treasury Dept., 1941-43; assoc. dir. research, statis. research group, war research div. Columbia Univ., 1943-45; assoc. prof. econs. and bus. adminstrn. Univ. Minn., 1945-46; assoc. prof. econs. Univ. Chgo., 1946-48, prof. econs., 1948-62, Paul Snowden Russell Disting. Service prof. econs., 1962-82, Paul Snowden Russell Disting. Service prof. emeritus, 1983–; Fulbright lectr. Cambridge Univ., 1953-54; vis. Wesley Clair Mitchell Research prof. econs. Columbia Univ., 1964-65; fellow Center for Advanced Study in Behavioral Sci., 1957-58; mem. Pres.'s Commn. All-Volunteer Army, 1969-70, Pres.'s Commn. on White House Fellows, 1971-74, Pres.'s Economic Policy Advis. Bd., 1981-; vis. scholar Fed. Reserve Bank, San Francisco, 1977; sr. research fellow Hoover Instn., Stanford Univ., 1977–; awards: John Bates Clark medal Am. Econ. Assn., 1951; Nobel prize in econs., 1976; Pvt. Enterprise Exemplar medal Freedoms Found., 1978; named Chicagoan of Year, Chgo. Press Club, Chgo. Press Club 1972; Educator of Year, Chgo. United Jewish Fund 1973; mem: Fellow Inst. Math. Stats., Fellow Am. Statis. Assn., Fellow Econometric Soc., Nat. Acad. Scis., Am. Econ. Assn. (exec. com. 1955-57, pres. 1967), Royal Econ. Soc., Western Econ. Assn. (v.p. 1982-3, pres. 1984-5), Am. Philos. Soc., Mont Pelerin Soc. (dir. 1958-61, pres. 1970-2); club: Quadrangle; author: Taxing to Prevent Inflation (w/ Carl Shoup and Ruth P. Mack) 1943; Income from Independent Professional Practice (w/ Simon S. Kuznets) 1946; Sampling Inspection (w/ Harold A. Freeman, Frederick Mosteller, W. Allen Wallis) 1948; Essays in Positive Economics, 1953; A Theory of the Consumption Function, 1957; A Program for Monetary Stability, 1959; Price Theory, 1962; (with Rose D. Friedman) Capitalism and Freedom, 1962, Free To Choose, 1980, Tyranny of the Status Quo, 1984; (w/ Anna J. Schwartz) A Monetary History of the United States, 1967-1960, 1963, The Great Contraction, 1965, Monetary Statistics of the United States, 1970, Monetary Trends in the United States and the United Kingdom, 1982; Inflation: Causes and Consequences, 1963; The Balance of Payments: Free vs. Fixed Exchange Rates (w/ Robert Roosa) 1967; Dollars and Deficits, 1968; The Optimum Quantity of Money and Other Essays, 1969; Monetary vs. Fiscal Policy (w/ Walter W. Heller) 1968; A Theoretical Framework for Monetary Analysis, 1972; Social Security (w/ Wilbur J. Cohen) 1972; An Economist's Protest, 1972; There Is No Such Thing As A Free Lunch, 1975; Price Theory, 1976; Milton Friedman's Monetary Framework (w/ Robert J. Gordon et al) 1974; Bright Promises, Dismal Performance: An Economist's Protest (w/ William R. Allen) 1983; editor: Studies in the Quantity Theory of Money, 1956; bd. eds. Am. Econ. Rev., 1951-53, Econometrica, 1957-69; columnist Newsweek mag. 1966-84, contbg. ed. 1972-84; contbr. arts. to profl. jours. Ofc: Hoover Instn Stanford Univ. Stanford 94305-2323

FRIEDMAN, PETER MICHAEL, aircraft products co. president; b. Sept. 17, 1944, Los Angeles; s. Harold Herman and Gladys Shirley (Kreeger) F.; children: David B. b. 1974, Stephanie Anne b. 1984; edn: Airframe & Powerplant/ Inspection Authorization, Masters Degree Applied Sci., Pacific Western Univ. 1980. Career: sales mgr. United Supply Co., Los Angeles 1965-71; pres. Aircraft Metal Products Corp., Venice 1971–; also FAA Cert. Comml. Pilot, Instrument Flight instr., ground instr., Advanced & Instrument repairman; FAA Accident Prevention Counselor Designate; mem: Aircraft Owners & Pilots Assn., Nat. Bus. Aircraft Assn., Experimental Aircraft Assn., designee inspector; holder of num. engrg., supplemental type certificates for aircraft modification cert. by FAA, sev. publ. articles in aviation trade publs. on aircraft hardware and systems; mil: USNR 1963-65; Republican; rec: flying, photog. Ofc: Aircraft Metal Products Corp., 4206 Glencoe Ave Venice 90292

FRIEDMAN, W. ROBERT, JR., investment banker, venture capitalist; b. May 1, 1942, NY,NY; s. William Robert and Erica deMeuron (Urich) F.; m. Jeanette Lascoume, July 9, 1983; children: Douglas b. 1968, Brian b. 1971, Catherine b. 1974; edn: BA, Univ. Pa. 1965; MBA, Wharton Sch. of Bus. 1970. Career: senior mktg. cons. Coca Cola Corp. 1971-73; senior securities analyst Investment Mgmt. Gp. Citibank 1973-76; v.p., health analyst L.F. Rothschild, Unterberg, Towbun 1976-78; ptnr. Montgomery Securities 1978–; prin. Montgomery Medical Ventures 1985–; dir. Health Care Corp. Fin. Gp.; trustee Alta Bates Corp.; dir. Hillsdale Group, Geri Med. of Am. Inc., honors: Top Institutl. Health care Analyst (Institutl. Invester Mag. 1977); mem: Am. Hosp. Assn., Health Care Fin. Mgmt. Assn., City Athletic Club (NY), Bay Club (SF); mil: 1st lt. US Army 1966-68; rec: skiing, biking, military & political history, health care. Res: 2545 Baker St San Francisco 94123 Ofc: Montgomery Securities 600 Montgomery St San Francisco 94111

FRIEND, REGINALD DAVID, hotelier, real estate development co. president; b. June 21, 1944, New Orleans, La.; s. Aaron David and Barbara Ann (Hensley) F.; edn: Pasadena Playhouse Coll. of Theatre Arts 1962-63. Career: pres./CEO Friend & Wolfe Hotels, Inc. (co. owns Sheraton-Bridgeport (Conn.) Hotel and 4 motor hotels in So. Calif.) 1969–; pres./CEO Friend & Wolfe R.E. Devel. (devel. luxury custom homes in So. Calif.); bd. dirs. Conn. Grand Opera; honors: City of Lompoc beautification award, Elks Club of Lompoc award for hist. flags display at hotel, Best Western Golden Crown award; mem. Am. Hotel Motel Assn., Calif. Hotel Motel Assn., Hollywood CofC; publs: design of home pub. Architl. Digest (July-Aug. 77); Republican; rec: collect 18th Cen. French & Italian furniture. Ofc: Friend and Wolfe Hotels Inc. POB 27009 Los Angeles 90027

FRIES, HERLUF BECK, ranching consultant; b. April 1, 1915, Easton; s. Christian P. and Emma A. (Beck) F.; m. Geraldine Wood, Aug. 14, 1954; children: Donna b. 1940, Doug b. 1942, Jean b. 1967, Benta b. 1969. Career: cons. Fidinam Corp., Luguna, Switz. and Investors of Ger. and Italy 1977-80; farmer, rancher, Oakhurst 1980-83; mem: Calcot Lamo, Fresno Co. Farm Bureau, Calif. Young Farmers (pres. 1948-49), honors: Hon. Degree State Farmer 1950; Grand Marshall, Caruthers Dist. Fair, 50 yrs.; rec: tennis, youth. Address: 49526 Meadwood Rd., P.O. Box 2326 Oakhurst 93644

FRIESEN, JERRY (GERALD), company president; b. Oct. 29, 1937, Elsie, Neb.; s. Henry A. and Elizabeth H. (Janzen) F.; m. Sally Zehner, Dec. 15, 1962; children: Dale b. 1966, Wendy b. 1969; edn: AA, Cerritos Coll. 1965; BA, CSU Fullerton 1978. Career: supv. No. Am. Rockwell, Inc., Downey 1962-69; self-employed 24 Hour Rent-A-Car, Inc., Whittier 1969-76, 24 Hour Airport Express, Inc., La Habra 1971–; guest spkr. bus. Biola Coll. 1981-82; honors: Cert. of Excellence (Assoc. Travel Nationwide); mem: Nat. Fedn. of Businessmen 1978-, La Habra Area CofC 1978-, Whittier Area CofC 1971-78; mil: sp4 US Army 1958-59, Good Conduct; Republican; Protestant; rec: skiing, biking, shooting, tennis. Res: 15536 Olivebranch Dr La Mirada 90638 Ofc: 24 Hour Airport Express, Inc., 491 E Lambert Rd La Habra 90631

FRIIS, CAROLE KAY, real estate broker, school administrative coordinator; b. July 1, 1944, Denver, Colo.; d. Stanley Floyd and Barbara Elizabeth (Shipley)

Self; m. Ronald Friis, Aug. 8, 1964; children: Eric b. 1967, Steve b. 1969, Michael b. 1971; edn: AA, Reedley Coll. 1964; UC Berkeley 1964-65; real estate sales Anthony Schools 1978, r.e. broker, 1982. Career: dir. therapeutic activities Hillview Hosp. Morgan Hill, Calif. 1973-79; real estate sales Red Carpet Real Estate Morgan Hill 1978-81, Value Realty 1981-82; r.e. broker, owner co. Morgan Hill 1982–; adminstrv. coord. Morgan Ctr. Los Altos 1981–; secty., bd. dirs. Morgan Ctr. 1983–; guest spkr. on autism Stanford Univ. psychol. dept. 1982-; honors: Top Producer (Red Carpet 1978, 79), Top Lister (1978, 79), Bausch & Lomb Hon. Science Award (1962); mem: San Jose Real Estate Bd., Calif. Real Estate Assn., Nat. Assn. Real Estate Bds., G.E. Co. Engr. Wives Club (pres. 1967-70), Calif. Assn. Neurologically Handicapped (chpt. v.p. 1974-75), Nat. Soc. Autistic Children & Adults (chpt. pres. 1981-); Republican; Protestant; avoc: medical research, human rights (esp. for disabled). Res: 2865 Thomas Grade Morgan Hill 95037 Ofc: Morgan Ctr. 201 Covington Rd Los Altos 94022

FROST, CHARLES EDWARD BRAMWELL, training director, co. president; b. Feb. 8, 1924, Los Angeles; s. Charles Edward and Vera Elizabeth (Brown) F.; m. Jeannie A., Aug. 12, 1943; children: Charlotte A. b. 1944, Nancy J. b. 1947, Jack E. b. 1953, Robert C. b. 1955; edn: electrical apprenticeship, Riverside City Coll. 1945-48; techtonic engring., San Bernardino Valley Coll. 1967-70; vocational tchg., UCLA 1970-71; Life Tchg. Cred., Calif. 1970. Career: journeyman electrician IBEW Lu #440, Riverside 1948-84; tchr. electrical apprenticeship Riverside City Coll. 1953-74, San Bernardino Valley Coll. 1979-84; owner, elec. contractor Frost Electrice, Riverside 1977–; training dir. Riverside/ San Bernardino Jt. Electrical Journeyman and Apprenticeship Training Ctr. 1984–; elec. cns. Power City Constrn.; mem: Elks, VFW; works: course outlines and materials, elecrical apprenticeship and journeyman training pgms.; chaired com. to rewrite and print Electrical Code for the City of Corona 1969; mil: radioman 1/c USN 1942-45, European Theatre, North Africa, Sicily, Tarawa, New Guinea, Philippines, So. Pacific, Pres. Unit Citation; Democrat; Lutheran; rec: bowling, bass fishing tournaments. Res: 4684 Brentwood Ave. Riverside 92506 Ofc: NECA/ IBEW Inland Training Fund, P.O. Box 6286 San Bernardino 92412

FROST, EDITH MAXINE, educator; b. Aug. 10, 1933, Morris, Okla.; d. Ira Jesse and Gladys Ethel (Vance) Norwood; children: Michelle b. 1954, Diane b. 1956, Estelle b. 1959; edn: AA, Foothill Jr. Coll. 1968; BA, CSU San Jose 1970, MA, honors, 1974; Calif. Tchg. Cred. (gen. secondary, minor Spanish), Adminstrv. Cred. Career: English tchr. Mountain View High Sch. 1971-72, tchr. gifted (GATE pgm.) and chair English Dept. Milpitas H.S. 1973-81, Rancho Middle Sch. 1981–, and Mentor tchr. Milpitas Sch. Dist. 1981–; honors: Epsilon Eta Sigma (1974); mem: Nat. Council Tchrs. of English, Calif. Tchrs. of English, Assn. for Supvsn. and Curriculum Devel., Santa Clara County Airmens Assn.; Democrat; Assembly of God; rec: pvt. pilot (1200 hrs. in Cessna 1982). Res: 1490 Gretel Ln Mt. View 94040 Ofc: Rancho Middle School 1915 Yellowstone Dr Milpitas 95035

FROST, JACK MC CABE, oral-maxillo facial surgeon; b. May 31, 1926, Los Angeles; s. George McCabe and Lola (Williams) F.; m. Julia Malesic, R.N. (dec. 1979), Aug. 16, 1952; children: Toni b. 1953, Gina b. 1956, Lisa b. 1958, John b. 1962, James b. 1964; edn: BA, UC Los Angeles 1946, grad. wk. 1957; DDS, USC 1951. Career: intern. oral/max. facial surgeon, Los Angeles County Gen. Hosp. 1952-53; oral surgeon US Army, Brooks Hosp., San Antonio and Korea, 1952-54; pvt. practice, Los Angeles 1955-77; disabled 1977; public rels. Urdoljak Motors, Van Nuys 1985–; mem. Am. Dental Assn., Calif. Dental Soc., Los Angeles Dental Soc., So. Calif. Soc. Oral Surgeons, LA CofC, Knights of Columbus; research: A Form of Oseous Implants (1960); mil: capt. US Army 1952-54, decorated 4 battle stars; Republican; Catholic; rec: fishing, hunting, sports car racing. Res: 4016 Old Topanga Cyn Rd Calabasas 91302 Ofc: Urdoljak Motors 15245 Burbank Blvd Van Nuys 91302

FRYE, DAVID BONNELL, electro-mechanical designer, entrepreneur; b. Feb. 17, 1952, Sacramento; s. Louis Bonnell and Elizabeth Davie (Cox); edn: AS, Foothill Jr. Coll. 1973, postgrad. Foothill & DeAnza Jr. Colls. 1973-80. Career: jr. mfg. techn., lead mfg. techn., R&D lab techn., senior R&D lab techn. National Semiconductor Corp. P.O.S. Div., Santa Clara 1973-79; corp. co-founder, mgr. of engring. support Onyx Systems Inc. (now Corvus Sys. Inc.), San Jose 1979-83; corp. co-founder, senior mem. tech. staff Arete Systems Corp., San Jose 1983–; works: prin. contbr. conceptual & detailed design approach for electro- mechanical pkg. of Onyx Sys. C8000 & C5000 (1979-83) and Arete Sys. 1100 & 1200 (1983-86) series computers; Republican; rec: electronic, mechanical and industrial designing, bowling, guitar. Res: 38790 Bell St. Fremont 94536

FRYE, JONATHAN SCOTT, civil engineer; b. Mar. 23, 1956, Aurora, Ill.; s. Charles Jerome and Gertrude May (Frank) F.; m. Andrea, Aug. 14, 1983; 1 dau. Eva Elizabeth b. 1986; edn: BS, Univ. Ill., 1978; Reg. Profl. Civil Engr., Calif. (1984). Career: engr. Geotech. Div. (analysis of slope stability and earth dam seepage in var. sites worldwide), Harza Eng. Co., Chgo. 1978-79; project and design engr. (residential, comml.) Flowers & Assoc. Inc., Santa Barbara 1981–; honors: Junior Citizen of Year, Aurora, Ill. Jaycees (1974), All-Chgo. Area H.S. Football (1973), Nat. Who's Who Among H.S. Athletes (1974); mem. ASCE; Republican; Christian; rec: bicycling, hiking, hockey. Res: 3375 Foothill Rd #1121 Carpinteria 93013 Ofc: Flowers & Assoc. Inc. 923 Olive St Ste 4 Santa Barbara 93101

FU, HORNG-SEN, electrical engineer; b. Nov. 26, 1936, Taiwan, nat. US cit. 1976; s. Te-Li and San-Mei (Liao) F.; m. Rosa, Aug. 27, 1966; children: Michael b. 1970, Carolyn & Irene b. 1974; edn: BSEE, Nat. Taiwan Univ. 1960; MSEE, Nat. Chiao-Tung Univ. Taiwan 1962; MEEE, Univ. Fla. Gainesville 1965; PhDEE, Univ. Ill. Champaign- Urbana 1971. Career: electrical engr. Allied Control Co. NYC 1965-66; research assoc., asst. prof. elec. engrg. dept. Univ. Ill. 1971-73; process engr. Texas Instruments Inc. Dallas 1973-78; r&d process engr. Hewlett Packard Co. 1978-82, proj. mgr. Silicon Process Lab. H-P 1982–; honors: Outstanding Paper (IEEE Internat. Solid State Circuits Conf. 1975); mem. IEEE; publs: num. articles in tech jours.; rec: electronics. Ofc: Hewlett-Packard Co. 3500 Deer Creek Rd Palo Alto 94304

FUHRMAN, ROBERT ALEXANDER, aerospace co. executive; b. Feb. 23, 1925, Detroit; s. Alexander A. and Elva (Brown) F.; m. Nan McCormick, Sept. 16, 1949; children: Lee Anne, Richard, William; edn: BS, Univ. Mich. 1945, MS, Univ. Md. 1952, UC San Diego 1958, Stanford Bus. Sch. Exec. Mgmt. Pgm. 1964. Career: project engr. Naval Air Test Center, Patuxent River, Md. 1946-53; chief tech. engring. Ryan Aero. Co., San Diego 1953-58; v.p./ asst. gen. mgr. Missile Systems Div., Lockheed Missiles & Space Co., Sunnvale 1966, v.p./gen. mgr. 1969, exec. v.p. 1973-76, pres. 1976–, chmn. 1979–; v.p. Lockheed Corp., Burbank 1969-76, senior v.p. 1976-83, group pres. Missiles, Space & Electronics System, 1983-85, pres./chief op. ofcr. Lockheed Corp. 1986–; also dir./pres. Lockheed Ga. Co., Marietta 1970-71; pres. Lockheed Calif. Co., Burbank 1971-73; chmn. bd. Ventura Mfg. Co. 1970-71; dir. Bank of the West; mem. FBM Steering Task Group 1966-70; mem. Def. Sci. Bd. (chmn. task force on indsl. responsiveness, 1980), San Jose Mgmt. Task Force (exec. com.), Ala. Space and Rocket Center (sci. adv. com.), Bay Area Council (bd. dirs.), Univ. Santa Clara Sch. of Bus. (adv. bd.), Federated Employees of Bay Area (bd. govs.), United Way of Santa Clara County (trustee 1975-), Atlanta Junior Achievement (bd. dirs), Stanford Univ. Sch. of Engring. (adv. council), Univ. Mich. Coll. of Engring. (adv. bd. 1981-), Univ. Tex. - Austin Coll. of Engring. Found. (adv. council 1983-); awards: Silver Knight award, Nat. Mgmt. Assn. (1979), John J. Montgomery award (1964), award, Soc. Mfg. Engrs. (1973), disting. citizen award, Boy Scouts Am. (1983), Donald C. Burnman Award, Soc. Mfg. Engrs. (1983), Eminent Engineer, Tau Beta Pi (1983); mem: Fellow AIAA (dir.- at- large, Von Karman 1978), Fellow Soc. Mfg. Engrs., Nat. Acad. Engring., AM. Astron. Soc. (sr.), Nat. Aero Assn., Ga. CofC (dir.), Am. Def. Preparedness Assn. (dir., exec. com.), Navy League U.S. (life), Air Force Assn., Assn. U.S. Army, Soc. Am. Value Engrs. (hon.), Santa Clara County Mfrs. Group (past chmn.), Beta Gamma Sigma; club: Burning Tree (Bethesda, Md.), Los Altos Country; mil: served to ensign USNR 1944-46. Res: 23455 Camino Hermoso Los Altos Hills 94022 Ofc: Lockheed Corp. 4500 Park Granada Blvd Calabasas 91399

FUIS, GARY STEPHEN, geophysicist; b. Feb. 29, 1944, Oak Ridge, Tenn.; s. Frank, Jr. and Hazel Lee (Stephens) Fuis; m. Stacey Andrews, Sept. 1, 1979; edn: BA honors, Cornell Univ. 1966; PhD, Calif. Inst. of Technol. 1974; geophysicist, USGS 1974. Career: geologist USGS Flagstaff, Ariz., Pasadena, Calif. 1966-74; chief scientist USGS Pasadena, supv. USGS-Caltech. seismograph network 1974-78; research sci. USGS Menlo Park, chief scientist for deep structure, Trans-Alaska Crustal Transect and Pacific to Arizona Crustal Experiment 1978–; honors: Disting. Lectr. (USGS 1983), Sigma Xi (1974), NSF Fellow (1966-70), Woodrow Wilson Fellow (honorary, 1966), Phi Beta Kappa (1964), Cornell Nat. Scholar (1962-66), other scholarships; mem: AM. Geophysical Union, Seismological Soc. of Am., Soc. of Economic Paleontols. and Mineralogists, Santa Clara County Horsemen's Assn., Woodside Trail Club, Barron Park Creek Com.; publs: num. tech. articles in sci. jours.; rec: running, horseback riding, backpacking, bicycling, construction. Res: 745 La Para Ave Palo Alto 94306 Ofc: USGS 345 Middlefield Rd Menlo Park 94025

FUKAWA, TAKIO, corporate executive; b. Feb. 21, 1930, Yokohama, Japan; s. Seikichi and Kimiko F.; m. Reiko Adachi, Oct. 3, 1957; 2 children: dau. Tamae, b. 1959, son, Jun, b. 1962; edn: grad. in internat. trade, Yokohama Coll. (presently Kanagawa Univ.) 1949; stu. Harvard Bus. Sch. 1974. Career: with Mitsui Orgn. since 1952, currently senior v.p. and gen. mgr. of Mitsui & Co. (USA), Inc., Los Angeles Office, 1981–; deputy gen. mgr. Mitsui Tokyo's Energy and Petrochem. Plant Div. 1978-81; previous assignments in San Francisco (4 yrs), NYC (3 yrs), London (7 yrs), and Okinawa; fmr. splst. in import & export of heavy machinery (chem., petrochem. and energy processing mach. & plants), Nippon Machinery Trading Co. (later merged with Mitsui); mem: Japanese CofC (bd. dirs., v.p. 1982, 85), Japan Business Assn. (bd. dirs., pres. 1984), Japan America Soc. (bd. dirs.), Japanese Am. Cultural and Community Ctr. (bd. dirs., orgnzr. Ambassador's Council 1984); mem. adv. com. L.A. Open Golf Tournament 1983, 84, bd. dirs. YMCA 1984-; clubs: University (LA), The Los Angeles, California CC,, Riviera CC; rec: golf, travel. Res: 335 South Hudson Ave Los Angeles 90020 Ofc: Mitsui & Co. (USA) Inc., 611 West Sixth St Los Angeles 90017

FUKUSHIMA, CRAIG TOSHIO, health care co. executive; b. Sept. 24, 1957, Los Angeles; s. Thomas Yoshitomi and Betti Kinuyo (Kurihara) F.; m. Judith Montemayor, Apr. 17, 1982; edn: BS, UC Davis 1981; MBA, Pepperdine Univ. 1983; lic. Nursing Home Adminstr., Calif. State Bd., 1982. Career: emergcy. med. tech. Superior Ambulance Service, Sacramento 1978-81; asst. adminstr. Fountain Conv. Hosp., Orange 1982; adminstr. Canyon Conv. Hosp. 1982-83, Fountain Conv. Hosp. 1983-85; regional v.p. Summit Health Ltd., Long Term Care Group, Los Angeles 1985–; mem: Calif. Assn. of Health Facilities, Orange Co. Assn. Health Facilities (bd. 1984-85), Am. Coll. Health Care Adminstrs., Am. Health Care Assn.; civic: Orange CofC (coms.), Kiwanis Club (Youth Svcs. com.), Boy Scouts Asm., Orange Co. Health Plnng. Council; Democrat; Christian; rec: sports, music Address: Los Angeles

FULLER, JAMES WILLIAM, financial co. president; b. Apr. 3, 1940, Rochester, Ind.; s. Raymond S. and Mildred B. (Ostemeir) F.; m. Mary Falvey, Aug. 21, 1981; children: Kristen Anne b. 1970, Glen Wm. b. 1973; edn: AA, San Bernardino Valley Coll.; BS, CSU San Jose 1962; MBA, CSU 1966. Career: mgr. Investment Industries Practice, SRI Internat. 1974-77; sr. v.p. NYSE 1977-80; sr. v.p. mktg. Charles Schwab & Co. Inc. 1980-84; pres. Jones Fuller & Co. (stockbrokerage) 1984-85; pres. Bull & Bear Group, NY, NY 1985 –; dir. Tools Are; honors: Beta Gamma Sigma (1966); clubs: Jonathan (LA), University (NY); research publ: The Future of the Securities Industry (1975); mil: lt. Supply Corps USN; Republican; (exec. com. Calif. State); Presbyterian; rec: tennis. Res: 2584 Filbert St San Francisco 94123 Ofc: Bull & Bear Group 11 Hanover Square New York NY 10005

FULLERTON, DIANE CAROLINE, property management co. executive; b. Feb. 6, 1943, Mnpls.; d. Carl Walter and Mildred Florence (Christensen) Hansen; div.; children: Scott b. 1969, Kristen b. 1971; edn: BA, Univ. of Minn. 1966. Career: spl. projects adminstr. Lend Lease National, Mnpls.; controller Imperial Oil, Los Angeles 1967-68; regl. mgr. Alta Property Management, Irvine 1975-79; exec. v.p. Mercury Property Management, 1980-85, pres. 1985–; cons. Donald R. Bren Co., Eastlake Devel. Co., Taylor-Woodrow Homes; featured speaker Bldg. Industry Assn. functions, and Calif. Assn. of Subdivision Consultants; mem: Building Industry Assn., Community Assns. Inst., Calif. Assn. of Sub-Division Consultants; Republican; Prot.; rec: aerobics, skating, travel. Ofc: Mercury Property Management 4670 Barranca Pkwy Irvine 92714

FULLERTON, GAIL JACKSON, university president; b. Apr. 29, 1927, Lincoln, Nebr.; d. Earl Warren and Gladys Bernice (Marshall) Jackson; m. Stanley Fullerton, Mar. 27, 1967; 2 children by previous marriage, Gregory and Cynde Putney; edn: AB, Univ. Nebr. 1949, AM, 1950; PhD, Univ. Ore. 1954. Career: lectr. sociology Drake Univ., Des Moines 1955-57; asst. prof. Fla. State Univ., Tallahassee 1957-60; prof. sociol. San Jose State Univ., 1963-72, dean, 1972-76, exec. vice pres., 1977-78, pres., 1978–; bd. dirs. San Jose Symphony 1979-, Associated Western Univs., Inc. 1981-; bd. govs. NCCJ of Santa Clara Co., 1981-; trustee Nat. Commn. Cooperative Edn., 1982-; awards: Carnegie fellow, 1950-51, Doherty fellow, 1951-52; mem: AAAS, Internat. Sociol. Assn., Am. Sociol. Assn., Western Coll. Assn. (pres. 1982), San Jose CofC (dir. 1978-); author: Survival in Marriage (1972, ed. ed. 1977); coauthor: The Adjusted American (1964). Res: 226 Wave Crest Ave Santa Cruz 95060 Ofc: San Jose State University, Washington Sq., San Jose 95192

FULTON, DANIEL A., writer, rancher, ret.; b. June 8, 1904, Minier, Ill.; s. William and Bertha E. (Fluss) F.; m. Mary Ann George, Feb. 21, 1931; children: M. Louise b. 1932, Dorothy b. 1933, D. George b. 1935; edn: Montana St. Coll. 1921-22. Career: mgmt. of family ranch in Montana (estab. by father in 1890), 1920-1959; dir. Bank of Baker, Baker, Mont. 1950-59; came to Calif. in 1975; apptd: chmn. Montana Grass Conservation Commn. 1949-51, chmn. Montana State Board of Equalization 1961-65; honors: Hon. Dr. of Sci., Mont. State Univ. (1959); mem: Soc. for Range Mgmt. (pres. 1951), US Chamber of Commerce (Natural Resources Com. 1954-57), Mont. Stockgrowers Assn. (pres. 1956-57), Mont. Woolgrowers Assn. (pres. 1958-59); Elks; author: Failure on the Plains (Big Sky Books, Mont. State Univ., 1982); num. articles on ranching subjects esp. on range mgmt. and land tenure; rec: amateur radio. Res: 27540 Grosse Point Dr Sun City 92381

FUNAKI, TOSHIYUKI K., co. executive; b. Aug. 30, 1947, Osaka, Japan; s. Tsuneo and Kimiko (Inoue) F.; m. Akemi, Feb. 11, 1973; children: Miho b. 1974, Takao b. 1975; edn: mech. engring., Kansai Univ. 1971. Career: engring., sales mgr. Rundel Components Inc., 1972-75; founder IDEC (from 0 to $15 million corp. 1975-76), now exec. v.p./COO IDEC Systems & Controls Corp. 1975–; founder/pres./CEO IDEC Canada, Ltd. 1985–; dir. internat. mktg. IDEC Izumi Corp. (selling to 60 fgn. countries), 1985–; club: Los Altos Golf & Country; rec: golf, water sports, ski. Res: 22791 Stonebridge Cupertino 95014 Ofc: IDEC Systems & Controls Corp. 1213 Elko Dr Sunnyvale 94089

FUOTI, JAMES CHARLES, insurance agent, broker; b. Jan. 13, 1951, Reading, Pa.; s. James and June Elizabeth (Witman) F.; m. Susan, June 24, 1972; edn: BS indsl. mgmt., Purdue Univ. 1972; Chartered Property Casualty Underwriter, Am. Inst. PLU 1976; Accred. Advisor Ins., Ins. Inst. of Am. 1983. Career: mktg. rep. Hartford Ins. 1972-74; surplus lines broker M.J. Hall & Co. Inc. 1974-77; v.p., ins. agent/ broker J.P. Burris Ins. 1977-82, Pickett, Rotholz & Murphy 1982-84, Nationwide Ins. 1984–; instr. San Joaquin Delta Coll. 1975-76; ins. assns. 1981-; asst. chmn. regl. mktg. action group Nationwide Ins. 1986; guest spkr. Rotary 1984-85; Risk Mgmt. Day Panelist 1983; honors: USNROTC Scholar 1968, Contg. Profl. Devel. (CPCU 1983-86), Ins. Profl. of the Yr. (Ind. Agents of No. Calif. 1984); mem: Chartered Property Casualty Underwriters (Sacto. Valley secty. 1981, pres. 1983, v.p. 1984, Risk Mgmt. Forum 1981-); North Ridge CC, Purdue Alumni Assn.; Catholic; rec: golf, music. Res: 5536 Camas Ct Orangevale 95662 Ofc: POB 1718 Orangevale 95662

FUQUA, JAMES BRIAN, investment-management co. president; b. Aug. 21, 1941, Santa Monica, Calif.; s. James H. and Julia E. (Campiglia) F.; m. Rachel, Nov. 9, 1985; children: Anne b. 1963, Beth b. 1964, Joe b. 1968, Pete b. 1969; edn: BS, Univ. Santa Clara 1963. Career: life ins. agent Penn. Mutual 1963-66; ptnr. Fuqua & Baptist Mgmt. Co. 1966-68, pres., chmn. bd. 1968 –; dir., CFO Focus Investment Corp.; dir., v.p. Agri-Versified Inc.; dir., v.p., CFO Four Point Investment Co.; dir., v.p. Planned Benefit Svcs. Inc.; Presidential Task Force; honors: Agent of the Yr. (Penn Mutual); mem: Nat. Ass. Securities

Dealers, Life Ins. Nat. Assn., Bronco Beach (Univ. Santa Clara), Presidents Club (Bellarmine, Univ. Santa Clara); Republican; Catholic; rec: tennis, racquetball, golf. Res: 14750 Sobey Rd Saratoga 95070 Ofc: Fuqua & Baptist Management Co. 150 E Campbell Ste 201 Campbell 95008

FURLONG, ROBERT JOHN BLANCHARD, real estate investment co. president; b. Nov. 20, 1932, Halifax, Nova Scotia, Canada, nat. 1962; s. John Aléxander MacDonald and Margaret Anderson (Rowlings) F.; neph., Hon. Flemming Blanchard McCurdy, M.P., first to fly a heavier -than-air aircraft in British Empire (1908); m. Vivienne Moss, Mar. 12, 1983; 1 son, Robert Jr., b. 1964; edn: BA, First Honors, 1958, law stu. Dalhousie Univ. 1958-60; MBA, honors, McGill Univ. 1962; econ., UC Los Angeles 1970-72. Career: pres. Commonwealth Realty Co. Ltd., Halifax 1962-68; chmn. Am. Mutual Investment Corp., Beverly Hills, Calif. 1969-74; chmn. Am. Standard Inv. Corp., 1969-74; chmn. Dominion Capital Corp., 1969-74; pvt. real estate investor nationally, 1974-83; pres. Kion Inc., Marina del Rey 1983 –; Dir. 20th Century Energy Corp., Can.; assoc. with Dr. Edward Teller on Methacoal Process, Dallas; coordinator annual conf. on Nuclear Medicine, Wash DC; promoting NASA space shuttles at Cape Kennedy and Edwards AFB; honors: First Award, Outstanding Student in Bus. & Econ. 1962, Canada; Phi Delta Theta Frat.; clubs: St. Bruno Riding (St. Bruno, Quebec), Bedford Basin Yacht (Bedford, Can.), Royal Yacht Squadron (Stockholm), Canadian Soc. of Los Angeles, Marina Yacht Club, Carleton (Ottowa); Republican; Presbyterian; rec: music and the arts. Res: 4267 Marina City Dr, Ste 204WTS, Marina Del Rey 90292 Ofc: 9701 Wilshire Blvd Ste 800 Beverly Hills 90212

GABLE, TOM POWELL, JR., marketing-public relations executive; b. July 4, 1944, San Diego; s. Dr. Tom Powell and Mary Ellen (Kilfoy) G.; m. Laura Lee, Dec. 17, 1966; children: Michelle Diane b. 1974, Brian Thomas b. 1978, Lisa Ann b. 1979; edn: BA journ., CSU San Diego 1967. Career: feature writer San Diego Tribune 1966-67, investigative reporter 1969-70, daily bus. columnist 1970-73, bus. ed. 1973-75; prin. The Gable Agency (pub. rels.), San Diego 1976–, pres./CEO The Gable Group of Cos. (The Gable Agency, Gable/Schoen Advt., Gable/Direct, and Gable/Sales Promotion), 1985 –; guest lectr. UCSD Ext. 1986, CSUSD 1984; honors: 50+ writing awards as a finl. journalist, nominee for the Pulitzer Prize (1974), The Gable Group recipient 125+ profl. awards for excellence in pub. rels., advt. & mktg.; mem: San Diego Press Club (past dir.), Sigma Delta Chi Soc. (past dir.), BPAA, S.D. Downtown Mktg. Consortium (charter, exec. com.), Greater San Diego CofC (bd., exec. com., v.chmn. Economic Research Bureau), Central City Assn. (v.p., exec. com.); current publs: monthly wine column in San Diego Mag., contbr. to Where To Eat in America (Random House), contbr. to The Best of San Diego (Rosebud Books); mil: combat corresp. US Army 1967-69, 2 Bronze Stars, 2 Army Commendn. medals, Vietnam; Republican; Presbyterian; rec: contemporary humor, ski, coaching youth sports. Ofc: 101 West Broadway Ste 1600 San Diego 92101

GABRIEL, HELEN TASHJIAN, realtor; b. July 28, Fresno; d. John H. and Pearl (Manger) Tashjian; m. Herond Gabriel, Feb. 6, 1944; children: Janet, b. 1945; John, b. 1950; edn: bus., Jr. Coll. Career: real estate broker 1953–: assoc. Bob Symonds Realty, No. Hollywood 1953-5; Ralph Masters Realty, No. Hywd. 1955-6; Charles Janssen Realty, Sherman Oaks 1957-8; Lamping- Handler Realty, Studio City 1958-77; White House Properties, Sherman Oaks 1977 –; Calif. Real Estate Assn., Dir. 1955-83 (Assocs. Com., Planning & Zoning Com., Profl. Standards Panel), chmn. Sgt.-at-Arms 1963, honored as Realtor-Assoc. of Yr. 1974; bd. dirs. San Fernando Bd. of Realtors, 1964-5, 1981-; candidate 40th Assy. Dist. Calif. 1984; honors: Calif. Mother of the Year (Am. Mothers Inc. of NY 1986); mem: Sherman Oaks CofC (bd. dirs. 1980-exec. com. 1982 3); San Fern. Valley Bus. & Profl. Assn.; Eastern Star; Tarzana Republican Women 1977-83; Valley Research Orgn. 1962-77; Pro-America; United to Serve Am. 1968-78; Republican (elected L.A. County Central Com. 1987-88, alt. 1985-86, exec. com.); Presbyterian; rec: gardening, singing (ch. choir 25 yrs.), cooking. Res: 5801 Ranchito Ave Van Nuys 91401 Ofc: Buddy Bernard's White House Properties, 17130 Ventura Blvd Encino 91316

GABRIELSON, EDWARD FRANCIS, civil engineer; b. Jan. 5, 1914, Spokane, Wash.; s. Frank Helmar and Tekla Rebecca (Franson) G.; m. Alice Maler, Jan. 22, 1938; children: Lyle b. 1940, Carol b. 1943, Edward b. 1944, William b. 1950; edn: BSCE, Univ. Calif. 1936; grad. AUS Command & Gen. Staff Coll. 1958. Career: sanitary engr. San Diego City and County, 1936-37, S.E. Washington, 1937-39; civil engr. US Corps of Engrs., 1939-42; civil engr. City of San Diego 1946-58, city engr. of S.D. 1958-72; v.p. Penasquitos Properties, 1972-80, ret.; honors: Chi Epsilon (1935), Tau Beta Pi (1936), James Monroe McDonald Fellowship (1936), Top Ten Men in Public Works (1970); mem: San Diego Engrs. Club (pres.), ASCE (pres. S.D. Sect.), League of Calif. Cities (pres. Public Works Sect.), Scottish Rite, Masons (32nd degree); works: designed/supvsd. constrn. of Mission Bay, San Diego; supvsd. constrn. of San Diego Metro Sewer System and Major Street System; mil: capt. US Army 1942-46, col. Army Corps of Engrs. 1968; Republican; Lutheran; rec: golf. Address: San Diego

GADDIS, MARSHALL LEWIS, educator; b. Oct. 27, 1942, Wash DC; s. Bevy Marshall and Claudelle (Lewis) Gaddis; edn: BA with honors, Univ. of Iowa 1967; MFA, Univ. of Mont. 1969. Career: instr. English, Univ. of Montana 1969-75; free-lance writer, film actor, radio prod., software developer, 1975 –; dir. computer studies National Univ., Sacramento 1983; coordinator of computers in edn./prof. of computer studies National Univ., Vista 1983-85; dir. computer sci. and info. sys., Nat. Univ., Palm Springs 1986; instr. computer tng. for Proctor and Gamble, Calif. Dept. of Energy, Kaiser Permanente and Sutter Hosps., Hughes Aircraft, Sacto. Utility Dist.; mem: Nat. Computer Graphics Assn., Assn. of Computing Machinery, Data Processing Mgrs. Assn.; Male lead actor (film): Slow Moves (Bay Area Filmmakers' Showcase 1983, L.A. Filmex 1984, London Film Festival 1984, Spl. Jury Prize, San Remo Italy Director's Festival 1985); star (film): Belle Diamond 1986; writer (story) Occupational Hazard, Antigonish Rev. (Nova Scotia) 1971; (screenplay) The Dolphin Conspiracy 1986; (software) The I Ching: Disk of Changes 1986; Democrat; Unitarian; rec: windsurfing, music. Res: 29650 Chihuahua Valley Rd Aguanga 92302 Ofc: National Univ. 2022 University Dr. Vista 92083

GADSBY, ROBERT CHARLES, security consultant; b. Sept. 29, 1951, Hammonton, NJ; s. Charlton Patrick and Mary Helen (Black) G.; edn: UC San Diego 1969-70; AS, in admin. of justice, Grossmont Coll. 1979; BS bus. adminstrn., Univ. Redlands 1986; Certified by Calif. Commn. on Peace Ofcr. Standards and Training 1979. Career: firefighter, Calif. Div. of Forestry, El Cajon 1971; engr. Naval Artic Research Site Fire Dept., Point Barrow, AK 1971-2; interpretive naturalist San Diego Wild Animal Park, Escondido 1972-6; corp. security Southland Corp. South Pacific Div., La Mesa 1977—; pvt. investigator/ cons. 1978—; mem.; spkr. crime prevention and justice; mem: Calif. Crime Prevention Ofcrs. Assn.; Calif. Robbery Invest. Assn.; Calif. Narcotics Ofcrs. Assn., Am. Soc. Indsl. Security, Reserve Police Ofcr., El Cajon 1974-7, 1983-; Reserve Deputy Sheriff, San Diego Co. 1978-9, 80; wildlife photog., freelance writer on natural history, arts. in Sports Afield, Zoonooz; Republican; rec: photog., firearms, shooting sports. Res: 1327 Hardin Dr El Cajon 92020 Ofc: 7839 University Ave La Mesa 92041

GADSON, BETTY WALKER, clinical social worker; b. Mar. 7, 1947, Fairfield, Ala.; d. Elijah James and Verna Rea (Calloway) Walker; widowed; edn: BA, Univ. of Ala. 1968; MSW, Atlanta Univ. 1970; Calif. LCSW, lic. clin. soc. wkr.; Community Coll. Counselor/ Instr. Credential in Public Svcs. & Adminstrn.; lic. real estate agent. Career: med. soc. wkr. Atlanta Southside Comp. Health Ctr. 1970; dir. soc. svcs. Trenton Neighboorhood Family Health Ctr, Trento, NJ 1970-3; dir. soc. svcs. Trenton Head Start Pgm. 1973-4; cons./ pgm. analysis & job tng. New Era Learning Corp., Greenvale, NY 1972-3; instr./ mgmt. & supvr. Los Angeles Southwest Coll. Evening div. 1976-9; child welfare wkr. Los Angeles Co., Dept. of Adoptions 1974—; Lic. Clin. Soc. Wkr./ cons./trainer, pvt. practice; honors: Delta Sigma Kappa; mem. L.A. chpt. Top Ladies of Distn., Inc.; asst. advisor L.A. chpt. Top Teens of Am., Inc.; bd. dirs. Exceptional Children's Opportunity Sch.; mem: Nat. Assn. Social Wkrs; Alpha Kappa Alpha Sorority, Inc.; Univ. of Ala. Alumni Assn.; local neighborhood Block Club; developed: techniques for mainstreaming spl. needs children into regular child care sys.; Democrat; Baptist; rec: acting, floral design, arts & crafts. Res: 1119 South Sycamore Ave Los Angeles 90019 Ofc: L.A. Co. Dept. of Children's Svcs., Adoption Div., 2550 W Olympic Los Angeles 90006

GAITHER, JAMES CASTLE, lawyer; b. Sept. 3, 1937, Oakland; s. Horace Rowan, Jr. and Charlotte Cameron (Castle) G.; m. Susan, Apr. 30, 1960; children: James b. 1962, Stanley b. 1964, Reed b. 1968, Kendra b. 1970; edn: BA econs., Princeton Univ. 1959; JD, Stanford Law Sch. 1964; admitted to practice: Calif. Supreme Ct. (1966), US Dist. Ct., (Dist. Col. 1966, No. Dist. Calif. 1972), US Ct. of Appeals (7th Cir. 1966, 9th Cir. 1975), US Supreme Ct. (1969). Career: intern, UN (ECOSOC), Geneva, Switz. 1957; clk. Draper, Gaither & Anderson, Palo Alto 1962; law clk. Orrick, Dahlquist, Herrington & Sutcliffe, San Francisco 1963; law clk. to Earl Warren, US Chief Justice, 1964-65; spl. asst. to John W. Douglas, Asst. Atty. Gen. Civil Div. US Dept. Justice, 1965-66; staff asst. to the President of the US, 1966-69; lawyer Cooley, Godward, Castro, Huddleson & Tatum, San Francisco 1969-, ptnr. 1971-, mng. ptnr. 1984—; bd. dir./exec. com. Varian Assocs., Inc.; bd. dir. Basic Am. Foods, S.F.; active: Carnegie Endowment for Internat. Peace (bd. trustees, exec. com.), Center for Biotechnology Research, S.F. (chmn. bd. trustees), Stanford Univ. (v.p. bd. trustees), Stanford Law Sch. (bd. visitors), The Rand Corp. (bd. trustees, exec. com.); honors: Distinguished Public Service Award, US Dept. HEW (1977), Order of the Coif, Hilman Oehlmann, Jr. Award, Phi Delta Phi (Graduate of the Year, 1964, Province 12), note ed. Stanford Law Review 6 qtrs.; mem. Am., Calif. and San Francisco Bar Assns.; mil: capt. USMCR 1959-61; Democrat; Presbyterian; rec: tennis, camping, fishing, photog. Ofc: Cooley, Godward, Castro, Huddleson & Tatum One Maritime Plaza Ste 2000 San Francisco 94111

GALINSON, MURRAY LAWRENCE, banker; b. May 8, 1937, Mpls.; s. Louis and Kay June (Lifson) G.; m. Elaine, Dec. 22, 1959; children: Laura b. 1963, Jeffrey b. 1965, Richard b. 1967; edn: BA cum laude, Univ. Minn. 1958; Stanford Univ. Law Sch. 1958-59; JD cum laude, Univ. Minn. 1961; PhD, US Internat. Univ. 1976. Career: asst. US atty. Dept. of Justice 1961-63; atty. Ericson, Popham, Haike & Schnobrich 1963-64; ptnr. law firm Mullin, Galinson & Swirnoff 1964-70; prof. law Calif. Western Law Sch. 1971-83; spl. asst. to US atty. So. Dist. Calif. 1979-81; dir. adminstrn. Mondale/ Ferraro Nat. Campaign 1983-84; pres., CEO San Diego Nat. Bank 1984—; dir. Riverforest Bancorp. 1966-72, S.D. Nat. Bank Financial Corp. 1981—; Democrat; Jewish; rec: jogging, scuba. Ofc: San Diego National Bank 1420 Kettner Blvd San Diego 92101

GALLAGHER, DEBORAH WRIGHT, co. president; b. Nov. 1, 1954, Kokomo, Ind.; d. George Wallace and Katherine Sue (Hardesty) Wright; m. Wm. Gallagher, May 24, 1981; stepchildren: William Jr. b. 1964, Robert b. 1966, Thomas b. 1968, Sarah b. 1975, Nathaniel b. 1979; edn: bus. mgmt. major, St. Mary's Coll. Career: interior designer/prin. Deborah Wright Ints., Oakland 1976-81; major account mgr. Robert Morry Inc. (contract furniture), San Francisco 1981-83; pres. Gallagher and Assocs., Oakland dba Computers Simplified Now (internat. tng. firm), 1983—; instr. int. design, Sunset Community Ctr. 1982; honors: Dean's list Coll. Alameda (1975); mem. Nat. Speakers Assn./No. Calif., Bay Area Bus. Womens Assn., Oakland Athletic Club, Mountain Movers (civic projects orgn.); publs: art., J. for Human Technology (1984), research- Mgmt. by Intuition (1986), poetry reading KMEL Radio (1981); Democrat; Jewish; rec: sailing, tennis, hiking. Address: Gallagher and Assocs. 6515 Saroni Dr Oakland 94611

GALLAGHER, NEIL DENNISON, physician, surgeon; b. Oct. 17, 1923, Scranton, PA; s. Leo Aloysius and Daisy Uzella (Belles) G.; m. Tally Rago, June 21, 1951; 1 dau: Michele, b. 1956; edn: DC, Penn. Coll. of Chiropractic, 1944; MD, Hahnemann Med. Coll. 1949. Career: research res. Gen. Practice 1950-60; genetics research Sonoma State Hosp. 1960-2; med. dir. classified research proj. NASA, Calif. Med. Facility 1963-4; fellowship, postgrad. med. and cons. Presbyterian Hosp., S.F. 1967-9; med. dir. Home Health Care Dept., Sacto. Med. Ctr. 1970-2; staff mem. Solano Co. Hosp. 1972-3; gen. practice 1974-8; med. dir. Physicians Weight Clinic 1978—; lectr. Am. Cancer Soc. 1964-9; cons. Presbyterian Hosp., S.F. 1968-9; awards: plaque of commdn., NASA 1964; Cert. of Excellence in Med. Edn., Am. Med. Assn. 1969; mem: Am. Med. Assn. of Family Practitioners; pres., Vacaville Chpt., Nat. Exchange Club; Am. Soc. of Bariatric Physicians (ASBF); author: med. column in local newspaper; med. dir. classified pgm. for NASA 1963-4; mil: USNR; Methodist; rec: music, magic, numismatics. Res: 119 Anita Ct Vacaville 95688 Ofc: Physicians Weight Clinic, 619 Buck Ave, Ste B, Vacaville 95688

GALLANT, ANN MARIE CAROLE, investment co. executive; b. June 3, 1950, Carbondale, Pa.; d. Raymond Francis and Elizabeth Barbara (Alecks) Dougher; div.; 1 dau. Sara Ann b. 1974; edn: BA, UC Irvine 1972; MPA in fin./ personnel, magna cum laude, CSU Fullerton 1977; cert. fin. & budget, Municipal Fin. Ofcrs. Assn.; cert., real estate inv., UC Irvine. Career: asst. city mgr. City of Santa Ana, 1977-83; v.p./ corp. dir. adminstrn. Butterfield Svgs & Loan, 1983-85; CEO David Hall Inc., Irvine 1985—; owner/gen. mgr. consulting firm Uptegraff, Gallant & Assocs.; mem. ICMA, World Trade Center of Orange Co., Am. Mgmt. Assn., Santa Ana CofC, Irvine CofC; research: on organizational behavior in public vs. pvt. sector; Democrat (O.C. Dem.); Catholic; rec: music (piano, guitar, sing), crewel. Ofc: David Hall Inc 18300 Von Karman Irvine 92806

GALLAWAY, ROBERT RUSSEL, real estate broker/developer; b. Jan. 21, 1942, Sacramento; s. A. Russel, Jr. and Betty Louise (Hill) G.; m. Pamela DuPratt, Nov. 14, 1977; children: Hunter b. 1967, Cameron b. 1970, Carey b. 1972; edn: grad. The Thacher Sch., Ojai 1969; BA pol. sci., Stanford Univ. 1963; Smaller Co. Mgmt. Pgm., Harvard Bus. Sch. 1979; Calif. lic. gen. contr. and real estate broker. Career: v.p./prin. broker/ mgr. real estate dept. Wright & Kimbrough (R.E. & ins. co. estab. 1893), Sacto. 1964-75; realtor/pres. Gallaway & Co., Sacto. 1975—, gen. contr. 1976—; dir. Guild Svgs & Loan Assn. 1970-80; apptd. by Gov. Reagan Cal-Expo Exec. Com. (1972-73); trustee (pres. 1975-76) Sacto. Country Day Sch. 1973-82; mem: Nat. Assn. of Real Estate Bds., Calif. Assn. of Realtors, Sacto. Board of Realtors (dir. 1981-86, pres. elect 1986), Stanford Assn. of Sacto. (pres. 1968-9); clubs: Masons, Sutter Butte Outing (dir. 1980-86), Rio Del Oro Racquet, Sutter, Beach & Tennis, Pebble Beach, Flatrock (Idaho); rec: tennis, fly fishing, hunting. Res: 1817 Parliament Circle Carmichael 95806 Ofc: Gallaway & Co 109 Scripps Dr Sacramento 95825

GALLEGO, JOSE MIGUEL, chemist; b. Nov. 5, 1955, Mexicali, Baja Ca., Mexico; nat. US cit. 1984; s. Waldemar Munoz and Josefina Baker (Garcia) G.; m. Leticia Osuna, Jan. 10, 1981; 1 dau. Kimberly b. 1985; edn: BS in chem., Univ. Autonoma de Guadalajara 1977, grad. work 1977. Career: ops. supr. of water plant, State Water Commn., Tijuana, B.Ca., Mex. 1978-79; research chemist Quimica Organica de Mexico, S.A. Mexicali, B.Ca., 1979-81; v.p./ chief chemist/ptnr. Labs. Industriales y Servicios Internat., S.A., Tijuana, B.Ca. 1981-84, also contract tech. cons. (svc. & maint. microcomputers Sci. Faculties) Univ. Autonoma de Baja Ca., 1982-84; owner G.C. Systems, Chula Vista, Ca. 1983-85; chemist Chemical Energy of Calif. (recycle processes, hazardous waste mgmt.), San Diego 198400; gounder/gen. mgr./ptnr. Innovative Computer Accessories (mfr. computer hardware/software), Imperial Beach 1985—; instr. chem., physics UAG, f.t. 1978, p.t. 1981-84; publs: sev. research arts. in sci. jours., arts. in computer jours., newsletter ed. Boletin Informativo, UAG Faculty of Chem. (1974-77); author book: Programming BASIC en Quimica (under review at UABC); num. tech. arts. for TI-59 PPC (pub. Texas Instruments Inc. 1978-82); mil: Mexican Army 1973-74; Catholic; rec: computer, coin collection, electronics. Res: 2302 D Ave Apt 104 National City 92050 Ofc: Innovative Computer Accessories 1249 Downing St Imperial Beach 92032

GALLEGUS, JESS JAMES, appliance industry executive; b. Sept. 9, 1951, Hayward, Calif.; s. Jess M. and Helen M. (Valencia) G.; m. Virginia Carol, June 24, 1979; children: Monica Marie b. 1982; edn: BA, UC Berkeley 1974. Career: claims adjuster Allstate Ins. Co. 1975-76; salesman Automatic Appliance 1976-77, sales mgr. 1977-78, jr. ptnr. 1978-80, full ptnr., v.p., gen. mgr. 1980—; pres. Elec. & Gas Inds. Assn. honors: Employee of the Yr. 1983; mem: Elec. & Gas Inds. Assn. (pres.), Trinidad Aero Club 1985; Democrat; Catholic; rec: golf, student pilot. Ofc: 37383 Fremont Blvd Fremont 94536

GALLO, JAMES ANDREW, lawyer; b. Feb. 6, 1950, Los Angeles; s. Jack and Margaret (Baiamonte) G.; m. Lesley Anne, June 27, 1981; 1 dau., Sara b. 1984;

edn: BA, Loyola Univ. of Los Angeles 1972, JD, 1976; admitted Calif. State Bar 1977; lic. Real Estate Broker 1983. Career: trial lawyer Ralston, Smith & Sullivan, 197-80, Clinnin, Siracuse & Belcher, 1980-82; assoc. atty./broker MacFarlane, Lambert & Co., 1982-85, senior vice pres. 1985–; ptnr. MacFarlane, Lambert, Sloat & Gallo, 1985–; judge pro tem Los Angeles Municipal Ct., L.A. Superior Ct.; mem: State Bar of Calif. (panelist State Bar Conv. 1977-; mem. real property sect., comml. & indsl. devel. subsect.); Los Angeles County Bar Assn. (arbitrator; mem. trial lawyers, real property sects.); Univ. Club (Pasadena); Democrat; Catholic; rec: tennis. Ofc: MacFarlane, Lambert & Co. Inc. 35 N Lake Ave 7th Fl Pasadena 91101

GALLUCCIO, FRED JAMES, physician and surgeon, educator; b. Jan. 11, 1952, Burbank; s. Fernando Joseph and Virginia Frances (Dawson) G.; edn: BS, Loyola Univ., L.A. 1974; MD, UC Irvine 1979. Career: family practice residency, UC San Francisco and Santa Rosa 1979-82, UCSF fellowship in family and comm. medicine, Serabu Hosp., Sierra Leone, West Africa/chief of Ob-Gyn Neonatal and Med. Wards, 1983; asst. clin. prof. Dept. of Family Medicine, UC Irvine 1983–, also dir. Inpatient Svcs., dir. UCIMC Family Medicine Clinic; clin. instr. Comm. Hosp. Sonoma Co. (UCSF) 1982-83; awards: honors pgm. Loyola Univ., summer research fellowship Calif. Heart Assn.; mem: Calif. Acad. of Family Physicians, Am. Acad. of Family Physicians, Phi Delta Epsilon, Soc. of Tchrs. of Family Medicine, Physicians for Social Responsiblity, Internat. Physicians for Prevention of Nuclear Warfare (Nobel Peace Prize Winner 1985), var. sports clubs, Nat. Peace Network, Hunger Project, Alliance for Survival, UCI Interfaith Found. (bd. dirs., Eucharistic minister); participant Physician's info. exchange group in Russia, Germany, G.B.; guest lectr. in china and Japan 1985; Catholic; rec: sports, peace. Ofc: 661 W First St Ste E Tustin 92680-2972; UCI/CCM Dept. of Family Medicine 101 The City Dr Orange 92668

GAMBOA, GEORGE CHARLES, educator, oral surgeon; b. Dec. 17, 1923, King City; s. George Angel and Martha Ann (Baker) G.; m. Winona Mae Collins, July 16, 1946; children: Cheryl, b. 1948; Jon, b. 1951; Judith, b. 1953; edn: DDS, Univ. of the Pacific Coll. of Phys. & Surgeons 1946; MS, oral surgery, Univ. Minn. 1953; AB, zoology, USC 1958; EdD, USC 1976. Career: assoc. clinical prof., grad. pgm. Oral Surgery, USC 1954–; assoc. prof., grad. pgm. oral surgery, Loma Linda Univ. 1958–; part-time practice Oral Surgery, San Gabriel; chmn. Dept. of Oral Surgery, Sch. of Dentistry, Loma Linda Univ. 1960-3; mem. exec. com. Profl. Staff Assn., LAC-USC Med. Ctr. 1977-; mem. (v.chmn. Profl. Edn. sub-com.) Calif. Div., Am. Cancer Soc. 1978-; chmn. Safety Svcs. Com., W. San Gabriel chpt. ARC 1981-; honors: Omicron Kappa Upsilon; mem: So. Calif. Soc. of Oral and Maxillofacial Surgeons; So. Calif. Acad of Oral Pathology; Marsh Robinson Acad. of Oral Surgeons; Am. Assn. Oral & Maxillofacial Surgeons; Internat. Assns. of Oral and Maxillofacial Surgeons; Diplomate, Am. Bd. of Oral and Maxillofacial Surgeons; Fellow Am. Coll. of Oral & Maxfl. Surg.; Am. Acad. of Dental Radiology; San Gabriel Valley Dental Soc. (pres. 1984-85); Alhambra Lions Club (pres. 1968); mil: lt. jg USNR, dental ofcr. 1946-8; Republican; Seventh-day Adventists; rec: golf, water skiing. Res: 1102 Loganrita Ave Arcadia 91006 Ofc: 132 So. Mission Dr San Gabriel 91776

GANDSEY, LOUIS JOHN, petroleum & chemical engineering consultant; b. May 19, 1921, Greybull, Wyo.; s. John Wellington and Leonora Francis (McLaughlin) G.; m. Mary Louise Alviso, Nov. 10, 1945; children: Mary b. 1946, Catherine b. 1948, John b. 1953, Michael b. 1958, Laurie b. 1960; edn: AA, Compton Jr. Coll. 1941; BS, UC Berkeley 1943; M.Eng., UCLA 1958; Profl. Engr., State of Calif. 1958. Career: var. positions with Richfield then ARCO 1943-69; with ARCO 1969-77: mgr. Supply & transport., Chgo. 1969-70; mgr., planning, NY 1970-1; mgr. coord. & supply, Los Angeles 1971-5; mgr. domestic crude, ARCO, 1975-77; v.p. Lunday- Thagard Oil Co., So. Gate 1977-82; cons. Templeton & Los Angeles 1982–; coll. tchr., chemistry, petroleum, petroleum refining; mem: Am. Chemical Soc.; Pacific Energy Assn.; publ: arts. in Petroleum Refiner, World Oil, Chemical Processing; mil: pvt. Corps of Engrs., US Army 1946; Republican; Catholic; rec: farming, horses, cattle. Res: Route 1 Box 16A Templeton 93465 Ofc: POB 1519 South Gate 90280

GANZ, CLAUDE L., biochemical research & development co. president; b. Aug. 5, 1931, Europe, nat. US cit. 1952; s. Arthur J. and Jetta I. (Brumlik) G.; m. Lynn Preisler, Sept. 15, 1979; children: Lionel b. 1969, David b. 1971, (nee Preisler): Stacy b. 1951, William b. 1954; edn: BS indsl. mgmt. Univ. Calif. 1956. Career: var. pos., bd. chmn./CEO (9 yrs.) DYMO Industries Inc., 22 yrs.; indep. cons. and pvt. investor; pres./CEO Aquanautics Corp., San Francisco 1984–; advis. council San Francisco State Univ. Bus. Sch.; dir. Esselte Bus. Systems (ofc. equip., supplies); past dir: Calif. Energy Corp. 1979-82, Shaklee Corp. 1977-79, Koracorp 1975-77; trustee Am. Conservatory Theatre (S.F.), KQED, S.F. Art Inst., S.F. Film Fest., Jerusalem Univ., Anti Defamation League (chmn.), S.F. Bicentennial Commn., S.F. Jewish Mus., Duke Univ. (pres.'s council); mil: US Army Intel. 1951-54; Jewish; rec: skiing, boating. Ofc: Aquanautics Corp. One Maritime Plaza Ste 1750 San Francisco 94111

GARBER, BERNARD JEFFREY, judge; b. June 6, 1946, Berkeley, Calif.; s. Philip and Martha B. (Highiet) G.; m. Elise Leveroni, Jan. 20, 1973; children: Matthew b. 1975; Stephanie b. 1980; Allison b. 1983; edn: AB, UC Berkeley 1967; JD, Golden Gate Law Sch. 1970. Career: dep. dist. atty. San Joaquin Co. Dist. Atty's Ofc. 1971-84; judge, Stockton Mun. Ct. 1984–; mil: capt. US Army field artillery. Ofc: 222 E Weber Stockton 95202

GARBER, CHESTER STANTON, businessman, lawyer (ret.); b. Nov. 28, 1943, Fresno; s. Chester and Virginia Lee (Trimmer) G.; m. Emilia Ting, MD, June 20, 1981; edn: BA, Univ. of San Francisco 1963; MA, 1968; JD, S.F. Law Sch. 1971; mem. Calif. State Bar; lic. Calif. Real Estate Broker; Registered Rep., SEC; Calif. Securities Agt. lic.; Insurance lic.: life, disability; lic. comml. pilot (multi engine and instrument ratings). Career: (past) pres./ CEO: John's Italian Restaurants Inc., Garmah Investments Co. Inc., Maurlee Investment Co. Inc., Stage Lounges Inc., 418 Geary Corp; currently: pres./ chmn. bd./ CEO: C.S. Garber, Inc.; Garber Petroleum, Inc.; Xanadu Mines, Inc.; Eldorado Mines, Ltd.; Golden Valley Aero, Inc.; pres., CEO Garber Svcs. Inc., Gen. Aviation Archives, Inc., Tingar Investments Inc.; asst. treas. of Emilia C. Ting, M.D., Inc. (lic. med. corp.); mem: Calif. State Bar; Aircraft Owners & Pilots Assn.; Nat. Assn. of Real Estate Brokers; Nat. Assn. of Security Dealers; Am. Mgmt. Assn.; Downtown Club, Fresno; nationally published profl. wildlife photg.; mil: capt. Spl. Forces, US Army, silver, bronze stars, DSC, Purple Heart (4); rec: gardening, martial arts, firearms. Ofc: C.S. Garber & Assoc., 510 W Kearney Blvd Fresno 93706

GARCIA, FERNANDO DOMINGUEZ, physician; b. July 22, 1948, Marfa, Texas; s. Federico C. and Consuelo D. Garcia; div.; 2 sons: Fernando David b. 1970, Juan Alejandro b. 1975; edn: Pharm.D., UC San Francisco 1973; MD, Univ. of Utah 1980. Career: founder, dir. Pharmacy Services, Orange Cove, 1973-76, United Health Center of San Joaquin Valley; pvt. practice Family Medicine, Farmersville 1981-84, Visalia 1984–; staff Kaweah Delta District Hosp.; lectr. on topics: nutrition, prenatal health, drug abuse, rheumatoid arthritis, hypertension, and diabetes; mem. AMA, CMA; charter bd. mem. Visalia Youth Club; past bd. Am. Cancer Soc. 1983-84, Club de Salud; advis. bd. mem. Tulare County Health Dept. 1984-85; past pres. State & Regional Migrant Edn. Parent Advis. Bd. 1974-76; Republican; Roman Catholic; rec: racquetball, water skiing, hunting. Ofc: Fernando D. Garcia, MD 1900 N Dinuba Blvd, Ste B, Visalia 93291

GARD, ZANE RONALD, physician-surgeon; b. Jan. 24, 1932, Denver, Colo.; s. Roy C. and Della Pearl (Morton) G.; m. ERma Jean Brown, Mar. 18, 1961; children: Keith b. 1952, Marlene b. 1953, Bruce b. 1958, Zane, Jr. b. 1963, Geneva b. 1966; edn: MD, UC Irvine 1961; MT & DO, Kansas City Coll. of Osteopathy and Surgery; postgrad. courses Family Practice, Allergy, Nutrition, Bariatrics, Environ. Medicine; diplomate Am. Board of Bariatric Medicine (1972). Career: intern Phoenix (Ariz.) Gen. Hosp. 1961-63; family practice residency, Tulare, Calif. 1962-63; group family practice, Modesto 1963-66, pvt. family practice 1966-72; pres. Zane R. Gard Med. Corp., 1972-76; cons. for Medical Risk Mgmt., ins. investigator 1976-79; pvt. family practice, 1979-81; group practice Livingston-Wheeler Clinic, San Diego 1981-82, Alvarado Allergy & Immunol. Group, 1983–, cons. Human Environmental Medicine, Inc. 1983-; speaker for num. orgns. re Environmental induced illness; honors: Friends award (1983); Fellow: Am. Acad. of Family Physicians (charter 1974), Am. Acad. of Environ. Medicine, Internat. Acad. of Metabolism, Internat. Coll. of Applied Nutrition; mem: Am. Acad. Otolaryngic Allergy, Pan Am. Assn. of Oto-Rhino-Laryngol., Am. Acad. of Med. Preventics, AMA, CMA; num. articles in med. jours.; Republican; SDA; rec: flying, sailing, dune buggy. Ofc: 6386 Alvarado Ct Ste 326 San Diego 92120

GARDNER, DAVID PIERPONT, university president; b. Mar. 24, 1933, Berkeley; s. Reed S. and Margaret (Pierpont) G.; m. Elizabeth Fuhriman, June 27, 1958; children: Karen, Shari, Lisa, Marci; edn: BS, Brigham Young Univ. 1955; MA, UC Berkeley 1959, PhD, 1966. Career: dir. Calif. Alumni Found., UC Berkeley, 1962-64; asst. chancellor UC Santa Barbara, 1966-69, vice chancellor, exec. asst., also assoc. prof. higher edn. UCSB, 1969-71; vice pres. Univ. of Calif. System, Berkeley 1971-73; pres. Univ. Utah, Salt Lake City 1973-83, prof. higher edn., 1973-83; pres. UC Berkeley, 1983–; vis. fellow Clare Hall, Cambridge Univ. 1979, assoc., 1979-; dir. Utah Power & Light Co., First Security Corp., Denver and Rio Grande Western RR Co.; mem. Presidents Council Nat. Assn. State Univs. and Landgrant Colls. 1973-, Western Athletic Conf. 1973-, bd. dirs. Am. Council on Edn. 1977-80, chmn. bd. trustees Tanner Lectures on Human Values, Salt Lake City 1978-, Nat. Commn. on Student Finl. Assistance 1981-, chmn. Nat. Commn. on Excellence in Education 1981-, chmn. George S. and Dolores Dore Eccles Found.; mem. Am. Assn. for Higher Edn., AAUP, Phi Kappa Phi, Phi Beta Kappa; clubs: Rotary, Alta, Timpanogos, Ft. Douglas, Century Assn.; author: The California Oath Controversy (1967). Address: 714 University Hall, 2200 University Ave., Berkeley 94720

GARDNER, NORD ARLING, management consultant; b. Aug. 10, 1923, Afton, Wyo.; s. Arling A. and Ruth (Lee) G.; m. Thora Marie Stephen, Mar. 24, 1945; children: Randall Nord, Scott Stephen, Craig Robert, Laurie Lee; edn: BA, Univ. Wyo. 1945; MS, CSU Hayward 1972; MPA, 1975; postgrad. Univ. Chgo., Univ. Mich., UC Berkeley. Career: Commnd. 2d.lt., advanced through grades to lt. col. US Army, 1942-64, ret. 1966, (Army Commendn. medal); personnel analyst Univ. Hosp. UC San Diego 1946-8; coord. manpower devel. UC Berkeley 1968-75; univ. tng. ofcr. San Francisco State Univ. 1975-80, personnel mgr. 1976-80; exec. dir. CRDC Maintenance Tng. Corp. (nonprofit), S.F. 1980-85; pres./dir. Sandor Assocs. Mgmt. Cons., Pleasant Hill; instr. Japanese, psychol., supervisory. courses, 1977-8; Advis. Council S.F. Comm. Coll. Dist.; mem: Retired Ofcrs. Assn.; Am. Soc. Tng. and Devel.; No. Calif. Human Rels. Council; Am. Assn. Univ. Adminstrs.; Internat. Personnel Mgrs. Assn.; Coll. and Univ. Personnel Assn. (W. Coast rep.); Internat. Platform Assn.; Am. Legion; clubs: Commonwealth of Calif., UCB Faculty, University (SF); listed nat., internat. biographical ref. books; author: To Gather Stones, 1978; Republican. Res: 2995 Bonnie Ln Pleasant Hill 94523 Ofc: Asian Resource Ctr., 310 Eighth St Ste 309 Oakland 94607

GARDNER, ROBERT ALEXANDER, human resource development consultant; b. Sept. 16, 1944, Berkeley; s. Robert Alexander and Eleanor (Ambrose) G.; edn: BA, UC Berkeley 1967, MA, CSU Chico 1974. Career: placement counselor Sonoma County Office of Edn., Santa Rosa 1975-76; personnel ofcr. Wells Fargo Bank, San Francisco 1977-80; dir. personnel Transam. Airlines, Oakland 1980-84; human resource devel. cons. Gardner Assocs., Oakland 1983–; instr. UCB Extension Div., 1980-; instr. Armstrong Coll., Bus. and Mgmt. Div. 1978-80; mem. Nat. Soc. for Performance and Instrn., Nat. Orgn. Devel. Network, Career Planning and Adult Devel. Network, Am. Assn. for Counseling and Devel., Calif. Assn. for Counseling and Devel., Rotary Internat., UC Alumni Assn.; publs: Time Management (Telelearning Systems, Inc. S.F., 1983); Achieving Effective Supervision (UCB, 1984), Managing Personnel Adminstrn. Effectively (UCB, 1986), The National Review Magazine: A Survey from 1955 to 1973 (CSU Chico 1974); mil: 1st lt. US Army Intel. 1970-71, Bronze Star, Cross of Gal. w/star cluster, Rep. of Vietnam Service medals; Republican; Congregational; rec: collect and study antique Chinese Snuff Bottles. Res: 6 Captain Dr #340 Emeryville 94608 Ofc: Gardner Associates 3873 Piedmont Ave Ste 3 Oakland 94611

GARDNER, ROBERT WILLIAM, physician; b. June 17, 1949, Phila.Pa.; s. Milton and Myra (Sacks) G.; 1 dau: Erica b. 1978; edn: Penn. State Univ.; MD, Thomas Jefferson Univ. 1974. Career: psychiatric resident 1975; phys. pvt. practice 1976-83; asst. health ofcr. Marin Co. 1982; pvt. practice, med. dir. Sonoma Co. Drug Abuse Council, Meml. Hosp. Chem. Dependency Unit. 1984–; honors: Phi Beta Kappa; mem: CMA, Calif. Acad. Prev. Med. (pres.), Sonoma Co. Med. Assn.; U.S. Draft Bd. (bd. mem.); publ: health column, For the Health of It. Res: 6600 Foothill Ranch Rd Santa Rosa 95406 Ofc: Oasis Health Ctr. 680 E Cotati Ave Cotati 94928

GARFINKEL, ARTHUR IRA, orthopaedic surgeon; b. Mar. 12, 1946, NY, NY; s. George and Henrietta (Zoffen) G.; m. Sandra Laites, Sept. 2, 1984; 1 son, David b. 1985; edn: AB, Columbia Univ. 1967; MD, State Univ. of N.Y., Downstate Med. Ctr. 1971; lic. phys. N.Y. 1972, Calif. 1975; Diplomate Am. Bd. Orthopaedic Surgery. Career: intern and gen. surg. resident Mount Sinai Hosp. Med. Ctr./CUNY 1971-73; postdoc. fellow USC, orthopaedic residency LA County/USC Med. Ctr., 1976-80; major, flight surgeon US Air Force 1973-75, chief flight medicine Udon Royal Thai AFB, Thailand and flt. surgeon to 555 Tactical Fighter Squadron, 1973-74, chief aerospace medicine, Ellington AFB, Tx. 1974-75; attending phys. Kaiser Permanente Med. Ctr., Los Angeles 1975-76; pvt. practice orthopaedic surgery, Newhall 1980–; mem: Santa Clarita Valley Med. Soc., L.A. County Med. Assn., Calif. Med. Assn., Profl. Stds. Review Orgn. (Calif. Area XX), Nat. Assn. of Disability Evaluating Physicians, USC Grad. Orthopaedic Soc., Aerospace Med. Assn., USAF Soc. of Flight Surgeons, Rotary Club; publ: Effect of Angulation in Both Bone Fractures, J. of Bone & Joint Surgery (1982); Jewish; rec: scuba, travel, photog. Ofc: 25050 Peachland Ave Ste 206 Newhall 91321

GARGANTA, NARCISO MERIOLES, librarian; b. Sept. 18, 1932, Masbate, Philippines; s. Francisco Legaspi and Leonor (Merioles) G.; edn: BLS, Arellano Univ. 1956; MLS, Pratt Inst. 1971; cert. profl. public librarian NY. Career: dir. tech. library United Drug Co. Inc., United Labs Inc., Manila, Phil. 1960-67; serials librarian Norris Med. Library, USC Medical Ctr. 1967-68; med. librarian Milton Helpern Library Legal Medicine, NYC 1970-72; curriculum devel. splst. RCA Resource Center, NYC 1972-77; asst. librn. VA Med. Ctr., West L.A. Brentwood Div. 1978-79, Patients and Audio Visual Librn. 1984–; dir. med. library Burbank Comm. Hosp. 1979–; cons. Calif. Acupuncture Coll., L.A., West Covina Comm. Hosp.; chmn. Local Bd., Selective Service, Local 24, L.A.; mem: Medical Library Assn., Am. Soc. Information Sci., Med. Group So. Calif. and Ariz., NYC Geneal. Soc.; publs: mng. editor Philippine Library Jour., 1959, Internat. Microform Jour. of Legal Medicine, 1970. Res: 4914 York Blvd., Los Angeles 90042

GAROUTTE, BILL CHARLES, physician, medical school professor; b. Mar. 15, 1921, Absarokee, Mont.; s. Bernard Clark and Anna (Kosir) G.; m. Sally Jeter, July 18, 1848; children: Brian b. 1949, Susanna b. 1951, David b. 1953, Katherine b. 1956; edn: San Diego State Coll. 1939-42; BA, UC Berkeley 1943; MD, UC San Francisco Med. Sch. 1945; PhD, UC Berkeley 1954. Career: lectr. to prof. anatomy & neurology UC Med. Sch. San Francisco 1952–; mem: Am. Acad. Neurology, Am. EEG Soc., Am. Assn. Electrodiagnosis and Electromyography; publ: Survey of Functional Neuroanatomy (1981), various scientific papers on function of central nervous system; mil: lt. j.g. USNR 1946-47. Res: 105 Molino Ave Mill Valley 94941 Ofc: UC San Francisco 94143

GARSIDE, BEN CHARLES III, securities investment advisor; b. May 25, 1925, Denver, Colo.; s. Ben Charles Jr. and Eloise Nadene (Eisele) G.; m. Charlyn Louise Pyles, Sept. 4, 1949; children: Pamela, b. 1953; Deborah, b. 1956; Victoria, b. 1957; Cynthia, b. 1958; edn: BA, Stanford Univ. 1949; AA, Control Data Inst. 1970; investment advisor, Sec. & Exch. Com. 1970. Career: 2nd Lt., Aerial Navigator, Army Air Corps., Europe 1943-5; dist. staff asst. Pacific Telephone, San Rafael 1949-51; 1st Lt., Aerial Navigator, USAF, Korea 1951-3; acct. exec. Dean Whitter & Co., Santa Ana 1954-70; ed./pub. The Garside Forecast, Tustin 1970–; sr. partner Garside & Co., (invest. mgmt.), Tustin 1975–; sr. v.p./ dir. Market Timing and Research, (var. annuity timing), Huntington Beach 1978–; guest lectr. Cal. State Fullerton, West Coast Univ., Golden West Coll., and Santa Barbara City Coll.; num. seminars and TV appearances related to securities; awards: Stock Market Timer of Yr. (1982) and Number One Gold Timer (1985), Timer Digest, Ft. Lauderdale, Fla.; Top 5 percent in Portfolio Performance out of 400 fin. publs., Select Info. Exch., NY, NY 1981-5; mem: Tech. Securities Analysts Assn.; Internat. Assn. of Fin. Planners; mil: 2nd Lt., Navigator, Army Air Corps. 1943-45 8th Air Force; 1st Lt., Navigator, USAF 1951-3 5th Air Force; Distng. Flying Cross, Air Medal w/ 3 Oak Leaf Clusters; Republican; Protestant; rec: golf, swimming, trout fishing. Res: 5200 Irvine Blvd, No. 370, Irvine 92720 Ofc: Garside & Co., 17772 Irvine Blvd, Ste 102, Tustin 92680

GARTNER, HAROLD HENRY, III, lawyer; b. June 23, 1948, Los Angeles; s. Harold H. and Frances Mildred (Evans) G.; m. Denise Young, June 7, 1975; children: Patrick Christopher b. 1977, Matthew Alexander b. 1982; edn: Pasadena City Coll. 1966-67; Geo. Williams Coll. 1967-68; CSU Los Angeles 1968-69; JD, cum laude, Loyola Univ. Sch. of Law 1972. Career: assoc. atty. Hitt, Murray & Caffray, Long Beach 1972; dep. city atty. L.A. 1972-73; assoc. atty. Patterson, Ritner, Lockwood, Zanghi & Gartner (and pred. firm) L.A., Ventura & Bakersfield 1973-79, ptnr. 1979–; instr. of law Ventura Coll. of Law 1981-; honors: Am. Jurisprudence Award (Trusts & Equity 1971), St. Thomas More Law Honor Soc. (bd. dirs. 1971-72), Law Review; mem: Am., Calif., Ventura Co. bar assns.; Ventura Co. Trial Lawyers Assn., Assn. of So. Calif. Defense Counsel, Nat. Assn. Defense Counsel, Direct Relief Internat. (bd. trustees), Pacific Corinthian Yacht Club; Republican; rec: sailing, scuba diving, skiing. Res: 6900 Via Alba Camarillo 93010 Ofc: Patterson, Rittner et al. 260 Maple Ct, Ste 231, Ventura 93003

GARTRELL, ROBERT SANFORD, dentist, dental educator- administrator; b. Dec. 28, 1944, Oakland; s. Thorold Ivan-Lance and Phyllis May (Smith) G.; m. Sloan M. Mcdonald, June 5, 1983; children: Amy-Beth Caroline b. 1974, Emily-Jean Katherine b. 1979; edn: BS, UC Berkeley 1969; DDS, Univ. of the Pacific Sch. of Dentistry 1974. Career: assoc. Ray J. Rucker DDS, San Mateo 1974; owner, practitioner pvt. practice, Yuba City 1975-79; clin. instr. community dentistry Univ. of the Pacific 1974-75, asst. prof. fixed prosthodontics 1979-82, asst. prof. operative dentistry 191-82; clin. adminstr. Univ. of the Pacific Sch. of Denistry 1980-82; asst. prof. Dept. of Gen. Dentistry, Louisiana State Univ. Med. Ctr. Sch. of Dentistry 1982-84; asst. prof., chmn. Dept. of Community Dentistry, dir. Div. of Cont. Edn., Univ. of the Pacific Sch. of Dentistry 1984–; grant/ pgm. dir. pvt. pracitice assoc. pgm. Am./ Calif. Dental Assn. 1984-; pvt. practice cons. 1979-; cons. Profl. Mgmt. Sciences Inc. 1984-; faculty del. House of Delegates Am. Assn. of Dental Schs. 1980-82; honors: Incentive Award, Univ. of the Pacific Sch. of Dentistry 1981; C. Edmund Kells Hon. Soc. 1984; Recogn. Award, Am. Dental Assn. 1986; mem: Am., New Orleans and Calif. Dental Assns., Butte-Sierra and Alameda Co. Dental Socs., Am. Assn. of Dental Schs., Acad. of Gen. Dentistry, Am. Soc. of the Aging, 20/30 Culb of Yuba City (past), Yuba City CofC, Toastmasters, The Univ. Club of San Francisco; works: co-author with Simmon, Modifications to Improve Retention of Acid Etched Bridges, Louisiana Dental Journ. 1984; co-author with. Friesenger, Getting Associated, Calif. Dental Assn. Journ. 1984; mil: splst. 5/c US Army 1964-65, GCM, Nat. Defense; Republican; Protestant; rec: duck hunting, fishing. Ofc: Univ. of the Pacific, Sch. of Dentistry, 2155 Webster St. San Francisco 94115

GARVIN, HAROLD WARD, obstetrician-gynecologist; b. Apr. 6, 1922, New Canton, Ill.; s. Wiley Boyce and Hazel Helen (Ward) G.; m. Shirley D. Mueller, Jan. 30, 1942; m. 2nd Vlasta Lupich, Jan. 10, 1986; children: Nancy b. 1943, Sharon b. 1944, Chuck b. 1949, Kim b. 1955; edn: BS, Univ. of Ill. 1942, MD, 1945; board certified OB-Gyn 1957. Career: physician US Navy, 1945-54; pvt. practice in obstets-gyn, Van Nuys 1954–; clin. prof. OB-Gyn, USC Med. Sch., 1955–; mem: Am. Coll. of OB-Gyn, Los Angeles County OB-Gyn Soc., LA County Med. Soc.; mil: lt. USN 1945-54; Republican; Protestant; rec: cycling, tennis, scuba diving. Ofc: OB-Gyne Medical Group 15243 Vanowen, Van Nuys 91405

GARZA, LYNN EDWARD, insurance brokerage executive, b. May 20, 1949, Sacramento; s. Eddie R. and Hazel M. Garza; m. Linda Reynolds, June 28, 1985; 1 son, Anthony, b. 1967; edn: BS, CSU Sacto. 1979; desig: CPA, Calif. Career: gen. mgr. Bouza's Inc., Sacto. 1969-79; auditor Price Waterhouse Co., Sacto. 1980; asst. v.p./ Trust Acctg. mgr. Granite Finl. Corp., Sacto. 1981; senior auditor John F. Forbes Co., Sacto. 1982; controller Rollins Burdick Hunter of N. Calif., Sacto. 1983-85; v.p., CFO Butler & Assocs. Ins. Agency Inc., Sacto.; honors: Beta Gamma Sigma 1978-9; mem: Am. Inst. of CPAs, Nat. Acctg. Assn., Acctg. Research Assn.; pres. Crestview Merchants Assn. 1978-9; works: designed accounting sys. to monitor the creation and servicing of the first successfully insured 2d Deed of Trust Mortgage Pool created on a comml. mktg. basis; Democrat; Methodist. Res: 542 La Purissima Ave Sacramento 95819 Ofc: Butler & Assocs., 8001 Folsom Blvd Ste 110 Sacramento 95826

GASTON, BRUCE WILLIAM, composer; b. Mar. 11, 1946, Glendale; s. Marcus Theodore and Evangeline Mary (Radley) G.; m. Sarapi Areemitr, July 9, 1976; 1 son: Theodore, b. 1982; edn: BA, USC 1967, MM, 1969; (ordained into 3d level of Thai Classical Music). Career: profl. organist, No. Hollywood Presbyterian Ch., La Canada Presbyterian Ch., St. Mark's Cathedral, Seattle, Wash. 1962-69; co-founder Payap Univ. Sch. of Music, Chiang Mai, Thailand 1970-80; spl. lectr. faculty of arts Chulalongkorn Univ. drama dept., Bangkok 1980–; dir. Siamese Music Ensemble 1981–; res. composer Butterfly Sound and Film Co., Bangkok 1981–, chmn. exec. com. 1983; currently musical dir. Bangkok Symphony Orchestra; adviser, Electronic music for Nitespot Prodns. 1985; awards: Danforth Scholar 1963-67, Danforth Fellow 1967-69; Golden Swan Award for Best Musical Score, motion picture The Primitive, 1981; Outstanding Musician of the Nation, Her Royal Highness Princess Sirinthorn 1982; works: CHAO Phraya Concerto for 5 orchestras and electronic tape; opera, Chuchok, premier Metamusik Festival, Berlin 1978; opera, Phra- Sang-

Iphigenie, premier Bangkok 1984; Ahnu for piano and electronic tape, premier Lincoln Ctr., Alice Tulley Hall, NY 1982. Res: 606/2 Soi Chayapreuk, Sukumvit 65, Bangkok 10110, Thailand Ofc: Butterfly South and Film Co. 96/6 Soi Prasarnmit, Sukumvit 23, Bangkok, 10110, Thailand

GATES, DARYL F., Los Angeles chief of police; b. Aug. 30, 1926, Glendale; edn: BS in pub. admin., USC, grad. Managerial Policy Inst. and Exec. Pgm. USC Grad. Sch. Bus. Adminstrn. Career: with Los Angeles Police Dept., 1949–, dep. chief 1968-69, asst. chief 1969-78, chief 1978–; adv. Nat. Adv. Commn. on Civil Disorder; adv. bd. Childrens' Village; Internat. Police Assn., Calif. Police Chiefs Assn., Internat. Assn. Chiefs Police (editorial cons.), Criminal Justice Group, Womens Peace Officers Assn. Calif., Rotary; mil: USN, WWII. Ofc: Los Angeles Police Department, P.O. Box 30158, Los Angeles 90020

GATES, LAURA JEANNE, artist/art-therapist; b. Aug. 1, 1946, Alhambra; d. Glenn B. and Martha M. (Petter) Gates; gr.grandmother, Minerva Herrick, M.D. (grad. Chgo. Med. Sch. 1910, first in class); grandmother, Laura Gates (internat. ballet troupe asst. mgr./costume designer); mother, Martha Gates (singer-evangelist); m. Aram Kazazian (architect/builder, grad. CalPoly SLO), 1985; two stepdaus: Christina, Alisa; edn: AA, Los Angeles Valley Coll. 1967; BA summa cum laude, Immaculate Heart Coll. 1976, MA, 1979. Career: screen cartoonist at Spungbuggy, Filmation, Bakshi, Hanna-Barbera, 1966–; dir. Boys Club of Hollywood 1976-77; psych./clinical art therapist, Marriage, Family & Child Therapist Intern 1977-, USC/L.A. Co. Med. Center 1977, VA Hosp. Sepulveda 1978, Glendale Adventist Med. Center 1979, Pasadena Comm. Hosp. 1980-81, Riverside Comm. Hosp. 1981-82; model Mary Webb Davis Agcy. 1981-83; chief estimator-bid coordinator Aram Kazazian Constrn. Inc., Glendale 1983–; honors: news featured alumni with biography, Immaculate Heart Coll. (1977), nat. recogn. for program excellence, also students ranked first in nat. competition, Boys Club of Am. (1977-78); mem: Am. Art Therapy Assn., Motion Picture Screen Cartoonist Union; civic: Glendale Symphony Orch. (Womens Com.), Glendale Hist. Soc., Glendale Repub. Womens Workshop Fedn.; works: fine art exhibits and sales of etchings, lithography, woodcuts, paintings, textile designs; book-cover art: Family Clinical Art Therapy by Helen Landgatens (1986); Republican; Lutheran; rec: doll collector, architecture, antiques, cats. Res: Glendale 91206

GATHERS, GEORGE ROGER, physicist; b. Feb. 1, 1936, Meridian, Okla.; s. George Walker and Eugenia Midian (Payne) G.; m. Christine, Apr. 5, 1969; 1 son, Kevin b. 1973; edn: AA, Pierce Jr. Coll., Woodland Hills 1957; BS, Univ. So. Calif. 1960; PhD, UC Berkeley 1967. Carer: staff physicist Lawrence Livermore Nat. Lab. 1967-68, asst. diagnostics gp. leader L-Div. 1968-69, diag. group leader L-Div. 1969, staff physicist 1969-71, staff physicist H-Div. 1972, senior staff phys. for isobaric expansion facility 1972-83, staff phys. H-Div. 1983–; mem: Am. Physical Soc., Am. Scientific Affiliation, Christian Businessmen's Com., Nat. Rifle Assn. (cert. instr. rifle, pistol, practical firearms), BSA (asst. scoutmaster), Radio Amateur Civil Emergency Svcs.; publs: num. tech. jour. articles, handbook on testing of nuclear weapons; main field of interest: liquid metal physics; mil: a 1/c Calif. Air Nat. Guard, AF Reserve 1954-62; Republican; Evangelical Free Ch. of Am.; rec: amateur radio, scuba, marksmanship, archery. Ofc: Lawrence Livermore Nat. Lab. POB 808 Livermore 92550

GATTONE, EDMOND, lawyer, certified public accountant, ret.; b. Sept. 18, 1907, Phila.; s. Dominico and Julia (Gulli) G.; m. Alberta Robertson, 1934; edn: AB bus. admin., Stanford Univ. 1928; LLB, Loyola Univ. 1939; CPA Calif. Career: Calif. Corporation Dept. (securities commn.) 1932-36; atty. pvt. practice L.A. 1939-43; Bechtel Corp. 1943-46; arbitrator Am. Arbn. Assn. 1970-78; mem: Calif. State Bar, Am. Bar Assn., Atty-CPA Assn. (pres. 5 yrs.), L.A. Stock Exchange Club; publ: An Accounting Perspective of Society (Journal of Accountancy); poetry; mil: US Army Engineers Civilian Capacity; Christian; rec: music. Res: 825 Weldon Rd Santa Barbara 93109

GAULTNEY, STEPHEN GLENN, business owner, investor; b. Feb. 26, 1947, Alameda; s. James O. and Freida R. (Hammond) G.; m. Ellene, Jan. 9, 1970; 1 dau. Jennifer b. 1971; edn: BA zool., Humboldt State Univ. 1969. Career: owner Steve Gaultney Investments (prop. devel. co.), and Carnival Time Supplies (fundraising and supply co.); store dir./opr. Big J Foods Inc. dba Hagstroms Supermarket, Petaluma; dir. Big J Foods Inc 1970-, v.p. 1985-; advis. bd. Big T Supermarkets 1978-; apptd. City of Petaluma Housing Allocation Bd. (1977), Downtown Design Com. (1985); trustee Petaluma Valley Hosp. Found. (1978-85); mem. Petaluma CofC (dir. 1978-83, pres. 1983-84), Calif. Groc. Assn.; Republican; Baptist. Res: 913 B St Petaluma 94952 Ofc: Hagstroms Supermarket 200 Douglas St Petaluma 94952

GAUT, GARY EDWIN, government auditor; b. Sept. 12, 1936, Lynn, Ala.; s. Arlie Dow and Pearl (Pendley) G.; m. Kaye Barnette, Dec. 18, 1955; children: Deborah b. 1956, Gary b. 1963; edn: undergrad. La. State Univ. 1954-5, Southeastern La. Univ. 1964-66; BS, Miss. St. Univ. 1967; MS, Univ. Ark. 1974; certified internal auditor Inst. of Int. Auditors Inc. (1973). Career: auditor Air Force Audit Agency (AFAA), Lackland AFB, Tx. 1967-72, RAF Upper Heyford, England 1972-74; resident auditor AFAA, Patrick AFB, Fla. 1974-76; supvsy. auditor Langley AFB, Va. 1976-77, Norton AFB, Calif. 1977-80, Offutt AFB, Nebr. 1980-82; pgm. mgr. AFAA, Norton AFB, 1982-84, chief AFAA Operations Reviews, 1984–; honors: disting. grad. Profl. Mil. Comptroller Sch. (1979), outstanding performer AFAA (1974, 1982), family of year Junior Womens Aux., Cocoa Beach, Fla. (1976), Barbershopper of year SPEBSQSA, Omaha (1981), Jaycee Man of the Qtr., San Antonio, Tx. (1970);

mem: Beta Alpha Psi, Soc. of Mil. Comptrollers, Assn. of Govtl. Accts. (v.p. 1976); civic: vol. tax cons. San Bernardino 1984-85; Inland Master Chorale (exec. dir. 1984-), Inland Empire Symp., Univ. of Redlands Comm. Chorus (v.p. 1984-86), Soc. for Preserv. of Barbershop Quartet Singing in Am., Comm. Concert Assn., 2 Gallon Blood Donor Club; sev. publs. in field (1973-); Republican; United Methodist; rec: music, travel. Res: 2931 Orange St Highland 92346

GAYLORD, ROBERTA IRENE, speech pathologist; b. Jan. 18, 1922, Detroit, Mich.; d. Lloyd Rutherford and H. Irene (Slagel) Worden; mother, Irene Worden, author, rec'd. internat. Mark Twain award for book 'Our Falling Image'; m. Richard Cody Marsh, July 5, 1941; m. 2d Harold Bernard Gaylord, Apr. 5, 1959; 1 dau. Sandra b. 1944; edn: BA, CSU San Jose 1969, MA in edn., 1973. Career: prod., writer commentator "Star's Stairway Radio Show" (reviewed stage prodns. and interviewed celebrities) Sta. KWKW, Pasadena 1949-54; v.p./co-owner Gaylord Constrn. Co., 1963-67; language, speech and hearing splst. Moreland Sch. Dist., Campbell 1969-82; cons. 1982-83; honors: Voice of Democracy Award, VFW (1973-74); mem: Calif. Speech-Language-Hearing Assn. (nominating com. 1976), Santa Clara Co. Speech Hearing Assn. (chair Hosp. com. 1974, secty. 1975, legislative chair 1976), CTA (life), Am. Fedn. TV Radio Artists, Sigma Alpha Eta, Pi Lambda Theta (chair Hosp. com. 1983, Newsletter ed. 1983-85), Internat. Platform Assn. (authors' com. 1983, 84), People to People Internat. (secty. 1983-85), Am. Assn. of Women (legis. chair 1985); publs: TORP Pgm., research in sp. pathol. (1978-79); Republican; rec: travel, dancing, bridge. Res: 3312 Sudbury Rd (POB 1067) Cameron Park 95682

GAYMAN, PATRICIA GYNETH H., chiropractor; b. Aug. 16, 1938, San Pedro; d. Norman Alan and Olive Delone (Jensen) Smith; m. Merrill Gayman, Mar. 29, 1969; children: Cheryl b. 1954, Robert b. 1956, Karla b. 1956, Kym b. 1957, Leland b. 1958, Deirdre b. 1960, Stacy b. 1962; edn: Monterey Peninsula Coll. 1958-9; DC, Palmer Coll. of Chiropractic 1964; Shasta Coll. 1971-3; DC, Calif. State Bd. of Chiropractic Examiners 1964. Career: chiropractic practice, Monterey Peninsula 1964-8; assoc. Dr. G.E. Anderson, D.C., Hayward 1968-9; assoc. Dr. Neal Swanson, D.C., Redding 1974-9; Gayman Chiropractic Ofc., Redding 1979–; Holistic Living Edn. classes 1979-83; Stress Reduction and Imagery classes 1980-3; guest lectr. Civic orgns. & TV and radio appearances; mem: Sigma Phi Chi Sor. (pres. 1962); Women of Chiropractic Profl. Soc.; Bus. & Profl. Women's Club of Redding; Regents Pacific States Chiropractic Coll.; Family Planning, Inc.; Quota Club of Redding; Acad. Parapsychology and Medicine; Redding CofC (var. coms.); Metaphysical Exploration Ctr.; Democrat; Ch. of Relig. Sci.; rec: cont. chiro. edn., metaphysical studies. Res: 7252 Churn Creek Rd Redding 96002 Ofc: Gayman Chiropractic Ofc., 1065 W Cypress Ave Redding 96001

GDOWSKI, DIANA, accountant; b. Aug. 16, 1951, Utica, NY; d. Michael and Frances Mary (Carzo) G.; edn: BA, Univ. of San Dieg7o 1972; MA, USC 1979, MBA, 1981, M.B.Taxation, 1986; Cert. Public Acct., Calif. 1985; Secondary Educator, Calif. 1973. Career: French tchr. Bishop Montgomery H.S., Torrance 1973-76; adult edn. tchr. Torrance Unif. Sch. Dist., Torrance 1976-78; French lang. instr. USC 1977-79; auditor Ernst & Whinney, Los Angeles 1981-82, mgmt. cons. 1982-83; tax splst. Fox & Co., Los Angeles 1983-84; senior tax splst. Kenneth Leventhal & Co., Los Angeles 1984–; honors: Calif. State Scholar 1968; Phi Delta Phi 1970; Beta Alpha Psi 1980; mem: Am. Inst. CPAs, Calif. Soc. CPAs, Am. Soc. of Women CPAs; Republican; Catholic; rec: Afghan hounds, French language and literature. Ofc: Kenneth Leventhal & Co., 2049 Century Park E. Ste. 1700 Los Angeles 90067

GEARY, JERYL ELAINE, business owner, fashion editor; b. Dec. 1, 1948, Long Beach; d. George and Ina Florence (Menetee) Woosley; edn: AA, Mt. San Antonio Coll. 1972; desig: classical pianist, MTA, 1967. Career: prop. Fresh Hair Beauty Salon, Mission Viejo 1977–, owner/pres. Fresh Face Cosmetics, M.V. 1983–; fashion editor Household Mag. 1985–; feature writer nat. trade jours. (Modern Salon, American Salon); beauty lectr. John Robert Powers Modeling Sch.; local TV show on beauty (in devel.); honors: Nat. winner solo pianist, MTA (1960), num. profl. awards for hair and make-up; mem. Calif. Cosmetology Assn.; works: hot oil cuticle stick (mktd. internat.), shampoo for hard water, (in devel.) moisturizer for sports-people; Republican; rec: writer/lectr. on bus. success and grooming. Res: 164 Ave Santa Margarita San Clemente 92672 Ofc: Fresh Hair/Fresh Face 28570 Marguerite Pky Mission Viejo 92692

GEE, HENRY W., real estate broker, investment consultant; b. Nov. 26, 1922; m. Eudora Ma, Mar. 16, 1952; children: Nancy Ann b. 1953, Faline J. b. 1958, Cindy D. b. 1959; edn: Western Bus. Coll., Albuquerque, NM; LaSalle Ext. Univ., Chgo., Ill. 1958; LLB, Am. Sch. of Law, Chgo. 1957; Univ. of New Mexico, Albuquerque 1960-3; MAI I., Univ. of Okla. 1967; MAI II., USC 1968; UC Berkeley 1972; grad. Realtor's Inst. 1975. Career: owner/ mgr. real estate ofc. Albuquerque, NM 1960-9; owner/ mgr. Gee Realty & Inv. Co., Mtn. View 1970–; dir.: Mtn. View Community Svc. 1974-6; Mtn. View CofC 1976-81; Downtown Bus. Assn., Mtn. View (pres. 1986); Calif. Assn. of Realtors 1979, 80; Mtn. View Chpt. United Way; Mtn. View Bd. of Realtors; mem: Mtn. View Bd. of Realtors (pres. 1980); San Jose Bd. of Realtors; Nat. Assn. of Realtors; Mtn. View CofC; Mtn. View Central Bus. Assn.; Chinese Am. Citizens Alliance (pres. Albuquerque Lodge 1961-2; pres. Peninsula Lodge 1971-2); Stanford Area Chinese Club; Mtn. View Kiwanis Club; rec: photog., bowling. Res: 891 Cascade Dr Sunnyvale 94087 Ofc: Gee Realty & Investment Co., 786 W Dana St Mountain View 94041

GEE, NANCY ANN, lawyer; b. June 30, 1953, Albuquerque, NM; d. Henry W. and Eudora L. (Ma) G.; edn: BS, UC Davis 1975; JD, Univ. of Santa Clara 1978. Career: lab. asst. NASA Ames Research Ctr.; atty. assoc. William K. Wilburn, a profl. corp.; currently, atty. at law, sely employed, Mountain View; honors: Calif. State Scholar; mem: Chinese American Citizens Alliance (pres. Peninsula Lodge 1980, 81); Chinese Am. Citizens Alliance, Grand Lodge (spl. asst. to the Grand Pres. on Women Affairs, 1981, 1st woman elected as a Grand exec. 1983, Grand secty. 1985); Santa Clara Co. Bar Assn.; Soroptimist Internat.; rec: photog., music, stained glass. Res: 891 Cascade Dr Sunnyvale 94087 Ofc: Nancy Ann Gee, atty. at law, 774 W Dana St Mountain View 94041

GEE, VIRGINIA CATHERINE, recruitment administrator; b. May 19, 1941, San Francisco; d. Chew Wing and Sue (Jeong) Hom; m. Herbert H. Gee, May 12, 1962; 1 son: Christopher Lawrence, b. 1963; edn: AS, San Francisco City Coll. 1959; BS, Univ. of San Francisco 1981. Career: supr. Bus. Ofc. Pacific Tel. Co., S.F. 1959-63, Public Office mgr. 1963-66, mgmt. instr. 1966-68, Urban Affairs rep. 1968-70, personnel staff mgr. 1970-74; recruitment adminstr. Stanford University, Stanford 1974–; Gov. Brown apptd. Appeal Hearing Ofcr./commnr. Calif. Apprenticeship Council, 1974-, Gov. Deukmejian apptd. 1983-, chair 1984-; commnr. Federal Com. on Apprenticeship 1975-84; Cert. Mediator, Nat. Ctr. for Collaborative Planning Public Service Appointments; Mayor Feinstein apptd. v.p. S.F. Pvt. Indus. 1980-82 and dir. S.F. Conservation Corp. 1984-; apptd. by gov. to exec. asst. to chief, Dept. of Indsl. Rels., Div. of Apprenticeship Stds. 1985-; adv. com. Chancellor of Calif. Comm. Coll. on Trade and Industry 1985-; hearing ofcr. S.F. Civil Svc. Commn. 1985-; adv. com. Coro Found. Pub. Affairs Pgm. 1985-; cons. Asian Art Mus. of S.F.; honors: Hon. Citizen of Louisville, Ky.; recogn., Stanford Fed. Credit Union, Chinese Am. Inst. of Engrs. (SF), TIDE Proj.-Calif. Dept. Edn., YWCA Central Hqtrs (SF); mem: Commonwealth Club of SF, Nat. Soc. for Fundraising Execs., Am. Soc. for Pers. Admin., No. Calif. Human Resources Council, Am. Soc. for Tng. & Devel., Northeast Medical Services (bd. vp), SF Squash Club, UC Alumni Assn. (life), Stanford Univ. Alumni Assn. (life), Museum Soc., Soc. for Asian Art, World Affair Council, S.F. Mus. of Modern Art, Calif. Comm. Coll. Placement Assn. (v.p.), Bay Area Profl. Womens Network (bd.), Chinese Am. Citizens Alliance (SF, bd.), YWCA (bd., treas.), Asian Pacific Personnel Assn. (pres.); Republican; Catholic; rec: model ship building. Res: 1422 Clay St San Francisco 94109 Ofc: 525 Golden Gate Ave Ste 500 San Francisco 94102

GEHLE, RICHARD WALTER, educator, engineer; b. Aug. 11, 1946, Indpls., Ind.; s. William Edward and Lucille Marie (Backus) G.; m. Claudia Jones, June 21, 1969; children: Deborah b. 1972, Timothy b. 1974; edn: BA, UC Irvine 1967; M.Div., Talbot Theol. Sem. 1972; MS, CSU Fullerton 1979; DD, So. Calif. Comm. Bible Coll. 1986. Career: pres. Infection Control Educational Products, Yorba Linda 1979–; senior mechanical engr. Rockwell Internat., Anaheim 1968-84, Hughes Aircraft Co., Fullerton 1984–; adj. prof. mech. engrg. CSU Fullerton 1979–; mem. nat. awards com. Soc. of Advancement of Materials and Processes; honors: Outstanding Engr. of the Year (Rockwell Internat. 1979); mem: Am. Soc. Heating, Refrigeration and Air Cond. Engrs., Assn. Practitioners in Infection Control; inventor, 3 US patents in microwave technol.; Republican; Quaker; rec: amateur radio. Res: 16961 Cumberland Cir Yorba Linda 92686 Ofc: Hughes Aircraft Co 1901 W Malvern Fullerton 92634

GEIGER, STEPHEN JOHN, real estate development co. president; b. Nov. 15, 1945, Denver, Colo.; s. Robert Howard and Eunice Marcine (McClain) G.; m. Vicki, Jan. 27, 1973; children: Stephen b. 1977, Catherine b. 1974; Realtor, Nat. Assn. Realtors 1975. Career: set lighting, Hollywood 1964-68; v.p. Geiger Distributing Inc., Chicago, Ill. 1969-75; seniorv.p. The Hanes Co., Los Angeles 1976-79; pres. Brokers & Builders Inc., Woodland Hills 1979-84; pres. Christiansen/ Geiger Inc., Los Angeles 1985–; founding dir. Malibu Savings & Loan, Malibu 1984; mem: Nat. and Calif. Assns. of Realtors, San Fernando Valley Bd. Realtors; mil: s/sgt. USAF 1964-70; Republican; Methodist; rec: golf. Ofc: 3907 W. Alameda Ave. Ste. 102 Burbank 91505

GEIL, SAMUEL BENTON, personnel executive; b. Aug. 4, 1953, Richmond, Calif.; s. James Sheldon and Ann Elizabeth (Robison) G.; m. Donna Lee Costa, Jan. 15, 1977; 1 son, Patrick Martin b. 1978; edn: AA, Merced Jr. Coll. 1975; BS in bus., CSU San Jose 1978; grad. seminar, USC 1986. Career: human resource senior analyst Xerox Corp. (Shugart Corp.), Sunnyvale 1979-83; area human resource mgr. Data General Corp., Manhattan Beach 1983–; civic: El Segundo PTA, Youth Soccer (coach), Homeowners Assn. (pres. Peppertree 1985-86, pres. Park Row III 1984-85); Democrat; Roman Catholic; rec: music, philately. Ofc: Data General Corp. 1500 Rosecrans Ave Manhattan Beach 90266

GEISE, HARRY FREMONT, meteorologist (ret.); b. Jan. 8, 1920, Oak Park, Ill.; s. Harry and Rosalind (Muser) G.; children: Marian Apgar b. 1955, Gloria Peterson b. 1943, triplets: Barry, Gary, Harry b. 1976; edn: Univ. of Chgo. 1938-9; Meteorologist Svc. Sch., Lakehurst, NJ 1943-4. Career: pvt. weather svc., Chgo. 1937–; chief meteorologist Kingsbury Ord., 1943; meteorol. radio sta. WLS and Prarie Farmer newspaper 1941, 42, 46; assoc. Dr. Irving P. Krick, meteorol. cons. 1947-9; media dir., dir. Pac. div. 1955-59; Army Air Corps. research, developed new temperature forecasting technique, Calif. Inst. of Tech. and Am. Inst. Aerological Research 1948-9; cond. weather and travel shows: WBKB- TV, Chgo,; radio sta. WOPA, Oak Park, Ill., 1950-1; pvt. weather svc. 1954; staff meteorol., San Jose Mercury and News: radio KSJO, KNTV, San Jose; KHUB, Watsonville; KGO-TV, S.F.; cond. 'The Weather and You' series, Columbia Pac. radio network 1956-8; Panorama Pac. Weather Show, KNXT- TV, CBS, L.A. 1957-8; prod. over 70 daily radio pgms. in U.S. 1959; est. Weather Center for CBS, NY (demonstrated forecasts 2 yrs. in advance), WCBS-TV 1966-7; pvt. weather svc., incl. commercial accts. and radio sta. 1962-81; Nat. Defense Exec. Reservist 1968-75; instr. meteorol.: Santa Rosa Jr. Coll. 1964-6; Sonoma State Coll. 1967-8; issued first week in advance forecasts to pub., also first month in advance and first year or more in advance; recognized relationship between specified solar emissions and maj. changes in earth weather pattern 1956; initiated thunderstorm warning sys. using radio static known as Sferics (1st discovered in 1936), which became model for US Ord. plants 1942; Calif. 1st tchg. cred. based on outstanding eminence in meteorol. 1964; discovered a relationship between a particular weather type and rash type tornado outbreaks in Midwest, US 1965; origin. transatlantic weather radio pgm. from Geneva, London and Paris to Calif., Dec. 1965-77. Author: USA: Voice of America 1968; sev. TV films, arts. publ. in newspapers, mags., trade and profl. journals, num. radio and TV stations.; spkr. environmental problems: Rotary; CofC; AAUW; Commonwealth Club of Calif.; CBS Stations; life foreign mem. Royal Meteorological Soc.; mil: Aerologist, USMC, 1943-5, WWII; rec: world travel, writing, reading. Res: 4100 Folsom, 3D, Sacramento 95819; 566 Rainbow Dr Napa 94558; 49-975 Avenida Obregon La Quinta 92253

GEISEN, WALTER MARTIN, engineer; b. Apr. 28, 1928, Elmwood Place, Ohio; s. George William Sr. and Charlotte Ann (Rogers) G.; m. June Koss, June 19, 1948; children: Nancy b. 1949, Eric b. 1951, Jeffrey b. 1955, Timothy b. 1957; edn: LLB, Williams Coll. 1965; reg. profl. engr. Calif. and Canada 1977. Career: with General Electric Co. 1953–; engring. supvr., Evandale, Ohio, 1953-8; field engring. supvr., L.A. 1958-63; mgr. svc. shops sales, Evandale, OH 1963-5; proj. engr., Edwards AFB 1965-7; design, drafting mgr., Edwards AFB 1967-70; pgm. mgr., Mojave 1970-80; mgr.- mfg. engring. 1980-2; Honorable Order of Kentucky Colonels 1964; mem: Soc. of Mfg. Engrs.; Soc. of Flight Test Engrs.; Antelope Valley Aero Museum (founder/ dir. 1968-72; pres. 1972-5); No. L.A. Co. Planning Council; Death Valley 49ers, Inc.; mil: Chief Warrant Ofcr., USAR 1949-60; Republican, Central Comm., Ohio 1954-8; Christian; rec: flying, hunting, community related activities. Res: 44526 Lowtree Ave Lancaster 93534 Ofc: General Electric Co., POB 700 Mojave 93501

GELBER, LOUISE CARP, lawyer; b. Oct. 24, 1921, Detroit, Mich.; d. Jacob and Gusta Carp; m. Milton (dec.), July 10, 1942; children: Jack b. 1947, Bruce b. 1949, Julie (McCoy) b. 1952; edn: BA, UC Berkeley 1943, JD, 1944; admitted bar: Calif. (1944), Supreme Ct. Calif. (1945), US Dist. Ct. (so. dist. Calif., 1946), US Supreme Ct. (1965). Career: research asst. to Justice Roger Traynor, Calif. State Supreme Ct. 1944-45; gen. practice of law, El Monte 1945–; judge pro tem El Monte Municipal Ct.; legislative advocate Calif. Bus. & Profl. Women's Club, 1949; mem: Am. Bar Assn., Calif. State Bar Assn., L.A. Co. Bar Assn., Pomona Valley Bar Assn., Citrus Bar Assn., Internat. Platform Assn., El Monte-South El Monte CofC (chmn. Speakers Bur.), Arcadia CofC (treas.), So. Calif. Womens Lawyers, Nat. Fedn. Bus. & Profl. Womens Clubs, Eastern Star, Tournament of Roses Assn., League of Women Voters, Am. Rec Cross, Community Chest, United Way, Cub Scouts, Girl Scouts; Democrat: nominee for Calif. State Senate (1968), asst. treas. LA Co. Dem. Com. (1968), mem. Calif. Dem. State Central Com. and exec. com./co-chair 24th Congl. Dist. (1968-70); Christian Sci. Address: Gelber Law Office 1225 Rancho Rd Arcadia 91006

GELMAN, GLENN M., accountant; b. April 28, 1954, Brooklynn, NY; s. Irvingand Rochelle (Smola) G.; m. Bernice, Dec. 25, 1982; children: Rebecca b. 1981 (step), Lisa b. 1983, Elana b. 1984; edn: BS, New York Univ. 1975; MS, in progress, Golden Gate; CPA, NY 1978. Career: audit supvr. Coopers & Lybrand, NYC, NY; audit mgr. Newport Beach CPA firm; pres. Glenn M. Gelman CPA, An Accty. Corp., Irvine currently; instr. of acctg. National Univ.; mem: Am. Inst. CPAs, NY, Calif. Socs. CPAs, Cantor- Chabad of Irvine (vol.). Res: 4 Almond Tree Ln. Irvine 92715 Ofc: Glenn M. Gelman CPA, An Accty. Corp., 2070 Business Center Dr. Irvine 92715

GENDREAU, JACQUES RENE, leasing co. president; b. May 14, 1942, Chambery, France, nat. US cit. 1970; s. Jacques and Yvonne G.; m. Odile, Apr. 20, 1973; children: Pierre b. 1977, Philippe b. 1979, Edouard b. 1981; edn: MS, Univ. of Lyon 1964; MBA, Univ. Chgo. 1970. Career: mktg. research mgr. Allis Chalmers, Chgo. 1966; asst. v.p. ops. Graco Corp., Mnpls. 1969; div. mgr. Cit Alcatel, Paris 1972; gen. mgr. Benson, Paris 1982; pres./CEO Businessphone Rentals, Mission Viejo 1983–. Res: 33571 Windjammer Dr Laguna Niguel 92677 Ofc: Businessphone Rentals 26522 La Alameda Mission Viejo 92691

GENO, RICHARD EARL, life insurance agency president; b. Mar. 20, 1942, Oakland; s. Claude Earl (dec.) and Florence Jacqueline Geno; m. Joan Horgan, June 14, 1964; children: Jennifer b. 1965, Deborah b. 1967, Kristin b. 1968, Richard II b. 1969, Lauren b. 1976, Jodi b. 1978, Stephanie b. 1980; edn: BS, UC Berkeley 1964; MS, The American Coll. 1979; CLU 1970; Chartered Fin. Cons. 1982; Cert. Fin. Planner 1983. Career: agent College Life Ins. Co. 1964-74; general agent 1974-82; pres. Richard E. Geno & Assoc. Ins. Svcs., Inc., San Jose 1979–; agency mgr. The Bankers Life 1982–; bd. dir. San Jose Gen. Agent's and Mgr. Assn. 1975- (pres. 1980-1); bd. dirs. San Jose Chpt. Chartered Life Underwriters 1981- (pres. 1986-87); bd. dirs. Leading Life Ins. Producers of No. Calif. 1978-80 (pres. 1979); bd. dirs. Peninsula Life Underwriters 1971-2; awards: Jack Richter Meml. Awd., Underwriter of the Year, San Jose Life Underwriters Assn. 1980; Million Dollar Round Table 1965-; Co. Sales Leader (1972, 76, 78) and No. One Agency (1978, 80, 81, 82), College Life Ins. Co.; mem: Nat. Assn. of Life Underwriters; Am. Soc. of CLUs; Leading Life Ins. Producers of No. Calif.; Internat. Assn. Financial Planning; Republican; Catholic; rec: Little League baseball, coaching basketball, tennis, bridge. Res: 12516 Arroyo De Arguello Saratoga 95070 Ofc: Richard E. Geno & Assocs., Ins. Svcs., Inc., The Geno Bldg, 1042 West Hedding San Jose 95126

GENTRY, WILLIAM OLIVER, land surveyor; b. Mar. 1, 1923, Ardmore, Okla.; s. Russell Hogue and Erma Mae (Camp) G.; m. Betty McCollum, Dec. 2, 1950; children: Norman Perry b. 1955, Katherine Jean b. 1961, Kenneth Dale b. 1962; edn: CSU Fresno 1968-71; UC Berkeley 1970-73. Career: surveyor, cost analyst, estimator So. Pacific Railroad 1942-48; surveyor R.E. White, civ. engr. Bakersfield 1948-49; surveyor, v.p. J.A. Ross & Assoc. 1949-68; owner W.O. Gentry, land surveyor 1969–; lectr. CSU Fullerton; assoc. dep. sheriff Jeep Rescue Squadron 1967–; mem: Am. Congress on Surveying & Mapping (life) 1954-, Calif. Council of Civil Engrg. & Land Surveyors 1956- (chap pres. 4 times), Calif. Land Surveyors Assn. (chap. pres., state pres.) 1967-, Fresno CofC 1960-; Republican; First Christian. Res: 5340 E Madison Ave Fresno 93727 Ofc: W.O. Gentry, Land Surveyor, 1822 H St Fresno 93721-1022

GEORGE, KENNETH ROBERT, securities co. executive; b. July 5, 1942, Pittsburgh, Pa.; s. Cecil Leroy and Ollie Grace (Quigely) G.; m. Frances Jean, Feb. 5, 1967; children: Tamara b. 1969, Jennifer b. 1973; edn: BA in bus. adminstrn., Grove City Coll. 1964. Career: indsl. sales Armstrong Cork Co., 1964-67; stockbroker Shearson Hammill & Co., 1967-70; asst. branch mgr. Paine Webber, 1970-72, branch mgr. Pasadena ofc., 1972-76; branch mgr. Los Angeles ofc., Sutro & Co. Inc., 1976-78, dir. of branch ofcs./ mem. bd. dirs./ dir. sales & mktg., 1978-82; gen. ptnr./ exec. v.p. Boettcher & Co., 1982-84; exec. v.p. Birr Wilson & Co., Inc. 1984-, dir./ pres. 1986–, also dir./ pres. Birr Wilson Securities, Inc., dir./ exec. v.p. Birr Wilson Group, Inc.; mem. Securities Industry Assn./Dist. 10 (1978-); arbitrator for NYSE and NASD; recipient num. sales awards: clubs: Pasadena Bond (1970-76), Los Angeles Bond (1976-78), Pasa. Rotary (1973-76), Commonwealth, Commercial (SF), Bankers (SF), Los Angeles Athletic (1976-78), Telegraph Hill (SF), Claremont Country; mil: E3 US Air Force Reserve, active duty 1966; Republican; Methodist; rec: golf, racquetball, boating. Res: 37 Caperton Ave Piedmont 94611 Ofc: Birr Wilson Securities Inc. 155 Sansome St San Francisco 94104

GERBER, SYLVAN Y., manufacturing co. president; b. July 20, 1928, Chgo.; s. Edward N. and Helen (Fink) G.; m. Gretchen, June 14, 1956; children: Robert b. 1958, Steven b. 1960, Helen b. 1963; edn: BA, Wright Jr. Coll. 1949; BSC, Roosevelt Univ. 1951. Career: sales mgr. Effenger Electric, Chgo. 1953-64; gen. mgr. Air King Corp., Chgo. 1964-74; founder/pres. Capri Mfg. dba Capri Lighting, Los Angeles 1974–; recipient pres.'s award, Am. Home Lighting Inst. (1981); mem: Am. Home Lighting Inst. (pres. 1985), Calif. Electric Alliance (pres. 1983-4), Illuminating Engring. Soc. (assoc.); mil: US Navy 1951-53. Address: Los Angeles 90040

GERBL, MARGARET, real estate broker; b. July 8, 1916, Winnepeg, Man., Can., nat. US cit. 1925; d. George Willis, Sr. and Esther (Jackson) Tyson; m. Lewis Gerbl, June 1, 1946; children: Larry b. 1949, Jack b. 1951; edn: McKay Bus. Coll. 1936, AS with distn., Mt. San Jacinto Coll. 1971; Mortuary Sci., Cypress Coll. 1982; real estate broker Calif. 1968. Career: dance instr., entertainer Hollywood Conservatory 1923-33; legal/med. soc. bookkeeper Los Angeles 1933-39; secty. Sears, Roebuck L.A. 1939-42; acct. Douglas Aircraft, El Segundo 1942-45; secty. to v.p. Hammond Lumber Co. L.A. 1945-46; co-owner M&L Auto Parts L.A. 1949-64; real estate broker San Jacinto Realty San Jacinto 1968-86; honors: All Time Best Student (McKay Bus. Coll. 1940); Pres.'s Honor Roll (Cypress Coll. 1982); mem: Hemet-San Jacinto Women's Council 1976-78, Calif. Assn. Realtors 1968-, Nat. Assn. Realtors 1968-, Grad. Real Estate Inst. 1968-, AARP; hostess at Ramona Pageant in Hemet 1971-; Republican; Ch. of Christ; rec: piano, dance, swimming, grandchildren. Res: 39109 Ramona Blvd San Jacinto 92383 Ofc: San Jacinto Realty 202 E Main St San Jacinto 92383

GERBO, PEGGY JEAN, semiconductor co. computer executive; b. Nov. 27, 1953, Palo Alto; d. Arnold and Dorrene Novella (Heath) Gerbo; edn: Calma GDSI, Calif. Acad. of Drafting, 1978, Calma GDSII, DeAnza Coll., 1980. Career: with Stewart Warner Microcircuits, Sunnyvale 1972-74; acctg. clerk Peninsula Building Matls., Menlo Park 1974-75; microphoto lithography step and repeat opr. NBK Corp., Santa Clara 1975-76; tooling supr. Computer Aided Design (CAD) supr. Microfab Systems, Palo Alto 1976-80; Computer Aided Design Integrated Circuit (CADIC) layout designer Micropower Systems, Santa Clara 1980-82; CADIC layout design supr. Teledyne Semiconductor, Mountain View 1982-83; CADIC layout design splst. Fairchild Camera and Instrument/ Linear Div., 1983-85; tng. mgr. CADIC Design Verification Software/ senior applications engr. ECAD, Inc., Santa Clara 1985–; tchg. layout designers CAD, 1980-; mem: NOW, ASCUS; Catholic; rec: raising, tng. dogs and horses, piano, camping. Res: 1201 Sycamore Terrace, Sp 159, Sunnyvale 94086 Ofc: ECAD, Inc. Santa Clara

GERLACH, CLINTON G., company executive; b. June 18, 1926, Rosemont, Nebr.; s. Herman F. and Lena (Knigge) G.; m. Juanita R. Sowers, Aug. 29, 1953; children: Kimberlee Ann b. 1955, Clinton G. II b. 1957; edn. BSBA, Univ. of Denver 1949. Cert. Public Acct. Career: Arthur Andersen & Co., Chicago, Ill. 1949-52; controller Penn- Union Electric Corp., Erie, Penn. 1952-58, pre-. 1958-67; group exec. Teledyne Co. 1967-79; founder, chmn. bd. Tannetics Inc., Erie, Penn. 1969-83; chmn. bd. Gerlach Industries Inc. 1983–; dir. Zero Corp. 1971-; mem: Beta Gamma Sigma, Masons, Shriners; Presbyterian; rec: 17 Holster Ln. Bell Canyon 91307 Ofc: P.O. Box 6070 Spartanburg, South Carolina 29304, 7435 Valjean Ave. Ste. 200 Van Nuys 91406

GERMAN, DANA J., certified public accountant; b. July 14, 1950, Fowler; d. Hans A. and Phyllis Elizabeth (Oxford) Jensen; m. Stephen German, June 24, 1972; children: Matthew, b. 1980; Sarah, b. 1983; edn: BS, CSU, summa cum laude, Fresno 1972; CPA; Am. Inst. CPAs; Calif. State Soc. of CPAs. Career: staff acctnt. Price Waterhouse, Los Angeles 1972-5; mgr. Design Furniture, Reedley 1975-7; secty./ treas. Stephen L. German Accountancy Corp., Reedley 1977–; instr. Reedley Coll.; guest lectr. Reedley Coll. 1978-; awards: Bank of Am. Achievement Awd. 1968; Good Citizenship Awd., DAR, 1968; Phi Kappa Phi; Beta Gamma Sigma; Beta Alpha Psi; mem: Am. Inst. of CPAs; Calif. State Soc. of CPAs; Am. Women's Soc. of CPAs; Bus. & Profl. Women; Calif. Women for Agriculture; Sierra Kings Hosp. Aux.; chmn. Reedley Parks & Rec. Commn.; Reedley Hist. Soc.; Kings River Arts Council; co-chmn. & judges chmn. Miss Reedley Pageant Com., affil. of Miss Calif., Miss Am. Pageants; Democrat; Mennonite Brethren; rec: gardening, cooking. Res: 19283 E American Reedley 93654 Ofc: Stephen L. German Accountancy Corp., 1423 11th Street Reedley 93654

GERMAN, ROBERT JOSEPH, auto dealer executive; b. Apr. 4, 1931, Milwaukee; s. Clifford Andrew and Anna Betty (Hidinovich) G., m. Donna, May 4, 1949; children: Marsha b. 1951, Tracy b. 1961, Robin b. 1962, Stephanie b. 1964, Scott b. 1965. Career: Thrifty Drug Store Lompoc, Calif. 1961-65, store dir. Zody's San Bernardino 1965-75; sales mgr. Weber Cooper Lincoln Mercury Pomona 1975-86; gen. mgr. Vreeland Cadillac Ventura 1986–; mem. Odd Fellows; Republican; Protestant; rec: computer, bike riding, sports cars. Res: 4948 Dolphin Way Oxnard 93035 Ofc: Vreeland Cadillac 6450 Leland St Ventura 93003

GERSON, JUDITH ELAINE, dancer, educator, youth counselor; b. May 27, 1938, Columbus, Ohio; d. Max and Pamela (Levine) Weiss; div.; 1 dau., Chandra b. 1966; edn: profl. dance tng. (Russian Ballet) w/Elizabeth Werblosky 1950-53, Lester Horton 1951, Rose Lorenze 1953-57; dance study tour Europe, Royal Acad. of Ballet, London, and Paris Opera, 1954; Conn. Coll. Sch. of Dance 1967; BS in dance/edn., USC 1960, MA in dance, CSU San Jose 1966; MA, ed. psych., CSU Northridge 1972; EdD, Brigham Young Univ. 1974; admin. cred., Loyola Univ. 1973; Career: profl. dancer: on tour with Keith Killinger Troupe from Chgo. 1953, var. TV pgms., Dallas 1957, with Richard Oliver Co., L.A. 1959-60; dance dir. City of Torrance Rec. Dept. 1958-60; dance instr. Westlake Sch. for Girls, L.A. 1959, instr. dance and P.E., Rosemead High Sch. 1961-64; instr., asst. prof. dance CSU San Jose 1964-67, instr. Peace Corps tng. pgm. 1966, Foothill Coll. 1965, 67-68; tchr./counselor Continuation Sch., L.A. Unified Sch. Dist. 1968-1974, 1978–, coord. program for asocial youth, 1971-74, devel. new programs for troubled youth (Criminal Justice grant) for LA Bd. of Edn. 1975-78, then requested re-assignment to cont. sch. classroom; postdoc. intern, psych. asst. Bert Labin, MD 1974-76, Stephen Rush 1977-79, John M. Stalberg MD 1979-, Harvard Univ. 1984; instr. instr. UCLA Ext. (1974-76) Pepperdine Univ. Ext. (1974-5), apptd. faculty Nat. Council of Juvenile and Family Ct Judges (1977); frequent guest speaker, t.v. and radio, on divergent youth; mem: Calif. State Psychol. Assn., English Council of L.A., Delta Kappa Gamma; clubs: Ebell, De Camera Soc.; mil: major Army Reserves, psychologist Med. Det. 1977-80; rec: tennis, writing (book in prog.), travel. Ofc: 2901 Wilshire Blvd Ste 431 Santa Monica 90403

GETTY, ROBERT MICHAEL, real estate broker, building contractor; b. July 14, 1941, Pittsburgh; s. Wm. Daniel and Annina M. (Hall) G.; m. Jacqueline, Dec. 18, 1965; children: Maria Louise, Robert Michael, Joseph Christopher; edn: AA, Pasadena City Coll. 1961; Woodbury Bus. Coll. 1964-69; real estate courses, Bakersfield Coll. 1968-70, Lumbleau R.E. Sch. 1969, Anthony Schs. 1967, Am. Appraisal Inst., Univ. Ind. 1969; lic. real estate broker; lic. general contr. Career: salesman Getty Investment Co., Pasadena 1961-63; sales rep. C.E. Niehoff & Co. Los Angeles 1963-64; real estate ops. supv. L.A. Fed. Savings & Loan Assn. 1964-68; asst. v.p., loan ofcr. Heritage S&L Assn. Bakersfield 1968-70; pres. Getty Land Co., Inc. Bakersfield 1970–; pres. Getty's Happyland, Inc., preschool and elem. sch. establishment 1971–; honors: Achievement Award (Soc. of Real Estate Appraisers 1968), Grad. Award (Woodbury Bus. Coll. 1968), Achievement Award (Am. Savings & Loan Inst. 1966); mem: Assoc. Bldrs. & Contrs. (chpt. dir. 1978-80), Bakersfield Bd. of Realtors, Toastmasters, Stockdale CC; mil: USAFR 1960-66; Republican; Catholic; rec: skiing, surfing, flying, reading, music, collecting classic cars. Res: 8009 Luces Corta Bakersfield 93309 Ofc: Getty Land Co. Inc. 920 Wible Rd Bakersfield 93304

GIBAS, NICHOLAS JOSEPH, financial planner; b. Oct. 27, 1956, Ann Arbor, Mich; s. Albert John and Helen Virginia (Andell) G.; m. Kimberly Ann, Dec. 10, 1983; 1 son, Garrett Wayne b. 1985; edn: Central Mich. Univ.; Gen. Securities Rep., NASD; Reg. Commodity Trading Advisor, Commod. Futures Trading Commn.; Tax Interviewer, Calif.; Life Underwriter Tng. Council Fellow; CFP cand. Career: CFO for IFP Advisors, Ltd., Ventura, Calif., developer and mgr. of Automated Acctg. Mgmt. System; bd. dirs. Ctr. for Human Devel., Inc.; mem: Internat. Assn. Financial Planning (charter mem.), Nat. Soc. Public Accts., Nat. Assn. Life Underws.; Republican; Lutheran; rec: boating, flying. Res: 2140 El Cajon Way Oxnard 93033

GIBBS, ANNETTE ALLSMAN, financial executive; b. Dec. 11, 1946, San Francisco; d. Paul E. and Anna Frances (Bellis) Allsman; children: Allison b. 1971, Johnson b. 1973, Anthony b. 1976; edn: BA art and history, San Francisco Coll. for Women 1969; MBA finance, Golden Gate Univ. 1980. Career: var. financial analytical positions; civic and nonprofit volunteer work; financial consulting var. cos.; prof. econs. Coll. of Marin; auditor Fireman's Fund Ins. Co. San Rafael; loan ofcr. Century Bank S.F.; currently asst. v.p. Latipac

Financial Corp. Oakland; advisor Golden Gate Bridge Hwy. and Transp. Dist.; mem: Paradise Property Owners Assn. (pres.), Who's Who Internat., Tiburon Peninsula Club, AMBA, League of Women Voters, var. sch. and other orgns.; works: professional oil portrait painter, impressionist pallette. Ofc: Laripac Financial Corp. 1321 Kaiser Bldg. 300 Lakeside Dr Oakland 94612

GIBBS, GEORGE KARROLL, b. June 9, 1911, Grace, Ida.; s. John Chester and Clara (McClellan) G.; m. Myrtle Trimmer, Jan. 29, 1939; children: Rose Marie, b. 1939, Gregory, b. 1949; edn: BS in agri., Univ. of Ida. 1934. Career: area dir. Rural Resettlement, Boise, Ida. 1934-37; soil scientist Calif. Soil Conserv. Svc., Berkeley 1937-52; soil conserv. expert UN Food and Agr. Orgn., 1952-53; soil conservationist Soil Cons. Service, Watsonville, Ca. 1953-56, Soil Cons. Service Area Fresno, 1956-72; soil scientist FMC Internat. Op., San Jose 1973-74; currently semi-ret., real estate broker, Fresno; cons. on soil conserv. for UN in Iraq 1952-3; cons. in irrigation devel., FMC Corp. in Nigeria 1973-4; awards: Union Pacific coll. scholarship 1930; appreciation, UN, 1953; award of merit, Calif. Assn. of Soil Cons. Districts; mem: Soil Conserv. Soc. of Am., Calif. (charter); publs: soil survey maps, project studies (Bonner Co., Ida.; San Diego Co.; Iraq; Hadejia Valley, Nigeria); Catholic; rec: gardening. Res: 1740 No Arthur Ave Fresno 93705

GIBBY, ALAN DAYLE, television sports producer; b. Dec. 22, 1957, Fullerton; s. M. Neal and Betty Rae (Bailey) G.; m. Sharon Eastwood, Sept. 22, 1979; children: Justin b. 1981, Jessica b. 1983; edn: bus. courses Saddleback Coll. 1980-82; grad. LDS Ch. Sem. 1972-76. Career: LDS missionary vol. in England and Wales, 1977-79; dir. mktg. Estate Planning Publs., Newport Beach 1980-81, Creative Audio and Video, Laguna Niguel 1981-82; owner/pres. Dynocomm Prodns. (prod. sports spls. for network affils. and cable t.v. stations incl. ESPN, USA Cable), Laguna Niguel 1982—, video cons. Ocean Pacific Sunwear 1983-; honors: Citizen of Year, Laguna Beach (1971), winner (TV sports) 4 Nielson Ratings; mem. Nat. Assn. of T.V. Program Execs. 1983-; Boy Scouts Am. (leader); Republican; Latter-Day Saints; rec: watersports. Ofc: Dynocomm Productions 27285 Las Ramblas Ste 130 Mission Viejo 92691

GIBSON, GAYNOR ALLISON, educator; b. Aug. 25, 1919, San Francisco; s. Ray Atherton and Alice Eleanor (Koehncke) G.; m. Manuela Gabellini, Oct. 19, 1947, Florence, Italy; children: Cynthia Rae b. 1948, Micaela b. 1953, Gregory b. 1954, Regina b. 1957, Randy 1963-1982; edn: Cert. Engr., Stanford Univ., 1942-3; Univ. of Md., 1959-60; hon. MA, UCLA Ext. Div. 1981; Calif. Life Teachers Cred., Jr. Coll. Career: grocery chain mgr. Keystone Grocers, San Francisco 1935-38; decorator florist Podesta & Baldocchi, S.F. 1938-42; enlisted man to lt. col. US Army Signal Corps, 1942-63 (instr. communications and Italian interpreter, 1942-45, contracting ofcr., world-wide 1945-63); asst. chief contracts, plans, procedures, tng. CalTech Jet Propulsion Lab., Pasadena (contract negotiator/adminstr. for "Ranger" Moon Pgm.) 1963-67; sr. contracts adminstr., Navy Phoenix F-14/AWG-9 Radar Pgm., Hughes Aircraft Co., 1967-81; dean of instrn., Procurement & Contracts Tng. Schs. & Consultants, Altadena 1981—; instr. Pasadena City Coll. 1962-, head Purch. & Contracting Dept.; master instr. UCLA, curriculum adv. com. UCLA Ext. Div.; instr. CSU Northridge 1980-, Northrop Univ. 1982-3; instr Hughes Aircraft Co., all sites, 1967-81; honors: Calif. Scholarship Soc. 1935; Fellow, Nat. Contracts Mgmt. Assn. 1981; National Educator of Year 1982-3; mem: The Retired Officers Assn. (chpt. pres. 1985, ROTC chmn.), Reserve Officers Assn. (ROTC chmn.); Mil. Order World Wars (ROTC chmn.); Navy League; CofCs- Pasadena, Altadena (bd. dirs.), Glendale (mil. affairs com.); Purch. Mgmt. Assn. of Los Angeles; dir. and asst. to dean to estab. Profl. MS degree in Acquisition and Contracts Mgmt., Northrop U. 1982-85; author textbooks in field; mil. decorations (11) incl. Army; Commend., Berlin Airlift, Presdtl. Cit., Korean Medal; Repub.; Catholic; rec: language studies, golf. Address: Procurement & Contract Tng Schools & Cons., 411 W. Altadena Dr Altadena 91001-1236

GIBSON, WELDON BAILEY, international economist; b. Apr. 23, 1917, Eldorado, Tx.; s. Oscar and Susie (Bailey) G.; m. Helen Mears, Mar. 1, 1941; children: Arthur 1943-1963, David b. 1947; edn: AB, Wash. State Univ. 1938; MBA, Stanford Univ. 1940, PhD 1950. Career: served to col./dir. of materiel requirements, US Air Force 1941-46; asst. dir. USAF Inst. of Tech., Dayton, Ohio 1946-47; joined SRI Internat., Menlo Park (fmr. Stanford Research Inst., non-profit research orgn.) as dir. econs. research/chmn. internat. pgms., 1947-, assoc. dir. 1955-, v.p. 1959-, exec. v.p. 1960-, senior dir. 1982—; originated the Internat. Indsl. Conf., major meeting of world bus. leaders held every 4 yrs in San Francisco; mem. gov. bds. of Pacific Basin Econ. Council, S.F. Bay Area Council; dir: Plantronics Inc., The Valley Nat. Bank (Ariz.), Valley Nat. Corp. (Ariz.), Technical Equities Corp. Inc.; govt. cons.: US Bur. of the Budget (1949-53), Nat. Security Resources Bd. (1949-53), White House Conf. on INdsl. World Ahead (1972); awards: Medal of the Legion of Merit, US Govt. (1946), Order of Comdr. of the British Empire (1947), Govt. of Indonesia Pres. Award (1978), Wash. State Univ. Disting. Alumnus; current mem: AAAS, Am. Econ. Assn., Western Econ. Assn., Soc. for Internat. Devel., Am. Arbitration Assn. (comml. panel), The Explorers Club; civic: Brit.-Am. CofC (dir.), Korean-Am. CofC (v.p.), Fedn. of Korean Indus. (hon.), Internat. Acad. of Mgmt. (fellow), Planned Parenthood, World Affairs Council/SF, SF Bay Area Council (past dir.), Internat. Mgmt. and Devel. Inst. (bd. adv.), Japan Soc. of No. Calif. (sr. advis. council), The Most Venerable Order of the Hosp. of St. John of Jerusalem (assoc. ofcr.), Epilepsy Found. of Am., Hoover Instn. (internat. assocs.), Am. Univ. of Beirut (trustee), Wash. State Univ. Found. (founding chmn.), Soodo Women's Tchrs. Coll., Korea (hon. trustee); mem. Beta Theta Pi, Alpha Kappa Psi, Phi Kappa Phi, Shriners, Masonic Order, Stanford Assocs.; author, SRI: The Founding Years (1980), SRI: THe Take-Off Days (1986), coauthor 3 books, num. monographs and articles. Res: 593

Gerona Rd Stanford 94305 Ofc: SRI International 333 Ravenswood Ave Menlo Park 94025

GIDDINGS, DAVID WIGHT, company executive; b. Feb. 5, 1954, Lynwood; s. Edwin and Manya (Koshko) G.; edn: CSU Fullerton, 1972-78. Career: pres. D.W. Giddings Co., Inc., Downey 1972—; dir. Elsinore Aerospace Services, Inc., Downey 1982—; owner Jet Set Enterprises, Irvine 1983—; mem: BBB of L.A. and Orange Co.; Republican; rec: computers, electronics. Res: 5151-38 Walnut Ave Irvine 92714 Ofc: Jet Set Enterprises, 14252 Culver Dr Ste A-302 Irvine 92714

GIERSCH, FREDERIC E., III, beverage co. president; b. July 28, 1952, Red Bank, N.J.; s. Frederic E., Jr. and Carlota (Busch) G.; m. Mary J., May 25, 1980; 1 dau., Christina b. 1983; edn: BS in bus., USC 1977; MBA, Pepperdine Univ. 1978. Career: mktg. analyst Anheuser-Busch, Inc. St. Louis, Mo. 1976-77; mgmt. trainee Exec. Devel. Pgm., Corp. Planning Dept., Anheuser-Busch Cos., St. Louis 1978-79; exec. asst. to V.P., Anheuser-Busch, Inc. St. Louis 1978-79, regl. adminstr. Region III, 1980-81; dir. plnng. and ops.-Europe, Anheuser-Busch Internat. 1981-84; owner/pres. Gold Cities Beverage (Anheuser-Busch distbr.), 1984—; mem. Nevada Co. Bus. Assn. (dir.), Nevada Co. CofC, Active 20/30 Club, Moose, Elks, Lake Wildwood Country Club; Republican; Catholic; rec: golf, tennis, karate. Ofc: Gold Cities Beverage Co 717 S Auburn St Grass Valley 95945

GIET, GEORGE ROBERT, librarian; b. Oct. 11, 1898, NYC; s. Daniel Nathanial and Laurina (Calyo) G.; m. Cary Ellis, July 14, 1928; edn: AB, Columbia Univ. 1921, EE, 1923. Career: with Am. Tel. & Tel. Co., NYC 1923-25; prof. radio engring. US Naval Postgrad. Sch., Annapolis, Md. 1925-42; prof. electronics engring. 1946-51, prof. electronics engring., Monterey, Calif. (introduced use of Laplace Transformation at PG Sch. for solution of transient electrical circuits, etc.) 1952-65, chmn. dept. electronics engring. 1954-62; librarian Allan Knight Maritime Mus. Library, Monterey 1970—, mem. ops. bd. 1973—; served to comdr. USNR, 1942-46, capt. Res. ret.; named fellow US Naval Postgrad. Sch. Faculty, 1962, first recipient Distinguished Professor award US Naval Postgrad. Sch., 1966; mem: IEEE (life, senior mem.), Am. Soc. Engring. Edn., Monterey Hist. and Art Assn., Nat. Ret. Ofcrs. Assn., Mil. Order World Wars, Navy League US, Tau Beta Pi; clubs: Monterey Peninsula CC, Ft. Ord Officers, Naval Postgrad. Officers and Faculty, Marines Meml. Res: 24702 Upper trail Carmel 93923 Ofc: 550 Calle Principal, Monterey 93940

GILBERT, ALORA JEAN GILES, marketing and sales; b. Oct. 23, 1947, Calexico; d. Clifford L. and Vera L. (Randles) Giles; m. Maurice Gilbert Jr., Mar. 28, 1983; edn: AA, Pierce Jr. Coll. 1967; BA in psych., UC Santa Barbara 1980. Career: statistical clerk So Calif. Gas Co. 1970-73; field merchandiser Warner Elektra, Atlantic Corp., 1977-79; promotion/mktg. mgr. Warner Bros. Records, San Francisco 1979-85; mktg. div. Primary Sales Acct. Ctr., AT&T Communications, Van Nuys; coordinator Eleanor Curry Fund, San Mateo; awards: Bay Area Promo. Dir. of Year 1983, Profl. Dance Music Assn.; Outstanding Young Women of Am. 1982; various Gold Records for promo., mktg. 1979-; mem: Nat. Assn. for Female Execs. Inc., Women in Mgmt. (chpt. v.p. pub. rels.); rel: A.M.E.; rec: writing (plays, poetry, short stories), theatre. Res: 855 35th St. Oakland 94608 Ofc: Warner Brothers Records 680 Beach St San Francisco 94109

GILBERT, LINDA MARIANNE, hospital management executive; b. Aug. 4, 1951, Altdorf, Germany; d. Wm. and Elizabeth Lina (Rupprecht) Krizansky; m. Jeffrey Gilbert, Jan. 20, 1979; children: Stephanie b. 1980, Matthew b. 1982. Career: nursing ward clerk City of Hope Med. Ctr., Duarte, Calif. 1969-71, outpt. dept. clerk 1972-75, outpt. dept. supv. 1975-77, clin. adminstr. 1977-79, adminstrv. coord. 1979-82, patient acct. coord. 1982-84; asst. dir. patient acct. Queen of the Valley Hosp., West Covina 1984-85, bus. ofc. mgr. 1985—; mem: Healthcare Financial Mgmt. Assn., Am. Guild of Patient Acctg. Mgrs., Healthcare Mgmt. Assn. of So. Calif., West Covina CofC (women's div.); Democrat; Catholic; rec: golf, reading. Ofc: Queen of the Valley Hosp. 1115 S Sunset Ave West Covina 91793

GILBERT, NANCI ELAINE, real estate broker/developer; b. Jan. 10, 1943, Honolulu; d. James Carl and Josephine Adell (Sullivan) Gilbert; gr.granddau. of founder of first real estate co. in Calif., McCarthy Real Estate, L.A. Edn: grad. Punahou Sch, Honolulu 1961; AS in Radio & TV, Endicott Coll. 1963; real estate courses, USC, 1981, Coll. of Marin, 1978; Calif. real estate sales lic. 1978, r.e. broker lic. 1981; "B" gen. contractors lic. 1985. Career: residential real estate sales, 1978-; currently devel. cost-efficient residential bldg. projects in Sacramento area; developer/owner/broker RRR Properties; pres./owner Crystal Bay Holding Co.; owner/broker Russian River Resort Properties; cons.: The Alexander Co. 1983-, Ward Ent. 1981-, Las Baulines Nurseries 1982-; bd. dirs. Shane Distbrs. 1983-. Recipient num. sales awards, President's Club, 1974, Multi-Million Dollar Club, 1983, Million Dollar Club, 1981-2. Mem: Sacramento, Sonoma Co., Marin Co. Board of Realtors; Nat. Assn. for Female Execs. Inc., Sacto. Women's Network, Women in Bus. in Sonoma Co., Bay Area Career Women, The Smithsonian Assocs (nat. mem.), Alpine Explorers and Adventurers Club (pres. 1984), Nat. Geographic Soc.; Republican; Episcopal; rec: x-c skier, class. guitar, scuba, wildlife photog. Res: 6670 Oakhill Dr Roseville 95678 Ofc: RRR Properties 8125 Sunset Ave, 251, Fair Oaks 95628

GILE, BARRIE AVERILL, financial planner; b. Dec. 18, 1938, Waltham, Mass.; s. Harold R. and Geraldine (Olmstead) G.; div.; 1 son: Jason B., b. 1961;

edn: Bowdoin Coll. 1956-57; BA, Boston Univ. 1961; reg. fin. plnnr., Internat. Assn. of Reg. Fin. Plnnrs. 1984. Career: sales mgr. P.F. Collier, Inc., Hartford, Conn., Springfield and Boston, Mass. 1961-65; sales rep. Prudential Ins. Co. of Am., Salem & Gloucester, Mass. 1965-68; sales mgr., sales rep. Mutual Mass. Life Ins. Co., Boston, Los Angeles and Long Beach 1969-85; res. fin. plnnr. M M L Inevstors Svcs., Inc., Los Angeles and Long Beach 1984-85; currently reg. fin. plnnr., Barrie A. Gile & Assocs., Long Beach; cons. Am. Fedn. of Tchr., ABC Unif. Sch. Dist., Cerritos 1981-85; honors: Million Dollar Round Table 1982-85; Nat. Sales Achiev. Award 1981-85, Nat. Quality Award 1967-68, 1981-85, Nat. Assn. of Life Underwriters; mem: Calif. Assn. of Life Underwriters; Internat. Assn. of Reg. Fin. Plnnrs.; Long Beach Life Underwriters Assn.; YMCA Bus. Mens Club; The Cousteau Soc., Inc.; L.A. Co. Mus. of Art.; Am. Film Inst.; Smithsonian Inst.; rec: music record collecting, sports. Res: 661 25th St., Manhattan Beach 90266 Ofc: Barrie A. Gile & Assocs., 100 Oceangate, Ste. 800, Long Beach 90801

GILES, JEAN HALL, business executive; b. March 30, 1908, Dallas, Texas; d. Clarence D. and Elizabeth (McInytre) Overton; m. Alonzo Russell Hall II, Jan. 23, 1923, dec.; m. 2d Harry Edward Giles, April 24, 1928, div. 1937; children: Marjorie Jean, Alonzo Russell III, Janice R., Marjean Ruth. Career: realtor-notary, Los Angeles Co. 1948-61; bldg. contractor- prop. Los Angeles Real Estate Exchange; ptr. Tech. Contractors Dir. Vol. Corps., Los Angeles Area War Chest; capt., commdg. ofcr., orgn. S.W. Los Angeles unit 1942; maj., nat. exec. ofcr. 1943-44; Children's Hosp. Benefit 1945-46; coord. Motor Corps., Los Angeles Area War Chest 1944-45; capt. Communications Corp., U.S. hdqtrs.; past mem: Los Angeles and Nat. Realty Bds.; Am. Inst. of Mgmt., Los Angeles CofC (Women's Div.), Los Fiesteros de Los Angeles, Nat. Fedn. of Bus. & Profl. Women (Hollywood chpt.), L.A. World Affairs Council, Hist. Soc. of So. Calif., Los Angeles Art Assn., Assistance League of So. Calif.; Democrat (inspector Precinct 747); Protestant; rec: golf (scorer, 18 yrs., Los Angeles Open). Ofc: P.O. Box 36474 Los Angeles 90036

GILL, ZORA SINGH, vascular surgeon; b. June 15, 1949, Phulewala, Punjab, India, nat. US cit. 1982; s. Balbir Singh and Dalip Kaur Gill; m. Lucille, June 24, 1984; 1 son, Zora b. 1985; edn: premed. R.S.D. Coll., 1967-70; MB, BS, Punjab Univ., Dayanand Med. Coll. Ludhiana 1975. Board Cert. in Gen. Surgery 1984; lic. in Md., Ill., Calif., Ariz. Career: resident in gen. surgery Union Meml. Hosp., Baltimore, Md. 1977-78, New Rochelle (NY) Hosp. Med. Ctr. 1978-79, Rush-Presbyn. St. Luke's Med. Ctr., Chgo. 1979-82; fellow in vascular and thoracic surg. White Meml. Med. Ctr., Los Angeles 1982-83; general & vascular surgeon in pvt. practice, Bakersfield; awards: Best Medical Grad. of Year (1975), Gold Medal, 1st pos. in surgery (1974), var. academic prizes; Fellow Internat. Coll. of Surgeons, mem. Calif. Med. Assn., Kern Co. Med. Soc.; Republican; rec: movies, hockey. Ofc: Zora S. Gill, MD, FICS 1615 First St Bakersfield 93304

GILLARD, CHANTAL SUZANNE, wedding consultant; b. July 27, 1948, France, nat. US cit. 1976; m. Jim Hager, 1969, div. 1976; Calif. Real Estate lic. (1983). Career: actress in Cyrano de Bergerac, La comedie Francaise, 1962, performances in sev. Am. movies filmed in Studio de Le Victorine, Nice, Fr.: Moment to Moment, The Liquidator, The Poppy is Also a Flower, Grand Prix; came to Calif. 1967; fashion model, appearances var. convs., San Francisco, incl. ARC State Conv., Nat. Western Restaurant Assn.; founder/owner The Wedding Secretary, San Francisco, 1974–; wedding cons., added custom design gowns and accessories 1984-, mail order custom design bridal shoes and purses under Chantal label, 1985-, publish quarterly bridal mag., 1986-; speaker bridal shows and schs. on "how to plan your wedding;" sev. interviews local and network TV (planned a real wedding 1-hr live for AM show Ch. 7, 1983, eve. news Ch. 7, 1986, Ch. 4, 1985, CBS, 1979) and print media (S.F. Mag. 1974, Money Mag. 1980, local newspapers); rec: violinist. Res: Burlingame Ofc: Wedding Secretary 668 Post St San Francisco 94109

GILLIAM, EARL BEN, federal judge; b. Aug. 17, 1931, Clovis, N.Mex.; s. James Earl and Lula Mae Gilliam; m. Barbara Jean, Dec. 6, 1956; children: Earl Kenneth, Derrick James; edn: BA, CSU San Diego 1953; JD, Hastings Coll. Law, 1957; admitted to Calif. State Bar 1957. Career: dep. dist. atty., San Diego 1957-62; judge San Diego Municipal Ct. 1963-74; judge Superior Ct. Calif., San Diego County 1975–; prof. law Western State Coll. Law, 1968-; honors: Commr. Gen. San Diego's 200th Anniversary, Jaycee Young Man of Year 1965; Democrat; Ofc: U.S. Courthouse, 940 Front St., San Diego 92189

GILLIGAN, DOREEN ELAINE, real estate broker; b. Canada, nat. US cit. 1958; d. Neil and Ada (Rothwell) McArthur; m. Timothy Gilligan, Oct. 18, 1952. Career: var. pos. Bank of Toronto, Vancouver BC; Lansdown Race Track, Vancouver; bank ofcr. Bank of Am.; American City Bank; current: Westwood real estate broker and owner interior improvement co.; mem. Toastmistress, Canon Explorers, Sierra Club, Twilite Hikers; rec: camping, hiking, travel. Address: 1422 S Bentley Ave Ste 201 Los Angeles 90025

GILLO, BENEDICTO JANOZO, company president; b. Feb. 21, 1937, Dinagat, Surigao del Norte, Philippines, nat. US cit. 1974; s. Juan Custodio and Crescencia Ecle (Janozo) G.; m. Carmen Baldueza, Dec. 12, 1964; children: Virginia b. 1958, Benedicto, Jr. b. 1963, George b. 1965, Roberto b. 1967; edn: BSIE, Adamson Univ. 1964. Career: jr. indsl. engr. United Textile Mills 1964-66, Universal Corn Prods. 1966-67; leadman map draftsman Title Ins. Co. 1969-71; survey mapping techn. County of Los Angeles 1971-78, equal opportunity compliance investigator 1978-81, deputy compliance ofcr. 1981–; pres. Phil-Cen Svcs. 1978–; award: Lynwood Jaycees 1985; mem: Assn.

Energy Engrs., Nat. Assn. Gen. Contrs., Am. Inst. Indsl. Engrs. (senior), Philippine Engrs. &.Scientists of So. Calif. (chmn.), L.A. Council Engrs. & Scientists, Lynwood Jaycees (pres. 1984-85), Optimist Club of Pasadena (bd. 1984-85), Filipino Am. Residents of Southeast L.A. (pres.), L.A. County Filipino Am. Employees Assn. (v.p.), Surigao Assn. of So. Calif. (vice chmn.), Filipino Am. Press Club (treas.), Fil. Am. Community of L.A. (v.p. 1977), Mindanao Assn. of Am. (bd. 1977), BSA (scoutmaster 1974-77); contbg. editor Filipino Catholic Newsmagazine, Phil-Am Times; mng. ed. The Motivator; Democrat; Catholic; rec: basketball, softball. Res: 3352 Seminole Ave Lynwood 90262 Ofc: Phil-Cen Svcs. 2115 Beverly Blvd Los Angeles 90057

GILMAN, RICHARD CARLETON, college president; b. July 28, 1923, Cambridge, Mass.; s. George Phillips Brooks and Karen Elise (Theller) G.; m. Lucille Young, Aug. 28, 1948 (dec. June 1978); children: Marsha, Bradley Morris, Brian Potter, Blair Tucker; m. Sarah Gale, Dec. 28, 1984; edn: BA, Dartmouth 1944; stu. New Coll., Univ. London (Eng.) 1947-8; PhD (Borden Parker Bowne fellow Philosophy, 1949-50), Boston Univ. 1952, LLD, 1969; LLD, Pomona Coll. 1966, USC 1968, Coll. Ida., 1968; LHD, Chapman Coll. 1984. Career: teaching fellow religion Dartmouth, 1948; faculty Colby Coll., 1950-56, assoc. prof. philosophy, 1955-56; exec. dir. Nat. Council Religion Higher Edn., New Haven 1956-60; dean coll., prof. philosophy Carleton Coll., 1960-65; pres. Occidental Coll., 1965–; counselor/exec. asst. to US Secty. Edn., 1979-80; mem. Intergovtl. Council on Edn. (1980-82), Pres.'s Commn. Nat. Collegiate Athletic Council (1984-); bd. dirs. Am. Council on Edn., Assn. Am. Colls., Council on Postsecondary Accreditation, Nat. Assn. Independent Colls. and Univs., Council Finl. Aid to Edn., Calif. Museum Found., LA World Affairs Council; Fellow Soc. Religion Higher Edn., Newcomen Soc., Calif. CofC (dir.); Phi Beta Kappa; clubs: University (NYC), California, Twilight, 100 (Los Angeles); mil: USNR 1944-46. Res: 1852 Campus Rd., Los Angeles 90041 Ofc: 1600 Campus Rd Los Angeles 90041

GINDER, STEVEN POWELL, mortgage banker; b. May 3, 1949, Inglewood; s. Paul and Marguerite Lucille G.; m. Deborah Ann, Aug. 27, 1972; children: Reid b. 1980, Grant b. 1982; edn: BA, UC Santa Barbara 1971; MBA, USC 1973; Real Estate Broker, Calif. 1985. Career: acct. exec. Dean Witter Reynolds, Long Beach 1973-76; v.p. Cal Fed Mortgage Co., Los Angeles 1976-80; founder/ pres. National Pacific Mortgage Co. 1980–; dir. Nat. Pacific Mortgage; chair CSULB Executive in Residency com.; mem. Fed. Mortgage Assn. Bus. Advy. Bd.; mem: Cerritos CofC, Mortgage Bankers Assn., Calif. Mortgage Bankers Assn., YMCA, AYSO, Sigma Chi; mil: E-4 Calif. Nat. Guard 1969-71; Republican; Lutheran; rec: skin diving, sailing, tennis. Res: 17521 Bates Huntington Beach 92649 Ofc: National Pacific Mortgage Co., 10900 E. 183rd Ste. 120 Cerritos 90701

GINDICK, JONATHAN FRANKLIN, writer, publisher, musician; b. Sept. 10, 1948, Hollywood; s. Franklin and Gladysann (Poffenberger) G.; edn: BA, UC Berkeley 1972; MA, Univ. for Profl. Students of San Diego 1982. Career: currently, pres. Cross Harp Press, Visalia; harmonica sems. to orgns.; instr. to people in hosps.; opr. mail order bus. for music enthusiasts; mem: Hollywood Hghts. Assn. (block capt.), Soc. for Preservation & Adv. of the Harmonica, Artists & Writers Workshop (Los Angeles); author: recorded (8) instructional cassettes for musical beginners 1977–; The Natural Blues and Country Western Harmonica, A Beginners Guide, 1977; Rock N' Blues Harmonica, Stories, Lessons, Record Index, 1982; Country & Blues Harmonica For the Musically Hopeless, 1984; rec: songwriting, story and screenplay writing, swimming. Res: 1939 Pinehurst Rd. Los Angeles 90068 Ofc: Cross Harp Press, 530 Ranch Rd. Visalia 93291

GINGERICH, THOMAS DALE, life insurance co. executive; b. Feb. 15, 1941, Wellman, Iowa; s. Glenwood E. and Catherine G. (Sitler) G.; m. Patricia Baum, Sept. 12, 1970; children: Lisa b. 1965, Jonathan b. 1974, David b. 1979; edn: BA, Univ. Iowa 1963; M.Div., Am. Baptist Seminary of the West 1968; CSU Stanislaus 1973-74; American Coll. 1976-86. Career: minister, counselor First Baptist Ch. San Carlos 1971-72; Calif. Inst. Family Relations Modesto 1973-74; acct. exec. Corplan Modesto 1975; mgr. brokerage Rudy Facciani Co. Fresno 1976; life ins. agent Crown Life Fresno 1977-80, assoc. gen. agent 1981, Monaco 1978, Vienna 1981, Athens 1984; unit mgr. The Principal Financial Group; mem: Assn. Life Underwriters (secty./treas. 1975, bd. 1982), Advis. Bd. on Alcohol Problems, Nat. Assn. Health Underw., Stanislaus County Estate Planning Council (bd. 1985-86), Young Republicans (pres. 1960), Modesto Rotary; mil: cpl. Nat. Guard 1956-64; Republican; Presbyterian; rec: camping, backpacking. Ofc: The Principal Financial Group 1800 Tully Rd Ste A Modesto 95350

GIORDANO, MICHAEL RALPH, securities co. executive; b. Oct. 5, 1946, Bronx, N.Y.; s. Michael James and Adele (Powers) G.; m. Elizabeth, June 8, 1968; children: James b. 1969, Jennifer b. 1971, Michelle b. 1974, Melinda b. 1980; edn: AS eng., Citrus Jr. Coll. 1966; BS aerospace eng., Cal Poly Pomona 1970; MBA in fin. & investments, Univ of Utah 1974; desig: reg. rep. SEC 1979. Career: capt. US Air Force, pilot, squadron cmdr. 2852nd Air Base Group, McClellan AFB, Sacto. 1970-79; bd. chmn./CEO Leo D. Fields Co. Inc. (aircraft parts co.), Los Angeles 1981–; mgr. Tax Advantaged Investment Dept., Kidder Peabody & Co. Inc., L.A. 1979–; clubs: Jonathan, Gr. Whittier Tennis; author book: 29 Ways to Retire Wealthy, & 37 Ways to Get Uncle Sams Hand Out of Your Pocket; num. mag. articles; frequent public speaker; Republican; Episcopal; rec: tennis. Res: 560 Santa Anita Ave San Marino 91108 Ofc: Kidder Peabody 333 S Grand Ave 2300 Los Angeles 90071

GIRAMONTI, ADRIANA AURORA, chef; b. May 24, 1929, Roma, Italy, nat. US cit. 1961; d. Umberto and Clotilde (Pascale) Silvestri; m. Frank Giramonti, July 7, 1960; children: Piero b. 1964, Roberto b. 1967; edn: Armando Diaz Coll. (Italy) 1944; shorthand/ typist, Berlitz Sch. 1952. Career: bkpg. helper, cashier First Class Ristorante Roma 1949-53; pvt., personal secty. Dr. Claudi Roma 1953-56; practical nurse, cook Serra Sanitarium Millbrae 1956; rubber pillow making factory 1957-58; waitress Little Joe Restaurant s.F. 1958-77; chief owner, pres. Giramonti Restaurant Inc. (Giramonti Rest. in Mill Valley and Adriana Rest. in San Rafael); demonstration classes Macy's S.F. 1984-85, La Cordon Rouge Sausalito 1983, Loni Khon Cooking Tour 1983-84, Culinary Carnival 1984-85; honors; Diploma and Medal (Great Chefs of S.F. 1984), Italian Chef of A.M. San Francisco ABC (1983, 84, 85, 86), Gourmet Mag., Pacific Sun of Marin; publ: Great Chefs of S.F. (from the PBS nat. TV series, Avon Books NY 1983); Catholic; rec: dressmaking. Ofc: Giramonti Restaurant Inc. 999 Anderson Dr San Rafael Dr San Rafael 94901

GISVOLD, DARRELL IVAN, psychiatrist; b. Dec. 12, 1933, Madison, Wis.; s. Ole and Evelyn (Nelson) G.; 1 son, Mark b. 1970; edn: BA, Univ. of Minn. 1955; MA, Univ. of Mont. 1957; MD, Creighton Univ. 1960; psychiatric residency, N.J. State Hosp., Hammonton, 1965; bd. certified Psychiatry, Nat. Boards. Career: chief psychiatrist US Army 1965-67; staff psychiatrist Community Mental Health 1967-71, Dept. of Corrections San Quentin 1971-73, chief psychiatrist Keokuk L- Facility, 1970-75; pvt. practice psychiatry, Kentfield and Petaluma, currently; cons. Workers Compensation, State Disability Examiner; assoc. prof. Univ. of Fla. (Canal Zone) 1966; mem: AMA, Am. Psych. Assn., Am. Trial Lawyers Assn. (assoc.), E. Vitus Clampus; publs: A Validity Study of the EPPS, Am. J. of Psychology (1957), A Clin. Study of Librium, Colo. J. of Med. (1960), A Case Report: Post Traumatic Stress, Sonoma County Physician (1985); mil: capt. US Army chief of psychiatry 1965-67, Medal of Honor; Republican (Nat. Com.); Lutheran; rec: golf, boating, music- chorus, violin. Ofc: 612 S Petaluma Blvd Petaluma 94952

GIUMARRA, JOHN GEORGE, JR., agricultural and wine industry executive; b. Oct. 13, 1940, Los Angeles; s. John George and Florence (Respoli) G.; m. Pamela Presley, Sept. 11, 1965; children: John, III b. 1968, Randall b. 1972, Juliana b. 1975, Joseph b. 1978, Jillian b. 1981; edn: BS, UC Berkeley 1962; LLD, Stanford Sch. of Law 1965; admitted Calif. State Bar 1965. Career: atty. law firm Rutan & Tucker, Santa Ana 1966-67; prin. and v.p. Giumarra Vineyards Corp. (largest grower of table grapes in USA) 1967–, and opr./owner of winery (12th largest in state); negotiated first major collective bargaining agreement between grape growers of Calif. and Cesar Chavez of United Farm Workers; active in drafting and enacting the Agri. Labor Relations Act; mem. var. wine tasting panels incl. LA Times Home Mag. panel; honors: book rev. editor Stanford Law Rev., award for excellence in legal writing (1965); mem: Calif. Grape & Tree Fruit League (bd. chmn. 1982), Wine Inst. of Calif. (bd.), Winegrower of Calif., Calif. Table Grape Commn.; trustee Gr. Bakersfield Meml. Hosp.; chmn. fundraising event for CSUB Athletic Found.; frequent speaker (1967-) produce and wine conventions and meetings nat. on agricultural wine, labor rels., mktg., fin. topics; Republican; Catholic; rec: golf, tennis, sailing. Res: 4224 Country Club Dr Bakersfield 93306 Ofc: Giumarra Vineyards PO Bin 1969 Bakersfield 93303

GIVANT, PHILIP JOACHIM, educator, real estate investment co. president; b. Dec. 5, 1935, Mannheim, Germany, nat. US cit. 1940; s. Paul and Irmy (Dinse) G.; children: Philip Paul b. 1963, Julie Kathleen b. 1965, Laura Grace b. 1968; edn: BA, CSU San Francisco 1957, MA, 1960. Career: math. prof. San Francisco State Univ. 1958-60, American River Coll. (Sacto.) 1960–; pres. Grove Ents. Real Estate Investment Co. 1961–; mem. Calif. Community Colls. (CCC) Academic Senate (v.p. 1974-77), Am. River Coll. Acad. Senate (pres. 1966-69), State Chancellor's com. on the Academic Calendar (1977-79); awards: spl. commendn. CCC Academic Senate, spl. human rights award for InterCultural Affairs, CCC (1977), human rights award Fair Housing Commn. Sacto. County; mem. CCC Faculty Assn. (1966-), Am. Soc. for Psychical Research (1965-); civic: founding mem. Sacto. Blues Soc. (1980-), Lake Tahoe Keys Homeowners Assn., Sea Ranch Homeowners Assn., Klamath River Country Estates Homeowners Assn., NAACP (life); works: founder/pres. & prod. Sacto. Blues Festival Inc. (1976-); prod. weekly music pgm. "Blues with Phil" on Public Radio St. KVMR, Nevada City; prod. musical festival Folsom State Prison (1979-81), Vacaville State Prison (1985); rec: tennis, music, boating. Address: Grove Enterprises 3809 Garfield Ave Carmichael 95608

GLASER, HERBERT, real estate developer, lawyer; b. Aug. 1, 1927, New Brunswick, N.J.; s. Samuel and Rosalind (Barenfeld) G.; m. Sharon, Jan. 20, 1957; children: Tamar Eileen b. 1955, Jonathan b. 1962; edn: AB, UC Los Angeles 1947; JD, Harvard Law Sch. 1951. Career: senior ptnr. Glaser & Glaser, 1951-1968; owner Glaser Devel. Co., Los Angeles 1968–; apptd. Real Estate Advis. Commn., Calif. Dept. Corps. (1972-74), L.A. City Bd. of Fire Commnrs. (pres. 1962-71); civic: Bur. of Jewish Edn./LA (pres.), Jewish Fedn. Council/LA (v.p.), Jewish Community Found. (trustee), Brandeis Bardin Inst. (dir.), Am. Assoc. Ben Gurion Univ. (co-chmn. exec. com. W. Region), Israel Tennis Centers Assn. (dir.), Calif. Chamber Symphony (dir.), UCLA Chancellor's Assocs.; clubs: Beverly Hills Tennis, Vail Athletic, Harvard of So. Calif.; mil: Sl/c USN 1944-45 (inactive duty); Jewish; rec: ski, mountaineering, biking, writing. Ofc: Glaser Development Co 924 Westwood Blvd Los Angeles 90024

GLASSMAN, ARTHUR JOSEPH, physicist; b. Apr. 4, 1948, NY, NY; s. Max Samuel and Ruth Rae (Gold) G.; edn: SB in physics, MIT 1968; MS in physics, Yale Univ. 1969; MA and PhD in physics, Columbia Univ. 1971, 1977. Career: senior pgmmr. Cubic Corp., San Diego 1978-79; engr. Linkabit (now Ma-Com Linkabit), 1979-80; senior scientist Jaycor, 1980–; mem. Am. Physical Soc., Am. Geophysical Union, IEEE, MIT Alumni Club, Yale Alumni Club, Young Bus. Profl. Council Steering Com.; coauthor sev. tech. articles in sci. jours.; rec: tennis, folkdance. Res: 8310 Regents Rd #2-B San Diego 92122 Ofc: Jaycor POB 85154 San Diego 92138

GLAVIANO, CHARLES ROY, manufacturing co. president; b. Dec. 19, 1923, Los Angeles; s. Nick and Alice (Guardia) G.; m. Diana, May 18, 1962; children: Michael b. 1950, Nancy b. 1953, Mark b. 1965; desig: Mfg. Technologist, Soc. Mfg. Engrs. Career: apprentice bronze & aluminum foundry, while in H.S.; machinist Baker Engring. Co., Hollywood 1939-40; owner Airborn Products, San Gabriel 1941-44, Nicson Engring. Co., City of Commerce 1945-61, owner/pres. Nicson Engring. Co. Inc., Santa Fe Springs 1961–; awards: named Marine Mfr. of Year, Vapor Trail's (1977), Designer of Year, Caesar's Marine Academy (1977); feature articles in Raceboat mag. (2/76), Hot Boat mag. (4/84); works: research, design, mfg. (1941-), photog.- catalog design (1941-); mil: US Navy 1944-46, Victory Medal, WWII; Republican; rec: classic cars, antique guns, gardening, boating. Ofc: Nicson Engineering Co. Inc. 11850 Burke St Santa Fe Springs 90670

GLEASON, GERALD T., hotel executive; b. July 15, 1943, Corning, N.Y.; s. Lawrence E. and Onalee E. (Hanrahan) G.; m. Linda Vancompernalle, July 1, 1983; 1 dau. Pamela b. 1967; edn: AA, Corning Comm. Coll. 1963; BA Russian lang., State Univ. of N.Y. at Albany 1968. Career: mgmt. Hyatt Corp. (Albany Hyatt; Mills Hyatt, Charleston; Hyatt Regency, O'Hare- Chgo.; Hyatt Regency, Houston; Hyatt Monterey; Hyatt Dearborn; Cherry Hill (N.J.) Hyatt), participant in opening of 4 Hyatt Hotels, 1968-78; regional v.p. Doubletree Hotels (Monterey, Dallas and Overland Park, Ks.), opening team leader for 5 Doubletree Hotels, 1978-84; mng. dir. La Costa Hotel & Spa, Carlsbad 1984–; mem: San Diego County Hotel Motel Assn. (dir. 1985-86), Soc. of Incentive Travel Execs. (dir. 1985-86), Am. Hotel Motel Assn., Calif. Hotel Motel Assn., (fmr): Kans. Hotel Motel Assn. (dir.), Overland Park Conv. & Vis. Bur. (founder), Overland Park CofC (bd.), Boulevard Club- Overland Park, Ks. (founder); mil: E4 USAF Intel. Service, Russian Linguist. Res: 1826 Hummock Lane Encinitas 92024 Ofc: La Costa Hotel & Spa Costa Del Mar Rd Carlsbad 92008

GLEASON, TERRY BRAINARD, mechanical engineer; b. July 18, 1936, Oakland; s. Roger Wendel and Harriet (Brainard) G.; m. Janice Hendren, Feb. 13, 1960; children: Brian b. 1965, Julie b. 1967; edn: BS, UC Berkeley 1959; Reg. Profl. Mech. Engr. Calif. 1968; Cert. Energy Mgr., Assn. of Energy Engrs. 1983. Career: trainee FMC Corp., San Jose 1956-58; engring. aide UC Berkeley 1957; US Steel Corp. 1959–; trainee 1959; engr. 1961; designer 1961; staff engr. 1962; power & fuel engr. 1965; supvr. project engring. 1966; conveyor belt engr. 1967; prodn. asst. 1970; foreman 1973; senior staff engr. 1975; senior design engr. 1980; project engr. 1980; currently, project engr. US Steel Corp., Pittsburgh Works 1985–; loaned exec. Governor's Task Force on Efficiency and Cost Control in State Gvt., State of Calif. 1967; honors: Chevalier, Order of DeMolay 1955; mem: Assn. of Iron & Steel Engrs. (San Francisco sect. chmn. 1978, Nat. bd. dirs. 1979), Calif. Mfrs. Assn. (Energy Steering Com. 1978-85), Y-Indian Guides, Cub Scouts (com. chair 1976-79), Boy Scouts Am. (scout master 1979-83), Order of DeMolay (1950-56); KQED Auction volunteer, First Presbyterian Ch. Handbell Choir; mil: sgt. E-6 USAR 1959-65; Republican; rec: flying, sailing.

GLEBERMAN, FRANK MARTIN, financial services co. principal; b. Jan. 26, 1938, Cincinnati, Ohio; s. Myron Fernando and Betty (McKim) G.; edn: USC Sch. of Business, 1955-60; desig: Chartered Life Underwriter (CLU), Am. Coll./Bryn Mawr (1969), Cert. Finl. Planner (CFP), Coll. for Finl. Plnng., Denver (1985), mem. Nat. Assn. Securities Dealers (NASD). Career: asst. advt. mgr. Carnation Co. 1961-62; life ins. agent New York Life Ins. Co., 1962-66, asst. mgr. 1966-70, supt. So. Pacific Region, 1971-74, gen. mgr. 1970-71, 1974-78; asst. gen. agent Mass. Mutual Life, 1978-80; prin. Manufacturers Financial Services, Los Angeles 1981–; dir: Westways Inc., Western-Mayflower Moving and Storage, Modern-Mayflower Moving and Storage, Great Amer. Moving & Storage, Lorentine Corp.; owner Frank M. Gleberman Gen. Mgmt. Consulting; writer, lectr., tch. seminars in finl. plnng. & ins.; chmn. LA Unified Sch. Dist. Underutilized Sch. Sites Com.; honors: resolutions, L.A. City Council and Co. Bd. Supvrs. 1973; KNX Radio Citizen of Week 1977; mem: Nat., Calif., L.A. Assn. of Life Underwriters; Inst. of Certified Finl. Plnnrs.; Am., L.A. Co. Soc. of CLU; NASD (chmn. The Finl. Plnng. Study Group); civic: Nat. Assn. for People with Disabilities (pres.), LA County Easter Seal Soc. (past pres./ bd. chmn.); LA Jr. Chamber of Commerce (past pres./ bd. chmn.; past pres. Charity Found.), LA Area CofC (past dir.), Commerce Assocs. of USC (past pres./ bd. chmn.), USC Assocs. (life), LA Civic Light Opera Assn. (past dir.), LA Open Golf Tournament Advis. Com. (past v.chmn.), Glen Campbell-LA Open Golf Found. (past pres.); club: Calif. Yacht (rear commodore); mil: E5 USCGR; Republican; Catholic; rec: sail, ski, travel. Res: 4314 Glencoe Ave Marina del Rey 90291 Ofc: Mfrs. Finl. Services, 3333 Wilshire Blvd Los Angeles 90010

GLENN, JAMES DRYDEN, II, executive; b. Jan. 29, 1934, Sharon, Penn.; s. James Dryden and Treva Irene (Hartman) G.; m. Lorraine, Dec. 18, 1954; children: James D. III b. 1958, Sharyn Diane b. 1956, Scott Douglas b. 1961, Steven Dale b. 1965; edn: BSCE, Carnegie Mellon Univ. 1955. Career: metalurgis' Crucible Steel Co., Pittsburgh, Penn. 1955; metalurgist US Army Corps of Engrs., Ft. Belvoir, Va. 1955-57; sales trainee, asst. prod. mgr. Crucible Steel Co., Pittsburgh, Penn. 1957-60, salesman, prod. splst., Chicago, Ill.

1960-64, dist. mgr., Rockford, Ill. 1964-68; dist. mgr. The Steel Corp. of Texas, Dallas, Texas 1968-69, v.p., Houston, Texas 1969-76, v.p., Los Angeles 1976-82; pres. Sun Belt Steel & Aluminum, Los Angeles 1982–; dir., part owner The Steel Corp. of Texas 1968-82; dir., part owner Sun Belt Steel & Aluminum 1982-; mem: Am. Soc. for Metals, Steel Svc. Ctr. Inst. (assoc.), Kappa Sigma, Kappa Sigma Alumni Assn. (v.p. Orange Co. chpt.); mil: 1st lt. US Army Corps of Engrs. 1955-57; Republican; Presbyterian; rec: racquetball, athletics, moutain home. Res: 18402 Jocotal Villa Park 92667 Ofc: Sun Belt Steel, 1645 W. Orangewood Orange 92668

GLENN, JOHN WILEY, transit district president; b. Dec. 2, 1927, Puxico, Mo.; s. Charles Thomas and Minnie Elizabeth (Hodge) G.; m. Betty Berry, June 30, 1951; children: John b. 1955, Sharon b. 1962, Karen b. 1966; edn: BS mktg., S.E. Mo. State Univ. 1952. Career: owner, gen. mgr. John Glenn Adjusters & Adminstrs., Oakland, San Rafael, San Jose, Calif. and Portland, Ore. 1966–; v.p. S.F. Bay Area Rapid Transit Dist. (BART) 1978, 85, pres. 1980, 86; dir. Royal Nufoam Corp. 1968-77; organizer and dir. CivicBank of Commerce, Oakland and Walnut Creek 1984–; trustee Holy Family Coll. 1983-86, Ohlone Coll. Found. 1986; honors: Alumni Merit Award (S.E. Mo. State Univ. 1986); mem: Calif. Assn. Independent Ins. Adjusters (pres. 1979-80), East Bay Adjusters Assn. (pres. 1970), Am. Public Transit Assn. (bd. dirs. 1981-), Central Coast Claims Assn.; Democrat; United Methodist; rec: gardening, photog., travel. Res: 36601 Cuenca Ct Fremont 94536 Ofc: John Glenn Adjusters & Administrators, 337 17th St, Rm 202, Oakland 94612

GLENN, PATRICIA MARVIS, escrow executive; b. Dec. 4, 1938, Owensboro, Ky; d. Joseph Marvin and Beatrice (Travis) Wedding; m. James Glenn, Oct. 26, 1981; children: Joseph Dane Wolfe b. 1964, Robert Darrel Wolfe b. 1965, Shandra Erin Wolfe b. 1971, Andrew Clifton Wolfe b. 1974; edn: BS real estate, San Diego State Univ. 1976; MBA mktg., Nat. Univ. 1985; real estate broker Calif.; Calif. Lifetime Tchg. Cert. (ltd.), Calif. Pvt. Postsecondary Edn. Cert. Career: foreclosure, escrow dept. mgr. Ben Hinkle Real Estate Inc., Apple Valley, Calif.; real estate instr. Victor Valley Coll.; mem: Kentucky Colonels, High Desert Toastmasters (pres.), Sun Country Toastmasters (adminstrv. v.p.), Women of the Moose; Democrat; So. Baptist; rec: square dancing. Res: 18020 Catalpa St Hesperia 92345 Ofc: Ben Hinkle Real Estate Inc., 21940 Hwy 18 Apple Valley 92307

GLENN, RICHARD ELDON, JR., insurance broker; b. June 15, 1931, Oakland; s. Richard Eldon and Aileen Margaret (Collier) G.; m. Rita Jean Kroner, Nov. 7, 1977; children: Richard III b. 1953, Leslie b. 1955, Matthew b. 1964; edn: AB, Univ. of Calif. 1956; Chartered Prop. & Casualty Underwriter, CPCU 1978. Career: West Coast prodn./ undw. mgr. Markel Service Inc., San Francisco 1966; asst. v.p. Johnson & Higgins, San Francisco 1980; owner, exec. v.p. Glenn, Nyhan & Assoc., San Francisco currently; honors: Sigma Phi Soc.; mem: Soc. of Ins. Brokers, Nat. & Western Assns. of Ins. Brokers, CPCU, San Francisco CofC; mil: 1st lt. US Army Transp. Corps; Republican; rec: tennis, gardening, outdoors. Res: 1181 Balclutha Dr. Foster City 94404 Ofc: GNA, 282 2nd St. 4th Flr. San Francisco 94105

GLESS, JOHN JEROME, citrus farmer; b. Oct. 12, 1937, Orange, Calif.; s. John Pierre and Mary Louise (Etchezahar) G.; m. Janet McCandless, June 22, 1958; children: John b. 1959, Betsy b. 1961, Jeff b. 1964, Jason b. 1970; edn: Orange Coast Coll. 2 yrs. Career: began farming with father El Toro, Calif. 1955; planted new groves in newly formed water dist. in Woodcrest 1962; planted new citrus in Riverside area through 1975; currently farming 3000 acres and oper. Gless Ranch Market and Christmas Tree Farm; dir. Fed. Land Bank of Calif.; honors: Outstanding Contbr. Soil Conservation 1975; mem: Calif. Pest Control Opers., Calif. pest Control Advisors, Western Farmers Assn., Olive Hts. Citrus Assn. (past. bd.), Victoria Ave. Citrus Assn. (past bd.), Riverside Co. Farm. Bureau (bd.), Citrus Heritage State Park Adv. Bd., Riverside CofC (bd.), Inland Empire Economic Council (bd.); Republican; rec: golf. Ofc: Gless Ranch 19985 Van Buren Riverside 92504

GLICK, ANDREW JUSTUS, computer systems engineer; b. Oct. 25, 1948, Los Angeles; s. George Gordon and Josephine (Griner) G.; edn: BA, CSU Long Beach 1969; BSEE, USC 1977. Career: quality engring. supvr. Thomas Organ Co. 1974-75; senior sys. analyst Tektronix Inc. 1979-81; tech. supvr. computer graphics Lockheed CALAC 1981-82; tech. support splst. Digital Research 1982-83; pres. Justus Engineering 1983–; prof. Computer Information Sciences, Northrop Univ. 1985-; honors: Outstanding Scholarship in Material Sciences Award, Am. Soc. of Testing Materials 1975; mem: Am. Assn. for Adv. of Sci., Assn. of Computing Machinery (Spl. Interest Gp. in Computer Graphics), Musical Arts Soc. of Los Angeles, Cambridge Singers; works: Interfacing the Chromatics CX-1536 Ultra- High- Resolution Graphics System to the Teledyne Camera Systems GFC-1 HDTV Video- to- Flim Recorder, Soc. of Motionpicture and Television Engrs. Conf. 1985; World Aerobatics Championships: 4054 Teams with Radar for Automated Boundary Judging; mil: splst. 4/c, E-4 US Army; Democrat; Unitarian; rec: music, bird watching, hiking. Ofc: Justus Engineering, P.O. Box 1451 La Canada 91011-5451

GLOBERMAN, LINDA MARYLIN, dermatologist; b. May 15, 1951, Los Angeles; d. Alfred A. and Helene C. (Schulz) G.; m. Gary Jackson, Aug. 19, 1984; edn: BA, UC Los Angeles 1972; MD, USC Sch. of Med. 1976; internship Mercy Hosp. Sch. of Medicine, San Diego 1977; resident in dermatology UC Irvine Affil. Hosps. 1980; Calif. lic. physician 1976; Board certified in Dermatology 1980. Career: physician group practice Valley Dermatologic Med. Group, Tarzana 1980-84; estab. solo practice derm., Irvine 1982–; clin. assoc. in medicine UC Irvine Dept. Derm. 1979-80, attending staff UCI 1985-; instr. derm. Northridge Family Practice, 1981-82; honors: Phi Beta Kappa (1972), Woman of Year-Physician, Tarzana CofC (1982); mem: Am. Acad. of Derm., Am. Soc. for Dermatologic Surgery, Soc. for Investigative Derm., Am. Med. Womens Assn. (sec.treas. branch 1979-80), Orange Co. Med. Assn., Salerni Collegium, Irvine CofC, Irvine Bus. & Profl. Women (pgm. com. 1985); contbr. articles med. journals; rec: music, travel, theater. Ofc: Linda M. Globerman MD 4902 Irvine Center Drive Ste 105 Irvine 92714

GLORIG, ARAM, physician; b. June 8, 1906, Manchester, Eng.; US citizen; s. Aram and Beatrice (Allen) G.; div.; children: Patricia b. 1947, Deborah b. 1951; edn: BS, Atlantic Union Coll. 1931; MD, Loma Linda Univ. 1938. Career: intern Lawrence Meml. Hosp., New London, Conn. 1937-8, res. Willard Parker Hosp., NYC 1939-40, Henrietta Egleston Hosp., Atlanta, Ga. 1940-1; major US Army M.C., chief, ENT, various hosps. Iceland, Eng., Ger., 1942-46; dir. Audiology and Speech Correction Ctr., Walter Reed Army Med. Ctr./ and dir. Tech. Resrch in Hearing Dept. of Army/ and chief, Audiol. and Speech Correction, VA, Wash DC 1947-53; dir. of resrch. The Los Angeles Found. of Otology, and Noise Resrch. Ctr., 1953-64; dir. Callier Ctr. for Communication Disorders, 1964-77, Dir. Emeritus 1977-; cons. indsl. and forensic otology Otologic Med. Group, Inc., L.A. 1977–, assoc. dir. resrch House Ear Inst., L.A. 1977–; teaching, num. med. instns., univs. 1949-; Dean Emeritus, Univ. of Texas, Dallas, 1977-; Calif. lic. Provider Cont. Edn. for RNs, 1981-3; mem: Acoustical Soc. of Am. (Fellow), Am. Acad. Opthalmol. and Otolaryngol. (Fellow), AAAS, Am. Auditory Soc. (founding pres. 1972), Am. Indsl. Hygiene Assn. (past pres. No Tex. Sect.), Am. Laryngol., Rhinol., Otol. Soc. Inc. (Fellow), AMA, Am. Otol. Soc. (Fellow), Am. Speech and Hearing Assn. (Fellow, life), Royal Soc. of Med., etc.; awards: Ignacio Berraquer (1968), Citizenship, WFAA (1969), Am. Acad. of Ophthal. and Otol. (1971), Amplifon Center for Resrch. Study, Milan, Italy (1979), Carhart Meml., Am. Auditory Soc. (1979), Mem. of Honor, XV Intl. Cong. of Audiol., Krakow, Poland (1980); author four books, num. med. arts.; Republican; Prot.; rec: golf, sailing. Res: 5400 The Toledo Long Beach 90803 Ofc: Otologic Med Gp. 2122 West 3rd St Los Angeles 90057

GLOUDEMAN, JOSEPH FLOYD, corporate president, scientist; b. Oct. 19, 1935, West Allis, Wis.; s. Martin Peter and Anna Marie (Kieweg) G.; m. Jeanette Therese Markert, June 14, 1958; children: Mike, Mark, John; edn: BSME, Marquette Univ. 1958; MSME, USC 1962; PhD, Univ. of Stuttgart, Germany 1970. Career: engring. trainee Kearney & Trecker Corp., Milwaukee 1955-58; engr. Norair Div. Northrop Corp., Los Angeles 1958-61; section mgr. The Aerospace Corp., L.A. 1961-67; dir./G.M. Data Mgmt., Rockwell Internat. Corp., Seal Beach 1967-78; v.p. mktg. The MacNeal- Schwendler Corp., L.A. 1978-83, pres./ CEO 1983–, mem. bd. dirs.; honors: USAF Space Systems Div. spl. achieve. award (mem. Aerospace Corp. Gemini Team, 1966), Apollo achieve. award, NASA (1969), award for contbns. to Space Div. pgms., No. Am. Rockwell (1973); mem: Am. Inst. of Aero. & Astro. (assoc. fellow 1984), Structural Mechanics in Reactor Technology (dep. orgn. chmn., mem. Internat. Sci. Com. 1977), Computer- Aided- Engring. for Reactor Structures (seminar co-organizer 1977); civic: pres.'s council Loyola Marymount Univ., pres.'s advis. council Univ. of La Verne, Newcomen Soc., Town Hall of Calif.; num. tech. publs. and mgmt.-oriented papers on structural analysis, computer scis., applied math., and advanced spacecraft structures concepts; Republican; Roman Catholic; rec: racquetball, running. Res: 731 Hillcrest La Canada Flintridge 91011 Ofc: The MacNeal-Schwendler Corp. 815 Colorado Blvd Los Angeles 90041

GLOVER, N. DOREEN, chiropractor, nutritionist, craniopathist; b. Fort Madison, Iowa; d. Marvin Henry and Ethel May (Miller) Cherry; children: Kendra Kay Glover b. 1963, Jana Lynn Glover b. 1969; edn: Iowa St. Univ., LA Chiro. Coll.; DC, Western State Chiro. Coll. 1977; lic. DC in Calif., Ore.; Certified Reichian Therapist; Career: chiropractor, pres., founder Inst. for Natural Health, Santa Monica; tchg. profl. seminars and schs. in US and Japan var. profl. techniques, 1979-; neurolinguistic programming/ unconscious restructuring instr.; mem: Am. Chiro. Assn., Calif. Chiro. Assn., Sacro Occipital Research Soc., Internat. Craniopathic Soc., Women Chiropractors of So. Calif., Ellen Clark Meml. Ctr. for Cancer Research, Am. Acad. of Holistic Chiropractic, LA World Affairs Council; rec: travel, tennis, skiing, sailing. Res: 1127 12th St, 305, Santa Monica 90403 Ofc: Institute for Natural Health, 1424 Lincoln Blvd Ste 200 Santa Monica 90401

GLOVNA, DOLORES CECILIA, real estate broker; b. Aug. 16, 1927, Providence, R.I.; d. Salvatore and Helene Bertha Dorothy (Racewicz) Iorio; m. Steve David Glovna, June 28, 1952; edn: BFA in fashion design & textiles, R.I. Sch. of Design 1949; Calif. lic. real estate broker (1980); GRI, Grad. Realtors Inst., NAR (1980). Career: footwear designer United States Rubber Co., Mishawaka, Ind. 1949-52; freelance designer and fiber artist, in Oakland, Lafayette, San Mateo, Belmont (14 yrs), Calif., 1952-77; active in Hillbarn Theatre (little theatre) as Hillbarn Angel (business) and in costume design assistance; instr. design, form & color in fiber arts & stitchery, also exhibiting artist (sev. awards, Bronze medals); real estate broker asso. Century 21-Lad Realty Inc., Aptos 1977–; mem. Santa Cruz R.E. Exchangors Assn., Santa Cruz Art Museum Assn.; club: Tennis (Rio Del Mar); pub. real estate newsletter (1977-); Democrat; Catholic; rec: walking, swim, fiber arts. Res: 1728 Cheryl Way Aptos 95003 Ofc: Century 21-Lad Realty Inc 9047 Soquel Dr Aptos 95003

GLUNTS, DONALD E., real estate co. president; b. Feb. 5, 1952, Chelsea, Mass.; s. James D. and Georgia (Gabor) G.; m. Jan, Sept. 16, 1979 (div.); edn: Santa Monica City Coll. 1969-71, Anthony R.E. Schools 1972, 74; Calif. lic.

R.E. Broker 1974, Alcohol Beverage Control lic. 1981. Career: mgr. Crown Realty, Venice 1972-76; pres. D.G. Realty, Inc., Venice 1976–; prop. Ports of L.A. Liquors, Pac. Palisades; founding dir. Executive Savings and Loan, Marina Del Rey, 1984-; dir. Venice/Marina del Rey Area Bd. of Realtors, 1978-84; awards: Venice of America, 1983; profl. recognition awards; Master Real Estate Appraiser 1982; mem: CAR, Venice/Marina del Rey Bd. of Realtors, Nat. Council of R.E. Exchangors, R.E. Appraisers Assn.; Jewish; rec: travel. Res: 2228 Prospect Ave Venice 90291 Ofc: D.G. Realty, Inc. 1009 W. Washington Blvd Venice 90291

GLYDON, JULIANA, nursing consultant; b. Oct. 26, 1947, St. Johann Bei Herbestien, Austria, nat. US cit. 1951; d. John and Juliana (Znidarcic) Penic; edn: grad. Allentown Hosp. Sch. of Nsg. 1969; Reg. Nurse (RN), Calif. Bd. Nsg. (1970). Career: health care supr. Brandon (Vt.) Tng. Sch. 1970-71; physician asst., counselor Planned Parenthood, Rutland, Vt. 1971-73, also charge nse. var. convalescent and nursing facilities, 1971-75; dir. of nurses Community Convalescent East (62-bed), Vallejo 1975-77, also Comm. Conv. West (37-bed), 1976-77; pres./bd. chpsn. The Living Centers Mgmt. Corp., 1977-85; nsg. care coord. The Living Centers (2 facilities, 99-bed total), Vallejo 1977-81, nsg. adminstr. Springs Road Living Ctr., Vallejo 1981–; pres. The Unicorn Consulting Services (cons. nsg. mgmt., long term care) 1981–; lectr. inservice tng. classes, Holy Names Coll. (Oakland), The Ombudsman Project (Alameda Co.); clin. supr., long term care, UC San Francisco Sch. of Nsg., and CSU Hayward; honors: named Whole Life Person of Month, The Whole Life Times nat. mag. (6/84), listed Who's Who in Am. Nsg., Soc. of Nsg. Profls. (1984); mem: Calif. Nses. Assn. (Holistic, Long Term Care interest gp.), Council of Nse. Healers, Nses. in Transition support gp. (chair); civic: Vallejo City Unified Sch. Dist. (pres. adv. council for work experience end.), Hospice Svcs. Solano Co. (chair nse. advis. com.), Solano Co. Ombudsman Project (advis. bd.), Vallejo Alzheimer Support Gp. (co-chair); Catholic; rec: English hist., needlework. Res: 1160 Green Valley Rd Napa 94558 Ofc: The Living Centers 1527 Springs Rd Vallejo 94591

GOBAR, ALFRED JULIAN, economist; b. July 12, 1932, Lucerne Valley; s. Julian Smith and Hilda Mary (Millbank) G.; m. Sally Randall, June 17, 1957; children: Wendy b. 1963, Curtis b. 1964, Joseph b. 1971; edn: BA, Whittier Coll. 1953, MA, 1955; PhD, USC 1963. Career: sales engr., asst. to pres., Microdot 1953-55; sales engr., sales mgr. Sutorbilt Corp. 1957-59; advt. and market research exec. Beckman Instruments Inc. 1959-63; corporate mktg. dir./ mgr. long-range plnng. Duetsch Co. 1962-63; senior economist Western Management Consultants Inc. 1963-66; pres. Alfred Gobar Assocs. Inc. 1966–; prof. of finance: USC (1963-64), CSU Los Angeles (1964-80), CSU Fullerton (1968-70); honors: selected Among 100 Most Disting. Living Graduates and Friends of Whittier Coll. (1986), Lambda Alpha, Omicron Delta Epsilon; mem. Am. Soc. of Real Estate Counselors, Town Hall of Calif.; publs: 200+ articles, 1960-; Republican; rec: Marlin fishing, travel. Res: 1100 West Valencia Mesa Dr Fullerton 92633 Ofc: Alfred Gobar Associates Inc 207 S Brea Blvd Brea 92621

GODDARD, HERBERT HARRY, real estate broker; b. June 25, 1903, Edgemont, S.D.; s. Herbert and Carrie (Lehr) G.; m. Bernice Boss, Mar. 31, 1928; children: Beverley, b. 1929, Joanne, b. 1930, James Herbert, b. 1941. Career: building trades (carpenter), L.A. 1923-28; trainee to mgr. S.H. Kress Co., No. & So. Calif., 1928-40; variety store owner, Long Beach area 1940-45; Shipyards fabrication splst., Wilmington 1942-45; real estate broker, Arcadia 1946–; dir. (pres. 1968) Arcadia Bd. of Realtors 10 yrs., Realtor of Year 1971, vice pres. Area 16, Calif. Assn. of Realtors; Civitan Citizen of Year 1959; Legion of Honor DeMolay 1975; mem: Masons, Scottish Rite, Shriners (S.G.V. pres. 1963), High Twelve Club Arcadia (charter pres. 1960, State pres. 1967), pres. Ensign Mayo High Twelve Loan Fund 1974-84, Rotary, Arcadia CofC (pres. 1954), Arcadia Hist. Soc. (pres. 1980); chmn. Arcadia Historical Commn., 1984; Republican; Prot.; rec: fishing, photog., club work. Address: 11 West Longden Ave Arcadia 91006

GODFREY, WILLIAM ROBERT, mortgage banker; b. Oct. 5, 1947, Norwalk, Conn.; s. Ronald George and Audrey (Ralston) G.; m. Louise, Dec. 28, 1973; 1 dau. Lauren b. 1976; edn: BS, Univ. Pittsburgh, 1969. Career: data proc. mgr. Louis Stores Inc., Emeryville 1970-72; data proc. mgr. Sheet Metal Workers of No. Calif., Oakland 1972-74; project mgr. Mason McDuffie Co., Berkeley 1974-78; mgr. mortgage banking div. Management Decision Systems, San Jose 1978-79; senior v.p./dir. mktg. (Risk Mgmt.) Weyerhaeuser Mtg. Corp., Republic Fed. S&L, Walnut Creek 1979–; bd. dirs. Republic Fed. S&L; mem: No. Calif. Mortgage Bankers, Calif. Mortgage Bankers Assn. (co-chair Single Family Com.), Mortgage Bankers Assn. (Single Family Com.); Prot.; rec: sailing, skiing, golf. Ofc: Mason McDuffie Mortgage Corp. 1550 Parkside Dr Walnut Creek 94596

GODWIN, STEPHEN B., rehabilitation counselor, industrial engineer; b. Feb. 11, 1930, Ozark, Ala.; s. Stephen B. and Elizabeth (Renfroe) G.; edn: BS, Auburn Univ. 1952; MA, CSU Northridge 1974; tchg. cred., Calif. Lutheran Coll. 1975; Reg. Profl. Engr., Calif. 1969. Career: standards engr. McDonnell Douglas, St. Louis, Mo. 1953-56; indsl. engr. Carter Carburetor & Union Camp Paper Co., St. Louis, Mo. 1956-62; indsl. engr. Warwick Electroncis 1963-68; senior rehab. counselor Build Industries, No. Hollywood 1972-78; rehab. splst. ADEPT, Panorama City 1978-84; rehab. counselor State of Calif. 1985–; Elem. & Spl. Edn. Tchg. Creds.; honors: Staff Mem. of the Year, ADEPT 1982; Crime Prevention Splst., Los Angeles Police Dept.; mem: Mountain Repeater Radio Club (secty. treas.), Am. Radio Relay League, Studio City Residents Assn. (past v.p.); publs: articles in Aquatic Life mag., Under Glass mag., World Radio; rec: amateur radio operator (Adv. Class Lic., Call KD6ZZ). Ofc: State of Calif., 6150 Van Nuys Blvd. Van Nuys 91401

GOEAS, BRUCE MICHAEL, military officer; b. Oct. 2, 1955, San Francisco; s. Edward Arthur and Nancy Rae (Walker) G.; m. Christina, Apr. 21, 1979; edn: BS bus. adminstrn./ mgmt., San Jose State Univ. 1979; MBA, Univ. So. Dak. 1983; MS human resource mgmt./ devel. (in progress), Chapman Coll. 1984-. Career: mem. AF Missile Combat Crew, flight cmdr., senior flight cmdr. Ellsworth AFB S.D. 1980-84; protocol ofcr. to cmdr. 1st Strategic Aerospace Div. Vandenbertg AFB, Calif. 1984-85, instr. Space & Missile Orientation Course 1985–; instr. bus. edn. Allan Hancock Coll.; honors: Base/ Wing/ Squadron Junior Ofcr. of the Year (Ellsworth AFB 1983), Base Jr. Ofcr. of the Month (Vandenberg 1984), Sect. Instr. of the Month (Vandenberg 1985), Jr. Ofcr. of the Quarter (1985); mem: Am. Mgmt. Assn., AF Assn. (life); currently researching/ writing a curriculum for a corporate univ.; mil: capt. USAF 1979–, AF Commdn., AF Achievement. Outstanding Unit, Combat Readiness; Republican; Catholic; rec: soccer (base varsity team), running. Res: 517 Ash Vandenberg AFB 93437-5000 Ofc: 4315 CCTS/ CMCM Vandenberg AFB 93437-5000

GOEHRING, ARNOLD, bank leasing co. executive; b. Mar. 9, 1939, Tarutine, Rutiania, nat. US cit. 1969; s. Johann and Adele (Mittelstadt) G.; m. Brigitte Binder, Oct. 25, 1963; children: Karen b. 1964, Andreas b. 1965; edn: BS in bus. adm., Bremen, 1958; CPA, Wash. (1973). Career: budget analyst The Boeing Co., Seattle 1966-69; acctg. officer Seattle First Nat. Bank, Seattle 1969-73; chief finl. ofcr. Western Bancorp Data Proc. Co., Los Angeles 1973-76; v.p./mgr. cost mgmt. Seattle First Nat. Bank, 1976-78; v.p./CFO Leasing Subs., Bank of Am., San Francisco 1978-83; exec. v.p./ chief ops. First Interstate Leasing, Inc., Pasadena 1983–, also dir., 1983-; mem. Nat. Assn. Accts., Nat. Assn. Equipt. Lessors (Fed. Govt. Rels. Com. 1986-), Calif. Assn. of Equipt. Lessors (dir. 1985-); Pasadena CofC; mil: 2d lt. West German Army 1960-62; Baptist; rec: golf, boating. Res: 19015 La Crosse Glendora 91740 Ofc: First Interstate Leasing Inc 245 S Los Robles Pasadena 91109

GOERGEN, JAN ROGER, financier; b. Dec. 11, 1935, Caledonia, MN; s. Cass Leon and Flavia Joyce (Evans) G.; m. Karen Rolli, June 25, 1977; edn: BA, Univ. of Minn. 1957; Harvard Bus. (Ext.) 1958-9, London Sch. of Econ. 1968-9, Univ. of Caracas 1977-82, PhD cand., Internat. Econ. Career: Merrill Lynch & Assocs. Investment Corp. 1959-62; vp-finance, sr. v.p., exec. vice pres., pres., pres./chief op. ofcr., currently chmn./chief exec. with Intercap, Ltd. and its affils.; (current) Congl. Advis. Council, US Senatorial Bus. Advis. Bd., Am. Economic Council Found., Nat. Found. for Philanthropy; honors: Eagle Scout, BSA 1950; John Sargeant - Pillsbury Fellow (Univ. Minn. Found. 1964); One of Minn.'s Outstanding (JC's 1967); Order of Bolivar (Venezuela 1980); listed Who's Who in Fin. & Industry; mem: Am. Soc. of Profl. Cons.; clubs: Rancho Santa Fe Garden Club, Univ. of Minn. Found., Eagle Scout Alumni Assn., Big Brother, Little League Football. Works: mng. an investment portfolio for an OPEC member nation (value $3 billion 1975, to over $15 billion value in 1985); devel. first program to achieve infinite leverage in the purchase of US equity securities (1962); estab. first co. to survey and accurately project mutual fund perf. (1964); asstd. in design of first series of US oil and gas lmtd. partnerships (1966); asstd. in design of first fgn.-based US real estate investment trust (1968), trust grew to be largest single owner/mgr. of US properties in just four years; designed first combination travel resort prop. ownership program (1972); mil: 2d lt. US Army (Battlefield Comm.) 1951-52, Purple Heart, Silver Star; Christian; rec: travel, tennis, fishing, swim. Res: POB 1485, Rancho Santa Fe 92067 Ofc: Intercap, Ltd. POB 607, Rancho Santa Fe 92067

GOERT, WILBUR HENRY, dentist, ret.; b. Apr. 24, 1915; s. John W. and Clara Charlotte (Windhorst) G.; m. Arline Richards, June 30, 1941; children: John b. 1945, Sharon b. 1946, Richard b. 1951; edn: BA, CSC Fresno 1938, Lite Cert. Gen. Ed. 1940; DMD, Univ. Ore. 1945. Career: teacher 1940-42; dentist Walla Walla, Wash. 1945-56, Fresno 1956-80; sch. bd., local church acad. finance com.; mem: Am. (life), Calif., Fresno-Madera Dental Assns., Boy Scouts of Am., Kiwanis, Youth Pathfinder Org., Brea Mensa Jurisprudence Assn.; mil: capt. USAF, USAR 1942-51; Republican; Seventh-Day Adventist; rec: farming. Res: 40634 Rd 56 Dinuba 93618

GOERTZEN, DOUGLAS RAY, accountant, hospital administrator; b. May 29, 1948, Hutchinson, Kans.; s. Clarence K. and F. Verna (Siemens) G.; edn: BS acctg., CSU Fresno 1978; Nursing Home Adminstr. Calif. 1983. Career: ops. supv. Crocker Bank Fresno 1970-75; loan ofcr. Pioneer Mortgage Co. Clovis 1975-76; acct. Moore, Grider, Griggs, Cowan & Sudjian CPAs Fresno 1978-81, Raikow & Lewis Accy. Corp. Woodland Hills 1981; acctg. supv./ auditor Beverly Enterprises Inc. Fresno 1981-83; adminstr. Greenhaven Country Place Sacto. 1983-84, The Hillhaven Corp. Woodland 1984-85, Longer Life Found. 1986–; honors: First Place (Central Calif. Speech Contest 1972); mem: Nat. Assn. Accts. (bd. dirs. 1979), Calif. Assn. Health Facilities 1983, Masons, Kiwanis; devel. Ancillary Variance Analsis Worksheet for nation's largest owner/oper. of nursing homes; mil: sp5 Calif. Army Reserve Nat. Guard 1969-78; Republican; Methodist; rec: fishing, boating, horseback riding, all outdoor sports. Ofc: Eagle Enterprises POB 1174 Wheatland 95692

GOINGS, WILLIE, JR., corrosion engineer; b. Aug. 20, 1938, St. Francisville, La.; s. Willie and Mary Lee (Noflin) G.; m. Hattie P., Mar. 10, 1963; children: Monique b. 1967, Fayvette b. 1969; edn: AS, L.A. Trade Tech. 1969, spl. courses CSULA 1975-77; Reg. Profl. Corrosion Engr., Calif. (No. 1003) 1978. Career: sr. fire control opr. Calif. Army Nat. Guard Nike Hercules Air Def. Missile System, Palos Verdes 1965-67; structure assembler Lockheed

Corp., Burbank 1967, McDonnell Douglas Corp., Santa Monica 1967-69; electronics techn. Northrop Nortronics Div., Hawthorne 1969-70; communication techn. So. Calif. Edison Co., Rosemead 1971-73, engring. asst. 1973-78, corrosion splst., 1978 – ; chmn. So. Calif. Cathodic Protection Com. 1981; honors: Alpha Gamma Sigma (1969), appreciation City of Los Angeles (1983); mem. IEEE, Nat. Assn. of Corrosion Engrs., Los Angeles Council of Black Profl. Engrs., Masons; mil: E5 US Army 1960-65, Good Conduct Medal, Army Commendn., Expt. Missileman; Democrat; Christian; rec: interior decor. Res: 15 Flintlock Ln Bell Canyon 91307 Ofc: So California Edison 2244 Walnut Grove Ave Ste 190 Rosemead 91770

GOLDBERGER, MARVIN LEONARD, educator, physicist; b. Oct. 22, 1922, Chgo.; s. Joseph and Mildred (Sedwitz) G.; cousin, Dr. Joseph Goldberger, discoverer of Pellagra cure; m. Mildred Ginsburg, Nov. 25, 1945; children: Joel S., b. 1952, Samuel M., b. 1949; edn: BS, Carnegie Inst. of Tech. 1943; PhD, Univ. Chgo. 1948. Career: asst., assoc. prof. Univ. Chgo., 1950-55, prof. 1955-57; Higgins Prof. of Mathematical Physics, Princeton Univ., 1957-77, chmn. Dept. of Physics, Princeton Univ., 1970-76, Joseph Henry Prof. of Physics, 1977-78; pres. Calif. Inst. of Tech., 1978 – ; bd. dir. Gen. Motors 1980; mem. Pres.'s Sci. Adv. Commn. 1965-69; adv. com. Ofc. of Sci. & Tech., 1959-69; chmn. Nat. Acad. of Scis. Comm. on Internat. Security and Arms Control, 1980; bd. mem. Arms Control Assn., 1985; honors: ScD, Carnegie-Mellon Univ. 1979, ScD, Univ. of Notre Dame 1979, DHL, Hebrew Union Coll. 1980, LLD, Occidental Coll. 1980, Heineman Prize for Mathematical Physics 1961, Pres. Award, New York Acad. of Scis. 1981; mem.: Nat. Acad. of Scis., Am. Physical Soc., Am. Acad. of Arts & Scis., Fedn. of Am. Scientists (chmn. 1972-73), Am. Philosophical Soc., Council on Fgn. Rels., Weizmann Inst. of Sci. (bd. govs.), Am. Com. on East-West Accord, Haskel, Inc. (bd. dirs.), Business-Higher Edn. Forum (adv. bd.), L.A. Children's Mus. (assoc.), Center for Internat. and Strategic Affairs-UCLA (trustee), Aspen Inst. of Humanistic Studies, Nuclear Safety Oversight Comm.; Nuclear Safety Oversight Com.; mil: ssgt. US Corps of Engrs. 1943-46; Democrat; Jewish; rec: gourmet cook, jogging, scuba. Res: 415 S Hill Ave Pasadena 91106 Ofc: Calif. Institute of Technology, Pasadena 91125

GOLDING, CHARLES GREGORY, newspaper publisher; b. Apr. 17, 1957, Fort Ord; s. Theo Harold and Betty Louise (Ricketts) G.; m. Gwendalyn, Nov. 2, 1979; children: Auburn b. 1981, David b. 1982, Greg b. 1984; edn: BA in journ., magna cum laude, Brigham Young Univ. 1981. Career: editor Perris (Calif.) Progress, 1971-75; served 2-yr LDS mission to Quetzaltenango Mission, Guatemala 1977-79; ed. BYU Daily Universe, Provo, Utah 1981; pub. Lake Elsinore Valley Sun-Tribune and Rancho News, 1981 – ; honors: CNPA Better Newspapers Contest 1st Place awards in Best Newspaper Promotion (1982), Best Spot News Photo (1983), Best Editl. Page (1984, 85), Outstanding Comm. Service (1985), and NNA 2d Pl. award Best Newspaper Promo. (1983); mem: Nat. Newspaper Assn. (Calif. state chmn. 1985-), Calif. Newspaper Pubs. Assn. (bd. dirs. 1986-, Seminar Com. 1985-, chmn. Basic Newsroom Tng. sem. 4/86), Am. Press Inst. (grad. Mgmt. of a Weekly Newspaper 1984); Ch. of Jesus Christ of Latter-day Saints; rec: coach Little League. Res: 409 Adobe St Lake Elsinore 92330 Ofc: Sun-Tribune 506 W Graham Ave Ste 104 Lake Elsinore 92330

GOLDMAN, E. B., marketing consultant; b. July 22, 1929, Springfield, Mass.; s. Samuel M. and Esther (Grant) G.; m. Barbara Ann Greene, May 2, 1952; children: Susan b. 1953, Elizabeth b. 1954, Linda b. 1955, Merril b. 1959, Robert b. 1973; edn: Syracuse Univ. 1948-49, Utica Univ. 1947-48, Am. Internat. 1951. Career: sales and purch., Mendolsohn Zeller Co., Los Angeles 1959; salesman Gilman Shandler Co., L.A. 1960-64; Calif. sales mgr. Crown Produce Los Angeles 1964-79; pres., treas., CEO Professional Marketing Consultants Inc., 1980 – ; also cons., v.p. and chief of finance Meridian Entertainment Corp. Hollywood 1986 – ; owner Two Hipp Stables (breeding Standardbreds); awards: Trading mem. Blue Book, BCA award Red Book; mil: s/sgt. US Air Force 1950-54; rec: patron and collector original oils by artist AB Makk. Address: Beverly Hills 90212

GOLDSMID, MICHAEL ALAN, optometrist; b. Feb. 15, 1958, Johannesburg, So. Africa; s. Julian Harry Walter and Eileen Hannelore (David) G.; edn: BS, cum laude, Univ. of Houston 1980, OD, 1982. Career: extern ocular pathology & diagnosis, Miami, Fla. 1982; pvt. practice optometry, San Diego 1983 – ; tng. in art of refraction and contact lenses; B.S.K. internat. honor grad. 1982; Fellow Am. Acad. Optometry 1984; Noteworthy Practitioner 1984; mem: Am., Calif. and Tex. Optometric Assns., Am. Acad. of Optometry, Royal Soc. of Health, Better Vision Inst., Am. Publica Health Assn., Lions Vision Clinic; mil: pvt. photo-journalist, Signals; rec: classical pianist. Ofc: Dr. Goldsmid, 3750 Sports Arena Blvd. Ste. 9 San Diego 92110

GOLDSTEIN, MICHAEL STUART, computer systems co. executive; b. Apr. 22, 1945, NYC, s. David and Ann (Klotz) G.; m. Penny J. Donaldson, May 4, 1968; children: David John b. 1971, Darren Stuart b. 1979; edn: BA, UC Los Angeles 1966. Career: promotions mgr. Transamerica Fin., Los Angeles 1966-70; Western regional mgr. Trans Union Systems Corp., Los Angeles, Chgo. 1970-78; pres. Mutogo Data Corp., Irvine 1978 – ; condr. num. seminars in field; cons. in computer systems; mem: Data Entry Mgmt. Assn., Data Processing Mgmt. Assn., Am. Mgmt. Assn. Ofc: Mutogo Data Corp. 15560-E Rockfield Blvd Irvine 92718

GOLDSTEIN, ROBERT STANLEY, contractor; b. Jan. 11, 1923, Kansas City, Mo.; s. Leo Roy and Doris (Binks) G.; edn: Northwestern 1946-47. Career: soldier of fortune Africa (8 yrs.), last personal envoy to US for Col. Ojuku,

Biafran War; pres./ chmn. bd. Federated Advtg., 1970-78; gen. contr./ pres./ chmn. bd. Pittsburgh Metals 1974-84; honors: TV and Radio Pub. Svc., Mayor Sam Yorty, City of L.A. 1973, and Calif. State Assemblyman Hank Arklin, 1970; mem. State Congl. Advsry. Bd.; mil: lt. col. US Army Air Corps; Republican; rec: flying, horse racing. Res: 7224 Hillside Los Angeles 90046 Ofc: Pittsburgh Metals, 808 S Vermont Los Angeles 90005

GOLDSTRAND, DENNIS JOSEPH, financial and estate planning executive; b. July 12, 1952, Oakland; s. Joseph N. and Frances M. G.; edn: BSBA, CSU Chico 1975; Chartered Life Underwriter 1986. Career: asst. mgr. Household Finance Corp. 1975-76; reg. rep. Equitable Financial Svcs. 1976-79, dist. mgr. 1979-85; ptnr. Goldstrand & Small Ins. & Financial Svcs. 1986 – ; honors: Million Dollar Round Table (1984-86), Nat. Champion (Equitable Fin. Svcs. 1982), Nat. Quality Award (NALU 1985-86), Nat. Sales Achievement (NALU 1986); mem: Stockton Assn. Life Underw. (bd. 1986-87, guest spkr. 1986), Life Underw. Political Action Com., Leading Life Ins. Producers of No. Calif., Million Dollar Round Table Found., Greater Stockton CofC, Mex. Am. CofC, Repub. Presdl. Task Force (trustee), Univ. Pacific Athletic Found.; publ: article in Life Insurance Selling (1986); Republican; rec: tennis. Res: 2828 Appling Cir Stockton 95209 Ofc: Goldstrand & Small 2155 W March Ln Ste 2C Stockton 95207

GOLPER, JOHN BRUCE, lawyer; b. Sept. 6, 1950, El Paso, Texas; s. Dr. Marvin Norman and Jean Rose (Becker) G.; m. Leslie Ann Lawry, Mar. 21, 1981; children: Matthew b. 1982, Brian b. 1983; edn: BA, honors, Indiana Univ. 1972; JD, UCLA Law Sch. 1975; admitted to Calif. State Bar (1975), US Supreme Ct. (1981), US Circuit Ct. Appeal (9th Cir. 1976, 3d Cir. 1982), US Dist. Ct. (Central, No., So., East Dists. Calif., 1976, 81, 81, 86). Career: law clk. Whittaker Corp., Los Angeles 1973-74; extern law clk. Calif. Ct. of Appeal (1st App. Dist.) 1974; summer law clk. Bodkin, McCarthy, Sargent & Smith, L.A. 1974, assoc. atty. 1975-78; ptnr. Parker, Milliken, Clark, O'Hara & Samuelian, L.A. 1978-86; ptnr. Ballard & Rosenberg (spec. labor and employment law rep. mgmt.), L.A. 1986 – ; apptd. by Gov. Deukmejian to Calif. Comparable Worth Task Force 1984-86; honors: Indiana State "Hoosier Scholar" (1968), Grable Meml. Scholar (1968), Honors Div. Merit Scholar (1971-72), recipient recogn. certs. Compensation Practices Assn. San Diego Co. (1983, 84), and Electronic Salary and Wage Assn. (1985), listed Who's Who in Am. Law (1986); mem: Am. Bar Assn., Calif. State Bar Assn., L.A. Co. Bar Assn., Indsl. Rels. Research Assn.; clubs: Jonathan, US Ski Assn., UCLA Law Sch. Dean's Council, UCLA Alumni Assn. (life), Indiana Univ. Alumni Assn. (life), Sigma Alpha Mu frat.; contbr. num. chapters and articles in law and labor law jours., contbg. ed. PMCO Labor Report (1982-86); Republican; Jewish; rec: tennis, alpine ski. Res: 650 Hampton Rd Arcadia 91006 Ofc: Ballard & Rosenberg, 1900 Ave of the Stars Ste 2300 Los Angeles

GOMEZ, ELEZIER CARDENAS, silversmith; b. Aug. 30, 1937, Jalisco, Mexico; s. Eufracio and Angelina C. (Onopa) G.; m. Norma Armenta, Apr. 16, 1968; edn: AA bus. data processing, East L.A. Coll. 1970. Career: worked in family silversmithing shop in Mexico making jewelry; Airstream Trailers 1962-63; M&O Engrg. Co. 1965-68; Quaker City Plating Silversmiths Whittier 1971-73; owner, oper. Eli Silversmiths La Habra 1974 – ; mem: Metal Finishers Assn., La Habra CofC; restored num. metal antiques for museums and pvt. collectors; designer of silver jewelry; mil: pvt. 4/c US Army 1963-65; rec: soccer (player & coach). Res: Hacienda Heights 91745 Ofc: Eli Silversmiths 113 W 1st Ave La Habra 90631

GOMEZ, JESSE SENOVIO, physician; b. Oct. 11, 1950, Corpus Christi, Texas; s. Jesse S., Sr. and Mercedes (Gutierrez) G.; edn: BS, Texas A&M Univ 1973; Univ. of Wash. 1973-74; MD, Univ. of Minn. 1980. Career: internship Univ. of N.Dak. 1980; medical director North Coast Industrial Med. Clinic of San Diego, 1983 – ; indsl. medicine consultant for 362 companies; honors: AMA Physicians Recogn. Award; mem. North County Jazz Musicians group; mil: lt. US Navy M.C. 1981-83; Republican; Catholic; rec: rock and jazz music. Ofc: No Coast Industrial Med. Clinic, 2461 Impala Dr Carlsbad 92008

GONDA, THOMAS ANDREW, physician; b. Aug. 24, 1921, Vienna, Austria, nat. 1929; s. Victor Emanuel and Ossy (Kopp) G.; m. Elizabeth Marie Chandler, July 3, 1944; children: Paul b. 1945, William b. 1948, Lynn b. 1953; edn: Univ. of Chgo. 1939-40; AB, Stanford Univ. 1942, MD, 1945. Career: clin. dir. psychiatry San Francisco Hosp. 1949-51; chief neurol. and psychiat. VA Hosp. San Francisco 1951-53; instr. Stanford Sch. of Med. 1953-55, asst. prof. 1955-58, assoc. prof. 1958-65, prof. 1965 – , assoc. dean 1967-75; dir. Stanford Univ. Hosp. 1968-74; med. dir. Stanford Univ. Med. Ctr. 1974-75; chmn. dept. psychiat. and behav. sci. 1975 – ; vis. prof. Inst. of Exptl. Psychol. Oxford Univ. England; awards: Am. Med. Writers Assn. 1984; outstanding achievement No. Calif. Psychiat. Soc. 1984; fellow: Am. Coll. of Psychiatrists; Am. Psychiat. Assn. (life); mem: AMA 1945-; author book: Dying Dignified (1984); over 50 med. and sci. jour. publs.; mil: capt. US Army 1946-48; rec: antique autos (Replicars), philately. Ofc: Stanford Univ. Stanford 94305

GONDO, YASUHIRO, banking executive; b. Feb. 25, 1936, Shinagawa, Tokyo; s. Shigemi and Kikue (Sawatari) G.; m. Yoko, May 25, 1967; 1 dau, Nozomi b. 1972; edn: Econs. MD, Tokyo Univ. 1962. Career: Nippon Credit Bank 1962 – ; Tokyo and Osaka; dept. gen. mgr. NY br., and gen. plnng. div., 3 yrs.; gen. mgr., agent Los Ageles Agency 1983 – ; mem: Japan Bus. Assn., Internat. Bankers Assn. of Calif., Univ. Club of L.A.; Buddhist. Res: 2695 Tura Ln. San Marino 91108 Ofc: Nippon Credit Bank Ltd., 800 Wilshire Blvd. Ste. 1460 Los Angeles 90017

GONZALES, LUCILLE CONTRERAS, educator; b. Nov. 30, 1937, Colton, Calif.; d. Antonio Colunga and Romona (Arroyo) Contreras; m. Enrique Gonzales, 1960; children: Leticia Maria b. 1961, Cecilia Maria b. 1963; edn: AA, San Bernardino Valley Jr. Coll. 1958; BA, UC Santa Barbara 1960; MA, Claremont Grad. Sch. 1969; adminstrv. credl., CSU Fullerton 1977. Career: Chino Unified Sch. Dist. 1960-85: classroom tchr. 1960-70, bilingual classroom tchr. 1970-74, coord. bilingual edn. 1974-76, coord. consolidated application & intergroup relations 1976-77, supr. spl. projects 1977-78, adminstr. spl. projects 1978-82, dir. spl. projects 1982-85; dir. state and fed. pgms. Pomona Unif. Sch. Dist. 1985–; rep. Calif. State Dept. of Edn. in Pgm. Reviews and Sch. Plan Review 1980-82; honors: Outstanding Elem. Tchr. (1972), Friend of Magnolia Jr. H.S. (1980), listed Who's Who: Am. Women, West, World WW of Women, others, listed 2000 Notable Americans, Dir. of Disting. Americans, 5000 Personalities of the World, Internat. Book of Honor, Biography of the Year; mem: Assn. of Calif. Sch. Adminstrs. 1974-, Chino Assn. of Mgmt. Personnel 1974-, Pi Lambda Theta 1966-, Delta Kappa Gamma 1972-, Phi Delta Kappa 1986-, PEO chpt. CS 1972-, Assn. San Bernardino Co. Adminstrs. of Consol. Application Pgms. (pres. 1981-82), Migrant Edn. (exec. bd. 1978-), Assn. of Secondary Spl. Projects 1980-82, Large Urban Directors 1985-, Calif. Assn. of Adminstrs. of State and Fed. Pgms. 1985-, Nat. Assn. Female Execs. 1979-; master trainer for program quality reviews; publs: ESL Handbook; Democrat; Catholic; rec: reading, gardening. Res: 4955 Tyler St Chino 91710 Ofc: Pomona Unified Sch. Dist., 800 S Garey Ave Pomona 91766

GOODBODY, TERRY GEORGE, computer executive; b. Aug. 18, 1944, San Diego; s. Francis and Jeanne (Lane) G.; m. Anita Miknuk, May 15, 1982; children: Sean b. 1969, Terri b. 1972; edn: Bach. equiv., Marine Corps Sch. Info. Mgmt. 1961-63. Career: project mgr. IBM, Poughkeepsie, NY 1968-72; mgr. fin. systems Nat. Steel & Shipbldg., San Diego 1972-76; cons. CACI, US Navy, Harrisburg, Pa. 1976-79; mgr. Carter Hawley Hale Stores Inc., Anaheim 1980-83; v.p. Calif. Fed. Svgs & Loan, Rosemead 1984-85; pres./CEO I-See Corp., Anaheim 1983–; dir. data proc. The Orange County Register, Santa Ana 1986–; guest lectr. on data proc. mgmt. for var. profl. assn. confs. 1975-, incl. DPMA Confs. (Tokyo 1985, Nice, Fr. 1983), Pharmaceutical Mgmt. Assn. (Phoenix, Az. 1984); frequent speaker local orgns. and clubs, 1986-; mem: Data Proc. Mgmt. Assn., Data Adminstrn. Mgmt. Assn.; author book: Managing the Three Resource of Data Processing (1985), art. in Computerworld mag. (2/83); mil: s/sgt. USMC 1961-68, Cuba crisis, Vietnam Campaign, Good Conduct, Pres. Cit.; Republican; Catholic; rec: boating, golf, ski, classic cars. Res: 5997 E Calle Principia Anaheim Hills 92807 Ofc: The Register 625 N Grand Ave Santa Ana 92701

GOODMAN, ROBERT CEDRIC, lawyer; b. Sept. 16, 1956, Burbank; s. William Arthur and Nancy Jane (Furbush) G.; edn: AB, magna cum laude, Brown Univ. 1978; JD, Univ. of Chicago Law Sch. 1983. Career: chief political reporter KJRH-TV, Tulsa, Okla. 1978-80; assoc. Feldman, Waldman & Kline, San Francisco 1983–; mem: Am. Bar Assn. (v.chr. Young Lawyers Div. Com. on Pro Bono and Delivery Legal Svcs. 1985-), State Bar of Calif. (edtl. bd. California Lawyer magazine 1985-), San Francisco Bar Assn., Phi Delta Phi, Commonwealth Club of Calif., Brown Univ. Club of No. Calif., Brown Univ. Alumni Schs. Pgm. (chr., Tulsa, Okla. chpt. 1978-80); Democrat; Catholic; rec: jazz, contemporary art, running. Res: 144 Carl St, No. 5., San Francisco 94117 Ofc: Feldman, Waldman & Kline, 235 Montgomery St San Francisco 94104

GOODNIGHT, BRADLEY ALAN, investment executive; b. May 22, 1954, Marysville; s. Clyde Lee and Marvin Gladys (Turner) G.; m. Bannie J., Aug. 13, 1977; children: Kelly b. 1980, Laurie b. 1983; edn: BS, CSU Chico 1977. Career: mktg. splst. computers Burroughs Corp., San Francisco 1977; stockborker Paine Webber 1978–; currently, acct. v.p. investments; John Nuveen Nat. Adv. Council; honors: (2) Pacesetter Sales Achiev., Paine Webber; Investment Co. Club, 1984, 1985; mem: Delta Sigma Pi, Native Sons of the Golden West (pres. elec.), Gold Country Lions; Republican (Nev. Co. Central Com.); rec: golf, skiing, gardening. Res: 629 Norlene Way Grass Valley 95949 Ofc: Paine Webber, 102 Banic St. Grass Valley 95945

GOODRICH, WILLIAM CHARLES, trade association executive; b. Nov. 16, 1943, Denver, Colo.; s. Herbert Lynn and Frances Luola (Turner) G.; m. Mary Louise, Jan. 30, 1963; children: Lori Lynn b. 1963, Lesha Raye b. 1963, Billie Louise b. 1969; edn: AA, Long Beach City Coll. 1976; BBA, Columbia Pacific Univ. 1980; courses UC Irvine 1982-83, Univ. Denver 1962-63; CLU, Chartered Life Underwriter, Am. Coll. 1975. Career: gen. agent Woodmen of the World, Downey 1968-76; v.p. American Finl. Union, Downey 1976-78; senior v.p. Western Growers Assn., Irvine 1978-83; pres. United Agric. Assn., Santa Ana 1983–; honors: nat. sales award (1974, 75, 76), nat. quality award (1975, 76) NALU, fraternal counsellor, Calif. State Frat. Assn.; mem: Orange County Soc. of CLUs (Edn. Com.), Am. Soc. of Assn. Execs., Am. Soc. CLUs, United Fresh Fruit & Vegetable Assn., Produce Mktg. Assn.; mem. Masons, Civil Air Patrol, Aircraft Owners & Pilots Assn.; speaker: Symposium Medicus (1981), TV show guest (1985), participant Internat. Reins. Conf., Bermuda (1984, 85); Republican; Prot.; rec: pilot, microcomputers. Ofc: United Agricultural Assn. 1570 Brookhollow Santa Ana 92705

GOODWIN, WALTER ARNOLD, co. executive; b. Jan. 31, 1922, Poca, W.Va.; s. Reverdy Elliot and Elizeth (Durst) G.; m. Deloise, Apr. 17, 1947; children: Walter A., Jr. b. 1948, Terry Deloise b. 1950; edn: Troy H.S. 1939. Career: owner Goodwin Vending Service, Los Angeles 1949-68, Serra Automatic Sales, Placerville 1969-72, Aero Pacific Sales, San Diego 1973–; clubs: Masons, Shriners, Elks; mil: 1st sgt. US Army Ordnance 1941-45; Republican; Prot. Res: 135 Pepper Tree Rd Chula Vista 92010

GORBIS, BORIS ZINOVJEVICH, lawyer; b. Aug. 29, 1950, Odessa, USSR, nat. US cit. 1985; s. Zinovy R. and Nelli (Goldenstein) G.; m. Eda Jacobashvili, Nov. 29, 1981; 1 son Andrew Rafael b. 1985; edn: bS, Odessa Inst. Tech. 1969; MA, Univ. Odessa 1972; JD, UC Berkeley 1980. Career: immigrated to US 1975; pres. RETTCO 1976-80; assoc. atty. Graham & James, Los Angeles 1980-82; founding atty. Law Offices of Boris Z. Gorbis, Los Angeles, San Francisco, Santa Ana 1982–; vis. prof. Stanford Univ. (1976); bd. dirs. Am. Jewish Congress SF (1976), Westside JCC, LA (1982-84), New Am. Talent Assn.; mem: ABA, Trial Lawyers Assn. of Am., Calif. Trial Lawyers Assn., LA Trial Lawyers Assn., past pres. (2 terms) Internat. Law Soc. of Boalt Hall 1977-79; civic: New Times, Guardians, Republican Senatl. Inner Circle, Russian Republican Club; publs. (5) in psycholinguistics and gen. theory of communication; rec: pol. and advt. button collector, New Americans contbn. to Am. culture. Res: 1531 N Crescent Hts Blvd Los Angeles 90046

GORDER, CHARLES FRANKLIN, JR., lawyer; b. Feb. 23, 1952, Mason City, Iowa; s. Charles Franklin, Sr., and Bonnie (Brunner) G.; m. Carol Lynn Griest, June 27, 1981; edn: BA, UC Riverside 1973; JD, UC Berkeley 1976; admitted Calif. Bar 1976. Career: law clk. US District Judge Samuel P. King, Honolulu, Hawaii 1976-77; assoc. Orrick, Herrington, Rowley & Sutcliffe, San Francisco 1978-79; Asst. US Attorney, So. District of Calif. 1980-, Spl. Prosecutions -Fraud, 1984–; awards: spl. commendation for outstanding service Dept. of Justice 1983; mem. San Diego County Bar Assn., S.D. Zoological Soc. US Atty's Office: 940 Front St, Rm 5-9-19, San Diego 92189

GORDIN, JAMES ALLAN, corporate financial executive; b. Apr. 30, 1950, Modesto; s. Clark Duane and Gertrude Mary (Jenck) G.; edn: AA, Modesto Jr. Coll. 1971; BA in bus. adm., CSC Stanislaus 1973; Certified Public Acct., Calif. (1977). Career: staff acct. Robert G. Martin Acctcy. Corp., Modesto 1973-75; auditor, supvg. senior Fox & Co., CPAs, Stockton 1976-80; asst. controller James Horn Constrn. Co., Modesto 1980-83; v.p./chief finl. ofcr./ controller CuraCare, Inc. (subs. National Medical Ents.), Modesto 1983–; instr. statistical sampling, Delta Coll., Stockton 1977-78; honors: acad. scholarship awards Foster Farms (1969), Modesto Board of Realtors (1968); mem. Am. Inst. of CPAs, Calif. Soc. of CPAs, Modesto Apartment Assn.; Modesto Men's Bowling Assn.; Democrat; Catholic; rec: bowling (av. 84-85, book 215). Res: 212 Parry Ave Modesto 95354 Ofc: CuraCare, Inc. 1400 Lone Palm Ave Modesto 95351

GORDON, BETTY HALSTEAD, publisher; b. Feb. 16, 1925, Ironton, Ohio; d. Ira Roosevelt and Peggy Elizabeth (Riley) Halstead; m. Richard MacKenzie, Aug. 10, 1944 (div. 1963); children: Peggy b. 1945, James b. 1947 (decd.), Matthew b. 1949, Anne b. 1950, Elise b. 1955; m. 2d Alvin Gordon, May 14, 1966; edn: Marshall Univ. 1942-43; El Camino Coll. 1957-58; Univ. Ariz. 1971-72. Career: social news columnist Charleston (WV) Daily Mail 1950-53; dir. McHenry Models Charleston 1953-55; ofc. mgr. Malcolm Marlis DDS Hawthorne, Calif. 1958-62; secty. to author Irving Wallace Brentwood 1964-66; freelance ed. Sonoma Calif. 1967-80; ed., publr. Meiklejohn Edn. Found. Quarterly 1982-86; owner, publr. Arcus Pub. Co. 1983–; dir. Meiklejohn Edn. Found. 1984-; corp. ofcr. El Paseo de Sonoma Corp. 1975–; trustee N.H. Gordon Corp. Trust 1970–; mem: Internat. Assn. Independent Publrs., Publrs. Mktg. Assn., Sonoma County Press Club, Sonoma League for Historic Preservation, Friends of Sonoma Library, Mus. Soc.; Democrat; Protestant; rec: gardening, birdwatching, reading, writing. Ofc: Arcus Pub. Co. POB 228 Sonoma 95476

GORDON, GARY BABCOCK, research and development manager, inventor; b. Nov. 16, 1939, Portland, Ore.; s. George Wm. and Francis Jean (Babcock) G.; m. Nicola Whitney, June 16, 1962; children: Kimberly b. 1963, Benjamin b. 1968; edn: BSEE, UC Berkeley 1962; MSEE, Stanford Univ. 1969; FCC lic. pvt. pilot, 1/C Comml. Radiotel. Cert. & Extra-Class Amateur Radio lics. Career: R&D mgr. Laser Measurements, Hewlett-Packard Co., Palo Alto 1971-73, R&D mgr. Logic Products, (credited with pioneering HP's entry into instrumentation for digital design, from the Logic Probe, thru to HP's 1st Logic Analyzer) 1973-79, project mgr. Laboratory Robotics, HP Labs., 1979–; assoc. prof. CSU San Jose; awards: NROTC Scholar, UCB (4 yrs), named one of HP's most noteworthy inventors in co. publ. (1986); Holder 16 patents in fields of instrumentation, controls and optics (including Logic Probe, Logic Clip, Logic Pulser, Signature Analyzer, Remote Laser Interferometer, and Sports-Camera Autofocuser), products have been featured on 7 mag. covers; author num. tech. articles and presentations; mil: lt. US Navy 1962-66, communs. and surveillance; Republican; Prot.; rec: flying, jogging, contemp. furniture and residence design. Ofc: Hewlett-Packard Co 1651 Page Mill Rd Palo Alto 94304

GORDON, LINDA R., health care co. executive; b. Sept. 10, 1941, Toledo, Ohio; d. Ralph H. and Juanita (Royster) Radabaugh; m. Andrew K. Gordon, Apr. 2, 1982; children: nee McCabe: Rebecca b. 1966, Melinda b. 1968; edn: BS in edn., Ohio State Univ. 1963; grad. Stanford Univ. Executive Pgm. 1985; Calif. lic. Preceptor/ Nsg. Home Adminstr. (1984). Career: founder, gen. ptnr./ exec. dir. two 150-bed convalescent hosps., two adult day care centers, Sacramento; preceptor, Calif. Board of Nursing Home Adminstrs.; developed tchg. hosps. for gerontology pgms. with Community Colls., Sacto.; mem: Am. Coll. of Health Care Adminstrs. (Calif. Chpt. Edn. Com. chair), Calif. Assn. of Health Facilities, Golden Empire Health Systems Agency (Policy Review Com.), Comstock Club; Republican; Protestant; rec: sailing, skiing, tennis. Ofc: Greenhaven 415 Florin Rd Sacramento 95831

GORDON, ROBERT CHARLES, JR., hospital administrator; b. Dec. 14, 1943, Wilkinsburg, Pa.; s. Robert Charles and Dorothy Mae (Denning) G.; m.

Yvonne C. Cordova, Aug. 22, 1969; children: Christy E. b. 1972, Anthony M. b. 1976; edn: AA pol. sci., Fullerton Jr. Coll. 1968; BA pol. sci. & pub. adminstrn., CSU Fullerton 1970; MPH hospital adminstrn., UC Los Angeles 1976; JD, Western State Univ. 1979. Career: adminstrv. asst. UC Irvine Med. Ctr. 1969-74; asst. adminstr. Hoag Meml. Hosp. Newport Beach 1975-80; c.e.o. Barstow Comm. Hosp. 1980-82, Hillside Hosp. San Diego 1982–; nom. Am. Coll. Health Care Execs.; mem: Am. Coll. Osteopathic Hosp. Admnstrs., So. Calif. Health Care Mktg. Soc., Independent Comm. Hosps. of San Diego (bd. 1983-), Hosp. Council Shared Svcs. (bd. 1983-), Univ. Club, Mid-City CofC, S.D. CofC; mil: Airman 1/c USAF 1962-66, AF Commdn.; rec: tennis, chess. Res: 11724 Negley St San Diego 92131 Ofc: Hillside Hosp. 1940 El Cajon Blvd San Diego 92104

GORINSTEIN, ISRAEL, physician; b. Jan. 10, 1943, USSR, nat. 1984; s. Moisei and Leyica (Preiger) G.; m. Rachel Sandler, Sept. 21, 1972; children: Janna, b. 1974, Eric, b. 1981; edn: MD, Orenburg 1965; neurology, UCLA 1983. Career: chief neurology Lvov State Hosp. 1965-78; res. UCLA 1980-83; solo practice Israel Gorinstein, MD, Inc., Los Angeles 1983–; mem: Am. Acad. Neurology, Los Angeles Soc. Neurology, Am. EEG Soc., Thalians; Republican; Jewish; rec: downhill skiing, chess. Res: 404 Laurel St Los Angeles 90048 Ofc: Israel Gorinstein, MD, Inc., 9201 Sunset Ste. 905, Los Angeles 90069

GORMAN, JAMES RADCLIFF, lawyer; b. May 12, 1944, Phila.; s. John Donald and Margaret M. (Meighan) G.; children: James Jr b. 1970, Margaret b. 1970, Brian b. 1980; edn: BS, Penn. State Univ.; JD, Univ. San Diego 1975; admitted Calif. State Bar 1976. Career: pilot USN 1966-73; USNR 1973-78; atty. law firm McDonald, Pulaski & Harlan 1975-78; self-employed Newport Beach 1978–; law instr. UC Irvine Sch. of Law 1977-78; mem: Am., Orange Co. bar assns., Exchange Club of Irvine (pres.), Newport Harbor Area CofC 1980-, Irvine CofC 1984-; mil: lt. cmdr. USN 1966-73, USNR 1973-78, Air Medal; rec: flying, skiing. Ofc: 4000 MacArthur Blvd, Ste 5500, Newport Beach 92660

GORRIE, PETER WILLIAM, chief operating officer; b. Dec. 30, 1942, Toronto, Ont., Canada, nat. US cit. 1963; s. Peter and Grace Evelyn (Daniels) G.; m. Dolores Garza, Dec. 25, 1966; children: Peter Scott b. 1969, Tami b. 1977; edn: BS, San Diego State Univ. 1968. Career: asst. mgr. Canuck, Inc. San Diego 1957-66; ofc. mgr. Garza Constrn., San Diego 1966-68; auditor City of S.D. 1968-69; mgr. acctg. Burroughs Corp., Carlsbad 1969-73; controller Psychology Today mag., Del Mar 1973-75; controller Calif. Instruments, S.D. 1975-78; senior v.p. Gremlin Inds., Inc., S.D. 1978-84; chief ops. ofcr. Omnar Technologies, Inc., S.D. 1984–; honors: merit awards (United Way/CHAD 1976, 80); mem: Soc. of Govtl. Accts. 1968-73, Nat. Assn. Accts. 1968-, Personnel Mgmt. Assn. 1976-81; mil: capt. USMC 1961-64, 2 Meritorious Masts for outstanding performance; Republican; Episcopal; rec: golf, gardening, photog. Res: 4460 Huggins St San Diego 92122 Ofc: Omnar Technologies, Inc., 9938 Via Pasar San Diego 92126

GOSDEN, FREEMAN F., JR., advertising agency president; b. July 12, 1928, Chgo.; s. Freeman and Leta G.; m. Dorothy Paxton, Nov. 29, 1954; children: Lee, b. 1956, Jill, b. 1958; edn: BA in econ., Princeton Univ. 1950. Career: account exec. Young & Rubicam Inc., 1954-56; acct. exec. BBDO, 1956-62; dir. corp. communications Dart Industries, 1963-67, v.p. Service Indus. Group, 1968-71, pres. MCRB Div., 1972-73, pres. Me-Books Div., 1973-75; pres. Smith- Hemmings- Gosden, Los Angeles 1976–, in 1984 SHG sold to Foote, Cone & Belding, remain pres. SHG and also pres. FCB/Direct, San Francisco 1984–; v.chmn. Direct Marketing Assn. (NYC, Wash DC); pres. Direct Mktg. Club So. Calif.; instr. CSU Northridge; conduct num. seminars on direct mktg. var. univs. and major corps.; trustee: Univ. of Redlands, Direct Mktg. Ednl. Found.; publs: direct mktg. columnist ADWEEK, contbg. ed. DIRECT MARKETING; mil: 1st lt, psy. warfare, US Army; mem. The Beach Club (pres. 1977). Res: 211 Barlock Ave Los Angeles 90049 Ofc: Smith-Hemmings-Gosden, 3360 Flair Dr El Monte 91731

GOSLINE, CARL ANTHONY, environmental planning and management consultant; b. Feb. 11, 1921, Beloit, Wis.; s. Carl Anthony, Sr. and La Rene (Halls) G.; m. Carol Tiffany, June 18, 1941; 1 son, Carl b. 1941; edn: BA zool., Univ. Iowa 1941; bus. adm. cert. Alexander Hamilton Inst. 1954; spl. courses Stanford Univ. Grad. Sch. Bus. 1967, 68. Career: bus. exec. w/ multi-functional, multi-industry experience in hazardous waste mgmt., environmental issues, planning, technol. transfer and troubleshooting; pres. Gosline Assocs.; past senior environmental ofcr. Occidental Petroleum Corp., pres./CEO Rollins Environ. Svcs., environ. staff exec. Chem. Mfrs. Assn., exec. v.p. Systems Assocs. Inc., v.p. Fibreboard Corp., exec. v.p. Hexcel Corp., exec. v.p. Univ. Patents, research engr./ dir. DuPont Co. Engring. Test Ctr., field supvr. Hanford Engr. Works - Univ. Chgo.; assigned to Manhattan Project, 1943, to devel. safeguard protocols for dispersion of stack gasses from plutonium separation plant ops.; bd. dirs: Lake County Energy Inc., Little Lake Devel. Corp. and Mendocino Devel. corp.; apptd. Mendocino County Solid Waste Mgmt. Bd. (public mem.) and Devel. Corp.; author 40+ scholarly publs., tech. papers, num. trade jour. and public forums; rec: history, fishing, dog. Res: 27280 Bear Terrace Willits 95490 Ofc: Gosline Associates POB 1567 Willits 95490

GOSNEY, JACK RAY, financial services co. president; b. Mar. 29, 1933, Portland, Ore.; s. Frank Russell and Mildred Lauelle (Wrisley) G.; m. Mary, June 20, 1959; children: John b. 1960, Daniel b. 1961, Elizabeth b. 1963, Karen b. 1964, Jennifer b. 1971; edn: BS, San Francisco State Univ. 1960; MBA, Cal. Poly. Univ. 1972; Certified Financial Planner, Cal. Lutheran Univ. 1986; real estate broker Calif. 1977. Career: asst. claims mgr. Kaiser Steel, Inc., Fontana, Calif. 1960-73; practicing tax cons. Riverside 1961–; owner acctg. firm Riverside 1973-81; owner real estate firm Riverside 1977-81; v.p. adminstrn. & fin. Dave Tucker & Assoc. Inc., San Bernardino 1981-83; owner acctg. & real estate firm Riverside 1983–; CFO Inland Mgmt., Inc., Riverside 1983-86, pres. 1986–; real estate assoc. Now Realty, Inc. 1977-79; honors: Realtor of the Year (Now Realty 1979); mem: Internat. Assn. Fin. Planners, Internat. Assn. Bus. Planners & Fin. Cons. 1983-86, Am. Mgmt. Assn. 1960-86, Calif. Sheriffs Assn. 1985-86, Riverside Bd. of Realtors 1977-81, Delta Sigma Pi 1958-60, Riverside CofC 1985-86; mem. spl. edn. com. for Riverside County Schs. 1982-84; spl. deputy County of San Bernardino Sheriff's Dept. 1984-86; developer and gen. ptnr. Woodcrest Profl. Ctr. Ofc. Complex, Riverside 1986; publr. Lifeline financial newsletter 1985-86; mil: AC3 USN 1952-56; Republican; Protestant; rec: classic sports cars, philately. Res: 16535 Rancho Escondido Riverside 92506 Ofc: Inland Mgmt. Inc. 17241 Van Buren Blvd Ste A Riverside 92504

GOSSARD, THOMAS WESTON, company president; b. Oct. 14, 1948, Glendale; s. Weston D. and Dorothy Eva (Fleming) G.; children: Jason Thomas b. 1970, Staci Lorraine b. 1972; edn: AA, Orange Coast 1974; CSU Fullerton. Career: carpenter, v.p. D.L. Godbey & Sons, Santa Fe Springs 1972-81; pres. The Gossard Corp., Huntington Beach 1981–; mil: E-4 USN 1968-72; Republican; rec: tennis, flying. Ofc: The Gossard Corp., 19171 Beach Blvd. Ste. D Huntington Beach 92698

GOTTESMAN, JUDITH D'VERA, real estate broker; b. Dec. 1, 1936, Chgo.; d. Harry and Helen Irene (Seltzer) Bilski; div.; 1 son, Howard b. 1960; edn: BA, UC Los Angeles 1958; Calif. lic. real estate broker; realtor. Career: tchr. L.A. City Schs., Portola Jr. H.S., 1970-76; realtor assoc. Fred Sands Realtors: one of Top 6 Producers in County 1976-77, asst. mgr. Brentwood ofc. 1978, assoc. mgr. Beverly Hills ofc. 1979, sales mgr. Woodland Hills, 1979-80; mgr./prin. Properties, Etc., 1980-82, Producers Realtors, 1982–; bd. chmn./prin. Escrow Resources, Inc.; instr. in-house real estate tng. classes (1978-); recipient Multi-Million Dollar sales honors in real estate annually (1976-); mem. San Fernando Valley Bd. Realtors, L.A. Bd. Realtors, Beverly Hills Bd. Realtors, Escrow Assn.; civic: Tarzana CofC, YMCA (Indian Guides), Scouts, Little League; Valley Beth Shalom (Sisterhood bd. dirs.); rec: folk dancing. Res: 2220 The Terrace, Brentwood 90049 Ofc: Escrow Resources Inc 12400 Wilshire Blvd Ste 1500 Los Angeles 90025

GOUGH, HARRISON GOULD, psychologist; b. Feb. 25, 1921, Buffalo, Minn.; s. Harry Betzer and Aelfreda (Gould) G.; m. Kathryn Whittier, Jan. 23, 1943; 1 dau. Jane Kathryn b. 1950; edn: BA, summa cum laude, Univ. Minn. 1942, MA, 1947, PhD, 1949. Career: asst. prof. psychol. UNiv. Minn. 1948-49; prof. psychol. and research psychol. UC Berkeley 1949–, chmn. psychol. dept. 1967-72, dir. Inst. of Personality Assessment and Research 1973-83; cons. clin. psychol. VA 1950–; dir. Cons. Psychols. Press 1956-; Governor's Advisory Com. on Mental Health 1968-72; Citizen's Advisory Council Calif. Dept. of Mental Health 1969-72; honors: Social Sci. Research Council Demobilization Fellowship 1946-47, Fulbright Research Fellowships 1958-59, 1965-66, Guggenheim Found. Fellowship 1965-66, Phi Beta Kappa; mem: Am. Psychol. Assn. 1946-, Internat. Assn. Cross-Cultural Psychol., Soc. for Personality Assessment, Commonwealth Club S.F., Soc. of Mayflower Descendants, Phi Kappa Psi; publ: psychol. tests, 200+ research papers and monographs on topics of psychol. assessment, perception, cognition and psychodiagnostics, editorial affil. 9 psychol. jours.; mil: 1st lt. US Army 1942-46; Protestant. Res: POB 909 Pebble Beach 93953 Ofc: Dept. of Psychol. UC Berkeley 94720

GOURLEY, JAMES WALTER, III, utility co. executive; b. Jan. 8, 1941, Los Angeles; s. James W., Jr. and Eleanor Mae (Kanel) G.; div.; children: Jennifer, b. 1970, Matthew, b. 1973; edn: BS in geology, cum laude, Univ. Redlands 1962, MS in geol., USC 1971. Career: with Standard Oil Co. of Calif. 1965-72: prodn. engr., Santa Fe Springs 1965-68, review team engr., La Habra 1968-69, devel. engr., Inglewood 1970, devel. geologist, La Habra 19717-72; Southern Calif. Gas Co., Los Angeles 1972–: supr. energy planning 1972-76, mgr. energy resources 1976-79, mgr. supply acquisition 1979-80, mgr. supply projects and forecasting 1980-82, mgr. underground storage 1982–, spokesman for So. Calif. Gas Co. on energy related matters, and frequent public spkr. on the natural gas industry and energy topics; mem. Soc. of Petroleum Engrs., Am. Gas Assn. (bd. dirs. Exploration & Prodn. Com. 1979-81), Pacific Energy Assn. (bd. dirs. 1985-86); club: Los Angeles Athletic; mil: gunnery sgt. USMCR 1963-75; Republican; Protestant; rec: skiing, surfing, travel. Res: 5132 Tierra Majorca Dr Whittier 90601 Ofc: So California Gas Co, 720 W Eighth ML 168, Los Angeles 90017

GOVIER, GEORGE ARTHUR, hospital administrator; b. Mar. 8, 1949, Vancouver, B.C., Can.; s. Oren Wheeler and Grace Marjorie (Turner) G.; m. Gretchen Kuehn, Dec. 29, 1972; children: Michael b. 1977, Melissa b. 1981; edn: BA pol. sci., CSU San Jose 1971; MA hosp. adm., Univ. Minn. 1973. Career: dir. Adminstrv. Svcs., Huntington Meml. Hosp., Pasadena 1973-77; asst. adminstr. Profl. Svcs., Mercy Hosp. of Sacto. 1977-83; chief op. ofcr. Mercy Medical Ctr., Redding 1983-85, bd. dir./CEO, 1985–; honors: finalist W. Glenn Ebersole Compet., Assn. of Western Hosps. (1973); mem. Am. Coll. of Healthcare Execs., Sacto. Healthcare Mgmt. Assn. (treas. 1983), Vis. Nurses Assn./Pasa. (bd. mem. 1976), Rotary Internat., United Way of Redding (bd. 1985); rec: golf, ski. Ofc: Mercy Medical Center POB 6009 Redding 96099-6009

GOWETT, EDWARD HENRY, wire and cable co. executive; b. June 10, 1952, Plattsburgh, NY; s. Francis Henry and Dorothy Lucille (Ryan) G.; single; 2 children: Michael Edward b. 1982, Cynthia Marie b. 1983; edn: BS-BA, Bryant Coll., RI 1974; MBA, Cal. Poly Univ. Pomona 1981; CPA Texas. Career:

internal auditor The Anaconda Co., NYC 1974-76, account mgr. wire and cable div., Los Angeles 1976-80; sales mgr. Houston Wire and Cable Co., Los Angeles 1980-82, v.p. 1982–; honors: Delta Mu Delta (bus.); mem: Am. Inst. CPAs, Kappa Tau Frat. 1973-74, Greek Letter Council 1973-74, Am. Mgmt. Assn.; Republican; Roman Catholic. Res: 6108 Ave De Castillo Long Beach 90803 Ofc: Houston Wire and Cable 1210B Kona Dr Compton 90220

GRAFF, ULRICH B(OEPPLE) aka DON, electrical engineer; b. Mar. 26, 1909, San Francisco; s. Ulrich Karl Ernst Eduard and Louise Marie (Boepple) G.; m. Lucille Josephine Knutson (dec.), Oct. 22, 1938; m. 2. Helen Rust Stricklen (dec.), Apr. 26, 1969; 2 daus: Susan Patrice Caton, Deborah Jane Coleman; edn: BSEE, Stanford Univ. 1934; Reg. Profl. Electrical Engr., Calif. (#292). Career: chief elec. engr. Kaiser Engineers, Aluminum Div., 1945-53, did all elec. design for Chalmette Aluminum Plant (then worlds largest aluminum reduction facility); chief elec. engr. Nobel Corp., 1953-59, designed Garrison Dam Cement Batch Plant; senior elec. engr. Plant Facilities, Lockheed Corp., Sunnyvale 1960-70; elec. design checker Nuclear Power Plants, Bechtel Corp., 1970-74, Nine Mile and Hope Creek Nuclear Power Plant Control Rooms; ret. 1974-79; senior elec. engr. Nuclear Control Rooms, General Electric Co., San Jose 1979-85; electrical cons. prin., 1985-; instr. EE, Heald Evening Engring. Coll.; past mem. AIEE (now AIEEE); vol. San Jose Museum; mil: capt. US Army, 1938-45, major Reserve 1945-53, EE. ops. and commun. ofcr. 474th Self Propelled Anti-Aircraft Arty. WWII, Bronze Star; Republican; Mormon; rec: model railroader, street car restoration. Res: 277 Bel Ayre Dr San Jose 95117

GRAHAM, DAVID MICHAEL, physician; b. Jan. 15, 1941, Chgo.; s. Jack and Geraldine Helen Graham; 1 son, Kenneth b. 1985; edn: BS, Univ. Ill. 1963; MS, Ill. Inst. of Tech. 1967; MD, Univ. of Mexico 1972; lic. phys. & surgeon in Fla. 1977, Calif. 1979. Career: Family Practice physician in San Diego; instr. University, Mercy and Balboa Hosps.; awards: Ill. State Scholarship, HEW Research Fellowship; mem. AMA, CMA, San Diego Med. Soc., Variety Club; mil: ROTC; Jewish; rec: boating. Res: 11348 Duenda Rd., San Diego 92050 Ofc: David M. Graham MD 2345 E 8th St, Ste 103, National City 92050

GRAHAM, JACQUELYN MAE, speech pathologist; b. Aug. 24, 1934, Los Angeles; d. Floyd Samuel and Pauline (Cook) Bradford; m. Thomas Graham, Nov. 20, 1982; children: Lynn b. 1954, Lori b. 1955, Cynthia b. 1959; edn: AA, Cerritos Coll. 1965; BA, CSU Fullerton 1967, MA, 1974; lic. Speech Pathol. Calif. 1974. Career: speech pathol. Buena Park Sch. Dist. 1968-79; dir. speech & hearing Tustin Learning Ctr. 1976; communicatively handicapped tchr. Buena Park Sch. Dist. 1979-83; faculty Biola Univ. 1983-84, Cerritos Coll. 1983-84; speech pathol. Buena Park Sch. Dist. 1984–; Awards: Cerritos Coll. Forensic Speech Squad 1960-65, Toastmasters Internat. 1985, nom. Women of Achievement San Gabriel Valley YWCA 1986; mem: Calif., Buena Park Teachers Assn., Nat. Edn. Assn., Calif. Speech & Hearing Assn., Am. Assn. Univ. Women, Soroptimists, Nat. Assn. Investment Clubs (local pres. 1985), Toastmasters Internat. (pres. 1986), Am. Cancer Soc. (vol. research proj. 1982-88), La Mirada Republican Women's Federated (chaplain 1980-85), Hacienda Colima Repub. Women's Fed. (legis. chmn. 1986), La Mirada Senatorial Campaign Organizer for S.I. Hayakawa 1976; publicity chmn. Charles House for Congress 34th dist. 1985-86; Republican; Baptist (deaconess); rec: swimming & skiing. Res: 15436 Circle Ridge Ln Hacienda Heights 91745 Ofc: Buena Park School District 6885 Orangethorpe Ave Buena Park 90620

GRAHAM, JANET ELLEN, real estate broker; b. Sept. 8, 1941, Oakland, Calif.; dau. Robert W. Murden and Ruth Ehmke; m. David T. Graham, June 22, 1979; stepchildren: Lisa, Jennifer; edn: Fresno City Coll. 2 yrs. Career: real estate sales Herald Realty 4 yrs.; owner Graham Realty 1982–; notary public; bd. dirs. Com. to Save the Kings River; Democrat; rec: wood carving, fly fishing. Ofc: Graham Realty 4588 E Washington Fresno 93702

GRALL, CARL JOSEPH, coin dealer, ret.; b. May 22, 1916, Detroit, Mich.; s. Peter Joseph and Cleona Lilly (Daugherty) G.; nephew of Carl V.P. Daugherty, dist. atty. Detroit; m. Mary Goodrich, 1942 (div. 1948); m. 2d Patricia Lorraine Gentle, 1963; 1 dau. Kristi, b. 1964. Career: owner, Farmer Joe's Mkt., Hawthorne, Calif. 1946-50; owner Farmer's Daughter Stamps &: Coins, Redondo Beach, 1951-60; owner The Money Bag, Torrance, 1960-67; pres. San Pedro Farms Inc., 1967-72; chmn. bd. Colorsound Inc., West Covina 1965-69; founding pres. Teletype Coin Dealers Assn. of Calif., 1963–; owner Lawndale Jewelry & Loan, 1973-78; also investment counseling, Teletype Coin Dealers; mem. Masonic Lodge West Adams 565, L.A. Golden West Comdry 43, L.A. Royal Arch Masons 33, Cryptic Masons of Calif. 35, Knight Templar of Cal. 35, Peace Ofcrs Shrine Club, So. Bay Shrine Club, L.A. Consistory, 32nd deg. Masons (life), Al Malaikah Temple (life); mil: chief warrant ofcr. USCG, 1943-45; Republican (supporting); Christian; rec: fishing, numismatics. Res: Star Route 1 Box 230 Rosamond 93560

GRAMATKY, W. HERBERT, merchandising executive, ret.; s. Bernhard A. and Blanche A. (Gunner) G.; m. Thelma Settle, June 12, 1940; 1 son, John b. 1946. Career: displayman, salesman Desmond's, Silverwood's, Phelph's-Terkel, Jerrems Ltd., and Columbia Hollywood, Los Angeles 1929-42; constrn. of bases US Army, Lemoore Air Base and Camp Beale, Marysville, timekeeping and paving material hauling foreman Gunner Corp. and M.W. Stanfield Co. 1942-46; timekeeping/ purchasing Gunner Corp. Hwy. Constrn., Merced and Fresno 1946-48; men's clothing dept. mgr. Monte Factor Ltd., Beverly Hills 1948-59; men's clothing buyer and dept. mgr. Bullock's at Bullock's Fashion Square, Sherman Oaks 1959-67; mgr. Desmond's Downtown Store then Desmond's Pasadena Store, Pasadena 1967-75; ret.; mng. personal

real estate investments; mem: Apt. Assn. of Gr. Los Angeles, Kiwanis of Pasadena; Republican; Vedanta Soc. of So. Calif.; rec: golf. Address: Los Angeles

GRANT, DOROTHY LUCIA, real estate sales executive; b. June 5, 1923, Biola, Calif.; d. John and Martha (Jaschiniak) Jerkovich; m. Charles Lindy Grant, May 27, 1959; 1 son, Bruce Charles b. 1948; edn: grad., Sawyer Sch. of Business 1942; various real estate courses, Lumbleau R.E. Sch.; Calif. lic. R.E. Broker Assoc. 1965. Career: bookeeper/secty. Harbor Belt Line R.R., San Pedro 1942-48; ofc. mgr. Victor Adding Machine Co., Long Beach 1950-59; broker assoc. Marcus W. Meairs Realtors, Riverside 1961-82, James W. Miller Real Estate Co., 1981-85; broker assoc. Shelter West Realty, Riverside 1985–; sales awards: Top Ten (1976, 77, 78, 79), Million Dollar Club (1979, 81, 82, 83, 84); mem. Riverside Bd. of Realtors 1961–; advis. bd. YWCA 1978-82; Republican; Lutheran (organist 1938-45, recording sec.); rec: travel, photog., int. decor., gourmet cook. Res: 4530 Toyon Rd. Riverside 92504 Ofc: Shelter West Realty 5885 Brockton Ave Riverside 92506

GRANT, JON BARTON, dentist; b. July 17, 1943, Elmhurst, Ill.; s. Russell Sutherland and Louise Winona (Brown) G.; edn: undergrad., Colo. State Univ. 1961-3; DDS, Univ. of Nebr. 1968. Career: group practice of dentistry, Colorado Springs, Colo. 1968-74, pvt. practice, Foster City 1974–; mem: FAGD, Fellow Acad. of Gen. Dentistry (pres. Colo., regional v.p., nat. dir.); Acad. of Dental Group Practice (founding, charter treas.); FAIDS, Fellow Acad. of Internat. Dental Studies; FADI, Fellow Acad. of Dentistry Internat.; Am. Assn. of Endodontists; Am. Soc. of Preventative Dentistry; Am. Acad. of Dental Gp. Practice; Nat. Analgesial Soc. (nat. v.p.); Am., Calif., San Mateo Co. Dental Socs.; Rotarian (pres. Foster City), Foster City CofC (pres.); awards: World Record in Parachuting 1977; San Francisco Mags. 100 Most Eligible Bachelors 1981; rec: water/snow skiing. Res: 653 Pitcairn Foster City 94404 Ofc: 1289 E. Hillsdale Blvd Foster City 94404

GRANT, THOMAS PATRICK, sales and marketing executive; b. Nov. 21, 1954, Marquette, Mich.; s. Norbert J. and Florence A. (Counsel) G.; m. Cynthia, July 28, 1985; edn: BA, Mich. State Univ. 1976; MBA, Pepperdine Univ. 1986. Career: ops. mgr. Marriott Hotels, Wash DC 1976; senior research analyst MIS, Inc., San Diego spec. in retail site eval., 1977-79; dir. mktg. National Decision Systems, San Diego 1980-82; sales mgr., regional sales mgr. Western Region, Donnelley Mktg., Fullerton 1982–; cons. direct mktg. and retail site eval.; honors: Phi Eta Sigma, Phi Beta Kappa; mem: Internat. Council of Shopping Ctr., Nat. Assn. of Corporate Real Estate Execs., Am. Stat. Assn., Am. Mktg. Assn., Direct Mktg. Assn., Market Research Assn., Acad. of Arts & Scis.; works: "Second Effort"- a guest rels. program designed for Marriott Hotels; "Trade Area Delineation - Franchises"- a technique for optimizing franchisee's geographic trade area; Republican; Evangelical Christian; avocation: alcohol/drug abuse counselor. Address: Fullerton 92635

GRANTON, SAMUEL RICHARD, real estate broker, consultant, professor; b. Sept. 3, 1922, Buffalo, NY; s. Frank Charles and Marie (Costanzo) G.; m. Esther Fracasso, May 10, 1950; children: Gregory S. b. 1951, Gina A. b. 1953; edn: BS in soc. sci., City Univ. of NY, 1950; dip., real estate acctg., appraising & law, Weaver Sch. of Real Estate, 1954; grad. studies, Claremont Grad. Sch. 1955-6; grad. US Armed Forces Inst. 1947-52, Anthony Sch. of Real Estate 1967; spl. courses, San Bernardino Valley Coll. 1955-67; MBA, PhD, Western States Univ. for Profl. Studies 1985; lic. real estate broker, Calif., Okla.; life teaching cred., real estate and social science, Calif. Comm. Colls. Career: land title searcher/ title examiner & sr. escrow ofcr. Security Title Ins. Co. (SAFECO), San Bernardino 1952-69; real estate counselor- exchanger, Nat. Assn. of Securities Dealers rep., 1969-71; asst. v.p./escrow mgr. First California Title Co. of San Diego, 1971-72; v.p./nat. escrow ofcr., Commercial Standard Title Ins. Co., S.D. 1972-75; owner, Gran Terra Realty & Mgmt. Services Co., Cardiff by the Sea 1975; internat. bus. cons. (hi-tech) Granton & Son & Assocs. 1982–; assoc. Creative Systems Engrs. (mech./elec. engring. mktg. cons.); real estate instr. Mira Costa, Palomar, Grossmont Colls., 1971-; US rep. Framag Inc., Italy; honors: Direct Commn. from Pres. Truman (1949); mem: Nat. Assn. of Realtors, Calif. Assn. Realtors, Calif. Escrow Assn. (Cert. Sr. Escrow Ofcr.), Am. Escrow Assn., Internat. Exchangers Assn.; SEAT (INEX) Internat. Investment & Bus. Exchg., London, Eng., (IREA) Internat. Orgn. of Real Estate Appraisers (Internat. Certified Appraiser, senior mem.), (NREC) Nat. Assn. Real Estate Cons. (master real estate cons.), (WWPU) Worldwide Properties Unlimited Inc. (life mem., state rep.); publs: arts. in real estate, escrow indus. mags.; rec: research analyst, internat. travel. Res: 1652 Traveld Way, Encinitas 92024 Ofc: 2157 Newcastle Ave, Ste A, Cardiff by the Sea 92007

GRASSE, WANDA GENE, lawyer; b. July 28, 1940, Baird, Tex.; d. William Eugene and Alta Roberta (Dickerson) George; m. John Grasse, Mar. 28, 1970; children: Karen b. 1971, Conrad Carriker b. 1965; edn: LLB, La Salle & Whittier Sch. of Law 1975. Career: hair stylist, beauty instr. Garland's of Texas 1956-60; traffic dir., continuity dir. West Tex. TV Network 1960-65; promo. writer KTTV L.A. 1965-66; promo., advertising, pub. rel. KCOP-TV 1966-71; atty. pvt. practice L.A. 1978-80; legal aid atty. Huntington Park 1980-81; atty. Laurence E. Clark APC (appellate & civil law) Monterey Park 1981–; honors: Woman of Achievement (Bus. & Profl. Women 1981); mem: Mensa, Bus. & Profl. Women, Am., L.A. Co., San Gabriel Valley bar assns.; Republican; Religious Science; rec: swimming, writing, reading, travel. Res: 1300 Fulton Ave Monterey Park 91754 Ofc: Laurence E. Clark APC 631 S Atlantic Blvd Monterey Park 91754

GRASSL, THEODORE PETER, newspaper executive; b. Nov. 12, 1931, Stratford, Wis.; s. Ferdinand V. and Rebecca M. (Fandre) G.; m. Marlene Palmer, Aug. 25, 1962; 1 dau. (adopted), Melody b. 1959; edn: BBA, Univ. Wis., Madison 1959. Career: sys. supr. Control Data Corp., Mnpls. 1967-69; bus. sys. mgr. Minneapolis Star & Tribune Co., 1969-71, data proc. mgr., 1971-74, dir. acctg., 1974-75; bus. mgr. Trenton Times Corp., Trenton, NJ 1975-76, v.p./gen. mgr. 1976-78; gen. mgr. Los Angeles Herald Examiner 1978-84; v.p. Hearst Community Newspapers, 1981-84; pres. TPG Mgmt. Svcs. 1984—; bd. dirs. New Trenton Corp. 1977; instr. Pillsbury Acctg. Devel. Pgm.; instr. Control Data's After Hours Pgm. Beta Alpha Psi, 1957; mem: Mercer Co. CofC bd. dirs. 1977, Nat. Campers and Hikers Assn. (Minn. state assn. pres. 1973-75), BSA Geo. Wash. Council bd. dirs. 1976-77; publs: num. arts. in field of data proc., project mgmt.; major seminar, Control Data, 1960s; mil: USN 1951-55; Republican; Roman Catholic; rec: tennis, oil painting, camping. Res: 17453 Caminito Canasto San Diego 92127 Ofc: POB 28586 San Diego 92128

GRATER, MARGERET KAY, educator; b. July 12, 1942, Cedar City, Utah; d. Russel K. and Evelyn P. Grater; edn: BA, CSU Long Beach 1966; MA, CSU Fresno 1972; PhD, Univ. So. Calif. 1975. Career: tchr. St. Mary's Jr. H.S., Augusta, Ga 1966 67, Adult Edn. Ctr., Camp Darby, Italy 1967, Woodlake H.S., Woodlake, Calif. 1968-69; staff devel. coord. Fresno Unif. Sch. Dist. 1971-73, 1975; instr., coord. Model Schs. Proj., Univ. S. Carolina 1973-75; prin. Norwalk, La Mirada Unif. Sch. Dist. 1975-80; coord. L.A. County Ednl. Resource Consortium (LACERC), L.A. County Supt. of Schs. Ofc., Downey 1980-84; cons., Mgmt. Devel. Ctr., L.A. County Ofc. of Edn. 1984—; pres. Grater & Assocs., Leaders in Excellence Cons. Firm 1986—; instr. sch. adminstrn., CSU Fullerton Grad. Sch. 1980—; instr. ext. classes CSU Fresno, Pepperdine Univ., UC Santa Cruz 1968-78; cons. var. states, dists. 1968-; honors: merit awards, Assn. of Calif. Sch. Adminstrs., Norwalk La Mirada Adminstrn. Assn., Am. Red Cross/Europe 10-Year Svc. Award; mem: CSU Fullerton Educ. Adminstrn. Adv. Bd. 1980-, Assn. of Calif. Sch. Adminstrs. (reg. dir. 1982-85, profl. stds. chair 1985-) ALACOSA (charter v.p. pgms. 1982-, pres. 1984), Norwalk La Mirada Adminstrn. Assn. (pres. 1978-79), L.A. CofC (Edn. Com. 1980-), Assn. of Supvn. & Curriculum Devel. (1977-), Phi Delta Kappa (CSUF chpt. v.p. mem. 1986-87), CSUF Partnership Acad. 1(982-), La Mirada Coord. Council (parliamentarian 1975-80), Dist. PTA 1975-80; co-author Task Force Report to Calif. Commn. for Tchr. Licensing (1981), Tchr. Preservice & Inservice (1982); Presbyterian; rec: tennis, music, art, writing. Res: 1023 Lawanda Placentia 92670 Ofc: L.A. Supt. of Schs., 9300 E Imperial Hwy Downey 90242

GRATNY, THOMAS JEROME, managerial economist; b. Apr. 1, 1944, Altadena; s. R. Emery and Margy C. (McBain) G.; m. Sandra Brooks, Jan. 13, 1974; children: Thomas J., II b. 1969, Kimberly Dawn b. 1979; edn: UC Santa Barbara 1963; Univ. of Ariz., Tucson 1966. Career: mgr. Prolight Industries, Fullerton 1971-77; mgr. ITT, Costa Mesa Div. 1977-79; senior ptnr. Shoreline Services (mgmt. consulting), 1979—; dir. Half Moon Bay Aquaculture Project (study comml. feasibility of lobster farming) 1983-; honors: Internat. Assn. of Chiefs of Police Hall of Fame for devel. safety equip. for law enforcement personnel; mem: Internat. Assn. of Chiefs of Police 1974-, Calif. Aquaculture Assn.; author outdoor survival book: One Way Out (1983); mil: cmd. sgt. major Academy US Army 1963-; US Army Key Member Consultant 1982; Democrat; Methodist; rec: fishing, camping. Res: 340 Shelter Cove Dr Half Moon Bay 94019 Ofc: Shoreline Services 700 Mill St Half Moon Bay 94019

GRAY, GILBERT JAMES, company president; b. May 31, 1928, New Castle, Pa.; s. Alexander Millar and Christina Hunter (Crieg) G.; m. Dolores Helen Vargas, Aug. 22, 1953; children: Kevin James, Kimberly Dee; edn: BA, Antioch Coll. 1952; Certified Fin. Planner (CFP), Coll. for Fin. Plng. 1976. Career: sales rep. Burroughs Corp., San Francisco 1952-56; district mgr. I. D. S., San Jose 1956-67; branch mgr. Powell/Johnson, San Jose 1967-69; vice pres. Belmont Reid & Co. Inc., San Jose 1969-77; pres. Lifetime Fin. Planning Corp., San Jose 1977—; pres. Internat. Vector Corp., Del. 1982-; mem. American Board of Trade, NY 1982-; regional dir. Internat. Fin. Exchange, London 1983-; seated mem. Inex, London 1982-; mem: Internat. Assn. of Fin. Planners (pres. 1970-71), Inst. of Cert. Fin. Planners, Rotary Internat. (Saratoga), past pres. (1963) Jr. CofC San Jose; Libertarian; Prot. Res: 18720 Harleigh Dr Saratoga 95070 Ofc: Lifetime Financial Planning Corp., 966 Saratoga Ave San Jose 95129

GRAY, JAN CHARLES, retail food chain executive; b. June 15, 1947, Des Moines, Iowa; s. Charles Donald and Mary C. Gray; BA econ., UC Berkeley 1969; JD, Harvard Law Sch. 1972; MBA, Pepperdine Univ. 1986. Career: assoc. atty. Halstead, Baker & Sterling, Los Angeles 1971-75; senior v.p. and gen. counsel/External Affairs, Ralphs Grocer Co., Los Angeles 1975—; judge pro tem, Los Angeles Municipal Court, 1977-; arbitrator, Amer. Arbitration Assn., 1977-; real estate broker, 1973-; instr. UCLA Ext. div.; Retail Food Mktg. Law, 1976-: Retail Food Mktg. Indus., 1977-; instr. Pepperdine Univ. MBA program, Legal & Regulatory Issues, 1984-; speaker, rent control, State Bar Conv., 1979; trustee So. Bay Univ. Coll. of Law, 1978-79; bd. vis. Southwestern Univ. Sch. of Law, 1983-; mem: Am. Bar Assn., var. sections: State Bar Calif. (del. Conv. 1976-81), L.A. Co. Bar Assn. (Corp. Law Dept. Exec. com. 1975-76, 1979-), Barristers (exec. com. 1974-75, 1979-81), L.A. Bar Journal (exec. com. 1973-75), San Fernando Valley Bar Assn. (chmn. Real Prop. section 1975-77); Calif. Retailers Assn. (Supermarket Com. 1977-); Food Marketing Inst. (Govt. Rels. Com., 1977-, Govt. Affairs Council, 1977-); govt. apptd. mem. L.A. County Private Industry Council (1982-), L.A. Co. Martin Luther King, Jr. Gen. Hosp. Commn. (1984-), L.A. Co. Aviation Commn. (1986-), L.A. Police Crime Prevention Advis. Council (1986); publs:

articles in legal periodicals, contbg. author, book: Life or Death: Who Controls? (Springer Pub. 1976); mil: USAR; Democrat (State and L.A. Co. Central Coms. 1980-; del. 1980 Dem. Nat. Conv.); Catholic; rec: tennis, travel. Res: POB 407, Beverly Hills 90213 Ofc: Ralphs Grocery Co., POB 54143 Los Angeles 90054

GRAY, RICHARD MOSS, college president; b. Jan. 25, 1924, Wash DC; s. Wilbur Leslie and Betty Marie Grey; m. Catherine Claire Hammond, Oct. 17, 1943; children: Janice Lynn, Nancy Hammond; edn: BA, Bucknell Univ. 1942; M.Div. summa cum laude, San Francisco Theol. Sem. 1961; PhD, UC berkeley 1972. Career: writer, creative dir. N.W., Ayer & Son Inc. advt. agcy., Phila. 1942-58; commd. to campus ministry United Presbyterian Ch., 1961; campus pastor Portland State Univ., 1961-68; pres. World Coll. of West, San Rafael, Calif. 1972—; trustee San Francisco Theol. Sem. 1968-, Lewis and Clark Coll., Portland, 1972-76; Ruling elder 1st Presbyn. Ch., San Rafael; mil: ofcr. USNR 1943-46; mem. Am. Assn. Higher Edn., Assn. World Edn., UN Assn. U.S. (dir. 1980-), Phi Beta Kappa; Republican. Address: P.O. Box 3060, San Rafael 94912

GRAY, SUZANNE STANIFER, medical secretary, civic worker, business owner; b. Jan. 5, Huntington Park, Calif.; d. Earle Thomas and Vonda Bernice (Newcomb) Stanifer; m. Charles E. Gray, Apr. 28; 1 son, Sean Earle b. 1969; edn: BA, Univ. Evansville 1963; Calif. lic. Notary (life). Career: past owner of night club Tamis, Canon City, Colo.; real estate sales agt., Huntington Park; sales rep. Tura of N.Y., in So. Calif.; current: interior design prin./owner Sangray, now Crickets (dealer rare prints and art); secty. VA Hosp., Loma Linda; secty. VA Public Employees Assn. (mem. chair 1986); contbg. writer hosp. monthly newspaper, Pettis Pulse, and mo. article for Riverside Nat. Cemetery; active in mil. affairs, Norton AFB; mem: Eastern Star, Daus. of Golden West, Desert Four Womens Club, Rape Crisis Ctr., Riverside Art Alliance (num. art awards), Sunnymead CofC (Ambassadors Club, Sunnymead Days & Parade), Calif. Optical Assn. (life), Gen. Pattons Memorial (fundraising); past mem. Picadilly Players (little theatre); fmr. vol. PTA, Cub Scouts, Boy Scouts, youth soccer and baseball; Republican; Christian. Address: Loma Linda 92357

GRAY, WILLIAM PERCIVAL, judge; b. Mar. 26, 1912, Los Angeles; s. Jacob L. and Catherine (Percival) G.; m. Elizabeth Polin, Nov. 8, 1941; children: Robin Marie, James Polin; edn: AB, UCLA 1934; LLB, cum laude, Harvard Univ. 1939; admitted to Calif. State Bar 1941. Career: legal secty. to judge US Ct. Appeals, Wash DC, 1939-40; with law firm O'Melveny & Myers, Los Angeles 1940-41; pvt. law practice, Los Angeles 1945-49; ptnr. firm Gray, Pfaelzer & Robertson, L.A. 1950-66; judge US Dist. Ct. Central Dist. Calif., 1966—; spl. asst. to US Atty. Gen., 1958-64; chmn. Calif. Conf. State Bar Dels., 1952; Fellow Am. Bar Found.; mem: Am. Law Inst., Los Angeles County Bar Assn. (pres. 1956), State Bar Calif. (bd. govs. 1960-63, pres. 1962-63); mil: 1st lt. to lt. col. US Army, 1941-45. Ofc: U.S. Courthouse, Los Angeles 90012

GRAYSON, JOHN NEWTON, manufacturing co. president; b. Sept. 4, 1932, Brooklyn, NY; s. Leroy and Doris (Stewart) G.; m. Dorothy Lane, Jan. 1, 1970; children: Lois Rene b. 1952, Dorothy Theresa b. 1953, Susan Ann b. 1955, April Doris b. 1958; edn: BSEE, Pacific States Univ. 1955-58. Career: prod. line mgr. Hughes Aircraft Co., El Segundo 1955-62; bus. mgr. Guidance & Navigation Labs. TRW, Redondo Beach 1962-71; pres. Univox- Calif. Inc., L.A. 1971—; bd. dirs: Univox, Unilog, Uniflex, Bank of Finance; deputy dir. Ofc. of Minority Bus. Enterprise; honors: Hon. Committee, 5th Annual King Birthday Celebration (1981), Disting. Svc., Nat. Assn. Black Mfrs.; mem: Nat. Assn. Black Mfrs., Black Bus. Assn. of L.A., Inst. Elec. Engrs., Am. Mgmt. Assn. (pres.'s assn.), Urban League, NAACP (life), Pres.'s Youth Motivation Task Force, Synod of So. Calif. United Presbyterian Ch. (past moderator); mil: sgt 1/c US Army 1950-55; Republican; Presbyterian; rec: archery, golf, horseback riding. Res: 1932 Virginia Rd Los Angeles 90016 Ofc: Univox-Calif., Inc., 12800 S Broadway Los Angeles 90061

GREBBIEN, LOUIS JOHN, U.S. Merchant Marine officer, ret.; b. June 17, 1922, San Diego; s. Henry William Sr. and Lena Marion (Rivers) G.; m. Lilliam Basney, Dec. 6, 1912, dec. Career: enlisted to P.O. 1/c USN, Reserve 1940-49; chief warrant ofcr. US Coast Guard 1949-64; purser, chief purser US Merchant Marine 1966-84; ret.; mem: USCG Chief Warrant & Warrant Ofcrs. Assn. (life), Marine Staff Ofcrs. Assn. (life); Republican; Protestant; rec: travel, computers. Res: 41717 Chadbourne Dr. Fremont 94539

GRECO, STEVEN LOUIS, sales executive; b. Dec. 5, 1949, Los Angeles; s. John Joseph and Theresa Marie (Musacco) G.; m. Mary Anne, Dec. 18, 1971; children: Laura b. 1974, Paul b. 1977, Mark b. 1979; edn: BA, Loyola Univ. 1972. Career: salesman Pfizer Inc. 1973-74; salesman Connecticut General, Los Angeles 1974; Boehringer Ingelheim Pharmaceuticals Inc., Ridgefield, Conn. 1975—; profl. sales rep. 1975-78; Los Angeles dist. sales mgr. 1978-82; nat. dir. sales tng. & devel. 1982-84; Western reg. sales dir. 1984—; coord. internat. tng. of bronchodilator materials; honors: Pi Gamma Mu, 1972; Diocese of Orange Area Coord., Catholic Renewal Svcs. 1982; mem: Nat. Soc. of Sales Tng. Exec., St. Elizabeth Ann Secton (Christina Svc. Coord., Prasih Council mem. 4 yrs.), Am. Youth Soccer Orgn. (referee); Democrat; Catholic; rec: soccer, chess, tennis. Res: 19401 Sierra Bello Irvine 92715 Ofc: 2070 Business Center Dr. Ste. 205 Irvine 92715

GREEN, ALLEN PERCIVAL, III, manufacturing co. executive; b. July 5, 1936, N.Y., N.Y.; s. Allen P., Jr. and Rita (Le Blanc) G.; m. Marieann Baratelli,

Jan. 7, 1971; children: Andrea b. 1972, Bianca b. 1975; edn: BS aero., Parks Coll. St. Louis Univ. 1957; FAA lic. comml. pilot. Career: naval aviator 1958-69; pres. PRD Inc., Seattle, Wash. 1969-76; prodn. control mgr. Sperry/New Holland, Fowler, Calif. 1976-83; plant mgr. Meyers-California, Visalia 1983-84; dir. of mats. Roto-Master Inc., N. Hollywood 1984—; cattle rancher, Arbuckle; dir. A.P. Green Found., Mexico, Mo.; mem: Colusa County Farm Bureau, Calif. Agric. Aircraft Assn., Am. Prodn. & Inventory Control Soc.; Los Angeles County Art Museum (patron); patent: Sperry/New Holland Round Bale Wagon; mil: lcdr. US Navy 1958-69, light attack pilot, Vietnam Vet., Nat. Def., Air Medals (3), Vietnam Service, Rep. of Vietnam Campaign, Armed Forces Meritorious Unit Cit.; Republican; Catholic; rec: aviation, sailing, fishing. Res: 3382 Coy Dr Sherman Oaks 91423 Ofc: Roto Master Inc 7101 Fair Ave North Hollywood 19605

GREEN, CYNTHIA JANE, underwriting and operations manager; b. Sept. 19, 1950, Wood River, Ill.; d. Francis Dean and Arminta Bell (Green) Whitcock; m. Russell Green, Aug. 24, 1977; 1 dau. Kimberly Dawn b. 1970; edn: Lewis & Clark Jr. Coll. 1967-68; bus., journ., Washington Univ. 1969-71; Santa Ana Coll. 1978-79, 81-82; Certified Profl. Ins. Woman 1985. Career: underwriter Foutch & Webb Ins. Wood River, Ill. 1964-68; exec. asst. Marsh McClennan Ins. St. Louis 1968-70, supv. Alexander & Alexander St. Louis 1970-73; acct. exec., mgr. Daniel Henry Ins. St. Louis 1973-77; mgr. Paul Muench Ins. Agcy. Orange, Calif. 1977-85, Pioneer Financial Ins. Svc. Costa Mesa 1985—; instr. ins. classes 1978—; honors: Ins. Woman of the Yr. (1985); mem: Ins. Women of Orange Co. (pres. 1984-85), Nat. Assn. Female Execs. 1986, Independent Ins. Agents (bd. 1985-86), Ins. Women Assn., Field Persons Assn., Job's Daughters (council); publ: monthly ins. newsletter 1984-85; R.L.D.S.; rec: painting, knitting, reading. Res: 3671 Upper Terrace Dr Riverside 92505 Ofc: Pioneer Financial Insurance Svc. 275 McCormick Costa Mesa 92626

GREEN, HOWARD CHESTER, judge; b. Sept. 6, 1916, Fresno; s. Thomas Butler and Ida B. (Bomar) G.; m. Jeanne McCarty, Apr. 26, 1944; 1 dau. Kelly, b. 1953; edn: JD, Baylor Univ. 1953. Career: deputy Fresno County Recorder, 1938-50 (except 1941-5); tchr. comml. subjects Fresno City Coll. Night Sch. 1947-8; atty., sole practitioner, 1954-82; judge pro tem Madera County Superior Ct., six yrs. (heard leading case on "in lieu" lands, Jay vs. Madera Lumber Co., decision upheld on appeal); judge Chowchilla Judicial Dist., 1958-82 (handled original appearances of defendants in the Chowchilla School Bus kidnapping case, 1976); as vis. judge Fresno Municipal Ct. declared the "No-Knock" provisions of Cal-OSHA unconstnl. in People vs. Salwasser, decision upheld by appellate courts, quoted in US Congl. Record, 4/4/77; honors: asst. editor Baylor Law Rev. 1952-3; awarded Internat. Order of DeMolay Chevalie Degree 1941, Legion of Honor Degree 1976; mem. Calif. State Bar, 1954-, Madera Co. Bar Assn., 1954-; American Legion, D.A.V., Delta Theta Phi Law frat. 1951-; past mem. Judges and Constables Assn., Rotary, Chowchilla Dist. CofC (secty. 1958-9); mem./Parade Announcer, Chowchilla Spring Festival, 25 yrs.; Chowchilla Plnng. Commn. 1957-8; chmn. March of Dimes 1956-60; dean of boys Madera Co. 4H Camp, 1965; exec. com. Sequoia Council BSA 1956; clubs: Madera Golf and Country, Masons, Scottish Rite, Fresno Bodies; mil: s/sgt US Army 1941-5 (insp., ct. reporter, Insp. Gen's Sect. Hq. 3d Army); Republican; Methodist; rec: antique car restoration, square dance, fish. Res: 604 Ventura Ave Chowchilla 93610

GREEN, JANET MARY, nurse-educator; b. Nov. 6, 1933, Sharpsburg, Pa.; d. Lawrence John and Agnes Petronella (Lanzino) Yoest; m. Cecil Green, July 1977; children: Donald Lawrence b. 1962, Denise Lynn b. 1965; edn: nurse dipl., Braddock Gen. Hosp. Sch. of Nsg. 1954; BA, Redlands Univ. 1974; MA, CSU Long Beach 1978; lifetime tchg. credl. Calif. Comm. Coll.- Nursing; Reg. Nse. Calif., Pa. Career: staff nse. oper. room Braddock (Pa.) Gen. Hosp. 1954-55; senior staff nse. oper. rm. Western Pa. Hosp., Pittsburgh 1955-58; head nse. Calif. Rehab. Ctr. for Drug Addicts, Norco 1964-65; oper. rm. asst. supv. Riverside Comm. Hosp. 1965-66; head nse. Riverside Gen. Hosp. Univ. Med. Ctr. 1966-77; mgmt. counselor, mgmt. seminars US, Canada; apptd. by gov. mem. State Adv. Com. on Emerg. Med. Svcs. 1976-80; adv. com. CSU Long Beach Emerg. Nse. Clinician Pgm. 1982-; mem. Riverside Emerg. Med. Care Com.; honors: appreciation, Riverside Rotary (1975), Calif. Sch. for Deaf (1976), AF Nse. for W. Pa. (1958), Woman of the Yr., Am. Bus. Woman's Assn.; mem: Calif. Emerg. Nses. Assn. (v.p. 1976-78, chpt. pres. 1973-75, bd. dirs. 1973-77), Medical Alert Assn. of Riverside County 1975-78, Calif. Hosp. Assn. of So. Calif. (tech. adv. com. for audit of hosp. emerg. depts. 1974-75), Public Employees Assn. of Riverside Co. (1st v.p. 1973-75), Nat. Emerg. Dept. Nses. Assn. (cred. com. 1975), Calif. Nses. Assn. 1975-, Calif. Assn. for Psychiatric Techn. Educators 1977-; Republican; Catholic; rec: travel, dancing, fishing. Res: 17334 Ranchero Rd Riverside 92504 Ofc: S.B. Valley Coll. 701 S Mt Vernon Ave San Bernardino 92403

GREEN, SUZANNE PHIPPS, (profl. name, Suzanne Fairly), interior designer; b. May 4, 1935, Carroll, Iowa; d. Joseph Montgomery and Mary Elizabeth (Grems) Phipps; m. Harold Paul Fairly, Mar. 21, 1955; children: Suzan Lyn b. 1956, Steven Paul b. 1957, David Carl b. 1959; m. 2d Harlan Russell Green, June 4, 1983; edn: Univ. of Denver 1958-60, UCLA 1975-79, spl. courses Santa Barbara City Coll.; BA communications, Antioch West Univ. 1985. Career: designer apprentice Cannell & Chaffin, Santa Barbara 1968-71; public rels. / staff designer Furniture Guild, 1972-74, also writer radio and t.v. commls. and did voice-overs on both medias; curriculum devel./coord. Interior Design Pgm., Santa Barbara City Coll., 1974-81, mem. design advis. bd. 1981-; design prin. Inside.Out Design Associates, 1981—; frequent speaker on design as a career in local high schs.; public service commls. on local radio and t.v. (KDB, KRUZ, KTMS); advis. bd., lectr., student advisor UCSB Interior

Design pgm. 1986-; honors: appreciation, Planned Parenthood and S.B. Sch. Systems (1978-81), S.B. Semana Nautica Fest., S.B. City Coll. Found. (1981); mem. ASID (assoc.), Interior Design Networking (lectr), S.B. CofC, Channel City Women's Club; civic: S.B. Museum of Art (docent), Semana Nautica (v.p.), Women's Support Group of S.B. (founder), The First Earth Run (Earth Ambassador)/ Olympics of Cooperation/NYC (S.B. chair); works: authored grant proposal to Nat. Endowment of the Arts, Livable Cities Div.; organized and devel. July 4th Arts Faire (S.B. Mission) and Symphony Solos pgm. (S.B. Symphony), YMCA (fundraiser); publ. design work "Creative Ideas for Your Home: Kitchens" (Knapp Press 1984); Democrat; Unitarian; rec: freelance writing, theatre, sculpting. Ofc: Inside.Out Design Associates 952 Miramonte Dr Ste 5 Santa Barbara 93019

GREENBAUM, RICHARD EDWARD, lawyer, importer, exporter; b. June 5, 1947, Chicago, Ill.; s. Bert F. and Ester (Mayer) G.; m. Judith, June 27, 1971; children: Mark b. 1975, Sabrina b. 1979; edn: BA, CSU Northridge 1969; JD, UC Hastings Coll. of Law 1972. Career: Dept. of Public Social Svcs., Los Angeles 1972-73; San Francisco Public Defenders Ofc., San Francisco 1971; US Atty Gen. Ofc., Los Angeles 1972-73; owner, mgr., legal counsel Ace Hy Sales Inc., Chatsworth 1973—; contbr. Associated Surplus Dealers Newpaper 1984; Calif. Community Coll. Techg. Cert. in Law 1972; honors: David E. Snodgrass Award for Outstanding Appellate Advocacy 1971; Percy E. Towne Scolarship Award 1971; mem: Am. and Calif. Bar Assns., Associated Surplus Dealers, Calif. Assn. Student Bookstores, Young Republicans, Boy Scouts of Am., Tau Epsilon Phi (CSU Northridge, charter, founding mem.), Phi Delta Theta (UC Hastings Coll. of Law), Phi Alpha Theta; works: Scout-O-Rama display, Pack 251, Canoga Park 1985; designer, new emblem UCLA and other major univs. 1981; major distributors Olympic caps 1984; Republican; Jewish; rec: numismatics, camping, gardening. Res: 7330 Pomelo Dr. Canoga Park 91307 Ofc: Ace Hy Sales Inc., 21541 Nordhoff St. Bldg. A Chatsworth 91311

GREENBAUM, ROBERT STRAUSS, mail order gift co. president; b. Dec. 29, 1955, New Orleans, La.; s. James Richard and Peggy (Strauss) G.; m. Andrea, June 30, 1985; 1 dau. Jolene b. 1986; edn: BA, Tulane Univ. 1978; lic. Calif. real estate broker. Career: pres. TMC of Las Vegas, Nev. (long-dist. tel. co.), 1978—; owner/realtor Greenbaum Realty, Palm Springs 1980—; pres. Andrea's California Farms (exec. mail order bus.), P.S. 1985—; mem. Nat. Assn. of Realtors; civic: Common Cause, Sane, Wilderness Soc., Greenpeace, Ctr. for Def., Jewish Fedn. (bd. 1985-86), Sierra Club, Cousteau Soc., B'nai B'rith; Jewish; rec: marathon runner, ski. Ofc: Andrea's California Farms 700 E Tahquitz Way Ste D Palm Springs 92262

GREENBERG, MYRON SILVER, lawyer; b. Oct. 17, 1945, Los Angeles; s. Earl W. and Geri (Silver) G.; m. Shlomit Gross, Aug. 23, 1985; children: David b. 1972, Amy b. 1975; edn: BS in bus. adm., UC Los Angeles 1967, JD, 1970; admitted Calif. State Bar (1971), CPA, Calif. (1972), certified tax splst., Calif. Bd. Legal Spec. (1980), admitted to US Dist. Ct. (Central) Calif. (1971), US Tax Ct. (1977). Career: staff acct. Touche Ross & Co., Los Angeles 1970-71; assoc. Kaplan, Livingston, Goodwin, Berkowitz & Selvin, Beverly Hills 1971-74; ptnr. Dinkelspiel, Pelavin, Steefel & Levitt, S.F. 1975-80; ptnr. Steefel, Levitt & Weiss, S.F. 1981-82; atty. prin., Larkspur 1982—; lectr. Golden Gate Univ.; planning com. Real Estate Tax Inst., Calif. Continuing Edn. of the Bar; honors: bd. editors UCLA Law Review; mem: ABA, Calif. Bar Assn., Marin County Bar Assn., Am. Inst. CPAs; civic: Am. Heart Assn. (bd. dirs., secty. Marin County chpt. 1983-), Am. Technion Soc. (bd. dirs. No. Calif. chpt.), Larkspur CofC (bd. dirs.), San Anselmo Planning Commn. 1976-77; author: California Attorney's Guide to Professional Corporations (1977, 1979); Democrat; Jewish. Ofc: Myron S. Greenberg, APC, 80 East Sir Francis Drake Blvd Ste 3E Larkspur 94939

GREENBERG, RICHARD SHELDON, merger and acquisition executive; b. June 6, 1934, Boston; s. Julius and Dora (Wolfe) G.; m. Sharon, Apr. 23, 1955; children: Mark b. 1959, Victoria b. 1962, Kenneth b. 1963; edn: BS bus. admin. UC Los Angeles 1957; CPA Calif. 1958. Career: pres. Lee Constrn. Co. 1962-77; ptnr. R.S. Greenberg CPA 1977-83; v.p. Corporate Finance Assoc. 1983—; trustee So. Calif. Constrn. Laborers Tng. Trust 1975-, Constrn. Teamsters Tng. Fund 1975-85; Mayor's Advisory Com. on Constrn. 1971-73; honors: Shalom Award (State of Israel 1975); mem: Engrg. & Gen. Contractors Assn. (pres. 1972), Engrg. Contractors Assn. (treas. 1975-77), Am. Inst. CPAs, Calif. Soc. CPAs, Soc. Calif. Accts., Nat. Assn. Pvt. Placement Syndicators, Nat. Asthma Ctr.; publ: mag. articles; mil: PO3 USCG 1953-56, Am. Defense Medal; Republican; Jewish (congregation pres.); rec: water skiing, reading, scuba. Ofc: Corporate Finance Assoc. 11645 Wilshire Blvd, Ste 650, Los Angeles 90025

GREENE, ALVIN, management consultant; b. Aug. 26, 1932, Pittsburgh, Penn.; s. Samuel David and Yetta (Kroff) G.; m. Louise Sokol, Nov. 11, 1977; children: Sharon b. 1959, Ann b. 1962, Ami b. 1964, Daniel b. 1965; edn: BA, Stanford Univ. 1954, MBA, 1959. Career: asst. to pres. Narmco Industries, So. Dakota 1959-62; corp. mktg. mgr., Whittaker Corp., Los Angeles 1962-67; senior v.p., group exec. Cordura Corp., Los Angeles 1967-75; chmn. bd. Sage Cons. Inc., Los Angeles 1975-79; exec. v.p., COO Republic Distributing Inc., Carson 1979-80; chmn. bd. Sage Cons. Inc., Los Angeles 1981; COO Memel, Jacobs & Ellsworth, Los Angeles 1981—; also, dir. Republic Distributors 1980, True Data Corp. 1976-77; vis. prof. Am. Grad. Sch. of Bus., Pheonix, Ariz. 1977-; chmn. Housing Authority Bd. of Commns., City of Los Angeles 1984-; awards: Historical Honor Society 1953; Polit. Sci. Honor Society, Stanford 1953; mem: Direct Mail Assn., Safety Helmet Mfgrs. Assn., Alpha Epsilon Pi; mil: 1st lt. US Army Infantry 1955-57; Jewish; rec: swimming, travel, photog.

Res: 16669 Charmel Ln. Pacific Palisades 90272 Ofc: 1801 Century Park E. Ste. 2500 Los Angeles 90067

GREENE, JOHN CLIFFORD, dental school dean; b. July 19, 1926, Ashland, Ky.; s. Ella R. Brawner; m. Gwen Greene, Nov. 17, 1957; children: Alan b. 1960, Laura b. 1962, Lisa b. 1962; edn: AA, Ashland Jr. Coll. 1947; DMD, Univ. Louisville Sch. of Dentistry 1952; MPH, UC Berkeley Sch. of Pub. Health 1961. Diplomate Am. Board of Dental Pub. Health (past pres.). Career: with US Public Health Service, 1952-81: intern, Chgo., Ill. 1952-53, staff PHS Hosp., San Francisco 1953-54, asst. regl. dental cons., S.F. 1954-56, Epidemic Intell. Service, CDC, Atlanta, Ga. and K.C., Mo. 1956-57, spl. cons. World Health Orgn., India 1957, Nat. Inst. of Dent. Resrch., NIH, Bethesda, Md. 1957-58, asst. to chief dental ofcr., PHS, Wash.DC 1958-60, chief Epidemiology Pgm., S.F. 1961-66, dep. dir. to dir. Div. Dent. Hlth., Bethesda 1966-73, acting dir. to dir. PHS, 1973-75, chief dent. ofcr. PHS, 1975-78, dep. surgeon general PHS, 1978-81; prof. and dean Sch. of Dentistry, UC San Francisco 1981–; vis. lectr. Univ. Calif. 1965-72, lectr. Univ. Pa. 1972-75, Univ. Mich. 1972-75; mem. Bd. of Consultants to the Comdr. Naval Medical Command 1983-, US Preventive Services Task Force 1985-; honors: Omicron Delta Kappa (1948), Omicron Kapa Upsilon (1952), Delta Omega (1961), Univ. Citation, Boston Univ. Sch. Grad. Dentistry (1971), Dept. HEW disting. service award (1972) and medal (1975), Federation Dentaire Internat. award of merit (1978), elected mem. Inst. of Medicine (1979); Alumnus of Year, Univ. Louisville (1980), UCB Sch. of Pub. Health (1984); hon. Dr. of Sci. degree, Univ. Ky. (1972), Boston Univ. (1975), Univ. Louisville (1980); mem: Am., Calif., San Francisco Dental Assns., Am. Assn. of Dental Schs. (v.p. Fed. Dental Svcs. 1978-80), Am. Assn. for Dent. Resrch. (pres. elect 1985), Internat. Assn. for Dent. Resrch, Fellow Am. Coll. of Dentists, Am. Assn. Pub. Hlth Dentists, Fedn. Dentaire Internat., WHO Panel of Experts on Dent. Hlth 1976-80, Inst. for Hlth Policy Studies, Am. Pub. Hlth Assn., Epidemic Intell. Service Alumni Assn., W. Conf. of Dent. Examiners and Dent. Sch. Deans (pres. 1985), Inst. for Advance. of Hlth, Inst. of Medicine of Nat. Acad. of Scis. (Sect. Leader 1983-); author num. profl. reports, journal articles, abstracts and book chpts. Res: 103 Peacock Dr San Rafael 94901 Ofc: School of Dentistry UCSF S-630, 515 Parnassus San Francisco 94143-0430

GREENE, KATIE ELLEN, real estate consultant; b. Aug. 11, 1941, Wash DC; d. Edward H. and Katherine (Cardwell) Guilford; m. Michael Greene, Jan. 1, 1982; children: Griffin b. 1961, Paul b. 1962, David b. 1966, Chris b. 1966. Career: real estate broker Century 21 Consultants Inc., San Diego 1975–, pres. National Real Estate Consultants, devel. unique mktg. program for lender reposessions nationwide, currently under contract to var. lenders: Home Federal, Security Pac. Nat. Bank, Security Pac. Fin. Corp., The Hammond Co., Westinghouse Credit Corp., Imperial Savings Assn.; frequent lectr. on REO mktg.; recipient Centurion Sales Award, Cen. 21 Internat. (1983, 84); mem. Century 21 Regional (bd. dirs.), C-21 Easter Seals San Diego (chair), Employee Relocation Council Wash DC, Rancho Bernardo CofC, C-21 VIP Soc. San Diego (pres.); works: Marketing Pgm. and Forms (copyright 1985); rec: travel. Res: 11571 Duenda Rd San Diego 92127 Ofc: Century 21 Consultants Inc. 11770 Bernardo Plaza Court Ste 116 San Diego 92128

GREENE, WAYNE MARK, research scientist; b. Feb. 21, 1963, Queens, N.Y.; s. Stanley L. and Renee Greene; edn: BS, Mass. Inst. of Tech. 1984. Career: research assoc. Dept. Chem. Engring., M.I.T., 1982-84; cons. Stone & Webster Corp. 1983; research intern Thomas J. Watson Research Center, IBM, 1984; research asst. Dept. Chem. Engring., UC Berkeley 1985–; awards: Eagle Scout, BSA (1977), Vigil Honor, Order of the Arrow (1979), Rodman McClintock Outstanding Thesis Award, M.I.T. (1984), NSF Fellowship (1984), Sigma Xi, Tau Beta Pi; mem. Am. Inst. of Chem. Engrs., Materials Research Soc., Electrochem. Soc.; civic: Boy Scouts Am., Order of the Arrow, Nat. Eagle Scout Assn.; publs. Photophoresis of Irradiated Spheres: Evaluation of the Complex Index of Refraction (ed. Langmuir; 1985), contbr. article J. Optical Soc. of Am. (1985); rec: Shotokan karate, racquetball. Ofc: University of California 201G Gilman Hall Berkeley 94720

GREENTHAL, DAVID W., lawyer; b. June 26, 1953, NY, NY; s. Monroe W. and Ruth (Davey) G.; m. Christine R. Mains, Sept. 16, 1983; edn: BA, magna cum laude, Univ. Colo. 1975; JD, UC Hastings Coll. of Law 1978. Career: atty. sole practitioner S.F. 1979-81; atty. Canterbury, Raub & Greenthal S.F. 1981–; bd. dirs. Friends Outside 1985; note & comment editor Hastings Coll. of Law Internat. and Comparative Law Jour. 1978; honors: Phi Beta Kappa 1975-; mem: Calif. State Bar 1978-, S.F. Bar Assn. 1981- (fee dispute panel 1985), Calif. Trial Lawyers Assn. 1983-, Hastings Alumni Assn. 1980-, Hist. Soc. US Dist. Ct. of No. Calif., World Affairs Council of No. Calif., S.F. Bay Club, Univ. Colo. Alumni Assn.; Democrat; rec: basketball, running, skiing, tennis. Ofc: Canterbury, Raub & Greenthal 60 Green St San Francisco 94111

GREENWALD, PAUL EVAN, lawyer; b. Sept. 28, 1944, Santa Monica; s. Alvin G. and Audree E. (Smolier) G.; m. Isabel Raboff, Sept. 16, 1973; children: Dianna-Jae b. 1975, Seth Benjamin b. 1976; edn: BS, USC 1968; JD, Southwestern Univ. 1972; admitted to practice Fla. bar, Calif. bar. Career: atty. assoc. Buchner, Gurland & Schwartz, London, England 1972; atty. assoc. Greenwald and Baim, Los Angeles 1973-76; ptnr. Greenwald & Greenwald, Los Angeles 1976-83; ptnr. Greenwald & Resnick, law corps. Century City and Newport Beach, 1983–; of counsel Hyman and Goodrich, Tampa, Fla.; splst. L.A. Police Dept. Reserves; honors: senior editor The Proponent, senior staff mem. of Law Review; mem. Calif., Fla., Los Angeles County, Beverly Hills, Orange County bar assns.; civic: Orange Co. Performing Arts Ctr., Huntington Harbour Philharmonic Com., Cancer League; club: Huntington Harbour Yacht (judge advocate); mil: boatswains mate 2/c USCGR; rec: sailing, yachting, skiing. Ofc: Greenwald and Resnick 4350 Von Karman Ste 450 Newport Beach 92660

GREENWALD, PAUL JEROME, institutional corporate bond sales executive; b. Oct. 28, 1949, N.Y.C.; s. Gustave Edward and Mildred (Ostrove) G.; m. Joan Alboum, Nov. 2, 1980; 1 dau., Anne b. 1984; edn: BA, Allegheny Coll. 1971; Certified Finl. Planner (CFP), Inst. of Cert. Finl. Plnnrs. (1985). Career: retail broker var. firms, 1974-85; institutional corp. sales, Shearson Lehman Bros., 1984–. Res: 541 Marin Ave Mill Valley 94941 Ofc: Shearson Lehman Bros. 1 Sansome St San Francisco 94104

GREENWOOD, STUART ALDEN, chiropractor; b. Feb. 24, 1950, Toronto, Canada; s. Morris and Anne (Tohn) G.; m. Mariangela Mammoliti, Feb. 12, 1985; 1 dau. Maxi Yvonne b. 1985; edn: BS, honors, Univ. Waterloo, Ont., 1973; Logan Coll. Chiro. 1974, Canadian Meml. Chiro. Coll. 1975-78; DC, Pasadena Chiro. Coll. 1980; Diplomate Nat. Bd. Chiro. 1980; lic. DC, Calif. (1981), Disability Evaluator (1986). Career: student clinic supr. 1978; assoc. Barstow (Calif.) Chiropractic Clinic, 1983, Victorville Chiropractic, 1983; dr. chiro./ prop. Knolls Family Chiro. Center, Apple Valley 1984–; mem: Calif. Chiro. Assn. (secty. San Bernardino Soc. 1985-86), Calif. Thermographic Soc.; civic: vol. Health Fair Expo (1986), Kiwanis, Victor Valley Concert Assn. (bd. 1984-); Jewish; rec: tchr. guitar/ piano, collect spl. interest autos. Res: 22129 Tehama #3 Apple Valley 92308 Ofc: 18182 Hwy 18 Ste 2 Apple Valley 92307

GREGG, NANCY VAN SANT, retail/wholesale co. president; b. Oct. 19, Fostoria, Ohio; d. Lester A. and Nella C. (Mellott) Van Sant; m. R. Calvin Gregg, Apr. 24, 1960; children: Roger b. 1962, Christian b. 1973; edn: No. Central Coll., Naperville, Ill. 1957-58, Ripon Coll. 1958-59, UC Santa Barbara 1962-64, Otis Art Inst. 1968-69. Career: med. secty., Fostoria 1959-60, then med. transcriber, Oxnard (Ca.) Comm. Hosp.; sales, mktg. rep. Tiny's, Inc., Oxnard 1972-74, v.p. advt. & mktg. 1974-85, pres. 1985–; frequent lectr., workshop leader; awards: Republican Found. Scholar (1958-59); mem: Ventura Co. Profl. Women's Network (bd. dirs., ed. Focal Points newsletter 1985-), Am. Bus. Womens Assn., Nat. Assn. of Female Execs., Nat. Fedn. of Independent Bus., Oxnard CofC, Better Bus. Bur., Nat. Assn. Retail Dealers; Prot.; rec: music, art, theatre. Ofc: Tiny's Inc. 1237 Saviers Rd Oxnard 93033

GREGORY, CALVIN LUTHER, insurance agent, educator, counselor; b. Jan. 11, 1942, Bronx, NY; s. Jacob and Ruth (Cherchian) G.; m. Rachel Anna Carver, Feb. 14, 1970, div. 1977; 2 daus: Debby Lynn, Trixy Sue; m. 2d. Carla Deaver, June 30, 1979; edn: AA, L.A. City Coll.; BA, CSU Los Angeles 1964; M.Div., Fuller Theol. Sem. 1968; M.Re.Edn., Southwestern Sem. 1969; D.D., Otay Mesa Coll, San Diego 1982; PhD in religion, Universal Life Ch., Inc. 1982; Ordained minister Am. Baptist Conv. L.A. 1970; real estate lic., Calif. 1969; Notary Public, Calif. 1969. Career: USAF Chaplain, Edwards AFB 1970; pastor First Baptist Ch., Boron, CA 1971; ins. agent Prudential Life Ins. Co., Ventura 1972; mgr. Prudential Ins. Co., Thousand Oaks 1973; casualty ins. agent Allstate Ins. Co., Thousand Oaks 1974; pres. Ins. Agcy. Placement Svc., Thousand Oaks 1975–; counselar Wilshire Presbyterian Ch., Los Angeles, fmrly. Hd. Youth Minister, 1974; tchr., polit. sci. Maranatha H.S., Rosemead; investor - owner apt. bldgs., real property 1974–; awards: president's citation, Prudential 1972; WLRT, Prudential 1972; Top- 20 Salesman awd., Southwestern Co. 1967; mem: Forensic Club, CSU, L.A. 1963; Apartment Assn. L.A. 1975-; Republican; rec: travel, video tapes, jogging. Res: 3307 Big Cloud Circle Thousand Oaks 91360 Ofc: Insurance Agency Placement Service, POB 4407 Thousand Oaks 91359

GREGORY, EVELYN ILENE, real estate broker; b. May 26, 1930, Canton, Ill.; d. Joseph Alfred and Gladys Irene (Benson) Kidd; m. Frank D. Gregory, Jr., Aug. 14, 1946; children: Donald b. 1952, Robert b. 1954, John b. 1956, Mark b. 1965; edn: AA, Santa Rosa Jr. Coll. 1950; BA, Sonoma State 1963; MA, 1970; GRI, Grad. Realtors Inst. 1976, CRS, cert. resl. spl. 1978, Nat. Assn. of Realtors; sr. cert. mem., IREA; Internat. Cert. Appraiser. Career: college instr. 1970-4; real estate salesprsn. 1973; owner/broker Real Estate Information Center, Inc., Sonoma 1975–; precentor (relig. soloist) First Ch. of Christ Scientist, Sonoma 1965-; honors: GRI; CRS; Million Dollar Club (life); mem. Women's Soc. of Christian Svc. for outstanding svc. 1965-; VFW Distng. Svc. 1983; mem: Nat. Assn. of Realtors; Sonoma Co. Multiple Listing Svc., Bd. of Realtors 1973- (dir. 1976-8, mem. Edn. Com., chmn. Million Dollar Club, Sonoma Council); soloist Sonoma Valley Chorale; recordings: relig. solo music, Infinite Power of Love; Republican; Christian Sci.; rec: music, writing, sewing. Res: 327 Napa Street E., Sonoma 95476 Ofc: Real Estate Information Center, Inc., 481 First Street W., Sonoma 95476

GREIFZU, CARL WARREN, lawyer, b. Jan. 27, 1943, Baltimore, Md.; s. Carl Warren and Gertrude (Morris); m. Kim-Dung, Oct. 2, 1971; edn: AB, Univ. of Md. 1965; JD, Georgetown Univ. Law Ctr. 1972, LLM, 1976. Career: economist Dept. of Labor Wash DC 1965-69, survey statistician 1971-72; legal asst., atty. advisor Office of Gen. Counsel, Price Commn. & Cost of Living Council Wash DC 1972-73; atty. gen. practice Law Offices of Edward T. Conroy, Upper Marlboro, Md. 1973-78; gen. and bus. atty. Cummings & Assoc. PC Wash DC 1978-80; pvt. practice Los Angeles 1980–; judge pro tem L.A. Mun. Ct. and Pasadena Mun. Small Claims 1982-; tchr. seminar How To Write a Will Pasadena City Coll. 1982-; honors: Phi Delta Phi, high honors arts & sci., honors econ., Phi Beta Kappa, Phi Kappa Phi; mem: Calif., L.A. Co., Pasadena bar assns.; Am. Red Cross (bd. dirs. Arcadia chap. 1985-), Mentor Palms Owners Assn. (pres.); mil: US Army 1969-71; Republican; Catholic; res: studying Chinese. Address: 300 S Mentor, No. 4, Pasadena 91106

GRETCHEN, EDWARD ANTHONY, physician; b. Jan. 20, 1930, Weirton, W. Va.; s. Anthony and Katherine (Kraina) G.; m. Judith Ann, Oct. 31, 1982; 1 dau. Lisa Jean b. 1968; edn: BS chem., Xavier Univ. 1952; MD, St. Louis Univ. Sch. of Med. 1956; grad. Air Univ.- Air Command & Staff Coll. (1977-78), Air War Coll. (1982-83); certified Am. Board Family Practice (1978, 1984). Career: intern Akron (Ohio) City Hosp. 1956-57; capt. USAF and chief Profl. Services, Charleston Air Force Base, S.C. 1957-60; pvt. practice of medicine/ surgery in Weirton, W.Va. 1960-65; family practice in Reno, Nev. 1966-76, staff St. Mary's Hosp. and Washoe Medical Center; re-entered USAF as major, and chief Clin. & Aeromed. Svs. at Hickam & Beale AFB, 1976-81, lt. col., col. 1978-, cmdr. USAF Clinic Norton AFB, 1981–; named Strategic Air Command Flight Surgeon of Year (1981), 9 decorations include Hamanitarian Svc. Medal, Meritorious Svc. (2), AF Commendn., Expt. Marksman; mem: Fellow Am. Bd. of Family Practice, Aerospace Med. Assn., Air Force Assn., Am. Mil. Surgeons of US, WV State Med. Assn. 1960-67, Hancock County (WV) Med. Soc. (pres. 1963-64) 1962-64, Nev. State Med. Assn. 1966-76, Washoe Co. Med. Soc. 1966-, AF Officers Clubs, Elks; rec: historical numismatics. Address: USAF Clinic Norton AFB92409

GREWAL, KULDIP SINGH, chiropractor; b. May 14, 1956, Tatanagar, Bihar, India, nat. US cit. 1975; s. Ranjit Singh and Sant Kaur (Mangant) G.; m. Darshan, Dec. 23, 1984; edn: BS nutrition sci., UC Davis 1979; DC, with honors, Palmer Coll. of Chiro. Davenport, Iowa 1983. Career: aide Dr. B. Singh Braintree, Mass. summer 1978; chiro. Milpitas, Calif. 1984–; honors: Most Outstanding Project in Indsl. Arts (Yuba-Sutter County Fair 1972 for floor plan of house); mem: Am. Chiro. Assn., Indian Students Assn. Yuba Coll. (pres. 1977), Indian Students Assn UC Davis 1979-80; Democrat; Sikh; rec: jogging, basketball, football, volleyball (capt. volleyball team H.S. & Yuba Coll. 1977). Ofc: 40 N Park Victoria Dr Ste F Milpitas 95035

GRICIUS, RAMONA MARIA, accountant, b. June 4, 1958, Los Angeles; d. Vytautas and Donna (Rusteika) Alseika; edn: BS in acctg., magna cum laude, USC 1981; MBA in bus. taxation pgm., USC in progress; Certified Public Acct., Calif. (1984). Career: sales clk. Broadway Dept. Store, Hollywood 1978-79; tax asst. mgr., tax splst. senior staff Peat, Marwick, Mitchell & Co., Los Angeles 1981–; honors: USC Dean's List all semesters 1976-81, Beta Gamma Sigma (1980); mem. Calif. Soc. of CPAs, Accounting Circle USC, Nat. Assn. for Female Execs.; civic: Town Hall of Calif., L.A. World Affairs Council, Smithsonian Inst. (nat. assoc.), L.A. County Mus. of Art, L.A. Olympic Organizing Com. staff (1984); works: classical ballet- tchg. cert. awarded, Tamara Maximov Sch. of Dance (1978), dance choreography works performed in local comm. theaters; Republican; Catholic; rec: dance (classical ballet, modern, folk), art collection. Ofc: Peat Marwick Mitchell & Co. 725 Figueroa St Los Angeles 90017

GRIEVES, JAMES JESTIN, marketing executive, ret.; b. Apr. 27, 1910, Mason, Nev.; s. Rufus Hill and Nettie Viola (White) G.; m. Ada Lou Landreth, Sept. 20, 1939; 1 son, James Philip b. 1947; edn: AA, Fullerton Jr. Coll. 1930; BA, Transylvania 1934. Career: mktg. Union Oil of Calif. 1934-39; self-employed ptnr. w/ W.H. Burton as mktg. commn. agents for Union Oil in N.E. Orange County 1939-57; mktg. & property mgmt. Westway Petroleum Co.- Pacific Coast 1957-67; real estate/ property mgmt. 1967-75, semi-retired; owner, founder, mng. dir. Casa Del Buen Amigo Convales. Hosp., Newbury Park, Calif. 1962-72; mem. Rotary; mil: lt. col. USAF, 3 Commdns.; Republican; Christian; rec: horses (riding & breeding). Res: 1714 Victoria Dr Fullerton 92631

GRIFFIN, GERALD DIETER, emergency physician, pharmacologist; b. Sept. 8, 1940, Staufenberg, Germany, nat. US cit. 1955; s. Delos Boardman and Liesel Elizabeth (Neun) G.; m. Carolyn King, Oct. 31, 1964; children: Katherine b. 1965, Renate b. 1966, Sarah b. 1970; edn: AB, UC Berkeley 1965; PharmD, Univ. of Pacific 1971; MD, Univ. of Juarez, Mex. 1977; lic. physician-surgeon, BMQA 1981; Calif. Comm. Coll. tchg. cred. (1971). Career: chief Pharmacy Service, USPHS Indian Hosp., Cass Lake, Minn. 1971; asst. prof. Univ. of N.M., Albuquerque 1973; intern Case Western Reserve Univ. 1978; staff physician, Ft. Sam Houston, Tx. 1979-80, Ft. Ord, Calif. 1982; resident in emerg. med. Brooke Army Med. Ctr. 1982, asst. chief E.M. Svcs., El Paso 1984; chief E.M. Svcs., Ft. Ord. 1985; emerg. phys. Salinas Valley Meml. Hosp., Salinas, Calif. 1985–; clin. instr. in surg. Texas Tech Sch. of Med. 1982–; honors: Rho Chi (1974), grad. speaker Univ. of N.M. Health Scis. (1974), guest lectr. series N.M. Pharmaceutical Assn. (1974), AMA recogn. award (1981); mem: AMA, Am. Coll. of Emerg. Physicians (Toxicology Com. 1983-84), Nat. Assn. of Residents and Interns, Assn. of Mil. Surgeons of US, Am. Radio Relay League, Case Western Reserve Univ. Med. Alumni Assn.; works: US Patent on new type toothbrush (1974), contbr. num. research articles in med. jours.; mil: major US Army Med. Corps 78-85, Merit. Svc. Medal; instr. Calif. Nat. Guard OCS Pgm. 1968-70; Republican; Unitarian; rec: Amateur Radio Opr. (W8MEP, 1958-). Res: 123 Forest Ave Pacific Grove 93950 ofc: EM Dept Salinas Valley Memorial Hosp. 450 E Romie Ln Salinas 93901

GRIFFIN, JAMES CLYDE, truck driver; b. Oct. 1, 1937, Tenn.; s. Dewey Sampson and Osa Nelson (Akers) G.; m. Rhea Lee, 1961; 3 children. Career: truck driver Milne Truck Lines, Inc. Whittier; honors: 2-Million Mile Safe Driving Record; Safety Pins and Awards from Milne Truck Lines annually for 25 yrs., num. awards incl. 6 1st Place Heavy-Semi at state and local truck driving rodeos, Driver of the Month (Calif. Trucking Assn. 7/81), Trucker of the Week (KLAC Radio 4/74), nom. Citizen of the Year (City of Norwalk 1975, 76, 77, 78, 79, 80); candidate for 33rd Congressional Dist. 1974, US Senate

1980, Gov. of Calif. 1982; elected 3rd term as chmn. Norwalk Citizens Action Council; mem. State Exec. Com. for Political Party, Central Com. chmn.; mem. Assem. Bruce Young's Advis. Panel; Dept. of Motor Vehicles Pub. Adv. Panel 1976-80; mem: Norwalk CofC, Moose, Elks, Norwalk Rod & Gun Club, Nat. Rifle Assn. Res: 5069 Bain St Mira Loma 91752 Ofc: Milne Truck Lines, Inc. 3200 Workman Mill Rd Whittier 90601

GRIGORESCU, OCTAVIAN, interior designer; b. Oct. 1, 1960, Bucharest, Romania; s. Radu and Ortansa (Turlea) G.; edn: Baccalaureate of arch., Saligny Sch. of Arch., Romania 1979; BA arch., Beverly Hills Univ. 1984. Career: librarian Mission Hosp., Huntington Park, Calif. 1980-81; proj. mgr. Thrifty Corp., La Palma 1980-83; dir. devel. Baker Healthcare Inc., Orange 1983-84; designer, prin. Avi Designs Co., La Mirada 1983–; designer, ptnr. F.P. Austin Co., W. Los Angeles 1985–; mktg. dir. Metamorphoses Magazine 1985-86; design cons. A.S. Design Co. 1983–; honors: 1st Prize Fine Arts (1976), 3rd Prize Fine Arts (1979), Excellence Awards (1975-79) for literature & participation in Math Olympiads, mem: Romanian Ministry of Edn., Assn. of Adventist Forums, The Summit Orgn., Orange County CofC; publ: creative editor for The Romanian Signs of the Times; mil: pvt. Romanian Army 1979-80; Republican; Seventh-Day Adventist. Address: 15300 Ocaso Ave, E-102, La Mirada 90638

GRIM, DOUGLAS PAUL, lawyer; b. May 12, 1940, Bellingham, WA; s. Paul R. and Vivian I. (McMillen) G.; children: Caryn, b. 1970; Devin, b. 1972; edn: BA, Lawrece Coll. 1962; LLB, Stanford Law Sch. 1965; LLM, taxation, NYU Sch. of Law 1966. Career: assoc. Hanna and Morton, L.A. 1966-72; of counsel Harris, Noble, Huler & Gallop, L.A. 1972-5; partner law ofcs. of Douglas P. Grim, L.A. 1975–; instr. Golden Gate Univ. Sch. of Law 1975; awards: Michael F. Tobey Awd., L.A. Jr. CofC 1972; listed: Who's Who in Am. Law, 1st, 2nd, 3rd eds.; honors: student body pres., Lawrence Coll. 1962; mem: Calif., L.A. Co., and Am. Bar Assns.; L.A. Area Council Boy Scouts; L.A. Jr. CofC; Wilshire Kiwanis; Uptown Investment Club (pres. 1978); Jonathan Club; Riviera Tennis Club; publs: arts. legal journals; Methodist; rec: tennis, polo, skiing. Res: 247 So Lorraine Blvd Los Angeles 90004 Ofc: Law Offices of Douglas P. Grim, 523 W Sixth Street Los Angeles 90014

GRIMES, RONNIE E., contractor, developer; b. Dec. 28, 1923, Peru, Ind.; s. John A. and Mary H. (Rockenbaugh) G.; m. Mamie Lee, Feb. 19, 1945; children: Terry b. 1946, Larry b. 1947, Gary b. 1948; edn: Univ. of Hong Kong 1950-70; Lic. Contractor, A.B. Calif. Career: Ronnie Grimes Trucking Co. 1947-58, pres. Ronnie Grimes Const. Co. 1958–; owner Pen-Ron Co.; tnr. G&W Financial Co. 1958-86; Republican. Res: 1540 N San Joaquin St Stockton 95204 Ofc: 1212 N El Dorado St Stockton 95203

GRIMM, LUCIEEN CHARLOTTE, fashion designer; b. Apr. 28, 1921, Berlin, Ger.; nat. USA 1962; d. Fritz George and Marie Charlotte (Mietz) Henschel; edn: attended Victoria Oberlyzeum (Berlin) 1931-36, stu. Coll. Fashion Design (Ger.) 1936-69. Career: fashion designer, Germany, 1940-52; fashion designer of Antiguelaces, bridal gowns, dresses, Los Angeles 1952–, bus. owner, Lucieen, L.A.; honors: listed as Fashion Designer of Berlin, 1952; mem. Art Guild (Berlin); Protestant. Res: 752 S. Wilton Place, Apt. 1, Los Angeles 90005 Ofc: Lucieen, 225 N. Larchmont Blvd. Los Angeles 90004

GRITTEN, DARRELL PAUL, lawyer; b. Oct. 13, 1944, Sheridan, Wyo.; s. Paul Hubert and Doris Louise (Conklin) G.; m. Jeanine Thompson, Jan. 9, 1966; children: Paul b. 1966, Mark b. 1967; edn: BA, Univ. Wyo. 1968, JD, 1973; admitted to Wyo. Bar. 1973, Calif. Bar 1976; Notary Public, 1977. Career: capt. AUS, Judge Advocate Gen. Corps 1973-76; assoc. atty. Amschel Law Corp., Hemet 1976–; instr. N.Mex. State Univ. 1975-76; mem: ABA, Calif. Bar Assn., Riverside County Bar Assn., Mt. San Jacinto Bar Assn., Wyo. Bar Assn., Kiwanis Club of Hemet Valley (past pres.), Downtown Hemet Bus. Assn., Inc. (past pres.); mil: capt. US Army 1973-76, major USAR 1976-; Republican (mem. Calif. Repub. Assembly, Hemet); Christian (Deacon); rec: motorcycling, travel. Res: 419 East Nolan Ave Hemet 92343 Ofc: Amschel Law Corp. 120 S Harvard St Hemet 92343

GRODIN, JOSEPH RAYMOND, judge; b. Aug. 30, 1930, Oakland; s. Michael and Celia (Falk) G.; m. Janet Sapper, July 20, 1952; 2 daus., Sharon, b. 1956, Lisa, b. 1961; edn: BA, UC Berkeley 1951; JD, Yale Law Sch. 1954; PhD, London Sch. Economics 1960. Career: practiced law, specializing in labor law, firm of Neyhart & Grodin, San Francisco 1955-71; law prof. Hastings Coll. of Law, 1972-79; assoc. justice Calif. Ct. Appeal, Dist. 1, Div. 1, 1979-80; presiding justice, Div. 2, S.F., 1982, associate justice Calif. Supreme Ct. 1982–; vis. prof. Stanford Law Sch. 1976-77; mem: Calif. Agric. Labor Relations Bd. 1975-76; mem. Phi Beta Kappa, Order of the Coif, Am. Jewish Congress; publs: Union Govt. & the Law, 1960, num. law rev. articles; Democrat; Jewish; rec: backpacking. Res: 2926 Avalon Ave Berkeley 94705. Ofc: State Building, San Francisco

GRODY, WAYNE WILLIAM, physician, biomedical researcher, film critic; b. Feb. 25, 1952, Syracuse, NY; s. Robert Jerome and Florence Beatrice (Kashdan) G.; edn: BA, Johns Hopkins Univ. 1974; MD, Baylor Coll. of Medicine 1977; PhD, 1981; lic. physician Texas (1978), Calif. (1982). Career: postdoc. fellow Dept. Cell Biology, Baylor Coll. of Medicine 1979-81; intern, resident UCLA Sch. of Medicine 1982-84, fellow Div. Medical Genetics 1984–; film reviewer and contbg. editor MD Magazine (monthly mag. for physicians, nat. circ. 180,000) 1981–; awards: First Prize, Roche Awards in clin. scis. (1980), Best Paper award LA Soc. of Pathology (1984), Co-investigator Univ.-wide Task Force on AIDS (1984-); mem: AAAS (1973-), Am. Soc. of Human

Genetics, Alpha Epsilon Delta, Motion Picture Assn. of Am. (Accredited Film Critic), Am. Film Inst., Internat. Physicians for Prevention of Nuclear War, ACLU; num. articles in scholarly publs. on molecular biology, biochem., AIDS research, cancer research, human genetics; Democrat; Jewish; rec: classical music. Res: 11645 Chenault St Ste 104 Los Angeles 90049 Ofc: Div. Medical Genetics UCLA School of Medicine Los Angeles 90024

GROSS, ADOLPH B., entrepreneur; b. Nov. 17, 1919, Sharon, Pa.; s. Jacob S. and Rosa (Schreiber) G.; m. Florence Scott, Jan. 28, 1945; 1 son, Richard b. 1946; edn: BA, Yale Univ. 1942; MBA, Wharton Sch. of Bus. 1944. Career: artist portraits of famous people, 1944-50; vice pres. Weather-wise Windows, Youngstown, Ohio 1950-56; gen. sales mgr. Alsco Anaconda, Akron, O. 1950-58; qualified finl. coordinator Investors Diversified Svcs., Akron 1958-73; pres. Window Supply Co., Orlando, Fla. 1973-76; ptnr. Money At Work Realty, La Jolla, Calif. 1976-82; founder/owner Hall of Success Gallery, San Diego current; awards: Nat. Salesman of Year, Anaconda Copper/Alsco, Inc. (1957), Rookie of Year, Investors Diversified Svcs. (1959), Horatio Alger Award (1974); life mem./founder Shrine Burn Hosp.; mem. Masons, Scottish Rite, Shriners; mil: Civilian Ferry pilot 1945. Res: 303 Coast Blvd Ste 19 La Jolla 92037

GROSS, BARRY, real estate developer; b. Jan. 25, 1950, N.Y.C.; s. J. George and Roslyn L. (Lippman) G.; m. Pat, May 14, 1977; edn: BA, Union Coll. 1972; MBA, Rutgers Grad. Sch. of Bus. 1974; Calif. CPA (1976) lic. R.E. Broker (1983). Career: acct. Kenneth Leventhal & Co., CPAs, Newport Beach 1974-77; corporate controller The Housing Group, Irvine 1977-81; indep. mgmt. cons., 1981-84; gen. ptnr. Concorde Devel., Irvine 1984—; mem. Building Indus. Assn. (subcom. chmn.), Performing Arts Frat.; club: Newport Beach Country; rec: golf, cycling, cabinetry. Ofc: Concorde Development 19752 MacArthur Blvd Ste 240 Irvine 92715

GROSS, STEVEN ALAN, candiologist; b. Sept. 27, 1946, Brookline, Mass.; s. Sumner A. and Jeanne (Freeman) G.; m. Joan E., June 20, 1971; children: Eric, b. 1973, Jennifer, b. 1976, Brian, b. 1980; edn: AB, Bowdoin Coll. 1968; MD, Boston Univ. Med. Sch. 1972; Bd. Cert., Cardiovascular Diseases 1977. Career: cardiology fellow Boston Univ. Med. Ctr. -1977; asst. dir. cardiology Mercy Hosp., San Diego 1977-81, assoc. dir. 1981-83; dir. coronary care unit and cardiology lab. 1983—; bd. San Diego Heart Assn.; named Tchr. of Year, Mercy Hosp. & Med. Ctr.; CPR instr.; mem: Am. Coll. of Cardiology, Am. and San Diego Echocardiographic Socs., Jewish Community Ctr. (bd.); publs: 10 research papers in cardiology 1977-; Republican; Jewish; rec: swimming, basketball, sports. Ofc: Mercy Cardiology Medical Group, 4077 Fifth Ave., San Diego 92103

GROSS, STEVEN HAROLD, lawyer; b. Jan. 2, 1944, Chgo., Ill.; s. Harold Max and Jeanne (Courshon) G.; m. Jacqueline Edelstein, June 4, 1966; children: Michelle b. 1968, David b. 1970; edn: BA, Stanford Univ. 1960; MBA, Columbia Univ. 1968; LLB magna cum laude (1st in class), Univ. of W. Los Angeles Law Sch. 1981; admitted Calif. State Bar 1981; C.P.A., Ill. 1970; C.F.A. (Chartered Financial Analyst) Fin. Anal. Assn. 1975. Career: accountant various firms 1968-70; security analyst Allstate Insurance 1970-71, Hambrecht & Quit 1971-73, Bateman Eichler, Hill Richards 1973-79; independent financial advisor 1979-81; atty. pvt. practice 1981—; instr. bus. law Woodbury Univ. 1983; instr. sec. anal. and bridge var. sch. in Calif. and Ill.; honors: U.S. Bridge Team (placed 35th mixed pairs 1981); Life Master Am. Contract Bridge League; mem: Am., Calif., Los Angeles bar assns. 1981-; Warner Center Tennis Club; Grand Prix Tennis Assn.; Republican; rec: bridge, tennis, golf, bowling. Address: 10040 Hanna Ave Chatsworth 91311

GROSS, SYDNEY, real estate developer; b. May 18, 1921, Czech., nat. 1943; m. Sarah Velick, Feb. 8, 1942; children: Harold b. 1948, Barry b. 1951, Lori b. 1955; edn: BA, business 1939. Career: owner Belknap Distbrs., Detroit, Mich. 1944; sales Calgate Corp., L.A. 1958; owner Blue Chip Realty Investments, L.A. 1959; pres. Gross Enterprises, Inc., Encino 1960—; awards: Fernando Awd., US CofC; mem: Encino CofC; B.P.O. Elks; Al Malaikah Shrine; mil: US Army 1942-4; rec: community planning, high rise office devel. and constrn., creative real estate devel. Res: 4169 Clear Valley Encino 91436 Ofc: 16000 Ventura Blvd, Ste 1200, Encino 91436

GROSSMAN, JERRY JAY, emergency physician; b. Apr. 16, 1949, Phila.; s. Martin O. and Esther Ethel (Jacobson) G.; m. Mary, Dec. 17, 1975; children: Lauren b. 1976, Rachel b. 1979; edn: BA, undergrad. Temple Univ. 1966-69, MD, Jefferson Med. Coll. 1973; certified Mental Health Profl. 1975; Diplomate Am. Board of Emergency Medicine 1985. Career: med. intern and resident Penna. Hosp., Phila. 1973-75, asst. instr. in medicine Univ. of Pa. Sch. of Med. 1974-75; emergency physician and assoc. dir. of emergency med. services, Los Alamitos Medical Ctr., Los Alamitos, Calif. 1975—; emerg. phys. Humana Westminster Comm. Hosp., Westminster 1979-80; instr. med. and nsg. staff in Advanced Cardiac Life Support, Los Alamitos and Humana Westminster Hosps., (semi-annually) 1979-; instr. Orange County Paramedics (monthly) 1975-; participant in Orange County Disaster Planning, 1975-; honors: Phi Eta Sigma, Alpha Omega Alpha; mem: Fellow Am. Coll. of Emergency Physicians, AMA, Orange County Med. Assn., Nat. Assn. of Interns & Residents; civic: YMCA Indian Princess Pgm. (chief of tribe 1985) 1982-; coach AYSO soccer orgn. 1982-; sev. research publs. (Azide Compounds) (Radiation Physics); Jewish. Ofc: Coast Emergency Physicians 3751 Katella Ave Los Alamitos 90720

GROSSMAN, REGINA VALDEZ, computer systems analyst, psychotherapist; b. Apr. 29, 1946, Oakland; d. Robert K. and Louisa (Valdez) Mitchell; m. Dr. Stephen Grossman, July 26, 1972; edn: MSW, UC Berkeley 1971; Postmasters cert. in Comm. Mental Health, 1973; MPH, 1973; JD, UCLA Sch. of Law 1980; Masters Pgm. Computer Sci., Univ. San Francisco; LCSW, lic. clin. soc. wkr., Calif. 1974. Career: soc. wrk. staff Children's Hosp. of Oakland 1973-4; Stanford Univ. Med. Ctr. 1974-6; dir. soc. wrk. Kaiser Hosp., So. San Francisco 1981-3; computer programmer Control Data Corp.l 1985; cons. to legal profession re psycho- social aspects of family law; pvt. practice 1983—; past adminstrv. research for Judge C. Reynoso (now Cal. Supreme Ct. Justice); UCLA Judicial extern in Marin Co. Superior Ct.; honors: California State Fellowship 1964; mem. Profl. Connections for Women, Palo Alto Chpt.; rec: computers, photog., sports. Res: POB 291 San Carlos 94070

GROVE, SYLVAN (Bud) EDWARD, computer consultant, administrator; b. Dec. 23, 1939, Detroit, Mich.; s. Sylvan Duward and Laura May (Beal) G.; div.; 1 dau: Cherie Kim, b. 1970; edn: Macomb Coll., Mich.; No. Montana Coll.; Maryland Univ. Career: served to E4, USAF 1958-65; electrician Chevrolet; electronic splst. Hughes Aircraft, 1958, Gen. Motors, 1965-72; electronic spec. Hughes Aircraft, El Segundo 1972-, equipment eng. 1979-80, adminstr. 1982—; pres. Topless Computer, Carson 1983—; computer cons. hardware and software; mem: Software Writers Internat. Guild; SME; IEEE; Nat. Computer Graphics Assn.; Hughes Aircraft computer Assn. (HESEA); mil: E-4, USAF 1958-65; rec: chess, computers, creating software. Res./ Topless Computer, 21111 Dolores, No. 146, Carson 90745 Ofc: Hughes Aircraft, 2060 Imperial El Segundo 90245

GROW, CAROLYN MARIE DAWSON, artist, biologist; b. Feb. 7, 1940, Pasadena; d. Charles Alexander, Jr. and Josephine Carolyn (Kayl) Dawson; m. Harry S. Grow, July 25, 1964; children: Lisa b. 1965, Harry II b. 1966, Diana b. 1968, Rachel b. 1969, Gavin b. 1970, Karin b. 1971, Bret b. 1973, Lara b. 1974, Catharine b. 1977, Anica b. 1979; edn: AA, Pasadena City Coll. 1959; BA, CSU Los Angeles 1961; MS, USC 1963; postgrad wk. Scripps Inst. of Oceanography 1963-64. Career: subs. tchr. San Dieguito Sch. Dist. 1964-65; piano tchr., 1965-82, also dir. L.D.S. church musical pgms.; cellist sev. orchestras incl. San Diego County Symp., Jewish Comm. Symp., 1980—; owner Cimarie Arts (silkscreening), Encinitas 1982—, biologist/ cons. Polychaete Worm I.D., Marine Ecological Consultants, 1984—; recipient awards, USC; mem. S.D. Art Mus.; works: paintings, musical compositions (1960-); contg. edn. UCSD Russian Studies 1986-; Republican; Ch. of Jesus Christ of L.D.S.; rec: chamber music. Address: Cimarie Arts 919 Doris Drive Encinitas 92024

GRUBBS, WILLIAM ROBERT, insurance agent; b. May 3, 1927, Los Angeles; s. Willaim Robert Sr. and Rachel (Dykes) G.; m. Carrie Susan, April 28, 1973; children: Sandra Lee b. 1957, Laura Ann; edn: Los Angeles City Coll. 1946; Long Beach City Coll. 1959-63; Chartered Life Underwriter, American Coll. 1968; Life Underwriting Tng. Council, 1986. Career: teller Security Bank, Los Angeles 1946-49; sales Roberts Supply Co., Bell Gardens 1950-52; sales ins. fin. E & James Buick, Los Angeles 1952-54; ins. agent State Farm Ins. 1954-86; currently, pres. Grubbs Ins. Agency Inc.; bd. dirs. Los Angeles Life Underwriters Assn. 1969-73; CLU instr. 1975; spkr. to ins. groups; honors: Presidents Club; Million Dollar Club; Nat. Sales Achiev. Award; Nat. Quality Award Life and Health; mem: Life Underwriter Assn. (pres. 1968), Downey Exch. Club (charter), Toastmasters; mil: seaman 1/c USN 1945-46; Republican; Religious Science; rec: body building. Ofc: Grubbs Insurance Agency Inc., 10846 Paramount Blvd. Downey 90241

GRZANKA, LEONARD G., writer; b. Dec. 11, 1947, Ludlow, Mass.; s. Stanley Simon and Claire (Rozauszka) G.; m. Jannette Donnenwirth, Sept. 3, 1982, div. 1986; edn: BA, Univ. of Mass. 1972; MA, Harvard univ. 1974. Career: sales promotion writer Tymshare Transactin Sources, Fremont 1981-82; acct. exec. Strayton Corp., Santa Clara 1981-82; mng. ed. Portable Computer Mag., San Francisco 1982-84; columnist California Farmer Mag., San Francisco 1984—; West Coast ed. Var Magizine, Camden Communications, Camden 1985—; colmunist PC Companion Mag., Camden Communications, Camden 1985—; prin. Grzanka Associates, San Francisco 1984—; lectr. Golden Gate Univ. 1985-; contbg. ed. Slicon Valley Mag. 1982-85; honors: Phi Beta Kappa (1972), Phi Kappa Phi (1972), Danforth Fellow (1972-74), Japan-US Friendship Commn. Literary Translation Award (1982); mem: Harvard Club of S.F., Press Club S.F. (admissions com.), Issues Network of Calif., Calif. Hist. Soc., Ivy Club of No. Calif.; author Neither Heaven Nor Hell (1978); ed. Maser Pieces of Contemporary Japanese Crafts, (1977); contbr. Manajo: Th Chinese Preface in Kokinshu: A Collection of Poems Ancient & Modern (Princeton 1984); mil: sgt. USAF Pararescue, Senior Jumpmaster, Vietnam Svc.; Democrat; Catholic; rec: writing. Res: 1324 Jackson Apt. 5 San Francisco 94109

GUBLER, RUSSELL MARION, accountant; b. Dec. 27, 1955, Salt Lake City, Utah; s. Marion Emil and Doris (McInnes) G.; edn: BS acctg. Brigham Young Univ. 1981; Certified Public Acct., Calif. Career: staff acct., senior acct. Audit Dept. Price Waterhouse, Los Angeles; continuing edn. instr. 1984-85; mem. Am. Inst. CPAs, Calif. Soc. CPAs, BYU Alumni Assn.; Republican; Latter Day Saints; rec: hunting, fishing. Ofc: Price Waterhouse 400 S Hope St Ste 2200 Los Angeles 90071

GUENTHER, CHARLES R., business executive, consultant; b. Apr. 21, 1948, Santa Ana; s. Stanley George and Wilma Eliza (Zentner) G.; m. Ann Marie Eyerly, Aug. 31, 1966; children: Andrea, b. 1967; Christian, b. 1978; edn: AA, Santa Ana Coll. 1968; BA, CSU Fullerton 1970; MA, 1974; Airline Transport

Pilot Cert. Career: pres./sr. cons. Wollack, Waibel and Guenther, Inc. (mgmt. conssultants), Fair Oaks 1974-7; dir. human resources, Mercy Health Care Orgn., Sacramento 1978-84; labor rels. cons. 1978-; dir. devel. and regl. ops. Foundation Health Plan, Sacto. 1984-85; exec. dir. Freeman Health Ventures, Los Angeles 1985-; lectr. Grad. Sch. Bus. Adm. Golden Gate Univ.; awards: NSF Research Fellowship 1970; frequent guest spkr. law enforcement, personnel & labor rels. and health care; arts. in profl. journals; Republican; Ch. of Jesus Christ L.D.S.; rec: aviation, sport fishing, alpine skiing. Res: 2039 Shelfield Dr Carmichael 95608 Ofc: Freeman Health Ventures 6053 Bristol Pkwy Culver City 90230

GUEST, KARL REED, lawyer; b. Sept. 29, 1951, Jacksonville, Fla.; s. Karl Macon and Lois (Reed) G.; m. Patricia Ontiveros, Oct. 20, 1984; edn: BA, Emory Univ. 1973; JD, Univ. of Pacific McGeorge Sch. of Law 1980; MBA, CSU Sacto. 1982; admitted Calif. State Bar 1980. Career: asst. controller Stone Container Corp. Atlanta 1974-77; atty. pvt. practice Sacramento 1981-83; atty. ptnr. Sehr, Lamb & Guest Walnut Creek 1983-; honors: Outstanding Young Men of Am. 1974; mem: Am., Calif., Contra Costa Co. bar assns.; rec: skiing, sailing. Res: 2100 Bay St, Apt 204, San Francisco Ofc: Sehr, Lamb & Guest 45 Quail Ct, Ste 300, Walnut Creek 94596

GUGAS, CHRIS, polygraphist, author; b. Aug. 12, 1921, Omaha, Nebr.; s. Nicholas and Vera (Henas) G.; m. Anne Claudia Setaro, June 27, 1942; children: Chris, Jr. b. 1943, Steven E. b. 1946, Carol (Hawker) b. 1951; edn: DD, Ch. of Living Sci. 1968; BA, pub. adminstrn. 1970; MA, USC 1977; postgrad. CSU Los Angeles; PhD behav. psychol., Univ. of Beverly Hills 1978. Career: asst. dir. L.A. School Security, Los Angeles Bd. of Edn. 1949-50; CIA agent, U.S. Govt. 1950-4; L.A. Bd. of Edn. 1955-7; dir. Central Bureau of Investigation, L.A. 1962; public safety dir. Omaha, Nebr. 1963-5; dir. Profl. Security Consultants, Hollywood 1966-; security cons.: business, t.v., motion picture industries; instr. L.A. Polygraph Inst.; Las Vegas Polygraph Inst.; exec. dir. The Truthseekers; mem: founder Nat. Bd. of Polygraph Examiners; Am. Polygraph Assn. (pres. 1971-2); Special Agents Assn. (pres. 1960); Marine Corps League (pres. 1945); Combat Correspondents Assn. (pres. 1970); Red Cross Council (pres. 1939); Calif. Peace Ofcr. Assn.; Silver Dollar Club; author: The Silent Witness: A Polygraphist's Casebook, Prentice-Hall 1979; columnist: Los Angeles Daily Journal, Security World Mag.; contrib. over 150 arts. on crimonology; newspapers, mags., trade journs.; mil: USMC 1940-9, decorated Presdtl. Unit Cit., 4 Battle Stars, 3 Navy Unit Cits.; Greek Orthodox; rec: electronics, writing, sports. Res: 4018 Dixie Canyon Ave Sherman Oaks 91423 Ofc: 6253 Hollywood Blvd Ste 311 Hollywood 90028

GUGGENHEIM, WOLF Z., physician, internist; b. Mar. 28, 1932, Western Europe; s. Willy and Betty (Schlesinger) G.; m. Vivian ; children: Arye b. 1967, Achiezer b. 1972, Schlomo b. 1984, Sharona b. 1985; edn: MD, Univ. of Zurich 1959; lic. MD, Switzerland (1959), NY (1964), Calif. (1966). Career: postdoc. research fellow Univ. Zurich Med. Sch. 1959-60; intern State Univ. New York, Glensfalls Gen. Hosp. 1960-1; res. physician, internal med. N.Y. Polyclinic Hosp. Med. Ctr. 1961-3; sr. res./NIH Fellow Joslin Diabetes Ctr., Harvard Med. Sch. 1963-4; physician/internist, solo pvt. practice 1964-; instr., asst. prof. Internal Med., N.Y. Med. Coll. 1964-7; prof. of medicine (Distinguished Professorship) Touro Coll. 1975-8; recipient Klaus Found. Postgrad. Merit Scholarship 1959-60; mem: Am. Diabetes Assoc., So. Calif. affil.; Graduate Council, Univ. of Zurich; mil: capt., inf./ field intell., I.D.F.; rec: classical music, swimming. Res: 2 Ketch St, Marina Peninsula, Marina Del Rey 90292 Ofc: 804 Venice Blvd Venice 90291

GULLICKSON, HOWARD MAXFIELD, lawyer; b. May 15, 1911, Great Falls, Mont.; s. John Albert and Hannah Gertrude (Nelson) G.; m. Ingeborg Bollmann, May 21, 1971; edn: JD, Univ. of Montana 1935; admitted to the bars of Mont., Calif., Colo. and Wyo. Career: gen. law practice, Billings, Mont. 1935-40; atty. gen. State of Montana 1941-42; staff atty. Shell Oil Co. 1946-53, gen. atty., Denver Colo. and Los Angeles 1954-63, mgr. land investments, NYC and Houston 1964-75; pvt. practice law, Rancho Santa Fe 1975-; pres. Plaza del Oro Corp. (Shell Oil subs.); asst. secty. Shell Oil Co.; chmn. Rocky Mountain Oil & Gas Assn. Legal Com. 1952-55; mem: Am. and Calif. Bar Assns., Am. Judicial Soc., Mont. State Bd. of Edn., San Diego Opera Assn.; San Diego Opera, San Digo Co. Seniors Golf Assn.; mil: lt. commdr. USN 1943-45, Bronze Star; Republican; Protestant; rec: golf. Res: 4835 El Mirlo Rancho Santa Fe 92067 Ofc: P.O. Box 1978 Rancho Santa Fe 92067

GUNDLACH, HEINZ L(UDWIG), investment banker; b. July 6, 1937, Dusseldorf, Germany; s. Heinrich and Ilse (Schuster) G.; div.; children: Andrew, b. 1971, Annabelle Kathryn, b. 1973; edn: LLD, Heidelberg Law Sch. 1963; JD, Wurzburg Law Sch. 1964. Career: Foreign Guest Tng. Pgm., The Chase Manhattan Bank, NA, NY, 1964; mgmt. trainee Dresdner Bank A.G., Frankfurt, 1964-65; financial v.p., Pipeline Constrn. Div., Thyssen A.G., 1965-66; v.p. and partner, Loeb, Rhoades & Co., Investment Bankers, 1967-75; dir. and mem. exec. com. Sunbelt Properties, Inc., 1975, v.chmn. of bd., 1976-, pres. 1978-81; mil: served in W. Ger. Army, sgt. ROTC, dischg. 1959; clubs: The Recess (NYC), Annabelle's (London); Prot.; rec: skiing. Ofc: 600 B Street San Diego 92110, 375 Park Avenue, NY, NY 10152

GUNDZIK, RICHARD MICHAEL, chemical engineering consultant; b. Nov. 10, 1930, Cleveland, Ohio; s. Michael and Anna (Petrus) G.; m. Arlene Geitz, Nov. 9, 1952; children: Sharlene b. 1958, Sharon b. 1961, Richard L.M. b. 1965; edn: BS, Case Western Reserve Univ. 1953; Reg. Profl. Engr., Calif.; Lic. Gen. Engring. Contractor, Calif.; DOD Fallout Shelter Analyst. Career: aeronautical research scientist National Advy. Com. for Aeronautics 1953-54; chem.

engr. American Steel & Wire, US Steel Corp. 1954-57; mgr. chem. engring. Kerr-McGee Corp. 1957-70; engring. v.p. Garrett Research & Devel. Corp. 1970-77; senior mgr. Occidental Research Corp. 1977-85; currently, chemical engring. cons. Grefco Inc., Torrance 1985-; honors: S.W. Smith scholastic prize in engring.; contbns. to Florida Plant Task Force, Occidental Research Corp. 1980; contbns. to Titanium Dioxide Plant, Am. Potash Corp. 1966; mem: Am. Inst. of Chem. Engrs., Am. Assn. of Cost Engrs., Sigma Xi, Tau Beta Pi; works: 31 patents 1966-78; 3 publs. 1954, 1974, 1982; mil: sgt. US Army 1955-56, (chief Chem. & Metallurgical Labs., Tokyo Ord. Depot); Republican; Catholic; rec: auto collecting, skiing. Res: 650 Nenno Ave. Placentia 92670 Ofc: Grefco Inc., 3435 W. Lomita Blvd. Torrance 90509

GURLING, GARY ALLAN, engineer-hybrid/microelectronics; b. Apr. 10, 1946, National City; s. Edward Francis and Anita May (Laird) G.; m. Beverly Ruskow, Jan. 27, 1979; edn: BSEE, CSU San Diego 1973. Career: tech. asst., draftsman, designer, assoc. engr. General Dynamics/Electronics Div., San Diego 1966-, currently senior engr. in hybrid/microelectronics, 1979-; mem: Internat. Soc. for Hybrid Microelectronics, Internat. Electronics Pkging. Soc.; Democrat; Christian; rec: photog., skiing, gardening. Res: 6821 Rolando Knolls Dr La Mesa 92041 Ofc: General Dynamics/ Electronics Div., POB 85310, M/Z 7234-R, San Diego 92138

GURNEY, KATHLEEN SUSAN, financial psychologist; b. June 25, 1946, Newark, NJ; d. Wm. John and Lily May (Curran) G.; edn: BA, Upsala Coll. 1968; MA, Seton Hall Univ. 1970; PhD, Univ. So. Calif. 1981; lic. Ednl. Psychol. & Marriage, Family, Child Therapist Calif. 1976. Career: rehab. counselor Orange County Rehab. Ctr.; psychologist Newark (NJ) Bd. of Edn., L.A. Unified Sch. Dist. 1976-86; asst. prof. Univ. So. Calif. 1981-85; pres. Kathleen Gurnay Assocs. 1982-; mem: Am. Psychol. Assn., Internat. Assn. of Financial Planners; pioneer new field in psychol.- financial psychology; author Financial Personality Profile (1982, 86); articles in national magazines, newspapers; national speaker and television guest; rec: oil painting, ballet, tennis, golf. Res: 240 Moreno Dr Beverly Hills 90212 Ofc: POB 10936 Beverly Hills 90213-3936

GURNEY, KATHLEEN SUSAN, financial psychologist; b. June 25, 1946, Newark, NJ; d. Wm. John and Lily May (Curran) G.; edn: BA, Upsala Coll. 1968; MA, Seton Hall Univ. 1970; PhD, Univ. So. Calif. 1981; lic. Ednl. Psychol. & Marriage, Family, Child Therapist Calif. 1976. Career: rehab. counselor Essex County Rehab. Ctr.; psychologist Newark (NJ) Bd. of Edn., L.A. Unified Sch. Dist. 1976-86; asst. prof. Univ. So. Calif. 1981-85; pres. Kathleen Gurney Assocs. 1982-; mem: Am. Psychol. Assn., Internat. Assn. of Financial Planners; pioneer new field in psychol.- financial psychology; author Financial Personality Profile (1982, 86); articles in national magazines, newspapers; national speaker and television guest; rec: oil painting, ballet, tennis, golf. Res: 240 Moreno Dr Beverly Hills 90212 Ofc: POB 10936 Beverly Hills 90213-3936

GUSTAFSON, KENNETH GENE, financial planner; b. Aug. 27, 1922, Akron, Ohio; s. Paul Runkle and Olive Everlyn (MacDowell) G.; m. Carol, June 6, 1959; children: Jeffrey b. 1962, Amy b. 1964; edn: BS, UC Berkeley 1948; desig: Chartered Life Underwriter (CLU) 1966, Chartered Finl. Cons. (ChFC) 1985, American Coll, Bryn Mawr. Career: life underwriter Penn Mutual Life 1949-; owner Property Casualty Agency 1957-83; reg. rep. 1969-; semi-ret.; mem: Am. Soc. CLU, Estate Plnng. Council of Diablo Valley (charter), Big C Soc. (pres. 1946), Phi Kappa Psi, Calif. Alumni Foresters (UC Berkeley); mil: USNR Air Corps active duty 1942-44, NROTC 1944-46, lt. j.g. Aviation Line Vol. Reserve, ret; Protestant; rec: golf, fishing. Res: 15 Snow Ct. Orinda 94563

GUTIERREZ, OLGA, psychiatrist/educator; b. Dec. 29, 1929, Buenos Aires, Argentina; d. Salvador and Soledad (Garcia Bueno) G.; granddau. of Jose San Roman, Dean, Sch. of Medicine, Spain; div.; 1 son, Luis Eduardo, b. 1961; edn: immunologist, Inst. Pasteur, Paris 1959; PhD in biochem., Univ. Buenos Aires 1954, MD, 1967; 3d. postgrad. phys. in psychiatry, USC 1980. Career: ednl. asst. Univ. Buenos Aires, 1953-58; research fellow, Inst. Pasteur, Paris, 1958-60; ednl. chief and research assoc. Univ. Buenos Aires, 1960-70; resrch. fellow Superior Council of Biol. Resrch, Madrid, Spain 1970-71; resrch. fellow, Reproductive Biol., OB-Gyn, USC, 1971-74; pvt. practice of med., Buenos Aires, 1975-77; postgrad. phys. tng. in psychiatry, USC 1978-80; adult psychiatrist LAC/USC Med. Ctr. 1981, child and adolesc. psychiatrist, 1982, forensic psychiatrist USC Inst. of Psychiat., Law and Behavioral Scis., Dept. of Psychiatry 1985-; awards: Golden Medal, Univ. of Buenos Aires 1952, Faculty of Med. awd. 1954, Acad. of Med. awd. 1966; Jr. Chamber awd. 1968; mem: Soc. of Chem. of Uruguay (corres. mem.); Acad. of Pharm. and Biochem., Arg.; Microbiol. and Immunol. Assn.; AMA; Biochem. Assn.; publs: over 15 sci. arts. rel. to medicine; guest appearances on t.v. and radio on psychiatric issues; Catholic; rec: sports, swimming, sailing, tennis. Res: 101 California Ave, Apt 507, Santa Monica 90403 Ofc: 746 W Adams Blvd Los Angeles 90007

GVILLO, FREDRICK HENRY, corporate development executive; b. Dec. 23, 1948, Alton, Ill.; s. Benjamin Fredrick H. and Pearl Francis (Mason) G.; m. Katherine Joanne Kacena, June 20, 1970; children: Michael b. 1972, Jeffrey b. 1975; edn: BS agriculture, Univ. Ill. 1971. Career: biol. prod. mgr. Pitman-Moore Inc. Wash. Crossing, NJ 1975-83; mkt. devel. mgr. Animal Health and Nutrition, Genentech Inc. S. San Francisco 1983-85; dir. corp. devel. Codon Inc. Brisbane, Calif. 1983-; mem: San Ramon Valley United Methodist Ch., Walnut Creek Little League; rec: fishing, woodworking. Ofc: Codon Inc. 430 Valley Dr Brisbane 94005

GYAN, VIJAY, physician, anaethesiologist; b. Nov. 2, 1946, Chaguanas, Trinidad and Tobago; s. William and Gautam (Mooleedhar) G.; edn: GCE, Queen's Royal Coll. 1965; BS, Univ. of the West Indies 1969, MBBS, 1974. Career: med. microbiologist Univ. of W. Indies, Kingston, Jamaica 1969; food microbiologist Bureau of Standards, Kingston, Jamaica 1970; grad. spl. Ambassador Coll., Pasadena 1974-76; cons. anaesthesiologist Community Hosp. of Los Angeles 1980-82; cons. anaesthesiologist Hosp. Del Pueblo, E. Los Angeles 1982−; honors: Geddes Grant Prize in Zoology 1963, 1964, 1965, and in science 1965; Distn. in Zoology, Univ. of Cambridge 1964, 1965; works: Isolation of Leptospirosis Jamaicii, Univ. of the W. Indies 1969; Biochemistry of the Irreversibly Sickled Cell, Univ. Fla. Papanicola Cancer Research Inst. 1970; NIL; World Wide Ch. of God; rec: pvt. pilot, comml. pilot, flight instr., jet co-pilot. Res: 17366 Sunset Blvd. #305B, Pacific Palisades 90272 Ofc: Hospital Del Pueblo, Pomona Blvd., E. Los Angeles

GYEMANT, INA LEVIN, judge; b. Aug. 2, 1943, San Francisco; d. Manuel and Mildred Lita (Woloski) Levin; m. Robert Ernest Gyemant, June 7, 1970; children: Robert Ernest, Anne Elizabeth; edn: AB, UC Berkeley 1965, JD, Hastings Coll. of Law 1968; admitted to Calif. State Bar 1969. Career: clk. chief justice Calif. Supreme Ct., 1969; dep. pub. defender City and County of San Francisco, 1970; individual practice law, San Francisco, 1971; dep. atty. gen. State of Calif., San Francisco 1972-81; municipal ct. judge, San Francisco 1980−; mem. Am., San Francisco bar assns., Calif. Judges Assn. (Executive Bd. 1985-), Queen's Bench (dir. 1976-80, pres. 1979), Calif. Women Lawyers, Foster Parents Assn., Alpha Epsilon Phi; Commonwealth Club of Calif. (ch. law enforcement sect. 1976-79), Barrister's, Criminal Trial Lawyers, SF Lawyer's Wives, Met., Variety Club of No. Calif. (SF); Republican. Ofc: City Hall, San Francisco 94102

HA, CHONG WAN, data processing executive; b. Oct. 26, 1938, Seoul, Korea, nat. US cit. 1977; s. Kyung S. and Gyung N. (Park) Ha; m. Karen, Aug. 19, 1968; children: Jean Frances b. 1969, Julie Anne b. 1972; edn: BA in econs., UC Los Angeles 1970; MA in mgmt., Claremont Grad. Sch. 1985. Career: systems pgmmr./analyst Transam. Corp., 1968-72; senior systems pgmmr. Atlantic Richfield Co., 1973-78; asst. v.p./mgr. Calif. Data Center, First Interstate Bancorp., 1978-85; v.p. D.P. Services, Ticor Title Ins. Co., 1985−; civic: Police Reserve, City of Monterey Park 1981-82; Democrat; Prot.; rec: music, golf. Res: 7801 Via Foggia Burbank 91504 Ofc: Ticor Title Insurance Co 6300 Wilshire Blvd Ste 686 Los Angeles 90048

HAAK, HAROLD H., university president; b. June 1, 1935, s. Harold John Andrew and Laura (Kittleson) H.; m. Betty Steiner, June 25, 1955; children: Alison, b. 1963, Janet, b. 1965; edn: BA, Univ. of Wisc. 1957, MA, 1958; PhD, Princeton Univ. 1963. Career: asst./assoc. prof. of political sci., San Diego St. Coll. 1962-69, prof. of public adminstrn. and urban studies and dean Coll. of Profl. Studies, 1969-71; academic v.p. CSU Fresno, 1971-73; chancellor Univ. of Colo. at Denver, 1973-80; president CSU Fresno, 1980−; chmn. Denver Metropolitan Study Panel, 1976-77; bd. dirs. Fresno Economic Devel. Corp., 1981-, Fresno Philharmonic, 1981-, Fresno Chamber of Commerce, 1981-; awards: Distinguished Service Award, Denver Regl. Council of Govts. 1978; mem: Phi Beta Kappa, Phi Kappa Phi, Blue Key; club: Sunnyside Country. Res: 4411 N. Van Ness Blvd Fresno 93704 Ofc: California State University, Fresno 93740

HAAS, RALPH LEWIS, chemical engineer; b. June 12, 1928, Meiningen, Germany; s. Justin and Babette (Schuhman) H.; m. Rita S., Mar. 27, 1955; children: Renee b. 1960, Mark b. 1958, Jeffrey b. 1956; edn: Ohio State Univ. 1947-49, 1950-51; BSChE, Wash. Univ. (St. Louis) 1953; Reg. Profl. Engr. Mo. 1953. Career: non- metallic materials research inland Mfg. Div. Gen. Motors Corp. Dayton, Ohio; research chem. engr. Nat. Distillers & Chem. Corp. Cincinnati; staff process engr. Koppers Co. Inc. Pittsburgh; senior devel. engr. Aerojet General Corp. Sacramento; senior research engr. Union Carbide Corp. South Charleston, W. Va.; senior process engr. Fluor Corp. L.A.; proj. engr. Ralph M. Parsons Co. Pasadena; senior proj. engr./ mgr. Hooker Chem. & Plastics Corp. Tacoma, Wash.; engrg. cons.; honors: Assistanceship (Engrg. Experiment Station, Ohio State Univ. Dept. Metallurgy 1950-51); mem: Am. Chem. Soc. 1955-70, Am. Inst. Chem. Engrs. 1950-70, BSA, UNited Fund, Boys Club; works: devel. early prodn. type silicone brake cylinder bladder (patent assigned 1953), process devel. of butadiene coupling and sodium reduction to produce a diabasic acid (1954), design of Minuteman Missile System ignition system (1959), space application devel. of ablative insulation materials (1962), seal failure correlations for static application o-rings (1965), part. in nat. award- winning design improvement of ammonia plants 1968, part. design & constrn. proj. mgmt. of North Slope Prudhoe Bay oil field devel. 1974-78; publs: tech. research articles, design manual; rec: philately. Res: 984 Berenice Dr Brea 92621

HABERBERGER, RICHARD LOUIS, JR., microbiologist; b. June 2, 1951, East St. Louis, Ill.; s. Richard L., Sr. and Patricia Ann (Henderson) H.; m. Cynthia Irby, June 30, 1973; children: Lori b. 1975, Sarah b. 1977, Amy b. 1979; edn: BS, Rockhurst Coll. 1973; MS, Northeast La. Univ. 1975; PhD, So. Ill. Univ. 1983; Reg. Microbiologist (1979), Splst. in Public Health and Med. Lab. (1984), Am. Acad. of Microbiol. Career: microbiol. supr. Herrin (Ill.) Hosp., 1976-83, also microbiol. cons. Bethesda Med. Ctr. 1980-83, Franklin County Hosp. 1981-82, and adj. instr. Rural Allied Health Manpower Pgm., So. Ill. Univ. 1978-80; microbiol. supr. Welborn Baptist Hosp., Evansville, Ind. 1983; microbiologist US Navy Medical Service Corps, Oakland 1983−, sci. ofcr. Naval Biosciences Lab.; honors: Dean's List (1970, 71, 73); mem. Am.

Soc. for Microbiol., Am. Public Health Assn., No. Calif. Am. Soc. for Microbiology; civic: Junior CofC, K.C., Elks, Masons, Scottish Rites, Shriners, PTA, Alpha Phi Omega (1973); research publs. (1983-86), Chlamydin Prevalence in Coll. Students (J. of Am. Coll. Health Assn. 1985); mil: lt. USNR 1983-; Republican; Catholic; rec: gardening, hunting, bowling. Res: 302A Nimitz Dr Yerba Buena Island San Francisco 94130 Ofc: Naval Biosciences Lab Bldg 844 Naval Supply Center Oakland 94625

HACKETT, OTIS EDWIN, real estate appraiser/broker; b. Jan. 14, 1950, Los Angeles; s. Otis Everett and Ruth Davenport (Myers) H.; m. Karen E. Bailey, Oct. 26, 1985; edn: BA, UC Los Angeles 1974; Real Estate Cert., W. L.A. Coll. 1976; Approved Appraiser, Fed. Nat. Mortgage Assn., and Calif. State Svgs. and Loan Commnr.; desig: MAI, Am. Inst. of R.E. Appraisers; SRPA, Soc. of R.E. Appraisers; ASA, Am. Soc. of Appraisers. Career: real estate appraiser Marina Federal Savings, Torrance 1976-77; senior appraisal ofcr. Calif. First Bank, L.A. 1977-83; senior analyst Lea Assocs. Inc., L.A. 1983−; owner/broker/ cons. prin., Woodland Hills 1984−; mem. Nat., Calif. Assn. Realtors, San Fernando Valley Bd. Realtors, SAR; Episcopal; rec: fishing, non-fiction lit., running. Ofc: Otis E. Hackett, Realtor 22131 Oxnard St Woodland Hills 91367; Lea Associates Inc 1635 Pontius Ave Los Angeles 90025

HADDAD, EDMONDE ALEX, public affairs executive; b. July 25, 1931, Los Angeles; s. Alexander Saleeba and Madeline Angela (Zail) H.; m. Harriet Lenhart, Dec. 22, 1955; children: Mark Edmonde b. 1956, Brent Michael b. 1959, John Alex b. 1964; edn: AA, Los Angeles City Coll. 1956; BA, Univ. So. Calif. 1958; MA, Columbia Univ. 1961. Career: editorial assoc. CBS-KNX Radio News L.A. 1957-58; staff writer WCBS News NY 1959-61; news reporter/ commentator KPOL AM & FM Radio News L.A. 1961-73; dir. public affairs KPOL 1967-73; exec. dir. L.A. World Affairs Council 1973-84, pres. 1984−; honors: Mayor Tom Bradley and City of L.A. Award for Contrbns. to Internat. Understanding (1983), Am. Pol. Sci. Assn. Award for Disting. Reporting of Foreign Affairs (1967), Golden Mike Award- Best Commentary (Radio & Television News Assn. of So. Calif. 1965), Outstanding Young Men of Am., US Jr. CofC (1966), CBS News & Public Affairs Fellowship, Columbia Univ. (1958); mem: Nat. Council World Affairs Orgns. (pres. 1980-83), Radio & TV News Assn. of So. Calif. (pres. 1965-67), Am. Friends of Wilton Park (v.p. 1976-82); founder, publr. World Affairs Jour.; author: Suggestions for the Reporting of Civil Disorders (Columbia Journalism Review 1967), contbg. author How Peace Came to the World (MIT Press, Christian Sci. Monitor 1986); Episcopal; rec: reading, people-watching. Ofc: Los Angeles World Affairs Council 900 Wilshire Blvd Ste 230 Los Angeles 90017

HADDAD, WISAM BOULOS, surgeon; b. Mar. 4, 1954, Amman, Jordan, nat. USA 1985; s. Boulos Somail and Taman M. (Hawatmeh) H.; m. Rozanne, June 12, 1977; children: Angie b. 1980, Laila b. 1982, Laura b. 1985; edn: BS, acad. distinction, Andrews Univ. 1976; MD, Loma Linda Univ. 1979; lic. phys. Calif. 1981. Career: gen. surgical residency Loma Linda Univ. 1980-85; attending surgeon Riverside General Hosp., University Medical Center; instr. in surg. Loma Linda Univ. 1985-; honors: Alpha Omega Alpha, LLU Sch. of Med. Alumni Assn. medal for Distinction in Quest of Excellence 1979; mem: AMA, CMA, candidate Am. Coll. of Surgeons; publs: Am. Jour. of Surgery 1985, papers presented Tri-County Surg. Soc. of So. Calif. Annual Clinic Day 1984, 85; Seventh Day Adventist; rec: travel, camping, fishing. Res: 12734 Dutch St., Grand Terrace 92324 Ofc: Riverside General Hospital, 9851 Magnolia Ave Riverside 92503

HADDEN, FRANCES ELIZABETH, data processing executive; b. Nov. 6, 1944, NY, NY; d. Alfred August and Mary Elizabeth (Lentz) Schuhsler; m. Earl F. Hadden II, Nov. 7, 1970; children: Elizabeth Patricia b. 1974, Amanda Ratliff b. 1977; edn: BS, honors, Chestnut Hill Coll. 1965; MS, Bucknell Univ. 1966. Career: with IBM Corp. 1966-78; sys engr. New Jersey Govt. & Svcs. branch office, Cranford, NJ 1966-67; sys. engr. Los Angeles Fin. & Ins., Los Angeles 1967-70; sys. engr., Custom Contract Svcs,. Los Angeles 1970-78; senior sys. analyst Western Airlines, Los Angeles 1978-81, supvr. personnel sys. & pgmmg. 1981-82, group supvr. personnel/ mktg./ revenue acctg. sys. & pgmmg. 1982-83, mgr. mktg. information sys. & pgmmg. 1983-84, mgr. fin./ adminstrv. sys. & pgmmg. 1984−; awards: Assistantship, Bucknell Univ.; Republican; Catholic; rec: travel, bridge. Ofc: Western Airlines, 6060 Avion Dr. Los Angeles 90045

HADLEY, RUTH BANDY, educator; b. March 28, 1925, Honolulu, Hi.; d. Edwin Reeder Powell and Ruth Marie (Bandy) Powell Millikan; edn: BA, Univ. Ariz. 1958. MA, Calif. Polytechnic Univ. 1967, postdoctoral pgm., 1982-; m. John Hadley, Oct. 9, 1948; children: John Craige b. 1949, Ruth Bandy b. 1952. Career: instr. Allan Hancock Coll., Vandenberg AFB 1958-59; lectr. Calif. Lutheran Coll., Santa Maria 1978-79; tchr. Lompoc Unif. Sch Dist. 1959-85; cons. Calif. State Dept. of Edn. 1985−; chair Calif. State Legal Compliance Com. 1984−; commnr. Curriculum Devel. & Supplemental Mat. Commn. 1981-84; mem. Calif. Assessment Pgm., Math. Advy. Com. 1978−; mem. writing team Calif. Dept. of Edn., honors: Commdn., Pres. Awards for Excellence in Sci. & Math. Tchg. 1985; Delta Kappa Gamma, 1976; mem: Nat. Council of Tchrs. of Math, Calif. Math Council (life), Math. Council (charter pres., Calif. Central Coast 1984), Nat. Council of Supvrs. of Math., Oregon Council of Tchrs. of Math., Delta Delta Delta (charter Phi Beta chpt.), Calif. Tchrs. Assn., Lompoc Edn. Assn. (pres. 1978); publs: Math. Handbook, 1982; Calif. Proficiency Assessment Sample Items (math.), 1978; Test Item Writing Com., 3rd., 6th., and 12th. Grade Calif. Assessment Pgm. Tests; Test Item Writing Com., Calif. Basic Ednl. Skills Test (math) 1983-; coord. Calif. State

Bd. of Edn. pubs: Raising Expectations: Model Graduation Requirements 1983 (math), Calif. Math. Framework Addendum 1980, Calif. Math. Framework 1985, Calif. K-8 Curriculum Guide Writing Com. 1985-86, Instrnl. Mats. Evaluation Panel for Math. Adoption cycle 1986-87; Concrete to Abstract, Manipulative Activities and Games in the Math. Classroom, NEA pub. 1978; Episcopal; rec: golf, computer. Res: 1414 So. Wallis Santa Maria 93454

HAENNELT, GLADYS GOLDEN, public accountant; b. Mar. 7, 1910, Golden, Colo.; d. Albert David and Weltha May (Ragan) Fletcher; m. Leon Haennelt (dec.), Sept. 28, 1927; children: David Lee (dec.) b. 1931, Gladys Catherine (dec.) b. 1935; edn: Hartnell Coll., Salinas 1965, contg. edn. Cabrillo Coll., Aptos 1972-; lic. Public Acct., St. of Calif. (1943). Career: teletype opr. Western Union, Salinas 1941-43; bookkeeper Hal Attenborough, P.A., Salinas 1942-43, Whitehill's Mens Store, 1942-43; self-empl. public acct., public stenographer, Salinas 1943-53, Watsonville 1953 –; mem. Bus. and Profl. Womens Club, Salinas 1945-53; civic: 4-H Clubs, PTA and sch. booster activities; Catholic (Altar Soc., instr. First Communion classes); avocation: writing for children, enrolled Inst. of Children's Literature. Address: 540 Lewis Rd Watsonville 95076

HAFTEL, ANTHONY J., physician, hospital emergency services director; b. Dec. 9, 1944, Philadelphia, Penn.; s. Samuel and Gladys (Frankenthal)e H.; m. Janiece, May 12, 1979; 1 dau: Ingrid b. 1984; edn: BA, Central H.S. 1962; BSME, Drexel Univ. 1967; MD, Univ. of Penn. 1971; Bd. Cert. Emergency Phys. 1983. Career: surgical res. UC San Diego, 3 yrs.; res. emerg. med. Univ. of Chicago; sub spec. fellowship, peaditric emerg. med. Univ. of Wash., Seattle; phys. emerg. med. Mercy Hosp., San Diego; currently, chief emerg. med. div. Children's Hosp., Los Angeles also dir. fellowship pgm. emerg. pediatrics and current chmn. Trauma Pgm., Critical Care Svcs. and Distaer Comm.; dir. pediatric edn. Los Angeles Co. Paramedics; mem: Los Angeles Pediatric Soc. (Com. on Emerg. Svcs.), Am. Coll. of Emerg. Phys.; author: Fifty Cases in Pediatric Emergencies, Aspen Publ., Rockville, Md. Res: 4923 Worster Ave. Sherman Oaks 91423 Ofc: Childrens Hosp. of Los Angeles, 4650 Sunset Ave. Los Angeles 90027

HAGAN, JONELLE JOAN, chiropractor; b. June 8, 1957, Castro Valley, Calif.; d. John William and Patricia A. (Duff) A.; edn: UC Berkeley 1975-77; Sherman Coll. opf Chiro. 1978; DC, Life Chiro. Coll. 1982; Diplomate Nat. Bd. Chiro. Examiners. Career: assoc. Van Born Chiro. Clin. Dearborn Heights, Mich. 1982-83, Family Chiro. Clin. Irvine 1983-84; owner/ dir. Hagan Chiropractic San Ramon & Fremont 1984 –; mem: Internat. Chiro. Assn., ICA Calif., Calif. Chiro. Assn., Lambda Delta Epsilon (founder, charter mem.), San Ramon CofC, Alpha Chi Omega Alumni, Mt. Diablo Club, Pilot Assn. (women's bus. grp.); publ: articles on low back pain (Barnstormer, Irvine 1983); Republican; rec: writing, tennis, volleyball. Res: 38323 Blacow Rd Fremont 94536 Ofc: Hagan Chiropractic 2570 San Ramon Valley Blvd San Ramon 94583

HAGEN, WILLARD LYLE, arboriculturist; b. Feb. 13, 1913, Woodlake, Neb.; s. Sylvester C. and Katie Bell (King) H.; m. Ruth Madsen, June 12, 1956; children: Alma b. 1957, Jarom b. 1958; edn: BS, Cal. Poly. Univ. S.L.O. Career: show card & sign painting; arboriculturist cons. and broker, tree service 30 yrs.; mem. L.A. County Arboretum (furnished them with many rare and unusual trees); imported Kamthoica tree from China, from which drug is extracted to treat leukemia; landscaped many homes and streets in Arcadia, San Marino and Pasadena; contbr. Nursery Mag.; mil: sgt. USAAC 4 yrs.; L.D.S.; rec: hi fi equip., video & home entertainment. Res: 135 Las Tunas Dr Arcadia 91006

HAGGSTROM, EDWARD JAMES, manufacturing engineer; b. Nov. 12, 1942, Blair, Neb.; s. August and Mildred Ruby (Shulte) H.; m. Alice Alford, May 25, 1966; children: Deborah b. 1951, April b. 1967, Edward b. 1970, Dusty b. 1974; edn: AA, Citrus Coll. 1977. Career: assembler Sawyer Inc. Arcadia 1964-65, research & devel. lab. 1965-66, qual. control mgr. 1966-69, supv. customer svc. dept. 1969-79; plant supv. Electra-Motion Inc. 1979-84, qual. control/ R&D engr. 1984–; civic: Azusa Jr. All American Football (pres. 1982, 83, 84), Azusa Youth Pgm. (pres. 1985); mem. Am. Legion; mil: USMC 1959-63; Catholic; rec: camping. Ofc: Electra-Motion Inc. 40 N Daisy Ave Pasadena 91107

HAGOPIAN, RICHARD AVEDIS, deli owner, artist; b. April 3, 1937, Fowler; s. Khosrof and Angel H.; m. Geraldine M. Simonian, Nov. 5, 1960; children: Kay b. 1961, Harold b. 1964, Richard b. 1966. Career: farmer, owner grape farm; prop. Hagopian's Internat. Delicatessen; profl. OUD player with sev. records; apptd. Resident Folk Artist, CSU Fullerton 1979; tchr. The World of Richard Hagopian, CSU Fullerton; honors: Named Oudi, Oudi Hrant of Instanbul, Turkey 1969; founder The Kef Time Band, 1967; mem: Knights of Vartan, Masons (num. pos.), Shriners; mil: splst. 4/c Calif. Army Nat. Guard 1959-65; Armenian Apostolic; rec: music (Middle Eastern, Armenian), fishing, collecting books on Armenian art minatures. Res: 633 Whitney Ln Visalia 93277 Ofc: Hagopian's Internat. Deli, 409 No. Willis St Visalia 93291

HAHN, BRIAN (YONG KUN HAN), real estate co. president; b. July 14, 1947, Seoul, Korea, nat. US cit. 1982; s. Seaduk (Park) H.; m. Grace, Mar. 18, 1974; 1 dau. Sarah b. 1974; edn: BA, Hanyang Univ. 1966; Calif. lic. real estate broker (1980); Cert. Business Opportunity Appriaser, Am. BUs. Consultants Inc. (1983). Career: oriental mktg. supr. Liberty Water Systems Inc., Pomona 1979-80; realtor asso./v.p. Chong Lee Investment Co., Los Angeles 1980-82; realtor assoc./bus. appraiser, Calif. Realty & Inv. Co., 1982-83; realtor/pres.

Zenith Props. Inc., Los Angeles 1983 –; honors: appreciation, Korean Am. Coalition (1986), Northwest Center (1985); mem. Nat. Assn. of Realtors, Calif. Assn. of Realtors, Los Angeles Board of Realtors, Greater L.A. Apt. Assn., Nat. Notary Assn.; civic: World Family of Bluebird (dir.); mil: sp4 US Army 1976-79; Republican; Baptist; rec: golf, bowling. Res: 213 S Martel Ave Los Angeles 90036 Ofc: Zenith Properties Inc. 601 N Vermont Ave Ste 205 Los Angeles 90004

HAHN, GORDON RYERSON, real estate brokerage president, ret.; b. Apr. 15, 1919, Kinderseley, Sask., Canada, nat. US cit. 1926; s. John Henry and Hattie Louise (Wiggins) H.; m. Donna Sunkler, Mar. 24, 1961; children: David Gordon b. 1962, Debra Louise (Andrews) b. 1964; edn: BS, US Merchant Marine Acad. 1944; BA, Pepperdine Univ. 1950; Calif. lic. R.E. Broker 1963. Career: dep. county clk. County of Los Angeles 1938-43; mem. Assembly, Calif. State Legislature, 66th Dist., 1947-53; elected Los Angeles City Council 1953-63; real estate broker, cons./pres. Gordon R. Hahn, Associates, Inc., 1963 –; fmr. instr. Pepperdine Univ.; honors: elected to John C. Fremont H.S. Hall of Fame (1986); mem. (fmr.) L.A. Bd. Realtors, Pepperdine Univ. Alumni Assn. (past pres.), Kings Point Merchant Marine Acad. Alumni Assn.; civic: Pacific Christian Coll., Fullerton (dir.), Billy Graham Crusade for L.A. (past exec. com.), L.A. Sister Cities Com., San Jose Bible Coll. (past dir.); mil: deck ofcr. US Merchant Marine WWII, ofcr. USNR; Republican; Christian Ch. Address: Torrance 90503

HAHN, JAMES KENNETH, city attorney; b. July 3, 1950, Los Angeles; s. Kenneth and Ramona (Fox) H.; m. Monica Ann Teson, May 19, 1984; edn: BA Eng. magna cum laude, Pepperdine Univ. 1972; JD, Pepperdine Sch. of Law 1975; admitted Calif. State Bar 1975. Career: prosecutor Los Angeles City Atty's Ofc. 1975-79; pvt. practice law Horner & Hahn, Marina Del Rey 1979-81; elected City of L.A. Controller 1981-85; elected L.A. City Atty. 1985 –; mem: Nat. Inst. Municipal Law Ofcrs. (chair litig. com.), Am. Bar Assn. (vice chmn. Govt. Tort & Liability Com.), United Way Corp. Allocations Com. (vice chair L.A. reg.); Democrat; Ch. of Christ. Ofc: L.A. City Atty's Ofc., 1800 City Hall East, 200 N Main St Los Angeles 90012

HAINES, GEORGE LAMAR, lawyer; b. Aug. 28, 1935, Harre De Grace, Md.; s. G. Lamar and Miriam Elizabeth (Lysle) H.; children: Heather, b. 1963; Brent, b. 1967; edn: BS, Penn. State 1957; BD, Princeton 1960; ThM, 1962; PhD, NY Univ. 1966; Calif. comm. coll. 1970; post doctorate, UCLA 1973; JD, Western State Univ. 1978. Career: prof. CSU Long Beach 1971-74; v.p. Anthony Schs. Newport Beach Education Corp. 1975-78; pres. Haines Financial Cons., Inc., Fullerton 1978 –; pres. George L. Haines Investments, Inc., Fullerton 1978; chmn. bd. H & A Internat. Investments Inc. 1983-; prof. Anthony Schs. 1974-; trustee Univ. of Penn. Presbyterian Hosp. 1968-70; trustee Bucks Co. Hist. Soc. 1968-70; honors: Delta Sigma Roe nat. pub. spkg. hon. soc., Penn. State 1957; Presidential Award, Princeton 1960; Founders Day Award, NYU 1966; mem: WRCV T.V., Phila. (t.v. moderator 1963); Save Headstart Ctrs. (chmn. 1966-68); Presbyterian; rec: music, theatre, travel. Res: 3062 Associated Rd., No. 14, Fullerton 92635 Ofc: Haines Financial Consultants, Inc., P.O. Box 18019, Irvine 92713

HAINSWORTH-STRAUS, CHRISTINE LOUISE, commercial real estate broker; b. Oct. 29, 1962, Alton, Ill.; s. Joseph Richard, II and Nola Jo (Harwood) Hainsworth; m. Michael W. Straus, Aug. 31, 1985; edn: bus. adminstrn., Eng. lit., Principia Coll. 1983; real estate broker Mo. 1984; real estate sales Calif. 1986. Career: leasing agent Murdoch & Coll Inc. St. Louis 1983-84, mktg. mgr. 1984-86; comml. real estate broker William D. Feldman Assocs. Culver City, Calif. 1986 –; candidate Am. Inst. Realtors; mem: Nat. Assn. Female Execs., Comml. Real Estate Women; publ: poems in Praxis (1983); Christian Science (sunday sch. tchr.); rec: tennis, soccer, Japanese & French impressionist art. Res: 140 S Mentor Ave Apt 211 Pasadena 91106 Ofc: William D. Feldman Assocs. 5995 S Sepulveda Blvd Culver City 90230

HAIRABEDIAN, MARTIN, JR., police chief; b. Aug. 18, 1932, Chgo.; s. Martin and Tamara (Kacutoff) H.; m. Pauline, Mar. 15, 1953; children: Pamela b. 1955, Penny b. 1957, Patricia b. 1961; edn: AA in police sci., 1963; Southwestern Univ. Law Sch. 1963-66; JD, South Bay Univ. 1976; admitted Calif. State Bar 1976. Career: ofcr. Los Angeles Police Dept., 1954-, sgt. 1960-, lt. 1964-, capt. 1969-, ret. L.A.P.D. 1977; apptd. chief of police, City of Fullerton, 1977 –; mem. Calif. Crime Resistance Task Force; commnr. Orange County Human Relations Commn.; honors: Honor Cadet No. 1, L.A. Police Acad. 1954, Man of the Year Pico Robertson Lions Club 1971; mem: Internat. Assn. of Chiefs of Police, Calif. Police Chiefs Assn., Calif. Peace Ofcrs. Assn., Orange County Chiefs Assn. (pres.), Police Mgmt. Assn.; Rotarian; Civil Air Patrol; Orange County Steering Com. to elect Gov. Geo. Deukmejian 1982; wks: implemented Neighborhood Watch Pgm. (1977), Police Community Council (1978), K-9 Program (1983), policed Team Handball Olympic Event, 1984; Republican; Orthodox; rec: golf, pvt. pilot, skiing. Ofc: Fullerton Police Dept. 237 W Commonwealth Ave Fullerton 92632

HAKIM, ALBERT, corporate finance and export executive; b. June 21, 1943, Alexandria, Egypt, French citizen, US resident; s. David and Allegra (Betito) H.; m. Barbara, Oct. 29, 1982; children: Thierry b. 1965, Sophie b. 1967, Martine b. 1970; edn: French CPA and MBA equivalent 1964. Career: mng. dir. French Investment Banking, Paris 1964-74; senior v.p. French Bank Metz, France 1974-77; exec. v.p./chief fin. ofcr., mfg., Paris 1977-79; chief exec. ofcr. Real Estate Constrn., Paris; chief exec. ofcr. Calif. Export & Devel. L.A. 1982 –; dir., bd. dirs. two cos. in France until 1982; mem. French Chamber of Financial Cons.; publ: book on the French Stock Exchange; mil: French Army 1962-63; Jewish; rec: boating. Ofc: Los Angeles

HAKIM, HOSNY F., engineer, general engineering contractor; b. March 1, 1946, El Maragha, Egypt, nat. US cit. 1983; s. Fawzy H. and Thoria (Ghali) H.; m. Soad, July 20, 1975; children: Marian Grace b. 1981, Rose Mary b. 1982; edn: BS, Univ. of Alexandria 1968; MS, Univ. of Toronto 1977; Reg. Profl. Engr., Wash. (1984), Calif. (1985); gen. engring. contractor, Calif. 1985. Career: research asst. Univ. of Toronto, Canada 1975-77; designer office of Jame Ruderman, NYC 1977-79; engr. Geiger Berger Assn., NY 1978-79; design engr. Ebasco Svcs. Inc., NY 1979-81, Wash. 1981-84; pres. Hakim & Habashi Inc., Pasadena 1984–; tchg. asst. Univ. of Toronto 1975-77; tchg. asst. Univ. of Alexandria, Egypt 1968-75; honors: Fellowship, Univ. of Toronto 1975-76; Univ. of Alexandria Scholarship 1963-68; publs: Automated Design of Rigid Steel Frames, Canadian Soc. of Civil Engrs., Conf. Montreal 1977; Christian. Ofc: Hakim & Habashi, 281 No. Altadena Dr. Pasadena 91107

HAKIM, SAID FRANCOIS, physician; b. Apr. 11, 1953, Beirut, Lebanon; s. Francois Said and Zariffe Nassib (Yammine) H.; edn: BS, Am. Univ. of Beirut 1974; MS, Univ. Nebr. Med. Ctr. 1977; MD, Univ. Nebr. Med. Sch. 1980. Career: resident pathol. Yale Univ. 1980-82, res. lab. med. Yale Univ. 1982-84; fellow hematopathol. UC Irvine/ Meml. Med. Ctr. Long Beach 1984-85; clin. instr. hematopathol. UC Irvine Med. Ctr. 1985-86, clin. adj. prof. 1986–; mem: Coll. of Am. Pathol., Am. Soc. Clin. Pathol., AMA; publ: papers in med. journs.; Christian-Maronite. Res: 6100 Edinger Ave, Apt 129, Huntington Beach 92647 Ofc: UC Irvine Med. Ctr. Pathol. Dept. 101 City Dr S Orange 92668

HALBERT, DOUGLAS JAMES, insurance co. executive; b. June 28, 1932, Porterville; s. Sherrill and Verna (Dyer) H.; m. Kay, Jan. 11, 1986; children: Douglas J., Jr. b. 1957, Richard A. b. 1958, Kimberlee L. (Young) b. 1961; edn: BS, Univ. of San Francisco; cert. Harvard Univ. Grad. Sch. Bus. Adminstrn., 1971. Career: secty. US Cong. LeRoy Johnson, 1954; mgmt. Aetna Casualty & Surety Co., 1958-70; asst. v.p. Aetna Life Insurance Co., 1971-75, regional dir. 1975-85, v.p./chief op. ofcr. Aetna Dental Care for Groups, Sherman Oaks 1985–; dir: Nicollet Eitel Family Health Plan (1971-75), Halbro Technologies (current); treas. Community Health Services (Hartford, Conn.) 1973-80 and commnr. Health & Welfare Commn. (Simsbury, Conn.) 1978-80; mem. Health Ins. Assn. of Am. (v.chmn. Calif. Council); clubs: Commonwealth Club of Calif., Hartford Club , Rotary Internat., Elks; mil: sgt. 1/c US Army Med. Corps 1951-54; Republican; Prot.; rec: computer tech. Res: 720 N Louise St Apt 314 Glendale 91206 Ofc: Aetna Dental Care for Groups 15260 Ventura Blvd Ste 2100 Sherman Oaks 91403-5307

HALBERT, SHERRILL, federal court judge, b. Oct. 17, 1901, Terra Bella, Calif.; s. Edward D. and Ellen (Rhodes) H.; m. Verna Dyer, Santa Rosa, June 7, 1927; children: Shirley Ellen (Mrs. Herbert M. Hanson, Jr.) b. 1929, Douglas James b. 1932; edn: AB, UC Berkeley 1924, JD 1927; admitted Calif. State Bar 1927. Career: estab. pvt. law practice, Porterville 1927-41; dep. dist. atty. Tulare County 1927-36, dep. atty. gen. State of Calif. 1942-44; assoc. with McCutchen, Thomas, Matthew, Griffiths & Greene law firm, S.F. 1942-44; pvt. practice law, Modesto 1944-49; asst. dist. atty. Stanislaus Co. 1944-49, dist. atty. 1949; judge Superior Ct., Stanislaus Co. 1949-54; apptd. U.S. Dist. Judge, No. Calif. 1954-69, senior judge 1969–; mem: Am. Bar Assn., Am. Judicature Soc.; past internat. pres. 20-30 Club, mem. Native Sons of the Golden West, Elks, Masons, Alpha Chi Rho, Phi Delta Phi, Lincoln Fellowship of So. Calif., Book Club of Calif., Rotary, Sutter Club (Sacto.), Commonwealth Club (SF); Republican (pres. Calif. Rep. Assoc. 1934-36, v.chmn. Young Rep. Nat. Fedn. 1938-42); rec: book collector, camellia hort., gardening. Res: 4120 Los Coches Way Sacramento 95821 Ofc: 2008 US Courthouse 650 Capitol Ave Sacramento 95814

HALBY, ANTHONY WAYNE, insurance agent; b. Nov. 22, 1949, Mesa, Ariz.; s. Tony and Linda H.; m. Charlene T., Aug. 21, 1971; children: Gabriella Marie b. 1982, Matthew James b. 1984, Mark Anthony b. 1986, Mark Alfred b. 1986; edn: BS in mgmt./mktg., Woodbury Univ. 1971. Career: ins. agt., Life, Health & Disability, 1972-, agency owner, La Crescenta 1973–, opened No. Calif. office, Nevada City, 1983–, splst. in Employee Benefits; mem: Los Angeles Assn. of Health Underwriters (charter mem. 1979, bd. dirs. 1981-83, pres. 1982-83), Nat. Assn. Health Underws. (mem. Leading Producers Round Table), Calif. Assn. Health Underws. (charter); Republican; Catholic; rec: fastpitch softball. Res: 11534 Country View Way Grass Valley 95945 Ofc: 206 Sacramento St Ste 302 Nevada City 95959; 3131 Foothill Blvd Ste H La Crescenta 91214

HALE, CAROLE DIANE JEZIORSKI GORDON, real estate appraiser/ consultant; b. Feb. 19, 1943, Los Angeles; d. Anthony John and Vivian (Smith) Jeziorski; m. 2d. Roger Hale, Feb. 14, 1982; 1 son (by previous m.), William Gordon, b. 1966; edn: AA, Orange Coast Coll. 1976; num. spl. profl. courses; Calif. lic. Real Estate Broker 1980-; MAI, Am. Inst. of R.E. Appraisers 1983. Career: secty./asst. Brabant Real Estate & Appraisals, Huntington Park 1971-73; sales agt. Tarbell Realtors, Costa Mesa 1974-75; assoc. appraiser Roger A. McInnes, MAI, Tustin 1974-76; asst. mgr./appraisal ofcr. Calif. First Bank, El Segundo 1976-78; asst. v.p. Appraisal Dept., So. Calif. Region, The Bank of California, L.A. 1978-84; prin., The Hale Co., Real Estate Appraisals & Consultation, 1984–; mem. Am. Inst. of Real Estate Appraisers (MAI), mem. admissions com. 1985; publs: arts. in trade publs.; Republican; Protestant. Address: The Hale Co. 12612 Central Ave Chino 91710

HALE, JACK VINCENT, insurance and investment co. president; b. Oct. 1, 1940, Fullerton; s. Harold "Vince" and Edith Marie (Nelson) H.; m. Patricia Ann Durbin, Nov. 21, 1959; children: Robin b. 1961, Wendy b. 1967, Jacquelyn b. 1970; edn: BA mktg., CSU Fullerton 1962; BS engring., CSU Long Beach 1972; MBA, UC Los Angeles 1979. Career: pres./gen. mgr. Hale Internat. (oilfield sales & service co.) 1973–, active in oil lease investments and ins. sales, corp. is 1/3 owner El Dorado Exploration (oil prodn. in Calif. and Columbia, S.A.), and owner subs. cos. Amerind Devel., other cos.; dir. Pioneer Research Inc.; mem. Soc. Petroleum Engrs., Am. Petroleum Inst., US Naval Reserve Assn., Masons; works: completed the first (under fed. guidelines projected) successful Affordable Housing Project; mil: comdr. USNR-R 1958-80, decorated; Republican; Prot.; rec: golf, water sports, flying. Ofc: Hale Internat. Inc. Insurance/ Investments 536 E Lincoln St Ste 6 Orange 92665

HALES, NORMA M., credit union executive; b. Feb. 7, 1933, Brooklyn, NY; d. Robert J. and Rita R. (Surrette) Jordan; m. Robert L. Hales, June 18, 1967; 1 son, Robert L., Jr., b. 1968; edn: stu. Am. River Coll. 1980-83, Dale Carnegie courses 1983. Career: working in credit unions since 1954; var. mgmt. positions, 1959–: mgr. Western Electric personnel credit union, NYC 1959, serviced NY-NJ Credit Unions on The Service Bureau Data Proc. System, 1968-70; mgmt., School Employees C.U., Sacramento 1970-, currently v.p. mgr. central ops., Golden 1 Credit Union, Sacto.; mem.: Sacto. Valley Chpt., Calif. Credit Union League (past bd. dirs. 5 yrs.; chmn. Edn./dir. Regl. Learning Ctr. 1984); Credit Women Internat.; Comstock Club; recipient spl. appreciation award for svc., Calif. C.U. League. Res: 5344 Maui Way Fair Oaks 95628 Ofc: The Golden 1 C.U., 1108 O Street Sacramento 95814

HALL, DOROTHY JONES, real estate broker; b. Apr. 18, 1931, Richmond; d. Phillip Rattenbury and Ruth H. (Vaslie) Jones; m. James M. Hall, Apr. 18, 1984; children (nee Wyman): Philip b. 1958, Katharine (Karstens) b. 1962, Robert b. 1965; edn: San Diego Jr. Coll. 1948-49, UC Berkeley 1950, Woodbury Univ. 1951; Calif. lic. real estate broker. Career: owner/mgr. Wyman's (dress shops), La Mesa and La Jolla, 1962-68; mgr. rental props. 1968-69, exec. secty. 1971-72, corp. secty., prin. Mobile Mart Inc. (mobilehome dealership w. 3 locations), San Marcos, Escondido, Ramona 1972-77; broker assoc. Forest E. Olson, Escondido 1977-80; adminstrv. asst. to dir. Corp. Tax Dept., Carter Hawley Hale Stores Inc., Los Angeles 1980–; broker/owner Wyman Realty, Palm Desert 1980–; campaign coord. (full-time) Muriel C. Watson (R.) for State Senate (40th Dist.) campaign, 1986; bd. dirs. Grossmont Shopping Ctr., La Mesa 1964-66; honors: Alpha Iota (1951), Million Dollar Club (1978); mem. Nat., Calif. Assn. of Realtors, Newport Beach/Costa Mesa, Escondido, and La Mesa Board of Realtors, Palm Desert CofC, DAR, Westport Hist. Soc. (Kansas City), Christian Voters League, Eisenhower Med. Ctr. Aux. (life); Republican; Presbyterian; rec: travel, genealogy. Res: 73-256 Highland Springs Dr Palm Desert 92260

HALL, FREDERICK FOLSOM, mechanical engineer; b. May 30, 1922, Boston, Mass.; s. Wilfred McGregor and Anne Gertrude (Jones) H.; m. Esther Deevers, Aug. 10, 1968; children: Frederick b. 1948, Richard b. 1950, Jeffrey b. 1951, Charles b. 1954, Gregory b. 1956; edn: grad., Columbia Midshipman Sch. 1945; BSME, cum laude, Tufts Univ. 1945; Reg. Profl. Engr., Mass., Calif. and Nebr. Career: ship supt. US Naval Shipyard, Portsmouth, Va. 1946; structural engr. Chas. T. Main Inc., Boston, Mass. 1947-49, mec. engr. 1950-61; head systems engr. Stanford Linear Accelerator Ctr. 1962-66, head plant engr. 1967-84, asst. tech. dir. 1985; currently, senior staff mem.; founder Hydrosol Corp. 1976; p.t. cons. egr.; honors: V.Chmn., Wellesley Adv. Com., Town of Wellesley, Mass. 1957-60; mem: Am. Soc. of Mech. Engrs., Internat. Assn. for Hydrogen Energy, Thomas Newcomen Soc. in No. Am.; works: 35 tech. papers on cryogenics, energy sources; 2 inventions, solar collector (1978) and electrolytic cell (1980); mill: lt. jg USNR 1943-46; Republican; Catholic; rec: history, cosmology, contract bridge. Res: 2452 Villaneuva Way Mountain View 94040 Ofc: Stanford University, P.O. Box 4349 Stanford 94305

HALL, JAMES M., governmental legal specialist; b. Jan. 22, 1915, Los Angeles; s. Charles S. and Lola Ruth (West) H.; m. Christine Sheedy, Oct. 9, 1922; children: James b. 1946, Glenda b. 1949, Joseph b. 1959; edn: pre-law, USC 1936-40; LLB, Southwestern Sch. of Law 1941; Dr. of Sci. (Adminstrn.) Luxembourg, 1967; Calif. Coll. of Trial Judges, U.S. Law Sch., 1971. Career: atty. Union Oil Co. 1947-50; pvt. practice of law, 1951-70; city atty. Maywood, 1968-69; judge County of Los Angeles, 1970-73; spl. counsel Cities of Hawthorne and Torrance, 1973–; atty. South Bay Hosp. Dist., and spl. counsel for Cities of Gardena, Redondo Beach, Hermosa Beach, Torrance, Palos Verdes Estates and Rolling Hills Estates, 1956-70; state inheritance appraiser 1960-67; Dir./v.p. Cabrillo Svgs. & Loan, and Guaranty Bank, Torrance, 1961-68; awards: two Presidential Citations; Ephebian; academic scholarship USC; mem: ABA, Am. Judicature Soc., LA County Bar Assn., San Diego County Bar Assn., Rotary Intl. (hon.); mil: cmdr. USNR, Intell.; Democrat; Protestant; rec: golf, tennis. Res: 1123 Los Campaneros Lake San Marcos 92069

HALL, MANLY PALMER, lecturer, author, educational organization executive; b. March 18, 1901, Peterborough, Ont., Can., nat. 1904; m. Marie Bauer, Dec. 6, 1950; Litt.D., John F. Kennedy Univ. 1981. Career: research scholar, lecturer and founder/president Philosophical Research Soc. Inc., Los Angeles 1934–, founder of The PRS Library containing more than fifty thousand select books, rare manuscripts, research mats. and related artifacts (has written introduction and commentaries to twenty reprints of rare books in the collection); author over 200 books and monograms incl. Ency. Outline of Masonic, Hermetic, Qabbalistic and Rosicrucian Symbolical Phiosophy (1928), Lectures on Ancient Philosophy (1947), First Principle of Philosophy (1949), Healing, The Divine Art (1950), Search for Reality (1967), Buddhism and Psychotherapy

(1967), Initiates of Greece and Rome (1981); num. articles, taped lectures, booklets; honored for distinguished service as lectr., author, tchr., City of Los Angeles Soc. (life), N.M. Hist. Soc. (life), Soc. Rosicruciana in Civitatibus Foederatis (hon. 8 deg.), Mark Twain Soc. (hon.), Indian Assn. of Am., Internat. Soc. Gen. Semantics, Am. Soc. Psychical Research, Fedn. Philat. Clubs of So. Calif. (past pres.), Scottish Rite Mason (33 deg.); rec: avid philatelist, his collection of India and Feudatory States (in 80 volumes) won the Grand Award for research in the Indian postal system and other exhib. awards. Address: Philosophical Research Society Inc. 3910 Los Feliz Blvd Los Angeles 90027

HALL, MARJORIE RUTH, certified public accountant; b. Mar. 4, 1950, Jamaica, West Indies, nat. US cit. 1980; d. Dudley C. and Vera E. (Reynolds) Grant; m. Colin Hall, Sept. 6, 1986; edn: BSBA, Roosevelt Univ. 1976, MSA, 1978; desig: CPA, Ill., Calif. (1983). Career: audit senior Arthur Andersen & Co., Chgo. 1979-83; CPA, audit supr. Oppenheim, Appel, Dixon & Co., Century City 1984-, Friedman Rosenthal Knell & Co., L.A. 1984-85, Coopers & Lybrand, L.A. 1986—; lectr. in acctg., UCLA (1985), Chgo. State Univ. (1978-83); recipient Fund Raiser Award, Free Arts Clinic (1984, 85); mem. Am. Inst. CPA, Calif. CPA Soc. (Oil & Gas Com.); civic: Free Arts Clinic for Abused Children (bd., pgm. com.), Grace Comm. Ch. (Sunday Sch. tchr.); rec: photog., tennis. Res: POB 10451 Beverly Hills 90213 Ofc: Coopers & Lybrand 1000 West 6th St Los Angeles 90017

HALL, MARTIN HAROLD, civil engineer; b. Feb. 16, 1951, Arkadelphia, Ark.; s. Harold and Agee (McGuire) H.; m. Beverly, June 12, 1982; children: Erik b. 1973, Matthew b. 1976; edn: BS, Calif. Polytechnic Univ. Pomona 1973; Reg. Profl. Civil Engr., Calif. (1976), Ariz. (1983) and N.Mex. (1984). Career: quality control engr. Guy F. Atkinson Co., San Luis Obispo 1974-75; roadway asst. Atchison, Topeka & Santa Fe Rwy. Co., 1975-76, asst. bridge & bldg. gen. foreman, San Francisco & Fresno 1976-78, asst. div. engr., San Bernardino 1979-80, constrn. engr., San Francisco, Los Angeles 1980—; cons. Hall Enging./ Devel. Co. 1984-; mem: Am. Railway Engring. Assn. (com. #15 1977); Roadmasters Maintenance of Way Assn., Bridge & Bldg. Assn.; Republican; Christian; rec: racquetball, skiing, sailing. Res: 37 Cedarwood Ave. Pomona 91766 Ofc: Atchison, Topeka & Santa Fe Railway Co., 5200 E. Sheila St. Los Angeles 90040

HALL, TED OLIVER, accounting co. executive; b. Sept. 11, 1942, Huntington Park; s. Charley and Mary Elizabeth (Shonkwiler) H.; m. Norys Beni, Aug. 25, 1969; children: Hanna b. 1967, Marcus b. 1970, Dax b. 1972; edn: BS, CSU San Jose 1965, MBA, 1969; JD, Golden Gate Univ. 1979; Certified Public Acct., Calif. 1985. Career: US Peace Corps vol. in Peru, 1966-68; mgr. var. finl. depts. of San Francisco hdqtrs. office, The Western Pacific R.R. Co., 1969-79; tax mgr. and prin., Arthur Young & Co., San Francisco office, 1979-85; tax mgr. Grant Thornton, Sacramento office 1985-86; tax prin./dir. ins. tax svcs., Arthur Young & Co. S.F. 1986—; instr. in tax research, Calif. Soc. of CPAs (1980), num. seminars on the taxation of life insurance cos. and their products, Arthur Young & Co.; mem: Am. Bar Assn. (Tax Sect. Student Div., 1979), Calif. Soc. CPAs; bd. dirs. Tri-Cities Children's Ctr., Fremont (1979-80); coauthor: Taxation of Life Insurance Companies and Their Products (pub. Arthur Young & Co.); Republican; Protestant. Res: 106 Shetland Ct Vacaville 95688 Ofc: Arthur Young & Co. 1 Sansome St San Francisco 94104

HALLADAY, KAREN SUE, real estate broker, financial planner; b. July 26, 1943, Stockton; d. Dr. Louis, Jr. and Eleanor Sue Keene (Sandberg) Jaques; m. Wayne Halladay, Feb. 4, 1967; edn: BA, 1965 and MA, 1967, with highest honors, CSU San Jose; postgrad. wk., philos., UC Berkeley 1970-76; Calif. tchg. creds. (Std. Elem., Comm. Coll. instr./counselor), lic. real estate broker, NASD reg. rep., reg. investment advisor, finl. planner (1984). Career: elem. sch. tchr. Lompoc Unified Sch. District, 1967-70; instr. Alan Han Jr. Coll., Santa Maria 1968-70; coll. instr./supr. student teachers, St. Marys Coll., Moraga 1974-76; real estate agt. Marcus Co. and Stephen R. Payne, Walnut Creek, 1977-81; realtor/prin. Halladay & Assocs., Concord 1982-83; finl. planner 1984-; broker Security Pacific Real Estate, Walnut Creek; acct. exec. WZW Financial Services; with Southmark Financial Svcs. 1984—; mem: Nat./ Calif. Assn. of Realtors, Contra Costa Bd. of Realtors (profl. stds. panel 1981-, chair ethics com. 1985, mediation com. 1986), Walnut Creek CofC (founding chair Speaker's Bur. 1984-85), Toastmasters Internat.; Democrat; Episcopal; rec: hiking, gourmet cooking, wine appreciation. Res: 2365 Hagen Oaks Dr Alamo 94507 Ofc: Sec. Pacific Real Estate, 587 Ygnacio Valley Rd. Walnut Creek 94596

HALLETT, BRUCE R., lawyer; b. Feb. 2, 1956, Covina, Calif.; s. Robert Kenneth and Dolores Jean (Bittner) H.; edn: BA, UC Irvine 1978; JD, UC Los Angeles 1981; admitted Calif. State Bar 1981. Career: asst. dean of students UCLA 1979-81; assoc. atty. Rutan & Tucker 1981-84, McKenna, Conner & Cuneo Costa Mesa 1984—; honors: Aldrich Scholar (UC Irvine 1977), Nat. Merit Scholar 1974; mem: Am. (corp., banking and bus. law sect.) Orange Co. (bus. sect.) bar assns.; rec: film, architecture, design. Ofc: McKenna, Conner & Cuneo 611 Anton Blvd, Ste 910, Costa Mesa 92626

HALLEY, STEPHEN ROBERT, hospital administrator; b. Nov. 27, 1953, El Paso, Tx.; s. Lionel Joseph and Grace Louisa (Hendershot) H.; m. Mary Dana Peterson, Dec. 31, 1979; children: Derek Brandon b. 1981, Danielle Elizabeth b. 1985; edn: pre-med. major CSU Sacto. 1972-74; UC Davis 1974-77; BS hum. relations/org. behav., Univ. of San Francisco 1984. Career: sales rep. Sacramento Graphics Systems, 1977-78; sales rep. Johnson & Johnson Baby Products, 1978-84, Western USA sales trainer 1983-84; dir. of mktg./hosps., Re-

public Health Corp., 1984-86, hosp. administr./coord. hosp. ops. in Las Vegas, Nev. 1985—; awards: Bank of Am. Sci. award (1972), Johnson & Johnson Baby Prods. Co. Ring Club (1980); mem. No. Sacto. CofC (pres. 1985-86), Friends of Light Rail (bd. 1985-), Gr. Sacto. Certified Devel. Corp. (bd. 1985-), Calif. State Enterprise Zone Task Force (1985-); works: Group Dynamics research UCD Primate Ctr. 1976-77; Republican; Baptist; rec: sailing, golf, woodworking. Res: 6844 Duckling Way Sacramento 95842

HALLIBURTON, GENE DENNIS, executive consultant; b. Sept. 7, 1919, Kennett, Mo.; s. Wm. Elija and Minnie Ola (Fowler) H.; m. May Gardner, Apr. 3, 1955; children: Randall Bryan b. 1959 Susan Marguerite b. 1969, Kathryn Elizabeth b. 1961, Gardner William b. 1963; edn: Univ. of Ind. 1939-41, Univ. of Calif. 1949-51. Career: passenger agent Transworld Airlines, Kansas City, Mo. 1939-44; instr. USAF Air Tng. Command, USA, 1944-47; mgr. Whitcomb Travel Agcy., San Francisco 1947-49; pres., dist. sales mgr. Nat. Automobile Club, S.F. 1949—, pres. and CEO, 1974—; v.p. Am. Automobile Touring Alliance; honors: Man of the Year, Eastbay Insurance Man's Assn. (1960, 61); vice chmn. Calif. commn. for Driver Edn. 1968-71; mem. adv. panel Gov.'s Traffic Safety Commn. 1969; dir. Calif. Traffic Safety Found. 1971; mem: Oakland Ins. Forum (pres. 1960), Ins. Fieldman's Assn. (pres. 1961), S.F. Pub. Rels. Round Table (chmn. bd. govs. 1967), Ins. Co. Mgrs. Assn. of No. Calif. (pres. 1976); works: prod./moderator Bay Area local radio pgm., How To Buy Insurance (1961); mil: s/sgt. USAF 1944-46; Republican; Protestant; rec: photog., travel, camping. Res: 300 Vernon St Oakland 94610 Ofc: National Automobile Club, One Market Plaza, Suite 300, San Francisco 94105

HALLINAN, PATRICIA, physician; b. Aug. 29, 1916, San Francisco; d. Patrick and Elizabeth (Sheehan) H.; div.; children: Charles, b. 1944, Stephen, b 1945, Michael, b. 1951, David, b. 1952, Patrick, b. 1958; edn: BA, Stanford 1941, MD, 1942. Career: (current) physician Agency for Infant Development, Marin Co. Community Mental Health, Kentfield; active in advocacy of abused children (num. court appearances); advisor for Assemblyman Ryan re Bill AB 850; TV appearances for Cerebral Palsy Telethons (1971, 75), and spoke on Fetal Alcohol Syndrome on Nat. Alcoholism pgm. (NBC Network 1985); honored by March of Dimes for Meritorious Svc. (1970s), listed Who's Who in Am. Women (1975), named 1 of Outstanding Women of Marin (1981); mem. Gov. Reagan's Citizen Com. on Welfare Reform (1971); publs: num. articles on battered children in newspapers, Pediatric Psychology (1976); poetry; Republican; Catholic; rec: poetry, piano. Res: 320 Via Casitas Greenbrae 94904 Ofc: Marin Community Mental Health 1030 Sir Francis Drake Blvd Kentfield 94904

HALLMAN, MIKKO NIILO KUSTAA, medical educator; b. Jan. 30, 1945, Helsinki, Finland; s. Niilo Oskar Birger and Helena Maria Margareta (Tuulio) H.; m. Marjo-Riitta, Oct. 7, 1967; children: Anne b. 1968, Anssi b. 1973, Lauri b. 1979; edn: MD, Univ. of Helsinki 1970, PhD, 1972. Career: Fogarty Internat. Fellow, Univ. Calif. San Diego 1973-75; asst. prof. pediatrics Univ. Helsinki, Finland 1975-77; asst. prof., assoc. prof. of pediatrics UC San Diego 1978—, cons. UCSD; senior investigator, research dir. Found. of Pediatric Research; pioneer in Human Surfactant Substitution; author 190+ sci. publs.; Lutheran. Res: 4363 Caminito del Diamante San Diego 92121

HALPERIN, WARREN LESLIE, management/executive search consultant; b. Apr. 12, 1938, Bklyn.; s. Abraham and Bertha G. (Aronowitz) H.; m. Sherry Weshner, Mar. 31, 1968; children: Jonathan b. 1969, Justin b. 1972; edn: grad. Bordentown Mil. Inst. 1955; BA in philos., Adelphi Univ. 1959. Career: research dir. West, Weir & Bartel, NYC 1962-67; mktg. dir. Faust/Day Advtsg., Los Angeles 1967-69; new product devel. mgr. Hunt Wesson Foods, Fullerton 1970-73; group v.p. Searchmasters, Fullerton 1973-79; ptnr. in charge, Exec. Search, McSweeney & Assocs., Newport Beach 1979-83; founder/CEO The Halperin Co., Inc., Newport Beach 1983—; mem. advis. bd. West Helena Svgs. & Loan Assn. 1985-86; past guest lectr. Pace Coll., UCLA, USC; mem: U.S. League of Savings Instns., Mortgage Bankers Assn. of Am. (Capital Markets Com.); civic: Leukemia Soc. of Am. (past pres. Tri-County Chpt. & mem. Exec. Com. Nat. Bd. of Trustees), Boys Scouts Am. (fmr. scoutmaster, Irvine); publs: articles in Savings Institutions, Bank Administration, Directors Digest; pioneered the concept of Strategic Exec. Search; Jewish; rec: travel. Res: 30962 Steeplechase San Juan Capistrano 92675 Ofc: The Halperin Co. Inc. 1601 Dove St Ste 205 Newport Beach 92660

HALPERN, HERB H., real estate investment co. owner; b. Mar. 24, 1937, McKeesport, Pa.; s. Sam and Pearl H.; edn: BS mech. engrg. and aero. engrg., Univ. Pittsburgh 1960; MS bus., UC Los Angeles, San Diego State Univ.; lic. real estate broker Calif. Career: General Dynamics San Diego 1960-63; Aerospace Corp. El Segundo 1963-78; owner K&H Ents. 1970—; owner Herb H. Halpern & Assoc. 1982—; mil: sgt. US Army 1951-53, 5 decs. for svc. in Korea; rec: collecting (coins, art, seashells), tennis, diving. Res: 4335 Marina City Dr 736 ETS Marina del Rey 90292 Ofc: K&H Ents. 16200 Ventura Blvd Ste 316 Encino 91436

HALVERSON, WARREN LYNN, mortgage banking co. executive; b. Apr. 23, 1941, North Platte, Nebr.; s. Floyd Leroy and Esther Adaline ((Oueale) H.; m. Ardith Yager, June 12, 1960; children: David b. 1963, Steven b. 1965; edn: grad. Torrington (Wy.) H.S. 1959; Grad. Inst. of Finl. Edn.; spl. courses UC Irvine, Alexander Hamilton Inst., banking schs.; lic. Ins. Broker, Mobile Home Sales (Colo.), Ins.- Fire and Casualty (Calif.). Career: v.p./ branch mgr. Colo. Springs Indsl. Bank, subs. Avco Finl. Services 1963-72; asst. v.p. Security Svgs. and Loan Assn., Colo. Springs 1972-75; v.p./mgr. consumer loan div. Otero Svgs and Loan Assn., Colo. Springs 1975-78; ptnr. Romin Homes Ltd. (mobile home sales) 1978-79; credit mgr. The Alumeco Co., Colo. Springs

1979-80; regl. mgr. mtn. states region, Greentree Acceptance Inc., Denver 1980-83; v.p. adminstrn. All Valley Acceptance Co. (mfd. housing fin.), Irvine 1983—; apptd. mem. Colo. Mobile Home Dealer State Licensing Bd.; mem: Inst. of Finl. Edn. (past pres. Pike's Peak chpt.), US Savings League (consumer loan com.), Colo. Springs Mobile Home Assn. (chmn.), Colo. Mfd. Housing Assn., Mortgage Lenders Assn., Savings & Loan Mid-Continent Computer Users Com.; civic: CofC, Red Cross (bd. Mile High chpt.), Kiwanis Intl. Ofc: All Valley Acceptance Co. 17911 Von Karman Ave Ste 410 Irvine 92714

HAMBRICK, KENNETH EDWARD, electronics/ telecommunications consultant; b. Mar. 24, 1928, Pueblo, Colo.; s. Daniel Edward and Lorene Lottie (Langley) H.; m. Donna Day, Nov. 14, 1980; children: William b. 1955, Joyce b. 1956, Patricia b. 1958, Jerome b. 1964, James b. 1975; edn: BS, UC Berkeley 1951; MBA, Golden Gate Univ. 1969. Career: var. mgmt. positions in oper. svcs. and tech. ops. Pacific Bell 1953-64; owner company 1964-66; div. mgr. var. tech. and engrg. ops. Pacific Bell 1966-82; dir. SRI Internat., mgmt. cons. in electronics, telecoms., ofc. automation, computers 1983—; mem: Boy Scouts, Peanut League (baseball); publ: The New Telecommunications Industry, Bus. Intelligence Pgm., SRI Internat. (1984); mil: 1st lt. US Army Signal Corps 1951-53, QM3 USN 1945-47; Republican, avoc: property devel., ltd. partnerships, constrn. Ofc: SRI Internat. Menlo Park

HAMILTON, AARON LAMAR, insurance agent; b. Mar. 7, 1930, Washington, Utah; s. Alvin LaVar and Elva (Sproul) H.; m. Ursuline Sherbs, Dec. 31, 1954; div.; children: Alan b. 1955, Erline b. 1957, David b. 1960, Daniel b. 1960, Marla b. 1963; edn: BS, UCLA Sch. of Bus. 1961. Career: claim rep. State Farm Mutual Auto Ins. Co., 2 years; founder/pres. Agency, Sunland 1978—; sales awards: Career Achievement Club (1978-); mil: US Army CIC, 1953-56; Restoration Ch. of Jesus Christ (founder, presiding bishop); rec: hang gliding, swim. Res: 8323 Owens St Sunland 91040 Ofc: 8119 Foothill Blvd Ste 5 Sunland 91040

HAMILTON, BRANDON LESLIE, system engineer; b. Nov. 26, 1947, Chgo.; s. Eugene Alexander and Gloria Lee (Gladney) H.; edn: AA, Kennedy-King Coll. 1975; BS, Univ. Ill. 1979. Career: nuclear engineer cons. Stone and Webster Engring., Boston, Mass. 1972-74; self empl. engineering tutor, Chgo. 1974-77; sci. research pgmmr., Univ. of Ill., Chgo. 1977; physics lab asst., Ill. Inst. of Tech., Chgo. 1977; tutor/instr. Inroads Inc., Chgo. 1975-78; strategic analyst Analytic Services, Arlington, Va. 1979-80; nuclear/computer engr. So. California Edison, San Clemente, Ca. 1980-84; satellite test dir. Aerojet Electrosystems, Azusa 1984—; mem. Operations Research Soc. of Am. 1978-80; mem. Mathematical Assn. of Am.; D.C. Student Math. Soc. (newsletter ed. 1979-80); Omega Psi Phi Frat.; Youth Motivation Task Force 1984-; publs: tech. papers, sci. reports; mil: E5 USN 1968-72, Nat. Defense Medal, Honorman; rec: jogging, scuba, swimming, modeling. Res: 211 Grand Ave, 412, Long Beach 90803 Ofc: Aerojet Electrosystems, 1100 West Hollyvale St, Azusa 91702

HAMILTON, JAMES MARVIE, automotive research & devel. co. executive; b. Jan. 2, 1950, Blythe; s. D.L. and Mary Elizabeth (Dekens) H.; m. Tracy, March 16, 1985; edn: BSEE, honors, Loyola Univ. 1972; MS, UCLA 1974; EIT Calif. 1972. Career: tech. staff Hughes Aircraft, Los Angeles 1972-76; group head 1976-80, sect. head, Irvine 1980-84; pres., CEO COAST Technologies Inc. 1984—; gen. ptr. Spectrum Investment Co. 1976-82; dir. COAST Technologies Inc. 1984-; honors: Tau Beta Pi Engrg. Hon. Soc., ASN Jesuit Honor Soc., Loyola 1970; mem: IEEE, Sigma Phi Delta, Loyola Engring. Alumni (v.p. 1977, pres. 1978), MSJH Inc. (dir. 1984-); works: author IEEE paper and (4) patents on integrated circuits; author IEEE paper and (3) patents (5 pend.) on automotive computerized suspension control; Republican; Christian; rec: inventing, study of physical sciences, skiing. Res: 1167 Loma Portal Dr. El Cajon 92020 Ofc: COAST Technologies, 11491 Woodside Ave. Santee 92071

HAMILTON, JOHN RICHARDSON, III, strategic data planner; b. May 13, 1952, Hagerstown, Md.; s. John Richardson, Jr. and Anne Sophia (Earley) Hamilton; m. Eileen Budnaitis, Feb. 11, 1984: children: Marna b. 1966, Darren b. 1969, Daniel b. 1973; edn: BSGS (comp.sci.), US Mil. Acad., West Point, 1974; MBA in progress, Univ. Santa Clara. Career: senior database analyst CTB/McGraw-Hill, Monterey, Ca. 1977-81; database adminstr. National Semiconductor, Santa Clara 1982; mgr. Database Adminstration, ESL, Sunnyvale 1983; senior cons. NDBS Inc., Redwood City 1983-84; strategic data-planner Amdahl Corp., Sunnyvale 1984—; tchg. Public Utils. Commn. 2/84; cons. GECC 3/84; cons. Charles Schwab Inc. 1983-84; cons. US Fleet Leasing 1984; mem. Cullinet Regl. Users Gp., Order of DeMolay, BSA, Am. Sportsmans Club, Assn. of (West Point) Graduates; mil: 2d lt. US Army 1974-76; Republican; rec: Gundogs (train, breed), hunting, microcomputer software. Res: 1130 Polk Ln San Jose 95117 Ofc: Amdahl Corp. 1250 E Arques Ave Sunnyvale 94088-3470

HAMLIN, CARL TED, gemologist-jeweler; b. Jan. 2, 1939.; s. Carl Cecil and Clara Savanna (Anderson) H.; m. Marilyn Miller, Mar. 11, 1980; children: Jay THomas b. 1957, Garrett Carl b. 1968; edn: San Diego Coll. 1964; tchr. cred., CSU San Diego 1974; cert. GIA, Gemological Inst. of Am. 1971. Career: owner/opr. manufacturing jewelry firm, Hamlin's Mfg. Jewelers, El Cajon, Calif. 1969-; lectr.; tchr. gemcutter and master jeweler; awards: for jewelry designs num. shows 1973-78; mem: Retail Jewelers of Am., Calif. Retail Jewelers Assn., San Diego Gemological Soc.; publs: num. gemological and jewelry technical articles 1973-85, research in field of gemology, goldsmithing and lapidary arts; mil: USAF 1956-60; Republican; Protestant; rec: travel. Res:

6150 Broadmoor Dr La Mesa 92041 Ofc: Hamlin's Mfg. Jewelers 2234 Fletcher Pkwy Ste F El Cajon 92020

HAMLIN, MERVYN RAY, physician; b. Aug. 25, 1919, Stockton; s. Ray Leo and Ada Elizabeth (Hildebrand) H.; m. Margaret Baer, April 24, 1943; children: Peter b. 1947, Robin Ann b. 1954; edn: BA, Stanford Univ. 1941; MD, Duke Univ. 1950. Career: physician solo practice 1952—; adminstr., co-owner Redwood Coast Hosp., Ft. Bragg 1965-71; chief of staff Mendocino Coast Dist. Hosp., Ft. Bragg 1971-72; asst. prof. family practice UC Davis 1975-77; mem: Am. Acad. of Family Practice (charter fellow), Diplomate Am. Bd. of Family Practice, Am. and Calif. (House of Dels. 1975-80) Med. Assns., Mendocino-Lake Co. Med. Soc. (pres. 1980-81), Mendocino Lake Found. for Med. Care (pres.), Stockton Scottish Rite F&AM (life), Spyglass Hill Golf Club; mil: lab tech. 5 US Army Med. Corps, WWII; Republican; Episcopal; rec: golf, fishing, travel. Res: 400 Winifred Fort Bragg 95437 Ofc: 120 W. Fir St. Fort Bragg 95437

HAMMER, ARMAND, industrialist; b. May 21, 1898, NY, NY; s. Julius and Rose (Robinson) H.; m. Frances Barrett, 1956; 1 son; edn: BS, Columbia Univ. 1919, MD, 1921. Career: pres. Allied Am. Corp., NY, NY 1923-25, A. Hammer Pencil Co., NY, London, Moscow 1925-30, Hammer Galleries Inc., NY, NY 1930—, J.W. Dant Distilling Co., NYC, Dant, Ky. 1943-54; pres., bd. chmn. Mutual Bdcstg. System, NY, NY 1957-58; bd. chmn., CEO Occidental Petroleum Corp., Los Angeles 1957—; chmn. M. Knoedler and Co., Inc. NY, NY 1972—; bd. dirs. Canadian Occidental Pet. Ltd. 1964—; founder, hon. chmn. Armand Hammer Coll., 1981-; mem. Grad. Sch. of Mgmt. Bd. of Visitors UCLA 1957-; mem. Los Angeles Petroleum Club 1960-; bd. govs. Eleanor Roosevelt Cancer Found. 1960-; apptd. mem. Nat. Petroleum Council 1968-; bd. trustees LA County Mus. of Art 1968-; bd. trustees, chmn. exec. com. Salk Inst. for Biol. Studies 1969-; bd. irs. LA World Affairs Council 1969-; adv. com. Com. for a Greater Calif. 1969-; founder LA Music Center; bd. dirs., bd. govs. UN Assn. of USA 1970-; bd. govs. Ford's Theatre Soc. 1970-; bd. dirs. Planned Parenthood World Pop./L.A. 1970-; hon. mem. Royal Acad. of Arts (Eng.) 1975-; bd. dirs. Assocs. of the Harvard Bus. Sch. 1975-; bd. dirs. Am. Petroleum Inst. (Wash DC) 1975-; LAC-USC Cancer Assocs. 1975-; bd. dirs. Calif. Roundtable 1976-; founder mem. Pepperdine Assocs. 1976-; nat. trustee National sym.; mem. James Smithson Soc., Smithsonian Nat. Assocs.; pres. Found. of the Internat. Inst. of Human Rights (Geneva) 1977-; bd. dirs. Century City Cultural Commn.; adv. com. Fogg Art Mus.; adv. council The Friendship Forces; bd. trustees United for California; exec. mem. Energy Resrch. and Edn. Found.; charter mem. Nat. Vis. Council of Health Scis. Faculties, Columbia Univ.; trustee The Capitol Children's Mus.; bd. dirs. Corcoran Gal. of Art; hon. mem. The Jockey Club; bd. dirs. Keep America Beautiful Inc.; mem. LA Council Navy League of the US; bd. dirs. Bus. Com. for the Arts (NYC); Fifty Year Club of Am. Medicine; Fellows for Life of New Orleans Mus. of Art; Com. on Artic Oil and Gas Resources; UNICEF Nat. Support Council; adv. council Am. Longevity Assn. Inc.; Univ. Okla. Assocs.; hon. mem. Royal Scottish Acad. (Edinburgh); adv. bd. Ctr. for Strategic and Internat. Studies, Georgetown Univ.; LA Olympic Citizens Adv. Commn.; Fine Arts Com. of US State Dept.; chmn. President's Cancer Panel 1981-; Mayor Bradley's Task Force for Africa/LA Rels. 1981-; internat. bd. govs. Bob Hope Internat. Heart Research Inst. 1982-. Life mem. AMA, NY Co. Med. Assns., Alpha Omega Alpha, Mu Sigma, Phi Sigma Delta; presented Pres. F.D.R.'s Campobello residence as US-Canadian Peace Park in presence of Pres. Kennedy and Prime Minister Lester Pearson (1964); mem. Lotos Club 1973-; mem. Internat. Inst. of Human Rights 1978- (spons. Peace Confs., Oslo, Norway 1978, Campobello Peace Park 1979, Warsaw, Poland 1980, Aix-en-Provence, France 1981; founded the Armand Hammer Ctr. for Cancer Biol, and Resrch., Salk Inst. 1969; estab. the Julius and Armand Hammer Health Scis. Ctr., Columbia Univ. 1977. Honors: hon. LL.D, Pepperdine Univ. 1978, Southeastern Univ. (Columbia Univ.), hon. DHL, Univ. Colo. 1979, hon. .Pub. Svc., Salem Coll. 1979, hon. LL.D, Aix-en-Provence Univ. (Fr.) 1981; decorated comdr. Order of the Crown (Belgium), comdr. Order of Andres Bellow (Venez.), Mexican Order of the Aztec Eagle, ofcr. Nat. Order of Legion of Honor (Fr.), Order of Friendship Among Peoples (USSR), Royal Order of the Polar Star (Sweden), Grand Officer to the Merit of the Republic (Italy), Knight Comdr's Cross (Austria); Internat. Achievement Award, World Trade Club of SF., 1982; Maimonides Award, LA Jewish Community, 1980; Entrepreneur of the Year, USC, 1980; author: The Quest of the Romanoff Treasure (1936); subject of books by Robt. Considine: The Remarkable Life of Dr. Armand Hammer, and Larger Than Life; mil: US Army Med. Corps 1918-19. Ofc: Occidental Petroleum Corp., 10889 Wilshire Blvd. Ste 1500, Los Angeles 90024

HAMMER, SAMUEL KEITH, accountant; b. Nov. 17, 1960, Miami, Fla.; s. Oscar J. and Barbara (Weiser) H.; edn: BBA, Emory Univ. 1982; Certified Public Acct., Fla. (1983), Calif. (1985). Career: staff acct. Price Waterhouse, Miami 1982-84; ptnr. in charge of acctg. services Sidney Stern Acctcy. Corp., Sherman Oaks 1984—; mem: Am. Inst. CPAs, Calif. Soc. CPAs, Nat. Soc. of Public Accts., Fla. Inst. CPAs, B'nai B'rith; works: prodn. exec.: Your Personal Guide to Love, Money & Fitness; Evel Knievel, The Last of the Gladiators; New Reform Temple; rec: tennis. Ofc: 14144 Ventura Blvd Ste 255 Sherman Oaks 91423

HAMPTON, COLETTE PIAT, high fashion designer; b. Sept. 21, 1933, Amiens, France; d. Andre Charles Julian and Hama (Micheline) Piat; div. Dr. Antoine Scheckenberger; children: Alexander Christian b. 1958, Antoine Eric b. 1959, Sophie Colette b. 1961; edn: Baccalaureate, Notre Dame, 1945-49;

deg., art hist., cum laude, Sch. of Ecoile Beaux-Arts 1950-52. Career: began art/design career traveling with architect father, with first couture design at age 13; awarded spl. authorization by Cambre des Metiers to conduct profl. bus. before age of 21 years; high fashion designer, Modiliste Haute Couture, with pvt. clientele in E. France, Paris, Carmel, San Francisco; pvt. fashion shows in Pebble Beach, currently; Catholic; rec: art hist., piano, literature. Address: Colette Piat High Fashion, POB 415, Carmel 93921

HAMZEY, ROBERT MANSOUR, JR., insurance agency president; b. Apr. 15, 1952, Detroit; s. Robert M. and Pauline E. H.; m. Marie Ann, Aug. 23, 1974; children: Brian b. 1977, Jennifer b. 1979, Amber b. 1983, Christina b. 1984; edn: Eastern Mich. Univ. 1970-72. Career: agent John Hancock 1972-77 (youngest leading agent for life 1976, property casualty 1977); started own agency 1977; moved to San Diego County 1982, pres. Insurance Unlimited of San Diego County Rancho La Costa 1982—; honors: President's Club (John Hancock 1976-77, Sun Life 1979-80), Agent of the Yr. (J.H. 1976), PIA Fine Mark Soc. (1979-82); mem: Independent Agents Assn. (secty. 1986), Nat. Assn. Life Underwriters (bd. 1976), Assn. for Financial Planning, Masons, Optomists (pres.), Westland CofC (pres.), Carlsbad CofC (m.c.), Rotary, YMCA (past bd.), Westland Mayors Task Force; Republican; rec: golf. Res: 2745 Argonauta Rancho La Costa 92008 Ofc: Insurance Unlimited 7750 El Camino Real Ste 2E Rancho La Costa 92008

HAN, MAN HI, acupuncturist, educator, clergyman; b. Apr. 18, 1934, Choong, Buk, Korea; edn: degree economics, Dongkuk Univ. 1966; PhD, Columbia Pacific Univ. 1979; PhD, OMD, S.A.M.R.A. Univ. Health Sci., 1983. Career: monk, Suh Duk Sah Buddhist Temple, Korea 1954; Dahl Mah master, Ven Monk Dahl Mah Beum Euh Temple, Korea 1966; abbot and chmn. Dahl Mah Sah Buddhist Monastery, Los Angeles, 1973, Suh Doh Sah Buddhist Temple of Am., Inc. 1976—; owner Oriental Acupuncture Clinic, L.A. 1977-, Oriental Acu. Beverly Hills Clinic, B.H. 1979-, Oriental Health Food & Herbs Co., L.A.; prof. Calif. Acupuncture Coll., 1981-; mem: Korean Am. Acupuncture Assn., Acu. Assn. of Am., Calif. Korea Acu. & Oriental Medicine Assn., Internat. Platform Assn.; mil: Rep. of Korea Army 1957; rec: mountain climbing. Res: 674 Crenshaw Blvd Los Angeles 90005

HANDLEY, MARGIE LEE, asphalt and aggregate mfg. co. president; b. Sept. 29, 1939, Bakersfield; d. Robert Eugene and Jayne Ann (Knoblock) Harrah; m. Leon Carl Handley, Sr. Oct. 28, 1975; children (nee Lovell): Steven b. 1956, David b. 1957, Ronald b. 1962; ed. Willits Union H.S. 1957; Calif. lic. Gen. Engring. Contr. (1983). Career: secty. to dist. supt. Montague Sch. Dist., 1968-85; owner/opr. Shasta Pallet Co. (mfr. gun boxes), Montague 1969-70, Lovell's Tack 'N Togs (retail W. clothing store), Yreka 1970-73; v.p. Microphor Inc. (indsl. prods. mfr.), Willits 1974-81; pres. Harrah Industries Inc. (real estate dev.), Willits 1981—; gen. ptnr. Madrone Profl. Group (profl. office complex), Willits 1982-; pres. Hot Rocks, Inc. (mfr. asphalt and aggregates), Willits 1983—; apptd: Calif. Transp. Commn. (1986-90), del. White House Conf. on Small Bus. (1986), del. Calif. State Conf. on Small Bus. (1984-86), Region IX SBA Advis. Council (chair Ops. Com. 1982-), elected clerk Bd. Trustees, Montague Sch. Dist. (1970-73); mem. Assoc. Gen. Contrs. of Calif. Inc. (state dir. North Bay Dist. Hwy Grading and Heavy Engring. Div. 1986), Calif. CofC, Geysers Geothermal Assn., Toastmasters Intl., No. Coast Bldrs. Exchange, CofC (Willits, Cloverdale); civic: Willits Comm. Scholarships Inc. (secty. 1962), Montague PTA (secty.), Montague United Methodist Ch. (trustee 1966-73); Republican (del. Nat. Conv. 1984, alt. del. 1976, 80; campaign chair Deukmejian 1982, Reagan/Bush 1980, 84; charter Senatl. Inner Circle 1980-). Res: 16000 Hearst Rd Willits 95490 Ofc: Hot Rocks Inc. 42 Madrone St Willits 95490

HANDWEILER, MARTIN CHARLES, lawyer; b. Jan. 26, 1940, Brooklyn, NY; s. Sidney and Elsie (Shapiro) H.; m. Beth, May 1, 1983; 1 son: Daniel b. 1984; edn: Univ. of Washington 1962; JD, Pepperdine Univ. 1972; admitted Calif. State Bar 1972. Career: insurance investig. 1961-67; investig. for atty. John K. Trotter, Jr., (currently pres. justice 2d div. 4th dist. ct. of appeals) 1967-72; atty. Trotter, Handweiler & Bahan, Inc. 1972-79; self-employed atty. pvt. practice spec. in trial of civil litigation 1979—; lectr. for cont. ed. of bar, Coll. of Trial Advocacy, Orange Co. Bar Assn.; judge pro tem Orange Co. Superior Ct.; mem: Am., Calif., Orange Co. bar assns.; Calif. and Orange Co. Trial Lawyers Assns.; mil: SP4 U.S. Army 1958-61; Democrat; Jewish. Res: 34 Pinewood Irvine 92714 Ofc: Martin C. Handweiler, Inc., 2372 SE Bristol, Ste. B, Santa Ana 92707

HANES, JOHN WARD, hydraulic engineer; b. June 5, 1936, San Francisco; s. Ward Herbert and Ruth Florence (Jacks) H.; m. Virginia Meadows, Nov. 27, 1957; children: Derek b. 1959, Kim b. 1960, Mark b. 1962, Ward b. 1970; m. 2d, Meda Walter, June 29, 1968; edn: undergrad. Santa Rosa J.C. 1956-58, Cal.Poly. State Univ. 1958-59; BS in agri. engring., UC Davis 1979; Reg. Profl. Civil Engr., Calif. 1982. Career: soil conservation techn. US Soil Conservation Service (Madera) 1961-62, civil engring. techn. (Davis) 1962-79, civil engr., 1979-82, hydraulic engr., 1982—; mem. Loyal Order of the Moose; Populist; Christian; rec: wood sculpture, stained glass, hunting, flying. Res: 29000 Mountain View Rd Boonville 95415 Ofc: US Soil Conservation Service 2828 Chiles Rd Davis 95616

HANN, GARY DEAN, insurance agent; b. Nov. 9, 1950, Trenton, NJ; s. Hollis Stanley and Patience Ruth (Wheeler) H.; m. Wendy Remick, Aug. 11, 1973; children: Justin Paul, b. 1977, Brandon Dean, b. 1982; edn: grad. Calif. Sch. of Insurance, TI. Career: ins. clk. Chase Ins. Agcy., Palm Springs 1974-75; ins. agt., office mgr. Garcia Ins., Palm Springs 1975-77; owner/prin. Hann Insur-

ance Agency, Yucca Valley 1977—; mem: Profl. Ins. Agts. Assn., Yucca Valley CofC (pres. 1982-3), Rotary Internat. of Yucca Valley (pres. 1984-5); Republican; Christian; rec: water/snow skiing. Res: 57855 El Dorado Yucca Valley 92284 Ofc: Hann Insurance Agency, 7355 Church St Yucca Valley 92284

HANNA, GORDIE (JACK) CONSYNTINE, olericulturist; b. July 1, 1903, Quannah, Texas; s. Welch Consyntine and Dossie Lee (McElroy) H.; m. Delia Webb, June 18, 1926; children: Jacqueline b. 1930, Margaret Anne b. 1933; edn: BS, Univ. of Calif. 1928. Career: (tchr., researcher) splst./ asst., assoc./ olericulturist UC Davis 1929-70; plant breeder Petoseed Inc., Woodland 1971—; awards: Calif. Tomato Growers Assn. 1963; Calif. Seed Assn. 1968; Forty-Niner Service award 1969; Man of the Year, Pacific Seedsman Assn. 1969; Canner League Hall of Fame, 1975; John Scott Award, 1976; Appreciation, UC Davis 1979; Distng. Achiev., Cal Aggie Alumni Assn. 1980; mem: Am. Soc. of Horticultural Sci., Commonwealth CLub, UC Faculty Club (pres. 1944-45), Rio Vista Lodge F&AM (Master 1941), Chancellor's Club, O.E.S.; works: num. papers rel. to plant beerding work on tomatoes, sweet potatoes and asparagus; developed tomatoes suitable for mechanical harvesting; inventor, patented UC-Blackwelder Tomato Harvester; Republican; Presbyterian; rec: gardening. Res: 526 Oak Ave. Davis 95616 Ofc: Petoseed Inc., Rt. 1 Box 1255 Woodland 95695

HANNA, MARY ELLEN MARTIN, real estate broker; b. Jan. 21, 1932, Winner, S.Dak.; d. Raymond Vincent and Clara Hazel (Talcott) Hughes; m. Donald Martin, 1949-77; children: Vicki, b. 1950, Debra, b. 1952, Michael, b. 1954, Gregg, b. 1957, Tamara, b. 1960; m. 2d. Richard G. Hanna, Jan. 14, 1979 (div. 1985); edn: stu. De Anza Coll. 1976-79, Foothill Coll. 1982, Univ. of Phoenix 1984; Calif. lic. Cosmetology 1965, Real Estate Broker 1979, Subject Tchr. Credential 1982. Career: hairdresser Reflections of Beauty, Mt. View; owner Mary Martins Coiffures, Sunnyvale, Hair-O-Scope Beauty Salon, Mt. View; sales assoc. Van Vleck Realtors, Sunnyvale, Condominium Splsts., Sunnyvale; broker assoc. J.M. Daley & Assocs., Palo Alto; v.p./branch mgr. Cornish & Carey Realtors, Cupertino; mng. gen. ptnr. MMH Investments, a lmtd. ptnrshp.; owner/broker Hallmark Properties, San Jose 1985—; tchr. adult edn. courses, Mt. View, Los Altos 1982-85; mem: Nat., and Calif. Assn. of Realtors; San Jose, Sunnyvale and Los Gatos/Saratoga Boards of Realtors; Women's Council of Realtors (Santa Clara Valley chpt. bd. dirs.); Internat. Order of Rainbow for Girls, Mothers Club (pres. Fremont, Ca. 1966, 68), Girl Scouts (ldr. 1959-63); Republican; Rel. Sci.; rec: travel, cooking. Res: 20730 Garden Crest Ct Cupertino 95014 Ofc: Hallmark Properties, 1084 S Saratoga/Sunnyvale Rd San Jose 95129

HANNA, PHILIP RUSH, engineering consultant; b. May 1, 1945, Pittsburgh, Pa.; s. Boyd Everett and Hazel Mae (Bauman) H.; m. Barbara Kreemer, Aug. 30, 1983; children: Win-Son b. 1959, Win-Sho b. 1961, Soo-Ling b. 1963, Shiao-Yu b. 1965, Mariel b. 1982; edn: BSEE, cum laude, Univ. of Ariz. 1972; Reg. Profl. Engr. (electrical) Calif. Career: instrument & control design engr. Bechtel Power Corp. (Los Angeles) 1972-73, electrical startup engr. (Ariz.) 1974-76, senior startup engr. (Calif.) 1976-78, asst. project startup engr. (Ariz.) 1978-80; pres. Philip-Rush Assoc. Ltd., Louisiana 1980, Calif. 1981—, cons./tech. splst. Startup Nuclear Inc.; honors: Tau Beta Pi; mem. Research Council of Scripps Clinic and Research Found.; works: poem "Joany's Flights" pub. Lehigh Literary Review; two dimensional art, drawing exhibited Saddleback Coll. 1985 Juried Art Exh.; mil: sgt. E5, US Marine Corps 1964-68; rec: drawing, photog., gardening. Address: Philip-Rush Assoc. Ltd. 126 Ave Dominguez San Clemente 92672

HANSEN, ARLEN RALPH, general building contractor; b. Apr. 6, 1928, Halfway, Ore.; s. Ralph L. and Zella V. (Herring) H.; m. Kaye Bailey, June 3, 1955; children: Kim b. 1956, Kelly b. 1957, Krista b. 1958, Kurt b. 1960, Karla b. 961, Kourtney b. 1962, Kaylene b. 1964; edn: Brigham Young Univ., Utah State Univ. Career: vol. missionary service in Ga., Fla., Miss., 1948-50; saw opr. Pilot Rock (Ore.) Lumber Co., 1951-52; supr. Multnomah Co. Dairy Herd Improvement Assn., Portland 1953; ptnr. in dairy farm, Portland 1953-54; mgr. Hoodview Holstein Dairy, Troutdale, Ore. 1954-57; constrn. carpentry, Los Angeles 1957-63; gen. building contr. prin., Saugus 1962—; recipient Santa Clarita Sch. PTA hon. service award (1972); civic: Pleasantview Achieve. Center workshop for handicapped (bd. dirs. 1969-, bd. pres. 2 terms), Wm. S. Hart Boys Baseball Team (mgr. 1966-74, bd. 1971-74), vol. num. youth pgms. for boys and girls; Republican; Ch. of Jesus Christ of Latter Day Saints (bishop 1978-83, High Council 1974-78); rec: sports, fishing, hunting. Address: Arlen R. Hansen, Gen. Contractor 27602 Santa Clarita Rd Saugus 91350

HANSEN, DANIELS DUBOSE, cardiologist, medical clinic director; b. Mar. 30, 1931, Denver, Colo.; s. Samuel Shirley and Louise (Tucker) H.; children: Genevieve b. 1964, Lindsay b. 1965; edn: AB, Princeton Univ. 1952; MD, UC Los Angeles 1956, postgrad., residency, 1959; research fellow Univ. of Colo., Denver 1960; bd. certified internist, cardiologist, Am. Board of Internal Medicine 1962. Career: research fellow Rockefeller Found. 1953; NIH fellow Univ. Colo. 1959; chief of profl. service USAF Hosp. (S.A.C.), Columbus, Miss. 1960-62, NIH fellow in psychiatry Menninger Found. 1962; asst. clin. prof. of medicine UCLA Med. Center 1962-78; pvt. practice of medicine and cardiology, 1978—, med. dir. Scripps Clinic, San Jacinto; chief dept. med. Hemet Hosp. 1981-84; awards: Nat. Scholarship, Princeton Univ. 1948-52), Grass Trust Fellow (1953), Bank of Am. outstanding stu. math. and sci. (1952); mem: Fellow Am. Coll. Physicians, Am. Coll. Cardiology, Am. Coll. Chest Physicians, So. Calif. Soc. Clin. Hypnosis, Hemet Hospice (pres. 1979); 9 sci. publs. in cardiology and psychosomatic medicine; mil: capt. USAF, Dist. Service Unit

Citation; Republican; Presbyterian; rec: flying, scuba diving, skiing. Res: 26811 Sol Court Hemet 92344

HANSEN, DAVID CARY, physician - dermatologist; b. May 10, 1956, Aberdeen, S.D.; s. Lloyd Milton and Ramona Leonardo (Lutter) H.; m. Anita Lee Bolden, Oct. 6, 1984; edn: BA magna cum laude, Univ. of S. Dak. 1978, MD, 1982. Career: Integrated Transitional housestaff ofcr., Univ. of Hawaii, 1983; chief dermatology res. King/Drew Med. Center, Los Angeles 1983-86; honors: E.M. Mumford Scholar 1976; Lovelace Found. Inhalation and Toxicology Research Inst. summer fellow 1976; Sanger English Scholar 1977; Phi Sigma Soc. 1978, Eta Sigma Phi 1978; mem: Am. Acad. of Dermatology, AMA, Hawaii Med. Assn., Nat. Assn. of Residents and Interns, Joint Counsel of Interns and Residents; publs: research in biology field 1974-78, profl. papers, Dermatopathology Symposia, Am. Acad. of Derm., Wash DC 1984; Lutheran; rec: salt water aquarist, dancing, snorkling., sports. Res: 8607 Tuscany Ave., No. 205, Playa del Rey 90293 Ofc: King/Drew Medical Center 12021 S Wilmington Ave Los Angeles 90059

HANSEN, DON CURTIS, envelope manufacturing executive; b. March 13, 1929, Marinette, Wisc.; s. Curtis Albert and Dagmar Anne (Johnson) H.; m. Joan Crant, Nov. 9, 1973; edn: bus. admin., Carroll Coll. 1952. Career: purchasing agent Prescott/ Sterling, Menominee, Mich. 1954-62; mfrs. rep. Don C. Hansen Assoc., Phoenix, Ariz. 1962-63; salesmgr. Karolton Envelope Co., San Francisco 1964-72; pres., owner San Francisco Envelope, San Francisco 1972-79; owner Curtis Swann Cards, San Francisco 1977-79; pres., owner Don C. Hansen Inc., San Francisco 1979 –; dir. Printing Industries of No. Calif. 1980 –; dir. Envelope Printing Splsts. Assn., NY, NY 1983 –; mem: Envelope Printing Splsts. Assn. (pres. 1983-84), San Francisco Litho & Craftsmans Club, Printing Industries of No. Calif., Masons, Harbor Point Tennis Club, San Francisco Tennis Club, Ahmed Shrine; mil: pfc US Army 1952-54; Republican; rec: tennis, skiing, bridge. Ofc: The Envelope Co., 750 2nd St. San Francisco 94107

HANSEN, DONNA DARLENE, real estate broker; b. Jan. 16, 1947, San Mateo; d. John Simpson and Marion (Lilly) Albright; m. Robert Noel Hansen, Aug. 7, 1971; children: Darin b. 1967, Daryl b. 1971, Hans b. 1974, Clinton b. 1981; edn: AA, Coll. of San Mateo 1966; counselor, Chattan Edn. Corp., 1981; Calif. lic. R.E. Agent (1976) Broker (1985). Career: secty. to the hd. librarian, City of Burlingame, 1966-76; agent Trotter Realty 1976-77, Grubb and Ellis 1977-81, J.M. Taylor & Co. 1981-85; broker/pres. Hansen Props., Woodside 1985 –; dir: Hansen Finl. Services, Hansen Properties; honors: Million Dollar Club; mem. San Mateo Bd. Realtors (prop. mgmt. com., Investment Exchange gp.), Menlo Park- Atherton Bd. Realtors (edn. com.), Peninsula Exchangers, Associated Inv. & Exchange Counselors; civic: Am. Womens Volunteer Services, Suicide Prevention; club: Peninsula Golf & CC; Republican; Christian; rec: writing, gardening. Ofc: Hansen Properties 2995 Woodside Rd Ste 400-322 Woodside 94062

HANSEN, JAMES TYLER, physician-gastroenterologist; b. Jan. 31, 1940, Upland; s. Jack Tyler and Beverly (Brantley) H.; m. Sharlyn, Aug. 27, 1966; children: Jennifer b. 1970, James b. 1971; edn: BA, Vanderbilt Univ. 1961; MD, USC 1965; certified Am. Board Internal Medicine (1971), Gastroenterology (1975). Career: rotating intern LA County/USC Medical Ctr. 1965, resident internal med. 1966-69; splst. internal med. (chief of medicine, Munich 1971-72) US Army Germany 1969-72; fellowship gastroenterology UCLA- Wadsworth VA Hosp. 1972-73; consulting splst. gastroenterology, Sacramento 1973 –; assoc. clin. prof. Int. Med., UCD 1975-; mem: Fellow Am. Coll. Physicians, Calif. Med. Assn., Sacto. Med. Soc., Am. Gastroent. Assn.; club: North Ridge Country; mil: major US Army 1969-72; Republican; Lutheran; rec: golf, ski, photog. Ofc: 5404 Laurel Hills Ste A Sacramento 95841

HANSEN, RAYMOND LAWRENCE, lawyer, labor organizer; b. Jan. 23, 1933, Crystal Lake, Ill.; s. Carl Anchor and Mary J. (Lobb) H.; div.; children: Erik, b. 1959; Gregory, b. 1960; Theresa, b. 1962; edn: AB, UCLA 1959; JD, UC Berkeley 1961; admitted, State Bar 1962. Career: v.p. Worldwide Books Inc., NYC 1969-70; v.p. Visual Resources Inc., NYC 1970-71; chief counsel Calif. Teachers Assn. 1972-85; mgmt. cons. (rels.) WOFAC GmbH, Europe; pvt. law practice; bd. dirs. Pipeline Experimental Theater, Los Angeles; mem: Am. Bar Assn. (chmn. Labor subcom. 1980-83); State Bar Exec. Com. (Labor), editor State Bar publ. Labor and Employment News; ACLU; Jobs With Peace; Amnesty Internat.; arts. in legal and labor journs.; mil: sgt. 1952-55; Independent; rec: computers, basketball, soccer. Res: 1966 Vestal Ave., Los Angeles 90026 Ofc: Peoples Muffinry, 827 S. San Julian, Los Angeles 90014

HARA, GEORGE, venture capitalist; b. Oct. 10, 1952, Osaka, Japan; s. Shinsuke and Mihoko (Kuroda) H.; edn: LLB, Keio Univ. Sch. of Law 1975, engring. stu. 1975-77; MS in engring., Stanford Univ. 1981, MBA, Stanford Bus. Sch., 1981; lic 1/c capt. for vessels, Japan Ministry of Transp. (1974). Career: fin. ofcr. UN Capital Devel. Fund, 1981; task force Kansai Com. for econ. devel., Osaka, Japan 1981; founder Gekee Fiberoptics 1982; mng. dir./ pres. Data Control Ltd. 1983 –; concurrent: mng. ptnr. DEFTA Partners (venture capital); v.p. Pacific Catalyst Group, Los Angeles 1984–; pres. evp, IDA Bldg. (USA) Corp. 1985-, bd. chmn. Networking Japan (Tokyo, Palo Alto, Boston) 1985-; dir: Japan Incubation Capital (Tokyo), Plantec Inc. (Tokyo), Control Technology Ltd. (Osaka), The Wollongong Group (Palo Alto), Software Connections Inc., (Santa Clara); apptd. spl. advisor to Gov. of Osaka, Japan (1986-); chmn. Alliance Conf. Bd. (US-Japan) 1986–; mem. Shotosha Found. (chmn. 1979-), Smithsonian Instn., Japan-El Salvador Assn., Japan-Costa Rica Assn., Stanford Alumni Assn., Japan-Central Am. Assn. (pres.

1976-78); civic: Shang Lira R.R. & Train Mus., Ashiya, Hyogo, Japan (dir.), mem. Central Am. Archaeol. Soc.; inventor: fiberoptic display systems (pat. pend., Japan 1986), computer wiring network system (pat. pend., Japan 1986); author: Multi-nat. Hightechnology Start-up Theory, Stanford Grad. Sch. of Bus.; rec: archaeol., trains & locomotives. Res: 3737 Fillmore St #105 San Francisco 94123 Ofc: Data Control Ltd. POB 51238, 1131 San Antonio Rd Palo Alto 94303; Marchant Capital Div. Four Embarcadero Ctr, 36th flr, San Francisco 94111

HARDING, CYRIL RICHARD BENNETT, civil engineer; b. Nov. 3, 1906, Torquay, Devon, England; s. Alfred Sidney Cowell and Florence Adeline Augusta (Hall) Harding; emigrated to Lynn, Mass. 1912 with parents, nat. US cit. 1920; m. Ruth Dorothea Jensen, Dec. 7, 1929; children: Richard Bennett, Robert Hall; m. 2d. Joanna Savage, Jan. 1, 1947; children: Joanna Candice, George Thomas; edn: BSCE, M.I.T. 1930. Career: chief engr. Lynn Park Dept. 1930-41 (designed and blt. the largest H.S. stadium in USA 25000 seats; also a cantilevered-roof grandstand for the Lynn baseball club, then a Boston Red Sox farm club; both designs pub. in Christian Sci. Monitor, var. trade publs., local and Boston newspapers); tech. cons., asst. dir. of engring. Stran Steel Div., Great Lakes Steel Corp., Detroit, Mich. (designed Quonset Huts for USN, patented expansion system enabled std. parts to build huge warehouses throughout S.Pac. during WWII; designed the light-wt. steel floats used in USN system for floating dry-docks, floating piers and wharfs, floating bridges; tech. asst. loaned to English Ministry for Reconstrn. 1945), 1941-48; mgr. middle east ops. Johnston Pump Co. of Los Angeles, HQ Athens, Greece 1949-50; design engr., senior design engr. Wing Group, No. Am. Aviation 1950-60; pres. Peerless Investment Co. (real estate brokerage), Hollywood 1957–; honors: bow oar, 8-oared crew 1923-25, Nat. Junior Championship, Poughkeepsie (1925), MIT swim team (1926) MIT rifle team (1927), MIT Drama Club (1928-29), Silver Ski Award, Sun Valley (1941), cert. scuba diver (1953); mem: Soc. of Am. Mil. Engrs. (awarded life mem. 1942), US/Los Angeles Power Squadron (comdr. 1969), MIT Alumni Assn. So. Calif., Hollywood Yacht Club. Address: 7454 Hillside Ave Hollywood 90046

HARDING, JOANNA SAVAGE (Savich), Olympic athlete, fencing school founder, real estate broker; b. Apr. 30, 1908, Detroit, Mich.; d. George Thomas and Gizella D'Aguillar (Vojner) Savich; m. Bela de Tuscan, May 9, 1931; m. 2d. Cyril R.B. Harding, Jan. 1, 1947; children: Joanna Candice and George Thomas Harding; edn: Detroit Sch. of Arts and Crafts 1926-29, Rhode Is. Sch. of Design 1929-30, pvt. stu. portrait painting w/John Hubbard Rich; Santelli Sch. of Fencing 1932-36; stu. ballet, Jessie Bonstelle Theater Group 1932-34; Chinese painting w/Rewena Ko Ming Fei 1980-82. Career: co-founder Salle de Tuscan Sch. of Fencing and Club (world's largest Salle d'armes; produced a national champion, Canadian champion, sev. Mid-west champions), Detroit 1930-43; US Nat. Champion Women's Foil (1936) and capt. US Womens Olympic Fencing Team (voted Most Beautiful Olympian, Olympic Games Berlin) 1936; fencing tchr. Wayne Univ. and the Cranbrook Sch., Bloomfield Hills, Mich. 1934-36; choreographer/performer in a fencing ballet for full-year run at the Palladium, London 1938-39; World Profl. Champion Women's Foil (1939); fencing exhibs. in prin. cities Europe and Balkan countries 1939-40 (on last convoy lv. France during German invasion WWII); entertainer featured act, fencing and dancing, Broadway musicals incl. Keep Off the Grass, others, NYC 1941-43; USO Sports Unit entertainer Armed Forces in Pacific 1944-45; fencing tchr. 20th Century-Fox Studios, Agnes Moorhead Sch. of Drama, movie double for stars in fencing scenes 1957-62; real estate broker, Hollywood 1945–, dba Peerless Investment Co. 1957-, incorporated, v.p. 1975–; mem. 1984 Olympic Speakers Bureau; mem. Nat. Assn. of Realtors, Calif. Assn. Realtors, Los Angeles Bd. Realtors, Calif. Art Club, Squadronettes aux. LA Power Squadron (pres. 1969-70), The Gingersnaps (fmr. Ziegfield, Earl Carol, Theatre dancers dance group for charity 1982-); first female fencer to wear trousers, subject of Paul Gallico column in the N.Y. News headlined "Pants is for Guys" w/3-col. cartoon; cited in Ency. Britannica (1941 supplement), and Black's Hist. of Aviation as the first person to lift off ground in a heavier-than-air machine using only her own power. Address: 7454 Hillside Ave Hollywood 90046

HARDING, JOHN MARTIN, business owner; b. Sept. 28, 1928, Earlimart; s. Marian Lee and Dorothea Mae (Holtzman) H.; m. Mary Partain, Dec. 1, 1951; children: Karen Christine b. 1952, Steven Douglas b. 1955. Career: subcontractor/owner/pres. J & L Cabinets Inc., Fullerton 1962 –, incorporated 1974; mem: So. Calif. Assn. Cabinet Mfrs., Nat. Fedn. Small Businesses; Republican; Christian; rec: gardening, camping. Res: 5911 Country View Dr. Yorba Linda 92686 Ofc: J & L Cabinets Inc., 1232 Orangethorpe Fullerton 92631

HARDING, MARY JOANN PARTAIN, business executive; b. Jan. 25, 1933, Palmdale; d. Joseph Henry and Cora Mae (Payne) Partain; m. John Martin Harding, Dec. 1, 1951; children: Karen Christine b. 1952, Steven Douglas b. 1955; grad. Antelope Valley Jt. Union High Sch. Career: accounting; v.p., prin. J&L Cabinets Inc., Fullerton 1962 –; civic: Girl Scouts Am. (Brownie leader), PTA (Drum & Bugle Corp); Republican; rec: cooking, camping, family. Res: 5911 Country View Dr. Yorba Linda 92686 Ofc: J & L Cabinets Inc., 1232 E Orangethorpe Fullerton 92631

HARDY, SANDRA KAY, chiropractor; b. May 10, 1947, Ottumwa, Iowa; d. Keith L. and Dorothy L. (Hunt) Miler; m. Donald W. Hardy, June 14, 1981; children: Devin b. 1965, Deanna b. 1969, Stephanie b. 1985; edn: Fullerton Jr. Coll. 1979-80; Central Oregon Community Coll. 1978-79; Santa Ana Community Coll. 1980; DC, Cleveland Coll. of Chiropractic 1983. Career: owner, opr. ladies clothing store, Mammoth Lake 1973-74; owner, opr. interior &

drapery store, Mammoth 1973; real estate salesperson Tolar Realty, Yorba Linda 1975-77; real estate sales, Oregon 1977; owner, opr. ladies clothing store, Oregon 1978; paramedical examiner, Santa Ana 1979-80; currently, chiropractor, Modesto; host weekly radio pgm., Your Health & You, KBEE FM 1984-; mem: Stanislaus Co. Chiropractic Soc., Womens Aglou, Christian Womens Club, Profl. Womens Network; Republican; Protestant; rec: skiing, boating, tennis sailing. Res: 18197 Sleepy Hollow Sonora 95370 Ofc: Early Chiropractic Office, 2937 Veneman Ste 105B Modesto 95356

HARDY, WILLIAM HOWARD, trust co. business development executive; b. Mar. 1, 1927, Omaha, Neb.; s. Howard Lewis and Carolyn Gertrude (Collins) H.; m. Doris Marie, Mar. 15, 1975; children: Candace b. 1950, Nancy b. 1952, Judith b. 1956, Rebecca b. 1960; edn: bus., Santa Ana Coll. 1946-48; LLB, LaSalle Extn. Univ. 1970. Career: ops. ofcr. Bank of Am. Newport Beach 1948-55; gen. agent John Hancock Mutual Life Long Beach 1955-63; mortgage broker Hardy Mortgage Co. Long Beach 1963-68; trust ofcr. mktg. Bank of Am. Santa Barbara 1968-73, First Interstate Bank Palo Alto 1973-84; v.p., trust ofcr. Pacific Trust Co. San Jose 1984–; ofcr., dir. Hardy TENS & Med. Supply 1977-; co-founder, treas. Electromediacl Pain Research Ctr. 1980-; mem: Estate Planning Council (county dir. 1983-84), Masons; mil: aviation ordnanceman 3/c USN 1944-46, Asiatic Pacific; Republican; Presbyterian; rec: botany. Ofc: Pacific Trust Co. 1245 S Winchester San Jose 95128

HARGARAY, ELIZABETH ANN, real estate broker; b. June 27, 1945, Toledo, Ohio; d. LeRoy and Mary Jane (Griswack) Kirkover; m. Norman C. Hargaray, Apr. 15, 1962; children: Michelle b. 1962, Cindy b. 1964, Billy b. 1969; edn: AA real estate, Sierra Coll. 1979; Grad. Realtors Inst. 1978. Career: sales & mgmt. Beeline Fashions Inc. 1966-80; real estate sales Realty Quest 1976-78, Mother Lode 1978-82, C-21 1982-85, Robinet Realty 1985–; mem: Placer County Bd. of Realtors (membshp. com., pol. action com.), Toastmasters, Bus. & Profl. Women, Parent Tchr. Club Loomis Schs., Sch. Advis. Com.; Republican; Protestant; rec: antiques, plates, books. Res: 3781 Taylor Rd Loomis 95650 Ofc: Robinet Realty 4877 Granite Dr Rocklin 95677

HARLAN, GEORGE HILARY, writer; b. July 4, 1916, Sausalito, Calif.; s. George Hillary and Esther (Greaves) H.; m. Kathleen Shannon, June 9, 1958; children: Sandra Kay Rose b. 1937, Kadeane Hilary b. 1949; edn: AA, Coll. of Marin 1935; BA, Univ. Nev. 1937. Career: naval architect Army Transport Svc. 1941-50; naval architect, supt. port engr., engrg. ofcr. USN Military Sealift Command 1950-80; self-employed writer; honors: Meritorious Civilian Svc. (USN 1954), NASA Apollo Achievement Award 1969; mem: Soc. of Naval Architects and Marine Engrs., Soc. of Port Engrs. of S.F., Corinthian Yacht Club; author: Oil Lamps and Iron Promises (1949), Of Walking Beams & Paddle Wheels (1951), San Francisco Bay Ferryboats (1967), An Island in Yosemite (1981), Those Amazing Cab Forwards (1983); rec: photog., model railroading. Res: 180 Via Lerida Greenbrae 94904

HARLEY, ROBISON DOOLING, JR., lawyer; b. July 6, 1946, Ancon (C.Z.) Panama; s. Robison Dooling and Loyde Hazel (Gouchenauer) Harley; m. Suzanne P. Bendel, Aug. 8, 1975; children: Arianne Erin, b. 1980, Lauren Loyde, b. 1982; edn: BA, Brown Univ. 1968; JD, Temple Univ. 1971; LLM (criminal law), Univ. of San Diego 1984; cert. criminal law splst. Calif. State Bar (1981); admitted to US Supreme Ct., US Ct. of Mil. Appeals, various Federal Dist. and Circuit Cts. throughout the US; Certified Criminal Trial Advocate, Nat. Bd. Trial Advocates 1982, Career: judge advocate (trial counsel, def. counsel, mil. judge, asst. staff judge adv.) USMC, 1971-75; asst. agency dir. Safeco Title Insurance Co., Panorama City 1975-77; criminal defense atty. law firm of Cohen, Stokke & Davis, Santa Ana 1977-85; Law Ofcs. of Robison D. Harley, Jr., Santa Ana 1985–; instr. Orange Co. Coll. of Trial Advocacy; judge pro tem Orange Co. Municipal Cts.; mem: Am., Calif., Penna, NJ and Dist. Columbia Bar Assns.; Calif. Attys. for Criminal Justice, Calif. Pub. Defenders Assn., Nat. Assn. of Criminal Defense Lawyers, Orange Co. Bar Assn. (Judiciary Com., Adminstrn. of Justice Com., Criminal Law Sect.), O.C. Trial Lawyers Assn., Assn. of Trial Lawyers of Am., Calif. Trial Lawyers; bd. dirs. Legal Aid Soc. of O.C.; mil: lt.col. USMC(R), cert. of congratulations, Commandant USMC, cert. of commendn., Comdg. General, USMC; Republican; Prot.; rec: sports, phys. fitness. Res: 12 Bayberry Way Irvine 92715 Ofc: 825 N Ross St Santa Ana 92701

HARLOW, LISA LAVOIE, psychological counselor, educator; b. Dec. 3, 1951, Hartford, Conn.; d. Jean Paul and Mary Bernadine (Heslin) Lavoie; m. Gary Russell Harlow, June 10, 1978; 1 dau. Rebecca b. 1986; edn: BA psychol., CSU Fullerton 1979, MA, 1981; PhD, UC Los Angeles 1985. Career: checker, bkpr. Von's Grocery, Rolling Hills & Yorba Linda, Calif. 1969-79; tchg. asst. in statistics, CSU Fullerton 1978-79, instr. stats. 1980; tchg. assoc., research assoc. UCLA 1980-85; asst. prof. psychol. Univ. Rhode Island, Kingston 1985–; psychol. counselor, pvt. tutor in statistics and research; guest lectr. in psychol. testing and advanced statistics; statistical cons.,; co-dir. microcomputer proj.; honors: Outstanding Grad. Student (CSUF 1980), Travel Grant (UCLA 1982, 84), Research Grant (UCLA 1984), Computer Grant (UCLA 1985), Summer Faculty Fellowship (URI 1986); mem: Am. Psychol. Assn., Am. Ednl. Research Assn., Psychometric Soc., Am. Statistical Assn., Soc. Psychols. in Addictive Behaviors, Assn. of Profl. and Academic Women in Psychol. (RI); publs: 6 research papers in psychol. jours. 1983-, 5 research presentations at regional, nat. and internat. confs. 1980-, topics incl. statistics, meaning in life, addictive behaviors, depression, social support and stress; Democrat; Christian; rec: piano, sewing, skiing, microcomputers. Res: POB 1497 Kingston, RI 02881 Ofc: Dept. of Psychol., Univ. R.I., Kingston, RI 02881-0808

HARMON, JEFFREY, sales executive; b. July 26, 1953, Santa Monica; s. Julius and Ruth (Neidelman) H.; edn: BS in Bus. Adm., Pepperdine Univ. 1975. Career: (current) district sales mgr. Oracle Corp. Los Angeles; (past): mktg. rep. Cognos Corp., L.A.; mktg. rep. Dun & Bradstreet Computing. Recipient journalism scholarship, Pepperdine Univ. (1974); mem. DECUS, Toastmasters, Concern II; Democrat; Jewish; rec: sailing, running, travel. Ofc: Oracle Corp. Ste 210 13160 Mindanao Way Marina Del Rey 90292

HARNSBERGER, THERESE COSCARELLI, librarian; b. Muskegon, Mich., d. Charles and Julia (Borrell) Coscarelli; m. Frederick Owen Harnsberger, Dec. 24, 1962; 1 son, Lindsey Carleton; edn: BA cum laude, Marymount Coll. 1952; MLS, USC 1953; postgrad. Rosary Coll., River Forest, Ill. 1955-56, UCLA Ext. 1960-61. Career: freelance writer, 1950–; librarian San Marino (Calif.) High Sch., 1953-56; cataloger, cons. San Marino Hall, South Pasadena 1956-61; librarian Los Angeles State Coll., 1956-59; librarian dist. lib. Covina-Valley Unified Sch. Dist., Covina 1959-67; librarian Los Angeles Trade Tech. Coll., 1972–; med. librarian, tumor registral Alhambra (Calif.) Community Hosp., 1975-79; pres., dir. Research Unltd., 1980–; freelance reporter Los Angeles' Best Bargains, 1981-; med. library cons., 1979-; chmn. spiritual values com. Covina Coordinating Council, 1964-66; mem. Calif. Assn. Sch. Librarians (ch. legis. com.), Covina Tchrs. Assn., AAUW (historian 1972-73), USC Grad. Sch. Library Sci. (life), Am. Nutrition Soc. (chpt. Newsletter ch.), Nat. Tumor Registrars Assn., So. Calif. Tumor Registrars Assn., Med. Library Assn., So. Calif. Librarians Assn., So. Calif. Assn. Law Libraries, Book Publicists So. Calif., Pi Lambda Theta. Ofc: 2809 W. Hellman Ave., Alhambra 91803

HARRELL, ROBERT ELLIS, rancher; b. Aug. 5, 1920, Vallejo; s. Andrew Jasper and Irma Lucille (Peachman) H.; m. Kathleen Varcoe, Feb. 12, 1961; children: Wm. Andrew b. 1946, David b. 1951, Christina b. 1953, Richard b. 1954, Paul b. 1955, Craig b. 1956; edn: BS, UC Davis 1942, M.Edn., 1946; UCB Boalt Hall Sch. of Law 1947-48. Career: voc. agric. tchr. Elk Grove High Sch. and Paso Robles High, 1947; fire underwriter Home Insurance Co., Los Angeles 1948-50; owner/mgr./ pres. Harrell Ranches Inc. (devel. 7,000 acres of diversified farming land), Tulare County 1950–; civic: Kaweah Delta Hosp. Found. (extensive fundraising; pres. 1979-), Coll. of Sequoia Found. (1986) School Board mem. (1962-66), Kaweah Water Conc. Dist. (1966-68), mem./ chmn. Tulare County Board Supvrs. (1968-81), Tulare County Water Commn. (1955-), Tulare County Planning Commn., Visalia YMCA (pres.), CofC, Visalia Rotary (pres.); club: Visalia CC (dir.); mil: m/sgt. US Army Med. Corps 1942-46; Republican; Episcopal; rec: golf, travel. Address: Harrell Ranches Inc. 510 Lombard Ct Visalia 93291

HARRINGTON, EUNICE PETERS, educator; b. Middletown, Conn.; d. Wm. J. and Eunice S. (Lowery) Peters; 1 dau. Lisa Beth b. 1965; edn: BA, Whittier Coll. 1951; MA, Azusa Pacific Univ. 1978; desig: Reading Splst., State Bd. Edn. (1978). Career: educator, 35 yrs., tchr. USAF in England, US Army in Germany and USA; owner/dir. Harrington Reading Lab, Azusa 1978–; recipient appreciation awards, Azusa H.S. (1981), Dalton Sch. (1976-77), Leukemia Soc. Am. (1976), LA County Heart Assn. (1970), Americanism Award, VFW Post 8070 (1972); civic: East San Gabriel Valley Regl. Occupational Pgm. (v.chmn.), City of Azusa Parks and Rec. Dept. (commnr.), Azusa Pac. Univ. (Comm. Advis. Council), Azusa U. Sch. Dist. (bd. govs. 1981-, past pres.); publs: handbook for parents of children entering Kindergarten; rec: music, creative arts. Address: Harrington REading Lab 230 Viewcrest Dr Azusa 91702

HARRINGTON, HARLAND JAMES, quality professional/quality engineering executive; b. Jan. 16, 1929, Johnson City, NY; s. Frank O. and Carri May (Sanders) H.; m. Marguerite Holtzmaster 1965; 1 son, James Steven b. 1968; edn: AA, electronics, Broom Tech. Coll. 1953; BS gen. engring., Univ. of Beverly Hills 1978, MBA, 1980; MS Quality Systems, Columbia Pacific Univ. 1981, PhD Quality Engring., 1982. Career: apprentice tool maker, IBM, 1947-, then worked in Devel. Engring., Mfg. Engring., Prod. Engring. depts.; cons. on reliability to IBM, San Jose (temporary assignment) 1963; var. mgmt. promotions to current position, Quality Profl./project mgr., IBM; honors: Benjamin Lubelsky Award as outstanding QC Profl. in Calif., 1978; ASQC Adminstrv. Applications Silver Ann. Award as outstanding contrib. to QC in Mgmt. Sci. field over past 25 years, 1980; IBM Awards Banquet, recognition for service in field of quality, 1981; John Delbert Award for outstanding contbns. to field of mgmt., Internat. Mgmt. Council, 1982; hon. mem. Chinese Soc. Quality Control, Brazil Soc. Quality Control; mem: Am. Soc. Quality Control (pres.), Internat. Mgmt. Council (v.p., dir.); chmn. adv. com. on Quality Reliability, CSU San Jose; chmn. adv. com. Mgmt. Studies, San Jose City Coll., West Valley Coll.; num. articles and tech. publs., USA and internat.; frequent speaker worldwide; mil: seaman 1/c USNR 1947-55; rec: fishing. Res: 16080 Camino Del Cerro Los Gatos 95030 Ofc: IBM, 5600 Cottle Rd San Jose 95193

HARRINGTON, LEROY RICHARD, trucking co. president; b. Jan. 31, 1933, Oneida, Kans.; s. Richard Neal and Susie Kathryn (Baer) H.; m. Fayetta Roberts, Sept. 26, 1952; children: Diana Lynn b. 1953, Yvonne Inez b. 1955; edn: A.V. Coll. 1951-52. Career: transp., Wilsons Hatchery, 1952-59; truck-dispatcher in trucking bus., 1959-62; owner/mgr. Antelope Valley Trucking Co., 1962–; speaker high sch. students on trucking indus., Palmdale H.S. (1984), Quartz Hill H.S. (1985); community service awards: A.V. Bd. of Trade (1985), Palmdale Elks (1973), Palmdale Emblem Club (1973), Lulu Award-Coord. Council (1797, 82); mem: A.V. Board of Trade (past pres.), Elks, SPIA (dir.), A.V. Fair Bd. (past pres.), Trade Club (dir.), Kiwanis (past pres.), Palmdale CofC (past v.p., dir.), Lancaster CofC, Cultural Ctr. (life), A.V. Press

Club (life), Palmdale Civic Authority Commn. (2 yrs), Traffic Survival Sch. (dir.), Nat. Fedn. Ind. Bus., Friends of Library, Lilac Fest. (com.), Hacienda Fiesta; sponsor num. youth and civic orgns.; Republican; rec: community service. Res: 39701 Makin St Palmdale 93551 Ofc: Antelope Valley Trucking Co POB 516 Palmdale 93550

HARRIS, BRUCE EUGENE, financial systems executive; b. jan. 14, 1950, Zanesville, Ohio; s. Harold Eugene and Ruth A. (Harbaugh) H.; m. Linda Elaine Vess, March 6, 1971; edn: BS, Ohio State Univ. 1974; Cert. of Data Processing, Data Processing Mgmt. Assn. 1982. Career: coal miner Peabody Coal Co. 1970-72; auditor Boyrin Ents. 1972-74; cost acct. Ashland Chemical, Dublin, Ohio 1974-76; gen. acct. Ohio State Univ., Columbus, Ohio 1976-78; sys. analyst Gulf Oil Corp., Houston, Texas 1978-81; cons. Deloitte Haskins & Sells, Houston, Texas 1981-82; fin. sys. mgr. Information Svcs. Group Div. of Mars Inc., Houston, Texas and Los Angeles 1982–; mem: Data Processing Mgmt. Assn., Inst. for Certification of Computer Profls., Citizens Choice, Smithsonian Inst.; Republican; Cathlic; rec: travel, theatre, tinkering. Res: 6949 La Presa Dr. San Gabriel 91775 Ofc: Information Services Group, P.O. Box 58853 Vernon 90058

HARRIS, DIANE JEANETTE, psychologist; b. Aug. 26, 1952, Kansas City, Mo.; d. Theodore R. and Leona N. Harris; edn: BA, honors, Univ. Calif. 1974; MA, Univ. Mich. 1976, Ed.S., 1978, PhD, 1980; lic. in Psychology, Mass. (1982), cert. in School Psychology, Mass. (1984), Calif. (1986). Career: psychologist Dorchester Counseling Ctr., Family & Childrens Svcs., Mass. 1982-83; clin./consulting psychologist Tufts-New England Med. Ctr., Child Psychiatry Dept., Mass. 1983-84; psychologist Boston Sch. Dept., Mass. 1980-84; psychologist Fresno (Calif.) Community Hosp., 1984-86, Youth Services, Fresno County Dept. of Health 1986–; lectr. CSU Fresno; bd. dirs. Douglas A. Thom Clinic, Inc. Boston (1983-84), Dept. of Social Service, Area 36, Boston (1983-84); recipient Outstanding Young Women of Am. Award (1981); mem: Fellow Am. Psychol. Assn., Am. Orthopsychiatric Assn., Am. Assn. for Counseling and Devel., Alpha Kappa Alpha Sor., NAACP, United Negro College Fund, Interagcy. Council for Children & Child Sexual Abuse Council; sev. local TV and talk radio appearances; interviewee, article in Fresno Bee newspaper (1985); Methodist. Address: Fresno 93711

HARRIS, ELLIOTT, business owner; b. Sept. 16, 1924, Providence, R.I.; s. Myer and Esther (Sholes) H.; m. Shirley, June 3, 1947; children: Barbara Ann b. 1947, Jeffrey b. 1952; edn: BBA, Univ. of Rhode Island 1944, MBA, 1948. Career: dir. of mktg. Toy Distbrs. Inc. 1948-52; eastern regl. mgr. Revlon Inc. 1952-74; nat. sales mgr. Lindy Pen Co. Inc. 1974-84; owner Harris Ofc. Supplies 1984–; Nominating Com. of the Bd. of Dirs., Better Bus. Bureau of San Diego; honors: Arbitrator, Better Business Bureau 1984-86; mem: Golden State Travelers Club (Ofc. Products Assn.), Better Bus. Bureau of San Diego; mil: sgt. US Army 1944-46, Silver Star, Bronze Star, Purple Heart, Pres. Combat Unit Citation; rec: sailing, boating. Res: 4624 Pavlov Ave. San Diego 92122 Ofc: Harris Office Supplies, 9628 Miramar Rd. Ste. 43 San Diego 92126

HARRIS, HERBERT LESLIE, III, manufacturing co. executive, winemaker; b. June 3, 1944, San Diego; s. Herbert L. and Nona (Edwards) H.; m. Patricia, Apr. 9, 1979; children: H. Leslie b. 1981, Cassie b. 1984; edn: BA, San Diego State Univ. 1968; M.Internat. Mgmt., Am. Grad. Sch. of Internat. Mgmt., Thunderbird Campus, Phoenix, Ariz. 1972. Career: sales rep. Kaiser Steel Corp. Oakland, Houston and L.A. 1973-83; asst. sales mgr. so. div. Lysaght-America Sausalito and L.A. 1983-86; prop., winemaker Palos Verdes Winery L.A. 1982–; west coast mktg. mgr. BHP Trading Inc. L.A. 1986–; honors: wine competitions: Gold Medal (Cal. Expo 1985), Silver Medals (San Jose Mercury News 1985, Riverside Fair 1985, Central Coast Growers 1985, S.D. Nat. Wine Comp. 1986), Silver Medal (Orange County Fair 1986); mem: Cellarmasters Winemakers (pres. 1981), Winegrowers of Calif.; mil: yn2 USN 1969-71, Vietnam Campaign; Republican; Protestant; rec: sailing. Res: 808 S Juanita Ave Redondo Beach 90277 Ofc: BHP Trading Inc. 5801 E Slauson Ave Ste 200 Commerce 90040; Palos Verdes Winery 10620-D S La Cienega Blvd Lennox 90304

HARRIS, JOHN D., judge; b. June 19, 1934, Los Angeles; s. Samuel A. and Virginia A. (Rose) H.; m. Marjorie Rosen, Nov. 15, 1969; children: Pamela, b. 1971, Anthony, b. 1973; edn: BA, UC Berkeley 1956, LLB, JD, Boalt Hall, UCB 1959; admitted Calif. State Bar 1960. Career: deputy city atty. Los Angeles City Atty's Ofc. 1960-73; municipal court commnr. Los Angeles Municipal Ct., 1973-84, judge, 1984–; honors: Phi Beta Kappa 1956; pres. Calif. Court Commnrs. Assn. (1981-84); mem. LA County Bar Assn., Criminal Cts. Bar Assn., Calif. Ct. Commnrs. Assn., Calif. Judges Assn.; mem. Profl. Mens' Club of L.A., Westgate Masonic Lodge, F&AM, Temple Israel Hywd., Vista del Mar Assocs., Guardian of Jewish Home for Aged; Democrat; Jewish; rec: sports, travel, theater, pub. speaking. Ofc: LA Municipal Court, 110 N Grand Ave, Div. 18, Los Angeles 90012

HARRIS, NORMA MARANI, welding co. president; b. July 1, 1925, Weed; d. Pietro and Matilde (Sbarbaro) Marani; grad. McClatchy H.S. 1943; m. Kent Harris, Oct. 6, 1946; children: Joanne b. 1947, Kathleen b. 1950, Marilee b. 1954, Kent b. 1962. Career: personnel bd. 1943-46, supr. mail room 1946-70, teacher aide Colfax Grammar Sch., Placer Hills Sch., Placer H.S., 1970-73; bookkeeper, counter clerk, 1973, pres. Harris Wldg. Inc., Citrus Hts. 1974–; mem. Placer H.S. Welding Adv. Bd. 1976-; Metals Adv. Bd., Sierra Coll. 1981-83; adv. dir. Alex Brown Bank 1979-82; exec. bd. Com. to Preserve the Courthouse for the Courts; honors: Annual Auburn Journal Award (1985), Woman of the Year (Auburn 1985); mem: Placer County Contractors Assn. (1st

Woman Dir.; Scholarship chpsn., nom. 2nd v.p.); Auburn Area CofC (pres. 1982); Golden Chain Council (pres. 1982-83); Sierra Coll. Found. Bd. (pres. 1976-83); Order Sons of Italy in Am. (Venerable 1st Woman, Roseville Lodge 1981-83); Bus. & Profl. Women (Woman of Achievement 1982); Soroptimist Intl. of Auburn (2d v.p. 1983); American Legion Aux.; Calif. Native Daughter; Auburn Merchants Council; Gold Country Fair Booster; Applegate Civic Ctr., past. dir. 20th District Agri. Fair Auburn; Citrus Hts. CofC; Roseville CofC; orgnzr. Applegate Well Baby Clinic 1958-68; Colfax Parents Club, Placer Hills PTA; publ: article Women in Non-Traditional Business (Soroptimist of the Americas 1985); Republican; Catholic (choir); rec: jogging, swim, poetry. Res: POB 238 Applegate 95703 Ofc: Harris Welding Inc. 8475 Auburn Blvd Citrus Hts 95610

HARRIS, RICHARD LOUIS, credit union controller; b. Nov. 1, 1954, Glendale; s. Louis Jay and Ruth Elizabeth (Weise) H.; m. Debra Salvo, Feb. 8, 1986; children: Michah Paul b. 1976, Rachel E. b. 1978; edn: stu. Pt. Loma Coll. 1972-74, CSULA 1974-75, Pasadena City Coll. 1977-78; Calif. R.E. Sales lic. (1985). Career: bookkeeper Roger A. Brown, CPA, Pasadena 1972-73; mng. ptnr. La Canada Htg. and Air Condtg., La Canada 1974-80; v.p./controller Nazarene Fed. Credit Union, Brea 1981–, mem. Cunadata Corp. steering com. (in-house computer div.) 1986-; bd. dirs. The Member Service Corp. (1986-), La Canada Youth House Comm. Center (1986-); reserve dep. sheriff L.A. County 1978-83; mem. Nat. Assn. Accts., Am. Mgmt. Assn., Credit Union Exec. Soc., Finl. Ops. Assn., Credit Union Finl. Mgrs. Assn. Res: 4442 Alta Canyada Rd La Canada 91011 Ofc: Nazarene Federal Credit Union POB 4000 Brea 92622

HARRIS, ROSELYN JACKSON, dietitian, consultant; b. Sept. 26, 1916, Ossian, Ind.; d. Glenn Franklin and Zura Maude (Weirich) Jackson; m. Haydn Bevan Harris, Oct. 18, 1941; children: Robert Haydn b. 1943, Douglas Glenn b. 1949; edn: BS nutrition, Purdue Univ. 1938; MS nutrition, Western Reserve Univ. 1940; grad. work UCLA, USC; Reg. Dietitian (RD), Am. Dietetic Assn.; Calif. Comm. Colls. Limited Svc. Cred. (Life) 1976. Career: internship University Hosp., Cleveland, O. 1940-42; staff L.A. County/USC Med. Center, L.A. 1956-61, Olive View Med. Ctr. 1961-67, Covina Inter-Comm. Hosp. 1967-72, Bay General, Chula Vista 1972, Huntington Meml. Hosp., Pasadena 1972-75, Psych. Center for Girls, Charter Oaks 1969-78; cons. Windsor Manor Retirement and Health Facility 1965-74, cons. in Santa Barbara area 1975-: Casa Dorinda Retirement Home (1 yr), La Cumbre Skilled Nsg. (5 yrs), Dos Pueblos Skilled Nsg. (4 yrs), Vista del Monte Ret. Tchrs. Home & Skilled Nsg. (4 yrs), Hillsides House Cerebral Palsy Home (6 yrs), Valle Verde Ret. & Skilled Nsg. Home (10 + yrs) 1976–; cons. on call for area hosps.; tchg. jr. coll. nutrition classes for student nses.; faculty Santa Barbara Jr. Coll., Ventura Comm. Coll., num. 1-day seminars for Am. Soc. Hosp. Food Service Adminstrs. (ASHFSA); charter mem. Dial-A-Dietitian pgm. (founding mem. San Gabriel Valley and 4 other chpts. L.A. area, 1961-71); originated State file of therapeutic diets in Chinese, Japanese, and other languages, authored first USC-LAC Diabetic Manual in English and Spanish; chaired City of Pasadena Task Force on Food and Nutrition for Elderly (1971); mem: Am., Calif. (Therapy chair), Tri-Counties (pres. 1980-81) Dietetic Assns., (past, charter) So. Calif. Chpt. ASHFSA, Soroptimist, Toastmistress, Order of Eastern Star (50-yr), Chi Omega Nat. Womens Frat. (50-yr pin); civic: Santa Barbara Mediation Task Force for Landlord and Tenant (1978-), past area chair for Altadena Red Cross and March of Dimes, Pasa. Urban Coalition League; contbr. num. articles to dietetic jours.; Blue ribbons for ceramic and art works, L.A. County Fair; Episcopal (pres. Ch. Women, S.B.); rec: handbells, gardening, seminars. Res: 4067 Via Zorro Santa Barbara 93110

HARRIS, TIMOTHY ARTHUR, retail co. president, investor; b. Dec. 27, 1954, Lafayette, Ind.; s. Ernest A. and Arline J. (Armantrout) H.; m. Carol Huffman 1979; 1 son, Christopher Allen b. 1972; edn: Antelope Valley Coll. 1974-77. Career: owner/pres. Pet Oasis, Inc. 1976–; real estate investor; mem. Antelope Valley Merchant Assn. (pres.); rec: sailing, scuba, ski. Res: 7523 Ave A Rosemond 93560 Ofc: Pet Oasis Inc. 43749 15th St Ste W Lancaster 93534

HARRIS von DASSANOWSKY, ROBERT, writer; b. Jan. 28, 1956, N.Y., N.Y.; s. Leslie and Elfriede Maria (Baroness von Dassanowsky) Harris de Erendred; edn: grad. American Acad. of Dramatic Arts, 1977; BA in pol. sci./ German, UC Los Angeles 1985, grad. work in German lit./ history, 1986-. Career: actor/dir. 1977–; free-lance playwright, poet and essayist, 1979–; pen name: "Robert Harris"; works include plays: The Birthday of Margot Beck (1979), Briefly Noted (1980), Vespers (1981), Tristan in Winter (1986), Songs of a Wayfarer (1986); book: Telegrams from the Metropole (1986); works pub. (in English and German) in USA, West Ger., Austria, France, England, Canada, India, Australia and Japan; co-dir. of independent theatrical prodn. company, Los Angeles 1981–; num. lectures and readings, 1981–; contbg. editor Rohwedder Mag. L.A. 1986; bd. advisors Com. Art for Olympia, N.Y. (1984-); awards: Found. Michael Karolyi Residency Award (France, 1979), UCLA Ralph Bunche Award (1984), UCLA Alumni Scholar (1985), Beverly Hills Theatre Guild Playwright Award (1984), Man of Achievement (I.B.C., Cambridge, U.K. 1986); mem: Dramatists Guild, Screen Actors Guild, Poet and Writers, World Literary Acad. Paneuropa Union (Ger. & Austria), Heinrich von Kleist Gesellschaft (Ger.), German-Am. Cong., Mensa, UCLA Dean's Council; Catholic; rec: genealogy/ heraldry, fencing, swimming, riding. Address: 4346 Matilija Ave Sherman Oaks 91423

HARRIS, WILLIAM DEVERE, scientist; b. Jan. 11, 1922, Kanawha, Iowa; s. David Francis and Daisy Mae (Hahn) H.; m. Genevra Howson, Aug. 30, 1969; edn: BSChE, Univ. Calif. 1947. Career: research chemist Best Foods Co.

1947-52, Calif. Ink Co. 1952-57; research engr. Research Specialties Co. 1957-61; engrg. cons. 1957–; assoc. prof. chem. UC Berkeley 1961-64; prof. phys. scis. Tahoe Paradise Coll. 1967-69; dean div. phys. scis. Sierra Nevada Coll. 1969-72; pres. Research Inst. for Science 1969–; honors: Hon. D.Ed (Columbia Univ. 1968), Hon. PhD (Univ. Calif. 1970; mem: Am. Chem. Soc., Am. Inst. Chem. Engrs., num. musical orgns., public svc. orgns.; publs: 150+ in tech. jours., 3 books, 30 science fiction articles; mil: tech. sgt. US Army 1941-46; rec: music, reading, skiing. Res: 1201 David Ave Pacific Grove 93950 Ofc: Research Inst. for Science 1328 Burton Ave SB-1 Salinas 93901

HARRISON, DIANNE, video producer; b. May 24, 1951, Oakland, Calif.; d. Gordon E. and Carole M. (Wilde) H.; edn: BS, Cal. Poly. Univ. Pomona 1973; MS, CSU Sonoma 1975; currently att. NY Univ. Dept. of Film & TV; Therapeutic Counseling Lic. Nev. 1979; provl. tchg. cred. Calif. 1976; Certified Police Ofcr. Nev. 1978. Career: therapist/counselor with strong wilderness background; extensive solo world travel to China, India, Malaysia, Borneo and Latin Am. formed basis for documentaries televised internat.; owner/ mgr. Three Mountain Video Prodns., Lone Pine 1985–; spkr., guest lectr. US and internat.; honors: Best Docum. Short, NY Film & Video Festival (for One Woman's China, 1985), Best New Producer, Internat. Video Arts Festival (1986), nominator for nat. NFLCP Best TV Station Gen. Mgr. (1986); mem. Nat. Fedn. of Local Cable Producers; video prodns. include: Song of the Heart (1986), One Woman's China (1985), China in the 80's (1985), A Place Called Brunei (1984), Goa, India: Historical Past, Colorful Present (1984). Res: Wolff Ranch Granite View Lone Pine 93545 Ofc: Three Mountain Video POB 1180 Lone Pine 93545

HARRISON, JOHN PAUL, insurance co. president; b. Feb. 3, 1931, NY, NY; m. Ann Patricia Hogan, Jan. 24, 1959; children: Gregory Scott b. 1959, Lynn Patricia b. 1961, Glenn Michael b. 1964; edn: BS acctg., Long Island Univ. 1951; lic. Reinsurance Intermediary, N.Y. (1977-). Gen. Ins. Broker, Calif. (1977-). Career: ins. div. W.R. Grace Co., NY, NY 1951-54; adminstrv. asst. Excess & Treaty Management Group, NY, NY 1954-55; exec. v.p., dir., trustee Delaney Offices Inc., NY, NY 1955-77; pres./dir. Harrison & Co., San Carlos 1977–; v.p. Hansen & Co., San Carlos 1977–; assoc. prof., Reinsurance course, Coll. of Insurance, NY, NY 1961-65; mil: US Army Arty., Korean War 1951-53; rec: swimming, wind sprints, sailing. Res: 320 Alvarado Ave Los Altos 94022 Ofc: 1091 Industrial Rd San Carlos 94070

HARRISON, KATHY M., marketing executive; b. Aug. 17, 1945, Alameda, Calif.; d. Nickolas Thomas and Mary (Phinos) Chester; children: Cynthia b. 1967, Michelle b. 1969, Carolyne b. 1970; edn: BA, CSC Long Beach 1967. Career: prodn. control clerk Max Factor 1975-76, prodn. control planner 1976-77, mgr. prodn. control 1977-78, master planner 1978-79, asst. prod. mgr. 1979-80, prod. mgr. 1980-81, senior prod. mgr. 1981-82; prod. mgr. Mattel 1982-84, dir. mktg. 1984–; mem: Am. Mgmt. Assn. 1986, Mattel Mgmt. Assn. 1982-, Mgmt. Action Pgm. 1983, Aesthetics Review Bd. 1986 (charter), Quality Improvement Pgm. 1984, Editorial Adv. Com. 1985; Republican; Greek Orthodox; rec: tennis, photog. Ofc: Mattel Toys 5150 Rosecrans Hawthorne 90250-6692

HART, CHARLES RICHARD, trucking company president; b. Mar. 13, 1915, Moose Lake, Minn.; s. Mr. and Mrs. Charles P. Hart; m. Corinne M. Cole, June 25, 1938; children: Charles R. Jr. b. 1939, Carol Ann b. 1940, John Robert b. 1945, William Louis b. 1950; edn: stu. Los Angeles Jr. Coll. 1934-36; transp. courses, UCLA and USC 1937-38. Career: var. pos. all depts. The Charles P. Hart Transportation Co., p.t. 1932, f.t. 1935–; apptd. mgr. Los Angeles Terminal, apptd. gen. mgr. 1940–; exec. v.p. and gen. mgr. 1950-57; sold to Watson Bros. Trans. Co. 1957; v.p., gen. mgr. Imperial Truck Lines Inc. 1958; pres. Shipper Express Co. 1959-69; pres. Peerless Trucking Co. 1970–; chmn. bd. 4H Mountain Valley Cup Co.; pres. MGN Equipment Co.; pres. Hart & Sons Trans. Co.; pres. Hart & Sons Enterprises; recipient, 50 yr. plaque, Calif. Trucking Assn.; mem: Gov.'s Traffic Safety Commn. (past), Calif. Trucking Assn. (statewide bd. sponsor Council of Safety Supvrs. and bd. sponsor So. Council of Safety Supvrs.; pres. 1957; bd. dirs.; num. coms.; past pres. Western Motor Tariff Bureau; Am. Trucking Assn. (Ops. Council), Trucking Employers Inc., Western Trucking Employers (past pres.), Interstate Freight Carriers Conf., Local Jt. Western Aea Com., Regular Route Common Carriers Conf., Western Hwy. Assn.; Santa Fe Springs CofC, Gr. Santa Fe Springs Indsl. League (past pres.), Shriners (past pres. Transp. Shrine Club), Los Angeles Athletic Club, Candlewood Country Club. Res. 8862 Lawrence Ave. Westminster 93683 Ofc: 5833 So. Malt Ave. Commerce 90040

HART, HOWARD ARTHUR, personnel outplacement co. executive; b. Oct. 20, 1934, Newark, NJ; s. Irving J. and Helen (Franklin) H.; edn: BS, Wharton Sch. of Fin. & Commerce Univ. of Penn. 1956; MBA, Fla. Atlantic Univ. 1973; doctoral cand., Golden Gate Univ. Career: mktg. mgr., coms. edn. tng. IBM, NYC 1956-64; tng. chief New Jersey Community Action Tng. Insts., Trenton, NJ 1965-66; corp. mgr. manpower devel. ESB Ray-O-Vac Mgmt. Corp., Phila. 1967-82; corporate tng. & devel. mgr. Atari, Inc., Sunnyvale 1982-83; current v.p. Drake Beam Morin, Inc., San Francisco; lectr., cons. in field; guest prof. Temple Univ. 1975-76; recipient, Leadership Conf. Achiev. Award, Am. Mgmt. Assn. (1970), DBM Profl. Excellence Award, Drake Beam Morin, Inc. (1984); mem: Indsl. Rels. Assn. (v.p. Philadelphia chpt. 1974-), Am. Soc. of Tng. & Devel., Am. Soc. of Personnel Adminstrs., No. Calif. Human Resources Council; mil: 1st lt. US Army QMC. Ofc: Drake Beam Morin Inc., One Embarcadero Ctr. Ste. 4100 San Francisco 94111

HART, LAWRENCE AUSTIN, consultant; b. Feb. 16, 1960, Hollywood; s. Robert Ray and Faye Irene (Wohlers) H.; edn: BS, CSU Fullerton 1982. Career: quality control supr. U.S. Polymeric, Santa Ana 1979-82; research & devel. chemist Xenotech Labs, Irvine 1982-85; cons. (computer) Authorized Supply of Calif., 1985-86; chemical and computer cons. Hart's Labs, 1986–; cons. US State Dept. 1980; listed Who's Who in Frontiers of Sci. and Technol.; Delta Sigma Phi frat.; Republican; Episcopal. Res: 15491 Pasadena Ave #82 Tustin 92680 Ofc: Hart's Labs POB 393 Brea 92622-0393

HART, TIMOTHY R., college administrator; b. Jan. 5, 1942, Portland, Ore.; s. Eldon V. and Wanda J. H.; m. Annette Hart, Aug. 8, 1981; children: Mark b. 1956, Matthew b. 1959, Marisa b. 1962, Martin b. 1965; edn: AA, San Jose City Coll. 1968; BA, San Jose State Univ. 1970; MA, Wash. State Univ. 1973; JD, San Joaquin Coll. of Law 1983; admitted Calif. State Bar, Fed. Dist. Ct. 1983. Career: police ofcr. City of Santa Clara, 1965-71; chief of police Univ. of Idaho, Moscow, Ida. 1971-73; crime prevention ofcr., City of Albany, Ore. 1973-75; instr. Coll. of Sequoias, Visalia 1975-81, coordinator Paralegal Dept. 1981-84, dir. and chair Adminstrn. of Justice Div., 1984–; atty. ptnr. Wichowski and Hart; awards: Outstanding Young Men of Am. 1981; J. Edgar Hoover Meml. Award 1983; listed Who's Who in Law Enforcement (1980), Who's Who in the West (1985); mem: Crime Prevention Assn. of Ore. (pres. 1972-73), Am. Criminal Justice Assn. (pres. Region 1, 1981-82), Academic Senate Coll. of Sequoias (pres.), NEA, CTA, Coll. of Sequoias' Tchrs. Assn., Nat. Assn. of Legal Assistant Educators, Delta Theta Phi law frat., Am., Calif. State, Tulare County bar assns., Calif. Assn. of Adminstrn. of Justice Educators, Calif. Academy Dir's Assn.; mil: E4 USAF 1960-63; Ind.; Mennonite Brethren. Res: 2301 S Dollner Visalia 93277 Ofc: College of Sequoias, 915 S Mooney Visalia 93277

HARTNESS, SANDRA JEAN, venture capitalist, developer; b. Aug. 18, 1944, Jacksonville, Fla.; s. Harold H. and Vi H.; edn: AB, Georgia Southern Coll. 1969; grad. work, San Francisco State Coll. 1970-71. Career: researcher Savannah Planning Commn. 1969, Environmental Analysis Group S.F. 1969-71; dir. Mission Inn Riverside 1971-75; developer self-employed 1976–; founder, ptnr., bd. dirs. Western Neuro Care Ctr. 1983–; pres., dir. Enviro-Sync; honors: Outstanding Renivation (Riverside 1983), num. leadership awards; mem: Riverside CofC, Downtown Devel. Group; Republican; rec: reading, golf. Res: 32612 Adriatic Dr Laguna Niguel 92677 Ofc: 301 Forest Ave Laguna Beach 92651

HARTY, RICHARD JAMES, financial advisor; b. Feb. 9, 1944, Chgo.; s. James John and Mary Rita (Cooke) H.; 1 son, Chad b. 1969; edn: Loras Coll. 1962-64; BS, Drake Univ. 1966; desig: lic. commodity pool opr., CFTC (1982), reg. rep., NASD (1985). Career: unit mgr. Proctor & Gamble, 1966-68; sales promotion mgr. Royal Crown Cola, 1968-72; sales mgr. Chicago Equities, 1972-76; v.p. TSI Finl., 1976-78; pres. Caliber Finl. Group, Ltd. 1978–; founding mem. Pacific Coast Commodity Exchange, Wash DC 1985; honors: Merit Award for Support of New Americans, Omega Group (1985), recogn. Free Afghanistan Com., Wash DC (1985), recipient bi-partisan congl. recogn. for assistance to Contra groups in Central Am., (1985); mem. Internat. Assn. of Finl. Planners, Nat. Futures Assn., Nat. Assn. Securities Dealers; civic: Internat. Inst. of Los Angeles (treas., bd. dirs.), Global Economic Action Inst., Young Conservative Alliance/Wash DC (bd.), Civilian Mil. Assistance, Nat. Com. to Restore Internal Security; clubs: Los Angeles Athletic, Riviera Country, Calif. Yacht; works: designed Forward Conversion Strategy utilized by sev. major U.S. banks and svgs. & loans for downside risk protection and income enhancement (1985); mil: USAR 1966-72, 118 JAG Corps. Res: 8440 Irondale Canoga Park 91306 Ofc: 15303 Ventura Ste 700 Sherman Oaks 91403

HARVEY, ALAN EUGENE, company president, contractor; b. July 7, 1940, San Diego; s. Eugene Victor Harvey and Orbee Virginia (Mellor) Milalek; m. W. Beth Harvey, Nov. 23, 1967; 1 son: Russell b. 1970; stepchildren: Sherri b. 1959, Beckie b. 1961, Tresa b. 1963; edn: AA prelaw, Palomar Coll. 1960, San Jose State Univ. 1960-61, San Jose City Coll. 1962; C-15 Floor Covering Contr. Calif. Career: salesman/ bkpr. Clark's Inc., Vista, Calif. 1965-75; contract sales mgr. Frederick's Sales, Inc., San Diego 1975-83; pres. Harvey Interiors, Inc., San Diego 1983–; honors: Outstanding Svc. (Vista CofC 1975), Singles Bowling Champion (Tripler Army Hosp. 1964); mem: S.D. County Floor Covering Assn. 1983-, Elks (21 yrs.), Lions Internat. 1966-75 (past treas., v.p.), YMCA (bd. dirs. 1976-77), Vista CofC (dir. 1974-75), Vista Nat. Little League 1978-83 (mgr., coach, head unpire, bd. dirs.); mil: sp4 US Army 1963-65, Good Conduct; Republican; Protestant; rec: fishing, bowling, golf. Res: 816 Cypress Dr Vista 92084 Ofc: Harvey Interiors, Inc. 7595 Carroll Rd San Diego 92121

HARVEY, JAMES ROBERT, missiles & space co. engineering executive; b. Aug. 25, 1931, Prescott, Ariz.; s. Francis Travis and Bernice Nora (Davis) H.; m. Shirley Scott, July 21, 1952; children: Greg b. 1954, Mark b. 1958, Chris b. 1960, Lisa b. 1962; edn: BSME, Univ. Ariz. 1958; Santa Clara Univ. 1985; Reg. Mech. Engr. Ariz. 1962, Calif. 1970. Career: jr. engr. Goodyear Aerospace Co. Litchfield Park, Ariz. 1958-60, analytical engr. splst. 1960-68; research engr. splst. Lockheed Missiles & Space Co. Sunnyvale 1968-75, supv. system engrg. 1975-82, pgm. mgr. data systems modernization 1982–; pres. Goodyear Mgmt. Assn. 1966; honors: Lockheed Mgmt. Inst. Cert. (Santa Clara Univ. 1985); mem: Am. Inst. Aero. and Astro. 1960-67, Armed Forces Communication Electronics Assn. 1976-, Toastmasters Internat. (chpt. pres. 1961), Lynbrook H.S. Boosters (pres. 1974), Dillworth Home & School Club 1970, Univ. Ariz. Alumni. Assn. (chpt. pres. 1985); publ: articles in tech. jours.; mil:

radioman l/c USN 1950-54, Korean Svc., Good Conduct, China Svc.; Republican; rec: square dancing, western dancing. Ofc: Lockheed Missiles & Space Co. 0/66 B/572 1111 Lockheed Way Sunnyvale 94086

HARVEY, JOSEPH BIVENS, superior court judge; b. Nov. 5, 1927, Hankow, China; s. Earle Rolston and Mary Lee (Mullis) H.; m. Donna Askins, Dec. 24, 1983; children by previous marriage: Jean, b. 1953, Warren, b. 1954, Thomas, b. 1956, Mary, b. 1962, Katherine, b. 1963; edn: BA, Occidental Coll. 1949; JD, Hastings Coll. of Law 1952. Career: research atty. Ct. of Appeal, First Appellate Dist., San Francisco 1953-54; dep. dist. atty. San Diego Co., 1954-56; assoc. counsel Dept. of Alcoholic Beverage Control, Sacramento 1957-59; dep. atty. State of Calif., Sacto. 1959; asst. exec. secty. Calif. Law Revision Commn., Stanford, 1959-67; ptnr. Herrick, Gross, Mansfield, Harvey & Miller and successor firms, Palo Alto 1967-70; sole practice, Susanville, Calif. 1970-77; ptnr. Harvey & Bradbury, Susanville 1977-78; judge Superior Ct. of Lassen County, 1979 –; lectr. Calif. Cont. Edn. of the Bar; honors: Order of the Coif, Thurston Soc.; mem. Calif. State Bar Assn. 1953-78, Palo Alto Bar Assn. 1967-70, Lassen County Bar Assn. 1970-78 (pres. 1975), Susanville Rotary Club 1971-, Lassen Co. Taxpayers Assn. 1976-78 (pres. 1977-8); publs. num. articles incl. Rights and Duties Upon Termination of a Lease (54 CA Law Rev. 14, 1966), Judicial Notice, Calif. Evidence Code Manual 375 (CEB 1966), Evidence Code Section 1224 - Are An Employee's Admissions Admissible Against his Employer? (8 Santa Clara Lawyer 59, 1967); author, coauthor legislation incl. Calif. Evidence Code (1965 Stat. Ch. 299), Calif. Arbitration Act (1961 Stat. Ch. 461), Rescission of Proceedings (1961 Stat. Ch. 1621), Taking Possession and Passage of Title in Eminent Domain Proceedings (1961 Stat. Ch. 1613), Separation of the Nondelinquent from the Delinquent Minor in Juvenile Ct. Proceedings (1961 Stat. Ch. 1616); mil: seaman l/C, USN 1945-46, 1st lt. USAF 1952-53; Democrat; Presbyterian (elder); rec: backpacking, choral dir., quartet singing. Res: 8 Fairway Dr Susanville 96130 Ofc: Superior Court, Courthouse, Susanville 96130

HASEGAWA, KEIKSUKE (KASEY), manufacturing co. president; b. Jan. 18, 1935, Fukuoka, Japan; s. Hichiro and Hatsuyo H.; m. Taeko; children: Noriko b. 1965, Keitaro b. 1967, Yuko b. 1970; edn: BS econs., Kyushu Univ. 1958. Career: sales and adminstrn. Daido Dyeing Co. Ltd. 1958-67; mgr. internat. sales div. Kyoto Ceramic Co. 1967-71; ops. mgr. Kyocera Internat. Inc., San Diego 1971-79, pres. 1979 –; senior mng. dir. Kyocera Corp., Kyoto, Japan; mem: Internat. Trade Commn. (bd. 1986), San Diego CofC 1986; San Diego Japan Club (pres.); rec: golf. Ofc: Kyocera Internat. Inc., 8611 Balboa Ave San Diego 92123

HASEGAWA, TONY SEISUKE, computer graphics executive, consultant; b. Dec. 21, 1941, Tokyo, Japan; s. Sukesaburo and Chiyo (Sano) H.; edn: BS commun. engring., Univ. of Electro-Communs. 1965; MS computer sci., Univ. of Santa Clara 1979. Career: project mgr. and systems analyst Control Data Far East, Tokyo 1967-74; computer graphics cons. Control Data Corp., Sunnyvale 1974-82; advanced project cons. NASA Ames Research Center, Moffett Field 1975-81; pres. Fine Technology Corp., Mountain View 1983 –; bd. dirs. VCI Internat.; awards: spl. scholarship of Japanese Govt.; mem: Computer Graphics Soc. (pres. 1984-85), Assn. Computing Machinery, ACM Siggraph, Am. Inst. Aero & Astro., CGS, IEEE; NASA Ames Ski Club; works: mag. cover of Scientific American (1/82); Republican; Roman Catholic; rec: ballroom dance, tennis, ski. Res: 33711 Quail Run Road Fremont 94536 Ofc: Fine Technology Corp. 2083 Landings Dr MOuntain View 94043

HASHIOKA, CHRISTOPHER EDWARD, real estate investor-developer; b. Jan. 19, 1948, Chgo.; s. Edwin T. and Pauline A. H.; m. Ethel, Dec. 23, 1979; children: Michelle b. 1967, Emily b. 1970, Kristen b. 1970, Oliver b, 1975; edn: BA, Harvard Coll. 1970; MBA, Univ. of Chgo. Grad. Sch. of Business 1972; Certified Public Acct., Ill. (1974); desig: Certified Property Mgr. (CPM), Inst. of Real Estate Mgmt. (1979). Career: assoc. Blyth Eastman Dillon, Chgo. 1972-73; senior v.p./prin. Balcor/American Express Inc., Skokie, Ill. 1973-84; owner/pres. Fairfield Investments, Inc. (real estate, investments and devel.), San Diego 1984 –; mem: Am. Inst. CPAs, Ill. Soc. CPAs, Inst. of Real Estate Mgmt.; clubs: Harvard (SD), Fairbanks Country; rec: swimming. Res: POB 1204 Rancho Santa Fe 92067 Ofc: Fairfield Investments 11199 Sorrento Valley Rd Ste H San Diego 92121

HASKELL, GREGG OWEN, structural engineer; b. Dec. 1, 1952, Oakland; s. Owen Wesley and Zelia Juanity (Ulrich) H.; edn: BSCE, No. Ariz. Univ. 1974; ME, UC Berkeley 1978, PhD cand., 1984-. Career: engr. in tng. H.J. Degenkolb & Assoc., Cons. Engrs., San Francisco 1972-75; proj. engr. Owen W. Haskell, Inc., Oakland 1977-78; civil engr. Ruthoff & Englekirk Inc. 1979-80; Forell/ Elsesser Engrs., Inc., S.F. 1980-83; strl. engr. Martin Middlebrook & Nishkian, S.F. 1984 –; tchg. asst. UC Berkeley 1974-75; awards: Outstanding Civil Engr., NAU Sch. of Civil Eng. & Tech. 1974; Outstanding Engr., NAU Coll. of Eng. 1974; mem: NAU Soc. of Eng. Exec. Council (pres. 1974); Am. Soc. of Civil Eng.; Structural Engrs. Assn. of No. Calif.; ASCE SEAONC (Cont. Edn. Com.); author: Free Vibrations and Near- Field Acoustic Radiation of a Simply Supported Cylindrical Shell; coauthor: w/ Gary W. Rogers, Acoustic Radiation of a Vibrating Rectangular Membrane, 24th Annual Am. Inst. of Aero. & Astro., Reg. IV Student Conf. 1974; Republican, Melones Dam Advoc. 1975; Methodist; rec: pvt. pilot, archery, skiing. Res: 2487 West St Berkeley Ofc: Martin Middlebrook & Nishkian 111 Townsend St San Francisco 94107

HASKINS, JANE RUTH, chiropractor; b. June 12, 1955, Ancon, Panama, C.Z.; d. Howard Earl and Ruth Margaret (Gamble) H.; m. Ernesto Paz Rey, June 19, 1982; edn: BA in health studies, UC Santa Cruz 1978; DC, Palmer Coll. of Chiropractic West 1982; lic. DC, Calif. 1982; postgrad. studies in applied kinesiology, certified in disability evaluation, 1985. Career: solo pvt. practice of chiropractic, Monrovia 1983 –; mem: Am., Calif., San Gabriel Valley Chiropractic Soc. (pres. 1985-86), Arcadia Toastmistress Club, Monrovia Leads Club, Monrovia CofC; Democrat; Rel. Sci.; rec: gardening, travel. Ofc: 109 N Ivy Ave Monrovia 91016

HASKINS, WILLIAM STEVEN, real estate broker; b. Mar. 16, 1953, San Francisco; s. Herbert Claude and Joan Theresa (Schunk) H.; edn: spl. courses Am. River Coll., Coll. of San Mateo, Skyline Coll.; Calif. lic. Real Estate Broker. Career: journeyman operating engr., 1969-76; currently 50% stockholder/ broker Oceana Investments, dba Better Homes Realty, Pacifica; recipient top producer awards: Century-21 and Better Homes Realty; mem. Nat., Calif. Assn. of Realtors, Pacifica Bd. Realtors (arbitration com.), Pacifica CofC; invention: earthquake detector (pat. pend.); Republican; Catholic; rec: skiing, bicycling, music. Address: 143 Dardenelle Ave Pacifica 94044

HASLER, GINO JOSEPH, artist, photographer, cinematographer; b. Mar. 16, 1941, Prague, Czech., nat. US cit. 1978; s. Gene Sidney and Bozena (Mirkova) H.; m. Susan Hartman, July 5, 1975; 1 son, Gino, Jr. b. 1976; edn: producer, cameraman, Charles' Univ. Film Faculty, Prague 1965. Career: news corresp./ newsreel cameraman Hessian Radio & TV, Frankfurt, W.Germany 1968-69; nat. tech. rep. Cinema Beaulieu, Los Angeles 1970-71; sci. photog./ endoscopy research asst. Cedars-Sinai Med. Ctr. Los Angeles 1971-76; cons. Endoscopic Cinematography to doctors nat. 1970-79; freelance cinematographer and art cons., 1977-79; senior photog./graphic artist Karl Storz, Inc. 1979-83, art director 1984; comml. artist/prin. G.H. Productions (Multimedia arts), Los Angeles 1985 –, projects incl. graphic design, product photog., med. illustr. for doctors worldwide, cinematography, sportswear design; honors: co-winner 1st place medal (design of sci. exhibit for Dr. Paul Ward), Internat. Cong. of Otolaryn., Toronto (1971); mem. Soc. of Motion Picture and TV Engrs., Am. Film Inst.; works: dir. of photog. "Ten Speed" feature movie for TV (1978), TV comml. for Glendale Fed. S&L (1979); Endoscopy over 150 photo illustrns. for med. book (1976), contbr. film footage "The Incredible Machine" Nat. Geographic TV spl. (1975); Republican; Catholic; rec: military modeling -dioramas. Res: 13630 Muscatine St Arleta 91331

HASSELL, FRANK RICHARD, optical-mechanical engineer; b. Feb. 12, 1953, Port Angeles, Wash.; s. Charles Richard and Lucille Hanna (Lonsdale) H.; m. Claudia Martinsen, July 2, 1982; 1 son, Charles b. 1983; edn: BSME engring., Wash. State Univ. 1975. Career: laser engr. Pratt & Whitney Aircraft, West Palm Beach, Fla. 1975-80; mem. tech. staff TRW, Redondo Beach 1981-83, section hd. 1983-85, senior staff engr. TRW Optical Engring. Dept., 1986 –; listed TRW Indep. Research and Devel. Roll of Honor (1982, 84); mem. AMSE, Masons; Republican; rec: sailing, scuba, skiing. Res: 2421 227th St Ste 22 Torrance 90501 Ofc: TRW One Space Park (MS 01/1240) Redondo Beach 90278

HASTINGS, JAMES HAYES, appellate court judge; b. Nov. 17, 1917, Los Angeles; s. James Neil and Monnie Lucy (Hayes) H.; m. Margaret Alman, June 9, 1941; Children: Gary b. 1943, Neil b. 1947, Dean b. 1949; edn: AB, Univ. of So. Calif. 1940, JD, 1948. Career: ptnr. Hastings, Blanchard & Hastings 1948-72; judge L.A. Superior Ct. 1972-73; judge 2nd Dist. Ct. of Appeals 1973 –; chmn. bd. Bank of Pasadena 1970-71; chmn. Com. of Unauthorized Practice of the Law 1969-70; instr. real property law Southwestern Law Sch. 1953-60; chmn. personnel bd. City of Arcadia 1965-66; honors: asst. ed. Law Review USC Law Sch.; Skull & Dagger USC; mem: Am. Bar Assn.; Calif. Bar Assn. (disciplinary bd. mem. 1971-72); Am. Coll. of Probate Counsel; Chancery Club of L.A.; Rotary; mil: capt. USNR, C.O. Naval Intelligence Reserve 11th Naval Dist. 1960-63, Pres. Unit Citation; Republican; Protestant; rec: scuba diving, yachting. Res: 3455 Starling Dr Rancho Palos Verdes 90274 Ofc: Ct. of Appeals 3580 Wilshire Los Angeles 90010

HASTINGS, SVEN NORDSTROM, banking administrator; b. May 19, 1947, Dallas, Tex.; s. Earle Grant and Virginia Mildred (Baker) H.; m. Susan, May 19, 1972; children: Sawyer b. 1976, Lindsay b. 1978, Cecily b. 1984; edn: BBA, Okla. Univ. 1973; M.Internat. Mgmt., w/ distinction, Am. Grad. Sch. of Internat. Mgmt. 1975; MBA, So. Methodist Univ. 1976. Career: v.p. Hasty Bake Co. Tulsa, Okla. 1976-78; comml. credit ofcr. United Calif. Bank San Francisco 1978-80; corp. loan adminstr. Pacific Valley Bank San Jose 1980-84, credit adminstr. 1984 –; honors: Beta Gamma Sigma (Okla. Univ. 1973); mem: Robert Morris Assocs., Calif. Comml. Finance Conf., Rotary Internat., San Jose CofC Leadership Pgm., Jr. CofC (Okla.), Soc. for Advancement of Mgmt., Delta Phi Epsilon, Beta Theta Pi; mil: E-5 USN Russian interpreter 1966-70, Naval Unit Commendn.; lt. comdr. USNR Intelligence 1979-, Admiral's staff mem. for nat. Dir. of Naval Reserve Intelligence; Republican; Presbyterian; rec: guitar, travel. Res: 1800 Phantom Ave San Jose 95125 Ofc: Pacific Valley Bank 333 W Santa Clara St San Jose 95113

HATCH, CHARLOTTE BALDWIN, rancher, ladies apparel store owner; b. Nov. 17, 1930, Oakland; d. Louis Gerlach and Helen Wheeler (Clowes) Baldwin; desc. Calif. Pioneer families Thomas Cooper (1848), Louis Gerlach (1852), Stockton; children (nee Hatch): Braddon B. b. 1961, Christopher B. b. 1963; edn: BA, UC Berkeley 1952. Career: ind. rancher, 1952-84; retail store owner, Just for You, Stockton 1985 –; honors: named Volunteer of the Year, Junior Girl, Am. Red Cross, Children's Home; Republican; Roman Catholic; rec: sports, hist., needlework. Ofc: Just for You 423 Lincoln Center Stockton 95207

HATCHELL, JOYCE CHRISTINE STRICKLAND, manufacturing co. executive; b. Sept. 16, 1945, Greensboro, N.C.; d. Paul Theodore and LaVern Inez (Coburn) Strickland; m. Ross B. Holler, Mar. 11, 1982; children: Cassandra, 1962-81; James, Jr., b. 1965; edn: stu. Old Dominion Univ. 1969-72; BA in psych., Memphis State Univ. 1975; MS in ops. mgmt., Univ. of Ark. 1981; ops. mgmt., Golden Gate Univ. 1983; current cand. Quality Control Engrs. cert., ASQC. Career: remedial diagnostic aide, Little Creek Primary Sch., Norfolk, Va. 1972; social counselor Tenn. Dept. of Human Svcs., Memphis 1975-77; Quality Control supr. Celotex Corp., Memphis 1977-81, Fremont, Calif. 1981–; cons. Celotex Central Quality Control, Roofing Prods. Div. 1981; honors: Phi Kappa Phi, Dobro Slovo, Liberal Arts Hon. Soc., Psi Chi, Memphis State Univ. 1975; mem: NOW (v.p. Memphis State chpt. 1974), ASQC, AAUW; adult sponsor BSA; Friends of the Norfolk Juvenile Court; Women of the Moose (charter mem. Chpt. 1822); Democrat; Prot.; rec: sailing, canoeing, travel. Res: 38036 Acacia St Fremont 94536 Ofc: Celotex Corp. 6400 Stevenson Blvd Fremont 94537

HATCHER, CARO CALDWELL, educator, speech pathologist, psychologist; b. June 25, 1904, St. Jo, Texas; d. Samuel West and Emma Gene (Whaley) Caldwell; m. O.E. Hatcher, Dec. 31, 1922, div. 1946; children: Evert b. 1923, Martin b. 1927, James b. 1935; edn: BA, Okla. State Teachers Coll., 1925; MA, Okla. A&M, Stillwater 1933; EdD and PhD, Univ. Denver 1950. Career: tchr. public schools, Okla. 1923-41; civilian instr. US Air Force, Lowry Field, Colo. 1942-44, Colo. Mil. Sch. and Univ. of Denver, 1944-48; speech pathol. Eugene (Ore.) Children's Hosp. 1948-50, State Sch. for Cerebral Palsied, Pasadena, Calif. 1950-54, Univ. of Norway Med. Sch., Oslo 1954-55, CSU Los Angeles 1955-71, Spastic Foundation L.A. 1971-82, ret.; cons. pvt. practice; lectr.; sponsored own pvt. sch. for the handicapped, Pasadena 1960-67; awards: Fulbright Lectr. Univ. of Norway (1954-55), Woman of Year, Soroptomist Club of Am. (1956), facility named for her: Hatcher Habilitation Ctr. (Chatsworth), outstanding prof. CSULA, state & local recognition awards for innovative tchg. materials; mem: Am. Psych. Assn., Am. Speech & Hearing Assn., Internat. Council of Psychol. (treas. 1966-68), Council Exceptional Children, Soroptimist Internat. of Am.; contbr. articles re handicapped ednl. journals; Democrat; Protestant; rec: writing. Res: 1621 E Commonwealth Fullerton 92631

HATELEY, DONALD PATRICK, investment banker; b. Sept. 28, 1957, Long Beach, Calif.; s. James Charles and Enid Ellen (Shephard) H.; m. Wendy J. Seretan, May 25, 1985; edn: BS, Univ. So. Calif. 1979; CPA Calif. 1982. Career: CPA Peat, Marwick, Mitchell & Co., Los Angeles 1979-82; assoc. ENI Corp., L.A.- Seattle, Wash. 1982-83; pres. Cambridge Resources Inc., L.A. 1983-84; chmn. The Cambridge Group Inc., L.A. 1984–; dir. City Resources Inc., L.A. 1984–; chmn. Coll. Ctrs. of So. Calif., L.A. 1984–; mem: Calif. Soc. CPAs (securities com. 1982), Am. Inst. CPAs, Town Hall of Calif., L.A. World Affairs Council, St. James Club- London; Republican; rec: tennis, golf, skiing. Res: 1316 Centinela Los Angeles 90025 Ofc: The Cambridge Group Inc., 10801 National Blvd Ste 600 Los Angeles 90064

HATFIELD, GREGORY ARTHUR, medical researcher; b. Oct. 31, 1953, Junction City, Kans.; s. Gervaise Archibald and Maxine Ruth H.; m. Janet L., May 20, 1983; edn: BEE, Univ. Minn. 1977; MS in engring., UC Los Angeles 1979; MD, Univ. Minn. 1983. Career: mem. tech. staff Hughes Aircraft Co., Los Angeles 1977-79; med. resident St. Mary's Hosp. & Med. Ctr., San Francisco 1983-84; pres./CEO M.D. Engineering, Inc., Foster City 1984–; awards: Hughes Fellow (1977-79), Zagaria Fellow (1982), Commencement Speaker (1977), Eta Kappa Nu, Tau Beta Pi, Kappa Eta Kappa; mem: Am. Med. Assn., Commonwealth Club of Calif.; patents: IV Strain Relief Bracelet, LM2000 Gen. Purpose Surgical Suction Monitor, Noiseless Suction Channel; research: In Vitro Rheographic separation of tissue and fluid, Non-invasive blood pressure measurement; rec: quantum physics, computer pgmmg., expert systems, artificial intelligence. Ofc: M.D. Engineering Inc. 214 Lincoln Centre Dr Foster City 94404

HATH, DAVID COLLINS, college dean; b. Mar. 13, 1944, San Diego; s. Collins Maxwell and Dorothy (Laird) H.; children: Derek Collins, Douglas Alan; edn: AA, Porterville Coll. 1964; BS, CSU Fresno 1966; MA, Chapman Coll. 1972; post grad. Pepperdine Univ., UC Irvine. Career: indsl. rels. rep. Ford Motor Co., Automotive Assem. Div. 1966-68; instr. Tustin Union H.S. Dist. 1968-69; instr./ counselor/ counseling psychologist Orange Unified Sch. Dist. 1969-75; dean cont. edn. div. Rancho Santiago Comm. Coll. Dist., Orange 1975-83; dean Orange Canyon Campus, Rancho Santiago Comm. Coll. Dist., Orange 1983–; mem. Orange Intercultural Edn. Commn. 1973-75; Rehab. Inst. of Orange Co. (Easter Seals Found.) 1979-; Vocational Edn. Adv. Com.; Calif. Dept. of Food & Agri. Regl. Edn. Accreditation Com. 1980-84; awards: Eagle Scout, Boy Scouts of Am. 1956; William T. Hornaday awd. 1958; Bus. Awd., Outstanding Achiev., Bank of Am. 1963; W.P. Bartlett Found. Awd. 1964; Mgmt. Commdn., Ford Motor Co. 1968; Comm. svc. awds; Outstanding Young Men of Am., Jaycees; mem: Rehab. Inst. of Orange Co. (Comm. Adv. Bd.); Assn. of Calif. Sch. Adminstrs.; Assn. of Calif. Comm. Coll. Adminstrs.; Calif. Assn. Marriage & Family Therapists; Calif. Comm. Coll. Cont. Edn. ASsn.; Calif. Personnel & Guidance Assn.; Phi Delta Kappa; Jr. Achiev. Adv. Rep.; Chapman Coll. Comm. Clinic Adv. Bd.; YMCA Indian Guides; Orange CofC; Republican; Presbyterian; rec: camping, gardening, jogging. Res: 10744 Rancho Santiago Blvd Orange 92669 Ofc: Rancho Santiago Comm. Coll. Dist., Orange Campus, 8045 E Chapman Ave Orange 92669

HATHAWAY, DOROTHY ELEANOR, antique dealer; b. Nov. 13, 1928, Los Angeles; d. Charles Willis and Eleanor Margaret (Breuning) Robbins; m. James Alderman Hathaway, Dec. 30 , 1950; children: Christine b. 1951, Linda b. 1953, Laurene b. 1954, James Jr., b. 1958, Cecile b. 1961; 12 grandchildren; edn: art major, Glendale City Coll. 1946-47; shorthand, Metropolitan Trade Sch. 1953. Career: secty. to TV comic Jim Hawthorne 1949-50; model Lola Whitehead Agcy. 1947-50; prodn./ stage mgr. Euterpe Opera Club (Dorothy Chandler Pavillion) 1965-69; owner Tioga Lodge Historical Site Resort 1969-80; owner Tioga Lodge Antiques 1970-, (name chg.) Hathaway House Antiques 1978–; tchr. antiques class, Malaga Cove Adult Sch. 1982; conducted auctions, Tioga Lodge 1970-77; mem: Catholic Daughters of Am. (25 year pin 1977); Am. Legion Aux. (Chaplain); columnist Bridgeport Chronicle, Mono Herald 1972-76; Republican; Catholic; rec: arts, crafts. Res: 4009 Milaca Pl Sherman Oaks 91423

HATHAWAY, ODELL S., II, (Jay), motion picture producer/director; b. Mar. 3, 1941, Los Angeles; s. James Lawrence and Lucille Marie (Harding) H.; m. Marjorie Berry, Dec. 10, 1960; chldren: Odell, b. 1961; Susan, b. 1963; Constance, b. 1964; James John, b. 1965; Robert, b. 1969; Ann E., b. 1977; edn: Columbia Coll., Chgo. 1959-60; grad., Van Nuys H.S. 1958. Career: prod./dir. Jay Hathaway Prodns., Sherman Oaks 1965–; exec. dir. Am. Acad. of Husband-Coached Childbirth, Sherman Oaks 1970–; bd. advs., Nat. Assn. Parents & Profl. for Safe Alternative Childbirth (NAPSAC); mem: Acad. TV Arts & Scis.; Soc. of Motion Picture & TV Engrs.; author: w/ wife, Children at Birth, and, The Bradley Method; prod./dir. more than 20 films on childbirth edn.; Republican; Episcopal; rec: pvt. pilot. Res: 4846 Katherine Ave Sherman Oaks 91423 Ofc: American Academy of Husband-Coached Childbirth, POB 5224 Sherman Oaks 91413

HATTAN, THOMAS STREUN, quality assurance auditor; b. May 3, 1946, Dayton, Ohio; s. Mark, III and Virginia Mae (Streun) H.; grandson of Wm. Cary Hattan (1875-1929) chief engr. of the Clinchfield R.R.; edn: BA, UC Los Angeles 1969; Pepperdine Sch. of Law 1970-71. Career: storekeeper Emerson Electric Co., Santa Ana 1975-77, labor contract negotiator U.A.W., 1976; senior insp. CMC Inc., Long Beach 1978-80; quality supr./engr. Canon Inc., Costa Mesa 1980-83; chief insp. Times Mirror Corp., Irvine 1983-84; qual. assur. auditor Northrop Aircraft Div., Hawthorne 1984–; awards: U.A.W. Award for Labor Rels. (1976), 5th Pl., Am. Legion solo snare drum champion (1964); mem. Am. Soc. Quality Control, Swiss Soc. for the Promotion of Quality (Bern, Switz.); civic: mem. Calif. Republican Assembly (v.p. Laguna Bch. chpt.), UCLA Alumni Assn., Soc. of Descendants of Washington's Army at Valley Forge (cmdr. Calif. Brigade 1986), Nat. Soc. of SAR (pres. Orange Co. chpt. 1980-82, Calif. State Soc. dir. 1980-81, historian 1980), Children of the Am. Rev. (state liaison ofcr. 1982), Mil. Order of the Stars and Bars (sec. John B. Hood Chpt. 1979), Sons of Confederate Vets. (1st lt. cmdr. 1979), Clan Campbell Soc., Clan Stewart Soc.; publs: Hist. of the House of MacGillechattan (1980); mil: pvt. US Army 1971-72, Nat. Def. Svc. medal, War Svc. medal, War Svc. Cross; Republican; Presbyterian; rec: history. Res: 23700-2 Cambridge Circle Laguna Niguel 92677 Ofc: Northrop Aircraft Div. 1 Northrop Ave Dept 7240/09 Hawthorne 90250

HAUG, KEVIN RICHARD, entrepreneur; b. Sept. 23, 1953, Dhahran, Saudi Arabia; s. Roy Keller and Mary Cecelia (Colon) H.; m. Christine, Oct. 25, 1980; edn: BS bus. mgmt., San Diego State Univ. 1975; M. Internat. Mgmt., Am. Grad. Sch. of Internat. Mgmt. 1979. Career: contracting adminstr. Arabian American Oil Co. (Aramco) Dhahran, Saudi Arabia 1975-78; owner, dir. Al-Hasa Exports Internat. Concord, Calif. 1980–; honors: Honors Award (Small Bus. Adminstrn. 1979), Small Bus. Exporter of the Year (1986); mem: Internat. Trade Council (v.p. 1985), US-Arab CofC, Calif. Council for Internat. Trade; Democrat; Protestant; rec: water & snow skiing, racquetball, squash, swimming, furniture restoration. Ofc: Al-Hasa Exports POB 635 Concord 94522-0635

HAUGHEY, DELL DEAN, physician, medical educator; b. Jan. 12, 1905, Otsego, Mich.; s. Allen Gilbert and Daisy Dean (Huffaker) H.; m. Ruth E. Ellwanger, June 10, 1932; children: Dell D. (Jr.) b. 1943, Susann Ruth b. 1947; m. 2d. Betty Evans Magill, May 9, 1956; m. 3d. Irene V. Miller (nee Dawson), Nov. 26, 1981; edn: BA (in absentia), Washington Missionary Coll. (now Columbia Union Coll.), Takoma Park, Md. 1937; MD, Loma Linda Univ. 1938; certified Am. Board of Obstetrics-Gynecology 1946. Career: full time prof. Dept. Ob-Gyn. (dept. exec. sec. 10 yrs.) Loma Linda Univ. Sch. of Medicine 1938-56; group practice in Orange and Los Angeles Counties 1956-67; dir. Obstetrical & Gynecological Services Tulare Co. Gen. Hosp., 1967-75, ret.; called back for 3 months (1978) as acting dir., clinician and surgeon at age 73; cons. and family planning practice 1970-72; med. dir. Tulare & Kings Counties P.S.R.O. 1972-75; fmr. chief of staff White Meml. & Tulare Co. Hosps.; chief of Ob-Gyn Services L.A. County Hosp. 1942-55, and physician CME Services 1941-56; honors: named honorary staff mem. Tulare County Hosp. (only hon. mem. in 50 yr. hist. of Tulare Co. Hosp.) 1980; mem: Founder Fellow Am. Coll. of Obstets. & Gyne., active mem. LA, Orange, Tulare County Med. Assns. 1944-80 (hon. mem. 1980-), LA OB-Gyn Soc. 1946-68; mem. McGrew-Kaweah Area Tumor Board (1980-), Commn. on Aging, City of Visalia (1980-); Republican; Seventh Day Adventist (Elder, SS tchr.); rec: music, gardening. Res: 3132 West Iris Ave Visalia 93277

HAUK, A. ANDREW, federal judge; b. Dec. 29, 1912, Denver; s. A.A. and Pearl (Woods) H.; m. Jean Nicolay, Aug. 30, 1941; 1 dau., Susan; edn: AB magna cum laude, Regis Coll. 1935; LLB, Catholic Univ. Am. 1938; JSD, Yale Univ. 1942; admitted to D.C. bar 1938, Colo. bar 1939, Calif. bar 1942, US Supreme Ct. bar 1953. Career: asst. to law librarian Library of Congress, summers 1935-38; spl. asst. to atty. gen., counsel for govt. antitrust div. US Dept. Justice, Los Angeles, Pacific Coast, Denver, 1939-41; instr. law Southwestern Univ. 1939-41; asst. US atty., Los Angeles 1941-42; assoc. firm Adams, Duque & Hazeltine, L.A. 1946-52; individual practice law, Los Angeles, also asst. counsel Union Oil Co., L.A. 1952-64; judge Calif. Superior Ct. Los Angeles County, 1964-66; judge US Dist. Ct. Central Dist. Calif., 1966-80, chief judge 1980-82, senior judge 1982—; lectr. USC Sch. Law, 1947-56, Southwestern Univ. Sch. Law 1939-41; vice chmn. Calif. Olympic Com. 1954-61; ofcl. VIII Olympic Winter Games, Squaw Valley, 1960; del. IX Olympic Winter Games, Innsbruck, Austria 1964; mem., dir. So. Calif. Olympic Com., 1973-; honors: recognition for civic and judicial achievements L.A. County Bd. of Suprs. 1965, 66, 76, 82; award Internat. Ladies Garment Wkrs Union 1938; Regis Coll. Alumnus of Year 1967; named to National Ski Hall of Fame, 1975; Sterling fellow, 1938-39; mem: Los Angeles County Bar Assn. (chmn. pleading and practice com. 1963-4, chmn. law day com. 1965-6), State Bar Calif. (corps. com.), Am. Bar Assn. (antitrust, criminal law sects.), Fed. Bar Assn., Nat. Conf. Fed. Trial Judges, Lawyers Club Los Angeles, Am. Judicature Soc., Am. Legion, Navy League, US Lawn Tennis Assn., So. Calif. Tennis Assn. (dir. 1972-), So. Calif. Tennis Patrons Assn. (bd. govs.), Far West Ski Assn. (past dir., vice pres. 1947-9), Yale Law Sch. Assn. So. Calif. (dir., pres. 1951-56), Town Hall of Calif., L.A. World Affairs Council, People to People Sports Com.; clubs: Yale of So. Calif. (dir. 1964-7), Newman, Valley Hunt (Pasadena), Jonathan (LA); num. pub. decisions and opinions; mil: lt. to lt. comdr. Intell., USNR 1942-46. Ofc: U.S. Courthouse, 312 No. Spring St., Los Angeles 90012

HAUN, RALPH EDWIN, commercial real estate investment co. president, restaurant owner; b. Dec. 10, 1940, Whittier; s. Ralph Edwin and Dorothy Maude (Utter) H.; m. Diane Butler, Jan. 25, 1964; edn: BS, CSU San Jose 1963; MS, 1964; postgrad. wk., Univ. Calif. 1972; Calif. Jr. Coll. Tchg. Credential 1972; Real Estate Broker Lic. 1978. Career: mgmt. analyst Hood Corp., Whittier 1969; gen. mgr. Auto Electric Eng. Co., Anaheim 1970-71; v.p./ gen. mgr. Trabaca Prods. of Calif., Costa Mesa 1971-78; comml. R.E. sales Stout & Assoc., Newport Beach 1978-80; pres. Haun Raab Webster & Co., Inc., Newport Beach 1980—; mem: Apart. Assn. of Orange Co.; R.E. & Ins. Club; Soc. for Adv. of Mgmt.; spkr., var. local govtl. meeting & functions; mil: 1st lt. US Army Infantry 1966-69, Bronze Star, Army Commdn. w/ V, Air medal, Purple Heart; Republican; Protestant; rec: drawing, painting, photog. Res: 21162 Castlerock Rd Laguna Beach 92651 Ofc: Haun Raab Webster & Co., Inc.. 5 Upper Newport Plaza Newport Beach 92660

HAUPT, JON RICHARD, real estate investment advisor and maintenance contractor; b. Aug. 31, 1942, Detroit, Mich.; s. Myron Merle and Emily Viola (Partney) H.; m. Giselle Best, July 17, 1965; edn: BA, UCLA 1965, MA, 1968. Career: owner The Cleaning People (TCP), Los Angeles 1970—; recipient, Woodrow Wilson Fellowship, UCLA 1967-68; mem. Los Angeles Bd. Realtors; co-author: with Leonard Arrington, Intolerable Zion, selected by Mormon History Assn. for Annual Periodical award as 'Most Disting. Scholarly Pub. in the Field of Mormon History' 1968-69; contbr. articles to publs. in the bldg. and residential maintenance field; co-ed., with Charles Wheeler Jr., The Contract Cleaner Companion, Am. Inst. of Maintenance 1979; Republican. Res: 1385 Brixton Rd. Pasadena 91105 Ofc: Red Carpet Real Estate, Harnsberger and The Winners, 6330 No. Figueroa St. Los Angeles 90042

HAVAS, MAURICE, logistician; b. Jan. 8, 1948, Amsterdam, Holland, nat. 1959; s. Gustav and Jeannette (Van Weezel) Havas; m. Patsy Edwards Dec. 30, 1981; children (by previous marriage): Jacki b. 1968, Carrie b. 1970, Daniel b. 1975; (stepdau.) Robyn Stettler b. 1968; edn: BS, Weber State Coll., Ogden, Ut. 1976; cert., Utah St. Univ. 1967, cert., Hill AFB, 1969; Certified Profl. Logistician, 1978. Career: card punch machine opr. Defense Depot, Ogden, Ut. 1966-7, aircraft flt. line mech., Ogden (Utah) Air Logistics Ctr., 1967-72, supply clk. to suprv. supply clk., 1972-74, inventory mgmt. splst., 1974-76, supply systems analyst, 1976-79, suprv. inventory mgmt. splst., 1979-81; AF Logistics Insp., AF Inspection and Safety Ctr., Norton AFB, 1981-84; maint. staff ofcr. Hqtrs USAF, Pentagon 1984-85; deputy chief of supply McClellan AFB, Calif. 1985—; honors: recipient suggestion awards, Def. Supply Agcy. 1968, USAF 1972, (2) 74, 1980; 3 performance awds., USAF, 1982, 83; Boss of Year 1980, Am. Bus. Women's Assn., Ogden chpt. 1980; appreciation, Fed. Employed Women and Spanish Spkg. Pgms., 1977; selection into AF Logistics Exec. Cadre, 1980; appreciation, Utah chpt. Soc. of Logistics Engrs. 1977; sr. mem. Soc. of Logistics Engrs. (Profl. Qualifications Rev. Bd.1980-; inventory control com. mgr. Tech. Activities Div. 1982-; Utah SOLE Bd. Advisors 1977-81; chmn. Ut. SOLE Chpt. 1, 1976-7); Jewish; profl. publs.; rec: computer pgmg., auto mechs., fgn. coins. Res: 8660 Blue Jay Way Citrus Heights 95610 Ofc: Sacramento Air Logistics Center/ DSD McClellan AFB 95652

HAVLICK, JOSEPH GEORGE, insurance co. executive; b. Mar. 21, 1931, Chgo.; s. Joseph George and Anna Mae (Horist) H.; m. Tanna Pauline Seger, Sept. 20, 1980; children: Elizabeth (Loder) b. 1954, Michael b. 1956, Lawrence b. 1957, Gloria b. 1962, Thomas b. 1964, Nicole b. 1973; edn: Loyola Univ., L.A. 1949-50; AA, Ventura Coll. 1953; UCLA 1953-54. Career: underwriter Zenith Nat. Ins. Co. (Encino) 1955, branch mgr. Fresno 1955-63, v.p. in charge of sales & underwriting 1963-69, exec. v.p. 1969-77; pres. Fairmont Ins. Co., Burbank 1977-85, bd. chmn. 1979—; bd. chmn. & pres. Fairmont Financial Inc. (1980-), Fairmont Leasing Corp. (1983-), F.I.C. of Bermuda Ltd. (1984-); bd. chmn. F.L.M. Insurance Agency Inc. (1983-), Alamos Corporation Bond and Ins. Services (1984-), South Coast Surety General Agency Inc. (1984-), Infantino and Company (1984-); mem: Toluca Lake CofC, Burbank CofC, Assn. of Calif. Ins. Cos. (dir.), City of Hope (Insurance Council); mil: US Air Force 1951-52; Catholic (K.C. 4th deg.); rec: golf, travel. Ofc: Fairmont Insurance Co 4111 West Alameda Ave Burbank 91505

HAWKINS, LELAND BARNES, III, real estate executive; b. Apr. 4, 1926, Moneta; s. Leland Barnes, Jr. and Jessie Geneva (Luckensmeyer) H.; m. Jane Louise Albrecht, Sept 26, 1959; children: Joanna Louise, b. 19061; Katherine, b. 1963; Frederick Barnes, b. 1967; edn: BA, Univ. of Redlands 1949; UC Davis 1983; cert. in real estate, Wharton Sch., Univ. of Penn. Career: power cons. indsl. sales Metropolitan Div. So. Calif. Edison 1952-56; coll. rep. Prentice Hall 1956-58; So. Calif. sales mgr. Occidental Chem. Co. 1958-76; gen. mgr. Brookside Properties 1977-83; dir. Foothill Investments 1983—; chmn. Calif. Delegation to European Congress celebrating the Bicentennial of the Treaties of Paris & Versailles 1983; awards: Meritorious Svc. Medal, Riverside Chpt. Sons of the Am. Revolution, Patriot Medal 1985; mem: SAR (National Soc. trustee 1984-86, v.p. 1986-, pres. Calif. Soc. 1983-84, del. to state and nat. annual mtgs., pres. Riverside chpt. 1979-80, secty. 1980-81, editor 1980-81); Affiliated Cities Rental Owners Assn. (past v.p., dir.); Affiliated Cities Apartment Assn.; Am. Legion; Redlands Hist. Soc.; Orange Belt Mineralogical Soc.; Redlands Gem & Mineral Soc.; Redlands Symphony Assn.; Ky., Va., Orange and Spotsylvania Hist. Socs.; Classic Car Club of So. Calif.and Am.; Hon. Order of Kentucky Colonels; Univ. of Redlands Fellow; City of Redlands Traffic Commnr. 1982-86; Winter Concert Assn.; works: ed. Patriot Volunteer 1983-84; mil: US Army 1943-45; USMCR 1947-52; Republican; Congregational; rec: desert exploration, opera, Am. & European history. Res: 1521 W Cypress Ave Redlands 92373 Ofc: Brookside Properties, POB 646 Redlands 92373

HAWKINS, RANDALL SEARLE, neurologist; b. Oct. 31, 1947, Los Angeles; s. Merrill Guyern and Belle (Searle) H.; m. Penelope, Dec. 19, 1981; 1 dau. Erica Jane b. 1985; edn: BS, UC Los Angeles 1970, MS in Computer Sci., UCLA, 1970; MD, Yale Univ. 1976; Board Cert. Am. Bd. of Psychiatry and Neurology. Career: assoc. engr. Litton Data Systems Div. 1968-71; assoc. instr. Dept. Computer Sci. UCLA 1969-71; neurologic cons. Sharp-Rees-Stealy Medical Group, San Diego 1980—; asst. clin. prof. of neuroscis. UC San Diego, 1981-; honors: Phi Beta Kappa 1970, Tau Beta Pi 1968; mem. Am. Coll. of Physicians, Am. Acad. of Neurology; mem. Physicians' Advisory Bd. CyCare Systems, Dubuque, Iowa; Democrat; rec: golf. Ofc: Sharp-Rees-Stealy Medical Gp. 2001 Fourth Ave San Diego 92101

HAWN, PEGGY JANE, financial services co. executive; b. May 8, 1956, Loma Linda, Calif.; s. George Donald and Margaret Mary (Mitchell) Rothgeber; children: Jody b. 1980, David b. 1978, Jamie b. 1965; edn: Cert. Activity Dir. Calif., Mt. San Antonio Coll. 1977; Cert. Fin. Planner Calif., Cal. Lutheran Univ. 1986. Career: dist. canvasser & rep. Congressman Geo. Brown, Colton, Calif. 1972; juvenile diversion dir. Pomona Valley YMCA 1977; activity dir., Marshall Convales. Hosp., El Monte 1976-78; collection ofcr. San Bernardino County Collections Dept. 1979; ptnr. JHA, San Bernardino 1979-81; developer/ adminstr. Prado Country Family Entertainment Park, S.B. 1980-83; v.p./ bd. dirs. Inland Mgmt., Inc., Riverside 1983—; bd. dirs: Prado Country 1983, JHA 1981; cons. Marshall's Convales. Hosp. 1978; mem: Internat. Assn. Fin. Planners 1986, Internat. Assn. Bus. & Fin. Cons. 1983-, Am. Mgmt. Assn. 1983-, Am. Entrepreneurs Assn. 1983, Riverside CofC 1985-; publr., editor Lifeline financial newsletter 1985-; developer, gen. ptnr. Woodcrest Profl. Ctr. Ofc. Complex 1986; Republican; Protestant; rec: music. Ofc: Inland Mgmt. Inc. 17241 Van Buren Blvd Ste A Riverside 92504

HAWTHORNE, DONALD BRUCE, bio technology co. financial executive; b. Dec. 31, 1955, Los Angeles; s. Donald Claire and Elene Ruth (Roussey) H.; edn: BS, Harvey Mudd Coll. 1977; MBA,. Stanford Univ. Grad. Sch. of Bus. 1981. Career: financial plnnr. Westinghouse Electric Corp., Sunnyvale 1978-79; summer intern Morgan Guaranty Trust Co., NY, NY 1980; summer cons. Arabian- Am. Oil Co., Dhahran, Saudi Arabia 1981; senior finl. analyst treasury dept. Atlantic Richfield Co., Los Angeles 1981-83; senior finl. analyst corp. plnng. Syntex Corp, Palo Alto 1983-84, finl. plnng. mgr., controller Syntex Corp. Ophthalmics Div., Phoenix, Ariz. 1984-85; mgr. fin. and admin. Gene Labs Inc., San Carlos 1985—; honors: Calif. State Scholar (1973-77), Pi Sigma Alpha (1977), Scholarship award, Stanford Bus. Sch. (1979-81); mem: Am. Soc. for Engring. Edn., Harvey Mudd Coll. Alumni Assn. (pres., bd. govs. 1984-86), Harvey Mudd Coll. (bd. trustees 1986-), San Francisco Young Republicans, Peninsula Republican Assembly; Res: 400 Davey Glen Rd No. 4621 Belmont 94002 Ofc: Gene Labs Inc., 871 Industrial Rd. Bldg. J San Carlos 94070

HAWTON, KENNETH JAMES, chiropractor; b. Feb. 8, 1950, Vallejo; s. James Samuel and Beverly Ann (Teed) H.; div.; children: Azure b. 1975, Seneca b. 1977; edn: CSU Los Angeles 1974; BS, Los Angeles Coll. of Chiropractic 1976, DC, 1978; Chiropractor, Calif. 1980. Career: cert. respiratory therapist, dept. head Respiratory Therapy Assn. Inc., Fox Hills 1970; dept. head cardio pulmonary lab West Adams Hosp., Los Angeles 1971; supvr. respiratory therapy dept. Hollywood Presbyterian Hosp., Los Angeles 1972; owner, dir. H.P.S. Inc., Canoga Park 1981; pvt. practice, Tarzana 1982; owner, dir. High Desert Health Ctrs., Victorville- Hesperia 1983—; honors: Diplomate, Chiropractic Bd. of Examiners 1976; mem: Calif. Chiropractic Assn., Internat. Acad. of Nutrition Cons., Internat. Acad. Holistic Health & Med., Internat. acad. Metabiology, Am. Assn. Acupuncture & Oriental Med., High Desert Gold Diggers; Republican; Christian; rec: prospecting, mining. Ofc: High Desert Health Center, 14270 7th St Ste 3 Victorville 92392

HAYDEN, WILLIAM GEORGE, physician; b. Dec. 10, 1934, NYC; s. Patrick Kelly and Mary Cecelia (Poye) H.; m. Johan Baker, July 11, 1970; 1 son, Patrick, b. 1984; edn: AB, Stanford Univ. 1963, MD, 1968. Career: instr. in cardiovascular angiography Stanford Univ. 1972, asst. prof., 1973-75, clin. asst. prof. cardiovascular angiography, 1975—; dir. Cardiovascular Lab. Sequoia Hosp. 1978—; cons. American Edwards Labs.; honors: Roche Award 1966, Alpha Omega Alpha 1967, Upjohn Award 1968; mem: Fellow Am. Coll. of Cardiology, Fellow Am. Heart Assn., Internat. Cardiovascular Surgical Soc.; inventor: Hayden Angioplasty Catheter, mfg. by American Edwards; 30 sci. publs.; rec: mem. Olympic Club Internat. Shooting Team. Ofc: 770 Welch Rd, Ste 201, Palo Alto 94304

HAYES, CLAUDE Q. C., engineer/scientist; b. Nov. 15, 1945, N.Y.C.; s. Claude and Celestine H.; edn: BA in chem., geol. sci., Columbia Univ. 1971, MBA pgm. Columbia Grad. Sch. of Bus. 1972-73; NY Law Sch. 1973-75, var. tech. courses 1975-; JD, Western State Law Sch. 1978; tchg. cred. Calif. Comm. Colls. (1976). Career: worked in areas of mfg. engring., project mgmt., systems analysis, R&D, automation, mktg., and edn.; tech. writer Burroughs Corp. (MCO) San Diego 1978-79; faculty mem. City Coll. 1979-79, Nat. Univ. 1980-81, Miramar Coll. 1975-82, Mira Costa Coll. 1985-86; senior systems analyst and prin. engr., Melting Point Control Project mgr., General Dynamics/Western Data Systems 1979-80, contract cons. Gen. Dynamics Convair 1983; current: defense contr., sci. & tech. consulting prin. to US Govt. and aerospace corps., 1981—; lectr. on technology transfer; patents: Solid State Heat Sink for Electronic Component Cooling, passive non-fluid endothermic cooling process (1984), 3 patents devel. at Gen. Dynamics: Dual Melting Point Solder, Improved Melting Means, and Controlled Melting Point Process for Solder Technology (1981); contbr. articles in num. tech. and trade publs. (1981-); honors: NYC Citizenship Award for science club activity (1969), Tchr. of the Year nom., Miramar Coll. (1982), listed Who's Who in Technology Today (1986); mem. Am. Chem. Soc.; rec: music, theater, art. Address 7980 Linda Vista Rd Ste 49 San Diego 92111

HAYES, JAMES CLYDE, artist; b. May 28, 1946, Clovis, N.M.; s. Christopher C. and Willow Grace (Hoyle) H.; edn: Univ. of NM 1966-9; stu. architectl. rendering w/ Yum Kee Fu, AIA Hong Kong, China (now in Albuquerque NM), portraiture w/ R.C. Gorman, Garo Antresian, w/ British sculptors Pearson and Young. Career: artist, painter spec. in combining history with art; reproduction prints of his paintings available in S.F. shops in St. Francis Hotel, Fairmont, The Opera Shop, Grace Cathedral, many others; one of his Windmill prints presented to Queen Beatrix of Holland by the ofcs. of S.F. Parks and Rec. Dept., 1982; his paintings of historically significant buildings in San Francisco printed as cards and prints for sale on site include: the Conservatory purchased by S.F. Garden Club to commemorate restoration and raise funds for maint.; oil painting of the Second Flood Mansion printed into cards for graduation ceremonies by the Hamlin Girls Sch., 1983; Stuart Hall Boys Sch. at Sacred Heart, the 3d. Flood Mansion, purch. watercolor of their sch. 1981; the San Francisco Opera House and Louis M. Davies Sym. Hall watercolor purchased by pres. of the War Memorial Bd. and was printed on Christmas cards for S.F. Opera; watercolor paintings of Grace Cathedral (in pvt. collection of Rt. Rev. William E. Swing) and Trinity Episcopal Ch. (blt. 1890, pre-earthquake structure), 1981. Address: 100 Harbor Blvd. Sp.4, Belmont 94002

HAYES, JEAN CLAIRE CHILDERS, real estate broker; b. Sept. 19, 1947, Kansas City, Mo.; d. Jesse Lee and Winona Lillian (Steffens) Childers, (mother dec.), stepmother, Roberta Ann Sevier Childers; edn: BA, Baker Univ. 1969; further studies, UCLA; Calif. lic. R.E. Broker (1985). Career: adminstrv. asst. Kansas City, Mo. Board of Edn. Public Sch. Dist.; mgr. Systems and Procedures, Bennett Respiration Prods. Inc., Culver City (subs. Puritan Bennett, K.C., Mo.); mgmt. systems Hughes Helicopters, Culver City; current: broker assoc. Sunset Co. Realtors; honors: debutante presented in the American Royal (BOTAR)1q, K.C., Mo. (1970); mem. Santa Maria Bd. Realtors (treas., dir. 1984-86), Multi-Million Dollar Club (1982, 84, 85, 86); civic: Santa Maria Valley Developers, AAUW (dir. 1980, 81), League of Women Voters (dir. Santa Maria Valley), Shelter Services for Women Advis. Council (pres. 1985), YMCA Youth Sponsor (1986), S.M. Symphony Aux.; Republican; Disciple of Christ. Ofc: 1660-B S Broadway Santa Maria 93454

HAYES, PETER ADDISON, computer marketing co. executive; b. June 4, 1956, Walnut Creek; s. Paul Monroe and Mary Martha (Waite) H.; m. Sandra, Aug. 11, 1979; children: Lindsay b. 1982, Addison b. 1986; edn: BS indsl. engr., UC Berkeley 1978. Career: research asst. Lawrence Berkeley Lab., 1978; systems engr., mktg. rep., IBM, San Francisco 1979-83; gen. mgr. Businessland, Inc., Oakland 1983-85, mktg. tng. mgr., Businessland Inc. San Jose, 1985, product line mgr. 1985—; guest lectr. MBA Program, CSU San Francisco (1982, 83); honors: Am. Legion School Award (1970), Eagle Scout (1972), Bay Area Engrs. Soc. School Award (1974); clubs: Rotary (Oakland), Zeta Psi frat.; avocation: pop music composer, recorded/prod. Record Album (1984); Republican; Methodist. Res: 6763 Pinehaven Rd Oakland 94611 Ofc: Businessland Inc 3600 Stevens Creek Blvd San Jose 95117

HAYMOND, DWIGHT CLARENCE, marketing, sales, contracts administrator; b. Sept. 8, 1932, Ventura, Calif.; s. Dwight Russell and Betty Edith (Bright) H.; m. Dorothy L. Haymond, June 26, 1972; children: Lesli b. 1951, Cynthia b. 1955, Stephen b. 1957; stepchildren: Robert E. Barron b. 1961, Brenda B. Barron b. 1962; edn: AA, Ventura Coll. 1950; BA, UC Los Angeles 1952. Career: 30 yrs. in comml., indsl., mil. and ordnance applications related to mfg., ops., mgmt., specializing in contract negotiations, product line devel., technical expertise, initiating major proposals, implementation of customer service programs, sales forecasting, corp. projections, contracts adminstrn.; mktg., sales mgr., dir. contracts Talley Corp. Newbury Park, Calif.; mem: Am. Mgmt. Assn., Elks, Moose, Lions; mil: USNR 1951; Republican; Methodist rec: sports, gardening. Res: 2516 Northpark St Thousand Oaks 91362 Ofc: Talley Corp. 3303 Old Conejo Rd Newbury Park 91320

HAYNES, VINCENT ARCHIBALD, physician; b. Dec. 8, 1947, Barbados, West Indies; s. John Milton and Gladys (Jordan) H.; m. Myrna Matthews, July 7, 1974; edn: MD, UC Los Angeles 1976; Diplomate Am. Board of Pediatrics. Career: resident pediatrics, Univ. So. Calif., 1976-79, chief res. 1979-80; emergency staff physician Childrens Hosp. Los Angeles 1980-82; editorial bd. L.A. Parent Mag., 1977—; pediatric cons. Glendale Adventist Family Practice Pgm., 1982-85; pediatrician Glendale Burbank Medical Group, 1981—; att. staff USC, Glendale Adventist, Childrens Hosp.; mem. Los Angeles Pediatrics Soc., Los Angeles County Med. Assn., Fellow Am. Acad. of Pediatrics; rec: photog. Ofc: Glendale Burbank Medical Group 801 S Chevy Chase Blvd Glendale 91205

HAYUTIN, DAVID LIONEL, lawyer; b. Apr. 19, 1930, Phoenix, Ariz.; s. Henry and Eva (Gaines) H.; m. Lee, June 15, 1951; edn: AB, USC 1952, JD, 1958; admitted Calif. State Bar and Fed. Cts. Career: assoc. and ptnr. Lillick McHose & Charles, Los Angeles 1958—; Dir: The Kyowa Bank of Calif., Scripto Inc., Tokai Internat., Calif. Fashion Publications, Anja Engineering, others; mem. Internat., Am., Calif. bar assns., Maritime Law Assn.; clubs: University (Los Angeles), Mountaingate Country; author var. legal articles; mil: lt jg USN 1952-55; Republican; Prot.; rec: opera, golf. Ofc: Lillick McHose & Charles, 707 Wilshire Blvd Los Angeles 90017

HAZEL, NORMAN WALLACE, consulting entomologist; b. Nov. 11, 1919, Huntington Park; s. Percy Nelson and Docia Belle (Chandler) H.; m. Ruth Wilcox, July 5, 1947; children: Marilyn b. 1949, Marcia b. 1950; edn: BS, UC Berkeley 1949. Career: entomologist Producers Cotton Oil, 1950-53; consulting entomologist prin., 1953-59; entomologist AFC, Inc. 1959-63; research entomologist Uniroyal Corp. 1964-69; cons. entomologist, research & applied, 1969-75, ret.; honors: Sigma Xi; mem: San Joaquin Ent. Soc. (pres.), Ent. Soc. of Am., AAAS, ARPE, Masons (32 deg.), Elks; publs: articles, J. of Economic Entomology (1967); mil: 1st lt. US Army 1942-46, So. Philippines, No. Solomon campaigns; Republican; Prot.; rec: computer, golf. Address: Valley Center 92082

HAZELTINE, HERBERT SAMUEL, lawyer; b. Dec. 12, 1907, Huntington Beach; s. Herbert Samuel and Emma (Phelps) H.; m. Frances Sue Coffin, Aug. 5, 1936; children: Susan b. 1940, Ann b. 1947, Lynn b. 1952; edn: AB, Stanford Univ. 1931, JD, Harvard Law Sch. 1934. Career: assoc. Evans & Boyle, Pasadena 1934-42; ptr. Adams, Duque & Hazeltine 1945—; currently, senior ptr.; past dir. Metropolitan Ins. Co., Norris Industries, Hoffman Electronics and Prepared Products; honors: Hon. JD, Univ. of So. Calif. (1979), USC life trustee and mem. bd. counselors USC Law Sch.; mem: Am. Bar Assn., Chancery Club, Sunset Club, Economic Round Table, Boys Club Found. of So. Calif. (life trustee), Am. Red Cross (dir., Los Angeles chpt.); mil: lt. commdr. USN 1942-45; Republican; rec: golf. Res: 495 Orange Grove Circle Pasadena Ofc: Adams, Duque & Hazeltine, 523 W. 6th St. Los Angeles 90014

HAZLEHURST, CHARLOTTE NICHOLLS, artist; b. Sept. 5, 1949, New Brunswick, NJ; s. Robert Purviance and Mary Marguerite (Kierulff) H.; edn: AA, Pine Manor Jr. Coll. 1969; San Francisco Acad. of Art 1 yr.; secty., Haddow Sec. Coll. Brighton, Eng.; pvt. study w/ Leonard Boden, Royal Portrait Painter, London (2 yrs.). Career: artist, production & sale of oil paintings (large, impressionistic landscape scenes of Calif. & Hawaii); honors: Third Place (Beverly Hills Art Show 1984), Hon. Mention (Studio City Rotary 1985), 2nd Place (Sacramento Suburban Kiwanis 1984); mem. San Francisco Artists Guild 1983-; art work appears on labels of Satori Tea Co. 1985-; rec: guitar, aerobic exercise. Address: Aptos 95003

HEADLEE, ROLLAND DOCKERAY, executive director, Town Hall of Calif.; b. Aug. 27, 1916, Los Angeles; s. Jesse William and Cleora (Dockeray) H.; desc. Thomas Wight, English emigrant to Mass. 1634; stu. UCLA; m. Alzora Burgett, May 13, 1939; 1 dau: Linda Ann (Pohl), b. 1946. Career: asst. mgr. Finance Assocs. 1946-59; fin. & bus. cons. R.D. Headlee & Assocs. 1959—; acct. exec. and cons. Walter E. Heller & Co. 1962-65; exec. v.p. Genrus Engring. Corp. 1965-67; exec. dir. Town Hall of California, 1967—; Dir.: Am. Internat. Bank, Mfrs. Assocs., Starfire Engring. Co.., (past) Genuss Engring., Jolie Cosmetics; Moderator, Town Hall on the Air, nat. radio pgm.; guest lectr. USC Sch. Eng. 1977, 78; tchr. Comparative Religions 1954-69; honored by formal resolution: US Senate, 92d & 95th Sessions; US Cong., 91st Session; Calif. State Assembly, 1971, 76; City of L.A. 1971; mem: Town Hall (life) Detroit Econ. Club; Mensa Internat.; L.A. World Affairs Council; L.A. Stock Exch. Club; US Power Squadron; US Coast Guard Aux., flotilla commdr.; Commonwealth Club; Newcomen Soc.; Com. on Foreign Rels.; Advisory Bd., L.A. Area Council, BSA; Oceanic Soc.; publs: ed. 11 anthologies concerning over 20 subjects; guest writer, var. trade publs.; mil: 1st lt., gen. staff ofcr., lt.jg USCGR, post WWII; Republican; Methodist (adult supt., v.chmn. bd.); rec: skiing, gem/mineral collector, sailing, equestrian. Res: 8064 El Manor Ave Los Angeles 90045 Ofc: Town Hall, R.D. Headlee Assocs., 523 W 6th St, Ste 232, Los Angeles 90014

HEALD, DAVID VINCENT, bank executive; b. Aug. 30, 1948, Pasadena, Calif.; s. Vincent Armond and Esther Marie (Lorenzen) H.; m. Jacqueline, Apr. 1, 1978; edn: BS, San Diego State Univ. 1971. Career: credit adminstr. Toronto Dominion Bank of Calif., S.F. 1972-76; asst. v.p., Calif. Canadian Bank, S.F. 1976-82; senior v.p. Coast Comml. Bank, Santa Cruz 1982—; mem: Calif. Bankers Assn. (regl. chmn. 1985-86), Robert Morris Assocs., Central Coast Group (dir. 1985); Democrat; Lutheran. Ofc: Coast Comml. Bank, 104 Walnut Ave Santa Cruz 95060

HEALY, BARBARA ANNE, financial planner; b. May 21, 1951, Chgo.; d. Wm. James and Eileen Mary (Dooley) Healy; edn: BA, No. Ill. Univ. 1973; MBA, De Paul Univ. 1976; desig: Cert. Finl. Plnnr. (CFP) 1984, admitted to IAFP Registry of Fin. Plnng. Practitioners 1986. Career: tchr./dept. hd. St. Benedict High Sch., Chgo. 1973-76; mktg. rep./sr. high volume sales exec. Xerox Corp. 1976-79; comm. coll. instr. var. colls., including Loop Coll., Northeastern Ill. Univ., Coll. of Dupage, Triton Comm. Coll., Chgo. area, 1976-80; W. Dist. mgr. McGraw-Hill Corp. 1979-81; dir. membership services San Diego Tchrs' Assn., also finl. plnnr. United Resources, 1981-83; San Diego Dist. mgr. United Resources 1983-84, exec. v.p. market devel. and finl. plnng. 1984-85, regional v.p. 1986–; instr. personal finl. plnng. Southwestern Comm. Coll. 1985; guest speaker var. orgns. incl. Lions Club, Coll. Univ. Personnel Assn., Am. Assn. of Coll. Registrars & Admissions Ofcrs.; listed Who's Who Financial Planning 1985; mem: Am. Soc. CLUs, Am. Mgmt. Assn., Inst. of CFPs, Internat. Assn. Finl. Plnnrs., Internat. Assn. Registered Finl. Plnnrs., Nat. Speakers Bur. for Nat. Center for Finl. Edn., Am. Assn. of Exec. Dirs., Calif. Assn. of Exec. Dirs., Am. Mgmt. Assn.; publs: Financial Planning for Educators (1987), contbr. articles var. tchr. assn. newspapers (Me., Mass., Va., Dela., San Diego) 1984-85; Republican; Catholic; rec: flying, ski, scuba. Res: 610 Bridge Port Foster City 94404 Ofc: United Resources 33879 Madison St Torrance 90505

HEALY, JOHN JOSEPH, JR., real estate consultant; b. Aug. 1, 1946, NY, NY; s. John Joseph and Katherine (Hohen) H.; m. Patricia Rich, Aug. 31, 1985; edn: BBA, fin., Hofstra Univ. 1969, MBA, 1975; desig: Counselor of Real Estate (CRE), ASREC, 1985; Mem. Am. Inst. (MAI), AIREA, 1978; Sr. Real Prop. Appraiser (SRPA), SREA, 1975. Career: account mgr., appraiser Ray Brower Assn., N.Y. 1973-78; v.p. real estate service Mfrs. Hanover Trust, N.Y. 1978-82; sr. v.p./dir. valuation svcs., N.Y. and San Francisco 1982-85; sr. v.p./chief op. ofcr. B.A. Appraisals, S.F. 1986; prin. Spectrum Evaluation Group 1986–; assoc. prof. N.Y.U. 1979-86, Golden Gate Univ. 1985–; certified instr. for AIREA and SREA, 1975-; mem: AIREA, SREA (past pres. Long Is. chpt. 1984-85, past pres. Appraisal Div. 1976), ASREC, ULI, NACOR, ICSC; club: New York Athletic; publs: Tax Effect on the Elderly of Reassessing at Market Value (N.Y. State Legis. Inst., 1975), num. profl. articles in Assessors Jour., The Real Estate Appraiser, The Real Estate Forum; rec: ski, jog, tennis, travel. Res: 2111 Hyde St #603 San Francisco 94109

HEALY, MICHAEL FITZGERALD, lawyer; b. Mar. 3, 1954, Burlingame, Calif.; s. Dr. Francis A. and Grace C. (Warner) H.; m. Andrea Wirum, Dec. 22, 1979; 1 dau. Carolyn Grace b. 1985; edn: BS, Univ. of Notre Dame 1976; JD, Hastings Coll. of Law 1980; admitted Calif. State Bar 1980. Career: tech. coordinator Camino Medical Lab., Burlingame 1976-77; summer intern/assoc. law firm Sellers, Conner & Cuneo (now McKenna, Conner & Cuneo), Wash DC 1979; ptnr. Sedgwick, Detert, Moran & Arnold, San Francisco 1980–; mem. ABA, San Francisco Bar Assn.; Catholic. Ofc: Sedgewick, Detert, Moran & Arnold One Embarcadero Ctr. 16th Fl San Francisco 94111

HEALY, ROBERT JOSEPH, certified public accountant; b. Nov. 19, 1916, Iowa City, Iowa; s. Joseph Ambrose and Anna Lillian (Zenishek) H.; m. Lee Prestage, July 24, 1948; children: Robert J., Jr. b. 1954, Anne E. b. 1955, Rosemary M. b. 1956 (dec.); edn: BS in commerce, State Univ. of Iowa 1938; acctg. major, UCLA 1950-52; controllership, Calif. Inst. of Tech. 1965; Certified Public Acct., Calif. 1956. Career: consultant Kerr Glass Mfg. Corp., Los Angeles 1982-84, asst. corp. controller 1969-82; control mgr. Kerr McGee Chem. Corp., L.A. 1947-69; var. mgr. and supvr. positions Am. Potash & Chem. Corp., L.A. 1957-69; loan analyst Union Bank & Trust Co., L.A. 1938-47, incl. 4 yrs military leave; mem. Tech. Review Panel, State Bd. of Accountancy; mem: Calif. Soc. of CPAs, L.A. chpt. 1956-, Nat. Assn. of Accts., S.F. Valley Chpt. 1955-; civic: Fallbrook Village Homeowners Assn. (bd. dirs., treas. & v.p., 2 yrs), Holy Name Soc. (ofcr., 3 yrs); mil: 267th Field Artillery, 3rd US Army, France ETO 1942-45, Bronze Star medal, 4 Battle Stars; Democrat; Catholic; rec: travel, High Sierra hiking, camping, fishing. Address: 1738 Woodlark Ln Fallbrook 92028

HEARST, RANDOLPH APPERSON, publishing co. executive; b. Dec. 2, 1915, NYC; s. William Randolph and Millicent (Willson) H.; m. Catherine Campbell, Jan. 12, 1938, div. 1982; children: Catherine; Virginia; Patricia; Anne; Victoria; m. 2d. Maria C. Scruggs, May 2, 1982; edn: student, Harvard 1933-34. Career: asst. to ed. Atlanta Georgian 1939-40; asst. to. pub. San Francisco Call-Bull. 1940-44, exec. ed. 1947-49, pub. 1950-53; pres./ dir./ CEO Hearst Consol. Publs., Inc. and Hearst Publ. Co. Inc. 1961-64; chmn. exec. com. The Hearst Corp. 1965-73, chmn. bd. 1973-, dir. 1975-; pres. San Francisco Examiner 1972-; trustee Hearst Found.; mem: Piedmont Union; Piedmont Driving (Atlanta); Burlingame Country Club; Pacific Union; Press (San Francisco); mil: capt. USAAF Air Transport Command 1943-45; Catholic. Ofc: 110 5th St San Francisco 94103

HEATH, TED HARRIS, research engineer; b. May 24, 1951, Durango, Colo.; s. Parrish Richard, Sr. and Dixie (Harris) Heath; m. Jane, Aug. 31, 1974; children: Geoffrey Edwin b. 1980, Sally Jane b. 1981, Anne Elizabeth b. 1984; edn: BS, CSU Long Beach 1979; Reg. Profl. Mech. Engr., Calif. Career: mech. engr. US Dept. of Navy, Mare Island Naval Shipyard 1980; research engr. So. Calif. Edison Co., Rosemead 1981–; mem: Tau Beta Pi; Am. Soc. of Mech. Engrs.; Pacific Coast Electrical Assn.; Zool. Soc. of San Diego; mil: P.O. 2/c (machinist mate), USN 1970-74, Nat. Defense; Republican; Episcopal; rec: sports, camping. Res: 1230 Cottowood St Ontario 91761 Ofc: Southern California Edison Co., 2244 Walnut Grove Ave Rosemead 91770

HEATH, THOMAS RICHARD, health care administrator; b. May 9, 1948, Battle Creek, Mich.; s. William Hoyt and Rose Geraldine (Braxmaier) H.; div.; children: John David b. 1971; Jennifer b. 1975; edn: BA, St. Mary's Coll. 1978; cert. UC Santa Cruz 1973; AA, CHabot Coll. 1977; lic. nursing home adminstr., 1972. Career: ast. adminstr. Aloha Conv. Hosp., Hayward 1972-73; purchasing agent Griffin Hosps. Inc., Hayward 1973-75; admistr. Charlene Conv. Hosp., Castro Valley 1975-80; adminstr., owner Goberly Green ICF, Oakland 1981; adminstr. Sunnyvale Conv. Hosp. 1982–; bd. mem. Cupertiono Senior Pay Svcs.; honors: Valuable Svcs., Bd. of Examiners of Nursing Home Adminstrs.; Outstanding Young Men of Am. 1981; mem: Fellow Am. Coll. Helath Care Adminstrs., Fellow the Royal Soc. of Health (Eng.), Santa Clara Med. Soc. (Ad-Hoc Com.), Am. Bowling Congress, Rotary; mil: E-5 aviation ordnanceman 2/c USN 1967-71, Nat. Defense, Vietnam Svc. and Campaign, Armed Forces Expedition; Republican; Christian; rec: bowling. Res: 35948 Nicolet Ct. Fremont 94536

HEBNER, ROBERT JOHN, lawyer; b. Nov. 21, 1948, Long Island, N.Y.; s. Robert Gross and Sarah Bridget (Roscoe) H.; m. Susan, Oct. 9, 1970; children: Heather b. 1971, Rachel b. 1973, Robert Jr. b. 1975; BA, CSU Fullerton 1974; JD, Western State Univ. Coll. of Law 1977; admitted Calif. State Bar, U.S. Dist. Ct. of Appeals 9th circ., U.S. Dist. Ct. cent. dist. 1980. Career: claims supvsr. Fremont Indemnity Co., Orange 1978-80; atty. Zonni, Ginocchio & Taylor Glendale 1980-82; ptnr./owner Kriner, Hebner & Vermes Santa Ana 1982–; v.p./shareholder VSO Inc. Santa Ana 1985-; v.p./major shareholder Fantasy Pie Inc. Santa Ana 1985-; mem: Am., Calif., Orange Co. bar assns.; Democrat; Catholic; rec: golf, fiction writing, art, family activities. Ofc: Kriner, Hebner & Vermes 2006 N Broadway, Ste 212, Santa Ana 92706

HECHT, BARRY E., hydrologist; b. Oct. 20, 1949, NY, NY; s. Dr. Herbert and Esther (Indman) H.; m. Ellen Dreyfuss, Sept. 21, 1975; children: Jory b. 1979, Brent b. 1983, Garin b. 1985; edn: BS in geol., UC Santa Cruz 1970, BA, geography/regl. plnng., 1970; MA, geography, UC Berkeley 1972, PhD cand., geog., UCB, 1975; Reg. Geologist (1981), Certified Engring. Geologist (1985), St. of Calif. Career: instr. UC Santa Cruz, 1974-75; hydrologist/ grad. stu. US Geological Survey, 1975-77; hydrologist/vice pres. H. Esmaili & Assocs., Inc. 1977-82; chief hydrologist/ptnr. J.H. Kleinfelder & Assocs., Inc., Walnut Creek 1982–; dir. SoHaR, Inc. 1978-82; Public member Calif. Dept. Fish & Game Upper Sacto. River Salmon and Steelhead Adv. Com., 1982-; honors: Woodrow Wilson Fellow (1970); mem. Am. Geophysical Union, Assn. of Am. Geographers, Sempervirens Fund, California Trout; v.p. Bay Area Wind Symphony, 1978-85; publs: approx. 15 articles on channel sedimentation and its effects on salmon and steelhead in Calif. streams. Res: 509 Pomona Ave Albany 94706 Ofc: J.H. Kleinfelder & Assoc., Inc. 1901 Olympic Blvd Ste 300 Walnut Creek 94596

HECHT, MORTON PEACE, graphics co. executive; b. Dec. 15, 1924, Los Angeles; s. Jack and Mollie (Green) H.; children: Michael b. 1953, Sondra b. 1955, Kevin b. 1956, Steven b. 1958, Ricky b. 1962, Chester b. 1965, Peggy b. 1968; edn: L.A. City Coll. Career: pres./bd. chmn. Hecht Custom Photo/ Graphics Lab, Inc., Hollywood 1956–, pres./bd. chmn. Krismor, Inc.; mem. Advt. Prodn. Assn., Am. Inst. of Archs., Assn. of Profl. Color Labs.; mil: seaman 2c US Coast Guard; Republican; rec: photog. Res: 23440 Via Barra Valencia 91355 Ofc: Hecht Custom Photo/ Graphics Lab 1711 N Orange Dr Hollywood 90028

HECK, OTTO LUDWIG, manufacturing co. executive; b. Aug. 10, 1920, Germany, nat. US cit. 1943; s. Ludwig and Hedwig Clementine (Schirmer) H.; m. Barbara, May 31, 1942; 1 dau. Susanne b. 1947. Career: mgr. customer svc. Angelus Sanitary Can Machine Co., 1960-, v.p. Customer Svc. 1969-, v.p. Ops. 1978-, exec. v.p./secty. 1980-, pres./chief ops. 1983–; dir: Angelus Sanitary Can Machine Co., Angelus Export Co., dir./pres. Angelus Corp. Internat., dir./sec.treas. Henry L. Gunther Found.; mem. Food Processing Mach. & Suppliers Assn., Old Guard Soc. (FPM & SA), Master Brewers Assn. of Am., U.S. Brewers Assn. (Beer Inst.), The Packaging Inst. of USA, Fgn. Trade Assn. of So. Calif.; mem. US CofC, Calif. CofC, Vernon CofC, Masons, Balboa Bay Club; mil: T5 US Army Engrs. 1943-46, Pres. Citation, Am. Theatre rib., European Theatre rib. w/clusters, Victory rib., Good Conduct Medal; Republican; Prot.; rec: golf, stamp collection. Ofc: Angelus Sanitary Can Machine Co 4900 Pacific Blvd Los Angeles 90058

HEDGES, PATRICIA ANN, psychologist, researcher; b. Aug. 23, 1955, Bellflower; d. Paul Willis and Helen (Atwood) Hedges; edn: BA psych., Pepperdine Univ. 1978; MA clin. psych., Antioch Univ., L.A. 1981. Career: psychiatric aide Charter Med. Hosp., Long Beach 1978-81; MFCC (marriage, family, child counselor) trainee, Helpline Youth Counseling, Bellflower 1981-82; MFCC reg. intern, So. Calif. Pain Control Inst., Long Beach 1981-82; coord./resrchr. Pain Control Pgm., Joseph Moskowitz, MD, Inc., Long Beach 1982-83; MFCC reg. intern Bernard Landes PhD & Assocs., Long Beach 1983-86; psychol. asst. Michael Harris PhD, Whittier 1983–; mem: Calif. Assn. of Marriage and Family Therapists 1981-, Biofeedback Soc. of Am. 1983-, TMJ Disorder Cons. Bd. 1985-, Century Club, USC Sch. of Dentistry 1985-; profl. presentations: W. Psychol. Conf. for Undergrad Research, Santa Clara 1978, Annual Conf. for Calif. Assn. of Marriage & Family Therapists, San Diego 1982, Annual Conf. Biofeedback Soc. of Am., New Orleans 1985; Democrat; Protestant; rec: sewing, swimming, tennis, writing. Res: 6533 Fairman St Lakewood 90713 Ofc: Ofc: 15111 E Whittier Blvd Ste 320 Whittier 90605

HEDRICK, DANIEL LEE, automobile dealer; b. Jan. 9, 1929, Portland, Ore.; s. Earle Wesley and Mary (Talmadge) H.; m. Mary Lou Cleland, Aug. 5, 1950;

children: Stephen b. 1951, Donald b. 1957; edn: LA City Coll. 1947-8; UCLA 1948-9. Career: service op. dept. Milliken Chevrolet, Culver City 1951-56, mgmt., Chevrolet Div., General Motors Corp. 1956-77, pres./dealer-opr. Dan Hedrick Chevrolet, Inc., San Fernando 1977—; bd. dirs. Quintec Mfg., Costa Mesa; recipient Comm. Svc. Award, San Fernando CofC 1980, 82, 83; mem: S.F. CofC (exec. bd.), S.F. Kiwanis Club (past pres.), Woodland Hills Country Club; Republican; Episcopal; rec: water ski, boating, old car restoration. Res: 4516 San Blas Ave Woodland Hills 91364 Ofc: Dan Hedrick Chevrolet Inc. 753 San Fernando Rd San Fernando 91340

HEFFERN, WILLIAM LEWIS, III, professor; b. Dec. 28, 1932, Endicott, NY; s. William Lewis, Jr. and Marie Cecelia (Wurzer) H.; m. Mary Ann Regan, Aug. 13, 1960; children: David b. 1961, William b. 1964, Thomas b. 1965, Timothy b. 1973; edn: BS, CSU Long Beach 1972, MA, 1975; reg. profl. engr., 1979. Career: senior elec.- mech. designer Litton Systems Inc. 1959-61; senior gyro designer Guidance Tech. Inc. 1961-63; senior mech. engr. Hughes Aircraft Co. 1963-66; senior eng. scientist McDonnel Douglas 1966-67; owner, pres. Enducation & Engineering Ent. 1983—; prof. drafting and eng. Los Angeles Harbor Coll. 1967—; lectr. eng. & indsl. tech., CSU Long Beach; mem: Soc. Mfg. Engrs. (sr.), Am. Soc. Eng. Edn., Phi Kappa Phi, Lo Alamitos Soccer Boosters Club (pres. 1981), Los Alamitos Junior Baseball (gen. mgr. 1976), West Orange Co. Soccer Club (pres. 1985); works: Drafting Syllabus I; Proposals & Specification Handbook; mil: PO 1/c USN 1952-56. Res: 11832 Davenport Rd. Los Alamitos 90720 Ofc: Los Angeles Harbor Coll., 1111 Figueroa Pl. Wilmington 90744

HEFFLEFINGER, CLARICE THORPE, real estate broker; b. Oct. 5, 1937, Oregon, Ill.; d. Ralph Wayne and Wyota A. (Nashold) Thorpe; m. Jack K. Hefflefinger; children: Kevin, Deborah, Jack, Kenneth; edn: AA, Coll. of the Sequoias 1967, certs. in Ins., R.E., Bus. courses; Fresno State Coll. 1956. Career: var. positions, banking & insurance, 1956-76; real estate 1977—; substitute tchr. Tulare City Schs. 1979—; rep. State Assemblyman Don Rogers, 33rd Dist., Tulare Co. 1982—; chmn. Tulare Co. Draft Bd.; awards: Realtor of the Yr. 1983 Tulare Bd. Realtors, appreciation cits. from Am. Legion, Amvets; mem: Nat. Assn. Realtors; Calif. Assn. Realtors (dir.); Tulare Bd. Realtors (pres. 1982, dir. 1984); civic: Republican Nat. Com. (sustaining), Rep. Womens Fedn. Tulare, League of Women Voters. Tulare CofC (Booster Club), Tulare Amvets Aux. (treas. 1983-84), Toastmasters; Protestant; rec: dancing, playing piano. Res: 1351 William Tulare 93274 Ofc: Lewis Real Estate, POB 1213 Tulare 93275

HEIECK, PAUL JAY, wholesale distributor co. executive; b. Aug. 6, 1937, San Francisco; s. Erwin N. and Ann C. (Retchless) H.; m. Kathleen Pawela, Oct. 14, 1967; children: Valerie b. 1959, Yvonne b. 1960, Elizabeth b. 1962, Krista b. 1971, Justin b. 1973; edn: Golden Gate Coll. 1957-58. Career: salesman Heieck & Moran, San Francisco 1958-63, sec.-treas. Heieck Supply, S.F. 1963-76, pres. 1976—, also dir.; pres., dir. Eureka (Calif.) Supply, 1972—, Heieck Supply, San Jose 1980—, Heieck Supply, Sacto. 1980—; mem. San Francisco Bd. Trade (bd. dirs. 1978-82, v.p. 1980-82); mem: Nat. Assn. Wholesalers, Am. Supply Assn. (dir. 1983-), No. Calif. Suppliers Assn. (dir. 1980-85, pres. 1981-83); civic: San Francisco Boys Club (bd. 1972-), Rotary, San Mateo County Mounted Posse; clubs: Olympic, Ingomar, Sharon Hts. Country; mil: US Army 1955-57; Republican; Episcopal. Ofc: 1111 Connecticut St San Francisco 94107

HEINDL, CLIFFORD JOSEPH, physicist, executive researcher; b. Feb. 4, 1926, Chgo.; s. Anton T. and Louise (Fiala) H.; edn: BS, Northwestern Univ. 1947; MA, 1948; MA, Columbia Univ. 1950; PhD, 1959; Oak Ridge Sch. of Reactor Tech. 1954-55. Career: sr. physicist Bendix Aviation Corp. Research Labs., Detroit, Mich. 1953-54; asst. sect. chief atomic energy div. Babcock & Wilson Co., Lynchburg, Va. 1956-58; supvr. nuclear & reactor physics gp. Jet Propulsion Lab., Pasadena 1959-65; tech. mgr. research & adv. devel. Jet Propulsion Lab., Calif. Inst. of Tech. 1965—; mem: Am. Inst. of Aero. & Astro., Health Physics Soc.; Am. Physical Soc.; Am. Nuclear Soc.; author: var. sci. & tech. papers; mil: sgt. US Army Med. Corps 1944-46, WWII. Res: 179 Mockingbird Ln, So. Pasadena Ofc: 4800 Oak Grove Dr Pasadena 91103

HELANDER, CLIFFORD JOHN, state government researcher; b. July 7, 1948, Lake Forest, Ill.; s. Orvo Axel and Thelma Viola (Kaski) H.; edn: BA, Occidental Coll. 1970; MPA, USC Sch. Pub. Adminstrn. 1979. Career: music business, Los Angeles 1970-76; mgr. Calif. Dept. Motor Vehicles in Escondido and Daly City, 1977-80, driver improvement analyst Calif. DMV, San Francisco 1980-81, research analyst, Sacto. 1981—; presentations include 4th Symposium on Traffic Safety Evaluation Projects, Nat. Safety Council, Chgo. (1985), 5th Inst. on Applied Research and Stats., Sacto. (1984); mem. coms. Gov.'s Advis. Council on Alcohol, Drugs, and Traffic Safety; awards: full fellowship grant USC (1977); mem. Am. Statistical Assn., Sacto. Chpt. (1981-); publs: research studies for Calif. DMV (3 in 1986), article in J. of Safety Research (Vol. 15, 1984); rec: music. Res: 22 Seaside Ct Sacramento 95831 Ofc: Calif. DMV Research & Devel. Sect., 2415 First Ave Sacramento 95818

HELD, BRUCE JAY, industrial hygienist; b. Apr. 10, 1933, Allentown, Pa.; s. Warren H. and Evelyn (Muschlitz) H.; m. Peggy Anderson (dec.); m. 2d. Beryl Siemer, Feb. 16, 1973; children: Karen, b. 1956, Bruce, b. 1958, Karl, b. 1961, Kurt, b. 1961, Glen, b. 1964, (step): Kenneth, b. 1961, Beryl Katherine, b. 1962, Kerrie, b. 1969; edn: BS, Cornell Univ. 1955; MPH (IH), Univ. of Mich. 1964; Calif. Reg. Profl. Safety Engr., Cert. Safety Profl. Career: indsl. hygienist Nat. Lead of Ohio, Cincinnati, 1956-59; indsl. hygienist US Atomic Energy Commn., Idaho Falls, Ida. 1959-63, Atomics International, Canoga Park, Ca.

1964-67, Sandia Labs., Livermore 1967-71, Allied Gulf Nuclear Corp., Barnwell, S.C. 1971-72; asst. group ldr. for R&D, Los Alamos (NM) Sci. Lab., 1972-75; leader Indsl. Hygiene Group, Lawrence Livermore Nat. Lab., Livermore, Ca. 1975—; bd. dirs. Board of Cert. Safety Profls. of the America 1974-79 (pres. 1978); mem. (apptd. Gov. Reagan) State Environmental Quality Study Council 1969-71; expert witness for OSHA sev. health std. hearings; faculty Environ. Sci. Dept., CSU Hayward 1976-; mem. Health and Safety Adv. Com., (past chmn. Breathing Apparatus Panel 1979) Internat. Assn. Fire Fighters; cons. on respiratory protection pvt. indus.; US rep. of the Internat. Atomic Energy Agcy. meeting to revise Respirator and Protective Clothing Std., Vienna, Austria 1982; mem. Am. Indsl. Hygiene Assn. (1959-), Am. Conf. of Govtl. Indsl. Hygienists (1959-), Veterans of Safety, Internat. Soc. for Respiratory Protection (1st pres. 1982); NFPA Fire Fighter Breathing Apparatus Com. 1978-; publs: author/ coauthor 6 books in field, num. journal arts., conf. papers; rec: model railroading. Res: 534 Yosemite Dr Livermore 94550 Ofc: LLNL, POB 5505, L-384, Livermore 94550

HELGESON, DUANE MARCELLUS, librarian; b. July 2, 1930, Rothsay, Minn.; s. Oscar Herbert and Selma Olivia (Sateren) H.; edn: BS, Univ. Minn. 1952. Career: librarian Chance-Vought Co., Dallas 1956-59, System Devel. Corp., Santa Monica, 1959-62, Lockheed Aircraft, Burbank 1962-63, C.F. Braun Co., Alhambra 1963-74; chief librarian Ralph M. Parsons Co., Pasadena 1974-79; pres. Mark-Allen/ Brokers-in-Information, Los Angeles 1976-80; phys. scis. librarian Calif. Inst. Tech., 1980-85; librarian James M. Montgomery, Consulting Engrs., Pasadena 1985—; mem. adv. bd. Los Angeles Trade Tech. Coll. 1974-79, USC Library Sch., 1974-79; mem. Special Libraries Assn. (chmn. nominating com. 1974); coeditor (with Joe Ann Clifton) Computers in Library and Information Centers (1973); mil: USAF 1952-54. Res: 2706 Ivan Hill Terrace, Los Angeles 90039 Ofc: James M. Montgomery, Consulting Engineers, 250 N Madison Pasadena 91101

HELLMAN, BARNET RICHARD, management information systems executive; b. Feb. 10, 1956, New Martinsville, W.Va.; s. J. Walter and Charlotte R. (Raimist) H.; edn: USAF Acad. 1974-78; BS, Worcester State Coll. 1980; MS, Univ. of New Haven 1984; cert. data proc., Worcester State Coll. 1980. Career: pgmr./ analyst R.R. Donnelley & Sons Co., Old Saybrook, Ct. 1981-82; data processing mgr. Allied Refrigeration Inc., Long Beach 1983; cons. J.D. Edwards & Co., Newport Beach 1984-85; dir. MIS Compusac Corp., Santa Ana 1985—; adj. lectr. Univ. of New Haven, Groton Ext. 1982; mem: DATA; mil: cadet USAF 1974-78; Jewish; rec: philatelist, sci-fi. Ofc: Compusac Corp. 200 W Columbine Ste B-8 Santa Ana 92747

HELLWARTH, GLEN ALLEN, real estate broker; b. Mar. 20, 1925, San Diego; s. Cornelius Allen and Grace Marie (Courser) H.; m. Harriet E., Sept. 23, 1947; children: Jo Anne b. 1948, Janis b. 1951, William b. 1955; edn: BS advt., USC 1947; Calif. lic. real estate broker (1975). Career: sales Coats & Clarks Sales Corp., 1947-75, dist. sales mgr. Portland, Ore. 1965-70, Los Angeles 1971-76; real estate sales Irvine and Costa Mesa, 1976-, broker/office mgr. Re/Max, 1976-81; broker/owner Re/Max of Irvine, 1981—; mil: US Navy 1943-46, 1950-52; rec: golf, travel. Res: 18 Canyon Ridge Irvine 92715 Ofc: Re/Max of Irvine 4482 Barranca Pkwy Ste 210 Irvine 92714

HEMMING, MICHAEL JOHN, lawyer; b. June 14, 1948, Los Angeles; s. Gerald Patrick and Catherine Ellen (Simpson) H.; m. Leoti Lynn, June 21, 1966; children: Michael G., b. 1966; Ryan, b. 1972; edn: AA, East L.A. Jr. Coll. 1969; BA, CSU L.A. 1971; JD, Western State Univ. Coll. of Law 1976; admitted to practice, Calif. State Bar 1977. Career: salesman ABC Stadium Concessions 1962-72; machinist apprentice Union Pacific Railroad 1966-69; meter reader So. Calif. Edison Co. 1969; constrn. acct. 1969; jr. acct. 1969; accountant 1970-71; jr. auditor 1971-73; assoc. auditor 1973-75; sr. auditor/ contract adminstr. 1975-79; gen. counsel DWD Mgmt. Co. 1981—; atty. at law 1977—; dir. DWD Mgmt. Co.; mem: Calif., Los Angeles Co. & Eastern Bar Assns.; Diamond Bar CofC; Republican; rec: chess, coin & stamp collecting. Res: 23560 Gold Nugget Diamond Bar 91765 Law Ofcs. of Michael J. Hemming, 22632 Golden Springs Dr, Ste 230, Diamond Bar 91765

HEMMINGER, PAMELA LYNN, lawyer; b. June 29, 1949, Chgo.; d. Paul Willis and Lenore Adelaide (Hennig) Hemminger; m. Robert A. Miller, May 9, 1979; edn: BA magna cum laude, Pomona Coll. 1971; tchg. cert. Claremont Grad. Sch. 1971-72; JD magna cum laude, Pepperdine Univ. Sch. of Law 1976; Calif. Tchr. Credential 1972; admitted Calif. State Bar 1976. Career: tchr. Etiwanda Sch. Dist. 1971-74; law clk. Gibson, Dunn & Crutcher, Newport Beach 1974-76, assoc. atty. L.A. Office, 1976-84, ptnr. spec. in labor and employment law rep. mgmt., 1985—; apptd. by Gov. Deukmejian to Calif. Comparable Worth Task Force (4/84); frequent lectr. on employment law (ABA, Calif. Mfrs. Assn., Calif. Employment Law Council, Nat. Assn. Mfrs., Am. Compensation Assn., Am. Banking Assn., others); appearances on TV and Radio rep. mgmt. viewpoint on equal employment law; honors: Phi Beta Kappa; mem: ABA, Calif., L.A. Co. Bar Assns., Calif. CofC (Indus./Labor Rels. Com. 1982-), Los Angeles CofC (chair Legis. Subcom. Human Resources Com. 1980-81), Indsl. Rels. Research Assn., Defense Research Inst.; Republican Assocs.; num. publs. in legal jours. in areas of employment law; Republican; Lutheran. Ofc: Gibson, Dunn & Crutcher, 333 S Grand Ave Los Angeles 90071

HEMPHILL, ALAN POLK, television broadcasting co. executive; b. Aug. 22, 1933, Montgomery, Ala.; s. Alan P. and Elizabeth Orr (Evans) H.; m. Jean Tilden Baker, June 8, 1957; children: Elizabeth, b. 1958, Alan, b. 1960, Laurie, b. 1964; edn: BSEE, US Naval Acad. Annapolis 1957. Career: served to Lcdr.

USN 1957-77; comdg. ofcr. US Naval Reserve Tng. Center, Vallejo, Ca. and ofcr. in chg. USS Pampanito, 1963-64; project ofcr. Information Flagship Data Sys. Devel., Naval Electronics Lab., San Diego 1967-69; nat. dir. Remember the Pueblo cmpgn. 1968; ofcr. in chg. Chollas Hts. Transmitter Sta., San Diego 1976-77; mgr./broker Prestige Properties Real Estate, San Diego 1977-80; founder/ gen. ptnr./ dir. of mktg. Orion Business Systems, S.D. 1981-82; pres./ CEO, Oak Broadcasting Systems, Glendale (Channel 52), 1981-82, chmn. bd. dirs. 1982-83, bd. dirs./trustee of 50% stock of Oak Industries, Oak Bdcstg. Systems (approved by FCC), 1982—; honors: qualifed for Submarines (ofcr. 1961), qual. for command of Submarines (1966); mem: Kiwanis Internat. (pres. Rancho Bernardo 1980-81), Green Valley Civic Assn. (pres. 1974, chmn. 1976), Junior Achievement of North County (bd. chmn. 1978); contbg. columnist Escondido Times Advocate (1980), regular columnist (Rancho) Bernardo News 1981-; Libertarian; rec: creative writing. Res: 16241 Del Norte, Poway 92064 Ofc: Oak Broadcasting Systems Inc. 1139 Grand Central Ave Glendale 91201

HEMPHILL, WILLIAM ALFRED, III, marketing executive; b. Mar. 3, 1949, Pittsburgh, Pa.; s. Wm. Alfred, II and Virgie Mae (Fisher) H.; m. Sandra L., Feb. 17, 1973; 1 dau., Michelle b. 1979; edn: grad. Marion Mil. Inst. 1968; BS poly. sci./gen. engring. USAF Acad. 1972; grad. work in bus. adm., Univ. of N. Colo. 1978-79, Ariz. State Univ. 1981-83; Air Command & Staff Coll., Air Univ. 1985-86. Career: navigator tng. 1972-74; B-52 radar navigator SAC/US Air Force, Blytheville, Ariz. 1974-77, Ellsworth AFB, S.D. 1977-79, AF Squadron Ofcrs Sch., Maxwell AFB, Ala. 1977; mktg. rep. Sperry Def. Syst. Div., Phoenix, Ariz. 1979-82, mktg. rep. Sperry Space Syst., 1982-83; mktg. mgr. Motorola GEG, Tempe, Ariz. 1983-84; dir. mktg. Conrac SCD, Duarte, Calif. 1984-; Reserve Assistance Ofcr. instr. Civil Air Patrol Cadet classes, Squad. 25, Cable Airport, Upland; cons. with individuals on resume preparation; frequent public speaking var. civic groups; awards: Falcon Found. Scholarship (1967); mem: AF Acad. Assn. of Graduates, Air Force Assn., Tech. Mktg. Soc. of Am.; mil: capt. USAF Reserve, active duty 1972-79, Nat. Def. Service Medal, AF Outstanding Unit Cit., Presidtl. Unit Cit., Navigator Wings; Republican; Episcopal; rec: golf, computers, raquetball, tennis. Ofc: Conrac SCD, 1700 S Mountain Ave Duarte 91010

HEMPSEY, WILLIAM CHARLES, chiropractor; b. Feb. 2, 1953, Chincoteague, Va.; s. Joseph M. and Mary K. (Gibbons) H.; m. Christine A. Meyer, Oct. 20, 1979; edn: RT, UCSD Sch. of Radiology, 1973; AA, San Diego Mesa Coll. 1979; BS, Cleveland Chiropractic Coll. 1981, DC, 1983; Calif. lic. DC, 1984. Career: radiological technol. UCSD University Hosp., San Diego 1971-73, Donald N. Sharp Hosp., San Diego 1973-76; supr. of Rd Technologists Bay Gen. Hosp., Chula Vista 1976-79; roentgenology instr. Cleveland Chiro. Coll., Los Angeles 1981-83; asst. prof. roentgenology Pasadena Coll. of Chiro., Pasadena 1984-85; chiropractor, Sherman Oaks 1984-, LA Suns Softball Team doctor; recipient appreciation award Am. Businesswomen Assn. (1983); mem: Gonstead Clin. Studies Soc. 1982-, Planetary Soc.; rec: golf. Ofc: 14629 Ventura Blvd Sherman Oaks 91403

HEMPSTEAD, MARJORIE SUNDEEN, business owner; b. Mar. 17, 1934, South Gate; d. Adrian George and Martha Aurora (Hanson) Sundeen; m. Walter Hempstead, Apr. 21, 1962; children: Debra-Sue b. 1958, Donald Allen b. 1965; edn: BA, Pepperdine Univ. 1956. Career: writer Editorial Dept., weekly column, and Society ed. Wave Publs. Newspaper, Los Angeles 1952-56; secty. So. Calif. Optical and Am. Safety Supply Co., 1956-57; army wife, symphony orch. in Germany 1957-58; secty. Rutherford Electronics Corp., Culver City 1959-62; pvt. tchg. of piano, 1946—; owner/mgr. Margie's Hallmark Shop (card and gift shop, US Post Ofc. contract station), Anaheim 1982—; honors: YMCA Woman's Spl. Service Award, Orange Coast Y, Newport Beach (1972), hon. life mem. Sonora Sch. PTA, Costa Mesa (1972); accompanied Ambassador Chorale (110-voice group) Lucerne, Switz. Music Fest. and European tour (1973-74); mem. Mu Phi Epsilon nat. music sor. (1953-5); civic: Anaheim CofC, Job's Daus. (pres. 1953, Bethel Exec. Council 1959), YMCA (Girls Youth Club leader 1965-74), Girl Scouts (leader 1968-74), PTA (bd. 1962-83, pres. 1978, Newport-Mesa Schs. Harbor Council PTA 1978-84), Am. Field Service Fgn. Exchange Stu. Pgm. (chpt. pres. 1974-83), sec.treas. in PTA, church & bus. bowling leagues (1962-83); works: Orange County Fair winner in baked goods, handcrafts, floral arrangement (1970-72); ed./pub. church cookbook (1984, 2d ed. 1985); Democrat; Presbyterian (S.S. tchr./supt., pianist); rec: collects owl figurines, daily diary (1945-). Res: 840 St. Clair St Costa Mesa 92626 Ofc: Margie's Hallmark Shop 1093 North State College Anaheim 92806

HENDERSON, CARL GREGORY, chiropractor; b. Feb. 21, 1947; s. Robert Milton and Vella Rose Henderson; children: Michael b. 1967, Jeanna b. 1970, Jennifer b. 1975; edn: DC, Los Angeles Coll. of Chiro. 1979; ND, DO, Anglo-Am. Inst. Career: fmrly. with Kaiser Gpysum Co.; self- defense instr.; currently, pvt. practice, doctor of chiropractic, Fallbrook Chiro. Ctr.; owner On-Guard Tng. Inst. (lagest teargas/ self defense sch. in Calif.); creator self defense sys. for women; lectr. worldwide on chiropractic, self defense and Boy Scouts; author/ pub. Deseret Alphabet Primer 1972; writer/ prod. movie, Women Be Aware, 1982; awards: Grand Champion, USFE Karate Championships, Europe 1968; num. presidential sports awds., Black Belt in Nippon Kenpo; mem: Am. Chiro. Council on Mental Health (past pres.); Phon- A-Thon organizer; Boy Scouts of Am. (asst. dist. commr., organizer awd., Scouters Key, Scouters tng. awd., Den Talk, Tng. Awd., Commnr. Arrowhead Awd., Awd. of Merit); Village Rotary Club (pres. 1985); mil: USAR, 3 yrs. Ofc: Fallbrook Chiropractic Center, 125 W Fig St Fallbrook 92028

HENDERSON, DANIEL ROBERT, business excutive; b. May 3, 1944, Indpls., Ind.; s. Robert Harry and Barbara Jacquiline (Maloney) H.; m. Ellen Veronica, June 24, 1967; children: Nicole b. 1972, Katherine b. 1975, Rory b. 1977, Emily b. 1978; edn: BS, Univ. of Cincinnati 1968; MBA, Univ. of Ariz. 1969; profl. engr., Ohio. Career: engr. Bechtel Corp., San Francisco 1969-71; analyst Well Fargo Bank, S.F. 1971-72; proj. mgr. Scott-Buttner Corp., Oakland 1972-73; contracts coord. Arabian Am. Oil Co., Saudi Arabia 1973-74, project & pgms. engr. 1974-75; asst. mgr. cost. control Davy McKee Inc., Cleveland, Ohio 1975-79; mgr. proj. control Sohio Constrn. Co., San Francisco 1979-82, ofcr. plng. & budgets 1982-84; bd. chmn. Hystrix Corp., Santa Clara, Ca. 1984—; pres. Neu Bros. Grading & Paving Inc., Santa Clara 1984; dir. AGC of Calif.; Republican; rec: golf, photog. Address: Hystrix Corp., 1390 Norman Ave Santa Clara 95054

HENDERSON, DAVID JOHN, computer co. executive; b. Sept. 22, 1945, San Francisco; s. John Murray and Hazel Martha (Dunbar) H.; edn: AA, Coll. of San Mateo 1965; AB, San Francisco State Univ. 1966. Career: ins. agent Metropolitan Life ins. Co., Hayward 1970-73; subrogation adjuster Ins. Co. of No. Am. dba Recovery Svcs. Internat., San Francisco 1973-75; gen. mgr. Pacific Pub. Carriers, S.F. 1975-77; acct. exec. Western Ins. Assoc., S.F. 1977-80; ins. investigator, Ins. Co. of No. Am., S.F. 1980-83; founder/ pres./ CEO Estate Design Sys., Inc., Fremont 1983—; computer cons. Estate Design Sys., Inc. 1983-; mem: Nat. Notary Assoc.; New Bus. Admin.; Marines Meml. Club, S.F.; sgt. USAF 1966-70, Reserve 1972, Air Force Svc., Air Force Commdn.; Republican (Pres. Task Force 1984); Episcopal; rec: music, yachting, travel. Res: 1205 Old Canyon Rd Fremont 94536 Ofc: Estate Design Systems, Inc., POB 7223 Fremont 94537

HENDERSON, ROBERT PAIGE, business owner; b. Nov. 10, 1919, Davenport, Iowa; s. Claude A. and Viola M. (Boley) H.; m. Phyllis, Feb. 11, 1984; children: Wayne b. 1950, Bruce b. 1953; stepchildren nee Anderson: Colleen b. 1951, Brad b. 1954, Joni b. 1956; edn: Portland Univ. 1940-43; Jamestown Coll. 1938-39. Career: desk clerk, night mgr. Heathman Hotel, Portland, Ore.; salesman Addressograph- Multigraph Corp. 1945-48; br. mgr. Bldg. Material Distrib. 1949-56; owner Bob's Supply Co., San Francisco 1956—; mem: Associated Volume Buyers, Am. Bldg. Contractors Assn.; mil: s/sgt. USMC 1942-45; Republican; Protestant; rec: golf. Ofc: Bob's Supply, 1665 Mission St. San Francisco 94103

HENDERSON, VICTOR WARREN, physician, behavioral neurologist; b. Aug 20, 1951, Little Rock, Ark.; s. Philip S. and N. Jean (Edsel) H.; m. Barbara Curtiss, May 24, 1975; children: Gregory b. 1978, Geoffrey b. 1980, Stephanie b. 1982; edn; BS, summa cum laude, Univ. of Georgia 1972; MD, Johns Hopkins Univ. 1976; diplomate, neurology, Am. Bd. of Psychiatry & Neurology 1981. Career: intern, internal med. Duke Univ. Med. Ctr., Durham NC 1976-77; res. neurology Wash. Univ. Sch. of Med., Barnes Hosp., St. Louis, Mo. 1977-80; fellow, behav. neurology Boston Univ. Sch. of Med. (Aphasia/ Neurobehavior Research Ctr., Boston Veterans Admin. Hosp.), Boston, Mass. 1980-81; instr. neurology Boston Univ. Sch. of Med., Boston, Mass. 1980-81; asst. prof. USC Sch. of Med. 1981-86, assoc. prof. neurol. 1986—; co-dir. USC Neurobehavior Clinic/ Bowles Ctr. for Alzheimer's and Related Diseases; cons. Adult Head Injury Svc., Rancho Los Amigos Hosp., Downey; awards: Nat. Merit Scholar, 1968-72; Stanley Grey prize in psychology, Univ. of Ga. 1972; Phi Beta Kappa 1972; mem: Acad. of Aphasia; Am. Soc. Neurol. Investigation; Am. Acad. of Neurology; Internat. Neuropsychology Soc.; Nat. Head Injury Found.; Behavioral Neurology Soc.; Los Angeles Soc. of Neurology and Psychiatry; publs: frequent contbr., med. arts., sci. publs. 1980-; coauthor: book, Neurologic Logic, 1985; Protestant. Ofc: USC School of Medicine, Dept. of Neurology, 2025 Zonal Ave Los Angeles 90033

HENDRICKS, NORMAN B., lawyer; b. Apr. 11, 1934, St. Anthony, Idaho; s. Alonzo James and Emma Mae (Blanchard) H.; div.; children: Monica b. 1965, Kim b. 1968; edn: JD, Univ. Utah 1961; admitted Calif. State Bar 1965; lic. Calif. real estate broker (1965-), lic. notary public. Career: atty., 1961—, pres. Law Offices of Norman B. Hendricks, P.C., Berkeley; instr. in law and real estate Peralta Coll. Dist.; judge pro tem Berkeley Municipal Ct.; vice mayor City of Emeryville 1975-79; arbitrator Am. Assn. Arbitrators, mem. Calif. Bar Assn., Calif. Teachers Assn., Calif. Trial Lawyers, Berkeley Board of Realtors; civic: KQED; mil: US Army, Korea 1953-5; Democrat; Latter Day Saints; rec: restoration Victorian houses, jogging. Res: 934 Rose Ave Piedmont 94611 Law Ofc: 2275 Shattuck Ave Berkeley 94704

HENDRICKSON, D. JOHN, lawyer; b. July 16, 1955, Berkeley, Calif.; s. J.W. and Ruth (Cumming) H.; edn: BA (w/distinction) Stanford Univ. 1977; UC Los Angeles Law Sch. 1977-78; JD cum laude, Pepperdine Univ. Sch. of Law 1981; admitted Calif. State Bar 1981. Career: ptnr. Wolf, Pocrass, Reyes and Hendrickson, Beverly Hills; adj. prof. of law Pepperdine Univ.; lectr. Calif. Contg. Edn. of the Bar; mem. ABA, State Bar of Calif., LA Co. Bar Assn.; clubs: Stanford Westside (dir.), Pepperdine Assocs.; Republican; Presbyterian; rec: pianist, golf. Ofc: Wolf, Pocrass, Reyes & Hendrickson 9454 Wilshire Blvd Ste 900 Beverly Hills 90212

HENDRICKSON, JO-L, software co. president; b. Dec. 16, 1941, Los Angeles; s. Jack Wilcox and Geraldine Mary (Selman) H.; children: Paul b. 1967, Matthew b. 1969; edn: BA in econs., UC Santa Barbara 1966, BS in chem. 1966; MS computer sci., UC Berkeley 1972, MBA, 1978. Career: pgmmr. Lawrence Livermore Lab. 1968-71; business unit mgr. Varian Assocs., 1971-77, research & devel. mgr. 1977-79, gen. mgr. 1979-81; v.p./gen. mgr. Xebec, Inc. 1981-82; pres./CEO/ founder Individual Software, Inc. 1982—; mem. Am. Electronic

Assn., ADAPSO, Assn. Computing Machinery, UC Berkeley Alumni; author: The Instructor, Professor DOS; Democrat; rec: travel, golf, tennis. Res: 24 Spinnaker Pl Redwood City 94065 Ofc: Individual Software, Inc. 1163-I Chess Dr Foster City 94404

HENDRICKSON, THOMAS ROY, architect; b. Sept. 29, 1951, Seattle, Wash.; s. Laurie John and Rose Josephine (Helina) H.; m. Lana Shull, Jan. 12, 1973; children: Aaron b. 1973, Charity b. 1975, Melody b. 1976; edn: BA environmental design, Univ. Wash. 1973; Reg. Arch. Wash., Calif. 1984. Career: arch. var. firms 1974-78; designer Olympic Assoc. Seattle & Richland, Wash. (nuclear projects incl. fusion reactor planning) 1978-82; proj. arch. Ehrlich-Rominger Archs. Los Altos (hi-tech microelectronics projects in Calif. NY, Mass.) 1982–; honors: Seattle Times Open House (1981); mem: Am. Inst. Archs. (contg. edn. com. 1985), Bay Vista Town Homes Assn. (bd. dirs., treas.); Solar Master Conserver Wash. State 1981; worked on US Solar Demonstration Project 1976; Christian; rec: internat. travel, skiing. Res: 1429 Marlin Ave Foster City 94404 Ofc: Ehrlich-Rominger 4800 El Camino Real Los Altos 94022

HENG, DONALD JAMES, JR., lawyer; b. July 12, 1944, Mpls.; s. Donald James and Catherine Amelia (Strom) H.; m. Kathleen Ann Bailey, Sept. 2, 1967; children: Francesca Remy b. 1975; edn: BA cum laude, Yale Coll. 1967; JD magna cum laude, Univ. Minn. 1971; admitted Calif. State Bar, US Dist. Ct. (no. dist. Calif.), US Ct. of Appeals (9th Cir.) 1971. Career: assoc. Brobeck, Phleger & Harrison 1971-73; atty.- advisor Ofc. of Internat. Tax Counsel, Treas. Dept. 1973-75; ptnr. Brobeck, Phleger & Harrison 1978–; honors: Fulbright Scholar (Italy 1967-68), Order of the Coif (1971), Am. Lawyer Award for Outstanding Performance (1981); mem: ABA, Calif. Bar Assn., Oakland Museum Assn. (bd. 1983-, pres. 1985-86); lectr., writer on tax related subjects, note & comment editor Minn. Law Review 1970-71; Republican; Congregationalist. Res: 914 Hillcroft Circle Oakland 94610 Ofc: Brobeck, Phleger & Harrison One Market Plaza San Francisco 94105

HENLEY, RICHARD MERLE, business executive, entrepreneur; b. Mar. 15, 1952, Portland, Ore.; s. Roy F. and Grayce L. (Roatch) H.; m. Jan Talbert, Feb. 14, 1984; edn: AA, Barstow Jr. Coll. 1972; BA cum laude, CSU Long Beach 1974, grad. wk. 1974; mgmt. Hubbard Tng. Acad.; cert. Drug Rehab. Splst., Narconon Tng. Ctr. 1974-75; Calif. State lic: Gen. Constrn. Contr., Plumbing Contr., Solar Contr.; Nat. Certified Water Splst. CWS-V. Career: clk. J.C. Penneys, 1966-68; mgr. gp. of Texaco Stations, 1968-72; Narconon, L.A. Rehabilitation Center (counselor up to 80 hrs. wkly. to rehab. drug addicts), 1974-76, nat. adminstr. Narconon U.S. (25 offices), 1976-77, estab. Delaware br. 1977; formed Henley Ents. 1975, became largest volume br. ofc. in Water Refining Co. Network 1979-80; founder/ bd. chmn. Northland Environmental Inc., Burbank 1980–, water purification, satellite TV, solarium and renewable energy field, So. Calif. Factory rep. for Sunland Solar and SATCO Satellite TV Systems, mfr. of ENER-G, Northland Pure Water and Northland Satellite TV Systems; chmn. bd. dirs. Sunland National Dealer Assn. 1982-84; sales and mgmt. cons. and trainer, 1986-; num. tv, radio, press interviews re solar industry; awards: Bus. Pioneer, Northland listed twice in top 100 pvt. cos. in INC. 500 mag. (1984, 85), recipient volume trophies & awards for 10 offices set up across USA, Sunland and Northland cos.; mem: Calif. Lic. Contrs. Assn., Solar Energy Industries Assn., Calif. SEIA, State CofC, Nat. Fedn. of Ind. Bus., US Dept. of Commerce Exporters Directory; spkr. Renewable Energy Technologies Symp. and Internat. Expo. (RETSIE 84); gen. secty. Nat. Assn. of People Who Care (NAPWC) 1979; publs: Employer's Bill of Rights, Employee's Bill of Rights (1983), Calif. CofC, and Nat. Fedn. Ind. Bus.; contbg. writer: Solar mag., Sun Up, Sunspots, Energy Collector, Apartment Reporter, Bnai Brith, Properity, WISE News; Inc. 500 Top 10% of 500,000 companies 1984; Expert marksman (NRA) Rifle team placed 3d in state; Republican; Scientologist; rec: flying (helicopter, ultralight), skiing. Res: 230 Bethany Rd Burbank 91506 Ofc: Northland Environmental Inc. 1115-1121 Chestnut St Burbank 91506

HENMAN, JAMES ORAL, psychologist; b. Nov. 5, 1947, Geneva, Nebr.; s. Oral Kenneth and Mary Jean (Haley-Reeh) H.; m. Sonia Magdich, Aug. 5, 1972; children: Jesse Michael b. 1981, Nathan Andrew b. 1983; edn: BA, CSU San Jose 1969, MA, 1972; PhD, Calif. Sch. of Profl. Psychology 1978; lic. clin. psychologist, Calif. 1980. Career: head tchr. Head Start Summer Pgm., Santa Cruz 1969; hd. tchr. Head Start, Santa Clara County, 1969-71, ednl. coordinator, 1970-71; supr. Ednl. Centers, Migrant Edn., Merced Co. 1971-72; dir. Stanislaus Co. Family Service Agcy. 1972-78; pvt. practice in clinical psychology, 1978–; tchg. CSU Stanislaus; cons. DMZ Project for Vietnam vets., San Joaquin County Emergency Food Bank; honors: Who's Who in Am. Jr. Colls. (1967), Pres.'s Scholar (1968), Phi Kappa Phi (1969); mem: Stanislaus County Psychol. Assn. (pres. 1980), Calif. State Psychol. Assn., Christian Assn. for Psychol. Studies; works: dev. new therapy approach, Cognitive Hypnotherapy; Democrat; Christian; avocation: translating Christianity into practical, living principles. Res: 2429 Teval Ct Modesto 95356 Ofc: 2909 Coffee Rd Ste 14 Modesto 95355

HENNIGAN, J(AMES) DAVID, superior court judge; b. Dec. 5, 1920, St. Louis, Mo.; s. James David and Matilda D. (Smith) H.; m. Mary Jane Ager, Mar. 15, 1946; children: James David (Jay) b. 1951, Lorinda Fields b. 1957; edn: BS in Jur., Washington Univ. 1942; JD, Washington Univ., St. Louis 1943. Career: pvt. practice St. Louis 1946-48; loyalty bd. U.S. Civil Svc. S.F. 1949; public defender Riverside Co. 1949-52; pvt. practice Riverside 1952-79; judge Sup. Ct. 1979–; honors: Order of the Coif; mem: Am., Riverside Co. (pres. 1965-66) bar assns.; various civic orgs.; mil: 1st lt. US Army 1943-46, battle ribbons; Republican; Episcopal; rec: scuba and skin diving, gardening. Res: 7065 Seville Way Riverside 92504 Ofc: Superior Ct. 4050 Main St Riverside 92501

HENRIKSEN, THOMAS HOLLINGER, senior research fellow; b. Nov. 16, 1939, Detroit, Mich.; s. Paul Friis and Irene (Hollinger) H.; m. Margaret Mueller, Sept. 7, 1968; children: Heather b. 1970, Damien b. 1979; edn: BA, Va. Mil. Inst. 1962; MA, Mich. State Univ. 1966, PhD 1969. Career: prof. State Univ. of N.Y. 1969-79; research fellow Hoover Instn., Stanford 1980-82, senior research fellow 1982-, assoc. dir. 1983–, and exec. secty. Nat. Fellows Program, Hoover Instn. 1984–; apptd. mem. Army Science Board (1984-); honors: Choice (lib. journal) Outstanding Book Award for "Mozambique: A History" (1979); Peace Fellowship, Hoover Instn. (1979-80); author five books, num. profl. and popular articles; mil: ofcr. US Army 1963-65; Republican. Res: 177 Lundy Ln Palo Alto 94306 Ofc: Hoover Institution, Stanford University, Stanford 94305

HENRY, H. LON, biotechnology corporate executive; b. Aug. 31, 1927, Santa Barbara, Calif.; s. Barney J. and Myrtle L. Henry; m. Beverly J., Aug. 19, 1950; children: Laura Diane b. 1952, Drake Allan b. 1954; edn: AA, Glendale Coll. 1948; BS, Univ. So. Calif. 1951, MS, 1953; MBA, San Diego State Univ. 1964; Clin. Lab. Bioanalyst 1956; Clin. Lab. Technologist Calif. 1951. Career: chief of labs. El Segundo Hosp./ Zeiller Labs, El Segundo 1958-61; dir. labs. So. Bay Hosp. Gp., Redondo Beach 1961-66; scientific sales & tech. splst. Aloe Scientific, L.A. 1966-68; dir. in-vitro diagnostics, Calbiochem, San Diego 1968-77; v.p., gen. mgr. Nichols Inst. Diagnostics, San Pedro 1977-80; v.p. mktg. & sales Internat. Diagnostics Technology, Santa Clara 1980-82; v.p., gen. mgr. B. Braun Instruments, Burlingame 1982–; assoc. prof. El Camino Coll. 1966; bd. dirs. Spectrolyte Corp. 1981-83; honors: Boy of the Year (F.D.R. 1943), Lodge Secty. Award (Calif. Freemasons 1970); mem: Am. Soc. Clin. Pathol., Am. Soc. Med. Technol., Am. Assn. Clin. Chemists, World Health Orgn., Nat. Com. for Clin. Lab. Stds., fellow Royal Soc. of Health, F&A Masons (past master); co-author: Clinical Methods of Enzymology (w/ Karmew, 1974); contbg. ed. Methods of Clinical Chemistry (1985); mil: lcdr. USNR -1950, PTO, Japanese Occup., Good Conduct; Republican; Methodist; rec: scuba, flying, writing. Ofc: Burlingame 94010

HENRY, THOMAS GRENFELL, stockbroker; b. Jan. 3, 1942, San Francisco; s. Frank Grenfell and Marjorie (Campbell) H.; m. Elizabeth Gibson, June 20, 1964; children: Richard b. 1967, William b. 1970; edn: BA, UC Berkeley 1965. Career: stockbroker/v.p. E.F. Hutton & Co. Inc., Oakland 1965–; mem. East Bay Street Club (pres. 1976-77), Rotary (Lafayette pres. 1979-80), Oakland Service Club (pres. 1978-79), Athenian Nile Club, Lincoln Child Center (bd., chmn. fin. com. 1982-), Boy Scouts of Am. (Eagle Advancement chmn. Mt. Diablo Council, Troop 243); Republican; Episcopal; rec: running. Res: 3422 Silver Springs Ct Lafayette 94549 Ofc: EF Hutton & Co Inc 300 Lakeside Dr Lobby Ste Oakland 94612

HERALD, MARCUS ALAN, material program administrator; b. Oct. 26, 1948, Centralia, Wash.; s. Raymond Hedley and Nelda Smith (Wolff) H.; m. Un Sun Park, Sept. 17, 1983; edn: BA in econs., honors, Univ. of Puget Sound 1970; desig: CPA, Ill. (1973), CIA, Inst. of Internal Auditors (1975). Career: sr. internal auditor Kemper Group, Long Grove, Ill. 1972-74, Zurich-Am. Group, Chgo. 1974; chief internal auditor ITT Harper, Morton Grove, Ill. 1974-76; corp. auditor Gulf Oil Corp., Los Angeles 1977-78; sr. internal auditor GTE Service Corp., Santa Monica 1978-80; materiel program adminstr. Lockheed-California Co., Burbank 1980–; mem: Phi Theta Kappa frat., Alpha Kappa Psi frat., Ill. CPA Soc., Am. Inst. CPAs, Inst. of Internal Auditors, Nat. Mgmt. Assn., Eagle Investment Club; mil: lt.jg US Navy 1970-72, Nat. Def. Service, Vietnam Service, Repub. Vietnam Campaign medals; Republican; rec: sailing. Ofc: Lockheed-California Co. POB 551 Burbank 91520

HERLIHY, JOHN FRANCIS, judge; b. Dec. 17, 1949, Atlanta, Ga.; s. James Thomas and Helen Marie (Savoie) H.; m. Mary Ann La Porta, Sept. 4, 1971; children: Shannon Colleen b. 1977, Jennifer Kathleen b. 1980; edn: BA with distinction, CSU San Jose 1971; JD, UC Hastings Coll. of Law 1974; admitted Calif. State Bar 1974. Career: atty. partner law firm Hansen & Herlihy (gen. civil practice, spec. in real estate & bus. litigation) 1974-76; dep. dist. atty. Santa Clara County, 1976-80; commnr. Santa Clara Co. Municipal Ct., 1980-82, judge Santa Clara County Municipal Ct. 1983–, presiding judge elect 1985-86; instr. in trial techniques, Univ. of Santa Clara Law Sch. 1984-; real estate instr. Foothill Coll. 1975-81; faculty Hastings Trial Advocacy Coll. 1979-81; pres. and chmn. bd. dirs. Sentencing Alternatives Program Bd.; bd. dirs. Justice System Advisory Bd. (advis. to County Bd. Supvrs.); honors: contbg. ed. assoc. Hastings Constnl. Law Qrtrly. 1973; recognition for contbn. to trial advocacy pgm. Univ. of Santa Clara Law Sch.; mem. Calif. Judges Assn. (Criminal Law Com.), St. Thomas More Soc., Calif. Ct. Commnrs. Assn. (bd. dirs. 1980-83); mem. Elks, Friends of Cupertino Library, San Jose Hist. Museum; publs: num. articles on real estate used in Calif. Community Colls. 1978-, law review art. on condemnation 1973; mil: capt. Calif. Army Nat. Guard 1980-85; Catholic; rec: skiing, tennis, gardening. Res: Cupertino Ofc: Santa Clara Co. Municipal Ct., 200 W. Hedding St., San Jose 95014

HERLIK, EDWARD CHARLES, military officer/aviator; b. July 31, 1958, Frankfurt, W. Germany; s. Querin Edward and Mary Josephene (Lemerond) H.; m. Cindy Strong, Aug. 14, 1982; edn: BS engring., USAF Acad. 1980; MA (Phi Kappa Phi) in nat. security studies, CSU San Bernardino 1986. Career: served to capt. US Air Force 1976–: engr. Space Command (satellite R&D) 1981-82, pilot tng. 1982-83, pilot 1983– (qualified to lead 4 fighter aircraft), currently a squadron supvr. and chief liaison ofcr. for USAF Academy in the High Desert (Victorville) 1984-; speaking & counseling area high sch. seniors on behalf of USAF; served in Cavalry unit guarding Inter-German border in Europe; mem. Am. MENSA Ltd. 1986; mil. awards: USAF Commendn. Medal (1982), US Army Achievement Medal (1986), var. ribbons; rec: photog., scuba, travel, camping. Address: Victorville 92392-5212

HERMAN, DEBORAH ANN, manufacturing co. executive; b. April 19, 1960, Los Angeles; s. Arthur Martin and June Eleanor (Graham H.; edn: BA, Brigham Young Univ. 1982. Career: v.p. sales Bedspreads of California, Huntington Park 1982-; honors: Distng. Student in Pub. Rels., BYU 1981; Outstanding Young Women of Am. 1982; mem: NEWH (charter), PRSSA, Sonance, Mercado; publs: ed., Beginning, BYU 1982; Missouri Music Fedn.- #1 Piano, Moderately Difficult Category, 1978; Republican; Jewish; rec: skating, softball, travel. Res: 1 Northstar Apt. 203 Marina del Rey 90292 Ofc: Bedspreads of Calif., 2067 Clarendon Ave. Huntington Park 90255

HERMIONE (Hermione Palmer Chase), artist, gallery owner; b. Apr. 8, 1905, San Francisco; d. Archie Leon and Alice Evelyn (White) Palmer; desc. John Alden & Priscilla, grandneice US Pres. James Buchanan; m. Kelsey David Chase, 1955 (decd.); edn: UC Berkeley 1923-27; spl. stu., Otis Art Sch. 1964-82. Art Career: feature writer, cartoonist Daily Cal (newspaper) and Pelican Mag. 1923-27; summer artist Montgomery Ward Oakland 1926; freelance artist I Magnin S.F.; freelance cartoonist Life Judge College Humor NYC 1928, NY American 1934, cartoon between O.O. McIntyre and Will Rogers (1935); Fashion Page, Society Section NY American 1935-36; artist Liebes S.F. Fashions 1937; ceramic designer, manufacture patent on wire hair and eyelashes on ceramic dolls and flower holders 1937-55; porcelain mfr. mirrors, lamps, boxes, bottles, lamps, jewelry 1945-; owner Hermione gallery and card shop Glendale 1955-; honors: Best of Show (open show La Mirada 1977), exhibit pastels (Paul Elder Gallery S.F 1937), paintings (Gallery Plus L.A. 1977), mem. Theta Sigma Phi (1927); life mem. Soc. of Illustrators NYC; Republican; Christian Scientist. Address: Hermione 418 W Los Feliz Rd Glendale 91204

HERNANDEZ, FERNANDO VARGAS, lawyer; b. Aug. 9, 1939, Irapuato, Mexico; s. Jose E. and Ana Maria (Vargas) H.; m. Bonnie Corrie, Jan. 1966; children: Michael b. 1966, Alexandra b. 1968, Marcel b. 1972; edn: BS, Santa Clara Univ. 1961, MBA, 1962; JD, UC Berkeley 1966; admitted Calif. State Bar 1967. Career: atty. pvt. practice, San Jose 1967-, spec. in trial practice; lectr. Lincoln Univ. Law Sch. 1968-69, Santa Clara Univ. Grad. Sch. of Bus. 1969-70; chmn. bd. trustees Calif. Rural Assistance, Inc. 1973-75; honors: CTLA recognition of experience in Personal Injury, Prods. Liability Law; mem: Am. Bar Assn. 1967-84, Calif. State Bar Assn., Am. Trial Lawyers Assn., Calif. Trial Lawyers Assn. (bd. govs. 1979-82); civic: West San Jose Optimist, San Jose Civic Light Opera (bd. dirs.); publs: contbg. ed. Calif. Pleadings (CTLA 1980-81), lectr. CTLA Seminars (1979-83), Jury Voir Dire, CTLA Forum; mil: USAR 1962-68; Democrat; Roman Catholic; rec: painting, tennis, racquetball. Res: 14098 Elvira St Saratoga 95070 Ofc: 690 Saratoga Ave Ste 9 San Jose 95129

HERNANDEZ, RICHARD F., lawyer; b. June 24, 1945; edn: BA in econs., Univ. of Tx., El Paso 1968; MS in adminstrn., Pepperdine Univ. 1972; JD, La Verne Univ. 1977; admitted Calif. State Bar 1977. Career: gen. law practice, law firm Mattier, Annigian, Minto & Hernandez; Richard F. Hernandez & Assocs., West Covina currently; past chief spl. asst. L.A. Co. Assessor's Office, legislative advocate in Sacto. rep. L.A. Co. Supt. of Schs., adminstr./pgm. supr. Azusa Unified Sch. Dist.; past adminstr. US Dept. of Labor funded job devel. & career counseling pgm. San Gabriel Valley; past recreation dir. City of Azusa; recipient recogn. awards: Los Angeles City Mayor, County Bd. of Supvrs., LA Co. Commn. on Human Relations, Azusa City Council, San Gabriel Valley Community Rels. Award, Outstanding Young Men Am., others; mem. Am. Bar Assn., Mex-Am. Bar Assn., East San Gabriel Valley Bar Assn., L.A. Co. Bar Assn., Adult Educators Assn. (past pres.), Internat. Assn. of Assessing Ofcrs., Assn. of Calif. Sch. Adminstrs., Calif. Assn. of Work Experience Educators; civic: LA Co. Manpower Council (chair), Mex Am Political Assn., Labor Council for Latin Am Advance., Mex-Am Educators Assn. (past pres.), LA Co. Youth Planning Council (chair), S.G.V. Human Rels. Commn. (chair), Catholic Social Svcs Council SGV (bd.), Teen Post Advis. Com. (bd.), Junior Civitan Club (founder), Civitan Internat.; Democrat (past pres. Azusa Dem. Club, del. State Conv.). Ofc: 818 West Cameron Ave West Covina 91790

HERRICK, ALBERT WILLIAM, investor, ret.; b. Mar. 4, 1906, Liccester, Eng., nat. US cit. 1930; s. Thomas and Harriet Ada (Smith) H.; m. Marian, Apr. 28, 1960; edn: Pasadena City Coll. 1940-48. Career: chemist's asst. Colonial Dames Cosmetics 1924-26; mgr. North East Svc. 1926-30; owner, mgr. H&H Automotive Los Angeles 1930-69, H&H Hardware 1940-69; rancher Tulare County 1969-80; real estate investor 1975-83; honors: Merit Award (Texaco 1965); mem: Rotary, Masons (master mason 50 yrs., Golden Veteran Pin 1986), Kiwanis, Exeter Meml. Hosp. Assn.; trustee First Presbyterian Ch. of Exeter 1972-75; inventor several mechanical devices (none patented); Republican; Baptist; rec: travel, woodworking. Res: 2193 W Visalia Rd Exeter 93221

HERRICK, DOUGLAS GEORGE, manufacturing co. executive; b. Feb. 5, 1953, Dayton, Ohio; s. George G. and Mildred (Mahland) H.; m. Victoria, June 6, 1961; edn: BSBA, Univ. of Denver 1976. Career: senior buyer Storage Technology Corp., Louisville, Colo. 1976; owner/op. Retreat Restaurant, Den-

ver 1976-78; mgmt. tng. Deutsch Metal Co., Los Angeles 1978-80, pres./mktg. dir. Deutsch Aerospace Fitting Co., Gardena 1980-; honors: Kappa Sigma frat. (pres. 1974) scholarship award (1974); Univ. of Denver Intrafrat. Council (v.p. 1974), Varsity Soccer Team; mem. Nat. Rifle Assn. (life), Trout Unlimited (life); bd. trustees Memorial Hosp. of Gardena; Republican; Methodist; rec: skiing, hunting, golf. Res: 2 Ranchero Rd Rolling Hills 90274 Ofc: Deutsch Aerospace Co. 14500 S Figueroa St Gardena 90248

HERRING, CHARLES DAVID, lawyer; b. March 18, 1943, Muncie, Ind.; s. Morris Jr. and Margaret Helen (Scherbaum) H.; m. DeLayne Riedberger, Oct. 8, 1977; children: Charles David Jr. b. 1966, Margaret b. 1967, Christopher b. 1979; edn: BA, Indiana Univ. 1965, JD, cum laude, 1968. Career: research asst Indiana Univ. 1965-68; clerk, prosecuting atty. Monroe Co., Ind. 1968; Us Army Judge Advoc. Gen.'s Corps 1968-72; with law firm Odorico, Franklin and Herring 1972-74; Herring and Stubel, San Diego 1976-; adj. prof. of law Western State Univ., San Diego 1972-; guest spkr. Calif. Escrow Assn. 1981, San Diego Escrow Assn. 1981, 1982; honors: Order of the Coif, 1968; Milton Award Outstanding Oral Advoc., Indiana Univ. 1968; mem: Indiana Bar Assn., Calif. Trial Lawyers Assn., Valle de Oro Plnng. Assn.; publs: co-author with Jim Wade, legal casework, Cases and Materials on Professional Responsibilty; mil: capt. US Army 1965-72, Army Commdn. (2); Republican; Protestant; rec: gardening, swimming, golf. Res: 1968 Treseder Circle El Cajon 92021 Ofc: Herring, Stubel & Lehr, 1670 Wells Fargo Bank Bldg., 101 W. Broadway San Diego 92101

HERRMANN, VICTOR ADAM, physician, ret.; b. Dec. 2, 1914, Osceola, Neb.; s. Adam John and Hannah Christine (Timm) H.; m. Jeanne Marjorie Palmer, July 27, 1938; children: Victor b. 1945, Sandra b. 1950; edn: BS, Univ. of Neb. 1938; MD, Univ. Neb. Coll. of Med. 1940. Career: flight surgeon Army Med. Corps 1942-46; pvt. practice internal med. Los Angeles 1946-82; pres. med. staff Hollywood Presbyterian Hosp. Med. Ctr. 1961; mem: Hollywood Acad. of Med. (pres. 1956); Masons; Scottish Rite; Knights Templar; Shrine; mil: major (USAAC) Army Med. Corps WWII; Republican; Presbyterian; rec: piano, golf. Res: 32 Lakeview Circle Palm Springs 92264

HERRON, ELLEN PATRICIA, judge; b. July 30, 1927, Auburn, NY; d. David Martin and Grace Josephine (Berner) H.; edn: AB, Trinity Coll. 1949; MA, Cath. Univ. Am. 1954; JD, UC Berkeley 1964. Career: asst. dean Catholic Univ. Am. 1952-54; instr. East High Sch., Auburn 1955-57; asst. dean Wells Coll., Aurora, NY 1957-58; instr. psychology and hist. Contra Costa Coll., 1958-60; dir. row SStandrd, 1960-61; assoc. Knox & Kretzmer, Richmond, Ca. 1964-65; admitted to Calif. bar 1965; ptnr. Knox & Herron law firm, Richmond, Calif. 1965-74, Knox, Herron and Masterson, 1974-77; judge Superior Ct. State of Calif., 1977-; mem. assembly Calif. Judiciary Com. for Court Improvement, 1979-80; gen. ptnr. Real Estate Syndicates, Calif. 1967-77; active num. civic orgns.; bd. dirs. Rhonoh Sch. (Richmond), YWCA, Econ. Devel. Council Richmond; alumnae bd. dirs. Boalt Hall UC Berkeley, 1980-; mem. ABA, Contra Costa Bar Assn. (exec. com. 1969-74), Calif. Trial Lawyers, Nat., Calif. assns. Women Lawyers, Nat. Assn. Women Judges, Applicants Attys. Assn., Calif. Judges Assn. (ethics com. 1977-79, criminal law procedure com. 1979-80), Queens Bench, Juvenile Ct. Judges Assn.; Democrat. Res: 51 Western Dr., Point Richmond 94801

HERRON, SANDRA WHITACRE, psychotherapist, speech therapist; b. July 1, 1935, Calumet, Mich.; d. Ahti John and Inga Aurora (Savela) Jaaskelainen; m. Jim Herron, Oct. 30, 1982; children: Lisa b. 1956, Lance b. 1958, Leslee b. 1961; edn: BA in speech and psychology, Whittier Coll. 1956; MA in speech path., CSU Fullerton 1969; MA psych., Sierra Univ. w/o Walls 1984; candidate PhD, Internat. Coll.; Calif. lic. (MFCC) Marriage Family Child Counselor. Career: speech therapist Whittier Sch. Dist. 1956-70, Magnolia Sch. Dist.- Lord Baden Powell Orthopedic Unit 1970-; counseling: MFCC, Crystal Cathedral Christian Counseling Service 1984-, Town and Country Psychological Services 1984-; seminars: annual Nat. Singles Conf. 1982-85; Crystal Cathedral instr. lay minister tng. classes 1980-85, and former dir. of Spiritual Life, Positive Christian Singles 1980-82; honors: Outstanding Profl. Woman of Year, La Mirada (1971); mem: Calif. Assn. Marriage Family Therapists, MEA, Nat. Edn. Assn., Calif. Tchrs. Assn., CSHA, ALIVE (v.p. bd. dirs., nat. suicide prevention org.); publs: (article) It's My Turn Now; (slide show) Zoo Who; Christian; rec: photog. Ofc: Garden Grove 92645

HERST, PERRY STERN, JR., real estate executive; b. Sept. 18, 1929, Chgo.; s. Perry Stern and Gertrude (Browarsky) H.; children: Perry III, b. 1965; Craig, b. 1966; edn: BA, Brown Univ. 1951, MBA, Harvard Grad. Sch. 1953. Career: loan ofcr. Equitable Finance Corp., Chgo. 1957; R.E. leasing & devel. broker Arthur Rubloff & Co., Chgo. 1958-64; v.p. Tishman- Gateway Inc., Chgo. 1964-68; sr. v.p. Tishman Realty & Constrn. Co., Inc., Los Angeles 1968-77; pres. Tishman West Mgmt. Corp., L.A. 1977-; awards: Humanitarian award NCCJ (1976); Civic Achiev. Awd., The Am. Jewish Com. 1979; mem: Lamda Alpha; Urban Land Inst.; L.A. area CofC (Long Range Plng. Com.); Los Angeles Mayor's Economic Council; Nat. Conf. of Christians & Jews; The Am. Jewish Com.; Jr. Achiev. of So. Calif.; UCLA Chancellor Assocs.; mil: lt. sr. grade USN 1954-56; Republican; Jewish; rec: fishing, hunting, tennis. Res: Malibu Ofc: Tishman West Management Corp. 10960 Wilshire Blvd Ste 700 Los Angeles 90024

HERTWECK, E. ROMAYNE, educator; b. July 24, 1928, Springfield, Mo.; s. Garnett P. and Gladys (Chowning) H.; m. Alma Louise Street, Dec. 16, 1955, 1 son: William Scott, b. 1970; edn: BA, Augustana Coll. 1962; MA, Pepperdine Coll. 1963; EdD, Ariz. State Univ. 1966; PhD, US Internat. Univ. 1978. Career:

night ed. Rock Island Argus Newspaper, Ill. 1961-62; grad. tchg. asst. Pepperdine Coll., Los Angeles 1963; counselor, VA, Ariz. State Univ., Tempe, Ariz. 1964; assoc. dir. conciliation ct. Miracopa Co. Superior Ct., Phoenix, Ariz. 1965; instr. Phoenix Coll. 1966; prof. psychol. Mira Costa Coll., Oceanside, Calif. 1967–; chmn. psychol. counseling dept. World Campus Afloat, S.S. Ryndam, spring 1970; instr. edn. dept., Univ. of San Diego, part- time 1968-69; lectr. bus. mgmt. dept., San Diego State Univ., part- time 1980–; instr. Chapman Coll. Residence Ctr., Camp Pendleton 1969-78; p-t lectr. Dept. of Bus. Adminstrn. San Diego State Univ. 1980-84, Scho. of Human Behavior US Internat. Univ. 1984–; pres. El Camino Preschools, Inc., Oceanside 1985–; bd. dirs. Christian Counseling Ctr., Oceanside 1970–; mem: Kiwanis; Carlsbad Club; Am., Western & No. San Diego Co. Psychol. Assns.; Am. Personnel & Guidance Assn.; Phi Delta Kappa; Kappa Delta Pi; Psi Chi; Republican; Protestant; rec: travel, golf, photog. Res: 2024 Oceanview Rd Oceanside Ofc: Mira Costa College, Oceanside

HERTZLICH, HENRY L., manufacturing executive, ret.; b. May 30, 1923, Warsaw, Poland, nat. US cit. 1956; s. Mark and Stefanie (Rozycki) H.; m. Christine Suk, Apr. 27, 1950; edn: BS commerce (equiv.) Balham Coll. of Comm., England 1948. Career: fin. analyst Litton Industries, Canoga Park; budget analyst Curtiss Wright (Caldwell Wright Div.), No. Hollywood; financial analyst Menasco Corp. Office, Burbank; mgr. cost acctg. Menasco- Calif. Div., Burbank, Menasco Canada Ltd., Montreal; v.p. fin. Menansco Inc. - Overhaul Div. (subs. Colt Industries), Burbank; ret. 1985; mem. Nat. Assn. of Accts. (1965), Polish Nat. Alliance, Polish-Am. Cultural Network; mil: CAD. ofcr. Polish 2nd Corps (Brit. VIII Army); Democrat; Roman Catholic; rec: photog., music. Res: 9753 Johanna Pl Sunland 91040

HERZBERG, RICHARD WILLIAM, superintendent of schools, b. Dec. 23, 1951, Elmhurst, Ill.; s. Wm. Charles and Joyce Ardythe H.; m. Marilyn Orcutt, Aug. 17, 1974; children: Michael b. 1979, Jason b. 1983; edn: BS, Univ. Ore. 1974; MS, CSU Fullerton 1978; PhD, UC Santa Barbara 1984. Career: tchr., learning splst. Los Alamitos Unified Sch. Dist., 1974-78; supt./prin. San Miguel Sch. Dist. 1978-79; asst. supt. Paso Robles Public Schs., 1979-85, supt. of schools 1985–; pres. Bureau of Edn. & Research; instr. num. colls. and univs.; mem. Assn. of Calif. School Adminstrs., Assn. for Supvsn. and Curriculum Devel., Am. Assn. of Sch. Adminstrs.; Rotarian; rec: outdoor sports, x-c skiing, camping. Ofc: 504 28th St Paso Robles 93446

HERZOG, SUSAN ROCK, librarian; b. Mar. 31, 1946, Phila.; d. Milton L. and Shirley Ruth (Cylinder) Rock; m. Richard Joseph Herzog, Aug. 5, 1967 (div.); 1 dau. Liza Devon; edn: BA, Univ. Mich. 1967, MA in Chinese Studies, 1969; MLS, UC Berkeley 1976. Career: Reference librarian Fresno County Free Library, 1976–; librarian Thomas, Snell et al law firm, Fresno 1977–, Baker, Manock, Jensen law firm, Fresno 1978–, US Dept. Agri., 1978–. Res: 623 E. Yale, Fresno 93704 Ofc: 2420 Mariposa Fresno 93721

HESS, ROBERT PRATT, tax lawyer; b. May 1, 1942, Evanston, Ill.; s. Robert Graves and Evelyn Marie (Pratt) H.; m. Kathryn, Dec. 17, 1966; children: Robert b. 1969, Michael b. 1972; edn: BA in econ., Lehigh Univ. 1964; LLB, Stanford Law Sch. 1967; Certified Splst. in Taxation Law, Calif. Bar 1973. Career: atty. law firm Hill, Farrer & Burrill, Los Angeles 1967–, senior partner Tax Dept.; secty., bd. dir. Presto-Tek; lectr. Calif. Contg. Edn. of the Bar; honors: Outstanding Young Man of Am. 1978; mem. Am., Calif., Los Angeles bar assns.; publs: Desk Book for setting up a Closely-Held Corporation (Inst. for Bus. Planning) 1979, 1985; num. articles on tax planning; Republican; Presbyterian; rec: tennis, golf. Res: 4273 Hampstead Rd., Flintridge 91011 Ofc: Hill, Farrer & Burrill, 445 S Figueroa St, Ste 3400, Los Angeles 90071

HESTER, EDWARD CLAY, lawyer; b. Apr. 2, 1948, Los Angeles; s. Clarence Carmen and Thelma Marie H.; m. Karen, June 23, 1973; children: Sienna b. 1981, Trevor b. 1983; edn: AA history, El Camino Jr. Coll. 1968; BA history, CSU Long Beach 1973; JD, Calif. Coll. of Law 1979; admitted Calif. State Bar 1980. Career: atty Stern, Baranov & Watkins Century City 1980-81; atty. pvt. practice Torrance 1981, Fair Oaks 1982-83, Citrus Heights 1983-84; atty. ptnr. Bernard & Hester ALC Citrus Heights 1985–; mem: Calif. State, Sacto. Co. bar assns. 1980-, Christian Legal Soc. of Sacto. (pgm. chair 1982-), Capital City Trial Lawyers Assn. 1982-, Christian Concilliation Svcs. of Sacto. (treas. 1983-), Masons; mil: CW2 US Army 1968-71, Dist. Flying Cross, Air Medal w. 25 devices, Bronze Star, Purple Heart w. 1 palm leaf; capt. Calif. Army Nat. Guard 1972-, Medal of Merit; Democrat; United Methodist; rec: helicopter flying, church work, reading. Ofc: Bernard & Hester ALC 8035 Madison Ave, Ste F-1, Citrus Heights 95610-7949

HEVENLY, JUDY ANN, author/psychic consultant, b. Feb. 1, 1938, Port Elizabeth, South Africa; d. Trevor and Mavis (Butt-Thompson) Doorly-Jones; m. Robert P. Heverly, 1968, div. 1970; ed. Holy Rosary Convent, Collegiate H.Sch. (Port Elizabeth); Asso. in Rel. Sci., United Ch. of Rel. Sci. 1976; D.Div., Ch. of Gospel Ministry Inc. 1978; Career: actress, London, Eng. appearing in such movies as Charles Chaplin's "Countess from Hong Kong," Dick Lester "The Knack," "Goldfinger" (James Bond), Francois Truffaut's " Fahrenheit 451," "Alfie" w/ Michael Caine, 1970-73; writer/catalogue designer Southeby Parke Bernet, Los Angeles 1973-74; asst. to rep. Hong Kong Trade Council, L.A. 1976-79; astrologist/ psychic/ metaphysician, dir. Los Angeles Wholistic Group, 1984–, pub. L.A. Wholistic Publishing Co., 1984–; author: Unlock Your Mind (novel) 1986; freelance writer Globe Newspapers (1979-), The Enquirer; psychic columnist for Eve's Weekly (Bombay, India); mem: Am. Fedn. of Astrologers, L.A. Press Club, Internat. Directory of Astrologers/ Psychics, Spiritualists Soc. of G.B., British Actors Equity Assn., Psychic Guide 1982-86, Hollywood CofC, Book Publicists of So. Calif.; works: accurately predicted more than 150 major nat. and internat. events, featured in publs. incl. The Nat. Enquirer, Star, Globe, Examiner, The London TV Times, Fate, Psychic Guide; interviews in The LA Times, Herald Examiner, Valley Daily News, Civic Center News, Israeli Times, Esoteric News, and overseas in THe Times of India, Bombay's Daily and Evening Outlook and Eve's Weekly of India; num. radio, TV appearances, Entertainment Tonight; Republican; Ch. Rel. Sci.; rec: politics, world travel, writing. Res: 14411 Kittridge Van Nuys 91405 Ofc: Los Angeles Wholistic Group, Ste 421, Box 6010, Sherman Oaks 91413

HEWITT, GEORGE E., foundation president, commercial real estate developer; b. July 2, 1921, NYC; married, four children; edn: BS in mech. engring., Columbia Univ. 1943; cert. in UHF techniques, radar, MIT 1943; spl. courses UCLA Ext., Orange Coast Coll.; Reg. Profl. Engr., Real Estate lic., Calif. Career: instr. Columbia Univ. 1941-42; staff MIT Radiation Lab. 1943-45; engr., project engr. (microwave radar antennas & systems) Gilfillon Bros. Inc., 1946-48; founder, v.p., gen. mgr., bd. dirs. Canoga Corp. (devel., engr. & mfg. radar antennas & systems) 1948-58, merged co. with Underwood Olivetti; founder, pres. V-N Mfg. Co. (mfr. microwave components) 1949-60; founder, gen. ptnr. Airad Co. (mfr. electronics sheet metal & structures) 1950-59; founder, pres., chmn. Radiatronics Inc. (devel., engr. & mfg. radar antennas & systems) 1959-69, merged with Wittaker Corp.; mgmt. consulting and personal estate mgmt., 1970–, developer comml., indsl. real estate 1970–; founder, pres., chmn. The George E. Hewitt Found. for Med. Research (funds postdoc. research fellows Salk Inst., Scripps Research, UCI), 1980–; bd. trustees Calif. Coll. of Medicine UCI; mem. bd. Center for Health Edn., Meml. Med. Center of Long Beach; mem. Exchange Club (dir.), Rotary, Newport Found., World Affairs Council, Navy League, Am. Defense Preparedness Assn., Internat. Oceanographic Found., Newport Harbor Art Mus., Orange Co. Performing Arts, Hoag 552 Club, Nat. Soc. for Immunology, UCI Med. Research and Ednl. Soc.; clubs: Lido Island Yacht, Balboa Bay. Address: 137 Jasmine Creek Dr Corona Del Mar 92625

HEWITT, ROBERT SPENCER, metallurgical engineer; b. Nov. 9, 1920, Gary, Ind.; s. Jess Sylvester and Lillian Love (Reid) H.; m. Elizabeth, Feb. 16, 1952; children: Ellen Leslie b. 1956, Paul Chandler b. 1960; edn: Colo. Sch. of Mines 1939-41; BS, honors, New Mexico Inst. of Mining and Tech., 1951; Reg. Profl. Engr. (met.) Calif. (1966), Nev. (1980). Career: consulting metallurgical engr.; project engr. for Bechtel Corp., responsible for design of num. domestic and overseas non-ferrous and ferrous mining and processing projects including: Copper Leach Plant for Kennecott, Salt Lake City (1966), Carbon Paste Plant for Reynolds Metals, Longview, Wash. (1967), Copper Concentrator for Palabora Mining Co., S.Africa (1970), Carr Fork Copper Plant for Anaconda, Tooele, Utah (1979), Nev. Molybdemum Plant for Anaconda, Tonepah, Nev. (1982); pre-constrn. engring. design and cost studies for: Homestake copper lead zinc plant, S.Africa (1974), Anaconda copper oxide leach plant, Ariz. (1972), Phelps Dodge copper lead zinc plant, S.Africa (1974); honors: Award of Merit, Bechtel Tech. Information Pgm. (1980); mem. Am. Inst. of Mining, Met. and Petroleum Engrs. (1949-); past pres. Lions Club, Morenci, Az. (1956-57); mil: chief petty ofcr. 3/c USN 1944-46, 15th and 36th Constrn. Batts., Asia-Pacific Theater and Am. Theater campaigns; rec: golf, photog., travel. Res: 2141 Ward Dr Walnut Creek 94596

HEWLETT, WILLIAM REDINGTON, industrialist; b. May 20, 1913, Ann Arbor, Mich.; s. Albion Walter and Louise (Redington) H.; m. Flora Lamson, Aug. 10, 1939, dec. 1977; children: Eleanor Louise b. 1942, Walter Berry b. 1944, James Sterry b. 1947, William Albion b. 1949, Mary Joan b. 1951; m. 2d. Rosemary Kopmeier Bradford, May 24, 1978; edn: BA 1934, E.E. 1939, Stanford Univ.; MS, Mass. Inst. of Tech. 1936; LHD, Johns Hopkins Univ. 1985; Hon. Degrees: LLD, UCB 1966, LLD, Yale Univ. 1976, DSc, Kenyon Coll. 1978, DSc, Polytech. Inst. of NY 1978, Eng.D, Univ. of Notre Dame 1980, Eng.D, Utah State Univ. 1980, Eng.D., Dartmouth Coll. 1983, LLd, Mills Coll. 1983. Career: co-founder/ptnr. Hewlett-Packard Co., Palo Alto 1939-46, dir. 1947-, exec. VP 1947-64, pres. 1964-68, pres./CEO 1969-77, chmn. Exec. Com./ CEO 1977-78, dir./chmn. of Exec. Com. 1978-83, v. chmn. bd. 1983–; dir. Utah International Inc. 1974-85, Chase Manhattan Bank 1969-80; trustee Calif. Acad. of Scis. (Hon.) 1969-; trustee (chmn. bd. trustees 1980-) Carnegie Inst. of Wash. 1971-; awards: Calif. Mfr. of Year 1969, Calif. Mfrs. Assn.; Business Statesman of Year 1970, Harvard Bus. Sch. of No. Calif.; Medal of Achievement, 1971, Western Electronic Mfrs. Assn.; IEEE Founders Medal 1973; Industrialist of Year 1973 (w/ David Packard), Calif. Mus. of Sci. & Indus. 1973; Herbert Hoover Medal, 1977, Stanford Univ. Alumni Assn.; Nat. Medal of Science 1985; mem: Nat. Acad. of Engring. 1965-, Nat. Acad. of Scis. 1977-, Fellow Am. Acad. of Arts & Scis. 1970-, Fellow IEEE (pres. 1954), Instrument Soc. of Am. (hon. life), The Franklin Inst. (life fellow); clubs: Bohemian, Pacific-Union, Menlo Country (Woodside), Century Assn. (NYC); coauthor sev. tech. arts.; holds patents on R.C. Oscillators and other electronic devices; mil: lt. col. US Army Signal Corps WWII 1942-45, Army Commendn.; Republican; Presbyterian; rec: ski, golf, photog. Ofc: Hewlett-Packard Co. 1501 Page Mill Rd Palo Alto 94304

HEYMAN, IRA MICHAEL, chancellor UC Berkeley; b. May 30, 1930, NYC; s. Harold Albert and Judith (Sobel) H.; m. Therese, Dec. 17, 1950; children: Stephen Thomas b. 1961, James Nathaniel b. 1963; edn: AB in govt. Dartmouth Coll. 1951; JD, Yale Law Sch. 1956; admitted State Bar of NY 1956, State Bar of Calif. 1961. Career: legislative asst. Sen. Irving M. Ives, Wash DC 1950-51; atty. assoc. Carter, Ledyard and Milburn, NYC 1956-57; law clerk Chief Judge

Charles E. Clark, Ct. of Appeals (2d Circuit) New Haven, CT 1957-58; chief law clerk Chief Justice Earl Warren, US Supreme Ct. 1958-59; acting assoc. prof. law, UC Berkeley 1959-61, prof. of law 1961-, prof. City and Regional Planning 1966-, vice chancellor 1974-80, chancellor UC Berkeley, 1980-; vis. prof. of law Yale Law Sch. 1963-64, Stanford Law Sch. 1971-72; num. govtl. consultantships 1964-; honors: LLD, Univ. of the Pacific 1981, DHL, The Hebrew Union Coll. 1984; mem: bd. trustees Lawyers Com. for Civil Rights under Law (1977-); bd. trustees Dartmouth Coll. (1982-), bd. dirs. (advis. mem.) Pacific, Gas and Elec. Co. (1983-), bd. dirs. Am. Council on Edn. (1984-86), Nat. Assn. of State Univs. and Land-Grant Colls. (pres. elect 1985-6), Pacific 10 Conf. (pres. Presidents' and Chancellors' 1984-5); past mem: US Commn. on Civil Rights (sec. Calif. Adv. Com. 1962-7), Oakland Inter-Agcy. Project (resrch. adv. com. 1964-5), State-wide UC Academic Assembly (chmn. 1972-3, chmn. UCB 1965-7), City of Berkeley Human Rels. & Welfare Commn. (chmn. 1966-8), Pres.'s Commn. on Violence (counsel 1968-9), Public Land Law Rev. Commn. 1968-70, Commn. on Isla Vista, UC Santa Barbara 1970; spl. arbitrator Ahtna v. Alyeska Pipeline Co. (1974-5, 79-80); publs: num. in areas of civil rights, constnl. law, land plng., metropolitan govt., housing, environmental law and mgmt., affirmative action; Democrat. Res: 2400 Hearst Ave Berkeley 94709 Office of the Chancellor UCB, 200 California Hall, Berkeley 94720

HIBERT, CHARLES LOUIS, metallurgist; b. Nov. 22, 1908, Latrobe, Pa.; s. Charles and Helena (Dorn) H.; m. Margaret Schenck, Aug. 23, 1930; children: Shirley b. 1934, Charles b. 1935; edn: metallurg., Univ. of Detroit, 1928, 1932; Reg. Profl. Metallurg. Engr. (No. 589), Calif. 1966. Career: test engr. US Air Corps, Wright Field, Dayton, Ohio 1932-35; Convair Div. of Gen. Dynamics 1935-70: supr. Heat Treat & Welding 1935-41, welding engr. Prodn. Engring. Dept. 1941-43, coord. mfg. problems for 13 divs. of Convair 1942-44, div. process engr./mgmt. 1944-52, process control supvr. Quality Control Dept. 1952-54, senior design engr. Productivity Group 1954-69; introduced spot welding of aluminum alloy at Convair (1935), introduced silver brazing, copper brazing, inert gas arc-welding, metal stitching at Convair; instr. San Diego Vocational Night Sch. (metallurgy) during WWII, num. in-plant shop tng. tech. lectures, lectr. San Diego State Coll.; mem. Am. Soc. for Metals (founder S.D. chpt. 1941, past chmn., pgm. chmn., life mem.), Soc. Am. Value Engrs., Am. Soc. for Quality Control (founder San Bernardino Sect.), Am. Welding Soc. (Handbook Com., Com. on Brazing and Soldering), served on sev. War Time Coms. on Welding and Brazing; rec: woodworking, collect early glass. Res: 10021 Sierra Madre Spring Valley 92077

HICK, KEN W., manufacturing company president; b. Oct. 17, 1946, New Westminister, B.C., Canada; s. Les W. and Mary I. (Warner) H.; 1 son, David W., b. 1969; edn: BA, E. Washington St. Coll. 1971; MBA, Univ. of Wash. 1973, PhD, 1978. Career: regional mgr. Hilti Inc., Stamford, Conn. 1975-79; gen. mgr. Moore Internat., Portland, Ore. 1979-80; v.p. sales/mktg. Phillips Inc., Anaheim, Ca. 1980; owner/pres./CEO KC Metal Products Inc., San Jose 1981-; mem. Bd. of Fellows Univ. of Santa Clara; mem. Am. Inst. of Timber Constructors, Nat. Assn. of Business Economists, Am. Mgmt. Assn.; mil: s/sgt. USAF 1963-66, Commendn. Medal; num. arts. in business journals; Republican; Catholic; rec: aviation/ pilot. Res: 2130 Hidden Oaks Danville 94569 San Jose Ofc: KC Metal Products Inc. 1960 Hartog Dr San Jose 95131

HICKERNELL, PHILLIP JAMES, concrete ready mix supply co. president; b. Jan. 13, 1960, Taft; s. Harry James and Glenda Lee (Heaps) H.; edn: AA, Taft Coll. 1981; bus. adm., CSU Bakersfield 1981-82. Career: var. pos. in local cement cos., 1978-85; founding ptnr. with brother Chris, plant mgr./v.p. Southwest Ready Mix, Taft 1985-; mem: Am. Concrete Inst., Nat. Fedn. Indep. Businesses, Taft CofC, Elks; Republican; United Methodist; rec: skiing, boating. Ofc: Southwest Ready Mix, Hwy 33 Taft 93268

HICKERSON, ANN SPENCER, company executive; b. Dec. 15, 1946, Columbia, Mo.; d. Samuel M. and Juanita Jean (Jones) Spencer; m. Joseph Hickerson, Aug. 24, 1968; edn: BA, Sacto. State Univ. 1969. Career: mgr. Marin County CHlif 1978; founder, v.p., CFO Northern Communications, Petaluma 1978-83; acctg. mgr. Calif. Div., Standard Telecom, Petaluma 1984; secty. CFO Sun Telecommuns. Inc., Petaluma 1984-; mem: Calif. Interconnect Assn.; Alpha Xi Delta Alumnae; Am. Assn. of Univ. Women; Am. Assn. of Bus. Women; Sportswoman Assn. of USA; Republican; Methodist; rec: tennis, travel, gardening. Res: 99 Center Rd., Petaluma 94952 Ofc: Sun Telecommunications, Inc., 201 Petaluma Way, Petaluma 94952

HICKIE, MELVIN RUSSELL, public relations agency owner; b. Nov. 30, 1949, Centerville, Iowa; s. John Russell and Mae Leona (Bennett) H.; m. Ruth Jackson, Sept. 1, 1972; 1 son, Brandon Jackson; edn: BA hist., Univ. Northeast Mo. 1972. Career: western div. mgr. Vance Publishing Co. Kansas City, Mo. 1972-78; pres. El Libro Verde La Canada, Calif. 1978-80; advt. mgr. Western Growers Assoc. Newport Beach 1980-84; owner Hickie, Ag Mktg. Svcs. Huntington Beach 1984-; honors: awards from Nat. Agra Mktg. Assn. West 1982, 83, 85; mem: NAMA West, Calif. Seed Assn., Soc. for Preservation of Vaudvcllc, Orange Apple Computer Club; author: El Libro Verde, Dict. to Agriculture in Mexico (Sp. and Eng.), num. smaller works and contbns. to consumer and profl. press; Republican; Methodist (church choir). Ofc: Hickie, Ag Marketing Services 20171 Inperial Cove Huntington Beach 92646

HICKMAN-MANOR, KIMBERLY KAY, veterinarian; b. July 23, 1956, Des Moines, Iowa; d. Charles Robert and Marcia Delores (Butcher) Hichman; m. Craig A. Manor, Dec. 7, 1984; 1 son, Nathan Allen b. 1985; edn: DVM, Iowa State Univ. 1981. Career: intern Tamarack Animal Hosp., Fort Lauderdale, Fla.

1980-81; assoc. veterinarian Bear Valley Animal Hosp., Big Bear Lake 1981-82; veterinarian, owner Bear City Animal Hosp., Big Bear City 1982-; awards: Scholarship, Iowa State Univ. Coll. of Vet. Med. (1979); mem: Am. Vet. Med. Assn., Orange Belt Vet. Med. Assn.; civic: youth vol., Big Bear Lake Sch. system in career modeling activities; Republican; rec: aerobic instr., bicycling, stitchery crafts. Res: 698 Menlo Big Bear Lake 92315 Ofc: Bear City Animal Hospital, 121 E Big Bear Blvd, POB 499, Big Bear City 92314

HICKS, THEODORE JOHN, corporation president; b. Apr. 1, 1939, Omaha, Neb.; s. Theodore C. and Antoinette J. (Kay) H.; edn: BA, Stanford Univ. 1961, MA, 1964. Career: Lester, Ryons & Co., Stockbrokers 1965-66; pres. Gramercy Escrow Corp. L.A. 1967-; dir. escrow Agents Fidelity Corp.; chmn. Republican Party of Los Angeles County 1983-84; mem. Electoral Coll. 1984; mem. exec. com. Republican Party of Calif.; mem: Republican Urban Counties Republican Chmn.'s Assn. of the US, Optimist Club of L.A. (past v.p.); Episcopal; rec: sailing, skiing, travel, politics. Ofc: Gramercy Escrow Corp. 3407 W 6th St Ste 711 Los Angeles 90020

HIGBEE, DONALD WILLIAM, electronics co. executive, lawyer; b. Jan. 7, 1931, Stonewall, Okla.; s. James Wm. and Nannie May (Driver) H.; m. Joan Diamond; children: Bradley b. 1954, Carter b. 1957, Phillip b. 1960, Lisa b. 1961; edn: AB cum laude, USC 1956; JD, USC 1962; admitted Calif. State Bar 1963. Career: acct. Pacific Press, Los Angeles 1956-60; controller Interstate Electronics Corp., Anaheim 1960-63; secty./treas. Utah R & D Corp., Salt Lake City 1964; dir. of contracts Interstate Electronics Corp., Anaheim 1965-74, dir. 1971-, v.p., secty. 1974-; dir. Silverado Water Dist. 1965-70, dir. Silverado- Modjeska Rec. & Park Dist. 1965-70; mem: State Bar Assn., Orange County Bar Assn., Nat. Contract Mgmt. Assn., Nat. Assn. of Accts. 1960-64, Machinery & Allied Prods. Inst., Nat. Security Indsl. Assn.; civic: VFW, Moose, Masons; mil: US Army 1946-48, US Marince Corps 1950-51, Purple Heart; Republican; Prot.; rec: gardening, computers, tennis, golf. Res: 3502 Cazador Ln Fallbrook 92028 Ofc: Interstate Electronics Corp 1001 E Ball Rd POB 3117 Anaheim 92803

HIGBIE, MICHELLE FARESHETIAN, accountant; b. Feb. 5, 1955, Los Angeles; d. Arthur J. and Helen (Pion) Fareshetian; m. Gerald Walter Higbie, Nov. 25, 1978; edn: BA in bus. adm., CSU Fullerton 1977. Career: sr. auditor Arthur Andersen & Co., Los Angeles 1977-81; dir. acctg. Flying Tiger Lines, Inc. 1981-83; project controller, then v.p./asst. treas. First City Industries Inc., Beverly Hills 1983-85; co-owner Higbie Sound Co., Long Beach 1985-; asst. treas. Bren Investment Props., Los Angeles 1985-; civic: Island Village Homeowners Assn. (dir.); Republican; Catholic; rec: music. Res: 7045 Seawind Dr Long Beach 90803 Ofc: Bren Investment Properties 11111 Santa Monica Blvd 20th Flr Los Angeles 90025

HIGGINS, STEPHEN DANIEL, physician; b. April 24, 1947, Huntington Park; s. Sam Lamar and Betty May (Briggs) H.; m. Margaret, Dec. 21, 1969; children: Samantha Leigh, b. 1973, Andrew Michael, b. 1977; edn: BA, USC 1970, MD, 1974. Career: research asst. Human Design Ctr., Rancho Los Amigos Hosp., Downey 1968-69; family plnng. physician Long Beach Commn. on Econ. Opportunities, Long Beach 1976; emerg. physician Downey Community Hosp., Downey 1976-77; hosp. physician Inglewood Hosp., Inglewood 1977-78; paramedic liaison physician St. Francis Med. Ctr., Lynwood 1980-82, med. dir. emerg. med. 1982-; asst. clin. prof. ob.-gyn. Harbor-UCLA Med. Ctr.; med. dir. Suspected Child Abuse & Neglect Com., St. Francis Med. Ctr.; mem: AMA, CMA, Los Angeles Co. Med. Assn.; Fellow Am. Coll. Emerg. Physicians; Am. Coll. Ob.-Gyn.; Am. Assn. for Hist. of Med.; publs: Caring for the Injured Pregnant Patient, Contemporary Ob-Gyn. 1983; Late Abruptio Placenta in Trauma Patients: Implications for Fetal Monitoring, Ob-Gyn. 1984; Essentials of Fluid Resuscitation & Blood Transfusion, Cont. Ob-Gyn. 1984; Protestant; rec: bicycling, swimming, hiking. Res: 5020 Rolling Meadows Rd., Rolling HillsEs 90274 Ofc: St. Francis Medical Ctr., 3630 E. Imperial Hwy., Lynwood 90262

HIGGINS, SUSAN OLSON, publisher; b. Dec. 23, 1946, Janesville, Wis.; d. Robert Philip Olson and Dorothy Jane (Foster) Williams; m. Daniel John Higgins, Nov. 29, 1969; children: Peter b. 1978, Joshua b. 1979; edn: BS in edn., Univ. Wis. 1971; Tchr. credential, 1972. Career: tchr. 1972, dev. splst. Univ. Wis. R&D Ctr., Madison 1972-74, reading cons. 1975-76, tchr. in one-room schoolhouse 1978-80, tchr. 1979-82; owner/adminstr./tchr. Educational Co-op (pvt. sch.), 1984-; owner/pub. Pumpkin Press Pub. House, 1984-; author: The Pumpkin Book (1983), The Thanksgiving Book (1984), The Bunny Book (1985), coauthor: Pre-Reading Skills Bilingual Supplement; mem. AAUW (1981-83), Nat. Reading Assn.; civic: PTA (pres.), Newcomers, Shasta Wildlife Rescue Ctr., Performing Arts Soc., Shasta Art Soc., Alpha Sigma Alumni Assn.; Congregational; rec: rafting, canoeing, skiing, travel. Ofc: POB 139 Shasta 96087

HIGGINS, THOMAS EDWARD, business valuation co. president; b. May 11, 1939, Hollywood, Calif.; s. John S. and Vera E. (McGrath) H.; 1 son, March Charles b. 1962; edn: BS, USC 1965, MBA, Pepperdine Univ. 1976; desig: ASA (senior mem. Am. Soc. Appraisers). Career: v.p., portfolio mgr. Los Angeles 1965-75; v.p. Valuation Research (nat. valuation orgn.), L.A. 1975-80; pres./CEO Higgins, Marcus & Lovett, Inc. (bus. valuation and asset analysis), L.A. 1980-; faculty Graduate Bus. Sch., Pepperdine Univ. 1976-; frequent speaker var. orgns. on Valuation of Closely-held business; mem: LA Soc. of Finl. Analysts, Western Pension Conf., Am. Arbitration Assn. (Comml. Panel of Arbs.); civic: Jonathan Club (pres. 1983), Rotary (LA 5), Republican Assocs., Pepperdine Assocs. (founding), Toastmasters Internat. (past area Gov.), United

Way, Citizens Task Force Juvenile Crime; mil: 1st lt. US Army; Republican; Catholic; rec: sailing, ski, photog. Ofc: Higgins, Marcus & Lovett Inc 800 S Figueroa St Ste 890 Los Angeles 90017

HIGHBERGER, WILLIAM FOSTER, lawyer; b. May 15, 1950, Suffern, NY; s. John Kistler and Helen Stewart (Foster) H.; m. Carolyn Barbara Kuhl, July 12, 1980; edn: AB, Princeton Univ. 1972; JD, Columbia Law Sch. 1975; admitted bars: Calif. (1976), Dist. Col. (1981), NY (1984), US Supreme Ct., US Cts. of Appeals (2d, 3d, 9th, and DC circuits), US Dist. Cts. (So. Dist. NY, So. Dist. Calif., Central Dist. Calif., East Dist. Calif. and D.C.). Career: law clerk Hon. Wm. H. Timbers, US Circuit Judge for US Ct. of Appeals (2d Circuit 1975-76; assoc. Gibson, Dunn & Crutcher, Los Angeles and Wash. DC 1976-82, ptr. 1983–; spkr. var. continuing edn. pgms. re labor, pension and equal employment opportunity; honors: James Kent Scholar, Columbia Law Sch.; Notes & Comments ed. Columbia Law Rev.; mem: Am. (Labor & Litigation Sects.), Indsl. Rels. Research Assn., Am. Judicature Assn., Princeton Club of NY, Nat. Trust for Historic Preservation, The Nature Conservancy; co-author: Labor Law Aspects of High-Tech Real Estate, High-Tech Real Estate, Dow-Jones Irwin 1985; Republican; Presbyterian; rec: skiing, architecture. Res: 11688 Picturesque Dr. Studio City 91604 Ofc: Gibson, Dunn & Crutcher, 333 So. Grand Ave. 49th Flr. Los Angeles 90071; 1050 Connecticut Ave. NW, Wash. DC 20036

HIGHTOWER, JAMES REID, engineer; b. Apr. 26, 1927, Benton, Ark.; s. John Rush and Ruby Belle (Adams) H.; m. Barbara Franck, July 5, 1982; children: Rebecca b. 1951, Barker b. 1954, Liza b. 1959; edn: BSME, Univ. New Mex. 1954; Reg. Profl. Engr. Calif. 1963. Career: proj. control engr. Honeywell Inc., San Francisco 1954-55; chief engr. Gen. Nailing Machine Corp., Sanger, Calif. 1955-59; plant engr. Sun-Maid Growers of Calif., Kingsburg 1959-69; chief engr. SWF Machinery Inc., Sanger 1969-76, dir. engrg. & mfg. 1976-81, senior v.p. 1981–; instr./ lectr. in engrg., Fresno City Coll. 1963-68; cons. engr. Teneco Inc., Indio, Calif. 1971; honors: Pi Tau Sigma (1952), Sigma Tau (1954); mem: Nat. Soc. Profl. Engrs., Calif. Soc. Profl. Engrs., Elks, E. Clampus Vitus, Westerners Internat., Fresno City & County Hist. Soc.; inventor high-speed variable-height case sealing machine for produce industry 1974; mil: s 1/c USN WWII; Republican; Protestant; rec: golf, fishing, gardening. Res: 413 S Arroyo Fresno 93727 Ofc: SWF Machinery Inc., 1324 Academy Ave Sanger 93657

HIGHTOWER, TROY DANIEL, aerospace computer software consultant; b. Sept. 23, 1957, Los Angeles; s. Rudolph L. and Maryilyn N. (Townes) H.; edn: elec. engring. courses Norfolk State Coll. 1975-76, computer pgmmg. Bakersfield Coll. 1979-82, pilot tng. Air Center Internat. 1984–; FAA lic. comml. pilot. Career: pos. with var. airlines incl. USAir and Aspen Airways, 1977-84; current: indep. software designer for aerospace applications for num. aviation and oil cos.; bd. chmn./pres. and dir. space technology and aeronautical research, Troy D. Hightower & Assocs., Bakersfield 1982-; founder/gen. ptnr. Airtrans (transport leasing co.); recipient Pilot Proficiency Award (1982); mem: Am. Soc. of Aerospace Pilots, Am. Inst. of Aero. and Astro., Am. Mgmt. Assn.; civic: Calif. Museum Found., Nat. Audubon Soc., National Travel Club, Digital Equip. Corp. Users Soc., The Smithsonian Assocs.; Baptist; rec: swimming, skiing, lacrosse, the Space Pgm. Ofc: Ming Ave Ste E Bakersfield 93309

HILADO, ROLANDO VILLARICO, instrument engineer; b. April 19, 1941, Bacolod City, Philippines; s. Aurelio Abogado and Aurora Poa (Villarico) Hilado; m. Pilar Illenberger, Sept. 5, 1970; 2 daus: Joy b. 1974, Cathy b. 1978; edn: grad. Negros Occidental H.S. 1957, prep. engring. Univ. of Negros Occidental-Recoletos, 1960; BS ChE, Mapua Inst. of Tech. 1964; MS ChE, Univ. So. Calif. 1977; Reg. Profl. Engr. (chemical & control systems), Calif. Career: instrument engr. Procon Inc., El Monte, Calif. 1977-80; project instrument engr. Norman Engineering, Los Angeles 1980-81; senior instrument engr. C.F. Braun & Co., Alhambra 1981-85; senior instrument engr. Ultrasystems, Inc. Irvine 1985–; mem: Instrument Soc. of Am.; patentee: Container with Cooling Capability (1984); developed new theory in structural mechs. (1980), devel. new concept and formula pertaining to application of Hooke's Law; contbr. sci. publs.; article: Space Velocity Determination of Point Emission Source (generalized form of Doppler's equation and mathematical formulas for locating the birthplace of the universal "Big-Bang"). Res: 2725 Pam Place West Covina 91792 Ofc: Ultrasystems, Inc., 16845 Von Karman Ave Irvine 92714

HILBE, JAMES D., investment advisor; b. Dec. 4, 1945, Santa Monica; s. James J. and Betty J. (Dow) H.; m. Betsey A. Walker, June 17, 1967; children: Laura b. 1968, Diana b. 1969, Janet b. 1970; edn: BA, and MBA, CSU Long Beach 1967, 1970; desig: CFP, Coll. for Finl. Planning, 1984. Career: corporate acct. Pacific Lighting Corp., Los Angeles 1973-75; mgr. finl. plnng. Carter Hawley Hale, L.A. 1975-79; asst. controller Aerojet Electrosystems, Azusa 1979-81; controller Monogram Aerospace, L.A. 1981; bd. chmn./CEO J.D. Hilbe & Co., Inc. 1982–; mem: Internat. Assn. for Finl. Plnng., Inst. of Cert. Finl. Plnnrs., Rotary Internat., Ontario CofC; Republican; Conservative Baptist; rec: pvt. pilot, tennis, art collector. Ofc: J.D. Hilbe & Co. 2151 East D St Ste 220-C Ontario 91764

HILDENBRAND, LAURENCE ALFRED, engineering/ managerial consultant; b. June 12, 1953, Portland, Ore.; s. Grover Loren and Martha Janet (Pottage) H.; m. Carolyn, Apr. 8, 1978; 1 son, Brian b. 1975; edn: BS engrg., San Jose State Univ. 1977. Career: systems analyst Gen. Elec. Co., San Jose 1973-77; sr. mfg. engr. IBM Corp. 1977-80; staff engr. GCA Corp., Sunnyvale 1980-81; software engr. mgr. Identronix Inc., Santa Cruz 1981-83; cons. prin./

pres. Foxfire Systems Corp., Scotts Valley 1983–; mem. IEEE, ACM, PATCA; Republican; Episcopal; rec: flying (comml. pilot). Ofc: Foxfire Systems Corp. POB 66168 Scott Valley 95066

HILGER, FREDERICK LEE, JR., bank president, lawyer; b. Feb. 17, 1946, Dallas; s. Frederick, Sr. and Maryann Taylor (Ayers) H.; m. Terri Lynn, May 13, 1984; 1 son, Matthew b. 1985; edn: BA, Univ. of Pacific 1967; JD, UC Berkeley 1970; admitted Calif. bar 1971. Career: staff CPA, Touche Ross & Co., San Francisco 1971-73; pres. Hilger Assocs. Ltd. in Eureka and Seattle, Wash. 1973-78; senior cons. Sites & Co., Seattle 1978-79; v.p. ops. U.S. Cruises Inc., Seattle 1980-82; chief finl. ofcr./pres. First National Bank, Chico 1982–; recipient ABA Outstanding Banker Award (1985); mem. Am. Bar Assn., Am. Mgmt. Assn.; clubs: Olympic, Riverview Golf & CC, Butte Creek CC; Presbyterian; rec: golf. Ofc: First National Bank POB 496 Chico 95927

HILL, HARRY DAVID, personnel management executive; b. Oct. 29, 1944, Whittier; s. Harry Boreman and Winifred Nell (Purvis) H.; m. Linda Price, Nov. 8, 1969; 1 son, Jon, b. 1979; edn: BA in pol. sci., UCLA 1966; MPA, Univ. of So. Calif. 1972. Career: personnel splst. City of Anaheim, 1966-67, personnel analyst 1967-71, senior staff asst. 1971-73, sr. personnel analyst 1973-76, personnel services mgr. 1976-83, asst. dir. Human Resources, City of Anaheim, 1983–; dir. So. Calif. Public Labor Relations Council 1981-; mem: Internat. Personnel Mgmt. Assn. W. Region (pres. 1983-84); So. Calif. Personnel Mgmt. Assn. (pres. 1978-79); mil: sp5 US Army Reserve 1966-72; Democrat; Prot.; rec: hiking, backpacking. Res: 551 So Reynolds Pl Anaheim 92806 Ofc: City of Anaheim, 200 So Anaheim Blvd Ste 332 Anaheim 92805

HILL, LAURINE JONES, teacher, ret.; b. Mar. 28, 1922, Spokane, Wash.; d. John Newton and Aldena Mary (Foumal) Jones; m. Elmer Clair Hill, Sept. 12, 1942; children: Gary Lee b. 1946, James Newton b. 1956; edn: BA, Holy Names Coll. 1964; grad. study edn., MoreFolkehojskole Oresta, Norway 1971, New Experimental Coll. Norden Fjord, World Univ., Snedsted, Denmark 1971, Univ. Heidelburg, Germany 1971; lifetime tchg. credl. 1971. Career: tchr. Oakland Public Schs. 1964-83 (ret.); mem: Calif. Tchrs. Assn. 1964-83, Oakland Edn. Assn. 1964-83, Calif. Retired Tchrs. Assn., Alpha Delta Kappa (chpt. pres. 1982, historian 1986), Children's Hosp. of East Bay, Holy Names Coll. Alumni Assn., Shrine; Republican; Christian; rec: gardening, travel, boating, reading, music. Res: 335 Deerfield Dr Moraga 94556

HILL, LELAND R., real estate appraiser, company owner; b. May 16, 1956, Santa Monica, Calif.; s. Leland R. and Phyllis Marie (Aydt) H.; m. Diane Carol, Aug. 25, 1984; 1 dau. Jessica LeAnne b. 1986; edn: BS acctg., real estate finance CSU Long Beach 1980; Certified Review Appraiser, Nat. Assn. Review Appraisers 1984. Career: staff appraiser Paul Jackle & Assocs. Huntington Beach 1980-81; senior appraiser Real Estate Appraisal Co. Newport Beach 1982-83; v.p. Real Estate Svcs. Huntington Beach 1983-84; owner Assoc. Appraisers of Am. 1984–; mem: Soc. Real Estate Appraisers, Nat. Assn. Review Appraisers (senior); Republican; Lutheran; rec: snow and water skiing, surfing. Ofc: Assoc. Appraisers of America 18652 Florida St Ste 200 Huntington Beach 92648

HILL, LESLIE CLYDE, insulation contractor; b. Aug. 9, 1934, Bell; s. Noble Clyde and Leona Pearl (Franks) H.; m. Gilda, Nov. 27, 1977; edn: Mt. San Antonio Coll. 1956-59. Career: pres./bd. chmn. Schmid Insulation Contractors, Inc.; pres. The Hill Cos., Inc.; bd. dirs. The Bank of Rancho Bernardo (San Diego); co-chmn. San Diego County Energy Conservation Orgn.; mem: Insulation Contrs. Assn. of Am. (bd. dirs., 1st v.p. 1978-80); club: The Golden Eagle (S.D.), De Anza Desert Country (Borrego Springs); mil: cpl. Army Security Agcy. 1952-55; rec: golf. Res: 230 W Laurel St #604 San Diego 92101 Ofc: The Hill Cos., Inc. 4555 Mission Gorge Pl San Diego 92120

HILL, LORIE ELIZABETH, psychotherapist; b. Oct. 21, 1946, Buffalo, NY; d. Graham and Elizabeth Helen (Salm) H.; edn: Univ. of Manchester, Eng. 1966-67; BA, Grinnell Coll. 1968; MA, Univ. Wisc. 1970; MA, CSU Sonoma 1974; PhD, Wright Inst. 1980. Career: English instr. Univ. of Mo. 1970-71; therapist trainee Valley Children & Youth, Pleasanton 1975-76; adminstr./ supvr. Antioch- West & Ctr. for Ind. Living, San Francisco & Berkeley 1975-77; dir. of tng. Ctr. for Edn. & Mental Health, S.F. 1977-80; exec. dir. 1980-81; instr. MA pgm. in psychol. John F. Kennedy Univ., Orinda 1981; psychotherapist, pvt. practice, Berkeley 1981-83, Oakland 1983–; organizer against nuclear war; found. mem. Psychotherapists for Soc. Responsibility; spkr. non- sexist psychology; mem: Nat. Abortion Rights Action League; Sane (Anti- nuclear orgn.); Nat. Orgn. Women; Demo. Socialist; Rainbow Coalition for Jesse Jackson's Pres. Campaign; Ron Dellum Reelection Com.; rec: sports, travel. Res: 310 Westline Dr, B302, Alameda 94501 Ofc: 312 Hudson St Oakland 94618

HILL, LOWELL STANLEY, designer, business owner; b. Feb. 5, 1934, Fort Sheridan, Ill.; s. Jack and Velma Opal (Borton) H.; m. Barbara Matilde Suarez, Nov. 9, 1957; children: Lowell b. 1958, Velma b. 1959, Barbara b. 1961, Sandra b. 1962, Stanley b. 1964; edn: Univ. of Mo. 1953-56; Chaffey Coll. 1959; AA, Mt. San Antonio Coll. 1962, tchrs. credential 1967. Career: illustrator US Army, Ft. Leonard Wood, No. 1953-56; mgr. Stout Sign Co., Long Beach 1957-58; lead man Circuit Bd. Div. Gen. Dynamics, Pomona 1959-63; tech. advr./ store mgr. E.W. Dorn Co., Gardena 1963-70; tchr. los Angeles Trade Tech. Coll., L.A. 1966-68; owner/ designer/ cons. Lowell S. Hill Enterprises, Ontario 1970–; guest spkr.: Cal Poly Univ., Pomona; Mt. San Antonio Coll., Walnut; Foundation Sch., Montebello; moderator and featured spkr. Screen Printing Internat. Convention, L.A. 1984; guest technical trainee Zurich Bolting Mfg. Co., Switz. 1975; honors: Hon. Chief, Nez Perce Nation 1970; mem: Screen Printing Internat.; Nat. Small Bus. Assn.; Calif. Assn. Independent Bus.; US CofC; Trade Adv. Com., L.A. Trade Tech. Coll.; Am. Indian Week (v.p 1968-); Boy Scouts of Am. (ldr. 1972-75); research: European methods as applied to design, mfg. of screen printing rel. prods.; original designs of metal frames; imported the first Harlacher screen stretcher from Switz. into USA, 1980; mil: sgt. E-5 AUS 1953-56, mem. Champion Pistol Team 1955; Republican; Catholic; rec: target shooting, hunting, archery. Res: 775 W 24th St Upland 91786 Ofc: Lowell S. Hill Enterprises, 5416 Mission Blvd Ontario 91762

HILL, RAY THOMAS, JR., import-export co. president; b. Dec. 4, 1926, Norfolk, Va.; s. Ray T. and Mary Eula (Benton) H.; m. Geraldine Stamos, Sept. 15, 1945; children: John b. 1947, Gary b. 1948, Ray, III b. 1951, Mark b. 1959; edn: bus./fin., Lee Coll. 1942-43. Career: sales rep. Royal Typewriter Corp., 1945-47; dist. mgr. Best Foods Corp. 1948-55; dist. mgr. S.W. USA, Internat. Latex Corp. (Playtex) 1956-59; regl. mgr. in S.W. and N.W. USA, Kayser-Roth Corp. (now Gulf & Western Corp.) 1959-72; regl. mgr. No. Calif. and Hawaii, Wayne Gossard Corp., 1972-76; founder/pres./CEO Hill-Umbach-Golematis, 1976-; bd. dirs. Grand Canyon State Travelers Assn. 1963-64; awards: Salesman of Year- USA, Internat. Latex Corp. (1958), Top Salesman of Year- USA, Kayser-Roth Corp. (1961, 62, 63, 64); mem. Nat. Rifle Assn. (life), Calif. Rifle & Pistol Assn. Inc.; inventor: two sight rests for long guns and handguns; Democrat; Lutheran; rec: hunting (took world record javelina- 64 lb., in Ariz., 1963), camping Address: H.U.G. Co. PO Box 1287 Alameda 94501

HILL, THELMA M., promotion and sales consultant, diet products distributor; b. Oct. 3, 1916, Ruleville, Miss.; s. Thomas and Eliza (Smith) H.; div.; 1 son, Lonnie C. Clark, III b. 1946; edn: Lewis Inst., Chgo 1935-37; spl. courses, Midwestern Bdcstg. Sch., Univ. Chgo. Career: bookkeeping clk., US Treasury Dept., Wash DC; research asst./statistician, Study of Negro Life in Chgo. (used in book, Black Metropolis); sales mgr., columnist Chicago Defender newspaper, and Conte-Cal mag.; consumer cons. Pet Mil Co.; host/ announcer Mary Therese Radio Show, Sta. KGFJ; owner cosmetics co. mfr./ distbr. Mary Therese Cosmetics; library clk. Tidewater Oil Co., Los Angeles; current: splst. in mktg. and sales tng. for reaching black pop. in metropolitan areas; indep. distbr. Cernitin Flower Pollen Products; awards: appreciation, Am. Cancer Soc., Cosmopolitan CofC; civic: Pasadena Lung Assn., Amvets, Hilton LXV 65 Club, Urban League, NAACP; Democrat; Seventh-day Adventist; rec: travel. Res: 415 E Poppyfields Dr Altadena 91001

HILLIS, MICHAEL SCOTT, company owner; b. Sept. 28, 1958, Chattanooga, Ten.; s. Ronald Agger and Vera Jennille (Yates) H.; m. Pamela Marie, July 12, 1980; 1 son, Michael Scott, Jr. Career: sales Factory Carpet House Chattanooga, Tenn. 1975-77; parts dept. mgr. Milo Equip. Corp. Santa Ana 1977-80; ptnr. Pacific Carpets Huntington Beach 1980-83; owner Universal Carpets Santa Ana 1983-; honors: Most Charitable Donations (Active 20/30 Club 1985); Republican; Baptist; rec: horseback riding, desert racing, ocean jet skiing. Res: 2884 El Rio Costa Mesa 92626 Ofc: Universal Carpets 3100 W Harvard Ste 3 Santa Ana 92704

HILLMAN, AARON WADDELL, educator, consultant, editor/ publisher, artist, writer, poet; b. Sept. 29, 1926, Chaffee, Mo.; s. Basil Emory and Erthel Dora (Pearman) H.; m. Rosemary Witherow, Aug. 6, 1953; edn: BA, San Francisco State Univ. 1960; ME, UC Santa Barbara 1973, PhD, 1973. Career: ednl. cons. self-empl. 1965-; tchr. Santa Maria H.S., Santa Maria 1965-68, Dos Pueblos H.S., Goleta 1968-; pres. Cedarc Inc., Santa Barbara 1974-80, secty. treas. 1981-84; pres. Bibliotherapy Inc., Santa Barbara 1981-86; publr./ ed: The Confluent Education Journal, The Santa Barbara Book Review 1986-; mil: warrant ofcr. US Army 1945-65; author: (plays) The Swagger Stick and others; (books) Concepts and Elements of Confluent Edn. and others; poetry; The Golden Rule Funeral Association and others; rec: writing, music, walking. Res: 833 Via Granada Santa Barbara 93103 Ofc: The Santa Barbara Book Review, 30 W. Calle Laureles Ste. 3 Santa Barbara 93105

HILLSBERG, SANFORD JAY, lawyer; b. June 20, 1948, NY, NY; s. Herbert and Madeline (Freedman) H.; m. Laurie, Nov. 1, 1975; edn: BA, summa cum laude, Univ. of Penna. 1970; JD, cum laude, Harvard Law Sch. 1973. Career: atty. assoc. Nossaman Krueger & Marsh, 1973-76; atty. Troy & Casden, Los Angeles 1976-, mng. ptnr. 1979-, spec. in corporate and securities law; honors: Phi Beta Kappa; mem. Am. Bar Assn.; club: Riviera Country; Republican; Jewish (Reform); rec: stockmarket, tennis. Res: 10355 Lorenzo Dr Los Angeles 90064 Ofc: Troy & Casden, 1801 Century Park East Los Angeles 90064

HILTON, WILLIAM BARRON, hotel executive; b. Oct. 23, 1927, Dallas, Tx.; s. Conrad Nicholson and Mary Barron H.; m. Marilyn June Hawley, Chgo., June 20, 1947; children: William Barron, Jr., b. 1948, Hawley Anne, b. 1949, Stephen Michael, b. 1950, David Alan, b. 1952, Sharon Constance, b. 1953, Richard Howard, b. 1955, Daniel Kevin, b. 1962, Ronald Jeffrey, b. 1963. Career: founder, gen. partner Vita-Pakt Citrus Products Co., 1946; vice pres./ dir. Hilton Hotels Corp., 1954-66, pres./CEO, chmn./ pres./ CEO 1979-; pres. San Diego Chargers Ltd., 1961-66; pres. Am. Football League, 1965; dir. Mfrs. Hanover Trust Co. (1970-), dir. Conrad N. Hilton Found.; trustee City of Hope; honors: Hon. Dr. of Humane Letters, Univ. of Houston (1986), Hotel Man of Year, Penn State Univ. (1969); mem: LA World Affairs Council, Chevalier Confrerie de la Chaine des Rotisseurs, Magistral Knights Sovereign Mil. Order

of Malta; clubs: Bel Air CC, Los Angeles CC, Desert Horizons CC, Bel-Air Bay; mil: photog. mate USN, 1946; rec: soaring, flying, photog., hunting & fishing. Res: 1060 Brooklawn Dr Holmby Hills 90024 Ofc: Hilton Hotels Corp. 9336 Santa Monica Blvd Beverly Hills 90212

HIMELSEIN, LEONARD, manufacturing/import-export co. executive; b. Oct. 21, 1945, Johannesburg, S.Africa; s. Abe and Sarah (Chaitowitz) H.; m. Sheila Joseph, Jan. 10, 1971; children: Felicia, b. 1973, Wayne, b. 1974; edn: Damelin Coll. 1964. Career: trainee mgr. O.K. Bazaars, Johannesburg 1965, dept. mgr./buyer Ackermans, 1968, dir. Taj Mahal Mfg. Co. (diamond dealers and jewellery mfrs.), Johannesburg 1969-74, mng. dir. 1975-80, bd. chmn. 1981-; mng. dir. Himelsein Prop. Co., Johannesburg 1977-; bd. chmn. Czar Jewellers, Boputhatswana, S.A. 1981-; pres. National Pacific Corp. dba Himelsein Inc., Los Angeles 1981-; dir. Internat. Wines & Spirits, Ariz. 1984-; pres. St. Paul Cleaners & Laundry, div. of L&R Dry Cleaning Inc., Santa Barbara 1985; honors: feature subject, Personalities In The Diamond Trade, The Diamond News and S.A. Jeweller (1971); mem. Diamond Club of S.A. 1973- (chmn. Dept. Manpower & Util. 1980), Jewelry Mfrs. Assn. (exec. com. 1973-81); v.p. Pacific Jewish Center; bd. Emmanuel Streisand Sch. Res: 1254 Bel Air Dr Bel Air Knolls Santa Barbara 93101 Ofc: Himelson Inc., Nat. Pacific Corp., 1235 Santa Barbara St Santa Barbara 93101

HINDERBERGER, PHILIP ROBERT, lawyer; b. June 22, 1943, East St. Louis, Ill.; s. Walter and Ouida H.; m. Clara Doyle, May 27, 1967; children: Kirk b. 1974, Brent b. 1977; edn: BA, Univ. of Ill. 1966; JD, magna cum laude, Univ. of San Diego Sch. of Law 1973. Career: EDP sales rep. Honeywell Inc., Los Angeles 1966-69; counsel Calif. Dept. of Insurance, San Francisco 1974-78; gov. affairs counsel Fireman's Fund Ins. Co., San Francisco 1978-79; senior v.p., gen. counsel, corp. secty. Beaver Pacific Corp. and subs., San Francisco 1979-; mem: Am., Calif., Marin Co. and San Francisco Bar Assns., Sierra Club, Common Cause, Assn. Calif. State Attys., Mill Valley Sch. Dist., Bay Area Soc. of Ins. Counsel, Mill Valley Sch. Found., Mill Valley Soccer Club (pres.), Banker's Club, Commonwealth Club; mil: maj. USMCR 1966-, Navy Commdn., Purple Heart (2), Vietnamese Cross of Gallantry. Res: 469 Live Oak Dr. Mill Valley 94141 Ofc: Beaver Pacific Corporation, 100 California St. Ste. 500 San Francisco 94111

HINDERY, LEO JOSEPH, JR., media co. executive; b. Oct. 31, 1947, Springfield, Ill.; s. Leo Joseph Sr. and E. Marie (Whitener) H; m. Deborah Diane, Feb. 20, 1980; 1 dau, Robin b. 1981; edn: BA, Seattle Univ. 1969; MBA, Stanford Univ. 1971. Career: asst. treas. Utah Internat. Inc., San Francisco 1971-80; treas. Natomas Co., San Francisco 1980-82; exec. v.p. fin. Jefferies & Co., Los Angeles 1982-83; chief fin. ofcr. and mng. dir. A.G. Becker Paribas, NY 1983-85; chief ofcr. plnng. and fin. Chronicle Publishing Co., San Francisco 1985-; dir. San Francisco Newspaper Agency; dir. Bay Area Bus. Devel. Co.; dir. San Francisco Renaissance; mem: Olympic Club, University Club; mil: US Army 1968-70; rec: hiking, climbing, golf. Res: 1272 Hardscrabble Rd. Chappaqua, NY 10514 Ofc: Chronicle Publishing Co., 901 Mission St. San Francisco 94103

HINDIN, MAURICE J., judge; b. Oct. 10, 1910, Los Angeles; s. Theodore J. and Ida Hindin; m. Dorothy Sweet, Salt Lake City, Aug. 11, 1938; children: Arthur T., b. 1943, Carol, b. 1950; edn: BS, USC 1933, LLB, 1935, LLD. Career: admitted to practice law, Calif. 1935, admitted US Supreme Ct., 1942; formerly senior partner Hindin, McKittrick, Marsh law firm, Beverly Hills; mem. Am., Los Angeles County bar assns., Am. Trial Lawyers Assn.; Friars Club; rec: owner/opr. amateur radio sta. W6EUV. Ofc: Court and Chambers, Los Angeles County Courthouse, Los Angeles

HINGARH, HEMRAJ K., semiconductor co. executive; b. Aug. 22, 1944, Rani, India, nat. US cit. 1984; s. Kundan Mal and Pain Bai (Ranka) H.; m. Lila H., April 11, 1970; children: Nisha b. 1971, Nilesh b. 1974, Viresh b. 1979; edn: BSEE, Birle Inst., Pilani, India 1966; MSEE, UC Berkeley 1967. Career: dir. Adv. Logic Div. Fairchild research Ctr., Palo Alto 1972-86; dir. design engirng. Fairchild Memory & High Speed Logic Div., Puyallup, Wash. 1986-; honors: Most Important Scientist (1980), Presidential Award (1981), Fairchild; mem. IEEE, PTA (Saratoga Sch. Dist.); works: 12 patents, 9 pend.; 20 papers publd.; Republican; Hindu; rec: running, tennis. Ofc: Fairchild MH5L, 1111 39th S.E., Puyallup, WA 98374

HINOJOSA, JAIME ALBERTO, financial planner; b. Jan. 25, 1955, El Paso, Texas; s. Porfirio and Martha Dolores H.; m. Brenda, Feb. 14, 1981; children (adoptive): Lawrence Brandley b. 1978, Timothy Stuart b. 1980; edn: BS, Univ. Texas, El Paso 1977; Certified Finl. Planner (CFP), 1983. Career: teller UCB Bank (1st Interstate) 1979-80; agent Equitable Life Ins. 1980-81; finl. plnnr. Capital Analysts Inc., Walnut Creek 1981-85, ptnr. 1985-; v.p. Capital Analysts Pension Accounting; pres. CAI Brokers Ltd.; v.p./bd. dirs. Besco Inc. and D & H Pump Service, 1979-; mem. Internat. Assn. of Finl. Plnnr., Nat. Assn. of Securities Dealers, Bus. Execs. for Nat. Security; publish qtrly finl. newsletter: Legislative and Economic Review; Republican; Baptist; rec: golf, tennis, racquetball. Res: 85 Coral Dr Orinda 94563 Ofc: Capital Analysts 2700 Ygnacio Valley Ste 360 Walnut Creek 94598

HIRSCHMAN, HENRY, eye surgeon; b. June 1, 1931, NY, NY; s. Jerome and Rebecca (Stein) H.; children: Jason b. 1960, David b. 1961, Harry b. 1963, Micah b. 1964; edn: undergrad. Seton Hall Univ. 1949-50, Mich. State Univ. 1954-55, MD, Univ. of Mich. 1959. Career: medical dir. Hirschman Eye Surgery Center, Long Beach; pioneered the use of introcular lenses in cataract surgery, gave first courses in USA on Lens Implant; cons. Intermedics; editor Ocular Surgery News (Intraocular Assn.); coauthor (first U.S. textbook on lens implants) Pseudophokos; mem./co-founder Am. Intra Ocular Implant Soc. (chmn. sci. advis. bd.); awards: Binkhorst Medal lecturer (1979); rec: photog., skiing, fishing, tennis. Res: 5800 Bayshore Walk Long Beach 90803 Ofc: Hirschman Eye Surgery Ctr 4100 Long Beach Blvd Long Beach 90807

HIRSEN, JAMES L., lawyer; b. Aug. 18, 1950, Chgo., Ill.; s. Carl A. and Erica G. H.; m. Margaret, Mar. 15, 1976; edn: BA, Northeastern Univ. 1972, JD, 1980; admitted Calif. State Bar 1980. Career: atty. Pizante, Gregg & Osborne Beverly Hills, Law Offices of James Hirsen Santa Monica; atty./office leasing specialist Grubb & Ellis Co. Sherman Oaks; legal panel Nat. Acad. Song Writers; honors: Bancroft Whitney Award for Academic Excellence, Delta Theta Phi Scholarship Award, Class Valedictorian, editor Law Review; mem: Am. Bar Assn., Assn. of Real Estate Attys., Nat. Assn. Recording Arts & Sci.; research: Solar Access Rights; Catholic; rec: music, sailing. Res: 19712 Merryhill St Canyon Country 91351 Ofc: Grubb & Ellis Co. 4827 Sepulveda Blvd, Ste 250, Sherman Oaks 91403

HIRSH, ROGER CAVANAUGH, acupuncturist; b. Aug. 31, 1948, Los Angeles; s. Dwight Charles and Margo Gail (Sage) H.; m. Marcia Lee, Aug. 13, 1983; edn: BA, UC Los Angeles 1971; B. Acupuncture, honors, Internat. Coll. of Oriental Medicine, London 1976; postgrad. study (constitutional medicine) Inst. of Oriental Studies, 1977-80; OMD (Dr. Oriental Medicine), Calif. Acupuncture Coll. 1984; Certified Acupuncturist, Calif. BMQA; Diplomate (NCCA) Nat. Commn. of Certified Acupuncturists (1985) Career: linguistic cons. Chariot Publishing Co., Los Angeles 1970-73; acupuncturist Hillside Clinic, London and research assoc. in chronic rhinitis, sinusitis 1975-76; pvt. practice Doynton Street Clinic, London 1974-76; pvt. practice, Santa Monica, Calif. 1977-80; resident acupuncturist Center for Orthomolecular Medicine, Palo Alto 1981-83; dir. Los Altos Acupuncture Clinic, Los Altos 1984 –; cons. Central Testing Unit, State Board of Consumer Affairs, 1983; lectr. Calif. Acupuncture Coll. 1977-78, adj. faculty Am. Coll. of Traditional Chinese Medicine 1982-84, San Francisco Coll. of Acupuncture 1983–; research advisor Am. Found. of Traditional Chinese Medicine 1984-; mem. Exam. Design Commn., Calif. BMQA Acu. Advis. Com. 1982-85; Exam. Design Commn., Nat. Commn. of Certified Acupuncturists; exam. commnr. Nat. Licensing Exam. (S.F.); mem: Calif. Acupuncture Alliance (bd. dirs. Legislative Com. 1983, secty. 1984), Oriental Healing Arts Inst., Acupuncture Assn. of Am., North Am. Acupuncture Assn., Kappa Sigma Frat.; publs: contbr. J. of the Am. Coll. of Traditional Chinese Medicine (1983-85); Democrat; rec: contemplative martial arts, photog., Chinese med. hist. Ofc: Los Altos Acupuncture Clinic 4546 El Camino Real Ste B Los Altos 94022

HLAVIN, ROBERT, petroleum refining process engineer; b. Jan. 14, 1927, Cleveland, Ohio; s. Joseph and Irene (Kreicher) H.; children: Dawn Michelle b. 1966, Robert Jan b. 1968; edn: BSChE, Univ. Mich. 1950, MSChE, 1952. process engr. Fluor Corp. L.A. 1952-56; pvt. cons. L.A. 1956-60; process engr. Ralph M. Parsons Co. L.A. 1960-68, Jacobs Engrg. Group Inc. Pasadena 1968 –; honors: Tau Beta Pi, Phi Lambda Upsilon; publ: Critical Pressure (Oil & Gas Jour. 1985); lt. USNR 1959-; Republican; Lutheran; rec: computers, stamps, music. Ofc: Jacobs Engrg. Group Inc. 251 S Lake Ave Pasadena 91101

HO, HANSON AN-HSIN, architect; b. Feb. 28, 1947, Nanking, China, nat. US cit. 1983; s. Wm. Wei-Ming and Lan-Ing (Kuo) Ho; m. Rachel Apostol, Oct. 1, 1952; children: Katherine b. 1980, Kristoffer b. 1982, Kevin b. 1984; edn: B.Arch., Tunghai Univ. 1969; grad. pgm. in urban/regional plnng., Univ. of Iowa 1970-72; Harvard Univ. Grad. Sch. of Design 1975; Reg. Architect, Calif. 1982. Career: research asst. Inst. of Urban & Regl. Research, Iowa City, Iowa 1970-72; plnnr. Space Mgmt. Consultants Inc., NYC 1973; chief designer Deck House, Inc. Acton, Mass. 1973-78; v.p. Arenco, Inc. (architecture, engring. cons.), Whittier 1979-82; pres. Hanson Ho & Assocs., Arch., Cerritos 1982 –; pres. Royal Constrn. Corp., Cerritos 1983-; dir. Richmark Devel. Corp., Alhambra 1984-; awards: for preliminary design of Civic Plaza, Iowa City, America the Beautiful Fund, Nat. Endowment of Art (1971), merit cert. for Elderly Housing Project, Mass. Housing Auth. (1975), for signific contbn. to internat. trade & devel., Belmont Coll., Tenn. (1974), hon. citizen, State of Tenn. (1974); mem. Am. Inst. of Arch.; Republican; Buddhist; rec: tennis. Ofc: Hanson Ho & Assocs. 11480 South St Ste 209 Cerritos 90701

HO, JAMES T., eye surgeon; b. Aug. 19, 1952, China, nat. 1984; s. Sze Pao and Mei Fung (Ng) H.; edn: BA, UC Santa Barbara 1974; MD, Albert Einstein Coll. of Med. 1978; eye surgeon Emory Univ. Sch. of Med. 1982, Stanford Univ. Sch. of Med. 1982; bd. certified, Diplomate Am. Bd. Ophthalmol. 1983. Career: dir. Am. Refractive Eye Surg. Ctr. San Francisco; attg. eye surg. St. Mary's Hosp. S.F., Pacific Med. Ctr. S.F. 1982 –; honors: in biochem. and molecular biol. research 1970-74, distinction during med. tng., The Distinguished Eye Surgeon (Soc. of Refractive Surg. 1985; mem: fellow Am. Acad. Ophthalmol, candidate Am. Coll. Surg., fellow Internat. Coll. Surg., Union Square Club; research: perfection of surg. techniques and technol. for the correction of near-, far-sightedness, and cataract lens implants; Theist; rec: Tennis, jogging, classical music. Ofc: Am. Refractive Eye Surg. Ctr. 490 Post St, Ste 950, San Francisco 94102

HOAGLAND, GRANT TAYLOR, lawyer; b. June 21, 1949, Los Angeles; s. Dallas Abram and Marydene (Oldham) H.; edn: BA, cum laude, CSU Long Beach 1974; JD, Western State Univ. Coll. of Law 1978; lic. real estate broker. Career: atty. law ofcs. Erwin Sobel 1979-80; Legal Clinic of Jacoby & Meyers, Cerritos 1980 –; awards: Am. Jurisprudence Awd. for Remedies II, Western

State Univ.; BSA Order of the Arrow, Eagle Scout; mem: Am. & L.A. Co. Bar Assns.; Am. & L.A. Trial Lawyers Assns.; Elks Club; commnr./chmn. South Gate Parks & Recreation Commn.; Latter Day Saints; rec: skiing, racquetball, musicianship. Res: 2882 W Rome Ave Anaheim 92804

HOBBS, MARCIA WILSON, zoo association president; b. June 23, 1947, Los Angeles; d. William Albert and Elizabeth Ann (Johnson) Wilson; children: Christian Choate b. 1970, Jeffrey Michael b. 1973, Nicholas William b. 1972; edn: UC Los Angeles 1965-67; UC Berkeley 1967-68. Career: pres, CEO Greater L.A. Zoo Assn.; mem: Calif. Tourism Corp. Exec. Com., State Rec. & Parks Commn., Calif. Travel Industry Assn. (bd.), Am. Assn. Museums, Am. Assn. Zoological Parks & Aquariums, Loyola- Marymount Bd. Regents, L.A.-Guangzhou Sister City Assn. (bd.), L.A. Council for Internat. Visitors (bd.), Am. Women for Internat. Understanding (bd.); Republican (del. to nat. convention 1976, 80, 84); Catholic. Ofc: 5333 Zoo Dr Los Angeles 90027-1498

HOBBS, RICHARD LEIGHTON, physicist; b. Nov. 3, 1942, Boston, Mass.; s. Irving Leighton and Gertrude Otilia (Peterson) H.; edn: BA, physics, Northeastern Univ. 1966; grad. courses, astronomy, comp. sci., Boston Univ. 1966-70. Career: senior systems engr. Rockwell Internat., Autonetics Strategic Sys. Div.; reentry physicist and weapon systems analyst: Peacekeeper (MX), Titan and Minuteman Intercontinental Ballistic Missiles (ICBMs), SR-71 and U2 spy planes, Space Shuttle, B-1 Bomber, Air Launched Cruise Missiles (ALCMs), and MK92 Fire Control Sys and 76mm Gun Mounts for FFG-7 Class frigates, Vandenberg AFB, Edwards AFB, FLTAC, Corona and the Kwajalein Missile Range; honors: Toward Excellence Inovative Idea Award, Rockwell 1985; Engr. of the Quarter, Fall 1983, Dynalectron Norco Div.; mem. Am. Inst. of Physics 1961-66 (treas.); Planetary Soc.; Urantia Found.; Am. and Orange Co. Mensa; Am. Assn. Individual Investors; Internat. Soc. of Cryptozoology; Am. Security Council's Congl. Adv. Bd.; num. sci. publs.; Ind.; Christian; rec: travel, archeol., nat. history, commodity futures trading, parapsychology, paleontology. Res: 4453 W Coast Hwy Newport Beach 92663 Ofc: Rockwell Internat. Defense Electronics Ops., 3370 Miraloma Ave Anaheim 92803

HOBDY, FRANCES LEAP (RADER), real estate broker; b. Mar. 1, 1920, Fresno; d. Edward Gerald and Emma (Tittle) L.; m. Robert J. Rader, (dec.), Jan. 19, 1943; m. Morris M. Hobdy, (dec.), May 27, 1972; children: Robert Rader, Jr. b. 1944, Judith Rader b. 1948; edn: Coll. of William & Mary 1969-69; AA, Palomar Coll. 1976; BA, Newport Univ. 1979; desig: GRI (Graduate Realtors Inst.), Calif. Assn. of Realtors; CRS (Cert Residential Splst.), CRB (Cert RE Brokerage), Nat. Assn. of Realtors. Career: legal secty. Hatchett & Ford, Hampton, Va. 1961-67; realtor assoc. Denny Realty, Escondido 1973-75; broker assoc. Mark, Realtors, Escondido 1975-78; owner/broker Hobdy, Realtors, Escondido 1978 –; dir. Fowble & Assocs., San Diego 1974-; trustee BORPAC, 1986-; honors: Calif. State Legislature commendn. for service to community (1983), Directory of Disting. Americans for services to community, ABI (1981); mem: Escondido Bd. of Realtors (past dir., pres.; mediator 1985-), Calif. Assn. of Realtors, Nat. Assn. Realtors, Nat. Mktg. Inst.; civic: Escondido CofC, Zool. Soc. of San Diego, Smithsonian Assocs., San Diego Opera, Golden Wives Club, Meadowlark Country Club; Republican; Prot.; rec: exercise, computer. Res: 910 Milane Ln Escondido 92026 Ofc: Hobdy, Realtors 510 N Escondido Blvd Ste 2A Escondido 92025

HOCTOR, ARTHUR EDWARD, psychiatrist; b. May 2, 1923, Lima, Ohio; s. Arthur Edward and Louise Frances (Labadie) H.; m. Patricia Lee Jones, Dec. 28, 1949; children: Susan b. 1950, Sally b. 1952, Sandra b. 1953, Timothy b. 1954, Michael b. 1956; edn: St. Joseph's of Indiana, Collegeville 1941-43, 1946-67; John Carroll Univ. Cleveland 1943; MD, St. Louis Univ. 1951; bd. eligible psych. 1955. Career: intern Jackson Meml. Hosp. Miami 1951-52; resident psych. Indiana Univ. Indpls. 1952-54, Camarillo State Hosp. 1955; dir. Ventura Co. Mental Health 1956-60, Day Treatment Ctr. and Aftercare Metro. State Hosp. Norwalk; pvt. practice psych. Santa Maria 1960-74; Santa Clara Co. Alcohol Pgm. San Jose 1974-75; dir. star Lodge Hosp. for Alcoholism Scotts Valley 1975-77; admissions coord. Metro. State Hosp. Norwalk 1977-80, Capitol Med. Grp. Sacto. 1981-82, Correctional Facility Lompoc, Calif. State Social Svc.; pvt. practice Oxnard 1982-84, Santa Maria 1984 –; staff local hosps.; mem: Am. Psych. Assn., CMA (pending); mil: ensign USNR 1943-46; capt. USAR (MC) 1952-64; Catholic; rec: collecting, travel, camping, sports & games. Res: 1036 Brookside Ave Santa Maria 93455 Ofc: 301 S Miller St Ste 215 Santa Maria 93454

HODGE, CHARLES STANLEY, engineer; b. Nov. 19, 1936, Waterton, NY; s. Gordon Levi and Isabelle Louise (La Pier) H.; m. Elizabeth Badalato, June 20, 1963; children: Beth b. 1965, Rebecca b. 1972; edn: BSCE, summa cum laude, Ind. Inst. of Technol. 1966; Reg. Profl. Engr. Calif. 1980. Career: engr. Erdman & Anthony Assoc. Rochester, NY 1966-72; dept. mgr. General Automation Anaheim 1972-74; engr. VTN Corp. Irvine 1974-78; engr., dir. computer svcs. Boyle Engrg. Corp. Newport Beach 1978 –; dir Profl. Cons. 1985 –; honors: Coswell Award (Ind. Inst. Tech. 1964, 65), Archie T. Keen Outstanding Civil Engrg. Student (IIT 1966); mem: AM. Soc. Civil Engrs. (chmn. tech. council computer practices 1981-82, chmn mgmt. grp. A 1984-85), Am. Red Cross (disaster vol. 1975-81), So. Orange Amateur Radio Assn. 1974-80 (pres. 1974-76), Beach City Wireless Soc. 1977-82; publ: num. papers and articles on computing in Civil Engrg.; mil: cpl. US Army 1959-61; Episcopal; rec: amateur radio, radio-controlled model aeronautics. Res: 23582 Duryea Dr El Toro 92630 Ofc: Boyle Engrg. 1501 Quail St Newport Beach 92660

HODGE, KATHLEEN SMITH, realtor; b. Nov. 2, 1932, Wenanchee, Wash.; d. LeRoy Agustus and Anna Louise (Brown) Smith; m. James Leonard, Feb. 14,

1959; children: Patricia Kay b. 1959, Keith Richard b. 1961, David Bruce b. 1963; stepson, Gregg Allen b. 1953; edn: De Anza Coll. Career: asst. cook Albertina Kerr Nursery 1946; founder fountain-lunch bus., Portland, Ore. 1951; asst. to order mgr. Hawaiian Pineapple Co. 1960; real estate lic. 1968; broker lic. 1974; broker, sole owner Preferred Realtors, Cupertino 1981–; tng. class for new lic. agents; honors: Preferred Realtors in Top 10 Percent in US, Nat. Statistical Research Co.; mem: San Jose and Sunnyvale Real Estate Bds.; Republican; Protestant; rec: breeding and showing Rottweiler dogs. Ofc: 10897 So. Blaney Ave. Cupertino 95014

HODGES, JAMES BROWN, III, engineer; b. Aug. 1, 1950, Charleston, S.C.; s. James Brown and Mary Johnny (Stevenson) Hodges, Jr.; edn: BSEE, Univ. of S.C. 1972, MBA 1974. Career: engr. Wilbur Smith and Assocs. Consulting Engrs., S.C., 1972-74; test adminstr. US Army, Ft. Jackson, S.C., 1974-75; served to capt. USAF, 1975-81; pilot, Columbus AFB, Miss. and McChord AFB, Wash., 1975-79; Space Shuttle Inertial Upper Stage Integration Activities, USAF Space Div., Los Angeles 1979-81; staff engr. Martin Marietta Corp., Denver Aerospace Div., 1981–; awards: So. Caro. Elec. & Gas Co. Scholar (1968-70), George I. Pair Scholar (1968-71), AF Reserve Ofcrs Tng Corps Scholar (1970-72), Thomas Moore Craig Leadership Award (1971); honors: Who's Who in Am. Colls. and Univs., Omicron Delta Kappa nat. leadership hon. soc. (pres., Outstanding Mem. Award 1972), Tau Beta Pi nat. engring. hon. soc., Eta Kappa Nu nat. elec. engring. hon. soc., Pi Mu Epsilon nat. hon. math. soc., Beta Gamma Sigma nat. bus. adminstrn. hon. soc.; mil: 7 mil. decorations, var. AF Reserve Ofcrs. Tng Corps decorations; mem: Nat. Space Inst. 1975–, Am. Inst. of Aero. and Astro. 1985–, Technical Mktg. Soc. of Am. 1985–, IEEE 1970, Arnold Air Soc. (comdr., outstanding mem. 1970-73), Air Force Assn. 1971, Huguenot Soc. 1978–, First Families of So. Caro. 1978–, United Fund vol.; Episcopal; rec: sailing, theatre, flying. Res: 14506 Yukon Ave Hawthorne 90250 Ofc: Martin Marietta Corp., 185 So Douglas St El Segundo 90245

HODGES, JOHN ATHANASIOU, lawyer; b. Oct. 10, 1898; s. Athanasios Geroge and Elizabeth (Dadacaredes) H.; m. Violet, May 23, 1937; edn: pre-legal, UCB, Stanford Univ.; LLB, Hastings Coll. of the Law, 1923; admitted Calif. State Bar 1923. Career: gen. practice of law, 1923-29, 1931–, currently semi-ret. from law, atty. for Greek Consulate; organized a dairy corp. mfg. var. cheese products, 1929-31; financial advisor, reg. rep. NYSE; patron Pythagoras Soc., non-profit health orgn.; awards: resolution, San Francisco City & Co. Board of Supvrs.; Selective Svc. Medal, US Congress; named Man of Year, Annunciation Cathedral of S.F. (1977), Ecumenical Patriarch Athenagoras, Greek Orthodox Archon. (1977). Res: 1545 Meadow Ln Burlingame 94010

HODGKIN, DEBORAH DALE, real estate broker; b. June 7, 1950, Denver, Colo.; d. Dale Wayne and Shirley Rita (Kellaher) Wagers; m. Peter Hodgkin, June 16, 1973; 1 dau. Cameron Jolene b. 1981; edn: Rio Hondo Coll. 1968-69; BS Cal. Poly. S.L.O. 1972; Calif. Secondary Std. Tchg. Credl. 1973; real estate sales Calif. 1978; real estate broker Calif. 1981. Career: mgr. games, asst. to concessions Olde Towne Mall Torrance, Calif. 1973-74; store mgr., clerk Scenic Coast Pet Shop Morro Bay 1975-78; realtor assoc., asst. mgr. House of Realty Morro Bay 1979-82; broker assoc., ofc. mgr. West Wind Realty Los Osos 1982–; honors: Million Dollar Producer (House of Realty 1981, West Wind Realty 1984), Two Million Producer (1985); mem: Nat. Bd. Realtors, Calif. Bd. Realtors, Scenic Coast Bd. Realtors, Multiple Listing Svc., Los Osos- Baywood Park CofC, Downtown Baywood Park Merchants Assn. (membership chair); rec: stained glass, bicycling, golf, camping, kiting, picnics. Ofc: West Wind Realty 1205 4th St Baywood Park 93402

HOECHLIN, DONALD ROBERT, physician, b. Oct. 14, 1946, Pasadena, s. Calvin Elton and Arleen Ernestine (Hoenk) H.; m. Bonny (dec.), June 3, 1972; children: Travis b. 1976, Carrie b. 1979; edn: BS, San Diego State Univ. 1972, MS, 1974, MD, UC Irvine 1977. Career: emergency physician Corona Community Hosp. 1978-85, dir. Outpatient Urgent Care, 1985–; paramedic instr.; physician Corona Child Abuse Pgm.; mem. Am. Coll. of Emergency Physician, Am. Ornithologists Union, Nature Conservancy; team physician Corona H.S. Football Team; publs: photographic essay of Golden Eagles (1975), and Note on Yellow-crowned Night Heron in California (1976) (West. Birds); mil: sp4 US Army 1967-68, Vietnam; Ind.; Baptist; rec: wildlife photog., wood carving, sports. Ofc: Corona Comm. Hospital 812 S Washburn Corona 91720

HOFERT, JACK, lawyer; b. Apr. 6, 1930, Phila., Pa.; s. David and Beatrice (Schatz) H.; m. Marilyn, Sept. 4, 1960; children: Dina b. 1963, Bruce b. 1966; edn: BS, UCLA 1952, MBA, 1954; JD, 1957; admitted to practice, Calif. State Bar 1958; CPA, 1959; lic. R.E. broker 1965. Career: fin. v.p. Pacific Theatres Corp., Los Angeles 1962-69; self- empl. bus. cons. & acquisitions finder, L.A. 1969-74; mgr. tax dept. Peat, Marwick, Mitchell & Co., L.A. 1974-77; dir. of taxation Lewis Homes, Upland 1977-80; atty. & bus. cons. 1980–; owner/pres. Di-Bru, Inc., L.A. (bus. consulting co.) 1981–; dir. Cinerama, Inc. 1965-69; tchr. income tax courses, UCLA Ext. pgm. 1962-69; honors: Order of the Coif, staff UCLA Law Review; mem: State Bar of Calif.; Am. Inst. CPAs (past); Calif. Soc. CPAs (past); publs: approx. 12 arts. in tax & bus. mags.; mil: seaman apprentice USN 1948-49. Address: 2479 Roscomare Rd Los Angeles 90077

HOFFER, DONALD CHARLES, optometrist; b. Sept. 6, 1946, Detroit, Mich.; s. Martin and Frances (Ross) H.; m. Robin, Aug. 25, 1968; 1 son, Antony b. 1970; edn: undergrad. Wayne State Univ. 1964-67; OD, So. Coll. of Optometry 1971. Career: general optometry practice, Detroit, Mich. 1971-73; head of optometry Bascom Palmer Eye Inst., Univ. of Miami, Fla. 1974-81;

tchg. and clin. splst. in low vision care; cons. Fla. State Board of Opt. 1979-81; optometrist pvt. practice limited to low vision care to partially sighted, Beverly Hills 1981–; Fellow Am. Acad. of Optometry; author/pub. self-taught method of guitar instrn. for the blind, 6-vol. course (talking books) disbtd. internat. by the Library of Congress; contbr. articles in Review of Optometry (1979, 84, 85) and Guitar Player (1/80); rec: piano, guitar, ham radio opr. Ofc: 8530 Wilshire Blvd Ste 206 Beverly Hills 90211

HOFFER, PAUL BARRY, financial consultant; b. July 20, 1951, Los Angeles; s. Aaron Samuel and Rose (Graver) H.; edn: BBA, MBA, CSU Northridge. Career: sales and mktg., Polygram Records, Inc. 5 yrs.; v.p. sales & mktg. Video Odyssey, Inc., Hollywood, 2 yrs; finl. planner Bretcourt, 3 yrs.; founder/pres. Hoffer/Dow Financial, and finl. cons. Merrill, Lynch, Pierce, Fenner & Smith, currently; lectr. on finl. planning var. civic and bus. groups; mem. Pro-Trac Financial Profl. Advis. Panel; mem. Internat. Assn. of Finl. Planners; publ: (booklet) Getting Financial Mileage out of Personal Retirement Plans (1985); Republican; Jewish; rec: automobiles, raising horses. Ofc: Merrill Lynch Hollywood 90028

HOFFMAN, CHARLES L(ARRY), business consultant; b. Aug. 6, 1938, Flint, Mich.; s. Charles L., Sr. and Loretta E. (Russell) h.; m. Carol Ann Mentor, July 11, 1981; children: Michele, b. 1967; Jacquie (adptd.); Danny (adptd.); Graydon Whelan (step), b. 1973; edn: AA, Saddleback Coll., Irvine 1978. Career: nat. sales mgr./ v.p. mktg. Washington West Trade Corp., Los Angeles 1969-75; owner C. Larry Hoffman & Assoc. 1975-80; chmn. bd./ CEO Hoffman Business Consultants 1980–; partner Irvine Meadows Amphitheatre; former chmn. Irvine City Plng. Commn.; mem: Irvine CofC (past pres.); Cystic Fibrosis, Orange Co.; mil: E-4 US Army 1961-63; Republican; So. Coast Comm. Ch.; rec: gourmet cooking. Res: 21 Rainstar Irvine 92714 Ofc: Hoffman Business Consultants, Inc., 2300 Michelson Dr, Ste 300, Irvine 92715

HOFFMAN, MARK BRUCE, computer co. president; b. Nov. 9, 1946, Windom, Minn.; s. Henry T. and Phyllis M. (Knutson) H.; m. Susan A. Van Wagner, Feb. 18, 1972; children: Annie b. 1978, Andrew b. 1980; edn: BS, US Mil. Acad. 1969; MBA, Univ. of Ariz. 1979. Career: sales Precision Toyota, Tucson, Ariz. 1976-78; mgmt. Amdahl Corp., Sunnyvale 1979-80; v.p. ops. Britton Lee, Los Gatos 1980-84; pres. Sybase Inc., Berkeley 1984–; CEO Sybase Inc. 1984–; mem: San Francisco Ballet (patron), San Francisco Zoological Soc. (guardian); mil: capt. US Army 1969-75, Commdn. w/ Oak Leaf cluster; Republican; Episcopal; rec: triathlete, skiing, tennis. Ofc: Sybase, 2910 Seventh St. Ste. 110 Berkeley

HOFFMAN, MARVIN, computer professional resource co. president; b. July 27, 1933, Wauwatosa, Wisc.; s. Sam and Anna (Cohen) H.; m. F. Evelyn Lazar, Sept. 28, 1955; children: Loren b. 1959, Darryl b. 1960; edn: BA in math., CSU Northridge 1962; postgrad. wk., CSU and UCLA; Life Tchg. Credential Bus. Data Processing. Career: systems supr. North Am. Rockwell 1961-66; dir. 6000 Software Devel., Control Data Corp. 1966-69; dir. software devel. Ampex Corp. 1969-72; mgr. software devel. F&M Systems Co. 1972-73; dir. R&D Div. Computer Machinery Corp. 1973-76; founder/pres./bd. chmn. XX-CAL, Inc. (multi-branch data processing consulting and human resource co.), Los Angeles 1976–; bd. mem. RIMTECH; instr./mem. adv. com. L.A. City Coll.; honors: Alpha Gamma Sigma 1958; mem: W.L.A. CofC 1981-, So/Cal/ Ten, Uaide & Sel Users Group (nat. past pres. 1962-72), past mem. DPMA, ACM; mil: AG2 USN 1952-56, Korean, Far East Cpgn., GC; Democrat; Jewish; rec: ski, golf, jogging. Res: 2423 S. Beverly Dr Los Angeles 90034 Ofc: XXCAL Inc. 11500 Olympic Blvd Ste 459 Los Angeles 90064

HOFFMAN, NANCY, judge; b. Sept. 13, 1933, San Francisco; d. Franz and Sara (Flaschen) Rosenfeld; m. Daniel N. Hoffman, Dec. 24, 1961; children: Sharon Lynne, b. 1963, Jeremy Franklin, b. 1965, Carolyn Miriam, b. 1967; edn: BA, UC Berkeley 1955; JD, summa cum laude, Univ. of Santa Clara Law Sch. 1974. Career: dep. pub. defender Santa Clara Co. 1975-80; judge of the municipal ct. Santa Clara Co. 1980–; instr. Hasting Coll. of Advocacy 1979; honors: Women of Achiev. Award, Commn. on the Status of Women and the San Jose Mercury News; mem: Calif. Judges Assn. (exec. bd.), Nat. Assn. of Women Judges, Calif. Women Lawyers (exec. bd.), REPAY (adv. bd.), Santa Clara Co. Law Rel. Edn. Com., Santa Clara Co. Lib. (bd. trustees); publs: Taming the Felony- Murder Rule, 14 Santa Clara Lawyer 1973; art., w/ McCarthy, Juvenile Detention Hearings: The Case for a Probable Cause Determination, 15 Santa Clara Lawyer 1975; Democrat; Jewish; rec: weightlifting, gardening. Ofc: 200 W. Hedding St., San Jose 95110

HOFFMAN, SUSAN LOUISE, lawyer; b. Oct. 28, 1948, Montreal, Quebec, Canada; d. Wm. and Sylvia (Lazarus) H.; edn: BA, UC Los Angeles 1969; PhD, psychology, Stanford Univ. 1974; JD, Yale Univ. 1979. Career: vis. lectr. Stanford Univ. 1973; asst. prof. Univ. Fla. 1973-76; research fellow Harvard Univ. 1977; adj. asst. prof. USC 1981; assoc. atty. Tuttle & Taylor Inc. 1979-84; ptnr. 1984–; awards: NSF undergrad. fellowship (1968), Canada Council doctoral fellowship (1971-73), Social Sci. Research Council postdoc. fellowship (1976-77); mem: Assn. of Business Trial Lawyers, Am. Psychology-Law Soc., L.A. County Bar Assn.; civic: bd. dirs. Los Angeles Contemporary Exhibitions (1982-83); bd. dirs. Mental Health Advocacy Services (1980-); bd. dirs. Community of Peace People, Inc. (1981-); contbr. articles to num. profl. journals; rec: skiing, hiking. Ofc: Tuttle & Taylor Inc., 355 S Grand Ave Los Angeles 90071

HOFFMAN, WILLIAM J., hotel management co. executive; b. Apr. 28, 1944, Chgo.; s. Charles A. and Marion F. (Johnson) H.; m. Judy M., July 3, 1970; children: Jennifer b. 1980, Eric b. 1983; edn: BS, Western State Univ. 1975, JD, 1977; certified hotel adminstr. Am. Hotel-Motel Assn. (1982). Career: with C&EI R.R., Chgo. 1962-66, Ill. Bell Tel. Co., Chgo. 1967-71, self-empl. Chgo. 1972; vice pres. Trigild Corp., San Diego 1973-82, pres. 1982–; dir. Calif. Lodging Indus. Assn.; mem. ABA, Calif. Bar Assn., Internat. Council of Hotel-Motel Mgmt. Cos., Calif. Hotel-Motel Assn., Calif. Lodging Industry Assn.; publs: contbr. articles Lodging Hospitality, Resort Management, Innkeeping World, Cornell Univ. Hotel & Restaurant Admin. Quartely; rec: camping, trout fishing. Ofc: Trigild Corp. 12760 High Bluff Dr San Diego 92130

HOFMANN, REVA BUTLER, contract engineering co. executive; b. Red Bud, Ill.; d. Allen Wm. and Bertha Elizabeth (Conway) Moore; div.; children: Kathy b. 1957, Dennis b. 1960; edn: BS in bus., Univ. Mo. 1967; desig: C.P.C. (Cert. Placement Counselor), Univ. Mo. 1970. Career: office mgr., then sales rep. medical instrument sales co., St. Louis, Mo.; sales & mktg. cons. to major corps. incl. Mobil, Standard, Johnson & Johnson, Coca-Cola; moved to Calif. 1976; founder/pres. Butler Packaging, 1976-82, clients incl. Monsanto Chem., McDonald Restaurants; owner/ pres./ CEO HTS Internat. Inc. (consulting engrs., providing temporary svcs. of qualified engrs. to the power industry), 1982–; mem. nuclear tech. delegation to China, Citizen Ambassador Pgm. (1985); speaker for Entrepreneur Night, SME Orange County Chpt.; honors: First woman in state of Mo. to receive C.P.C. desig. (1970), num. product pkg. design awards, MidWest Pkg. Assn. (1976-82), First Lady of the Day, St. Louis radio station WORTH (1975); mem: Sales & Mktg. Execs. Internat. (bd. dirs., Man of the Year Award), Nat. Employment Assn. (ethics com.), CEO (execs. com.), Am. Nuclear Soc., Am. Mgmt. Assn. (bd. dirs., com. chair); civic: Cystic Fibrosis (sponsor many golf tournaments), Muscular Dystrophy, March of Dimes (sponsor fund drive); rec: golf, sailing. Ofc: HTS International 30012 Ivy Glenn Dr Ste 280 Laguna Niguel 92677

HOGUE, DAVID BRUCE, manufacturing co. executive; b. Aug. 20, 1949, Dermott, Ark.; s. Russel Guy and Janie Jo (Whitaker) H.; m. Dana Robinson, Aug. 30, 1975; children: Robinson b. 1979, Austin b. 1984; edn: BS mktg. Univ. of Ark. 1973; desig: cert. supvr. Dana Univ., Toledo, O. 1986. Career: sales rep. mat. handling equip. Bigelow Robinson Co., 1973-74; sales rep. Orgill Bros/ Little Rock Arkansas Wholesale Appliances & TVs, 1974-76; dist. sales mgr. Dana Corp./ Gard Div. LRAR (sales of NAPA filters thru NAPA) 1976-81, dist. mgr. sales & mktg. of NAPA Filters, New Orleans, La. 1981-83, Western Div. mgr. Dana Corp./ Gard Div., Fresno 1983–, also Gard Div. manager trainer, 1979–; honors: Univ. of Ark. Football Letterman (1969-71, capt. 1971), mem. Gard Pres.'s Club (5 yrs), and Top Growth in Sales (1985, 1986); mem. Univ. Ark. Alumni Assn. and Lettermen Club; civic: PTA, coach Lawless Sch. Youth Soccer, YMCA Youth Football, Youth Baseball; Republican; Baptist; rec: golf, woodworking, furniture refinishing, travel. Res: 5624 N Hazel Ave Fresno 93711 Ofc: Gard Corp. 83 E Shaw Ave Ste 250 Fresno 93710

HOLDER, GEORGE H., co. executive; b. June 24, 1936, Lafayette, Ind.; s. George A. and Carolyn J. (Switzer) H.; m. Suzanne L. Lamb, Nov. 26, 1976; edn: BS in ag., Purdue Univ., 1957. Career: asst. advt. mgr. Nat. Livestock Producer mag., Chgo. 1960-63; sales rep., advtsg. mgr., sales mgr. product mgr., mktg. mgr., country mgr. for Thailand, all with Elanco Products Co. div. Eli Lilly and Co., 1963-80; v.p. mktg. Syntex Agribusiness, 1980-83, v.p./gen. mgr. Syntex Agribusiness USA 1984-85, pres. 1985–, and v.p. Syntex Corp.; bd. dirs. Animal Health Inst.; mil: 1st lt. US Army Arty. 1957-59, Korea Svc. Address: Palo Alto 94304

HOLDER, WILLIAM WALLACE, college professor; b. July 2, 1945, Colorado Springs, Colo.; s. Wallace and Florence Kathryn Holder; m. Carolyn S., May 22, 1983; 1 son, Mark b. 1974; edn: BS, Okla. State Univ. 1969; M.Acctg., Univ. Okla. 1972, Dr. of Bus. Adminstrn., 1974; CPA Okla. 1971. Career: asst. prof. Texas Tech.; vis. assoc. Univ. Tenn.; dir., master acctg. pgm., assoc. prof. Univ. So. Calif.; chair audit com., bd. dirs. Community Counseling Ctrs.; honors: Beta Alpha Psi, Beta Gamma Sigma, Deloitte Haskins & Sells Doctoral Fellowship; mem: Am. Inst. CPAs (council), Am. Acctg. Assn. (chmn. public sector sect.), The Acctg. Circle, Univ. Okla. Alumni Assn.; author: Audits of Small Governments (vols. I and II, Practitioners Pub. Co. 1986), Intermediate Accounting (Harcourt, Brace, Jovanovich 1984), The CPA Examination: A Complete Review (vols. I and II, Houghton, Mifflin & Co. 1985), Local Management Accounting, Management Policies in Local Government Finance (Internat. City Mgmt. Assn. 1981), num. articles in acctg. jours.; mil: E-Y US Army Nat. Guard 1966-72; Republican; Protestant; rec: scuba, sailing. Res: 111 Geneva Walk Long Beach 90803 Ofc: Univ. So. Calif. Sch. of Acctg. Rm 113 Los Angeles 90007

HOLGATE, GEORGE JACKSON, university president; b. Feb. 19, 1933, Lakewood, Ohio; s. George Curtis and Melba (Klein) H.; 1 dau. Leigh M.; edn: BM, Baldwin-Wallace Coll. 1953; MS, Univ. So. Calif. 1955, EdD, 1962; PhD, Riverside Univ. 1970, LLD. Career: exec. v.p. Sierra Found., 1953-56; tchr. Oxnard High Sch. and Ventura Coll., 1956-62; campus coord. Congo Polytech. Inst., 1962-64; pres. Riverside Univ., 1965–; bd. dirs. Lincoln General Corp. 1972-77. Music condr.: Ojai Festival, 1945, Ventura Co. Concert Chorale and Chamber Singers, 1956-60, Ventura Bach Festival, 1958, Columbia Orch. 1960; awards: US Jr. CofC Distinguished Service Award 1962; bd. dirs: Riverside Sym. Orch., Riverside Opera Assn., Calif. Assn. for Pvt. Edn., Calif. Council of Business Schs.; mem. Phi Mu Alpha Sinfonia, Phi Delta Kappa, Sigma Phi Epsilon, Delta Epsilon; mil: flotilla comdr. USCG Aux. 1983-; Democratic State Central Com. of Calif. 1962, Dem. nominee for Cong.

1962; rec: music, fishing, sailing, flying. Ofc: 890 Indian Hill Blvd Pomona 91767

HOLIAN, DARWIN KENNARD, general surgeon; b. Apr. 9, 1923, Maynard, Minn.; s. Kenneth Edwin and Jessie (Kuiper) H.; m. Eleanor Eastvold, Nov. 11, 1944; children: Charlotte b. 1948, Barbara b. 1952, Steven b. 1954, Ann b. 1956; edn: BA, St. Olaf Coll. 1945; MB, Univ. Minn. 1947; MD, Univ. Minn. Med. Sch. 1948; Diplomate Am. Bd. Surg. Career: gen. surgeon Albert Lea (Minn.) Med. Surg. Ctr. 1954-68; gen. surg. Santa Barbara 1969–; chief of staff Goleta Valley Comm. Hosp. 1979-82; fellow Am. Coll. Surg.; mem: Disabled Am. Vets., Boy Scouts of Am., YMCA (pres.), Kiwanis; num. research papers on biliopancreatic bypass for morbid obesity; mil: USN 1943-45, capt. US Army (MC) 1949-51, Korean War, Combat Med. Badge, 2 Battle Stars; Republican; Protestant; rec: computers, woodworking, fishing. Res: 1066 Via Los Padres Santa Barbara 93111 Ofc: 5333 Hollister Ave Ste 210 Santa Barbara 93111

HOLLADAY, WILLIAM LEE, consulting engineer; b. Dec. 9, 1901, Fayette, Mo.; s. Robert Lee and Estella Adelaide (Redman) H.; m. Louise Helen Cook, Sept. 24, 1925; children: William Lee b. 1925, Richard Lee b. 1934, Nancy Lee (Mrs. Kenneth J. Weger) b. 1936; edn: stu. So. Branch, Univ. Calif. 1920-22; BS in E.E., honors, Calif. Inst. of Tech. 1924; grad. wk. UC Los Angeles 1956-57; Reg. Profl. Engr. (Mech. 1948, Electrical 1956) Calif. Career: test mgr. and engr. sales, Gen. Electric Co., Schenectady, NY 1924-25, dist. refrigerator splst. G.E. Co., Dallas 1925-26; product mgr. Geo. Belsey Co., Los Angeles 1927-41; mgr. central repair, Montgomery Ward & Co., Oakland 1941-44; purch. agt. Gen. Htg. & Air Conditioning, Oakland 1944-46; mgr. field service, Drayer-Hanson Inc., Los Angeles 1946-47; v.p. engring. Hieatt Engineering Co., Burbank 1947-52; co-founder, v.p., pres., chmn. Holladay Eggett & Helin, Los Angeles 1952-72; cons. in pvt. practice, Altadena 1972–; adj. prof. mech. engring. USC, 1948-52; honors: Tau Beta Pi, Cal Beta 1924; ASRE-Wolverine Diamond Key, best paper award, 1950; mem: IEEE (life), Fellow ASHRAE (life mem.), pres. 1968-69), Assoc. Energy Engrs. (charter mem, Certified Energy Mgr.), Caltech Alumni Assn. (pres. 1963), Pasadena Lung Assn. (pres. 1970); publs: papers on low temperature refrigeration, weather data, heat transfer; editor: Recommended Design Temperatures, So. Cal., Ariz., Nev. (1957, 1959, 1964, 1972); coeditor: Climatic Data ASHRAE Region X (1982); co-author: Numbers (handbook for Air Con Engrs.); Democrat; Protestant; rec: walking, camping, photog. Res: 2173 Mar Vista Ave Altadena 91001

HOLLAND, HARVEY GLENN, real estate developer/investor; b. July 8, 1917, San Pedro, Calif.; s. Harvey White and Amelia Ida (Landsberg) H.; m. Carolyn Wyatt, Nov. 23, 1939; children: Pamela b. 1945, Mark b. 1947; edn: AA, Compton Coll. 1936. Career: real estate devel., investor, broker 1947–; developer, oper. Club San Moritz, Lake Gregory, Calif.; founder, pres. Santa's Village Resorts, Lake Arrowhead, Santa Cruz, Calif. and Dundee, Ill.; cons. to gen. mgr. Am. Machine and Foundry Monorail Exhibit NY World's Fair 1962-64; pres., gen. mgr., prin. Sierra Dawn Mobile Home Estates, Hemet, Calif.; prin. Crown Hill Properties, Los Angeles; founder, dir. Bank of Hemet; mem. Calif. Club L.A.; mil: USN A/C Reserve 1936-40; Republican; rec: sailing. Res: 3655 La Canada Rd Fallbrook 92028

HOLLEMAN, JOHN JOSEPH, college president; b. Oct. 25, 1932, Oakland, s. Joseph W. and P. Grace (Kingham) H.; m. Nancy Bracken, Mar. 1956; children: Jennifer, b. 1960; Linda, b. 1962; John, b. 1964; edn: BA, UC Berkeley 1956; MA, 1958; EdD, Nova Univ. 1983. Career: instr. Merritt Coll. (designed new biology curriculum; intro. oceanography & marine biol. pgms.) 1957-74; chmn. Dept. Biological Sci. 1966-70; coord. instrn. 1967-70; chmn. Sci. & Math. Div. Merritt Coll. 1975-77; pres. Vista Coll. (264 locations, 600 courses, 13,500 students), Berkeley 1977–; cons./ environ. biologist Dames & Moore, Soil Engrs. & Geologists 1971-78; mem: Nat. Task Force of 2-yr. Coll. Biologists, Am. Inst. Biological Sci. 1970-71; dir. HEW Urban Chem. Tech. Itern Proj. 1973-75; dir. NSY Human Beings & Their Environ. 1977-80; Task Force, locally funded constrn. projs., Chacellors Ofc., Calif. Comm. Colls. 1980; cons. Am. Inst. Biol. Scis. 1974-75; mem: Am. & Calif. Assns. of Comm. & Jr. Colls.; Am. Assn. of Higher Edn.; Ecological Soc. of Am.; Nat. Assn. Biology Tchrs.; Am. Inst. Biol. Scis. (adv. council Proj. Biotech 1971-76); Biol. Soc. of Wash.; Calif. Malacazoological Soc.; W. Soc. of Natuarlists; W. Soc. of Malacologists; Calif. Acad. of Scis.; So. Calif. Soc. of Scis.; Peralta Found.; Rotary; Berkeley Breakfast Club; Berkeley & Oakland CofC; Herrick Health Care Found.; num. arts.in scholarly journs. mil: cpl. US Army 1950-52; rec: youth soccer coach, referee. Res: 164 Greenbrook Dr Danville 94526 Ofc: Vista College, 2020 Milvia St, Ste 480, Berkeley 94704

HOLLEN, DONALD WILLIAM, private investigator, polygraph examiner; b. Dec. 27, 1936, San Francisco; s. Mac Martin and Ruby Grace (Mobley) H.; children: Eric b. 1965, Heidi b. 1968; edn: AA, Cabrillo Coll. 1971; BS, CSU San Jose 1974; cert. FBI Nat. Acad. 1975; Calif. lic. Polygraph Examiner, Pvt. Investigator. Career: police lt. Santa Cruz City Police Dept. 1965-82, ret.; prin. Hollen Pvt. Investigation, Santa Cruz 1983–; recipient profl. commendns. FBI, S.F. (1967, 1972), heroism in line of duty, Santa Cruz City Police Chief (1972), S.C. Co. Bd. Supvrs. (1980), outstanding svc. Marello High Sch. (1981); mem. FBI Nat. Acad. Assocs., Calif. Acad. of Polygraph Scis., Calif. Assn. of Polygraph Examiners, Calif. Assn. of Lic. Investigators; Elks Club. Ofc: Hollen Private Investigations 107 Dakota Ave Ste 1 Santa Cruz 95060

HOLLINGSWORTH, CRAIG D., insurance agent; b. Apr. 18, 1946, Corning, Calif.; s. Elby F. and Mary E. (Craig) Bowman; children: Shari b. 1968, Brent b. 1970, Jared b. 1975, Jodi b. 1977; edn: BA, Pacific Union Coll. 1967; desig: LUTC. Career: dist. pastor Iowa Conf. Seventh Day Adventist Ch., 1967-75,

So. Dakota Conf. SDA, 1975-77; owner/agt. Farmers Ins. Group Agcy., Ceres 1977—; profl. awards: 1985 Dist. Comml. Splst. and Comml. Masters Club, Farmers Ins. Gp. (1985); rec: pvt. pilot, musician (guitar, sax.), restore antique autos. Res: POB 898 Ceres 95307 Ofc: Craig D. Hollingsworth Farmers Ins. Group 2101 Central Ave Ceres 95307

HOLLOWAY, CORRIE VANSHERE, chiropractor; b. Apr. 27, 1929, Los Angeles; parents: Wm. Raymond and Orleans Virginia (Young) Holloway; children: Renee' b. 1957, Rosie b. 1964; edn: undergrad. Sinclair Coll., Los Angeles Technical Coll.; BS, Winsor Univ. 1958; DC, Cleveland Coll. of Chiropractic 1973; postgrad., UC Los Angeles Sch. of Med. 1978; Diplomate Am. Coll. of Chiropractic Orthopedists 1984. Career: owner Holloway's Landscape Constrn. Co., Los Angeles 1954-68; resident roentgenologist Imperial Med. Ctr. 1972-77; pvt. practice chiropractic, Allied Health & Associates, Los Angeles 1978—; lectr. Calif. Coll. of Health Profls.; Calif. Disability Evaluator; mem. City of Los Angeles Med. Panel, L.A. Kidney Found. (past pres.), Calif. Alcoholism Found. (bd. chmn.); awards: Greater L.A. Occupational Achievement award, City Beautiful, Los Angeles Bus. League (1966); mil: served in 555th Airborne Corps; Democrat; Christian; rec: stained glass designer. Ofc: Allied Health & Assocs. 3850 West Santa Barbara Ste 103 Los Angeles 90008

HOLLOWAY, ROBERT ANTHONY, clinical psychologist; b. Aug. 30, 1946, Okla. City, Okla.; s. Maurice Earl and Gertrude (Van Hooser) H.; 1 son: Justin Anthony, b. 1982; edn: BA, honors, Chapman Coll. 1979; MA, 1981; PhD, Calif. Grad. Inst. 1982; tchg. credentials, Calif. St. Dept. Edn. 1980, Calif. Real Estate Lic. 1982. Career: currently pres./ CEO Camelot Communications Inc., Clear Advantage Travel Inc.; founder cameo for Singles; past owner Great Expectations Franchise, Sausalito; dir. Drug & Alcohol Pgm., Germany 1977-78; staff therapist Capistrano by the Sea Psychiatric Hosp. 1981-82; pvt. practice, Tustin 1981-82; mem: Am. Psychological Assn.; Am. Testing & Evaluation; Am. Mgmt. Assn.; Boy Scouts of Am.; Pop Warner Football; Kids Against Alcohol & Drugs; publs: arts., Single in Orange Co. Mag. 1981; conduct sems. on self devel. & wealth consciousness; mil: hospitalman 3/c USN 1964-67; capt. US Army 1970-78: Purple Heart, Vietnam, Joint Svc. Commdn. for valor, Navy Achiev. for valor & Commdn., Vietnamese Cross of Gal., MC Combat Action, Combat Medic; Republican; Protestant; rec: stamps, ice skating, skiing, travel. Address: Robert A. Holloway, PhD, 336 Dolphin Isle Foster City 94404

HOLMEN, GARY LYNN, lawyer; b. Apr. 3, 1944, Rice Lake, Wis.; s. Albert and Evelyn Jane (Tallman) H.; div.; children: Brian b. 1971, Barrett b. 1972, Jenna b. 1980; edn: undergrad. Univ. Wis. 1962-63; BS, USAF Academy 1967; JD, Univ. Denver Coll. of Law 1975. Career: served to capt. US Air Force 1967-74, office of spl. investigations doing criminal investigations in US and intell. work in Japan; with ins. defense firms Archbald & Spray, Santa Barbara and Henderson and Smith, S.B. 1975-81; trial lawyer, ptnr. Pattillo & Holmen, S.B. 1981-85, rep. plaintiffs in major personal injury, malpractice and comml. litigation; prin. Knapp, Paterson & Clarke, ins. defense firm, Universal City 1986—; honors: Am. Jurisprudence Award, evidence, (1973); mem: State Bar of Calif., Calif. Trial Lawyers Assn. (speakers bur. 1983-85), Santa Barbara County Bar Assn.; civic: helped estab. AYSO soccer dept. Santa Barbara, Channel City Club; Republican; Protestant; rec: skiing, boating, soccer. Ofc: Knapp, Petersen & Clarke 70 Universal City Plaza Universal City 91608

HOLMES, HENRY W., lawyer; b. Apr. 1, 1943, Malden, Mass.; s. Henry W., Sr. and Sue (Rossetti) H.; edn: BA, UC Berkeley 1966, JD, 1969; admitted Calif. State Bar 1970. Career: atty. law firm Cooper, Epstein & Hurewitz, Beverly Hills (handled well-known copyright cases- Ellison v ABC, Gerber v Marvel; co-counsel in Marilyn Barnett v King; mem. advis. bd. Nat. Women's Sports Found., gen. counsel to Sci. Fiction Writers of Am.); lectr. on copyright and representing artistic talent at USC Law Sch., Southwestern Law Sch., UCLA Law Sch.; frequent speaker bar assns. on copyright infringement and plagiarism; honors: Ford Found. grant in constnl. law, New Delhi, India; Dean's Honor Award, Boalt Law Sch. UCB; mem: L.A. County Bar Assn., Beverly Hills Bar Assn., Calif. State Bar Assn., Bar Assn. of Am. Samoa, L.A. Copyright Soc., ACLU; author Rules of Civil Procedure for High Ct. of Am. Samoa; contbr. arts. in law jours.; Democrat; Catholic; rec: ship wreck diving, surfing, contemp. art. Res: 3315 Ocean Front Walk Marina Del Rey 90291 Ofc: Cooper, Epstein & Hurewitz 9465 Wilshire Blvd Ste 800 Beverly Hills 90212

HOLMES, MARIA L., organizational consulting firm executive; b. Mar. 2, 1944, San Francisco; d. Tracy S. and Nini(Lyddy) Holmes; edn: BA in creative writing/journ., CSU Long Beach 1967; grad. stu. Columbia Pacific Univ. Career: tchr. Los Angeles Unified Sch. Dist. 1967-80; prin. Maria Holmes Co. (pub. rels.), Harbor City 1980-81; ptnr. Davidson & Holmes Assocs. (orgnl. consultants), Harbor City 1982—; dir. bus. and program devel., TranSyn Ltd. (orgnl. consulting firm), Venice 1982—; lectr. in bus. and psychol., Torrance Adult Sch. 1980-81, Harbor Coll., Wilmington 1982-; consultant: Child Focus Pub. Co., Los Angeles Co., South Bay-Harbor Volunteer Bureau, Woman Space Mag., L.A. Unified Sch. Dist., Denny's Restaurants, Computer Learning Ctr., Incolay Mfg., Shuper Photogs.; mem: AAUW, COTO, The Centers Network, Alpha Omicron Pi; author: Dealing with Difficult People; Soaring (Through Plate Glass Windows), A Handbook of Personal Evolution; rec: sailing. Ofc: Maria Holmes Communication Services, 760 W Lomita Blvd, Ste 144, Harbor City 90710

HOLT, DONALD GENE, tool & die co. president; b. Mar. 24, 1934, New Bloomfield, Mo.; s. Paul G. and Nellie Ethel (Blythe) H.; children: Karen b.

1960, Darrell b. 1962, Douglas b. 1964; edn: USN Machinist Sch. 1953. Career: tool room foreman Grow Value, 1957-68; founder/pres. Diamond Tool & Die Inc., 1972—; mem. Soc. Mfg. Engrs., Masons, Elks; patent: Inmation Quickchange Tooling; mil: MR1 US Navy 1953-57; Republican; Prot.; rec: camping. Res: 1328 Fernside Blvd Alameda 94501 Ofc: Diamond Tool & Die Inc 508 29th Ave Oakland 94601

HOLTSMARK, ERIC B., architect; b. July 25, 1937, Malmkoping, Sweden; s. Bent Erling and Birgit (Egerstrom) H.; m. Aase Kristoffersen, Sept. 5, 1975; children: Devon b. 1963, Eric, II b. 1964, Mindi b. 1977, Jenni b. 1979, Nicole b. 1984; edn: Midland Sch., 1950-55; B.Arch., UC Berkeley 1963; cert., Inst. d'Urbanisme (1960-61), L'Ecole des Beaux Arts (1960-61), Paris. Reg. Architect, ca. 1978; Reg. EIT, Ca. 1965; NCARB, 1982. Career: journeyman carpenter (7 yrs), var. constrn. trades, 1951-63; resident engr. Masonic Home, Union City (hosp. project) 1963-64; proj. coordinator Bechtel Internat. San Francisco for Tarapur Nuclear project, India 1964-66; field engr. Bechtel Pacific Corp. Ltd., Tasmania (iron mine & townsite) 1966-67; sr. engr. var. hotel projects, Bechtel Corp., NY 1968-69; proj. mgr. and architect Bechtel Internat. Ltd., Helsinki, Finland (Hotel Inter-Continental) 1969 72; proj. mgr. Bechtel Intl. Ltd., London, England (Hotel Inter-Continental) 1972-76; proj. mgr. Bechtel Inc., S.F. (Saudi Arabia projs.) 1976-78; architect/ owner/ founder Commercial & Hotel Development, S.F. (Holtsmark Architects after 1985, hotels and other projects in USA, Europe, West Indies, Mid East) 1978—; dir. and part owner Eurocal Hotel Devel., Ltd., London, Eng. (hotel devel., renovation and operation) 1985—; owner/ founder Mark-Bentland Properties (property inv. co.) 1975—; mem: Phi Kappa Tau (1955-7), Project Mgmt. Inst., S.F. 1977-79, AIA No. Calif. 1978-81, Soc. of Am. Reg. Architects 1980-82, Nat. Trust for Hist. Preservation 1980-; Republican (Presdtl. Task Force 1982-); author: Putyshestvinik (accts. of travel alone through Russia 1960), pub. in Paris 1960; Ind.; rec: tennis, skiing, swimming, yachting. Res: 321 Scenic Ave Piedmont 94611 Ofc: Holtsmark Architects, 1 Market Plaza, Spear St Tower, Ste 346, San Francisco 94105

HOLTZCLAW, BYRON PAUL, manufacturing co. executive; b. May 1, 1931, Vallejo; s. Paul Watson and Josephine (Lanzi) H.; m. Laura, Mar. 10, 1957; children: Mark b. 1958, Mia b. 1968; edn: bus. courses Valley Coll. 1956, Anthony Real Estate Sch. 1973. Career: plant mgr. Western Globe (Globe A-1 Spaghetti), Los Angeles 1963-72; plant mgr. Internat. Foods., Commerce 1972-74; currently plant mgr. Globe Prods. and v.p. Robert William Realty; civic: Friendly Hills Homeowners Assn.; inventor: new packaging system (Pasta Bag) for pkg. macaroni products which doubled prodn., sys. still in use (1974); mil: yeoman US Navy 1951-55, Nat. Def., Pres. Unit Cit., Korean Service, UN Service 2 stars, China Service Extended; Republican; Catholic; rec: golf, tennis, photog. Ofc: Western Globe Inc 8985 Venice Blvd Los Angeles 90034

HOM, YOW O., restaurant owner; b. Mar. 7, 1922, Canton, Kwangtung, China; s. Ming and Shee (Lee) H.; m. Natsumi Terasaki, Dec. 16, 1961; children: Dex b. 1950, Gary b. 1958, Ronald b. 1960, Jim, Jr. b. 1962, Lisa b. 1964; edn: AA, San Diego City Coll. 1948. Career: worked in Chinese Grocery, San Diego 1948-50; opened China Land restaurant, S.D. 1950-73; owner Jim Hom's Restaurant, Spring Valley 1973—; mem: Masons, San Diego Uplifters Inc., Spring Valley CofC, San Diego Tavern and Restaurant Assn.; works: made award winning model airplane for USN during WWII (1941-42); mil: s/sgt US Air Force 1943-45, Good Conduct, Sharp Shooter, So. Pacific Ops., Mariana Campaign; Republican; Prot.; rec: landscaping, woodworking. Res: 3293 Altadena Ave San Diego 92105 Ofc: Jim Hom's Restaurant 9330-Jamacha Blvd Spring Valley 92077

HOMEL, LEONARD, sales co. owner; b. June 7, 1917, Chgo.; s. Harry L. and Dorothy (Belson) H.; m. Margaret Chirillo, Jan. 9, 1953; children: Steven b. 1944, Daniel b. 1953, Kevin b. 1955, Jeffrey b. 1957; edn: Univ. of Ill. 1934-38. Career: gen. sales 1945-72; gen. mgr. Heaven Hill Distillery Sales Co. 1972-81; owner Heaven-Hill Williams Distillery Sales Co. 1981-86; originated and taught sales tng. seminars; past pres. Nat. Profl. Bowling League (1962); mem. Series Book Collectors Club, Horatio Alger Soc., Henty Soc.; ofcl. editor Edgar Rice Burroughs - Amateur Press Assn.; mil: 2d lt. US Army Transp. Corps 1941-45; rec: book collecting. Ofc: Heaven Hill-Evan Williams Co. POB 3217 Thousand Oaks 91359

HONEYMAN, BETTY, executive secretary; b. July 26, 1938, Clintonville, NY; d. Guy and Cora M. (Carpenter) Everest; m. David Honeyman, Nov. 5, 1955; children: David Jr. b. 1956, Scott b. 1959, Daniel b. 1960. Career: bookkeeper State Bank of Albany, Plattsburgh, NY 1957-59; bookkeeper National Commercial Bank, Plattsburgh, NY 1959-60; acct. clerk Plattsburgh Press Republican, Plattsburgh, NY 1960-63; acct. clerk Valley Paper Co., Sacramento 1967-71; bookkeeper, office mgr., bd. dirs. J.B. Specialty Sales, Sacramento 1972-75; office mgr., bd. dirs. Valley Cabinet & Mfg. Inc., Sacramento 1975-81; corp. v.p., secty., bd. dirs. Sacramento Valley Cabinet 1981—; honors: pres. award Internat. Assn. of Jim Beam Bottle & Specialties Club (1985), Golden Fox award Council of Golden Foxes (1985); mem. Camellia City Jim Beam Bottle Club; publs: Jim Beam Bottles a Pictoral Guide (1982), supplement update (1983, 1985), A Regal Collection of Jim Beam Go Withs (1983); Republican; Catholic. Ofc: 2500 Citrus Rd. Rancho Cordova 95670

HONG, SOON KYUNG, electrical engineer; b. July 13, 1930, Seoul, Korea, nat. US cit. 1979; s. Jang Sung and Zakun Soon (Zee) H.; m. Myung, Nov. 5, 1954; children: John b. 1960, Richard b. 1963; edn: BS, Seoul National Univ. 1957; Reg. Profl. Engr., Calif. 1978. Career: chief Electrical Sect., Korea

Electrical Co., Seoul 1958-73, in charge of design and constrn. for power plants; supvsg. engr. Bechtel Power Corp. and Bechtel, Inc., San Francisco, responsible for the elec. system design work for a fossil plant, hydro plant, nuclear plant and an airport, 1973—; honors: Merit Awards (3), Prime Minister of Korea (1971), Pres. of Korea Elec. Co. (1967), Comdr. Engineering Div. of Korea Army (1955); mem: IEEE, Korean Am. Scientist and Engr. Assn.; mil: capt. Korea Army 1950-55; Methodist; rec: mountain climbing. Res: 35344 Dover Ct Newark 94560 Ofc: Bechtel Inc. 50 Beale St San Francisco 94119

HONIG, BILL, educator, state official; b. Apr. 23, 1937, San Francisco; s. Louis and Miriam (Anixter) H.; m. Nancy Catlin, June 2, 1973; children: Michael, Carolyn, Steven, Jonathan; edn: BA, UC Berkeley 1958; JD, UCB Boalt Hall 1963; MA, San Francisco St. Univ. 1972; admitted Calif. State Bar; Calif. Teaching Credential. Career: clerk Calif. Supreme Court 1963-64; atty. State of Calif. Dept. of Finance 1964-67; atty. Pettit & Martin, San Francisco 1967-71; elementary sch. tchr. San Francisco Unified Sch. Dist. 1972-76; dir. Staff Devel. Project, San Francisco 1977-79; supt. Reed Union Elem. Sch. Dist., Tiburon 1979-82; elected supt. of public instrn., State of Calif., 1983—; mem. Calif. State Board of Edn. 1975-, exec. ofcr. and secty. 1983-, regent Univ. of Calif. 1983-, trustee Calif. State Colls. and Univs. 1983-; honors: Law Review (1963), Order of Coif (1963), num. awards as Calif. Supt. of Public Instrn.; orgs: Californians Preventing Violence (bd. dirs.), Carnegie Forum on Edn. (Task Force on Teaching as a Profession), Chamber of Commerce (State Edn. Com.), PTA (Calif. State Advisory Bd.), YMCA (Model Legislature Advisory Com.); author: Last Chance for our Children (Addison Wesley, 1985); coauthor instrnl. manual, Handbook for Planning an Effective Reading Program (1983, 4th printing); num. articles on ednl. issues in state and nat. publs. including Education Week, American Spectator, Phi Delta Kappan, and Los Angeles Times; mil: 2d lt. US Army Med. Service Corps 1958-59; Jewish; rec: running, swimming, piano. Ofc: State Dept. of Education, 721 Capitol Mall Sacramento 95814

HONIG, EMANUEL M., psychiatrist-psychoanalyst; b. Feb. 1, 1915, Bklyn.; s. Louis and Minnie (Metzger) H.; m. Muriel Mosler, June 14, 1942; children: Madalyn b. 1946, Sheila b. 1949, Jeffrey b. 1948; edn: BS, Bklyn. Coll. 1935; M. Hebrew Lit., Rabbi, Jewish Inst. of Religion 1939; MD, Univ. Ore. 1950; PhD, So. Calif. Psychoanalytic Inst. 1977. Career: rabbi Temple Bethel, Binghamton, NY 1939-41; chaplain US Army and Air Force 1941-46; medical student 1946-51, fellow Menninger Found. 1951-54; pvt. practice of psychiatry, 1954—; asst. clin. prof. Dept. Psychiatry UC Los Angeles 1956-; bd. dirs. Cardiovascular Research Corp.; honors: Alpha Omega Alpha 1950; mem: Life Fellow Am. Psychiatric Assn., Life Mem. Am. Psychoanalytic Assn., LA County Med. Assn., CMA; bd. dirs. Jewish Fedn. Council; bd. govs. Univ. of Judaism; publs: papers in psychiatry and religion; mil: major Chaplains Corp, AUS, USAF 1941-46, Mediterranean Theater, 4 Battle Stars; Democrat; Hebrew; rec: tennis, travel, community. Ofc: Emanuel M. Honig MD Inc. 300 S Beverly Dr Ste 312 Beverly Hills 90212

HONOROF, MARC PAUL, electronic/computer marketing executive; b. Feb. 20, 1957, Queens, N.Y.; s. Daniel M. and Gladys Honorof; edn: BBA, Adelph Univ. 1979; MBA, CSU Dominguez Hills 1983. Career: insurance adjuster G.A.B., 1980-83; mktg. dir., Cal-Abco (computer distbr.), 1983—; CFO Bakari Internat. import/ export 1986; honors: Dean's list CSUDH; mem. Long Beach CofC; rec: small bus. consulting. Res: 5354 Lindley Ave Encino 91316 Ofc: Cal-Abco 6041 Variel Ave Woodland Hills 91367

HONZIK, MARJORIE PYLES, developmental psychologist; b. May 14, 1908, Johannesburg, So. Africa, parents US citizens; d. Jay Franklin and Maude Ethel (Knickerbocker) Pyles; m. Charles H. Honzik, Aug. 7, 1935; children: Eleanor b. 1938, Elizabeth b. 1941; edn: BA, UC Berkeley 1930, MA 1933, PhD 1936. Career: research fellow and nursery sch. tchr. Nat. Child Research Center, Wash DC 1931-32; asst. research psychologist Inst. Child Welfare, UC Berkeley 1932-38; Rockerfeller fellow 1938-42; research assoc. to asst. research psychologist UC Inst. of Child Welfare 1942-54; assoc. to research psychologist and lectr. in psychology, UCB Inst. of Human Development 1954-75, research psychologist and lectr. in psych. emeritus 1975-; cons. with neurologists, Presbyterian Hosp., S.F. and Childrens Hosp., S.F.; honors: G.Stanley Hall Award for distinction in research, Div. Developmental Psychology, Am. Psych. Assn. (1983); mem: Am. Psych. Assn., Soc. for Research in Child Devel., Internat. Soc. for Study of Behavioral Devel., Fellow AAAS; co-editor of 3 books, co-author 1 book, contbr. 27 articles in sci. jours., 9 chapters in books; Democrat; Unitarian; rec: symphony concerts, opera, play piano. Res: 2614 Street Berkeley 94705 Ofc: Institute of Human Development, Univ. California Berkeley 94720

HOOD, VALERIE, computer consultant; b. July 23, 1954, El Paso, Texas; d. Frank E. and Ruth (Matkin) H.; 1 son, Cameron b. 1982; grad. Simi Valley H.S. 1971. Career: contracts adminstr. ABC-TV, Los Angeles 1978-83; pres. Independent Data Services, W.L.A. 1983—; workshop leader (Microcomputers) Women In Film, 1983-; tech. writing cons. MICOM Technologies, Inc. 1984-; Software quality assurance cons. Epson America 1984-85; mem: Women in Film (recipient Contribn. Award 1984-85), Assn. of Entertainment Industry Computer Profls., L.A. Framework User's Gp. (exec. bd. 1984-), Los Angeles Paralegal Assn. 1980-, Assn. for Women in Computing, Women Writer's Computer Gp., Nat. Software Review Board (1983-); author: The Computer Consultant's Consultant (1985), Baby's Mother's Book (1983), num. articles in field; 3 appearances on "Famous Computer Cafe" radio show; SysOp of The Computer Consultant's Network BBS in Los Angeles. Ofc: Independent Data Services, 12021 Wilshire Blvd Ste 396 Los Angeles 90025

HOOD-GIBSON, BETTY, real estate co. executive; b. April 6, 1945, Ft. Worth, Texas; s. Cecil and Edna Lou (Brock) Hood; m. David Gibson, March 23, 1978; 1 dau, Anne b. 1980; edn: BBA, cum laude, Texas Christian Univ. 1966; MBA, Pepperdine Univ. 1981; CPA, Texas (1968) and Calif. (1976). Career: senior auditor Arthur Young Co., Dallas, Texas 1966-72; controller Inter City Investments Co., Dallas, Texas 1972-74; cash mgr. Crown Zellerbach Corp., San Francisco 1974-78; v.p. Consolidated Capital Cos., Emeryville 1978-81; real estate and tax cons., San Francisco 1981-84; senior v.p. public pgms., finance and ops. Cosolidated Capital, Emeryville 1984—; adj. lectr. MBA Financial Plnng., Golden Gate Univ., San Francisco; honors: Beta Gamma Sigma; Beta Gamma Psi; mem: Am. Inst. CPAs, Texas and Calif. Socs. CPAs; Nat. Assn. Real Estate Investment Trusts, Bridgemont H.S. (bd. trustees, San Francisco 1982-84), Central YMCA (bd. mgr., San Francisco 1984-); works: publn., Characteristics of Sucessful Entrepreneurs- Northern California Bay Area - 1981; Protestant; rec: Cellar Soc. of San Francisco (wine tasting). Ofc: Consolidated Capital Cos., 2000 Powell St. Emeryville 94608

HOOKO, MARK DAVID, restaurateur; Aug. 26, 1952, NYC, NY; s. David John and Clara Marie (Paull) H.; m. Sherry Lynn, Sept. 29, 1977; edn: BSEE, New York Univ. 1974; MS, San Diego Culinary Acad. 1978. Career: restaurant mgr. Hyatt Hotels Inc., Miami Beach, Fla. 1973-76; owner, opr. Marin Mobile Munchies 1981—; currently, owner, opr. Marco's; prof. microwave cookery Litton Microwave Co.; tchr. microwave tech.; mem: San Francisco Chef's Guild, Calif. Restaurant Assn. (San Marin Valley Assn); supporter Marin Art & Garden Ctr.; midl: food svc. ofcr. USN 1976-81, Navy Exploration Award; Democrat; Catholic; rec: backgammon, polo, auto collector. Address: Marin Mobile Munchies, 7 Rosemary Ct. Novato 94947

HOOPER, LOUIS GORDON, candy manufacturing co. executive; b. March10, 1908, Milbrae; s. Rupert Thomas and Elsie Muriel (Pagan) H.; m. Barbara, June 15, 1924; children: L. Gordn b. 1935, Robin b. 1937. Career: candy mfg. bus. 1921, plant supt. 1930-39; founder international chocalate business 1939; currently, pres. Hooper's Conf. Inc., Oakland; honors: Legion of Honor, De Molay; mem: Retail Conf. of U.S. (pres. 1956), Assn. Retail Mfg. of U.S. & Canada (pres.), De Molay, Masons, Scottish Rite, Shriners, Elks, Jesters; Republican; rec: flying, horse patrol. Res: 15 El Sereno Rd Orinda 94605 Ofc: Hooper's Conf. Inc., 4632 Telegraph Oakland 94609

HOOSE, WINSTON PETTUS, financial planning executive; b. Oct. 3, 1946, Los Angeles; s. Harned Pettus and Elisabeth S. (Smith) H.; edn: BA, Whittier Coll. 1968; JD, USC Law Ctr. 1971; CLU, cand. Career: Vista volunteer lawyer, Ctr. for Law & Poverty, Los Angeles 1971-72; trust ofcr. United Calif. Bank L.A. 1973-75, trust ofcr., S.F. Hdqtrs. & secty., Trust Investment Com. 1975-77, mgr. pension trust accts., S.F. 1977-78; credit ofcr./ analyst, L.A. Hdqtrs. & S.F. Main Ofc. 1978-79; fin. plng. exec., Levine Financial Group, San Francisco 1979—; Whittier Coll. Endowment Com. 1984; bd. dirs. San Francisco Jaycees 1979-80; awards: New Agent in the Country for Mutual Benefit Life Ins. Co. in Number of Cases, 1980; New Assoc. of Year 1980, Investment Leader 1984, Levine Fin. Gp.; Delta Sigma Rho- Tau Kappa Alpha, nat. spkg. frat. 1968; Phi Sigma Alpha, polit. sci. frat. 1968; mem: S.F. & Nat. Life Underwriters Assns.; Million Dollar Round Table; Phi Alpha Delta, Ross chpt.; Nat. Spkrs. Assn.; S.F. Rotary (Oct. div. chmn.); Big Brothers of the Bay Area; Whittier Coll. No. Calif. Alumni chpt.; William Penn Soc.; Whittier Coll. Frat.; publs: United Calif. Bank Trust Mgmt. Tng. Pgm. 1973; Democrat; Ch. of Relig. Sci.; rec: biking, phys. fitness, youth orgns. Res: 441 Via Hidalgo, 20, Greenbrae 94904 Ofc: Levine Financial Group, 1 California St, Ste 2400, San Francisco 94111

HOPE, HARRY, producer, director, writer; b. May 26, 1926, Elmhurst, Long Island; s. Felix Pelziger; m. Nancy, July 4, 1958; children: Margot b. 1958, Mark b. 1962; edn: BA, UC los Angeles 1949; MA, Univ. Houston (USAF Pgm.) 1954; PhD pol. and soc. scis., Etudes Universetaires Internationales, Brussels 1965. Career: spl. effects, stuntman Republic Studios; producer, writer Star Prodns.; producer, dir. Exploitation Films; founder Blue Bird Films, Taiwan and Hong Kong; owner Inter-Associates; producer Columbia Studio; exec. v.p. in chg. of prodn. First Leisure Corp. (merger of Inter-Associates and Western Internat.) 1970-72; owner, operator (writer, producer, director) Inter-Associates 1972—; honors: Hong Kong Cinema Critics Award (for producer/ writer No. 13 Sin Alley, 1961), Best Picture Asian Film Festival (producer The Little Widow 1967), Honors Award (Acad. of Sci. Fiction, Fantasy and Horror Films 1980); mem: Am. Film Inst., Mus. of Natural History, Smithsonian Inst.; films: Smokey and the Judge, Sunset Cove, Doomsday Machine, Death Dimension, Thunderfist, Tarzana, The Mad Butcher, Death Blow; mil: capt. USAF, major USAFR; rec: horseback riding, swimming, running, basketball, volleyball, badminton, stunt driving. Ofc: Harry Hope Productions Hollywood 90028

HOPKINS, BARBARA P., public relations executive; b. Sept. 26, 1948, Santa Monica; d. Philip Rising and Caroline Jean (Dickason) Peters; m. Philip J Hopkins, May 23, 1981; Edn: AA, Santa Monica Coll., 1971; BS, San Diego State Univ. 1976; grad. stu., UCLA, 1981-2. Career: gen. partner, Signet Properties, Los Angeles 1971-85; tech. editor, C. Brewer & Co., Hilo, Hawaii 1975; ed. Aztec Engineer, San Diego, 1976; regional publicist, YWCA, San Diego 1977; Campaign Cons. Repub. Congl. and Assem. Candidates, San Diego 1978-79; Public Opinion Pollster, Los Angeles Times, 1982; pres., Humbird Hopkins Inc., Los Angeles 1979—; ASCE 1975-76, Am. Soc. of Mag. Photo. 1980. Listed in: Who's Who Among Students in Am. Univ. & Coll. 1976; Personalities of Am.; Personalities of the West & Midwest; The Directory of Distinguished Americans; mem: IEEE 1974-76; Internat. Assn. of Bus. Communicators; Sales & Mktg. Exec. Assn. Orgns: Mayor's Council on Libraries, Los Angeles; Wilshire Blvd. Property Owners Assn.; Comml. & Indus. Props. Assn. (founding mem.); docent Mus. of Sci & Indus. Publs: The Layman's Guide to Raising Cane - An Overview of the Hawaiian Sugar Industry, 1976; The Students' Survival Guide, 1977, 2d ed. 1978. Rec: writing, travel, opera. Ofc: Humbird Hopkins Inc., POB 49813, Barrington Station, Los Angeles 90049

HOPKINS, CECILIA ANN, college administrator; b. Feb. 17, 1922, Havre, Mont.; d. Kost L. and Mary (Manaras) Sofos; m. Henry E. Hopkins, Sept. 7, 1944; edn: BS, Mont. State Coll. 1944; MS, San Francisco St. Coll. 1958, 2d. MA, 1967; PhD, Calif. Western Univ. 1977. Career: business tchr. Havre H.S., 1942-44; secty. George P. Gorham Real Estate, 1944-45; escrow secty. Fox & Carskadon Realtors, 1945-50; escrow ofcr. Calif. Pacific Title Ins. Co. 1950-57; bus. tchr. Westmoor H.S., 1957-58; instr. Coll. of San Mateo, 1958–, chpsn. Real Estate Dept. 1963-76, dir. Div. of Business 1976-86, post-retirement dir. real estate dept. 1986–; cons. Calif. State Dept. Real Estate, Sacto.; chpsn. Comm. Coll. Adv. Commn., 1971-72; adv. com. Comm. Coll. Chancellor 1976-; adv. com. Comm. Coll. R.E. Edn. Endowment Fund 1977; project dir. Career Awareness Consortium Com. 1976-; appt. to State Dept. of R.E. Commnrs. Adv. Com. for Edn. and Resrch. 1983-; awards: RECI (Real Estate Certificate Inst.) Award, Calif. Assn. of Realtors 1982; RECI Geo. Thuss Award 1982, 86; CBEA (Calif. Bus. Education) Commendn. for devel. real estate curriculum and devotion to bus. edn. 1978; Soroptimist Intl. (San Mateo - Burlingame) Woman of Achievement 1979; mem: Delta Pi Epsilon (nat. secty. 1968-9), Calif. Assn. of Real Estate Tchrs. (state pres. 1964-5, hon. dir. 1965-), S.F. State Coll. Counseling and Guidance Alumni Assn., Calif. Bus. Tchrs. Assn., Alpha Gamma Delta, Theta Alpha Delta, Phi Lambda Theta, AAUW; coauthor: Calif. Real Estate Principles (John Wiley & Sons 1980); rec: travel, antiques, hiking. Res: 504 Colgate Wy San Mateo Ofc: College of San Mateo 1700 W. Hilldale Blvd San Mateo 94402

HOPKINS, MARGARET EDITH, advertising agency executive; b. Dec. 4, 1940, Los Angeles; d. Harold James and Beatrice Elizabeth (Fry) Schlarman; m. Franklin L. Hopkins, July 17, 1977; children: Darin b. 1960, Jeff b. 1961, Lisa b. 1963; stepchildren: Frank b. 1962, Gary b. 1963, Jodi b. 1965, Kelly b. 1966; edn: AA, Cerritos Coll. 1976; personnel mgmt. cert., UC Irvine 1976; supermarket mgmt. cert., Univ. So. Calif. 1977. Career: dept. mgr. Broadway Dept. Stores 1965-68; employment mgr. Vons Grocery Co. 1968-78; v.p. Hopkins & Assocs. Inc. advtg. agcy. 1978–; honors: John Kelly Award (Fountain Valley CofC 1984), Bd. Mem. of the Year (FV CofC 1983), District Checker of the Year (Vons 1970, 71, 72); mem: Fountain Valley CofC (fiesta dir. 1984, num. coms. and task force), Omni Bus. Club (pres. 1985-86, v.p. 1985-86, treas. 1984-85), Little Miss Softball (mgr. 1975-78), Little League (secty. 1973), Rainbow Girls (worthy advisor 1956), Cerritos Coll. Women's Pres. 1959; Republican; Baptist. Res: 8111 Atwater Cir Huntington Beach 92646 Ofc: Hopkins & Assoc. Inc. 10101 Slater Ave Ste 245 Fountain Valley 92708

HOPMANN, DAVID EDWARD, lawyer; b. Aug. 31, 1943, St. Louis, Mo.; s. Edward Louis and Agnes Alma (Aurin) H.; edn: BA, Yale Coll. 1965, JD, Yale Law Sch. 1968; admitted to State Bar of Calif. 1969. Career: assoc. atty. Pillsbury, Madison & Sutro, San Francisco 1972-76, partner, 1977–; mil: capt. US Army Intell. Br. 1968-71. Res: 64 Graystone Terrace, San Francisco 94114 Ofc: Pillsbury, Madison & Sutro, 235 Montgomery St San Francisco 94104

HOPPING, RICHARD LEE, college president; b. July 26, 1928, Dayton, Ohio; s. Lavon Lee and Dorothy Marie (Anderson) H.; m. Patricia Vance, June 30, 1951; children: Ronald, b. 1952, Debra, b. 1954, Jerrold, b. 1956; edn: BSc and D.Opt., So. Coll. of Optometry, 1952, hon. D.Ocular Sci., 1972. Career: practice optometry, Dayton, Ohio 1953-73; pres. Southern California Coll. of Optometry, Fullerton 1973–; past pres. Assn. of Schs. and Colls. of Optometry, 1982-85; trustee Assn. of Independent Calif. Colls. and Univs., 1973–; chmn. Adv. Research Council, Am. Opt. Found., 1976-; chmn. Awards Com. Am. Acad. of Opt., 1981-; vice chair Nat. Acad. of Practice in Optometry, 1983-; honors: Disting. Service award Am. Public Health Assn., Vision Care Sect. (1984), Vision Optometrist of Year, Am. Public Health Assn. (1962), Ohio State Opt. Assn., Optimist of Year (1956), Dayton View Optimist Club, Ohio's Ten Outstanding Young Men of Year 1960, Junior CofC, Sigma Alpha Sigma, Beta Sigma Kappa; mem: Fellow Am. Acad. of Opt., Fellow Am. Public Health Assn., Am. Opt. Assn. (pres. 1971-2, bd. trustees 1966-73, Referee in Practice Mgmt. Jour. 1977-), Ohio Opt. Assn. (pres. 1964-65), Miami Valley Opt. Soc. (pres. 1958-59), Calif. Opt. Assn. (Long Range Plnng. Com. 1974-77, 81-); num. publs. on vision and health care; Republican; Presbyterian. Res: 2741 Anacapa Pl Fullerton 92635 Ofc: Southern Calif. Coll. of Optometry, 2001 Associated Rd Fullerton 92631

HOPPY, DANIEL L., real estate broker; b. Apr. 6, 1946, Seattle, Wash.; s. Lawrence E. and Evelyn C. (Evans) H.; m. Marcia, July 11, 1971; children: Amy Lynn b. 1976, Jill b. 1981; edn: BA, CSU Fullerton 1969; JD, Western State Univ. 1978. Career: owner/broker Dan Hoppy Realty (resales) and Dan Hoppy & Assocs. (mktg. and sales new home tracts in N. Orange Co.), also comml. real estate brokerage in Calif., Ariz. and Nev.; mem: Huntington Beach/F.V. Bd. Realtors (past dir.), Calif. Assn. Realtors (past dir.), Nat. Assn. Realtors, Nu Beta Epsilon legal frat.; civic: Rotary (dir. internat. svcs.), F.V. Chamber of Commerce, F.V. Planning Commnr., Bethany Christian Acad. Sch. Bd. (chmn.); mil: US Army staff Judge Advocate (mem. def. counsel for 1st lt. Wm. L. Calley Court Martial re My Lai massacre in Vietnam); Republican (O.C. Central Com.); Christian; rec: golf, tennis, pvt. pilot. Res: 17432 Winemast St Fountain Valley 92708 Ofc: Dan Hoppy & Associates 10221 Slater Ste 201 Fountain Valley 92708

HORAN, CAROLE PUGH, school administrator/ boutique owner; b. July 1, 1944, Chgo.; d. Hillard B. and Goldie L. (Lawson) Williams; children: Scott b. 1965, Deborah b. 1968, Danielle b. 1978, Anthony b. 1980; edn: BA, Central State Coll. 1966. Career: dir. Winner Business Sch. 1971-73; dir. Holoman Career Inst. 1973-75; adminstr. Dorothy Brown Sch., spl. edn. sch. 1975–; owner Little Like Me Fashion Petite Boutique 1982 –; ptnr. in limo. svc. Yours, Mine and Ours, specializing in English Classic Limo. Svc.; awards: Comm. Svc. awd., C.I.T.I.E.S. 1981; mem: Urban League; NAACP; Calif. Assn. Pvt. Spl. Edn. Schs. (CAPSES); Black Edn. Assn.; Carson CofC; publs: Reach Out and Touch $$$, 1982; Ch. of Relig. Sci.; rec: golf, swimming, balloon decorations. Res: 1783 Gladwick St Carson 90746 Ofcs: Little Like Me, 111 E Carson St, Ste 6, Carson 90745; Dorothy Brown School, 3502 S Normadie Ave Los Angeles 90007

HORN, (JOHN) STEPHEN, university president; b. May 31, 1931, Gilroy; s. John Stephen and Isabelle (McCaffrey) H.; m. Nini Moore, Sept. 4, 1954; children: Marcia (Yavitz), Stephen; edn: AB with great distinction, Stanford Univ. 1953, PhD, 1958; MPA (Administration fellow), Harvard Univ. 1955. Career: adminstrv. asst. to US Secty. Labor James P. Mitchell, 1959-60; legis. asst. to US Sen. Thomas H. Kuchel, 1960-66; senior fellow Brookings Inst., 1966-69; dean grad. studies and research American Univ., 1969-70; vice chmn. US Commn. on Civil Rights, 1969-80, commr. 1980-82; pres. CSU Long Beach, 1970 –; fellow Inst. Politics Harvard Univ., 1966-67; bd. dirs. Nat. Inst. Corrections (chmn. 1984-), Inst. Internat. Edn.; vice chmn. Long Beach Promotion Com.; mem. Calif. Republican League; Congl. fellow Am. Polit. Sci. Assn. 1958-59. Mem. Stanford Alumni Assn. (pres. 1976-7), Stanford Associates, Calif. Scholarship Fedn. (chpt. pres.), Phi Beta Kappa, Pi Sigma Alpha; author: The Cabinet and Congress (1960), Unused Power: The Work of the Senate Committee on Appropriations (1970), (with Edmund Beard) Congressional Ethics: The View from the House (1975). Ofc: 1250 Bellflower Blvd., Long Beach 90840

HORN, IRENE, hypnotherapist; b. Nov. 24, Los Angeles; d. Milton Harold and Elsie (Kaye) Gutterman; m. Howard Horn, Feb. 15, 1953, div. 1974; children: Robin Elyse, Matthew Steven; edn: Univ. of Miami, Fla.; Maryland Coll. for Women, Baltimore, Md.; desig: Ordained Minister of Metaphysics (1978), Cert. Hypnotherapist (1980). Career: owner/dir. Tree of Life Hypnosis Counseling Center, North Hollywood 1979–; lectr. hypnosis, metaphysics, psychic awareness classes, crystal energy & meditations; mem. Assn. for Past Life Research and Therapy, Am. Council of Hypnotherapist Examiners; contbr. article Valley Hi Mag. (2/86). Ofc: Tree of Life Hypnosis Counseling Center 5200 Laurel Canyon Blvd North Hollywood 91607

HORN, LARRY ALAN, financial consultant; b. Jan. 20, 1952, Oakland; s. Paul E. and Elvis D. Horn; m. Mary K., Aug. 26, 1972; children: Paul b. 1980, Michelle b. 1982; edn: BA in bus. adm., Azusa Pacific Univ. 1975; MBA, Pepperdine Univ. 1983. Career: cons. Borg Warner Acceptance Corp., Santa Ana 1978-79; loan ofcr. Merit Mortgage, Montclair 1977-80; sales coordinator 3M AC&S, Los Angeles 1980-84; pres. Financial Concepts Ltd., Montclair 1984–; condr. Effective Fin. Mgmt. Sem. 1984; recipient cert. of achievement, 3M, 1982; mem. Internat. Assn. of Bus. & Fin. Consultants; dir. of Learning Center, Chaparral Hts. Comm. Ch. (1984); publs: Fin. Concepts No. 1 to 8 (series of reports of capital mgmt.) 1984; Republican; Baptist; rec: travel, photog. Res/Ofc: Financial Concepts Ltd., 9832 Snowmass Montclair 91763

HORNADAY, WILLIAM H.D., clergyman, civic leader; b. Apr. 26, 1910, Carson City, Nev.; s. Rev. William H.D. Sr. (Meth. Minister) and Mary (Leaming) H.; desc. 7 generations of ministers; m. Louise Clara Wright; 1 son, Wm. H.D., III; edn: M.Humanities, CSU Long Beach; fellow, Calif. Lutheran Coll.; DD, Whittier Coll.; Dr. Relig. Sci. & Phil., (study under Dr. Ernest Holmes, dean/ founder relig. sci.); Jungian Inst. (personal student of Dr. Carl Jung). Career: Methodist Minister; assoc. w/ Dr. Ernest Holmes, This Thing Called Life (L.A. radio pgm.), Ch. of Relig. Sci.; author: Prayer for Universal Peace; Sucess Unlimited, 1955; Life Everlasting, 1957; coauthor (w/ Dr. Ernest Holmes) Help for Today, 1958, (w/ Harlan Ware) The Inner Light, 1964; honors: Humanitarians Awd., Albert Schweitzer Coll., Switzerland 1956; Terra Sancta, State Medal of Israel 1965; Paul Harris Fellow 1974; Freedoms Found. Awd. 1963; decorated, Kim Khanh of Vietnam (highest civilian awd.) 1970; mem: Multiple Schlerosis Soc., So. Calif. chpt. (past. chmn. bd. trustees); Commn. on Civil Rights & White House Conf. on Health (past pres., 3 terms); Cancer Prevention Soc. (bd. dirs.); Jonathan Club; Guest Chaplain, U.S. Senate. Ofc: Church of Religious Science, 3281 W 6th St Los Angeles 90020

HORNADAY, WILLIAM HARRY DELYN, lawyer, business consultant; b. Oct. 20, 1945, Los Angeles; s. William H.D. and Patricia Lee (Leach) H.; edn: BA, UCLA 1974; JD, UCLA Law Sch. 1977; admitted to State Bar of Calif. 1977. Career: asst. dean students UCLA 1975-77; atty. Columbia Pictures 1977-78; exec. dir. Creative Affairs, Avco Embassy Pictures Corp. 1979-80; currently atty./bus. cons. in pvt. practice, partner Alcanter & Hornaday, A Profl. Law Corp., Beverly Hills; coord. UCLA Entertainment Symposium (Exec. Com.) 1976; honors: UCLA Law Review 1976-77; mem: Beverly Hills & Los Angeles Bar Assns.; Los Angeles Copyright Soc.; Am. Film Inst.; works: ed. The Legal and Related Business Aspects of Independent Film Production, 1976; Republican; Relig. Sci.; rec: creative writing, racquetball. Res: 7566 Rosewood Ave, 8, Los Angeles 90036 Ofc: Alcanter & Hornaday, 9701 Wilshire Blvd, Ste 550, Beverly Hills 90210

HORNBECK, MARGUERITE ELMA, educator; b. Oct. 4, 1901, Great Bend, Kans.; d. Richard Elmer and Jonette Still (Cowgill) Hornbeck; Gr.Grandfather

Andrew Still, MD, the founder of Osteopathy; Gr.Grandniece of Robert Louis Stevenson; m. Don Carlos Barrett, atty. (dec.), June 3, 1938; edn: BA, UC Berkeley 1926, MA, 1931; postgrad. wk., edn., Stanford Univ. 1954, Univ. of the Pacific 1956, 57; Gen. Life Sec. Tchr. Credential. Career: general science tchr. (gr. 8, 9), and Visual Aid coordinator, San Francisco Unified Sch. District, 1927-67, ret.; orgnzr. school Science Fairs, had youngest Grand Award winner in S.F. Sci. Fairs; vol. Sabin Polio Public Immunization Cpgn.; vol. Fed./State tax counselor for the Elderly; honors: First tchr. recipient Conservation Tng. Scholarship in Calif.; Pi Lambda Theta; photographed the burning of the Carrier of Sputnik I in skies over Los Angeles (the only photo of the event, US Govt. has copy); life mem: Univ. Calif. Alumni Assn., Stanford Univ. Alumni Assn., Calif. Tchrs. Assn., Nat. Tchrs. Assn., Nat. Retired Tchrs. Assn., Calif. Retired Tchrs. Assn., Calif. PTA (hon. life mem.); mem: US Intl. Secretariat; Service Info. Dir. for UN Conf. on Internat. Orgn., S.F. 1945; vol. civilian service in 2d Army Secret Command, WWII; dir. school First Aid Ctr., WWII; author 5 major research studies in field of edn. incl: 'The I.Q.-Classroom Mental Test Study that was inspired at Stanford in 1954 and which it has completely ignored then and now' (1982), 'Intro. the Specific Formula and Its Methods of converting Achievement Test Scores to Final Sch. Grades' (1985); Republican; Episcopal; club: Past Matron OES; rec: photog., breeding Fancy Siamese cats, creating (prize winning) crochet patterns. Res: 101 Laidley St San Francisco 94131

HORNE, ERNA ANNA, dentist, writer; b. Aug. 22, 1938, Marata, Santa Caterina, Brazil; d. Joseph and Anna (Rehme) Konrad; m. John Horne, Aug. 17, 1947; 1 son, Eric b. 1948; edn: AA, distinction, Riverside City Coll., 1970; BS, cum laude, Loma Linda Univ., 1973; DDS, Univ. Calif., 1977. Career: exec. secty. Riverside (Ca.) City Schs. 1964-66; exec. secty. to mktg. mgr. ACOA, Sydney, Australia 1966-68, AMAX, Riverside, Ca. 1968-71; dentist practitioner, 1977 –; mem: Am. Dental Assn., Calif. Dental Assn., Orange Co. Dental Soc., Nat. Womens Political Caucus, AAUW; Indep.; rec: needlework, swim, fine arts. Ofc: Erna A. Horne, DDS, 305 Orange Ave Ste C Huntington Beach 92648

HORNSBY, JOHN DANIEL, company executive; b. Nov. 6, 1953, Long Beach, Calif.; s. Joseph Thomas and Dorthea Ann (Price) H.; edn: BS in bus. mgt., Radford Coll. 1978; cert. Traffic & Transp. Mgt., Transp. Tng. Corp. 1978. Career: mgmt. trainee with Rampart General Inc., Orange Co., Calif. 1978, now gen. mgr. in estab. sheetmetal fireplaces mfg. factory, Fireplace Mfg. Inc., Santa Ana (7th largest fireplace mfr. in USA), apptd. sec.treas. F.M.I., 1983 –; partner Empire Fireplace Co. & Empire Products Co. (fireplace distbn. and mfr. fireplace grates & componets for gas products indus.), Ontario; own/lease indsl. equip.; Republican; Catholic; spl. interest: solar energy projects. Res: 1566 Tam O'Shanter Ontario CA 91761 Ofc: Fireplace Mfg. Inc., 2701 So Harbor Santa Ana CA 92704; Empire Fireplace, 10799 Fremont St Ontario CA 91761

HORNSTEIN, MARK, manufacturing co. president; b. Mar. 18, 1941, Bklyn.; s. Hyman and Arlene (Charnow) H.; m. Carmella, Feb. 28, 1970; stepdau. Sheri b. 1958; edn: USC 1958-61; Calif. lic. contractor. Career: draftsman Welton Becket & Assocs., L.A.; senior plnnr. Litton Industries, Woodland Hills 1970-73; Hyatt Hotel coord. (coord. 6 openings nat.), Elster, Inc. 1973-76; office and ops. mgr. DEC Assocs. (mfr. hotel and rest. furnishings), Compton 1977-81; mfrs. rep./owner CHM Assocs., Los Alamitos 1981 –; pres. Designing Manufacturing Installation, Inc. Buena Park 1983 –; mem. Buena Park CofC; works: aided in devel. glass fibre reinforced gypsum and sanding gelcoats for fibreglass industry; rec: tennis, water ski, equestrian. Ofc: Designing Manufacturing Installation Inc 7379-A Orangethorpe Ave Buena Park 90621

HORNWOOD, SANFORD W., lawyer, writer, author, investor; b. Sept. 14, 1909, Chicago, Ill.; s. Benjamin W. and Louise Louise (Green) H.; m. Rita, Sept. 14; children: Steven b. 1940, Richard b. 1945; edn: JD, Southwestern Univ. 1931; JD, American Univ. 1942. Career: law instr. American Univ. 1940-43; law practice in personal injury field; author law books: Systematic Settlements (Lawyer Co-Op, 1970, 2d ed. 1986); author: No. 1 Investments-Real Estate, No. 1 Investments- Mortgages, No. 1 Investments- Shopping Centers (all Prentice Hall, 1986); currently, v.p./bd. chmn. Westmark Group, A Realty Co., Nevada; past pres., current v.p. Lilliputians; lectr. LUTC; lectr. medical convs. in Europe and the Orient; mem: NY, Calif. and Los Angeles Trial Attys. Assns., Calif. Bar Assn., Elks, Shriners; mil: ROTC; Republican; Metaphysical; rec: miniature liquor bottle collection, photog., raising orchards, golf, deep sea fishing. Res: 2030 Bagley Ave. Los Angeles 90034

HOROWITZ, DAVID CHARLES, consumer correspondent; b. June 30, 1937, NY, NY; s. Max Leo and Dorothy (Lippman) H.; m. Suzanne E. McCambridge, 1973; 2 daus.; edn: BA, hons. journ., Bradley Univ. 1959; MSJ, Northwestern Univ. 1960; CBS Fellow, Columbia Univ. 1962-63. Career: editor-in-chief Tazewell Co. (Ill.) Newspaper, 1956; reporter Peoria (Ill.) Journ. Star, 1957-60; reporter, columnist Lerner Newspapers and Chgo. City News Bureau, 1959-60; newscaster KRNT Radio-TV, Des Moines 1960-62; news writer/ prod. ABC Radio Network, NYC 1963; Far East corr. NBC News, 1963-64; pub. affairs dir. WMCA, NYC 1964-66; corr.-edn. editor, Consumer Ombudsman, KNBC News Action Reporter, L.A. 1966 –; spec. features: Consumer Guideline, Of Consumer Interest, Consumer Close/Up; nat. syndicated pgm. David Horowitz Consumer Buyline, Fight Back! with David Horowitz; worldwide Apollo 15 splashdown, 1971; Calif. earthquake 2/9/71; Dem. Conv. 1972; host/exec. prod./dir. of home videotape: The Baby Safe Home (distbd. Embassy-McGraw Hill); synd. columnist Cowles Synd. 1981-; author: Fight Back

and Don't Get Ripped Off (1979); advis. UCLA publs. Awards include Natl. Radio-TV Daily Award, 1963, Emmy for consumer ombudsman, KNBC Newsservice, Emmy awards for comsumer reporting 1973, 75, 77, 82 (two), 83, citations, City and County of L.A., and State of Calif., 1979, recognition, City of Hope Spirit of Life Awd. 1979, US Postal Insps. 1981, Calif. State Disting. Citizen 1982, US Consumer Product Safety Commn. 1982, Calif. Consumer Affairs Assn. 1982, Vista Del Mar 1981, Jewish Fedn. Council 1981, media award Nat. Soc. of Consumer Affairs Profls. 1982, Humane Soc. of the US, LA Press Club, LA Co. Commn. on Alcoholism, Work Tng. Pgm. for Devel. Disabled Young Adults; frequent TV talk show guest; feature subject in Time Mag. (1/4/82), TV Guide (5/15/82); mil: USNR 1954-62; mem. Child Passenger Safety Assn.; bd. mem: Nat. Bdcst. Edn. Conf., Am. Cancer Soc. Calif. Div., LA Jewish Home for Aged, The Silent Network, The Young Musicians Found. Inc.; adv. bd. S.H.A.R.E., Inc.; patron LA Co. Art Mus.; mem. Acad. TV Arts and Scis., Internat. Radio-TV Soc., Radio-TV News Dirs. Assn., Nat. Edn. Writers Assn., The Guardians, Sigma Delta Chi, Phi Delta Kappa, Overseas Press Club of Am., Friars Club. Ofc: 3000 W. Alameda Ave Burbank 91523

HORTON, HILDA MAE, business owner; b. Nov. 15, 1915, Canyon, Tex.; d. Joseph Edward and Minnie Mae (Thomas) Patterson; m. Troy Horton, Aug. 31, 1931; children: Peggy b. 1932, Poy b. 1934, Robert b. 1936. Career: anchor strap maker Goodyear Tire & Rubber WWII; wholesale sandwich bus. No. Calif. 1961-84; Democrat; rec: reading, crossword puzzles, travel. Res: POB 222 Chico 95927

HORTON, MICHAEL LYNN, mortgage banker; b. Oct. 19, 1961, Pasadena, Calif.; s. Jerry Stanley and Mary Louise (Harmon) H.; edn: BA econs., Claremont McKenna Coll. 1983; realtor Calif. 1986. Career: ops. mgr. I.W.S. Pasadena 1977-78; exec. asst. to pres. Harris Constrn. Co. La Verne 1979-80; founder NBB Svcs. 1980; senior mortgage banker Sycamore Financial Group Ontario 1984 –; instr. mortgage finance workshop; honors: life mem. CSF, Outstanding Student of Yr. (Chaffey Comm. Coll. econ. dept. 1980), Calvin G. Justice Meml. Scholar (1980), Doris D. Lepper Meml. Scholar (1981), Outstanding Bus. Student (Chaffey 1981), Dean's List (Chaffey, Claremont Men's Coll.), acad. scholarship (Claremont McKenna 1981), Calif. State Scholar (1981); author: A Real Estate Professional's Reference Guide to Mortgage Finance (1985), Money Talks (newsletter); Republican (Calif. Central Com. 1981-86, nom. by Pete Wilson to Republican Senatorial Inner Circle 1985); rec: basketball, racquetball, tennis, water sports. Ofc: Sycamore Financial Group Utica, Rancho Cucamonga 91730

HORVATH, PATRICK STEPHEN, metallurgical engineer, co. president; b. MAr. 23, 1945, Daggett, Mich.; s. Stephen William and Thelma Olivia (Fleetwood) H.; m. Carol Ann "Eddy"; children: Holly Lynn b. 1973, Heidi Ann b. 1975; edn: BS metallurg. engrg., Mich. Technol. Univ. 1967; MBA, CSU Long Beach 1973. Career: engr. Wyman Gordon Co., Mass. and subsid. Reisner Metals, South Gate, Calif. 1967-76; gen. mgr. Atlas Testing 1976-79; founder, pres. Accurate Metallurg. Svcs., Santa Fe Springs 1979 –; pres. H&H Heat Treating 1981 –; pres. Aluminum Heat Treaters of Am. 1985 –; honors: ASM-Westec 82; mem: Am. Soc. for Metals, Am. Inst. Materials Engrg., Mich. Tech. Fund Mich. Technol. Univ. (trustee); Republican; Catholic; rec: golf, skiing, tennis, travel. Ofc: Accurate Metallurg. Svcs. Inc., 10005 Freeman Ave Santa Fe Springs 90670

HORWITCH, MICHAEL RICHARD, real estate broker; b. July 1, 1941, Chicago, Ill.; s. Albert A. and Celia Brill H.; m. Niki, Aug. 26, 1973; children: Lauren b. 1975, David b. 1976; edn: BS, USC 1963, MBA, 1965; desig: CCIM (cert. investment real estate broker). Career: nat. sales mgr. Deena Inc., Los Angeles 1965-83; senior v.p., mng. broker Sun Cal Properties Inc., Los Angeles 1984 –; leader real estate seminars; mem. Center City West Associates/ downtown L.A. (founder/exec. com.); author; pub. fiction; mil: capt. US Army 1965; Democrat; rec: travel, tennis, golf. Ofc: Sun Cal Inc., 233 S Beaudry Ave Los Angeles 90012

HORWITZ, LARRY STUCKEY, inventor, engineer, physicist; b. July 11, 1949, Port Arthur, Tex.; s. Herman and Mary Jane (Stuckey) H.; m. Mary MacAdam, July 16, 1983; edn: BSEE, Lamar Univ. 1972; MSEE, Univ. So. Calif. 1974; M. Optical Scis., Univ. Rochester NY 1974. Career: mem. tech. staff Hughes Aircraft Co. 1972-77; research engr. Ford Aerospace and Communs. Corp. 1977-82; senior staff engr. TRW 1982-85; senior scientist Rockwell Internat. 1985 –; pres. Applied Medical Technologies; pgm. mgr. Strategic Defense research for high energy lasers, proposal mgr., dir. research; honors: Eta Kappa Nu, Tau Beta Pi, Sigma Pi, Phi Mu Alpha; mem: Inst. Elec. Electron. Engrs. (past. chpt. pres.), Optical Soc. of Am., Am. Inst. Physics; publ: 30+ tech. articles in profl. jours.; inventor ophthalmic device for automatic vision correction; 8 patents; Republican; Jewish; rec: clock and wine collections. Address: 6232 Malaga Ct Long Beach 90803

HORWITZ, ROBERT PERRY, engineering executive, real estate broker; b. Dec. 2, 1932, Los Angeles; s. Gus and Doris A. (Roe) H.; div.; children: Lori, b. 1953; Robert, b. 1955; Jamie, b. 1961; James, b. 963; edn: BSME, honors, CSU Los Angeles 1958; Calif. Reg. Profl. Engr. Calif. (1965), lic. R.E. broker (1970). Career: mech. engr./senior project engr. Peerless Pump Div., FMC Corp., Los Angeles 1955-66; prod. supvr. Hydroaire Div., Crane Co., Burbank 1966-68; project mgr. Task Corp., Joy Mfg. Co., Anaheim 1968-73; senior project engr. ITT J.C. Carter Co., Costa Mesa 1973-74; eng. mgr. Airco Cryogenics, Irvine 1974-78; eng. mgr. Aurora Pump, Gen. Signal Corp., City of Industry 1978-80; R.E. broker Newport Harbor- Costa Mesa Bd. Realtors

1978–; senior project engr. ITT Jabsco Prods., Costa Mesa 1981-85, mktg. mgr. 1985, dir. of engring. 1986–; mem: Nat. & Calif. Assns. Realtors; Am. Soc. of Mech. Engrs.; Instrument Soc. of Am.; Mensa Soc.; works: patents in field of turbomachinery 1963-83, num. arts. in tech. journs.; Republican; Protestant; rec: skiing, boating, bridge, vintage sports cars. Res: 2047 Sea Cove Ln Costa Mesa 92627 Ofc: Select Properties 3130 Harbor Blvd Costa Mesa 92626

HOSKINS, BARBARA BRUNO, speech-language pathologist, consultant language/learning disabilities; b. Feb. 21, 1948, Havre de Grace, Md.; d. Onofrio Pasqual and Marjorie Helena (Goertler) Bruno; edn; BS, magna cum laude, Syracuse Univ. 1970; MS, So. Ill. Univ. 1972; PhD, Northwestern Univ. 1979. Career: speech therapist Norwalk Public Schools Conn. 1975-76; speech & lang. splst. L.A. Co. Supt. of Schools 1976-79; adj. asst. prof. CSULA 1976-79; cons. and assessments lang., learning disorders 1976–; cons. Las Encinas Psych. Hosp. 1976–; vis. prof. Univ. of Redlands, Whittier Coll. 1979–; dir. of tng. & research Almansor Edn. Ctr. 1979–; ed. cons. speech, lang., hearing svcs. in schools; affil. staff Ingleside Psych. Hosp. ; mem: Am. Speech Lang. Hearing Assn., Internat. Neuropsych. Soc.; publ: articles in profl. jours. Res: 285 W California Pasadena 91105 Ofc: Almansor Education Center 9 N Almansor St Alhambra 91801

HOSPODOR, ANDY D., engineer; b. Oct. 20, Ithaca, N.Y.; s. Andrew Thomas and Rose Marie (Pitarra) H.; m. Dolores Crosby, Apr. 20, 1985; edn: BS in computer sci., Lehigh Univ. 1981; MS in C.S., Santa Clara Univ. 1986. Career: software engr. Digital Equip. Corp., Tewksbury, Mass. summers 1979, 80; system devel. engr. Nat. Semiconductor, Sunnyvale 1981-82; design engr. Scientific Micro Systems, Mt. View 1982-85; dir. engring. Micro Consulting Assocs., Santa Clara 1985–; prof. elec. engring. and computer sci., Santa Clara Univ.; awards: student research grantee Lehigh Univ. (1980); mem. IEEE, ACM, Sigma Phi Soc.; research: in communication and mass storage; Republican; rec: restoration classic sports cars. Res: 292 Maria St Santa Clara 95050 Ofc: Micro Consulting Associates 1556 Halford Ave Ste 316 Santa Clara 95051

HOTCHKIS, PRESTON, lawyer; b. 1893; edn: Univ. of Calif.; hon. LLD, Whittier Coll. (1957), Pepperdine Coll. (1955); m. Katharine Bixby S. 1923; two daus. and two sons; m. 2d Georgina Mage, Feb. 1981. Career: seaman to ensign US Navy, WWI, 1918-19; co-founder, dir., vice pres. Pacific Finance Corp. 1920; dir., exec. v.p. Pacific Indemnity Co. 1926; dir. exec. com. Consolidated Western Steel Corp. 1929; dir. pres. Central Business Properties Inc. 1929; dir. pres. vice-chmn. Founders Insurance Co. 1946; chmn. bd. Bixby Ranch Co. Los Angeles. Mem: pres. Calif. Alumni Assn. 1934-36; regent Univ. of Calif. 1934-36; War Manpower Board for S. Cal. 1942-45 US Rep. Econ & Social Council 1954-55; past mem. Hoover Commn. Task Force Fed. Lending agencies; Official Host, City of Los Angeles; chmn. Greater LA Area War Chest Campaign; current: trustee Mills Coll., Harvey Mudd Coll., Southwest Museum, Good Hope Med. Found. (v.p.); co-founder Hon. Dir. Past Pres. LA World Affairs Council; Japanese Philharmonic Soc., LA; mem. Mayors Adv. Com.; Girl Scouts of US Nat. Ad. Council; chmn. Local Agcy. Formation Commn. LA County; Southland Water Com.; pres. bd. Pepperdine Coll.; adv. council Univ. of Redlands; adv. council Calif. State Parks Found.; dir. Property Owners Tax Assn. of Calif. Inc.; dir. Metropolitan Water Dist. of So. Calif. 1978; trustee Calif. Alumni Found., Univ. Calif.; mem. Am. Business Council publs: History of Lost Angels Camp; clubs: California (LA), University (LA), Valley Hunt (Pasa.), Pacific Union (SF), Bohemian (SF), Twilight (SF);. Res: 1415 Circle Dr San Marino 91108 Ofc: 523 West Sixth St Los Angeles 90014

HOUCHIN, ROBERT JAMES, dentist; b. March 22, 1947, Minneapolis, Minn.; s. Orlo Lee and Mary Eileen (Cannon) H.; m. Linda Coral (Little) Barber, Dec. 9, 1971; children: Kelly Jocelyn b. 1976, Elizabeth Lee b. 1978; edn: UC Berkeley 1965-66; AS, Citrus Coll. 1971; BS, Loyola Univ. Los Angeles 1973; CSU Los Angeles 1973-74; DDS, Georgetown Univ. Sch. of Dentistry 1978. Career: pvt. solo practice dentistry, Covina 1978–; annual guest lectr. Georgetown Univ. Sch. of Dentistry, Wash. DC; honors: Alpha Gamma Sigma 1971; Golden Key of Knowledge 1971; Chemistry Student of the Year, Citrus Coll. 1970; mem: Rotary Internat. (pres. Covina 1986-87), Am. and Calif. Dental Assns., San Gabriel Valley Dental Soc., Dist. of Columbia Dental Soc., Acad. of General Dentistry, U.S. Senatorial Bus. Advy. Bd., Ronald Reagan's Presdtl. Task Force; works: Spl. Olympics Com. Research; neurobiological reserch, City of Hope Nat. Med. Ctr., Duarte and Naval Med. Researh Inst., Bethesda, Md. 1973; mil: hosp. corpsman 2/c USN 1966-69, Nat. Defense, Vietnamese Defense, Vietnam Campaign w/ 5 clusters, Presdtl. Unit Citation, Navy Achiev. w/ Combat V; Democrat; rec: investments, sports, politics. Res: 912 So. Heritage Dr., West Covina 91791 Ofc: Robert J. Houchin DDS, 153 W. College St. Covina 91723

HOUDE, JOSEPH W., JR., communication co. executive; b. Jan. 4, 1944, Attleboro, Mass.; s. Joseph W. and Lillian Viola (Halliley) H.; m. Christine, July 11, 1970; children: Lincoln b. 1971, Jessica b. 1972; edn: BBA magna cum laude, Nat. Univ. 1978. Career: mgr. Singer San Leandro, Calif. 1969-76; dept. mgr. TRW San Diego 1976-81; v.p. Omex Santa Clara 1981-82; cons. Zatyko Assocs. Santa Ana 1982-84; chmn. Network Decisions Inc. Santee 1984–; mem. AMA; rec: psychology, ancient history, trekking, camping. Res: 11032 Summit Ave Santee 92071 Ofc: Network Decisions 25461 Barents Laguna Hills 92653

HOUGARDY, ROBERT GRAY, certified financial planner, stockbroker; b. Feb. 24, 1931, Henryetta, Okla.; s. Oscar Daniel and Evelyn Mildred (Gray) H.; m. Jeanne Grove, Dec. 28, 1957; children: Peter, b. 1959; Nevin, b. 1960; Elizabeth, b. 1961; Matthew, b. 1963; edn: USAF Univ. Ext. 1952-53; BBA, Woodbury Univ. 1955; UCLA Ext. 1957-58; CFP, Coll. for Fin. Plng. 1980. Career: mktg. assoc. Frito Co. 1955-58; mktg. analyst Frito Lay 1958-67; stockbroker Reynolds Securities- Mitchen Jones & Templeton 1967-79; fin. cons. Shearson American Express 1979-82; v.p./ asst. mgr. 1982–; tchr. mktg. San Jose State 1959, Cabrillo Coll. 1970-83; mem: Coll. for Fin. Plng.; Assn. of Fin. Plnrs.; Rotary; Soquel Dist. Unified Sch. Bd (pres. 1971-75); mil: currently capt. Calif. state Mil. Reserve; t/sgt US Army Air Force 1947-53, Distng. Unit Citation w/ 3 Bronze Stars, Korean Svc., United Nations Svc.; Republican (Central Com.); Catholic; rec: tennis. Res: 133 Kenny Ct Santa Cruz 95065 Ofc: Shearson American Express, 555 Soquel Ave Santa Cruz 95062

HOULE, SUE, photographer; b. Nov. 27, 1940, Lowell, Mass.; d. Dr. Emile A. and Gertrude (Dozois) H.; edn: BFA, Boston Univ. Sch. Fine & Applied Arts 1961. Career: photographer and model 1956-68: was the original Breck Shampoo Girl, a Rheingold Girl, completed 55 t.v. commls. incl. Prell Shampoo, Toni Home Permanent, Ford Motors, Schick Razor Blades, Max Factor Cosmetics, Polaroid Corp.; photojournalist, 1968–, articles in num. publs. including Petersen's Photographic Mag., Popular Photog., U.S. Camera Annual, var. museum publs.; one-woman exhibs: Africa Portraits (180 prints, 17 murals, sponsored by Levin Found.), L.A. Zoo (1970); Amazon Images, Am. Soc. of Mag. Photogs. (1972), Africa Portraits, L.A. Pub. Library (spons. Petersen Pub. Co., 1973), Aeriel Archaeol., Oxford Univ., Worcester Coll. (1973), Amazon Images (60 prints), Eastman Kodak Co., Rochester, N.Y. (10/74), The Eyes of Ancient New Guinea, Boston Mus. of Sci. (spons. Cultural Survival Inc., 1978), The Eyes of Modern Psychics, Royal Photog. Soc. of G.B. (1980-81), The Eyes of Success (1984) and Ancient Dowsers (1985), Addams Booksellers, Cambridge, Mass.; participant num. internat. photog. exhibns.; awards: Levin Found. Photog. Grant (1970), Carol Channing Diamond Achievement Award, Hollywood Women's Press Club Golden Apple Awards (1977), Oxford Univ. scholarship (1973), Emmy Award for "Amazon Images" and "Africa Portraits" NBC-TV (10/75); mem. Am. Soc. of Mag. Photogs., Royal Photog. Soc. of G.B., Hollywood Women's Press Club, Women in Show Business. Address: Sucoy Photography West 2418 Tesla Ter Los Angeles 90039

HOUSER, JOE JAMES, insurance broker; b. April 17, 1916, Udall, Kansas; s. John Jefferson and Elsie Mae (Effner) H.; m. Sherry Lindberg, July 10, 1978; children: Joe James II b. 1948, Jeffrey Jay b. 1946; edn: var. studies USC, UCLA 1941-46. Career: asst. buyer Bullocks, Los Angeles 1938-41; supvr. North American Aviation, Los Angeles 1941-46; v.p. J.E. Wells Co.Inc., Los Angeles 1946-57; pres., owner Houser Ins. Agency, Los Angeles 1957–; fmr. dir. Insurance Brokers Assn.; honors: Resolutions for civic and community svc., Los Angeles City and County 1968, 1970; Boys Club of Am. Medallion Award 1975; Goodwill Industries award 198; Los Angeles Elks Lodge (1957, 67, 74), Wilshire CofC (1968), Beverly Hills Shrine Club (1964, 67), Elks Roses for the Living award 1980; Hyatt House Comm. award 1977; pres., bd. chmn Boys Club of Hollywood; dir. Goodwill Indus.; dir. Los Angeles- Bombay Sister City Com.; dir. Los Angeles area U.S.O.; mem. Independent Ins. Agents & Brokers Assn., Ins. Borkers Assn. of Calif., US Navy League (life), F&AM Masons (life), L.A. Commandery Knights Templar, L.A. Scottish Rite, Al Malaikah Shriners, L.A. Elks Lodge (past pres., fmr. Dist. Deputy Grand Exalted Ruler), BPOE of US, Wilshire CofC (past pres.), Wilshire Rotary Club, L.A. Royal Arch Masons, Trojan Shrine CLub, Western Assn. of Ins. Brokers, Ind. Ins. Agents Assn. of L.A., L.A. Philanthropic Found., Am. Film Inst., Los Angeles Breakfast Club; Republican (Nat. Com., Presdtl. Task Force). Res: 11039 Wrightwood Pl. Studio City 91604 Ofc: Houser Insurance Agency, 12025 Ventura Blvd Studio City 91604

HOUSTON, KENNETH EUGENE, state engineering executive, ret.; b. Sept. 10, 1920, Colby, Kans.; s. Phillip Mathew and Dicy Alice (Braden) H.; div.; children: Phillip Kenneth b. 1949, Tamara Jeanne (Pierson) b. 1950, Robert Kent b. 1953; edn: Fort Hays State Coll. 1938-39, Kans. State Univ. 1940-41, var. engring. courses on corrosion UC Davis, num. spl. tech. courses; Reg. Profl. Engr. (Quality Engr.), Calif. Career: asst. to consulting engr., Aircraft Accessories, Kansas City, Kans. 1941-43; ind. rancher (Angus cattle and small grains), Colby, Kans. 12 years; engring. asst. to chief of Governor Section, also Field Erection Engr., equipt. installed in hydraulic structures, Pelton Water Wheel (San Francisco), B.L.H. (Eddystone, Pa.), 10 yrs.; supvr. E&M Section, insp. equipt. for hydraulic structures, State of Calif. 1965-86 (retd.); instr., control of hydraulic structures, Governor Sch.; club: Elks No. 6; Republican; Baptist; rec: woodworking. Res: 1390 Munger Way Sacramento 95831 Ofc: Dept. Water Resources, 1801 Seventh St Sacramento 95802

HOUSTON, NICHOLAS BRANDON, chiropractor; b. Feb. 2, 1958, Encino; s. Edward Theodore and Marcia Elizabeth (Darnell) H.; edn: AS, L.A. Pierce Jr. Coll. 1980; BS, biol., Cleveland Chiropractic Coll., L.A. 1984, DC, 1984; MS, biol./nutrition, Univ. of Bridgeport, Ct. 1985; grad. Parker Sch. of Profl. Success 1984, Applied Kinesiology (100 hr. course) 1985, Steward Seminars nutrition courses, 1984-85; lic. DC, Calif. St. Board, 1985. Career: intern Dr. Alfred Garbutt, DC, Los Angeles 1983-84, clin. intern Cleveland Chiro. Coll. LA, 1983-84; assoc. doctor Gordon Chiropractic Health Center, 1984-85; prin. Houston Chiropractic, Encino 1985–; mem: Am. Chiro. Assn., Calif. Chiro. Assn., Sacral Occipital Research Soc., CCC Alumni, LACC Alumni, Encino CofC, United Chambers of Commerce San Fernando Valley, Nat. Health Fedn.; Democrat; Christian; rec: dancing, wt. lifting, martial arts. Res: 5425 Bellingham, 6, No Hollywood 91607 Ofc: Houston Chiropractic, 16161 Ventura Blvd Ste 227 Encino 91436

HOUSTON, WILLIAM ANDREW, real estate broker/appraiser; b. Aug. 20, 1910, Okolona, Miss.; s. Wm. Andrew and Margaret Damron (Darden) H.; m. Juanita Crouse, Sept. 27, 1952; children: Wm. Andrew, III b. 1953, Mary Anne (Thompson) b. 1956; edn: LLB, La Salle Extension Univ. 1948; MBA, Univ. of Beverly Hills 1983, PhD 1984. Career: real estate broker, developer, appraiser dba William A. Houston, Real Estate, 1947–; real prop. appraiser/mem. VA Panel of Independent Fee Basis Appraisers, 1972–; mem. Buena Park Dist. Bd. Realtors (Realtor of Year 1973), Am. Legion, VFW; mil: cpl. Army Air Force 1942-45, combat ribbons; Christian. Address: W.A. Houston 7122 Bon Villa Circle La Palma 90623

HOVING, GARY LLOYD, forensic scientist, investigator; b. Sept. 30, 1953, Redlands, Calif.; s. Lloyd E. and Glenna E. (Gareis) H.; m. Karla M. Raidy, June 9, 1977; children: Stephanie b. 1978, Jill b. 1980, Gregory b. 1984; edn: AA police sci., San Bernardino Valley Coll. 1973; BA criminalistics, Columbia Pacific Univ. 1984. Career: dep. sheriff Orange County Sheriff's Dept. 1975-79, San Luis Obispo Sheriff-Coroner's Ofc. 1979; detective S.L.O. Sheriff-Coroner's Crime Lab. 1979–; instr. Allan Hancock Coll. Santa Maria 1981–; honors: Disting. Svc. (S.L.O. Co. Deputy Sheriffs' Assn. 1985), Acad. Award (Peace Ofcrs. Research Assn. of Calif. 1973); mem: S.L.O. Deputy Sheriff's Assn. (pres. 1986), Central Coast Investigators Assn. (pres. 1981), Internat. Assn. for Identification (So. Calif. dir. 1986-87), Internat. Assn. Bomb Technicians and Investigators; author: Crime Scene Investigations - A Manual for Patrol Officers; instrumental in use of ground penetrating radar for buried body searches in Calif.; Republican; Lutheran; rec: computers, restore sports cars. Ofc: San Luis Obispo County Sheriff-Coroner's Dept. POB 32 San Luis Obispo 93406

HOWARD, BRUCE WAYNE, petroleum engineer; b. Sept. 22, 1958, Lawrence, Kans.; s. Billy Glen and Flavia Leah (Dunn) H.; m. Elaine Ball, June 11, 1963; edn: BSChE, Univ. Kans. 1980; Reg. Profl. Petroleum Engr. Calif. Career: engr. in training ARCO Oil & Gas Co., Lafayette, La. 1980-81; ops/analytical engr. ARCO Bakersfield 1981-85; senior petroleum engr. ARCO Internat. Co., Jakarta, Indonesia 1985–; mem. Soc. Petroleum Engrs. 1981-; Republican; rec: bowling, camping, gardening. Address: POB 63/JKT Jakarta 10002 Indonesia

HOWARD, DUNCAN LENT, government administrator; b. Sept. 4, 1940, San Francisco; s. Lot Duncan, Jr. and Elizabeth (Lent) H.; m. Madeline Ann Domning (dec. 1983), June 18, 1967; children: Lent b. 1968, Lyman b. 1969; edn: AA, Pre-law, San Francisco City Coll. 1968; BA, govt., Univ. of S.F. 1970; Calif. lic. R.E. Broker, Realtor. Career: gen. supt. George Howard Trucking & Excavating Co., Marin Co. 1962-65; asst. to sales mgr. Engs Motor Truck Co., Hegenberger Rd, Oakland 1965-67; real estate sales, resdtl., Coldwell Banker & Co., S.F. 1971-72; R.E. sales/mgr. S.F. office, W. Bruce Shafer & Co., Realtors 1972-73; asst. to the pres. Cushman & Wakefield of Calif., S.F. 1973-76; exec. v.p., chief adminstrv. fin. and ops. ofcr. Owen Ent. Inc. (R.E. Dev. and Fin.), S.F. 1978-80; owner/pres. Duncan Howard Co., Real Estate 1976-84; deputy assoc. dir. White House Personnel 1984; regional adminstr. Dept. of Housing & Urban Devel. 1984–; mem. Nat. Adv. Council Small Bus. Adminstrn. (subcoms. on Women in Bus., Taxation) 1981-83; fund raiser for Big Brothers, Boy Scouts of Am., United Way (chmn. 1979), Burks Sch. of S.F.; candidate for US Congress 1983 (5th Congl. Dist. of S.F.); mem: S.F. Chamber of Commerce (Crime Prev. Com.); Nat., Calif. Assns. of Realtors, S.F. Bd. of Realtors; Cow Hollow Homeowners Assn. (bd. dirs.); Assocs. of Childrens Hosp. of S.F. (past pres.); adv. bd. chmn. Inst. of Neurobehav. Scis. of Frank Gerbode Resrch. Found.; bd. dirs. S.F. Zoo Soc.; pres. St. Luke's Sch.; bd. chmn. Cathedral Sch. for Boys; Republican (S.F. Central Com.; S.F. Fin. Com.; campaign wkr.); bd. trustees Grace Cathedral 1985; Episcopal; rec: jog, tropical fish, fishing, duck hunting. Res: 1961 California St San Francisco 94109 HUD Ofc: 450 Golden Gate Ave San Francisco 94102-3448 Personal Ofc: Howard Family Investments 505 Sansome St Ste 1502 San Francisco 94111

HOWARD, GAIL P., accounting executive; b. March 31, 1959, Los Angeles; s. John Jerry and Judith Nazima (Levy) H.; edn: BSBA, USC 1981; USC Grad. Sch. of Bus. 1984; CPA, Calif. 1984. Career: senior acct. Gelfand, Rennert & Feldman, Century City 1982-83; audit ofcr. Security Pacific Nat. Bank, Los Angeles 1984; senior acct. American Med. Internat., Beverly Hills 1984-85; gen. acctg. mgr. Wherehouse Entertainment, Gardena 1985–; AIESEC Job Internship, Bilbao, Spain 1980; Co: Tubacex, S.A.; honors: Alpha Lambda Delta 1977; mem: Am. Inst. CPAs, Toastmasters, Chi Omega (treas.), AIESEC, USC Acctg. Soc. Res: Los Angeles Ofc: Wherehouse Entertainment, 19701 Hamilton Ave Los Angeles

HOWARD, MURRAY, realty co. president; b. July 25, 1914, Los Angeles; s. George A.J. and Mabel (Murray) H.; edn: BS, UCLA 1939; lic. pub. acct. Career: mgr. Foundries, Inc. 1945-59; pres./chmn. bd. Howard Mach. Prods., Inc. 1949-63; chmn. bd. Murray Howard Realty, Inc. 1961-62; pres./chmn. bd. 1962–; pres./chmn. bd. Ranch Sales, Inc. 1968–; pres./chmn. bd. Murray Howard Devel., Inc. 1969–; bd. dirs. Shur-Lok Corp. 1969–; dir. Airshippers Pub. Corp., La Brea Realty & Devel. Co.; mem: Gov. Warren's Calif. Minority Commn.; Nat. Assn. Cost Accts. (past v.p./ dir.); Nat. Assn. Mfrs.; Delta Tau Delta. Res: 3771 Lockland Dr Los Angeles 90008 Ofc: 1605 W Olympic Blvd, Ste 404, Los Angeles 90015

HOWARD, RANDY DE WAYNE, hospital adminstrator; b. Apr. 19, 1934, Athens, Tx.; s. Jesse Hardy and Jessie Viola (Harrison) H.; div.; children: Daniel Edward b. 1957, Frederick Dale b. 1959; edn: BBA, Northwood Inst., Midland, Mich. 1972; M.Hosp. Admin., Cornell Univ. 1974. Career: dir.

mgmt. services (4 small rural hosps.) for Saginaw (Mich.) Gen. Hosp., 1969-76; adminstr. Brotman Med. Ctr., Culver City 1978-81, Beverly Hills Med. Ctr., L.A. 1981-82, Los Banos Community Hosp. 1982-85; hosp. adminstr. Mee Meml. Hosp., King City 1985–; mem. Am. Coll. Healthcare Execs.; Rotarian; mem. King City CofC; publs: (book) $2.5 Million Dollar Plan; Republican; Seventh Day Adventist; rec: tennis, golf. Res: 45025 Merritt St King City 93930 Ofc: Mee Memorial Hospital 300 Canal St King City 93930

HOWARD, RICHARD EARL, manufacturing co. president; b. Dec. 3, 1932, Springfield, Ill.; s. P.H. and Garnet (Neher) H.; m. Evalyn Sharon Pitts, Nov. 28, 1957; children: Angela D. b. 1958, Susan E. b. 1963, Richard B. & Sherilyn A. b. 1968, Rebecca S. b. 1971; edn: St. Louis Univ. 1951; BSE, Ariz. State Univ. 1958; MBA work, Ariz. State Univ. and Northeastern Univ. 1959-80; MSME, Univ. of Mass. 1977; ops. mgmt. Penn. State 1978; Reg. Profl. Engr., Calif. Career: senior engr. Motorola Inc., Ariz. 1959-64; senior staff UACSC, Conn. 1964-66; mgr. Transitron Elects., Mass. 1966-69; senior mgmt. Polaroid Corp. Electronics Div. , Mass. 1969-80; v.p. Calma Co. (subsidiary of General Electric), Milpitas 1980-82; div. pres. J.C. Schumacher Co., Oceanside 1982-86; pres./CEO Xinix, Inc., Santa Clara 1986–; co-founder, dir. Amelcon Inc. 1982; p.t. faculty Northeastern Univ. Grad. Sch. 1967-80; mem: IEEE, Assn. of Media Based Cont. Edn. for Engrs. (orignal Ind. adv. bd. 1977-80), Boy Scouts of Am.; author, textbook, Northeastern Univ. 1975; sev. patents; mil: USAF 1951-55; Republican; Ch. of Jesus Christ LDS. Res: 3408 Apostol Rd. Escondido 92025 Ofc: Xinix, Inc. Santa Clara 95054

HOWARD, SCOTT H., government lawyer; b. May 22, 1950, Los Angeles; s. Harold I. and Janet H.; edn: BS, USC Sch. of Bus. 1972; JD, Southwestern Univ. Sch. of Law 1976; admitted Calif. State Bar (1976), Federal Dist. Ct. (Central Dist.), US Claims Ct. Career: legal intern, dep. city atty., Los Angeles Dist. Atty., 1975-79; asst. city atty., senior asst. city atty. City of Glendale, 1979–; lectr. for Calif. Parks & Rec. Soc. Inc. annual, and regional seminars (1984-), frequent lectr. annual meetins var. nat. assns.; arbitrator, judge protem Glendale Municipal Ct.; guest tchr. local high schs. annual Law Day activities; mem: Am. Bar Assn. (chmn. Subcom. on Regulation), Calif. Bar Assn., Glendale Bar Assn., Calif. Dist. Atty.'s Assn.; civic: Glendale Comm. Coll. Dist. (pres. Edn. Advis. Com. legal sectl.); works: obtained precedent setting Ct. decisions in the area of municipal taxation and licensing; the Constnl. limitations on use of muni. streets for news publs.; the rights of public agencies re police use of firearms and med. retirement benefits; Republican; rec: sports, skiing. Ofc: City of Glendale 613 East Broadway Ste 220 Glendale 91205

HOYE, WALTER, college administrator; b. May 19, 1930, Lena, Miss.; s. William Horace and LouBertha (Stewart) H.; m. Vida M. Pickens, Aug. 28, 1954; children: Walter II b. 1956, JoAnn b. 1957; edn: BA, Wayne State Univ. 1954. Career: sports ed., columnist Michigan Chronicle Newspaper, Detroit 1965-68; asst. dir. pub. rels. San Diego Chargers Football Co., San Diego 1968-76; media coord. at large Nat. Football League 1972-75; pub. info. ofcr. San Diego Urban League/ Neighborhood House 1976; comm. vcs. ofcr. Ednl. Cultural Complex, San Diego 1980, placement/ pgm. support supvr. 1981; also, bd. dirs. Neighborhood House Assn.; pres. Black Communications Ctr. San Diego State Univ.; bd. dirs. Community Video; recipient: United Way/ CHAD Award of Merit 1974; nominator for Outstanding Men of Am., Outstanding Young Women of Am., mem: Assn. Calif. Comm. Coll. Adminstrs., Nat. Mgmt. Assn., Internat. Assn. of Bus. Communicators, San Diego Career Guidance Assn., Am. Soc. Tng. & Devel., Coll. Placement Council Inc., Am. Personal Guidance Assn., Council for Adv. & Support of Edn.; Protestant; rec: tennis, skiing, jogging Res: 6959 Ride Manor Ave. San Diego 92120 Ofc: Educational Cultural Complex, 4343 Ocean View Blvd. San Diego 92113

HOYNAK, BRYAN CLIFFORD, physician/ professional golfer; b. June 13, 1957, San Antonio, Tex.; s. Peter Xenephon and Barbara (Jones) H.; m. Martha Spenler, Jan. 14, 1983; edn: BA biology, magna cum laude, Wilkes Coll., Wilkes Barre, Pa. 1978; MD, Washington Univ. Sch. of Med., St. Louis, Mo. 1982. Career: res. gen. surg. Richland Mem. Hosp. Columbia S.C. 1982-83; emerg. phys. McCleod Reg. Med. Ctr. Florence, S.C. 1984, Washington Hosp. Culver City, Calif. 1984-85; Merced Co. Med. Ctr. 1985; Needles Desert Comm. Med. Ctr. Needles, Calif. 1985–, Santa Marta Hosp. 1985–; profl. golfer 1984–, NGA tour,South African PGA Tour; PGA tour sch. 1985; working for unification of ground/air ambulance svcs. for the High Desert of San Bernardino Co., SW Ariz., SW Nev., to better serve needs of tri-state area; honors: winner 7 intercollegiate golf events 1976-78; Dan Donnely Mem. Golf Tourn. winner 1977; mem: AMA, Am. Coll. Emergency Phys.; El Niguel Country Club; Republican; Catholic; rec: running, civil war history, cycling, history of surgery. Res: 33701A Blue Lantern Dana Point 92629

HOYT, DARLENE PRANDINE, police psychologist; b. Sept. 9, 1942, Canonsbury, Penn.; d. Bruc P. and Louise Esther (DeAngelo) Pradine; m. Charles A. Hoyt, III, Feb. 8, 1964; children: Stacey b. 1968, Stephanie b. 1971; edn: nursing diploma, Wash. Hosp. Sch. of Nursing 1963; BS, magna cum laude, Christopher Newport Coll., Coll. of William & Mary 1979; MA, MFCC, US Internat. Univ. 1981; PhD, Calif. Sch. of Profl. Psychology 1984. Career: nurse therapist Guam Community Mental Health Ctr., Agana, Guam 1979-80; tchg. asst. US Internat. Univ. 1981; pvt. practice with Dr. Michael Mantell spec. in law enforcement consultation 1983–; psychologist San Diego Police Dept. 1985–; adj. faculty National Univ.; tchr. diversion pgm. San Diego Police Dept. Juvenile Intervention Pgm.; sponsor Peer Resource Group, San Diego Police Dept.; honors: Cert. of Achiev., Departmental Distn. in Psychology 1979; mem: Am. Psychological Assn., Calif. Psychological Assn., Navy Wives Club, Supply Corp Wives Club; research: police stress 1983-84; post shooting trauma; Democrat; Catholic; rec: golf, jogging. Res: 14433 Yazoo St. San Diego 92129 Ofc: San Diego Police Dept., Psychological Svcs., 2615 Camino del Rio So. Ste. 300 San Diego 92129

HOYT, GORDON WESLEY, public utilities executive; b. Dec. 8, 1925, Santa Monica, Calif.; s. Raymond Earl and Edna Lenora (Campbell) H.; m. Joan Kenney, Sept. 10, 1947; children: Gordon b. 1948, Sally b. 1953, Claire b. 1958; edn: BSEE, Univ. Texas 1947; reg. profl. elec. engr. Calif. 1958. Career: elec. engr. Pacific Gas & Elec. Co. 1947-61; elec. supt. City of Santa Clara 1961-64; public utilities gen. mgr. City of Anaheim 1964—; mem: Am. Public Power Assn. (pres. 1985-86, v.p. 1983-84, bd. dirs. 1976-82), Calif. Municipal Util. Assn. (pres. 1971-73, v.p. 1969-71, bd. govs. 1968-77), Western Energy Supply & Transmission Assoc. (v.p. 1981-83, bd. dirs. 1975-84), Am. Inst. Elec. & Electron. Engrs. (senior) 1960-, Rotary, Anaheim Ichthylogical, 5-Card Draw & Sour Mash Soc. 1965-; publ: num. articles in Public Power Mag., num. presentations to profl. orgs.; mil: lt. j.g. USNR 1942-46, Am. Theatre Ops.; Democrat; Catholic; rec: sailing, fishing. Res: 432 Cedarhaven Way Anaheim 92807 Ofc: City of Anaheim 200 S Anaheim Blvd Anaheim 92805

HOYT, JACK W., educator; b. Oct. 19, 1922, Chgo.; s. Claire A. and Fleta (Wheeler) H.; m. Helen Erickson, Dec. 27, 1945; children: John b. 1948, Katheryn b. 1952, Annette b. 1959, Denise b. 1964; edn: BS, Ill. Inst. of Tech. 1944; MS, UCLA 1952, PhD 1962. Career: engr. Nat. Advis. Com. on Aeronautics, Cleveland, Oh. 1944-48; engr. Naval Ocean Systems Center, San Diego 1948-79; prof. mech. engring. US Naval Acad., Annapolis 1976-77, Rutgers Univ. 1979-81, CSU San Diego 1981—; honors: Freeman Scholar, ASME (1971), Gilbert Curl Award, USN (1975); mem: ASME, NY Acad. of Scis., Soc. of Naval Architects and Marine Engrs.; num. tech. publs. in hydrodynamics; rec: jog, woodworking, stamps. Res: 4694 Lisann St San Diego 92117 Ofc: San Diego State University, San Diego 92182-0191

HSIA, FREDERICK TSU, civil engineer; b. Oct. 8, 1941, Beijing, China, nat. US cit. 1974; s. Cheng Yin and Han Yin (Lin) H.; m. Min, Apr. 6, 1968; children: Constance b. 1970, Eric b. 1976; edn: BS hydraulic engring., Nat. Cheng Kung Univ., Taiwan 1963; MSCE, Texas A&M Univ. 1967; PhD, Mich. State Univ. 1977; Reg. Profl. Engr., Mich. (1975), Calif. (1978). Career: bridge design engr. Mich. Dept. of State Hwys & Transp., Lansing, Mich. 1967-74; transp. research engr. 1974-77; project geotechnical engr. US Forest Service, Pleasant Hill, Calif. 1977—; awards: Nat. Highway Inst. Research Fellowship (1973-74); mem: Assn. of Asphalt Paving Technologists, I.A., Transp. Research Board, Triaxial Inst.; publs: over 30 tech. papers and reports re pavement engring. and geotechnical engring.; rec: skiing, tennis, movies. Ofc: US Forest Service 2245 Morello Ave Pleasant Hill 94523

HSIEH, CARL CHIA-FONG, educator; b. Jan. 5, 1939, Taiwan, nat. US cit. 1974; s. Chun Yen and Chen (Hsu) H.; m. Shu-Mei Chuang, Nov. 10, 1962; children: Janet b. 1963, Louis b. 1964, Helen b. 1969, Christine b. 1977; edn: BS, Nat. Taiwan Univ. 1961; MS, So. Dak. Sch. of Mines & Tech. 1965; PhD, Northwestern Univ. 1968; Reg. Profl. Engr. (Civil) Calif. Career: structural engr. Taiwan Public Works Bureau, Taiwan 1962-64; body research engr. Chrysler Corp., Detroit 1968-70; senior engr. Bechtel Corp., San Francisco 1974, engring. splst., 1977; prof. of arch. engring. Calif. Poly. State Univ. 1970-82, prof. civil engring. 1982—; awards: ARPA research assistanceship (1965-68), Grad. Research Fellowship (1965), scholarship award China Found. for Promotion of Edn. and Culture, NY (1965), NASA-ASEE summer faculty fellow 1974, 79, 85; mem: ASCE (v.p. San Luis Obispo Br. 1981-82; dir. L.A. Sect. 1982-83), Am. Soc. for Engring. Edn., Chinese Assn. Cal Poly SLO (founding v.p. 1979, pres. 1980), Nat. Soc. Profl. Engrs. (1973-76), Calif. Soc. Profl. Engrs. (1973-76), Calif. State Employees Assn. (1979-82), United Profs. of Calif. (1982-83), Calif. Faculty Assn.; 9 tech. publs., contbr. Internat. J. of Engring. Sci., Oxford, Eng. (1973); Democrat; rec: jogging, tennis. Res: 1730 Jalisco Ct San Luis Obispo 93401 Ofc: Calif. Poly. State University, Civil Eng. Dept., San Luis Obispo 93407

HSIEH, SHAO-RONG "RON", engineering executive; b. Feb. 6, 1944, Shanghai, China; s. Ming-De and Liu H.; m. Suk#kuen, Dec. 18, 1981; 1 son, Larry b. 1984; edn: BS in physics, Nanking Univ. 1968; MS in E.E., UC Irvine 1981; Reg. Profl. Engr. (elec. eng.) Calif. 1983. Career: electronic/ mech. engr. Ser-Chu Ball Bearing Mfg. Co., Nanking 1973-78; assoc. prof. Nanking Univ. 1968-80; vis. lectr., research scientist UCI 1980-82; electr-mech. engr. (computerized automatic mfg.) VHD Disk Mfg. Co., Irvine 1981-82; project engr. Data Tech Co., Santa Ana 1982-83; senior engr., electronics engring. dir. Vitacomm Inc., Orange 1983-85; mil. electronic design supv. Del Mar Avionics, Irvine 1985—; Res: 3034 Cheryllyn Ln Anaheim 92804

HSU, JOHN YUAN-PO, professional engineer; b. May 26, 1939, Nanking, China, nat. US cit. 1977; s. Gin Hin and Fang Ling (Jen) H.; m. Yunmei, June 29, 1946; children: Nancy b. 1973, Lucy b. 1977; edn: BS, Chung Yuan Univ. 1963; MS, Tenn. Tech. Univ. 1971; reg. profl. engr. Calif. 1978. Career: shift supv. Taiwan Fertilizer, Taipei 1964-68; tchg. asst. Tenn. Tech. 1968-70; product researcher American Excelsior Co. Chicago 1971-73; engr. H.K. Ferguson Co. Cleveland 1973-74; instrumentation engr. Fluor Engrs. Inc. No. Calif. div. Redwood City 1974-76; control & instr. engr. Brown & Root Co. San Ramon 1976-78; control syst. engr. Fluor Engrs. No. Calif. div. 1978-79; sr. control syst. engr. Dav McKee Engrg. San Ramon 1979-80, sr. engr. Bechtel Inc. S.F. (main process control of defense waste processing facilities proj., a $2.5 billion proj.); dean edn. Fremont Chinese Saturday Sch.; mem: Chem. Products Research Bd. 1977, Instrument Soc. of Am. 1976, Bay Area Toastmasters, Chung Yuan Univ. Alumni Assn. of No. Calif., Assn. of Bay Area Chinese

schools (v.p.); established bylaws for Assn. of Bay Area Chinese Schs. (1983), Fremont Chinese School (1985); mil: 2nd lt. ROTC Taiwan 1963-64; Republican; Christian; rec: skiing, football, tennis, swimming, bridge, guitar, piano. Res: 4340 Peregrine Way Fremont 94536

HSU, LAMBERT, investment firm president; b. June 12, 1962, Okinawa, Japan; s. Hugo C.K. and June (Takekawa) H.; edn: Univ. of Miami 1980-81; elec. engring., San Diego State Univ. 1981-; Reg. securities broker, SEC 1985. Career: assoc. engr. Solar Turbines Inc. 1983-84; computer cons. Convoy Computers 1984-85; investment mgr., founder, pres. Pioneer Investments, San Diego 1985—; mem. Assoc. Students SDSU, exec. dir. 1985 Spring Fiesta (adm. $100,000 budget, mobilized 1000 stu. vols.); honors: Nat. Hon. Soc. (1980-81), Tau Beta Pi (1983), Eta Kappa Nu (1984), Outstanding Greek Award (1985), scholarship awards: Am. Womens Welfare Assn. (1980), Univ. of Miami Pres.'s Merit Scholar (1980), Alpha Tau Omega Found. (1983); Southwestern Co. sales awards (1982); mem. Assoc. Students Univ. of Miami 1980-81 (coord. Carni Gras Frat. Ops.), Alpha Tau Omega Frat. (alumni rels. ofcr., spl. events coord., pub. rels. ofcr., rush-social chmn., soc. svc. chmn.; Brother of Year 1985), Internat. Missing Children's Found. (Dance Event Coord.); organizer of Battle of the Bands Pgm., San Diego (features 12 local bands, full media support local radio KGB-FM) 1982-; Republican; rec: sports, flying, travel. Ofc: 6765 Alvarado Rd Ste 9 San Diego 92120

HU, GENDA JAMES, microelectronics device physicist; b. Jan. 20, 1952, Taipei, Taiwan; s. Su-Hung and Chang-Chi (Wan) H.; m. Wen-ming Shen, July 23, 1977; children: An-swol b. 1980, An-yen b. 1982; edn: BSE, National Cheng Kung Univ. 1973; MS, Princeton Univ. 1977, PhD, 1979. Career: research staff mem. IBM T.J. Watson Research Ctr., Yorktown Hts., NY 1979-83, Xerox Palo Alto Research Ctr. 1983-84, proj. mgr. device design and simulation 1984; dept. mgr. device engrg. Sierra Semiconductor Corp., San Jose 1984—; honors: Invention Achievement Award (IBM 1983), Spl. Recogn. Award (Xerox PARC 1984); mem: IEEE (senior), Electro-Chemical Soc.; publs: 20 articles in tech. jours. and confs.; 1 US patent issued 1984; Republican; rec: sports, music. Res: 776 Carlisle Way Sunnyvale 94087 Ofc: Sierra Semiconductor Corp. 2075 N Capitol Ave San Jose 95132

HUANG, BING YUAN, acupuncturist; b. July 19, 1936, Canton, China, nat. US cit. 1986; s. You Chong Wong and Ming Fong Huang; m. Shu Chin, Feb. 2, 1983; 1 dau., Sing b. 1985; edn: MD, Hunan Med. Coll., China 1959; Cert. Acupuncturist, Calif. 1982. Career: MD, China 1959-81; cert. acupuncturist and herbalist, Calif. 1982—; mem: Calif. Acupuncturist Assn.; rec: sports, plants.

HUANG, CARL KUO-CHANG, hotel owner; b. Sept. 22, 1937, Taiwan, Republic of China; s. Tien Hsi and Yon Pong Huang; m. Show Chin, Jan. 24, 1964; children: James b. 1966, Jane b. 1968; edn: BA, Nat. Taiwan Normal Univ. 1962; MA, 1970; MA, UCAL 1971. Career: primary sch. tchr., Taiwan 1955-57; H.S. tchr., Taiwan 1965-67; coll. instr., Taiwan 1965-67; owner Manhattan Motel, Glendale 1975-81; owner Glendale Motel 1978-81; owner Town House Motel, Van Nuys 1978-79; mng. partner New Orlean Hotel 1979, joined franchise of Travelodge, sole owner Inglewood Airport Travelodge 1981—; mem. bd. First Bank of Inglewood (Orgn.); pres. Taiwan Benevolent Assn. of Calif.; dir. Taiwan Benevolent Assn. of Am.; mem: Inglewood CofC; Westchester/ LAX CofC; Calif. Hotel & Motel Assn.; LA Chinatown Lion Club; publs: Dr. Sun Yat Sen' Theory of Political Power, 1970; From Man to Class; Karl Marx's Key Idea 1972; rec: writing. Res: 1508 E Orange Grove Glendale 91025 Ofc: Inglewood Airport Travelodge, 3900 W Century Blvd Inglewood 90303

HUANG, WILLIAM WEI-WEN, enologist; b. Jan. 26, 1938, Kuang Tung, China, nat. US cit. 1976; s. Ching Chiu and Yun Ping (Chang) H.; m. Sue, Mar. 20, 1965; 1 dau. Tammy b. 1982; edn: dipl. Taiwan Provincial Inst. of Agri. 1962; BS, UC Davis 1969, MS, 1970. Career: mgr. Taiwan Pineapple Co., Taipei 1963-67; food research cons. Sawyer-Adecor Internat. Inc., Los Angeles 1971-74; senior enologist United Vintners Inc., Madera 1974-77; mgr. of quality control The Wine Group Co., Ripon 1977—; owner W.H. Eggs Farmers, Modesto 1984—; dir. Dynasty Fed. Svgs Bank, San Mateo (1986-); cons. food and beverage indus.; mem. Inst. of Food Technols. (1971-), Am. Soc. of Enologists (1974-); Republican; rec: fishing. Res: 1908 Chelwood Way Modesto 95355 Ofc: POB 6322 Modesto 95355

HUBBARD, CHARLES RONALD, corporate programs executive; b. Feb. 4, 1933, Weaver, Ala.; s. John Duncan and Athy Pauline (Lusk) H.; m. Betty McKleroy, Dec. 29, 1951; 1 son: Charles Ronald II b. 1957; edn: BSEE, Univ. of Ala. 1960. Career: engr./ mktg. & pgm. mgr. Sperry Corp., Huntsville, Ala., 1960-71; sect. head 1971-74; sr. staff engr. Honeywell, Inc., Clearwater, Fla. 1974-76; mgr. 1976-79; chief engr., Honeywell, Inc., W. Covina, Calif. 1979-82, assoc. dir. engr. 1982-84, assoc. dir. Advanced Products, 1984—; dir. S&H Office Supplies, Huntsville, Ala. 1972-74; mem: IEEE (Govt. Rels. Com.,sect. chmn.); publs: Saturn V/ Apollo and Beyond, Am. Astronautical Soc., 1967; mil: USAF 1953-57; Methodist; rec: jogging, golf. Res: 5460 Willowick Cir Anaheim 92807 Ofc: Honeywell, Inc., 1200 E San Bernardino Rd, West Covina 91790

HUBBS, THOMAS WILLIAM, technology co. executive; b. Nov. 22, 1944, Cumberland, Md.; s. Thomas Caudy and Marian Viola (Bartlett) H.; m. Helen Pak, Oct. 6, 1973; children: Bryna b. 1979, Megan b. 1981; edn: BS in bus. adm., Lehigh Univ. 1966; MBA, Univ. Santa Clara 1977. Career: staff acct. Price Waterhouse & Co., Phila. 1965-67; acctg. mgr. Hewlett Packard Co.,

Palo Alto 1970-73; dir. acctg., asst. controller Four Phase Systems Inc., Cupertino 1973-80; v.p. fin., Ungermann-Bass Inc., Santa Clara 1980-84; senior v.p. fin. & admin., Atasi Corp., San Jose 1984-85; co-founder, dir., v.p. Phoenix Technology, Santa Clara 1985 —; dir. Linkware Inc., Wellesley, Mass. (1983-84); mem. Financial Executive Inst., Beta Gamma Sigma (1977); mil: 1st lt. US Army 1967-70, Army Commendn. Medal; Republican; rec: inv. analysis, real estate, ski, racquetball. Res: 10340 W Loyola Dr Los Altos 94022 Ofc: Phoenix Technology Inc. 2803 Bunker Hill Dr Santa Clara 95054

HUBKA, MARK ALAN, chiropractor; b. Sept. 28, 1958, San Diego; s. Verne Robert and Corinne Vernetta (Rens) H.; m. Janet Wilsie, Dec. 16, 1979; children: Joshua b. 1982, Thomas b. 1986; edn: BS, San Diego State Univ. 1978; DC, summa cum laude, Los Angeles Coll. of Chiropractic 1981. Lic. Disability Evaluator, 1985; Career: owner, dir. Kearny Mesa Chiropractic Center; indsl. cons. to ins. companies and San Diego Police Ofcrs. Assn.; mem; Am. Chiropractic Assn., Found. for Chiropractic Edn. & Research, Councils on Orthopaedics/ Roentgenology/ Neurology, Entrepreneur Club of San Diego; works: conducting study on cost effectiveness of chiropractic treatment in industrial related injuries; 1980 study on the Relationship Between Vitamin C and the Adrenal Glands; Republican; Catholic; rec: basketball, skiing, body surfing. Ofc: Kearny Mesa Chiropractic Center, 4626 Mercury St. San Diego 92111

HUDSON, EDWARD GORDON, real estate development co. executive; b. Feb. 20, 1950, Seattle, Wash.; s. Edward G. and Ruth (Gordon) H.; edn: BBA, Univ. Wash. 1973, MBA, 1974. Career: project mgr. McKeon Devel. Co., San Mateo 1974-77; exec. v.p. DeMonet Indus., Los Angeles 1977-84; pres. West Anaheim Profl. Center Devel., Anaheim 1985 —; exec. chmn. Town and Country Constrn., Sacto., 1981-; instr. real prop. devel. UC Los Angeles; civic: Mission Rescue Ctr. (1980-), Am. Cancer Soc. (1981-). Res: 10505 Sandal Ln Bel-Air 90077 Ofc: West Anaheim Professional Center 408 S Beach Blvd Ste 208 Anaheim 92804

HUETTENHAIN, HORST, engineering executive; b. Jan. 17, 1937, Csnabrueck, Ger, nat. US cit. 1973; s. Hermann and Irene (Zietemann) H.; m. Carolyn; children: Philipp b. 1962, Petra b. 1963, Barbara b. 1964, Todd b. 1964, Neil b. 1966; edn: Dilpoma Ing., T.U. Clausthal 1963; bus., LaSalle Univ. 1974; Reg. Profl. Mining Engr., Penn. 1968. Career: research engr. Kloeckner-Humboldt- Deutz, Cologne, Ger. 1963-67; devel. engr. Dravo Corp., Pittsburgh, Pa. 1967-73; v.p. internat. sales McNally Pittsburgh, 1973-77; group mgr. Bechtel Group Engring., San Francisco 1977-85, mgr. coal technology 1985 —; honors: (8) Awards of Merit, Bechhtel 1977-85; Presidential Achievement Award, 1982; mem: Am. Inst. Mech. Engrs., Am. Inst. Chem. Engrs., Engring. Found., Benicia Yacht Club, Peutsche Burschenschaft; patents in field of coal processing; sev. tech. publs.; rec: sailing, philately. Res: 411 Mills Dr. Benicia 94510 Ofc: Bechtel National Inc., So. Beale St. San Francisco 94119

HUFF, NORMAN NELSON, educator; b. Apr. 22, 1933, San Diego; s. Cmdr. George P. (USN ret.) and Norma Rose (Nelson) H.; m. Sharon Kay Lockwood, Sept. 1980; edn: Masters Tech. Cert., UCLA 1969-72; AA bus., Victor Valley Coll. 1972; BS chem. engr., Univ. San Diego 1957; MBA, Golden Gate Univ. 1972; lic. Profl. Engr. (chem.) Calif. 1958. Career: deep sea salvage ofcr., petroleum engr., CALCO, Venice, Louisiana 1950-51; research chemical/ astrophysics engr. Gen. Dynamics Convair, San Diego 1955-56; entomologist insp. State of Calif. 1956; chem. engr., field surveyor US Gypsum, El Centro 1957-58; USAF 1958-67: pilot, flight test ofcr., fighter pilot, quality control, maint. ofcr., chief of maint., nuclear weapons ofcr., tng. ofcr., pub. relations ofcr.; system programmer, State of Calif.; system programmer Pfizer Inc., Victorville 1972-73; lectr., dept. chmn. computer sci., Victor Valley Coll. 1967 —; p.t. lectr. Golden Gate Univ. and Chapman Coll., 1972-74; cons. finl. trusts; ednl. critic, edit computer software; honors: Instr. of Year (1968), fellowship (1972) Victor Valley Coll., VFW shooting award (1951), athletic awards in swimming, tennis, track, wrestling, shooting, mil. aerial combat (1949-65), Presidential Achievement Award (1982); mem. Nat. Advis. Bd. Am. Security Council, Am. US Congressional Advis. Bd.; mem: Calif. Bus. Edn. Assn. 1969-73, Inst. of Aero Sci. (pres. 1956-57), Calif. Edn. Computing Consortium (bd. mem., chmn. engring. 1979-), Internat. Platform Assn., Life Fellow Internat. Biographical Assn. (U.K.), Life Patron Am. Biog. Inst.; author five Computer Sci. texts; contbr. articles in chem., engr. jours. (1975); patent on Fusion Engine Application for Space Travel (Lockheed Aircraft Corp. 1976); mil: mil: USNAR 1950-53, USAFR 1953-57, capt. USAF 1957, decorated Air Medal; Republican (Nat. Com.); Catholic; rec: viticulture, writing, model bldg., skiing. Res: 16173 Rimrock Rd Apple Valley 92307

HUGHES, DAVE JEFFREY, industrial technology modernization specialist; b. May 9, 1960, Bellingham, Wash.; s. Clyde Marvin and Kay Hazel (Anguick) H.; edn: BSIE, Ore. State Univ. 1983; Reg. Profl. Engr. Career: mfg. methods engr. McDonnell-Douglas, 1983-85; senior indsl. technology modernization splst., Leach Corp., Los Angeles 1985 —; mem: Soc. of Mfg. Engrs. (senior), Inst. of Indsl. Engrs.; civic: Long Beach Jaycees (dir.), Long Beach Toastmasters; works: devel. statistical ops. research tool for lumber inventory control (1983), devel. Leach Corp. indsl. strategic plan (1985); Republican; rec: fitness (triathlete). Res: 576 Bellflower #222 Long Beach 90814 Ofc: Leach Corp. 5915 Avalon Blvd Los Angeles 90003

HUGHES, EDWIN JAMES, librarian; b. Nov. 30, 1922, Adrian, Wash.; s. Guy Allen and Lucy (Norman) H.; m. Edith Luverne Carter, June 17, 1951; children: James, Nancy, David; edn: stu. Eastern Wash. State Coll. 1948-49; BA,

Univ. Minn. 1952, MA, 1961; BS, Mankato State Coll. 1962; MPA, USC 1973. Career: senior clerk US Post Office, Ephrata, Wash. 1941-43, 46-48; county librarian Martin County Library, Fairmont, Minn. 1954-69; library dir. Oxnard Public Library, 1969 —; mem. faculty Library Inst. Seminar, Univ. Minn. 1956; pres. Minn. Library Film Circuit Corp., 1966-68; mem. state adv. council Inter-Library Coop., 1967-68; incorporator So. Minn.-No. Iowa Edn. TV Corp., 1967; v.p. Total Inter-Library Exchange Network, 1978-79, pres. 1979-80; chmn. Martin County Red Cross, 1957-59; dist. finance chmn. Boy Scouts Am., 1960-66; fund chmn. Fairmont Community Chest, 1965; bd. dirs. Ventura County Mental Health Assn.; mem. ALA, Minn. (chmn. sect. 1958), Calif. library assns., Public Library Execs. Assn. So. Calif. (sec. treas. 1982-83), Jr. CofC (sec. 1957, named Key Man 1955), Alpha Phi Omega, Nat. Exchange Club (sec. 1958-60 Fairmont); mil: US Army 1943-46, ETO; Methodist. Res: 1021 Ivywood Dr., Oxnard 93030 Ofc: 214 South C St Oxnard 93030

HUGHES, ELIZABETH, real estate broker; b. Apr. 11, 1920, Macon, Ga.; d. Charles Mason and Claire Elizabeth (Ward) Huguley; m. Harold G. Hughes, July 19, 1961; 1 dau. Valerie Hunken b. 1947; edn: AB, Emory Univ. 1940; lic. real estate broker Calif. 1950. Career: owner Hughes Realty, 1950 —; mem. com. to bring water to Las Virgenes Area (75,000 acres), L.A. County, 1955-58; elected first bd. dirs. Las Virgenes Municipal Water Dist. 1958-62; apptd. mem. (by L.A. County Bd. Supervisors) Los Angeles Co. Citizens Planning Council 1972-77; apptd. (by City Council) Traffic Com. City of Coronado 1979-81; mem. Las Virgenes CofC, Agoura CofC (secty.), Las Virgenes Hist. Soc., The Nature Conservancy (life), Monterey Peninsula Mus. of Art, Monterey Co. Symphony Assn., Mont. Bay Symphony Assn., Monterey Aquarium Assn.; mil: lt. USNR 1942-46; Republican; Catholic; rec: travel, reading gardening. Address: POB 222171 Carmel 93922

HUGHES, RICHARD KECK, film producer, director; b. Apr. 28, 1945, Ft. Madson, Iowa; s. Raymond H. and Roberta (Keck) H.; m. Wynne Gragg (div.); 1 son Justin R., b. 1970; edn: BA, Brooks Inst. 1972. Career: pres. October Film Prodns. Inc. 1972 —; num. profl. awards including 3 CLIO Award nominations; mem. Directors Guild of Am.; mil: sgt. US Army, Vietnam Svc. Ofc: October Prodns. Inc. 9 Ashley Ave Santa Barbara 93103

HUGHMANICK, DOUGLAS B., lawyer; b. Oct.15, 1919, Burlingame, Ca.; s. John H. and Mildred E. (Brown) H.; m. Dorothy Dalton, Jan. 21, 1943; children: Michael b. 1943, Douglas b. 1946, Gail b. 1949, Susan b. 1950, Robin b. 1953, John b. 1956; edn: BA, UC Berkeley 1948; JD, Stanford Univ. 1951; admitted Calif. bar and Federal Cts., 1951, US Tax Ct. 1979. Career: atty. assoc. Thelen, Marrin, Johnson & Bridges, San Francisco 1951-, ptnr. 1961 —; judge pro tem San Francisco Municipal Ct. 1980-; Fellow Am. College of Trial Lawyers, Fellow Am. Bar Found.; mem. San Francisco Bar Assn., Am. Bar Assn.; mil: major USAF 1940-46; Republican; Catholic; rec: cycling, swimming, tennis, travel. Res: 289 Park Lane Atherton 94025 Ofc: Thelen Marrin Johnson & Bridges, Two Embarcadero Ctr San Francisco 94111

HULSE, CHARLES N., real estate broker, investment consultant; b. Oct. 3, 1927, South Gate; s. George Lee and Hazel Virginia (Thompson) H.; m. Betty J., Nov. 23, 1950; children: Lee b. 1951, Chuck b. 1953; edn: Compton Coll. 1949-50; Cerritos Coll. 1971-74. Career: profl. race car driver 1949-68, Indy 500 race driver 1960-68, ret. from racing at Indianapolis 1968; instrument tech., tire devel. and pub. relations Firestone and Good Year; current: medical center developer/ owner/ adminstr. Pepper Tree Plaza; cons. real estate devel. & investments; cons. tire devel. Firestone and Goodyear; mil: sgt. US Army Air Force; Republican; Protestant; rec: flying, boating, travel. Res: 7341 Spruce Circle La Palma 90623 Ofc: C.N. Hulse Real Estate, 7851 Walker St. Ste. 100 La Palma 90623

HUMPHERYS, KENT C(IO), research scientist, radiation chemist; b. Jan. 17, 1932, Thayne, Wyo.; s. Willard Davis and Rhoda (Clark) H.; m. Vonzzaa Dursteler, June 11, 1952; children: Shauna b. 1953, Debra b. 1955, Brett b. 1958, Bryan b. 1960, Diana b. 1962, Brenda b. 1967; edn: undergrad. Utah State Univ. 1950-52, BS, Univ. of Utah 1954; grad. stu. Univ. N.Mex. 1957-58. Career: scientist Radiobiology Lab., 1952-55; nuclear research ofcr. USAF 1955-57; staff scientist Sandia Nat. Labs. 1957-62; sci. exec. E G & G Inc., 1962-73; v.p. Far West Technology Inc., Goleta 1973 —; cons. Kemp Reduction Corp. 1976-78; awards: Honor Soc., Univ. Utah (1954), Silver Beaver, Boy Scouts Am. (1982); mem. Am. Soc. for Testing & Mats. (1958-), Assn. for Advance. of Medical Instrumentation (1983-), Am. Nuclear Soc., Am. Chem. Soc.; civic: Mission Council BSA (v.p. 1978-), LDS Bus. & Profl. Assn. (pres. 1985-86); contbr. approx. 60 research arts. in sci. jours. (1955-); mil: capt. USAF 1955-57; Republican; Latter Day Saints; rec: church service, scouting, gardening. Res: 6262 Ave Ganso Goleta 93117 Ofc: Far West Technology Inc 330 S Kellogg Ste D Goleta 93117

HUMPLE, CAROL SEGRAVE, educator; b. Nov. 9, 1942, South Amboy, N.J.; d. Francis D. and Alice M. (Seeman) Segrave; m. George, Aug. 28, 1965; children: Alise b. 1967, Brodie b. 1972; edn: BA, Coll. of St. Elizabeth 1964; M.Ed., and cert. in ednl. gerontol., Rutgers Univ. 1979. Career: pres. Life Planning Managment (provider retirement life plnng. pgms. to major Fortune 500 cos.), Irvine 1979 —; instr. Saddleback Comm. Coll., 1981-83; lectr./writer on mid and late life planning and adjustment issues; advis. bd. Stonebridge Inst.; honors: Sigma Phi Omega (nat. gerontol. hon. soc.), Kappa Delta Pi; mem. Internat. Soc. of Retirement Plnnrs. (dir. Profl. Devel. Publs. 1981-83), Older Womens League; author: Retirement Life Designs (self-study ret. plnng. manual) (Ret. Designs, 1985), Mgmt. of the Older Worker Policies & Programs

(LPS 2050-Ret. Plnng. Video Series); Democrat; Catholic. Res: 13 Elderberry Irvine 92715 Ofc: Life Planning Management 2102 Business Center Dr Ste 130 Irvine 92715

HUNG, NGUYEN PHU, research and development engineer; b. Aug. 23, 1953, Hanoi, Vietnam; s. Son Phu and Thanh Thi N.; m. Lien Ha, July 3, 1981; edn: engring., Nat. Inst. of Tech. Vietnam 1972-75; BSME, Univ. of Mich. Ann Arbor 1978, MS, mfg. eng., 1979; Optical Tech., Santa Rosa Jr. Coll. 1982; PhDME, UC Berkeley 1987. Career: research asst. Univ. of Mich., Ann Arbor 1977-79; process engr. Hewlett Packard, Santa Rosa 1979-83, research & devel. engr.; multi div. cons. Hewlett Packard 1983-; honors: ASM Scholastic Achiev. Award, 1984; Hewlett Packard Fellowship, 1983; Univ. of Mich. Scholarship, 1978; mem: Am. Soc. of Mech. Engrs., Soc. Mfg. Engrs.; works: inventor, manufacturing processes, 1983; publs: num. tech. mags. 1984-86; Buddhist; rec: camping, photog. Ofc: Hewlett Packard, 1400 Fountain Grove, Santa Rosa 95401

HUNG, WILLIAM W., physician; b. Nov. 11, 1949, Tainan, Taiwan; s. Chin-Swei and Chun-Yu H.; m. Patricia, July 1977; children: Jennifer b. 1979, Steven b. 1980; edn: MD, Nat. Taiwan Univ. 1974; MPH, Harvard Univ. Sch. of Pub. Health 1978; Diplomate Am. Board Internal Medicine 1984. Career: physician in internal medicine, Downstate Medical Ctr., Kings County Hosp., 1978-81; pvt. medical practice in Montebello, Monterey Park, 1981–; bd. dirs. Beverly Community Hosp., Montebello; mem: AMA, Am. Coll. Physicians; Republican. Ofc: 1920 West Whittier Blvd Montebello 90640

HUNN, DWAYNE LAWRENCE, housing developer; b. June 18, 1943, Cleveland, Ohio; s. George Stephen and Martha Jane (Donoskovich) H.; edn: BA, St. Joseph's Coll. 1965; MA, Claremont Grad. Sch. 1969; MA, San Francisco State 1974; PhD, Claremont Grad. Sch. 1984; Lic. Real Estate Salesperson 1978-79. Career: vol. urban community devel. Peace Corps, Bombay, India 1966-68; tchr. Glendora H.S./ Citrus Coll 1969-76; ptr. Recycled Bldg. Co., Marin Co. 1975-78; mgmt. California Conservation Corps 1976-79; ptr. Solar Energy Retirement Community, San Rafael 1979-82; asst. exec. dir. Novato Ecumenical Housing, mgr. condo devel. 1982–; tchr. Owner Bldr. Ct. of Berkeley; pvt. cons. bus.; landlord 1976-; foreman Lollop Constrn. Co., St. John, Virgin Islands 1970; honors: Lincoln Sch. Fellowship (1969), appreciation, S.F. Police Chief (1974), Who's Who in Am. Colls. & Univs. (1965); civic: Marin Housing Devel. Trust Fund Com. (chair 1986-), mem. People's Lobby Steering Bd. (1970-76), Big Brother, Canal Community Alliance; works: helped build Castle at Rubelia (5-yr proj.) now on Calif. Historic Mus. list; contbr. articles in newspapers & mags.; prod./host of 36 TV & radio Public Affairs pgms.; Democrat; Catholic; rec: carpentry, gardening, hiking, baseball, basketball, biking. Res: 359 Jean St. Mill Valley 94941 Ofc: Novato Ecumenical Housing, P.O. Box 428 Novato 94947

HUNT, DAVID CARLTON, inventor, marketing executive; b. Jan. 6, 1949, Danville, Va.; s. David Cisero and Loraine (Robertson) H.; m. Deborah Suzanne, Nov. 19, 1977; 1 son, David Christopher b. 1985;q edn: AA, Davison Community Coll. 1968; Long Beach City Coll. 1971; UCLA 1972. Career: admisions ofcr. Brooks Coll. for Women 1971; founder Am. First Alert Security 1973; founder Commex Telesystems 1980; founder Far West Community Devel Inc. 1977; formed Commwatche Systems 1982; currently, owner Commex Telesystems; founders Club Dial One Region, Advy./ Focus Bd. Tie Communications; compositions: Everything is Possible, Am. Song Festival Winner 1976, 1978; The Light At The End Of The Tunnel, theme song for RP 1982; works: inventor, patentee, Commwatch, alarm device against cut telephone lines; rec: tennis, skiing, camping. Res: 19642 Ballinger St. Northridge 91324 Ofc: Commex, 9349 Melvin Ave. Ste. 4 Northridge 91324

HUNT, ERNEST WOODROW, JR., ophthalmologist; b. Aug. 7, 1938, Greenville, N.C.; s. Ernest Woodrow and Mary King (Fountain) H.; m. Coley Drohomer, June 22, 1962; children: Lisa b. 1966, Jennifer b. 1969, Melissa b. 1972; edn: BS, Davidson Coll. 1960; MD, Univ. of N.C. 1964; Navy Flt. Surgeon Sch., Pensacola 1965-66; Diplomate Am. Bd. Opthal. 1972. Career: intern Nat. Naval Medical Center, Bethesda, Md. 1966; naval flight surgeon Carrier Air Wing 15, 1966-68; resident in ophthal. Naval Hosp., San Diego 1968-71; staff ophthalmologist Naval Hosp., Camp Pendleton 1971-74; pvt. practice, La Jolla 1974–; staff (chmn. Section of Ophthal. 1979) Scripps Meml. Hosp. and first medical dir. Mericos Eye Inst., 1984–; mem: Fellow Am. Acad. of Ophthal., Fellow Am. Coll. of Surgeons, AMA, CMA, San Diego Co. Med. Soc., S.D. Eye Bank, S.D. Co. Acad. of Ophthal., Soc. of Mil. Ophthalmologists, Calif. Assn. of Ophthal., Am. Intraocular Implant Soc., Contact Lens Assn. of Ophthalmologists, Ophthalmic Outpatient Surgery Soc., Soc. for Office Based Surgery; mil: cmdr. US Navy Med. Corps 1964-74, Air Medal, Navy Achieve., Navy Unit Commendn. w/star, Nat. Def. Svc., Armed Forces Exped., Vietnam Cross of Gal. w/Frame and Palm, Vietnam Campaign w/4 stars, Rep. of Vietnam Campaign; Republican; Presbyterian; rec: flying. Ofc: Eye Care of La Jolla 9834 Genesee Ave Ste 200 La Jolla 92037

HUNT, JERRY DUNCAN, real estate consultant, author, investor; b May 21, 1941, Twin Falls, Ida.; s. Richard Gerald and Lucile Della (Duncan) H.; children: Bryan b. 1973, Laurel Ann b. 1975; edn: BS, UC Berkeley 1963; real estate broker Calif. 1970. Career: auditor Arthur Anderson & Co. S.F. 1963-65; portfolio mgr. UC Pension Fund Berkeley 1965-69; exec. v.p. Pacific States Housing Co. San Mateo 1969-73; regl. mgr. PMI Mortgage Ins. Co. S.F. 1973-79; pres. Calif. Housing Properties San Jose 1979-85; chmn., CEO Equity- Sharing Inc. Palo Alto 1985–; senior real estate cons. Stanford Research Inst.; bd. dirs. Bay Area Mortgage Investments, Cornish & Carey

Mortgage Co. 1984-85; honors: Merit Awards (Pacific Coast Builders Conf. 1979, PMI Mortgage Ins. 1977); mem: Am. Banking Assn., Mortgage Bankers Assn., Univ. Club (bd. 1980-85), Boy Scouts of Am., Babe Ruth Baseball, Engrs. Club of S.F.; publs: num. real estate articles; author: Equity- Sharing - The Key to Real Estate Success (1986); Republican; Ch. of Rel. Sci.; rec: tennis, skiing. Ofc: Equity- Sharing Inc. 3790 El Camino Real Ste 334 Palo Alto 94306

HUNT, MARGARET VIRGINIA, educator; b. March 24, 1938, Orange; d. Henry Lynn and Margaret Helene (Lehnhardt) H.; edn: BA, magna cum laude, Chapman Coll. 1961, MA, 1970; Elem. Life Cred. and Elem. Admin. Cred., Calif. Career: tchr. Alamitos Sch. Dist., Garden Grove 1961-63; tchr., sch. plnng. mem., tchg. pilot pgm. Tustin Sch. Dist. 1963-69; tchr. 1st Baptist Sch., Pomona 1969-79; designer, developer learning disabilities pgm. 1980; currently, dir. Ctr. for Creative Edn., 1st Baptist Sch., Pomona; mem: Dela Kapap Gamma Internat., Orton Dyslexia Soc., CANHC/ ACLD, Baptist Day Sch Assn., Fish of Fullerton, League of Women Voters; works: workshops presented at Baptist Day Sch. Confs. and Calif. Assn. of Pvt. Schs.; Republican; Baptist; rec: theatre, travel. Ofc: 1st Baptist School, 521 No. Garey Pomona 91767

HUNT, ROBERT G., oral maxillofacial surgeon; b. July 10, 1945, San Diego; s. Harvey G. and Pauline A. (Nazarovic) H.; m. Diane, Apr. 26, 1975; 1 dau: Christine b. 1981; edn: AA, Mesa Coll. 1971, DDS, USC 1976; BS, Univ. Nebr. 1979; MD, 1979. Career: physician, surgeon & dentist; currently, pvt. practice oral maxillofacial & reconstructive surgery of the jaws, San Diego; chmn. Blood Reserve Com. San Diego Co. Dental Soc.; v.p. Nat. Cred-A-Chek, Inc.; diplomate: Nat. Bd. Med. Examiners, Nat. Bd. Dental Examiners, Am. Bd. Oral Maxillofacial Surgery; fellow, Am. Assn. Oral Maxillofacial Surgeons; mem: Am. Med. Assn.; Am. Dental Assn.; So. Calif. Acad. of Oral Pathology; Paul Revere Study Club (pres.); Phi Kappa Phi; Omikron Kappa Upsilon; Mensa; contbr: San Diego Co. Cancer Soc. publs.; mil: s/sgt. USAF 1965-70, ret. Res: 4205 Trias St San Diego 92103

HUNT, STEVEN JAMES, financial executive; b. Nov. 3, 1944, Scottsbluff, Nebr.; s. Robert Sumner and Frances Maria (Burnham) H.; m. Debbie Hummel, Aug. 13, 1966; children: Suna b. 1968, Ryan b. 1974; edn: BA, Doane Coll. 1967; MBA, Univ. of Nebr. 1968. Career: finl. mgmt. trainee Gen. Elec. Co. 1968-70, corporate audit staff 1970-75, mgr. fin. GE Credit Corp. 1975-79, mgr. ops. analysis Consumer Prods. Sect. 1979-81, senior v.p. fin./planning VHD Programs Inc. (GE joint venture) 1981-83; exec. v.p./chief fin. ofcr. Chiat/Day Inc. Advertising, Los Angeles 1983–; dir. Venice Operating Co. (1986-); club: Los Angeles Athletic. Res: 9902 Currand Ave Fountain Valley 92708 Ofc: Chiat/Day Inc. Advt. 517 S Olive Los Angeles 90013

HUNTER, ART, stock broker; b. Apr. 24, 1933, Fairport Harbor, Ohio; s. Albert Dexter and Mary (Kapostasy) H.; m. Chip Aquino; children: Terry, b. 1958; Caroline, b. 1963; edn: BS in finance, Univ. of Notre Dame 1954. Career: profl. football, L.A. Rams, Green Bay Packers, Pittsburgh Steelers, Cleveland Browns, 11 yrs ; currently, acct. exec. Merrill Lynch, Santa Ana; awards: All American; All-Pro; mcm: NFL Players Assn.; NFL Alumni Assn.; mil: pfc US Army 1955-56; rec: sunning, gardening, arts. Res: 1376 S.E. Skyline Dr Santa Ana 92705 Ofc: Merrill Lynch, 1000 N Main St Santa Ana 92702

HUNTER, DUNCAN LEE, congressman; b. May 31, 1948, Riverside; m. Lynne Layh, 1973; children: Ducan Duane, Robert Samul; edn: JD, Western State Univ. 1976; admitted to Calif. State Bar 1976. Career: practiced law in San Diego; mem. 97th Congress from 42d Dist. of Calif., 98th Congress from 45th Dist. Calif., asst. regional whip; mem. Navy League; mil: 1st lt. US Army 1969-71; Republican; Baptist. Ofc: 117 Cannon House Office Bldg., Wash. DC 20515

HUNTER, JAMES GALBRAITH, JR., lawyer; b. Jan. 6, 1942, Phila.; s. James Galbraith and Emma Margaret (Jehl) H.; m. Pamela Ann Trott, July 18, 1969, div.; children: James b. 1973, Catherine b. 1978; edn: BS in eng. sci., Case Inst. of Tech. 1965; JD, Univ. Chgo. 1967; admitted to Ill. State Bar (1967), Calif. State Bar (1980), US Supreme Ct. (1979), US Cts. of Appeals for the 7th (1967), 4th (1978), 9th (1978), 5th (1982) and Federal (1982) Circuits, US Claims Ct. (1976), US Dist. Cts. Ill. (No., 1967, Central, 1980) and Calif. (So., 1980, Cent., 1980, and No., 1982). Career: atty. assoc. law firm Kirkland & Ellis, Chgo. 1967-68, 70-73, partner 1973-76; partner Hedlund, Hunter & Lynch, Chgo. 1976-82; partner Latham & Watkins, Hedlund, Hunter & Lynch, Chgo. 1982-84; partner Latham & Watkins, Los Angeles 1982–, and Chgo. 1984–; mem. Am., Chgo., Calif., Los Angeles County bar assns., Metropolitan Club, Chgo. Athletic Assn.; honors: exec.ed. Univ. Chgo. Law Rev. 1966-67; mil: lt. USNR 1968-70, Navy Commendn. with combat distg. device, Vietnamese Cross of Gall. with Palm, Vietnam Service, Vietnam Campaign, Nat. Def. Service medals. Ofc: Latham & Watkins, 6900 Sears Tower, Chicago IL 60606 Latham & Watkins, 555 So. Flower St. Ste. 4500, Los Angeles 90071

HUNTER, JEFFREY CHARLES, technical manager, educator; b. Oct. 19, 1938, San Diego; s. Theodore Lee and Dorothea (Wilson) H.; m. Doreen E. Lonergan, Nov. 26, 1983; edn: BS, CSU San Diego 1962, MS, 1964; postgrad. wk. Univ. Wash., Seattle 1964-65, MAM, Univ. Redlands 1979. Calif. Comm. Coll. Tchr. credentials in bus. and chem. Career: all with Avery International: senior chemist 1966-71; lab. supv. 1971-76; research dept. Avery Label Div. product devel. splst. 1976-79; project mgr. 1979-84, echnical mgr. 1984–, Avery Consumer Products Div., Consumer and Office Products Group, Avery Internat.; undergrad and grad. instr. in bus. and sci. Coll. of Profl. Studies,

Univ. of San Francisco 1981-; state chmn. curriculum design com. Coll. of Profl. Studies 1982, 83, 84; co-dir. E. San Gabriel- Pomona Valley Back in Control Ctr. 1985-; mem: Am. Chem. Soc., Council of Reprographics Execs., Assn. of MBA Execs., Tech. Assn. of the Pulp & Paper Indus., Kiwanis Intl.; co-author curriculum handbooks, Introduction to Organizational Behavior, and Research in Organizations; contbr. articles in field to profl. jours.; patentee in field; Republican; Episcopal; rec: numismatics, scuba diving. Res: 9744 Lehigh Ave Montclair 91763 Ofc: Avery Consumer Products Div., Avery Internat., 777 E Foothill Blvd Azusa 91702

HUNTER, LAURIE KIMBERLY, certified public accountant; b. Sept. 4, 1953, Des Moines, Iowa; d. Jess Evan and Naomi Irene (Wade) H.; m. Robert Leslie Tiedemann, Apr. 28, 1984; edn: BS magna cum laude, Univ. Ariz. 1975; MBA, UC Los Angeles 1980; MBT (taxation), Univ. So. Calif. 1983; CPA Calif. 1977. Career: senior acct. Deloitte, Haskins & Sells L.A. 1975-80; cons. Xerox Computer Svcs. L.A. 1980-83; senior financial mgr. L.A. Olympic Organizing Com. 1983-85; self-employed tax & mgmt. cons. 1985–; honors: Davre Davidson Fellow (UCLA Grad Sch. of Mgmt. 1979); mem: Am. Inst. CPAs, Calif. Soc. CPAs, USC MBA Alumni Assn., UCLA Mgmt. Alumni Assn., USC Acctg. Circle, UCLA Grad. Sch. Mgmt. Dean's Council, Gamma Phi Beta; Republican; Christian Science; rec: skiing. Res: Manhattan Beach Ofc: Manhattan Beach 90266

HUNTER, LYLE W., financial planner; b. June 26, 1956, San Diego; s. Mel and Eleanor Diane (Miller) H.; m. Vicki, Aug. 26, 1984; edn: AS law, Southwestern Coll. 1977; San Diego State Univ. 1978-79; financial planner 1985. Career: mgr. B&W Auto Parts Inc. National City 1980-83; ins. agent, fin. planner, investment advisor self-employed 1982–; mem: Calif. Assn. Financial Planners, Internat. Assn. Financial Planners 1984-, Am. Legion; Republican (supporter Presdl. Task Force); Christian; rec: automobile racing. Address: 6735 Parkside Ave San Diego 92139

HUNTLEY, DONALD EDWARD, commercial real estate broker; b. Nov. 14, 1947, Modesto; s. Alfred Daniel and Clara Jane (Hubbs) H.; m. Carol, Jan. 13, 1979; children: Scott b. 1975 (previous marriage), Michelle b. 1979, Jennifer b. 1984; edn: AA, Modesto Jr. Coll. 1970, AA in R.E., West Valley Coll. 1979; BS, CSU San Jose 1974, MBA, 1976; desig: R.E. Broker (1978), Notary Public (1976). Career: mgmt. trainee Macys Calif., 1974; sales asso. Allstate Realtors, 1974-82, ofc. mgr. 1980-82; comml. real estate broker splst. in sales and leasing, Schneider Commercial, San Jose 1982–; instr. in principles of R.E. and license prep. Century 21 Real Estate 1984-; awards: co. sales achievement awards (1974-); mem. Nat. Assn. Realtors, Calif. Assn. Realtors, San Jose Bd. Realtors, Nat. Notary Assn.; mil: s/sgt. US Air Force 1968-72; Republican; Catholic; rec: pvt. pilot, hunt, fish, travel. Res: 1816 Kirkmont Dr San Jose 95124 Ofc: Schneider Commercial 2635 North First St Ste 116 San Jose 95134

HURD, WALTER LEROY, JR., product assurance executive; b. July 8, 1919, Columbus, Mont.; m. Ann C., Sept. 26, 1941; children: David b. 1949, Caroline b. 1952, Drew b. 1953, Bruce b. 1954, Kevin b. 1957; edn: BA, hist., pol. sci., Morningside Coll. 1940; MA, guidance & counseling, San Jose State Univ. 1977; Reg. Profl. Engr., Calif. (1975), Cert. Quality Engr., ASQC (1966), Cert. Reliability Engr., ASQC (1972). Career: engr. Philippine Airlines 1945-54, Federal Mogul Corp. 1954-58; reliability and quality engring. mgr. Lockheed Missiles and Space Co. 1962-65, dir. product assur. Space Systems Div., 1966-77; corporate dir. product assurance Lockheed Corp., Burbank 1977–; honors: B.L. Lubelsky Award (1972), E.L. Grant Award (1975), E.J. Lancaster Award (1984), ASQC; Merit Award, San Fernando Valley Engrs. Council (1979); hon. mem. Philippine, Australian and New Zealand nat. quality control orgns.; mem: Fellow ASQC (nat. pres. 1977-78), Nat. Soc. Profl. Engrs. Assn., Fellow Am. Inst. Astro. & Aero., Internat. Acad. for Quality (Academician), Fellow British Interplanetary Soc., Nat. Space Inst. (charter life), Asia Pacific Orgn. for Quality Control (charter life); co-author two books: Reliability Handbook (McGraw-Hill, 1966), and 50 tech. publs. on reliability and quality control; mil: brig. gen. (ret.) USAF Active duty 1941-46, Reserve 1946-79, D.F.C. (3), Air Medal (4); Protestant; rec: speaking on space industrialization, swimming. Res: 1840 Dalehurst Ave Los Altos 94022 Ofc: Lockheed Corp 2555 N Hollywood Way Burbank 91520

HURFORD, DAVID DEAN, JR., realty services co. executive; b. July 4, 1951, Los Angeles; s. David Dean and Patricia Jean (Woodard) H.; edn: AB, Stanford Univ. 1973; MA, Occidental Coll. 1974; lic. real estate broker, Calif. 1976. Career: Coro Foundation Fellow, San Francisco 1974; municipal fin. cons. Bartle Wells Assocs., S.F. 1975-76; with Coldwell Banker & Co., Los Angeles 1976–: staff salesman 1976-80, sales cons. 1980-82, senior sales cons. 1982-83, v.p. institutional realty svcs. 1983–; awards: Top Salesman Awd. 1982, 83; Distng. Achiev. Awd., Coldwell Banker; fellow, Rotary Internat. Found. 1980; mem: Urban Land Inst.; Los Angeles Bd. Realtors; Town Hall; Coro Assocs.; United Way; Jonathan Club; Explorers Club; rec: backpacking, travel, photog. Res: Pasadena Ofc: Coldwell Banker & Co., 533 Fremont Ave Los Angeles 90071

HURLEY, EMMET DANIEL, lawyer; b. July 24, 1923, Buffalo, N.Y.; s. Emmet Daniel and Irene Maston (Lee) H.; m. Elizabeth Hamilton-White, June 8, 1979; children: Kathleen Fox b. 1951, Stephanie Funk b. 1955, Irene L.M. b. 1972; edn: BSS, Georgetown Univ. 1947; JD, Harvard Law Sch. 1951. Career: assoc. atty. Pittsburgh 1957; ptnr. law firms in L.A. and San Diego counties since 1957, currently sole practitioner Borrego Spgs.; dir., pres. Odyssey Computer Corp.; mem: Am., Calif., S.D. Co. bar assns.; other profl. orgs., Harvard Law Sch. Alumni Assn., Harvard Club of S.D., De Anza Desert CC; mil: USAAF 1942-46; rec: golf. Address: Borrego Springs 92004

HURT, ROBERT GLENN, investment securities co. executive; b. Jan. 31, 1919, Pasadena; s. Dr. Leslie M. (past pres. AVMA) and Effie Mae (McKim) H.; edn: AB, USC, 1940; postgrad. Harvard Bus. Sch. 1941. Career: trainee Calvin Bullock, Ltd., NYC 1946; asst. to west coast head, L.A. 1946-49; northern div. head, 1949-53; resident and senior v.p. Calvin Bullock, Ltd., San Francisco 1954–; honors: Order of Kentucky Colonels; mem. Alpha Delta Sigma, Phi Kappa Psi, Andreas Canyon Club, Stock Exchange Club of San Francisco, Stock Exchange Club of Los Angeles, Harvard Club, Pres. Circle USC, Am. Legion, Reserve Officers Assn.; mil: pvt. to lt. col. AUS Inf. 1941-46; comdr. Mil. Order of World Wars; Cathlic. Res: 937 Ashbury St San Francisco 94117 Ofc: Calvin Bullock, Ltd., 931 The Mills Bldg., 220 Montgomery St San Francisco 94104

HUTCHESON, JERRY DEE, marketing research executive; b. Oct. 31, 1932, Hammon, Okla.; s. Radford Andrew and Ethel Mai (Boulware) H.; brother, Radford Roland Hutcheson, NM Dir. of Missions, So. Baptist Conv.; m. Lynda Weber, Mar. 6, 1957; edn: BS, Eastern NM Univ. 1959; postgrad., Temple Univ. 1961-62; postgrad., Univ. NM 1964-65; reg. elec. engr., Calif. Career: research engr. RCA 1959-62; sect. head Motorola 1962-63; research physicist Dikewood Corp. 1963-66; sr. tech. staff Signetics Corp. 1966-69; eng. mgr. Littons Sys. 1969-70; eng. mgr. Fairchild Semiconductor 1971; eqpt. eng. gp. mgr. Teledyne Semiconductor 1971-74; dir. eng. D.C.A. Reliability Labs. 1974-75; founder, pres./ CEO VLSI Research, Inc., San Jose 1975–; mem: Masonic Lodge (Master Mason); Nat. & Calif. Socs. of Profl. Engrs.; Profl. Engrs. in Pvt. Practice; Profl. & Tech. Cons. Assn.; Semiconductor Eqpt. & Materials Inst.; coauthor/ pub: The VLSI Manufacturing Outlook, 1980; contbr: var. arts. in profl. journs. 1960-; research, integrated circuits and process equipment 1960-; mil: USAF 1951-55; Democrat (Precinct Com. 1964-66); Presbyterian; rec: philately, oil painting, tennis. Res: 5950 Vista Loop San Jose 95124 Ofc: VLSI Research Inc., 1754 Technology Dr, Ste 226, San Jose 95110

HUTCHESON, LYNDA LOU, co. executive; b. Nov. 26, 1936, Clovis, N.M.; d. John S. and Iva (Neff) Weber; m. Jerry D. Hutcheson, Mar. 9, 1953; children: Gera[illegible] b. 1954, Lisa Marie (Shufelt) b. 1956, Vicki Lynn (Verducci) b. 1957; edn: spl. courses Foothill Coll. Career: ofc. mgr., adminstrv. asst., office publications methods analyst, Technical Ventures, 1976-81; co-founder/v.p. adminstrn. VLSI Research Inc., 1981–, bd. dirs. 1983-; Republican; Presbyterian; rec: interior design, gardening, tennis. Res: 5950 Vista Loop San Jose 95124 Ofc: VLSI Research Inc 1754 Technology Dr Ste 117 San Jose 95110

HUTCHINS, JERRY JOHN, artist, photographer; b. May 1, 1962, Chula Vista, Calif.; s. Roland Thomas and Bertha Irene (MacDougall) H.; edn: Southwestern Coll. 1980-82. Career: custom black & white printer Visual Prodns. San Diego 1982-83, Photodyne S.D. 1983-84; yearbook photographer Naval Tng. Center, Sch. Pictures Inc. S.D. 1984-86; owner, photog. Jerry Hutchins Photo S.D. 1986–; mem: Photog. Soc. of Am. 1980-, Friends of Photog. 1982-, Aerospace Mus., Hall of Fame 1981-; Democrat; Catholic; rec: photog., camping, nature. Ofc: Jerry Hutchins Photog. POB 84899 San Diego 92138

HUTCHINSON, DOROTHE DEANE, college president; b. July 11, 1927, Burwell, Nebr.; d. Ralph Winfred and Viola Emelia (Horner) Haas; m. Wilbur E. Hutchinson, Nov. 23, 1947; 1 dau. Kathryn Louise b. 1949; edn: Pacific Union Coll. 1945-47. Career: business mgr. Santa Rosa Med. & Surg. Clinic, Santa Rosa 1950-52; staff acct. Ashton Hayes, CPA, 1952-54; treas. Sonoma Mtg. Corp., 1954-60, v.p. 1960-75; senior v.p. Wells Fargo Mortgage Co., San Francisco 1975-83, cons./bldg. project mgr. 1982-83; pres. Empire College, Santa Rosa 1983–; dir: Luther Burbank Savings (1983-), Geyser Peak Winery (1983-), v.chmn. bd. Empire College (1982-), trustee St. Helena Hosp. and Health Care Center (1976-); honors: Woman of Distinction, Santa Rosa Jr. Coll. (1984); mem. No. Calif. Mortgage Bankers Assn. (pres. 1981-82), Mortgage Bankers Assn. of Am. (bd. govs. 1980-83); mem. Assn. of Indep. Colls. and Schs. (1983-), Pres.'s Associates Sonoma State Univ. (1985-); civic: S.R. CofC (dir. 1984-, v.p. Community Devel. 1986-), United Way (dir. 1983-), YMCA (dir. 1983-), No. Calif. Found. (dir./v.p. 1984-), Community Found. of Sonoma Co. (dir. 1985-), March of Dimes (Teamwalk chair 1984); Republican; Seventh-day Adventist; rec: skiing, boating, needlepoint. Ofc: Empire College 3033 Cleveland Ave Santa Rosa 95401

HUTCHINSON, LORRAINE KAY, marriage, family and child therapist; b. Aug. 27, 1951, Pittsburg, Calif.; d. Louis V., Sr. and Alice G. (Jackson) Green; m. Chester Hutchinson, Feb. 22, 1975; children: Treasure b. 1976, Reginald b. 1976; edn: BS, Univ. Santa Clara 1973; MA, Azusa Pacific Univ. 1983; marriage family child counselor, Calif. BBSE 1983. Career: marriage, family, child counselor, Inst. for Marital Family Studies 1983–; admissions counselor Azusa Pacific Univ., San Jose Extn. 1983-; instr./ counselor Opportunities Industrialization Ctr. 1973-74; dir. presch. pgm. Emmanuel Baptist Ch. 1978-81; marriage, family & child counselor intern Center For Family Learning, San Jose 1983; volunteer cons./ marriage, family & child therapist, Arbutus Youth Assn. 1982-; cons. Dept. of Health & Human Svcs. Wash. DC 1985; honors: life mem. Calif. Scholarship Fedn. 1969; mem: Internat. Soc. for Prevention of Child Abuse & Neglect; Calif. Assn. Marital & Family Therapy; Christian Assn. for Psychological Studies; Democrat; Baptist. Res: 3579 Rowley Dr San Jose 95132 Ofc: Inst. for Marital Family Studies, 5150 Graves Ave, Bldg 6D, San Jose 95129

HUTCHISON, GWENLYN LEE WINKLER, entrepreneur; b. May 15, 1939, Los Angeles; d. Max Louis and Ruby Avanell (Barker) Winkler; m. Dudley Hutchison, July 13, 1958; children: Celeste Colleen b. 1959, Wendy Lee b. 1961; edn: AA, Ventura Coll. 1975; BS, UC Santa Barbara 1978. Career: prodn. mgr. Spec Tech Publs., Oxnard 1977-82; prodn. control splst Stanwick Corp.

Sys. Engrg. Group, Ventura 1979; owner Hutchison Graphics, Ventura 1982—; honors: var. profl. awards, 1st Pl. Typesetting (1986), Ad Club of Ventura, Blue Ribbon- Calligraphy (1982) and 2d. Pl. Oil Painting (1981), Ventura County Fair; mem: Gr. Ventura CofC, Ventura County Profl. Women's Network (newsletter), Ventura County Roots & Wings Reading Pgm. for Adults (adv. bd.); rec: oil painting, needlework, fishing, study of physical scis. Res: 523 Skyline Rd Ventura 93003 Ofc: Hutchison Graphics 2734 Johnson Dr Ste 101 Ventura 93003

HUTH, DIANE MAE, manufacturing co. executive; b. Feb. 23, 1935, Chgo.; d. John Francis and Helen Lorene (Stevens) Seymour; m. Gerald Huth, Apr. 26, 1958; children: Sharon b. 1959, Gerald, II b. 1961, Carol b. 1962, Kathleen b. 1964; edn: AA, Goldenwest Jr. Coll. 1970; BBA, UC Fullerton 1972. Career: acct. Ansel E. Young, CPA, Tustin 1972-73; acct., senior acct. Swedlow Inc., Garden Grove 1973-75, acctg. supr. 1975-79, gen. acctg. mgr. 1979-82, asst. controller 1982—, asst. secty. 1985—; mem. Swedlow, Inc. Benefits Com. 1979-, Pension Com. 1979-; honors: Leadership of Women in Econ., Civic & Cultural Life of Orange Co., YWCA (1983); mem. Nat. Accts. Assn. (treas. 1978), Inst. of Mgmt. Acctg., Women in Mgmt., West Garden Grove Women's Club; Republican; Catholic; rec: ski, water sports, bridge, needlework. Res: 9382 Russell Ave Garden Grove 92644 Ofc: Swedlow Inc. 12122 Western Ave Garden Grove 92642

HUTTENBACK, ROBERT ARTHUR, university chancellor; b. Mar. 8, 1928, Frankfurt, Germany; s. Otto Henry and Dorothy (Marcuse) H.; m. Freda Braginsky, July 12, 1954; 1 dau. Madeleine Alexandra; edn: BA, UC Los Angeles 1951, PhD, 1959; postgrad. Sch. Oriental and African Studies, Univ. London (Eng.) 1956-57. Career: faculty Calif. Inst. Tech., 1958-78, asst. prof. 1960-63, assoc. prof. 1963-66, prof. history, 1966-78, master student houses, 1958-69, dean students, 1969-72, chmn. div. humanities and social scis., 1971-77; chancellor Univ. Calif., Santa Barbara 1978—; cons. Jet Propulsion Lab., Pasadena 1966-68; mem. Assn. Asian Studies, Am. Hist. Assn.; author: British Relations with Sind, 1799-1843, An Anatomy of Imperialism (1962), (with Leo Rose, Margaret Fisher) Himalayan Battleground -Sino-Indian Rivalry in Ladakh (1963), The British Imperial Experience (1966), Gandhi in South Africa (1971), Racism and Empire (1976). Res: 543 Channel Islands Rd., Santa Barbara 93106

HUTTON, JOEL DEAN, import co. owner; b. May 29, 1956, Vermillion, S.D.; s. Dean Ellwood and Joanne Mabel (Schmidt) H.; edn: Miami Univ., Oxford, Ohio; real estate courses, Coll. of Colo. Career: real estate agent, Denver until 1978; founder, senior v.p. Burtram Corp., Santa Monica 1979—; cons. var. real estate firms; subject of interviews and tv spots for entrepreneurial publs.; mem. Santa Monica CofC; clubs: Trident, Interlachen Country; Republican; Methodist; rec: tennis, golf. Ofc: Burtram Corp. 1321 Ocean Ave Ste 201 Santa Monica

HYDRICK, DONALD FRANCIS, small business consultant; b. June 23, 1918, Danbury, Conn.; s. Wm. John and Florence May (Nichols) H.; m. Gay Nichols, Mar. 15, 1946; children: Gay Marsh Nichols St. Clair b. 1947, Elizabeth Lee Kelley b 1951; edn: BS chem. engring. Tri State Univ. 1938, grad. UCLA Sch. of Mgmt. 1952; grad. work Columbia, Cal Tech, Univ. Calif., 1940-60. Career: small bus. consulting prin./owner D.F. Hydrick & Assocs., Inc. 1957—; founder/bd. dir. Soniform, Inc., San Diego (1970-74), Cut 'N Jump, Inc. (1970-74); founder/v.p. prodn. Spectral Dynamics Corp. of San Diego (1960-70); founder/v.p. Transformer Engineers, Pasadena (1950-57); mil: lt.jg USNR 1942-46; Republican; Congregational; rec: Am. hist., family hist. (13th gen. Connecticut). Res: 4055 Couts St San Diego 92103 Ofc: D.F. Hydrick & Assocs. Inc. 814 Morena Blvd Ste 102 San Diego 92108

IANCU, LEON, structural engineer; b. Jan. 26, 1935, Bucharest, Romania; s. Moise and Zoe (Tzadik) I.; m. Inda, May 20, 1965; 1 son: Andrei b. 1968; edn: BA, Mathematic Univ. Bucharest 1959; MS, Construction Univ. Bucharest 1957; Structural Engr. (1984) and Civil Engr. (1982), Calif. Career: Iprolam Engring. & Design Inst., Bucharest, Romania 1958-80; structural engr. 1958, senior structural engr. 1961, prin. stuctural engr. 1964, project engr. 1968; senior structural engr. C.F. Braun, Alhambra 1981; cons. structural engr. self-empl., Los Angeles 1982; senior structural engr. Delon Hampton & Assoc., Los Angeles 1983—; mem: Structural Engrs. Assn. of So. Calif., Am. Soc. of Civil Engrs.; rec: travel. Res: 6148 Lindenhurst Ave. Los Angeles 90048

IBA, SHOZO, radiologist; b. Nov. 10, 1918, Los Angeles, Calif.; s. Kennosuke and Sumie (Misumi) I.; children: Nadine Sumiye b. 1955, Diane Akiko b. 1956, Lynn Etsuko b. 1957, Wayne Shozo b. 1959, Elaine M. b. 1961; edn: BA, Univ. So. Calif. 1940, MS, 1941; MD, Boston Univ Sch. of Med. 1945. Career: intern USPHS 1946, N.Y. State Hosp. Ray Brook, N.Y. 1946-47; res. City Hosp. Cleveland, Ohio 1948-51, asst. radiol. 1952; instr. Western Reserve Med. Sch. Cleveland 1952; staff L.A. County Harbor Gen. Hosp. Torrance, Calif. 1953-57, St. Francis Hosp. Lynwood, offices Huntington Park and Downey, Calif. (semi-retired); honors: Rotary Club awards; mem: AMA, Am. Coll. of Radiol.; Radiol Soc. of N.Am.; Trudeau Soc.; Calif. Radiol. Soc.; Los Angeles Radiol. Soc.; CMA; LA Med. Assn.; Rotary Club; Republican; Protestant; rec: fishing, stamps. Res: 9201 Marina Pacifica Dr Long Beach 90803

IBBETSON, EDWIN THORNTON, development co. president; b. Apr. 17, 1923, Los Angeles; s. Robert Edwin and Ann E. (Thornton) Ibbetson; m. Harriett Alice Hudson, Dec. 28, 1947; children: Elizabeth Ann (Mrs. Phillip Hitchcock), Douglas Hudson, Gregory Bruce, Timothy Edwin, Julia Katherine (Mrs. Martin Zilinskas), Erika Alice (Mrs. Tor Hertzog). Career: with Union Devel. Co., Cerritos 1944-, pres. 1961—; partner Paramount Constrn., Cer-

ritos 1948-; v.p. Valley Properties Inc., Imperial Valley 1962-; pres. Union Farms Inc., Cerritos 1962-81; chmn. bd. dirs. Dutch Village Bowling Ctr. Inc., Lakewood 1965-; partner Ibbetson-Marsh Realtors 1975-; vice chmn. bd. Equitable Svg.& Loan Assn. 1977-85; bd. dirs.(chmn. 1977-9) Garden State Bank 1974-79; bd. dirs.(sec. 1979-82, chmn. 1983-) Met. Water Dist. So. Calif., 1959-; chmn. Bellflower Water Devel. Com. 1965-; chmn. Los Angeles Co. Real Estate Adv. Com. 1974-; bd.dirs. Armed Services YMCA, Long Beach 1962-72; trustee St. Mary's Hosp., Long Beach; honors: Young Man of Year 1959, Bellflower Jaycees; Hon. Pres. for Life, Calif. Assn of Realtors, 1980; Realtor of Year, Bellflower Dist. Bd. Realtors, 1962, 67, 71; Bellflower Kiwanis Man of Year 1983; mem: Am. Soc. Real Estate Counselors (fov., pres. 1977), Calif. Assn. Realtors (treas. 1972-7, dir.), Internat. Real Estate Fedn., Nat. Assn. Realtors (dir.), Nat. Inst. Real Estate Brokers (cert. comml. investment men.), Inst. Real state Mgmt. (cert. property mgr.), Urban Land Inst., Rancho Los Cerritos Bd. Realtors 1949- (pres. 1961), Central Basin Water Assn. (dir.), Calif. Real Estate PAC, Internat. Council Shopping Centers; clubs: Elks, Kiwanis (pres. 1958), Internat. Traders, So. Calif. Tuna (Long Bch). mil: USNR 1943-46. Roman Catholic. Ofc: 16550 Bloomfield Ave, Cerritos 90701

IBBETSON, GREGORY BRUCE, real estate executive; b. Nov. 7, 1951, Long Beach; s. Edwin Thornton and Harriett Alice (Hudson) I.; m. Trudy, Sept. 11, 1971; children: Gregory b. 1973, Eric b. 1976; edn: AA, Long Beach City Coll. 1976; BA, CSU Dominguez Hills 1978; Lic. Real Estate Broker, Calif. 1981. Career: air traffic controller USAF 1970-73; maintenance crew Union Devel. Co. 1973-74, property mgr. 1974—; dir. Union Devel. Co. 1976; dir., v.p. Dutch Village Bowl 1980-; secty. Union Devel. of Hawaii Inc. 1985-; honors: Hon. Svc. Award, Bellflower Unif. Sch. Dist. 1984; Realtor of the Year, Rancho Los Cerritos Bd. Realtors 1985; Referee of the Year, AYSO 1982; mem: Calif. Assn. of Realtors (chmn. Pension & Retirement 1986), Rancho Los Cerritos Bd. Realtors (treas. 1984, pres. elec. 1985, pres. 1986), Bellflower Kiwanis, AYSO (referee), SPMA, Washington Elem. Sch Site Council (chmn. 1985-86), CSU Dominguez Hills Económic Club (charter pres.); mil: E-3 USAF, decorated Fgn. Conflict, Marksmanship; Republican; rec: surfing, swimming, skiing. Ofc: Union Development Co. Inc., 16550 Bloomfield Cerritos 90701

ICHIUJI, JOHN KIYOSHI, dentist; b. Oct. 5, 1954, Carmel; s. Mickey Nakakiyo and Edith Yoshiko (Yonemoto) I.; edn: AS, Monterey Peninsula Coll. 1974; DDS, Univ. of Pacific 1978; lic. dentist, State Boards in Calif., N.J., Bds. in N.E. Regional USA; Career: asst. mgr. Walden Book Store 1972-74; tchr. asst. Monterey Peninsula Coll. 1973-74; gen. dental ofcr. US Air Force, McGuire AFB, N.J. 1978-81; gen. prac. Tri-Valley Dental Arts, San Ramon 1981—; lectr. in dental assisting, emergency dental care for physicians; mem: Am. Dental Assn., Calif. Dental Assn., Contra Costa Dental Assn., Acad. of Gen. Dentistry (fellow), Acad. of Dental Group Mgmt.; civic: Rotary (dir. Club Service), Japanese-Am. Citizens League (pres. 1984), Dublin Hist. Preservation Assn., San Ramon CofC; mil: capt. USAF 1978-81; Presbyterian; rec: volleyball, tennis, skiing. Ofc: Tri-Valley Dental Arts 9260 Alcosta Ste D30 San Ramon 94583

IDRIS, NOOR MOHAMMED, computer systems consultant; b. Jan. 21, 1953, Massawa, Eritrea, nat. US cit. 1985; s. Mohamed K. and Nura A. Idris; m. Majda H. Sultan, May 26, 1983; 1 child, Idrees b. 1985; edn: H.S. dip., Massawa, Eritrea 1972; cert. Jr. Acct., London, Eng. 1974; AS computer sci., Long Beach City Coll. 1982; AA computer mgmt., Cypress Coll. 1983; BBA MIS, National Univ. 1984, MBA exec. computer mgmt., 1986. Career: acctg. clerk Massawa, Eritrea 1972-73; Letter of Credits clerk Bank of Cairo, Riyadh, Saudi Arabia 1976-77; controller Compagnie Francaise de Metalique, Riyadh 1977-78; cashier, night auditor Holiday Inn, Universal City, Philadelphia, Pa. 1978-79; computer ops. supr. Cortes Corp. Long Beach, Calif. 1980-82; DP mgr. Certified Data Systems, Huntington Beach 1982-83; computer ops. coord. MDB Systems Inc., Orange 1983-84; computer systems cons. Internat. Energy Systems Inc. 1984—, cons. to var. cos. including Economy Inns of Am. Fullerton, Ramada Inn Disneyland, Onward Traders Anaheim; mem: Independent Computer Consultant Assn., Internat. Assn. for Finl. Planning, Finl. Profl. Advisory Panel (1984), Am. Mgmt. Assn., Data Proc. Mgmt. Assn., Internat. Assn. Computer Cons., Assn. Computing Machinery, Internat. Trading Assn., Nat. Univ. Student Alumni Assn., Islamic Soc. of Orange County, secty. Eritrean Student Union- Greece (1973-76), Saudi Arabia (1976-78), Eritrean Relief Com. 1978-81); amateur sport reporter Asmara Radio Station (1970-73) Democrat; Muslim; languages: English, Arabic, Tigrinia, Italian, Greek; rec: soccer, tennis, jog, world travel. Ofc: International Energy Sys. Inc. POB 202 Cypress 90630

IKEDA, CLYDE STEVEN, dentist; b. Sept. 18, 1956, San Luis Obispo; s. Seirin and Marion Masa (Mana) I.; edn: BS in biol., Loma Linda Univ. 1978, DDS, LLU Sch. of Dentistry 1982. Career: dentist Queens Medical Center, Honolulu 1982; prin. dental practice, Santa Maria, Calif. 1983—; honors: Omicron Kappa Upsilon (1982); mem: Central Coast Dent. Soc., Calif. Dent. Assn., Am. Dent. Assn., Acad. of Gen. Dentistry, Santa Maria Valley Kiwanis (dir., secty.); Republican; Methodist; rec: skiing, biking, fishing. Res: 160 Stagecoach Rd Arroyo Grande 93420 Ofc: Clyde S. Ikeda DDS 504 E Church St Ste A Santa Maria 93454

IKEDA, REX KANICHI, corporate customer services executive, b. Oct. 31, 1943, Hilo, Hawaii; s. Richard Sueki and Esther (Kimura) I.; m. Marian Toshiko Mitsuda, Feb. 14, 1964; children: Laurie b. 1965, Kemlyn b. 1969; edn: undergrad. Purdue Univ. 1961-63; BBA, magna cum laude, National Univ. 1984, grad. bus. pgm. 1984-. Career: field engr. NCR Corp., Los Angeles

1964-76, field technical mgr., then branch mgr., Santa Ana 1977-79, dist. mgr., NCR Customer Services Div., San Diego 1979 –; awards: Top Ten Dist. (1979, 81, 83), Best Dist. (1985), NCR Corp.; rec: golf, archery, computers. Ofc: NCR Corp. 5040 Shoreham Pl San Diego 92122

ILLING, LILLIAN BAKER, real estate broker, insurance agent; b. April 29, 1922, Bronx, NY; d. William C. and Esther (Berman) Ulrich; m. 2d. Hans Illing, April 19, 1962; 1 son, Theodore Lloyd Baker b. 1952; edn: Los Angeles City Coll. 1939-42. Career: real estate broker, ins. agent self-empl. Advisory Mortgage Loan Svc., Los Angeles 1962 –; vol. Santa Monica Westside Hotline 1980-; Crime Prevention splst. 1982-85; recording secty. Wilhelm Furtwangler Soc. 1978-; Shaklee distbr.; Democrat; Baptist; rec: piano (performed w/ LACC orch. 1941), artist (oil painting). Address: Advisory Mortgage Loan Service, 6112 W. 77th St. Los Angeles 90045

IMPARATO, NICHOLAS J., management consultant, educator; b. Feb. 3, 1944, NY, NY; s. Michael and Clara; edn: BA, St. Bonaventure Univ. 1965; MA, Bowling Green State Univ. 1967, PhD, 1970. Career: mktg. and personnel cons. prin./ pres. NJI Resources Corp., San Francisco 1976 –; cons. Coit Cos., Burlingame 1977-80, exec. v.p./chief op. ofcr. 1981-83,bd. dirs. 1983-85; prof. of mgmt. McLaren Coll. Bus. Adm. Univ. of San Francisco, 1970 –, chair McLaren Lecture Series, 1983-; research cons. Stanford Univ. 1980; vis. prof. Boston Coll. 1976-78, UC Berkeley 1973-75, vis. scholar Stanford Univ. 1979-80; dir. Voicemail Internat. Inc. (1985-), Nat. Group Telecomm. of Burlington (N.C.) Inc. (1980-84); cons. Santa Clara Co. Housing Authority, 1983-; commnr. Calif. State Psychology Exam. Com., BMQA 1979-84; publs: (18) in organizational behavior, telecommunications; Roman Catholic; rec: tennis. Res: 180 N Balsamina Way Portola Valley 94025 Ofc: McClaren College of Business USF San Francisco 94117

INGHAM, GEORGE GRAEFE, manufacturing co. executive; b. May 27, 1925, Ajo, Ariz.; s. George Reed and Hildegarde Louise (Graefe) I.; m. Carol Kidd, Feb. 10, 1952; children: Jeffrey b. 1953, Marianne Leslie b. 1954, Suzanne Ingham b. 1957; edn: BS chem., Stanford Univ. 1949; UC Berkeley 1950-51; Reg. Profl. (Mfg.) Calif. 1978. Career: jr. chemical engr. Cutter Laboratories, 1951-53, assoc. chem. engr. (R&D) 1953-58, senior chem. engr. (R&D) 1958-63, senior chem. engr. (mfg.) 1963-71, supr. process engring. 1971-74; mrg. chem. processing Teledyne McCormick, 1974-75; senior process engr. Miles Labs. (subs. Cutter Group), Berkeley 1975 –; v.p. Cutter Employees Credit Union 1971; mem: Am. Chem. Soc. 1951-76, Am. Inst. of Chem. Engrs. 1952-85 (chmn. AIChE Symp. 1978; com. Bay Area Sci. Fair 1964-72), Geographical Soc. of Am., Toastmasters; leader Cub Scouts; research: Characterization and prevention of precipitates in intravenous solutions (1953-63), Ethylene Oxide sterilization parameters defined (1957-63), Filtration of intravenous solutions (1963-74), Validation of Biological Processes (1975-85); mil: pfc US Army 1943-46, Merit Cert.; Democrat; rec: bridge, bicycling, gardening. Res: 6640 Monte Verde, POB 921, El Sobrante 94803 Ofc: Miles Laboratories 4th & Parker Sts Berkeley 94803

INGLEDUE, ELWOOD MARTIN, travel executive; b. June 21, 1899, Lima, Ohio; s. Charles Wilson and Sybil Maude (Whitney) I.; m. Mary Elizabeth Rich, June 24, 1928 (dec. 1972); children: Richard (dec.), Ronald; m. 2d Alice Lee Gregg, 1973; edn: BA, Occidental 1923. Career: publisher of travel directories for profl. travel agents: hotel information, hotel-travel index, travel horizons, tours and cruises, internat. golf directory; founder Am. Soc. Travel Agents in So. Calif.; founder So. Calif. chpt. Hotel Sales Mgrs. Assn.; honors: Man of the Year (Am. Soc. Travel Agents 1960), ASTA Hall of Fame (1986); mem: Am. Soc. Travel Agents, Oakmont CC, Masons, Kiwanis, Verdugo Club, Glendale Old Settlers Assn. (pres.); founder Golf Oriented Travel Agents (GOTA) 1986; publ: Internat. Golf Directory for Golf-Oriented Travel Agents (1986); author: 180 Days Around the World; mil: S.A.T.C. 1917; Republican; rec: photog., golf, travel. Res: 1897 Starvale Rd Glendale 91207

INSTITORIS, EMIL ZOLTON, consulting co. president; b. July 27, 1927, Detroit, Mich.; S. Michael and Margaret (Dont) I; m. Shirley Melton, Oct. 24, 1978; 1 dau: Paulette Mueller b. 1945; edn: BA, Jackson State Univ. 1972; MBA, 1974; PhD, Thomas A. Edison 1976; clin. psychologist, Palm Beach Tng. Center 1976. Career: process engr. quality stds. Gen. Motors Fisher Body Div., Detroit, Mich. 1950-58, asst. supt. quality control 1958-63, supt. quality control 1963-68; dir. ops. Skyways Airport Hotel 1969-70; bd. chmn./pres. Skyways Ent., Inc. 1971 –, cons. to major hotel chains, UCLA & USC Continuing Edn. Pgm.; mem: fellow Am. Acad. Behav. Sci., fellow Assn. for Soc. Psychology, fellow Am. Coll. of Clinic Adminstrs., mem. Am. Bd. Examiners in Psychotherapy; Nat. Psychological Assn., Am. Psychotherapy Assn., Am. Assn. Profl. Hypnologists, Nat. Psychiat. Assn., United Assn. of Christian Counselors, Am. Assn. of Rel. Counselors, Am. Mgmt. Assn., Am. Entrepreneurs Assn., Alphi Psi Sigma, Delta Epsilon Omega; mil: tech. 4th gr. US Army 1945-48, Euro., Am. Theatre, Occ. Forces Ribbon, GCM; Republican (Pres. Task Force); Catholic; rec: writing, collect firearms, restore mil. vehicles. Res: 447 W Via Escuela Palm Springs 92262 Ofc: Skyways Ent., Inc., POB 1572 Palm Springs 92262

INTHAVONG, ONSY JAMES, manufacturing co. executive; b. July 1, 1942, Luangprabang, Laos; s. Thit Phoumy and Sao Bouasy I.; m. Syvay Naophianekham, Apr. 1978; children: Liane b. 1960, Thong b. 1965, Meng b. 1975; edn: BA Univ. Srisavangvong 1965; cert. T.E.S.L., Univ. Hawaii 1968; BS, Univ. Wis. 1975, grad. work 1975. Career: English tchr. Coll. of Edn., Vientiane, Laos 1966-68, dean Student Coll. of Edn., 1968-70; asst. dir. of tchr. tng. Ministry of Edn., Vientiane, Laos 1970-73; salesman Graystone Block Co.

Inc., Modesto 1977-81, dispatch/ops. mgr. 1981 –; civic: Lao Lane Xang Assn. of Calif. (pres.); publ: handbook - tchg. aide for refugee students (Calif. State Dept. Edn.); rec: outdoor sports. Res: 12101 Lambuth Rd Oakdale 95361 Ofc: Graystone Block Co. Inc. 316 W River Rd Modesto 95351

IRICK, PATRICIA CAMILLE, fast foods co. executive; b. Nov. 18, 1936, Los Angeles; d. John Richard and Dorothea D. (Pearce) Collins; edn: BS in Edn., Univ. of Houston 1958; M.Ed., Stephen F. Austin, 1964; Texas Tchr. Cert. (life): Supvsn/Adm., Elem., H.S.; pgmmg. tech. Control Data Inst. 1973. Career: math. instr. Dallas (Tx.) Independent School Dist. 1961-70; supr. Lower Sch. Math Dept. The Hockaday Sch., Dallas 1970-72; data center coord., mgr. I/O Control Dept., Gambles Datamation Ctr, Burbank, Ca. 1973-79; mgr. computer ops./tech. support Collins Foods Internat. Inc. 1979 –; honors: Hockaday Study Grant (Stanford 1971), Outstanding Young Educator, Dallas Jr. CofC 1969, listed Who's Who in Am. Edn. 1970; rec: writer short stories, oil painting, bridge. Res: 6500 Green Valley Circle, 135, Culver City 90230 Ofc: Collins Foods Inter. Inc. 5400 Alla Rd Los Angeles 90066

IRICK, ROBERT LEE, educational and business executive; b. Aug. 14, 1930, Competition, Mo.; s. Melvin Hollege and Delphia Ruth (Handley) I.; edn: BA, Southwest Mo. State Univ. 1955; cert. Yale Ins. of F.E. Languages, 1951-52; MA, Harvard Univ. 1958, PhD, 1971. Career: rep. The Hannaford Co., Inc.; pres. Chinese Materials Center, Hong Kong, 1978 –; pres. Chinese Materials Center Publications, S.F. 1982 –; gen. mgr. Taiwan Ent. Co., Ltd., Taipei, 1970 –; res. dir. Calif. State Internat. Programs, Taipei, 1966 –; v.p., mng. dir. Chinese Mats. and Res. Aids Service Center, Inc. Taipei 1964-74; also adj. assoc. prof./prof. Nat. Chengchi Univ. 1976-79, Nat. Chengkung Univ. 1974-75, adj. prof. Nat. Taiwan Univ. 1982-83; v.p. Sen Bin Chem. Indus. Corp., 1985 –; advisor Nat. Anti-Counterfeiting com., R.O.C.; instr. Yale Univ. 1957; secty. Adv. Bd., Sino-Am. Commn. workshop on coop. in scis. and humanities, Taipei 1965-71; hon. director World-Wide Ethical Soc. 1981-; honors: Boys Nation, Lebanon H. Sch. No. 1 grad., Debate Letter 1951, Who's Who Among Students in Am. Colls. and Univs. 1955, Intl. Who's Who in Edn., Men of Achievement, Who's Who in the World, Intl. Director of Scholars & Splsts. in the Third World, Who's Who in Library and Information Services, Directory of Am. Scholars, The Intl. Book of Honor; mem: past pres. Harvard Club of Taipei, Am. Univ. Club (Taipei), Assn. for Asian Studies Inc., Ann Arbor (Com. on East Asian Libraries), Chinese Lang. Tchrs. Assn., Kappa Alpha Order No. 1, 1950-51, Presidents Club Southwest Mo. State Univ., Smithsonian Assocs.; num. publs. incl. 50th Ann. edition SMSU Ozarko; mil: TSgt. USAF 1951-55, Commendn.; Republican; Methodist; rec: collect cookbooks. Res: 1610 Sutter Apt 202 San Francisco 94109 Ofc: 655 Post Ste 151 San Francisco 94109

ISHII, IONE LA RAE, semiconductor association executive; b. Dec. 19, 1950, Harvey, No. Dak.; d. Ben August and Elsie Rosinna (Schweitzer) Wutzke; m. Hiroshi Ishii, July 24, 1982; 1 dau. Vanessa Ayumi b. 1984; edn: AA bus. Monterey Peninsula Coll. 1974; Worcester Coll., Oxford Univ. summer 1977; BS Info. Sys. Mgmt., Univ. San Francisco 1986. Career: tech. administr. Science Applications Inc. Palo Alto 1975-79; tech. editor, writer Kozo Keikaku Tokyo, Japan 1979-81; sales analyst NEC Electronics Inc. Mtn. View 1981-83; corp. mktg. analyst Advanced Micro Devices Sunnyvale 1983-85; mgr. statistical pgms. Semiconductor Industry Assn. 1985 –; editor Stanford PhD cand. theses 1978-81; tutor statistics USF students 1985-86; mem: Forum for Corp. Communications, Women's Networking Group (co-chair 1985), Young Mothers Club 1985-86; publ: short stories in Eng. newspaper in Japan 1979-81; creator abstract art; Democrat; Protestant; avoc: archeology (var. excavations in Calif. and England); rec: travel. Ofc: Semiconductor Industry Assn. 4320 Stevens Creek Blvd Ste 275 San Jose 95129

ISHII, WILLIAM CLIFFORD, engineer; b. Mar. 7, 1951, Los Angeles; s. William Rin and Hoshiko (Matsumoto) I.; m. Becky Tsujioka, Jan. 11, 1975; 1 dau., Kamerin b. 1980; edn: BS, Univ. So. Calif. 1973, MPA, 1977; Reg. Mech. Engr. Ariz., Wash.; Reg. Profl. Engr. Ala., Fla., Calif., Ore., Tex. Career: jr. mech. designer Wm. R. Ishii & Assocs. Inc., Long Beach, Calif. 1976-77, electrical designer 1977-78, mech. designer 1978-79, v.p. ops. 1979-85, pres. 1985 –; tech. v.p. WRICO Internat., Long Beach; v.p. WRICO Inc., Long Beach; mem: Calif. Soc. Profl. Engrs. (chpt. secty., 2nd v.p., 1st v.p., pres.), Asian Am. Architect & Engrs. (chpt. secty., v.p., pres., dir.), Am. Soc. Plumbing Engrs., Nat. Soc. Profl. Engrs., Illuminating Engrg. Soc., Optimist Internat.; Republican; Christian. Res: 8845-5 Hoffman St Buena Park 90620 Ofc: William R. Ishii & Assocs., Inc., 1165 E. San Antonio Ste E Long Beach 90807

ISHIWATA, BYRON JUN, accountant; b. Dec. 20, 1956, San Jose; s. Shigeru and Haruko Helen (Yamada) I.; edn: BS in commerce, cum laude, Santa Clara Univ. 1978; MBA, Golden Gate Univ. 1982; Certified Public Acct., Calif. (1980). Career: staff acct. Hamilton & Bradshaw, CPAs, San Jose 1978-80; tax mgr. Brookshire, Rowinski, Plette & Kado Acctncy. Corp. 1980-83; tax mgr. Johanson & Yau Acctncy. Corp. 1983 –; honors: Beta Gamma Sigma (1978); mem: Am. Inst. CPAs, Calif. Soc. CPAs, Nat. Assn. of Accts.; mem. Northside Theatre Council of San Jose (treas.); Democrat; Konkokyo (bd.); rec: trivia, tennis, coins. Ofc: Johanson & Yau Acctncy. Corp. 701 Miller St Ste 240 San Jose 95110

ISSAKHANIAN-STONER, ALICE, civil engineer; b. June 22, 1948, nat. US cit. 1977; d. Bartooghemyus and Sima (Masihi Nejad) Issakhanian; m. Stephen Stoner, Mar. 5, 1973; 1 child Armineh b. 1983; edn: AA, Chiba Univ. Japan 1970, BS arch.-engrg., 1973; Reg. Profl. Civil Engr. Calif. 1982. Career: arch.

Nikken Sekkei Ltd. Japan 1973; drafting tech. City of Sacramento 1975-78, asst. strl. engr. 1978, asst. civil engr. 1978-83, assoc. civil engr. 1983−, acting senior civil engr. 1985; honors: Scholarship (Japanese Ministry of Edn. 5 yrs.); mem. Western Council of Engrs.; Republican; Christian; rec: oil painting, reading, piano. Ofc: City of Sacramento Engrg. 915 I St Sacramento 95814

IWATAKI, MIYEKO, financial executive; b. July 18, 1921, Los Angeles; d. Matsutaro and Makino (Uyeki) Hiraishi; m. Osamu Iwataki (dec. 1962), Nov. 1, 1947; children: Sandra Misaye b. 1948, Gregory Osamu b. 1950, Patricia Gail (Iwasaki) b. 1951; edn: grad. Theodore Roosevelt H.S. 1938; num. banking courses. Career: with Bank of Am., 1961−, clerk 1961, note hd. (signing ofcr.) 1962, lending ofcr. 1968, loan ofcr. Inglewood Main Ofc. 1971, supr. note dept. 1973, asst. mgr. Hermosa Beach Ofc. 1975, asst. mgr. Normandie-Redondo Beach Ofc. 1978, sr. loan ofcr. Gardena Main Ofc., then asst. v.p. urban affairs dept. 1979, apptd. liaison ofcr. (serving cities in So. Calif.) for City Improvement & Restoration Pgms., 1985−; honors: appreciation UCLA Chancellor's Circle (1981), corporate award for Bank of Am., Business Devel. Assn. of So. Calif. (1985); mem: Asian Bus. Assn., Latin Bus. Assn. 1981-84 (trustee 1983-84), Asian Pacific Network (charter), Tuesday Niters Womens Club (charter 1948-); civic: advis. bd. Mayor Bradley's Office of Small Bus. Assistance (sec.treas.), Asian Pac. Am. CofC (steering com.); Democrat; Protestant; rec: stamp and coin collection. Ofc: Bank of America NT/SA Corporate Comm. Development Ste 4763 555 S Flower St Los Angeles 90071

JAACKS, JOHN WILLIAM, aerospace executive; b. Sept. 3, 19−, Chgo.; s. Oren Ernest and Matilda (Dritlein) J.; m. Marilyn Walker, Sept. 24, 1952; children: John W. II b. 1954, Jeffrey A. b. 1955, Holly W. b. 1956; edn: BS indsl. adminstrn., Univ. Ill. 1949, BS indsl. engrg., 1962; MS bus. adminstrn., Univ. So. Calif. 1971, MA lib. arts, 1983; Reg. Profl. Indsl. Engr. Calif. 1985. Career: navigator/ intercept ofcr. USAF 1952-55, interceptor pilot 1955-60, chief avionics and maintenance Soisterberg, Holland 1962-65, chief pgm. mgmt. Space Systems Div. 1966-67, dir. pgm. control Space Launch Vehicles, Space and Missile Systems Orgn. 1967-73; proj. mgr. Support Systems Div. Hughes Aircraft Co. 1973−, currently logistics pgm. mgr. F/A 18 Pgm.; honors: Chi Gamma Iota 1962; BSA Award of Merit 1971, Silver Beaver 1977; mem: Am. Inst. Indsl. Engrs., Am. Inst. Aero. and Astro., Air Force Assn., USC Alumni Assn., Univ. Ill. Alumni Assn., Boy Scouts of Am.; author: Contrails (autobiography, unpubl.); mil: lt col. USAF 1950-73, Meritorious Svc.; Republican; Lutheran; rec: sailing, skiing. Res: 3310 Seaclaire Dr Rancho Palos Verdes 90274 Ofc: Hughes Aircraft Co. POB 92426 Bldg R7/MS 312 Los Angeles 90009

JABIN, LELIA HONIG, developer, lawyer; b. Mar. 13, 1932, Albany, NY; d. Jacob Lyon and Rose (Greenspan) H.; m. Marvin (Mark) Jabin, May 13, 1952; children: Valerie b. 1957, Gregory b. 1958, Anthony b. 1965, Desiree b. 1970; edn: NY Univ. 1949-52; AB, UC Los Angeles 1952, JD, UCLA Sch. of Law 1956; admitted to Calif. State Bar 1957. Career: corporations counsel Dept. of Corps., State of Calif., Los Angeles 1962-67; senior counsel Calif. Div. of Labor Law Enforcement, L.A. 1967-78; adminstrv. law judge Calif. Unemployment Ins. Appeals Board, Upland 1978-79; current: land developer/syndicator; partner Monterey Views, 1979-, New West Constrn. Co., 1983-, Montebello Properties, 1984-, Beacon Properties and La Plaza Properties, 1985-; founder/dir. Omni Bank, N.A. (fmrly Monterey Park Nat. Bank) 1980-; founder/chair Golden Security Thrift & Loan, 1982; mem. Women Lawyers Assn. of Los Angeles (pres. 1976-77); Democrat; rec: art collector. Ofc: 701 S Atlantic Blvd Monterey Park 91754

JABIN, MARVIN (MARK), lawyer; b. Mar. 28, 1929, Brooklyn, NY; s. Sol and Belle (Paikoff) J.; m. Lelia Honig, May 13, 1952; children: Valerie, b. 1957; Gregory, b. 1958; Anthony, b. 1965; Desiree, b. 1970; edn: AB, NYU 1952; BS, UCLA 1954; JD, UCLA 1957. Career: partner law firm Jabin & Jabin, Monterey Park 1958−; v.p. CVJ Constrn., Inc., Monterey Park 1977−; partner sev. real estate devel. cos. in Los Angeles Co. 1979−; asst. prof. bus. law SCU Los Angeles 1972-75; patent counsel Hoffman Electronics L.A. 1958-62; dir. Golden Security Thrift & Loan Assn. 1983-; arbitrator, Am. Arbitration Assn. 1963-80; Judge Pro Tem, Alhambra Municiple Ct. 1981-82; mem: ABA 1958-82, Los Angeles Co. Bar Assn.(trustee 1975-77), San Gabriel Valley Bar Assn. (pres. 1975),Monterey Park CofC (dir. 1982-85), Monterey Park Rotary 1964-84; CSU Los Angeles ch. of Bus. Adv. Council 1971-76; mil: tech. 5th gr. M.C., US Army 1946-49; rec: reading, music, chess, photog., racquetball, art collecting. Ofc: Jabin & Jabin, 701 S Atlantic Blvd Monterey Park 91754

JACKSON, JOSEPH, physiotherapist; b. Feb. 25, 1935, Greenville, Miss.; s. Mose and Lola B. (Duncan) Jackson; children: Dwight, b. 1960; Toni & Terri, b. 1961; edn: AA, Los Angeles City Coll. 1963; BS, CSU Long Beach 1970; lic., Bd. Med. Examiners 1971. Career: currently, dir. physical therapy dept. Manor West Hosp., L.A.; pres./owner Community Physical Therapy Ctr., Inc. 1975−; dir. physical therapy dept. Edgemont Hosp., Hollywood 1981-; owner, dir. La Rhea Med. & Physical Therapy Ctr. Long Beach; awards: Spl. Citation, Post Ofc. 1969; Suggestion Awd., L.A. Postal Svc. 1969; mem: Am. Physical Therapy Assn.; UCLA Alumni Assn.; Calif. Guest Home Owners Assn.; CSU Long Beach Alumni Assn.; Am. Red Cross; A I A frat.; founder: Jackson's Found. for the Disabled 1969; Republican; SDA; rec: basketball, carpentry. Res: 1934 W 22nd Street Los Angeles 90018 Ofc: La Rhea Med. & Physical Therapy Ctr., 1954 Atlantic Ave Long Beach

JACKSON, MARY CHRISTINE, restaurant owner; b. Dec. 24, 1937, Bonham, Tx.; d. A.C. and Margie Ray (Marshall) Reed; m. Wilburn Wayne Jackson, May 5, 1956; children: Jeffrey Wayne b. 1957, Kim Nanette b. 1962, Marlin

Linn b. 1968, Stephanie Dian b. 1972; edn: Coll. of Sequoia 1956-58. Career: bookkeeper var. cos. 1956-66, self-empl. 1966-71; owner/opr. restaurant, 1971-, estab. T's Farmhouse Restaurant, Earlimart 1981−; mem. Small Bus. Assn.; active in church and youth activities; Democrat; Prot. Res: 7651 Rd 144 Earlimart 93219 Ofc: T's Farmhouse Restaurant 853 Armstrong St Earlimart 93219

JACOBS, LEO H., real estate investor-developer, rancher; b. Nov. 19, 1902, Des Moines, Iowa; s. Moses and Elizabeth Clara (Byoir) J.; edn: N.W. Mil. Acad., Lake Geneva, Wis.; undergrad. Univ. Iowa 1921-24, UC Los Angeles 1924-25; AB, USC 1926. Career: real estate sales agt. 1926-27; bd. chmn., pres., dir. American Gear and Parts Co. Ltd., San Francisco 1928-34; real estate broker and building contr./owner Advance Co., 1935−; pres., dir. Laurel Valley Devel. Co., Dallas, Tx. 1960-82; honors: Eagle Scout (1918), att. Boy Scout Jamboree, London, Eng. (1920); mem. Soc. of Automotive Engrs., S.F. 1930-34; mem. Univ. of Iowa Found. (Pres.'s Club, Old Gold Capitol Club), Phi Epsilon Pi frat. (1921-24), Masons, Scottish Rite, Shriners; rec: raising horses. Res: Escondido 92025

JACOBS, MICHAEL CONRAD, photographer; b. Feb. 10, 1948, Los Angeles; s. Oscar and Dorothy Ray (Weiss) J.; m. Christine Sherry, July 31, 1970; edn: Univ. of Miami 1966-67; AS, Long Beach City Coll. 1976; BA, CSU Long Beach 1983, MA; instr. art & design, photography, Bd. Govs. of Calif. Communitcy Coll. Career: warranty analyst American Honda Motor Co. Inc., Gardena 1972-73, traffic asst. 1973-75; instructional media producer Long Beach City Coll. 1976-79, instructional assoc. 1979−, instr. of photog. 1980−; owner American Audio Visuals; mem: Profl. Photographers of Am., Pi Kappa Phi (Univ. of Miami); Democrat; Jewish; rec: mechanics. Res: 2411 Roswell Ave. Long Beach 90815 Ofc: Long Beach City College, 1305 E. Pacific Coast Hwy. Long Beach 90806

JACOBS, RAYMOND GORMAN, advertising art director; b. June 4, 1943, Bklyn.; s. Harry Leonard and Grace (Grosser) J.; m. Sylvia, Jan. 8, 1962; children: Scott b. 1965, Christopher b. 1969; edn: Art Center Coll. of Design 1962-65. Career: prodn. artist Gumpertz, Bentey & Dolan, Los Angeles 1962-65; art director Tilds & Cantz Adv. 1965-68; Fuller, Smith & Ross, Inc. 1968-69; Jannson Adv. 1969-70; art dir./mgr. L.A. office Wilton, Coombs & Colnett 1970-71; ptnr. Nashick & Jacobs 1971-74; exec. v.p./ptnr. Jacobs & Gerber Inc., L.A. 1974−; guest lectr. local colls.; instr. Otis Inst. of Design; num. profl. awards 1968-, incl. Broadcast Designer's Assn. (6 nat. awards, 2 gold- 85), CEBA Awards, B/PAA West Awards, CLIO awards (80, 84), Emmy regl. (1975, 83), Internat. Film & TV Fest. of NY (3- 84), Annual Belding Awards (78, 79, 80), num. gold and silver awards, var. ad clubs in Chgo., LA, NY, Indpls., Boston, Detroit; mem. Art Directors Club of L.A. (pres. 1973); works: cover photography, "Fast Forward" (1984); Smithsonian Inst./Pac. Outdoor Advt.- Outdoor Hall of Fame, Wash DC (KIIS Radio painted bulletin board, displayed 5 yrs.); mil: sgt. US Army Reserve 1961-67; Democrat; Jewish; rec: astronomy, writing sci-fi, poetry, musician (9 instruments). Res: 13501 Chetenham Dr Sherman Oaks 91423 Ofc: Jacobs & Gerber Inc. 731 N Fairfax Ave Los Angeles 90046

JACOBSSON, LARS, automobile dealer; b. July 7, 1950, Stockholm, Sweden; s. Lars Olof and Anna Greta (Barck) J.; m. Andrea, Oct. 13, 1985; edn: bus., Taby Coll. 1972. Career: owner, pres., c.e.o. Jacobsson Automobile Corp. Sweden 1972−, Jacobsson Finance Ltd. Sweden 1973−; ptnr. Villa Auto Sales L.A. 1977-81; owner, pres. JAMA Auto House Hermosa Beach 1982−; honors: Best Driver (British Petroleum 1968), Bosch Driver 1976; Republican; rec: auto racing, tennis, skiing. Ofc: JAMA Auto House 700 Pacific Coast Hwy Hermosa Beach 90254

JACOBY, DAVID, chemical co. president; b. Oct. 14, 1929, King City, Silesia, Poland, nat. US cit. 1973; s. Chayim and Rivka J.; m. Janine Volk, June 10, 1956; children: Naomi Ruth b. 1959, Daniel Ron b. 1965; edn: AA, Los Angeles City Coll. 1953; BS, honors, Univ. of Ill. 1955; MS, UC Berkeley 1956. Career: food technologist Gerber Baby Foods, Oakland 1956-60; asst. dir. of research Richmond Chase Co. (Cal-Can), San Jose 1960-63; asst. dir. of research, prod. devel. & quality control Adolph's Food Products Co., Burbank 1963-65; v.p. research Specialty Coatings & Chemicals Inc., No. Hollywood 1965-74; pres. J.B. Chemical Co. Inc. and J.B. Chemical Co. Internat. Inc. 1974−; Company Recogn. for the canning of cottage cheese as baby food to be stored at room temperature, Gerber Baby Foods 1958; mem: Sigma Xi, Inst. of Food Technologists, Automotive Parts & Accesories Assn., Am. Friends for the Weizmann Inst. of Science (Israel), Am. Friends for the Tel Aviv Univ. (Israel); works: US patents, meat additives 1969, vinyl repair process 1974; mil: sgt. maj. Israel Defense Forces 1948-50; Democrat; Jewish; rec; painting, gardening. Ofc: J.B. Chemical Co. Inc., 7314 Varna Ave. No. Hollywood 91605

JACOBY, JANINE VOLK, educator; b. May 4, 1935, Brooklyn, NY; d. Armin and Claire Volk; m. David Jacoby, June 10, 1956; children: Naomi Ruth b. 1959; Daniel Ron b. 1965; edn: BA, UC Berkeley 1952-56; Masters pgm., Univ. of Judaism 1981-; Elem. Sch. Tchg. Cred., Calif. 1957. Career: elem. sch. tchr. Lockwood Elem. Sch., Oakland 1957-59; Sunday sch. tchr. Temple Emanu- El, San Jose 1961-63; master kindergarten techr. Abraham Joshua Heschel Day Sch., Northridge 1973−; v.p. J.B. Chemical Co. Inc., No. Hollywood 1974−; workshop leader Bureau Jewish Edn., Los Angeles 1974-; workshop leader CAJE Conf. Coalition for Alternatives in Jewish Edn., Irvine 1978, Santa Barbara 1980; honors: Dolores Kohl Award for Exemplory Tchg. in No. Am., Dolores Kohl Found., Wilmette, Ill. 1985; Hayil Award for Excellence, Heschel Day Sch., Northridge 1986; mem: PTA Hancock Park Elem. Sch.

(pres. 1965-66), Temple Aliyah (v.p. edn. 1968-71), Hadassah, ORT; works: development of fourth grade curriculum for Sunday sch.; recogn. of unit of biblical study for kindergarten, Kohl Inst., Wilmette Inst. 1986; Democrat; Jewish; rec: music (guitar, composition), writing stories for young children, travel. Ofc: Heschel Day School, 17701 Devonshire St. Northridge 91325

JACOBY, RICHARD DOWNING, international airline executive; b. Dec. 12, 1942, Long Beach; s. Ned Levering and Barbara Moffett (Downing) J.; m. Carolyn Martin (dec.), Aug. 6, 1966; children: Markus b. 1971, Jennifer b. 1971; edn: BA, CSU Northridge; LLB, La Salle Law Sch., Chgo.; PhD, Univ. of Oriental Studies, L.A.; desig: Calif. Life Tchg. Cred., lic. Real Estate and Mortgage Loan Broker; FAA lic. Airline Transport Pilot; Airline Capt., FAA, GWA, BAA. Career: lawyer Edwin G. Davies & Assocs., Los Angeles 1968; contract capt. US Navy, Jet Propulsion Labs., 1970; capt. Golden West Airlines, 1971-82; pres. Downing Land Co., Inc., Newport Beach 1979-81; founder British Am. Air (1st internat. airline for both Atlantic and Pacific in 18 yrs approved by US Dept. Transp.), capt. 1982-85, pres. 1982-84, bd. chmn. 1984–; dir. General Air Transport 1986-; mem. Airline Pilots Assn., Masons; mil: 1st lt. US Army Reserve; Republican; Presbyterian; rec: travel, karate. Address: British American Air, LAX 90045

JACQUEZ, DAVID MICHAEL, tax consultant, real estate broker, systems designer; b. Oct. 30, 1951, Oakland; s. Ray and Ruth (Townes) J.; edn: BA, CSU Hayward 1975; Calif. lic. Real Estate Broker; Enrolled Agent IRS. Career: founder, owner Western Income Tax 1976–; founder, broker New World Real Estate 1979–; founder, chmn. pres. Tax Flow 1982–. Res: 37810 3rd St Fremont 94536 Ofc: Western Income Tax, 37275 Niles Blvd Fremont 94536

JAFF, SHERRI RAI, accountant; b. Sept. 4, 1958, Belleville, Ill.; d. Gene Ralph Keck and Leona M. (Karban) Blaes; m. Sarchel Jaff, June 29, 1985; edn: BA acctg., Ill. State Univ. 1978; bus. major, Grossmont Coll. 1978-81, Mesa Coll. 1981-84, San Diego St. Univ. 1984-. Career: sales clk. May Co. Ventura 1975-76; library asst. Withers Public Lib., Bloomington, Ill. 1976-77; exec. sec., acctg. clk. Ralston Purina Co., Bloomington 1977-78; credit adminstr. Datagraphics Inc., San Diego 1978-80; exec. bkkpr. Torrey Ents., La Jolla 1980-81; ofc. mgr. Elegance Interiors, S.D. 1981-82; comptroller Phone Ware Inc., La Jolla 1982–; honors: Youth of the Month, Exchange Club (1976), leadership award Am. Legion (1972), v.p. Distributive Edn. Club of Am. (1975-76); mem. S.D. Business Womens Club, Exchange Network; Republican; Catholic; rec: Middle Eastern cuisine. Res: 3750 La Jolla Village Dr La Jolla 92037 Ofc: Phone Ware Inc 7534 La Jolla Blvd La Jolla 92037

JAINCHILL, MARSHALL LEWIS, co. president; b. Apr. 19, 1947, Hartford, Conn.; s. Charles and Edythe (Lavine) J.; m. Lynne, Mar. 23, 1984; children: Elkhanah b. 1972, Bianca b. 1975; edn: BSBA, Northeastern Univ. 1970; Calif. lic. real estate agt. 1985. Career: owner/opr. 3 restaurants, St. Louis, Mo. 1977-83; pres./bd. chmn. Sweat Equity Inc. dba Bubba's Diner, San Anselmo 1984–; realtor assoc. Frank Howard Allen & Co., San Anselmo; dir. Barah Pub., Barah Guidebook Series (1985, 86); mem. Nat. Assn. of Realtors, Calif. Assn. of Realtors, Marin County assn. of Realtors; Jewish; rec: ski, sailing, biking, golf. Address: PO Box 2827 San Anselmo 94960

JAMES, BERT ALAN, architect; b. April 24, 1955, San Fernando; s. Charles Wendel and Elsie (Fred) J.; edn: B.Arch., Calif. Polytechnic Univ. SLO 1978; Project Architect, Calif. Career: designer, draftsman Froelich & Kow Architects, Beverly Hills 1978-79; designer, draftsman Howard R. Lanes Assoc., Woodland Hills 1979-80; project mgr. Nash Brown Assoc., Bakersfield 1980-81; project mgr. Roger Grulke Architects, Bakersfield 1981-82; project architect KSA Group Architects, Bakersfield 1982-85; project architect Milazzo & Assoc., Bakersfield 1985–; mem: Am. Inst. Architects (corperate), Kern Co. Offcls. Assn. (football ref. 1983-85); rec: oil painting, photog. Res: 3612 Sampson Ct. Unit C Bakersfield 93309 Ofc: Milazzo & Associates, 1200 Truxtun Ave. Ste. 120 Bakersfield 93301

JAMES, DOT, non-profit organization consultant; b. Sept. 14, 1938, San Antonio, Tex.; d. Royal Percy and Eloise (Ohlen) J.; edn: BA, So. Methodist Univ. 1960; MA, Stanford Univ. 1962; MPA, Univ. of San Francisco 1986; gen. secondary tchg. cred., Calif. 1962. Career: mgmt. analyst, Dept. of Navy 1963-65; H.S. English tchr. Gilroy H.S. & Caldwell (ID) H.S. 1965-71; travel mag. ed., Boise Cascade 1971-73; chief editor Venus mag. 1973-75; partner/CEO F.S. Button Mfg. Co. 1975-83; freelance writer/ ed. 1965–; exec. dir. AIDS Found., Santa Clara Co. 1983-84; currently self-employed; awards: NDEA Inst. in Eng. Fellowship 1967; Coe Found. Inst. in Am. Studies Fellowship 1969; mem: NEA/ CTA/ GTA; AFT/ CFT; Nat. Assn. Female Execs.; Bay Area Career women; Stanford Bay Area Profl. Womens Club; San Jose & Los Gatos CofC; BBB of Santa Clara Co.; NOW, Calif.; Womens Athletic Assn., San Jose; Alpha Delta Pi (v.p. 1956); commnr. City of San Jose Parks & Recreation Commn. 1972-73; works: Biography of John Knott, Tex. Hist. Soc. Archives; creator/mfr. Feminist-slogan buttons 1975-83, housed in Womens Collection, Smithsonian Instn. 1975-83; Democrat; Humanist; rec: cartooning, golf, philately. Address: 4260 Camden Ave San Jose 95124

JAMES, ENEZ THERESA, dietitian, ret.; b. Feb. 26, 1926, Brooklyn, NY; d. Massimo (Max) and Madeline Maria (Frugoni) Pordon; m. Edward James, Jr., May 13, 1967; edn: BS diet & nutrition, Brooklyn Coll. 1947; reg. dietitian, Am. Dietetic Assn. Career: clin. dietitian Long Island Coll. Hosp., Brooklyn 1947-51; dietitian NY City Sch. Lunch 1952-55; head dietitian Kings County Hosp. NYC 1955-61; asst. dir. dietary svcs. Beekman Downtown Hosp. NYC

1961-67; dir. dietary svcs. Brookdale Comm. Hosp. Oakland, Calif. 1968-73; clin. dietitian VA Hosp. Livermore 1975-82; retired; cons. Albany (Calif.) Hosp. 1974, num. convales. hosps. 1972-74; mem: Am. Dietetic Assn., Calif. Dietetic Assn.,, Diablo Valley Dietetic Assn. (edn. chmn. 1974-76, pres. 1977-78, parliamentarian 1978-79), Food Svc. Exec. Assn.; Republican; Protestant; rec: travel, hiking. Res: 1085 Peary Ct Livermore 94550

JAMES, SONDRA DIANE, ballet dancer/teacher; b. Feb. 14, 1952, Long Beach; d. Emerson George and Dorothy Louise (Ebbert) James; edn: AA, honors, Long Beach City Coll. 1974; BFA, cum laude, U.S. Internat. Univ. 1976; MBA, National Univ. 1978. Career: ballet dancer Lakewood Philharmonic Dance Co. 1960-64, Ballet Gala 1965-67, The Royal Ballet Co. 1967-68, International Ballet Co. 1973-76; asst. ballet tchr. Audrey Share Sch. of Dance, Long Beach 1966-69; artistic dir./tchr. Greta Anderson's, Los Alamitos 1967-69; artistic dir. Ice Capades Chalet, San Diego 1976-79; asst. to the pres. Nat. Univ., San Diego 1977-79; owner/dir. The Ballet Conservatory, Spring Valley 1979–; honors: Outstanding Young Women of Am. (1977), Who's Who Among San Diego Women (1982), Alpha Gamma Sigma, Horizon Club Award (1967); mem: The Royal Acad. of Dancing 1966-, The San Diego Watercolor Soc., Western Fedn. of Watercolor Socs., Gr. San Diego CofC, Entrepreneur Club of S.D., Better Bus. Bureau; works: creator and choreographer 3 ballets; dir. Internat. Folk Ballet of San Diego (1981-); published in Profl. Ice Skaters Mag. (1978), Horizon Club (1967); Democrat; Presbyterian; rec: watercolor, clay sculpture, golf. Ofc: The Ballet Conservatory 8300 Paradise Valley Rd Spring Valley 92077

JANG, ALLEN WAI, school administrator; b. Aug. 18, 1950, Los Angeles; s. Bock Chong and Kau Ngook (Chiang) J.; m. Loan, Aug. 31, 1974; children: Timothy b. 1975, Julie Kau b. 1986; edn: BA, Pepperdine Univ. 1974, MA, 1978; cert. counseling UC Los Angeles 1978; PhD, Columbia Pacific Univ. 1984; profl. tchg. cert., Assn. of Christian Schs. Internat. 1983, adminstrv. cert., 1984; law enforcement instr., Bur. of Collection & Investigative Svcs. 1983. Career: adminstr. Normandie Christian Sch., Los Angeles 1981-83; h.s. prin. Calif. Christian Sch., Sepulveda 1983-86; adminstr. Orange County Christian School, Cypress 1986–; faculty mentor Columbia Pacific Univ. 1985-; assoc. minister San Gabriel Ch. of Christ 1983-; law enforcement instr. US Sch. of Law Enforcement, L.A. 1981-; honors: Dean's List (CSULA, Pepperdine), Stipend from NSF/Am. Chem. Soc. for tng. to improve quality of h.s. chem. instrn. at San Jose State Univ. (1985); mem: Am. Scientific Affil., Nat. Sci. Tchrs. Assn., Christian Martial Arts Assn., Ptnrs. for Christian Edn., Inc.; Republican; Ch. of Christ; rec: martial arts, reading scientific literature. Res: 1712 Azalea Dr Alhambra 91801 Ofc: Orange County Christian Sch. 5400 Myra Ave Cypress 90630

JANOFSKY, LEONARD S, lawyer; b. Oct. 13, 1909, Los Angeles; s. E. and Ida (Schwartz) J.; m. Nancy Neilson, Dec. 29, 948; children: (Dr.) Irene (Hartzell) b. 1940, John b. 1951; edn: AB, Occidental Coll. 1931; LLB, Harvard Univ. Law Sch. 1934. Career: senior regional atty. Nat. Labor Rels. Bd., 21st Region, Ariz. and So. Calif., 1937; spl. trial counsel Eminent Domain Proceedings, Housing Authority of City of Los Angeles, 1951; partner Paul, Hastings, Janofsky & Walker, 1951–; del. US Dept. of State to Internat. Labor Organization Conf., Geneva, Switz. 1969-70; mem. Senior Advis. Bd., US 9th Circuit Ct. of Appeals; Fellow Am. Coll. of Trial Lawyers; Fellow Am. Bar Found.; honors: LLD, Occidental Coll. 1981; LLD, Pepperdine Coll. 1981; Shattuck-Price Award of Los Angeles County Bar Assn. 1977; recipient Medallion Award, St. Thomas More Law Hon. Soc., Loyola Univ. Sch. of Law 1977; mem: Am. Bar Assn. (pres. 1979-80; chmn. ABA Labor Rels. Law Sect. 1975; chmn. ABA Action Commn. to Reduce Costs and Delay 1982-84), Nat. Conf. Bar Presidents (pres. 1974-75), State Bar of Calif. (pres. 1972-73), Los Angeles County Bar Assn. (pres. 1968-69); trustee (chmn. 1960) Occidental Coll.; publs: num. legal articles; mil: lt.cmdr. USNR, WWII. Res: 661 Thayer, Los Angeles 90024 Ofc: Paul, Hastings, Janofsky & Walker, 22nd Fl. 555 S Flower St Los Angeles 90071

JANSSEN, FRANK WILLIAM, stock brokerage executive; b. July 17, 1929, Buffalo, NY; s. Franz Janssen and Rose W. Hamann; m. Mary Louise McGehee, Oct. 25, 1965; children (by previous marriage): Robert F. b. 1958, David A. b. 1960, Christina b. 1961; edn: BA w/distinction, Univ. Va. 1953; MPA, Geo. Washington Univ. 1967; grad. Squadron Ofcr. Sch. (1958), Air Command and Staff Coll. (Disting. Grad. 1963), Air War Coll. (Disting. Grad. 1971). Career: served to col. USAF 1953-78: AF pilot (C-47s, L-20s) Osan, Korea and (C-119s) Yokota AB, Japan, 1955-57, (C-124s) Larson AFB, Wash. 1957, (C-130s) with 317th Tactical Airlift Wing, Evreaux AB, France 1963, pilot in Europe 1963-66, Vietnam 1967-68; served in Pentagon; faculty Air War Coll.; comdr. 314th Tactical Airlift Wing, Little Rock, Ark.; chief of staff Air Univ., Ala.; asst. commandant Defense Language Inst., Monterey, Calif. 1977-78, ret.; account exec., asst. v.p. Merrill Lynch Inc., Carmel 1978–; mem. Air War Coll. Found., Retired Ofcrs. Assn., Air Force Assn., Airlift Assn., Sigma Chi frat.; num. mil. decorations inc. Legion of Merit w/cluster, Bronze Star, Defense Merit. Service Award; Republican; Prot.; rec: golf, gardening, bridge. Res: Sonado Road Box 970 Pebble Beach 93953 Ofc: Merrill Lynch Box 22320 Carmel 93922

JANUARY, DELLMAN, auditor; b. Oct. 30, 1919, Blodgett, Ore.; s. Otto David and Ollie Mabel (Henderson) J.; m. Oleda Thorson, June 15, 1947; edn: BS, Ore. State Univ. 1949; Certified Internal Auditor, The Inst. of Int. Auditors (1973). Career: mgr. Western Union Office, Fort Peck, Mont. 1940-42; secty. to pres. McCloud River R.R., McCloud, Calif. 1949-51; postal insp. Western Region, San Bruno 1968-80, ret.; mem: Govt. Accts. Assn. (pres. San Bernardino Chapt. 1966-67), Inst. of Internal Auditors 1970-75; mil: major USAF Auditor General 1951-68, decorated Disting. Unit Cit., AF Commendn. Medal, Asiatic-Pacific w/2 bronze stars; Republican; Presbyterian; rec: philately, bowling, golf. Res: San Mateo 94403

JARVINEN, RICHARD STANFORD LARSEN, economic analyst; b. Nov. 7, 1954, Santa Monica, Calif.; s. Richard Stanford and Lois (Lindborg) Larsen; father: Harry Allen Jarvinen; m. Suzanne, Mar. 21, 1986; edn: BA econs., UC Los Angeles 1977; MBA, San Diego State Univ. 1986. Career: dir. ops. Escondido Travel Agcy. Inc. 1978-80; regl. ops. mgr. Ask Mr. Foster Travel San Diego 1980-81; research analyst S.D. Gas & Elec. 1984-85, econ. analyst 1985–; v.p. ops. Jarvinen Vacations Escondido 1985–; honors: Beta Gamma Sigma 1985; mem: Ops. Research Soc. of Am. (secty. 1986), Rotary (charter dir. 1980). Res: 10055 Dauntless St San Diego 92126 Ofc: S.D.G.& E. 110 West A St POB 1831 San Diego 92112

JARVIS, DONALD BERTRAM, judge; b. Dec. 14, 1928, Newark; s. Benjamin and Esther (Golden) J.; m. Rosalind C. Chodorcove, June 14, 1954; children: Nancy, Brian, Joanne; edn: BA, Rutgers Univ. 1949; JD, Stanford Univ. 1952; admitted to Calif. State Bar 1953. Career: law clk. Justice John W. Shenk, Calif. Supreme Ct. 1953-54; assoc. Erskine, Erskine & Tulley, 1955; assoc. Aaron N. Cohen, 1955-56; law clk. Dist. Ct. Appeals, 1956; assoc. Carl Hoppe, 1956-57; adminstrv. law judge Calif. Public Utilities Commn., San Francisco 1957–; pres. Calif. Adminstrv. Law Judges Council, 1978-83; mem. faculty Nat. Jud. Coll., Univ. Nev. 1977, 78, 80; chmn. pack BSA 1967-69, chmn. troop, 1972; class chmn. Stanford Law Sch. Fund, 1959, mem. nat. com., 1963-65; dir. Forest Hill Assn. 1970-71; mem. Am., Calif., San Francisco bar assns., Calif. Conf. Public Utility Counsel (pres. 1980-81), Nat. Panel Arbitrators, Am. Arbitration Assn., AF Assn., Res. Officers Assn., De Young Mus. Soc. and Patrons Art and Music, San Francisco Gem and Mineral Soc., Stanford Alumni Assn., Rutgers Alumni Assn., Phi Beta Kappa (pres. No. Calif. 1973-74), Tau Kappa Alpha, Phi Alpha Theta, Phi Alpha Delta. Res: 530 Dewey Blvd., San Francisco 94116 Ofc: State Bldg 350 McAllister St San Francisco 94102

JARVIS, SUZANN, financial analyst; b. Mar. 14, 1935, San Antonio, Tx.; d. Harvey Bernhardt and Waldine Louise (Price) Persch; edn: BS, Univ. of Texas, Alpine 1955; MBA, Pepperdine Univ. 1979. Career: jr. geophysicist Shell Oil Co., Abilene, Tx. and Roswell, N.M., 1955-65; dir. finl. adminstrn. Sizzler Franchise Div., 1979-81, controller Sizzler Family Steak House- Retail Div. 1981-82, dir. finl. planning & reporting Sizzler Restaurants, Inc. 1982-84; owner Sue Jarvis & Assocs., Los Angeles 1984–; asst. treas. Laura Lynn Cosmetics, Inc.; asst. treas. So. Calif. KFC Advtsg. Assn.; mem. Roswell Desk and Derrick (secty.), Nat. Assn. of Women Bus. Owners; mem. All City Band, San Antonio, Tx. (1950-52); Republican (Young Repubs.); Lutheran; rec: spectator sports. Res: 12426 Beatrice Los Angeles 90066 Ofc: Sue Jarvis & Associates 5300 Beethoven Los Angeles 90066

JARZOMBEK, STANLEY JOSEPH, JR., military officer, information systems specialist; b. May 27, 1955, McAllen, Tex.; s. Stanley J. and Virginia Anna (Pfeifer) J.; m. Paula Jeannine Zaedow, July 27, 1974; edn: BA in computer sci., Univ. of Tex., Austin 1980, and BBA in data proc. & anal., 1980; MS, info. sys., AF Inst. of Tech. 1982; grad. wk. in systems mgmt. USC 1982-. Career: served to capt. USAF 1980–: systems devel. ofcr. AF Inst. of Tech. (AFIT), Wright Patterson AFB, 1980-82; systems integration ofcr., currently Network Integration Branch Chief , Sunnyvale AFS, Calif. 1982–, chmn. AF Satellite Control Network Configuration Mgmt. Gp. 1983-84, chmn. AF Satellite Control Facility Change Control Wkg. Gp. 1983-84, v.p. AF Inst. of Tech. Engineering Council 1980-81; mem. AF Language Control Bd. 1982-; Software Quality Assurance Seminar lectr. 1983-; pres. Sunnyvale AFS Co. Grade Officers Council 1983-84; honors: White House Fellow, Regional Finalist (1985-86), listed in Who's Who in Computer Graphics (1984), AF Assn. CGOY, Co. Grade Officer of Year (1984), AF Satellite Control Facility CGOY (1983), listed in Jane's Who's Who in Aviation and Aerospace (1983), Outstanding Young Men of Am., US Jaycees (1982), Omicron Delta Kappa, Scabbard & Blade, Mortar Board, CACTUS Outstanding Student and Disting. Grad., Univ. of Texas at Austin (1980), AFROTC Corps Cmdr., UT; mem: ACM, IEEE, AIAA, DPMA, AFA, Ada/Jovial Users Group, UT Data Proc. Alumni Assn., UT Ex Students Assn.; civic: US Jaycees, Toastmasters Int. (ATM, Toastmaster of Yr. 1983, Area F4 gov. 1984-85, Div. F lt. gov. 1985-86, currently v.p. Adv. Speakers Club and pres. Pub. Rels. Club), Boy Scouts Am. (Order of the Arrow; asst. scoutmaster and Santa Clara Co. Council Unit Trainer); authored/ coord. a Space Div. regulation; published the Jovial J73 Pgmmg. Stds. and Convs. (now used by USAF and DoD contrs. as the std. for Jovial software devel.); contbr. articles Daily Texan, UT Air Force Newslwctter; contbr. to 8th West Coast Computer Faire (1983); mil: AF Commendn. Medal, GCM; Republican; Catholic; rec: backpacking, camping, public spkg. Res: 112 Falkirk Ct Sunnyvale 94087 Ofc: USAF Satellite Control Facility, POB 3430, Sunnyvale AFS 94088-3430

JASKIEWICZ, WOJTEK ANDRE, dentist; b. Nov. 26, 1943, Lasotka, Poland; nat. US cit. 1974; s. Josef and Honorata (Dragan) J.; m. Elizabeth Jolanta Akacka, Feb. 24, 1978; 1 dau. Emanuella Joanna b. 1980; edn: tchg. credentials, Teacher Coll. 1962; BA, Art Center 1964; DDS, Med. Acad. Div. Dentistry 1980; lic. DDS, Calif. Bd. Dental Examiners, 1982. Career: asst. prof. Medical Acad., Warsaw, Poland 1980-82; practicing dentist, Anatomicum Dental Clinic, Los Angeles 1982–; mem. Calif. Dental Service, Wilshire CofC; Democrat; Roman Catholic; rec: architectural design. Res: 2313 Moreno Dr Los Angeles 90039 Ofc: Anatomicum Dental Clinic 550 N Larchmont Blvd Ste 103 Los Angeles 90004

JAVAHERIAN, HADI, engineer; b. Sept. 3, 1956, Mashhad, Iran, nat. PR 1982; s. Ahmad and Moulood (Milanizadeh) J.; m. Linda Preuninger, Jan. 30, 1982; 1 son, Ivan M. b. 1985; edn: BSME, Univ. of Wash., Seattle 1980; postgrad. degree in energy, Swiss Fed. Sch. of Tech., Lausanne, Switz. 1981. Career: research engr. asst. Applied Thermal Lab., Lausanne, Switz. 1980-81; vice pres./rep. So. Calif., Robertson & Assocs. Inc., Canoga Park, 1982-83; gen. mgr. Willy Loi Enterprises Inc., Van Nuys 1983-84; energy inspector DMC Energy Inc., Anaheim 1984–; mem. ASME (assoc.); rec: jewelry, soccer, travel. Res: 7439 Woodman Ave, No. 29, Van Nuys 91405 Ofc: DMC Energy Inc., (Hqtrs.) 31 Milk St Ste 610 Boston, MA 02109

JEFFERIS, ALLEN L., engineering training director; b. Jan. 26, 1938, Eaton, Ohio; s. Raymond H. and Glenna D. (Younce) J.; edn: BSEE, Ohio Univ. 1961, MSEE, Univ. Santa Clara 1967; Bus. Mgmt. Cert., Coll. of Notre Dame 1977. Career: senior system engr. Lockheed Missile & Space Co. 1962-68; prod. support/ customer tng. mgr. Hewlett Packard Co. 1968-77; microprocessor tng. mgr. Nat. Semiconductor 1977-78; customer tng. mgr. Intel Corp. 1978-85; dir. Bay Area Technol. Ctr. Northeastern Univ. 1985–; independent tng. cons. 1985–; instr. num. courses on missile electronics, microcomputers, automatic test systems, microprocessors; honors; Tau Beta Pi, Eta Kappa Nu; mem: Inst. Elec. Electron. Engrs., Am. Soc. Tng. and Devel., Am. Soc. Engrg. Edn., Sierra Club; rec: fishing, skiing, hiking, reading. Res: 1025 Wonderlich Dr San Jose 95129 Ofc: Northwestern Univ. 2620 Augustine Dr Santa Clara 95054

JEFFERSON, ROLAND SPRATLIN, physician, author, film producer; b. May 16, 1939, Wash DC; s. Bernard S. and Devonia Helen (Spratlin) J.; m. Melanie, July 26, 1966; children: Roland Jr. b. 1967, Rodney Earl b. 1969, Shannon Devonia b. 1971, Royce Bernard b. 1975; edn: BA, USC 1961; MD, Howard Univ. Coll. of Med. 1965. Career: staff psychiatrist United Health Plan, Watts Health Foundation, 8 years; assoc. prof. psychiatry Martin Luther King, Jr. Gen. Hosp. (3 years), also cons. Calif. State Dept. of Rehabilitation; currently in pvt. practice medicine; film producer, novelist, screen writer and film reviewer; novels: The Secret Below 103rd Street (1976), A Card for the Players (1978), 559 To Damascus (1985); films: Disco 9000 (1976), Pacific Inferno (1977), Angel Dust: The Wack Attack (1980); awards: NAACP Image Award 1980 for filmmaking; Black Filmmakers Hall of Fame award for filmmaking 1980; mem. Nat. Med. Assn., Assn. of Black Motion picture and TV Producers, Writers Guild of Am.; Democrat; Prot.; rec: aviation, automobiles, swimming. Address: 3870 Crenshaw Blvd. #215, Los Angeles 90008

JEFFERSON-BRAMHALL, RONA LEE, tax preparer, executrix of estates; b. Nov. 26, 1900, Salisbury, Tenn.; d. John Thomas and Margaret Ann (Moore) Tice; m. Ray Carlton Bramhall, Dec. 24, 1982; 1 dau. Colette b. 1924; edn: Univ. So. Calif. 1937-40; enrolled agent IRS 1978; reg. parliamentarian. Career: clerk Cencus Bureau Wash. DC 1941; clerk, ed. Corps of Engrs. L.A. 1942-49; USAF clerk, prodn. splst, indsl. splst. contractor plants Hawthorne, Inglewood, Culver City 1950-70; income tax preparer. executrix self-employed 1960–; mem: Calif. Assn. Parliamentarians (state treas.), Nat. Assn. Parliamentarians, Internat. Toastmistress Club (all local ofcs., regl. treas.), Eastern Star (Grand Rep. of Ky. 1984-85), White Shrine (line ofcr. 1986), Viennese 200 Club (secty., treas., pres.); Protestant; rec: stamps, dancing, travel. Res: 5537 Littlebow Rd Palos Verdes 90274

JEKUMS, THEODORE JAMES, surgeon; b. June 12, 1943, Riga, Latvia; s. Julius and Helen (Bogdans) J.; m. Sonia, Dec. 21, 1969; children: Lara b. 1970, Theodore Jr. b. 1973, James b. 1974, Erick b. 1976; edn: BS, McGill Univ. 1965; MD, CM, McGill Univ. Med. Sch. 1968; Diplomate Am. Board of Surgery 1977. Career: pvt. practice in surgery, Anaheim, Calif. currently; Fellow Am. Coll. of Surgeons (1985); mem. Calif. Med. Assn., Orange Co. Med. Assn.; Roman Catholic; rec: tennis. Ofc: Theodore J. Jekums MD Inc. 1211 West La Palma Ste 408 Anaheim 92801

JELLEY, JOSEPH G., real estate co. president; b. Apr. 19, 1937, Blairsville, Pa.; s. Joseph G. and E. (Freidline) J.; m. Patricia A. Tremellen, July 29, 1982; children: Joseph b. 1957, James b. 1959, Joanna b. 1961, John b. 1962; edn; BS, cum laude, Tri- State Univ. 1957; GRI, Calif. 1978; Cert. Residential Splst., Nat. Assn. Realtors 1979; cert. R.E. broker, mgr., N.A.R. 1980. Career: sale mgr. Robert Hall Co., NY 1962-64; merchandising supt. Sears Roebuck & Co., NY 1964-70; Midwest dist. sales mgr. Melville Shoe Co., Foxmoor Div., NY 1971-74; sr. regl. v.p. V.E. Howard & Co., Del Mar 1975-76; founder/ pres. Western State Pacific Pines Corp., Del Mar 1976–; pres. The Jelley Co., Inc. (R.E. brokerage, comml./ res.); pres. Pacific Pines Devel. Corp.; pres. Del Mar Morgage Co., Inc.; fin. dir. Patjel Ltd., Inc. 1981; profl. lectr./ cons., fin., mktg., mgmt.; recipient num. corp. awds.; mem: Nat. & Calif. Assns. Realtors; Internat. Assn. Real Estate Appraisers (senior); No. Co. Youth Svcs. Bureau; publs: num. arts. on fin. and real estate, San Diego Co. newspapers, periodicals; rec: creative design, writing. Res: 13635 Pine Needles Dr Del Mar 92014 Ofc: The Jelley Co. Inc., 1312 Camino Del Mar Del Mar 92014

JEMISON-SMITH, PEARL DOROTHY, nurse epidemiologist; b. Feb. 15, 1938, England, nat. US cit. 1970; d. Arthur Henry and Ethel Gladys (Chaplin) Rider; m. Burton Smith, Feb. 22, 1978; children (nee Jemison): Jamie b. 1958, Keri b. 1960, Darren b. 1962, Linda b. 1964; edn: AA, RN, Fullerton Comm. Coll., 1971; comm. colls. utchg. cred., Long Beach City Coll. 1979; Cert. in Infection Control (CIC), 1984. Career: Intensive Care Unit nse., Orange Co. Med. Center 1971; hd. nse. Respiratory Intensive Care Unit, UC Irvine Med. Center 1974-78, nse. epidemiologist, 1978–; honors: Alpha Gamma Sigma (1969), Zonta Woman Award (1970), Woman of the Year, Fullerton Coll. (1971), Student Nse. of Year/So. Calif. (1971), UCI Laurels for comm. svc. (1984),

Bishop Daniel Corrigan Award (1986); mem. AIDS Coalition Orange Co. (chair 1985), AIDS Task Force O.C.; Am. Lung Assn. (nat. bd. dirs. 1985-; Calif. State pres. 1985-86, bd. 1980-; Orange Co. pres. 1983-85, bd. 1977-), Assn. for Practitioners in Infection Control (bd. 1983-85), Nat. Critical Care Inst. (editorial cons. 1979-82, editl. advis. bd. 1982-), Nat. Intravenous Therapy Assn. (editl. bd. 1981-), Trainex Corp. (bd. advisors 1975-76); frequent guest lectr. var. health care orgns., TV and radio guest, lectr. symposiums internat.; contbr. num. articles in med. jours.; Republican; Prot.; rec: gardening. Res: 11531 Montlake Dr Garden Grove 92641 Ofc: UCI Medical Center 101 The City Drive Ste 171 Orange 92668

JENKINS, LEW, II, computer software co. president; b. Dec. 27, 1947, Antioch; s. Lew and Lupie (Galarza) J.; m. Linda M. Hubbert, Jan. 25, 1970; children: James b. 1972, Stephanie b. 1974, John b. 1980; edn: BS electronics eng., CSU San Jose 1971; MBA Program, USC 1974, UC Berkeley 1975. Career: techn. IBM Corp. San Jose, 1969-71; data proc. mgr. Cordon Internat., Los Angeles 1973-75; systems & pgmmg. mgr. Emporium/ Capwell, San Francisco 1975-76; v.p. information systems Fritzi of Calif., S.F. 1976-78; pres. Apparel Computer Systems, Concord 1978-; mil: 1st lt. US Army 1971-73; Republican; rec: amateur radio opr., sailing. Ofc: Apparel Computer Systems, Inc. 1485 Enea Ct Concord 94520

JENKINS, THOMAS M., judge; b. Mar. 7, 1921, Benton, Ill.; s. Thomas M. and Ruby (Lasley) J.; m. Anne Oakhill, July 13, 1944; children: Thomas Mark, III b. 1949, Jo Anne b. 1950, Dirk b. 1954; edn: B.Ed., Chgo. State Univ. 1943; LLD, UC Hastings 1949. Career: atty. Hanson, Bridgett, Marcus & Jenkins, 1950-75; judge Superior Ct., State of Calif., County of San Mateo, 1975-; elected mayor and councilman City of San Carlos, 1962-74: bd. dirs. League of Calif. Cities, 1970-74; mem. Gov.'s Hosp. Advis. Council 1963-67; chmn. bd. Calif. Ctr. for Judicial Edn. 1982-86, mem. Calif. Judicial Council 1972-76; mem. Calif. Judges Assn. (exec. bd. 1979-83), State Bar of Calif. (v.p., bd. govs. 1969-72, chmn. Conf. of Dels. 1967), Am. Bar Assn. (House of Dels. 1959-64); civic: Peninsula Comm. Found. (bd. 1985-), Mills-Peninsula Hosp. Senior Care Pgms. (v.chmn., bd. 1985-), Friends Services for Aging, Phila. (advis. bd. 1984-), Living at Home Pgm., N.Y. (advis. bd. 1985-), United Way of Calif. (pres. bd. dirs. 1976-77), Am. Assn. of Homes for the Aging (pres. 1966-67, bd. 1962-68), No. Calif. Presbyn. Homes (bd., pres., 1977-86), S.F. Assn. for Mental Health (bd. 1971-76), Campfire Girls (vice chmn., nat. bd. dirs. 1962-66); Democrat; Prot. Res: 711 Terrace Rd San Carlos 94070 Ofc: Superior Court Hall of Justice Redwood City 94063

JENKINS, WILLIAM, III, certified public accountant; b. Sept. 9, 1932, Clayton, Mo.; s. William Jr. and Holetha (Hollins) J.; m. Sharion Mc Donald, Dec. 23, 1967; children: William IV b. 1968, Samara Y. b. 1971; edn: BS, Calif. State Colls. 1965; MBA, Univ. of Calif. 1966; CPA, Calif. 1970. Career: staff acct. Haskins & Sells, St. Louis, Mo. 1966-70, senior acct., Los Angeles 1970-72; prin. self-empl. William Jenkins III CPA, Los Angeles 1973-; dir. Los Angeles Council of Boy Scouts; Black Agenda Adv. Bd. of Senate Select Com. on Small Bus. 1982 & 1983 of Los Angeles Inc.; past dir. Family Svc. Inc., svc. Los Angeles Unif. Sch. Dist. 1984, 1985; honors: Appreciation, The Coll of the Ins. 1981; Appreciation, Charles Drew Scholarship Loan Fund Inc. 1975; mem: Am. Inst. CPA, Calif. Soc. CPAs, Black Agenda of Los Angeles Inc. (secty., treas.), 100 Black Men of Los Angeles Inc., Rotary, Town Hall of Calif. (past dir.),; mil: sgt. US Army 1953-55; Democrat; Catholic; rec: tennis, chess. Res: 1051 So. Ridgeley Dr. Los Angeles 90019 Ofc: William Jenkins III CPA, 408 So. Spring St. Ste. 712 Los Angeles 90013

JENSEN, DOUGLAS BLAINE, lawyer, b. Feb. 10, 1943, Fresno; s. Rodger Blaine and Margaret Mae (Roberts) J.; m. Lesley Smith, Sept. 4, 1967 (div. 1982); children: Clayton b. 1971, Kelly b. 1973; edn: AB cum laude, Stanford Univ. 1964, JD, 1967; admitted Calif. State Bar 1967. Career: law clk. to Judge Gilbert Jertberg, US Ct. of Appeals (9th Cir.) 1967-68; fellow Internat. Legal Center, Santiago, Chile 1968-70; assoc. atty. law firm Miller, Groezinger, Pettit, Evers & Martin, 1970-72; assoc. Baker, Manock & Jensen, 1972-74, ptnr. 1974-; adj. prof. Water Law, San Joaquin Coll. of Law; mem. ABA, Calif. Bar Assn., Fresno County Bar Assn. (pres. 1983), Stanford Assocs; Rotarian; chmn. Bd. of Trustees Valley Childrens Hosp.; secty. The Academy; publs: Chile's New Water Code and Agrarian Reform: A Case Study (Univ. Wis. Land Tenure Ctr. Research Paper 41); Republican; Protestant; rec: hunting, fishing, mountain sports. Res: 1309 West Robinwood Fresno 93711 Ofc: Baker, Manock & Jensen 600 Security Bank Bldg Fresno 93721

JENSEN, GERALD RANDOLPH, editor, graphic artist; b. Aug. 12, 1924, Kalispell, Montana; s. Hans Clemen and Mabel E. (Everson) J.; m. Helen Levine, Dec. 11, 1943; 1 dau: Marjorie, b. 1955; edn: G.Th., Life Coll. 1945; Litt.D., Internat. Acad. 1970; MA, Union Univ. 1976; PhD, 1978. Career: regl. & nat. dir. youth & Christian edn. Internat. Ch. Foursquare Gospel, Los Angeles 1946-54; dir. San Francisco area Youth for Christ 1955-60; v.p. Sacred Records, Whittier 1960-63; dir./ed. internat. publs. Full Gospel Businessmen's Fellowship 1963-69, 1985-; pres. Triangle Productions, Burbank 1970-79; pres. Claiborne/ Jensen Adv. 1980-82; pres. Jerry Jensen & Assocs., Santa Fe Springs 1982-85; bd. dirs.: Friends in the West, Seattle, Wash.; Internat. Bible Inst., Santa Fe Springs; Outreach Korea, Torrance; World Missioary Assistance Plan; Wings of Healing; Total Health Mag.; Am. Bible Soc.; Revival Fires; The Methodist Hour; Jimmy Snow Evangelistic Assoc., Nashville, Tenn.; awards: design, Dynamic Graphics, 1961; Christian Edn. Awd., Internat. Bible Inst. 1980; Spl. Svc. Awd., Golden Gate Univ. 1983; works: acts, Asian ed., Scandanavian, European & Spanish eds. Voice Mag., Full Gospel Businessmens Fellowship 1977-; youth mags., Vision, Young America, Today's

Youth, Campus, View, Charisma Digest; Republican; Protestant; rec: art collection, golf, travel. Res: 12402 St. Mark Garden Grove 92745 Ofc: Full Gospel Business Men's Fellowship Internat., 3150 Bear St Costa Mesa 92626

JENSEN, HELEN MARIE, real estate broker; b. Apr. 10, 1923, Waxahachie, Tex.; d. Ben S. and Johnnie L. (Thedford) Likins; widow; two daus: Charlotte b. 1942, Jeanne b. 1946; stu. Long Beach Jr. Coll., Delta Coll.; Calif. lic. real estate broker. Career: sales mgr. Don Schneider Realty, Downey 1956-60; broker/owner Candlewood Realty, Whittier 1960-63, Foothill Realty, Fullerton 1963-76, specialized in exchanges with Landmark Homes, repossessions, residences, land, income devel.; fmr. realtor assoc. Riverboat Realty, Abbott Realty; currently owner/broker Classic Realty, Stockton 1985-; mem: Stockton Bd. of Realtors, (past) Downey Bellflower, Whittier, No. & E. Orange County Bds. of Realtors; names Salesman of Year (2 times), Downey Bd. Realtors, Hometown Speech Contest finalist, State of Calif.; mem: Bus. & Profl. Women, 1956-59; num. exchange groups; publs: stories, poems in Delta Showboat mag.; Baptist; rec: squaredancing (Lodi Promenader, Boots & Bonnets clubs). Res: POB 99466 Stockton 95209 Ofc: Classic Realty 41 W Yokuts Ste 125 Stockton 95207

JENSEN, JAMES LESLIE, educator; b. Oct. 17, 1939, Tulare, Calif.; s. Lester E. and Mabel I. (Brown) J.; m. Nancy Ruth Peterson, Aug. 13, 1960; children: Randall Mark b. 1964, Linda Suzanne b. 1969; edn: BA chem., Westmont Coll. Santa Barbara 1961; MA chem., UC Santa Barbara 1963; PhD chem., Univ. Wash. Seattle 1967. Career: instr. Westmont Coll. 1962-64, Univ. Wash. 1968; asst. to full prof. CSU Long Beach 1968-, assoc. dean Sch. of Natural Scis. 1983-; vis. scientist Brandeis Univ. 1974-75; vis. prof. UC Irvine 1981-82; publs: num. tech. articles in sci. jours., presentations at profl. mtgs.; Republican; Protestant. Res: 3301 Huntley Dr Los Alamitos 90720 Ofc: Sch. of Nat. Scis. CSU Long Beach 90840

JENSEN, JOHN PAUL, JR., engineer, consultant; b. Feb. 27, 1917, Sioux City, Iowa; s. John Paul and Bertha (Jorgensen) J.; m. Judith Karker, Nov. 1, 1981; edn: Iowa State Univ. 1937-38, Morningside Coll. 1939-40. Career: vol. Royal Canadian Air Force, 1940-41; served in US Air Force 1941-45, with 6th Photogrammetry Sq., aerial maps and bomb charts in 35 countries; cons. engr. Communications Cons. Inc., Burlingame; sales & advt. dir. Seagrams Distillery, San Francisco; owner John's Back Bay (retail food & liquor), Lodi 1976-83; independ. cons., 1984-, Sunworks Solar Electronics Inc. 1984, Nat. Micro Systems Inc. 1984; mem. Lions Internat., Delta Tau Delta (1937), Lodi CofC (1977-83), Woodbridge Golf & Country Club; Republican; Worldwide Ch. of God. Address: POB 810 Pine Grove 95665

JENSEN, LYNDA, real estate broker; b. March 11, 1941, Los Angeles; d. Edward J. and Helena (Kohut) Friedlander; children: Hans Brett b. 1967, Tamara Lynn b. 1971; edn: BA, Ohio State Univ. 1963. Career: subs. tchr. Hillsboro Va. Elem. Sch 1961-62, London County H.S. 1962; sales assoc. Mooney Real Estate, Salt Lake City; broker assoc. Merrill Lynch (fmrly. MacElhenny & Levy & Co.) 1973-83; mgr. Merill Lynch Financial PLaza Ofc. Santa Barbara 1981-; dev. 1st real estate class for h.s. Santa Barbara H.S. 1976-79; instr. real estate principles and practices Santa Barbara City Coll. 1976-80; adult edn. real estate cont. edn. classes 191-; honors: Bd. of Realtors Svc. Award 1977; Most Inspirational 1976; Most Listings 1978-79; MVP Award 1980; Million Dollar, Multi-Million Dollar & Exec.'s Club awards; Mgr. of Year., MLR Santa Barbara 1984; Soc. of Excellence Award, Merrill Lynch 1985; Spl. Contbns. to Ed. award, Santa Barbara Bd. Realtors; mem: So. Santa Barbara Bd. of Realtors (Pub. Rels. Com., Edn. Com.), MLS Com. Santa Barbara; rec: needlework, writing, racquetball. Res: 1057 Monte Dr. Santa Barbara 93110 Ofc: Merrill Lynch, 3938 State St. Santa Barbara 93105

JENSEN, RITA PAULA, real estate broker; b. May 22, 1932, Los Angeles; d. Lawrence Charles and Marguerite Willeta (Thomas) Fox; m. Leroy Jensen (dec.); 1 dau: Tamara, b. 1968; edn: Long Beach City Coll. 1951-54; Long Beach State Univ. 1955-56. Career: reliability engr. Vickers Eng., Torrance 1960-64; math. analyst McDonnell Douglas, Huntington Beach 1966-69; real estate sales, Real Estate Store, Long Beach 1971-75, Coltrane & Co., Long Beach 1975-77, Top Sail Properties, Long Beach 1977-80; broker/pres. JTM Brokerage, Long Beach 1980-; bd. dirs. St. Francis Hosp. Lynwood; mem. Relocation Agency City of Long Beach; bd. dirs. Long Beach Bd. Realtors; mem: Nat. & Calif. Assn. Realtors; Civic Light Opera; Republican; Catholic; rec: travel. Res: 37 61st Pl Long Beach 90803 Ofc: JTM Brokerage, 312 Redondo Ave Long Beach 90814

JENSEN, RODGER BLAINE, farming executive; b. Sept. 12, 1920, Parlier; s. Chris B. and Edna L. (Peterson) J.; m. Margaret, Dec. 28, 1941; children: Douglas b. 1943, Marjorie (Brand) b. 1946; edn: BA, CSU Fresno 1941. Career: v.p. S & J Ranch, Inc., Fresno 1948-70, pres. 1970-; pres. Earlibest Orange Assn., Inc., Exeter 1972-; pres. San Joaquin Citrus Co., Clovis 1975-; co-chmn. bd. T.M. Duche Nut Co., Inc., Orland 1979-; honors: Citrus Farmer of the Year, America USA (1964), outstanding achieve., CSU Fresno Ag Sch. (1980); apptd: Calif. Commn. on Ag. (1978-82), Calif. Pistachio Commn. (1981-); mem: Am. Soc. of Farm Mgrs. & Rural Appraisers, Calif. CofC (dir.), Calif. Citrus Nurserymens Soc. (Thermal pres. 1970-71), Fresno County Farm Bur. (dir. 1950-60), Fruit Growers Supply Co. (dir. 1980-), Mid-Calif. Citrus Exchange (dir. 1980-), Sunkist Growers Inc. (dir. 1980-); civic: CSU Fresno (dir. Ag One Boosters 1979-83, dir. Ag. Found. 1965-, dir. Bus. Advis. Bd. 1980-84, dir. CSU Fresno Found. 1984-), Fresno City/Co. CofC (dir. 1974-78), Fresno Metropolitan Mus. (dir. 1985-), No. Fresno Rotary (pres. 1977-78, mem. 1951-), St. Agnes Hosp. Found. (dir. 1984-), Sequoia Council Boy Scouts

Am. (dir. 1960-78), Valley Children's Hosp. (dir. 1955-65); mil: 1st lt. US Air Force 1942-46, B-29 pilot, Air Medal; Republican; Prot.; rec: fishing. Res: 5476 N Parrish Way Fresno 93711 Ofc: POB 3347 Pinedale 93650

JENSEN, SCOTT KIMBALL, auditor; b. Sept. 7, 1951, Salt Lake City, Utah; s. Jack Monson and Winona (Simonsen) J.; m. Debra Woolley, April 17, 1974; children: Rachel b. 1975, Edward b. 1977, Michelle b. 1978, Melissa b. 1981, Gail b. 1983; edn: BA, Brigham Young Univ. 1978; BS, Univ. of Utah 1980, MBA, 1981; CPA, Calif. 1983. Career: acct. Price Waterhouse, Los Angeles 1981-83; auditor Lockheed Corp., Burbank 1983-84, systems and fin. analyst 1984-85; senior internal auditor Conrac Corp., Alton Div., Duarte 1985−; mem: Am. Inst. CPAs, Calif. Soc. CPAs; Republican; Ch. of Jesus Christ LDS. Res: 11116 Lynrose St. Arcadia 91006 Ofc: Conrac Corp., Alston Division, 1724 So. Mountain Ave. Duarte 91010

JEPPESEN, BETTY LENA EGEBERG, lawyer; b. Aug. 29, 1952, Skive, Denmark, nat. 1973; d. Ejner Egeberg and Gerda Marie (Holgersen) J.; dn: BA, French, BA in German, UC Santa Barbara 1974; JD, Santa Barbara Coll. of Law 1980. Career: librarian UCSB 1974-75, librn./internat. liaison Am Bibliographical Center - CLIO Press, S.B. 1975-80; law clk., atty. law firm Goux, Romasanta & Cappello, S.B. 1980-82; in-house atty. Islay Investments, S.B. 1982−; awards: Lions Club (1970), Rotary Club (1970), NEDT (1969), S.B. Scholarship Fedn. (1970), Calif. Scholarship Fedn. (1967-70, life mem., sealbearer); mem: ABA (Real Property Sect.), Calif. State Bar Assn., Santa Barbara Co. Bar Assn., Barristers Club; Student Bar Assn. (pres. 1978-80); Republican; Lutheran; rec: judo. Res: 1504 Eucalyptus Hill Rd Apt A2 Santa Barbara 93108 Ofc: Islay Investments, 800 Garden St Ste K Santa Barbara 93108

JEPPESON, WILLIAM WAYNE, educator; b. Apr. 21, 1946, Cincinnati, Ohio; s. William Donald and Jacqueline Lee (Ruwe) Jeppeson; div.; children: Jennifer Layne b. 1969, Kara Lynn b. 1983; edn: BA, Univ. of Cinn. 1972, M.Ed (honors), 1974; Calif. tchr. credential; lic. Marriage, Family and Child Counselor (MFCC) 1978. Career: supvry. social wkr. Hamilton County Welfare Dept., Cinn., O. 1972-74; psychiat. soc. wkr. Longview State Hosp., Cinn., O. 1974-75; supvsg. mental health wkr. Marin Gen. Hosp., 1975-78; staff mental health wkr. Peninsula Hosp. 1979-81; staff counselor Pacifica Youth Svc. Bur., 1981-82; tchr. spl. edn./mental hlth, San Mateo Union High Sch. Dist., 1982−; mem: Tri-State Group Psychotherapy Assn. 1970-74; Group Child Care Consultants, N.C. 1973-74; mem. Calif. Marriage Family Child Counselors Assn.; mil: served in USMC, decorated Purple Heart (Vietnam), Viet. Cross of Gal. w. Gold Palm, Pres. Cit., Weapons Expert; rec: softball player; pers. computers. Res: No.6 Morningside Dr San Anselmo 94960

JEROME, FREDERICK R., medical device mfg. co. president; b. Feb. 16, 1945, Sharon, Pa.; s. Anthony and Theresa (Bayer) DeGerolamo; m. Patricia A. Falvo, July 29, 1967; children: Alicia Ann, b. 1974, Aaron Richard, b. 1976; edn: BS cum laude, Youngstown State Univ. 1967; PhD in chem., USC 1971. Career: research scientist Inter Science Research, Los Angeles 1972-73; sr. research scientist Hyland Labs., Costa Mesa 1973-75; mgr., Immunology, Oxford Labs., Foster City 1975-77; founder/pres. Monobind, Inc. (spec. in the in-vitro diagnostic market), Costa Mesa 1977−; awards: Inst. of Chemist Scholastic Award (Youngstown Univ. 1967), NSF Fellowship (USC 1968-70), NASA Fellowship (USC 1970-71); mem. Am. Assn. of Clinical Chemists, Am. Chem. Soc.; patentee: Diagnostic Reagent System; contbr. profl. jours.; rec: racquetball, golf, basketball, tennis. REs: 29406 Ivy Glenn Dr Laguna Niguel 92677 Ofc: Monobind Inc. 729 West 16th St Costa Mesa 92627

JERVES, WAYNE EDWARD, consultant/programmer; b. Oct. 11, 1941, Lihue, Hawaii; s. Albert and Ida (Francisco) J.; m. Julie Freeman, Sept. 12, 1970; children: Lisa b. 1974, Tracy b. 1975, AnnMarie b. 1972; edn: BS, Univ. San Francisco 1963; UC Berkeley. Career: with IBM 1963−: systems engr., distbn. ind. splst., San Jose 1963-64, sys. engr., railroad ind. splst., S.F. 1967-70, railroad ind. cons., London, Eng. 1970-73, advsy. programmer, mgmt. of distributed systems in networks, Palo Alto 1973-80, senior ind. devel. analyst, Rome, Italy 1980-81, senior programmer, staff cons. to IBM mgmt. on computer network mgmt., Palo Alto 1982−; instr. IBM 1969-70; mem: Assn. for Computing Machinery, Am. Cancer Soc.; mil: communications security USN 1964-70, active duty 1965-67; Republican; Catholic. Ofc: IBM, 1501 California Ave Ste MS33G Palo Alto 94304

JESAITIS, ALGIRDAS JOSEPH, research biologist; b. Aug. 21, 1945, Freiburg, W.Ger., nat. US cit. 1954; s. Kestutis Joseph and Jadvyga (Kalinauskas) J.; m. Ellen Feeney, March 31, 1979; children: Anna Marie b. 1980, Christina Jadvyga b. 1981, Andrew Victor b. 1985; edn: BS, New York Univ. 1967; PhD, Calif. Inst. of Tech. 1973. Career: EMBO postdoctoral fellow, Univ. of Freiburg, Freiburg, FRG 1973-75; NIH postdoctoral fellow, UC San Diego 1975-79; senior research assoc. Scripps Clinic & Research Found., San Diego 1979-83, asst. mem. 1983−; honors: EMBO Postdoctoral Fellowship 1973-75; NIH Postdoctoral Fellowship 1976-79; Am. Heart Asst. Establish Investigator 1984-85; NIH Individual Research Grant 1985-88; mem. Am. Soc. for Cell Biology, Biophysical Soc.; publs: Journ. Gen. Physiol., Plant Physiol., Journ. Biol. Chem., Journ. Cell Biol., Journ. Cell Biochem. 1973−; Catholic; rec: skiing, surfing, outdoor activities. Ofc: Dept. of Immunology IMM-12, Scripps Clinic & Research Foundation 10666 No. Torrey Pines La Jolla 92037

JESCH, PHILIP MATTHEW, computer programmer/consultant; b. Feb. 29, 1964, Fullerton; s. Carl D. and Lillian V. (Winkley) J.; identical twin brother, David Lawrence J.; m. Thuy Do, Feb. 2, 1985; 1 dau. Christina b. 1985; edn:

bus. info. systems, Orange Coast Coll. 1980-82. Career: computer opr. Orange Coast Coll., Costa Mesa 1982−; computer pgmmr./analyst prop. Skyline Business Systems, Costa Mesa 1983−; computer cons. ILAR Systems, Newport Beach (1984-85), Pulizzi Engineering Inc., Santa Ana (1984-), pgmmr./analyst PCI/Turbodata, Anaheim (1986-), The Geneva Cos., Costa Mesa (1985-); honors: Software Product of the Year, Family Computing Mag. (1985), Dean's List OCC (1980); civic: musician with community stage band in Orange County 1979-83; works: devel. public domain software pgm. "FOTOGRAF", devel. graphics software product "Bottomline GRAF", co-devel. software products: Bottomline CAPITALIST, Bottomline LOAN, Bottomline TAX; Republican; Christian; rec: computer Bulletin Bds., jogging, racquetball. Ofc: Skyline Business Systems POB 3737 Costa Mesa 92628

JESSEN, RAY ALLEN, real estate executive; b. Nov. 12, 1944, San Diego; s. Jesse Altho and Beatrice Lorreta (Zimmer) J.; m. Rebecca Kunkel, Sept. 27, 1975; children: Cara b. 1978, Meagan b. 1979; edn: Univ. San Francisco 1963; San Diego State Univ. 1964; Chartered Life Underwriter. Career: br. mgr. Transamerica Corp. 1965-68; dist. agent Northwestern Mutual Life Ins. 1968-72; pres. Jessen Devel. Co. 1972−; dir. Bank of Commerce 1984, Housing Opportunities Inc.; mem. Mayor's Task Force on Housing; trustee Constrn. Industry Promotion Trust; honors: SAM Awards from Bldg. Ind. Assn. of San Diego (1982, 83, 84); mem: Nat. Assn. Home Bldrs. (dir.), Calif. Bldg. Ind. Assn. (dir.), Bldg. Ind. Assn. of San Diego (pres. 1983), Nat. Assn. of Independent Ofc. Parks, Constrn. Ind. Fedn. (chmn. Legis. Com.), San Diego CofC, 20/30 Club (pres. 1980), City of Hope of S.D. (chmn. bd. trustees 1984-), Make A Wish Found. (dir. 1984-); Republican; Presbyterian; rec: golf, racquetball. Ofc: Jessen Development Co. 7297 Ronson Rd Ste E San Diego 92111

JESSUP, WARREN T., patent lawyer; b. Aug. 1, 1916, Eureka; s. Thurman Warren and Millie (Johnson) J.; m. Evelyn Via, Sept. 13, 1941; children: Thurman, b. 1943; Paul, b. 1947; Stephen, b. 1950; Marilyn, b. 1952; BSEE, USC 1937; JD, George Washington Univ. 1942. Career: engr. General Electric Co., Schenectody, NY 1937-38; patent assoc. Gen. Elec. Co., Wash. DC 1938-42; patent counsel Eleventh Naval Dist., Pasadena 1946-50; patent atty. Huebner, Beehler, Warrel, Herzig, Los Angeles 1950-56; patent atty., Los Angeles 1956-68; patent atty. Jessup & Beecher 1968-85, Jessup, Beecher & Slehofer 1985−; instr. UCLA Engring. Ext. 1951-65; instr. UCLA Grad. Engring. Sch. 1965-75; honors: Eta Kappa Nu; Phi Delta Phi; Order of Coif; Tau Beta Pi; mem: Am. & Los Angeles Patent Law Assns.; Hidden Valley Municipal Water Dist. (pres. 1978-); Conejo Valley Hist. Soc.; publs: arts, Jour. Patent Office Soc., contbr., Ency. of Patent Practice (Reinhold); mil: commdr. USNR 1942-46; Baptist; rec: equestrian, cartography. Res. Thousand Oaks Ofc: Jessup, Beecher & Slehofer, 875 Westlake Blvd, Ste 205, Westlake Village 91361

JETT, RICHARD JAMES, banker; b. May 7, 1940, South Gate; s. Artie Richard and Evelyn C. (Tuksbre) J.; m. Michelle, Oct. 25, 1984; children: Sandi b. 1966, Teri b. 1968, Richi b. 1970; cdn: Mt. San Antonio Jr. Coll. 1957-59, dipl. Univ. of Va. Grad. Sch. of Banking 1977. Career: collector Dial Financc 1960-62; v.p. United Calif. Bank 1962-79; exec. v.p. Citrus State Bank 1979-82; pres./CEO Empire Bancorp (holding co.) and Empire Bank (nat. bank), 1982−; mem: Calif. Bankers Assn. (bd. drs.), Am. Inst. of Banking (bd. dirs.), Independent Bankers Assn. of So. Calif. (bd. dirs.), Am. Bankers Assn. (retail advis. com.), Western States Law Advis. Group (exec. com.), Purdue Univ. Credit Research Center Communications Council (advis. council), Consumer Bankers Assn. (past bd. dirs. and edn. policy com.); civic: Covina CofC (pres. elect 1986), Covina Host Lions Club, Masons; mil: capt. Calif. Army Nat. Guard 1959-76; Republican; Lutheran (ch. treas.); rec: ski, public speaking. Res: 646 Chaparro Rd Covina 91724 Ofc: Empire Bank POB 1059 Rancho Cucamonga 91730

JEWELL, JOHN HUTTSELL, librarian; b. May 13, 1940, Kansas City, Mo.; s. Jack Huttsell and Corrinne Elizabeth (Fye) J.; m. Carol Thompson, June 16, 1961; 1 dau: Teresa Elizabeth, b. 1972; edn: BA, Univ. of Ks. 1961; MA, Univ. of Denver 1969. Career: dir. WTTV, Bloomington, Ind. 1962-64; intern, Fresno Co. Free Labrary 1967-69; science librarian 1970-76; coord. reference svcs. 1976-82; principal librarian reference svcs. 1982−; honors: Phi Betta Kappa; Beta Phi Mu; mem: Calif. Alliance of Info. & Referral Svcs.; Spl. Libraries Assn.; Am. & Calif. Library Assns. Res: 2901 N Teilman Ave Fresno 93705 Ofc: Fresno County Free Library, 2420 Mariposa Fresno 93721

JHAWAR, MANOJ KUMAR, co. president; b. Aug. 15, 1965, Nagpur, India; s. Makhanlal and Vimla (Daga) Jhawar; edn: mktg. major, CSU San Diego 1984-. Career: sales rep., sales mgr. Infotainment Computers, Encinitas 1982-85; pres. Industrial Water Technology, Leucadia 1985−; sales/gen. mgr. San Diego ops. Net Profit Computers, Anaheim 1986−; cons. Toma Ltd.; founder/owner Business Computer Systems; ptnr./founder Comml. Computer Systems; dir. Indsl. Water Technology; honors: Bank of Am. Bus. Student of Year (1983); mem., co-founder Kohinoor (cultural assn. of S.Asia); Republican; Hindu; rec: Comic book collector, model rocketry, computers. Ofc: 1018 Oldham Way Encinitas 92024

JIMENEZ, STEPHEN VICTOR, banking executive; b. Apr. 14, 1952, Orange; s. Narcizo Davis and Rose Amelia (Acosta) J.; edn: AA, Cypress Coll. 1974, BA, CSU Fullerton 1979. Career: program dir. Anaheim Family YMCA, 1976-79; sales and mktg. rep. Everest Electronic Equip., 1979-80; credit mgr. Norwest Finance, 1981-82; asst. mgr. Security Pacific Finance, Laguna Hills 1982-83; retail banking ofcr. Crocker Bank, Fullerton 1983−; sales mgr. Wells

Fargo Bank; mem. bd. dirs. Martin Luther Hosp. Medical Center, Anaheim; awards: coll. scholarship CSUF 1975-79, Crocker Bank Circle of Excellence award for comm. volunteer; civic: Kiwanis Club of Anaheim (pres. 1985-86, Rookie of the Year Award), Anaheim Comm. Services Bd. (past chmn.), Anaheim Museum (bd.), Anaheim Found. for Culture and Arts (bd.), past chmn. City of Anaheim Comm. Block Grant Allocation Com., past mem. Co. of Orange Spl. Allocation Com. Revenue Sharing; Democrat; Catholic; rec: golf, politics. Address: Fullerton 92632

JIN, GORDON, data processing center director; b. Aug. 10, 1949, San Francisco; s. Hung B. and Ngar F (Lee) J.; edn: BSEE, Heald Eng. Coll. 1971; DeVry Sch. of Electronics 1968. Career: messenger Fed. Reserve Bank of Chgo. 1967; data assembly clerk Wells Fargo Bank, San Francisco 1968, A.V.P. mgr. 1978; dir. Fed. Home Loan Bank of S.F. 1980, A.V.P. dir. 1982–; mem. IEEE 1970; bd. dirs. San Francisco Volunteers Bureau; Junior Achievement S.F.; Democrat; rec: skiing, boating, outdoor activities. Res: 1535 S Diamond Bar Diamond Bar 91765 Ofc: Federal Home Loan Bank, 19935 E Walnut Dr Walnut 91789

JODY, GILBERT STEVEN, orthopedic surgeon; b. Dec. 16, 1948, NY, NY; s. Boris A. and Lillian R. (Zloto) J.; m. Dianne, Mar. 27, 1976; children: Sean b. 1982, Ryan b. 1986; edn: BS, Washington Coll. 1969; MD, Univ. Autonoma Guadalajara 1973. Career: orthopedic resident, then chief res. orthopedic surgery, New York Univ. Med. Ctr. and Bellevue Hosp., 1976-79; pvt. practice, indsl./orthopedic, Century Medical Group, cons. for num. cos. (i.e. Rockwell Internat., TWA, Pan Am. Airlines, Western Airlines, others), 1979-85, orthopedic cons. Olympian Med. Group, 1985–; dir. orthopedic surgery Ambulatory Health Systems, Inc., 1985–; Jewish; rec: travel. Res: 14550 Deervale Pl Sherman Oaks 91403 Ofc: Olympian Medical Group 500 N Nash El Segundo 90245

JOHANNING, CLIFFORD CARLOS, financial planner, fund raiser; b. Mar. 4, 1952, Dallas, Tex.; s. Douglass Henry and Phyllis May (Saunders) J.; edn: BS Ed., Stephen F. Austin State Univ. 1976; Coll. for Financial Plnng. Denver; NASD Securities Series 7 license 1983; Calif. Life & Disabil. 1981. Career: reg. dir. Easter Seals 1978; promotions dir. for Athletes in Action Internat. Basketball Team Tustin 1978-80; founder, pres. Pro-Players West, Inc. Irvine 1980-82; investment exec. Univ. Securities Irvine 1981-82; acct. exec. Baraban Securities Fullerton 1983; ptnr., fin. plnnr. Financial Service Corp. Costa Mesa 1984–; devel. dir. Rancho Damacitas, Temecula 1984–; bd. dirs. Thessalonika Found. 1980-84, Christian Adoption & Family Services Inc. 1984–; Fieldstead Inst. 1980-84; mem. Internat. Assn. of Financial Planning 1985; publ: contbr. Inland Empire Mag. (Dec. 1985); Republican; Independent Bible; rec: travel, skiing, teaching. Ofc: Rancho Damacitas 27715 Jefferson Ste 103 Temecula 92390 FSC Securities Corp. 695 Town Center Dr Ste 800 Costa Mesa 92626

JOHNN, RENE, counseling psychologist; b. Sept. 16, 1943, Woodland, Calif.; d. Lester O. and Verna (Lemenager) McKinney. Career: dist. mgr. Elaine Powers Figure Salon; owner, pres. Rene Johnn Enterprises Inc.; adminstr. Happy Acres Ranch; pres., owner Great Northern Investments Inc.; exec. dir. No. Calif. Children's Home Inc.; adminstr. Rene Hospitality House for the Elderly, Country Confidential Alcohol Recovery, Cottonwood Ranch Youth Ctr.; exec. dir. Constructive Youth Assessments Unlimited; Sen. S.I. Hayakawa Calif. Constituency Council (apptd. 1979); mem: Women's Ednl. Svc. Assn. (No. Calif. dir.), Calif. Assn. Residential Homes, Women's Profl. Rodeo Assn.; instrumental in adoption of Youth-Animal Incentive Pgms. for physically abused children; Republican; Catholic; rec: horses, livestock, tennis, sailing, swimming. Ofc: Cottonwood Ranch Youth Ctr. 7667 Rodden Rd Oakdale 95361

JOHNS (USTER), ROBERTA ANN, real estate broker; b. Nov. 23, 1944, Chgo.; d. Robert Otis and Patricia Emily (Thompson) Uster; 1 son, Marc b. 1967; edn: AA, Rio Hondo Coll. 1979; BS, Calif. State Polytech. Univ., Pomona 1981. Career: sales rep. Leggs Hosiery 1968-69, Kraft Foods 1970-72; real estate appraiser, self-empl. 1975-84; sales assoc. Hinrichs Realty San Jose 1984–; instr., motivational spkr.; honors: Sales Award (Hinrichs 1986); Republican; Catholic; rec: singing, writing. Res: 7652 Marine Cucamonga 91730 Ofc: Hinrichs Realty 5120 Campbell Ave San Jose

JOHNS, GARY DENNIS, film director; b. Mar. 3, 1946, Natrona Hts., Pa.; s. Ernest Francis and Martha Emily (Gregory) J.; edn: BS, Ohio State Univ. 1968, grad. wk. Geo. Washington Univ. 1969-70. Career: art director Ketchum, MacLeod & Grove, Pittsburgh, Pa. 1971-75; N.W. Ayer, Chgo. 1975-78; v.p., assoc. creative dir. Della Femina, Travisano, L.A. 1978-81; assoc. creative dir. Chiat-Day Advt., Los Angeles 1981-85; dir. Johns + Gorman Films; consulting prin. 1975-; exhibs: Art Store (1984), UCLA (1984); awards: num. advertising indus. profl. awards incl. Bronze Lion at Cannes (1985), CLIO, NY Art Director's Show, One Show, CA Awards, Beldings, Obies, L.A. Art Directors Show, CEBA's, others; mem. Graphic Artists Guild; pres. Wilshire-Olympic Comm. Assn. 1981-84; Independent; rec: antique cars, rare Rythm & Blues records, photog. Res: 940 S Ogden Dr Los Angeles 90036 Ofc: Johns + Gorman Films 5006 Franklin Ave Los Angeles 90027

JOHNS, W(ILLIAM) LLOYD, university president; b. May 25, 1930, East St. Louis, Ill.; s. Wm. C. and Beatrice G. (Schoenen) J.; m. Dorene Ann Hill, Oct. 11, 1975; children: Victoria (Parsons), Michelle Lynn, Terri Lee; edn: BS, N.E. Mo. State Coll. 1952, MA, 1956; EdD, USC 1966; postgrad. Inst. Ednl. Mgmt., Harvard Univ. 1974. Career: tchr. music schs., Mo., 1950-54, Calif., 1958-59;

prin. schs. in Mo., 1954-58, Calif., 1958-65; prof. ednl. adminstr. CSU Northridge, 1965-75, asst. to dean edn., 1968-70, dir. audiovisual services, 1970-72, assoc. v.p. bus. and adminstrv. affairs, 1972-75; v.p. adminstrv. affairs and ednl. services, then acting pres. Sonoma State Coll., Rohnert Park 1975-77; exec. v.p. CSU Sacramento, 1977-78, pres. 1978–; chmn. accreditation com. Western Assn. Schs. and Colls., 1965-76; chmn. mgmt. adv. com. Calif. State Univs. and Colls., 1972-, chmn. public safety adv. com., 1978-; tng. inst. dir. Leadership Tng. Area of Deaf, Rehab. Services Adminstrn., 1967-70; pres. bd. dirs. Helping Hand Fund, Sacto.; adv. bd. Sacto. Salvation Army; bd. dirs. Sacto. United Way; chmn. membership subcom., long-range plnng. com. Golden Empire Council BSA; mem. Am. Mgmt. Assn., Phi Delta Kappa, Comstock Club; coauthor: Systematic Instructional Strategy (1971); coeditor: Readings in Educational Leadership (1969); contbr. articles to profl. publs. Ofc: California State University, 6000 J St., Sacramento 95819

JOHNSEN, GEORGE E., electronic sound co. owner; b. June 28, 1953, Eugene, Ore.; s. Duane Ellis and Patricia Elsie (Daugherty) J.; m. Roberta Liebreich, July 31, 1977; 1 son, Adam b. 1982; edn: Univ. Ore. 1971-73. Career: pioneer in electronic music and production techniques for film; spl. sound effects production for Star Trek-The Movie, The Black Hole, and Altered States; design cons. Audio Digital, Audio Technica, Biamp Systems, BTX Synchronizers, EMU Systems Digital Div., Fender-Rogers-Rhodes, Sony Profl. Prods., Sony Broadcast; acoustic designer 27 recording studios, shooting stages and video editing suites incl. Falcon Video, Paramount, Panavision and Michael Sembello; owner, chief sweetening engr. EFX Systems, Burbank 1981–; internationally renowned expert in time code technique; honors: Eagle Scout (BSA 1966, youngest in country), Scholarship to Art Inst. of Chgo. (1971); mem: Audio Engrg. Soc. 1977-, Soc. for Preservation of Variety Arts (founding mem. 1977); interviewed in audio trade magazines: Mix Mag., Pro Sound News, Recording Engr. and Producer; Libertarian; rec: radio control race cars, computers, music. Ofc: EFX Systems 919 N Victory Blvd Burbank 91502

JOHNSON, ANGA LEEO ANDERSON, real estate broker; b. Oct. 17, 1899, Jerico Springs, Mo.; s. James Isaac and Dora (Lee) Anderson; m. Ivon Carles, April 20, 1921; m. 2d. Carl Johnson, April 16, 1948; edn: Springfield Tchrs. Coll.; Calif. lic. Real Estate Broker (1953). Career: bookkeeper Farmers Exch., Everton, Mo. 1921; in charge of stationary dept. Herr's Dept. tore, Springfield, Mo. 1922; clerk, hd. ready-to-wear dept. Archers Dept. Store, Lindsay 1924-28; packer Orange Package's Houses 1928-30; sales assoc. Evans Real Estate 1950-52; realtor/prin., Lindsay 1953–; honors: Outstanding Realtor of the Year (1975); mem: Orange Belt Bd. Realtors (pres. 1962), CofC, Farm Bureau, AARP (VIP award 1986), Am. Legion Aux. (pres.), Eastern Star of Lindsay (Rob Morris Merit Award), Acacia Garden Club, Lindsay Hosp. Guild; Orange Grove Management; Democrat; Methodist; rec: needlework, bridge, gardening. Address: Johnson Real Estate, 733 Hamlin Way Lindsay 93247

JOHNSON, BARBARA JEAN, superior court judge; b. Apr. 9, 1932, Detroit, Mich.; d. Clifford Clarence and Orma Cecile (Boring) Barnhouse; m. Ronald Johnson, June 24, 1965; 1 dau: Belinda b. 1955; edn: BS, Univ. So. Calif. 1953, JD, 1970. Current pos: superior ct. judge Los Angeles. Ofc: Los Angeles Superior Court 111 N Hill St Los Angeles 90012

JOHNSON, CAROLYN (HASSLER), librarian, educator; b. May 29, 1921, Oakland; d. Ferdinand Oren and Clara Wells (Humphrey) Hassler; m. Benjamin Alfred Johnson, Feb. 12, 1943; children: Robin, Rebecca, Anne Elizabeth, Delia Mary; edn: grad. in journalism, UC Berkeley 1946; MLA, Immaculate Heart Coll., L.A. 1968; State sch. library credentials. Career: asst. children's librarian Fullerton Public Library, 1951-58, coordinator children's services, 1958-80, city librarian, 1980–; instr. Rio Hondo Jr. Coll. 1970-72, Grad. Sch. Librarianship CSU Fullerton, 1972-77; pres. So. Calif. Council on Literaturae for Children and Young People, 1977-79; life mem. PTA; mem. LWV, YWCA, ALA, Calif. Library Assn. (pres. Children's Services sect. 1979), Calif. Media Educators Assn., AAUW, Phi Beta Kappa, Theta Sigma Phi. Ofc: 353 W. Commonwealth Ave., Fullerton 92632

JOHNSON, CHARLES WAYNE, engineer, manufacturer, consultant; b. Feb. 7, 1921, Vinita, Okla.; s. Charles Monroe and Willie Mae (Hudson) J.; m. Cleo Fay Witter (dec.) 1940; m. 2d Genevieve Hobbs (dec.) 1960; m. 3d Susan Gates Johnson, 1986; 1 dau. Karen Candace (Limon) b. 1946; edn: PhD theol., Ch. of Ancient Christianity, Glendale 1972; BE, Kensington Univ. 1974, ME, 1975, PhD eng., 1976. Career: owner El Monte Mfg. Co., 1946-56; co-owner Anjo Pest Control, Pasadena 1946-56, Hoover-Johnson Cons. Co., Denver, Colo. 1956-59; pres. Vanguard Chem. Co., Denver 1957-61; pres. Mineral Prods. Co., Boise, Ida. 1957-61; owner Crown Hill Meml. Park, Dallas 1959-61; chief geologist, research dir. Bekins Mineral Resources, Palmdale 1961-63; cons. prin. Johnson Engring., Long Beach, San Bernardino, Victorville 1961–; gen. mgr. Cal Pacific Corp., San Bernardino 1975-82; owner J & D Mining Co., Victorville 1977–; pres. Astro Minerals, Victorville 1985–; instr. theol., Ch. of Ancient Christianity 1972-75; park dir. Fun-Fair Amusement Park, San Diego 1970-72; awards: Navy unit cit. for outstanding achieve. for bldg. instrument repair shop on Guam (1945), award for weekly radio pgm. "Garden Chatter", East Pasa. Businessmens Assn. (1948); mem. Assn. for Finishing Processes (sr. engr.), Soc. of Mfg. Engrs. (sr. engr.), Computer & Automated Systems Assn. (charter); US patent: Metallurg. Vacuum Furnace (1970), num. profl. papers; mil: US Navy 1941-45; Republican; Ch. of Ancient Christianity; rec: prospecting, assaying, environ. pollution research. Res: Wrightwood Ofc: Johnson Engineering 12277 Marter-White Rd Victorville 92392

JOHNSON, CHERYL LEE, lawyer; b. June 9, 1950, Burlington, Wash.; d. Percy and Jean Carolyn (Wick) J.; m. Marc Marmaro, July 11, 1981; children: Ashley Johnson b. 1983; edn: BA, honors, Barnard Coll. 1971; EdM, Harvard Grad. Sch. of Edn. 1972; JD, Columbia Law Sch. 1975. Career: assoc. Morrison & Foerster, San Francisco and Los Angeles 1971-81, ptr. 1981-83; v.p., senior mng. counsel Crocker Nat. Bank, Los Angeles 1984–; honors: Bd. of Editors, Columbia Law Sch. 1974-75; mem: Am. Bar Assn., San Francisco Fee Arbitration Panel, San Francisco Lawyers Baseball League (prize commnr. 1978-80), Queens Bench, San Francisco Lawyers Assn., Los Angeles Trial Lawyers; publs: ed., Columbia Barnard Course Guide, 1971; Bar and Merger in Patent Consent Decrees, 74 Columbia Law Review; co-author, Geographical Restrictions in Patent Licnesing Arrangements, PLI-78; co-author, Functional Discounts and the Availability Doctrice, PLI Annula 1979; Advanced Antitrust Seminar. Res: 4970 Cromwell Ave. Los Angeles 90027 Ofc: Crocker Bank, 333 So. Grand Ste. 5100 Los Angeles 90071

JOHNSON, DARRELL KURT, financial executive; b. Mar. 2, 1950, Waukegan, Ill.; s. Kurt Charles and Verna Naomi (Richards) J.; edn: BA, Greenville Coll. 1972; MIM, Am. Grad. Sch. of Internat. Mgmt. 1977; MBA, So. Methodist Univ. 1977; BA, Baptist Christian Coll. 1984, MA, 1986. Career: business cons., Peace Corps, Colombia, S.A. 1973-75; finl. advisor to credit coops. Peace Corps, Nicaragua 1978-79; advisor in fin. & adminstrn. to agric. coops. Peace Corps, Guatemala 1979-80, fin. & adminstrn. advisor to ag. co-ops. Ag. Co-op. Devel. Internat. Bolivia 1980-81; Asia Regional fin. assoc. World Vision Internat., Philippines 1982-84, mgr. field acctg. World Vision Internat., Monrovia 1984–; awards: Nat. Honor Soc. (1968), full scholarship Ill. State (1968-72), internships SMU, AGSIM (1976-77), Outstanding Young Men of Am. (1985); mem. Soc. for Internat. Devel., Evangelicals for Social Action; Nazarene Ch.; rec: classical guitar, languages, tennis. Ofc: World Vision Intl. 919 W Huntington Dr Monrovia 91016

JOHNSON, DAVID DEAN BRIAN, structural engineer; b. Feb. 7, 1956, No. Hollywood; s. Charles Walton and Marcia Miriam (Baile) J.; great-great grandson of San Fernando Valley pioneers Neils and Ann Wilden Johnson; edn: BS, CSU Northridge 1980; grad. studies, UCLA 1986-; Reg. Profl. Civil Engr. 34859, Calif. 1982. Career: design draftsman Aircraft Component Repair Co., Sun Valley 1977-79; struct. designer/ draftsman John Chan & Assoc., Struct. Engrs., Van Nuys 1979-80; proj. struct. engr. KPFF Consulting Engrs., Santa Monica 1980–; mem: Am. Soc. Civil Engrs.; Structural Eng. Assn. of So. Calif.; Am. Concrete Inst.; Republican; Methodist; rec: handball, racquetball, wine tasting. Res: 19241 Nordhoff St, 27, Northridge 91324 Ofc: KPFF Consulting Engineers, 2121 Cloverfield Blvd Ste 200 Santa Monica 90404

JOHNSON, DEANNA DEWENE, airline sales executive; b. Mar. 14, 1941, Benkelman, Nebr.; d. Dewey Daniel and Annie Marie (Gunther) Gerdes; 1 dau: Cara, b. 1973; edn: spec. courses, Weaver Airline Sch. 1960-61, Braniff Tng. Sch. 1961, Northwest Airlines 1961. Career: opr. and accts. receivable Benkelman Telco, Nebr. 1957-61; ticket agent Braniff Airways, Mpls.- St. Paul, Minn. 1961; reservations/ sales Northwest Airlines, Mpls.- St. Paul 1961-77, Los Angeles 1977-78, reservation mgr. (temp.) 1978-79, reservation supvr. 1979–; instr. Travel & Tourism, Mpls. Vocational Sch. 1972; apptd. mem. Adv. Bd. Bloomington (Minn.) Outreach Homes 1975; honors: sev. Mrs. Jaycee of the Month (1972-77); mem: BRAC Union; Bloomington (Minn.) Mrs. Jaycees (state del. 1974); Stadium Queens Bowling League (pres. 1975-77); John Muir Jr. H.S. PTA; Burbank Dialogue Gp. NCCJ 1981-; Burbank Vikings Youth Cheerleader pgm. (team mother 1982, cheer dir. 1984); Democrat; Methodist; rec: needlework, people, travel. Res: 824 E Groton Dr Burbank 91504 Ofc: Northwest Airlines. 11101 Aviation Blvd Los Angeles 90045

JOHNSON, DOROTHY DAVIES, pediatrician; b. Sept. 26, 1945, Denver, Colo.; d. Maurice Brown and Margaret Kaiser (Rauch) Davies; m. Henry C.L. Johnson, Jr., Dec. 29, 1973; 1 son: Charles b. 1978; edn: BA, The Colorado Coll. 1967; MD, Pritzker Sch. of Med. 1971; Diplomate Am. Bd. Pediatrics 1976. Career: pediatric intern, resident, Strong Meml. Hosp., Rochester, NY 1971-74; pvt. practice, ptnr. North Coast/ Torrey Pines Pediatrics Med. Group, La Jolla; instr., asst. clin. prof. Dept. Ped., UC San Diego Sch. of Med. 1974-81; instr., 1979-80, cons., 1981-, Health Services and DIS, San Diego City Schs.; lectr. Univ. San Diego Sch. of Nursing, 1981-; staff (chief ped. 74-76) Southeast Health Ctr., (chief ped. 76-79) Comprehensive Health Ctr.; mem. Calif. Med. Assn., Am. Acad. of Ped. (chair S.D. Chpt. subcom. on SADD-Students Against Driving Drunk); University City United Ch. (choir); rec: family, music. Ofc: North Coast/ Torrey Pines Pediatrics Med. Group, 9834 Genesee Ave Ste 312 La Jolla 92037

JOHNSON, DOUGLAS WAYNE, technical services executive; b. Feb. 26, 1946, Pittsburgh, Pa.; s. Clarence Harold and Shirley Lou (March) J.; m. Jolene Anderson, June 25, 1971; 1 dau: Andrea, b. 1974; edn: AA, Bakersfield Coll. 1967; BS, CSU Fresno 1973; adv. cert., The Commn. on Peace Ofcr. Stds. & Tng. 1981. Career: computer sys. cons./ sem. lectr.; police ofcr./ dir. tech. svcs. Madera Police Dept., Madera 1974–; exec. dir. Public Safety, Micro-Software, Madera 1983–; instr. Calif. Dept. of Justice, Inves. Computer Crimes 1985-; assoc. dir. Insight Research Group L.A. 1985-; awards: Distinguished Profl. Police Service, Hanford Police Dept. 1983; Tho Noble Order of Field Mice, USAF, Strategic Air Command, Grand Forks AFB 1970; Meritorious Conduct, Madera Police Dept. 1975; mem: Calif. Law Enforcement Assn. (pres. Records Supvrs., Central chpt. 1980-81); Madera City Peace Ofcrs. Assn.; Peace Ofcrs. Research Assn. of Calif.; Civil Air Patrol (Mission pilot 1972-74); publs: writer/ publisher: Public Safety micro-Software "ANALYST", S.T.A.R.S. (Subpoena Tracking & Reporting Sys.), March 1984 (software for law enforcement); contbg. writer (title cover art.) Law & Order Mag. 5/79; Texas Instruments Profl. Pgm. Exch.: Offender Census, Investigative Manpower, Patrol Workload Analysis, others; Technology Transfer Directory of People, Minority Bus. Devel. Agcy. of Dept. of Commerce & Fed. Lab. Consortium for Technol. Transfer 1981-; mil: sgt. E-4 USAF 1967-71, Nat. Def., Unit Cit. (2), GCM; Republican; rec: painting, computer pgmmg., photog. Res: 25575 Sybil Way Madera 93638 Ofc: Madera Police Dept., 203 W Fourth St Madera 93637

JOHNSON, EARL JR., appellate judge; b. June 10, 1933, Watertown, So. Dakota; s. Earl Jerome and Doris Melissa (Schwartz) J.; m. Barbara Yanow, Oct. 11, 1970; children: Kelly Ann, b. 1961, Earl Eric, b. 1964, Agaarn, b. 1976; edn: BA, Northwestern Univ. 1955; JD, Univ. of Chicago 1960; LLM, Northwestern Univ. 1961; admitted to the Bars of ILl. 1960, Ninth Circuit 1964, Dist. of Columbia 1965, U.S. Supreme Ct. 1966, Calif. 1972. Career: trial atty. Organized Crime Sect., US Dept. of Justice 1961-64; dep. dir. Neighborhood Legal Svcs., Wash. DC 1964-65; dep. dir. DEO Legal Svcs. Pgm., Wash. DC 1965-66, dir. 1966-68; vis. scholar Ctr. for the Study of Law & Soc., UC Berkeley 1968-69; prof. law USC Law Ctr. and sr. research assoc. USC Soc. Sci. Research Inst. 1969-82; assoc. justice Ct. of Appeals, Los Angeles 1982–; honors: 1st Annual Loren Miller Legal Svc. Award, Calif. State Bar 1977; Justin Dart Award for Acad. Innovation, USC 1971; So. Calif. Citizen of the Week, KNX News Radio 1978; Jackson Lecturer, Nat. Judicial Coll. 1980; Order of the Coif 1974; Ford Fellow in Criminal Law 1960-61; mem: Calif. Judge Assn. (Appellate Ct. Com. 1983-, Judicial Ethics Com. 1985), Law & Soc. Assn., Am. Bar Assn.; publs: Justice and Reform, Transaction Books, 1978; co-author, Toward Equal Justice, Oceana, 1975; co-author, Outside the Courts, Nat. Ctr. for State Cts., 1977; co-author, Dispute Resolution in America, Corp. Press, 1984; num. arts. and book chpts. on organized crime, legal svcs. and admin. of justice; mil: lt. j.g. USN 1955-58; rec: reading, writing, history, mysteries, tennis. Res: 1627 Monterey Blvd., Hermosa Beach 90254 Ofc: California Court of Appeal, 3580 Wilshire Blvd., Los Angeles 90010

JOHNSON, ERIC RAY, public utility executive; b. Aug. 4, 1952, Fresno; s. Raymond Paul and Jean Carol (Will) J.; m. Pamela Person, Oct. 30, 1976; children: Adam b. 1981, Emily b. 1985; edn: AA, Fresno City Coll. 1980. Career: ofc. mgr. Great Pacific Leasing 1972-75; opr. Pacific Telephone 1975-76, svc. rep. 1976-79, pub. svc. cons. 1979-82, mgr. res. order ctr. 1982–; commr. Fresno County Landmarks and Historical Records Commn.; honors: Cert. of Achiev. for Academic Performance, Fresno City Coll. 1982; mem. Natives Sons of the Golden West (past pres. Parlor 25, Fresno); Republican; Protestant; rec: videography, photog. Ofc: Fresno 93762

JOHNSON, FLOYD OLIVER, office equipment co. president; b. Aug. 10, 1929, Berwyn, Ill.; s. Oliver R. and Lena J.; m. Marie L., Sept. 12, 1976; children: Floyd, Jr. b. 1952, Mark b. 1959, Karen b. 1961; edn: BS engring., UC Los Angeles 1960; grad. work in E.E., Stanford Univ.; std. tchg. cred. designated subject, UC Berkeley 1962. Career: mgr. engring. Varian Assocs., Palo Alto 1960-77; program mgr. Satellite Earth Systems, Hughes Aircraft, Torrance 1977-81; pres./CEO More Copy Systems Inc., Santa Barbara (1980-), San Luis Obispo (1982-85), Ventura (1982-); cons. Hughes Aircraft 1981; instr. engring. Foothill Coll. 1961-71; honors: Tau Beta Pi (1959); mem. Carpinteria CofC; works: 8 patents (1960-77), approx. 35 tech. paper presentations nat. and internat. confs.; mil: electronic techn., 1/c p.o. US Navy 1948-55; Republican; Seventh-day Adventist. Res: 1705 La Mirada Dr Carpinteria 93013 Ofc: Mor Copy Systems Inc 1001 Mark Ave Carpinteria 93013

JOHNSON, HAROLD, judge; b. Oct. 8, 1928, Syracuse, NY; s. Harold Oscar and Elizabeth Lulu (Kittell) J.; m. Kay Reilly Blair, June 35, 1950; children: Michael b. 1952, Kevin b. 1954, Kristin b. 1958, Linda b. 1963; edn: undergrad. Syracuse Univ. 1945-46; BS pol. sci., Northwestern Univ. 1951; Calif. tchr. credential, UC Los Angeles 1954; JD, Southwestern Univ. Law Sch. 1961; admitted Calif. State Bar 1963. Career: mgmt. trainee Provident Mutual Life Ins. Co. 1951-52; tchr. Simi Valley Unified Sch. Dist. 1954-56, 1960-61; staff asst. mat. & contracts adminstrn. depts. No. Am. Aviation Inc. 1956-60, 61-63; deputy dist. atty. San Luis Obispo County 1963-64, 65-66; assoc. Muller & Woolpert, San Luis Obispo 1964-65; city atty. City of San Luis Obispo 1966-71; justice court judge S.L.O. County 1971-75, judge San Luis Obispo County Municipal Ct. 1975–, presiding judge 1985-; instr. bus. law Cuesta Coll. 1964-66; instr. legal aspects of real estate Univ. Calif. Ext. 1964-65; mem. Am. Bar Assn., Calif. Judges Assn., Phi Alpha Delta legal frat., Rotary, Zeta Psi frat.; wks: Radio actor, Stations WFBL and WSYR, Syracuse, NY 1937-43; mil: ET3 USN 1946-49 WWII Victory Medal; Republican; Protestant; rec: tennis, bowling. Res: 1567 Bee Canyon Rd., Arroyo Grande 93420 Ofc: SLO County Municipal Court, Box 1247, San Luis Obispo 93406

JOHNSON, JAMES EARL, sales & marketing executive; b. July 21, 1942, Evansville, Ind.; s. James P. and Ethel L. J.; m. Victoria A., Dec. 13, 1968; children: Franz b. 1964, Darryl b. 1965, Donald b. 1967; edn: AA, Palomar Coll. 1973; BA, Univ. Redlands 1977, MA, 1979. Career: chief criminal investigator; real estate agent Bob Thacher Realty 29 Palms, Calif. 1975; polygraph examiner for fed. govt. 1976-80; FBI Acad. Quantico, Va. 1978; pres. Juf 1978-80; real estate broker Walker & Lee, Golden West Realty 1980; dir., pres. J & B Investment Assn. 1980–; owner, dir. Time Mortgage 1981–; owner Golden State Escrow 1980–; instr. Santa Ana Coll.; mem: Nat. Assn. Realtors, Am. Polygraph Assn., Am. Red Cross, Alpha Gamma Sigma 1973, The In Club, CofC; mil: gy. sgt. USMC; rec: golf, reading, sports. Res: 13192

Silver Birch Tustin 92680 Ofc: J & B Investment Assocs. 202 Fashion Ln Ste 211 Tustin 92680

JOHNSON, JAMES LAWRENCE, psychotherapist, writer; b. Sept. 17, 1953, Devils Lake, No. Dakota; s. Lawrence and Irene Johnson; m. Paula Sechler, Aug. 1981; 1 son, Daniel b. 1985; edn: AA, Lake Region Jr. Coll. 1973; BA, Univ. of No. Dakota 1975; MA, Azusa Pacific Univ. 1980. Career: freelance writer 1977-78; marriage, family and child counselor intern and trainee, Foothill Community Mental Health Ctr., Glendora 1978-81; lic. marriage, family and child counselor pvt. practice, Pomona, Glendora and Covina ofcs. 1981–; social worker LeRoy Boys Home, La Verne 1981-3; cons., trainer Stephen Ministries 1985–; cab. leader, incl. pres., tchr. and advr. Singles Ministry of the First Baptist Ch. 1980-82; honors: sports ed., ed.-in-chief, college newspaper 1971-73; drama scholarship, 1973; mem: Am. and Calif. Assns. Marriage and Family Therapists; author: 36 articles, Worldwide Challenge Mag. (one recognized by Los Angeles Police Chief Ed Davis on Crime), 1975-77; play, sev. short stories and poems 1977-80; doctoral research on intimacy, United States Internat. Univ. 1985-; Christian; rec: basketball, backpacking, photog. Res: 3409 Duke Ave. Claremont 91711 Ofc: Jim Johnson, 101 So. Barranca Ave. Ste. 208 Covina 91723

JOHNSON, JEFFREY DON, engineering executive; b. July 19, 1949, Fort Worth, Tx.; s. Charles Lillard and Ruth Marie (Kenkel) J.; m. Kristen Kvitky, June 23, 1973; children: Keely Piper b. 1974, Ben David b. 1977; edn: AS metallurgy, Don Bosco Tech. Inst. 1967; BS in ceramics, BS in metallurgy, UC Berkeley 1973. Career: metallurgist U.S. Steel, Torrance 1967-69; materials research engr. Intel Corp., Santa Clara 1973-74; engring. mgr. Bechtel Corp., San Francisco 1974-84; dir. metallurgy and quality assurance Teledyne Corp., City of Industry 1984-85; div. quality assurance mgr. Hexcel Corp., City of Industry 1985, engring. mgr. 1986–; mem. Am. Welding Soc., Am. Soc. for Metals, Am. Soc. for Nondestructive Testing, ASME; inventions: Electronic Image Analysis Instrumentation (1984), Soluble Spacer Gasket (1982), Electrothermal Diffusion Bonding (1973), E-Prom Semiconductor Packaging (1973), Al-Fe Cast Iron Alloy Devel. (1972). Res: 1501 South Bluff Court Diamond Bar 91765 Ofc: Hexcel/MCI 140 N Orange Ave City of Industry 91744

JOHNSON, JERRY LYNN, industrial designer, furniture designer; b. Feb. 15, 1927, Grand Rapids, Mich.; s. C. Evan and Louise E. (Kies) J.; m. Mary Louise, July 7, 1982; children: Laura Lynn b. 1960, Craig Evan b. 1962; edn: BA, Mich. State Univ. 1950. Career: furniture designer Lightfoot Studios, Pasadena; independent designer; designed for num. firms incl: Tropical Sun, Pasadena, Landes Mfg., Gardena, Charton Co. of Calif. & Mass., Lane Co. Va., O.W. Lee Co., Azusa, Plus-Aviante, Cypress, Earthwoods, Gardena, Calif. & Mexico; honors: Golden Key Award, Nat. Home Fashions League (1962), Poly Award, Soc. of Plastics Ind. (1968, 70), num. Calif. Design Selections, Cologne Furn. Fair, Eurodomus, Italy; mem: Calif. Furn. Designers Assn. (past pres.), Greater Potrero Assn. (past pres.); num. design patents, 1st to use PVC plastic for outdoor furniture; included in Innovative Furn. in Am., Cooper-Hewitt Mus./Smithsonian; mil: rdm 3/c USN 1945-46; Republican; Protestant; avoc: ranching. Res: 24463 Hwy 94 Potrero 92063 Ofc: Jerry Johnson Enterprises, POB 50 Potrero 92063

JOHNSON, KEITH ALAN, residential developer; b. July 4, 1942, Wash. DC; s. Charles Revere and Harriett (Wheeler) J.; m. Jane Preston, Mar. 10, 1967; children: Brian b. 1971, Todd b. 1973; edn: BSME, Purdue Univ. 1963; MBA, Stanford Univ. 1969. Career: asst. mgr. Joint Venture Div. William Lyon Devel., Newport Beach 1969-70, eastern regional mgr. Wash. DC 1970-72; proj. mgr. Wm. Lyon Co., San Jose 1973-74, v.p., regl. mgr. San Diego 1975-81; dir., exec. v.p. The Fieldstone Co. San Diego 1981–; adv. bd., guest lectr. San Diego State Univ. Sch. of Bus., UC San Diego 1981-; honors: Constrn. Industry Leader of the Year (1981), Spirit of Life Award (City of Hope 1983); mem: Bldg. Ind. Assn. (chmn. arbitration com. 1977,), BIA of San Diego (pres. 1982, dir. 1977-83), BIA Homebuilder's Council 1980-, BIA President's Council (founder 1983, pres. 1985), Constrn. Industry Fedn. (chmn. comm. rels. com. 1978, dir. 1983-85, chmn. 1985), Hardhats Toastmasters (pres. 1977), Concord Group 1978–, Republican Assoc. 1979-, Golden Eagle Club 1984-, Pres's Club UC San Diego 1985-, Chancellor's Assocs. UCSD 1985-, Ducks Unlimited (chpt. chmn. 1981, steering com. 1976-), Housing Opportunities Inc. 1980- (pres. 1981, dir. 1980-83); mem. Mayor's Growth Mgmt. Task Force 1985, S.D. County Water Conservation Task Force 1977-78, City of S.D. Sch. Availability Task Force 1979; adv. bd. Friends of Handicapped Children 1978-84; mil: lt. USN 1964-67, Vietnam Svc. (6), Nat. Defense, Rep. of Vietnam Medals; Republican; Presbyterian (elder, choir mem., music com., organ task force, bldg. com. Solana Bch. Pres. Ch.); rec: scuba, fishing, skiing, hunting. Ofc: The Fieldstone Co. 8340 Clairemont Mesa Blvd Ste 211 San Diego 92111

JOHNSON, LAWRENCE WILFORD, JR., manufacturing co. executive; b. June 6, 1953, Newton, NJ; s. Lawrence W., Sr. and Teresa Mary (Ripp) J.; m. Marie Stolz, July 16, 1983; edn: BS bus. adminstrn. and public adminstrn., Nichols Coll. 1975. Career: tech. product splst., OEM Medical Inc., Edison, NJ 1976-77; western regl. sales mgr. 1977-79; western regl. govt. sales mgr. Poloroid Corp. 1979-82, western regl. mgr. electronic imaging 1982-84, nat. accts. mgr. 1984; currently European mktg. mgr. Polarizer Div., Poloroid Corp.; tech. spkr. for western aerospace industry rep. Poloroid to such firms as: Lockheed, Rockwell Internat., Hughes Aerospace, Ford Aerospace; honors: mem. Poloroid Corp. Achiever Soc. 1982-; Republican; Episcopal; rec: skiing, sailing, photog. Res: 177-F Riverside Dr Newport Beach 92663 Ofc: Poloroid (Europa) BV 24 Markt 7511 GB Enschede The Netherlands

JOHNSON, LINDA ROSEMARY, product marketing engineer; b. Nov. 2, 1951, Guildford, England; d. Ivor Percy and Esme Josephine (Pitts) J.; edn: dipl. bilingual secty. (French, German), Polytechnic of Central London, England 1971. Career: bilingual secty. Gulf Oil Chem. Co., London, England 1971-75; adminstrv. asst. Siliconix Inc., Santa Clara, Calif. 1977-78, internat. customer service supr. 1978-81, product mktg. splst. 1981-84; product mktg. engr. Intersil Inc., Cupertino 1984–; mem. Sierra Club, Planetary Soc., Rosicrucians; rec: hiking, camping, classical music. Res: 188 Truckee Ln San Jose 95136

JOHNSON, LISA ANNETTE, dentist; b. Feb. 5, 1956, Montgomery, Ala.; d. Gene Bass and Vera May (Hobdy) J.; edn: BS chem., UC Berkeley 1977; BS dental sci., UC San Francisco 1981, DDS, 1981. Career: dental asst. with x-ray lic. Dr. Sadler, Berkeley, Dr. Johnson, Oakland, and Dr. Brockstein, Montclair 1974-75; research chemist, Dr. John Beneman, Algea Project 1974-77; dentist, Public Health of Alameda Co. 1981; pvt. practice, San Leandro 1982–; staff St. Rose and Valley Meml. Hosps. 1982; advisor/ cons. Skilled Nursing Facility 1983; mem: Am. and Calif. Dental Assns., SACDS. Ofc: Lisa Johnson, DDS 505-B Estudillo Ave. San Leandro 94577

JOHNSON, MARILYN ALTHEA, makeup artist-designer; b. Jan. 1, 1954, Chgo.; d. Wm. Herbert Johnson and Marguerite Althea Johnson Bayliss; edn: BS in pub. health edn., Ind. Univ., Bloomington 1975; grad. Master make-up artistry, fashion & design, London Sch. of Make-Up 1986; MBA (cand.), Armstrong Univ. Berkeley 1987; lic. cosmetol., Alameda Beauty Coll. (1984). Career: mktg. mgr. cosmetic & hair care prod. sales, So. Ind. territory (first woman to hold pos.) Schering Pharmceuticals 1976-79; western regl. mgr. Revlon Realistic NY, NY, Kenilworth, N.J. 1979-82; free lance cons./make-up artist & designer skin care & cosmetics, total image design, for var. orgns. and individuals, 1982-85, founder Rainbow Moods Cosmetics & Skincare (natural formulation cosmetic prods.), Oakland 1985–; educator/trainer/cons. Alexander & Assocs., Fashion Fair Cosmetics, 1982–; honors: Delta Sigma Theta Sor. (1986), Nat. Master Bus. Adminstrn. Club; Unity; rec: travel in search of new healthful prod. ingredients. Res: 433 Perkins St Apt 210 Oakland 94610 Ofc: Rainbow Moods 516 Oakland Ave Oakland 94611

JOHNSON, MARVIN W., fish farmer-geneticist; b. Dec. 8, 1938, Elmdale, Mich.; s. Rev. Raymond C. and Eunice L. (Henry) J.; m. Loretta Frailey, Aug. 24, 1958; children: James S. b. 1959, Thomas R. b. 1962; edn: dipl. Jt. Services Language Sch., Monterey Presidio 1961-62; AA bus., S.F. City Coll. 1969; BS pol. sci., CSU San Francisco 1973; grad. work Waseda Univ., Tokyo 1972-73. Career: Nat. Security Agcy., Taiwan; Two Rock Ranch, Petaluma; supvr. D.P./ Computer Div., United Airlines, S.F. Intl. Airport; adm. asst. in San Francisco, Cong. Wm. Mailliard (R. 6th Dist.), US House of Reps.; v.p. market promo. US Trade Ctr., Tokyo; current: owner Lone Pine Hatchery, Sebastopol; author: Goldfish Standards- GFSA, GSGB; attend nat. competition, Goldfish & Koi, Europe, US, Japan; awards: Top Producer 1973-1978, All Japan Lionhead Assn., Breeder of the Year 1974, 75, 76, 77 (All Japan), Award of Merit 1980, Goldfish Soc. of Great Britain; mem: Mensona Kennel Club/ Santa Rosa (dir.), Afghan Hound Club of No. Calif., Goldfish Soc. of Am., All-Japan Goldfish Assn., Goldfish Soc. of G.B. (fellow); publs: Goldfish in Color (1986), contbr. var. GF & Koi periodicals; mil: US Army Security Agcy 1957-61; Republican; Prot.; rec: ornamental pheasants, peafowl, pigeons, afghan hounds. Address: Lone Pine Hatchery 5570 Lone Pine Rd Sebastopol 95472

JOHNSON, MERLIN ELMER, lighting consultant; b. Nov. 22, 1931, Sebastopol; s. Wm. Elmer and Mary Louise (Pierini) J.; m. Peggy Jean, Oct. 4, 1952; children: Duane b. 1953, Glenn b. 1956, Eric b. 1959; edn: undergrad., Phoenix (Ariz.) Coll. 1950; Mech. Engring. Degree, USAF Chanute Field, Ill. (Univ. of Ill. affil.) 1952; spl. courses, Santa Rosa Jr. Coll. 1954, I.C.S. 1955, elec. engring., Samuel Gompers, 1960; Calif. lic. gen. electrical contractor 1968. Career: plant supt. (classified govt. wk.) Rudolf Wendel Inc., Santa Rosa 1953-59; custom lighting design, installations Casella Lighting Co., San Francisco 1959-69; pres. Artistic Lighting Corp., San Rafael 1969-80; pres. Merlin Johnson & Assocs., Palm Desert 1980–; creating custom lighting designs/ installations nationwide, Canada, and Japan; patents pending for optical framing projection equip.; mem: Assoc. Builders & Contrs., Am. Bldrs. & Contrs. Assn., Illuminating Engring. Soc.; Masons; Scottish Rite, Shriners; mil: A2C USAF; rec: music. Res: 44-8o5 San Clemente Cir Palm Desert 92260 Ofc: Artistic Lighting Design & Mfg. Co. 958 Vella Road So. Palm Springs 92264

JOHNSON, NORMA ISABELLE, county government administrator; b. Mar. 9, 1947, San Diego; d. Acklin C. and Lucille F. (Beckett) J.; m. Otis Bailey, Sept. 15, 1976; 1 son, Conrad b. 1970; edn: UC San Diego 1965-68; BA, CSU Long Beach 1972, MPA, 1974. Career: instr. CSU Long Beach 1974-75; exec. asst. to dean, instr. Tex. Southern Univ. Houston 1975-78; assoc. dir. WCIC Sacramento 1978-79; employment & tng. analyst III 1979-80; chief independent monitoring unit/ AA/EEO Ofcr. 1980-82; head start dir. Sacramento County, Sacto. Employment & Tng. Agency 1982–; workshop presenter Nat. Head Start Conf. San Juan, Puerto Rico 1985, Portland, Ore. 1986; honors: Outstanding Svc. (City/ County of Sacto.), academic scholarship (UC San Diego 4 yrs.), grad. fellow (So. Calif. Assn. of Govts.); mem: Am. Soc. Public Adminstrs., Nat. Head Start Dirs. Assn., Women's Ctr., Women's Civic Improvement Ctr. (com. chair, secty. bd.), Blacks Organizational Leadership & Devel. (secty.); Democrat; Catholic; rec: reading, chess, sports, political and civic activities. Res: 19 Stampede Ct Sacramento 95834 Ofc: Sacto. County SETA 1510 J St Sacramento 95814

JOHNSON, PEGGY E., convention service coordinator; b. July 25, 1954, Oak Park, Ill.; d. Lando J. and Cora J. (Cesaretti) Lenzi; m. James Johnson, Aug. 24, 1985. Career: acctg. and control supv. OAG Oakbrook, Ill. 1973-76; conv. coord., mtg. planner OAG Travel Magazines div. NY, NY 1976-78; dir. tour & travel Atlas Hotels San Diego 1978-82; nat. sales mgr. Town & Country Hotel San Diego 1982-84, senior conv. svc. coord. 1984—; honors: Salesperson of the Yr. (Hotel/ Motel Assn. of S.D. 1980), Excellence in Sales (Atlas Hotels 1980); mem: Hotel Sales & Mktg. Assn. (2nd v.p., 1st v.p., pres., chmn. bd.), Nat. Assn. Female Execs., Am. Soc. Assn. Execs.; rec: tennis, bicycling, volleyball, baseball. Ofc: Town & Country Hotel 500 Hotel Circle N, San Diego 92108

JOHNSON, RALPH EMSLEY, manufacturing co. executive; b. Dec. 2, 1934, Long Beach; s. Ralph Newton and Irene Johnson (Garside) J.; m. Rose Ann, July 3, 1957; children: Renee, Ralph, Robin, Rosanne; edn: UCLA 1968-69; Long Beach City Coll. 1952-54. Career: gen. mgr. Los Angeles Miniature Products, Gardena 1967-70; v.p. Lamps Inc./ Oak Electronetics, Torrance 1970-74; gen. mgr. electronics div. GTI Corp., Pittsburg, Penn. 1974-76; exec. v.p. Carley Corp., Torrance 1976-81; mng. dir. Carley of Calif. Hong Kong Ltd., Hong Kong, BCC 1978-81; gen. mgr. Mag Instrument Inc., Ontario 1981—; corp. dir. Mag Instrument, Ontario 1981-86; dir. Aqua Spa Mfg. Co., Long Beach 1967-72; mem: Soc. for Adv. of Mgmt., Commodore- Long Beach Boating Club; works: Computer Mulitplexing for Airborne Instrumentation Incandescent Lamps, Aircraft Instrument Lighting Inst. of the Soc. of Automotive Engrs. 1974; mil: splst. 2 US Army Signal Corps 1955-57; rec: boating, diving. Res: 11791 Harrisburg Rd. Los Alamitos 90720

JOHNSON, RICHARD ALLEN, telecommunications executive; b. Oct. 23, 1943, Mobile, Ala.; s. Raymond Richard and Helen Louise (Caldwell) J.; m. Carolyn Murphy, Oct. 23, 1965; children: Sherril b. 1967, Richard b. 1970; edn: AA, Harris Jr. Coll. 1963; BSEE, Washington Univ. 1965; St. Louis Univ. 1966-69; MS engrg. mgmt., Univ. Mo. 1981; Reg. Profl. Engr. Calif. 1984, Mo. 1970. Career: engr., senior engr., supv. engr. Southwestern Bell Tel. Co. St. Louis, Mo. 1965-69, equipment engr., dir. Personnel Assessment Ctr. Kansas City 1969-74, dist. staff mgr. St. Louis 1974-79; regional dir. GTE Corp. Los Gatos, Calif. 1979-81, hdqs. dir. Stamford, Ct. 1981-83; mgr. Telecomns. Pacific Gas & Elec. Co. San Francisco 1983—; honors: Upper Div. Honor Scholarship (Wash. Univ. 1963), Top Ranking Graduate (Nat. Bell Sys. Ctr. for Advanced Commn. Sys. Tng. 1968); mem: IEEE (senior mem., chpt. chmn. 1985-86), Smithsonian Inst., Telecommns. Assn., Telecommns. Edn. Council (chmn., dir. 1984-), Commonwealth Club of Calif.C; youth baseball and basketball coach and adminstr.; publ: articles in telecomns. field, author training course Equipment Engrg. Mgmt. 1973; Republican; Catholic; rec: manual crafts, golf, oil painting, coaching. Res: 1096 Lehigh Valley Circle Danville 94526 Ofc: Pacific Gas & Electric Co. 245 Market St Ste 246 San Francisco 94106

JOHNSON, RICHARD LLOYD, physician; b. Feb. 16, 1918, Weaverville, Calif.; s. Lloyd Godfrey and Elizabeth Avis (Henderson) J.; div.; children: Elizabeth, Ellen, Victoria, Caroline; edn: AB, UC Berkeley 1939; MD, UC Med School, San Francisco 1942. Career: intern Sacto. Co. Hosp. 1942-43; residency Internal Med., Milwaukee Co. Hosp., Wis. 1946-48; solo practice Internal Medicine, Sacramento 1949—; senior staff mem. Sutter Comm. Hosps., chief Dept. of Med. 1965-66, 1975-76, chair of staff 1966; senior staff Mercy Gen. Hosp., chief Dept. of Med. 1960; participant White House Conf. on Aging (1961, 81), mem. Gov.'s Advsry. Com. on Aging (1958-68), Board of Medical Examiners, State of Calif. (1965-69); mem. AMA (alt. del. 1985-), CMA (del. 1977-), Sacto. Co. Med. Soc. (pres. 1978; editor 1955, 79-), Sacto. Soc. Int. Med. (pres. 1975), Calif. Soc. Int. Med. (pres. 1980), Masons, Scottish Rite, SAR; mil: capt. US Army M.C. 1943-46; Episcopal; rec: genealogy, Calif. hist. Res: 1500 4th St Apt 16 Sacto. 95814 Ofc: 2600 Capitol Ave Ste 301 Sacramento 95816

JOHNSON, ROBERT CHARLES, association executive; b. Aug. 24, 1935, Detroit, Mich.; s. Wm. A. and Verna M. (Outhwaite) J.; m. (Clementine) Tina Johnson, May 19, 1964; children: Gary R. b. 1965, Craig W. b. 1968; edn: BS, Wayne State Univ. 1958, MS, 1962; Reg. Pharmacist, Mich. 1959. Career: mgr. McUmber Pharm., Trenton, Mich. 1959-60; spl. instr. pharm. adminstrn. Wayne State Univ. 1959-60; field dir. Mich. Pharmacists Assn. 1960-62, executive dir. 1962-69; exec. v.p. Calif. Pharmacists Assn., 1969—; adj. assoc. prof. Wayne State Univ. 1969; treas. Calif. Pharmacists Ednl. Found. (1969-), exec. ofcr. Nevada Pharmacists Assn. (1980-85); honors: Troy C. Daniels medal Univ. of Calif. (1984), Executive of Year, Sacto. Soc. Assn. Execs. (1982), Pharmacist of Year award, Mich. (1969), disting. alumni award Wayne State Univ. (1975), Hon. DPS, Univ. of Pacific (1974); mem. Am. Pharmaceutical Assn. (pres. 1974-75), Sacto. Soc. Assn. Execs. (pres. 1984-85), Am. Council Pharmaceutical Edn. (v.p. 1986), Internat. Pharmaceutical Fedn. (council mem. 1974, 77), Medic-Alert Found. (bd. trustees 1985-, chmn. fin. com. 1986-); civic: Stanford Home Found. (pres. 1982), Phi Delta Chi frat. (hon. pres. 1978), Rho Chi Soc., Comstock Club (1972-), Sacto. Safety Council (trustee 1984-85); publs: Remarkable Pharmacists (1973), num. articles in profl. jours.; Republican; Catholic; rec: travel, music. Res: 114 Harber Ct Sacramento 95825 Ofc: California Pharmacists Assn 1112 I St Sacramento 95814

JOHNSON, ROGER OWEN, trading co. executive; b. Oct. 12, 1930, Downers Grove, Ill.; s. Elmer Owen and Leta Frances (Smith) J.; m. Barbara King, Nov. 23, 1953; children: Stephen b. 1957, Douglas b. 1960, Scott b. 1962; edn: BA, Univ. of Ill. 1954. Career: v.p. Grant Advertising Inc., internat., 1958-70; pvt.

mgmt. cons. in Singapore 1970-73; mng. dir. Far East, Campbell Soup Co., Tokyo 1973-79; pres., Far East, Owens-Illinois Inc., Tokyo 1979-83; pres. Morgan Trading Co., San Francisco 1983—; advisor Fgn. Experts Bureau, State Council, People's Rep. of China, Beijing 1985; mem. Singapore Am. Assn. (founding gov. 1969-73), Am. CofC in Japan (gov. 1975-76), Mansfield Center for Pacific Affairs/S.F. (advisor 1985); trustee American Sch. in Japan; trustee American Sch. in Singapore; clubs: Manila (Phil.) Polo, Singapore Is. Country, Tanglin (Singapore), Singapore American (Singapore), Tokyo American (Tokyo); mil: lt. US Navy 1954-58; Republican; Presbyterian; rec: light aviation (power and glider), scuba, amateur theatricals. Res: 84 Malta Dr San Francisco 94131-2816

JOHNSON, RONALD JOHN, commodity broker, market analyst; b. Oct. 3, 1946, Long Branch, NJ; s. Wilbur W. and Adeline G. Johnson; m. Nancy Eileen Murphy, Sept. 25, 1982; edn: AA, Pasadena City Coll. 1966; BS, CSU Los Angeles 1968; grad. bus. pgm., CSULA 1970; desig.: Assoc., Commodity Futures Trading Commn. & Nat. Futures Assn. Career: research anal. Market Research Assoc. Inc., Pasadena 1965-68; commodity broker M.S. Commodities/ Rosenthal & Co., Pasadena 1970-72; commodity broker Enterex Commodities/ Kipnis Commodities, Newport Beach 1972-74; commodity mgr. Hornblower & Weeks, Hemphill Noyes, Orange 1974-79; pres. Mages & Johnson Inc. dba Archer Commodities, Santa Ana 1979—; host daily TV show, The Futures & Options Review, KSCI (Ch. 18) 1982-84; host Today's Future (Ch. 22, 1985-); nat. spkg. tour, Am. Entrepreneurs Assn. Fin. Opportunity Expo. 1980-81; honors: Traders Club, Hornblower & Weeks (3 yrs.); mem: Santa Ana CofC; publs: spl. reports & newpaper arts. on economic matters; guest spkr. Financial Inquiry, nat. TV show, E.F. Hutton; mil: E-5 USNR, reserve 1963-68, active 1968-70; Republican; Catholic. Res: 2325 Heliotrope Dr Santa Ana 92706 Ofc: Archer, 970 W 17th St, Ste F, Santa Ana 92706

JOHNSON, STANLEY, lawyer; b. Apr. 25, 1915, Oakland; s. Elliott and Hope (Mathews) J.; m. Bruener, Mar. 12, 1949; 1 dau. Joey Carolyn; edn: BA, UC Berkeley 1937; JD, Harvard Law Sch. 1940; admitted Calif. State Bar 1940. Career: tax practice atty., assoc. McCutcheon, Olney, Mannon and Green, San Francisco 1940-43; ptnr. Johnson Ricksen and Johnson, Oakland 1943-54; ptnr. Bledsoe Smith, Cathcart, Johnson and Rogers, S.F. 1954-71, ret. 1971, of counsel Bledsoe Cathcart Boyd Curfman and Eliot, 1971-; dir. Fink and Schindler Co., S.F. (1951-), dir. (bd. chmn. 1981-84) EMS Group, Oakland (1978-84); honors: Phi Beta Kappa (1937); mem: Am. Bar Assn., Calif. Bar Assn., Calif. Trial Lawyers Assn., Assn. of Railroad Trial Counsel, Assn. of Am. Trial Lawyers (Advocate); mem. Oakland CofC 1941-54, University Club (SF), Olympic Club, SF Fly Casting Club (Truckee), SF Symphony Assn., Alpha Delta Phi; mil: lt. USNR 1943-45; Republican; rec: trout fishing, chess. Res: 66 Brushwood Ln San Rafael 94901

JOHNSON, THOMAS REED, education administrator; b. Apr. 26, 1951, Youngstown, Ohio; s. Quentin LeRoy and Mary Jane (Scarmuzzi) J.; m. Catherine Virginia, May 18, 1982; 1 son, Aaron, b. 1983; edn: BA, San Jose State Univ. 1974; MA, lang. pathol., Humboldt State Univ. 1975; MA, edn., Calif. Lutheran Coll. 1978. Career: speech pathologist Bakersfield City Schs. 1975-79; lang. splst. Dept. of Youth Authority, No. Calif. 1979-83; dir. edn. Lincoln Christian Acad., Stockton 1983—; estab. spl. edn. in 10 schs., Dept. Youth Authority; lectr. on juvenile delinqcy. and spl. edn.; mem: Am. Speech, Lang. & Hearing Assn. (Cert. of Clin. Competence, 1978); Council of Exceptional Children; Assn. of Christian Schs., Internat.; State Legis. Com. on Edn.; Republican; Protestant; rec: ship design & model bldg., Mid. East hist. Res: 8260 Bennett Rd Stockton 95212 Ofc: Lincoln Christian Academy, 1700 Porter Way, Stockton 95207

JOHNSON, WALTER WILLIAM, librarian; b. Oct. 21, 1925, Grand Rapids, Mich.; s. Carl and Dewey (Vander Mass)J.; m. Marcelon Cadeaux Matteson, Apr. 9, 1948; children: Koe Johnson-Orneles, Brook, Camille, Leigh, Stacy Ferl, Chad; edn: BA, Mich. State Univ. 1949, MA in Art, 1950; MLS, USC 1957. Career: tchr. art Poly. High Sch., Long Beach 1950-51, Artesia High Sch., 1952-53; librarian CSU Long Beach 1956-58; dir. Library Information and Cultural Resource Center, Huntington Beach 1958—; sec. to Allied Arts Bd.; liaison to Allied Arts Assn.; past pres. Orange Coast Unitarian -Universalist Ch.; mem. Public Adminstrs. Orange County (past pres.), Orange County Library Assn. (past pres.), Public Library Execs. So. Calif., Calif. Library Assn., ALA, Rotary; mil: US Army 1944-45, decorated Bronze Star, Purple Heart. Ofc: Library Information Center, 7111 Talbert St., Huntington Bch. 92646

JOHNSTON, BRUCE TODD, construction materials co. executive; b. Dec. 26, 1927, Delano; s. Ted Y. and Josephine E. (Todd) J.; m. Sue, May 19, 1951; children: Joell Diane b. 1957, Mark Todd b. 1959; edn: BS, Calif. Maritime Acad. 1948, spl. courses USN War Coll., 1968-73; lic. deck ofcr. US Merchant Marine, USCG. Career: sales and mgmt. Pacific Cement & Aggregate, No. Calif. 1953-55, 1967-67; asst. to the pres. Precision Technology Inc., Livermore 1955-57; gen. sales mgr. Port Costa Prods. Co. div. Homestake Mining Co., Port Costa and San Francisco, 1967-72; v.p./mgr. Teichert Aggregates, Sacto. 1972—; chmn. bd. of govs. Calif. Maritime Acad.; chmn. bd. dirs. Sacto. Safety Council; mem. Aggregate Producers Assn. of No. Calif. (v.p., dir.), Soc. of Am. Mil. Engrs., Engrs. Club of S.F., Engrs. Club of Stockton, Assoc. Gen. Contrs. (past dir.), Naval Reserve Ofcrs. Assn. (past v.p.); civic: Eskaton (dir.), Sacto. Disaster Commn., Civil Military Forum of Sacto., Calif. CofC (nat. resources com.), Sutter Club, Comstock Club, Rotary; mil: capt. USNR-R 1948-82, num. decorations; Republican; Prot.; rec: tennis, travel. Ofc: Teichert Aggregates 3500 American River Dr Sacramento 95864

JOHNSTON, CYNTHIA LEA, professional skater, amusement park owner; b. Sacramento; d. Samuel Franklin and Pearl Jane (Gordon) J.; edn: AA, Sacto. City Coll. 1969; stu. Univ. of Pacific, Humphrey's Law Sch., 1971-. Career: owner, dir. Johnston Amusements Inc., Lodi 1976—, opr. amusement park 1976-86 (now leased); currently self-empl.: prod. songs and jingles; entertainer watersports and profl. skater, performer National Sports Show tour with Walk on Water Sport, entertainer Marin County Fair and Calif. State Fair; co-inventor and 1st Woman to "Walk on Water" across San Francisco Bay in invention (seen on CBS-TV show That's Incredible, KCRA Weeknights and PM Magazine, Exotic Sports Expo in Los Angeles, S.F. Bay promotion for Pier 39); awards incl. Newport Beach Commodores Club Water Parade, Stockton Jaycees Canal Cup Challange (1st Pl.), Sacrament Water Festival Award; mem: Internat. Assn. of Amusement Parks & Attractions, Am. Recreation Equipt. Assn., Am. Guild of Variety Artists, Show Folks of Am., Outdoor Amusement Bus. of Am., Am. Mgmt. Assn., Roller Skater Rink Operators of Am. (mem. & judge of events), San Joaquin Spring Festival Club, Sigma Phi Kappa sor.; songster (Pantherette) at college games; Christian; rec: music, sports, bodybuilding. Ofc: Johnston Amusements Inc. 11793 N Micke Grove Rd Lodi 95240

JOHNSTON, GERRY PASCOE, speech pathologist; b. Apr. 26, 1951, Oakdale, Calif.; d. Harold L. and Anita Elizabeth (Larrieu) Pascoe; m. Glenn Michael Johnston, Aug. 6, 1977; edn: undergrad. Shasta Coll., Coll. of Marin; BA, CSU Sacto. 1977, MA 1979; Calif. lic. Sp./Language Pathologist; Cert. Clin. Competence, Am. Sp.-Lang.-Hearing Assn. (1980). Career: grad. asst. CSU Sacto. Speech and Hearing Center, 1978-79; language, speech and hearing splst. (elem. schs.), Sacto. County Office of Edn. 1979-82, Sutter County Schs. (pre-sch. through high sch.), Yuba City 1982-86; speech & language pathologist in pvt practice, ptnr. Goldsworthy & Johnston, Yuba City 1984—; honors: Dean's Honor List CSUS; mem. Am., Calif. (Dist. 2 Nominating Com. 1985-87), Sacto. (Coord. Council 1983-85) Speech-Language-Hearing Assn.; civic: Children's Home Soc. of Calif.; Democrat; rec: tennis, ski, cooking. Res: 1764 Clark Ave Yuba City 95991 Ofc: Goldsworthy & Johnston, Speech & Language Pathology 951 Live Oak Blvd Ste 15 Yuba City 95991

JOHNSTON, THOMAS JOHN, management consultant; b. Nov. 2, 1922, Oak Park, Ill.; s. John J. and Helen J. (Gilmore) J.; m. Elaine Berger, Feb. 16, 1946; children: Elene (Kapp), Molly, Ann (Gardner), Karen, John; edn: BS, St. Mary's Coll. 1943; postgrad., Columbia Univ. 1943. Career: personnel analyst Western Electric Co., Inc., Chgo. 1946-49; retail personnel mgr. Montgomery Ward & Co., Chgo. 1949-54; mgr. personnel Panellit, Inc., Chgo. 1954-56; assoc. Heidrick & Struggles, Inc., Chgo. 1956-60, director in chg. West Coast ops. 1960-70, pres./chief exec. 1970-78, bd. chmn. 1978—; apptd. mem. Univ. Redlands Pres.'s Adv. Council (1968-73), Pres.'s Commn. White House Fellows (1971-76), bd. trustees (bd. chmn. 1984-) Robert Louis Stevenson Sch., Pebble Beach (1977-); clubs: California, University, Annandale Golf, San Francisco Yacht, Belvedere Tennis, mem. Knights of Malta; mil: lt. USNR 1942-46, PTO, ATO; Republican; Roman Catholic. Res: 29 Westshore Rd Belvedere 94920 Ofc: PO Box 768 Calistoga 94515

JONES, BETTY DE WITT, computer programming executive; b. June 24, 1933, Logan, Kans.; d. Loren Leroy and Virga Hazel (Coombs) DeWitt; m. Wilmer L. Jones, Nov. 24, 1982; children: Stephen J. and Karyn Sue Washburn. Career: sr. pgmmr. Varian Assocs. Palo Alto 1968-75; project leader R. L. Polk, Detroit, Mich. 1977-78; owner Custom Computer Consultants, Carson City, Nev. 1978-80; dir. MIS/asst. v.p. Gits Ents., Chgo. 1980; sr. pgmmr./analyst Harrah's Reno 1980-81; sr. analyst Dillingham Constrn., Pleasanton, Calif. 1981-83; mgr. pgmmg. Atherton Indus., Menlo Park 1983-84; mgr. fin. acctg. sys., Fox & Carskadon Financial Corp., San Mateo 1985—; Orion, Mich.; asst. tchr. pilot pgm. Head Start, summer 64; vol. instr. arthritis self-care class Mills Meml. Hosp., San Mateo; tchg. asst. in statistics and computers Coll. of Notre Dame, Belmont. Res: 355 Nevada Moss Beach 94013 Ofc: 2755 Campus Dr San Mateo 94403

JONES, BILL RAY, manufacturing co. executive; b. Feb. 26, 1944, Porterville; s. Ray E. and Myrtle Evelyn (Mann) J.; m. Rosemary, Dec. 12, 1965; children: Tracie Ann b. 1965, Trent Michael b. 1967; edn: Porterville Coll. 1961-62. Career: pres., corp. owner Porterville Ready Mix 1966—; honors: Distng. Svc., Jaycees 1977; Cert. of Recogn., Lions Club 1973-74; M Award, Monache H.S. 1984-85; mem: Park Commn. (chmn. 1968-75), School Bd. Stannes (chmn. 1975), Breakfast Lions (pres. 1973-74), Portervill Fair (dir. 1976-86, chmn. 1986), Elks, Lions, Monache Booster Club, Jaycees, ECV; mil: E-4 USN 1961-62; Republican; Protestant; rec: woodworking, skiing, golf. Res: 20582 Ave 164 Porterville 93257 Ofc: Porterville Ready Mix Inc., 22157 Ave. 152 Porterville 93257

JONES, CHARLES EARL, judge; b. June 8, 1934, San Antonio, Tex.; s. Earl Austin and Vivian (Monroe) J.; m. Evangelina, Aug, 8, 1985; children: Kevin b. 1958, Steven b. 1959, Dana b. 1971, Tajin b. 1972; edn: AA, San Diego Jr. Coll. 1959; BS, S.D. State Univ. 1961; JD, Univ. of S.D. Law Sch. 1967. Career: deputy dist. atty. San Diego Co. 1968-72; atty. pvt. practice S.D. 1972-80; asst. dist. atty. Imperial Co. 1980-81; judge El Centro Mun. Ct. 1981—; mem: Calif. S.D. Co. bar assns.; Calif. Judges Assn.; Lions Club; Elks; El Centro CofC Los Vigilantes; mil: cpl. USAF 1952-56, Good Conduct, Defense medals; Democrat; Protestant; rec: reading, fishing. Ofc: Imperial County Municipal Court 852 Broadway El Centro 92243

JONES, CHARLIE, television sportscaster; b. Nov. 9, 1930, Ft. Smith, Ark.; s. Ira Fulton and Mary Virginia (Norris) J.; m. Ann, June 16, 1954; children:

Chuck b. 1958, Julie b. 1963; edn: undergrad., USC; JD, Univ. of Ark. Law Sch. 1953. Career: sports dir., then station mgr. KFPW, Fort Smith, Ark. 1955-60, dir. t.v. and radio, AFL Dallas Texans 1960, began network bdcstg. with ABC-TV (3 AFL Championship Games) ABC's Wide World of Sports, and sports dir. WFAA-TV, 1960-65; sportscaster NBC-TV, 1965—, NBC Host-Announcer for 1986 World Cup Soccer, Mexico City (largest internat. sports event ever); actor (1951-) in over 30 t.v. series incl. Ironside, McMillan, Colombo, The Dick Van Dyke Show, Rich Man - Poor Man, and in 12 + Movies of the Week; hosted t.v. series "Almost Anything Goes" and sports-game show "Pro-Fan;" honors: Emmy award (1973) as writer/prod. and host of documentary "Is Winning The Name of the Game?"; Cine Golden Eagle (1982), bronze medal, N.Y. Film & TV Festival (1982), Freedom Found. Award (1982) for PBS series "The American Frontier" (co-prod., co-wrote, co-host w/Merlin Olsen, 1982); Toastmasters Intl. Speech Champion (1956); mem. USC nat. championship tennis team (1949-50); mil: 1st lt. USAF 1953-55; Christian; rec: golf, tennis. Address: C-M Productions, 8080 El Paseo Grande La Jolla 92037

JONES, HAZEL BELLE, business executive; b. Feb. 23, 1925, Talpa, Texas; d. Clyde Lafayette and Nina Lorene (Westphall) Rayburn; m. Garland Henderson Jones, Aug. 22, 1942; children: Maxine Gail (Loustalot), Jerry Dale, Ronald Gene, Pamela Lynette (Fernandez), Richard Keith; edn: spl. courses in real estate, bus. machines, stu. Bible Baptist Coll.; Calif. Real Estate Sales lic. Career: retail sales clk. 1975-78; prop. Garment Exchange, Richmond 1978—; real estate sales agt.; Democrat; Res: 2435 Wright Ave Pinole Ofc: Garment Exchange 250 Pacific Ave Rodeo 94572

JONES, JAMES HAROLD, corporate executive; b. Aug. 26, 1930, Harrison, Ark.; s. Charlie and Pearl M. (Wood) Jones; m. Peggy Lou Bort, Apr. 2, 1960; children: James Bort b. 1963, Cliff b. 1965, Lee b. 1967, Kenneth Carson b. 1974; edn: BSBA, banking/fin., Univ. of Ark. 1953; S.W. Grad. Sch. of Banking at So. Methodist Univ., Dallas 1960; Harvard Bus. Sch. Adv. Mgmt. Pgm. 1966. Career: mgmt. trainee Lakewood State Bank of Dallas, 1953-54; asst. cashier, v.p., exec. v.p. Republic Nat. Bank of Dallas, 1958-69; bd. chmn./ pres./ CEO: First Commerce Corp., New Orleans and subs. First Nat. Bank of Commerce, and First Commerce Realty Investors, 1969-75; dep. chmn./ pres./ CEO Bancal Tri State Corp., S.F. and subs. The Bank of Calif., 1975; current: owner/ bd. chmn. First Resources Corp., San Mateo 1975—, and Jameson Pharmaceutical Corp., San Mateo 1983—; dir. Wal-Mart Stores Inc. (1970-); apptd. public boards: New Orleans Aviation Bd. and Bd. of City Trusts, Louisiana Superport Task Force and Gov's Com. on Offshore Revenue Sharing (1970-75), US Dept. of Commerce nat. and regl. (chmn. Gulf South) Minority Purchasing Council (1972-74), US Savings Bonds (LA chmn. 1973-75), US Dept. of Labor Nat. Alliance of Businessmen (metro chmn. 1974-75); honors: New Orleans Pub. Rels. Soc. of Am. 1974 Hornblower Award, Nat. Cystic Fibrosis Resrch Found. service award, New Orleans CofC service award (1972), Carnation Award for outstanding volunteer service; mem: Young Pres's Orgn., Assn. of Reserve City Bankers, Am. Bankers Assn., LA Bankers Assn., Miss. Valley World Trade Council, Internat. Trade Mart Assn., Ala. Bankers Assn., Mid-Continental Oil & Gas Assn., Mid-Continental Oil & Gas Assn., Miss. Bankers Assn., New Orleans Bank Clearing House (pres. 1972-73), The Newcomen Soc., Tex. Mtg. Bankers Assn., Mtg. Bankers Assn. Am., Dallas Homebuilders Assn., num. civic orgns.; clubs: Alpine, Bienville, Banqueros de Mexico, Confrerie de la Chaine des Rotisseurs, Dallas Athletic, Dallas Country, Dervish (Dallas), Internat. House, Lakewood Golf (Pt Clear, Ala.), Metairie Country (New Orleans), Petroleum (N.O.). Address: 862 Chiltern Rd Hillsborough 94010

JONES, JENNIFER VEE, public relations/ marketing communications co. executive; b. May 28, 1953, Lancaster, Pa.; d. James Victor and Beatrice Carolyn (Beal) J.; m. David McMullin, June 11, 1983; edn: BA, Univ. Colo. 1975. Career: assoc. producer Hallmark Cards Kansas City, Mo. 1975-76; assoc. news producer KNXT-TV L.A. 1976-77; news reporter/ producer KSL-TV Salt Lake City 1978; news producer KPIX-TV San Francisco 1978-80; acct. supv. Manning, Selvage, Lee S.F. 1980-82; v.p., group mgr. Ketchum Pub. Rels. S.F. 1982-84; v.p., gen. mgr. Regis McKenna Inc. Palo Alto 1984—; honors: Twin Recipient (YWCA 1986); mem. Am. Mgmt. Assn.; Democrat; Episcopal; rec: horses, skiing, tennis. Ofc: Regis McKenna Inc. 1800 Embarcadero Rd Palo Alto 94062

JONES, LOLA MARIE, insurance agency owner; b. Dec. 20, 1930, Pierce, Col.; d. Edwin Thomas and Bertha Violet (Nicks) Smith; children: Jerry b. 1949, Stephen b. 1952, Penelope b. 1954. Career: US Fidelity & Guaranty 1961-68; Paris R. Masek Ins. Svc. 1968-75; Miner Harkness Ins. 1975-80; Christian Ins. Agcy. 1980-83; owner, Lola M. Jones Ins. Svc., Sierra Madre 1983—; elected (first woman) bd. govs. Am. Agents Alliance; named Underwriter/ Agent of the Yr. 1981 for Calif., Nat. Auto & Cas. Co.; mem. Am. Agents Alliance; Republican; Baptist; rec: quilting. Res: 136 W Montecito Sierra Madre 91024 Ofc: Lola M. Jones Insurance Service, 55 ½ N Auburn Sierra Madre 91024

JONES, LOUIS WORTH, management analyst, journalist, ret.; b. Jan. 8, 1908, St. Louis, Mo.; s. Ed C. and Vida Pearl (Wrather) J.; m. Pauline Marie Ernest, May 24, 1947; children: David Worth b. 1948, Roger Louis b. 1949, Ethan Ernest b. 1956, Faye b. 1932, Arthur Carlyle b. 1936; edn: Washington Univ. 1925-27. Career: trainee, adminstrv. ofcr. Farm Security Admin., US Dept. of Agriculture, Wash. DC 1934-46; mgmt. analyst War Assets Admin., San Francisco 1946-48; mgmt. analyst Atomic Energy Commn., Los Alamos, N.Mex. 1948-50; mgmt. analyst U.S. Naval Radiological Defense Lab., San Francisco 1950-68; vol. alternate Civil Defense Cord., San Mateo

Co. 1957-58; honors: Nat. Honor Soc. 1925; Member of Year, Unitarian-Universalist Ch., San Mateo 1977; mem: Am. Soc. for Pub. Admin. (past), Western Govtl. Research Assn. (past), Nat. Assn. of Intergroup Rels. Offcls. (past), Am. Assn. of Ret. Persons, Internat. Platform Assn., Mid-Peninsula Council for Civic Unity (pres. 1959-60), Bi-County (San Mateo- Santa Clara) Comm. on Human Relations, Intergroup Rels. Assn. of No. Calif.; works: ed., creator, Lou Jones Newsletter 1959-70; Unitarian- Universalist (trustee 1958); rec: music (piano), photog. Res: 511 Verano Ct. San Mateo 94402

JONES, NAPOLEON A., JR., judge; b. Aug. 25, 1940, Hodge, La.; s. Napoleon A., Sr. and Lillie Burdette (Taylor) J.; 1 dau. Lena Laini b. 1972; edn: AB social welfare, CSU San Diego 1962, MA 1967, JD 1971. Career: staff atty. Calif. Rural Legal Assistance, Modesto 1972-73, Office of Defender Services, San Diego 1973-75; atty. pvt. practice, Jones & Adler, S.D. 1975-77; judge San Diego Municipal Ct., 1977-82, Superior Ct. Judge, State of Calif., 1982–, presiding judge San Diego Juvenile Ct.; apptd: S.D. Integration Task Force (1980), faculty Continuing Judicial Studies Pgm., Indigent Defense Police Bd.; awards: USF Law Rev. (1970-71), Kappa Alpha Psi frat., Varsity Wrestling Team; Minority Group Scholar (1968-71), Grantt-Richardson Award, Book Award for achieve. in labor Law (1971) Univ. of San Diego, Regional Herber-Smith Fellow (1971-73), USF Sch. of Law disting. alumni (1981), S.D. Trial Lawyers Assn. Municipal Ct. Judge of Year (1981), spl. commendn. S.D. City Council (1982), NAACP disting. svc. (1984), Earl B. Gilliam Bar Assn. Thurgood Marshall Award (1984); mem. Calif. Judges Assn. (Criminal law and Procedures Com.), Calif. and S.D. Black Attys. Assn., USD bd. vis., bd. mem. SE Criminal Justice Coalition, bd. Grad. Sch. for Comm. Devel., S.D. Urban League, Sigma Pi Phi, Kappa Alpoha Psi; coauthor chpt. 17, Calif. Criminal Procedure Handbook, contbr. articles in law revs. Ofc: 2851 Meadow Lark Dr San Diego 92123

JONES, PROCTOR PATTERSON, diplomat, Honorary Vice Dean, San Francisco Consular Corps; b. May 25, 1916, Cleveland, Oh.; s. John Beverly and Ferne (Patterson) J.; desc. William Whipple, signer Declaration of Independence; desc. of the family de Savignac who settled Detroit in 1701 with Cadillac; desc. John Jones, first English-born child in Montreal (1760); m. Martha Martin, Nov. 29, 1947; children: John, Martha, Proctor Jr., Jessica, Melinda, Greta; edn: AB, Western Reserve Univ. 1937, LLB, JD, 1948; grad. wk. Harvard and Stanford Univs., 1949. Reg. with US Treasury Dept., admitted to practice US Tax Ct., 1951, US Supreme Ct., 1965. Career: owner, mgr. Summer Theatre, Cedarhurst, Long Is.; tchr. Western Reserve Univ., Cleveland Coll., 1947; exec. dir. Experiment in Internat. Living, 1949; tax counsel, Redwood City, Ca. 1951-52; adv. dept. S.F. Newspaper Agcy., 1953; legal ed. Bancroft Whitney Publ. Co., S.F. 1954-59; owner Proctor Jones Photog. Studio, S.F. 1959-77; hon. consul general of Tunisia, 1977–; bd. chmn. Proctor Patterson Jones-Ferne Beverly Ford Found.; awards: num. profl. photography awards, DFA (hon.), Baldwin-Wallace Coll. 1976; One of 50 Outstanding Californians, 1951, Fortnight Mag.; mem. bd. dirs. French-Am. Bilingual Sch.; bd. Seadrift Prop. Owners Assn.; past pres. Presidio Hts. Assn. of Neighbors 1976; mem. Republican State Central Com. 1949-52; past mem. Young Republicans of Calif. (treas.; pres. San Mateo Co. chpt.); bd. dirs. Stinson Beach Co. Water Bd.; bd. dirs. Calif. Water, Transit & Defense Proj. 1952; mem: SF Opera, SF Symphony, The Book Club of Calif.; clubs: Bohemian, Union (Cleveland), St. Francis Yacht; author: Ransom of the Golden Bridge (1983), Idylls of France (1982), Classic Russian Idylls (1985); mil: capt. USAF 1941-46, Spl. Svcs. Div. War Dept. Staff WWII; Democrat (Nat. Fin. Com.); Episcopal; rec: collect travel materials. Res: 330 Seadrift Rd Stinson Beach 94970 Ofc: Consulate General of Tunisia, 3401 Sacramento St, San Francisco 94118

JONES, ROBERT RICHARD, consultant; b. Sept. 13, 1925, Canton, Oh.; s. Robert Hall and Clara (Channell) J.; div.; children: Melinda Lou b. 1953, Christopher b. 1955; edn: BA, UCLA 1951; MA, NY Univ. 1962; postgrad. wk. Univ. of Pa. Wharton Sch. of Bus. 1974; PhD Cand., Golden Gate Univ. 1979-; Ga. State Univ. Sch. of Ins. 1966; CLU, Chartered Life Underwriter, Am. Coll. 1978. Career: info. ofcr. US Dept. of State, news corres. Voice of Am., NYC, 1950-53; nat. mgr. mktg. NY Life Ins. Co., NYC 1953-66; asst. v.p. and pres. Fla. Growth Fund, Gulf Life Ins. Co., Jacksonville, Fla. 1966-69; asst. v.p. Aetna Variable Annuity Life in Wash. DC, Hartford, Conn., 1969-72; dir. specialized mktg. Hartford Variable Annuity Life, Hartford Ins. Gp. (subs. ITT), Hartford, Conn. 1972-78, planned, devel. internat. ops. 1975; cons. Robert R. Jones and Assocs., San Francisco, Burlingame 1978–, splst. in devel. of life and health sales through property-casualty firms; senior cons. to SRI Intl., Finl. Industries Center, Intl. Mgmt. & Econs. Gp.; expert testimony in life/health ins. litigation Tech. Advsry. Service for Attys. (TASA), 1980-; adj. faculty Finl. Plnng., SFO State Univ. (1986); finl. plnng. advsy. bd. Golden Gate Univ. (1986); acad. honors: J.N. Flint, and NBC Radio Scholarships, UCLA, 1949, 1950; Ednl. Theater Awd., UCLA, 1950; TKA (forensics hon.), Phi Mu Alpha Sinfonia (profl. music hon.), Debate and Oratory Champion, 1946-7, Ohio State Oratory, 3d Pl. 1946; mem: NY Univ. Alumni Assn. (pres. 1964), Wharton Club, Parents Without Partners (intl. pres. 1961), UCLA Alumni Assn, NY (pres. 1965), Old First Concerts, SF (dir. 1983-85), Internat. Assn. for Finl. Plnng., SF (pres. 1984-85, chmn. 1985-86; Disting. Svc. Award 1984, Leadership Award 1985), Peninsula Chpt. Am. Soc. of CLUs (pres. 1986-87), Nat. Assn. Life Underws.; mil: Communications Div. AFRS 1943-46, Am. Cpgn., Victory, Euro- Middle Eastern and African Cpgn. medals; rec: pvt. pilot, Jaguar XKE. Address: POB 489 Burlingame 94011

JONES, RON L., office furniture mfg. co. president; b. Sept. 6, 1942, Joplin, Mo.; s. Melvin Levine and Mary Belle (Hackler) J.; m. Nancy Young, June 2, 1962; children: Ron Jr., Valori Lee, Jennifer Lee, Matthew; edn: BA, Central Methodist Coll. 1972. Career: gen. mgr. Ithaca Gun Co., 1974-78; exec. v.p. Chisum Industries, 1978-79; gen. mgr. Material Handling Div./ Beverage Container Div., Hoover Universal, 1979-83; pres. The Hon Co., Muscatine, Iowa 1983–; dir. Booth, Inc., Dallas 1983-; cons. var. beverage industry related cos.; civic: Four Rivers Comprehensive Health Care Council (dir.), University Extension Council (pres.), Kiwanis Club (pres.); publs: Industrial Safety for Mid-Sized Companies; article, Performance Appraisals for Hosp. Administrators; Republican; Ch. of Jesus Christ of Latter-day Saints (high priest). Address: South Gate 90280

JONES, ROY STEVEN, printing management executive; b. Dec. 22, 1944, Weston, W.Va.; s. Lloyd Hall and Ethel Marie (Flinn) J.; m. Rebecca Piercy, Apr. 26, 1964; children: Stephanie b. 1964, Allyson b. 1965; edn: AA, Santa Barbara City Coll. 1970; BA, UC Santa Barbara 1973; Calif. DOE Vocational Tchg. Cred. Career: hwy. insp. techn. W.Va. State Road Commn., 1964-66; shipping clk. Automated Bus. Forms Inc., Goleta 1966-67, collator opr. 1967-69, pressman 1969-72, prodn. mgr. 1972-78, plant mgr./owner 1979–; bd. chmn. Entrepreneur Funding (1985-), dir./treas. Solar Gate Inc. (1985-), dir. Instant Printing SBCC (1983-85); voc. instr. in public schs. 1976-80; honors: Goleta Good Guy award Goleta CofC (1985); mem. Goleta Valley CofC (pres. 1983-4, 86), founder/pres. Center for Santa Barbara Small Bus. Devel.; clubs: Channel City, Montecito Country; Democrat; Baptist; rec: philately, golf. Res: 6171 Verdura Ave Goleta 93117 Ofc: Automated Business Forms Inc 137 Aero Camino Goleta 93117

JONES, THOMAS FRANK, family holding co. executive; b. June 25, 1937, Los Angles; s. Frank Kemon and Cordelia Esther (Renard) J.; m. Louise Annette Agee, June 19, 1964; children: Suzanne b. 1976, Kevin b. 1978, Jeffrey b. 1981; edn: BS, CalPoly Pomona 1959; MBA, UC Los Angeles Grad. Sch. of Mgmt. 1964; MA, Claremont Grad. Sch. 1983, PhD in exec. mgmt. 1986. Career: mgmt. trainee/ plant engr. GT&E, Santa Monica 1965-67; founding ptnr. Rodriguez, Jones & Co., Anaheim 1967–; pres. and dir., LNS Corp., New Orleans, La. 1982–; founder/bd. chmn. Jonescorp, Pasadena 1985–; dir. Betty Zane Corp. (1982-85); civic: reserve ofcr., cons. L.A. Co. Sheriff's Mgmt. Projects Div.; dir: Ch. of Our Savior Endowment Fund, San Gabriel (1983-), Pasadena Library Found. (1986-), Claremont Grad. Sch. Corporate Roundtable (1982); mem. bd. of fellows Claremont Univ. Ctr. & Grad. Sch., Caltech Ad Hoc Com. on Bus., Econs. and Mgmt. (1985), Dean's Council of the Jacoby Assocs.- UCLA Grad. Sch. Mgmt., UCLA Chancellor's Assoc., United Way San Gabriel Valley (co-chmn. Major Gifts 1981), L.A. Music Ctr. (founder), Huntington Library (Fellow 1978-), Cal Tech Pres.'s Circle Assoc.; clubs: Regency, Jonathan, San Gabriel CC, University (Pasa.); PhD dissertation: An Exploration of Owner-Founder Mgmt. Practices; mil: US Army 1960-62, ETO; Republican; Episcopal; rec: classic autos, golf. Ofc: 440 Wells Fargo Bank Bldg 350 West Colorado Blvd Pasadena 91105

JONES, WYMAN, city librarian; b. Dec. 17, 1929, St. Louis, Mo.; s. Jay Hugh and Nina Marie (Dallas) J.; sons: Gregory Foster, Mark Jay, Manson Matthew, Ross Christopher; edn: BA, Adams State Coll. 1956; MLS, Univ. Tex. 1958. Career: chief sci. & industry dept. Dallas Public Library 1958-59; chief of Branches 1956-64; dir. Ft. Worth City/ County Public Lib. Sys. 1964-70; dir. Los Angeles Public Library System, 1970–; library building & system planning cons. 1963-; mem: Am., Calif. Library Assns.; author: (with E. Castagna) The Library Reaches Out (1964); publs: monthly column in Library Journal 1964), arts. in profl. pubs.; mil: USAF 1951-55. Res: Promenade West, 880 W First St Los Angeles 90012 Ofc: Los Angeles Public Library, 630 W Fifth St Los Angeles 90071

JORDAN, DANIEL ARTHUR, real estate developer; b. Mar. 18, 1956, Fresno; s. Philip Anselm and Marion Leona (Durman) J.; edn: BS, Calif. Lutheran Univ. 1978; MBA, USC 1981; Calif. lic. real estate broker. Career: senior sales assoc. Brown/Realtor, Thousand Oaks 1978-82; v.p. TB & A Devel. Co., Los Angeles 1982-84; pres. Auto Spectrum Inc., L.A. 1985–, Jordan Ents., Inc. 1985–, ptnr. Jordan Eisen Industries 1985–; bd. dirs. Poipu Kai Resorts (Kauai, HI), Stonebridge (Deer Valley, Utah); honors: Alpha Mu Gamma, Calif. Scholarship Fedn. (Life), Who's Who Among Am. Univ. & Coll. Students (1978), Million Dollar Cir., Nat. Assn. of Homebuilders; mem: Nat., Calif. Assn. Realtors, Los Angeles Bd. Realtors, Fresno Bd. Realtors, USC Career Services (dir.), USC Real Estate Assn.; Republican; Lutheran; rec: ski, mt. climbing, tennis. Res: 2408 Moreno Dr Los Angeles 90039 Ofc: Jordan Eisen Industries 1520 Wilshire Blvd 5th Flr Los Angeles 90017

JORDAN, RACHEL PHYLLIS, architect; b. Dec. 16, 1945, Chicago, Ill.; d. Robert Efram and Belle Lavina (Hoy) J.; 1 dau. Camille b. 1967; edn: B.Arch., Univ. of Ill. 1974; M.Arch., Univ. of Utah 1976. Career: draftsperson Skidmore, Owings & Merrill, Chicago, Ill. 1968-74; project mgr., job capt. Architects- Planners Alliance, Salt Lake City, Utah 1978-79; project mgr., designer Dolven, Larson & Daniels, Reno, Nevada 1979-80; project mgr. Whisler-Patri, San Francisco 1980-82; prin. San Francisco Design Resource Ctr., San Francisco 1982–; honors: Tchg. Fellowship, Univ. of Utah 1974; Graham Found. Grant for Undergrad. Thesis Proposal and Devel.; mem. Am. Inst. Architects; Democrat; rec: drawing, computer programming, photog. Ofc: Design Resource Center, 973 Mission St. San Francisco 94110

JORDAN, ROBERT FREDERICK, certified public accountant, ret.; b. Mar. 16, 1916, Brockton, Mass.; s. John Francis and Annie Frances (Creed) J.; m. Helen C. Killory, July 2, 1941; children: Barbara (Haupt) b. 1944, Robert F., Jr. b. 1947, Margaret (Budd) b. 1951, Peter M. b. 1953; edn: BA, Bentley Coll.,

Boston 1939; CPA, Calif. (#2723, 1948). Career: chief Fiscal Div. Fed. Nat. Mortgage Co., 1946-50; controller First Fed. Svgs & Loan, Altadena 1950-57; senior ptnr. Jordan, Hebert & Co., CPAs 1957-74; ptnr. Alexander Grant & Co., CPAs 1974-76, ret.; dir: Consyne Corp. (ASE), Republic Fed. Svgs., Westwood Svgs & Loan, Glendora Country Club, El Niguel Country Club; instr. Savings & Loan Inst.; mem. Soc. of Svgs. & Loan Controllers/L.A. (past pres.), Am. Inst. CPAs, Calif. Soc. CPAs; fmr. mem. Exchange Club, Rotary; founder El Niguel Country Club (1976), founder Palm Beach Park Home-owners Assn. (1979); mil: USNR, WWII; rec: golf. Res: 206 Breaker Dr San Clemente 92672 Ofc: Niguel Investment 2738 Camino Capistrano Ste 1 San Clemente 92672

JORDAN, WILBERT CORNELIOUS, physician; b. Sept. 11, 1944, Wheatley, Ark.; s. William and Annie Mae (Tolson) J.; edn: AB, Harvard 1966; MD, Case Western Reserve 1971; MPH, UCLA 1978. Career: physician, Govt. of India, World Health Orgn. Smallpox Eradication Pgm. 1973-74; assoc. epidemiologist, Dist. of Columbia 1973-76; pub. health chief, South area, Los Angeles County, 1977-80; actg. chmn. Dept. of Community Med., Charles R. Drew Postgrad. Med. Sch. 1978-80; practitioner, infectious disease, Los Angeles; assoc. prof. Chas Drew Med. Sch.; asst. prof. UCLA; UCLA Med. Sch. Admissions Com.; dir. ofc. of quality assurance, Martin Luther King Gen. Hosp. 1977—; mem: Nat. Med. Assn.; Assn. of Am. Med. Colls.; Am. Pub. Health Assn.; Am. Coll. of Physicians; NAACP; publs: sev. arts. on infectious diseases; mil: USPHS 1973-76; Democrat; Baptist; rec: jogging, gospel music, jazz. Res: 2380 Venus Dr Los Angeles 90046 Ofc: 3200 S Susana Rd, Ste 304, Compton 90221

JORSS, EMMA BARBARA, university president; b. Odessa, Russia; foster dau. Jacob and Wilhelmina Bauman; m. Harry Charles Jorss, 1932; 1 dau. Margaret; edn: stu. Dakota Wesleyan Coll., 1930-31, UC Berkeley 1931-32, USC 1932-37, Univ. Omaha 1964-65; JD, Lincoln Univ. 1950. Career: mgr. Eversharp Inc., San Francisco 1939-45; bus. mgr. YWCA, San Francisco 1945-53; exec. vice pres. Lincoln Univ., S.F. 1953-78, pres. 1978-83, pres. emeritus, 1983—, bd. trustees, 1953-80, founding mem., dir. Lincoln Univ. Found., founder Lincoln Univ. Law Sch., Sacramento; referee, public mem. State Bar Court 1985; mem. Nat. Assn. Higher Edn., AAUP, Commonwealth Club; exec. prod. cable TV series This Is Your Law (1974); Republican; Episcopal. Address: 281 Masonic Ave., San Francisco 94118

JOSEPH, JEFFREY ALAN, lawyer; b. Aug. 3, 1947, Chgo.; s. Bryan Kenneth and Carol Maxine (Jackson) J.; m. Valerie Pearson, Sept. 12, 1981; edn: AB in hist., UC Berkeley 1969; JD, UC Davis 1972; admitted to Calif. State Bar 1972. Career: deputy atty. general, Criminal Div., Office of Atty. General, State of Calif., 1972-78, principal atty. Spl. Prosecutions Unit, 1978-79; atty., Calif. State Dept. of Transp., 1979—; honors: capt. UCD State Moot Court Team (1st Pl. and Best Brief, 1971 Roger Traynor Competition), mem. UCD Nat. Moot Ct. Team (3d Pl. and Best Brief, 1971 Western Regionals); Outstanding Young Man of Year 1979, U.S. Jaycees; arbitrator (Personal Injury), San Diego Superior Ct. Arbitration Pgm.; mem. Calif. State Bar Com. on Jury Instructions 1978; mem: Assn. of Calif. State Attys. (bd. dirs., collective bargaining rep. 1982-3), Assn. of San Diego Deputy Attys. General (pres. 1976, 1979); UC Davis Law Sch. Alumni Assn. (bd. dirs. 1973-7); mem. S.D. Hist. Soc., S.D. Zool. Soc., S.D. Public Radio and TV; Democrat; Catholic; rec: bass player/ singer. Res: 4018 Mt. Barnard Ave. San Diego 92111 Ofc: 110 West C St, Ste. 1502, San Diego 92101

JOYCE, STEPHEN MICHAEL, lawyer; b. Mar. 19, 1945, Los Angeles; s. John Rowland and Elizabeth Rose (Rahe) J.; m. Bernadette, Aug. 18, 1973; children: Natalie b. 1982, Vanessa b. 1983; edn: BS, CSU Los Angeles 1970; JD, Univ. San Fernando Valley 1976; admitted to Calif. State Bar 1976, US Ct. of Claims 1981. Career: atty., Beverly Hills 1976—; bd. dirs. Safety Edn. Treatment Ctr., San Fernando Valley; mem: Los Angeles Trial Lawyers Assn.; Calabasas Racquetball Club; Calabasas Athletic Club; Appeals pub. Joyce v. U.S. (2 Ct. Cl. 226, 1983), Rolon v. Kulwitzky (153 Cal. App. 3d 288, 200 Cal. Rptr. 217, 1984); mil: pvt. US Army; Democrat; Catholic; rec: running, racquetball, golf, fishing. Res: 4724 Barcelona Ct Calabasas Park 90302 Ofc: 241 S Beverly Dr Beverly Hills 90212

JOYCE, THOMAS THEODORE, lawyer, real estate co. executive; b. Aug. 16, 1940, Pasadena; s. Howard Theodore and Leonora Mary (Pridham) J.; m. Diane Coover, Sept. 27, 1957; chldren: Christopher b. 1958, Patrick b. 1960, Kimberly b. 1962, Julie Ann b. 1964, Elizabeth b. 1966; edn: AA, Pasadena City Coll. 1964; BBA, Univ. of Wisc. 1966; JD, Blackstone Sch. of Lab 1969; LLB, 1986. Career: pres., Joyce's Market 1960-71, v.p. mgmt. 1971—; bd. chmn. Tom Joyce Investments 1975-; pres. A.A. Recreation Inc., Cabo San Lucas, Mex. 1980-; estab. Tom Joyce Realty 1982; chmn. Old Fashion Days Parade & Community Bicentennial; Project Area Com., West Altadena Redevel.; chmn. Kite Day U.S.A., Pasadena Centennial Com. 1986; exec. secty. Pasadena City Coll. Found. 1985; dist. gov. Junipero Serra Internat. 1985; honors: Calif. Scholarship Fedn. 1966-68; All C.I.F. Football Left Tackle 1965; No. One Sales Nat. Top Producer 1973, 1974; Youth Opportunity Award, Indsl. Assocs. 1974; Outstanding Young Men of Am. 1975; Outstanding Citizen of the Year, Altadena; mem: Altadena CofC (pres. 83), Pasadena CofC), Pasadena Bd. Realtors, Pasadena Exch. Club (pres. 1976), Knights of Columbus, Pasadena Serra Club (pres. 1977), United Service Clubs Ofcr. Assn. (pres. 1978), Tournament of Roses Assn., Elks, Capistrano Surf Side Inn, Good Sam R.V. Club, Navy League; publs: ed., Junipero Serra's Camino Real, 1981; ed., Guide to Recreation Vehicle Enjoyment, 1980; How to Leave your Employer Creatively, 1985; Tom Joyce the Jury's Choice, 1986; Re Joyce, 1986; mil: USCG 1960; Republi-

can (Central Com.); Catholic; rec: fishing, scuba, video taping. Res: 1045 E. New York Dr. Altadena 91001 Ofc: Tom Joyce Realty, 1530 No. Lake Ave. Pasadena 91104

JOYNER, CRANDON NEIL, chiropractor; b. Dec. 20, 1954, Anchorage, Alaska; s. Clifford Mervyn and Karma Leoan (Fickes) J.; m. Carmen Abigail Pineda, Nov. 11, 1976; children: Jennifer b. 1977, Jamie b. 1978, Jonathan b. 1980, Jared b. 1981, Jazmine, b. 1984; edn: undergrad. Brigham Young Univ. 1972-3, 1977-8; DC, cum laude, Life Chiropractic Coll. 1982; lic. Chiropractor, Calif. 1983, Ga. 1983. Career: missionary for Mormon Ch. in Mexico 1976-79; restaurant mgr. Pipes & Pizza, Provo, Ut., 1976-79, and Mauldins Pizza, Marietta, Ga., 1980-82; assoc. doctor Wright Chiropractic Clinic, Rocklin, Calif. 1983; prin. Alta Sierra Chiropractic Office, Citrus Heights 1983—, opened 2d. ofc., So. Sacramento 1985—; recipient Outstanding Service to Family & Chiropractic Award, Life Chiro. Coll. 1982; mem: Placer County Concilio (pres. 1985), Rocklin Area CofC (bd. 1983-4, secty. 1984), Rotarian; Ch. of Jesus Christ of LDS; rec: all sports. Res: 2041 Swetzer Rd. Penryn 95663 Ofc: Alta Sierra Chiropractic, 8224 Auburn Blvd Citrus Hts 95610 and 27315 Stockton Blvd Sacramento 95823

JU, CHANG D., real estate broker; b. Apr. 10, 1931, Jung Ju, N. Korea; d. Byung S. and Chung M. Chu; m. Jung Ju, Apr. 16, 1972; children: Jay b. 1961, David b. 1963, Anne b. 1969; edn: USMC Supply Ofcr's Sch., Camp Lejeune 1960; engring. Catonsville Comm. Coll. 1968; BS acctg., Woodbury Univ. 1973; real estate broker, Anthony Sch. 1974; desig: realtor. Career: supply ofcr. Korean Marine Corps, 1955-64; realtor assoc. Red Carpet, Los Angeles 1974; v.p. Royal World Inc. 1974-76; realtor/pres. Happy Realty and Investment Co., L.A. 1976—; honors: academic honor award Korea Minister of Defense, appreciation, Prime Minister Rep. of Korea, pres. Korean Amateur Sports Assn.; mem: Nat. Bd. of Realtors, L.A. Bd. of Realtors, Korean Marine Corps Vets. Assn. (dir.), Korean Vets. Assn. (v.p.); mil: capt. Korean Marine Corps, num. decorations; Republican; Presbyterian (steward Chung Hyun Mission Ch.); rec: sports, golf. Res: 2615 N Commonwealth Ave Los Angeles 90027 Ofc: Happy Realty and Investment Co 2978 Wilshire Blvd Ste 303 Los Angeles 90010

JUAREZ, REINA MARIA, clinical psychologist; b. Jan. 6, 1956, Managua, Nicaragua; d. Jorge Alfredo and Zela Esperanza (Navarrete) J.; edn: BA, UCLA 1977; MA, Calif. Sch. of Profl. Psychology 1980, PhD, 1982. Career: asst. dir. Los Angeles Co. Dept. of Mental Health, Roybal Family Mental Health 1981—; clin. psychologist Cedars Sinai Community Mental Health Ctr. 1985—; Mental Health Adv. Bd.; research; media presentations; CSPP Alumni founding member; mem. Am. Psychological Assn.; publs. in Journ. of Psychotherapy 1985; rec: Nautilus, scuba diving, hiking, French literature.

JULIAN, ROBERT DENNIS, mortgage loan broker; b. Mar. 1, 1939, San Francisco; s. John Meredith and Ethel May (Butler) J.; m. Susan, May 17, 1958; children: Stuart b. 1959, Brian b. 1960, Theresa b. 1961, Sean b. 1976, Kevin b. 1978; edn: Coll. of San Mateo 1962-63, Columbia Coll. 1981, Modesto Jr. Coll. 1983; var. certs. Sears Tng. Inst. 1960-75; Calif. lic. real estate broker (1984). Career: mgmt. trainee Sears, Roebuck & Co., 1958-76; s/s clk. Hales and Symons Inc. 1976-77; loan ofcr. Calif. Housing Securities 1977-80; loan ofcr. Key Real Estate Loans Inc., Sonora 1981-82, pres./broker 1983—; mem. Nat. Assn. Realtors, Calif. Assn. Realtors, Tuolumne County Bd. Realtors; civic: Couple to Couple League (w/wife tch. natural family planning), Toastmasters Internat., Parent Faculty Club (pres.), Cubscouts Master, Worldwide Marriage Encounter (w/wife dist. scheduling coords.) marriage prep. instrs., St. Patrick's Catholic Ch. (choir dir. 1976-80, pres. Parish Council 1977); Republican; rec: music, woodworking, drawing portraits. Res: 20383 Brook Dr Sonora 95370 Ofc: Key Real Estate Loans Inc 2107A Mono Way Sonora 95370

JULIUS, JAY ROBERT, physician; b. Apr. 3, 1937, NY, NY; s. Abraham Juris and Betty (Friedman) J.; m. Ulla, Dec. 14, 1976; children: Ami b. 1962, James b. 1966, Erik b. 1981, David b. 1983; edn: BA history, Univ. of Vermont 1958; MD, Univ. Louisville Sch. of Med. 1962. Career: intern Univ. Louisville Hosp. 1962-63; resident in med. Seton Hall Coll. of Med. 1963-65; fellow in med. Univ. Ill. Hosp. 1965-66; pvt. practice int. med. San Leandro 1968—; asst. clin. prof. med. UC San Francisco; chief-of-staff Vesper Meml. Hosp. 1975-76; pres.-elect Meml. Hosp. of San Leandro 1985; Interamerican fellow Tropical Med. Louisiana State Univ. 1961; mem: CMA, Am. Soc. Tropical Med., Am. Soc. Internal Med., Alameda Co. Med. Assn.; mil: lt. USN (MC) 1966-68; Republican; Jewish; rec: photog. Res: 140 Estates Dr Piedmont 94611 Ofc: Jay R. Julius MD Inc. 237 Estudillo Ave San Leandro 94577

JULIUS, JOHN LOY, dentist; b. Oct. 24, 1945, Iowa City, Ia.; s. Loy Luvern and Louise Anne (Stedeford) J.; m. Linda, June 25, 1977; edn: undergrad. USAF Acad. 1963-65; BS, Univ. Iowa 1967; MA, Marycrest Coll. 1972; DDS, Creighton Univ. 1979. Career: high sch. tchr. and coach, Moline, Ill. 1967-74; dental ofcr. US Air Force Dental Corps 1979-85, chief of prosthetic dentistry USAF Hosp. Castle AFB, Calif. 1984-85; dentist pvt. practice, Merced 1985—; tchg. staff dental asst. pgm., Merced Comm. Coll. 1981-; honors: 6-sport high sch. letterman All-State football, swimming, class pres. dental sch. 4 years (1975-79), Alpha Sigma Nu; mem. Am. Dental Assn.; mil: maj. USAF Dental Corps 1979-85, Res. 1985-, AF Commendn. Medal; Protestant; rec: tennis, golf, triathlons. Res: 3434 Wathen Ave Merced 95348 Ofc: 3071 College Green Dr Merced 95348

JUNCHEN, DAVID LAWRENCE, pipe organ builder; b. Feb. 23, 1946, Rock Island, Ill.; s. Lawrence Ernest and Lucy Mae (Ditto) J.; edn: BSEE, highest honors, Univ. of Ill. 1968. Career: founder/ owner Junchen-Collins Organ Corp., Woodstock, Ill. 1975-80; mng. dir. Baranger Studios, South Pasadena 1980-81; contbr. Ency. of Automatic Musical Instruments; awards: key to City of Rock Island, Ill. 1957; Outstanding Freshman in Engring., Univ. of Ill. 1963; mem: Am. Inst. of Organbldrs.; Am. Theatre Organ Soc.; Musical Box Soc.; Automatic Musical Instrument Collectors Assn.; Tau Beta Pi; Eta Kappa Nu; composer/ arranger over 100 music rolls for automatic musical instruments; author: Encyclopedia of Am. Theatre Organs, 1985. Address: 280 E. Del Mar, Ste 311, Pasadena 91101

JUNG, JACK J., manufacturing co. executive; b. July 9, 1937, Freeport, NY; s. Jacob and Margaret Ester (Danielson) J.; m. Joyce, Aug. 7, 1965; children: Steven b. 1967, Stacy b. 1971; edn: BSEE, Univ. Fla. 1960. Career: design engr. Calbest Electronics Co. L.A. 1964-65, Airesearch Mfg. Co. Torrance 1964-65; field sales engr. Hewlett Packard Co. No. Hollywood 1965-69, computer sys. 1969-72, dist. sales mgr. 1972-75, regl. sales mgr. calculator prods. 1975-79, area computer mgr. Lawndale 1979-84, gen. mgr. southwest area Fullerton 1984–; adv. bd. Am. Microwave Systems; mem: So. Cal. Ten (exec. orgn.) 1984-; honors: Top Salesman (worldwide, Hewlett Packard 1971), Spl. Recogn. (Toastmasters Internat. 1985), Outstanging Svc. (H.P. Customer Orgn. 1982); mem: IEEE 1966, Jr. Achievement, Little League; mil: USAR 1960; Republican; Lutheran; rec: music (play piano), sports, golf, running. Res: 18151 Vintage St Northridge 91325 Ofc: Hewlett Packard 1421 S Manhatten Ave Fullerton 92631

JUNG, JIMMIE D., insurance broker, real estate broker; b. Aug. 26, 1926, Canton, China; s. Frank N.Q. and N. Y. (Der) J.; m. Pauline Foy, Nov. 19, 1951; children: Paula b. 1952, Roberta b. 1955; edn: BS, USC 1951; Gen. & Life Ins. Broker, Real Estate Broker, Calif. 1951. Career: chmn. bd., pres. Dynasty World Corp., Los Angeles 1963–; gen. and life ins. broker; real estate broker; honors: Pres.'s Club Award, Security Life of Denver 1962; 25 yrs. Distng. Svc. Award 1979; Chinese Am. Citizen Alliance Honor Award, 1960; mem: Lions, Masons, Internat. Footprint Assn., Optimist, Ind. Ins. Assn. of Calif., Nat. Notary Assn., Chinese Consolidated Benevolent Assn., Lung Kong 4 Family Assn., Lung Kong World Fedn., Lung Kong Pan Am. Fedn., Chinese Am. Citizen Alliance (pres.); mil: motor machinists mate 3/c USN 1944-46; Republican; Presbyterian; rec: shooting, huntng. Res: 2387 W. Silverlake Dr. Los Angeles 90039 Ofc: Dynasty World Corp., 1011 No. Broadway Ste. 201 Los Angeles 90012

JUNOD, DAVID HENRY, landscape designer/contractor; b. Jan. 7, 1939, Mnpls.; s. David Louis and Valerie Mae (Durand) J.; m. Maria Guadalupe, May 28, 1983; children: Kim b. 1960, Mark b. 1962, Darla b. 1966, Dane b. 1968, Brandy b. 1975; edn: Glendale Coll., Pierce Coll., CSU Los Angeles, CSU Northridge; Calif. lic. lndscp. contr. 1982; Calif. Certified Nurseryman (#37). Career: empl. Sheridan Gardens Nursery, Inc. 1959-, ptnr./v.p. 1970-82, founding ptnr./pres. Sheridan Landscaping, Inc. 1982–; instr. Polytechnic High Sch. Sun Valley 2 yrs.; guest lectr. to garden clubs, womens clubs, civic gps.; served on organizing com. to estab. Calif. Certified Nurseryman Pgm. (pgm. now has been instituted in 10 other states); mem: Calif. Assn. of Nurserymen/ San Fernando Valley Chpt. (dir. and ofcr. 1968-73, pres. 1974-76), Calif. Landscape Contractors Assn./SFV Chpt. (bd. dirs. 1979-, pres. 1986-); Republican; Rel. Sci.; rec: scuba, stamps, 1930 Model A Ford. Address: Sheridan Landscaping Inc 8714 Glenoaks Blvd Sun Valley 91352-2895

JUSTUS, ADALU, designer, writer, lecturer; b. Aug. 5, 1928, Lawrenceville, Ill.; d. Edward G. and Zerma E. (Johnston); m. Gary H. Justus, Jan. 8, 1974; children: Rick b. 1948, Marlene b. 1950, Jeff b. 1952, Jamie b. 1954, Melinda b. 1955, Brett b. 1968. Dip. in custom-fitting, Symbra-Ette. Career: designer of custom undergarments, brassieres, etc.; original pattern maker, prototypes in custom-bra and prosthesis field; opr. lic. Child-Care Center, 1968-73; owner The Elegante Lady, Hesperia 1973 –: direct sales Symbra-Ette (Calif.), 1974–, held tng. seminars 1977; designer undergarments (2 patent appls.) incl. strapless bra for large sizes and exclusive side-hook design bra, and direct sales, Command Performance (mfg. co. Waco, Tex.) 1977–; free-lance writer, author book for women on Self-Image; other publs: In the Shadow of Death (1960), Body & Soul (TV screenplay 1963), Mommy, Please Don't Kill Me (1983), You Are Elegant in God's Sight (1984), Generation Faith (play 1985), My Son, My Mother (book co-authored w. Ira James Marlin 1985); instr. Breast Clinic, Victor Valley Hosp., instr. classes for nurses in breast self-exam., V.V. Hosp., St. Mary's of the Desert (Apple Valley); Am. BSE instr., Mastectomy Adv. V.V. Br. American Cancer Soc.; respons. for obtaining grant from the Irvine Found. to estab. blood donor center for Hemophilia Found. in Orange Co.; counselor to approx. 15,000 women and husbands re mastectomies; designer custom undergarment patterns for Bjene' Inc. 1985; honors incl. Miss America Pageant Award (1978, 79), recognition from num. civic orgns. as speaker for Hemophilia Found.; mem: ASTM, Hesperia CofC, Hemophilia Guild (bd. mem. L.A. 1967-71; pres. O.C. chpt. 1969-71), Am. Cancer Soc., founder Victor Valley Women Against Abortion; Republican; Presbyterian; rec: doll clothes patterns, 7 grandchildren. Address: The Elegante Lady, 18019 Danbury Ave Hesperia 92345

KADAR, ANDREW GABOR, physician; b. July 25, 1948, Budapest, Hungary, nat. 1964; s. Nicholas Miklos and Magda (Izsak) K.; m. Christine Gregory, Jan. 9, 1984; 1 son: Kenneth b. 1984; edn: BS, magna cum laude, UCLA 1969; MD, Yale Univ. 1973; bd. certified in anesthesiology 1979. Career: surgical res. UC San Diego 1974; anesthesia resident Stanford Univ. 1975, Harvard Univ. 1976;

attending physician Cedars-Sinai Medical Center, Los Angeles 1976–, chmn. Edn. Com., CSMC Dept. Anesthesiology; clin. instr. in anesth. UCLA Sch. of Medicine, 1978-; owner Fantasy Travel Co. (tour opr. spec. in trips to the Orient); honors: Phi Beta Kappa (1968), Physics Honor Soc. (1967), 3-year varsity letterman in gymnastics (1966-69); mem: Calif. Med. Assn., Am. Soc. of Anesthesiologists, Calif. Soc. of Anes., L.A. County Soc. of Anes., Sierra Club; publs: Pediatrics 51:36-43 (1973), Gymnast 9:21 (1967); Democrat. Res: 10535 Wilshire Blvd Ste 807 Los Angeles 90024 Ofc: Cedars-Sinai Medical Center 8700 Beverly Blvd Los Angeles 90048

KADAU, ROBERT LANE, engineer; b. Feb. 11, 1922, Long Beach; s. Carl J. and Elma L. (Lane) K.; 1 dau. Patricia (Mrs. Henry R. Dressendorfer, III); edn: AA, Fullerton Coll. 1942; BS engring., US Merchant Marine Acad., Kings Point, NY; MBA, USC 1962; Reg. Profl. Engr. (indsl.), Calif. (1959). Career: plant engr. U.S. Steel, Torrance 1947-49; indsl. engr. Johns/Manville, Long Beach 1949-60; indsl. chief engr. Safeway Stores, Oakland 1960-69; founder/ pres. K-R-B Engineers, Inc. Los Angeles 1969 –; currently semi-ret., consulting engr.; mem: Am. Inst. of Indsl. Engrs. (senior mem.); mem. Federal Technical Panel (engineered workshops for the handicapped in Calif., Nev., Ariz., Kans., Colo., Utah) 1975-, active in Lutheran Ch., Boys Club, P.T.A.; works: designs systems for factories and installs control pgms., largest installation covered 75,000+ employees; mil: lt. USNR 1942-45; Republican; Protestant; rec: golf, sailing, travel, tennis, performing arts. Address: 911 Ronda Sevilla Laguna Hills 92653

KADEVARI, RAMAN, international trade executive; b. July 21, 1960, Hyderabad, India; s. Babiah and Rudramma (Koppula) K.; edn: B.P.C. Vivek Vardhini, 1979; bus. adm. pgm. Univ. of Redlands 1979-81, West Coast Univ. 1981-82, USC 1985-86. Career: internat. trade splst., cons. to med. industry; founder/ pres. East India Trading Co. Ltd. (import, export leather and leather goods), and Omnimed Internat. Inc. (mfg. medical supplies internat.); mem. Assn. for Advance. of Med. Instrumentation, Taipei Med. Mfrs. Assn., Telugu Assn. of No. Calif., Am. Kidney Found (Coachella Valley br. treas.), Nat. Kidney Found. (patron); Hindu; rec: tennis, swim. Res: POB 1125 Rancho Mirage 92270 Ofc: Omnimed International Inc 870 Research Dr Bldg 5 Palm Springs 92262

KAFFL, ASRES, dentist; b. Feb. 15, 1950, Asmara, Eritrea, Ethiopia; s. Kaffl and Medhin (Tewelde) G-Dinghil; edn: AA, Wayne Co. Coll. 1976; San Francisco State Univ. 1979-80; BS, DDS, UC San Francisco 1984. Career: mgr. The Hot Tubs, San Francisco; asoc. Dr. Winfield Scott, San Jose 1984; assoc. Dr. George Forneret, Oakland 1985; dental clinic dir. Drew Health Found., East Palo Alto 1985 –; honors: Letter of Appreciation, Dean of San Francisco State Univ.; mem: mem. NDA, BSHA, CDS, Eritrean Med. Assn. (chpt. chmn. 1984-85); civic: fundraising band mem. (base player) to drought victims in Eritrea, East Africa, being sold internationally; rec: billards, music, martial arts (4th gup, Red Belt, Tae Kwan Do). Res: 1250 48th Ave. San Francisco 94122 Ofc: Drew Health Foundation, 211 University Ave., East Palo Alto 94303

KAHANE, DENNIS SPENCER, lawyer; b. Oct. 28, 1947, N.Y.C.; s. Aaron and Frances (Asheroff) K.; edn: BA, Tulane Univ. 1969; JD, honors, George Washington Univ. 1972; admitted bar: Dist. Col. (1973), La. (1980), Calif. (1982), US Supreme Ct., US Circuit Cts. (D.C., 5th, 7th, 9th, 11th) and num. US Dist. Cts. Career: senior atty. Federal Communications Commn., Wash DC 1973-80; atty. assoc. Jones, Walker, Waechter, Poitevant, Carriere & Denegre, New Orleans 1980-82; assoc., of counsel, ptnr. Pillsbury, Madison & Sutro, San Francisco 1982 –; gen. counsel Calif. Bdcstrs. Assn. Sacto. 1982 –; mem. Com. of Bar Examiners, State Bar of Calif. 1984- (chair subcom. on moral character 1985-), State Bar Consortium on Lawyering Performance; mem. Am. Bar Assn., Federal Communs. Bar Assn.; publs: "Colonial Origins of Our Free Press," ABA Jour. (2/76); mil: capt. USAR -1980; Republican; rec: travel. Ofc: Pillsbury, Madison & Sutro 225 Bush St San Francisco 94104

KAHLER, ARTHUR REYNOLD, ophthalmologist; b. Feb. 20, 1900, Perham, Minn.; s. Conrad and Mary Frances (Matz) K.; m. Frances, July 18, 1931; children: John b. 1937, Mary b. 1938, Helene b. 1941, Virginia b. 1952; edn: BA, Univ. of Iowa 1921, MD, 1928. Career: tchg. asst. Dept. of Ophthalmol. Univ. of Iowa 1934-35; pvt. practice (first ophthalmologist in Sacramento) 1935 –; staff ophthalmol. Sacto. Co. Hosp. 1935-45; dir. 1st ophthalmol. surg. svc. Mercy Hosp. Sacto. 1936, staff Mercy Hosp. 1935-83, Sutter Hosp. 1935-86; German translation gen. ophthalmol. & glaucoma research; honors: member Governor's Traffic Safety Conf. 1959; mem: MAM, CMA, Alta Calif. Ophthalmol. Soc., Research Study Club of L.A. 1935-86; publ: tech. art. in ophthalmol. jour. and textbook; Republican; Catholic; rec: gardening, geneology. Ofc: Sacramento 95819

KAHN, EDWIN WALTER, construction co. president; b. June 3, 1922, Pittsburgh, Pa.; s. Theodore and Helen Henrietta (Meyers) K.; m. Sandra, Aug. 10, 1985; children: Gregory b. 1952, Julie b. 1955, David b. 1956; edn: BS in civil engring., UC Berkeley 1948; FAA lic. comml. pilot; Reg. Profl. Engr., Calif. (1953), lic. Gen. Contr. (1954). Career: civil engr. General Engring. Service Co., Los Angeles 1948-50, chief structural designer 1950-54; ptnr. Pollack-Kahn & Assocs., L.A. 1954-56; ptnr. Mogil-Kahn Constrn. Co., L.A. 1956-60; consulting civil engr./ real estate developer/ pres. Kahn Constrn. Co., L.A. 1960 –; mem. Am. Soc. Civil Engrs., Am. Concrete Inst.; civic: Town Hall of Calif., L.A. World Affairs Council, Inter-American Soc., Natural Hist. Museum Alliance, Smithsonian Assocs., Air Force Assn., Varsity Club UCLA, Masons, Scottish Rite, Shriner, Aircraft Owners and Pilots Assn., Civil Air

Patrol; mil: lt. USAAF, pilot instr.; rec: travel, flying, camping. Res: 13029 Mindanao Way #3 Marina Del Rey 90292 Ofc: Kahn Construction Co. 1535 Sixth St Ste 105 Santa Monica 90401

KAKUK, TED, co. president; b. Oct. 16, 1937, NYC; s. Theodore S. and Jessie E. (Dean) K.; m. Roseann, May 9, 1959; children: Anthony b. 1960, Kim b. 1962, Tracy b. 1964, Stephen b. 1965; edn: BA, Brooklyn Coll. 1965; Calif. lic. contractor. Career: owner/pres. Custom Design Masonry & Concrete Co. (subs. Kakuk Inc.), Glendora; profl. photog. (comml.) dba Custom Design Photo Factory; pres. Custom Design Import & Export Co.; former New York disc jockey and TV host, fmr. profl. boxer and trainer; awards: Home Owners Assn. Award- design, workmanship, Anaheim (1981), Gold Nugget "Best in the West" merit award for masonry, landscape, wood structure, design & workmanship, Moscone Center, S.F. (1983); mem. Profl. Photogs., Am. Legion/ W.Covina (v.cmdr., chaplain); mil: USN Spl. Services 1954; rec: boxing. Ofc: Custom Design Masonry & Concrete Co. POB 1030 Glendora 91740

KALINA, JOHN MARION, real estate broker; b. May 13, 1930, Table Rock, Nebr.; s. Joseph Wm. and Vincis Helen (Foale) K.; mat. gr. grandfather, Peter O. Foale, one of first settlers Nebr.; m. Marianne, May 23, 1954; 1 dau. Lizbeth Ann (Miss Escondido 1981, California Universal Girl 1982); edn: BA in gen. edn., Univ. Nebr., Omaha 1960; Calif. lic. real estate broker. Career: served to lt. col. US Army 1951-75, helicopter pilot Korea and Vietnam, decorated Disting. Flying Cross; owner/broker Kalina and Assocs., Realtors, Escondido 1971-76; pres. John Kalina, Inc. (investment real estate and oil & gas investments), 1977–; mem. Escondido Bd. Realtors (past chmn. Ethics Com., mem. pres.'s advis. bd. 1984-); civic: Am. Security Counsel, Christian Business Men of Escondido, Gideons Internat.; invention: Swinging Singer (plastic toy); Republican; So. Baptist; rec: flying, restoration antiques. Ofc: John Kalina Inc 403 West 5th Ave Ste C Escondido 92025

KALINOWSKI, IRENE KARCZ, real estate broker; b. Apr. 13, 1928, Nieswiez, Poland, nat. US cit. 1959; d. Stanislaw and Leonarda (Piekutowska) Matuszak; m. Jerzy Karcz, June 14, 1950; m. 2d. Marian Kalinowski, Dec. 28, 1979; children: Jan b. 1951, Maria b. 1953, Jerzy b. 1955, Bartholomew b. 1959, Joseph b. 1962; edn: BA, Kent State Univ. 1951; Calif. lic. R.E. Broker 1974. Career: served in Polish Forces in Great Britain 1946-49, nurse Mil. Coll. for Women; real estate agt. Gribin, Vandyl, 1973-74; broker/prin., Santa Barbara 1974–; awards: coll. scholarship, Polish Nat. Alliance (1949-50); civic: Smithsonian Instn., Nat. Museum of Women in Arts, Koscinszko Found., Polish Am. Art Assn., Am. Contract Bridge League; Democrat; Roman Catholic; rec: painting, photog., ceramics, books. Address: 3855 Foothill Rd Santa Barbara 93110

KALLENBERG, JOHN KENNETH, librarian; b. June 10, 1942, Anderson, Ind.; s. Herbert August and Helen Elizabeth (Suttles) K.; m. Ruth Ann Barrett, Aug. 19, 1965; children: Jennifer Ann, Gregory John; edn: AB, Ind. Univ. 1964, MLS, 1969. Career: Reader's adv. Fresno County Library, 1965-67, librarian Fig Garden branch, 1967-70, county librarian, 1976–; asst. dir. Santa Barbara Public Library, 1970-76; chmn. adv. council, bd. dirs. Calif. Authority for Systems and Services, 1978-80; mem: ALA, Calif. Library Assn. (adminstrv. council 1975-77, 1984-85, v.p. 1986), Am. Soc. Public Adminstrn., Calif. County Librarians Assn. (pres. 1977), Kiwanis (treas. 1974-5, v.p. 1975-6 North Santa Barbara, dir. Fresno 1977-8, 79-80, v.p. 1980-1, pres. 1981-2); Presbyterian. Ofc: Fresno County Free Library, 2420 Mariposa St., Fresno 93721

KALLMAN, STEVEN, endodontist; b. May 5, 1943, Napa, Calif.; s. Walter and Lottie (Robert) K.; m. Trudy, June 15, 1979; edn: DDS, Univ. So. Calif. 1967; cert. in endodontics, Univ. Ill. 1969. Career: endodontist L.A. 1969–; clin. instr. USC Sch. of Dentistry 1969-72; profl. staff L.A. Free Clinic 1969-71; chief endodontics Cedars Sinai Hosp. 1984–; lectr. to various dental students; honors: Endodontic Award (USC 1967), Endodontic Table Clinic Honor (Univ. Ill. 1969), Cert. of Appreciation (Hebrew Univ. 1976); mem: Alpha Omega (undergrad. pres. 1966, chmn. edn. seminar 1983, editor grad. bulletin 1984-), Calif., L.A., Western Dental Soc., Am. Dental Assn., Am. Assn. Endodontics, So. Calif. Acad. Endo. (secy. 1973-74), Century City CofC, Bev. Hills Theatre Guild, Century Club-USC Alumni, several Hebrew orgs.; publ: articles in dental jours.; Jewish; rec: photog., reading, spectator sports, gardening. Ofc: 2080 Century Park E, Ste 1710, Los Angeles 90067

KALMAN, ELEONORA AGNES, transportation broker; b. July 3, 1937, Hungary, nat. US cit. 1977; d. Lajos Karoly and Karola (Kudelich) Roganyi; children: Nora b. 1958, Charles b. 1960, Vicky b. 1962; edn: acctg. courses Citrus Coll. 1972-74, data proc. courses Control Data Network 1975. Career: part time clerk, later ofc. mgr. J.S. Shafer Trucking, Baldwin Park 1968-82; mng. ptnr. Magyar Trucking, El Toro 1982–; awards: Miss Congeniality, Budapest, Hungary (1956); mem. Associated Gen. Contractors of Am.; Republican; Christian; rec: performing arts, visiting shut-ins. Res: 3 Taywood Ct Laguna Niguel 92677 Ofc: Magyar Trucking 23331 El Toro Rd Ste 107 El Toro 92630

KALMIKOV, JOHN PETER, investment property acquisition executive; b. Apr. 23, 1960, Whittier, Calif.; s. John Peter and Joann (O'Day) Adriance; stepfather: Michael Steven Kalmikov; m. Claudia, Nov. 2, 1985; edn: BA bus. fin., CSU Fullerton 1983; real estate broker 1984. Career: ops. supv., United Parcel Svc., Anaheim, Calif. 1980-83; broker/owner Basics Realty, Brea, 1982-86; v.p. investment property acquisition Basics Financial Planning & Investments Inc., Anaheim 1986–; mem: Rho Epsilon (pres. 1983), Realty

Investment Assn. of Calif.; rec: water skiing, tennis. Ofc: Basics Financial Planning & Investments Inc., 1717 E Lincoln Ave Ste A Anaheim 92805

KALTENBACH, HUBERT LEONARD, newspaper executive; b. Jan. 3, 1922, Sandoval, Ill.; s. Adolph Leo and Elizabeth Margaret (Nagel) K.; m. Theodora S. Hunt, June 15, 1946; children: Shirley Jean, b. 1948; Jeffrey Leo, b. 1951; edn: USN Aviation Cadet Sch., 1942; BA, UCLA 1947. Career: Copley Newspapers: News-Pilot, San Pedro 1946-78: asst. circulation mgr. 1946-56, circulation mgr./ indsl. rels. dir. 1956-64, asst. to publisher and indsl. rels. dir. 1963-65, publisher 1965-78; The Daily Breeze, Torrance 1969-78: asst. to pub. 1969-70, publisher 1970-78, pres. The Copley Press Inc., 1978–, dir. 1968-, Exec. Com. 1979-; pres. So. Calif. Assn. Newspapers 1972-74; mem: Calif. Newspaper Pubs. Assn. (pres. 1979); Western Newspaper Industrial Relations Bureau (pres. 1973, 74); Calif. Pres. Assn. (pres. 1983, 84); US Navy League; Assn. of Naval Aviation (life); US Naval Inst.; Am. Newspaper Pubs. Assn.; La Jolla Country Club; Point Ferman Masonic Lodge; San Pedro & Torrance CofC; San Diego Press Culb; United Way, L.A., S.D. Counties; mil: lt. USNR 1942-46, naval aviator; Republican; Protestant. Res: 1630 Valdez Dr La Jolla 92037 Ofc: Copley Newspapers 7776 Ivanhoe Ave (POB 1530) La Jolla 92038

KAMEN, CHRISTOPHER R., dental plan executive; b. Oct. 28, 1950, Chicago, Ill.; s. Bernard and Natalie Jane K.; div.; children: Jason Russell, Travis Russell; edn: DDS, USC 1978. Career: pvt. practice dentistry, Van Nuys 1979-83; prin., obtained Calif. Knox-Keene lic. 1981; prin. shareholder, dental dir. Gr. Calif. Dental Plan and Nat. Dental Svc. 1981–; cons. PPO claims, Pacific Mutual Life Ins. Co.; honors: O.K.U. hon. dental frat., USC 1974; Scholarship, CSU; mem: Am. and Calif. Dental Assns., San Fernando Valley Dental Soc.; Republican; rec: racquetball, scuba diving. Ofc: Greater California Dental Plan, 7009 Owensmouth Canoga Park 91303

KAMERER, PHILIP FINLEY, real estate broker, consultant, developer; b. Dec. 6, 1938, Lima, Ohio; s. Henry Alden and Madge (Mitchell) K.; m. Gail Young, Aug. 19, 1966; children: Nancy b. 1970, Shelley b. 1972; edn: BA, Ohio State Univ. 1960, MBA, UC Berkeley 1968; real estate broker, Calif. Dept. Real Estate 1984. Career: right of way agent Calif. Div. Highways S.F. 1964-66; land acquisition agent Boise Cascade Bldg. Co. Hayward 1968-71, Hofmann Co. Concord 1971-75; real estate mgr. Shortstop Stores Benicia 1975-77; devel. mgr. Citation Builders San Leandro 1977-84; owner Ramsgate Realty & Devel. Co. San Ramon 1984–; honors: Glenn Willaman Found. Award (Calif. Real Estate Assn. 1968); mem: Contra Costa Bd. Realtors, Bldg. Ind. Assn. of No. Calif., Commonwealth Club (SF), Crow Canyon Athletic Club (San Ramon); mil: lt. USNR 1960-66; Democrat; Episcopal; rec: whitewater rafting, aerobics, swimming. Res: 615 Logan Ln Danville 94526 Ofc: Ramsgate Realty & Devel. Co. 2092 Omega Rd Ste C-2 San Ramon 94583

KAMINE, BERNARD SAMUEL, lawyer; b. Dec. 5, 1943, Okla. City, Okla.; s. Martin and Mildred Esther K.; m. Marcia P. Haber, Sept. 9, 1982; children: Jorge H. b. 1973, Benjamin H. b. 1983, Tovy H. b. 1985; edn: BA, Univ. of Denver 1965; JD, Harvard Univ. 1968. Career: deputy atty. general Calif. dept. of Justice, 1968-72; asst. atty. gen. Colo. Dept. of Law, 1972-74; assoc. Shapiro & Maguire Law Corp., 1974-76; Law Offices of Bernard S. Kamine, 1976–; instr. Glendale Univ. Coll. of Law, 1970-72; lectr. Calif. Continuing Edn. of the Bar 1979, 82, 84, 85; judge pro tem Municipal Cts. 1974-; panel of arbitrators, Am. Arbitration Assn. 1976-; mem. Calif. Judicial Council Adv. Com. on Legal Forms, 1978-82; mem: Am., Calif. Bar Assns., Los Angeles Bar Assn. (chpsn. Superior Cts. Com. 1977-9; chpsn. Constrn. Law Subsect., Real Prop. Sect. 1981-3; exec. com. of delegation to State Bar Conf. of Dels. 1980-2), Reserve Officers Assn. (chpt. pres. 1977-8), Assoc. Gen. Contractors of Calif., Engrg. Contractors Assn. (dir. 1985, chpsn. APWA com. 1983-), So. Calif. Contractors Assn., Anti-Defamation League (regional bd. Pac. S.W. Region); co-author chpt. in Calif. Forms of Jury Instruction (Matthew Bender 1985); contbr. profl. jours., law revs. Mil: maj. USAR. Democrat (L.A. Co. Dem. Central Com. 1982-85). Jewish. Rec: jogging. Law Offices of Bernard S. Kamine, 350 S. Figueroa, Suite 250, Los Angeles 90071

KAMINSKI-DA ROZA, VICTORIA CECILIA, human resources consultant; b. Aug. 30, 1945, E. Orange, N.J.; d. Victor and Cynthia Helen (Krupa) Hawkins; m. Robert da Roza, Nov. 25, 1983; 1 dau. Sarah Hawkins Kaminski, b. 1976; edn: BA, Univ. of Mich. 1967; MA, Univ. of Mo., 1968. Career: elementary public sch. tchr., Mich. 1968-70; middle sch. tchr. Banning Unified Schs., Calif. 1970-72; mgr. of contract compliance City of San Diego 1972-75; v.p. personnel Bank of Calif., San Francisco 1975-77; human resources splst. Lawrence Livermore Lab. 1978-86; human resources cons./prin., 1986–; mem. Am. Soc. on Aging (Employment Com.), Am. Soc. of Tng. & Devel., Gerontol. Soc. of Am.; civic: Greenbrook PTA (v.p.), Livermore Mayor's Social Concerns Com.; contbr. num. articles in profl. jours.; audiotape: Optimizing Older Workers, A Tng. Design (ASTD, 1984); videotape (7 tape series): Careers, Phase II (sponsored nat. by IEEE); contbr. poems in poetry anthologies (1980, 82); Protestant. Ofc: Victoria Kaminski-da Roza & Assocs. 385 Borica Dr Danville 94526

KAN, HENRY, engineering executive; b. Oct. 10, 1921, China, nat. US cit. 1975; s. Sing-Yuek and Wai-Sing (Li) K.; m. Linda, May 5, 1951; children: Grace b. 1952, John b. 1954; edn: BS, Nat. Sun Yat-Sen Univ. 1945; MS mech., City Univ. of NY 1967; MBA, Golden Gate Univ. 1976; Reg. Profl. Engr., Calif. 1972. Career: asst. to v.p., dist. chief engr. Taiwan Sugar Corp., Taiwan 1946-67; adminstrv. mgr. Foremost Dairies Ltd., Taiwan 1967-69; proj. eng. supvr. Bechtel Inc., San Francisco, Petroleum and Nuclear Projects 1969-85; Congo Sugar Refinery Revamping & Op. 1961; Singapore Sugar Refinery

Construction Proposal 1965; productivity studies, India & Japan 1965; citations: excellent achiev. & bonus awards, Ministry of Economic Affairs, ROC 1956; Taiwan Sugar Corp., Taiwan 1965, Bechtel Inc., San Francisco 1980; listed: Who's Who in the west 1980, Men of Achievement 1982, Dict. of Internat. Biog. 1982, Personalities of Am. 1985; mem: Am. Soc. Mech. Engrs.; AAAS, Salvation Army, Am. Security Council, Internat. House; publs: contb. ed., Taiwan Sugar Hand Book; mil: lt. reserve ofcr. Chinese Army 1941-45; Republican; Christian; rec: philately, gardening, travel, swimming, boating. Res: 1666 34th Ave. San Francisco 94122

KANE, MARGARET MC DONALD, lawyer; b. June 2, 1944, Long Beach; d. James LaSalle and Nora Margaret (Foley) McDonald; 2 children (both adopted 1969), Elyse Caron Vosburg, b. 1954; Lawrence Andrew Hoytt, b. 1952; edn: AB, USC 1967; JD, Southwestern Univ. Sch. of Law 1980; USC Sch. of Bus. Admin. 1976-78; admitted to practice Calif. State Bar (1980), US Dist. Ct., Central Dist. (1981), US Ct. of Appeals, 9th Circuit (1981). Career: atty. ptnr. Silver & Freedman, Los Angeles 1981–; investment advr. McDonald & Co., L.A. 1970-81; honors: Dean's Scholar (USC); mem: L.A. Co. Bar Assn. (Bus. & Corp. Law Sect. 1981-), Century City Bar Assn. (Bus. Orgns. Sect. 1985-), ABA (Corp., Banking and Bus. Law Sects. 1981-), Coro Assocs. 1975-85, Tax Law Soc. (Curriculum Com.), Southwestern Univ., Los Angeles World Affairs Council. Ofc: Silver & Freedman, A Profl. Law Corp., 1925 Century Park E, Ste 2100, Los Angeles 90067

KANE, ROBERT WILLIAM, auto club district manager; b. Nov. 9, 1943, NY, NY; s. John Birchman and Catherine Rita (Fleming) K.; m. Marilyn Guillen, July 17, 1965; children: Denis b. 1966, Thomas b. 1967, Sean b. 1967, Bridget b. 1972; edn: AA, East L.A. Coll. 1976; BS, Pepperdine Univ. 1979; MS, USC 1981; cert. Rio Hondo Police Acad. 1986. Career: Automobile Club of So. Calif. 1966-, sales rep., claims adjuster, atty. negotiator 1966-70, claims supr. 1970-71, asst. mgr. Los Angeles Facility 1971-75, sales & mktg. mgr. L.A. Hq. 1975-81, dist. mgr. Temple City Office 1981, dist. mgr. Alhambra-San Gabriel Office 1982–; dist. mgr. Alhambra-San Gabriel and Temple City ofcs. 1985–; mem. L.A. Co. Transp. Commn. (Intergovtl. chmn. 1985-86); co-founder Alhambra Econ. Devel. Corp. (pres. 1985-86); honors: Golden Eagle, Boy Scouts Am. San Gabriel Valley Council (1985), City of Alhambra proclamation, pres. Sister City Taiwan R.O.C. Assn. (1984), Resolutions Calif. State Legislature and L.A. County Bd. of Suprs. (1985); mem. Direct Mktg. Club of So. Calif., Industry Edn. Council (San Gabriel Valley Council 1984-86), Town Hall of Calif. (mem. com. 1981-84), San Gabriel Valley Pvt. Industry Council, SG Comm. Coord. Council, Alhambra Comm. Hosp. (life mem. 1985), Alhambra CofC (pres. 1985), Rotary (SG pres. 1984-85, dist. rep. 1985-86), Long Beach Freeway Assn. (intergovt. rels. chair 1981-86), Alhambra Police Dept. Assn. (reserve ofcr. 1986), YMCA (SGV campaign chmn. 1985), Asian-Am. Friendship Assn. (co-founder 1984), Chinese Am. PTA of So. Calif. (advisor 1986), CSULA (Bus. Advis. com. 1984-86); mem. Calif. Fedn. of Chaparrel Poets (merit award 1981, 86); Catholic; rec: poetry, jogging. Ofcs: Auto Club of So. Calif. 215 S Mission Dr San Gabriel 91776; 9810 Las Tunas Dr Temple City 91780

KANEKO, TSUNEO, acupuncturist; b. Sept. 4, 1947, Tokyo, Japan; s. Hideo and Kimie K.; m. Heloisa Da Paz, Dec. 5, 1975; 1 dau. Lisa; edn: BA econs., St. Paul Univ. 1970; Toyo Acupuncture Coll., 1970; OMD, SAMRA 1985, PhD oriental medicine 1985. Career: Shiatsu Anma therapist; Acupressure therapist; dir. Ido Clinic and Workshop for Oriental Medicine; dean Shiatsu Massage Sch. of Calif., and dir. Tao Healing Arts Center, Santa Monica; instr. Calif. Acupuncture Coll., Santa Barbara; mem. Shiatsu Assn. of Am. (vice pres.); publs: Shiatsu Manual (1984); Nishinen Shoshu; rec: Tai Chi Chuan, sports, Tea Ceremony. Res: 2712 Highland Ave Apt 3 Santa Monica 90405 Ofc: Shiatsu Massage School of California, Tao Healing Arts Center, 2309 Main St Santa Monica 90405

KANG, TAE WHA, research institute president; b. Feb. 18, 1945, Chejoodo, Korea; s. Chan Bok and Kap Soon (Song) K.; m. Young Ae, Aug. 10, 1973; children: Joon b. 1976; Susie b. 1978; edn: BS, Yonsei Univ., Korea 1970; grad. wk., So. Ill. Univ. 1970-71; PhD in biol., Ill. Inst. Tech. 1976; Lic. Med. Tech., Calif. Career: postdoctl. fellow, Univ. of Edinburgh, Scotland 1975-76; chmn. Chem. Dept. Bio-Technics Labs. Inc., Los Angeles 1976-77; med. tech. Baldwin Park (Calif.) Comm. Hosp. 1978-79; lab. director and pres. Bio- Science Research Inst. Inc., Chino 1979–; consulting microbiologist, UHI Corp., L.A. 1983-; honors: British Med. Fellowship 1976-77; Predoctl. Research Grant, US Army Research Ofc. 1975; Nat. Sci. Found. Trainee 1971-75; mem: Sigma Xi; Am. Soc. for Microbiology; Am. Assn. for Clin. Chem.; num. arts. & conf. presentations; rec: mountain climbing. Res: 3007 Adrienne Dr West Covina 91792 Ofc: Bio-Science Research Inst., 4813 Cheyenne Way Chino 91710

KANNIKE, MUSA BABATUNDE, manufacturing & marketing co. executive; b. Sept. 15, 1936, Lagos, Nigeria, nat. US cit. 1978; s. Alimi and Tawakalitu (Olowu) K.; m. Vida Lovan, Mar. 10, 1960; children: Paula b. 1961, Musa Jr. b. 1966, Lukeman b. 1972; edn: BS in mech. eng., London Univ., England 1963. Career: instruments engr. Cambridge Instruments, Tally Ho, London, England 1963-65; Brush Instruments, Pasadena, Ca. 1965-66; process engr. Microsemiconductor Corp., Culver City 1966-68, Internat. Rectifier, El Segundo 1968-71; mng. dir. Nat. Salt Co. of Nigeria Ltd., Nigeria 1973-77; pres. Kannike-Martins Assocs., Inc., Los Angeles 1977–; dir. Los Angeles Mayor's Task Force for LA/Africa Relations; mem. The Research Council, Scripps Clinic & Research Found.; Rotarian (Paul Harris Fellow); Democrat; Catholic; rec: golf, swimming. Ofc: Kannike-Martins Associates Inc. 3712 W 54th St Los Angeles 90043

KAPLAN, SHELBY JEAN, executive- company owner; b. May 2, 1947, Quantico, Va.; d. James Sharpe and Jean Rita (Catusco) Williams; children: James David, b. 1962; Jean Louise, b. 1963; edn: BS, UCLA 1959; MBA, summa cum laude, Pepperdine 1976. Career: v.p. P.P.I., Los Angeles 1976-83; v.p. P.I.S.I., Los Angeles 1976-83; exec. v.p. N.I.D.C. 1976-84; pres., chmn. bd. Securities Placements, Inc., Los Angeles 1979–; guest lectr. to profl. socs.; advr. to Presidential Candidate on Housing 1984; mem: West L.A. CofC (fin. com.); Chancellor's Assocs., UCLA; Homeowners Assn.; clubs: Rancho Las Palmas, Riviera; Democrat; Catholic; rec: equestrian, tennis. Res: Two Latimer Rd., Santa Monica 90402 Ofc: Securities Placements Inc., 11777 San Vincent Blvd., Ste. 601, Los Angeles 90049

KAPP, BRUCE ERVIN, teacher; b. Aug. 19, 1951, Frankfurt, Germany; s. Ervin John and Rose Marie (Lipp) K.; edn: AA bus., Monterey Peninsula Coll. 1971; BS bus., CSU Fresno 1975; secondary tchg. credl. Calif. 1976. Career: business tchr. Ripon H.S. 1976–; football coach: asst. 1976-81, head coach 1981-85; bd. dirs. Cowtronics Inc.; profl. tutor; honors: Best Freshman Football Coach (1977), Coach of the Yr. (So. League 1982, 83), Coaching Excellence, Outstanding Community Contbn. (Budweiser 1983), Coach of the Yr. (Modesto Bee 1983), head coach South in North-South All-Star Game sponsored by Lions Club- No. 1 team in Calif. 1982-83; mem: Lambda Chi Alpha, HALT Orgn., Nat. Rifle Assn.; publ: book on coaching football in progress; Catholic; rec: music, guitar, songwriting, sports. Res: 1900 Cheyenne Way Modesto 95356 Ofc: Ripon H.S. 301 N Acacia Ripon 95366

KARAMATI, FARIDOON, electronic engineer; b. July 11, 1941, Tehran, Iran; s. Nosratollah Karamati and Tahereh Malekbanoo Taherzadeh; edn: BSEE, UC Santa Barbara 1970; MSEE, San Jose State Univ. 1972; EE, UCLA 1976; post grad., UC Irvine 1976-80; VLSI design, Helman's Assocs. 1981; Dept. of Defense VHSIC wkshp., Pallisades Inst. 1983; tng. Daisy's computer aided eng. wk. stas., Daisy Corp. 1984; Investment in excellence course, Litton/ Dept. HRD, 1984-85. Calif. Comm. Colls. Instr. (engrg., math.) Credential, 1972. Career: prod.- design engr. Signetics Crop., Sunnyvale 1972-74; design engr. Rockwell Internat., Anaheim 1979-80; design engr. Western Digital Corp., Irvine 1980-81; proj. engr. Mattel Electronics, Hawthorne 1981-82; gp. ldr. Custom Microelectronics Sect., Components Eng. Dept., Litton Guidance & Control Sys., Woodland Hills 1982–; honors: Campbell Scholar, UC Santa Barbara 1967, scholarship awards, UC Santa Barbara 1968, San Jose State Univ. 1971; research asst., tchg. asst. Dept. of Elec. Engrg. UC Irvine, tchg. vol. MITE Pgm. (Minorities Intro. to Engrg.) 1978; cofounder, first treas. UCI Internat. Students Assn., 1978; mem: IEEE; research: in field of magnetic bubble memories, UC Irvine 1979-80; rec: tennis, skiing, backgammon. Res: 12 Spring Buck, Irvine 92714 Ofc: Litton Guidance & Control Systems, 5500 Canoga Ave, Woodland Hills 91365

KARATZ, BRUCE E., real estate executive; b. Oct. 10, 1945, Chgo.; s. Harry Robert and Dearie (Goldstein) K.; m. Janet Louise Dreisen, July 21, 1968; children: Elizabeth b. 1970, Matthew b. 1971, Theodore b. 1978; edn: The Blake Sch. 1963; BA, Boston Univ. 1967; JD, USC Law Sch. 1970; admitted Calif. State Bar 1971. Career: atty. Keatinge & Sterling, Los Angeles 1970-72; assoc. corporate counsel Kaufman and Broad, Inc., L.A. 1972-73; dir. Forward Planning, Irvine 1973-74; pres. Kaufman and Broad Provence, Aixen Provence, France 1974-76; pres. Kaufman and Broad France, Paris, France 1976-80; pres./CEO Kaufman and Broad Home Corp., Los Angeles 1980–; dir. Kaufman and Broad Inc., L.A.; honors: Humanitarian, Man of the Year, NCCJ, Los Angeles (1982); mem. Young Pres.'s Orgn.; civic: Coro Found. (dir.), Pitzer Coll. (trustee), USC Law Sch. (Bd. of Councilors), Cedar Sinai Med. Ctr. (Bd. Govs.); Jewish; rec: travel, modern art, skiing. Res: 160 S Thurston Ave Los Angeles 90049 Ofc: 11601 Wilshire Blvd 11th Fl Los Angeles 90025

KARLAN, KENNETH ALLAN, financial planning executive; b. Feb. 15, 1941, N.Y.C.; s. Samuel S. and Edna (Levine) K.; m. Rene, Oct. 4, 1962; children: Bryan b. 1965, Beth b. 1969; edn: BA, City Univ. of N.Y. 1962; desig: Chartered Life Underwriter (CLU) The Am. Coll. 1976, Chartered Finl. Cons. (ChFC) 1983; Reg. Principal, SEC 1985. Career: sales rep. Hallmark Cards, 1967-69; finl. planner CIGNA Finl. Services, White Plains, NY 1969-71, asst. mgr. 1971-76, assoc. mgr. 1976-81, sales mgr. 1981-84, regional v.p. CIGNA, Newport Beach 1984–; mem: Newport/ Irvine Estate Planning Council, Orange County Charitable Giving Council, Internat. Assn. of Finl. Planners, Nat. Assn. of Life Underws., Am. Soc. of CLU/ ChFC; mil: capt. US Air Force 1962-67; Republican; Jewish; rec: tennis, sailing. Res: 1362 Galaxy Dr Newport Beach 92660 Ofc: CIGNA Individual Financial Services, Inc. 19000 MacArthur Blvd 4th Fl Irvine 92715

KARLTON, LAWRENCE K., judge; b. May 28, 1935, Bklyn.; s. Aaron Katz and Sylvia (Meltzer) K.; m. Mychelle Stiebel, Sept. 7, 1958; edn: stu. Washington Sq. Coll., LLB, Columbia Univ. 1958; admitted to Fla. bar 1958, Calif. bar 1962. Career: acting legal ofcr. Sacramento Army Depot, Dept. Army, 1959-60, civilian legal ofcr., 1960-62; solo law practice, Sacramento 1962-64; mem. law firm Abbott, Karlton & White, 1964, Karlton & Blease, until 1971, Karlton, Blease & Vanderlaan, 1971-76; judge Calif. Superior Ct. for Sacramento County, 1976-79; judge US Dist. Ct. Eastern Dist. Calif., 1979–, chief judge, 1983–; mem. Am. Bar Assn., Sacto. County Bar Assn., Am. Trial Lawyers Assn., Assn. Criminal Def. Attys., B'nai B'rith (past pres.; co-chmn. Central Calif. Council Anti-Defamation League Commn. 1964-65); Sacto. Jewish Comm. Relations Council (treas., chmn. 1967-68). Ofc: 650 Capitol Mall Sacramento 95814

KARPPINEN, ANNE-LEA, lawyer; b. Oct. 24, 1947, Helsinki, Finland, nat. 1963; d. Urho Veikko and Vieno Angeli (Heikkinen) K.; edn: BA, Calif. State Univ. Northridge 1969; JD, Southwestern Univ. 1978; admitted Calif. State Bar 1979. Career: secondary sch. tchr. 1969-70; social services wkr. (Spanish speaking) 1970; environmental designer L.A. Co. Regional Planning Commn. 1971-75; atty.- real estate defense (prin. client Transam. Title Ins. Co.), Smolker & Maas, Beverly Hills 1979-80; research atty. for Hon. Eli Chernow, Superior Ct. L.A. Co. 1980-81; civil atty. spec. in medical and pharmaceutical liability litigation, law firm Butler, Jefferson, Dan & Allis, Los Angeles 1981–; guest lectr. and speaker on women, medicine and the legal process 1981-; instr., coordinator Tort Litigation for Legal Personnel annual course, UCLA and LATLA, 1982-; honors: mng. editor Law Rev. 1977-78, Outstanding young women of Am. 1977-78, award of merit Women Lawyers Assn. of L.A. (1984); mem: Calif. State Bar Assn. (standing com. on Rules and Procedures of Ct. 1983-), Women Lawyers Assn. Los Angeles (bd. govs. 1985-); bd. dirs. Westside Womens' Clinic, Santa Monica 1985-; publs. in law jours.; rec: skiing, scuba. Ofc: Butler, Jefferson, Dan & Allis 626 Wilshire Blvd Ste 914 Los Angeles 90017

KASARI, LEONARD SAMUEL, quality control engineering executive; b. Sept. 22, 1924, Los Angeles; s. Kustaa Adolph and Impi (Sikio) K.; m. Elizabeth Keplinger, Aug. 25, 1956; children: Lorraine b. 1959, Lance b. 1961; edn: Compton Coll. 1942-43; UC Los Angeles ext. 1964-70; reg. profl. engr. Calif. 1977. Career: gen. bldg. & constrn. 1946-61; supv. inspection svc. Osborne Testing Labs 1961-64; mgr. cust. svc. Lightweight Processing Co. 1965-77; dir. technical svcs. Crestlite Prods. 1977-78; quality control mgr. Standard Concrete Prods. 1978–; YMCA High Sierra summer camp dir. 1969-80; reg. spl. inspector for reinforced and prestressed concrete L.A., Orange Co.; honors: Hon. Life Member Calif. PTA 1983; mem: Am. Concrete Inst. 1967-, Torrance Family YMCA (bd. mgrs.); mil: aviation ordnanceman USN 1943-46; Democrat; Lutheran; rec: skiing, backpacking, fishing, hunting. Res: 2450 W 233rd St Torrance Ofc: Standard Concrete Prods. POB 15326 Santa Ana 92705

KASE, STEVEN GERALD, university president; b. Feb. 10, 1923, Santa Barbara; s. George and Etta (Ricketts) K.; m. Manon, 1952; children: Monte b. 1952, Mark b. 1954, Donald b. 1956; edn: BA, Pepperdine Univ. 1948; D.Sc. Pacific States Univ. 1971; DBA, Ind. Northern Univ. 1974; Reg. Indsl. Engr. Calif. Career: dir. planning Kemmerer Engrg. Co.; tech. advisor to Air Forced Space Technical Labs.; indsl. engr. Autonetics Corp. (No. Am. Aviation); pres. and chief adminstr. Pacific States Univ.; honors: Disting. Service Award (USAF), Diploma of Honor, Phi Kappa Phi (USC); mem: Calif. Soc. Profl. Engrs., Nat. Soc. Profl. Engrs., Council for Private Post Secondary Educational Institutions, Calif. Assn. State Approved Colls. and Univs., Am. Assn. Private Schools and Colls., Assn. of Independent Schools, Assn. Internat. Colls. and Univs., Com. to Conserve Chinese Culture, Chinese Am. Christian Friendship Alliance, La Mirada Planning Commn. (past chmn.); works: created 10-20 zoning in city planning, master planned two university campuses; mil: USN; Republican; Protestant; rec: equestrian, travel, gardening. Res: 13203 Calle de Maya Rd La Mirada 91638 Ofc: Pacific States Univ. 1516 S Western Ave Los Angeles 90006

KASSEL, TICHI WILKERSON, publisher; b. May 10, 1932, Los Angeles; d. Albert Clarence and Beatrice (Velderrain) Noble; m. Arthur M. Kassel, Aug. 23, 1983; children: William Wilkerson Jr., Cynthia; edn: Sacred Heart Convent, Mexico Univ.; HHD, Columbia Coll. 1976. Career: pub./ ed. in chief Hollywood Reporter 1962–; pres. Hollywood Reporter Corp; dir. Imperial Bank; Exec. Com., Los Angeles Mayor's Com. Internat. Visitors and Sister Cities 1966-; founder Internat. Festival Advy. Council 1971-; bd. dirs: Friends of USC Libraries, Inst. Advy. Plnng. Bd. Edn. for Senior Adults, Los Angeles Music Ctr.; exec. bd. dirs. bilingual Children's TV; founder, sponsor Mktg. Concept Awards 1981-; sponsor Make It on Your Own, Hollywood Reporter Key Art Awards 1975-; civic: Motion Picture Country Home, Motion Picture and TV Relief Fund, Los Angeles Orphanange; honors: named Ofcl. Hostess City of Los Angeles 1974; recipient award, Treasury Dept. 1966; Nat. Theatre Owners Award 1967; Cert., Am. Women in Radio & TV 1968; Distng. Philathropic Svc., Nat. Jewish Hosp., Denver; Citations: Will Rogers Hosp., O'Donnell Meml. Research Labs., Montague Library & Study Ctr., Los Angeles City Council; Letter, Pgm. Youth Opportunity, Hubert H. Humphrey 1968; Golden Flame Award, Calif. Press Women 1970; Women of the Year, Girl Fridays of Show Bus. 1972, Personal Mgrs. Ind. 1976; Bronze Plaque, Mayor of Los Angeles 1972; Award of Excellence, Imperial Bank; Star on Wall, Hollywood CofC 1975; Shofar Award, United Jewish Appeal 1976; ShoWest commdn., consec. 1977-86; mem: printing Ind. of Am., Cinema Circulus, Women of Motion Picture Ind., Am. Women in Radio & TV, Calif. Press Women, Nat. Acad. TV Arts & Scis., UN Assn., Internat. Newspaper Promotion Asn., Western Publs. Assn., Dames del Champagne, Calif. Thoroughbreeders Assn., Hollywood CofC, Women in Film (founder, pres.), Los Angeles Film Ind. Council, Delta Kappa Alpha. Ofc: Hollywood Reporter, 6715 Sunset Blvd. Hollywood 90028

KATES, GEOFFREY RAYMOND, computer co. executive; b. Aug. 23, 1956, London, Eng., nat. US cit. 1982; s. Raymond Wm. and Doreen Margaret K.; edn: BSc honors, Bath Univ., Eng. 1978. Career: software mktg. mgr. National Semi 1981-83, Televideo 1983; bus. unit mgr. Micro Focus 1983-85; v.p.-sales & mktg., Genesis Microsystems 1985-86; pres. Camelot, Inc. 1986–; mem: AMIEE (IEE, Eng.); publ: num. tech. papers at shows; Republican; Ch. of Eng. Res: 8 Mayflower Lane San Carlos 94070

KATIRAIE, KAMYAR, manufacturing co. executive; b. Apr. 5, 1960, Tehran, Iran; s. Haraun and Mahin (Darshy) K.; BSEE, honors, UC Irvine 1981, MSEE, honors, 1983, postgrad. work in econs. 1985-86. Career: research design and devel. engr. Philips Ultrasound 1982-83, Systec Bus. Systems 1984, Hycom Corp. (dev. 300 bit per second modem) 1984-85; founder/pres. Kamyco, 1985–; tchg. asst. UCI 1982, UCLA 1983; honors: Eta Kappa Nu (pres.); mem. IEEE; patentee: digitally controlled Sonar System with LED display; Jewish. Res: 433 Heliotrope Ave Corona del Mar 92625

KATZ, DAVID HARVEY, physician, biomedical research co. president; b. Feb. 17, 1943, Richmond, Va.; s. Benjamin Samuel and Gertrude Anne (Siegel) K.; m. Lee Richmond, Aug. 1, 1963; children: Lisa Dawn b. 1967, Danica Lauren b. 1969; edn: BA, Univ. of Virginia 1963; MD, Duke Univ. 1968. Career: intern Osler Med. Svc. and fellow Dept. of Med. Johns Hopkins Univ. 1968-69; staff assoc. Lab. of Immunology Nat. Inst. of Allergy and Infectious Disease, NIH 1969-71; instr,. asst. prof., assoc. prof. Dept. Pathology Harvard Med. Sch. 1971-76; clin. mem. Scripps Clinic and Research Found., La Jolla 1977– (chmn. Dept. Cellular & Developmental Immunol. 1976-81; Dept. of Med. 1977-82; Dept. of Molecular Immunol. 1981-82); pres., CEO Medical Biology Inst., La Jolla 1982–; chmn., pres., CEO Quidel, La Jolla 1982–; honors: Phi Beta Kappa (1963), Alpha Omega Alpha (1968), Phi Sigma Soc.; Cancer Spl. Pgm. Advy. Com., Nat. Cancer Inst. 1981-; trustee Leukemia Soc. of Am. 1981- (Med. and Sci. Advy. Com. 1981-); publs: assoc. ed., Journ. of Immunol.; edtl. bd. mem., CRC Critical Reviews in Immunol., Immunopharmacology, Immunol. Today, CRC Monoclonal Antibodies, Clinical Immunol. Reviews; author 209 publs. incl. textbook, Lymphocyte Differentiation, Recognition and Regulations; mem: AAAS, Am. Assn. of Immunologists, Am. Fedn. for Clin. Research, Am. Inst. of Biological Scis., Am. Soc. for Clin. Investigation, Am. Soc. for Exptl. Pathology, Collegium Internat. Allergologicum, Nat. Bd. of Med. Examiners, Diplomate NY Acad. of Scis., The Fedn. of Am. Scientists, The Johns Hopkins Med. & Surg. Assn., The Reticuloendothelial Soc.; mil: col. USPHS 1969-71; Jewish. Res: 1775 La Jolla Rancho Rd. La Jolla 92037 Ofc: Quidel, 1107 No. Torrey Pines Rd. La Jolla 92037

KATZ, RONALD S., lawyer; b. May 1, 1945, St. Louis, Mo.; s. Isadore and Lillian (Goldman) K.; widowed; children: Jason b. 1979, Elliot b. 1982; edn: BA, New York Univ. 1967; MA, Oxford Univ. 1969; JD, Harvard Univ. 1972; admitted bar: Dist. Col. 1973, Calif. 1979. Career: overseas fellow (Bandung, Indonesia), Internat. Legal Ctr., N.Y. 1972-75; atty. US Dept. Justice Antitrust Div. 1975-77; dep. dir. Law of the Sea negotiations US State Dept. 1977-78; atty., assoc. McCutchen, Doyle, Brown & Enersen, San Francisco 1978-82; ptnr. Gaston Snow & Ely Bartlett, Palo Alto 1982-86; ptnr. Kadison, Pfaelzer, Woodard, Quinn & Rossi 1986–; adj. prof. trial practice, internat. antitrust, Univ. Santa Clara Sch. Law; awards: Rhodes Scholar (1967-69), Tchg. fellow Harvard Coll., Hon. Woodrow Wilson Fellow (1967), Phi Beta Kappa; mem. Am. Bar Assn., State Bars of Calif. and Dist. Col., Bar Assn. S.F. (chmn. Law of the Sea com.); co-editor, contbr. Jowett Papers (Oxford: Blackwell's, 1970), contbr. num. articles in law jours. and reviews, newspaper arts. in S.F. Chronicle (8/6/83), Christian Monitor (2/1/82). Res: 1160 Stanley Way Palo Alto 94303 Ofc: Kadison, Pfaelzer, Woodard, Quinn & Rossi 660 Hansen Way Palo Alto 94304

KAUFMAN, GORDON RAYMOND, owner/pres. air conditioning, refrigeration, heating co.; b. July 15, 1925, Youngstown, NY; s. Raymond Monroe and Clara (Banks) K.; m. Doris Mae Gilbert, Aug. 21, 964; children (by previous marriage): Fraser b. 1947, Bruce b. 1949, Ellen b. 1959; stepchildren (by wife Doris): Wayne, Barbara (Fraser), Harry, Roger, Patricia (Reid), Nancy (Sharrow), and Marilyn Howden; credentials: Calif. jr. coll. teaching cred. 1968. Career: in refrigeration indus. since 1947; constrn. and svc. mgr. (supvr. 65 men) for Calif. firm, 1963-68; founder/owner Weather Systems Service Inc., Palo Alto 1968-, now pres. Weather Systems Mechanical Inc., Santa Clara; instr. (adv. refrigeration) San Jose City Coll. 1968-73, Union Tng. Center, San Jose 1973-; mem: Refrigeration Service Engrs. Soc. 1956- (charter pres. and certificate mem. RSES chpt., London, Ont., Can.; unanimously elected internat. pres. RSES 1983-84); Local 393 (past mem. Apprentice Bd., chmn. Journeyman Tng. Com.); ASHRAE; Air Condtg. and Refrig. Contractors Assn. of No. Calif. (past pres.); Nat. Environmental Contractors Assn. (now ACCA); Am. Inst. of Plant Engrs.; Masons; mil: torpedoman, Royal Canadian Navy 1944-46; Baptist; rec: philately. Res: 51 Callie Ln Menlo Pk 94025 Ofc: Weather Systems Mechanical Inc. 2125 Ronald St Santa Clara 95050

KAUFMAN, HAROLD, management consultant; b. June 20, 1939, N.Y.C.; s. Max and Clara (Soberman) K.; m. Frances, June 24, 1961; children: Michael b. 1965, Benjamin b. 1967; m. 2d Hedi S., May 25, 1976; edn: AB, honors, Hunter Coll. 1961, MA, 1963; postgrad. work New York Univ. 1962-65. Career: research fellow, lectr. Hunter Coll. 1961-65; asst. dean Univ. of Delaware 1965-67; exec. dir. Delaware H.E.L.P. 1965-67; chief program devel., US Office of Edn., Wash DC 1967-70; v.p. Academic Finl. Services Assn., N.Y.C. 1970-72; exec. dir. Cooperative Cost Study- Dartmouth Coll.; pres. Financial Aid Assocs. and SRM Corp., N.Y.C. 1973-778; pres. University Concepts, 1977-83; Systemwide Loan coord. Univ. Calif. 1979-81; dep. dir. Fine Arts Museums of San Francisco 1981-83; pres. Harold Kaufman & Assocs., S.F. 1983–; dir. AFSA Data Corp.; faculty Mitchell Coll., Long Island Univ., Hunter Coll., Univ. Del., Washington Saturday Coll.; awards: Jean Bennett Webster Grad. Scholar (1961), Departmental Honors (1961), Woodrow Wilson Nat. Fellowship nominee (1960-61); mem: Bus. Execs. for Nat. Security, S.F. Economic Roundtable (pgm. chmn.), Nat. Assn. of Student Personnel Adminstrs., Nat. Assn. Student Finl. Aid Adminstr. (var. regl. divs.), Am. Assn.

of Museums, Assn. Museum Devel. Adminstrs., Nat. Assn. Coll. & Univ. Business Ofcrs.; civic: S.F. Friends of the Arts, Leukemia Soc. of No. Calif. (trustee), Presidio Terrace Assn. (pres.), S.F. CofC, S.F. Symphony Marathon (fin. com.), Hamlin Sch. (trustee, PTA pres.); contbr. num. articles in higher edn. profl. publs.; regular contbg. writer 2 small newspapers in S.F.; Democrat; Jewish; rec: writing (restaurant critic). Ofc: Harold Kaufman & Assocs. San Francisco 94118

KAUFMAN, K. RICHARD, association executive; b. Aug. 26, 1936, NY, NY; s. Jack Arthur and Beulah (Greenburgh) K.; m. Lois K., Sept. 7, 1958; children: Jeffrey b. 1960, Gary b. 1963; edn: AB, cum laude, Brown Univ. 1957. Career: with Credit Managers Assn. of So. Calif., Los Angeles 1963–, asst. mgr., then mgr. Estates 1963-71, asst. corporate secty. and mgr. Adjustment Bureau 1971-83, exec. v.p. 1984–; v.p./dir. United Affiliates, Inc. 1985-; chmn. NACM Adjustments/ Bankruptcy Procedure Com. 1984-; chmn. bd. trustees Calif. Business Credit PAC (1984-); mem. Bankruptcy Study Group of Los Angeles Inc. (co-founder 1976, dir. 1976-84, treas. 1976-78, v.p. 1978-80, pres. 1980-82, dir. emeritus 1984-); civic: Boy Scouts Am., Little League, Rotary; clubs: Los Angeles Athletic, Candlewood Country; mil: Calif. Army Nat. Guard 1957-62; rec: golf. Ofc: Credit Managers Assn. of So. California 2300 W Olympic Blvd Los Angeles 90006

KAUFMAN, TOBY, asset management co. executive; b. Dec. 17, 1941, Bklyn.; d: Morris H. and Hannah (Meislich) Talish; div.; children: Sharyn b. 1966, Debra b. 1969; edn: BA, Bklyn. Coll. 1962; bus., acctg. courses UCLA. Career: tchr. elementary schs. in New York, Mo., 1962-66; ofcr. mgr. SDA, Inc. (retail shoe chain), Los Angeles 1977-81; senior staff acct., staff supv., asst. controller Goldrich & Kest Indus. (devel. & prop. mgmt. co.), Culver City 1981-85; asst. controller Maguire/Thomas Ptnrs. (asset mgmt. co.), Los Angeles 1985–; seminar instr. Assn. of HUD Mgmt. Agents (1984, 85); mem. Assn. of HUD Mgmt. Agents, Women in Mgmt., Bklyn. Coll. Alumni Assn.; Jewish. Res: 439 S Oakhurst Dr Beverly Hills 90212 Ofc: Maguire/ Thomas Partners 355 S Grand Ave Ste 4300 Los Angeles 90071

KAUFMANN, GEORGE OSCAR, chiropractor; b. July 9, 1951, Buenos Aires, Argentina, nat. US cit. 1969; s. Oscar and Antonia (Stiffel) K.; m. Angela D., Dec. 20, 1980; edn: AA in sci., Cerritos Coll. 1980; BS in human biol., Cleveland Chiropractic Coll., 1982, DC, 1983; Calif. lic. DC, 1984. Career: musician, 1964-70; electronic video techn. Sanyo Elect., 1971-77; chiropractor Alondra Chiropractic, Bellflower 1984–; honors: Nat. Hon. Profl. Soc. (1982); mem. Bellflower CofC, Kiwanis, Christian Businessmen's Com.; Christian; rec: musician. Ofc: Alondra Chiropractic 10106 Alondra Blvd Ste C Bellflower 90706

KAUS, OTTO MICHAEL, judge; b. Jan. 7, 1920, Vienna, Austria; s. Otto F. and Gina (Wiener) K.; came to US, 1939, nat. 1942; m. Peggy A. Huttenback, Jan. 12, 1943; children: Stephen D., Robert M.; edn: BA, UCLA, 1943, LLB, Loyola Univ. Los Angeles, 1949; admitted to Calif. State Bar, 1949. Career: pvt. practice law, Los Angeles, 1949-61; judge Superio Ct. Calif., 1961-64; assoc. justice Calif. Ct. Appeal, 2d Appellate Dist., Div. 3, Los Angeles, 1965-66, presiding justice Div. 5, 1966-81; assoc. justice Calif. Supreme Ct., San Francisco 1981–; mem. faculty Loyola Univ. Law Sch. 1950-75, USC 1974-77; mem. Am. Law Inst., Phi Beta Kappa, Order of Coif; mil: US Army 1942-45. Ofc: California Supreme Court, State Building, San Francisco 94102

KAVITKY, STEVEN MARK, chiropractor; b. Jan. 27, 1953, Los Angeles; s. Simon and Sophie (Camhi) K.; m. Susan, June 30, 1984; edn: AA, Pierce Coll. 1977; BS, Cleveland Chiropractic Coll. 1981, DC, magna cum laude, 1982; lic. chiropractor, Calif. 1984. Career: owner Kavitky's Custom Metal Artifacts 1970; designer, owner Funky Frog Prodns. 1972; owner Kavitky's Custom Picture Framing 1977; designer, pres. Physio-Tronics 1980; doctor of clinic Steven M. Kavitky Chiropractor, Arleta 1984–; seminars on spinal bio-mechanics 1984-; seminars on stress reduction and biofeedback 1980-; honors: Delta Tou Alpha Scholastic Excellence award 1981; 3rd place photog. trophy, Van Nuys Optimist Club, 1970; Diplomate Nat. Bd. of Chiropractic Examiners; mem: Delta Tau Alpha; designer: portable biofeedback module, 1980; greeting card line, 1972; metal sculptures; rec: inventing, tennis, photog. Ofc: Dr. Steven M. Kavitky Chiropractor, 8940 Woodman Ave. Ste. A, Arleta 91331

KAY, HOWARD A., manufacturing co. executive; b. ec. 29, 1941, Los Angeles; s. David Kay and Francine P. (Weinstock) K.; m. Marilyn, Aug. 1979; children: Bryan b. 1971, Marja b. 1980, Annika Eve b. 1982; edn: AS electronics, L.A. Trade Tech. 1962; BA in edn., CSU Los Angeles 1965. Career: field rep. Litton Industries, 1961-68; field rep., data analyst Computicket Corp./ Computer Scis. Corp., El Segundo 1968-70; engring. cons. Computicket, Ltd., London, Eng. 1970-72; project mgr., sr. engr. Tempo/GTE Info. Systems, Anaheim 1972-74; W.Coast dist. mgr. No. Telecom Spectrum Div., Moorestown, N.J. 1974-81; regl. mgr. (9 W. States) Datacomm. Mgmt. Scis., East Norwalk, Conn. 1981-82; W. regl. mgr. Sensitek Corp., Moorestown, N.J. 1982; regl./internat. sales mgr. Halycon Comm., 1982–; pres. Communications Data Systems Inc.; faculty West Coast Univ.; honors: commendn. City of Placentia for contbns. city planning, 10-year Top Sales award; mem. Telecomm. Assn., (fmr.) HTCA, US Coast Guard Aux.; civic: City of Placentia (Heritage Parade Com., Indsl. Plnng. Com.); mil: electricians mate 3/c p.o. USNR; Democrat; rec: pvt. pilot, Karate (black belt cand.), boating. Address: Fullerton 92631

KAY, SAUL H., real estate development & management executive; b. April 8, 1932, NY, NY; s. Jack B. and Ruth K.; m. Rima Sherwood, June 28, 1953;

children: Lawrence b. 1955, Paul b. 1957, Leslie b. 1959, Mike b. 1962; edn: BS, UCLA 1954; Exec. Pgm. GSM, UCLA. Career: v.p. plnng. & fin. Kaysons Internat. (subs. Intermark Investing Inc.), Los Angeles 1956-71; pres. C.D.I. Constrn. (div. Capital Dynamics Inc.), Los Angeles 1971–; ptr. Kay Proper-ties, Woodland Hills; ptr. URSA Co., Ventura; honors: Silver Beaver, BSA 1975; life mem., PTA 1974; mem: Boy Scouts of Am. (Exec. Com Great Western Council, El Camino dist.), Al Malaikah Shrine, Masons, Ventura Arts Council; mil: 1st lt. US Army 1954-55, spl. asst. to commdg. gen. White Sands Proving Grounds, N.M. on G-4 staff 1955-56; Democrat; Jewish; rec: wood-working, hiking. Res: 18134 Chardon Circle Encino 91316 Ofc: Kay Properties, 5525 Oakdale Ave. Ste. 240 Woodland Hills 91364

KAYAJANIAN, JACK J., lawyer; b. Aug. 22, 1950, Fresno; s. Haig and Esther K.; edn: BA, CSU Fresno 1972; JD, Western State Univ. 1976; Cert. Family Law Splst., Calif. St. Bd. of Legal Specialization 1983; prof. of law, Western State Univ. Career: currently, atty., cert. family law splst., Santa Ana; prof. of law, Western State Univ.; mem: West Orange Co. Bar Assn. (bd. trustees); No. Orange Co., West. Orange Co., Orange Co., Central Municipal and Harbor Bar Assns.; Triple X Frat. (recording secty.); publs: United State Trust Co. vs. New Jersey, WSU Law Review, Vol. 5, No. 2, 1978; Republican; Episcopal. Res: 21721 Hilaira, Huntington Beach 92646 Ofc: 1605 Fourth St., Santa Ana 92701

KAYE, RICHARD J., chiropractor, b. Apr. 11, 1946, Bronx, N.Y.; s. Albert and Mildred K.; m. Arlene; 1 son, Jonathon Edward; edn: undergrad. North-eastern Univ. 1964-67; BS, C.W. Post Coll., Long Island Univ. 1973; DC, Columbia Inst. of Chiropractic 1976; Diplomate Nat. Bd. Chiro.; Board cer-tified in Craniopathy; lic. in Ariz., N.J., Fla., Calif.; grad. Parker Chiro. Research Found.; cert. instr. Internat. Systemic Health Orgn., Sacro Occipital Research Soc. Internat. Career: dir. Kaye Chiropractic Group, San Diego; adj. instr. Los Angeles Coll. of Chiropractic; honors: Phi Chi Omega, Robert B. Botterman Award (1982, 85) S.D. County Chiro. Soc.; mem: Fellow Internat. Craniopathic Soc., Sacro Occipital Research Soc. Internat. (chmn. bd. dirs.), Internat. Systemic Health Orgn. Inc. (pres.), Am. Chiropractic Assn. (Coun-cils on Sports Injuries, Roentgenology), Calif. Chiro. Assn., San Diego County Chiro. Soc. (pres. 1981-83; alt. state dir.), Chiro. Information Bureau (pres.), Rotary; rec: running (instr. Mission Bay Marathon Clinic), scuba diving. Ofc: 6612 Mission Gorge Rd San Diego 92120-2309

KAZANJIAN, JAMES MEHRAN, gemologist; b. Jan. 26, 1899, Turkey; s. Garabed and Anna (Yakligian) K.; m. Euphrates Pashgian, Sept. 2, 1933; children: Michael James b. 1937, Stanley Myron b. 1939. Career: owner Kazanjian Bros. Inc., Beverly Hills; internat. gem merchant, gemologist, appraiser; founder Kazanjian Found. of Pasadena (scholarships to foreign students at Occidental Coll., USC); creator four sapphire heads of U.S. presi-dents, representing George Washington, Abraham Lincoln, Thomas Jefferson, Dwight Eisenhower, also the Star of Queensland created from five largest sapphires in the world, presented through Kazanjian Found. to people of U.S., on view Smithsonian Inst.; creator Ruby Liberty Bell, Smithsonian Inst.; rec: collecting fine gems, tennis, jogging. Res: 150 Fern Dr. Pasadena 91105 Ofc: 332 No. Rodeo Dr. Beverly Hills 90210

KAZAZIAN, EDWARD VAHAN, investor, entrepreneur; b. Jan. 17, 1939, Toledo, Ohio; s. Haig H. and Hermine A. (Papelian) K.; m. Linda Rittenhouse, June 24, 1961; children: Nina b. 1964, Lisa b. 1966; edn: BS, Northwestern Univ. 1961; CCIM, Nat. Inst. of Real Estate Brokers. Career: real estate agt., Denver, Colo. 1964-67; co-owner The Sheman Agency Inc., Denver 1968-76; investor real estate, Denver 1976-83; investor, entrepreneur, Rancho Mirage 1983–; mil: spl. agent US Army Intelligence Corps 1961-64; rec: golf. Res: 548 Desert West Dr. Rancho Mirage 92270

KAZMI, SYED A.M., psychiatrist, b. Mar. 25, 1952, Rawalpindi, Pakistan; s. Syed Manzoor Ali Shah and Syeda Aijaz Begum (Bokhari) K.; m. Farzana, Apr. 20, 1975; 1 child Raza b. 1977; edn: F.Sc. Gordon Coll. 1968; BS, Punjab Univ. 1971; MD, King Edward Med. Coll. 1974. Certified, Am. Board of Psychiatry & Neurology 1981. Career: resident in gen. psychiatry Eastern Va. Med. Sch., Norfolk, Va. 1975-78; chief of mental health Castle AFB, Merced, Ca. 1978-81; staff psychiatrist Stanislaus County Mental Health Dept., Modesto 1981-85, staff psychiatrist San Joaquin Mental Health Dept., Stockton 1985–; pvt. practice; cons. to courts, Workman's Comp., Social Security Disability Eval. Dept.; mil: major USAF 1978-81; Muslim; rec: singing, music, physical fitness. Ofc: 615 Fifteenth St Ste E Modesto 95354

KEADY, PETER, company president; b. Aug. 15, 1932, Evanston, Ill.; s. William Leo and Maragret Jennings K.; m. Lynne Brooks, June 14, 1961; children: Ann Jennings; Kate M.; Peter J.; edn: BA, Claremont Men's Coll. 1957. Career: sales & prodn. Phila. Steel & Iron 1957-59; Union Oil Co. of Calif. 1959-60; Balloon Tire Mould Corp. 1960-68; sales mgr. Super Mold Corp., Lodi 1968-70; pres. Viking Container Co. 1970–; mem: Tech 24; San Jose Athletic Club; Republican; Catholic. Res: 10 Campo Bello Ln., Menlo Park 94025 Ofc: P.O. Box 1067, 620 Quinn Rd., San Jose 95108

KEALY, ARTHUR PHILIP, service co. executive; b. Aug. 1, 1945, Chgo.; s. John Arthur and Grace Genevieve (Harris) K.; m. Kathleen, Oct. 19, 1968; children: John Arthur b. 1969, Patrick Michael b. 1971; edn: BS aerospace engring., US Naval Acad. 1967; MBA, fin., CSU San Francisco 1978. Career: salesman Monogram Indus., Elkhart, Ind. 1971-72; stockbroker Shearson Hay-den Stone, San Francisco 1972-76; logistics analyst Lockheed Missiles & Space Co., Sunnyvale 1978-79, program cost controller DIALOG Information Services, Inc. (subs. Lockheed Corp.), Palo Alto 1979-81, mgr. finl. plnng. & controls 1981-84, asst. to the pres. 1984—; mem: Soc. of Logistics Engrs., Lockheed Mgmt. Assn., No. Am. Soc. for Corporate Plnng., Navy League, US Naval Academy Alumni Assn.; coach AYSO Boys Soccer, Little League Baseball; mil: lt. cdr. USN 1967-71 Active, Reserve 1971-76, Vietnam Svc.; Catholic (pre-marriage counselor, mem. Social Justice Com.); rec: golf. Res: 1166 Denton Ave Hayward 94545 Ofc: DIALOG Information Services Inc 3460 Hillview Ave Palo Alto 94304

KEARNEY, ELIZABETH I., human resources consultant; b. Dec. 7, 1933, New Burnside, Ill.; d. E. W. Edmondson and V.P. (Grier) Eppley; children (nee Kearney): Kim b. 1958, Michael Lee, Jr. b. 1955; edn: BA, UC Los Angeles 1954; MA, Univ. of Penna. 1959, postgrad. work 1959. Career: program dir. Pasadena Unified School Dist. 1971-83; v.p. Western Div. Managex, 1984, pres. Kearney Enterprises, 1984—, present seminars: Creative Problem Solving, Team Building, Strategic Communications; awards: NDEA Fellow, Johns Hopkins Fellow, Am. Library Assn. award as author of Outstanding Reference Work (1968); mem: Los Angeles Business Visitors Bureau (Internat. Affairs com.), Nat. Speakers Assn., L.A. Area Hist. Preservation Group, Los Angeles CofC; author 9 books, 200+ articles, currently regular contbg. writer to bus. journal and magazines; Republican; Episcopal; rec: travel, hist. preservation. Ofc: 1866 West Fourteenth St Los Angeles 90006

KEATHLEY, JACKSON PHILLIP, agricultural consultant; b. Mar. 22, 1942, Dustin, Okla.; s. Luster and Stella (Liles) K.; m. Florence Paulsen, Sept. 2, 1967; children: Laura Beth, b. 1970; Craig Phillip, b. 1973; edn: BS, Okla. State Univ. 1965; MS, 1966; PhD, Univ. of Ga. 1972. Career: sr. research biologist Dow Chem. Co., Walnut Creek 1872-74; field research & devel. rep. Gulf Oil Chem. Co., Concord 1974-80; devel. rep. E.I. du Pont de Nemours & Co., Menlo Park 1980-82; agricultural cons./ pres. Keathley Agricultural Svcs., Concord 1982-83, pres. J. Phillip Keathley, Inc., Concord 1983-84, Ripon 1984—; mgr. Jr. Optimists Baseball League 1982, 83, 84; honors: Am. Legion Award 1960, Sigma Xi 1970, Gamma Sigma Delta 1972; mem: Entomological Soc. of Am.; Weed Sci. Soc. of Am.; Au. Phystopathological Soc.; Am. Mosquito Control Assn.; Am. Regis. of Profl. Entomologists; AAAS; Calif. Council of Agri. Prod. Consultants Assn.; Council of Agri. Sci. & Tech; Calif. Weed Conf.; Calif. Pest Control Advrs.; Ripon CofC; pub: papers in sci. and trade journals; mil: lt. commdr. USN 1966-78; Democrat; Baptist; rec: softball, basketball, woodworking. Address: J. Phillip Keathley, Inc., 25330 S Ruess Rd Ripon 95366

KEAY, LOU CARTER, writer; b. Mar. 28, 1927, Oceanside; d. Frank Leslie and Ota Belle (McCain) Carter; m. David Warren Keay, June 11, 1948; children: David b. 1949, Monica b. 1956; edn: Texas Womens Univ. 1944-46, Emerson Coll., Boston 1947-48, Texas Christian Univ. 1950-51, Texas Tech. Univ. 1976; Cert. in Public Rels., Univ. of Texas 1958. Career: TV Continuity dir. KLBK-TV, Lubbock, Tex. 1959-61; pub. rels. dir. United Fund of Lubbock, Inc. 1961-64; field rep./pub. rels. coordinator The Museum of Texas Tech. Univ. 1964-71; owner Costume Studio, Lubbock 1970-78; owner Apropos Public Relations, Lubbock 1971-78, Studio City, Calif. 1978—; ptnr. Investors Mgmt. Services (Midland) 1970-76, Tri-Ad Publications, (Lubbock) 1972, Media Tours (Lubbock) 1972-77; current: writer Columbia Pictures Television, Burbank; honors: World Poetry awards (1971), Burke Award for poetry (1970, 71); mem: Calif. Writers' Roundtable (pres.), Women's Nat. Book Assn. (past nat. bd. dirs.; past pres. Los Angeles Chpt.), Mensa, Book Publicists of So. Calif.; publs: former columnist "Cabbages & Kings" in weekly Texas newspaper, monthly entertainment and dining features in mag.; author: Beggars Would Ride, a collection of poetry (incl. in Pleasures, Vol. II, ed. by Lonnie Barbach, PhD Doubleday, 1986); Republican; Episcopal; rec: collector rare books, prints and etchings, sailing, travel. Res: 11684 Ventura Blvd Ste 807 Studio City 91604-2652

KEELER, RICHARD LEE, college executive assistant; b. July 19, 1958, Pomona; s. Robert Lee and Lucille Mae (Sarafian) K.; edn: BA, magna cum laude Univ. of La Verne 1980, MA 1983. Career: publicity coordinator Univ. of La Verne, 1980-81; Gen. assignment reporter Claremont Courier newspaper, Claremont 1981-82; assoc. dir. communications Nat. Energy Research & Info. Inst., Univ. of La Verne, 1983-86, instr. Journalism and Communications, 1985-86; asst. to pres., acting dean Colo. Mtn. Coll., Leadville campus 1986—; honors: cert. Creativity 1984 Contest, Cogeneration World Mag., listed Who's Who in Am. Colls. and Univs. (1980), Sigma Delta Chi; mem: Los Angeles Cogeneration Assn., Internat. Cogeneration Soc. (contbg. ed. Cogeneration World mag.); Republican; Prot. (chmn. Christian Edn.); rec: kayaking. Res: 381 Baseline Rd Claremont 91711

KEENEY, EDMUND LUDLOW, Scripps Clinic president emeritus; b. Aug. 1908, Shelbyville, Ind.; s. Bayard G. and Ethel (Adams) K.; m. Esther Cox Loney Wight, Mar. 14, 1950; children: Edmund L. Jr., Eleanor (Smith); edn: AB, Ind. Univ. 1930; MD, Johns Hopkins Univ. 1934. Career: intern Johns Hopkins Hosp., 1934-35, res. 1935-36, instr. in med. 1940-48; est. medical practice, spec. in allergy, San Diego 1948-55; pres., dir. Scripps Clinic and Research Found., La Jolla, 1955-77, pres. Emer. 1977—. Bd. trustees, Univ. of San Diego, 1974-; dir. Allergy Found. of Amer.; author: Practical Medical Mycology (publ. Charles C. Thomas, 1955), contbr. articles, papers in allergy, immunology, mycology to profl. jours.; ed. bd. Journ. of Allergy; dir. research on fungus infections Ofc. of Sci. Research and Devel., USN, WWII, 1942-46; mem: AMA 1938- (sec. Sect. on Allergy 1964-65); fellow Am. Acad. of Allergy 1940- (pres. 1963-64); Soc. for Clin. Investigation 1945-; Fellow Am. Coll. of Phys. 1946-; Diplomate Am. Bd. of Internal Med., subspecialty

allergy; Western Soc. for Clin. Research 1948-; Western Assn. of Phys. 1955-; Calif. Med. Assn. (sci. bd. dirs.); Rotarian; Eldorado CC; Phi Beta Kappa, Alpha Omega Alpha, Beta Theta Pi; Republican; Presbyterian; rec: golf, fishing, swim. Res: 338 Via del Norte La Jolla Ofc: 10666 N. Torrey Pines Rd La Jolla 92037

KEIBLE, EDWARD ANTHONY, JR., corporate executive; b. Sept. 30, 1943, Port Chester, NY; s. Edward Anthony and Anna Leora (Wardell) K.; m. Terry Wehmueller, July 3, 1982; edn: BA, Dartmouth Coll. 1965, BS engrg., 1966, MS engrg., 1967; MBA, Harvard Univ. 1973. Career: mgmt. cons. Resource Planning Assocs., Boston 1972-73; prod. mgr. Raychem Corp., Menlo Park 1973-75, mktg. mgr. 1976-78; internat. regl. mgr., Mid-East/Africa, Raychem Corp., Bahrain 1978-81; gen. mgr. Europe/ Africa/ Mid-East, Raychem, Milan, Italy 1981-83; v.p., gen. mgr. Internat. Group, Raychem, Menlo Park 1983-85, group v.p., gen. mgr. electronics group 1985—; dir: Alpha Wire & Cable Co., Remtek Corp., Bentley-Harris Corp; honors: Goodyear Fellow, Dartmouth Coll. (1966), Loeb Rhodes Fellow and Baker Scholar, Harvard (1973); mem: Dartmouth Soc. of Engrs., Am. Mensa; mil: capt. USAF 1967-71; Republican; rec: tennis, skiing, golf. Res: 261 Walter Hays Dr Palo Alto 94303 Ofc: Raychem Corp., 300 Constitution Dr Menlo Park 94025

KEITH, MICHAEL VAN, communications co. president; b. Mar. 5, 1952, St. Louis, Mo.; s. Solomon Leon and Josephine Ruth (Mays) K.; edn: Lincoln Univ. 1970-71; communications, Stephens Coll. 1972-73; BA comms./journ., Univ. Mo./ Columbia 1974. Career: pgm. dir. KCBJ-TV Columbia, Mo. 1974-75; asst. mgr. Wherehouse Records San Diego 1975-76; pub. rels./ mktg. Zool. Soc. of San Diego 1976-79; acct. exec. Chapman & Warwick Advtg., Conv. & Visitor's Bureau S.D. 1979; staff assoc. corp. communs. Wickes Cos. Santa Monica (formerly San Diego) 1979-81; founder., pres. Omnicommunications Inc. 1981—; mktg. instr. Southwestern Coll. Chula Vista; freelance script writer; honors: Dean's List (Univ. Mo.), Leadership Award (UNCF 1980), Outstanding Young Man of Am. (1980); mem: Am. Cancer Soc. (planned gift giving com.); mil: ROTC Lincoln Univ.; rec: Latin percussionist. Ofc: Omnicommunications Inc. 225 Broadway Ste 1500 San Diego 92101

KELLEHER, ROBERT JOSEPH, judge; b. March 5, 1913, NYC; s. Frank and Mary (Donovan) K.; m. Gracyn W. Wheeler, Aug. 14, 1940; children: R. Jeffrey, Karen Kathleen; edn: AB, Williams Coll. 1935; LLB, Harvard Univ. 1938; admitted to practice NY bar, 1939, Calif. bar, 1941, US Supreme Ct. bar, 1954. Career: atty. US War Dept. 1941-43; asst. US atty. No. Dist. Calif., 1948-50; pvt. practice law,. Beverly Hills 1951-71; judge US Dist. Ct. Central Dist. Calif., 1971—; mem: So. Calif. Com. for Olympic Games 1964; capt. US Davis Cup Team, 1962-63; treas. Youth Tennis Found. So. Calif., 1961-64; mem. So. Calif. Tennis Assn. (v.p. 1958-64), US Lawn Tennis Assn. (pres. 1967-68), Am., Los Angeles County, Beverly Hills, Fed. bar assns., Am. Judicature Soc., Delta Kappa Epsilon; clubs: Williams (NYC), Harvard of So. Calif.; mil: ensign to lt. USNR 1942-45. Ofc: U.S. Courthouse, 312 No. Spring St., Los Angeles 90012

KELLEY, MARY VIRGINIA, real estate broker; b. Sept. 27, 1920, Johnson City, NY; d. Roderic and Margaret Griswold (Hall) Pierce; m. Alfred Kelley, Oct. 29, 1945; children: Christopher b. 1946, Glen b. 1948, Margaret b. 1950; edn: BS, Syracuse Univ. 1942. Career: tchr. Guilford (NY) Central Sch. 1942-43, Calif. Public Schs. 1970-78; real estate agent 1978—; lic. broker 1982; currently broker/assoc. Grubb & Ellis Co. Oakland; honors: Salesman of the Yr. (Century 21-Clevenger Realtors, Oakland 1980); mem: Nat. Assn. Realtors, Calif. Assn. Realtors, Oakland Bd. Realtors (8 yrs.), Pi Lambda Theta, Chi Omega, Omicron Nu; social dance instr. w/husband 1956-69, 1985-86; mil: lt. j.g. USNR 943-46, Victory Medal, Atlantic Theatre; Republican; Episcopal; rec: dancing, choir. Res: 1945 Cortereal Ave Oakland 94611 Ofc: Grubb & Ellis, 2077 Mountain Blvd Oakland 94611

KELLOGG, BRUCE MICHAEL, real estate investor; b. Jan. 3, 1947, Buffalo, NY; s. Harlan Wood and Hilma Moore (Yarrington) K.; m. Diane Mancuso, Dec. 25, 1979; children: Jeremy b. 1972, Catherine b. 1974, Michael b 1980, Elizabeth b. 1982, David b. 1985; edn: BS, Rutgers Univ. 1969; MBA, Golden Gate Univ. 1976. Career: real estate investor 1973—; proprietorship in 5 Bay area counties, spec. owning & rehabilitating low income properties; 1982 inventory approx. 200 properties; trader stocks & commodities using advanced statistics & computers, -1973; mem: Nat., Calif. & Tri-Co. Apartment Assns.; Nat., Calif. Assn. Realtors; San Jose Bd. Realtors; Internat. Platform Assn.; publs: arts. in Commodity Journal Mag. (7/72, 1/ 73, 3/73) on computer comparison of systems for commodity trading; Republican; Catholic; rec: family outings; Address: POB 18966 San Jose 95158

KELLOGG, HUSTON GLENN, pediatrician; b. Apr. 6, 1924, Los Angeles; s. William Pitt and Thelma Bernice (Huston) K.; m. Dorothy Zulick, Jan. 13, 1951; children: Jacob b. 1951, Paul b. 1953; edn: BS, Yale Univ. 1944; MD, Washington Univ. Med. Sch. 1947. Career: intern St. Luke's Hosp. St. Louis 1947-48; res. pediat. St. Joseph Infirmary Louisville 1948-49, St. Louis Univ. 1949-50; pvt. practice pediatrics in San Diego, La Mesa 1952—; asst. clin. prof. pediat. UC San Diego Med. Sch. 1969-; chief pediat. S.D. Co. Hosp. 1957-61; med. dir. Home of Guiding Hands 1967-79, 2nd v.p. bd. 1979-; staff Grossmont Hosp. (chief. pediat. 1967,72,76), El Cajon Valley, Mercy, Children's, Sharp, University hosps. mem: Naval Reserve Assn., Reserve Ofcrs. Assn., Assn. of Mil. Surg. U.S., S.D. Co. Med. Soc., CMA, AMA, fellow Am. Acad. Pediat., Navy League (bd. dirs.), Rotary (pres. La Mesa 1980-81, pres. San Diego Council 1984-85); publ: art. in med. journ. 1951; mil: capt. USNR (ret.) 1942-84, Nat. Award of Merit (Naval Reserve Assn. 1984), J.J. Pershing Club

Award (Res. Ofcrs. Assn. 1985), National Surgeon (R.O.A. 1976-77); Republican; Presbyterian; rec: swimming, diving, real estate. Res: 3404 Cromwell Pl San Diego 92116 Ofc: 5565 Grossmont Ctr Dr, Ste I-116, La Mesa 92041

KELLY, CARL HALL, III, pharmacist/consultant; b. July 27, 1945, Henderson, Nev.; s. Carl Hall and Dorothy Dean (Mason) Kelly; m. Barbara Brown, Mar. 3, 1973; children: Erin b. 1977, Brent b. 1979, Brandon b. 1982; edn: Linfield Coll. 1963-4, BS, Ore. State Univ., 1969; desig: R.Ph. Career: pharmacy intern Salem (Ore.) Meml. Hosp., 1966-69; pharmacist Sav-On Drugs, Chula Vista, Ca. 1969-71; pharmacy mgr. White Front Pharmacy, La Mesa 1971-75; co-developer Santa Ana/Tustin Clinic Pharmacy, Santa Ana 1973; owner/pharmacist White Front Pharmacy/K&L Nutrition, La Mesa 1975-; co-founder Pink's Plantation Tree Farm, Mill City, Ore. 1977-; pres. Telbat, Inc., Santa Ana 1979-; pharmacy cons. US Dept. of Justice Fed. Bur. of Prisons, San Diego Metropolitan Correctional Center, 1985-; mem. S.D. County Drug Abuse Advisory Com.; profl. advisor Advisory Bd. for Alternative Pursuits Inst., Inc. 1977; Kappa Psi frat. (v.p. 1969); works: You and Your Nutrition, a TV interview, Ch.8, San Diego (1978); Republican; Roman Catholic; rec: aquatic sports, numismatics, skiing. Res: 351 Ave De Las Rosas Encinitas 92024 Ofc: White Front Pharmacy/ K&L Nutrition 5280 Baltimore Dr La Mesa 92041

KELLY, DANIEL GRADY, JR., corporate executive, lawyer; b. July 15, 1951, Yonkers, N.Y.; s. Daniel Grady and Helene Patricia (Coyne) K.; m. Annette Susan Wheeler, May 8, 1976; children: Elizabeth b. 1982, Brigid b. 1985; edn: Choate Sch. 1969; BA, magna cum laude, Yale Univ. 1973; JD, Columbia Univ. Sch. of Law 1976; admitted to New York State Bar and Fed. Cts. (1977). Career: law clerk Hon. I. R. Kaufman, chief judge US Ct. Appeals (2d Cir.) N.Y. 1976-77; assoc. Davis Polk & Wardwell, N.Y. 1977-83; senior v.p. investment banking, Shearson Lehman Bros., N.Y. 1983-85; senior v.p./gen. counsel Kaufman & Broad, Inc., Los Angeles 1985-; honors: Notes & Comments ed. Columbia Law Rev. (1976), Honors in hist. Yale (1973); publs: Indian Title: The Rights of Am. Natives in Lands They Have Occupied Since Time Immemorial (Col. Law Rev. 4/75). Res: 417 Cascada Way Los Angeles 90049 Ofc: Kaufman & Broad Inc 11601 Wilshir Blvd 12th Fl Los Angeles 90025

KELLY, ELBERT ERIN, mechanical engineer; b. Nov. 9, 1921, Lebanon, Ore.; s. Arthur Lee and Mary Agnes (Densmore) K.; m. 2d Dorothy Mausser, Apr. 6, 1973; children: Nita b. 1949, Nicki b. 1951, Timothy b. 1955, (stephil.) nee Heintz: Carl b. 1952, Christine b. 1954, Barbara b. 1953; edn: BSME, Ore. State Univ. 1947. Career: assoc. J. Donald Kroeker Assocs., Portland, Ore. 1947-56; chief mech. engr. Chas Luckman Assocs., Los Angeles 1956-60; v.p. Thomas H. Parry Assocs., Pasadena 1960-67; project engr. Levine & McCann, L.A. 1967-70; assoc. Dahl-Taylor Assocs., L.A. 1970-71; chief engr. Johnson-Joeckel Assocs., Long Beach 1971-74; v.p. Syska & Hennessy, L.A. 1974-; mem. var city and nat. code coms.; mem. Am. Soc. Htg., Refrig., and Aircondtg. Engrs. (award of merit ASHRAE Reg. X 1979, Fellow 1981, Life Mem. 1986, pres. Ore. chpt. 1954, pres. So. Calif. chpt. 1971, mem. nominating com. 1977-78, 81-85); mil: capt. USAF 1942-46, USAFR 1946-60; Republican; Prot.; rec: woodworking, photog., golf, camping. Res: 3737 Vigilance Dr Rancho Palos Verdes 90274 Ofc: Syska & Hennessy 11500 W Olympic Blvd Los Angeles 90064

KELLY, FAITH B., opportunity program director, computer consultant, b. July 2, 1953, Long Beach; d. William M. and Suzanne F. (Fisher) Brennan; m. Matthew J. Kelly, July 16, 1977; children: W(illiam) Luke b. 1980, Kathleen Lyra b. 1984; edn: BA, Calif. Polytechnic Univ. Pomona 1975, Ryan Tchg. Cred., 1977; MA, CSU San Bernardino 1985, Admin. Cred., 1985; Tchr./Adminstr., Calif. Credential System 1977-1986. Career: admin. liason UCLA-Exptl. Lng. Ctr./ Spadra Hosp., Pomona 1975-76; student tchr., coop. pgm. Nogales H.S., Calif. Polytechnic Univ. Pomona 1976-77; subst. tchr. Rim of the World Unif. Sch. Dist., Lake Arrowhead 1977; coord./ supvr. Behavioral Intervention Ctr., Frisbie Jr. High, Rialto 1977-78; girls track & field and volleyball coach 1978-84; social studies tchr. (dept. chair 1978-80) Frisbie Jr. High 1977-83; Sabbatical 1984; Opportunity Pgm. tchr. 1984-, and asst. to the v.p. Rialto Jr. High 1985-86; honors: Univ. Scholar, CalPoly Pomona (1973-76), nom. Student of the Year, CSUSB (1985); mem: Assn. for Supervision & Curriculm Devel., Nat. Assn. of Secondary Sch. Principals, Calif. Tchrs. Assn., Rialto Educators Assn.; civic: Catechistical tchg. & curricula devel. for Our Lady of the Lake Catholic Ch. (Lake Arrowhead) and St. Annes Catholic Ch. (Running Springs) 1977-84; guest spkr. var. ednl. & computer rel. topics, Rialto Dist.; author: Character Edn. Curriculum, and Opportunity Pgm. Guide & Reference; Republican; Catholic; rec: world travel, equestrian, doll collecting. Ofc: Computers to Boot, Grand Terrace 92324

KELLY, MICHAEL PATRICK, chiropractor; b. June 10, 1950, Kansas City, Mo.; s. Dean B. and Mary A. Kelly; m. Joyce, Feb. 10, 1978; children: Marsha b. 1973, Megan b. 1983, Aubrey b. 1985; edn: AA, Southwest Mo. State Univ. 1974; DC, Cleveland Chiropractic Coll. 1979. Career: intern Pacific Beach Chiropractic Assocs.; dir. Santee Chiropractic Clinic, Santee currently; honors: merit award, Nat. Bd. of Chiropractic Examiners; mem. Acupuncture Soc. of Am., Internat. Acad. of Clin. Acupuncture, Exchange Club; mil: sgt. US Air Force; Republican; rec: golf. Res: 10300 Pebble Beach Dr Santee 92071 Ofc: Santee Chiropractic Clinic 9317 Mission Gorge Rd Santee 92071

KELLY, WILLIAM W., insurance broker; b. July 9, 1918, La Salle, Ill.; s. James Wm. and Helen Katherine (Whitmarsh) K.; m. Phoebe (dec.), Sept. 4, 1940; children: William P. b. 1942, Thomas J. b. 1946, Kathryn b. 1950, James J. b. 1955; edn: BS, Univ. Ill. 1940. Career: ins. broker Duncan Insurance, La

Salle, Ill. 1940; asst. mgr. C.E. Canfield & Son (ins. brokers) Santa Cruz, Calif. 1946-50, ptnr./mgr. 1950-70; bd. chmn./CEO Wm. W. Kelly & Co., Inc. (ins. brokerage), Santa Cruz 1970-; owner/devel. shopping center 1965, office complexes 1980-86; instr. Stanford Univ. 1959-61; vice foreman 1968 Grand Jury; mem. Independent Ins. Agents of Calif. (dir. 1958, 60; pres. Santa Cruz chpt. 1967, 70), Lions, Elks, Commonwealth Club of S.F.; mil: capt. US Air Force; Republican; Catholic; rec: golf, tennis, duck hunting. Res: 610 Graham Hill Rd Santa Cruz 95060 Ofc: Wm. W. Kelly & Co. 211 River St Santa Cruz 95060

KELNER, HARRON, art therapist; b. Dec. 16, 1928, NY, NY; d. Joseph Louis and Pearl (Schwind) K.; div.; children: Jill b. 1952, Peri b. 1959, Dean b. 1961; edn: BA, Antioch Univ. West 1976, MA, 1977; PhD cand., Cambridge Grad. Sch. Psychology 1983-; ATR (Art Therapist Reg.), Am. Art Therapy Assn. 1977. Career: art therapist in pvt. practice, 1975-; art therapy supr. and trainer of students and mental health profls., 1975-; adj. prof. Antioch Univ. West, 1976-; asst. prof., art therapy, CSU Los Angeles, 1979-; set decorator and costume dresser ednl. films: Albert Einstein (1970), Helen Keller and Her Teacher (1969), McGraw-Hill; art exhibits, one person shows: Ryder Gallery, L.A. (1964), Valley Ctr. of Arts, Encino (1965, 66), num. group shows (1957-83) incl: Daley Civic Ctr. (Chgo.), CSULA Fine Arts Gal., Frye Art Mus. (Seattle), Laguna Beach Mus. of Art, Cerritos Coll. Art Gal., LA Co. Mus. of Art, Pasadena Mus. of Art, Oakland Mus. of Art, Long Beach Mus. of Art, Otis Art Inst. (LA), Santa Barbara Mus. of Art, Mount St. Marys Coll. (LA), Springfield (Ohio) Art Mus.; art reviews and articles in L.A. Times (1957, 64), la Revue Moderne, Paris, Fr. (1960, 65), others; mem: Western Psych. Assn., Am. Psych. Assn. (student afil.), Am. Art Therapy Assn., So. Calif. Art Therapy Assn. (v.p. 1978-79), Nat. Watercolor Soc., Womens Inter-action Network; Democrat (Nat. Com.). Address: 22445 Lassen St Chatsworth 91311

KELSAY, WILLIAM MILLARD, superior court judge; b. July 24, 1941, Oakdale, Calif.; s. Daniel Paul and Josephine (Pitti) K.; m. Claire Biancalana, Mar. 10, 1985; children: Anne b. 1968, Daniel b. 1971; edn: BA, UC Davis 1963; JD, UC Hastings Coll. of Law 1969. Career: asst. dist. atty. Santa Cruz Co. 1969-77; mun. ct. judge 1977-85; sup. ct. judge 1985-; bd. dirs. Santa Cruz Com. Counseling Ctr., Women's Crisis Support, Monterey Bay Salmon-Trout Proj.; mem: Calif. Judges Assn. Ofc: Santa Cruz Superior Court 701 Ocean St Santa Cruz 95060

KELSEY, LEO HAROLD, manufacturer's agent; b. Mar. 27, 1952, Casper, Wyo.; s. Harold Franklyn and Audrey (Cohee) K.; m. Pamela Baird, Jan. 14, 1978; 1 child, Eryn, b. 1976; CKD (cert. kitchen designer), Soc. Certified Kitchen Designers 1982. Career: sales/designer Everitt Kitchen Center, Ft. Collins, Colo. 1972-73; owner Cabinet Creations Unlmtd., Greeley, Colo. 1973-78; sales/designer Elm Distbrs. Denver, Colo. 1978-7-9; pres. KB Associates, Foster City, Ca. 1980-; nat. bd. dirs. National Kitchen and Bath Assn. 1983-86, recipient NKBA merit award for svc. to indus. (1982, 83, 84, 85), past pres. NKBA Mtn. States Chpt. 1978, pgm. chmn. No. Calif. Chpt. 1981. Res: 135 East O'Keefe, 3, Menlo Park 94025 Ofc: KB Assocs. 1169 Chess Dr, Ste. I, Foster City 94404

KELSO, CAROL LEE, construction co. owner; b. Dec. 17, 1949, Inglewood, Calif.; d. Ferd Allan and Emma Lucille (Mills) Rombaugh; m. David Kelso, Apr. 27, 1974; children: Russell David b. 1977, Kristine Carolyn b. 1980; edn: Pasadena City Coll. 1968-69; CSC Los Angeles 1970-72; BA art edn., CSU Long Beach 1974. Career: model, fashion dir. asst. May Co. 1965-70; display dir., fashion coord. Ivers Dept. Store 1970-72; dir. youth art svcs. for parks & schools City of Long Beach 1972-74; art teacher City of Carlsbad Year Round Schools 1974-76; self-employed interior decoration, remodeling 1977-86, owner C&D Construction Vista 1984-; computer cons. Crestview Sch. 1986; art, interior design cons. to var. small cos. in No. San Diego County; honors: Ephebian Soc., West Coast finalist Seventeen mag. model contest (1970), Citizen of the Year (Oceanside 1976), hon. mention- Decoration (Metropolitan Home Mag. 1985), Woman of the Year (Vista Jr. Women's Club 1981); mem: Interior Design Profls. (asso.), Nat. Assn. of Felmale Execs., Internat. Apple Corp., No. San Diego Apple Club (dir.), A.P.P.L.E. Coop.; civic: Carlsbad Firefighters Firewives Aux. (co-founder 1970), Vista Jr. Women's Club, Cymbidium Soc. of Am., Palomar Orchid Soc. (Blue ribbon for specimen orchid, 1986), Crestview PTA, Vista Soccer Club (team mom), Vista Little League (team mom); Republican; Presbyterian; rec: orchids, dress designing, children. Ofc: C&D Construction 1171 Phillips St Vista 92083

KELSO, LOUIS ORTH, investment banker; b. Dec. 4, 1913, Denver, Colo.; s. Oren S. and Nettie (Wolfe) K.; m. Betty Hawley; m. 2d.n Patricia Hetter, Feb. 14, 1980; children by 1st marriage: Martha Jennifer and Katherine Elizabeth; edn: BS, cum laude, Univ. of Colo. 1937, JD, 1938; DSc, Araneta Univ. 1962. Career: atty. assoc. Pershing, Bosworth, Dick & Dawson, Denver, Colo. 1938-42; ptnr. Brobeck, Phleger & Harrison, San Francisco 1946-59; senior ptnr. Kelso, Cotton, Seligman & Ray, S.F. 1959-70; mng. dir. Louis O. Kelso, Inc., S.F. 1970-75, bd. chmn. Kelso & Co., Inc., San Francisco/New York, 1975-; invented Employee Stock Ownership Plan (ESOP) financing and other financing methods; mem. ABA, Calif. Bar Assn., San Francisco Com. on Fgn. Rels.; clubs: Bohemian, Pacific-Union, Villa Taverna (SF), Chicago (Chgo.); author (with Mortimer J. Adler) The Capitalist Manifesto (1958), The New Capitalists (1961); (with Patricia Hetter) Two-Factor Theory: The Economics of Reality (1967); (with Patricia Hetter Kelso) Democracy and Economic

Power (1986); contbr. (with Patricia Hetter Kelso) num. articles to profl. jours. and other publs.; mil: lt. USNR 1942-46; Episcopal. Ofc: Kelso & Co. Inc. 505 Sansome Street 16th Floor San Francisco 94111

KENARNEY, RICHARD BRIAN, architectural & interior design consultant; b. Jan. 3, 1938, Princeton, NJ; s. Henry William and Arline Brian K.; m. 2d. Judy, Nov. 6, 1980; children: Kathryn M. and Megan E., Richard B. Jr.; edn: BABA, Rutgers Univ. 1960; MBA (in progress), Amos Truck Grad. Sch. of Bs. Career: sales Federal Electric Co., Surban, NY and Conn.; sales, sales mgmt. Ward Leonard Electric Co., Philadelphia and Chicago; sales, sales mgmt. McGraw Hill Publg. Co., Chicago and St. Louis 1967-72; sales to pres. Medical Economics Co. (Hudson Publg. Co.), Chicago, NJ and Los ALtos 1972-80; ptr. Design Associates West 1980–; pres. Design Comm. Inc.; tchr. Louis Allen mgmt. tng., Med. Economics Co. 1977; pvt. an group bus. cons. to small design firms around the country 1985-; honors: Salesman of the Year, Medical Economics Co. 1973; Lansing Chapman Award, Medical Economics Co. 1974; mem: Pharmaceutical Advtg. Club (past), Midwest Pharmaceutical Advtg. Club, Newsletter Assn., Chicago Athletic Club, Am. Soc. of Interior Designers, ASID Industry Found., Los Alto Athletic Club; works: developed bus. mktg. and opg. sys. packaged into a concise usable manual, sales & mgmt. devel. pgms.; Republican; Catholic; rec: calliscal music, tennis, ice hockey. Res: 10594 Creston Dr. Los Altos 94022 Ofc: 401 Florence Ave. Palo Alto 94301

KENDALL, ARTHUR, mine manager; b. Nov. 16, 1893, Quincy Mine location, Hancock, Mich.; s. Matthew Charles and Charity Ann (Chegwin) K.; m. Annie M. Giles, June 2, 1917; chidlren: Giles b. 1918, Loraine b. 1920, Robert b. 1922, Nancy b. 1941; edn: engr. of mines, Mich. Coll. of Mines, 1917; desig: Profl. Engr. (P.E.), Assn. of Profl. Engrs., Toronto, Ont., Canada. Career: mine surveyor Quincy Mine, Hancock, Mich. 1914-15, mine supv. Quincy Mining Co. 1918-21; mine supv. Nevada Consol. Mining Co., Ruth Mine, Ruth, Nev. 1923-27; mine engr. North Star Mining Co., Grass Valley, Ca. 1927; mine supv. Woodward Iron Co., Bessemer, Ala. 1927-31; with Newmont Mining Corp. 1934-44: mine supt. North Star Mine, Grass Valley, Ca. 1934-37, gen. mgr. Tombill, Northern Empire, Magnet & Elmos mines, Little Long Lac area, Ontario, Can. 1937-41, gen. mgr. Resurrection Mining Co., Leadville, Colo. 1941-44; gen. mgr. Magnet Consol. Mines, Ltd., Geraldton, Ont., Can. 1946-50; mine supt./mgr. Central Eureka Mining Co., Sutter Creek, Ca. 1950-53; project mgr. Utah Consol. & Mining Co. rehabilitation (after war) Diamond Drilling Project, Korea Tungsten Mining Co., Korea Central R.R. Co. and Dai Han Coal Co., 1953-58; mining cons., gold mines, Grass Valley area, 1958–; honored by Rep. of South Korea for rehabilitation and modernization of mining & milling plants (Korea Tungsten Mng Co. Sangdong Mine, and start-up op. Cons. Synthetic Scheelite Plant), and tech. assistance on constrn. (num. tunnels and bridges) of 50 miles Korea Central R.R.; mem. Empire Mine Park Assn., Empire State Park, Empire Mine, Grass Valley; works: devel. safety method underground drill-hole blasting with fuse & dynamite; mil: civilian instr. army troops in drilling, blasting techniques; Republican; Baptist; rec: baseball, hockey, golf; baseball team mgr. (Ruth, Nev. and Grass Valley). Res: 543 Scadden Dr Grass Valley 95945

KENDRA, JOHN MARK, neuropsychologist; b. Aug. 3, 1942, Punxsutawney, Pa.; s. George and Winifred Joan (O'Leary) K.; m. Starley White, Sept. 16, 1964; children: Mark b. 1976, Kathleen b. 1979; edn: BA, San Francisco State Univ. 1968; MA, Temple Univ., Phila. 1970, PhD, 1974; Calif. lic. Clinical Psychologist, Std. Tchg. Credential (life), Calif. Community Colls.- Psych. (life). Career: school psychologist Bonsall Sch. Dist., Camden, N.J. 1969; research asst. Audiology & Speech Pathology Dept., VA Hosp., Phila. 1969-70; mental health wkr. Suicide Prevention Ctr., Phila. summers 1970, 71; intern clin. psychol., VA Hosp. Palo Alto, Calif. 1972-73; clinical psychologist: Santa Clara County Mental Health Dept., San Jose 1973–, staff Guidance Clinic, Juvenile Probation Dept. 1974-75; pvt. practice, Sunnyvale 1975–; tchg. asst. Temple Univ. 1971-72; adj. faculty Calif. Sch. Profl. Psychology; dir. of tng. and field placement supvr. Blossom Hill Mental Health Ctr. internship program, 1974-, and chmn. Quality Assurance Com. 1979-, chmn. Quality Assurance Exec. Council 1980-83; mem. Am. Assn. of Suicidology, Soc. for Personality Assessment, Internat. Neuropsychological Assn.; contbr. articles profl. jours.; mil: E5 sonarman, US Navy 1959-63; rec: golf, music hist. Big Bands. Res: 1381 Pauline Dr Sunnyvale 94087 Ofc: Blossom Valley Mental Health Center 5671 Santa Theresa Blvd San Jose 95123

KENNEDY, DONALD, university president, educator; b. Aug. 18, 1931, NYC; s. Wm. Dorsey and Barbara (Bean) K.; m. Jeanne Dewey, June 11, 1953; children: Laura Page, Julia Hale; edn: AB, Harvard Univ. 1952, AM, 1954, PhD, 1956. Career: faculty Syracuse Univ. 1956-60, Stanford Univ. 1960-77, prof. biol. scis., 1965-77, dept. chmn., 1965-72, vice pres., provost, 1979-80, pres., 1980–; commr. FDA (1977-79), senior cons. Office of Sci. and Tech. Policy, Exec. Office of the Pres. (1976-77); bd. overseers Harvard Coll. (1970-76); mem: Fellow Am. Acad. Arts and Scis., Fellow AAAS, Nat. Acad. Scis., Am. Physiol. Soc., Soc. Gen. Physiologists, Am. Soc. Zoologists, Soc. Exptl. Biology (U.K.); author: (with W.H. Telfur) The Biology of Organisms (1965); editor: The Living Cell (1966), From Cell to Organism (1967), editorial bd. Jour. Exptl. Zoology (1965-71), Jour. Comparative Physiology (1965-76), Jour. Neurophysiology (1969-75), Science (1973-77). Office of the President, Stanford University, Stanford 94305

KENNEDY, REBA RENICE, real estate broker; b. Sept. 5, 1916, Benton County, Ark.; d. James Berry and Frances Melvina (Boydstun) Hegwood; m. Anthony Kennedy, Oct. 27, 1940; 1 dau. Gloria b. 1942; edn: Woodbury Coll. 1937-38; real estate sales, R.E. Coll. L.A. 1957; r.e. broker, R.E. Coll. Santa Ana 1965. Career: bakery and ofc. Continental Baking Co. L.A. 1936-41, ofc. only Santa Ana 1959-60; secty. Aaragon Elementery Sch. L.A. 1953-54; real estate sales 1957-65, broker 1965–; mem: Nat. Bd. Realtors 1975-80, Senior Citizen Club, Am. Assn. Retired Persons; formerly active PTA, speaking and dramatics, Girl Scout leader 1950-51; Democrat; Christian; rec: writing, swimming, oil painting. Address: 12781 Sholic Rd Apple Valley 92308

KENT, JAMES JOSEPH, career school president, b. Dec. 4, 1924, Bklyn.; s. James Joseph and Gertrude (Lee) K.; m. Anna Helene Powell, Feb. 28, 1951; children: Craig b. 1953, Baden b. 1954, Dean b. 1956; edn: BA voc. edn., CSU Long Beach 1971; Hon. DD, Universal Univ., Modesto 1978, PhD religion, 1979; Calif. Life Tchg. Cred. (1970); FAA lic. pilot comml./instrument (1973). Career: assoc. optics engr. Research Opt. Lab. Nortronics Div. Northrop AC Corp., Hawthorne 1955-59; engr., opt. devel. engring., Aerojet Gen. Corp., Azusa 1959-64; engr./mgr. Opt. Test Facility, Electro-Optical Corp., Pasadena 1964-66; mgr. research optical test facilities Pacific Optical Corp., 1966; pgm. dir./instr. optics, Citrus Comm. Coll., 1966-80; current: pres. J/H and Sons, Inc.; pres. John Robert Powers Career Coll., Upland 1980–; optics cons. Optical Craftsman (1970), Electro-Optical Systems subs. Xerox (1978), Gen. Dynamics (1979), Optico Glass Fabrication Inc. (1972-); honors: Keeper of the Flame award (6th award recipient in 50 years) Pasadena Playhouse Alumni (1986), best actor, Theatre Americana (1960-61), best actor Ninth Ann. Play Tour- Riverside (1968); mem: Calif. Soc. of Ophthalmic Dispensers (hon. life), Calif. Tchrs. Assn., Nat. Edn. Assn., Calif. Nat. Guard Council, Pasa. Playhouse Alumni and Assocs. (adminstr.); trustee Republican Presdl. Task Force 1985-86; inventor: Single Wire Test for fast aspheric mirrors, patents: Dying Spider Web, and Mechanism for Live & Cinema Stage Prodns.; fabrication of spl. scanning radiometer optics for 200' Palomar scope and 158' Ciero-tololo in Chile; mil: capt., fighter pilot WWII 1942-45, Calif. N.G. 1947-55, Aide-de-Camp Comdg. Gen. 40th Armd Div. Korea 1950-52, Aviation Ofcr. Combat Command "C" 1952-55, Merit Service Medal; Republican; rec: boating, hunting, camping. Ofc: John Robert Powers Career College 2133 W Foothill Blvd Ste C7D Upland 91786

KENTERA, MILO KRIS, mortgage banker, b. May 9, 1936, Globe, Ariz.; s. Kris L. and Eva K. K.; m. Lois Ann, Oct. 24, 1954; children: Marie Kristene, b. 1955; Milo Kirk, b. 1958; edn: BS, Univ. of Ariz. 1960; R.E. Lic., CSU San Jose 1974; R.E. Broker, 1979; Pharmacist, Calif., Ariz. 1960; R.E. Broker, Calif. 1978. Career: owner/ pharmacist Los Gatos Pharmacy and Los Gatos Rx Pharmacy, Los Gatos 1967-73; mgr./ pharm. Walgreen's Pharmacy, San Jose 1973-77; loan ofcr. Calif. Mortgage Svc., San Jose 1977-78; loan ofcr. Banco Mortgage Co., San Jose 1978-79; regl. v.p. Medallion Mortgage Co., Santa Clara 1979–, branch mgr. 1982–; mem: Am., Calif. and Santa Clara Pharm. Assns.; Mortgage Bankers Assn.; Elks Club; Republican; Protestant; rec: sports, jogging, golf. Res: 1902 University Ave., San Jose 95126 Ofc: Medallion Mortgage Company, 3600 Pruneridge, Ste. 300, Santa Clara 95055

KENYON, DOUGLAS ALAN, safety and environmental health executive; b. Jan. 8, 1953, Binghamton, NY; s. Douglas W. and Edith (Noble) K.; m. Marsha Smith, Mar. 17, 1973; 1 son, Jared b. 1981; edn: cert., Ohlone Coll. 1978; AS, Merrit Coll. 1979; BS, Univ. Redlands 1983. Career: safety coord., Washington Hosp., Fremont 1975-77; safety & health asst. Stanford Med. Ctr. 1977-78; mgr. safety & environmental health Pacific Med. Ctr. S.F. 1978-83, safety mgr. Browning Ferris Industries, San Jose 1983–; instr. safety studies Cogswell Coll., S.F. 1980-; exec. dir. Instnl. Safety Mgmt. Assocs. 1980-; recipient Tri-Cities Stamp Out Crime Award 1968; mem: Nat. Safety Council (chmn. reg. O, Healthcare Sect. 1980-83), Profl. Healthcare Safety Assn. (chmn. exec. bd. 1978-83), Am. Soc. Safety Engrs., No. Calif. Indsl. Safety Soc., Nat. Safety Mgmt. Soc., World Safety Orgn., publs: arts. in var. profl. publs.; mil: E4 USN 1970-74, E5 USAR 1976-82, Presdl. Unit Cit., Good Conduct, Vietnam Svc., Navy Unit Cit., Armed Forces Expeditionary, Vietnam Cross of Gallantry, Vietnam Campaign; Protestant; rec: woodworking, wine tasting. Res: 42848 Everglades Park Dr Fremont 94538 Ofc: Browning Ferris Industries, 1995 Old Oakland Rd San Jose 95131

KERIM, TAMARA NICKOLA, international trade consulting co. president; b. March 18, 1936, Odessa, Ukraine, USSR, nat. US cit. 1954; d. Nickolas R. and Vera F. (Stelingovska) Kerimly; edn: BA, UCLA 1958, Calif. Secondary and Jr. Coll. Tchg. Creds., 1962; MA, CSU Sacramento 1972. Career: tchr. gen. secondary sch., Hampton, Va. 1958-61; tchr. (orgn. fgn. language lab., devel. new curriculum for German & Russian langs.), Culver City Unif. Sch. Dist. 1961-66; tchr. (curriculum devel. for fgn. langs.), San Ramon Valley Unif. Sch. Dist. 1966-71; pres., CEO Intertorg Inc., Los Angeles and Moscow, USSR 1972–; honors: charter mem. of US-USSR Trade and Econ. Council (invited to Kremlin dinners with Pres. Brezhnev, 1979, Pres. Gorbachev, 1985, as a traditional part of bus. dialogue between two countries); Republican; Orthodox; rec: interior decorating, modern dance, painting. Res: 940 Sagamore Way Sacramento 95822 Ofc: Intertorg Inc., 10889 Wilshire Blvd. Ste. 1270 Los Angeles 90024

KERN, WILLIAM HENRY, pathologist; b. Dec. 25, 1927, Nurnberg, Germany, nat. USA 1957; s. Judge Wilhelm and Julie (Maedl) K.; m. Lynn Williams, Aug. 14, 1966; children: Julie Lynn b. 1969, Lisa Catherine b. 1970; edn: Univs. of Erlangen, Vienna and Munich, 1947-52; MD, Univ. of Munich 1952; bd. certified Am. Bd. of Pathology 1958. Career: intern Good Samaritan Hosp. Cincinnati 1952-53, res. in pathology Good Sam Hosp. Cinti and Univ. of Colo., 1953-56; dir. of pathology Hosp. of the Good Samaritan, Los Angeles 1966–, v.p. bd. of trustees (1975-) and chmn. medical staff (1972-74); clin.

prof. of path. USC Sch. of Medicine 1972 – ; v.p. bd. dirs. Am. Red Cross, L.A. Chapter 1983-, and chmn. Blood Op. Com. of L.A. and Orange Counties; mem: L.A. Acad. of Medicine (pres. 1980-81), L.A. Soc. of Pathologists (pres. 1968), Am. Soc. of Cytology (pres. 1980-81), Fellow Coll. of Am. Pathologist; clubs: Saddle & Sirloin (pres. 1980), Jonathan, Rancheros Visitadores (Charro Camp); publs: over 100 sci. papers & book chapters in field of pathology and cancer; mil: capt. M.C. USAR 1956-58; Republican; Prot.; rec: riding, skiing, history, writing. Res: 2321 Chislehurst Dr., Los Angeles 90027 Ofc: Hospital of the Good Samaritan, 616 S Witmer St Los Angeles 90017

KERNAN, REDMOND F., III, redevelopment agency executive; b. May 27, 1934, NYC; s. Redmond F., Jr. and Marguerite Rose (Ghelfi) K.; m. Deidre Jay, Sept. 19, 1964; children: John b. 1965, Julia b. 1967, Michael b. 1965; edn: BCE, Univ. of Santa Clara, 1956; Reg. Profl. Civil Engr., Calif. 1966. Career: civil engr. City and County of San Francisco Dept. of Public Works, 1958-69; chief engr. San Francisco Redevelopment Agency, 1969-72, dir. of engring. 1972-75, deputy exec. dir. Planning & Devel. 1975-78, senior deputy exec. dir. 1978 – ; dir. San Francisco Planning and Urban Research (SPUR); dir. Planning Assn. for the Richmond Dist. (PAR); mem. Am. Soc. of Mil. Engrs.; mil: lt. col. US Army 1956-58, Reserv. 1958-84, ret.; rec: sailing (racing), skiing, jogging. Res: 35 Sixth Ave San Francisco 94118 Ofc: San Francisco Redevelopment Agency 939 Ellis St San Francisco 94109

KERNS, "BETTY" (ELIZABETH) KAYTON, computer manufacturing co. executive; b. July 4, 1957, Lowell, Mass.; d. Myron and Paula Ann (Erde) Kayton; m. William Ross Kerns, March 30, 1980; edn: BA, Pomona Coll. 1977; MBA, USC 1983; CPA, Calif. (1982). Career: audit staff Arthur Young & Co., Los Angeles 1977-79; controller Customer Services Div., Carte Blanche Corp. (div. Citicorp), Los Angeles 1979-81; finl. planning mgr. TRW-Fujistu Co., Los Angeles 1981-83; co-founder, vice pres. sales/mktg. Zoltech Corp., Los Angeles 1983 – ; income tax consultant; honors: Beta Gamma Sigma, Delta Sigma Pi; mem. IEEE; participant career counseling pgm. for liberal arts grads.; mem. Pasadena Ballroom Dance Assn.; works: developed Z/MIS, acctg. software package for small to mid-size mfr. firms. Res: 344 South La Peer Dr Beverly Hills 90211 Ofc: Zoltech Corporation 7023 Valjean Ave Van Nuys 91406

KERWIN, JOHN KEVIN, co. executive; b. Feb. 2, 1943, St. Paul, Minn. s. Frank Leo and Jean Delores (Mindrum) K.; edn: BA, Univ. of Minn. 1967, EE, 1970; FAA lic. pilot (1960). Career: branch mgr. Dictaphone Corp., Rye, N.Y. 1967-69; pres. College Painters, Fargo, N.D. 1969-74; sales rep. Van Dusen Aircraft, Mnpls. 1974-79; pres. Aviation Directory, St. Paul, Minn. 1979 – ; pres., CEO Magnasign, Inc., Laguna Hills 1985 – ; founder/dir. West Side Devel. Corp., 1982-; honors: Man of the Year, Wells Fargo CofC (1971); mem. U.S. Jaycees (state dir., chapter pres.), Toastmasters, Lions, Am. Legion, VFW, Mountain Pilots, Aircraft Owners & Pilots Assn., Profl. Pilots Assn.; Republican; Catholic; rec: flying, sailing. Res: Plaza 9 Treasure Island Laguna Beach 92651

KESSLER, JUDD STUART, computer software co. president; b. Dec. 17, 1952, Orange, NJ; s. A. D. and Ruth S. K.; m. Andrea Carol, Feb. 14, 1982; 1 son, Alexander Judson b. 1986; edn: BA, UC San Diego 1972; Calif. Real Estate Broker (1972), Cert. Finl. Plnnr. (1983). Career: real estate broker 1972 – ; pres. Space Bldg. Assoc. 1972-75; dir. mktg. Profl. Edn. Found. 1976-80; pres. Timeshare Resorts Internat. 1980-82; pres. Abacus Data Systems Inc. 1983 – ; spkr., guest lectr. IAFP & ICFP regl. and nat. events; mem: Internat. Assn. for Finl. Plnng., Inst. of Cert. Finl. Plnnrs.; publs: articles in Finl. Plnng. Mag., Journ. of Finl. Plnng., Inventor of Fastplan, Finl. Plnng. Software; Republican; rec: flying, skiing, scuba. Res: P.O. Box 8873 Rancho Santa Fe 92067 Ofc: Abacus Data Systems Inc. 2775 Via de la Valle Ste. 101 Del Mar 92014

KEVER, J. WARREN, agronomist; b. Jan. 24, 1923, Valdasta, Tex.; s. Autie Travis and Bonnie Katherine (Combest) K.; m. Yvonne McIntosh, Sept. 16, 1950; children: Tom b. 1953, Kathy b. 1954, Leslie b. 1954, Connie b. 1962; edn: BS in agronomy, Texas A&M, 1947, M.Horticulture, Univ. Mo., 1950. Career: tchr. Veterans Agriculture Sch., McKinney, Tex. 1958-59; agri. researcher UC Davis, 1950-52; sales rep. John Pryor Fertilizer Co., Salinas 1952-54, Hayes-Simmons Co., Mission, Tex. 1954-55, The Triangle Co. (fertilizer), Salinas 1955-59; sales, research, prin, bd. dirs. The John Pryor Co., Salinas 1969 – ; mem: Elks, Combest Family Assn. (pres. 1975-77), Calif. Fertilizer Assn.; publs: The Story of John Pryor Co., Solutions Mag. (1980), agronomic research rel. to local fertilizer usage; mil: pfc US Army Arty. 1943-45, Germany; rec: geneology. Res: 531 Ambrose Salinas 93901 Ofc: John Pryor Co. 1505 Abbot St Salinas 93902

KEYES, JUDITH DROZ, lawyer; b. Jan. 16, 1946, Pittsburgh, Pa.; d. Blair Guthrie and Barbara Jane (Tilden) Huddart; m. Donald Droz May 25, 1968 (decd. 1969), m. David Keyes, June 6, 1970; 1 dau: Tracy b. 1969; edn: BS, Penn. State Univ. 1966; MA, Univ. of Missouri 1970; JD, UC Berkeley Boalt Hall 1975. Career: law clerk/extern Judge Stanley A. Weigel U.S. Dist. Ct. S.F. 1974; field atty. Nat. Labor Rel. Bd. 1975-76; atty./member Corbett & Kane S.F. 1976 – ; prof. Cuna Mgmt. Sch. 1985; honors: Order of the Coif 1975, Sigma Tau Delta 1966, Phi Delta Kappa 1966, Calif. Law Review 1974-75; mem: Am., Calif. bar assns. (labor law assn.); S.F. Bar Assn.; publ: Roe & Doe & the Shape of Things to Come (Wash. Univ. Law Quarterly 1974); Democrat; Unitarian Universalist; rec: ballet, swimming. Res: 6442 Hillegass Ave Oakland 94618 Ofc: Corbet & Kane APC 2200 Powell St, Ste 500, Oakland 94608

KEYS, CHRISTOPHER WILLIAM, chief financial officer, accountant; b. Apr. 20, 1959, Hackensack, N.J.; s. Clement Marvin and Helga Analise (Hartkopf) K.; edn: BA bus. econs., UC Santa Barbara 1981; CPA Calif. 1983. Career: senior acct. Arthur Young & Co. Costa Mesa 1981-84; c.f.o./controller Profl. Community Mgmt. Inc. El Toro 1984 – ; dir. PCM Escrow Svcs. Inc. Newport Beach; honors: Dean's List (4 quarters UCSB), Third Place (5-color silkscreen, N.J. Art Fair 1974); mem: Am. Inst. CPAs, Calif. Soc. CPAs, National Wildlife Fedn.; Republican; Episcopal; rec: outdoor sports, reading, music. Ofc: El Toro

KEYS, MERELD D., educator, consultant; b. June 22, 1932, Los Angeles; s. Thomas O. and Sarah F. (Walker) K.; m. Patricia Sebern, Apr. 4, 1952, div.; children: Karen b. 1954, Sheryl b. 1955, David b. 1958; m. Mary Ann Moore Saves; stepdau. Allison Saves b. 1962; edn: AA, San Bernardino Valley Coll. 1961; BA cum laude, Univ. of Redlands 1962; MA, Claremont Grad. Sch. 7 Univ. Ctr. 1966, PhD 1967; desig: Operator (Small Passenger Vessels) USCG; Instr./Adminstr., Calif. Dept. Edn. Career: instr. Idaho State Univ., Pocatello 1965-67; assoc. prof./ chmn. Philosophy Dept., State Univ. of New York, Potsdam 1967-71; pgm. chmn./ vis. prof., Nat. Humanities Series, Princeton 1970-71; grantee Nat. Endowment for the Humanities 1971-72; dir. Nat. Project Ctr. for Film & the Humanities, 1972-76; exec. dir. N.J. Edn. Consortium 1976-79; cons./ tng. rep., Princeton and Lawrence, 1979-83; owner/opr. Mereld Keys: Marine Training Programs, Westminster, Calif. and cons. prin., M. Keys: Consulting Services & Programs (small bus. & microcomputer applications), 1983 – ; cons. Coastal Piloting, Houston Marine, Louisiana 1981-83; cons./grants adminstr. Earth House, N.J. 1981-83; mem. SUNY Faculty Senate gov. com. 1969-70; recipient Distinguished Service Award, USCG Aux., Sandy Hook, N.J. (1981); mem. AAUP (pres. SUNY, Potsdam 1969-70); USCG Auxiliary (operational mem., Div. vice capt. Grp. Sandy Hook, NJ 1975-83; Long Beach, Ca. 1983-85); publs: "Justice…Trial & Error," Nat. Humanities Series (1970-), gen. editor 3 books and 27 film guides, Nat. Project Ctr. for Film & Humanities (1972-75), "Sea Lore" a hist. series in 4 East Coast monthlies (1975-82), General Boating Series (monthly), Burges Mag. (1983-), num. reviews and misc. articles; mil: 1st lt. US Army Arty. 1953-58; Ind.; rec: computers, sailing. Res: 5422 Shrewsbury Ave Westminster 92683 Ofc: Mereld Keys: Marine Training Programs, 5835-B Westminster 92683

KEZIRIAN, GREGORY EDWARD, furniture restorer, cabinetmaker; b. Mar. 19, 1948, Fresno, Calif.; s. Edward and Adeline Mary (Ganzinotti) K.; m. Kathaleen Sorensen, Mar. 19, 1979; edn: BA psychol., UC Santa Barbara 1971; indsl. arts, Fresno City Coll. 1975, CSU Fresno 1977. Career: produce material handler George Arakelian Farms Blythe, Calif. 1967-76; owner Krikor's Furniture Repair and Refinishing Fresno 1976 – ; honors: G.B. Noakes Outstanding Wood Craftsman (CSU Fresno 1977); mem. Fresno Metropolitan Museum of Art, History & Sci.; works: complete restoration of two 8-ft. tall Goddess of Justice Statues and bldg. bases for Fresno City & County Hist. Soc. 1985; Democrat; rec: music (trumpet, classical & popular), travel. Res: 836 E Clinton Fresno 93704 Ofc: Krikor's Furniture Repair & Refinishing 9555 W North Fresno 93706

KHALIL, HANY ROSHDY, physician; b. June 18, 1948, Cairo, Egypt; s. Roshdy Georgy and Marcel (Erian) K.; m. Margaret, Aug. 31, 1974; children: James b. 1977, Andrew b. 1981; edn: MD, Cairo Univ. 1971; bd. cert. Am. Board of Internal Med. 1981. Career: intern Cairo Univ. Hosp. 1971-72; internal med. resident Harts Health Authority, Harts, U.K. 1972-73; hematology res. Liverpool Area Heart Authority, U.K. 1973-75, internal med. res. 1975-76; internal med. res. Case Western Reserve, Cleveland, Oh. 1976-79; oncology res. Emery Univ., Atlanta, Ga. 1979-80; oncology res. Liverpool Area Health, U.K. 1980-81; pvt. practice oncology/ hematology/ internal medicine, Simi Valley/ Thousand Oaks 1982 – ; honors: Junior Nat. champion in tennis (Egypt) at ages 14, 16, 18, and represented Egypt on jr. & sr. tennis team (Orange Bowl) 1964-71; mem. AMA; rec: sports, beach. Res: 31720 Kentfield Ct. Westlake 91361 Ofc: 2925 Sycamore Dr Ste 101, Simi Valley 93065

KHALSA, AKAL SINGH, chiropractor; b. July 24, 1957, Detroit, Mich.; s. Edward and Helen Mary (Rakos) Koc; m. Siribani Tobin, Sept. 30, 1981; edn: undergrad. Oakland Comm. Coll. 1979; DC, cum laude, Life Chiropractic Coll. 1980. Career: yoga instr. Univ. of Ga., Life Coll., Ga. State Prison, 1977-84; founder, cons. Stress Away of Georgia, Atlanta, Ga. 1979-84; asst. dir., treas. Health, Happy, Holy Organization of Ga. Inc., 1981-84; chiropractor, G.R.D. Chiropractic Clinic, Atlanta 1981-84; tour doctor Michael Jackson Victory Tour No. Am. 1984, Paul Young World Tour, No. Am. 1985; pvt. practice chiropractic, Cedars-Sinai, Los Angeles 1985 – ; cons. Atlanta Public Schs. Fitness Ctr., Profl. Karate Assn.; Atlanta Sch. of Massage, Fulton County Juvenile Treatment Ctr. 1980-84; mem. Calif. Chiro. Assn.; publs: contbr., Beads of Truth (Sikh rel. mag.), Today's Chiropractic mag.; Sikh Dharma; rec: Martial Arts (Green Belt), marksman, stamps & coins. Ofc: Cedars-Sinai Medical Towers 8631 West 3rd St Ste 1135E Los Angeles 90048

KHAN, GULAMMOHEMMED CHAND, dental surgeon; b. Apr. 1, 1936; Bombay, India, nat. US cit. 1975; s. Chand Ahmed and Badrunnissa Kassim (Herekar) K.; m. Christine Leicht, May 24, 1975 (div. 1979); edn: BS, Inst. Sci. Coll. Bombay Univ. 1956; DDS, Govt. Dental Coll. Bombay Univ. 1962; fellowship clin. pedodont., Guggenheim Dental Clin. N.Y. 1964; MPH, Columbia Univ. 1965; LLB, Newport Univ. L.A. 1982; dentist Calif. 1980. Career: resident oral surg. Govt. Dental Coll.; research Univ. Toronto; spl. foreign student pgm. Univ. So. Calif.; assoc. Dr. Oscar Krater L.A. 1980, Dr. Louis Serpa 1981-82; solo practice Montrose 1982 – ; honors: Currimbhoy Ebrahim Scholar, Guggenheim Fellow; mem: Am., Calif. Dental Assns., Am. Public

Health Assn., Am. Endodontic Soc., Acad. of General Dentistry, Greater New England Acad. of Hypnosis, Alpha Omega, India Dental Soc. USA, Kiwanis, Montrose-Verdugo City CofC; publ: article in Bombay Dental Jour. 1962; Republican; Muslim; rec: photog. Ofc: 2435 Honolulu Ave Montrose 91020

KHAN, MOHAMMED A., national park service executive; b. in 1933, Peshawar, Pakistan ; came to USA in 1954, nat. 1959; m. Garnett K. Samples (fmr Peace Corps vol. Colombia, S.A. 1962-64); two sons: Mo Khan, Jr. and Marcus; edn: Sind Muslim Coll., Pakistan, Western Kentucky Univ., Bowling Green, and American Univ., Wash DC; evening courses, The Dept. of Agriculture Grad. Sch., Wash DC; Peace Corps tng., Utah State Univ., Logan and Calif. Poly Tech., San Luis Obispo. Career: US Peace Corps Vol./ agri. extension splst. in Morocco, North Africa, 1962-64; with US Nat. Park Service 1967 –, served as youth counselor, safety ofcr., asst. pub. rels. ofcr., with Job Corps Civilian Conservation Pgm.; served as urban projects coordinator for Nat. Capital Parks, East; coordinator Summer in the Parks Pgm. in Wash DC area,1 1969-72; apptd. Equal Employment Opportunity Splst. for the Nat. Park Svc. and coord. of Pres.'s 16-Point Pgm. for Spanish speaking of Nat. Park Svc.; apptd. 1st area mgr. for devel. of Staten Is. Unit, Gateway Nat. Recreation Area, NY and NJ Urban Parks Pgm., 1974; 1st supt. Springfield (Mass.) Armory Nat. Historic Site, 1977; 1st US Park Supt. assigned to asst. in devel. of the Asir Nat. Park, Abha, Saudi Arabia, 1980; asst. supt./Comm. Rels. and Urban Affairs mgr. Santa Monica Mtns. Nat. Recreation Area in Calif., 1984 –; honors: Recognition Certificates, 1970, 1971; Dept. of the Interior Unit Award, 2d World Conf. on Nat. Parks 1973; Conservation Award, Staten Is., NY 1974; youth award, Staten Is. Football League, 1976; Americanism medal, DAR, 1977; mem: Kiwanis Internat. 1974-, Club Internat. 1977-78, Community Leaders Club of Calif., Lutheran Coll. 1984-; rec: tennis, golf, fishing. Ofc: National Parks Service, Santa Monica Mountains National Recreation Area, 22900 Ventura Blvd, Suite 140, Woodland Hills 91364

KHAN, ZAHID SALIM, advertising agency executive; b. Mar. 5, 1935, Lahore, Pakistan, nat. US cit. 1973; s. Abdul Salim and Mahmooda Salim (Hyat) K.; children: Chris b. 1963, Robert b. 1965, Elizabeth b. 1966, Timothy b. 1967; edn: S.C. (Sr. Cambridge) Aitchison Coll. 1951; AA, City Coll. of San Francisco, 1953; BA, Univ. Calif., 1955. Career: art dir. E.T. Howard, New York 1956-58; advt. mgr. Pakistan Tobacco, Karachi 1958-68; mktg. communs. mgr. British Am. Tobacco 1968-73; cons. to Botsford Ketchum, San Francisco 1974; advt. & sales promotion mgr. Hewlett Packard, Palo Alto 1975-80; v.p. Bonfield & Assocs. Advt., San Francisco 1981–, bd. dirs. 1985-; honors: C.B.C. award, BPAA (1985), awards for Best TV comml. (1968), award for photograph, Cremona Salon of Photog. (1965); mem. Bus. Profl. Advt. Assn. (dir. No. Calif. Chpt.); works: 'The Island Story' audio-visual essay on South Pacific (1969); Liberal; rec: photog., cooking. Ofc: Bonfield & Assocs. 666 Howard St Ste 401 San Francisco 94105

KHANNA, MOHAN D.S., civil engineer; b. Nov. 1, 1930, Dhariwal, India, nat. 1975; s. Jai D.S. and Bhagwant (Kaur) K.; m. Satwant, Jan. 28, 1955; children: Kiran b. 1956, Simi b. 1959, Simar b. 1962, Suresh b. 1974; edn: dip. civil engring., Roorkee (India) Univ. 1955; BSc structural & highways, Heald Engring. Coll., S.F. 1967; var. spl. courses, UCSF, UCB; Reg. Profl. Civil Engr., State of Calif. 1971. Career: constrn. supr. Punjab State, India 1956-64; design engr. US Steel Corp. (Am. Bridge Div.), So. San Francisco 1967-69; asst. chief engr. Assoc. Constrn. Co., So. S.F. 1970-73; consulting engr. Leeds, Hill, and Jewett Co., S.F. 1973-74; prin. structural engr. Fluor Corp., San Mateo 1974-78; design engring. mgr. Raymond Kaiser Engineers Inc., Oakland 1978-84; pres. Khanna Consulting Engineers Inc. (engring. design, constrn. mgmt. and field insp. of indsl. and comml. projects), Oakland 1978-84, Redwood City 1984 –; splst in mfg. plants of Cement, Steel, Aluminum, and Power prodn. including co-generation (Power + Steam); honors: recipient Gold Watch awarded by Prime Minister of India (1957), appreciation from Pres. of India (1959), Govt. of Punjab, India (1962); mem: Am. Concrete Inst., Struc. Engrs. Assn. of No. Calif.; mem. Building Review Bd. of Redwood City; mem. adv. bd. to Senate Select Com. on Small Bus. Ents.; Democrat; Sikh; rec: religious lit., photog. Res/Ofc: Khanna Consulting Engineers, 583 Seahorse Lane Redwood City 94065

KHORRAMIAN, ABID, medical technologist; b. July 30, 1952, Teheran, Iran, nat. US cit. 1984; s. Nourollah and Anice (Cohansedgh) K.; edn: BS, Cal. Poly. Pomona 1974; MS, CSU Los Angeles 1976; acupuncture cert., Emperor Coll. 1986; med. technologist, Dept. Pub. Health 1977; real estate broker Calif. 1980. Career: tchr. Azusa Pacific Coll. 1978; med. technol. Foothill Presbyterian Hosp. 1978-81; independent real estate broker 1980 –; med. technol. Washington Med. Ctr. Culver City 1981 –; honors: Dean's List (Cal. Poly. Pomona, Emperor's Coll. Santa Monica); mem: Calif. Assn. Realtors, Calif. Acupuncture Alliance; rec: chess, backgammon, coins & stamps. Res: 11820 Mayfield Ave Apt 321 Los Angeles 90049 Ofc: Washington Hosp. 12101 Washington Blvd Culver City 91230

KHOSLA, ANAND PRAKASH, engineer; b. May 7, 1933, Simla, India, nat. US cit. 1979; s. Mulkh Raj and Sita Wati (Sarin) K.; m.Asha L., Nov. 18, 1957; 1 son, Rakesh K. b. 1958; edn: BE (Elec.), Univ. of Delhi, India 1955; ME (Elec.), Univ. of Roorkee, India 1962; Reg. Profl. Engr. (Elec.), Mich. (1973), Calif. (1976). Career: project engr. (switchgear), G.E.C., Calcutta, India 1956-70; elect. designer on contract to Union Carbide Corp., Niagara Falls, N.Y. 1970-71; elect. engr. designer Wilson Klaes Brucker & Worden, Buffalo, N.Y. 1971-72; senior elect. engr. Bechtel Power Corp., Ann Arbor, Mich. 1972-75; prin. elect. engr. Ralph M. Parsons Co., Pasadena 1975 –; honors: Martin Marietta Corp. subcontractor employee of the year (1984) for the

Ground Support Systems Pgm. at Vandenberg AFB, Launch honoree NASA Manned Flight Awareness Pgm. (9/84); mem. IEEE, Power & Indsl. Appl. Socs.; rec: swimming, photog. Res: 990 Pepperhill Rd Pasadena 91107 Ofc: Ralph M. Parsons Co. 100 W Walnut St Pasadena 91124

KHOURY, MICHEL SADALAH, construction senior engineer, purchasing/ contracts executive; b. Jan. 1, 1942, Abadieh, Lebanon, nat. US cit. 1974; s. Sadalah Elias and Victoria (Mikael) K.; m. Gladys El, Feb. 1984; children: Tarek b. 1976, Vicky b. 1985; edn: BS civil engring., cum laude, Laval Univ., Quebec, Canada 1967; MSCE, Univ. Ill. 1969; Dipl. Bus. Mgmt., La Salle Ext. Univ. 1973; MBA, UC Berkeley 1983; Reg. Profl. Engr., Calif. 1971. Career: senior engr. Bechtel Corp., San Francisco 1969-70; design supr. Bechtel Power Corp., S.F. 1970-74; asst. to VP & Mid-East Devel. mgr. International Bechtel Inc., Beirut, Lebanon 1974-75; area contracts adminstrn. supr. for New Riyadh Internat. Airport, Saudi Arabian Bechtel Co., Riyadh, Saudi Arabia 1975-81; project contracts mgr. for New Istana (Palace) Project, Bechtel Internat. Constructors Inc., Brunei, Borneo 1981-82; senior contracts/ purchasing supr. Bechtel Petroleum Inc., San Francisco 1984-86; real estate broker, Albany 1986 –; mem. ASCE (assoc.), Canadian Engring. Inst., Red Cross (Emergency Preparedness), Univ. Calif. Amateur Radio Club, Bechtel Amateur Radio Club (v.p.); publs: Engineering Design Innovation, Seismic Soils - Structural Interaction (Design Innovation Digest, Bechtel Corp., pub. 1972, 1973); research in Finite Element Techniques and Mathematical Modeling for Nuclear Power Plants; Roman Catholic; rec: amateur radio, tennis, camping. Res: 903 Ventura Ave Albany 94707 Ofc: Bechtel Inc. 50 Beale St San Francisco 94105

KHOURY, SAMI ERNEST, physician-surgeon; b. May 26, 1953, Cairo, Egypt; s. Ernest S. and Jacqueline H. (Abouzakhm) K.; m. Josiane, May 11, 1980; children: Joelle b. 1981, Michelle b. 1982; edn: BS (biol. & chem.) Am. Univ. of Beirut 1974; MD, USC 1978; lic. Bd. of Med. Quality Assurance 1980. Career: panel physician Prudential Ins. Co. 1982-85; med. cons. Calif. Social Security Disability Evaluation Div., Los Angeles 1984 –; panel physician for State of Calif. Health & Welfare Agcy., Employment Devel. Dept., L.A. 1984; pvt. practice general/family practitioner in Bell, 1980 –; staff phys. Mission Hosp. (Huntington Pk.), La Mirada Hosp. (La Mirada); mem. Calif. Med. Assn., Los Angeles County Med. Assn.; Orthodox; rec: tennis, chess, football. Res: 2519 Sleepy Spring Way Hacienda Hts 91745 Ofc: Sami Khoury MD Inc. 5101 E Florence Ave Ste 3 Bell 90201

KHWARG, STEVEN GURN J., ophthalmology/vitreoretinal surgeon; b. Mar. 23, 1956, Seoul, Korea; s. Edward S. and Susan D. K.; m. Jung Ran, May 10, 1981; children: Juewon b. 1982, Jueyoung b. 1985; edn: BS, Northwestern Univ. 1977, MD, 1981. Career: physician Huntington Meml. Hosp./USC, Pasadena 1981-82; staff phys. Jules Stein Eye Inst./UCLA Med. Center, 1982-85, vis. lectr./faculty mem. VitreoRetinal Div., 1985-87; honors: Heed Nat. Ophthalmic Found. Fellow (1985-86), Heed/Knapp Award (1986-87), Abe Meyer Fellow of Vitreoretinal Div., Jules Stein Eye Inst. (1985), best research paper award (3) for "Operating Microscope Light-Induced Maculopathy" (1985) from Jules Stein Eye Inst. Residents and Fellows Day, Pharmacia Nat. (Stockholm, Sweden) competition, Pacific Coast Oto-Ophthalmic Soc. (San Diego) competition; mem: AMA, Am. Acad. Ophthal., Calif. Assn. Ophthal., Nat. Bd. Med. Examiners; Prot. (choir); rec: classical music, tennis. Res: 3326 Sawtelle Blvd Los Angeles 90066 Ofc: Jules Stein Eye Institute 800 Westwood Plaza Los Angeles 90024

KIDD, BRIAN, educator; b. June 8, 1948, San Bernardino; s. Archie Cyril and Jean Catherine (Eakin) K.; m. Kathryn Klausner, June 22, 1974; children: Jennifer b. 1979, Jason b. 1982; edn: BA sociol., UC Santa Barbara 1970; MS counseling, CSU Fullerton 1974; MA edn., Claremont Grad. Sch. 1983; PhD 1984; Calif. Community Coll. Counselors Cred. (life), Std. Designated PPS (life). Career: instrnl. counselor Calif. Sch. for the Deaf, Riverside 1971-74; hd. counselor Yucaipa Jt. Unified Sch. Dist. 1974-80; faculty assoc./psych. cons. Univ. of Redlands 1978-80; counselor, instnl. researcher, dir. spl. projects, Mt. San Jacinto Comm. Coll. Dist., 1980 –; honors: Calif. Tchrs. Assn. Legal Award, Calif. P.T.S.A. scholarship (1973) service award (1977); mem: So. Calif. Comm. Coll. Instnl. Researchs Assn., San Bernardino Co. Counseling/ Guidance Assoc. (pres. 1978-9), Redlands- Yucaipa Guidance Clinic (bd. pres. 1977-9); author num. acad. programs, profl. presentations, art. Jour. of Rehabilitation of the Deaf (5/74); Democrat; rec: arts patron, human rights legal advocate. Res: 1705 Shirley Ln Redlands 92374 Ofc: Mt San Jacinto College 1499 N State St San Jacinto 92383

KIEFER, ELSE MARIE, gerontologist, health care administrator; b. Feb. 4, 1938, Hamar, Norway; d. Gunnar and Ingrid (Hekneby) Lie; m. Christie W. Kiefer, Dec. 20, 1980; children: Ingrid b. 1959, Rolf Gunnar b. 1963, Kristiane b. 1966; edn: BA, Queen Maud's Coll. 1960; MA, Univ. Amsterdam 1975; MA, St. Louis Univ. 1983. Career: child devel. splst. 1960-68; nutrition centers dir. AAA, Mo. 1968-73; cons. in gerontological motivation, State of Missouri, 1975-78; exec. dir. John Knox Village, Waynesville, Mo. 1978-81; pres./CEO, Mercy Retirement and Care Ctr., Oakland 1981 –; lectr. in gerontology var. univs.; cons. in gerontology; honors: Young Woman of the Year, Rolla, Mo. (1973), 7C Penny award (1985), CAHA annual award for community service (1985); mem: Calif. Assn. of Homes for the Aged (bd. mem., chair No. Region CAHA), Am. Soc. on Aging, Am. Gerontology Soc., Nordic Gerontology Soc., Catholic Health Care Assn.; civic: Diocese of Oakland Retirement Task Force, St. Mary's Hosp. Geriatic Task Force (S.F.); publs: Cross cultural study of ten European countries of care for the aged (1975), Therapeutic Community Concepts in LTC (1976, 77), New model for LTC; invited speaker many internat. confs. in Europe, US, Australia; rec: music, hiking, skiing, family. Res: 1275 Aspen Dr Pacifica 94044 Ofc: Mercy Retirement & Care Center, 3431 Foothill Blvd Oakland 94601

KIEFER, ROBERT JOHN, engineer; b. Dec. 7, 1936, Cleveland, Ohio; s. Paul Everette and Beulah Elizabeth (Moore) K.; m. Aura Ann (Nan) Knosbe, Sept. 4, 1982; children: Kelly b. 1961, Paul b. 1964; edn: BSME, cum laude, The Ohio State Univ. 1959, MS, cum laude, 1959; reg. profl. engr. (mech.) Ohio 1963, Calif. (mech. 1964, nuclear 1974). Career: proj. ofcr. Bomb Devel. Branch USAF Kirtland AFB Albuquerque 1959-62; anal. engr. General Atomic Co., San Diego 1963-71, nuclear fuel proposal mgr. 1972-75; mgr. tech. tng. Scientific Atlanta S.D. 1976–; cons. on vibration measurement and mech. diagnostics; honors: Tau Beta Pi 1958, Pi Tau Sigma 1957, Sigma Xi 1959, Phi Eta Sigma 1955, Citation Highest Ranking ROTC Student (Dean of Engrg.), Gold Medal (Soc. Am. Mil. Engrs. 1959); mem: Am. Soc. Profl. Engrs., Am. Soc. Mech. Engrs.; num. technical publs.; mil: lt. col. USAFR; Republican; Southwest Baptist Conf.; rec: tennis, skiing, hiking, jogging, bicycling. Res: 10215 Saunders Dr San Diego 92131 Ofc: Scientific Atlanta 4255 Ruffin Rd POB 23575 San Diego 92123

KIESSIG, CAROL ANN, resort operator; b. Feb. 11, 1944, Chgo.; d. Gunnar Otto and Bernice Aluilde (Johannessen) Hansen; m. Russell Kiessig, Oct. 12, 1968; children: Priscilla Anne b. 1970, Randall Otto b. 1973, (step): Richard Scott b. 1959, Stephanie Lynn b. 1961; edn: BA, honors, CSU San Jose 1966. Career: secty. Scott, Foresman & Co., Palo Alto 1966-68; administrv. asst. Mellonics Div., Litton Ind., Sunnyvale 1968-69; owner Profl. Resource Associates, Mt. View 1969-75; owner Sycamore Mineral Springs (resort), San Luis Obispo 1975–; owner/ed. Central Coast Times, S.L.O. 1977-78; owner San Juan Hot Springs (resort), San Juan Capistrano 1981–; civic: San Luis Obispo Comm. Health Council, AAUW, Las Buenas Amigas (Family Svc. Assn.), PTSA, San Juan Cap. CofC, San Juan Hist. Soc.; Republican; Lutheran; rec: creative writing. Ofc: San Juan Hot Springs POB 58 San Juan Capistrano 92693

KILIAN, OTTO HENRY, architect; b. July 1, 1923, Glendale; s. Henry O. and Elise (Hillabold) K.; m. Virginia Zerman, Sept. 15, 1945; children: Diane b. 1949, Christine b. 1950, Linda b. 1953; edn: BA, USC Sch. of Architecture 1951. Career: designer Pereira & Luckman, Los Angeles 1952-56, v.p. 1956-58; v.p. Charles Luckman Assocs., Los Angeles 1958-61, v.p. gen. mgr. 1961-70, exec. v.p. 1970-73; pres. Kilian Assocs., Glendale 1973-75; sr. v.p. William Pereira Assocs., Los Angeles 1975-78; div. mgr. Albert C. Martin Assocs., Los Angeles 1978-80; pres. Kilian Assocs., Glendale 1980–; bd. dirs. Charles Luckman Assoc. 1970-73; bd. dirs. USC Architectural Guild; honors: Commercial Design Award, Glendale Beautification Com. 1985; mem: Am. Inst. Architects, CCAIA (chmn. ins. com.), Rotary, Wilshire Country Club (bd. dirs. 1973-76); mil: CPO, athletic specialist, USN 1943-45; Republican; Episcopal; rec: golf, woodworking. Res: 1860 Las Flores Glendale 91207 Ofc: Kilian Associates, Architects, 251 No. Brand Blvd. Ste. 201 Glendale 91203

KILLEBREW, MIRIAN CLAIRE (SHARPE), sales company president; b. Oct. 25, 1920, Indianapolis, Ind.; d. Randle Percy and Lucille Edith (Horton) Sharpe; m. James Artell Killebrew, Sept. 14, 1940; children: Dorothy Jean b. 1942, Deborah Jean b. 1957; edn: AA, Placer Coll. (now Sierra Coll.) 1940. Career: v.p. K & H Sales Inc., pres. 1946-76, 1976–; mem: O.E.S. (Castro Valley chpt.), San Leandro CofC, Alta Mira Club, Oakland Mus. Assn., Nat. Right to Work Comm., Better Bus. Bur. (Eastbay), Nat. Fedn. of Ind. Bus.; Anglican-Episcopal (treas. Alter Guild); rec: golf, needlepoint, reading. Res: 18397 Magee Way Castro Valley 94546 Ofc: K & H Sales Inc., 1800 Williams St. San Leandro 94577

KILPATRICK, ALAN T., chartered life underwriter; b. Oct. 4, 1941, Los Angeles; s. Paul Wm. and Lillian Pauline (Jackson) K.; m. Jo Ann Kubasek, Apr. 6, 1968; children: Laura, b. 1972, Jason, b. 1979; edn: UC Berkeley 1959-62; BS, CSU Hayward 1970; CLU, Coll. of Life Underwriters 1969. Career: ins. agt. Mutual of Omaha, 1965-70; ins. agt. Allstate Ins. Co., 1970-73; ins. broker, Kilpatrick Insurance Agency, 1973-76; ins. broker/pres. C/K Ins. Agency, 1976–; acct. exec. Poulton Assocs., 1980–; finl. plnnr. Independent Financial Planners, 1976–; real estate inv. mgr. own co. 1971-; pres. Action Internat. (wholesale/retail distbn. co.) 1979–; gen. ptnr. Rental Properties Assocs. 1983–; formed var. real estate limited partnerships 1984-; real estate mortgage lender 1985-; lectr. on real estate topics; mem: Internat. Assn. of Fin. Planners Inc., Ind. Insurance Agts. Assn., Contra Costa Bd. of Realtors (affil. 1985-), Oakland CofC (affil.), Apt. Owners Assn. of Contra Costa County 1984-, United Profl. Investors 1984-, Small Yacht Racing Assn., commodore Venture 24/25 Fleet of No. Calif. (1984); mil: sp4 US Army 1966-67, Parachutist Badge, Vietnam Cmpgn., Viet. Svc., Nat. Def. medals; Republican (past pres. Oakland Young Repubs.); Congregational; rec: soccer coach, sailing, travel. Res: 806 Matadera Cir. Danville 94526 Ofc: Poulton Associates 140 Franklin St Oakland 94607

KIM (HARRIS), SUE ANN, county administrator; b. Mar. 12, 1924, Daegu, Korea, nat. US cit. 1965; d. Dong Hwan and Ok Chung (Choi) Kim; m. Gilbert Harris (dec.) Sept. 8, 1961; edn: BA in home econs., Women's Coll., Tokyo, Japan 1944; BA in counseling, CSU Los Angeles 1965; MA in Edn., UC Los Angeles 1967, PhD in Edn. 1970. Career: pres. Korean-Am. Fgn. Scholarship Fedn., UCLA, 1970-72, and post doctoral research staff 1970-75; research dir. Science and Technology Inc., Santa Monica 1970-75; treatment counselor Dept. of Children Services, County of Los Angeles, 1975–, dept. adminstr. 1985–; founder/ chmn. bd. dirs. Pacific Asian Consortium of Employment 1975-79; elected mem. L.A. Unified Sch. Dist. Asian-Am. Ed. Commn.

1975-76; vol. worker (8 hrs. wkly.) Korean Community Ctr. in Counseling Svcs. of newly arrived immigrants 1976-84; mem. Pvt. Post-sec. Edn. Council, Calif. State Dept. Edn. (1982-), Dean's Council mem. UCLA Grad. Sch. of Edn. (1978-), consulting advisor Korean Am. Assn. of Edn. Inc. U.S.A. (1980-); awards: recogn. Korean Consul-Gen. in Los Angeles and from the pres. Korean Assn. of So. Calif. (1972, 75, 80, 83), Korean Minister of Fgn. Affairs (1973), honored in Bicentennial Salute to Los Angeles Women of the Year by L.A. City Human Rels. Commn. (1976); mem: Profl. Womens Assn., Am. Edn. Assn., Korean-Am. Coalition, Korean-Am. Democratic Caucus/So. Calif. (v.p. 1980-83), Korean Community Ctr., Korean Womens Assn. of So. Calif. (founding pres. 1972-4); sev. scholarly publs. in field; Presbyterian; rec: piano, music appreciation. Res: 334 Anita Dr Pasadena 91105 Ofc: MacLaren Childrens Center 4024 Durfee Rd El Monte 91732

KIM, CHONG-SOO, import-export co. president; b. Jan. 27, 1941, Pyung Yang, Korea; s. Keun Su and Keun (Shin) Kim; m. Myung-Ai, Apr. 24, 1970; children: John b. 1970, Patty b. 1973, Edward b. 1977; edn: BS, Korea Univ. 1963, MBA, 1966; MBA, CSU Hayward 1974; desig: Bus. Analyst, Korea Univ. (1963). Career:gen. mgr. Jeil Moolsan Ind. Co., Ltd., Seoul, Korea 1963-70; payroll analyst United Parcel Service, Oakland, Calif. 1971-74; faculty mem. Sch. of Business, CSU Hayward 1974-75; pres. Kim Pacific Trading Corp. Inc., San Leandro 1974–; also gen. mgr. Tri Gem Computer, Inc. and acting chmn. Han ONe Electronics, Inc.; honors: award, City of Seoul (Korea) Commerce and Industries Dept., World Tae Kwon Do Fedn.; mem: Korean Am. Assn. of San Francisco and Bay Area (past v.p., chmn. Com. to Condemn USSR), Korean Am. CofC; contbr. newspaper articles to Korea Times, San Francisco; Republican; Catholic; rec: martial arts, speed skate, ski. Ofc: Kim Pacific Trading Corp. Inc. 1451 Doolittle Dr San Leandro 94577

KIM, DUKE DONG-BACK, physician; b. Jan. 29, 1941, Pusan, Korea, nat. US citizen; s. Joo Yeon and Suk Soon (Shin) K.; m. Bonnie Ryu, Dec. 29, 1963; children: Janet b. 1969, Tim b. 1976; edn: pre-med., Pusan Nat. Univ. 1960, 1964; certified Am. Board of Pediatrics 1974. Career: pediatric residency tng. UC Irvine Med. Center 1968-71; pvt. practice pediatrics, Mission Viejo 1972–; clin. instr. Dept. Ped., UCI; pastor Korean Fellowship Calvary Chapel, Costa Mesa; Fellow Am. Acad. of Pediatrics; mil: lt. Med. Corps Navy, ROK; Christian; rec: pianist. Ofc: 27800 Medical Center Rd Ste 116 Mission Viejo 92691

KIM, EDWARD, superior court judge; b. Jan. 17, 1923, Riverside; s. David and Maria (Melendrez) K.; m. Lucille Martin, June 8, 1966; children: Nancy b. 1954, Gloria, b. 1963, Maria, b. 1963; edn: AA, Reedley Coll. 1948; AB, UC Los Angeles 1950; LLB, JD, Hastings Coll. of Law 1954. Career: atty. Tulare County Dist. Atty. Office, 1955-58; Tulare County Public Defender, 1959-70; Juvenile Referee, 1972-74; judge Dinuba Justice Ct., 1975-78; judge Tulare County Superior Ct., 1978–; mem. Tulare Co. Bar Assn. (pres. 1973), Tulare Co. Legal Services (chmn. 1974), Rotary Club Dinuba (pres. 1972); Democrat; Ofc: County Courthouse, Civic Center, Visalia 93277

KIM, EDWARD (YOUNG-KI), manufacturing- packaging export co. president; b. March 23, 1932, Busan, Korea; s. Ee-Mann and Keum An Su K.; m. Nam Sook, Dec. 28, 1959; childrcn: Dong Su b. 1961, Yoon- Hee b. 1962, Sung Su b. 1965; edn: BSChE, Seoul Nat. Univ. 1955. Career: founder, pres. Hap-Sung Inc., Korea 1956-70; founder, pres. Bestway Recycling Co. Inc., Los Angeles 1971–; honors: cash prize in mfg., Pres. Rhee, Korea; num. awards, KAC/ KYC; mem: So. Calif. Sherriff's Support Group, Seoul Nat. Univ. Alumni Assn. of So. Calif. (past chmn.), Waste Paper Assn., Korean- American Trade Assn. (past); patentee: indsl. part, Korea; mil: Korean Airforce; Democrat. Rec: 3751 Westfall Dr. Encino 91436 Ofc: Bestway Recycling Co. Inc., 2268 E Firestone Blvd Los Angeles 90002

KIM, EDWARD WILLIAM, ophthalmic surgeon; b. Nov. 25, 1949, Seoul, Korea; s. Shoon Kul and Ellen Clara (Kim) K.; m. Carole Takemoto, July 24, 1976; children: Brian b. 1979, Ashley b. 1982; edn: BA, Occidental Coll. 1971; post grad, Calif. Inst. of Tech. 1971; MD. UC San Francisco 1975; MPH, UC Berkeley 1975. Career: intern S.F. Gen. Hosp. 1975-76; clin. fellow/res. ophthalmol. Harvard Med. Sch./Mass. Eye and Ear Infirmary, Boston 1977-79; clin. fellow retina, Harvard Med. Sch. 1980; pvt. practice ophthalmol. S. Laguna, Calif. 1980–; vice chief of Staff So. Coast Med. Ctr. S. Laguna; honors: Reinhart Scholar 1972-73, R. Taussig Sholar 1974-75; mem: fellow Am. Coll. of Surg., fellow Am. Acad. of Ophthalmol., fellow Internat. Coll. of Surg., Am. Intraocular Implant Soc., Kerato Refractive Soc., CMA, Harvard Alumni Assn., Orange Co. Ctr. for Performing Arts (founding mem.), Laguna Bch. Summer Music Festival (pres. 1984), MENSA; publ: arts. in ophthalmol. journs. Ofc: Ophthalmic Assoc. 31872 Coast Hwy, Ste. 203, S Laguna 92677, 655 Camino Los Mares, Ste 117, San Clemente 92672

KIM, EDWARD Y(OUNG-KI), manufacturing- packaging export co. president; b. March 23, 1932, Busan, Korea; s. Ee-Mann and Keum An Su K.; m. Nam Sook, Dec. 28, 1959; childrcn: Dong Su b. 1961, Yoon- Hee b. 1962, Sung Su b. 1965; edn: BSChE, Seoul Nat. Univ. 1955. Career: founder, pres. Hap-Sung Inc., Korea 1956-70; founder, pres. Bestway Recycling Co. Inc., Los Angeles 1971–; honors: cash prize in mfg., Pres. Rhee, Korea; num. awards, KAC/ KYC; mem: So. Calif. Sherriff's Support Group, Seoul Nat. Univ. Alumni Assn. of So. Calif., Waste Paper Assn., Korean- American Trade Assn. (past); patentee: indsl. part, Korea; mil: Korean Airforce; Democrat. Rec: 3751 Westfall Dr. Encino 91436 Ofc: Bestway Recycling Co. Inc., 2268 E. Firestone Blvd. Los Angeles 90002

KIM, FRANK, judge; b. Jan. 15, 1931, Marysville, Calif.; s. Edwin and Helen (Tom) K.; m. Patricia, Aug. 15, 1959; children: Karen b. 1960, Allison b. 1963, Robin b. 1967, Christian b. 1968, Ashley b. 1976; edn: AA, Yuba Coll. 1952; LLB and JD, Hastings Coll. of Law 1959; admitted Calif. State Bar 1959. Career: dep. dist. atty. San Joaquin County 1960-62; pvt. law practice 1962-71; apptd. by Gov. Ronald Reagan judge Stockton Municipal Ct. 1971; apptd. by Gov. Jerry Brown judge Superior Ct. of San Joaquin Co. 1979—, asst. presiding judge, 1985—; Stockton Planning Commnr. 1965-71, chmn. 1967; named Traffic Court Judge of Year 1976, Sacto. Safety Council; mem. Chinese Assn. of Stockton (English secty. 1966-71), Stockton Cathay Club (pres. 1969-70), Gee Deck-Sam Deck Assn. (pres. 1968-69), Calif. Judges Assn., Calif. Judges Found.; mil: s/sgt. US Army 1952-54; Catholic; rec: tennis. Ofc: Superior Ct., 222 E. Weber Ave., Stockton 95202

KIM, HENRY, accountant; b. Sept. 5, 1946, Korea; s. Harvart R. and Sook Young (Park) K.; m. Yon Kim, Oct. 27, 1976; children: Christopher b. 1978, Catherine b. 1980; edn: BS acctg., CSU Los Angeles 1975; CPA Calif. Career: govtl. auditor III State of Calif. 1975-83; owner Henry Kim CPA firm; advisor Korean/Am. Garment Industry Assn.; spkr. on tax issues to profl. and civic orgs.; mem: Am. Inst. CPAs, Calif. Soc. CPAs (chmn. discussion group), Korean CPA Soc. (vice chmn.), Middle Age Club (United Meth. Ch., chmn.); mil: sp5 US Army 1969-73, Army Commdn. Medal; Republican; Methodist; rec: travel. Res: 12339 Gettysburg Dr Norwalk 90650 Ofc: Henry Kim CPA 955 S Vermont Ave Ste M Los Angeles 90006

KIM, JAMES JAE HO, electrical engineer; b. Mar. 5, 1962, Seoul, S. Korea, nat. US cit. 1975; s. Sa Man and Chong Hui (Lee) K.; edn: BSEE, cum laude, Univ. of the Pacific 1985, grad. stu. MSEE, Univ. of Santa Clara 1985-. Career: student engr. (GS-4) NASA Ames Research Ctr., Moffett Field 1983; lab. asst. UOP Sch. of Engring., Stockton 1984-85; assoc. engr. Lockheed Missiles & Space Co., Inc. Sunnyvale 1984—; honors: UOP Dean's List (1983, 85), Nat. Dean's List (1983, 85), Eta Kappa Nu (1983-85); mem: IEEE, Assoc. Engring. Students UOP (1980-5), UOP Alumni Assn., UOP Korean Students Assn. (1984); Republican; rec: Tae Kwon Do (Black Belt), sports, nature. Res: 10154 Parkwood Dr #1 Cupertino 95014 Ofc: Lockheed Missiles & Space Co Inc POB 3504 0/81-86 B/15 Sunnyvale 94088-3504

KIM, JONG WAN, educator, doctor of Oriental Medicine; b. July 14, 1937, Kyonggi-Do, Korea (South); s. Myong Kwan and Gui Jeon (Lee) K.; 1 son, Andrew Bong; edn: AS, Laney Coll., Oakland 1976; BA, Dong-Gook Univ., Korea 1962; MA, No. Ill. Univ. 1970; PhD SAMRA (Chinese Medical) Univ. 1983; OMD, San Francisco Coll. of Acupuncture 1984; lic. Certified Acupuncturist, Calif. BMQA 1977. Career: director/ acupuncturist Jong Inst. of Acupuncture Medicine, Oakland 1977-79; dir./ acupuncturist and herbalist Family Acupuncture Clinic & Herbs Center, San Lorenzo 1980—; prof. of acupuncture and oriental med., San Francisco Coll. of Acupuncture, 1981—; mem. Korean Acupuncture & Herbs Assn. of No. Calif. (pres. 1985); honored speaker 2nd Internat. Congress of Chinese Medicine, 7/85; research: on Blood Groups A B O and relationship to Korean Constitutional Acupuncture (10 years); mil: ROK Army 1957-58; Buddhist; rec: Zen, gardening, community health. Res: 160 Sparrow Dr Hercules 94547 Ofc: 17259 Hesperian Blvd, Ste 3, San Lorenzo 94580

KIM, JUNG CHUL, business owner; b. Apr. 6, 1926, Seoul, Korea; nat. 1974; s. Ri Hyon and Do Hyon (Hong) K.; m. Jang Ho, Apr. 10, 1957; children: Yong Sung, b. 1958; Yong Rim, b. 1959; Yong Joo, b. 1961; Masters Degree, Gunkook Univ. 1959. Career: Katusa personnel ofcr. Korea Mil. Adv. Gp. (KMAG) 1963-68; camp mgr. Chulai Base, Philco Ford Corp. 1968-70; owner Meadowmaid Farms, Los Angeles 1974-79; owner, Long Beach Suzuki, Long Beach 1979-84, Long Beach Suzuki- Kawasaki 1984—; personnel mgmt., Adjutant Gen. Sch. 1959; honors: Master Achiev., US Suzuki Corp. 1982, 83; Achiev., Personnel Mgmt., KMAG 1963; mil: maj. Adjutant Gen. Corps; Presbyterian. Res: 7501 Los Trancos Cir La Palma 90623 Ofc: Long Beach Suzuki, 2441 Long Beach Blvd Long Beach 90806

KIM, KWANG EUN, acupuncturist/chiropractor/herbalist; b. Sept. 15, 1938, Seoul, Korea, nat. 1974; s. Ick Chae and Tan (Ock) K.; m. Kyung Sook Yoo, Jnue 17, 1966; children: Sion, b. 1967; Yale, b. 1969; Royle, b. 1975; edn: BA, Union Christian Coll., Seoul 1960; MA, Yonsei Univ., Seoul 1962; DC, Cleveland Chiropractic Coll. 1973; M.Herb., Emerson Coll. of Herbology 1981; PhD, cand., Donsbach Univ. 1982. Career: pvt. practice acupuncturist, chiropractor, herbalist, nutritionist; pres. Dr. Kwang Eun Kim, DC, Inc., Los Angeles; clin. asst. tchr. Cleveland Chiro. Coll., L.A. 1972-73; bd. dirs. New Internat. Mortgage Corp.; apptd. by Calif. State Senate as mem. Council on Technology Edn.; mem: Am. Chiro. Assn., Found. for Chiro. Edn. & Research/ USA, Fellow Research Council on Botanic Medicine/ Canada, Am. Acupuncture Assn., Am. Nutrition & Herbal Med. Assn., Korean Chiropractic Assn. of US (pres.), Korean-Am. Christian Bus. Mens Com. of So. Calif., Korean Ch. Music Assn.(pres.); Republican; Presbyterian; rec: pictures, coins, stamps. Res: 645 Hillcrest Ave, Flintridge 91011 Ofc: Dr. Kwang Eun Kim, DC, Inc. 252 S Oxford Ave Los Angeles 90004

KIM, KWANG KEUN, dentist; b. June 15, 1941, Seoul, Korea, nat. US cit. 1980; s. Chang Hoon and Bong Soon K.; m. Kyung Sook, Mar. 9, 1965; children: Sandy b. 1965, Paul b. 1969, Joseph b. 1971; edn: DDS, Seoul Nat. Univ. Sch. of Dentistry 1965, MS, SNU Postgrad. Sch. 1967, PhD 1975; lic. DDS, Calif. 1976. Career: own dental practice Seoul Korea 1968-69, dental ofcr. R.O.K. Army 1969-72; own practice, Arleta 1978-80, ptnrship practice, La Puente 1980-84, own practice, Los Angeles 1984—; mem. Korean Dental

Assn. of USA (v.p.); contbr. dental publs., Korea; rec: photog. Res: 1011 Matilija Rd Glendale 91202 Ofc: Dr. Kim's Dentistry 2900 W 8th St Ste 2 Los Angeles 90005

KIM, SUNG HO, acupuncturist; b. June 18, 1936, Inchon, Korea; s. Young OK and Bok Soon (Yu) K.; m. Young, Jan. 4, 1982; 1 child, Tammi Young b. 1984; edn: grad. Dong Yang Oriental Med. Univ. 1961-64; grad. Tong Han Acupuncture Inst. for Specializing Five Elements Tech. Acup., Seoul 1964-66; R&D for acup. and herbal medicine with Dr. Seung Y. Han, East-West Med. Research Ctr., Seoul 1966-70; grad. Korean Finger Therapy Research Inst., Seoul 1971-72; PhD health scis., Columbia Pacific Univ. 1983; OMD, San Francisco Coll. of Acup. & Oriental Medicine 1984. Career: acupuncturist Oriental Herbal Art Gymnasium, Phila., Pa. 1972-73; Kims Acupuncture Offices, Honolulu, Hawaii 1974-79; Dr. Sung Ho Kim, PhD/C.A., Acupuncture Clinic, Sunnyvale 1980—; oral examiner State of Calif. Acup. Examiner 1981, acupuncturist examiner 1984; prof. San Francisco Acup. Coll. 1983-; mem: United Acupuncture of Calif. Assn., Hawaii State Acup. Assn., Korean Acup. Assn., CofC of No. Calif.; publs: research on cancer; Christian; rec: golf. Res: 854 Durshire Sunnyvale 94087 Ofc: Kim's Acupuncture Clinic 970 West El Camino Real Ste 2 Sunnyvale 94087

KIM, YEONG JO, investment co. president; b. Aug. 2, 1938, Daegu, Korea, nat. US cit. 1979; s. Hyeong Shoo and Goe (Buhk) K.; m. Hong Ja, Dec. 27, 1967; children: Hyeon J. b. 1965, Seong H. b. 1967, Hyeon S. b. 1969; edn: BA, Kyung-puk National Univ. 1964; spl. courses Premier Real Estate Sch., Los Angeles City Coll.; Calif. lic. R.E. Broker 1980. Career: real estate broker assoc. Coldwell Banker, Glendale, later with Am. Realty Centre, Los Angeles; current owner/ pres. Daisy Group Investor, and Daisy Ridge Garment Industry; mem. Korean-Am. Garment Industry Assn. (profl. awards), Calif. Assn. Realtors; rec: tennis, hiking. Res: 1811 Morton Ave #308 Los Angeles 90026 Ofc: Daisy Group 714 S Hill St Te 605 Los Angeles 90014

KIM, YOON HAN, accountant; b. Nov. 9, 1954, Seoul, Korea; s. Yong Jin and Ki Cheol (Shin) K.; m. Keum Kyu, June 3, 1978; children: Yoo Dong b. 1979, Hyo Dong b. 1982; edn: BBA, Sung Kyun Kwan Univ. 1977; MBA, Seoul National Univ. 1981; MPA, Ga. State Univ. 1984. Career: researcher Korean Devel. Inst. Seoul 1977-78; CPA Coopers & Lybrand Seoul 1978-81; CPA/mgr. Cho, Cho & Yoo 1984-86; Yoon Han Kim & Co., CPA 1986—; instr. Hankook Univ. of Fgn. Studies; pres. Korean Student Assn. at Ga. State Univ.; honors: Dean's Scholar (Sung Kyun Kwan Univ.), Univ. Scholar (Seoul Nat. Univ.); mem: Korean Inst. CPAs, Am. Inst. CPAs, Calif. Soc. CPAs; publ: Interperiod Allocation of Income Tax, Korean translation of Montgomery's Auditing; Presbyterian; rec: tennis, golf, travel. Address: Yoon Han Kim & Co., CPA 435 S Gramercy Pl #16 Los Angeles 90020

KIMBALL, DOUGLAS EUGENE, financial consultant; b. Feb. 18, 1945, Newark, N.J.; s. Edward and Mary Elizabeth (Drake) K.; m. LaVone, Aug. 6, 1962; children: Kelly Ann b. 1965, Michele b. 1966; edn: BBA, Jackson State Univ. 1966; Becker CPA Review 1973, Univ. Texas Grad. Sch. 1975. Career: internal auditor/ asst. v.p. fin. Dallas County Comm. Coll. 1973-78; asst. internal auditor Univ. Texas S.W. Medical Sch. 1970-73; chief fiscal ofcr. Better Valley Services, 1978-85, South Bay Free Clinics, 1983—; mem. bd. dirs. Better Valley Services and Victims Anonymous (comm. services orgns.); honors: community recogn., Sen. Allan Robbins (1981, 82, 83); mem. Nat. Assn. Accts. 1972-78, Nat. Assn. Notary Publics 1981-85, Profl. Bowlers Assn. 1960-66, Lions Club; mil: E4 USAR 1961-67; Republican; Lutheran; rec: golf, bowling. Res: 2200 Vanderbilt Ln #20 Redondo Beach 90278 Ofc: South Bay Free Clinics 1807 Manhattan Beach Blvd Manhattan Beach 90266

KIMBALL, ROGER STANLEY, physician; b. May 18, 1935, Portland, Ore.; s. Stanley and Sylvia (Seymore) K.; m. Patricia Wadsworth, April 20, 1970; children: Keri Ann b. 1971, Dyana b. 1975; edn: BA, Stanford Univ. 1957; MA, UC Berkeley 1958; MD, Albany (NY) Med. Coll. 1962. Career: pvt. medical practice, San Francisco; asst. clin. prof. med. Dept. of Med., Univ. of Calif. Med. Ctr., San Francisco; awards: Outstanding Intern of the Year 1962; mem: Am. Med. Assn., ASIM; mil: capt. USAR; Republican; Protestant. Res: 183 Los Robles Dr. Burlingame 94010 Ofc: 350 Parnassus Ave. San Francisco 94117

KIMBLE, THOMAS MICHAEL, bank executive; b. Mar. 2, 1949, Highland Park, Mich.; s. James Walter and Martha (Eshleman) K.; m. Sandra, Aug. 15, 1970; children: Brent b. 1975, Ryan b. 1979; edn: BA econs., Judson Coll. 1971; No. Ill. Univ. 1974; Nat. Sch. of Bankcard Mgmt. 1982; Pacific Coast Banking Sch. 1985-87. Career: br. mgr. Household Finance Corp. Chgo. 1974-77, asst. to v.p./ spl. assignments HFC Hdqs. Chgo. 1977-78, proj. mgr./ mktg. Prospect Hts., Ill. 1978-80; dist. mgr. HFC Industrial Bank & Thrift Group Colo. & Utah 1980-81; spl. assignment Valley Nat. Bank Salinas, Calif. 1981-82, v.p., controller 1982-83, senior v.p. br. adminstrn. 1983-85; senior v.p. Household Bank fsb, Newport Beach 1985—; dir: Valley Nat. Bank, The Household Bank- Salinas; honors: Dean's List (Judson Coll. 1971); mem: Salinas Area CofC (dir. 1985-86, v.p. econ. devel. 1986), Rotary, Elks (ofcr. 1984-85); mil: sp4 US Army Nat. Guard 1971-77; Republican; Protestant; rec: golf, refinishing furniture and golf clubs. Ofc: Household Bank fsb POB 80032 Salinas 93912

KIMM, YOUNG MOON, computer high technology co. executive; b. July 20, 1931, Korea, nat. US cit. 1961; s. Duk Sun and Kyung Shim (Park) K.; m. Christine Lee, Dec. 20, 1980; children: Curtis b. 1959, Anthony b. 1963, Lorissa b. 1963, Susan b. 1970; edn: BSEE, Univ. of Wisc. 1961; dip., Stanford Univ. Grad. Sch. of Bus. 1974. Career: regl. mgr. for Asia, Control Data Corp.

of Minneapolis, Minn. 1961-70; exec. dir. Contral Data Japan Inc., Japan 1971-74; pres. Control Data Korea Corp., Korea 1971-75; ind. cos. computer ind. 1975-77; v.p. Pacific/ Latin Am. mktg. Data Products Corp. 1977-81; v.p., gen. mgr. Comrex Internat. Inc., Torrance 1981-85; pres., CEO Peripheral Technology Inc., Simi Valley 1985—; dir: Control Data Far East, Control Data Japan, Internat. Leasing Corp. 1970-75; cons: Data-100, Epson, DataProducts, Sumitomo Corp., Contro Data 1975-77; recipient, Presdtl. Citation for export bus., Repub. of Korea 1970; mem. IEEE (v.p. Computer Group Japan chpt. 1973-74); publs: U.S. Business vs. Japanese Business, 1972; Space Navigational Techniques, 1952; Republican; Methodist; rec: golf, skiing. Res: 11849 Susan Dr. Granada Hills 91344 Ofc: Peripheral Technology Inc., 685 E Cochran St Simi Valley 93065

KIMMEL, LYNN ANN, accountant; b. July 3, 1958, Rochester, N.Y.; d. Ronald Kenneth and Gudrun Anna Berta (Degel) Kimmel; edn: BS acctg., Loyola Marymount Univ. 1980; Certified Public Acct., Calif. (1983). Career: staff acct. Ernst & Whinney, Los Angeles 1980-84, supvr. 1984; chief finl. ofcr. Fremont Insurance Services, Los Angeles 1984—; honors: Loyola Marymount Univ. Business Alumni award (1980); mem. Am. Inst. CPAs; Ponderosa Homeowners Assn. (CFO 1984-85); treas. Campaign to elect George Nakano, Torrance City Council; Republican; rec: travel, fgn. languages. Ofc: Fremont Insurance Services 1709 West 8th St Los Angeles 90017

KIMMELMAN, PHILIP, architect; b. Sept. 14, 1910, Trenton, N.J.; s. Louis and Rose (Kluger) K.; m. Anne, Dec. 28, 1943; children: Lawrence b. 1946, Janis b. 1947, Walter b. 1949; edn: B.Arch, USC 1936; pre-med. UCLA 1935-37; structural engring., Wm. Porsch 1948; cert. fallout shelter analysis (1967), protective constrn. design (1967), environmental engring. (1968), US Dept. Def. Office of Civil Defense; Reg. Arch., Calif. (1949). Career: designer/draftsman var. arch. firms., Los Angeles 1935-38, Universal Picture Studios, L.A. 1937-38, Calif. State Div. of Arch., Sacramento 1938-41; architect War Dept. US Engineers, Sacramento, Los Angeles 1941-43; architect: Projects, Welton Becket Assocs., Los Angeles 1945-85, dir. Supvsn. Architects, Engineers; types developed: auditoriums, convention, sports, banks, univs., cemeteries, dept. stores, hosps., hotels, medical, clinical, parking, office, residtl., restaurants, shopping ctrs., air terminals, airfields, airports, federal, state & city, detention, religious; practicing consulting architect, Los Angeles, architl. cons.: Calif. State Energy Resources & Devel. Commn. to estab. new Energy Stds. for new non-residential bldgs. (1974-77), Los Angeles Dept. of Bldg. & Safety Code coms. to estab. new codes (for heating, ventilating, air condtg. & refrig., electrical, elevators) (1966-); awards: for Welton Becket projects include The first US Spiral Ramp Parking Structure for Gen. Petroleum Corp. (1948) used as model; first new dept. store concept, Bullocks Pasadena (1947); AIA commendations as Code & Planning Com. chmn. & mem. (1955-); mem: Am. Inst. of Archs., Wash DC, Calif. Council A.I.A., Sacto., So. Calif. Chpt. A.I.A., Los Angeles, 1955-; mem. AARP 1985-; mil: tech5 Detached Engr. Sect. US Army 1943-45, Asiatic Pacific campaign medal; Democrat; Jewish; rec: tennis, art. Address: Philip Kimmelman Architect AIA, 8973 Wonderland Park Ave Los Angeles 90046

KIMPORT, DAVID LLOYD, lawyer; b. Nov. 28, 1945, Hot Springs, S.D.; s. Ralph E. and Ruth N. (Hutchinson) K.; m. Barbara Buggert, Apr. 2, 1976; children: Katrina b. 1978, Rebecca b. 1981; edn: AB, Bowdoin Coll. 1968; Univ. of London 1970-71; JD, Stanford Univ. 1975; admitted Calif. State Bar. Career: assoc. atty. Baker & McKenzie San Francisco 1975-82, ptnr. 1982—, admin. ptnr. 1983-84; honors: Phi Beta Kappa 1967; mem: Am. (bus., commercial and internat. sects.), Calif. and S.F. bar assns. 1975-; Bar of U.S. Supreme Ct. 1978-; S.F. Planning and Urban Research Assoc. 1979-; Commonwealth Club of Calif. 1984-; mil: sgt. US Army 1968-70, Bronze Star, C.I.B.; Democrat; Episcopal; rec: piano, reading, trains. Ofc: Baker & McKenzie 580 California St, Ste. 500, San Francisco 94104

KINCAID, JOHN EDWARD, psychologist, administrator; b. Dec. 11, 1948, Cleveland, Ohio; s. Walter Perry and Rose Dravoe (Keim) K.; m. Arlene Rae Marcus, Sept. 8, 1984; 1 son, Jason M. b. 1985; edn: BA, biol., edn., Dickinson Coll. 1970; MS in counseling, CSU Hayward 1974; PhD, Calif. Sch. of Profl. Psychology, Berkeley 1980; Lic. Psychologist, Calif. 1982. Career: clin. psychologist in public sector and pvt. practice, Lafayette 1983—, pvt. splst. in school aged children, adolescents, adults and forensic issues; var. positions with Contra Costa County Health Services Dept., 1975—, currently supr. Mental Health and Substance Abuse Pgms., Main Detention Facility, Martinez; consult. and tng. Standards for Training in Corrections (STC) 1983-; mem: Am. Correctional Health Services Assn. (bd. dirs. Calif. Chpt.), Calif. Assn. of Psychology Providers (bd. dirs., v.p. 1983-84), Am. Psychological Assn., Contra Costa County Psychol. Assn., Assn. for the Advance. of Psychology; med. staff Merrithew Meml. Hosp., Martinez; publs: profl. papers and articles, research; Democrat; rec: construction, mechanics. Ofc: Detention Facility Mental Health/ Substance Abuse Programs, 1000 Ward St Martinez 94553

KING, BENJAMIN EARL (Tom), lawyer; b. July 10, 1929, Camden, Ark.; s. Ben E. and Henrietta (Weitzman) K.; edn: BS, Univ. of Ore. 1951; LLB, UCLA Sch. of Law 1956; admitted State Bar of Calif. (1957), US Supreme Ct., US Ct. of Appeals (9th Cir.), US Dist. Cts. (So., Central, No., Eastern dists. Calif.). Cert. Civil Trial Splst., Nat. Bd. of Trial Advocacy. Career: Deputy Attorney General, State of Calif. 1957-60; prin. law firm of Buchalter, Nemer, Fields, Chrystie & Younger, APC, Los Angeles 1963—; mem. L.A. County Commn. on Judicial Procedures 1975-78; Vol. Hearing Referee, State Bar Courts, 1978-; lectr. Calif. Contg. Edn. of the Bar; Fellow Am. Coll. of Trial Lawyers 1982-; mem: Am. Bar Assn., Assn. of Bus. Trial Lawyers (bd. govs. 1983-85, editor

ABTL Report 1980-82), L.A. County Bar Assn. (edtl. bd. Bar Bull. 1966-71), UCLA Law Alumni Assn. (pres. 1959-60), Lawyers Advisory Council, Constnl. Rights Found. 1981-; articles in Am. Bar Assn. Jour., Calif. Lawyer, Los Angeles Lawyer, other profl. publs.; contbr. chapters in Calif. Condemnation Practice and Calif. Civil Procedure During Trial, (Calif. CEB); contbg. ed. Civil Litigation Reporter (Calif. C.E.B.) 1985-; author: In the Shadow of the Giants-Mountain Ascents Past & Present (A.S.Barnes & Co. Inc. 1981); articles in Sport, Summit, Carte Blanche, Travel, Sir, Scholastic Coach, L.A. Times, Mainichi (Tokyo), Nippon Times (Tokyo), The Statesman (Calcutta), other publs.; clubs: American Alpine, L.A. Athletic; Democrat; Jewish; rec: skiing, mountaineering. Ofc: Buchalter, Nemer, Fields, Chrystie & Younger, APC, 700 S. Flower St, Ste 700, Los Angeles 90017

KING, CLIFTON W., clergyman; b. June 9, No. Carolina; s. Samuel Walton Sparks and Anne Elizabeth King; m. Loriene Chase, May 24, 1974; Dr. of Humane Letters; ordained, Internat. Fedn. of Divine Sci. Chs. Career: Chase-King Personal Development Ctrs.; minister Santa Anita Ch., Arcadia; minister Divine Sci. Ch., Beverly Hills; minister Encino Community Ch., Tarzana 1977—; pres. Chase/ King Productions Inc.; lectr. on stress; wkshps. on motivation and successful living; pvt. counseling; fmr. staff USC Stress Ctr.; splst. dream analysis and meditation as healing aids; mil: chaplain US Army USC, WWII; author: Two-Way Prayer; Happiness Through the Beatitudes; co-author, The Human Miracle; mem: Internat. Assn. Ch. Bus. Adminstrs., Order of St. Luke the Physician, Internat. Platform Assn., Navy League, Bel Aire Council (life), Confrerie de la Chaine des Rotisseurs, Lakeside Country Club, Beverly Hills CofC. Res: 4925 Tarzana Woods Dr. Tarzana 91356 Ofc: 5955 Lindley Ave. Tarzana 91356

KING, COLLEEN ELIZABETH, company president; b. Jan. 11, 1944, Alberquerque, N.Mex.; d. Kenneth Joseph and Mary Jeannette (Ingraham) Quigley; m. Wayne King, Aug. 8, 1964; children: Patricia b. 1965, Kenneth b. 1977, Geoffrey b. 1979; edn: Long Beach State Coll. 1961-64; Brigham young Univ. 1985-. Career: v.p. Quigley Corp., Fullerton; treas. Resort Enterprises Inc., Big Bear Lake 1975-80; pres., chmn. King Services, Victorville 1979—; mem: Young Presidents Orgn., Victor Valley CofC; Ch. of Jesus Christ LDS; rec: golf, tennis. Ofc: King Services Inc., 15345 Bonanza Victorville 92392

KING, CURTIS HOWARD, realty co. president; b. July 4,. 1949, Great Falls, Mont.; s. Robert Carl and Ione Marie (Randolph) K.; m. Sharon Ann Jones, July 30, 1977; children: Steven b. 1983, Kristin b. 1984; edn: BS, Cal Poly 1971, Secondary Tchg. Credential, 1972, MS, 1974; Calif. Real Estate Sales lic., 1978, R.E. Broker lic., 1981. Career: secondary tchr. Fairfield- Suisun Unif School Dist. 1972-79; sales agent Allstate Realtors, Vacaville 1978-80; pres. K & K, Inc., dba American West Realty 1981— and Ashland Properties 1979—; counselor/ tchr. Am. Inst. for Foreign Study 1976-77; investment counseling/ cons. Allstate Realtors 1978-80, Am. West Realty 1981-; honors: v.p. Fairfield-Suisun Unif. Tchrs. Assn. 1978, Salesman of the Yr., Allstate Reltors 1979, 80; mem: No. Solano Co. Bd. Realtors; Nat. & Calif. Assns. Realtors; Inst. Real Estate Mgmt.; Vacaville Cofc; Calif. Real Estate PAC; Issues Mobilization PAC; Democrat; Lutheran; rec: pvt. pilot, skiing, travel. Res: 179 Cheyenne Dr Vacaville 95688 Ofc: American West Realty (Ste. B) Ashland Properties (Ste. C) 501 E Monte Vista Vacaville 95688

KING, CYNTHIA ELAINE, word processing specialist; b. Nov. 10, 1950, Berkeley; d. Charles Olney and Christine Miles (Thomas) King; edn: BA, Univ. of Puget Sound, 1972. Career: reader for visually handicapped Berkeley Unified Sch. Dist. 1966-68; temp. typist Kelly Svcs. in Redding, Calif. and Tacoma, Wash., 1968-73; asst. to exec. secty. Corp. Plnng. Group, Crown Zellerbach Corp., San Francisco 1973-75, adminstrv. asst. Corp. Information Ctr. 1975-76; exec. typist self-empl., 1975-80; live-in governess, 1976; adminstrv. asst. Cutter Labs. Inc., Berkeley 1977-79; secty. Altus Corp., Palo Alto 1979-80; owner/cons. Cindy's Typing & Organizing Svc., 1980-83, Cindy's Typing & Word Processing Service, Los Altos 1980—; cons. in new bus. startups (word processing bus.), trainer, computer users; frequent lectr. Peninsula Bus. Svcs. Assn. and var. computer users groups; mem: Peninsula Bus. Svcs. Assn. (pres. 1983), Nat. Assn. of Secretarial Svcs. (conv. del. 1986), Nat. Alliance of Homebased Businesswomen; rec: photog. Address: Cindy's Typing & Word Processing Service 2108-A Fallen Leaf Lane Los Altos 94022

KING, FORBES, real estate broker; b. Sept. 5, 1911, Portland, Ore.; s. Lorne Pierce and Alice (Forbes) K.; m. Julia, Mar. 10, 1951; children: Patricia b. 1952, Brian b. 1955. Career: BA, UC Berkeley 1936. Career: mgr. acct./ underwriting Motors Insurance Corp., Long Beach 1936-41; mgr. engring. analysis Permanente Metals Corp., Richmond 1942-43; supr. field dirs. & hosp. workers, China Theater, Am. Red Cross, China 1944-46; adminstrv. mgr. Indsl. Indemnity Co., San Francisco 1946-76; real estate broker Davey Props., San Carlos 1976—; mem. Redwood City Bd. of Realtors (chmn. Profl. Stds. com.), San Carlos CofC (dir.), Rotary, Commonwealth Club of Calif., Chi Psi Frat.; Republican; Presbyterian (elder); rec: community svc. Res: 7 El Sereno Dr San Carlos 94070 Ofc: Davey Properties 100 El Camino Real San Carlos 94070

KING, FRANKLIN W., lawyer; b. Aug. 8, 1942, Alexandria, La.; s. William F. and Helen Kathleen (Weaver) K.; edn: BA, Univ. of Ala. 1965; JD, Duke Univ. Law Sch. 1972. Career: law practice, San Francisco; listed Who's Who in American Law, 1980; mem: Am., Calif. Bar Assns.; Am., Calif. Trial Lawyers

Assns.; Phi Delta Theta legal frat.; Pi Kappa Phi; mil: USAF 1965-69, major Judge Adv. Gen. Dept. Reserve 1974-; rec: sports, music, theatre. Ofc: 899 Ellis St San Francisco 94109

KING, GARY ALLEN, research and development executive; b. Nov. 24, 1960, San Francisco; s. John M. and Sandra Gloria (Serian) Addison; m. Luz Gloria King, Oct. 15, 1983; 1 son, Allen b. 1985; edn: BS mktg., CSU Long Beach 1982; real estate broker Calif. 1983. Career: senior analyst Am. Savings Stockton 1984; sys. design analyst Eureka Fed. Savings S.F. 1985; v.p./ research & devel. mgr., dir. LoanCorp USA Inc. S.F. 1986—; cons. San Joaquin Mgmt. Co. 1982-86; honors: Business Honor Soc. (CSU Long Beach 1981-82); mem: Stockton Bd. Realtors, Calif. Assn. Realtors, Nat. Assn. Realtors; inventor computer database logic systems, telecommunication sys.; Republican; Catholic; rec: iterative formulations, photog. Res: POB 7954 Stockton 95207 Ofc: LoanCorp USA 870 Market St Ste 628 San Francisco 94102

KING, GEORGE (H.S.H. Prince de Santorini, Count de Florina), Archbishop; b. Jan. 23, 1919, Wellington, Shropshire, Eng.; s. George and Mary King; m. Dr. Monique Noppe, Jan. 30, 1971; edn: Guisborough Public Sch., Eng.;. Career: author 30 pub. books; lectr./tchr./broadcaster on religious subjects; prod./dir. num. 16mm docu. films and video-tape prodns.; prod. num. ednl. cassettes; founder/pres. The Aetherius Soc., (reg. relig., sci., and edn. orgn.) and Metropolitan Archbishop, The Aetherius Churches; founder/pres. and Grand Master, Mystical Order of St. Peter (reg. relig. and charitable orgn. and reg. UCCI); founder/pres. Coll. of Spiritual Scis., London, Eng.; Deputy Grand Master, Grand Chancellor for USA, Royal Knights of Justice (reg. charity); Lt. Grand Master, grand Chancellor, The Grand Sovereign Dynastic Hospitaller Order of St. John, Knights of Malta (reg. UCCI); Grand Collier, mem. Supreme Council, The Sovereign Mil. Orthodox Dynastic Imperial Constaninian Order of St. Georges (reg. UCCI); prof. human rels., mem. North-West London Univ. Reg. of Adv. Consultants for schools and colls.; internat. adv. bd./ordained minister Internat. Evangelism Crusades Inc., Calif.; nat. adv. bd. Nat. Chaplains Assn. USA; honors: recipient Peace Prize (1982), Intl. Evangelism Crusades Inc., Peace and Justice Awd. (1981), UCCI; num. chivalric titles and awards incl. Gold Medal for outstanding svc. to humanity, Imperial House of Byzantium; D.Sc., D.Lit. North-West London Univ.; 1st vice chancellor gen. USA, Accademia delle Scienze di Roma (Italy); mem. Confedn. of Chivalry, Eng.; nat. adv. bd. Nat. Chaplains Assn. USA; Internat. Acad. of Criminology (patron); mem: Am. Fedn. of Police, Royal Nat. Lifeboat Instn. (Brit. Govt.), Nat. Rifle Assn., Calif. Rifle and Pistol Club, Republican Presdl. Task Force, Royal Soc. for Promotion of Health (Brit., affil.), Order of Ky. Colonels; nat. adv. bd. Am. Security Council Found.; state adv. US Congl. Adv. Bd. mil: Hon. Amb.-at-Large, Rep. of Poland (in exile); Hon. Army Gen. Polish Armed Forces (in exile); WWII Def. Medal (Brit), Cross of Merit w/ Swords (Poland). Address: 6216 Afton Place Hollywood 90028

KING, JOHN DOUGLAS, human resources consultant; b. June 1, 1934, Beckenham, Kent, Eng.; s. Douglas Stanley and Mary (Carpenter) K.; m. Shirley Spencer, Feb. 13, 1971; children: Douglas b 1957, Lynn b 1960, Linda b. 1955, Alan b. 1957, Pamela b. 1959, Gary b. 1961; edn: BS, Oglethorpe Univ. 1956; MAOM, USC 1969; DBA, US Internat. Univ. 1980. Career: ops. analyst Davlyn Enterprises, San Diego 1977; mgmt. analyst Northrop Svcs. Inc., San Diego 1977-78; mem. tech. staff Intercon Corp., Camp Pendleton 1978-79; tech. staff PE Sytems Inc. 1979-83; lab. coord. U.S. Internat. Univ., San Diego 1981-83; adj. faculty National Univ. 1983—; senior systems scientist Computer Sciences Corp. 1983-85; human resources cons. The Consultants Group, San Diego 1985—; dir. bus. admin. pgms. La Jolla Univ., La Jolla 1986—; honors: Lowry Meml. Scholar,. 1952-53; mem: Am. Assn. of Profl. Cons., Am. Mgmt. Assns., Assn. of Old Crows, The Retired Ofcrs. Assn., Scripps Ranch Community Theatre; mil: lt. commdr. USN 1956-77, Navy Commdn.; Ch. of England; rec: x-country skiing, travel. Res: 10287 Grayfox Dr. San Diego 92131 Ofc: The Consultants Group, 3855 Avocado Blvd Ste 230 La Mesa 92041

KING, JOHN LAFAYETTE, historical economist; b. Oct. 16, 1917, Douglas, ARiz.; s. William David and Lillian (Nolan) K.; div.; children: Sherri b. 1946, William D. b. 1948, John R. b. 1958; edn: BSE, distng., Univ. of Penn. Wharton 1938; grad. studies, Univ. of Chicago, USC, Northwestern 1938-41; MBA, Calif. Coast Univ. 1985, PhD, 1986. Career: prof. Sawyer Coll., Los Angeles 1964-70; instr. CSU Fullerton, 1972-73; founder Future Economic Trends p.t. 1970-73, f.t. 1973—; currently, ed., publisher; also pres. Economic Behavior Inst. Ltd. Reseach; economist Chicago Daily News 1938-41; economist Mutual Life of NY 1946-48; misc. publishing jobs in So. Calif. 1948-64; honors: Beta Gamma Sigma 1938; mem: University Club (Santa Barbara and Los Angeles); publs: book, Human Behavior & Wall Street, Swallow Press 1973; book, The Ostrich Society Ends, Trends Publ. 1985; mil: capt. US Army, gen. staff George S. Patton II Armored Corps, European gen. staff ofcr. 8th Armored Div. 1941-46; Democrat; Episcopal; rec: oil painting. Res: 135 Valerio St. Santa Barbara Ofc: Future Economic Trends, 29 W. Anapamu St. Santa Barbara 93101

KING, MAUREEN CAROLE VICTORIA, psychotherapist; b. Oct. 28, 1955, Los Angeles; d. Jeremiah and Elsie (Berman) King; edn: BA, UC Santa Barbara 1977; MA, honors, CSU Los Angeles 1979; doctl. pgm. Calif. Grad. Inst. 1980-; Calif. lic. MFCC, Marriage Family Child Counselor. Career: recreational therapist Children's Hosp. of L.A. 1979; senior staff clinician Wilshire West Sch., Santa Monica 1979—; psychotherapist pvt. practice; cons. Palmer Drug Abuse Program, and Cry Help; honors: Psi Chi; mem. Calif. Assn. of Marriage Family Therapist (West Side afil.), Am. Psychoanalytic Soc., Am.

Psych. Assn., City of Hope; rec: equestrian, sailing, skiing. Ofc: 1640 Durango Ave Los Angeles 90035

KING, PATRICK JAMES, dentist, b. May 5, 1949, Alameda; s. James Franklin and Elaine Gerrard (Ward) K.; m. Janna Marilyn, July 4, 1979; children: Christopher Patrick b. 1982, Tara Kathline b. 1985; edn: BA, UC Los Angeles 1972; DDS, USC 1977. Career: general dentistry practice, Greenfield 1977—; asst. clin. prof. Fixed Prosthodontics, UC Dental Sch. 1983-84; mem: Am., Calif., Monterey Bay (Dental Health chmn. 1978-79) Dental Socs. 1977-, No. Calif. Gnatholleigy Soc., Salinas Dental Study Group, Peter K. Thomas Study Group; mem. CofC, Local Devel. Corp. Greenfield (treas. 1978), Rotary, Toastmasters; Democrat; Episcopal; rec: golf, gardening. Ofc: 847 Oak Ave, POB 1447, Greenfield 93927

KING, ROY EDWARD, safety engineer, educator; b. Apr. 2, 1921, San Francisco; s. Walter John Hartman and Ella Anna (Kauck) K.; m. Marilyn A., Sept. 22, 1946; 1 son, Brian Edward b. 1953; edn: engring. grad., US Merchant Marine Acad. 1943; AA, pre law, Oakland City Coll. 1957; pre law, Univ. Calif. 1959; Reg. Profl. Engr. (Indsl. Safety); Calif. Comm. Coll. life tchg. credentials. Career: mgr. of safety Sacramento Branch, Transam. Ins. Co., 1969—, loss control splst. San Francisco Branch, 1966-69; personnel and safety dir. Am. Manganese Steel Co., Oakland 1952-58; cons. for safety, City of Sacto., School Dept. Cities of Lodi, Rio Vista, and Univ. of the Pacific; dir. of public speaking, Learning Exchange; awards: Man of the Year, Transam. Ins. Co. (1977), World Golf Hall of Fame mem. Hole-in-One Club (1976); mem: Am. Soc. Safety Engrs. (Mgmt. Div.; Assembly del.; Legislative com.), No. Calif. Indsl. Safety Soc. (past pres.), Engrs. Club of Sacto., Univ. of Calif. Alumni, Oakland 20-30 Club (past pres.), Oakland Real Estate Bd. Toastmasters Club (past pres), Nat. Family Opinion for product testing (1949-), Nat. Republican Soc.; mil: cadet, midshipman USNR and USMM 1942-43, 1st asst. engr. USMM, 1943-46, Pacific and Atlantic Zone Ribbon, Philippine Liberation w. Bronze Star; Officially acted and signed for the US Secty. of War for first US ship to be sold to the Repub. of China by US Govt. (1946); rec: golf, tchg. pub. speaking. Address: Sacramento

KING, WILLIAM RICHARD, dentist; b. May 15, 1930, Inglewood; s. William Dunn and Ruth Avalon (Bell) K.; m. Jan Ergenbright, Dec. 19, 1951; children: William E. b. 1955, Jon C. b. 1957, Kristin S. b. 1967; edn: stu., UCLA 1948-49, CSU Los Angeles 1952-53; AA, Los Angeles City Coll. 1952; DDS, USC 1957. Career: ins. claims investigator/ adjuster Automobile Club of So. Calif. 1949-57; US Army Dental Corps, 34th Gen. Hosp., La Chapelle, France 1957-59; pvt. dental practice, Fullerton 1959—; honors: Fellow Am. Coll. of Dentists 1980; Am. Prosthodontic Soc. 1981; Fellow Acad. of Internat. Dental Studies; Pierre Fouchard Acad. 1976; Alpha Tau Epsilon 1957; Spl. Svc. Award, Orange Co. Dental Soc. 1971; mem: Am. and Calif. Dental Assns., Orange Co. Dental Soc., Delta Sigma Delta, Am. Prosthodontic Soc., Am. Endodontic Soc., Fedn. Dentaire Internat. (life), USC Alumni Assn., USC Dental Alumni Assn., USC Century Club, Mariners Ch. (founding bd., elder, Newport Beach); mil: capt. US Army 1957-59; Republican; So. Coast Comm. Ch.; rec: sailing, skiing, sm. group counseling. Res: 415 Redlands Ave. Newport Beach 92663 Ofc: William R. King DDS, 2651 E. Chapman Ste. 208 Fullerton 92631

KINGSLEY, ROBERT, Court of Appeal Justice; b. Oct. 8, 1903, Cedar Falls, Iowa; s. Frank Amos and Angeline (Van Niman) K.; m. Doris Field Forbes-Manson, June 12, 1937; m. 2d. Ninon M. Hogan, July 3, 1976; edn: AB, AM, Univ. of Minn., 1923; LLB, 1926; S.J.D., Harvard Univ. 1928. Career: instr. in law, Univ. of Minn., 1926-27; Thayer Fellow Harvard Law Sch. 1927-28; asst. prof. law, USC, 1928-30, prof. 1930-, vice dean Sch. of Law 1947-51, assoc. dean 1951-52, dean 1952-63; justice, Ct. of Appeal, 1963—; mem: Junior CofC (past pres.), Music Found., L.A. Music Guild (past pres.), L.A. Civic Light Opera Assn. (secty. 1948-77, pres. 1977-); L.A. Co. Bar Assn. (trustee 1963); Delta Theta Phi frat., University Club (L.A.), Nat. Lawyers Club (Wash DC); Congregational. Res: 231 S. Citrus Ave Los Angeles Ofc: 3580 Wilshire Blvd Los Angeles 90010

KINSELLA, KEVIN JOHN, venture capitalist; b. Dec. 23, 1945, NY, NY; s. Walter Aloysius and Jane Andrew (Davis) K.; edn: BS, Mass. Inst. of Tech. 1967; MA, Johns Hopkins Sch. of Adv. Internat. Studies 1969. Career: mathematics tchr. Am. Community Sch., Beirut, Lebanon 1969-70; writer Stockholm Internat. Peace Research Inst. Yearbook of World Disarmament 1970; applications engr. Adage Inc., Boston, Mass. 1972-74; senior assoc. Transcentury Corp., Wash. DC and Peru 1974-75; dist. dir. Western States, Leadership Campaign, Mass. Inst. Tech. 1975-78; gen. mgr., vp. Pacific Solar Design, San Diego 1978-79; mgr., regl. devel. Solar Turbines Internat., San Diego 1979-81; dir. venture devel. NuCorp Energy, San Diego 1981-83; founder, mng. gen. ptr. Avalon Vetures, La Jolla 1983—; dir. Spectragraphics Corp., San Diego; chmn. bd. NeoRx Corp., Seattle, The Meno Corp., San Jose, GourMate Restaurants, La Jolla; publs: 24+ columns in the Boston Globe, Boston Herald American, Boston Sunday Globe, 1976-78; Siberian Journey, NY Times 1971; In the Eye of the Storm, MIT Literary Mag. 1971; Computer Graphics, Digital Design 1972; Democrat; (San Diego Co. Central Com.); Catholic; rec: tennis, swimming, hiking. Ofc: Avalon Ventures, 1020 Prospect St. Ste. 405 La Jolla 92037

KINSEY, THOMAS DU WAYNE, direct mail specialist; b. July 4, 1937, Gerrett, Ind.; s. Elza DuWayne and Teresa Virgilia (Moran) K.; m. Suzanne, June 20, 1959; children: Keith b. 1960, Kerryn b. 1961, Kevin b. 1964; edn: BA, CSU Long Beach 1959. Career: nat. accts. mgr. CompuCorp. Santa Monica 1971-74; owner Thomas D. Kinsey & Assocs. Fillmore 1974-75; shareholder, nat. mktg. mgr. Delphi Info. Sciences Corp. Santa Monica 1975-81; owner Ergo Mktg. & Advtg. Thousand Oaks 1981−; evening bus. div. Moorpark Coll.; lectr. UCLA Entrepreneurial Pgm.; mem: Bardsdale Homeowners Assn. (dir. 1984-), Rotary (mem. com.), Fillmore CofC (bd.); co-author: Business Today, Small Business Section (Random House textbook), ed. Compound Interest Tables, Complete Compound Interest Tables (Contemporary Books); Republican; Catholic; rec: tennis, bicycling. Res: 1401 Pasadena Ave Fillmore 93015 Ofc: Ergo Marketing & Advertising 240 Lombard Ste 208 Thousand Oaks 91360

KIRK, CASSIUS LAMB, JR., lawyer, investor; b. June 8, 1929, Bozeman, Mont.; s. Cassius L. and Gertrude V. (McCarthy) K.; edn: AB, pol. sci., Stanford Univ. 1951; JD, UC Berkeley 1954; lic. real estate broker. Career: assoc. law firm of Cooley, Godward, Castro, Huddleson & Tatum, San Francisco 1956-60; staff counsel business affairs, Stanford Univ. 1960-78; chief bus. ofcr., staff counsel, Menlo Sch. and Coll., Menlo Park 1978-81; pres. Elberli-Kirk Properties, Inc., Menlo Park 1981−; faculty, UC Santa Barbara Wkshop for Coll. Adminstrs. 1965-73; pres. Menlo Towers Assn., 1978-79, 82-83; mem. Palo Alto CofC (v.p. for community affairs 1969-70); mem. Calif. Bar, Order of the Coif, Phi Sigma Alpha, Phi Alpha Delta, Stanford Faculty Club; law rev. arts.; mil: sp3 US Army, Occ. Ger., GCM; Republican; rec: jogging, travel, opera. Address: Eberli-Kirk Properties Inc. 1330 University Dr, No. 52, Menlo Park 94025

KIRKLAND, BERTHA THERESA, asst. project engineer; b. May 16, 1916, San Francisco; d. Lawrence and Therese (Kanzler) Schmelzer; m. Thornton Crowns Kirkland, Jr. (dec. 1971), Dec. 27, 1937; children: Kathryn Elizabeth b. 1943, Francis Charles b. 1945. Career: supr. hospital operations, American Potash & Chemical Corp., Trona, 1953-54; office mgr. T.C. Kirkland, Electrical Contractor 1954-58; sec.treas., dir. T.C. Kirkland Inc., San Bernardino 1958-74; electrical estimator/engr. ADD-M Electric, Inc. San Bernardino 1972-82; vice pres. 1974-82; elec. estimator, engr. Corona Industrial Electric, Inc. Corona 1982-83; asst. project engineer Fischbach & Moore, Inc. Los Angeles 1984−; mem. Arrowhead Country Club; Episcopal. Res: 526 East Sonora St San Bernardino 92404 Ofc: Fischbach & Moore, Inc. 4690 Worth St Los Angeles 90063

KIRKPATRICK, CRAIG GILBERT, professional engineer; b. Jan. 22, 1928, Fairfield, Iowa; s. Walter Craig and Berniece Olaf (Buchanan) K.; edn: BS metallurg. engrg., Univ. Ariz. 1953; Law, Univ. Wash. Seattle 1955; reg. profl. engr. (metallurg.) Calif. 1966. Career: asst. supt. American Smelting & Refining Co. 1953-55; research engr. Collins Radio 1956-57; metallurg. engr. Nuclear Corp. of Am. 1957-58; senior research engr. autonetics div. No. American Aviation 1958-59; chief metallurgist Nuclear Corp. of Am. 1959-62; senior research engr. autonetics div. No. Am. Aviation 1962-63, research specialist 1963-64, sr. tech. splst. 1964-66; tech. staff No. American Rockwell 1966−; pres. Orange Co. Microfilm Inc. 1980; metallurg. cons. 1955−; fellow: Inst. for the Advancement of Engrs., AAAS; mem: Am. Inst. Mining & Metallurg. Engrs., Am. Soc. Metals, Sigma Xi, Tau Beta Pi, Am. Inst. Mgmt., Nat. Mgmt. Assn., N.Y. Acad. of Sci., Girl Scouts Orange Co. (properties chmn. 1975-80); patents: rare earth, dynamic strain measurements; publs: rare earths, electronics, logging, semiconductors, lasers; mil: 2nd lt. USAF, U.N. Medal, Korean Campaign (Battle Star); sgt. US Army Paratroops, Occupation, Victory Medal; Libertarian; Presbyterian; rec: Scottish history, Scot. mil. hist. Res: 812 Ride Out Way Fullerton Ofc: Rockwell Internat. 3370 Mira Loma, mail code GA40, Anaheim 92803

KIRKPATRICK, GARY EUGENE, real estate development/contruction co. president; b. Aug. 27, 1952, Long Beach, Calif.; s. Eugene Reese and Betty Anne (Stewart) K.; edn: BA bus./ fin., Univ. So. Calif. 1974, MBA, 1976. Career: asst. adminstrv. dir. Santa Fe Servicos e Purfuracao Ltda., Vitoria, Brazil 1976; chief ops ofcr., v.p. Kirgo Inc. Long Beach, Calif. 1977-79; pres., founder Kirkwood Development Inc. 1979−; mem: Commerce Assocs., Bldg. Ind. Assn., Home Builders Council, Jr. CofC, Long Beach Yacht Club, Committee of 300 (L.B. Grand Prix); rec: travel, skiing, tennis, golf, sailing. Address: 3464 Glorietta Pl Sherman Oaks 91423

KIRLIKOVALI, ERGUN, polymer scientist, co. president; b. Oct. 31, 1952, Izmir, Turkey; s. Ratip and Munire K.; m. Juliana Marian, Apr. 22, 1978; edn: BS, Bogazici Univ. of Istanbul; M.Polymer Sci., Univ. of Manchester, England. Career: dev. chemist Adhesive Engineering, 1978-81; sr. dev. chemist Narmco/Celanese, Costa Mesa 1981-82; v.p. Quality Control/R&D Belzona Molecular Internat., Inc. N.Y. 1982-85; pres. Integrated Polymer Industries, Inc., Santa Ana 1985−; recipient Top Exec. Award, Belzona Molecular Internat. Inc.; mem. Soc. of Plastic Engrs., Am. Concrete Inst., ASTM; civic: Fedn. of Turkish-Am. Socs. Inc./NY (chmn. P.R. com. 1984-85), Am.-Turkish Assn. of So. Calif. (pres. 1982); 2 patent disclosures, Adhesive Engring.; contbr. paper on Polymer Concrete, Modern Plastics Ency. (1981, 1982 eds.); mil: lt. Turkish Navy 1975-77; Republican; rec: folk dancing (Turkish Nat. Team 1970, 71, 72). Res: 507 Harbor Woods Pl Newport Beach 92660 Ofc: 1430-P Village Way Santa Ana 92705

KISHIMOTO, YORIKO, US-Japan business consultant; b. Sept. 8, 1955, Shizuoka, Japan, nat. US cit. 1977; s. Yasuo and Miyoko (Nishikawa) K.; m. Leland Collins, Aug. 4, 1979; edn: BA, Wesleyan Univ. 1977; MBA, Stanford Univ. 1981. Career: Internat. Fellow, Nomura Research Inst., Japan 1979-80; founder, mng. prin. Japan Pacific Assoc. 1981−; num. cons. assignments; organizer couse on Japanese Business, Stanford Bus. Sch.; spkr. num. confs. on mktg., Japan; venture mktg., Japan; works: author, Rising Sun, Japanese

Entrepreneurs, Inc Mag. 1984; co-author, Theory F, Inc Mag. 1986; publisher, Biotechnology in Japan Newsservice, monthly; rec: hiking, writing. Res: 1797 Juarez Ave. Los Altos 94022 Ofc: Japan Pacific Associates, 467 Hamilton Ave. Ste. 2 Palo Alto 94301

KITADA, SHINICHI, biochemist; b. Dec. 9, 1948, Osaka, Japan; s. Koichi and Asako (Seki) K.; edn: MD, Kyoto Univ. 1973; MS in biol. chem., UC Los Angeles 1977, PhD in biol. chem., 1979. Career: intern Kyoto University Hosp. 1973-74; resident physician in Chest Disease Research Inst. 1974-75; research scholar Lab. of Biomedical and Environmental Scis., UCLA 1979−; awards: Japan Soc. for the Promotion of Sci. Fellow (1975-76), Edna Lievre Fellow of Am. Cancer Soc. (1981-82); mem: Am. Oil Chemists Soc., Sigma Xi, N.Y. Acad. of Scis.; contbr. articles in profl. jours.; Presbyterian; rec: swimming, tennis. Res: 478 Landfair Ave No. 5, Los Angeles 90024 Ofc: Lab. of Biomedical and Environmental Sciences 900 Veteran Ave Los Angeles 90024

KITAMURA, ROBERT EDWARD, architect; b. June 12, 1950, Los Angeles; s. Kazuo Eddie and Helen (Hifumi) K.; m. Janice Marie, Feb. 11, 1978; 1 son, Christopher b. 1981; edn: Los Angeles City Coll. 1968-70; B.Arch., Calif. Polytech. State Univ. 1975; Reg. Architect Calif. 1978. Career: chief designer Richmond Rossi Montgomery Inc. San Luis Obispo 1976-78; v.p./assoc. Richard Dodd & Assoc. Newport Beach/S.L.O.; corp. secty., bd. dirs., senior v.p. RRM Design Group Inc. S.L.O. 1980−; instr. arch. and CRP depts. Sch. of Arch. & Environmental Design CSUSLO 1977-81; honors: CCCCAIA Award of Merit 1985, Obispo Beautiful Awards 1980, 81, 82, 83, Kiwanian of the Year (S.L.O. Kiwanis 1981), mem: Am. Inst. Archs. (corp. mem.) 1978-, CCCCAIA (dir. legislation 1980-81), Interfaith Forum on Art and Arch. 1978-79, Constrn. Specs. Inst. (profl. mem.) 1983, 85, Kiwanis; publ: drawings in Presentation Drawings by Am. Archs.; Democrat; Ch. of the Nazarene; rec: guitar, Christian youth work. Res: 3030 Johnson Ave San Luis Obispo 94301 RRM Design Group 416 Higuera St San Luis Obispo 93401

KITCHEN, LYNN ELIZABETH, financial securities broker-dealer; b. July 31, 1951, Danville, Ill.; d. Richard Stanley, Sr. and Pollyann (Castle) K.; edn: BS in mktg., CSU Long Beach 1976; Reg. Securities Prin., NASD (1981), Reg. Options Prin. (1985). Career: regl. sales mgr. Challenge Systems Inc., Atlanta, Ga. 1972-74; account exec. Dean Witter Reynolds Inc., Los Angeles 1976-78; Oppenheimer & Co. Inc., L.A. 1978-80; branch mgr. Private Ledger Finl. Services Inc., L.A. 1980-85; securities broker-dealer/ pres. Lynn Kitchen Inc., 1985−; mem. Pi Sigma Epsilon sales & mktg. frat. 1975-76 (Mktg. Award 1976); mem. Nat. Assn. Securities Dealers Inc. 1985-, Securities Investors Protection Corp. 1985-, W.L.A. Chamber Commerce, CSU Alumni Assn., Women In Bus.; Republican; Methodist; rec: fencing, swimming. Address: Los Angeles 90064

KITCHENS, JOEL, engineering executive; b. Nov. 12, 1922, Bristow, Okla., s. George Riley and Gertrude Agnes (Schwartz) K.; m. Lois Dean, June 18, 1949; children: Kathryn b. 1950, Dean b. 1952, James b. 1957, Carolyn b. 1964; edn: BSEE, UC Berkley 1948, MS, bus. mgmt. 1974; Reg. Profl. Engr., Calif. (1954) and Ariz. (1973). Career: elec. engr. Pacific Gas & Electric Co., San Francisco 1948-55; elec. engr. Anaconda Co., San Francisco and NYC 1956-60, chief cable engr., NYC 1960-62, gen. mgr. cable sys. div. 1963-65; project engr. Bechtel Corp., San Francisco and Toronto 1965-76; engring. mgr., Wash. DC and Los Angeles 1977−; honors: Distng. Engring. Achiev., Soc. of Mfg. Engrs. 1985; mem: IEEE (sect. chmn. 1971, 1977), Inst. for the Adv. of Engring. (pres. 1985), Town Hall of Calif., Am. Mensa Ltd.; num. tech. papers related to profession; mil: sgt. US Army 1943-46, Southeast Asia Campaign, Philippines Campaign; Democrat; Protestant; rec: amateur radio (N6DTH). Res: 1232 Fawnridge Dr. Brea 92621 Ofc: Bechtel Corp., 12440 E. Imperial Hwy. Norwalk 90650

KITE, DENNIS S., institutional securities sales executive; b. May 10, 1945, Chgo.; s. Allen M. and June T. (Hillman) K.; m. Aleta Lindbeck, Feb. 14, 1982; 1 dau. Debra b. 1968; edn: BBA, Univ. Wisc. 1967; MBA, Univ. Chgo. 1973; desig: Prin., Municipal Securities Rulemaking Bd. (1985). Career: trainee, mail clk., teller Nat. City Bank, now Mfrs. Nat. Bank, Chgo. 1967-68; adminstrv. asst. Inv. Div. Am. Nat. Bank, Chgo. 1968-70; asst. v.p./regional mgr. Montgomery Ward Credit Corp., Chgo. 1970-77; account exec. Bank of Am., Bank Investment Sec. Div., Los Angeles 1977-79, v.p./ Houston regional sales mgr. 1979-82, v.p./regl. sales mgr./dir. BA Asia Ltd., Tokyo, Japan 1982-84, v.p./mgr. retail securities sales So. Calif., Bank of Am. Capital Markets Group, 1984-86, v.p./sr. acct. exec. 1986−; mem. Municipal Bond Club of L.A., Univ. Chgo. Grad. Sch. of Bus. Alumni Club, Univ. Wisc. Alumni Assn., Stock Exchange Club of L.A.; civic: Zool. Soc. San Diego, L.A. Art Museum, Smithsonian, Save the Children (sponsor); contbr. material to Marcia Stigum's book: The Money Markets, Myth Reality & Practice (1978); mil: s/sgt. USAFR 1968-73; Jewish; rec: music, golf, swim, racquetball. Res: 27115 Comba Mission Miejo 92692 Ofc: Bank of America 555 S Flower Dept 422291 Los Angeles 90071

KITTA, JOHN NOAH, lawyer; b. Aug. 26, 1951, San Francisco; s. John E. and Norma Jean (Noah) K.; edn: BS, Univ. of Santa Clara 1973, JD, 1976; admitted Calif. State Bar 1976. Career: Fleet Service clk. American Airlines, San Francisco 1975; intern, Calif. State Assem. Allister McAllister, 1975-76; asst. mgr. Transam. Title Ins. Co., 1977-78; atty. assoc. Rhodes, McKeehan & Bernard, 1978-79; atty. prin., 1979−; owner Seven Seas Yachting Co. Inc. 1984-; elected trustee Alameda Co. Bd. of Edn.; apptd. by gov., commnr. Calif. Crime Resistance Task Force; mem: ABA, Alameda County Bar Assn., Washington Township Bar Assn., Chamber of Commerce, 100 Club, National Sch.

Board Assn.; publ: article on wrongful discharge pub. by CofC; Democrat; Protestant; rec: active sports, philately, equestrian, yachting. Res: 2135 Ocaso Camino Fremont 94539 Ofc: 39261 Liberty St Fremont 94538

KITTLESON, HAROLD ALVER, electronic mfrs. representative; b. Jan. 9, 1912, Malta, Ill.; s. Elon Edwin and Anna Olena (Hobbet) K.; Great Uncle Ole Kittleson invented and patented barbed wire (1875); m. Ella Hartshorn, Apr. 5, 1941; 1 dau. Betty Ann (York) b. 1942; edn: tchr. cred. Iowa State Tchrs. Coll., Cedar Falls 1932; elec. engrg. Iowa State Coll., Ames 1934-38; cert. Microwave Engring., Cal. Tech., 1941; cert. USN Radar Sch., Phila. 1943; tech. & bus. courses, Lockheed Co., Sperry Electronic Corp. (NY), MIT, UCLA; bus. mgmt. certs., Stanford Univ., 1961-62. Career: wk. on family farm, Woden, Iowa, -1932; country school tchr., Iowa, 1932-34; resrch. asst., E.E., Iowa State Coll, 1936-39; chief elec. engr. American Pubs. supply, Lynn, Mass. 1939-40; hd. electronic test equip. engring. an design, Lockheed Aircraft, No. Hollywood, Ca. 1940-43; coordinating engr. AEW Proj., MIT Radiation Lab., Cambridge, Mass. 1944-45; founder/owner/pres. Kittleson Co. (electronic mfrs. rep), Los Angeles 1946–, Continental Components 1955-60; lectr. Lockheed Aircraft 1943; cons. No. Am. Phillips Co. 1957, Gen. Equip. Corp. 1958, Fairchild Recording Equip. Corp. 1960, Airtron 1965; recipient appreciation profl. orgns., Presbyn. Ch.; guest of honor sev. banquets; No. 1 Booth Choice (1000 exhibitors), WESCON Show and Conv. 1969. Mem: Internat. Platform Assn., Electronic Reps Assn. (pres. 1950), Mfrs. Agents Nat. Assn. (pres. 1955), Precision Measurement Assn. (charter, internat. pres. 1970-72), Meals for Millions Found (bd. trustees 1975-80); active in charity fundraising; publs: tech. reports, mkt. studies; book on family recollections (3 vols. completed); US patent applicant (1983); Republican (Election Bd.); Presbyterian (commnr. Gen. Assem.); rec: painting, cosmology, exptl. gardening. Address: 20315 Runnymede Canoga Park 91306

KLAHS, DONALD RICHARD, lawyer; b. May 24, 1945, Long Beach; s. Curtis L. and Lillian M. (Marino) K.; m. Sherry, Dec. 3, 1971; children: Dana b. 1974, Erica b. 1980; edn: AA, Orange Coast Coll. 1966, BA, CSU Long Beach 1969, JD, Southwestern Univ. Sch. of law 1976; admitted Calif. State Bar 1976. Career: medical research 1969-73; atty. prin. in pvt. law practice, Glendale 1976–, areas of practice incl. personal injury (plaintiffs), business, probate, family law and criminal defense; recipient commendation, State Bar of Calif. Bd. of Govs. for pro bono legal services; mem. Calif., Los Angeles County, San Fernando Valley, Glendale and Burbank bar assns.; contbr. articles on post-tranfusion hepatitis in The Lancet (9/73), Gastroenterology (1973); mil: sgt. Calif. Army N.G. 1966-70; Republican; Methodist; rec: hunting, fishing, scuba diving. Res: 25682 Velan Dr Valencia 91355 Ofc: 401 N Brand Blvd Ste 726 Glendale 91203

KLAVINS, VILIS ARNOLDS, opera singer; b. Feb. 6, 1924, Jelgava, Latvia, nat. US cit. 1957; s. Vilis Andrejs and Zelma (Burgelis) K.; edn: grad., Herzog Peter Gymnasium, Latvia 1943; studied music w/ Arno Niitof, Estonian baritone of the Tallin Opera and Prof. Tallin Music Acad. 1950-51, Victor Stots, singer w/ opera house and prof. of Music Acad. in Riga, Latvia 1951, Norbert Ardelli, soloist and mem. Metropolitan Opera in NY; hotel and apt. mgmt., Pacific Hotel Schs. 1970; lic. real estate sales Calif. 1971. Career: singer The Mathison Singers, Culver City 1970-75; singer in concerts for clubs, churches, opera groups, radio, etc.; songwriter, composer; owner Latvis Music publ. co. 1984–; real estate broker; honors: 1st and 2nd Place (Annual Composers & Writers Contest, Manuscript Club of L.A. 1982), 2-Star Double Ribbon Award (Parade of Am. Music Contest, Nat. Fedn. of Music Clubs 1985), 2nd Place (Composers & Writers Contest, MCLA 1985); mem: Manuscript Club of L.A. 1980-, ASCAP, Nat. Inventors Found.; songs: Have A Heart Full of Sunshine (1982), Evening Bells Are Ringing (1982), My Heart Is Crying For Homeland (1984), The Little Shamrock (1985), My Song To The Ocean (1985); languages: Latvian, German, Russian, English, also sing in French, Italian, Old Latin, Spanish; Republican; Lutheran; rec: inventions. Ofc: Latvis Music 12028 Venice Blvd Ste 4-249 Los Angeles 90066

KLEIER, MITCHELL PAUL, banker; b. Aug. 8, 1953, San Francisco; s. William Richard and Pauline Corin (Barton) K.; m. Linda, Oct. 3, 1982; children: Matthew b. 1983, Sean b. 1985; edn: BA, honors, UC Berkeley 1977; MBA, USC 1979; Calif. Community Coll. Cred. in Acctg., Banking and Mgmt. Career: loan ofcr. Bank of Lake County 1979-81; asst. v.p., controller Bank of Marin, San Rafael 1982; v.p., controller Westamerica Bank, San Rafael 1982; v.p., cashier Valley Commercial Bank, Stockton 1983; v.p., CFO Valley Commercial Bank, Stockton 1984, CEO 1985–; instr. Mendocino Coll.; mem: Calif. Bankers Assn. (County Key Banker 1982), Big Brothrs & Sisters of Lake Co.; Republican; Seventh-Day Adventist; rec: running. Res: 9206 Decatur Dr. Stockton 95209 Ofc: Valley Commercial Bank, P.O. Box 9700 Stockton 95208

KLEIN, ALAN RICHARD, lawyer; b. July 24, 1950, Chgo.; s. Clarence and Lois Beverly (Jacobson) K.; m. Susan Lynn, June 10, 1973; children: Jonathan b. 1981, Kimberly b. 1982; edn: BA in hist., UC Los Angeles 1972; JD, Univ. of San Fernando Valley 1973; admitted Calif. State Bar 1976. Career: atty. law firm Sidney M. Kaplan 1976-82, ptnr. Kaplan, Klein & Kaplan, Los Angeles 1982-85, spec. in field of immigration and nationality law, entertainment law (as it relates to fgn. born) and personal injury, Kaplan, Klein, Kaplan & Steinberg 1985–; mem: Am. Immigration & Nationality Soc., Los Angeles County Bar Assn. (Immigration & Nat. Sect.), Beverly Hills Bar Assn. 1976-82; Republican; Jewish; rec: sports, boating, fine art. Ofc: Kaplan, Klein, Kaplan & Steinberg, A Law Corp., 3600 Wilshire Blvd, Ste 2230, Los Angeles 90010

KLEIN, ALFRED, lawyer; b. Oct. 22, 1946, Stuttgart, Germany, nat. USA 1954; s. Gerson and Viola (Greenberger) K.; m. Beth Greenberg, Sept. 22, 1984; edn: BA in English, Univ. Mich. 1968; JD, UC Boalt Hall 1971; admitted Calif. State Bar 1972. Career: field atty. Nat. Labor Relations Board, Los Angeles 1971-72, San Francisco 1972-73; instr. Legal Writing & Research, UC Hastings Coll. of Law, S.F. 1973-74; labor mgmt. atty. Musick, Peeler & Garrett, L.A. 1973-75; atty. (asst. to Corp. Employee Rels. Counsel) Atlantic Richfield Co. 1975-79, senior atty. ARCO Petroleum Products Co. div. Atlantic Richfield Co. 1979-85; prin. Law Office of Alfred Klein, Los Angeles 1985–; lectr./ moderator UCLA Ext., Am. Arbitration Assn., Town Hall of Calif. (Indsl. Rels. Sect.), OC Indsl. Rels. Research Assn., San Gabriel Valley Bar Assn., Merchants and Mfrs. Assn., Bur. of Nat. Affairs; honors: recognition awards, Los Angeles Unified Sch. Dist. (1978), Constnl. Rights Found. and LA County Bar Assn. (1978); mem: Am. (Sect. on Labor and Employment Law), Calif. (Sect. on Labor and Employment Law), Los Angeles County (Sect. on Labor and Employment Law, Exec. Com. 1984-86, Symposium Planning Com. 1985, chair Legislative Monitoring Com. 1986) bar assns., Town Hall of Calif., Los Angeles Athletic Club, Sierra Club; publs: Solicitation Rules Will Need Revision, J. Am. Hosp. Assn. (1975), reprinted in Hosp. Organization and Mgmt. (Rakich and Darr 2d ed.); contbr. ABA Antitrust and Labor Com. Report (1977, 78); contbg. ed. The Developing Labor Law (2d ed.); photog. award, LA Athletic Club Art Exhib. 1981; Independent; Jewish; rec: hiking, camping, backpacking. Law Ofc. Alfred Klein, 624 S Grand Ave, Ste 2900, Los Angeles 90017

KLEIN, LAWRENCE ROBERT, securities broker; b. May 27, 1938, NY, NY; s. George Samuel and Miriam Gertrude (Billig) K.; m. Joan Kramer, Sept. 17, 1960; children: Lisa, b. 1962; Amy, b. 1965; Randi, b. 1970; edn: MBA, Adelphi Univ. 1965; BA, NYU 1960; MCFP, UCLA 1981; R.I.A., SEC. Career: Merrill Lynch Pierce Fenner & Smith 1960-80; Shearson American Express 1980-84; v.p. E.F. Hutton & Co. Woodland Hills 1984–; instr. UCLA Grad. Sch. of Business; honors: Instr. of the Yr. UCLA 1982; mem: Beverly Hills Mgrs. Assn.; Scottish Rite; Masons; Jewish; rec: working with handicapped. Res: 4390 Charlemont Ave Woodland Hills 91364 Ofc: E.F. Hutton & Co. 5945 Canoga Ave Woodland Hills 91365

KLEIN, LESLIE, lawyer; b. Jan. 7, 1947, Hungary, nat. US cit. 1964; s. Imre and Magda (Goldman) K.; m. Erika, June 22, 1970; children: Kenneth b. 1971, Sherri b. 1975, Richard b. 1976, Jason b. 1985; edn: BS, UC Los Angeles 1968, MBA, 1969, JD, 1971; Certified Public Acct. (CPA) 1969; admitted Calif. State Bar 1971. Career: staff acct. Kenneth Leventhal & Co., 1968-71; atty. prin. Mackey & Klein, (current) Klein & Cutler, 1971–; founder Bay Area Devel. Co. (real estate holding co.); honors: pres. Yeshiva Torath Emeth; mem. Calif. Soc. CPAs, Calif. Bar Assn., Los Angeles County Bar Assn., Attorney-CPA Soc.; Republican. Ofc: 15250 Ventura Blvd Ste 518 Sherman Oaks 91403-3274

KLEIN, MARK FRANKLIN, computer systems consultant; b. April 29, 1952, Flint, Mich.; s. Alfred E. and Barbara J. K.; m. Sherralyn, Nov. 19, 1978; children: David b. 1983, Rachel b. 1985; edn: BBA, Univ. of Mich. 1975. Career: AFG Financial Systmes 1975-76, acquired by Standard & Poor's, mgr. sys. & pgmmg. 1976-78; vp. sys. Abacus Systems Inc. 1978-83; pres. info. sys. div. DIS Internta. Ltd. 1983–; dir. DIS Internat.; spkr. Hewlett-Packard User's Group Meetings 1978-; mem: Assn. for Computing Machinery, Aircraft Owners & Pilot's Assn., Marin Pilot's Assn. (bd. mem. 1983-84); accomplished musician; rec: music, aviation, photog. Ofc: DIS International, 505 San Marin Dr. Novato 94947

KLEPPE, KRISTIN, vocational school owner; b. Apr. 17, 1955, Milwaukee, Wis.; parents: Thomas H. and Beverlee D. Sorenson (Dobbe) K.; edn: BS, Univ. Fla. 1977. Career: counselor Banking Inst., Los Angeles 1977-, dir. 1979-, owner/pres. 1985–; v.p. L.R. Sorenson Inc., Ariz.; cons. check cashing ops.; guest speaker var. credit union functions; mem: Calif. Assn. of Private Post-Secondary Schs. (bd.), Calif. Check Cashers Assn., So. Calif. Credit Union Collectors Assn.; author teller tng. book; Republican; Lutheran. Ofc: Banking Institute 6300 Wilshire Blvd Ste 1460 Los Angeles 90048

KLINE, J(OHN) ANTHONY, judge; b. Aug. 17, 1938, NYC; s. Harry and Bertha (Shapiro) K.; m. Susan Sward, Nov. 25, 1982; edn: BA with honors, Johns Hopkins Univ. 1960; MA, Cornell Univ. 1962; LLB, Yale Univ. 1965; admitted to NY State Bar, Calif. State Bar. Career: law clk. to Justice Raymond Peters, Calif. Supreme Ct., 1965-66; assoc. Davis Polk & Wardwell, NYC 1966-69; chief litigating atty. Nat. Housing and Econ. Devel. Law Project, Boalt Hall, UC Berkeley, 1969-70; co-founder, mng. ptnr. Public Advocates Inc., San Francisco 1970-75; apptd. legal affairs secty. to Gov. Calif., 1974-80; apptd. Superior Ct. judge, San Francisco 1980-82; apptd. presiding justice Calif. Ct. Appeals, Dist. 1, Div. 2, San Francisco 1982–; bd. dirs. San Francisco Private Indus. Council; bd. dirs. No. Calif. Div. Am. Jewish Congress; awards: Alfred P. Sloan fellow Cornell Univ., 1960-62; Cherini and Sutherland Cup Prizes, Yale Univ.; mem. Calif. Judges Assn.; publs: articles in legal jours. Democrat; Jewish. Ofc: California Court of Appeals, State Building, San Francnisco 94102

KLINE-CZERNIAK, ALLENE SUZANNE, manufacturing co. executive; b. Mar. 10, 1951, Allentown, Pa.; d. Irvin H. and Alice Kline; m. Martin Czerniak, Oct. 24, 1970; children: Justin b. 1974, Kara b. 1976; edn: Am. Univ. 1972-74; CSU Los Angeles 1980-81. Career: founder, pres. A. Kline Chocolatier; cons., lectr. on chocolate industry to colleges and small businesses; subject of feature articles in L.A. Herald Examiner, L.A. Times, L.A. Home & Entertaining Mag., San Gabriel Valley Mag.; guest on KNX and KABC radio; panelist "The Entrepreneur" forum presented by Claremont Economics Inst.; mem: Retail Confectioners Internat. 1982-, Am. Assn. Candy

Technols. 1982-, Nat. Assn. Female Execs. 1985-; creator of recipes for full line of chocolate confectionary products; devel. unique store licensing and mdsg. concepts. Res: 3871 Chelsea Dr La Verne 91750 Ofc: A. Kline Chocolatier POB 756, 111 S College Ave Claremont 91711

KLING, PETER HELMAR, advertising executive; b. Feb. 5, 1931, Rockford, Ill.; s. Helmar G. and Orpha (Halleen) K.; children: Steven b. 1953, David b. 1956, Timothy b. 1958, Pamela b. 1961; edn: BS, USC 1955. Career: sales mgr. Wylde & Sons Printing, 1960-63; sales mgr. Emtec, Pico Rivera 1962-65; pres. Media IV Advtsg. (prod. indsl. films; pub. sev. indsl. publications), Long Beach 1965-75; pres. Trimagination Creative Services, Santa Ana 1975-79; pres. Custom Business Systems, Santa Ana 1979-82; v.p. Smith & Myers Advtsg., Santa Ana 1982–; honors: Certified Business Communicator, BPAA (1985); mem. Sales and Mktg. Execs. (bd.); mil: US Army 1952-54; Republican; Evangelical Free Ch. (mem. Nat. and S.W. Dist. boards); dir. Summit Experiences, Covina; mem. Am. Bd. of Missions to the Jews; rec: golf, photog., tentmaking, backpacking. Ofc: Smith & Myers 2020 First St Ste 320 Santa Ana 92705

KLINGENSMITH, ARTHUR PAUL, relocation and redevelopment consultant; b. May 23, 1949, Los Angeles; s. Paul A. and Hermine Elinore (Wacek) K.; edn: AA soc. sci., Indian Valley Jr. Coll. 1976; BA indsl. psych., San Francisco State Univ. 1979; MA indsl. psych., Columbia Pacific Univ. 1980; desig: senior right of way cand., Internat. Right of Way Assn. Career: USAF radio ops. instr., Biloxi, Miss. 1968-72, air traffic controller, Novato, Ca. 1972-74; right of way agent Calif. Dept. Transp., San Francisco 1978-85, senior right of way agent, Sacto. 1985–; relocation and redevel. cons. var. cities (San Jose, Pacifica, San Pablo), 1984–; tech. cons. computerization of Right of Way process, CalTrans; course instr. Internat. Right of Way Assn. (1980-); mem: Am. Arbitration Assn., Internat. Right of Way Assn., Marin Co. Bd. of Realtors; mil: s/sgt. US Air Force 1968-74, merit service award; Republican; Prot.; rec: auto. restoration, painting, study of light. Res: POB 1050 Novato 94948

KLIVANS, CRAIG LYLE, chiropractor; b. Nov. 20, 1955, L.A.; s. Harvey and Marcia Sue (Linker) K.; m. Janet Epstein, Nov. 30, 1985; edn: BA, Hofstra Univ. 1978; BS, Pasadena Chiro. Coll. 1983, DC, 1983. Career: assoc. Yerman Chiro. Grp. 1983-84; clinician and instr. Pasadena Chiro. Coll. 1984-85; pvt. practice Klivans Chiro. Ofc. 1985–; p-t instr. Pasadena Chiro. 1985–; honors: Sigma Chi Psi 1983; mem: Am. Chiro. Assn., Calif. Chiro. Assn., Internat. Chiro. Assn., Encino CofC; publ: Effects of Low Back Pain on American Business; Republican; Jewish; rec: skiing, sailing, horseback riding. Ofc: Klivans Chiropractic 16100 Ventura Blvd, Ste 9, Encino 91436

KLUDJIAN, VAHE ZAREH, engineer; b. Feb. 27, 1947, Tripoli, Lebanon, nat. US cit. 1977; s. Zareh Nicola and Efronia (Berejkilian) K.; edn: BS in engring., CSU Long Beach 1975, MS engring., 1981; Reg. Profl. Engr., Calif. Career: product test engr. Ford Motor Co., Dearborn, Mich. 1978-80; engr. Mazda (No. America), Inc., Irvine 1980-81, senior engr. 1981-82, asst. mgr. R&D Div. 1982–; mem: ASCE, Soc. Automotive Engrs., Armenian Engrs. and Scientists of Am.; life mem. Ulysses S. Grant Assn.; Democrat; Congregational; rec: movies, auto racing, music. Res: 1101 Elm Ave Apt 203 Long Beach 90813 Ofc: Mazda (North America), Inc. 1444 McGaw Ave Irvine 92714

KLUG, ROBERT J., insurance co. exceutive, ret.; b. May 15, 1931, Philadelphia, Penn.; s. Rudolph J. and Ida J. (Wolf) K.; children: Leslie J. b. 1958; David J. b. 1961; edn: BA, Penn. State Univ. 1954, MS, 1956; Chartered Life Underwriter (CLU), Am. Coll. Life Underws. Career: Mutual Benefit Life Ins. Co. of Newark, NJ 1958-83: sales 1958, sales supvr. 1962, mgr. Phila. 1966, asst. dir. of agency fin. 1969, gen. agent Orange Co. 1971-, corp. adminstrv. v.p. 1976, ret. 1983; mem: Gen. Agents & Mgrs. Assn., Orange Co. Agents & Mgrs. Assn. (dir.), Nat. Assn. of Life Underwriters (PAC), Mastework Music & Art Found.; rec: music, classical pianist. Res: Oakland 94604

KLUGER, ANDREW MICHAEL, financial adviser, management consultant; b. Sept. 6, 1951, Mexico City, Mex.; s. Sidney and Mildred (Gerber) K.; div.; children: David b. 1981, Alexander b. 1982, Jonathan b. 1984; edn: BA, UC Davis 1973; JD, Univ. San Francisco 1978. Career: law clk. Hon. Leland J. Lazarus, Superior Ct. Judge 1972-73; moderator KNBR-NBC Radio, San Francisco 1973-74; exec. asst. Office of the Mayor, S.F. 1973-74, dir. of pub. information 1974-76; pres. Dos Mundos Inc. 1976-78; founder/pres. Kluger & Assocs. 1978-81, 1983–; finl. plnnr./ staff atty. Dean Witter Reynolds Inc. 1981-83, devel. the Select Account Executive Seminars on Financial Planning; dir. Agritec Ltd., 1985-88; finl. adv. Pro-Trac; adj. prof. Lone Mountain Coll.; mem: Internat. Assn. of Finl. Planners, Calif. Assn. Finl. Planners, Univ. of S.F. Law Assembly, CalAggie Alumni Assn.; civic: Boys Town Jerusalem, B'nai B'rith, Adoption of Spl. Kids- Shaar Zedek Hosp., Hadassah; Democrat; Jewish; rec: swim, writing. Ofc: Kluger & Assocs Inc 68 Paul Dr Ste B San Rafael 94903

KMET, EUGENIA RUTH (aka Rebecca), pharmacist; b. June 17, 1948, Ellisville, Miss.; d. Eugene Roberts and Ruth Winn (Pettis) Patterson; m. Joseph Kmet, March 29, 1969; edn: BS, Univ. of Ariz. 1971; MBA, National Univ. 1980. Career: pharmacist Defender Star Community Pharmacy, Tucson, Ariz. 1971-72, Santa Monica Bldg. Profl. Pharmacy, Santa Monica 1972-73; US Veteran's Admin., Wadsworth VA Hosp., W. Los Angeles 1974-75; pharmacist spec. Kaiser San Diego Med. Ctr., San Diego 1979-82; community svc. lectr. in field; cont. edn. instr.; honors: Participant, Current Strategy Forum, Naval War Coll., Newport, R.I. 1981; Rho Chi; mem: Naval War Coll. Found., Am. Defense Preparedness Assn., San Diego Aerospace Mus., Smithsonian Assn., Am., Calif. & San Diego Socs. of Hosp. Pharmacists, Kappa Epsilon; mil: lt. USN Med. Svc. Corps 1975-78, USNR 1978-82; Republican; Episcopal; rec: stu. govt. def. indus., theology, pub. speaking needlepoint, bicycling. Res: 5619 Camber Pl San Diego 92117

KNECHT, JOHN RICHARD, computer sales executive; b. June 4, 1944, Los Angeles; s. John F. and Shirlee M. (Hardcastle-Lethin) K.; children: Jana L .b. 1966; Scott b. 1970; edn: UCLA 1966. Career: computer sys. engr., dist. sys. engring. mgr. Sanders Data Systems Div. of Sanders Assocs. 1967-71; senior sales engr. Sanders Data Systems 1971-72; owner, mng. ptr. Capital Mktg. Corp. 1972-76; sales engr., acct. exec. Data General Corp. 1976-81; sales rep., acct exec., br. sales mgr., br. mgr. Prime Computer 1981-86; sales mgr. Pyramid Technology 1986–; honors: Golden Circle, Sanders Associates 1972; Million Dollar Culb, Data General 1978; Spl. Achiev., Data General 1978; Million Dolar Club, Data Gen. Corp. 1979; 2 Milliom Dollar Club, Data General 1980; Top Producer, Prime Computer 1983; 100 Club, Prime Computer 1984; mem: DPMA, Toastmaster, Data General Grey Eagles, Prime Alumni Assn. (PALS), Boy Scouts of Am.; works: short stories, 'IF' Science Fiction 1962-64; rec: backpacking, hiking, fishing. Ofc: Pyramid Technology, 1862 MacArthur Blvd. Ste. 200 Irvine 92715

KNIGHT, VIRGINIA FRANCES, writer, former first lady of California; b. Oct. 12, 1918, Fort Dodge, Iowa; d. Lawrence Frederick and Emma Julia (Miller) Piergue: stepfather: 1923-, E. B. Hershberger, advt. exec. Internat. Harvester Co.; 2 bros: Ralph Gotch Piergue (dec. 1982), Richard B. Hershberger, atty. San Marino; mother wrote ofcl. welcome song for 1933 LA Olympic Games; m. C. Lyle Carlson (lt. 15th AF, killed in action WWII 1944), June 28, 1940; m. 2d Goodwin Jess Knight (Superior Ct. judge 1935-46, lt. gov. Calif. 1946-53, gov. Calif. 1953-59; stepchildren: Marilyn (Stubbs) b. 1927, Carolyn (Weedman) 1933-1970; grad. Los Angeles H.S. 1937. Career: fashion model Warner Bros. theatres, radio 1937-42, pioneer TV pgms. KHJ, Don Lee Network 1937; Douglas Aircraft 'accomodation sales & emergency procurement/ civic and vets rehabilitation work/ entertainment pgms. for vets. hosps., "Victory House" Pershing Sq./ active war bond drives, WWII; assoc. prod./ participant TV Tele-Forum and Freedom Forum, 1947-54; First Lady of Calif. 1954-59, ofcl. hostess Nat. Republican Conv., S.F. 1956, planted Virginia Knight Camellia Capitol Park 1958, estab. collection of portraits of Calif. First Ladies for Gov.'s Mansion forseeing it would become a museum; current owner/ opr. Elephant-Eagle Gold Mines, Mojave; honors: nat. cit. for sale of war bonds (1941-46), Nat. Viola Queen, Mil. Order of the Purple Heart (1954-55), Dr. in Metaphysics, St. Andrews Ecumen. Coll., London (1955), Hon. Poet Laureate State of Del. (1955), Outstanding Woman of Calif. press award (1956), Ten Best Dressed Women list So. Calif. Fashion Council (1959), fellow (poetry) Am. Inst. of Fine Arts (1969), life mem. Internat. Clover Poetry Assn., Soc. of Literary Designates, Wash DC (1970), Dame Commander, Order of the Crown of Thorns, San Luigi "Disting. Humanitarian" (1977); mem: Am. Legion Aux. (past pres.), VFW Aux. (hon), Edwin Markham Poetry Soc.; civic: founder The Music Center Building Fund Com., Soc. of Arts & Letters (nat. advy. council 1956-58), Ettie Lee Homes for Youth (nat. advy. com.), Stanford Univ. Libraries, Navy League (life mem.); author: The Golden Heritage of Goodwin Knight (1975), series of oral hist. interviews Bancroft Library, UCB (1977-80), mss. Reflections on Life with Goodwin J. Knight; Republican; rec: writing verse, tennis, swim. Res: 540 S Arden Blvd Los Angeles 90020

KNOOP, VERN THOMAS, civil engineer; b. Nov. 19, 1932, Paola, Kans.; s. Vernon Thomas and Nancy Alice (Christian) K.; edn: BS in civil engring., Kans. State Univ. 1959; Reg. Profl. Engr., Calif. (1966). Career: surveyor James L. Bell, Surveyors and Engrs., Overland Park, Kans. 1954; engring. asst. to county engr. Miami County (Kans.) Hwy Dept. 1955; civil engr. State of Calif. Dept. of Water Resources (DWR), Los Angeles 1959–, program mgr. Water Quality Pgm. 1965-67, unit chief Relocations Unit 1968-74, pgm. mgr. (acting section chief) Statewide Planning Pgm. 1974–; indep. cons. engr.; hydrology tchr., state DWR 1984; awarded two DWR unit citations: for outstanding quality of ground water basin investigation (1964), for work in Design and Constrn. Branch, State Water Project (1975); mem: Am. Soc. Civil Engrs. (dir. L.A. Sect. hydraulics and water resources mgmt. tech. group), Profl. Engrs. in Calif. Govt.; civic: Internat. Cultural Activities Singles, Smithsonian Soc., Am. Assn. of Individual Investors; publs: research in ground water pub. in tech. jours. in US and Israel (1964); prin. investigator, author reports: Ground Water Study of Homeland and Green Acres - Riverside Co. (1983), Pyramid Lake Master Waste Water System Plan (1984); mil: sp3 US Army 1955-57, Good Conduct Medal; Young Republicans; Baptist; rec: gardening, skiing, sailing, photog. Res: 116 N Berendo St Los Angeles 90004

KNOPINSKI, KENT J., service company executive; b. Jan. 7, 1941, Kansas City, Mo.; s. George M. and Gladys C. (Ogle) K.; m. Judith A. Baba, Feb. 22,1 986; edn: BA, Univ. of Missouri 1965. Career: ptr. bldg. svc. firm 1971-74; exec. v.p. Bekins Bldg. Maint. Co. Inc. 1974-77; CEO Bekins Svc. Group Inc. 1978-82; chmn., CEO Pedus Svcs. Inc., Los Angeles; dir. sev. Bekins subs. and currently Pedus; mem. Bldg. Svc. Contractors Assn. Internat., Jonathan Club, Sigma Chi Alumni Assn., Univ. of Missouri Alumni Assn.; Republic. Ofc: Pedus, 3500 W. 1st St. Los Angeles 90004

KNOTT, LESLIE WHITESTONE, physician; b. June 14, 1911, San Francisco; s. Fred and Agnes Maud (Thomas) K.; m. Gertrude Reeves, Sept. 3, 1935; children: Sylvia b. 1941, Roxanna b. 1943, Leslie Jr. b. 1947; edn: AB, Occidental Coll. 1933; MD, USC 1940; MPH, Johns Hopkins Univ. 1942. Career: commd. USPHS 1940, asst. to state health dir., Ill. 1942-47, deputy dir. Dept. of

State Aid to Greece, Athens 1947-49, asst. dir. and chief Health Manpower, then med. dir. and chief Chronic Disease div., USPHS, Wash. DC 1949-62; ret.; senior fellow Rehab. Med. Stanford Univ. 1962-64, asst. prof. rehab. 1964-67; pvt. practice of med. 1967-77; dir. physical med. O'Connor Hosp. 1972-77; honors: Phi Beta Kappa (1933), Phi Kappa Phi (1939); Gold Cross Order of George I. Kingdom of Greece 1949; Silver Medal, Hellenic Red Cross, Greece 1949; mem: Bay & Valley Habitat for Humanity (bd.), Biblical Archaeological Soc., Nat. Geographic Soc.; past mem: Am. and Calif. Med. Assns., Santa Clara Co. Med. Soc., Fellow Am. Coll. of Preventitive Med. & Public Health, Fellow Am. Bd. of Physicial Med. & Rehab.; publs: num. articles in med. journs.; A Study of Chumash Teeth, Journ. of New World Archaeology 1979; mil: med. dir. USPHS 1945-52; Democrat; Ch. of Religious Sci.; rec: woodworking, archaeology, photog. Res: 110 Wood Rd. J-101 Los Gatos 95030

KNOX, DONNA LEE LAWSON, manufacturing co. executive; b. Apr. 10, 1944, South Gate; d. Donald Franc and Edith Louise (Richards) Lawson; m. Michael Knox, Mar. 1, 1963; div. 1985; children: Jeffrey b. 1963, Kimberly b. 1966, Steven b. 1971; edn: spl. courses var. colls. Career: secty. (security clearance) mil. def. dept. Aerojet Gen., Downey 1962-64; p.t. fashion modeling; instr., sales, Mirror, Mirror Co., Phoenix, Ariz. 1969; real estate props. renovation, Phoenix and Scottsdale, Ariz. 1973; media rels. (radio, t.v., print) for var. charitable orgns., Ariz. 1981; mfg. and mktg. (wholesale & retail) of invention: Vehicle Door Shield (pat. app. 1982) sold as the Ding Wing, 1982 –; instr. Marilyn Shore Studios, Agoura and John Robert Powers Sch., Woodland Hills, 1986; dir. Academy West Modeling & Talent Sch., Santa Barbara; mem. Internat. Arabian Horse Assn. 1978-84, Paradise Valley Farms Homeowners Assn. 1978-84 (v.p.); Republican (precinct com. 1982-84); Christian Sci.; rec: fitness, art. Res: 4740 Park Granada #247 Calabasas 91302 Ofc: D. Wings POB 8201 Calabasas 91302

KNUDSON, KARL JAMES, lawyer; June 17, 1945, New Brunswick, N.J.; s. Richard F. and Eleanor M. (Van Doren) K.; m. Ruth E. Rodisch, June 15, 1968; children: Robert b. 1977, Richard b. 1979; BA, Lehigh Univ. 1967; grad. pgm. chem., Univ. of Wisc. 1967-68; JD, Univ. So. Calif. 1975; admitted Calif. State Bar 1975, federal 1978. Career: atty. Clerk, Sullivan, Brown, Pickell & Smith 1975, Pickell & Brown 1976-79, Robert J. Pickell & Assoc. 1979-80, sr. atty., v.p. Pickell & Knudson A Law Corp. 1981 –; judge pro tem Riverside Municipal Ct.; arbitration panel, mandatory settlement conf. panel Riverside Superior Ct. Indio 1983-84; honors: Hale Moot Ct. Competition, Written Advocacy (USC 1974); mem: Am., Riverside Co. bar assns.; AYSO (referee 1984-); author: various briefs on appeal; mil: ssgt. USAF 1968-72, AF Commendation, Good Conduct; Republican; Presbyterian (elder); rec: swimming, camping. Ofc: 7145 Magnolia Ave, Ste 200, Riverside 92514-4760

KOBAYASHI, WENDY N., comptroller; b. Apr. 27, 1961, Los Angeles; d. Woodrow Y. and Rose (Takahashi) Kobayashi; edn: BS CSU Long Beach 1983. Career: appeals clk. Internal Revenue Service, Los Angeles 1980-82; acct. Ken Graves CPA, Glendale 1982-83; comptroller Stursberg & Hewitt, Inc., L.A. 1983 –; vol. income tax preparer, IRS 1982-; honors: Noteworthy contbn., IRS (1982); mem. Beta Alpha Psi, Alpha Delta Kappa, Young Buddhist Assn.; creative: Miss Sansei of California candidate (1979), Theatre dancer in Asian Showcase (1982), Nisei Week (1985); Buddhist; rec: dance, ski. Res: 766 Topacio Dr Monterey Park 91754 Ofc: Stursberg & Hewitt Inc. 6671 Sunset Blvd Ste 1525 Los Angeles 90028

KOBLICK, MAURY ALLAN, lawyer; b. May 16, 1931, San Francisco; s. Louis and Frances (Horowitz) K.; m. Jane Ward, June 28, 1953; children: Geoffrey b. 1954, Andrew b. 1957, Theodore b. 1959, James b. 1964; edn: BA, Univ. Calif. 1952; LLB, UC Boalt Sch. of Law 1955; admitted Calif. State Bar 1955. Career: teaching fellow Stanford Law Sch. 1955-56; lectr. San Francisco Law Sch. 1956-71; reader Calif. State Bar 1972-78; senior atty. Supreme Court of California, San Francisco 1956 –; Chief Justice Phil S. Gibson (1956-64), Justice Raymond Peters (1965-73), Justice Wm. P. Clark (1973-81), Justice Allen Broussard (1981-); honors: Order of the Coif (1955). Res: 195 Fairway Dr San Rafael 94901 Ofc: Supreme Court of California, State Bldg Ste 4236 San Francisco 94102

KOBZA, DENNIS JEROME, architect; b. Sept. 30, 1933, Ullysses, Nebr.; s. Jerry Frank and Agnes Elizabeth (Lavicky) K.; m. Doris Mae Riemann, Dec. 26, 1953; children: Dennis Jerome, Diana Jill, David John; edn: BS, Healds Archtl. Engring. 1959. Career: draftsman, designer B.L. Schroder, Palo Alto 1959-60; senior draftsman, designer Ned Abrams Architect, Sunnyvale 1960-61; Kenneth Elvin Architect, Los Altos 1961-62; ptr. B.L. Schroder Architect, Palo Alto 1962-66; pvt. practice architecture, Mountain View 1966 –; recipient, Solar PAL Design Award, 1983; mem: CofC, Am. Inst. Architects, Constrn. Specifications Inst., Am. Inst. of Plant Engrs., Nat. Fedn. Ind. Bus. Orgn.; Rotary (pres. 1986-87); mil: USAF 1952-56. Res: 3840 May Ct. Palo Alto 94303 Ofc: 2083 Old Middlefield Way Mountain View 94043

KOCH, GEORGE BYRON, software company executive; b. Nov. 5, 1946, Chicago, Ill.; s. George Oscar and Patricia (McCormick) K.; m. Victoria Cole, May 3, 1979; children: George August b. 1981, Isaiah James b. 1984; edn: BS, Elmhurst Coll. 1968. Career: asst. chief engr. Aaron Stevens Corp., Chicago 1968-69; v.p. Tommorrow Inc., Los Angeles 1969-70; pres. Koch Research & Devel. Corp. (fmrly. Koch Engring. 1970-78), San Francisco 1970-83, chmn., CEO Koch Systems Corp. 1983 –; chief cons. engr. Sattwa Corp. Los Angeles 1971-76, Sportoys Corp., Los Angeles 1971-72; cons. Bank of Am.; mem: Am. Physical Soc., AAAS, Am. Conservative Union, Four Sigma Soc.; publs: ed., Journ. of Four Sigma Soc. 1980-82; author num. mag., newspaper articles,

anthologies, etc. on number theory, science, philosophy and political thought; patentee, ednl. devices, furniture, energy storage, chemical equip., computer peripherals; Republican; Episcopal; rec: number theory, music. Ofc: Koch Systems Corp., P.O. Box 2510 San Francisco 94126

KOCH, PETER RUTLEDGE, typographic designer; b. Nov. 15, 1943, Missoula, Mont.; s. Stanley Heiberg and Dorothy (Fergusen) K.; div.; 1 son, Peter Morgan; edn: BA in philos., Univ. of Mont. 1970. Career: book designer/ letterpress master printer, 1973 –, pub. Montana Gothic (literary mag.) 1972-78, Black Stone Press books, 1974-82; owner prin. Peter Koch & Assocs., Typographic Design, Oakland 1983 –; lectr. Calif. Coll. of Arts & Crafts, UC Santa Cruz, Montana State Univ. symposium 1984; cons. Montana Arts Council 1984; awards: AIGA Award of Merit (1978), Nat. Endowment for the Arts grantee (197, 78, 80), Rounce & Coffin Club Design Award (1979, 81, 85); mem. Am. Printing Hist. Assn., Roxburghe Club of S.F., Colophon Club, The Book Club of Calif.; publs: reviews on printing design in Fine Print Mag., poetry and essays on lit.; Democrat; rec: trout fishing, philosophy, reading the Classics. Ofc: Peter Koch & Associates 439 23rd St Oakland 94612

KOEHLER, LLOYD K., regional personnel executive; b. Dec. 30, 1942, Spring Valley, Ill.; s. Lloyd F. and Martha Pauline (Campbell) K.; div.; children: Chuck b. 1960, Scott b. 1963, Kristy b. 1972; edn: BA, psych., Univ. of So. Fla. 1968; PhD cand., Kensington Univ. 1986. Career: counselor Youth Opportunity Center, St. Petersburg,Fla. 1964-69; personel rep., then Equal Empl. Opp. coordinator GTE Data Services, Tampa, Fla. 1969-73; div. personnel supr. Eckerd Drugs Inc., Clearwater, Fla. 1973-75; pers. mgr. Gulfstar Yachts Inc., St. Pete., 1975-79; pers. mgr. United Div. of Howmedica (Pfizer Inc), Largo, Fla. 1979-81; regional pers. mgr. Pfizer Inc., Lucerne Valley, Ca. 1981 –; honors: Equal Emply. Opportunity Award, Tampa Urban League (1972, 73), mem. Com. of 100, Pinellas County, Fla. (1980, 81); dir. Lakewood Jr. Spartans Youth Football 1972-77 (pres.'s awd. 1972, 73); vol. youth sports: baseball, football, track and field; Republican; Presbyterian; rec: sports, phys. fitness. Res: 20012 Talihina Rd Apple Valley 92307 Ofc: Pfizer Inc., POB 558, Lucerne Valley 92356

KOEHN, SAMUEL PETER, project engineer, building contractor; b. Nov. 13, 1953, Merced, Ca.; s. Samuel C. and Ida V. (McCollum) K.; m. Dr. Mary L. Coelho, June 11, 1983; edn: Bach. Urban Geog., CSU San Jose 1975, Masters, 1980; grad. bus. adm. pgm., CSU Fresno, currently; Calif. lic. Real Estate Broker 1981, Gen. Building Contractor 1982; Reg. Profl. Engr. 1984. Career: engineering assoc., asst. city plnnr., City of Atwater, 1977-79; assoc. plnnr., acting plnng. dir., City of Madera, 1980-84; bldg. constrn. and real estate bus. owner, Northwest Development Co., Can-Am Devel. Co.; project engr. County of Monterey; guest spkr. var. service clubs, profl. assns.; honors: Sigma Iota Epsilon (bus. hon.); mem: Nat. Soc. Profl. Engrs., Calif. Soc. Profl. Engrs., Am. Soc. Civil Engrs., Nat. Assn. Realtors, Soc. of Calif. Accts., Am. Planning Assn., Calif. Inst. of Technology Transfer; Ex-officio mem. City of Atwater Plnng. Commn., 1978-79, City of Madera Plnng. Commn. 1982-83; publs: Calif. Environmental Quality Act: A tool for geographic planning (1979); Republican; Catholic; rec: sailing, skiing. Res: 310 Spencer Monterey 93940 Ofc: 855 E Laurel Dr Salinas 93902

KOEPPEL, DONALD ALLEN, b. Oct. 17, 1917, Chgo.; s. Joseph John and Ethel Mae (Cowley) K.; m. Gloria Allan, Mar. 20, 1948; children: Bruce Allan b. 1952, John Paul b. 1956, Robert James b. 1959; edn: BS, Northwestern Univ. 1949; JD, Chicago-Kent Coll. of Law 1954; admitted Ill. State Bar 1955. Career: mgmt. trainee Swift & Co., Chgo. 1937-42; gen. counsel, secty. Belnap & Thompson, Chgo. 1947-56; pres., dir. Blue Chip Stamps, Los Angeles 1956 –; past dir: Buffalo Evening News, Precision Steel Inc.; mem: Chgo. Bar Assn. (1955-), Ill. Bar Assn. (1955-), Greater Los Angeles Urban Coalition (pres. 1970-77), Los Angeles Regional Purchasing Council (chmn. 1974-79); civic: Cancer Research Assocs. USC (dir., past pres. 1977-), Univ. of Redlands (Exec. Com. 1971-84, trustee emeritus), LA Area CofC (dir. 1970-74), Hispanic Urban Ctr./LA (dir. 1970-79), United Way of LA (dir. 1975-77), Rotary of LA (mem. 1968-, pres. 1980-81); clubs: California, Annandale Golf; mil: asst. insp. gen. HQ US 8th Army 1943-46, SE Asia-Pacific Theater, Bronze Star; Congregational. Res: 1445 Caballero Rd Arcadia 91006 Ofc: Blue Chip Stamps POB 54109 Los Angeles 90054

KOFF, HOWARD MICHAEL, financial services co. president; b. Dec. 4, 1947, Bronx, NY; s. Philip and Sara K.; m. Marcia, Aug. 23, 1970; children: Stacy b. 1974, David b. 1977; edn: BA, Bowling Green Univ. 1969; Series 7 Lic., Nat. Assn. of Securities Dealers 1971; Life, Disability, Variable Annuity Lic. 1970; Reg. Investment Advisor 1982. Career: marketer 1970-78; pres./CEO HMK Financial, Beverly Hills 1978-82; pres./CEO Integrated Financial, Encino 1982 –; guest speaker Ten Million Dollar Forum, San Fernando Valley Estate Plnng. Conf., Chief Exec. Forum, Young Presidents Orgn., Calif. Contg. Edn. for CPAS, var. life ins. cos.; honors: Phi Eta Sigma Leadership Award, Sidney Frohman Scholarship Award, Omicron Delta Kappa, and Phi Kappa Phi, Bowling Green Univ.; mem: Million Dollar Round Table (charter mem. The Top of the Table 1978-), ALIGNPAC (bd. dirs. Indus. PAC 1983), Assn. for Advanced Life Underwriters (bd. dirs. 1985-), Ten Million Dollar Forum (pres. 1984-85), Young Pres.'s Orgn., Jewish Big Brothers and Camp Max Straus (secty., bd. 1978-); clubs: Regency, Sand & Sea, Center, Brentwood Country, Ironwood Country, US Senatorial; Republican; Jewish; rec: sports. Res: 3604 Hayvenhurst Ave. Encino 91436 Ofc: Integrated Financial, 16530 Ventura Blvd. Ste. 500 Encino 91436

KOFFORD, CREE, lawyer; b. July 11, 1933, Santaquin, Utah; s. Cree C. and Melba N. (Nelson) K.; m. Ila Jean Macdonald, Sept. 11, 1953; children: Kim b. 1954, Jane b. 1957, Bradley b. 1962, Quinn b. 1965, Tracy b. 1966; edn: BS, Univ. of Utah 1955; JD, USC 1961. Career: partner Munns and Kofford, San Marino 1962-68; mng. partner Munns, Kofford, Hoffman, Hunt & Throckmorton, Pasadena 1969–; frequent spkr. construction related topics, var. engrg. socs. & constrn. indus. convs.; recipient appreciation certs: Constrn. Consultants Bd. of Ch. of Jesus Christ of Latter-day Saints, 1981; Am. Soc. of Plumbing Engrs.; Refrigeration Svc. Engrs. Soc.; mem: Boy Scouts of Am., San Gabriel Valley Council; ABA (constrn. ind. sect.), Calif. & L.A. Co. Bar Assns.; University Club; publs: num. arts. in profl. journs.; reg. contbr. under title "Legal Briefing," Plumbing Engineer pub. by Am. Soc. of Plumbing Engrs. 1973–; "Real Estate and the New Tax Law," pub. in the Real Estate Mkt. Advr. 1982; Republican; Ch. of Jesus Christ of Latter-day Saints; rec: equestrian. Res: 1330 Rodeo Rd Arcadia 91006 Ofc: Munns, Kofford, Hoffman, Hunt & Throckmorton, 199 N Lake, Ste 300, Pasadena 91101

KOGER, STEVEN ALLEN, manufacturing technology engineer; b. Feb. 9, 1960, Terre Houte, Ind.; s. Garmon Winford and Barbara Ann (Anderson) K.; m. Jennifer, Aug. 25, 1984; 1 dau, Amber b. 1981; edn: BS, Ball State Univ. 1981, MA, 1983, Univ. of Mich. 1983; Brigham Young Univ. 1986; USC 1986. Career: prodn. supvr. Internat. Packings Corp., Scottsburg, Ind. 1981-82; plastics lab. supvr. Ball State Univ. Dept. of Indsl. Tech., Muncie, Ind. 1982-83; mfg. tech. engr. senior Northrop Corp. Adv. Sys. Div., Pico Rivera 1983–; project tech. advr. Northrop Corp. 1985–; honors: admitted with distn., Ball State Univ. 1978; mem: Soc. of Mfg. Engrs., Soc. of Plastics Engrs. (pres., charter), Gamma Theta Upsilon (life); research papers: Integrated Composites Center Manufacturing Simulation, 1985; Integrated Composites Center Scheduling Using Expert Systems, 1986; Republican; rec: numismatics, technical research, travel. Res: 287 S Dallas Ave San Bernardino 92410 Ofc: Northrop Corp. Adv. Systems Div., 8900 E. Washington Blvd. M120/3M, Pico Rivera 90660

KOJAK, WILLIAM A., JR., engineer; b. Nov. 1, 1952, Beaumont, Texas; s. William A. Sr. and Earlene (Kellum) K.; m. Renee, March 26, 1981; children: Keasha b. 1971, Karleen b 1974, Julie b. 1981; edn: BA, Univ. of Houston 1975. Career: therapist psychiatric Bellaire Gen. Hosp., Houston, Texas 1975-76; head counselor Because of Youth, San Jose 1977-78; counselor Eastfield Children's Ctr., Campbell 1978-79; freelance writer, Bouder Creek 1980; engring. aide Underwriters Labs. Inc., Santa Clara 1980-83; product safety engr. Santa Clara Research, Santa Clara 1983-85; compliance engr. Robinton Products Inc., Sunnyvale 1985–; product safety cons. 1985; works: short story, Song for the Dragon, Pulse 1975; short story, Letters to Lucy Bell, Forms 1979; poem, Come On In, Am. Poetry Anthology 1983; Democrat; rec: computers, programming and digital electronics, writing. Ofc: Robinton Products Inc., 580 Maude Ct. Sunnyvale 94086

KOKKONEN, KIM ROLF, computer scientist, physicist; b. Aug. 9, 1952, Norfolk, Va.; s. Ralph Melvin and Wilifred Ann (Fair) K.; m. Anita R., Dec. 26, 1985; edn: BA math, physics, Univ. Colo. 1973; MSEE, Ariz. State Univ. 1976. Career: physicist Motorola Semiconductor Phoenix 1974-76; physicist, integrated circuit designer Intel Corp. Santa Clara 1976-77; designer Maruman Integrated Circuits Sunnyvale 1977-79; proj. mgr., senior scientist Intel Corp. 1979-85; owner, chief scientist Turbopower Software Campbell 1985–; independent cons. var. semiconductor cos. 1979-82; vis. scientist Stanford Univ. 1984; honors: Phi Beta Kappa (1973), Boettcher Found. Scholar (1978); mem: IEEE 1975-, Assn. Computing Machinery 1985-; 4 patents in semiconductor field, 2 copyrighted software products, num. papers and presentations; rec: science fiction, woodworking, flute. Ofc: Turbopower Software 478 W Hamilton Ste 196 Campbell 95008

KOLENDER, WILLIAM BARNETT, police chief; b. May 23, 1935, Chgo.; s. David Solomon and Esther (Dickman) K.; children: Michael, Myrna, Joy, Randie, Dennis; edn: stu. San Diego City Coll. 1963, BA in pub. adminstrn., San Diego State Univ. 1964. Career: with San Diego Police Dept., 1956–, chief of police 1976–; tchr. UC San Diego 1971-, SDSU 1972-; mem. Commn. on Peace Officers Stds. and Tng. Calif.; bd. dirs. Police Exec. Research Forum; mem. exec. com. San Diego County Council BSA; mem. Mayor's Crime Control Commn.; pres. Boys Clubs of San Diego; awards: SDSU Alumnus of Year 1973, Outstanding Young Man of Year San Diego 1970, Man of Year 1981 Irish Congress of So. Calif. Man of Year 1981 Charter 100 Profl. Womens Club, City of San Diego Mayor's Award for Human Relations and Civil Rights 1971, Am. Jewish Com. Human Relations award 1975, Diogenes award S.D. chpt. Pub. Rels. Soc. Am. 1978, Histadrut award Am. Trade Union Council 1981, S.D. Urban League equal opportunity award 1981; mem. Calif. Police Chiefs Assn., Calif. Police Officers Assn., Internat. Assn. Chiefs of Police, Rotary; Republican; Jewish. Res: 6370 Rancho Park Dr. San Diego 92120 Ofc: 801 W Market St San Diego 92101

KOLIN, WILLIAM MICHAEL, lawyer; b. Apr. 1, 1948, Chgo.; s. Theodore W. and Lillian M. Kolin; m. Shirley, July 22, 1972; children: Jennifer b. 1982, Michael b. 1985; edn: BA, No. Ill. Univ. 1970; JD, Kent Coll. of Law 1974; admitted Calif. State Bar 1974. Career: clerk to Presiding Judge, Circuit Ct., Cook County, Ill. 1972-74; atty. assoc. law firm B. Mackenzie, Berkeley 1974-75; Clancy, Wright & Laws, Oakland 1975-78; founding senior ptnr. Morgan & Kolin (first law firm in state devoted exclusively to rep. plaintiffs in legal malpractice court cases), Oakland 1978–; consulting atty. num. law firms and corps. on legal malpractice law; recipient award for pro bono services, Alameda Co. Bar Assn. (1984); mem. Am. Trial Lawyers Assn., Calif. Trial Lawyers Assn., Alameda County Bar Assn.; Catholic; rec: restoration vintage autos. Res: 124 Hardy Cir Pleasant Hill 94523 Ofc: Morgan & Kolin, 436 14th St Ste 1105 Oakland 94612

KOLLAR, JOSEPHINE PENCE, civic leader; b. Mar. 3, 1913, Hillsboro, Ohio; d. Wm. Henry and Lida Lee (Lewis) Pence; m. Theodore J. Kollar, Nov. 21, 1981; 1 son, August J. Minke III b. 1943; edn: R.N., Christ Hosp. 1931-1934. Career: stewardess American Airlines 1938-41; Community service, 1950s-: Am. Field Service (placing fgn. exchange students in homes); Palmdale High Sch. PTA (pres. 1961, hon. life); Antelope Valley Fair (Floriculture Com. 1958-, chmn. 1976-); South Antelope Valley Coord. Council (treas. 1986, service awards 1964, 72) area chair March of Dimes and area chair Tuberculosis and Health; Antelope Valley Coll. (charter mem. patron club); Am. Red Cross (bd. dirs.); Calif. Fedn. Women's Clubs (State Bd. 1972-78, Sierra Cahuenga Dist. pres. 1972-74), Palmdale Womens Club (pres. 1964-66; Junior coord., dist. coord., hon. life mem. 1968), Parliamentary Law Club (cert. 1977); Lutheran Women's Missionary League (Zone pres. 1963); Republican; rec: gardening. Res: 35750 41st St East Palmdale 93550

KOLTAI, STEPHEN M., consulting engineer; b. Nov. 5, 1922, Ujpest, Hungary, nat. US cit.; s. Maximilian and Elisabeth (Rado) K.; m. Franciska Gabor, Sept. 14, 1948; children: Eva b. 1951, Susanne b. 1955; edn: M. Engring., Tech. Inst. of Budapest 1948; MBA econs., Univ. of Budapest 1955. Career: engring. cons., var. European countries, 1948-58; economic adviser/secty. Hungarian Embassy, Rome, Italy 1958-62; engring. exec. in Switzerland 1963-76; cons. engr./ pres. Pan Business Consulting Corp., Palm Springs 1977–; patentee inventions in computer & printing process; Republican (Presdtl. Task Force); rec: tennis, golf. Res: 740 Sonora Road Palm Springs 92264

KOMYATHY, GABOR, hotelier; b. Mar. 10, 1944, Budapest, Hungary; s. Dr. Aladar and Maria (Fuzessery) K.; edn: Masters, F.Liszt Acad. of Music, Bpest, 1963-68; Masters, Coll. for Hotel & Food Indus., Bpest 1975-78; desig: CTC, Cert. Travel Counselor, ICTA, Wellesley, Mass. 1983. Career: regl. mng. dir. Ibus Travel Co., Lake Balaton Region, Hungary 1972-75; dir. sales and mktg. Danubius Hotel & Spa Co., Budapest, 1975-78; dir. internat. mktg. The Beverly Hilton Hotel, Beverly Hills, Ca. 1979-83; dir. National Olympic Com. Relations, LAAOC, Los Angeles, 1984; gen. mgr. El Encanto Hotel and Garden Villas, Santa Barbara 1984–; honors: commendn., County of Los Angeles, 1983; mem: ATME, AH&MA, AIWF (chpt. bd., Conf. & Visitors Bur., S.B.); guest lecture series spkr., USC, 1982; rec: classical music, sports, literature. Res: Santa Barbara Polo and Racquet Club Ofc: 1900 LaSuen Rd Santa Barbara 93103

KONKOFF, HERBERT JEROME, physician, urological surgeon; b. Apr. 7, 1934, San Francisco; s. Leon Joseph and Sima (Altshuler) K.; m. Arlene Weinberg, June 20, 1959; children: Stephen b. 1961, Lisa b. 1963; m. 2d Beverly Ostwald, Mar. 14, 1976; stepchildren: Mitchell b. 1957, Karen b. 1959, Gregory b. 1962; edn: BA, UC Berkeley 1955; MD, Univ. Calif. Med. Sch. 1959. Career: internship 1959-60, gen. surgery resident 1960-61; capt. AUS Med. Corps active duty 1961-63; urology resident 1963-66; pvt. practice of urological surgery, San Franciscow 1966–; staff mem. French Hosp., (asst. chief urol.) Mt. Zion Hosp., Marshall Hale Hosp., Franklin Hosp.; fmr. chief urology Golden Gate Hosp.; mem: Tamalpais Med. Edn. Soc. (bd. dirs.), Pan Am. Med. Soc., No. Calif. Urological Soc., Am. Urol. Soc./ Western Sect., San Francisco Med. Soc., Calif. Med. Assn.; civic: Calif. Heritage Council (pres. 1984-), Calif. Hist. Soc., Tiburon Landmarks Soc., Purple Heart Assn., Order of the Compassionate Heart, Regular Veterans Assn., San Francisco Symphony Assn., S.F. Ballet Guild; publs: clin. research pertaining to urology, mil; capt. US Army, Reserves 1961-66. Res: Four Berke Ct Tiburon 94920 Ofc: 2340 Sutter Ste 105 San Francisco 94115

KONOVALOV, VLADIMIR, engineer; b. Feb. 7, 1939, Baranowitch, Russia, nat. US cit. 1960; s. Valentin and Maria (Klimova) K.; m. Olga, Nov. 14, 1964; children: Gregory b. 1967, Paul b. 1971; edn: BS mech. engring., CSU Los Angeles 1970; Reg. Profl. Engr. (Control Sys.). Career: senior design engr. machine tool indus. (10 yrs.), proj. engr. high tech. electronics (6 yrs), chief engr. semiconductor indus. (10 yrs.): Litton Indus., Interstate Electronics, Bridgeport Mach., Advanced Control Corp., West Bond Inc., Alpha Micro, Hughes Aircraft; current: dir. engring. Excellon, Torrance; invention: 1st machine for semiconductor "Pull Tester" application for chips; mil: E5 US Army; Eastern Orthodox; rec: classical guitar, chess, soccer, karate. Res: 6862 Evening Hill St Huntington Beach 92648 Ofc: Excellon 23915 Garnier St Torrance 90509

KONWIN, THOR W., entrepreneur, corporate executive; b. Aug. 17, 1943, Berwyn, Ill.; s. Frank and Alice S. (Johnson) K.; m. Carol Svitak, Aug. 4, 1967; 1 son, Christopher b. 1970; edn: AA, Morton Jr. Coll. 1966; BS, Northern Ill. Univ. 1967; MS, Roosevelt Univ. 1971. Career: Sunbeam Corp. 1968-81; cost acct. Sunbeam Appliance Co., Chicago, Ill. 1968-71; controller General Molded Prods., Des Plaines, Ill. 1971-75; asst. controller Sunbeam Appliance Co., Chicago, Ill. 1975-78, controller 1978-81; CFO Bear Medical Systems Inc., Riverside 1981-84; CFO, v.p. fin. Bird Products Corp., Palm Springs 1984–; designer, devel. high tech. bldg., Bear Medical Corp. hdqtrs.; structered LBO acquisition Bird Corp. form 3M Corp.; founder The Flowers n More; mil: E-4 US Army 1969-71; rec: buying and selling antiques. Res: 3254 Pachappa Hill Riverside 92506 Ofc: Bird Corporation, 3101 E. Alejo Rd. Palm Springs 92263

KOONIN, JOSEPH, industrial safety & security professional; b. May 10, 1937, Baltimore, Md.; s. Leon and Ida (Weisman) K.; m. Winifred Ruth, June 17, 1967; children: Marc b. 1968, Rachel Elizabeth b. 1971, Rebecca Jennifer b. 1974; edn: BS in sociol., Univ. Nebr. 1971; MEd psychol., Georgia State Univ. 1973; num. seminars in health, safety and security; desig: CPP (Cert. Protective Profl.), The Am. Soc. of Indsl. Security, Wash DC (1975-). Career: with Wells Fargo Bank, N.A., San Francisco 1978–: asst. bank security ofcr. 1978-81, asst. mgr. Safety Dept. and prin. facilitator Disaster Recovery Plan 1981-83, mgr. Safety Dept. 1983–; adj. prof. Federal Emergency Mgmt. Inst.; instr. Golden Gate Univ.; honors: apptd. senior banking industry advisor, President's Nat. Defense Executive Reserve, Fed. Emergency Mgmt. Agcy.; recogn. by US House of Reps. for his leadership in moving Calif. Clearing House Assn. towards major disaster preparedness; mem. Calif. Gov.'s Finl. Monetary & Ins. Earthquake Task Force, Bankers Clearing House Assn. Earthquake Recovery Task Force, Emergency Preparedness Task Force; mem. Calif. Bankers Assn., San Francisco CofC (Public Safety Com.); contbr. articles in banking mags.; coauthor: Guideline for an Emergency Preparedness Program (Calif. Bankers Assn.); assisted 30+ cos. in corporate disaster recovery planning; mil: major, M.P., US Army Inf. 1955-78, Disting. Service Cross, Bronze Star, 3 Purple Hearts, Sr. Parachute Wings, Combat Inf. Badge, Vietnamese Silver Star; Ind.; Jewish; rec: historical novels, nature walks. Res: 4541 Shellflower Ct Concord 94518 Ofc: Wells Fargo Bank, N.A. 343 Sansome 13th Floor San Francisco 94163

KOOS, BRIAN JOHN, physician; b. Mar. 23, 1949, Los Angeles; s. John Raymond and Marian Irene (Averrett) K.; m. Mary Pat Spikes, Jan. 24, 1971; children: Samantha b. 1978, Jordan b. 1976; edn: BA, Loma Linda Univ. 1971, MD, 1974; D.Phil, Univ. of Oxford 1982. Career: intern and res. Brigham & Womens Hosp., Boston 1975-79; fellowship in maternal- fetal medicine, Women's Hosp. USC- Los Angeles County Med. Ctr. 1983; asst. prof. of physiology and obstets. & gyn. Loma Linda Univ. 1983–; researcher Div. of Perinatal Biology, and instr. med. students and residents; honors: Alpha Omega Alpha, USPHS Postdoctoral Fellow, research grantee: Basil O'Connor Starter Research, March of Dimes; mem: AMA, NY Acad. of Scis., AAAS, Am. Fedn. for Clin. Research, Perinatal Research Soc.; contbr. article in J. Physiol. (1985). Res: 22950 DeBerry Grand Terrace 92324 Ofc: Perinatal Biology, Loma Linda University Loma Linda 92350

KOPENY, LOUIS CLARENCE, lawyer, indsl. engineer, mgmt. consultant; b. Mar. 31, 1926,Chgo.; s. Louis Joseph and Caroline (Zapfel) K.; m. Elizabeth Macaluso, Nov. 23, 1946; children: Betty Lou (Wojciechowski) b. 1948, William J. b. 1950, Carol Anne (Jones) b. 1954, June Ellen (Havlena) b. 1956, Robert L. b. 1957; edn: Ph.B., Northwestern Univ., 1951; MBA, CSU Fullerton, 1970; JD, Western State Univ. 1980. Calif. Reg. Profl. Engr.; Calif. Jr. Coll. Tchr. Credential; admitted to Calif. State Bar. Career: indsl. engr. Motorola Inc. and Motorola Canada, Ltd., Toronto 1951-55; chief indsl. engr., Radio-TV Div., Westinghouse Elec. Corp., Metuchen, NJ, 1955-57; mng. assoc. Mgmt. Services Dept., Arthur Young & Co., Los Angeles and NYC, 1957-61; mgmt. cons., self-empl., Sepulveda, Ca. 1961-62; asst. to Oper. V.P., Autonetics Div. Rockwell Internatl., Anaheim 1962-70; prin. (mgmt. cons.) Arthur Young & Co., Santa Ana 1970-75; ops. mgr./indsl. engr. Knott's Berry Farm, Buena Park 1975-82; atty. pvt. practice, Yorba Linda, 1982-83; internal mgmt. cons. MCA Inc., Universal City 1983–; instr. UCI Ext. 1969-73; adj. prof. National Univ. 1982-83; honors: Beta Gamma Sigma 1970; mem: Am. Inst. of Instl. Engrs. (sr.), State Bar of Calif., Masons; mil: yeoman USNR 1943-46, ATO, Asia-Pac. Theater (1 star), Philippine Liberation (1 star), Victory Medal; Republican; Lutheran; rec: gun collector, fishing, barbershop singing. Address: 9649 Hayvenhurst Ave Sepulveda 91343

KOPIT, MARK JAY, veterinarian; b. Feb. 13, 1954, Stillwater, Okla; s. Harold and Phyllis Florence (Wissoff) K.; edn: BA in biol. scis., CSU Fullerton 1976; DVM, Okla. State Univ. Coll. Vet. Med. 1981. Career: intern Angell Mem. Animal Hosp., Boston, Mass. 1981-82; resident Tufts Univ. Sch. of Vet. Medicine, Boston 1982-84; staff veterinarian Stanton Pet Hosp., Stanton 1984–; advisory bd. Orange County Animal Shelter; honors: Phi Kappa Phi (1981), Phi Zeta (1981), Upjohn Award clin. proficiency (1981); mem: Am. Animal Hosp. Assn., Am. Vet. Med. Assn., Acad. Vet. Cardiology, Am. Heartworm Soc., Stanton CofC; works: use of ivermectin as a heartworm preventative (1984); Democrat; Jewish; rec: cycling, running, exercise. Ofc: Stanton Pet Hospital 8591 Katella Ave Stanton 90680

KOPPEL, JOH F., accountant; b. Oct. 3, 1940, NY, NY; d. George and Elena (Zito) Gallina; children (nee Koppel): Kimberly Ann, Guy Joseph; edn: CSU Sacramento 1958-59, Am. Inst. of Banking 1958-74, UC Los Angeles Ext. 1980-81; desig: Class IV Counselor/Minister, Hubbard Guidance Ctr., Ch. of Scientology. Career: branch auditor Bank of America Downtown Plaza and Sacramento Main Offices, 1968-80; mktg. planning dir. Bridge Publications, Hollywood 1981; acct./controller Moctesuma Esparza Prodns. and BuenaVision Cable T.V., Los Angeles 1981-83; controller, corp. secty., dir. fin. & adminstrn. Kresser, Craig/D.I.K., Los Angeles 1983–; acct. for The Ballad of Gregario Cortez, American Playhouse (released by Embassy, 1982); mem: Basic Computer Systems Users Group (del. 1983-), The American Film Inst., Internat. Assn. of Scientologists for Rel. Freedom (lifetime mem. 1973-); civic: lectr. for young offenders, Sacto. Youth Authority (1973), Narconon, lobbyist for Medical Ethics bill (1979), pub. rels. advisor Applied Scholastics, Sacto. (1974-76); Democrat; Scientologist; rec: writing, art work, hiking. Ofc: Kresser, Craig/D.I.K. 2029 Century Park East Fifth Flr Los Angeles 90067

KORF, HAROLD EDWARD, university library director; b. Oct. 28, 1925, Osakis, Minn.; s. Herman and Elizabeth (Reller) K.; gr.grandson of Graf von Korf of Russia; m. Evelyn Parsons; edn: BA, UC Berkeley 1949, BLS, 1953. Career: assoc. director Humanities and Social Scis., Stanford Univ., 1957; librarian Business Sch., Golden Gate Univ., 1960-70; assoc. prof., Humanities, Golden Gate Univ., 1965–, director Golden Gate Univ. Library, 1970–; bd. dirs. Strybing Arboretum Soc., S.F.; res. World Trade Library, 1977–; mem: AAUP, Special Libraries Assn.; Unitarian; rec: gardening. Res: 1549 Beach St. San Francisco 94123 Ofc: Golden Gate University, 536 Mission, San Francisco 94105

KORNBLUM, GUY ORVILLE, lawyer; b. Oct. 29, 1939, Indpls.; s. Guy Joseph and Gilmette Gilberta (Damart) K.; m. Mary Victoria Adams, Apr. 15, 1977; children: Anna Victoria b. 1978, Guy Laurence b. 1980; edn: BA, Indiana Univ. 1961; JD, UC Hastings Coll. of Law 1966. Career: atty. pvt. practice Indpls. 1966-67, S.F. 1967-72; ptnr. law firm Pettit & Martin 1972-79; senior member firm Kornblum, kelly & Herlihy APLC 1979–; prof. of law UCSF Hastings 1970-78, asst. dean 1970-72, co-founder Hastings Coll. of Advocacy, dir. 1970-72; lectr. Calif. Ctg. Edn. of Bar 1972-, The Rutter Grp. 1982-; honors: Ford Found. Fellow (N.Y.U. 1971), Phi Eta Sigma, Order of the Coif, Thurston Honor Soc.; mem: Fellow Am. Bar Found., Nat. Conf. Commrs. for Uniform State Laws, Am. Bar Assn. Nat. Inst., various bar assns. and profl. groups, Defense Research Inst. Intern Assn. Ins. Counsel (bd. of ed.), Fedn. of Ins. Counsel, Olympic Club S.F., S.F. Yacht Club; publ: ed. Civil Advocates Manual 1971-78, bd. eds. Hastings Law Jour. 1964-66, Defense Law Jour. 1979-; mil: 1st lt. US Army counter intelligence corps 1960-61; Republican; Episcopal; rec: jogging, yachting, tennis, photog. Res: 2083 Pacific Ave San Francisco 94109 Ofc: Kornblum, Kelly & Herlihy 445 Bush St, 6th floor, San Francisco 94108

KORSHAK, MARVIN STANLEY, manufacturing co. executive; b. Sept. 27, 1921, Chgo.; s. Charles Isador and Frances (Silverman) K.; m. Lourdes Zambrano, Apr. 10, 1985; children: Steven Teren b. 1949, Leslie White b. 1956, Todd Eliott b. 1959; edn: BSME, highest honors, Purdue Univ. 1943; Reg. Profl. Engr. (mech.) Calif. 1943. Career: design engr., security clearance design group- B51 Mustang, El Segundo, Calif. 1943-44; USNR ofcr., N.A.C.A., Moffet Field 1944-46; aero stress analysis AVRO Aircraft, Toronto, Ontario, Can. 1946-48; pres. Stanmar Mfg. Co., San Jose; pres. Pelican Co. 1986–; honors: Eagle Scout, BSA (1938); play 1st clarinet, San Jose Symphony Orch.; inventions: reed holder for clarinet & saxophone, Pelican molded bib, self-righting Up Cup, potty seat, bottle cradle, convertible infant seat & high chair; mil: ensign USNR 1943-45; rec: sports, music, dancing. Address: 7593 State Hwy 70 Marysville 95901

KORTKAMP, RONALD DALE, financial services co. president; b. Dec. 18, 1942, Los Angeles; s. Perry Reading and Zelda Jean (Thompson) K.; m. Hanh Vo, June 22, 1980; children: Craig, b. 1971, Candice, b. 1980; edn: AA, Pasadena City Coll. 1965; BA, UC Berkeley 1967; Chartered Life Underwriter (CLU) 1973, Chartered Fin. Consultant (ChFC) 1984. Career: cons. (MIC) Metropolitan Life Ins. Co., Pasadena 1967-69; assoc. Shelton Group (New England Life), Los Angeles 1970, developed & dir. Physician Planning Services for co.; founding ptnr. Money Direction (fin. & ins. svcs.), Los Angeles 1971-75, incorporated 1975; pres./ chief exec. ofcr. Money Direction: Financial & Insurance Services, 1975–, Money Direction: Intercontinental Trade (USA) Inc. (import-export mgmt.), 1984–, Money Direction: Intercontinental Services Inc. (fin. svcs.), 1984–; ptnr. Internat. Helicopter Export; mem. Pres.'s Council- Guardian Life Ins. Co.; mem. Chief of Staff Council- Lafayette Life Ins. Co.; speaker profl. orgns. on pension/ fin. plng./ exec. compensation plans; honors: mem. New England Life Hall of Fame, Life and Qualifying mem. Million Dollar Round Table, Am. Soc. of CLU; mem: Nat., Calif., Los Angeles assns. of life underwriters, Amway Distbrs. Assn. (voting mem.), L.A. CofC, Pi Kappa Phi Frat. Gamma Chpt. (pres. 1967-8), UCB Alumni Assn., Bear Backers (donor); clubs: LA Athletic, Riviera Country, Calif. Yacht; Republican (1984 Repub. Task Force); rec: sailing, tennis, hist. research. Res: 2850 Montrose Ave La Crescenta 91214 Ofc: Money Direction, 3440 Wilshire Blvd, Ste. 610, Los Angeles 90010

KOSIOREK, KENNETH WILLIAM, marine engineer, metal sculptor; b. Feb. 25, 1957, Batavia, N.Y.; s. Wm. Anthony and Leora Ruth (Schoenbachler) K.; edn: USN spl. courses 1975, 76; AAS mech. engring. Monroe Comm. Coll. 1982. Career: hull technician US Navy, 1975-80; designer Hoffend & Sons Theatrical Staging, 1980-82; mats. and plnng. div., Eastman Kodak Co., 1982-84; solar salesman (while touring west coast by motorcycle) Great Western Solar, 4 mos. 1984; tech. support engr. Naval Ocean Systems Center, San Diego 1984–; awards: Eastman Kodak Art Show 2d Pl. and Rochester Annual Indsl. Art Show 3d Pl. for Frankenstein Metal Sculpture (1983), 7 First Pl. trophies racing flat track motorcycles, NY (1974); mem. Am. Welding Soc., Am. Motorcycle Assn., Honda V-4 Motorcycle Assn.; civic: Dig-Sig (computer users group for the impaired, vol. instr.); Boy Scouts; works: Metal Sculpture commn. for Case-Hoyt Printing, Rochester, NY (1983); bldr. Human Powered Vehicle for SDSU engrg. students; article, Popular Mechanics (1980); mil: p.o. USN 1975-80; rec: metal sculpture, inventions, motorcycle touring. Address: POB 60551 San Diego 92106-8551

KOSKINEN, CAROLYN LOUISE, advertising account executive; b. Oct. 7, 1957, Seattle, Wash. ; d. William Conrad and Phyllis Marie (Blanchard) K.; edn: B.Commun., Univ. of Wash. 1979. Career: pub. rels. intern The Olympic Hotel, Seattle, Wash. 1976; advtg./mktg. intern Sunset Mag., Seattle, Wash. 1977; advtg./pgmmg. intern K101 Radio Sta., Golden West Broadcasting 1978; advtg. sales rep. The Weekly, Seattle, Wash. 1980-81; mktg. asst. Sunset Mag., Seattle, Wash. 1981-82; merchandising coord. Sunset Mag., Menlo Park 1982-85, advtg. sales acct. exec. 1985–; advr. San Francisco Ad II 1985-86;

honors: Outstanding Sophmore, Chi Omega, Univ. of Wash. 1977-78; mem: Seattle Advtg. Fedn., San Francisco Ad Club, Children's Orthopedic Hosp. (San Francisco), Children's Hosp. Ball, Chi Omega Alumnae Assn., Guide Dogs for the Blind Assn.; works: handpainting needlepoint design; rec: skiing, tennis, contemporary American art. Ofc: Sunset Magazine, 625 Market St. San Francisco 94105

KOST, GERALD JOSEPH, physician, research scientist; b. July 12, 1945, Sacramento; s. Edward Wm. and Ora Imogene (Casey) K.; m. Angela, Sept. 9, 1972; children: Christopher b. 1982, Laurie b. 1985; edn: BS and MS in engring., Stanford Univ., 1968, 69; PhD bioengring., UC San Diego 1977; MD, UC San Francisco 1978. Diplomate Clin. Pathol., Am. Board of Pathology. Career: electrical engr. Bechtel Corp. 1965; tchg. asst. Stanford Univ. 1966-69; faculty Clin. Blood Gas Edn. Pgm., San Diego 1976, lab. asst. Bioengring. 1976-77; resident UC Los Angeles Dept. Medicine 1978-79, Dept. Neurology 1979-80; res., chief res. Univ. of Wash. Dept. of Lab. Medicine 1980-82, research (cardiopulmonary bioengring. and clin. chem.) 1982-83; asst. prof. pathol., faculty, Biomed. Engrg. and dir. clin. chem. UC Davis Sch. of Medicine, 1983–; cons. Earth Resources Satellite Project, Indsl. Engring. Dept., Stanford Univ.; honors: Phi Kappa Phi, Sigma Xi, Calif. Scholarship Fedn. Highest Honor (1963), recipient 20+ fellowships, awards and research grants incl: Bank of Am. Fine Arts Award (1963), C.K. McClatchly Outstanding Student Award (1963), M.O.P. award, US Rep. in Engring., Internat. Scholar, Venezuela (1967), Grad. Engring. Fellow, Stanford (1967-68), Nat. Research Service award in bioengring., NHLBI, UCSD (1972-77); hon. mem. ASTM (1967), ASCE Stanford outstanding student award (1968), Millberry Art Award, One-Man Show UCSF (1970), vis. lectr. Univ. Utah (1979), Univ. Penn. (1982); Young Investigator Award, Acad. of Clin. Lab. Physicians and Scientists (1982, 83); Nuclear Magnetic Resonance Award, UCD (1984, 85); trumpet soloist univ. bands and orch., var. musical ensembles; mem: AAAS, Am. Assn. for Clin. Chem., Acad. of Clin. Lab. Physicians and Scientists, Am. Heart Assn., Assn. Clin. Sci., Biomed. Engring. Soc.; author num. sci. papers, monographs, med. & sci. journal articles; rec: music, photog., outdoors. Address: Davis 95616

KOSTENKO, GLORIA JOYCE, fashion consultant/designer; b. Mnpls., Minn.; d. Merritt William and Inez Remilia (Gaustad) Johnson; m. Wash, Aug. 26, 1950; children: Jill Marie b. 1951, Michael Merritt b. 1955, Lynda Kay b. 1956, Kris Nicholas b. 1960; edn: stu. Univ. of Minn. 1947-48. Career: exec. secty Santa Cruz County, 1970-76; designer/owner Kos Ko Designs Ltd., 1978– (a women's couture collection of fashions shown in the privacy of the home, features individual color analysis and tailoring to customer's measurements), fashion show presentations of the collection are seen statewide incl. Thunderbird Country Club, (Palm Springs) and The Springs (Rancho Mirage), TV Ch. 26 (San Francisco) and TV Ch. 44 (Monterey), and presentations for charity fund raisers; orgn: Newcomers of Santa Cruz (pres. 1961), Santa Cruz CofC, Quota Club, Stanford Alumni Mothers Club, Am. Cancer Assn., Aux. of Dominican Hosp. (fundraising 1983), Symphony Guild of Santa Cruz, Miss Calif. Orgn. (hostess 1986); Republican; Lutheran; rec: Surf Twirlers and Lucky Steppers square dance clubs, ball room dancing, bridge. Address: Kos Ko Designs Ltd., One Brooktree Ln Santa Cruz 95060

KOSTRZEWSKI, W. R., television cable co. executive; b. July 18, 1952, Deventer, Netherlands; s. Ryszard and Gonda (De Nooy) K.; edn: BS, Mich. State Univ. 1976. Career: customer service mgr. Continental Cablevision, Lansing, Mich. 1976-79; with Warner Cable Communications, Barstow, Calif. 1980–, currently gen. mgr. in Barstow/Kingman (rebuilt system from 12 svc. channels to 40 ch., and 6 premium svcs., one-way addressable, converters in all homes); mem. Calif. Cable TV Assn. (bd. 1981-85), Cable PAC, Barstow Area CofC, Kiwanis (pres. 1983-84), rec. ski, dirt biking, photog., golf. Res: 500 S First St Barstow 92311 Ofc: Warner Cable Communications 305 E Main St Barstow 92311

KOTOWSKI, MICHAEL FRANKLIN, commercial artist, graphic designer; b. Aug. 3, 1941, Wyandotte, Mich.; s. Michael Florin and Minnie Elris (Ford) K.; m. Claire James, Aug. 5, 1967; children: Andrew Franklin b. 1973, Matthew Stephen b. 1981; edn: AA, Alan Hancock Coll., Santa Maria 1965; BA, San Jose State Univ. 1967, MA photog., 1970. Career: sports announcer/columnist and photographer 1960-69; owner, dir. Visual Communications Svcs. (VICOM) 1968–; mng. art dir. Stor Ad Publrs. 1969-71; asst. prof. West Valley Comm. Coll. 1975-78; mayor City of Campbell; past chair Campbell Planning Commn.; Intercity Council Santa Clara County; '85 Policy Bd.; past Transp. Commr.; honors: num. Disting. Awards (Campbell CofC), Campbell Citizen of the Year (1982), spl. commdns. from var. cities and community orgns.; mem: Campbell CofC (past pres.), Soc. of Steam Artists of Am. (charter), Billy Jones Wildcat RR (v.p. ops.), West Valley Mayors & Mgrs.; art work is represented in pvt. and public collections worldwide; mil: airman 1/c USAF 1960-64, Airman of the Month sev. times, mem. Airman's Council; Democrat; Catholic; rec: prototype steam and model railroading, photog. Ofc: VICOM Svcs. 21 N Harrison Ste 200 Campbell 95008

KOTTE, JOHN EUGENE, stockbroker; b. Oct. 30, 1946, Fargo, N.D.; s. Hovin Jalmer and Dorothy Marie (Askegaard) K.; m. Susan Cook, May 21, 1980; 1 dau., Sarah b. 1981; edn: BS edn., Moorhead State Univ., Minn. 1968; MA in edn., Pepperdine Univ. 1976, MBA 1980; desig: stockbroker, SEC (1984). Career: capt. US Marine Corps 1969-78; sales rep. Container Corp. of Am., Los Angeles 1978-80, field sales mgr. 1980-84; account exec. Prudential-Bache Securities, Newport Beach 1984–; Republican; Lutheran (treas.); rec: skiing, golf. Res: 1430 Easy Way Anaheim 92804 Ofc: Prudential-Bache Securities 1301 Dove St Newport Beach 92660

KOTULA, MITCHEL LEE, military officer, educator; b. Aug. 11, 1946, Phila.; s. Mitchel and Hilda Wilhelmina (Lee) K.; m. Marilyn Witmer, July 4, 1969; children: Mitchel Lee, Jr. b. 1973, Clark Ramsdell b. 1977; edn: BS soc. sci., Calif. Poly. Univ. 1968; M.Ed guidance, Winthrop Coll. 1979; MA mgmt., Webster Univ. 1984; Organizatl. Effectiveness Cons., OECS 1982. Career: career Army ofcr. Infantry, Airborne, Ranger Assignments 1968-82; organizatl. effectiveness cons. team chief 82nd Airborne Div., Ft. Bragg, NC 1982-83; Sys. Integration Futures Team, USAOECS, Ft. Ord., Calif. 1983; chief instr., sys./organizatl. behavior br. chief USAOECS 1985; dir. mgmt. sci. dept. and external cons. div. USAOECS 1985; chief spl. task force Soldier Support Ctr. 1985–; adj. faculty Vermont Coll. 1984-; founder, dir. Development Plus, a consortium of cons. and tng. profls. 1984-; honors: Fourth Estate Award (1983), Leo A. Codd Award (1978), Who's Who Am. Colls. & Univs. (1968); mem: Phi Delta Kappa, Am. Profl. Guidance Assn., Assn. of US Army, Am. Soc. Tng. & Devel., Am. Mgmt. Assn., Internat. Soc. for Gen. Sys. Research, Lions Club Internat.; publ: articles in Army, The Jogger, The Organizational Effectiveness J.; mil: lt. col. US Army, Airborne Inf. 1968-, Bronze Star (3), Purple Heart (3), Meritorious Svc. (4), Air Medal (3), Army Commdn. (5), Humanitarian Svc., Vietnamese Cross of Gallantry w/Star; Republican; Protestant; rec: writing, pottery, beer brewing. Res: 683 Santa Cruz Salinas 93901-3926 Ofc: Development Plus 1900 Garden Rd Ste 140 Monterey 93940

KOVACHY, EDWARD MIKLOS, JR., psychiatrist; b. Dec. 3, 1946, Cleveland, Ohio; s. Edward Miklos and Evelyn Amelia (Palenscar)K.; m. Susan LIght, June 21, 1981; edn: BA magna cum laude, Harvard Coll. 1968; JD, Harvard Law Sch. 1972, MBA, Harvard Bus. Sch. 1972; MD, Case Western Reserve Med. Sch. 1977. Career: intern, resident in psychiatry, Stanford Univ. Med. Ctr. 1977-81, chief res. in psychiat. 1980-81; pvt. practice of psychiatry, mediation and mgmt. consulting, Menlo Park 1981–; cons. Mid Peninsula H. Sch., Palo Alto 1983-; chair Symp. on Co-Mediated Divorce by a Psychiatrist and an Atty., Am. Psychiatric Assn. 1984 Ann. Meeting; awards: Falk Fellowship, Am. Psychiat. Assn. 1978-80; mem. Am. Psychiat. Assn., No. Calif. Psychiat. Soc., Assn. of Family and Conciliation Cts., No. Am. Soc. for the Psychology of Sport and Physical Activity, S.F. Acad. of Hypnosis; mem. Harvard Club of S.F. (schools and scholarships com.; co-prod. 15th Reunion Class Show, Harvard Coll. Class of 1968, 1983); columnist The Peninsula Times Tribune, Palo Alto 1983-85; Presbyterian; rec: personal and social activism, musical comedy, athletics. Ofc: Edward M. Kovachy Jr., MD, JD, MBA 1187 University Dr Menlo Park 94025

KRAFT, GARRY G., chiropractor; b. Oct. 6, 1945, San Francisco; s. Basil and Frances Gannon; edn: Orange Coast Coll. 1971-72, Univ. of Colo. 1975-77; DC, Los Angeles Coll. of Chiropractic 1982; lic. chiropractor Calif. and Colo. Career: parts dept. mgr. Hueberger Volkswagen, Colorado Springs, Colo. 1972-75; veterans counselor, Vets. Outreach Pgm. of Univ. of Colo., 1976-77; salesman Santa Monica (Ca.) Volkswagen 1978; lab. and tchg. asst. L.A. Coll. of Chiropractic, 1980-81; staff chiropractor Hobson Chiropractic/Medical Clinic, Glendale 1982-83; co-owner/ staff chiropractor Citrus Health Center (chiro./med. clinic) Azusa, 1973-85; owner Anacapa Health Care Ctr., Port Hueneme 1985–; awards: grantee, Springwell Research and Trust for emergency med. care pkg.; Outstanding Senior Awd., LA Coll. of Chiro. 1981; Who's Who in Am. Colls. & Univs. 1981; listed: Who's Who in Calif. 1984, Men of Achievemet 1984, Who's Who in Internat. Med. 1985; Diplomate Nat. Bd. of Chiro. Examiners 1981; mem: Am. Chiropractic Assn. (past pres. Student Chpt. LACC); Calif. Chiro. Assn.; Am. Pub. Health Assn.; Alumni Assn. of Sigma Chi Psi (past pres. LACC chpt.); CofCs: Glendora, Azusa, Port Hueneme, Oxnard; Red Cross vol.; mil: sgt. US Army 1977-79, Army Commendn., Nat. Def., Vietnam Svc., Vietnam Cpgn. medals; Democrat, rec: off road racing, sailing. Res: POB 43 Port Hueneme 93041 Ofc: 325 W Channel Islands Blvd Port Hueneme 93041

KRAFT, KATHLEEN ANN, operations executive; b. June 29, 1942, Oak Park, Ill.; d. Bernard and Dorothy (Coffey) Coleman; m. Tedd R. Kraft, Jan. 25, 1964; children: Alexander b. 1972, Erin Courtney b. 1975; edn: BS journ., Bradley Univ. 1964; MBA cand., Golden Gate Univ. Career: editor Field Enterprises Ednl. Corp. (World Book) 1964-68, Litton Inds. 1968-70, CTB/ McGraw-Hill 1970-72, freelance 1972-80, The Hampton-Brown Co. Inc. 1980-85, ops. mgr. 1985–; dir. The Lyceum of the Monterey Peninsula; mem: United Presbyterian Women (dir.), The New Forum, Profl. Women's Network; avoc: group facilitator, communications. Ofc: Carmel

KRAGEN, ADRIAN ALBERT, law professor; b. June 3, 1907, San Francisco; s. Simon and Minnie (Hables) K.; m. Billie Bercovich, June 4, 1933; children: Kenneth, b. 1936, Robin, b. 1942; edn: AB, UC Berkeley 1931, JD, 1934; admitted Calif. State Bar 1934. Career: pvt. practice of law, Oakland 1934-39; deputy atty. general Calif., 1940-44; partner law firm Loeb & Loeb, L.A. 1944-52; Shannon Cecil Turner Prof. of Law UC Berkeley 1952-73, prof. of law UC Hastings 1974-81, prof. of law emeritus (on recall) UC Berkeley, currently; vice chancellor UC Berkeley 1960-64; general counsel Calif. Retailers Assn. 1946-; cons. to various motion picture cos. 1952-75; honors: Phi Beta Kappa, Order of Coif, Boalt Hall Alumni Citation, UC Berkeley Citation, Univ. Calif. Alumni Service Award, Alta Bates Hosp. distinguished service award, Berkeley Fellows; mem. Am., Calif. bar assns., Internat. Fiscal Assn., others; author: Kragen & McNulty, Materials on Federal Income Taxation (4th ed. 1985), var. articles in law reviews; Republican; Hebrew; rec: golf, reading. Ofc: UC Berkeley, 308 Law Bldg., Berkeley 94720

KRAJCAR, STEPHEN ROBERT, financial services co. executive; b. May 16, 1947, Allentown, Pa.; s. Stephen Joseph and Irma (Kuronya) K.; m. Antoinette

Freitas, July 4, 1980; edn: BA, Muhlenberg Coll. 1969; Chartered Life Underwriter 1979; Chartered Financial Cons. 1986. Career: exec. mgmt. trainee Equitable Life NYC 1969-70, agent Allentown, Pa. 1970-73, dist. mgr. L.A. 1973-79, agcy. mgr. S.F. 1979-84; field dir., CFO Northwestern Mutual S.F. 1984-86; exec. H.L. Financial Group San Jose 1986—; instr. mgmt. classes; honors: Nat. Champion (Equitable 1982, 83), Mgmt. Devel. Award (Equitable 1981, 82, 83, 84); mem: Nat. Assn. Life Underwriters, Am. Soc. Chartered Life Underws. and Chartered Financial Cons., Gen. Agents & Mgrs. Assn., S.F. Zool. Soc., Matro. Mus. Soc. NY, S.F. Ballet Assn.; mil: sgt. US Army 1969-71; Republican; Lutheran; rec: competition trap and pistol shooting. Res: 2065 Spyglass Dr San Bruno 94066 Ofc: Home Life 2150 N First St Ste 330 San Jose 95131

KRAL, KEVIN MICHAEL, allergist, b. July 29, 1951, Wash. DC; s. Louis Martin and Margaret Cecilia (O'Malley) K.; edn: BA summa cum laude, honors in math.,, Univ. Penna. 1973; MD, Univ. Va. 1977; bd. certified Am. Board of Pediatrics (1981), Am. Board of Allergy and Immunology (1981). Career: intern and resident, pediatrics, NY Hosp.-Cornell Univ. Medical Ctr., NY, NY 1977-1979; fellow allergy-immunology UC Medical Center, San Francisco 1979-81; chief of allergy Eglin Regl. Hosp., Eglin AFB, Fla. 1981-83; staff allergist David Grant Med. Center, Travis AFB, Calif. 1983-85; chief of allergy Kaiser Permanente Clinic, Fairfield 1985—; honors: Phi Beta Kappa (1973), First Prize for paper presentation Carl Tempel Mil. Allergy - Pulmonary Symp., Denver (1984); mem: Fellow Am. Acad. of Allergy and Immunol., Allergy Assn. of No. Calif., Assn. of Mil. Allergists; contbr. articles med. jours.; mil: major USAF Med. Corps 1981-85; rec: gardening, food and wine, skiing. Res: 2267 Clear View Circle Benicia 94510 Ofc: Allergy Clinic Kaiser Permanente 1550 Gateway Blvd Fairfield 94533

KRAM, HARRY BERNARD, physician; b. June 14, 1954, Newark, N.J.; s. Philip and Brenda (Stein) K.; edn: BS magna cum laude, Univ. Fla. 1977, MD, 1981. Career: gen. surgery intern LSU-Charity Hosp., New Orleans, La. 1981-82; gen. surg. resident Harbor-UCLA Medical Center, Torrance 1982-84, critical care fellowship 1983-85; trauma fellowship, Dept. Surg., Hollywood Presbyn. Med. Center, L.A. 1984-85; research fellow Dept. Surg., King-Drew Med. Center, L.A. 1985—; awards: academic scholarship, St. Petersburg Comm. Coll. (1974), Sigma Tau Sigma (1976), Phi Kappa Phi (1977), Alpha Epsilon Delta (1976), research award Internat. Soc. for Biomaterials (1984), 1st pl. So. Calif. chpt. (2) Am. Coll. of Surgeons Com. on Trauma Residents' Papers Competition (1984, 85), 2d pl., Soc. of Critical Care Medicine Surgeon's Award (1984); mem: The Soc. of Critical Care Medicine, Acad. of Surgical Research, Research and Ednl. Inst. Harbor-UCLA Med. Ctr. (1982-85); publs: num. abstracts, book chapts., med. jour. articles; Jewish; rec: sports. Ofc: Dept. of Surgery, King-Drew Medical Center 12021 S Wilmington Ave Los Angeles 90059

KRAUS, JAMES ALAN, lawyer; b. Dec. 30, 1947, Long Beach; s. Morrie Stanley and Kay Fanny (Penn) K.; edn: BS in laws, Western State Univ. 1975, JD, 1976; admitted to Calif. Bar 1977, US Federal Ct. (So. Dist.) 1977, US Ct. of Appeals 1977, US Supreme Ct. 1981, US Tax Ct. 1981, US Claims Ct. 1983, US Ct. of Internat. Trade 1983. Career: legal intern US Dept. of Justice (first internship granted to W.S.U.) 1976; law clerk Sheela, Lightner, Hughes, Castro & Walsh (first internship granted to W.S.U.) 1976; chief trial counsel to Tolman, Lefebvre & Kraus, 1977-80; sole owner of Law Offices of James A. Kraus, 1980—; judge pro tem San Diego Municipal Ct. 1980-; counsel to San Diego Police Officers Assn., former US Cong. Clair Burgener, former S.D. Co. Supr. Lou Ridgeway, Security Pacific Nat. Bank, Calif. First Bank, Aztec Finl. Corp., Calif. Real Estate Assn., Westland Title Co., Nat. Am. Title Ins. Co., and Bara Farms; mem: Am. Trial Lawyers Assn., S.D. Co. Trial Lawyers Assn., Calif. Bar Assn., Am. Bar Assn., S.D. Co. Bar Assn.; W.S.U. alumni patron to Criminal Justice Journal; clubs: Mensa, San Diego Track, University (S.D.), Arabian Horse Registry, B'nai Brith (past v.p., chmn. Anti-Defamation League); mil: USN 1967-71, cryptographer Spl. Intell.; publs: contbr. law revs., editor U.S.I.U. student newspaper; Democrat; Jewish; rec: own, breed and train Arabian Horses. Res: 4611 Conrad San Diego 92117 Law Ofc: James A. Kraus 160 Thorn St Ste 3 San Diego 92103

KRAUS, VINCENT JOHN, real estate broker; b. Mar. 20, 1951, Pittsburgh, Pa.; s. Vincent, Sr. and Aldona C. (Barzoloski) K.; edn: AA, El Camino Coll. 1982; Calif. lic. R.E. Broker. Career: engr. Gruman Aerospace (F-14s), 1975; staff Transamerica, Gen. Electric Credit; current: real estate broker/mgr. J & P Management, Torrance; mem: Nat., Calif. Assn. Realtors, Naval Reserve; club: Fairwind Yacht (fleet cmdr.); mil: E5 USNR 1971-81, 4 years active duty, 5 ribbons, C.N.O. Spl. Award; Republican; Catholic; rec: sailing. Res: 1101 W MacArthur Blvd #192 Santa Ana 92707 Ofc: J & P Managment 1024 Crenshaw Blvd Torrance 90501

KRAUSE, DORIS MARCELLA, real estate broker; b. Jan. 17, 1928, Flushing, NY; d. John M. and Bernadine L. (Guarneri) Pryer; m. Edmund Fairfax Krause, Sept. 26, 1982; children: John Jay Nicholas b. 1953, Beth Ann b. 1955; edn: Texas A&I 1956-57; FAA, Alabama Tech. Inst. 1968. Career: instrument ground instr. FAA Dothan, Ala.; Live Oak Realty Ojai, Calif.; broker Doris M. Krause Ojai; mem: Calif. Bd. Realtors 1978, Ojai Valley Bd. Realtors (ethics com. 1975), Calif. Dressage Assn., Deep South Dressage Assn. (charter); publs: Pony Club of Am. (1964), Fitzpatrick Hunt (1966); Republican; Episcopal; rec: classical dressage. Res: 10248 Ojai Santa Paula Rd Ojai 93023 Ofc: Doris M. Krause POB 502 Ojai 93023

KRAUSE, LAWRENCE ALLEN, personal financial advisor; b. Oct. 28, 1939, Chgo.; s. Leo and Sylvia Harriet (Bergman) K.; m. Donna Ferkel, Aug. 14, 1971; children: Danielle b. 1976, Alexis b. 1981; edn: BA, State Univ. of Iowa 1961; CFP, Coll. of Fin. Plnng. 1978; admitted to Registry of Financial Planning Practitioners 1984; Real Estate Broker, State of Ill. 1967; Reg. Securities Principal, SEC, 1980. Career: exec. v.p. JOBS Inc., Waukegan, Ill. 1961-62; pres. Inventory & Bus. Controls, Inc., Waukegan 1963-66; real estate broker Shoen Realtors, Rockford, Ill. 1967-69; reg. rep./ investment banker Reynolds & Co., San Francisco 1970-75; dir./ coord. fin. plnng. dept. Sutro & Co., Inc., S.F. 1975-79; chmn. Lawrence A. Krause & Assocs. Inc., S.F. 1979—; pres. KW Securities Corp., pres. KW Financial Svcs. Inc.; adj. prof. fin. plnng. San Francisco State Univ. 1982-; adv. com. Golden Gate Univ.; faculty USC 1984; adv. bd. Technology Funding, Inc. 1984; adv. bd. Physicians Guide To Money Management 1984, Digest of Financial Planning Ideas 1984; honors: elected Fin. Plnnr. of the YR., San Francisco 1982; Fin. Writers Awd., Financial Plnnr. Mag. 1981; mem: Nat. Center for Fin. Edn. Inc.; Internat. Assn. for Fin. Plnng. Inc. (pres. S.F. chpt. 1980-82); Inst. CFPs; Am. Canecr Soc. (S.F. Unit); Concordia- Argonaut Club; publs: monthly column, Krause on Financial Planning, Calif. Bus. mag. 1979-; author: The Money-Go-Round; co-author Lawrence A. Krause on Marketing; author chpt., Financial Planning for the Professional, in Your Book of Financial Planning, 1983; author sect., Forms and Planning Aids Volume, Financial and Estate Planning, Commerce Clearing House; mil: sp5 US Army 1961-67; Republican; Jewish; rec: equestrian, skiing, golf. Res: 198 Shooting Star Isle Foster City 94404 Ofc:.Lawrence A. Krause & Assocs., Inc., 500 Washington St, Ste 750, San Francisco 94111

KRAVA, BESSE FLORINDA HOOD, real estate associate; b. Aug. 24, 1916, Hastings, Nebr.; d. Harry G. and Florence May (De Conley) Feist; m. 2d. Roy A. Krava, Jr. Dec. 20, 1980; 1 dau. Diane Mae (Banker); edn: night classes, Denver Univ. 1943-47; interior decoration, Green River Coll., Auburn, Wisc. 1967-71; Calif. real estate lic. 1977. Career: mng. exec. secty. Public Service Co. of Colo. (Denver), exec. bd. for women employees 1940-50; currently active real estate, San Diego, assoc. S.D. Bd. Realtors (1976-); honors: appreciation comm. service, S.D. Parks & Rec. Dept., Spring Valley Park & Advis. Council, Spring Valley CofC (1985); civic: Auburn (WN) Gen. Hosp. (dir. vols. 1968-69), Spring Valley Womans Club (mem. 1952-, pres. 1956-7, 1985-6, 1986-7); clubs: Singing Hills CC El Cajon (charter), Overland Park GC, Denver (pres. 1938-42); awards: 1st pl. statewide sewing contest, Federated Womens Clubs Calif. (1956), runnerup 1st class championship, Singing Hills CC (1957), champion Willis Park GC (1937); cons. to writer and instrumental in publication of book, My Friend the Indian (sold internat.); Republican; Episcopal (soloist); rec: golf, painting, vol. work. Res: San Diego

KREBSBACH, MICHAEL LARRY, manufacturing co. sales representative; b. Jan. 25, 1951, Devil's Lake, No. Dak.; s. Larry Ambrose and Monica (Boehm) K.; edn: AA, West Valley Jr. Coll. 1972; 1BS, Calif. Polytechnic Univ. SLO 1979. Career: sales rep. I Monsanto Agricultural Co., San Francisco Bay area 1979, sales rep. II 1981, sales rep. III 1983, sales splst. 1985—; Monsanto Mktg. Task Force 1984-86; Monsanto Career Rep Task Force 1983; Monsanto Recruiting Ofcr., Calif. Polytechnic Univ., San Luis Obispo 1984-86; honors: Master Salesman, Monsanto 1984; Monsanto Achiev. Award, 1984; Silver & Branze Medalist, US Men's Nat. Rowing Championships 1984; 350+ Awards & Records for Swimming 1960-70; mem: Calif. Agric. Prod. Consultants Assn. (chpt. pres. 1985, 1986), CAPCA, Calif. Weed Conf. Pgm. Com., Nat. Agric. Mktg. Assn., Los Gatos Rowing Club (Masters Liaison); publs: rowing articles in nat. publ. 1985; contbg. master salesman to book, The Master Salesman 1984; Democrat; Catholic; rec: crew rowing, snow skiing, swimming. Res: 46 Heritage Village Ln. Campbell 95008 Ofc: Monsanto Agricultural Products, 24551 Raymond Way Ste. 285 El Toro 92630

KREGER, PHILIP, educator; b. Jan. 18, 1908, W. Seneca, NY; s. Benjamin and Anna (Lipman) K.; m. Bernice Gerstman, June 19, 1932; children: Lois Arlene b. 1934, Melvin Joseph b. 1937, Linda F. b. 1940; edn: BSBA, Univ. of Buffalo 1958; MBA, State Univ. of NY 1962; CPA lic. NY (1961), Calif. (1983); Cert. Purchasing Mgr., Nat. Assn. Purchasing Mgmt. 1975. Career: office mgr. Wagner Folding Box Corp., Buffalo, NY 1935-45; v.p. Falls View Box Co. Inc., Nigara Falls, NY 1945-49; asst. comptroller Permalite Awning Co. Inc., Buffalo, NY 1949-55; staff acct. Samuel Goldman CPA, Buffalo, NY 1955-62; assoc. prof. acctg. Canisuis Coll., Buffalo, NY 1962-81; mgmt. cons. self-empl., Buffalo, NY 1981-82; mgmt. cons. and lectr. self-empl., Van Nuys 1982—; lectr. on purchasing mgmt., India 1969-70; purchasing proceedures reviewer, CIty of Buffalo Sch. Bd. 1981; honors: Gamble Award, Purchasing Mgmt. Assn. of Buffalo 1978; Achiev. in Literary Field of Acctg., nat. Assn. Accts. 1975; mem: Am. Inst. CPAs, Calif. Soc. CPAs, NY Soc. CPAs, Shut-In Soc. of Western NY, Blind Found. of Buffalo, Buffalo Adv. Com. for Charitable Orgns. (acctg. ons.); publs: author acctg. textbook, Control Accounts, 1980; num. articles, Nat. Assn. of Accts. Bulletin, The Enrolled Agent Mag. and Niagara Frontier Purchaser; mil: cpl. US Nat. Guard 1927; Republican; Jewish; rec: piano, organ. Address: Philip Kreger, CPA, 6939 Woodman Ave., Ste 310, Van Nuys 91405

KREITENBERG, ARTHUR, orthopaedic surgeon; b. Apr. 24, 1957, Los Angeles; s. Sam and Irene (Deutsch) K.; edn: AB magna cum laude, UC Los Angeles 1978; MD, UC San Diego 1982; Grad. Certif. Biomed. Engr., UC Irvine 1984. Career: summer intern NASA, Johnson Space center, Houston 1979; general surgery resident UCI Medical Center, Orange 1982-84; orthopaedic surgery resident, 1984-; awards: Samuel Hamburger Award for outstanding thesis, UCSD (1982); club: Zeta Beta Tau frat.; publs. in med. jours., Am. J. of Cardiology (1982), Paraplegia (1984); US patent (1983) for Neck Venous and Arterial Examination Teaching Instrument; spl. interest in devel. of space for benefit of man.

KREITZBERG, FRED CHARLES, engineering management co. president; b. June 1, 1934, Paterson, N.J.; s. William and Ella (Bohen) K.; m. Barbara, June 9, 1957; children: Kim b. 1959, Caroline b. 1962, Allison b. 1964, Bruce b. 1968, Catherine b. 1969; edn: BS in civil engring., Norwich Univ. 1957; Reg. Profl. Engr. in Aka., Ariz., Calif., Colo., Conn., D.C., Ill., Ind., Md., Mass., Nev., N.J., N.M., N.Y., Oh., Ore., Pa., Va., Wash. Career: asst. supt. Turner Constrn. Co., N.Y.C. 1957; project mgr. for Project Mercury before first astronaut launching, RCA, N.J. 1958-62; schedule and cost mgr. Catalytic Constrn. Co., Pa. 1963-65; 1965– : owner, now pres./mem. bd. dirs. O'Brien-Kreitzberg and Assocs., Inc. (OKA) a profl. constrn. mgmt. firm responsible for San Francisco Cable Car rehabilitation, S.F. Airport expansion, Silicon Valley Rail System, world's largest wind tunnel for NASA, Library of Congress, Bellevue Hosp. and Walter Reed Hosp.; leading nat. authority and expert witness in constrn. mgmt. claims; lectr. annually Stanford Univ. and UC Berkeley engineering students; honors: ASCE Construction Mgr. of the Year (1982), Engineering News Record Man of Year nominee (1984); mem: ASCE (Fellow 1956), Am. Arbitration Assn., Constrn. Mgmt. Assn. of Am. (founding mem. 1982, bd. dirs.), Soc. of Am. Value Engrs.; civic: Alden Partridge Soc., Norwich Univ. (Bd. dirs.), Community Field Assn. (Marin Co. bd. dirs.), Ross Hist. Soc., Marin Charitable Assn., Council for Internat. Visitors; clubs: San Francisco Tennis, Palm Springs Tennis, Marin Tennis; works: designed catenary support system for World's largest radio telescope, patent app. by RCA (1960); contbg. author to Critical Path Method Scheduling for Contractor's Management Handbook (1971); key articles: Repetitive Scheduling (ASCE J. 1984), Cable Car Renovation Project: On Time and On Budget (Proceedings of the Splty. Conf. on Orgn. & Mgmt.); mil: 1st lt. Corps of Engrs. (Airborne) 1957-58; Cong. Rodef Sholom; rec: running, biking, tennis, scuba, tropical fish. Res: 19 Spring Rd (POB 1200) Ross 94957 Ofc: O'Brien-Kreitzberg & Associates, Inc. 188 The Embarcadero San Francisco 94111

KRIEGSMAN, JAMES W.C., transportation co. president; b. May 13, 1944, Pekin, Ill.; s. John C. and Juanita (Martin) K.; m. Sandra J. Cunningham, Nov. 28, 1985; 1 son, John Doherty b. 1978; edn: Univ. of Wyo. 1963-65. Career: sales Kriegsman Warehouses, Inc. 1968-69, dir. 1969-; mng. dir. Crown Pacific, Ltd., Hong Kong 1969-78; pres. Camel, Inc. Jeddah, Saudi Arabia, 1978– ; mng. dir. Camel Holdings, Ltd., Hong Kong and O.E.M., Ltd., Singapore, 1978– ; pres. Empire Van & Storage, Inc., 1986– ; mem. American CofC, Hong Kong (dir.), Am. Club of Hong Kong (dir.), Servicemens Guides Assn., Hong Kong (chmn.), Kiwanis Club, Hong Kong (dir.); mil: sp5 US Army 1966-68, Vietnam Svc.; Republican; Prot.; rec: boating, golf, tennis. Address: 2170 Chianti Dr Santa Rosa 95401

KRIENKE, CAROL BELLE, realtor; b. June 19, 1917, Oakland; d. George and Ethel Lucretia (Purdon) Manikowske; m. Oliver Kenneth Krienke, June 4, 1941; children: Diane (Denny) b. 1944, Judith (Giss) b. 1947, Debra (Davalos) b. 1950; edn: stu., Nat. Bus. Tng. Coll., Univ. of Mo.; BS, Univ. of Minn. 1940. Career: youth leadership State of Minn., Congregational Conf., Univ. of Minn. 1940; demonstrator General Foods, Minneapolis, Minn. 1940-41; war prodn. workers Airesearch Mfg. Co., Los Angeles 1944; tchr. Los Angeles City Schs. 1945-49; realtor dba Ethel Purdon, Manhattan Beach 947-65; buyer Purdon Furniture & Appliances, Manhattan Beach 1949; realtor O.K. Krienke Realty, Manhattan Beach 1965– ; honors: Hon. Life Mem., Mira Costa PTA 1964; Hon. Life Mem. (1974) and Appreciation (1981), South Bay Bd. of Realtors; recipient with husband the Rose & Scroll Award for Outstanding Community Svc., Manhattan Beach CofC (1985); mem: South Bay Council of Girl Scouts USA, Manhattan Beach Coordg. Council, Long Beach Area Children's Home Soc. (pres. 1969), Beach Pixies (charter, pres. 1967), United Way, Beach Cities Sym. (sponsor), DAR, Colonial Dames 17th Century (charter, Jared Eliot chpt., pres. 1979-81), Friends of the Library, Torrance- Lomita Bd. Realtors, South Bay Bd. Realtors, Internat. Platform Assn.; Republican; Congregational; rec: travel. Res: 924 Highview Ave. Manhattan Beach 90266 Ofc: O.K. Krienke Realty, 1726 Manhattan Beach Blvd. Ste. A Manhattan Beach 90266

KRIGMONT, HENRY VALENTINE, manufacturing co. executive; b. July 18, 1948, Odessa, USSR, nat. US cit. 1979; s. Valentine David and Feiga (Litvinsky) K.; m. Ada, Oct. 10, 1980; 1 son, James Robert b. 1982; edn: equiv. MSEE, Kishinev Politechnic Inst., USSR 1974; equiv. PhD, Moskow Thermotechnic Inst., USSR 1979. Career: senior applications engr. Joy Mfg. Co. Los Angeles 1980-83, chief tech. engr. 1983-86; dir. spl. projects. Wahlco Inc., Santa Ana 1986– ; co-owner, v.p., gen. mgr. Applied Computer Systems; mem: IEEE, APCA, Am. Assn. for Aerosol Research; patents: 1 US, 3 USSR; rec: chess. Res: 3600 Marigold St Seal Beach 90740 Ofc: Wahlco Inc., 3600 W Segerstrom Ave Santa Ana 92704

KRIMM, DAVID R., management consultant; b. Oct. 12, 1953, Ann Arbor, Mich.; s. Samuel and Marilyn Marcy (Neveloff) K.; edn: AB, Brown Univ. 1975; MPPM, Yale Univ. Sch. of Orgn. & Mgmt. 1981. Career: asst. bus. mgr. Roundabout Theatre, NY, NY 1976-77; bus. mgr. Twyla Tharp Dance Fedn. NY, NY 1977-79; assoc. public finance Donaldson, Lufkin & Jenrette, NY, NY 1981-82; assoc. The Mac Group, San Francisco 1983-84, senior assoc. 1985– ; bd. dirs. Alumni Assn. Yale Sch. of Orgn. & Mgmt. 1981 ; Democrat; rec. skiing, kayaking, sailing. Res; 100 Parker Ave. San Francisco 94118 Ofc: The Mac Group, 1000 El Camino Real St. 250 Menlo Park 94025

KRINDLE, DANIEL JASON, lawyer; b. Jan. 6, 1940, Winnipeg, Manitoba, Can.; s. Sam E. and Sophie (Rosen) K.; edn: BA, honors, Univ. of Manitoba 1961, LLB, 1965; Barrister and Solicitor, 1965, Man., Can. Career: assoc. D'Arcy, Irving Haig & Smethurst, Barristers & Solicitors, Winnipeg 1965-70; assoc. law firm of Gibson, Dunn & Crutcher, Los Angeles, Ca. 1971-73, law firm of Haight, Dickson, Brown & Bonesteel, L.A. 1973-78; atty., Daniel Jason Krindle A Profl. Law Corp., Los Angeles 1978– ; arbitrator: Los Angeles Superior Ct., Fee Dispute Com. (L.A.), and Am. Arbitration Assn.; recipient commendns. for legal articles, Atty. Gen. of Manitoba (1963), Govt. of Canada (1976); mem: Law Soc. of Manitoba, Manitoba Bar Assn., Am. Bar Assn. (sustaining), LA Trial Lawyers Assn. (sustaining), Calif. Trial Lawyers (sustaining); mem. Beverly Hills, Century City Bar Assns. (bus. litigation, personal injury, medical malpractice & product liability sects.); Cert. of Experience Products Liability, P.I., Med. Malpractice, Domestic Relations (Calif.); author: Medical Illustrations for the Purpose of Settlement & Trial (1984); mem. Thalians Pres. Club, Bev. Hills Mens Charities Orgn., Soc. of the Founders of Hebrew Univ. of Jerusalem; rec: football, aerobics, wt.lifting. Res: 1284 Monte Cielo Dr Beverly Hills 90210 Ofc: Daniel Jason Krindle APLC, 10880 Wilshire Blvd, Ste 1900, Los Angeles 90024

KRINSKEY, IRA WALTER, consultant; b. Jan. 15, 1949, Long Beach, NY; s. Rubin and Lillian Evelyn (Tucker) K.; m. Susan, June 6, 1971; 1 son, Brian b. 1975; edn: BA, Hofstra Univ. 1972; MA, NY Univ. 1975; EdD, Harvard Univ. 1979. Career: tchr. Monticello Public Schs. NY 1972-73; tchr., adminstr. Huntington Public Schs. NY 1973-75; doctoral cand. Harvard 1975-77; asst. supt. Levittown Public Schs. NY 1977-78; deputy supt. Pomona Public Schs. Callif. 1978-82; v.p., ptnr., head edn. div. Korn/ Ferry Internat. 1982– ; trustee Southwestern Univ. Sch. of Law L.A. 1985; honors: PHI Delta Kappa 1978; mem. Harvard-Radcliffe Club of So. Calif. (bd. 1985-86); mil: sp5 US Army Airborne Inf. 1966-69, Bronze Star w/ OLC, Combat Inf. Badge, Army Commdn., Parachute Badge, Vietnam Svc.; rec: stamps. Ofc: Korn/ Ferry Internat. 1800 Century Park East Ste 900 Los Angeles 90067

KRIPANARAYANAN, KOLADI MUTHERI, construction engineering executive; b. July 25, 1943, New Delhi, India, nat. US cit. 1981; d. K. M. N. and K. M. (Janaki) Kurup; m. Nirmala Kripanarayanan, Aug. 29, 1980; children: Unni b. 1968, Rajesh b. 1971, Girija b. 1971, Vijay b. 1973; edn: B.Tech., Indian Inst. of Tech., Madras 1965; MS, Univ. of Iowa 1967, PhD, 1970; Reg. Structural/ Civil Engr. in Calif., Iowa, Ohio, Ill. Career: senior struct. engr. PCA, Skokie, Ill. 1971-76; head struct. engr., Procon, Chgo. 1976-81; project mgr. M.W. Kellogg Co., El Monte, Calif. 1981-85; project mgr. E & L Engring., Long Beach 1985– ; honors: Academic Distinction (1965), J.N. Tata Found. Fellow (1966), Outstanding New U.S. Citizen, Citizenship Council of Metropolitan Chgo. (1981); mem. ASCE, ACI, SEAOSC; publs: over 25 tech. publs., 9 computer pgms. (6 pub. by PCA, 3 prop. by PROCON); Hindu; rec: editorial bd. Philosophy Mag. Ofc: E&L Engineering 3711 Long Beach Blvd 90807A

KRIZ, JOSEPH ALOIS, educator, writer, business consultant; b. Mar. 16, 1920, Oshkosh, Wisc.; s. Rudy Aloyious and Catherine Ann (Klemmer) K.; m. Doloris Hesser, Aug. 5, 1944; children: Susan Terese (McKechnie),b. 1955, Mary Kay (Cox), b. 1957; edn: BS, US Naval Acad. 1942; MBA, Columbia Univ. 1952; postgrad. stu. GBS Harvard, UC Berkeley. Career: served to Comdr. Supply Corps, USN, 1942-63; tours as Comptroller/Supply Dir. of two major Navy air stations; Supply Ofcr. of Aviation Supply Ship during Korean War, prof., four years, US Navy Postgrad. Sch. (estab. 1st grad. bus. sch. in US Mil.); lectr. Univ. of Texas, Arlington, 1 yr.; lectr. UC Berkeley, 2 yrs.; prof./ Small Bus. Coord. Diablo Valley Coll., Pleasant Hill 1965-84, ret.; guest lectr. 1984-; vol. SCORE/ACE pgm. of the Small Bus. Adminstrn. 1970-; creator/ instr. course in Logistics fr Peruvian Naval Acad., Lima, Peru 1949; vol. cons. to Contra Costa County Bd. of Suprs. (new civil svc. personnel code) 1969-71; mem. PROBE study group of the Commn. for Study of Higher Edn. 1972-75; past cons. Allis Chalmers Corp., and Santa Fe Indus.; honors: num. ltrs of commendn., (6) area ribbons from mil. duty WWII, Korean War; Beta Gamma Sigma (bus. hon.), Beta Alpha Psi (acct. hon.), Bus. Tchr. of Year 1973-4 (Diablo Vly Coll), Fellow Found. of Econ. Ed. (1969, 1974); mem: Am. Mgmt. Assn., Soc. for Advanced Mgmt., Western Mktg. Assn. (bd. govs. 1979-81); author: Your Dynamic World of Business (McGraw Hill 1974), other texts and short arts.; author suspense novel: Conch Chowder (1984); Republican; Catholic; rec: bridge, sports. Res: Palma Vista 25 (Box 256) Diablo 94528

KRUEGER, EDNA ELIZABETH, optical & sporting goods co. executive; b. July 24, 1922, Detroit, Mich.; d. John Morgan and Lillian Winifred (Doherty) Thomas; m. Dr. Richard H. Krueger; children: Richard Heinrich, Thomas Edward, Paul Eric; edn: BS, Wayne State Univ. 1942; grad. wk. UCLA 1975-77; Calif. Inst. Tech. 1977-84; USC 1973-83; Loyola Marymount 1980-81. Career: owner/ gen. mgr. Krueger Constrn. Co., Airjet Ventilator Co., S.C. Steel Fabricators, and S.C. Heating & Ventilating Co., 1943-66; ofc. mgr. Pacesetter Homes 1964-66; dir. personnel Salfed Corp. Kentucky Fried Chicken 1966-70, asst. gen. mgr. 1968-70; personnel mgr. Bushnell 1970-, dir. personnel, 1979, dir. human resources 1985, v.p. community rels. Bushnell, Div. of Bausch & Lomb 1966; v.p. So. Coast Comm. Hosp.; Capistrano Beach Club bd. dirs.; personnel mgmt. instr. Pasadena City Coll. 1980; honors: Woman of Achievement (Bus. & Profl. Women 1986), Woman of the Year (Women in Mgmt. 1985), Cert. of Recogn. (San Gabriel Valley Daily Tribune 1985); mem: Personnel & Indsl. Rels. Assn. (exec. bd. dirs. & chprsn. Dist. III; moderator 1983, 84, 85 Annual Confs.); Exec. Women Internat.; Am. Mgmt. Assn.; Am. Soc. for Personnel Admin.; San Gabriel Employers Adv. Bd.; Womens Civic League; West Point Army/ Navy '83 Found.; Nat. Assn. for Female Execs.; Soroptomist; Internat. Assn. of Personnel Women; L.A. Basin Equal Opportunity League; Calif. Inst. Tech. Svc. League Bd.; Pasadena Urban League; East Pasa. Human Resources Assn. 1982-86; E. Pasa. Improvement Assn. 1983-86; bd. dirs. Pasa. CofC; Independent Bus. Affairs Com. chair Bus. & Econ. Div. 1982-86; pub. rels. Am. Cancer Soc. League West 1986; corp. adv. bd. Women at Work 1985-86; publs: newsletter, Bushnell Banner

1972-80, Bushnell Insight 1985-86; newsletter, Three's A Crowd, Personnel & Indsl. Rels. Assn. 1983; featured L.A. Daily News, Go For It column 1983; mil: observer USAF 1962-63, So. Calif.; Republican (Central Com.); rec: swimming, bicycling, desert living. res: 2263 C Mira Monte Circle Palm Springs; 1150 Fairview Ave Arcadia 91006 Ofc: Bushnell, Div. of Bausch & Lomb, 2828 E Foothill Blvd Pasadena 91107

KRUG, FRED ROY, motion picture & television producer-director; b. Aug. 30, 1929, Bern, Switz., nat. US cit. 1954; s. Adalbert and Margot Panchaud de Bottens-Krug; m. Rosemary Wehner, Feb. 25, 1956; 1 dau. Vivian b. 1956; edn: BA communs., Columbia Coll. 1962, postgrad. 1963. Career: cinematographer & writer Switzerland 1945-51; station mgmt. KCOP-TV L.A. 1963-68; producer, v.p. prodn. Bill Burrud Prodns. L.A. 1968-72; producer- dir. Walt Disney Studios 1972-74; freelance producer- dir. 1974–; mem: Dirs. Guild of Am. 1974-, Producers Guild of Am. 1981-, Nat. Acad. TV Arts & Scis., Rotary (bd. 1984-87), Bob Hope USO Club (bd. 1984-86), Salvation Army/ Hollywood Adv. Council; films: assoc. producer Across the Great Divide, exec. producer Mountain Family Robinson; TV: cinematographer CHiPs MGM/NBC, num. articles on film in European and US mags., translated novel Dracula into German (1951); mil: Swiss Army 1950, US Army Intelligence Germany 1953-56; rec: flying. Res: 5911 McDonie Ave Woodland Hills 91367

KUCERA, ELOISE LABERTA, health care executive; b. Nov. 26, 1917, Seiling, Okla.; d. Charles Ralph and Ada Bell (Fall) Harphamp; m. Lada Kucera, 1937; children: Winafred Anita (Stephens) b. 1945, Frank Lada b. 1949; edn: Northwestern Okla. State Univ. 1935-36; Contra Costa Coll. 1975-77; spl. courses, Univ. Calif., Birmingham (Eng.) Univ. 1980. Career: supr. US Govt., Medical, San Francisco 1940-45; adminstr. Kyakameena Sanitorium No. 1, Berkeley 1945-49; owner/adminstr. The El Lade Home 1949-65; adminstr./ofcr. Harpham, Inc., Kyakameena No. 1 and 2 1965-74; founder-dir. Long Term Health Care Edn., Inc., (non-profit) 1975–; tchr. Vallejo Unif. Sch. Dist. 1980; ARC (vol.) instr. Berkeley 1980-; mem: El Cerrito Com. on Aging, County Adult Day Health Care Com., East Bay Nursing Home Assn. (pres.), Girl Scouts of Am. (leader); dir. church blood bank; youth leader; research: participant Univ. Ohio Long Term research proj. 1978; editor LTHCE 1977-; Republican; Protestant; rec: entertaining, knitting, research. Ofc: Long Term Health Care Edn., Inc., 737 Avila Pl El Cerrito 94530

KUHL, ANNA F., educator, forensic psychologist; b. Sept. 1, 1941, Seattle, Wash.; d. John N. and Marie Anna (Phillips) Belcher; m. Wesley C. Kuhl, June 10, 1977; children: Robert David Lyle b. 1961, Donna Marie Kuhl b. 1962, John Michael Lyle b. 1963; edn: BA, Ft. Wright Coll. 1977, MA, 1978; PhD, Wash. State Univ. 1981. Career: therapist Spokane Mental Health Clinic, 1966-76; dir. Alternatives to Violence, 1978-81; asst. prof. San Jose State Univ., 1981-84, assoc. prof. 1984–, chair Adminstrn. of Justice 1985-; forensic psychologist, prin. Anna F. Kuhl & Assocs., San Jose; honors: Phi Kappa Phi, Phi Delta Kappa, Psi Chi, Danforth nominee (1980); mem. Am. Soc. Criminology (Women's Div. secty.), Acad. of Criminal Justice Scis., Am. Psychol. Assn., Western Soc. Criminol.; publs: Community Responses to Battered, Personality Traits of Battered Women, Expert Testimony in Sexual Abuse Evaluation, Damned If She Does, Research Methods in Criminal Justice; Democrat; Unity; rec: golf. Res: 35 S Terrace Ct San Jose 95138 Ofc: California State University, San Jose 95192

KUHN, CHARLES E., corporate executive; b. Nov. 29, 1919, Cincinnati, Oh.; s. Leo and Vivian K.; m. Elma Jane Smith, Nov. 17, 1944 (div.); m. Patrica L. McVicar, Nov. 27, 1974 (div. 1980); m. Rena Horten, Jun. 1, 1980 (div. 1983); children: Karen Jo Ann, James Roland. Edn: Purdue Univ., 1938-39. Career: v.p. Fansteel Metal Corp., 1950-55; Hills McCanna Co. 1955-58; v.p. Dresser Mfg. Div. of Dresser Ind., Inc., 1958-60, pres. 1960-64; group v.p./dir. Parent Co., 1964-65, exec. v.p. 1965-68, pres./chief op. ofcr. 1968-70; pres./dir. Wylain Inc., Dallas. chmn. bd. and CEO 1970-82; bd. dirs.: General Portland, Inc., Dallas Bay; Beer Distr., Redondo Bch; Am. First Corp., Oklahoma City; chmn. bd. Michigan General Corp., Dallas. Mem: Am. Gas Assn., Florida Council of 100, Pennsylvania Soc., Canadian Gas Assn.. Mil: USNR 1940-42. Res: 1654 Mandeville Canyon Rd. Los Angeles 90049. Ofc: POB 800443 Dallas Texas 75380

KUHN, RALPH CLIFFORD, JR., certified public accountant; b. June 23, 1947, Marysville, Kans.; s. Ralph C. and H. Ann (Gamble) K.; m. Carole A., Oct. 17, 1969; 1 son, Derek Alden b. 1972; edn: BA in acctg. Ft. Lewis Coll., Durango, Colo. 1972; MBA in tax., Golden Gate Univ. 1981; CPA, Calif. 1975. Career: staff acct. Kenneth Leventhal & Co., CPAs, Century City 1971-72; mgr. finl. and forecasting, Toscopetro, Bakersfield 1972-74; senior tax ptnr. Carpenter, Kuhn & Sprayberry, CPAs, Bakersfield 1974–; faculty Master of Tax program for Golden Gate Univ. and Calif. Soc. of CPAs; contbg. writer: Practicing C.P.A., Practical Accountant, and The Management of an Accounting Practice Handbook; mem: Am. Inst. of CPAs, Calif. Soc. of CPAs, Rotary (pres. No. Bksfld. 1985-86), Apartment Owners Assn. (past bd. mem.), Kern County Republican Central Com. (Caucus chmn. 1978-82); mil: sgt. US Army 1967-69, Viet Nam 1968 101st Airborne Div. Res: 6510 Kane Way Bakersfield 93309 Ofc: Carpenter, Kuhn & Sprayberry, CPAs, 5601 Truxtun Ave Ste 200 Bakersfield 93309

KUISK, HANS, radiologist; b. Oct. 16, 1913, Tallinn, Estonia, nat. USA 1955; s. Aleksander and Elvine (Gutman) K.; m. Harda Ivask, Oct. 14, 1939; edn: MD, Univ. Tartu, Estonia 1939, D.Sc, 1941; Diplomate Am. Board of Radiology 1964; certified Am. Bd. Radiology 1964. Career: asst. to chief asst. Inst. Microbiology, Univ. of Tartu 1939-44; residency in radiol. Univ. of Minn.; asst. prof. Univ. of Minn. 1967-72, assoc. prof. 1973, and chief of therapeutic radiology VA Hosp. Mpls.; current: adj. prof. Radiation Oncology, UC Los Angeles; also asst. chief Radiation Therapy Service, Vets. Adm. West Los Angeles Medical Center; mem: Fellow Am. Coll. of Radiology 1965, Radiological Soc. of N. Am., Fellow Am. Coll. of Radiology, Am. Soc. of Therapeutic Radiol. and Oncol., Los Angeles Radiological Soc., So. Calif. Radiation Therapy Soc., Estonian Learned Soc. (NY); author (med. textbook): Technique of Lymphography and Principles of Interpretation (1971); (with Falz M. Khan) Nominal Standard Dose (NSD) and Tumor Std. Dose Tables for Radiation Therapy Planning and Analysis (1975); Republican; Lutheran; rec: skiing. Ofc: Vet. Adm. West Los Angeles Medical Center, Los Angeles 90073

KUKLIN, JEFFREY PETER, talent agency executive; b. Dec. 13, 1935, NY, NY; s. Norman Bennett and Deane Kuklin; m. Jensina Olson, 1960, div. 1969; son, Andrew b. 1967; m. 2d. Ronia Levene, June 22, 1969; children: Adam b. 1971, Jensena b. 1974, Jeremy b. 1975; edn: AB, Columbia Coll. 1957; JD, Columbia Law Sch. 1960. Career: program atty., Am. Broadcasting Co., NYC 1969-72, L.A. 1972-73, also assoc. dir. contracts 1970-73; bus. affairs atty. Internatl. Famous Agency, Los Angeles 1973-74, v.p. bus. affairs & law, West Coast 1974-75; v.p. legal & bus. affairs, Billy Jack Ent., Culver City 1975-76; bus. affairs exec. William Morris Agency Inc., Beverly Hills 1976-79, hd. TV bus. affairs 1979-81, vice pres./hd. TV Bus. Affairs Dept. 1981–; listed, Who's Who in Am. Law; mem. Acad. of TV Arts & Scis. 1973-, L.A. Copyright Soc. 1973-, Am. Bar Assn. 1962-. Res: 30312 Eaglebrook Dr Agoura Hills 91301 Ofc: William Morris Agency Inc. 151 El Camino Dr Beverly Hills 90212

KULKA, PHYLIS CHRISTINE, psychotherapist; b. Dec. 6, 1921, Auckland, N.Z., nat. 1948; d. Trevor Francis and Olive R. (Bray) McCarthy; m. Frank L. Kulka (dec. 1981), Aug. 11, 1944; children: Kathleen b. 1947, Ronald b. 1950; edn: BA, National Univ. 1980; MA, Profl. Sch. of Psychol. Studies, 1982; PhD, Golden State Univ. 1983; desig: Marriage, Family, Child Counselor Calif. 1983. Career: primary grade school tchr. in sev. states and Hawaii, 22 years; pvt. practice psychotherapy, Vista, Calif. 1983–; cons. EternalHills Mortuary; instr. Profl. Sch. for Psychol. Studies 1982; honors: recogn. for outstanding public svc. as mem. Crime Prevention Commn., City Council of Vista; mem: Assn. for Humanistic Psychology, No. County Psychol. Assn., Am. Psychol. Assn. (assoc.), Senior Citizens, Disabled Am. Vets., Lifeline Comm. Svcs.; author: Psychic Surgery: A study to determine correlation of specific personality traits and successful psychic surgery (6/83); Democrat; Catholic; rec: gardening and preserving the harvest. Address: 1044 Prospect Pl Vista 92083

KULKARNI, GOPALRAO BINDUMADHAV, civil engineer; b. June 2, 1941, Hangal, India, nat. US cit. 1985; s. Bindumadhav Gangadhar and Laxmibai Tirumalrao (Desai) K.; m. Geetha Krishnappa, Aug. 22, 1971; 1 child, Raghavendra b. 1973; edn: BE (civil), Coll. of Engring., Poona, India 1960; MBA, Inst. of Mgmt. Research and Devel., Poona 1979; Reg. Profl. Civil Engr., Calif. (1982). Career: field engr., resident engr. Corps of Engrs., India 1969-80; project engr. Ralph M. Parsons Co., Pasadena 1980-83; project mgr. Condor Constrn. Corp. (and A-E div. Control Design Systems), Los Angeles 1983-84; design rev. engr. TRW, Redondo Bch. (1 mo.) 1984; project mgr., Facilities Engring. & Constrn. Mgmt. Sect., Jet Propulsion Lab (NASA), Pasadena 1985–; vis. prof., cons. Defense Inst. of Workstudy, Mussoorie, India and Coll. of Mil. Engring., Poona, India (1974-78); apptd. Minority Business Advis. Subcom., So. Calif. Rapid Transit Dist. (1983-); mem. ASCE, Instn. of Engrs. (India); publs. in profl. jours.; Hindu; rec: ice skating, fishing, photog. Res: 246 Greencroft Ave Glendora 91740 Ofc: JPL 4800 Oak Grove Dr (200-213) Pasadena 91109

KUMAR, K. PREAM, physician; b. Jan. 4, 1943, Hyderabad, India; s. Kadevari Babiah and Kadevari Rudramma (Koppula) K.; m. Connie, Mar. 21, 1975; 1 child, Raja b. 1976; edn: MD, Osmania Med. Coll. India 1969; bd. certified Am. Bd. Int. Med. 1984. Career: intern Cook Co. Hosp. Chgo. 1971-72; resident int. med. VA Hosp. Long Beach, UC Irvine 1972-74, fellowship 1974-76; owner, med. dir. Desert Dialysis Med. Ctr. Palm Springs; affil. Eisenhower Meml., Desert, Indio Comm. Hosps. and Hi-Desert Med. Ctr.; honors: Phys. Recognition Award (AMA); mem: AMA, CMA, Internat. Soc. of Nephrol., Riverside Co. Med. Assn., Am. Soc. Parenteral and Enteral Nutrition; Hindu. Res: 562 Desert West Dr Rancho Mirage 92270 Ofc: Desert Dialysis Med. Clin. 345 Tachevah Dr, Ste 9, Palm Springs 92262

KUNEY, KENNETH ALBERT, lawyer; b. Jan. 8, 1920, Tulare, Calif.; s. Harry Albert and Clara May (Kendall) K.; m. Patricia Rosson, Oct. 16, 1941; children: Douglas b. 1948, Jean b. 1950, Scott b. 1956; edn: BS, UC Berkeley 1946; JD, UC Hastings Coll. of Law 1949; admitted Calif. State Bar, US Dist. Ct. (no. eastern, central dist. Calif.), US Ct. of Appeal 9th circ. US Supreme Ct. 1950. Career: atty. pvt. practice spec. in water rights law, representation of water agcys., rep. fed. Central Valley Proj. water svc. contractors in all principal ct. and admin. agcy. proceedings 1955–; honors: Sheffield Sanborn Scholar (Hastings 1948), Order of the Coif 1948; mem: Am., Calif., Tulare Co. (pres. 1960) bar assns.; Tulare CofC (pres. 1961), Tulare Co. Heart Assn. (founder), Tulare Econ. Devel. Corp. (founder), Calif. State CofC (Water Resources Com.), Hastings Alumni Assn. (bd. govs. 1967-80, pres. 1979-80), Lions Club, VFW, Boy Scouts of Am., Tulare Library Board (pres. 1955-70); mil: lt. USNR 1942-46, PTO; Republican; Episcopal; rec: gardening, hunting, needlepoint. Res: 830 Sycamore Tulare 93274 Ofc: 145 North N St Tulare 93274

KUNG, GARY WEI, manufacturing co. executive; b. Oct. 7, 1959, Taipei, Taiwan, nat. US cit. 1973; s. Yao Hua and Jiar Ming (Wong) K.; edn: AB engrg., Lafayette Coll. 1981; MBA, Univ. Santa Clara 1985. Career: sales rep., mgr.

distbn. sales Dupont Connector Systems, Santa Clara 1984; acct. mgr. Teradyne Connection Sys. Sunnyvale 1985; v.p. sales & mktg., co-owner I.O. Interconnect San Jose 1985—; bd. dirs. Shanghai Pearl & Gems; honors: Million Dollar Sales Club (Dupont 1983, 84), Big Hitter Mktg. Award (Dupont 1983); Republican; rec: skiing, fishing, reading, hunting, investments. Res: 390 S 15th St San Jose 95112 Ofc: I.O. Interconnect 1590 Old Oakland Rd Ste B101 San Jose 95131

KUNS, KAY SUSANNE, lawyer; b. Aug.2, 1951, Wareham, Mass.; d. Denzil Ira and Mary Ann (Kempton) K.; m. Michael Christiansen, Mar. 20, 1983; edn: BA, highest honors, UC San Diego 1973; JD, cum laude, Univ. of San Diego 1976; admitted Calif. State Bar 1976. Career: deputy city atty., trial deputy, asst. supr. of Bauchet Street Branch, Los Angeles City Atty's Office, 1976-79; atty. prin. pvt. practice, Santa Ynez, 1979—; staff instr. Calif. Youth & Govt.'s model court program; honors: Appellate Moot Court Board, Order of the Barristers, best oralist Calif. State Moot Ct. Competition (1975); mem. Calif. Bar Assn.; civic: Youth & Govt. (sponsored by Calif. YMCAs); rec: sports, travel. Res: POB 971 Santa Ynez 93460 Ofc: Kay S. Kuns ALC, POB 69, Santa Ynez 93460

KUNZ, R. KENT, company executive; b. July 11, 1940, Montpelier, Idaho; s. George S. and Edith B. (Bills) K.; m. Barbara Jean Creasy, Feb. 14, 1976; chidren: Michael P. b. 1967, Julie Ann b. 1970, Tiffany Jean and Tyler John (twins) b. 1979, R. Kent II b. 1981; edn: BA, Univ. of Utah 1964. Career: secty., treas. Los Angeles Lathing Co., Los Angeles 1964-70; secty., treas. Pierce Enterprises, Fresno 1970—; bd. dirs. six corps.; mem: Sunnyside Counry Club, Star Valley Ranch Country Club, Sequoia Council Boy Scouts of Am. (bd. dirs. 1981-85), East Fresno Rotary, Fresno State Bulldog Found., Clovis H.S. Cougar Found., Ducks Unlimited; mil: pfc USAR 1959-65; rec: golf, skiing, fishing. Res: 7818 E. Nees Ave. Clovis 93612 Ofc: 2651 E. Byrd Ave. Fresno 93706

KUO, CHANG KENG, engineering executive; b. March 14, 1935, Tachia, Taiwan, nat. US cit. 1970; s. Chin Quen and Chin Chiaw (Lee) Kuo; m. Chung-Yu, Jan. 22, 1962; children: Jane b. 1963, John b. 1966, Alfred b. 1969; edn: BSEE, Nat. Taiwan Univ. 1957; MSEE, Univ. of Tenn. 1963; PhDEE, cand. UC Berkeley 1968-73; Reg. Profl. Elec. Engr., Calif. (1975) and Ore. (1976). Career: jr. elec. engr. Taiwan Sugar Co. 1959-62; elec. designer Kocher Consulting Engring. Co., Los Angeles 1964-66; asst. elec. engr. Dept. of Water Resources, State of Calif., Sacramento 1966-68; elec. design engr. Pacific Gas & Elec. Co., San Francisco 1972-74; elec. engr. Bechtel Power Corp., San Francisco 1974-76; senior elec. engr. 1977, engring. supvr. 1978, engr. splst. 1984, currently, electrical group supvr. Saltstone/ DWPF Project 1985—; mil: lt. Chinese Air Force, Taiwan 1957-59; Democrat; Buddhist; rec: fishing, swimming, research of history. Res: 2836 Buckskin Rd. Pinole 94564 Ofc: Bechtel National Inc., 50 Beale St. 45/2/B18 San Francisco 94105

KUO, FRAUKE G., court reporter; b. Dec. 29, 1946, Eutin, West Germany, nat. US cit. 1970; d. August and Frauke (Rasul-Linde) Feistl; m. Dinluh Kuo (dec.), Sept. 23, 1965; children: Mathias b. 1967, Bianca b. 1970; edn: Abitur, W. Ger. 1965; AA, magna cum laude, Rutledge Coll. 1982; Reg. Profl. Reporter, Nat. Bd., certified shorthand reporter, Calif., New Mexico; Notary Public. Career: court reporter, 1982—; translator/ interpreter, English-German; mem. Certified Shorthand Reporters Assn./Calif., Nat. Shorthand Reporters Assn., German-Am. Socs. of San Diego; Republican; rec: philately. Address: Chula Vista 92010

KURAHASHI, TEISEI, company executive; b. Jan. 3, 1934, Tokyo, Japan; s. Sadamu and Tazuko (Fukano) K.; m. Kazuko, Oct. 19, 1958; 1 child, Michiko b. 1959; edn: BA, cum laude Keio Univ. 1957. Career: with Nippon Steel Corp. 1969-81, Nippon Steel USA, Inc. 1981—; mgr. export sales 1969; mgr. corp. plng. 1974; deputy gen. mgr. corp. plng. 1978; exec. v.p. 1981—; v.p. Japan Bus. Assn. of So. Calif.; mem: Japan Bus. Assn. of So. Calif.; Calif. CofC; University Club; Breamar Country Club; Los Coyotes Country Club; Methodist; rec: classical music. Ofc: Nippon Steel U.S.A., Inc., 611 W 6th St, Ste 2900, Los Angeles 90017

KURTZ, ALVIN AGEE, administrative law judge, ret.; b. Dec. 30, 1906, Salem, Ore.; s. E.A. and Rose (Agee) K.; m. Virginia Dean Beall, July 8, 1933; children: Janet Virginia (Cook) b. 1936, Judith Lu (Suor) b. 1940; edn: JD, Willamette Univ. 1929; admitted to bar: Ore. Supreme Ct. and Fed. Dist. Cts. (1929), US Supreme Ct. (1938), US Cts. of Appeal (3d. dist. 1955, 9th dist. 1941, 10th dist. 1946) and Dist. Col. (1946). Career: gen. counsel Public Utilities Commn. of Ore. 1935-43; senior atty. Securities and Exchange Commn. 1943; senior atty. and adminstrv. law judge Federal Power Commn., Wash DC 1943-73, ret.; honors: Meritorious Service Award for outstanding public service, Federal Power Commn. (1973); mem: Ore. State Bar (Adminstrv. Law Com. 1942-43), Interstate Commerce Commn. (jt. board mem. 1935-43), Nat. Assn. of R.R. and Utils. Commnrs. (spl. com. on regulatory law devels. 1941), Administrv. Law Judges Conf.; mem. Masons, Scottish Rite orgns., The Jamestowne Soc. of Va., Sun City Golf Club; Ind.; Episcopal; rec: golf, fishing. Res: 28055 Grosse Point Dr Sun City 92381

KUSTURA, JOHN BRINSLEY, aerospace engineer, executive; b. Sept. 13, 1956, Detroit, Mich.; s. John Joseph and Elizabeth Jean (Sheridan) K.; m. Kathleen, Mar. 24, 1984; edn: BS aerospace engrg., cum laude, Parks Coll. of St. Louis Univ. 1977; MS Aeronautics & Astronautics, Purdue Univ. 1978; MBA, Univ. So. Calif. 1985; Reg. Engr.-In-Tng. Ind. 1978. Career: engr. III Jet Propulsion Lab., Pasadena 1979-80; engr. senior, unit mgr. Northrop Elec-

tronics Div., Hawthorne 1980-86; staff engr. TRW Space & Technol. Group, Redondo Beach 1986—; instr. IMU Familiarization Course, Northrop Elec. Div. 1983-86; var. personnel and mgmt. devel. tng. courses; honors: Outstanding Student (Parks Coll. SLU 1977), Alpha Sigma Nu (1976-77), Pi Mu Epsilon (1977), Student Govt. Pres. (Parks Coll. 1975-76), Dean's List (Parks Coll.- 5, USC- 2), Who's Who Among Students in Am. Colls. & Univs. (1976-7), Employee of the Quarter (Northrop Electronics Div. 1981), TEAM Award (Northrop Elec. Div., Engrg. Dept. 1985); mem: Am. Inst. Aero & Astro (fmr), Youth Motivation Task Force, High Sch. Involvement Pgm. (instr.); publ: co-author paper presented at 12th Biennial Guidance Test Symposium (1985); Catholic; rec: softball, basketball, golf, skiing, bowling. Res: 6291 Priscilla Dr Huntington Beach 92647 Ofc: TRW Space & Technol. Gp., Mail Stn M2/2131, 1 Space Park Redondo Beach 90278

KUTNER, (S.) JEROME, psychologist; b. Mar. 7, 1938, NY, NY; s. Abraham L. and Frances A. (Gorelick) K.; m. Kathleen, May 21, 1982; edn: BS, New York Univ. 1960; MA, The New Sch. for Social Research 1964, PhD, 1966; Cert. mem. Nat. Acad. of Neuropsychologists; Calif. Tchg. Cred. Career: asst. prof. psych. State Univ. of New York, Fredonia 1965-66, Fort Hays Kans. State Coll. 1966-67; research psychologist Kaiser Found. Research Inst., Oakland 1967-72, UC Sch. of Medicine, Langley Porter Psychiat. Inst., San Francisco 1972-75; pvt. practice splst. in testing (pshcyol. and neuropsychol.), San Jose 1975—; mem. Forensic Panel, Superior Ct., Santa Clara County (1981-); instr. personality assessment, Calif. Inst. of Transpersonal Psychol. (1984-85); honors: for community service re substance abuse, Pathway Soc.; mem: Am. Psychol. Assn. div. Neuropsychol., Calif. State Psychol. Assn., Santa Clara Co. Psychol. Assn., Forensic Mental Health Assn. of Calif.; contbr. articles in med. jours. (1971-); mil: pfc Army Security Agency 1960-62; Jewish. Res: 166 Middlefield Rd Palo Alto 94301 Ofc: S. Jerome Kutner PhD, 2444 Moorpark Ave Ste 116 San Jose 95128

KUWAHARA, STEVEN SADAO, biochemist; b. July 20, 1940, Lahaina, Maui, Hawaii; s. Toshio and Hideko (Sasaki) K.; m. Rene M. Miyajima, June 24, 1972; children: Daniel T. b. 1974, Sara S. b. 1978; edn: BS, Cornell Univ. 1962; MS, Univ. Wisc. 1965, PhD, 1967. Career: research asst. Univ. Wisc. 1962-66; research assoc. Univ. Wash. Seattle 1966-67; asst. prof. CSU Long Beach 1967-71; asst. research biol. UC Irvine 1971-73; unit chef Mich. Dept. of Public Health, Lansing 1973-76, sect. chief 1976-82; mgr. test technol. Hyland Therapeutics, L.A. 1982—; adj. research assoc. Coll. of Human Med., Mich. State Univ. 1980-82; honors: Award of Merit (Long Beach Heart Assn. 1969), Spl. Research Fellowship (NIH 1971-73); mem: AAAS, Am. Assn. Blood Banks, Am. Chem. Soc., Am. Fedn. Clin. Research, Am. Soc. Microbiology, Soc. for Exptl. Biol. & Med., NY Acad. of Scis., Hemophilia Found. of So. Calif., BSA (scoutmaster); publ: 25 sci. papers, 15 presentations; Buddhist (treas. W. Covina Buddhist Ch.); rec: stamps, gardening. Res: 975 W Amador St Claremont 91711 Ofc: Hyland Therapeutics 4501 Colorado Blvd Los Angeles 90039

KWASKY, ALBERT JOSEPH, naval architecture and marine engineering co. president; b. Nov. 2, 1919, Manistee, Mich.; s. Joseph Albert and Antonia Regenia (Krasniewski) K.; m. Virginia Moore, Aug. 26, 1949; edn: BA, Columbia Coll.; postgrad. electrical engring. 1943, electronics engring. 1945, Univ. Calif.; Reg. Profl. Engr., Calif. (1946). Career: electrical engr. Hurley Marine Works, Oakland 1942-45; elec. engr. Pillsbury & Martignoni, Inc., San Francisco 1946-51, marine engr. 1963-71, marine engr. supvr. 1972-78, mgr. 1979-81, pres. 1982— (only the third pres. of firm founded in 1901, as the first pres. Capt. Albert Pillsbury lived to age 94, and 2d pres. Walter L. Martignoni lived to 101 yrs); ed. Electronics Systems Tech. Manual for USS Hancock (CVA-19) and USS Oriskany (CVA-34); mem: US Naval Inst., Navy League of the US, Soc. of Naval Archs. and Marine Engrs.; civic: The Nature Conservancy, Nat. Audubon Soc., Sierra Club, New England Anti-Vivisection Soc.; publs: The Old Lady in Dubuque, The Old Lady in Dubuque's Other Son, The Old Lady in Dubuque's Town; Catholic; rec: tennis, chess, mtn. climbing, bird watching. Res: 2418 Ashby Ave Berkeley 94705 Ofc: Pillsbury & Martignoni, Inc. Pier 1 San Francisco 94111

KWOCK, BERRY, lawyer, certified public accountant; b. Aug. 26, 1946, Sanger; s. Hing and Louise (Tsang) K.; m. Teresa Yep, Apr. 20, 1975; children: Tiffany b. 1979, Nicole b. 1981; edn: AB, Chinese, Stanford Univ. 1968; JD, Columbia Univ. Sch. of Law 1971; MBA, tax, USC 1984; admitted to bar: NY 1972, Dist. Columbia 1972, Calif. 1974; lic. CPA, Calif. 1984. Career: atty. law firm Anderson, Martin & Cable, NY, NY 1971-72; vis. assoc. prof. of law National Chengchi Univ., Taipei, Taiwan, 1973; atty. law firm James F. Wagner, P.C., Fresno 1974-81; tax mgr. acctg. firm Touche Ross & Co., Los Angeles 1982—; honors: Beta Gamma Sigma (1985); mem: Am. Inst. of CPAs, Calif. Bar Assn., Am. Bar Assn., Los Angeles County Bar Assn. (exec. com. Internat. Law Sect. 1985), So. Calif. Chinese Lawyers Assn.; publs: supplement to Touche Ross Investment and Tax Book on People's Republic of China (1983); Republican; rec: computers, karate. Res: 519 South Orange #E, Monterey Park 91754 Ofc: Touche Ross & Co, 3700 Wilshire Blvd Los Angeles 90010

KWONG, EDWARD SHIU-YING, civil engineer; b. Dec. 4, 1937, China; s. Lee Chung and Siu King (Ngan) K.; m. Ida Ping-Ming, Oct. 18, 1970; children: Frank b. 1971, Ben b. 1974, Charles b. 1982; edn: dipl. in struc. engring., Brixton Sch. of Building, London, Eng.; Reg. Profl. Engr., Calif.; Chartered Civil Engr., Engring. Council, U.K. Career: engr. Greater London Council, England, Blyth Borough Council, England; civil engr. Scott Wilson Kirkpatrick & Ptnrs., Hong Kong; pvt. practice Edward S.Y. Kwong, Architects & Engineers, Hong Kong; civil engr. Sverdrup & Parcel and Assocs., San

Francisco; current: civil engr. Martin, Middlebrook & Nishkian, S.F.; mem. Instn. of Civil Engrs. (U.K.). Res: 2965 19th Ave San Francisco 94132

KYLE, H. JAMES, JR., commodity broker; b. Mar. 22, 1946, Uniontown, Pa.; s. Henry James, Sr. and Mary Zulla (Culleton) K.; m. Janet Trunzo, Mar. 23, 1972; 1 son: Robert b. 1972; edn: BS, Calif. State Univ. 1968; JD, Western State Univ. 1977; MBA cand., Pepperdine Univ. 1984-; assoc. Commodity Futures Trading Commn. 1976. Career: broker Hornblower, Weeks San Diego 1976-78, Clayton Brokerage 1978-79; pres., chief exec. HJK & Assocs. Irvine 1980-; motivation teacher, speaker 1979-; dir. Infinity Co. Inc. 1986; honors: Am. Jurisprudence Awards- Torts & Trial Practice (1974, 77), Nu Beta Epsilon (past. pres.); mem: First Marine Div. Assn., Force Recon. Assn., Sickle Cell Anemia Found., Marine Corps Reserve Ofcrs. Assn., S.D. CofC; mil: capt. USMC 1968-76, Combat Action, Navy Commdn. w/ Valor; Catholic; rec: running, boxing, swimming. Res: 7219 El Fuerte St Carlsbad 92008 Ofc: HJK & Assoc. 2691 Richter Ave Ste 130 Irvine 92714

KYLE, ROBERT DUVAL KIM, real estate broker; b. July 22, 1950, Fargo, No. Dak.; s. Robert Duval and Loris Marlys (Haugen) K.; m. Maryann Heredia, April 2, 1977; 1 dau: Kathryn, b. 1983; edn: AA, West Valley Coll. 1971, Real Estate Cert. 1973; USAF Noncommnd. Officer Acad. 1978; Real Estate Cert. Inst. 1977. Career: sales rep. Liggett & Myers Tobacco Co., Inc., Carmel/ Monterey 1973-75; loan ofcr. United Calif. Mortgage Co., Campbell 1975-77; real estate broker Kyle Realty, San Jose 1977-; res. mktg. dir. National Smoke Detector Sys. 1983-85; recipient commendation, The Crippled Children's Soc. of Santa Clara Co. 1981; mem: Los Gatos- Saratoga Bd. of Realtors; Calif. Assn. Realtors; Nat. Fedn. of Ind. Bus.; Internat. Real Estate Fedn.; Nat. Assn. Realtors; West Valley Svc. Club (pres. 1981-82); Campbell Progressive Srs. (dir. 1981-84); works: selected by USAF with consent of the gov. to work at Logistics Readiness Ctr., Pentagon, Wash. DC 1977; mil: staff sgt., USAF Calif. Air Nat. Guard 1971-83; Air Reserve Forces Meritorious Svc. Award; Cammand Generals Award; Presidential Unit Citation; Republican; Lutheran; rec: NASCAR sprint auto racing (sponsor, dir. Robinson Racing). Res: 5293 Taft Dr., San Jose 95124 Ofc: Kyle Realty, 2100 Los Gatos- Almaden Rd., San Jose 95124

LAALY, HESHMAT OLLAH, construction materials scientist; b. June 23, 1927, Kermanshah, Iran; s. Jacob and Saltanat (Afshani) L.; m. Parivash Farahmand, Feb. 7, 1982; children: Ramesh b. 1964, Edmond b. 1967; edn: B.Chem., Univ. Stuttgart, West Germany 1956, M.Chem., 1959, PhD Chem., 1962. Career: textile chief chemist E.F. Kren, Solme, W. Germany 1963-67; analytical chemist Gulf Oil Research, Canada 1967-70; material scientist Bell-Northern Research, Canada 1970-71; research officer National Research Council of Canada 1972-83; cons., author, educator 1984-; tech. dir. of Roofing Materials Science & Technology; plastic expert UN Indsl. Devel. Orgn. 1975-; honors: Cert. of Merit (Canadian Gen. Stds. Bd.); mem: Assn. of Profl. Engrs. of Ontario, Assn. for Advancement of Sci. in Canada, Am. Chem. Soc., Chem. Inst. of Canada, Spectroscopic Soc. of Canada, Canadian Soc. Chem. Engrs., Am. Soc. Testing & Materials, Canadian Gen. Stds. Bd.; publs: 15 sci. papers; 50+ speeches; Bahai, Jewish. Address: 9037 Monte Mar Dr Los Angeles 90035

LA BARBERA, BARRY THOMAS, district attorney San Luis Obispo County; b. Aug. 14, 1944, Mt. Vernon, NY; s. Frank Michael and Mary Angelina (Leggierre) La B.; m. Jeanne, July 15, 1967; 1 dau. Lisa b. 1970; edn: BA, Ohio State Univ. 1967; JD, Univ. San Diego 1970; admitted Calif. State Bar 1971. Career: Disciplinary atty. State Bar of Calif. 1971-72; dep. dist. atty. Orange County 1972-79; deputy and chief deputy dist. atty. San Luis Obispo County 1980-85, dist. atty. 1985-; bd. mem. Rape Crisis Pgm., Sexual Assault Response Team, Women's Shelter; advis. bd. County Drug Pgm., Alcohol Services Pgm.; recipient Am. Jurisprudence Awards (evidence, constnl. law); mem: ABA, Calif. Bar Assn., S.L.O. County Bar Assn., Nat., Calif. Dist. Atty. Assns.; Rotarian; past pres. Lions Club; past mem. Exchange Club; rec: golf, basketball, jogging. Ofc: SLO County District Attorney County Government Center San Luis Obispo 93408

LA BASH, LOUIS LEE, inventor, precious metals co. owner; b. Mar. 25, 1938, Los Angeles; s. Martin Jr. and Svea Leannea Ingeborg (Sjostrand) LaB. Career: owner LaBash Metals Newbury Park, Calif., gold & silver refining; owner Anacapa View Nursery (specimen plants, tropical and subtropical plant stock, Mediterranian nature plants), Anacapa Koi Farm (breeding of fancy carp); mem: Sierra Club, Ventura County Koi Club, Salt Flat Racing Assn., So. Calif. Timing Assn., Silver Inst.; inventor high-purity silver cells, precious metals refining membranes; owner, developer historically designated home in Butte, Montana; mil: AE-3 USNR disch. 1969; Methodist; rec: salt-flat racing, restoration of historical structures, antique silver and bronze statuary collecting. Res: 15634 Tierra Rejada Moorpark 93021 Ofc: LaBash Metals 3479 Old Conejo Rd Newbury Park 91320

LA BORDE, MICHAEL RAY, airline pilot; b. Oc.t 15, 1958, Killeen, Texas; s. John and Glenda Gail (Meredith) L.B.; edn: AABA, Orange Coast Coll. 1982; BABA, CSU Fullerton 1983; Airline Transport Pilot (1984), Flight Engr.-Turbojet (1981), Flight Instr. airplane single and multi engine- insturment airplane (1982), Ground Instr. Adv. and Instrument (1983), FAA. Career: cable patrol pilot Pacific Telephone, Santa Ana 1981-82; asst. chief flight instr. Martin Aviatin, Santa Ana 1982-84; capt. Desert Sun Airlines, Los Angeles 1984; 2nd ofcr. B-727 Continental Airlines, Houston, Texas 1984, 2nd ofcr. DC-10, Los Angeles 1985, 1st ofcr. DC-9 1985, 1st ofcr. B737-300, Los Angeles 1986-; honors: Employee of the Month, Martin Aviation 1983; Republican; Catholic;

rec: tennis, running, swimming. Res: 601 Lido Park Dr, #1-D, Newport Beach 92663 Ofc: Continental Airlines, 7300 World Way West R.A.T.O. 337 Los Angeles 90009

LABOUNTY, HUGH ORVICE, university president; b. Sept. 22, 1927, Chgo.; s. Hugh Orvice and Dorothy (Cooper) La B.; widowed; children: Brian, Mark, Kim, Paul, Eric; edn: BA, Univ. Redlands 1950, MA 1951; EdD, UCLA 1961. Career: faculty Citrus Coll., Azusa 1950-53; faculty dept. social sci. and history Calif. State Poly. Univ., Pomona 1953-, v.p. acad. affairs 1967-77, acting pres. 1977-78, pres. 1978-; cons. Tanzania, Greece, United Arab Emirates, South Korea; mem. AASCU Com. on Internat. Programs, Consortium for Internat. Devel., Pacific Rim Task Force Advis. Group; civic: bd. trustees: Univ. of Redlands, Pomona Economic Devel. Corp., Casa Colina Rehab. and Health Found., L.A. Co. Fair Assn., College Div. II Director for United Way. Office of the President, Calif. State Polytechnic University, Pomona, 3801 W. Temple Ave., Pomona 91768

LACAYO, CARMELA GLORIA, community development co. president; b. June 28, 1943, Chihuahua, Mexico, nat. US cit. 1968; d. Enrique Luis and Maria Louisa (Lacayo) Velazquez; edn: BA social welfare, Immaculate Heart Coll.; BA psychol., Regina Mundi Univ. Rome. Career: mem. Sisters of Social Service L.A. 1961-71; prof. urban devel. and sociology Univ. San Buenaventura (Colombia) 1973-74; adminstrv. coord. Ofc. of Mayor L.A. 1974-75; pres., exec. dir. Nat. Assn. for Hispanic Elderly L.A. 1975; pres. Nat. Hispanic Inst. of Public Policy 1978;, Nat. Hispanic Research Ctr. 1980, El Pueblo Community Devel. Corp. 1985-; honors: Latina Woman of the Year (L.A. 1976), Nat. Woman of the Year (Latin Am. Profl. Women's Assn. 1977), Fellow Gerontological Soc. of Am. (1981); mem: Nat. Council on Aging, Am. Soc. on Aging, Indirect Sector, Am. Public Health Assn. Res: 4225 Villa Arbolada Apt 573 Los Angeles 90042 Ofc: Nat. Assn. for Hispanic Elderly 2727 W 6th St Ste 270 Los Angeles 90057

LACHS, STEPHEN M., judge; b. Sept. 227, 1939, NY, NY; s. Irving and Irene (Balogh) L.; edn: BA, UC Los Angeles 1960, LLB, 1963; admitted Calif. State Bar 1964. Career: atty. pvt. practice 1964-69; atty. Public Defender's Office 1969-75; superior ct. commr. 1975-79; superior ct. judge Los Angeles County 1979-; adj. prof. law Whittier Coll. Sch. of Law; lectr. Calif. Cont. Ed. of the Bar, Am. Family Law Inst., Rutter Grp., etc.; mem: Am. Bar Assn., L.A. Co. Bar Assn. (exec. com. Faculty Law Sect.); Lawyers for Human Rights; bd. dirs. AIDS Project Los Angeles; L.A. Gay & Lesbian Community Svcs. Ctr.; founder Municipal Elections Com. of L.A.; L.A. Co. Art Museum; publ: art. in Calif. State Bar Journ. and Whittier Law Review. Ofc: Los Angeles Superior Court 111 N Hill St Los Angeles 90012

LACK, FRED SEVIER, III, distributing co. executive; b. Oct. 4, 1947, Los Angeles; s. Fred S., Jr. and Ruth Munro (Reynolds) L.; m. Barbara Ann Bell, June 19, 1971, div. 1978; 1 dau., Kelly Suzanne b. 1975; edn: BS, USC 1970. Career: sales mgr. San Tong Inc. 1970-71; account mgr. Mattel Toys Inc. 1971-72; pres. Fredmark Distbg. Co. Inc. 1972-76; nat. sales mgr. F.D.I., Inc. 1976-78; account mgr. Flecto Inc. 1978-81; owner Fred S. Lack III Distributing, and Atlantis Ents., Culver City 1981-; mem. Internat. Jet Ski Boating Assn. (trade orgn.), Culver City CofC (Rose Parade com.), Sigma Alpha Epsilon; Republican; Presbyterian; rec: racquetball, scuba, jet skiing, guitarist. Ofc: 5900 Canterbury Dr Ste A107 Culver City 90230

LACKEY, DAVID MOORE, stockbroker; b. April 29, 1947, Oakland; s. Jack Jr. and Helen Tidd L.; m. Leigh, Sept. 28, 1986; children: Mark b. 1970, Jeffrey b. 1973, Jake b. 1975, Mollee b. 1978; edn: BA, Pacific Univ. 1968. Career: salesman Frist California Co. 1968; salesman Blyh & Co. Inc. 1970; ptr., dir., salesman Hammerbeck & Co. 1974; A.G. Edwards & Sons 1983; founder, pres. Tidd, Lackey & Co. 1985-; dir. Chancellor Computer Systems; honors: Blue Key Honorary; mem: Rotary of Chico, Chico CofC, Chico Economic Plnng. Corp.; Republican; Episcopal; rec: sports. Res: 3457 Bell Rd. Chico 95926 Ofc: Tidd, Lackey & co., 430 Broadway Chico 95928

LACKEY, JACK, JR., securities co. owner; b. Aug. 26, 1919, Kansas City, Mo.; s. Jack, Sr. and Esther (Landau) L.; m. Helen Tidd, July 11, 1940; children: John b. 1940, David b. 1947, Ruth Helen b. 1950, Harry b. 1952; edn: AB, Univ. of Mo. 1940. Career: securities sales agt. First California Co., San Francisco 1946-59; v.p. Dempsey-Tegeler & Co., Inc. 1959-70; v.p. Birr-Wilson 1970-71, ret. 1971; v.p. WZW Financial Corp. (fmr Zeal Corp.), 1972-, currently bd. chmn. Tidd, Lackey & Co., Inc., Chico; mil: lt. US Navy 1942-45, decorated; Republican; Episcopal. Res: 25357 Tierra Grande Dr Carmel 93923 Ofc: Tidd, Lackey & Co. Inc. POB 3314 Chico 95927

LACKMANN, ERNEST ALBIN, lawyer; b. Nov. 12, 1902, San Francisco; s. Ernest August and Eugenie Emilie (Coursinoux) L.; widower; 2 step children; edn: AB, UC Berkeley 1923, Boalt Hall of Law 1921-25; admitted Calif. State Bar 1926; Certified splst. in Workers' Compensation Law. Career: atty. pvt. practice, Sacramento and Modesto, 1926-36; dep. labor commissioner 1936-38, atty. for state labor commnr. 1938-45, referee Indsl. Accident Commn. and Workers' Compensation Appeals Board 1945-71, referee in charge, Los Angeles 1970-71, presiding referee, Southern Calif., 1971; atty. prin., Los Angeles 1972-; mem: Coordinating Council, San Diego 1937-38, Los Angeles County Bar Assn. (Workers' Comp. Sect., sect. chmn. 1979-80), Phi Alpha Delta, Elks, UC Berkeley Alumni (secty. Class of 1923); publs: chapter on Limitations of Time in Calif. Workmen's Compensation Practice, 1973 Ed.; Democrat; Lutheran; rec: dogs, walking, bridge. Address: Los Angeles 90068

LA COURTE, MATTHEW P., mobile radio co. president; b. June 7, 1938, Jersey City, N.J.; s. James and Constance LaC.; children: James b. 1959, Matthew Jr. b. 1961, Mark b. 1965, Kevin b. 1966; edn: electronic techn., RETS 1964; Ocean County Coll. 1976-82; 1st class radio tel. lic., FCC 1961. Career: mobile radio communications tech. 1961-69; lead tech. Radio Communications Co., Freehold, N.J. 1969-75; branch mgr. Syntonic Technology Inc. 1975-79; dist. service mgr. Gen. Electric Co., Lynchburg, Va. 1979-82; pres. Bay Area Service Center Inc., Santa Clara 1982 — ; charter mem. Customer Quality Advisory Bd., GE; mem. SMR Assn. (charter), Friendly Wednesday Club; mil: 1st lt. US Marine Corps 1952-57; Republican (charter Pres. Task Force); Catholic; rec: sailing, model planes and boat bldg., equestrian. Ofc: Bay Area Service Center Inc 858 Aldo Ave Santa Clara 95054

LA CROSBY, JOSE, hairstylist, executive; b. Nov. 16, 1926, E. St. Louis, Ill.; s. Willie M. and Dorothy (Spell) LaC.; children: Emma b. 1944, Dorothy b. 1945, Kim b. 1960, Guy b. 1964; edn: Laney Trade Coll. 1954; lic. Charm Beauty Sch. 1955; cert. Perma-Hair of Hollywood 1960; lic. cosmetol. instr. Calif. 1974; certs.: Clairol, Summit Lab., Al Tate of Hollywood. Career: opened first shop 1957 and operated 5 shops simultaneously; currently own and operate one beauty salon and a school in advanced hair styling, LaCrosby Style House and LaCrosby Budget Salon, San Francisco; frequent lectr., guest artist; honors: Gold Shield Award (1955-56), HOPE Stylist Award (1962), Top Hair Stylist, Texas Alumni (1962-63), Man of the Yr., Sun Reporter Merit Award (1st runnerup 1962-63), Bonat Gold Trophy (1965), 1st Pl. Hair-Strate Perm. Contest (1960), West Coast Top Stylist (1964), Who's Who in Coiffure (1974), and many others; mem. Nat. Hairdressers & Cosmetol. Assn., hon. mem. Sickle Cell Anemia Research & Edn., Nat. Small Bus. Assn., Tchrs. Ednl. Council of Nat. Assn. Cosmetol. Schs., Inc., NAACP (life), NCCA, CCA, United Brotherhood Grand Lodge, Beauty Culture League, past mem: Hunters, Point Boys Club, YMCA, others; invented new method dry pressing (1955), inventor and manufacturer Soul Products (1969), Mus-Hav-It Products (1978) and LaCrosby Curl (1978); work has appeared in var. newspapers and mags.; mil: hon. discharge 1954, Nat. Defense, Korean Svc. w/ 4 bronze svc. stars, UN Svc., Pres's Unit Citn. Korea, Good Conduct, Sharpshooter Badge w/ Carbine & Rifle bars; Baptist; rec: dancing, cooking, singing. Ofc: LaCrosby Style House 1415 Divisadero St San Francisco 94115

LAD, PRAMOD MADHUSUDAN, research scientist, executive; b. Dec. 25, 1948, Bombay, India, nat. US cit. 1985; s. Madhusudan Mangesh and Lila Madhusudan (Nadkarni) L.; m. Urmila Desai, Mar. 31, 1978; 1 child, Shivanand b. 1979; edn: BSc, Kings Coll., London Univ., (UK); MS, Cornell Univ. 1972, PhD, 1974. Career: research fellow Nat. Inst. Health, Bethesda, Md. 1975-77, senior staff scientist 1977-80; coord./dir. Kaiser Found. Hosps. Research Lab. 1981 — ; adj. assoc. prof. Univ. So. Calif. 1986; research faculty Calif. Inst. of Technol. 1981; cons. Amicon Corp. 1975-76; honors: Prize, Am. Heart Assn. (1986), chmn. Symposium on Receptor Pharmacology 1986, Symposium on Receptors of Immune & Endocrine Systems 1985; mem: Sigma Xi, AAAS, Am. Chem. Soc., Biophysical Soc., Endocrine Soc., Am. Soc. for Pharmacol. & Exptl. Therapeutics, Am. Acad. Allergy & Immunol., Cornell Club L.A.; publs: 40+ articles in med. and sci. jours.; rec: cinema, poetry, hiking. Res: 520 N San Marino Ave North San Gabriel 91775 Ofc: KFH Research Lab., 4953 Sunset Blvd Los Angeles 90027

LA DOW, CHARLES REYNOLDS, educator, author; b. Nov. 18, 1907, Hermosa Beach; s. Charles Stephen and Elizabeth Mae (Reynolds) La Dow; m. Ruth E. Brown, Mar. 9, 1930; children: Peter b. 1931, Jerome b. 1935, Stephen b. 1943; edn: BA, Pomona Coll. 1928; MA, Claremont Grad. Sch. 1939; grad. study UCLA 1960-65. Career: trainee Far Eastern Div. National City Bank of New York, 1929; self-empl., mgr. La Dow Co. (agri-bus.) 1930-37; tchr. of hist. and govt., Calif. public schs. 1940-71; freelance writer (topics incl. intellectual hist., economics, yachting) 1972 — ; awarded fellowships: So. Calif. Economics Conf. (1960), Gen. Elec. Corp. - C.M.C. Econ. Conf. (1964), Found. for Econ. Edn. (1969); mem. San Diego Tchrs. Assn. (dept. chmn. Hist.-Govt. 28 yrs., pub. rels. chmn. 1955); civic: San Diego Hist. Soc., S.D. Maritime Mus., Maritime Research Soc., S.D. Yacht Club, S.D. Zool. Soc., S.D. Aerospace Mus., Nockean Soc., Warner's Ranch; publs: Presuppositions of a Social Philosophy (1939), The Genius of Western Man (1965), contbr. num. articles in The Freeman, etc.; contbg. editor Sea Mag., The Ships, The House and The Men (1975 hist. of S.D. Yacht Club), Aristotle's Secret (1986); mil: Calif. State Guard, instr. aircraft recogn.; Constitutionalist; non-sectarian; rec: study, boat building, gardening. Address: 3735 Trudy Ln San Diego 92106

LAFFERTY-HERNANDEZ, GILBERT, pro-football team marketing executive; b. May 3, 1949, El Paso, Tx.; s. Hilario and Soccoro H.; m. Nancie Carolyn Roberts, July 21, 1983; children: Gilbert, Jr., Michael David, Christian Andrew, Vincent Anthony; edn: BS, Univ. of Tx. 1973; MA, Central Mich. Univ. 1977; postgrad. work in sports psych., Loyola Marymount Univ. Career: nat. products mgr. Bristol Myers Prods., El Paso, Tx. 1978-80; dir. of mktg./ Spl. Markets, Strohs-Schlitz Brewery, Milwaukee; dir. of mktg./community affairs Los Angeles Raiders, current; honors: 1984 Super Bowl XVIII Ring, World Champion L.A. Raiders, Olympic Organizing Com. youth support participation medal and Olympic Med. Team Psychologist Cert. award (1984); hon. mem. Hispanic Caucus interacting with Fed. and State Ofcls. for legislation; mem. Am. Mktg. Assn. of Calif.; civic: Boys Club and Boy Scouts (counselor), Santa Marta Hosp. (bd. dirs.), vol. cons.: United Way Campaign, BSA Golf Tournament, Cystic Fibrosis, Am. Lung Assn., Child Abuse, Am. Diabetes Assn., Heart Assn., Christian Fellowship for the Blind, El Centro Comm. Agency, La Familia, St. Patrick's Youth Parade, Raider's Stay-in-Sch.,

Anti-Drugs, Anti-Vandalism Pgms., Am. Cancer Soc., Muscular Dystrophy, Children's Hosp., Camp Good Times for Children with Cancer, Starlight Found., VA Hosp. pgms.; publs: First Bilingual Guide to Profl. Football, Psychology of Winning According to the Raiders, "If I Could Only Touch You Now" (collection of songs); mil: capt. US Army Air Def. Reserves 1973-, Army Commendn., Nat. Def.; Christian; rec: poetry, music, youth work. Res: 1447-C Manhattan Beach Blvd Manhattan Beach 90266 Ofc: Los Angeles Raiders 332 Center St El Segundo 90245

LAGARDE, JACQUES, manufacturing co. president; b. May 2, 1938, Rennes, France; s. Gaston and Charlotte (Bequignon) L.; m. Marie Christine, Sept. 4, 1965; children: Marion b. 1967, Charlotte b. 1968, Cecile b. 1969, Antoine b. 1982, Julie b. 1983; edn: MBA, Ecole Des Hautes Etudes Comm. 1960; AMP, Harvard Bus. Sch. 1975. Career: var. to product line mgr. The Gillette Co., France 1963-68, regl. sales mgr. 1968-70; internat. product line mgr. Bran AG, W. Ger. 1970-72; dean Lyons Grad. Sch. of Bus. Admin., France 1972-81; gen. mgr. Gillette Co., France 1981-85; pres. Oral-B Laboratories Inc. 1985 — ; Knight, French Nat. Order of Merit; mil: Naval Ofcr. in Algeria 1961-62; rec: mountain climbing, tennis, jogging. Ofc: Oral-B Laboratories Inc., One Lagoon Dr. Redwood City 94065

LA GRANGE, CLINTON JOHN, physician; b. June 1, 1934, Belle Rose, La.; s. Dozelian P. and Lucy Marie (Portier) LaG.; m. Erin F., Oct. 3, 1964; children: Michele b. 1965, Clinton J. b. 1966, Liesl b. 1967, Erik b. 1969, Edward b. 1974; edn: BS edn., L.S.U. 1956, BS premed., 1960; MD, L.S.U. Sch. of Med. 1964; Diplomate Am. Acad. of Ophthalmol. and Otolaryngol. 1970. Career: intern Charity Hosp. New Orleans 1964-65, resident ENT, 1965-69, trainee otologic research 1969-69, asst. clin. instr. 1969-69; pvt. practice otorhinolaryngol. Oxnard, Calif. 1969 — ; chief of surgery St. John's Hosp. Oxnard; mem: Ventura County Med. Soc., Calif. Med. Assn., AMA; mil: 1st lt. US Army 1956-58; Humanitarian; rec: oil painting, hiking, skiing. Ofc: Clinton LaGrange MD, 500 Esplanade Dr Ste 720 Oxnard 93030

LAH, DAVID DOOSUP, physician; b. May 4, 1947, Pyungnam, Korea, nat. 1982; s. Seon Hyo and Kil Woo (Kim) L.; m. Nancy Y., Feb. 6, 1975; children: Benjamin b. 1976, Carol b. 1980; edn: MD, Seoul Nat. Univ. Coll. of Med. 1973. Career: flex. intern Jewish Meml. Hosp. NY, NY 1977-78; pediat. resident Lincoln Med. Ctr. Bronx 1978-81; pvt. practice pediat. Cass City, Mich. 1981-83, Garden Grove, Calif. 1983; pediat. staff So. Calif. Permanente Med. Grp. Fontana 1983 — ; mem: Am. Acad. Pediat. Res: 959 Deborah St Upland 91786 Ofc: So. Calif. Permanente Med. Grp. 9985 Sierra Ave Fontana 92335

LAIDLAW, DOUGLAS MC NEILL, JR., printing co. executive; b. Nov. 16, 1954, Los Angeles; s. Douglas McNeill and Jean Metcalf (Monroe) L.; m. Kathleen Mary Laudenback, Sept. 20, 1986; edn: BS in bus. adm., USC 1978. Career: prodn. mgr. MacDermott & Chant, Welshpool, Wales, G.B. 1977; field rep. Southland Corp., Dallas, Tx. 1978-80; dir. of sales Creative Web Systems, Los Angeles 1980-83, gen. mgr. 1984, v.p./gen. mgr. 1984-86, pres./CEO 1986 — ; instr. Dale Carnegie courses 1984-85; honors: Eagle Scout, BSA (1969); mem: Printing Industries Assn./So. Calif. (dir. 1986-); Master Printers Sect. P.I.A. (dir. 1986-), Young Printing Execs. of So. Calif. (pres., dir. 1986-), Western Publs. Assn. (dir. 1980-84), USC Gen. Alumni Assn., Inglewood CofC, L.A. World Affairs Council, Phi Kappa Psi frat.; Republican; Christian; rec: volleyball, ski, golf, woodworking. Res: 230 S Guadalupe Ave #1 Redondo Beach 90277 Ofc: Creative Web Systems 371 N Oak St Inglewood 90302

LAING, CLAYTON HUGH, retirement home executive; b. Nov. 19, 1953, Saco, Maine; s. Alan and Dorothy Lucille (Houghton) L.; m. Nancy Culver, Aug. 11, 1979; children: Cody, b. 1982; Kelly, b. 1984; edn: AS, Grossmont Coll. 1976; BBA, National Univ. 1985. Career: dept. hd. Handyman Retail Stores, San Diego 1972; store mgmt. 1975; corp. purchasing agent, Handyman Corp. Ofcs., San Diego 1980; supvr. Am. Alliance Cleaning Corp., San Diego 1982; dir. Eldorado Ch. of God Home, Inc., Oceanside 1983 — ; del. Cali. Assn. fo Homes for the Aged; mem: Am. Assn. Homes for the Aged; Oceanside CofC; Oceanside Ch. of God (bd. trustees, v.chmn.); Republican; Protestant; rec: firearms, fishing, golf. Address: Eldorado Church of God Home Inc., 115 So. Clementine, No. 101, Oceanside 92054

LAM, DONALD Y-K, accountant; b. Apr. 5, 1957, Hong Kong, nat. US cit. 1985; s. Andrew and Carol (Ling) L.; edn: BS, CSU Los Angeles 1980; CPA, Calif. (1983). Career: intern Kenneth Leventhal & Co., L.A. 1980-81, staff acct. 1981-82, semi-senior 1982-83, senior 1983-85; ptnr. Kirkpatrick, Lam & Isaac, L.A. 1985 — ; ptnr. New Universe Co., a real estate investment cons. firm 1983; bd. dirs. Genexus Mktg. Inc., an importing mktg. firm 1985; honors: Dean's List (1977-80), Nat. Assn. Accts. Scholar (1978), Beta Alpha Psi (co-chmn. editl. com. 1979); mem: Calif. Soc. CPAs 1983-, Am. Inst. CPAs 1983-, Beta Alpha Psi 1978-, Phi Kappa Phi 1980-, Beta Gamma Sigma 1981-; rec: tennis, Chinese painting. Res: 1385 Avenida de Cortez, Pacific Palisades 90272 Ofc: Kirkpatrick, Lam & Issac, 1900 Ave of the Stars Ste 2625 Century City 90067

LA MACCHIA, MARIO J., business owner; b. Feb. 15, 1930, Phila.; s. Sylvestro and Maria Liberata (Cassotti) La M.; m. Mary Rose Abono, Sept. 17, 1950; children: Joe b. 1951, Sylvester b. 1956, Mary Ann (Girard) b. 1959; edn: spl. courses, US Army 1948, IRE electronic tng. 1952-53. Career: owner/mgr. Mario's TV & Video, Pittsburg 1957 — ; apptd. mem. (chmn. 2 terms) Pittsburg Planning Commn. 1971-73; clubs: Pittsburg Elks, Italian Am., Sons of Italy,

Foresters of Am.; mil: cpl. US Army 1948-51; Ch. of the Good Shepherd. Res: 23 Barrie Ct Pittsburg 94565 Ofc: Mario's TV & Video 200 Atlantic Ave Pittsburg 94565

LAMBERT, AMANDA WAITE, interior designer; b. Mar. 21, 1928, Yreka; d. Charles Edwin and Amanda Seran Waite; m. Clement Bernard Lambert, Aug. 21, 1948; children: Susan b. 1950, Daniel b. 1952, Peter b. 1953; edn: San Luis Jr. Coll., Coll. of the Pacific. Career: head designer Fletchers Home Furnishings, Santa Maria 1965-75; owner/designer Interiors by Amanda, Arroyo Grande 1975 –; curriculum advis. com. Cuesta Jr. Coll.; participant in Apprentice Pgm., Calif. Polytechnic St. Univ., S.L.O.; mem. Arroyo Grande CofC, Arroyo Grande Village Assn.; civic: hold benefits for the Mozart Festival, Hist. Soc., Am. Assn. Univ. Women, and CALM (Child Abuse Listening Mediation); works: purch. and restored the 100 yr old Methodist Ch. and parsonage in Arroyo Grande (to be designated Calif. Hist. Monuments), 1979-, published in Designer's West Mag. (2 arts.), and Sunset Mag.; participant in 3 showcase houses (Montecito, San Luis Obispo, Santa Barbara); Republican; Prot.; rec: tennis, sewing, knitting. Ofc: Interiors by Amanda 124 W Branch Arroyo Grande 93420

LAMM, JULE DAVID, optometrist; b. Sept. 21, 1923, Los Angeles; s. Joseph and Rose Lilly (Dachis) L.; m. Judy, Dec. 15, 1956; children: Randy b. 1960, Brett b. 1961, Wendy b. 1964; edn: AA, UCLA, 1947; BS, No. Ill. Coll. of Optometry 1948, OD, 1950; grad. work UCLA, So. Calif. Coll. of Opt.; lic. Optometrist, Calif. 1950. Career: optometrist pvt. practice, Los Angeles; mem: Am. Opt. Assn., Calif. Opt. Assn., Los Angeles County Opt. Soc. (pres. 1966); civic: Brentwood Optimist Club, Culver City Breakfast Optimist Club (past pres.), Brentwood Bus. & Profl. Assn. (pres. 1967-68, chmn. Citizen Transp. Com. 1967-72, co-chmn. Brentwood Picnic Parade 1976-85), Santa Monica Long Range Plan com. 1974-75, World Health Volunteers (vol. optometric svcs., Mexico 1976-85); mil: 1st lt. Army Air Corps 1943-46, pilot Troop Carrier SW Pacific; Democrat; Hebrew; rec: aviation, pilot vol. emergency services. Res: 212 16th St Santa Monica 90402 Ofc: Jule D. Lamm, OD, 11657 San Vicente Blvd Los Angeles 90049

LAMM, MARCIA GINGER, psychological intern; b. Apr. 19, 1952, Chgo.; d. Alvin J. and Betty A. Lamm; edn: BS, Univ. Ill. 1975; MA, U.S. Internat. Univ. 1982, PhD (honors grad.), 1985; Calif. Comm. Coll. Tchg. Credential (1985-6). Career: (current) psychotherapist/dir. of tng. Clinical & Consulting Assocs., Encino 1983 –; divorce mediator/dir. of tng. Am. Assn. for Mediated Divorce, Encino 1983 –; AMEND psychological advisor/ therapist Valley Chpt. (support for parents of neonatal death); guest lectr. CSU Los Angeles 1983-84; mem. So. Calif. Mediation Network, Am. Assn. for Mediated Divorce, affil. mem. Am. Psych. Assn., WPA; co-author: Divorce Mediation (Trial Mag. 1983); contbr. book chapt. in Emerging Issues in Child Psychiatry and the Law (D. Schetky, MD, E.P. Benedeck, MD, editors); adult edn. tchr. Temple Judea, Encino 1983-84. Address: Encino 91316

LA MONK, CHARLES SAMUEL, graphic artist; b. Apr. 22, 1910, Kemmerer, Wyo.; s. George Wm. and Louise Fredrica (Potter) La M.; widowed; children: Mary b. 1929, Geren b. 1931, Janice b. 1940, Robert Charles b. 1945; edn: art stu. L.A. Trade Tech. 1926-29, postgrad. 1930-31, Chinouard Art Inst. 1941-43, Will Foster Assoc. of Nat. Acad. 1943-50; Calif. tchg. cred., 1976-80. Career: theatrical apprentice poster artist Fox West Coast Theatre, 1927-28; bulletin artist George Gillette Advt. Co., 1930-34, Foster & Kleiser Advt. Co., Los Angeles 1934-47; graphic artist/mgr. Art Dept., Al Metz Advt. Co., 1947-55; designer/mgr. Art Dept., Martin Outdoor Advt. Co., Lancaster 1955-76; volunteer pioneer field artist/cons. Archeol. Survey Assn. of So. Calif. (ASA), p.t. 1952 –; freelance portrait painter and artist splst. pictographs and prehistoric Indian rock graphics, 1952 –; art instr. Antelope Valley High Sch., 1976-80, lectr. to sch. children on art throughout L.A. and San Bernardino Cos.; guest lectr. A.V. Coll. Anthropol. Dept.; guest research assoc. S.B. Co. Museum Div. of Anthropol.; exhib. num. one-man shows; Pictograph and Petroglyph facsimiles shown throughtou USA and through Cultural Exchange Show in Japan, Scandinavia and Brussel's World Fair; partipant Death Valley 49er's Art Exhib. 15 yrs.; awards: many ribbons in art shows, Gold & Silver medals, Am. Indian and Cowboy Artist Soc. (1978, 77), April 22 declared Charles LaMonk Day, City of Palmdale (1979), Resolution, State of Calif. (1985); mem. Archeol. Survey of So. Calif. (life mem. 1985-), Am. Indian & Cowboy Artist Soc. (1974-84), Leona Valley Hist. Soc. (life), Archaeol. Soc. A.V. (life), Friends of A.V. Indian Mus., Wyo. Art Assn., A.V. Allied Artists Assn. (1962-), Toastmasters Int. (CTM); works: first one-man show Lancaster Museum/ Art Gellery 1986; devel. facsimile of stone for pictographs; contbr. chapt. on Indian Rock Art in A Prehist. of Black Canyon by Clayton Howe; subject of 2 audiovisual films on ancient Indian Rock Art; Republican. Studio: 809 West Ave J-13 Lancaster 93534

LAMPSON, FRANCIS KEITH, metallurgist/materials engineer; b. Aug. 7, 1924, Mnpls.; s. Albert Dean and May (Miner) L.; m. Margaret, Sept. 30, 1945; children: Michael b. 1949, Jan b. 1952, Andrea b. 1953, Kevin b. 1958; edn: BS, met. engr., Univ. Ill. 1949. Career: jur. met., N.E.P.A. Div., Fairchild Eng. & Airplane Co., Oak Ridge, Tenn. 1949-51; metallurgist Allison Div., G.M.C., Indpls. 1951-54; group leader mats. & proc. engr. Marquardt Co., Van Nuys 1954-57; Pacific Coast Area tech. rep. Allegheny-Ludlum Steel Corp., Los Angeles 1957-65; mgr. mats. & proc. dept. Marquardt Co., Van Nuys 1965 –, dir. Materials Engring. Dept.; pres. F.K. Lampson Assocs., a mats. engring. consulting co.; awards: Engr. of Year, Marquardt, 1981; Engr. Achievement award, S.F. Valley Engr. Council, 1982; mem: Fellow Am. Soc. for Metals (bd. trustees 1979-81), Soc. for Advancement of Mats. & Proc.

Engring., Am. Inst. of Mining & Met. Engring., Air Force Studies Bd. (Net Shape Technol. Com. 1984-86), Masons, Scottish Rite, Shriners; works: num. tech. papers and presentations; devel. thermo-mechanical forging process for cobalt-base super alloy; co-devel. cobalt-free Maraging Steel; Republican; Protestant; rec: photog., travel. Res: 10000 Aldea Ave Northridge 91325 Ofc: Marquardt Co. 16555 Saticoy St Van Nuys 91409-9104

LANAHAN, DANIEL JOSEPH, lawyer; b. Jan. 13, 1940, Brooklyn, NY; s. Daniel J. and Mary (Maguire) L.; m. Suzanne Sheehan, Aug. 18, 1962; children: Mary Patricia b. 1963, Karen Marie b. 1964, Maureen Claire b. 1966, Daniel Joseph III b. 1983; edn: JD, San Francisco Law Sch. 1969; admitted to Calif. State Bar 1970; Life Comm. Coll. Tchg. Cred. (Law), Calif. 1971. Career: claims adjuster/ claims mgr. Consolidated Insurances Co., NYC, Phila., San Francisco 1961-68; staff asst. Insurance Del Monte Corp. 1968; claims mgr. El Dorado Ins. Co. 1968-70; lawyer/ dir. Ropers, Majeski, Kohn, Bentley, Wagner & Kane, S.F. 1970 –; corp. secty./ dir. Bay Area Bank 1979 –; secty. San Francisco- Cork Sister City Com.; tchr. law San Mateo Comm. Coll. Dist. 1971-74; mem: San Mateo, San Francisco, Calif. & Am. Bar Assns.; Assn. of Defense Counsel; Defense Research Inst.; Redwood City CofC; S.F. CofC; publs: handbook, Laws of Arrest, Search and Seizure, Firearms, 1975; mil: sp4, US Army 1957-61, GCM; Republican; Catholic; rec: equestrian, golf. Res: 1540 Cordilleras Rd Redwood City 94062 Ofc: Ropers, Majeski, et al., 655 Montgomery St, Ste 1600, San Francisco 94111

LAND, JUDY, real estate broker; b. Oct. 6, 1945, Phoenix, Ariz.; d. Stanford Karl and D. Latanne (Hilburn) L.; children: Neal McNeil, III b. 1973; Tahnee McNeil, b. 1975; edn: AA, Merritt Coll. 1968; R.E. Broker Lic., Anthony's Real Estate Sch. 1976; MBA, Burklyn Bus. Sch. 1981. Career: gen. mgr. Ace Rent-A-Car, San Francisco 1968-72; R.E. agent, J.W. Welch Co., San Diego 1972-76; v.p. mktg. & land acquisitions Brehm Communities, San Diego 1977; pres. land sales The Land Co., Del Mar 1978-83; asst. v.p. land acquisition Harry L. Summers, Inc., La Jolla 1983-85; pres. The Land Co., Land Devel. & Sales, Carlsbad 1985 –; honors: The Spike Club, Building Indus. Assn.; mem: Home Builders Council (pres.), Building Indus. Assn. (mem. com.), San Diego Econ. Devel. Corp., Women in Comml. Real Estate, San Diego Republican Businesswomen, San Diego Bd. Realtors, San Dieguito Bd. Realtors, Olympics Exec. Com., City Club San Diego; Republican; rec: decorating, shopping, flying. Address: 916 Begonia Ct Carlsbad 92008

LANDAKER, STEPHEN DAVID, physician; b. Dec. 2, 1951, Charleston, S.C.; s. Chester Lavaughn and Mary Catherine (Hogan) L., Sr.; edn: Ore. State Univ. 1969-70; BS, Univ. of Nev., Reno 1973; MD, Tufts Univ. Sch. of Medicine 1978. Career: internship, Navy Regl. Medical Ctr., San Diego 1978-79; Naval flight surgeon, Naval Aerospace Med. Inst., Pensacola, Fla. 1979-80; USN Branch Clinic, El Toro MCAS, Santa Ana, Ca. 1980-83; residency orthopedic surg. Naval Hosp., San Diego 1983 –; awards: AMA Physicians Recognition awd. 1982; mem: AMA, Soc. of Naval Flight Surgeons, Aerospace Med. Assn.; mil: lt. comdr. USN Medical Corps 1978 –; Democrat; Episcopal; rec: swimming, skiing, sailing. Res: 4660 Huggins St San Diego 92122 Ofc: Naval Hospital, San Diego

LANDERS, NEWLIN J., contractor/ business executive; b. July 10, 1906, N. Salem, Ind.; s. De Loy and Pearl (Paige) L.; m. Margaret Richart (dec.); children: Larry, Marlin; m. 2d. Vernette Trosper, May 2, 1959; edn: Bus. Contractors Sch.; courses in personnel mgmt. Career: fmr. owner/mgr. Landers Mach. Co., Bell Gardens and E.L.A.; owner Havasu Landing, Ca.; ptnr. Selwyn-Landers Valve Co., E.L.A.; owner/mgr. Navajo Tract, Apple Valley; prop. Landers Air Strip, Gas Sta. and Water Delivery Co.; founder, Landers, Calif. (donated land for fire sta. and Homestead Valley Womens Club). Awards: Bus. Man of Week, KJST Radio Sta., Joshua Tree, Ca. 1969, Silver Medal-1st 500, Int. Biog. Ctr., Cambridge, Eng. 1985, Dir. of Notable Americans and 2000 Notable Americans, ABI Hall of Fame 1985; mem. Sheriff Rangers, Yucca Valley (recogn. for 13 years service with search and rescue, 1972); hon. mem. Landers Vol. Fire dept.; bd. dirs. Landers Moose Lodge; life mem. Intercontinental Biographical Assn.; Am. Biog. Inst. Research Assn. Life Fellow Awd. (1981); Comm. Leaders of Am. 1972; Landers Community Dinner in honor of founder on his 75th birthday (1981); mem. Nat. Wildlife Fedn.; rec: pvt. pilot, Citizens radio band. Res: 904 Landers Ln Landers Ofc: 1105 Landers Ln Landers 92284

LANDERS, THOMAS WILLIAM, III, systems-software engineering consultant; b. June 8, 1944, Dodge City, Kans.; s. Thomas Wm., Jr. and Dorothy Eileen (Mosty) L.; m. Jan S., July 8, 1967; children: Laura M. b. 1971, Alison L. b. 1974; edn: MBA, Pepperdine Univ. 1980, BA, Univ. Tex., Austin 1967; Certified Profl. Mgr. 1982. Career: software engrg. unit supv. Philco-Ford Corp., Houston 1967-72; software proj. engr. Rockwell Internat., Anaheim 1972-76, mgr. advanced systems 1979-81, mgr. systems engrg. 1977-85; pres. Systelogic Corp., Tustin 1985 –; nom. Rockwell engr. of the Yr. Award (1979), nom. Who's Who in the West (1974); secty., bd. trustees Am. Overseas Sch. of Rome 1983-84; mem. Nat. Mgmt. Assn.; publs: articles in profl. jours. and presentations at profl. confs.; Republican; Presbyterian; rec: golf, skiing, music. Res: 4418 E Fernwood Orange 92669 Ofc: Systelogic Corp., 17291 Irvine Blvd Ste 311 Tustin 92680

LANDERS, VERNETTE, author/school district counselor (ret.); b. May 3, 1912, Lawton, Okla.; d. Fred and La Verne Trosper; m. Maj. Paul A. Lum (dec.), 1955; 1 son, William Tappan; m. 2d. Newlin Landers, May 2, 1959; children: Larry, Marlin; edn: AB, honors, UCLA 1933; MA, 1935; EdD, 1953; tchg. life diploma 1940; gen. pupil personnel svcs. life diploma 1970. Career:

tchr. Montebello (Ca.) schs., 1935-45, 1948-50, 1951-59; prof. Long Beach City Coll. 1946-47, Los Angeles State Coll. 1950; dean of girls 29 Palms H.S., 1960-65; dist. counselor Morongo Unified Sch. Dist., 1965-72; coord. Adult Edn., 1965-67; dir. Guidance Proj., 1967; chg. clk., vol. Landers Post Office, 1962-83; secty. Landers Volunteer Fire Dept. 1972; v.p. Landers Assn. Inc., 1969-71; dir., secty. Desert Ears, emerg. radio serv. 1970-73; contbg. writer var. mags., jours. 1944-; recogn. awards: Intl. Biog. Centre (1973), Intl. Acad. of Poets, London, Eng. (1973), hon. dip. Univ. of Arts, Parma, Italy (1982), hon. dip. Leonardo DaVinci Intl. Acad., Rome, Italy (1982), Intl. Personnel Research Assn. (1972), Intl. Who's Who in Poetry (1980), Golden Year Bruin UCLA (1983), Golden Palm Diploma of Honor in Poetry, Leonardo Da Vinci Acad. (1984), World Culture Prize (1984), Diploma of Merit & Titular Member Internat. Com. of Internat. Ctr. of Cultural Studies and Exchanges, Rome (1984), Appreciation Plaque, USPS (1984), Appreciation, Morongo Unif. Sch. Dist. (1984), Recogn., San Gorgonio G.S. Council (1984-85), Hon. Cultural Doctorate, World Univ., Tucson, Ariz. (1985), Silver Medal-1st 500, Int. Biog. Ctr., Cambridge, Eng. (1985), num. others; life fellow: World Literary Acad., Cambridge, Internat. Biog. Assn., Cambridge; author: Impy (74), Talkie (75), Impy's Children (75), Nineteen O Four (76), Little Brown Bat (76), Slo Go (77), Who and Who Who (78), Sandy The Coydog (79), The Kit Fox and the Walking Stick (80), Poems in New Voices in Amer. Poetry (74, 75), An Anthol. on World Brotherhood and Rainbow People (81); mem: Am., Calif., Personnel and Guidance Assns., Am. Assn. for Counseling & Devel., NEA, Calif. Tchrs. Assn., Nat. Wildlife Fedn., Nat. Hist. Soc., Internat. Platform Assn., Nat. League of Am., World Inst. of Achievement (life 1985), Penwomen, Bus. and Profl. Womens Club (pres. Montebello 1940), Toastmistress (pres., Whittier 1957), Soroptimist (Soroptimist of Year, 29 Palms 1967, life mem. 1983), Landers Area CofC (secty. 1983), Desert Mem. Hosp. Guild (life), Hi Desert Playhouse Guild (life), Homestead Valley Womens Club (life), Phi Beta Kappa, Pi Lambda Theta, Sigma Delta Pi, Pi Delta Phi, Mortar Bd. Prytanean Spurs, Landers Garden Club; Community Ch.; rec: wild animals, flying. Res: 905 Landers Ln Landers 92284

LANDES, ROBERT ALTON, clinical pharmacist; b. Aug. 31, 1942, Inglewood; s. Glenn Alton and Edith Irene (Demmon) L.; edn: AA, Compton Coll. 1962; D.Pharm., USC 1966; UCLA 1981-83; MBA pgm., CSU Los Angeles 1983-; reg. pharmacist, Calif. 1966, Nevada, 1966. Career: staff pharmacist Titus Pharmacy, Santa Ana 1966-68; owner/ pres. Robert's Reports, Torrance 1983-; clin. pharmacist St. Francis Med. Ctr., Lynwood 1968-; exec. bd. Inst. for Adv. in Human Svcs.; preceptor Calif. State Bd. Pharmacy 1975-; clin. instr. USC Sch. of Pharm. 1976-80; honors: Rho Chi 1965; Horton and Converse Awd. for Excellence in the practice of pharmacy 1966; mem: Am. & So. Calif. Socs. Hosp. Pharmacists; Am. Mktg. Assn.; Orange Co. Soc. Hosp. Pharmacists (Clin. Svcs. Com.); Phi Delta Chi; S.F. Med. Ctr. Critical Care Com.; Am. Assns. for Adv. of Sci.; USC Alumni; Southwood Homeowners Assn.; Am. Running and Fitness Assn.; presentations: Devel. of Clinical Pharmacy Svcs., ASHP, San Antonio, Tex. 1978; Hand- Held Calculators and Clinical Pharmacokinetics, ASHP, San Francisco 1980; Digoxin Predictability, ASHP, New Orleans 1981; arts. in profl. journals; Republican; Baptist; rec: cycling, weight training, philatcly. Res: Robert's Reports, 21321 Marjorie Ave Torrance 90503 Ofc: St. Francis Medical Center, 3630 Imperial Highway Lynwood 90262

LANDESS, B. ROSS, health care physician, executive; b. Aug. 5, 1941, Tucumcari, N.M.; s. William H. and Lalla D. (Deatherage) L.; edn: BA, Baylor Univ. 1963; MD, Univ. of Tex. Med. Branch 1968; Diplomate Am. Bd. Family Practice 1978. Career: adult med. practitioner Ariz. Health Plan 1973-84, dir. alcohol & drug dependency 1975-84, chmn. health maint. svcs. 1981-84; v.p. CIGNA Healthplan of Ariz. 1982-84; v.p./ staff med. dir. CIGNA Healthplans of Calif. 1984-; dir. Mgmt. Alternatives Santa Fe, N.M. 1980-84; cons. Ariz. Bd. Med. Examiners 1982-84; dir. Diversified Counselors Inc. Phoenix 1977-79; alcoholism advisor mayor Phoenix 1975-79; honors: Alpha Epsilon Delta 1961; mem: Am. Acad. Family Practice, Am. Med. Soc. on Alcoholism, Phi Chi Med. Frat., Am. Acad. of Med. Dirs.; mil: capt. US Army Med. Corps 1970-72; Republican; Episcopal; rec: sailing, skiing, gardening. Res: 4785 Cromwell Ave Los Angeles 90027

LANDRY, CALISTE JOHN, JR., engineer, teacher; b. Aug. 28, 1941, Glendale; s. Caliste John and Evangeline Priscilla (Wright) L.; m. Cathy Marie Peterson, May 5, 1983; edn: BS, UC Santa Barbara 1966, PhD, 1972. Career: lectr. UC Santa Barbara 1971-; tech. staff General Research Corp., Santa Barbara 1976-80; research splst. Lockheed Research Lab., Palo Alto 1980-82; project engr. Santa Barbara Research Ctr., Santa Barbara 1982-85; pres. Electro-Optics Consultants, Santa Barbara 1983-; head mechano-optics research Ctr. for Robotic Systems UC Santa Barbara; exec. dir. Santa Barbara Sci. Discovery Ctr. 1984-; faculty Brooks Inst. of Photog., Santa Barbara 1978-; honors: Outstanding IEEE Tech. Paper, Los Angeles Dist. 1966; Cert. of Leadership, Los Angeles Dist. IEEE 1978; mem: Optical Soc. of Am., Seismological Soc. of Am., Sigma Xi, Science & Engrng. Council of Santa Barbara, Santa Barbara CofC, Aircraft Owners & Pilots Assn., Santa Barbara Science Fair Council Bd. Dirs.; works: num. tech. papers optical and acoustic holography; patent, Aerial Image Display; Democrat; Lutheran; rec: sailing, flying. Res: 663 Wakefield Rd. Goleta 93117 Ofc: UCSB Robotic Systems, 6740 Cortona Dr. Goleta 93117

LANDRY, EDWARD ANTHONY, lawyer; b. March 29, 1939, New Orleans, La.; s. Edward L.and Ellen L. (Landry) L.; m. Madeleine Rodde., June 9, 1962; children: Monique b. 1963, Lucette b. 1964; edn: BA, Louisiana State Univ. 1961, JD, UCLA Law Sch. 1964. Career: ptnr., head Probate, Trust & Estate Plnng. depts. law firm Musick, Peeler & Garrett, Los Angeles 1964-; lectr. UCLA Law Sch.; mem. bd. dirs: Music Ctr. Opera League, So. Calif. chpt. Arthritis Found., The Dan Murphy Found., Northridge Hosp. Devel Assn., trustee Harvey Mudd Coll., and CSU Northridge Trust Fund.; honors: Beta Gamma Sigma (1960), Order of the Coif (1964); mem: Am., Calif. and Los Angeles Co. Bar Assns., Chancery CLub, Am. Coll. of Probate Counsel, UCLA Law Alumni Assn., UCLA-CEB Estate Plnng. Inst., Kappa Alpha Order, Phi Delta Phi, Calif. Club, Wine & Food Soc. of So. Calif., Calif. Vintage Wine Soc., CHevalier Du Tastevin, Breakfast Panel, Northridge Tennis Club; works: author num. articles in continuing edn. law publs. rel. to estate plnng. and taxation; Republican; Catholic; rec: tennis, theater, art. Res: 9040 Newcastle Northridge 91325 Ofc: Musick, Peeler & Garrett, One Wilshire Blvd. Ste. 2000 Los Angeles 90017

LANDRY, WAYNE CHARLES, physician-surgeon; b. July 22, 1937, Easton, Pa.; s. Wm. Robert and Marguerite (Hoffman) L.; m. Kay Jean, Aug. 22, 1980; children: Curtis Wayne b. 1981, Tiffany Amber b. 1982; edn: BS, Albright Coll. 1961; MS, UC Irvine 1971; MD, Calif. Coll. of Medicine UCI 1974. Career: gynecologist and cosmetic surgeon in pvt. practice, Tustin 1980-; pres. Orange County Liposuction Medical Clinic Inc. 1985-; mem. Am. Acad. Cosmetic Surgery, Am. Soc. of Liposuction Surgery Inc., Am. Coll. Obstets. & Gynecols., Calif. Liposuction Soc. (charter), Orange Co. Liposuction Soc. (charter); Republican; Prot.; rec: old cars. Ofc: Wayne C. Landry MD Inc 14591 Newport Ave Ste 111 Tustin 92680

LANDUN, HOWARD STEPHEN, insurance underwriter; b. July 6, 1949, Montreal, Canada; s. Bob and Sylvia L.; m. Doreen, Dec. 22, 1973; children: Brian b. 1977, Jason b. 1981; edn: BA, CSU Northridge 1974. Career: life ins. agent Mass. Mutual Life Insurance Co., 1974-; named Agent of the Year, S.F.V. Agcy. (1982, 84, 85), Life and Qualifying mem. Million Dollar Round Table; mem. San Fernando Valley Life Underws. Assn. (pres. 1983-84), Calif. Life Underws. Assn. (trustee 1985-); civic: Newbury Park AYSO youth soccer (bd.); Republican; rec: soccer coaching, ins. writing & speaking. Ofc: Howard S. Landun 22801 Ventura Blvd Woodland Hills 91364

LANE, DON VALENCION, photographer; b. May 24, 1953, Newport News, Va.; s. Paul and Louise R. Lane; edn: AA photog., San Francisco City Coll. 1973; BA flimmaking, San Francisco State Univ. 1977, MA cinematography, 1983. Career: owner Don Lane Photographs, San Francisco; lectr. film history, SFSU 1979-80; dir. Channel 25 S.F. public access TV station 1981; honors: 2nd Place Drama div. Black Filmmakers Hall of Fame Film Competition (1979), mem: Profl. Photogs. of Am., Profl. Photogs. of S.F., Black Filmmakers Hall of Fame, Am. Bowling Congress, Profl. Central Calif. Bowlers; works: film drama: Decisions; film documentary: Attitude; Democrat; rec: bowling, swimming. Address: 2429 Diamond St San Francisco 94131

LANE, GEORGE IRVING, lawyer; b. Feb. 1, 19-, San Francisco; s. George W. and Helen (Green) L.; m. Lourdes Sevilla, Nov. 28, 1981; 1 dau. Jani b. 1984; edn: AA, San Jose State Univ. 1955; JD, Univ. San Francisco 1963; admitted Calif. State Bar 1964. Career: tchr. Campbell H.S. 1955-56; claims rep. Calif. State Auto Assn. 1956-64; atty. pvt. practice 1964-85; city atty. City of Live Oak, Calif. 1969-78; dep. dist. atty. Yuba County 1971-74; defense counsel Cal-Farm Ins. Co. 1978-; honors: Phi Kappa Phi; mem: Calif., Fresno Co. bar assns.; mil: sgt. US Army 1948-52, Bronze Star, Korean Svc. w/ Silver Battle Star; Catholic. Res: 851 E Decatur Fresno 93710

LANE, JOHN WILLIAM, instrumentation sales co. president; b. Oct. 14, 1931, Phila.; s. Thomas Joseph and Annie (Rotzell) L.; m. Virginia Patterson, Aug. 4, 1984; edn: mech. engring., Pa. State Univ. 2 yrs. Career: calibrator, order ed., project engr., salesman Fischer & Porter Co., Warminster, Pa.; mfg. rep. coordinator Fluidyne, Oakland, Calif.; product mgr. ITT Barton Instruments, City of Industry; area mgr. Transmation, Buena Park; dist. mgr. Rochester Instrument Systems, Inc.; current: prin. John W. Lane & Assocs. Inc., Fullerton; senior mem. Instrument Soc. of Am., contbr. to first ISA Exhib., Anchorage, Alaska (1980); mil: s/sgt. US Air Force 1949-53, Korean Theatre; Republican; Roman Catholic; rec: golf. Res: 15140 Granada Ave La Mirada 90638 Ofc: John W. Lane & Associates Inc. 2742 West Orangethorpe Ste P Fullerton 92633-4269

LANEY, WILLIAM CHARLES, international funding executive; b. Aug. 14, 1922, Frederick, Okla.; s. Willis Earl and Ina Adeline (Parish) L.; m. Elizabeth Swanson, Mar. 27, 1943; children: Karen b. 1952, William b. 1956; edn: mech. engring., USC 1942. Career: tool design engr. Lockheed Aircraft 1942-44; tech. supvr., US Atomic Energy Commn. Phillips Petroleum Corp. 1950-65; nuclear fuels engr., US AEC, United Nuclear Corp. 1965-70; dir. Calif. ops., oil prodn., Am. Resources Mgmt. Corp. 1970-75; v.p./ dir. engring. Hydro-Combo Corp. 1973-77; mem. tech. staff, environmental test, classified satellites, Rockwell Internat. 1981-82; fin. and internat. funding coord., 1979-; agt. Estate and Trust Properties, Sunset Co., Santa Barbara 1985-; dir. Kemp Reduction Corp. 1985-; mem. Santa Barbara Bd. of Realtors; patents: relating to Oil Producing Indus., Oil Well completion safety system (202), Mining dredge; tech. paper presented Internat. Nuclear Symp., Gatlinburg, Tenn. (1956); mil: cadet USAF 1944-45, GCM; Republican; Ch. of Jesus Christ of Latter-Day Saints (Bishop); rec: Native Am. hist. & archaeol., Legend Mines, hunting. Res: 902 El Rancho Rd Santa Barbara 93108 Ofc: Sunset Co 140 Hot Springs Rd Santa Barbara 93108

LANG, JAMES DELMER, Entomologist; b. Feb. 13, 1942, Santa Monica; s. Delmer Theide and Mary Jane (Gillespie) L.; edn: BA, Univ. of No. Dakota

1969; MS, Univ. of Ariz. 1972, PhD, 1975; postgrad. research assoc. in entomology, UC Riverside 1975-78. Career: grad. asst. in research Dept. Entomology Univ. Ariz., Tucson 1971-74, tchg. asst. 1974-75; postgrad. research assoc. Dept. Entomology Univ. of Calif., Riverside 1975-78; public health entomologist Riverside Co. Health Dept. 1978—; reviewer Journ. of Medial Entomology; ed. authors' manuscripts of medical entomological topics; Riverside Co. Health Dept. rep. for the Co. Poultry Advy. Com.; county rep. Fly Abatement Com.; recognized authority on human lice and house dust mites; cons. Calif. State Health Svc.; 8 month butterfly survey of a nature preserve near Palm Springs, Nature Conservancy Assn.; honors: three different species of mites new to science named for when found on beetles collected in Vietnam; mem: Entomological Soc. of Am., Soc. of Vector Ecologists, Am. Mosquito and Control Assoc., Aubudon Soc., Am. Mus. of Natural History, Nature Conservancy, Nat. Wildlife Fedn.; works: senior author or co-author 25 scientific publications dealing with medical or public health entomological topics pub. in entomological journs.; author of children's short story, The Little Frog; mil: splst. 4/c US Army 1967-69, Air Medal, Army Commdn., GCM, Vietnamese Honor Medal (II Class); Democrat; Lutheran; rec: butterfly collecting, oil and watercoloring painting, camping. Res: 2839 Wyoming Way Riverside 92506 Ofc: Riverside County Health Dept., 3575 Eleventh St. Mall Riverside 92502

LANG, PATRICK JAMES, chiropractor; b. Jan. 30, 1951, St. Paul, Minn.; s. Mathias Aloysius and Katherine Ann (Condon) L.; edn: West Los Angeles Coll. 1974-75; AA, Santa Monica Call. 1976; BS, Los Angeles Coll. of Chiropractic 1978, DC, 1979. Career: dir. of clinics Beyerle Chiropractic Corp., El Monte 1980-81; clinic dir. Parker Chiropractic Group, El Cajon 1981-83; clinic dir. So. Bay Chiropractic Center (Spector Chiropractic Corp.), National City 1983—; Erhardt X-Ray Seminars 1979; Parker Sch. for Profl. Success 1985; mem: Am. Chiropractic Assn., Parker Chiropractic Research Found., Found. for Chiropractic Edn. and Research, Los Angeles Coll. of Chiropractic Alumni Assn.; rec: fishing, camping, hiking. Ofc: South Bay Chiropractice Center, Spector Chiropractic Corp., 1722-F Sweetwater Rd. National City 92050

LANG, TZU-WANG, professor of medicine; b. Apr. 15, 1929, Hsiang-Shan, Hsien, Chekiang Provind, China, nat. US cit. 1977; s. Wang-Chieh and Chun-Hsiang (Chang) L.; grandson of Jing-Bang Lang, the Scholar of the Ching Dynasty (1884-1950); m. Winnie Chi, Apr. 15, 1960; children: Daniel b. 1962, Cathy Mae b. 1972; edn: MB, Nat. Defense Medical Center 1955; MD, Nat. Acad. Bd. in Med. 1955. Career: research fellow Am. Coll. of Cardiology, 1963-65; prin. investigator Cardiovascular Research, VA Gen. Hosp., Taiwan 1966-68; chief of cardiology, Tri-Service Gen. Hosp., Taiwan 1967-69; senior research scientist Dept. Medicine Cedars-Sinai Med. Center, Los Angeles 1969-78; adj. assoc. prof., assoc. clin. prof. medicine UC Los Angeles, 1976—; awards: Gold Medal in sci., Taiwan (1962), Young Investigator award finalist, Am. Coll. Cardiology, Boston (1965); mem: Fellow Am. Coll. Cardiology, Am. Heart Assn., Am. Soc. of Echocardiography, AMA, Calif. Med. Assn.; works:one of the pioneers of synchronized retro-perfusion (SRP) for the treatment of coronary artery disease (Am. Jour. Cardiol. 1976, 78); author over 90 sci. papers and contbr. chapters to 4 textbooks on cardiology; Confucianism. Res: 301 N Elm Dr Beverly Hills 90210 Ofc: 8920 Wilshire Blvd Ste 104 Beverly Hills 90211

LANG, W(ILLIAM) HAROLD, entomologist; b. Nov. 27, 1901, Tulare; s. Edmund David and Ruth (McNeely) L.; m. Helen Thompson, March 25, 1925; children: Barbara b. 1926, Gilbert b. 1932, Lawrence b. 1942; edn: BS, Univ. of Calif. 1924. Career: sales Calif. Spray Chem. Corp. 1928-46; citrus rancher 1926-70; citrus cons. 1946—; dir. Bridgford Foods 1958—; trustee Fullerton H.S. & coll. 1948-52, bd. pres. 1951-52; mem: Fullerton Kiwanis (pres. 1946), Elks, Orange Co. Hist. Soc. (pres. 1969-70), County Admin. Dir. Bicentennial; publs: historical writing 1970-; author, Island of the Pacific, Great Western Pub. Co. 1983; Great Explorers of the Sailing Era; Orange County Stories; Republican; Protestant; rec: travel, writing, athletics. Res: 700 Ocean View Dr. Fullerton 92632

LANGE, CLIFFORD E., library director; b. Dec. 29, 1935, Fond du Lac, Wis.; s. Elmer H. and Dorothy Brick (Smithers) L.; m. Janet M. LeMieux, June 6, 1959; children: Paul, Laura, Ruth; edn: stu. St. Norbert Coll. 1954-57; BS, Wis. State Univ. 1959; MSLS (Library Services Act scholar), Univ. Wis., 1960, PhD (Higher Edn. Act fellow), 1972. Career: head Extension Dept. Oshkosh (Wis.) Public Library, 1960-62, head Reference Dept., 1962-63; asst. dir. Jervis Library, Rome, NY 1962; dir. Eau Claire (Wis.) Public Library, 1963-66; asst. dir. Lake County Public Library, Giffith, Ind., 1966-68; asst. prof. Sch. Library Sci. Univ. Iowa, 1971-73; dir. Wauwatosa (Wis.) Public Library, 1973-75; asst. prof. USC, 1975-78; state librarian New Mexico State Library, Santa Fe, 1978-82; dir. Carlsbad (Calif.) City Library, 1982—; mem: ALA, Calif. Library Assn.; mil: US Army 1958. Res: 3780 Garfield St., Carlsbad 92008 Ofc: 1250 Elm Ave Carlsbad 92008

LANGE, KELLY, television anchorperson; b. Flushing, Long Island, NY; d. Edmund V. and Alice (Reason) Scafard; 1 child, Kelly Snyder; edn: BA, English, Merrimack Coll., N. Andover, Mass. Career: Ladybird reporter from helicopter, KABC Radio, Los Angeles 1967-72; news reporter and co-host Sunday Show, KNBC-TV, 1w1-81; weather caster, KNBC News, 1971-76; anchorperson, 1976—, anchor 4 and 6 p.m. hour news Mon. thru Fri.; host: Strange As It Seems 1981, Take My Advice 1975-76, NBC's Rose Parade 1975-82, Kelly's LA 1975-; interviews: film stars, politicians, govt. leaders; Vacation anchor, NBC's Nightly News, 1976—; Vacation host, Today Show, 1976—, Tomorrow Show 1976-81; speaker num. clubs and orgns.; rec: fgn. travel, restoring antiques, cars, skiing. Ofc: 3000 W. Alameda Ave Burbank 91523

LANGENEGGER, BRUCE FRED, equipment rental co. executive; b. Apr. 18, 1936, San Francisco; s. Fred John Charles and Esther Elizabeth (Sippo) L.; m. Audrey, Dec. 16, 1961; 1 dau. Kristin b. 1962; edn: Whitworth Coll. 1954-55, Univ. of Wash. 1955-58; Vernon Sch. of Real Estate 1964; Calif. lic. R.E. sales 1964. Career: prodn. control mgr. Watkins-Johnson, Palo Alto 1964-69, Calif. Microwave, Sunnyvale 1970-71, Nat. Semiconductor, Santa Clara 1972-73, Sierra Electronics, Redwood City 1974, Eimac (div. Varian), San Carlos 1975-77; exec. v.p. Wilkinson Equip. Co., Inc., San Jose 1978—; honors: univ. scholastic scholarships (1953, 54), Alpha Epsilon Delta nat. premed. hon. soc. (1957); mem. Am. Prodn. & Inventory Control Soc. (1962-), Calif. Rental Assn., Univ. Wash. Alumni Assn., Sigma Alpha Epsilon Frat. (1954-), Sunnyvale Mens Golf Club; Republican; Presbyterian; rec: golf. Res: 1441 Kyle Ct Sunnyvale 94087 Ofc: Wilkinson Equip. Co. Inc. 2150 O'Toole Ave San Jose 95131

LANGLEY, MATTHEW GREGORY, business owner; b. April 7, 1954, Santa Cruz; s. Glenn Marvin and Dona Louise (Weeks) L. Career: Martys Catering Svc., San Carlos 1967-69; Sams Family Steakhouse 1970-72; sales clerk Donas Hallmark, San Carlos 1973-74; mgr. Hallmark, San Carlos 1973-74; mgr. Donas Hallmark, Menlo Park 1975; sales clerk Target Surplus, Redwood City 1976; driver, shipping clerk Consolidated Publs. 1977-78; owner Donas Hallmark, San Carlos 1979—; honors: Beautification Award, San Carlos CofC 1979; mem. Nat. Assn. of Watch and Clock Collectors 1979-80; Republican; Presbyterian; rec: collecting coca-cola memorabilia, neon beer signs, antiques. Res: 152 Belvedere San Carlos 94070 Ofc: Donas Hallmark, 701 Laurel Ave. San Carlos 94070

LANNI, J. MICHAEL, financial services co. president; b. Mar. 14, 1943, Los Angeles; s. Anthony Warren and Mary Lucille (Leahy) L.; m. Margaret Ellen, July 31, 1976; children: John Michael b. 1979, Melissa Ann b. 1982; edn: BS, USC 1965, MBA, 1967. Career: asst. comml. credit supr. United California Bank, Los Angeles 1965-67; dir. bus. devel. Great Western Finl. Corp., Beverly Hills 1967-70; v.p. mktg. Computing and Software, L.A. 1970-71; dir. mktg. Kaiser Aetna, Rancho Calif. 1971-78; pres./chief exec. Western Finl. Group, Newport Beach 1978—; v.p., dir. Eagle Valley Water Dist.; dir. Home Sell of America Inc.; honors: Karl Frederick Gauss Mathematics Award; Commerce Assocs. (dir. 1977-; v.p. 1982; Outstanding service awards 1980, 81, 82, 83); mem. Calif. Thoroughbred Breeders Assn., Horsemens Benevolent and Protective Assn., Los Angeles Turf Club, Hollywood Park Turf Club; Los Angeles Bachelors (1970-76), Los Solteros (1970-76, pres. 1976); civic: Boys Republic (dir. 1975, bd. trustees 1976); Republican; Roman Catholic. Res: 1907 Yacht Truant Newport Beach 92660 Ofc: Western Financial Group 4041 MacArthur Blvd Ste 170 Newport Beach 92660

LANNI, MARY LOU, educator; b. Los Angeles; d. Anthony Warren and Lucille (Leahy) Lanni; dir. desc. of Israel Putnam (one of four maj. gens. of Am. Revolution) and Rufus Putnam (built armaments at West Point, led settlers to Ohio); edn: Immaculate Heart Prep.; BSc, MS, USC. Career: tchr., pvt. schs., Los Angeles Co. chs. 1960; L.A. Unif. Sch. Dist. 1961—; supvg. tchr. UCLA Tchr. Tng. 1961-64; master tchr., USC Tchr. Tng. Pgm. 1965-79; partner Greenhill Stables (Thoroughbred horse racing), 1967-70; dir. pub. rels. Delta Design 1981—; cons. for ednl. film. 1972; filmed interview for Japaneses TV, American Education: Science Applications, 1974; tchr. math., sci. and soc. sci. insvc. classes for tchrs. 1965—; author part of teachers exam. for Sch. dist. 1970; awards: UCLA Math. Conf., Computer Programming Am. Legion Essay Awd.; USC awds. for svc. to tchg. profession 1972-76; NSF Marine Edn. Pgm. Grant & Cert. 1978-79; Eng. as a Second Lang. Tng. Pgm. Cert. 1980-81; mem: L.A. Opera Assocs.; Commerce Assocs.; USC Intergreek Soc.; Trojan Club; editor for publs: Americans, Then and Now, and Geometry, Use It; contbr. Computers And Kids; rec: skiing, painting, antiques. Res: POB 5496 Beverly Hills 90210

LANS, CARL GUSTAV, architect; b. Oct. 19, 1907, Gothenburg, Sweden; s. Carl and Ida (Sjon) G.; m. Iris Meyer, Dec. 21, 1935; children: Douglas, b. 1937; Randolph, b. 1938; edn: City Coll. of NY 1925-26; Columbia Univ. 1926-30. Career: chief engr. inspector U.S. Dept. of Agriculture, Wash DC 1935-38; supvg. architect Federal Housing Adminstrn., 1938-48; partner John H. Graham & Assoc., Architects, 1947-55; tech. dir. Nat. Assn. of Home Bldrs., 1948-52; V.P. Architecture, Earl W. Smith Orgn., Berkeley, Calif. 1952-55; internat. practice architecture w/ ofcs. in Seoul, Korea 1955—; research, lectr. real estate economics, Hotel consultation; recipient Citation & Medal of Achiev., Pres. of Korea; mem: Am. Inst. of Architects; Bldg. Research Adv. Bd., Nat. Acad. of Scis.; Southwest Research Inst.; Seismological Soc. of Am.; Prestressed Concrete Inst.; Urban Land Inst.; works: thesis, Earthquake Constrn. 1954; advr. on urban redevel. to Pres. of Korea post-Korean War/ dir. ednl. pgm. 1955-56; guest lectr. var. univs. 1949-62. Address: Carl G. Lans, A.I.A., Architect, 21821 Fairlane Cir Huntington Beach 92646

LANSFORD, WILLARD DALE, manufacturers representative; b. June 2, 1940, Checotah, Okla.; s. Daniel Madison and Doris Ilene (Clay) L.; m. Virdean Janie, Sept. 12, 1963; children: Jeffrey Todd b. 1965, Nichole Holli b. 1968; edn: Assoc., Los Angeles Trade Tech. 1964; San Mateo Coll. 1966; Compton Coll. 1967; Alexander Hamilton Sch. 1968-69. Career: with Sigler Inc. 1964-69; junior engr. Holly Div., South Gate 1964; mgr. testing lab., San Francisco 1965; lab testing and equipment design air condition equipment, South Gate 1967; prodn. mgr. hydronic fan coils 1968; prod. mgr. air condition and forced air heating equipment Holly div. 1969; junior ptr. W.O. Johnson & Asoc. Mfg. Rep. orgn. 1970; currently, sole owner AVR Asociates; mem: ASHRAE, RSES, Am. Soc. of Gas Engrs., Toastmasters, YMCA, Bobbysox

(Cer-ART-Nor); mil: USAF 1958-62; Democrat; Ch. of Jesus Christ LDS; rec: tennis, golf. Ofc: AVR Associates, Artesia 90701

LARGE, DAVID JAMES, electrical engineer; b. Dec. 31, 1940, Puyallup, Wash.; s. Wm. Henry, Jr. and Alice Arminta (Cox) L.; m. Sally Jo Shepherd, June 28, 1963; children: Sean, b. 1970, Cynthia, b 1972; edn: BSEE, Calif. Inst. of Tech. 1963; CSU San Jose 1964-5, DeAnza Coll. 1975, West Valley Coll. 1976. Career: project engr. Eimac Div. Varian Assocs., San Carlos 1963-67; sr. devel. engr. Varian Assocs., Palo Alto 1967; section hd. Instrument Devel., Kruse Electronics div. Systron Donner Corp., Sunnyvale 1968-73; senior mem. tech. staff Avantek Inc., Santa Clara 1973-78; chief engr. Gill Cable TV, San Jose 1978-82; v.p. engring. Gill Industries, San Jose 1982 —; bd. dirs. Mtn. Charlie Water Co. 1981-; mem: IEEE (senior), Soc. of Cable TV Engrs. (sr.), Nat. Cable TV Assn. (engring. subcom. on consumer interconnection), Calif. Cable TV Assn. (telecomm. policy com.), Alumni Assn. Caltech, inventions: Cavity Input Tuner (1965), Active Diode Oscillator (1971); publs: 15 tech. arts. in nat. mags., 1966-83; 10 tech. papers, regl. & nat. confs. 1976-83; Ind.; rec: house constrn., electronic musical instr. design. Res: 26175 Pierce Rd Los Gatos 95030 Ofc: Gill Industries 234 E Gish Rd San Jose 95112

LARGE, TIMOTHY WALLACE, administrator, accountant; b. Feb. 23, 1942, Palo Alto, Calif.; s. Charles Delano Henry and Jean Eleanor (Parker) L.; m. Vickie Olson, Aug. 6, 1978; children: Jonathan b. 1980, Sarah b. 1982; edn: BS bus. adminstrn., Menlo Coll. 1964; MBA, Univ. Santa Clara 1966; M.Divinity Talbot Theol. Seminary, Biola Univ. 1978; CPA Calif. 1984. Career: dir. stewardship Instituto Evangelico La Puente, Calif. 1978 —; acct. Conservative Baptist Assn. of So. Calif. 1978-83, H. Canaday Public Acctg. Santa Fe Springs 1983-85; adminstr. Temple Baptist Ch. and Temple Christian Sch. Perris 1985 —; instr. acctg. Univ. Md. 1967-68, Biola Univ. 1977-78, Calif. Baptist Coll. 1983-84; fellow ch. bus. adminstrn. (Nat. Assn. Ch. Bus. Adminstrs. 1982); mem: Am. Mgmt. Assn., Christian Mgmt. Ministries Assn., Nat. Assn. Ch. Bus. Adminstrs., Founder's Chpt. Kidney Found. of So. Calif. (treas.); mil: sp5 US Army 1965-72; Republican; Conservative Baptist. Res: 26928 Potomac Dr Sun City 92381 Ofc: Temple Baptist Church 745 N Perris Blvd Perris 92370

LARGMAN, KENNETH, strategic analyst, strategic defense analysis co. executive; b. Apr. 7, 1949, Phila.; s. Franklin Spencer and Roselynd Marjorie (Golden) L.; m. Suzanna Forest, Nov. 7, 1970; l child, Jezra b. 1971; edn: State Univ. NY, Old Westbury 1969-70. Career: independent strategic analyst 1970-80; c.e.o. World Security Council 1980 —; extensive research in strategic defense; cons. to top US political and military leaders 1985; working to arrange meetings with US and Soviet leaders; plays US/ Soviet move- counternove simulation games in Pentagon, Soviet Embassy, Capitol Hill; mem: Air Force Assn., Am. Inst. Aero. and Astro., Am. Astronautical Soc., Commonwealth Club, World Affairs Council; author: num. books on prevention of nuclear war; rec: mountaineering, nature, fgn. travel. Ofc: World Security Council 303 World Trade Center San Francisco 94111

LARIVEY, ROBERTA MARIE, manufacturing co. executive; b. June 29, 1950, Buffalo, N.Y.; d. Robert E. and Marie Ellen (McNiff) Larivey; edn: AA bus. adm., Erie Comm. Coll. 1972; BS bus. adm., State Univ. N.Y. at Buffalo 1976; MBA, Pepperdine Univ. 1980. Career: chemistry techn. Cancer Research, Roswell Park Meml. Cancer Res. Inst., Orchard Park, N.Y. 1968-77; export sales, Moody Sprinkler & Irrigation Co., Costa Mesa, Calif. 1977-78; cofounder/ pres./ gen. mgr. Calif. Orthopaedic Lab. Inc., Lakewood 1978 —; mem. Modern Plastics advis. bd. (1980); mem. US CofC, Long Beach CofC, Soroptomists Internat.; Republican; rec: womens softball, co-ed softball, biking. Ofc: California Orthopaedic Lab. 3710 Industry Ave Ste 201 Lakewood 90712

LARKINS, MARION L., federal management executive; b. May 16, 1949, Desoto, Mo.; d. Daniel O. and Mary Frances (Tyus) Meadows; m. William M. Larkins, May 10, 1980; 1 dau, Melanie b. 1982; edn: BS, Univ. of Arkansas 1971. Career: with Social Security Admin.; claims rep., St. Louis, Mo., Atlanta, Ga., and Independence, Kans. 1971-77; ops. supvr., Monrovia 1977-78; ops. ofcr., Glendale 1978-79; area admin. asst., Los Angeles 1979-82, dist. mgr. 1983-85; dist. mgr. Glendale 1985 —; mgmt. workshop trainer; mem. Regl. SSA Los Angeles/ Orange Co. Combined Fed. Campaign, chmn. 1980-85; Mgmt. Com. 1984-86; Regl. Merit Pay Com. 1985; honors: High Quality Awards, SSA 1977, 82; Merit Pay Awards, 1984, 85, 86; mem: Mgmt. Assn. (SSA), Women Execs., Wadsworth Ch. of God. (Sunday sch. tchr.), Foothill Jobs, Reading Tutor; publs: potery, Combined Fed. Campaign Newspaper 1984-86; Democrat; rec: writing. Ofc: Social Security Adiminstratior, 318 W. Wilson Ave. Glendale

LARNER, JULES, physician-surgeon, ret.; b. Oct. 24, 1910, Los Angeles; s. Max and Esther Larner; m. Ruth Genss, Feb. 9, 1955; children: Douglas b. 1950, Jakki b. 1951; edn: MD, Calif. Coll. of Med. 1962; DO, Coll. Osteopathic Physicians & Surgeons. Career: staff physician, founder Sequoia Hosp., Fresno (1942), San Gabriel Valley Hosp., San Gabriel (1948); attending staff Dept. Surgery, L.A. County Gen. Hosp., Los Angeles 1953-58; bd. chmn. and pres. Glendora Hosp., Glendora 1960-67; ret.; named Bonds for Israel Man of Year (1968); recipient disting. service awards: San Gabriel Valley Hosp. (1973), Jewish Big Brothers (1975), Jewish Fedn. Council E. Area (1983); mem. San Gabriel Valley Osteopathic Soc. (pres. 1958-59); past mem. Fresno Rotary, Elks, Odd Fellows; mem: Pasadena Bnai Brith, Jewish Fedn. Council United Jewish Fund, Fellow Anti-Defamation League, Del Rey Yacht Club (past bd.); established Larner Educational Trust and Larner Chapel at Temple Shaarei Tikvah, Arcadia; publs: article on San Joaquin Fever; Republican; Jewish; rec: yachting, golf. Res: 3491 Lombardy Rd Pasadena 91107

LARSEN, CARTER LAWRENCE, investor; b. Feb. 10, 1919, Phila., Penn.; s. John Lawrence and Caroline (Miller) L.; m. Carita Martin, June 6, 1952; children: Carter, Jr., b. 1955; Martin Scott, . 1953; Brett F.M., b. 1957; Caroline, b. 1959; edn: BS, Bucknell Univ. 1940; MBA, Harvard Univ. 1947. Career: banker, investor, vineyardist; currently, owner/ mgr. vineyard; dir. Eastern Ore. Land Co.; dir. Stearns Ranchos; pres. Taunton Inc.; mem: Pacific Union Club, University Club, Harvard Club of NYC; mil: commdr., USNR, Ltr. Commdn. WWII, 4 battle stars; Protestant. Res: 3621 Washington St., San Francisco 94118 and Alexander Valley, Sonoma County

LARSEN, HENRY ALBERT, co. executive; b. Oct. 15, 1912, Farwell, Nebr.; s. Rudolph and Anna (Mikelsen) L.; m. Helen L. Wolcott, Mar. 16, 1985; children: Brooke (Garlock) b. 1952, Candace (Templeton) b. 1955; edn: BS in econs. and fin., Univ. Nebr. 1935. Career: v.p. Greater Mountain Chemical Co., Monterey Park; personnel dir. J.W. Robinson Co., L.A.; sales mgr. Burlington Mills, L.A.; current: corp. mgr. John L. Fellows & Son, Burbank; pres. Larsen Imports, Pasadena; prof. of retailing Lewis & Clark Univ.; awards: "E" citations (2) for organizing the most effective war bond drive in Chgo., US Army and USN; listed Los Angeles Social Blue Book Registry; civic: (Chgo.): Kiwanis (dir.), CofC (dir.), YMCA (dir.); club: Valley Hunt (Pasadena); Democrat; rec: writing, hunting, fishing. Res: 3535 Locksley Dr Pasadena 91107 Ofc: John L. Fellows & Son 3100 W Magnolia Blvd Burbank 91505

LARSON, GARY DWAYNE, architect; b. Aug. 5, 1944, Nevada City; s. Roy W. and Alice M. L.; m. Sherrill Ann Smiley, Dec. 13, 1968; children: Britta b. 1973, John b. 1981, Sarah b. 1983; edn: AA, Am. River Coll. 1965; Calif. State Polytechnic Univ. 1966-70; reg. architect, Calif. 1977. Career: assoc. McCarthy Assocs., Paso Robles 1969-71; devel. coord. Condominiums West inc., Tahoe City 1971; assoc. Richard Dorman FAIA and Assocs., Los Angeles 1971-76; facilites plnnr. The Church on the Way, Los Angeles 1976-78; dir. of design Theodore Barry & Assoc., Los Angeles 1978; principal Larson Architects, Los Angeles 1978 —; mem. bd. of regents Calif. Theological Seminary 1986; honors: Merit Award for design, San Fernando Valley chpt. Am. Inst. Architects 1983, 84, Honor Award for design, 1984 mem: Am. Inst. Architects (San Fernando Valley chpt. bd. dirs. 1982-, treas. 1985), Salvation Army (San Fernando Valley adv. bd., bd. chmn. 1985), Joni and Friends (bd. dirs.); mil: splst. 5 USAR 1968-74; Republican; Christian. Ofc: Gaede & Larson Architects, 95 N Marengo Ave Pasadena 91101

LARSON, H. PHILLIP, marketing co. executive; b. Jan. 18, 1938, Onawa, Ia.; s. Dale Newton and Mary Ethel Bell (Kimble) L.; children: Teri Lynne, b. 1959; Steven Dale, b. 1962; edn: Coll. Equiv., 1 yr., Mil. GED. Career: v.p. Liqui-Brush Corp. 1966-68; pres./ owner Pacific Prods. 1969-72; v.p. Friendly, Inc. 1972-73; sales mgr. Bookkeepers Svc. 1973-76; group coord. Ideal Inc. 1976-78; nat. tng. dir. Golden Youth Mktg. 1978-80; gen. mgr. Herbalife Internat. Inc. 1980 —; mil: E.G. USN 1955-66, Nat. Defense, GCM, Vietnam Svc.; rec: sports, ednl. reading. Res: 9416 Zelzah Ave Northridge 91325 Ofc: 5721 Slauson Ave Culver City

LARSON, MARION LEE, healthcare executive; b. Dec. 14, 1941, Cornwall, N.Y.; d. Charles Earle and Ruby Lee (Manning) Matthews; m. Emmett Larson, Mar. 18, 1967, div. 1984; edn: Ridgewood Sch. of Bus. 1960-62. Career: asst. mgr. Blue Shield of California, San Francisco 1966-71, mgr. Provider Certification and Profile 1971-74, dir. CHAMPUS Ops. 1974-83, dir. Medicare Ops. 1975-83, dir. CHAMPUS Ops., Escondido 1983-85, dir., mgmt. splst. Blue Shield of Calif., S.F. 1985 —; mem. Nat. Assn. for Female Execs.; Republican; Methodist; rec: sports enthusiast, problem solving. Res: 554 Windlass Ln Foster City 94404 Ofc: Blue Shield of California 2 North Point San Francisco 94133

LARSON, THALIA LYDA, speech and hearing consultant, ret.; b. Mar. 15, 1912, Foraker, Okla.; d. Hugh Curtis and Magnolia (Hart) Wilson; m. Carl Olof Larson, Aug. 17, 1935; children: Curtis Carl b. 1939, Carol Lynn b. 1946; edn: BA, Univ. So. Calif. 1932; MA, CSU Long Beach 1958. Career: principal Mecca Elem. Sch. Mecca, Calif. 1934-36; tchr. Newport Elem. Schs. Newport Beach 1948-57; speech therapist Santa Ana Schs. 1958-64; faculty CSU Fullerton speech communication 1964-70, special edn., tchr. tng. 1973-76; cons. pvt. practice speech pathol. 1964-77; honors: Delta Zeta Lamplighter of So. Calif. Award (Women of Achievement); mem: Am., Calif. Speech & Hearing Assns. (life), Zeta Phi Eta, Calif. Teachers Assn. (life), Eastern Star, Parkinsons Support Group, China Painters Originals; publ: article in Academic Therapy (1971), book: Communication for the Nonverbal Child (1973); Presbyterian; rec: travel, china painting. Res: Laguna Hills

LARSON, WILLIAM JOHN, manufacturing co. financial executive; b. May 1, 1941, Elkhorn, Wis.; s. Walter August and Helen Louise (Woodford) L.; m. Jean Ann, Oct. 2, 1981; children: Mark b. 1966, Susan b. 1969; edn: BBA, Univ. of Wis. 1964; Certified Public Acct., Wis. (1967). Career: staff acct. Price Waterhouse, Milwaukee, Wis. 1964-80, San Jose, Calif. 1980-83, ptnr. of firm 1975-83; with Verbatim Corp., Sunnyvale 1983-84, senior v.p. fin., 1985 —; mem. Masters of Taxation Advis. Council, CSU San Jose 1984-; mem. Am. Inst. CPAs (chmn. Milwaukee Chpt. 1977), Tax Execs. Inst.; civic: Boy Scouts. Am., Santa Clara County Council (treas. 1981-85, v.p. admin. 1986); Republican; Methodist; rec: golf, camping, bridge, outdoor sports. Res: 7060 Elmsdale Dr San Jose 95120 Ofc: Verbatim Corp. 323 Soquel Way Sunnyvale 94086

LA SALVIA, TONY, farmer, wholesale meat packer; b. Sept. 11, 1911, Los Banos; s. Joseph Fortunato and Maria (Lagrutta) LaS.; m. Laura Iacopi, July 28, 1935; children: Antonia Marie (Ebner) b. 1941, Nicola Claire (Smith) b.

1943, Steven Joseph b. 1948. Career: meat packing bus. 1930-, ptnrship owner Los Banos Abattoir (slaughtering plant) 1940-, owner/pres. 1966—; mem. Lions Club, Volunteer Fire Dept.; Catholic; avocation: farming, livestock. Res: 1227 California St Los Banos 93635 Ofc: Los Banos Abattoir POB 949 Los Banos 93635

LASH, HARVEY, plastic surgeon, b. Sept. 19, 1926, Lorain, Ohio; s. Harry and Helen (Milner) L.; children: Alan D. (M.D.) b. 1953, Robert E. (M.D.) b. 1957; edn: DDS, cum laude, Ohio State Univ. 1951, MD, cum laude, 1955; MS, Univ. Minn. 1961; lic. physician and surgeon, Calif. 1960. Career: pvt. practice of dentistry, Columbus, O. 1951-56; instr. Ohio State Univ. Coll. of Medicine, Columbus 1951-54, Ohio State Coll. of Dentistry, 1952-55; intern University Hosp., Columbus, O. 1955-56; resident gen. surgery Western Reserve Univ., Metropolitan Gen. Hosp., 1956-58; fellow in plastic surg. Mayo Clinic 1958-61; clin. asst. prof. plastic surg. Stanford Univ. 1961—; chmn. Dept. Plastic & Reconstructive Surg., Palo Alto Med. Found., Palo Alto 1961—; mem: Am. Soc. of Maxillofacial Surgeons (pres. 1982; bd. trustees 1977-), Am. Soc. for Laser Medicine and Surgery (founding mem; editor J. of Laser Medicine and Surgery), Santa Clara Co. Med. Soc., Calif. Med. Assn., AMA, Am. Soc. of Plastic & Reconstructive Surgery, Calif. Soc. of Plastic Surg., Am. Soc. for Aesthetic Plastic Surgery, Education Found.; author: 65 profl. publs., 7 motion pictures- video tapes; research: Surgical mgmt. of impotence, laser surgery, oral implants; patents held on Oral Implant and Penile Silicone Implant; mil: Cadet Army Air Force, Hon. Disch. 1945; rec: sculpting. Ofc: Palo Alto Medical Foundation 300 Homer Ave Palo Alto 94301

LASH, ROBERT EVAN, medical electronics co. executive, b. Jan. 23, 1957, Cleveland, Ohio; s. Dr. Harvey and Rose (Gold) L.; m. Wendie, July 22, 1979; edn: BS, EE and Computer Sci., UC Berkeley, 1979; MD, UC San Diego Sch. of Medicine, 1983; lic. physician, BMQA, 1984. Career: engr. in tgn. Stanford Linear Accelerator Center, 1974; engr. in tgn. IBM, 1977; gen. ptnr. Computer Magic, Palo Alto 1982; physician St. Mary's Hosp. and Med. Center, San Francisco 1983-84; bioengineer/co-pres. & CEO, M.D. Engineering, Inc., Foster City 1984—; awards: Kraft Prize for academic excellence, Univ. Calif. (1976), Phi Beta Kappa (1979), Tau Beta Pi (1979), Eta Kappa Nu (1979); active mem. Assn. for the Advancement of Medical Instrumentation, 1984-; patron KQED and KTEH Public T.V., Calif. Acad. of Sci.; papers: A Microprocessor-Based System for Visual Evoked Potential Measurement (1979), A Computer Algorithm to Control Walking Function in Paraplegics (1983); Democrat; Jewish; rec: classical music, guitar, cooking. Ofc: M.D. Engineering, 214 Lincoln Centre Dr Foster City 94404

LASH, THOMAS ALLEN, military officer; b. Apr. 2, 1956, Shelby, Ohio; s. Marvin E. and Harriet G. (Haley) L.; m. Teresa Pfeifer, Aug. 15, 1981; edn: BS, US Air Force Academy 1978; MBA, Santa Clara Univ. 1981; MS, USC 1985; Reg. Profl. Engr., Colo. 1983. Career: capt. US Air Force, 1978—, satellite command engr. 1978-79, chief Spacecraft Ops. Team 1979-82, chief Adv. Plans Devel. 1982-83, Sunnyvale AFS; chief Mission Control 1983—, Los Angeles AFS; mem. Am. Inst. of Aeronautics & Astronautics, AF Assn.; decorated AF Commendn., AF Achievement medals; Republican; Methodist; rec: scuba, skiing. Address: Redondo Beach 90278

LASKA, PAUL B., hardware co. president; b. Sept. 8, 1939, Pittsburgh, Pa.; s. Sol and Lena I. (Berman) L.; m. Judith, Aug. 6, 1972; children: Laura b. 1962, Jeff b. 1962, Sheryl b. 1964, Jodi b. 1964, Shelley b. 1977; edn: AA, L.A. City Coll. 1965. Career: salesman, buyer, mgr., treas., v.p., now pres. Peerless Hardware Inc., Los Angeles 1962—; civic: active in community and local business; Cedar Sinai Hosp. Blood Donor Pgm.; mil: pfc US Army 1958-60, 61-62; Republican; rec: photog. Ofc: Peerless Hardware 2011 Sunset Blvd Los Angeles 90026

LA SOTA, NANCY ROSE, health care executive; b. Jan. 12, 1939, Indpls.; d. Anthony George and Dorothy Doris (Capes) Lee; m. Michael LaSota, Sept. 13, 1981; children (nee Kotzbauer): William b. 1961, Karen b. 1962; edn: stu. Marion Coll. 1957-58, RN, St. Vincent's Sch. of Nursing 1960; BS, Chapman Coll. 1981. Career: hd. nse. VA Hosp., Indpls. 1960-64, ofc. nse. Robert Parr, MD, Indpls. 1965-67; staff nse. West Park Hosp., Canoga Park, Calif. 1972-73, asst. supvr., then supvr. D.O.U., 1973-83, dir. of edn. 1983-85, dir. community edn. and rels. Nu-Med HealthSource (community edn. and resource ctr.), Nu-Med Medical, Inc., Canoga Park 1985—; instr. for Am. Red Cross, Am. Heart Assn.; awards: appreciation for Health Fair Expo 1984, West Park Hosp.; commendn. for service to senior community, County of Los Angeles (1985); mem. Women in Health, West Valley Council for Senior Concerns (Health Adviser 1985-), Valley Edn. Council 1982-84, Hosp. Public Relations Mktg. Assn. 1986-, CofC (Canoga Pk., Woodland Hills); works: devel. tchg. program for cont. edn. units and community lectures, var. health fair expos and senior pgms.; Republican; Catholic; rec: bowling, aerobics, snorkling. Res: Chatsworth 91311 Ofc: Nu-Med HealthSource 22323 Sherman Way Ste 9 Canoga Park 91307

LATHROP, MITCHELL LEE, lawyer; b. Dec. 15, 1937, Los Angeles; s. Alfred Lee and Barbara Isabella (Mitchell) L.; children: Christin b. 1964, Alexander b. 1967, Timothy b. 1971; edn: BS, US Naval Acad. 1959; JD, USC Law Sch. 1966; admitted bar: Calif., New York, Dist. Col.; Cert. Civil Trial Splst., Nat. Board of Trial Advocacy. Career: dep. county counsel Los Angeles County, 1966-69; atty., assoc., then ptnr. Brill, Hunt, DeBuys & Burby, L.A. 1969-71; ptnr. Macdonald, Halsted & Laybourne, L.A. and San Diego, 1971-80; senior ptnr. Rogers & Wells, S.D., L.A., N.Y., 1980—; presiding referee Calif. State Bar Court (1985-), lectr. in law, Calif. State Bar, Univ. of San Diego, Calif. Western

Univ., Practising Law Inst.; mem. Am., Calif., N.Y., D.C. bar assns., San Diego County Bar Assn. (v.p., dir. 1983-85), Am. Board of Trial Advocates, S.D. County Bar Found. (dir.), Internat. Assn. of Ins. Counsel; civic: Metropolitan Opera Assn., N.Y. (dir.), Met. Opera Nat. Council (com. chmn., dir.), S.D. Opera Assn. (v.p., dir.); num. legal publs.; mil: capt. JAGC, USNR, active duty 1959-63, Vietnam Svc.; Republican; Catholic; rec: classical music, scuba. Res: 706 Stafford Pl San Diego 92107 Ofc: Rogers & Wells 101 West Broadway San Diego 92101

LATTER, MITCHELL CURTIS, ophthalmologist; b. Oct. 29, 1952, Cleveland, O.; s. Marvin and Ilene Rose (Bregman) L.; edn: BS, Univ. of Cincinnati 1974, MD, 1978; Diplomate Am. Bd. of Ophthalmology 1985. Career: intern med. Long Beach VA Hosp. 1978-79; resident in ophthalmology Hollywood Presbyterian Med. Center, Los Angeles 1980-83; pvt. solo practice in ophth. 1983—; clin. instr. Hollywood Presbyterian Med. Ctr. 1985-; Fellow Am. Acad. of Ophthalmol.; mem. AMA, CMA; Republican; Jewish; rec: photog., aerobics. Res: 3245 Anne Circle, Huntington Bch. 92649 Ofc: 10230 E Artesia Blvd, Ste 204, Bellflower 90706

LAU, DAVID T., human relations representative; b. Apr. 26, 1939, Hong Kong, nat. US cit. 1976; s. George Yau-Yuen and Nancy Tak-Chi (Eng) L.; m. Cecilia, Jan. 28, 1967; children: Michael b. 1970, Michelle b. 1975; edn: BS, Idaho State Univ. 1965; MBA, Pace Univ. 1968. Career: supv. direct pay Kaiser Found. Health Plan Inc. L.A. 1973-75; equal employment opportunity coord. Kaiser Permanente Pasadena 1975-85, human relations rep. 1985—; commr. Rec. & Parks Commn. Monterey Park 1985—; honors: Asian Am. Achievement Award for Leadership Devel. in Equal Opportunity (Orgn. of Chinese Americans 1985), Amigos de Ser Award for Outstanding Support of SER Employment Pgms. (1979); mem: L.A. Basin Equal Opportunity League (spl. affairs com. 1984-86; United Chinese American League (bd. 1985-86), Chinatown Svc. Ctr. (treas., bd. 1985-86, past pres. (2 terms), past bd. chmn.), United Way (budget allocation and agcy. rels. coms. 1982-84), Amigos de Ser (steering com. 1978-), Pacific Asian Consortium in Employment (bd. 1976-78), Career Counseling Adv. Com. L.A. Valley Coll. 1979-81; Catholic; rec: sports, music, readings, chess, travel. Res: 835 Abe Way Monterey Park 91754 Ofc: Kaiser Permanente 393 East Walnut Pasadena 91188

LAU, STANLEY KWOK, chemist; b. June 3, 1923, Kobe, Japan (Chinese parentage), nat. US cit. 1943; s. Shiu Kwong and Yui Ying (Ho) L.; m. Dora, Jan. 29, 1949; edn: BS, UC Los Angeles 1949. Career: chemist Gasparcolor, Hollywood 1952-54; research chemist Specialty Resins, Lynwood 1955-56; chemist American Latex, Hawthorne 1956; project chemist Aerojet-General, Downey 1956-60; chief chemist Torginol of Am., Maywood 1963-66; research chemist Rezolin, Santa Monica 1966-67; chief chemist Resins Research, Paramount 1967, Chem. Seal Corp., L.A. 1967-68; chemist, City of Los Angeles 1968; computer pgmmr. L.A. Dept. Water & Power, 1968—; mem. L.A. Adv. Affirmative Action; honors: Phi Beta Kappa (junior year), Phi Lambda Upsilon, Alpha Mu Gamma; mem. Chinese Hist. Soc. of So. Calif. (founding pres.), L.A. City Employees Asian Am. Assn. (past pres.), Chinese Am. Citizens Alliance, Pasadena Crown City Optimist Club; mil: cpl. US Army 1943-45; Republican; Prot.; rec: spectator sports, ski, bowl. Res: 3850 Monterey Rd Los Angeles 90032

LAUDENSLAGER, WANDA LEE, speech pathologist/ real estate broker/ building contractor; b. July 22, 1929, San Jose; d. Victor Vierra and Florence Lorene (Houck) Silveria; m. Leonard Laudenslager, Apr. 26, 1952; children: Leonard II, b. 1953, Dawn Marie, b. 1954; edn: AA, Coll. of San Mateo 1960; BA, CSU San Jose 1962; BA, 1965. Calif. tchr. credential 1962, std. supvn. 1971, std. designated svcs. 1971; lic. audiometrist, 1966, speech pathologist 1974; lic. real estate broker 1978, gen. bldg. contractor 1979. Career: speech pathologist, Newark Unif. Sch. Dist. 1962-65, 1983— dist. coord. Speech, Lang. and Hearing Dept. 1965-83; self- empl. R.E. broker, gen. bldg. contractor; honors: Alpha Gamma Sigma 1960; Phi Kappa Phi; Pi Lambda Theta; Kappa Delta Pi 1962; mem; Am. Speech Lang. & Hearing Assn.; Assn. of Calif. Sch. Adminstrs.; Nat./ Calif. Assns. Realtors; So. Alameda Co. Bd. Realtors; Republican; Presbyterian. Res: 3773 Logan Dr Fremont 94536 Ofc: Newark Unified Sch. Dist., 5715 Musick Ave Newark 94536

LAUFER, LOUIS HENRY, physician; s. Sept. 8, 1929, Brooklyn, NY; s. William and Elsie (Bard) L.; m. Vivian Evelin, Nov. 26, 1953; children: Brian Andrew b. 1956, Keith Alan b. 1960, Deena Manette b. 1963; edn: AB, Washington Square Coll. of NY Univ. 1950; DO, Coll. of Osteopathic Phys. & Surgeons 1954; MD, UC Irvine Sch. of Med. 1962; Diplomate Am. Bd. Family Practice. Career: intern L.A. Co. Gen. Hosp. 1954-55, resident 1955-56; phys. Belvedere Med. Clin. L.A. 1956-57; instr. anatomy lab. Calif. Coll. Med. 1956—; chief of staff Comm. Hosp. No. Hollywood 1957—; preceptor Coll. of Osteopath. Med. of the Pacific 1982—; fellow: Am. Acad. Family Practice, Acad. Preventive Med.; mem: Am. Occupational Med. Assn., AMA, CMA, LACMA, Phi Delta Epsilon, Tau Epsilon Phi. Ofc: Vanowen Med. Group 11432 Vanowen St N Hollywood 91605

LAUGHLIN, JERRY (WILLIAM) MARION (JOSEPH), financial planner; b. Dec. 16, 1930, Cleveland, Ohio; s. James J. and Geraldine (Milligan) L.; m. Judy, Nov. 1, 1969; children: Jennifer b. 1972, William b. 1973; edn: BA English, St. Bonaventure Univ. 1952, grad. work, Eng., 1960-64; B.Theol., Catholic Univ. of Am. 1964; grad. work, rel. edn., Loyola Univ. 1968-69, study of consciousness, J.F.K. Univ. 1976-78; Cert. Finl. Planner (CFP), Coll. Finl. Plnng. (1982), Reg. Principal, NASD. Career: mfrs. rep., Houston, Tx. 1954-57; Franciscan seminarian/student in NYC and Wash DC 1957-64; Franciscan priest/assoc. pastor, Atlanta, Ga. 1964-66; Franciscan Retreat dir., Boston 1966-69; sales agent New York Life Ins. Co., Burlingame, Calif. 1969-75; pres. Laughlin Financial Corp., San Ramon 1976—; awards: Million Dollar Round Table (1973, 74, 75), NY Life Top Club (1972, 73, 74), Pres.'s Council, Great Am. Life Ins. Co. (1978), Finl. Planners Equity Corp. Top 100 (17) recognition (1985); mem. Internat. Assn. of Finl. Planners, San Ramon CofC; unpub. paper: Carl Jung as a Spiritual Master; mil: 1st lt. US Army Arty. 1952-53, Far East, Korea; Republican; Catholic; rec: swimming, biking, travel. Res: 1025 Ocho Rios Dr Danville 94526 Ofc: Laughlin Financial Corp. 18 Crow Canyon Ct Ste 205 San Ramon 94583

LAUSEN, P. SANDER, optician; b. Oct. 29, 1934, Aarhus, Denmark, nat. 1973; s. Daniel Severin and Ragnhilde (Faurholt) L.; m. Jytte Rasmussen, Jan. 25, 1958; children: Pia, b. 1960; Rene, b. 1963; edn: BS, Inst. of Tech., Copenhagen, Denmark 1956; M.Ophthalmic Optics 1972; bd. cert. Am. Bd. Opticianry 1967; Fellow Nat. Acad. Opticianry 1967. Career: dispensing optician Corne4lius Knudsen, Aarhus, Denmark 1952-57, C.F. Mc William Ltd., Auckland, NZ 1957-65; dispensing optician/ mgr. Superior Optical Co., Newport Beach 1965 74; mgr. Victor Optical, Laguna Hills 1974-76; ownr Continental Eyewear, Newport Beach 1976—; awards: Man of the Month (2), and Awd. of Merit Hi-Lite, Superior Optical Co. 1971; mem; Calif. Soc. Ophthalmic Dispensers; Newport-Balboa Rotary Club 1977- (sgt. at arms 1983), Newport Beach Tennis Club; Newport Ctr. Toastmasters; Conservative Caucus; research: Aniseikonia and Iseikonic Lenses; Republican; Lutheran; rec: soccer (chief referee Newport-Irvine AYSO 1972-77, bd. dirs. AYSO 1972-77), tennis. Res: 725 omingo Dr Newport Beach 92660 Ofc: Continental Eyewear, 3901 E Coast Hwy Corona Del Mar 92625

LAVERNE, MICHEL MARIE-JACQUES, manufacturing co. executive; b. June 1, 1928, Paris, France; s. Charles Henri Andre and Anne Marie Henriette (Bour) L.; m. Genevieve, June 29, 1963; children: Beatrice b. 1954, Thierry b. 1956, Loic Heaulme b. 1960, Christophe b. 1965, Matthieu b. 1966; edn: MBA equiv., Ecole des Hautes Etudes Commerciales, 1953; Centre de Perfectionnement dans l'Adminstrn. des Affaires, 1960. Career: var. mktg., adminstrn., and finance pos. Shell group of cos., internat. 1954-73; acct. exec. Union D'Etudes et Investissements (subs. Credit Agricole, Paris, Fr.), spec. in the baking industry, and involved in forming Generale Biscuit (now 3d largest cookie group in the world), 1973-76; v.p. fin. Salmon et Cie (family-held paper group), Paris, Fr. and also CEO Cartonneries de Saint Germain (pkg. and box mfr.) and CEO Papeteries Maunoury (printing & paper distbn. co.), 1976-81; exec. Generale Biscuit, Athis-Mons, France 1983—, fmr. bd. chmn. Generale Biscuit, Italy (subs. co.), current pres./CEO Mother's Cake & Cookie Co. (subs. co.), Oakland, Calif.; civic: Peralta Colls. Found. (dir.), Alumni Assn. of No. Calif., Hautes Etudes Commerciales (pres.), Oakland Mus. Assn. (dir.), French-Am. CofC/S.F. (v.p.), St. Mary's Coll. H.Sch./Berkeley (regent), Holy Names Coll./Oakland (regent); Catholic; rec: sail, ski, photog., hunting. Ofc: Mother's Cake & Cookie Co. 810 81st Ave Oakland 94621

LAVERTY, BEN WILLIAM, III, agricultural consultant; b. Oct. 26, 1945, Taft; s. Ben Wm., Jr. and Marilyn Edith (Kruger) L.; m. Tamara Anderson, Dec. 20, 1966; children: Ben, IV, Bret, Tim, Terra, Tallie; edn: Bakersfield Jr. Coll. 1964-65; BS, Brigham Young Univ. 1967. Career: tree crop supt. Belridge Farms, Bakersfield 1968-73; bd. dirs./owner Willow Creek Farms, Oakley, Ida. 1973-80; current: pres./CEO Lamco-Ben Laverty, Inc., Bakersfield 1980—; v.p. Alma Oil Co. 1984—; mgr./agt. Cal Farm Invest; irrigation cons. Kester Bros. 1978-80, agri. cons. Mobil Oil Corp. 1982-; bd. dirs. Western Kern Resource Conservation Dist. 1982-; mem: Calif. Agricultural Prodn. Consultants Assn., Am. Consultants League, Am. Mgmt. Assn.; civic: LDS Businessmen Assn., Boy Scouts Am. Explorer Post Advisor, Bakersfield Coll. Alumni Assn. and Helmet Club (mbrship. chmn. 1983-), BYU Cougar Club; publs: agri. economic outlook 1986, Bakersfield Lifestyle mag.; Republican; Ch. of Jesus Christ of L.D.S.; rec: Masters Track Pgm., woodworking, geneology. Address: Lamco-Ben Laverty Inc., 1720 Calloway Bakersfield 93312

LAWDER, JOHN ORMSBY, physician; b. March 23, 1932, Durban, So. Africa; s. Eward F. and Therese (Junque) L.; m. Marion Russell, Aug. 22, 1964; children: Shelley T., b. 1966, Shannon L., b. 1969; edn: Columbia Coll. 1958; Univ. British Columbia 1965; Lic. Doctor, Canada 1966, Calif. 1980. Career: med. practice, B.C., Canada 1965-80; pres. Fort Health Manor Ltd., Can.; currently owner, pres. John D. Lawder MD, Inc., Torrance; v.p., dir. N.A.T. Labs Santa Ana; med. dir. Vitafax Inc., Doctors Nutrition Guidance Labs, Inc., Seattle; honors: Fellow Price-Pottinger Nutritional Found. 1982; mem: Canadian Med. Soc., Torrance Meml. Hosp. Med. Ctr. Staff; author: Dr. John Lawder's "I.N. Diet" - Individualized Nutritional diet program; rec: golf, running, swimming. Res: 333 Palos Verdes Dr., Redondo Beach

LAWLESS, JANET EVELYN, insurance executive; b. Dec. 8, 1943, Fresno, Calif.; d. Edward Victor and Lucille Miriam (Skoegard) Rosenthal; m. William Lawless, Sept. 28, 1974; children: Don b. 1966, Jerry b. 1967; edn: Central Calif. Comml. Coll.; Calif. lic. insurance agt. Career: secty. Valley Ford Sales Inc. 1963-65; customer svc. rep. Sears Roebuck & Co. 1965-70, Calif. Casualty 1970-77; personal lines supv. Eaton & Eaton Ins. Brokers Inc. 1977-83, Lundberg & Assocs. 1983-86; personal lines mgr. Eaton & Eaton 1986—; corp. secty. Cal-Rose Inc. 1981—; honors: Cecil L. Sawyer Award (1973), Cert. of Achievement (1974), Cert. of Excellence (Univ. Ore. 1980); Republican; Episcopal; rec: antique collecting, creative cooking. Ofc: Eaton & Eaton Fresno 93621

LAWRENCE, ROBERT RAYMOND, orthopaedic surgeon; b. Feb. 9, 1932, Philadelphia; s. James Robert and Mabel Clareace (Hunter) L.; children: Jonathon b. 1961, Peter Robert b. 1962, Jennifer Rae b. 1972, Megan Elizabeth b. 1979, Brett Tyler b. 1982; edn: BS, Penn State Univ. 1954; MD, Univ. of Penn. 1958; Bd. certified orthopaedic surgery (1967), Am. Acad. of Neurol. and Orthopaedic Surgeons (1984), Independent Medical Examiner (1982). Career: intern gen. surgery L.A. Co. Gen. Hosp., 1958-59; resident gen. surg. Univ. of Penna. Hosp. 1959-60, Orthopaedic Hosp., Los Angeles 1960-64; fellowship in hand surg., 1963; pvt. practice in orthopaedic surgery, active staff 3 hosps., 1964—; mem: Am. Fracture Assn., Fellow Internat. Coll. of Surgeons, Diplomat Pan Am. Med. Assn., Pan Pacific Surg. Assn., Am. Acad. Neurol. & Ortho. Surgeons, Internat. Doctors in AA, Lancaster CofC; Republican; rec: fishing; recovering alcoholic. Res: 2128 Ave N-4 Lancaster 93550 Ofc: 43847 N Heaton Lancaster 93534

LAWRENCE, SANFORD HULL, physician; b. July 10, 1919, Kokomo, Ind.; s. Walter Scott and Florence Elizabeth (Hull) L.; edn: BA, Indiana Univ. 1941, MD, 1944. Career: intern Rochester (NY) Gen. Hosp.; chief Medical Service, Regional Hosp., Ft. Ord; resident Halloran Hosp., Staten Is., NY; dir. Biochemistry Research Lab., VA Hosp. San Fernando, Calif.; instr., asst. prof. Dept. of Infectious Diseases, UCLA; consultant Internal Medicine and Cardiology, US Govt., and Los Angeles County; hon. vis. colleague Immunochem., Univ. London; lectr. Immunochem., Protides of the Biological Fluids, Bruges, Belgium and Faculte de Med. Sorbonne, Univ. of Paris, France; recipient research awards, Calif. T.B. and Health Assn., L.A. County Heart Assn., Pres.'s Award; mem: NY Acad. of Scis., Am. Fedn. for Clin. Research, AAAS, Am. Assn. for Clin. Pathology, Am. Assn. of Clin. Chem., AMA, CMA, LACMA, Employees Assn. Halloran VA Hosp. (pres.); Whitley Hts Civic Assn.; author: The Zymogram in Clinical Medicine (Charles, Thomas), 75 sci. arts. in sci. journals; mil: capt. US Army M.C. 1946; Republican; Prot.; rec: comml. airplane pilot, piano, organ. Res: 2014 Whitley Ave., Hollywood 90068 Paris Address: 160 Rue St. Martin Paris 75003 France

LAWS, JOHN TERRELL, finance executive; b. Nov. 2, 1938, Lockhart, Tx.; s. John Thomas and Nelda V. (Simon) L.; 1 son, David L. b. 1960; edn: BA, Univ. of Texas 1961, MBA, 1965. Career: finl. staff Exxon 1963-69; finl. mgmt., senior v.p. Fin. & Adminstrn. Dataproducts Corp., Woodland Hills 1969—; mem. Am. Mgmt. Assn., MAPI; Republican; rec: music. Res: 21465 Iglesia Dr Woodland Hills 91364 Ofc: Dataproducts Corp. 6200 Canoga Ave Woodland Hills 91365

LAWSON, BARBARA LOCKHART, corporate executive; b. Apr. 15, 1933, Columbus, Ohio; d. Leo Osel and Mildred Annalee (Dowell) L.; 2 children: Robin b. 1956, Stacey b. 1958; edn: Bach. Gen. Studies, Capital Univ., 1981; MBA, International Coll. 1984; PhD in Franchising, Internat. Coll. (cand. 1985); spl. studies, Univ. of Toledo, W.L.A. Coll., NY Univ., UCLA Grad. Sch. of Mgmt. Career: advt. mgr. Lazarus, Columbus, Oh. 1967-76; advt. director Macy's, Toledo, Oh. 1976-81; v.p. of mktg. Quickprint of America, L.A. 1981-83; asst. v.p. pub. rels. Postal Instant Press, L.A. 1983—; research- The Inst. for the Study of Adult Devel., 1983—; self-empl. cons., Toledo, Oh. 1/81-11/81; awards: Creative Advertising Writing, Lazarus (Federated Dept. Stores) 1968, 69, 70; Scholarship for ToledoScape (yr long civic leadership sem. for corporate execs.) 1980-81; mem: Internat. Assn. of Business Communicators, Pub. Rels. Soc. of Am., Direct Mktg. Club of So. Calif., AAUW, Alpha Gamma Delta Frat.; publs: resrch. papers on communication, corp. news mags. (for Quickprint and PIP), ghost-write for var. trade publs.; listed in California Workbook 1982-; Democrat; Methodist; rec: Victorian homes, create china dolls, collect hearts. Res: 1011 4th St, 102, Santa Monica 90403 Ofc: Postal Instant Press, 8201 Beverly Blvd Los Angeles 90048

LAWSON, CARROLL MC KINLEY, III, lawyer; b. Mar. 30, 1946, San Diego; s. Carroll M., Jr. and Elaine Rosalie (Ennis) L.; m. Brooke Herrick, May 28, 1977; children: Trinda b. 1970, Tricia b. 1973, Carroll M., IV b. 1983, Kelli b. 1984; edn: BA, Loma Linda Univ. 1967; JD, Calif. Western Sch. of Law 1970; admitted Calif. State Bar 1970. Career: atty. Office of Legal Counsel, Loma Linda Univ. 1970-71; ptnr. Lunsford, Hopp & Lawson 1971-73; senior ptnr. Lawson & Hartnell, Redlands 1973—; founder/pres. Loma Linda College of Law; prof. of law Loma Linda Univ., Riverside City Coll.; honors: mng. editor law sch. student bar journal; merit award ABA (1974), appreciation award San Bernardino County Bar Assn. (1974); elected mem. Loma Linda City Council (1984-), mem. Redlands Police Reserve (1974-85), League of Calif. Cities (Pub. Svcs. Com.); Rotarian; works: founder, developer of Tel-Law (1974); Republican; 7th-Day Adventist. Res: 11452 Iris St Loma Linda 92354 Ofc: Lawson & Hartnell 25757 Redlands Blvd Redlands 92373

LAWSON, DONNA JOYCE, trucking co. executive; b. May 22, 1949, San Bernardino; d. Donald O'Neal and Joyce Marie (Poole) Rouse; div.; children: Stacy Marie Kammerer, b. 1967, and Steven Floyd Kammerer, b. 1969; edn: Nurse, Chaffey Coll., 1972-3, bus. law, Mt. San Antonio Coll. 1979-81. Career: vice pres. R.D. Nickell Trucking Co., Inc. San Dimas 1982-84, office mgr., computer op./dir., legal and claims rep. for corp.; pres., owner Trans Continental Consolidators, 1984—; awards: Bank of Am. Achievement Award, Home Econs., 1968, Mrs. Inland Empire Queen 1982; mem. Calif. Trucking Assn. 1983-, San Antonio Nurses Assn. 1974-78; mem. Upland Pop Warner bd. dirs. and cheerleader coordinator, 1978-83; booster sch. related sports 17 years (team mother for football, baseball, softball, cheerleading, soccer, basketball); publs: team song: Upland Pop Warner Football 1981; Democrat; Baptist (youth supr.); rec: swim, equestrian, bowling league. Res: POB 1284, Upland 91785

Ofc: Trans Continental Consolidators, 10664 Acacia St Rancho Cucamonga 91730

LAWSON, HEDLEY, banker, author, investigator; b. Sept. 2, 1923, Los Angeles; s. William James and Edith Blanche (Beesley) L.; m. Julia A.B. Lawson, May 29, 1944; children: Hedley Jr. b. 1947, Carol b. 1950, Paul b. 1951, Mimi b. 1953, Craig b. 1954, Blake b. 1962; edn: bus. adminstrn., Mt. San Antonio Coll.; Sonoma State Univ. 1 yr.; grad. Calif. Sch. Ins. 1953-59; cert. Am. Inst. Banking; lic. investigator Calif. 1975. Career: cons. FDIC; senior assoc. Dick Spencer & Assocs. Inc.; pres., CEO Am. Commerce Nat. Bank; senior v.p., loan adminstr. Mechanics Nat. Bank; oeo calif. Enterprises; licensed investigator real estate and ins.; advisor to atty. gen. and dist. atty.; mem: CofC (v.p.), Jr. CofC (v.p., treas.), Yorba Linda CC, VFW, Lions, Rotary, Moose, YMCA, BSA (dist. organizer); publ: num. articles in banking jours., career outline courses for bankers; mil: tsgt. US Army armored div. WWII, Unit Citn., 2 Battle Stars, Purple Heart; Republican; Christian; rec: golf, painting, spectator sports. Ofc: Calif. Enterprises 2735 A E Hill St Signal Hill 90804

LAWTON, GEORGE MARION, physician; b. Dec. 18, 1927, Lowell, Mich.; s. Walter M. and Gladys Amanda (Wicks) L.; m. Barbara J., Jan. 13, 1973; children: Walter b. 1952, Evert b. 1954, John b. 1960; stepchildren - Gwynn: B. Anne b. 1946, Virginia b. 1951, William b. 1957; edn: premed., Mich. State Univ. 1951-54; MD, Wayne State Univ. 1958; Occupational Medicine residency, Univ. of Cinti. 1961-64; Diplomate Am. Board of Preventive Medicine, Certified in Occupational Medicine (1965). Career: served to Capt., Med. Corps, US Navy 1957-78: US Naval Hosp., Pensacola, Fla. 1958-59; med. ofcr. USS Nereus (AS-17), 1959-61; resident occupational med., Kettering Lab., Coll. of Med., Univ. of Cincinnati., 1961-63, USPHS Research and Tng. Facility, Cinti. 1963-64; med. ofcr., 1964-68, then dir. Naval Ordnance Systems Command Environmental Health Ctr., US Naval Ammunition Depot, Crane, Ind., 1968-70; Dir. Occupnl. & Environmtl. Health Div., Bureau of Med. and Surgery, Navy Dept., Wash DC 1970-76, Dep. Dir. Occupnl. & Preventive Med. Div., 1976-78; Medical Dir. JRB Assocs., McLean, Va. 1978-82, Lawrence Livermore Nat. Lab., Univ. Calif., Livermore 1982–; assoc. clin. prof. Dept. Med. UC San Francisco, 1983-; v.p. Employee Health Services, Inc. 1982-; honors: Gorgas Medal, Assn. of Mil. Surgeons of the US (1976), Navy Commendn. Medal (1970), Navy Meritorious Service Medal (1978), Inaugurated the Capt. George M. Lawton, MC, USN Lecture Series of the USN Environmtl. Health Ctr. (March 1986); mem: AMA, Am. Occupnl. Med. Assn., Am. Acad. of Occupnl. Med., Am. Indsl. Hygiene Assn., Am. Conf. of Govt. Indsl. Hygienists, Soc. of Consultants to the Armed Forces, Assn. of Consultants to the Mil. Surgeons of the US; contbr. num. articles on environmtl. health in trade jours.; Republican; Episcopal; rec: farming, travel, bird watching. Res: 3264 Cheryl Circle Pleasanton 94566 Ofc: Lawrence Livermore National Laboratory, POB 808 (L-423), Livermore 94550

LAYFIELD, ELWOOD BAKER, engineering co. executive, ret.; b. June 23, 1908, Chgo.; s. Elwood Norman and Mabel Pearl (Baker) L.; m. Teresa Jamieson, Oct. 22, 1985; children (by previous marriage): Barbara (MacCallum) b. 1938, Sharon (Harrington) b. 1941, James b. 1949, Pamela (Speirs) b. 1951; edn: Bach. Chem. Engring., Ohio State Univ. 1929; MS in chem. engring., USC 1931. Career: chief chemist Northwest Stellarene Co., Coutts, Alta., Can. 1931-33; chief chemist Big West Oil Co., Kevin, Mont. 1934; chief engr. The Ralph M. Parsons Co., Los Angeles 1934-60, cons. 1975-; bd. chmn./CEO, The Ralph M. Parsons Co. Ltd., London, Eng. 1960-75, ret. 1975, corp. dir. and cons. 1975-; honors: Tau Beta Pi, Phi Lamba Upsilon, Sigma Xi, Phi Kappa Phi; mem. Am. Inst. of Chem. Engrs.; club: El Niguel Country; mil: civilian mng. engring. dept. War Petroleum Products; Republican; Methodist; rec: railroads, rail travel, Nat. Railway Hist. Soc. Res: 32581 Adriatic Dr Laguna Niguel 92677-3507

LAYTON, EDWARD NORMAN, construction co. president; b. June 29, 1928, Kellogg, Idaho; s. Ernest Alfred and Ruth Eloise (Thwing) L.; . Mary Katherine Ketchum, June 29, 1948; children: Norman b. 1950, Cheryl b. 1954, Terri b. 1957, Dennis b. 1958; edn: cert. bus. mgmt., UCLA 1957; lic. General Contractor B1, Calif. 1958. Career: cowboy for Davis Ranch, Ariz. 1944; shop foreman Fiat Metal Products 1948; carpenter 1949-52; carpenter supt. Casnor Constrn. 1952-63; v.p./ part owner 1964-77; founder/ pres. Ed Layton Constrn. Co. 1978–; bd. chmn. Tri-County Investment Gp. Inc. 1976-; Building Industry Assn. So. Calif. (dir. 1976-84, v.p. labor 1981-83, chmn. Labor Negotiation Com. 1982-83); elected bd. Walnut Valley County Water Dist. 1985; awards: Citizen of Yr., Walnut Valley 1975; Cabrillo awd. for excellency of constrn. (La Mirada City Hall), Architects Inst. of Am. 1970; Gold Nuggent awd. of merit, Pacific Coast Bldrs. Conf. 14 Western States, for excellence of comml. remodel 1981; mem: Bldg. Indus. Assn., Pasadena San Gabriel Valley chpt. (Comml. Indsl. Council); Nat. Assn. Home Bldrs.; Men's Club Queen of Valley Hosp.; N.A.H.B. Spike Club (So. Calif. labor policy dir.); So.Calif. Aracheol. Survey Assn.; Kiwanis Internat. (Cal-Nev-Ha Found.); Calif. Country Club; works: first fiberglass domed bldg. for projection and display of stellar films of spac flights 1965; rewrote master labor agreement for B.I.A. 1980; constrn. over 200 million projs.; Republican (Pres. Task Force); Protestant; rec: amateur archeologist, lapidarist, minerologist. Res: 404 S Lemon Ave Walnut 91789 Ofc: Ed Layton Construction Co., Inc., POB 60, Walnut 91789

LAZAN, clothing designer; b. Oct. 9, 1957, Sn Francsco; d. Richard Burdon and Janet Kay (Smith) Deal; m. Kent Smith, Dec. 4, 1975; edn: cert. tailoring, Chesapeake (Va.) Tech. & Voc. Center 1973-4; AA, Tidewater Comm. Coll. 1976; BFA, Virginia Commonwealth Univ. 1980; cert. diver, NASLI 1975. Career: seamstress/tailor Leggetts (dept. store) Norfolk, Va. 1974-76; supvr. alterations Thalhimers (dept. store) 1976-77; freelance designing, tailoring, fashion cons. for pvt. clients in Virginia and Wash DC area, 1972-80, in greater Los Angeles area, 1980–; designer, owner Lazan boutique in Malibu, 1981-82; designer, patternmaker Charles Ray Limited Creations Inc., Topanga 1983-84; pvt. clients include sev. champion figure skaters (internat.), the 1974 Buffalo Bills' Linebackers, num. show business celebrities; costume designer credits: Matchmaker (graduate film, CSU Long Beach 1983), Future World Expo '83 (L.A. Conv. Ctr.), The Seduction (feature movie 1981), Jim Bray Roller Boogie (roller skating show 1981), Longshot (feature movie 1981); num. profl. awards incl. First Pl. Best use of Fabric, Burlington Industries (1978); mem. Toastmasters Intl., Malibu CofC; publs: Dad's Car Cure Schedule Book (1983); Sci. of Mind; rec: dream analysis, jogging, photog. Res: 22660 PCH No. 13, Malibu 90265 Ofc: Malibu Alterations POB 612, Malibu 90265

LAZANSKY, ELENORE MAY, educator, pyschologist; b. May 1, 1909, Manila, Philippine Islands; s. Milton William and Carrie May (Ward) L.; edn: AB, UC Berkeley 1931, MA, 1932; Secondary Sch. Tchr., Calif. 1932; Sch. Psychologist, Calif. 1956; Psychologist, Calif. 1959. Career: mathematics tchr., counselor, testing Oakland Schs. 1935-74; Oakland Schs. Gifted Pgm. 1957-61; instr. Merritt Coll., Oakland 1956-57, 1961-62; head math dept. Castlemont H.S. 1968-69; tchr. Univ. of Calif. Summer Demonstration Secondary Sch. 1943, 1944, 1951; The Learning Ctr., Lafayette 1976-82; pvt. pracitce edn. psychology Learning Difficulties in Mathematics, Lafayette 1974–; advr., dir., treas. Calif. Scholarship Fedn. 1967-74; honors: Nat. Science Found. Fellowship, 1963-65; Fellow, Am. Assn. for Adv. of Science; Phi Beta Kappa, Sigma Xi, Pi Lambda Theta, Pi Mu Epsilon; mm: Am. Ednl. Research Assn., Calif. and Contra Costa Co. (secty., treas. 1976-77) Psychological Assns., Nat. Council of Tchrs. of Mathematics (past dir.), Nat. Edn. Assn., Calif. Tchrs. Assns., Mt. Diablo Iris Soc., San Francisco Bay West Highland White Terrior Club; publs: articles and reports, talks at confs. on mathematics, curriculum materials, Oakland's Gifted Pgm.; Republican; Protestant; rec: handcrafts, Victorian houses and costumes, writing.

LE, KHOA VAN, artist; b. June 10, 1933, Cantho, South Vietnam; s. Ut Van and Tram Thi (Do) Le; m. Ha Ngoc Phan, Jan. 26, 1976; children: Kim b. 1979, Khanh b. 1981, Kieu b. 1983; edn: BA (equiv.) Univ. Saigon 1957. Career: (Vietnam): composer, conductor: Ca Doan Co-Doc 1962-75, Ca Doan Trung Duong 1969-74, Tieng Nhac Tram Tu, Vietnam TV 1968-75, and writer/ed. Vietnam Pub. Co. 1968-75; came to USA in 1975: asst. prof. advanced photog. Salisbury State Coll., Md. 1976-77; Superfast Photo, San Diego 1984–; printing mgr. Paradise Valley Hosp., S.D.; founder/pres. Artistic Photographic Assn., Vietnam (1969-75), reorganized, elected pres. Artistic Photography Assn., USA 1978-; exhib. One man show, selected group, Faculty show, Juried show throughout USA; contbr. num. Viet. mags. in photog. columns; awards: num. prizes in photog.; Honor Fellowship awards: APA (1971), KBC (1972), MPC (Hong Kong 1973), award of excellency in mass media Vietnam Govt. (1973), leadership toward cultural exchange award Fullerton Coll. (1979-80); musician/condr. concerts throughout Calif. and nat.; prod. music cassette tape "Tieng Chieu Roi" (1983); author: Thanh Ca Co Doc (3d ed. Pacific Press 1978), Con Duong Giai Thoat (4th ed. Pacific Press 1982), Giao Duc Tre Con (6th ed. 1984); composer/pub. num. songs, translator/pub. Viet. hymnal "Thanh Ca Codoc" (1978); film actor in Tri Star Picture "Alamo Bay" and ABC-TV "Call to Glory;" Seventh Day Adventist; rec: video prodn. Res: 2901 E 8th St National City 92050

LE, LAC VAN, certified quality engineer; b. July 5, 1943, Dalat, South Vietnam, nat. US cit. 1980; s. Tan Van and Cau Thi (Ho) L.; m. Xuan An Nguyen, April 1971; children: Hieu Hahn b. 1972, Phuc Van b. 1973, Hau Hien b. 1974, Peter Tho Long b. 1976, Thomas Binh b. 1983; edn: equiv. MS, Saigon Univ. 1966; MSEE, CSU Long Beach 1980; Mfg. Mgmt. & Q.C., Matsushita Overseas Tng. Ctr., Osaka, Japan 1973; var. mgmt. courses, Am. Mgmt. Assn.; Cert. Quality Engr., ASQC 1979. Career: asst. plant mgr. National Panasonic factory, Saigon, Vietnam 1970-75; Pioneer Electronics of Am., Long Beach 1976-80; prodn. procurement plnnr. 1976-77; mgr. prodn. plnng., scheduling & material control 1977-78; quality assurance & assembly scheduling mgr. 1978-79; project engring. mgr. 1979-80; quality assurance mgr. Pioneer Electronics (USA), Long Beach 1980-83; quality assurance & engring. div. mgr. Pioneer Electronics Svc. & Engring. Inc., Long Beach 1983–; asst. prof. Vietnam Nat. Inst. of Tech. 1970-73; awards: 2nd Prize for Outstanding Preformance of the Year (1973), 1st Prize for Outstanding Contrib. Co. (1974), Nat. Panasonic Co., Saigon, Vietnam; mem: ASQC, Electronics Industries Assn., Vo Vi Meditation Friendship Assn. (founder, pres.-elec.); publs: ed., Vo Vi Friendship Assn. monthly newsletter; Buddhist; rec: meditation. Res: 9224 Buttercup Ave Fountain Valley 92708 Ofc: Pioneer Electronics Svc. & Engring. Inc., 1925 E Dominguez St Long Beach 90810

LE, TRUC HUY, international quality assurance and technical service manager; b. Apr. 10, 1952, Hanoi, Vietnam, nat. US cit. 1975; s. Chinh Tri and Nhieu Thi (Cong) Le; m. Kim-Hoa Hoang, July 29, 1976; edn: BS, Univ. Saigon 1971; BSME, Kanto Univ., Yokohama, Japan 1976; BSME, Cal. Poly. Univ. Pomona 1981; MBA, Univ. Redlands 1983. Career: mech. engr. Cal Best Corp., Los Alamitos 1977-78; qual. control engr. Pioneer Electronics Tech., Duarte 1978-79; qual. control, test dept. mgr. General Dynamics, Upland 1979-82; internat. qual. assurance and tech. svc. mgr. IOLAB Corp., div. of Johnson & Johnson, Claremont 1982–; qual. circle trainer General Dynamics 1981; honors: Nat. Dean's List (1981-82); mem: Am. Soc. Qual. Control, Am. Mgmt. Assn., Soc. Plastics Engrs., Vietnamese & Am. Student Assn. (secty., Tokyo, Japan); Buddhist; rec: soccer, swimming, computer programming. Res: 878 W Oak-Knoll Brea 92621 Ofc: IOLAB Corp., 500 IOLAB Dr Claremont 91711

LEA, DIXIE, consultant; b. Dec. 12, 1943, Lakeville, Ind.; d. John T. and Marietta A. Frick; edn: BS, Purdue Univ. 1966; MA, Mich. State Univ. 1970; PhD, Univ. Wis. Madison 1982. Career: faculty Purdue Univ. 1966-69, Mich. State Univ. 1969-72, prof. Univ. Wis., Madison 1972-82; pres. Lea Assocs., San Diego and senior cons./publisher InterPhase: Interaction Skills Training, 1982–; internal cons. (positive choice pgms.) Kaiser Permanente Health Care Systems, 1983-; awards: Robert W. Amick Award for outstanding tchg. (1968), MSU Team award for excellent ednl. pgm. (1971); mem: Nat. Speakers Assn., Am. Soc. for Tng. & Devel., Am. Home Econs. Assn.; civic: San Diego Symphony, Zeta Tau Alpha; coauthor (w/Richard Brostrom, PhD): Pre-FAX (Pre-Employment Interviewing Guide), O-SCAN (Orgn. Style Indicator), IPSI (InterPhase Style Inventory), Dynamics of Interpersonal Exchange, Managing Technical Professionals; rec: boating, walking, biking. Res: 4627 Ocean Blvd Pacific Beach 92109 Ofc: Lea Assocs POB 9675 Pacific Beach 92109

LEA, JONATHAN DISMUKES, accountant, auditor; b. Jan. 14, 1952, Charlottesville, Va.; s. Luther David and Alma Lyle (Marshall) L.; edn: BS, acctg., Univ. Va. 1974; postgrad. Golden Gate Univ. 1980-82; Certified Public Acct., Va. (1982), Calif. (1983). Career: lt. US Navy, payroll disbursing ofcr. USS Bainbridge, Bremerton, Wa. and San Diego 1975-77, audit team West Coast USN, 1977-80; staff auditor Pannell Kerr Forster CPAs, San Francisco 1980-82, The Bekins Co., Internal Audit Dept., Glendale 1982-83; Medicare Provider auditor, senior auditor Blue Cross of Calif., Woodland Hills 1983–; bus. mgr. Shadow Ranch Condominium Assn., Canoga Pk.; awards: NROTC Scholar (1974), Honor grad. USN Supply Corps; mem: Am. Inst. CPAs, Calif. Soc. CPAs (Health Care com.); mil: lt. cmdr. US Navy, Reserves 1980-; Republican; Episcopal; rec: travel, education, movies. Res: 7137 Shoup Ave Apt 44 Canoga Park 91307 Ofc: Blue Cross of California 21555 Oxnard St Woodland Hills

LEACH, ROBERT DALE, boat manufacturer; b. April 24, 1940, Saginam, Mich.; s. James Ditz and Mildred Marie (Ruffle) L.; m. Claudia, May 18, 1981; children: Brent b. 1963, Bryant b. 1965, Brandie b. 1982, Briana b. 1985. Career: sales Chun King, Duluth, Minn. 1962-64; sales Kellogg's, Battle Creek, Mich. 1964-70; pres. Eliminator Boats, Anaheim 1970–; honors: (6) Awards for Product Excellence, Power Boat Mag.; rec: water skiing, flying, fishing. Res: 1314 Sunview Dr. Orange 92665 Ofc: Eliminator Boats, 1010 No. Grove St. Anaheim 92806

LEADER, DANIEL BRUCE, manager of financial reporting; b. Nov. 5, 1958, San Jose; s. Charles C. Jr. and Catherine R. (Ross) L.; m. Jeffie, Feb. 12, 1983; edn: BSBA, honors, San Jose State Univ. 1981; CPA, Calif. 1983; Notary Public, Calif. 1985. Career: fin. admin. asst. IBM Corp., San Jose 1979-81; audit senior Coopers & Lybrand, San Jose 1981-83; corp. controller DH Technology Inc., Sunnyvale 1983-86; mgr. financial reporting Glenborough Corp. San Mateo 1986–; mem: Am. Inst. CPAs, Calif. Soc. CPAs (San Jose chpt.), Nat. Notary Assn., Am. Mgmt. Assn.; rec: skiing, white water rafting. Res: 4451 Calle de Arroyo San Jose 95118 Ofc: Glenborough Corp. 4 W Fourth Ave San Mateo 94402

LEAHY, JOSEPH PATRICK, chiropractor; b. Jan.14, 1949, San Jose; s. Joseph F. and Helen E. Leahy; m. Candace, June 25, 1977; children: Sean b. 1982, Megan b. 1985; edn: BS Los Angeles Coll. of Chiropractic, 1982, DC, 1982. Career: chiropractor, Hamilton Ave Chiropractic Center, Campbell; instr. Palmer Coll. of Chiropractic-West 1984-85; faculty advisor for sports injury club; cons. var. exercise equipment cos. and health clubs; team chiropractor San Jose Earthquakes profl. soccer team; chiropractor for Swiss Olympic Track and Field Team; honors: cited by Special Olympics for benefit service; mem: Calif. Chiropractic Assn. (dir. Coll. liaison pgm. 1984, Long Range Plnng. com, 1984), Santa Clara County Chiro. Assn. (v.p. 1985), Rotary; research: devel. techniques for enhancement athletic performance thru steroids, nutrition, tng. methods; Democrat; Christian; rec: Decathlon, golf. Ofc: Hamilton Ave Chiropractic Center 286 East Hamilton Ste K Campbell 95008

LEATHERWOOD, JERRY LANE, JR., manufacturing co. executive; b. June 6, 1946, Oakland; s. Jerry L., Sr. and Helen Marie (Gartner) L.; m. Karol Hemphill, Nov. 28, 1970; 1 son, John b. 1984; edn: BSCE, Univ. of Tenn. 1970; MBA, Univ. of N.C. 1975; Reg. Profl. Engr., N. Caro. (1979), reg. PE in 24 states. Career: engr. trainee Pittsburgh-Des Moines Steel, Pitts. 1970-71; engr. assoc. Duke Power Co., Charlotte, N.C. 1975-77; chief design engr. Varco-Pruden Buildings, Winston-Salem 1977-79, customer service mgr. 1979-80, engring. mgr. 1980-84, engring. mgr. Varco-Pruden Buildings, Turlock, Calif. 1984–; master instr. Defense Mapping Agcy. US Army, Ft. Belvoir, Va. 1972-73; awards: Most Valuable Player/ Best All Around Player- Basketball, Baseball, Football (1964); mem. Nat. Soc. of Profl. Engrs., Profl. Engrs. of N. C., Lions Club; mil: sgt. E5 US Army 1971-73, Jt. Svc. Commendn., Good Conduct; Democrat; Baptist; rec: golf, tennis, numismatics , woodworking. Res: 2500 Marie Dr Turlock 95380 Ofc: Varco-Pruden Buildings POB 1824 Turlock 95381

LE BAKER, EDWIN HARRISON, III, tax consultant, financial analyst, contracts adminstrator; b. Dec. 23, 1945, Oakland, Calif.; s. Edwin Harrison, Jr. and Clara Francis (Page) LeB.; m. Deborah Kilkenny, July 18, 1981; 1 son: David b. 1982; edn: BS, CSU Hayward 1973; MBA, Golden Gate Univ. 1982. Career: indsl. acct. Varian Assocs., Inc., Palo Alto 1973-77, acctg. mgr. 1977-79; senior financial analyst EIMAC, San Carlos 1979-80; cost acctg. mgr. Varian Assocs. 1980-82; bus. mgr., contracts adminstr. ARACOR, Sunnyvale 1982-85, dir. finance & adminstrn. 1985–; owner, LeBaker Tax & Financial Cons. Svc. 1980–; mem: Veterans Club (pres. 1973); mil: seaman USN

1966-69, Vietnam, Pistol & Rifle Marksmanship; Republican; Protestant; rec: jogging, coin collecting. Res: 10582 Esquire Pl Cupertino 95014 Ofc: ARACOR, 425 Lakeside Dr Sunnyvale 94086

LE BARON, CONSTANCE PEARSON, game manufacturing co. president and owner; b. Apr. 5, 1922, Kansas City, Mo.; d. John Elmer and Eva Marie (Rogers) Pearson; m. David G. LeBaron, Nov. 8, 1947; children: Rogers b. 1948, Catherine b. 1950, Clyde b. 1951, Constance b. 1953, Paul b. 1954, Nancy b. 1956, Mary b. 1957, Joanne b. 1960, David, Jr. b. 1961, Timothy b. 1966; edn: grad., Marymount Coll. (now Loyola/Marymount, CA). Career: with engring. div. Douglas Aircraft Co., Westwood 5 years (won "A" suggestion award 1944); owner/pres. Twinson Co. (mfr. unique toys and games for all ages), 1936– (first game invented in 1936, published in 1937, and sold at Kansas City Union Station Toy Shop), legally estab. bus. in ptnrship with twin sister, Catherine, in Los Angeles (4/6/46), bought twin out, sole prop. bus.; civic: Children of Mary, Children's Home Soc., Federated Womens Club; honors: Family of the Month, Los Altos (1958); works: approx. 40 original toys and games (1936-); prod./dir. St. Williams Variety Show, 1962; Republican; Catholic; rec: all sports, writing. Res: 433 La Prenda Rd Los Altos 94022 Ofc: Twinson Co 1289 Reamwood Ave Ste E Sunnyvale 94089

LE DAO QUANG, engineer, nuclear power plant consultant; b. Sept. 11, 1947, Phuoc-Hai, Vietnam, nat. US cit. 1981; s. Dieu Van and Tai Thi (Nguyen) L.; m. Bi Vuong, July 1, 1973; 1 dau. Serena b. 1985; edn: BA math, W.J. Bryan Coll. 1971; BS, Univ. Tenn. 1972; MS, UC Berkeley 1976, M.Engrg., 1979. Career: mathematician Tenn. Valley Authority Knoxville, Tenn. 1969-73; assoc. engr. Duke Power Co. Charlotte, NC 1973-75; prin. engr. EDS Nuclear Inc. S.F. 1976-77; cons. Gen. Elec. San Jose 1977-81; cons. Bechtel Corp. S.F. 1981-84, Advance Engrg. Corp. Sweden 1984, Sargent & Lundy Engrs. Chgo. 1985; independent cons. 1985–; honors: Tau Beta Pi, Chi Epsilon, Phi Kappa Phi, Outstanding Young Men of Am. (1977); mem: UC Berkeley Engrg. Assn., Republican Presdl. Task Force (trustee); publs: num. tech. reports; Republican; Protestant; rec: travel, home remodeling, gardening. Address: 723 Key Route Blvd Albany 94706

LEDEEN, WILLIAM PRESENT, mechanical engineer; b. Oct. 26, 1954, Pasadena; s. Howard Lee and Phyllis (Present) L.; edn: BSME, Stanford Univ. 1976, MSME, 1977; MBA, UC Berkeley 1986; Reg. Profl. Engr. (mech. engr.) Calif. Career: project engr. Digital Dynamics Inc., Sunnyvale 1977-78, gen. mgr. 1978-80; engring. splst. Energy Equipt. & Systems Inc., San Francisco (subs. NOVA Corp., Canada) 1980–; instr. radio prodn. Stanford Univ. 1978; dir: Digital Dynamics Inc. (1978-80), Pipeline Hydraulics, Engr., Inc., Houston (1981-); mem: ASME 1977- (exec. com. Santa Clara Sect. 1978-79), Instrument Soc. of Am. 1978-; patents: Precise Valve Positioning (1981), Design for a Throttling Ball Valve (1983); Democrat; Jewish; rec: photog., FM radio pgmmg. & news prodn. Res: 10265 Parkwood Dr, 1, Cupertino 95104

LEDFORD, GARY ALAN, designer, builder, developer; b. Dec. 30, 1946, San Diego; s. Loren Oscar and Madge Francis (Condon) L.; m. Linda Halbert Barker, Jan. 7, 1979; children: Kelly b. 1969, Jeanne b. 1970, Robert b. 1972, Kevin b. 1973; edn: CE, US Army Engrg. Sch. 1967; grad. courses in structures, Univ. of Colo. 1969. Career: platoon dr., co. comdr., Battalion Civil Engr., US Army Corps of Engrs. (Airborne), Vietnam, 1969; pres. Mastercraft Contractors, Inc., Colorado Springs 1969-73; v.p./ gen. mgr. K.L. Redfern, Inc., Orange, Calif. 973-75; 1975–: pres. Mojave Feed & Fuel Corp., mng. partner Apple Valley Mall; current projects: retirement community, residential developments, shopping ctr., ofc. park; instr. (Command & Staff), Us Army Eng. Sch., Ft. Belvoir, VA 1966 (Nike Missile Support Sys.); awards: 2nd pl. design, Colo. Springs Parade of Homes 1972, mem. Urban Land Inst.; Nat. Assn. home Bldrs.; Nat. Rifle Assn.; Nat. Plnng. Assn.; Bldg. Industry Assn.; VFW; Internat. Council of Shopping Ctrs.; works: design, engineering, constrn. projects incl. 26 shopping ctrs., 44 restaurants, 3 Edwards Theatres, 3 schools (L.A. Bd. Edn), Malibu Grand Prix (Pomona), over 100 svc. stations, num. indsl. bldgs., medical facilities, and var. mil. projects; design & devel. contractor computer software (copyrighted 1979), Tuffcore Bldg. Sys. (pat pend. 1981); mil. decorations: Bronze Star (2), Army Commdn. (2), Purple Heart; Republican; Protestant; rec: hunting, equestrian, chess. Res: 14415 Erie, Apple Valley 92307 Ofc: Jess Ranch Development Co., 11401 Apple Valley Rd Apple Valley 92308

LE DOUX, MARK ANTHONY, vitamin manufacturing co. president; b. March 19, 1954, Los Angeles; s. Victor Emke and Marie (Altmann) L.D.; m. Elinor Ann, Feb. 14, 1976; edn: BA, cum laude, Univ. of Okla. 1975; JD, Western State Univ. Coll. of Law 1979. Career: exec. v.p. Fovac Labs. Inc. 1975-80; CEO, pres. Natural Alternatives Inc. 1980-85, pres. 1985–; honors: Pres.'s Leadership Award, Univ. of Okla. 1972; mem: NNFA (Exec. Mfg. Council 1983-85), Council for Responsible Nutrition, Drug Chemicals & Allied Trades Assn.; works: guested on 300 + radio and television talk shows re proper nutrition for optimum health; Republican; Catholic; rec: golf, racquetball, sailing. Ofc: Natural Alternatives Inc., 11850 Linda Vista Dr San Marcos 92069

LEE, ANABELLE CAROLINE, corporate real estate broker; b. Apr. 20, 1938, Amery, Wisc.; s. Elmer Theodore and Lillian Matilda (Anderson) L.; edn: BA, Univ. Minn. 1960. Career: pres. Lee/ Sugita Inc. L.A. 1976-80; v.p. sales & mktg. Villa Florenze Devel. Co. 1980-82; senior v.p. sales & mktg. Indivest Inc. 1982–; corp. real estate broker; instr. real estate ethics Santa Monica City Coll. 1978-79, motivation in real estate 1979-80; part owner Stowebridge Farms 1984–; mem: Beverly Hills Bd. Realtors 1979-, Multiple Listing Svc. 1976-,

Young Republicans 1960-70, Nat. Kidney Found. 1965-; Republican; Religious Sci.; rec: music, ranching, politics. Res: 835 S Lucerne Blvd Los Angeles 90005 Ofc: Indivest 969 Hilgard Ave Los Angeles 90024

LEE, ANDY TAY, (Tay Hon Ly), insurance/business financing executive; b. Feb. 8, 1951, Saigon, Vietnam, nat. US cit. 1986; s. Huu and Ha Bich (Su) Ly; m. Annie Lee, Jan. 22, 1969; children: Chad b. 1970, Celia b. 1972; edn: AA cum laude, Los Angeles City Coll. 1982; cert. of completion, digital business machine, Abram Friedman Occupational Ctr. L.A. 1980; cert. of proficiency in Eng., Vietnamese Am. Assn., Saigon 1967; cert. English lang., Central Tng. Inst., Dept. of Army 1968. Career: interpreter's supr. Ofc. of the Provost Marshal, Dept. of Army 1968-72; gen. mgr., owner Huu-Cuong Plastic Co., Saigon, Vietnam 1973-74; gen. mgr., owner Huu-Cuong Transp. Co. 1975-78; agent Cal Western Life, Monterey Park, Calif. 1981-83; sales mgr. Mony Finl. Svcs., Pasadena 1983–, and nat. cons. mktg. com. 1985-; finl. plnng. cons. Asian Am. Assn.; sales awards: Million Dollar Round Table -4, Nat. Sales Achievement -3, Nat. Quality -2, Health Ins. Quality, Man of Year Cal Western Life (1982), Agcy. Man of Year (1983), co. Pres.'s Council (1984) and Top Club (1985, 86); mem: L.A. Life Underwriter Assn. 1981-, S.E. Asian Chinese-Am. CofC (dir), So. Calif. Fukienese Assn. (dir.); Buddhist; rec: basketball, swimming, reading. Res: 1529 Walnut Creek Pkwy West Covina 91791 Ofc: Mony Financial Svcs., 936 E Green St Pasadena 91106

LEE, CHONG SER, architect; b. June 1, 1940, Seoul, Korea, nat. 1978; s. Eui Young and Im Young L.; m. Kim Inbong, July 16, 1970; children: James, b. 1971; Brian, b. 1976; edn: BS, Hanyang Univ., Seoul, Korea 1964; reg. architect, Calif. 1979. Career: installation ofcr. Korean Air Force Hdqtrs., Korea 1964-68; proj. arch. H.S. Lee Eng. Cons., Seoul, Korea 1968-70; chief arch./mgr. Kuzo-sa Architects & Engrs. Co., Seoul 1970-72; senior draftsman Architectural Prodns. Inc., Newport Beach 1973-77; job capt. William L. Pereira Assoc., Corona del Mar 1977-80; arch./ job capt. Austin Co., Irvine 1980-84; currently, prin. Chong S. Lee A.I.A. & Assocs., Newport Beach; honors: 1st pl. design, NCARB Architect's Lic. Exam.; mem: Calif. Council Am. Inst. of Architects; mil: capt., Korean Air Force 1968; Protestant; rec: reading. Res: 3701 Baylor St., Irvine 92714 Ofc: Chong S. Lee & Assocs. AIA, 4500 Campus Dr Ste 520, Newport Beach 92660

LEE, CHONGKOO CHARLES, insurance executive; b. Feb. 2, 1948, Kosung, Korea, nat. US cit. 1985; s. Kyu Jae and In Ja (Chung) L.; m. Hyera, Oct. 29, 1978; children: Dennis b. 1980, Edna b. 1982; edn: BS in fisheries biol., Nat. Fisheries Univ. of Busan, Korea 1969, MS in fisheries biol. 1973; MS in marine sci., Univ. of Alabama 1979; desig: Reg. Rep., NASD (1982); LUTC (1984), enrolled CLU pgm. (1985-), Nat. Assn. Life Underwriters. Career: research assoc. Nat. Fisheries Univ. of Busan, 1970-73, Univ. of Ala. Dauphin Island Sea Lab. 1975-79; ins. agent Equitable Life Assurance Soc. of U.S., Los Angeles 1980-, dist. mgr. 1984–; awards: Nat. championship awards, Equitable Life (1982, 84), Nat. Quality and Nat. Sales Achieve. awards, NALU (1983, 84), Million Dollar Round Table (1984, 85); mem. Nat. Assn. Life Underws.; clubs: Queen-Anne Tennis, L.A. (pres.), Korean Tennis Assn. USA, Scuba Diving Assns. (YMCA, PADI), Kyung Nam Alumni Assn. So. Calif. (secty.); publ: The Seasonal and Spatial Setting of Oyster Spat and other settling organisms in Mobile Bay (thesis, 1979; Sea Grant); Presbyterian (choir, deacon); rec: tennis, scuba, travel. Res: 6149 Encinita Ave Temple 91780 Ofc: The Equitable Financial Services 3435 Wilshire Blve Ste 1114 Los Angeles 90010

LEE, DAURENE, financial planner; b. Feb. 2, 1952, Stockton; d. Harry Lyle and Mary Wong Lee; edn: BS, summa cum laude, CSU Fresno 1971; desig: CFP, Cert. Finl. Plnng. Inst. (1986). Career: div. mgr. Sears, Stockton and Fresno, 1971-76; ins. agent/finl. planner Prudential Life Ins. Co. 1976-79, state bond sales 1979-82; acct. exec. Drexel Burnham 1982-84; owner/ prin./ branch mgr. Daurene Lee, A Financial Planning Firm, Fresno 1985–; speaker seminars and local orgns. on finl. plnng. topics; awards: Prudential Rookie of Year (1977), Women's Million Dollar Round Table (1979), pres.'s club (1985) chairman's club (1986) Southmark Finl. Svcs.; mem. Internat. Assn. Finl. Planners (secty. Fresno chpt. 1985), Fresno Career Women (v.p. 1981), Cofc, Womens Trade Club; civic: St. Agnes Hospice (vol.), Girl Scouts Am. (fundraiser); Democrat; Rel. Sci.; rec: play piano, guitar, clarinet. Ofc: Daurene Lee, A Financial Planning Firm 333 W Shaw Ste One Fresno 93704

LEE, DAWN RENEE, accountant; b. Sept. 15, 1956, Bakersfield; d. Donald Ralph and Betti Jo (High) Geivet; m. Larry Lee, Apr. 24, 1981; 1 son, Aaron b. 1981; edn: AS, Bakersfield Coll. 1976; BS, CSU Fresno 1978; Certified Public Acct., Calif. (1983). Career: staff acct. David Wm Tuttle, CPA, Fresno 1978-79; staff acct., senior acct. Davis & Vogl, CPAs, Fresno 1979-83; senior acct. Blohm, Gilman, Lozano & Harris, CPAs 1984–; also payroll clk. p.t., 1979-83; mem: Am. Inst. of CPAs, Calif. Soc. of CPAs; Democrat; Episcopal. Ofc: Blohm, Gilman, Lozano & Harris, 320 West Oak Visalia 93291

LEE, DONALD ALFRED, computer consulting co. executive; b. Mar. 10, 1930, Methuen, Mass.; s. Alfred and Louise Pierson (Goddard) L.; widowed; children: Susan b. 1954, Donald Jr. b. 1956, Carol b. 1957, Nancy b. 1963; edn: BSEE, Northeastern Univ. 1952. Career: design engr. IBM, Poughkeepsie, N.Y. 1952-55; project mgr. IBM SAGE System, MIT, Bedford, Mass. 1955-60, IBM liaison mgr. SAGE System, SDC, Santa Monica, Calif. 1960-65; IBM project mgr. AWACS Computer System, Westlake, Calif. and Seattle, Wash. 1965-69; var. mgmt. pos. while forming a new IBM computer consulting orgn., Westlake & Glendale, Calif. 1969-74; IBM regl. mgr. and Western Area mgr., Information Systems, 1974-85, ret.; v.p. Pinkerton Computer Consultants Inc. (W. ops.), Burbank 1985–; Computer Literacy Adv. Bd., Loyola Marymount

Univ.; recipient IBM recogn. awards for outstanding achievement, mgmt. and sales mgmt. (1979, 80, 82, 85); mem. Assn. of Data Proc. Profls.; civic: founder and fmr. bd. mem. Half Way House for recovering alcoholic women; fmr. bd. mem. Half Way House for alcoholic men; current bd. mem. Sch. for Developmentally Disabled Adults (Tierra del Sol), pres. Am. Liver Found./So. Calif. Chpt., mem. Burbank CofC; publs: tech. paper on Digital TV, sev. classified papers on Soviet threat; mil: cpl. US Army 1952-53; Republican; Prot.; rec: golf, skiing, vol. work with the disabled. Res: 1313 Valley View Rd Glendale 91202 Ofc: Pinkerton Computer Consultants 333 N Glenoaks Blvd Ste 600 Burbank 91502

LEE, ERNEST GIN, insurance broker/employee benefits consultant; b. Nov. 3, 1955, San Francisco; s. Hall Sik and Pearl Sheung (Yue); edn: Palo Alto Mil. Acad., 1970; dip. Bellarmine Coll. Prep., 1974; stu. St. Mary's Coll., Moraga 1974-76. Career: sales cons. Mass. Mutual, Oakland 1979-81; gen. partner Benefit Design Co., Oakland 1981-82; director Reliance Group Administrators, Oakland 1982-83; pres. E.G. Lee & Company Insurance Services, Inc. 1979–; honors: Rookie Agt. of Yr. 1979, General Agents Mgrs. Assn. Presidents Club, Mass. Mutual, 1979-80; Leaders Assn., Hall of Fame, New England Mutual, 1981; mem. Nat., Oakland-East Bay Assn. of Life Underwriters; club: Moraga Country; Catholic; rec: ski, tennis, racquetball. Res: 317 Elliot St San Francisco 94134 Ofc: E.G. Lee & Co. Inc., POB 29469, Oakland 94604

LEE, GARRETT, physician; b. June 23, 1946, San Francisco; s. Frederick B. and Josephine (Woo) L.; edn: BA genetics, UC Berkeley 1968; MD UC Davis Sch. of Med. 1972. Career: intern Duke Univ. Med. Ctr. 1973; res./cardiology fellow UC Davis 1976; asst. prof. of med. UC Davis Sch. of Med. 1975-77; dir. card. cath. lab. UC Davis 1977-83; dir cardiovasc. laser research lab. Cedars Med. Ctr. Miami, Fla. 1983-84; dir. research Western Heart Inst. San Francisco 1984–; honors: student research award 1972; Alpha Omega Alpha 1972; phys. recog. award 1984; mem: fellow Am. Coll. of Clin. Pharmocol.; fellow Am. Soc. for Laser Med. And Surg.; fellow Am. Coll. of Angiology; Am. Heart Assn.; Am. Fedn. for Clin. Research; publ: 100+ arts. on treatment of cardiovasc. disease. Ofc: 900 Alice St Oakland 94607

LEE, GEORGE MING-CHI, engineer; b. Feb. 22, 1932, Hahn-Kow, Hurbeei, China, nat. US cit. May 27, 1986; s. Tsu-Fen and Annie Chie-Yun (Chao) L.; m. Ming-Fen, Sept. 8, 1958; edn: BS, Tsin-Hwa Univ. Peking 1953, MS, 1956; reg. mech. engr. Calif. 1982. Career: asst. prof. Harbin Civil Engrg. Inst. China 1956-79; design engr. Fluor Engrs. Inc. Mining and Metals Div. 1980-83; mechanical drafter CHA Industries, Menlo Park 1984–; mem. Am. Soc. Mech. Engrs. 1981-; works: domes calculations (dev. formulas for computing the maximum no. of holes on any size of spherical substrate domes, 1984); rec: microcomputers, classical music, bridge. Ofc: CHA Industries 3565 Haven Ave Menlo Park 94025

LEE, JAE KU, company president; b. Mar. 20, 1938, Seoul, Korea; s. Chung Hee and Chin Hee (Cho) L.; m. In Pin Kim, May 27, 1964, 1 dau: Elisa b. 1968; edn: BA, Kun Kuk Univ. 1964; MA, 1968. Career: exec. dir. Hwashin Retail & Mfg. Co., 1967; pres. Moolim Bldg. Material Prods. Co., Inc. 1969; pres./ CEO Dai Ocho USA, Inc. 1975; mem: Korean Am. Assn. (pres.); Korean Comm. Orgn. (S.F & Bay Area rep. 1979); Northwestern US Dist. of the Adv. Council on Peaceful Unification Policy, R.O.K. (pres.); orean Am. Edn. Ctr.; Korean Am. Political Assn.; Multi Svc. Ctr. for Koreans; S.F., Seoul Sister City Commn.; No. Calif. Korean Soccer Assn.; mil: R.O.K. Army 1959-61; Republican; Baptist; rec: music, table tennis. Address: 800 Sea Spray Ln, 102, Foster City 94404

LEE, JAMES WOOILDO, architect; b. March 2, 1945, Hadong Gun, Korea; s. Byung-Moo and So Aha L.; m. Sun-Duck, Feb. 2, 1969; children: Jon Jeung-Hoon, Doli Jeung-Kyu; edn: BS, Univ. of Hanyang 1966; cert., UC Berkeley 1978; Profl. Lic. Architect, Calif. 1980. Career: project architect Project USTS: San Francisco Internat. Airport, Riydh Internat. Airport, Eastern Province Internat. Airport, Jubail Industrial City Project: Residential & Commercial Group, Hope Creek Power Plant Project, Cerra Motoso Nickel Project; currently, project architect, architectural spec.; Bechtel Engring./ Constrn.; honors: Terminal Area Master Plan, San Francisco Internat. Airport, City & Co. of San Francisco 1979; mem: Am. Inst. Architects; Republican; (Nat. Congl. Com. 1982-85); Catholic; rec: golf, leadership. Res: 636 Telford Ave., So. San Francisco 94080 Ofc: Bechtel, 50 Beale St. San Francisco 94119

LEE, JEFFREY CHUCK, lawyer; b. Sept. 25, 1954, Los Angeles; s. Young and Rose Suey (Jong) L.; m. Julia, Sept. 3, 1983; children: Lindsay Nicole b. 1985; edn: BS, USC 1976, JD, Univ. of Santa Clara 1980; admitted Calif. State Bar 1982. Career: atty. assoc. law firm Senzaki, Osajima & Nishimura, 1982-83; prin. solo law practice, 1983-84; ptnr. law firm Turchin & Lee, Glendale 1985–; founding mem. Asian Law Alliance (non-profit legal aid orgn.); mem: ABA, LA County Bar Assn., Los Angeles Trial Lawyers Assn., Chinese Am. Bar Assn., Japanese Am. Bar Assn., Japanese Am. Optimist Club; Democrat; Christian; rec: jogging, swimming, literature. Ofc: Turchin & Lee, 516 Burchett St Ste 103 Glendale 91203

LEE, LAWRENCE B., educator; b. June 4, 1917, Chgo.; s. Judson F. and Jessie Bacon Lee; m. Frances Egger, Apr. 17, 1949; 1 son, Thomas E., b. 1952; edn: BS, Ill. Inst. of Technol. 1939; MA, Univ. Chgo. 1941, PhD, 1957. Career: prof. pol. sci., history Ft. Hays State Coll., Hays, Kans. 1947-49; prof. AFROTC Univ. of Detroit 1951-53; prof. Commerce Sch., Northwestern Univ. 1954-57; prof. history San Jose State Univ. 1957-83, prof. emeritus 1983–; mem: Am. Hist. Soc., Orgn. of Am. Historians, Calif. Hist. Soc., Western Hist. Assn.,

Ag. Hist. Soc., Sierra Club, Audubon Soc., Nat. Resources Defense Council; author: Kansas and the Homestead Act 1982-1905 (Arno Press 1979), Reclaiming the American West (Clio Press 1980), article in Calif. Water Atlas (1979); mil: lt. col. USAF 1942-46, 1951-53; Democrat; Methodist; rec: hiking, gardening, reading, photog., travel. Res: 640 S 14th St San Jose 95112

LEE, MARK CLAYTON, furniture designer/manufacturer; b. Mar. 22, 1949, Fullerton; s. Robert and Audre Wynnette (Minnier) L.; m. Cynthia, Sept. 8, 1975; children: Rachel b. 1967, Lean b. 1970, Seth b. 1976, Ryan b. 1979; grad. Servite Prep Sch. Anaheim 1967. Career: self-taught, furniture designer, mfr., owner Mark Lee Willow Designs, Crescent City; designer original furn. for Knotts Berry Farms, sev. MGM films, num. hotels, pvt. homes; work featured in newspaper articles in The San Francisco Chronicle, L.A. Times Home Mag. (cover illus., Calif. Furniture Craftsmen), L.A. Examiner; avocation: eradication of world hunger thru global cooperation; Esoteriscism; rec: family. Res: 4101 Hwy 101 N Crescent City 95531 Ofc: Mark Lee Willow Designs POB 1454 Crescent City 95531

LEE, NEIL YUN-LIU, engineer; b. Apr. 16, 1947, Kwong-Tung, China, nat. US cit. 1974; s. To Yee and Kim Fon (Chin) L.; m. Sharon F., Sept. 11, 1970; children: Stephanie b. 1971, Abraham b. 1972, Christine b. 1977, Bryan b. 1978; edn: BS, Chu Hai Coll. (Hong Kong) 1969; BS, CSU Los Angeles 1977, MS, 1979; cert. sci. & engring. mgmt., West Coast Univ. 1982; reg. E.I.T., Calif. (1976). Career: asst. struc. engr. Chau Lam Arch. & Assocs., Hong Kong 1969-70; structural dynamic analyst, mem. tech. staff Rockwell Internat., Downey, Ca. 1976—; honors: Tau Beta Pi (1975), Chi Epsilon (1975), Dept. outstanding student LACC (1972), dean's list CSULA (1975, 76), ALT Award, ASTP Award, Flag was flown aboard STS2, NASA; mem. ASCE (assoc.), Nat. Rifle Assn., Smithsonian Assocs.; publs: Two Degrees of Freedom System with Harmonic Base Motion (Nastran Pgm.), Rockwell Intl. (11/84); rec: jogging. Res: 3473 S Falcon Ridge Rd Diamond Bar 91765 Ofc: Rockwell International 12214 Lakewood Blvd (MC AB97) Downey 90241

LEE, PAMELA GINNY, financial planner, b. Sept. 21, 1952, Lodi; d. Sam and Chow Choung (Siu) Lee; edn: BA, UC Berkeley 1974; desig: Cert. Finl. Planner, Coll. for Finl. Plnng. (1983). Career: affirmative action ofcr. Chinese for Affirmative Action, San Francisco 1974-75; comm. liaison Human Rights Commn. 1975-76, Commn. on Study of Women 1976-78; reg. rep./ cert. finl. plnnr. Investors Diversified Svcs., San Rafael 1978-81, AIS Finl. Svcs., Oakland 1981—; mgr. Plnng. Div.; instr. Vista Coll. 1985-; adj. faculty Coll. for Finl. Plnng. 1985; honors: Outstanding Young Woman of Am. (1980); mem. Internat. Assn. Finl. Plnnrs.; civic: The Womens Found. (bd. 1983-85), active var. womens and comm. orgns., 1974-; Democrat. Res: 62 Lobos St San Francisco 94112 Ofc: AIS 300 Lakeside Dr Ste 1300 Oakland 94612

LEE, PETER BINGHENG, acupuncturist, herbalist; b. June 21, 1931, Shanghai, China, nat. US cit. 1985; s. Louis Zhi Tak and Lih Ming (Ling) L.; m. Meiwan, Oct. 24, 1980; 1 son, Thomas C.K. b. 1961; edn: MD, Shanghai Second Med. Coll. 1954; D.Oreintal Med., San Francisco Coll. of Acupuncture & Oriental med. 1984; Cert. Acupuncturist, Calif. Career: resident St. Mary's Hosp., Shanghai, China 1955; MD, First Hosp. of Shanghai Textile Industry Bureau, Shanghai, CHina 1956; lectr. Shanghai Texetile Hosp. Nurse's Sch. 1956; clin. instr. Shanghai Med. Coll., Shanghai, China 1957; prof. of anatomy & surgery Pudu Community Med. Coll., China 1958; clin. prof. San Francisco Coll. of Acupuncture & Oriental med., San Francisco 1983—; currently, pres. Sutter Acupuncture Clinic and acupuncutrist College Medical Clinic; mem: Chinese Acad. of Med. Sciences, United Acupuncturists of Calif., Calif. Cert. Acupuncturists Assn., San Francisco Tung Hwa Benevolent Assn.; works: a concept of idiopathic facial paralysis in T.C.M. 1985; Catholic. Res: 1655 Pacheco St. San Francisco 94116 Ofc: 447 Sutter St. Ste. 417 San Francisco 94108

LEE, ROBERT ANDREW, librarian; b. Dec. 7, 1923, Wash.; s. Frederic Edward and Edna (Stewart) L.; edn: BA, Oberlin Coll. 1947; MLS, USC 1966; Career: jr. cataloger, Columbia Univ. Law Lib. 1950-51; reference librarian N.Y. Daily Mirror 1952-54; researcher for Dore Schary, MGM, Culver City 1955; with Universal Studies 1955—; research librarian 1960-69; head research dept. 1969—; mil: AUS 1943-46, Bronze Star w/ Oak Leaf cluster; mem: Acad. Motion Picture ARts and Scis. (gov. 1973-75); Acad. TV Arts and Scis.; Am. Film Inst.; Los Angeles Internat. Film Expositions; Spl. Libraries Assn.; author: arts. in field. Res: 2212 Cahuenga Blvd. Apt. 104,Los Angeles 90068 Ofc: 100 Universal City Plaza, Universal City 91608

LEE, ROBERT HOPE, gem stone cutter; b. Mar. 15, 1947, Seoul, Korea; s. Yoo Soo and Ki Soon (Chang) L.; m. Carol Sook, Nov. 27, 1974; children: James b. 1977, Sharon b. 1981; edn: BA, Korean Union Coll. 1975. Career: gem cutter/ supv. Mehdi Gem Co., 1975-83; owner R. Lee Gem Co., Los Angeles current; mem. Wholesale Jewelers Assn. of Los Angeles Inc.; mil: Korean Army 1968-70; Republican; Christian; rec: mineral rock, golf, travel. Ofc: R. Lee Gem Co. 607 S Hill St Ste 924 Los Angeles 90014

LEE, SAMMY, physician-surgeon; b. Aug. 1, 1920, Fresno; s. Soonkee (Rhee) and Eunkee (Chun) L.; m. Rosalind Wong, Oct. 1, 1950; children: Pamela Alicia b. 1955, Sammy, II, b. 1960; edn: AB, Occidental Coll. 1943; MD, USC 1947. Career: physician and surgeon, practice limited to diseases of the ear, Santa Ana currently; also diving cons. Mission Viejo (Calif.) Nadadores, and to Korean National Diving Team, 1984—; Gold medallist high diving and Bronze medallist 3 meter springboard 1948 London Olympics; Gold Medallist high diving 1952 Helsinki Olympics; US Sports Ambassador to S.E. Asia 1954;

personal representative of Pres. Eisenhower to 1956 Melbourne Olympics; personal rep. of Pres. Nixon to 1972 Munich Olympics; US Olympic diving coach to 1960 Rome Olympics; apptd. by Pres. Nixon, 1970, to Pres.'s Council on Physical Fitness & Sports, re-apptd. to PCPFS by Pres. Ford, 1975, and by Pres. Carter, 1976; apptd. to Pres. Reagan's Commn. on White House Fellows, 1981; Olympic Torch Runner eve of 1984 Los Angeles Olympic Games, and one of official Olympic Flag Bearers at the Opening Ceremony; awards include: James E. Sullivan Award 1953, voted Outstanding American born Korean, Korean Am. Soc. 1967, inducted into Swimming & Diving Hall of Fame 1984, named USC Sch. of Medicine outstanding alumnus 1984, Occidental Coll. hon. degree Doctor of Science 1984, awardee of Asian Pacific Am. Soc./ USC and Asian Alliance/ Univ. Penn., 1985; mem. AMA, Orange County Med. Assn., Korean Am. Republican Soc. of Orange County (hon. pres.); coauthor book, Diving (Atheneum Books 1979); mil: major US Army M.C.; Republican; Protestant; rec: coaching fancy diving, tennis. Res: 16537 Harbour Ln Huntington Beach 92649 Ofc: Sammy Lee, MD Inc. Ste 559N, 125 E 17th St Santa Ana 92701

LEE, SI KON, college president, clergyman; b. May 15, 1937, Kyungbuk, Korea, nat. US cit. 1976; s. Hun Bong and June Ya (Bang) L.; m. In, Jan. 7, 1967; children: Daniel b. 1969, Susan b. 1972; edn: BA, Keimyung Univ., Taegu, Korea 1965; MS, CSU Fullerton 1975; PhD, Calif. Grad. Sch. of Theology 1974. Career: English tchr. Joong-ang Commerce Secondary Sch., Taegu, Korea 1966-67; tchr. Harbor City (Calif.) Christian Elem. Sch. 1969-70; prof. Defense Language Inst., Fgn. Lang. Ctr. Presidio of Monterey, Calif. 1981-83; bd. trustees/ pres./ prof. Agape Bible Coll., Los Angeles 1983—; vis. prof. Taegu (Korea) Univ. summers 1985-, hon. bd. trustees 1982-; recipient appreciation award Korean Ch. of Pomona Valley, Ontario (1981); doc. dissertation: Orffschulwerk as a technique for the rel. tng. of mentally retarded children; Republic; World Agape Mission Ch./LA (asst. pastor); rec: music appreciation, swimming. Address: Los Angeles 90006

LEE, STANLEY TAK, dentist; b. Mar. 1, 1946, Chungshan, China, nat. US cit. 1973; s. Man Hoy and Bo Yuk (Lau) L.; m. Rita S. Chin, July 3, 1976; children: Winnie b. 1978, Jennie b. 1981; edn: AS, City Coll. of San Francisco 1971; BS, UC Berkeley 1973; DDS, Loma Linda Univ. 1977; lic. to practice dentistry, Nat. Bd. (1976), Calif. Bd. (1978), Canada Bd. (1978). Career: dentist/ owner Family Dental Center, 1978—, and 3 Star Dental Center, 1984—, both in San Jose; honors: Alpha Gamma Sigma (1971), Beta Gamma Sigma (1973), Honor Student Soc. (1973); mem: Santa Clara Dental Soc. (Dental Career Com. 1984), Calif. Dent. Assn., Am. Dent. Assn., Acad. of Gen. Dentistry, Am. Endodontic Soc.; civic: Chinese Culture Assn., Chinese Am. Assn. of Engineers and Scientist, Chungshan Benevolence Assn., Lions Club; research: in Surgical Periodontics, UOP (1983-84), for similarity in response between eye tissue and teeth nerve tissue to inflammation and regeneration (1981-); Republican; Christian; rec: friends. Res: 1317 Echo Valley Dr San Jose 95120 Ofc: 1095 Branham Ln San Jose 95136; 2139 Tully Rd San Jose 95122

LEE, SUNG HEE, acupuncturist; b. Mar. 18, 1932, Seoul, Korea; d. Chong Koo and Hwa Sun (Kwun) Yhee; m. Soon Lee, 1959; children: Jongsoo b. 1960, Choon b. 1963; edn: BA, Su-Do Women's Teachers Coll. 1957; cert., Kyung-Hee Univ. Acad. of Acupuncture 1974; OMD, Samra Univ. of Oriental Med. 1984-85, PhD, 1985; lic. Calif. 1978. Career: acupuncturist Wi-Kang Med. Clin. Seoul, Korea 1961-77, Chinese Herbs & Mercantile Co. 1978-80; operator Han-Chung Oriental Herbs & Acupuncture Clinic 1980-82, Han-Kook Or. Med. & Acup. Clin. 1982—; honors: Award (Kyung-Hee Univ. Acad. of Acupuncture 1974), Certificates (seminars 1982, 84, cert. pgm. 1960, 74); mem: Internat. Acupuncture Assn., Korean-Am. Oriental Med. Doctors & Acupuncturinst Assn.; research: Acupuncture Treatment of Headache, Five-Element Acupuncture; presbyterian; rec: reading, music, children. Ofc: Han-Kook Oriental Med. & Acupuncture Clinic 809 S Vermont Ave Los Angeles 90004

LEE, THOMAS WAY, physician; b. Dec. 20, 1943, Bhamo, Burma, nat. US cit. 1973; s. Way Yway and Daw (Kin) L.; m. Rita, Mar. 31, 1967; children: Patricia b. 1973, Jeffrey b. 1977; edn: BS, Univ. of Rangoon, Burma 1962; MB, BS, Inst. of Medicine, Rangoon, 1967; Bd. cert. Am. Bd. of Obstets. and Gynecols. 1974. Career: med. intern Rangoon Gen. Hosp., Rangoon, Burma 1967-68; intern St. Mary's Hosp., Phila. 1968-69; resident, chief res. ob-gyn., Millard Fillmore Hosp., Buffalo, N.Y. 1969-72; pvt. practice in ob-gyn., Easton, Pa. 1972-73, Upland, Calif. 1973-84, solo practice in Rancho Cucamonga 1984—; asst. clin. instr. SUNY (1970-72); mem: Fellow Am. Coll. Obstets and Gynecols., Fellow Am. Coll. of Surgeons, Fellow Internat. Coll. of Surgeons, Am. Fertility Soc., San Bernardino Co. Med. Soc., San Bernardino-Riverside Ob-Gyn Soc., Calif. Med. Soc., Am. Med. Assn., Am. Assn. Gynecologic Laparoscopists, Burma Med. Soc. (pres. 1984-85); publ: J. of Reproductive Medicine (Oct. 71); Republican; Buddhist; rec: table tennis, swimming, basketball. Res: 1746 Palm Ave Upland 91786 Ofc: 7388 Carnelian St Ste B Rancho Cucamonga 91730

LEE, YUEH-TSEN, acupuncturist; b. Mar. 23, 1943, Ling Seng Ct. Fu-Chien Prov., China; d. Yu-Keng and Chin-Chai (Yao) Wang; m. Chi-Wen Lee, Dec. 12, 1965; children: Huai-Tsu (Mike) b. 1968, Hui-Lang (Diana) b. 1971; edn: BA, Tamkang Univ. 1971; Internat. Research Ctr. for Acupuncture Sci., Inst. of Chinese Culture, 1978-79; AMD, Asian Am. Acupuncture Medicine Univ. 1985; lic. Acupuncturist, Calif. (1979). Career: acupuncturist Kou Seng Clinic, Taipei 1968-79; acupuncturist, ptnr. Wang's Acupuncture, Chula Vista 1981—; acupuncturist, owner Wang's Acupuncture and Herb Center, Solana Beach 1984—; honors: appreciation, Chinese Social Service Ctr. Inc. (1981), Internat.

Acupuncture Soc. (1976); mem: Acupuncture Medicine Assn. of So. Calif. (dir. 1985), Chinese Acupuncture Assn.; civic: Chula Vista CofC, Solana Beach CofC, San Diego Zool. Soc. (asso. 1982); Baptist; rec: cooking. Ofc: Wang's Acupuncture Center, 234 Landis Ave Chula Vista 92010

LEEB, CHARLES SAMUEL, psychologist; b. July 18, 1945, San Francisco; s. Sidney Herbert and Dorothy Barbara (Fishstrom) L.; m. Storme Gilkey, Apr. 28, 1984; edn: BA, psych., UC Davis 1967; MS, CSU San Diego; PhD, edn., psych., Claremont Grad. Sch. 1973. Lic. Psychologist Nev. (1979), Kans. (1980), Calif. (1983). Career: cons. psychologist Palm Hosp., 1975, Golden State Rehab. Ctr., 1974-75, Mar Linda West Hosp., 1975-, Glenhaven of LaVerne Hosp., 1973-75; hosp. adminstr. Glenhaven of Pomona Hosp., 1975-; expert witness L.A. County Superior Ct., 1975-76; assoc. southern reg. dir. Mental Retardation Ctr., Las Vegas, Nev. 1976-78; pvt. practice psychology, Las Vegas 1978-79; dir. Biofeedback and Athletics, and dir. Childrens Div. Biofeedback and Psychophysiol. Ctr., the Menninger Found., 1979-82; chief psychologist Raleigh Hills Hosp., San Gabriel, Calif. 1982-83; pvt. practice Newport Med. Group, San Gabriel 1982-83, Claremont 1984—; tchg. Claremont Grad. Sch., 1970-, San Diego St. Univ. 1967-69; num. seminars, workshops, invited lectures, var. profl. groups, 1973-; num. TV and radio appearances; contbr. to profl. journals; mem: AAAS, Biofeedback Soc. of Am., Nev. Psychol. Assn. Res: 4822 Rodeo St Ontario 91762 Ofc: Clinical Psychologists of Claremont 250 West First St Ste 252 Claremont 91711

LEERSKOV, WILLIAM S., health services administrator/Dr. Indsl. & Orgnl. Psychology; b. Oct. 20, 1943, San Bernardino; s. Wm. Wesley and Jean Louise (Howell) L.; edn: AA, Valley Coll. 1975; BA, CSU San Bernardino 1976, MA, 1980; PhD, Columbia Pacific Univ. 1984; cert. Valpar Nat. Rehab. Tng. Inst.; Spl. Edn. Tchg. Credential (lifetime), Calif. Comm. Colls.; Pupil Personnel Svcs. Credential; Calif. lic. Marriage, Family & Child Therapist (MFCT). Career: 1976—: counselor Genesis II, Human Services, Inc., San Bernardino/ Fontana; profl. student intern Riverside Co. Mental Health -Children's Therapeutic Gp. Home Svc.; counselor/evaluator/job devel. splst. Fontana Rehab. Wkshop, Fontana; rehabilitation counselor/ wkr's comp. splst. Dept. of Rehab., State of Calif., San Bernardino; occupnl. hlth coordinator County of San Bernardino Occupnl. Health Unit; dir. Counseling & Psychological Consultants, San Bernardino; also tchr./counselor Beaumont Boys Mil. Acad.; rehab. cons. var. non-profit agencies; mem. Rehab. Advisory Com. (State); mem. County Gov.'s Task Force DP 37 (state-wide); mem: Am. Cancer Soc. (exec. bd.), Inland Empire Rehab. Assn. (assoc.), Calif. Assn. of Rehab. Profls.; publs: Supervisor's Guide to Employee Aid Program (1982); mil: medic USN, fleet USMC; Republican; rec: photog., writing, skiing. Address: POB 1506 San Bernardino 92402

LEFEBVRE, GEORGE ALFRED, lawyer; b. Feb. 13, 1929, Ft. Huachuca, Ariz.; s. Charles and Mary C. (Figeroa) L.; m. Rebecca M., May 1, 1976; children (prior marriage): Roxanne b. 1952, Suzanne b. 1953, Thomas b. 1955, David b. 1959; edn: BSBA, Ohio State 1952; JD, Univ. of San Diego 1963; admitted to Calif. Bar 1966. Career: mgr. contracts dept. General Dynamic, San Diego 1952-66; atty. self-empl., San Diego 1966-81; mgr. procurement, contracts & legal depts. General Dynamics Svcs. Co., temp. Cairo, Egypt 1981—; honors: del. San Diego Fedn. of Musicians 1976-77; mem: San Diego Co. Bar Assn. (qualified), Calif. State Cts., Fed. Dist. Cts., U.S. Ct. of Clains, Am. Fedn. of Musicians (life); copyrights: composer 3 songs; mil: staff sgt. USMC 1952, Korean conflict; Democrat; Catholic; rec: music. Res: 9358 Crest Dr. Spring Valley 92077 Ofc; General Dynamics Services Company, 105 Omar Ebn El Khattab, Cairo, Egypt

LEFF, ALEXANDER, management consultant, lawyer; b. San Francisco; s. Walter and Muriel (Lerner) L.; edn: BA, Stanford Univ. 1979; JD, Yale Law Sch. 1983. Career: spl. asst. to dir. President's Commn. for a National Agenda for the Eighties, The White House, Wash. DC 1980-81; currently, assoc. McKinsey & Co., New York; mem: Calif. Bar Assn. Ofc: McKinsey & Co., 55 East 52nd St. New York, NY 10022

LEFFERTS, GEORGE LINDSAY, insurance executive; b. Jan. 14, 1932, Jersey City, N.J.; s. George L. and Claire E. (Glassmeyer) L.; m. Joann Smith, July 6, 1955; children: John b. 1957, Carolyn b. 1960; edn: BS, Univ. of Idaho 1953, M.Edn., 1954; desig: CLU, Am. Coll. of Chartered Life Underwriting. Career: coached football and baseball, Calif. Western Univ. (now U.S. Internat. Univ.), 1958-66; life insurance sales agt./mgr. Equitable Life, N.Y. 1968-71, gen. agent Aetna Life & Casualty 1971-78, dist. mgr. Equitable Finl. Services, San Diego 1978—; honors: Jr. College All-American (1951), Community Action Award (1975), Million Dollar Round Table; mem: Nat. Assn. Life Underws., San Diego CLU Chpt., Internat. Assn. of Finl. Planners, Seattle Life Mgrs. Assn. (past pres.), Portland Life Mgrs. Assn. (past pres.); clubs: Downtown San Diego YMCA, Lions, San Diego Athletic; num. articles in life ins. profl. jours.; mil: capt. US Marine Corps 1954-58; Republican; Lutheran; rec: golf, tennis. Res: 6054 Via Regla San Diego 92122 Ofc: Equitable Financial Services 701 B St Ste 855 San Diego 92101

LE GRANDE, PATRICIA DARLENE, artist, teacher; b. Kansas City, Kans.; d. Hugo Ernest and Orteaze Athlene (Sharpe) DeClaudre; m. Sergei Bongart; children: Eric, Lance; edn: Coll. of the Sequoias; Fresno Coll., Bongart Sch. of Art. Career: feature artist Artist of the Rockies and Golden West 1983; artist, teacher Bongart Sch. of Art; honors: Best of Show (Calif. Art Club), 2nd Place (Columbia Greene Nat. Juried Show NY 1981), 3rd Place (JWA 1982), 2nd Place (River Side State Wide Juried Show), 3rd Place (Santa Rosa State Wide Juried Show 1981); mem: Calif. Art Club, Soc. Western Artists; publ: art

featured in Masterworks of Impressionism (1985); feature film featuring work and demonstration shown on PBS-TV (Metropolitan Library Sys. of Okla.); Res: 533 W Rustie Rd Santa Monica 90402

LEHOCZKY, JOHN, III, aerospace-manufacturing co. executive; b. Dec. 23, 1955, Detroit, Mich.; s. John Jr. and Elizabeth Grace (Balla) L.; edn: BS, Eastern Coll. 1977; MBA, Pepperdine Univ. 1981; Cert. in Mfg. Eng., UCLA 1984, Cert. in Purchasing Mgmt., 1985, Cert. in Govt. Contracts Mgmt. 1986; Cert. Purch. Mgr., NAPM, Cert. Mfg. Engr., Soc. of Mfg. Engrs. Career: quality contrtol statistician, analyst, supvr. Mack Trucks Inc., Allentown, Penn. 1977-79; senior acctg. splst. AiResearch Mfg. Co., Torrance, Calif. 1980-81, supvr. mfg. engring. 1981-83, mfg. pgm. mgr. 1984-85, supvr. materiel plnng. 1985, product procurement mgr. 1986—; tchg. mgmt. devel. pgm. AiResearch 1984-; reporter corporate newspaper, Garrett Corp. AiReporter; mem: Soc. of Mfg. Engrs. (senior), Assn. of MBA Execs., Am. Soc. of Quality Control, Jr. Achiev. of So. Calif., Los Angeles Olympics Alumni Assn. (vol.), Delta Pi Epsilon of Eastern Coll.; Republican; Baptist; rec: bicycling, running, education. Res: 4140-159 Workman Mill Rd. Whittier 90601 Ofc: AiResearch Manufacturing Co., 2525 W. 190th St. Torrance 90509

LEIDY, PHILIP BRUCE, clinical psychologist; b. Dec. 30, 1949, Los Angeles; s. Charles William and Norma Ruth (Rosendale) L.; m. Colleen, June 1, 1972; children: Kimberly, b. 1976, Melinda, b. 1979; Lindsey, b. 1983; edn: Rio Hondo Coll. 1968-72; BA, Westmont Coll. 1972; MA, Fuller Theological Sem. 1976; PhD, Fuller Grad. Sch. of Psychology 1979; lic. Psychologist, Calif. BMQA 1981. Career: psychological asst. Creative Counseling Ctr., Hollywood 1979-80; psychol. asst. Live Oak Counseling Ctr., Glendora 1978-81; psychol. asst. Hacienda Psychological Svcs., Hacienda Hghts. 1979-81, clin. psychologist 1981—, jr. partner 1983—; clin. asst. prof. Fuller Grad. Sch. of Psychology 1981-82; honors: Outstanding Young Men of Am., Jaycees 1983; mem: Am. Psychological Assn.; Christian Assn. for Psychol. Studies; Whittier Area Baptist Fellowship (Bd. Overseers, var. coms., tchr. on death, divorce & step families); Republican; Baptist; rec: jogging, racquetball, photog. Res: 9949 Winfield Ave Whittier 90603 Ofc: Hacienda Psychological Services, 2440 S Hacienda Blvds, Ste 104, Hacienda Heights 91745

LEIGHTON, ALAN JOHNSTONE, consulting engineer; b. Nov. 9, 1933, Ft. Lewis, Wash.; s. Harry Raymond and Theola May (Alexander) L.; m. Bonnie Teague; m. 2d. Erma Ann Herzer Bluder, Sept. 1, 1974; 1 dau, Cheryl b. 1968; edn: BS, UC Berkley 1956, MS, 1961; Reg Profl. Engr., Calif. 1965. Career: research engr. Kobe Pump Co., Los Angeles and UC Berkeley 1956-57; US Bureau of Mines, San Francisco 1958-75; research pgm. mgr. US Energy Research & Devel. Admin., Oakland 1975-82; cons. engr. Leighton Consulting Svcs., Walnut Creek 1982—; vis. lectr. in mech. engring. UC Berkeley 1980; chmn. Soc. of Petroleum Engrs. Reg. I, 52nd Annual Calif. Regl. Meeting 1982; career counseling in engring. Bay Area public schs.; honors: Sect. Svc. Award, Soc. of Petroleum Engrs. 1975; Superior Performance awards, US Bureau of Mines 1960, 1968, US Dept. of Energy 1978; Tau Beta Pi (life); mem. Am. Inst. Mech. Engrs., Soc. Petroleum Engrs. (Golden Gate sect. chmn. 1965, v.chmn. 1964, secty. 1966-70), Alpha Shattuck Stephens Masonic Lodge (master 1967, trustee 1968-75), First Congregational Ch. (asst. treas. 1972-78); author or co-author 24 tech. papers in engring. journs., 11 biomathematical papers in optometry journs., contbr. popular tech. article, Calif. Engineer 1980; mil: sp4 US Army Nat. Guard 1957-60; Republican; Presbyterian; rec: hiking, nature study, philosophy. Address: 1816 Holland Dr. Walnut Creek 94596

LEIVERS, ALFRED EMERY, physician; b. Mar. 6, 1908, Benedict, Nebr.; dec. May 18, 1986; s. George Wesley and Cynthia Elizabeth (Blackburn) L.; m. Irma Fesenmeyer, Aug. 21, 1938; children: George Kenneth b. 1946, Christianne b. 1948; edn: BA, UC Los Angeles 1932; MD, Leland Stanford Univ. 1938. Career: chief otorhinolaryngologist Woodland Clinic, Woodland 1941-56; solo pvt. practice, 1956—; otology cons. Crippled Childrens Service 1949-69, Calif. State Dept. of Rehab. 1982-; founding chmn. Enloe Hosp. 1966-; secty. treas. Yolo County Med. Soc. 1951-55; mem: Calif. Acad. of Medicine, Butte Glenn Med. Soc. (bd. dirs. 1977-80, chmn. Med. Ins. Review Com. 1977-81), Calif. Med. Assn., Am. Med. Assn.; publs: Archives of Otol. (1968); Presbyterian. Res: 17 Pebblewood Pines Chico 95926 Ofc: 500 Cohasset Rd Ste 23 Chico 95926

LEMBURG, DAN MICHAEL, business executive; b. Dec. 2, 1947, Fremont, Nebr.; s. Roger Frederick and Yvonne (Seeber) L.; m. Bo, Aug. 23, 1970; children: Matthew b. 1972, Jennifer b. 1973, Benjamin b. 1975; edn: AA, Golden West Coll. 1969. Career: pres. CTA Distbg. Corp., Buena Park 1970-86; pres. Lemburg Devel., Fullerton 1975-86; ret., pvt. investments mgmt., current; civic: Melodyland Young Marrieds Fellowship (founder, leader), Lighthouse Christian Fellowship (founding mem., bd. chmn.), Hotline Help Center (advis. bd.); Republican; Prot.; rec: golf, tennis. Res: 1512 Robin Way Fullerton 92635

LEMONS, HAROLD L., publications co. owner, lecturer; b. Oct. 18, 1921, Terre Haute, Ind.; s. Charles R. and Jenny (Madden) L.; m. Nancy Vaughn, Aug. 26, 1984; edn: BS journ., Univ. Ill. 1948. Career: thirty years in mktg., advtg., and tech. publs. for pvt. industry and aerospace industry; owner, mgr. Associated Publications & Graphics Torrance 1979—; instr. UCLA extn. course, Production Art for the Writer; senior mem. Soc. for Technical Communication (formerly Soc. for Tech. Writers & Publrs.); mil: ensign USN Air Corps 1942-46, pilot flight instr.; Republican. Res: 8100 Glider Ave Los Angeles 90045 Ofc: Associated Publications & Graphics 3825 W 226th St Torrance 90505

LENHART, LAWRENCE DONALD, physician; b. Jan. 31, 1937, Youngstown, Ohio; s. Milton Stephen and Anne (Vansuch) L.; m. Gerry A. Brown, Sept. 2, 1961; children: Jennifer b. 1971, Mark b. 1969, Colette b. 1964, Scott b. 1962; edn: BA, Ohio State Univ. 1958, MD, 1962. Career: intern San Diego Co. Univ. Hosp. 1962-63; med. resident VA, Univ. Miami Hosps. 1965-67; cardiol. res. Cleveland Metro. Hosp. 1967-68; pvt. practice int. med. & cardiol. San Mateo; honors: Alpha Epsilon Delta, Phi Eta Sigma, Physicians Recognition Award (AMA 1985); mem: Calif. Med. Soc., Physicians for Social Responsibility, Psi Chi med. frat., Hillsborough Schs. Found., Mills-Peninsula Hosp. Found. Assoc., Commonwealth Club; patent: method of heart lead tracings 1976; mil: capt. USAF (MC) 1963-65; Republican; Byzantine Catholic; rec: travel, tennis, skiing. Ofc: 36 S El Camino Real, Ste 208, San Mateo 94401

LENOVER, KATHLEEN, financial counselor; b. Sept. 21, 1945; d. Russell and Henrietta (Kuper) Lenover; edn: BA in edn., Mt. St. Joseph On the Ohio 1967; MEd, St. John Coll., Cleveland 1970; desig: MGA, Master Graphoanalyst (1972); Life & Disability Ins. lic.; reg. rep. NASD (Series 6, 7, 22, 63); CFP cand., Coll. for Finl. Plnng., Denver. Career: sch. tchr. in Albuquerque, N.M. and Aurora, Colo., 1967-73, Denver, 1973-79; mgr. major markets, A.B. Dick Co., Denver 1979-82; finl. services rep./ dist. mgr. United Resources, Las Vegas and San Diego, 1982–; dir. membership svcs. and finl. advisor San Diego Teachers Assn.; recipient Golden Circle Award for top sales achieve., Un. Resources; mem. Internat. Assn. for Finl. Plnng., Bus. & Profl. Women, Internat. Graphoanalysis Soc. (Chgo.), Exec. Womens Assn., University Club (S.D.); works: devel. video tng. pgm. for AB Dick Co., sales tng. cassette audio for Un. Resources; Democrat; rec: golf, tennis, handwriting anal. Res: 10669 Porto Ct San Diego 92124 Ofc: United Resources Financial 10393 San Diego Mission Rd San Diego 92108

LENZ, PETER NORRIS, sales executive; b. Dec. 15, 1956, Stockton; s. Howard O. and Alice (Goodwin) L.; edn: BA in acctg., CSU Chico. Career: ofc. mgr. Pace, 1980-81; regl. coll. coord. Adolph Coors Co., 1981-83; spl. project mgr./div. sales mgr. Western U.S., California Cooler, Stockton 1984–; honors: Phi Kappa Tau Alumni of Year (1983, 84, 85); Republican; rec: freelance sports writer, video & hi-fi, photog. Ofc: California Cooler 2601 Teepee Dr Stockton 95205

LEO, ROBERT JOSEPH, association executive; b. Nov. 24, 1939, Paterson, NJ; s. Dewey J. and Jean (Bianco) L.; m. Margaret Elena Ingafu, Aug. 5, 1962; children: Christopher, Nicholas; edn: BA, Temple Univ. 1960, MA, 1962; PhD, Univ. of Wash. 1968. Career: instr. Mammoth Coll., West Long Branch, NJ 1962-64; spl. asst. to chancellor Dallas Co. Comm. Coll. Dist. 1968-71, dir. spl. svcs. and gov. rels. 1971-76; assoc. exec. dir. League for Innovation in the Community Coll., Los Angeles 1976-80, exec. dir., Dallas 1980-82; gen. mgr. Los Angeles Jaycees 1982–; founding pres. Nat. Council Resource Devel., adj. assoc. proj. East Tex. State Univ. 1975-76; chmn. Tex. Health Plnng. Council; honors: distng. svc., Oak Cliff Jaycees 1973; spl. recogn., Nat. Counicl Resource Devel. 1981; Significant Contbr. to Fair Housing, Gr. dallas Housing Opportunity Ctr. 1973; mem: Am. Soc. Tng. and Devel.; Am. Soc. Assn. Execs.; Nat. Council Resource Devel.; AAAS; Fgn. Policy Assn.; Am. Youth Soccer Orgn.; Porter Valley Country Club; Los Angeles Athletic Club; author: arts. in field; Catholic. Res: 11934 Gerald Ave., Granada Hills 91344 Ofc: Jr Chamber of Commerce, 404 So. Bixel St., Los Angeles 90017

LEONE, KENNETH CHARLES, JR., hotel/restaurant chain president; b. Marhcl 9, 1955, San Francisco; s. Kenneth C. Sr. and Elizabeth Joann (Brondon) L.; m. Kimberly Sue, June 18, 1977; children: Sheryl Renee b. 1978, Michele Denise b. 1982; edn: BS, CSU Chico 1978; Cert. Hotel Adminstr., Am. Hotel & Motel Assn. 1982. Career: gen. mgr. Westwater Hotels, Olympia, Seattle, Wash. 1977-84; gen. mgr. Stockton Hilton, Stockton 1984; pres. Wednesdays Restaurants Inc., Stockton 1985-86; currently, exec. v.p. Matteo Hotel Corp./ Matteo Entertainment Corp.; v.p., dir. Matteo Investment Corp.; mem. Rotary, Am. Hotel Assn.; mil: sgt. USMC 1977-80; Republican; Catholic. Ofc: 445 W. Webor Stockton Ln. Ste. 128 Stockton 95203

LEONE, LOUIS MICHAEL, company president; b. May 8, 1948, Waterbury, Conn.; s, Louis Michael and Vivian (Ciccio) L.; m. Irma Rose Heffernan, May 24, 1986; edn: AA, Mattatuck Coll. 1972; BA, UCLA 1975; MA, CSU Northridge 1977. Career: sales, asst. dist. mgr. Clairol Inc., NYC 1968-71; dir. sales evon Mathieu Internat. 1978-79; mgr. Foreign Affair Ltd. 1977-79; owner, pres. Aqua Purity Sentinel 1980–; also: T.A. UCLA 1974; owner, pres. Digital Flotronics Corp., Los Angeles; dir. Digital Automotive Systems inc., Garden Grove; Fortune 500 Ambassador, Statue of Liberty Restoration; owner, Whitefeathers Restaurant, Playa del Rey; honors: Golfer of the Year, Golf Digest 1971; Outstanding Merit Achievs., asst. ed. Arrow, Dean's Advy. Bd., Mattatuck Jr. Coll. 1971; mem: Phi Alpha Rho, So Cal Ten, RimTech, Ferrari Owners Club; publs: Job Satisfaction & Work Productivity, Ind. Research Psychology, UCLA 1976-77; Repulbican; Catholic; rec: golf, squash, boating. Ofc: Aqua Purity Sentinel, 12530 Beatrice St. Los Angeles 90066

LEONG, MARGARET ELIZABETH WOO, psychiatric social worker; b. June 23, 1943, Peoria, Ill.; d. Herbert Ying Yick and Kate H. (Jue) Woo; m. Dr. Tony Chan Leong Jr., Feb. 9, 1974; edn: AA, Merritt Coll. 1965; BA, San Francisco State Univ. 1968; MSW, UC Berkeley 1974; PhD, Wright Inst. 1983; LCSW, Calif. 1980. Career: Teacher's Corp intern, Urban Tchr.'s Corp., Chgo., Ill. 1968-69; tchr. Martin Luther King In-Community Sch., Berkeley 1969-70; field work asst. East Bay Chinese Youth Council, Oakland 1970-72; comm. aide Oakland Pub. Schs., Oakland 1970-71; comm. liaison Alameda Co. Mental Health Svc., Oakland 1975-76; patients rights advoc. 1976-80; psychiatric soc. wkr. 1976–; Alameda Co. Mental Health Asian Caucus & Ethnic Minority Employees Caucus; Alameda Co. Health Care Svcs. Affirmative Action Com. & Tng. Com.; recipient NIMH Grant 1972-74, Carnegie Grant 1972-74, Univ. Grant In-Aid 1973-74; mem: Social Services Union 535; UC Berkeley Alumni Assn; NIMH Sub-com. (E. Oakland Mental Health Citizens Com.); UCB Sch. of Soc. Welfare Counseling Proj. (comm. cons. Calif. Ctr. Proj.); Cub Scouts (den mother); History, Culture & Current Problems of Racial & Ethnic Minorities Com.; Democrat; rec; teddy bear collection, gardening. Res: 334 Newton Ave Oakland 94606 Ofc: Alameda Co. Mental Health, Asian Unit, 285 17th St, 3rd Flr, Oakland 94612

LEPORIERE, RALPH DENNIS, quality engineer; b. Nov. 8, 1932, Elizabeth, NJ; s. Maximo and Christian Leporiere; m. Judith Louise Crowhurst, Nov. 19, 1960; children: Bonnie Ann, b. 1961; David Anthony, b. 1964; edn: BS, Rutgers Univ. 1954; postgrad. Rutgers Statistics Center 1955-6, 1958-9; Coll. of the Holy Names, Oakland 1965-66; Reg. Profl. Quality Engr. Career: chemist NY Quinine & Chem. Works, Inc., Newark NJ 1954-55; asst. to chief chemist/qual. control C.D. Smith Pharmaceutical Co., New Brunswick, NJ 1955-56; asst. supvr. qual. control White Labs, Inc., Kenilworth, NJ 1958-60; staff cons. qual. eng. Calif. & Hawaiian Sugar Co., Crockett, Calif. 1960–; chmn./ instr. Qual. Control Dept. Laney Coll., Oakland 1967–; chmn./ asst. prof. JFK Univ., Martinez 1967-72; instr./mem. adv. com., Annual Stat. Short Course, UC Davis 1969-; mem: Fellow ASQC (S.F. & East Bay Sects.), Toastmasters (Vallejo chpt. pres. 1965), Am. Statistical Assn., Am. Chem. Soc.; civic: Am. Canyon Co. Water Dist. (pres. 1973-83, v.p. 1971-73); Listed: Who's Who in the West 1970-; mil: Med. Svc. Corps, US Army Environmental Health Labs, Edgewood, MD 1956-58. Res: 618 Kilpatrick St Vallejo 94589 Ofc: Calif. & Hawaiian Sugar Co., 830 Loring Ave Crockett 94525

LEQUANG, JOHN CUONG, lawyer, business brokerage co. president; b. Apr. 27, 1945, Hue, S. Vietnam, US cit.; s. Ngoan Q. and Quyen Thi (Tonnu) Le; m. Roma H., 1968; children: Binh, Hoang, minh; edn: JD, Magna Carta Univ. 1979; admitted State Bar S. Vietnam 1968. Career: atty., head law firm S. Vietnam; pres. Computerlaw Realty Torrance; corp. ofcr. United Bus. Investments Garden Grove; mem. tech. staff Rockwell Internat. Lakewood. Ofc: Computerlaw Realty 22300-1 S Vermont Ave Torrance 90502

LERNER, LAWRENCE, interior architecture design co. president; b. Sept. 21, 1923, NY, NY; s. Abraham and May (Epstein) L.; m. Leslie, June 1, 1950; 1 son, Erik b. 1951; edn: BA, Brooklyn Coll. 1948. Career: pres. Environetics Internat. Inc. (and predecessor cos.) 1948-84; pres. Erg Inc.; chmn. emeritus Environetics Internat. Inc.; pres. LDC Cal.; past vis. prof. Ohio Sch. of Arch., Parsons Sch. of Design; bd. advisors Fashion Inst. Technol.; honors: Interior Design Hall of Fame charter member 1985; mem: Young Presidents Orgn. 1963-73, Chief Execs. Orgn. 1973-; mil: lt. US Army Infantry 1942-46. Res: 516 N Beverly Dr Beverly Hills 90210 Ofc: Environetics Internat. Inc. 11110 Ohio Ave Los Angeles 90025

LERNER, RICHARD ARTHUR, corporate and individual financial consultant; b. Apr. 8, 1951, NY, NY; s. Philip and Esther Weinreb (Stern) L.; edn: BS, highest honors, UC Berkeley 1973; MBA, Harvard Business Sch. 1977; CPA Calif. Career: tax mgr. Arthur Anderson S.F.; self-employed financial cons., financial guarantee expert systems design (MIS), emphasis on capital, reserves and liquidity; portfolio mgmt., taxes; fiduciary; honors: Phi Beta Kappa 1973, study published by Harvard (double-weighted excellent, 1977), Mensa 1968; mem. Harvard Bus. Sch. Club No. Calif.; misc. publs. for Industrial Indemnity Fin. Corp. (cons.); Libertarian; Jewish; rec. philosophy, piano, karate. Address: 1134 Green St San Francisco 94109

LERNER, SHELDON, plastic surgeon; b. Mar. 3, 1939, NYC; s. Louis and Lillian Lerner; edn: AB with honors, Drew Univ., 1961; MD, Univ. Louisville 1965. Career: intern, resident Albert Einstein Coll. Medicine, 1965-73; practice medicine, spec. in plastic surgery, Plastic Cosmetic and Reconstructive Surgery Center, San Diego 1973–; mem: AMA, Am. Soc. Plastic and Reconstrv. Surgeons, CMA, San Diego County Med. Soc., San Diego Internat. Plastic Surgery Assn., Masons, Shriners; mil: USPHS 1968-70. Ofc: 3399 1st Ave San Diego 92103

LESHER, DEAN STANLEY, publisher; b. Aug. 7, 1902, Williamsport, Md.; s. Dr. David T. and Margaret E. (Prosser) L.; m. Kathryn E. Crowder, Nov. 23, 1929 (dec. Mar. 7, 1971); m. 2d Margaret L. Ryan, Apr. 2, 1973; children: Dean S., II b. 1934, Melinda Kay b. 1945, Cynthia Ann Rice b. 1947; edn: BA, magna cum laude, Univ. of Md. 1924; LLB, Harvard Law Sch., 1926; admitted bar: Mo., Kans., Nebr., Calif., U.S. Fed. Cts. and Treas. Dept. Career: atty. pvt. practice, Kansas City, Mo. 1926-40, Merced, Calif. 1942-46; owner/pub. newspapers, 1938–, currently hd. newspaper groups with 40 publications (daily and weekly): bd. chmn./pub. Lesher Communications Inc. (Walnut Creek), Calif. Delta Newspapers Inc. (Antioch), No. Calif. Publications Inc. (Walnut Creek and Santa Rosa), pres./pub. Lesher Newspapers Inc. (Merced), Madera Newspapers Inc. (Madera); honors: Phi Kappa Phi, Phi Delta Theta, Sigma Delta Chi, Phi Sigma Kappa, named Publisher of Year in Calif. (1977), Businessman of Year Walnut Creek (1978-79), Best Daily Newsp. in Calif., the Contra Costa Times, CNPA (1979), Outstanding Edn. Publisher in Calif., Gov. of Calif. Comm. Colls. Assn. (1979-80), CSU Trustee (1973-81, 1985-93), Calif. Post-Secondary Edn. Commn. (1978-81), Publisher of Decade, Suburban Newspapers of Am. (1982), Disting. Service Award presented at the White House by Pres. Reagan and V.P. Bush, Nat. Newsp. Assn. (1983), named Mr. Contra Costa County (1985, 86); buildings named: Dean and Kathryn Lesher Library, Merced Coll. (1971), Dean Lesher Outpatient Clinic, Children's Hosp., Oakland (1982), Dean and Margaret Lesher Teaching Auditorium, Mt. Diablo Hosp., Concord (1979); civic: (current) Alameda-Contra Costa Cos. Better Bus. Bur. (dir. 1968-), East Bay BBB (dir.), Bay Area Council (dir. 1970-), East Bay Children's Hosp. Found. (dir.), sponsor accredited H.S. Journalism Classroom at Contra Costa Times, Walnut Creek (1973-), Contra Costa Council (pres.); clubs: Rotary (pres. Merced 1951-52, Cent. Calif. dist. gov. 1958-59, fmr. Internat. Nominating Com.), Blackhawk CC, Round Hill CC, Lakeview. Res: 6 Sally Ann Rd Orinda 94563 Ofc: 2640 Shadelands Dr (POB 5166) Walnut Creek 94596

LESSARD, ARTHUR GILBERT, meteorologist; b. Apr. 18, 1929, New Bedford, Mass.;s. Arthur P. and Juliette M. (Montminy) L.; m. Maria G. Konrad, Dec. 19, 1960; 1 son: Arthur Jr. b. 1963; edn: Eastern N. Mex. Univ. 1964-66; BS atmospheric sci., Univ. of Hawaii 1971. Career: meterologist Nat. Weather Service, Wake Island 1971-72, Nat. Weather Service Severe Storms Forecast Ctr., Kansas City, Mo. 1972-73; leading forecaster Nat. Weather Service, Topeka, Kans. 1973; quality control ofcr. Nat. Weather Service, San Francisco 1973-77; dep. meterologist in charge Nat. Weather Serv. Los Angeles 1977-79; area mgr., meteorologist in chg. Nat. Weather Serv. Forecast Office, L.A. 1979–; govt. liaison to Los Angeles 1984 Olympic Games Orgn. Com.; So. Calif. Nat. Weather Serv. liaison to the Fed. Emergency Mgmt. Agency; mem. Los Angeles Federal Exec. Bd.; On US Dept. of Commerce, Nat. Weather Serv. Line Forecasters Honors List 1971, 73; mem: Am. Meteorol. Soc., Fellow Royal Meteorological Soc., Nat. Weather Assn., Aircraft Owners and Pilots Assn., Nat. Pilots Assn., Nat. Geographic Soc.; contbg. writer Nat. Geographic Soc. publications; mil: SMS (E-8) USAF 1951-71, Korean Service, UN, Nat. Defense Service medals, USN Merit. Service Commendn.; Roman Catholic; rec: flying, philately. Res: 12221 San Vicente Blvd. Los Angeles 90049 Ofc: NOAA/National Weather Service, RM 11102, Fed. Bldg., 11000 Wilshire Blvd Los Angeles 90024

LESTER, DON KEVIN, orthopaedic surgeon; b. July 21, 1950, Chgo.; s. Donald C. and Bonna E. (Esterson) L.; m. Linda, June 7, 1979; 1 son, Tyler b. 1982; edn: BA, UC San Diego 1973; MD, UC Irvine Coll. of Med. 1979. Career: orthopaedic intern L.A. Co.-USC Med. Center 1980, grad. orthopaedic residency Penn. State Univ. Hershey Med. Center, Div. Orthopaed. Surg., 1984; orthopaedic surgeon in pvt. practice, Fresno 1984–; mem. Orthopaedic Research Soc., Fresno Madera Med. Assn.; contbr. 18 publs. in med. jours., num. presentations nat. profl. meetings (1979-); mil: sgt. USAF Nat. Guard, hon. disch. 1973. Ofc: D. Kevin Lester, MD, Inc. 6095 N First St Fresno 93710

LEUNG, DENNIS BEECHAI, import & wholesale co. president; b. Sept. 1, 1942, Hong Kong, nat. US cit. 1972; s. Martin Shiuwing and Sau Hing (Wong) Leung; m. Teresa, Oct. 4, 1966; 1 dau. Christina b. 1968; edn: BA, Hong Kong Univ. 1967; BA, Calif. Coast Univ. 1978, MBA, 1980. Career: senior acct. Levi Strauss & Co. 1969-75; acctg. mgr. Levi Strauss Export Sales Corp. 1976-77; controller Levi Strauss Eximco S.A. 1978-80; v.p. Mon Sac Ltd. 1981-82, pres. 1983–; Levi Strauss Found. Advisory Com. 1976-77; mem: Nat. Assn. Accts. 1973-74, Soc. Chinese Am. Accts. 1978-81, Blackhawk CC; Republican; Catholic; rec: tennis, jogging, golf. Address: Blackhawk, Danville

LEUNG, VINCENT C.L., orthopedic and hand surgeon; b. Mar. 1, 1952, Hong Kong, nat. US cit.; s. Ming-Hin and Kwan-Ying (Chan) L.; m. Karen Chan, 1978; children: Nicky b. 1980, Jonathan b. 1981, Tiffany b. 1984; edn: BS and MS in mech. engring., MIT, 1974; MD, Mount Sinai Sch. of Med. 1979; physician lic. Calif., Conn. Career: grad. research asst., MIT 1974-75; chief resident, Yale Univ. Sch. of Med. 1983-84, instr. in orthopedics; hand surgery fellow Loma Linda Univ. Sch. of Med. 1984-85; orthopedic & hand surgeon, pvt. practice, Stockton 1985–; honors: Tau Beta Pi, Pi Tau Sigma, Clapp & Poliak cash award for biomed. engring. design (1974); mem: AMA, Calif. Med. Assn., San Joaquin County Med. Soc.; publs: research publs. in NSF Hard Materials Research (1974), J. of Dental Research (1976), Yale Univ. Sch. Medicine (1984), J. Pediatric Orthopedics (1985), Orthopedics (1986). Ofc: 333 E Alpine Stockton 95204

LEUNG, VINSON YUE-HON, mechanical engineer; b. Oct. 10, 1953, Canton, Kwongtung Province, nat. US cit. 1984; s. Chin Pang and Kim Kwawn (Lau) L.; m. Annette Chan, Aug. 25, 1979; children: Michael b. 1984, Allison b. 1986; edn: BS, Dalhousie Univ. 1977; B.Eng., Technical Univ. of Nova Scotia 1979; Reg. Profl. Engr., Calif. 1983. Career: pressure vessel engr. Ralph M. Parsons Co., Pasadena 1980-81; apparatus engr. C.F. Braun & Co., Alhambra 1981-83; applications engr. Futura Metal Technology, Westlake Village 1983-84; project mechanical engr. J.C. Schumacher Co., Oceanside 1984–; mem. ASME, Assn. of Profl. Engr. of Nova Scotia; mem. J.C. Schumacher Co. sports team, orgnzr. of co. tennis team; works: devel. pilot plant of producing electronic grade silicon and wafer; Roman Catholic; rec: auto mechanics, sports, music. Ofc: J.C. Schumacher 396 Via El Centro Oceanside 92054

LEUTY, GERALD JOHNSTON, osteopathic physician-surgeon; b. July 23, 1919, Knoxville, Iowa; s. Johnston William and Mable Geraldine (Johnston) L.; m. Norma Jean Hindman, Dec. 30, 1964; children: Barbara, b. 1970; Patrick, b. 1975; edn: AA, Kemper Mil. Sch. 1939; Coll. of Mortuary Sci. 1941; Drake Univ. 1946; DO, Coll. of Osteopathic Med. & Surgery 1949; lic. Osteopathic Physician & Surgeon, Calif. 1975. Career: mortician/ embalmer, Des Moines, Ia. 1940; aeronautical engr. Boeing Aircraft Co., Wichita, Ks. 1942; bacteriologist US Army Med. Corp. 1942, 46; osteopathic physician- surgeon, Knoxville, Ia. 1949, 56; clin. dir. Leuty Osteopathic Clinic, Earlham, Ia. 1956-77; osteopathic physician- surgeon, gen. practice, Santa Rosa, Ca. 1977– ; lectr. Coll. of Osteopathic Med. & Surgery, Des Moines, Ia. 1975; assoc. preceptor instr. Coll. of Osteopathic Medicine of the Pacific, Pomona 1981-83, prof. clin. med. 1985; honors: Life mem. Am. Med. Soc. of Vienna 1970; Fellow, Internat. Coll. of Angiologiae 1980; OPSC Awd. 1981; mem: Iowa Osteopathic Soc. (pres. 6th dist. 1974); Soc. of Osteopathic Physicians; No. Calif. Osteopathic Med. Soc. (pres. 1981); Osteopathic Physicians & Surgeons of Calif. (pres. 1982); Am. Osteopathic Assn. (House of Delegates); Am. Acad. of Osteopathy Calif. Div.); Lions Club, Knoxville, Ia. (pres. 1946); Am. Legion, Ia. (6th dist. commdr. 1974-75); works: Eitiology of Primary Atypical Pneumonia 1944; mil: sgt. US Army M.C. 1942-46, Respiratory Disease Commn.; Republican; Presbyterian; rec: travel, photog. Res: 5835 La Cuesta Dr Santa Rosa 95405 Ofc: 4275 Montgomery Dr Santa Rosa 95405

LE VECQUE, CHARLOTTE ROSE, psychiatric social worker; b. Nov. 11, 1944, Darby, Penn; d. George Alfred and Charlotte Vivian (Bunsart) L.. Edn: BS, Western Michigan Univ., 1966; MSW, Adelphi Univ., 1968.; LCSW, lic. clin. soc. wkr. NY 1968, Calif. 1974; ACSW, NASW, 1970. Career: psychiat. social worker Patton State Hosp., Patton, CA, 1968; Sr. psychiat. soc. wkr. dept. mental health San Bernardino Co. Hosp., 1971-74; dept. psychiat. So. Cal. Permanente Med. Grp., Fontana, San Bernardino and Canyon Crest, 1974–; LCSW, dept. psychiat. So. Cal. Prmanente Med. Grp.; Nat. Assn. of Soc. Wrks. (mem. at large); guest lectr. Clin. Psycho Internship; speaker health topics seminars. Awards: Orange Empire Dog Club service award (1983), cert. of merit (1984); mem: NASW; fellow, SCSW; Nat. Registry Health Care Providers (charter); ASCW. Orgns: Palm Springs Kennel Club; Am. Fox Terrier Club; Western Fox Terr. Breeders Assn. (bd. govs., ed. Kliptails); Santa Ana Valley Kennel Club; San Bedo. Humane Soc; San Bedo. Horseman's Assn; publs: Terrier Chit Chat, Front & Finish, Down to Earth; Democrat. Rec: Fox Terrier breeding, exhibs., tng., horseback riding. Res: 3465 E. Holly Circle Dr Highland 92346 Ofc: SCPMG, 5225 Canyon Crest Dr Riverside 92507

LE VESQUE, GERALDINE A., finance management official; b. May 24, 1935, St. Paul, Minn.; d. Joseph Arthur and Anna Charlotte (Kohls) Le Vesque; desig: spl. mgmt. and tech. course certs: Am. Inst. of Banking (1965), Nat. Assn. of Bank Women (1978), The Forum (1980), Citibank (1981), Inst. for Adv. Technology (1984). Career: audit ofcr. Bank of California, N.A. 1968-70, asst. auditor 1970-79, asst. v.p./mgr. Fund Mgmt. 1979-81, asst. v.p./project leader Corp. Services 1981-82, asst. v.p./mgr. Correspondent Bank & Payroll Services 1982–; honors: First woman auditor at Bank of California in 104 years, First individual to qualify for Mgmt. Certification by NABW Ednl. Found.; mem. Nat. Assn. of Bank Women, Nat. Assn. of Female Execs., Toastmasters (past pres.); civic: Deafness Research Found., Animal Protection Inst. of Am., Peninsula Humane Soc.; publs: educational modules for NABW Ednl. Found. (1st non-profl. author accepted); Democrat; Lutheran; rec: oil painting. Ofc: Bank of California, N.A. 400 California St San Francisco 94115

LEVINE, STANLEY BRYANT, pathologist; b. June 27, 1942, St. Louis, Mo.; s. Morris Harold and Frances Ida Levine; edn: BS, Tufts Univ. 1963; MD, Harvard Univ. 1967; Career: anatomic pathol. res. Yale New Haven Med. Ctr. 1967-69; clin. pathol. res. Walter Reed Army Med. Ctr., Wash. DC 1969-71; chief pathol. US Army Hosp., Saigon, So. Vietnam 1971-72; chief clin. pathol. Letterman Army Med. Ctr. San Francisco 1973-74; chief of hematol. Metropolitan Hosps., Portland, Ore. 1974-77; chief clin. pathol. O'Connor Hosp., San Jose 1977–; asst. clin. prof. clin. pathol., nuclear med. Univ. Ore. Med. Sch. 1977; lectr. hematopathol. course Armed Forces Inst. of Pathol. 1977-80; mem: Am. Soc. Clin. Pathols., Coll of Am. Pathols., Soc. of Nuclear Med., AMA, CMA, Santa Clara Co. Med. Soc., Am. Assn. Clin. Chem. (pres. No. Calif. Div. 1987, Roundtable co-chair 1987), Phi Delta Epsilon; publ: papers in Clin. Nuc. Med. (1977), Archives of Pathol. (1973, 74, 77), Am. J. Surg. (1970), JAMA (1985); mil: major US Army 1969-74, Bronze Star, Vietnam Svc.; rec: softball, tennis, racquetball. Res: 3180 Loma Verde Dr Apt 11 San Jose 95117 Ofc: O'Connor Hosp. 2105 Forest Ave San Jose 95128

LEVY, MARGARET, lawyer; b. March 11, 1951, Louisville, Ky.; d. Henry A. and Grace (Ades) L.; edn: BA, Mich. State Univ. 1972; JD, UCLA Law Sch. 1975. Career: assoc. Adams, Duque & Hazeltine, Los Angeles 1975-81, ptr. 1981–; honors; UCLA Law Review 1974-75; UCLA Moot Ct. Honors Pgm. Exec. Bd. 1974-75; Nat. Merit Scholar 1969; mem: Am. Bar Assn. (Torts & Ins. Practice sect.), Los Angeles Co. Bar Assn. (Trial Lawyers sect.), Assn. of Bus. Trial Lawyers, Women Lawyers Assn., Contstitutional Rights Found. (Lawyers Adv. Council), Public Counsel; Democrat; Jewish; rec: tennis, golf, bicycling. Ofc: Adams, Duque & Hazeltine, 523 W. Sixth St. Los Angeles 90014

LEWELLEN, ROYCE RUTLEDGE, judge; b. Sept. 25, 1930, St. Louis, Mo.; s. Ursul Garnet and Helen Frances (Rutledge) L.; m. Margaret Ruth, Dec. 10, 1977; children: Mark b. 1958, Michael b. 1961, David b. 1970; edn: BA, distn., Univ. of Mo. 1952; LLB, UC Boalt Hall Sch. of Law 1957; admitted to Calif. Bar 1957; US Dist. Ct. (so. dist.) Calif. Bar 1958. Career: assoc. Arden T. Jensen, Solvang 1957-59; sole practice law, Solvang 1959-71; ptr. Lewellen & Kersten 1971-73, Lewellen & Canter 1974-75; judge Solvang Judicial Dist. of Santa Barbara 1968-75, superior ct. County of Santa Barbara, Santa Maria 1975–; trustee Solvang Sch. Bd. 1966-74; pres., dir. Solvang Bus. Assn. 1970-75; moderator Presbytery of Santa Barbara United Presbyterian Ch. Synod of Calif. 1968-69; cmmr. Gen. Assembly, United Presbyterian Ch. 1970; dir., v.chmn. bd. Central Freighters Inc., Joplin, Mo. 1970-; mem: Calif. Judge Assn. (dir. 1982-85, exec. bd. 1982-85), Calif. Judges, Marshals & Constables Assn. (dir. 1974-75), Criminal Law Procedure Inst. (chmn. 1984), Rotary (pres. Santa Ynez Valley 1969-70); YMCA (dir. Santa Maria Valley 1981-83);

mil: 1st lt., USAF 1952-54; rec: backpacking, gardening. Res: 5745 Oakhill Dr. Santa Maria 93455 Ofc: Superior Court No. 1, 312 E. Cook St. Santa Maria 93454

LEWIS, DENNIS CARROLL, public relations executive; b. Jan. 7, 1940, Milwaukee, Wis.; s. Cappy and Alyce Mae (Bryce) L.; div.; 1 son, Benoit b. 1975; edn: undergrad. Univ. Wis. 1957-61; BS in philos./rel., CSU San Francisco 1964. Career: computer pgmmr./analyst Levi Strauss, San Francisco 1969-72; freelance book ed., S.F. 1972-73; book ed. Miller Freeman Publs. 1973-76; public rels. writer/ account exec. Paul Purdom & Co., S.F. 1977-81; co-pub. Computer Publicity News, 1981–; co-founder, ptnr. Hi-Tech Publicity Consultants, 1981-84, pres. Hi-Tech Public Relations, Inc. 1984–; mem: Pub. Rels. Soc. of Am., Pub. Rels. Roundtable, Internat. Assn. of Bus. Communicators, Bus. Profl. Advt. Assn., S.F. CofC; co-editor (w/Jacob Needleman) two books: On The Way To Self Knowledge (Knopf, 1976), Sacred Tradition & Present Need (Viking, 1975), contbr. num. book reviews and articles in bus., trade and gen. interest publs.; Democrat; rec: tennis, chess. Res: 523 Valley St San Francisco 94131 Ofc: Hi-Tech Public Relations, Inc. 444 DeHaro St San Francisco 94107

LEWIS, GERALD JORGENSEN, judge; b. Sept. 9, 1933; s. Norman Francis and Blanche Myrtle (Jorgensen) L.; m. Laura S. McDonald, Dec. 15, 1973; children: Michael D.G., Mark J.; edn: AB, magna cum laude, Tufts Univ. 1954; JD, Harvard 1957; admitted State Bar of Calif. 1962, D.C. Bar 1957, NJ Bar 1961. Career: atty. Gen. Atomic, La Jolla 1961-63; mem. firm Haskins, Lewis, Nugent & Newnham, San Diego 63-77; lectr. bus law San Diego State Coll. 1961-62; Calif. Cont. Edn. of Bar 1971, 1976; tchr. evidence law Western State Univ. Coll. Law 1977–; city atty. City of Del Mar 1963-74, City of Coronado 1971-77; spl. counsel San Diego Co. Comprehensive Plnng. Orgn. 1972, San Diego Co. Med. Soc. 1976-77; judge protem San Diego Co. Superior Court 1975-76; judge El Cajon Municipal Court 1977-78, Superior Court of Calif., San Diego Co. 1978-84, Associate Justice, Calif. Court of Appeal, 1984–; exec. bd. Western State Univ. Coll. of Law; mem: Nat. Inst. Municipal Law Ofcrs.; San Diego Co. City Attys. Assn.; Calif. and San Diego Co. Bar Assns.; Am. Arbitration Assn. (panel of arbitrators); Calif. Judges Assn.; Rotary; mil: lt. commdr. USNR 1958-61. Res: 6505 Caminito Blythefield,La Jolla 92037 Ofc: San Diego County Courthouse, San Diego 92101

LEWIS, GLEN ALAN, pulp and paper manufacturing executive; b. June 22, 1958, Willows; s. Lee Francis and Carole Diane (Carlile) L.; m. Jill Christine Medwid, 1986; edn: undergrad. Cal Poly S.L.O. 1976-78, Harvard Univ. 1978; BA, UC Los Angeles 1980; pilot USAF Sch., Tx. 1981. Career: tech. supr., paper mill, Container Corp. of Am. (Mobil Corp.), Los Angeles 1981-82, tech. supt. 1983, prodn. supt. 1984-85, prodn./tech. supt. paper mill prodn. & tech. ops., 1985–; cons. in field; awards: Walter Wells Meml. Scholar (1976), Calif. State Scholar (1976-80), Disting. Citizen Award, Willows, Calif. (1972), Air Force ROTC Grad. UCLA (1980); mem. Tech. Assn. of the Pulp and Paper Industry, Am. Chem. Soc., L.A. World Affairs Council, Lambda Chi Alpha frat.; mil: capt. USAFR 1980-; Republican (Nat. Rep. Congl. Com.); Baptist; rec: nature, sports, flying. Ofc: Container Corporation of America 2001 E 57th St Los Angeles 90058

LEWIS, HOWARD DAVIS, software co. president; b. Nov. 5, 1935, Doyle, Tenn.; s. Howard Wilson and Mildred Louise (Davis) L.; m. Patricia Franklin, Oct. 9, 1970; children: Lise b. 1956, Quinn b. 1957, David b. 1962, Mildred b. 1963, Cassandra b. 1968, Kristianna b. 1972; edn: BSEE, Indiana Inst. of Tech. 1961; MBA, CAF, Harvard Bus. Sch., 1964. Career: engr. Rockwell Internat. 1969; engr. supvr. Lockheed Corp. 1972; software mgr. Hughes Aircraft 1975; const. to IBM 1976; mktg. rep. for Raythoen 1977; vice pres./chief scientist Intercon Systems Corp. 1979; co-founder/pres. Systems Software, Inc., Anaheim 1979–; asst. prof. CSU Long Beach 1972; recipient num. achievement awards from employer cos.; mem. Assn. of Old Crows Engring. Soc., Fellow IEEE, Anaheim CofC; mil: US Air Force; Republican; Lutheran; rec: golf, books, amateur chef. Res: 1662 Aspen Grove Ln Diamond Bar 91765 Ofc: SSI 1532 East La Palma Anaheim 92805

LEWIS, JERRY, U.S. congressman; b. Oct. 21, 1934; divorced; children: Jerry, Jennifer, Jeff and Dan (twins); edn: BA, UCLA 1956. Career: life insurance underwriter; field rep. for former US Rep. Jerry Pettis; mem. Calif. State Assembly, 1968-78 mem. 96th-99th US Congresses (Appropriations Com.) from 35th Dist. Calif.; past mem. San Bernardino Sch. Bd. Ofc: 326 Cannon House Office Bldg., Wash. DC 20515

LEWIS, MARVIN ELLIS, lawyer; b. July 14, 1907, San Francisco; s. Ellis and Selena (Cohen) L.; m. Frederica, June 15, 1935; children: Joelle b. 1939, Marvin K. b. 1942; edn: LLB, San Francisco Law Sch. 1929. Career: commnr. Office of the US Price Adminstrn. for 9th Circuit, 1942-44; supervisor City and County of San Francisco 1945-55, legislative rep. of San Francisco in Wash DC, 1955; second pres. of Bay Area Rapid Transit Dist. (BART); trial atty. in pvt. practice, prin. Lewis & Lewis, San Francisco currently; author of book: Psychic Injuries; lectr. in law schools and to practicing trial attys. throughout USA; mem. Law Sci. Acad.; mem. Coll. of Advocacy Hastings Coll. of Law, Harvard Law Sch. and Mich. Law Sch.; advis. bd. NY Inst. of Legal Research; awards: Trial Lawyer of the Year (1983) Am. Board of Trial Advocates, Man of the Year (1975) City of Hope, recognition awards: Law Student Div. of ABA, San Diego Trial Lawyers Assn., Bay Area Rapid Transit (1986); mem: ABA, Internat. Acad. of Trial Lawyers (fellow 1975-; bd. dirs.), Calif. Trial Lawyers Assn. (founding v.p. 1961-), Western Trial Lawyers Assn. (pres.); clubs: DeMolay (Internat. Supreme Council), Moose, Scottish Rite (Knight Comdr. Ct. of Honor 1985), Shriners, Moskovitz Luncheon Club; Democrat; Jewish. Res: 2020 Geri Ln Hillsborough 94010 Ofc: Lewis & Lewis 690 Market St, Penthouse, San Francisco 94104

LEWIS, MICHAEL WILLIAM, county administrative executive; b. May 29, 1951, Pasadena, Calif.; s. Wm. S. and Mary E. (Enyart) L.; m. Lorraine, Dec. 30, 1955; edn: pol. sci., CSU Fullerton 1970-72; bus. adminstrn., CSU Los Angeles 1973-74. Career: student intern to staff asst., asst. deputy, deputy, asst. chief deputy, chief of staff County of Los Angeles 1973–; former bd. mem., pres. So. Calif. Rapid Transit Dist.; chmn. adv. bd. Joint Ctr., Rice Univ.; former mem. South Coast Air Qual. Mgmt. Dist.; honors: Eagle Scout, Outstanding Public Svc. Award (Urban Mass Transp. Adminstrn. 1982); mem: Jonathan Club, San Dimas Planning Commn., Young Execs. of Am. (bd.); author: Moving People- A Layman's Guide to Improving Public Transit; Republican; Catholic; rec: photog. Res: 843 Calle Arroyo, San Dimas 91773

LEWIS, NORMAN, author, educator; b. Dec. 30, 1912, NY, NY; s. Herman and Deborah (Nevins) L.; m. Mary, July 28, 1934; children: Margery b. 1942, Debra b. 1949; edn: BA, City Coll. of N.Y. 1939; MA, Columbia Univ. 1941. Career: instr. City Univ. of N.Y. 1943-52; assoc. prof. of English, N.Y. Univ. 1955-64; instr. Compton (Ca.) Coll. summers 1962-64, UCLA Ext. 1962-69; prof. of English (communs. dept. chmn. 1964-75), Rio Hondo Coll., Whittier 1964–; honors: pres. Academic Senate R.H.C. (1966-68), Outstanding Tchr., Alpha Gamma Sigma, R.H.C. (1980, 82, 84); mem. Authors League of Am.; author 29 books and textbooks (1941-) including the R.S.V.P (Reading, Spelling, Vocabulary, Pronunciation) series, How to Read Better and Faster (4th ed. 1978), The New Roget's Thesaurus in Dictionary Form (revised ed. 1978), Word Power Made Easy (rev. ed. 1978), Instant Word Power (rev. ed. 1982); contbr. articles nat. mags. 1939-63, incl. Cosmopolitan, Coronet, Saturday Evening Post, Harper's, Ladies Home Jour., Reader's Digest, Vogue; editor Correct English Mag. 1946-52; rec: bridge, chess. Ofc: Rio Hondo College Whittier 90608

LEWIS, OREL EASTLICK, civil engineer, ret.; b. May 3, 1903, Orofino, Calif.; s. Wm. Lincoln and Belinda Ann (Eastlick) L.; m. Eleanor Ashley, Oct. 6, 1935; children: Janet b. 1938, William b. 1941; edn: BSME, UC Berkeley 1932; BSCE, Oregon State Univ. Corvallis 1948; Reg. Profl. Engr. Calif., Ore. Career: engr. US Indian Svc. 1948-49; engr. incharge of road pgm Siskyou Co. 1949-58; cons. engr. pvt. practice 1958-79; honors: Citizen of the Year (Scott Valley CofC 1983); mem: Am. Soc. Civil Engrs. (life), Nat. Rifle Assn., Commonwealth Club, Siskyou Co. Hist. Soc., Sierra Club, Wilderness Soc., Audubon Soc., Scott Valley Jr. Rifle Club (leader, coach 1950-80); mil: capt. US Army 1941-45; Republican; Methodist; rec: local history, working with youth groups. Res: 5726 Lighthill Rd Fort Jones 96032

LEWIS, ROBERT LEE, III, medical laboratory executive; b. Sept. 20, 1949, San Francisco; s. Robert, Jr. and Dolores Patricia (Brady) L.; m. Kimberly G. Hawkins, June 24, 1972, div. 1981; edn: BS, CSU Fresno 1971, MBA 1978; adv. mgmt., Stanford Univ. 1983. Career: admin. asst. to regional v.p./ops. ofcr. Security Pacific Nat. Bank, Valley Div., 1971-74; service chief Fresno County Health Dept., Rehab. Svcs., 1974-79; adminstrv. dir. Clinical Labs., Stanford Univ. Hosp., 1979-84; pres. Western Div., Internat. Clin. Lab., Dublin 1984–; mem. hiring boards State of Calif. and Fresno County, 1978-79; hosp. mgmt. cons. 1982-, cons. Syva Co. (1983-84), Nichols Inst. (1984), Abbott Diagnostics (1984-86), Performance Health Care (1986); mem: Clin. Lab. Mgmt. Assn. (founder No. Calif. Chpt. CLMA 1985), Calif. Clin. Lab. Assn. (bd. 1984-86), Pi Omega Pi frat. (v.p. 1970-71), Goodwill Industries (adv. bd. 1977-78), Fresno County Council for Devel. Disabled (ofcr. 1975-79), Calif. Assn. for Rehab. Facilities (co-chmn. 1976 State Conf.), Mayor's Com. on Hiring the Handicapped (1976-79); civic: YMCA Century Club (1985), Stanford Buck Club (1980-), Fresno Assn. for the Retarded (dir. 1975-78); publs: Optimizing Productivity: Capital Equipment Acquisition (106 pp., 1985) and ednl. video tape: Tools for Success (1985) pub. Am. Assn. Clin. Chemistry; lectr. profl. confs. (1984-); mem. editl. bd. Syva Monitor (1984); mil: Calif. Army Nat. Guard 1971-76; Republican; Roman Catholic; rec: tennis, collect S.W. Art. Res: 108 Durham St Menlo Park 94025 Ofc: ICL-Western 6511 Golden Gate Dr Dublin 94568

LEWIS, RONALD GEORGE, automotive corporation executive; b. Sept. 14, 1942, Orange; s. George Oliver and Phyllis Eleanor (Alfrey) L.; m. Nora Kathleen Lee, Aug. 26, 1967; children: Kristine b. 1969, David b. 1972; edn: AA, Santa Ana Coll. 1962; BA, San Jose State Univ. 1965; post grad., 1965-66; post grad., Pepperdine 1968, 1969-70; Spl. Secondary (1965), Gen. Secondary (1966), and Standard Life (1972) tchg. credentials, Calif.; Automotive Smog Equip. Installers Lic., Bureau of Auto Repair 1972-77. Career: dir. aquatics City of Santa Ana 1963-69; automotive instr. Sunny Hills H.S., Fullerton 1966-72; with Nissan Motor Corp. 1972–; tech. tng. instr., Los Angeles Reg. 1972-74; dist. svc. mgr. 1974-75; consumer rels. mgr. 1975-76; regl. svc. mgr. I, Nissan Motor Corp., San Francisco region 1976-81; regl. svc. mgr. II, Los Angeles region 1981-82; nat. mgr. Consumer Relations, Carson 1982–; automotive adv. bd. Rio Hondo Coll. 1975; advis. com. Career Expo, Humbolt County Schs. 1978; awards: Eagle Scout, BSA 1959; Man of the Year 1962, Santa Ana Coll.; Tech. Awd., Hon. Mention, Nissan Motor Corp. 1976; mem: Epsilon Pi Tau (pres. 1965-66); Calif. Indsl. Edn. Assn.; Soc. of Automotive Engrs.; Soc. Consumer Affairs Profls. (treas.); Automobile Importers of Am. (chmn. consumer rels. com.); Am. Mgmt. Assn.; Sigma Chi frat. (v.p.); Homeowners Assn.; Parent Tchr. Orgn.; works: devel. & implemented current Nissan Customer Care Pgm., incl. Mediation/ Arbitration Dispute Resolution Mechanism 1982-83; implemented a consumer assistance 800 hotline system and automated consumer rels. tracking system; Republican; rec: bicycling, swimming, restoration of vehicles. Res: 7562 Indigo Ln La Palma 90623 Ofc: Nissan Motor Corporation, 18501 S Figueroa St Carson 90248

LEWIS-BALLARD, TWINKLE LURENE, real estate broker; b. Oct. 30, 1951, San Diego; d. Martin Franklin and Eula B. (Goddard) Lewis; m. Michael Ballard, May 29, 1981; children: Mark b. 1977, Heather b. 1984; edn: real estate courses, Anthony Profl. Sch. 1981; real estate broker 1981. Career: real estate sales Century 21 George Higgins Realty, Santee, Calif. 1976-79; real estate sales, co-owner Lewis, Rose & Lewis Real Estate, Santee 1979-81; broker, co-owner Lewis & Lewis Realty, Santee 1981–; honors: Bank of Am. Award for Music (1969); mem: East County Bd. of Realtors 1976-81, Delta Chi Omega (Harding Coll., Ark.); Republican; Ch. of Christ; rec: ceramics, flower arranging, crafts, music. Ofc: Lewis & Lewis Realty, 9237 Prospect Ave Santee 92071

LEZAK, DANIEL SHERWIN, corporate executive; b. Dec. 1, 1933, Chgo., Ill.; s. Nathan and Jeanette Lezak; m. Cheryl Corol, Nov. 19, 1983; children: Jeffrey, Gary, Scott; edn: BS in acctcy., Roosevelt Univ.; Certified Public Acct., Calif. 1963. Career: tax dept. Armour & Co., Chgo. 1957; internal auditor Revel Inc., Venice, Calif. 1958; controller and treas. Remanco Inc., Santa Monica 1962; empl. with Hughes Aircraft; sec.treas., then asst. to the pres. Winsco Instruments and Controls (merged into Genisco Tech. Corp.); empl. with John Reitz & Co., Los Angeles; pres. Internat. Recreation & Sports Inc., -1971; splst. in revitalizing troubled cos. 1970–; current: pres. Lezak Group, Inc. (OTC); dir. Lezak Group Inc., General Residential Corp., Bio Recovery Technology Inc., Five Star Energy Corp, Tellus Inds., West Coast BanCorp., Indian Earth Cosmetics, Super Video Inc.; mem. Calif. Soc. of CPAs; mil: splst 1/c US Army 1953-55; Republican; Jewish. Res: 987 Tahoe Blvd Incline Village NV 89450 Ofc: Lezak Group Inc. 23501 Park Sorrento Calabasas 91302

LI, CHAO SHIH, structural engineer; b. Nov. 22, 1938, Foochow, Fulkien, China; s. Ching Hsiang and Chih Ju (Lin) L.; m. Ai Jung, Aug. 14, 1973; 1 son, Perry b. 1979; edn: BS agri. engrg., Nat. Taiwan Univ. 1962; MSCE, Univ. Tex. El Paso 1971; PhD engrg., Univ. Tex. Arlington 1978; Reg. Profl. Engr. Calif. 1979. Career: civil engr. Taiwan Power Co. 1965-70, Perez & Assoc. Cons. Engrs. El Paso, Tex. 1971-72, DeLeuw Cather Internat. Cons. Engrs. Taiwan 1973; grad. assoc. Univ. Tex. Arlington 1973-77; senior structural engr. Walton Becket Assoc. Archs. L.A. 1978-80; Procon Inc. L.A. 1980-81; group leader Engrg. Mechanics C.F. Braun & Co. L.A. 1981–; mem: Tau Beta Pi, Alpha Chi, Chi Epsilon; designer: Beverly Shopping Ctr. Beverly Hills 1978-80; presentation at engrg. mechanics conf.; rec: swimming, fishing, travel, music. Res: 1933 Tillie Ct West Covina 91792 Ofc: C.F. Braun & Co. 1000 Fremont Alhambra 91802

LI, HSIAO-PAO, acupuncturist; b. Jan. 28, 1949, Taiwan; s. Chao-ying and Chuan-ying (Fu) Li; m. Chih-hua, May 26, 1973; children: Melinda b. 1977, Patricia b. 1978; edn: MD, China Med. Coll. 1978; PhD, DOM, SAMRA Univ. of Oriental Med. 1986. Career: res. physician Taichung Air Force Hosp., Taiwan 1978-83; research asst. Center for Asian Studies, Long Beach, Calif. 1983-85; counselor of Taichung Med. Research Ctr., Taiwan 1985; acad. dean, prof. Asian Am. Acupuncture Med. Univ., San Diego 1985; currently dir. Golden Pacific Acupuncture & Med. Ctr., Torrance, prof., dir. Chinese Med. Dept., SAMRA Univ. of Oriental Med., L.A.; honors: Cert. of Excellence (Yen-Nien Sch. of Acupressure 1979); mem: Acupuncture Med. Assn. of So. Calif., Taiwan Med. Soc. of So. Calif., So. Bay Chinese Am. Assn., Torrance Area CofC; author: Traditional Chinese Medicine & Menopause Syndrome (1985), Traditional Chinese Medicine & Acute Glomerulonephritis (1985), Traditional Chinese Medicine & AIDS (1986); Christian; rec: fishing, swimming, tennis, golf. Res: 7011 Coventry Circle La Palma 90623 Ofc: Golden Pacific Acupuncture and Med. Ctr. 2670 Pacific Coast Hwy Torrance 90505

LIANG, TOM YUAN-TONG, artificial intelligence uncertainty reasoning expert for computer vision systems; b. Aug. 7, 1943, Mei-Hsien Kwangtung, China, nat. US cit. 1983; s. Jing-Kuang and Hsieh-Fei (Hsiung) L.; m. Chu-Ching Wang, Aug. 11, 1974; children: Jungber b. 1977, Jahming b. 1978, Jengyee b. 1983; edn: BSEE, MSEE, Nat. Taiwan Univ. 1965, 67; PhD in applied math & stat., SUNY Stony Brook 1973; MS ops. research UC Berkeley 1977; Engring. Exec. Pgm., UC Los Angeles 1980; Cert. Electrical/ Electronic Engr., ROC, 1967. Career: var. tchg. pos. Nat. Taiwan Univ., SUNY at Stony Brook, Univ. Wis. Madison, UC Berkeley, 1967-77; electronics engr. Oits Mat. Handling Div., Va. 1975; reliability analyst UC Berkeley/ Lawrence Berkeley Lab. 1976-77; reliability engr., mgr. System Integration & Test, mgr. Software Tools Dev., Systems architect, Xerox Corp., El Segundo 1977-84; mgr. Parallel Systems Simulation, Hughes Aircraft Co., Long Beach 1984-86; artificial intelligence uncertainty reasoning expert for computer vision systems Hughes Aircraft Co., El Segundo 1986–; indep. cons. Modeling/ Simulation, 1983-, cons. Japa Tech Info Serv, Penn., 1985-, abstracter for high tech. Japanese Jours., Univ. of Mich. Microfilm; honors: Dr. Chung Yung Yin Award, Dr. C.Y. Yin Found., Taiwan (1966), listed Marquis Who's Who in Frontiers of Sci. & Tech. (1985); mem. IEEE (affil. Reliability Soc., 1977-83), senior mem. Computer, Commu., Eng. in Med. & Biology, Reliability Socs. (1984-); coauthor textbook of electrical machinery (1968), 5 tech. papers in var. IEEE publs. (1978-), Internat. Computer Symposium (1984); mil: 2d lt. ROC Army 1966-67; rec: Chinese chess, Western chess, children's lit. Ofc: Hughes Aircraft Co MS E52/D220 POB 902 El Segundo 90245

LIAW, LUNG-DEN, investment management specialist; b. June 23, 1947, Taipei, Taiwan, nat. US cit. 1980; s. Ru-Shing and Chin-Mei (Chang) L.; edn:

BS, Nat. Taiwan Univ. 1970; M.Ed., Long Island Univ. 1974, MBA, 1976. Career: pres. Banker's Finance Co. Orange 1976–, No. Am. Real Estatk,Co. 1978–, Internat. Investment Cons. Co., Internat. Bus. Cons. Co. Orange 1980–; cons. Pan Pacific Internat. Co. S.F. 1984–, A-P Japanese Enterprises Tokyo 1976–, Pacific Research Inc. NY 1977–; senior instr. Am. Bus. & Mgmt. Inst.; prof. Southwest Motivation Inst. 1984–; inner circle mem. US Senatorial Com.; advisor US Senatorial Bus. Advisory Bd.; mem: Nat. Assn. Property Exchange (gold card mem.), Am. MBA Execs., Toastmasters, Achievers Club, Multi-Million Dollar Club; books: How To Invest in the US (1981), Creating Financing & Investment (1982), Doing Business With China (1986), Your China Business Blueprint (in print); mil: capt. Taiwan Army; Republican; rec: 19511 Sierra Seco Irvine 92715 Ofc: Internat. Investment Cons. Co. 500 S Main St Ste One Orange 92668

LIBANOFF, ARTHUR, podiatrist; b. May 17, 1931, Chgo.; s. Leo and Sylvia (Goddman) L.; m. Erliss Ruff, 1955; edn: BS, Univ. of Ill. 1953; DPM, Ill. Coll. of Podiatry 1959. Career: pvt. practice podiatry, La Habra 1960–; residency pgm. and credential com., Podiatric Surg., Beach Comm. Hosp.; honors: Univ. Ill. Dean's List (1949), pres. German Club (1950), pres. Durlacher Honor Soc., Ill. Coll. Podiat. (1955); mil: cpl. US Army 1955-57; Jewish. Ofc: 740 W La Habra Blvd La Habra 90631

LIBIEN, JAMES ROSS, lawyer; b. Oct. 7, 1941, NY, NY; s. Benjamin H. and Hanna K. Libien; m. Patricia, May 9, 1975; children: Stephanie b. 1980, Jessica b. 1981; edn: AB, UC Berkeley 1964; JD, Univ. of San Francisco 1973; admitted to practice Calif. State Bar, US Dist. Ct. (N. Dist. Calif.), US Ct. Appeals (9th Cir.); Certified Splst. in Workers' Compensation, Calif. Bd. of Legal Specialization. 1979. Career: assoc. counsel Firemen's Fund Ins. Co. 1974-75; assoc. atty. Hanna, Brophy, MacLean, McAleer & Jensen, Oakland 1975-78; ptnr. 1978–, mng. ptnr. Santa Rosa, currently; mem: Calif. Compensation Defense Attys. Assn. (pres. elect 1985), Indsl. Claims Assn. SF (Seminar chmn.); A.V. Rating, Martindale-Hubbell; mil: 1st lt. USAR 1965-67, Thailand svc.; Republican; Jewish; rec: racquetball. Res: 95 Pacheco Creek Dr Novato 94947 Ofc: Hanna, Brophy, MacLean, McAleer & Jensen, 1221 Farmers Ln Ste B Santa Rosa 95405

LICHTENSTEIN, CHASE WALTER, management consultant; b. Sept. 22, 1936, Meriden, Conn.; s. Harry Charles and Josefa Rose (Weil) L.; m. Marie Sullivan, June 11, 1959; children: Helen b. 1960, Paul b. 1961, Jeremy b. 1962, Caroline b. 1966; edn: BS, chem. eng., Cornell Univ. 1959; Reg. Profl. Engr., NJ 1969. Career:project mgr. M&T Chemicals (subsid. American Can Co.), Rahway, NJ 1961-68; prodn. mgr. ER Squibb & Sons, New Brunswick, NJ 1968-74; plant mgr. MediPhysics (subsid. Hoffman LaRoche), So. Plainfield, NJ 1974-75; dir. engring. Hyland Div. Travenol Labs., Los Angeles 1975-85; owner Planning Masters, Thousand Oaks 1985–; pvt. cons. project mgmt. and tech. ops. mgmt. 1980–; mem: Nat. Soc. Profl. Engrs., Am. Inst. Chem. Engrs., Am. Soc. Tng. & Devel., Internat. Soc. Pharmaceutical Engrs. (charter), Knights of Columbus; mil: 1st lt. US Army Intelligence Corps 1959-61; rec: piano, swimming. Address: Planning Masters, 3343 William Dr. Newbury Park 91320

LIDDELL, BARNEY RAYMOND, musician, orchestra contractor; b. Aug. 13, 1921, Gary, Ind.; s. Raymond Paul and Beatrice Rosella (Sullivan) L.; m. Ethel Powell, Oct. 24, 1942; m. 2d Arlene March, Sept. 16, 1956; children: Terrence b. 1943, Patrick b. 1945, Susan b. 1949, Rachel b. 1959, Matthew b. 1961 (dec.), John b. 1963; edn: music stu. Univ. of Notre Dame 1 yr.; engring. courses Univ. of Chgo. 2 yrs. Career: musician/trombonist, played behind Billie Holiday 1946; 1st trombonist Les Elgart Orch. 1946, then with Glen Gray and Casa Loma Orch. 1946, then Elliot Lawrence Orch. 1946-48; 1st trombonist Lawrence Welk Orch., 1948-83; freelance musician/ musical contr. Bob Crosby Orch., Bob Keane Orch., Joe Moshay Orch., Myron Floren Orch. 1982–; instr. Sch. Clinics; mem: am. Fedn. of Musicians/ L.A. Local 47, Santa Ana Local 7; Knights of Col.; mil: T/5 US Army, decorations; Democrat; Roman Catholic; rec: golf, photog. Address: 22525 Sherman Way Ste 401 Canoga Park 91307

LIDDIARD, GLEN EDWIN, transducer co. president, physicist; b. Nov. 4, 1919, San Diego; s. Thomas Philip and Ruth Elizabeth (Durfee) L.; m. Roberta, June 21, 1942; children: Donald E. b. 1945, Carol Anne b. 1957; edn: BA, San Diego State Univ. 1942. Career: physicist US Naval Ornance Lab., Wash. DC 1942-46; supvy. physicist US Navy Electronics Lab., San Diego 1946-61; asst. chief engr. Bendix Corp., No. Hollywood 1961-63; supvy. physicist US Navy Electronics Lab., San Diego 1963-64;q v.p., div. head Ametek-Straza Corp., El Cajon 1964-78; pres. Internat. Transducer Corp., Santa Barbara 1978–; dir. ITC Corp. 1978–; mem: Acoustical Soc. of Am., IEEE, Sigma Pi Sigma; works: classified publus., Naval Underwater Sound Journ. 1960-61; Republican; Presbyterian; rec: philately, numismatics, gardening. Ofc: Internatioal Transducer Corp., 869 Ward Dr. Santa Barbara 93111

LIEBER, ROBERT MASON, labor relations lawyer; b. Jan. 29, 1942, Bklyn., NY; s. Milton D. and Hermene L. (Dryer) L.; m. Lucille Ablan, Sept. 8, 1985; children: Terry Ellen b. 1965, Hilarie Anne b. 1968; edn: AB, Antioch Coll. 1963; LLB, Boalt Hall UC Berkeley 1966; admitted to Calif. State Bar 1967, Calif. Supreme Ct., US Supreme Ct., US Ct. of Appeals (6th, 7th, 9th, 10th and D.C. Circuits). Career: atty. Office of the General Counsel, Nat. Labor Relations Bd., Wash DC 1966-69; senior partner Littler, Mendelson, Fastiff & Tichy, San Francisco 1969–; honors: listed, The Best Lawyers in America, Naifeh and Smith (Seaview/Putnam, NY, 1983); mem. Am., Calif., San Francisco bar assns., Meadowood Country Club; contbg. author: The McGraw-Hill

Construction Business Handbook (1985); Independent; rec: wine collecting, skiing. Ofc: Littler, Mendelson, Fastiff & Tichy, 650 California St San Francisco 94108

LIEBERT, ALLAN H., lawyer, investor; b. Jan. 24, 1936, St. Louis, Mo.; s. Samuel and Leona (Ketcher) L.; m. Sandra Appleman, June 17, 1955; children: Jody b. 1958, Norman b. 1960, Deborah b. 1961; edn: JD, Southwestern Univ. 1960; admitted Calif. State Bar 1962. Career: pvt. law practice, 1962–; pres. Liebert Corp. (real estate devel.); pres. Remington Prodns.; dir. Westport Savings Bank; judge pro tem Los Angeles and Beverly Hills Municipal Cts.; referee State Bar Ct.; mem: ABA, Calif. Bar Assn., Beverly Hills Bar Assn., LA Co. Bar Assn.; City of Hope (past pres. Med. Ctr. Aids); clubs: La Costa Country, Marina City; Republican; Jewish; rec: boating, tennis, photog. Law Ofc: Allan H. Liebert 1033 Gayley Ave Ste 200 Los Angeles 90024

LIEN, ALAN L., healthcare administrator; b. Mar. 15, 1955, Stevens Point, Wis.; s. Arthur Lowell and Arlene Edna (Keffner) L.; m. Constance L. Bailey, Aug. 14, 1976; edn: BS in Bus. Admin., Univ. of Wis., 1977; lic. Healthcare Adminstr. in Calif., Fla., Ind., Ill. and Wis. Career: adminstr. Iola Hosp. and Nursing Home, Iola, Wis. 1974-81, Healthquest Corp., South Bend, Ind. 1981-82, Beverly Ents., Merrillville, Ind. 1982-84, area adminstr. Hillhaven Corp., Modesto, Calif. 1984-85; adminstr. Canoga Care Center (200-bed facility), Canoga Park 1985–; instr. contg. edn. programs in healthcare mgmt. for NHAs, RNs, LVNs; mem. Am. Coll. of Healthcare Adminstrs., Healthcare Finl. Mgmt. Assn., Calif. Assn. of Health Facilities, Calif. Assn. of Homes for the Aging; bd. dirs. Stroke Resources (Modesto); Lions Club Internat.; United Methodist (Certified Lay Speaker). Res: 3416 Norton Ave Modesto 95350 Ofc: PO Box 1315 Canoga Park 91304

LIGAR, GEORGE FRANK, architect; b. Jan. 1, 1918, Odessa, Russia of Hellenic ancestry (parents both Greek); s. Frank (originally Ligaris) and Katerine Helen (Iliades) L.; edn: AA, Compton Jr. Coll. 1938; B.Arch., USC 1941; num. coll. courses to present. Career: studied with wellknown artist Tavoularis in Athens, Greece to age 12; came to US in 1930; exhib. one man show of his paintings in Detroit (Mich.) Public Library, for one month (at age 12), 1930; worked for var. architects 1941-48; lic. architect and bldg. contractor self-empl. 1948–; founder/owner/instr. Ligar Sch. of Architecture 1982–; instr. bldg. design USC Graduate Sch. of Engring., interior design Hollywood Art Center; honors: recognition, Frank Lloyd Wright (1957); publs: Round House, (1954-55), Diamond House (original owner: La Perle; current owners Carolyn Weaver and Barbara Lang) (1952), Block House (1948), plus others in Beautiful Houses & Gardens in California by Weiskamp; Round House in Fireplaces by Famous Architects (UCLA textbook); Newsweek (1955); T.V. (2) George Putnam, News All Over the World (Warner Bros.), and United Press publs. in 27000 newspapers & mags.; Republican; Greek Orthodox; rec: art (all media), photog., music, philosophy. Res: 6537 Abbottswood Dr. Rancho Palos Verdes 90274 Ofc: George Frank Ligar-Architect, 4626 Presidio Dr. Los Angeles 90008

LIGHTFOOT, WILLIAM HUGH, lawyer; b. Sept. 3, 1925, Minneapolis, Minn.; s. William Homer and Elva Asenith (Albright) L.; m. Trudi, July 30, 1965; edn: BA, Drake Univ. 1949, JD, 1951; admitted to practice US Supreme Ct. Career: atty. Law OFcs. Ted L. Mackey, W. Los Angeles 1972; atty. William H. Lightfoot, San Jose 1973–; tchr. Landlord-Tenant Law, Cont. Edn. of Bar; mem: Calif. and Santa Clara Co. Bar Assn., Masons, Scottish Rite, Shriners, Eagles, Am. Legion; mil: 2nd lt., USMC 1951-54, UN Medal, Korean Svc., Presidential Unit Citation; Republican; Christian; rec: exercise, politics, social problems. Ofc: Law Ofc. William H. Lightfoot, 95 So. Market St. Ste. 300 San Jose 95113

LILLIE, MILDRED L., presiding justice State Court of Appeal; b. Jan. 25, 1915, Ida Grove, Ia.; d. Ottmar A. and Florence E. (Martin) Kluckhohn; m. Cameron L. Lillie, Mar. 18, 1947 (dec. 1959); m. 2d A. V. Falcone, Aug. 27, 1966; edn: AB, UC Berkeley 1935; JD, UC Boalt Hall of Law 1938; hon. degrees: LLD, Western States Univ. Coll. of Law 1966; LLD, Pepperdine Univ. 1979; admitted to practice, State Bar of Calif. 1938, Fed. Ct. 1942, US Supreme Ct. 1961. Career: with the City Atty.'s Ofc., Alameda 1938-39; pvt. law practice Fresno, 1939-42, Los Angeles 1946-47; asst. US Atty., Los Angeles, 1942-46; judge, Municipal Ct., City of L.A. 1947-49; judge, Superior Ct., Co. of L.A. 1949-58; Justice, Ct.of Appeal, State of Calif. 1958-84, Presiding Justice, 1984–; assoc. Justice Pro Tem, Calif. Supreme Ct. 1961, 77, 79, 81, 82, 85; mem: L.A. area CofC (bd. dirs. 1975-82), L.A. Athletic Club, Western State Univ. Coll. of Law. (exec. & admissions bd.), Ebell Club of L.A., Am. Heart Assn., Civic Light Opera Assn., Les Dames de Champagne, Fed., Am. and L.A. County Bar Assns., Calif. Judges Assn., Nat. Assn. of Women Judges, Women Lawyers Asssn., Pepperdine Univ. Assocs., NCCJ (bd. dirs.); Catholic; rec: painting, cooking, writing. Res: 510 S Burnside Ave Los Angeles 90036 Ofc: 3580 Wilshire Blvd Los Angeles 90010

LIM, ALLEN, consulting civil engineer; b. Aug. 13, 1918, San Francisco; s. Sing T. and Gum Young (Lee) L.; m. Lilly Chow, Aug. 18, 1943: 1 son, Dr. Victor A. Lim, b. 1944; edn: BSCE, UC Berkeley 1942; M. Public Admin., Golden Gate Univ. 1984, postgrad., public admin., 1984-; Reg. Profl. Civil Engr. (1949), lic. Gen. Engring. and Building Contr. (1950), Calif. Career: military pilot, asst. dir. pilot tng., cmdr. of cadets, var. Army Air Corps bases, 1942-45; civil engr. Design Div. Corps of Engrs., San Francisco 1945-52; chief struc. engr. US Navy Engring., S.F. and San Bruno 1952-58; chief Tech. & constrn. Mgmt. Div. USAF Regional Civil Engring. office, 1958-84, ret.; cons. civil engr. prin., El Cerrito 1984–; honors: named Outstanding Engr. of the

Year (1983), Hq. USAF, Wash. DC and Hq. Nat. Soc. of Profl. Engrs.; recogn., US House of Reps., US Congl. Record (1983); Fellow ASCE (1964); mem: Chinese Am. Inst. of Engrs. and Scientists (pres. 1969), Struc. Engrs. Assn. of Calif., ASCE (life), Soc. of Mil. Engrs., UC Alumni Assn. (Chinese Chpt. pres. 1973, dir.), UC Chinese Alumni Found.; (dir.); coauthor, Seismic Std. for Federal Buildings (1/81); author, The Improvement of Communications in Public Orgns. (12/81), sev. tech. articles; mil: 1st lt. Army Air Corps 1942-45; Democrat; Protestant; rec: fitness, home repairs. Res: 619 Ashbury Ave El Cerrito 94530

LIM, EUSEBIO GAN, otolaryngologist; b. Aug. 14, Manila, Philippines; s. Bien Liong and Bella (Gan) L.; edn: MD, Univ. Santo Tomas, 1947, AA, 1947; Fellow Internat. Acad. of Cosmetic Surgery. Career: otolaryngologist Union Medical Clinic, Huntington Park, Calif.; mem. Los Angeles County Med. Assn.; Catholic; rec: photog., car racing. Res: 11730 Sunset Blvd Los Angeles 90049 Ofc: Union Medical Clinic 5421 Pacific Blvd Huntington Park 90255

LIM, LOOI (FRANK) K., financial services executive; b. Dec. 27, 1944, Alor Setar, Malaysia; s. Seng C. and Hai (Lee) L.; m. Shiow C., Feb. 10, 1972; 1 son, Richard b. 1979; edn: BA philosophy, Nat. Taiwan Univ. 1969. Career: news editor Shin Min Daily News Malaysia 1970-75; self-employed trade bus. 1976-79; gen. mgr. Asia Journal (newspaper) Calif. 1980-81; agent Equitable Financial Svcs. L.A. 1982-83, mgr. 1984–; honors: Top Agent (Equitable 1982, 83), Founders Award (Equitable 1984), No. 1 Dist. Mgr. in Nation (Equitable 1985); mem: Life Underwriters Assn. of L.A., Million Dollar Round Table, Lim's Family Assn. L.A.; rec: reading, travel, writing. Ofc: The Equitable Financial Svcs. 3435 Wilshire Blvd Ste 800 Los Angeles 90010

LIN, ALBERT KUNTUNG, accountant, real estate investor; b. Oct. 28, 1936, Taichung, Taiwan, nat. US cit. 1974; s. Tsu-Hong and Yeh-Lee (Chang) L.; m. Michiko Kadota, Aug. 26, 1967; children: Carol b. 1968, Selina b. 1970, Albert Jr. b. 1971; edn: LLB, honors, Soochow Univ. Law Sch., Taiwan 1961; MBA, New York Univ. 1965; Certified Public Acct., Calif. (1985). Career: internal auditor Am. Express Co., N.Y.C. 1966; senior auditor Touche Ross & Co., Los Angeles 1967-70; audit supvr. Blue Cross of So. Calif., Los Angeles 1971-74; dir. of reimbursement General Health Services, Culver City 1976-80, Hospital Corp. of Am., Tenn. 1981, Advanced Health Systems, Inc., Irvine 1982-83; reimbursement cons., CPA practitioner and real estate investor, Los Angeles 1983–; mem. Calif. Soc. of CPAs, Taiwanese-Am. Citizen League; mil: cpl. Taiwan Army 1956; Republican; Methodist. Address: 3139 Waverly Dr Los Angeles 90027

LIN, AMBROSE CHI-SHAN, acupuncturist; b. Apr. 6, 1935, Shan Tung, China; s. Pu-Chien and Maria Tsui-O (Mou) L.; m. Lanny Hendro, Sept. 29, 1981; children: Rosalie b. 1963, Cecilia b. 1964, Scott b. 1982; edn: Dr. of Acupuncture, Tung's Acupuncture Inst. Taipei, Taiwan 1962. Career: certified acupuncturist Tung's Meml. Acupuncture Clinic Costa Mesa; awards: Recipient (China Assn. of Acupuncturists Taiwan 1963); mem: Lions Club (dir. L.A. Chinatown 1979, dir. Taipei, Taiwan 1962), Am. Acupuncture and Herbs Research Inst. (dir. 1976), United Acupuncturists of Calif. 1976, Internat. Assn. of Acupuncturists 1972; research: stroke, lumbago pains and arthritis, hernia disc; Catholic; rec: music, travel, swimming. Res: 10211 Halawa Dr Huntington Beach 92646 Ofc: Tung's Meml. Acupuncture Clinic 569 W 19th St Costa Mesa 92627

LIN, CHARLIE CHUNG-SING, controller, property manager; b. Jan. 17, 1951, Hong Kong, nat. 1982; s. Henry Yuk Man and Deborah Hui- Chou (Chou) L.; m. Jacqueline Wu, Feb. 29, 1980; edn: BS, Woodbury Univ. 1977; Cert. Property Mgr., IREM (1983); Calif. lic. Tax Practitioner (1980), Notary Public (1984). Career: owner Capricorn Assocs. Internat. 1979-80; real estate broker Prime Realty & Devel. Co. 1980–; controller/ cert. property mgr. Tenants & Owners Devel. Corp. 1980–; pres. Ideal Entertainment Corp. dba Faces Faces (a discotheque) 1984–; mem: Nat. Assoc. of Acctg. Svc., San Francisco Bd. Realtors, Inst. of Real Estate Mgmt., Nat. Assn. of Asian American CPAs; founder Calif. Chinese Celebrity Club (social & sports club for young Chinese profls.); mil: cpl. Chinese Mil. Police; Republican; Christian; rec: music, sports. Res: 145 Marlin Ct., San Francisco 94124 Ofc: Tenants & Owners Development Corp., 230 4th St., San Francisco 94103; Faces Faces: 1550 California St San Francisco 94109

LIN, SHIRLEY HSUNMAN, dentist; b. Oct. 24, 1956, Kaohsiung, Taiwan, ROC; d. Rei Jen and Chin Yeh (Wei) Chen; m. Wayne L. Lin, Dec. 13, 1980; 1 son, Jeff b. 1985; edn: BDS, Chun San Medical & Dental Univ. Career: dentist in pvt. practice, owner Rei-Jing Dental Clinic, 1979-81; La Punte Family Dental Ctr., 1982-83; Dr. Thanh Dental Clinic, 1983-84; owner general dentistry practice, Dr. Shirley Lin Family Dental Center, Monterey Park 1984–; mem: R.O.C. Taiwan Dental Assn., Am. Dental Assn., Kiwanianne Club of San Gabriel Valley (ofcr. 1985), Southeast-Asian Chinese-Am. CofC (ofcr. 1985); rec: reading. Res: 2700 Winthrop Ave Arcadia 91006 Ofc: Dr. Shirley Lin Family Dental Center, 790 S Atlantic Blvd Ste 106 Monterey Park 91754

LIN, SUE HSIAO YUAN, acupuncturist; b. Oct. 13, 1936, Shanghai, China, nat. US cit. 1985; d. Su Tang and Hsin Yuan (Yu) Lin; m. Daren Chen, June 25, 1961; children: Edwin b. 1963, Ian b. 1965; edn: Doctor of Medicine, Peking Univ. Sch. of Medicine 1959. Career: doctor in charge Peking Childrens Hosp., 1959-78; medical cons. ACM Health Center, San Mateo 1979, 80, 82, executive dir. 1983–; pres. Academy of Chinese 1983–; mem: Calif. Certified Acupuncturist Assn.; contbr. sev. medical articles profl. jours. 1960-82. Res: 220 Duck Ct Foster City 94404 Ofc: ACM Health Center 111 Saint Matthews Ave San Mateo 94401

LINCOLN, JOHN, JR., chartered life underwriter; b. May 13, 1931, San Francisco; s. John and Rosalie M. (Dallman) L.; m. Marjorie Ellen Jones, April 20, 1957; 2 sons: John Spencer, b. 1958, Robert Emery, b. 1961; edn: Chartered Life Underwriter (CLU), The American Coll., Bryn Mawr, Penn. 1967. Career: field rep. Guardian Life Ins. Co., 1962—; also currently exec. v.p./dir. John Lincoln Co./ Lincoln Shoe Polish Co., Sunnyvale; mem. State of Calif. Advis. Commn., Senate Insurance & Indemnity Com. 1983-; honors: Guardian Life New Man of Yr. 1963, Guardian Life West. Region V.P. Group Sales (1975), The Million Dollar Round Table qualifying mem. 1964, 65, 67, 78, 82, 83; mem: San Jose Life Und. Assn., Santa Clara County CLU Assn. (pub. rels. ofcr., ednl. chmn., bd. dir. 1970-74), Santa Clara Co. Estate Planning Council; mem. Rotary, Masons, Saratoga Mens Club, Soc. of Calif. Pioneers, USCG Aux. (pub. rels. ofcr. 71-74); mil: USNR 1953-55 active duty; Republican; Prot.; rec: photog., skiing, flying. Res: 18650 Farragut Ln Los Gatos 95030 Ofc: Guardian Life Ins. 1602 The Alameda, Ste 204, San Jose 95126

LIND, TERRIE LEE, child and adolescent development center executive; b. June 5, 1948; Spokane, Wash.; d. Clifford and Edna Mae (Allenbach) Presnell; children: Erica b. 1976, Reid b. 1978; edn: BA, cum laude, Wash. State Univ. 1970, MA, 1971; tchg. cert. Wash. 1972, Ariz. 1983; speech pathol. Calif. 1982; cert. clin. competence Am. Speech, Lang., Hearing Assn. 1982. Career: tchg. asst. Wash. State Univ. 1970-71; communication disorders splst. Univ. Tex. Houston, Grad. Sch. of Biomed. Sci. (Houston Speech & Hearing Inst.) 1971-73; clin. supv. The Battin Clinic Houston 1973-76; career sabbatical Spokane, Wash.; communication splst. Spokane Guild's Sch./Neuromuscular Ctr. 1980-82; coord. Learning Devel. Ctr. Comm. Hosps. of Central Calif. Fresno 1982—; cons. Adolescent Chem. Dependency Unit; other communication related projects; honors: Award for Continuing Education (Am. Speech and Hearing Assn. 1982); mem: Am. Speech, Lang., Hearing Assn., Wash. Sp., Hearing Assn. (state conv. 1981, co-chair pgm. com.), Am. Assn. Univ. Women (ofcr.), Fresno Mental Health Assn.; research: language abilities among urban and agrarian children; Protestant; rec: sailing, skiing, flying, photog. Res: 7625 N First, No 121 Fresno 93710 Ofc: Comm. Hosps. of Central Calif. POB 1232 Fresno 93715

LINDEN, MARGARET JOANNE, librarian; b. Berkeley; d. Arthur William and Johanna Gesina (Zuydhoek) Dickie; m. Roy J. Linden, Jan. 6, 1965; edn: AB, Swarthmore Coll. 1960; mls, UC Berkeley 1962. Career: librarian Hans Kelsen Grad. Social Scis. Library, UC Berkeley 1962-66; librarian Giannini Found. Agrl. Econs. 1966-70; social scis. librarian Idaho State Univ. 1970-71; librarian Standard Oil Co. of Calif, San Francisco 1971-74, asst. chief librarian 1974-77, mgr. corp. library 1978—; mem: Spl. Libraries Assn.; Calif. Library Assn. Ofc: 225 Bush St. Rm. 1410, San Francisco 94104

LINDERMAN, GLENN ROLLAND, financial analyst; b. June 23, 1959, Trenton, Mich.; s. George Calvin and Doris Tabatha (Dale) L.; m. Mary Rutland, Aug. 9, 1986; edn: BSBA, Oakland Univ. 1981; UC Los Angeles 1984; MBA, Pepperdine Univ. 1986; stockbroker NASD 1980. Career: bank teller Mich. Nat. Bank Bloomfield Hills, Mich.; 1977-78; inventory control analyst Ford Motor Co. Dearborn, Mich. 1978-80; acct. exec. Merrill Lynch Pierce Fenner & Smith Southfield, Mich. 1980-82; financial analyst CCH Computax Inc. Torrance 1982—; gen. mgr. Linderman Speculative Partnership; mem. Big Brothers of Greater L.A.; avoc: commodity futures speculation, computer programming. Res: 3950 W 226th St Apt 70 Torrance 90505 Ofc: CCH Computax Inc. 21535 Hawthorne Blvd Ste 410 Torrance 90503

LINDLEY, F. HAYNES, JR., lawyer; b. Oct. 15, 1945, Los Angeles; s. Francis H. and Grace (McCanne) L.; m. Hollinger McCloud, Apr. 1, 1977; edn: BA, Claremont Men's Coll. 1967; MFA, Claremont Grad. Sch. 1972; JD, Southwestern Univ. Sch. of Law 1976; admitted Calif. State Bar 1976. Career: dep. public defender Los Angeles County 1977-79; staff atty. Dept. of Trial Counsel, State Bar of Calif. 1979-81; pvt. practice law, spec. estate mgmt., Santa Monica 1981—; dir. So. Calif. Assn. for Philanthropy, 1985-; dir. TreePeople (Calif. Conservation Project) 1985-; trustee, v.p. The John Randolph Haynes and Dora Haynes Found., 1978-; mem. ABA, LA County Bar Assn. Ofc: F. Haynes Lindley, Jr., Atty. 644 East Channel Road Santa Monica 90402

LINDQUIST, MARK ALAN, co. executive, architect; b. Nov. 21, 1951, Oakland; s. Lloyd v. and Elsie H. (Larson) L.; m. Patricia R., April 8, 1978; children: Lindsay Elisabeth b. 1979; Peter Mark b. 1983; edn: grad. study, Univ. of Copenhagen, Denmark; B.Arch., Calif. Polytechnic Univ. 1975; Reg. Architect (1979) and Lic. Gen. Contractor (1984), Calif. Career: project architect Jordan, Casper, Woodman, Dobson 1977-80; Lindquist- McNely Co. 1980-84; pres. M.A. Lindquist Co. 1984—; mgmt. com. Vickerman/ Zachary/ Miller Architects- Engineers; v.p. Western Balmoral Funds Inc.; honors: Remodeling Designer of the Year, Interior, Exterior, Commercial 1979; Outstanding Achiev., Boy Scouts of Am. 1982, 1983, 1984; mem: Associated Gen. Contractors of Calif., Boy Scouts of Am. (chmn. Career Awareness Com. 1982-85), Rotary Club of Oakland (internat. svc. com.); works: conversion of historic Overland Hotel into restaurant, shops and offices, Oakland; Democrat; 1st Covenant Ch., Oakland (deacon); rec: fishing, boating, skiing. Ofc: M.A. Lindquist Co. Inc., 383 Fourth St Ste. 200 Oakland 94607

LINDSAY, RODGER, insurance executive; b. Apr. 12, 1933, Phila.; s. F. Rodger and Geraldine C. (Swind) L.; m. Mary D. Flanagan, Apr. 8, 1980; edn: BA, Duke Univ. 1955; MBA, Columbia Univ. 1964; Chartered Life Underwriter (CLU), Am. Coll. 1967. Career: ofcr. US Navy 1955-62; Metropolitan Life Ins. Co. (NY, NY) agent, Cherry Hill, N.J. 1964-66, sales dir. G.B., London, England 1966-69, dist. mgr. Greenwich, Conn. 1969-74; branch mgr. Canada Life (Toronto), Stamford, Conn. 1974-78; gen. agent National Life (Vt) New Canaan, Conn. 1978-82; branch mgr. Metro. Life Ins. Co., Chula Vista, Calif. 1982—; honors: Outstanding Young Men of Am. (1969), comm. service award City of Stamford, Conn. (1978), NALU Nat. Mgmt. Award (1980, 81, 82, 85) and leadership awards (local assn. 1978, state assn. 1980); mem: Conn. State Life Underws. (pres. 1978-79), S.W. Conn. Life Underws. (pres. 1976-77), Gen. Agents & Mgrs. Assn. (pres. 1973, 74, 76); civic: San Diego Symphony (dir. 1983-86), St. Vincent De Paul Center S.D. (dir. 1986-89), Chula Vista Public Library (trustee 1986-90), Gr. S.D. CofC, Crippled Childrens Hosp., Phila. (Crescent Shrine life mem. award for Xmas visits to hosp.), Timken Art Gallery, S.D. (donor, patron Albert Bierstadt Exh. 1986); mil: cmdr. USNR, Ret. 1955-81. Res: 28 Center St Chula Vista 92010 Ofc: Metropolitan Life Insurance Co. 296 H St Ste 302 Chula Vista 92010

LING, WILLIAM S., dentist; b. Oct. 16, 1900, Honolulu, Hawaii; s. Kui and Shee (Lau) L.; m. Annie Leong, Apr. 26, 1919; 1 dau. Gayle L. (Chu) b. 1932; edn: DDS, Coll. of Physicians & Surgeons (now Univ. of Pacific), 1922. Career: dental practise in Honolulu 1922-37, San Francisco 1937—; mem. St. Mary's Catholic Chinese School Board (dir. 1940-73, treas. 14 years); mem. Tsung Tsin Benevolent Assn. (hon. pres.), Chinese Haka Soc.; Republican; Catholic; rec: golf. Res: 1515 Pine St San Francisco 94109 Ofc: 700 Sacramento St San Francisco 94108

LINGLE, ROBERT LEO, savings and loan executive; b. Nov. 27, 1941, Dubuque, Ia.; s. Leo Albert and Ruth Evelyn (Bruesch) L.; m. Bonita Bilbery, June 30, 1979; children: Darrin b. 1968, Todd b. 1970; edn: AA, Pasadena City Coll. 1962; BS, CSU Los Angels 1964; CFA, Inst. of Chartered Fin. Analysts 1974; Real Estate Broker, Calif. 1975. Career: mgmt. trainee Security Pacific Nat. Bank, Los Angeles 1964, portfolio mgr. 1965-68; trust investment ofcr. Union Bank, L.A. 1968-77, v.p. real estate lending 1977-80; v.p./ real estate mgr. Bank of Calif., San Bernardino 1980-82; v.p./ mgr. Beverly Hills S&L 1982-83; exec. v.p. Cal American Svgs. & Loan 1983—, mem. sr. loan com.; awards: SPOKE Awd., Jaycees 1972; mem: Inst. CFAs; Soc. Real Estate Appraisers (L.A. chpt.); Certified Review Appraisers; RIM Real Estate Internat.; Bldg. Ind. Assn. (Orange Co.); Hacienda Hghts. Drug Abuse Council (past) YMCA Fund Raising, San Bernardino; San Bernardino CofC; Republican; Lutheran; rec: skiing, travel. Res: 1234 Nashport La Verne 91750 Ofc: Cal American Savings and Loan Assn., 888 S West St, Ste 201, Anaheim 92802

LINHART, EDDIE G., aerospace manufacturing co. executive; b. March 8, 1941, Leachville, Ark.; s. Edward C. and Della I. (Towell) L.; m. Claudia Benninger, May 25, 1962; children: William b. 1968, Bonnie b. 1970; edn: AA, Fullerton Coll. 1970; BA, CSU Long Beach 1975, MA, 1977; Profl. Engr., Calif. 1978. Career: branch mgr. mfg. engring. McDonnell Douglas, Long Beach 1962-79; mgr. mfg. engring. Fairchild Republic, Farmdale, NY 1979-80; v.p. prodn. Avco Aerostructures, Nashville, Tenn. 1980-81; v.p. central mfg. Northrop Aircraft Div., Hawthorne 1981-85; v.p., gen. mgr. Wester Gear Corp., Industry 1985—; adv. bd. CSU, Los Angeles and Long Beach 1984-; honors: Bob Hope Award, Los Angeles Council Boy Scouts of Am. (1985), Disting. Engrg. Achievement Award, San Fernando Valley Engrs. Council (1986), Fellow Inst. for Advancement of Engrg. (1986); mem: Westec (chmn. adv. bd. 1986), Soc. of Automotive Engrs. (chmn. Mfg. Activity Aerospace Sect. 1984-86), Boy Scouts of Am. (exec. bd. Los Angeles Council); works: copyrighted thesis, Diffusion Bonding of Metals in Southern California Industries; mil: E-5 USN 1958-62; Republican; Lutheran; rec: golf, fishing, coin collecing. Ofc: 14724 E. Proctor City of Industry 91749

LINN, DAVID AUEN, lawyer; b. Aug. 8, 1948, Pittsburgh, Penn.; s. William Anthony and Margaret Irene (Auen) L.; m. Ellen Delaney, Sept. 15, 1973; edn: BS, Purdue Univ. 1970; MBA, CSU Dominguez Hills 1985; JD, Pepperdine Univ. 1976; admitted to Calif. Bar 1976, US Dist. Ct. (Central and East. Dists. Calif.) 1976, US Ct. of Claims Bar 1983. Career: pvt. practice atty. in Santa Ana, 1976-81; senior ptnr., civil litigation, Lindley, Linn & Walton, Oakhurst 1981—; guest lectr. Fresno City Coll.; mem: ABA (Natural Resources Sect.), Calif. State Bar Assn., Madera Co. Bar Assn., Mariposa Co. Bar Assn., Naval Reserve Assn., US Naval Inst., Eastern Madera Co. CofC (dir. 1985), Rotary (pres. elect Oakhurst-Sierra Club 1985); pres. Oakhurst Community Fund, Inc. (1985); chmn. Oakhurst Comm. Park Com. (1985); publs: Water Pollution and the Land Resource Manager/ Prairie Farmer Mag. (9/70); mil: cmdr. USNR 1970-73, active Ready Reserve 1973-, Nat. Def. Medal, Vietnam Service Medal, Service Warfare Designator; Republican; Roman Catholic; rec: golf, tennis, fishing. Address: Lindley, Linn & Walton, POB 2328 Oakhurst 93644

LINN, JOY, financial & media conglomerate president; b. Nov. 8, 1936, Monterey Park; d. Herbert A. and Kathleen L. (Reynolds) Shuttleworth; edn: AA, Fullerton Coll. 1974; desig: Cert. Senior Escrow Ofcr., Calif. Escrow Assn. 1980; Life Comm. Coll. Tchr. (real estate) Credential. Career: personnel dir. Camac Corp., Bristol, Va. 1970-72; escrow ofcr. Walker & Lee, Whittier 1972-74; adminstrv. dir. Christ Church, Anaheim 1974-76; escrow br. mgr. Tarbell, Buena Park 1976-77; mgr. escrow dept. Chartered Bank of London, Vista 1977-79; mgr. loan & escrow depts. Hawthorne Savings & Loan, Vista 1979-81; pres./chief exec. Pathways Assocs. Inc., Anaheim 1981-85; pres., CEO Pillar Enterprises 1985—; mem: CEA (regl. pres. & dir. State Bd. of Calif. Escrow Assn.), ASCAP, Jobs Daughters, Young Republicans, Abingden Soc. for Preservation of Native Art; works: composed/ preformed, The Story Lady (record for children), & The Star (a Chirstmas Story); contbg. mem. Calif. Christian Inst. of Human Rels. (4 yrs.); dir. Pathways to Happiness (non profit svc. orgn.); mil: s/sgt. USAF 1954-55; rec: writing, directing. Res: 1100 N Acacia, Unit 10, Anaheim 92805 Ofc: Pillar Enterprises, 12460 Euclid Ave Ste 103 Garden Grove 92460

LINN, THOMAS RICHARD, financial executive; b. June 29, 1956, France, nat. US cit. 1956; s. Gerald R. and Nancy J. (Kidd) L.; m. Kevil M., May 2, 1982; edn: BA, honors, Claremont McKenna Coll. 1978; BS, CSU Long Beach 1981; Enrolled Agent, IRS; CPA, Calif. Career: staff acct. Sherril Moore CPA, Long Beach 1980-82; senior staff acct. Squar & Clarke, An Accty. Corp., Irvine 1982-84; CFO DHA Dental Group, Santa Ana 1985–; bd. dirs. Mango Sportswear Inc., Huntington Beach; exec. cons. Victory Wetsuits Inc. Hunt. Bch.; mem: Am. Inst. CPAs, Calif. Soc. CPAs; rec: surfing/ kneeriding (3rd pl. (1985) and 4th pl. (1981) U.S. Amateur Surfing Championships).

LINN, WALLACE DEWEY, banker, b. Feb. 19, 1939, Mt. Union, Pa.; s. Wm. D. and Ella Esther (Shank) L.; m. Vicki McDaniel, May 15, 1970; children: Lisa (Markley) b. 1965, Faith Ann b. 1974, Joy Christine b. 1976; edn: Central Penn Bus. Coll. 1957, Shippensburg State Coll. 1958-61, Pacific Sch. of Banking, Univ. of Wash. 1979-82; DHL, Mid Am. Bible Coll. 1986. Career: v.p. Lloyds Bank of Calif., Los Angeles 1970-80; v.p. El Camino Bank, Anaheim 1980-82; pres./CEO New City Bancorp and New City Bank, Anaheim 1982–; frequent speaker on bus., fin., money mgmt., weekly radio talk show host of "Lets Talk About Money," KBRT, Century City (1985), guest on num. nat. TV talk shows; awards: Spirit of Life Award, City of Hope (1983); mem. Anaheim Bd. Realtors, Anaheim CofC (Ambassadors, bd. dirs., exec. com., chmn. edn. com.), Kiwanis (past pres.), James Madison Club (past pres.); civic: trustee Azusa Pacific Univ., So. Calif. Billy Graham Crusade (fin. chmn. 1985), served on bds. of Dino Media Ministries (Newport Bch), Christian Research Inst. (El Toro), Am. Liberties Inst. (Anaheim), Turning Point (Garden Grove); book in progress: Money Matters (1986); Republican; Christian; rec: golf, music, fine arts. Res: 8431 Meadowlark Ln La Palma 90623 Ofc: New City Bank 100 Anaheim Blvd Ste 100 Anaheim 92805

LIOU, REN-JEI, aerospace engineer; b. July 2, 1950, Tainan, Taiwan, nat. US cit. 1986; s. Tsun and Yuan (Shou) L.; m. Yeh-Chyn, June 10, 1975; children: Jethro b. 1977, Celeste b. 1981, Camilla b. 1984; edn: BS, National Central Univ., Taiwan 1972; MS, Univ. of Ill. 1977, PhD, 1980; profl. mech. engr. Calif. 1983. Career: instr. Kuan-Shan Inst. of Tech., Tainan, Taiwan 1974; research and tchg. asst. Univ. of Ill. 1975-80; cons. GDS Consulting Eng. Assoc., Chicago, Ill. 1981; engr. Bechtel Power Corp., Norwalk 1983; currently, tech. splst. Servocontrols Div., HR Textron Inc.; cons. Sargent & Lundy Engrs., Chicago, Ill. 1980; honors: Tau Beta Pi, 1980; Phi Kappa Phi, 1977; Lin Shun-Jean Meml. Fellowship 1969-72; mem: Am. Soc. of Mech. Engrs., Sigma Ki, The Scientific Research Soc. of No. Am., Univ. of Ill. Alumni Assn. (life); publs: Bend Flow Calculational Methods Compared, Journ. Eng. Mechanics 1984; Numerical Simulation of the Hemodynamics at a Arterial Asymmetric Stenosis, Journ. of Biomechanics 1981, The Dynamics of Unsteady Bifurcation Flow, Proc. 2nd Mid-Atlantic Conf. on Bio-Fluid Mechanics, VPI, Blacksburg 1980–; rec: reading. Res: 20102 Donway Dr. Walnut 91789 Ofc: HR Textron Inc., 25200 W. Rye Canyon Rd. Valencia 91355

LIPARI, STEVEN RAND, restaurant owner; b. July 2, 1951, Los Angeles; s. Carl John and Patricia Louie (Castles) L.; m. Virginia Huffman, Aug. 24, 1985; edn: Moorpark Coll. 1969-73. Career: mgr. Associated Hosts Inc. 1973-75; real estate devel. prin., S.R. Lipari & Assocs., 1972-80; trustee and finl. cons. to estate of Lillian Nichols, 1981-85; pres. HNL Co., 1983–; owner/gen. mgr. Livingstone's Restaurant, Fresno 1985–; awards: Bank of America scholarship award, Art (1969); civic: Susana Knolls Homeowners Assn. (pres. 1977-79); works: jazz composer/musician; artist and repertoire dir. Mystic Sound Studios, Los Angeles; rec: sport fishing. Res: 4750 N Van Ness Fresno 93704 Ofc: Livingstone's Restaurant & Pub 831 E Fern Fresno 93728

LIPPITT, ELIZABETH CHARLOTTE, writer; b. San Francisco, d. Sidney Grant and Stella Lippitt; edn: Univ. Calif., Mills Coll. Career: writer, performer satirical monologues, popular singer; contbg. writer to 80 newspapers, 1960s–: Shreveport Journ., Miami Herald, St. Louis Globe-Democrat, Jackson News, Union Leader, Orlando Sentinel, Phoenix Republic, Tampa Tribune, Birmingham Post Herald, Speak Up (Toronto, Can.), num. other publs.; honors: Congress of Freedom Awards (6) for arts. on national affairs; listed in Marquis- Who's Who in the World (1984-5), num. biog. refs.; vocalist performer Internat. Biog. Congress, Los Angeles (1981), NYC (1983); mem: Metropolitan Club, Olympic Club, Nat. Adv. Bd. Amer. Security Council, IPA, Commonwealth Club, Nat. Assn. R.R. Passengers, Nat. Trust for Historic Preserv., Amer. Conservative Union, Guide Dogs for the Blind, humane and anti-vivisection orgns. (9), Friends of Animals, Com. for Humane Legislation, Amvets, Childrens Village Home Soc., Congressional Club, Young Americans for Freedom, Freedoms Found., Com. for Free Afghanistan; Catholic; rec: swim (50 mi. swim for ARC). Res: 2414 Pacific Ave San Francisco 94116

LIPSCOMB, JAMES LOUIS, lawyer; b. Feb. 14, 1947, Albany, NY; s. Eric and Vinel (Motley) L.; m. Nancy, Nov. 27, 1971; children: Kathryn b. 1974, Julie b. 1977, Angela b. 1979; edn: AAS, Hudson Valley Comm. Coll., Troy, NY 1967; BA, Howard Univ., Wash. DC 1969; JD, Columbia Law Sch. 1972; LLM, NY Univ. Law Sch. 1977. Career: atty. Metropolitan Life Ins. Co. 1972-79, asst. gen. counsel 1979-81, assoc. gen. counsel 1981–, in charge of real estate investments in 10 western states; expert in field of real estate law; mem. num. local and state panels concerning real estate transactions; vis. prof. Nat. Urban League Black Executive Exchange Pgm.; honors: Spl. Achievement Award (Metro. Life 1984); mem: Calif. State Bar (vice chmn. Exec. Com. Real Property Law Sect. 1984), Am. Bar Assn., Am. Coll. Real Estate Lawyers, NY State Bar; book in progress on complex real estate transactions; Democrat; Baptist; rec: racquetball, carpentry, photog. Ofc: Metropolitan Life Ins. Co., 101 Lincoln Centre Dr Foster City 94404

LIPSCOMB, PAUL ROGERS, orthopaedic surgeon, consultant; b. Mar. 23, 1914, Clio, S.C.; s. Paul Holmes and Mary Emma (Rogers) L.; m. Phyllis Oesterreich, July 20, 1940; children: Susan Lovering b. 1943, Paul Rogers, Jr. b. 1944; edn: BS, Univ. S.C., 1935; MD, Medical Univ. of S.C., 1938; MS in Ortho. Surgery, Mayo Found., Univ. Minn. 1942. Career: intern Cooper Hosp., Camden, N.J. 1938-39; resident in ortho. surg. Mayo Clinic, Rochester, Minn. 1939-43, staff Mayo Clinic 1943-69, faculty Mayo Graduate Sch., Univ. Minn. 1943-69; prof. ortho. surg. Univ. Minn. Medical Sch., 1961-69, prof. emeritus 1969–; prof. and chmn. Dept. Ortho. Surg., Sch. of Medicine, UC Davis 1969-81, prof. emeritus 1981–, staff pres. UCD/Sacto. Med. Center 1980-81; surgery of the hand and cons. orthopaedic surg. Woodland Clinic Medical Group, Woodland, Calif. 1981–; vis. prof. at 13 univs. in US, Rhodesia, Brazil, Iran, New Zealand and Australia; member num. profl. coms., ten chairmanships; trustee Sterling Bunnell Found. 1983-; mem. (pres. 1984-85) Woodland Clinic Research & Edn. Found.; chmn. Leadership Fund Com. UCD Sch. of Med. 1984-85; honors: Alpha Omega Alpha, Sigma Xi; mem: Am. Acad. Ortho. Surgeons, Am. Bd. of Med. Splties., Am. Bd. of Ortho. Surg. (pres. 1971-73), Am. Coll. of Surgeons, AMA (chmn. Ortho. Sect. 1965), Am. Ortho. Assn. (pres. 1974-75), Am. Rheumatism Assn., Am. Soc. for Surg. of the Hand, Am. Trauma Soc., Clinical Ortho. Soc., Ortho. Research Soc., Calif. Med. Assn., Central Ortho. Soc., Texas Ortho. Assn. (hon.), Western Ortho. Assn./ Sacto. Valley Chpt., Wilson Interurban Club, New Zealand Ortho. Assn. (corresp. mem.), Internat. Soc. Ortho. Surg. and Traumatology, Internat. Ortho. Soc., Sacto. County Med. Soc. (assoc.), Yolo County Med. Assn., Mayo Alumni Assn., Bay Area Joint Replacement Soc. (hon.); author over 140 publs.; Protestant. Res: 749 Sycamore Ln Davis 95616 Ofc: Woodland Clinic Medical Group 1207 Fairchild Ct Woodland 95695

LIPTRAP, WILLIAM HERBERT, pathologist; b. Sept. 18, 1927, Glendale; s. Wm. Harrison and Jeannette Elizabeth (Booth) L.; m. Evelyn C. White, June 1952, div. 1973; children: William b. 1954, Robert b. 1957, Carolyn b. 1958, James b. 1961; edn: AB, Stanford Univ. 1950; DO, Coll. of Osteopathic Physicians & Surgeons 1955; MD, Calif. Coll. of Medicine 1962; State of Calif. 1st Physician & Surgeon lic., July 1956. Career: worked as med. technologist; independent gen. practice of medicine, 1956-64; surgical fellowship, McGill Univ. 1962; resident physician in anatomic pathology, fellow in anatomic pathology, Stanford Univ. Med. Center, 1965-71, also clin. teaching asst., Stanford Med. Sch. and med. research Veterans Adm. Hosp., Palo Alto 1968-71; physician & surgeon spec. in anatomic pathology, largely forensic 1971–, founder/owner pathology lab., Susanville 1971; anatomic pathology exams., Lassen Meml. Hosp. 1971-77; medical examiner County of Lassen, and fmrly. for Plumas and Sierra Counties; mem. Quad County Med. Soc.; fmr. Rotarian; life mem. Stanford Alumni Assn.; publs: article in Jour. Ultrastructure Research (1968); mil: T/5 US Army Signal Corps 1946-47; rec: med. laboratory work. Address: 455 Ash St, POB 1317, Susanville 96130

LISONI, JOSEPH LOUIS, lawyer; b. Mar. 13, 1947, Los Angeles; s. Joseph Arthur and Frances Genevieve (Minna) L.; m. Gail, Mar. 24, 1984; edn: BA, St. Mary's Coll. 1969; JD, UC Hastings Sch. of Law 1972; admitted Calif. State Bar 1972. Career: founding ptnr. law firm Lisoni & Lisoni, Los Angeles 1973–, spec. in personal injury; arbitrator (pers. injury) Am. Arb. Assn.; honors: Who's Who in Am. Colls. & Univs.; mem. ABA, Calif., Los Angeles, Italian-Am., Wash DC Bar Assns.; mem. Am., Calif., Los Angeles Trial Lawyers Assns; mem. Sons of Italy in Am.; Democrat; Catholic; rec: swim, golf, travel. Ofc: Lisoni & Lisoni, 3701 Wilshire Blvd Ste 700 Los Angeles 90010

LITTLE, FANNING MILES, neurological surgeon; b. May 13, 1948, Spartanburg, S.C.; s. Herbert Lindsay Little and Belle Little Smith; edn: BA, cum laude, Wash. & Lee Univ. 1970; MD, Medical Univ. of S.C. 1974. Career: med. intern L.A. Co.-USC Medical Center, Los Angeles 1974-75, surgical intern 1978-79, resident in emergency medicine 1976-78, res. in neurosurgery 1979-84; asst. prof. Dept. of Neurosurgery, USC Sch. of Medicine 1984–, also att. neurosurgeon Childrens Hosp. of Los Angeles, LAC-USC Med. Center, Norris Cancer Center, Rancho Los Amigos Hosp., Huntington Meml. Hosp.; mem. Congress of Neurol. Surgeons, AMA, L.A. Co. Med. Assn., Calif. Med. Assn., Calif. Assn. of Neurological Surgery, So. Calif. Neurosurg. Soc.; sev. articles in med. jours., profl. presentations nat. and local; Republican; Episcopal; rec: sports, travel, sports cars. Res: 800 W First St Ste 2007 Los Angeles 90012 Ofc: Childrens Hospital of Los Angeles 1300 N Vermont Ave Ste 906 Los Angeles 90027

LITTLE, JOHN NEWELL, physician, surgeon; b. Nov. 18, 1917, Logansport, Ind.; s. Dr. John Alexander (MD) and Blanche Elise (Mitchell) L.; edn: BS, Northwestern Univ. 1940, MD, 1944; lic. phys. & surgeon, Calif. (1947), Ill. (1949), USCG to Merchant Marine (1961); Fellow (life) Am. Coll. Surgeons (1982), Fellow Am. Coll. Chest Physicians (1972), Assoc. Fellow Aerospace Med. Assn.. Career: physician VA Hosp., San Fernando and med. office Lyman A. Brewer, Los Angeles 1952-55, 57; group med. practice Ross-Loos, Glendale 1959-60; pvt. med. practice in No. Hollywood, and Northridge, 1958, 61-66; ship surgeon S.S. Matsonia and S.S. Monterey, 1961, 66; surgeon L.A. Receiving Hosp., City of Los Angeles 1967-70; med. dir./plant phys. GMC Auto Assembly Plant, South Gate 1974-75; ship med. ofcr. M.V. Glomar Challenger, NSF/GMI, 1977; attend. physician Plasma Phoresis Ctr., 1979; recipient appreciation awards Nat. FOP (76), Nat. APA (1983), US Navy Commendation, SS Marine Lynx at sea (1945), and Army AF Commendation, 308th B.W. Kimlo AFB (1946); mem: AFA (life), NI (life), ADPA, Am. Legion, ALEOA, AFP, APA, ASC, SIF, NRSC, AIAA, Jane's Defence (1984), USC Alumni Assn. (life), Sigma Chi frat. (life); mil: 1st lt. Med. Corps, flt. surgeon AAF 1942-46; Republican; Presbyterian. Res: 507 California Ste 106 Santa Monica 90403

LITTLE, LAWRENCE ALAN, hospital pharmacy services director; b. Jan. 23, 1947, Downey; s. Eugene R. and Naomia L. (Murphy) L.; edn: Long Beach City Coll. 1964-66; Pharm.D., UC San Francisco 1970; Reg. Pharmacist, Calif., Nev. Career: staff pharmacist French Hospital, S.F. 1970-76, asst. dir. of pharmacy, 1976-79, dir. of pharmacy, 1979-80; assoc. dir./dir. of pharmacy svcs., Herrick Hospital, Berkeley 1980—; asst. clin. prof. of pharmacy UCSF 1982—; cons. Pharmacy Group Purchasing Pgm., Hospital Council of So./No. Calif. 1979-; pres. Herrick Hosp. Credit Union; mem: Am. Soc. of Hosp. Pharmacists, Calif. Soc. of Hosp. Pharmacists, Diablo Soc. of Hosp. Pharmacists; publs: art. Am. J. of Hosp. Pharm. (3/82, 8/84); rec: photog. Res: 100 London Ct San Bruno 94066 Ofc: Herrick Hospital & Health Center, 2001 Dwight Way Berkeley 94704

LITTLE, PHILIP WAYNE, private investigator, security co. president; b. June 7, 1942, Mercer, Mo.; s. Frank E. and Bertha M. (McConnell) L.; m. Marvella Renno, Dec. 22, 1962; children: Philip Wayne II b. 1963, Wade Alan b. 1964; edn: spl. courses Whitman Tech. Tng. Ctr. 1960, CSU San Jose 1981-82; Calif. lic. Pvt. Investigator 1972. Career: dep. sheriff San Bernardino 1963-70; prin. Phil Little Investigations, San Bernardino 1970-77; owner/pres. West Coast Detectives (120+ agents internat.), No. Hollywood 1977—; num. TV and Radio appearances include 3-hr series on crime prevention Pub. TV, 700 Club (CBN-TV), 22 Views (KWHY-TV), Midmorning L.A. (KHJ-TV), rel. pgmmg. (KTBN-TV); recipient 220 awards for community involvement, The Prince of Peace award (for work in Middle East) High Adventure Ministries; mem: Nat. Assn. of Chiefs of Police, World Assn. of Detectives, Internat. Police Cong., US Chamber of Commerce; civic: Police Activity League Supporters/ assoc. LAPD (pres.), 1984 Olympics Security Pgm. (cons.), Middle East Relief and Peace Pgm. (cons.), High Adventure Ministries (bd. dirs.), Youth Intervention and Guidance Inc. (bd. dirs.). Address: West Coast Detectives 5113 Lankershim No Hollywood 91601

LITTLE, RICHARD CARUTHERS, entertainer; b. Nov. 26, 1938, Ottawa, Ont., Can.; s. Lawrence Peniston and Elizabeth Maud (Willson) L.; m. Jeanne Worden, Oct. 16, 1971; 1 dau. Bria, b. 1977; edn: dip. Lisgar Collegiate, Jr. Matrick, 1958. Career: television: Rich Little Christmas Carol, Rich Little Washington Follies, Great Pretenders I, and II, Jimmy Stewart Tribute, Jack Lemmon Tribute, Fantasy Island, Hawaii 5-0, Judy Garland Show, var. talk shows; feature films: Another Nice Mess and Dirty Tricks; nightclubs: all major clubs in USA incl. MGM Grand in Las Vegas, Sahara Tahoe, Riviera Hotel, Boardwalk Regency, Mill Run Theatre; benefits incl. Amy Karen Cancer Benefit, spokesman for Share, and Boy Scouts. Honors: Entertainer of the Year, Las Vegas, AGVA Comedy Star of the Year, Cleveland Amory Best Guest of a TV Talk Show, Ottawa's Favorite Son, Montreux Festival Golden Rose for Rich Little's Christmas Carol; mem. AFTRA, SAG, ACTRA, AEA, AGVA, ATAS; Anglican; rec: tennis, skiing, video. Ofc: Rich Little Prodns. Inc., 9200 Sunset Blvd Suite 607, Los Angeles 90069

LITTLEHAILES, RICHARD, keyboard training co. chief executive; b. Nov. 30, 1934, Beckenham, Kent, Eng.; s. Richard and Josephine Nina (John) L.; m. Edmee; children: Richard b. 1968, Roderick b. 1970. Career: founder/bd. chmn. Keyboard Training Ltd., England 1964—, has since started cos. in 26 countries. Ofc: Keyboard Productivity Inc. 6035 Bristol Pkwy Culver City 90230

LITTLEJOHN, EDWARD CHARLES, orthopedic surgeon; b. Sept. 28, 1954, Berkeley, Calif.; s. Charles Henry and Marjorie Arloa (McNew) L.; edn: BS cum laude, Calif. State Univ. Hayward 1975; MD, UC Irvine 1979. Career: orthopedic residency UC Los Angeles 1979-84; pvt. practice orthopedic surgeon, San Jose/Los Gatos 1984—; honors: Alpha Omega Alpha (1978), Lange Award for outstanding performance (1979); mem. Santa Clara County Med. Soc., Santa Clara Co. Orthopedic Club; publs: Orthopedic Rev. 12/83; rec: skiing, former club racer. Ofc: 14911 National Ave Ste 3 Los Gatos 95030

LIU, GRACE S. C., acupuncturist; b. Oct. 18, 1924, Fon Hua, Chekiang, China; d. Yu Shu and Woo-Chyn (Wu) Ger; m. Chi-Seng Liu, June 26, 1948; children: Maria b. 1950, Han Hsiung b. 1951, Han Kwan b. 1952, Steve b. 1957, Frank b. 1957; edn: MD, Fukien Provincil Medical Coll., China 1948; OMD, San Francisco Coll. of Acupuncture and Oriental Medicine 1984; desig: Certified Acupuncturist, Calif. (1976), Dr. of Oriental Medicine (1984). Career: interne Taiwan National Univ. Hosp. 1948-49; doctor General Tri-Service Hosp. 1949-050; chief doctor Med. Dept. and physiological instr. Girls Normal Coll., Taipei 1950-52; doctor, vice-chief, superior splst. dr. Med. Dept. Central Bank of China 1952-75; owner Dr. Liu's Private Physician and Acupuncturist Clinic, Taipei 1958-75; dir./chief dr. Acupuncture Clinic and Research Ctr. of The City of 10,000 Buddhas 1976—; prof. (acupunc. anat., acumassage) Dharma Realm Buddhist Univ., 1977-; honors: Silver Medallion highest honor; 23-year outstanding achievement in field of medicine, The Central Bank of China (1975); listed Who's Who Calif. (1981-2); mem: Drs. Assn. of Taipei, Acupuncture Assn. of the Rep. of China, The Sino-Amer. Buddhist Assn., The United Acupuncturist of Calif., Calif. Certified Acupuncturist Assn.; publs: Theory of Acupuncture (1979); Research on hay fever and treatment by acupuncture (1984); sev. inventions involving weight loss and smoking, alcohol and drug cures; Republican (Repub. Nat. Com. sustaining mem. 1980); Buddhist; rec: reading. Res: 15 Cottage Lane (POB 655) Talmage 95481 Ofc: Acupuncture Clinic of the City of 10,000 Buddhists, Talmage 95481

LIU, REX MINGCHAO, investor, co. executive; b. Oct. 10, 1940, Taiwan, R.O.C.; s. Jui An and Ah Jyu (Tzeng) L.; m. Alias, Sept. 9, 1970; children: Rex, Jr. b. 1973, Alex b. 1976; edn: B. Commerce, Nat. Chengchi Univ., Taiwan

1966. Career: lectr. Hsin-Wu Coll. of Commerce, Taiwan 1972-74; chief acct. Philips Electronic Industries (Taiwan) Ltd., Taiwan 1974-78; asst. to v.p. fin. Taiwan Polypropylene Co. Ltd., Taiwan 1978-81; gen. ptnr. Chase House Motel, Calif. and pres. Nutel Motel and Best Western Uplander Motor Hotel, 1981—; honors: Gold award Hong Kong Amateur Fencing Assn. (1970), head coach Fencing Dept. Martial Arts Assn. R.O.C. (1968-72); mem: Am. Inst. CPAs (assoc.), Nat. Fencing Coach Assn. of Am. (assoc. 1980-84); clubs: Lions (Taipei), Rotary (Taipei), Kiwanis (Taipei), Shriners (Taiwan and Tacoma, Wash.); publs: Fencing with Foil (Chinese ed.); mil: 2d. lt. China Army Reserve 1966-67; Republican; Buddhist; rec: classical music, sports, travel. Address: Rancho Palos Verdes 90274

LIU, SHIN-TSE, chemist; b. Sept. 27, 1932, Taipei, Taiwan, nat. US cit. Aug. 6, 1976; s. Teng-mien and Alee (Chen) L.; edn: BS chem. engring., Taiwan Univ. 1956; MS chem., Technische- Hochschule Aachen, Ger. 1962, PhD 1966. Career: research chemist ITT Rayonier, N.J. 1967; research engr. Jet Propulsion Lb., Pasadena 1970; chemical cons. prin./pres. S.T. Liu & Co., Los Angeles 1974—, chemical cons. for cos. in USA, Europe and Asia; agent for No. America for The Chemical Daily (Japanese chem. newspaper); mem. Am. Chemical Soc.; works: Synthesis of insuline peptide, publs. in polymer chemistry, inventions in waste effluent treatments. Ofc: S.T. Liu & Co., POB 17457 Los Angeles 90017

LLOYD, LANCE JOHN, chemical engineer; b. Aug. 5, 1936, Sydney, N.S.W., Australia; s. Walter William Scott and Ella Beatrice (Hobden) L.; m. Judith Ann Garnock, Dec. 5, 1964; children: Kylie b. 1966, Jaimie b. 1968, Andrew b. 1970; edn: B.Eng., honors, Univ. of Sydney 1958; M.Eng. Univ. of New. So. Wales 1966; Cert. of Eng., Inst. of Chem. Engrs.; fellow, Inst. of Dirs., Australia. Career: var. chem. engr. pos., U.K.; in charge A.C.I. Dimet & Brick Facilities, Univ. of New So. Wales; currently, reg. pres. A.C.I. America Inc., Newport Beach; dir. ACI Am., Inc., Kintruss Corp., Inc., McCullough Sys., Inc., ACI Galls Prods., Inc., DTH Ent., Inc., Overmyer Corp., Inc., ACI Am. Holdings Inc., ACI Internat. Bv, Am. Consolidated Industries Inc.; mem: Inst. Chem. Engrs., U.K.; Balboa Bay Club; Liberal (Australia); Methodist; rec: rugby football, field hockey. Res: 1845 Port Stanhope Pl Newport Beach 92660 Ofc: ACI America Inc., 1811 Quail St, 2nd Flr, Newport Beach 92660

LO, GLADYS GOH, physician, radiologist; b. March 28, 1950, London, England; d. Kenneth Kok-Aun and Irene Siu-Kwong (Wong) Goh; m. Richard Lo., Sept. 6, 1973; 1 dau, Christine b. 1983; edn: BA, UC Berkeley 1972; MD, UCLA Sch. of Med. 1976; Diplomate Am. Bd. of Radiology 1981. Career: chief div. of computed tomography and ultrasound Dept. of Radiology Hong Kong Sanitorium & Hosp. Ltd., Hong Kong 1981-85; radiologist Valley Radiology Med. Group Inc., San Jose 1985—; tech. com. Valley Radiology Med. Group Inc. 1986-; clin. tchg. staff Valley Med. Ctr., Santa Clara 1985—; mem: Radiological Soc. of No. Am., Am. Assn. of Women Radiologists; Protestant; rec: tennis. Ofc: Valley Radiology Inc., P.O. Box 2F San Jose 95109

LO SCHIAVO, JOHN JOSEPH, S.J., university president; b. Feb. 25, 1925, San Francisco; s. Joseph and Anna (Re) Lo Schiavo; edn: AB, Gonzaga Univ., Spokane 1948, MA, 1949; STL (Licentiate in Sacred Theol.), Alma Coll., Los Gatos 1962; Ordained priest Roman Catholic Ch. (1955). Career: vice principal Brophy Coll. Prep, Phoenix, Ariz. 1958-61; instr. Philos. and Theol., Univ. San Francisco, 1950-52, 1956-57, 61-62, dean of students 1962-66, v.p. Student Affairs 1966-68; pres. Bellarmine Coll. Prep., San Jose 1968-75; rector Jesuit Community Univ. San Francisco 1975-77; pres. Univ. San Francisco 1977—; mem. USF Bd. Trustees (1964-68, 1969-, bd. chmn. 1970-73), San Francisco Consortium (trustee 1977-), Assn. of Jesuit Colls. and Univs. (dir. 1977-), Assn. of Independent Calif. Colls. and Univs. (exec. com. 1978-), Bellarmine Coll. Prep. (bd. trustees 1968-78), Jesuit Secondary Edn. Assn. (bd. dirs. 1973-75), Jesuit High Sch., Sacto. (bd. trustees 1975-78); mem. Retirement Bd., Calif. Province of the Soc. of Jesus (1971-78), Novitiate Wines (bd. dirs. 1973-78), Senate of Priests, Archdiocese of S.F. (1969-71); honors: Alpha Sigma Nu (life), Nat. Jesuit Honor Soc.; civic: Red Cross, Santa Clara Co. (bd. dirs. 1969-70), Catholic Social Service of SC Co. (bd. dirs. 1974-75), Sacred Heart Schs. (bd. adv. 1972-75), NCCJ Inc. (bd. dirs. S.F. 1982-), The Olympic Club, The Bohemian Club, Il Cenacolo; Republican; rec: golf. Address: Univ. of San Francisco, Ignatian Hts. San Francisco 94117

LO, WILLIAM WEI-HSING, engineer; b. Apr. 15, 1950, Hong Kong, China; s. Tao-Haim and Fu-Shien (Hwang) L.; m. Emily Feng, Jan. 16, 1978; children: Jeniffer b. 1982, Benjamin b. 1985; edn: BS, Taipei Inst. of Tech. 1971; MS, Kansas State Univ. 1979. Career: elec. engr. Taiwan Power Co., Taipei, Taiwan 1976; research asst. Kansas State Univ., Manhattan, Bs. 1978; sr. engr. Control Data Corp., Omaha, Nebr. 1982; sys. engr. Ibis Sys. Inc., Westlake Village 1983; currently, principal engr. Pertec Peripherals Corp., Chatsworth; awards: tech. excellence, Control Data Corp. 1981; mem: IEEE; Christian; rec: research in computer based robotic systems field. Res: 2779 N Velarde Dr Thousand Oaks 91360 Ofc: Pertec Peripherals Corp., 9610 De Soto Ave Chatsworth 91311

LOBDELL, ROBERT C., legal executive; b. Jan. 1, 1926, Mankato, Mn.; s. Darwin Norman and Hilda Cecelia (Peterson) L.; m. Nancy Lower, July 12, 1952; children: Teresa (Johnson), b. 1953; Robert John, b. 1955; William Scott, b. 1960; James Marston, b. 1962; edn: AB, Stanford Univ. 1948; LLD, 1950; admitted to practice, State Bar of Calif. 1951, US Supreme Ct. Bar 1964. Career: atty., legal dept. Bank of America, Los Angeles 1951-52; atty./ corp. ofcr. Youngstown Sheet & Tube Co., Youngstown, Ohio 1952-65; asst. gen. counsel/ asst. secty. The Times Mirror Co., Los Angeles 1965-70, v.p./ asst.

secty. The Times Mirror Co. and v.p./ gen. counsel Los Angeles Times 1970-84; v.p. and asst. to senior v.p., gen. counsel Times Mirror Co. 1985–; secty./trustee Pfaffinger Found.; mem Inst. for Corp. Counsel (gov.); Constitutional Rights Found. (Lawyers Adv. Council); Am., Calif., Los Angeles County Bar Assn.; dir.L.A. Co. Bar Found.; Am. Soc. of Corp. Sectys.; Beta Theta Pi; Univ. Club; publs: co- ed., Southern California Conference on The Media and the Law, 1977; mil: pfc Army Air Corps 1944-45, 1st lt. USAR 1951-52; Episcopal; rec: tennis, jogging, music. Res: 925 Hillside Dr Long Beach 90815 Ofc: Times Mirror Co., Times Mirror Square Los Angeles 90053

LOBNER, KNEELAND HARNESS, lawyer; b. Feb. 2, 1919, Sacramento; s. Leo and Laura (Roberts) L.; m. Adele Frances Ohe, Dec. 20, 1941; children: Breton K., Robert K., Susan A. (Schroeder); edn: AA, Sacto. City Coll. 1939; JD, Hastings Coll. Law 1944; admitted Calif. State Bar 1946, US Supreme Ct. 1960. Career: atty. City of Auburn 1946-47; assoc. atty. law ofc. of K.D. Robinson, Auburn 1946-47; dep. dist. atty. Sacramento County 1947-49; litigation and membership atty. Calif. Automobile Assn.-No. Calif., Sacto. 1949-52; pvt. practice of law (incl. litigation and bus., property and probate), 1952–, prin. Lobner & Bull, Sacto.; elected councilman City of Sacramento 1957-62, vice mayor 1962; mem. Sacto. Met. Adv. Com. 1957-59, Sacto. Redevel. Agency 1964-73, chmn. 1970-72; mem. Sacto. Estate Planning Council 1960-; mem. Defense Research Inst. 1965-; bd. dirs. (pres. 1963-64) Am. Cancer Soc. Sacto. 1956-64; bd. dirs. (pres. 1969-71) Calif. Mus. Assn. 1968-73; bd. govs. (pres. 1966) Hastings Law Coll. 1960-, Hastings 1066 Found. (pres. 1976); bd. dirs. Hastings Coll. of Law (apptd. by Gov. Deukmejian) 1985-; bd. dirs. Sacto. Sym. Found.; pres. Crystal Shores West Assn. 1982-; honors: oustanding alumnus Hastings Coll. Law (1976); mem: Fellow Am. Coll. Probate Counsel, Am. Bd. Trial Advocates (pres. Sacto. chpt. 1985-86), ABA, Sacto. County Bar Assn. (pres. 1973), State Bar Calif., Am. Judicature Soc., Better Bus. Bur. (pres. 1967), Sacto. Zool. Soc. (pres. 1965), Am. Legion, Sacto. County Bar Council; clubs: Del Paso Country, Elks; Republican (Sacto. County Central Com. 1955-57, Calif. Rep. Central Com. 1962-68); Episcopal. Ofc: 717 20th St Sacramento 95814

LOCATELLI, PAUL LEO, university administrator; b. Sept. 16, 1938, Santa Cruz; s. Vincent D. and Marie J. (Piccone) L.; edn: BSc, Univ. Santa Clara 1961; M.Div., Jesuit Sch. of Theol., Berkeley 1974; BDA, USC 1971; Cert. CPA, Calif. 1965. Career: profl. acct. Lautze & Lautze (Wolf & Co.) 1960-64, 74; lectr. Jesuit Sch. of Theol., Berkeley 1973-74; with Univ. of Santa Clara 1974–: prof. of acctg. 1974–; assoc. dean Sch. of Bus. 1976-78; academic v.p. 1978–; bd. trustees: Seattle Univ., Seattle, Wash. 1983; Univ. of San Francisco 1979-85; Bellarmine Coll. Prep. 1975-; bd. dirs. and Senior Commn., Western Assn. of Schs. and Colls.; chmn. jury for Calif. Mus. Sci. and Industry 1978-79, and chmn. for selection of Industrialist of the Yr. 1979; honors: Teacher of the Yr. 1977-78, Beta Gamma Sigma 1978; mem: Am. Inst. & Calif. Soc. of CPAs, Am. Acctg. Assn.; Democrat; Roman Catholic Jesuit Priest; rec: photog. Address: University of Santa Clara, Santa Clara 95053

LOCKE, JOHN CLAYTON, telecommunications engineering executive; b. March 15, 1956, Glendale; s. Marvin Clayton and Irene (May) L.; m. Cynthia M. Roos, Feb. 18, 1978; 1 son, Jeffery, b. 1982; edn: BS in elec. & electronics eng., cum laude, CalPoly Univ. 1981; computer tech., Control Data Inst. 1975; EMBA pgm., Claremont Grad. Sch. 1985-; part-time teaching cred., Calif. 1983. Career: engrg. aide Alston Div. Conrac Corp., 1975-79; v.p. engrg./prin. Dimas Corp., 1979-82; v.p. engrg. Telcom Technologies, Ontario 1982–, bd. dirs. 1983-85; instr. computer tech. Mt. San Antonio Coll. 1983-4; honors: full scholastic scholarship, Control Data Inst. 1974; guest spkr. CalPoly Univ.; Eta Kappa Nu (mem. 1980, spkr. 1980, 81); resrch: fiber optics in telecommunications, 1980. Republican; Baptist; rec: x-c runner, racquetball. Res: 1101 Eaton Rd San Dimas 91773 Ofc: Telcom Technologies 3072 East G St Ontario 91764

LOCKE, JOHN WHITEMAN, III, corporate financial executive; b. Oct. 17, 1936, Melrose, Mass.; s. John W., Jr. and Lucille (Jones) L.; children: Stephanie b. 1962, Christine b. 1965, Nancy b. 1966; edn: BA, Williams Coll. 1959; MBA, Harvard Univ. 1965; Certified Public Acct., Calif. (1967). Career: auditor Price Waterhouse, San Francisco 1965-68, Peat Marwick Mitchell, S.F. 1969; group controller Kaiser Aluminum, Oakland 1970-81; comml. mgr. Bechtel Group, S.F. 1981-84; dir. finance and controller General Parametrics Corp., Berkeley 1984–; mem. Am. Inst. CPAs, Harvard Business Sch. Assn.; mil: USN 1959-63, lcdr USNR (Ret.). Res: 1451 Marchbanks Dr Apt 3 Walnut Creek 94598 Ofc: General Parametrics 1250 Ninth St Berkeley 94710

LOCKHART, JAMES BICKNELL, JR., manufacturing co. president; b. Mar. 27, 1918, Taunton, Mass.; s. James Bicknell and Charlotte Bradford (Babbitt) L.; m. Mary Ann Riegel, Oct. 2, 1943; children: Joan Riegel b. 1944, James B., III b. 1946, Ann Murchie b. 1948, Brenda Margaret b. 1950; edn: BS, Yale Univ. 1940, MBA, Northwestern Univ. 1941, MS, US Naval Acad. 1945. Career: cost acct. Gen. Electric Co., Mass. 1941-43; mgmt. cons. MacDonald Bros., Mass. 1945-48; chief indsl. engr. Riegel Paper Corp., N.J. 1948, purchasing agt. 1948-50, asst. to v.p. Prodn. 1950-51, mill mgr. 1951-54, N.Y. mgr. indsl. & merchant sale 1954-57, dir. 1952-67, corp. secty. 1955-63, corp. controller 1958-63, v.p. 1957-63; pres./CEO, dir., Conwed Corp., Minn. 1963-71; pres./ CEO Lockhart & Co., Minn., 1971-74; dir. 1971-82; pres./CEO, dir. Monier Co., Calif. 1974-78; pres./CEO, Isolite Corp., Hawthorne, Calif. 1978–; past dir: Ridge Water Co. Inc., N.J.; Bartelt Engring., Ill.; Conwed Internat., Minn.; Fiber Conversion Co., Ga.; Sonic Engring. Corp., Conn.; Internat. Acoustical Testing Labs Inc., Minn.; Wood Conversion Industries, Minn.; Magnus Products Corp., Mich.; Mica-Wood Corp., Wisc.; First Trust Co., Minn.; exec. com. Specialty Paper & Board Assn., NY 1957-58. Honors: permanent exhib. named in honor, Minn. Science Mus. 1974; award of honor, The Wisdom Soc. 1975; service awards, Big Brothers of St. Paul, Minn. (1975), Big Brothers/Big Sisters of Am. (1977); key to City of San Bernardino, Calif. (1977); listed, Who's Who in Amer.; founder/dir. Old Town Restorations, Minn. 1970; mem: Mayflower Soc., Nat. UN Day Com., 1978; mil: lt. USNR 1942-46, cmdr. minesweeper, Victory, Pacific Theatre, Amer. Theatre, Phil. Liberation medals; Republican; Episcopal; rec: travel. Res: 635 E. Palmdale Ave Orange 92665 Ofc: Locknell Corp., 1400 E Katella Ave Ste 224 Orange 92667

LOCKNESS, DORIS ESTELLE, aviatrix; b. Feb. 2, 1910, Bryant, Pa.; d. Lewis Watson and Harriette Estelle (Myers) Erwin; m. 2d. Robert Lockness, Apr. 10, 1948; children: Donna b. 1928, Paul b. 1930, David b. 1932, Ronald b. 1933. Career: student pilot, Wilmington, CA 1938; pvt. pilot, Long Beach 1939-40; WWII service military pilot, Women's Airforce Service Pilots (WASP), 1943; comml. pilot, Long Beach 1962; flight instr., Long Beach, Santa Monica, Van Nuys 1964-68; qual. in single and multi-engined airplanes, seaplanes, helicopters, hot air balloons and gliders; commd. ofcr. Confederate Air Force, 1982, grade Col.; Received Fedn. Aeronautique Internat. sporting lic. (FAI) Balloon Fedn. of Am. 1982; comml. pilot instr. hot air balloons 1983, gliders 1984; continues flying activities in personal aircraft; honors: OX5 Aviation Pioneers Legion of Merit (1984, first woman recipient); mem: Ninety-Nines Internat. (treas. Cameron Park chpt. 1983); chair Direct Relief Found., San Fernando Valley chpt. Ninety-Nines, 1980-82; OX5 Aviation Pioneers (life), OX5 Golden Gate Wing (bd. govs. 1985-); Whirly-Girls, Internat. Womens Helicopter Pilots Inc.; Seaplane Pilots Assn.; Air Force Assn.; CAF; WASPs; Balloon Fedn. of Am.; Soaring Soc. of Am.; Sacto. Jaguar Car Club; Republican; Lutheran; rec: cross country flying, soaring; exhibits Jaguar sports cars in concour'd' elegance events (num. 1st pl. trophies). Res: 312 Ogden Way Vacaville 95688

LOCKWOOD, DOROTHY ERNESTINE, real estate broker; b. Jan. 26, 1917, Clay Center, Neb.; d. Archie E. and Mildred E. (McClanahan) Leopold; m. Ernest E. Lockwood, Feb. 27, 1937; childern: Ronna b. 1941, Sandra b. 1947, Scott b. 1948; edn: secondary tchg. cert., Kearney State Teachers Coll. Neb. 1934-36; real estate broker Calif. Career: tchr. Phelps County, Neb. 1936-37; real estate sales, broker Fairfield, Calif. 1961–; state sales rep. No. Solano Bd. Realtors; mem: Nat., Calif. Realtors Assns., Bus. & Profl. Women; works: smuggled 40 bibles into Red China in 1983; Republican; So. Baptist (bible teacher); rec: golf, choir, photog. Res: 355 E Wyoming Fairfield 94533

LOEFFLER, ROBERT ALLAN, plastic and reconstructive surgeon (ret); b. Aug, 8, 1921, Avoca, Mich.; s. Arthur John and Pearl May (Green) L.; m. Betty Glaves, Sept. 23, 1944; children: Paula b. 1947, Pamela b. 1949; Diane b. 1952; Janice and Julie b. 1956; edn: BS, Oregon State Univ. 1943; MD, Univ. of Oregon Med. Sch. 1945; Diplomate Am. Bd. of Surgery 1957, Am. Bd. of Plastic Surg. 1959. Career: intern USN Oakland and Aiea Hts. Hawaii 1945; surg. trng. USNH San Diego and Wm. Milton Adams, Memphis, Tenn. 1955; chief plastic surg. Portsmouth, Va. Naval Hosp., Oakland Naval Hosp. 1956-63; pvt. practice plastic and reconstr. surg., staff of 6 local hosps. 1963-83; cons. in plas, surg. and urology USNM Ctr. Oakland; mem: AMA, CMA, Alameda Contra Costa Med. Assn.; Am. Soc. Plastic and Reconstr. Surg.; Am. Soc. Aesthetic Plastic Surg.; Calif. Soc. Plastic Surg.; Castlewood; publs: J. Urology 1956; mil: capt. Med. Corps USN 1943-63, decorated Combat Inchon, mem. surgical team II, Korea-Japan; Presbyterian; rec: ceramics, sculpture, fishing, boating, golf. Res: 4591 James Ave Castro Valley 94546 Ofc: 1856 Harvest Rd Pleasanton 94566

LOGAN, KENNETH R., personnel executive; b. June 6, 1943, St. Louis, Mo.; s. Lee and Lucille L.; m. Cynthia; 1 son, Jeffrey; edn: BS chem., Univ. of Mo. 1966; MBA, Unic. So. Calif. 1974; Calif. Comm. Coll. Tchg. Credl. (life) 1974. Career: production mgr. Paper Mate Pen Co., Santa Monica 1970-73; mgr. compensation TRW Energy Prods. Group, Los Angeles 1973-76; asst. personnel dir. Rand Corp., Santa Monica 1976–; honors: Curator's Award (Univ. Mo. 1965), Williams Award (USAF 1969), Medallion Award (Boys Clubs of Am. 1986); ofcr., bd. dirs. Venice Boys & Girls Club 1977-; steering com. L.A. Youth Motivation Task Force 1980-85; So. Calif. Tech. Personnel Com. 1978-; Employer Advis. Com. EDD 1983-; United Way Allocation Com. 1986; mem. L.A. Urban League 1985-86; mil: capt. USAF 1966-70; Methodist; rec: tennis, travel, youth work. Res: 5638 Canterbury Dr Culver City 90230

LOGAN, LYNNE, psychotherapist; b. Nov. 8, 1946, Houston; d. Robert Lloyd and Bonnie Mae (Herod) Exum; children: Lynette Marie b. 1966, Denise Dawn b. 1969, Wendy Jean b. 1973; edn: Moorpark Coll., Pierce Coll. 1976-79; BA psychol., Newport Univ. 1980; MA, Internat. Coll. 1981, PhD, 1985; lic. Marriage, Family, Child counselor. Career: currently in pvt. practice specializing in individual and family treatment; psychotherapist on staff of Corona Comm. Hosp., Charter Grove Hosp., Corona; host TV talk show A Slice of Life 1984; has appeared on num. AM Los Angeles TV broadcasts 1983-85; featured as One of Orange County's Women on the Move by Herself Mag.; listed Who's Who of Exec. Women of Calif. 1984; mem: Calif. Assn. Marriage Family Therapists, Assn. for Television & Radio Artists. Ofc: The Medical Ctr., 500 Anaheim Hills Rd Ste 206 Anaheim Hills 92807

LOGAN, WILLIAM FRANKLIN, real estate broker; b. Mar. 13, 1960, Frankfurt, Germany, US cit.; s. Theophilus A. and Martha R. (Nash) L.; edn: USAF Acad. 1978-80; BA econs., CSU San Diego 1983; Calif. lic. Real Estate Broker. Career: real estate broker Logan Realty Co., San Diego 1980–; instr. R.E. econs., Southwestern Jr. Coll. 1985-; mem. San Diego Bd. Realtors (chmn.

Housing Advis. Com., bd. dir. 1986-88), San Diego Indep. Baseball League; Democrat; Presbyterian; rec: sports, travel. Ofc: Logan Realty Co 4490 Logan Ave San Diego 92102

LOGANBILL, G. BRUCE, logopedic pathologist, educator; b. Sept. 6, 1938, Newton, Ks.; s. Oscar J. and Warrene (Rose) L.; edn: BA, Bethel Coll. 1956; MA, Univ. Ks. 1958; PhD, Mich. State Univ. 1961; postdoc. Inst. of Logopedics, 1965. Career: logopedic pathologist, professor CSU Fresno 1966-68, CSU Long Beach 1968–; lectr. on speech communication and logopedics in So. Am. (1971), Denmark (1973), Switz. (1974), Paris (1975), Switz. (1977), India (1981), Egypt (1982), Univ. of Edinburgh, Scotland (1983), Korea (1983), Russia (1984), China (1984); cons. in speech comm. for pvt. industry; mem: Speech Communication Assn., Speech Comm. Assn. of Pacific, World Comm. Assn., Western Sp. Comm. Assn., Am. Sp. & Hearing Assn., Internat. Assn. of Logopedics & Phoniatrics, Norsk Logopedic Assn., Phonetic Soc. of Japan, Assn. of CSU Professors (pres. 1984), Am. Assn. of Phonetic Scis., Calif. Sp. & Hearing Assn.; mem. Big Ten Club of So. Calif.; author: The Bases of Voice, Articulation, Pronunciation (3d ed. 1983); contbr. 28 articles in profl. journals: Folio Phoniatrica, J. of the Communication Assn. of the Pacific, others; Republican; Episcopal; rec: piano, bridge, travel. Res: 101 Claremont Ave Long Beach 90803 Ofc: CSULB 1250 Bellflower Blvd Long Beach 90840

LOGOTHETIS, LAMBROS C., manufacturing co. executive; b. Nov. 14, 1922, Alexandria, Egypt, nat. US cit. 1962; s. Thomas C. and Anthee M. (Sakell) L.; m. Kiki Carson, Aug. 20, 1961; children: Christine Patricia b. 1964, Caroline Anthe b. 1967; edn: BBA, Baruch Sch. NY 1964; Sorbonne Paris 2 yrs.; Baccalaureate, Coll. St. Marie 4 yrs.; CPA NY. Career: chief auditor Suez Canal Egypt, W.R. Grace NY; asst. controller Remington Conn.; controller, v.p. adminstrn. & finance Pirelli Tire Corp. NY; mem: NY State Soc. CPAs, Am. Inst. CPAs, Automobile Importers Assn. (dir.), Darien CC, Saratoga CC, Alliance Francaise; proficient in 5 languages; mil: Greek Royal Navy WWII; rec: tennis, philosophy. Res: 20856 Verdemoor Ct Saratoga 95070 Ofc: 2001 Gateway Pl San Jose 95110

LOGUE, MURL FRANCIS, manufacturing engineer, co. president; b. Feb. 9, 1921, Pittsburgh, Pa.;. s. Fred D. and Mary Ellen (Crawley) L.; m. Charlene Brown, Mar. 11, 1978; children: Kathleen b. 1946 (dec.), Michael Francis b. 1949, (step): Karen (Mrs. Gary Gervase), David Bobitt b. 1959; edn: cert. mgmt. engring., Pittsburgh Tech. Inst., 1953; stu. data proc. & computer pgmmg., San Joaquin Delta Coll. 1964-65; stu. and instr. USN Machinists Sch., Norfolk, Va. 1943; Reg. Profl. Engr., Calif. (1978-). Career: supr. West Penn Machine Shops, Pittsburgh 1946-53; supr. of methods engring. Lewis Mach. Div., Blaw Knox Corp., 1953-56; chief tool engr. Bucyrus Erie Corp., Erie, Pa. 1956-57; chief mfg. engr. Tel Autograph Corp., Los Angeles 1957-60; chief engr. Anderson Die Casting Co., L.A. 1960-62; senior tool engr. Norris Industry, L.A. 1962-64; mgr. mfg. engring. Super Mold Corp., Lodi 1964-66; chief machine tool engr. Norris Industry, Riverbank Army Ammo. Plant (responsible engr. for plant layout & equip. of largest US facility, 60 and 81 mm mortar shells; engr. responsible in planning & constrn. of most advanced facility in world, prodn. of hot pressed tech. ceramics, cermets and sialons) 1966-67; mfgrs. rep. 1967-71; pres. Logue Assocs. Inc. (successor to M.F. Logue Assoc.), mfg. engrs. & consultants, Newman 1971–, currently devel. new equip. and improved technology for prodn. of tech. ceramics and ferrites; dir. Fan-Fi Corp. 1972; mem. Soc. of Mfg. Engrs. (senior mem. 1965-, nat. lectr. 1970-76), Masons, US Congl. Adv. Bd. (1981-82); works: designer prodn. mach. for mil. hardware (Sparrow, Shrike, and other missiles), Patent (applicant) for new energy saving shower head; mil: MM1/c, acting CMM, US Navy 1942-45; Republican; Baptist; rec: boating, fishing, hunting. Address: Logue Associates Inc. 29435 Sanches Rd Newman 95360

LOHN, RAYMOND CHRISTIAN, restaurateur, b. July 27, 1935, Baltimore, Md.; s. Raymond Christian, Sr. and Mabel G. (Zoeller) L.; m. Elizabeth Mowbray, Apr. 23, 1958; children: Henrietta Swing b. 1959, Raymond C., Jr. b. 1963; edn: BS, Johns Hopkins Univ. 1965; mil. classified schs. nuclear weapons, 1954-57. Career: sales promotion Food Fair Stores, Balto. 1958-66; mgr. Brunswick Corp., Balto. 1966-67; corp. analyst finl. div. Arlens Realty Inc., Balto. 1967-72; adminstrn. mgr. Utica Tool Co. Inc. Orangeburg, S.C. 1972-73; adminstrn. mgr. Alex Colman Inc., Los Angeles 1974-78; owner Indian Creek Cafe, Happy Camp 1978–; profl. awards: "Better Homes and Gardens" mag. quote "terrific backwoods eatery" (1984), recognition by Calif. Restaurant Assn. and menu selected to tour Germany for a year to represent a typical Calif. menu (1984); appreciation for outstanding service, Senior Citizens orgn. (1984); mem: Assn. for Systems Mgmt. 1968-78, Calif. Restaurant Assn. 1984-; works: acquired a Frosty rest. (games & sandwiches) in 1978, without prior rest. experience (and in an economically depressed area) devel. bus. into a restaurant with large (one of largest) menu of primarily homemade food; mil: s/sgt. USAF 1954-58; Republican; Prot.; rec: water color painting, outdoors. Address: POB 687, 106 Indian Creek Rd Happy Camp 96039

LOLLI, ANDREW RALPH, consulting industrial engineer; b. Oct. 15, 1917, Seatonville, Ill.; s. Joseph Fredrick and Adolfa (Fiocchi) L.; m. Mary H. Tatsapaugh, Jan. 14, 1983; edn: Armed Forces Staff Coll. 1948, Nat. War Coll. 1957, N.Y. Inst. Fin. 1971; BS, Dickinson Coll. 1952; postgrad. Fordham Univ. 1952. Career: enlisted in US Army 1940, advanced through grades to maj. gen., 1960; chief plans and priorities Allied Forces So. Europe 1952-56; comdr. Air Def. units, N.Y. and San Francisco, 1957-60; comdr. XX U.S.A. Corps 1961-62, XV, 1962-63, comdr. Western NORD Region, Hamilton AFB, Calif. 1963-66, ret. 1966; exec. asst. Hughes Aircraft Co., Fullerton 1967; dir. gen. services State of Calif., Sacramento 1967-70; v.p. Sigmatics, Newport Beach 1970-73, Intercoast Investments Co., Sacto. 1975-76; pres. Andrew R. Lolli Assocs. Inc., San Francisco 1973–, Lolman Inc., S.F. 1976–; pres. bd. trustees Commonwealth Equity Trust 1974-80; v.chmn. Calif. Pub. Works bd. 1967-69; mem. adv. panel Nat. Acad. Scis. and Engring. in Research, Wash DC 1968-70; mem. fed., state and local govt. adv. panel Fed. Gen. Services, Wash DC 1968-69; bd. dirs. Columbia Boys Park Club (S.F.), Lab. for Survival (S.F.); awards: decorated D.S.M., Legion of Merit with oak leaf cluster, Bronze Star with oak leaf cluster; named Man of Year, Italian Sons of Am. (1964); mem: Nat. Assn. Uniformed Services, Assn. US Army, Ret. Ofcrs. Assn.; club: Presidio San Francisco, Golf; works: devel. Short Notice Inspection System for Army Air Def. Missiles (1960). Res: 1050 North Point San Francisco 94109 Ofc: 286 Jefferson St San Francisco 94133

LOMAS, ALICE SULLIVAN, dance choreographer; b. Sept. 19, 1907, San Francisco; d. George Henry and Amanda Adaline (Battenfeld) Sullivan; m. James Lomas, Apr. 7, 1940; children: James III b. 1941, Carol b. 1942; edn: Paul Gerson Sch. of Drama 1911-13; Talma Zeta Wilbur Drama 1913-18; O'Neill Sisters Dance Sch. 1914-16. Career: instr., dance dir. O'Neill Sisters Dance Sch. 1916-23; chorus line dancer Fanchon & Marco S.F. 1923, line captain 1926, asst. choreographer 1928; toured US 1929-30; stage mgr. Grauman's Chinese 1931; choreographer asst. to Gae Foster Dir. of Roxyettes, Roxy Theatre NY 1932-46; brought to Hollywood by Daryl Zanuck to direct finale of Betty Grable's "Pin-Up Girl" 1942; dir. Alice Sullivan Girls, Date Festival S.B. 1950; dir., choreographer N. Lake Tahoe Baltabarin Club stage shows 1954; dance dir. Laguna Moulton Playhouse "Anything Goes" 1964; real estate broker 1962-72; instr. cotillion, ballroom dance classes public school system San Clemente, Dana Point, San Juan Capistrano, Alice Lomas Dance Studios San Clemente, Costa Mesa; Republican; Christian Science; rec: skiing. Res: 2249 A Mariposa- East Laguna Hills 92653

LONDON, BRETT GEORGE, government lawyer; b. Aug. 18, 1951, Ogden, Utah; s. George Hillman and Vivian (Stromberg) L.; m. Donna Danielsen, Jan. 17, 1976; children: Jessica b. 1977, Alexis b. 1978, Joanna b. 1981, Chelsea b. 1984; edn: BA, high honors, CSU Fullerton 1976; JD cum laude, Brigham Young Univ. 1979; admitted Calif. State Bar 1979. Career: dep. dist. atty. Orange County Dist. Atty., Santa Ana 1979–; adj. prof. of law Western State Univ. Coll. of Law 1984-; honors: Phi Kappa Phi; mem. Calif. Bar Assn., Orange County Bar Assn., Calif. Dist. Attys. Assn.; dist. commnr. at large Boy Scouts Am.; publ: Western St. Univ. Law Rev.; Republican; Ch. of Jesus Christ of Latter-day Saints (Bishop). Ofc. of District Attorney 700 Civic Center Dr West, Santa Ana 92702

LONERGAN, JOHN BARTOW, lawyer, ret.; b. Oct. 5, 1908, Ravenna, Ohio; s. Pierce Hart and Olive Freeman Ratliff L.; m. Kathleen Eleanor Guthrie (dec.), June 25, 1948; children: Michael b. 1950, James b. 1953; m. 2d. Dorothy Sandlin (Marvin), Apr. 29, 1978; edn: JD (spl. student status), Univ. Calif. Hastings Coll. of Law 1933; admitted Calif. State Bar 1933, US Supreme Ct., US Ct. of Appeals (9th Cir.), var. US District Cts., Calif. Superior and Appellate Cts. Career: traveling secty. to Calif. Gov. C.C. Young, 1928-30; estab. pvt. law practice, San Bernardino County 1933-, partner in successive law firms: Guthrie, Lonergan & Jordan; Lonergan & Jordan; Lonergan, Jordan, Gresham, Varner & Savage, ret. 1975; mem: State Bar of Calif. (bd. govs. 1957-60, v.p. 1959-60), San Bernardino County Bar Assn. (secty. 1935-38, pres. 1951), Am. Bar Found. (life); clubs: California (LA), Los Angeles Country (LA), Newport Harbor Yacht (Orange Co.); mil: major US Army Engrs. WWII; Republican; Roman Catholic (Knights of Equestrian Order of the Holy Sepulchre of Jerusalem). Res: 1103 Bel-Air Pl., Los Angeles 90077

LONG, ALBERT LOUIS, physician; b. Jan.2, 1922, New Albany, Ind.; s. John Henry and Ida Philippina (Will) L.; m. Beatrice Devine, July 5, 1947; children: Kathy b. 1948, Cheryl b. 1950; edn: AB, Miami Univ. (Ohio) 1945; MA, Columbia Univ., 1946; MD, Univ. of Cinn. Coll. of Med. 1956; bd. certified Am. Board of Family Practice 1971, 1983. Career: pvt. practice family medicine, Paso Robles; staff physician Atascadero State Hosp. 1957; chief of staff Paso Robles Dist. Hosp. 1970-74; mem: AMA, Calif. Med. Assn., San Luis Obispo Co. Med. Soc. (bd. dirs. 1980), Am. Assn. of Family Physicians, Calif. Acad. of Family Physicians (pres. SLO Co. chpt. 1973), Central Coast Hypnosis Soc.; clubs: Rotary, SAR; publs: articles, The Science Teacher (1951), Cinn. J. of Med. (1955); mil: pfc US Army, Good Conduct Medal; Republican; Methodist; rec: skiing, Baritone Horn, numismatics. Res: POB 1948 Paso Robles 93447 Ofc: Albert L. Long MD 522 13th St Paso Robles 93446

LONG, JOYCE ARLINE, wildlife rehabilitator and artist; b. Apr. 6, 1934, San Francisco; d. Adolph H. and Grace (Folger) Noeth; m. Dennis M. Long, Sept. 24, 1955; 2 daus: Lori Anne, b. 1959, Sharon Anne, b. 1962; edn: stu. Univ. of Ore. 1952-5. Career: flight attendant American Airlines, 1955; personnel Toni Co., St. Paul, Minn. 1955; stitchery kit designer Creative Crafts, Chgo. 1967; profl. freelance artist, 1967–; sales, Down Home Arts and Crafts Stores, Mt. View, Calif. 1976-79; active volunteer/bd. mem. Wildlife Rescue, Inc. (recipient hon. life mem. award), 1976–: past pres. (1980, 81), newsletter ed. (1981-), instr. tng. classes for volunteers, personally raise and care for approx. 250 wild birds and animals yearly; mem. Wildlife Rehabilitation Council - Walnut Creek, Defenders of Wildlife, Internat. Wildlife Fedn., Kiwi (retired AAL flt. attendants, secty. 1977), Fed. Womens Club of Los Altos (past v.p.); works: create new diets for difficult care song birds; publs: 2 species papers (Blackbirds, Starlings), 3 spl. care papers for Wildlife Rescue; Signs of Illness of Song Birds. Democrat; Catholic; rec: wildlife, art, dollhouse miniatures. Res: 676 Camellia Way Los Altos 94022 Ofc: Wildlife Rescue Inc. 4000 Middlefield Rd Palo Alto 94303

LONG, ROSALEE MADELINE, law librarian; b. Aug. 27, 1931, Concordia, Kans.; d. James Allen and Mary Clara (McConnell) Vincent; m. Robert Long, 1954; edn: AB in L.S., Kans. State Univ. at Emporia, 1953; JD, Univ. of Santa Clara 1973; admitted to Calif. State Bar, 1976. Career: cataloger San Jose State Univ., 1954-56, hd. Cataloging Dept. 1956-58; cataloger Stanford Law Library, Stanford Univ., 1958-60, hd. Cataloging Dept. 1960-74, spl. projects librarian 1974-75, assoc. law librarian 1975–; faculty Am. Assn. of Law Libraries Inst., Univ. Minn. 1974; awards: law sch. scholarship, Am. Assn. of Law Libraries; mem. State Bar of Calif., Am. Assn. of Law Libraries; coauthor (w/Merryman): Notation (1966), Stanford Law Classification (1968); contbg. author: Law Librarianship, a handbook (1983). Ofc: Stanford Law Library, Rm 220, Stanford 94305

LONGENBERGER, DIANA JO, certified public accountant; b. April 29, 1948, Waxahachie, Texas; d. Ewell Madison and Ouida Laurene (Kuykendall) Prather; m. Rodney Longenberger, Feb. 14, 1981; edn: BA, Univ. Texas Austin 1970; MBA, CSU Long Beach 1982; stu. UCLA 1971-74; Southern Methodist Univ. 1966-68; USC 1968; Texas Christian Univ. 1967; Cert. Real Property Broker, Calif. 1980; Lif. Secondary Tchg. Cred., Calif. and Texas. Career: mathematics instr. Covina Valley Sch. Dist., Covina 1970-71; revenue ofcr. Collections div. IRS, Los Angeles 1971-75; internal revenue agent Large Case Examination div., IRS, Laguna Niguel Dist. 1975–; awards: Sustained Superior Performance, 1981; Spl. Achiev. (1982), Spl. Act (1983), IRA; mem: Beta Gamma Sigma, Phi Delta Gamma, Kappa Mu Epsilon, Alpha Lambda Delta, Gamma Phi Beta, So. Calif. Assn. CPAs in IRS; publs: num. profl. papers; Republican; Protestant; rec: travel. Ofc: Internal Revenue Service, P.O. Box C-8 Laguna Niguel 92677-0800

LONGFELLOW, JOHN PATRICK, corporate marketing director; b. Aug. 20, 1953, Roseburg, Ore.; s. John Jay and Rosemaree (McPolin) L.; m. Lynn Marie, March 6, 1982; 1 son Zachary Wade b. 1984; edn: BS, Univ. of Oregon 1975; MS, Univ. of Utah 1980. Career: recreation dir. Black Butte Ranch Resort, Oregon 1976-79; communications dir. Snowbird Ski & Summer Resort, Utah 1980-82; communications dir., sales asst. Park City Ski Resort, Utah 1982-84; Western reg. sales dir. Rockefeller Found.- Rockresorts Inc., Los Angeles 1984; nat.sales dir. Pierre Cardin's Maxim's de Paris Suite Hotels, Los Angeles 1985; corp. mktg. dir. Friden Hotel Company, Santa Barbara 1985–; bd. dirs. Santa Barbara Conf. & Visitors Bureau; honors: Outstanding Grad. Student of the Year, Univ. of Utah 1980; mem: Meeting Planners Internat., Hotel Sales & Mktg. Assn., Am. Soc. of Assoc. Execs., Am. Soc. of Travel Agents, Santa Barbara CofC, Beta Theta Pi Alumni Assn.; works: freelance writer, var. consumer & trade publs.; Democrat; Catholic; rec: equestrian, tennis, running, swimming. Res: Santa Barbara Polo & Racquet Club, 3375 Foothill Rd. No. 111 Santa Barbara 93013 Ofc: Friden Hotel Co., 2020 A Alameda Padre Serra, Santa Barbara 93103

LOO, DENNIS JAN, financial planner; b. May 24, 1938, San Francisco; s. James M. and Claire (Soo) L.; div.; children: Diana Lynn b. 1965, Valerie Denise b. 1969; edn: BA cum laude, Macalester Coll. 1960; M.Div., Union Theol. Sem. 1964; ChFC, American Coll. 1985; NASD (Series 7) Securities lic., Life & Disability lic. Career: minister United Presbyterian Ch., USA 1965-73; exec. dir. Asian Comm. Mental Health Services, Oakland 1973-77; exec. dir. Devel. Disabilities Council, San Francisco 1977-80; assoc. D/A Financial of Calif., Orinda 1980-83; assoc. Curtis Finl. Group, Walnut Creek 1983-86; indep. finl. planner/ reg. rep. Cypress Capital Corp., Walnut Creek 1986–; instr., Finl. Plnng. for the Business Owner, CSU Hayward Ext. 1985-; awards: Million Dollar Round Table (1982, 83); mem. Internat. Assn. Finl. Planners, Nat. Assn. Life Underws.; civic: CEO-Contra Costa, comm. entrepreneurs org. (coordinator), W.C. Chamber of Commerce (bus. seminar com.), Asian Bus. Assn., MAC Users Gp., Keys Condo Owners Assn. (fin. com.); publ: Why an Asian Am. Theology of Liberation?, Church & Soc. Mag. (2/74); Prot.; rec: jogging, aerobics, Tai-chi. Res: 340 N Civic Dr #305 Walnut Creek 94596 Ofc: 2940 Camino Diablo Ste 200 Walnut Creek 94596

LOO, ROBERT YIU-YUEN, electrical engineer; b. June 20, 1943, Shanghai, China, nat. US cit. 1977; s. Yuen-Chun and Jane Zer-ing (Cheng) L.; m. Mabel Shen, Jan. 7, 1982; edn: BA, Monmouth Coll. 1968; MS, State Univ. New York, Buffalo 1970; PhD, UC Los Angeles 1976. Career: research asst. UCLA 1970-76; tech. staff p.t., Jet Propulsion Labs, Pasadena 1972-74; mem. tech. staff, senior staff physicist Hughes Research Labs., Malibu 1976–; vis. lectr. in E.E., UCLA 1976-; honors: Sigma Xi, cert. for outstanding tech. paper IEEE (1974); mem. Chinese-Am. Engrs. and Scientists Assn. of So. Calif.; U.S. Patent: Accelerated Annealing of GaAs Solar Cells (1/85), sev. publs. on GaAs solar cells; Christian; rec: sports, cinema. Ofc: Hughes Research Labs. 3011 Malibu Cyn Rd Malibu 90265

LOOMIS, ROBERT LINDSEY, magazine publishing co. executive; b. May 2, 1942, Visalia, Calif.; s. Robert Gillis and Peggy L.; m. Jan, Feb. 10, 1985; children: Robert b. 1966, Richard b. 1967; edn: BA govt., Claremont Men's Coll. 1965. Career: insurance sales 1970-72; v.p. Santa Monica Land & Water Co. 1972-76, pres. 1979-83; CEO Santa Monica Bay Printing & Publishing Co. 1983–; mem: Ad Club So. Calif., Magazine Publrs. Assn.; mil: capt. US Army field artillery 1965-70; Bronze Star, Army Commdn.; Republican; Catholic. Address: Pacific Palisades

LOONG, ERIC SEE KIN, corporate controller; b. July 8, 1956, Malaysia; s. Lee Soong and Low (Loy) L.; m. Khau Kam, Mar. 7, 1981; edn: MBA, Claremont Graduate Sch. 1983; desig: FCCA, Fellow Chartered Assn. of Certified Accts., U.K. (1976); CPA, Calif. (1985). Career: audit asst. Michael

& Assocs., Malaysia 1976-77; senior acct. Wallins H.K. Ltd., Saudi Arabia 1977-81; v.p./controller DeVore Industries, Los Angeles 1983-86; CFO, controller Ri-Maf Ents., San Gabriel 1986–. Res: 114-D North Fourth St Alhambra 91801

LOPES, THOMAS ATHERTON, oil co. owner; b. Feb. 25, 1923, San Jose; s. Frank Xavier and Florence Mae (Pyne) L.; m. Janet Lilly, June 17, 1950; children: Shelly b. 1951, Stephen b. 1951, Jeffrey b. 1958; edn: AA, San Mateo Jr. Coll. 1942; AB, San Jose State Coll. 1949; petroleum jobber 1956. Career: trainee Signal Oil Co. 1951-53, distbr. 1953-56; founder, pres. Western States Oil Co. 1956–, Spartan Tank Lines 1960–; owner Talco Leasing 1978–, Tom Lopes Properties 1974–; advisory bd. San Jose State Univ. Sch. of Bus., President's Council; honors: Man of the Month (Jr. CofC 1956), Disting. Award (Sch. Bus. San Jose State Univ. 1982); mem: Calif. Oil Jobbers (pres. 1969-70, bd. dirs. 1965-75), Pacific Oil Conference (chmn. 1970), Rotary, United Way (div. chmn. 1982-83, bd. 1978-), Salvation Army (adv. bd.); mil: lt. USN Aircorps 1943-45, USNR 1946-57; Republican; Protestant; rec: golf, tennis, travel. Ofc: 1790 S 10th St San Jose 95112

LOPEZ, ANTHONY BONILLA, city manager; b. Dec. 12, 1945, El Paso, Tex.; s. A. Tafoya and Ophelia (Bonilla) L.; edn: AA, Long Beach City Coll. 1973; BS, CSU Long Beach 1974; postgrad., para-legal cert. Univ. San Diego 1975; Personnel Mgmt. & Employee Rels. cert., Univ. Calif. 1980. Career: adminstrv. services dir. City of Coachella, 1982–84; city mgr. City of Corning, 1984–; mem. State of Calif. Gov.'s Advis. Com. on Ednl. Block Grant; fmr. dir. Human Services and Grants Ofcr., City of Desert Hot Springs; cons. nonprofit orgns., dir. Anthony B. Lopez and Assocs.; program dir. Stanton Reachout Pgm.; campus minister, orgnzr. Newman Club, Golden West Coll.; adminstrv. intern Long Beach City Police Dept. and City of Paramount, intern L.A. County Harbor Patrol, Marina del Rey; asst. mgr. TransAm. Corp. Honors: Phi Kappa Phi, Gold Nugget Award, CSULB; mem: Municipal Finance Officers Assn., Internat. Personnel Mgmt. Assocs., Internat. City Mgmt. Assn. (afil.), Public Risk & Ins. Mgmt. Assn., Calif. Soc. of Municipal Finance Ofcrs., Am. Soc. for Pub. Adminstrn., Am. Mgmt. Assn., Municipal Mgmt. Assts. of So. Calif., Internat. City Managers Assn., Toastmasters Intl., Coachella Valley Rotary Club; Catholic; rec: tennis. Address: PO Box 1214, Corning 96021

LOPEZ, ELVA MARIE, real estate broker, insurance underwriter; b. Oct. 1939, Dallas, Texas; d. Andrew and Josefa Marie (Rodriguez) Hernandez; m. Phillip Lopez, June 29, 1957; children: David Joseph b. 1958, Terri Anne b. 1960; edn: BS, St. Mary's Coll. 1961; profl. tng. courses underwriting 1974, real estate 1979, Dale Carnegie sales tng. 1980; Calif. lic. R.E. Broker. Career: nun, Sisters of Holy Cross, tchr. elem. school and social worker; pub. relations (new bus. welcoming service), San Francisco 1970; agent New York Life Ins. 1974–; real estate agent Merrill Lynch Realty 1979; real estate broker/owner EML Realty (splst. comml. R.E.), San Mateo 1986–; awards: Million Dollar Round Table, Ins. (1974, 75, 76), Million Dollar Club, R.E. (1978-86), Health Leader Award (1980), Manpower Growth Leader (1980), Dale Carnegie achieve. cert. (1982); mem. Nat. Assn. Women in Comml. R.E., San Mateo, Burlingame Bd. of Realtors, Nat. Assn. Female Execs., Found. of Human Understanding; civic: City Recreation Dept. (instr. Yoga), San Mateo Social Club (Reading), vol. social work (teens & elderly); Republican; Christian. Address: San Mateo

LORBEER, HOWARD BURWELL, entomologist, citrus grower; b. May 16, 1899, Pomona; s. Charles Irving and Mary Helen (Coe) L.; m. Lilliam May Smith, Oct. 18, 1930; 1 son, James W. b. 1931; edn: BA, Pomona Coll. 1923. Career: tree surgeon Coit Agric. Svc., Pasadena 1923; L.A. Co. horticultural inspector Covina Dist. 1923-25; lab. asst. L.A. Co. Inspectory, Rivera 1925-26; lab. tech. Fillmore Citrus Protective Dist. 1926-27, mgr. 1927-74; ret. citrus grower 1942-84; honors: Award of Honor, Lemon Men's Club of Calif. 1973; Citizens Award for Agric., Fillmore CofC 1966; Citation of Appreciation, Future Farmers of Am., Fillmore chpt. 1966; Appreciation & Recogn., Fillmore Citrus Protective Dist. 1974; Resolution of Appreciation, Ventura Co. Farm Bureau 1974; mem: Entomological Assn. of So. Calif., Lemon Men's Club of Calif., Council of Calif. Growers, Internat. Soc. of Citriculture, Entomological Soc. of Am., Am. Inst. of Biological Scis., Fillmore Rotary Club; publs: regular contbr., Fillmore Herald 1926-74; var. contbns., Calif. Citrography 1931-65; works: supvr. Red Scale Eradication pgm. using cyanide gas fumigation in citrus orchards; research and prodn. pgm. in insectary and members orchards for integrated biological control of citrus pests; mil: pvt. Cavalry 1918; stu. Army Tng. Corp., Ore State Coll. Corvallis; Republican; Methodist. Res: 558 Mountain View St. Fillmore 93015

LORD, JACK, actor, director, producer, artist, writer; b. Dec. 30, 1930, NYC; s. William Lawrence and Ellen Josephine (O'Brien) Ryan; m. Marie de Narde, Apr. 1, 1952; edn: BS, NYU 1954. Career: exhibits: Cocoran Gallery, Nat. Acad. Design, Whitney Mus., Brooklyn Mus., Lib. of Congress, Biblioteque Nationale, Paris, France; rep. in perm. collection Metropolitan Mus. of Art., appearances on Broadway: Traveling Lady (Theatre World awd. 1954) and in starring role Cat On A Hot Tin Roof; motion picture performances: Court Martial of Billy Mitchell, Williamsburg - the Story of a Patriot, Tip on a Dead Jockey, God's Little Acre, Man of the West, Hangman, True Story of Lynn Stuart, Walk like a Dragon, Doctor No.; leading roles in TV prodns: Constitution series Omnibus, Playhouse 90, Goodyear Playhouse, Studio One, U.S. Steel; TV film appearances: Have Gun Will Travel (pilot), Untouchables, Naked City, Rawhide, Bonanza, Americans, Route 66, Gunsmoke, Stagecoach West, Dr. Kildare, Greatest Show Earth, Star Stoney Burke series; TV appearances: Combat, Chrysler Theater, 12 O'Clock High, Loner, Laredo, FBI, Invaders, Fugitive, Virginian, Man from Uncle, High Chaparral, Ironside, Twilight Zone, Grad Hotel (pilot), You Are There, Danger, Suspense, The Web; star: Hawaii 5-O; creator TV shows: Tramp Ship, Yankee Trader, McAdoo, The Hunter series; writer orig. screenplay Mellissa 1968; pres. Lord & Lady Ent., Inc. 1968—; awards: St. Gauden's Artist Awd. 1948; Fame Awd. 1963; named to Cowboy Hall of Fame 1963; mil: 2nd ofcr., navigator US Merchant Marine; grad., Ft. Trumbull Acad., New London, Ct.; rec: running, swimming. Ofc: Hawaii Five-O Studios, Ft. Ruger, Honolulu, Hi. 96816; c/o J. Wm. Hayes, 132 S. Rodeo Dr Beverly Hills 90212

LORENTZEN, KAY WILBUR, veterinarian; b. Mar. 31, 1920, San Francisco; s. Dr. Kay Gustav and Carolyn Frieda (Stettin) L.; m. Barbara Nunes, June 24, 1945; edn: AA, San Benito Jr. Coll. 1939-41; VMD, Univ. of Penn. 1943-47; grad. Command and Gen. Staff Coll., US Army 1972; Stanford Univ. 1941-43. Career: pvt. practice, Santa Rosa 1947-50; Col. US Army Veterinary Corp, (USA, Alaska, Germany, Vietnam) 1950-77; retired as Western Regl. Army Veterinary Consultant Letterman Army Med. Ctr. 1977; mem: Nat. Eagle Scout Assn.; Am. & Calif. State Vet. Med. Assns.; Ret. Ofcr. Assn.; mil. decorations: Legion of Merit, Bronze Star, Meritorious Svc. w/ Oak Leaf Cluster, Vietnam Svc. w/ 4 campaign stars, Vietnam Campaign w/ yr. bar, Armed Forces Hon. Medal 1/c, Vietnam Unit Cit., Cross of Gallantry; Republican; Protestant; rec: golf, swimming, model trains. Res: 211 Donald Dr Hollister 95023

LORRAINE, EVA, ballet company artistic director; b. Jan. 5, Chicago; d. Yoseph Fortuna (composer, conductor) and Sara (White) Cassatta (changed to Cassidy); edn: grad. St. Xavier's Acad.; AB in Eng. Lit., Univ. Chgo. (assoc. tchrs. hn. deg.); stu. with Adolph bolm, Bronislava Nijinska, Mordkin, Ambrozini and Preobrajenska, Paris, Fr.; accredited tchr.-choreographer. Career: actress Essanay Studios, 20 motion pictures incl. Mary McAllister pic. "Pants," before age of 12 yrs; Broadway debut as Eva Lynn in Earl Carroll Vanities, Naughty Riquette, Passing Show; star of film: It Happened in Paris; ballet soloist Chgo. Opera (at age 16); apptd. George White's Scandals; dir., choreographer of seven Broadway shows, Shubert Theaters; prima ballerina, Manhattan Mary; staged ballet, Down, Simple Simon (Ziegfeld), 1931-33; Orphans of the Storm, Ft. Lee Studios, 1933; ballet soloist, Michael Mordkin Ballet in Les Sylphides, Giselle; Euro. tour w/David Appolon for Paramount, Our American Pavlova, 1936-39; Ziegfeld Follies, 1937-40; contract with MGM, Republic Studios, protege-asst. to Maria Ouspenskaya, 1940-49; Carnegie Hall debut, 1948; founder, dir., choreographer Calif. Ballet Co. of Los Angeles, debut Hollywood Bowl 1954; artistic dir. L.A. Festival Ballet, Pasadena Civic Ballet; guest choreographer, ballerina Vienna and London Fests., 1971, Chgo. Ballet Ctr., 1972; currently artistic dir. American Ballet Ctr. Performing Arts, Oak Park Civic Ballet (repertory opera): "The Magic Flute," "Tannhauser," "Merry Widow," "Nutcracker Ballet"; created orig. choreography for ballets: Boccaccio, Command Performance, Rhapsody in Blue, Western Symphony, Concerto, Mischief Maker, Mukunda; recipient Gov.'s Award for outstanding merit (1979), L.A. Critics Art Award for first Calif. Childrens' Ballet (1954); mem: Dance Masters of Am., SAG, AEA, AFTRA, CofC; rec: writing, costume design, painting. Res: 136 N. Marion, Oak Park, IL 60302

LOSCHIAVO, JOHN JOSEPH, university president; b. Feb. 25, 1925, San Francisco; s. Joseph and Anna (Re) LoSchiavo; edn: AB, Gonzaga Univ., Spokane 1948, MA, 1949; STL, Alma Coll., Los Gatos 162. Career: instr. philosophy, theol., Univ. San Francisco, 1950-52, 61-62, dean of students, 1962-66, v.p. for student affairs 1966-68; pres. Bellarmine Coll. Prep., San Jose 1968-75; pres. USF, 1977—, trustee USF, 1964-68, 1969-, chmn. 1970-73; dir. assn. of Jesuit Colls. and Univs., 1977-; exec. com. Assn. of Independent Calif. Colls. and Univs.; mem: NCCJ Inc. (bd. mem. No. Calif. 1982-), Alpha Sigma Nu (life), The Olympic Club 1977-, The Bohemian Club 1978-, Il Cenacolo 1977-; Democrat; Roman Catholic, ordained RC priest. Rec: golf, swimming. Res: Xavier Hall, Univ. of San Francisco, San Francisco 94117 Ofc: University Center, 424, Univ. of S.F., San Francisco 94117

LOUGEAY, DENIS H., electric power engineering consultant; b. Sept. 27, 1943, Belleville, Ill.; s. Howard E. and Jean L. (Snyder) L.; m. Denruth Barre, Aug. 14, 1965; children: Stace b. 1970, Gregg b. 1973; edn: BS in C.E., Univ. of Ill. 1966, MBA, 1968;l Reg. Profl. Engr., Calif. (1973). Career: supr. Material Control, General Dynamics-Electronics, San Diego 1969-72; consultant Enviromed, Inc., La Jolla 1972-73; mgr. Project Support Services, San Diego Gas & Elec. Co., 1973-81; sr. cons., elec. power, Pickard, Lowe Garrick, Inc., Irvine 1981-85 (on leave of absence 1982-83), ind. consultant State Elec. Commn. of Victoria, Melbourne, Australia, 1982-85; pres. DHL Assocs., Inc., Encinitas 1985—; mem: Am. Assn. of Cost Engrs. (elec. utility cost group, chmn. instrn. manual com.), Order of DeMolay, Legion of Honor; rec: waterski, backpack, duplicate bridge. Address: DHL Associates Inc 404 Alviso Way Encinitas 92024

LOUGEAY, DENRUTH COLLEEN, psychotherapist; b. Nov. 7, 1943, Chicago, Ill.; d. Denzil Gordon and Ruth Marian (Bergstrom) Barre; m. Denis Lougeay, Aug. 14, 1965; children: Stace b. 1970, Gregg b. 1973; edn: BS, Univ. of Ill. 1965, M.Ed., 1968; PhD, U.S. Internat. Univ. 1986. Career: spl. edn. tchr., Urbana (Ill.) Public Schs., 1965-68; ednl. diagnostician, founding tchr., The Clinical Classroom, Joliet (Ill.) Public Schs., 1968-69; counselor, Women's Resource Ctr., San Luis Rey, 1980-82; psychologist, Delmont Pvt. Hosp. for Alcohol Drug Rehab., Victoria, Australia, 1982-83; group therapist Parents United of No. San Diego Co., San Luis Rey, (1984), Parents United of El Cajon (1982-84); psychologist, Palomar Coll., San Marcos, 1984—; splst. eating disorders, incest families, battered spouses, alcohol and drug abuse; mem: Am. Psychol. Assn., Acad. of San Diego Psychologists, Am. Mensa Ltd.; dissertation: The Relationship of Jealousy to Defensiveness and Anxiety: A Correlational-Descriptive Study; profl. presentation, On Founding of the Clinical Classroom- Program Mgmt. in The Clinical Classroom, Ill. Council for Exceptional Children state conv. (Chgo. 1969); rec: pvt. pilot for hot air ballooning, genealogy, travel. Res: 404 Alviso Way Encinitas 92024 Ofc: Palomar College, 1140 W. Mission Blvd. San Marcos 92069

LOUGHEED, ARTHUR LAWRENCE, insurance agency president; b. Aug. 11, 1944, Fresno; s. Evan A. and Irene E. (Westby) L.; m. Nancy L. Sanderson; children: Christopher, b. 1967; Jennifer, b. 1969; Evan, b. 1975; edn: Albion Coll. 1963-64; AA, Orange Coast Coll. 1964; USC Grad. Sch. of Law 1964-65; MS finl. svcs., American Coll., Bryn Mawr 1980, MS mgmt., 1985; desig: CLU, Am. Soc. Chartered Life Underwriters 1973; Chartered Property and Casualty Underwriter, Soc. of Ch. Prop. & Cas. Und. 1980. Career: Farmers Ins. Gp., Los Angeles, served Santa Ana, Calif. & Pocatello, Idaho; agent./ Div. Agcy. mgr./ Regional life mgr. Aetna Life & Casualty Ins. Co., Hartford Conn., served Los Angeles 1974-77; mgr. of estate, bus. & pension sales CNA Ins. Cos., Chgo., Ill., served Los Angeles & Chgo. 1977-81; reg. dir. life sales ofcs./ nat. dir. mktg. & sales tng. Arthur L. Lougheed & Assoc. 1981—; currently, pres./ gen. agnet The Bershire Life Ins. Co., San Diego; lectr. on ins. Glendale Coll., Univ. of Ill., Chgo., De Paul Univ., Chgo., UC San Diego, UC Irvine; reg. instr./ sem. leader Ins. Ednl. Assn. of San Francisco; honors: Alpha Gamma Sigma 1964; Toppers Club, Farmers Ins. Gp. 1965-69; Regionaire, Aetna Life & Casualty 1975-; Nat., Calif., San Diego & Glendale/ Burbank Assns. of Life Underwriters; Am. Soc. CLUs; Soc. Chart. Property & Casualty Underwriters; Internat. Assn. of Financial Plnng.; Saddleback Kiwanis, Mission Viejo; San Diego CofC; editor assoc. CALUnderwriter mag. 1976, contbr. articles in finl. field various nat., regl. publs.; photog. work pub. var. newspapers and mags.; Republican; Luthern; rec: fishing, history, literature. Res: 4793 Panorama Dr San Diego 92116 Ofc: Arthur L. Lougheed & Assocs., 2515 Camino del Rio S., Ste 226, San Diego 92108

LOUIE-KAI, DORINDA GAY, nutritionist; b. Nov. 4, 1952, Los Angeles; d. George Calvin and Doris (Chinn) Louie; m. George Kai, Mar. 29, 1980; edn: BS dietetics, UC Berkeley 1973; dietetic intern, Univ. Iowa 1974, MS prev. med. and envirmtl. health, nutrition, 1975. Career: therapeutic dietitian Univ. Iowa 1974; cons. dietitian Senior Citizen's Meals Pgm. Iowa City 1974-75; clin. dietitian Fresno Comm. Hosp. 1975-79, chief clin. dietitian 1980-83; nutritionist Assoc. Indian Svcs. Inc. 1984-85, Central Calif. Diabetes Ctr. Fresno 1984—; honors: Omicron Nu (1973); mem: Am. Assn. Diabetes Educators, Am. Diabetes Assn. (council on nutrition and food sciences), Am. Dietetic Assn. (diabetes care and edn. practice group, newsletter reviewer 1986), Calif. Dietetic Assn./ Central Valley Dist. (rep. to dist. council 1986-89, diet therapy chair 1975-76, convention pgm. chair 1979, qual. assurance chair 1979-80, treas. 1984-86); rec: swimming, skiing, sewing, gardening. Res: 868 E Serena Ave Fresno 93710 Ofc: 4005 N Fresno St Fresno 93726

LOUIS, JOSEPH ELIAS, civil engineer; b. May 11, 1941, Homs, Syria, nat. US cit. 1973; s. Elias E. and Khanom (Khozam) L.; m. Najah, July 16, 1974; children: Elham b. 1975, Maher b. 1976, Leila b. 1977, Mazen b. 1979; edn: BSCE, San Jose State Coll. 1969; Reg. Profl. Civil Engr., Calif. 1975, Nev. 1982, Ariz. 1982, Wash. 1982, Ore. 1982. Career: jr. engr. City of Saratoga Public Works Dept., Saratoga 1969-71; project engr. Ruth & Going Inc., San Jose 1971-73; project engr. Creegan & D'Angelo Inc., San Jose 1973-77; pres., civil engr. Louis & Diederich Inc. Cons. Civil Engrg., San Jose 1977—; pres. MJM Land Devel. Co. Inc. 1982—; honors: Engr.'s Week chmn., Calif. Soc. of Profl. Engrs. 1982; Outstanding Performance in Mem. Devel., Santa Clara Co. chpt. Calif. Soc. Profl. Engr. 1982; mem: Calif. Soc. Profl. Engrs. (pres. Santa Clara Co. chpt. 1982), Am. Public Works Assn., Calif. Soc. Profl. Engrs., Engrs. Club of San Jose, Am. Soc. Civil Engrs.; chaired num. engring. and public works coms. establishing standards, procedures and guidelines to constrn. and devel.; Republican; Christian; rec: golf, tennis, swimming. Ofc: Louis & Deiderich Inc., 778 No. First St. San Jose 95112

LOVATT, ARTHUR KINGSBURY, JR., manufacturing co. executive; b. Mar. 12, 1920, Ventura; s. Arthur K., Sr. and Flora Mercedes (Dominguez) L.; m. Juanita Gray, Feb. 1, 1946; children: Sherry b. 1952, Tim b. 1959; edn: BS, USC 1941; MBA, Queens Univ. 1943. Career: leaseman Shell Oil Co., Los Angeles 1946-51; dir. indsl. rels. Willys-Overland Motors, Inc., Los Angeles 1952-55; asst. to pres. and gen. mgr. Pastushin Aviation Corp., L.A. 1955-57; pres. Lovatt Assocs., L.A. 1957-66; chmn. bd., pres., gen. mgr. Lovatt Tech. Corp., Santa Fe Springs, 1966—, also dir.; chmn. bd. Lovatt Sci. Corp., Santa Fe Springs; dir. Lovatt Industries, Inc., others; mem. Am. Soc. Metals, AAAS, Am. Space Inst., N.Y. Acad. Sci., Los Angeles CofC, USC Alumni Assn. (life), Am. Legion (post comdr. 1946), Am. Defense Preparedness Assn., Nat. Advis. Bd. Am. Security Council, U.S. Naval Inst., Disabled Am. Vets. (life), Am. Ordnance Assn., U.S. Senatorial Club, Nat. Hist. Soc. (founding asso.), Internat. Oceanographic Found., Am. Mus. Natural Hist. (asso.), Planetary Soc., Masons (past master; Shriner); inventor: devel. Banadize, Sheradize, Timadize, Ebacolor, Ebadize, and Akadize, electrochemical metal surface processes; Republican; Protestant; rec: fishing, hunting, travel. Res: 13649 Valna Dr Whittier 90602 Ofc: Lovatt Technology Corp. 10106 Romandel Ave Santa Fe Springs 90670

LOVE, ALBERT, architect/poet; b. Jan. 20, 1927, Philadelphia, Penn.; s. Samuel and Esther (Israel) Love; m. Lilly, Nov. 15, 1964; children: Sherie b. 1953, Michael b. 1959; edn: architecture, Drexel Univ. 1953; Reg. Architect,

Penn. (1959), Md. (1967), Calif. (1968), NCARB (1977). Career: tng. and drafting/ design assignments with noted firms incl. Kling Partnership & Swineburne Assocs., Phila. 1953-65; project architect/ specifications engr. Pereira Assocs., Luckman Partnership and Ralph M. Parsons Co., Los Angeles 1965-75; facilities design cons. for U.S. Postal Svc., IBM Corp., Jet Propulsion Lab., Northrop Corp., others, 1975-81; architect Northrop Corp., Advanced Systems Div., Pico Rivera 1981 — ; honors: Golden Poet Award for 1986, World of Poetry Press; mem: Nat. Council of Architectural Registration Bds. (Nat. Cert. 1977), Soc. of Am. Reg. Architects (mem. 1962), Constrn. Specifications Inst. (profl. mem. 1980), Britannica Soc. (1973); mil: Sgt. US Army 1945-46; Republican; Jewish; rec: music, aerobics, travel. Res: P.O. Box 10816 Beverly Hills 90213

LOVELACE, JON B., JR., investment company executive; b. Feb. 6, 1927, Detroit, Mich.; s. Jonathan Bell and Marie L. (Anderson) L.; m. Lillian Pierson, Dec. 29, 1950; children: Carey, James, Jeffrey, Robert; edn: AB, cum laude, Princeton Univ. 1950; hon. LLD, Claremont McKenna Coll. 1976. Career: bd. chmn: Am. Mutual Fund, dir. 1959 — , exec. v.p. 1961-68; Capital Research Co., dir. 1966 — , mng. assoc. 1978-81; The Investment Co. of Am., dir. 1959 — ; Capital Strategy Research Inc. 1977 ; pres. Capital Research & Mgmt. Co., dir. 1957 — , exec. v.p. 1962-64; New Perspective Fund, dir. 1973 — ; research responsibilities: (current) international; (fmr.) automobiles, aerospace, elec. & electronic, forest products & paper, data processing; air and rail transportation 1953-65; mem: Los Angeles Soc. of Fin. Analysts, Calif. Inst. of the Arts (trustee), Claremont Univ. Center, Claremont McKenna Coll., Santa Barbara Com. on Fgn. Rels., Town Hall, The Sierra Club (life), J. Paul Getty Mus. (trustee). Res: 800 W. 1st St. Los Angeles 90012 Ofc: Capital Research & Mgmt. Co., 333 So. Hope St. Los Angeles 90071

LOW, ARTHUR WONG, optometrist; b. Aug. 5, 1948, Sacramento; s. Raymond and Yvonne L.; m. Stella Dea, June 6, 1976; children: Ryan b. 1981, Evan b. 1983; edn: BS, UC Davis 1970; OD, UC Berkeley 1975. Career: staff optometrist Family Health Found. of Alviso 1975 — ; pvt. practice partnership Drs. Leong & Low 1975 — ; honors: Young OD of Yr., Calif. Optometric Assn. 1979; Lion of Yr., Campbell Golden Lions 1985; mem: Santa Clara Co. Optometric Soc. (secty. 1980-82), Campbell Golden Lions (pres. 1979-80), Am. Public Health Assn., Campbell CofC, Am. and Calif. Optometric Assns.; publs: Patient Response to PMMA Contact Lenses, Journ. of the Am. Optometric Assn. 1975; Democrat; rec: tennis, fishing, skiing. Res: 1322 Nancarrow Way San Jose 95120 Ofc: 621 E. Campbell Ave. Ste. 11-B Campbell 95008

LOW, DICK CHOY, retail food and restaurant co. president; b. June 8, 1940, China, nat. US cit. 1961; s. Howard and Mon Hueng (Kong) L.; m. May, May 3, 1958; children: Darrin b. 1969, Michelle b. 1970, Derrick b. 1981; edn: UC Berkeley 1958-59. Career: owner small grocery store, Nevada City, Calif. 1965-72, purch. supermarkets in Sacramento 1972-, Healdsburg 1977-, incorporated, pres. JD-Mart Inc., 1978 — , owner Tip Toe Cafe 1980 — ; mem: Redwood Empire Restaurant Assn. (dir.), Healdsburg CofC (dir. 1982, 84); mil: A2c US Air Force, 1965. Ofc: D-Mart Inc. 1345 Healdsburg Ave Healdsburg 95448

LOW, HARRY W., appellate court presiding justice; b. Mar. 12, 1931, Oakdale; s. Tong and Ying (Gong) L. m. May Line Jue, Aug. 24, 1952; children: Lawrence b. 1953, Kathleen b. 1957, Allan b. 1962; edn: AA, Modesto Jr. Coll. 1950, AB, UC Berkeley 1952, LLB, 1955. Career: tchg. assoc. Boalt Hall 1955-56; dep. atty. gen. Calif. Dept. of Justice, 1956-66; commnr. Workers' Compensation Appeals Bd. 1966; municipal ct. judge 1966-74, presiding judge 1972-73; superior ct. judge 1974-82, supvg. judge Juvenile Ct. 1981-82; presiding justice Ct. of Appeal, San Francisco 1982 — ; speaker, instr. var. judicial seminars and study coms.; faculty Calif. Judges Coll. 1976-83, Nat. Coll. of Judiciary 1977-79, Inst. of Ct. Mgmt. 1976-81; bd. CJER Journal; conf. guest lectr. at meetings of Ida., Wash., Ariz., Va., Mich. and Nev. Judiciaries; cochmn. past confs. on Media and the Law; editor Courts Commentary 1973-76; chmn. bd. vis. US Mil. Acad., West Point 1982; mem: Calif. Judges Assn. (pres. 1978-79), Calif. Council on Criminal Justice, Edn. Center for Chinese (bd. chmn. 1969-), S.F. City Coll. Found. (pres. 1978-), Chinese-Am. Citizens Alliance (Grand Bd., past pres.), Calif. Jud. Council 1979-81, Chinese Am. Bilingual Sch. (chmn. 1980-); mem. bd. dirs: Salesian Boys Club, St. Vincent's Home for Boys, Friends of Rec. and Parks, S.F. Zoological Soc., Law in the Free Soc., NCCJ, World Affairs Council, Chinatown Youth Task Force, Mayor's China Gateway Com.; Democrat; rec: gardening, S.F. hist. Res: 104 Turquoise 94131 Ofc: Court of Appeal 350 McAllister, Rm 4154, San Francisco

LOWE, WARREN, research chemist; b. June 4, 1922, San Francisco; s. Lung and Jean L.; m. Caroline L., Nov. 30, 1958; edn: BS, UC Berkeley 1945. Career: researchassoc. Manhattan Project, Radiation Lab., UC Berkeley 1943-45; senior research assoc. Chevron Research Co. 1945 — ; honors: Fellow Am. Inst. of Chemists; mem: Am. Chemical Soc., Sigma Xi, AAAS, Am. Inst. of Chemists, Am. Research Soc., Missions of Pacific Presbytery, Nat. Bd. of Missions, UC Alumni Assn., Adv. com. Mount Hermos ASsn., YMCA, El Sobrante Boys CLub, Tung Sen Benevolent Assn.; works: holder 170 patents in field of chemistry; contbr. scientific articles to var. profl. mags. incl. Journ. of Am. Chem. Soc.; Republican; Presbyterian; rec: gardening, sports, photog. Res: 5619 Jordan Ave. El Cerrito 94530 Ofc: Chevron Research Co., 578 Standard Ave. Pt. Richmond

LOWRY, RONALD RALPH, architect; b. Jan. 1, 1937, Oakland; s. Ralph Clair and Desiree A. (Queyrel) L.; m. Roberta Lynn Coffield, Oct. 31, 1964; children: Rhonda Lynn b. 1967, Julie Ree b. 1970, Joel Justin b. 1971; edn: AA,

Sacramento City Coll.; Calif. State Polytechnic Coll.; BA, CSU Sacramento; Reg. Architect, Calif. (1972) and Nat. Council of Archtl. Regis. Bds. (1980). Career: archtl. asst. Calif. Dept. of Water Resources 1961-69; archtl. plnnr. Calif. Dept. Gen. Svcs. 1969-71; retirement ofcr. Calif. Tchrs. Retirement System 1971-72; govt. pgm. analyst, architect Calif. Dept. Gen. Svcs. 1972-76; deptl. const. & maint. supvr. Calif. Dept. of Devel. Svc. 1976-80; chief facilities plnng. Calif. Youth Authority 1980 — ; currently, owner Ronald R. Lowrey Arhitect; mem: Constn. Specification Inst. (Sacramento chpt.), Consumnes Area Comm. Plnng. Advy. Council, Sloughhouse Fire Protection Dist., Sheldon Hills Homeowners Assn. Inc. (pres. 1974-80); mil: USNR 1962; Republican; Agnostic; rec: local govt., hunting, camping. Res: 7515 Lakehill Ct. Elk Grove 95624 Ofc: Calif. Youth Authority, 4343 Williamsborough Dr. Sacramento 95823

LOWRY, WILLIAM GEORGE, consulting engineer; b. Feb. 10, 1909, Cincinnati, Ohio; s. Harvey Jackson and Augusta Blanche (Koch) L.; m. Blanche Rose Zinsle, Sept. 21, 1907; children: Joy Elaine b. 1932, George Wm. b. 1933; edn: BSCE, Univ. Cinti. 1940; Reg. Profl. Engr. (Civil 1945, Mech. 1948), Calif. Career: gen. foreman Hwy Maint. Dept., City of Cinti., O. 1932-41; senior design engr. Lockheed Aircraft Corp. 1941-45; indep. consulting engr. (clients incl. Lockheed Aircraft, No. Am. Aviation, Douglas Aircraft, So. Counties Gas Co., Haliburton Corp., others) 1945-60; project engr. Lockheed Aircraft Corp., 1960-74; chief engr. Plant Engineering Co. 1944-46, FAB Constrn. Co. 1946; apptd. city councilman City of Beaumont 1981-85, bd. mem. Riverside County Transit Agcy. 1983-85; honors: Mu Pi Kappa (1937); mem. Structural Engrs. Assn. 1945-51; inventions: patents- Pipe Cleaning Tools while with City of Cinti. Hwy. & Sewer Maint. Dept.; num. unpatented devices for lifting & assembling aircraft components for Lockheed Hudson Bombers, P-38s, the Constellation Airplane, the Electra Airplane, the L1011 Airplane and Agena Rocket parts, others; Republican; Seventh-day Adventist; rec: golf. Address: Beaumont 92223

LU, WUAN-TSUN, biotechnology co. executive; b. July 8, 1939, Taichung, Taiwan; s. Yueh and Jin-Mien Lu; m. Rita, July 25, 1970; children: Dorcia b. 1973, Loretta b. 1977; edn: BS agrl. econs., Nat. Taiwan Univ. 1960; MS microbiol., Brigham Young Univ. 1968; PhD, microbiol. & immunol., Health Med. Ctr. Univ. Okla. 1978. Career: research asst. Chung Hsing Univ. 1961-63; research asst. microbiol. dept. Brigham Young Univ. 1966-68; microbiol., chemist Murray Biol. Co. L.A. 1969-71; microbiol. Reference Labs. N. Hollywood 1971-73; research assoc. microbiol. & immunol. dept. Univ. Okla. 1976; supv. Reference Med. Lab. Cupertino 1980; toxicologist Smithkline 1981; founder, pres. United Biotech Inc. Mtn. View 1983-85, dir., chmn. 1985 — ; bus. advisor Health Medical Industries Inc. San Mateo; mem: Am. Soc. Clinical Pathol., Am. Soc. Clin. Chem. Chinese Club, Delta Group; publs: tech. articles on microbiology; mil: 2nd lt. Taiwan ROTC; rec: fencing, horseback riding. Ofc: United Biotech Inc. 1300 C Spacepark Way Mountain View 94043

LUCAS, BRUCE JAY, optometrist; b. Mar. 20, 1957, St. Louis, Mo.; s. Jules Martin and Shirley Rae (Rosen) L.; edn: BS, Univ. of Mo. 1979; BS, So. Calif. Coll. of Opt., 1981, OD, 1983. Career: optician Jules Martin Ty-Roler Opticians, St. Louis, Mo. 1970-79; optician/mgr. California State Optical, Newport Beach 1979; optician FedOptics, Costa Mesa 1980, Dr. Joshua Kaye, Santa Ana 1981-83; optometrist/prin. Woodland Hills 1983 — ; tchg. asst. ophthalmic optics 1981-83; honors: Nat. Dean's List (1981), Phi Eta Sigma (1976), Beta Sigma Kappa (life mem. 1980, pres. 1982-83); mem: Am. Optometric Assn., Contact Lens Sect. of AOA, Calif. Optometric Assn., San Fernando Valley Optometric Soc., Kiwanis- Woodland Hills; research: Fresnel Prisms: Their effects on visual acuity and contrast sensitivity (presented Am. Acad. of Opt., Houston 1983); Democrat; Jewish; rec: sports, music. Ofc: Dr. Bruce J. Lucas, 19828 Ventura Blvd Woodland Hills 91364

LUCE, EDGAR A., JR., lawyer; b. Aug. 9, 1924, San Diego; s. Edgar Augustine and Carma (Coppard) L.; m. Barbara Remy, June 26, 1947; children: Constance Marian (Jubb) b. 1949, Edgard A., III b. 1951, Jennifer Susan (Howard) b. 1954, Deborah Jean (Thurman) b. 1958; edn: BA, Stanford Univ. 1946, LLB, 1948; admitted Calif. State Bar 1949. Career: atty. gen. bus. practice, assoc. law firm Luce, Forward, Hamilton & Scripps (firm founded by pat. grandfather, Moses A. Luce, in San Diego in 1873), San Diego 1948 — , ptnr. 1955, mng. ptnr. 1978-83; dir. San Diego Trust & Savings Bank (chmn. Audit Com.); lectr. Continuing Edn. of the Bar programs; arbitrator, mediator Am. Arb. Assn.; arbitrator San Diego County Bar Assn., Fee Com.; bd. vis. Stanford Univ. Law Sch.; mem: S.D. County Bar Assn. (past v.p., dir.), State Bar of Calif. (past asst. secty.; past exec. com. Conf. of State Bar Delegates, Pub. Rels. Com., and Accident Reparations Com.), Am. Bar Assn.; civic: S.D. Center for Children (dir.), S.D. Conv. and Vis. Bur. (dir.), McDonald Center for Alcoholism & Drug Addiction Treatment (dir.), Stanford Univ. Buck Club (dir.), Univ. Club (past pres.); past dir: Stanford Univ. Alumni Assn., S.D. Childrens Hosp., Dodson Home for the Aged, YMCA Mgmt. Com., S.D. Downtown Assn., Mission Valley Tennis Club, Merchants Credit Assn., Presidio Little League; Republican; Prot.; rec: Little League Baseball. Res: 2461 Presidio Dr San Diego 92103 Ofc: Luce, Forward, Hamilton & Scripps 110 West A Street San Diego 92101

LUCKEY, JOHN MANLEY, dental surgeon; b. Sept. 11, 1952, San Bernardino; s. Manley J. and Jean J. Luckey; m. Elaine F., Feb. 11, 1980; children: Jonathan M. b. 1983, Craig John b. 1984; edn: DDS, Loma Linda Univ. 1981. Career: dental surgeon in solo practice, San Diego 1981 — ; owner Photo Decor Co.; pres. JML Ent. a greeting card co.; distbr. sobriety testing equip.; mem: Am. Dental Assn., Calif. Dental Assn., San Diego Dental Soc., Nat. Rifle Assn.,

Assn. of Pilots of Am.; author book: The Last Night on Earth; Republican; SDA; rec: photog. (scenic), flying, tennis, golf, skiing. Ofc: 4230 30th St San Diego 92104

LUDWIG, CARL LAWTON, engineer/product assurance executive; b. Nov. 22, 1930, San Francisco; s. Carl Lawton Sr. and Alberta (Cook) L.; m. Patricia Anabo, Dec. 31, 1953; children: Debra Kim b. 1954; Michael Jon b. 1957; edn: BSEE, Western State Coll. of Engring. 1958; Reg. Profl. Engr., Calif. Career: gen. supvr. Ryan Areo Electronic Div. 1962; mgr. quality assurance Litton Ind. Guidance Control 1970; dir. reliability & quality Amecom, College Park, Md. 974; dir. quality assurance Litton Ind. Guidance & Control 1985; v.p. product assurance Pacesetter Systems Inc., Sylmar 1985–; mem: Am. Soc. Quality Control, Nat. Conf. of Standards Lab., Nat. Security Ind. Assn., Highpoint Homeowners Assn. (dir.), YMCA (Indian Guide dir. 1968), Boy Scouts of Am. (life, Sea Scout); mil: s/sgt. USAF 1950-54; Republican; Protestant; rec: flying, tennis, artistic hobbies. Res: 4256 Antigua Way Mandalay Beach Oxnard93030 Ofc: Pacesetter Systems Inc., 12884 Bradley Ave. Sylmar 91342

LUDWIG, ROLF MARTIN, physician; b. June 3, 1924, Bautzen, Germany, nat. USA 1958; s. Max Martin and Dora Thea Franziska (Metz) L.; m. Shirley Jean Ray, Oct. 26, 1956, div. 1983; 1 son, Mark Stephen b. 1965; edn: MD, Eberhard Karl's Univ. Med. Sch., Tuebingen, Ger. 1953; lic. phys. and surgeon, Calif. 1955. Career: intern Mary's Help Hosp., San Francisco 1953-54, res. in internal med. Mary's Help Hosp., Franklin Hosp., S.F., 1954-55, chief res. Huntington Meml. Hosp., Pasadena 1955-56; phys. US Army Med. Corps, Fort Myer, Arlington, Va. 1956-59; res. int. med. Wadsworth VA Gen. Hosp., Los Angeles 1959-60; pvt. practice int. med., Yucaipa 1963-72; phys. So. Calif. Permanente Med. Group, Kaiser/Permanente, Fontana 1960-63, 1973–; staff phys. Dept. Internal Med., Kaiser Found. Hosp., Fontana; mem. Am., Calif., Inland Soc. of Internal Medicine, Union of Am. Physicians and Dentists; mil: capt. US Army MC 1956-59; Republican; Lutheran; rec: photog. Res: 11711 Holmes St., Yucaipa 92399 Ofc: S.C.P.M.G., 9985 Sierra Ave Fontana 92335

LUEBTOW, JOHN GILBERT, artist, educator; b. Apr. 2, 1944, Milwaukee, Wisc.; s. Gilbert J. and Evelyn Lucille (Pohl) L.; div.; 1 son, Matthew b. 1968; edn: BA, Calif. Lutheran Univ. 1967; MA, UC Los Angeles 1969, MFA, 1975; cert., Zr. Maria Regina Coel Language Sch., Vught, Netherlands 1970. Career: instr., sculpture Calif. Lutheran Univ., Thousand Oaks 1969, p.t. instr. painting, 1972-73; dir. Architl. and Exptl. Ceramics Depts. "De Porcelyne Fles" The Royal Delft (Netherlands) Factory 1969-71; ednl. exchange artist with Tamagawa Gakuen, Tokyo, Japan 1976; instr. in the arts (dept. chair 1980-) Harvard Sch., No. Hollywood 1971–; indep. artist Primary Media Glass Sculpture, lectrs., exhibs., commissions throughout USA, the Orient and Europe; commnd. works by Marshal Fields, Saks Fifth Avenue stores (Calif., Ill., Fla.), Hilton, Sheraton, Hyatt Regency, Ana (Tokyo) hotels, H.S.H. Princess Caroline of Monaco for Intercoiffure Maison des Nations, Redken Corp., Huntcor, Trammell-Cro Co. (Pasadena), The Koll Center Irvine, Cumberland Center (GA), others; awards include: R.I. Sch. of Design Scholar (1984), Calif. Lutheran Univ. Alumni career achievement award (1983) and CLU Athletic Dept. Football Hall of Fame; mem. Calif. Art Edn. Assn., Nat. Art Edn. Assn., Calif. Assn. of Indep. Schs., Nat. Assn. of Indep. Schs., Glass Art Soc.; civic: L.A. County Museum of Art, Craft and Folk Art Mus., L.A. Inst. of Contemp. Art, Am. Crafts Council; Democrat; Lutheran. Res: 18411 Hatteras #148 Tarzana 91356 Ofc: Harvard School 3700 Coldwater Canyon North Hollywood 91604

LUHN, ROBERT KENT, editor, writer; b. Nov. 25, 1953, Oakland; s. Joel Adrian and Norma Jeanne (Arnold) L.; m. Alison B.K., Oct. 12, 1983; edn: AB, UC Davis 1976. Career: free lance writer; contbr. to The New Yorker, American Film, PC World, PC, The Hudson Review, New West, The San Francisco Chronicle, Dramatics, Paper Cinema, Book Forum, The Nantucket Review, Computerworld, Media and Methods, Boardroom Reports, Executive Update, Small Press Review, Unisphere; author of Collected Works, Vol. III; contbr. anthologies, Horizon Press Editions; (current) assoc. editor PC World Magazine; honors: New West Writer's Award (1977); listed Who's Where Among Writers (1983), Who's Who in the West (1984-85); mem: No. Calif. Science Writers Assn., Am. Film Inst., ACLU, Common Cause, Found. for Nat. Progress, NOW; Democrat; Pre-episcopal; rec: music, tennis, hist., anthropol. Ofc: PC World 555 De Haro St San Francisco 94107

LUI, ELWOOD, appellate court justice; b. Feb. 4, 1941, Los Angeles; s. Hong and Ho Ngun (Toy) L.; m. Mari Crystaline Jung, Mar. 7, 1964; children: Bradley b. 1964, Christopher b. 1969; edn: BS, UC Los Angeles 1962, MBA, 1964, JD, 1969; CPA, Calif. (1966). Career: CPA, Deloitte, Haskins & Sells and Kenneth Leventhal & Co., Los Angeles, 1964-69; deputy atty. general, Los Angeles, 1969-71; pvt. practice of law, L.A. 1971-75; municipal court judge, L.A. 1975-80; superior court judge, L.A. 1980; assoc. justice Calif. Court of Appeal, L.A. 1981–; adj. prof. USC Sch. of Bus., 1977-; mem. Judicial Council of Calif.; mem. L.A. County Domestic Violence Commn.; recipient Pres.'s Award, Calif. Judges Assn. (1984); mem: Calif. Judges Assn. (exec. bd.), UCLA Law Alumni Assn. (pres. 1985), So. Calif. Chinese Lawyers Assn., Chinatown Service Center Advis. Bd.; publs: contbr. to Continuing Edn. of the Bar Seminar, Center for Judicial Edn. and Research; mil: sgt. USAR 1962-68; Republican; Presbyterian; rec: jogging. Ofc: Court of Appeal, 3580 Wilshire Blvd Los Angeles 90010

LUKE, JAMES ALBERT, III, financial executive; b. Sept. 15, 1950, San Mateo; s. James A., II and Lillian Ann (Moyer) L.; m. Linda, May 15, 1971; 1 child, Sunshine b. 1977; edn: BS, Univ. Santa Clara 1971, grad. work in bus. adminstrn. Career: pharmaceutical chemist Syntex Corp. 1971-75, Alza Corp. 1975-77; adminstrv. analyst, CETA pgms., Tulare County, 1977-78; comptroller, personnel dir. Proteus Training, Visalia 1978–; guest instr. govt. acctg., CSU Fresno; honors: Calif. Honor Soc. (life), Calif. Scholarship Fedn. (life), Tulare County Business Assoc. Boss of the Year (1983); mem. Am. Chem. Soc. (1971-80), Nat. Comptrollers Group (1985-); civic: co-founder Visalians Interested in Affordable Housing (sec. treas. 1983-84), YMCA, Tulare Co. Lawyers Wives; works: devel. innovative non-profit fund accounting procedures, sev. publs. on Indirect Costs and Joint Cost Allocation (1980-85); contbg. writer criminology publ. "Rapid Identification of Restricted Dangerous Drugs through Microcrystalline Techniques (1976); actor, singer in community theatre and events; mil: s/sgt. Calif. Nat. Guard 1971-77; Catholic; rec: jog, marathon runner (26 mi.). Res: 1422 W Monte Vista Visalia 93277 Ofc: Proteus 4612 W Mineral King Visalia 93291

LUKE, SHERRILL DAVID, judge; b. Sept. 19, 1928, Los Angeles; s. Mordecai David (dec.) and Venye Alfasetta (Richards) L.; m. Anne Bradford, Aug. 22, 1959; children: David, b. 1960; Melana, b. 1962; edn: BA, UCLA 1950; MA, UC Berkeley 1954; JD, Golden gate univ. 1960. Career: asst. city mgr., Richmond 1953-61; urban affairs secty., Gov.'s Ofc., Sacto. 1961-65; atty. at law, L.A. 1965-67; dir. pgm. devel. Mayor's Ofc., Wash. DC 1967-69; urban affairs dir. Aetna Life & Casulty, Hartford, Ct. 1969-73; atty. at law, L.A. 1973-78; chief. dep. assessor, L.A. Co. 1978-81; judge of the municipal ct., L.A. Judicial Dist. 1981–; con. Ford Found. 1966; dir. Urban Design & Devel. Corp. 1969-70; adj. prof. Loyola Law Sch. 19979-; student body pres., UCLA 1949-50; pres. L.A. City Plng. Commn. 1973-76; lectr. Cont. Edn. of the Bar 1980-81; mem: Kappa Alpha Psi, Upsilon chpt. (pres. 1948-50); UCLA Alumni Assn. (gen. counsel 1966-67; v.p. Scholarships & Admissions 1975; v.p. Awards & Reunions 1984-86); The UCLA Found. (Trustee 1976-); Lambda Alpha land econs. hon.; mil: 1st lt. USAF 1954-56; Democrat (Calif. Demo. Council); Unitarian; rec: tennis, running. Res: 286 Trino Way Pacific Palisades 90272 Ofc: Los Angeles Judicial District, 110 N Grand Ave Los Angeles 90012

LUKES, ALBERT ISADOR, real estate agent; b. Jan. 22, 1917, Sumner, Nebr.; s. Carl Emanuel and Ann Eve (Kruml) L.; m. Claudia Mae Ward, May 30, 1941; children: Laberta Ann, b. 1957; Carl Aden, b. 1962; edn: BA, Nebr. State Teachers Coll. 1947; grad. wk. USC 1947-48; Elem., Sec. Tchg. Credential, Nebr.; Calif. Real Estate lic./CREA 1973. Career: with So. Calif. Gas Co., 1947-72: successively clk., customer contact supr., telephone service supr., 1947-54, mgr. South Bay area, Redondo Beach 1954-71, mgr. Santa Monica area 1971-72; real estate agt. Las Lomas Realty, Torrance 1973–; current mem: Redondo Beach CofC (pres. 1955, Citizen of the Year 1957), Redondo-Riviera Rotary (pres. 1958), Am. Field Service So. Bay chpt. (pres. 1957-58), Community Concert Assn. (pres. 1961-62), USS Chester Alumni Assn.; past mem. vol.: South Bay chpt. UN Assn. (dir.), Am. Cancer Soc. (drive chmn. Redondo 1954, So Bay Area 1955), Salvation Army (dir. 1958), South Bay YMCA (pres. 1962-63, dir.), Redondo Beach Community Chest (chmn. 1956), Redondo Youth Canteen (chmn. Adult Adv. Bd. 1956-57); mil: seaman to lt. jg USN 1938-46, WWII Vet., Commendn. for saving ship torpedoed in the Coral Sea; Republican; Rel. Sci.; rec: woodworking, football. Res: 1227 So Helberta Ave Redondo Beach 90277 Ofc: Las Lomas Realty 24217 Hawthorne Blvd, Ste 1, Torrance 90505

LUM, THEODORE, insurance co. executive; b. Apr. 6, 1951, San Francisco; s. George F. and Wanda Sui Wai (Chew) L.; m. Trudy, Feb. 21, 1976; 1 son, Bryan b. 1983; edn: BS in bus. adm., CSU San Jose 1974; desig: CLU, Chartered Life Underwriter (1981), ChFC, Chartered Finl. Cons. (1984), Am. Coll. Career: spl. agt. for Prudential Ins. Co., San Jose 1972-74, devel. mgr. 1974-80, regional field cons. Pacific N.W. Region 1980-81, gen. mgr. Prudential, 1981–; profl. awards include Rookie of Year, San Jose (1973), pres.'s citation (1976, 78, 79, 81, 83), senior vice pres.'s award (1978); mem: Nat. Assn. of Life Underw. (PAC), Gen. Agents and Mgrs. Assn. (bd. dirs. 1981-), Am. Soc. of CLU (dir. 1983), Alameda CofC; rec: travel, cycling, aerobics, martial arts. Res: 308 Livorna Hts Rd Alamo 94507 Ofc: The Prudential 1080 Marina Village Pkwy Ste 410 Alameda 94501

LUNDBERG, DONALD LEE VERN, educator; b. Aug. 11, 1915, Red Oak, Iowa; s. Charles A. and Ada B. (Swanson) L.; m. Mildred Peaslee (dec. 1976); m. 2d. Verna Stover Aug. 4, 1983; children: Suzanne b. 1948, Carl b. 1950, Eric b. 1958; edn: BA, State Univ. of Iowa 1938; BS in BA, USC 1941; MA, CSC Stanislaus 1966; Nat. Univ. of Mexico (summer) 1937; Tchg. credentials: Iowa (1938), Calif. (1955), Pupil Personnel Counseling (1957). Career: high sch. tchr. Arthur, Iowa 1938-39, H.S. & Jr. Coll. tchr. Creston, Iowa 1948-54; Fulbright tchg. grantee, Aleppo, Syria 1954-55; tchr. Thomas Downey H.S., Modesto, Calif. 1955-57, counselor, 1957-65, estab. the Am. Field Svc. Program and Tchr. Asst. Pgm.; counselor Modesto Jr. Coll. 1965-76, estab. the Peer Tutoring Pgm., dir. Internat. Student Pgm.; ret.; owner/mgr. 3 ranches; honors: 9th fastest marathon runner in 65-69 age group nationally and fastest 10K runner age 68 in 1982, Nat. Data Running Center, Tucson; life mountain climber, all peaks in Mexico, all 14,000 ft. peaks on West Coast, many climbs in Europe, S.A., and Himalayas; mem: Nat. Assn. of Foreign Student Affairs, local, state, nat. edn. assns.; pres. Modesto Toastbreakers Toastmasters 1960; pres. Waterford Lions Club 1982-3; ch. YMCA World Service Com. 1981-82; Audubon Soc. (donor $100,000 to buy land for wildlife refuge Stanislaus County 1978); active lifelong in conservation projects; mil: s/sgt. USAF 1942-46, S.W. Pacific. Res: 2113 Patterson Rd Modesto 95355

LUNDGAARD, STANLEY HOWARD, defense contractor, budget analyst; b. May 10, 1939, Mpls.; s. Alvin Clarence and Clara Amelia (Peterson) L.; m.

Beverly Cross, June 21, 1969; children: Sara b. 1969, Sonja b. 1974; edn: BSBA, Univ. Minn. 1962; MBA, Univ. Santa Clara 1971. Career: ins. broker self-employed Campbell 1967-70; instr. USN NAS Moffett Field 1970-72; import/ export bus. Mt. View 1972-74; agcy. supv. Travelers Ins. Co. San Jose 1974-77; ins. broker, fin. planner San Jose 1977-84; budget analyst Lockheed Missiles & Space Corp. Sunnyvale 1984—; mem. Calif. State Senate Advis. Com. on Life Ins. 1982-83; honors: Letter of Commdn. (Calif. State Senate 1983); mem: Assn. of Naval Aviation (life), Naval Reserve Assn. (life), Sons of Norway, Univ. Santa Clara MBA Alumni Assn. (bd. dirs., treas. 1981-84); mil: capt. USNR 1956-, aviator, Armed Forces Exped., Meritor. Svc., Vietnam Svc., Navy Unit Commdn., Nat. Defense Svc., Armed Forces Reserve - 30 yrs.; Republican; Lutheran; rec: reading, cooking, investment mgmt.; Res: 1210 Rousseau Sunnyvale 94087

LUNDIE, GEORGE JOHN, artist; b. Dec. 27, 1922, Chgo.; s. John and Nettie L.; m. Loreene Kunz, Oct. 5, 1945; children:L Cynthia b. 1953, Craig b. 1954, Deborah b. 1958; edn: Art Inst. of Chgo. 1944-46; Ray Vogue Sch. of Art 1946. Career: art dir. Western Lithography L.A. 1950-59; owner, pres. Lundie & Assocs and Production Art Service Inc. L.A. 1960—; mil: sgt. USAF 1941-45; Republican; Catholic; rec: oil painting, art research. Ofc: Production Art Svc. Inc. 5551 Jillson St Los Angeles 90040

LUNDIN, DAVID ERIK, lawyer; b. May 8, 1949, Middletown, Conn.; s. Irving Erik and Majorie (Walker) L.; m. Gayle, June 25, 1977; 1 son: Erik Stewart b. 1985; edn: BA, Univ. of Redlands 1971; JD, UCLA 1974; admitted to Calif. Bar 1974. Career: assoc. atty. Haight, Dickson, Brown & Bonesteel, Los Angeles 1974-75; atty. advisor Fed. Trade Commn., Wash DC 1975-76; assoc. atty. Fredman, Silverberg & Lewis, San Diego 1976-78, ptnr. 1978-85; ptnr. Sternberg, Kidder, Eggers & Fox 1985—; mem: ABA (Sects. on Antitrust, Litigation), Calif. Bar Assn., San Diego Co. Bar Assn.; Bd. of Fellows Univ. of Redlands; Trustee San Diego Art Center; clubs: University (S.D.), Cotillion (S.D.). Res: 11779 Fuerte Dr El Cajon 92020 Ofc: Sternberg, Eggers, Kidder & Fox 19th floor Central Savings Tower 225 Broadway San Diego 92101

LUNDQUIST, JAN LOFTON, microcomputer & aerospace industries consultant; b. Mar. 6, 1950, Brookhaven, Miss.; d. Raz and Billie Jean (Keene) Lofton; edn: BA hist., Auburn Univ. 1971; grad. work in adminstrn. & systems mgmt., Univ. of W. Fla., CSU San Diego, USC, 1972-80; MBA cand., Nat. Univ. 1986. Career: govt. sales rep. SCM Office Equip., San Diego 1974; logistics engr. Cerberonics Inc., San Diego 1975-78; mgr. spl. projects Support Systems Assocs. Inc., Dayton, Ohio 1978-80; mgr. F/A-18 Aircraft Logistics, Support Systems Assocs., San Diego 1980-82; cons. prin./pres. Jan L. Lundquist & Assocs. (systems cons.- mktg., tng., edn. & quality assur.), La Mesa 1981—; co-founder Co-op Computers, Systems Integrators; honors: session chair Autotestcon (1979, 1980), appreciation cert. Naval Air Systems Command (1979), Dean's List, Auburn (1969-71), National Univ.; charter mem. Soc. for Software Quality (1984-); mem. San Diego Comm. Colls. Qual. Assur. Technology Advis. Com. (1984-); publs: Comdex Show Daily (1984), Computer News of San Diego, The Oasis Times, (1985), recipient Calif. Press Womens (So. Dist.) Poetry Award for "The Blind Man" (1983); Ind.; Taoist; rec: bicycling. Res: 5826 Nagel St La Mesa 92041 Ofc: Jan L. Lundquist & Associates 5826 Nagel St La Mesa 92041

LUNT, STEPHEN WILLIAM, media corporate financial controller; b. June 4, 1948, Stockton; s. Wm. Norton and Elizabeth Kirk (Campbell) L.; edn: BS, UC Berkeley 1970. Career: auditor State of Calif., Oakland 1970-75; controller Design Five Assocs. Inc., Lafayette 1975-81; controller Gannett Outdoor Co. Inc. of No. Calif., Berkeley 1981—; mil: E5 Calif. Army Nat. Guard 1970-76; Democrat; Prot.; rec: gardening, music, computers. Res: 1534 Saint Charles Alameda 94501 Ofc: Gannett Outdoor Co Inc 1695 East Shore Hwy Berkeley 94710

LUPTON, RALPH LEANDER, workers compensation appeals board judge, ret.; b. May 31, 1906, Toledo, Ia.; s. John Lawrence and Susan Louise (Clark) L.; grandfather, Leander Clark, co. judge, Tama Co., Ia. (legislator, Ia. House Reps., lt. col. Union Army, Civil War); m. Winifred Lowe, Dec. 30, 1933, dec. 1970; children: Leslie Ann b. 1938, William b. 1942; edn: Cornell Coll., Ia. 1024-26; BS, Northwestern Univ. 1928; JD, 1931. Career: gen. law practice, Iowa 1931-38; asst. auditor Occidental Coll., L.A., Calif. 1938-39; auditor Sales tax div. State Bd. of Equalization, L.A. 1940-41; head legal dept. 1942; sr. trial atty./ head of subrogation dept. State Compensation Ins. Fund, in Law of Subrogation 1944-57; judge Workers Compensation Appeals Bd. 1957-69, ret.; instr. Claims Dept. State Compensation Ins. Fund, Law of Subrogation 1944-47; awards: Gold Medal, winner Big Ten & Nat. Wrestling Championship 1926-29 (125- pound class); Hall of Fame, Cornell College 1974, All American Honor Roll, Northwestern Univ. 1928; mem: Phi Delta Theta; Beta Gamma Sigma; Phi Alpha Delta; Elks; Lions (Lion Tamer); Sierra Club; Wilderness Soc.; Audubon Soc.; Nat. Parks & Conservation Assn.; Nat., Calif. & Iowa Bar Assns.; publs: contbr. law journals and revs.; Workmens Compensation Law, Due Process: Conduct of Trial, Examination and Cross Examination, for judges of state compensation appeals bd., 1969; Democrat; Methodist (deacon); rec: mtn. climbing (Mt. Whitney 10 times), dancing, bridge, historical novels. Res: 1516 Rock Glenn Ave 208, Glendale 91205

LURIE, ABRAHAM M., property management co. president; b. Nov. 21, 1923, Des Moines, Iowa; s. Nathan and Tillie (Livingston) L.; m. M. Katherine, May 1, 1983; children: Leslie Ralston b. 1951, Scott Lurie b. 1956; edn: BS, Ohio State Univ. 1948; grad. work Loyola Law Sch. 1952-53, UCLA Law Sch. 1953-54; admitted Calif. State Bar, Certified Public Acct. Career: CPA,

Leonard & Jacobson; CPA, Touche, Niven & Co. 1948-53; acctg. prin. solo practice 1953-57, dual practice as atty./CPA, 1957-64; senior ptnr. Lurie & Skaug, CPAs, Beverly Hills 1963-68; CPA, Braveman, Lurie & Co., Beverly Hills 1968-73; bd. chmn./pres. Real Property Management, Inc., Marina Del Rey 1973—; honors: Man of the year, Boys & Girls Club Venice (1981), Citizen of Year, Marina Del Rey CofC (1981); mem. Calif. Bar, Am. Assn. of Atty./ CPAs (past dir.); civic: County of Los Angeles Economy & Efficiency Commn., Community Relations Task Force of E & E Commn., County of Los Angeles Land Devel. Coordinating Ctr. Advis. Com.; mil: pvt. US Army Inf. 1943-46. Ofc: Real Property Management, Inc. 444 Washington Marina Del Rey 90292

LUSTER-CARPENTER, MARY JOAN, speech-language pathologist; b. June 18, 1951, Waukon, Iowa; d. Ernest J. and Alice D. (Mullarkey) L.; 1 dau. Amy b. 1984; edn: BA, Coll. of St. Teresa 1973; MS, Univ. of Wisc.-Madison 1975; Cert. of Clin. Competence, ASHA (1977). Career: dir. Information, Dissemination & Tng., Trace Center, Univ. of Wisc.-Madison 1974-75; speech-lang. pathologist Edgerton (Wisc.) Comm. Schs. 1975-77, Green Schs., Ohio 1977-78, Baldwin Park (Ca.) Unified Sch. Dist. 1978—, chair speech-lang. pathol. Baldwin Park Univ. Schs. 1982—; honors: ACE, ASHA (1986), Who's Who in Health Services (1986); mem. Delta Kappa Gamma, Am. Speech-Lang. Hearing Assn., Calif. Speech-Lang.-Hearing Assn.; civic: South Pasa.-San Marino YMCA (fund raising com., Enfant Movement Pgm. vol.); sev. publs. in area of non-vocal communication; rec: music, art. Res: 620 S Euclid Ave Pasadena 91106 Ofc: Baldwin Park Unified School District 3699 N Holly Ave Baldwin Park 91706

LYDICK, LAWRENCE TUPPER, judge; b. June 22, 1916, San Diego; s. Roy Telling and Geneva (Lydick) L.; m. Gretta Grant, Aug. 7, 1938; children: Gretta Grant, Lawrence Tupper; m. 2d. Martha Martinez, Oct. 1969; 1 son: Chip; edn: AB, Stanford 1938, LLB (Crothers law scholar), 1942; postgrad. (Sigma Nu exch. scholar), Univ. Freiburg, Germany 1938-39, Harvard 1943, Mass Inst. Tech. 1943-44; admitted State Bar of Calif. 1946; practice in Los Angeles 1946—; dir. disputes div. 10th region Nat. War Labor Bd., San Francisco 1942-43; asst. to pres., gen. counsel U.S. Grant Export-Import, Ltd., Los Angeles 1948-53, partner 1953-71; U.S. dist. ct. judge Central Dist. calif. 1971—; mem: Am. Calif. and Los Angeles Bar Assns.; Sigma Nu.; Commonwealth (San Francisco); mil: ensign to lt. USNR 1943-46. Ofc: US Court House, Los Angeles 90012

LYE, RONALD, import/export co. president; b. Aug. 30, 1940, Singapore; s. K.H. and Boh Lin (Loh) L.; m. Irene Chia, Dec. 8, 1966; children: Coleen, Linda; edn: BS, honors, Leeds Univ. 1965; MS, Cranfield Inst. of Tech. 1969; desig: M IEE, IEE, U.K. (1969), AFRAES, RAES U.K. (1970). Career: deputy mng. dir. Singapore Airlines, Ltd., Singapore 1960-77; exec. vice pres. Indamerica Internat., Inc. 1977—, pres./chief exec. 1979—; pres./ chief exec. CIGNA UMW Finance, Inc., 1983—; instr. Singapore Polytechnic; club: Singapore Island Country, Porter Valley Country; Anglican; rec: golf, music. Ofc: 4151 Beverly Blvd Los Angeles 90004

LYLE, ROBERT, investor; b. Jan. 16, 1944, Cheyenne, Wyo.; edn: BA, UC Los Angeles 1965, PhD econs., 1977. Career: stock analyst H. Hentz & Co.; ptnr. Zik & Co.; senior counselor of finance for the Bahamas; senior ptnr. Herman & Co.; current: owner Humphrie Lyle Inc.; cons. HVS Telecommunications Investments Inc.; dir: Popkin Investments Inc., Nuero Medical Group Inc., PMS Medical Group; mem. Freedom Train Commn. (1976), AASK Com. (1985); author: Real Money (Doubleday 1976); Jewish; rec: showing Bulldogs; art collector incl. Modigliana, Picasso, Chagall, Dali. Address: San Francisco

LYMBERIS, PETER, psychiatrist; b. Nov. 18, 1949, Athens, Greece, nat. 1980; s. Joseph and Ismini (Castalia) L.; edn: MD, Univ. of Athens 1980; PhD, Free Univ. of Brussels, Belgium 1976. Career: dir. family hosp., Castalia Inst., Athens, Greece; dir. Psychiatric inst., Los Angeles; recipient Achiev. award for work in alcohol & drug rehab.; mil: capt. US Army 1979-80, Bronze Star 1980; rec: guitar, sound recording. Res: 105 Via La Circula, Redondo Beach 90277

LYNCH, BERNICE JOAN, psychologist; b. Aug. 21, 1941, Chgo.; d. Joseph and Genowefa (Mieszczak) Fijak; m. 2d George Anthony Bajada, Sept. 25, 1986; children (by previous m.): Christopher Emmett b. 1964, Eric Daniel b. 1966, Julie Elizabeth b. 1970, Zachary Joseph b. 1972; edn: BA, Mt. St. Mary's Coll. 1963, gen. sec. tchg. cred. 1965; MFCC, PPS, Univ. of Santa Clara 1978. Career: marriage, family, child therapist Assoc. Psychologists of Santa Clara 1979-86, Ontos Therapy Inst., Santa Clara 1986—; trainer/therapist Nat. Tng. in Treatment of Sexual Abuse, Child Sexual Abuse Treatment Center, San Jose 1976-83; counselor Santa Clara Co. Alcohol & Treatment Center, 1980-; cons. Center for Self-Reliant Edn. (1981-), Holy Family Counseling Center, San Jose (1986-); instr. divorce/custody edn., De Anza Coll. (1980-83), seminars: Univ. of S.F., Univ. of Santa Clara (1980-81); awards: academic scholarships Univ. Santa Clara and Mt. St. Mary's Coll., appreciation Santa Clara County Bd. Suprs. (1979); mem: Calif. Assn. Marriage, Family Therapists, Equal Rights for Fathers, Am. Psychol. and Law Soc., Assn. for Transpersonal Psychol., Nat. Council on Alcoholism; publs: contbr., Manual for Prevention of Sexual Abuse (Wash DC), two books in progress: From Addiction to Wholeness, and Controlling Your Own Destiny (1986); Republican; Siddha Yoga; rec: ski, sailing, dancing, tennis. Res: 1214 Washoe Dr San Jose 95120 Ofc: Ontos Therapy Inst. 160 Saratoga Ave Ste 42 Santa Clara 95051

LYNCH, ROBERT LEON, insurance executive; b. June 28, 1940, Junction City, Wisc.; s. Glenn A. and Betty Bell (Darrar) L.; m. Wanda Magnum, 1961;

children: Robert Leon II, Vance Lee; m. 2d Dandy Deen, May 3, 1986; edn: Am. River Coll. 1965; life, health, disability underwriter 1975. Career: mgmt. family business 1966-74; agent Bankers Life Co. 1974-, currently with Allstate Ins. Co., Turlock, Calif. 1983 –; instr. LUTC I 1980-81, LUTC II 1981-82; honors: Eagle Scout (BSA 1955), also Bronze, Gold & Silver Palms, God & Country, Emerg. Svc., Order of the Arrow (BSA 1954-56), Rookie of the Yr. and other sales awards (Banker's Life 1975-76), Honor Ring (Allstate 1983), Outstanding Young Men of Am. (1975), num. other achievement and appreciation awards; mem: March of Dimes (county chmn. 1969-70, 3-co. chmn. 1971, 9-co. chmn. 1972, campaign chmn. 1970), Jaycees (num. awards and ofcs. held incl. chpt. pres. 1969-70, dist. gov. 1969-70, lt. gov. 1970-71); mil: radioman 3/c USN 1958-63; rec: gardening, photog., writing, sailing, collecting Am. art (pottery). Res: 2220 Jason Way Modesto 95380

LYNCH, URBAN HARRISON DEHOFF, aerospace engineer, research co. president; b. Nov. 30, 1938, Baltimore, Md.; s. Frederick Constantine and Helen (Kaline) L.; m. Janet Fabrick, Oct. 7, 1961; children: Andrew Michael Patrick b. 1964, Matthew Paul b. 1967; edn: BSME, Univ. Md. 1961; MS aeronautical engring., Air Force Inst. of Tech. 1963, PhD aerospace engring. 1973; Def. Systems Mgmt. Sch., Naval Postgrad. Sch. 1977; Combined Air Warfare Sch., Air War Coll. 1978. Career: served to lt. col. USAF, 1961-81, pgm. mgmt. (Blue Goose rocket vehicle and Satellite Data System spacecraft) assigned to AF Studies and Analysis Hq., The Pentagon and USAF Space Div.; founder/pres. U.H.L. Research Assocs. Inc., 1981 –, design/mfr. software for personal computers in home & church applications, also engring. svcs. for US Govt.; prin. staff mem. modeling & simulation, The BDM Corp., 1984 –; also mem. staff, minister of evangelism, The Bellflower Ch. of the Nazarene 1981-86; currently cons. to churches in tng. laymen, church growth and computer applications; honors: Pi Tau Sigma, Tau Beta Pi, Omicron Delta Kappa, Who's Who in Am. Colls. & Univs. (1961); mil. decorations: AF Commendn. medal w/o.l.c., Meritorious Service medal w/2 o.l.c.; Republican; Ch. of the Nazarene; rec: guitar, writing computer software. Address: UHL Research Associates Inc. 7926 Berner St Long Beach 90808

LYON, BILLY RAY, chiropractor; b. Nov. 28, 1941, San Bernardino; s. Charles Raymond and Geneva (Lamar) L.; m. Shirley, April 30, 1964; children: James b. 1971, Tammy b. 1966; edn: BA, Kansas Newman Coll. 1974; DC, Palmer Coll. of Chiropractic 1983. Career: chiropractor self-epml., Highland 1984 –; honors: grad., Parker Chiro. Research Found. 1984; Diplomate, Nat. Bd. Chiro. Examiners 1982; mem: Christian, Am. and Calif. Chiropractic Assns.; mil: m/sgt. USAF 1960-80, Bronze Star; Pentecostal; rec: auto mechanics, CB radio. Ofc: Christian Family Chiropractic Center, 6956 Palm Ave. Highland 92346

LYONS, BILL, trust co. president; b. June 26, 1937, N.Y.C.; s. Wm. Patrick and Lucy Ann (Flatley) L.; m. Noreen Corkerry, June 26, 1965; children: Kerry b. 1966, Luann b. 1968, Nora b. 1970, Billy b. 1972, Siobhan b. 1978; edn: BBA, Manhattan Coll. 1962; MBA, New York Univ. 1968; CPA, N.Y., Calif. (1972). Career: gen. ptrn. Wellington & Co., N.Y. 1971-78; v.p./treas. Cantor, Fitzgerald & Co., Beverly Hills 1978-80; pres. Wall Street Trust California, Los Angeles 1980 –, bd. dirs. 1981-; instr. Fordham Univ. 1975-77; mem. Am. Inst. of CPAs, New York Soc. of CPAs, Calif. Soc. of CPAs (Banking and Finl. Instns. coms.), Assn. of Western Securities Mgmt. (pres. 1986, bd. 1984-86); civic: AYSO youth soccer coach (1979-84), Most Blessed Sacrament Sch. Board (pres. 1976); mil: sgt. US Marine Corps 1954-57; Republican; Catholic; rec: tennis, swim, travel, dancing. Res: 15330 Albright St Pacific Palisades 90272 Ofc: Wall Street Trust California 510 W 6th St Ste 1115 Los Angeles 90014

MAC ALLISTER, DONALD, manufacturing representative co. president; b. Nov. 26, 1932, Hollywood, Calif.; s. Donald and Ruth (Waidlich) MacA.; m. Marilyn Jean Simmons, Sept. 25, 1955; children: Denise b. 1956, Gayle b. 1960, Michelle b. 1963; edn: AA, Pasadena City Coll. 1958; CSU Los Angeles, 2-½ yrs.; grad. (top 10%), USN Aviation Prep. Sch. and Electronics Sch. 1950. Career: electronics tech. Collins Radio, Burbank 1954-57; engrg. prodn. mgr. C.A. Rypinski Co., Pasadena 1957-59; mgr. planning and sch. Wiancko Engrg. Co., Pasadena 1959-60; sales engr. A-F Sales Engrg. Inc., Pasadena 1960-65; ops. mgr. No. Andros Devel. Co., Bahamas 1965-67; reg. & internat. sales mgr. Duncan Electronics, Costa Mesa 1967-69; v.p., A-F Sales Engrg. Inc., Pasadena 1969-83; pres. founder Seevid Inc., Huntington Beach 1983 –; dir. Huntington Nat. Bank 1982-; honors: Outstanding Jaycee (Costa Mesa Jaycees 1968), PTA Hon. Svc. Award (Hunt.Bch. H.S. 1974), Citizen of the Year (HBHS 1974); mem: Electronics Representatives Assn., Soc. for Information Display, Am. Soc. for Indsl. Security, Elks 1959-, Huntington Valley Boys & Girls Club (dir. 1982-), BSA (area chmn. 1987); mem. City Council Hunt. Bch. 1978-86, mayor 1979-80, 82; bd. trustees H.B. Union H.S. Dist. 1976-79, pres. 1978-79; mem. Public Cable TV Authority 1978-86, chmn. 1981; commr. Harbors, Beaches & Parks Commn. Orange County 1983-86; mil: aviation electronics tech. 3/c USN 1951; Republican; Protestant; rec: politics, woodworking, photog., computers. Res: 1121 Park St Huntington Beach 92648 Ofc: Seevid Inc., 15178 Transistor Ln Huntington Beach 92649

MACBRIDE, THOMAS JAMISON, judge; b. Mar. 25, 1914, Sacramento; s. Frank and Lotta (Little) MacB.; m. Martha Harrold, Nov. 7, 1947; children: Peter, Thomas Jamison, David, Laurie; edn: AB, UC Berkeley 1936, LLB, 1940; admitted to Calif. State Bar 1940. Career: dep. atty. gen. State of Calif., 1941-42; practiced in Sacramento, 1946-61; mem. Calif. House of Reps., 1955-60; US dist. judge for Eastern Dist. Calif., Sacramento 1961-, chief judge 1967-79, senior judge, 1979 –; mem. US Fgn. Intelligence Surveillance Ct., 1979-80; mem. US Temporary Emergency Ct. Appeals, 1982-; pres. Town Hall, Sacto. 1952; pres. N.E. area YMCA, Sacto. 1960, bd. dirs. 1956-68; mem. Nat. Commn. Reform Fed. Criminal Laws; mem. US Jud. Conf. 1975-78, chmn. Criminal Justice Act Com. 1979-; bd. dirs. KVIE Ednl. TV; founding mem. League to Save Lake Tahoe; mem. Am. Bar Assn., Univ. Calif. Alumni Assn. (v.p. 1955, 60), Phi Delta Phi, Kappa Sigma, Masons (33 deg.), Shriner KCCH), Rotary (pres.), University Club (pres. Sacto. 1953), Sutter, Comstock (bd. dirs., pres. 1975-6), Senator Outing; mil: lt. USNR 1942-46. Res: 1800 Rockwood Dr., Sacramento 95825 Ofc: US Courthouse Sacramento 95814

MAC CAULEY, HUGH BOURNONVILLE, stockbroker, banker; b. March 12, 1922, Mt. Vernon, NY; s. Morris Baker and Alma Orcutt (Gardiner) M.C.; m. Felice Cooper, Dec. 2, 1980; edn: Rutger Univ. 1939-40; Texas Christian Univ. 1948-50; Omaha Univ. 1957-59. Career: acct. exec. Dean Witter, San Bernardino 1974-79; v.p. Great American Securities, San Bernardino 1980 –; chmn. bd. Desert Community Bank, Victorville 1980 –; chmn. bd. KIST Corp., Riverside 1982 –; dir. Air Force Villago West Inc. 1986-, chmn. fin. com.; mem: Dadaelian Soc., Riverside Rotary (dir.), Victoria Country Club; mil: capt. US Army 1943-48; col. USAF 1949-73, Legion of Merit w/ Oak Leaf Cluster, Air Medal w/ (2) Oak Leaf Clusters, Air Force Commdn. w/ Oak Leaf Cluster; Republican; Presbyterian; rec: golf, aviation, equestrian. Res: 1630 Monroe St. Riverside 92504 Ofc: Great American Securities Inc., 334 W. Third St. Ste. 201 San Bernardino 92401

MAC DONALD, DONALD KEITH, inventor, electronics co. president; b. May 20, 1944, Annapolis, Md.; s. Frank Wadsworth and Henrietta Maria (Scott) MacD.; edn: AA, Foothill Coll. Career: chem. tech. research US Geol. Survey, Menlo Park 1963-70; inventor/mfr. Puzzlepaper (US patent 1970), 1968 –; inventor, owner MacDonald Co., MacDonald Controls and Schematic Control, 1967 –; inventions: programmable mirrors & power seat (for Ford), Abstract Painting & Woodwork Desk-Table & Lamp (1970), Two-Conductor Remote Switching and Transmitting Control System (pat. 1971), Indicator and Shutoff for Cartridge Type Tape Recorders, Laser Disc Programmable Record Player (for IBM), others; Republican; Catholic; rec: hi-fi, electronics. Address: MacDonald Controls 20400 Brook Dr Sonora 95370

MAC DONALD, RICHARD ROSS, information systems consulting co. executive; b. Aug. 20, 1945, Annapolis, Md.; s. Frank Wadsworth and Henrietta Maria (Scott) M.; m. Cheryl A. Peffer, Aug. 31, 1968; children: Brian R. b. 1972, Garrett C. b. 1975; edn: BS, US Naval Acad. 1967; MBA, Golden Gate Univ. 1979. Career: proj. engr., nuclear engr., eng. supvr., proj. eng. mgr., Bechtel Power Corp. 1971-79; sr. proj. mgr. TERA Corp. 1980-82; v.p. ops. TERA Info. Engrg. Corp. 1982-84, pres. 1984 –; cons. TERA Corp. 1980-; mem: Sigma Pi Sigma; works: Evaluating Decommissioning Costs for Nuclear Power Plants, Decontamination and Decommissioning of Nuclear Facilities, Plenum Press 1980; mil: LCDR N 1967-71; Republican; Catholic. Res: 14 Mt Eden Pl Clayton 94517 Ofc: TERA Information Engineering Corp., 2150 Shattuck Ave Berkeley 94704

MAC DONALD, SANFORD ROBERT, investment co. pres.; b. Jan.12, 1941, Los Angeles; s. Sanford Christian and Carrie (Nolton) M.; m. Linda Cardillo, Feb. 10, 1962; 1 dau. Lisa Lorraine b. 1963; edn: El Camino Coll. 1959-61. Career: insurance broker Pacific Fidelity Life Ins. Co. Los Angeles 1963-69; op. mgr. Airport Parking Co., LA Intl. Airport 1961-69; regl. mgr. Ampco Auto Parks, Phoenix, Ariz. 1969-74; gen. mgr. United Auto Parks, Denver, Colo. 1974-76; ops. dir. Parking Concepts Inc., Los Angeles 1976 –; pres. Diversified Investments Co., L.A. 1982 –; sales cons. Southwestern Petroleum Corp., Ft. Worth, Tx. 1984 –; honors: Bronze Medal of Merit awarded by Pres. Reagan for extraordinary participation and support as mem. Rep. Presidential Task Force (1984), top sales award Pacific Fidelity Life Ins. (1964), top regl. mgr. ABMI Parking, Phoenix (1972); mem./ pres. Phoenix Parking Assn. 1972-74, Bus. & Govt. Council 1973-74, Phoenix Metro. CofC; mem: Am. Mgmt. Assn. (NY), The Am. Film Inst. (Wash DC), Nat. Geographic Soc. and Smithsonian Instn.; apptd. to Govt. Affairs Council Denver Co. 1975; mem. Youth for Christ USA Found. 1984; Republican (mem. Rep. Nat. Com. 1984-, charter mem. Rep. Pres. Task Force); Christian; rec: music, theater, water

MAC ALLISTER, DONALD, manufacturing representative co. president; b. Nov. 26, 1932, Hollywood, Calif.; s. Donald and Ruth (Waidlich) MacA.; m. Marilyn Jean Simmons, Sept. 25, 1955; children: Denise b. 1956, Gayle b. 1960, Michelle b. 1963; edn: AA, Pasadena City Coll. 1958; CSU Los Angeles, 2-½ yrs.; grad. (top 10%), USN Aviation Prep. Sch. and Electronics Sch. 1950. Career: electronics tech. Collins Radio, Burbank 1954-57; engrg. prodn. mgr. C.A. Rypinski Co., Pasadena 1957-59; mgr. planning and sch. Wiancko Engrg.

sports. Res: 5772 Garden Grove Bl, 197, Westminster 92683 Ofc: Diversified Investments Co. 11925-F Grevillea, Hawthorne 90250

MAC FADEN, WILLIAM HUGH, merchant shipmaster; b. June 22, 1943, Santa Monica; s. John Raymond and Moya Louise (Langan) MacF.; children: Michael Robert b. 1965, Hugh Lantry b. 1966; edn: BS nautical sci., Calif. Maritime Acad. 1966; lic. Master/Pilot Steam & Motor Vessels Unlimited Tonnage, USCG (1973). Career: var. pos. as draftsman, carpenter, sales clk.; ordinary seaman California Shipping Co.; 2nd mate, 3rd mate Chevron Shipping Co. (tanker ops.) 1966-69; loading master Phillips Petroleum Co. 1969-70; relief chief mate and master Marine Transport Lines, Inc. 1971-77, permanent master 1978–, master SS Marine Chemist (chemical carrier) 1985-86; indep. marine surveyor/cons., pres. Port Services Unlimited Inc., 1983–; devel. micro-computer pgms. to analyze vessel charter performance, fuel consumption, calculate payroll and maintain personnel records; honors: excellence in seamanship, Shipowners & Merchants Towboat Assn. (1966), awards for rescues at sea, Am. Inst. of Merchant Shipping (1979, 1984); mil: comdr. USNR 1967-; Republican; rec: sailing, surfing, Scuba, skiing. Res: 922 18th St Hermosa Beach 90254 Ofc: Marine Transport Lines Inc 150 Meadowland Pkwy Secaucus NJ 07094

MAC GILLIVRAY, JOHN FRASER, rancher, real estate broker; b. Aug. 6, 1932, Grass Valley, Calif.; s. John Fraser and Dorothy Caroline (Smart) MacG.; m. Sandra Hawkins, Sept. 25, 1965; children: John b. 1967, Robert b. 1970, James b. 1975; edn: Calif. State Poly. Univ. 1950-53. Career: owner, oper. MacGillivray Ranches 1956–, McGillivray Airport 1965–; real estate broker 1979–; dir. transportation Port-A-Port Inc. 1971-73, mktg. and sales 1985–; Monterey- San Luis Obispo B-County PLanning Commn. 1967-68; S.L.O. County Master Plan Advis. Com. 1967-75; bd. dirs. Adelaida Land Owners Protective Assn. Inc., S.L.O. County Farm Bureau Inc.; mem: Calif. Assn. Realtors 1982-, Soc. of Los Alamos, Paso Robles Area Hist. Soc., Santa Ynez Hist. Soc., S.L.O.County Hist. Soc., Central Coast Geneal. Soc., Arizona Natures Conservancy, Republican Central Com.; Protestant; rec: hist. research and writing. Res: 8910 Adelaida Rd Paso Robles 93446 Ofc: Port-A-Port Inc. Rt 1 Box 14K Paso Robles 93446

MACINTYRE, DONALD J., college president; b. Aug. 19, 1939, Detroit, Mich.; s. Donald Maclellan and Ellen (McGrath) Macintyre; m. Antoinette Shen, June 2, 1979; chil: Honey, b. 1962, James, b. 1964, Michele, b. 1964, John, b. 1965; edn: AB, Univ. of Detroit 1961, MA, Univ. of Iowa 1963, PhD, 1966. Career: history prof. Univ. of the Pacific, Stockton 1966-73; dean/acting pres. St. Francis Coll., Biddeford, Me. 1973-75; v.p. academic affairs Univ. of San Francisco, 1975-79; pres. Metropolitan State Coll., Denver, Colos. 1979-81; pres. Canada Coll., Redwood City 1981-83; pres. Skyline Coll., San Bruno 1983-85; pres. John F. Kennedy Univ., Orinda, 1985–; labor/mgmt. rels. cons.: Indsl. Rels. Workshop Seminars, Inc. 1978-, assoc. John A. Scalone and Assocs., Orinda 1977-, cons. Colo. State Bd. of Agriculture 1979, chief negotiator Univ. of San Francisco 1975-79; frequent keynote speaker, panelist, workshop leader ednl. confs.; num. talks, comm. groups. Awards: research grants, UOP, 1969, 70, 70-1; distinguished tching. award, students of UOP 1971; Henry Clay Award, Univ. of S.F. 1976; hon. mem. Internat. Cultural Soc. of Korea 1979; Don Quixote Awd., Nat. Hispanic Univ. Convocation 1983; hon. mem. World Trade Center Club, Nanjing, China, 1985; Mem. Nat. Adv. Council on Telecommunications Edn., Wash DC 1984; bd. dirs. Chinese Culture Found., S.F. 1983-; adv. bd. European Univ. of Am. 1982-; trustee Nat. Hispanic Univ. 1982-. Publs: editorial bd. The State of Hispanic Am. (1981-), journal arts. Rec: tennis. Res: 27 Midway, Mill Valley 94941 Ofc: JFK University, 12 Altarinda Rd Orinda 94563

MACK, BRENDA LEE, company executive; b. Mar. 24, Peoria, Ill.; d. William James and Virginia Julia (Pickett) Palmer; 1 son, Kevin; edn: AA, Los Angeles City Coll.; BA sociol. CSU Los Angeles 1980. Career: secty. bus facilities So. Calif. Rapid Transit Dist. 1974-81; pres. Brenda Mack Enterprises 1981–; founder, ptnr., dir. Innermedia Corp. 1985–; lectr., writer, sociologist, radio & TV personality, artists' rep.; co-originator Vee/Dee Advtg. Concept; mem: Women For 1974-, CSULA Alumni Assn.; mil: pfc US Women's Army Corps; rec: travel, languages, reading, tennis, flying. Ofc: POB 5942 Los Angeles 90055

MACK, MARILYN LOTZ, financial services marketing executive; b. May 28, 1945, Oakland; d. Edward S. and Marjorie M. (David) Ageno; children: John b. 1969, Kim b. 1971; edn: UC Berkeley 1966. Career: regional mgr. Urban Management Consultants, San Francisco 1980-81; br. mgr. Equitec Securities Co., Oakland 1981-84; v.p. retail mktg. Certified Financial Services, Irvine 1984–; honors: recogn. for dedicated service, Town of Moraga (1984), Outstanding Young Women of Am. (1976), Who's Who in Am. Women (1984); mem. Internat. Assn. of Finl. Planners; civic: Junior League of Newport Harbor; Republican; Catholic. Res: 8 Bellezza Irvine 92720 Ofc: Certified Financial Services 18300 Von Karman Ste 620 Irvine 92715

MAC KENZIE, ALBERT HAROLD, government lawyer; b. Aug. 18, 1944, Willows, Calif.; s. Harold Lincoln and Blanche (Covert) MacKenzie; edn: AA, Harbor Coll. 1964; BA, CSU Long Beach 1966; JD, Glendale Coll. of Law 1970; cert. Lawyers Post Graduate Clinic 1972; admitted to Calif. State Bar 1971, US Supreme Ct. 1980. Career: deputy dist. atty., Los Angeles County 1973–; spec. in major fraud prosecutions Major Fraud Div., 1979–; spl. asst. to US Atty. 1984, 85; mem. So. Calif. Fraud Investigators Assn., Am. Ins. Assn., Nat. Dist. Attys. Assn., Calif. Dist. Attys. Assn., Peace Officers Shrine Club, Al Malaikah Shrine Temple, Scottish Rite, Masons; profl. presentations on insurance fraud prosecutions: Am. Ins. Assn. (1983), So. Calif. Fraud Investigators (1984), Calif. Hwy Patrol (1985); Republican; Protestant; rec: tennis. Ofc: District Attorney, POB 2766, Rolling Hills Estates 90274

MAC KENZIE, JEANNE L., geriatric nurisng consultant; b. Apr. 28, 1939, Calif.; d. Stanley Fuller and Jeannette Barbara (Quast) Davis; children: John Douglas b. 1960, Gary Gordon b. 1962; edn: BS, San Francisco State Coll. 1960; MPA, Univ. San Francisco 1984; Med. Surg. Nsg., Stanford Univ. 1958; tchr., edn. series, UC Ext., Santa Cruz 1974; grad. studies, Geriatric Nursing, San Jose State Univ. 1978–; lic: R.N., Pub. Health Nse., Nursing Home Adminstr., (life) Std. Designated and Comm. Coll. (nsg. edn.) Tchg. credentials. Career: aide Sequoia Hosp., Redwood City 1957-60; RN, 1960-64; nurse Devenshire Oaks Conv. Hosp. 1964-66; Grays Harbor Comm. Hosp., Aberdeen, Wash. 1967; Redwood City Sch. Dept., Redwood City, Calif. 1968; Drs. Richards, Porter & Levenson 1969; dir. nirs. svc. Capitola Extended Care Hosp., Capitola 1970; Lark Manor Conv. hosp., Los Gatos 1971- 78; relief adminstr., Inservice Edn., dir. nursing svc. Marcus Manor Conv. Hosp., San Jose 1978-79; instr. nsg. assts. San Jose Regl. Vocational Ctr. 1979-; staff nurse San Jose Hosp. 1979-; nsg. cons. num. extended care facilities, Los Gatos areo 1979-, honors: Lucina K. Lordon Nursing Awd. 1978; Resolution of Commdn., League of Friends of Santa Clara Co. Commn. on the Status of Women 1981, 82, 84; Lic. Provider for Cont. Edn., BRN and BENHA 1982; mem: Calif. Nurses Assn.; Am. Coll. of Nursing Home Adminstrs.; Peninsula Long Term Nurses Assn.; Republican; Protestant; rec: beekeeper. Address: POB 415, Redwood Estates 95044

MAC LACHLAN, JANET LYNN, lawyer; b. Oct. 9, 1956, Chgo., Ill.; d. Donald R. and Joan G. (Bartels) Krahn; edn: BS, San Diego State Univ. 1978; JD, UC Los Angeles Sch. of Law 1983; admitted Calif. State Bar 1983, US Ct. of Appeals, Ninth Circ., US Dist. Ct., Cent. Dist. Calif. 1984. Career: atty. Rutan & Tucker Costa Mesa, Calif. 1983–; mng. ed. and contbr. Fed. Communications Law Journal 1982-83; honors: Paula Lubic Scholarship 1980; Outstanding Marketing Student (San Diego State 1979); Phi Kappa Phi; Beta Gamma Sigma; mem: Orange Co. Bar Assn.; Orange Co. Financial Soc.; Phi Alpha Delta; rec: stained glass. Ofc: Rutan & Tucker 611 Anton Blvd, Ste. 1400, Costa Mesa 92626

MAC QUIDDY, THOMAS MALCOLM, insurance broker; b. Apr. 13, 1906, Watsonville; s. Thomas Smith and Lou Vivien (Englehart) MacQ.; m. Gertrude Flint, Nov. 5, 1977; children: Barbara Lou b. 1941, Jean Elizabeth b. 1943; edn: AB, Stanford Univ. 1928. Career: insurance broker MacQuiddy Ins., Watsonville; mem. Indep. Inc. Agents and Brokers of Calif., Watsonville Assn. of Ins. Agents, Rotary, Elks, Masons, Scottish Rite; Episcopal; rec: photog. Res: 410 Stanford Watsonville 95076 Ofc: MacQuiddy Insurance 966 E Lake Ave Watsonville 95076

MACRI, PAULINE FRANCES, pharmacist; b. Oct. 25, 1957, San Francisco; d. Frank Rocco and Anna Macri; edn: BS, Univ. of the Pacific 1980; RPH (Reg. Pharmacist) lic. in Calif. 1980, Nev. 1981. Career: intern pharmacist Los Altos Pharmacy, Los Altos 1980; chief pharmacist Clifford's Pharmacies, Menlo Park 1980-82; chief pharmacist Walgreens, Santa Clara 1982–; pharmacy cons. Adult Day Health Ctr., Visiting Nurse Assn. of San Mateo Co., Inc. 1981-; bd. dirs. San Mateo Pharmacists Assn., Inc. 1981-82; v.p. 1982-; TV comml. actress 1976-80; fashion model 1982-; honors: UOP Cheerleader 1979-80; Leadership Awd., Cheerleading Camp 1979; mem: Lambda Kappa Sigma (profl. frat.); Am. & San Mateo Co. Pharmaceutical Assns.; Calif. Pharacists Assn.; Calif. Pharmacists PAC; San Jose Jaycees; works: Choosing the proper sunscreen, art. printed & distbd. in community 1980, 82; Republican; Cathoic; rec: tennis, dancing. Res: 755 Arlington Rd Redwood City 94062 Ofc: Walgreens, 2012 El Camino Real Santa Clara 95050

MACY, KIMBERLY ANN, public relations and advertising executive; b. Dec. 19, 1956, Westwood, Calif.; d. Ernest Richard and Roberta Jean (Schlichting) Macy; edn: BA, UC Los Angeles 1980. Career: pub. rels. coord. Kaplan/ McLaughlin/ Diaz Architects & Planners, San Francisco, 1980-84; dir. corp. communications, Tishman West Mgmt. Corp., Los Angeles 1984–; advis. bd. Building Owners & Managers Marketing Guide (1985); recipient achievement award, YWCA of Los Angeles (1985), also awards from Internat. Assn. of Bus. Communicators and L.A. Publicity Club; mem: Pub. Rels. Soc. of Am., Ad. Club of Am., Soc. of Mktg. Profls. (1983-84), San Francisco Plnng. & Research Assn. (1984), Media Alliance (1984), Greater Los Angeles Press Club, Publicity Club of L.A., Kappa Kappa Gamma Alumni; publs. in real estate jours.; Republican; Prot.; rec: oil painting, sailing, skiing. Res: Hermosa Beach 90254 Ofc: Tishman West Mgmt. Corp. 10960 Wilshire Blvd Ste 700 Los Angeles 90024

MADANAT, GEORGE MICHAEL, pediatrician; b. Jan. 21, 1944, Karak, Jordan; s. Michael Suleiman and Jameelah Salman (Sunnaa) M.; m. Maha Zabaneh, Oct. 14, 1979; children: Michael b. 1980, Jumana b. 1981, Fadi b. 1983, Lana b. 1985, Bassil b. 1986; edn: MD, Damascus Sch. of Med. 1969; Diplomate, Am. Bd. of Pediatrics, Tulane Univ. 1976; Fellow, Am. Acad. of Pediatrics 1976. Career: intern and pediatric resident Charity Hosp. of LA in N.O. Tulane div. 1971-73; attndg. pediatrician 1974; instr. pediatrics Tulane Med. Sch. 1973; pvt. practice pediatrics, Glendora, W. Covina, San Dimas 1975–; cons. pediatrician, Diamond Bar 1981–; chief of pediatrics San Dimas Community Hosp. 1976, 1981, bd. dirs. 1977–; awards: Physicians Recogn. Award for cont. med. edn., Am. Med. Assn.; mem: Am. and Calif. Med. Assns., Los Angeles Pediatric Soc. (life, Council), Calif. Perinatal Assn., Fellow Am. Acad. of Pediatrics, Arab Am. Med. Assn.; publs: edl., Journ. of

Calif. Perinatal Assn.; Republican; Orthodox; rec: swimming, tennis, classical music. Res: 22835 Ridgeline Rd Diamond Bar 91765 Ofc: Geo. M. Madanat, MD, FAAP, 1330 W. Covina Blvd. Ste. 106 San Dimas 91773 and 750 No. Diamond Bar Blvd. Diamond Bar 91765

MADDY, KENNETH LEON, state senator; b. May 22, 1934, Santa Monica; s. Russell T. and Anna M. (Balzer) M.; m. Norma Foster, Nov. 28, 1981; children: Deanna, Donald, Marilyn, (step): Jayne, Ron, Janet, Suzi, Carrie, Lori; edn: BS, CSU Fresno 1956; JD, UC Los Angeles Law Sch. 1963. Career: atty. ptnr. law firm Chinello, Chinello & Maddy, Fresno 1963-77; elected rep. Calif. State Assembly, Sacramento 1970-78, Calif. State Senator 1979–, chmn. Senate Republican Caucus (1979-83); honors: named Alumnus of the Year (1981) CSU Fresno, Alumnus of the Year (1985) UCLA Sch. of Law; invited participant (1 of 50 legislators throughout USA) Rutger Univ. Legislators' Conf. (1972); bd. mem. Mental Health Assn. of Greater Fresno, Fresno Philharmonic Assn.; mem. CSUF Bulldog Found. and Pres.'s Club; Rotarian; mil: 1st lt. USAF 1957-60; Republican; rec: golf, tennis, horses. Ofc: 3433 West Shaw Ste 119 Fresno 93711

MADLAING, ART GABOT, real estate broker, notary public; b. Aug. 18, 1947, Binalonan, Pangasinan, Philippines, nat. US cit. 1981; s. Emilio Baguilat and Elena Sampatan (Gabot) M.; m. Virginia Barte Jimenez, May 6, 1974; children: Darlene Vi b. 1975, Wynema Joy b. 1978; edn: Assoc. Forestry, Univ. Philippines 1967; Cert., Phil. Bible Coll. 1973; Cert., Chamberlin Real Estate Sch. 1980; PhD economics (real estate), World Univ. Tucson, Ariz. 1984. Career: co. forester Taggat Industries Philippines 1967; forest station warden, timber mgmt. ofcr., asst. rgl. info. ofcr. Bureau of Forestry Manila 1968-75; community editor Forum Philippines San Francisco 1976; acct. exec. Putnam Financial Svcs. San Rafael 1976; mgr. Internat. Realtors Corp. S.F. 1979-80; pres., broker Equity Internat. Real Estate Inc. S.F. 1980-81; agcy mgr. Am. Bankers Ins. Group Miami, Fla. 1981; owner, broker Am. Bankers Realty 1981–; v.p. adminstrn. Calif. Examiner 1985–; pres., chmn. bd. Internat. Land Investment Inc. 1985–; real estate columnist Philippine News S.F. 1978-80, Calif. Examiner S.F. and L.A. 1980–; honors: Entrance & Coll. Scholar (Univ. Phil. 1964, 67), Bureau of Forestry Scholar (1964-67), Outstanding Editor (Daly City Jaycees 1979), Outstanding Ofcr. (Baguio- Californians 1982), Ten Outstanding Filipinos of No. Calif. (FANCO 1984); mem: S.F. Bd. Realtors, Calif. Assn. Realtors, Nat. Assn. Realtors, Nat. Notary Assn., Zeta Beta Rho, Binalonians of No. Calif., United Pangasinanes of Am., UP Alumni Assn. of No. Calif., Daly City Jaycees, Toastmasters Internat., Baguio-Californians (secty.); author books: Real Estate & You (1984), No Guts, No Glory (1985); Democrat; Ch. of Christ; rec: reading, writing, travel. Ofc: Am. Bankers Realty & Internat. Land Investment Inc. 6777 Mission St Daly City 94014

MADNI, ASAD MOHAMED, engineering executive; b. Sept. 8, 1947, nat. US Citizen 1983; s. Mohamed Taher and Sara Alimohamed (Wadiwalla) M.; m. Gowhartaj, Nov. 11, 1976; 1 son, Jamal A. Madni b. 1984; edn: dip. in advanced electronics RCA Insts. Inc., NY, NY 1968; BS, UC Los Angeles 1969, MS 1973; Stanford Exec. Inst. 1984. Career: engring. reader (undergrad. and grad. courses) UCLA, Los Angeles 1969-73; senior electronics instr. Pacific State Univ., Los Angeles 1969-71; senior electronics auditor Pertec Corp., Chatsworth 1973-75; proj. engr. Systron Donner Corp. Microwave Div., Van Nuys 1975-80, senior engr. 1980-81, engring. mgr. 1981-82, dir. of Engring. and dir. of Advanced Programs Technology, 1982-85, dir. engrg., gen. mgr. 1985–, respons. for devel. of num. industry firsts in the field of intelligent instrumentation and subsystem conceptualization and design; West Coast chmn. editl. review bd. MSN mag. (EW Communications, Palo Alto) 1983-; tech. adv. to Test and Measurement World mag. (Interfield Pub. Co., Boston); profl. presentations worldwide (incl. the Pentagon), workshop ldr., track ldr.; senior mem. IEEE 1976-, mem. Assn. of Old Crows, Nat. Rifle Assn. of Am. (life); works: 3 U.S. Patents (6 pats. pend. in area of electronic warfare), num. tech. articles in sci. publs.; rec: art collector, music. Res: 3582 Greenfield Ave Los Angeles 90034 Ofc: Systron Donner Corp. Microwave Div. 14844 Oxnard St Van Nuys 91411

MAGEE, ALBERT DENNIS, Indian Health Council administrator; b. Oct. 9, 1937, Pala; s. Raymond Milton and Prudence Theresa (Golsh) M.; edn: San Diego Jr. Coll. 1955-57; Bus. Admin., CSU San Diego 1957-61. Career: wholesale Droschel Inc., San Diego 1962-66; wholesale Stanley Andrew Sports Outfitters, San Diego 1967-69; adminstr. Indian Health Council Inc., Pauma Valley 1970–; developed health delivery sys. for Am. Indians on 17 reservations in rural San Diego Co.; expert witness, appropriations, Senate and House subcoms. Wash. DC 1971-82; guest spkr. 10th Anniversary Meml. Svcs. for Robt. F. Kennedy, Arlington Nat. Cemetery 1978; appeared in panel debate with Sen. Barry Goldwater on 'The American Indian Today' (1972), CBS TV spl., asst. San Diego Chargers Profl. Football Team fund raising health pgm. (1973); honors: San Diego Jr. Coll. Football, Jr. Coll. All American 1956; CSU San Diego All Conf. selection, Freshman Football coach 1957-59; Robert F. Kennedy Meml. Fellowship, 1970; Ten Outstanding Young Men of San Diego 1971; San Diego No. Co. Man of Year, CofC 1971; Calif. State Senate Resolution 1972; hon. degree, Palomar Coll. 1973; Nat. Distng. Community Svc. Award, Nat. Social Wkrs. Techni-Culture Coalition 1973; Indian Health Center, dedicated to Dennis Magee, Oct. 16, 1976; Letter of Commdn., Pres. Jimmy Carter 1980; mem: Native Am. Tng. Assocs. Inst. (Sacramento), Pauma Valley Community Assn., Nat. Social Workers Techni-Culture Coalition (Cincinnati), Masters in Public Health Pgm. for Native Americas (UC Berkeley), San Diego Co. Mental Health Advy. Bd. (Com. on Ethnic Minorities), San Diego Co. Regl. Criminal Justice Plnng Bd., San Diego Co. Minority Elderly Research Plnng. Com., Calif. Assn. for Indian Helth Adminstrs., Robert F. Kennedy Meml. Found. (bd. trustees), CSU San Diego Athletic Found., CSU San Diego Alumni Assn.; Democrat; Catholic; rec: sports enthusiast, bullfight aficionado. Res: P.O. Box 86, Mission Rd. Pala 92059 Ofc: Indian Health Council Inc., P.O. Box 406 Pauma Valley 92061

MAGNUSON, RICHARD R., manufacturing co. sales executive; b. Nov. 8, 1930, Detroit; s. Frank and Adeline (Latvala) M.; m. Carol, Nov. 10, 1956; children: Debra b. 1957, Richard Jr. b. 1958, Eric b. 1965, Julie b. 1970; edn: BS, CSU Long Beach 1970, MBA, 1971; real estate broker Calif. Career: salesman Moore Bus. Forms Detroit 1954-55, IBM Electric Typewriter Div. Detroit 1955-57, Svc. Bureau computer svcs. 1957-58, 3M copy div. Chgo. 1959; mgr. Recording Mach. Div. Dictaphone Corp. 1959-65; lessee western region, mgr. Oscar's Restaurant Long Beach 1965-66; creator, owner The Zoo. Restaurants 1967-71; real estate sales Coldwell Banker 1971-72; real estate negotiator Dept. Water & Power City of L.A. 1973; regl. sales mgr. Dictaphone Corp. 1974–; honors; Life Master (Am. Contract Bridge League), 10 Achievement Clubs (Dictaphone Corp.), Regl. Mgr. of the Month (16 times), Sales Mgr. of the Yr. (2 times); mem: Nat. Sheriff's Assn., Assn. Police Communications Ofcrs., Calif. Ambulance Assn., Internat. Assn. Chiefs of Police, Am. Mgmt. Assn., Sales Execs. Assn.; mil: PO1 USN 1948-50, 1952-54, Korean Svc., UN Svc.; Republican; Catholic; rec: bridge. Res: 2800 Neilson Way Apt 1415 Santa Monica 90405 Ofc: Dictaphone Corp. 3101 Ocean Park Blvd Ste 303 Santa Monica 90405

MAGOWAN, PETER ALDEN, grocery chain store executive; b. Apr. 5, 1942, NY, NY; s. Robert Anderson and Doris (Merrill) M.; m. Deborah Johnston, Aug. 14, 1982; children: Kimberley b. 1967, Margot b. 1969, Hilary b. 1972; edn: BA, Stanford Univ. 1964; MA, Oxford Univ. 1966; Johns Hopkins Sch. of Adv. Internat. Studies, 2 yrs. Career: store mgr. Safeway Stores, Inc., Wash DC 1968-70, dist. mgr., Houston 1970, retail ops. mgr. Phoenix 1971-72, div. mgr. Tulsa, Okla. 1973-76, mgr. Internat. Div., Toronto, Can. 1976-78, Western regl. mgr., San Francisco 1978-79, chmn. bd./CEO, 1980–; dir: Pacific Gas & Elec., S.F. 1981-, Chrysler Corp. 1986-; trustee Johns Hopkins Univ. (1984-) and mem. adv. council John Hopkins Sch. of Adv. Internat. Studies; mem. US CofC (dir. 1984-), Food Mktg. Inst. (dir. 1984-), Bus. Roundtable. Ofc: Safeway Stores Inc. 4th and Jackson Sts Oakland 94660

MAGUIRE, JOHN DAVID, educator, university president; b. Aug. 7, 1932, Montgomery, Ala.; s. John Henry and Clyde (Merrill) M.; m. Lillian Louise Parrish, Aug. 29, 1953; children: Catherine Merrill, Mary Elizabeth, Anne King; edn: AB, magna cum laude, Washington and Lee Univ. 1953; Litt.D, hon., 1979; Fulbright scholar, Edinburgh Univ., Scotland 1953-54; BD, summa cum laude, Yale 1956, PhD, 1960; postdoctoral research, Yale Univ. and Univ. Tubingen, Germany 1964-65, UC Berkeley 1968-69, Silliman Univ., Philippines, Chinese Univ., Hong Kong 1976-77. Career: actg. chaplain Washington and Lee Univ. 1952-53; actg. dir. Internat. Student Ctr., New Haven 1956-58; asst. in instrn. systematic theology Yale Div. Sch. 1958-59; mem. faculty Wesleyan Univ., Middletown, Conn. 1960-70, assoc. provost 1967-68; vis. lectr. Pacific Sch. Religion 1968-69; pres. State Univ. N.Y. Coll. at Old Westbury 1970-81; pres. Claremont Univ. Ctr. and Grad. Sch. 1981–; Conn. Adv. Com. U.S. Commn. Civil Rights 1961-70; participant White House Conf. on Civil Rights 1966; mem. Assn. of Am. Colls. 1966-, dir. 1981-, chair bd. dirs. 1984-85; dir. NAACP Legal and Ednl. Defense Fund, Inc. (West Coast) 1981-; permanent trustee and dir. Martin Luther King Ctr. for Soc. Change, Atlanta 1968-; pres., bd. dirs. Nassau Co. Health and Welfare Council 1971-78; trustee Inst. Internat. Edn., United Bd. for Christian Edn. in Asia; bd. dirs. Assn. Am. Colls.; honors:China Inst. Am. recipient Julia A. Archibald High Scholarship award, Yale Div. Sch. 1956; Day fellow, Yale Grad. Sch. 1956-57, Kent fellow, 1957-60; Howard Found. postdoctoral fellow, Borwn Univ. Grad. Sch. 1964-65; Fenn lectr., 7 Asian countries 1977; Conn. Prince Hall Masons' awd. for outstanding contbs. human rights in Conn. 1965; E. Harris Harbison Gt. Tchr. prize, Danforth Found. 1968; mem: Soc. Religion Higher Edn. (bd. dirs. 1967-, pres. 1974-81); Hazen Theol. Discussion Group; Phi Beta Kappa; Omicron Delta Kappa; author: The Dance of the Pilgrim: A Christian Style of Life for Today, 1967; num. arts.; Democrat. Ofc: Office of the President, Claremont Univ. Ctr. & Grad. Sch., Claremont 91711

MAHAJAN, RAJINDER NATH, physician; b. Dec. 16, 1950, Batala, India; s. Ram C.and Sushila M.; m. Shashi, Dec. 31, 1977; 1 child, Neha b. 1984; edn: MBBS, Govt. Med. Coll., Amritsar, India 1974; Cert. Spec. in Internal Med. (1977) and Rheumatology (1980), Am. Bd. of Internal Med. Career: intern, resident, chief resident Lutheran Medical Ctr., Cleveland, Ohio 1974-78; rheumatology fellow Louisiana State Univ. Sch. of Med., New Orleans, La. 1978-80; rheumatology- internal med. practice with OPMG, Cleveland, Ohio 1980-83; practicing physician with SCPMG, Harbor City 1983–; mem. Am. Rheumatism Assn.. Ofc: SCPMG, 25825 So. Vermont Ave. Harbor City 90710

MAHALATINIA, ALI GHAHREMAN, engineer; b. July 6, 1958, Tehran, Iran; s. Ahmad and Gohar-Malek (Abtahi) M.; edn: undergrad. Geo. Wash. Univ., Miami Dade Jr. Coll., Tulsa Univ.; BSCE and BS mats. sci. & engring., UC Berkeley 1980; MS struc. engring., CSU San Jose 1983; spl. courses UCB, CSU Humboldt, UC Davis; Reg. Profl. Engr., Calif. Career: interpreter US Dept. of Justice, San Francisco 1979-80; tchg. asst. Univ. Calif., Berkeley 1980; assoc. earthquake engr. Tera Corp., Berkley 1981-82; structural engr. Tenera Corp., Berkeley 1983-84; civil engr. Dept. of Public Works, City and County of San Francisco, 1984-86; pres. Mahalat Engring. Corp., Vallejo 1986–, cons. civil/struc. engineering; mem. ASCE; Moslem; rec: jogging. Ofc: Mahalat Engineering Corp. 607 Georgia St Vallejo 94590

MAHER, JEANMARIE, law office administrator; b. Couer d'Alene, Idaho; d. Richard Bonaventure and Celine Catherine (Chainey) M.; edn: BA, Univ. Santa Clara 1964. Career: spl. asst. The Asia Found. S.F. 1965-69; exec. asst. to chmn. Calif. Democratic Party 1971-74; owner Jeanmarie Maher & Assocs. S.F. 1974-75; staff Brobeck, Phleger & Harrison S.F. and L.A. 1975-79; adminstr. Lasky, Haas, Cohler & Munter S.F. 1979-86; adminstrv. mgr. Calif. Brown & Wood 1986—; occasional lectr., cons.; mem: Assn. Legal Adminstrs. (chpt. pres. 1985-86, treas. 1984-85, ed. newsletter 1982-83, mem. dir. 1981-82), Nat. Assn. Legal Adminstrs. (ed. newsletter 1983-85), Am. Mgmt. Assn., Am., Calif. Bar Assns. 1983-, THe Irish Forum (bd.), Women's Council Democratic Nat. Com., rec: music, writing. Res: 570 Union St Apt 206 San Francisco 94133 Ofc: Brown & Wood 555 California St 50th flr San Francisco 94104

MAHLER, VICTOR GEORGE, instrumentation and controls engineer; b. July 17, 1920, Vienna, Austria, nat. US cit. 1943; s. Joseph M. and Fritzi (Forster) M.; m. Wynnaretta Wilson, Nov. 6, 1943; 1 dau: Margaret Mary (Burnham) b. 1946; edn: BS, Univ. of London 1940; DD, Universal Church 1977; profl. engr., Calif. 1977. Career: sr. sales & svc. engr. The Foxboro Co., Foxboro, Mass.; asst. corp. mktg. mgr. Envirotech Corp., Mountain View; principal instrument engr. Ralph M. Parsons Corp., Pasadena; ret.; consultant; instr. instrumentation, Savannah Vocational Sch., Savannah, Georgia; mem: Instrument Soc. of Am. (v.p. reg. 3); works: design of major control systems for Petrochemical & Paper Industry; mil: temp. lt. col., perm. tech. sgt. US Army Intelligence Corps; Republican; Episcopalian.

MAJMUNDAR, HASMUKHRAI HIRALAL , geologist, geochemist; b. Nov. 18, 1932, Baroda, India; nat. US cit. 1974; s. Hiralal Bhagwanji and Jekorben Hiralal (Parikh) M.; m. Vasanti Parikh, Mar. 9, 1962; children: Ami (MD) b. 1963, Kalyan (mech. engr.) b. 1966; edn: BS, honors, M.S. Univ. of Baroda, India 1955; MS, Banaras Hindu Univ., India 1957; PhD, Univ. de Nancy, France 1961; Reg. Geologist, State of Calif. Career: prof. geology (dept. chmn. 1959-60) M.S. Univ. of Baroda, 1957-64; research assoc. Goddard Space Flight Ctr., NASA, Greenbelt, Md. 1964-66; prof. geochem. and head Geochem. Sect., Dalhousie Univ., Halifax, Nova Scotia, Canada 1966-68; prof. geol. Appalachian State Univ., Boone, N.C. 1968-70; mgr. Geochem. Sect., Calif. Div. of Mines and Geology, 1970-84, geologist Surface Mining and Reclamation pgm., 1984—; instr. var. colls. and univs., S.F. Bay area 1970-; mem. Indo-Am. Soc.; publs: 60+ articles in field of geology, geochemistry; Democrat; Hindu; rec: camping, photog., handi-work. Ofc: State of Calif. Div. Mines & Geology, 610 Bercut Dr Sacramento 95814

MAKEPEACE, DARRYL LEE, manufacturing co. executive; b. Oct. 24, 1941, Pittsurgh, Pa.; s. Thomas Henry and Nevada Ruth (Wagner) M.; m. Maryanne, Aug. 16, 1977; children: Krisanne b. 1965, Erin b. 1973; edn: BSIE, Penn State, 1969; MBA, Pepperdine Univ., 1982; desig: CPIM, APICS (1981). Career: journeyman machinist Gen. Elec., Erie, Pa. 1961-66; dept. mgr. Proctor & Gamble, Cinti. 1969-72; plant mgr., prodn., Columbia Bdcstg. Systems, Fullerton, Calif. 1972-76; dir. ops. Federal Sign/ Signal, L.A. 1976-77; dir. mfg. Frigid Coil/ Wolf Range, La Mirada 1977-79; mgr. mfg., Nat. Supply, Los Nietos 1979—; adj. prof. mgmt. CSU Fullerton 1984-; mfg. cons. Businiss Kinetics; honors: Alpha Pi Mu, Tau Beta Pi, Sigma Tau, Kentucky Cols., Who's Who (Am. Sci. & Industry, West, Orange County); mem: IIE, ASME, Am. Prodn. Inventory Control Soc. (ednl. staff 1984-); contbr. articles P&IM Mag. (9/82), Mini-Micro (10/85), Today's Office (12/85), Am. Machinist (10/85), Computer Decisions (10/86), Computer Advances (1/86); mil: splst E4 Army Arty. 1960-61; Republican; Presbyterian. Res: 10541 Fredrick Dr Villa Park 92667 Ofc: National Supply 9100 S Norwalk Blvd Los Nietos 90610

MAKOWSKI, PETER EDGAR, hospital executive; b. Nov. 21, 1953, Milwaukee; s. Edgar Leonard and Patricia Mae (Nock) M.; m. Cynthia R.E., Apr. 7, 1979; edn: BA, Whittier Coll. 1976; MPH, UC Los Angeles 1980. Career: adminstrv. intern Calif. Med. Ctr. L.A. 1977, unit mgr. emgcy. dept. 1977-78; adminstrv. resident Presbyterian Intercommunity Hosp. Whittier 1979-80, adminstrv. dir. support svcs. 1980-82, v.p. ambulatory/ spl. svcs. 1982-84, v.p. diagnostic/ therapeutic svcs. 1984-85; v.p., 1985, senior v.p. Calif. Med. Ctr. L.A. 1986—; bd. dirs. Haas Corp. 1986; honors: Nat. Honor Soc. (1972), Who's Who Students in Am. Univs. & Colls. (1975-76), West (1984-85); mem: Am. Coll. Hosp. Adminstrs. (nominee), Health Care Execs. of So. Calif., Am. Hosp. Assn., UCLA Hosp. Adminstrn. Alumni Assn., Lions Club, Whittier Coll. Alumni Assn. (bd.); Republican; Catholic; rec: 1308 Calle Galante San Dimas 91773 Ofc: California Medical Ctr. L.A. 1414 S Hope Los Angeles 90015

MALAN, RANDY, insurance broker; b. Oct. 1, 1951, Eugene, Ore.; s. Lex A. and Margaret (Lee) M.; m. Christine Rasmussen, Nov. 7, 1975; children: Andrea b. 1976, Sara b. 1978, Stephen b. 1980, Megan b. 1983; edn: BS, Weber State Coll. 1974; desig: LUTCF, Life Underwriters Tng. Council (1986). Career: self-empl. sales, 1976-78; sales rep. for Allied Van Lines, 1978-80; ins. agt. Guardian Life, 1981, current: Bankers Life, San Diego; guest speaker National Univ.; honors: Intermountain Ski Instrs. Assn. cert. ski tchr. (1973), Premier Club Bankers Life (1982, 84, 85), Rookie of the Yr. (1982); mem. Nat. Assn. Life Underws., S.D. Assn. of Life Underws.; civic: Smithsonian Instn., LeTip of Pacific Beach (pres. 1983-84), LeTip of El Cajon (bd. 1985-86); Latter Day Saints Ch.; rec: active in Boy Scouts, church service, ski, leatherwork. Res: 1291 Whitsett Dr El Cajon 92020 Ofc: Bankers Life 1450 Frazee Rd Ste 515 San Diego 92108-1337

MALCOLM, MACKEY H., judge; b. July 20, 1929, Hoboken, N.J.; s. William Gasden and Winifred Walker (Hamilton) M.; m. Sharon Scovill, Sept. 1963 (div. 1980); children: Michael b. 1969, Kristie b. 1973; edn: AB, New York Univ. 1951; JD, Southwestern Univ. 1958; admitted Calif. State Bar 1959. Career: sales rep. Tidewater Oil Corp. 1951-54, Richfield Oil Corp. 1954-55; claims rep. Allstate Insurance Co. 1956-57; assoc. atty. Dalton, Groff & Dunne 1958-59; trial lawyer pvt. practice 1959-78; elected judge Los Angeles Municipal Ct. 1978-84, reelected 1984-1990; mem: Calif., L.A. County (trustee 1978-79) bar assns.; L.A. Co. Mun. Ct. Judges Assn. (treas. 1985-86); Lawyers Club of L.A. (past-pres.); Calif. Judges Assn.; Presiding Judges Assn. of L.A. Co.; Masons; Am. Fed. of Radio & TV Artists; publ: wrote Small Claims Procedural Manual for L.A. Mun. Ct.; mil: cpl. USMC 1946-84, Navy Good Conduct and Occupational medals; Democrat; Church of Religious Science. Ofc: 110 N Grand Ave Los Angeles 90012

MALDONADO, JUAN, insurance agency president; b. Dec. 17, 1942, Falfurrias, Tex.; s. Gilberto and Anita (Garza) M.; m. Maria M. Kennedy, Aug. 12, 1967; chldren: J. Eric b. 1969, Andrea Marie b. 1971, Aaron Gilbert b. 1975; edn: stu. Santa Ana Coll. 1966-71, Orange Coast Coll. 1969-70, profl. courses USC. Career: with Union Central Life Insurance Co. 1970—: agent, Santa Ana 1970, Orange Co. unit mgr. 1973, asst. mgr. Los Angeles agency 1975, mgr. of Orange Co. for UCL 1979, mgr. Spl. Mktg. Agency 1982—; pres. Juan Maldonado Insurance Assoc., Inc. 1984—; mem. Knights of the Round Table; mem. Golden Key Soc.; honors: Presidents Club (1973-), Leaders Circle (1982-), Inner Circle (1983-), Union Central Life Ins. Co.; mem: Orange Co. Life Underwriters Assn.; Million Dollar Round Table; Pres.'s Field Adv. Cabinet, Union Central Life; Orange Co. Latin Am. Businessmen Assn.; Baja Oso Homeowners Assn.; Viejo Little League Bowling League (pres.); mil: USMC 1961-65; Republican; Catholic; rec: racquetball, bowling, travel. Res: 26952 Marbella Mission Viejo 92691 Ofc: Juan Maldonado Insurance Associates, 1600 N Broadway, Ste 960, Santa Ana 92706

MALDONADO, ROBERTO, sales and marketing executive; b. Jan. 26, 1935, Madrid, Spain, nat. 1963; s. Andres and Meri (Bermejo) M.; m. Dolly Torres Figueroa, Aug. 18, 1956; children: Robert, b. 1959; Eric, b. 1963; edn: AA, Univ. of Madrid 1953; BS, physics, NY Univ. 1959; BS, math., 1959; MS, 1961. Career: dist. mgr. IBM, The Svc. Bureau Corp. 1959-70; v.p. mktg. System Develop. Corp. 1970-80; v.p. internat. mktg. Pertec Computer Corp. 1980-82; v.p. mktg. 1982-85; v.p. computer mktg. Tandon Corp. 1985—; dir. Bantam Computer Corp.; awards: 100 Percent Club of IBM 1967, 68, 69; mem: NY Univ. Foreign Student Dept. (Cultural chmn.); orgns: Cub Scout Master, P.V. (1966-69), Beconsfield, Quebec, Can. (1972-73); P.V.E. Men's Club; soccer coach, P.V. 1965-70, 1974-76; Republican; rec: exercise, golf. Res: Topanga Cyn Ofc: Tandon Corp. POB 2107 Chatsworth 91313-2107

MALI, DINESH BHAGWANJI, engineering executive; b. Jan. 9, 1946, Karachi, W. Pakistan, nat. US cit. 1981; s. Bhagwanji L. and Shantaben; m. Purnima, July 19, 1980; children: Sandip b. 1972, Sonal b. 1976, Ketan b. 1983, Milan b. 1986; edn: BSME, Univ. of Mo., 1969; MSME, Washington Univ., St. Louis, Mo. 1976; Reg. Profl. Engr. in Calif., Mo., Ill. Career: design engr. Bendy Eng., St. Louis, Mo. 1970-73; mech. designer Wm. Tao Assoc., 1973-74; mech. engr. Fruin-Colnon Corp., 1974-76; project engr. Allen & Garcia Co., Chgo. 1976-79; project engr. D.R. Warren Co., Los Angeles 1979; mgr./pres. Shanta Eng. Co., Cerritos 1979—; awards: curator grant-in-aid, Univ. of Mo. (1967-69), Pi Tau Sigma (1969); mem. mining assns. of Calif., Alaska, Colo., Utah; Hindu; rec: tennis, golf, travel. Ofc: Shanta Engineering Co. 11110-C Artesia Blvd Cerritos 90701

MALKOFF, DONALD BURTON, researcher in artificial intelligence; b. July 10, 1935, Pittsbutgh, Pa.; s. Louis and Shirley (Lippock) M.; m. Margaret Ellen Aldridge, June 16, 1980; edn: Harvard Univ. 1953-56; MD, Univ. Pittsburgh Sch. of Med. 1960; MS computer sci., UC San Diego 1983; certified Am. Bd. Psychiatry & Neurol. 1970; med. lic. Pa. 1961, Md. 1962, Ala. 1966, Fla. 1973, Calif. 1968. Career: research asst. Univ. Pittsburgh Sch. of Med. 1956-60, Marine Biol. Inst. Woodshole, Mass. 1958-59; intern neurol. Univ. Mich. 1960-61, resident 1963-66; research NIH Nat. Heart Inst. gerontol. branch Baltimore 1961-63; pvt. practice neurol. Birmingham, Ala. 1966-68, San Marino, Calif. 1968-69, Bethlehem, Pa. 1969-73, Ft. Meyers, Fla. 1973-78; computer programmer Navy Personnel Research & Devel. Ctr. San Diego 1981, research psychol. 1982, cons. Ofc. Scientific Advancement & Command & Support Systems 1982-83, computer sys. analyst 1983—; instr. clin. neurol. Univ. Ala. Hosp. Birmingham 1967-68; tchg. asst. Univ. Mich. Med. Sch. 1964, elec. engrg., computer sci. UC San Diego 1981-83; rep. stroke task force Greater Del. Valley Regl. Med. Pgm. Pa. 1972; bd. dirs. Lee County Mental Health Guidance Ctr. Ft. Meyers, Fla. 1975-78; pres. Lodos Oil Corp. London, Paris, Hamburg 1979-80; honors: sustained Superior Performance (Navy Personnel R&D Ctr. 1984), Outstanding Performance (1984), Alpha Omega Alpha, Pauline W. Albert Meml. Award; mem: Am. Assn. Artificial Intelligence, Soc. Neuroscience, Computer Applications in Neurol. Am. Med. Electro- Encephalographic Assocs., Am. Acad. Neurol., Am. Assn. Med. Sys. and Informatics, Assn. Computing Machinery, Am. Soc. Naval Engrs., Harvard Club of San Diego, IEEE, Internat. Test & Evaluation Assn.; publs: num. articles in profl., med. jours., num. presentations at univs., profl. assns. and confs.; mil: USPHS 1961-63, reserves 1963-80; rec: photog. Res: 10960 Worthing Ave San Diego 92126 Ofc: Naval Personnel Research & Devel. Ctr. Code 41 San Diego 92152-6800

MALLINGER, MICHAEL J., marketing/ sales executive; b. Nov. 14, 1940, Fort Didge, Iowa; s. Thomas Michael and Eloise Catherine (Bendit) M.; m. Jenik Esrailian, Feb. 10, 1973; children: Michelle b. 1975, Gregory b. 1977; edn: BSEE, Iowa State Univ. 1966; MBA, Santa Clara Univ. 1968. Career:

senior engr. Fairchild Semi Mtn. View 1966-69; dir. mktg. Communications Transistor Corp. San Carlos 1969-78; founder, v.p. mktg. Acrian Inc. San Jose 1978—; mem: Am. Mgmt. Assn., IEEE; publ: articles in trade jours. 1974-; mil: lt. Iowa Air Guard 1959-66. Res: 13039 Ten Oak Way Saratoga 95070 Ofc: Acrian 490 Race St San Jose 95126

MALMSTROM, DOROTHY ELVIRA, financial corporation executive; b. April 4, 1945, Guatemala City, Guatemala; d. Carl Olof and Esther (Butler) Malmstrom; edn: AA, Chaffey Coll. 1966; BA in sociol., honors, UC Riverside 1969; MA in social sci., honors, Azusa Pacific Coll. 1980; PhD in progress, US Internat. Univ. 1983-. Career: resrch. sociologist UC Riverside, 1969-70; adminstrv. coordinator Yamaha of Indio (Calif.), 1971-73; mktg. exec. Good Stuff Natural Bakery, Los Angeles 1974-81; founder/pres. Health Network Inst., Santa Monica 1981-82; internat. finance exec./co-founder Advance Financial Services Inc., Santa Monica 1982—; mem: AAAS, The Am. Orthopsychiatric Assn., The Assn. for Women in Sci., Ocean Park Comm. Center (Santa Monica); rec: music, dance, art, beach jogging. Res: 2727 Sixth St, 301, Santa Monica 90405 Ofc: Advance Financial Services Inc. 2210 Wilshire Blvd, Ste 247, Santa Monica 90403

MALOOLY, BARBARA ELLEN, real estate co. executive; b. Jan. 26, 1940, Ackley, Iowa; d. Wilke J. and Dorothy Geraldine (Wagner) Eilders; m. Richard Malooly, 1957, div.; children: Cynthia b. 1959, Carol b. 1960, William b. 1962, Richard b. 1966; edn: stu. Mt. San Antonio Coll. 1971-76, real estate courses 1974; certs: exchange, Nat. Inst. of Exchange (1978), condo. devel., Calif. Assn. of Realtors (1982). Career: waitress, mgr. Diamond Bar (Calif.) Country Club, 1963-71; real estate sales Diamond Bar Realty 1971-72, Red Carpet Realty, Diamond Bar 1972-74; owner/broker Gallery of Homes, Diamond Bar 1974; pres. Malooly Realty Inc., 1977; trainer/tchr. real estate for So. Calif. Regional Gallery of Homes, 1977-78; honors: Top listing and sales award (1971), Top sales and listing, and Top overall award (1974), So. Calif. Regl. Red Carpet; mem. Hacienda Bd. Realtors (chair Polit., Legislative & Local Govt. Affairs 1980-81), No. Orange Co. Bd. Realtors, West San Bernardino Co. Bd. Realtors; civic: Walnut Valley CofC (1975-), Diamond Bar Womens Club (1977), Am. Bus. Womens Assn.; Presbyterian; rec: sailing, golf, fishing, ceramics. Res: 870 Golden Prados Diamond Bar 91765 Ofc: Gallery of Homes 574 N Diamond Bar Blvd Diamond Bar 91765

MALQUIST, GRANT LOUIS, insurance underwriter; b. Nov. 6, 1923, Salt Lake City; s. Grant Leonard and Grace Kelly (Sims) M.; m. Alice Niven, Dec. 30, 1950; children: Carolyn b. 1958, Kenneth b. 1962; edn: BA, Coll. of Pacific 1944; grad. work Univ. of Mo. 1945, Univ. Calif. 1946, Hastings Law Sch. 1947. Career: field underw./ registered rep./ mentor agent TAI: New York Life Ins. Co., 1946—, New York Life Securities Corp., 1984—; honors: Top of the Table (1985), Qualifying and Life mem. Million Dollar Round Table (28 yrs.), Nat. Quality Award winner (30 yrs.), Chairman's Council NYLIC (charter, current), San Francisco office NYLIC Agent of Year (1984) and Leading Producer (1985); mem. S.F. Estate Planning Council, Leading Life Producers of No. Calif.; active Boy Scouts Am., 25 + yrs. (cubmaster, scoutmaster Troop 215 1975-79); mil: lt. jg US Navy 1942-46; Republican; Ch. of Jesus Christ of Latter Day Saints (High Priest Quorum, exec. secty. Menlo Park); rec: waterskiing, surfing, tennis, photog. Res: 1060 Lemon St Menlo Park 94025 Ofc: New York Life 100 Pine St Ste 2900 San Francisco 94111

MAN, DEBRA CHING, environmental engineer; b. June 14, 1953, Honolulu; d. Robert Quon Kin and Constance Mew Oi (Chang) Ching; m. Guy Kee Man, Dec. 15, 1979; edn: BSCE honors (1st in class), Univ. Hawaii 1976; MS environmental engrg., Stanford Univ. 1977; Reg. Profl. Civil Engr. Calif. 1980, Hawaii 1981. Career: environmental engr. Pacific Div. Naval Facilities Engrg. Command Pearl Harbor, Hawaii 1977-80; proj. mgr. Space Div. Los Angeles AFB 1980-81; proj. environmtl. engr. Kennedy/ Jenks Engrs. Irvine 1981-83; proj. mgr., engr. CH2M Hill Inc. Newport Beach 1983-86; senior engr. Metropolitan Water District of So. Calif. (state water project) L.A. 1986—; honors: Phi Kappa Phi, Chi Epsilon, Outstanding Senior Engrg. Student Award (ASCE 1975-76), Superior Achievement (cmdr. Naval Facilities Engrg. Command 1979); mem: Am. Water Works Assn., Water Pollution Control Fedn., Soc. Women Engrs., Orange County Water Assn., So. Calif. Utilities Assn., Orange Co. Indsl. League; rec: reading, hiking, tennis. Res: 5331 Bridgewood Dr La Palma 90623 Ofc: Metropolitan Water District of So. Calif. 1111 Sunset Blvd Los Angeles 90054

MAN, GUY KEE, engineer; b. May 27, 1951, Hong Kong, nat. US cit. 1985; s. Hon-Kwong and Sau-Ching (Luk) M.; m. Debra Ching, Dec. 15, 1979; edn: BS, honors, Univ. of Redlands 1974; BS, Stanford Univ. 1975; Engr., 1978; PhD, 1979; Reg. Profl. Engr. (mech.), Calif. Career: tchg. asst. Dept. of Mech. Eng. Stanford Univ. 1975-78; senior engr. Jet Propulsion Lab Guidance & Control Sect., Caltech Pasadena 1979-81, tech. gp. leader Control Analysis Group, 1981-83; tech. gp. supv. Galileo Guidance and Control System Analysis Gp. 1983—; cons. in Dynamics, Controls and Seismic Analysis 1982-84; mem: Am. Soc. of Mech. Engrs.; Calif. Soc. of Profl. Engrs.; Nat. Soc. of Profl. Engrs.; Sigma Xi; publs: arts. in var. tech. journs.; rec: painting, hiking, photog. Res: 5331 Brisgewood Dr La Palma 90623 Ofc: Jet Propulsion Lab, Caltech, 4800 Oak Grove Dr Pasadena 91109

MANAHAN, MANNY CELESTINO, accountant; b. Apr. 6, San Miguel, Bulacan, Philippines; edn: BBA acctg., Univ. of the East, Manila, Phil. 1963; MBA mgmt., Golden Gate Univ. 1968, contg. edn. MBA (tax) 1984; CPA Calif. 1983. Career: loan counselor Lomas & Nettleton Co. S.F. 1967-68; acctg./ ofc. mgr. Henry Irving & Assocs. S.F. 1968-73; owner Manny Celestino Manahan

CPA firm 1973—; p-t instr. acctg. S.F. Comm. Coll. Dist. 1974-78; honors: Disting. Svc. (Golden Gate Univ. 1983), Outstanding CPA in Comm. Svc. & ist Quarter Award (PICPA 1983), Man of the Year (Men's Club of St. Anne's of the Sunset S.F. 1982), Presidential Awardee (Phil. Inst. CPAs 1982); mem: Am. Inst. CPAs, Calif. Soc. CPAs, Am. Acctg. Assn., Calif. Soc. Enrolled Agents, East Bay S.F. Assn. Enrolled Agents (bd. 1983-84, chmn. finance, buget & audit 1983-84), Filipino Accts. Assn. of Calif. (pres. 1974-75), Financial Planning Profl. Practices Adv. Panel, Nat. Assn. Enrolled Agents, Nat. Assn. Self Employed, Nat. Assn. Small Bus., NAt. Soc. Public Accts. (awards com. 1983-84), Soc. Calif. Accts., Phil. Inst. CPAs (sustaining life mem., nat. dir. 1984, chmn. profl. devel. com. 1983, accred. com. 1982, co-chmn. 1984 conv.), Golden Gate Univ. Alumni Assn. (council 1976-, chmn. devel. com. 1982-, pres. 1980-82, v.p. 1978-80, treas. 1977-78), Fil-Am Soc. St. Anne's (bd. 1976-, pres. 1981), Men's Club St. Anne's (treas.), Golden Gate Univ. Assocs., Am. Biographical Inst. (bd. advisors), ABI Research Assn., Citizen's Choice, Repub. Presdl. Task Force, US Republican Senatorial Club; Catholic; rec: bowling, dancing, outing, swimming, travel. Address: 2020 Judah St San Francisco 94122-1531

MANAVIAN, YERVANT, computer services executive; b. July 8, 1957, Benghazi, Lybia, nat. US cit. 1963; s. George M. and Flora (Alagiagian) M.; edn: BS acctg., bus. adminstrn., Univ. So. Calif. 1979; CPA, Calif. 1983. Career: staff acct. Price Waterhouse & Co. L.A. 1979-80; senior auditor AVCO Corp. Newport Beach 1980-82, supv. mgmt. audit 1982-84; mgr. internal audit Automatic Data Processing San Dimas 1984, exec. in tng. (funds mgmt.) 1984-85, dir. cash ops., funds mgmt. 1985—; mem: Am. Inst. CPAs 1983-, Acctg. Soc. USC 1979-, Inst. Internal Auditors 1984-, Laguna Village Homeowners (treas.), Jr. Achievement, Century II Pledge Drive USC; Republican; Catholic; rec: sports, creative writing, history, art, music. Res: 22307 Caminito Arroyo Seco Laguna Hills 92653 Ofc: Automatic Data Processing 502 Covina Blvd San Dimas

MANDEL, BENJAMIN JORGE, dentist; b. May 13, 1944, Mexico City; nat. 1975; s. Mauricio and Victoria (Eskenazi) M.; m. Olga Sherr, Dec. 27, 1970; children: Joshua b. 1980, Jonathan b. 1983; edn: BS, chem., UC Berkeley 1966; MS, chem., Polytech. Inst., Mexico 1969; postgrad. biochemistry advanced studies, Univ. of Wisc. 1970-71; DDS, NY Univ. 1975. Career: research assoc. Univ. of Wisc. 1970-72; gen. practice resident VA Hosp., Martinez, Ca. 1975-76; pvt. practice dentistry, Santa Clara 1976—; cons. Mission Convalescent Home, 1976-77; fmr. cons. Child Health & Disability Prevention Pgm.; KRON Health Fair volunteer 1980, 81; founder, chmn. Santa Clara Co. Periodontology Study Club; lectr. on T.M.J. disorders and relationship to headache, back and neck pain, (Hawaii, and internat.) 1982; guest spkr. TV show People and Progress 1/85 and 5/85; elected mem. Calif. Dental Bd. of Examiners; listed Who's Who in the West (1985); mem: Santa Clara Dental Soc. 1975- (hosp. com. 1977, dental health com. 1982); Western Soc. of Peridontol. (bd. dirs. Santa Clara Co. Orthopedic Study Club); Am. Soc. of Clin. Hypnosis; Am. Dental Assn.; Calif. Dental Assn. (table clinic presentation 1983 Anaheim meeting); Hispanic Amer. Dental Assn.; Amer. Acad. of Periodontology (assoc.); Alpha Omega frat. publs: art., Australian J. of Chem. 1970; presentation Calif. Dental Assn. mtg. in S.F. 1984; resrch. in pain control 1971-2; rec: cello player, opera, ballet, painting. Ofc: Ben Mandel, DDS, Inc. 74 Harold Ave San Jose 95117-1080

MANDEL, MAURICE, II, lawyer; b. Hollywood, Calif.; s. Maurice and Wynne Mandel; edn: BS, Univ. So. Calif. 1971, MS Ed., 1972; JD, Western State Univ. 1979; lifetime cred. tchr. Calif. Career: elementary sch. tchr. Orange Co. 1972-82; lawyer pvt. practice Irvine 1982—; honors: Honored Senior (USC); mem: Am., Calif., Orange Co., Federal bar assns.; Am. Trial Lawyers Assn., Women Lawyers, USC Alumni, Mensa; rec: sailing, skiing. Res: POB 411 Balboa Island 92662 Ofc: 359 San Miguel Dr Ste 301 Newport Beach 92660

MANDERS, ROBERT HAROLD, system development executive; b. Mar. 12, 1941, Evansville, Ind.; s. Harold Carl and Marabel (Cross) M.; m. Beverley Ware, Nov. 29, 1963; children: Michael b. 1969, Mathew b. 1972; edn: BS aerospace engrg., Iowa State Univ. 1963. Career: lead engr. Douglas Aircraft Co. 1963-65; NASA task mgr. Space Technol. Lab. 1965-68; section head TRW Systems Group 1968-72, work package mgr. site defense pgm. 1972-75, proj. mgr. 1975-77, proj. mgr. TDRSS 1977-85, deputy pgm. mgr. I-S/A AMPE Pgm. 1985—; honors: NASA Apollo Achievement Award (1969), Apollo Flight Safety Award Silver Snoopy (1969), Apollo XVII Achievement Award (1972), NASA TDRSS Commdn. (1983); mem. Pi Kappa Alpha; TDRSS Control Network, Internat. Tlemetering Conf. 1981; Republican; Episcopal; rec: distance running, oil painting, bridge. Res: 22816 Pepper Tree Pl Torrance 90501 Ofc: TRW One Space Park Redondo Beach 90278

MANER, ETHRIDGE LESTER, realtor/ business owner; b. Sept. 24, 1932, Knoxville, Tenn.; s. Ethridge Lee and Katherine Elizabeth (Webb) M.; m. Emily Caraway, July 3, 1954; children: Lisa Ann b. 1962, Mark Lester b. 1964; edn: BS, Univ. of Tenn. 1959; Adv. Mgmt., Ohio State 1970. Career: v.p. Curlee Clothing Co., St. Louis, Mo. 1960-72; Mono Co. Bd. Supvrs., Mono Co. 1980-82; chmn. 1981-82; owner Mono County Realty, Mammoth Lakes 1972—; co- owner High Sierra Travel Svc., Bishop and Mammoth Lakes 1982—; Tch. Adv. Com., Apparel Industry; apparel indus. cons. Adv. Com. to Devel. Sports Interest in The Nat. Forests of Calif.; awards: Awd. of Spl. Merit in recgn. of faithful svc. and contbns., Am. Apparel Mfrs. Assn. 1974; Pres.'s Awd., Mammoth Lakes CofC; recipient commendations, Calif. Senate Rules Com. and Calif. Ofc. of Emergency Svcs., 1983; Resolution, Calif. State Assembly

1983; mem: Rural Counties Supvrs. Assn. of Calif. Co. Supvrs. Assn. of Calif.; Mammoth Lakes Lions Club (pres. 1979-80); Mammoth Lakes CofC (pres. 1978-79); Elks; Jaycees; works: Nat. Adv. Com. to Develop Metric Standards for USA and Canada; mil: USAF 1951-55 (incl. 25 combat missions in B-29 over Korea), Air Medal w/ Oak Leaf Cluster, Korean Svc., Nat. Defense, UN Svc.; Republican; Episcopal; golf, aviation, skiing. Res: 280025 Grindelwald S Mammoth Lakes 93546 Ofc: High Sierra Travel, 621 West Line St Bishop 93514

MANGANO, ROBERT J., executive consultant; b. May 1, 1945, N.Y.C.; s. Constantino Louis and Adele (Dergentis) M.; div.; children: Robert b. 1973, Kelly Michelle b. 1974; edn: BS, N.Y. Inst. Technol. 1967; Pace Coll. Career: v.p. A.P.W.U., Novato; pub. relations cons., exec. cons.: 1001 Home Ideas Mag., Le Monde d'Amour, Love and Desire, Inc., Disco Inferno (current) Camarro Ents.; civic: Roman Am. Soc. (v.p.), Sons of Italy, Am. Legion, Francis Lewis Civic Assn., Dixie-Terra Linda Little League, Cub Scouts; mil: sp5 US Army 1968-70; Democrat; Catholic; rec: baseball, basketball, racquetball, flying. Res: 1610 Merritt Dr Novato 94947 Ofc: Camarro Enterprises Box 923 Novato 94947

MANGER, CHARLES CHRISTIAN, III, physician- ophthalmologist; b. Jan. 16, 1944, Mare Island; s. Charles C. and Helen Frances (Alexander) M.; m. Carol Granone, June 4, 1977; edn: BS, USN Acad., Annapolis 1965; premed., Harvard Univ. 1971; MD, USC 1976; internal med. intern, LAC/ USC Med. Ctr. 1976-77, ophthalmology resident, 1977-80. Career: fully qualified in submarines/ electrical and reactor ofcr. Nuclear Submarine Force 1965-70; Ballistic Missile Submarine USS Nathan Hale, 3 yrs.; researcher in Hypertension Lab., NYU Med. Ctr 1971-72; pvt. practice ophthalmology, Laguna Hills 1980−; clin. instr. ophthalmology USC; advy. council Nat. Hypertension Assn.; med. staff: Western Medical Center, Tustin; Saddleback Community Hosp., Laguna Hills; Mission Community Hosp., Mission Viejo; honors: Student Body Pres., USC Sch. of Med. 1973-74; Diplomate, Am. Bd. Ophthalmology 1981; mem: Orange Co. Med. Assn., Orange Co. Soc. of Ophthalm- ology, Am. and Calif. Med. Assns., Am. Acad. of Ophthalmology; publs: hypertension research (3), clin. ophthalmology research (1); mil: lt. USN 196570, Polaris Patrol Medal; Republican; Catholic; rec: golf, swimming, tropical and saltwater aquariums. Res: 13 South Peak Laguna Niguel 92677 Ofc: C.C. Manger III MD Inc., 23561 Paseo de Valencia Ste. 46 Laguna Hills 92653

MANGUM, DANNY LEE, quality assurance and engineering chief; b. July 26, 1933, Salt Lake City, Utah; s. Cleddy Merrill and Lillian Beatrice (Schell) M.; m. Jacqueline Louise Cordle, Mar. 4, 1955; children: David, b. 1956; Sandra, b. 1957; Angela, b. 1959; Leslie, b. 1962; Teresa, b. 1964; edn: AA, Allan Hancock Coll. 1976. Career: field insp.: Convair Astronautics Div. Gen. Dynamics Corp., Palmdale 1957-60, Fairchild AFB, Wash. 1960-61, RCA Svc. Co., Beale AFB, Calif. 1961-62, Martin Marietta Corp., Vandenberg AFB 1962-64, Rocketdyne, Div. NAA Rocket Site, Edwards AFB 1964-66; with Martin Marietta Corp., Vandenberg AFB 1966−; insp. field site 1966-69, engr./ sr. engr. quality field 1977-81, lead Quality Assurance & Engring., 1981−, (aerospace pgms. involved with: Titan 34D, Peacekeeper, Titan III, Apollo, Gemini, Titan II, Titan I, Atlas E, F-106, & F-102); honors: Annual Awds., Operational Performance, Martin Marietta Corp., Denver, Colo. 1983; Gold Medallion Awd., Martin Marietta 1976, 83; Engr. of the Yr., Air Force Assn., Robert H. Goddard chpt. 1982; Director's Award, Martin Marrietta 1985; life mem., Alpha Gamma Sigma, Aquarius chpt., Allan Hancock Coll. 1976; mem: Martin Marietta Mgmt. Club; Nat. Mgmt. Assn.; Youth Football League, Lompoc (Ways & Means chmn. 1970); Youth Softball League (mgr./ coach 1967-77); mil: sgt. US Army 1951-54, Combat Inf. Badge, UN Svc., Korean Svc. w/ Bronze Star, Nat. Def. Svc.; Republican; Protestant; rec: home computer, camping, fishing. Res: 209 North W St Lompoc 93436 Ofc: Martin Marietta Corp., POB 1681, Vandenberg AFB 93437

MANION, MARTHA LISA, librarian, bibliographer; b. Feb. 2, 1949, San Francisco; d. Roy R. and Maxine F. (LeDoux) M.; m. Ronald Allen Powell, Feb. 8, 1975; edn: BA, cum laude, San Jose State Univ. 1971, MA, 1974; MLS, UC Berkeley 1976. Career: cert. tchr., Calif. Research asst., Univ.-Wide Library Automation Project, Berkeley 1976; reference librarian Santa Clara Co. Library, Sunnyvale 1977; asst. librarian Sci. and Eng. Library, San Jose State Univ. 1977-80; librarian Mt. View Research Ctr., Stauffer Chemical Co. 1980−; mem: Spl. Libraries Assn.; San Francisco Bay Area Online User's Group; Pi Lambda Theta; Beta Phi Mu; Kappa Delta Pi; author: Writings about Henry Cowell: An Annotated Bibliography, 1982. Ofc: Mt View Research Ctr., Stauffer Chem. Co., 1195 W. Fremont Ave., Sunnyvale 94087

MANLEY, PATRICIA ANN, telecommunications consultant; b. July 30, 1939, Los Angeles; d. Herbert Allen and Eva Phyllis (Neiburger) M.; 1 dau. Jennifer Christie Arriola, b. 1973; edn: undergrad. Valley Coll., LACC; BS, UC Los Angeles 1962; Reg. Nurse. Career: paralegal and law office mgr. Rowen & Schweitzer, Louis S. Edelberg 1972-78; indep. cons. in telecommunications nat., 1966−; co-owner Earline Reeves & Assocs., Palmdale 1978−; mem. Am. Heart Assn.; rec: sign language, hypnosis, youth wk. Address: 38722 Yucca Tree Palmdale 93551

MANN, JAMES RICHARD, communications co. president, ret.; b. Sept. 20, 1926, Covington, Ky.; s. Walter Richard and Viola Elizabeth (O'Brien) M.; m. Loraine Bens, Feb. 5, 1949; children: James b. 1949, Michael b. 1951, Christine b. 1953, Terrence b. 1955, Donna b. 1958, Lynn b. 1960, Patrick b. 1962, Mary b. 1964; edn: NY Tech. Inst. 1946-48. Career: v.p. sales & promo. NY Tech Inst. 1948-53; mktg. mgr. telecomm. div. RCA 1953-62; mgr. commun. div.

Fairchild Camera & Instrument 1962-63; pres. Mann C&E Inc., pres. Intrastate Radio Telephone Inc. of L.A. 1963−; dir., chmn. bd. IRT of L.A. and Mann C&E Inc. 1963-86, ret.; investment mgmt. currently; honors: Mem. and Fellowship award, Radio Club of Am.; Kentucky Colonel, Admirals Club (1960), Ambassador Club (1962), United Airline 100,000 Mile Club (1962); mem: Hollywood Park, Del Mar, and Oak Tree Turf Clubs, Turf Club, Calif. Thoroughbred Breeders Assn. of L.A., Jockey Club, Radio Club of Am.; works: Mexicana A.C. Pioneer in one-way paging field, first units in 1952; mil: cpl. US Army 1944-46; Republican; rec: breeding and racing Thoroughbreds, golf, investments. Res: 5882 E. Sunnyvist Ave. Agoura 91301

MANN, MAURICE, investment banker; b. Feb. 22, 1929, Peabody, Mass.; s. Abram S. and Jennie (Goldberg) M.; m. Betty M. Melnick, Sept. 6, 1953; children: Deborah Ellen b. 1955, Pamela Sue b. 1957; edn: BA, Northeastern Univ. 1951; MA, Boston Univ. 1952; PhD, Syracuse Univ. 1955; LLD, Northeastern Univ. 1977. Career: tchg. and govt. svc. 1955-60; v.p./gen. economist Federal Reserve Bank of Cleveland 1960-69; asst. dir. Office of Mgmt. & Budget, Wash DC 1969-70; exec. v.p. Equibank, Pittsburgh, Pa. 1970-72; pres. Federal Home Loan Bank of San Francisco 1973-78; v. chmn. Becker Paribas Inc., S.F. 1978-84; pres./v.chmn. Merrill Lynch Capital Markets, S.F. 1984 ; dir. Blackman, Garlock Flynn & Co. Inc.; chmn. Advis. Com. Freddie Mac; chmn. Policy Advis. Bd., Ctr. for Real Estate & Urban Economics, UCB; mem. Bankers Advis. Council - Am. Gas Assn.; honors: Hon. Degree and Alumni citation Northeastern Univ., Chancellor's medal for disting. achievement in banking Syracuse Univ., Academy of Disting. Grad. Sch. Alumni- Boston Univ.; mem: Am. Econ. Assn., Am. Fin. Assn., Nat. Assn. of Bus. Economists; clubs: Bankers (SF), Concordia-Argonaut, Commonwealth, Nat. Alumni Council of Northeastern Univ., Lambda Alpha frat.; Republican; Jewish; rec: tennis. Res: 3255 Jackson St San Francisco 94118 Ofc: Merrill Lynch Capital Markets 101 California St Ste 1140 San Francisco 94111

MANN, SANTA SINGH, corporate executive; b. June 28, 1933, Ganga Nagar, Rajputana, India, nat. US cit. 1968; s. Sardar Dalip Singh and Katar Kaur (Sahota) M.; m. Balbir Kaur Sandhu, July 1951; children: Sohan b. 1952, Mohan b. 1954, Babu Weryam b. 1964, Sahib Bhagwan b. 1967, Prem Eileen b. 1969; edn: BA, BS, Rajputana Univ. 1954; BSEE, Univ. Ariz.; MS, MS PhD, MBA, LLB equiv. var. univs. in US 1955-65. Career: mgr. Transdata Inc. San Diego; senior staff engr. Hoffman Elec. Corp. L.A.; exec. v.p. Electro technol. Inc S.D.; CEO, chmn. var. corps.; cons. num. corps.; owner 25,000 acre subdivision in Lassen County; real estate investor; mem: Am. Mgmt. Assn., var. bus. realtors, tax cons., ins. orgns.; pres., chmn. Sikh Temple, Nat./ Internat. World Sikh Orgn.; proposed 4-way clock tower of golden tower (Sikh) in San Jose; author book (1985); Republican; Sikh; rec: reading, writing. Ofc: 2103 S King Rd San Jose 95122

MANNING, DIANE LOIS, winery owner-administrator; b. Dec. 21, 1940, Bklyn.; d. Wm. and Louise Margaret (Backer) Pfuhl; m. Thomas F. Manning, Apr. 9, 1960; children: Craig b. 1961, Scott b. 1964, Dawn b. 1965, Corey b. 1969; edn: bus. major Hofstra Coll. 2 yrs. Career: owner, pres., adminstr. Chateau Diana, Healdsburg 1978−; pres. Manning & Assocs. (wine imports); bd. chmn. Grapevine Express (freight co. servicing wineries); awards: Gold Medal (1984) for Napa Valley Chardonnay, Silver Medal (1965) Port; mem. Sonoma County Wine Growers Assn., Calif. Wine Growers Assn., Dry Creek Valley Assn., local Chambers of Commerce; past pres. PTA; Republican; Catholic; rec: golf, tennis, jog. Ofc: Chateau Diana 6195 Dry Creek Rd (POB 1013) Healdsburg 95448

MANNING, HAROLD WESLEY, accountant; b. May 9, 1952, Tacoma, Wash.; s. William Wesley, Jr. and Frances Ella (Schenk) M.; edn: BA bus. adminstrn., Univ. Wash. Seattle 1974; CPA, Wash. 1976, Calif. 1983. Career: senior acct. Deloitte Haskins & Sells Seattle 1974-78; audit supv. Sharp, Taylor, Hughes & Woodring Tacoma, Wash. 1978-80; audit mgr. Peterson, Sullivan & Co. Seattle 1980-82; ptnr. Killeen & Manning Ridgecrest, Calif. 1982-83; br. mgr. Burkey & Cox Accountancy Corp. Lancaster 1983−; p-t instr. Cerro Coso Comm. Coll., advis. council; financial advisor Maturango Mus., endowment fund com.; organized Ridgecrest's first Networking Party; sch. bd. Fife H.S. Wash.; honors: Delta Chi, Scholarship for Highest GPA (1971); apptd. (by Gov. Deukmejian) to Desert Empire Fair Bd. 1986; mem: Wash. Soc. CPAs, Calif. Soc. CPAs, Am. Inst. CPAs, Exchange Club of Ridgecrest, Lions Club (past pres.); Republican; Lutheran; rec: antique cars, theatre and dance, sailing. Res: POB 2025 Ridgecrest 93555 Ofc: Burkey & Cox Accountancy Corp. 1240 S China Lake Blvd Ridgecrest 93555

MANNING, MICHAEL M., certified public accountant; b. Nov. 23, 1939, Los Angeles; s. Earl Francis and Isabel Mary (Hanley) M.; father, Capt. Earl F. Manning, US Merch. Marine, WWII (veteran of 2 sinkings, 19 days and 1200 mi. in lifeboat to safety); m. Phyllis M.H. Underwood, 1963; children: Phyllis E., b. 1964; Helen, b. 1965; twins, Patrick and Michael G., b. 1969; edn: BS, Golden Gate Univ. 1961-64; CPA, 1971; FAA Cert. comml. pilot Instrument Rating (Land & Sea). Career: pub. acct., staff acct. 1960-64; res. auditor in charge States Steamship Co., Maritime Admin., Dept. of Commerce 1965-70; principal, pub. acctg. firm Michael M. Manning, CPA 1971-80; partner, pub. acctg. firm. Manning & Carroll, CPAs 1980−; dir. of Nat. Real Estate Fund ($20,000,000 R.E. Investment Trust); mem: Fed. Govt. Acct. Assn., Am. Inst. of CPAS; Soc. of Calif. Accts. (No. Bay pres. 1976-77, pres. elec. 1975-76); Calif. Soc. of CPAs, S.F.; Marin Estate Plng. Council; Rotary, Mill Valley (pres. 1985-86); Elks, San Rafael; Native Sons of the Golden West; mil: SK3 USNR 1957-65; Republican; Catholic; rec: music (active in var. Dixieland & big bands), flying, jogging. Address: Manning & Carroll, CPAs, 169 Miller Ave Mill Valley 94941

MANNING, OWEN JOHN, govt. postal service executive; b. Oct. 12, 1942, Pittsburgh, Pa.; s. Richard Coleman and Nellie (Conroy) M.; edn: stu. Washburn Univ. 1961-63, Univ. of Md. (USAFE) 1964-66, Victor Valley Coll., Victorville 1968; AA, Skadron Coll., San Bernardino 1975. Career: mailhandler, distbn. clk. USPS, San Bernardino 1968-71, postal source data techn. 1971-73, acctg. techn. 1973-74, cost ascertainment splst. 1974, postal systems splst. 1974-76, supvr. Mails, 1976-78; gen. supvr. Mails, San Diego 1978-80; supt. National City 1980; postmaster Trona, Calif. 1980-81, ops. mgr. in Phoenix, Az. 1981-83, mgr. Distbn. (EAS-20), Stockton, Calif. Mgmt. Sectional Ctr., 1984—; instr. var. Postal Svc. Employee Mgmt. Workshops; num. profl. awards include: recogn. for unusual achievement (25 suggestions) Postal Suggestion Pgm. (1970), Key to City of San Bernardino for Credit Union wk. (1975), recogn. awards (2) as Postal Ops. mgr., Phoenix (1982), Vietnam Veteran Award for devel. USPS Pgm. to recognize Ariz. Postal Vietnam Vets. (1982), 2 EEO awards, Stockton P.O. (1984, 85); civic: Hesperia Mobile Home Owners' Assn. (pres. 1970, 72), Skadron Coll. Alumni (v.p. 1972), Nat. Assn. Postal Supvrs./San Brdo (v.p. 1974-75), Postal Credit Union of San Brdo (secty. 1970, treas. mgr. 1971-75); publs: Facility Activation Handbook for Phoenix, Az. gen. mail facility (1983); mil: s/sgt. USAF 1960-68, SAC ednl. achieve. award Forbes AFB, Kans. (1965), USAF Europe ednl. achieve. award, Ankara, Turkey (1965); rec: philately. Res: 8114 Grenoble Way Stockton 95210 Ofc: U.S.Postal Service 3131 Arch Rd Stockton 95213-9701

MANNING, RAY TUCKER, JR., vocational counselor; b. Oct. 14, 1942, Santa Rosa; s. Ray Tucker Sr. and Alice Lotsi (Thomas) M.; m. Connie, April 30, 1976; children: Michael b. 1967, Noal Shewcraft (step) b. 1970, Jasen b. 1974, Stephanie b. 1978; edn: BA, Calif. State Coll. Bakersfield 1972, MS, 1978. Career: data entry, programming Standard Oil Co. 1967-71; cons. group therapy Calif. Correctional Inst., Tehachapi 1972-75; dir., clinician Bakersfield Communty Mental Health 1975-76; biofeedback technician self-empl. 1975-80; consultation, edn. cons. Henrietta Weill Child Guidance Clinic 1980-82; owner, dir. Manning Rehabilitation Svcs., Bakersfield 1982—; vocational expert, Social Security Admin. 1984; mem: Nat. Rehabilitation Assn., Nat. Rehabilitation Counseling Assn., Kern Co. Bar (Family Law Subcom. 1980-), Booster; works: The Myth of Drea Interpretation, WPA 1972; mil: E-5 USN 1961-65, GCM, Expeditionary Forces, Vietnam Svc.; Repubilcan; Protestant; rec: flying, tennis. Ofc: Manning Rehabilitation Services, 1601 H St. Ste. 4 Bakersfield 93301

MANNING, TIMOTHY CARDINAL, archbishop; b. Oct. 15, 1909, Cork, Ireland, ant. 1945; s. Cornelius and Margaret (Cronin) M.; edn: stu., St. Patrick's Sem., Menlo Park 1928-34; DCL, Gregorian Univ. 1938; Ordained priest, Roman Catholic Ch. 1934. Career: asst. pastor Immaculate Conception Ch., Los Angeles 1934-35; consecrated bishop 1946; aux. bishop and chancellor Roman Cath. Archdiocese of Los Angeles 1946—; 1st bishop of Fresno 1967-69; titular bishop of Capri 1969-70; arch bishop of Los Angeles 1969—; cardinal, 1973. Address: 1531 W. 9th St., Los Angeles 90015

MANNINO, ANTHONY VINCENT, executive; b. June 11, 1917, Brooklyn, NY; s. Mateo and Jennie (Mannino) M.; m. Rose, June 22, 1946; children: Maryam b. 1947, Joanne b. 1950, Matthew b. 1951; edn: BS, Univ. of Arkansas 1940; Manhatten Coll. 1936; Louisiana State UNiv. 1939. Career: owner M&M Electronics, Morristown, NJ 1947-62; owner Anthony's Stereo, Daytona Beach, Fla. 1962-63; owner Antonio's Restaurant, Daytona Beach, Fla. 1962-63; owner Beatles for Him & Her, Daytona Beach, Fla. 1962-63; currently, owner M&M Electronics, San Francisco; co. dir. M&M Electronics 1963-; recipient profl. awards in electronics; mem: Lions Club (pres., deputy dist. gov.), All Souls Hosp. (bd. mem.), CofC Hosp. Bd.; research: loudspeakers 1947-86; mil: elec. techn. USN 1943-45; Republican; Catholic; rec: golf. Res: 470 Imperial Dr. Pacifica 94044 Ofc: M&M Electronics 338 N Canal St, So. San Francisco 94080

MANOUGIAN, EDWARD, physician; b. Apr. 11, 1929, Highland Park, Mich.; s. George and Vera M.; children: Tasha b. 1963, Yon b. 1968; edn: BS, Wayne Univ. 1951; MD, Univ. Mich. 1955. Career: intern San Bernardino County Charity Hosp. 1955-56, Patton State Hosp. Medical Service 1956-59; capt. Med. Corps US Army, Korea 1957-59; NIH postdoc. fellow biophysics, Donner Lab., UC Berkeley 1960-62, research assoc. Donner Lab. 1962-77; emergency physician Peralta Hosp., Oakland 1979-81; current: pvt. practice, Hospice of Contra Costa; mem: AAAS, Am. Math. Soc., NY Acad. Sci., Alameda Contra Costa Med. Assn., Calif. Med. Assn.; invention: (patent pend.) Medical device for home use; mil: major USAR, Letterman Army Inst. of Research, 1982-; rec: sprinting. Res: 1517 Summit Rd Berkeley 94708

MANSFIELD, LAWRENCE VICTOR, naval officer, accountant, real estate broker; b. Apr. 21, 1919, Sioux City, Iowa; s. Leo John and Dena (Millette) M.; m. Dolores Grocott, Mar. 10, 1958; children: John b. 1947, James b. 1948, Maribeth b. 1949, Sharon b. 1959, Gordon b. 1960, Francis b. 1961, Sarah b. 1962; edn: Morningside Coll. 1948; Calif. lic. real estate broker (1966). Career: credit mgr. Firestone Tire & Rubber Co., Los Angeles 1949; supply ofcr., US Navy 1950-58; sec. treas./gen. mgr. Arcee Foundry Inc., Norwalk 1958-66; ofc. mgr. Wood-Geringer Realty, Fullerton 1966-70; owner, P.O. clk., Mill Creek (Calif.) Resort, 1970-76; civil svc. US Air Force, Norton AFB, San Bernardino 1977-85; mgr. Shadow Mt. Mobile Home Park, Mt. Shasta 1985—; mem. Fullerton Bd. of Realtors (1966-70), Calif. State Mil. Reserve (major Supply Sect. 1983-84), Placentia Lions Club (pres. 1969); mil: lcdr. USNR, Good Conduct, Am. Theater, Asia-Pac. Theater, Korean Svc 2 stars, UN, WWII Victory, Nat. Def., Reserve medals; Democrat; Catholic; rec: golf, comm. service. Address: Shadow Mt. Mobile Home Park #29, 1934 S Old Stage Rd Mt. Shasta 96067

MANTOR, CATHARINE E(LIZABETH), film studio accountant/senior financial analyst; b. Oct. 8, 1950, Drumheller, Alberta, Canada; d. Clarence Edward and Helen (Poworoznyk) Holmes; edn: BA in English, Univ. of Alberta. Career: retail dept. mgr. Hudson's Bay Co., Edmonton, Alberta, Canada 1973-79; senior dept. mgr. Bullock's Dept. Stores, Carlsbad (Calif.) Store, 1980-83; mdse. distbr. Bullock's corp. hqtrs., 1983-84; disaster preparedness coord. Bullock's (also emergency plnng. resource person for var. cos.), 1984, staff analyst Research & Long Range Plnng. Dept., 1984; senior finl. analyst Twentieth Century Fox Film Corp., Beverly Hills 1985—; honors: Bullock's Dept. Mgr. of the Year (1982); mem: Financial & Adminstrv. Mgmt. in Entertainment, Bus. & Indus. Council for Emerg. Preparedness. Ofc: 20th Century Fox POB 90 Rm 1005 Beverly Hills 90213

MAPES, BRUCE R., bank executive; b. Nov. 22, 1946, Sacramento, Calif.; s. Roscoe R. and Maxine M. (Jansen) M.; m. Helen Buzolin, Mar. 31, 1978; 1 dau. Aimee b. 1973; edn: CSU Sacramento 1964-67. Career: trainee Bank of Am. Sacramento 1967-69, ops. ofcr. Colusa 1969-71, Sacramento 1971-72, ofc. mgr. regl. HQ Sacramento 1972-73, asst. mgr. Santa Cruz Main Ofc. 1972-75, tng. ofcr. personnel dept. S.F. 1975-77, asst. v.p. Calif. div. adminstrn. S.F. 1977-80, v.p. mgr. spl. proj. Calif. div. 1980-82, v.p. mgr. br. ops. & coord. S.F. 1982-85, v.p. mgr. br. automation S.F. 1985—; mem: Am. Bankers Assn. (Task Force on Delayed Funds Availability (1982-83), S.F. Museum Soc. (sustaining); devel. and implemented BofA's check truncation svc. Time Saver Space Saver 1981-84; Republican; rec: wine tasting and collecting, hunting, fishing. Ofc: Bank of America 201 Mission St, 22nd floor, San Francisco 94105

MAPES, SALLY JANE, commercial artist; b. Dec. 13, 1947, Susanville; d. Julian Ward and Evelyn Louise (Carr) M.; childen: Analisa and Annette (twins), Heather; lic. Calif. Real Estate Sales (1972). Career: real estate sales agent, 1972—; comml./graphic artist and designer, owner Whiz King Graphics, Redding; creator floats for parades, designer back drops for vaudville plays and rel. ents., designer all forms of printing, signs, silkscreening & logos; awards: 1st Place Western Fairs Sweepstakes, Co. of Lassen (1983); mem. Redding CofC; past mem. Soroptimist; works: pulbr., ed. College Literary Mag., Lassen Coll. 1968; ed. Lassen H.S. literary mag., El Escribano 1966; designer, frachise logo, registered 1985; rec: oil painting. Ofc: Whiz King Graphics, 2165 Pine St. Redding 96001

MARCHAND, DANIEL WELLS, realtor-appraiser; b. Nov. 13, 1951, Oakland; s. Claude Charles and Marilyn (Wells) M.; edn: real estate courses, Chabot Jr. Coll. 1973-74; (GRI) Graduate Realtors Inst., CAR 1975; (CRS) Cert. Residential Splst., NAR 1979. Career: gen. real estate brokerage firm, incl. sales (res., comml., & indsl.), develop., appraisals, property mgmt., investment counseling, estate plng. & mortgage lending 1971—; currently, pres. MW Assoc., Inc., A. Calif. Real Estate Corp.; advr./ cons. Alameda Co., City of Hayward, attys., developers, realtors, banks, pvt. individuals & bus., & mortgage cos.; appraiser I.R.S., gen. real estate values, probate of estate; expert witness, Superior Ct, Alameda & Contra Costa Co.; honors: Named Who's Who in Resdtl. Real Estate, Nat. Assn. Realtor 1981-84; life mem. Million Dollar Club; life mem. Achievement Club, So. Alameda Co. Bd. Realtors; mem: Alameda Co. Assessment Appeals Bd.; Calif. Assn. Realtors (Interbd. Arbitration Com.); Internat. Orgn. of R.E. Appraisers; So. Alameda Co. Bd. Realtors; Nat. Assn. Realtors; Contra Costa Bd of. Realtors; Alameda Co. Apart. Owners Assn.; Alameda Co. Property Owners Assn.; Hayward Rotary; St. Rose Hosp. Adv. Bd.; Alameda Co. 100 Club; mil: airman USAF 1970; Republican; Protestant; rec: equestrian, skiing. Res: 2625 Warwick Pl Hayward 94542 Ofc: MW Associates, Inc., 1122 B St Ste 300 Hayward 94541

MARCUSSEN, ROGER STEVEN, commercial real estate lender; b. Feb. 18, 1941, Bklyn.; s. Rolf I. and Sophie (Nerheim) M.; div.; children: Keith Eric b. 1966, Kari Lisa b. 1970; edn: BA, Augustana Coll., S.D. 1963; MBA, UC Los Angeles 1965, Comm. Coll. Tchg. Pgm. 1966; Calif. Community Colls. Life Tchg. Cred. (1966); Calif. lic. Real Estate Agt. (1976), Insurance Agt. (1982). Career: mktg. cons., analyst Price Waterhouse & Co., 1967-69; sales rep. Xerox, Inc., Century City 1973-75; dist. sales mgr. Bank Building Corp. (constrn. package) 1976-80; inv. sales real esstate broker Marcus & Millichap (selling apt. and comml. props. to instnl. investors and syndicators) 1980-82; pres./CEO MM & Associates (comml. real estate loan origination), Irvine 1982—; instr. comm. colls., El Camino, LA Harbor, UC Irvine Ext.; cons. to finl. instns. on comml. real estate, permanent loans; honors: academic scholarship UN/Treas. Dept. (1962); mem. Building Indus. Assn., Town Hall of Calif.; author: Commercial Real Estate Financing- Permanent Loans (1986); Republican; Lutheran; rec: photog., cinematog., marathon runner. Address: Newport Beach 92660

MARDIAN, ROBERT CHARLES, JR., restaurant corporation executive; b. Feb. 1, 1947, Orange; s. Robert Charles and Dorothy Driscilla (Denniss) M.; m. Kathleen, Oct. 13, 1984; children: Robert, III b. 1975, Alexandra b. 1986. Career: BA, Stanford Univ. 1969; MBA, Pepperdine Univ. 1986. Career: founder/pres./bd. chmn. Wind & Sea Restaurants, Inc. (op. restaurants in Calif. and Hawaii), 1970—; dir. Woodie's Restaurants, Inc. Tucson, Az. 1985; mem: Young Presidents Orgn., Waikiki Rod & Gun Club, Nat. Restaurant Assn., Stanford Alumni Assn., San Onofre Surfing Club; Republican; rec: surfing, skiing, volleyball, Hawaiian Ironman Triathalon (1984). Res: 26391 Via California Capistrano Beach 92624 Ofc: Wind & Sea Restaurants Inc. 34699 Golden Lantern Dana Point 92629

MARHOEFER, GORDON JOSEPH, chartered life underwriter, lawyer; b. Aug. 25, 1932, Detroit, Mich.; s. Edwin Louis and Lucy Cecilia (Cavanaugh) Marhoefer; m. Patricia Black Nutter, 1978; children: George, b. 1956;

Clifford, b. 1956; Thomas, b. 1958; Robert, b. 1960; (step) Darci, b. 1969; edn: BA, Loyola Univ., L.A. 1954; CLU, Am. College 1966; JD, Loyola Law Sch. 1972; ChFC, Am. College 1983. Career: Pacific Mutual Life Ins. Co., L.A.: adminstrv. trainee 1955-7, agent (Sherman Oaks) 1957-9, adminstrv. asst. 1959-61, mgr. of conservation 1961-4, mgr. advanced underwriting, 1964-7, dir. estate & bus. planning, 1967-72; life underwriter/atty., Newport Beach 1972–; CLU instr.; Life Mgmt. Assn. instr.; mem: Million Dollar Round Table, Life and Qualifying mem. 1977-85; Newport Bch-Irvine Estate Planning Council (founding dir., finl. ofcr. 1982-3, secty. 1983-4, v.p. 1984-86); Calif., Orange Co. Bar Assns.; Am. Soc. of CLUs; Nat. Assn. Life Underwriters; Mensa; Alano Club of Costa Mesa (v.chmn. 1975-6); Burbank Parochial Baseball League 1968-71. Publs: arts. in profl. jours. Republican (first pres., Burbank Young Repubs.). Catholic. Rec: photog., camping. Res: 342 Sydney Ln Costa Mesa 92627 Ofc: Massachusetts Mutual Life Ins. Co., 610 Newport Ctr Dr, Ste 1300 Newport Bch 92663

MARINCOVICH, KAREN IRENE, interior designer; b. Oct. 9, 1949, San Francisco; d. Peter John and Irene Roberta (Jansen) M.; edn: AA in mdsg., Santa Rosa Coll. 1969; Rudolph Schaeffer Design Sch. 1973. Career: interior designer, owner KM Assocs., Tiburon 1974–, pres. Karen Marincovich Inc. 1982–; pres. Crown Towers Corp.; pres. Hill Investment Co. Corp.; honors: recogn. Edgewood Children's Center (AASK) Aid to Adopt Special Kids; civic: Nob Hill Assn. (conservation gp.); publs: Better Homes & Gardens, Galleria Floors, Ltd. (1983), Interior Design (1982, 84, 85, 86), Casa Claudia (1981), Grubb & Ellis Premier Pub. (1984); design Xmas Sets for Am. Conservatory Theatre (1983, 84); Republican; Catholic; Address: Tiburon 94920

MARINKOVICH, PAUL GEORGE, restaurateur, chef; b. Oct. 10, 1912, Komiza, Jugoslavia, US cit.; s. George and Vinka M.; m. Geneva Cranston, Sept. 3, 1939; children: George b. 1940, Molo b. 1946, Winefred b. 1951; edn: Classic Realka, Yugoslavia 1924-28; celestial navigation, Capt. Thorsen Nav. Sch. 1930. Career: master ocean vessels; navigator var. vessels; chef in his own restaurants; ret.; num. awards include Three Star Award, L.A. Restaurant Writers Assn. (1982, 1983, 1984), recipient the only Three Star Award for Seafood, L.A. County (1982); Cordon Bleu Award, Hollywood Wine & Food Soc. (1959); Crown Award, Pasadena Wine & Food Soc. (1983); Chef of the Year, L.A. Restaurant Writers Assn. (1980); mem. Calif. Chef De Cuisine, Master Knight of the Wines and Vines; Democrat; Catholic; rec: cooking adventures in food, cookbooks, collect art objects, wine maker and wine critic. Res: 1739 S Grand Ave San Pedro 90731

MARKER, CLIFFORD H., company president; b. Apr. 3, 1899, Ligonier, Pa.; s. Denny C. and Nancy Maude (Clifford) M.; (the Clifford and Marker families came to W. Penna. prior to 1800, see Hist. of Westmoreland Co., Pa.); m. Beryl Schuler, 1924 (dec.); m. 2d. Voris Linthacum, 1936, (dec.); children: Clifford b. 1925, Charles b. 1926 (dec.), Marc L. b. 1941; edn: BA, Amherst Coll. 1921 (Delta Upsilon frat.); USC Law Sch., Calif. Inst. Tech. Career: pres. Selected Investments, Inc. 1930s; pres. Internat. Engring. Co. 1937-42; spec. personnel rep. Lockheed Aircraft Corp. 1942-43; personnel dir. The Owl Drug. Co. 1943-48; indsl. rel. dir./ v.p./ corp. dir. Sav-On Drugs, Inc. 1948-82; pres./ chmn. bd. Refiners Petroleum Corp. 1965-81; pres./ dir. Voris, Inc., Reno, Nev. 1947–; commnr. Dept. of Water & Power, L.A. 1960-64, pres./ mem. bd. 1962; 1st v.p./dir. L.A. Water & Power Assocs. 1977-83; former chmn. adv. bd. Booth Meml. Hosp., L.A.; mem: Metro L.A. Salvation Army (adv. bd. 1966-84); mem. Pepperdine Univ. Assocs. Founding 400; President's Circle of L.A. County Mus. of Art; The Univ. Club of L.A.; L.A. Country Club; pvt. turf clubs of Santa Anita & Del Mar; mil: SATC Ofcrs. Tng., Plattsburgh, NY 1918, hon. disch. US Army 1918; Republican; Presbyterian. Res: 2401 Bowmont Dr Beverly Hills 90210

MARKER, MARC LINTHACUM, bank executive, lawyer; b. July 19, 1941, Los Angeles; s. Clifford Harry and Voris (Linthacum) M.; m. Sandra Yocum, Aug. 28, 1965; children: Victor b. 1970, Gwendolyn b. 1974; edn: Harvard Sch.; AB, UC Riverside 1965; JD, USC 1967. Career: asst. v.p., asst. secty. Security Pacific Nat. Bank, Los Angeles 1970-73; chief counsel Security Pacific Leasing Corp., San Francisco 1973– and secty. 1980–; pres., secty., counsel Security Pacific Leasing Services Corp., 1977–; dir. Refiners Petroleum Corp. (1977-81), dir., secty. Voris Inc. (1973-); instr. comml. law Am. Inst. of Banking (1971-72); mem. Am. Assn. of Equip. Lessors Lawyers Com. (1977-81); Presentations: Practicing Law Inst., Am. Assn. of Equip. Lessors, 1976-; mil: cmdr. USCGR 1966-; Republican; Lutheran; rec: scuba, mountaineering. Res: 41 Lakeside Dr Corte Madera 94925 Ofc: Security Pacific Leasing Corp. 4 Embarcadero Center Ste 1200 San Francisco 94111

MARKLAND, FRANCIS SWABY, JR., biochemist, educator; b. Jan. 15, 1936, Phila.; s. Francis S. and Willie Lawrence (Averitt) M.; m. Barbara Blake, June 27, 1959; children: Cathy b. 1961, Mark b. 1964; edn: BS, Penn State Univ. 1957; PhD, Johns Hopkins Univ. 1964. Career: postdoc. fellow UCLA Sch. of Medicine, Los Angeles 1964-66, asst. prof. biochem. 1966-73; vis. asst. prof. medicine/biochem., USC Sch. of Medicine 1973-74, assoc. prof. biochem. 1974-84, prof. biochem. (acting dept. chmn. 1986-) USC Sch. of Med. 1983–, cons. CLMG Los Angeles (1977-), Cortech Denver (1983-); mem. NIH Study Section (1986-90); editl. bd. Toxicon (Intl. J. of Toxinology); awards: USPHS NIH Research Career Devel. Award, UCLA (1968-73), USPHS grants from Nat. Cancer Inst. (1979-) and Nat. Heart, Lung and Blood Inst. (1984-); mem: Am. Chem. Soc., Am. Soc. Biological Chemists, Sigma Xi, Internat. Soc. of Toxicology, Am. Assn. for Cancer Research, Endocrine Soc., Am. Soc. of Hematol., Am. Heart Assn., Internat. Soc. of Thrombosis and Haemostasis; civic: Masterworks Chorale, Northridge, SAR, Soc. of the Cincinnatti; author 64+ papers in sci. books and jours., co-editor 1 book; mil: capt. USNR-R 1957-, Active duty 1957-59; Republican; Prot.; rec: ski, jog, tennis, sing. Ofc: USC School of Medicine, Cancer Research Lab. Ste 106, 1303 N Mission Rd Los Angeles 90033

MARKLE, GEORGE BUSHAR, computer co. executive; b. June 9, 1950, Rochester, Minn.; s. Dr. George B., IV and Mildred Donna (Umstead) M.; edn: stu. Lafayette Coll. 1968-71, N.M. State. Univ. 1971, grad. (ASEET) No. Am. Tech. Inst. 1974; desig: Cert. Engring. Techn. (CET), Nat. Inst. CET 1974; FCC lic. 1/c RTO (1970). Career: bdcst. announcer, reporter, KGGM, KRKE, Albuquerque, N.M. 1972-73; bdcst. engr. KABQ and N.M. Bdcstg. Co., Albq. 1973-74; senior electronics engring. techn. Exptl. Engring. Electronics Devel. Lab., Lockheed Missiles & Space Co., Sunnyvale 1974-77; cons., slave processor communications software devel. SRI Internat. 1979; cons. for analog/digital converter product testing, CPS, 1980; pres. Am. Computer Consultants (ACC), Mt. View 1978–, pres. ProAccess Software (subs. ACC), 1984–; rep. W. Computer Dealers Assn. (WCDA) in Calif. State Assembly computer indus. hearings, 1985; recipient award for Pioneering Role in birth of Microcomputer Industry, WCDA (1986); mem: Am. Soc. CET, Nat. Radio Inst. Alumni Assn., Am. Radio Relay League, WCDA (secty., founding mem. 1978-), Nat. Fedn. of Indep. Business, Software Entrepreneurs' Forum (1984-), Nat. Office Machine Dealers Assn.; civic: Cypress Pt Lakes HOA Assn. (bd. 1983), Community Theatre (actor), Teen CofC (advisor 1970), Junior Achievement (advisor 1977), Am. Heart Assn. (area fund coord. 1975-78); author: File-works File Processor (P.C. software) (ProAccess, 1984); rec: scuba, model rocketry, psychology. Res: 505 Cypress Point Dr #110 Mountain View 94043 Ofc: 883 Stierlin Rd Ste B120 Mountain View 94043

MARKOTA, IVAN STEPHEN, JR., producer, acting academy owner; b. Apr. 26, 1927, Los Angeles; s. Ivan and Clothilde (Szymanski) M.; m. Frieda Lippitt, July 4, 1976; two children: Cindy b. 1959, Mitchell b. 1961; edn: BA, Columbia Coll. 1962, MA, 1964; Dip. D. Rouzer Sch. of Motion Picture Prodn.,, 1970. Career: constrn. industry, 1958-73; professional actor, 1963-73; producer, stage (theatre), 1974–, also prod. for Cable-TV; exec. dir./owner Van Mar Acad. of Motion Picture & TV Acting (250 students), schs. in Hollywood and Dallas, 1967–; recipient Bronze Halo Award for Outstanding Contbn. to the Motion Picture Indus. (1984); mem: Acting Coaches & Teachers Assn. (pres.), Calif. Private Sch. Assn., Am. Theatres Assn., Am. Film Inst., Nat. Am. Film Inst., Screen Actors Guild, AFTRA, Actor's Equity Assn., The Actors Fund (life), Am. Theatre Council, Calif. Theatre Council, Internat. Platform Assn., Planetary Soc. (charter), Hollywood Stuntmen's Hall of Fame (charter), Am. Legion, Hollywood CofC, L.A. CofC, W. Hollywood Comm. Alliance, Better Bus. Bur.; mil: US Merchant Marines; sgt. US Paratroopers WWII, 307 Combat Engrs., 82 Airborne, 1945-47; Democrat; Catholic; rec: study, helping people. Res: 950 N. Kings Rd, 218, Los Angeles 90069 Ofc: Van Mar Academy of Motion Picture & TV Acting, 7710 Santa Monica Blvd Hollywood 90046

MARKOVICH, EDWARD, financial advisor; b. Sept. 4, 1940, Lundale, W.Va.; s. Joseph and Julia (Dixon) M.; m. Mary Lou Spangler, Aug. 23, 1969 (dec.); edn: BA, cum laude, Bethany Coll. 1967; MBA, Indiana Univ. 1969; CFP, Coll. for Fin. Plnng., Denver 1984. Career: assoc. mgmt. cons. Touche Ross, Bailey & Smart, Chgo. 1969-70; div. mgr. Johnson & Johnson, Sherman Oaks 1970-73; asst. v.p. Merrill Lynch, Sherman Oaks 1973-83; v.p. investments Prudential- Bache, Westlake Village 1983–; mem: Inst. of CFPs, Internat. Assn. for Fin. Plnnrs.; mil: cpl. USMC 1958-63; rec: jogging, tennis, skiing. Res: 6248 McLaren Ave, Woodland Hills 91367 Ofc: Prudential- Bache, 125 Auburn Ct., Westlake Village 91362

MARKS, ALAN BARRY, real estate brokerage president; b. Apr. 7, 1943, Los Angeles; s. Louis and June (Furstman) M.; children: Lisa b. 1967, Kim b. 1970; edn: L.A. Valley Coll. 1961-63, UC Berkeley 1965-67, Lumbleau Sch. Real Estate; Calif. lic. real estate broker 1966. Career: broker/pres. Alan B. Marks & Assocs., offices in San Fernando Valley (R.E. investments, prop. mgmt., estate plnng.), 1966–; honors: Gold Seal Award, Allied Svcs. com. Bd. of Realtors (1971); mem. Nat. Assn. Realtors, Calif. Assn. Realtors, S.F. Valley Bd. of Realtors; founder Gama Delta Phi frat.; charter v.p. Marty Young Bnai Brith youth orgn.; charter mem. Akivva Bnai Brith Mens Gp.; mil: USAR 1961-69; rec: pvt. pilot, ham radio opr. Address: Tarzana 91356

MARKS, MARY DEBORAH, chiropractor; b. Oct. 19, 1943, Tucson, Ariz.; d. Norval Lee and Patricia Josephine (Waltz) Gill; m. Keith Marks, Aug. 2, 1963 (div. 1973); children: Joseph b. 1965, Erik b. 1966, Alice b. 1969; edn: New Mex. Inst. of Mining & Technol. 1960; Antioch Coll. Yellow Springs, Ohio 1961-63; grad., Automation Inst. Sherman Oaks 1968; UC Los Angeles 1974-75; Pasadena Coll. of Chiropractic 1975; DC, L.A. Coll. of Chiro. 1979; chiro. New Mex. 1979, Calif. 1980, Ariz. 1980; Phys. Therapy Cert. Ariz. 1982; adminstr./ instr. Calif. Dept. Pvt. Postsecondary Edn. 1982; Diplomate Nat. Bd. Chiro. Examiners 1979. Career: lab asst. NIH Bethesda, Md. 1962; ednl. resources asst. Am. Friends Svc. Com. 1963; computer programmer CSU Northridge 1968; co-owner Smilite Co. Giftware 1970-72; adminstr./ instr. Touch for Health Found. Pasadena 1973-83; freelance graphic arts prodn. L.A. 1976-78, 1983-85; chiropractor Phoenix 1980-82, Pasadena 1982–, Costa Mesa 1985–; ednl. cons. 1980–; editor var. ednl. materials and publs. Touch for Health Found. Pasadena 1982-83; adminstr., assoc. producer CAM-TV Prodns. Pasadena 1983; archivist Ofc. of Charles & Ray Eames Venice; assoc. Sunrise Chiro. Clin. 1980; co-treas. Mothers Club Coop. Nursery Sch. 1970; guest lectr.; mem. sch. bd. Wide Horizons Edn. Ctr. 1980-81, Desiderata 1981; honors: Silver Thimble (DAR 1958), NSF Scholar (1960), S. Paul Ward Chem. Engrg. Scholar (1961), Calif. State Scholar (1961), Antioch Coll. Scholar (1961-62), freshman class rep. Pasadena Coll. Chiro. (1975), Dean's List (L.A.

Coll. of Chiro 1979); mem: Am. Acad. Pediats., Chiro. Assn. of Ariz., Internat. Chiro. Assn., Calif. Chiro. Assn., So. Calif. Head Injury Found.; co-author: Touch For Health (w/ John F. Thie 1973), A Brief Guide to Cognitive Style Mapping (w/ Barbara Buchanan 1980), Basic Applied Kinesiology Workshop Manual (w/ Gordon Stokes 1983); contbg. author Teach Only Love (Gerald Jampolsky 1983); author Touch For Health Workbook (1983); editor: In Touch For Health, Touch for Health Times, Instructor Training Manual (TFH Found. 1983); Protestant; rec: art, music, science, literature, computers. Address: 3756 E Elma Rd Pasadena 91107

MARKS, MICHAEL BRUCE, international personnel agency executive; b. Nov. 1, 1940, Charlotte, N.C.; s. Leo Mitchell and Jeanne (Fine) M.; m. Susan Roy, Dec. 27, 1985; children: Leo b. 1971, Zachary b. 1977; edn: BS psych., Stanford Univ. 1961; MBA, Pepperdine Univ. 1977. Career: nat. accounts mgr. Univac Div., Sperry Rand Corp. 1968-74; pres. Martronics, Inc. and Universal Consulting, Inc., 1974-85; bd. chmn./CEO Overseas Unlimited Agency, Inc. 1981—, also pres. Overseas Advisory, Inc. and OUA of Idaho, Inc.; bd. dirs: Calif. dir. Overseas Unlimited Agcy., Overseas Advisory Corp.; Idaho dir. OUA of Idaho, Inc.; Fla. dir. TRT, Inc.; N.J. dir. TRT of N.J., Inc.; honors: Michael Marks Golf Classic (to fight diabetes) estab. Riviera Country Club, May 1986; var. awards for Charities Inc. Centro De Ninos (1985), City of El Centro (1985), L.A. Childrens Museum (1985); mem: Calif. Assn. of Personnel Consultants, Nat. Assn. of Pers. Consultants; civic: bd. trustees L.A. Childrens Museum, bd. dirs. L.A. Chap. American Diabetes Assn.; mil: capt. US ARmy 1961-68; rec: contract bridge, deep sea fishing. Ofc: Overseas Unlimited 3460 Wilshire Blvd Ste 908 Los Angeles 90010

MARKSTEIN, ALBERT CARL, wholesaler distributor executive; b. Sept. 26,1914, Richmond; s. Albert Robert and Elsie Mary (Class) M.; m. Bertha, May 8, 1943; 1 son, Robert Carl b. 1949; edn: UC Berkeley 1933; DC, Calif. Chiropractic Coll. 1939; Univ. of San Francisco 1941. Career: ptr. Albert R. Markstein & Sons, Albany 1933; v.p. Markstein Beverage Co., Oakland 1947; chmn. Markstein Beverage Cos. of Union City & Pittsburg 1982—; pres. Albert Markstein & Son, Danville 1982—; pres. Calif. Beer Wholesalers Assn. 1953; pres. Nat. Beer Wholesaler's Assn. 1968-70; honors: U.S. Dimensions of Excellence Awards, Anheuser Busch Brewery Inc. 1984, 85; Calif. Legis. Resolution No. 32, 1969; mem: Elks Club, Eagles, Druids, Masons, Am. Legion, VFW, Herman Sons Soc., Nat. Beer Wholesaler's Assn. (dir. emeritus); mil: chief pharm. mate USN 1942-45; Lutheran; rec: golf, hunting, fishing. Res: 20 Tarry Ln. Orinda 94563 Ofc: Markstein Beverage Company of Union City, 2900 Volpey Way Union City 94587

MARLOWE, WILLIAM RILEY, JR., research co. business development executive; b. Nov. 17, 1930, El Paso, Texas; s. Wm. Riley and Dorathy Margaret (Gardner) M.; m. Elizabeth, Nov. 11, 1982; edn: BS, Texas Tech. Univ. 1954; BS, Univ. of Colo. 1963, MS, 1964. Career: pilot, missile man, engr. US Air Force 1954-75, NASA Apollo flight controller 1968-71; ops. mgr. SAI Internat., El Segundo 1975-80, expert witness 1977; vice pres./mem. bd. dirs. SRS Technologies, Newport Beach 1980-85; dir. bus. devel. & plnng. Access Research Corp., Encinitas 1985—; honors: Tau Beta Pi (1964), Sigma Tau (1963); mem. System Safety Soc. (chmn. profl. devel.), Technical Mktg. Assn., Am. Soc. Safety Engrs., Amvets, The Am. Legion; mil: lt. col. USAF 1954-75; Republican; Methodist; rec: racquet ball, target shooting (pistols). Res: 3651-K Bear St Santa Ana 92704 Ofc: Access Research Corp 527 Encinitas Blvd Encinitas 92024

MARON, MILFORD ALVIN, judge; b. Jan. 21, 1926, Chgo.; s. Martin and Anna (Newman) M.; m. Esther Kass, Dec.24, 1966; children: Steven, Dean, Melissa, Adam; edn: BA cum laude, USC 1949, MA, 1953, LLB, 1954, LLM, 1958; admitted to Calif. State Bar 1955. Career: dep. commr. corps. Calif. Div. Corps., Los Angeles 1955-57; trial counsel SEC, Los Angeles 1957-61, Calif. Div. Labor Law Enforcement, 1961-63; adminstrv. law judge Calif. Office Adminstrv. Hearings, Los Angeles 1963—; mil: US Army Air Corps 1944-46; Democrat; Jewish. Ofc: 314 W. 1st St., Los Angeles 90012

MARRANO, JOSEPH R., electrical engineer/contractor; b. Mar. 24, 1920, Chgo.; s. Saverio and Chiara (DeBono) M.; m. Frances E. House, Dec. 28, 1953; children: Joseph Jr., Sharon Lee, Cheryl Lynn, Rick J., Saverio, Chiara; edn: AA, East Los Angeles Coll., 1982; courses, Lincoln Tech. Inst., Radio-TV of Los Angeles, US Postal Svcs mgt.; Reg. Profl. Engr. (Controls), lic. Electrical Contr., Calif. Career: electrical design engr./supr., 1944-, supr. engring. Control Mation, Chatsworth 1971-73; elec. power & equipment engr. US Postal Service, Bell 1973—; instr. in systems troubleshooting USPS personnel; recipient 2 profl. recogn. awards, US Postal Service; mem: Am. Mgmt. Assn., Electrical Indus. Evaluation Panel for E,C & M Periodical; mil: pvt. US Army Engrs. 361st Regt. 1943; Democrat; Catholic; rec: prospecting, bowling, fishing, numismatics. Res: 10525 Victoria Ave Whittier 90604-2448 Ofc: US Postal Service, Tech Staff, 5555 E Bandini Blvd Bell 90201-9997

MARSH, CRISTINA, real estate broker, building designer/builder; b. May 23, 1939, Boston, Mass.; d. Antonio and Madeline (Marano) Sardo; m. John W. Marsh, Apr. 27, 1963; children: Cristina b. 1964, Gina b. 1965, Johnny b. 1967, Davey b. 1969, Gary b. 1973, Anna b. 1975; edn: var. courses, Chabot Coll., San Jose City Coll., (honors in music) Cabrillo Coll., 1965-86; Calif. lic. R.E. Broker 1984. Career: secty., bookkeeper Sardo's Auto Seatcovers, Malden, Mass. 1954-55; teller Bank of Am., Pasadena 1956-60, Citizens Nat. Bank, Atwater 1961-62, Wells Fargo Bank, Oakland 1963; real estate investor, Alameda/Santa Cruz Co., 1963-86; realtor prin., Aptos 1984—; designer/builder John Marsh, Contractor, Aptos 1979-86; awards: 1st pl. Hayward Art Show (1972), exhibs: Palmer Art Shows, No. Calif. (1972); mem. Calif. Assn.

Realtors, Santa Cruz Board Realtors; civic: singer with Santa Cruz Symphony Orch. and Community Chorus (1980) and 25/25 (1986), Aptos Comm. Chorus (1978-80), Resurrection Ch. Choir/Aptos (1983), theatre prodn. Louden Nelson Ctr. Santa Cruz, Cabrillo Coll. Theater prodns. (1979-80), Barn Theater (1980-81), communications 1981-82 S.F. and Aptos; Democrat; Catholic; rec: theater, dancing, art. Address: Cristina Marsh, Realtor POB 1181 Aptos 95001

MARSHALL, CONSUELO BLAND, judge; b. Sept. 28, 1936, Knoxville, Tenn.; d. Clyde Theodore and Annie (Brown) Arnold; m. George Edward Marshall, Aug. 30, 1959; children: Michael Edward, Laurie Ann; edn: BA, Howard Univ. 1958, LLB, 1961; admitted to Calif. State Bar 1962. Career: atty. City of Los Angeles, 1962-67; assoc. law firm Cochran & Atkins, Los Angeles 1968-70; commr. Los Angeles Superior Ct., 1971-76; judge Inglewood Municipal Ct. 1976-77, Los Angeles Superior Ct., 1977-80, US Dist. Ct. Central Dist. Calif., Los Angeles 1980—; mem. adv. bd. Richstone Child Abuse Center; research fellow Howard Univ. Law Sch. 1959-60; mem. State Bar Calif., Calif. Women Lawyers Assn., Calif. Assn. Black Lawyers, Calif. Judges Assn., Black Women Lawyers Assn., L.A. County Bar Assn., NAACP, Urban League, Beta Phi Sigma; publs: articles in profl. jours., notes editor Law Jour. Howard U.; Ch. Religious Sci. Office: U.S. Courthouse, 312 No. Spring St., Los Angeles 90012

MARSHALL, MARILYN MAE, psychotherapist, educator; b. Feb. 20, 1936, Omaha, Nebr.; d. Paul Ellsworth and Edith Mae (Nairn) McCandless; m. 1956, separated; children: Teresa b. 1957, Joseph b. 1959, Anne b. 1960, Jeanette b. 1961, Danny b. 1962, David b. 1964; edn: AA, cum laude, San Diego Comm. Coll. Dist. 1978; BA behavioral scis., summa cum laude, National Univ. 1980, MA counseling, with Distinction, 1982; lic. Marriage, Family, Child Counseling (MFCC), Calif. 1985. Career: pub. rels. Community Services Office, San Diego Community Coll. Dist., Mesa Coll. 1973-80; counselor & coord. VEA/CETA/JOVE pgms., San Diego Comm. Coll. Dist. E.C.C. Campus, 1980-83, instr. psychology 1982; MFCC intern, 1980-84; MFCC therapist in pvt. practice, Counseling Services Center, San Diego 1984—; workshops on marriage bonding, destructive cults, relationships, psychol. of religion, stages of faith devel., 1976—; founder/dir. Spiritual Life Conf., Catholic Diocese of San Diego 1976—; guest appearances on tv discussing cults, suicide, marital bonding; mem: Calif. Assn. of Mariage, Family Child Counseling/ San Diego Chpt. (student rep 1979-82, profl. affairs com. 1982), Assn. Christian Therapists; civic: Wilson Jr. High Citizens Adv. Council (mem. 1971-75, pres. 1973-74), Opti-Mrs. Internat. (pres. 1973-77); research: dialogue with and between Psychology & Religion; Republican; Roman Catholic, Secular Franciscan; rec: dream analysis, public speaking, running. Res: 4175 Norfolk Terrace San Diego 92116 Ofc: Counseling Services Center 4274 Meade Ave San Diego 92116

MARSHALL, STEVEN KENT, television writer-producer; b. July 19, 1943, Los Angeles; s. Willard Denver and Lorraine Lee (Waltman) M.; m. Vicki K. Marshall, 1986; 1 dau. Kareen b. 1974. Career: disk jockey, pgm. dir., cons. in broadcasting, creator first soft rock format for KNX/FM and CBS/FM stas. 1967-79; story ed., producer WKRP In Cincinnatti 1979-81; prod. Gloria-Co-Executive 1982; co-creator, exec. prod. Off The Rack, 1984, Growing Pains,1985—; ptr. Mugwump Prodns.; film scripwriting; honors: Emmy nom., producer WKRP in Cincinnati; Scott Newman Drug Abuse Prevention Award 1981; mem. Acad. of Television Arts and Scis.; mil: USNR, 2 yrs. active, Vietnam; Democrat; rec: short story writing.

MARSHALL, THOMAS C., private investor; b. Mar. 14, 1929, Deming, N.M.; s. Carolyn Caldwell; m. Helen V., Sept. 1, 1949; children: David b. 1951, Pamela b. 1953, John b. 1963, Robert b. 1965; edn: mil., Harvard Sch. 1946; BA econ./govt., Pomona Coll. 1950; BS hotel admin., Cornell Univ. 1952. Career: prop. Dana Point Hotel 1953-54; gen. mgr. Handlery Hotels 1954-58, Hotel Woodland, 1954, and Alexander Hamilton Hotel, S.F., 1955-58; owner/opr. hotel co., Continental Pacific Hotels 1958-82 (Lombard H., Continental H., and H. Victorian, S.F.; H. Claridge, Lakehurst H., Oakland; H. Fresno, H. Californian, Fresno; H. Commodore, Rossmore House H., Los Angeles), sold co. 1982; pvt. investor 1982-; mem. Calif. No. Hotel Assn. (pres. 1962), Calif. Hotel & Motel Assn. (pres. 1974); trustee Joseph Drown Found.; clubs: Marin Yacht, Meadow Club (past dir.); Republican; Episcopal; rec: golf, boating, fishing. Res: One Orchard Way Kentfield 94904 Ofc: Marshall Management POB 308 Kentfield 94914

MARSTON, RICHARD WELDEN, lawyer; b. May 8, 1933, Ithaca, NY; s. Winthrop Simon and Sylva Orabelle (Jones) M.; m. Margaret Scholz, Feb. 20, 1960; children: John b. 1962, Ann b. 1964, Robert b. 1965; edn: BS, UC Berkeley 1955; JD, UC Hastings Coll. of Law 1963. Career: pvt. practice law, San Jose 1964-68; municipal atty. San Jose, Glendale, Beverly Hills & Burbank 1968—; currently, senior asst. city atty., Burbank; judge pro tem Los Angeles Municipal Ct.; mem: Calif. Bar Assn. (Pub. Law Sect.); Los Angeles Co. Bar Assn.; Kiwanis, Glendale; Sons of the Am. Revolution; So. Calif. Genealogical Soc.; mil: capt. USAFR 1971; Republican; Catholic; rec: dist. running, backpacking, geneology. Res: 1224 Imperial Dr Glendale 91207 Ofc: City of Burbank, 275 E Olive Ave Burbank 91502

MARTELLA, VINCENT NICHOLAS, engineer; b. Sept. 12, 1935, New York City; s. Michael and Anna (D'Andrea) Martella; nephew of Dr. Luigi Martella (1911-1971), distinguished Italian architect, professor, educator and artist; m. Jean Wright, June 29, 1963; children: Denise, b. 1967, Paul, b. 1970, JoAnne, b. 1978; edn: BSME, Polytech. Inst. of New York, 1966; MSME, Loyola Univ. of Los Angeles, 1972; Reg. Profl. Engr., Mech., State of Calif., 1978. Career:

stress analyst, F-5 supersonic fighter and 747 comml. jet, Northrop Corp., Hawthorne 1966-68; stress analyst, mil. and comml. helicopters incl. advanced rotorcraft design, Hughes Helicopters Inc., Culver City 1968-71; stress analyst, B-1 Bomber, Rockwell Internat., Los Angeles Div., El Segundo 1971-72; lead engr., San Onofre nuclear power plant, Bechtel Power Corp., Norwalk 1972-77; prin. engr., oil refineries, gas-oil separation units and nuclear power plants, C.F. Braun & Co., subs. Santa Fe Internat., Alhambra 1977-85; senior engr., F-20 Tigershark aft fuselage structural analysis and loads test, Northrop Corp., Aircraft Div., Hawthorne 1985–; civic: Town Hall of Calif.; Republican; Catholic; rec: reading, amateur astronomy. Res: 5308 Vista Del Mar, Cypress 90630 Ofc: Northrop Corp., Aircraft Div., One Northrop Ave., Hawthorne 90250-3277

MARTIN, ALEXIS ARLIS HARLAN, physician and linguistics specialist; b. April 2, 1945; s. Arlis Harlan and Margaret (Dickson) M.; m. Eleutheria Mingou, June 19, 1972; 1 son, Demetrius Taxiarches b. 1974; edn: BA, Southern Methodist Univ. 1968, BS, 1968; MD, USC 1971; intern, resident, Cedars Sinai Med. Ctr. 1973. Career: senior ptr. Friendly Hils Med. Group 1973–; splst.as language expert on ancient languages of the Near East (Hurrian, Urartian, others) Inst. of Archaeology, UCLA; tchg. preceptor Dartmouth Sch. of Med. 1984-85; honors: annual acad. awards, Calif. Med. Assn. 1973-; mem: Am. and Calif. Med. Assns., Inst. of Archaeology (UCLA), La Habra CofC, Physicians for Human Rights, Inst. for Mesopotamian Area Studies; works: author, num. articles on med. topics; linguistic text, A Comparative Phonology of Hurrian and Caucasic Languages, Journ. of Hurrian & Caucasic Studies, Inst. for Mesopotamian Area Studies 1985-86; Democrat; Orthodo; rec: archaeology of the Mediterranean basin. Res: 2 Barlovento Ct. Newport Beach 92663 Ofc: Friendly Hills Medical Group, 951 So. Beach Blvd. La Habra 90631

MARTIN, CARL WINSTON, private investigator; b. May 6, 1940, Houston, Tx.; s. Carl and Addie Mae (Burnley) M.; m. Charlotte Ann, Nov. 24, 1979; edn: cert., Title Escrow Sch. 1966; spl. courses, L.A. City Coll. 1968; lic. Pvt. Investigator 1969. Career: dep. court clk. US Dist. Ct., Los Angeles 1961-64; title searcher Am. Title Ins. of Miami, Los Angeles 1964-65; staff investigator Equifax Services (former Retail Credit Co.), Glendale 1965–; splst. in forensic genealogy/W. Coast investig. Am. Archives Assn., Wash DC 1970–, W.C. Cox & Co. (internat. probate research), Tucson, Az. 1970–, Am. Research Bur., L.A. 1970-75, Infosearch Inc., Albany, NY 1986-; past mem. Calif. Assn. of Lic. Investigs. (1975); active in church work, bd. mem. Fellowship West, Inc.; Democrat; Baptist (deacon); rec: tennis, Bible study & tchg. Ofc: Carl Martin Investigations POB 4266 West Covina 91791

MARTIN, CLYDE VERNE, psychiatrist; b. Apr. 7, 1933, Coffeyville, Kansas; s. Howard Verne and Elfrieda Louise (Moehn) M.; m. Barbara McNeilly, June 24, 1956; children: Kent b. 1959, Kristin b. 1960, Kerry b. 1962, Kyle b. 1965; edn: BA, Univ. Kansas 1955, MD, 1958; MA, Webster Coll. 1977; JD, Thomas Jefferson Coll. of Law 1985; bd. certified Am. Bd. Psychiatry & Neurol. 1982. Career: med. dir. Midcontinent Hosp. Olathe, Kans. 1972-83; chief psych. residency pgm. Atascadero State Hosp. Calif. 1984-85; chief psych. Calif. Med. Facility Vacaville 1985-86; med. dir. Hillcrest Hosp. San Diego 1986–; clin. prof. UC San Francisco, Fresno Med. Sch. 1985-86; fellow: Royal Soc. Health (London), Am. Assn. Mental Health Profls. in Corrections, World Assn. Social Psychiatry, Am. Orthopsychiatric Assn.; mem. Carriage Club; publs: author 3 books and 23 articles; mil: col. USAFR; Republican; Methodist; rec: classic cars. Ofc: Hillcrest Hosp. 345 W Dichson Box 85524 San Diego 92138-5524

MARTIN, DAVID WILLIAM, engineer, project manager; b. Dec. 29, 1943, Niagara Falls, N.Y.; s. Robert Wm. and Muriel (Irving) M.; m. Evelyn, July 12, 1972; children: Bruce b. 1965, Douglas b. 1966, Jennifer b. 1973; edn: BS in chem. engring., Univ. of Rochester 1965; cert. bus. mgmt., UCLA 1985; Reg. Profl. Engr. (chem.) Calif. 1979. Career: chemical engr.; prodn. supt./process engr. Amax, West Va. and Colo., 1966-75; senior process engr. Ralph M. Parsons, Pasadena 1975-80; project mgr. C.F. Braun, Alhambra 1980–; honors: Nat. Honor Soc. (1959), D.A.R. (1961); mem. Am. Inst. of Chem. Engrs. Res: 2395 Monte Vista Pasadena 91107 Ofc: C.F. Braun 1000 S Fremont Alhambra 91802

MARTIN, DUMAS, JR., manufacturing co. executive; b. Apr. 26, 1948, Natchez, Miss.; s. Dumas, Sr. and Arsulia (Brown) M.; m. Peggy Ann, July 7, 1973; children: Angela Monique b. 1975, Dumas b. 1978; edn: undergrad. Citrus Coll. 1969-70, CalPoly Pomona 1970-71; grad. Electronic Computer Pgmmg. Inst. 1968; LUTC grad. Life Underwriter Sch. 1973-76; lic. Notary Public (1981). Career: ins. key agt. Pacific Mutual, Los Angeles 1971-72; agt./sales mgr. Liberty Nat., Pomona 1972-81; agt. Prudential Ins., 1981-82; owner Dumas Martin Ins. Agcy. 1982-83; owner Sport.A.Pad Ents. (sports products mfg. co.) 1984–; cons. prin., Mind To Market (new prod. devel.) 1985–; awards: Calif. Fedn. of Chaparral Poets (1986), United Negro Coll. Fund vol. (1985); mem. Nat. Sporting Goods Assn.; civic: Booster Clubs of Am., UNCF (vol.), United Way, Ontario CofC; inventor: Adjustable lounge chair (10/83), Lounge 'N Games (T.M.) (10/84), devel. line of therapeutic cushions for medical field (1986); Democrat; Baptist; rec: athletics, new product devel. Ofc: Sport.A.Pad Enterprises POB 9073 Ontario 91762

MARTIN, HARRY M. (aka Joe), advertising agency executive; b. July 19, 1931, Detroit, Mich.; s. Harry M. and Irene Louis (McClung) M.; m. Linda Garn, Feb. 15, 1976; children: Monique b. 1960, Michael b. 1963, Jeffrey b. 1972; edn: BA, Mich. State Univ. 1957. Career: advtg. agcy. mgr. Gate City Sash & Door Co. Ft. Lauderdale, Fla. 1955-56; advt. brand mgr. Coca Cola Co. 1958-59; founder, pres. Martin Advtg. Inc. Tustin 1960–; mem: Western States Advtg. Agencies Assn. (bd.), Pub. Rels. Soc. of Am., Nat. Assn. Home Builders, Sales & Mktg. Council, Bldg. Ind. of Am., Tustin Area Republican Assembly, Constrn. Ind. Alliance for City of Hope (chpt. v.p.); clubs: Lincoln, Pacific, Center, Balboa Bay, Shark Island Yacht, Irvine Racquet; adv. bd. El Dorado Bank, Platt Coll.; mil: USCGR, active 1953-55, Svc. Medal; Republican; Christian; rec: sailing, photog. Ofc: 18141 Irvine Blvd Tustin 92680

MARTIN, JOSEPH, JR., lawyer; b. May 21, 1915; edn: BA, Yale Univ., 1936, LLB, Yale Law Sch. 1939; mem. State Bars of Calif., NY, and D.C. Career: assoc. Cadwalader, Wickersham & Taft,NY, 1939-41; USN (to Lt. Cmdr.) 1941-46; ptnr. Wallace, Garrison, Norton & Ray, San Francisco 1946-55; ptnr. Allan, Miller, Groezinger, Keesling & Martin, 1955-70; Pettit, Evers & Martin 1973-, (Pettit & Martin); Gen. Counsel, Fed. Trade Commn., Wash DC 1970-71; US Rep., Geneva Disamarment Conf. (rank, Ambassador) 1971-76. Fellow, Am. Bar Found.; mem. Pres's Advis. Com. for Arms Control & Disarmament, 1974-78; pres. S.F. Public Utilities Commn. 1956-60; Repub. Natl. Committeeman for Calif. 1960-64; dir. Nat. Fair Campaign Practices Com. 1965-; dir. Arms Control Assn. 1977-; dir. Legal Assistance to the Elderly; Arcata Corp., 7/28/82; dir. Barber-Greene co. 1983; Shaughnessy Holdings Inc., 1983; treas. Repub. Party of Calif. 1956-58; dir. Patrons of Art & Music, Calif. Palace of Legion of Honor, 1958-70, pres. 1963-68; clubs: Pacific-Union (S.F.), Burlingame CC, Yale (of N.Y.); honors: Official Commendation, Outstanding Service as Gen. Counsel, FTC, 1973; Disting. Hon. Award, US Arms Control & Disarm. Agcy. 1973; Lifetime Achievement Awd., Legal Assistance to the Elderly, 1981. Address: c/o Pettit & Martin, 101 California St, 35th Fl., San Francisco 94111

MARTIN, LOUIS HAROLD, labor relations executive; b. Apr. 30, 1916, Joplin, Mo.; s. John L. and Mabel (Smith) M.; m. Vineta R. Babb, June 16, 1936. Career: founder, editor, publr. Contra Costa LABOR News 1960-78; founder, adminstr. Contra Costa Labor Blood Bank 1959-78; founder, exec. secty. Contra Costa Labor Health & Welfare Council 1956-78; svc. ofcr. Contra Costa Bldg. Trades Council 1953-78, secty. emeritus 1978–; founder Martinez Health Ctr. Inc., exec. treas. 1971-76; founder Martinez Med. Arts Bldgs. Inc., exec. treas. 1972-76; founder Pre-Paid Comprehensive Health Svcs. Corp., exec. treas. 1972-76; vice chmn. adv. com. Adobe Savings & Loan Assn. 1978-81, v.p., dir. 1983–; cons., editor Contra Costa, Napa- Solano Labor News 1980–; US marshall No. Dist. Calif. 1968-69; pres., dir. West Contra Costa Water Dist. 1955-59; pres. Richmond Boys Club 1959, Martinez Boys Club 1962-65; bd. dirs. Martinez Comm. Hosp. 1967-73; honors: Medallion & Keystone (Boys Clubs of Am. 1962-65), Resolution & Commdn. (Calif. Legislature 1966, 73, 79), Award of Merit (Frat. Order of Eagles 1967), Commdn. (US Dept. Justice 1969, US Bureau of Prisons 1969), Cert. Commdn. (Contra Costa County Bd. Supvs. 1979), Proclamation of Appreciation (City of Martinez 1979), Labor Man of the Year (Contra Costa County 1973), First Man of Year (Martinez 1972); mem. Elks (exalted ruler 1962-63); mil: USMC 1942-45. Res: 320 Lindsey Dr Martinez 94553

MARTIN, ROBERT BROOKS, JR., lawyer; b. July 12, 1944, Akron, O.; s. Robert B. and Margie E. (Wymer) M.; m. Kathleen, Dec. 13, 1969; children: Elysia b. 1973, Robert b. 1975; edn: AB, Kent State Univ. 1966; JD, USC 1969; admitted Calif. State Bar, Certified Specialist Taxation Law. Career: assoc. atty. Keatinge & Sterling 1969-70; ptnr. Richards, Martin & McLaughlin 1970-73, Bergland, Martin & McLaughlin 1973-76; assoc. atty. Meserve, Mumper & Hughes 1976-77, ptnr. 1977-83; ptnr. Martin, Davis & Deacon 1983-84, ptnr. Martin & Deacon 1984–; dir.: Permanent Portfolio Fund, Mansion Industries Inc., United Investment Groups; advisory bd. Tax Shelter Insider; frequent lectr. on taxes and tax sheltered investments, USC Inst. on Federal Taxation, Calif. CPA Found., var. profl. groups; mem. ABA, Calif. State Bar; author num. articles on taxation in profl. publs.; Libertarian; Congregational. Res: 370 West Del Mar Blvd Pasadena 91105 Ofc: Martin & Deacon, 350 W Colorado Ste 320 Pasadena 91105

MARTIN, ROBERT THEODORE, chiropractor; b. Dec. 24, 1956, NY, NY; s. James George and Irene (Karas) M.; edn: BS, biology, Seton Hall Univ., N.J. 1978; DC, magna cum laude, Los Angeles Coll. of Chiropractic 1982; lic. DC, Calif. and N.J. (1983), X-ray supr. & Opr. cert. (1983). Career: physical therpy asst. Delridge Nsg. Home, Paramus, N.J. 1978-79, Emerson Convalescent Ctr., Emerson, N.J. 1978-79; chiropractor, assoc. Gramercy Health Group, Los Angeles 1984, Bixby Knolls Chiropractic Arts, Long Beach 1985–; mem: Delta Sigma Hon. Scholastic Soc. of the Healing Arts, LACC and Seton Hall Univ. alumni assns.; rec: astronomy, photog., music. Res: 442-B Riverdale Dr Glendale 91204 Ofc: 3726 N Atlantic Ave Long Beach 90807

MARTIN, SCOTT ALFRED, lawyer; b. Apr. 21, 1946, Grand Rapids, Mich.; s. Alva Cecil and Mary Albertine (Walz) M.; m. Gail Margaret Russell, July 12, 1975; children: Brooke b. 1977, Matthew b. 1979; edn: BA, UC Riverside 1968, JD, UC Hastings Coll. of Law 1973; admitted Calif. State Bar 1973. Career: atty. assoc. Reid, Babbage & Coil, Riverside 1973-74, Hillsinger & Costanzo, Los Angeles 1974-79, ptnr. 1979-81; ptnr. Gardner & Martin, Newport Beach 1981–; mem: ABA, Calif. State Bar Assn., Orange County Bar Assn., Am. Trial Lawyers Assn., Assn. of So. Calif. Defense Counsel; mil: s/sgt. US Army Reserve 1968-74; Republican; Christian. Ofc: Gardner & Martin, Attys. 4400 MacArthur Blvd Ste 200 Newport Beach 92660

MARTIN, WILLIAM WILEY, psychotherapist, vocational consultant; b. Mar. 24, 1951, Albany, Ga.; s. William Wiley Sr. and Lynne (Durham) M.; m. Diana, Nov. 7, 1981; 1 son, Christopher William b. 1983; edn: AA, Clayton Jr. Coll. 1973; BS, Ga. State Univ. 1975; MS, Chapman Coll. 1978; MA, MFCC, Pepperdine 1980; PhD, Internat. Coll. 1983. Career: vocational cons. IRA

Orange 1978-80, Atlanta, Ga. 1980-82, V.E.S. Orange 1984; psychotherapist pvt. practiceCypress 1978-80, Atlanta 1980-83, Los Alamitos, Huntington Beach, Tustin 1983–, exec. dir. Consolodated Health Svcs. Atlanta 1982-83; vocational cons., owner Comprehensive Vocational Svcs. Los Alamitos 1984–; honors: listed various Who's Whos, Personalities of Am., Men of Achievement, Biog. Roll of Honor in the Hist. Preservations of Am., Directory of Disting. Americans, Dictionary of Internat. Biography, World Biographical Hall of Fame, Internat. Directiory of Disting. Leadership, Disting. Leadership Award, Internat. Book of Honor; mem: Am., Calif. Psych. Assn., Child Sexual Abuse Network, Calif. Assn. of Marriage and Family Therapists, Am. Assn. for Sex Educators, Counselors and Therapists, Nat., Calif. Assn. of Alcoholism and Drug Abuse Counselors, Nat. Rehab. Assn., Calif. Assn. of Rehab. Profls., So. Calif. Rehab. Exchange, Phobia Soc. of Am.; Democrat; Unitarian; rec: skiing, martial arts, gourmet cooking, reading, aerobics, dancing. Ofc: Clinical Psychology Group 3772 Katella Ave Ste 212 Los Alamitos 90270

MARTINEZ, BENJAMIN JOHN, medical laboratory technologist, chiropractor; b. May 24, 1955, Antioch, Calif.; s. Benjamin J. and Mary Eva (Abowd) M.; edn: AS in physical sci., honors, Los Medanos Comm. Coll. 1975; BS in biol. scis., honors, CSU Sacramento 1979; lic. M.T. (ASCP) 1980; DC candidate, Palmer Coll. of Chiropractic-West 1984-1987. Career: lab. asst. Sutter Meml. Hosp., Sacto. 1977-79; med. lab. technologist, intern Valley Children's Hosp. and Guidance Clinic, Fresno 1979-81; med. lab. techn. Los Medanos Comm. Hosp., Pittsburg 1981-82; asst. lab. mgr. Internat. Clinical Labs., Dublin 1982-84; supr. of lab. ops. Palo Alto Medical Clinic, 1984–; honors: Class pres., Palmer Coll. of Chiro.-West (1984-85); mem. Am. Chiropractic Assn. (assoc.), Calif. Chiropractic Assn. (assoc.), Calif. Assn. of Med. Lab. Technologists; civic: vol. Jr. High Sch. sci. instr. Holy Rosary Catholic Sch., Antioch (1981), Santa Clara County Crippled Childrens Soc. (counselor 1986); research: Acute lymphocytic leukemia, Valley Childrens Hosp., Fresno (1981-82); Republican; Roman Catholic; rec: boardsailing, skiing, backpacking. Res: Sunnyvale 94086

MARTINEZ, EUGENE JOHN, lawyer; b. Aug. 18, 1944, Santa Barbara; s. John Sanchez and Catherine Ann (Smith) M.; m. Margaret, April 12, 1965; 1 son, E. Theodore b. 1983; edn: BA, UC Santa Barbara 1971; JD, Univ. of Santa Clara Sch. of Law 1975; admitted to Calif. Bar 1976. Career: law clerk, atty. Public Defender Santa Clara Co. 1973-76; deputy dist. atty. Dist. Atty., San Mateo Co. 1976-79; deputy dist. atty., deputy-in-chg. Consumer Bus. Law Sect., Santa Barbara Co. 1979–; honors: Outstanding Civic Achiev., Univ. of Santa Clara Law Sch.; mem: Nat. and Calif. Dist. Attys. Assns.; mil: sgt. E-5 US Army 1965-67, (CIB); Republican; Catholic; rec: infantry, light weapons rock climbing, jogging. Ofc: Dist. Atty.'s Ofc., Santa Barbara Co., 115 Civic Center Plaza Lompoc 93436

MARTINEZ, FRANK R., college president; b. Dec. 28, 1921, Los Angeles; s. Frank and Caroline (Bassett) M.; m. Lois M. Martinez, March 16, 1951; children: Larry F., b. 1953, Jay, b. 1955, Mark, b. 1956, Barbara, b. 1960; edn: BA in pol. sci., Univ. Redlands 1947; MA, hist., USC 1953, EdD, 1963. Career: instr., counselor Citrus Coll., 1947-52; adminstrv. dean, 1962-64, asst. supt. Ednl. Services, Cuesta Coll., 1964-77, pres./supt., 1977–; mem. San Luis Obispo County Civil Service Commn. 1974-8; mil: USMC 1942-6, served in South Pac.; Rotarian (pres. 1959-60); Presbyterian (Elder); rec: bullfighting. Res: 2383 Sunset Dr San Luis Obispo 93401 Ofc: POB J, San Luis Obispo 93406

MARTINEZ GANDARA, JULIO ANTONIO, librarian; b. Oct. 4, 1931, Santiago, Cuba; nat. 1968; s. Julio and Maria (Gandara) M.; edn: BA, So. Ill. Univ. 1963; MALS, Univ. Minn., 1967; MA, Univ. Minn.; PhD, UC Riverside, 1980. Career: asst. librn. San Diego State Univ., 1973-76, senior asst. librn. 1976-78, assoc. librn. 1980–, also coord. Chicano Collection, S.D.S.U. Library; ed. Cognition and Brain Theory Jour.; awards: So. Ill. tuition & activity awards, 1958-61; cons. Nat. Endowment for the Humanities, 1985-, and Calif. Council for the Humanities, 1985-; mem: Nat. Librns. Assn., Calif. Lib. Assn., Soc. for the Interdisciplinary Study of the Mind, Mensa; author: Chicano Scholars and Writers (Scarecrow Press, 1979), Chicano Literature: A Reference Cuide (Greenwood Press, 1985), Dictionary of Contemporary Cuban Literature (Greenwood Press, forthcoming); 28 book revs.; Democrat; rec: chess, Beethoven. Res: 5642 Hamill Ave San Diego 92120 Ofc: University Library, Gen. Ref. Dept. SDSU, San Diego 92182

MARTINEZ, GLENN ADAM, artist, designer; b. Mar. 12, 1957, Pound Ridge, NY; s. John Robert and Violet Mary (Vallejo) M.; m. Coleen Schuman, Aug. 16, 1985; edn: Maryland Inst. Coll. of Art. 1973-75; Kansas City Art Inst. 1975; San Francisco Art Inst. 1975-77. Career: artist, The New Studio, NY, NY 1972; art dir. California Builder & Engineers 1975-76; art. dir. Sonoma Business, Santa Rosa 1976-77; publisher Scope Mag., Santa Rosa 1978-80; owner Glenn Martinez & Assocs. Inc. 1977–; owner Zenitram Gallery- Modern and Contemporary Fine Art; bd. dirs. Profl. Communication Design, Santa Rosa 1981-; mem: Am. Inst. of Graphic Arts, Santa Rosa CofC, Execs. Assn. of Sonoma Co., Nat. Fedn. of Independent Bus.; designer: wine labels, brochures, graphic designs for U.S. and French wineries; anarchist; atheist; rec: drawing, travel, skating. Res: 4709 Sheehan Ln., Santa Rosa 95404 Ofc: Glenn Martinez & Associates Inc., 15 Third St., Santa Rosa 95401

MARTINEZ, IVAN PICADO, physician; b. May 14, 1944, Leon, Nicaragua, nat. US cit. 1975; s. Salomon and Maria Luisa (Picado) M.; m. Margarita Lanzas, Mar. 27, 1969; children: Richard b. 1971, Felipe b. 1979; edn: pre-med. Natl. Auto. Univ. of Nicaragua 1966, Med., 1970; phys. cert. Calif. 1974.

Career: rotating intern St. Clare's Hosp. Schtdy., N.Y. 1972; residency, fellowship Long Beach VA Hosp. 1973-77; pvt. practice Anaheim 1977–; dir. diabetology unit, chmn. med. dept. Placentia Linda Hosp.; co-dir. Diabetic Treatment Ctrs. of Am., Western Med. Ctr., Santa Ana; honors: Phys. of the Year (Canyon Gen. Hosp. 1977), Phys. Recogn. Award 1977-87; mem: Orange Co. Med. Assn., CMA, Orange Co. Endocrine Soc., Calif. Soc. Internal Med., Am. Diabetes Assn, Hispano-Am. Assn.; publ: research papers 1976, 1977, 1982; Republican; Catholic; rec: pvt. pilot. Ofc: 500 S Anaheim Hills Rd, Ste 230, Anaheim 92807

MARTINEZ, JESUS FLORES, banking executive; b. Mar. 16, 1931, Santa Ana; s. Jesus Caldera and Leonor (Flores) M.; children by previous marriage: Cynthia b. 1953, Sylvia b. 1954; edn: AA, LA City Coll. 1952; BS, CSU Los Angeles 1966; indsl. mgmt. Univ. of Calif. 1969-72; MBA, Univ. of Redlands 1979; creds: Profl. Engr., Calif. 1970; Cert. Data Processor (CDP) 1965. Career: mgr. Civil Engr. Systems, AMCO Engrs., Los Angeles 1962-65; cons. Project Mgmt., US Navy, Far East, 1965-68; systems mgr. Xerox Data Systems, Santa Monica 1968-75; senior staff, Constrn. Mgmt., Northrop Corp., Middle East and Calif., 1975-80; v.p., Constrn. Mgmt., Bank of America- Latin Am. Div., Caracas, Venez. 1981–83, S.E. United States, 1984–; lectr., Proj. Mgt. Systems, US Navy 1965-68, and for pvt. indus. 1968-77; instr., Data Proc. Systems, UCLA 1970-72; panel mem. Am. Arbitration Assn. 1976; mem: Am. Soc. of Civil Engr. 1956-, Am. Soc. Indsl. Engr. 1965-77, Data Proc. Mgmt. Assn. 1962-75, Soc. of Hispanic Profl. Engrs. (chmn. nom. com. 1979-81); dir. Fathers Club, Ramona Convent Girls Sch. 1968-72; dir. Coll. Internat. de Caracas 1981-82; publs: instruction texts in proj. mgmt. (incl. CPM, PERT, LOB), Spanish translations; mil: lst lt. Army Corps of Engrs. 1952-56; Republican; Catholic; rec: tile mosaics, travel, history. Res: 273 Glenarm St. Unit 1, Pasadena 91106 Ofc: BA Appraisals Inc., 3220 Rosemead Blvd El Monte 91731

MARTINEZ, JOSE ANTONIO, physician; b. June 10, 1938, Santa Ana, El Salvador, Central Am.; s. Manuel A. and Mercedes (Sandoval) M.; m. Gloria Bendeck, 1966; children: Jose Antonio b. 1967, Evelyn b. 1969d,; Leslie b. 1973, Carlos Manuel b. 1980; edn: Bach. in Letters & Sci., Nat. Inst., El Salvador 1957; MD, Sch. of Med., El Salvador 1967. Career: ob-gyn. splst. Alma Med. Gp., Panorama City 1971-76; ob-gyn. tng., Baltimore (4 yrs.); pvt. practice 1976–; ob-gyn. residency, El Salvador 1966-69; asst. prof. El Salvador Sch. of Med. 1969-71; mem: Am. Coll. of Ob-Gyn.; Am. Fertility Soc.; Am. & Calif. Med. Assns.; Assn. of Gyn-Laparoscopists; L.A. Obstetrical Soc.; Med. Coll. of El Salvador; L.A. County Med. Soc.; Catholic. Res: 116 Fullbright Ave Chatsworth 91311 Ofc: Serra Medical Clinic, 14673 Parthenia St Panorama City 91402

MARTINEZ, JULIAN B., ship chandler; b. Jan. 9, 1917, Long Beach; s. Jesus Diaz and Ester (Kujasky) M.; m. Floriza N. Garcia, Apr. 15, 1971; grad. Poly H.S., 1936. Career: police ofcr. Long Beach Police Dept., 1940-44; founder/ owner Julian Ship Supplies, Long Beach 1944–; awarded Hon. mem. L.B. Police Officers Assn.; mem: Masons, Shriners, Scottish Rite, Latin Am. Club of L.B.; Republican; Catholic; rec: fishing, philanthropy. Ofc: Julian Ship Supplies 505 W Broadway Long Beach 90802

MARTINEZ, OLGA, restaurateur, travel consultant; b. Oct. 4, 1959, Fresno; d. Faustino and Frances Martinez (Gonzalez) M.; edn: BS, CSU Fresno 1982; desig: Calif. real estate lic. (1986), cert. travel agent (1986), environmental sanitarian (1982). Career: survey interviewer Cal Trans, Fresno 1978; admitting interviewer Valley Med. Ctr. 1978-79, Community Hosp. 1980, Clovis Comm. Hosp. 1980; acctg. asst. Paul Schletewitz, CPA 1979; vol. Amigos de las Americas, Santo Domingo, Dominican Republic 1980; owner Martinez Drive Inn, Mendota, Calif. 1980–, and Mendota Taqueria, 1984–; travel cons. Elegant Journey, San Jose 1986–; engring. asst. Fresno Dept. of Health Svcs. 1980-83, environ. health aide 1983-84; real estate investor 1980-, promoter Latin Music groups 1986–; honors: Bus. Woman of Year, Hispanic CofC (1985), Most Improved Bus. of Year, City of Mendota (1983); mem: Nat. Rest. Assn., Calif. Environ. Health Assn., Nat. Environ. Health Assn., CSUF Alumni Assn., Amistad Assn., Small Bus. of Am., Fresno CofC, Mendota CofC, Community Alliance for Better Water Policy/ Kesterson, Hispanic CofC, Latin Am. Bus. Club, League of Mexican Am. Women; Democrat; Catholic; rec: photog. Res: 1520 Third St Mendota 93640 Ofc: Mendota Taqueria 570 S Derrick Mendota 93640

MARTINEZ, ROBERT JAMES, chiropractor; b. Oct. 25, 1950, Brooklyn, NY; s. Michael and Hortencia (Rodriguez) M.; m. Heather Glass, Nov. 27, 1982; edn: AS, El Camino Coll. 1976; DC, Cleveland Chiropractic Coll. 1982. Career: supvr. radiological dept. Cleveland Chiropractic Coll., Los Angeles 1982-83; dir. Santa Maria Chiropractic Ofc., Santa Maria 1983-84; currently, chiropractor pvt. practice; tchr. radiological physics, normal radiographic anatomy Cleveland Chiropractic Coll., Los Angeles 1982-83; mem: Am., Calif. and Santa Maria (pub. rels. ofcr. 1985) Chiropractic Assns., Central Coast Chiropractic Soc., Delta Tau Alpha, Elks, Santa Maria CofC, G.I. Forum, YMCA; mil: sgt. E-4 USAF 1968-82; Republican; Catholic; rec: snow skiing, fishing, racquetball. Res: 1296 Ken Ave. Santa Maria 93456 Ofc: Central City Chiropractic, 920 So. Broadway Ste. B Santa Maria 93454

MARTINI, ELMO ERNEST, vintner; b. Nov. 28, 1910, San Francisco; s. Narciso A. and Linda (Vannucci) M.; m. Harriet Bohn, Mar. 2, 1940; children: William, b. 1941, James, b. 1944, Thomas, b. 1948; edn: BS, St. Mary's Coll. 1929-33. Career: part owner R. Martini Wine Co.; prodn. mgr./ v.p. W.A. Taylor & Co.; mgr. Sebastopol Apple Growers Union; current: pres. Martini &

Prati Wines Inc. and Fountain Grove Vineyards; mem: Wine Inst.; Nat. Apple Assn.; Calif. CofC; U.S. CofC; Elks; Republican; Catholic; rec: fishing. Res: 2101 Laguna Rd., Santa Rosa 95401 Ofc: Martini & Prati Wines, 2191 Laguna Rd., Santa Rosa 95401

MARTINSON, JOHN ELWYN, metallurgical engineer, ret.; b. Feb. 8, 1919, Astoria, Ore.; s. John and Ellen Amanda (Hanson) M.; m. Betty Fruehling, Apr. 1, 1946; children: John, Jr. b. 1959, Julia b. 1951, Mina b. 1953; edn: BS in met. engring., Univ. of Nev., Reno 1948. Career: metallurgist Union Carbide Corp. Metals Div., (research, plant trouble shooter, process devel., ore and concentrate purch., environmental control) 1948-82, ret.; mem. AIME (chmn. Los Angeles Subsect. 1950s); civic: Lions (past pres. Pine Creek), Elks, Cub Scouts Cubmaster (1953-60), 4-H Leader (1962-66); tech. paper presented nat. AIME conv. (Pulp Density Meters); mil: 1st lt. US Army FA 1942-46, 1950-52; Republican; Lutheran; rec: travel, stamps & coins, walking. Res: 301 N Mt View Rd Bishop 93514

MARVIN, ARTHUR ELTON, real estate investment broker; b. Feb. 22, 1936, Troy, NY; s. Frank Charles and Mary Katherine (Aiken) M.; edn: AA, Eric Tech. 1959; BS, Univ. of Ariz. 1966; Calif. lic. Real Estate Broker 1982; Nat. Exchanger, NCE. Career: metallurgical engr. Atomic Energy Commn., Los Alamos, NM 1966; engr. McDonnell Douglas 1970; pres. Steelmans, Inc., Huntington Park 1976; broker/ owner Century 21 Carrington Realty 1982–; instr. real estate seminars; honors: Top Salesman, Whitaker Metals 1968; President, Pony/ Colt/ Thoroughbred League, Garden Grove; mem: Nat. Council Exchangers; Huntington Beach- Fountain Valley Bd. Dirs.; Elks; Boys Club com.; works: founder, Real Estate Club of Calif.; author: Foreclosing-Profits and Pitfalls; mil: sgt. US Army 1956-57; Catholic; rec: golf. Address: Marvin Investments POB 5425 Garden Grove 92645

MARVIN, LAWRENCE WARREN, JR., superior court judge; b. Dec. 25, 1927, Sacramento; s. Lawrence W., Sr. and Lillian (Hateley) M.; m. Roberta Renth, July 28, 1956; children: Lawrence, III b. 1957, Katherine b. 1960, Thomas b. 1962; edn: AA, Sacto. Jr. Coll. 1947; AB, UC Berkeley 1949; LLB, JD, Univ. San Francisco 1953; admitted to Calif. State Bar 1954. Career: research atty. Third Dist. Court of Appeal of Calif. 1955-58; dep. dist. atty. Sacramento 1958; assoc. law firm Fitzwilliam, Memoring & McDonald 1958-62; senior ptnr. Barrett, Marvin, Good & Newlan 1962-69; judge Sacramento Municipal Ct. 1969-85, judge Sacramento Superior Ct. 1985–; faculty Judges Coll. of Calif. (1977), lectr. New Judges Orientation (1975-80), lectr. on landlord-tenant sem. McGeorge Sch. of Law (1982), moot court judge num. competitions; mem. Barristers Club of Sacto. (founding pres. 1957, secty. 1958), Legal Aid Soc. (treas. 1961-62), 20-30 Club (1957-64), Rotary Club, Park Terrace Swimming & Tennis Club (pres. 1969); publs: contbr. to Calif. Legal Forms; art. on landlord-tenant law in McGeorge Law J.; mil: P.O./2 USCG 1953-55; Presbyterian (Deacon); rec: fishing, hunting. Ofc: Sacramento Superior Court 720 Ninth St Dept. 20 Sacramento 95814

MARX, ROBERT STUART, manufacturing co. president; b. Aug. 19, 1930, N.Y.C.; s. Gummo and Helen (Theaman) M.; m. Gilda, June 30, 1972; children: Gregg b. 1955, Christopher b. 1962, Tracy b. 1964; edn: USC 1948-50. Career: prod./dir. Screen Gems Inc., CBS Radio, and Filmcraft Prodns., 1952-56; pres./CEO Marval Constrn. Co. Inc., Palm Springs 1956-62, Twin Castle Restaurants Inc., Los Angeles 1962-70; sales mgr. Pennsylvania Life Ins. Co. and Penn Securities Corp., Santa Monica 1970-76; pres./CEO Flexatard, Inc. (mfr. leotards), West Los Angeles 1976–; v.p./CEO Body Designs by Gilda Inc. (exercise studios); recipient Key Man award, Junior CofC (1960); club: Desert Circus, P.S. (pres. 1960); mil: yeoman 1/c US Coast Guard 1950-52; Jewish; rec: photog. Ofc: Flexatard, Inc. 11755 Exposition Blvd Los Angeles 90064

MASH, BARRY DANE, stockbroker; b. Apr. 17, 1958, Pine Bluff, Ark.; s. Michael Charles and Annie Ruth (Doss) M.; edn: BA in pol. sci., Univ. Ariz. 1979; grad. stu. La. State Univ., Shreveport 1980-81; MA internat. rels., Univ. San Diego 1983. Career: comml. lines underwriter Royal Ins., 1980-82, Great Am. Ins., 1982-83; stockbroker Bateman Eichler Hill Richards, San Diego 1983-84, Prudential Bache Securities, La Jolla 1984–; honors: Outstanding Young Men of Am. (1985); mem. Bachelor Club of S.D.; Republican; Prot.; rec: jog, tennis. Res: 701 Gage Dr San Diego 92106 Ofc: Prudential Bache Securities 888 Prospect Ste 301 La Jolla 92037

MASON, DEAN TOWLE, cardiologist; b. Sept. 20, 1932, Berkeley, Calif.; s. Ira Jencks and Florence Mabel (Towle) M.; m. Maureen O'Brien, June 22, 1957; children: Kathleen, Alison; edn: BA chem., Duke Univ. 1954, MD, 1958; Diplomate Nat. Bd. Med. Examiners, Am. Bd. Internal Med. (cardiovascular diseases). Career: intern, med. resident Johns Hopkins Hosp. 1958-61; clin. assoc. cardiol., senior asst. surgeon USPHS, Nat. Heart Inst., NIH 1961-63, asst. sect. dir. cardiovasc. diagnosis, attg. phys., sr. investigator cardiol. 1963-68; prof. med., physiol., chief cardiovasc. med. UC Davis Med. Sch.-Sacto. Med. Ctr. 1968-83; chief phys. Western Heart Inst., St. Mary's Med. Ctr. S.F. 1983–; co-chmn. cardiovasc.-renal drugs US Pharmacopeia Com. Revision 1970-75; mem. life scis. com. NASA; med. research review bd. VA, NIH; vis. prof. num. univs.; cons. in field; mem. Am. Cardiovasc. Splty. Cert. Bd. 1972-78; awards: Recipient Research (Am. Therapeutic Soc. 1965), Theodore and Susan B. Cummings Humanitarian (State Dept.-Am. Coll. Cardiol. 1972, 73, 75, 78), Skylab Achievement (NASA 1974), Merit (World Cong. Vascular Diseases 1976), UC Faculty Research (1978), Sci. Citation (Inst. Sci. Info.), Recognition (for svc. to internat. cardiol. 1978); Tex. Heart Inst. (1979), Disting. Alumnus (Duke Univ. Med. Sch. 1979), Outstanding Prof. (UCD Med.

Sch. 1972); honors: Phi Beta Kappa, Alpha Omega Alpha; fellow: Am. Coll. Cardiol. (pres. 1977-78), Am. Coll. Phys., Am. Heart Assn., Am. Coll. Chest Phys., Royal Soc. Med.; mem: Am. Soc. Clin. Investigation, Am. Physiol. Soc., Am. Soc. Pharmacol. and Exptl. Therapeutics (exptl. ther. award 1973), Am. Fedn. Clin. Research, NY Acad Scis., Am. Assn. Univ. Cardiols., Am. Soc. Clin. Pharmacol. and Therapeutics, Western Assn. Phys., AAUP, Western Soc. Clin. Research (past pres.), El Marcero CC; author: Cardiovascular Management (1974), Congestive Heart Failure (1976), Advances in Heart Disease (Vol. 1 1977, Vol. 2 1978, Vol. 3 1980), Cardiovascular Emergencies (1978), Clinical Methods in Study of Cholesterol Metabolism (1979), Principles of Noninvasive Cardiac Imaging (1980), Clinical Nuclear Cardiology (1981), Myocardial Revascularization (1981), Love Your Heart (1982), Cardiology (1981, 82, 83, 84, 85, 86), num. articles, ed. Clin. Cardiol. Jour., ed.-in-chief Am. Heart Jour., ed. bds. sci. jours.; Republican; Methodist. Res: 3015 Country Club Dr El Macero 95618 Ofc: Western Heart Inst., St. Mary's Med. Ctr. 450 Stanyan St San Francisco 94117

MASON, KENNETH ALLEN, audit services executive; b. June 25, 1942, Albany; s. Harold R. and Hazel V. (Blakemore) M.; 1 dau, Kendra b. 1964, edn. BS, cum laude, Armstrong Coll. 1976; Golden Gate Univ. 1985-86. Career: acct. Andrews, Williams & Co., John H. Williams CPA and George C. Westenrider CPA 1971-76; auditor Jt. Legislative Audit Com., State of Calif. 1976-78; pres. TAB Management Corp. 1978-79; prin. Kenneth A. Mason & Assoc. 1979-80; dir. audit svcs. IKON Financial Sys. Inc., San Mateo 1980–; mem: Inst. of Internal Auditors (past edl. chair 1984-85), Am. Mgmt. Assn.; works: assisted in the writing of legislation affecting mass transportation in Calif. 1977-78; Luthran; rec: golf. Res: 3392 Manchester Common Fremont 94536 Ofc: IKON Financial Systems Inc., 2855 Campus Dr. San Mateo 94403

MASON, ROTHWELL BRISBANE, superior court judge; b. July 7, 1927, Hagerstown, Md.; s. James Gratton and Sudie S. (Clopper) M.; m. Barbara Lee Cochran, Dec. 31, 1964; edn: AB, George Washington Univ. 1951; JD, Fordham Univ. 1956; admitted NY Bar 1957, Calif. Bar 1963. Career: naval aviator 1945-49; FBI agent 1951-54; asst. US Attorney 1963-67 partner law firm Crow, Lytle, Schleh & Mason, Sacramento 1968-73; judge Sacramento Municipal Ct. 1973-76, Sacto. Superior Ct. 1977–; honors: Phi Beta Kappa, Pi Gamma Mu, Delta Phi Epsilon, Phi Delta Phi; publs: Gardner: The Second Gallery, 24 Santa Clara Law Rev., Fall 1984; mil: cdr. USNR, active duty 1945-49, reserv. 1950-70; Republican; rec: gen. aviation, travel. Res: 724 Commons Dr., Sacramento 95825 Ofc: Superior Court, 720 Ninth St Sacramento 95814

MASSA, EDWARD CLEMENT, real estate/insurance broker; b. May 7, 1907, Hayward; s. Manuel Maria and Camilla (Cotta) M.; widower; two children: Michael b. 1938, Valerie (Lozowicki) b. 1948; edn: AB, St. Mary's Coll., Moraga 1929; JD, Univ. of Notre Dame 1933; grad. stu. Stanford Univ. Career: realtor, insuror, developer, cattle ranch owner; handled real estate transactions for num. corporations, developers, public utils., insurance cos., corp. and individual investors; connected family ins. agcy. estab. in the late 1890s; mem. Bd. of Regents St. Mary's Coll. 1970-80; mem. Community Council Sch. of Bus. and Economics, CSU Hayward, mem. CSUH Affiliates, Pres. Circle; secty. Past Presidents Assn. U.P.E.C. (a Portuguese Frat. Life Ins. Co., Calif. -Nev.); mem. Com. of Four rep. Portuguese of origin or birth in Calif. on mission to Fayal, Azore Is. (volcanic eruption mercy mission, 1958); mem. Nat. Ital. Am. Found.; (past): chmn. US Small Bus. Adminstrn. San Francisco Dist. Advis. Council (48 counties); mem. SBA Nat. Advis. Council; awarded citation for svc., SBA (1977); past orgns: pres. St. Mary's Coll. Nat. Alumni Assn. 1957-8, dir. Notre Dame Univ. Alumni Club of No. Calif., chmn. Infantile Paralysis Com. (Hayward), CofC (ofcr., coms.), United Crusade (bd. dirs.), So. Alameda Co. Bd. of Realtors, Hayward Merchants Assn. (pres.), others; book in prog.; Republican; Catholic; rec: writing, music, lecturing, travel. Ofcs: 22566 Norwood Dr Hayward 94541; World Trade Center, Ferry Building, Ste 275C, San Francisco 94111

MASSIE, GEORGE THOMAS, magazine publisher/editor; b. Sept. 1, 1939, Norfolk, Va.; s. Chester James and Constance M. (Berry) M.; m. Wilma Kuypers, Oct. 22, 1960; children: Perry b. 1962, Thomas b. 1965; edn: BSEE, UC Los Angeles 1964. Career: publisher/ed. 1980–, pub. Gold Prospector Mag. (86,000 cir.); pres./CEO Global Resources Inc. (Public Co.); founder/ pres. Gold Prospectors Assn. Inc. (65,000 mem.); founder/pres. Lost Dutchman's Mining Assn. Inc. (1500 mem.); author two books on prospecting for gold in Calif. and Alaska, over 3000 articles Gold Prospector Mag.; honors: Gold Prospector of the Year (5); TV guest, the Merv Griffin Show (1983); mil: airman 1/c USAF; rec: bush pilot (Cessna 206). Res: 2814 Olive Hill Rd Fallbrook 92028 Ofc: Gold Prospector Mag. POB 507 Bonsall 92003 Ofc: 205 N Main St Fallbrook 92028

MASSIER, PAUL FERDINAND, engineering manager; b. July 22, 1923, Pocatello, Idaho; s. John and Kathryn (Arki) M.; m. Miriam Parks, May 1, 1948 (decd. 1975); children: Marilyn b. 1951, Paulette b. 1953; m. 2d Dorothy Hedlund Wright, Sept. 12, 1978; edn: mech. engrg. cert., Univ. Idaho So. Branch (now Idaho State Univ.) 1943; BSME honors, Univ. Colo. 1948; MSME, M.I.T. 1949. Career: engr. Pan Am. Refining Corp. Texas City, Tex. 1948; design engr. Maytag Co. Newton, Iowa 1949-50; research engr. Boeing Co. Seattle, Wash. 1950-55; senior rsch. engr. Jet Propulsion Lab. CalTech Pasadena 1955-58, group supv. 1958-82, exec. asst. 1982-83, task mgr. 1983–; honors: Sigma Xi, Tau Beta Pi, Pi Tau Sigma, Sigma Tau, Life Mem. Svc. Award, PTA of Calif. (1970), Apollo Achievement Award, NASA (1969), Basic Noise Research Award, NASA (1980), Sustained Svc. Award, AIAA (1980-81), Layman of the Yr., Arcadia Congreg. Ch. (1971); mem: assoc. fellow Am. Inst.

Aero. and Astro. (var. coms.), AAAS, Planetary Soc., Am. Biographical Research Assn. (life fellow), Internat. Biographical Assn. (fellow); publs: num. articles in tech. jours., reviewer 7 tech. jours.; mem. plnng. coms./ session chmn. for num. tech. confs.; mil: T/4 US Army 1943-46, Good Conduct, Unit Citn.; Congregational; rec: prod. motion picture travelogs, antiques, collectibles. Res: 1000 N First Ave Arcadia 91006 Ofc: Jet Propulsion Lab. 4800 Oak Grove Dr Pasadena 91109

MASSIHPOUR, SHAHRIAR, structural engineer; b. July 6, 1956, Tehran, Iran, nat. US cit. 1985; s. Hassan and Tahereh (Mirzaabedin) M.; m. Kathleen Ott, Jan. 16, 1981; edn: BS in C.E., CSU San Jose 1978, MS in structural engring., with honors, 1980; Reg. Profl. Engr. (Civil), Calif. 1983. Career: structural designer Cabak Assocs., Menlo Park 1979-83; project mgr. Kee Wong Engineering, Inc., Santa Clara 1983-; struc. cons. Advanced Structual Engineering (ASE), 1985-; assoc. mem. Am. Inst. of Steel Constrn.; rec: books, tennis. Address: San Jose 95124

MASUCCI, VINCENT JOSEPH, insurance co. executive; b. Sept. 3, 1947, Oneida, N.Y.; s. Vincent Samuel and Josephine (Setticase) M.; edn: BA, Univ. of Madrid 1968; BA, King's Coll. 1969; MBA internat. mgmt., Am. Grad. Sch. Internat. Mgmt. 1971. Career: casualty ins. underwriter, Am. Internat. Underwriters, New York (USA) 1972-73, cas. mgr. Latin Am., AIU Guatemala (Central Am.), cas. mgr. Europe, AIU London (UK) 1974-77, asst. worldwide casualty mgr. AIU New York (USA) 1977-78, sr. v.p./mgr. AIU So. Calif. 1978-83, pres. AIU (West Coast) Inc., Los Angeles 1984-; dir. AIU Corp. NY, NY; dir. AIU (West Coast) Inc.; honors: Alpha Mu Gamma; mem. Surplus Lines Assn., Fgn. Trade Assn., LA CofC, British Am. CofC, Calif. Com. for Internat. Trade; clubs: Jonathan, Los Angeles; mil: NY Army Res. Nat. Guard 1969-74; Republican; Roman Catholic; rec: hist., biking, travel. Ofc: American International Underwriters 3699 Wilshir Blvd 3d Flr Los Angeles 90010

MATERDOMINI, DANIEL, dental ceramist; b. Sept. 26, 1941, Brooklyn, NY; s. Domonick and Salvatrice M.; m. Christine, Dec. 26, 1971; children: Damian b. 1974, Chasin b. 1980; edn: Dental Ceramist, Kerpell Sch. of Dental Tech. 1961. Career: dental ceramist Nu-Dent Porcelain Studio NYC 1961-64, dental ceramist and mgr. 1964-69, adminstr. and quality control supv. 1969-70; ptnr. Dental Studio in So. Calif. Fine Arts Dental Lab 1970-73; merged w/ Ceramic Science, new name Fine Arts & Science 1973-76; pres., owner DaVinci Dental Lab./Studios Topanga Cyn. 1976-; splst. in epoxy, aluminum porcelain, blending porcelain, porcelain veneers; lectr., instr., clinician to dental profession, Johnson & Johnson, DaVinci Dental Studios 1984, 85, 86; mem: SCDLA, Mus. of Contemp. Art of L.A., Nat. Audubon Soc., Natural History Mus.; mil: sp4 US Army 1964; Republican; Catholic; rec: boating, flying. Ofc: DaVinci Dental Studios 7355 Topanga Cyn Blvd Ste 200 Topanga Canyon 91303

MATHAUDHU, SUKHDEV S., engineer; b. Sept. 11, 1946, Dhamtan Sahib, India, nat. US cit. 1979; s. Kesho Ram and Channo Devi (Dhiman) M.; m. Veena Chand, Aug. 20, 1972; children: Suveen b. 1975, Suneel b. 1976; edn: BSME, Walla Walla Coll. 1970; Reg. Profl. Engr., Calif. and Penn. Career: project engr. McGinnis Engring. Inc., Portland, Ore. 1970-71; campus engr. Canadian Union Coll., College Hts., Alberta, Can. 1971-72; project engr. H.D. Nottingham & Assocs., McLean, Va. 1972; project engr. Shefferman & Bigelson Co., Silver Springs, Md. 1973-77; mech. engr. Buchart Assocs., York, Penn. 1977-78; senior mech. engr. Gannett Flemming, Harrisburg, Penn. 1978-80; chief mech. engr. Popov Engrs. Inc., Newport Beach 1981-83; pres. Mathaudhu Engring. Inc., Riverside 1983-; bd. dirs. La Sierra Acad. & Elem. Sch.; mem: Nat. and Calif. (pres. Riverside- San Bernardino chpt. 1985, state dir. 1986) Socs. of Profl. Engrs., ASHRAE, Am. Soc. Plumbing Engrs., Soc. of Am. Mil. Engrs.; Republican; Seventh-Day Adventist (lay advy. com. Southeastern Conf.); rec: woodworking, camping, photog. Res: 5394 College Ave. Riverside 92505 Ofc: Mathaudhu Engineering Inc., 3903 Brockton Ave. Ste. 5 Riverside 92501

MATHIAS, BETTY JANE, communications and community affairs consultant, lecturer, b. Oct. 22, 1923, East Ely, Nev.; d. Royal F. and Dollie B. (Bowman) M.; 1 dau. Dona Bett; edn: Merritt Bus. Sch. 1941-42; San Francisco State Univ. 1941-42. Career: asst. publicity dir. Oakland Area War Chest and Community Chest 1943-46; pub. rels. staff Am. Legion Oakland 1946-47; asst. to pub. rels. dir. Central Bank of Oakland 1947-49; pub. rels. dir. East Bay chpt. Natg. Safety Council 1949-51; proprietor, mgr. Mathias Public Relations Agcy. Oakland 1951-60; gen. assignment reporter and teen news editor Daily Review Hayward 1960-62; freelance pub. rels. and writing Oakland 1962-66, 67-69; dir. corp. communications Systech Fin. Corp. Walnut Creek 1969-71; v.p. corp. communs. Consol. Capital Cos. Oakland 1972-79, v.p. community affairs Emeryville 1981-84, v.p. spl. projects 1984-85; v.p., dir. Consol. Capital Realty Svcs. Inc. Oakland 1976-77; communs. cons. 1979-; bd. dirs. Oakland YWCA 1944-45, ARC Oakland, So. Alameda County chpt. 1967-69, Family Ctr. Children's Hosp. Med. Ctr. No. Calif. 1982-85, March of Dimes 1983-85; adult and publs. adv. Internat. Order of the Rainbow for Girls 1953-78; communs. arts adv. com. Ohlone Coll. 1979-85 (chmn. 1982-85); mem. adv. bd. dept. mass communs. CSU Hayward 1985; pres. S.F. Bay Area chpt. Nat. Reyes Syndrome Found. 1981-; honors: Grand Cross of Color Award (Internat. Order of Rainbow for Girls 1955); mem: Women in Communs. (dir. 1979-83), East Bay Women's Press Club (pres. 1960-61, 83-85), Order of Eastern Star (state publicity chmn. 1955); Editor East Bay Mag. 1966-67, TIA Traveller 1969, Concepts 1979-83. Res: 20575 Gopher Dr Sonora 95370

MATHIAS, CORINNE FLORENCE, consulting co. president; b. June 10, 1926, Buffalo, N.Y.; d. Sidney and Florence (Vincent) O'Neill; m. Richard C.

Mathias, Sept. 4, 1947; children: Richard b. 1948, Michael b. 1950, Corinne b. 1953, Marc b. 1954; edn: AA, Citrus Coll. 1979. Career: supr. Von's Grocery Co., El Monte 1960-72, adminstr. 1973-78; pres. Direct Delivery Data, Glendora 1978-85, bd. chmn., 1986-, cons. Alpha Beta Grocery Co., Lucky Stores Inc., Hughes Markets, Ladd Ents., Boys Markets; recipient scholarship award, Women in Mgmt./ San Gabriel chpt. (1979); mem. So. Calif. Grocers Assn.; civic: L.A. County Museum of Arts, Redlands Comm. Music Assn., Com. Against Govt. Waste, NOW; publs: Receiving Clerk's Manual (1969); Democrat; Roman Catholic; rec: photog., bridge, golf, travel. Res: 4575 Romana #2 La Verne 91750 Ofc: Direct Delivery Data 935 E Myrtle Ave Glendora 91740

MATHISON, LAWRENCE GEORGE, telecommunications/ distribution co. executive; b. May 13, 1946, Newton, Mass.; s. Francis Christy and Helen (Kavanagh) M.; m. Pamela, May 25, 1980; edn: BS in bus. Adm., Univ. New Hampshire 1968; MBA program, Pepperdine Univ. 1984-. Career: mgr. budgets & forecasts, major account mgr., dist. sales mgr., area sales mgr., branch gen. mgr. Western Union Tel. Co., 1969-85; nat. sales mgr. and div. mgr. Coast to Coast Terminals Inc., 1985-; profl. awards as Top Area Sales Mgr. nat. (1982, 83) and Top Dist. Sales Mgr. (1979, 80), Western Union; mem. Sales & Mktg. Execs. (1980-81); Republican; Prot.; rec: golf, basketball, tennis. Res: 7 Copper Hill Irvine 92714 Ofc: Coast to Coast Terminals 17752 Skypark Cir Ste 180 Irvine 92714

MATSON, JOHN WILLIAM, II, publisher; b. Sept. 15, 1944, Nashville, Tenn.; s. John Wm. and Janet Louise (Reese) M.; edn: AB, William Penn Coll. 1968; AM, Creighton Univ. 1971. Career: security ofcr. Pinkerton Inc., Los Angeles Office, 1972-76; title clerk TransAm. Title Ins. Co., L.A. 1976-80; owner John William Matson III, A.M., Publr., Beverly Hills, 1980-; honors: History Award, William Penn Coll. (1968), appreciation certificates: L.A. Co. Heart Assn. (1964), Nat. Police Ofcrs. Assn. (1972), Second Amendment Found. (1983), United Service Orgn. (1984); mem. Fla. Assn. of Pvt. Investigators (1977-); preceptor Glendale Chpt. Order of DeMolay (1959); works: currently composing acrostic poetry on the deities and values of the religion of Asatru; Libertarian; Episcopal; rec: hist. research, European folk music. Res: POB 9201 Glendale 91206 Ofc: John William Matson II, A.M. Publshr. 256 S Robertson Blvd Ste 5350 Beverly Hills 90211

MATSUI, ROBERT TAKEO, congressman; b. Sept. 17, 1941, Sacramento; s. Yasuji and Alice (Nagata) M.; m. Doris Kazue Okada, Sept. 17, 1966; edn: AB in polit. sci., UC Berkeley 1963; JD, UC Boalt Hall of Law, 1966; admitted to Calif. State Bar 1967. Career: legal intern Calif. State Dept. Water Resources, Sacto. 1966; practice law, Sacto. 1967-78; elected mem. Sacramento City Council 1971-78; elected rep. 96th Congress from 3d Calif. Dist., 1979-, mem. com. on ways and means; city rep. Sacto. Area CD and Disaster Council, 1972-; campaign chmn. Cong. John E. Moss re-election campaign, 1972, 74, 76; mem. Calif. Democratic Central Com. 1973-4, 75-6, 77-8; awards: Jaycees Young Man of Year 1973, Distinguished Service Award 1973; mem. Sacto. Japanese Am. Citizens League (pres. 1969), Sacto. Met. CofC (dir. 1976), 20-30 Club (pres. 1972), Rotary. Ofc: 231 Cannon House Office Bldg., Wash. DC 20515

MATSUURA, ALVIN M., accounting executive; b. Feb. 1, 1949, Wailuku, Hawaii; edn: BS honors, Cal. Poly. S.L.O. 1971; MBA, CSU Dominguez Hills 1985. Career: gen. acct. gen. acctg., accts. payable, audit, payroll Gen. Motors Van Nuys 1972-78, gen. acct. product cost 1978, senior acct. in chg. freight sect. 1979, senior acct. in chg. factory cost, accts. payable supv. 1981-86, factory cost supv. 1986-; honors: President's Cup (Cal. Poly. 1971); mem: AM. Mgmt. Assn., Assoc. Photogs. Internat., Japanese American Citizens League; mil: capt. infantry USAR, CANG 1972-79; rec: photog. Ofc: General Motors Van Nuys 91409

MATTA, LORENE GENEVA, electronics co. president; b. Aug. 27, 1943, San Jose; d. Willie Manuel and Lorene (Baxter) Dean; m. Dallas Matta, May 18, 1959; children: Tina b. 1963, Heidi b. 1966, Preston b. 1969 (decd.). Career: electronic assembler Sylvania Santa Cruz 1961-63; motel mgr. 1963-64, waitress Holiday Inn Santa Cruz 1969-70; co-owner, oper. Dallas Union 76 Bainbridge, Ga. 1973-74; electronic assembler self-employed Santa Cruz 1975-81; pres., co-owner Dallas Electronics Santa Cruz 1981-; mem. PTA (Santa Cruz 1968-82, Bainbridge 1973-74); Democrat; Protestant; rec: writing, sewing, knitting, gardening, cooking. Res: 1351 High St Santa Cruz 95060 Ofc: Dallas Electronics 1201 Shaffer Rd Ste B Santa Cruz 95060

MATTESON, WILLIAM ROBERT, real estate co. president; b. July 14, 1922, Kellhier, Minn.; s. Charles James and Maude Jesse (Jones) M.; children: Robert b. 1952, Lorraine b. 1962; edn: BS, Bryant A. & Stratton Coll. 1948; PhD in bus. mgmt., Internat. Coll. 1982; Calif. lic: Road Builder, Gen. Contractor, Real Estate Broker. Career: past pres. Title Realty Co.; past chmn. bd. Portafone Corp.; past chmn. bd. S.U.S. Ents., Diversified Corp.; current: pres. P.S. I Love You Realty; pres. Matteson Constrn. Co.; pres. P.S. Devel. Group; bd. dirs. num. mutual funds, and other corps.; author, lectr. var. colls. statewide; awards: Mexico-US Cultural Exch. Award; mem: Internat. Congress of Shopping Ctr. Developers, Palm Springs Bd. of Realtors, Palm Springs CofC, Aircraft Owners & Pilots Assn., The Magic Castle; civic: Angleview Crippled Childrens Hosp. (past bd. dirs.); author, 1st Am. book on Timeshare: The Prepaid Vacation; inventor and developer of the cordless telephone; mil: US Army 1942-45, ETO, Bronze Star, Purple Heart, Pres. Citation (2); Republican (pres. The Rep. Club, So. Calif. co-chmn. the Pres.'s Club, Reagan coord. counsel, 3d Dist. Rep. Central Com., pres. P.S. Rep. Assem.); Presbyterian; rec: pilot, golf. Ofc: 2825 E Tahquitz-McCallum Way Palm Springs 92262

MATTEUCCI, LOUIS ALFRED, real estate broker; b. Apr. 1, 1927, San Francisco; s. Aladino and Stella Domenica (Pastorini) Panelli; m. Gloria Colombo, Sept. 20, 1954; children: Paul b. 1955, Glenn b. 1958; edn: UC Berkeley 1947-48; real estate, Skyline Jr. Coll. 1972-74 ; lifetime lic. jr. coll. real estate instr., City Coll. S.F. 1978; real estate broker Calif. 1974. Career: sole prop. retail-food market 1968-72; financial planner Putnam Financial Svcs. 1968-72; real estate agent 1972-74; sole prop. Matteucci & Co. Realtors So. San Francisco 1974—; instr. real estate classes Skyline Coll. 1977-82; mem. Downtown Parking Commn. So. S.F.; mem: Sam Mateo Bd. of Realtors (pres. 1980, bd. dirs. 1978, 81, 82, v.p. 1979, chmn. edn. 1983, other coms.), Italian Family Club (pres. 1955), Monte Cristo Club (pres. 1965-69), El Camino Boosters (pres. 1971, 73), So. S.F. Merchants Assn., CofC; mil: sgt. USAF 1945-46; Republican; Catholic; rec: fishing. Res: 648 Joaquin S San Francisco 94080 Ofc: Matteucci & Co., 439 Grand S San Francisco 94080

MATTHEWS, LESTER ORR, educator, ret.; b. Dec. 17, 1901, Pendleton, Ore.; s. Arthur Thomas and Lulu May (Wilson) M.; m. Onda Glunt, Feb. 9, 1926; 1 dau: Donna May b. 1927; m. 2d Grace C. Huus, 1948 (decd. 1977); m. 3d Frances Evelyn Carter; edn: BS, Oregon State Coll. 1925; supvry. & adminstrn., Univ. So. Calif. 1937, MS edn., 1955. Career: mgr. A.T. Matthews & Son Constrn. Co. 1925-29; elem. sch. tchr. L.A. City Schools 1929-30; h.s. tchr. Fremont H.S. 1930-47; supv. of jr. and sr. h.s. agriculture pgm. 1947-65 (84 schs., largest pgm. in US); in charge edn. pgm. for Los Angeles Beautiful 1950-65; honors: Alpha Zeta, Gamma Sigma Delta, Hon. Calif. Future Farmers of Am., L.A. Beautiful Award for Community Svc.; mem: L.A. Teachers Assn., NRTA, NEA, AARP, Calif. Vocat. Agri. Tchrs. Assn., Calif. Bureau of Agri. Educators (ex-officio), Kappa Delta Rho frat., L.A. Co. Poultrymen's Assn. (past pres.), L.A. CofC, Masons; past pres. Mutual 15 & Mutual 12, Leisure World, Laguna Hills, Calif. publ: articles for nat. vocat. ednl. jours. on agri. edn. in urban schools; Republican; Episcopal; rec: gardening, landscaping, golf. Res: 17343 Lakeshore Dr Weed 96094

MATZ, KENNETH FRANCIS, paper co. president; b. Nov. 1, 1924, Los Angeles; s. Peter and Ella Rose (Farnham) M.; m. Louise Nobs, Nov. 23, 1947; children: Larry b. 1950, Fred b. 1961; edn: L.A. City Coll., Loyola Univ. 1943. Career: founder/pres. Matz Paper Co., Inc. Van Nuys 1946—, customers in 6 Western states; mem. Van Nuys CofC, YMCA; mil: sgt. US Army Inf. 1943-46, 89th Div.; Republican; Lutheran; rec: golf, music, bowling. Res: 5843 Costello Ave Van Nuys 91401 Ofc: Matz Paper Co. Inc. 14122 Aetna St Van Nuys 91401

MATZ, RUDOLPH WALTER, transit mix co. president; b. Oct. 21, 1919, Newark, Ohio; s. John and Frances Helen (Mattern) M.; m. Maxine E. Wilson, Sept. 23, 1944; children: Carolyn b. 1945, Linda b. 1948, Rudolph, Jr. b. 1951, Eric b. 1964; edn: Univ. Ga. 1942; Navy Flight Sch. Pensacola 1943; Temple Univ. 1946-47; BS indsl. mgmt., Ohio State Univ. 1958. Career: pres. Poway Lumber Co. 1960-74, Padre Transit Mix 1974—; honors: President's Award (Lions Internat. 1981); mem: Assn. Building Contrs., Am. Concrete Inst., Poway Lions Club, Silver Eagles Assn.; mil: cmdr. USN 1939-60, 3 Disting Flying Crosses, 8 Air Medals, 2 Pres. Citns.; Republican; Protestant; rec: fishing, travel, woodworking. Res: 16692 Espola Rd Poway 92064 Ofc: Padre Transit 10975 Beeler Cyn Rd Poway 92064

MAUK, MERLIN HAROLD, physician; b. Aug. 25, 1928, Arroyo Grande, Calif.; s. Harold Harrison and Evelyn Mathilda (Haglund) M.; m. Doreen Ham, Aug. 29, 1953; children: Mitchell b. 1957, Russell b. 1958, Glenn b. 1963; edn: BA, Pacific Union Coll. 1949; MD, George Washington Univ. 1957. Career: pvt. practice family med. 1958—; asst. prof. clin. med. UC Davis; honors: Paul Harris Fellow Award (Rotary Club); mem: AMA, CMA (del. 1985), Am. Acad. Fam. Phys., Calif. Acad. Fam. Phys. (spkr, House of Delegates, bd. dirs., treas.), Rotary Club, Rancho Cordova CofC; co-author: A Study of Drugs Used for Preanesthetic Medication 1956; mil: corpl. US Army (MC) 1950-52; Republican; Protestant; rec: sailing, skiing, racquetball. Ofc: 2828 Mills Park Dr, Ste. A, Rancho Cordova 95670

MAXHAM, LAWRENCE ARTHUR, patent lawyer; b. Jan. 4, 1938, Framingham, Mass.; s. Harold W. and Ellen C. (Orton) M.; children: Heidi b. 1963, Tanya b. 1967; edn: BS in E.E., Tufts Univ. 1960; JD, Boston College Law Sch. 1966; admitted to bar: Mass. (1966), Calif. (1982). Career: atty. assoc. Weingarten, Orenbuch & Lahive, Boston 1966-67, Joseph Weingarten Law Offices, Boston 1967-70; ptnr. Weingarten, Maxham & Schurgin, Boston 1970-81; of counsel Dike, Bronstein, Roberts, Cushman & Pfund, Boston 1981; assoc. atty. Brown & Martin, San Diego 1981-84; atty. ptnr. Baker, Maxham, Callan & Jester, S.D. 1984-85, Baker, Maxham & Jester 1986—; honors: Tau Beta Pi engring. hon. soc. (1959), Order of the Coif (1966); mem: Boston Patent Law Assn. (chmn. coms.; ofcr; pres. elect 1981), San Diego Patent Law Assn. (v.p. 1985), ABA, Am. Intellectual Property Law Assn., US Trademark Assn., State Bar of Calif. (Patent, Trademark and Copyright Sect.); publs: two law review articles; hundreds of patents written for clients; mil: lt. US Navy 1960-63; rec: golf, tennis. Res: 13661 Mango Dr Del Mar 92014 Ofc: Baker, Maxham & Jester 110 West C Street Ste 1202 San Diego 92101

MAY, ROGER ANDREW, accountant; b. Aug. 29, 1946, Hartford, Conn.; s. Henry Andrew and Evelyn Emma (D'Amour) M.; edn: Glendale Coll. of Law 1974-76; BS, CSU Northridge 1971; CPA, Calif. 1975. Career: jr. acct. Gursey Morgan & Co. CPAs, Los Angeles 1972-73; acct. Gilbert Vasquez & Co., CPAs, Los Angeles 1973-74; suvpr. acctg. Harry Nourse & Co., PAs, Santa Monica 1974-76; CPA, solo practice, Panorama City 1976-77; tax senior, CPA, Philip Bartmasser & Co. CPAs, Beverly Hills 1977—; cons. J.L. Bunner Co. 1985; sole practitioner 1976-; honors; Silver Star for Scholastic Achiev. 1964;

mem: Phi Sigma Kappa Alumni (CSU, treas., secty.), Calif. Soc. CPAs; mil: sp4 US Army 1968-70; Republican; rec: body building, bicycling, jogging. Res: 8179 Wakefield Ave. Panorama City 91402 Ofc: Philip Bartmasser & Co. CPAs, 8913 W. Olympic Ste. 205 Beverly Hills 90211

MAYALL, ROBERT BAILEY, electrical engineer; b. July 2, 1926, Los Angeles; s. James Samuel and Mildred F. (Bailey) M.; m. Patricia Laurene Smith, Dec. 27, 1952; children: Carol Laurene b. 1955, James Harley b. 1956; edn: Univ. of New Mexico (USNR V-12) 1944-46; BE in E.E., USC 1948; var. grad. courses USC 1949-56; Reg. Profl. Engr. (elec.) Calif. Career: jr. engr. to supv./ senior engr. So. Calif. Edison Co., Rosemead 1948—, held var. engring. and supvsry. positions in engring. design, system ops., computer applications, involved in power contracts negotiation and adminstrn., 1964-; honors: Phi Kappa Phi, Sigma Tau, 2d Prize for Papers, Am. Inst. of Elect. Engrs., Pacific Dist. 8 (1961-62); mem: IEEE, Pacific Coast Elect. Assn., Am. Legion, Sigma Chi Frat., USC Alumni Assn., L.A. County Mus. of Art, Smithsonian Assocs.; author: Comput-A-Grade (1985), computer gradebook pgm. for tchrs.; mil: ensign USNR 1944-47; Republican; Episcopal; rec: golf, tennis, genealogy. Res: 17075 Knapp St Northridge 91325 Ofc: Southern California Edison Co. PO Box 800 Rosemead 91770

MAYBURY, JOHN EDWARD, psychologist, counselor; b. Sept. 10, 1922, Phila.; s. John Wesley and Irene (Dapp) M.; m. Thelma M., May 23, 1946; children: Patricia, Suzanne, Stephen, Kim Ann; edn: BA, Eastern Nazarene Coll. 1945, ThB, 1946; BD, Nazarene Theol. Seminary 1955; MA, Eastern New Mex. Univ. 1965; MA, Chapman Grad. Sch. 1975; PhD, Calif. Coast Univ. 1985. Career: minister Ch. of the Nazarene 1946-70; hosp. chaplain Long Beach Meml. Hosp. 1970-71; med. social worker Pacific Hosp. Long Beach 1971-74; adminstr. Riviera Convales. Hosp. Pico Rivera 1974, Internat. Inst. Orange County 1975-82; pvt. practice family counselor 1982—; mem. Santa Ana CofC; Republican; Protestant; rec: golf, creative weddings. Res: 7055 Creekside Ln Anaheim 92807 Ofc: Virginia Foster & Assoc. 2220 E Fruit St, Ste 109, Santa Ana 92701

MAYEDA, BRYAN, veterinarian; b. Sept. 1, 1922, Loomis, Calif.; s. Sanjiro and Kin M.; m. May Satsuki Mizobe, Apr. 5, 1953, children: Elaine Tsuruyo b. 1955, Phyllis Naomi b. 1958; edn: DVM, Mich. State Univ. 1949; lic. Calif. 1950. Career: diag. lab. vet. Calif. Dept. of Food & Agriculture Sacramento Lab. 1949-64, asst. dir. Sacramento Lab.1964-83, dir. Petaluma Lab. 1983-85; emerg. on-the-farm vet. diag. svc. for poultry and game bird growers 1986—; lectr. Sch. of Vet. Med. UC Davis 1964-81; pgm. chmn., pres. Western (No. Am.) Poultry Disease Conf. 1963-65; honors: Disting. Svc. Award (Cosumnes River Coll. Sacto. 1974), Disting. Svc. Award (Western No. Am. Poultry Disease Conf. UC Davis 1985), Appreciation Award (Calif. Dept. of Food & Ag. 1985); mem: Am. Vet. Med. Assn. 1949-, Am. Assn. Avian Pathologists 1958-, Calif. Vet. Med. Assn. 1983-, Explorer Scouting (assoc. advisor 1971-72, advisor 1973-74), advisory com. Animal Health Technol. Pgm. Cosumnes River Coll. 1971-75; publ: 11 sci. articles in poultry medicine 1961-83; mil: lt. USAR 1949-54; Democrat; Presbyterian; rec: photog., gardening, home improvement, bird watching. Res: 6521 13th St Sacramento 95831

MAYER, BRUCE EDWIN, mechanical design engineer; b. Mar. 24, 1955, Ipswich, S.Dak.; s. Frank Felix and Marcella Virginia (Mohr) M.; m. Susan, May 19, 1979; edn: AA, Cabrillo Coll. 1976; BS, UC Berkeley 1978; MS, Stanford Univ. 1983; Reg. Profl. Engr. (Mech.); Calif. Community Coll. Lmtd. Service Credential (Engring.). Career: research tech. Lawrence Berkeley Lab., 1978-79; engring. instr., Cabrillo Coll. 1980-81; project engr. Watkins-Johnson Co., Scotts Valley 1979—; honors: Pi Tau Sigma, Tau Beta Pi; mem: ASME (assoc.), Santa Clara Valley Chpt. ASME, ASHRAE (assoc.), Soc. for Am. Baseball Research; Republican; rec: baseball, microcomputer pgmmg. Res: 4424 Starboard Ct Soquel 95073 Ofc: Watkins-Johnson Co. 440 Kings Village Rd Scotts Valley 95066

MAYER, JAMES BRADLEY, optometrist; b. March 22, 1957, Beloit, Wisc.; s. Melvin William and Mary Elizabeth (Lenges) M.; m. Suzanne K. Nakama, June 29, 1980; edn: BS, Pacific Univ. 1981, OD, 1983. Career: optometrist, independent contractor, var. 1983-84; vision therapist Dr. William Ludlam, Hillsboro, Ore. 1981-83; pres. Pacific Prisms, Forest Grove, Ore. 1982-83; chief of staff Dr. James B. Mayer, Thousand Oaks 1984—; bd. dirs. Senior Concerns, Conejo Community Svcs. Ctr., A Total Learing Ctr., Sports Vision of Am. 1983-; honors: Donald Bybee Award, Excellence in Vision Therapy, Pacific Univ. 1983; J. Harold Bailey Award, Best Senior Thesis, Am. Optometric Found. 1983; Acceptance for Profl. Presentation, Calif. Optometric Assn. 1985; mem: Am. Optometric Assn. (Contact Lens and Sports Visions sects.), Optometric Extension Pgm., Coll. of Optometrists in Vision Development, Nat. Acad. of Sports Vision, Sports Vision Assn. of Am., Orthon Soc., Assn. of Children with Learning Disabilities, Rotary of Thousand Oaks, Conejo Valley CofC, Conejo Valley Senior Concerns, Conejo Valley Community Svcs. Ctr., A Total Learning Ctr.; author: sev. articles in local media on contact lenses and visually related learning problems 1984-; Christian; rec: racquetball, bicycling, photog. Res: 263 Gazania Ct. Thousand Oaks 91362 Ofc: Dr. James B. Mayer, Optometry, 1329 E. Thousand Oaks Blvd. Thousand Oaks 91362

MAYER, PATRICIA JAYNE, financial executive; b. Apr. 27, 1950, Chgo.; d. Arthur and Ruth J. (Greenberger) Hersh; m. Wm. A. Mayer, Jr. Apr. 30, 1971; edn: BS in acctg., CSU Hayward 1975; CPA (1978). Career: auditor Elmer Fox, Westheimer CPAs, 1976; supvsg. auditor Alameda County Auditors Office, 1976-78, devel. and wrote new auditing procedures 1976; asst. mgr. Gen.

Acctg. Dept., CBS Retail Stores dba Pacific Stereo, 1978-79; controller Oakland Unified Sch. Dist., 1979-84; v.p./controller YMCA of San Francisco 1984 – ; instr. in-house acctg. seminars; mem. Nat. Assn. of Accts.; civic: Dep. County Registrar of Voters (1971-76), draft counselor Mt. Diablo Peace Ctr. (1971-73); Democrat; rec: Dalmation dogs. Res: 2395 Lake Meadow Circle Martinez 94553 Ofc: YMCA of San Francisco 220 Golden Gate Ave 3d Fl San Francisco 94102

MAYFIELD, EVELYN JOYCE, word processing services consultant; b. July 21, 1933, Hutchinson, Kans.; d. Chester Marvin and Kathryn (Nickel) Dauber; m. Joseph Hoyle Mayfield, Sept. 12, 1952; children: Keith b. 1953, Dennis b. 1956, Cynthia b. 1960 (decd. 1976); edn: Pierce Coll. 1962-63. Career: secty. First Baptist Ch. Taft, Calif. 1952-53; direct sales rep. Emmons Jewelry 1967; secty. Phillips Petroleum Co. 1967-68, Litton Inds. 1967; owner, mgr. Mayfield Svcs. 1968 – ; cons. secretarial svcs., thesis preparations, office sys. acquisitions; lecturer, seminar leader; honors: Dedicated Svc. Award (Profl. Assn. of Sec. Svcs. 1983); mem. Nat. Assn. Secretarial Svcs. (formerly Profl. Assn. Secretarial Svcs., internat. v.p. pgms. 1981-83); lectr. Christian Women's Clubs, L.A. Baptist Mission Soc. Aux.; publ: articles in profl. mags., nat. newsletters; Baptist; rec: puppetry, reading, writing. Address: 23860 Friar St Woodland Hills 91367

MAYMAN, EVELYN WINIFRED, physician, ret.; b. Apr. 5, 1900, Sauk Rapids, Minn.; d. Edward W. and Harriet A. (Rockwell) M.; edn: BS, Univ. Minn. 1924; MD, Univ. Minn. Med. Sch. 1927. Career: physician pvt. practise in Modesto 1930-71; active staff (chief anesthesiologist 10 years) McPheeter's Hosp. (1930-50), St. Mary's Hosp. (1930-45), Memorial Hosp. (1950-71), Modesto Hosp. (1945-71); consulting phys. Stanislaus Co. Hosp.; mem: AMA, Stanislaus Co. Medical Soc., Calif. Med. Assn., Modesto Branch Nat. Penwomen (pres. 1968-70); charter mem. Modesto Branch Internat. Soroptomist Club; Senior Activities Inc. (1977-); Shakespeare Club of Modesto; publs: contbr. J. Pediatrics (1940); Republican; Episcopal; rec: watercolor painting, silkscreen painting. Res: 900 Brady Ave Modesto 95350

MAYNARD, MICHAEL ERNEST, manufacturing co. president; b. Mar. 17, 1943, Franklin, N.H.; s. Charles Leonel and Ruth Evelyn (Doyle) M.; m. Sally Provost, Nov. 8, 1963; children: Michael Jr. b. 1964, Stephen b. 1966, Shelena b. 1966; edn: US Armed Forces Inst. 1960-63. Career: mgr./ food supvr. Howard Johnson Restaurant 1963-65; svc. mgr., prod. mgr., v.p. research & devel., pres. Automation D.S.S., Inc. 1966-82; pres./ engr. Misa Mfg., Inc., Design 1982 – ; pres./ dir. mktg. Automatic Dishwashing Sys., Inc. 1983 – ; mem: Retail Bakers Assn. of Am.; Calif. Restaurant Assn.; Golden Circle Club of Am. R.B.A.; US CofC 1984-85; charter contbr. Statue of Liberty Ellis Island Found.; Royal Order of Moose; inventions: Egg Master, Helper I, Helper II; mil: E-4 USN 1960-63; Republican; Catholic; rec: spl. project research, organist. Res: 11401 Jacalene Ln Garden Grove 92640 Ofc: Misa Manufacturing, Inc., 14752 Franklin Ave Tustin 92680

MAYNARD, NANCY HICKS, journalist, consultant; b. Nov. 1, 1946, NY, NY; d. Alfred W. and Eve K. (Keller) Hall; m. Robert C. Maynard, Jan. 1, 1975; children: Don b. 1958, David b. 1971, Alex b. 1979; edn: BA cum laude, Long Island Uni. 1967; Stanford Law Sch. 1984-. Career: news asst., reporter NY Post 1966-68; reporter (edn., science news, Wash. bureau) NY Times 1968-77; dir. Inst. for Journalism Edn., Berkeley 1977-79, pres. 1979-83; reporter, commentator KTVU Oakland 1983-84; freelance journalist, consultant 1984 – ; dir. Kaiser Found. Health Plan Inc. 1981-, Oakland Tribune Inc. 1983-, KQED Inc. 1982-85; trustee Mills Coll. 1982-86; selection com. Nieman Fellowships for Journ., Harvard Univ. 1984; panelist Wash. Week in Review, PBS 1977-79; contbg. editor Black Enterprise Magazine 1978-79; guest panelist Face The Nation, CBS, Meet The Press, NBC 1975, 76; honors: Marsh Disting. Prof. of Journ., Univ. Mich. (1978), Achievement Awards: Coro Found. (1984), Women in Communs. (1981), Advocates for Women (1982); author Rep. Shirley Chisholm, Congresswoman from Brooklyn (1971); writer Understanding Pregnancy & Childbirth by Sheldon Cherry, MD (1972); composer lullaby (1958); Lutheran. Ofc: 5960 Broadway Terrace Oakland 94618

MAYNE, J. LEE, industrial/ aerospace executive; b. Nov. 26, 1931, St. Anthony, Idaho; s. George M. and Myrtle M. (Lutz) M.; m. Diane Myers, May 27, 1955; children: Kim b. 1957, Craig b. 1959, Chad b. 1962, Kevin b. 1964, Kathy and Stacy b. 1974; edn: AA, DeAnza Coll. 1968; BS, Coll. of Notre Dame 1970; Exec. Mgmt. Pgm., Penn. State Univ. 1975; Lockheed Exec. Inst., Kellog West 1979; Cert. Mgr., Inst. of Cert. Profl. Mgrs. 1977. Career: with Lockheed, Sunnyvale 1966 – ; mgr. procurement control 1966-71; mgr. space engring. & control 1972-76; dir. energcy 1976-82; dir. plant svcs. 1980-82; div. mgr. 1982 – ; chmn. bd. Dirs. Mgmt. Assn. 1984-85; dir. Mgmt. Assn. 1983-84; mem: Am. Inst. of Indsl. Engrs. (senior), Inst. of Cert. Profl. Mgrs., Park Com. (exec. bd.); mil: m/sgt. US Army 1950-52, Bronze Star w/ Battle Stars; Republican; Ch. of Jesus Christ LDS; rec: tennis, church activities. Res: 20357 Clay Cupertino 95014 Ofc: Lockheed, 1111 Lockheed Way Sunnyvale 94086

MAYO, JOHN BLOUNT, public relations agency owner/ educator; b. Jan. 9, 1938, Richmond, Va.; s. John B. and Lillian (Hargrave) M: M. Nita Louise Kellam, May 30, 1965; children: Carolyn Lee b. 1962, Sara Louise b. 1967, John Kellam b. 1969, Kathleen Elizabeth b. 1974; edn: BA, Univ. of N.C. 1960; MA, Univ. of Tex., Austin 1966; MA, Am. Univ., Wash. DC 1976. Career: Cdr, USN (ret.), active duty USN as Spl. Duty (Public Affairs) Ofcr. 1960-80: deputy pub. affairs ofcr. Submarine Force Atlantic 1966-68; asst. pub. affairs ofcr. First Naval Dist. 1968-69; pub. affairs ofcr. Naval Material Command 1969-70, Naval Air Sys. Command 1980-81, Naval Forces Vietnam 1971-72;

dir. research & evaluation Naval Internat Rels. Activity 1972-73, dir. print media 1973-75; dir. audiovisual ops. Ofc. of Info., Navy Dept. 1975-76; asst. chief of staff Eleventh Naval Dist. 1977-80; dir. pub. rels./ prof. mktg. National Univ., San Diego 1980-82; corp. commn. dir. Robert Keith & Co., Inc. 1983; pres. Mayo & Assoc., Inc. 1983 – ; awards: Donald M. Mackey Awd., Navy League of US 1981; No. San Diego Co. Press Club Publicity Awd. 1982; PR Casebook, Special PR Event of the Year Awd. (King Kong), 1983; mem: Navy League of US (San Diego Council bd. dirs.); Pub. Rel. Soc. of Am. (chpt. pres.); San Diego Press Club; S.D. Computer Soc. Investors Gp.; Rotary Internat.; author: Bulletin From Dallas: The President is Dead (Banner Books 1967); Methodist; rec: personal computing, photog. Res: 17023 Cloudcroft Dr Poway 92064 Ofc: Mayo & Assoc. Inc., 16776 Bernardo Center Dr, Ste 110B, Rancho Bernardo 92128

MAYS, ALFRED GLEN, accountant, ret.; b. Dec. 8, 1917, Wakita, Okla.; s. William Oliver and Pearl (Grant) M.; m. Frances Harper, Feb. 3, 1940; edn: stu. Okla. A&M Coll. 1935-38, George Washington Univ., Wash DC 1940-41. Career: acctg. clerk Farm Security Admin., Wash DC 1939-41, acct. US Govt., Wash DC 1941-61, Reconstrn. Fin. Corp. 1941-46, War Assets Adminstrn. 1948, Gen. Svcs. Admin. 1958-60, NASA 1960-61, ret. 1961; Examiner, wrote recommendns. to bd. dirs. Defense Plant Corp. (RFC) 1943-46; honors: Knights of Phythias (hon. mem. 1935), won individual All College Golf (1937); mem. Nat. Assn. of Ret. Federal Employees (chapt. pres. 1972); publs: addressed US Senate Fgn. Rels. Com. (1962) as a friend of Pres. Harry S. Truman, remarks were read into the record of the House Fgn. Rels. Com., and quoted by Life Line for 8 minutes on 300 radio stations reaching possible 12 million listeners; mil: 2d lt. ROTC 1938; Republican; Baptist; rec: golf. Res: POB 787 Vista 92083

MAYS, JAMES ARTHUR, cardiologist; b. May 1, 1939, Pine Bluff, Ark.; s. Talmadge and Edna Clara (Motley) M.; div.; children: James A. b. 1963, James E. b. 1967, James O.T. b. 1975, James E. b. 1983; edn: BS, Univ. of Ark. Pine Bluff 1960; BS in med., MD, Univ. of Ark. Sch. Med. 1965. Career: physician US Army, Vietnam; completed internal medicine splty. and 2-yr cardiology fellowship UC, Irvine; staff UCI/Wadsworth VA Hosp., 1972; first chief of cardiology Martin Luther King Hosp., Los Angeles; current: splst. cardiology/ internal medicine pvt. practice, L.A.; med. dir. Compton Hypertension Found. and Compton Sickle Cell Center; chancellor Technical Health Careers Sch.; frequent speaker on Effects of PCP on Hypertensive Risk Population, and How to know when your child is really sick; num. interviews on TV (incl. Today, Phil Donohue, 2 On the Town), print media (incl. LA Times, NY Times, Washington Post, Atlanta Constitution); awards: Freedoms Found. at Valley Forge award for individual achievement (1984), L.A. City Council outstanding citizen of year (1980-83), KNX Radio citizen of week (1983), HUD spl. achievement (1984), LA Co. human rels. achieve. (1983), S.E. Health Region Citizen award (1979), Ark. State Legis. (1984), Women for Good Govt. (1976), Willing Workers Vol. (1981), Calif. State Senate resolution (1978), LA Co. Jr. Olympics Vol. (1983), Calif. War on Drugs (1981); civic: founder/devel. L.A. Co. High Blood Pressure Found., (nat. pgm.) Adopt-A-Family Endowment Inc., and RADIAN's Anti-Crime/Anti-Drug Campaign; Operation PUSH (LA chpt. pres.); works: research on breakdown of family in urban America; author 8 books and num. songs; 33 deg. Mason; mil: capt. 1st Air Calvary Div., Combat Medics badge, Bronze Star, Gal. Cross, Pres. Cit.; Prot.; rec: sports, writing. Ofc: 9214 S Broadway Los Angeles 90003

MAYS, JOYCE BOEGE, investment executive; b. July 29, 1940, Orange; d. Dr. John Niels and Dorothy Dixon (Russell) Boege; 4th gen. Californian (Boege family settled Anaheim 1848); m. Paul Rabbitt, Aug. 25, 1979; children: Victoria Lynn b. 1962, Sherry Ann b. 1967; edn: BA, CSU Fullerton 1976; MBA (Presidential Key Exec.), Pepperdine Univ. 1986, stu. under Dr. Art Laffer and Dr. Demos Vardiabasis (Pacific Rim economist). Career: account exec. Sutro & Co. Inc. 1976-79; v.p. Lehman Brothers 1979-82; account exec.-investments & fin./ v.p. Oppenheimer & Co. Inc. 1982 – ; guest lectr. Saddleback Coll.; honors: life mem. Calif. Scholastic Fedn., Fullerton Coll. Woman of Year (1959), Junior Nat. Ski Team (1958), American Legion Ski Team (1958), Alpha Lambda Sigma; civic: Marshall McLuhan Found. (dir. 1981-83), Orange Co. Childrens Hosp. (fundraising com. 1981), Sierra Club, NOW; works: photog. exhib., Women & Mothers as Artists (CSUF 1977); Episcopal; rec: ski, photog., swim. Res: 3305 Pine Ave Manhattan Beach 90266 Ofc: Oppenheimer & Co 2029 Century Park E Ste 35 Los Angeles 90067

MAYTUM, HARRY R., physician; b. Jan. 25, 1913, Alexandria, S.Dak.; s. Wellington James and Lillian May (Syferd) M.; m. Louetta Stoltz, Apr. 23, 1937; children: James b. 1941, Nancy b. 1947, Joan b. 1951; edn: BS cum laude, Univ. Wisc. 1936, MD, 1938; Fellow Am. Acad. of Family Practice 1974. Career: asst. command surgeon 19th Tactical Aid Cmd. USAF 1941-46; asst. resident and res. surgeon 1939-41, 1946-67; ptnr., physician and surgeon Merced Medical Clinic, Merced 1947-84, geriatrician independent practice, 1984 – ; honors: Phi Beta Kappa (1935), Alpha Omega Alpha (1937); mem. AMA and local med. socs. (past pres. county soc.) 1939-; Am. Acad. of Family Physicians (past pres. co. soc.) 1949-; Merced Kiwanis Club (pres. 1953), Merced CofC (bd. 73-77, chmn. Health Affairs Com.), Merced Co. Mosquito Abatement Dist. 1954-64; mil: lt. col. USAF 1941-46, ETO, five campaign ribbons, Unit Citation w/two o.l.c., Bronze Star; Republican; Protestant; rec: woodcarving, furniture restoration, lapidary. Res: 2887 Forist Ln Merced 95340 Ofc: 650 W Olive Ave Merced 95340

MAZAREI, HOSSEIN, industrialist; b. Mar. 17, 1935, Shiraz, Persia; s. Bagher M. and Naier (Shariah) M.; m. Fereshteh Banu, Apr. 6, 1958; two sons:

Victor B. b. 1962, Richard B. b. 1963; edn: grad. Nemazi, 1957; AA, Pierce Coll. 1961; BS engrng. Calif. Polytech. Univ. SLO 1963; MA in cinematography, Columbia Univ. 1965; JD/LLB, La Salle Univ. 1973. Career: pres. Hossco Petroleum Inc. offices in Kuwait, Abu Dabi, Geneva, Riyahd, and London; import/export bus. liason between heads of state of various Middle Eastern countries; past cons. to OPEC (pre-Khoemeni); owner two corps. (textile indus.): Westher Financial Inc. dba Texprint Internat. and CIM (Corp. Indsl. Mgmt.); owner/landlord of chain of service stations; real estate investor; recipient Gold Medal award for contbns. to Persia's 2,500 Year Centennial; mem. Optomist Club Intl.; works: drawings of ancient Persopolis; Republican; Agnostic; rec: flying, tennis, golf. Res: 4419 Valley Spring Dr North Ranch Westlake Village 91362 Ofc: Hossco Petroleum Inc. 16311 Ventura Blvd, Ste 1080, Encino 91436

MAZZONE, GARY ANTHONY, telemarketing executive; b. June 18, 1949, NY, NY; s. Russ Boardman and Ann King; m. Chris, Dec. 11, 1968; children: Tracie b. 1969, Marc b. 1971, Jenny b. 1974, Mike Henry b. 1967; edn: Long Beach City Coll.; Santa Monica City Coll.; CSU Long Beach. Career: various mgmt. positions in retail trade; dir. telemktg., nat. sales mgr. C.R. Laurence Co. L.A.; cons. telemktg. field, mem: SEMA, APAA, Nat. Van Conversion Assn., volunteer Red Cross, Jerry Lewis M.D. Telethon, Patrick Henry Boys League; Republican; Catholic; rec: camping. Res: 1955 Pattiz Ave Long Beach 90815 Ofc: C.R. Laurence Co. 2503 E Vernon Ave Los Angeles 90058

MC ADAMS, LAWRENCE L., graphic designer; b. Apr. 26, 1952, Fontana, Calif.; s. Samuel R. and F. Ruth (Poore) McA.; m. Joyce Hebestreit, June 1, 1974; children: Paul b. 1976, Lara b. 1979; edn: AA, Golden West Coll. 1972; BA magna cum laude, CSU Long Beach 1974. Career: pres. Larry McAdams Design Inc. Newport Beach 1975—; ptnr. Adlink & Measure Mark (advt. agcys.) 1985—; instr. CSU Long Beach 1984—; honors: Soc. of Illustrators (Illustration West 1976), Champion Award (El Torito), Western Lighting Collateral (1980), Potlatch 1985 Inkspot Calendar, Ad Awards (Art Dirs. Club 1976, 83); mem: Art Dirs. Club of L.A., Am. Inst. Graphic Arts, Christian Communication Artists Assn. (founder, pres.), Breakfast Club of Champions, Calvary Ch. Christian Sch. Bd.; publ: designs in Menu Design (PBC Internat. 1985), Print's Regional Design Annual (1982, 83), Print Mag. (May/June 1986); Republican; Christian; rec: surfing, swimming, tennis, skiing, gardening, teaching. Ofc: Larry McAdams Design Inc. 1400 Bristol St N Ste 220 Newport Beach 92660

MC ALISTER, RALPH KNIGHT, real estate tax service executive; b. Aug. 1, 1929, Bakersfield (3d gen. Calif.); s. Wyllie Robert and Virginia Lorice (Knight) McA.; m. Marilyn Clarke, 1946; children: Karen, Daniel, David, Ann, Virginia; m. 2d. Kathy Krider, Oct. 26, 1961; stepchildren: Michael, J. Joseph, Ruth, Kay. Career: empl. Tehachapi Supply Co. 1947-48, Sears 1949-51; searcher, sr. searcher Transam. Real Estate Tax Service 1951-65, asst. mgr. San Francisco Div. 1966-67, mgr. Los Angeles Div. 1967-73, mgr. New York Div. 1973-76, nat. mktg. mgr. 1977—, asst. v.p. 1966, v.p. 1968, senior v.p. 1983—; instrumental in devel. tape to tape system of payment of municipal taxes in Calif. (saving municipalities $ millions), system now being devel. nat.; mil: cpl. US Army and Calif. Nat. Guard 1949-51, sharpshooter; Republican; rec: bowling (past pres. Palo Alto Bowling Assn. 1966-67, sr. dir. O.C. Bowling Assn. 1986), golf. Res: 14950 Tacuba Dr La Mirada 90638 Ofc: Transamerica Real Estate Tax Service 101 S. 1st St Ste 300 Burbank 91502

MC ANALLY, DON, editor, publisher; b. Oct. 27, 1913, Sewell, NJ; s. James C. and Ina (MacLeod) M.; m. Edith P. McKinney, Dec. 11, 1934; 1 dau: Shirley Ann English; edn: John Wanamaker Cadet Inst., Phila.; Sales Analysis Inst., Chgo. Career: reporter/ed. Woodbury Daily Times, NJ 1932-45; ed. Owens-Illinois Co. Publs., NJ and Ohio 1945-47; asst. advtg. mgr. Libbey- Owens-Ford Glass Co., Toledo, Oh. 1947-53; sales promotion mgr./ prod. sales mgr. LOF Glass Fibers Co., Toledo 1953-59; ed. Pacific Oil Marketer, Los Angeles 1960-66; owner Hovercraft of So. Calif. 1975-76; pub. Calif. Businesswoman 1978; ed./pub. O & A Mktg. News 1966—, Calif. Senior Citizen News 1977-85, The Automotive Booster of Calif. 1974—; awards: Man of the Year, Pacific Oil Conf. 1977; Spl. Award, Printing Plant House Craftsmen 1950; Good Neighbor award, Toledo, Oh. 1948; Dinner guest of honor, So. Calif. Petroleum Indus. Golf & Tennis Tournament 1984; mem: Nat. Spkrs. Assn., Internat. Platform Assn., Lions Club, Calif. Indep. Oil Marketers Assn., Masquers (Hywd.), Silver Dollar Club (S.F.Vly), Roorag (L.A.), Automotive Booster Club of Greater L.A., OX 5 Aviation Pioneers, Nat. and So. Calif. Wing, Greater L.A. Press Club. Address: 4409 Indiana Ave La Canada 91011

MC ATEE, GARY LEE, medical electronics service co. owner; b. Oct. 13, 1949, Marion, Ind.; s. Dallas Wilbur and Hazel Mae (Flook) M.; m. Debra Saegar, Aug. 2, 1980; children: Katherine b. 1972, Michael b. 1974, Jonathan b. 1982, Kimberly b. 1983; edn: ASEET, Purdue Univ. 1971; desig: BMET, 1980. Career: regl. svc. mgr. Alpex Computer Co. 1971-74; tnr. regl. svc. coord. Internat. Medical Corp. 1974-80; owner Medical Repair Svcs. Co. 1980-81; owner Western Electronic Sales & Tech. 1981—; mem: Med. Equip. Repair Assn.; Christian; rec: raising Dobermans, salt water fishing. Res: 662 Kingman Dr Vacaville 95688 Ofc: W.E.S.T., POB 1313 Vacaville 95696

MC BAIN, ANGUS WILLIAM, investment banker; b. June 21, 1938, Los Angeles; s. Angus Carlson and Rose Ethel (Stava) McB.; m. Lucy Ann Quirk

Toberman, May 27, 1978; 1 dau. Barbara Elizabeth; edn: BA in econs., honors, UC Los Angeles 1961; MA in pol. sci., Stanford Univ. 1964, MBA, 1976. Career: investment exec., L.A., then corporate finance assoc., NYC, Shearson Hammill & Co., 1967-73; vice pres. and regl. mgr. of corporate finance, Kidder Peabody & Co., N.Y.C. and L.A., 1976-80; vice pres. and area mgr. Merchant Banking, Citicorp., N.Y.C. and L.A., 1982-84; founding ptnr. McBain, Rose Partners, Los Angeles 1985—; bd. chmn. Spaulding Fibre Co., Inc., Buffalo, N.Y. (1984-), Automation Industries, Greenwich, Conn. (1985-); honors: Pi Gamma Mu; founding dir. Hollywood Presbyterian Medical Ctr. Found.; dir. Hathaway Home for Children; clubs: California, Los Angeles Country; publs: contbr. to PAC Directory, a complete guide to Political Action Coms.; founder/ pres. Corporate Political Action Mgmt., Inc. 1980-82; mil: 1st lt. US Army Arty. 1961-63; Republican (Lincoln Club of LA); Christian; rec: golf, tennis, travel, music. Res: 227 Muirfield Rd Los Angeles 90004 Ofc: McBain, Rose Partners 523 West Sixth St Ste 524 Los Angeles 90014

MC BRIDE, ALLISON BURNS, civic volunteer; b. May 21, 1920, Redlands, Calif.; d. John Scott and Marion Elsie (Wilmot) Burns; m. Henry Lesley McBride, June 18, 1955; children: Marion Theresa b. 1956 (dec.), Cameron Lesley b. 1957, Lucy Scott b. 1960; edn: BA, UC Berkeley 1942. Career: research analyst USAF Mil. Intelligence, Wash. DC 1942-43; ferry pilot Air Transport Command, Romulus Army Air Field, Romulus, Mich. 1943-45; asst. mgr. Ontario Airport 1945-46; social worker II San Diego County Welfare Dept. 1946-48; real estate broker Hill Rockey Co., La Jolla 1948-55; pres. Las Patronas 1972-73, raised $300,000 per yr. for many charities and hosps., schs., zoo, Old Globe Theatre; pres. Mothers & Parents of La Jolla Country Day Sch. 1968-69, trustee 1970-73; mem: Women's Air Force Svc. Pilots of World War II, La Jolla Beach & Tennis Club, La Jolla CC, Ironwood CC, San Diego Mus. of Art, Nat. Hist. Mus., Aerospace Mus., Athaneum; mil: civil svc. USAF WWII, Victory and Campaign medals; Republican; Episcopal; rec: tennis, golf, art, oil painting, gardening. Res: 2466 Vallecitos Ct La Jolla 92037

MC BRIETY, JEFFERSON DAVIS, aerospace industry program manager; b. Jan. 23, 1948, Salisbury, Md.; s. Lewis Jefferson and Margaret Elnora (Davis) McB.; m. Linda Sue Beers, Aug. 16, 1975; 1 dau. Jamie Lynn b. 1978; edn: BS phys. sci., USAF Acad. 1971; MS sys. mgmt., Univ. So. Calif. 1981; postgrad. MBA, Univ. Lincoln Neb. 1979. Career: pilot SE Asia, Alaska, Middle East, sqdn. cmdr. March AFB 1973-76; aircraft maint. ofcr. Offutt AFB Omaha, Neb. 1976-79; 15th AF hdqtrs. staff ofcr. recon. aircraft March AFB 1979-81; proj. engr., pgm. mgr. Aerojet Azusa 1981—; pgm. mgr. spaceborne passive microwave sensor system ($20 million); asst., acting exec. dir. US Army Ball 1985; honors: W.C. Brownfield Jaycee Award 1978, AFA Junior Ofcr. of the Year 1st Runnerup 1978, 15th AF Crew of the Year Copilot 1973, nom. Jabara Award 1980, 3rd Place Statewide Competition Neb. Toastmasters 1979; mem: Soc. Logistics Engrs., Jaycees (v.p. indiv. dev. 1978), Aerojet Mgmt. Club 1984-86, Toastmasters 1977-79, AF Assn., Calif. PTA, Phiddleharmonics Bluegrass Band, So. Calif. Inland Empire Bluegrass Assn. 1984—; author: I Grew Up with Linda (1982), editor- in- chief SOLE Newwsletter 1982-83; song: Mush Creek (1977); helped restore Mission Inn B-29 Bomber for March AFB Museum 1980; mil: capt. USAF 1971-81, Meritorious Svc., AF Commdn., Vietnam Svc., Nat. Defense, AF Longevity, Small Arms Expert, Army Good Conduct, Republican; Presbyterian; rec: military history, Am. Bluegrass music, competitive sports, sailing. Res: 2872 Sulky Ct Riverside 92504 Ofc: Aerojet ElectroSystems 1100 W Hollyvale St Ste 59/1661 Azusa 91702

MC BROOM, LARRY EDWARD, bank executive; b. July 17, 1947, Houston, Tex.; s. Robert Edward Lee and Rachel Irene (Atkinson) McB.; edn: Univ. Houston 1965-66. Career: var. positions First City Nat. Bank 1966-73; credit ofcr. Houston Nat. Bank 1973-77, asst. v.p. 1977, Security Pacific Nat. Bank 1977-85; v.p. 1985—; mem: Nat. Assn. Credit Mgmt. (NCC)(dir. 1981-82, 86), Houston Assn. Credit Mgmt. (dir. 1975-77, treas. 1976); Democrat; Baptist; rec: bowling (mem. Amateur Bowlers Tour). Res: 1851 15th St Apt 3 San Francisco 94103 Ofc: Security Pacific Nat. Bank 1105 Battery St San Francisco 94111

MC CAFFREY, STANLEY EUGENE, university president; b. Feb. 26, 1917, Taft, Calif.; s. Joseph Cormack and Dorothy (Bunyard) M.C.; m. Beth Conolley, July 6, 1941; children: Stephen Conolley, Nancy; edn: AB, Univ. Calif. 1938; LLD, Golden Gate Univ. 1972; Pepperdine Univ. 1978; Korea Univ. 1981. Career: personnel Standard Oil Co. of Calif. 1939-40; coord. vets. affairs UC Berkeley 1946, v.p. exec. asst. 1957-60, exec. mgr. Alumni Assn. 1948-56; advtg. mgr. Kaiser Aluminum, Oakland 1946-48; exec. asst. to. Vice Pres. of U.S. 1960; pres. Univ. of Pacific, Stockton 1971—; pres., exec. ofcr. San Francisco Bay Area Council 1961-71; chmn. Vets Bd. Calif. 1956; del. Gov.'s Conf. on Children and Youth 1956; v.p Berkeley Recreation Commn. 1957; Oakland Manpower Commn. 1967-68; State Commn. on Govt. Orgn. & Economy 1966-68; bd. dirs. Berkeley Community Chest. 1953-55, Berkeley YMCA 1953-54, Internat. House; pres. Berkeley Service Club Council 1954-55, pres. San Francisco Bay Area Council 1960-71; trustee Peralto Jr. Coll. Dist. 1962-68, pres. 1964-66; v.chmn. trustee Golden Gate Coll., San Francisco 1965-71; trustee Univ. Calif. Alumni Found., Pacific Med. Ctr.; bd. Regents Coll. Holy Names; mem: Am. Alumni Council, Assn. Ind. Calif. Colls. & Univs. (pres. 1976-78), Ind. Colls. of No. Calif., Western Coll. Assn. (pres. 1979-), Big C Soc. Univ. Calif., Internat. House Assn., Navy League, Order of Golden Bear, Phi Beta Kappa, Pi Sigma Alpha; clubs: Rotary Internat. (pres. Berkeley club 1966-67, now hon. mem., also hon. mem. Stockton club, mem. internat. bd. dirs. 1969-71, internat. 1st v.p. 1970-71, research com. 1976, nominating com. 1976, 79, internat. pres. 1981-82), Berkeley Fellows, Family, Commonwealth of Calif. (qtrly. chmn. 1955, gov.), Bohemian, St. Francis Yacht (SF); mil: lt. commdr. USNR 1940-45, Silver Star, Legion of Merit; Congregational. Res: President's Home Univ. of the Pacific Stockton 95211

MC CALL, JAMES ANDREW, software technologist; b. Apr. 1, 1947, Paterson, NJ; s. James Andrew and Grace Marie (Schultheis) McC.; m. Carol, July 25, 1981; children: Andy b. 1973, Julianne b. 1983, Chris b. 1985; edn: BS engrg., US Mil. Acad. 1969; MS ops. research, engrg., Stanford Univ. 1971. Career: info. sys. analyst Gen. Elec. Space Div. Sunnyvale, mgr. technol. pgms.; software technol. section mgr. Science Applications Internat. Corp., software engrg. dept. mgr., v.p.; honors: Undergrad. Dean's List 4 yrs., Hon. Mention All-Am. Football (1969), NCAA Scholar- Athlete (1969), One in a Thousand (GE Space Div. 1980); mem: Assn. Computing Machinery, IEEE; publs: 50+ tech. articles, contbr. Software Quality Management (Petrocelli, NY); mil: capt. US Army 1969-75, Bronze Star; rec: sports, camping. Res: 3132 Verde Ave Carlsbad 92008 Ofc: Science Applications Internat. Corp. 1200 Prospect St La Jolla 92038

MC CALL, PATRICK ANTHONY, lawyer; b. Feb. 9, 1958, Santa Barbara, Calif.; s. Verlin R. and Sally M. (Recupio) M.; m. Christina M., Aug. 25, 1984; 1 dau: Brittany Ann b. 1985; edn: BS CSU Long Beach 1979; JD, Western State Univ. Sch. of Law 1982; Orange Co. Coll. of Trial Adv. 1982; admitted Calif. State Bar 1983. Career: research cons. Assem. Ronald Cordova 1977-81; research clerk Orange Co. Dist. Atty's. Ofc. 1981; atty. Lais & Luetto Santa Ana 1982 - ; judge pro tem Superior Ct. of Calif. County of Riverside 1985 - ; adj. prof. Saddleback Comm. Coll. 1985-; mem: Calif. and Orange Co. bar assns. (1983-); Orange Co. Barristers (1983-); Calif. and Orange Co. Trial Lawyers assns. (1983-); Nat. Ski Patrol Sys.; Am. Red Cross; first aid advisor Snow Summit Ski Patrol; cert. first aid instr. Nat. Ski Patrol; Republican; Catholic; rec: skiing, flying. Ofc: Lais & Luetto Inc., 1200 N Main St, Ste. 916, Santa Ana 92701

MC CARTHY, EDWARD JOSEPH, III, computer co. president; b. Jan. 22, 1955, Chgo., Ill.; s. Edward Joseph, Jr. and Diane Marie (Paschen) McC.; m. Carolyn Jean Brown, Sept. 7, 1980; edn: BS, CSU Long Beach 1977; MBA, 1979. Career: sales mgr. Quikdata (computer timesharing firm), Long Beach 1976-78; dir. Delphi Systems Inc. (computer sys. house), No. Hollywood 1978-81; Western US mgr. Computer Sharing Svcs. (computer timesharing firm), Denver Colo.; pres./ CEO Promethean Sys., Inc. (computer sys. house), Santa Monica 1981 - ; dir. Western Reserves (oil exploration & drilling co.); mem: Los Angeles CofC; Santa Monica Kiwanis; Republican; Catholic; rec: skiing, ice hockey. Res: 8970 W 25th St Los Angeles 90034 Ofc: Promethean Systems, Inc., 1800 S Robertson Blvd Ste 411 Los Angeles 90035

MC CARTHY, FRANCIS MICHAEL, JR., (DICK), real estate broker; b. Aug. 21, 1918, Aberdeen, So. Dak.; s. Francis Michael and Frances Katherine (Higgins) McC.; m. Mary Larmon, Aug. 7, 1948; children: Sheila b. 1951, Michael b. 1953, John b. 1954, Patrick b. 1955, Francis b. 1960, Anne b. 1963, Maureen b. 1965; edn: Loyola Univ. L.A. 1937-38; USN Physical Instrs. Sch. 1945; spl. tchg. credl., Calif. 1946; UC extn. 1947; real estate broker Calif. 1964. Career: var. positions to gen. foreman Allis Chalmers Mfg. Oxnard 1939-44, 1946-54; swimming instr. Ventura Coll. 1946; owner, prop. Dick McCarthy's Sporting Goods Oxnard 1954-64; real estate broker 1964 - ; tennis pro Las Posas CC 1958; tennis coach Moorpark H.S. 1957, Santa Clara H.S. 1961-63; past pres., dir. K of C Hall, Inc. 1966-; honors: Realtor of the Year (Oxnard- Harbor Bd. Realtors 1976), Athletic Scholarship (Loyola Univ. L.A. 1937-38), Oxnard Festival Awards (1981-86), tennis coaching awards 1961-63; mem: Nat. Sporting Goods Dealers Assn., Oxnard Harbor Bd. Realtors (pres. 1972), Calif. Real Estate Assn. (state dir. 1972), Nat. Assn. Realtors, Nat. Farm Brokers Assn., Santa Clara H.S. Guild (pres. 1977), Calif. Parks & Rec. Soc., Oxnard Parks & Rec. Commn. (chmn. 1982-83), Calif. Parks & Rec. Commrs. (bd.), Oxnard CofC (dir. 1959-61); clubs: Oxnard Tennis (pres. 1952, secty. 1983-86), Knights of Columbus (Grand Knight 1965); past mem: Oxnard Exchange, Elks, Ventura County Tennis, Cabrillo Racquet; co-authored several compositions of popular music in the 1940's; was one of original founders/ organizers of Little League Baseball and Junior Tennis in city of Oxnard; was Oxnard's first tennis pro; mil: sp-a 2/c USNR 1944-46, Am. Area Victory WWII; Republican; Catholic; rec: tennis, golf, creative writing, music, poetry, boating, fishing, hunting, camping, all sports. Res: 329 Roderick Ave Oxnard 93030 Ofc: F.M. "Dick" McCarthy- Realtor Inc. 741 Richmond Ave Oxnard 93030

MC CARTHY, KEVIN JOSEPH, business machine co. executive; b. Nov. 16, 1945, NY, NY; s. Timothy and Beatrice Hester McC.; children: Jennifer Lynn b. 1969, Kevin Joseph b. 1971; edn: AS, Cuesta Coll. 1981; BA, Antioch Univ. 1982; MA, Pepperdine Univ. 1986. Career: adminstrn. & sales NYC 1966-69; sales, mktg. & mgmt. Office Machines, So. Calif. 1970-79; gen. ptnr., sales mgr. Trinity Ofc. Prods. Los Alamitos 1983-86, CEO 1986 - ; co-facilitator growth-oriented workshops and seminars through Cal. Poly. SLO and facilitator workshops through Laguna Beach Community Clinic; honors: Nat. Honor Soc. in Psychol.; mem: Nat. Ofc. Machine Dealers Assn., Western Ofc. Machine Dealers Assn., So. Calif. Ofc. Machine Dlrs. Assn., Phi Chi frat., St. Joseph Hosp. Hospice Pgm.; Democrat; Christian; rec: travel, fishing, sailing, camping. Res: 212 Fifth St Seal Beach 90740 Ofc: Trinity Ofc. Products 4772 Katella Los Alamitos 90270

MC CARTNEY, RICHARD LEE, entepreneur; b. July 7, 1938, Hood River, Ore.; s. Howard Eugene and Dorothy Mary (Hiday) McC.; m. Faye Auvon Woodruff, Feb. 24, 1968; children: Celeste b. 1959, Debbie b. 1961, Adrian b.

1962; edn: AA, Chabot Coll.; LLB, LaSalle Univ. 1968; real estate broker Calif. 1962; Calif. Comm. Coll. tchg. credl. 1975; notary public; reg. practitioner ICC 1975, Fed. Maritime Commn. 1976. Career: asst. pchsg. agent Enterprise div. De Laval Turbine Oakland 1959-66; pchsg. agent Gen. Elec. Co. San Leandro 1966-69; commodity splst. Fairchild Semiconductor Mtn. View 1969-70; self-employed real estate 1970-72; mgr. pchsg. Ecolair Environmental Pleasant Hill 1972-80, Instru. div. Varian Assocs. Palo Alto 1980-81; owner, mgr. Camaraderie (art gallery & custom frame shop) 1981 - ; cons. in physical distbn. 1981 - ; instr. phys. distbn. courses Chabot Coll. and UC Berkeley Extn. 1974 - ; mem: Nat. Fedn. of Indep. Bus., Assn. Transp. Practitioners, Am. Pchsg. Soc. (life), So. Alameda County Bd. Realtors, Calif. Acad. Scis. (life), S.F. Museum Soc., S.F. Zool. Soc.; mil: cpl. USMC 1956-59; Republican; The Interim Ch. of Jesus Christ (pastor); rec: computer pgmmg. Res: POB 1605 San Leandro 94577 Ofc: Camaraderie 1481 Solano Ave Albany 94706

MC CARTY, GERALD FRANCIS, co. president; b. June 29, 1934, St. Louis, Mo.; s. Carl Stokley and Ann Marie (Bosnack) McC.; m. Roberta Lee Sherman, Sept. 27, 1963; children: Heather b. 1966, Shannon b. 1973; edn: BA, Roosevelt Univ. 1972; MBA, Pepperdine Univ. 1974; Reg. Profl. Engr., Calif. 1985, R.E. Broker lic. 1986. Career: indsl. engr. mgr. Aerojet General, Placentia 1964; corporate engring. mgr. Litton Ind., Zurich, Switz. 1979; mfg. engring. mgr. Foote Jones, Chgo. 1973; div. mgr. Electra Motors, Anaheim 1976; mng. dir. Dresser So. Africa 1980, v.p. Internat., Dresser Ind., Houston, Tx. 1983; pres. TEC Services, Anaheim 1986 - ; honors: Nat. Honor Soc. (1952), Dean's List (1972); mem. Calif. Assn. Profl. Engrs., Nat. Assn. Profl. Engrs., Soc. of Applied Indsl. Engrs.; clubs: Yorba Linda Country, Pine Forest Country; Republican; Methodist; rec: ski, golf, tennis, flying. Address: TEC Services 1781 W Glenoaks Anaheim 92801

MC CARTY, PAULA ANNE, investment banker; b. Oct. 21, 1957, Medford, Mass.; d. Charles Francis and Stella Priscilla (Forti) McC.; edn: Univ. of Colo. Semester at Sea, 1978; BA pol. sci./econs., Tufts Univ. 1985; grad. certif. in adminstrn. & mgmt., Harvard Univ. 1985. Career: concert violinist with num. orchestras incl. Boston Civic Sym., Boston Pops Orch. Festival, Marlboro Sym., Harvard-Radcliffe Univ. Orch., and Greater Boston Youth Sym. Orch./ toured Colombia, S.A./ taught and composed music, 1970-81; advt. director Tufts Univ. Opera, Medford, Mass. 1977-79, conference facilitator 1979, fundraiser 1979-80; mktg. asst. Mobil Oil Corp., Los Angeles 1981-83; acct. exec. R.R. Johnson Corp., San Clemente and also bus. mgr. Dana Point Foreign Car, Dana Pt. 1983-85; investment banker Morgan, Olmstead, Kennedy & Gardner, Los Angeles 1985 - ; violin tchr., independent finl. consultant, 1983-; honors: Nat. Honor Soc. 1973-75, Outstanding Teenager of Am. (New England regional winner) 1975, recipient Tufts Univ. scholarship awds. 1975-80, Mass. State Scholarship winner; mem: Nat. Orgn. of Women Musicians & Composers, Nat. Assn. for Female Execs., Harvard Alumni, Tufts Alumni, Gr. Boston Sym. Alumni, Orange County Womens Soccer League; works: 1975-83 music compositions: Concerto in D for 2 Violins and Harp; jazz music for violin arrangements; Republican (Young Repub. Club); rec: chess, x-c skiing, travel. Res: 17 Hidden Valley Rd Rolling Hills Estates 90274 Ofc: Morgan, Olmstead, Kennedy & Gardner, 606 S Olive St Los Angeles 90014

MC CLAIN, GEORGETTE, specialty paving co. president; b. May 18, 1927, Ventura; d. George W. and Harriet Josephine (Hanawalt) Floyd; m. James Weston McClain, Sept. 3, 1950; children: David b. 1952, Paul b. 1954, Mark b. 1961; edn: BA, Mills Coll. 1949; grad. Sawyer Bus. Coll. 1975; Calif. lic. Gen. Engring. Contractor. Career: self-empl. piano tchr., Grass Valley 1950-74; office mgr. Gabe Mendez Inc., Newcastle 1976-79, Livingstons Grading & Paving Co., Newcastle 1979-81; founder/pres. Specialty Paving, Inc. and owner A.C. Dike Co., 1981 - ; mem. Associated Gen. Contractors of Am., Assoc. Gen. Contrs. of Calif.; Republican; Episcopal (ch. organist). Res: 7021 Lincoln- Newcastle Hwy Newcastle 95658 Ofc: A.C. Dike Co., POB 1113 Loomis 95650

MC CLANAHAN, MICHAEL N., software engineer, systems analyst; b. Oct. 28, 1953, Cincinnati, Ohio; s. Roland Nelson and Jeanne Ann (Stevens) M.C.; m. Tina Swiecki, March 8, 1986; edn: Univ. of Cininnati 1973-74; Goldenwest Coll. 1980-81; Riverside City Coll. 1982-85. Career: photographer, digital image splst. Arrow Blue Co., Cincinnati, Ohio 1972-78; publr. Barefoot Inc., Cincinnati, Ohio 1978-81; pgmmr., analyst Blue Lustre Home Care of Calif., Ontario 1981-83; owner Riverside Mktg., Riverside 1984 - ; honors: VFBC Golden Plume Award for Excellence in Algorithm Simplification; mem: VFBC (Western U.S. chpt., hon. life mem.); works: devolped multi- user system and application software for IBM & Compatible Microcomputers in Real- Time Applications; Republican; rec: photography. Ofc: Riverside Marketing, P.O. Box 3850 Riverside 92519

MC CLATCHY, JAMES, newspaper publisher; b. Sacramento; s. Carlos and Phebe (Briggs) McC.; edn: AB, Stanford Univ.; MS, Columbia Univ. Career: newspaper reporter, editor and publisher; chmn. bd. McClatchy Newspapers; publisher: Tiburon Ark, Tahoe World; mil: pilot US Air Force. Ofc: 21st & Q Streets Sacramento 95813

MC CLELLAN, JOAN LURELLE, direct mail marketing executive; b. Aug. 13, 1946, Santa Monica; d. Clarence Stuart III and Virginia Lois (Woodruff) M.C.; m. Kurt P. Kupper 1974-82; m. 2d. Benedictus H. Bolsman, Feb. 6, 1983; children (nee Kupper): Kristopher Parnell b. 1966, Damon Stuart b. 1968; edn: Los Angeles Pierce Coll. 1964-66; San Francisco City Coll. 1966-67; Cuesta Coll. 1969-70; BS, honors, Calif. Polytechnic Univ. 1973; Standard Tch. Cred., Calif. 1974. Career: vis. instr. Calif. Polytechnic State Univ. 1972-73; dir. of ops. McClellan Corp. Internat. 1974, v.p. 1979, pres. 1981 - ; honors:

Outstanding Mem. of the Year, Hotel Sales Mktg. assn. 1981; mem: Travel & Tourism Research Assn. (So. Calif. chmn. 1986), Calif. Gov.'s Conf. on Tourism Plnng. Com. (pgm. chmn.), Calif. Travel Industry Assn. (exec. ofcr), Postal Customer Council (ofcr. 1981-82), Pacific Area Travel Assn., Am. Soc. of Travel Agents, TTRA, Caribbean Tourism Assn., Assn. of Travel Mktg. Execs., Hotel Sales & Mktg. Assn. (dir. 1982, secty. 1980), Mktg. Assn. (dir.), MPI, Woodland Hills CofC (Pres.'s Adv. Council 1983); works: research survey (1985), wk. in progress 1986; newsletter pub./ed. Travel & Tourism Research Assn. and Hotel Sales & Mktg. Assn. 1980-84; Democrat; Presbyterian; rec: antique clocks collection, printmaking, Japanese print collection. Ofc: McClellan Corp. Internat., 21318 Dumetz Rd. Woodland Hills 91364

MC CLELLAN, ROBERT EDWARD, consulting engineer; b. Feb. 27, 1922; s. Robert Edward and Maria Elizabeth (Ameln) M.; m. Mary Billetter, Oct. 21, 1944; children: Kathleen b. 1947, M. Elizabeth b. 1948, Patricia b. 1949, Eileen b. 1951, Robert III b. 1952, Mary b. 1955, Thomas b. 1956; edn: BSCE, USC 1947, MSCE, 1956, PhD, 1970; Structural Engr., Calif. 1955. Career: engring. assoc. Los Angeles City Public Works Dept., Los Angeles Dept. of Water and Power, Los Angeles 1948-56; structural engr. Calif. State Div. of Architecture, Los Angeles City Sch. Dist., Los Angeles 1956-59; gen. supvr. of design Rocketdyne, Canoga Park 1959-62; tech. staff The Aerospace Corp., El Segundo 1962-69; chief tech. staff The Ralph M. Parsons Co., Pasadena 1969-80; mgr. strategic studies The Aerospace Corp., El Segundo 1980-85; currenty, cons. engr., Woodland Hills; dir. Apollo Systems Technology Inc., Canyon Country 1985; honors: Outstanding Civil Engring. Grad., USC 1977; mem: Am. Inst. of Aero. & Astro., Am. Defense Preparedness Assn., Structural Engrs. Assn. of So. Calif., Am. Soc. for Indsl. Security, Chi Epsilon, Tau Beta Pi, Sigma Xi, Los Angeles Athletic Club; publs: Assessment of Seismic Survivability, Shock and Vibration Bulletin, Naval Research Lab. 1984; Ground Shock Effect of Soil Field Inclusions, Shock & Vibration Bulletin, Naval Research Lab 1984; Gaseous Nuclear Fission Rockets, AIAA Jt. Propulsion Conf., Cleveland, Ohio 1982; mil: lt. j.g. CEC USNR, Asiatic- Pacific Theater, WWII; Republican; Catholic. Ofc: R.E. McClellan PhD, PE, Consulting Engineer, P.O. Box 6168 Woodland Hills 91365

MC CLINTOCK, THOMAS WILLIAM, hospital administrator; b. May 20, 1940, Phila.; s. Thomas W. and Margaret Mary (Dolan) McC.; m. Judy F. Ernst, Jan. 3, 1961; children: Linda b. 1962, Stephen b. 1963; edn: BS, George Washington Univ. 1971; MA, Chapman Univ. 1974. Career: exec. dir. Harbor View Med. Ctr. San Diego; CEO El Centro Comm. Hosp.; assoc. exec. dir. San Diego PSRO; ofcr. in chg. Regl. Med. Ctr. Annex Naval Tng. Ctr. San Diego; adminstr. San Clemente Gen. Hosp.; asst. prof. San Diego State Univ. 1975–; co-dir. health care pgm., prof. Nat. Univ. San Diego 1976-79; bd. dirs. So. County Comm. Clin. San Juan Capistrano; mem: Am. Coll. Health Care Execs. 1976-, Health Sys. Agcy. (planning & facilities, service coms.), Am. Lung Assn. (bd.), Blue Ribbon Com. of San Clemente 1985-86; mil: lcdr. USN Med. Svc. Corps 1959-78, Navy Achievement; Republican; Lutheran; rec: skiing, racquetball, jogging. Res: 3104 Calle Qieto San Clemente 92672 Ofc: San Clemente Gen. Hosp. 654 Camino de los Mares San Clemente 92672

MC CLUNG, JOHN ROBINSON, JR., advertising executive/editor; b. Sept. 14, 1914, Sewanee, Tenn.; s. John Robinson and Mary Merle (McCall) McC.; m. Edith Eve Logue, Feb. 3, 1944; children: John b. 1946, Bonnie b. 1948, Marilyn b. 1951; edn; BA, Kansas State Univ. 1937. Career: reporter Manhattan Mercury, Kansas 1934-36; editor Kansas State Royal Purple (awarded All American Pacemaker) 1936-37; advtg. staff & editor, home office house mag., Aetna Life & Casualty, Hartford, Ct. 1938-41; acct. exec./ assoc. mgr. Kirschner & Co. (advtg. agcy./ publ. firm), San Francisco & Palo Alto, 1946-61, Palo Alto 1962-65; ed. Nat. Insurance Adjuster Mag. 1963-65; v.p. Art Blum Agcy. (Pub. Rels.), San Francisco 1966; founder/ chmn./ pres. McClung Avtg. Agcy., Inc., Palo Alto 1967–; current ed. The Beta Theta Pi (founded 1872, oldest continuously pub. fraternity mag.) 1977-; mem: Beta Theta Pi (past pres. S.F. Bay Area Alumni Assn., Beta Theta Calif. Dist. chief 1954-72, elected pres. of Nat. Convention 1965); Sigma Delta Chi; S.F. Advtg. Club; S.F. Adcrafters (pres. 1955); Peninsula Advtg. Club; P.A.L.O. Club; Fraternity Editors Assn.; mil: capt. Signal Corp. 1941-45, ofcr. in chg of Gen. MacArthurs GHQ Intercept Ctr. (1944) & GHQ Signal Ctr. (1945), Hollandia, New Guinea, Pacific Theater Commun. Ctrs.; Republican; Methodist; rec: sports, travel. Res: 746 Josina Ave Palo Alto 94306 Ofc: McClung Advertising Agency, Inc., POB 60699 Palo Alto 94306

MC CONNELL, JUDITH DOBSON, judge; b. Feb. 10, 1944, Lincoln, Nebr.; d. Raymond A., Jr. and Maren E. (Dobson) McC.; m. Randall Collins, June 1970; children: Anthony b. 1975, Maren b. 1977; edn: undergrad. Scripps Coll. 1962-3, Pomona Coll. 1963-4, BA, UC Berkeley 1966, JD, 1969; admitted Calif. State and Fed. bars. 1970. Career: atty. Calif. Dept. of Transp. 1970-76; ptnr. law firm Reed, McConnell & Sullivan 1976-77; apptd. municipal court judge 1977-80; apptd. judge Superior Court of San Diego, 1980–, presiding judge Appellate Dept. 1985; adj. prof. of law Univ. San Diego 1973-76; lectr. Juvenile Ct. Inst., Contg. Edn. of the Bar; honors: Phi Beta Kappa 1966; dir. Found. for Women Judges; dir. San Diego County Bar Found.; mem. Nat. Assn. of Women Judges, Calif. Judges Assn., Lawyers Club of San Diego, Dimensions. Ofc: Superior Court 220 W Broadway San Diego 92101

MC CORMACK, JOSEPH ANDREW, executive search consultant; b. Dec. 15, 1944, NY, NY; s. Joseph and Cecelia (Posch) McC.; m. Patty Hall Neff, Sept. 12, 1981; children: Annette b. 1982, Caroline b. 1984; edn: Univ. Santa Clara 1962-64; BA, UC Berkeley 1967. Career: Am. Heritage Publishing Co. NY, NY 1967-68, 1971-72; coord. comm. relations Rockefeller Ctr. NY, pgm. adminstr. Young Presidents' Orgn. NY 1972-76; exec. search cons. Kiernan & Co. NY 1976-78; exec. search cons./ mgr. Arthur Young & Co. NY 1978-80; v.p. Billington, Fox & Ellis NY 1980-82; v.p. Paul R. Ray & Co. L.A. 1982-83; founding ptnr. McCormack & Farrow, Exec. Search Cons. Long Beach 1983–; mem: Nat. Assn. of Corp. & Profl. Recruiters, Rotary Club of Long Beach, Greater L.B. Area CofC, Town Hall of L.A., Univ. Club NY, L.A. Athletic Club; mil: lt. s.g. USN 1968-71, asst. public affairs ofcr. for commdr. US 2nd fleet; Republican; Episcopal; rec: running, fitness, history, choral singing. Ofc: McCormack & Farrow 211 E Ocean Blvd Ste 225 Long Beach 90802

MC CORMICK, DENNIS K., psychologist; edn: BA, Calif. Western Univ. 1969; MA, USIU 1971, PhD, leadership & human behav., 1974, PhD, psychol., 1978. Career: dir. Jr. Frogman Sch., life guard, swimming and diving instr., Coronado Rec. Dept. summers 1962-66; grad. asst. USIU Calwestern 1966-69; phys. edn. instr. asst. track coach, dir. San Diego Holiday Basketball Tournament 1968; asst. football coach Grossmont Union H.S. Dist. 1969-71, math instr. 1969-76, dist. psychologist 1976-77, alternative sch. coord. 1977-79; pvt. practice Individual and Family Therapy 1975–; cons. La Jolla Weight Control Med. Clinic 1982–; personal and crisis counselor/ encounter group facilitator United Methodist Ch. of Coronado 1973-75; freq. guest spkr. on stress and stress reduction, interpersonal relationships, church and svc. orgns.; chmn. City of Coronado Plnng. Commn. 1978-; Land Use Com. 1979-80; bd. dirs. Coronado CofC 1981-; chmn., Pastor/ Parish/ Personnel Rels. Com., St. Paul's Methodist Ch., Coronado 1978-81; mil: USN 1956-65; Underwater Demolition and Seal Teams France, Norway, Greece, Hawaii, Taiwan, Okinawa, Japan, Korea, Phil., Vietnam; Combative Measures instr. 1962-64, Seal Team Operational instr. 1964-65; GCM (2), Armed Forces Expedition, Navy & Marine Corps Parachutist Insignia, Expert Pistol. Res: 827 Tolita Ave. Coronado 92118 Ofc: P.O. Box 583 Coronado 92118

MC COY, BOWEN HADLEY, investment banker; b. June 5, 1937, San Francisco; s. Ord Bowen and Berneice Virginia (Hadley) McC.; m. Janice Arthur, Aug. 26, 1961; children: Anne b. 1965, Elizabeth b. 1968, John b. 1970; edn: BA, Stanford Univ 1958; MBA, Harvard Univ. 1962; Counsellor of Real Estate, Am. Soc. of Real Estate Consellors. Career: with Morgan Stanley 1962–; assoc. in corp. fin., internat. fin. and mergers 1962-70; ptr., mng.dir. 1970; in charge of real estate 1973-85; currently, responsible for West Coast ops.; mem: Urban Land Inst. (trustee), Nat. Real Estate Com. (dir.), Stanford Univ. Alumni Assn. (pres.), Pacific Sch. of Religion (trustee), Hoover Institution War, Revolution & Peace (overseer), Downtown Los Angeles United Way (v.chmn), YMCA Los Angeles (bd. dirs.); publs: articles in Harvard Bus. Review, Appalachia, Urban Land Journ., Am. Mgmt. Assn., Theology Today; mil: ofcr. US Army Intelligence, Korea, Army Commdn.; Republican; Presbyterian (Elder, Bd. of Pensions), rec: mountaineering, Explorers Club. Ofc: Morgan Stanley, 515 So. Figueroa Los Angeles 90071

MC COY, RAYMOND CLARENCE, business/program management consultant; b. Mar. 30, 1939, Cedarfalls, Iowa; s. Raymond Stephen and Edna Josephine (Tingelstad) McCoy; m. Carol, Oct. 24, 1981; children (by wife's previous m.): Richard Glugatch b. 1963, Daniel Glugatch b. 1965; edn: Ft. Belvoir, Va. Engring. Sch. 1957-58, Def. System Mgmt. Coll. 1984. Career: aerospace- pgm. plnng. and mgmt. control, 23 yrs. (Lockheed Aircraft Corp. 1958-61, 65-77, 83-85, mgmt. cons. 1985-86; Rockwell Internat. 1981-83; Philco/Ford Aerospace 1961-63; Hi-Shear 1963-64); mgmt. staff internat. and domestic constrn., 6 yrs. (Ralph M. Parsons Inc. 1977-81; Holmes & Narver 1964-65); bus. cons. prin., McCoy Ents. 1970-77, Caray Assos. 1983–; project planner US Pavillion and rel. facilities for the EXPO '64 World Fair, Spokane Wash.; prin. planner for complete mid-Eastern city and indsl complex; lead planner PP&C op. for facility activation of Trident Complex at Bangor, Wash.; senior planner to organize Integrated Mission Control Ctr. Houston; mgmt. advisor B1-B Pgm.; honors: Indsl. Arts/Architecture award 1952, Calif. Scholarship Fedn. 1953-57, num. profl. commendns.; mem. Nat. Mgmt. Assn.; creative: dance instr., choreographer, musician, radio perf. 1946-65; author num. tech. publs. and tng. aids; mil: E6 splst. US Army 1957-65; Democrat; Lutheran (Walther League 1950-57); rec: mind games, tennis, golf, dancing. Address: Caray Associates 20751 Berdon St Woodland Hills 91367

MC CRARY, BARBARA JO, mobile home sales co. owner; b. Jan. 6, 1934, Quinton, Okla.; d. Ben H. and Nan V. (Murrell) Brackett; m. m. Bill Johnston, div.; children: Julie b. 1952, Terry Ellen (Hauff) b. 1954, Vickie Lynn b. 1956; m. 2d. Jerry Lee McCrary, Oct. 19, 1973; desig: Calif. Ins. Lic. (life) Fire & Casualty, Calif. lic. Contractor, P.U.C. lic. for freight of mobile homes, etc.; lic. Mobile Home Dealer, Calif. Career: retail sales clk., Merced 1968-69; automobile sales Town & Country Chrysler, Merced 1969; sales Travelon Trailer Co., Modesto 1973; ptnr. Bill's Trailer Sales, Merced 1974-77; owner McCrary's Mobile Homes, Merced 1977–; mem. Merced, Mariposa Horsemans Assn.; Republican; Prot.; rec: dance, fish, gardening. Res: 2799 Branco Merced 95340 Ofc: McCrarys Mobile Homes, 1950 N. Ashby Rd Merced 95340

MC CRAVEN, CARL CLARKE, mental health center president; b. May 27, 1926, Des Moines; s. Marcus Harry and Buena Vista (Rollins) McC.; m. Eva, Mar. 18, 1978; 1 son, Carl Bruce b. 1948; edn: BSEE, Howard Univ. 1950; MS health svc. adminstrn., CSU Northridge 1976; Certified Mental Health Adminstr. 1983. Career: radiation physicist Nat. Bureau of Stds. Wash. Dc 1950-55; senior research engr. Lockheed Calif. Co. Burbank 1955-63; mem. tech. staff Space Elec. Power Engrg. Dept. TRW Sys. 1963-72; asst. prof. CSU Northridge 1974-76; assoc. adminstr., v.p. Pacoima Meml. Hosp. Lake View Terrace 1972-73; exec. dir. Hillview Mental Health Ctr. Lake View Terrace 1973-84, pres., exec. dir. 1985–; regent, dir. Casa Loma Coll. 1970-85;

honors: recipient Citation (Calif. Senate & Assembly, City of L.A. 1971), Cert. of Appreciation (Councilman Bob Ronka 1979); fellow Assn. Mental Health Adminstrs.; mem: Am. Pub. Health Assn., NAACP (nat. bd. 1970-76, pres. So. Area Calif. Conf. 1967-71), Am. Mgmt. Assn. 1978-, Nat. Assn. Health Svcs. Execs. 1976-, SFV Girl Scout Council (bd. 1980-82), Rotary (past pres.), Sigma Phi Xi Boule 1984-; publs: research reports for Nat. Bureau Stds. and Dept. HEW; mil: US Army 1945-46. Res: 17233 Chatsworth St Granada Hills 91344 Ofc: Hillview Mental Health Ctr Inc. 11630 Eldridge Ave Lake View Terrace 91342

MC CURRY, EDNA A., business owner; b. Feb. 15, 1920, Arona, Pa.; d. Harry Wilson and Bertha Amanda (Shotts) Anthony; raised by aunt, Daisy Dermore; m. Leonard McCurry (dec.), Dec. 22, 1940; 1 dau. Kathy Dale b. 1944; edn: grad. Norwin H.S. 1938. Career: var. pos. Douglas Aircraft and Associated Tel. Co., Calif., 1943; owner Geni Laundra-Magic, Tarzana 1966–, owner Geni Jeannes Trees (xmas tree farm), Thousand Oaks; breed, raise and show poodles (Best in Show awards); Republican; Christian; rec: art, fishing, nature. Res: 18235 Burbank Blvd Tarzana 91356 Ofc: Geni Laundra-Magic 18147 Ventura Bl Tarzana 91356

MC CUTCHEN, CHARLOTTE BARNWELL, physician; b. Oct. 31, 1944, Camp Lejeune, N.C.; d. James Malcolm and Emily Strother (Dunovant) McC.; edn: BS, Univ. of S.C. 1966; MD, Med. Coll. of Va. 1970. Career: residency tng. Vanderbilt Univ. 1972-74; instr. neurology & lab. medicine, Univ. of Wash. Sch. of Med., Seattle, 1974-77; asst. clin. prof. neurosciences UC San Diego 1977-84; cons. UCSD Internal Med. Gp. 1980-84; bd. dirs. Western Electroencephelo- graphic Soc. 1983-86; secty. Am. Epilepsy Soc. 1982-88; mem: San Diego Neurological Assn.; S.D. County Epilepsy Soc.; Western EEG Soc.; Am. EEG Soc.; Am. Acad. of Neurology; A.U.R.A.; publs: num. arts. in med. journs.; Episcopal; rec: sailing, backpacking, gardening. Res: 5559 Dalen Ave San Diego 92122 Ofc: S.D.V.A.M.C., 3350 La Jolla Village Dr San Diego

MC CUTCHEON, NORMA JOHNSINE, professional writer; b. Oct. 27, 1932, Oskaloosa, Iowa; d. Selmer M. and Irene (Reid) Muhl; m. Kenneth A. McCutcheon, Aug. 29, 1954; children: Michael K. b. 1956, Brian D. b. 1962, Craig S. b. 1964; edn: BA, State Univ. of Iowa 1954. Career: soc. ed. Daily Iowan, Iowa City, Iowa 1953, 1954; asst. soc. ed. and gen. news. Oskaloosa Daily Herald, Oskaloosa, Iowa 1953, 1954; freelance publicity PTA, Boy Scouts, Little League, AYP; articles publd. Azusa Herald and San Gabriel Tribune; mgr. Profl. Resume Service, Covina 1977-84; owner, mgr. Inland Empire Resume Service, Upland 1984–; career cons.; participant Women's Expo, Red Lion Inn., Ontario 1985 and Rancho Cucamonga Bus. Expo 1986; mem: State Univ. of Iowa Alumni Assn., Zeta Tau Alpha (life, past pres., Quad Cities Alumnae, Alpha Omicron chpt.), Upland CofC, Azusa Nat. Little League, Azusa Yout Pgm., PTA Orgns.; Republican; Protestant; rec: creative crafts, home decorating, gardening. Res: 7315 Ambrosia Rd. Rancho Cucamonga 91730 Ofc: Inland Empire Resume Service, Executive Office Center, 517 No. Mountain St. 102 Upland 91786

MC DANIELS, DAVID BENJAMIN, chiropractor; b. May 28, 1956, Tulsa, Okla.; s. David B., Sr. and Maria Luiza (Vidal) McD.; m. Laurie, May 18, 1985; edn: AA, Modesto Jr. Coll. 1976; BS, Los Angeles Coll. Chiropractic, 1978, DC, 1980; lic. DC, Calif. State Board 1980. Career: staff wholistic practice in Woodland Hills 1980-81, apprenticeship in jin sing do and shiatzu oriental pain relief techniques; sports chiropractic practice under Leroy Perry D.C., Olympic team doctor; currently owner chiropractic practice The Back Institute, Modesto; frequent lectr. var. groups, instr. Dale Carnegie Courses; mem: Stanislaus Chiro. Assn., Calif. Chiro. Assn., Am. Chiro. Assn., F.A.R.E., Chamber of Commerce; rec: sports, chiropractic research. Res: 3209 Harbor Modesto 95355 Ofc: The Back Institute 2813 Coffee Rd Ste F Modesto 95355

MC DANIELS, JOHN LEA, lawyer; b. May 30, 1940, San Francisco; s. John Hale and Vivian Marie (Lea) McD.; edn: BA, Stanford Univ. 1962; JD, San Francisco Law Sch. 1969. Mem: Internat. Bar Assn.; Am. Bar Assn.; Commonwealth Club; Cercle de l'Union; The Wine & Food Soc. of S.F.; Internat. Food & Wine Soc.; Inns of Court Society in Calif.; The Assocs. of the Stanford Univ. Libraries (adv. council); The Friends of the Bancroft Library; St. Thomas More Soc. of S.F.; Comanderie de Bordeaux des Etats-Unis; Soc. of Mayflower Descendants; bd. dirs. Bay Area USO; mil: Spec. 4/c AUS 1962-64; Catholic. Res: 1250 Jones St San Francisco 94109 Ofc: John Lea McDaniels, 40 First St, 3rd Floor, San Francisco 94105

MC DERMOTT, MICHAEL JAMES, firefighter, mariner, maritime safety specialist; b. June 16, 1956, San Francisco; s. James E. and June E. (Noyes) McD.; edn: US Coast Guard Acad. 1974-75; BS nautical indsl. technol., Calif. State Maritime Acad. 1979; Maritime Inst. of Technol. & Grad. Studies 1984; Firefighter I & II Cert., Alan Hancock Coll. 1985; lic. deck ofcr., US Merchant Marine (USCG). Career: boilermaker San Francisco 1975; licensed deck ofcr. Internat. Orgn. Masters, Mates & Pilots 1979-85; ofcr. mgmt. trainee Am. President Lines 1979-81; firefighter Santa Barbara County Fire Dept. 1985–; research, reports re. offshore oil safety problems; honors: Order of the Golden Shellback; mem: Internat. Assn. Fire Fighters, Nat. Fire Protn. Assn., Common Cause, Men's Rights advocate; mil: cadet USCG 1974-75, Nat. Defense Svc. Medal; rec: sailing, rowing, hiking, reading, current events. Res: 236 San Julian Santa Barbara 93109 Ofc: 5598 Corte Sonora Pleasanton 94566

MC DERMOTT, THOMAS J., JR., lawyer; b. Mar. 23, 1931, Santa Monica; s. Thomas J. and Etha Irene (Cook) McD.; m. Barbara, Dec. 6, 1972; children:

Jodi Friedman b. 1955, Kimberly Elizabeth b. 1973; edn: JD, UCLA Sch. of Law 1958. Career: assoc. Gray, Binkley & Pfaelzer 1959-64, ptnr. 1964-67, Kadison, Pfaelzer, Woodard, Quinn & Rossi 1967–; prof. law Southwestern Univ. Sch. of Law; arbitrator; judge pro tem; lectr.; honors: Order of the Coif; fellow Am. Coll. Trial Lawyers; mem: Assn. Bus. Trial Lawyers (pres. 1980-81), Am. Bar Assn., Calif. Bar Assn., L.A. Co. Bar Assn., UCLA Law Alumni Assn. (pres. 1961-62); author num. publs.; mil: US Army; Jewish; rec: reading, music, magic. Res: 505 N Foothill Rd Beverly Hills Calif. 90210 Ofc: Kadison, Pfaelzer et al. 707 Wilshire Blvd 40th floor Los Angeles 90017

MC DONALD, GARY T., mortgage banker, lawyer; b. Aug. 22, 1953, Stuttgart, Germany; H.R. and E.L. McDonald; 1 son, Matthew b. 1982; edn: BA honors, CSU Hayward 1976; JD, Golden Gate Univ. Law Sch. 1979; admitted Calif. State Bar; real estate broker Calif.; Calif. Comm. Coll. instr. (law). Career: atty. Law Ofc. of Gary T. McDonald, San Leandro; mng. atty. Calif. Legal Plan, Walnut Creek; pres. US Nat. Finance, USNF Svc. Corp.; instr. law Chabot Coll. 1982; bd. dirs. US Nat. Finance, USNF Svc. Corp., Columbia Properties and Investments 1985-; honors: Eagle Scout w/ Bronze Palm (1968), 5 Presdl. Sports Awards; mem: Assn. of Profl. Mortgage Womenb (pres.), Alameda Contra Costa Bar Assn., Calif. Trial Lawyers Assn., Am. Bar Assn., Assn. of Trial Lawyers of Am., So. Alameda County Bd. of Realtors; assoc. advisor Explorer Post 626 San Leandro. Ofc: 21119 Redwood Rd Ste 4 Castro Valley 94546

MC DONALD, JAMES EARL, horticulturist, pomologist; b. May 20, 1931, Oceanside; s. Baylis Morse and Opal B. McD.; m. Virginia Ann Ray, June 18, 1960; children: Lisa b. 1961, Roderick b. 1966, Robert b. 1970; edn: undergrad. UC Berkeley 1949-52; BS in fruit scis., Calif. State Polytech. Univ. 1957; Calif. lic. Pest Control Advisor. Career: participant in family avocado and citrus orchard/ nursery bus., Fallbrook -1949; quality control chemist Sunkist Growers, Inc. 1957-61; tech. writer Beckman Instruments Inc. 1961-65; farming ops. mgr. Calavo Growers of Calif. 1965-72; cons. prin. McDonald Agriscience (agric. mgmt. and cons.), Fallbrook 1972–; lectr. (f.t.) in fruit scis., Cal Poly Pomona 1985–; expert witness in agric. litigation and insurance; honors: honors award Sunkist Lemon Mens Club (1957), Calif. State Assem. Resolution No. 718 (1971), appreciation cert. San Diego Co. Dept. Edn. for leadership as mem. Vocational Plnng. Com. for S.D./ Imperial Cos. (1974); mem: AAUP, Calif. Agric. Tchrs Assn., Calif. Agric. Prodn. Consultants Assn., Citrus Research Com. UC Coop. Extension, Calif. Rare Fruit Growers, No. Am. Fruit Explorers, Calif. Avocado Soc., Assn. of Applied Insect Ecologists, Fallbrook Hist. Soc., Clan Donald Soc.; publs: write/pub. The McDonald Report (avocado mktg. newsletter); contbr. arts. Avocado Grower Mag. (10/77), Calif. Avo. Soc. Yearbook (1982); mil: US Army 1952-54; Republican; rec: travel, host to farm advisers and grad. students on study tours. Address: 2536 Valerie Dr Fallbrook 92028

MC DONALD, JOHN GREGORY, finance education; b. May 21, 1937, Stockton; s. Earl and Dora (Mitchell) M.D.; s. Melody June 19, 1973; edn: BS, Stanford Univ. 1960, MBA, 1962, PhD, 1967. Career: with Stanford Univ. Grad. Sch. of Bus., Stanford; asst. prof. 1968-71; assoc. prof. 1971-75; prof. of fin. 1975-78; The Joseph McDonald prof. of fin. 1979–; dir: Investment Co. of Am., Growth Fund of Am., New Perspective Fund, Europacific Growth Fund, Scholastic Inc.; vis. prof. Univ. of Paris 1972, Columbia Univ. 1975, Harvard Univ. 1986; honors: Fulbright Fellow, Paris 1967-68; mem: Adv. Bd. InterWest Venture Capital, Pension Bd. Varian Assoc.; mil: 1s lt. US Army 1962-64. Res: 1098 Vernier Pl. Stanford 94305

MC DONOUGH, PATRICK JOSEPH, lawyer; b. Oct. 11, 1943, Los Angeles; s. Thomas John and Cecilia Veronica (Roach) M.D.; m. Susan Singletary, Dec. 30, 1967; 1 dau, Coleen b. 1971; edn: BA, CSU Northridge 1969; JD, Loyola Univ. Sch. of Law. 1971. Career: House of Reps., US Congressman Ed Reinecke 1966-68; corp., secty. assoc. counsel Automobile Club of So. Calif. Mgmt. Svcs. Inc. (wholly owned subs.) and Interinsurance Exch. of the ACSC 1971-85; v.p., gen. counsel Johns & Higgins of Calif. 1986–; bd. govs. Inst. for Corp. Counsel 1981-86; exec. com. Los Angeles Bar Assn. Sect. for Corp. Law; bd. dirs. Assn. Calif. Tort Reform (1986), Am. Corp. Counsel Assn. (1985-86); honors: Delta Sigma chpt. pres., Phi Sigma Alpha 1965; mem: Am., Calif. and Los Angeles Bar Assns., Conf. of Insurance Counsel, Phi Delta Phi, Town Hall; Republican; Catholic; rec: fishing, sailing. Res: 18726 Nau Ave Northridge 91326 Ofc: Automobile Club of So. Calif., 2601 S Figueroa St Los Angeles 90007

MC DOWELL, CHARLES S., accountant; b. Feb. 18, 1942, Indpls.; s. Glen Earl and Dorothy Maxine (Stewart) McD.; m. Mary Jo Masulli, Jan. 4, 1964; children: Shannon b. 1967, Suzanne b. 1970. Career: AA, Los Angeles Valley Coll. 1966; BS in acctg., CSU Northridge 1968; MBA in acctg., Woodbury Univ. 1984. Career: mgr. acctg. and finance Unocal ops. in N.W. Europe until 1980, mgr. corp. acctg. Unocal Corp. 1980-83, asst. corp. comptroller Unocal Corp., Los Angeles 1983-86, apptd. corporate comptroller 1986–, mem. bd. dirs. 1983–; instr. undergrad. pgm. in acctg., Woodbury Univ. 1985-; honors: Wall Street Journal award for outstanding grad. Woodbury Univ. (1984), Phi Beta Kappa (1984); mem: Finl. Execs. Inst./LA Chap. (chmn. FEI Com. on corp. reporting 1985-86, bd. dirs. 1986-87), Am. Petroleum Inst. (acctg. & fin. com.), USC Accounting Circle (bd.), Union Royal Toastmasters Club (charter pres.); publs: thesis on var. mgmt. styles in the petroleum industry (pub. by several univs. 1984); Republican; Catholic; rec: sports enthusiast, tennis, jogging. Res: 3175 Emerald Isle Dr Glendale 91206 Ofc: Unocal Corp. 1204 West Fifth St (POB 7600) Los Angelees 90051

MC DOWELL, JENNIFER, publisher/composer; b. May 19, 1936, Albuquerque, NM; d. Willard A. and Margaret (Garrison) McDowell; grandfather, Lemuel Addison Garrison, fmr. pres. Central College (Pella, Iowa); mother, Margaret F. Garrison, author; uncle Lon Garrison, supt. Yellowstone Nat. Park 1955-63. Edn: BA, UC Berkeley 1957; MA, CSU San Diego 1958; MLS, UCB 1963; PhD, Univ. Ore. Eugene 1973; m. Milton Loventhal, July 2, 1973. Career: high sch. tchr. Abraham Lincoln H.S., San Jose 1960-61; freelance ed., Soviet field, 1961-63; resrch. asst., sociol., Univ. Ore. 1964-66; ed./ pub. Merlin Papers, San Jose 1969−; ed./pub. Merlin Press, 1973−; res. cons. sociol., San Jose 1973−; music publisher Lipstick and Toy Balloons Pub. Co., San Jose 1978−; resrchr., writer Merlin Research and Writing Center, 1980−; co-creator musical comedy: Russia's Secret Plot to Take Back Alaska (1983); tchr. writing workshops 1969-73; manuscript reader for Journ. of the Sci. Study of Religion, 1974−; on the list of composers for Paramount Pictures, 1981−; co-prod. radio shows, Sta. KALX, Berkeley 1971-72; songs (3) featured in Survey of Am. Music for Bicentennial Year; Awards: doctoral fellowship 1971-73, AAUW; Calif. Arts Council grant 1976-77; profl. awards: Am. Song Festival (1976-79), Poetry Orgn. for Women (1979), Bill Casey Meml. Award (1980), listed in Directory of Am. Poets and Fiction Writers 1980; composer for Harold C. Crain Award (1980) winning play, Simple Gifts by Nancy Gilsenan; honors: Kappa Kappa Gamma, Sigma Alpha Iota, Phi Beta Kappa, Beta Phi Mu; mem: Soc. for the Sci. Study of Relig., Soc. for the Study of Relig. under Communism, Am. Sociological Assn., Poetry Orgn. for Women, Feminist Writers Guild, Internat. Womens Writing Guild; author: Black Politics (1971), Contemporary Women Poets an Anthology (1977); contrib. many arts. in Bulletin of Bibliography, Jour. for the Sci. Study of Religion, San Jose Studies; contbr. poems, essays to num. mags. incl. Women's World, Women Talking, Women Listening, X a Journal of the Arts, others; composer over 60 songs. Democrat; Prot.; rec: tennis, Calif. native plants, hiking. Ofc: Merlin Press, POB 5602, San Jose 95150

MC EACHRON, EDGAR LINDSLEY, architect; b. Dec. 23, 1948, Wausau, Wisc.; s. Edgar Desnoyers and Elizabeth (Burchard) McE.; m. Mary K., June 22, 1974; 1 dau: Elizabeth Lindsley, b. 1982; edn: BA, cum laude, Yale Univ. 1971; Cert., Universite de Lyon, France 1972; M.Arch., UC Berkeley 1974; Reg. Architect, Mass. (1978) and Calif. (1979). Career: designer The Architects Collaborative, Boston, Mass. 1977; designer, project mgr. Huygens & Tappe, Moston, Mass. 1978-79; v.p. Backen, Arrigoni & Ross Inc., San Francisco 1979-84; pres. McEachron Associates Architects Inc., San Francisco 1984−; mem: Am. Inst. of Arhitects, Edgewood Neighborhood Assn. (pres.), Found. for San Francisco's Architectural Heritage, Nat. Trust for Historic Preservation, Calif. Acad. of Sciences, San Francisco Opera Guild, San Francisco Museum Soc.; painting and architectural work exhibited, New Haven, Conn., NYC, Berkeley and San Francisco; Democrat; Unitarian; rec: skiing, bicycling, hiking. Res: 100 Edgewood Ave. San Francisco 94117 Ofc: McEachron Associates Architects Inc., 100 Edgewood Ave. San Francisco 94117

MC ELHANEY, VOL GENE, real estate broker; b. Mar. 21, 1924, Claremore, Okla.; s. Vol Wilson and Bonnie (Casey) McE.; m. Roberta Sparks, July 8, 1948; children: Suzanne b. 1951, June b. 1952; edn: AA, Modesto Jr. Coll. 1949; BE, CSU Sacramento 1964; FBI Acad., Wash. DC 1975. Career: sheriff's inspector Stanislaus County 1951-53, chief vice & narcotics and asst. to sheriff 1953-57; senior spl. investigator San Joaquin, Alameda, Contra Costa counties 1957-61; spl. agent (to asst. chief) Calif. Dept. of Justice 1961-77; real estate broker, investor 1977−; owner, mgr. Faubus Motel and Madison County Real Estate, Huntsville, Ark.; honors: Spkr. of the Year (Pre Legal Club, Modesto Jr. Coll. 1951), Honorary Colonel (State of Tenn. Nat. Guard, Ala. Nat. Guard); mem: Calif. Spl. Agents Assn., FBI Nat. Acad. Assocs., AARP, Calif. Retired Tchrs. Assn., Stanislaus Co. Deputy Sheriffs Assn., Internat. Assn. Chiefs of Police, Calif. Policewoman Assn., Masons, Elks, VFW; founder Calif. Narcotics Assn. (1952); helped create and was first supv. agent of Calif. Dept. of Justice Tng. Acad.; organized, trained and supervised (w/ Harold McKinney) first Stanislaus County Sheriff's Reserve (1952); Protestant; avoc: computer sci., business. Res: 658 Shadowview Ct Turlock 95380 Ofc: Madison County Real Estate Rt 5 Box 1 Huntsville AR 72740

MC ELROY, LEO FRANCIS, public relations executive; b. Oct. 12, 1932, Los Angeles; s. Leo Frances Sr. and Helen Evelyn (Silliman) McE.; m. Dorothy Montgomery, Nov. 3, 1956 (div. 1981); children: James b. 1961, Maureen b. 1964, Michael b. 1967, Kathleen b. 1969; edn: BS Eng., Loyola Univ. 1953. Career: broadcast newsman Ill., Calif. 1954-63; broadcast news exec. Los Angeles 1964-73; television host, producer PBS 1967-74; pres. media cons. firm L.A. 1973-74; political editor, investigative reporter, news anchor KABC-TV L.A. 1974-81; pres. McElroy Communications Sacramento, L.A. 1981−; spl. asst. to Lt. Gov. of Calif. 1983-84; prin. cons. Assembly Com. on Aging and Long-Term Care 1983; chmn. Calif. Task Force on Emgcy. Info. 1973-74; crim. justice cons. Calif. Dept. Justice 1971-74; honors: Emmy (L.A. Acad. TV Arts & Scis. 1968), Golden Mike (L.A; Radio- TV News Soc. 1973), Commdn. (Calif. State Assembly 1981); mem: Am. Assn. Political Cons. 1985-, Am. Soc. Composers, Authors & Publishers 1963-, Am. Fedn. of TV-Radio Artists 1958-, Concern Over Surplus Technol.- Med. Ethics (exec. dir.), Steroids Out of Sports (co-exec. dir.); plays: To Bury Caesar (1952), Mermaid Tavern (1956); book: Uneasy Partners (1984); num. songs incl. Melanie Goodby (1963), Wanderin' Song (1964); mil: 1st lt. USAF 1954-56; Republican; Catholic; rec: tennis, archery, writing. Res: 1325 O St Apt 2 Sacramento 95814 Ofc: McElroy Communications 2410 K St Ste C Sacramento 95816; 603 E Green St Ste 200 Pasadena 91101

MC EVERS, DUFF STEVEN, lawyer; b. Apr. 21, 1954, Los Angeles; s. Milton Stoddard and Virginia Mary (Tongue) McE.; m. Jeannine, July 14, 1984; 1 child, Tay b. 1985; edn: BA, USC 1976; JD, Western State Univ. 1980; admitted Calif. State Bar 1981. Career: atty. assoc. Donald B. Black, Inc. Laguna Beach 1981-85, sole practitioner in Laguna Beach 1985−; of counsel, Donald B. Black, Inc.; volunteer Amicus Publico; honors: Skull and Dagger (1976), Outstanding Student Senior (1976), Law Review (1980), Participant Oral Advocacy, Jessup Competition (1980); mem: Am., Calif., Orange County bar assns., Am. Soc. Internat. Law, Am. Trial Lawyers Assn., Breakfast Club of Newport Beach, Alzheimer's Disease and Related Disorders Assn.; Republican; Episcopal; rec: sailing. Law Offices of D. Steven McEvers, 301 Forest Ave Laguna Beach 92651

MC EVOY, PAMELA THOMPSON, psychotherapist; b. March 8, 1937, NYC; d. Reynolds Thomas and Pamela Shipley (Sweeny) M.E.; children: Michael Anderson b. 1955, Jeffrey Thomas b. 1956, Candy Anderson (Smith) b. 1959, Kenneth Anderson b. 1960; edn: AA, Allen Hancock Coll. 1974; BA, Univ. of Laverne 1976, MS, 1979; PhD, US Internat. Univ. 1982. Career: guidance and data processing coord. Ernest Righetti H.S., Santa Maria 1975-78; mental health worker Santa Barbara Co. Alcohol Svcs., Lompoc 1978; instr. Allan Hancock Coll., Santa Maria 1976-78; gen. mgr., controller Profl. Suites, San Diego 1978-81; grad. tchg. asst. (research coord. 1981-82), US Internat. Univ., San Diego p.t. 1979-82; psychotherapist pvt. practice, Chula Vista Counseling Ctr. 1978-86, currently, Rancho Bernardo; awards: Calif. State Fellowship Award, consec. 1978-82; Calif. State Scholarship Award, 1976; mem: Am. Psychological Assn., Calif. Assn. of Marriage & Family Therapists, Am. Personnel & Guidance Assn.; co-author: with E.J. Hunter and S. Whitworth, Annotated Bibliography on Military Family Literature, Praeger pub.; Republican; Catholic; rec: Hypnosis, parapsychology, ballet. Res: 17452 Ashburton Rd. San Diego 92128 Ofc: Bernardo Psychological Services, 16776 Bernardo Center Dr. Ste. 204 San Diego 92128

MC FADDIN, DON EVERET, mechanical engineer consultant; b. July 17, 1906, San Dimas; s. Eugene Josiah and Nettie Ethel (Brown) McF.; m. Daisy, Sept. 1, 1928; edn: BS, Calif. Inst. of Tech. 1928; Reg. Profl. Engr., Calif. (1946). Career: engr. Union Oil Co. of Calif., 1930-38, designed processes and initiated ops. of several gasplants and refinery plants incl. lube oil plants at Oleum, Calif.; field engr. Union Oil Co. of Calif. at Orcutt, Santa Maria Area, 1938-51; supvr. of plants, Prodn. Dept., Home Office, Los Angeles 1952-69; engr. consultant prin., 1970−, engring. and tech. cons. to major public utility on underground natural gas storage, engring. and tech. cons. on var. landfill gas projects in So. Calif., Central U.S. and East Coast areas; honors: Service Award of Merit (1957) Calif. Natural Gasoline Assn. (later became Western Gas Processors and Oil Refiners Assn., now known as Pacific Energy Assn.); mem: ASME, Petroleum Prodn. Pioneers, Pacific Energy Assn. (pres. 1977-78), Tau Beta Pi, CalTech Alumni Assn. and Athenaeum Club, Pasadena; works: contbd. fundamental data based on research and oilfield ops. and tests for the phenomenon of retrogade condensation; participant in Jersey-Union-Indiana-Kellogg patent pool; mil: commnd. 2d lt. US Army Corps of Engrs. 1928, assigned to Roster of sci. and tech. personnel (frozen in his job) 1942; Republican; Presbyterian (pres. bd. deacons 1986; pres. bd. dirs. El Calvario Comm. Ctr., El Monte 1986). Address: 735 Irving St Apt 5 Alhambra 91801

MC FARLAND, DANIEL JOSEPH, physician; b. Dec. 16, 1951, El Reno, Okla.; s. James Lawrence and Mary Margaret (Moore) McF.; m. Nancy Chadwick, June 25, 1977; edn: AB in human biol., Stanford Univ. 1974; MD, UC San Diego Sch. of Med. 1978; certified anesthesiologist, Am. Board of Anesthesiology 1985. Career: intern in internal medicine, Stanford Univ. Med. Center 1978-79, resident and chief res., neurology, 1979-82, resident and chief res., anesthesiology, 1982-84; staff anesthesiologist Sequoia Hosp., Redwood City 1984−; asst. clin. prof. of anesthesia Stanford Univ. Sch. of Med.; honors: Phi Beta Kappa (1974); mem. AMA, Calif. Med. Assn., San Mateo Co. Med. Soc., Am. Soc. of Anesthesiologists, Calif. Soc. of Anes., Sierra Club. Res: 2019 White Oak Way San Carlos 94070 Ofc: Redwood Medical Clinic 2900 Whipple Ave Redwood City 94062

MC FARLAND, LEE CRAIG, oil company executive; b. Aug. 16, 1920, Long Beach; s. John and Edna Christina (Fehrm) McF.; m. Ruth Smails, June 22, 1943; children: John b. 1947, Stuart b. 1949, Andrew b. 1951, William b. 1960; edn: BS, UC Berkeley 1942. Career: petroleum engr. Tidewater (Getty) Oil 1946-47; petroleum engr., geologist Universal Consolidated Oil 1947-64; mgr. prod. & exploration Gulf Oil 1964-66; cons. L.A. Basin, Occidental Petroleum 1966-68; pres., CEO McFarland Oil Corp. 1968-72; pres., CEO McFarland Energy Inc. 1972-82, bd. chmn., CEO 1982−; mem: Am. Inst. Mech. Engrs., API, AAPG, IPAA, CIPA, Los Angeles and Bakersfield Petroleum Clubs, The Calif. Club, Sigma Nu frat.; Republican; rec: old cars, philately, fishing. Ofc: McFarland Energy Inc., P.O. Box 3608 Santa Fe Springs 90670

MC GADDEN, JOSEPH RAYMOND, author, logistician, cryptologist; b. Apr. 2, 1935, Lowell, Mass.; s. Joseph Walter and Elizabeth Grace (Foster) M.; m. Ruth Marie Albee Dunn (dau. Sir Clarence J. Albee, mem. Royal French Order of Soldats de Verdun 1918; rel., poet/playwright Edward Albee; desc. of Adm. Byrd), 10/6/84; children: William, Charles, Robert, Scott; and Alan, Sheila, Gary Dunn; edn: Lowell Tech., 1967-71; Fla. Inst. of Tech. 1976; Orange Coast Coll. 1964; Chapman Coll. 1965; Adult Voc. Teaching Cert., Mass. 1970; Cryptologist, NSA/CSS 1978; (cand. 1985) Cert. Profl. Logistician (CPL). Career: avionics supr. USMC 1953-66; with GTE Systems, 1966−: proj. supr. communication satellites, GTE, Waltham, Mass. 1966-70, supr. LEAA Projects 1970-72; mgr. EW & Recon Projects, Ops. Group, GTE Mountain View, Ca. 1973-79, mem. tech. staff SIGINT Improvement Pgms, 1980-82, tech. support/ logistics/ configuration mgr. 1982-3, logistics mgr. Space Resrch. Projects 1983–; cryptologic ofcr. USNR Security Gp., cons. to Naval Weapons Sta., Newport, RI 1969; awards: Cryptol. Svc. to Country, USNCVA 1979; mem. Internat. MENSA, Soc. Logistics Engrs., SALT, NRA, NRA Polaris Chpt., US Naval Inst., Am. Soc. for Tng. & Devel., USN Cryptol. Assn.; GTE Employees Assn. (vp 1979); sponsor San Jose Civic Light Opera, S.J. Performance Group; publs: sev. tech., sci. publs.; book: FOES, Fundamentals of Electronic Surveillance (1986/87); mil: USMC 1953-66, USAF 1968-1972; chief warrant ofcr. USNR 1982-; Air Crewman Wings, combat action, Vietnam svc., Valorous unit (28 combat and svc. decorations); rec: theatre, jogging. Res: 687 London Dr Milpitas 95035 Ofc: GTE Systems, 100 Ferguson Dr Mountain View 94039

MC GEATH, MICHAEL HARLOW, restaurateur; b. Apr. 8, 1948, Evanston, Ill.; s. Harlow Higenbothem and Ruth (Bachofen) McG.; edn: BA in hist., CSU San Diego 1972; Western State Univ. Law Sch. 1973-75. Career: gen. mgr. Old Spaghetti Factory Internat./ San Diego 1974-76; gen. mgr. Stoneridge Country Club Rancho Bernardo 1976-78; gen. mgr. San Diego Yacht Club, 1978-80; gen. mgr. San Diego Culinary Concepts Inc.- Harbor House Restaurant 1980-82, Papagayo Rest. 1982-85; gen. mgr., ptnr. Silas St. John Rest., San Diego 1985–; ptnr. California Rest. Consultants, S.D. 1985–; honors: under his mgmt. both Harbor House and Papagayo listed by Esquire Mag. Top 50 Restaurants in U.S., and Papagayo named one of best seafood restaurants Calif. Rest. Writers Assn.; student body pres. (CSU San Diego), Eagle Scout (BSA); mem. Les Amis Du Vin, Nat. Rest. Assn., Sigma Chi frat., S.D. Co. Dep. Sheriffs Assn., Boy Scouts Am. (scoutmaster), Easter Seals (wine auction chmn.), S.D. Charger Backers (bd. dirs. 1973-76), S.D. Nat. Wine Competition (dir.), Riverside Co. Fair in Wine (judge); Republican; Episcopal; rec: enology, western art and artifacts, Porsche. Res: 3893-8 California St San Diego 92110 Ofc: Silas St. John Restaurant Inc. 4720 Kensington Dr San Diego 92116

MC GILLOWAY, THOMAS RICHARD, management consultant; b. July 27, 1946, Phila.; s. Edward John and Helen Catherine (Sawchynsky) M.G.; m. Beverly J., Jan. 8, 1980; 1 dau, Jennifer b. 1971; edn: BA, Temple Univ. 1973; So. Illinois Univ. 1984-85. Career: plant mgr. Book Craftsmen Ltd., Bridgeport, Penn. 1973-78; project mgr. Byrne Mgmt. Corp., Medford, NJ 1978-82; mgmt. cons. Coopers & Lybrand, Los Angeles1 1982-83; mgr. mgmt. advisory svcs. Deloitte Haskins & Sells, Los Angeles 1983–; steering com. Los Angeles Aerospace & Defense Spl. Interest Group 1986; orgn. com. Calif. Tech.-MIT Forum 1985; honors: cand., Upland City Council; mem: pres. Am. Prodn. & Inventory Control Soc. (Inland Empire chpt.), Ops. Mgmt. Assn., Industry Hills Mfrs. Council, Upland CofC, Friends of Ontario Airport; works: seminar, Computer Integrated Manufacturing- Strategy for the Future, APICS Sem. Circuit 1985-86; Republican; Methodist; rec: tennis, reading. Res: 1352 Clark St. Upland 91786 Ofc: Deloitte Haskins & Sells, 21600 Oxnard St. Woodland Hills

MC GINN, JANE LEOCHA, real estate broker; b. Oct. 14, 1948, Annapolis, Md.; d. Victor Stanley and Nancy Irr (Clarke) Leocha; children: John, b. 1968; David, b. 1970; Daniel, b. 19785; edn: AA, West Hills Coll. 1982; Meridian Jr. Coll. 1968; Reedley Jr. Coll. 1978; Univ. of Md. 1966-67; Calif. Reg. Dental Asst. (1978), lic. R.E. Broker, 1984. Career: sales assoc. ERA Town & Country Realtors, Lemoore 1980-82; sales assoc. Centurion Realtors, Lemoore 1982; broker/ owner Century 21 Creative Realty, Lemoore 1983-85; Kings Harvest Savings & Loan div. of Westport Savings Bank 1985–; dir./ chmn. grievance com. Kings Co. Bd. Realtors 1982-; secty. Pioneer Square Merchants Assn. 1983-85; honors: Outstanding Young Women of Am. 1983; mem: Kings Co. Womens Trade Club; Kings Co. Navy League; Assn. Naval Aviation; Lemoore CofC; campaigner: Pashayan for Congress (Steering Com. 1983-); Maroot Supvr. Com. 1982; Republican (Central Com., Steering Com.); Catholic; rec: equestrian, golf, riflery. Res: Lemoore Devel. Corp. 30 B Faun Ln Lemoore 93245 Ofc: Kings Harvest Savings & Loan 106 E Seventh St Hanford 93230

MC GINTY, BRIAN DONALD, lawyer/ writer; b. June 22, 1937, Santa Barbara; s. Donald Bruce and Natalia Vallejo (Haraszthy) McG.; edn: AB,. UC Berkeley 1959; JD, 1962. Career: practicing atty., Monterey County, Ca. 1963-73; journalist and writer 1973–; author: Haraszthy at the Mint; The Palace Inns; 125+ arts. in scholarly and profl. journs. & popular mags.; contbg. author: Calif. Legal Forms; Calif. Real Estate Law and Practice; lectr., polit. sci. Hartnell Coll., Salinas 1963-64; legal writer Matthew Bender & Co., S.F. & Oakland 1984-. Res: San Francisco 94101 Ofc: 2101 Webster Oakland 94612

MC GRAIN, JOHN PATRICK, investor; b. Aug. 23, 1945, Los Angeles; s. Jack Freeman and Muriel Teresa (Arnold) Runyon; m. Nancy H. Abel, Dec. 28, 1968; edn: BA, UCLA 1967; Reg. Options Principal, NASD Principal, Br. Ofc. Mgr., 1979. Career: v.p./ dir. R.M. Evans & Co., Los Angeles 1969-71; securities broker Bateman, Eichler, Hills, Richard & EF Hutton, L.A. 1972-77; nat.'s fixed income mgr. Loeb Rhoads Hornblower/ Shearson, L.A. 1977-79; v.p./ mgr. Wagenseller & Durst, L.A. 1979-80; sales mgr. Bache, Halsey, Stuart, Shields, L.A. 1980-81; v.p./mgr. Thomson McKinnon Securities, Inc., L.A. 1981-84; pres., chmn. Conversion Industries Inc. 1984–; dir: Plant-Minder 1981-, Pacific Waste Mgmt., Pasa. 1983-, Conversion Industries USA, Inc., Pasa. 1983-, Jeha Resources Ltd., Vancouver, BC 1985, Patrick-Riley Securities Inc., Western Congeneration, Inc., Pasa. 1983-; awards: Leadership Awd., Nat. Elks Club 1963; Calif. recipient Hearst Senate Youth Pgm. 1963; State Pres. Calif. Assn. of Student Councils 1963; Leadership Awd. Am. Legion 1962; mem: Pasadena Bond Club; rec: equestrian, golf. Res: 707 Sierra Meadow, Sierra Madre 91024 Ofc: Conversion Industries Inc., 255 S Marengo Ave Pasadena 91101

MC GRUDER, CHARLES THOMAS, consultant; b. July 29, 1949, Bethesda, Md.; s. Herbert George and Dorothy Elizabeth (Kennedy) McG.; m. Jane Marie, Sept. 6, 1969; children: Karen b. 1970, Justin b. 1974; edn: BA, Johnston Coll./ Univ. Redlands 1973; MA, PhD, Claremont Grad. Sch. 1976, 1978. Career: instr., researcher, proposal writer, Citrus Coll. 1977-79, Blaisdell Inst. 1978-79; pgm. advisor (Internat. Place) Claremont Colls. 1980-82; modernernization pgm. NI Industries 1981-83; cons. prin./pres. co-founder Ergodotics, Claremont 1975–, cons. Menke Marking Devices (1975-), Blaisdell Inst. (1976-82), Broco Inc. (1982-), American Honda (1983-), Clayton Industries (1983), Communications Cos. Internat. (1983-84); awards: fellowship Claremont Grad. Sch. 1974-76, Golden Apple Award (1978); conf. presentor: Fortis Imaginato (1982), Philosophical Research Soc. (1982, 83), Pepperdine Univ. (1983), Training Fair, ASTD (1983); mem: Am. Soc. for Tng. and Devel. (ASTD), Am. Soc. for Performance Improve., Application of Psychological Type (bd.), Hastings Inst. for Study of Soc., Ethics and the Life Scis., Soc. of Mfg. Engrs. (edn. chmn. 1981-82), The Philos. Research Soc.; avocation: practicing ideas of Peter Drucker (entrepreneurship and innovation) and David Kersey (type theory); rec: read, skateboard, conversation. Ofc: Ergodotics POB 1141 Claremont 91711

MC GUIRE, MICHAEL JOHN, water quality manager, b. June 29, 1947, San Antonio, Tx.; s. James Brendan and Opal Mary (Brady) McG.; m. Deborah Marrow, June 19, 1971; children: David b. 1980, Anna b. 1985; edn: BSCE, Univ. of Penna. 1969; MS, environmtl. engring. Drexel Univ. 1971, PhD, 1977; Reg. Profl. Engr. Calif., New Jersey, Penna. Career: proj. engr. Philadelphia (Pa.) Water Dept. 1969-73; research assoc. Drexel Univ. 1976-77; prin. engr. Brown and Caldwell Consulting engrs., Pasadena, CA 1977-79; water quality engr. The Metropolitan Water Dist. of So. Calif., L.A. 1979-84, Water Quality Mgr. 1984–; consulting environmtl. engr. 1979-; cons. to Nat. Acad. of Sci., Safe Drinking Water Com. 1978-79; bd. trustees Am. Water Works Assn. Research Found. 1983-; honors: academic achieve. awd. Am. Water Works Assn. 1978, Sigma Xi, Sigma Tau (eng. hon.) 1969, Diplomate Am. Acad. of Environmtl. Engring.; listed Who's Who in the West 1981-85; mem: Am. Water Works Assn. (chmn. Edn. Div. 1982, v. chmn. Jt. Tng. Coordinating Com. 1982, Calif-Nev. Sect. Edn. Adminstr. 1978-81 and chmn. Water Qual. and Resources Div. 1983-84, bd. trustees 1985-); Am. Chemical Soc.; ASCE; Internat. Assn. on Water Pollution and Control 1972-; Water Pollution Control fedn.; Sigma Nu 1966-; publs: co-editor w/ I.H. Suffet: Activated Carbon Adsorption of Organics from the Aqueous Phase (2 vols., 1980), and Treatment of Water by Granular Activated Carbon (1983); author over 50 tech. publs. on trace contaminant control in the water treatment process; rec: swim, scuba dive, personal computers. Ofc: The Metropolitan Water Dist. of So. Calif. POB 54153, Los Angeles 90054

MC HUGH, KEVIN DOUGLAS, civil engineer-land surveyor; b. Dec. 30, 1934, Ottawa, Ont., Canada, nat. US cit. 1971; s. Joseph and Margaret (Carroll) McH.; m. Patricia Ann, June 26, 1970; children: Patti b. 1955, Erin b. 1956, Patrick b. 1957, Kevin Jr. b. 1958, Michael b. 1961; edn: Carleton Coll., Algonquin Coll., Santa Ana Coll., Univ. Calif.; certs: Reg. Engring. Technician, Profl. Engrs. Assn. Ontario (1960); Reg. Profl. Civil Engr., Calif. (1983); Reg. Land Surveyor in Calif. (1971), Nev. (1978), Colo. (1980). Career: survey crew mem., supr., constrn. insp. McRostie & Assocs., Ottawa 1950-57, chief of party No. Quebec wilderness survey for proposed railway line, Canadian Aero Svcs. 1957-58, engring. tech., chief survey crew Div. Water Works Dept. City of Ottawa, 1958-65; survey analyst engring. dept. Williamson & Schmid, Santa Ana 1965-69; dir. land title and record maps, subdiv. survey dept. Raub, Bein, Frost & Assocs., Newport Beach 1969-71; pres., ptnr. McHugh-Norris, Inc., engring. and surveying, Tustin 1971-76; v.p. Surveying Dept., Jack G. Raub Co., Mission Viejo 1976–; instr. Cal Poly Univ., Pomona; mem: Am. Cong. on Surveying & Mapping, Calif. Land Surveyor's Assn. (past pres.), Calif. Council of Civil Engrs. & Land Surveyors (pres.-elect), So. Calif. Assn. of Civil Engrs. and Land Surveyors (past dir., gov.), Calif. Found. for Land Surveying Edn. (past pres.), Orange Co. Engrs. Club; Republican; Episcopal; rec: pvt. pilot, skiing, guitarist. Res: 27703 Ortega Hwy, 38, San Juan Capistrano Ofc: Jack G. Raub Co. 24741 Chrisanta Dr Mission Viejo 92691

MC INTOSH, GREGORY CECIL (PRINCE), engineering co. president; b. Dec. 19, 1949, Ft. Hood, Tx.; Prince (hereditary title), Principality of Outer Baldonia, 1966; (nat. citizen, Principality of Outer Baldonia); s. Horace Samuel and Phyllis Mary (Mountford) McI.; m. Carol Ann Hackett, Oct. 14, 1978; edn: BA, philos., honors, CSU Dominguez Hills 1975-81; att. El Camino Coll. 1971, L.A. Harbor Coll. 1968-70; Cert. APT Pgmmr., UCC 1981; Cert. Compact II Pgmmr., MDSI 1980. Career: mgr. Lundquist-McDonalds, San Pedro 1968-70; salesman United-Overton, Inc. El Segundo 1970-73; supr. International Rectifier, El Segundo 1973-75; salesman Volume Shoe Corp., Gardena 1975-76; mgr. Levitan Mgmt. Corp., Gardena 1976-79; substitute tchr. Lawndale Elem. Sch. Dist., 1979; pres./CEO H.M.S. Engineering Inc., Gardena 1979-80; machine shop foreman/ maint. supr./ numerical control pgmmr. Essick-Hadco Mfg. Co. Div. Figgie Internat. Inc., 1980-84; mfg. engr. Electro-Optical Data Systems Group, Hughes Aircraft Co., El Segundo 1984–; mem: Assn. for Integrated Mfg. Technol. (AIM Tech, chpt. pres. 1984-85), US Chess Fedn. 1985-, The Non-Canonical Calabashes (Sherlock Holmes Soc. of L.A.) 1985-, Soc. for Philosophy of Sex and Love 1985-, Soc. for History of Discoveries 1985-, Numerical Control Soc. (pres. L.A. Chpt. 1982-3, 1983-4), North Am. Nietzsche Soc.; past pres. CSU-DH Philosophy and Chess Clubs; orgns: Holiday Project; publs: Joniper, The Littlest Elf (radio play bdcst.

12/83); Keynote spkr. Grad. Class, Wilshire Computer Coll. (6/83); Libertarian; Zen Buddhist; rec: painting, chess, poetry. Res: 2929 W. 190th St, 101, Redondo Bch 90278 Ofc: ESDG, Hughes Aircraft Co., POB 902 El Segundo 90245

MC KAY, NAN A., company executive, consultant; b. Aug. 14, 1942, Peoria, Ill.; d. John S. and Mary A. Brewer (Jameson) Norton; m. James D. McKay, June 15, 1968; children; Molly b. 1970, John b. 1972; edn: Bradley Univ. 1960-62; BA, Metro State Univ. 1976; postgrad., Mankato State Univ. 1976-78; Exec. Leadership & Mgmt. Pgm., Federal Execs. Inst. 1978; Cert. Housing Mgr., Nat. Ctr. for Housing Mgmt. 1980. Career: flight attendant American Airlines, Chicago, Ill. 1962-63; secty., admin. asst. Minneapolis Housing & Redevel. Authority, Minneapolis, Minn. 1963-67; admin. asst., mgr., asst. exec. dir. So. St Paul HRA, So. St. Paul, Minn. 1967-72; exec. dir. Dakota Co. HRA, Hastings, Minn. 1971-80; pres. Nan McKay & Assoc. Inc., San Diego 1980−; pres. McKay Computer Svcs. Inc., San Diego 1985−; bd. dirs. Nat. Leased Housing Assn., Wash DC 1980−; instr. Univ. of Minn., St. Paul 1979-80; instr. HUD pgms., Wash. DC 1983; instr. HUD, San Francisco; honors: Cert. of Appreciation, Metropolitan Council 1979; Honorary Citizen, West St. Paul City Council 1980; Nan McKay Bldg. 1979; McKay Manor 1980; Allan Anderson award 1981; Pres.'s Award, Nat. Assn. of Housing & Redevel. Offcls. 1981, Outstanding Young Women of Am. 1974, Who's Who Am. Women 1986; mem: Women in Housing (founder 1978), Am. Soc. for Tng. & Devel., Nat. Assn. of Female Execs., Nat. Assn. of Bus. Owners, Nat. Leased HSA Assn., Nat. Assn. of Housing & Redevel. Offcls. (pres., Minn. chpt.), Inver Hills Jr. Coll. Adv. Bd., Profl. Ethics Com. for Attys. (Dakota Co.), Dakota Area Referral & Transportation for Seniors (pres. adv. bd., founder); Public Svc. Bd. Vocational- Technical Schs.; Coop. Community Manpower Planning Commn., Twin Cities Camps; author coursebooks on housing: Creating Positive Performance; Creative Supervisor; A Guide to Assisted Housing Management; How to Do It Guide for Section 8; Multifamily Housing Management; Executive Directors Handbook; rec: bridge. Res: 1544 Shadow Knolls Dr. San Diego 92020 Ofc: McKay Computer, 3855 Avocado Ste. 110 La Mesa 92041

MC KEAN, GROVER L., investment banker; b. Mar. 7, 1949, Los Angeles; s. John Gilbert and Dorothy Marie (Grady) McK.; m. Judith Laing, May 15, 1980; children: Benjamin L. b. 1980, Jacob L. b. 1983; edn: BA, Loyola Univ. 1971, JD, Loyola Univ. Law Sch. 1975. Career: majority cons. Calif. State Assembly, 1972, adm. asst./press sec. Speaker of Assem. 1972-74, asst. state treas. Calif. State Treasury 1975-78, dep. state treas. 1978-81; 1st VP, sr. VP, mng. dir. Shearson/Am. Express 1981-84; West Coast regl. mgr. L.F. Rothschild, Unterberg, Towbin, 1984-85, mng. dir. 1986−; bd. dirs. Pacific Toxicology Lab.; mem. Calif. State Bar, Beafeaters Club, bd. dirs. Calif. Mus. of Sci. & Indus.; Democrat; rec: English Hist. Res: 2648 N Commonwealth Ave Los Angeles 90027 Ofc: L.F. Rothschild, Unterberg, Towbin 3250 Wilshire Blvd Ste 1314 Los Angeles 90010

MC KECHNIE, C. LOGAN, lawyer, writer; b. Sept. 29, 1942, Monticello, Ky.; s. Glenn Logan and Jean Alva (Eads) M.; m. Barbara Allan, Apr. 3, 1979; children: Amanda b. 1974, Roxanne b. 1977; edn: W. Texas State Coll. 1960-61; Amarillo (Tex.) Coll. 1961; fgn. lang. degree, German, Goeth Inst., Germany 1967; LLB, JD, Western State Univ. Coll. of the Law 1973-77. Career: reporter/ed. News-Texan Grand Prairie, Tex. 1959-60, KGNC-TV, Globe-News Amarillo, Tex. 1960-61; cryptologist Army Security Agency/Nat. Sec. Agcy. 1962-64; correspondent UPI Europe 1964-67; reporter/anchor The Republic, KTAR-TV Phoenix, Ariz. 1967-71; reporter/ed. The Evening Tribune San Diego 1971-72; spec. asst. to the Dist. Atty. San Diego 1972-80; atty. pvt. practice San Diego 1981−; lectr. San Diego State Univ., Western State Univ Coll. of Law, Nat. Coll. of Dist. Attys., Univ. of Houston Coll. of Law; honors: Distinguished Public Svc. Award ABA (1970); Cert. of Merit U.S. Jaycees (1969); 14 local and state writing awards (1960-70); mem: ABA (vice-chmn. crim. law 1985), Calif., San Diego bar assns.; Nat. and Calif. Dist. Attys. Assns.; Nu Beta Epsilon; publs: 500+ art. in Am. Europ. and So. Am. mags. (incl. Sports Ill., TV Guide, Quick); mil: capt. U.S. Army 1961-67; Republican; Protestant; Res: 11875 Rocoso Rd Lakeside 92040 Ofc: Law Offices of C. Logan McKechnie 4926 La Cuenta, Ste. 200, San Diego 92124

MC KEE, ROGER CURTIS, U.S. magistrate; b. Feb. 11, 1931, Waterloo, Iowa; s. James Arthur and Leonace Burrell M.; m. Roberta Jeanne, Sept. 3, 1954; children: Andrea, b. 1959, Brian, b. 1961, Paul, b. 1961; edn: BA, Univ. of No. Iowa 1955; MA, Univ. of Ill. 1959; JD, Univ. of San Diego Law Sch. 1968; admitted to Calif. Bar 1970. Career: agent, operator Illinois Central Railroad 1950-55; tng. asst. Northern Illinois Gas 1958-60; indsl. rels., purchasing General Dynamics Corp. 1960-70; pvt. practice, law, San Diego 1970-83; apptd. U.S. magistrate, So. Dist. of Calif. 1983; labor arbitrator, panel mem. Am. Arbitration Assn.; adj. prof. of law and bus. Nat. Univ. 1972−; mem: Calif. and San Diego Co. Bar Assns., San Diego Council Navy League, Reserve Ofcrs. Assn., Naval Researve Ofcrs. Assn., Nat. Rifle Assn. (life), Univ. of Ill. and Univ. of San Diego Alumni Assns., Kiwanis, Presbyterian So. Calif. Homes Inc.; mil: capt., USNR, ret. 1985, Meritorious Svc., Navy Commdn.; Presbyterian (past moderator, San Diego Presbytery); rec: hiking, camping, historical research. Res: 4881 Mt. Alifan Dr., San Diego 92111 Ofc: U.S. Courts Building, 940 Front St., San Diego 92189

MC KELVEY, GEORGE IRWIN, III, college administrator; b. May 5, 1925, Glen Ridge, NJ; s. George and Florence McK.; m. Velma Vergara, 1959; 1 son, George Stuart b. 1965; edn: AB, Univ. Rochester 1950, MA, 1957. Career: exec. secty. Alumni Assn., Univ. Rochester, 1950-54; dir. Alumni rels., 1954-56, assoc. dir. Alumni Council, 1956-57, dir. devel. Harvey Mudd Coll.,

1957-58, v.p. devel. and planning, 1968−; dir. Bates Found. for Aeronautical Edn. Raymond M. Alf Museum; mem: Council for the Advance. and Support of Edn., University Club (LA), Mens Garden Club (LA), Psi Upsilon; mil: aviation cadet USNR 1943-44, ensign USMS 1945-46; Presbyterian. Ofc: Harvey Mudd College, Claremont 91711

MC KENNA, THOMAS J., aerobatic pilot; b. May 12, 1908, Meadowbrook, Pa.; s. John and Bridget (Cassidy) McK.; grad. Catholic Schs., Berwyn, Pa. 1927; grad. flying sch., Wilmington, Del. 1938; soloed a Jenney Airplane, Camden, NJ 1928; pvt., comml. & instr. rating 1938. Career: pilot instr. combat flying to Royal Air Force pilots 1940-42, to US Army Cadets 1942-44, War Eagle Field, Lancaster, Ca.; currently, only aerobatic flight instr., Santa Barbara Airport (1976 150 h.p. Citabria), Mercury Air Ctr. 1981−; (most famous pupil, Frank Tallman whose movies incl. The Great Waldo Pepper, and TV series Baa-Baa Black Sheep); subject of arts. in num. publs. incl. Pvt. Pilot, Gen. Aviation News and sev. books.; mem: Quiet Birdmen; Santa Barbara Pilots Assn.; OX5 Pioneers of Am.; Santa Barbara Flying Club; S.B. Aero Club Inc.; Antelope Valley Aero Mus. Inc.; Republican; Catholic. Res: 1312 Shoreline Dr Santa Barbara 93109 Ofc: Mercury Air Center, Santa Barbara Airport

MC KENZIE, MEREDITH CHRISTINE, entrepreneur, public relations executive; b. Nov. 1, 1952, Warren, Ohio; d. William L. and Joan (Howell) Green; m. Nelson Bradford Hussey, May 5, 1984; 1 dau. Christina Joan b. 1975; edn: BA Am. Studies cum laude, Bowling Green State Univ. 1975; grad. study mass communication, Ohio State Univ. 1977-79; MA telecoms., Kent State Univ. 1980. Career: researcher The Social Security Adminstrn. Columbus, Ohio 1975-77. Ohio State Univ. 1977-79; producer/ dir. WNEO-TV Kent, Ohio 1979-80; assoc. dir. pgm. mktg. KCET-TV Los Angeles 1980-84; pres. McKenzie Communications L.A. 1984−; honors: Bronze Award (Internat. Film & Video Festival of NY 1981), Disting. Svc. Award (Bowling Green State Univ. 1975); mem: Acad. TV Arts & Scis. 1984- (judge student film competition), L.A. Jr. CofC (dir. 1983-84, v.p. 1984-86, pres. 1986-87), Premiere Patrons of Am. Cinematheque (exec. council 1984-), L.A. Open Golf Found. (trustee 1984-87), HLC Child Care Svcs. (bd. 1981-84, pres. 1983-84); Republican; Episcopal; rec: travel, music (pianist, contralto). Ofc: McKenzie Communications POB 8627 Universal City 91608-0627

MC KINNEY, GEORGE DALLAS, clergyman; b. Aug. 9, 1932, Jonesboro, Ark.; s. George Sr. and Rosie Anna (Thompson) McK.; m. Jean C., June 15, 1957; children: George b. 1958, Grant b. 1961, Gregory b. 1962, Gordon b. 1966, Glenn b. 1969; edn: BA, magna cum laude, Ark. State Univ. (Pine Bluff) 1954; MA, Oberlin Sch. of Theol. 156; PhD, Calif. Grad. Sch. of Theology 1974; Qual. tchr./coll. (life); Calif. Lic. MFCC (Marriage Family Child Counselor) 1969, Ordained Elder, Ch. of God in Christ 1954. Career: dir. Chagrin Falls Park (Ohio) Comm. Center 1955-56; Protestant Chaplain, Toledo State Mental Hosp. 1956-57; counselor Family Court, Toledo, O. 1957-59; senior probation ofcr. San Diego County Prob. Dept. 1959-65; asst. dir. Economic Com., San Diego 1965-71; minister St. Stephen's Ch. of God in Christ, San Diego 1962−; author: The Theology of the Jehovah's Witness (Zondervon Pub. House 1962), Pastoral Counselor Handbook (1981), Christian Marriage, I Will Build My Church (1977, 85), Rejoice (1985), var. relig. pamphlets. Honors: one of 20 authors who made significant contbn. to Evangelical Christian Literature, Christianity Today (1962); community svc. awd. Bus. & Profl. Women; Outstanding Man of Year 1969, Internat. Aerospace Wkrs. Dist. 50; J.F. Kennedy Awd. for service to Youth; Outstanding Pastor, SDSU Black Students; NAACP Award for contbns. in relig. field, San Diego 1975, 85; Democrat; Pentecostal; rec: swimming. Res: 5848 Arboles San Diego 92120 Ofc: St. Stephen's Ch. of God in Christ, 5825 Imperial Ave San Diego 92114

MC KINNON, ROBERT STEVEN, certified public accountant; b. Oct. 20, 1944, Burbank, Calif.; s. George and Helen Merrill (Chase) McK.; m. Ratsamee, Mar. 29, 1969; children: Kelly b. 1970, Malanee b. 1975; edn: BA hist., CSU Chico 1967, BS bus. admin. (acctg.), 1981; CPA Calif. 1985; instr. cred. Calif. Comm. Colls. 1982. Career: mgr. Shakey's Pizza Parlor Chico 1971-72; founder, owner Red Lion Family Pizza Parlor Paradise 1972-78; acct. David E. Worley Accountancy Corp. 1978-84, John A. Powell CPA Inc. Paradise 1984−; tchr. acctg. Butte Comm. Coll.; mem: Calif. Soc. CPAs, Paradise Little League (bd. dirs., mgr./coach), Paradise Tennis Club; mil: sp/5 US Army Signal Corps 1968-71, Vietnam Svc., Army Commdn.; rec: fishing, tennis. Res: 1675 Cameo Ln Paradise 95969 Ofc: John A. Powell CPA Inc 7030 B Skyway Paradise 95969

MC KONIC, MARC MICHAEL, medical co. founder, president; b. July 1, 1938, Port Vue, Penn.; s. Marco and Mary (Kolic) M.K.; edn: BS, Duquesne Univ. 1960; Wheeling Coll. 1956-57. Career: exec. mgmt. trainee R.H. Donnelley Corp., Chicago; acct. exec. O.K. Pulications, Los Angeles; dist. mgr. Hyland Div. Baxter Travenol, Los Angeles; div. mgr. Hycel Inc., Houston, Texas; v.p. H.M.O. Internat., Los Angeles; currently, founder, CEO, pres. Biocell Laboratories, Los Angeles; investor, cons. to sev. medical related companies; real estate developer; mem: Am. Assn. of Clin. Chemists, Tissue Culture Assn., Manhattan Country Club, Knights of Columbus; mil: E-4 USAR 1961-62; Republican; Catholic; rec: tennis, skiing. Res: 2708 Deep Canyon Dr. Beverly Hills 90210 Ofc: Biocell Laboratories, 1117 E. Janis St. Carson 90746

MC LAUGHLIN, ELLIOT CHARLES, manufacturers representative; b. Apr. 10, 1906, Monticello, N.Y.; s. George Lewis and Grace (Ennis) McL.; m. Madlyn H., Feb. 16, 1929; children: Jean b. 1934, Susan b. 1938, Linda b. 1942; edn: Ch.E., Rensselaer Polytechnic Inst. 1928. Career: mgr. compounding B.F.

Goodrich Co. 1938-44; H.M. Royal Inc. 1946-55, gen. mgr. 1955-71; owner, mfg. rep. Natural Rubber & Plastic Tote Boxes 1971—; dir. The L.A. Rubber Group Inc. 1947-51, chmn. 1950-51; mem: TLARGI, Am. Chem. Soc. (rubber div.); Republican; rec: music, relaxation. Address: 43 Drake St Newport Beach 92663

MC LAUGHLIN, IAN ERIC, management consultant; b. Nov. 21, 1915, Grand Mere, Quebec, Canada, nat. US cit. 1940; s. Wm. James and Dorothy Margaret (High) McL.; m. Olga Cendrier, Feb. 18, 1939; children: Heather b. 1944, Eric b. 1950, Leslie Margaret b. 1951; edn: Golden Gate Coll. 1937, 47, 48. Career: var. pos. to nat. retail sales mgr., dir. tng. Del Monte Corp., 1934-76; pres. bd. chmn. Training and Education Consultants, Inc. 1976-84; pres. Olian Corp., Diablo 1985—; adj. prof. Golden Gate Coll. 1947-51; vis. lectr. Univ. Wis., Cornell, Univ. Georgia; awards: Gold medals, Nat. Soc. Sales Tng. Execs. (1959, 1969); mem. Nat. Soc. Sales Tng. Execs. 1952- (pres. 1966), Soc. of Am. Magicians #112; bd. dirs. Boy Scouts Am. Mount Diablo Council (v.p. 1975); author: Executive Guide to Personnel (1963), Successful Sales Training (1983); mil: col. USAF, ret., Am. Svc., European Svc. 3 Stars; Republican; Episcopal; rec: magic, music, gardening. Ofc: Olian Corp. POB 524 Diablo 94528

MC LEAN, BONNIE SHEPHERD BUTT, acupuncturist, registered nurse; b. Mar. 9, 1945, New Orleans; d. Arthur J. and Barbara Mason (McCravy) Butt; children: Cameron b. 1969, Doug b. 1971; edn: BS nursing, Duke Univ. 1967; MA counseling, Pepperdine Univ. 1977; lic. acupuncturist, Calif. Acupunctire Coll. 1983, OMD, 1986. Career: nursing positions in Switzerland, Fla., Miss., Calif., So. Carolina 1967-77; supv. outreach dept. Beaufort-Jasper Comprehensive Health Svcs. (SC) 1977-78; clin. supv. Lindora Med. Ctr. El Toro, Calif. 1978; orthopedic floor staff nse. UC Irvine Med. Ctr. 1979, float pool RN 1980; lab. supv., counselor Wholistic Med. Clin. El Toro 1980; RN Nursing Svcs. Internat. 1980-82; RN Woodview Calabasas Psychiatric Hosp. 1982-84, Beverly Glen Hosp. for drug and alcohol abuse- adolescent unit West L.A. 1984—; acupuncture cons. Bresler Ctr. Santa Monica 1983—; instr., public spkr. and radio guest on pain control, guided imagery, acupuncture, acupressure- massage; honors: class pres. Duke Univ. Sch. Nursing 1967, Alpha Delta Pi; mem: Am. Assn. Acupuncture and Oriental Med. 1985, Oriental Healing Arts Inst. 1985, Junior League (Fla.), Cousteau Soc., Greenpeace, Sierra Club, Tree People; publ: A Manual of Chinese Medicine and Massage; Democrat; Episcopal. Res: 19711 Valley View Dr Topanga 90290 OFc: Bresler Center 2901 Wilshire Blvd Ste 345 Santa Monica 90403

MC MAHON, JO ANN FERGUSON, shipping industry executive; b. Dec. 28, 1941, Upland, Pa.; d. Samuel Garfield and Margith Naomi (Larsen) Ferguson; m. John Arthur McMahon, June 17, 1967; children: Kristen b. 1970, Brian Paul b. 1972, Colin Joseph b. 1975; edn: BA, Penn. State Univ. 1964. Career: teacher NJ, Calif., Conn., Wash. 1964-70; v.p. ops. Unicon Internat. Inc. 1970—; rec: watercolor and oil painting. Res: 60 Panoramic Way Berkeley 94704 Ofc: Unicon Internat. Inc. 2020 Milvia St Ste 302 Berkeley 94704

MC MANUS, JOHN HENRY, manufacturing co. executive; b. June 5, 1944, Los Angeles; s. David James and Hellen Laureen (Luhr) M.M.; m. Joan, Jan. 30, 1965; children: Kevin b. 1965, Kara b. 1969; edn: AA, Modesto Jr. Coll. 1964; BS, CSU Sacramento 1966, MBA, 1967. Career: sales mgmt. trainee Carnation Co., St. Louis, Mo. 1967-69; C&H Sugar, San Francisco 1969—; senior analyst grocery & ind. mktg. plnng. 1969-72; supvr. grocery prods. mktg. plnng. 1972-75; mgr. mktg. plnng. grocery & idnl. prods. 1975-82; asst. ind. prods. sales mgr. 1982-83, indsl. prod. sales mgr. 1983—; bd. dirs. Am. Mktg. Assn. San Francisco chpt. 1981-83; mem: Am. Mktg. Assn. (pres. San Francisco chpt. 1969-), Lake Chabot Golf Club; rec: golf, tennis, travel. Res: 1758 Indian Way Oakland 94611 Ofc: C&H Sugar, 1 California St. Ste. 2000 San Francisco 94111

MC MASTER, FRANK MICHAEL, citrus grower, nurseryman; b. Oct. 25, 1921, San Francisco; s. Wm. Peters and Lena (Katz) McM.; m. Marian McNitt, Dec. 30, 1964; edn: AA, Porterville Coll. 1942. Career: citrus nurseryman, owner, 1946-71; citrus grower, owner, 1946—; appt. dir. Central Calif. Tristeza Eradication Agency (1978-83), dir. Terra Bella Irrigation Dist. (1983-); mem. Calif. Citrus Nurserymen's Soc. (dir. 1962-72); mem. Nature Conservancy; research: Citrus variety and Rootstock (1946-); mil: cpl. US Air Force 1942-46; rec: horticulture, photog. Res: 26562 Ave 80 Terra Bella 93270

MC MASTER, MARY JANE, educator; b. Feb. 15, 1943, Nunda, NY; d. Earl and Marion C. (Stewart) McM.; edn: BS, SUNY Oswego 1965; MS, Univ. Ore., Eugene 1970; PhD, Univ. Wisc., Madison 1975; grad. work, Puskin Inst., Leningrad and Univ. Moscow, Russia 1975. Career: math tchr. Goshen (NY) H.S. 1966-69; tchg. asst. Univ. Wisc. 1970-74; prof. Univ. No. Iowa, Cedar Falls 1974-75; col. math tchr. Saddleback & Orange Coast Colls. 1977-79; prof. math L.A. Valley Coll. 1979-80; prof. math W. L.A. Coll., Culver City 1980—; honors: NSF Grant (1969-70), presenter at Nat. Council of Math Mtgs., Iowa (1975), mem. Edn. Honor Soc. (1973); mem: Calif. Coll. Tchrs., Wilderness Soc., Sierra Club, Canyon Explorers Club, sev. animal protection groups; Republican; Unitarian; rec: biking (rode across USA summer 1985, leader bike trips), hiking, travel, running, triathlon, backpacking. Res: 21931-J Rimhurst Dr El Toro 92630 Ofc: West L.A. Coll. Freshman Dr Culver City

MC MASTERS, JAMES HOWARD, real estate executive; b. Aug. 8, 1944, San Mateo; s. Howard James and Florence Marie (Neilsen) McM.; m. Ann Johnsen, Aug. 14, 1977; children: Rayna b. 1979, Kendra b. 1981; edn: AA, Foothill Jr. Coll. 1967; BS, CSU San Jose 1970; lic. Calif. Real Estate Broker 1973. Career: sales agt. Grubb & Ellis Co., Oakland 1972-76; principal owner

McMasters Realty Inc., Walnut Creek 1977; ptnr./pres. McMasters & Westland Commercial Real Estate Inc., Walnut Creek 1977—; ptnr. Consol. Regional Equities 1980—; ptnr. Asian Assocs. 1981—; pres., bd. dirs. Pro's for Kids; prin. Shepson Financial Corp./ McMasters & Westland 1985, McMasters & Westland Prop. Mgmt. Inc. 1984; awards: American Spirit of Honor Award 1971, Wall Street Journal Awd. 1970; listed, Who's Who Am. Colls. & Univs. 1970, Who's Who in Real Estate in Am. 1981-2; mem: Contra Costa Bd. of Realtors, Calif. Assn. of Realtors, East Bay Brokers Assn. (pres. 1983), Internat. Council of Shopping Centers (pgm. chmn. 1981-2), Walnut Creek Civic Arts Regional Center Com. 1981 (bd. dirs.), BSA Regl. Advis. Com. 1981-3; works: chief statistician US Army Proj. Volar (All Volunteer Army) 1971; mil: sp4 Human Resources Research Orgn. 1971; Republican; Episcopal; rec: Black Belt Karate. Res: 1633 Rocksprings Place Walnut Creek 94596 Ofc: McMasters & Westland, 1777 Oakland Blvd, Ste 300, Walnut Creek 94596

MC MILLAN, HORACE JIM, physician, b. Oct. 30, 1919, Mineola, Tx.; s. Lemon Columbus and Joann Aletha (Zollars) McM.; m. Jessie, Oct. 21, 1942, (div.); children: Yvonne Camille (Sawyer) b. 1943, Michelle Louise b. 1972; edn: BS, Prairie View A&M Coll. 1942; MD, Meharry Medical Coll. 1950; grad. wk. St. Louis Univ. 1945-46; H.M.O. Cert., UC Los Angeles 1975. Career: family practice in Santa Barbara, 1952—, semi-ret. 1978; prin. Family Medical Center, v.p. Physicians Inv. Corp.; staff mem. St. Francis Hosp., S.B. Cottage Hosp., Goleta Valley Comm. Hosp., Pinecrest Hosp.; founder (1 of ten), bd. dirs. (1967-77) Goleta Valley Comm. Hosp.; first chmn. Mayor's Advis. Com. on Human Relations, 1968; chmn. Community Health Task Force, 1973-81; mem: Am., Calif., Santa Barbara County Acad. Family Practice (1982-); NAACP (life); Am. Assn. for Clin. Immunology and Allergy; honors: recognition by City of Santa Barbara as innovator of the Franklin Neighborhood Service Center (charity) on its 10th ann. (9/28/85); mil: chief p.o., chief pharmacist mate USN 1942-46; Democrat; Methodist; rec: travel, sports. Res: 2439 Vista Del Campo Santa Barbara 93101 Ofc: Family Medical Center 101 West Arrellaga St Santa Barbara 93101

MC MILLEN, MARY LOU, real estate broker; b. June 22, 1935, Washington, Pa.; d. Clyde Johnson and Mary Cecile (Cochran) Henry; children: Lynda b. 1956, Kenneth b. 1957, Robert b. 1960, Gregory b. 1964; edn: BA, CSU Long Beach 1965; undergrad. (hons.) CSU Fullerton 1962-64, Stanford Univ. 1953-55; Calif. Gen. Elem. Tchr. Credential 1965; R.E. Broker lic. 1978. Career: tchr. in Mission Viejo 1966-69; real estate sales Alpine Realty, Big Bear Lake 1975-76, Lomas Santa Fe, Realty Execs., and McMillen Investments, in San Diego North County, 1976-84; currently, broker/ inv. counseling/ fin. plng. Mc Millen Investments, Encinitas; awards: Million Dollars Club, Realty Executives 1978, 79; mem: Calif. Assn. Realtors; Docent of Marine Biology, Scripps Inst. of Oceanography; AAUW; Toastmistress; Childrens Hosp.; Republican; Presbyterian; rec: horticulture, skiing, art. Address: McMillen Investments, 840 Val Sereno Dr Encinitas 92024

MC MILLION, CHESTER LEE, sales engineer; b. Jan. 27, Malden, Mo.; s. Charles and Stella (Willmurth) McM.; m. Kathryn Ritter, Oct. 13, 1962; children: Kathryn Ann b. 1964, Chester Lee, Jr. b. 1966; edn: USC 1942-44. Career: sales mgr. Marshall Tool & Supply; nat. sales mgr. Steco Corp.; dist. mgr. L & I Pacific; current: pres. Chet McMillion Mfrs. Representative, Inc.; mem. Exec. Sales Club 1949-53, Westerner's Club 1964-76 (pres. 1973), Elks, Navy League; Republican; Baptist. Res: 15514 High Knoll Rd Encino 91436 Ofc: 422 S San Fernando Blvd Burbank 91502

MC NALLY, SEAN PATRICK, government lawyer, b. Aug. 5, 1953, Scranton, Pa.; s. John Patrick and Elizabeth Jane (Hines) McN.; m. Diane, June 29, 1985; edn: AA, Citrus Coll. 1973; BA, UCLA 1975; JD, Western State Univ. Sch. of Law 1979; Adv. Criminal Practice, USC, 1981, 83; admitted to Calif. State Bar 1980, US Dist. Ct. (cent. div. 1980, so. div. 1981), US Ct. of Appeals 9th Cir. 1980, US Tax Ct. 1981. Career: law librarian Orange County Law Library, Santa Ana 1976-79; para-legal/atty. law offices of Leon Najman, Costa Mesa 1979-81; dep. dist. atty. San Bernardino County D.A., 1981—, currently felony trial deputy; honors: Delta Tau Delta, Delta Theta Phi, Alpha Gamma Sigma; mem: ABA, Calif. State Bar, Calif. Dist. Attys. Assn., San Bernardino Co., Riverside Co., Orange Co., L.A. Co. Bar Assns., Orange Co. Barristers Assn., Criminal Cts. Bar Assn., Am., Calif., L.A. Co. Trial Lawyers Assns., Irish Am. Bar Assn. of L.A., Constnl. Rights Found. (assisted high sch. mock trial pgm. 1984-85); Republican; Catholic; rec: bicycling, skiing, football, volleyball. Ofc: San Bernardino County District Attorney, 316 Mt. View Ave San Bernardino 92415

MC NAMARA, JOHN JOSEPH, college professor; b. Dec. 6, 1909, Rochelle, Ogle County, Ill.; s. John Joseph and Grace Elizabeth (Campbell) McN.; m. Hazel Dionne, Aug. 11, 1936; children: Denise b. 1938, John b. 1941, Carole b. 1943, Michael b. 1945, Terrence b. 1950, Kevin b. 1952; edn: BE, No. Ill. Univ. 1931; MA, Univ. Iowa 1932; PhD, Purdue Univ. 1941. Career: instr. math. St. Albans Acad. 1932-34, St. Viator Coll. 1934-37; asst. prof. bus. adminstrn. Univ. Detroit 1937-43; head supervisory and employee tng. Republic Aviation Corp. 1943-45; pres. M&M candy 1945-59; chmn. bd. Uncle Ben's Rice 1959-62; corp. mktg. advisor Warner- Lambert Pharmaceutical Co. 1966-70; prof. mktg. No. Ill. Univ. 1970-78, CSU Bakersfield 1978—, chmn. ag. mktg. dept. 1978; bd. dirs. M&M Mars 1952-62; writer tng. courses, policy manuals, handbooks; honors: Calcott-Kennedy Disting. Prof. (Calcott Cotton Co-op. 1980), Outstanding Svc. (NIU Alumni Assn. 1971), Football Hall of Fame (NIU 1985), Chick Evans Award (NIU 1971); mem. Stockdale Country Club; author: Marketing An Interdisciplinary Practical Approach (1985), Product Innovation and Brand Management (1985), articles in psychol. jours. (1941); Republican;

Catholic; rec: hunting, fishing, golf. Res: 508 Malibu Ct Bakersfield 93309 Ofc: CSU 9001 Stockdale Hwy Bakersfield 93309

MC NEIL, MALCOLM STEPHEN, lawyer; b. Jan. 7, 1956, San Francisco; s. Henry Stephen and Adeline Elizabeth (LaVoie) McN.; children: Jennifer b. 1975, Geoffrey b. 1977; edn: AA, L.A. City Coll. 1976; BA, Antioch Univ. 1980; JD, Loyola Law Sch. 1983; admitted Calif. State Bar 1983. Career: sales mgr. Metropolitan Life Ins. Co. 1977-82; law clerk Gilbert, Kelly, Crowley & Jennett 1982-83; atty. law firm Briedenbach, Swainston, Yokaitis & Crispo 1983-84, law offices of Brian F. Zimmerman 1984; self-empl. atty. Law Offices of Malcolm S. McNeil, Los Angeles 1984–; corp. counsel D & D Express Internat. Inc., Corporate Capital Resources Inc.; honors: Sigma Tau Sigma (1975), Deans Honor List, Loyola Law Sch. (1982), pres. Republican Law Forum (1981-83), Phi Alpha Delta; mem. Westchester CofC, Marina del Rey CofC; publs: legal article on pre-judgment interest (1982); Republican; Catholic; rec: Judo, skiing, book collecting. Ofc: 5757 West Century Blvd Ste 700 Los Angeles 90045

MC NERNEY, ROBERT JAMES, educator, ret.; b. May 2, 1916, Fairbury, Neb.; s. Harry A. and Blanche (Pantier) McN.; m. Jennie, June 9, 1937; children: R. James b. 1938, Sharon b. 1940, George b. 1941; edn: AB, Univ. Neb. 1938, MA (cand.), 1960-61; counseling cert., UC Riverside 1974; pupil personnel svcs. credl. Calif. Career: inspector US Maritime Commn. Oakland 1941-44; cost analyst 12th Naval Dist. Ind. Mgr. Mare Island 945-46; real estate developer, planner Lincoln, Neb. 1947-51; asst. dir. Neb. State Real Estate Commn. 1952-57; instr. Neb. Public Schs. 1957-59; admissions counselor Iowa Wesleyan, Univ. Dubuque 1960-64; asst. dir. admissions Park Coll. 1965; registrar, dir. admissions UCLA Coll. of Med. 1966-68; exec. mgr. Solano County Taxpayers Assn. Fairfield 1969-70; counselor, attendance ofcr. Perris Union H.S. Dist. Sun City 1971-81; real estate broker 1982–; elected dir. dist. hosp. bd. and trustee Mt. San Jacinto Coll. bd. Hemet; mem. (gov. apptd.) Calif. State Sunset Review Com. on Edn. 1983-85, Calilf. State Advisory Commn. on Aging 1986-89; mem: Calif. Retired Tchrs. Assn., Sons Am. Revolution (chpt. v.p. 1986), Calif. Comm. Coll. Trustees, Am. Comm. Coll. Trustees, Lions, Masons, Scottish Rite, Shrine; Republican (Calif. Central Com.); Christian. Res: 791 Oleander Hemet 92343

MC NICHOLAS, JOHN PATRICK, (III), lawyer; b. Aug. 18, 1936, Los Angeles; s. John P., Jr., and Rosemary Helen (Hurley) McN.; m. Diane Sawaya, Dec. 16, 1937; children: Erin, b. 1958, Brigid Nigg, b. 1959, Patrick, b. 1961, Courtney, b. 1962, Monica, b. 1965, David, b. 1966, Matthew, b. 1972; edn: BA, UCLA 1958; Loyola Law Sch. 1958-62; admitted to Calif. Bar 1962. Career: senior ptnr. Law Offices of Morgan, Wenzel & McNicholas Profl. Corp., 1964–; lectr. Contg. Edn. of the Bar, State Bar of Calif.; Am. Bar Assn. Nat. Inst. on Litigation in Aviation, 1985; Diplomate Am. Bd. of Trial Advocates; Fellow Am. Coll. Trial Lawyers, London 1985; mem. Am., Calif. State bar assns., Jonathan Club, Los Angeles CofC; Republican; Roman Catholic. Res: 516 So. Hudson Ave., Los Angeles 90020 Law Ofc: Morgan, Wenzel & McNicholas, 1545 Wilshire Blvd, Ste 800, Los Angeles 90017

MC NICHOLS, STEPHEN LUCID ROBERT, JR., lawyer; b. June 5, 1943, Denver; s. Stephen L.R. and Marjorie Roberta (Hart) McN.; children: Justin b. 1969, Chelsea b. 1972; edn: BA, Pomona Coll. 1965; JD, UC Berkeley Boalt Hall 1968; stu. Monterey Inst. of Fgn. Studies 1964-65; admitted bar: Colo. (1968), Calif. (1969). Career: dep. dist. atty., San Luis Obispo, 1965-72; assoc. law firm Varni, Fraser in Hayward 1972-76, ptnr. 1976-86, current firm name McNichols & McCann; awards: George Burgess Prize, Pomona Coll., Claremont (1965); apptd. mem. Calif. State Bar Com. on the Adminstrn. of Justice (1975-77); mem: Am. Bar Assn. (Litigation Sect.), Alameda Co. Bar Assn. (dir. 1985-), So. Alameda Co. Bar Assn. (dir. 1975-77), Assn. of Trial Lawyers of Am., Calif. Trial Lawyers Assn., Alameda & Contra Costa Co. Trial Lawyers Assn. (dir. 1976), Alameda Co. Barristers Club (dir. 1974-75); civic: Morro Bay Planning Commn. (1970-73, chmn. 1972), Childrens Hosp. Found. (bd. dirs.); Republican; rec: ski, run, golf. Res: 947 Redwood Dr Danville 94526 Ofc: McNichols & McCann 18 Crow Cyn Ct Ste 395 San Ramon 94583

MC WALTERS, JAMES G., commercial brokerage co. executive; b. Oct. 7, 1940, NYC; s. John and Mary McWalters; m. Patricia Rohweller, Apr. 19, 1975; edn: Midshipman/BS in Aeronautical Engr. and Nuclear Sci. (top 2% in grad. class), US Naval Acad., Annapolis 1964. Career: precision machinist, Arizona Gear, Tucson 1958-60; prodn. supr. No. Am. Aviation, Downey, Calif. 1960; founder/pres. Advanced Protective Systems, Inc., San Diego 1969-71, merged with Sterling Security Svc., 1971; with Grubb and Ellis Comml. Brokerage Co. 1972-78: investment mktg. 1972-3, mgr. new tract sales, San Diego 1973-4, Los Angeles sales mgr. 1974-5, mgr. Investment Bus. Devel. 1975-6, Investment Div. coordinator 1974-8, mgr. L.A. Comml. Brokerage Co. 1975-8, vice pres. 1974-8, bd. dirs. 1976-8; pres. Vistar Comml. Brokerage Co., 1978-80; exec. vice pres./regional dir. Merrill Lynch Commercial Real Estate (developed commercial real estate brokerage network in western states), 1981–; mil: served in USN 1960-69; conducted first boarding and search opns. on minesweeper Excel, Vietnam 1964-5, 3 yrs. abd. nuclear submarine Snook, Vietnam Service Star; rec: flying, golf, tennis, ski. Res: Glendale Ofc: Merrill Lynch Comml. Real Estate, 400 S Hope St Ste 2400 Los Angeles 90014

MC WATTERS, EDD DAVID, film producer, writer, director; b. Oct. 27, 1930, Ottawa, Ont., nat. US cit. 1980; s. Vernon Wm. and Irene Elizabeth (Langdon) McW.; m. Josie B., Oct. 14, 1976; edn: spl. courses Western Univ., cert. Brooks Inst. of Photog. 1962. Career: editor, cameraman of 108 T.V. shows; prod./dir./ writer of num. films including 25 of his own prodns., 1962-82; disabled auto injury 1982; currently writing poetry (3 pub. in separate books, 1986), and books (novel to be pub. 1986); instr. motion picture prodn. Brooks Inst. Photog., Santa Barbara; writer series of articles on movie making, SAC Movie News and arts. in var. photographic periodicals; judge 3 film festivals, PSA/ MPD, Canadian Internat., Santa Barbara Internat.; lectr. in US, Australia, Canada; honors: Masters Degree in Cinematography (awarded on Queen Mary, 1980, 1420 points earned in internat. competitions), Fellowship award (FSAC) Soc. of Amateur Cinematographers (1985); Poetry Award (1986); 75 Film Awards (nat. & internat.), for films: The Highwayman (comedy), Egghead Meets Vampire (spl. effects), Bikini Capers (comedy), MagicBottle (fantasy), Widdlest Surfer (humor), The Hungry Kook Goes Bazook (comedy, won 26 internat. film festival awards incl. A Ten Best- Christchurch, N.Z. Film Fest., Silver cup- the Cannes, Fr. Film Fest., Silver cup- Australian Internat. Film Fest., Melbourne, 1st Pl.- Scottish Internat.). Mem: Photographic Soc. of Am., Soc. of Amateur Cinematographers, Rifle Club, AARP; exhibition ballroom dancer in younger yrs.; underwater photog. late 1950s; rec: photog. Ofc: Movin Pitchures Co. POB 397 Van Nuys 91408

MEAD, ALBERT EDWARD, JR., lawyer; b. April 20, 1950, Los Angeles; s. Albert Edward and Barbara Elizabeth (Duque) M.; edn: BA, magna cum laude, Amherst Coll. 1972; JD, USC Law Ctr. 1977; admitted to Calif. Bar 1977. Career: assoc. atty. Allen & Kimbell, Santa Barbara 1977-81; assoc. atty. Darling, Hall & Rae, Los Angeles 1981-82; sole prop., Los Angeles 1982-83; in-house counsel, asst. to pres. Air Logistics Corp., Pasadena 1983–; dir., counsel First Stage, Los Angeles; mem. Los Angeles Athletic Club; author: The Duques of Los Angeles, a family history from 17th Century to present, 1983; rec: writing, arts, literature. Res: 192 Ramona Pl Pasadena 91107 Ofc: Air Logistics Corp. 3600 E. Foothill Blvd. Los Angeles 91109

MEAD, SEDGWICK, physician; b. July 2, 1911, Guymon, Okla.; s. Redmond Boyd and Bertha Mabel (Hunter) Corbett; m. Marjorie Chick, Sept. 22, 1940; children: Sedgwick Jr. b. 1943, Marshall b. 1946; edn: SB cum laude, Harvard Coll. 1934; MD, Harvard Med. Sch. 1938; Diplomate Am. Bd. Phys. Med. & Rehab. Career: intern Mass. Gen. Hosp. 1938-40, resident pathol. 1940-41, neurol. 1941-42, Baruch fellow 1946-47; asst. neurol. Harvard Med. Sch. 1941-42; assoc. prof. phys. med. Washington Univ. Sch. of Med. St. Louis 1948-54; med. dir. Kaiser Found. Rehab. Ctr. Vallejo 1954-69; asst. clin. prof. Stanford Univ. 1955-60; chief of neurol. Kaiser-Permanente Med. ctr. Vallejo 1969-77 (ret.); clin. prof. phys. med. and rehab. UC Davis 1969-72; cons. Letterman Gen Hosp., Martinez VA Hosp., Sacto. Med. Ctr.; staff Mass. Gen., Barnes (St. Louis), Kaiser Found. Hosps. No. Calif.; med. dir. Easter Seal Rehab. CTR OF Alameda County Oakland; honors: Honor Freshman (ROTC Univ. Ariz. 1931), Harvard Coll. Scholar (1932); mem: Am. Acad. Neurol., Am. Acad. Cerebral Palsy (pres. 1967), Assn. Rehab. Ctrs. (past pres.), AMA, CMA, Mass. Med. Assn., World Med. Assn., AAAS, White House Council on Health, Faculty Club (UCB), Harvard Club of S.F., Commonwealth Club of S.F.; trustee Contra Costa Co. Mosquito Abatement Dist.; publs: author 45+ sci. articles and chpts. physiol., phys. med., neurol., geriatrics, rehab., editl. bd. Am. J. of Phys. Med.; mil: US Army WWII 1942-45, col. USAR (ret. 1971); Unitarian- Universalist; rec: travel, sailing, flying, languages. Res: 1530 Arlington Blvd El Cerrito 94530 Ofc: Easter Seal Rehab. Ctr. 2757 Telegraph Ave Oakland 94612

MEANS, FLETCHER WEST, II, financial planner; b. Aug. 16, 1935, Portland, Maine; s. Fletcher West and Laura Foster (Soule) M.; m. Patricia, Oct. 15, 1983; children: Kimberly b. 1966, Malanie b. 1967, Scott b. 1971; edn: AB, Bowdoin Coll. 1957. Career: reg. rep. Kidder, Peabody & Co. San Francisco 1960-68; v.p. inst. sales W.E. Hutton & Co. S.F. 1968-72, sales mgr. 1972-74; options mgr. Loeb, Rhoades & Co. San Jose 1974-76; asst. mgr., financial planner, dir. tax-sheltered investments Bache & Co. San Jose 1976-81; senior ptnr. Means, Hutchinson, Wood & Assocs. San Jose 1981-83; owner Fletcher, WEst, Means & Assocs. San Jose 1983–; mem: Nat. Assn. Life Underwriters, Internat. Assn. Financial Planners, Street Club of S.F. (pres. 1971), Kiwanis (social chmn. 1983); publs: widely quoted in newspapers, magazines, jours.; financial planning interviewer for Channel 48 TV San Jose 1981-82; mil: 1st lt. US Army Infantry 1958-60; Protestant; rec: singing, acting, piano, sports. Res: 1840 Ashmeade Ct San Jose 95125 Ofc: Fletcher, West, Means & Assocs. 4030 Moorpark Ave Ste 122 San Jose 95117

MECHIKOFF, ROBERT ALAN, university professor, author; b. Nov. 7, 1949, Whittier, Calif.; s. Alex Vacily and Aileen Marie (Loving) Mechikoff; 1 child: Kelly Lee b. 1975; edn: BA, CSU Long Beach 1971, MA, 1975; PhD, Ohio State Univ. 1977. Career: asst. prof., head swimming coach, asst. football coach Univ. Minn. Duluth 1975-79; asst. prof. Tex. Tech. Univ. 1979-81; assoc. prof. phys. edn. and sportsmedicine San Diego State Univ. 1981–; pres., CEO USA Volleyball Inc., US Olympic Team 1982-83, bd. dirs. 1982-86; honors: One of 84 to Watch in 1984 (San Diego Magazine), Outstanding Young Men of Am. (1985); mem: Am. Assn. Univ. Profs., Calif. Faculty Assn.; publs: Sport Psychology: The Coach's Perspective (Charles C. Thomas Pub. 1983), Sport Psychology for Women (Harper & Row Pub. 1986); Republican; Protestant; rec: Formula One Grand Prix racing, yachting, travel, writing, gourmet cooking. Res: 45457 Clubhouse Dr Rancho California 92390 Ofc: Coll. of Profl. Studies SDSU San Diego 92182

MEDLAND, MAURICE B., business executive; b. Sept. 29, 1936, Centerville, Iowa; s. Wm. C. and Avis N. (Blue) M.; m. Karen A. McFarland, Aug. 7, 1965; children: Melissa b. 1968, Steven b. 1970; edn: BS, N.E. Missouri State Univ. 1961; MBA, Pepperdine Univ. 1977. Career: mgmt. systems analyst Rockwell

Internat. Corp., Space Div., Downey 1961-70; dir. planning and reporting Fluor Corp., Irvine 1970-85; v.p. PacifiCare Health Systems Inc., Cypress 1985−; dir. Saddleback Coll. Found. 1979-81; awards: Apollo Achieve. Award, NASA (1969), tech. presentation award, Fluor Corp. (1977); mil: US Navy 1954-57, China Service Medal. Res: 19842 Villager Circle Yorba Linda 92686 Ofc: PacifiCare Health Systems Inc. 5995 Plaza Dr Cypress 90630

MEDLEY, NANCY MAY, registered nurse; b. Oct. 8, 1948, Knoxville, Tenn.; d. Donald Raymond and Josephine Ruth (Blakely) M.; edn: AA, Riverside City Coll. 1970. Career: medical staff nurse Riverside Gen. Hosp. 1970-71; staff nurse neonatal unit Kaiser Permanente Hosp., Hollywood 1971-72; critical care nurse neuro unit, Harbor- UCLA Med. Ctr. 1972-78, head nurse cardiac care unit 1978−; mem. Am. Heart Assn.; Republican; Presbyterian; rec: gardening, bike riding. Res: 636 Manhattan Ave. Apt. G Hermosa 90254 Ofc: 1000 Carson St. Harbor- UCLA Medical Center

MEEHAN, PAULA KENT, cosmetic co. executive; b. Aug. 9, 1931, W. Los Angeles; d. Richard and Lois Martin (Hobbs) Moorehead; m. John E. Meehan, Apr. 20, 1973; children: Michael Miller, Chris Meehan, Matt Meehan; edn: bus. law & mgmt. courses, UCLA 1960-62. Career: founder, exec. v.p. Redken Labs., Canoga Park 1960-67, pres. 1967-72, bd. chmn. 1972-84, founder chmn. 1984−; awards: Hall of Fame award Nat. Hairdressers & Cosmetologists Assn., St. Louis, Mo. (1985), "100 Top Corporate Women" Business Week mag. (1977), "Savvy 60" top corp. women, Savvy Mag. (1985, 86); mem. Beauty & Barber Supply Inst., ICD-Intercoiffure Am/Can.; civic: regent Loyola Marymount Univ., bd. councilors USC Sch. of Bus. Mgmt., mem. Trusteeship for Betterment of Women; Republican. Ofc: Redken Labs Inc 6625 Variel Ave Canoga Park 91303

MEEKS, DASHIELL SHAWN, utilities co. supervisor; b. Apr. 2, 1948, Newark, NJ; s. Charles Augustus and Ada Lucille (Roberts) M.; m. Carol Miller, Oct. 11, 1974; edn: BS, Lehigh Univ. 1969; MBA, Murray State Univ. 1979; Engr. In Tng., Calif. 1980; Reg. Profl. Engr. Calif. (mech. 1982, indsl. 1983). Career: research engr. Kaiser Aluminum & Chem. Corp., Oakland 1969-73; proj. engr. W.R. Grace & Co., Lexington, Mass. 1973-79; maint. supv. San Diego Gas & Elec. Co., San Diego 1979−; spkr. Career Day, S.D. Jt. Council of Eng. Socs. (1980-81), Links Internat. (1982), S.D. Council of Black Engr. (1980, 81, 82, 83, 84), Serra Jr. H.S. (1983); judge, San Diego Nat. Student Sci. Competition, S.D. Elem. Inst. of Sci. 1982; awards: Scholastic Scholarship, Frat. Order of Masons 1969; Outstanding Young Men of Am., Jaycees 1983; mem: S.D. Council of Black Engrs.; Am. Inst. of Indsl. Engrs.; Proj. Mgmt. Inst.; Ops. Research Soc. of Am.; Assn. of MBA Execs. Inc.; Am. MENSA Ltd.; Sigma Alpha Mu, Sigma Kappa chpt.; works: presentation, Pacific Coast Elec. Assn. Conf., L.A. 3/83; paper presented Internat. Conf. of Inst. of Indsl. Engrs., Chgo. 5/84; Presbyterian; rec: basketball, bridge, chess. Res: 6432 El Perico Ln Carlsbad 92008 Ofc: San Diego Gas & Electric Co., POB 1831 San Diego 92101

MEEKS, DONNA JEANNE, chiropractor; b. Sept. 15, 1951, Reno, Nev.; d. Oren and Gladys Marie (Kangas) Meeks; edn: BA, Univ. Nev. 1973; postgrad., Inst. of European Studies in Vienna, Austria 1 yr.; DC, Cleveland Chiropractic Coll. 1983; Calif. lic. D.C., 1984. Career: chiropractor prin., Sherman Way Chiropractic Center, Canoga Park 1984−; Preferred Provider for Prudential and Blue Shield; wkr.'s compensation chiropractor for Saga Corp.; CPR instr. Am. Red Cross; organizer of restaurant health & safety seminars; cons. sport injuries var. sport shops; mem: Am. Chiro. Assn., Calif. Chiro. Assn., Council on Sports Injuries and Physical Fitness, San Fernando Valley Chiro. Soc., Woodland Hills CofC; Republican; Protestant; rec: horses, sports. Ofc: Sherman Way Chiropractic Center 22048 Sherman Way Ste 103 Canoga Park 91303; 221 W Los Angeles Ave Moorpark 93021

MEENA, EDWARD J., real estate - author; b. Apr. 2, 1922, Vicksburg, Miss.; s. Elias and Mamie (Abraham) M.; m. Warene Shurden 1951, div. 1956; edn: AA, Miss. State Univ. 1946-48. Career: Meena Landscaping and Floral Co., Clarksdale, Miss. 1948-55; MGM Studio, Culver City 1955-74; Tempa Geiger-Century 21 Realtors, Brentwood & Encino 1974−; dir. of S&S Pub.; honors: founder, Pet Defenders; mem: Theta Xi; L.A. Co. Mus. of Art; Royal Oaks Found.; L.A. World Affairs Council; Nat. Exchange; coauthor: Star Maker, Star Breaker; author: Bride of Annadale and The Prodigal Daughter; Methodist. Res: 5748 Saloma Ave Van Nuys 91411 Ofc: Tempa Geiger & Assoc., 16430 Ventura Blvd Encino 91436

MEGUIAR, MALCOLM FLOYD, manufacturer; b. June 16, 1915, Pasadena; s. Frank Jr. and Sadie Jane (Habenicht) M.; m. Mabel Ruth Hudson, Nov. 27, 1934; children: Larry Gordon b. 1935, Barry James b. 1942; edn: Pasadena City Coll. Career: bd. chmn. Meguiar's Mirror Bright Polish Co. Inc., Irvine (sales nationwide and 7 foreign re-packaging plants); co. was founded in 1901 by father, Frank Meguiar, Jr., son, Barry is current corp. president. Charter pres. Pasadena Lancer Club, charter v.p. Pasa. (now Pt. Loma) Coll. Crusader Club, charter mem., dir. Pasa. Quarterbacks; bus. advis. bd. Pasa. City Coll. and chmn. bd. govs. of Alumni Assn. (awarded lifetime Gold Pass to all coll. events); charter rep. Troop 21, Boy Scouts of Am.; past pres. Pasa. Boys Club (hon. lifetime mem.); awarded Orv Mohler Trophy, for contbn. to sports in So. Calif., Sports Ambassadors, 1961; mem: Tournament of Roses Com. (hon. life mem.); Jr. CofC (life); Pasa. Kiwanis Club (senior mem.); Salvation Army (Man of Year 1968); Pasa. University Club; Pasa. CofC; Balboa Bay Club; patron: YMCA (N.E. Br.), athletic teams (45+ years) Softball, Baseball, Little League, AAU Basketball, Bowling, Track and Field, Volleyball, Indianapolis 500 and Riverside Grand Prix. Ofc: Mirror Bright Polish Co. Inc. 17275 Daimler Ave Irvine 92714

MEHIN, RASHID, accountant; b. Feb. 16, 1951, Kerman, Iran; s. Mehraban and Banoo (Khanizadeh) M.; m. Homa S. Zartoshty, Mar. 1982; edn: BS, N.I.O.C. Coll. of Accountancy 1974; desig: ACMA, The Inst. of Cost & Mgmt. Accts., U.K. (1981), RIA, The Soc. of Mgmt. Accts., B.C. Canada (1984). Career: treas., controller Markel-Johnson Poultry Co. Inc., San Diego 1983−; mgmt. cons. Dana & Co., Brit. Col., Canada 1982-83; acct. Schlage Canada 1981-82; co. acct. Glenhill Furnishing Co., London, Eng. 1980-81, Lesser Services Ltd. 1977-80; auditor Plan and Orgn., Tehran, Iran 1970-74; treas., controller Markel Johnson Poultry Co. Inc., San Diego currently; recipient scholarship award in devel. orgn. (1975); mem. Am. Mgmt. Assn.; Zoroastrian; rec: tennis, badminton, chess. Res: 3670 Carmel View Rd San Diego 92130 Ofc: Markel Johnson Poultry Co Inc 2697 Main St San Diego 92113

MEHRAN, MASUD RAFAHI, co. executive; b. Feb. 6, 1920, Tehran, Iran, nat. US cit. 1951; s. Hasan R. and Zibandeh Mehran; m. Nov. 7, 1942; children: Ghaisar b. 1944, Alexander b. 1950; edn: high sch. grad. American Coll. of Tehran (Iran) 1939; BS, Cornell Univ. 1946. Career: founder/bd. chmn. Sunset Devel. Co., San Ramon 1951−, blt. Sunset-Town (planned community for 16,000+ residents, with homes, businesses and industry), currently bldg. Bishop Ranch Business Park (major suburban bus. park); honors: hon. LLD, Honoris Causa, Golden Gate Univ.; named Outstanding Immigrant to U.S.; recogn. awards Boy Scouts Am., YMCA, Calif. State Legislature; mem: Nat. Assn. of Home Builders (life dir. 1953-), Real Estate Research Orgn. (dir.), Lambda Alpha Profl. Land Economics Frat. (past dir.), Home Builders Assn. (past pres.), Urban Land Inst. (trustee 1983), CofC; civic: Dominican Coll. (bd. trustees), Childrens Hosp. (bd. trustees), Boy Scouts Am. (exec. bd); club: Olympic (SF); Republican (Pres. Task Force); Presbyterian; rec: swim, water ski, tennis. Res: 1750 Taylor St San Francisco 94133 Ofc: Sunset Development Co One Annabel Ln Ste 201 San Ramon 94583

MEHTA, PRATAP K., company executive; b. Dec. 21, 1940, Bombay, India, nat. US cit. 1979; s. Krishnaji J. and Sunderbai K. Mehta; m. Chetna, May 4, 1973; children: Rana b. 1973, Ashish b. 1981; edn: BS engrg., CSU Los Angeles 1967; MS sys. mgmt., West Coast Univ. L.A. 1970; Reg. Profl. Engr. Calif. Career: engr., scientist McDonald Aircraft; western regl. sales mgr. Control Systems Research; mktg. mgr. Texas Instrument; major acct. mgr. Intel Corp.; western regl. sales mgr. Summa Graphic Corp.; western area sales mgr. Calcomp Corp.; pres. Mehta Assoc.; honors: Pres. Award (Calcomp), 100% Quota Club; mem: Quality Control Engrs., Computer Graphic, India Cultural Assn.; Democrat; Hindu: Rec: flying, photog. Address: Walnut 91789

MEIER, LLOYD ALAN, cabinetmaker, ret.; b. Nov. 15, 1921, Chico, Calif.; s. Adolph Harry and Ethel May (Nixon) M.; m. Norma Anderson, Sept. 23, 1944; children: Karen b. 1951, Mindy b. 1954; edn: CSU Chico 1939-42. Career: bookkeeper Union Oil Co. 1946-48; builder 1948-60, cabinetmaker 1960-78; real estate broker 1978-85; restored old homes 1971-83; past mem. Delta Psi Frat. and Kiwanis; mem. Chico Historical Soc.; mil: pfc USAAC 1942-46; Republican; Protestant; rec: blacksmithing, jewelry making, knifemaking, wood carving. Res: 1615 Dayton Rd Chico 95928

MEINSEN, MILTON PETER, co. president; b. Jan. 22, 1944, Tucson, Ariz.; s. Milton Peter and Glennis Glee (Goodwin) M.; edn: mech. engrg., Marquette 1961-63. Career: proj. mgr. Elloit & Black Omaha 1969-73; owner Design Internat. Pasadena 1973-79; pres., chmn. bd. Future Timing Inc. Pasadena 1985−; pres., c.e.o. MPM Inc. Pasadena 1979−; mil: E-4 USAF Security Svc. 1964-68. Address: 787 E Washington No. 7 Pasadena 91104

MEISTER, RICHARD BURNS, ophthalmologist; b. Apr. 20, 1948, Okla. City; s. Stanford Harry and Cleo Lacy M.; m. Tricia Hutchcraft, July 30, 1980; 1 son, Chase Aaron b. 1984; edn: BS zool., Univ. Okla. 1971; BS med., Univ. No. Dak. 1978; MD, UC Davis 1980; bd. certified Am. Bd. of Ophthalmol. 1986. Career: cardiac technician Mt. Zion Hosp. San Francisco 1972-73; research assoc. II, supv. neonatal blood gas lab. Cardiovascular Research Inst., Moffett Hosp., UCSF 1973-74; senior research technol., supv. exptl. surgery lab. Mt. Zion Hosp. 1974-76; intern int. med. UCLA Harbor Gen. Hosp. 1980-81; resident ophthalmol. Univ. Texas, Houston affil. hosps. 1981-84, chief res. 1983-84; pvt. practice ophthalmol. Fair Oaks, Calif., spec. in keratorefractive surgery, cataract, corneal transplant and anterior segment surgery 1984−; honors: Most Outstanding Resident (UT 1983-84), Sequoyah Scholar (Univ. Okla. 1967), 1st Place sculpture, art in biology (Univ. Okla. 1968), Sigma Xi, President's Honor Roll (UO 1970); mem: AMA, CMA, Am. Acad. Ophth., Keratorefractive Soc., Assn. Am. Indian Physicians, Alta Ophth. Soc., speakers bureau for civic orgns. at several local hosps.; publs: tech. articles in med. jours.; rec: sailing, tennis, backpacking, alpine skiing, travel. Ofc: 6600 Mercy Ct Ste 100 Fair Oaks 95628

MELDON, GERI MICHELLE, jewelry designer; b. Feb. 4, 1944, Cleveland, Ohio; d. Paul E. and Rhoda (Goldberg) M.; edn: Stephens Coll. 1962-63; Parsons Sch. of Design 1963-64; 4-yr dipl. silversmithing, Cleveland Inst. of Art 1968; grad. gemologist in residence dipl., Gemological Inst. of Am. (GIA) 1969; BA, Calif. State Univ. 1975; Calif. Life Tchg. Cred. (adult edn.), UCLA 1972. Career: fine jewelry designer, 1970−; instr. jewelry making and design, Los Angeles Dept. of Rec. and Parks 1970-76; fine jewelry sales: May Co., L.A., Tiffany and Co., Bev. Hills, Slavicks, L.A., 1974-77; instr. jewelry retailing GIA, instr. Am. Gem. Soc. selling and mdsg. pgm., 1977-78; mem. Calif. Jewelers Assn., Nat. Assn. of Jewelry Appraisers; Ch. of Rel. Sci.; rec: cake decorating (winner num. competition awards), candy molding. Ofc: Geri Michelle Meldon, Bldg 1 Ste 316, 1187 Coast Village Rd Montecito 93108

MELIA, ANTHONY FRANCIS, JR., insurance broker; b. Sept. 3, 1933, Gretna, Nebr.; s. Anthony Francis Sr. and Hazel (Bishop) M.; edn: BA, Univ. of Nebr. 1957; cont. edn. UCLA & Los Angeles City Coll.; desig: CIC, Soc. of Cert. Ins. Counselors 1980; Notary Pub., Calif. 1967. Career: founder/ owner Melia Ins. Inc. 1967; changed to Nat. Bus. Ins. Agency upon acquisiton of Titan Agencies 1980; pres./ owner National Business Insurance Agency, Los Angeles 1967–; lectr./ author; mem: Profl. Ins. Agents of Calif. & Nev.; Metropolitan Elections Com. of L.A.; L.A. Bus. & Profl. Assn. (pres. 1981-); West Hollywood CofC (bd. dirs.); contbg. writer: NEXUS Mag. 1984, frequent interviews & arts in Bay Area Reporter (1982), Frontiers Mag. (1983), & L.A. Times (1/84); mil: corp. US Army 1953-55, Nat. Defense Svc., GCM, Army of Occupation Medal; Democrat; rec: photog., collector historic autographs/ signatures; Res: 1020 Carol Dr West Hollywood 90069 Ofc: NBIA, 1017 N La Cienega, Ste 306, West Hollywood 90069

MELLOTT, SHARON LEE, chiropractor; b. Nov. 9, 1939, Thief River Falls, Minn.; d. Melvin Ingolf and Evelyn Irene (Olson) Sabo; m. Keith D. Mellott, Aug. 11, 1962; 1 son, Kevin Gerard, b. 1965; edn: Pacific Lutheran Univ. 1957-58; Reg. Radiologic Technologist, Univ. of Ore. Med. Sch. 1960, DC, Palmer Coll. of Chirop. West 1982; postgrad. roentgenology, Western State Coll. of Chirop. 1982-85; postgrad. indsl. cons., L.A. Chirop. Coll. 1985; Diplomate Am. Bd. Chiro. Examiners 1982; DC lic. State Bds. Maine, Calif. (1982), Nev., Idaho, Colo. & Wyo. (1983). Career: radiologic tech., Seattle, Sacto., So. S.F. bay areas 1960-79; owner/ opr. The Transcriber, med. sectl. svc., Sunnyvale 1975–; chiropractor/ clin. dir./ owner Sierra Chirop. Clinic, Saratoga 1982–, chiropractic roentgenologist, chiropractic indsl. cons.; instr. anatomy & physiology, East- West Ctr. for the Healing Arts (1983), guest lectr. Palmer Coll. of Chirop.-West; honors: hon. Dr. Chirop., No. Calif. Coll. of Chirop. (1980); mem: Internat. Chiropractors Assn. (Congl. dist. dir. ICA 1984-85), Am. Chirop. Assn. (Council on Roentgenology), Internat. Chirop. Assn. of Calif., Am. Public Health Assn., Internat. Acad. Chirop. Indusl. Consultants, Nat. Council for Internat. Health, Community of Saint Luke; civic: Saratoga CofC, Soroptimist Internat., Saratoga Breakfast Network, Civitan Club, Good Shepherd Home Aux., Found. for Hearing Research, World Police and Fire Games, San Jose (vol. profl. services 1985); needlework exhibitor: var. local comm. shows; author/ presentor: monologue, Kate Luther-A Woman for All Ages; Republican; Lutheran; rec: needlework, music. Res: POB 492 Saratoga 95071 Ofc: Sierra Chiropractic Clinic, 12021 Saratoga-Sunnyvale Rd Saratoga 95070

MENDE, HOWARD SHIGEHARU, mechanical engineer; b. Nov. 19, 1947, Hilo, Ha.; s. Tsutomu and Harue (Kubomitsu) M.; edn: BSME, Univ. of Hawaii 1969; MSME, USC 1975; Mass. Inst. of Tech. 1978; lic. profl. mech. engr., Calif. 1981. Career: tech. staff I autonetics div., Rockwell Internat., Anaheim 1970-71, tech. staff II B-1 div., Los Angeles 1971-77; devel. engr. AiResearch Mfg. Co. of Calif., Torrance 1977-83; tech. staff IV No. Am. aircraft ops., Rockwell Internat., Los Angeles 1984–; lectr. Pacific State Univ., electronic thermodynamics 1974 and computer programming 1975; honors: book acknowledgement, Philosophy and Unified Science, Dr. George Robert Talbott 1977; mem: Pi Tau Sigma, Am. Soc. Mech. Engrs., Internat. Platform Assn.; Democrat; Buddhist; rec: gardening. Res: 1946 West 180th Pl. Torrance 90504 Ofc: Rockwell International, P.O. Box 92098 Los Angeles 90009

MENDELOW, SAMUEL MARVIN, educational computer software co. president; b. June 27, 1931, Buffalo, NY; s. Albert and Frida M.; children: Donna b. 1953, Debra b. 1957, Robert b. 1964; edn: bus. adm./ music, Univ. Fla. 1947-9, Univ. Miami 1950-52. Career: vice pres. General Aerospace Materials Corp., Plainview, NY 1952-62; pres. Aerodynamics Indus. Inc., Farmingdale, NY 1962-67; founder/v.p. EDP Indus. Inc., Los Angeles 1967-76; pres. QC Resources Group, L.A. 1977-82; pres. NET Systems, Inc., L.A. 1977-82; pres. Compass Software Corp., Encino 1984–; pres. CourseWare Research Corp., Encino 1984–; dir. Publishers Support Group, Inc., Encino 1984–; chosen by Govt. of Israel to exclusively rep. all indsl. products mfd. in Israel for export to US (1966); rep. (various tech. products mfd. for export to Israel) Grumman Internat. Corp.; honors: bus. chmn. United Cerebral Palsey (NY 1954), student guest condr. Tampa (Fla.) Sym. Orch. (1948); mem: Am. Soc. of Composers, Authors and Pubs.; Am. Soc. for Nondestructive Testing, Inc.; Masons, Pi Lambda Phi. Guest panelist 8th Ann. W.Coast Computer Faire, S.F. 1983; rec: music, golf, tennis, swim. Res: 133 N Almont Dr Beverly Hills 90211 Ofc: Compass Software Corp. 17000 Ventura Blvd Ste 220, Encino 91316

MENDENHALL, EDWARD VAN HORN, JR., industrialist; b. Jan. 8, 1917, Sioux City, Iowa; s. Edward V.H. and Mable (Hanna) M.; m. Betty Houston, July 25, 1961; 1 son, William Morgan b. 1947; edn: BSEE, US Naval Acad. 1940. Career: fmr. chief exec. Manganese Corp. of Ariz., 1950s; past pres. Arguello Constrn. Co. (contr. USAF missile launch facilities, Tucson); (current) leader in new industry, the thermoforming of large diameter PVC pipe fittings, and ten year pioneer innovator in drip irrigation technology; founder/ bd. chmn./ pres. Resource Water Technology and subs. cos.; bd. chmn./pres. Double Eagle Fittings Co.; dir. Galloway Internat. Farms; honors: Disting. service award, ASTM; mem: Am. Soc. Testing and Mats. (chmn. stds. com. F-17.10 Plastic Pipe Fittings), Soc. Plastic Engrs., Naval Acad. Athletic Assn., Tail Gate Soc., Assn. of Naval Aviators, Navy League, Masons; 6 patents: Thermoformed PVC Fittings and Drip Irrigation; mil: combat aviator, test pilot, squadron comdr., lt. col. USMC 1940-54, WWII, Korea, decorated D.F.C. w/star, Air Medal w/8 stars; Republican; Prot.; rec: golf, sky diving, fly fishing, polo. Res: 43 Margarita Camarillo 93010 Ofc: Resource Water Technology 333 N Dawson Camarillo 93010

MENDEZ, JOHN FRANK, horticulture co. executive; b. Sept. 12, 1942, Eureka, Nev.; s. John George and Neva June (Tognoni) M.; div.; 2 sons: Damon b. 1971, Derek b. 1973; edn: BA in acctg. Golden Gate Univ. 1968; MBA, Harvard Grad. Sch. of Bus. 1970; Certified Public Acct., Calif. 1975. Career: chief acct. Golden Gate Univ. 1968; audit mgr. Deloitte, Haskins & Sells, 1976; vice pres. of audit Amfac Distbn. Group, 1978; controller Amfac Electric Supply, 1980; asst. v.p./ asst. controller Amfac, Inc., 1982; pres. Amfac Garden Products, 1983; exec. v.p. Amfac Horticulture Group, 1984; founder, pres., CEO, bd. chmn. Tri-West, Inc. (one of largest horticulture firms in USA), San Mateo 1985–; instr. Golden Gate Univ. Grad. Sch. of Bus.; honors: Outstanding acctg. student 1968, Chi Pi Alpha; Chess Champion, Golden Gate Univ. (1967, 68); mem: Am. Inst. CPAs, Calif. Soc. CPAs; civic: soccer coach and commnr. AYSO 1981-85, vol./ leader YMCA Indian Guides, Cub Scouts and Youth Baseball, 1978; mil: sp4 US Army 1960-63; Republican; Episcopal; rec: golf, chess, bridge. Ofc: Tri-West, Inc. 1875 South Grant St Ste 520 San Mateo 94402

MENDOZA, JESUS CRUZ, physician; b. Aug. 18, 1948, Bamban, Phil., nat. USA 1984; s. Jose Espinosa and Belen Lagman (Cruz) M.; m. Helen Grace Cortez, June 1, 1985; edn: BS, Univ. of Santo Tomas 1968, MD, 1972. Career: general med. practice Philippines 1973-77; rotating intern Elyria Memorial Hosp., Ohio 1977-78; surgical resident St. Agnes Hosp., Baltimore 1978-79; 2 yr. res. emergency medicine Martin Luther King, Jr. Hosp., Los Angeles 1979-81; gen. practice HMO Group, Long Beach 1981-82; emerg. phys. Sta. Marta Hosp., East L.A. 1982-84; staff Emerg. Rm. West Hollywood Community Hosp., 1982–, Industrial & Urgent Care Clinic, Dalton Medical Grp., S.El Monte 1984–; mem. Am. Coll. of Emergency Physicians 1979-81; orgn: Knights of Columbus, Aquino Movement for Freedom in the Philippines, Anaheim Chess Club, choir St. Linus Ch. Norwalk; works: chess columnist, Phil. Asian News L.A.; Democrat; Catholic; rec: chess, tennis, jogging. Ofc: Dalton Medical Grp. 10414 Vacco St South El Monte 91733

MENDOZA, RAYMUNDO JOSE GONZALEZ, optometrist; b. July 21, 1954, Havana, Cuba; s. Jose Antonio M.; edn: Georgia Coll. 1973-74; Univ. of Miami 1975; BS, environmental health, Univ. of Georgia 1979; OD, Southern Coll. of Optometry 1984. Career: county health inspector, Jackson Co., Georgia 1979-81; assoc. optometrist RTS Inc. 1984–; cons. Sentro research and devel. co.; pres. Student Volunteers of Optometric Svcs. to Humanity 1984; mem: Am. and Calif. Optometric Assns., Lions Club; research: microbiological & biochemical fields; Democrat; Catholic; rec: skiing, painting, fly fishing. Res: 2028 Thomas Ave. San Diego 92109

MENNIG, JAN COLLINS, police executive; b. Oct. 9, 1927, Pasadena, Calif.; d. Christian Percival and Lucile (Collins) M.; m. Mary Harmelink, June 9, 1979; 1 dau. Lucy Marie; edn: BS, Univ. So. Calif. 1959, MS, 1964; PhD, Pacific Western 1983; US Army Command Gen. Staff Coll. 1972; Air War Coll. 1978; Certified Logistician, US Army 1977; Police Exec. Certification POST 1971. Career: police ofcr.-lt. Pasadena Police Dept. 1950-65; asst. chief Culver City Police Dept. 1965-69, chief 1970-75, asst. chief 1975–; instr. USC Sch. of Pub. Adminstrn. 1962-75, CSULA Sch.of Police Sci. 1974-75; cons. mgmt. and tng. govt. and pvt. industry 1965–; past chmn. L.A. County Regl. Crim. Justice Planning Bd. 1974-75; past pres. Police Chief's Dept. League of Calif. Cities; honors: Pi Sigma Alpha, Skull & Dagger (USC), Senior Leadership Award (United Way 1984), Golden Book Award (YMCA 1985), Man of the Year (YMCA 1971, Elks 1985); mem: Internat. Asn. Chiefs of Police, L.A. County Peace Ofcrs. Assn., Am. Soc. Public Adminstrs., SCAPA Practors, Internat. Police Assn., Calif. Peace Ofcrs. Assn., Calif. Police Chiefs Assn. (past exec. com.), Lions Club (past pres.), Masons, Shrine, Elks, YMCA (past chmn., bd.); past pres. Didi Hirsch Comm. Mental Health Ctr.; bd. Behavioral Health Svcs. L.A.; publ: Elements of Police Supervision (Melnicoe & Mennig, Glencoe Press 1969), and others; mil: col. US Army and USAR 1944-82, Legion of Merit, Meritorious Svc. (3), others; Republican; Protestant; rec: fishing, hiking. Ofc: Culver City Police Dept. POB 808 Culver City 90232

MENO, GLENN ANTHONY, printed circuit board designer, financial planner; b. Jan. 11, 1957, San Diego; s. Jesus Cruz (dec.) and Brigida (Javier) M.; m. Patricia Ann. Borja Pereira, Apr. 2, 1977; 1 dau. Alana Monet b. 1984; edn: San Diego City Coll. 1975-79; San Diego Mesa Coll. 1979; desig: Reg. Rep., NASD (Series 6) 1981; Life Only Agent, Calif. 1981. Career: eng. draftsman 32nd St. Naval Sta., San Diego 1974-78; elec. drafter NCR, Rancho Bernardo 1978-80; PCB designer Manpower co., San Diego 1980-81, Spin Physics 1981-82, Dynair Electronics 1982-83, TSA 1983; PCB designer, Senior Design 1983-84; consulting/finl. plnng. prin. GNP Docuservice, eng. svcs., Spring Valley 1984–; mem: Sons & Daughters of Guam Club, San Diego; Republican; Christian; rec: racquetball, basketball, computers, chess. Address: GNP Docuservice, 8243 Warmwood Ave Spring Valley 92077

MENSINGER, PEGGY BOOTHE, mayor; b. Feb. 18, 1923, Modesto; d. Dyas Power and Margaret (Stewart) Boothe; m. John Logan Mensinger, May 25, 1952; children: John B., Stewart I., Susan B.; edn: AB in polit. sci., Stanford Univ. 1944. Career: reporter San Francisco Red Cross Chpt. News Bur., 1944; acting mgr. Boothe Fruit Co., Modesto 1945; asst. dir. Stanford Alumni Assn., 1947, exec. secty. public exercises com. Stanford Univ., 1949-51; elected mem. Modesto City Council, 1973-79, mayor, 1979–; bd. dirs. League of Calif. Cities; mem. energy and environ. com. US Conf. of Mayors; bd. dirs. Nat. Council Girl Scouts USA; ch. Citizens Com. for Internat. Students, 1965-70; pres. Modesto PTA Council, 1967-69, Modesto chpt. Am. Field Service, 1969-70, Stanislaus County Hist. Soc., 1970-71; state bd. Common Cause, 1973-75; ch. Modesto City Cultural Commn. 1968-73, del. White House Conf.

on Families, Los Angeles 1980; ch. Stanislaus Area Assn. Govts., 1976-77; honors: Woman of the Year, 1980, VFW Aux.; mem. Nat. League Am. Pen Women (assoc.), LWV (hon.), Calif. Elected Womens Assn. for Edn. and Research, AAUW (grant honoree Edn. Found. 1978), Soroptomist (Women of Achievement award 1980); Stanford Associates, Phi Beta Kappa, Gamma Phi Beta. Res: 1320 Magnolia Ave., Modesto 95350 Ofc: 801 Eleventh St Modesto 95354

MERA, CSABA LESLIE, pediatrician; b. Sept. 28, 1949, Szeged, Hungary, nat. American; s. Zoltan and Klara Iren (Jobba) M.; m. Patricia Anne, June 27, 1981; children: Steven b. 1985, (by previous marriage) Todd b. 1969, Trent b. 1970; edn: BA, Andrews Univ. 1968; MD, Loma Linda Univ. 1972; FRCP(C), Fellow Royal Coll. of Physicians, Canada (1983); Diplomate Am. Acad. of Pediatrics (1984). Career: pediatric intern Loma Linda Univ. Med. Ctr. 1972-73, instr., asst. prof. LLU Emergency Dept. 1975-80, pediatric residency 1980-82; pediatric hematology/oncology fellow Hosp. for Sick Children, Toronto, Ont., Can. 1982-83; pediatrician in pvt. practice, San Luis Obispo 1983-85, Lompoc, 1985 –; staff ped. Lompoc District Hosp.; honors: Alpha Omega Alpha (1971); mem. Calif. Med. Assn., Mensa Intl.; publ: paper on Fanconis Anemia and Liver Abscess; Independent; rec: writing, soccer, cooking. Ofc: C. Mera, M.D. 601 E Ocean Ave Ste 8, Lompoc 93436

MERCHANT, LOREN KEITH, II, landscape contractor, designer; b. March 31, 1958, Bakersfield; s. Loren Keith and Verda Jo (Johnson) edn: AA, Bakersfield Coll. 1979. Career: supvr. No. Bakersfield Park and Recreation CETA pgm. supvr.; founder Treasure Cove Ltd. Landscpae Constrn. 1980 –; tchr. landscape Bakersfield Coll. 1980; Junior Exhibitors Council Pres., Kern Co. Fair 1977-79; cons. var. park and recreation dists. 1980 –; honors: Freedom Found. Valley Forge, 1976; Kern Co. Allstar 1978; Calif. Diamond Star Cand. 1979; John Philip Souza Award, 1976; mem: Kern Co. Bldrs. Exch., Barc, Kern Co. 4-H Club; Arvin United Pentecostal Ch. (dir. Sunday sch.); Democrat; rec: music. Res: Rt. 1 Box 114-L Arvin 93203

MERCHANT, ROLAND SAMUEL, SR., hospital administrator; b. Apr. 18, 1929, NY, NY; s. Samuel and Eleta (McLymont) M.; m. Audrey Bartly, June 6, 1970; children: Orelia b. 1971, Roland, Jr. b. 1972, Huey b. 1973; edn: BA, NY Univ. 1957, MA, 1960; MS, Columbia Univ. 1963, MS hosp. adminstrn., 1974. Career: asst. statistician NYC Dept. of Health 1957-60, statistician 1960-63, NY TB & Health Assn. 1963-65; biostatistician, adminstrv. coord. Inst. for Surgical Studies Montefiore Hosp. Bronx, NY 1965-72; resident hosp. adminstrn. Roosevelt Hosp. NY 1973-74; dir. health & hosp. mgmt. NYC Dept. of Health 1974-76; asst. adminstr. West Adams Comm. Hosp. Los Angeles 1976, adminstr. 1976; spl. asst. to assoc. v.p. for med. affairs Stanford Univ. Med. Ctr. 1977-82, dir. ofc. of mgmt. and strategic planning Stanford Univ. Hosp. 1982-85, dir. mgmt. planning 1986 –; lectr. div. of health adminstrn. Columbia Univ. Sch. of Pub. Health 1975-76, dept. of family, community and preventive med. Stanford Univ. Med. Sch. 1977-83, clin. asst. prof. 1983 –; honors: USPHS Fellow (Columbia Univ. 1962-63); fellow: Am. Pub. Health Assn. 1965, Am. Coll. Healthcare Execs. 1985; mem: Am. Hosp. Assn., Nat. Assn. Health Svcs. Execs., NY Acad. Scis.; author: Tuberculosis in New York City (1964), Tuberculosis Morbidity Resumes Decreasing Trend (1965), articles in med. and adminstrv. jours.; mil: US Army 1951-53; Democrat; Baptist (deacon); rec: bowling, fishing. Res: 953 Cheswick Dr San Jose 95121 Ofc: Stanford Univ. Hosp. Stanford 94305

MERINO, FRANK QUINONES, lawyer; b. Apr. 23, 1933, Santa Rita, New Mex.; s. Jesus Alvarez and Gregoria (Quinones) M.; m. Carmen Perez, Dec. 23, 1956; children: Ronald b. 1957, Theresa Ann b. 1962, Mark b. 1964, Patricia Lyn b. 1969; edn: BA, Western New Mex. Univ. 1956; JD, Univ. San Francisco 1965; admitted Calif. State Bar 1966. Career: maintenance planning ofcr. FASRON NAS Alameda 1957-59; legal ofcr. AIRTRANSRON 8 NAS Moffett Field 1959-64; ops. control ctr. ofcr. Treasure Island 1964-66; atty. gen. practice law 1966 –; arbitrator Superior Ct. Santa Clara County 1976 –; honors: Letter of Commdn. (6th Army Hdqs. 1964), Volunteer of the Year (United Way 1985), Hispanic Volunteer of the Year nominee; mem: Calif., Santa Clara Co. bar assns., Sunnyvale-Cupertino Bar Assn. (bd. trustees), Calif. Applicants Attys. Assn., La Raza Lawyers Assn. Naval Reserve Lawyers Assn., Pueblo de San Jose Kiwanis (past pres.), United Way Santa Clara Co. (vice chmn. chpt. coordination, exec. com.), New Mexico Club (founder, 3-term pres.), Am. G.I. Forum, Kenna Club, Naval Reserve Assn.; mil: comdr. USNR 1966-84, National Defense, Naval Reserve medals; Democrat; Catholic; rec: sports, esp. baseball. Res: 1638 Manitoba Dr Sunnyvale 94087 Ofc: Frank Q. Merino 433 S Murphy Ave Sunnyvale 94086

MERRICK, CYNTHIA SUNDAE, health consultant, educator; b. July 27, 1951, Oak Park, Ill.; d. George Edward and Lois Marie (Stoller) Flood; edn: AA, honors, Glendale Comm. Coll. 1971; BA, honors, Ariz. State Univ. 1973. Career: tchr., phys. ed., Phoenix Sch. for Deaf Children 1972-73, biol. scis., Camelback H.Sch. 1973-74; area sales rep./systems rep. Xerox Corp. 1974-79, mktg. rep. 1982-84; exec. dir. Peak Performance Corporate Fitness, 1984 –; creator of "CynErgetics" a unique, non-impact exercise system; founder/ pres./ bd. chair Universal Health (non-profit ednl.), 1985 –; mem. LA World Affairs Council, Am. Film Inst.; Self Realization Fellowship; rec: acting, dancing, biking, skating. Ofc: Peak Performance Corporate Fitness 14005 Palawan Way Ste 215 Marina Del Rey 90292

MERRICK, LOUISE EMILY, convalescent hospital administrator; b. July 2, 1956, New Bedford, Mass.; d. Robert Linwood and Antoinette (Fernandes) M.; edn: BS, Univ. Mass. Amherst 1978; nursing home adminstr. 1984. Career:

dir. Manatee Opportunity Council Home Care Pgm. Bradenton, Fla. 1978-80; recreation supv. Manatee Parks & Rec. Dept. 1980-83; adminstr. Hillsdale Group Inc. San Mateo 1983 –; bd. Manatee County Council on Aging 1978-83; honors: Alpha Lambda Delta, Phi Kappa Phi (Univ. Mass. 1974-78); mem: Calif. Assn. Health Care Facilities 1983-, Schoebers Athletic Club (So. S.F.), Calif. Marine Mammal Ctr.; Democrat; Catholic; rec: marathon running, aerobics. Res: 232 Nevada St San Francisco 94110 Ofc: Hillsdale Group 101 S San Mateo Dr San Mateo 94401

MERRIFIELD, DONALD PAUL, S.J., university chancellor; b. Nov. 14, 1928, Los Angeles; s. Arthur S. and Elizabeth Marian (Baker) M.; edn: BS (physics) Calif. Inst. of Tech. 1950; MS (physics) Univ. of Notre Dame 1951; Ph.L. (philosophy), St. Louis Univ. 1957; PhD (physics) Mass. Inst. of Tech. 1962; STM (theol.), Univ. of Santa Clara 1966. Career: instr. physics Loyola Univ. of L.A. 1961-62; lectr. Univ. of Santa Clara Eng. Sch. 1965; cons. theoretical chem. Jet Propulsion Lab, CalTech, 1962-69; pres. Loyola Univ. of L.A. (now. Loyola Marymount Univ.) 1969-84, chancellor 1984 –; awards: S.T.D., USC (1969), service award CalTech (1971); Soc. of Sigma Xi (sci. hon.); mem: Assn. of Independent Calif. Colls. & Univs. (exec bd., past pres.), Santa Marta Hosp. Found. (pres. bd.), mem. bd. trustees Univ. S.F., St. Joseph Univ., Interfaith Ctr. to Reverse the Arms Race; Catholic priest, Soc. of Jesus; rec: sailing, swimming. Address: Loyola Marymount Univ., Loyola Blvd at W. 80th St Los Angeles 90045

MERRILL, CHARLES MERTON, U.S. judge; b. Dec. 11, 1907, Honolulu; s. Arthur M. and Grace Graydon (Dickey) M.; m. Mary Luita Sherman, Aug. 28, 1931; children: Julia Booth Stoddard, Charles McKinney; edn: AB, Univ. Calif. 1928; LLB, Harvard Univ. 1931; admitted to Calif. State Bar 1931, Nev. Bar, 1932. Career: law practice in Reno, 1932-50; judge Nev. Supreme Ct., 1951-59, chief justice 1955-56, 59; judge US Ct. of Appeals, 9th Circuit, San Francisco 1959 –; gov. State Bar Nev. 1947-50; mem. Am. Bar Assn., Am. Law Inst. (council 1960-). Ofc: U.S. Court of Appeals, P.O. Box 547, San Francisco 94101

MERRIMAN, WILLIAM PAUL, dancer, manufacturing co. president; b. Jan. 22, 1945, Phila.; s. Alva Paul and Wilma (Sykes) M.; edn: BS (physics) Los Angeles City Coll. 1961; Rickard Sch. of Ballet 1961; Lichine- Riaboujinska Sch. of Ballet 1963. Career: dancer The Lido Paris 1963-64, Paris Opera World's Fair Montreal 1967, Festpielhaus Salzberg, Austria 1968, Festival Ballet Edinburgh, Scotland 1968, Ballet de San Juan Puerto Rico 1969, Am. Concert Ballet 1970, Ariz. Ballet 1978; tchr. Sch. of Am. Concert Ballet, Ballet Petit, Palos Verdes Ballet Arts, Lichine Sch. of Ballet, Whittier Civic Ballet, Newport Civic Ballet; pres., founder Primiere Dancewear Santa Rosa; honors: Ford Found. Grant (by Violette Verdi 1963); mem. Santa Rosa CofC 1984; creator and choreagrapher full act ballet The Firebird, Ariz. Ballet 1978 season; Mosaic; rec: viewing Russian ballet, videotaping for documentaries on Russian ballet. Ofc: Premiere Dancewear Santa Rosa 95401

MERTA, PAUL JAMES, cartoonist, engineer, logistics program manager, business owner, restaurateur; b. July 16, 1939, Bakersfield, Calif.; s. Stanley Franklin and Mary Anna (Herman) M.; edn: AA, Bakersfield Jr. Coll. 1962; BS engrg., San Jose State 1962. Career: cartoonist for nat. mags. 1959 –; civilian electronics engr. for USAF/ missiles San Bernardino 1962-65; electronics countermeasures engr. 1965-72, pgm. mgr. for logistics acquisition Sacramento Air Logistics Area 1972; TV/ film aminator, owner Merge Films 1965 –; photog., owner THe Photo Poster Factory Sacramento 1971 –; owner La Rosa Blanca Mexican Restaurant Sacto. 1980 –; ptnr. Kolinski and Merta Hawaiian Estates 1981 –; political cartoonist Calif. Journal 1958-59, Sacto. Union 1979, Sacto. Legal Journal 1979 –; rec: flying, skiing. Res: 4831 Myrtle Ave Sacramento 95841 Ofc: The Photo Poster Factory 1005 12th St Sacramento 95814, La Rosa Blanca Mexican Restaurant 3032 Auburn Blvd Sacramento 95821

MESBAH, SHAWN SHAHRAM, computer systems analyst; b. Oct. 15, 1955, Tehran, Iran, nat. US cit. 1976; edn: AA, Miami Dade Community Coll. 1975; BSCIS, Univ. of Fla. 1978, MSMIS, 1980; PhDMIS, UCLA 1985; Cert. Prodn. & Inventory Control Mgmt., APICS 1985; Cert. Data Processing, 1985; Cert. IBM Series 1 EDX Facility, IBM 1983. Career: asst. prof. Univ. of Florida, Gainesville, Fla.; adj. prof. Hillsborough Community Coll., Tampa, Fla. 1979-80; d.p. supvr., program analyst Rotoflow Cor.p, Los Angeles 1980-81; d.p. mgr. Gas Power Systems, Irvine 1980-82; founder, pres. SMC Data Systems, Los Angeles 1982 –; pres., founding ptr. SMC Data Systems 1982; ptr., dir. Superior Office Systems 1985; cons., project leader M.T.O. Publication Ctr. 1984; cons. Design Co. 1984; mem: Assn. of Computing Machinery, IEEE, Micro Computer Mgmt. Assn., Am. Prodn. & Iventory Control Soc., Mathematical Assn. of Am., Am. Mgmt. Assn., Smithsonian Inlst., Com. to Restore Statue of Liberty; publs: ed., Dolco Byte 1983; SMC Newsletter 1984; Republican (Pres. Task Force 1984). Res: 20019 Ingomar St. Canoga Park 91306

MESCHI, MICHAEL JOSEPH, electrical contractor/engineer; b. April 9, 1957, Los Angeles; s. Fred J. and Jacqueline J. M.; m. Karen, April 5, 1981; children: Michael R. b. 1984, Lauren Nichole b. 1986. Career: founder Mountain Electric 1979, Inc. 1984, currently, pres., CEO; cons. elec. engring.; mem: IES, NECA, AOPA, IEEE; rec: flying (pvt. pilot instrument rated), music (recording musician), skiing. Res: 3021 Caldwell Dr. Camino 95709 Ofc: Mountain Electric, 6201 Enterprise Dr Diamond Springs

MESFIN, WOND WOSSEN, computer scientist; b. Feb. 23, 1952, Addis Ababa, Ethiopia; d. Mesfin and Yechemebeth (Guma) Seleshi; 1 dau. Meckedelina, b. 1978; edn: BSEE/CS, 1974; UC Santa Barbara Grad. Sch. of

Math. Career: senior sys. pgmmr. Tym Share 1978-80; information sys. splst. C.S.C. 1980-82; senior engr. Raytheon 1982-83; prin. mem. tech. staff Citicorp TTI 1983-84; pres. TCT 1984—; works: TCT 1984—; works: R&D Computers; Othodox Ethopian. Res: 390 S Hauser Blvd Los Angeles 90036 Ofc: TCT, 2183 Fairview Rd. Ste. 216 Costa Mesa 92627

MESSNER, HAROLD DALE, patent lawyer; b. Jan. 19, 1935, Darrouzette, Tx.; s. Walter Burgette and Evelyn Mary (Lawson) M.; m. Barbara Bridges, July 13, 1978; children: Suzanne b. 1954, Matthew b. 1955, Steven b. 1956, Gregory b. 1958, Lynne b. 1962; edn: BSME, Stanford Univ. 1958; JD, Golden Gate Law Sch. 1964; admitted Calif. Bar 1965, US Supreme Ct. Bar 1980, US Fed. District 1965, US Patent Bar 1961, US Ct. of Appeals (8th Cir.) 1983. Career: engineering designer, FMC, San Jose 1958-59; patent liaison engr. General Telephone, Mt. View 1959-63; corp. research patent lawyer Standard Oil Co. of Calif. 1963—, senior Patent lawyer Chevron, currently; Appellant counsel in US Supreme Court arguing for independence of jurys from presiding trial judges; adminstrv. lawyer and co-Appellant counsel on appeal to US Supreme Ct. arguing for patentability of computer-dominated processes; mem. Vallejo CofC, Chinese YMCA, AM. Bar Assn., S.F. bar Assn., S.F. Patent Lawyers Assn., Diamond Club (Stanford Block 5); US patentee in computer-dominated processes. Independent, rec: antique collection and evaluation, sports, brass/music performer. Res: 1021 Nebraska St Vallejo 94590 Ofc: Chevron Research, 555 Market St, Ste 423, San Francisco 94105

METCALF, WANDA CHARLENE, real estate broker; b. May 29, 1931, Shawnee, Okla.; d. Charlie Columbus and Martha Beulah (Armitage) H.; m. Raymond Metcalf, Oct. 30, 1948; children: Debra Jean b. 1951, Ronnie b. 1955; Real Estate Broker, Calif. 1965; GRI, 1975. Career: ofc. mgr. Katzakian & Schaffer 1965-68; broker, ofc. mgr. Real Estate by Metcalf 1969—; bd. dirs., chmn. by laws Tehama Co. Bd. Realtors; honors: Million Dollar Sales Award; mem: Nat. and Calif. Assns. Realtors, Tehama Co. Bd. Realtors, Am. Assn. of Ret. Persons; Republican; Assembly of God; rec: water skiing, oil painting, crochet. Ofc: Route 2 Box 22 PR, Red Bluff 96080

METCALFE, ARTHUR G., research executive; b. June 12, 1922, London, Eng., nat. US cit. 1960; s. Henry John and Mabel Eugenie (Ford) M.; m. Sallie Troy, Dec. 30, 1978; children: Jeannette Susan Xaveria b. 1950, Jacqueline Eugenie b. 1952; edn: BA, Univ. Cambridge, Eng. 1942, MA, 1947, PhD, 1950. Career: metallurgist in England, Canada, and USA; supr. physical metallurgy Ill. Inst. of Tech. 1953-59; assoc. dir. research Solar Turbines Inc. (subs. Caterpillar Tractor Co.), San Diego 1959-81, dir. 1981—; assoc. prof. CSU San Diego 1961-, tchg. UCLA, Univ. of Utah, others; cons. MRB; awards: Foundation Scholar, Queens' Coll. Cambridge Univ., NASA spl. award, Sigma Xi; mem: Fellow Am. Soc. Metallurgy (chmn. San Diego Chtp. 1967-69), ASME (coms.), AIMME; 15 US Patents; author: Interfaces in Metal Matrix Composites (1974, Russian translation 1978), approx. 100 profl. publs.; rec: history. Res: 2108 East 24th St National City 92050 Ofc: Solar Turbines, Inc. 2200 Pacific Hwy San Diego 92138

METZLER, YVONNE LEETE, travel agency owner; b. Jan. 25, 1930, Bishop; d. Ben Ford and Gladys Edna (Johnson) Leete; m. Richard Metzler, June 2, 1950; children: David b. 1951, Regan b. 1953, Erin b. 1957; edn: UC Berkeley. Career: vocational instr. Ukiah Jr. Acad., Ukiah 1963-64; acct. W.W. Woodward, P.A./ Clarence White CPA, Ukiah 1971-73; partner/ owner Redwood Travel Agency, Ukiah 1973-76; owner/ mgr. A-1 Travel Planners, Ukiah 1976—; owner A-1 Travel Planners, Willits 1979—; mem: Ukiah Plnng. Commn. ; Ukiah CofC (pres. 1981, 1982); Ukiah Bus. & Profl. Womens Club 1964-79 (treas. 1977-8); Am. Soc. of Bus. & Profl. Womens Clubs 1968-9; Soroptimists (Ukiah pres. 1977-78); Am. Soc. of Travel Agents 1973—; Mendocino Co. CofC (dir. 1981); Republican (Central Com. 1979-80); Protestant; rec: travel. Res: 1112 W Standley St Ukiah 95482 Ofc: A-1 Travel Planners, 505 E Perkins St Ukiah 95482

MEYER, JAMES HENRY, university chancellor; b. Apr. 13, 1922, Fenn, Idaho; s. Carl A. and Anita (de Coursey) M.; m. Mary Regan, Aug. 20, 1980; children: Stephen J., Susan T., Gary C., Joan K., Teresa A.; edn: BS in agri., Univ. Idaho 1947; MS in nutrition (fellow Wis. Alumni Research Found), Univ. Wis. 1949, PhD, 1951. Career: research asst. Univ. Wis., 1949-51; faculty UC Davis, 1951—, prof. animal husbandry, 1960—, chmn. dept., 1960-63, dean Coll. Agri. and Environment, 1963-69, chancellor university, 1969—; mem. Commn. Undergrad. Edn. in Biology; honors: Am. Feed Mfr.'s award in nutrition, 1960; mem. AAAS, Am. Soc. Animal Prodn., Western Colls. Accrediting Assn., Sigma Xi; mil: USMCR 1942-46. Address: 16 College Park, Davis 95616

MEYER, KARIN THERESIA, real estate broker, notary; b. Nov. 29, 1926, Augsburg, West Germany, nat. US cit. 1960; d. Georg and Schallermeier Katharina (Braun) Fuermetz; m. Edward D. Meyer, Apr. 19, 1956; 1 dau., Sylvia Alexandra b. 1964; edn: bookkeeping, Kaufmaenische Privat Schule Augsburg 1946-47; AA, Delta Jr. Coll. 1969; real estate courses; Revere Acad. Jewelry Arts; S.F. Gemological Inst. of Am. Career: clerk, secty. Post Exchange Augsberg 1947-48; owner book store and Leihbuecherei Augsburg 1949-53; owner store Gonsenheim, Germany 1953-56, drive-in restaurant Ft. Hood, Tex. 1956-57; supv. Kellogs Variety Stores Oakland, San Leandro, Alamo, Calif. 1957-61; real estate sales 1962-69, owner r.e. ofc., property mgmt., notary, investment counseling 1969—; owner jewelry store Manteca 1981—; honors: num. sales, listings awards, Master Salesman Award, Million Dollar Club; mem: Manteca Bd. Realters (bd. dirs. 1982-85), Real Estate Certificate Inst., Nat. Notary Assn., Manteca Organ Club (v.p. 1980-83),

Order of Hermann Sons (Stockton, protocol secty. 1982-), Heimat Choir (Stockton); Republican; Catholic; rec: dance, music, opera, travel, swimming. Ofcs: Meyer's Realty 370 N Main St Manteca 95336; The Jewel Box 370 N Main St Manteca 95336

MEYER, RICHARD WALTER, retail business owner; b. Jan. 29, 1947, Monterey; s. Raymond Paul, Sr. and Dorthy (Dewers) M.; m. Christine Peterson, June 22, 1969; children: Kelly b. 1974, Mark b. 1978; edn: AA, Foothill Comm. Coll. 1967; Univ. Nevada, Reno 1968-69; BS, CSU San Jose 1970. Career: gen. mgr. sales & service, bd. chmn. Meyer Electric Co., Mt. View; honors: named Maytag Red Carpet Service Man of Year (1974); Key to the City of Mt. View (1985); civic: Jaycees (bd. chmn. 1981), Kiwanis (dir. 1985), Mt. View CofC (dir. 1986), Downtown Merchants Assn. (pres. 1983), City of Mt. View (serve on var. commns.; chmn. Parking Com. 1986), AYSO Soccer (coach); Republican; Christian; rec: ski, baseball. Res: 505 Pine Ln Los Altos 94022 Ofc: Meyer Electric Co 278 Castro St Mountain View 94040

MEYERS, RONALD WILLIAM, chiropractor; b. Mar. 27, 1942, San Francisco; s. Edward Clarence and Laura Alice (Lee) M., m. Maria Teresa Piratoni, Aug. 17, 1981; children: Ronald b. 1962, Alisa b. 1963, Randall b. 1968, Sean b. 1981, David b. 1983; edn: DC, Cleveland Coll. of Chiro. L.A. 1974; Diplomate Nat. Bd. 1975. Career: postgrad courses sacral occipital technique Dr. David Denton 1974, in radiol. and diversified technique L.A. Chiro. Coll. 1975; asst. dir. Black Chiro. Corp. 1976-77; assoc. Hayes Chiro. Corp. 1977-78; clin. dir. Static Chiroterapeutica S.I.L. Rome, Italy 1979-84; postgrad course motion palpation spinal mechanics Palmer Coll. of Chiro. 1981; clin. dir. Meyers Clinic of Chiro. Fairfield, Calif. 1985—; instr. peripheral neurol. Cleveland Chiro. 1974, differential diagnosis Univ. Pasadena 1975; chiro. cons. to Prof. Silvano Silvij; orthopedist and specialist for Italian Olympic teams 1980, 84; chiro. cons. and assoc. to Prof. Caruso and Prof. Jacovazzo Sch. of Med. Univ. Rome 1980-84; hon. mem. Alumni Assn. Sherman Coll. of Chiro. 1975; mem: Internat. Chiro. Assn. (dir. 4th Cong. Dist. 1985), Am. Chiro. Assn. 1978 (council on roentgenology), Parker Chiro. Research Found. 1977, Am. Coll. Chiro. Orthopedists 1985 (assoc.), Kiwanis, Fairfield CofC, Masons (3rd degree master), Scottish Rite (32nd degree), Knights Templar, European Shrine, Shrine, Nat. Health Fedn. (chpt. founder, pres.); research: invertebral disc syndrome and sciatica, presentation at World Chiro. Conf. Venice, Italy 1982; Republican; Ch. of Jesus Christ of L.D.S.; rec: chess, running. Ofc: Ronald W. Meyers, Sr., DC, 1550 Webster St Ste A Fairfield 94533

MEZA, CARLOS ENRIQUE, physician; b. July 15, 1948, Cortes, Honduras, nat. US cit. 1975; s. Modesto Alfonso and Trinidad Antonia (Palma) M.; m. Susan Baldwin, June 22, 1969; children: Daniel b. 1971, Robert b. 1980; edn: BA, Univ. of the Pacific 1969; MD, U.A.G. Sch. of Med. 1975. Career: 5th Pathway Pgm. St. Joseph's Hosp. Paterson, N.J. 1975-76; residency internal med. St. Michael's Med. Ctr. Newark 1976-79; ambulatory care ofcr. Letterman Army Med. Ctr., Sharpe Depot, Lathrop, Calif. 1979-80; attg. phys. St. Joseph's and Dameron Hosps., Stockton 1980—; chief of med. St. Joseph's Oak Park Hosp. 1982; bd. dirs. San Joaquin Found. for Med. Care 1984; honors: Recognition Award (United Way 1983-84); mem: Am. Coll. Phys. 1981, San Joaquin Co. Med. Soc., CMA, Stockton Rotary, Pacific Athletic Found., Su Salud (founder, charter mem.); works: founder Su Salud Inc., non-profit orgn. (public svc. TV and radio pgms.) 1983; Catholic; rec: music appreciation, reading. Ofc: 645 Harding Way Ste 5 Stockton 95204

MICHAELSON, ALVIN STUART, lawyer; b. May 13, 1939, Jersey City, N.J.; s. Adrian and Lillian (Schneider) M.; edn: BA, Columbia Coll. 1960; JD, Harvard Law Sch. 1963; admitted N.J. State Bar 1964, Calif. 1969. Career: asst. prosecutor Hudson Co. N.J. 1964-67, trial atty. U.S. Dept. of Justice Anti-Trust Div. L.A. 1967-69; atty. pvt. practice, Los Angeles 1969—; judge pro tem L.A. Mun. Ct. 1983-85; mem: Calif. Attys. for Crim. Justice; Am., Calif., L.A. Trial Lawyers Assns.; Criminal Cts. Bar Assn.; Nat. Assn. Criminal Def. Lawyers; ACLU; Anti-Defamation League; B'nai Brith; Am. Jewish Congress; Am. Jewish Com.; L.A. Museum of Contemp. Art (founder); rec: sports, art, music. Ofc: Michaelson & Levine 1900 Ave of the Stars, Ste. 2512, Los Angeles 90067

MICHAN, ALBERTO, real estate executive; b. June 22, 1957, Mexico City; s. David and Cecilia M.; m. Silvana, Aug. 14, 1982; 1 dau. Natalie b. 1985; edn: BBA cum laude (honors in real estate), CSU San Diego 1979; Calif. lic. real estate broker (1980). Career: comml. and residential real estate profl.; current: broker/ptnr. Usamex Real Estate Services (comml. brokerage), owner/pres. Home Mart Partners (residtl. brokerage), pres. Strata Equity Corp. (R.E. inv. co.), chief finl. ofcr. Blue House Financial (currency exchange), R.E. supv. Dolphin Investments, N.V.; mem. Beta Gamma Sigma, San Diego Tennis & Racquet Club; rec: jog, tennis, soccer, golf, boxing. Res: 5037 Maynard St San Diego 92122 Ofc: USAMEX 3211 Holiday Ct Ste 101 La Jolla 92037

MICHEL, HERBERT LEON, JR., lawyer; b. Nov. 16, 1949, Chgo.; s. Herbert Leon and Helen Ann (Levinthal) M.; edn: BA, UC Los Angeles 1971, JD, Univ. San Diego Sch. of Law 1974; admitted Calif. State Bar 1974. Career: trial atty., senior partner Herbert L. Michel, Jr., A Profl. Law Corp., 1974—; mem: Assn. of Trial Lawyers of Am., Calif., Beverly Hills, Century City, Los Angeles County bar assns.; rec: pvt. pilot, skiing. Ofc: Herbert L. Michel, Jr. APLC, 9911 W. Pico #990, Los Angeles 90035

MICHEL, VICTOR JAMES, librarian; b. Feb. 2, 1927, St. Louis, Mo.; s. Victor James and Bernadette (Fox) M. m. Margaret A. Renaud, Feb. 3, 1951;

children: Dennis W., Daniel J., Catherine A., Denise M.; edn: stu., St. Louis Univ. 1946-48. career: asst. librarian McDonnell Aircraft Corp., St. Louis 1948-55; mgr. Anaheim Information Ctr., Electroncis ps., Rockwell Internat. Corp. 1955–; secty. Placentia Devel. Co. 1964-71; plnng. commdr., Placentia 1957-60, city councilman 1960-70, v.mayor 1960-64, mayor 1964-68; trustee, Placentia Library Dist. 1970-79, pres. 1974-79; city historian, Placentia 1976–, city treas. 1980-; chmn. Placentia Fine Arts Commn. 1978-80; honors: Citizen of the Year, Placentia 1979; mem: Placentia-Tlaquepaque Sister City Orgn. (charter 1964-); St. Louis Browns Fan Club (founder, pres. Placentia chpt.); Calif. Library Assn.; Placentia CofC (v.p. 1960); Placentia Jaycees (hon. life); Calif. and Orange Co. (pres. 1976) Library Assns.; West Atwood Yacht (hon. yeoman emeritus w/ citation 1970, ship's librarian); author: Pictorial History of the West Atwood Yacht Club, 1966; Placentia– Around thWorld, 1970; arts. in profl. journs.; mil: staff sgt. AUS 1945-46; Res: 419 Somerset Dr.,Placentia 92670 Ofc: 3370 Miraloma Ave., Anaheim 92803

MICHELSON, DEAN RICHARD, management consultant; b. May 9, 1946, St. Paul, Minn.; s. Julius Clarence and Elizabeth Dean (Nolan) M.; 1 dau. Heather b. 1979; edn: BA, Univ. Minn. 1968; MA in indsl./ orgnl. psych., Univ. N.Dak. 1971. Career: personnel dir. Jonathan Club, Los Angeles 1972-75; employee rels. mgr. Am. Medicorps, L.A. 1975-76; mgmt. cons. W.C.I.R.A., Santa Clara 1976-81; mgmt. cons. Modern Mgmt. Inc., Chgo. 1981-83; mgmt. cons./ CEO DHS, Inc., San Jose 1983–; adj. prof. DeAnza Jr. Coll. (1979-); bd. dirs. Cut Flower Exchange (1984-85), Women's Community Clinic (1980-85), Hillbrook Sch.; named Cons. of the Year, W.C.I.R.A. (1981); mem. A.H.P., A.P.G.A., O.D. Network; clubs: Jonathan (LA), Decathelon (Santa Clara), CofC (Saratoga, San Jose); creative: toy mfg. "Throw A Fit" TM, Expressworks, Inc. (1984-); mil: capt. US Air Force 1968-72; Republican; rec: tennis, racquetball, ski. Ofc: DHS Inc. POB 2485, 1740 Technology Dr Ste 290 San Jose 95110

MICKEY, NORMAN LEE, social work supervisor, singles dating organization owner; b. Oct. 2, 1939, Antioch, Calif.; s. James Raymond and Jennie Virginia (Moglie) M.; m. Deanna Rolerson, 1961, div. 1968; 1 dau: Cathy, b. 1965; edn: BA, psy., San Jose State Coll. 1964; AA, Diablo Valley Coll. 1959. Career: social wkr. Contra Costa Co. Soc. Svc. Dept., Pittsburg & Pleasant Hill 1964-69, supr. soc. wrk. Contra Costa Soc. Svc. Dept. 1969–; founder/owner/ dir. Video Introductions (singles video dating orgn.), Concord 1977–; mem: Contra Costa Co. Central Labor Council (exec. bd. 1972-75, del. 1970-72); Soc. Svc. Union S.E.I.U., AFL-CIO (Contra Costa Co. chpt., founding pres. 1967-68); Contra Costa Housing Authority tenant appeal referee 71-81; author/ pub. Romantic Reminders (1980), A Modern Alternative (1986). Res: 420 Brookside Dr Antioch 94509 Ofc: Video Introductions, 1810 C Willow Pass Rd Concord 94520

MIDDLEMAS, ARTHUR BLAISDELL, trucking co. consultant; b. Sept. 17, 1921, Helena, Mont.; s. George Noel and Mary Alice (Blaisdell) M.; m. June Claire Kuntz, June 20, 1947; children: Dawn Maree b. 1948, William Cary b. 1956; edn: Long Beach City Coll., USC, 1951-56. Career: locomotive engr. No. Pacific R.R. (now Burlington), Mont. 1946-51; div. mgr. United Parcel Service, L.A. 1951-67; owner/opr. Middlemas & Son Ents., La Habra 1967-81, cons. 1981–; mem. Retired Ofcrs. Assn., Masons; mil: pilot, major US Air Force 1944-46, Reserve 1946-81, Air Medal w/6 clusters, 3 Battle Stars; Republican; Prot.; rec: photog., walking. Res: 710 S Mariposa St La Habra 90631

MIDDLETON, JULIE BARKER, real estate executive; b. Apr. 29, 1946, Peterborough, N.H.; d. Richard Charles and Gertrude Elizabeth (Mueller) Odell; edn: BA, Univ. Denver 1967; MA in journ., Univ. Ill. 1970; Summer Exec. Pgm., USC 1979; Tuck Exec. Pgm., Dartmouth Coll. 1980; Calif. lic. real estate broker 1980. Career: dir. of devel. Rocky Mountain Center on Environ., Denver, Colo. 1970-73; mgr. community & media rels. Atlantic Richfield Co., Denver 1973-74, mem. nat. advt. team, Los Angeles Ofc., 1974-75, dir. Consumer Affairs 1973-77, mgr. Advocacy Response 1977-80; v.p. Cushman Realty Corp., Los Angeles 1980–, mng. dir. Denver ofc. 1981-82; mem: Soc. of Consumer Affairs Profls. (pres. 1976), Orgn. of Women Execs. (v.p. 1981), Am. Petroleum Inst. (chair Environ. Com.), Urban Land Inst.; civic: Calif. Mus. of Sci. & Industry (trustee), Pasadena Heritage Found., Sierra Club, Downtown Denver Inc. 1981, Denver CofC 1981; club: L.A. Athletic; Prot.; rec: ski, backpack, tennis, piano. Res: 370 S Orange Grove Blvd Pasadena 91105 Ofc: Cushman Realty Corp. 333 S Grand Ave 4000 Los Angeles 90071

MIDDLETON, VINCENT FRANCIS, manufacturing co. executive; b. June 24, 1951, N.Y.C.; s. Vincent Aloysius and Mary Hilda (Lehane) M.; edn: BSCE, So. Methodist Univ. 1974; MBA, Golden Gate Univ. 1986; Reg. Profl. Engr. (Civil) Calif. (1977); lic. gen. building and constrn. contractor throughout U.S. Career: structural engr. Bechtel, Inc. 1974-77; project mgr. Fisher Development Inc. 1977-80; constrn. engring. mgr. Ecodyne Cooling Products Co., 1980-81, mgr. of projects 1981, dir. of constrn. 1981-84, mgr. engring. & constrn. Custodis-Ecodyne, Inc., Santa Rosa 1984–; honors: Outstanding Senior Student (1st in Class) So. Meth. Univ. (1974), S.M.U. Grad. Fellowship (1974), Chi Epsilon, Tau Beta Pi, Sigma Tau, Chi Epsilon, Texas Public Works Scholarship; mem: ACI, ASCE, Junior Achievement (bd. dirs.), AASCE, Young Republicans; works: structural concept for New Riyadh Internat. Airport, Saudi Arabia; Republican; Roman Catholic. Res: 1945 Knolls Dr Santa Rosa 95405 Ofc: Custodis-Ecodyne Inc. (POB 1267) Santa Rosa 95402

MIECKE, GARY G., engineer/manager; b. March 22, 1946, Buffalo, N.Y.; s. Erwin A. and Ella (Duell) M.; edn: AA, Los Angeles City Coll. 1972; BA, Cal

Poly Pomona 1976; Reg. Profl. Engr., Calif. Career: engr./mgr. Selective Services Corp. 1972–; cons. engr., pres. Ella/Omni & Co., Inc. (predecessor co. Omni Corp.) 1975–; mem. Inst. of Indsl. Engring.; civic: Easter Seal Found./Orange (research, cons.); mil: sgt. US Army 1967-69; rec: sailing, swimming. Address: Selective Services POB 17697 Los Angeles 90017

MIKALSON, ROY G., college president; b. July 21, 1921, Eureka, Mont.; s. Lawrence and Barbara M.; m. Eva M. Johnson, July 31, 1949; children: Steven A., b. 1950, Barbara G. (Brownstne), b. 1953, Jeffrey R., b. 1949, Thomas L., b. 1960; edn: BA, Univ. Wash. 1947, MA, 1948; PhD, UC Berkeley 1964. Career: instr. Montana Univ., Missoula 1948-49, Lower Columbia Coll., Longview, Wash. 1950-62; Dean of evening coll., Coll. of Marin, Kentfield, Calif. 1964-66; pres. Clackemas Comm. Coll., Oregon City, Ore. 1966-68; pres. Modesto Jr. Coll. 1968-71; pres./supt. Santa Rosa Jr. Coll., 1971–; mem. bd. dirs. YMCA, Family Information Center, Calif. Community Colls. Chief Exec. Officers; mil: Inf. US Army, 1940-45, South Pac., 7 campaigns, 4 decorations; mem. Elks, Rotary Internat., Commonwealth Club; rec: writing, hiking, golf, swimming. Res: 4050 Alta Vista Santa Rosa Ofc: 1501 Mendocino Ave Santa Rosa 95401

MIKKELSEN, JUANITA LESLIE HILL, ranch owner; b. July 4, 1926, Fresno; d. Leopold Pete and Eveline Ily (Osterode) Hill; div.; two children: Sheila Karen, b. 1950; John Paul, b. 1952; edn: Holmby Coll., L.A. 1943-44; lic. real estate sales, Calif. 1965. Career: asst. bookkeeper, Family Creamery 1942-46; co- owner/ mgr. Mikkelsen Butane Co. 1949-62; real estate sales 1965-82; antique shop owner 1970-75; owner/ mgr. rentals 1972 – ; owner/ mgr. ranch 1975 – ; mem: Ladies Oriental Shrine of No. Calif.; Bus. & Profl. Women; Calif. Women for Agric.; Farm Bureau; Nat. Fedn. of Independent Bus.; AQHA; Pacific Coast Quarter Horse Assn.; U.S. Equestrian Team; Senatorial Club; Pres. Task Force; Republican; Episcopal; rec: remodeling/ designing homes, animals, civic affairs. Res: 34600 Road 140 Visalia 93291

MILAZZO, DAVID Y., architect; b. Feb. 27, 1945, Bakersfield; s. Anthony Alfred and Reeba Allen (Young)M.; m. Linda Gold, Aug. 21, 1968; 1 son, David Anthony, b. 1974; edn: AA, Bakersfield Jr. Coll. 970; BA, Cal Poly State Univ.,S.L.O., 1974; cert. Nat. Council of Archit. Reg. Bds. Career: draftsman, designer, Fisher & Wilde Archs., Ventura 1974-75; Ken Sorensen Arch., Bakersfield, 1975-76; prin. ptnr. in charge of design Clement/Milazzo & Assocs., 1976-83; Milazzo & Assocs., Archs., 1983 – ; cons. to City of Bakersfield: Zoning Ordinance Review Adv. Com., Planning Commnr., Redevel. Agcy. Design Rev. Bd.; bd. dirs. Kern River Found.; awards: Golden Empire Chpt./AIA design of excellence (1981), citation (1984), merit (1984), Bakersfield CofC awards for most attractive comml. bldg. (1982, 83, 1984), & comml. landscaping (1982, 83); mem: AIA, (corp.mem.), Golden Empire Chpt.; Downtown Business Assn. (bd. dirs.); Italian Heritage Dante Assn. (bd. dirs.); Pres.'s Assn. of CSU Bakersfield; works: design and constrn. of contemporary arch.; mil: s/sgt USAF 1965-69, Vietnam, France; Republican; Prot.; rec: photog. Res: 2432 Spruce St Bakersfield 93301 Ofc: Milazzo & Assocs., Architects 1200 Truxtun Ave, Ste. 120, Bakersfield 93301

MILES, BRETT MALLORY, manufacturing co. executive; b. Jan. 7, 1955, Clarksville, Tenn.; s. Jack Beam Jr. and Kay (Ford) M.; m. Eleni Deam, May 13, 1984; chilren: Chris (Drakos), b. 1969; Tammy (Drakos), b. 1976; edn: BA, Johns Hopkins Univ. 1977; MS, USC 1983. Career: mktg. rep. Control Data Corp., Newport Beach 1981-84; senior sales rep. California Computer Prods., Anaheim 1985–; exec. v.p. Success Seminars 1983-85, pres. Profl. Success Systems, 1985–; honors: 100% Club (1983-84), Profl. Mktg. Award (1984), Control Data Corp.; Dist. Salesperson of the Year (1985), ranked no. 2 in nat. sales (1985), Marketing Excellence Award (1985), Calif. Computer Products; mem: Sales & Mktg. Execs. of Orange Co., Nat. Speakers Assn., Kiwanis; mil: capt. U.S. Army 1977-81, Parachutist Badge 1977, Disting. Mil. Grad.; Republican (Nat. Com.); rec: basketball, profl. sales tng. Res: 1718 W. Flower St., Fullerton 92633 Ofc: CalComp, 2411 W. La Palma, P.O. Box 3250, Anaheim 92803

MILES, JAMES FREDERICK, co. executive; b. Nov. 5, 1942, El Paso, Tx.; s. James B. and Kathleen (Bogardus) M.; m. B. Lynn, July 9, 1977; children: James b. 1971, Megan b. 1978, Courtney b. 1981; edn: BBA, Univ. of Texas, El Paso 1965. Career: engr./plant traffic depts. Western States Tel., Phoenix, Az. 1965-69; traffic planning dept. Contel Service Corp., Victorville 1969-70; v.p./ gen. mgr. Western States Tel., Phoenix 1970-72; asst. v.p. fin. Contel Service Corp., Bakersfield 1972-75, pres./gen. mgr. Contel of Texas, Dallas 1975-84, pres./gen. mgr. Contel of California, Victorville 1984–; mem: Calif. Tel. Assn. (v.p., bd. dirs.), Texas Tel. Assn. (pres., bd. dirs. 1984), United for Calif. (trustee); Republican; rec: golf, tennis. Ofc: Contel of California 16071 Mojave Dr Victorville 92392

MILES, MICHAEL EDWARD, construction co. sales executive; b. Jan. 28, 1954, Tucson; s. Kenneth James and Mary Genivieve (Milby) M.; m. Constance Watters, Feb. 16, 1980; 1 son, Michael b. 1984; edn: BSCE, Univ. Ariz. 1976; Reg. Profl. Engr., Colo. (1982). Career: plant engr. Pittsburgh-Des Moines Steel Co., Sacto. 1976-77; field engr. PDM Steel Co., Richland, Wash. 1977-79; contracting engr. PDM Steel Co., Santa Clara, Calif. 1979-80; struc. engr. Business Devel., Harrison Western Corp., Denver 1980-82; senior contracting engr. Pitt-Des Moines, Inc., San Mateo 1982-85, dist. sales mgr. 1985–; honors: outstanding senior, Univ. of Ariz. Found. (1975-76), Theta Tau outstanding engring. student (1975-76), Tau Beta Pi (v.p. 1975-76); mem: ASCE, Am. Inst. of Aero. and Astro., Soc. of Am. Mil. Engrs., Am. Inst. of Mining, Metallurg. and Petroleum Engrs.; Republican; United Presbyterian;

rec: golf, ski, guitar, scuba. Res: 116 13th Ave San Mateo 94402 Ofc: Pitt-Des Moines Inc. 66 Bovet Rd Ste 385 San Mateo 94402

MILES, PATRICIA ANN, teacher, businesswoman; b. Oct. 29, 1942, Vicksburg, MS; d. William McKinley and Hazel Lucille Thomas; children: RaJendra b. 1964, Shawndra b. 1972; edn: Bach. Music Edn., Jackson St. Univ. 1963; Pepperdine Univ. 1966-68, CSULA 1966. Career: substitute tchr. Fontana Schools, 1965-72j, Special Edn. tchr./ dept. chair 1970-72; Summer Girl Friday, Kelly Girls, 1966, 1974 – ; acctg., White Front Stores (part-time), 1967; Los Angeles City Schs. Home Tchr. 1974-79; ER Tchr., Jefferson High Sch., Poly Tech, Mulholland Jr. H.S., 1980; Amway Distributor 1982 – ; lectr., A Positive Thinker; beauty cons.; mem: CTA, NEA, UTLA, Delta Sigma Theta Sor., Council of Exceptional Children 1966-72, Music Educators Nat. Conf. 1964-74, National Council Negro Women, Order of the Eastern Star; mil: P.O. USNR/ CINCPAC/ WWMCCS ADP 119, Encino; rec: swimm, travel, helping people. Res: 3727 W. 107th St Inglewood 90303 Ofc: Pat's International, POB 4838, Inglewood 90302

MILKES, MILTON, superior court judge; b. Aug. 19, 1929, Long Beach, Calif.; s. Edward S. and Bella M.; children: Kevin b. 1971, Davida b. 1985, Seth b. 1985; edn: BA, UC Los Angeles 1951; JD, Stanford Sch.of Law 1954; postgrad. Jurisprudence, Univ. of Madrid, Spain 1960. Career: atty. 1960-76; apptd. municipal ct. judge South Bay San Diego Co. 1976; judge superior ct. 1979 – , reelected twice; mem: Calif. Judges Assn.; rec: travel, language. Res: 3032 Spearman Ln Spring Valley 92078 Ofc: Superior Court 220 W Broadway San Diego 92101

MILLER, ALFRED LEE, dairyman, rancher, investment broker; b. Feb. 5, 1924, Ontario, Calif.; s. Ora Lee and Ethel Harriet (Pettitt) M.; m. R. Jacqueline Smith, July 25, 1958; 1 child, Terry b. 1959; edn: BS, animal sci., UC Davis 1950; supv. cert., CSU Sacto. 1952-56. Career: owner/mgr. dairy 1950-74, owner/mgr. cattle ranch 1974 – ; civilian supvr. Electronic Div., Army 1951-59; indep. cons. animal sci., finl. investments; youth advisor 4-H and FFA activities; honors: Dairy of Merit 1964-1974; mem. Calif. State Grange (steward 1978-86), Dairyman Feed and Supply Coop. (bd. dirs. 1962-74), Galt CofC, Calif. Milk Producers (bd. dirs. 1964); publs: research paper, Economic Cycles and their Relation to Investments (1985); mil: pharm. mate 1/c US Navy 1943-46, Good Conduct, Am. Theater, Mid-East Theater w/4 stars, Far-East Theater w/3 stars; Republican; Christian Ch.; rec: gardening, equestrian, consulting. Address: 9650 Harvey Road Galt 95632

MILLER, BUSTER E., private investigator; b. Apr. 2, 1928, National City; s. Thomas Raymond and Rozella Marie (Dean) M.; m. Betty Jo Rodgers, Jan. 22, 1949; children: Judy Lynn b. 1949, Janice Linda b. 1956; edn: AS, Modesto Jr. Coll. 1980; BS, Columbia Pacific Univ. 1986. Career: spl. agent US Army, 1946-48, 1949-53, port security investigator in Bremerhaven, Germany, spl. investigator Provost Marshal's Office in Germany, Korea, and Pittsburg, Calif.; Criminal Investig. Div. (CID), Texas; owner/mgr. Advance Information Research Agcy. (investigations and mgmt. svcs.), Ceres, Calif. current; mem. Calif. Assn. of Licensed Investigators (dist. gov. Sacto. Dist. 1986), Nat. Council of Investig. and Security Services, Calif. Security Mgrs. Assn., Internat. Intell. & Organized Crime Investigators Assn., Nat. Rifle Assn. (cert. Pistol, Rifle and Shotgun instr.); civic: Little League Baseball (sponsor), Lions Internat., Vol. Fire Dept. (boosters), Police Reserve, CofC, Boy Scouts Am. (master); Republican; Prot.; rec: photog. Address: 3200 Vernal Dr Ceres 95307

MILLER, C. DUANE, corporate president; b. Aug. 24, 1941, Tulare; s. Carl D. and Ida Ferne (Martin) M.; m. Cheryl Rae, Mar. 29, 1961; children: Kelli b. 1962, Lori b. 1964, Craig b. 1965; edn: Coll. of the Sequoias 1959-60, Am. Inst. of Banking 1964-69, mgmt. courses 1977. Career: op. supvr. Crocker Citizens Nat. Bank, Tulare 1964-69, American Nat. Bank, Tulare 1969-70; Modesto Terminal mgr. Kings County Truck Lines 1970-75; Fresno Outbound supvr. California Motor Express 1975-77; Tulare Terminal mgr. Systems 99 1977-80; pres./gen. mgr. Tulare Terminal, Cal-Western Transport 1980 – ; Dir: Silver Arrow Express, Regency Transport Inc.; elected City Council ((mayor 1983-), City of Tulare 1979-, mem. Tulare County Economic Devel. (exec. bd.), League of Calif. Cities (transp. com.), Tulare Bd. of Public Utils.; mem. Am. Mgmt. Assn., Elks, Lions, Amvets (life), N.R.A.; mil: airman 1c US Air Force 1960-64, Good Conduct, Turkish Govt. medal; Republican; Prot.; rec: golf. Ofc: Cal-Western Transport 1517 South J St Tulare 93275

MILLER, CHARLES MAURICE, lawyer; b. Sept. 7, 1948, Los Angeles; s. Samuel C. and Sylvia Mary Jane (Silver) M.; m. Terri Senesac, Mar. 25, 1979; children: Samuel, b. 1980, Seth, b. 1982; edn: BA, cum laude, UCLA 1970; USC Law Ctr. 1970-71; JD, Univ. of Akron Sch. of Law 1975; admitted to bar assns. of Supreme Ct. of U.S. 1981, U.S. Dist. Ct. for Central Dist. of Calif. 1977, U.S. Ct. of Appeals Ninth Circuit 1978, Supreme Ct. of Ohio 1975, Supreme Ct. of Calif. 1977. Career: gen. atty. US Dept. of Justice Immigration & Naturalization Svc., Los Angeles 1976-79; owner Law Ofcs. Charles Miller, Studio City 1979 – ; honors: Univ. of Akron Law Review 1973-75, bd. eds., arts. ed. 1974-75; mem: Am. and Los Angeles Co. Bar Assns., Trial Lawyers of Am., Am. Immigration Lawyers Assn., Tau Epsilon Phi; Democrat; rec: computers, tennis. Ofc: Law Ofc. Charles Miller, 12441 Ventura Blvd., Studio City 91604

MILLER, DAVID MEANS, manufacturing co. executive; b. May 18, 1914, Mansfield, La.; s. Harry Alexander and Louise (Means) M.; m. Alice Klauber, Dec. 2, 1942; children: Laurence A. b. 1944, Grace L. b. 1947, David M., Jr. b.

1952; edn: Louisiana St. Univ. 1932-35; MBA, Peppedine Univ. 1976. Career: v.p. Security Title Ins. Co., San Diego 1945-54; v.p. Western Salt Co., S.D. 1954-60, pres. 1960-, also pres. H.G. Fenton Material Co. 1970-, and pres. Pre-Mixed Concrete Co. 1970-, bd. chmn. all 3 cos., 1986 – ; mem. Calif. Mfrs. Assn. (dir.); civic: Rotary, S.D. Mus. of Natural Hist., S.D. Zool. Soc., UCSD Board of Overseers, Sch. of Medicine Assocs., Inst. for Research on Aging; mil: major US Army Anti-Aircraft 1940-45, Soldiers Medal; Democrat; Episcopal; rec: fishing, gardening. Ofc: H.G. Fenton Material Co. POB 64 San Diego 92112

MILLER, DENNIS GENE, manufacturing/ construction co. executive; b. Sept. 25, 1951, Wasco; s. Douris Gene and Theresa Wiepkje (Visser) M.; m. Jeri Darby, Aug. 18, 1973; 1 dau: Jessica, b. 1984; edn: BS, CSU Fresno 1976. Career: transp. splst. Hodges Trucking, Wasco 1976-77; agric. engr. Visser Farms, Wasco 1977; sales, design engr. Thompson and Gill Inc., Madera 1977-85; sales engr. Calif. Mill Equip., Modesto 1985 – ; mem: Calif. Grain and Feed Assn.; Kiwanis; Republican; Protestant; rec: pvt. pilot, golf, scuba. Res: 2614 Greenwood Dr., Madera 93637 Ofc: California Mill Equipment, Modesto

MILLER, DIANE MARIE, financial planner; b. July 18, 1945, Burbank, Calif.; d. Garnett Addison and May Hope (Doeg) Smith; children: Nicole b. 1968, Tony b. 1969; edn: BA, UC San Diego 1972, MA, 1974; Certified Financial Planner 1982. Career: juvenile probation ofcr. San Diego County 1974-78; Conn. Gen. Ins. Corp. San Diego 1978-80; capital growth planning, financial planni S.D. 1980-81; founder, pres. Executive; Financial Planning S.D. 1981 – ; instr. UCSD, Nat. Univ.; cons. Home Federal Trust 1982-84; honors: Probation Volunteer Award (1977), listed Who's Who Am. Women, Personalities of the Southwest; mem: Internat. Assn. Financial Planners, Inst. Certified Financial Planners, UCSD Alumni, Women Bus. Owners, S.D. CofC; Republican; Episcopal. Res: 13754 Recuerdo Dr Del Mar 92014 Ofc: Executive Financial Planning 2250 4th Ave Ste 201 San Diego 92101

MILLER, ELVA RUBY, homemaker, civic worker; b. Oct. 5, 1907, Joplin, Mo.; d. Edward and Ada America (Martin) Connes; m. John R. Miller (decd. 1968), Jan. 17, 1934; student Pomona Coll. p-t 1936-56. Career: entertainer var. night clubs, supper clubs, Hollywood Bowl 1967; TV appearances; rec. artist Capitol Records 1966-, Amaret Records 1969-; appeared in motion pictures; active Girl Scouts USA 1933-58; hon. mem. Mayor's Com. for Senior Citizens L.A. 1966; honors: Thanks Badge (Girl Scouts 1956), Key to City (mayor San Diego 1967), plaque (Dept. of Defense for trip to Vietnam 1967); mem: Gen. Alumni Assn. USC, Repub. Nat. Com. (life), Calif. Repub. Party, Disabled Am. Vets., Commanders Club, Women for the Music Center/Los Angeles, L.A. County Mus. of Art, KCET; Presbyterian; rec: reading (history), cooking. Res: 9585 Reseda Blvd Northridge 91324

MILLER, EMERSON WALDO, accountant, financial and management consultant; b. Jan. 27, 1920, Green Island, Jamaica, W.I., nat. 1957; s. Adolphus Eustace and Catherine Sarah (Dixon) M.; m. Olive Claire Ford, Apr. 10, 1945; children: Cheryll b. 1945, Hellena b. 1947, Emerson b. 1949, Oliver (Rhodes Scholar 1978) b. 1953, Donald b. 1957, Selwyn b. 1960; edn: student Univ. of Toronto Ext. 1938-43, UC Berkeley 1950-61; BS, State Univ. of NY, Albany 1976; BA, Charter Oak Coll. 1979; ACI dip., Inst. of Commerce (London, Eng.) 1941; FAE dip., (cf. MBA/ CPA), Intern. Acct. & Exec. Corp. of Can. 1945; FFCS dip., Faculty of Sec. & Admin. (Guilford, Surrey, Eng.) 1945; ACEA dip., Assn. of Cost. & Exec. Accts. (London) 1982. Career: cost acct. Poirier & Mclane Corp., NYC 1941-42; principal Emerson Miller & Co., Intern. Acct., Chartered, Kingston, Jamaica W.I. 1942-49; lectr., acctg. & bus. law, Jamaica Sch. of Commerce, Kingston, Jamaica W.I. 1945-48; Tax Examiner/ Conferee Internal Revenue Svc., S.F. 1963-64, sect. chief 1965-70, branch chief 1970-84; maj. segment fin. mgmt. activities Gen. Svc. Admin., US Govt., S.F., Credit Com. chmn. 1969-81, treas. 1981 – ; dir. 1982- VARO-SF Fed Credit Union, S.F.; prin. Emerson W. Miller, Tax, Financial, Business & Mgmt. Svcs.; Edn. VP, GSA-SF chpt., Internat. Toastmasters Club 1965-68; instr., govt. acctg., GSA-SF 1966-69; mem. Mgmt. Improvement Com., Fed. Exec. Bd. 1973-74; pres. S.F. chpt. Assn. of Govt. Accts. 1973-74; honors: GSA Special Achiev. Awd. 1969; mem: Am. Acct. Assn.; Nat. Assn. Accts.; Assn. of Govt. Accts. (SF chpt. pres. 1973-74); Am. Mgmt. Assn.; Fin. Mgmt. Assn.; British Inst. of Mgmt.; Am. Judicature Assn.; NY Acad. of Scis.; AAAS; British Social and Athletic Club 1970; Inst. of Commerce (assoc.) 1941; Fellow, Internat. Accts. & Execs. Corp. of Canada 1945; Fellow, Faculty of Sec. & Admin. 1945; Assn. of Cost & Exec. Accts. (assoc.) 1982; Fellow, Royal Economic Soc. 1962; publisher: Classified Buyers Dir. (Jamaica) 1948; rec: gardening, cricket. Res: 505 Coventry Rd Kensington 94707 Ofc: POB 471 Berkeley 94701

MILLER, GAIL F., art gallery owner, b. July 7, 1940, Chgo.; d. Sol and Evelyn R. (Brenner) M.; edn: Univ. Ill. 1959, lab. tech. Cook County Sch. of Medicine 1960-61. Career: biochemist Cook County Hosp., Chgo. 1962-78; founder/ pres. Karen Asher Galleries (paintings and sculpture), Palm Springs 1978 – , representing 9 internat. artists; mem. Register Am. Med. Technician (AMT), Internat. Soc. of Registered Med. Technician (RMTI); Jewish; rec: guitar (fmr. instr.), art, real estate, tennis. Res: 2178 Aurora Dr Palm Springs 92262 Ofc: Karen Asher Galleries 265 S Palm Canyon Dr Palm Springs 92262

MILLER, J. SANFORD, investment banker; b. May 27, 1949, NY, NY; s. Michael and Loretta May (Lindquist) M.; m. Constance Corcoran, Aug. 25, 1979; children: Christine b. 1981, Charlotte b. 1986; edn: BA, Univ. of Va. 1971, MBA Stanford Univ. Grad. Sch. Bus. 1975, JD, Stanford Univ. Sch. of Law 1975. Admitted Calif. State Bar 1975. Career: atty. Pillsbury Madison & Sutro,

San Francisco 1975-78; mgr. Corporate strategy consulting, Bain & Co., Menlo Park 1978-82; v.p. investment banking, Donaldson, Lufkin & Jenrette (NY, NY) 1982-84, senior v.p. Inv. Banking (San Francisco) 1984—; honors: Phi Beta Kappa (1971); mem. St. Francis Hosp., S.F. (Bd. Assocs.); clubs: Olympic (SF), St. Francis Yacht (SF), Union Boat (Boston); Episcopal. Res: 2929 Washington St San Francisco 94115 Ofc: Donaldson, Lufkin & Jenrette One Montgomery St San Francisco 94104

MILLER, JEAN RUTH, librarian; b. Aug. 4, 1927, St. Helena; d. William Leonard and Jean (Stanton) M.; edn: BA, Occidental Coll. 1950; MS, USC 1952. Career: base librarian U.S. Air Force, Wethersfield Edn. 1952-55; post librarian U.S. Marine Corps Air Sta., El Toro 1955-63; data systems librarian Autonetics (later Rockewell Internat.), Anaheim 1963-65; chief librarian Beckman Instruments, Inc., Fullerton 1966—; chmn. Fullerton area scholarship alumni interview program, USC 1974-; adv. commn. library technician program, Fullerton Coll. 1969-; honors: Superior Performance, U.S. Marine Corps Air Sta., El Toro 1957, 1961; mem: So. Calif. Assn. Law Lbirarians; Am. Soc. Info. Sci.; Orange Co. Library A Assn. (past pres.; IEEE; Spl. Libraries Assn. (pres. So. Calif. chpt. 1975-76); author: Bibliography on Electrical Shock Hazards, 1974; Bibliography on Field Air Traffic Control, 1965; Republican. Res: 17901 E. Chapman Ave., Orange 92669

MILLER, JEFFREY CRAIG, manufacturing co. president; b. Jan. 7, 1948, Phila., Pa.; s. Bernard and Sylvia (Weizer) M.; edn BA, cum laude, Glassboro State Coll. 1974. Career: dist. sales mgr., div. sales mgr., national sales trainer I.C.S. 1976-80; dist. sales mgr. throughout Calif. I.C. Systems 1980—; currently, founder/ pres./ chmn. bd. Vital-Link Inc., Encino; mem: Phi Epsilon (pres. 1971); coach Fresno State Womens Gymnastic Team 1979; coach Glassboro State Coll. Gymnastic Team 1971; designed Vital-Link Lifesaving System 1980; mil: E-6 USN; Jewish; rec: windsurfing, flying, diving. Address: 15508 Camarillo St Encino 91436

MILLER, KENNETH RUSSELL, JR., financial planning co. president; b. Mar. 7, 1946, Bellevue, Pa.; s. Kenneth Russell, Sr. and Velma Jean (Barto) M.; edn: LUTC, Life Underwriters Tng. Council 1979; lic: Life, Disability, Health, NASD 6 & 22, Real Estate Sales. Career: radio & TV Announcer 1967-70; trucking indus. mgmt. with AllTrans Express, Watsonville and then whse. mgr. Bekins Moving & Storage, Burlingame -1973; ins. agt. Mass Mutual, San Jose 1973-79; individual financial planning firm, 1979-81; joined Money Concepts, Internat. Inc., 1982-, founder/pres. and finl. planner Money Concepts of Santa Clara County, 1982—; awards: Rookie of Year nom. San Jose Life Underwriters, Presidents Club 1978, Salesman/Year 1982 for USA, Money Concepts Internat., MCI Millionaires Club, MCI Eagles Club, 1983 Opportunity Seminar of the Year Presenter; mem: San Jose Life Underwriters Assn., San Jose Real Estate Board, Internat. Assn. Fin. Planning, Reg. Rep. IFS Capital (Mem. firm NASD); mil: cpl. USMC 1964-67, Vietnam Vet.; Prot.; rec: organic gardening, youth soccer. Res: 1949 Wright Ave Sunnyvale 94087 Ofc: Money Concepts/Santa Clara County, 1434 Wright Ave Sunnyvale 94087

MILLER, LEONARD WILLIAM, insurance broker; b. Oct. 17, 1929, NY, NY; s. Jack Eugene and Hjordis Theresa (Larsen) Miller; m. Mary Ann, Oct. 22, 1971; children: Scott b. 1956, Alison b. 1958, Todd b. 1962, Bryan b. 1965, Maryn b. 1966; edn: BA, San Jose State Univ. 1951; lic. ins. agent and broker. Career: Boston Ins. Co. San Francisco 1952-54; Safeco Ins. Co. L.A. 1954-55; Crum & Forster Ins. Co. L.A. 1955-62; owner Len Miller & Assocs. Tustin 1962—; exec. advis. bd. Calif. City Bank; v.p., dir. MRES UC Irvine; former city councilman Tustin, park commr., water commr.; mem. Profl. Ins. Agents Assn.; clubs: Balboa Bay, Indian Wells Racquet, Magic Island, Silver Circle-Republican Party, 552, Theta Chi; patent: voice calendar; Republican; Presbyterian; rec: tennis, photog., boating, magic. Res: 501 W Edgewater Newport Beach 92661 Ofc: Len Miller & Assocs. 18121 Irvine Blvd Tustin 92680

MILLER, MARY ANN SONIA, insurance agent; b. June 17, 1935, Detroit, Mich; d. Griffith Ray and Sally (Bord) Howell; m. Leonard W. Miller, Oct. 22, 1971; children: Scott b. 1956, Alison b. 1958, Todd b. 1962, Bryan b. 1965, Maryn b. 1966; edn: BA, Wayne State Univ. Career: State Farm Ins., Detroit, Mich.; B.S. Kendall Agcy., Detroit; St. Paul Fire & Marine, Santa Ana, Calif.; co-owner Len Miller & Assoc., Tustin; pres. Assessment Treatment Svc. Ctr.; v.p., bd. dirs. UC Irvine Coll. of Med.; honors: Tustin City Award; mem: March of Dimes (bd.), Pgm. for Women's Found. (bd.), Cystic Fibrosis Guild, So. Coast Repertory, Search Found. (bd.), Orange County Performing Arts, 552 Hoag Hosp.; Republican; rec: skiing, tennis, boating, art. Res: 501 W Edgewater Newport Beach 92661 Ofc: Len Miller & Assoc. 18121 Irvine Tustin 92680

MILLER, MILTON ARNOLD, ophthalmologist; b. Sept. 15, 1929, Eugene, Ore.; s. Ralph E. and Clara Mae (Christopherson) M.; m. Joyce, Dec. 24, 1981; children: Stephen b. 1954, Thomas b. 1957, Lori b. 1959, Meghan b. 1975, Mark b. 1985; edn: BA, Pacific Union Coll. 1952; MS, Loma Linda Univ. 1956, MD, 1957; bd. certified Am. Board of Ophthalmology. Career: pvt. practice ophthalmology; senior ophthalmic surgeon San Antonio Comm. Hosp., Upland and Corona Comm. Hosp., Corona; cons. Copeland Intralens Corp., Cilco Corp.; honors: Alpha Omega Alpha; mem. AMA, Calif. Med. Assn., Am. Acad. Ophthalmology; co-author two books on radial keratotomy; designer of Miller Intraocular Lens (mfd. by Copeland Intralens Corp., NY, NY); mil: capt. US Army Med. Corps 1957-61; Republican; Seventh-day Adventist; rec: golf. Res: 881 St. Andrews Upland 91786 Ofc: 1330 San Bernardino Rd Upland 91786

MILLER, PAUL R., financial executive; b. Dec. 5, 1947, New London, Conn.; s. Jesse R. and Imogene (Kirkwood) M.; m. Constance Groux, Jan. 30, 1971; children: Eric b. 1974, Jason b. 1977; edn: AA, El Camino Jr. Coll. 1972; BS magna cum laude, CSU Long Beach 1973; Certified Public Acct., Calif. 1976. Career: auditor, CPA, Arthur Young and Co., 1974-77; internal auditor Western Region, AMI, Inc. 1978, audit mgr. 1978-79, controller, asst. v.p. 1979-82, v.p./dir. of fin. Raleigh Hills Hosps., Div. AMI, Inc. 1983, v.p./dir. of fin. AMI Ambulatory Centers, Inc. 1983, v.p./chief finl. ofcr. Am. Emergicenters, Inc. 1983-84; v.p./controller Pandick California, Inc., Los Angeles 1984—; mem. Calif. Soc. CPAs; mil: sgt. US Air Force 1966-70; Democrat; rec: golf, fishing, boating. Res: 903 Firmona Ave Redondo Beach 90278 Ofc: Pandick California, Inc. 1900 S Figueroa St Los Angeles 90007

MILLER, PHOEBE AMELIA, computer software marketing consultant; b. Jan. 13, 1948, Evanston, Ill.; d. William Prescott and Elizabeth Helen (Lucker) Miller; edn: BA, honors, Univ. of Wisc. 1970; grad. work, Stanford Univ. 1973; MBA work, Golden Gate Univ. 1978; ICP Sales Tng. 1979. Career: optics analyst Coherent Radiation, Palo Alto 1970-72; engr. Bechtel Inc. 1972-77; asst. div. mgr. Rand Info. Systems, San Francisco 1977-79; sr. mktg. rep. Computer Scis. Corp., S.F. 1979-81; sr. mktg. cons., mgr. VAR/ distbr. Cognos Corp., Walnut Creek 1981—; awards: Cognos Pres.'s Awd., 1982, 83; V.P. Achiev. Club, Computer Scis. Corp. 1981; Awd. of Merit, for tech. contbn., Bechtel Corp.; publs: contbr. Nat. Structural Engring. Conf. 1976. Res: 101 Lombard San Francisco 94111 Ofc: Cognos Corp., 1801 Oakland Blvd, Ste 100, Walnut Creek 94596

MILLER, R. DANIEL, manufacturing co. executive; b. Nov. 23, 1943, Eureka, Kans.; s. Richard Ross and Lillian Bell (Matlock) M.; m. Shirley Kay Robertson, Oct. 2, 1976; edn: BA, CSU Long Beach 1973; MBA, USC 1975. Career: finl. analyst Mattel Toy, Hawthorne 1974-76; vice pres. Metaframe; Mattel Inc., Elmwood Park, N.J. 1977-79; gen. mgr. Marsh Mfg. Inc., Garden Grove 1980-82; gen. mgr. Umpco Inc., Garden Grove 1982—; dir. First Quality Vending, Inglewood (1974e-), Dream Machine, Garden Grove (1985-); cons. Monogram, Morton Grove, Ill. 1979; mil: E5, US Navy (SS); Republican; Catholic; rec: scuba, woodworking. Ofc: Umpco, Inc. POB 5158 12300 Industry St Garden Grove 92645

MILLER, STANLEY RAY, sound system consultant; b. Oct. 25, 1940, Lincoln, Nebr.; s. Maurice Winston and Blanche Fern (Mosier) M.; div.; two children: Cordie Lynne b. 1967, Neil Andrew b. 1971; edn: BA, Kearney State Coll. 1965. Career: founder/pres./chief exec. ofcr. Stanal Sound Ltd., 1962—, cons. engr./ audio mixer for sound systems and concerts; chief live concert mixing engr. for Neil Diamond, 1969-, designed, mfd. and toured large sound systems, worldwide 1964-, has toured sound systems for Simon & Garfunkel, Johnny Cash, Christy Minstrels, Young Americans, Bill Cosby, Mac Davis, Dolly Parton, Pink Floyd, Bob Dylan, John Denver, The Osmond Brothers, Donnie & Marie Osmond, Tom Jones and Englebert Humperdink, 1964-; dir. sound svcs. at the Universal Amphitheatre, Greek Theatre, Pantages Theatre, and the Wilshire Theatre (L.A.), Pacific Amphitheatre (Costa Mesa), Golden Gate Theatre (S.F.), Poplar Creek Music Theatre (Chgo.); respons. for functional design of more than ten different models of Yamaha Sound Mixing Consoles, as well as other Yamaha products for Concert Sound Indus.; lectr. num. colls., Audio Engring. Soc. nat. convs., Altec Sound Contractor Dealer Nat. Tng. Meetings; mem. Audio Engring. Soc. 1958-, Profl. Entertainment Prodn. Soc. (treas.), BPOE Lodge 984; Democrat; Lutheran. Res: 3336 Primera Ave Hollywood 90068 Ofc: Stanal Sound, Ltd., 7351 Fulton Ave N Hollywood 91605

MILLER, STEVEN HENRY, advertising agency owner/executive; b. Jan. 9, 1948, Madison, Wis.; s. LaVerne Henry and LaVona Ella (Hamilton) M.; m. Mary Elizabeth, Aug. 16, 1969; edn: AA, advt. commun., Madison Area Coll. 1968; spl. courses No. Ariz. Univ. 1975, Kimball Art Ctr., Park City, Utah 1978, Center for Humanistic Devel., Aspen, Colo. 1980. Career: staff artist J. Jerred Advt., Madison 1968-72; internat. mgr. Rath Mfg., Janesville, Wis. 1972-76; art dir./designer Bruneau Studios, Phoenix, Ariz. 1976-78; senior art dir. Gilliam Advt., Salt Lake City, Utah 1978-81; v.p. Willis Advt., Newport Beach 1981-83; CEO Miller & Miller Advt., Huntington Beach 1983—; chmn. bd. dirs. St. Albans Assn. 1982-85; advertising judge D.E.C.A., Calif. Awards Competition (1986); awards: Marsy Award, Am. Mktg. Assn. (1983), gold, silver awards, Utah Advt. Fedn. (1978, 79, 80), Golden Orange, Orange Co. Advt. Fedn. (1982), awards of excellence & merit, Bus. Profl. Advt. Assn. West Awards (1985), award of excellence, Orange Co. Advt. Fedn. (1986); mem. Nat. Advt. Agency Network 1978-81, Utah Advt. Fedn. 1978-81, Orange Co. Advt. Fedn. 1981-; civic: Orange County Arts Alliance (chmn. Design Discipline), O.C. CofC, Indsl. League of O.C., Newport Harbor CofC, Huntington Beach CofC; Republican; rec: astronomy, basketball, jogging. Ofc: Miller & Miller Advertising Design 3661 Bear St Ste C Santa Ana 92704

MILLER, THOMAS EUGENE, legal editor, author; b. Jan. 4, 1929, Bryan, Texas; s. Eugene Adam and Ella Lucille (Schroeder) M.; edn: BA, Texas A & M Univ. 1950; MA, Univ. of Texas 1956, JD, 1966; postgrad. work Univ. of Houston 1956-58, UC Berkeley Ext. 1984; admitted Texas State Bar 1966. Career: research tech. Univ. of Texas M.D. Anderson Hosp. and Tumor Inst., Houston 1956-58; claims examiner trainee Social Sec. Adminstrn., New Orleans 1964; trademark examiner trainee Patent Office, Dept. of Commerce, Wash DC 1966; ed. Bancroft-Whitney Co., San Francisco 1966—; honors: Phi Eta Sigma (1947), Texas A&M Scholarship Honor Soc. (1950), Phi Kappa Phi (1950), Psi Chi (1952), Disting. Student (1947-50); mem. Am. Bar Assn., Texas Bar, Nat. Writers Club, Commonwealth Club of Calif., Press Club of San Francisco; civic: Common Cause, ADA, Independent Action; author book pub.

under pseudonym (Libra Pubs.); Democrat (Nat. Com. 1981-86); Methodist; rec: travel, music, theater. Res: 2293 Turk Blvd Apt 5 San Francisco 94118 Ofc: Bancroft-Whitney Co 301 Brannan St San Francisco 94107

MILLETT, ARCHIE HERMAN, research scientist; b. Apr. 27, 1924, Lovell, Wyo.; s. Archie Calvin and Mary Isabelle (Asay) M.; m. Margaret Beck, Sept. 20, 1945; children: Cheri b. 1946, Carolyn b. 1948, Diana b. 1951, Becky b. 1954, Steven b. 1956, Bret b. 1961; edn: BS, Brigham Young Univ. 1951. Career: aircraft electrician (civil service), Hill Field, Ogden, Utah 1942-43; farmer, sole prop., inventor, 1951-72; ptnr. in large comml. greenhouse bus., Sacto. 1972-79; owner/opr. Millett's Mfg. Co., Davis 1956–; staff research assoc. (Fresh Market Tomato Breeding) UC Davis 1956–; cons. Calif. Greenhouse Growers, 1972-80; honors: Spl. Performance Award, Univ. Calif. (1981); civic: Vol. Fire Dept. (1959-73); research: assisted in devel. 13 varieties of tomatoes or peppers (tomatoes: Sequoia, 1959; Imperial, 1959; Earliana F-56, 1959; Pakmor, 1967; Calmart, 1967; Royal Red Cherry, 1977; Short Red Cherry, 1977; T175 hybrid, 1977; Cali Grande hybrid, 1977; Tomato resistant to 7 major diseases to be released 1986; peppers: Caloro Yellow Wax, 1967; Garden Sunshine Bell, 1982; spinach: Califlay, 1961); inventions sold commercially: Millett's Wet Vegetable Seed Separator, Pollen Collector, Flower Emasculator, misc. Plant Breeding Tools; contbr. research papers in agri. jours.; mil: US Army 1944-45, Purple Heart; Ch. of Jesus Christ of Latter-Day Saints (bishop 1979-85). Res: 921 Craig Pl Davis 95616

MILLIGAN, NITA RAMONA, real estate/ mineral, oil and gas broker; b. Oct. 25, 1929, Union City, Okla.; d. George S. and Reta Jane (Cook) Howard; m. Caleb Ross Milligan, Mar. 28, 1963; edn: spl. courses, Anthony Schools, USC, Bakersfield Coll.; Calif. lic. Mineral, Oil & Gas Broker (1982), Real Estate Broker (1979), Gen. Building Contractor lic. Class B (1984). Career: Texas to Bakersfield, Ca. in 1948; mgr. Stan's Drive-In, 1960; mgr. Freddie's Skyway House Restaurant 1960; owner of Ramada franchise: Ramada Inns of Am., La Ramada Restaurant 1965; owner of Hilton franchise: Hilton Inns of Am., Ambassador Rest. 1972; owner of Roadway franchise: Roadway Inns of Am., Regency Rest. 1977; real estate sales assoc. Paul Jacobs Myers, Bksfld. 1979, Community Mktg. Inc., Bksfld. 1980, Mr. Ken Colley, Tehachapi 1981; currently real estate broker Great American Mktg., and mineral oil & gas broker Paris Energy, Bakersfield; honors: recogn., Nat. Found. March of Dimes 1976, Kern County Shrine Club 1974, Advertising Club of Kern Co. 1976, Junior Achievement 1974, 75; mem: Am. Assn. of Petroleum Landmen, Bakersfield Assn. Petroleum Landmen; Nat., Calif. Assn. of Realtors, Bakersfield Bd. of Realtors; Republican; Presbyterian; rec: golf, swim, bowling. Res: 937 Panorama Dr Bakersfield 93305 Ofc: Paris Energy, POB 1569, Bakersfield 93301; Great American Marketing, POB 1569, Bakersfield 93301

MILLS, EUGENE SUMNER, college president; b. Sept. 13, 1924, West Newton, Ind.; s. Sumner Amos and Lela (Weatherly) M.; m. Dorothy Frances Wildman, Oct. 22, 1945; children: David Walden, Sara Anne; edn: AB, Earlham Coll. 1948; MA, Claremont Grad. Sch. 1949, PhD, 1952; postgrad. Harvard Univ. 1958-59; LLD, N.H. Coll. 1979. Career: instr. psychology Whittier Coll. 1950-52, asst. prof. 1952-55, assoc. prof. 1955-60, prof. psychol. 1960-62, dept. chmn. 1952-62; prof. psychol. Univ. N.H., Durham, 1962-79, chmn. dept. 1962-65, dean Grad. Sch. and coordinator research, 1963-67, dean Coll. Liberal Arts, 1967-70, acad. vice pres., 1970-71, provost, 1971-74, provost, acting pres., 1974, pres., 1974-79; pres./ prof. psychology Whittier Coll., 1979–; vis. prof. Univ. Victoria (BC) summers 1958, 60; bd. dirs. Elderhostel, Inc. 1977-, chmn. 1985; bd. dirs. Independent Colls. of So. Calif. 1979-; exec. com. Western College Assn. 1985-; trustee Southwest Mus. 1979-82; awards: Danforth Found. grantee 1956-57, NSF grantee, 1963-66, Sigma Xi, Phi Kappa Phi, Omicron Delta Kappa; mem: Fellow Am. Psychol. Assn., Western Psychol. Assn., Eastern Psychol. Assn., N.H. Psychol. Assn. (pres. 1969-70, dir. 1967-70), Town Hall of Calif., LA Area Council BSA (exec. bd. 1981-), past bd. dirs. N.H. Council on World Affairs 1976-79; clubs: California, Los Angeles; author: George Trumbull Ladd: Pioneer American Psychologist (1969), arts. in profl. jours.; Quaker. Res: 13952 Summit Dr., Whittier 90602 Ofc: Whittier Coll. 13206 Philadelphia St Whittier 90608

MILLS, L. BRUCE, physician; b. Jan. 22, 1951, Huntington, W. Va.; s. Troy and Imogene (Kirk) M.; edn: BS, cum laude, Yale Coll. 1972; MD, Stanford Univ. Sch. of Medicine 1979. Career: residency Stanford Univ. Dept. Dermatology, 1979-83, research fellow 1979-81; dermatologist in pvt. practice, San Francisco currently; awards: Nelson Paul Anderson lectr. Pacific Dermatol. Assn. (1980), fellowship awards Stanford Univ. Sch. Medicine (1979-81), Nat. Psoriasis Found. (1980-81); contbr. articles (6) in med. jours.; rec: microcomputers. Ofc: L. Bruce Mills, M.D. 450 Sutter St Ste 2304 San Francisco 94108

MILLS, TOM NELSON, administrator/ psychotherapist; b. Sept. 30, 1938, Konawa, Okla.; dec. May 9, 1985, Fontana, Calif.; s. Robert Alvin and Mary Emma (Brinlee) M.; m. Hannelore Schmidt, May 24, 1969; children: Eric, b. 1972; Jessica, . 1975; edn: BA, CSU Fullerton 1965; MSW, Fla. State Univ. 1970; PhD, United States Internat. Univ., San Diego 1980; LCSW, Calif. 1971; Lic. Marriage, Family & Child Counselor 1970. Career: psychiatric techn. State of Calif. Metropolitan State Hosp., Norwalk 1959-61, 1963-65; psych. soc. wk. splst. U.S. Army 1961-63; soc. svc. wkr. Co. of Riverside, Corona 1965-66; supvg. soc. wkr. Residential Treatment Ctrs. So. Calif. 1966-68; psych. soc. wkr. State of Calif. Dept. Soc. Welfare, Upland 1970; exec. dir. counseling & psychotherapy Tom N. Mills & Assocs., Upland 1971-79; exec. dir./ psychotherapist Tom N. Mills, Ph.D. Consulting, Upland 1979-84; pres. TLM Assocs. Consultants, Upland 1984-85; adminstr. Kaiser- Permanente Dept. of Psychiatry, Fontana 1970-85; counselor, psychotherapist and consultant in pvt. practice 1971-85, mgmt. cons. 1979-85, cons. child care residential pgms. 1967-85; chmn. Adminstv. Review & Referral Com., Peer Review/ Quality Assurance Com., Kaiser Premanente 1982-85; chmn. Eligibility Review Com. 1982-84; mem. Regl. Mental Health Task Force; awards: VA Traineeship 1968-69, USPH grantee 1969-70; mem: Nat. Registry of Health Car Providers; Kaiser- Permanente Mgmt. Assn.; Upland Sch. Dist.; City of Upland Parks & Recreation Com.; Calif. Sch. Bds. Assn.; AYSO; research: computer applications in mental health, mental health svc. delivery sys., provision of emergency psychiatric svcs; mil: sp5, US Army 1961-62, GCM; Democrat; Baptist; rec: golf, tennis, writing. Address: Upland 91768

MILNER, HOWARD M., real estate broker/developer; b. Sept. 21, 1937, Los Angeles; s. David and Rose (Devron) M.; children: Mara Lynn b. 1967, Debra Faye b. 1971; edn: AA, L.A. City Coll. 1957; cert. in real estate, UCLA 1962; Calif. lic. Real Estate Broker. Career: senior store planner Broadway Dept. Stores 1959; exec. dir./property mgmt. Palm Properties, 1960; nat. real estate dir. Fotomat Corp. 1968; dir. of real estate Copper Penny Coffee Shops, 1970; v.p./dir. real estate & constrn. Jerry Lewis Cinema Theatres, 1972; real estate broker/devel. prin. Milner Properties, Los Angeles 1980–; v.p./investment adv./bd. dir: Swiss Am. Finl. Corp. (Geneva), HESA Global Investments Ltd. and HESA Global Mortgage Corp., 1980-85; prop. mgr. Hersch and Co., Los Angeles, 1985, mng. dir. for multi-unit apt. bldgs. and K-Mart Shopping Ctrs. throughout U.S.; pres./CEO Lyons Internat. Inc. and Lyons Internat. Devel. Co. (entertainment, motion picture, R.E. devel. conglomerate) 1986; lectr. var. profl. orgns.; mem. L.A. Mayor's comml. devel. com.; honors: Eagle Scout, BSA (1952), Ford Motor Scholar (Arch.); mem: Am. Inst. of Indsl. Engrs., Am. Soc. of Mil. Engrs., Internat. Council of Shopping Centers, A.I.A., Toastmasters, Shriner, 32 deg. Mason, Scottish Rite, City of Hope (life); mil: US Army Corps of Engrs. 1957-59; rec: jogging, racquetball, golf. Ofc: Howard M. Milner 9200 Sunset Blvd Ste 820 Los Angeles 90069

MILO, MORYT NATALIE, pension administration executive; b. July 6, 1953, N.Y.C.; d. Zachary and Claire Sylvia (Cohen) Milo; m. Raymond Budriunas, May 9, 1952; edn: BA in sociol., cum laude, Case Western Reserve Univ. 1975. Career: student coordinator Case Western Reserve Univ., Cleveland, Ohio 1975-76; tech. asst. Pension Adminstrn., FM Financial, Los Angeles 197-80; pension mgr. Federated Profit Systems, San Jose 1981-82; v.p./prin. Creative Benefit Services, 1982–; honors: Spl. postgrad. pgm. in sociol. in junior year, Case Western Reserve; mem. Am. Soc. Pension Actuaries; Republican; rec: creative writing, piano, tennis. Res: 120 Saratoga Ave #85 Santa Clara 95051 Ofc: Creative Benefit Services 2025 Gateway Pl #85 Santa Clara 95110

MILTON, JUDITH ANN, computer consultant; b. Mar. 8, 1957, San Francisco; d. Robert Elwin and Gwin (Miller) M.; m. Peter Challinger, June 9, 1984; 1 son, Michael b. 1985; edn: BS in computer sci., CSU Sacramento 1983, grad. work CSUC. Career: software engr. Sound Imaging Inc. Folsom 1982-83; software engr. Grass Valley Group, Inc. 1984; owner Computer Image Consultants, Grass Valley 1985–; honors: Upsilon Pi Epsilon (chpt. pres. 1982), Golden Key Nat. Hon. Soc.; mem. IEEE, Assn. for Computing Machinery, Soc. of Motion Picture and T.V. Engrs.; Republican; Episcopal; rec: tennis, gardening, travel. Ofc: Computer Image Consultants POB 2108 Grass Valley 95945

MINDELL, EARL LAWRENCE, nutritionist, author; b. Jan. 20, 1940, St. Boniface, Manitoba, Can.; s. William and Minerva Sybil (Galsky) M.; m. Gail Jaffe, 1971; children: Alanna, b. 1972; Evan Louis Ashley, b. 1976; edn: BS, pharmacy, ND State Univ.; PhD, nutrition, Univ. of Beverly Hills 1980. Career: pres. Kis Min Inc. 1965-71; secty./ treas. Natural Organics Inc. 1971–; pres. Adanac Mgmt. Inc. 1979–; bd. dirs. Nat. Bancorp. 1981-; Dale Carnegie instr.; bd. dirs. Western L.A. Regl. CofC; awards: L.A. City Proclamation Awd. of Achiev. 1981; mem: Masons, Scottish Rite, Shrine, Kappa Psi pharm. frat., Am. Nutrition Soc., Nat. Health Fedn., Am. Pharmaceutical Assn., Calif. Pharmacists Assn. (charter), Am. Acad. of Gen. Practice of Pharmacy, Internat. Coll. of Applied Nutrition, Nutrition Found.; author: Earl Mindell's Vitamin Bible, (nat. best seller) (Warner Books 1980, paperback reprint 1981); Earl Mindell's Vitamin Bible For Your Kids (Rawson-Wade, paperback reprint, Bantam Books 1982); Earl Mindell's Quick and Easy Guide to Better Health (1982); Earl Mindell's Pill Bible (Bantam Books 1984); Earl Mindell's Shaping Up With Vitamins (Warnerbooks 1985); rec: antique collecting, racquetball, golf. Address: Adanac Management Inc., 709 N Hillcrest Rd Beverly Hills 90210

MINKOW, BARRY JAY, company president; b. Mar. 22, 1966, Los Angeles; s. Robert Irwin and Carole Marie (Winkelman) M. Career: pres., owner ZZZZ Best, Inc., Reseda, Calif. 1981–; began co. at age of 15 in his garage, today it encompasses 8 locations servicing from San Francisco to San Diego and beyond, it is one of the 5 largest cos. of its sort in Am. and the largest in Calif.; instr. seminars L.A. Valley Coll. 1985-; honors: L.A. Dist. & Region IX Young Entrepreneur (1986), Commdn. from Mayor Bradley (1985); mem: Reseda CofC, Conejo Valley CofC, San Diego CofC, Soc. of Cleaning Techs., SBA, ACE; supporter West Valley Family YMCA, AFAM Ariz., Mex. Relief Fund; Republican; Jewish; rec: weight-lifting, little league asst. coach. Ofc: ZZZZ Best Inc., 7615 Darby Ave Ste 206 Reseda 91335

MINOR, HAROLD MARVIN, insurance agent, broker; s. Lionel E. and Juanita C. (Carlisle) M.; m. Teddi Minor, May 10, 1975; children: Hal b. 1960, Sonja b. 1962, Russell b. 1967; edn: Univ. Calif. 3 yrs. Career: agent Allstate Ins. Co. 1966-67, Sentry Ins. 1967-70, gen. sales mgr. 1970-76; pres. Watrons McClory & Minor Ins. 1976-80; pres., owner Minor Ins. Agcy. Inc. 1980–;

sales tng. instr. Sentry Ins. 1970-76; adv. council Aetna Ins., Zurich Ins. Co.; honors: Man of the Yr. (Sentry Ins. 1969-70), other prodn. awards; mem: Profl. Ins. Agents, Independent Ins. Agents, Kiwanis, United Way (campaign chmn., dir.); mil: ssgt. USAF 1954-66, youngest AF recruiter at age 20; Republican; Baptist; rec: golf. Res: 7844 Jon Way Roseville 95678 Ofc: Minor Ins. Agcy. Inc. 11294 Coloma Rd Ste D Rancho Cordova 95678

MINOR, ROBERT H., court reporter, ret.; b. June 6, 1918, San Jose; s. Orval L. and Lilias Anne (Vining) M.; m. Martha Campbell, July 25, 1942; children: Richard W. b. 1943, Thomas A. b. 1946, Trudy J. b. 1956; edn: AA, San Jose State Coll. 1938. Career: clerk Work Projects Adminstrn (WPA), San Jose 1939-41; stenographer Fed. Bureau Investig., San Francisco 1941-45; court reporter, Stenotype Reporting Co., S.F. 1945-46, Moore & Minor Court Reporters, San Jose 1947-64, official reporter Santa Clara County Superior Court, San Jose 1964-80; mem: Calif. Court Reporters Assn. (pres. 1955), Santa Clara County Superior Court Reporters (pres. 1970-73) Santa Clara Court Reporters Assn. (pres. 1972-75), Retired Public Employees Assn. (bd. dirs., historian, San Jose chpt.), Palo Alto Historical Assn., Elks; mil: yeoman 2/c USNR 1943-44; Republican; Episcopal; rec: home recording. Res: 601 Marion Ave Palo Alto 94301

MINUDRI, REGINA URSULA, librarian, consultant, lecturer; b. May 9, 1937, San Francisco; d. John C. and Molly (Halter) M.; edn: BA, San Francisco Coll. for Women 1958; MLS, UC Berkeley 1959. Career: reference librarian Menlo Park Public Library, 1959-62; regional librarian Santa Clara County Library, 1962-68; project coordinator Fed. Young Adult Library Services Project, Mountain View 1968-71; dir. profl. services Alameda County Library, 1971, asst. county librarian, 1972-77, library dir. Berkeley Library, 1977–; lectr. Univ. San Francisco, 1970-72, UC Berkeley, 1977-81; cons., 1975–; mem. ALA (pres. 1986-87, exec. bd. 1980-87, council 1979-87, Grolier award 1974), Calif. Library Assn. (pres. 1981, council 1965-69, 79-82), LWV (dir. Berkeley chpt. 1980-81); author: Getting It Together, A Young Adult Bibliography (1970); contbr. to School Library Jour., Wilson Library Bull. Ofc: 2090 Kittredge St., Berkeley 94704

MIRJAHANGIR, FRANK FAROKH, consulting engineer; b. June 15, 1942, Tehran, Iran; s. Habib and Malek (Afrashtem) M.; m. Maureen Hicky, Dec. 1971; children: Michael b. 1972, Christopher b. 1974, Patrick b. 1979; edn: MBA, CSU Long Beach 1971; BS in C.E., Cal Poly Pomona 1966. Career: owner Amiran Const. Co.; civil structural engr. Bechtel Corp., Norwalk 1966-69; asst. civil engr. City of Long Beach 1970-71; struc. plancheck engr. County of Ventura 1972-73; chief struc. plancheck engr. City of Huntington Beach 1973-82; currently cons. engr., civil struc. engring.; past pres. Huntington Beach Municipal Employees Assn.; listed Who's Who in Orange County; civic: Kiwanis Internat.; Republican; rec: fishing, skiing. Address: 5942 Brassie Circle Huntington Beach 92649

MIRZA-MOGHADAM, ALEXANDER VICSON, research engineer; b.Oct. 18, 1956, Elizabeth, NJ; s. Victor Alexander and Germaine Malick (Davoud-Nejat) M.; edn: BSME, UC Santa Barbara 1979; MSME, UC Berkeley 1980; PhDME, UCLA 1986; Reg. Profl. Engr., Calif. and Penn. Career: gas turbine devel. engr. Solar Turbines Inc., San Diego 1980-81; research engr. Penn. State Univ. Applied Research Lab., University Park, Penn. 1981-83; research engr. UCLA Sch. of Egrs. & Applied Sci., Los Angeles 1983–; mathematics instr., Penn. State Univ. 1982-83; mem. Jr. Achiev. pgm., San Diego 1980-81; honors: mech. engring. scholarship, Getty Oil Co., UC Santa Barbara 1977-78; mem: Am. Soc. Mech. Engrs., Am. Inst. Aero. & Astro., ASM, Am. Inst. Chem. Engrs., UCLA Internat. Stu. Club (organized soccer team 1983), Semi-Profl. Los Angeles Soccer Team Bahman (SCPSL); works: Heat Transfer Conf. presentation, Denver, Colo. 1985, Miami Beach, Fla. 1985; thesis presented, Internat. Heat Transfer Conf. 1986; Iranian Christian; rec: athletics, internat. rels. Res: 3625 Glendon Ave. #105, W. Los Angeles 90034 Ofc: UCLA, Box 256- 308 Westwood Plaza, W. Los Angeles 90024

MISKUS, MICHAEL ANTHONY, electrical engineer; b. Dec. 10, 1950, East Chicago, Ind.; s. Paul J. and Josephine (Forstra) M.; m. Jeannie Ellen Dolmanni, June 24, 1949; edn: BS, elect. engring. tech., Purdue Univ. 1972; cert. mgmt. Ind. Central Coll. 1974, cert. mgmt. Ind. Univ., Purdue Univ., 1975. Career: maint. mgr./supr. Diamond Chain Co., Indpls. 1972-76; plant and primary elec. engr. Johnson Baby Products Co., Park Forest South, Ill. 1976-81; plant engr. Sherwin-Williams, Emulsion Plant, Chgo., Ill. 1981-82; prin. Miskus Consultants, Industrial and Commercial Electrical Consultants, Olympia Fields, Ill.; staff facilities engr., acting director plant engring. Bourns Inc., Riverside 1982–; instr., elect. tech. pgms., Moraine Valley Comm. Coll., Prairie State Coll., 1978; recipient P & Q Cost Reduction Award 1983, Bourns Inc., "Utility Rate Analysis"; mem: IEEE, Industrial Applications Soc., Indsl. Electronics & Control Soc. (sr.), Assn. of Energy Engrs., Illumination Engrs. Soc. of North Am., Internat. Platform Soc.; research: electrostatic precipitator, Purdue Univ. 1971-72; Republican; Lutheran; rec: skiing, sailing. Res: 5215 Glenhaven Ave Riverside 92506 Ofc: Miscon Assocs., POB 55353 Riverside 92517; Bourns Inc., 1200 Columbia Ave Riverside 92507

MISTRY, DHANSUK VITHALDAS, manufacturing co. president; b. July 9, 1927, Bilimora, Gujarat, India; s. Vithaldas Govindji and Deokorben Vithaldas Mistry; m. Bhanu, Dec. 2, 1948; children: Rohit b. 1950, Jayant b. 1952, Nermant b. 1954; edn: GD, Sirj.J. Inst. of Applied Arts 1948. Career: founder, owner Mishban Design Studio, Bombay 1948; creative dir. S.F. & Partners, England 1963-64; mktg. & prod. mgr. Eng. 1964-68; co-dir. Aquilla Plastics, Eng. 1968-70; founder, CEO Jayco Plastics Ltd., Eng. 1971–, Orange, Calif.

1978–; vis. lectr. Art Inst. Bombay 1952-55; honors: 1st, 2nd, 3rd Prize winner Art in Industry Show (1947); mem: Am. Svc. To India (trustee, dir.), SRV Sharda Ramakrishna Vivekananda NY (trustee, dir.), Gujarati Soc. (com. mem.); works: developed ind. laminates component- Compratex 1965; Vedantist; rec: classical music. Res: 543 Loyola Dr Placentia 92670 Ofc: Jayco Plastics of Calif., Inc., 507 W Blueridge Ave Orange 92665

MITA, JOYCE AIKO, government real estate loan specialist; b. June 20, 1946, San Francisco; d. David Kiyoshi and Shizu (Negishi) Yamakawa; m. Roy Mita, Sept. 17, 1977; children: Ryan b. 1980, Allison b. 1983; edn: BA, Univ. Calif. 1972, var. real estate courses, 1975-; Calif. lic. R.E. Broker 1981. Career: equal employment opportunity asst. Dept. HEW 1973; realty techn. Dept. HUD 1974-76, HUD mgmt. intern, Region IX 1976-77, HUD loan mgmt. ofcr., San Francisco 1977–; workshop leader Housing Issues, Nat. Conf. of Asian Americans (6/78), public speaker for HUD, 1977-; elected EEO Counselor, HUD Region IX (1979-80); awards: UC Alumni Assn. Scholar (1964), UC Honor Soc. (1965); civic: active in PTA, Employee Union, Community Food Coop., church, youth work; vol. housing cons. var. non-profit orgns.; Democrat; Methodist; rec: sewing (design/sew children's wear), aerobics. Res: 336 Oleander Ave Alameda 94501 Ofc: Dept. of HUD 450 Golden Gate Ave San Francisco 94102

MITCHELL, DARNELL, photographer, educator; b. Oct. 7, 1941, Cleveland, Ohio; s. John and Beatrice (Parsons) M.; m. Loretta C., Nov. 26, 1966; children: Leslie b. 1968, David b. 1972; edn: BFA, Ohio Univ. 1965; grad. New York Inst. Photog. 1981-82; cert. photog. Famous Photogs. 1975, Nikon Sch. Photog. 1979; Calif. Comm. Colls. tchg. cred. 1976. Career: photog. City of Cleveland, 1964; chief photog. Inst. of Regional Devel., Athens, Ohio 1965; freelance pub. rels. photog., radio/t.v. announcer for Ohio Univ. in Cleveland, O. and in So. Calif., 1965; photog. US Army 1966-68; chief photog. City of Cleveland, 1968-69; pub. rels. photog. Dept. of Recreation, Long Beach 1970-73; chief photog. Charles R. Drew Med. Sch., 1973-76; prof. photog. (dept. hd.) Compton Comm. Coll., 1976–; honors: finalist Olympic Trials-800m (1964, 68), All Army World Record Distance Medley Relay Team (9:33.4), Ohio Univ. Hall of Fame (1979), trackman in All-Mid Am. Conf. (1962-65) and MAC winner of the 880 & the mile races (1962), mem. Ohio Univ. MAC x-c Championship team (1965), and set new Am. record 800 meter event (1:47.6); Tchr. of the Year, CCC (1985), apptd. photog. and fine arts advisor 1984 L.A. Olympics Adv. Com.; mem. Profl. Photogs. of Am., Profl. Photogs. of Calif., Assn. of Internat. Photogs., Profl. Magazine Photogs. of Am., Nat. Assn. Photo Instrs.; works: research & grant appl. resulting in $50,000 photo equip. for coll.; mil: cpl. US Army 1966-68, Vietnam, Good Conduct Medal; Republican; Baptist; rec: photog., track, scuba. Res: 6739 Harbor Ave Long Beach 90805 Ofc: Compton College 1111 E Artesia Blvd Compton 90221

MITCHELL, EARL LAMONT, corporate president; b. Feb. 12, 1912, Sacramento; s. John Wesley and Hilda Maude (Schvalle) M.; m. Doris Aagaard Becker, Sept. 14, 1934; children: Earl, b. 1937; Mary, b. 1940; Jean, b. 1944; att. Jr. Coll. 2 years. Career: Pacific Coast sales rep. Scovill Mfg. Co., San Francisco 1932-45; pres./ treas. Mitchell Ent. Inc., owner State Plumbing & Heating Supplies, San Carlos 1942–; mem: Assn. of US Army (civilian status); Elks; Spy Glass Hill Golf Club; Palo Alto Hill Golf & Country Club; No. Calif. Seniors Golf Club; Senior Assn. NCGA; Seniors Assn. of Am.; Republican; Christian Science; rec: golf, work. Res: 3950 Sand Hill Rd Woodside 94062 Ofc: State Plbg. & Htg. Supplies, 1000 American San Carlos 94070

MITCHELL, MICHAEL CHARLES, lawyer; b. Feb. 13, 1947, Los Angeles; s. Dominic Chester and Dorothy Marie (Dolmage) M.; m. Ingrid Burkard, June 21, 1969; children: Daniel b. 1974, Alicia b. 1974; edn: BA, Loyola Univ., L.A. 1969; JD, Loyola Univ. Sch. of Law 1972; admitted to Calif. State Bar 1972. Career: law clerk Hanna & Morton, Los Angeles 1970-72; assoc. atty. 1972-79; partner Anglea & Burford, Pasadena 1979-82; counsel for Appellee, Darusmont v. United States, US Supreme Ct. 1980; sr. partner MacFarlane, Lambert & Mitchell, Pasadena 1982-85; legal advr. Lions Eye Found. of So. Calif. 1978-; legal advr. L.E.F. Meml. Trust 1980-; area chmn. Scout- O- Rama, San Gabriel Valley Council, Boy Scouts of Am. 1982, 83; bd. dirs. Escalon (sch. for developmentally disabled students in Altadena & Pasadena) 1985 –; pro bono legal counsel for The Dorland Mountain Colony, The Lions Eye Found. Meml. Trust, The Lions Eye Research Ctr., Pasadena Lions Philanthropy Corp.; legal advr. Tournament of Toys & Star News Charities; trustee Pasadena Lions Meml. Trust; awards: Distng. Svc. Awd., Pasadena Jaycees 1982; mem: Am., Calif., Los Angeles Co. & Pasadena Bar Assns.; Phi Alpha Delta; Pasadena Lions Club (pres 1980-81); Pasadena Tournament of Roses Assn.; Arcadia Elks Club; Pasadena CofC; Pasadena Univ. Club; Quarterbacks Club of Pasadena; publs: arts. in L.A. Co. Bar Journ. (11/77), L.A. Lawyer (12/78); Republican; Catholic; rec: philately, racquetball, photog. Res: 1007 Entrada Way Glendora 91740 Ofc: Michael C. Mitchell, APC, 35 N Lake Ave Pasadena 91101

MITCHELL, PETER JOHN, marketing consultant; b. Sept. 14, 1956, Bklyn.; s. John B. and Nancy A. Mitchell; m. Rosemary, May 1, 1977; children: Jacinthe, Peter; edn: CSU Fullerton 1978. Career: past gen. mgr. San Clemente Inn, hotel and timeshare facilities, San Clemente, later sales agt. Timeshares; pres. Mitchell Consulting & PMI, Mission Viejo 1984–, cons. Timesharing Marketing Co., San Clemente; recipient var. sales awards; civic: Boy Scouts Am. (com.); rec: NY Met (baseball) memorabilia. Ofc: Mitchell Consulting POB 3543 Mission Viejo 92690

MITCHELL, ROBERT RALPH, city manager; b. July 19, 1928, Emporia, Ks.; s. Ralph B. (dec.) and Susan Hazel (Ace) M.; m. Lois Amerine, Apr. 11, 1954;

children: Janice b. 1955, Julia b. 1957, R. Brian b. 1959, Edith Susan b. 1964; edn: certs., Univ. of Chgo. and Penna. State Univ.; BS, Emporia State Univ. 1950; MPA, Univ. of Ks. 1958. Career: admin. asst. to city mgr., Ferguson, Mo. 1954-56; borough mgr./secty. Holidaysburg, Pa. 1956-59, Sharpsville, Pa. 1959-63; city mgr. Webster City, Io. 1963; municipal financial analyst J.B. Hanaur & Co., Beverly Hills 1964-65; Marche & Co., Los Angeles 1965; city mgr. Coachella, Calif. 1965-68; city mgr, Duarte 1968-75; city mgr. Baldwin Park 1975-76; city mgr., Loma Linda 1977 –; adj. faculty Ctr. for Pub. Policy & Admin., CSU Long Beach 1976-; pgm. adv. bd. Calif. State Univ. San Bernardino 1983; honors: 25 Yr. Svc. Cert., Internat. City Mgmt. Assn.; Commdns. from City Council of Loma Linda, Mayor of Baldwin Park, City Council of Duarte, City Council of Coachella, The Burgess & Council of Sharpsville, Pa.; mem: Internat. City Mgmt. Assn.; Inland Empire City Mgrs. Assn. (pres. 1982-83); Am. Soc. for Pub. Admin.; Rotary, So. San Bernardino (pres. 1985-86); Masons, Yorkrite, Scottish Rite; mil: spl. agent US Army Counter-Intell. Corp 1951-54; Presbyterian (elder); rec: old cars, Wedgwood. Res: 11721 Martin St Loma Linda 92354 Ofc: City of Loma Linda, 11128 Anderson St Loma Linda 92354

MITCHELL, WILLIAM EDMUND, company president; b. Mar. 13, 1944, Los Angeles; s. John Stewart and Helen Fine M.; m Ian Schreyer, Feb. 16, 1968; children. Alden b. 1975, Amanda b. 1977, Alyssa b. 1985; edn: BSE, Princeton 1966; MSE, Univ. Mich. 1967. Career: analyst Exxon Corp. NY 1967-72, tech. mgr. Baton Rouge, La. 1972-73; ops. mgr. Raychem Corp. Menlo Park 1973-78, gen. mgr. Latin America 1978-81; senior v.p. Raychem Internat. Corp. Menlo Park 1982-85, pres. 1985 –; chmn bd. trustees Phillips Brooks Sch.; honors: Phi Beta Kappa 1966, Tau Beta Pi 1966; NSF Fellow 1967, finalist Rhodes Scholar Competition 1967; mem: Ops. Research Soc. of Am. 1967-74, Am. Mgmt. Assn. 1979-, Ladera Oaks Swim & Tennis Club, Princeton Club of NY; publ: Jockeying in Queues (J. of Naval Research 1967); Republican; Episcopal; rec: swimming, tennis, reading. Ofc: Raychem Corp. 300 Constitution Dr Menlo Park 94025

MITLER, MERRILL MORRIS, research scientist; b. Jan. 6, 1945, Racine, Wisc.; s. Benjamin and Dorothy Ann (Farrell) M.; m. Elizabeth Ann McClements, Aug. 27, 1976; children: Marc b. 1975, Morris b. 1979, Maximilian b. 1980; edn: BA, Univ. Wisc. 1967; MA, Mich. State Univ. 1968, PhD, 1970; Postdoc. Cert., Stanford Univ. 1973; lic. psychologist, NY (1981), Calif. (1982). Career: research assoc. Stanford Univ. Med. Sch. 1973-78; research prof. State Univ. of NY at Stony Brook, 1978-82; senior staff scientist Scripps Clinic and Research Found., La Jolla 1982 –; mem: Scripps Clinic Med. Group, 1982 –; clin. prof. psychiatry UC San Diego, 1985-; advis. bd. American Health mag.; bd. dirs. Am. Narcolepsy Assn.; pres. Wakefulness-Sleep Edn. and Research Found.; exec. secty.-treas. Assn. of Sleep Disorders Centers; recipient Nathaniel Kleitman Prize, Assn. of Sleep Disorders Centers; mem: Am. Psychol. Assn., AAAS, NY Acad. of Sci., Mensa; author: The Science of Sleep (textbook, in preparation); over 100 publs. in sci. and scholarly journals. Ofc: Scripps Clinic and Research Foundation, 10666 North Torrey Pines Rd La Jolla 92037

MITREVSKI, PAVLE JOVANOV, anesthesiologist; b. June 10, 1934, Bitola, Yugoslavia, nat. USA 1981; s. Jovan M. and Stojna Riste (Risteva) M.; m. Pandora, July 16, 1961; children: Jovan b. 1971, Julia b. 1975; edn: MD, Univ. Skopje, Yugoslavia 1959; Anesthesiologist, Yugislav St. Bd. of Anesthesiol. 1965; Diploma Anethesiologiae, Univ. Copenhagen, Denmark 1968; Calif. bds. 1972, 74; Fellow Am. Coll. of Anesthesiologists 1976. Career: intern General Hosp., Bitola Yugo. 1960-62, gen. pract. University Hosp. Skopje & Belgrade, resident anesthesiology 1962-65; chief anesthesiology dept. Medicinski Center Bitola 1965 68; fellowship in anethesia Anesthesiology Center Copenhagen 1968; chief anesth. dept. Medicinski Center Bitola 1968-73; res. in anesth. Maimonides Med. Ctr. Bklyn., NY 1973-75; anesthesiologist Staten Is. Hosp., NYC 1975-76; self empl. anesthesiologist Los Altos Hosp., Long Beach 1976 –; mem: Anesthesiol. Soc. of Macedonia, Yugo. (pres.), Yugoslav Soc. of Anesth., Am. Soc., of Anesth., Calif. Soc. of Anesth., Alumni Assn. Maimonides Med. Ctr., Nat. Writers Club, Internat. Platform Assn., Internat. Reading Assn.; publs: Why and How to Make English Phonetic (1982), Can the Enlish Language Become Phonetic (1984), How to Teach Johnny to Read (in prog.); mil: in Yugoslavia 1960; Christian; rec: sports, langs. Res: 17083 Westport Dr Huntington Beach 92649 Ofc: Spring Anethesia Group, POB 22222, Los Angeles 90022

MITTAL, MANMOHAN, electrical & computer engineer; b. Sept. 5, 1950, Muzaffarnagar, UP India; s. Kedar Nath and Prakash Wati M.; m. Shashi, Jan. 28, 1976; children: Vivek b. 1977, Vibhav b. 1981; edn: BSc electronics engrg., Inst. of Technol., Bhu, India 1971; M.A.Sc. electrical engrg., Univ. of Ottawa, Canada 1981; PhD electrical & computer engrg., Wash. State Univ. 1984. Career: electronics engr. IIMS, Bhu, Varanasi, India 1971-73; design engr. Bharat Heavy Electricals Ltd., Haridwar, UP India 1973-79; grad. research/ tchg. asst. Wash. State Univ., Pullman, Wash. and Univ. Ottawa, Canada 1979-84; supvg. DA engr. Silicon Systems Inc., Tustin, Calif. 1984 –; honors: Univ. Medal for 1st Place in B.Sc. Electronics Engr. Course (1972), Sigma Xi, Tau Beta Pi; mem: NY Acad. of Scis., IEEE (tech. pgm. com. of IEEE Bipolar Circuits & Technol. Mtg.), IEEE Computer Soc., IEEE Circuits & Systems Soc. (exec. com. 1986), Assn. Computing Machinery, Indian Hindu Temple Assn.; publ: 4 papers in IEEE Transactions & Conferences; devel. new VLSI Simulation Tools for design verification; Hindu; rec: travel, sports. Res: 8 Deerwood West, No. 44D, Irvine 92714 Ofc: Silicon Systems Inc., 14351 Myford Rd Tustin 92680

MO, YOKE KONG, chemist, engineer, food products co. president; b. Aug. 15, 1943, Ipoh, Malaysia, nat. US cit. 1974; d. Yee Chong and How Sam (Look) Moh; m. Ngoc Mo, Oct. 2, 1971; 1 dau. Wennie b. 1972; edn: BS in chem., Nat. Taiwan Univ. 1966; MS, Univ. of Saskatchewan, Canada 1969; PhD, Case Western Reserve Univ. 1972. Career: tchg. asst. Nat. Taiwan Univ. 1966-67, Univ. Sask. 1967-69, research asst. Case Western Reserve Univ. 1969-72; postdoc. fellow Case Western Reserve Univ. 1972-73, Stanford Univ. 1973-74; senior chemist Raychem Corp., Menlo Park 1974-76; pres. Menlo Food Products, East Palo Alto 1976 –; mem. Inst. of Food Technology; 42 sci. publs. (chemistry). Res: 1737 University Ave Palo Alto 94301 Ofc: Menlo Food Products 175 Demeter Street, E. Palo Alto 94303

MOBACH, MAARTEN, JR., co. president; b. May 11, 1945, Netherlands, came to US 1974; s. Maarten and Mathilda H. (Malmberg) M.; m. Mary, Apr. 17, 1971; children: Ursula b. 1972, Sharon b. 1975, Beau-Deanne b. 1980; edn: PhD in econs., Univ. Rotterdam 1974. Career: mgr. European Port Ops., Sud Americana and Zim, based in Rotterdam, The Netherlands, 1968-71; overseas mgmt. port ops. in Paramaribo, Suriname, S.A. 1972-75; econ. advisor/mem. mgmt. team Royal Dutch Steamship Co., 1975-80; sales mgmt. Preferred Risk Ins. Co. in Seattle, Wash. and San Jose, Calif. 1980 , and pres. Ark-Line Insurance Services, Inc., San Diego; honors: Boss of Year, N. San Diego County Woman Assn. (1982-83), top ins. sales Preferred Risk Mutual (1975, 76, 77) and 2d life producer nat. Prefereed Risk Ins. Co. (1976); contbr. articles on mergers, cost calculations, acquisitions in trade jours.; mil: Netherlands Army Spl. Forces; Republican; Prot.; rec: military orgs. Res: 13104 Old West Ave San Diego 92129 Ofc: Ark-Line Insurance Services Inc. 7080 Miramar Rd San Diego 92121

MOBLEY, ROBERT WESLEY, aerospace company administrator; b. Dec. 5, 1925, Jerome, Idaho; s. Frank Kenneth and Blanche Alice (Wasson) M.; m. Rosalie Naglik, June 3, 1950; children: Mark b. 1951, Diane b. 1952; edn: McDonnell Aircraft Co. schs. on aircraft sys. maint. 1964-65; Litton Ind. solid state computer sch. 1979; mil. schs. on electric/ electronic theory and aircraft sys. maint. Career: field svc. engr., assoc. McDonnell Aircraft Co., St. Louis, Mo. 1964-66; field svc. assoc. engr. AiResearch Mfg. Co., Torrance 1966-71; electronics tech. supvr. Naval Aviation engring. Svc. Unit., Dept. of Navy, Philadelphia, Penn. 1971 –; train mil. technicians in electronic computer & sys. installed in aircraft; lectr. pilots on sys. fundamentals and ops.; honors: num. letters of accomplishment from military commands; mem: USN Fleet Reserve Assn., Internat. Order of Foresters, Internat. Platform Assn.; works: designed new test bench and wrote test procedures to improve opn. of aircraft computers; mil: E-7 Chief USN 1943-64, gen. medals; Democrat; Lutheran; rec: model trains. Res: 27271 Nubles Mission Viejo 92692 Ofc: Naval Aviation Engineering Service Unit, MCAS El Toro, Santa Ana 92709

MOCERI, RONALD ALAN, investment-insurance co. executive; b. Jan. 30, 1946; m. Carol Ann; children: Michelle Lynne, Michael Alan. Career: mktg. mgmt. field, 1968-78; founding prin./CEO Financial Services Unlimited, Inc. (finl. plnng., investment & ins. co.; reg. NASD; mem. Securities Investor Protection Corp.), Newport Beach; frequent spkr. on finl. plnng. topics; mem. Interna. Assn. for Finl. Plnng., Orange County Life Underwriters Assn., Newport Harbor Area CofC (chmn. Bus. Asst. & Devcl. Com.), Million Dollar Round Table. Res: 41 Lindberg Irvine 92720 Ofc: Financial Services Unlimited Inc. 1601 Dove St Ste 270 Newport Beach 92660

MOCK, AMELITA GALICIA, life insurance agent; b. May 11, 1957, Philippines; d. Isidro P. and Leoncia R. G.; m. Richie S. Mock, Oct. 8, 1983; 1 dau. Pamela b. 1984; edn: BA, UC Berkeley 1979; Certified Financial Planner (in progress); bus. ins. courses, Life Underwriters Tng. Council 1985-86. Career: agent Coll. Life Ins. co. of Am. 1981-82, Principal Financial Group Bankers Life Co. Des Moines 1982 –; honors: Outstanding New Underwriter of the Year (San Jose Life Underw. Assn. 1983), mem. Million Dollar Round Table (1981-84); mem: Premier Club 1986, Prin. Financial Group, Women Life Underws. Conf. of Nat. Assn. Life Underws.; Democrat; Catholic; rec: piano, reading, cooking. Ofc: Principal Financial Group 1042 W Hedding St Ste 200 San Jose 95126

MODJTAHEDI, PARVIZ MODJI, marketing/administration executive; b. June 11, 1939, Tehran, Iran; USA Perm. Res.; s. Mahammed Ali and Suzanne Jeanne (Van De Nostande) M.; children: Bijan b. 1961, Susan b. 1969; edn: BA, London Univ. 1966, MSc, 1968. Career: asst. London Univ. 1968; mgr. productivity svcs. Iran Nat. Airline, Tehran 1969-72; dir. of tng. IDRO, Tehran 1972-76; v.chancellor Farabi Univ., Tehran 1976-79; assoc. prof. mktg. Tehran Univ. 1970-79; mktg. exec. Bowmont Corp. Corp., London & Calif. 1979-82; chief exec./ pres. Firstworld Travel of Orange Co. Inc., Newport Beach 1982 –; honors: 1st Class Honors, London Univ. 1968; Paul Harris Fellow, Rotary Internat. 1978; mem: Am. Mgmt. Assn.; British Inst. of Mgmt. (assoc.); Indsl. Mgmt. Inst.; fellow, British Soc. of Commerce; Rotary Club, Tehran West (past pres.); CofC; Balboa Bay Club; publs: var. mktg. & mkt. research papers 1970-80; rec: music. Res: 3110 Park Newport Newport Beach 92660 Ofc: Firstworld Travel of Orange County Inc., 567 San Nicolas Dr, St 210, Newport Beach 92660

MOE, STANLEY ALLEN, architect; b. May 28, 1914, Fargo, N.Dak.; s. Ole Arnold and Freda Emily (Pape) M.; m. Doris Lucille Anderson, July 25, 1937; children: Willa Joanne b. 1939, Myra Doris b. 1945; edn: stu. Univ. of N.Dak. Sch. of Engring. 1930-32; BA in arch., Univ. of Minn. 1936. Career: project designer/arch. var. firms in Mid-west, 1936-43; ptnr. H.S. Starin, Archs. & Engrs., Duluth, Minn. 1943-47; senior ptnr. Moe and Larsen, Archs. & Engrs.,

Los Angeles 1947-53; ptnr., gen. mgr., exec. v.p. Daniel Mann Johnson and Mendenhall, Archs. & Engrs., Los Angeles 1953-71, ret. 1971-72, corp. v.p. 1972-79; pres. Associated Design, Planning and Art Inc., Los Angeles and Columbus, Ohio 1972-73; prin. Stanley A. Moe, AIA, architl. and constrn. cons., 1979–; hd. design and/or mgmt. teams for large projects incl: Cairo Internat. Airport (1943), Titan I Missile Facilities (1958-63), Space Shuttle Maint. & Ops. facilities on East and West Coasts (1973-79), major med. facilities pgm. for Saudi Arabia Ministry of Def. and Aviation (1975-78); honors: disting. svc. award Van Nuys Jr. CofC (1949), Sioux Award, Univ. of N.Dak. Alumni Assn. and Found. (1985); mem: Am. Inst. Archs. (LA Chpt., Calif. Council AIA), Archs. of San Fernando Valley (pres. 1948-49), Far East Soc. Archs. and Engrs. (charter); civic: Van Nuys Jr. CofC (life), Van Nuys Kiwanis (v.p. 1952), Van Nuys CofC (dir. 1948-52), Wilshire Ctr Community Involvement Assn. (1983-84), LA Rotary (1963-), Young Republicans of SFV (pres. 1952); Republican; Presbyterian (bd. pres.). Address: 447 S Plymouth Blvd Los Angeles 90020

MOFFET, DONALD PRATT, computer co. executive; b. Jan. 30, 1932, St. Paul, Minn.; s. William Theodore and Dorothy (Pratt) M.; m. Sally Hullsiek, June 1, 1955; children: Kerry b. 1956, Kenneth b. 1959, Mark b. 1963; edn: BBA, MBA, Univ. Minn. 1954. Career: dir. computer svcs. Honeywell Inc. Mpls. 1957-72; v.p. mktg. AM Internat. Chgo. 1972-77; pres. Sycor Inc. Ann Arbor, Mich. 1977-80; v.p., gen. mgr. Computer Sys. div. Perkin- Elmer Corp. Oceanport, NJ 1980-81; pres. Zenith Data Sys. St. Joseph, Mich. 1981-84; pres., c.e.o. Fujitsu Sys. of Am. San Diego 1984–; dir. Wells Electronics Inc. South Bend, Ind. 1962–; mem: Bernardo Hts. CC (SD), Chancellor's Assocs. UCSD; publ: byline sports news articles Rochester (Minn.) Post- Bulletin 1948-49; mil: 1st lt. USAF 1955-57; Republican; Presbyterian; rec: golf, skiing. Res: 12833 Lunada Pl San Diego 92128 Ofc: Fujitsu Systems of Am. Inc. 10995 Torreyana Rd San Diego 92121

MOGLIOTTI, SHARON LYNN, mortgage banker; b. Aug. 1, 1946, Merced; d. Domenic and Vivian Helen (Mudgett) Mogliotti; div.; 1 dau., Darlene Sousa b. 1971; edn: AA, Merced Coll. 1966; Calif. lic. real estate agt. (1975) broker (1981). Career: bookkeeper Sousa Realty, 1966-68; loan dept. processor, supr. Guarantee Svgs., 1968-71, Am. Svgs. Vallejo/San Pablo, 1972-74; loan ofcr. Am. Svgs., Modesto Br., 1976-78; bus. devel. Transam. Title, Merced 1978-79, Suburban Coastal 1979-83, helped form new branch, name change to FPM Inc., currently branch mgr. FPM Inc., Merced 1983–; instr. Merced Coll., contg. edn. in fin.; mem. Merced County Bd. of Realtors (bd. chair 1986, Realtors Award 1985), Merced Trade Club (head trader 1984-86, 1st woman hd. trader), Soroptomist Internat., Venture Club of Merced (charter pres. 1978-79); Catholic; rec: swim, biking, equestrian. Res: 2750 Saratoga Ave Merced 95340 Ofc: FPM Inc 860 W Olive Ave Ste C Merced 95348

MOHAMED, JOSEPH, SR., business owner; b. Mar. 19, 1928, Omar, WV; s. Mose (Moski Mohamed Al Habal) and Minnie Elizabeth (Martin) M.; gr.grandfathers Jesse Testerman and Cable Martin fought in the Civil War; m. Shirley Medeiros, June 22, 1979; children (by previous marriage): Joseph Jr. b. 1948, James R. b. 1951, John W. b. 1951, Leslie Louise b. 1957; edn: AA, Sacramento Jr. Coll. 1951; BA, CSU Sacto. 1954. Lic. Calif. State Contractor, engring., gen., landscape, excavating-grading-paving, solar; Agri. Pest Control Opr.-Contractor, Agri. Pest Control Adviser, R.E. Broker, lic. Common Carrier hwy. transp.; lic. comml. pilot, rotor, instrument, flight instr. Career: worked on family ranches, farms in Lodi and Stockton areas, -1945; estab. a comml. trucking opn., hauled produce and lumber, Calif. and Nev., 1949-52; estab. the Mexican Co. of Agri. and Livestock, Ltd., Ensenada, Baja, Calif., Mex., devel. 2500 acres raising grain & row crops, 1953-57; opr. air charter service, Baja Calif., Mex. 1953-57; owner Quintair Inc. of Calif., an air charter service, 1957–; small scale farming in Sacto. Valley area, hay, orchard crops, raise and show horses, 1958–; R.E. investor, 1949–; R.E. subdivider, developer, 1970–. Mem: Masons, Shriners, Scottish Rite, Elks, Sacto Univ. Alumni Assn., Sacto City and Co. Mus., Elk Grove Hist. Soc., Sacto. and Calif. State Horsemans Assns., Amer. Heart Assn., Sacto Metro CofC, 1972-, Landscape Contractors Assn. 1952-58 (past pres.), Navy League of US (past pres.), Reserve Ofcrs. Assn. (v.p.), Assn. of US Army, Nat. Rifle Assn. (life), Calif. State Hwy. Patrol Aux., Sacto Co. Sheriff's Dept. Reserve Deputy, Sacto. Co. Sheriff's Mounted Posse (dir. active riding mem.), Elk Grove CofC, Sacto Safety Council, Ore. Shakespeare Festival Assn., Sacto. Regl. Arts Council, Civil Affairs Assn., Calif. Rental Assn., Sacto./Calif./Nat. Apartment Assn., Sacto. Country Music Assn. (life), Friends of Sacto. Hist. Soc. (contrib.), McClellan Aviation Mus. Found. (dir.), Easter Seal Soc. for Crippled Children (contrib.), Comstock Club of Sacto, Commonwealth Club SF, Sacto Bd. of Realtors, Calif./Nat. Assn. of Realtors, Am. River Coll. Found., Salvation Army, YMCA; apptd. mem. Gov's Emergency Drought Task Force 1977; mil: enlisted US Army 1946, commnd. 2d lt. 1947, ret. col. USAR 1978; Legion of Merit, Merit Svc., 2 Army Commendn. medals; Republican (Pres. Task Force); Moslem; rec: photog., hunting, riding. Address: 4405 College Oak Dr Sacramento 95841

MOHAMED, JOSEPH, JR., contractor, developer; b. June 25, 1948, Ft. Monroe, Va.; s. Joseph and Patricia Louise (Olmstead) M.; m. Shirley Irene Seastrand, Jan. 14, 1978; children: Stacey Lynn b. 1968, Joseph Paul III b. 1980, Michael Christopher b. 1982; edn: BS bus. adminstrn., Sacramento State Coll. 1971; Command & Gen. Staff Coll., US Army Coll. 1985; landscape contractor Calif. 1971, Nev. 1975; gen. contr. Calif. 1976. Career: owner Joseph Mohamed Jr. Landscape Contr. Carmichael, Calif. 1972, Property Mgmt. 1973, Sunrise Growers & Landscape 1983; honors: Family of the Year (YMCA 1985), Cert. of Appreciation (Elks 1984); mem: Am. River Coll. Alumni, Better Bus. Bureau, YMCA (area bd.), Elks, Carmichael CofC, Camelia Soc., Reserve Ofcrs. Assn., Masons, Scottish Rite, Shrine, Sacramento Receiving Home Guild, Navy League; publ: article on draught tolerant landscape (1981); mil: major USAR infantry (psychological ops.) civil affairs 1967-, Overseas Svc., Nat. Defense; Republican; Christian; rec: camping, motoring, lapidary. Ofc: Joseph Mohamed Jr. Constrn. & Devel. 4321 Walnut Ave Carmichael 95608

MOHANTY, PRABIR KUMAR, computer engineer; b. Sept. 7, 1960, Balasore, Ind., perm. res. 1985; s. Raj Kishore and Sabitri M.; edn: Utkal Univ. 1977; BS, honors, Indian Inst. of Tech. 1982; MS, NY State Univ. 1983. Career: currently, mem. Tech. Staff, Workstation Software, Xerox Corp., El Segundo 1985–; computer engr. A- series mainframe devel., Burroughs Corp., Mission Viejo 1983-85; cons. engr. Computronics India 1979; research engr. Space Borne Central Command Control Computers Devel., Indian Space Research Orgn., India; honors: Best orator- debator, F.M. Coll., Utkal Univ., India 1976. 1977; secty. Technology Spkrs. Forum, Indian Inst. of Tech., India; mem: Computer Soc. Indian Inst. of Tech (pres. 1980-82); Assn. of Computing Machinery; works: a cost/ preformance study of computer peripherals, Journ. of Computer Soc. of India; rec: soccer, water polo, skiing. Res: 4217-E Rosecrans Hawthorne 90250 Ofc: Xerox Corporation, A3-75, 701 S Aviation Blvd El Segundo 90245

MOINI, JASMINE, physician, biochemist; b. May 24, 1953, Tehran, Iran, nat. USA 1983; d. Abdol Hamid and Fatimeh Heidari (Zangeneh) M.; edn: BS cum laude, Findlay Coll., Ohio 1975; PhD in biochem., USC 1981; MD with honors, USC 1983. Career: physician in pvt. general medical practice, So. Calif. Medical Group, Los Angeles; awards: full academic scholarship (1972-75), fellowship in oncology USC Cancer Center (1978, 1980), research asst. in biochem. USC Dept. of Biochemistry (1977, 80); sci. seminar presented USC Sch. of Medicine Hoffman Med. Research Inst. (1981); rec: pianist (classical). Res: 3901 Highland Ave Manhattan Beach 90266 Ofc: Southern California Medical Group 2214 South Hoover St Los Angeles 90007

MOLINO, GERALD ANGELO, veterinarian; b. Jan. 2, 1937, San Francisco; s. Angelo and Josephine (Picchi); m. Alejandra, Jan. 29, 1972; children: Monique b. 1974, Veronica b. 1976; edn: AA, Coll. of San Mateo 1956; BS, UC Davis 1959, DVM, 1961; Lic. Calif. Vet. Md. Bd. of Examiners 1962; Accredited U.S. Dept. of Agriculture 1961. Career: veterinary med. ofcr. U.S. Dept. of Agriculture, San Francisco 1961-62; vet. med. ofcr. Calif. Dept. of Agriculture, San Francisco and Berkeley 1962-64; senior scientist biomedical div. Lawrence Livermore Lab. 1964-65; staff clinician Animal Hosp. SFSPCA, San Francisco 1965-71; assoc. pvt. veterinary practices, Bay Area and Los Angeles 1971-78; currently, emergency clinician and relief veterinarian, pvt. practice; recipient, Rotary Club Scholarship, San Mateo 1956; mem: Am. Vet. Med. Assn., New York Acad. of Sciences, St. Vincent de Paul Soc. (pres., Daly City Conf. 1970-71); Democrat; Catholic; rec: automobile mechanics, restoration and collectible cars. Res: 100 West 39 Ave. San Mateo 94403

MOLLETT, GEORGE HUNTER, orthopedic surgeon; b. Aug. 13, 1941, Van Nuys; s. Byron Hendrix and Margaret Louise (Hunter) M.; m. Sandra, May 27, 1979; children: Michael b. 1969, Darrin b. 1972, Scott b. 1981, Christian b. 1983; edn: BA, Stanford Univ. 1963; MD, UC San Francisco 1967; resident orthopedic surgery UC San Francisco 1971-74; cons. Mario Andrade Hosp., Dominican Republic, 1976; cons. Janhuriate Hosp., Kabul, Afghanistan 1977; orthopedist Kaiser Hosp. Martinez, Calif. 1977–; mem. Am. Acad. Orthopedic Surgery, Am. Coll. of Surgeons, Internat. Coll. of Surgeons; mil: lt. USN 1969-71; Republican; Catholic; rec: rugby, ski, triathalete. Res: 3664 Happy Valley Rd Lafayette 94549

MOLNAR, EUGEN MICHAEL, plastic surgeon; b. Sept. 27, 1942, Bratislava, Czechoslavakia, nat. US cit. 1974; s. Eugen and Augusta (Strelkova) M.; m. Gabriela, Dec. 10, 1970; 1 dau: Michele, b. 1974; edn: state jr. coll., Bratislava 1957-59; MS, Univ. of Ill. Med. Ctr. 1975; MD, Univ. of Komensky Med. Sch., Bratislava 1965. Career: res. County Hosp., Nitra, Czech. 1965-69, cons. 1969; intern Thomason Gen. Hosp., El Paso, Tex. 1970; res. Santa Fe Meml. Hosp., Los Angeles 1971; res. Eye & Ear Infirmary Univ. of Ill. Med. Ctr. 1972-75; pvt. practice, Los Angeles 1975–; currently, pres. E. Michael Molnar MD, Inc.; asst. prof. Drew Med. Sch., Los Angeles; honors: grad. with honors, first in class, from med. school; mem: AMA, CMA, LACMA, Am. Acad. Facial, Plastic and Reconstrv. Surg., fellow Am. Acad. Otolaryngol. - Head and Neck Surg., fellow Am. Acad. Cosmetic Surg.; works: book, Forever Young, practical handbook of youth extension 1985; host, Youth, Health & Beauty Show, KDOC channel 58, 1985; mil: lt. Czechoslavachia svc.; Republican; Catholic; rec: classical music, theater, skiing. Res: 13555 D'Este Dr., Pacific Palisades 90272 Ofc: E. Michael Molnar, MD, Inc., 8760 Sunset Blvd., Los Angeles 90069

MONEDERO, CARLOS CHARLES, hospital nursing home administrator; b. May 29, 1932, El Paso, Tex.; s. Gonzalo and Aurelia (Irigoyen) M.; edn: BBA, Univ. Tex. El Paso 1958; MS hosp. admin., Northwestern Univ. 1960; Nursing Home Adminstr. Calif. 1975. Career: asst. adminstr. Providence Meml. Hosp. El Paso, Tex. 1961-63; adminstr. Mercy Hosp. St. Petersburg, Fla. 1964; assoc. adminstr. Univ. Tex. Med. Branch Hosps. Galveston 1964-68; assoc. dir. Loyola Univ. Hosp. Maywood, Ill. 1969-70; adminstr. S.F. Gen. Hosp. 1970-75; pres. C. Charles Monedero Inc. dba Jones Rest Home & Convales. Hosp. San Leandro 1975–; honors: Men of Mines, Wall St. Jour. Award, Delta Sigma Pi Scholarship Key 1958, Rotary Found. Fellow 1959, Cert. of Merit (NE Med. Svcs. S.F. 1972); mem: Am. Hosp. Assn. 1958, Am. Coll. & Healthcare Execs. 1961, Calif. Hosp. Assn. 1970, Assn. of Western Hosps.

1970, Calif. Assn. of Health Facilities 1977 (secy., Community Care Conf. 1980-82, vice chmn. 1983, 84, 85, reg. v.p., bd. dirs. 1985, chap. pres. 1980-82), Am. Cancer Soc. (unit pres. 1979-81, state bd. dirs. 1980-84, personnel com. 1985); mil: PO2 USN 1951-55 hosp. corpsman; Republican; Catholic; rec: organ. Res: 2101 Shoreline Dr, No 294, Alameda 94501 Ofc: Jones Convalescent Hospital 524 Callan Ave San Leandro 94577

MONEMPOUR, FARAMARZ (Fred), architect; b. Sept. 2, 1946, Tehran, Iran; s. Khalil and Ferdous M.; married Fereshteh, Sept. 13, 1973; children: Farbod b. 1974, Fardad b. 1976, Michael David b. 1986; edn: BA in archtl. engring., Univ. Tehran, 1968, Master of Archtl. Engring., 1970; lic. architect Iran (1970), Israel (1979), Calif. (1983). Career: prin. arch., chief of tech. office major constrn. & urban devel. co. (design, constrn. 28,000 residtl. units), Tehran, Iran 1970-79; prin. architect var. residential projects, Israel 1979-82 (in Eilat, Rehovot, Ramat-Hasharon, Hertzelia); prin. architect F. Monempour AIA & Assocs, Los Angeles 1982–, projects: Havenhurst Plaza, Sunset Plaza, Ventura Plaza, Vermont Plaza, Laural Plaza, and 29 unit apt. bldg. Costa Mesa; cons. architect; recipient 1st honor awards for Commercial Bank 13-story office bldg., Tehran (1973), low-income residential, Tehran (1977), 1-story single residential units for Bney-Bitkha project, Eilat, Israel (1980), mem: Am. Inst. of Archs., Constrn. Specification Inst., Town Hall of Calif., Nat. Trust for Hist. Preservation, Smithsonian Inst.; mil: lt. Iranian Army 1970-71; rec: art, archtl. studies, sports. Res: 304 S Elm Dr Ste 203 Beverly Hills 90212 Ofc: F. Monempour AIA & Assoc., 626 S Spring St Ste 300 Los Angeles 90014

MONROE, MANUS BERNARD, chemist, instructor; b. March 20, 1942, Brooklyn, NY; s. Marvin and Helen (Moskovitz) M.; m. Rachel Hawk, June 20, 1980; 1 son, Nathaniel Hawk; edn: BA, San Francisco State Coll. 1967; PhD, Univ. of Utah 1972, postdoctoral fellowship, 1972-73. Career: dean Science Coll. Indian Valley Colls. 1975-77, senior chem. instr. 1973–; cons. Carol-Denise Labs., Ross 1984-85; recipient, Catalyst Award, Chem. Mfrs. Assn. 1984; mem: Am. Chem. Soc., The Royal Chem. Soc. (Eng.), Sonoma Co. Synagogue Ctr.; works: co-author, A Course in Experimental Chemistry, 2 vols. 1983; co-author, Our Chemical Environment, 1972; chemical patent for electrochemical device for tchg. of and doing research with battery cells; mil: E-4 US Army 1961-63, GCM; rec: cooking, developing new recipies, landscaping. Ofc: Chemistry Department, Indian Valley Colleges, Novato 94947

MONTANA, MONTIE, JR., show producer; b. Dec. 28, 1934, Los Angeles; s. Montie Sr. and Louise A. (Archer) M.; m. Linda, Oct. 25, 1980; children: Kelly b. 1959, Jess b. 1962, Dorothy b. 1965, Jeff b. 1977; edn: BS, UC Davis 1957. Career: rodeo performer, trick roping and riding with family 1938-; US rep. to foreign tours, Western Show to Sweden, Belgium, Spain, Japan, Australia, and others late 1960s; restarted Buffalo Bill's Wild West Show, pres. 1971–; cons. num. western oriented shows; honors: Appointed Vis. USA Ambassador, US Asst. Secty. of Commerce 1974; mem: Internat. Assn. of Fairs & Expositions, Internat. Assn. of Arena & Auditorium Managers, Internat. Assn. of Amusement Parks & Attractions; mil: 1st lt. US Army 1957-59; Republican; Protestant; rec: flying. Ofc: Buffalo Bill's Wild West, P.O. Box C Newhall 91321

MONTECALVO, JOSEPH, JR., college professor; b. June 12, 1949, Providence, RI; s. Joseph and Christine (De Simone) M.; m. Laura Harkey, Aug. 28, 1971; 1 son, Joseph III b. 1984; edn: BS food chem., Univ. R.I. 1972, MS food & nutrition sci., 1975, PhD food sci. & nutrition, 1980. Career: proj. leader corp. research Frito-Lay, Inc., Irving, Tex. 1979-81; asst. prof. food processing and food sci. Univ. Ill., Urbana 1981-83; asst. prof. Food Sci. & Nutrition Dept. Calif. Polytechnic State Univ., San Luis Obispo 1983-85, assoc. prof. 1985–; cons. San Luis Innovations 1983-84, Cabott Chemical Co. 1983, Warner & Pfleiderer Corp. 1983, B&M Seed Cleaning Inc. 1983-, Loomix Inc. 1985, Taco Works 1985; faculty advisor to Food Science Club; honors: Phi Kappa Phi, Sigma Xi, Undergrad. Tchg. Award (Univ. Ill. 1982); mem: Am. Chem. Soc., Inst. Food Technologists, Am. Assn. Cereal Chemists, Volvo Sports Am., Volvo Club of Am.; publs: num. articles in food sci. jours. and presentations at sci. mtgs.; patent pending: process for producing puffed, expanded seed product from hulless varieties of "Curcurbita pepo"; Catholic; rec: sports car restoration, model plane and ship building, hunting, furniture refinishing. Res: 510 Fresno Ave Morro Bay 93442 Ofc: Cal. Poly. Dept. of Food Sci. and Nutrition, San Luis Obispo 93407

MONTGOMERY, ERNESTO ALEXANDER, clergyman; b. Oct. 2, 1925, Kingston, Jamaica, nat. US cit. 1965; s. Isaac and Emily (Smith) M.; edn: DD, West Indies Baptist Sem. 1946; journalism, Jamaica Coll. 1946-48; Calif. Dental Coll. 1960-63. Career: Jamaica Volunteer Tng. Corp. (Army) 1939-40; Jamaica Battalion 1940-46; Jamaica Defense Force (Police Dept.) 1946-50; Jamaica Police Dept., Constabulary Force 1950-60; Minister of Religion, exec. dir. CHristian Fund 1963–; honors: appreciation, Mayor Tom Bradley (1981), LA City Councilman Michael Woo (1985), Councilman Zev Yaroslavsky (1985), Councilman Gilbert Lindsay (1984), Councilman Dave Cunningham (1984), LA Co. Supr. Kenneth Hahn (1984), Gov. Deukmejian (1984), Sen. Allan Cranston (1984), US Senate, Sen. Pete Wilson (1984), US Cong., Cong. Mervyn Dymally (1984), Resolutions: Calif. State Senate, Sen. Roberti (1984) and State Assembly (1983, 1984), Community Svc. award Jamaica Progressive League of NY (1985), Spirit of So. Calif. award for comm. service KNBC-TV, NBC (1986); mem: Hollywood Chorale, Orgn. of West Indies American Peoples Inc., Hollywood, El Monte and Los Angeles CofCs; author: Psychic Spy, Double Day & Co. 1978; mil: lt. British Jamaican Army, War, Star and Defense medals; Democrat. Res: 5333 Russell Ave. Apt. 110 Los Angeles 90027 Ofc: Jamaica Christian Fund, 1258 No. Highland Ave. Ste. 200 Hollywood 90038

MONTGOMERY, JOHN WARWICK, educator, theologian; b. Oct. 18, 1931, Warsaw, NY; s. Maurice Warwick and Harriet (Smith) M.; m. Joyce Ann Bailer, Aug. 14, 1954; children: Elizabeth Ann, David Warwick, CAtherine Ann; edn: AB with distinction, Cornell Univ. 1952; BLS, UC Berkeley 1954, MA, 1958; M.Div. Wittenberg Univ. 1958, MST, 1960; PhD, Univ. Chgo. 1962; Docteur de l'Universite, mention Theologie Prot. (ThD), Univ. Strasbourg (France) 1964; LLB, LaSalle Ext. Univ. 1977; Diplome cum laude, Internat. Inst. Human Rights, Strasbourg, 1978; M.Phil. in Law, Univ. Essex (England) 1983. Admitted to Va. bar 1978, Calif. bar 1979, US Supreme Ct. bar 1981. Career: librarian gen. reference service Univ. Calif. Library, Berkeley 1954-55; instr. Bibl. Hebrew, Hellenistic Greek, Mediaeval Latin, Wittenberg Univ., 1956-59, ordained minister, Lutheran Ch. 1958; head librarian Swift Library Div. and Philosophy, mem. federated theol. faculty Univ. Chgo. 1959-60; asso. prof. /chmn. dept. history Univ. Coll. Sir Wilfred Laurier Univ., Ont., Can. 1960-64; prof./chmn. Div. Ch. Hist. Trinity Evang. Div. Sch., Deerfield, Ill. 1964-74, dir. European seminar pgm. 1966-74; prof. law and theol. Internat. Sch. Law, Wash. 1974-75; theol. cons. Christian Legal Soc., 1975-76; lectr. Melodyland Christian Ctr., Anaheim, Ca. 1976-80; dean/ dir. library/ prof. jurisprudence Simon Greenleaf Sch. Law, Orange, Ca. 1980–; dir. studies Internat. Inst. Human Rights, 1979-81; vis. prof. Concordia Theol. Sem. 1964-7, DePaul Univ. 1967-70; hon. fellow Revelle Coll. UC San Diego 1970; mem. curatorium Free Univ. Hamburg (Germany) 1976-, rector 1981-. Honors: Phi Beta Kappa, Phi Beta Phi, Beta Phi Mu; invited participant, Cons. on Evang. Concerns, Colorado Springs, Colo. 1965; Nat. Luth. Ednl. Conf. fellow 1959-60; Can. Council postdoctl. sr. research fellow 1963-4; Am. Assn. Theol. Schs. faculty fellow 1967-8; Diplomate Med. Library Assn., Am. Assn. Law Libraries; Fellow Victoria Inst. (Eng.). Mem: Middle Temple (Eng.), World Soc. Law Profs., Internat. Bar Assn., Union Internat. des Avocats, Am. Bar Assn., Va. Trial Lawyers Assn., Calif. Bar Assn. (Human Rights Com. 1980-3), Internat. Real Estate Fedn., Tolkien Soc. Am., C.S. Lewis Soc., Am. Theol. Library Assn., Am. Soc. Internat. Law, Bibliog. Soc. U. Va., Evang. Theol. Soc., Acad. de Gastronomie Brillat-Savarin, Chaine des Rotisseurs, Confrerie St.-Etienne, Soc. des Amis des Arts (Strasbourg, Fr.), Occidental Order St. Martin, Order Des Chevaliers Du Saint-Sepulcre Byzantin. Author: The Writing of Research Papers in Theology (1959); A Union List of Serial Publications in Chicago Area Protestant Theological Libraries (1962); Chytraeus on Sacrifice: A Reformation Treatise in Biblical Theology (1962); The Shape of the Past: An Intro. to Philosophical Historiography (1962, 2d edit. 1975); The 'Is God Dead?' Controversy (1966); (with Thomas J.J. Altizer) The Altizer-Montgomery Dialogue (1967); Crisis in Lutheran Theology (2 vols., 1967, 2d ed. 1973); Es confiable el Christianismo? (1968); Ecumenicity, Evangelicals, and Rome (1969); Where Is History Going? (1969); History and Christianity (1970); The Suicide of Christian Theology (1970); Computers, Cultural Change and the Christ (1970, German trans. 1973); In Defense of Martin Luther (1970); Damned through the Church (1970); The Quest for Noah's Ark (1972, 2d ed. 1974); (with Joseph Fletcher) Debate on Situation Ethics (1972); La Mort de Dieu (1972); Principalities and Powers: The World of the Occult (1973, 2d ed. 1975); Christianity for the Toughminded (1973); Cross and Crucible (2 vols. 1973); Internat. Scholars Directory (1973); Myth, Allegory and Gospel (1974); How Do We Know There Is A God? (1974, Spanish trans. 1975); The Inerrant Word of God (1974); Jurisprudence: A Book of Readings (1974, 2d ed. 1980); Demon Possession (1975); The Law Above the Law (1975); The Shaping of America (1976); Weltgeschichte wohin? (1977); Law and Gospel (1978); Sensible Christianity (1978); Faith Founded on Fact (1978); Slaughter of the Innocents (1981). Editor at large Christianity Today; contbg. editor Raamattu Ja Scurakunta, Lutherischer Rundblick; contbr. articles to US and fgn. acad., theol. and legal jours., book chpts. Res: 2530 Shadow Ridge Ln Orange 92667

MONTGOMERY, MARY ANN E., real estate broker; b. Sept. 12, 1934, Detroit, Mich.; d. Jach H. and Daisy Mae (O'Steen) Shires; m. Victor A. Montgomery, Dec. 4, 1977; children (nee Norby): Carey b. 1953, Steven (DDS) b. 1957; edn: Glendale Comm. Coll. 1952, pre-med. stu., UCLA 2 yrs.; Calif. lic. real estate broker (1980). Career: spl. staff crime prevention, Juvenile Div., Sacto., then with County of El Dorado Probation Dept., Tahoe; current: owner/ broker West Wind Realty, Baywood Park; mem. Baywood Bd. of Realtors (ethics chair), CofC (bd.), Baywood Merchants (dir.), Profl. Womens Network; rec: writing, ski, travel. Res: 1587 14th St Baywood Park 93402 Ofc: West Wind Realty 1205 4th St Ste A Baywood Park 93402

MONTIJO, BEN, housing commission director; b. Feb. 28, 1940, San Jose; s. Gabriel S. Sr. and Margaret (Gomez) M.; m. Patricia Martinez, Sept. 18, 1965, div. 1981; children: Randy b. 1968, Kelly b. 1970; edn: AA, Coll. of Sequoias 1961; BS, Ariz. State Univ. 1963; grad. cert., urban studies, Yale Univ. 1971; MS, urban studies, Occidental Univ. 1972. Career: personnel & tng. dir. Ariz. Migrant Opportunity Pgm., Phoenix 1963-68; mgmt. cons. Western Training, San Francisco 1970-71; dep. city mgr. City of Scottsdale, Ariz. 1971-75; exec. dir. Fresno Housing Authorities, Fresno 1975-79; exec. dir. San Diego Housing Commn., San Diego 1979–; loan comm. mem. State Rental Housing Constrn. Pgm.; honors: Nat. Urban Fellowship, 1971; Named 1982 San Diegans to Watch, San Diego Mag.; mem: Am. Soc. for Tng. & Devel. (dir. Nat. Bd., Comm. Devel. Div.), Jobs for Progress Inc., Internat. City Mgrs. Assn., Am. Mgmt. Assn.; works: developed var. tng. & mgmt. materials; Democrat; Protestant; rec: tennis, jogging, motorcycling. Res: 1249 Fallbrook Ct. Bonita 92002 Ofc: San Diego Housing Commn., 1625 Newton Ave. San Diego 92113

MOODY, DANIEL, computer scientist; b. Dec. 4, 1946, Oak Park, Ill.; s. John H. and Antoinette M. M.; edn: BS, Univ. W. Mich. 1968; MSEE, M.I.T. 1970; PhD, ScD, Calif. Inst. Technol. 1972. Career: pres. Fedn. of Computer Users in

Medical Science; dir. Research Health Systems Information Exchange; chmn. UN Advisory Com. on Emerging Nations Technology; honors: Research Scientist of the Yr. (NSF 1979), Computer Scientist of the Yr. (Internat. Assn. Computer Scientists 1984); mem: AAAS, Calif. Physics Club, Computer Users of Am., AAMSI; research: protocols for paraphysic experiments, proj. involving interactive video in medical & dental databases; co-developer Josephson Logic Circuit Junction (microcircuit under study by IBM for use in their 5th generation computers); 38 patents in area of microcomputers & microcircuitry; mil: telemetrics/ orbit control NASA 1972-75; rec: photomicrography, audiophile. Ofc: FOCUS, The Computer Soc. for Doctors, Pacific Technology Ctr, Box 15579 San Francisco 94115

MOODY, HAMILTON MARK, psychologist; b. Dec. 17, 1920, Athol, Mass.; s. Edmund K. and Ida (Hamilton) M.; edn: BA, Emory Univ. 1942, MA, 1943; PhD, UC Los Angeles 1951. Career: clin. psychologist in pvt. practice, Long Beach; instr. UCLA 1951-72; mgmt. consultant 1951-70; dir. Harbor Bank 1975-; Diplomate ABPP, ABPH- Hypnosis; mem: Am. Psych. Assn., CSPA, WPA, Los Angeles County Psych. Assn., Sigma Xi; publs: num. articles on hypnosis. Res: 5901 East Bayshore Walk Long Beach 90807 Ofc: 3815 Atlantic Blvd Long Beach 90807

MOOERS, HARRELL DOUGLAS, JR., life insurance broker; b. June 27, 1930, Oakland; s. Harrell Douglas, Sr. and Betty (Gunar) M.; m. Janet, June 16, 1956; children: James Douglas b. 1957, Nancy Diane b. 1961; edn: BS, UC Berkeley 1953; desig: Chartered Life Underwriter (CLU). Career: pres. H.D. Mooers & Co., Lafayette 1956–; chmn. organizing com. (1981-83), bd. chmn. (1983-) Nat. Assn. of Independent Life Brokerage Agencies (this orgn. now presents an annual award called The Douglas Mooers Award of Excellence); mem. Soc. of Underwriting Brokers (founding mem.), Oakland- East Bay Life Underws. Assn. (pres.), Calif. Assn. of Life Underws. (regl. v.p.); civic: Planned Parenthood of Contra Costa Co. (bd. chair); mil: lt. USNR 1953-56; rec: tennis, walking. Res: 19 Richelle Ct Lafayette 94549 Ofc: 3688 Mt Diablo Blvd Lafayette 94549

MOON, STEVEN L., chiropractor; b. Nov. 16, 1950, Oakland; s. Robert R. and Hazel I. M.; edn: AA, Merrit Coll. 1972; DC, Western States Chiro. Coll. 1983; postgrad. course chiro. orthopedics 1984-86; Diplomate Nat. Bd. Chiro. Examiners 1982, Calif. Bd. 1983. Career: radiol. technol. Levine Hosp. Hayward 1972-74; head spl. procedures sect. radiol. dept. Kaiser Permanente Walnut Creek 1974-80; chiropractor pvt. practice Concord 1983–; honors: Yearbook Com. and Student Council Awards (1983); mem: Calif. Chiro. Assn., Contra Costa Soc. of Calif Chiro. Assn., Found. for Chiro Research and Edn., Am. Chiro. Assn. (Councils on Roentgenology, Chiro Orthopedics, Sports Injuries), Parker Research Found., Am. Coll. Chiro. Orthopedics (assoc. mem.), Toastmasters Internat., Concord CofC, Trade Club Com., Envoy Com., Nat. Exchange Club (secty. 1985); Republican; rec: photog dancing (swing dance instr.), water & snow skiing, scuba, reading. Ofc: Moon Chiropractic 5400 Ygnacio Valley Rd, Ste M, Concord 94521

MOORE, BERNIECE ANDERSEN, real estate broker, teacher, ret.; b. May 29, 1915, Cozad, Neb.; d. Frederick William and Cora May (Wallace) Andersen; m. George S. Moore, Oct. 3, 1937; children: Sheryl Lynne b. 1944, Douglas Andersen b. 1949; edn: BS, Neb. WEsleyan Univ. 1937; San Jose State Univ. 1960; Foothill Comm. Coll. 1969-71; real estate broker Calif. 1971. Career: early career included teaching and secretarial positions and work with husband arranging lecture tours and fundraising for churches; real estate sales Wold Realty Palo Alto 1969-71, sales mgr. 1971-76, broker 1976-84 (ret.); honors: Phi Kappa Phi (1937), Pi Gamma Mu (1937), Theta Alpha Phi (1935), Psi Chi (1937), Arc of Epsilon Pi (Alpha Gamma Delta 1981); mem: Nat. Real Estate Assn. 1971-84, Palo Alto Aux. to Children's Home Soc. (pres.), Palo Alto Pan-Hellenic (founder, pres.), Peninsula Alumnae Club of Alpha Gamma Delta (founder, charter pres.), PTA, Am. Assn. Univ. Women, DAR, Spring Valley Improvement Assn., var. ch. orgns.; author & publr: Wallace Family History (rev. 1983), Jorgensen Family History (rev. 1982); feature columnist Mt. Miguel Covenent Village Voice; Republican; United Methodist; rec: reading, bridge, choir, genealogy, writing, sewing. Res: 325 Kempton St Apt 817 Spring Valley 92077

MOORE, CAROLINE M., lawyer; b. Apr. 19, 1956, San Diego; d. James M. and Patricia E. (Lynch) M.; edn: BA, St. Mary's Coll., Notre Dame, Ind. 1978; JD, Univ. San Diego Sch. of Law 1982; admitted to Calif. Bar 1983; lic. Real Estate Broker, Calif. 1984. Career: project coordinator, 1982-83, research atty., Center for Criminal Justice Policy & Mgmt., Univ. of San Diego Sch. of Law, 1984–; mem. San Diego County Bar Assn., St. Mary's Coll. Alumni Club; Catholic; rec: tennis. Ofc: Center for Criminal Justice, Univ. of San Diego Sch. of Law, Alcala Park, San Diego 92110

MOORE, DAVID RICHARD, electrical contractor; b. Dec. 11, 1955, Los Angeles; s. Arby Raymond and Janet Marlene (Sandbeck) M.; m. Gail Le Moore, July 7, 1981; children: Nicholas Richard b. 1980, Jennifer Anne b. 1984; edn: grad. Electrical Estimator Sem. 1981, cert. L.A. Co. Sheriff Dept. 1984; lic. Elec. Contr. (1976). Career: elec. contr. asst. during H.S.; maint. and elec. wk. Azusa Pacific Univ., 1974-76; lic. elec. contr. 1976 (youngest licensee then on record); owner Moore Electric 1976–; civic: San Dimas CofC, Glendora Police Reserve Ofcr. (1982-84), Bethany Baptist Ch., W.Covina (prop. commn. chmn. 1984-86); Republican; Baptist; rec: photog., golf, sound & lighting. Ofc: Moore Electric 466 West Arrow Hwy Ste D San Dimas 91773

MOORE, FAYRE CYNTRESE, investment consultant; b. Apr. 24, 1958, Chgo.; d. Carl Brady and Lucy Beatrice (Roby) M.; edn: AA, San Joaquin Delta Coll. 1978; BS, USC 1981; MS, Golden Gate Univ. 1985; Calif. lic R.E. Broker (1985), SEC Reg. Rep. (1984), lic. Ins. Agent (1986). Career: cost acct. Stauffer Chem. Co., San Francisco 1981-83; investment cons. prin. Inter-City Investments, Oakland 1983–; mem. Internat. Assn. Finl. Planners, Calif. Planners, Bay Net Inc., Nat. Assn. of Black Accts.; civic: participant in sporting event benefits for youth scholarships; Baptist. Res: 777 Rand Ave Oakland 94610 (POB 32043 Oakland 94604) Ofc: Inter-City Investments POB 32043 Oakland 94604

MOORE, HENRY T., JR., superior court judge; b. Dec. 28, 1932, El Paso, Tex.; s. Henry Trumbull and Bonnie (Platt) M.; m. Lynda Doughty, Nov. 8, 1963; 1 son: Michael, b. 1967; edn: BA, USC 1954; LLB, 1957; LLM, Harvard Univ. 1958; Judge of the Superior Ct., Calif. 1984. Career: assoc./ partner, law firm Moore & Trinkaus 1958-62; partner, law firm, Moore & Moore 1962-76; sole practitioner, Century City & of counsel Ward & Heyler 1976-79; sole practitioner (gen. civil & trial practice), Santa Ana 1979-84; judge Superior Court, County of Orange 1984–; So. Coast Regl. Coastal Commn. 1979-80; L.A. Superior Ct. Panel of Arbitrators, Orange Co. Superior Ct. Panel of Arbitrators 1979-84; judge pro tem L.A. Municipal Ct. 1979; Orange Co. Tax Reform Com. 1976-77; Citizens Adv. Com. to L.A. City Plnng. Dept. (1971-72), to L.A. City Atty. Burt Pines (1973-74); honors: Phi Beta Kappa, Phi Kappa Phi, Order of the Coif; mem: Mandeville Cyn. Property Owners Assn. (pres. 1971-73); State Bar of Calif. (chmn. local admin. com. 1972) Beverly Hills, L.A. Co. (chmn. pub. rels. com. 1972-74), Orange Co. bar assns.; Am., L.A. & Orange Co. Trial Lawyers Assns.; Assn. of Bus. Trial Lawyers; Internat. Acad. of Law & Sci.; Am. Judicature Soc.; Newport Balboa Rotary Club; Hoag Hosp. 552 Club; Republican; Presbyterian; rec: racquetball, boating, tennis. Ofc: Courthouse, 700 Civic Center Dr W, Santa Ana 92701

MOORE, PATRICK WAYNE, corporate executive; b. Nov. 2, 1947, Portland, Ore.; s. Patrick Ray and Audrey Kathleen (Smith) M.; children: Eric b. 1973, Brian b. 1971, Julie b. 1969; edn: BA econs., cum laude, Willamette Univ. 1969. Career: manpower coord. Mid Willamette Valley Community Action Agency Salem, Ore. 1969-71, dir. coop. area manpower planning sys. 1973-75; staff assoc. Nat. Commn. for Employment Policy Wash. DC 1975-76; dir. Mid Willamette Valley Manpower Consortium Salem, Ore. 1976-81; exec. dir. San Diego Regional Employment & Tng. Consortium 1981-83; pres. San Diego Pvt. Industry Council 1983-86; senior v.p. Southwest General Industries 1986–; honors: Equal Opportunity Award (San Diego Urban League 1985); mem: Nat. Job Tng. Partnership Inc. (Wash. DC, pres. 1984-86), Nat. Assn. County Employment and Tng. Officials (Wash. DC, pres. 1976-77), Nat. Council Employment Policy (Wash. DC 1984-86), Nat. Acad. Sciences (Youth Employment Com., Wash. DC 1985-86), Labor- Indsl. Rels. Advis. Com. (San Diego Univ.), Vietnam Vets of San Diego (assoc.), Job Tng. Assn. of San Diego 1984-, Western Job Tng. Partnership Assn. (past pres.), Navy League; mil: sp5 US Army Nat. Guard 1969-75. Res: 2130-D Orinda Dr Cardiff By The Sea 92007 Ofc: Southwest General Industries 2105 Industrial Ct Ste A Vista 92083

MOORE, RICHARD F., JR., real estate investor; b. Mar. 18, 1943, Los Angeles; s. Richard F. and Marycile (White) M.; m. Linda M., Aug. 28, 1976; edn: Univ. Nacional de Mexico 1962, USC 1961-65. Career: var. mgmt. assignments Anthony Industries, Inc. in USA, S.E. Asia and Australia, 1967-78; real estate redevel., Long Beach area 1976–, pres. Denmore Financial Inc. and pres. Locust House Inc. Res: 2099 Locust Ave Long Beach 90806 Ofc: Locust House Inc. POB 16134 Long Beach 90806

MOORE, SCOTT DAVID, financial services co. executive; b. Apr. 28, 1960, Oakland; s. Robert James and Arlene Ellen (Banta) M.; m. Kimberly A.B., Oct. 15, 1983; edn: internat. corp. mgmt., Univ. Ore. 1978-79; Reg. Rep. NASD 1984. Career: reg. rep. Chesapeake Financial Group Danville 1980-81; pension splst. Capital Analysts Inc. S.F., Houston ofcs. 1981-83; cons., pension asset mgr. Equitec Securities Co. 1984; ops. mgr. retirement plans div. NPCI Cos. 1984–; pres. Securities Group (subsids. of NPCI Cos.); dir. NPCI, Securities Group Subsids., Calif. Danish Cheese Co.; honors: Paul Harris Sustaining Fellow (Rotary 1982), Exceptional People in Business (A Closer Look Prodns. 1984), Century Club (Fox Capital Corp. 1985), Excellence Award (Keystone Mass. Distr. 1985), Outstanding Athletic Achievement (Nat. Prestige Classic-cycling 1978); mem: NASD Nat. Bd. Arbitration, Internat. Assn. Financial Planners, Rotary (dir. internat. svc. 1983), CofC; contbg. author Network newsletter 1985-; guest appearance A Closer Look TV talk show 1984, 5; Republican; Episcopal; avoc: mfr. fine gold jewelry. Res: 115 Gleneden Ave Piedmont 94611 Ofc: NPCI 1330 Broadway Ste 500 Oakland 94612

MOORE, STEPHEN ALLEN, accountant; b. Oct. 14, 1952, Stockton; s. Thomas J. and Margaret V. (Tyrrell) M.; m. Robin R., Jan. 30, 1971; edn: AA, Canada Coll. 1976; BA, CSU San Francisco 1979; Certified Public Acct., Calif. (1981). Career: bookkeeper Merrill Higham & Co., CPAs, Belmont 1975-78; staff acct. Goss & Marcussen, CPAs, San Carlos 1978-79; staff acct. C.G. Uhlenberg & Co., CPAs, Redwood City 1979-82, ptnr. 1982-84; CPA prin. acctg. and tax practice, Redwood City 1984–; apptd. mem. Technical Review Panel, State Bd. of Acctncy. 1984-; apptd. mem. AICPA subcom. on Independence/ Behavioral Standards 1985-; mem: Am. Inst. CPAs, Calif. Soc. CPAs (State Ethics Com. 1985; Peninsula Chpt. chmn. Ethics Com. 1985)), Soc. of Calif. Accts. (Peninsula Chpt. pres. 1985-86), Nat. Soc. of Public Accts., Internat. Assn. for Finl. Planning; bd. dirs. Cartoon Art Mus. of Calif.; mil: sgt. USAF 1970-74; Catholic; rec: collect original art (cartoon, sci-fi/fantasy, animation art, etc.). Ofc: Stephen A. Moore, CPA, 1900 Broadway Ste 203 Redwood City 94063

MOORE, THOMAS WALDROP, rancher, viticulturist; b. Sept. 17, 1918, Meridian, Miss.; s. Thomas Miller and Abita Josephine (Stroble) M.; m. Claire Stirrat, Feb. 18, 1943; children: Thomas W. Jr. b. 1946, Jean Anne b. 1951; edn: Miss. State Univ. 1935-38; Univ. Mo. 1938; hon. LLD, Univ. Ala. 1966. Career: salesman CBS Radio & Tv 1946-55; sales mgr. CBS Film Sales 1955-57; v.p. sales ABC TV 1957-60, v.p. pgmmg. 1960-61, pres. 1961-69; founder Ticketron, Inc. 1969; founder Tomorrow Entertainment Inc. 1974; owner Moore Vineyards, St. Helena, Calif. 1970—, full-time mgmt. 1984—; bd. dirs: ABC TV 1960-69, GE Venture Capital 1971-73, GE Broadcasting Corp. 1971-73, Corp. for Public Broadcasting 1971-77; producer 32 2-hr. TV motion pictures, 30 TV series; honors: 5 Emmys, 2 Geo. Peabody Awards, 2 Christopher Awards, Horatio Alger Award; mem: TV Acad. (dir.), Bohemian Club S.F., Boone & Crockett Club, L.A. CC, Thunderbird CC, Meadowood CC; creator "Lifeline" and "Body Human" series for NBC and CBS; mil: lt. USNR, naval aviator 1941-45; Republican. Res: Sonoma Tree Ranch, Palm Springs 92264 Ofc: Moore Ranch, 1740 Conn Valley Rd St Helena 94574

MOORE, WILLIAM MODZELEWSKI, mechanical engineer; b. Dec. 27, 1946, Staten Island, N.Y.; s. Edward Paul and Eleanor (Beyer) Modzelewski; edn: Staten Island Comm. Coll. 1971; AA, Am. River Coll. 1972; Cal. Poly. S.L.O. 1972-73; BSME, CSU Sacramento 1976; Reg. Profl. Engr. (mechanical) Calif. 1978. Career: design engr. Am. Automatic Fire Protection Inc. Sacramento 1975-77; plant engr. Lawrence Livermore Lab. 1977-79; self-employed mech. engr. practicing fire protection engrg. for firms in Calif. and Hawaii 1978—; developing computer software, tech. references; honors: Honor Roll (Am. River Coll. 1971, 72); mil: ssgt. USAF 1966-70, Good Conduct, Marksman; Republican; rec: soccer player and referee, youth sports. Ofc: 3500 Clayton Rd Ste B-193 Concord 94519

MOORHEAD, CARLOS JOHN, congressman; b. May 6, 1922, Long Beach; s. Carlos Arthur and Florence (Gravers) M.; m. Valery Joan Tyler, July 19, 1969; children: Theresa, Catharine, Steven, Teri, Paul; edn: BA, UC Los Angeles 1943; JD, USC 1949; admitted to Calif. State Bar 1949. Career: dir. Lawyers Reference Service, Glendale Bar Assn., 1950-66; law practice, Glendale 1949-72; elected rep. Calif. Assembly, 1967-72; elected mem. 93d-99th Congresses from 22d Dist. Calif.; mem. Calif. Law Revision Commn. 1969-73; pres. 43d Dist. Republican Assembly, Glendale Young Repubs., 1957; mem. Los Angeles County Repub. Central Com. 1966-, Calif. Rep. Central Com., 1966-; bd. dirs. Glendale La Crescenta Camp for Girls; mem. Verdugo Hills Council BSA; mem. Calif., Los Angeles County, Glendale (past pres.) bar assns., CofC, Mason, Shriner, Lion, Elk; mil: 1st lt. US Army 1942-46, lt. col. Reserv. 1946-75. Ofc: 2346 Rayburn House Office Bldg, Wash. DC 20515

MOORMAN, JERRY DALE, financial services executive; b. May 7, 1941, Mangum, Okla.; s. Jack and Audrey (Sands) M.; m. Betty Jo Anderson, Dec. 2, 1972; childen: Deborah b. 1962, Christina b. 1963, Timothy b. 1968, Kristopher b. 1974; edn: AA, American River Coll. 1984; GRI, 1979. Career: real estate broker, owner Firm New Horizon Realty 1975-85; currently, reg. NASD for Fans Inc. and life agent A.L. Williams, San Jose; tchr. USN, USN Recruiter; tch real estate tng.; honors: Sacramento Bd. of Realtors awards; Coloma Crescent Players, Pres.'s Award; mem: Calif. Assn. Realtors, Grange Master, Coloma Theater (pres. 1985), Boy Scouts of Am., Parks and Recreation Lotus/ Coloma; El Dorado Arts Councl; reseach and devel: telecommunications systems, Yokosuka, Japan; mil: E-6 USN 1959-74, (4) GCM, Vietnam Cros of Gallantry, Secty. of Nav. Accomodation, Combat Action, Vietnam Campaign, Vietnam Svc., Nat. Defense; Republican; Protestant; rec: acting, pubic speaking. Res: 6721 Carver Rd. Coloma 95613 Ofc: A.L. Williams, 180 E. Gish Ste. C San Jose 95112

MOOSSA, A. R., academic surgeon; b. Oct. 10, 1939, Port-Louis, Mauritius; s. Yacoob and Maude (Rochecoute) M.; m. Denise Willoughby, Dec. 28, 1973; children: Pierre b. 1977, Noel b. 1981, Claude b. 1984; edn: BS, Univ. of Liverpool 1962, MD, 1965; postgrad. tng. Johns Hopkins Univ. 1972-73, The Univ. of Chgo. 1973-74; FRCS, Royal Coll. of Surgeons of England (1970); FRCS Royal Coll. of Surgeons of Edinburgh (1970); FACS, Fellow Am. Coll. of Surgeons. Career: asst. prof. of surgery Univ. of Chgo. 1974, assoc. prof. of surgery 1975, prof. of surg., dir. Surgical Research, and chief Gen. Surgery Service, vice chmn. Dept. of Surgery, Univ. of Chgo. 1977-83; prof. and chmn. Dept. of Surgery, UC San Diego and surgeon-in-chief UCSD Medical Center, 1983—; awards: Hunterian Prof., Royal Coll. of Surgeons (1977), Litchfield lectr. Univ. of Oxford, Eng. (1978), Praelector in Surgery, Univ. of Dundee, Scotland (1979); mem: Am. Coll. of Surgeons, Am. Surgical Assn., Soc. of Univ. Surgeons, Soc. of Surgical Oncology, Am. Soc. of Clin. Oncology, Soc. for Surgery of the Alimentary Tract; club: Fairbanks Ranch CC; Roman Catholic; rec: travel, soccer. Ofc: Dept. of Surgery, UCSD Medical Center 225 Dickinson St 92103

MORALES, ERNESTO J., orthopaedic surgeon; b. Feb. 25, 1930, Matagalpa, Nicaragua; s. Vicente and Victoria (Estrada) M.; m. Barbara Francis, June 9, 1956; children: Vincent D. b. 1957, John R. b. 1958, Ernest J. b. 1959, Thomas G. b. 1961; edn: MD, Univ. of Nicaragua 1955; bd. eligible orthopaedic surgeon 1965; bd. certified Medical Legal Analysis. Career: res. orthopaed. surg. N.Y. Med. Coll. 1961-64; fellow orthopaed. surg. Hosp. for Special Surgery 1964-65; pvt. practice, pres. E.J. Morales M.D. Inc. Santa Rosa, Calif. 1965—, spec. interest in Hand and Reconstructive Surgery of Upper Extremities; mem:

fellow Am. Acad. Neurol. and Orthopaed. Surgery; AMA; Rotary Club (past); Republican; Catholic; rec: golf, bicycling. Ofc: 1144 Sonoma Ave Santa Rosa 95405

MORAN, EDGAR M., physician, educator; b. Apr. 28, 1928, Constantza, Romania, nat. 1972; s. Leon and Catty (Rosenblatt) Mayersohn; m. Huguette M. Leger, MD, June 11, 1968; children: Daniel G. b. 1969, Andre A. b. 1971; edn: Baccalaureate (scis.) Nat. Coll. 'St. Sava' Bucharest 1946; MD, cum laude, Univ. of Bucharest Sch. of Med. 1952; cert. Splst. in Pathology, Israel. Career: staff phys. Dept. of Pathology, Hadassah Univ. Hosp., Jerusalem, Israel 1962-65, instr. pathol., Hebrew Univ. 1963-65; asst. in medicine Mt. Sinai Med. Ctr., NY 1968-69; instr. med., Univ. Chgo. Pritzker Sch. of Med. 1969-71; asst. assoc. prof. Pritzker Sch. of Med. and Franklin McLean Meml. Research Inst., 1971-76; dir. Dept. Oncology, City of Hope Nat. Med. Ctr., Duarte 1976-77; assoc. clin. prof. med. USC, 1977-78; prof. med. UC Irvine, also chief Hematol.-Oncol., Long Beach VA Med. Ctr., 1978—; awards: Outstanding new citizen of year Citizenship Council of Metro. Chgo. (1972), AMA Physician Recogn. (1969, 73, 76, 79, 84), Searle award 13th Internat. Cong. of Chemotherapy, Vienna, Austria (1983), Tchr. of year Long Beach VA Med. Housestaff Assn. (1985); mem: Am. Fedn. for Clin. Research, Am. Soc. of Hematology, Fellow Internat. Soc. of Hematology, Am. Assn. for Cancer Research, Am. Soc. of Clin. Oncology, Internat. Soc. of Chemotherapy, Fellow Royal Soc. for the Promotion of Health, Fellow NY Acad. of Scis., AAAS, Am. Soc. of Preventive Oncology (founding mem.), Soc. for Hematopathology; research grants: Mayo Found. 1979-82, Nat. Cancer Inst. 1979-83; num. sci. publs. (90+); research grants: Epstein-Barr Virus Markers in diagnosis of nasopharyngeal carcinoma, Mayo Found. (1979-82), Effect of total parenteral nutrition on chemotherapy of small cell anaplastic carcinoma of lung, Nat. Cancer Inst. (1979-83); rec: gardening, photog., numismatics. Res: 885 Palo Verde Ave Long Beach 90815 Ofc: Veterans Administration Medical Ctr. 5901 E. 7th St Long Beach 90822

MORAN, HUGH ANDERSON, III, lawyer; b. May 30, 1912, Shanghai, China (parents US citizens); s. Hugh A. (PhD) and Irene May (Hornby) M.; children: Winifred (Jasper) b. 1948, Pauline (Reed) b. 1951, Hugh A, IV, b. 1953, Robert Breck b. 1953; edn: undergrad Stanford Univ. 1931-33; BS, Cornell Univ. 1936; LLB and JD, Stanford 1939; admitted Calif. State Bar 1941, Federal Bar 1942. Career: law clerk firm Robert Beale, San Francisco 1939-40; Land Dept. Shell Oil Co., Los Angeles 1941-43; assoc. firm Salisbury, Robinson & Knudsen, L.A. 1942-46; individual practice law, Los Angeles 1945-52; partner firm Stone, Moran & Anderson, Pasadena (and predecessor firm Stone & Moran), 1952-66; individual practice law, Pasa. 1966—; ofcr., dir., general counsel Caine, Farber & Gordon, Inc.; honors: Phi Alpha Delta, listed Who's Who in Am. Law, Who's Who in the West; mem. Am., Calif., Los Angeles County, Pasadena bar assns., Am. Arbitration Assn. (Nat. panel arbitrators), Delta Upsilon frat.; Republican; Protestant. Address: 72 Arlington Dr Pasadena 91105

MORENO, ATHELINE MARIE, marketing executive; b. Mar. 5, 1944, Orange; d. Robert Gonzales and Margaret (Arroyo) Moreno; edn: Pacific Inst. of Comml. ARt 1972, spl. courses Fullerton Coll. 1969-71, Saddleback Coll. 1982. Career: art director Datum Inc., Anaheim 1969-79; cons. designer Marie Moreno Advt., Brea 1979-80; senior graphic designer Hughes Aircraft, Santa Fe Springs 1980-82; mktg. communications mgr. Media Systems Technology Inc., Irvine 1982-85; mktg. communs./projects mgr. Media Duplication Services Inc., Irvine 1985—; instr. sales tng. seminars; mem. Am. Mktg. Assn.; awards: advertisement award Mini-Micro Pubs.- readership voting (1985), staff award for mgmt. MST (1984); civic volunteer: Hope (unwed mothers), convalescent hosps. (resident helper), Fairview State Mental Hosp. (Mongoloid area), Little League; Democrat; Catholic; rec: oil painting, restore antiques, tennis, biking. Res: 11571 Azalea Ave Fountain Valley 92708 Ofc: Media Duplication Services Inc 1692 Deere Ave Irvine 92714

MORGAN, CHARLES EDWARD PHILLIP, bank executive; b. Nov. 3, 1916, Wichita, Kansas; s. Wells Carrol and Mary Elizabeth (Brown) M.; m. Elisabeth Ann Brown, 1943; children: Valerie G. b. 1947 Renee b. 1950; edn: Univ. of Wichita 1935; UC Berkeley Grad. Sch. of Bus. Admin. Career: First National Bank, Wichita 1936-38; teller First Nat. Bank, Santa Fe, N.Mex.; safety ofcr. Libby McNeil Libby, Sacramento 1946-67; Wells Fargo Bank 1948-76; var. pos. teller to v.p. and br. mgr. Capitol Bank of Commerce 1976—, senior v.p.; mem: Sacramento Lodge No. 40 F&AM, Scottish Rite of Free Masonry (Sacramento), Ben Ali Temple (Sacramento); mil: 1st lt. USAF, rated pilot (1943), rated navigator (1944); Democrat; Christian; rec: fishing, woodworking. Res: 6371 Granger's Dairy Dr. Sacramento 95831

MORGAN, EARL WAYNE, research veterinary toxicologist; b. Oct. 7, 1951, Seymour, Ind.; s. Marion Earl and Emma Belle (Harrell) M.; m. Hyo Kang, Nov. 5, 1977; children: Elizabeth b. 1979, Earl II b. 1980; edn: BS in agric., Univ. Mo. Columbia 1973, DVM, 1976; Diplomate Am. Coll. Vet. Preventive Med. 1984. Career: pvt. vet. practice Richland, Mo., Okla. City 1981-83; prin. investigator in applied toxicology research Letterman Army Inst. Research, Presidio of S.F. 1983—; honors: NSF Scholar in physics (1967), Am. Animal Sci. Assn. Scholar (1970), AF Health Professions Scholar (1973-76), Disting. Grad., Am. Vet. Med. Assn. Outstanding Student (AF Vet. Ofcr. Basic 1976); mem: Am. Vet. Med. Assn., Mo. Vet. Med. Assn., Am. Coll. Vet. Prev. Med., Am. Assn. Food Hygiene Vets., Mo. Alumni Assn. (activities com.); publs: num. tech. reports, paper presented 1985; mil: capt. US Army 1983-, USAR 1982-83, USAFR 1981-82, USAF active 1976-81, USAFR 1973-76; Republican;

Christian; rec: competitive shooting, coin collecting, hunting, fishing. Res: 788 A Vista Ct Presidio of San Francisco 94129 Ofc: SGRD-ULV-T, Letterman Army Inst. Research, Presidio of San Francisco 94129

MORGAN, KILE, elected city official; b. Mar. 22, 1920, Hancock County, Tenn.; s. George Preston and Geneva Mary (Barnard) M.; m. Donna Wilcox, July 28, 1944; children: Janice b. 1945, Kile, Jr. b. 1946, Robert b. 1950; H.S. grad. Ava, Mo. 1938; Calif. lic. real estate broker (1946). Career: prop. used car dealership, 1944-46; real estate builder/devel., 1946-66; elected National City City Council, 1960-66, city mayor 1966-86; club: Kiwanis; Democrat; Baptist; rec: golf. Res: 1223 J Ave National City 92050

MORGAN, W. ROBERT, lawyer; b. Jan. 6, 1924, Arkansas City, Kans.; s. Luois S. and Betty Mae (Starner) M.; m. Willia, Mar. 11, 1945; children: Marilyn, Robert Hall; edn: BA, Stanford Univ., LLB, 1948. Career: ptnr. Morgan, Morgan, Towery, Morgan & Spector; organizer: Triton Ins. Co., radio station 1040 AM Perry, Okla.; mem: Calif. Bar (past v.p.), Santa Clara Bar Assn. (past pres.), Internat. Acad. Trial Lawyers (past pres.), Am. Morgan Horse Assn. (v.p.), No. Calif. Club (pres.), Nat. Morgan Horse Club (pres.), Rotary, Mason (33rd degree), Triton Museum of Art (past pres.); works: reprinted many Morgan Horse books.; mil: 1st lt. US Army infantry, Commendation Ribbon; Democrat; Presbyterian; rec: art, Morgan horses. Res: 9500 New Ave Gilroy 95020 Ofc: Morgan, Morgan et al. 210 S First St, Ste 500, San Jose 95113

MORI, JUN, lawyer; b. Dec. 13, 1929, San Francisco; s. Isamu Arthur and Hide M.; m. May Tsutsumoto, Apr. 29, 1954; children: Richard Isamu, Ken Arthur; edn: BA, UC Los Angeles 1955; LLB, Waseda Univ., Tokyo 1951; JD, Univ. So. Calif. 1958; admitted to Calif. bar 1959, US Supreme Ct. bar 1971, Dist. of Col. bar 1979. Career: deputy commnr. of corporations State of Calif., 1959-60; senior mem. law firm Mori & Ota, Los Angeles 1960-84, ptnr. Kelley Drye & Warren, L.A. 1984−; legal advisor Sumitomo Bank of Calif.; trustee UCLA Found.; mem. Commn. on Pacific Basin Studies UCLA; mem. Bd. of Harbor Commnrs. City of Los Angeles; mem. Pres.'s Export Council; mem: ABA, Am. Judicature Soc., Am. Soc. of Internat. Law, Assn. of Immigration & Nationality Lawyers; mem. LA World Affairs Council, Japan Am. Soc. of So. Calif., Japanese Am. Jr. CofC (pres. 1962-63), chmn. Los Angeles-Nagoya Sister City Affil. (1966-67). Res: 2219 Cheswic Ln Los Angeles 90027 Ofc: Kelley Drye & Warren 624 S Grand Ave Ste 2600 Los Angeles 90017

MORIKAWA, THOMAS MASAYUKI, marketing consultant; b. May 19, 1945, Honolulu; s. Yoshio Morikawa and Janette K. Morikawa Minami; edn: BBA, Univ. Hawaii 1968. Career: restaurant mgr. Disneyland Anaheim 1968, Kahala Hilton Hotel Honolulu 1968-70; dir. sales, mktg. Holiday Inns- Hawaii 1970-72; v.p. Hawaii Star Bakery Inc. 1972-76; dir. sales Holiday Inns- San Francisco Dist. 1976-79, worldwide sales mgr. 1979-80; regnl. dir. of sales Hyatt Hotels Hawaii S.F. 1980-81; senior acct. exec. Focus Communications Group San Jose 1981-82; dir. mktg. Queen Anne S.F. 1982-83; pres. Morikawa Group Inc. S.F. 1984−; mktg. seminars and presentations var. assns. and colls.; mem: Hotel Sales Mktg. Assn. Internat. (chpt. pres. 1981), S.F. Convention & Visitors Bureau, Calif. Hotel & Motel Assn., Travel & Tourism Assn., former Optimists Internat. (Hawaii chpt. pres. 1976); rec: theater, painting. Ofc: The Morikawa Group 675 California St San Francisco 94108

MORINELLO, CARMEN ANGELO, lawyer; b. Feb. 19, 1955, Niagra Falls, NY; s. Angelo and Grace (Scerbo) M.; m. Susanne, Nov. 27, 1977; children: Michael Angelo b. 1982, Joseph Carmine b. 1983; edn: BA, Niagra Univ. 1977; JD, Pepperdine Univ. Sch. of Law 1980. Career: mng. ptr. Mare Tow & Assoc. 1981-84; mng. ptr. Morinello, Barone, Holden & Nardulli Newport Beach 1984−; dir. Nat. Copaitor Corp.; mem: Am. and Orange Co. Bar Assns., Orange Co. and Newport CofCs, Order Son of Holy in Am. (trustee); Catholic; rec: golf, mountain climbing. Res: 228 No. Highland Ave. Orange 92660 Ofc: Morinello, Barone, Holden & Nardulli 4921 Birch St. Ste. 100 Newport Beach 92660

MOROSO, MICHAEL JOSEPH, senior aerospace engineer, scientist; b. Jan. 26, 1923, Centerville, Iowa; s. John and Antoinette (Sartor) M.; m. Jody, June 16, 1951; children: Barbara b. 1953, Michael Jr. . 1956, Robert b. 1957, Philip b. 1960; edn: naval aviator, Pensacola Flight Sch. 1945; BSME, Univ. Wisc. 1952; Univ. So. Calif. 1968-69. Career: flight instr. USN Pensacola, Fla. 1945-47; designer Douglas Aircraft Co. Santa Monica 1952-65; engr./ scientist McDonnell Douglas Launch Ctr. Vandenberg 1965-70; engr./ scientist splst. McDonnell Douglas Astronautics Co. Huntington Beach 1970-76; senior propulsion engr. Northrop Corp. Hawthorne 1976-79; senior engr./ scientist Douglas Aircraft Co. Long Beach 1979−; honors: Hon. Bausch & Lomb Science Award (1941); assoc. fellow Am. Inst. Aero & Astro. (1982); mem: AIAA 1956-, Douglas Mgmt. Club (membership booster 1965-), Am. Legion, St. John's Men's Club, Little League, Assn. Naval Aviation, Boy Scouts of Am., Retired Ofcrs. Assn.; mil: lt. USN 1943-47, NAval Reserve Medal; Democrat; Catholic; rec: bicycling, tennis, hiking, dancing, coins. Res: 964 Lansing Lane Costa Mesa 92626 Ofc: Douglas Aircraft Co. 3855 Lakewood Blvd Long Beach 90846

MORRELL, JAMES WILSON, food service co. executive; b. Feb. 13, 1931, Kalamazoo, Mich.; s. Wilson and Evelyn Jewel (Anderson) M.; m. Marilyn Eck, June 21, 1952; children: Martha Jo b. 1956, David James b. 1958; edn: BA, Kalamazoo Coll. 1953. Career: Saga Corp. 1955−, food svc. mgr. Kalamazoo (Mich.) Coll. 1955-57, dist. mgr. edn. div. Kalamazoo 1958-61, reg. v.p. edn.

div. Menlo Park 1962-66, exec. v.p. adminstrn. 1966-68, pres. Scope 1970-71, pres. Saga Enterprises 1971-78, exec. v.p. & chief op. ofcr. Menlo Park 1978-82, exec. v.p. & member ofc. of the pres. 1983-85, vice chmn. 1985−; dir., bd. trustees Kalamazoo Coll. 1985−; dir., bd. overseers Fdsv. Ctr. NY Univ. 1980−; co-chair Stanford Univ. Hosp. Modernization Proj. 1985; mem: World Bus. Forum (chmn. 1981-), World Bus. Council 1978-; Am. Mgmt. Assn. (bd. dirs.), Calif. Restaurant Assn. (bd.), Culinary Acad. of Am. (bd. overseers), Nat. Restaurant Assn., March of Dimes (Teamwalk chmn. San Mateo Co. 1983-85), Resource Ctr. for Women (chmn. 1976-77); mil: sgt. US Army 1953-55; Republican; Presbyterian; rec: golf, tennis, swimming, photog., gardening, opera, sports. Res: 2 Mesa Ct Atherton 94025 Ofc: Saga Corp. One Saga Ln Menlo Park 94025

MORRELL, LAWRENCE DEAN, psychotherapist; b. Sept. 25, 1934, Galesburg, Ill.; s. James Edward and Doris Dean (Youngquist) M.; m. Deborah Joan Birner, Apr. 19, 1980; children: Elizabeth b. 1961, David b. 1963, Karis b. 1969; edn: BA, California Baptist Coll. 1962; MA, Pepperdine Univ. 1975; PhD psych., US Internat. Univ. 1981; Lic. Marriage, Child & Family Therapist, Calif. 1977. Career: public school tchr. Ocean View Sch. Dist., Huntington Beach 1965-73; psychotherapist pvt. practice, Orange 1970−; cons. Orange County Comm. Drug Council, 1970-71; cons. Orange County Teen Challenge, 1971-73; instr. Lay Minister Tng. Inst., Crystal Cathedral, Garden Grove 1975-80; dir. Christian Edn., FCCA, 1981; honors: Alumnus of Year, Calif. Baptist Coll. (1970), Teacher of Year, Ocean View Sch. Dist. (1970-71), Outstanding Young Men of Am. (1971); mem: Calif. Assn. Marriage, Family and Child Therapists/ Orange County Chpt., Am., Calif., Orange Co. Psychological Assns., Am. Assn. for Therapy, Marriage and Family, Clin. Western Psychol. Assn., Rotary, Marine Corps Assn., Am. Legion; publs: Attitudes of Adolescents toward Psychotherapy (1981), Psychic Controversies and the Christian Faith (1979); mil: sgt. USMC 1953-61, Nat. Def., Good Conduct, Meritorious Service; Republican; So. Baptist; rec: photog., writing, Am. Indian relics. Res: 3230 N Hartman St Orange 92665 Ofc: 1301 E Lincoln Ave Ste E Orange 92665

MORREY, ROBERT A., educator; b. Mar. 31, 1941, Berkeley; s. Charles B., Jr. and Frances E. M.; m. Barbara, July 3, 1966; children: Christina b. 1971, Charles B, III b. 1973; edn: BA and MA in German, Stanford Univ. 1964, 65, MA in edn. 1966, PhD in fgn. lang. edn. 1970. Career: high sch. tchr. Mission San Jose H.S., Fremont 1966-68, Capuchino H.S., San Bruno 1971, Cupertino H.S., 1971−; instr. CSU Hayward 1970, Coll. of San Mateo 1971, 72, 73, Coll. of Notre Dame 1972, 74; edn. dir. Radio Shack Computer Ctr., San Jose 1980-82; book salesman p.t. Newbury House Pubs., Rowley, Mass. 1977-83; pioneer in devel. computer-aided fgn. language programs in Calif. (1979-): obtained grant and dist. funding for devel. fgn. language technology center at Cupertino H.S. (34 microcomputers in 5 fgn. lang. classrooms), devel. inservice tng. of tchrs. in use of microcomputers in fgn. language classroom; lectr. local and nat. confs. (1982-); mem. sev. local, state and nat. profl. assns. incl. Calif. Fgn. Lang. Tchrs. Assn. and Fgn. Lang. Assn. of No. Calif.; works: num. lectures, sev. articles, 3 book chpts. on fgn. language pedagogy (1979-), devel. computer pgms. for learning German for classroom use, French & Spanish versions w/ co-authors; Republican; Prot.; rec: ski, backpack, gardening. Res: 3404 Merrimac Dr San Jose 95117 Ofc: Cupertino High School 10100 Finch Ave Cupertino 95014

MORRILL, L. MICHAEL, savings & loan association president; b. Sept. 3, 1948, Los Angeles; s. Dr. Lewis V. and Betty Jane (Miller) M.; edn: BS gen. mgmt., CSU Sacto. 1971. Career: loan ofcr., ops. ofcr., asst. mgr. Calif. Fed. Svgs & Loan Assn., Los Angeles 1971-75; mgr. Home Svgs & Loan Assn., Vacaville 1975-76, senior tng. ofcr. No. Calif., (Oakland) 1975-76, mgr. No. and So. Calif., 1977-78; pres./CEO Redding Svgs & Loan Assn., 1978-80 (achieved top ranking in US based on return on av. assets); cons. New Horizons Svgs & Loan Assn., San Rafael 1980; dir./ pres./ CEO Washington Svgs & Loan Assn., Stockton 1980−; instr. Inst. of Finl. Edn.; past instr. Savings and Loan Inst.; apptd. by Gov. Brown to var. task forces on industry guidelines; honors: at age 27 was the youngest Savings & Loan pres. in the US; mem. Calif. Savings and Loan League (t.v. and radio spkr), Soc. for Advance. of Mgmt., Kiwanis, Lions; mil: sp5 Army Med. Corps; Prot.; rec: water and snow skiing, bicycling, photog. Res: 9308 Single Tree Ct Stockton 95209 Ofc: Washington Savings & Loan Assn 526 W Benjamin Holt Dr Stockton 95207

MORRIS, EFFIE LEE, library consultant/lecturer; b. Apr. 20, Richmond, Va.; d. William H. and Erma (Caskie) M; m. Leonard Jones, Aug. 25, 1971; edn: BA, Case Western Res. Univ., 1945; BLS, 1946; MSLS, 1956; EdD, in progress, Univ. of San Francisco 1978-. Career: childs splst. Library for the Blind 1958-63; coord. Childrens Svcs., San Francisco Pub. Lib. 1963-78; senior ed. Harcourt Brace Jovanovich 1978-79; lectr. Childrens Literature, Mills Coll. 1981−; contbg. writer var. profl. publs. honors: The San Francisco Pub. Lib. designated The Effie Lee Morris Hist. & Research Collections of Childrens Literature, Nov. 1981; recipient 1984 Women's National Book Assn. Award; mem. Advis. Council, Mayor's Office of Child Care 1979-; apptd. Calif. Lib. Svcs. Board 1982-84, 1984-88; mem: Childrens Svcs. Lib., Calif. Lib. Assn. (pres. 1969-71); Am. Lib. Assn. (mem. Council 1984-88, pres. Public Library Assn. 1971-72); The Center for The Book of the Library of Congress (Adv. Bd. 1979-); Alpha Kappa Alpha sorority; Commonwealth Club. rec: reading. Res: 66 Cleary Ct San Francisco 94109

MORRIS, GRETCHEN JULIANA, financial executive; b. Dec. 23, 1948, San Francisco; d. John W. and Helen W. M.; 1 son, Timothy b. 1968; edn: BA psychol., CSU Los Angeles 1971, tchg. credl., 1974; MA behav. sci., CSU

Dominguez Hills 1983; Certified Am. Soc. Psychoprophylaxis in Obstetrics (UCLA) 1980. Career: tchr. L.A. Unified Sch. Dist. 1973-85; prepared childbirth instr. Rogers Park, Southwest Coll., Maxie Care, Watts Health Found. 1977-85; life & disability ins. agent 1983–; gen. securities reg. rep. NASD, advis. rep. Southmark Financial Svcs. Inc. 1985–; mem: Am. Soc. Psychoprophylaxis in Obstets., Internat. Assn. Financial Planners, Alpha Kappa Alpha, Ebony Guild; author: Personality Characteristics of Participating and Non-participating Fathers During Childbirth, contbr. to article in Wave Newspaper, IRAs Gain Popularity with Blacks, Minorities Seeking Tax Relief and Retirement Security; Democrat; rec: crafts, music, reading, coins, stamps. Res: 1936 W 73rd St Los Angeles 90047 Ofc: 2425 Colorado Ave Santa Monica 90404

MORRIS, JEFFREY ALBERT, investor; b. Mar. 2, 1955, San Mateo, Calif.; s. Mervin G. and Roslyn L. (Grossman) M.; m. Debra Ziegler, Sept. 11, 1977; children: Kimberly b. 1980, Matthew b. 1982, Jeffrey, Jr. b. 1984, Andrew b. 1986; edn: AB econs., Stanford Univ. 1977; MBA acctg. & finance., UC Los Angeles 1979. Career: v.p. Morris Mgmt. Co. Menlo Park; dir. The Pacific Bank, Buck Club (Stanford Univ.), Big Brothers/ Big Sisters; mem: Urban Land Inst., Menlo Circus Club; rec: athletics. Ofc: Morris Mgmt. Co. 3000 Sand Hill Rd Menlo Park 94025

MORRIS, JOHN HARVEY, architectural engineer; b. May 11, 1946, Los Angeles; s. Howard Denver and Marilee (Minor) M.; m. Sharon D., June 4, 1968; children: Traci Michelle b. 1969, Nicole Kristine b. 1970; edn: AA, Los Angeles Trade Tech. Coll. 1966; BS, CSU Los Angeles 1976; Cert. in Reinforced Concrete Design, UCLA 1977; Cert. in Flood Flow Frequency Analysis, UC Davis 1976, Cert. HE6-2 Water Surface Profile Computation, 1977; Reg. Profl. Engr., Calif. 1981. Career: design engr. Benito A. Sinclair & Assoc., Los Angeles 1975-81; staff engr. Psomas & Assoc., Santa Monica 1981-82; pres., owner Morris & Assoc. Cons. Engrs. Los Angeles 1982; physical devel. mgr. Community Redevel. Agency, City of Compton 1982-83; ptr., co-owner Architects, Engineers, Planners, Inc., Santa Monica 1983-84, pres., 1984–; bd. dirs. Route 2 Community Housing Corp.; co-founder Council for Black Engring., Math and Science Students, CSU Los Angeles 1980; honors: Martin L. King Award, CSU Los Angeles Sch. of Engring. 1974; mem: Am. Soc. Civil engrs., Los Angeles Council of Black Profl. Engrs., Cons. Structural Engr Soc., Constrn. Specifications Inst., Nat. Orgn. Minority Architects, Kenwood Neighborhood Assn., West Adams Heritage Assn., Los Angeles Athletic Club; works: with Benito Sinclair, Hydrology for Flood Insurance Studies in Southeast Arizona in Conjunction, Fed. Emerg. Mgmt. Admin. 1970; mil: splst. 4/c US Army 1966-68; rec: batik, tie-dyeing, ceramics. Res: 3014 Kenwood Ave. Los Angeles 90007 Ofc: A.E.P. Inc., 2221 Neilson Way Santa Monica 90405

MORRIS, PAUL J., state prison warden; b. June 28, 1929, Chgo.; s. Paul A. and Catharine (Summers) M.; m. Marva Daly, Dec. 1976; children: Paul J., II, b. 1952, Catherine Solis, b. 1954, Marie Rubio, b. 1957, Candy, b. 1965; ed. var. colls. Career: correctional officer, San Quentin 1951, promoted to sgt., Tehachapi 1955, lieut., Camp Minnewawa in San Diego Co., 1958, apptd. supr. of camp tng. Calif. Instn. for Men, Chino 1961-63, promoted to capt., Calif. Rehabilitation Center, 1964; served as Jail Insp., Bd. of Corrections; program adminstr. in charge of central camps, Sierra Conservation Camp; assoc. supt. CIM, 1970; asst. in reorganization of Soledad facility, then deputy supt.; apptd. by Gov. as supt. Calif. Correctional Center 1975-76; warden Folsom State Prison, 1976–; mem. Folsom CofC, Folsom Hist. Soc., Folsom Sports Complex Blue Ribbon Commn., Economic Devel. Council, Am. Correctional Assn.; mil: pfc USAF; rec: reading, fishing, camping. Address: Folsom State Prison, PO Box W, Represa 95671

MORRIS, ROBERT RUSSELL, physician and surgeon; b. Jan. 30, 1919, Hong Kong, BCC, Am. citizen by birth; s. Clarence Coat and Florence May (Christman) M.; m. Carol Campbell, Dec. 21, 1944; children: Charles b. 1946, Leonard b. 1948, Liana b. 1949; edn: BS, Columbia Union Coll. 1946; MD, Loma Linda Univ. 1947, pathology residency LLU 1947-50; Pathologist, Bd. Certified in Anatomic (1954), Forensic (1961), Clinical (1963) Path.; med. lic. Calif. (1947), Ariz. (1981). Career: started practice of pathology, Eureka 1950-75 (ret.), senior pathologist until 1975: Humboldt Path. Lab. Med. Group, Inc. and St. Joseph, General, Humboldt County, Redwood Meml., Mad River, Seaside (Crescent City), Garberville Comm. hospitals, med. dir. No. Calif. Blood Bank; (current) pathologist for Coroner of Humboldt County, 1982–; awards: Owen Thomas Award, Calif. Blood Bank System 1977; mem. AMA, CMA, Humboldt Del Norte Co. Med. Soc.; past pres. Kiwanis Club Eureka; publs: art. in J. of Forensic Scis. (1985); Republican; Prot.; rec: ham radio opr. Res: POB 6149 Eureka 95502 Ofc: Coroner, 3012 I St Eureka 95502

MORRISON, DARYL EUGENE, business executive; b. Feb. 5, 1931, Marysville; s. John Eugene and Irlene Alberta (Cook) M.; children: Terrie Lynn b. 1953, Eugene Scott b. 1955. Career: farming, food processing, 1954-61; real estate devel./constrn., 1961–; pres: Yuba City Refrigeration Co. Inc., 1972–, Hillcrest Water Co. Inc., 1962–, Morrison Orchard Suply Co., 1950–, Calif. Kiwi Products, 1985–; mil: US Navy 1950-54; Republican; Prot.; rec: hunt, ski, flying, boating. Res: 680 Jones St Yuba City 95991 Ofc: Morrison International POB 89 Yuba City 95991

MORSE, ROBERT MORETON, engineering and construction executive; b. Dec. 6, 1937, Pasadena; s. Barnard Alexander and Muriel Secor (Moreton) M.; m. Karen Lee Zeiders, June 28, 1986; children: Erin b. 1969, Heather b. 1970, Chelsea b. 1975, Megan b. 1979; edn: AA, Pasadena City Coll. 1957; BS, USC 1961. Career: acct. Twentieth Century, 1958, 61; purchasing agent Bechtel Power Corp., 1964-66, senior engr. 1966-67, bus. devel. mgr. 1967-76, mgr. of div. bus. devel., Internat. and Domestic, 1976-82, mgr. Internat. Ops., 1982-84, regl. v.p. and gen. mgr. (Southwestern U.S.) Ebasco Services Inc., Santa Ana; pres., dir. E&L Technologies Long Beach; dir. Pacific Transportation Svcs. Inc. Irvine 1986–; dir. Bechtel Adv. Group 1977-78, v.chmn. 1977, chmn. 1978, Bechtel Corp. Bus. Devel. Com.; mem: ASME, Atomic Indsl. Forum (dir.), Am. Nuclear Soc. (library mem.), Pac. Coast Elec. Assn. (com. chmn.), Los Angeles CofC (Water & Power Com.), Iran-Am. CofC, Masons, Knight Templar; clubs: Valley Hunt, Pacific, Center, Newport Beach Country, Balboa Bay, Silverado Country; mil: capt. USMC 1960-64; Republican; Episcopal; rec: tennis, golf, upland game shooting, fly fishing. Res: 3405 N Marengo Ave Altadena 91001 Ofc: Ebasco Services Inc. 3000 W MacArthur Blvd Santa Ana 92704

MORTON, ROBERT LEROY, oilfield contractor; b. Mar. 9, 1941, Taft; s. Samuel Mahlan and Belva Imogene (Jameson) M.; m. Sandra, Jan. 14, 1942; children: Dianna (Given) b. 1963, Denise b. 1967, Suzanne b. 1970; edn: AA, Taft Coll. 1962. Career: worked in the oil fields 1960s–, bought family firm (local work w/20 employees), devel. co. into internat. firm (225 empl.); owner: Bob Morton Const. Inc., R.L. Morton Welding Inc., co-owner South West Ready Mix Inc., McKittrick Oilfield Supply; founder/dir. Taft Nat. Bank; honors: Jefferson Sch. Volunteer of Year (1978), Boy Scout Patron Award, Pyles Boys Camp service award; mem. Taft CofC (v.p.), West Kern Oil Museum (bd.), R.M. Pyles Boys Camp (v.p. bd. dirs.), NSCA (bd.); Republican; rec: game hunter, sand racing, fisherman. Res: 716 Vista Via Dr Taft 93268 Ofc: Bob Morton Const., Inc. 27506 Hwy 119 (POB N) Taft 93268

MOSES, STEPHEN DAVID, investment co. executive; b. Nov. 24, 1934, Phila.; s. Lester Jacob and Rosalie (Berg) M.; m. Katherine Cone Keck, 1984; children: Kathryn b. 1963, K. Robert (Bobby) b. 1969; edn: BS in econ., Franklin & Marshall Coll. 1955; JD cum laude, Harvard Law Sch. 1958. Career: atty. Fran Bernstein Gutberlet and Conaway, Baltimore, Md. 1960-65; dir. Balt. Metro. AREA Study Comm., 1961-63; dir. Urban Development Div., Action Inc., Wash DC 1963-65; City Reconstrn. Corp. 1965-67; Boise Cascade Corp. 1967-70; Transcontinent Realty Corp. 1971-73; Nat. Devel. Corp. 1975–; apptd. by gov. Creative Financing Advisory Panel of State of Calif.; dir. Nat. Housing Conf.; mem. nat. advisory bd. Center for Nat. Policy; honors: Housing Man of the Year (1970); civic: Hebrew Union Coll. (bd. govs.), Franklin & Marshall Coll. (bd. trustees), Pitzer Coll. (bd. trustees), UCLA Found. (bd. trustees), Leo Baeck Temple (pres., trustee), Brentwood Sch. (chmn., trustee), Frat. of Friends of L.A. Co. Music Center (v.p.), Menorah Housing Found.; publs: num. articles in trade periodicals, lectr. var. colls. and univs.; mil: pfc. US Army 1959; Democrat (nat. fin. vice chair Dem. Nat. Com.; advis. com. Dem. Caucus Housing Task Force); Jewish; rec: tennis, classical music. Res: 12850 Marlboro St Los Anglees 90049 Ofc: Stephen Moses Interests, 11812 San Vicente Blvd 6th Flr Los Angeles 90049

MOSHER, SALLY EKENBERG, company president; b. July 26, 1934, NY, NY; d. Leslie Joseph and Frances Josephine (McArdle) Ekenberg; m. James Kimberly Mosher (dec. 1982), Aug. 13, 1960; edn: B.Mus., Manhattanville Coll. 1956; postgrad. Hofstra Univ. 1958-60, USC 1970-73; JD, USC Sch. of Law 1981; admitted to State Bar of Calif. 1982; Calif. lic. R.E. Broker 1984. Career: musician: pianist, tchr., critic (newspaper), coach, concert mgr., New York and Los Angeles 1957-74; rep. Occidental Life, Pasadena 1975-78; v.p. James K. Mosher Co. Inc., Pasadena 1961-82, pres. 1982–; pres. Oakhill Enterprises, Pasadena 1984–; assoc. White-Howell Inc., Pasadena 1984–; awards: Full Honor Scholarship, Manhattanville Coll. (1952-56), spl. election Mu Phi Epsilon (1970); mem: Kappa Gamma Pi, Mu Phi Epsilon, Phi Alpha Delta, Assocs. of CalTech, Athenaeum; Am., Calif., Los Angeles and Pasadena bar assns.; Am., Calif. and Pasadena (board of) assns. of realtors; civic: Pasadena Athletic Club, Upper Rancheros Rd. Assn. (pres. 1981-83), Pasadena Arts Council (ofcr. 1966-8, dir. 1986), Junior League Pasadena (dir. 1966-7), Encounters Concerts (dir. 1966-72), USC Friends of Music (dir. 1973-6), Pasadena Chamber Orch. (dir. 1986); publs: articles and music reviews 1966-72; Republican; Christian; rec: graphic design. Res: 1260 Rancheros Rd Pasadena 91103 Ofc: 711 E Walnut Ste 407 Pasadena 91101

MOSK, STANLEY, state supreme court justice; b. Sept. 4, 1912, San Antonio, Tex.; s. Paul and Minna (Perl) M.; m. Edna Mitchell, Sept. 27, 1936 (dec); 1 son: Richard Mitchell; m. 2d. Susan Jane Hines, Aug. 27, 1982; edn: stu. Univ. of Tex. 1931; PhB, Univ. of Chicago 1933, stu. Law Sch. 1935, Hague Acad. Internat. Law 1970; LLD, Univ. of the Pacific 1970, Univ. of San Diego 1971, Univ. of Santa Clara 1976; admitted State Bar of Calif. 1935. Career: practicing atty., Los Angeles 1935-39; exec. secty. to gov. Calif., 1939-42; judge superior ct. Los Angeles County, 1943-58; pro tem justice Dist. Ct. Appeal, Calif., 1954; state atty. gen., also head state dept. justice, 1959-64; justice Calif. Supreme Ct., 1964–; vis. prof. Santa Clara Univ. 1981-82. Mem. Calif. Commn. Jud. Qualifications, Calif. Disaster Council, Colo. River Boundary Commn., Calif. Commn.; Peace Ofcr. Stds., Dist. Securities Commn., Calif. Commn. Ofcl. Reports of Cts., Calif. Reapportionment Commn.; state chmn. Thanks to Scandinavia Fund, 1967-8; chmn. S.F. Internat. Film Festival, 1967; bd. regents Univ. Calif., 1940; pres. Vista Del Mar Child Care Svc., 1954-8; recipient disting. alumnus award Univ. Chgo., 1958; mem: Nat. Assn. Attys. Gen. (exec. bd.), Western Assn. Attys. Gen., pres. 1963), ALA, Los Angeles, Santa Monica, San Francisco, Korean bar assns., Am. Judicature Soc., Am. Legion, Manuscript Soc., Univ. Chgo. Alumni Assn. (pres. No. Calif. 1966-8), Phi Sigma Delta, Phi Alpha Delta, Bnai Brith; clubs: Lawyers, Town Hall (LA), Commonwealth (SF), Beverly Hills Tennis; mil: served in US Army WWII;

mem. Democratic Nat. Com. 1960-64. Res: 1200 California St San Francisco 94109 Ofc: State Bldg San Francisco 94102

MOSKOWITZ, ALLYN MARK, certified public accountant; b. Jan. 24, 1959, Little Neck, N.Y.; s. Bernard and Lorraine (Feldman) M.; edn: BS acctg., State Univ., of N.Y. Albany 1980; CPA N.Y. 1982, Calif. 1984. Career: Dean Witter Reynolds stockbrokerage Manhattan 1978, Loeb Rhoades Hornblower 1979; senior acct. Deloitte, Haskins & Sells N.Y. 1980-82, Touche, Ross & Co. San Jose 1982-83; controller Arbco Assoc. Beverly Hills 1983-84; treas., bd. dirs. Paragon Partnership Svcs. Inc. 1984-85; chmn. bd., pres. Moskowitz Financial Svcs. Inc. L.A. 1984–; founder, sr. ptnr. A.M. Moskowitz & Co. L.A. CPA firm spec. in real estate and taxation 1985–; honors: Regents Scholar 1976, Dean's List (SUNY Albany 1977-80); mem: Am. Inst. CPAs 1982-85, Community Assns. Inst. 1985; rec: microcomputer systems, investment analysis, athletics. Ofc: Moskowitz Financial Svcs. 9348 Santa Monica Blvd, Ste 101, Beverly Hills 90210

MOSS, CHARLES NORMAN, physician; b. June 13, 1914, Los Angeles; m. Margaret Louise; 1 dau., Lori Anne b. 1967; edn: AB, Stanford Univ. 1940; MD, Harvard Med. Sch. 1944; MPH, UC Berkeley 1955; Senior Flight Surgeon, USAF 1956; Dr.PH, UC Los Angeles 1970; Aviation Med. Examiner, FAA (1970). Career: surg. intern Peter Bent Brigham Hosp., Boston 1944-45; med. ofcr. US Army 1945-49: female ward, Birmingham Gen. Hosp., Van Nuys, 1945; Battalion surg., Shanghai and Peiping, China 1945-47 (responsible med. care for 2500, supr. 18 personnel); med. ofcr. US Air Force 1949-65: Wing Base surg., Wing Flight surg. and Med. Group comdr. 86th Fighter-Bomber Wing, Germany 1949-52, med. care 6000, supr. 48 personnel; surg., flight surg., and med. group comdr. San Antonio Air Material Area, Kelly AFB, Tx. 1952-54, med. care for 45,000, supr. 65 personnel; Preventive Med. Div., Communicable Disease Ofcr., Office of AF Surg. Gen., Wash DC 1955-59, supr. preparation & publ. of num. AF regulations and pamphlets, served on var. boards and coms. incl. Nat. Acad. of Sci., Nat. Research Council, Army-AF Master Menu Bd., US Civil Service Examiners; hosp. comdr. and flight surg. NATO Hdqtrs., AF & Army, Izmir, Turkey 1959, med. care for 10,000, supr. 45 med. personnel; chief Missile Test and Range Support Div., Staff Surgeon's Ofc., Atlantic Missile Range and Cape Canaveral 1959-61, med. care for 18,000, supr. up to 80; safety ofcr. and occupational med., Orlando AFB, Fla. and Lookout Mtn. AF Station, Los Angeles, 1961-64, ret. lt. col. 1965; med. dir. No. Am. Rockwell Corp., L.A. div. 1969-70; physician, Los Angeles Co. 1970–: Occupational Health Svc., Dept. of Personnel 1970-73, chief Med. Adv. Unit L.A. Co. Bd. of Retirement, Community Health Servs. 1973-79, med. cons. Health Facilities div. Dept. Health Servs. 1979-81; recipient Physician's Recogn. Awards, AMA, 1969, 72, 76, 79, 82; team physician Am. Weightlifting Team winner World Championships in Paris (1950), and Milan (1951); Presbyterian; rec: nutrition, wt.lifting, photog. Res: 7714 Cowan Ave Los Angeles 90045

MOSS, MIKE, economist; b. Feb. 6, 1943, N.Y.C.; s. Ed and Rose (Goldstein) M.; m. Sally Schneider, Dec. 12, 1984; edn: Miami Dade Coll. 1961-62, Univ. of Miami, Fla. 1963-64; Chartered Life Underwriter (1972). Career: div. mgr. Nat. Cash Register, Miami, Fla. 1964-69; asst. gen. mgr. Mass. Mutual Life Ins. Co., Miami 1969-74; mgr. Home Life Ins. Co. of New York, Coral Gables, Fla. 1974-80; pres. Moss Group, San Diego 1982–; awards: Order of the Nail brotherhood award, Yosemite Nat. Park (1981), Personality of the South, Miami (1979-80); mem. Market Technicians Assn., The Duck Club, San Diego Computer Soc., Soc. for the Investigation of Reoccurring Events, Commodity Research Bur. (1983-); past mem. Fla. Gen. Agents & Mgr's Assn. (Fla. State Ram Award 1979), Nat. Gen. Agts. & Mgrs. Assn./Fla. (nat. mgmt. award 1976, 77, 78); civic: Nat. FMCA, Calif. FMCA, Good Sam Club, Masons, Scripps Clinic & Research Found. (Research Council), Balboa Park Mus. of Art (San Diego), Cassidy's Mission Beach Bike Patrol, Cinema Soc. of San Diego; author novel: Snow White; rec: camping, biking, tennis, boating. Res: POB 90566 San Diego 92109

MOTAMENI, MEHDI, importer-exporter; b. Dec. 19, 1931, Iran; s. Safar Ali and H. M.; m. Zahra, Aug. 20, 1962; children: Mercedeh b. 1963, Alireza b. 1968, Ahmad reza b. 1983; edn: BA in Eng. lit., Univ. of Teheran 1955, BA in mgmt. 1956, MA in sociol. 1960; PhD econ., Walden Univ. 1976. Career: economic research, Univ. of Teheran; exclusive agt./distbr. internat. for sev. indsl. and prodn. cos.; elected to bd. dirs. Iran Chamber of Commerce Industries & Mines; headed Iran Economic Mission to several countries and traveled to 60+ other countries; current: pres. World Overseas, and was mng. dir. Iran Industrial Vehicle Mfg. Co.; honors: Commendatore, Pres. of Italy (1976) Edn. and Sci.; Homayoon (1975); mem. Internat. Chamber of Commerce/Paris 1967- (v.p. Irananian Com.; ICC del. to Istanbul 1969, Vienna 1971, Rio de Janeiro 1973, Madrid 1975, Orlando 1978, Manila 1981, Seoul 1976, Amsterdam 1975); publs: Social Problems of Teheran (1964), A Study of Residential Problems (1964); Islam. Address: Los Angeles 90077

MOUCK, NORMAN GARRISON, JR., retired community college superintendent- president; b. Sept. 9, 1928, Omaha, Nebr.; s. Norman G. and Madge Arvilla (Bossoh) M.; m. Dorothy Davis, Jan. 3, 1949; children: Susan, b. 1949; Richard, b. 1952; Teresa, b. 1956; edn: BS, Edinboro State Coll. 1953; M.Ed, UCLA 1956, doctoral studies, 1956-58; MBS, Univ. of Colo. 1959-60; doctoral cand., UCLA 1965-67. Career: dept. chmn./ tchr. math., physics, chem., earch scis. & geography, Fontana H.S. 1954-61; lectr./ supvr. tchr. edn. USC Santa Barbara 1965-66; dir. research & devel./ asst. dean of instrn./ div. chmn./ prof. math. Santa Barbara City Coll. 1961-68; asst. supt. instrn. Santa Clarita Comm. Coll. Dist./ v.p. Coll. of the Canyons 1968-79, interim supt./ pres. Santa Clarita Comm. Coll. District, College of the Canyons 1979, math. instr. 1979-82, supt.-pres. 1982–; cons. Stanford Univ. 1963-64; writer School Mathematics Group, Stanford Univ. 1964; visting asst. prof. of math., Edinboro State Coll.; honors: Nat. Sci. Found. Fellowship, UCLA 1957, Univ. of Colo. 1959-60; Ebell of Los Angeles Scholarship 1953-54; mem: Kiwanis Club (pres. 1978-79); United Crusade; publs: Elementary Algebra for College Students, H.S. Bear & N.G. Mouck; Mathematics Through Science, Revised Parts I-II; mem. writing team Stanford Univ. 1964; mil: surveying and draftsman US Army 1946-49, cartographer 1950-51; Democrat; Presbyterian; rec: swimming, skiing. Res: 28414 Winterdale Dr Canyon Country 91351

MOUREY, RICHARD WARREN, manufacturing co. owner; b. June 13, 1951, Los Angeles; s. Alfred Warren and Geraldine (Rundle) M.; m. Caroline Dunn, Oct. 5, 1985; edn: Rio Hondo Comm. Coll. 1969-71. Career: profl. photographer Watson Studios Whittier 1969-70; chief op. ofcr. L&L Thread Grinding Inc. Paramount 1969-74; qual. control mgr. W.M.C. Grinding Inc. Downey 1974-79; owner, CEO W.M.C. Grinding Inc. Santa Fe Springs 1979–; honors: nom. Business Citizen of the Year (Santa Fe Springs 1986), Svc. Award (LA Unified Sch. Dist. 1985, Metal Trades Advis. Com.); mem: Nat. Tooling & Machining Assn. (chpt. pres. 1986, bd. dirs., trustee nat. com.), US CofC, Nat. Fedn. of Independent Bus., Calif. Assn. Independent Bus., LA Dept. of Apprentice Stds. (apprent. com.), Downey YMCA, Town Hall Calif.; REpublican; Presbyterian; rec: photog., golf, deep sea fishing, big game hunting. Res: 10904 La Mirada Blvd Whittier 90604 Ofc: W.M.C. Grinding Inc. 13721 Milroy PL Santa Fe Springs 90670

MOURI, CAROLE DIANE, private investigator; b. Dec. 10, 1947, Chgo.; d. Nello Mario and Anne Delores (Skrobot) Monterastelli; m. Robert Mouri, Apr. 16, 1974; children: Nealan b. 1965, Monti b. 1968, Lawrence b. 1985; edn: AA, Mt. San Antonio Jr. Coll. 1966; BS, CSU Los Angeles 1970, MS, 1977; Calif. lic. Pvt. Investigator, 1984; Tch. cred. (security, retail sales, mgmt.) 1982. Career: pvt. investigator A. Conrad Investigations, Covina 1970-77; security investig. Mayfair Markets, Los Angeles 1971-73, Fazio's Markets, City of Industry 1973-78; substitute sch. tchr., Baldwin Park 1979–; owner/prin. C.D. Mouri Investigations, 1984–; awards: Top Real Estate agt Century 21 (1979), Top Investig. Fazio's Mkts (1977); mem. Lambda Alpha Epsilon law enforcement frat. 1960-77; civic: Northshore Animal League, Save the Animals Found.; publs: cartoons in weekly antique paper (1979, 80); Republican; Catholic. Address: West Covina 91790

MOY, CARL F., electrical contractor, dairy scientist; b. June 17, 1933, Mondovi, Wis.; s. Lester C. and Deva J. (Wiemer) M.; m. Loida D. Dipple, Sept. 9, 1955; children: Daniel b. 1965, Michelle b. 1968; edn: BS, Univ. of Wis. 1957, Grad. Sch. 1958, 1970. Career: quality control supr. The Borden Co., Rock Is., Ill. 1958-60; cultured products mgr. Penn Supreme Dairies, Inc., Harrisburg, Pa. 1960-64; quality control dir. The Borden Co., Milwaukee, Wis. 1964-68; prof. Dairy Mfg./ mgr. Campus Dairy Plant, Calif. Polytechnic State Univ., San Luis Obispo 1968-84; gen. ptnr. Societe Fromageon, Los Osos 1982-84; indep. electrical contr., Los Osos 1984–; presentations Am. Dairy Sci. Assn. annual meetins, East Lansing, Mich. (1971-), speaker UC Davis Dairy Conf., Creamery Oprs. Assn., Calif. Sanitarians; research publ: Darison Ultrasound Milk Analyszer, research on moisture content of Cheddar Cheese throughout the making process; mil: AC/lt. US Air Force 1953-55; Republican; Prot.; rec: golf, flying, fishing. Address: C. Moy Electric, 2149 Lariat Dr Los Osos 93402

MOY, PETER KARYEN, oral and maxillofacial surgeon; b. Oct. 23, 1951, Hong Kong, nat. US cit. 1977; s. Kein Wee and Bo Shui (Chan) Moy; m. Irene Wong, July 1, 1979; 1 dau. Janine b. 1983; edn: BS, Univ. Pittsburgh 1973, DDM, 1978; splty. in hosp. dentistry, Queen's Med. Ctr. 1979; splty. in oral & maxillofacial surg., UCLA Med. Ctr. 1982; bd. eligible oral & maxillofacial surg. 1982. Career: assoc. Dr. Robert Pittman, Thousand Oaks, Calif. 1982; pvt. solo practice Los Angeles 1982–; asst. clin. prof. Oral & Maxfl. Surg. UCLA 1982–; West Coast cons. for Nobelpharma, Swedish technique for osseointegration; honors: Award for Significant Contbn. to Dental Profession by a Grad. Student (Internat. Coll. of Dentists 1978), Dean's Honor Convocation (1979), Univ. Scholar, Cert. of Merit (Am. Assn. Endodontics 1978), Outstanding Table Clinic Award (Hawaii Dental Assn. 1981); mem: Am. Dental Assn. 1982-, Fellow So. Calif. Soc. of Oral Pathol., Am. Assn. Oral & Maxfl. Surgs., Delta Sigma Delta (secty. 1974-78), Supreme Chpt. Delta Sigma Delta 1978-, Pacific Coast Study Club; invention: localizing and surgical splint for the osseointegration technique 1985; publs: tech. articles in med. and dental jours.; Democrat; Episcopal; rec: photog. Ofc: 10921 Wilshire Blvd Ste 501 Los Angeles 90024

MRAZ, PATRICIA, nurse, home health director; b. Sept. 3, 1954, Lowell, Mass.; d. Joseph J. and Katherine (Backoff) M.; edn: nurse, Fall River Diploma Sch. of Nursing 1975; BS, health sci., Chapman Coll. 1982; public health nsg., honors, CSU Long Beach 1983; MBA, Chapman Coll. 1986. Career: nurse Faulknor Hosp. Boston 1975-76, Hawthorne Comm. Hosp. 1976, Riviera Hosp. Torrance 1976; dir. So. Calif. Comm. Health Assn. L.A. 1977-80; staff nse. So. Bay Hosp. Alcohol Rehab. Unit 1980-81; Home Health dir. Midway Hosp. 1981-84, Internat. Health Ents. 1984, Daniel Freeman Hosp. Inglewood 1984–; lectr. Japanese businessmen re. Home Care implementation in their country; vol. Alcohol Rehab. Harbor Gen. Hosp. 1977; Democrat; rec: running, flute. Ofc: Daniel Freeman Hosp. 333 N Prairie Ave Inglewood 90301

MUCCIGROSSO, DANIEL ANTHONY, bank real property executive; b. July 28, 1931, Elmira, N.Y.; s. Anthony N. and Genevieve (Cassetta) M.; edn: BA, Bowling Green State Univ. 1953. Career: asst. mgr. Display Div., Stuart Sauter

Co., San Francisco 1956-57; asst. prop. mgr. Milton Meyer & Co., S.F. 1960-68; prop. mgr. Callan Stroud & Dale, S.F. 1968-77; mgr. corp. premises/ facilities leasing asst. v.p. The Hibernia Bank (oldest chartered bank in state estab. 1859), S.F. 1978–, incl. hist. landmark, 1 Jones St; real estate cons. City of Mill Valley (1973), Pacific Coast Stock Exchange (1976); founding pres. Art Guild of Ohio (1953); awards for sculpture: 1st Pl. and hon. mention Bowling Green St. Univ. (1952, 53), scenery design, Frankfort Theatre (1955); mem: Bldg. Owners & Mgrs. Assn., BOMA Internat., Frankfurt (Ger.) Playhouse, Washington St. Playhouse (S.F.) 1957-58, S.F. Fairway Golf Club (tournament chmn. 1986); mil: draftsman US Army 1953-55; Republican; Catholic; rec: art, golf, tennis, theatre. Res: 1470 Willard St San Francisco 94117 Ofc: The Hibernia Bank 1 Jones St San Francisco 94102

MUH, ROBERT A., investment banker; b. Jan. 7, 1938, NY, NY; s. Irving and Freida (Glenn) M.; m. Berit, Dec. 19, 1968; childen: Alison b. 1974, Carrie b. 1976; edn: BS, Mass. Inst. of Tech. 1959; MBA, Columbia Univ. 1961, M.Phil., 1965. Career: cons. McKinsey & Co. 1966-69; chmn. Newburger, Loeb & Co. Inc. 1970-72; pres. Financial Svcs. Internat. Inc. 1973-78; mng. dir. Bear, Stearns & Co. Inc., San Francisco 1978–; dir. Certron Corp.; mil: 1st lt. US Army 1961. Ofc: 333 Market St. 29th Flr. San Francisco 94105

MULLAN, JACK W., real estate developer; b. Sept. 17, 1924, Ft. Dodge, Iowa; s. Paul B. and Florence (Zeller) M.; m. Beverly Fortner, Feb. 8, 1951; children: Lori Lee, Jill Ann; edn: BS, USC 1950; postgrad. Univ. J.W. Goathe, Frankfurt, Ger. 1953-54; PhD, San Gabriel Univ. 1970. Career: co-pilot United Airlines 1951-53; mgr. Aero Exploration, Frankfurt, Ger. 1954-55; pres. Mullan R.E. and other real estate devel. cos. 1955–; founding chmn. Orange Co. Econ. Devel. Conf. 1963; bd. dirs. Project 21 Orange Coast Assn., pres. 1986-87; Orange Co. Met. Area Com. 1963; chmn. City Newport Beach Air Traffic Advy. Com. 1967-68; fin. steering com. Orange Co. BSA 1959; trustee So. Calif. Aviation Council pres. 1980-81; pres. 1st Redevel. Agency Orange Co. 1986; mem: Calif. Real Estate Assn., Newport Harbor Bd. Realtors (pres. 1960), Aircraft Owners & Pilots Assn., So. Calif. Aviation Council, Delta Tau Delta; works: co-developer 1st horizontal condominium devel. in Calif.; mil: capt. US Army Air Force 1942-46, PTO. Res: 2031 Mesa Dr. Santa Ana Heights 92707 Ofc: 3400 Irvine Newport Beach 92660

MULLEN, DONALD RICHARD, mechanical engineer; b. May 15, 1947, Urbana, Ill.; s. John Raymond and Juanita Ava (Baker) M.; m. Katherine Latson, Oct. 2, 1983; edn: BSME, CSU San Jose 1971; Reg. Profl. Engr., Calif. (1978). Career: design engr. Peterbilt Motors Co., Newark 1970-74; maintenance engr. Bay Area Rapid Transit, Hayward 1974-77; staff scientist Lawrence Berkeley Lab., Berkeley 1977-80; senior engr. Elliott Control Co., Burlingame 1980-83; staff engr. Amdahl Corp., Sunnyvale 1983–; guest speaker UC Berkeley Engring. Students Career Speaker's Panel, 1985; honors: Tau Beta Pi (1971), ASME appreciation cert., 1985; mem: ASME (chmn. San Francisco Sect. 1984-85, var. coms. 1971-), Engineers Club (S.F.); publs: Locomotive Data Acquisition (1980), Bay Area Rapid Transit Disk Brake Improvement (1977), Air-Cooled Computer (1985); Democrat; Catholic; rec: electronics, photog., R.R. hist., model building. Res: 1901 Briscoe Terrace Fremont 94539 Ofc: Amdahl Corp. 1250 E Arques Ave Sunnyvale 94088

MULLEN, TERRI, educational administrator; b. St. Louis, Mo.; m. Thomas P. Mullen; children: Dabid and Mark b. 1966, Debi b. 1969; edn: BS (valedictorian), Southeast Mo. State Univ. 1964; Univ. Mo. 1964-65; MS sch. adminstrn., CSU Fullerton 1978, MS spl. edn., 1982; EdD instnl. mgmt., Pepperdine Univ. 1985. Career: dir. K-12 Tutoring Svc., Mission Viejo, Calif. 1968-72; chair practical arts and fgn. lang. depts. (gr.8, 9) Irvine Unif. Sch. Dist. 1972-78, site level curric. coord./resource splst. (gr. 9-12) 1981-84; English instr. Coastline Comm. Coll., 1981-82; asst. high sch. prin. Moreno Valley Unif. Sch. Dist. 1984-85; adminstr. spl. svcs. Centralia Sch. Dist., Buena Park 1985–; cons., instrnl. mats. in math and Eng., devel. proficiency tests 1980-82; awards: voted Outstanding Educator of the Year, S.E.L.F. High Sch. staff/ Rotary Award (1984), honors in 5 exams. in doctoral pgm. (1983), honored as tchr. of winning essayists, Herald Examiner (1976, 78), Gregory Fellowship in Eng. (Univ. Mo. 1964); mem: Assn. of Calif. Sch. Adminstrs. 1984, So. Counties Women Mgrs. in Edn. 1983-, Phi Kappa Phi 1978-, Calif. Council Adminstrs. of Spl. Edn. 1986-, Kappa Delta Pi 1963-, Soroptimist; author: Tips of the Trade for the Classroom Aide (1982), Understanding the Handicapped (1981); rec: roller/ice skating. Res: 2359 Engle Dr Riverside 92506 Ofc: Centralia Sch. Dist., 6625 La Palma Ave Buena Park 90620

MULLER, RICHARD ROBERT, cable television executive; b. Mar. 5, 1947, Hollywood, Calif.; s. Robert Harold and Helen Janet (Carty) M.; m. Lee Ann, Jan. 6, 1980; edn: BS finance, magna cum laude, Univ. So. Calif. 1969, MBA, 1970; real estate broker Calif.; class A gen. contractor Calif. Career: dir. mktg. Gill Cable TV Inc. San Jose 1975-77; pres. Trans Pacific Cable Inc. San Jose 1977-78; exec. v.p., gen. mgr. Indiana Cablevision Corp. So. Bend, Ind. 1978-79; v.p. Buford Television Inc. Tyler, Tex. 1979-80; v.p. The Security Channel L.A. 1980-82; v.p. Times Mirror Cable TV Irvine 1982–; bd. dirs. Homeguard of Am. Inc. L.A.; honors: Addy Award (Am. Mktg. Assn. 1979); mem: Cable Television Adminstrn. & Mktg. Soc., Am. Mktg. Assn., USC Alumni Assn., Toastmasters Internat., Braille Inst. (sustaining patron), Oceanaut Dive Club of Bev. Hills; publ: Calif. Legislature's Joint Subcommittee on Telecommunications Cable Report, Orange County Bus. Magazine; Republican; Catholic; rec: boating, scuba, jogging, travel, communications. Res: 1528 Santiago Dr Newport Beach 92660

MULLINER, DAVID KING, chemical engineer; b. Apr. 15, 1921, Twin Falls, Ida.; s. Sidney Jones and Viola Mae (Doll) M.; m. Margaret Maughan, Nov. 1, 1947; children: Stephen b. 1950, Bruce b. 1952, Donna b. 1954, Paul b. 1964; edn: BS chem., San Diego State Univ. 1949, postgrad. 1953-55; Reg. Profl. Engr. Calif. 1976. Career: chemist San Diego Gas & Elec. Co. 1949-51; photo lab supv. USAF 1951; measurement engr. SDG&E 1953-62, gas instrument supv. 1962-72, senior engr. 1972-82; geothermal cons. Mulliner Assoc. 1982–; instr. marine biol. PADI Coll. 1980; mem: Pacific Coast Gas Assn. (life) 1950-, Am. Chemical Soc. 1950-55, Instrument Soc. of Am. 1960-82, Western Soc. Malacologists (pres. 1965), San Diego Shell Club (v.p. 1965, pres. 1966), Boy Scouts of Am. (leader 1966), San Diego Natural History Museum (research assoc.); patent: apparatus and method for odorizing Liquid Natural Gas with Thiophene 1974; publ: research articles for S.D. Nat. Hist. Mus.; mil: msgt USAAF 1942-45, USAF 1951-53, EAME Theater, Air Medal w/ 2 olc, Unit Citation w/ olc; Republican; rec: marine biol., scuba, photog. Address: 5283 Vickie Dr San Diego 92109

MUMAW, JAMES WELSEY, funeral director; b. May 26, 1916, Lancaster; s. Roy S. and Florence M. (Rector) M.; m. Marian, May 29, 1953; 1 son, Jim b. 1955; edn: grad. Antelope Valley H.S. 1934; grad. Calif. Coll. Embalming, L.A. 1936, Calif. lic. (No. 2570) Funeral Dir., Embalmer. Career: youthful asst., later firm's ambulance man/embalmer, now owner/funeral dir./embalmer Mumaw Funeral Home (3d generation owner family bus. estab. 1913, with son Jim as 4th gen.), Lancaster 1913–; charter mem. Lancaster Elks Lodge 1625; works: co-devel. w/son the first profl. car for the funeral industry, winner top honors in class at custom car show, and featured in nat. mag. article; mil: tech. sgt. US Army, WWII; Republican; Prot.; rec: family R.V. travel. Ofc: Mumaw Funeral Home 44663 N Date Ave (POB 1067) Lancaster 93534

MUMBY, EDWARD SHELDON, mechanical engineer; b. Sept. 18, 1955, Tura, Assam, India; s. Winston Westly and Carol Elizabeth (Downs) M.; m. Maria, July 21, 1984; 1 son, James Winston b. 1985; edn: BS, Davidson 1977; MS, Ga. Inst. of Technol. 1978. Career: mech. engr. Exploration Logging Sacramento 1978-84, senior mech. engr. 1984–; mem. Am. Soc. Mech. Engrs.; patents: servo value for well logging telemetry (1983), apparatus for well logging while drilling (1983), apparatus for well logging telemetry (1985); Republican; Presbyterian; rec: racquetball, skiing, volleyball. Res: 5084 Tonya Way Carmichael 95608 Ofc: Exploration Logging 1770 Tribute Rd Sacramento 95815

MUNDHENK, ALVIN ROBERT, physician, surgeon; b. Nov. 27, 1914, Gildford, Mont.; s. Norman and Ethel Odessa (Harwood) M.; m. Dorothy Hare, Sept. 10, 1941; children: Norman b. 1943, Neil b. 1945; edn: No. Montana Coll. 1936-38; BA, Linfield Coll. 1940; MD, Univ. of Ore. 1948; diploma OB-Gyn St. Vincent's Hosp. Portland 1950; diploma surg. Emmanuel Hosp., Portland 1965. Career: phys. in charge Satribari Christian Hosp. northeast India, apptd. by Am. Baptist Ch. USA Bd. of Internat. Minist. 1950-65, Clough Meml. Hosp. Ongole, Andhra Pradesh, India, emphasis on family planning 1965-71; Pilgrim Baptist Hosp. Nigeria, Prog. Nat. Baptist Conv. 1971-81; Indian Health Svc. USPHS 1981–; phys./surg. pvt. practice Calif. 1983–; mem: Christian Med. Assn. of India (secy. 6 yrs.), Indian Med. Assn., Nigerian Med. Assn. 1972-81, Rotary Internat. (past pres. Gauhati 1955-64, Ongole 1965-71), publ: research papers on malaria, vaginal hysterectomy; mil: pharm. mate USNR 1942-45, decorations: Am. Area, Asiatic Pacific Area, Good Conduct; Democrat; Protestant; rec: group singing, golf, jogging, reading. Res: 212 S Atlantic Blvd, Apt N, Alhambra 91801

MUNN, ALAN JACOB, lawyer; b. Oct. 19, 1949, NY, NY; s. Ben and Grete (Samson) M.; edn: BA, UC Los Angeles 1970; MA, CSU Northridge 1974; JD, Univ. of La Verne 1977; admitted Calif. State Bar, Calif. Supreme Ct. 1980. Career: lawyer in solo practice, San Jose; instr. West Valley Comm. Coll. and De Anza Comm. Coll.; apptd. to Panel of Arbitrators, Am. Arbitration Assn., 1983; mem. Calif. Bar Assn., Santa Clara Co. Bar Assn.; won criminal appeal: People v. Cardoza (1984) 161 Cal. App. 3d adv. 40; rec: reading. Ofc: Alan J. Munn, Esq. 111 West St John St Ste 230 San Jose 95113

MUNOZ, JOSE EMILIO, JR., international fisheries consultant; b. Mar. 3, 1946, San Juan, Puerto Rico; s. Jose Emilio and Maria Victoria (Vallecillo) M.; m. Lindy McCollum, Feb. 6, 1971; children: Esther b. 1980, Rachel b. 1984; edn: BS finance, BS mgmt., Fla. State Univ. 1968, MBA finance, 1970; CPA Texas 1973. Career: budget analyst State of Fla. 1969-71; senior staff fin. analyst Exxon Corp., Baytown and Houston, Tex. 1972-74; v.p. fin. & adminstrn. Zapata Ocean Resources, San Diego 1974-76; controller Solar Turbines Internat., San Diego 1976-78; v.p. fin. adminstrn. and treas. Sun Harbor Industries, San Diego 1978-81; owner, pres. Morris Whaley, Inc., Chula Vista 1978–; owner, ptnr. Tuna Clipper Marine, S.D. 1978–; pres., owner Jose E. Munoz, Jr., Inc., S.D., internat. fisheries cons. firm 1985–; instr. Univ. Richmond, Ft. Lee, Va. 1971-72, Prairie View A&M Univ., Houston 1972-73, San Diego State Univ. 1976–, Peninsula Bank Mgmt. Tng. Seminars, S.D. 1984-85; honors: Internat. Who's Who of Contemp. Achievement (1984), Who's Who Calif. (1983); mem: Am. Inst. CPAs, Sigma Chi Alumni, Fin. Execs. Inst., Tex. Soc. CPAs, Calif. World Trade Assn., Calif. Council Internat. Trade, Am. Assn. Hispanic CPAs, Soc. Marine Mammalogy, Rotary, Propeller Club, US Triathlon Fedn.; bd. dirs. Am. Lung Assn. of S.D. & Imperial Cos.; past VIP panelist United Cerebral Palsy Telethon Fund Drive; mil: 1st lt. US Army QM Corps 1971-72, Army Commdn.; Republican; Catholic; rec: triathlon (competed in 1983 Ironman, Hawaii), travel, reading, photog. Res: 5961 Lomond Dr San Diego 92120 Ofc: Jose E. Munoz, Jr., Inc., 2040 Harbor Island Dr Ste 202 San Diego 92101

MUNSON, ALEXANDER LEE, management consultant; b. Aug. 22, 1931, Hempstead, NY; s. Alexander Lawrence and Bertha Louise (Geer) M.; m. Betty Shideler, Dec. 14, 1957; div. 1978; children: Eric L. b. 1960, Genevieve S. b. 1963, Anna L. b. 1966; edn: BA, Amherst Coll. 1953; MBA, Harvard Bus. Sch. 1960. Career: mgmt. trainee credit anaylst Mellon Nat. Bank & Trust Co., Pittsburgh, Pa. 1953-54; assoc. Cresap, McCormick & Paget, mgmt. consultants, NYC 1960-62; finl. adv., internat. fin. Mobil Oil Corp., NYC 1962-64, Melbourne, Australia 1964-65; mgr. spl. projects, NYC 1965-66, mgr. treasury reports and analysis, 1966-67; treas. Mobil Latin America, Inc., NYC 1968-70; v.p., treas. Fairchild Camera & Instrument Co., Mountain View, Calif. 1971-72; v.p., treas. Crown Zellerbach Corp., San Francisco 1972-82; pres. A.L. Munson & Co., 1982—; commnr. San Francisco Civil Service Commn.; mem. Mayor's Fiscal Advis. Com. (exec. com. 1976-); Recipient SBA Advocate of the Year award, 1976; civic: Harvard Bus. Sch. Assn. of No. Calif. (exec. v.p 1977-), Minority Bus. consulting group (founder, chmn. 1971-75), Phi Gamma Delta, Univ. Club; mil: lt. USCGR 1955-58; Republican (bd. dirs., treas. NY Young Repub. Club 1965-68); Presbyterian; rec: tennis, photog. Address: A.L. Munson & Co. 3369 Jackson St San Francisco 94118

MUNSON, DOUGLAS CROW, judge; b. Nov. 4, 1938, Modesto; s. Merrill Crow and Sybol Jean (Blankenship) M.; m. Baerbel A.E., Dec. 16, 1978; edn: BA, Stanford Univ. 1960; JD, UC Hastings Law Sch. 1966. Career: assoc. at law with law firm Mullen & Filippi, San Francisco 1967; trial atty., Ofc. of Dist. Atty. S.F. 1968, senior atty. 1969, principal atty. 1970, homicide div. 1972, head atty. Ofc. of the Dist. Atty., S.F. 1982-85; apptd. judge Municipal Ct. of San Francisco, by Gov. Deukmejian, May 22, 1985; faculty Coll. of Criminal Justice Advocacy Hastings Ctr. for Practice Courses; guest lectr. Hastings Law Sch., USF Law Sch., Calif. District Atty. Assn. advanced Prosecutors Sch, S.F. Coroners Ofc. (medical jurisprudence series), S.F. Police Acad.; honors: Outstanding Appellate Advocacy, David E. Snodgrass Moot Ct. Comp., Hastings Law Sch. 1964; Outstanding D.A., S.F. Police Assn. 1981; Outstanding Prosecutor, Calif. Dist. Attys. assn. 1982; mem: Calif. Bar Assn.; Calif. Dist. Attys. Assn.; S.F. Lawyers Club; Phi Delta Phi (Pomeroy Inn chpt.); mil: sp4 Calif Army Nat. Guard 1963; Republican; Protestant; rec: modeling, sailing, skiing. Res: 870 Pacheco St San Francisco 94116 Ofc: 850 Bryant St, Rm 320, San Francisco 94103

MURANAKA, HIDEO, artist; b. Feb. 4, 1946, Mitaka-shi, Tokyo, Japan; s. Nobukichi and Hisae Muranaka; edn: BFA, Tokyo Nat. Univ. of Fine Arts & Music 1970, MFA, 1972; research stu., traditional Japanese painting 1972-73; mural painting, Fresco 1973-74; faculty of Fine Arts. Career: artist, painting, printmaking, traditional calligraphy; art tchr. tradl. Japanese style painting; awards: Second Prize, Internat. Art Exhibition for Museo Hosio, Capranica-Viterbo, Italy (1984), Kasaku Prize, Shell Oil Co. (1971), purch. prizes: Wesleyan Coll. Intl. Exhib. of Prints and Drawings (1980), Owensboro Mus. of Fine Art, Ky. Mid-Am. Bienniel (1982); pencil drawing accepted for The Pacific Coast States Collection, Vice Pres. Mondale's res. in Wash DC, exhib. Nat. Mus. of American Art; art works accepted for Eberhard Faber Art Contest 1974, Rockford Internat. '83 Print and Drawing Biennial, Alabama Works on Paper Exhibn. (touring show) 1983, 18th Nov. Annual- Coos (Ore.) Art Mus.; S.F. Art Festival 1974-77; Two-man Show at Soker-Kaseman Gal., S.F. 1975; mem: Art Exhibn. of Inten, designated Inyu (assn. for artists of traditional Japanese style painting); Lepidopterists Soc.; publs: City Mag. (5/75), S.F. Chronicle (5/75); Christian; rec: music, collecting butterflies. res: 179 Oak St, Apt W, San Francisco 94102

MURATA, DEVANEY, advertising artist; b. June 13, 1948, Los Angeles; s. Ralph and Catherine (Kobashi) M.; edn: BFA, cum laude, Chouinard Art Inst. 1970. Career: freelance graphic artist, self empl., 1970-71; art dir. Charles Eames, 1972; v.p. Interrobang Inc., 1973-78; ptnr. Kertesz Assocs., 1979-81; creative cons. prin., 1982—; tchr. seminars Calif. Inst. of the Arts, instr. art related classes for var. charitable orgns.; cons. to U.N.; recipient num. internat. awards incl. Cannes Film Fest., Art Directors Club of LA, Public Access Video; mem. LA Creative Club, ADLA, Japanese Am. Cultural Orgn., UCLA Alumni Assn. (life), Cal Arts Alumni Assn.; rec: running. Address: 17125 S Dalton Ave Gardena 90247

MURINE, GERALD EDWARD, software co. executive; b. Feb. 24, 1934, Struthers, Ohio; s. John George and Agnes Marie (Majzun) M.; m. Carol Edna Jacque, Nov. 22, 1956; children: Kurt b. 1960, Lynn b. 1961, Brian b. 1963, Eric b. 1969; edn: BS, Kent State Univ. 1956, M.Ed. 1959, MA, 1960; postgrad. work, Univ. of Texas 1961-62, Marquette Univ. 1963. Career: software engr. North American Aviation, Downey 1963-65; computer scientist Computer Scis. Corp., El Segundo 1965-69; systems engr. Aerojet Electrosystems, Azusa 1969-70; software mgr. McDonnell Douglas, Monrovia 1970-79; dept. mgr. Softech Inc., San Diego 1979-81; pres. Metriqs, Inc., Carlsbad 1981-86; asst. prof. John Carroll Univ.; asst. prof. USC; internat. seminar lectr. State of the Art Seminars; mem: IEEE, Assn. of Unmanned Vehicles, Am. Soc. for Quality Control; over 30 tech. publs. (1971-86); rec: music, writing. Ofc: Metriqs Inc 390 Oak Ave Ste G Carlsbad 92008

MURPHY, A. JOHN, JR., lawyer; b. August 13, 1950; s. Arthur John, Sr. and Joan Marie (von Albade) M.; m. Joanne, Feb. 24, 1952; children: Arthur John, III b. 1982, Matthew Newsom b. 1985; edn: BA, Univ. San Diego 1972, JD, 1975; admitted Calif. Bar 1975. Career: atty. US Securities and Exchange Commn., Wash DC 1975-78; assoc. law firm Bronson, Bronson & McKinnon, San Francisco 1979-82, ptnr. 1983—; honors: Franklin Award, Outstanding Graduate Class of 1972, USD; Who's Who in Am. Colls. & Univs. (1972), Who's Who in Am. Law (1985); mem. Am. Bar Assn., Calif. Bar Assn. (chair Edn. Com. Bus. Law Sect. 1985-86), San Francisco Bar Assn., Olympic Club; publs. profl. articles in corporate, real estate and securities law journals; Roman Catholic; rec: skiing, tennis, gardening. Ofc: Bronson, Bronson & McKinnon, 555 California St San Francisco 94104

MURPHY, FREDERICK CLINTON, lawyer; b. Oct. 25, 1922, Willows; s. Frederick Cox and Emma Elizabeth (Fell) M.; m. Ethel Corinne Holland, Aug. 21, 1948; children: Corinne Lee, Kristine Elizabeth, Frederick Clinton; edn: AB in pol. sci., UC Berkeley 1947; Hastings Coll. of Law 1947-50; LLB, McGeorge Coll. Law 1951; admitted to Calif. State Bar 1953; cert. splst. in Worker's Comp. 1973. Career: prin. and tchr. Garden Valley Sch. Dist., 1950-51; investigator Indsl. Indemnity, Sacto. 1951-52; lawyer prin., W. Sacto. 1953-1958; atty. State Compensation Ins. Fund, Sacto. 1958-61; referee Indsl. Accident Commn., Eureka 1961-62; lawyer, Hanna & Brophy, Sacto. 1962-71, Twohy & Murphy, 1971-76, lawyer prin., F. Clinton Murphy Inc., Sacto. 1976—; bd. trustees Washington Unified Sch. Dist. 1956-59; honors: Theta Xi, Phi Phi, Delta Theta Phi; mem. Am., Calif. State, Sacramento County, Yolo Co. bar assns., Am. Judicature Soc. 1960-81, Calif. Compensation Defense Attys. Assn., Valley Indsl. Claims Assn.; Mason, Order of Eastern Star; mil: s/sgt. US Army 1942-45, Purple Heart, Bronze Star; Republican (Yolo County Rep. State Central Com. 1954-61, dir. Rep. State Central Com. 1961). Res: 1460 Meredith Way Carmichael 95608 Ofc: F. Clinton Murphy, 9700 Business Park Dr Ste 204 Sacramento 95827

MURPHY, GEORGE JAMES, brokerage account executive; b. Sept. 18, 1923, Weed; s. George G. and Bertha A. (McLaughlin) M.; m. Elaine Kozicki, Jan. 14, 1950; children: Patrick b. 1951, Michele b. 1953, Maureen b. 1955, Kathleen b. 1955; edn: BA journ., UC Berkeley 1950; Chartered Life Underwriter, American Coll. 1974. Career: mng. editor California Livestock News, Calif. Wool Grower Assn., San Francisco 1950-60; field ed., Western Livestock Journal, Anaheim 1960-69; life underwriter New York Life, Walnut Creek 1969-82; acct. exec. and life splst. E.F. Hutton, Walnut Creek 1982—; mem: Million Dollar Round Table (life and qualifying mem.), Top of the Table (1985), Soc. of Chartered Life Underwriters, Century Club of Contra Costa Co., Sonoma Co. Trial Blazers; mil: cpl. US Army Air Corps 1943-45, ETO; Republican; Catholic; rec: golf, hunting, fishing, trail riding. Res: 1302 Sanderling Island Point Richmond 94801 Ofc: E.F. Hutton, 1441 Locust Walnut Creek 94597

MURPHY, JOHN LEONARD, physicist/audio engineer; b. Mar. 31, 1950, La Plata, Md.; s. Francis Joseph and Sarah Elizabeth (Dameron) M.; m. Sharon L. Alsup, Dec. 24, 1980; edn: BS, physics, Lowell Tech. Inst. 1972; MS, physics, Univ. of Dayton 1974. Career: commnd. ofcr., space systems analyst USAF, 1974-78; chief engr. Ford Audio & Acoustics, Okla. City, Ok. 1978-81; chief engr. Carvin Mfg. Co., Escondido 1981—; mem. Audio Engring. Soc., Acoustical Soc. of Am., IEEE; publs: technical ed./contbg. writer (31 arts. audio topics) Modern Recording Mag. 1978-81; mil: capt. USAF 1974-8, Jt. Svcs. Commendn. Medal; rec: music and recording, computing. Res: 341 Cypress Crest Terrace Escondido 92025 Ofc: Carvin Mfg. Co. 1155 Industrial Ave Escondido 92025

MURPHY, W. MICHAEL, business executive; b. Oct. 28, 1945, San Jose; s. William C. and Jane B. (Burke) M.; m. Suzanne, Oct. 4, 1969; 1 dau. Meghan F. b. 1981; edn: BS, Memphis State Univ. 1967; MA, Univ. Iowa 1969. Career: dir. real estate western US Holiday Inns Inc. 1973-81; exec. v.p., dir. acquisitions Montgomery Realty Investors 1981—; exec. mgmt. com. Fox Group of Cos., bd. dirs. Fox & Carskadon Financial Corp. 1986—; participant UCLA Hospitality Investment Conf. L.A., Hampton Inn System Conf. Memphis 1986; mem: Am. Hotel & Motel Assn. (industry real estate finance adv. com.), Urban Land Inst. (urban devel./ mixed use council), Calif. Trout Orgn.; rec: tennis, fishing. Ofc: Montgomery Realty Investors 155 Bovet Rd 2nd floor San Mateo 94402

MURRAY, ALLEN KETCIK, biochemist; b. Dec. 2, 1944, Santa Monica; s. Allen Riddell and Josephine Elizabeth (Ketcik) M.; edn: BS, USC 1966; PhD, Mich. State Univ. 1971. Career: research asst. Mich. State Univ., E. Lansing, Mich. 1967-71; USPHS postdoctoral fellow in biol. chem. Wash. Univ. Sch. of Med., St. Louis, Mo. 1971-74; asst. adj. prof. biochem. genetics UC Irvine 1974-79; asst. dir. research devel. Muscular Dystrophy Assn., NY, NY 1979-81; cons., ind., Irvine 1981-82; pres. GLYCOZYME, Inc., Santa Ana 1983—; bd. mem. Coll. of nat. Sci. Alumni, Mich State Univ.; cons. ICN Biomedicals, Inc., Irvine and Costa Mesa 1984-; honors: Someone Special, for Heritage Park Aquatic Complex, City of Irvine Community Svcs. Dept., 1984; mem. Soc. for Inher. Metabolic Disorders; Soc. of Sigma Xi; Western Soc. for Pediatric Research; NY Acad. of Scis.; Am. Soc. of Plant Physiologists; Am. Chem. Soc.; Am. Assn. for Adv. of Sci.; Irvine Novaquatics; US Coast Guard Aux.; US Masters Swimming; publs: Cell wall enzymes, 1975; Human liver -glucosidase, 1978; Enzyme replacement therapy using -glucosidase-LDL complex, 1980; Composition and Function of Cell Membranes in Muscle Diseases, 1981; rec: photog., scuba, sailing. Res: 5 Juniper, Irvine 92715 Ofc: GLYCOZYME, Inc., 3873 S. Main St., Santa Ana 92707

MURRAY, GILMAN YOST, corporate executive; b. Dec. 26, 1923, Springfield, Mass.; s. Arthur Frederick and Barbara Aramenta (Gilman) M.; m. Winifred Tipping, June 15, 1947; children: Scott b. 1951, Craig b. 1954, Victoria b. 1961; edn: BS chem. eng., MIT 1944, MS metallurg., 1948; Reg. Profl. Engr. (metallurg.) Calif. Career: research and devel., tech. sales Allis-Chalmers, 1948-54; product and bus. devel. mgr. Wemco and W.K.E. -McKee, 1954-61; v.p., dir., mktg. ptnr. Bradberry Assocs. (natural resources cons. engring. firm) 1961-68, handled merger with Bendix Corp.; v.p., dir., mktg.

ptnr. Hallanger Engrs. (petroleum refining, petrochem. and chem. engring. and constrn. firm), 1968-71, handled merger with Zapata and sale to Kaiser Engrs.; first v.p. mining and metals div. (3 mos.), to v.p. and gen. mgr. world-wide ops. and senior v.p. mktg. Fluor Utah, Inc. (engring. and constrn. subs. Fluor Corp.), 1971-77; senior v.p., div. mgr., dir. Ralph M. Parsons Co., 1977-79; pres., chief op. ofcr., dir. Lurgi Corp. (subs. Metallgesellschaft, Lurgi Group, Frankfurt, W.Ger.), 1979-84, developed new US co. from startup; current: pres. Martinique Homes, Inc. (devel. and constrn. co.), 1985–; pres. Unipon Group, Inc. (internat. mktg. of high tech mats. and services), Mt. View 1985–; independent cons. Furukawa Electric Co., Ltd., Tokyo, Japan; honors: award of merit Colo. Mining Assn. (1959); mem: Sigma Xi, Alpha Chi Sigma, AIME, AMC, MMSA, Commonwealth Club, Engrs. Club, Univ. Club, Monterey Penin. Country Club, past pres. Menlo Park Comm. Theatre, past dir. Los Altos Hills Little League bd. mem. LCEF Mental Hlth. orgn. (San Jose), founding dir. Los Altos Village Assn.; mil: ret. ofcr. USN; rec: tennis, golf, skiing. Res: 12355 Stonebrook Los Altos Hills 94022

MURRAY, JAMES ACKLEY, (JR), educational executive; b. Dec. 11, 1923, Merced (3d gen.); s. James Ackley and Edna May (Erwin) M.; m. D. Jeanne Gooderham, Sept. 27, 1947; children: Susan Lee b. 1950, James Carleton b. 1952; edn: grad. Moler Barber Coll., Oakland 1942; grad., honors, Calif. Flyers Inc. Sch. of Aviation Mechs., L.A. 1943; Calif. lic. Barber, Barber Instr. (1984). Career: mgr. Moler Barber Coll., Fresno 1948-56; dir. Moler Barber Colls. in Fresno, Oakland, Sacto. and Stockton, 1956-75; owner/dir. Moler Barber Coll. and Modern Barber Coll., San Francisco 1959-68; onwer/dir. Moler Barber Colls. in Sacto. and Stockton, 1984–; bd. dirs: Mt. Reba Corp. (ski resort Bear Valley), Stockton Plastice Inc. (Galt); farming interests: cattle, raisin grapes, rice; breed and race Standardbred (Harness) race horses; mem. Nat. Assn. of Barber Schs. (pres. 1970), Calif. Barber Coll. Assn. (legislative advocate 1950-79; pres. 1965-79), Am. Angus Assn., Calif. Alumni Assn. (life), Calif. Harness Horse Breeders Assn., Far West Ski Assn. (life), Rice Growers Assn. of Calif., Siskiyou Co. Hist. Soc. (life), U.S. Trotting Assn., Western Standardbred Assn.; mil: US Army Air Force 1943-46, Guam; Methodist (trustee). Ofc: Moler Barber College 727 J Street Sacramento 95814

MURRAY, MARION A., clinical hypnologist; b. Oct. 20, 1942, Tulare, Calif.; d. Willis Lewis Sr. and Melvie Margorie (Wilson) Adams; m. Robert L. Murray, Jr., 1959; div. 1979; children: Robert Craig b. 1960, Karyn Michelle b. 1970; edn: AA, El Camino Coll. 1975; BA, psychol., CSU Dominguez Hills, 1977, MA, clin. com. psych., 1979; PhD hypnotherapy, Am. Inst. Hypnotherapy 1985; Calif. LMFCC (Lic. Marriage Family & Child Counselor); Comm. Coll. instr. cred. (life); Certified & Reg. Clin. Hypnotherapist 1985. Career: secty., cons. The Rand Corp., Santa Monica 1966-72; counselor Mid-Cities Comm. Rehab. Ctr., Compton 1978-79; voc. evaluator & coord. Mid-Cities Comm.Rehab.Ctr., 1979; instr. Compton Comm. Coll. 19b7p80; dir. Marion Murray & Assocs., L.A., 1979–; therapist Counseling and Psychol. Assocs., Inglewood 1980-83; v.p. Network Found. Inc. 1979-83; estab. comprehensive instrnl. pgm. for developmentally disabled; designed and implemented a Behavior Modification pgm. for the Exceptional Children's Opportunity Sch. (residentl. facility, L.A. Unif. non-public sch.) 1983; mem: Am. Psychol. Assn. Div. of Comm. Psychol. (27); Western Psychol. Assn.; Calif. Assn. of Marriage & Family Therapists; author: The Complete Travel Training Manual (self-pub. 1981); Democrat; Christian; rec: writing, modern dance, travel. Ofc: Marion A. Murray, PhD, 8615 Crenshaw Blvd Ste 202 Inglewood 90305

MURRAY, MICHAEL JOSEPH, investment sponsor; b. June 23, 1958, Castro Valley; s. Daniel Joseph and Sheila Lee (Stribley) M.; m. Catherine Ruth Douat, Dec. 29, 1984; edn: BA in hist., UC Los Angeles 1980; MS in internat. bus., St. Mary's Coll. 1985; Calif. lic. Real Estate. Career: finl. ofcr., bd. dirs. UCHA Inc. (non-profit coop. housing coop.) 1978-80; investment loan ofcr. The MoneyLenders (mortgage brokerage), San Francisco 1980-81; acquisitions agent Highsmith Investments (R.E. syndication co.), Burlingame 1981-83; splst. in apartment complexes, assoc. Merrill Lynch Comml. Real Estate, 1983-84; mng. ptnr. Park Central Investments, 1984–; mem. Internat. Sales & Mktg. Execs. (1982-83); Republican; Catholic; rec: fencing, public speaking. Res: 3016 Lincoln Ave Alameda 94501 Ofc: Park Central Investments 2424 Central Avenue Alameda 94501

MURRAY, SONYA LEVER, financial planner, sales trainer; b. Aug. 12, 1939, Phila., Pa.; d. Herman Emil and Lillian (Jurman) Lever; children (nee Sarachek): Joel Ivan b. 1966, Laurel Eve b. 1968; edn: BA, Mills Coll. 1961; desig: lic. Med. Technologist (MT), Am. Soc. Clin. Pathologists 1961-73; Calif. lic. R.E. agt. (1974-76), broker (1976-); GRI, Grad. Realtors Inst. (1978), Reg. Rep. NASD (1982). Career: med. tech. var. hosps. in Los Angeles, San Francisco, Martinez and Concord, 1962-74; real estate sales assoc. Newman Realtors, Walnut Creek 1974-82; real estate broker American Realty, Concord 1982-86; finl. planner, stockbroker, No. Calif. regl. sales mgr. Dan McBride & Assocs., 1985–; honors: Outstanding Young Women in Am. (1972), Million Dollar Club/R.E. (1975-80); mem. Nat., Calif. Assn. of Realtors, Contra Costa Bd. Realtors (spl. events com.), Nat. Speakers Assn./N. Calif., Womens Network Contra Costa Co.; civic: S.F. Symphony 500 (vol.), Mt. Diablo Mills Club (student referral com.), World Affairs Council, Who's Who Internat. (East Bay chair 1981-82), Mensa, AAUW 1965-74 (past pres.), Hadassah (life); creative: design/ mfr. jewelry- num. shows and sales; Jewish; rec: swim, sail. Ofc: Dan McBride & Assocs. POB 4871 Walnut Creek 94596

MURRAY, WILLIAM EDWARD, electrical engineer; b. March 14, 1924, Chickasha, Okla.; s. William Clifford and Blanche Winifred (McIntyre) M.; m. Jeannie Morris, April 27, 1946; children: Robert b. 1947, Richard b. 1948, Daniel b. 1953, John b. 1955, Alan b. 1962; edn: BS, UC Berkeley 1947; MSEE, USC 1954; postgrad. stu., UC Irvine 1978-80. Career: br. chief McDonnell Douglas Astronautics Co., Huntington Beach 1969-74; senior engr., scientist Douglas Aircraft Co., Long Beach 1974-78, prin. engr., scientist 1978-84, senior staff engr.1984-85, prin. staff engr. 1985–; instr. engring. UC Irvine 1978-84, UCLA 1960-66, 1985–, Golden West Coll. 1972-76, CSU Northridge 1974, Los Angeles Dept. of Edn. 1960-84; honors: IEEE Centennial Medal 1984, elected fellow, Inst. for the Adv. of Engring. 1982; IEEE- AES Internat. Tech. Paper Award, Wash. DC 1963; mem: Eta Kappa Nu (nat. pres. 1973-74, Western Rep. Award Orgn. Comm. 1983-, nat. v.p. 1972-73, nat. dir. 1970-72, pres. L.A. Alumni chpt. 1965-66), IEEE (Los Angeles Council, chmn. 1985-86, v.chmn., secty. 1984-85, treas. 1983-84, chmn. Sects. Com. 1982-83; Orange Co. sect., chmn. 1981-82, v.chmn. 1979-81, secty. 1978-79; gen. chmn. 1982 Reg. 6 Conf., awards chmn. Power Electronics Splsts. Conf. 1977-85, secty. Elec. Power/ Energy Sys. Panel 1977-, senior mem. 1970–), Tau Beta Pi, Pi Tau Pi Sigma, Pi Kappa Alpha, Aerospace Electrical Soc., Am. Inst. Aero. & Astro.; author, 8 engring. papers presented and publ. at confs.; mil: 1st lt. US Army Signal Corps 1943-45, 1950-52; Republican; Methodist; rec: literature, technology, travel. Res: 1531 Wyndham Court Rd. Santa Ana 92705 Ofc: Douglas Aircraft Co., 3855 Lakewood Blvd. Long Beach 90846

MURTOUGH, STEPHEN BENEDICT, lawyer; b. July 1, 1944, Liverpool, Eng., nat. US citizen 1964; s. Geoffrey B. and Eileen Grace (Halstead) M.; m. Francine, June 18, 1971; children: Gary, b. 1972, Graham, b. 1975; edn: BA, San Diego St. Univ. 1968; JD, Western St. Univ. Coll. of Law, 1980. Career: senior social wkr., San Diego County Social Svcs., 1968-82; lawyer pvt. practice, Chula Vista 1982–; adj. prof. Western St. Univ. Coll. of Law, 1983-; honors: Am. Jurisprudence Award 1978, Nu Beta Epsilon, law rev. staff Criminal Justice Jour. (1978); mem: Calif. State Bar, Am. Bar Assn., Assoc. of Trial Lawyers of Am., San Diego Trial Lawyers Assn., S.D. County Bar Assn.; vol. leader BSA; Republican; rec: horse training. Ofc: Stephen B. Murtough, Atty. at Law, 44 Third Ave, Ste H, Chula Vista 92010

MUSACCHIO, KIRK ANTHONY, lawyer; b. Nov. 11, 1955, Fresno; s. Theodore Alphonsus and Darlene June (Mirigian) M.; edn: BA, Univ. of San Francisco 1977; JD, Univ. of Santa Clara 1980; admitted to State Bar of Calif. 1982. Career: legal editor Matthew Bender & Co., San Francisco 1981-82; senior v.p.-Legal Counsel, Centennial Svgs & Loan Assn., Santa Rosa 1982-84, exec. v.p., gen. counsel 1984-85; pres. KTM Corp., S.F. 1986–; honors: Univ. of Santa Clara Law Review comments ed., bd. (1980), Pi Sigma Alpha (ofcr. 1976-77), St. Ives Law Soc. (1976-77), acad. honors for best resrch. paper in Sch. of Bus. (1977) Finl. Execs. Inst., academic scholarship USF 1976-77; mem: American Bar Assn., State Bar of Calif., Assn. of Trial Lawyers of Am., Calif. Trial Lawyers Assn., Commonwealth Club of Calif., Masons, Triple X Frat.; publs: contbr. law revs.; Republican; Catholic; rec: musician. Res: 4703 Tee View Ct Santa Rosa 95405 Ofc: KTM Corp 1750 Montgomery St San Francisco 94111

MUSE, JAMES WILLIAM, military pilot (ret.); b. Apr. 1, 1940, Chickasha, Okla.; s. Raymond Daniel and Elva Ophelia (King) M.; m. Paulina Tayaban, June 1, 1974; children: Jamie b. 1975, Jennifer b. 1976, Jessica b. 1978; edn: N.Mex. Inst. of Mining & Tech. 58-60; Univ. of the Philippines 1972-73; BS, CSU San Diego 1973-74. Career: served to lt. col. USAF 1960-84: navigator 1960, electronic warfare ofcr. on B-52 aircraft 1961-66, pilot US, Vietnam, Thailand, Laos, 1966-69; instr. pilot in T-37 aircraft, 1969-71; comdr. Jungle Survival Sch. of Clark AB, Philippines, 1971-73; directed estab. of Inanarro Negrito Village to incl. 1st Nigrito elem. sch., adult edn., medical dispensary, metal foundry and coop. farming, 1972-73; assisted Philippine Armed Forces estab. their 1st Mil. Arms Mus., 1972-73; comdr., 23rd Transp. Squadron, Eng. AFB, LA, 1974-76; chief of aircrew tng., 374 Tactical Air Wing (C-130 aircraft) Clark AB, Phil. 1976-77; chief. of affil. tng. (airlift) for all Armed Forces, Phil., Okinawa, Japan, Korea, 1977-78; exec. ofcr. and instr. pilot on CT-39 aircraft, Norton AFB, Calif. 1978-82; dir. of misc. aircraft mgmt. group/ fgn. mil. sales aircraft, AF Logistics Cmd., McClellan AFB, Calif. 1982-84; v.p. Treasurtron Inc., 1982–; logistics cons. 1984–; awards: USAF Humanitarian Medal for civilian flood relief, San Bernardino, Calif. 1981; Transp. Staff Ofcr. of Year 1976, Tactical Air Cmd.; 2 Phil. Citations 1972-73; Thailand and Vietnam Civic Actions medals 1969, 68; Silver Star, DFC w/oak leaf, Merit Svc. w/ 3 oak leaf, Air Medal w/12 o.l.c.; RVN Gallantry Cross w/Palm, Laos Order of Million Elephants (for Gallantry), Laotian Jump Wings; mem: Hist. Soc. of Phil. 1972-, Assn. of Old Crows (1963-73), Nat. Rifle Assn. (life), Calif. Scholarship Fedn. (life), CofC (Mesa, Ariz. chmn. mil. affairs com. 1970); Republican; So. Baptist; rec: archaelogy, lapidary, camping. Res: 12501 Wanderer Rd Auburn 95603

MUTSCH, MARTIN GEORGE, cogeneration and small power plant development; b. Apr. 5, 1952, NY, NY; s. Martin and Frances (Conway) M.; edn.: BSME, Lehigh Univ. 1975; BA econs., Univ. Pa. 1979; MME, Villanova Univ. 1981. Career: foreman, application/ sales engr. steel industry Pa. 1975-82; cons., devel. small power plant projects Fountain Valley, Calif. 1982–; honors: NSF Research Grant; mem: L.A. Cogeneration Assn. (bd., treas.), Internat. Cogeneration Soc. (chpt. bd., ed. newsletter), Pacific Energy Assn., Outdoor Singles Club; Republican; Catholic; rec: karate, guitar, skiing, golf. Res: 17150 San Mateo D-19, Fountain Valley 92708

MYATT, BRUCE CARLTON, engineering manager- consultant; b. Jan. 17, 1952, Oakland; s. Bert Jr. and Euteva Lee (Pugh) M.; m. Lydia Susan, June 17, 1979; edn: BSME, Univ. So. Calif. 1975; Reg. Profl. Engr., Calif. 1981. Career:

senior engr. EDS Nuclear Inc., San Francisco 1975-79; engring. cons., mktg. rep. Dynatech, San Francisco 1979-84; project engr., mktg. rep. Impell Corp., Walnut Creek 1984—; honors: Senior Recognition, Order of the Palm, USC 1974; pres. stu. chpt. Pi Tau Sigma 1974; pres. stu. chpt. Sigma Phi Deta 1973; pres. stu. chpt. Order of Omega 1974; v.p. Engring. Student Council 1973; Navy ROTC Scholarship 1970-74; Indsl. Scholarship, Royal Industries of Pasadena 1974; Commendation for Community Service, Lt. Gov. of Calif. 1974; Western Province Councilor, Sigma Phi Delta 1976; Varsity Letter, Soccer, USC 1972; mil: midshipman USNR 1970-74; rec: sports. Ofc: Impell Corp., 350 Lennon Ln. Walnut Creek 94598

MYERS, DON STEVEN, telecommunications executive; b. Dec. 22, 1942, Burbank; s. Harry Raymond and Mildred Lee (Leggett) M.; m. Audrey Beryl Sopansnik, Feb. 24, 1961; children: Deborah b. 1961, Scott b. 1965; edn: BSE, honors, UCLA 1964; MSEE, Bell Labs 1968; MS, Pace Univ. 1977. Career: dis. mgr. AT&T 1973-76; dist. mgr. Pacific Bell 1977-79, div. mgr. 1980-84; exec. v.p. Polaris Intelecom 1984-85; pres. Polaris Telesis and Polaris Intelecom 1985—; dir. Polaris Intelecom 1984-; honors: Svc. Commdn., Calif. State Senate 1984; mem: UCLA San Fernando Valley Alumni (pres.), Northridge CofC, Woodland Hills CofC, UCLA Alumni Council; rec: boating, tennis. Res: 19633 Hiawatha St. Chatsworth 91311 Ofc: Polaris Telesis, 3500 W. Olive Ave. Ste. 560 Toluca Lake 91505

MYERS, DOUGLAS GEORGE, administrator; b. Aug. 30, 1949, Los Angeles; s. George Walter and Daydeen (Schroeder) M.; m. Barbara, Nov. 30, 1980; 1 dau. Amy b. 1984; edn: BA, Christopher Newport Coll. 1981. Career: staff Anheuser-Busch and Busch Entertainment Corp., 1970-81; exec. dir. Zoological Soc. of San Diego, 1981—; mem. Am. Assn. of Zool. Parks & Aquariums (Profl. Fellow), Internat. Assn. Amusement Parks & Attractions, Internat. Assn. of Quality Circles, Rotary. Ofc: Zoological Society of San Diego POB 551 San Diego 92112A

MYERS, GORDON JEROME, company president; b. Apr. 28, 1935, Seattle, Wash.; s. Julius Moscovici and Florence (Warshal) M.; 1 dau. Eedelle b. 1962; edn: AS, Marion Mil. Inst. 1955; US Naval Acad. 1955-57; BA, Univ. Wash. 1958; MA, Kennedy Western Univ. 1985. Career: gen. mgr. Financial Svc. Co. Vancouver, BC Canada 1962-65; pilot Zantop Air Transport Detroit 1965; pilot Pan Am. World Airways (707, 747) 1965—, United Airlines 1986; founder, pres. Air Bahia Airlines San Diego 1978-80; founder, CEO L.A. Helicopter Airline 1980; faculty advisor Kennedy Western Univ. Sch. of Bus., airline mgmt. dept.; mem: Charge Account Bankers Assn. 1961-63, Rotary 1980, Regional Airline Assn., Air Courier Conf. of Am., L.A. Air Cargo Assn., Profl. Helicopter Pilots Assn. (hon.), Assn. Aero. Internat.; mil: lt. USCG 1958-68, Nat. Defense, Sea Command; rec: tennis, swimming, biking. Ofc: L.A. Helicopter Inc. POB 92934 Los Angeles Internat. Airport 90009

MYERS, HAROLD LLOYD, lawyer; b. Mar. 27, 1931, Evansville, Ind.; s. Daniel Andrew and Ethel (Hobbs) M.; edn: Pomona Coll. 1954; JD, Southwestern Univ. 1958. Career: atty. pvt. practice spec. in adoptions; mem: Round Table Internat. (Knight of the Year 1967, pres. 1968); num. publs. on adoption; mil: sgt. Combat Engrs. 1946-49; Republican; Protestant; rec: weightlifting, hiking, sailing, fishing, woodworking, sculpturing, diving. Address: 1487 ½ E Chevy Chase Dr Glendale 91206

MYERS, MARK GREGORY, accounting executive; b. May 25, 1956, Harvey, Ill. s. Hal Lemen and Eunice Jean (Stoltenberg) M.; edn: BS, internat. finance, Univ. So. Calif. 1979. Career: v.p. Meyers Enterprises Inc., Long Beach 1972-79; proj. cost adminstr., TRW/DSSG, Redondo Beach 1979-81; prime cost auditor Hughes Helicopters, Culver City 1981; internal auditor Hughes Aircraft Co., El Segundo 1981-86; auditor Holmes & Narver Inc., Orange 1986—; honors: Cal. State Scholarship recipient (1976-78), Civic Eagle Scout (BSA 1974), USC Band Grant (1976-78); mem: Alpha Kappa Psi 1976-, Gen. Alumni Assn. USC 1980-, Trojan Helmet Club (exec. dir. 1982); United Ch. of Christ; rec: music, cars, computers, enology. Res: 20454 Gilmore St Canoga Park 91306 Ofc: Holmes & Narver Inc., Orange

MYERS, STANLEY T., silicon co. president, consultant; b. Dec. 10, 1936, McPherson, Kans.; s. Thomas Coleman and Ada Viola (Rodgers) M.; m. Joan, Sept. 8, 1957; children: Tom b. 1960, Rebecca b. 1962, Jennifer b. 1967; edn: BS, Univ. Kans. 1960. Career: proj. engr. to plant supt., proj. mgr., plant mgr. Monsanto Corp. 1960-79; v.p. internat. ops. Siltec Corp. 1979-85, pres., CEO 1985—; pres., gen. mgr. Cybeq Systems; cons. to US Govt. Semiconductor Tech. Advisory Com.; bd. dirs. ACS; chmn. SAI Materials Advis. Com.; mem: Am. Electronics Assn., Am. Mgmt. Assn., Semiconductor Equipment & Materials Inst., Episcopal Ch. Vestry, St. Francis Men's Club Bd.; Republican; Episcopal; rec: jogging, tennis. Res: 482 Levin Ave Mountain View 94040 Ofc: Siltec Corp., 190 Independence Dr Menlo Park 94025

MYERS, VERNE STEELE, consultant; b. Apr. 11, 1907, Hillsdale, Mich.; s. Harry Silas and Ellen Mae (Steele) M.; m. Edna Cottle, Nov. 12, 1932; children: Monica b. 1936, Virginia b. 1942; edn: undergrad. Univ. Mich. 1928; BS, Hillsdale Coll. 1930; BS, Columbia Univ. 1932, MS, 1935; Reg. Profl. Engr., Calif. 1945. Career: indsl. engr. R.A. Lasley and R.W. Kelsey Consults., NYC 1934-35; econometric asst. to the pres. Tide Water Ass'd Oil Co., NYC 1935-41; supvrsg. statistical engr. Lockheed-Cal. Co., Burbank 1941-71; prof. (Statistical Decision-Making for Graduate Engrs.) USC, 1958-68; statistical scientist C.W. Whitston Assoc., Pasadena 1969-70; cons. mgmt. engr. prin., La Canada Flintridge 1950—; honors: Bridgham Fellow, Columbia Univ. (1939), Alumni Achievement Award, Hillsdale Coll. (1973), humanitarian

award, Advocates for the Quiet Minority (1969); mem: Greater L.A. Mgmt. Club (pres. 1944-49), Econometric Soc. 1935-65, Ops. Rsch Soc., Am. Indsl. Engring. Soc., Nat. Soc. Profl. Engrs. (chmn. edn. com.), Am. Soc. Engring. Educators, Delta Sigma Phi; Assocs. of Villa Esperanza (pres. 1985-86), SAR (pres. 1950-52), Mayflower Soc., Pasadena League for Spastic Children (chmn. Parents Aux. 1949-51), Cancer Control Soc. (bd. 1984-); publs: Reversible Relationship between GNP and R&D, J. IE Soc. (1964), num. articles on Wellness and Objective Enumerative Interpretation, Townsend Letter for Doctors, and Nutritional Consultant; America's Elliptical and Square Wheel Economy, L.A. Times; rec: working with Handicapped, Wellness, Senior Olympics swimming. Address: Verne S. Myers, P.E., 4610 Commonwealth, La Canada Flintridge 91011

MYERS, WALLACE JAMES, U.S. merchant marine engineering officer, ret.; b. Nov. 25, 1920, San Francisco; s. James Ira and Gertrude (Phillips) M.; m. Betty, June 25, 1960; 1 dau, Debra b. 1954; edn: BA, UC Berkeley 1951. Career: engring. ofcr. aboard seagoing passenger and cargo vessels, States Line, Am. President Lines, Matson Lines, Sealand Svcs., etc. 1942-1985; ret.; mem: Masons, Long Beach Scottish Rite, Shrine, Newport Harbor Elks, Sierra Club (life), Calif. Alumni Assn. (life), Palm Springs Desert Mus., Am. Radio Relay League; mil: lt. s.g. USN Ready Reserve; Republican; Lutheran; rec: amateur radio (call N6QM). Res: 1635 E. Ocean Blvd. Long Beach 90802

MYRAH, DENNIS LEE, bank officer; b. Dec. 16, 1954, Elmhurst, Ill.; s. Truman Leslie and Irene Geraldine (Matysak) M.; m. Patricia, Aug. 28, 1985; 1 dau. Shannon b. 1977; edn: BS, UC Los Angeles 1978; cert. data processing, Inst. Certification of Computer Profls. 1984. Career: sys. rep. Sperry Univac L.A. 1978-79; sys. analyst Great Western Savings Beverly Hills 1979-80; asst. v.p. Imperial Bank L.A. 1980-84; proj. mgr. Bank of the West Santa Clara 1984—; honors: Chess Champion (UCLA Chess Club 1973), Phi Eta Sigma (1974); mem: Assn. Computing Machinery 1975-, Data Proc. Mgmt. Assn. 1981-, Am. Mgmt. Assn. 1981-, Mensa, US Chess Fedn.; works: wrote chess playing computer pgm. (1974); Libertarian; Lutheran; rec: chess. Res: 10534 N Blaney Ave Cupertino 95014-2455 Ofc: Bank of the West 3233-1 Scott Blvd Ste 462 Santa Clara 95050

NAGENGAST, STEVEN JOHN, ocean engineer; b. Aug. 16, 1957, San Jose; s. Thomas George and Carol Elizabeth (Rankin) N.; edn: AA lib. arts, West Valley Comm. Coll. 1982; BSAE, Calif. State Polytechnic Univ. Pomona 1985. Career: electronics engr. Pacific Missile Test Ctr. Pt. Mugu, Calif. 1985—; honors: Program Involvement, Junior Profl. Program 1985; mem. Am. Inst. Aero. & Astro. 1984-; mil: E4 USCG 1977-80; Democrat; Catholic; rec: sailing, swimming, cycling. Res: 3600 S Harbor Blvd, No 96, Oxnard 93030 Ofc: Pacific Missile Test Ctr. code 3144 Pt Mugu 93042

NAGINENI, CHANDRASEKHARAM NAIDU, biologist; b. July 1, 1945, India; s. Changaiah Naidu and Seshamma Naidu (Dagupati) N.; m. Vijayakumari, Aug. 8, 1974; 1 child, Sahrudaya b. 1980; edn: BS, Sri Venkateswara Univ., India 1967, MS, 1969, PhD, 1976. Career: lectr. A.K.N. PG Coll., Hyderabad, India 1974; postdoc fellow UC Los Angeles 1982, asst. research physiologist 1983-85, PG research biologist 1985—; instr. biology to grad. students 6 yrs.; honors: Advanced Research Fellowship (Am. Heart Assn. 1980-82); publ: sev. research articles in var. nat. and internat. biol. scis. jours. and mags.; Hindu; rec: reading scientific books and research articles. Res: 8825 Woodman Ave, No. 20, Arleta 91331 Ofc: UC Jules Stein Eye Inst. Los Angeles 90024

NAHIN, BRUCE ALLAN, lawyer; b. Oct. 10, 1953, Los Angeles; s. Melville and Alice (Socola) N.; m. Debrah Ely, Mar. 25, 1984; 1 son: Jacob Stering b. Apr. 15, 1985; edn: BA, UC Los Angeles 1974; JD, Loyola Univ. 1977; admitted Calif. State Bar 1977, Pa. 1985. Career: ptnr. Nahin & Nahin Law Corp. 1977—; mem: Sylmar Mtn. Rescue Team; Masons; Shrine; Jewish; rec: hiking; helicopters. Res: 28021 Florence Canyon Country 91351 Ofc: Nahin & Nahin 6399 Wilshire Blvd, Ste. 1000, Los Angeles 90048

NAKAI, TSUYOSHI ROY, pediatric dentist; b. June 23, 1943, Manzanar; s. Noritatsu and Mistuyo (Nishida) N.; 1 dau: Leslie Akemi, b. 1975; edn: DDS, UC San Francisco Dental Sch. 1968; M.S.D., Univ. of Wash. 1972. Career: gen. dentist, pvt. practice 1968-70; pediatric dentist 1972—; dental kinesiology & nutritional counseling 1978-; guest lectr. UCLA Sch. of Dentistry 1976-77, 82; adv. com. (chmn. 1977), Long Beach City Coll. Dental Asst. Dept. 1975-; dental staff, Childrens Hosp., Long Beach 1974-; Meml. Hosp., Long Beach 1974-; St. Josephs Hosp, Orange, Dental & Oral Surgery Detp. staff Cert. Am. Bd. of Pedodontics 1972; mem: Am. Acad. of Pedondontics; Internat. Acad. of Microendocrinology; Am. Assn. of Dentistry for the Handicap; Calif. Assn. Pediatric Dentistry; rec: racquetball, jogging, skiing. Res: 12501 Camus, No. 5, Garden Grove 92641 Ofc: 4132 Katella Ave, Ste 202, Los Alamitos 90720; 4950 Barranca Pkwy, Ste 306, Irvine 92714

NAKAJIMA, HIDEYUKI, video game manufacturing and design co. president; b. March 11, 1936, Tokyo, Japan; s. Sadayuki and Mieko (Itoh) N.; m. Satoko, Nov. 17, 1969; children: Mina b. 1975, Yuko b. 1978; edn: BA, Aoyama Gakuin Univ. 1958. Career: mgr. mktg. Nippon Art Paper Mfg. Co., Tokyo, Japan 1958-66; dir. overseas dept. Japan Synthetic Paper Co., Tokyo, Japan 1966-69; exec. v.p. Atari Japan Corp., Tokyo, Japan 1969-78; pres. Namco America Inc., Sunnyvale, Calif. 1974-85; pres. Atari Games Corp., Milpitas 1985—; mem: No. Calif. CofC, San Jose Country Club, Musashi Country Club (Tokyo); rec: golf. Res: 97 Laburnam Rd Atherton 94025 Ofc: Atari Games Corp., P.O. Box 361110 Milpitas 95035

NAKAMOTO, REGINALD TSUTOMU, research structural engineer; b. Dec. 16, 1957, Honolulu, Hawaii; s. Isoji and Tsugie N.; edn: BSCE, Univ. of Hawaii at Manoa, 1979, MSCE, 1981; Reg. Profl. Engr. (Civil) Calif. 1984. Career: structural engr. SSFM Engineers, Inc., Honolulu 1979; research asst. Univ. of Hawaii 1980-81; research structural engr. Naval Civil Engring. Lab., Port Hueneme, Calif. 1982–; honors: Chi Epsilon (1978); mem. Am. Soc. of Civil Engrs., Am. Concrete Inst.; contbr. article in ASCE J. Struct. Engrg., Investigation of Wind Effects on Tall Guyed Tower (11/85); rec: bowling. Res: POB 426 Port Hueneme 93041 Ofc: Naval Civil Engineering Laboratory Code L51 Port Hueneme 93043

NAKAMURA, HIROMU, psychologist; b. Nov. 6, 1926, Los Angeles; s. Genjiro and Misao (Kamura) N.; m. Tamaye Yumiba, March 27, 1955; children: Glenn Vernon b. 1957, Colleen Patricia b. 1962; edn: AB, Univ. of Redlands, 1948; MA, UC Los Angeles 1951; PhD, USC 1973. Career: clin. psychologist intern Massillon (Ohio) State Hosp., 1951-52; clin. psychol. Patton (Calif.) State Hosp., 1952-58; clin. psychol. Pacific State Hosp., Pomona 1958–; pgm. dir. Lanterman Hosp. and Devel. Center Pomona 1971–; mem: Fellow Royal Soc. of Health, Calif. State Psychol. Assns., Am. Assn. on Mental Deficiency, Am. Pub. Health Assn., AAAS, New York Acad. of Scis., Town Hall of Calif., L.A. World Affairs Council, Psi Chi; contbr. articles to profl. jours.; Presbyterian. Res: 3861 Shelter Grove Dr Claremont 91711 Ofc: POB 100 Pomona 91768

NAM, HENRY H., architect, developer; b. June 25, 1941, Seoul, Korea, nat. US cit. 1976; s. Kyu Byuck and Yang Ok (Yoon) N.; m. Bonnie Yang, Aug. 15, 1969; children: Joanne b. 1971, Glenn b. 1976; edn: BS, Seoul National Univ. 1963; M.Arch., Okla. State Univ. 1970, MA, 1971. Career: designer H. Kim Architects & Assoc., Seoul, Korea 1963; designer Mu Ae Architects & Assoc., Seoul 1967; designer Cecil E. Stanfield Architect & Assoc., Tulsa, Okla. 1969; asst. prof. architecture Okla. State Univ. 1971, Calif. Polytechnic Univ., Pomona 1975; v.p. Revco Industres Inc., Los Angeles 1976; pres. Redin Devel. Inc., Los Angeles 1977; mem: Phi Kappa Phi, Am. Soc. for Engring. Edn., Korean American Theater Ensemble, Los Angeles Central Lions Club; publs: work package for architectural graphics, 1972; designer, K.I.S.T., Inchon stadium, CIA bldg., others, Korea 1963-68; Republican; rec: music. Res: 1445 No. Virginia Ave. Glendale 91202 Ofc: Redin Development Inc., 4422 Beverly Blvd. Los Angeles 90004

NAQVI, HIMAYAT HUSSAIN, botanist, ecologist-geneticist; b. June 16, 1936, Peshawar, Pakistan, nat. US cit. 1982; s. Wilayat Hussain-Shah and Nawab Begum (Jafary) N.; m. Patricia Palmer, July 17, 1971; 1 son, Jamil b. 1973; edn: BS, Univ. of Peshawar, 1958, MS, 1960; PhD, UC Santa Barbara 1969. Career: asst., assoc. prof. botany, Univ. of Peshawar, Pakistan 1969-76; senior research assoc. California Arboretum Found., Arcadia 1977-82; guayule research splst. Dept. of Botany and Plant Sci., UC Riverside 1982–; co-investigator Guayule Rubber Plant Devel. Project (devel. of a source of natural rubber in US), and founder-editor El Guayuleros (profl. mag.); mem. Guayule Rubber Soc. (dir. 1981-), Botanical Soc. Am., Crop Sci. Soc. Am., Am. Soc. of Agronomy, Ecological Soc. Am., Am. Soc. of Horticultural Scis., Sigma Xi, Am. Inst. Biol. Scis., Internat. Soc. Chem. Ecology; publs: 50+ articles in sci. internat. jours. (1972-), t.v., radio and print media interviews; rec: tennis, nature, photog. Ofc: Dept. Botany and Plant Scis. University of California Riverside 92521

NARAYAN, RANDHIR KUMAR, data processing professional; b. May 11, 1945, Patna, India, nat. 1984; s. Vishnu Deva and Kailash Basini (Chuadhury) N.; m. Neera Jaiswal, May 11, 1973; children: Nimesh, b. 1976; Nishant, b. 1978; edn: BS, physics, honors, Patna Univ., Patna, India 1962; BSME, B.I.T. Ranchi, India 1966; MS, computer sci., Wayne State Univ. 1978; cert. data processing, ICCP, Ill. 1984. Career: process engr. Hindustan Motors, Calcutta, India 1966-70; prod. engr. Chrysler Corp., Detroit, Mich. 1970-73; pgmmr. analyst Blue Cross of Mich., Detroit 1974; sys. pgmmr. Chrysler Corp., Highland Park, Detroit 1974-75; sys. pgmmr. Huck Mfg. Co., Detroit 1975-80; mgr. of sys. & pgmmg. Huck Mfg. Co., Irvine 1980-83, data processing mgr. 1983-85; sys. engr. ind. splst. IBM Corp., Santa Barbara 1985–; mem: Assn. of Computing Machinery; Data Processing Mgmt. Assn.; works: efficient software technique of error detection in communication of messages using parallel tables, 1978; Democrat; Hindu; rec: photog., travel. Res: 4043 Cliffrose Ave Moorpark 93021 Ofc: IBM Corporation 3820 State St Santa Barbara 93105

NASH, ED, investor/real estate developer; b. June 22, 1942, Hampton, Va.; s. Ed. Lawton Sr. and Esther Sarah (Morris) N.; edn: BA, CSU Los Angeles 1964; MA, Pepperdine Univ. 1968; AA, El Camino Coll. 1977; desig: (CCIM) Cert. Comml. Investment Mem., Realtors Nat. Mktg. Inst. 1980. Career: corp. mgr. compensation & orgn. plnng. Continental Airline 1971-77; pres. Prime Realty, Inc. 1978–; pres. ELN Development Co., Inc. 1978-81; chmn. bd./ CEO Enco Internat. Inc. 1983–; pres. Ed Nash, Inc., 1985–; former advisory dir. American City Bank; corp. dir./ chmn. investment com. Continental Fed. Credit Union; advisory dir. South Bay Bank; mem: Los Angeles CCIM Chpt. (dir.); Realtors Nat. Mktg. Inst.; Nat. Council of Exchangors; publs: Effects of Manifest and Induced Anxiety and Experimenter Variability on Simple Reaction Time, Perceptual & Motor Skills Journ. 1966; Republican; rec: boating, skiing, tennis, travel. Res: 600 The Strand Hermosa Beach 90254 Ofc: 605 Beach Dr Hermosa Beach 90254

NASONE, GEORGE H., construction consultant, civil engineer; b. July 1, 1923, Bayonne, NJ; s. Joseph and Emma (Zeis) N.; m. Shirley Winifred Zucker, May 16, 1943; edn: BSCE, Columbia Univ. 1948; certified arbitrator Calif. Career: constrn. engr., ptnr., dir. of constrn. cos. 1948-67; exec. v.p. A.A. Matthews Inc. Arcadia 1968-76; pres., CEO George H. Nasone & Assocs. Inc. Del Mar 1976–; mem: NY Soc. Profl. Engrs., Nat. Soc. Profl. Engrs., Profl.Engrs. in Pvt. Practice, US Com. on Large Dams, Am. Arbitration Assn., Soc. Am. Mil. Engrs., State Constrn. Arbitration Panel, Hazardous Substance Cleanup Arb. Panel; author several profl. and govt. publs.; mil: USN Constrn. Battn. 1941-45. Res: 284 Surf View Ct Del Mar 92014 Ofc: George H. Nasone & Assoc. Inc. POB 1041 Del Mar 92014

NASSAB, RICHARD GEORGE, chiropractor; b. Jan. 15, 1957, Boston, Mass.; s. Sam A. and Nadia K. N.; edn: AA, Chabot Coll. 1972; DC, Palmer Coll. of Chiropractic West 1981. Career: chiropractic cons. family practice, Burlingame; treating doctor, Gillne Chiropractor, Castro Valley; currently, faculty, Life-West and pvt. practice Eat Bay Chiropractic, San Leandro; tchr. Golstead Sems.; honors: named Chiropractic Faculty Pioneer for devotion to profession; mem: Internat. and Calif. Chiropractic Assns., Kiwanis of San Leandro; Catholic. Res: 3820 Almond Hill Pl. Castro Valley 94546 Ofc: East Bay Chiropractic, 120 Juana Ave. San Leandro 94577

NATER, ROBERT A., management consultant, retired transportation co. executive, computer communications consultant; b. June 25, 1940, Los Angeles; s. Abe and Jean (Cornblith) N.; div.; two children: Dan b. 1968, Katrina b. 1975; edn: stu. UC Los Angeles 1958-9; AA, LA Valley Coll. 1961; BS in electronic engring., Calif. St. Polytech. Univ., SLO 1964; desig: EIT, State of Calif. 1964; FCC 1st Class Radio-telephone lic. Career: consultant, ret. owner/ pres./bd. chmn. NJS Associates, Inc. (60 Truck intrastate trucker of live turkeys); owner/pres./bd. chmn. ULC Systems, Urban Leasing Corp. (supplier of software systems to mortgage loan indus.; automobile leasing); prop. R.A. Nater Communications Consultant (Data Proc. cons.); bd. dirs. Cal Valley Insur. Serv & Micom Systems 1972-73; past dir. sys. engr. American Data Systems; project engr. WED Enterprises (Disney), devel. Audio-Animatronic Animated Figure Control Systems, Maint. Monitoring and Telephone Plant for Walt Disney World and Disneyland (28 patents); transmission engr. Pacific Tel. Co.; mem. IEEE (award for Best Tech. Paper IEEE, 1964); Republican; rec: computer applications to business, photg. Res/Ofc: 97 Wilderness Dr Sanger 93657

NATHAN, MELVILLE CHARLES, auditing executive; b. July 12, 1922, San Francisco; s. Melville Clarence and Reta Martha (Golinsky) N.; gr.father, Herman Nathan was 1st Postmaster/ Wells Fargo agt. in Grangeville (1875); m. Bobette, Apr. 30, 1944; children: Lorie b. 1947, Terry b. 1949; edn: Univ. Calif. 1939-40, Univ. San Francisco 1940, S.F. Inst. Acctncy. 1940-41, Golden Gate Coll. 1941-42, 46-67; desig: collateral examination mgr. splst. Career: ptnr. M.C. Nathan & Co., Pub. Accts., San Francisco 1946-78; asst. v.p./exam. mgr. First Interstate Bank of Calif., S.F. 1978-85; asst. v.p./exam. mgr. Jennings & Jones, Inc., S.F. 1985–; dir: Bradford Oil Co., Del Sable Oil Co., (1957-); honors: winner Calif. State Handicap Golf Championship (1937), No. Calif. Masonic Golf Champion (1954-60), num. philatelic & research awards; clubs: Masons (past master), Lake Merced Golf & Country (jr. mem. 1928, now club historian); publs: asst. ed. Western Express 1951-74 (asstd. father in authoring Pony Express and Western Express Co. books); mil: chief storekeeper US Navy 1942-46, Victory, Good Conduct, Okinawa Invasion, Asiatic Pac., Am. Theater; Republican; rec: philatelic covers, S.F. & Calif. hist./1st edition books, golf. Ofc: Jennings & Jones Inc. 120 Montgomery St Mezz. Flr San Francisco 94104

NAVALTA, GLORINO MEMBRERE, real estate broker; b. Feb. 5, 1945, Bacnotan, La Union, Philippines, nat. US cit. 1978; s. Puturno N. and Patricia A. (Membrere) N.; m. Ludivica B., Sept. 23, 1968; children: Pati Dominic b. 1969, Christopher b. 1976; edn: BSIE, Nat. Univ., Manila, Phil. 1965; long range planning, UC Berkeley 1974; info. sys. planning, IBM Sys. Inst. 1975; real estate broker Calif. 1983. Career: assoc. indsl. engr. Oscar L.S. Sarte & Assocs. Manila 1960-68; tech. rep. 3M Co., Phil. 1960-68; indsl. engr. Safeway Stores, Bellevue, Wash. 1968-69; dir. corp. planning Blue Cross of No. Calif., Oakland 1969-81; realtor Solano County 1980–; pres. Navalta Inc., real estate and financial svcs., Vallejo 1984–; mgmt. cons. Southeast Asia Devel. Corp. 1984-; tech. advis. gp. on Medicare/ Medi-Caid Stds. & Performance 1978-81; mem. Calif. Coast Containment Council 1980-81; honors: Sigma Upsilon Sigma (1965), Cert. of Distn., Student Writer of the Year (Nat. Univ. 1965); mem: Calif. Assn. Realtors 1980-, Nat. Assn. Realtors 1985-, Am. Inst. Indsl. Engrs., Assn. for Sys. Mgmt., Planning Execs. Inst., Coll. Editors Guild of the Phils., Assn. of Mgmt. & Indsl. Engrs. of Phils.; mem. community adv. bd. Redwood Bank, Vallejo; publ: articles in J. of Sys. Mgmt.; mng. editor Technological Trends, Nat. Univ., Manila 1964-65; ed.-in-chief THe 1965 Nationalian, Nat. Univ., Manila; Republican; Catholic; rec: freelance writing. Ofc: Navalta Inc. 1051 Rollingwood Dr Vallejo 94591

NAY, SAMUEL W., JR., consulting engineer; b. May 29, 1914, Steamboat Springs, Colo.; s. Samuel W. and Josephine L. (Bartz) N.; m. Edythe L. Winberg, May 31, 1942; 1 son, Samuel W. III b. 1943 (decd.); edn: BS engrg., CSU Los Angeles; Reg. Mech. Engr. Calif., Fire Protection Engr. Calif. Career: tooling Lockheed Aircraft Burbank 1940-47; mech. engr. assoc. Dept. of Water & Power L.A. 1947-78; tchr. UCLA Extn. 1978-81; cons. engr. S.W. Nay Assoc., owner/ ptnr. in cons. engr. & parliamentary law firm 1978–; mem: Soc. Fire Protection Engrs. (past chpt. pres.), Am. Soc. Mech. Engrs., Inst. for Advancement of Engrs. (past treas.), Toastmasters Internat. (past area gov., able toastmaster), Brookside Men's Golf Club; editor: The Flame (tech. soc.

publ. 1978-81); mil: sgt. USAAF 1942-45, Meritorious Svc.; Republican; Protestant; rec: golf, photog. Ofc: POB 4663 Glendale 91202

NAYAK, BANNANJE RAVINDRA, physician; b. Apr. 28, 1948, Hyderabad, India; s. Devdas and Varada (Rao) N.; m. Sunanda, Aug. 15, 1980; children: Nita b. 1983, Priya b. 1986; edn: HSC, Nrupatunga Jr. Coll. 1965; MD, Gandhi Med. Coll. 1972; MD Calif. 1979. Career: intern, resident int. med. Inst. Med. Sci. Osmania Univ. Hyderabad, India 1972-75; intern Elyria Meml. Hosp. Ohio 1975-76; resident phys. med. & rehab. Univ. Texas Med. Sch. San Antonio 1976-79; physiatrist 1979–, presently Kaiser Permanente Med. Ctr. Hayward; cons. chronic pain pgm.; fellow Am. Acad. Phys. Med. & Rehab. 1982-; Hindu. Res: 3516 Pinewood Dr Hayward 94542 Ofc: Permanente Med. Grp. 27400 Hesperian Blvd Hayward 94545

NAYMARK, SHERMAN, engineering and consulting co. executive; b. May 12, 1920, Duluth, Minn.; s. David and Lena N.; m. Bettey Mintz, Sept. 2, 1984; children: Ronald L. b. 1945, Janet (Stone) b. 1948; edn: BS, engring., US Naval Acad. 1941; MS, engring./constrn., M.I.T. 1946; Reg. Profl. Engr. Calif., N.Y., Ill., Iowa, Wis., Minn., Pa. Career: engring. ofcr. US Navy 1941-48; senior scientist Argonne Nat. Lab. 1948-52; dir. Schnectady Office, KAPL proj. engring. mgr., Reactor Div. AEC, 1952-56; mgmt. Gen. Electric Co., 1956-70; pres. Quadrex Corp., Campbell 1970-85, bd. chmn. 1985–; lectr. Univ. of Va., M.I.T., and US Naval Reserve Tng. Schools; advisor to US Delegation, 3d Internat. Conf. on Peaceful Uses of Atomic Energy, Geneva, Switz., 1964; senior examiner Profl. Engrs., State of Calif., 1960-; awards: Distinguished citizen City of San Jose (1970), Torch of Liberty award ADL (1982); mem: US Naval Inst. (Hon. Life), US DOE/FPCC, Fellow Am. Nuclear Soc., ANS (bd. dirs. & exec. com.; nat. treas. 1979-80; bd. govs. Nuclear Technology; gen. chmn. 1977 ANS Annual Meeting), Am. Public Power Assn. (assoc.), AAAS; publs: contbr. 60+ tech. papers on nuclear research, dev. & engr. in Reactor Handbook (2d ed.), and Nuclear Reactor Engineering (Glasstone and Sesonske); mil: US Navy 1941-54; capt. USNR, ret.; Democrat; Jewish; rec: tennis, jogging, travel. Res: 218 Forrester Rd Los Gatos 95030 Ofc: Quadrex Corporation 1700 Dell Ave Campbell 95008

NAZEMI, REZA, neurologist; b. Nov. 25, 1947, Tehran, Iran; s. Abolghassem and Massoumeh (Barazandeh) N.; m. Mandana Shakerin, June 22, 1980; children: Navid b. 1981, Cameron b. 1983; edn: MD (Distinguished Grad.) Tehran Univ. 1973; Diplomate in neurology, Am. Board of Neurology & Psychiatry; certified Am. Assn. of Electromyography & Electrodiagnosis. Career: intern Burington County Meml. Hosp., Mt. Holly, NJ 1974-75; resident in physical med. & rehabilitation, Tufts Univ., Boston 1975-76; resident in neurology, Northwestern Univ., Chgo. 1976-79; fellow in neuromuscular diseases & electromyography Univ. of Calif., San Diego 1979-80; neurologist in pvt. practice, Palm Springs 1980–; active staff Desert Hosp. (P.S.) and Eisenhower Med. Ctr. (Rancho Mirage); mem: Am. Acad. of Neurology, Am. Assn. of Electromyography & Electrodiagnosis, Am. Soc. for Evoked Potential; contbr. Archives of Physical Medicine and Rehabilitation, Vol. 63 (1982); rec: running, swimming, hiking. Ofc: 1080 N Indian Ave Palm Springs 92262

NEAL, JAMES GARY, investment planning executive; b. May 5, 1956, Fresno; s. William Albert and Shirley Jean (Painter) N.; m. Mary Pamela, Jan. 23, 1982; children: Nicolin Jennifer b. 1983, Megan Sheriann b. 1985; edn: AA, Fresno City Coll. 1976; stu. CSU Fresno 1976-7, San Jose 1977, Hayward 1978; The American Coll. 1978-; grad. Conn. Mutual Grad. Sch. 1983. Life and Disability Lic. 1978-, Nat. Assn. of Securities Dealers 1982-. Career: life and disability ins. salesman, investment plng. exec. Connecticut Mutual Life (CML), Fresno 1978–; spkr., ins. class, CSU Fresno 1981; rep. to The Agents Advis. Com., CML 1983; honors: MVP, St. Mary's Coll. Baseball Sch. (1971), Co. Leaders Club, CML (1980, 81, 82), Agent of Year, Fresno Life Underwriters Assn. (1981), Nat. Sales Achieve. Award (1981, 82, 83), Million Dollar Round Table (Qual. mem. 1985), Bates Citation award for agency leader, CML/ Fresno (1985), CML Blue Chip Assn. pres. (1979-); mem: Nat., Calif. Assn. of Life Underwriters, FLUA, Rotary, Fresno Breakfast Tip Club (founder 1980), Lambda Chi Alpha (exec. com.), Aircraft Owners and Pilots Assn., San Joaquin Country Club, Sierra Sport and Racquet Club; works: invented a New Life Ins. Service (Trademark pend. 1984); founder/co-owner of the Fresno Indians, semi-pro baseball team; publ: article in Life Ins. Selling mag. 8/85; Republican; Christian; rec: numismatics, pvt. pilot, golf, baseball (coach Babe Ruth). Res: 3610 W. Locust Fresno 93711 Ofc: Conn. Mutual Life 5070 N. Sixth, Ste 189, Fresno 93710

NEASE, LARRY EDWARD, real estate investment analyst; b. June 13, 1950, Long Beach, Calif.; s. Francis Evans and Bernice Ann (Cooper) N.; m. Marile Anne, July 29, 1972; children: Michael b. 1976, Lindsey b. 1982; edn: BS, CSU Long Beach 1977; MBA, Pepperdine Univ. 1983; MSBA, Univ. So. Calif. 1985; real estate broker Calif. 1984. Career: senior title ofcr. World Title Co. Studio City 1981-82; senior internal auditor Safeco Title Ins. Co. 1982-84; asst. v.p. Real Estate Transaction Analysis, Beverly Hills S&L Mission Viejo 1984-86; owner LEN Analytics Lakewood 1985–; financial analyst August Financial Corp. Long Beach 1986–; honors: Beta Gamma Sigma, Dean's List (Pepperdine, CSULB); mem. BSA (cubmaster); publ: wrote REIA, a computer pgm. to analyze real estate investment alternatives; Republican; Catholic; rec: competitive cycling. Res: 6028 Eberle St Lakewood 90713 Ofc: August Financial Corp. 3545 Long Beach Blvd Ste 500 Long Beach 90801

NEAT, EUGENE, JR., photographer; b. June 16, 1945, Jackson, Miss.; s. Eugene and Annie Mae (Jenkins) N.; m. Lorraine, Sept. 14, 1969; children: Nila Jean b. 1970, Gina Michelle b. 1971, Melissa Rose b. 1975; m. 2d Juana Maria, Aug. 31, 1978; Mia Lynn b. 1979; edn: grad. Sch. of Modern Photog. 1973, spl. courses Nikon Sch. of Photog. 1976, grad. Photo Corp. of Am. tng. course 1977, grad. N.Y. Inst. of Photog. 1979; BA, Roosevelt Univ. 1974; BA, Columbia Coll. Chgo. 1975; MA, Governors State Univ. 1981; BA, Chgo. State Univ. 1982. Career: asst. photog. Playboy Studios, Chgo. 1975-76; profl. photog. Photo Corp. of Am., Downers Grove, Ill. 1976-77; staff photog. Disco Gossip Mag., Chgo. 1977-79; pres. Neat Photography Inc., Venice, Calif. 1979–; instr. photog. Beverly Hills Comm. Orgn. 1985; honors: Who's Who Among Students in Am. Jr. Colls. (1970-71), dean's list, talent scholarship, and outstanding senior award, Chgo. St. Univ. (1982); mem: US Marine Corps Combat Correspondents Assn., Nat. Press Photogs., Profl. Photogs. of Am., Am. Soc. of Mag. Photogs., Nat. Historian Montford Point Marine Assn. Inc., TWA Round the World Club (1973), Kappa Alpha Psi frat., Phi Beta Lambda; exhibs: Photog. Mus. of Sci. and Industry (1982), Santa Monica Coll. (1984); mil: sgt. USMC 1965-69, Combat Action Ribbon, Pres. Unit Cit., GCM, Nat. Def. Svc., Vietnam Svc. w/2 bronze stars, Rep. of Vietnam Merit. Unit Citations (2 awards), Rep. of Vietnam Campaign Medal, Combat Action Rib.; Democrat; Prot.; rec: photog., running (America's Marathon, 1985, L.A. Marathon, 1986). Ofc: POB 742 Venice 90291

NEAULT, CHARLES CAREY, chiropractor; b. July 26, 1951, Muskegon, Mich.; s. Earl Henry and Elfriede E. (Weber) N.; m. Jeannie Worley, April 5, 1985; children: Sara Elizabeth b. 1981, Jacqueline Rene b. 1983; edn: BA, New Coll. of Calif. 1977; MS, Bridgeport Univ. 1981; DC, Cleveland Chiropractic Coll. 1977. Career: founder practice, Simi Valley 1978; cert. disability evaluator, independent medical examiner, inc. 1980; currently, pres. Neault Chiropractic Corp.; research statistician Internat. Acad. of Chiropractic Low Back Pain Study; faculty Cleveland Chiropractic Coll.; founder So. Calif. Back School; honors: Prof. of the Year, Ventura Co. Chiropractic 1982; Outstanding Young Men of Am., 1983; Rober S. Botterman Award for Public Svc. 1983; mem: Am. Chiropractic Assn. (Council on Nutrition, Roentgoenology, Sports Injuries, Neurology and Research) and Calif. Chiropractic Assns., Ventura Co. Chiropractic Soc. (past pres.), Am. Assn. for the Adv. of Sci., Found. for Chiropractice Edn., Internat. Acad. for Chiropractic Low Back Pain Study, Cleveland Chiropractic Coll. Alumni Assn. (past chmn.), Boys & Girls Club of Simi Valley (past mem., bd. dirs.), Rotary, Businessmans Council for Simi Valley, Chiropractic Students Assn. of Calif. (past chmn. and founder); works: Tri-Valent Chromium as a Factor in the Treatment of Cardiovascular Atherosclerotic Disease and Glucose Intolerance; mil: s/sgt. USAF, Marksman, Vietnam Vets; Republican; Episcopal; rec: snow skiing, wind surfing, music. Res: 2707 Bitternut Circle Simi Valley 93063 Ofc: Neault Chiropractic Corp., 2345 Erringer Rd. Ste. 210 Simi Valley 93065

NEEL-DE SALVO, PAMELA LEA, chiropractor; b. Dec. 16, 1954, Albany, Calif.; d. James Wilfred and Evelyn Rosemily (Schlee) Neel; m. Robert Anthony DeSalvo, Jan. 29, 1984; edn: BS, magna cum laude, Cal. Poly. S.L.O. 1978; DC, magna cum laude, Palmer West 1983; DC Calif. 1984. Career: pvt. practice DeSalvo Chiro. 1984–; part-time faculty Palmer West 1986; honors: class valedictorian (Palmer Coll. 1983), Phi Kappa Phi, Tri Beta; mem: Am. Chiro. Assn., Calif. Chiro. Assn., Chiro. Council on Roentgenology; Lutheran; rec: aerobic dance, running, skiing. Ofc: DeSalvo Chiropractic 716 Kiely Blvd. Santa Clara 95051

NEELSEN, JENS KLAUS, hotel/real estate executive, b. Jan. 16, 1945, Berlin, W. Ger.; s. Dr. John H. and Erika O. (Sens) N.; m. Karin Bauer, Aug. 20, 1978; children: Nina b. 1968, Jennifer b. 1984; edn: grad. Hotel Mgmt. Sch., Reichenhall, W. Ger. 1964-65; spl. courses in law, tax and real estate. Career: gen. mgr. Hotel Europaeisher, Berlin 1966-69; credit and first trust deed dept. Dresdner Bank, Berlin 1969-70; cons. World Bank, Dubrovnik, Yugo., mgmt. advisor to India Tourism Devel. Corp., 1970-71; dir. gen. Ravenna Hotels, Mallorca, Spain 1972; senior cons., loding indus., Laventhol, Krekstein, Horwath & Horwath, Los Angeles 1973-74; pres./chief finl. ofcr. Paul-Weil Mgmt. Corp. (mgmt. 12 hotel props. and var. real estate in US) 1974-78; pres./owner Nina Limited (hotel and real estate acquisition and mgmt.), 1974–; mng. gen. ptnr. Neelson-Weil, Essex House (150 rm hotel, Lancaster), Thornwood Partners Limited (117 unit housing devel., Lancaster), Essex Center Ltd. (office bldg., Lancaster); honors: Kentucky Colonel; mem. Calif. Hotel-Motel Assn.; civic: City of Lancaster Center Site Dev. Com. (past chmn.), CofC (past chmn. Tourist Bur.); Lutheran; rec: gardening, art collection, travel. Ofc: 44916 North 10th St West Lancaster 93534

NEFF, HOWARD L., semiconductor equipment co. executive; b. Dec. 26, 1941, Connersville, Ind.; s. Charles Lowell and Thelma Grace (Brauchla) N.; m. Cheryl Bartholomew, Jan. 23, 1971; 2 daus. Stacey b. 1973, Simeon b. 1976; edn: BA, Dartmouth Coll. 1966; grad. work (toward MBA) Seton Hall 1968. Career: from prodn. supr. to plant mgr. Johnson & Johnson, assignments in mfg. & distbn. mgmt. in New Jersey, Calif., U.K., Chgo., 1966-77; corp. dir. distbn. Consol. Aluminum and exec. v.p. (COO) of subs. transp. co., St. Louis, Mo., 1977-80; var. opns., mfg., gen. mgmt. pos., currently v.p. ops. Applied Materials, Santa Clara 1980–, also v.p./gen. mgr. Deposition Products Div.; bd. dirs. Associated Shippers Inc. (1978-80), Traffic Com. Aluminum Assn. Wash DC (1977-80), Contract Carrier Conf. Wash DC (1978-80); mem. Japan Soc.; civic: Rotary (1975-77), AYSO soccer (referee 1978-); mil: sgt E5 US Army 1961-64; Republican; Methodist (ch. coms.); rec: tennis, travel. Res: 38040 Elena Rd Los Altos Hills 94022 Ofc: Applied Materials 3050 Bowers Ave Santa Clara 95054

NEFF, NANCY, educational purchasing executive; b. Sept. 9, Mich.; d. John M. and Helen A. (Snyder) Westrick; edn: ASc, Grossmont Coll. 1973; BSc,

Western State Univ. 1975; JD, 1977; DD, 1980. Career: airline hostess, model in NY, NY prior to 1971; personnel mgr. Buffums Dept. Store, Fashion Valley 1971-74; aerospace contractor/ contract analyst Rockwell Internat. 1974-77; small & minority bus adminstr. corp. agreement/ corp. agreement coord. (interfaced w/ all Rockwell divs. in Western reg.) 1977-79; deputy dir. Purchasing & Contracting County of San Diego 1979-83; dir. of Purchasing 1983–; spkr: Nat. Assn. Women in Constrn. (1982), Nat. Conf. Public Purchasing Officials, Grossmont Coll. Career Fair; honors: Outstanding Woman of the Yr. 1982; hon. awards: City of San Diego Personnel (1980-81), San Diego Minority Devel. Council (1982); mem: S.D. County Womens Network (pres.); Calif. Women in Govt. (exec. bd. 1981); Nat. Assn. Female Execs. (dir.); Nat. Notary Assn.; Purchasing Mgrs. Assn.; Calif. Pub. Purchasing Officials; San Diego Trial Lawyers Assn.; Delta Theta Phi; S.D. Career Guidance Assn.; No. Co. Connectiens; Presidents Council; Nu Beta Epsilon; No. Co. Repertory Theatre; Young Friends of S.D. Symphony; Young Connoiseurs of S.D. Art.; Calif. Trial Lawyers Assn.; sev. articles in profl. publs; hon. mention, Newsday NY, poetry; rec: theatre arts, flying, aero sports, travel. Res: 10216 Vultee St, 212, Downey 90241 Ofc: Nancy Neff, J.D., Compton Unified School Dist. Purch. Dept., 604 S Tamarind Ave Compton 90220

NEGRON, DENNIS, lawyer; b. Dec. 4, 1948, NY, NY; s. Dionisio and Mercedes (Martinez) N.; m. Maurine Claudia, June 19, 1980; children: Thomas, Bambi, Dennis, Tappi; edn: AA, Rio Hondo Coll. 1974; BS in law, Western State Univ. 1977, JD, 1978; MS in mgmt., Pacific Christian Coll. 1980; Certified Purch. Mgr., NAPM; Calif. Community Colls. tchg. cred.; admitted Calif. State Bar (1979), Supreme Ct. of Calif., US Ct. of Appeals, US Ct. of Claims, US Customs Ct., Central Dist. Ct. of Calif., US Tax Ct., US Ct. of Internat. Trade. Career: foreman Ford Motor Co.; contract adminstr. Fluor Engrs. & Constrs.; contracts splst. Bechtel Power Corp.; purch. mgr. Kal Kan Foods Inc.; current: atty. assoc. Law Offices of Evan L. Ginsburg, Fullerton; instr. Cerritos Comm. Coll.; mem. Nat. Assn. of Purch. Mgmt., Am. Bar Assn., Calif. Bar Assn.; mil: E5 US Navy 1968-70, Vietnam; Republican; Christian; rec: golf, tennis, racquetball, shooting. Res: 6051 Magnolia Ave Whittier 90601 Law Ofcs of Evan L. Ginsburg 704 N Harbor Blvd Fullerton 92632

NEILL, MARY HELEN, co. executive; b. July 30, 1929, Humboldt, Tenn.; d. James Vester and Mary Lily (Petty) Sisco; m. Austin Duane Neill, Apr. 27, 1946; children: Vickie L. b. 1953, Sandra R. b. 1955. Career: career placement advisor Reed & Assoc., Fresno 1967-69; prop. Alta Loma Trading Post, Alta Loma 1969-74; corp. ofcr. Eastland Market, Inc., Ontario 1974–; mem. Nat. Assn. of Self-Employed, Alta Loma Equestrian Club (pres. 1968-74); civic: Alta Loma Master Plan Com. (1972-73); Democrat; Christian; rec: golf, ski, equestrian. Res: 5617 Della Alta Loma 91701 Ofc: Eastland Market 1072 East G St Ontario 91764

NELSON, ANNE ROBERTS, television executive; b. July 6, 1922, San Francisco; s. Howard Hyde and Catherine Gwendolen (Gaynor) R.; m. Harmon Oscar Nelson, Jr. (decd. 1975), Nov. 1, 1946; children: Gaye Nelson b. 1952, Harmon Oscar III b. 1955, Amy Nelson b. 1955; edn: BA journ., Univ. Calif. 1944. Career: reporter Pasadena Star-News 1939-42; guest editor Madamoiselle Mag. 1942; freelance ports writer in coll.; research writer cartoon Strange as It Seems by John Hix 1942-44; exec. assoc. sales svc. dept., pgm. dept. and bus. affairs CBS 1945-50, dir. bus. affairs 1950-59, var. bus. affairs exec. positions, currently dir. bus. affairs, talent & pgm. acquisitions CBS Entertainment 1959–; mem: Acad. TV Arts & scis., Pacific Pioneer Broadcasters, CBS 40 Year Club, Am. Women for Internat. Understanding (bd. dirs.), Calif. Mus. of Sci. and Industry, Los Angeles Beautiful (var. advis. bd. positions), Crenshaw Neighbors Inc. (past v.p.); publ: historical book in progress; Republican; Congregational (Sunday school tchr.); rec: photog., travel, tap dancing, tennis, windsurfing, coin collecting, gardening, sewing, cooking. Ofc: CBS Entertainment 7800 Beverly Blvd Los Angeles 90036

NELSON, BRUCE LESLIE, allergist; b. July 12, 1948, Hilo, Hawaii; s. Henry Clement and Betty Theresa (Chan) N.; m. Marcia Jean Kubota, Oct. 31, 1948; children: Sara b. 1977, Brian b. 1979, Jason b. 1981; edn: BA, Boston Univ. 1970; MD, John A. Burns Sch. of Med., Univ. HI 1975; bd. certified Am. Bd. of Internal Medicine 1979, Am. Bd. of Allergy & Immunology 1981. Career: intern, resident in int. medicine, fellowship in allergy & immunology, Wilford Hall USAF Medical Center, San Antonio, Tx. 1975-81; staff and asst. chief allergy & immunol. Dept. of Med., David Grant USAF Medical Ctr., Travis AFB, Calif. 1981-83; pvt. practice in allergy & immunol. Thomas-Davis Clinic, Tucson, Ariz. 1983-84, Allergy & Asthma Assocs. of So. Calif., Mission Viejo & El Toro, 1985–; clin. asst. prof. UC Irvine Med. Center 1985-; mem: Fellow Am. Coll. of Allergy, Fellow Am. Coll. of Physicians, Am. Acad. of Allergy and Immunol., AMA, CMA, Orange County Med. Soc., Orange County Allergy Soc., Western Soc. of Allergy, Assn. of Mil. Allergists, AF Soc. of Physicians; contbr. articles to med. journals; mil: major USAF 1975-83; Republican; Roman Catholic; rec: gardening. Ofc: Allergy & Asthma Associates of Southern California 24432 Muirlands Blvd Ste 131 El Toro 92630

NELSON, C(ARL) ALLEN, specialty merchandise mail order co. owner; b. Feb. 14, 1920, Newton, Kans.; s. Carl Raymond and Marguerite Alice (Allen) N.; m. Betty Jane Johnson (dec. 1978), June 21, 1940; 1 son, Richard Allen, b. 1950; edn: Fort Hays Kans. State Coll. 1938-9, Salt City Bus. Coll. 1939-40; lic. Fire & Casualty/Life & Dis. Insurance Agt., Calif. 1948-53, 1965-85. Career: central ofc. equipt. instlr. (Long Beach and Whittier 1947-56), supply supr. (Whittier 1956-64), computer opr. (Santa Monica (1964-66), General Tel. Co., 1947-66; prin. (Farmers Ins. Gp.) Al Nelson Insurance Agency, Long Bch. 1948-53, Whittier 1966-69, Atascadero 1969-75, Al & Rick Nelson Ins. Agcy. 1975-78; owner Nelson Ents. dba Allen's World of Gifts, Knobby Horse, retail & wholesale - splty. mdse., 1983–; design patent (1953) prodn. & mail order of childrens' clothes hanger "Knobby Horse"; past pres. Whittier A.M. Y's Mens Club (YMCA) 1964-65, Man of the Year 1965. Helped wage successful battle to repeal the Calif. State Inheritance Tax (1982), testified before Calif. Assem. for AB 264 (bill to repeal tax), gave num. media interviews to arouse public awareness on behalf of INHERIT (Initiative to Help Ensure the Right to Inherit without Tax); mil: s/sgt. US Army Air Corps 1944-46, assigned to 10th AF 313th Wing, 6th Bomb Group, 24th Sqdrn. B-29 Central Fire Control, North Field AB, Tinian, Mariannas (then largest base in world from which the "Enola Gay" took off to bomb Hiroshima and Nagasaki), GCM, WWII Victory, Asia-Pac. Cpgn. w/ 4 battle stars, Disting. Unit Cit.; Republican; Congregational; rec: photog., growing (400+) hybrid poplar trees. Res: 15325 Lake Side Lane, Hornbrook 96044 Ofc: Nelson Ent. 15325 Lake Side Lane, POB 10, Hornbrook 96044

NELSON, CAESAR, JR., journalist, entrepreneur; b. Nov. 11, 1959, Sacramento, Calif.; s. Caesar and Clara R. (Benbow) N.; edn: BA Eng., UC Los Angeles and CSU Sacto. 1983. Career: publicist, mgr. of first black American to swim Eng. Channel; correspondent, journalist for Sacto. Observer Newspaper 1976-84; publr., ed. Capitol Currents Newsletter Mag. 1983-85; pres. Cesare & Assocs. Advt. & Pub. Rels. 1986–; editor VIP Mag.; founder, dir. first Water Safety Day Sacto. 1985; PR cons., Eng. tutor; honors: Outstanding Young Men of Am. 1980-81; mem. Sacto. City Coll. Forensic Dept.; book in progress; rec: travel, tennis, literature, piano. Ofc: Cesare & Assocs. Box 38412 Sacramento 95838

NELSON, DAVID ELDEN, software co. president; b. Feb. 7, 1938, Duluth, Minn.; s. Yngvar Englebrecht and Frances Alvilda (Elden) N.; m. Gloria, Sept. 1, 1962; children: Jennifer b. 1966, David b. 1969; edn: AA, Cerritos Jr. Coll. 1963; BS indsl. tech., CSU Long Beach 1968, MS in mgmt., 1971. Career: program coord. Philco-Ford, 1966-68; indsl. engr. Collins Radio 1968-69; mfg. engr. Varian Data Machines 1969-70; Data Pac cust. service mgr., 1970-71, PC material mng. 1971-75, Cal Comp spl. projects mgr. 1975-76, senior advisory mkt. rep. Control Data Corp. 1976-78, systems analyst Rolm Corp. 1978; sales mgr. W. region, IAI (Interactive Appli), 1978-80, pres. 1981–; mem. OMA; mil: FT3 USNR 1956-58; Republican; rec: woodworking, sailing, badminton. Ofc: IAI 2316 Walsh Ari Santa Clara 95051

NELSON, DON ALDEN, certified public accountant; b. Nov. 28, 1927, San Diego; s. Ernest Elmer and Lora Ellen (Swearengin) N.; m. Roslyn Reps, Feb. 12, 1949; children: Linda b. 1953, Adelaide b. 1954; edn: BA, UCLA 1948; CPA, Calif. 1951. Career: Deloitte Haskins & Sells, Los Angeles Ofc. 1948, partner 1963–; pres. L.A. chpt. Calif. Soc. of CPAs 1972-73; pres. Calif. Soc. CPAs 1983; Council of Am. Inst. of CPAs; trustee Methodist Hosp. of So. Calif.; dir./ pres. So. Calif. chpt. Nat. Multiple Sclerosis Soc.; dir. Partners Pgm., UCLA Grad. Sch. of Mgmt.; Jacoby Assocs. of UCLA Grad. Sch. of Mgmt.; mem. UCLA Chancellor's Assocs. (chmn. 1972-73); mem: Calif. Soc. CPAs (pres. 1983-84); Calif. CPA Found. for Edn. & Research (pres. 1981-83); L.A. Rotary Club; Calif. Club; L.A. Country Club; Jonathan Club (former); Republican; Methodist; rec: paddle tennis, golf. Res: 147 Granville Ave Los Angeles 90049 Ofc: Deloitte Haskins & Sells, 333 S Grand Ave, Ste 2800, Los Angeles 90071

NELSON, DOROTHY WRIGHT, judge; b. Sept. 30, 1928, San Pedro; d. Harry Earl and Lorna Amy (Wright) m. James Frank Nelson, Dec. 27, 1950; children: Franklin Wright, Lorna Jean; edn: AB, UCLA 1950, JD, 1953; LLM, USC 1956, LLD, 1983; admitted to Calif. Bar 1954. Career: with USC 1953-80; research assoc. 1953-56; instr. 1957-58; asst. prof. 1959-51; assoc. prof. 1961-67; prof. 1967; assoc. dean 1965-67; dean 1967-80; judge U.S. Ct. of Appeals 9th Circuit, Los Angeles 1980–; cons. Project STAR, Law Enforcement Assistance Admin.; co-chmn: Confronting Myths in Edn., Pres. Nixon's White House Conf. on Children; Pres. Carter's Commn. for Pension Policy 1979; UN Day in Calif. 1982; bd. dirs: Council on Legal Edn. for Profl. Responsibility, Constnl. Rights Found., Am. Nat. Inst. for Social Advancement; Pasadena Dispute Resolution Ctr. 1982-; advy. bds: Nat. Ctr. for State Courts 1974; Bd. Visitors, USAF Acad. 1976-78; Elizabeth Frye Ctr. 1973; Jr. League, Los Angeles 1976-79; advy. coms: Nat. Judicial Edn. Pgm. to Promote Equality for Women and Men in Cts. 1982-; Guardian ad Litem Pgm., Superior Ct. Los Angles 1982-; del. Internat. Women's Conf. 1975; mem. Los Angeles Employees Rels. Bd. 1974-79; honors: Law Alumnus of the Year, UCLA 1967; Profl. Achiev. Award, 1969; named Times Woman of the Year, 1968; Univ. of Judaism Humanitarian Award, 1973; AWARE Internat. Award, 1970; Ernestine Stalhut Outstanding Woman Lawyer Award, 1972; Coro Award for Edn., 1978; Pax Orbis Award, World Peace Through Law Center, 1975; mem: Fellow Am. Bar Found., Am. and Calif. Bar Assns., Am. Law Inst., Am. Judicature Soc., Assn. Am. Law Schs., Supreme Ct. Hist. Soc., Nat. Assn. of Public Adminstrn., Phi Beta Kappa, Order of Coif, Baha'i; author: Judicial Administration and the Administration of Justice, 1973; contbr. articles to profl. jours. Ofc: 312 No. Spring St. Los Angeles 90012

NELSON, ELLIS RICHARD, trade union apprenticeship training coordinator, b. Sept. 4, 1942, Portland, Ore.; s. Clifford Andrew and Dorothy Marie (Peterson) N.; m. Nancy Collins, Mar. 20, 1971; children: Neal b. 1974, Gwendolyn b. 1977; edn: steamfitter cert. San Diego Pipetrades Apprenticeship 1963-68; AA, San Diego Mesa Coll. 1968; voc. edn. cred. UCLA 1975; BS in voc. edn., CSU Long Beach 1983. Career: constrn. foreman Honeywell, San Diego 1972-80, mem. nat. constrn. field com. 1979; asst. dir. Apprentice &

Journeymen Tng. Trust Fund, L.A. 1980-82, dir. 1982-83; curriculum coord. Pipetrades Tng. Center (for Santa Clara and San Benito Counties), San Jose 1984–; awards: for meritorious service State of Calif. Apprenticeship Council (1980); mem. S.D. Pipetrades Joint Apprenticeship Com. (co-chmn. 1975-77), S.D. Pipefitters Joint Apprent. Com. (chmn. 1977-79), Calif. State Pipetrades Apprent. Advis. Com. (mem. 1980-), Instrument Soc. of Am., 82nd Airborne Div. Assn.; mil: s/sgt. US Army 1968-70, Commendn. w/V device, Bronze Star w/o.l.c.; Democrat; Lutheran; rec: ski. Res: 5251 Sunny Orchard Ln San Jose 95135 Ofc: Pipetrades Training Center 780 Commercial St San Jose 95112

NELSON, JEANIE MARLENE, chiropractor; b. Oct. 16, 1955, Fresno; d. Jean Marie Castleberry; edn: BA magna cum laude, CSU Fresno 1976, grad. stu. Univ. Wash. 1977-78; DC magna cum laude (valedictorian), Palmer Coll. of Chiropractic West 1984; lic. DC, Calif. State Bd. Career: self-empl. prin. Kingsburg Chiropractic Center, Kingsburg currently; faculty, research div. Palmer Coll. of Chiropractic West, 1984-; honors: Clarence S. Gonstead Ednl. Trust Scholar (1983-84), A.A. Adams Research Fellow (1983), Palmer/West 1984 Student of the Year, Calif. Chiro. Assn. 1983-84 Student of Year; mem: Am. Public Health Assn., Assn. for Chiropractic Hist., Calif. Chiro. Assn., Am. Chiro. Assn., Internat. Chiro. Assn.; publs: num. conf. presentations, profl. journal articles (1983-); Republican; Ch. of Jesus Christ of LDS; rec: collector humor books. Res: 2261 Fourteenth, 101, Kingsburg 93631 Ofc: Kingsburg Chiropractic Center, 1454 California St Kingsburg 93631

NELSON, KENNETH AAGE, business executive; b. Jan. 6, 1926, Oakland; s. Aage Swan and Elsie Louise (Skarp) N.; m. Viola Swanson, June 19, 1947; children: Druann b. 1950, Duane b. 1952; edn: courses, CSU Stanislaus, USC ext. Career: served in US Merchant Marine 1944-45; var. pos. building trades 1946-; lic. general contractor/prin. 1952–, swimming pool contr. 1958–, owner swimming pool related retail and service bus. 1967–, bd. chmn. Nelson Industries, Inc.; pres. Ken Nelson Aquatech Pools, Turlock (1970s-) and bd. dir., sec. treas. Aquatech Corp. Inc. (Del.) with offices in Huntington Beach and Tucson, Ariz.; awards: Swimming Pool Age pool design awards (1 silver medal, 13 hon. mentions), Nat. Spa & Pool Inst. nat. and internat. awards for design excellence (9 gold, 7 silver, 3 bronze medals; 30 merit awards); mem. Nat. Spa and Pool Inst., Nat. Spa & Pool Inst. (dir. 1971-74, nat. pres. 1980, hon. life); civic: Emanuel Medical Ctr. (bd.), Evangelical Covenant Ch. of Am. (Benevolence Plng. Bd.), Turlock Comm. Concert Assn. (bd.), Stanislaus County Arts Commn. (grants com.), Calif. Hosp. Assn. (liaison trustee network), Turlock CofC (past dir.), Lions (past secty.); Republican; Turlock Covenant Ch. (chmn. 1986); rec: music, swim, Bible study, travel. Ofc: Ken Nelson Aquatech Pools 323 W Canal Dr Turlock 95380

NELSON, MARY ALICE, entrepreneur, credit analyst; b. Aug. 25, 1955, Palo Alto; d. Anthony Andrew and Marian Edith (Etcheberry) Ciriscioli; m. T. Knute Nelson, Nov. 20, 1976; children: Kirsten b.1981, Tanya b. 1984; edn: CSR, Humphreys Coll. 1978; CSU Fresno 1973-75. Career: legal secty. Richard Harriman Atty. at Law, Modesto 1975; senior credit analyst Foster Farms, Livingston 1979–; owner, opr. Top Banana, Delhi 1976–; Svc. Mems., Western Fairs Assn.; var..project team membership Foster Farms 1984-86; spkr. Credit and its Relationship to Transporation, Foster Farms 1983; acquisition project team Top Banana 1982; mem: Western Fairs Assn., Nat. Assn. of Credit Mgrs., Agri Bus. Group, Exec. Com., Kappa Kappa Gamma Alumni; works: logo design, Top Banana 1977; advtg. campaign, Top Banana 1986; new product devel. & promotion, Top Banana 1986; Republican; Catholic; rec: gardening, music. Ofc: Livingston 95334

NELSON, RANDALL ERLAND, surgeon; b. Dec. 28, 1948, Hastings, Nebr.; s. Marvin Erland and Faith Constance (Morrison) N.; m. Carolyn Nelson, Feb. 28, 1976; edn: BS chem., cum laude, Bethany Nazarene Coll., Bethany, Okla. 1971; MD, Univ. of Nebr. Coll. of Medicine, Omaha 1975; MS, Univ. of Ill. at the Medical Ctr., Chgo. 1979. Diplomate Nat. Board of Med. Examiners (1976), Am. Board of Surgery (1983). Career: intern gen. surgery Strong Meml. Hosp., Univ. of Rochester 1975-76, gen. surg. resident Univ. of Rochester Affiliated Hosps. 1976-78, Rush-Presbyterian-St. Luke's Med. Ctr., Chgo. 1978-81, also tchg. 1978-80, and adj. attending surgeon 1980-81; pvt. practice gen. surgery, Surgical Group of San Jose, San Jose, Calif. 1981–; instr. gen. surg. Univ. of Rochester Sch. of Med. & Dentistry 1975-78; honors: Phi Delta Lambda (1971); mem: AMA, Calif. Med. Assn., Santa Clara County Med. Soc., Santa Clara County Surgical Soc., Am. Coll. of Surgeons (fellow 1985), San Jose Surg. Soc.; mem. Circle-K Club 1968-71, U.S. Chamber of Commerce; research: wound infection & host defense mechanisms (1979), article in J. Current Surgery (9/80); Republican (Rep. Nat. Com.); Protestant; rec: photog., model rocketry, coin & stamp col. Res: 5919 Porto Alegre Dr San Jose 95120 Ofc: Surgical Group of San Jose Inc. 2101 Forest Ave Ste 124 San Jose 95128

NELSON, RUSSELL WILLIAM, orthopedic and spinal surgeon; b. Jan. 7, 1952, Belvedere, Ill.; s. Everett Wm. and Thelma June (Cole) N.; m. Dawn Westrom, Sept. 21, 1985; edn: BS chem., Univ. of Ill., Champaign 1974; MD, Rush Univ. 1977. Career: orthopedic surg. resident Univ. Calif. San Francisco 1977-82; spinal surg. fellow USC/Rancho Los Amigos Hosp. 1983; surgeon, ptnr. Channel Islands Orthopedic Med. Group, Oxnard and Downey Orthopedic and Spinal Surgery Group, Downey; asst. clin. prof. USC Med. Sch.; honors: Phi Beta Kappa (1974); mem. Ventura County Med. Soc., Salerni Collegium; num. articles in med. journals; rec: own and race thoroughbred racehorses. Ofc: Channel Islands Orthopedic Group 300 South A Street Oxnard 93030

NELSON, TENA M., psychotherapist, educator; b. Oct. 30, 1934, Raleigh, N.C.; d. William Russell, Jr. and Frances Louise (Caldwell) Middleton; m. George Nelson, June 7, 1957 (div. 1972); children: Carl, b. 1959; Lisa, b. 1961; Paul, b. 1966; edn: BA, Agnes Scott Coll. 1956; MSW, San Diego State Univ. 1972; lic. Marriage, Family & Child Counselor, 1973, LCSW, 1978. Career: social service casewkr. Dept. of Pub. Soc. Svcs., Corona 1963-67; soc. svc. supvr. 1967-69; tng. supvr., Riverside 1969-70; soc. svc. supvr., spl. pgms. 1972-75; soc. svc. supvr. Juvenile Ct. Dependency Investigation and supvr. Shelter Home Pgm.; currently, staff devel. ofcr. Dept. of Pub. Soc. Svcs., Riverside; assoc. clin. prof. USC Sch. of Soc. Wk.; p.t. faculty Chapman Coll.; psychotherapist in pvt. practice 1973–; co-owner/ dir. Professional Symposiums 1977–; co-owner/dir. Southern Calif. Ctr. of Psychotherapy & Counseling, Riverside 1981-84; mem: Nat. Assn. of Soc. Wkrs.; Am. Soc. of Tng. & Devel.; Orthopsychiatric Assn. (past); Nat. Bus. & Profl. Women's Club (past); Democrat; Episcopal; rec: hiking, skiing. Res: 3401 Donder Ct., Riverside 92507 Ofc: Department of Public Social Services, 1111 Spruce St., Riverside 92507

NELSON, THOMAS ADAMS, electrical engineer; b. Aug. 26, 1921, Berkeley; s. Thomas Fleming and Mabel Margaretta (Adams) N.; m. Mary Anne Mares, July 12, 1958; edn: AA, Los Angeles City Coll. 1942; grad. Yale Univ. Aviation Cadet Sch. 1943; BE, USC 1949, MS, 1953; Cert. in Bus. Mgmt., UCLA Grad. Sch. of Mgmt. 1970; Reg. Profl. Engr., Calif. 1957. Career: Los Angeles Dept. of Water and Power 1950-80; design engr., Los Angeles 1950-53; quality assurance engr., Eastern US, Europe and Japan 1953-65; asst. chief quality assurance engr., Los Angeles 1965-68; chief quality assurance engr. 1968-72; senior engr., sect. head 1972-77; mgr. of communications, transmission lines, station maint., distribution trouble 1977-80; currently, cons. engr. and transp. cons.; Nat. Standards Com. rep., Los Angeles Dept. of Water & Power 1956-72, Calif. Power Pool rep., 1975-77, Rail Transp. cons. 1973-79; honors: Seal Bearer, Calif. Scholarship Fedn. 1940; Eta Kappa Nu (1948), Tau Beta Pi (1948), Phi Kappa Phi (1949); mem: IEEE (senior), Vehicular Technology Soc., Pacific Railroad Soc. (dir. 1977-80, 1982-85, v.p. 1986), Metro Rail Hollywood Citizens Com., Ephebian Soc.; works: ed., major author, Railroad Chronology Compendium, 1976; author num. rail transportation articles 1973-85; publs. in L.A. Downtown People Mover, Metro Rail, L.A. County Light Rail Environmental Reports 1979-85, L.A. City Coll. Celebrates (50th anniversary) 1979; ed./ prin. author "50 Years of Railroading in Southern California" (1986); mil: capt. USAF 1942-45, European Theatre w/ (7) Battle Stars, Pres. Unit Citation; Protestant; rec: travel, transp. facilities.

NEMIR, DONALD PHILIP, lawyer; b. Oct. 31, 1931, Oakland; s. Philip F. and Mary Madelyn (Shavor) N.; edn: AB, UC Berkeley 1957; JD, UC Berkeley Boalt Hall 1960. Career: senior atty. Law Ofcs. Donald Nemir, San Francisco 1961–; bd. dirs. Summit Found.; mem: Am. Bar Assn.; Phi Delta Phi; Univ. Club, S.F.; mil: USNR 1949-54. Res: 370 Marion Ave Mill Valley 94941 Ofc: Law Offices of Donald Nemir, One Maritime Plaza San Francisco 94111

NERIO, LELAND KAZUMI, lawyer; b. Sept. 16, 1948, San Francisco; s. Toyo and Tokie N.; edn: BA, San Jose State Coll. 1971; MA, CSU San Jose 1975; JD, UC Hastings Coll. of Law 1979; admitted to Calif. Bar. Career: student activities coord. De Anza Community Coll., Cupertino 1973-76, instr. p.t. 1973-78; law clerk State Bar of Calif., San Francisco 1978; law clerk to Assoc. Justice Wiley W. Manuel, Calif. Supreme Ct. 1979; law clerk to the Presiding Judge Alan Haverty, Law and Motion Dept., Superior Ct. of San Mateo Co., Redwood City 1979; of counsel Law Ofcs. Nordin F. Blacker, San Jose 1981-83; prin. atty. Law Ofcs. Leland Nerio, San Jose 1983–; coll. and univ. lectr.; mem: Am., Calif., Santa Clara Co., Los Angeles Co. and San Francisco Bar Assns., Santa Clara Co. Mental Health Adv. Bd. (co-chair Budget Com. 1976); Democrat; Presbyterian; rec: golf, sailing, tennis. Law Offices of Leland Nerio, 95 So. Market St. Ste. 250 San Jose 95113

NESBITT, PATRICK MICHAEL, lawyer; b. Feb. 7, 1944, Detroit, Mich.; s. Frederick Henry and Marie (Labadie) N.; div.; children: Elizabeth Paige b. 1977, Patrick Michael Jr. b. 1978; edn: BS, USAF Acad. 1967; MS, Univ. of Mich. 1968; JD, Whittier Coll. 1981. Career: research engr. USAF 1967-71; pres./chmn. bd. Patrick M. Nesbitt Assocs. 1971–; mng. ptr. Nesbitt/Freshman Devel. Co. 1977–; chmn. bd. Academy Savings & Loan Assn. 1983–; pres. Nesbitt Hotel Properties Inc. 1983–; chmn. bd. Charter Properties Inc. 1983–; honors: Congl. appt. to USAF Acad., grad. scholarship Univ. Mich., Exellence in design award, A.I.A. (1981); clubs: Jonathan, Columbus Athletic, Marina City; mil: capt. USAF 1963-81; Republican; Catholic; rec: skiing, flying, polo. Res: 273 S Glenroy Ave Los Angeles 90049 Ofc: 924 Westwood Blvd Ste 905 Los Angeles 90024

NESBITT, PAUL EDWARD, government historian; b. Dec. 25, 1943, Baltimore, Md.; s. William E. and Margaret Caroline N.; m. Anita, Dec. 8, 1984; children: Erik Paul b. 1968, Janelle M. b. 1972; edn: AB, Univ. Wash. 1965; MAA, Wash. State Univ. 1968; PhD, Univ. Calgary 1972. Career: staff interior designer and cons. Calif., Wash., Alberta 1961-70; prof. Wash. 1968-69; research dir., tchg. asst. Univ. Calgary 1969-71; senior exec. Hudson's Bay Co. Canada 1971; prof. Western Ore. Coll. Monmouth 1971-73; dir. Am. Sch. of Interior Design S.F. 1974; state historian Calif. 1974–; exec. mgr. UCSEC 1986; cons. energy planning devel. Smith Petrol Corp. 1986; honors: Hon. D.Phil. (Rochdale Coll. 1970), Am. Legion Award, var. awards United Way; fellow Am. Anthropological Assn.; mem: Calif. Hist. Soc., Com. for Preservation of History; publs: var. profl. monographs and articles; Republican. Ofc: Sacramento 95811

NEUFELD, REYNOLD WAYNE, financial planner; b. Apr. 16, 1937, Shafter, Calif.; s. Harvey and Esther Blondina (Nikkel) N.; m. Jean, Aug. 2, 1958; children: Christy Jean, Cheryl Diane; edn: BA, Northwestern Christian Coll. 1959; M.Div., Pacific Sch. of Religion 1965; Chartered Financial Cons. 1983; Chartered Life Underwriter 1983; Accredited Pension Adminstr. 1983. Career: founder, pres. Neufeld & Assocs. Inc. 1973−, Neufeld Ins. Svcs. Inc. 1980−; honors: Top Ring Club (Northwestern Nat. Life Ins. Co. 1980-); mem: NW Nat. Life Field Assn. (pres. 1986), Million Dollar Round Table (life 1986), Rotary 1986, Ednl. Found. for Black Americans (secty. 1986); Republican; Christian. Ofc: Neufeld & Assocs. Inc. POB 2949 Pomona 91769-2949

NEUMANN, PACITA BARBOSA, physician; b. Jan. 28, 1938, Iriga City, Philippines; d. Bonifacio Balang and Paula Crescini (Cabaltera) Barbosa; m. 2d. Walter Neumann, Feb. 16, 1981; children: (Lee) Jesus, b. 1962, Renato, b. 1963, Emmanuel, b. 1964, Maria Theresa, b. 1967, Jesus Alfonso, b. 1968, Peter, b. 1969, Michael, b. 1973; edn: AA, cum laude, Colegio de San Juan de Letran, Philippines 1957; MD, Univ. of St. Tomas, Philippines 1963;. Career: internship, res. Univ. of St. Tomas and affil. hosps., Manila 1962-63, Chinese Gen. Hosp., Manila 1963-64, Quirino Labor Hosp., Quezon City 1964-65; gen. med. rural practice in Iriga City, Phil 1965-70; asst. pathology lab., Dr. John Kwittken, Englewood, NJ 1970-71; res. phys. dept. of pathology Ospital Ng Maynila (City Hosp.), Phil. 1975-76; tchr. Coll. of Nursing and Midwifery, med. techn. St. Francis Xavier and Las Pinas Gen. Hosp., Manila 1976-78; gen. med. practice, sch. physician, Manila 1978-79; med. asst. Pulmonary Disease Inst., Redondo Beach 1980-81; res. Univ. of Med. and Dentistry Univ. Hosp. Newark, NJ 1981-82, Cedars Sinai Med. Ctr. Los Angeles 1982-83, Calif. lic. phys. 1983; gen. med. practice Long Beach 1983−; mission work; mem. Philippine Med. Assn., Manila Med. Soc.; AMA, Am. Women's Med. Assn., Phil. Women's Med. Soc.; mil: capt. USAR (MC); Catholic. Res: 5343 Bindewald Rd., Torrance 90505 Ofc: General Med. Clin. Inc. 12225 South St Ste 102 Artesia 90701

NEVINS, MICHAEL DAVID, public relations co. president; b. Sept. 3, 1953, Glendale; s. Gene Richard and Margaret Louise (Birdwell) N.; m. Margaret Hagen, Apr. 15, 1978, 1 dau. Martha Hagen b. 1984; edn: BA in English, summa cum laude, Seattle Univ. 1975. Career: freelance writer var. advt./pub. rels. agencies, opened Calif. office 1984, incorporated 1985, pres. Michael Nevins Communications Inc., Newport Beach 1985-86; prin. Green, Martin & Nevins Inc., Costa Mesa 1986−; cons. Frank Lloyd Wright Found., Taliesin Assoc. Architects, Taliesin Gates Devel. Co.; organizer "Inland Empire West" pgm. in coord. with L.A. Times and Orange County Register newspapers; mem. Nat. Assn. of Home Builders, Building Indus. Assn. So. Calif., BIA Orange County (Speakers Bur. 1985, 86); publs: contbr. fiction, Fragments (Seattle U. literary mag., 1974); sang role Melchoir in Amahl & Night Visitors" NBC-TV, Seattle (1975); rec: writing, music (piano, guitar, voice, composition). Ofc: Green, Martin & Nevins Inc. 3194 Airport Loop Ste D Costa Mesa 92626

NEWACHECK, DAVID J., lawyer; b. Dec. 8, 1953, San Francisco; s. John Elmer and Estere Ruth Sybil (Nelson) N.; edn: AB English, UC Berkeley 1976; JD, Pepperdine Univ. Sch of Law 1979; MBA, CSU Hayward 1982; admitted Calif. State Bar 1979, US Supreme Ct. Bar 1984, Dist. of Columbia Bar 1985. Career: tax consultant Pannell Kerr Forster, San Francisco 1982-83; atty. at law, legal writer, Matthew Bender & Co., San Francisco 1983−; dir: Aztec Custom Cos. 1982-, Garnish, Ltd. 1984-; mem. Am. (Law Office Mgmt. sect.), Calif., Alameda County bar assns., Mensa, Calif. Alumni Assn., Pepperdine Law Alumni; staff author & consultant: California Taxes, Collier Bankruptcy Package, Illinois Tax Service, New Jersey Tax Service (pub. Matthew Bender) 1983−; Republican (life mem. Repub. Nat. Com.); Lutheran (deacon); rec: music, competitive running, youth work. Res: 21 Tappan Ln., Orinda 945631310 Ofc: Matthew Bender & Co., 2101 Webster St Oakland 94612

NEWBURN, REX D., police polygraphist; b. Dec. 2, 1934, Malta, Ohio; s. Clancy E. and Ida Christine (Dougan) N.; edn: BS, State Coll. of Wash. 1958; MA, Wash. St. Univ. 1961; desig: Expt. Polygraphist, Nat. Tng. Ctr. of Lie Detection, NY (1968); lic. Calif. Polygraph Examiner 1985. Career: police ofcr. San Jose Police Dept., 1964-, police sgt. Bur. of Field Ops., 1970−; bd. dirs. San Jose Police Union, Local 170, 1983-86; mem: Am. Polygraph Assn., Calif. Assn. of Polygraph Examiners, Am. Assn. of Police Polygraphists, Acad. of Certified Polygraphists Inc.; Republican; Christian Ch.; rec: reading. Ofc: San Jose Police Dept POB 270 San Jose 95103-0270

NEWMAN, ANITA NADINE, physician-otolaryngologist; b. June 13, 1949, Honolulu, Hawaii; d. Wm. Reece Elton and Margie Ruth (Pollard) N.; m. Frank Burkett, Dec. 30, 1978; children: Justin b. 1982, Chelsea b. 1984; edn: AB, Stanford Univ. 1971; MD, Dartmouth Med. Sch. 1975. Career: resident surgery 1975-76, otolaryngology 1976-78, Northwestern Meml. Hosp., Chgo.; staff physician USC Student Health Ctr. 1979; resident, head and neck surgery, UCLA Hosp. 1979-82; staff surgeon Wadsworth VA Hosp., 1982-84; asst. prof. head and neck surgery UC Los Angeles 1982-84, postdoctoral scholar 1984, instr. adjunct series Head and Neck Surg., UCLA, 1984−; mem. Admissions Support Com. Dartmouth Med. Sch. 1982-; awards: Shirley Baron Meml. Research Award, Acad. of Otology, Rhinology and Laryngology (1986), 1st Pl. Research award Dept. Otolaryngology, Northwestern Meml. Hosp. (1978), Stanford Women Hon. Soc.; mem: Am. Acad. of Otolaryngology, Acad. of Research Otolaryngologists, LA County Medical Womens Soc., Am. Med. Womens Assn.; contbr. articles to med. jours.; Democrat; Protestant; rec: violin, piano, running. Ofc: Pasadena 91104

NEWMAN, FRANK C., educator/ former Supreme Court of California Justice; b. July 17, 1917, Eureka; s. Frank J. and Anna (Dunn) N.; m. Frances Burks, 1940; children: Robert; Julie; Carol; edn: AB, Dartmouth 1938; LLB, UC Berkeley 1941; LLM, Columbia Univ. 1947; JSD, 1953; LLD, Univ. of Santa Clara 1978. Career: atty. OPA, NYC and Wash. DC 1942-43; ofc. gen. counsel Navy Dept. 1943-46; prof. of law UC Berkeley 1946-77; dean UC Berkeley Law Sch. 1961-66; Jackson H. Ralston prof. internat. law 1974-77; assoc. justice Supreme Court of California 1977-82; vis. prof. to law schs. of Harvard (1953-54), Univ. of Wash. (1952), Salzburg Sem. in Am. Studies, Austria (1954, 64), Strasbourg Inst. of Human Rights (1970, 71, 75, 77), Ctr. Adv. Study in Behav. Scis. (1957-58); law book editorial bd. Little, Brown & Co. 1956-77; counsel Gov. Calif. Commn. on Unemployed Compensation 1952; cons. Gen. Acctg. ofc. 1959; bd. dirs. Fed. Home Loan Bank, S.F. 1962-70; mem. exec. com./ chmn. drafting com. Calif. Constn. Revision Commn. 1964-72; mem. nat. adv. council Amnesty USA; mem. Am. Soc. of Internat. Law; v.p. Internat. Inst. Human Rights; mil: ensign to lt. USNR 1943-46. Ofc: UC Berkeley Sch. of Law (Boalt Hall), Berkeley 94720

NEWMAN, RALPH SCARBROCK, JR.; food cooperative executive; b. Jan. 25, 1939, Bunkie, La.; s. Ralph S. and Annie Mae (Gremillion) N.; m. Ann Boyd Miller, Apr. 29, 1962; children: Paul b. 1964, Jonathan b. 1969; edn: BS (outstanding grad. Coll. of Agric.), La. State Univ. 1960. Career: organizer/ CEO American Rice, Inc. (rice milling and mktg. coop.), Houston, Tx. 1969-83; pres./CEO Farmers' Rice Cooperative, West Sacto. 1983−; v.chmn./ bd. dirs. New Orleans Commodity Exchange (chmn. Rice Com.); mem: Rice Millers Assn. (bd. dirs., past pres.), Calif. Rice Promotion Board; mem. US Sen. Pete Wilson's Agric. Advis. Com.; honors: Lambda Chi Alpha, Phi Kappa Phi, Scabbard and Blade, Alpha Zeta; mil: capt. US Army, 3 yrs active duty, aviator (Helicoptor) 125 Combat Missions in Vietnam. Ofc: Farmers' Rice Cooperative POB 696 West Sacramento 95691

NEWMARK, MILTON MAXWELL, lawyer; b. Feb. 24, 1916; s. Milton and Mary (Maxwell) N.; m. Marion Irene Johnson, July 31, 1941; children: Mari Anderson, Lucy Sammons, Grace M. Lucini; edn: AB, UC Berkeley 1936, JD, 1947; admitted Calif. State Bar 1941. Career: practiced law with father in San Francisco, 1940-56; pvt. practice S.F., 1956-62, Lafayette 1962-80, Walnut Creek 1980−; lectr. bankruptcy State Bar of Calif. Contg. Edn. Program; mem: Alameda County Bar Assn., Am. Bar Assn., Bar Assn. of San Francisco, Calif. State Bar Assn., Contra Costa County Bar Assn.; mil: US Army 1942-46, lt. col. USAR (ret.); clubs: Am. Legion, Scabbard and Blade, Mason (Shriner); Republican (Alameda County Rep. Central Com. 1940-41, pres. Alameda Rep. Assem. 1950). Res: 609 Terra California Dr No. 6 Walnut Creek 94595 Ofc: 1900 Olympic Blvd, Ste 103, Walnut Creek 94596

NEWPORT, EUGENE NORMAN, mayor of Berkeley; b. April 5, 1935, Rochester, NY; s. Leon and Bertha (Richardson) N.; m. Claudine Smith, Feb. 1958; 1 son, Kyle; m. Maria Luisa Vigo, Nov. 9, 1974; 1 dau, Maria Mercedes; edn: BABA, Internat. Coll. 1975. Career: Splst. Employment Tng., US Dept. of Labor 1971-74, 1977-79; dir. youth employment svcs. City of Berkeley 1975-76, senior adminstrv. analyst 1976, mayor 1979−; cons. Ofc. of Research, Calif. Assembly; mem: U.S. Conf. of Mayors (chmn. Subcom. on Edn. advy. bd. 1983-84), U.S. Peace Council (co-chmn.), World Peace Council (del.), Assn. Bay Area Govt. (regl. plnng. commn., regl. housing commn.), SANE (bd. dirs.), NAACP (life); mil: US Army 1958-60; Democrat. Ofc: 2180 Milvia St. Berkeley 94704

NEWTON, KARL LAVERNE, real estate broker-developer; b. Aug. 23, 1916, Veedersburg, Ind.; s. Ora Madison and Lilly Ann (Dobbs) N.; m. Ada L. Locknane, May 10, 1941; children: James Ernest b. 1944, Douglas Karl b. 1948, Deborah Jean b. 1953; edn: AA, Coll. of the Sequoias 1937; BA, Fresno State Coll. 1940; sec. edn. credl., UC Berkeley 1941; real estate broker Calif. 1946. Career: joined father's real estate bus. in 1946 and helped establish Newton Ins. Agcy. in Dinuba; became broker, owner of Newton & Sons Realty 1963−; subdivision & devel. bus. w/ brother 1953−, built over 300 homes and first major shopping center in area (1972), also involved in major developments incl. other shopping ctrs., subdivisions nd indsl. parks; honors: Junior Citizen of the Year (Dinuba CofC 1965), Svc. Award (Tulare County YMCA 1973), mem. Great Performance Club (Aetna Ins. Co. 1976, 78); mem: Nat. Assn. Realtors, Calif. Assn. Realtors, Visalia Bd. Realtors, Dinuba-Reedley Multiple Listing Svc. (pres. 1980, 81), Rotary (chpt. pres. 1965-66, Paul Harris Award 1985), Dinuba CofC (pres. 1950-51, num. coms.), Commonwealth Club of Calif. (fmr.), Bulldog Found.; publs: contbr. local newspaper, photos published also; mil: yeoman 3/c USN 1945-46; Republican; Protestant; rec: music, photog., travel, gardening, reading. Res: 520 Vermont Ave Dinuba 93618 Ofc: Newton & Sons Real Estate 170 E Tulare St Dinuba 93618

NEWTON, LEROY KENNETH, stockbroker; b. Feb. 20, 1949, Bad Tolz, Germany; s. Leroy Albert and Erna Edith N.; m. Christine Ann, Apr. 15, 1978; edn: BA honors, Linfield Coll. 1971; grad. work Portland State Univ. 1973-74; Northwest Outward Bound Sch. 1974. Career: mgr. Ketchum (Ida.) Drug and Gift Ctr., 1974-81; finl. cons., stockbroker Merrill Lynch Pierce Fenner & Smith, Santa Rosa 1981−; mem. Merrill Lynch Exec.'s Club (1983), Profl. Investment Assn. of Santa Rosa (charter), Santa Rosa Breakfast Club, CofC, Linfield Coll. Alumni Assn.; Republican; rec: travel, hiking, collects football cards. Ofc: Merrill Lynch 90 South E St (POB 4660) Santa Rosa 95402

NG, ERIC SIU-WAH, pharmacist; b. May 26, 1951, Hong Kong; s. Keung and Oi (Lee) Ng; edn: AA, Coll. of the Sequoias 1973; BS, pharm., Idaho State

Univ. 1977; BS, biology, 1977; Reg. Pharmacist, Calif. & Nev. 1978. Career: staff pharmacist Physician Med. Pharmacy, Indio 1978; pharmacy mgr., Gemco Pharmacy San Bernardino 1978-80, staff pharmacist, San Gabriel 1980-81; pharmacy mgr./ owner Crossroads Med. Pharmacy 1981-85; pharm. mgr./ owner Willowbrook Pharm. 1985—; mem: Am., Calif. & East L.A. Pharmaceutical Assns.; Republican; Christian; rec: jogging, tennis. Res: 400 S Garfield, 4, Monterey Park 91754 Ofc: Willowbrook Pharmacy 1901 E Imperial Hwy Los Angeles 90059

NG, SHEK WOON, acupuncturist; b. Aug. 16, 1913, People's Republic of China; s. Kwong Cheung and Ngan (Chang) Ng; m. Mei Yu, Apr. 15, 1931; children: Bing Fun b. 1932, Chui Ngor b. 1934, Chui Un b. 1939, Ping Sai b. 1944, Chui Chun b. 1950, Jonathan b. 1961, Florence b. 1963; edn: completed apprenticeship herbal medicine and acupuncture under brother Dr. Cheng Leng Ng, 1931-37; OMD, San Francisco Coll. of Acup. & Oriental Medicine 1984; Certified Acupuncturist, Calif. State Bd. 1979. Career: pvt. practice herbalist and acupuncturist, Toi Shan County, China 1937-54, Canton, China 1955-57, two offices in Hong Kong 1970-77, San Francisco, Calif. 1979—; pres. Internat. Acupuncture Coll., Hong Kong 1955-77; mem: Kowloon Assn. of Practitioners of Chinese Medicine 1958-, United Acupuncturists of Calif. 1978- (chmn. of supvrs. 1985-); works: first herbalist & acupuncturist to specialize in treatment of stroke with satisfactory results (1957-); rec: field-trips, reading, music. Ofc: 710 Grant Ave Ste 203 San Francisco 94108

NGUYEN, AN THI, real estate broker; b. May 3, 1940, Saigon, Vietnam; s. Voi Van and Dieu Thi (Tran) N.; m. Tung Vinh, Dec. 27, 1974; edn: AA, Fullerton Coll. 1979; BA, CSU Fullerton 1982; R.E. Broker, Anthony Sch. 1983; R.E. Broker, Calif. Career: writer/ reporter biggest newspaper in Vietnam, escaped from Communists, refugee in America 1976-; staff writer Hornet Newspaper & staff writer Ngawi Viet Newspaper, Orange Co.; curretly, R.E. broker Coldwell Banker, Fullerton; honors: Top Selling Units, Reg. I 1983; Activity Awds.; Quota Buster Awds. 1983; mem: Triing Viiong Assn. (chmn. of press com. 1982-83, 1983-84); works: pub. novel, Vietnam 1966; Buddhist; rec: economics, news, ping pong. Res: 14366 Brookhurst St Garden Grove 92643 Ofc: Coldwell Banker, 529 N. Harbor Blvd Fullerton 92632

NGUYEN, GIAO, psychologist; b. Oct. 15, 1922, Luang Prabang, Laos; s. Kien Huy and Thao Thi (Do) N.; m. Mai Truong, Apr. 10, 1958; children: Loan b. 1959, Phuongdung b. 1963; edn: clin. tng. Ecole Normale Superieure, Saint Cloud, France 1954-55; MA, Columbia Univ. Tchrs. Coll. 1959, profl. dipl. 1960; PhD, UC Berkeley 1969. Career: prof. of psychology & statistics, and chmn. Dept. of Psychol., Faculty of Letters, Saigon, Vietnam 1969-76; prof. of psychol. Faculty of Medicine, Saigon 1970-72; prof. of social psychol. & statistics, Grad. Sch. of Bus. Adminstrn., Saigon 1971-73; cons. (pgm. in social ecology) UC Irvine 1977-79; staff psychologist Stockton State Hosp., Stockton 1980—; awards: participant in 20th Internat. Cong. of Psychol., Tokyo, Japan (1972), Seminar in Exptl. Psychol., Williamstown, Williams Coll., Mass. (1973), 19th Internat. Con. of Applied Psychol., Montreal, Canada (1974); research and tchg. grantee, Ford Found. S.E. Asia Fellowship Pgm. (1975), the Asia Found. Grant (1971); mem. Am. Psychol. Assn., Am. Statistical Assn., Soc. D'Honneur Francaise; works: created the first Dept. of Psychol., Univ. of Saigon; estab. the first Psycho-Laboratory, Saigon; innovative and exptl. pgms. in behavioral and social scis.; Buddhist; rec: music, travel. Res: 4540 Romano Dr Stockton 95207 Ofc: Stockton State Hospital 510 E Magnolia Stockton 95202

NGUYEN, KHANH T.L., physician; b. Apr. 3, 1944, Vietnam, nat. US cit. 1981; d. Dung D. and Hanh T. (Pham) Nguyen; m. Tien Le, Feb. 5, 1972, div. 1983; m. 2d. Paul Hamblin, Sept. 15, 1985; children: David Le b. 1973, Michael Le b. 1974; edn: MD, Faculty of Medicine, Saigon 1968; pediatrics interne Clinique Infantile de Geneve, Switz. 1968-72; residency, Huntington Mem. Hosp., Pasadena 1978; lang. studies: Chinese 3 yrs., Spanish 2 yrs., East Los Angeles Coll., 1981-85. Career: staff physician Children's Hosp., Vietnam 1972-75; active in rescuing orphans and wounded children, Terre Des Hommes (charity orgn.) in Switz. and Vietnam, 1968-75; staff physician Queen of Angels Clinic, Los Angeles 1978—, caring for refugees from all countries; recipient recognition for her dedication in caring for the poor in newspaper articles in L.A. Times, The Tidings, num. local newspapers; frequent speaker on the plight of refugees, achievement of Asian women and minorities to high schs., health profls. groups; Buddhist; rec: fgn. languages and different cultures. Res: 992 S Ynez Ave Monterey Park 91754 Ofc: Queen of Angels Clinic 2859 Glassell St Los Angeles 90026

NGUYEN, MAI, engineer; b. June 13, 1947, Saigon; s. Ngat Van and Le Thi N.; m. Thanh-Mai Pham, July 29, 1975; children: Hoai-Huong b. 1976, Minh Quang b. 1981; edn: BS in chem. eng., CalPoly Pomona 1979, ME, 1986; Reg. Profl. Engr. (PE) Calif. 1984. Career: mem. tech. staff Rockwell Internat. Inc., Downey 1979—, system analyst Space Shuttle Main Propulsion System; honors: Tau Beta Pi (1979); mil: lt. Vietnamese Navy 1975; Republican; Buddhist; rec: movies, swim, music. Res: 10305 Muroc St Bellflower 90706 Ofc: Rockwell Int. 12214 Lakewood Blvd Downey 90241

NGUYEN, NHON THI, physician; b. Jan. 7, 1947, Nhatrang, Vietnam, nat. US cit. 1982; s. Thanh Qui and Hiep Thi N.; m. Anh Nong, June 27, 1980; children: Chantal b. 1981, Dominique b. 1983; edn: MD, Univ. Saigon faculty of Med. 1972. Career: instr. in med. Univ. Saigon 1972-74; resident in med. Univ. Okla. Coll. of Med. 1974, fellow Cardiol. 1974-78, 1978-80; staff cardiol. San Bernardino County Med. Ctr. 1980—; asst. prof. med. UCLA Sch. of Med. 1980—; non-invasive cardiac lab. staff S.B. Co. Med. Ctr. 1980—; honors:

Laureate in Medicine (Univ. Saigon Sch. of Med. 1972); mem: Am. Heart Assn. (bd. dirs. S.B. Co. chpt.); publ: Torsade de Pointes (1980), Ayphoid Hepatitis (1973); Catholic; rec: costume design. Ofc: Dept. of Med. 780 E Gilbert San Bernardino 92404

NGUYEN, QUOC DUOC, engineering project manager; b. Jan. 10, 1953, Saigon, Vietnam; s. Thinh Van and Oanh Kim (Le) N.; m. Bich-Nga, Oct. 15, 1983; edn: BSME, Phu-Tho Poly Technic Univ. 1984. Career: design engr. JB&B, Los Angeles 1977, project engr. 1979; project mgr. Store, Matakovich & Wolfberg, El Monte 1982—; asosc. mem. ASHRAE; Republican; Buddist. Res: 75 Hidden Valley Rd. Phillips Ranch 91766 Ofc: Store, Matakovich & Wolfberg, 9650 Flair Dr. El Monte 91734

NGUYEN, THU THE, chiropractor; b. July 7, 1935, Vietnam, nat. 1981; s. Chung Tac and Thoa Thi (Tran) N.; m. Phuong Ngo, Jan. 4, 1960; children: Thuyen, b. 1963; Huy, b. 1965; Nang, b. 1971; Richard, b. 1975; Phan The Daniel, b. 1982; edn: 2nd Lt, Dalat Mil. Acad., Vietnam 1954; BA, Saigon Univ. 1962; AA, Black Hawk Coll. 1977; BA, St. Ambrose Coll. 1981; DC, Palmer Coll. of Chiropractic 1981; Doctorate of Sci., Medicina Alternative, Colombo 1984; PhD nutrition, Donsbach Univ. 1985. Career: in Vietnam: platoon leader and co. cmdr. 6th Airborne Battalion 1955-57; 1st Lt., 34th Mortar C Co. Comdr. and Chief, G5 of 22nd Infan. Div. 1957-63; Capt. Intell., Chief Indoctrination Sector 1963-67; Maj., asst. of Deputy Chief of Staff of Op. of Third Corps and Third Mil. Region 1967-70; Col., Chief of Psychol. Warfare Third Corps and Third Mil. Region 1970-72; Di-An Dist. Chief and Sub-Sector Comdr. of Bien Hoa Province, 1972-75; came to USA as refugee, 1975; student, security guard Davenport (Ia.) Art Gallery 1975-81; Doctor of Chiropractic, Garden Grove, Calif. 1981—. Decorated Order National 4th gr. with palm, Army Distinguished 1st gr., 6 Gallantry w/gold, silver stars, 12 other mil. awards; US Army Commendn., Repub. of China Army Merit Decoration. Mem. Internat., Amer., Calif. chiropractic assns.; Buddhist. Res: 2454 Medford Pl Fullerton 92635 Ofc: 10244 Westminster Ave Garden Grove 92643

NGUYEN, TRUNG BUU, plastic surgeon; b. June 19, 1937, Tanan, S. Vietnam; parents: Buu Van and Thinh Thi (Ngo) N.; m. Hang, Aug. 6, 1966; children: Alison Ngoc b. 1947, Amy Nga b. 1948, Alain Huy b. 1949, Andy Hoang b. 1950; edn: MD, Saigon Med. Sch. 1966. Career: res. gen. surg. Columbia Univ. 1978-81; res. plastic surg. Cornell Med. Ctr. 1981-83; chief hand surg. Cong Hoa Mil. Hosp. Saigon 1973-75; plastic surg. Kaiser Med. Ctr. Bellflower, Calif. 1983-85, chief plastic surg. 1985—; awards: N.Y. City Health and Hosp. Corp. 1983; Am. Soc. for Surg. of the Hand 1975; Am. Soc. Plastic Reconstr. Surg. (cand. 1985); Am. Coll. of Surg. (cand. 1981); publs: arts. in med. journs.; mil: capt. Vietnamese Army 1974, Army Valiant Medal; Republican; Buddhist; rec: travel. Res: 5262 Van Dyke Cir La Palma 90623 Ofc: So. Calif. Permanente Med. Grp. 9400 E Rosecrans Ave Bellflower 90706

NICHOLAS, IRVIN DURAND, JR., insurance executive, consultant; b. May 14, 1937, Pryor, Okla.; s. Irvin D. and Helen M. (Milroy) N.; m. Sigrid Knudson, 1960; children: Jim, b. 1969; Amy, b. 1972; Mike, b. 1974; edn: BS, Ore. State Univ. 1961; MBA, Golden Gate Univ. 1974. Career: fin. analyst UC systemwide, Berkeley 1965-69; ins. & risk mgr. 1969-75; v.p. Fred S. James & Co. of Calif., San Francisco 1975-80; sr. v.p. 1980-85; pres. Applied Risk Mgmt. Inc. 1985—; guest lectr. risk mgmt. UC Grad. Sch. of Bus. 1974, 75; pres. Univ. Risk & Ins. Assn. 1975, dir. 1973, 74; mem: Calif. Hosp. Assn. Inst. Mgmt. Com.; Am. water Works Assn.; Risk & Ins. Mgmt. Soc.; Univ. Risk & Ins. Mgmt.; Am. Risk & Ins. Assn.; Alpha Tau Omega; Olympic Club; publs: arts. in profl. publs.; Managing the Library Fire Risk, 1975; Medical Profl. Liability Risk Mgmt. Guidelines, 1974; Accountants Profl. Liability, 1980; mil: capt. USMC 1961-64. Res: 120 Montecito Crescent Walnut Creek 94596 Ofc: Applied Risk Mgmt. Inc., 505 Sansome San Francisco 94111

NICHOLAS, JOHN GREGORY, II, lawyer; b. July 4, 1949, Palo Alto, Calif.; s. John Gregory, Sr. and Marche Ruth (Hand) N.; m. Martina N., MD, OB-GYN; edn: BS, Univ. Santa Clara 1971; M.Internat. Mgmt., Am. Grad. Sch. of Internat. Mgmt. 1973; cert. Serbo-Croatian language, Univ. Zagreb 1977; JD, Ocean Univ. Coll. of Law 1977 Career: contracts adminstr. Singer-Link Sunnyvale 1979-80, Kaiser Electronics San Jose 1980-81; internat. contracts adminstr. Applied Technol. Mtn. View 1981-83; contracts adminstr. Sun Microsystems Inc. Mtn. View 1984-85; self-employed 1985-86; public defender, Napa 1986—; mem: Am., Calif. Bar Assns., Nat. Contract Mgmt. Assn., Commonwealth Club of Calif., Republican; rec: beekeeping. Address: 1172 Castro St Mountain View 94040

NICHOLS, ARTHUR, investment/real estate co. president; b. Oct. 23, 1921, Springfield, Mass.; s. Max and Bertha N.; m. Patricia Hermes, Dec. 13, 1983; 1 dau. Susan b. 1952; edn: BS, Dartmouth Coll. 1946; Executive Pgm., Stanford Univ. Career: vice pres. Kurt Orban Co., Wayne, N.J. 1950-80; pres. Florida Wire Products Corp., Miami, Fla. 1957-77; pres. Southwest Wire Products Corp., Dallas, Tx. 1958-77; pres. Southeast Steel & Wire Corp., New Orleans, La. 1959-77; pres. Texas Steel & Wire Corp., Houston 1960-77; pres. Arthur Nichols Co., Inc., Los Angeles 1948—; clubs: Bel-Air Country (LA), Forest (Houston); mil: lt. USNR 1941-44, decorated Bronze star, Purple Heart, Presidential Cit. Address: Los Angeles 90024

NICHOLS, NORMAN PAUL, teacher, industrial supervisor; b. March 21, 1919, Vancouver, B.C., Can., nat. US cit. 1958; s. Paul William Marshall and Louise (Laueheart) N.; m. Alberta Goode, Nov. 22, 1962; edn: BS, Univ. of British Columbia 1950; M.Ed., Univ. of Idaho 1960. Career: inspector Aeronautics Directorite, Ottawa, Can. 1942-46; supvr. B.C. Forest Products Ltd.,

Victoria, B.C., Can. 1950-57; tchr. of science Eureka Sch. Dist., Eureka 1960-66; tchr. of mathematics Folsom Cordova Sch. Dist. 1966-80; ret.; bd. dirs. Credit Union, Eureka Sch. Dist. 1962-64; pres. Calif. Tchrs. Fedn., Sacramento Area 1972-74; chmn. Math Dept. 1965-66; honors: Phi Delta Kappa 1960; Nat. Science Found. Awards (6) for Mathematics 1960-65; Computer Pgmmg., Nat. Science Found. and Texas Instruments 1966; mem: Calif. Tchrs. Assn. (Eureka), Calif. Tchrs. Fedn. (pres., Sacramento 1972-74), Fair Oaks Community Club (pres. 1971-76), Chess Club (organizer 1970), Elks; mil: pvt. Calif. State Reserve 1962-64; vol. RCAF 1942-46, Medal of Honor; Republican; Protestant; rec: financial research, home construction, auto mechanics. Res: 2219 Warrenton Dr. Rancho Cordova 95670

NICKEL, THOMAS ROY, editor, publisher, author; b. Nov. 8, 1900, Everton, Mo.; s. James Benjamin and Clara Ellen (Collins) Nickel); m. Fannabelle Ford, July 29, 1927; m. 2d. Ruth Dowell, Aug. 13, 1961; children: Robert Bruce b. 1928, Sharon June b. 1932, William Wallace b. 1934, James Douglas b. 1936; edn: AB, Southwest Mo. State Univ. 1927; postgrad. stu., Tibetan Language, UC Berkeley 1944-5. Career: sold first news story to Saturday Blade, Chgo., 1912 (at age 12); owner/ed./pub. Dade County Journal, Everton, Mo. 1917-23; published Midget Mag. (World's Smallest Periodical) 1923-27, invented Nickeliner; staff mem. SMSU, Springfield, Mo. 1924-27 (student dir. publicity; ed. Southwest Standard 1924-27; assoc. ed. Ozarko, sch. annual); asst. gen. mgr. Haynes Corp. Publishers, Los Angeles 1927-30; produced promotional literature for founding of cities of San Clemente and Atascadero, 1928; Notary Public and Publicist, Hollister, Mo. 1932-36; founded Union Mission, Springfield, Mo. 1937; co-founder Full Gospel Business Men's Fellowship Internat. and Voice Mag., 1952; current: founder/pres. Great Commission Internat. and editor Testimony Mag., Hanford; staff mem. Monte Vista Christian Sch., Watsonville, Ca. 1950-55; published: Christianity, All the Recorded Words of Jesus Christ (1925), In Those Days, Upon All Flesh, Miracles Do Happen, Dying Buddhist Korean, God and America (1962-72), Azusa Street Outpouring, The Very Beginning (1981); honors: Medal of Merit presented by Pres. Ronald Reagan 1982, charter mem. Pres. Task Force; Israel State Medal for 25 years service to Israel (1982); mem: Golden Bears, SMSU (life); The Pres.'s Club; founder Hanford chpt. FGBMFI; ofcl. advisor Women's Aglow Fellowship Internat., Lemoore; mil: Civilian Employee as field ofc. mgr. on Defense Projects at Benicia, Woodland, and Arbuckle, Calif. and prodn. of blood plasma for Armed Forces at Cutter Labs., Berkeley 1943-48; Republican; Assemblies of God; rec: writing, philately. Res: 1300 Whitmore Hanford 93230 Ofc: Great Commission International, 1033 West 7th, Hanford 93230

NICOLET, MARGARET WIGLESWORTH, real estate broker; b. Sept. 20, 1957, San Bernardino; d. Donald Wayne and Anna Alice (Schapp) Wiglesworth; edn: AA in real estate, San Bernardino Valley Coll. 1979; Calif. lic. R.E. Broker. Career: sales rep. Safeco, San Bernardino 1976-79; broker/owner Earth Investments, S.B. 1979-84, sold co. 1984; broker/owner Miller Associates of San Bernardino - Property Mgmt., 1984–; instr. residential prop. mgmt., Univ. of Riverside, Valley Coll. (1982-); honors: Calif. Jaycees Humanitarian award (1978); mem. Inland Empire Apartment Assn. (pres. 1980-81), Affiliated Cities Apt. Assn., S.B. Board of Realtors, S.B. CofC (chair Business Expo. 1983), Calif. Jaycees 1976-79; Republican; Baptist; rec: softball, racquetball, tennis, golf. Res: 1750 Garden Dr San Bernardino 92404 Ofc: Miller Associates 715 N Arrowhead Ave Ste 213 San Bernardino 92410

NIEDERFRANK, KATHERINE LEE, educator; b. Nov. 28, 1955, Sanger; d. Christian Alfred, Jr. and Beverly (Gist) Sorensen; m. Edward P. Niederfrank, Aug. 11, 1984; edn: BS in phys. edn., Calif. Polytech. St. Univ. S.L.O. 1977, tchg. cred. and grad. work in counseling, 1978; bus. tchg. credential, CSU Fresno 1980; grad. work in computer edn., Fresno Pacific Coll. 1981-83; Calif. Sec. Tchg. Credential (Phys. Edn., Business). Career: tchr. Washington Union High Sch., Fresno 1978–: J.V. Girl's Basketball coach 1978-80, head softball coach 1979-85; adv. Pep Squad 1979-82, Future Bus. Leaders of Am. 1982-; mem. Nat./Calif. Bus. Educators Assn. (Central Sect. pres. elect., secty. 1985-86, Public/Profl. Rels. chair 1984), Calif. Tchrs. Assn./ local Faculty Assn. (1st woman elected pres. 1984-); works: devel. pgm. for high sch. students in entrepreneurship (1985), co-devel. a model office pgm., H.S. Bus. Dept.; Republican (sustaining); Prot.; rec: politics, ednl. law, dancing, cooking. Ofc: Washington Union High School 6041 South Elm Ave Fresno 93706

NIELSEN, LYNNE CATHERINE, consulting firm executive; b. Aug. 8, 1955, Castro Valley; d. Oliver Andrew and Helen Barbara (Cadil) N.; edn: Mass. Commun. Maj., CSU Hayward 1973-78. Career: bus./ advtg. mgr. Daily Pioneer newspaper, CSU Hayward 1974-78; computer ops. mgr. Daughtney's Dept. Store, Castro Valley 1974-78; customer svc. mgr. Mini Systems Inc., Pleasanton 1978–; consulting, devel. curriculum & instrn. IBM personal computers; pub. spkg. engagements; cons. purchasing- implementing a computer; mem: Alpha Phi Gamma; Alpha Phi Omega; Diablo Valley IBM PC Users Gp.; KQED pub. tv.; Republican; Lutheran; rec: computers, backpacking, gourmet cooking. Res: 313 Scottsdale Road Pleasant Hill 94523 Ofc: Hunt & Associates, 2250 Morello Ave Pleasant Hill 94523

NIELSON, MARGARET MAE, (Margie), insurance broker; b. Nov. 30, 1922, Stockton, Calif.; d. Ernest P. and Emma Joan (Boltzen) Hansen; m. Douglas S. Bean, Sept. 23, 1984; children: Pat b. 1947 (dec.), Clinton b. 1949, Pamela Joan b. 1955; edn: San Jose State Coll. 1940-42; property & casualty ins. broker, 1976. Career: claims secty. Globe Indemnity Ins. Co. 1942-46; asst. mgr. Cass & Johansing Ins. Agcy. 1965-68; life agent Penn. Mutual 1968-69; sales Earl Goldman Ins. Co. 1969-75, Fisher Agcy. 1970-75; broker, owner Nielson Ins. Agcy. 1975–; honors: Woman of the Yr. (Orinda, Lafayette BPW 1977); mem: Independent Agents of Contra Costa County, Orinda/Lafayette Bus. & Profl. Women's Club (past pres.), social Arts & Culture Soc., Discovery Bay Yacht Club, Discovery Bay Tennis & Racquet Club, Discovery Bay CC; publ: weekly newspaper column Insurance Echoes, Brentwood News; Republican; Methodist (lay person); rec: singing, dancing, gardening, boating. Res: 5843 Drake Dr Discovery Bay Byron 94514 Ofc: Nielson Insurance Agency 5901 Marina Rd Discovery Bay Yacht Harbor Byron 94514

NIGRO, DENNIS MICHAEL, physician; b. July 29, 1947, San Francisco; edn: art, UC Los Angeles 1967-68; BS chem., Univ. Notre Dame 1969; MD, Creighton Med. Sch. 1974. Career: extern Shriner's Nat. Burn Unit Galveston, Tex., Ben Taub Hosp. Emerg. Svc., Parkland Hosp. Trauma Svc. 1973; surgical intern Creighton affil. hosps. Omaha, Neb. 1974-75; resident gen. surg. UC San Francisco 1975-77; chief resident extremity svc., burn unit San Francisco Gen. Hosp. 1977; plastic surg. resident UC San Diego 1977-79, chief res. 1979; emerg. room phys. Scripps Encinitas Hosp. 1978; attg. phys. COAD Internat. Plastic Surg., UCSD group servicing Mexicali, La Paz and Guaymas 1979–; pvt. practice Encinitas 1979–; chief plastic surg. Scripps Hosp. Encinitas 1980–; clin. prof. plastic surg. UCSD 1980–; tennis instr. Neb. 1972-74; Disaster Svc. S.F. Internat. Airport 1977; phys. in chg. St. Luke's Intensive and Coronary Care 1976-77; res. dir. Mexicali Field Pgm. 1978-79; lectr. on plastic surg.; honors: Outstanding Young Men in Am. (1982), AMA Award for Postgrad. Med. Edn. (1985); mem. Multiple Sclerosis Soc. bd. 1983-, adv. bd. Am. Cancer Soc. 1984-; publs: research papers, presentations, newspaper article. Res: 1428 Eolus Leucadia 92024 Ofc: 351 Santa Fe Dr Ste 1 Encinitas 92024

NIKKEL, BARBARA JEAN, school administrator; b. Feb. 6, 1938, Hutchinson, Kans.; d. John E. and Emma (Siemens) Weins; m. Wilbur Nikkel, July 30, 1960; chidlren: Mark b. 1963, Lori b. 1966; edn: BA, highest honors, CSC Fresno 1959; grad work CSC Fresno 1961-62, LaVerne Coll. 1975, Christian Heritage Coll. 1976, CSU San Diego 1977-78, UC San Diego 1978; Calif. Life Tchg. Credentials (gen. K-8, Adminstrv., splst. in reading). Career: elem. tchr. public schs. Shafter, 1959-62, substitute tchr. 1964-67, remedial tchr. 1967-68; substitute tchr. San Diego City Schs. 1972-73; master tchr. (4th gr.) Christian Elem., San Diego 1974-78, v.principal (K-6th gr.) 1978-79, principal 1979–, also Elem. Dist. Curriculum Coord. Christian Unified Schs., El Cajon 1980–; tng. instr. for elem. tchrs. in Christian Unified Schs. Dist.; seminars on curriculum devel. & sch. adminstrn., Tchr. and Adminstrv. convs.; honors: Phi Kappa Phi (1959), Kappa Delta Pi (1959), Outstanding Leader in Elem. & Sec. Edn. (1976); mem: Assn. of Christian Schs. Internat. (mem. So. Calif. Accreditation Commn. 1985-87), Assn. of Supvsn. & curriculum Dev.; author: (4th gr. Character Foundation book) Willing to Wait (Revell 1981); Republican; Baptist; rec: skiing, gardening. Ofc: Christian Elementary 6747 Amherst St San Diego 92115

NILES, ALBAN ISAAC, judge; b. June 10, 1933, St. Vincent, West Indies, nat. May 1956; s. Isaac N. and Elsie (Lovell) N.; children: Maria, b. 1962, Gloria, b. 1964, Angela, b. 1969; edn: BS, UCLA 1959, JD, 1963. Career: auditor Div. of Corporations, State of Calif., 1959-60; auditor AF Auditor General, 1960; auditor Ernst & Ernst 1963-64; pvt. practice law, 1964-82; judge Los Angeles Municipal Court, 1982–; pres., gen. counsel Kedren Community Mental Health Center 1971-79; pres. L.A. County Civil Serv. Commn. 1980; lectr. Lawrence Univ.; secty. Nat. Council of Community Mental Hlth Ctrs.; honors: UCLA Law Rev. 1961-63; MVP, UCLA Soccer Team; capt. L.A. Cricket Team 1965-69; citations, Calif. Legislature 1978, Los Angeles City Council 1976; mem: Bus. Devel. Center of So. Calif. (chmn. 1976-), Orgn. of Caribbean Am. Peoples, Inc. (pres. 1978-), Caaribbean Action Lobby (pres. So. Calif. chpt. 1982-), Marina City Club (life, bd. govs. 1981-), Calif. Judges Assn., Langston Bar Assn. (trustee), Phi Alpha Delta; mil: USAF 1951-55; Catholic; rec: tennis, boating, skiing. Res: 3859 Lenawee St Culver City 90230 Ofc: Los Angeles Municipal Court, 1633 Purdue Ave Los Angeles 90025

NILES, JUDITH ELLEN (BLACKETER), financial planner; b. Aug. 24, 1947, Chgo.; d. Raymond James and Winifred Jean (Carlisle) Porter; children: Shannon b. 1970, Raymond b. 1965; edn: BSBA, fin., cum laude, Cal Poly Pomona 1975; Certified Fin. Planner (in prog.), Coll. of Denver, USC, 1983-; CPA, Calif. (1982); NASD Reg. Rep. (1982), Reg. Prin., Series 63, Life & Disability (1984), Life & Dis., Calif. (1985). Career: office mgr. H&R Block, Riverside 1973-75; acct. Touche Ross & Co., Los Angeles 1975-76; mgr. tax dept. Ross Landis & Pauw, CPAs, Riverside 1976-77; owner Profl. Business Mgmt., Riverside 1977-81; owner J. Niles, CPA, Corona 1981–; branch mgr. Am. Pacific Securities, Corona 1982-85, assoc. v.p. 1985–; tchr. Successful Money Mgmt. Seminars; named Woman of the Year, Fullerton J.C. (1968); clubs: Corona Womens, Corona Tennis, Yorba Linda Country; Republican; Reformed Ch. in Am.; rec: photog., needlepoint, camping. Address: 1720 Fairview Dr Corona 91720

NISICH, ANTHONY JOSEPH, construction co. executive; b. Apr. 19, 1951, San Jose; s. Louis Marco and Lena D. (Passantino) N.; m. Patricia Massi, Aug. 30, 1975; 1 dau. Kelli Lyn b. 1968; edn: BS in C.E., Univ. of Santa Clara 1973; MS in C.E., CSU San Jose 1978; Reg. Profl. (Civil) Engr., Calif. Career: civil engr. Calif. State Office of Archit. & Constrn., 1973-74; land devel. engr. Environmental Mgmt./ Gen. Services Agcy., Santa Clara County 1974-78, asst. mgr. Building Insp. Div., 1978-79; chief Bldg. Insp. and Land Use Enforcement Div., Dept. Pub. Works, County of Sacto. 1979-82; dir. Bldg. & Safety, City of Beverly Hills 1982–; vice pres. Lou Nisich Constrn. Co. Inc., San Jose 1975–; mem. DOE, HUD, and Nat. Assn. of Counties task force on Bldg. Energy Perf. Stds., Wash. DC (1978-81); tech. advis. com. Sacto. County

Overall Econ. Devel. Pgm. (1979-82); Calif. Energy Commn. advis. com. on Insulation Stds. (1978-84), Bldg. Ofcls. Advis. Com. (1979-82); mem: Am. Planning Assn., Nat. Inst. of Bldg. Scis. (Consultative Council), Calif. Bldg. Ofcls. Assn. (pres. 1985), Internat. Conf. of Bldg. Ofcls. (v.p. L.A. Basin chpt. 1985), Internat. Conf. of Bldg. Ofcls. (co-parlimentarian 1984), Am. Concrete Inst., Nat. Soc. Profl. Engrs., Calif. Soc. Profl. Engrs., ASCE (past chair Nat. Engrs. Week, Santa Clara Co.), Constrn. Spec. Inst., Am. Pub. Wks. Assn., ASHRAE, Santa Clara Co. Engrs. and Archs. Assn. (pres. 1977-79). Ofc: City of Beverly Hills, 450 N Crescent Dr Rm 301 Beverly Hills 90210

NIZAM-ALDINE, ZUHAYR, engineer; b. Nov. 20, 1948, Damascus, Syria, nat. US cit. 1980; s. Toufic and Ismat N.-A.; m. Tami Genton, July 4, 1984; edn: MS, Am. Univ. of Beirut, 1973; PhD, UC Berkeley 1976; Calif. Reg. Profl. Engr. (Civil), lic. Gen. Building Contr., lic. Real Estate Broker. Career: research engr. UC Berkeley 1973-76; structural analyst Cygna Energy Services, San Francisco 1976-80; supvsg. engr. Bechtel, San Francisco 1980-84; aerospace splst. engr. Northrup Co., Los Angeles 1984-85; aerospace staff engr. Physics Internat., San Leandro 1985–; dir. and cons. Dynatech Corp. 1979-80; mem: ASCE, Structural Engrs. Assn.; publs: 3 tech. papers and 12 reports, UCB, ASCE Struc. Div. (1975-85); designed and built four unusual houses on extremely steep hills (1979-81); rec: designing & bldg. spl. houses, restoration antiques, movies. Ofc: Physics International 55 Sutter Ste 509 San Francisco 94104

NOBLE, ANNA BETH, jewelry wholesaler/retailer; b. Sept. 30, 1926, Oakhurst, Madera Co., Calif.; d. Gustave Adolph and Grace Hannah (Hand) Schneider; m. Kenneth C. Noble, July 14, 1946; children: Diana Beth 1947-1981, Sandra Lee b. 1949; grad. Sierra Union H.S., Auberry, 1943; num. spl. courses, 1969-79. Career: land co. office mgr., Fresno 1965-69; co. exec.'s wife in Malaysia, Hawaii, So. Calif., 1969-79; owner/opr. Jewelers Warehouse (wholesale and retail), Santa Rosa 1980–; instr. porcelain doll-making; mem. Mfg. Jewelers of Am., mem. Jewelry Inst.; recipient service awards GTDC Wives Club (1965-80), El-o-win Council of Girl Scouts (1955-65); mem. Daughters of Am. Revolution; civic: Lady Lions, Rotary of W. Malaysia Wives, Wives of Barbershop Harmony; Protestant; rec: porcelain doll-making, genealogy, writing, painting. Res: 4356 Cox Dr Santa Rosa 95405 Ofc: 880 Piner Rd Ste 55 Santa Rosa 95401

NODDINGS, JAMES ARTHUR, high tech construction co. marketing executive; b. Mar. 21, 1929, Great Falls, Mont.; s. William Clayton and Sarah Stephenson (Cox) N.; m. Nel, Aug. 20, 1949; children: Howard b. 1952, Laurie b. 1952, James b. 1954, Nancy b. 1955, William b. 1957, Edward b. 1958, Victoria b. 1961, Timothy b. 1966; edn: commerce & engrg., Drexel Univ. 1953; AA real estate, Foothill Coll. 1976. Career: fac. mgr. Bendix, NSC, Revlon, Plantronics, and others 1953-73, Sperry Univac Santa Clara 1973-79; dir. fac. engrg. Signetics Sunnyvale 1979-83; dir. mktg. Carl N. Swenson Co. San Jose 1983-86; v.p. sales K.O. Swanson Milpitas 1986–; honors: Silver Beaver (BSA 1968); mem: Am. Inst. Profl. Engrs., SMPS, Rotary, Boy Scouts of Am., Masons; several patents in semiconductors 1967, various engrg. articles; mil: t/s US Army (MC) 1946-48, Victory Medal; rec: children. Res: 340 Arboleda Dr Los Altos 94022 Ofc: K.O. Swanson 194 S Hillview Dr Milpitas 95035

NODDINGS, SARAH E., lawyer (entertainment law); b. Jan. 19, 1944, Matawan, N.J.; d. Wm. Clayton and Sarah Stephenson (Cox) Noddings; 1 son, Christopher, b. 1982; edn: BA, Douglass Coll.- Rutgers Univ. 1965; MSW, Rutgers Univ. Grad. Sch. of Soc. Wk. 1968; JD, cum laude, Seton Hall Univ. Sch. of Law 1975; admitted to practice Calif., 1976, Nev., 1976, N.J., 1975, US Fed. Dist. Ct., (Central Dist.) Calif., 1976, N.J., 1975. Career: Peace Corps field work placement, Puerto Rico 1964; Vista field work placement, Ore. 1965; Vista Vol., Hanford, Calif. 1965-66; Graduate Sch. field work placements, N.J. 1966-8; dir. County Youth Program, Santa Rosa, Calif. 1968-9; School social wkr. Carteret Bd. of Edn., N.J., 1970-75; law clk. Eighth Judicial Dist. Ct., Nev. 1975-76; atty. (litigation) O'Melveny & Myers, Los Angeles 1976-78; atty. (entertainment/contracts) International Creative Mgmt., 1978-81, Russell & Glickman, 1981-83; and Lorimar Productions Inc., Culver City 1983–; ch. Small Claims Ct. sub-com., Municipal Cts.; mem. L.A. County Bar Assn.; co-chair Barristers Settlement Officer Pgm., awarded 2d pl. nat. for all Barrister sponsored pgms.); recipient Centennial Scholarship 1971-75; mem. Women in Films, Copyright Soc.; publs: arts. in legal jours.; rec: tennis, skiing. Res: Torrance Ofc: 3970 Overland Ave Culver City 90232-3783

NOLAN, DENNIS PAUL VINCENT, engineer; b. Dec. 8, 1954, Detroit; s. James Vincent and Anastasia Theresa (Kulick) N.; edn: BS fire protection engrg., Univ. Md. 1977; MS syst. mgmt., Fla. Inst. of Tech. 1979; grad., Sch. of Offshore Ops., Univ. Tex. Austin 1981; Reg. Profl. Engr. Calif. 1984. Career: fire protection engr. 1977-80 Boeing Aerospace Kennedy Space Ctr. (designed shuttle facilities fire protection systems) 1977-80; risk engr. Marathon Oil Co. Findlay, Ohio 1980-84; senior engr. Lockheed Vandenburg AFB (ops. of shuttle launching) 1984–; honors: Aerospace Awareness Award (NASA 1979); mem: Nat. Mgmt. Assn., Mil. Vehicle Collectors Club; research: Mathematical Comparison of Friction Losses in Plastic, Copper, Steel Pipes 1977, Fired Heater Losses and Prevention 1980, LC-39A Fire Protection Assessment 1979, Ground Safety Plan VLS STS 1985; Republican; rec: restoration of antique military vehicles. Res: 473 Hartnell Rd Santa Maria 93455 Ofc: Lockheed LSOC/SLC-6/76-12 Vandenburg AFB 93437

NOLAN, KATHLEEN KING, real estate broker; b. Dec. 13, 1942, Pasadena; d. J. Harold and Jeannette Louise (Geller) Mitchell; m. John Nolan, May 26, 1983; children: Michelle b. 1966, Stacy b. 1969, Allison b. 1973; edn: BA, CSU Los Angeles 1964; lic. R.E. broker (Calif., Texas). Career: prin./exec. v.p. King Realty, Sherman Oaks 1974–; v.p. Allan Erdy Escrow 1980-, dir. Escrow Services Plus 1983-; mem. San Fernando Valley Bd. Realtors (chair Forms Com., mem. MLS Com., 1983-84); civic: San Fernando Valley Girl Scout Council (fin. advis. com. 1980-83); publs: Real Estate column, L.A. Times (1981-83), Radio Talk Show (1985); Republican; Methodist; rec: ski, tennis, running. Res: 4201 Windsor Pkwy Dallas Tx 95205 Ofc: King Realty 13369 Ventura Blvd Sherman Oaks 91423

NONG, ANH THE, physician; b. Oct. 25, 1940, Haiphong, Vietnam, nat. US cit. 1982; d. Dang Van and Boi Thuy N.; m. Nhon Nguyen, June 27, 1980; children: Chantal b. 1981, Dominique b. 1983; edn: MD, Univ. Saigon faculty of Med. 1970. Career: asst. prof. med. Univ. Saigon 1971-72, Univ. Okla Coll. of Med. 1975-80; assoc. prof. med. UCLA School. of Med. 1975-80, clin. prof. med. 1985–; dir. div. of gen. med. San Bernardino Co. Med. Ctr., tchr. med. dept. 1980–; honors: Best Teacher of the Year (S.B. Co. Med. Ctr. 1981); fellow Am. Coll. Phys.; works: postgrad. edn. for Indochinese refugee physicians 1975-77, 80; Republican; Catholic; rec: foreign lang. Ofc: Dept. of Med. 780 E Gilbert San Bernardino 92404

NONG, painter-sculptor; b. Oct. 10, 1930, Seoul, Korea, nat. 1958. Career: pres. Nong Gallery, San Francisco; painter, sculptor; major one-man exhibs. include: Fort Lauderdale (Fla.) Mus. of the Arts, Santa Barbara Mus. of Art, E.B. Crocker Art Gal. (Sacto.), 1965; Georgia Mus. of Art (Athens, Ga.), El Paso (Tex.) Mus. of Art, 1967; Galerie Vallombreuse (Baritz, Fr.) 1970; Nat. Mus. of History (Taipei, Taiwan), Nihonbashi Gal. (Tokyo), Shinsegye Gal. (Seoul) 1971; Nat. Mus. of Modern Art (Seoul), S.F. Zool. Garden, 1975; Tongin Art Gal. (Seoul) 1978; Hartman Rare Art (Dallas) 1981; Korean Cultural Service (L.A.), Choon Chu Gal. (Seoul) 1982; group exhibs. incl. Smithsonian Instn., 1961, Conn. Acad. of Fine Arts, Charles and Emma Frye Art Mus. (Seattle), 1962, Denver Art Mus., 1965, Jersey City Mus., Univ. of Santa Clara (Calif.), 1967, UC Berkeley, 1968, Oakland Art Mus., Gal. des Champs Elysees (Paris), Nt. Sculpture Soc. (NYC), Taipei Provincial Mus., 1971, Gal. Hexagramme (Paris), 1975, Gal. de Arte Misrachi (Mexico City) 1979; rep. in permanent collections: E.B. Crocker Art Gal., Nat. Mus. Hist. (Taipei), Mus. Nat. des Beaux-Arts (Monte Carlo), Inst. de Cultura Puertoriquena (San Juan), Nat. Gal. Modern Art (New Delhi), Asian Art Mus. (S.F.), Nat. Mus. Modern Art and Nat. Mus. (Seoul), Santa Barbara Mus. Art, Consulate Gen. Rep. of Korea (S.F.), Presidential Palace (Seoul), Anchorage Hist. and Fine Arts Mus., Bankers Mtg. Co. of Calif. (S.F.), IBM (San Mateo), Security Pac. Nat. Bank (S.F.), Govt. of the People's Repub. of China (Beijing, and Shanghai), Govt. of Peru, Museo De Arte (Lima), The Korean Emb. (Lima, Peru). Honors: appreciation Repub. of Korea, disting. achievement cert. State of Calif., proclamation City & Co. of San Francisco, hon. mem. Art Soc. Repub. of China; patents: chest of drawers, building; mil: served with AUS and USAF, 1956-60. Res: 999 Green St, 2701, San Francisco 94133. Ofc: Nong Gallery Inc. Hyatt on Union Sq. San Francisco 94108

NOONKESTER, VIRGIL RAY, metereological researcher, consultant; b. June 11, 1929, Princeton, W.Va.; s. Albert Edgar and Lydia Ethel (Howell) N.; children: Dale b. 1958, Scott b. 1960, Pamela b. 1962; edn: BS magna cum laude, Concord Coll. 1950; MS, M.I.T. 1956, grad. work 1956-57. Career: comml. and mil. weather forecaster Langley AFB, Va. and Goose Bay, Labrador, analyst Nat. Weather Analysis Ctr., Silver Spgs., Md. 1952-55; meteorol. research asst. M.I.T. 1955-57; research scientist Naval Ocean Sys. Ctr., San Diego 1957–; cons. forensic meteorol. 1979-; mem. interview panel to select pollution control meteorol. for S.D. County 1975, 80, 85; honors: 4-yr. Scholarship to W.Va. Coll. (declined), Chi Beta Phi (Concord Coll. 1948), Blue Key (1948), Outstanding Performance Awards (Naval Ocean Sys. Ctr. 1960, 61, 65, 67, 78, 83, 84, 85); mem: Am. Meteorol. Soc. 1952-, AMS Nat. Com. on Meteorol. of the Coastal Zone 1977-82 (chmn. 1981), AAAS 1966-71, Commn. F of Internat. Radio Sci. Union 1975-85, RB Chorale (v.p.), resident's group to preserve city canyons for natural openland parks; publ: 18 papers in sci. jours., 40 lab. reports, 20 conf./symposium reports, presented 38 papers at profl. mtgs.; developed computer model which will be used by Dept. of Defense; mil: 1st lt. USAF 1951-56, Good Conduct; Democrat; Protestant; rec: choral singing, physical fitness, reading, sketching, oil painting. Res: 4274 Mt Henry Ave San Diego 92117 Ofc: Naval Ocean Systems Ctr. Catalina Blvd San Diego 92152

NOORDA, CAREY BRUCE, orthodontist; b. May 24, 1957, Salt Lake City, Utah; s. Dr. Norman and Janie Sharon (Datwyler) N.; m. Cynthia Ann Heaps, Jan. 5, 1979; children: Bryan Paul b. 1979, Stacie Anne b. 1981, Cami Marie b. 1984; edn: BS, Brigham Young Univ., Provo 1981; DDS (Valedictorian), Univ. of the Pacific 1984, MSD (dentistry), 1986. Career: dentist, practice limited to orthodontics; recipient academic awards for highest scholarship: Arthur Roscoe McDowell Award, Clinical Excellence Award, Harry A. True Award (operative dentistry), Bernard C. Kingsbury Award (fixed prosthodontics), Alpha Omega Internat. Dental Frat. Award, Pacific Alumni Assn. Award; honors: Tau Kappa Omega (pres. 1984), Omicron Kappa Epsilon; mem: Am. Denta. Assn., Calif. Dental Assn., Am. Assn. Orthodontists, Pacific Coast Soc. Orthodontists; Republican: Ch. of Jesus Christ of Latter Day Saints (missionary Zurich, Switz.); rec: water and snow skiing. Res: 1490 Sacramento St San Francisco 94109 Ofc: Dept. Orthodontics University of the Pacific San Francisco 94109

NORCROSS, JOE L., lawyer; b. Oct. 19, 1950, Inglewood, Calif.; s. Leland J. and Katie Mae (Lane) N.; 1 dau: Rebecca Anne b. 1984; edn: AA, El Camino Coll. Torrance, Calif. 1970; BA, CSU Dominguez Hills 1972; JD, Pepperdine Univ. Sch. of Law 1975; admitted Calif. State Bar 1975. Career; atty. Elliot &

Norcross 1976-78; legal counsel State Comp. Ins. Fund 1978-79; deputy dist. atty./ dep. co. counsel Kings County 1980; atty. pvt. practice Hanford, Calif. 1980—; awards: service Orange County Bar/ Orange Co. Sch. Bd. 1978; mem: Kings Co. Bar Assn.; Acad. of Model Aeronautics 1961-; Nat. Free Flight Soc. charter mem 1966-; FFMAASC (pres. 1980-82, svc. award 1979); SPEBSQSA 1970-; Toastmasters 1982-; Hanford CBMC 1980-83; Republican; Salvation Army (sgt. maj.); rec: model aircraft, barbershop quartet, band music. Res: 1048 E Hoover Way Hanford 93230 Ofc: 584 S 11th Ave PO Box 65 Hanford 93232

NORDLUND, DONALD CRAIG, corporate lawyer; b. May 23, 1949, Chgo.; s. Donald E. and Jane H. N.; m. Sally Baum, Sept. 7, 1975; 1 child, Courtney b. 1981; edn: AB, Stanford Univ. 1971; JD, Vanderbilt Univ. 1974; admitted Calif. State Bar 1974. Career: atty., assoc. Ware, Fletcher & Freidenrich, Palo Alto 1974-77; atty., Hewlett-Packard Co., Palo Alty 1977-, asst. secty./senior atty. 1980-81, asst. secty./corp. counsel 1981-85, secty./corp. counsel 1985—; secty. Hewlett-Packard Co. Found. and Hewlett-Packard Finance Co., dir. Hewlett-Packard Hellas; panelist Practising Law Inst. 1982-86; mem: Am. Corp. Counsel Assn. (dir. SF Bay Area chpt. 1984-), Am. Soc. of Corp. Secretaries (treas. SF chpt. 1985-86); club: Foothills Tennis & Swimming (Palo Alto); contbg. author: (course handbook) Preparation of Annual Disclosure Documents 1982 (also 1983, 1984, 1985, and 1986 eds.); Republican; Presbyterian; rec: tennis, golf, sailing, ski. Res: 764 Garland Dr Palo Alto 94303 Ofc: Hewlett-Packard Co 3000 Hanover St Palo Alto 94301

NORRIS, JACK MILFORD, b. June 3, 1912, Rock Island, Ill.; s. Pearl and Alice Gertrude (Visser) N.; m. Barbara Williams, Nov. 26, 1949; children: Susan b. 1945, Mary b. 1950, Barbara b. 1952, Catherine b. 1955, Patricia b. 1956, Laura b. 1962; edn: Univ. Texas Austin 1932-36; UCLA short course engrg. & mgmt. 1965; reg. profl. quality engr. Calif., Ill.; certificated instr. Quality Engring. Columbia Basin Coll., Pasco, Wash. 1970-73. Career: sr. project engr. Electromotive Div. G.M.C., La Grange, Ill 1946-52; asst. mgr. Quality Control Ofc., Ford Motor Co. Aircraft Div., Chgo. 1952-58; factory mgr. Marquardt Aircraft Co., Ogden, Utah 1958-60; mgr. Sacramento Plant Quality Control, Aerojet General, Sacto. 1960-68; mgr. quality assur. and stds. Battelle Mem. Inst., Richland, Wash. 1968-70, Wadco Corp., 1970-73; mgr. dev. quality assur. Westinghouse- Hanford, Richland, Wash. 1970-73; dir. qual. assur./ exec. engr./ mgr. Qual. Assur. Dept., NUS Corp., Rockville, Md. 1973-77; v.p. Management Analysis Co. 1977-85; v.p. Norris, Norris & Quixote, Inc. 1985—; internat. cons. in quality assurance, Taiwan, Korea, Yugoslavia 1974-; Fellow ASQC (chmn. Nuclear Div.); publs: over 30 profl. papers; presentation, Japan-USA Technol. Exchange, Technology Transfer Inst., Tokyo (1980); Republican; Catholic; rec: antique autos, painting (water colors). Ofc: Norris, Norris & Quixote, Inc. San Diego

NORRIS, STEPHEN NICHOLAS, aerospace engineer; b. Mar. 28, 1955, NY, NY; s. John Joseph and Angela Louise (Leggiero) N.; m. Sherrie, Nov. 30, 1981; edn: AAS civ. technol., Westchester Comm. Coll. 1975; BE civil engrg., summa cum laude, Manhattan Coll. 1977; MS civ. engrg., Lehigh Univ. 1979; reg. profl. civil engr. Utah 1982. Career: research asst. Fritz Engrg. Lab Lehigh Univ. Bethlehem, Pa. 1977-79; design engr. Fuller Co. Bethlehem 1979-81; chief engr. S&W Constrn. Co. Salt Lake City 1981-83; cons. engr., pvt. cons. Salt Lake City 1983-84; engr. General Dynamics Space Systems Div. San Diego 1984—; honors: Dean's List, Builders Inst. of Westchester Co., Mathematics, Am. Inst. Arch. Awards 1975; mem: Am. Soc. Civ. Engrs. 1977-84, Am. Concrete Inst. 1981-84, Fritz Engrg. Research Soc. 1977-, Countryview Homeowners Assn. (c.f.o.), Community Assn. Inst.; publ: article on bridge design in tech. jour. 1981; Catholic; rec: weightlifting, softball. Ofc: General Dynamics Space Systems Div. San Diego

NORRIS, WILLIAM A., judge; b. Aug. 30, 1927, Turtle Creek, Pa.; m. Merry Wright, 1974; children: Barbara, Donald, Kim, Alison; edn: BA, Princeton Univ. 1951; JD, Stanford Univ. Sch. of Law 1954. Career: law clk. to Justice Wm. O. Douglas, US Supreme Ct. 1955-56; atty. senior mem. Litigation Dept., Tuttle & Taylor, Inc. 1956-80; circuit judge US Ct. of Appeals (9th Circuit) 1980—; govtl. apptments: spl. counsel Pres. Kennedy's Commn. on the Airlines Controversy 1961; mem. (v.p. 1965-67) Calif. State Board of Edn. 1961-67; bd. trustees Calif. State Colleges 1966-72; pres. L.A. Board of Police Commnrs. 1973-74; honors: Phi Beta Kappa (1951), Order of the Coif, exec. editor Stanford Law Rev. (1954); civic: Stanford Law Sch. Alumni (charter Bd. Visitors 1958-61, mem. 1981-), Constnl. Rights Found. (bd. dirs. 1968-71), LA Co. Bar Assn. (chmn. Com. on Juvenile Justice 1975-76, Com. on Judiciary 1977-80), Craft and Folk Art Mus. LA (bd. trustees 1979-), Mus. of Contemporary Art LA (founding pres., bd. trustees 1980-); political: del. to Democrat Nat. Conv. (1964, 68, 72, 76; mem. Rules Com. 1968); Dem. nominee for Atty. General of Calif. (1974); gen. counsel Jimmy Carter for Pres. com., Calif. (1976); campaigner: Rudd Brown for Cong. (1960), Pat Brown for Gov. (1962), No on 14 (1964), Robt. Kennedy for Pres. (1968), Tom Bradley for Mayor (1969, 73, 77), Wilson Riles for Supt. of Public Instrn. (1970).. Ofc: United States Courthouse 312 North Spring St Los Angeles 90012

NORTON, BARRY A., corporate executive, publisher; b. May 4, 1933, Fort Ann, NY; s. Roy Charles and Beatrice (Hayes) N.; m. Kay V., July 23, 1974; children: Jonathan b. 1959, Meredith b. 1962, David K. b. 1962; edn: Norwich Univ. 1951-53; BA, Univ. Colo. 1956; UC Los Angeles 1957-58. Career: exec. v.p./ publisher Self Development Inc. WSAN Jose 1968-71; nat. sales mgr. Responsive Environment Corp. Englewood Cliffs, NJ 1971-73; exec. v.p. Prentice-Hall Learning Systems Englewood Cliffs 1973-76, pres., dir. 1976-82; pres./ publisher Mitchell Information Svcs. Inc. San Diego 1982—; v.p. Cordura Publs. Inc. (parent co.); mem: Calif. Assn. Vocat. Edn., Am. Vocat. Assn., Am. Mgmt. Assn., Automotive Svc. Ind. Assn., Univ. Colo. Alumni; producer: Of Course I Can (1972), Creating A Learning Environment (1978), Mitchell Automechanics (1986); Republican; Protestant. Ofc: Mitchell Information Services Inc. 9889 Willow Creek Rd POB 26260 San Diego 92126

NORTON, ROBERT LEON, association executive; b. Jan. 9, 1926, Jackson, Mich.; s. Oral Alfred and Irene Bertha (Hamaker) N.; m. Carol, Oct. 21, 1984; 1 son, Terry Lee b. 1945 (asst. atty. gen. State of Mich.); edn: Ferris State Coll. 1949-50, Univ. Mich. 1956-58, E. Mich. Univ. 1962-64; Cert. Profl. Mgr. (CPM) Inst. Cert. Profl. Mgrs. Career: indsl. engr. Clark Equip. Co., Jackson, Mich. 1950-65; staff exec. Nat. Mgmt. Assn., Dayton, Ohio 1965—, safety dir. -1967, dir. of tng. 1967-76, dir. of profl. devel. 1976-78, v.p. mktg. 1978-81, v.p. Western Ops., Calif. office 1981-85, staff v.p. 1985—; instr. Jackson Comm. Coll. (1967-76), So. Mich. State Prison (1974-76); profl. speaker and seminar leader (1974-); honors: Life mem. and past pres. Nat. Mgmt. Assn., Lifetime Cert. Profl. Mgr. and past exec. dir. Inst. of Cert. Profl. Mgrs.; mem. Nat. Speakers Assn., So. Calif. Soc. of Assn. Execs., Los Angeles CofC; works: Speech writer, author of Leader Guides, Motivational Guides, Manuals and texts for Leadership and Motivational workshops and seminars, involved in the devel. of leadership and mgmt. skills; mil: flight ofcr. US Army Air Force 1944-45; Republican; Prot.; rec: photog., travel, sailing, public speaking. Ofc: National Management Assn. 28261 Marguerite Pkwy Mission Viejo 92691

NOSCE, ABEL LENES, bank executive; b. Jan. 7, 1926, Tayabas, Quezon, Philippines; s. Donato Nosce and Brigida Lenes; m. Aurora Pineda, Apr. 17, 1954; children: Romarico b. 1958, Hideliza b. 1959, Abel Jr. b. 1962, Wilhelmina b. 1964, Maria Aurora b. 1966; edn: BS in commerce, Luzonian Univ. 1952, hon. PhD econs., 1981. Career: bookkeeper Phil. Nat. Bank, 1955-57; supvr., chief acct. Phil. Banking Corp. 1957-61; asst. v.p., chief acct., v.p. The Manila Banking Corp., 1961-65, v.p. 1961-66, 1966-71, senior v.p. 1971-73, exec. dir. US Investments currently, also bd. chmn. Manilabank Calif.; pres. BF Homes Inc. (realty) 1967-73, bd. chmn. BF Computers Svcs Inc. 1969—; bd. chmn. Abel L. Nosce Managers Inc.; pres. Pagibig Townhouse Devel. Inc.; dir. V.E. Finance, Inc.; past pres. Manila Integrated Data Svcs Inc. (EDP) 1971-73, Banco Filipino Svgs & Mortgage Bank 1974-81, Filipino Pensione Inc. 1976-82; frequent seminar lectr. on banking; recipient num. profl. and acad. awards; mem: Internat. Bankers Assn. (fellow 1978), Savings Bankers Assn. of Phil. (pres. 1981), Chamber of Thrift Banks (v.p.), Bank Mktg. Assn. of Phil. (charter pres. 1974; first hon. life mem.), Nat. Assn. for Bank Auditors & Controllers/ Phil. (pres. 1965-66); civic: Goodwill Industries Inc./Phil. chpt. (charter pres. 1977, hon. bd. chmn. 1982-), Rotary of Manila (dir. 1981-82), Tayabas Assn. Address: Los Angeles 90071

NOTAR, BETTY BRIDGES, educator; b. Dec. 7, 1923, New Orleans, La.; d. Daniel Edward and Helen Ethaline (Bridges) Sanders; m. Charles A. Notar, Sept. 1, 1945; children: Cathie Jo, b. 1946; Bonnie Kae, b. 1951; Toni Ann, b. 1957; Remi Su, b. 1961 (dec.; edn: BS, Seattle Univ. 1949; MEd, Univ. of Wash. 1966; PhD, US Internat. Univ. 1975. Career: secondary tchr. Quilcene (Wash.) High Sch. 1949-50; elem. tchr. Edmonds (Wash.) Grade Sch., 1952-54; sec. tchr. Mojave (Calif.) High Sch. 1955-59, counselor 1959-78, dir. of guidance 1978-84, guidance cons. 1984—; honors: Phi Delta Kappa, Pi Lambda Theta, NDEA Scholarship, Univ. of Wash. 1960; mem: Am. Sch. Counselors Assn.; Am. Personnel & Guidance Assn.; Nat. Vocational Guidance Assn.; Calif. Counseling & Guidance Assn.; Nat. & Calif. Edn. Assns.; Mojave Faculty Assn.; Kern County Juvenile Justice Commn.; Kern Co. Delinquency Prevention Commn.; Order of Eastern Satr, P.M.; Mojave Mineralogical Assn.; World Congress of Profl. Hypnotists; works: Relationship of Self Concepts Congruence to Achievement of High School Students, 1975; mil: PFC USMC; Democrat; Methodist; rec: lapidary, travel. Res: 2038 Trinity St Mojave 93501 Ofc: Mojave High School, 15732 O St Mojave 93501

NOVAK, GLORIA JEAN, librarian; b. Aug. 31, 1934, Detroit, Mich.; d. Julius and Rose (Bortnick) Berkowitz; m. Stefan Novak, Dec. 27, 1957; 1 dau: Genya, b. 1960; edn: Univ. of Mich. 1952-53; UCLA 1953-54; BA, UC Berkeley 1958; MLS, 1968. Career: admin. asst. McCue & Assoc., Archs., San Francisco 1959-66; head current serials East Asiatic Library, UC Berkeley 1969-71, head Engring. Library 1979-81, library space planning 1972—; library building cons: Johns Hopkins Univ. 1980-, Univ. of Md. 1982-, Mills Coll. 1983-, Naval Postgrad. Acad. Monterey 1983-, San Francisco Chronicle 1984, UCSF 1985; AIA/ ALA Library Bldg. Award, S.F. Univ. High Sch. 1985; mem: Am. Library Assn. (Coll.- Univ. Lib. Bldgs., Bldg. & Equip. Sect., Lib. Bldg. Awds., Lib. Bldg. Cons. List); publs: editor (book), Running Out of Space, 1976; contbg. writer: art., Information Bulletin, Western Association May Libraries (11/81), chpt., Austerity Management in Academic Libraries (1984). Res: 6925 Balsam Way Oakland 94611 Ofc: Univ. of California, Main Library, Berkeley 94720

NOVICK, BENJAMIN HASKELL, private investigator; b. Feb. 27, 1959, NY, NY; s. Alfred and Dorothy Dina (Goldberg) N.; edn: dipl. Alliance Francais, Tel-Aviv 1974; splst. in improvised battlefield ordinance. Career: trainee with 2 pvt. investigators, Howard Wilson, Joseph Kurtz; security cons. and pvt. investigator (clients in entertainment and defense indus.), pres. B.H. Novick & Assocs., Los Angeles; mem: Smithsonian Assocs., Air Force Assn., Cousteau Soc; sev. publs. in mil. scis. field; mil: Israel Spl. Forces 1977-81; Republican; Jewish. Address: B.H. Novick & Assocs. 2421 Hidalgo Ave Los Angeles 90039

NUCKLES, KATHLEEN JOYCE, orthodontist; b. Sept. 22, 1951, Burbank, Calif.; d. Thomas Frank and Joyce Ellen (Freeman) N.; m. Richard Hoard, July 28, 1984; edn: BA, UC Irvine 1973; RDH, L.A. City Coll. 1975; DDS, cum laude, UC Los Angeles 1981; Orthodontic Cert. UC San Francisco 1983. Career: pvt. practice orthodontics L.A. 1983–; honors: Omicron Kappa Upsilon 1981; mem: Am., Calif. Dental Assns., Am. Assn. Orthodontists, Am. Soc. Dentistry for Children, Am. Assn. Women Dentists; Republican. Res: 202 San Vicente Blvd Santa Monica 90402 Ofc: 10921 Wilshire Blvd, Ste 1003, Los Angeles 90024

NUGENT, JOHN WILLIAM, manufacturing co. executive; b. July 21, 1945; Sharon, Pa.; s. John William and Lillian Elizabeth (Rigby) N.; m. Nancy, Dec. 25, 1967; children: Derric James b. 1968, Shane Elden b. 1972; edn: Univ. Cincinnati 1963-64; BS, Youngstown State 1968. Career: corp. sales N/S Corp. Sharon, Pa. 1968-70, nat. acct. sales mgr. 1970-73, mktg. mgr. 1973-75, v.p. mktg. Inglewood 1975-82, exec. v.p. 1982–; dir: N/S Corp. 1975-, Nugent Convalescent Home Inc. 1979-, Nat. Car Wash Council 1981-82; honors: Disting. Svc. (NCC 1982), Paul Harris Fellow (Rotary 1985); mem: Advertising Frat. 1967-68, Am. Pub. Works Assn. 1983-85, Assn. School Bus. Officials 1981-83, Internat. Car Wash Assn. 1970-, Rotary (dir. 1986-); patent: vehicle washing machine; Republican; Lutheran; rec: horticulture, art. Res: 7335 Vista Del Mar Playa Del Rey 90293 Ofc: N/S Corp. 235 W Florence Ave Inglewood 90301

NUNENKAMP, DAVID CARL, mining co. executive; b. Aug. 4, 1943, Astoria, Ore.; s. Victor Louis and Mary Christobell (Burlingame) N.; m. Katherine Jo Clyde, Aug. 7, 1965; 1 son, Adrian Victor, b. 1972; edn: BS, Ore. State Univ. 1965. Career: indsl. engr. The Boeing Co., Seattle, Wash. 1966-69; div. mgr. Bio Consultants, Inc., South gate 1969-72; ind. cons., associations with Mgmt. Svcs. Co., Sacto., J.J. Davis Assocs., Inc., Mclean, VA and Ketron, Inc., Wayne, Penn. 1972-77; mgr. tch. svcs., gen. mgr. Glenrock Coal Co., gen mgr. Bridger Coal Co., Merco, Inc. 1977-83; v.p./ gen. mgr. California Nickel Corp., 1983–; dir. Area Ind. & Devel. Corp.; dir. Resource Ctr., Del Norte, Humboldt; mem: Am. Soc. of Mining & Metallurgical Engrs.; Rotary, Crescent City; num. tech. works in fields of mining and environmental science; mil: 2nd lt., USAFR; Republican; rec: fishing, hunting, golf. Res: 100 Middle Fork Rd., Gasquet 95543 Ofc: California Nickel Corp., 2550 Via Tejon, Ste. 3C, Palos Verdes Estates 90274

NUNIS, DOYCE BLACKMAN, JR., historian, author, educator; b. May 30, 1924, Cedartown, Ga.; s. Doyce B., Sr. and Winnie Ethel (Morris) N.; edn: BA, UCLA 1947; MS in edn., USC 1950, M.Ed, 1952, PhD in hist., 1958. Career: tchr. Calif. public schools 1948-51; grad. fellow USC, 1951-53, lectr. Dept. of Am. Civilization & Instns., 1953-56; instr. in hist. El Camino Coll., 1956-59, UCLA, 1959-65; prof. history, USC, 1965–; trustee Santa Barbara Mission Archive Lib., 1971-, pres. 1972-; author pub. books: Andrew Sublette, Rocky Mountain Prince, 1808-53 (1960), Josiah Belden, 1841 California Overland Pioneer: His Memoir and Early Letters (1962), The Golden Frontier: The Recollections of Herman Francis Rinehart, 1851-69 (1964), The California Diary of Faxon Dean Atherton, 1836-39 (1964), The Gold Rush Letters of Jasper Smith Hill (1964), The Letters of a Young Miner, 1849-52 (1964), Journey of James H. Bull, Baja Calif. Oct. 1843 to Jan. 1844 (1965), The Trials of Isaac Graham (1967), A Med. Journey in Calif. by Pierre Garnier, M.D. (1967), Hudson's Bay Company's First Fur Brigade to the Sacramento Valley, 1829-30 (1967), Past is Prologue: A Centennial Profile of the Pacific Mutual Life Ins. Co. (1968), A Journey on Two Oceans (1971), The Vigilance Committee of 1856: Three Views (1971), Los Angeles and Its Environs in the 20th Century (bibliography) (1973), The Westerners Brand Book Number 14 (1975), History of American Political Thought, 2 vols. (1975), The Mexican War in Baja, California (1977), coeditor, A Guide to Historic Places in Los Angeles County (1978), editor, A Frontier Doctory by Henry F. Hoyt (1979), Los Angeles From the Days of the Pueblo by W.W. Robinson (1981), The Letters of Jacob Baegert (1982), The 1769 Transit of Venus in Baja Calif. (1982), ed. Men, Medicine and Water (1982), ed. Frontier Fighter by George W. Coe (1984), A Southern California Historical Anthology (1985); num. arts. in scholarly hist. mags.; ed. So. Calif. Quarterly, 1962-; awards: Del Amo Found. Grant for research abroad 1967, Henry E. Huntington Library grantee 1960, John Simon Guggenheim Meml. Fellow 1963-4, award of merit Am. Assn. State and Local Hist. 1965, fellow Am. Philosophical Soc. 1969, fellow L.A. Chancery Archives 1976, fellow Calif. Hist. Soc. 1981; Distinguished Teaching Award 1975, Raubenheimer Disting. Faculty Award 1983, USC; Benemerenti Pedal (Papal honor) 1984; Am. Antiquarian Soc., 1984; mem. num. historical socs., L.A. Corral of Westerners, Phi Alpha Theta, Pi Sigma Alpha, Zamorano Club, The Athenaeum (London), research assoc. LA County Mus. of Natural Hist., 1972; Ofc: Dept. of History, USC, Los Angeles 90089-0034

NUNN, ERNEST EUGENE, company executive; b. Feb. 16, 1935, Parma, Mo.; s. Ernest F. and Rosa Lee (Pope) N.; m. Jo Ellen Neely, Jan. 25, 1957; children: Julie, b. 1959; Jeffrey, b. 1966; edn: BS, Indiana Univ. 1961. Career: v.p. to chmn. Lazarus Dept. Store (div. of fed. dept. store), Columbus, Oh. 1961-75; pres. Drapery Mfg. Inc., Columbus, Oh. 1975-77; pres. New Ideal Dept. Store, Birmingham, Ala. 1977-80; regl. mgr. Nat. Revenue Corp., Columbus, Oh. 1980-82; pres. Jani-King of Calif. Inc., 1982–; bd. dirs. Better Bus. Bureau, Indpls., Ind. 1973-75; dir. Birmingham CofC 1977-79; mil: sgt. US Army 1956-58; rec: woodworking, golf. Res: 5081 Pine Circle La Palma 90623 Ofc: Jani-King of California Inc., 14700 E Firestone Blvd, Ste 112, La Mirada 90638

NUNZIATO, RALPH JOSEPH, venture capitalist; b. Sept. 19, 1920, NY, NY; s. Ralph and Philomena (Coppola) N.; m. Shirley Rooks, June 12, 1943; children: Gail (Celentano) b. 1949, Margo (Santino) b. 1950; edn: B. Aeronautical Engring., Daniel Guggenheim Sch. of Aero., NY Univ. 1942. Career: assoc. Laurance S. and David Rockefeller, Belgium 1960-65; v.p. Emerson Electric, St. Louis, Mo. 1967-70; pres. Optics Technology Inc., Redwood City, Calif. 1972-77; pres. Rodenstock Instruments Corp., Sunnyvale 1978-81; mng. ptnr. Advanced Technology Ventures, Menlo Park 1981–; dir. Vestar Research Inc. (1981-), Quidel (1981-); clubs: Stock Exchange (SF), University (NYC), Menlo Country (Redwood City); mil: col. USAF 1942-60, Army Commendn. Medal 1944, Legion of Merit 1957, AF Commendn. Medal 1960; Republican; rec: golf. Res: 181 Forest Lane Menlo Prk 94025 Ofc: Advanced Technology Ventures 1000 El Camino Real Ste 210 Menlo Park 94025

NUTTER, BEN EARL, port planning and management consultant; b. May 17, 1911, Baldwin, Kans.; s. John Alva and Lillian Capitola (Boggs) N.; m. Leone Rockhold, Nov. 26, 1936; edn: Glendale City Coll. 1929-31; BSCE, Oregon State Univ. 1936; Reg. Civil Engr. Calif. 1938, Hawaii 1946. Career: asst. engr. materials to Chief of Engrg. Div. US Army Corps of Engrs., mil. constrn. to harbor and flood control 1941-52; asst. mgr., asst. chief engr. Hawaii Harbor Bd. 1952-53; chmn. Hawaii Irrigation Authority and planning and constrn. for Hawaii Aeronautics Commn. 1953-57; supt. of public works Terr. of Hawaii, chmn. Hawaii Harbor Bd., hwy. engr., mem. Honolulu Bd. of Water Supply 1953-57; chief engr., asst. exec. dir. Port of Oakland 1957-62, exec. dir. 1962-77; cons. port devel. & mgmt. to ports and steamship cos. 1977–; honors: Civil Govt. Award (Soc. Civil Engrs. 1971), Public Works Man of the Year (Kiwanis Internat./Am. Public Works Assn. 1967), Meritorious Civilian Service Overseas (War Dept. 1943), Sigma Xi Sigma, Tau Beta Pi; mem: Am. Soc. Civil Engrs. (past sect. pres.), Am. Assn. Port Authorities (pres. 1974-75), Regional Export Expansion Council, Nat. Defense Exec. Reserve, Internat. Assn. Ports & Harbors (chmn. containers com.), Internat. Cargo Handling Coord. Assn., Nat. Defense Trans. Assn., Rotary Internat., Masons, Scottish Rite, Beta Theta Pi, Propellor Club; Republican; Christian. Res: Santa Rosa

NYBO, L. BRUCE, consulting civil engineer; b. Mar. 6, 1944, Glendale, Calif.; s. Luverne Bernard and Elise Nybo; m. Jean W., May 29, 1965; children: Elisabeth b. 1967, David b. 1969, John b. 1970, Joy b. 1972; edn: Bakersfield Coll. 1961-63; Christian lib. arts Highland Coll. 1965; BSCE UC Los Angeles 1966; Reg. Profl. Engr. Miss. 1977, Reg. Civil Engr. Calif. 1978. Career: transp. ofcr. US Naval Base Adak, Alaska 1966-67; asst. resident ofcr. in charge of constrn. USMCAS Cherry Point, N.C. 1967-69; constrn. engr. The Kroger Co. Houston, Tex. 1969-71; dir. of engrg. Jitney Jungle Stores of Am. Jackson, Miss. 1971-75; corp. dir. engrg. Peter J. Schmidt Co. Buffalo, NY, Erie, Pa. 1975-78; gen. mgr., dir. engrg. and surveying svcs. Smith & Assoc. Bakersfield 1978-79; pres. L. Bruce Nybo Inc., pres. Nybo & Walker Inc. civil engrg. and land surveying Bakersfield 1979–; pres. Crown Block Petroleum & Mining Corp.; mem: Calif. Council Civil Engrs. and Land Surveyors (past chpt. pres.), Am. Soc. Civil Engrs., Nat., So. Calif. Soc. Profl. Engrs., Profl. Engrg. Assn. of Antelope Valley, Am. Petroleum Inst., Christian Businessmen's Com. of USA, Full Gospel Men's Fellowship Internat., Bakersfield CofC (econ. devel. com.), Nautilus of Bakersfield; mil: lt. USNR Civil Engrg. Corps, active duty 1966-69; Republican; Assembly of God. Ofc: L. Bruce Nybo Inc. 4200 Easton Dr Ste 2 Bakersfield 93309

NYHAN, CHRISTINE, community volunteer; b. Dec. 13, 1923, Portland, Maine; d. Clifford John and Marcia Somers (Cunningham) Murphy; m. William L. Nyhan, Nov. 20, 1948; children: Christopher b. 1951, Victoria 1953-1976, Abigail b. 1955; edn: Westbrook Coll. 1942-44; BS, St. Joseph's Coll. 1944-47. Career: dir. Junior Red Cross Portland, Maine 1947-48; field dir. Girl Scouts of Greater NY 1948-49; vol. work League of Women Voters Lombard, Ill. 1956-58; Planned Parenthood Bd. San Diego 1977-83; fundraiser Alliance for Mental Illness 1985–; honors: Margaret Sanger Award 1986, Girl Scout Achievement Award 1969; mem: Mus. of Natural History, S.D. Field Ornithologists, Wednesday Club, La Jolla Beach Tennis Club, Sierra Club, Audubon Soc., Experiment in Internat. Living; Democrat; rec: birding, travel, sketching. Res: 1825 Spindrift Dr La Jolla 92037

OAKES, THOMAS WARREN, corporate chief executive officer; b. Jan. 12, 1928, Salt Lake City; s. Eugene Turley and Mary Leona (Mendenhall) O.; m. Phyllis Ann Randall, Dec. 28, 1953; children: Kenton T. b. 1957, Robert E. b. 1960, Mark R. b. 1963; edn: BA, Brigham Young Univ. 1954, MA, 1955; PhD, Univ. of Utah 1970. Career: health care research Kaiser Found. Research Inst., Med. Methods Research, Oakland 1969-73; asst. prof. No. Ariz. Univ., Flagstaff 1973-77; founder, CEO Fuzetron Inc., La Mesa 1978–; dir. Calif. Small Bus. Innovation Network 1986-87, Ariz. State Health Planning Council 1973-76; listed: Who Is Publishing in Science 1975; awards: 3 Competitive Small Bus. Innovative Research 1983-86; senior mem. Soc. Mfg. Engrs. 1984-; 2 US patents; 7 profl. articles in health care field 1970-74; mil: USMC 1946-48; Republican; L.D.S.; rec: skiing, ocean swimming, aerobics. Res: 10303 Centinella Dr La Mesa 92041 Ofc: Fuzetron Inc., 1100 N Magnolia Ste J El Cajon 92020

OAKES, W. RICHARD, JR., commercial real estate development co. executive; b. Oct. 31, 1951, Norwich, Conn.; s. Wm. Richard and Mary Bernice (Thurston) O.; m. Cheryl, Sept. 30, 1978; 1 son, Austin b. 1984; edn: BS, cum laude, USC Sch. Bus. Adminstrn. 1973; desig: CRA (Cert. Review Appraiser). Career: v.p./br. mgr. Keystone Mortgage Co., Los Angeles and Irvine, 1973-80, dir. Profit Sharing Plan; ptnr. Johnson, Oakes & Co., Newport Beach 1980-81; v.p. State Savings & Loan Assn., Santa Monica 1982-83; v.p. Birtcher, Laguna Niguel 1984–; guest lectr. UC Irvine Ext., frequent speaker realtor groups; mem: Am. Indsl. R.E. Assn., Calif. Assn. Realtors, Building Indus. Assn. (Orange Co. Comml. Indsl. Council founding dir.), Internat. Council Shopping Ctrs., Long Beach Dist. Bd. Realtors, LA Area CofC (indsl. devel.

com.), LA Realty Bd. (Young Realtors com.), Nat. Assn. Indsl. and Office Parks, Nat. Assn. Realtors, Nat. Assn. Rev. Appraisers, So. Calif./Orange Co. Mortgage Bankers Assn., Urban Land Inst.; civic: Citizens for Excellence in Edn., Commerce Assocs. USC, Disciples Inc. (fin. adv. bd.), Gr. Santa Ana CofC (chmn.'s circle), Young Exec. Am. (life); Republican (Young Execs. Am.); Christian; rec: tennis, backpacking, ski. Res: 25212 Bentwood Laguna Niguel 92677 Ofc: Birtcher 27611 La Paz Rd POB A-1 Laguna Niguel 92677-1078

OBERG, MERRILL CHARLES, computer dealer/consultant; b. June 3, 1933, Sidney, Mont.; s. Hugo E. and Myrtle Grace (Green) O.; m. Harriet Sundheim, Jan. 20, 1952; children: Kathryn b. 1952, Sandra b. 1955, Michael b. 1961. Career: paymaster LaLonde Constrn., Sidney, Mont. 1951-55; asst. mgr. Gambles Stores, Miles City, Mont. 1955-57; controller Noble Land & Cattle, Kerman, Ca. 1957-65; owner/pres. Intrastate Data Processing, also Online Computers Plus, 1965-, cons. IBM, var. accounting firms (devel. 5000+ acctg. type computer programs for over 100 different industries, 1965-); honors: listed in top 100 computer dealers in U.S., Computer Merchandising Mag. (1985); mem. var. acctg., data proc., computer assns., Jr. CofC (past pres), Lions (past pres., dist. ofcr.); mil: m/sgt. Mont. N.G. 1951-57, Calif. Army N.G. 1957-63; Republican; Prot.; rec: golf, camping, travel. Ofc: Online Computers Plus 6789 N Blackstone Fresno 93710

OBRADOVITCH, MILOSH (MIKE) M., aircraft co. executive, engineer; b. May 11, 1944, Belgrade, Yugoslavia, nat. US cit. 1964; s. Miodrag M. and Milena V. O.; m. Barbara M., Apr. 11, 1981; children: Rob b. 1986, Mio b. 1983; (step) Andrea b. 1973, Lara b. 1969; edn: BSME, Univ. So. Calif. 1966, MSME, 1969, MBA, 1971; reg. profl. engr. Calif. Career: var. tech. mgmt. positions in engineering, mktg. and systems/program office environments; worked on Defense Dept. devel. projects incl. High Energy Laser Systems devel., F-15 Radar prodn., TOW Missile Subsystem for Bradley Fighting Vehicle; fmr. senior engr. Bendix-Electrodynamics; program mgr. BFVS-TMDE, Hughes Aircraft Co., El Segundo currently; lectr. CSULB, USC, and num. seminars within industry on productivity, strategic planning, project mgmt., 1974-83; civic: Los Alamitos Municipal T.V. Access Producers, Groups and Victims for Enforcement of Laws (GAVEL), PTA; coauthor Project Management Systems Development & Productivity (Daniel Spencer Pubs., 1985); num. tech. reports; Republican; Serbian Orthodox; rec: tennis, tchg./writing. Ofc: Hughes Aircraft Co. 2000 El Segundo Blvd El Segundo 90245

O'BRIEN, GREGORY CHARLES, JR., judge; b. June 22, 1945, Alhambra; s. Gregory C. and Mary Jane (McLeod) O'B.; m. Carolyn, Jan. 29, 1972; children: Kelly b. 1972, Jeffrey b. 1974, Tricia b. 1977; edn: AB, USC 1968; JD, Whittier Coll. Sch. of Law 1972; admitted Calif. State Bar 1972. Career: deputy city atty., City of Los Angeles 1972-78; atty. So. Calif. Edison Co., 1978-85; gov. apptd. judge Citrus Municipal Ct., West Covina 1985; honors: Man of the Year Award, US Jaycees 1979; mem. Whittier Coll. Alumni (bd.), Foothill Presbyn. Hosp. Mens Club (bd.), W. Covina Rotary Club; Republican (chmn. 62nd Assembly Dist. Central Com. 1981, 82); Roman Catholic; author: Lenin Lives! (novel pub. Stein & Day, 1984). Ofc: Citrus Municipal Court, 1427 West Covina Pkwy West Covina 91790

O'BRIEN, KEVIN JAMES, real estate investment banker; b. July 19, 1957, Tucson, Ariz.; s. Murray Andre and Sigrid (Kostoff) O'B.; edn: BS in fin., No. Ariz. Univ. 1979; JD, Loyola Univ. 1982; LLM in internat. taxation, Univ. San Diego 1985; desig: Splst. in Real Estate Securities, R.E. Sec. & Syndication Inst. (1985), Reg. Investment Advisor, Senior Certified Valuer, Calif. lic. Contr., R.E. Broker. Career: internat. tax. atty., investment advisor to offshore investors; prin. Amerinvest Capital Corp. (sponsor internat. inv. fund for fgn. instnl. investment in U.S. real estate), 1985-; mem. Am. Assn. of Atty.-CPAs, Internat. Bar Assn., Internat. Inst. of Inv. Banking, Mensa, Toastmasters Intl.; civic: vol. income tax asst. for elderly, fmr. leader flying club (pre- flight instrn.) for H.S. seniors; guest interviewee PBS-TV re fgn. investment in US real estate (1985); Republican; Catholic; rec: aviation, writing. Ofc: Amerinvest Capital Corp. 4525 Texas St Ste 7 San Diego 92116

O'BRIEN, PHILIP MICHAEL, librarian; b. Jan. 5, 1940, Albion, Nebr.; s. Lawrence J. and Mar Helen (Ruplinger) O.B.; m. Christina Bartling; children: Tara, Kirsten; edn: BA, Whittier Coll. 1961; MS, USC 1962, PhD, 1974. Career: asst. librarian Whittier Coll. 1962-66, spl. collections librarian 1974-; head bus. and social scis. dept. Chico State Coll. Library 1966-67; US Army librarian, Europe 1967-70 mem: ALA, Calif. Acad. and Research Libraries, Rounce and Coffin Club, Univ. Club (Whittier); Democrat. Res: 11724 Dorland St. Whittier 90601 Ofc: Whittier Coll. Library, Whittier 90601

O'BRIEN, WILLIAM SAMUEL, publisher, educator; b. Aug. 7, 1932, Atlanta, Ga.; s. Louis Mansfield and Ada (Miller) O.; m. Gwendolyn Jan Plummer, Feb. 14, 1959; children: Timothy b. 1960, Sherri b. 1962, Shelly b. 1964, William b. 1967, Jana b. 1970; edn: AA, Truett McConnell 1953; AB, Mercer Univ. 1955; MA, Redlands Univ. 1970; General Elem. Secondary Tchg. Credl. Career: pastor, music tchr. for ch. orgns. 1953-70; elem. sch. tchr. 1955-56; music, spl. media tchr. 1956-69; spl. media coord. MGM pgm. 1959-69; instr. publications, history, Eng., art, music Curtis Jr. H.S. 1969-75; instr. publications, advertisement, history, Eng., performing arts, psychology, creative writing Pacific H.S. 1975-81; instr. middle school Del Vallejo 1981-82, computers Riley Elem. Sch. 1982-83; owner, oper. Calif. Church Press; devel. Personal Touch Bridal Dept. Store; freelance advertisement display 1970-; honors: Innovative Teacher Award (Calif. Tchrs. Assn. 1979), Outstanding Contribution (Pacific H.S. senior class 1980), Apple Award (for innovative

programming 1980), Outstanding Contribution (Riley Sch.), Award of Contribution for public svc. work for USMCR; mem: Journ. Assn. of So. Calif., Nat. Journ. Assn., Nat. Forensic Assn. (hon.), Assoc. Journ. of Pacific, San Bernardino Tchrs. Assn. (pub. rels. 7 yrs.), Screen Writers Guild, PTA, YMCA; works: designed diorama for Nat. Educators Assn. convention in S.F.; publ. musical for elementary students, What Happened to Willie?; devel. art curriculum for Ghana, Africa, chools; devel. Speech Box for Linguistic Troubled Youths; Baptist; rec: painting, music. Address: 480 North D St San Bernardino 92401

OCHELTREE, RICHARD LAWRENCE, lawyer; b. Oct. 9, 1931, Springfield, Ill.; s. Chalmer M. and Helen M. (Camm) O.; m. Ann Washburn, Apr. 11, 1958; children: Kirstin, b. 1960; Lorraine, b. 1963; Tracy, b. 1966; edn: AB, Harvard Coll. 1953; LLD, Harvard Law Sch. 1958. Career: v.p. admin./ secty./ gen. counsel American Forest Products Co. Res: 1446 Floribunda Ave Apt 102 Burlingame 94010 Ofc: American Forest Products Co., 2740 Hyde St San Francisco 94109

O'CONNELL, FRANCIS ALOYSIUS, JR., lawyer, writer, lecturer; b. Apr. 4, 1914, NY, NY; s. Francis A. and Mary Colette (Cavanagh) O'C.; m. Eleanor Blair, Oct. 13, 1972; children: Ann (Knippenberg) b. 1952; stepsons: Arthur, William, and Anthony Grant (1942, 1946, 1950), Blair (1946-86) and Roy Tremoureux (1949); edn: pre-law, Fordham Univ. 1932-34, LLB. Fordham Law Sch. 1938; admitted New York State Bar 1939. Career: atty. assoc. Cravath, Swaine & Moore, NY, NY 1939-46; mgr. labor rels. Standard Brands Inc., NY, NY 1946-52; deputy dir. Office of Indsl. Rels., US Dept. of Defense, Wash DC 1951-53; cons. Anna M. Rosenberg Assocs., NY, NY 1953-57; (successively) Labor counsel, dir. Indsl. Relations, v.p. Employee Rels., Olin Corp., N.Y.C. and Stamford, Conn., 1957-77; exec. dir. John M. Olin Found., NY, NY 1974-79; (current) consultant, writer, lectr; vis. lectr. Cornell Univ. (1973-74), Univ. Calif. Regents' Prof., UCLA (1977); dir. National Review mag. (1975-), Inst. for Contemporary Studies (1982-), Public Research Syndicated, Claremont (1980-); honors: recogn. For Outstanding Service in Labor-Mgmt. Rels., Pace Univ. (1974); mem. Am. Bar Assn., Mont Pelerin Soc., Philadelphia Soc., Commonwealth Club, New York Athletic Club; publs: num. articles, speeches and lectures on labor-mgmt. rels. (1953-77), author "Plant Closings: 'Worker Rights', 'Management Rights' and the Law" (Fall 1986); mil: capt. Military Intell. 1942-45, capt./dep. dir. Office of Indsl. Rels., DOD 1952-53, awarded War Dept. Staff Cit. (1945); Republican; Roman Catholic; rec: fishing, photog. Res: 427 Seaview Dr Aptos 95003

O'CONNELL, JOHN JOSEPH, III, company executive; b. Apr. 4, 1959, Boston, Mass.; s. John Joseph and Ann Margret (Marandett) O'C.; edn: BA mktg., CSU Fullerton 1981; MBA, Chapman Coll. 1983. Career: sales rep. Hoke Inc., Anaheim 1981-84; account mgr. Taylor Instrument, Cerritos 1984-85; branch mgr. Patten Corp., San Diego 1985-; gen. ptnr. Computeck, Mission Viejo 1986-; mem. Instrument Soc. of Am., Chi Psi Frat. Alumni Assn., Knights of Columbus; Democrat; Roman Catholic; rec: dist. running, landscaping, swim. Res: 23321-B La Glorieta Mission Viejo 92691 Ofc: Patten Corporation 1259 Hornblend Ste 1 San Diego 92138

O'CONNOR, GREGORY MICHAEL, optometrist; b. April 8, 1952, South Bend, Ind.; s. Joseph Bernard and Irene Ellen (Kearney) O'C.; m. Patricia Ranville, Dec. 30, 1977; edn: BS, Univ. of Mich. 1973; BS, Ill. Coll. of Optometry 1975, OD, 1978; Reg. Optometrist, Calif. 1979. Career: staff optometrist Chicago Eye, Ear, Nose & Throat Hosp., Chicago, Ill. 1977-78; chief of optometry svc., Naval Regl. Med. Ctr., Barstow 1978-81; pvt. practice, Malibu 1981-; tchg. asst. Ill. Coll. of Optometry 1977-78; awards: State of Mich. Undergrad. Scholarship, Univ. of Mich. Honors Convocation, Armed Forces Health Professions Scholarship, Tomb & Key, Beta Sigma Kappa; mem: Am. and Calif. Optometric Assns., Mojave Desert and Los Angeles Co. Optometric Socs., Optimist (Flint, Mich.; bd. dirs., Malibu 1982), Rotary of Barstow (bd. dirs. 1979-80), Malibu CofC; works: Cataractogenesis and Exposure to Non-ionizing Radiation Sources, Dept. of Defense Study 1979; mil: lt. USN 1976-81, Letter of Commdn.; Republican; Catholic; rec: writing, hiking, woodworking. Res: 5460 White Oak Ave. C-210 Encino 91316 Ofc: 29169 Heathercliff Rd. Ste. 220 Malibu 90265

ODEKIRK, E. BARTON, business owner; b. June 2, 1929, Fort Stockton, Texas; s. Clair Barton and Oma Mae (Ray) O.; m. Joan Kazmer (decd.), Jan. 16, 1952; children: Jan b. 1955, Donna b. 1957, Eileen b. 1958, Thomas b. 1960, Paul b. 1963, Mary Ann b. 1964; edn: AA indsl. supvn., Riverside City Coll. 1960. Career: owner antique bus. Riverside 1965; personal property appraiser Riverside 1972-; owner Odekirk's Appraisal Svc. Riverside 1972-, Black Bart's Antique Shop Riverside 1986-; honors: Svc. Award (Volunteers of Riverside 1984); mem: Riverside Geneal. Soc. (charter), Volunteers of Riverside (bd.), Knights of Columbus (past); mil: US Army 1950-52, Korea; Democrat; Catholic. Ofc: 3634 Elizabeth St Ste 6 Riverside 92506

O'DONNELL, ROBERT JOHN, chemical engineer; b. May 23, 1924, Pawtucket, R.I.; s. Joseph James and Gladys Louise (Savoy) O'D.; m. Marie Davidek, Oct. 10, 1953; children: Sean b. 1955, Hugh b. 1957, Erin b. 1958, Joseph b. 1961, Megan b. 1963; edn: BS, M.I.T. 1946. Career: research engr. Chevron Research Co., 1946-63, senior research engr. 1964-80, senior engring. associate 1980-85, ret. 4/85; mem. Am. Inst. of Chem. Engrs.; fmr. treas./ pres. No. Calif. Henry George School; publs: sev. articles on laboratory analysis of crude petroleum; mil: pvt. US Army Air Force 1943; rec: photog. Res: 2190 Danberry Ln San Rafael 94903

OEI, KOK-TIN, investor; b. Jan. 10, 1924, Indramayu, Java, Indonesia; s. Han Siong and Ie Boen (Tjan) O.; m. Christina Khoe, June 21, 1952; children: John, b. 1955; Tony, b. 1957; edn: degree, textile engr. Hogere Textile Sch., Netherlands 1952. Career: weigher to asst. mgr. in fathers rice mills, Indonesia; agent, textile dyes, Indonesian import-export firm, Hamburg, Germany (3 yrs.); emigrant to Calif. 1971; investor in apartment bldgs., Northern Calif. 1971–; clerk, Metropolitan Life 1971-80; linguist: Indonesian, Dutch, French, German, English; rec: philately, coins. Res: 2054 Sloat Blvd San Francisco 94116

O'FARRELL ROBERT ANTHONY, superior court judge; b. July 2, 1941, NY, NY; s. John B. and Bernadette T. (des Garennes) O.; m. Maria, Dec. 29, 1973; children: Michael b. 1974, Anne b. 1976, Peter b. 1977, Meghan b. 1980; edn: AA, Ventura Coll. 1962; BA, CSU Fresno 1964; JD, UC Hastings Coll. of Law 1967. Career: deputy public defender Ventura Co. 1968-69, Monterey Co. 1969-74; justice ct. judge Castroville 1974-75; municipal ct. judge Monterey Co. 1975-81, superior ct. judge 1981–; mem: Calif. Judges Assn. (exec. bd. 1980-81); Democrat; Catholic. Ofc: Superior Ct. 240 Church St Salinas 93901

OFFENHAUSER, BOB RAY, architect; b. Feb. 8, 1927, Los Angeles; s. O.D. and Laura (Putney) O.; m. Katherine, Apr. 17, 1958; 1 son, Madison b. 1960; edn: B.Arch., USC, 1952. Career: architect prin. Bob Ray Offenhauser & Assocs., archtl. and interior design co., 1982-, incorporated, now pres. Offenhauser Assocs., Inc. (archtl. firm), and Offenhauser Decorating Corp. (int. design); mem./founder L.A. Music Center, New Mus. of Contemporary /Art,, L.A. County Art Museum, Fellow of Contemporary Art; club: Valley Hunt (Pasadena); mil: USCG; Republican; rec: gardening. Res: 445 Columbia St South Pasadena 91030

OGBODO, CHRISTOPHER CHIME, accountant; b. April 5, 1952, Enugu Anambra, State of Nigeria; s. James Ngene and Comfort Nneoge (Nkwuo) O.; m. Ukamaka, Dec. 30, 1981; child: Ifeoma b. 1984; edn: BS, Armstrong Coll. Berkeley 1979; MBA, cand., CSU Hayward; CPA, Calif. 1982. Career: auditor Adams, Grant, White & Co. CPAs, Oakland 1979-82; controller Powell Chemicals Inc., So. San Francisco 1982-83; sole practitioner Christopher Chime Ogbodo & Co. CPA, Oakland 1983–; mem: Am. Inst. CPAs, Calif. Soc. CPAs. Res: 6853 Simson St. Oakland 94605 Ofc: Christopher Chime Ogbodo & Co., CPA, 4223 Telegraph Ave. Oakland 94609

OGG, WILSON REID, poet, curator, lawyer, educator; b. Feb. 26, 1928, Alhambra; s. James Brooks and Mary Newton (Wilson) O.; edn: BA, UC Berkeley 1949; JD, UCB Boalt Hall Sch. of Hall 1952; admitted Calif. State Bar (1955), lic. R.E. Broker (1974), Calif. Comm. Colls. tchg. creds., law, real estate and social scis. (1976). Career: psychology instr. 25th Station Hosp., Taequ, Korea, also English instr. Taequ English Language Inst., 1953; pvt. practice of law, 1955-78; arbitrator Am. Arb. Assn., 1963-; senior ed. Continuing Edn. of the Bar, Univ. of Calif., 1958-63; secty. and mem. bd. trustees First Unitarian Ch. of Berkeley 1957-58; pres. Calif. Soc. of Psychical Study, 1963-65; treas. The World Univ. 1977-79; dir. of admissions The Internat. Soc. for Philosophical Enquiry 1981-84; poet, curator-in-residence Pinebrook, 1964–; honors: Cultural Doctorate in Philosophy of Law, The World Univ. Roundtable (1984), life patron Internat. Biographical Assn.; mem. State Bar of Calif., Am. Arb. Assn., Am. Assn. of Finl. Profls., World Future Soc. (profl. mem.), Bar Assn. of S.F., City Commons Club of Berkeley, Am. Soc. for Psychical Research, AAAS, Parapsychol. Assn., Berkeley Archtl. Heritage Assn., Artists Embassy Internat., The World Literary Acad., THe Ina Coolbreth Circle, Am. Biographical Inst. Research Assn. (deputy gov.), Grand Ambassador of Achievement, ABIRA, Press Club of S.F., Commonwealth Club, Town Hall of Calif., Faculty Club (UCB), Elks, Masonic Orders, Am. Legion, VFW, Amvets, Mensa, Triple Wine Soc., Lawyers in Mensa; publs: senior editor var. law handbooks (UC Regents, 1958-63), var. articles in J. of the Internat. Soc. of Philosophical Enquiry (1981-84), poem: My Escaping Self (2d pl. winner, World Inst. of Achievement Newsletter, 12/85), poems: Springtide, Bitter Harvest, & Lost Innocence (pub. WLA Newsletter 11/85), poems: To Touch with Love, & Interlude (pub. IBC Newsletter Winter 85); mil: cpl. US Army 1952-54, Commendn. Rib.; Libertarian; Unitarian; rec: theater, gardening, landscape & archtl. design. Address: 1104 Keith Ave Berkeley 94708-1607

OGLE, PROCTOR EDWARD, JR., investment executive; b. Dec. 20, 1936, Inglewood; s. Edward Proctor and Allene Emma (Blumenthal) O.; m. Elizabeth Myers, March 28, 1958; children: Kathryn, b. 1959; Wendy and Terry (twins), b. 1961; edn: BA, USC 1964; MA, Claremont Grad. Sch. 1980, Exec. Mgmt. Cert., 1979; Career: transp. engr. State of California, Los Angeles 1956-64; zone mgr. Investment Diversified Svcs., Pasadena 1964-66; acct. exec. Merrill Lynch, Pierce, Fenner & Smith, Pasadena 1966-72; mgr. capital placement dept. Clark Dodge, Los Angeles 1972-74; v.p. Security Pacific Nat. Bank, Los Angeles 1974-84; sr. v.p. The Pacific Century Gp., Newport Beach 1984-86; deputy mgr. Brown Bros. Harriman & Co. L.A. 1986–; corp. accts. coord. United Way; pres. Claremont Grad. Sch. Alumni Assn.; honors: Sales Execs. Club, Merrill Lynch, 1971, Millionaire Club and Presidents Club, Investors Diversified Svcs. 1965; mem: Pasadena Bond Club; Town Hall of Calif., Pasadena Tournament of Roses Assn., Los Angeles Bond Club, LA Soc. of Fin. Analysts, Fin. Analysts Fedn., USC Commerce Assocs., Balboa Bay Club, Jonathan Club; Lincoln Club; publs: art., Los Angeles Mag 1979; Republican; Protestant; rec: golf, tennis, photog. Res: 3336 Alderly Lane, Orange 92667 Ofc: Brown Bros. Harriman & Co. 444 S Flower St Los Angeles 90071

OGLESBY, MYRNA LEE, lawyer; b. Sept. 29, 1935, Ukiah; d. Earl Victor and Ruby Alice (Phillips) Snook; m. Neal V. Oglesby, June 13, 1964; children: Keith b. 1951, Deborah b. 1953, Gerald b. 1956, Donald b. 1956, Linda b. 1959; admitted Calif. State Bar 1983. Career: office mgr. law firm Rawles, Hinkle, Carter, Brigham, Gaustad & Behnke in Ukiah, 1976-83, assoc. atty., 1983-85, partner 1985–; (studied for the bar exam. in-house with law firm; first to pass in sev. years without formal schooling) mem. bd. dirs. Lawyer Referral Service of Lake & Mendocino Counties; hearing ofcr. panel Mendocino Co. Dept. Mental Health; mem. Mendocino County, Calif., Am. Bar Assns., Calif. Women Lawyers, Calif. Trial Lawyers Assn., The Assn. of Trial Lawyers of Am.; clubs: Toastmasters Internat., Soroptimist Internat., Bus. & Profl. Women; Democrat; Prot.; rec: travel, cruises. Res: 34 Fairview Ct., Ukiah 95482 Ofc: Rawles, Hinkle, Carter, Brigham, Gaustad & Behnke 169 Mason St, Ste 300, POB 720, Ukiah 95482

O'GRADY, JAMES EMMETT, II, certified public accountant; b. Nov. 7, 1947, Glendale; s. James Emmett and Ruth Hertha (Haas) O'G.; m. Janelle, Feb. 28, 1970; children: Deborah b. 1972, Kristen b. 1975, Bryan b. 1980, James b. 1985; edn: AA, Glendale Coll. 1967, BS, Fresno State Univ. 1970; CPA, 1973. Career: jr. to audit supvr. Coopers & Lybrand CPAs 1970-76; acctg. mgr. Am. Broadcasting Co. Inc. 1976-77, asst. dir. of acctg. 1977-79; dir. fin. controls ABC Television, West Coast 1979-82; dir. fin. controls ABC Television and ABC Entertainment, West Coast 1982–; treas., bd. dirs. Tel-Rad Employees Fed. Credit Union 1977-; mem: Am. Inst. CPAs, Fin. and Mgmt. Employees in Entertainment Assn., Calif. Inst. CPAs; mil: sgt. USAR 1970-76; Republican; Catholic; rec: family, camping, woodworking. Res: 4809 Grand Ave. La Canada Flintridge 91011 Ofc: Capital Cities/ABC Inc., 2040 Ave of the Stars Century City 90067

O'HALLORAN, LAVERNE M. KATHLEEN, realtor; b. Nov. 15, 1921, Laurium, Mich.; d. Joseph W. and Della K. (Gervais) Shaffer; m. John R. O'Halloran Jr., July 15, 1942; children: Sheila Anne (Stoll), Gregory John, Michael John, Maureen Therese (Benelli), Sean Thomas, Margaret Eileen. Career: pres. C&R Investments 1973-74; currently, realtor Kathy O'Halloran Realty, Fresno; mem: Infant of Prague Adoption Agency Aux. 1954-, secty. 1955; pres. Central Calif. CDL 1959-64; pres. Calif. Citizen for Decent Lit. 1961-63; bd. dirs. Nat. Citizens for Decent Lit. 1963-64; Calif. Arts. Soc.; Fresno Art. Ctr.; Republican: chmn., Fresno Co. United Republicans 1962; area coord. Clean Campaign Ballot Initiative 1966; Catholic: pres. Sacred Heart Mothers Club; secty. Sacred Heart Altar Soc.; St. Agnes Svc. Guild 1983; secty. Deanery, Nat. Council Catholic Women; pres. Legion of Mary, Jr. Presidium; rec: gardening, sewing, golf. Address: 3503 N Bond Fresno 93726

OHLUND, RHYNER JAY, company president; b. Nov. 22, 1926, Los Angeles; s. Rhyner John and Mabel Violet (Anderson) O.; m. Lois Rath, Sept. 14, 1958; chidren: Kathryn b. 1960, Robert b 1961; edn: BBS, Woodbury Univ. 1952. Career: br. mgr. Lamson & Gilbert 1952-58; photog. Edwards Sch. of Photog. 1958-61; bus. forms salesman Moore Business Forms 1961-63, Dataform Inc. 1963-71; ptr. Calco Co. 1971-79; pres. Calco Business Systems Inc. 1979–; Cert. Forms Cons. 1978-; bd. dirs. Nat. Bus. Forms Assn. 198-; chmn. Buckle Up Video Assn.; recipient Outstanding Svc. Award, Angelus Sanitary Can Machine Co. (1980-82); mem: Phi Theta Pi (pres. 1951), Pot O'Gold Investment Club (pres. 1963, 1965, 1967, 1969), Nat. Bus. Forms Assn. (Board mem. of Year 1971; Conv. Plnng. Com., Conv. Hospitality Com., Future Plnng. Com.); civic: Buckle Up Video Assn. pub. service orgn. (chmn. 1986); publs: contrib. ed., Form Mag. 1979-; mil: signalman USN 1944-46; Republican; rec: sailing, skiing, golf; raise and breed Arabian horses on Rancho, Bar-O Arabians. Res: 10671 Quail Springs Rd., Rancho Carillo, Murietta (Mail: P.O. Box 128 San Juan Capistrano 92693-0128) Ofc: Calco Business Systems Inc., 231-C Foundation Ave. La Habra 90631

OKAMOTO, MASAO, architect; b. Aug. 20, 1949, Tokyo, Japan; s. Shigekazu and Midori (Kosaka) O.; m. Kaeko, Feb. 16, 1982; children: Lisa b. 1983, Louie b. 1986, Mickie b. 1986; edn: B.Eng., Waseda Univ. 1974; Reg. Architect, Calif. 1985. Career: lectr. Sch. of Arch., Univ. of Natal, Rep. of South Africa 1972; chief arch. Shimizu Constrn. Co. Ltd, Tokyo, Japan 1974-81; v.p. Shimizu America Corp., Los Angeles 1981-84, v.p./principal architect 1985–; awards: Residential Design competition (1973); mem. Am. Inst. of Arch., Japanese Inst. of Arch.; publ: Architect's Data Book (Japanese Inst. of Arch.). Ofc: Shimizu America Corp. 261 S Figueroa St Ste 120 Los Angeles 90012

OKANO, STEVEN YASUAKI, executive search co. president, financial planner; b. Feb. 24, 1955, Berkeley; s. William K. and Kimi (Mizuhara) O.; m. Hiroko C. Nishikado, July 28, 1979; children: Jennifer Kiyomi, b. 1980, Lindsey Takimi, b. 1983; edn: BA in environmental/ urban plnng., CSU San Jose 1977, grad. work in cybernetics, 1978-9; Regis. Rep., SEC 1984; grad. TMSI, Total Money Mgmt. Tng. 1982. Career: profl. employment cons. (PEC)/ br. mgr. General Employment Enterprises Inc. (oldest emplymt firm USA), 1978-82; sr. exec. recruiter EDP World Inc. (Bay Area exec. recruiting firm), 1982-83; acct. exec./ finl. plnnr. Thomson McKinnon Securities Inc., San Francisco 1983–; seminar spkr on career plnng., fin. plnng.; pres. Strategic Pursuits Personnel Svcs. 1984–; prin. S.Y. Okano & Assocs. Exec. Search 1984–; awards: num. profl. awards, Presidents Club (2), Dale Carnegie Sales Presentation Award; 1st Pl. Architl. Design, City of Berkeley 1973; mem: Rotary Internat. (youth career fair orgnzr.), Asian Pacific Personnel Assn., Nat. Assn. Securities Dealers (NASD), Asian Business Network, PEC, San Francisco CofC; past bd. dirs. Japanese Am. Citizens League; Japanese Am. Youth advisor; basketball coach Asian Am. League; mem. Mid-Penin. Citizens for Fair Housing (investigator); orgnzr. youth-oriented volleyball tournaments; fundraiser/vol. various sr. citizen projects; Democrat (cand. El Cerrito City Council 1980); Buddhist. Res: 100 Aralia Ct. Hercules 94547 Ofcs: Strategic Planning Personnel Svcs./ Exec. Search, 2554 Martin Luther King Ave

Berkeley 94704; S.Y. bkano & Assocs. Exec. Search, 180 Grand Ave Ste 1060 Oakland 94612; Thomson McKinnon Securities Inc. 50 Fremont St. San Francisco 94105

O'KEEFE, JOHN DUGAN, aerospace technical manager and research scientist; b. Nov. 7, 1937, Anaconda, Mont.; s. John Michael and Elda Kathleen (Lundgren) O.; m. Christina Morey, Apr. 11, 1965; two sons, Ian, b. 1969, Cameron, b. 1973; edn: BS in physics, CSU Long Beach 1962, MS in physics, USC 1965; PhD, planetary physics, UCLA 1976. Career: research physicist Space Sciences Labs., North American Rockwell, Downey 1962-69; research physicist Systems Group Research Staff, TRW, Redondo Beach 1976-80, program mgr. High Energy Laser Projects, 1980-83, chief optical scientist for High Energy Lasers, 1981, mgr. Optics & Directed Energy Lab., TRW (leading orgn. in USA in High Energy Lasers), 1983-; research assoc. in planetary scis., Calif. Inst. of Tech.; mem. Optical Soc. of Am., Am. Geophysical Union; works: invention of a laser resonator concept for space based lasers; research papers on the role of meteorite impact on the evolution of the solar system and the periodic extinction of biota on Earth; Republican; Catholic; rec: minicomputers. Res: 418 Prospect Ave Manhattan Beach 90266 Ofc: TRW, One Space Park, Redondo Beach 90278

OKEN, STAN, co. executive; b. Aug. 14, 1928, Chicago, Ill.; s. Harry and Bertha (Goldberg) O.; children: Larry b. 1951, Roy b. 1954, Nancy b. 1955, 4 step children, 6 foster children; edn: BS, CSU Los Angeles 1954; Pepperdine Univ. 1984. Career: pres., chm. bd., CEO Western Camps Inc. dba Wonder Valley Ranch Resort, River Way Ranch Camp, Valley West Advtg. Co.; pres. Fresno City Co. Visitor Bureau; pres. Internat. De SKAL; former tchr./ baseball & basketball coach Los Angeles Sch. Dist. and Los Angeles City Coll.; honors: named outstanding mem. Central Calif. Hospitality Assn. (1985), Merit award Fresno City Co. CofC (1985), appreciation for support of pvt. independent camps, Am. Camping Assn. (1985); mem: Internat. De SKAL, Fresno City Co. CofC, Visalia CofC; mil: pfc US Army 1947-48; Republican; Jewish; rec: tennis, golf. Res: 6450 Elwood Sanger 93657 Ofc: Western Camps Inc., P.O. Box 71 Star Route Sanger 93658

OKUDA, KARL KAORU, acupuncturist, fisheries technologist; b. Oct. 24, 1929, Kyoto, Japan, nat. US cit. 1978; s. Chozaburo and Sada (Hata) O.; m. Tazuko Motohashi, Jan. 29, 1961; children: Mika b. 1962, Kathelen b. 1962, Mari b. 1970; edn: BS, Tokyo Univ. of Fisheries 1953, MS, 1954; OMD, PhD, Samra Univ. of Oriental Med. 1985. certified acupuncturist Calif. 1976. Career: captain, fleet mgr. Aurora Austal S.A. 1954-60; Argentina fleet & ops. mgr. Shinyo Fisheries Co. Ltd. Japan, Surinam 1960-65; mng. dir. Toyo Shrimp Co. Ltd. Japan, Malaysia 1965-67, Kagawa Godo Fisheries Co. Japan, Guyana 1966-70; v.p. Banoku Fisheries Inc. USA 1967-71; pres. Okuda Sea Foods Inc. USA 1971-85; owner Okuda's Acupuncture Ctr. 1979-; mktg. advisor, proj. mgr. Food & Agriculture of UN, Rome, Italy, Brazil, Tanzania 1977-79; mem: No. Am. Acupuncture Assn. 1983, Japan Consulting Engr. Assn. 1965; research: diagnosis by Digital O-Ring Test and selection of applicable treatment in acupuncture 1984; mil: Japanese naval aviation 1945; Republican; Zen Buddhist; rec: flying, fishing. Res: 13534 Rockway Dr Baldwin Park 91706 Ofc: Okuda's Acupuncture Ctr. 15541 Beach Blvd, Ste B, Westminster 92683

OLDHAM, MAXINE JERNIGAN, realtor; b. Oct. 13, 1923, Whittier; d. John K. and Lela H. (Mears) Jernigan; m. Laurance Oldham, Oct. 28, 1941; children: John Laurence, b. 1942; edn: UC San Diego 1951-80; Western State Univ. 1976-77; LaSalle Ext. 1977-78; AA, San Diego City Coll. 1974. Desig: GRI, Grad. Realtors Inst., CAR 1978. Career: Pacific Telephone, S.D. 1952-57; US Civil Svc. Commn., US Naval Aux., Air Sta., Brown Field, Chula Vista 1957-58; San Diego Bd. of Edn., 1958-59; real estate sales 1966-; realtor Shelter Island Realty, S.D. 1977-; mem: Nat. & Calif. Assns. Realtors; Apt. Owners Assns.; S.D. Bd. Realtors; Calif. Assn. GRI; S.D. Genealogical Soc.; Internat. Fed. Univ. Women; Native Daus. of Am. Revolution; Colonial Dames Seventeenth Century; Republican; Catholic; rec: painting, music, theater. Res: 3348 Lowell St San Diego 9106 Ofc: Shelter Island Realty, 2810 Lytton St San Diego 92106

OLIVA, REMEDIOS DY M., accountant; b. Feb. 17, 1940, Philippines, nat. US cit. 1980; d. Juan M. and Dulce T. (Dy Soco) Martinez; m. Jesus Oliva, Sept. 24, 1965; children: Vince b. 1966, Jessica b. 1968, Jesus, Jr. b. 1976; edn: BSBA in acctg., Ateneo de Naga, 1961. Career: chief acct. Manhattan Mdsg. Co. Inc., Phila. 1961-64; senior auditor Merchants' Aid Bus. Agency, CPAs, Phila. 1965-69; senior acctg. analyst Continental Ill. Nt. Bank, Chgo. 1969-77; senior acct., asst. acctg. mgr., then gen. acctg. mgr. Japan Line U.S.A. Ltd., Los Angeles 1978-82; billing mgr. Marine Terminals Corp., L.B. 1982-84; acct., tax preparer, acctg. & bookkeeping License Bus. Agency, Cypress 1985-; A/R mgr. LAACO Inc., 1985-; mem: Water Transp. Assn. (acctg. ofcr. 1980-84), Internat. Hospitality Accts., Filamerican Assn. (named outstanding treas., Chgo. 1976), Phil. Accts., Bicol Assn.; rec: reading, writing. Res: 9292 Grindlay St Cypress 90630 Ofc: LAACO Inc. 431 Seventh St Los Angeles 90017

OLIVEIRA, MANUEL JOHN, architect; b. Dec. 5, 1946, Hanford; s. Manuel Maria and Elizabeth O.; m. Evelina Pedro, June 25, 1983; children: Nellie b. 1965, Manuel b. 1970; edn: AA, Coll. of the Sequoias 1973; Reg. Architect, Calif. St. Board 1982. Career: draftsman E.H. Wilkerson, Visalia 1972-74; draftsman, project mgr. Octagon Assocs., Visalia 1974-85; architect prin., Tulare 1985-; mem. Am. Inst. of Architects, San Joaquin Chpt. (pres. Sequoia Sect. 1985); works: photographs for book "Exeter Now-Then" by John A. Mangini (1976); mil: s/sgt. US Air Force, Commendn. medal; Republican;

Catholic; rec: photog., computer pgmmg. Address: Manuel J. Oliveira 817 North N Pl Tulare 93274

OLIVER, ANTHONY THOMAS, JR., lawyer; b. July 19, 1929, San Jose; s. Anthony T. and Josephine G. (Bem) O.; m. Beverly J. Wirz, Jan. 27, 1952; 2m. Margaret E. Gurke, Mar. 31, 1984; children: Jeanne M. Hall, b. 1953; Marilyn M. Oliver, b. 1954; Cynthia M. Eschardies, 1958; Michelle M. Rogan, b. 1960; edn: BS, Santa Clara Univ. 1951; JD, 1953. Career: asst. counsel Bank of America Legal Dept., Los Angeles 1953-57; assoc. atty. Taylor & Barker, Los Angeles 1957-58; assoc. atty. John F. O'Hara, Los Angeles 1958-63; senior ptr. Parker, Milliken, Clark, O'Hara & Samuelian 1963-; honors: Edwin J. Owens Lawyer of the Year Award, Univ. of Santa Clara Coll. of Law 1976; mem: Am., Calif. and Los Angeles County (chmn. Labor Law Sect. 1985-86) bar assns., Am. Arbitration Assn., Chancery Club, Indsl. Rels. Research Assn., Nat. Guard Assn., Town Hall of Calif., University Club (LA); bd. vis. Santa Clara Coll. of Law; co-author: Affirmative Action Programs and Compliance, Advising Calif. Employers, Calif. CEB; contbg. ed. Personnel Journ.; mil: lt. col. USAR ret.; Republican; Catholic. Res: 2606 Canada Blvd., Unit 201, Glendale 91208 Ofc: Parker, Milliken, Clark, O'Hara & Samuelian, 333 So. Hope St., 27th Floor, Los Angeles 90071

OLIVER, MICHAEL, lawyer, creative management co. executive; b. March 15, 1930, London, England; s. Joshua and Cecilia (Balen) O.; edn: grad. St. Paul's Sch., London 1947, The Law Soc. Sch. of Law, London 1952; Solicitor of Supreme Ct. of England & Wales, 1952; admitted State Bar of Calif. 1983. Career: founding/sr. partner Berger, Oliver & Co., Solicitors, London 1961-82, cons. 1982-; assoc. Armstrong, Hendler & Hirsch, attys., Los Angeles 1982-83; exec. vice pres. Internat. Creative Management Inc., Los Angeles 1983-; chmn. and mem. Council- Nat. Youth Theatre of G.Brit.; mem. Council, Fin. and Gen. Purposes Com.- The London Acad. of Music and Dramatic Art; chmn., trustee Theatre Projects Trust Ltd.; mem. The Brit. Acad. of Film and TV Arts Assn. of Independent Producers, The Copinger Soc. (entertainment indus. lawyers), The Permanent Com. of the Entertainment Indus.; dir. Calif. Youth Theatre; rec: music, reading. Res: 2270 Maravilla Dr., Los Angeles 90068 Ofc: 8899 Beverly Blvd Los Angeles 90048

OLMOS, MARIO GUERRA, superior court judge; b. July 24, 1946, Nogales, Ariz.; s. Fidel Ramirez and Dolores Amaro (Guerra) O.; m. Mary Louise Frampton; children: Daniel b. 1978, Margaret b. 1981; edn: AA, Reedley Coll. 1966; AB, UC Berkeley 1968, JD, Boalt Hall 1971. Career: staff atty. Calif. Rural Legal Assistance 1971-74; ptnr. law firm Olmos & Frampton, 1974-83; justice court judge Parlier Justice Ct. 1975-77, Parlier-Selma Judicial Dist. 1977-83; superior ct. judge, Fresno County 1983-; mem. Calif. Judicial Council 1983-: Ct. Mgmt. and Superior Ct. (chmn. 1985-) coms., Exec. Com. (1985-); mem. Calif. Judges Assn. 1975-; honors: Phi Beta Kappa; citizen of year Latino Peace Ofcrs. Assn. 1983; Democrat; Catholic; rec: travel, reading. Ofc: 1100 Van Ness Ave, Rm 550, Fresno 93721

OLOUMI, MOSTAFA, engineer; b. Oct. 8, 1956, Gorgan, Iran; s. Khalil and Raya O.; m. Peggy Dowd, July 6, 1980; edn: BSCE, CSU Long Beach 1980; MSCE, Univ. So. Calif. 1984; Reg. Profl. Engr. Calif. 1982; Reg. Structural Engr., Calif (1986). Career: engr. Gouvis Engrg. Long Beach 1978-81; senior engr. Moffatt & Nichol Engrs. Long Beach 1981-83; prin. ADS Consulting Engrs. Sunset Beach 1983-; mem: Am. Soc. Civil Engrs., Strl. Engrs. Assn. of So. Calif.; rec: reading, travel. Ofc: 16431 Pacific Coast Hwy Sunset Beach 90742

OLSASKY, JOANN MARIE, real estate broker; b. Dec. 31, 1933, Des Moines, Iowa; d. Andrew Joseph and Genevieve (McKeigh) Feeley; m. Robert Olsasky, Sept. 26, 1953; children: Connie Louie b. 1956, Summer Marie b. 1959; edn: spl. courses, West Valley Coll., Saratoga; Calif. lic. Real Estate Broker, Notary; profl. desig: Realtor, CREA. Career: real estate sales Andrews Realty, Des Moines, Iowa 1967; escrow clk. Duc & Elliott Constrn. Co., San Jose 1970; real estate broker (comml. & indsl.) Value Realty, San Jose 1974; R.E. broker (new subdiv. sales) Jules Duc Constrn. Co., Los Gatos 1980, Shapell Industries of No. Calif., Milpitas 1984; owner/broker Olsasky & Co. (spec. in sales, mktg., subdiv. devel.), San Ramon 1984-; recipient Mame awards, Sales and Mktg. Council of No. Calif.; mem. Contra Costa Bd. of Realtors; past mem. Iowa, Los Gatos, and San Jose bds. of realtors, Los Gatos Exchange Club; Republican; Catholic; rec: gardening, renovation of old Victorian historical bldg. Res: 140 Via Santa Maria, Los Gatos 95030 Ofc: Olsasky & Company 19799 San Ramon Valley Blvd San Ramon 94583

OLSEN, DOUGLAS CRAIG, mechanical contractor; b. May 22, 1948, Eureka; s. Galen B. and Lilly Marie O.; m. Dera Novelo, Aug. 22, 1970; children: Matthew b. 1972, Jason b. 1974. Career: sheet metal wkr. 1966; v.p. Olsen's Heating & Sheet Metal, Eureka 1971, pres. 1977-; mem. Humboldt County Builders Exchange; club: Baywood Golf & Country; Republican; Episcopal; rec: golf, fishing. Res: 691 Hilma Dr Eureka 95501 Ofc: Olsen's Htg & Sheet Metal 417 W Wabash Ave Eureka 95501

OLSEN, STEVEN KENT, dentist; b. Nov. 20, 1944, Spanish Fork, Utah; s. Earl Clarence and Adela (Faux) O.; m. Karin Hurst, Oct. 5, 1984; 1 son, Christopher Steven b. 1984; edn: L.A. Valley Coll. 1969-70, Univ. of Utah 1967-68; BS, Brigham Young Univ. 1969; DDS, Univ. of Pacific 1974. Career: ptnr., practice dentistry spec. in surg. and endodontic procedures Brooks & Olsen, Salt Lake City, 1974; gen. practice dentistry, San Francisco 1974, solo 1974-76, ptnr. Olsen, Hack & Pooley 1977-83, ptnr. Olsen & Bergloff 1984-; chmn. bd. Am. Dentists Ins. Corp., Grand Cayman, W.I., 1978-81; dir. Wilks

& Topper, Inc., S.F.; instr. Univ. of Pacific, (1978-), cons., dir., editor corr. course, Calif. Inst. for Continuing Edn., S.F. (1981-), instr. Stanford Inst., Palo Alto (1979-82); med. staff Latter-day Saints Hosp.; honors: Alpha Epsilon Delta (life), Good Citizenship medal SAR (1963); polio pioneer 1954 initial group; mem: Assn. Coll. of Physicians and Surgeons, Am. Dental Assn., Calif. Dental Assn., Utah Dental Assn.; club: Physicians and Surgeons (SF). Res: 385 Old La Honda Rd Woodside 94062 Ofc: 1 Embarcadero Center 2205 San Francisco 94111

OLSEN, VIGGO NORSKOV, university president; b. July 18, 1916, Copenhagen; m. Sept. 1949; edn: BA, Andrews Univ. 1948, MA, 1950, B.Div., 1951; Th.M., Princeton Theol. Sem. 1960; PhD, Univ. of London 1966; Th.D., Univ. Basel, Switz. 1968. Career: chmn. dept. of Religion, academic dean Newbold Coll., Bracknell, England 1954-59, pres. 1960-66; prof. church history Loma Linda Univ. 1968–, chmn. dept. of Religion 1971-72, dean Coll. of Arts & Scis., provost 1972-74, pres. 1974–; Riverside City Mgrs. Group 1974-; Inland Empire Higher Edn. Council 1974-; Inland Action Bd. 1974-; honors: Distng. Faculty Lectr., Loma Linda Univ. 1972; Andrew Univ. Alumnus of the Year, 1973; American of Year, Am. Religious Town Hall Inc. 1981; mem: British Ecclesiastical History Soc., Am. Church History Soc., Soc. for Reformation Studies, Am. Council on Edn., Am. Assn. of Presidents of Ind. Colls. and Univ., Assn. of Ind. Calif. Colls. & Univs.; author: The New Testament Logia on Divorce, 1971; John Foxe and the Elizabethan Church, 1973; Seventh-Day Adventist;. Res: 24958 Huron St. Loma Linda 92354 Ofc: Loma Linda Univ., Loma Linda 92350

OLSON, CARL ALEXIUS, consultant; b. Oct. 24, 1919, Newcastel; s. Carl Alexius and Anna Antonia (Olsen) O.; em. Monna Latta, June 14, 1942; children: Chris b. 1946, Carol b. 1949; edn: BSCE, UC Berkeley 1941; Profl. Engr., Calif. 1978. Career: jr. engr. to chief engr. Kaiser Shipyards 1941-46; chief insp. to chief engr. engring. div. Kaiser Fraizer Corp. 1946-54; chief engr. to exec. v.p. & dir. of ops. Industrias Kaiser, Argentina 1955-68; mgr. aluminnum projects Kasier Engrs. 1968-69, v.p. aluminum & chem. projects 1969-83; pres. MTR Internat., Alamo 1983–; dir. Indsl. Kaiser, rgentina 1964-68; dir. Hallanger Rngrs. 1972-77; dir., treas. Am. Baptist Homes of the West; mem: Am. Inst. Mining Engrs., Soc. of Automotive Engrs., Diablo Country Club, Berkeley Engring. Alumni; mil: 2nd lt. US Army 1941; Republican; Baptist; rec: gardening, golf. Res: 11 Margaret Ln. Danville 94526 Ofc: MTR Internat., 3158 Danville Blvd. Alamo 94507

OLSON, DAVID ALFRED, marketing executive; b. June 6, 1957, Minneapolis, Minn.; s. Roy Hugo and Cammie Louise (Nelson) O.; edn: BSBA, Univ. of Colo. 1980, BS, Arch.Eng., 1980; MBA, cand., Univ. of San Diego 1981-; Reg. Profl. Engr., Calif. Career: design engr. Ellebrbe Assoc., Minneapolis, Minn. 1977-80; assoc. engr. Randall/ Lamb Assoc., San Diego 1980-82; mktg. engr. Honeywell Inc., San Diego 1982–; dir. South Platte Devel. Corp. 1981-; honors: Distng. Young Men Among Collegiate Frats. 1979; Honeywell Corp. VIP and SOQ Club Awards 1983; mem: Soc. for Mktg. Profl. Svcs., Illuminating Engring. Soc., City Club, Kappa Sigma (v.p.), Edina Country Club, St. Croix Yacht Club (v.commodore), Child Abuse Prevention Found. of San Diego; works: Roadway Lighting research paper, Illuminating Engring. Soc. 1979; Republican; Lutehran; rec: golf, skiing, ice hockey. Res: 8304 Via Sonoma #97 La Jolla 92037

OLSON, SCOTT BRADLEY, SR., computer consulting co. executive; b. July 26, 1956, St. Paul, Minn.; s. Lawrence Stanley and Patricia Lorraine (Sedin) O.; m. Paula Diane Butcher, Jan. 14, 1978; children: Scott Jr. b. 1978, Kenneth b. 1980; edn: BSBA, CSU Sacramento 1978; Ltd. Svc. Tchg. Cred., Calif. Career: sys. pgmmr. Cable Data, Sacramento 1975-79; sys. installation mgr. System Integrators Inc., Sacramento 1979-80; corp. sys. analyst J.P. Scripps Newspapers, San Diego 1980-85; owner, CFO The Mail Room, Redding 1983–; currently, owner, ptr., dir. software devel. Advantage Computer Sys., Redding; tchr. Am. River Coll., Sacramento 1979-81; Republican; Assemblies of God. Ofc: Advantage Computer Systems, 1800 Pine St. Redding 96001

OLSON, THOMAS FRANKLIN, lawyer; b. July 8, 1930, Red Oak, Iowa; s. Merrill Arthur and Ruth Jane (Wilson) O.; m. Jeanne Rodenberg, July 10, 1954; children: Jane b. 1961, Paul b. 1964; edn: BA, St. Univ. of Iowa 1952; LLB, Boalt Hall UC Berkeley 1958; admitted Calif. State Bar (1959), US Supreme Ct. (1974), US Ct. Appeals (D.C. Circuit 1980, 9th Circuit 1959), US Dist. Ct. (No. Dist. Calif. 1959, E. Dist. Calif. 1977). Career: asst. counsel Calif. Farm Bureau Fedn. and affil. cos., 1958-70, general counsel, 1970–; mem: Nat. Assn. of Independent Insurers, Des Plaines, Ill. Medical Malpractice Com. (1974-76), Gen. Liability Market Com. (1976-80); vol. atty. Berkeley Neighborhood Legal Services 1966-70; honors: Hon. Life mem. Berkeley City Commons Club (1980), Omicron Delta Kappa (1951), Phi Eta Sigma (1949); mem: Calif. Bar Assn. (chair Corp. Law Depts. Com. 1983-84), Phi Alpha Delta profl. legal frat. 1956-58 (v.p. 1957-58), Berkeley-Albany Bar Assn. (pres. 1979-80); civic: Rotary, Berkeley City Commons Club (dir. 1977-80, pres. 1979), Calif.- Nev. United Methodist Found. (dir. 1978-86, chair 1980-86), Fred Finch Youth Ctr. (dir. 1972-80, pres. 1979-80), United Ministries in Higher Edn. of No. Calif. and Nev. (dir. 1968-70, pres. 1970); publs: chapter "Risks and Liabilities," Calif. Farm and Ranch Law (Calif. CEB 1967), contbr. law reviews; mil: 1st lt. US Air Force 1952-54; Republican; United Methodist; rec: philately (Egypt, Bermuda, Sweden), atty. Brit. Caribbean Philatelic Study Group (1973-), regl. dir. Scandinavian Collectors Club (1971-86), pres. Golden Gate Chpt. 21 (1971-73). Res: 4 Woodmont Ct Berkeley 94708 Ofc: California Farm Bureau Fedn. 1601 Exposition Blvd Sacramento 95815

OLSON, THOMAS H(ILTON), psychologist; b. Nov. 5, 1945, Oak Park, Ill.; s. Theodore F. and Juanita K. Olson; 1 dau., Erika b. 1973; edn: BS, Univ. Utah 1967; MBA, UC Los Angeles 1969; DBA, USC 1977; lic. Psychologist, Calif. BMQA 1983. Career: psychologist and consultant, self empl.; past pos. Arthur, Young & Co. 1968-69, Booz-Allen & Hamilton 1969-70, Los Angeles Technical Services 1970-73, Calif. State Univ. 1973-76, Univ. Calif. 1976-77, San Diego St. Univ. 1977-78, Gen. Telephone & Electronics 1978-80, Rockwell Internat. Corp. 1980-86; vis. lectr. USC; honors: Beta Gamma Sigma, NSF grant co-investigator; mem: Acad. of Mgmt., Am. Psychol. Assn., Human Resources Planning Soc., Organization Devel. Network, Personnel Testing Council of So. Calif.; civic: commnr. Board of Zoning Adjustment, City of Manhattan Beach; publs: 15+ empirical & theoretical studies, papers, book chapts. Ofc: POB 3166 Manhattan Beach 90266

O'MALEY, OWEN EUGENE, JR., pilot, flight operations executive; b. Dec. 28, 1926, Culver City; s. Owen E., Sr. and Mary Margaret (Springmann) O'M.; m. Chris, Mar. 30, 1968; children: Mary b. 1957, Owen b. 1959, Julianna b. 1974; edn: AA, Los Angeles City Coll. 1956; spl. courses Westlawn Sch. of Yacht Design, Embry-Riddle; desig: FAA lic. Flt. Instr. (1961), Air Transport Pilot (1966), Helicopter Pilot (1968), Pilot Proficiency Examiner (1985). Career: clk. Von's Grocery 1951-60, sales Libby Foods 1960-61, Bell Brand Foods 1961-62; flt. instr. Santa Monica Flyers, 1962-65; pilot Continental Air Service, S.E. Asia 1965-67; pilot Garrett Corp., 1967-81; self empl. cons. Corporate Aviation Services, 1981-83; mgr. flt. ops. Global Airways Inc., 1981–; mgr. Shillelagh Rock Ranch 1981-, plt. Mail, Etc. Ltd. 1985-; Proficiency Examiner 1985-; honors: NBAA Million Miler, sev. internat. awards for flt. safety; apptd. El Dorado County Aviation Com.; mem: NBAA, Flight Safety Found., Shingle Springs CofC, Am. Quarter Horse Assn., Ponderosa Equestrians, Jet Squires, Santa Monica Yacht Club; creative: copyrights in aviation related computer pgms., aircraft & auto restorations (1954-); mil: cpl. US Army 1956-59, Combat Inf. Unit Award; Republican; rec: sailing, computers, quarterhorses. Ofc: Global Airways Inc. 7415 Hayvenhurst Pl Van Nuys 91406

O'MALLEY, JESSE ROBERT, lawyer, ret.; b. Apr. 27, 1913, Brown City, Mich.; s. Anthony and Louise (Wilson) O'M.; m. Caroline Congdon, Apr. 6, 1941; children: Shawn b. 1942, Mary (Seliger) b. 1943, Barbara (Floyd) b. 1947, Kathleen (Yeager) b. 1949, Michael A. b. 1952, Charles T. b. 1955; edn: AB, Univ. of Mich. 1939; JD, Univ. Mich. Law Sch. 1941; admitted Mich. bar 1941, US Supreme Ct. 1944, Ariz. bar 1947, Calif. bar 1948. Career: trial atty. US Dept. of Justice 1941-49; chief trial counsel for U.S., U.S. v. National City Times, 1949; assoc. law firm Cosgrove Cremer Dielher & Kindge, Los Angeles 1949-52; ptnr. Musick, Perler & Garrett, Los Angeles 1952-78, ret.; since 1978: prof. of law Univ. of San Diego (2 terms); lectr. Sch. of Mgmt., Calif. State Univ., and Calif. Polytechnic State Univ.; mem: Am. Bar Assn., Fellow Am. Coll. of Trial Lawyers; Democrat; Catholic; rec: history. Address: 2816 Sunset Hill Dr., West Covina 91791

OMHOLT, BRUCE DONALD, design/manufacturing co. president; b. Mar. 27, 1943, Salem, Ore.; s. Donald Carl and Violet Mae (Buck) O.; m. Darla Faber, Oct. 27, 1972; children: Madison, b. 1964; Natalie, b. 1969; Cassidy, b. 1975; edn: BSME, Heald Coll. of Eng. 1964. Career: real estate salesman R. Lea Ward & Assoc., San Francisco 1962-64; sales engr. Repco Engring., Montebello 1964; var. mfg. eng. & mgmt. pos. Ford Motor Co., Rawsonville, Saline, Owosso & Ypsilanti, Mi. 1964-75; chief engr. E.F. Hauserman Co., Cleveland, Oh. 1975-77; dir. of design & eng. Am. Seating Co., Grand Rapids, Mi. 1977-80; principal Trinity Engring., Grand Rapids, Mi. 1980-81, Rohnert Park, Calif. 1981-84; pres. Trinity Engrg., Rohnert Park 1984–; patentee: 5 US patents, 1 Japanese, 3 Japanese patents pending. Res: 1034 Holly Ave Rohnert Park 94928 Ofc: Trinity Engineering, 71 Utility Ct Rohnert Park 94928

ONEAL, WILLIAM JAMES, physician; b. June 17, 1914, Chicago; s. James Laughlin and Mildred Dorothy (Jones) Oneal; m. Helen Wheeler, Jan. 12, 1942; children: James b. 1947, Barbara b. 1948, Sally b. 1949, Billy b. 1952, Susan b. 1956; edn: AB, Stanford Univ. 1938, MD, 1942; MS, surg., Coll. Med. Evan. 1954. Diplomate American Bd. of Surgery (1957). Career: intern Los Angeles County Gen. Hosp., 1941-43; resident surg. Henry Ford Hosp., Detroit 1943-45; pvt. practice surgery, Pasadena 1946-53, 1956-58; resident in surg., Calif. Hosp., Los Angeles 1954-56; mem. Los Angeles Tumor Inst.; senior ptnr. and senior mem. surgical staff Calif. Hosp., L.A. 1958-78, ret. 1979-; clin. instr. in medicine USC Sch. of Medicine 1950-54; Fellow Am. Coll. of Surgeons 1959; mil: lt. USNR 1945-46; Republican; Presbyterian; rec: golf (local & nat. tournaments), medalist Calif. State Amateur, 1954-57. Res: 671 Bradford St Pasadena 91105

O'NEEL, THOMAS EDWARD, restaurant owner; b. May 14, 1954, Stockton, Calif.; s. Ramon Oliver and Elizabeth Jean (Bradley) O'Neel; m. Diana, May 7, 1983. Career: mgr., tng. mgr. Denny's Inc. 1971-83; mgr. Far West Svcs. (W.R. Grace Co.) 1983-85; owner O'Neels Cafe Stockton 1985–; mem. Presdl. Commn. 1986; hon. mem. US Senatorial Club 1984; trustee Rep. Pres. Task Force 1982; mem: Nat. Restaurant Assn. 1973-, Nat. Fedn. of Independent Bus., CofC; Republican; Catholic. Ofc: O'Neels Cafe POB 284 Woodbridge 95258

O'NEILL, ROBERT JAMES, superior court judge; b. July 25, 1940, Los Angeles; s. Robert Matthew and Virginia Marie (Phelps) O.; m. Elizabeth Ann Gingery, Jan. 4, 1944; children: Laura b. 1969, Michael b. 1975; edn: BS, Univ. San Francisco 1962; JD, USF Law Sch. 1965. Career: dep. dist. atty. San Diego Dist. Atty's Office 1967-78; judge San Diego Municipal Ct. 1978-80, San Diego Superior Ct., 1980–, presiding judge Juvenile Ct. 1983-84, trial judge, 1985-, mem. Superior Ct. Executive Com., chmn. Golden Hills Mediation Center 1983-; mem: Calif. Judges Assn., San Diego Judges Assn., advis. bd. S.D. Organizing Project; publs: articles: Common Areas of Ethical Concern for Prosecutors (1977), Insurance Fraud (1976), Reunification Services (1985); mil: capt. US Army Counter Intell. Corps; Democrat; Catholic; rec: mountaineering, cabinetry, photog. Ofc: 220 West Broadway San Diego 92101

ONG, LILLIAN SIAOMAN, dentist; b. March 20, 1955, Surabaya, Indonesia, nat. US cit. 1985; d. Sadrach and Paula (Wurangian) Siaoman; m. Rio Sutikno Ong, Dec. 19, 1972; 1 dau: Olvia Rachel b. 1985; edn: DDS, Loma Linda Univ. 1981. Career: assoc. Dr. Robert Klein DDS, Whittier 1981; owner pvt. practice, West Covina 1982-; honors: Ali Lassen's Lead's Club; mem: Am. and Calif. (Spkrs. Club) Dental Assns., Acad. of Gen. Dentistry, Am. Straight Wire Assn.; rec: music, reading. Res: 1550 Cambridge Ct., W. Covina 91791 Ofc: Lilian S. Ong DDS, 820 W. Merced Ave., W. Covina 91790

ONSKT, NANCY RAE, engineer; b. Apr. 17, 1939, Findlay, Ohio; d. Raymond E. and Bonita M. (Leary) O.; edn: BS bus. adm., Toledo Univ. 1966. Career: senior systems analyst Owens Corning Fiberglass, Toledo 1966-74; order entry supvr. Four-Phase Systems, Cupertino, Calif. 1974-76; mgr. MIS Marketing Systems, Fairchild, San Jose 1976-82; senior product mgr. Savin, Sunnyvale 1982; MIS mgr., Inmac, Santa Clara 1982-85; engr. Hewlett- Packard, Santa Clara 1986-; cons. System Application Computer Services, 1978-; mem: Am. Mgmt. Assn., Assn. System Mgmt., Nat. Womens Found.; NOW, Women Entrenpreneurs; Democrat; Catholic; rec: golf, ski, tennis. Res: 2404 Golf Links Circle Santa Clara 95050 Ofc: Hewlett-Packard 3300 Scott Blvd Santa Clara 95054

ONSTOTT, LARRY LEE, co. president; b. July 26, 1940, Hollywood; s. Horace T. Onstott and Geri L. (Marts) Witthaus; m. Laura L., Sept. 10, 1984; children: Renee b. 1967, Larry, Jr. b. 1971, Tommy b. 1974. Career: prodn. mgr. M.R.M. Enamelers, Sepulveda 1960-68; gen. mgr., supr. Interlink Corp., Chatsworth 1968-70; owner/pres. Cir-Mac Inc., Sepulveda 1970-81; founder/ owner/pres. Advanced Surface Technology, Inc. 1984-, L & L Aviation, Inc. 1984-, Const. Indsl. Systems, Inc. 1986-; mem. Nat. Dray Boat Assn. (treas. 1962-66), S.D. Marlin Club; mil: cpl. US Army 1957-60; rec: bass fishing, helicopter pilot, dune buggy. Res: 1863 Sefton Pl San Diego 92113 Ofc: Advanced Surface Technology Inc 3134 Main St San Diego 92113

OPIE, BILL MONTEE, real estate broker; b. April 10, 1932, Sandusky, Ohio; s. Albert Lee and Mary Elizabeth (Montee) O.; m. Selma, Oct. 7, 1984; children: Milo b. 1950, Barry b. 1952, Eric b. 1958, Robert b. 1960, Catherine b. 1961; BSBA, Bowling Green State Univ. 1957, BA, 1957e; Lic. Real Estate Broker, Calif. 1976. Career: pres., dir. O-P Craft Co., Sandusky, Ohio 1960-74; pres., dir. The Service Team Inc., San Diego 1976-; dir. Stone Ridge Home Owners Group; mem: Rancho Bernardo Broker's Assn. (pres. 1985), San Diego Bd. Realtors, Poway Broker's Assn., Escondido Bd. Realtors, Rancho Bernardo Rotary; works: publs. re plastic devices in var. trade journs. 1960-74, and re residential real estate 1976-; inventor, 13 plastic patents; mil: US Army 1953-55; Republican; Presbyterian; rec: bridge, writing, Macintosh computer devices. Res: 12936 Rios Rd. Poway 92064 Ofc: The Service Team Inc., P.O. Box 28216 San Diego 92128

OPPERMAN, HENRY JAMES, educator, writer; b. Mar. 15, 1925, Long Beach; s. Henry Kasper and Mary Frances (Riddle) O.; m. Barbara Donaldson, June 11, 1950; children: Michael b. 1952, Donna b. 1954, Teresa b. 1958; edn: BA, UC Santa Barbara 1948, MA, Stanford Univ. 1965; Calif. Life Tchg. Cred. (1948). Career: automotive industry, 1943-54; tchr. Santa Barbara H.S., 1947-48, Santa Maria Union H.S. and Jr. Coll., 1948-51, Hartnell A&M Coll., Salinas 1951-54; tchr. trainer/vocational edn. advisor Fgn. Ops. Adminstrn. US Dept. of State, Managua, Nicaragua 1954-59; Internat. Cooperation Adminstrn., Cali, Colombia 1959-61; Agcy. for Internat. Devel., Tehran, Iran 1961-64; splst. Occupational Edn., Office of t Chancellor, Calif. Comm. Colls., Sacto. 1965-69; assoc. dean, Vocational Edn, coord. Cooperative Edn., Bakersfield Coll. 1969-81; current: writer/pub. BJIS Publishing; cons. Calif. State Comm. Colls. Longitudinal Study (1979-81); honors: Epsilon Pi Tau (1946), Kappa Delta Pi (1947); mem. Latin Americanist, Latin Am. Studies Assn., Christian Businessmens Com. of USA (regl. chmn.); publs: No Illusions Philatelic Numismatic Combinations Catalog (1985) (also available as a Data Base), Career Challenge- Motivational Tng. Manual (1986); mil: sgt. USAAF 1946-47; Republican; Calvary Bible Ch.; rec: computers, photog., travel. Res: 4805 Manor Dr No. 21 Bakersfield 93308 Ofc: BJIS Pub. POB 6718 Bakersfield 93386

ORDOG, GARY JOSEPH, physician, educator; b. June 2, 1954, New Westminster, B.C., Canada; s. Joseph and Jean Ordog; m. Cindy Solodki, June 2, 1979; edn: BS, Univ. of Brit. Columbia 1976, MD, 1979. Career: rotating internship Vancouver General Hosp., 1978-79; Family Practice residency 1979-80; Emergency Medicine res., Martin Luther King Jr. Gen. Hosp. and Charles R. Drew/UCLA Postgrad. Med. Sch., Los Angeles, 1980-82; Emerg. Med. Fellowship, King/Drew Medical Ctr., 1982-84, Neurosurgery Research Fellowship, 1982-83; Trauma Fellowship 1983-85; asst. prof. Charles R. Drew/ UCLA Postgrad. Med. Sch., 1982-; physician Emergency Medicine, 1982-; honors: Award of Merit, Royal Life Saving Soc. of Canada (1969); Board Certified or Eligible: Am. Bd. of Emergency Med., Royal Coll. of Physicians an Surgeons of Canada (Emerg. Med.), Canadian Coll. of Family Physicians (Emerg. Med. and Family Practice), Am. Bd. of Med. Toxicology; fellow: Am. Coll. of Emerg. Physicians, Am. Acad. Clin. Toxicol.; mem. Canadian Coll. of Family Physicians; med. resrch: diving medicine, hyperbaric resrch., trau-

matology; publ: 120 articles, 8 books. Ofc: MLK, Jr. Hospital 12021 S. Wilmington Ave Los Angeles 90059

ORINGER, HOWARD, business executive; b. Apr. 26, 1942, NY, NY; s. Arnold and Belle (Tansky) O.; m. Janice Koppenhofer, Aug. 15, 1964; children: Jason b. 1967, Derek b. 1969; edn: BEE, Stevens Inst. of Tech. 1962; MSEE, Calif. Inst. of Tech. 1963; MBA, Univ. of Santa Clara 1966. Career: finl. mgr. Am. Tel. & Tel. Co. 1964-69; v.p. Rockwell Internat. 1969-76; dir. Plantronics Inc. 1976-78; exec. v.p. Calif. Microwave Inc., Sunnyvale 1978-; Dir: RJE Communications, AVC Inc., TXR Inc., STS Inc., Financial Center Bancorp.; prof. CSU San Jose; honors: Beta Gamma Sigma; mem. IEEE. Res: 12262 Goleta Ave Saratoga 95070 Ofc: California Microwave, 990 Almanor Ave Sunnyvale 94060

ORLANDO, MICHAEL PETER, real estate broker; b. Carl P. and Barbara Lee (Schulte) O.; edn: BS food sci., UC Davis 1978. Career: mgr. distbn. United Vintners Madera, Calif. 1980-81; salesman retail properties Charles Tingey Assocs. 1981-83, Grubb & Ellis Co. Fresno 1983-; honors: Rookie of the Year (Charles Tingey Assocs. 1982), Salesman of the Year (Grubb & Ellis 1984); mcm: Internat. Council of Shopping Centers, Bulldog Found. (CSUF), SJM Men's Boosters Club; Republican; Catholic; rec: running, cycling, travel. Res: 239 E Cole Fresno 93710 Ofc: Grubb & Ellis Co. 5250 N Palm Ste 120 Fresno 93704

ORLANDO, ROBERT ANTHONY, pathologist; b. Mar. 5, 1938, NYC, NY; s. Lawrence E. and IdaErnst (Karnikofsky) O.; m. Joan Crofut Weibel, Nov. 29, 1981; children: William, b. 1959; Robert, b. 1969; Vivian, b. 1971; edn: BA, NY Univ. 1960; MD, NJ Coll. of Med 16; PhD, Univ. of Chgo. 1971. Career: faculty, Univ. of Chicago 1966-71; UC Irvine 1971-81; So. Calif. Coll. of Optometry 1972-85; chief of pathology svcs. Mercy Gen. Hosp. 1972- ; Canyon Gen. Hosp. -1981; chief of pathology Whittier Hosp. Med. Ctr. 1981-; dir. of scientific affairs NMS- Pharmaceuticals; Med. Jurisprudence Cons., Prof. of Pathology 1972-85; rec: trumpet, Los Angeles Doctors Symphony Orchestra. Ofc: Whittier Hospital and Medical Center, 15151 Janine Dr., Whittier 90605

ORMSBY, LIONEL, advertising agency owner; b. Jan. 16, 1909, Oakland; s. Edgar L. and Georgia Council Ormsby; m. Myrtez Rush Boehmer (dec.); m. 2d Lola B. Ensminger, 1982; children: John Rush (stepson) b. 1933; Jean Garringer b. 1946; edn: AB, UC Berkeley 1932;. Career: ed. Pelican Mag., Univ. Calif. 1932; asst. prodn. San Francisco News, 1933-40; asst. acct. exec. McCann-Erickson, Los Angeles 1940-42; acct. exec. Shaw Advt., Los Angeles 1942-46, 56-60; acct. exec. Dozier Eastman & Co., Los Angeles 1946-56; owner Hammer & Ormsby Advt., Los Angeles, Santa Rosa, 1960-; tchr. journ., Alameda H.S. 1932-34, copywriting, LA City Coll. 1950-53; editor Rexall Reporter 1962-76; ed./publr. BankAmericard Trade Secrets 1970-78, Sales Talk (nationwide newsletter for ad agencies) 1958-; contbg. writer: Better Homes & Gardens, Am. Home, Readers Digest, Advt. Age, Printers Ink, Sunset, Western Advt., LA Times, LA Herald-Examiner, Seattle Post Intelligencer; mem: Kappa Sigma (UC, 1930); chmn. Bev. Hills Council BSA 1945; chmn. pub. com. LA TV & Health Assn. 1955-60; bd. dirs. LA Advt. Club (1st vp 1955-65), bd. mem. L.A. Beautiful (pub. dir. 1969-78); rec: golf, bridge, fishing, writing. Address: Hammer & Ormsby Advt., 476 Hillsdale Dr Santa Rosa 95405

O'ROURKE, EUGENE LAWRENCE, public utility executive; b. Aug. 12, 1929, San Antonio, Tx.; s. Lawrence F. and Rose (Lackey) O'R.; m. Marilyn, June 25, 1955; children: Ronald b. 1957, Kenneth b. 1959, Craig b. 1962; edn: BSME, UC Los Angeles 1955. Career: sales engr. Am. Standard Indsl. Div., Los Angeles 1955-60; exec. Coswell Corp., Newport Beach 1961-62; gen. mgr. Coastal Publications Corp., Fullerton 1962-64; v.p. So. Calif. Gas Co., L.A. 1964-; civic: Young Republicans/O.C. (pres. 1961), Newport Harbor Union H.S. Dist., N.B. (pres. 1964), scoutmaster BSA, N.B. (1969-71), mem. World Affairs Council; clubs: The Los Angeles (pres., dir 1986), Balboa Bay N.B.; Republican; Presbyterian; rec: tennis, bridge. Res: 1039 Tiller Way Corona Del Mar 92625 Ofc: So. California Gas Co. 810 S Flower St Los Angeles 90017

O'ROURKE, JAMES CLINTON, corporate financial executive; b. Oct. 23, 1937, San Francisco; s. Joseph F. and Mary J. (Creedon) O'R.; m. Ann, Sept. 9, 1961 (dec. 1979); 1 son, James B. b. 1971; edn: BS, Univ. of San Francisco 1961; Certified Public Acct., Calif. 1966; Calif. Community Colls. (Life) Spl. Skills (bus. related) tchg. credential. Career: acct. Peat, Marwick, Mitchell & Co., San Francisco 1960-67; v.p. fin. Tar Gard/Venturi Cos., S.F. 1967-70; asst. v.p./ mgr. fin. rpt. Sutro & Co., S.F. 1970-73; mgr. Moss, Adams & Co., CPAs, S.F. 1973-76; controller/CFO Exchange Linen Service, S.F. 1977-; dir. Plasti-Tie, Inc.; mem: Am. Inst. CPAs, Calif. Soc. CPAs, Rotary Club of S.F. (Paul Harris Fellow), Merchants Exchange Club (bd. dirs.); club: Olympic (bldg. com.); mil: US Coast Guard 1957-59, Reserve 1955-57, 59-61; Republican; Catholic; rec: boating, hunting, fishing, travel. Res: 435 Green Hills Dr Millbrae 94030 Ofc: Exchange Linen Service 1575 Indiana St San Francisco 94107

ORR, GEORGE VERNON, JR., secretary, US Air Force; b. Nov. 12, 1916, Des Moines, Ia.; s. George Vernon and Wilhelmina (Van Niewall) O.; m. Joan Peak, Mar. 31, 1941; children: Carolyn, b. 1947; Robert, b. 1949; edn: BA, Pomona Coll. 1937; MBA, Stanford Univ. 1939. Career: mgmt. trainee Bullocks Dept. Store, Los Angeles 1939-42; partner, Verne Orr Motors 1946-59; partner Verne Orr Co. 1959-62; pres. Investors S&L Assn. 1962-66; Calif. dir. Motor Vehicles 1967-69; Calif. dir. fin. 1970-75; secty. of the Air Force 1981-; past pres: Pasadena Merchants Assn., Family Assistance of Pasadena; L.A. Co. United Way 1963; foreman, L.A. Co. Grand Jury 1962; awards: Man of the Yr.,

Salvation Army of Pasadena 1970; mem: Kiwanis Club, Pasa. (pres. 1951); Rotary; Carmelita Lodge F&AM; Phi Beta Kappa; Alpha Delta Mu; Univ. Club; Methodist (chmn. bd. stewards, ofc. bd.); mil: ensign, USNR 1942, supply ofcr. Naval Tng. Sch., Chgo. 1943; lt. commdr. USS Mercury AK-42, S. Pacific 1944-45; rec: amateur radio, photog. Res: 1444 Hillcrest Ave Pasadena 91106 Ofc: The Pentagon, Wash. DC 20330

ORRISS, DAVID ANTHONY, oil co. executive; b. May 21, 1938, Gt. Shelford, Eng., nat. US cit. 1957; s. Flt. Lt. Clifford Walter (MBE, RAF ret.) and Eileen Mary (Brown) O.; m. Frieda Liakos, Apr. 25, 1963; children: David Jr. b. 1966, George b. 1968, Clifford b. 1970, Mary Ann b. 1972, Eileen b. 1975, Elena b. 1975; edn: BS engrg., US Naval Acad. Annapolis 1962; BSMe, US Naval Postgrad. Sch. Monterey 1968; Reg. Profl. Engr. (mech.), Calif. 1984. Career: served to comdr. (ret.) US Navy 1956-1980, splst. in op., repair, modernization, and overhaul of naval warships and nuclear submarines; assigned comdg. officer of USS Impervious (MS0449), asst. project mgr. frigate modernization pgm., Naval Sea Systems Command Hdqtrs., Wash DC 1972-75; asst. repair supt. Mare Island NSY, 1975-80; Surface Warfare Ofcr, Comdr. Command at Sea Qualified, Engrg. Duty Ofcr. Qualified in Submarines; currently maint. mgr. Martinez Mfg. Complex, 1984—: senior engr. (mech.) Shell MMC 1980-82, senior startup engr. Flexicoker 1982-83, process mgr. Hyrogen/ Dimerization Complex 1983-84; mem: US Naval Acad. Alumni Assn., US Naval Inst., Pacific Energy Assn.; mil. decorations: Vietnam Service, Meritorious Unit Commend.; Republican; Greek Orthodox; rec: gardening, repairing autos. Res: 1024 Loma Vista Dr Napa 94558 Ofc: Shell Oil Co. 3485 Pacheco Blvd Martinez 94553

ORTA, MYRA SLAVIN, interior designer; b. Aug. 21, 1933, N.Y.C.; d. Robert H. and Gussie (Blanc) Slavin; m. Carl Orta, Apr. 24, 1954; children: Lisa b. 1955, Leslie b. 1957; edn: BA cum laude, Syracuse Univ. 1954; tchg. cred. San Jose State Univ. 1963, grad. stu. int. design 1965-67. Career: interior design prin. Myra Interior Designs, Los Altos 1967—; honors: Psi Chi (1953), Kappa Delta Pi (1963); mem: Internat. Soc. of Int. Designers (sec. 1982-84, treas. 1986-88), Am. Soc. Int. Designers (asso.), Nat. Home Fashions League; civic: Los Altos CofC, Women in Bus. Club of Los Altos; work pub. in mags. incl. Designers West mag. (4/82), Hudson Home Guide (9/79), num. newspaper home sect. features in Times Tribune, San Jose Mercury News, Los Altos Town Crier; rec: violin, travel, tennis, jog. Ofc: Myra Interior Designs 1225 Via Huerta Los Altos 94022

ORTH, DAVID JOHN, agribusiness consultant, supply co. owner; b. July 22, 1922, Los Angeles; s. John Henry and Henrietta Helena (Schober) O.; m. Eloise Orr (dec. 1971), Oct. 5, 1946; children: John Wm. b. 1948, Alan David b. 1949, Philip Leslie b. 1951; m. 2d Darla Bancroft, Nov. 21, 1971; edn: AA, Modesto Jr. Coll. 1942; USAF cert. aircraft mech. (1943), flt. engr. (1945). Career: owner Orth Ranch, Hughson 1946-71, Orth Cling Peach receiving station (Calif. reg. #346), 1953-74, Orth Hydrocooler Svc. 1954-74, R.R. removal svc. 1954-80; Public Weighmaster 1953—; owner/pres. Big Valley Transport, 1971-72, Orth Indus. & Orth Ranch Supply, 1971—, cons., expert witness in agribusiness; honors: champion Hughson Tractor Rodeo (1964), State Comp. Fund award of excellence (1975, 76), KCEY "Top Hand" (1972), Hughson FFA Hon. Chapter Farmer (1979), Castle Air Mus. hon crew chief C-46 (1980); mem: Calif. Cling Peach Assn. (1946-74, dir. 1961-66), Calif. Freestone Peach Assn. (1953-81, dir. 1962, 63, 71-79), Growers Harvesting Commn. (1947-59, dir. 1963, del. to US Cong. briefings, Wash DC 1962, 66, 74, Statewide Com. for Mkg. Order 1965, Nat. Co-Op. conf. Wash DC 1966), Hughson Young Farmers (1947-59, pres. 1955), Calif. Farm Bur. (1946-66), Calif. Almond Growers Assn. (1965-75), Valley Nitrogen Producers (1965-78), Top Farmers of Am. (1970-78); orgns: Hump Pilots Assn. (life, bd. chmn. 1982, 83), C.B.I. Vets. Assn. (life), Air Force Assn., VFW, Elks, Antique Truck Assn., E. Clampus Vitus, Modesto Trade Club (1965-75 dir. 4 yrs.), Empire Toastmasters (1960), Turlock Sportsman's Club (dir. 1957-59); works: 1st cling peach tilt, bulk trailer sys. (1959-74), 1st curved D-9 shank & drain slot technique for fruit & nut trees, patented 3-pt. linkage (1985); pubs: contbg. author China Airlift - The Hump, Vol. 1 (1983), co-editor, author Vol. II (1984); mil: s/sgt. USAF 1942-45, Pres. Unit Cit., Air Medal, CGM, WWII Victory, Asiatic-Pac. Campaign, Am. Theatre, China War Meml., Gold Gratitude by people of Hankow, China; Republican; Prot.; rec: preserv. WWII aircraft, collect R.R. Tie brands, mule & ox shoes, antique barb wire. Address: Orth Industries 11506 E Whitmore Ave Hughson 95326

ORTIZ, LEOPOLD, engineering executive; b. May 1, 1926, El Paso, Tx.; m. Josephine Lomeli, July 5, 1952; children: Louise b. 1955, Leo b. 1959, Thomas b. 1962, Joann b. 1965; edn: BA w/ distinction and dept. honors, indsl. arts, San Jose State Univ. 1951; MS engring. mgt., Columbia Pacific Univ. 1979, PhD resources mgt./pub. admin., 1980; spl. courses AF Inst. of Tech. 1968, Indsl. Coll. of Armed Forces, Wash DC 1975-77, US Army Engr. Sch. 1978, 85; Calif. Life Std. Tchg. Credential (1967), Cert. Plant Engr. (CPE) AIPE (1985). Career: served in US Navy, WWII; col. US Air Force (ret.), Berlin Crisis, Pueblo Crisis, Vietnam Era; base civil engr./squadron comdr., 96th Civil Engring. Sq., Dyess AFB, Tx. 1968-69, chief Pgms. Br., 1969-70; spl. asst. for Reserve Affairs to the Dir. of Civil Engring., HQ USAF, Pentagon, 1971-75; chief Engring. Resources Mgmt., HQ MTMCWA, Oakland (Calif.) Army Base 1976-80, 1981—, chief engring. plans and svcs. 1980-81; p.t. faculty mentor Columbia Pacific Univ. (1982-); honors: AF ROTC Disting. Mil. Student and Graduate, Epsilon Pi Tau (1950), AF Scroll of Appreciation, Dept. of the Army Commendn.; mem. Am. Inst. of Plant Engrs. (chpt. secty.), Soc. of Am. Mil. Engrs. (past nat. v.p.), Nat. Assn. of Indsl. Tech., Reserve Ofcrs. Assn., Phi Sigma Kappa (life), San Jose State Univ. Alumni Assn. (past chpt. pres., life),

Disabled AmVets (life), Assn. of Iron and Steel Engrs. 1954-56, Martinez Jaycees 1955-60 (past chpt. pres.), Joint Commn. on CATV 1978-80; mil. decorations: Merit Svc. (1975), AF Commendn. (1970), AF Outstanding Unit w/3 olc, Navy GCM, Asia-Pac Campaign, WWII Victory, Nat. Def., AF Longevity Svc. w/olc, Armed Forces Reserve w/hr. glass device, Small Arms Expt. Marksman; Democrat; Catholic. Res: 725 Ulfinian Way Martinez 94553 Ofc: HQ MTMCWA (MTW-ENG) Oakland Army Base Oakland 94626

OSBERG, JAMES DENNIS, computer systems sales executive; b. Aug. 2, 1951, Monrovia; s. Harvey J. and Myrtle C. (Jenson) O.; m. Elizabeth I. Rennison, b. Apr. 9, 1983; 1 dau: Lacey Elizabeth, b. 1983; edn: AA, Pasadena City Coll. 1971; BS, CSU Los Angeles 1974; Real Estate Broker, Calf. 1974. Career: v.p. Robert Lowe Associates/Prominent Properties, Los Angeles 1973-76; acct. mgr. Agency Records Control Inc., L.A. 1977-79; sales mgr. Delphi Sys. Inc., L.A. 1979-80; owner James Osberg & Assoc., L.A. 1980-81; regl. v.p. Insurnet, Inc. 1981-85; honors: Top Exec. Sales Award, Insurnet 1981; Winners Circle, Insurnet, 1981, 82, 83; mem: Am. Mgmt. Assn.; Alpha Kappa Psi; Republican; Catholic; rec: golf. Res: 636 Birchwood Ct Danville 94526 Ofc: Insurance Systems Inc., 16815 Von Karman Irvine 92714

OSBORNE, CAROL ANN, lawyer; b. Aug. 26, 1938, Erie, Pa.; d. Clarence Henry and Grace Louise (McLaughlin) Bronson; children: Dwight b. 1966, Joy Louise b. 1969; edn: JD, Western State Univ. Coll. of Law 1977; admitted Calif. State Bar 1978. Career: pvt. practice, emphasis on probate, Downey, Calif. 1978—; seminars on wills, probate admin. 1983-85; mem: Calif. and Orange Co. bar assns.; Orange Co. Women Lawyers; Am. Business Women's Assn.; local PTAs; Republican Nat. Com. 1982-; Republican; Christian; rec: music. Ofc: Carol A. Osborne, Esq., 8221 3rd St, Ste. 201, Downey 90241

OSBORNE, LARRY WALTER, realtor; b. May 11, 1939, San Pedro; s. Clarence Raymond and Jeanette Marie (Seperski) O.; m. Sofia, July 29, 1961; children: Sharon b. 1963, Valerie b. 1965, Margaret b. 1966; edn: BA, San Jose State Univ. 1961; Cert. Comml. Investment Mem., Nat. Assn. Realtors; Cert. Comml. Investment Mem. and Cert. Residential Splst., Nat. Assn. of Realtors 1985. Career: cost analyst Ford Motor Co. 1962-66; sales Morrison Homes 1966-70; real estate broker Allied Brokers 1970-72; pres. Osborne Real Estate Inc. 1972—; v.chmn. Mission Valley Bancorp; bd. chmn. Bank of Pleasanton; dir. Founders Title Co.; mem: Nat. Assn. of Realtors, CCIM, Masons, CofC; Republican; Episcopal; rec: sailing, skiing, games. Ofc: Pleasanton 94566

OSHINSKY, LARRY A., health services administrator; b. March 5, 1952, NY, NY; s. Albert and Rhoda M. (Newman) O.; m. Alicia Rosas, Dec. 19, 1981; 1 dau: Suzanne b. 1983; edn: BA, City Univ. of NY Queens Coll. 1974; MS, State Univ. of NY Stony Brook 1976; nursing home adminstr., Calif. Career: adimstrv. res. Saint Charles Hosp., Port Jefferson, NY 1976; adminstr. Memorial Hosp., Greeley, Colo. 1977; asst. adminstr. Topanga Terrace Convalescent Ctr., Canoga Park 1979; adminstr. Longwood Manor Sanitarium, Los Angeles 1980; currently, mgr. environmental svcs. Cedars Sinai Med. Ctr.

OSHIRO, STEPHEN YEIICHI, financial executive; b. June 21, 1946, Honolulu, Hawaii; s. Seie and Evelyn Sumiko (Akamine) O.; edn: BA, Univ. of Hawaii 1969, MBA, 1977; CPA, Hawaii 1977. Career: ofc. mgr. Paramount Enterprises Inc., Honolulu, Ha. 1972-75; staff acct. Peat Marwick Mitchell & Co., Honolulu, Ha. 1977-79; unit controller, senior auditor Amfac Inc., San Francisco 1979-81; senior acct., fin. reporting Taco Bell, Irvine 1981-82; asst. treas. Knudsen Corp., Los Angeles 1981—; mem: Am. Insnt. CPAs, Los Angeles Cash Mgmt. Assn.; mil: radioman 2/c US Army; rec: guitar, microcomputers. Res: 170-D Casuda Canyon Dr Monterey Park 91754 Ofc: Knudsen Corp., 231 So 23rd St Los Angeles 90011

OSTER, MICHAEL CROLY, corporate insurance broker; b. Nov. 1, 1944, Los Angeles; s. Otto and Irene Evelyn (Croly) O.; m. Linell, Oct. 1, 1985; edn: BS, Calif. State Univ. 1969; desig: Chartered Life Underwriter (CLU), Am. Coll. CLU (1981), Cert. Ins. Cons. (CIC), Orange Coast Coll. (1975). Career: engring. cost data analyst McDonnell Douglas Aircraft, Long Beach 1966-70; sales rep. Continental Can, Los Angeles 1969-72; v.p. mktg. Calif. Casualty Mgmt., San Mateo 1972-79; v.p. Frank B. Hall & Co., San Francisco 1979—; publs: arts. on risk mgmt. and insurance in Photovoltaics Internat. (5/84), Cogeneration World (10/84), Alternative Sources of Energy (12/85); mil: s/sgt. USAFR 1966-72, Calif. Commendn.; Republican; rec: scuba, ski, travel. Res: 712 Steiner St San Francisco 94117 Ofc: Frank B. Hall & Co. One Market Plaza Ste 2100 San Francisco 94105

OSTERN, STANLEY, physician; b. Mar. 22, 1935, Stryj, Poland, nat. USA 1951; s. Henry (M.D.) and Yetta (Seliger) O.; m. Edie Tanner, July 18, 1975; children: Jill b. 1963, Vicki b. 1966, Penny b. 1968; edn: BA, NY Univ. 1956; MD, NY Medical Coll. 1960. Career: chief medicine Castle Air Force Base, Merced 1964-6; pvt. practice internal medicine, Santa Barbara 1966—; chief int. med. Pinecrest Hosp.; mem. Am. Soc. Internal Med., Calif. Med. Assn., Santa Barbara Co. Med. Soc., Calif. Soc. for Treatment of Alcoholism; publs: J. of AMA (1965); mil: capt. Med. Corps USAF 1964-66; rec: tennis, African mask collector. Ofc: Stanley Ostern MD, Inc. 504 W Pueblo St Ste 101 Santa Barbara 93105

OSTLER, JACK MARION, service co. owner; b. April 10, 1927, Rawlins, Wyo.; s. Marion Addison and Ruby Belle (Behunin) O.; m. Vera May, Feb. 13, 1953; children: Christina Hileman b. 1954, Jon Arther b. 1956; edn: Healds Engring. 1945. Career: customer engr. apprentice Burroughs Adding Machine Co. 1947; customer engr. IBM Corp., San Francisco & Hononlulu 1948-59;

owner, opr. Special Ostler Svc. 1959–; mem: Common Cause, Food First, Nat. Health Fedn., Organic Farming Club of Sonoma Co. Regenerative Agriculture Assn., Sierra Club, United Way; mil: fireman 1/c USN Pacific Fleet 1945-46; Democrat; Unitarian; rec: farming. Res: 317 Poinsettia Ave. San Mateo 94401 Ofc: Special Ostler Service, 135 So. B St. San Mateo 94401

OSTRENGA, JAMES ALLEN, pharmaceutical co. executive; b. Jan. 21, 1941, Green Bay, Wisc.; s. Anthony Paul and Verna (Holewinski) O.; m. Linda Mary Johnston, May 12, 1974; children: Sarah Matisse b. 1980, Andrew Yates b. 1983; edn: BS pharm, Univ. Wisc. Madison 1962, PhD, 1967; lic. pharmacist Wisc. (1964), clin. lab dir. Calif. Dept. Health (1971), US Dept. Health Ctr. for Disease Control (1972). Career: instr. physical chem. Sch. of Pharm. Univ. Wisc. 1966-67; senior scientist Syntex Research, Palo Alto 1967-71; founder, pres. PharmChem Research Found., Menlo Park 1971-78; founder, pres., chmn. bd. PharmChem Labs. Inc., Menlo Park 1971–; editor, founder PharmChem Newsletter, PharmChem Research Found. & PharmChem Labs. 1972-78, publr. 1978–; cons. Stanford Research Inst. psychobiol./physiol. sect., Menlo Park 1973-83, Westwood Pharmaceuticals, Buffalo, NY 1975-76; editl. bd. DO IT NOW Found., Phoenix 1976-79; cons. Pres. Carter's Ofc. of Drug Abuse Policy 1977-78; lectr. in elem. and high schs. on illicit drugs 1972-79; founder, dir. Analysis Anonymous, testing svc. for street drugs as a public svc. 1971-84; honors: Rennebohm Tchg. Award, Sch. of Pharm., Univ. Wisc. 1966, Rho Chi Hon. Soc. 1965; mem: Calif. Assn. Toxicologists 1978-, Acad. Pharmaceutical Scis. 1965-73, Delta Upsilon frat.; publs: num. arts. in pharm. jours.; rec: fly fishing, piano, flute, music appreciation, travel, golf, softball. Res: 829 Hermosa Way Menlo Park 94025 Ofc: PharmChem Labs., 3925 Bohannon Dr Menlo Park 94025; pvt. ofc: 120 Florence, 3rd floor, Palo Alto 94301

OSTROFE, ALLEN FRANCIS, financial consultant; b. Jan. 12, 1948, San Francisco; s. Frank Joseph and Colleen Margaret (Riley) O.; m. Sabine, Oct. 18, 1981; children: Shaun b. 1984, Nicole b. 1986; edn: BA, Univ. Portland, Ore. 1970; M. Internat. Mgmt., Am. Grad. Sch. Internat. Mgmt. 1972; lic. NASD securities 1984, lic. life, disability and variable annuity ins. 1986; Certified Financial Planner, Univ. So. Calif. (Coll. for Financial Planning, Denver, Colo.) 1986. Career: air traffic controller Anchorage Airport 1969-70; mgmt. trainee J. Walter Thompson Co. NY 1972-73, acct. supv. J. Walter Thompson Co. West Germany 1973-80, dir. J. Walter Thompson Co. Argentina 1980-84; financial cons. self-employed 1984–; honors: Cert. of Appreciation (League of Women Voters, Lions Club 1985); mem: Internat. Assn. Financial Planners, Inst. Certified Financial Planners, Nevada County Bus. Assn., Nevada County CofC, Sierra Nevada Meml. Hosp. (corp. mem.), Greater Grass Valley Devel. Corp. (pres.); thesis (The Art of Living in a Cybernetic Age) presented Internat. Symposium of Cybernetics, Switz. 1970; Democrat; Catholic; rec: sailing, windsurfing, investments; Res: 120 Pammy Way Grass Valley 95949 Ofc: Ostrofe Financial Consultants 10565 Brunswick Rd Ste 15 Grass Valley 94945

O'SULLIVAN, SHEVAUN EILEEN, antique and arts dealer; b. Dec. 28, 1937, Albuquerque, N.Mex.; d. William Twiss and Sofia Ann (Fedison) O'Sullivan; edn: Univ. of N.Mex. Career: antiques and arts dealers, Los Angeles 1967–; past pres. So. Calif. Orgn. of Antique Dealers; secty. co-ordinator St. Patrick's Day Parade, Los Angeles; mem: Magic Castle, Variety Arts Ctr.; So. Calif. Orgn. of Antique Dealers; Harp & Shamrock Club; Golden State Boxers & Wrestlers Assn. (secty.); publs: Bradbury Building Mag. 1977-78; Democrat; Catholic; rec: preserving arts and antiques. Address: 2623 Kent St, Los Angeles 90026

OSWAL, ABHAYA K., computer products manufacturing co. CEO; b. Jan. 12, 1946, Delhi, India; s. Sitab C. and Vidya D. (Parakh) O.; m. Pammi Jain, Jan. 9, 1950; children: Rajal b. 1974, Rishi b. 1977; edn: BS, Ill. Inst. Tech. 1967; MS, Northwestern Univ. 1972. Career: tech. staff Bell Labs., Napaville, Ill. 1970-75; cons. First Nat. Bank Chgo. 1975-76, Honeywell Inc. Arlington Hgts., Ill. 1976-78, Conic Data Sys. San Diego 1980-81; c.e.o. Micromax Sys. Inc.; designer: Gallery Accounting & Bus. Mgmt. Software Series for Macintosh. Ofc: Micromax Systems Inc. 6868 Nancy Ridge Dr, Ste H, San Diego 92121

OTANI, ROBERT HIROMU, electrical operations executive; b. Nov. 8, 1942, Topaz, Utah; s. Noboru and Tomoye (Hiruo) O.; m. JoAnn T., Aug. 7, 1966; children; Robin b. 1969, Scott b. 1974; edn: AE, Cogswell Poly. Coll. 1963; BSEE, San Jose State Univ. 1971. Career: elec. draftsman Jack D. Todd Inc. San Jose 1969-70; elec. engr. Owens Corning Fiberglas Santa Clara 1971-74, elec. ops. supv. 1974–; mem: Elec. Maint. Engr. Assn. (state v.p. 1978-79, pres. 1980-81 chpt. chmn. 1975-76), VFW, Indsl. Mgmt. Council; mil: E-5 US Army infantry 1963-66; Republican; Buddhist; rec: fishing, woodworking. Ofc: Owens Corning Fiberglas 960 Central Expwy Santa Clara 95050

OTIS, PETER T., hematologist/oncologist, internist; b. Mar. 23, 1938, Boston, Mass.; s. Terry Peter and Julia O.; m. Peggy T., Dec. 29, 1968; children: Terry P., Stevie Anastasia, Kathryn Christina; edn: BS, Northeastern Univ. 1960; MD, Tufts Univ. 1964; Diplomate Am. Bd. Internal Medicine (1972), Am. Bd. Hematol. (1972), FACP/Fellow Am. Coll. Physicians (1980). Career: intern Albany Med. Ctr., Albany, N.Y. 1964-65; resident VA Hosp./New England Med. Ctr., Boston 1965-66; phys. US Army 1966-68, charge of medical ward in 2 evacuation hosps. and comdr. of POW hosp., Vietnam 1966-67; resident in medicine USC-L.A. Co. Med. Ctr., Los Angeles 1968-70, fellow Div. of Hematology, USC 1970-72, asst. prof., assoc. prof. Dept. Medicine USC 1972–, mem. bd. (chmn. 1978-80) USC Cancer Mgmt. Network 1978-; pres.

Central Orange Co. Coagulation, Hematology, and Oncology Med. Group, Anaheim 1980–; bd. dirs. (pres. 1984-85) Med. Group of So. Calif., 1984–; med. cons. Alameda Co. Health Dept., and Blue Cross of No. Calif., 1967-68; dir. Hemophilia Ctr. Anaheim Meml. Hosp., 1973–, chief of medicine 1976-78, bd. dirs. 1985-; awards: med. research grantee Univ. Calif. (1972), Nat. Cancer Inst. (1974), O.C. Heart Assn. (1973, 74), USC (1980); mem: Am. Soc. Hematol., Am. Soc. Clin. Oncologists, Am. Assn. for Cancer Research; coauthor num. research publs.; Republican; Greek Orthodox; rec: yachting, hunting. Ofc: 1211 W La Palma Ave Ste 404 Anaheim 92801

OUGH, SE YUN, trading company president; b. April 18, 1937, Seoul, Korea, nat. US cit. 1979; s. Kyung Eun and Yoon Soon (Noh) O.; m. Kyung Park, Oct. 12, 1968; edn: B.Lang., Korea Univ. Foreign Language 1959; M.Journ., Maryland Univ. 1961. Career: gen. mgr. Sears, Roebuck & Co., Seoul, Korea 1967-73; asst. v.p., chemical export mgr. Marubeni America Corp., Chicago, Ill. 1973-79; senior v.p. California Overseas Inc., Los Angeles1 979-80; pres. Penta Internat. Co., Torrance 1980–; mem. South Bay Lions Club; Domacrat; Presbyterian; rec: hiking, skiing. Res: 1500 Hickory Ave. Torrance 90503 Ofc: 3451 Torrance Blvd. Ste. 212 Torrance 90503

OVANDO, LYNN ELLEN, lawyer; b. Dec. 10, 1957, Ann Arbor, Mich.; sd. Paul John and Charlotte Ann (Kearns) O.; edn: BA, summa cum laude, St. Mary's Coll. 1980; JD, Rutgers Univ. Sch. of Law 1983. Career: law clerk Christensen, Fazio, McDonnel, et al, La Habra 1981; research asst. Rutgers Law Sch. prof., Camden, NJ 1981-82; law clerk Law Ofcs. Robert Christensen, Fullerton 1982; legal intern Superior Ct. of New Jersey, Chancery Div., Camden, NJ 1982-83; law clerk Law Ofcs. Robert Christensen, Fullerton 1983; atty. Knneth A Satin & Assoc., Newport 1983-85; atty. Buck, Molony & Ammirato, Long Beach 1985–; history tchr. asst. 1977-80; honors: Blecha History Award; Sr. History Award; mem: Phi Alpha Theta (pres. 1980), Kappa Gamma Pi, Am. and Orange Co. Bar Assns., Orange Co. Barristers, Los Angeles Trial Lawyers Assn.; Democrat; Catholic; rec: tennis, golf. Res: 180 Cabrillo Unit 4A Costa Mesa 92626 Ofc: Buck, Molony & Ammirato, 4401 Atlantic Ave. Long Beach 90807

OVERALL, JESSE U., IV., university dean; b. Mar. 13, 1943, Harriman, Tenn.; s. Jesse U., IV., and Lucile B. (Bunch) O.; m. Katherine S. Coffman, May 12, 1984; edn: BS, USAF Acad. 1965; MA, UCLA 1968, PhD, 1977; MSBA, CSU Dominguez Hills 1979. Career: asst. prof. of Eng., USAF Acad. 1967-69; research assoc. UCLA 1970-72; ext. pgm. coord. UCLA 1972-73; academic plnnr., CSU Dominguez Hills 1973-74; dir. pgms. in admin. 1973-80; mgr. evaluation & personnel research, USC 1980-82; prof. exec. MBA pgm. and assoc. dean Golden Gate Univ. 1983; academic dean National Univ. 1984–; prof. exec. MBA pgm. Golden Gate Univ. 1982-; vis. lectr. UCLA Grad. Sch. of Mgmt. 1984–; honors: outstanding research award, UCLA Doctoral Alumni Assn. 1983, honor grad., Indsl. Coll. of the Armed Forces, Ft. McNair, VA 1983; mem: Am. Assn. of Higher Edn.; Am. Ednl. Research Assn.; Assn. for Instnl. Research; mil: Lt. Col. USAFR, current dept. commdr. USAF Acad. Admission Liaison Ofcr. Gp., Orange Co. rec: admissions rep. USAF Acad., Colo. Springs. Res: 6156 Palau St., Cypress 90630-5666 Ofc: National University, 2112 Business Center Dr., Irvine 92715

OW, GORDON Y. W., engineer; b. Oct. 11, 1931, Wailuku, Maui, Hawaii; s. Yong W. and Sue E. Ow; children: Steven b. 1954, Gail b. 1956, Mark b. 1958, Rick b. 1968; edn: MS, Air Force Inst. of Tech. 1960; MBA, Pepperdine Univ 1985. Career: lt. col. US Air Force (ret) 1953-73; v.p. N P Inc. 1974-76; pres. G S Inc. 1976-82; mem. tech. staff Advanced Engineering Div., Rockwell Internat., 1983–; honors: Deans List AFIT, Tau Beta Pi (life); civic: Waimanalo Neighborhood Bd., Honolulu; works: 4 US Patents (mechanical) issued; designed, built ½ acre swimming pool at Hyatt Regency Maui- winner of the 1982 NSPI (Nat. Swimming Pool Inst.) Gold Medal for commercial pools.; Republican; Christian; rec: flying, golf. Res: 628 W Imperial Ave #105 El Segundo 90245

OWENS, DAVID, psychiatrist; b. Jan. 19, 1925, Moscow, Penn.; s. William J. and Emma (Emerson) O.; edn: BS, Loyola Coll. Baltimore 1950; MD, Univ. Maryland 1954; Diplomate Am. Bd. Psychiatry and Neurol. 1969. Career: gen. med. practice Baltimore 1955-58; chief med. ofcr. Calif. Med. Facility Vacaville 1958-63, chief psychiat. 1966-69; chief psychiat. Calif. Inst. for Women Frontera 1969-70; coord. cntg. care San Diego Co. Mental Health Svcs. 1970-78; pvt. practice psychiat. S.D. 1978–; cons. Salk Inst., Heartland Senior Day Ctr.; assoc. clin. prof. UC San Diego; mem: San Diego Psychiat. Soc., Am. Psychiat. Assn., S.D. Med. Soc., CMA, AMA; publ: arts. for med. journs.; mil: ssgt. US Army infantry 1943-46, Silver Star, Combat Inf., Pres. Unit Cit., ETO w/ 5 battle stars; Deist; rec: gardening, surfing, swimming, beachcombing. Res: 13725 Choisser Ln Lakeside 92040 Ofc: David Owens MD Inc. 6386 Alvarado, Ste 118, San Diego 92120

OWENS, JAMES ALLEN, construction and manufacturing co. executive; b. Oct. 8, 1945, Richmond, Calif.; s. James Carl and Joyce Jewell (Eller) O.; m. Virdena Lea Boyer, Oct. 18, 1968; children: Dean b. 1969, Michael b. 1976; edn: bus. admin., Santa Ana Coll. 1973; ASME cert. for Pressure and Heat Exchangers; Calif. tchg. credential. Career: office mgr. Petrolane, Long Beach 1971-73; millwright constrn. worker 1973-79, millwright constrn. supvr. for var. contractors, 1979-81; founder/CEO Craftsmen Construction, Inc., Ventura 1981–; restaurant owner 1979-81; mem: Am. Mgmt. Assn., Pacific Energy Assn., Mfrs. and Processors Assn., Ventura County Economic Devel. Assn., Ventura County CofC, Los Angeles CofC, Smithsonian, Masons, Scottish Rite, Shriners; mil: cpl. USMC 1963-67; Democrat; Protestant; rec: racquetball, scuba. Res: 6644 Ralston St Ventura 93003 Ofc: Craftsmen Construction Inc. 2432-B Palma Dr Ventura 93003

OWENS, JOSEPHINE IRWINE, cosmetics co. president; b. Nov. 7, 1952, San Francisco; d. Wm. Levy and Loma Farr- (Riser) Owens; edn: dental tech., Bay City Coll. 1970-71; bus. courses Skyline Coll., Columbia Pacific Univ., 1984-86. Career: pres./ chief exec. and team coord. Owens Ents. Inc. (jewelry co. w/a 700 in sales force), Foster City 1980-83; dir. Park Lane Jewelry Co. (w/100 sales gp), Chgo. 1983-84; founder/ pres. and CEO Topaz Cosmetics and Skin Care Inc., Pacifica 1984–, dir. mktg., design cosmetics (24 new ultra-say lipstick colors, 1985), also dir. public rels. Diamite-Owens Ents.; recipient num. sales and profl. awards incl. Black Female Chief Exec. San Francisco Bay Area (1985), Top Cosmetic Design Catalog Award of Bay Area (for 1984 Topaz Cosmetics Cat., 25 pp.), Best-Dressed Female (S.F. Bay Area Bizzle Exec. Senior Div. 1982), Top Photog. Model in grad. class (Barbizon Modeling Sch. 1971) ; founder Skyline Pre-Sch. Ctr. (for 50 children), Pacifica 1983-; Democrat; Mormon; rec: dance, travel, art collector, collect yellow objects. Address: Topaz Cosmetics and Skin Care Inc. (POB 1722) 2450 Skyline Blvd Pacifica 94044

OXX, WILLIAM GARDNER, III, educator, writer, illustrator; b. Jan. 19, 1923, Newport, R.I.; s. Wm. G. and Mary Elizabeth (Bjorkman) Oxx; desc. John Howland of Plymouth Colony; Wm. Arnold, 2d Gov. of R.I.; King David of Scot.; lineage incl. Bliss, Gardner, Greene, Lindsay, Munro families of Bristol and Newport, R.I.; m. May Isobel Anderson, Feb. 11, 1956; children: William IV, (lt. j.g. USN), Sheri Lynn, Jonathan Howland. Edn: AB, hist., Univ. Redlands, 1949, MA, 1951; postgrad. Inst. of Russian Affairs, Columbia Univ.; 6 Calif. State Adminstrv. and Tchg. Credentials, San Fernando Valley State Coll. 1955-61. Career: fellow/instr. hist., Univ. Redlands, 1947-51; L.A. City Schs., instr. US Govt., Russian Hist., Mil. Naval Sci., 1954-84; coached num. So. Calif. Debate League varsity forensic teams (won 75 sweepstakes trophies, 303 gold, silver and bronze medals); apptd. Task Force for Studying Physical Attacks on Calif. Tchrs. 1969-71; dist. asst. chmn. Mayor's Task Force on Narcotics and Drugs, 1970; approx. 250 speeches, TV, radio appearances, 1951-. Publs: contbg. ed. (books) Vanguard of Freedom, 1975; The Oxx Family in America, 1973; Bible and Christianity (Lakeside Press) 1952, A Hist. of Flight, 1953; Pictorial Hist. of the World (Simon & Schuster), 1956, America (Ency. Brit. Press), 1954; (coauthor) Brig. Gen. Francis Hudson Oxx, USA (Ret.), The Descendants of Samuel Oxx, Bristol Plymouth Colony; 23 historical, mil. hist. articles; airbrush illustrator Warships of the World, 1946; Army-Navy Jour. of Recognition (vols. 1-24), 1942-45; US Naval Intelligence, Navy Dept., 1941-45; USNR 1947-54; mem. Naval Intelligence Team under Cmdr. in Chief Adm. Ernest J. King, Pearl Harbor Trial, US Senate, 1945; Rear Commodore, 11th Dist. USCG Aux., 1983-84; chief dockmaster XXIII Olympiad 1984; awards: 2d place Intercollegiate Western States Championship; James W. Kyle Award for Excellence in Journalism 1949; 1st and 2d Diamond Awards, Nat. Forensic League, 1966, 71. Mem: Univ. Redlands Varsity Debate Team, 1948-50; Pi Kappa Delta (pres.), Alpha Phi Gamma, L.A. Westlake-Wilshire Toastmasters (founder, pres., hon. life pres. 1968), Gen. Soc. Colonial Wars (dep. gov. gen.), Calif. Soc. S.R., SAR (past pres. Gen. Patton chpt.), Soc. Mayflower Descendants, Pilgrim John Howland Soc., Soc. Sons & Daus of the Pilgrims, Soc. War of 1812, Hereditary Order, Desc. of Colonial Govs., Mil. Order of the World Wars; hon. life mem. PTA 1959; Republican; Prot.; rec: hist., research, marine art, pvt. library (4000 vols.). Sum. Res. The Whaler, 2481 Kaanapali Pkwy, Lahaina, Maui, HI 96761; No. 162, 439 Ali Wai, Lake Tahoe Keys, So.Lake Tahoe 95705; Res: 2429 Leeward Cir Westlake Village 91361

OYGAR, AHMET E., neurosurgeon; b. Apr. 26, 1944, Istanbul, Turkey, nat. 1976; s. Prof. Ismail Hakki and Zeynep (Torgan) O.; children: Ruikye b. 1979, Sezen Z. b. 1981; edn: MD, BS, Hacettepe Univ. Med. Sch., 1964-71. Diplomate American Board of Neurological Surgery (1982), lic. phys. Fla. (1978), Calif. (1979). Career: surgical internship Jacksonville (Fla.) Univ. Hosp., 1971-72; neurosurgical residency, chief res. 1977-78, Kings Co. Hosp./Downstate Med. Center, Bklyn. 1972-78; pvt. practice, Palm Springs 1979–; mem: AMA, Calif. Med. Assn., Riverside Co. Med. Assn., Palm Springs Acad. of Medicine, Cong. of Neurol. Surgeons, Calif. Assn. of Neurol. Surgeons, Chevalier de la Confrerie de la Chaine des Rotisseurs Bailliage des U.S.A.; awards: Ofcr. du Palm Academique of French Govt., Merite Civique of Fr. Govt.; publs: articles in med. jours., profl. presentations med. confs.; First Application of Dorsal Column stimulator in England (1976); Republican; Moslem; rec: photog., painting, philately. Ofcs: A.E. Oygar MD, Kiewit Bldg. Ste 207, 39000 Bob Hope Dr Rancho Mirage 92270; 555 Tachevah Dr, Ste 101-2 East, Palm Springs 92262

OZELL, CHARLES SYLVAN, lawyer, real estate developer; b. Sept. 29, 1923, Chgo.; s. Nathan Sylvan and Sylvia (Isenberg) O.; m. Sally Phyllis Weber, Sept. 15, 1946; children: Robert Michael b. 1953, Sheri Beth (Drews) b. 1955, Patti Lynn b. 1958; edn: BS, Univ. of Ill. 1947; JD, De Paul Univ. 1950; spl. courses Univ. Chgo. 1955, Northwestern Univ. 1961; admitted Ill. State Bar 1951. Career: atty., assoc. with architect Roy M. Schoenbrod in co-op apt. devel., Hyland Builders Corp. (bldg. & mdsg. co-op. apts., forerunner of condominium concept), Chgo. 1951-71; devel. large multi-unit condominiums in San Francisco, Sacramento, and Marin County 1971-83, ret.; bd. chmn. Zell-O, Ltd. (real and personal prop. co.), S.F.; honors: pres. Northwest Builders Assn., Chgo./North Shore (1959, 60, 61); civic: S.F. Heart Assn. (1969-71), Cancer Soc. (1972-74), Kiwanis of S.F., Cong. Beth Sholem, S.F. (dir.); works: created new constrn. techniques: flat slab concrete pad (1963-65); mil: US Merchant Marine Cadet Corps; Jewish; rec: walking, tennis, equestrian. Ofc: Zell-O, Ltd. 550 Battery St Ste 102 San Francisco 94111

OZORKIEWICZ, RALPH LEO, electronics distributing co. executive; b. June 26, 1946, Wash. DC; s. Leo Edward and Frances Joyce (Sanders) O.; m. Marie Tuholski, Dec. 18, 1977; children: Laura b. 1967, Joy b. 1970, Ryan b. 1980, James b. 1981; edn: BS, engring. mgmt., Univ. of Mo. at Rolla, 1969. Career: district mgr. Texas Instruments, Ft. Wayne, Ind. 1975, Chicago 1975-77, Southwest area mgr., Costa Mesa 1977-80; v.p. Southwestern Gp. Kierulff Electronics, Tustin 1980-81, v.p. mktg., 1981-83, senior v.p. corporate mktg., 1983-84, exec. v.p., chief op. ofcr. 1984; pres. Wyle Laboratories, Electronics Mktg. Group, Irvine 1985–; elected founding mem. Acad. of Engineering Mgmt., 1980. Mem: Soc. of Engring. Mgmt., Amer. Electronics Assn., Amer. Mgmt. Assn.; Republican; Catholic; rec: golf. Res: 11912 Skyline Dr Santa Ana 92705 Ofc: Wyle Labs., Electronics Mktg. Group 18910 Teller Ave Irvine 92715

PACE, RUSSELL BROWN, JR., lawyer/insurance co. executive; b. March 6, 1929, Palmyra, Va.; s. Russell B. and Clara Virginia (Jones) P.; m. Margaret Caselli, Aug. 15, 1943; children: Jefferson b. 1954, Nancy b. 1957, Russell III b. 1979, Courtney b. 1982, Bradford b. 1985; edn: BA, Univ. of Va. 1950, LL.B, 1956; admitted to practice US Supreme Ct., US Ct. of Appeals (D.C. Circuit, Tenth Circuit), US Dist. Cts. (D.C., Colo.), Colo. Supreme Ct. Career: pvt. law practice with Davis, Graham & Stubbs, Denver, Colo. 1956-59; with Hogan & Hartson, Wash DC, 1959-68; pvt. law practice in Wash. DC and own investment bus., 1969-73; exec. v.p., gen. counsel, secty. and co-owner of Security First Group, Inc. and Security First Life Insurance Co., Los Angeles 1973-81, vice chmn. bd., co-owner, 1982–; honors: Theta Chi (pres.), Jefferson Soc. (pres.), Lambda Pi, O.D.K., Raven Soc., Baseball (1946-50); Law Rev., Nat. Moot Ct. Competition, John Bassett Moore Soc., Order of the Coif (1953-56). Gov. appointee, Calif. Economic Devel. Commn. 1982-87; co-chmn. The Earthquake Preparedness Com. (L.A. City and Co.) 1984-; pres. Internat. Found. for Learning Disabilities 1983-; founder L.A. Music Center; chmn. bd. Edmund G. "Pat" Brown Inst. of Govt. Affairs 1982-84; chmn. bd. Palmer Drug Abuse Pgm., L.A., Inc. 1981-84, mem. nat. bd. trustees 1981-84; fmr. fin. chmn. Princess Grace Gala (1981); mem. The Friends of the Anthony and Elizabeth DuQuette Found. for the Living Arts, Am. Art Council, LA County Mus. of Art, Town Hall, Bel Air Bay Club; mil: s/sgt. to 1st lt. US AF 1950-53, capt. Reserve, Commendn. Medal; Democrat: co-chmn. Nat. Platform Com. (1984), charter mem./dir. Bus. Council, Dem. Nat. Com. (1981-) and chmn. Task Force on Budget and Taxation Matters (1983-); Presbyterian (elder, treas.). Res: 364 N. Bristol Los Angeles 90049 Ofc: Security First Group, (POB 29193, L.A. 90009) 1800 Ave of the Stars, Ste. 1400, Los Angeles 90067

PACHECO, RONALD HOWARD, accountant; b. Aug. 2, 1936, Honolulu, Hi.; s. William Joseph and Alsie (Demotta) P.; m. Lorraine, Aug. 17, 1957; children: Stephen b. 1958, Paul b. 1961, Paula Ann b. 1962, Teresa b. 1963, Michael b. 1965; edn: BS, Univ. Santa Clara 1958; MBA tax, cum laude, Golden Gate Univ. 1975; CPA Calif. 1974. Career: agent Internal Revenue Service 1962-74; acct. Brandon & Tibbs CPAs 1974-76, Ronald H. Pacheco CPA 1976–; mem: Am. Inst. CPAs, Calif. Soc. CPAs, Soc. Calif. Accts. (chpt. pres.), Lions Club 1968-76; num. dissertations on fed. and state income tax matters including two constl. queries presently reflected in petitions before the US Tax Ct.; mil: 1st lt. US Army Infantry 1958-62 (Service in Korea); Republican; Catholic; rec: Baltimore Oriole baseball fan. Res: 22326 Davenrich St Salinas 93908 Ofc: Ronald H. Pacheco & Sons 737 S Main St Salinas 93901

PACKARD, RONALD C., congressman; b. Jan. 19, 1931, Meridian, Idaho; s. Forrest LeRoy and Esther (Carter) P.; m. Roma Jean Sorenson, July 18, 1952; children: Chris, Debre, Jeff, Vicki, Scott, Lisa, Theresa; edn: stu., Brigham Young Univ., Portland State Univ.,; DMD, Univ. of Ore. 1957. Career: gen. practice dentistry, Carlsbad 1959–; ofcr. Packard Devel. Corp., Carlsbad 1965–; mem. 98th Congress, 43d. Dist. Calif.; v.chmn., dir. First Nat. Bank of North County 1981-; trustee Carlsbad Unif. Sch. Dist. 1962-74, chmn. 1968-69, 1972-74; dir. North County Transit Dist. 1978-82; mayor City of Carlsbad 1978-82; mem: Carlsbad CofC, Calif. League of Cities, San Diego Assn. Govts., Am. Dental Assn., Calif. and San Diego Co. Dental Socs.; mil: lt. USN 1957-59; Republican; Mormon. Address: Carlsbad

PADEREWSKI, CLARENCE JOSEPH, architect; b. July 23, 1908, Cleveland, Ohio; s. Johan Tomasz and Barbara (Klebowska) P.; m. Maxine, May 3, 1969; children: Colette (McCanna) b. 1939, Coleen (Floyd) b. 1952; edn: BA arch., UC Berkeley 1931; postgrad. courses UC Ext., CSU San Diego; Reg. Architect, Calif. 1945; Fellow AIA, 1962. Career: designer, engring. draftsman for Wm. J. Moran, Struc. Engr., Los Angeles 1932-33; asst. mgr. Marlo Inv. Co., San Diego 1934-38; chief draftsman for Samuel Hamill Arch., S.D. 1939-44; architect prin. 1945-78, cons. architect 1978–; designer approx. 3,000 building projects (1930-); instr. archtl. drawing, San Diego Schs. Adult Edn. 1939-44; instr. math., UCSD Ext. Div. 1945-57; recipient merit awards (Design of S.D. Gen. Hosp.; Design of S.D. Internat. Airport East Terminal) AIA, San Diego Chpt.; honor award (Design S.D. Internat. Airport) Portland Cement Assn.; two First Prize Golden Trowel awards, Plastering Inst.; 5 awards, Unit Masonry Inst.; spl. 30 year service (1979), and disting. 50 year service awards, Calif. Council AIA; Pres.'s medal, Nat. Council of Archtl. Registration Boards (1966); knighthood and Order of Polonia Restituta Cross, Polish Govt. in Exile (1982); mem: Fellow AIA, Nat. Council Archtl. Registration Bds. (pres. 1965), Calif. Council AIA (sch. plnng. com. 1955-64), apptd. mem. Calif. State Bd. Archtl. Examiners 1949-61 (pres. 2 yrs), Am. Arbitration Assn. (Panel of Arbs. 1953-); civic: San Diego CofC (bd., chair coms.) 1954-59; S.D. Downtown Assn. 1962- (pres. 1973, emeritus mem. 1982); Bayside Social Ctr. 1950-65 (adv. bd.); Camp Oliver Adv. Bd. 1953- (chmn. 1963-5); S.D. Symphony Orch. Assn. (past bd.); Am. Nat. Red Cross (bd. S.D. chpt. 1969-75); Salvation Army 1969- (bd. 1985); Father Serra Club 1947-53 (charter, pres.); Lions Club;

Ignacy Jan Paderewski Soc. (hon. bd.); S.D. Mayor's Urban Design Com. 1983; Polish Am. Assn.; contbr. num. arts. in profl. mags. and newspapers; mil: cpl. ROTC 1927-28; Republican; Roman Catholic; rec: golf, gardening. Res: 2837 Kalmia Pl San Diego 92104

PADILLA, VINCENT PETER, college president ret.; b. May 29, 1925, San Jose; s. Vincent R. and Blanche (Ynostrosa) P.; m. Joyce Mathiesen, Feb. 15, 1947; children: Claudia, b. 1947; Thomas, b. 1954; edn: BA, San Jose State Univ. 1951; MA, CSU Sacto. 1967; Secondary Sch. Admin., Calif. Career: secondary sch. tchr. Sacto. City Unif. Sch. Dist. 1953-68; secondary sch. vice prin., principal 1968-71; with Los Rios Comm. Coll. Dist. 1971–; asst. dean instrn. Cosumnes River Coll. 1971-75, assoc. dean admin. svc. 1975-77; dean of admin. Sacto. City Coll. 1977-79; pres. Cosumnes River Coll. 1979-84; commnr. Bay Valley Athletic Conf. 1984–; mem: Assn. Calif. Comm. Coll. Adminstrs.; Epsilon Pi Tau; Calif. Indsl. Edn. Assn., Sacto. chpt. (pres. 1966); Sacto. Regl. Com. on Cont. Edn.; Calif. Comm./ Jr. Coll. Assoc., Reg. I; Am. Assn. Comm./ Jr. Coll. Adv. Com.; Calif. Comm. Colls. State Commn. of Athletics; Mexican Am. Edn. Assn.; Rotary, Elk Grove; Sacto. Yacht Club; Methodist Hosp., Sacto.; Los Rios Comm. Coll. Dist. Found. Cosumnes River Coll. Found.; mil: hosp. corpsman USNR, active 1943-46, 1951-52, reserve 1947-51; Catholic; rec: golfing, boating, cycling, fishing. Res: 8187 Gandy Dancer Way Sacramento 95823; Ofc: Cosumnes River Coll., 8401 Center Pkwy Sacramento 95823

PAFFHAUSEN, JAMES VOLNEY, mortgage banker; b. Aug. 3, 1925, Grand Rapids, Mich.; s. Joseph Francis and Helen Barbara (Ish) P.; m. Louise Shrader, June 15, 1957; children: James Jr. b. 1959, Laura b. 1962; edn: Grand Rapids Jr. Coll. 1947-48; Mich. State Normal 1948-49; DePaul Univ. 1951-52; UCLA 1958. Career: exec. v.p A.H. Greutzmacher & Co. Inc., Chicago, Ill. 1952-67; pres. Metropolitan Financial Corp., Los Angeles 1967-70; v.p. Campana Co., San Diego 1970-76; v.p. Southland Capital Corp., SanDiego 1976-80; pres. Presidio Captila Corp., San Diego 1980–; dir. Ill. Svc. Life. Isn. Co. 1963-64; guest lectr. State of Missouri Devel. Commn. 1962-65; mem: Mortgage Bankers Assn. of Am., Income Property Com., Urban Land Inst., Comml. Ind. Council; mil: sgt. 1/c US Army 1943-46, 1950-51; Republican; Episcopal; rec: piano, cooking, furniture restoration. Res: 5850 Sagebrush Rd. La Jolla 92037 Ofc: Presidio Capital Corp., 2550 5th Ave. Ste. 178 San Diego 92103

PAGEN, WILLIAM ROLAND, petroleum co. president; b. Feb. 26, Los Angeles; s. Roland Jocelyn and Minnie (Meyer) P.; m. Barbara M. Pauley; children: Patrice b. 1953, Robert b. 1955, John b. 1957; edn: BS, UCLA Sch. of Bus. Adm., 1946. Career: joined Edwin W. Pauley orgn. as accountant in 1946, treas. and dir., 1958, exec. vice pres. 1959, pres./chief exec. ofcr. Pauley Petroleum Inc., 1963–, chmn. bd./pres./CEO, currently; trustee The Edwin W. Pauley Found., Pauley Lifetime Trust, Barbara McHenry Pauley Trust; bd. chmn./CEO Newhall Refining Co. Inc.; pres./dir. Athens Oil Corp., Bayou Oil Co.; pres./dir. Gourmet Concessions, Via Verde Devel. Co.; bd. chmn./dir. Blacktop Materials Co., Pauley Pacific Inc., Pauley Transp. Inc.; mem. American Petroleum Club (incl. 25-Year Club), Petroleum Accountants Soc., Tax Executives Inst.; nat. dir. Mexican CofC; bd. trustees UCLA Found. (pres. 1975-78, chmn. 1978-80, Exec. Com.); vice chmn. UCLA 200 Million Dollar Capital Fund Campaign, chmn. Coll. of Letters and Sci. Campaign Steering Com.; mem: LA County Commnr. Small Craft Harbors (chmn. Rent Control Commn., mem. Mediation Com.), Orthopaedic Hosp. bd. of trustees (chmn. Investment Com., Adv. Council, Lohman Club, Resources bd. dirs.), L.A. Council for Internat. Visitors (dir.), John D. French Found. for Alzheimer's Disease (dir.); clubs: Petroleum, California, California Yacht (Staff Commodore), Marina City; mil: sgt. USAF 1942; Episcopal; rec: boating, photog., ham radio opr. Res: 9521 Sunset Blvd Beverly Hills 90210 Ofc: 10000 Santa Monica Blvd Los Angeles 90067

PAIGE, EDWARD JAY, communications co. president; b. Apr. 15, 1956, Los Angeles; s. Morton Lewis and Ruth May Pura (Goldman) P.; edn: grad. USN Comms. Sch. 1974, US State Dept. Comms. Sch. 1975, spl. courses, 1975-. Career: petty ofcr. US Navy 1974-79; mem. Presidential Communs. Team, Wash DC 1980-81; pres. Paige Communs. and Consultants, 1981-82, pres. Paige Communs., 1982–; pres./CEO Paige Communs. Corp. 1983-, Fast Eddie Ents. 1984-, FEE Finl. Services 1985-, Entrepreneurial Mgmt. Inc. 1985-; mem. No. Am. Telecomm. Assn., So. Calif. Technol. Execs. Network (charter), Statue of Liberty-Ellis Centennial Com., Nat. Electronics Assn., Rotary Internat., var. Chambers of Commerce; author: The Benefits of Ownership, Survival of the Quickest (1985), contbr. articles in var. mags., cover feature story in Business to Business Mag. (1984); mil. decorations: Nat. Def., Good Conduct, Pres. Merit. Award, Unit Cit., Naval Expedition; Republican (Pres. Task Force); rec: boating, water sports, travel, exotic autos. Ofc: 2620 Walnut Ave Tustin 92680

PAIGE, RICHARD ALAN, registered nurse; b. Sept. 27, 1955, Wichita, Kans.; s. Clarence and Marilyn Dezaree (Lagneau) P.; edn: AA, L.A. Pierce Coll. 1982; AS, State Univ. N.Y. 1982; Univ. of La Verne 1984-86; R.N., Calif. Bd. Career: critical care nse. Burbank Comm. Hosp., 1976-78; emergency nse. Riverside Hosp., No. Hollywood 1978-80, Western Park Hosp., Los Angeles 1979-80; nsg. educator/adminstr. Trauma Care Edn. Assocs., No. Hollywood 1979-80; multi-splty. nse. Professional Staffing, Northridge 1980-82; emerg. nse. Sherman Oaks Comm. Hosp., 1982-83; trauma nse. coord./ Paramedic Liaison nse. Henry Mayo Newhall Hosp., Valencia 1983–; recipient recogn. awards L.A. County Pediatric Soc. (1985), C.R.O.P. Walk for Hunger (1985); mem. Emergency Nurses Assn. (S.F.V. chpt. pres. 1985, State Membership chair 1986, assn. nominee to Calif. State Emerg. Med. Svcs. Commn. 1985), Am. Assembly of Men in Nsg. (1982-84), Assn. of Paramedic Liaison Nses. LA Co., Assn. of Trauma Nse. Coordinators L.A. Co., Am. Heart Assn.; Republican; Baptist; rec: photog., ski, computers. Ofc: Henry Mayo Newhall Memorial Hospital 23845 W. McBean Pkwy Valencia 91355

PALAFOX, BRIAN A., general thoracic & cardiovascular surgeon; b. Feb. 9, 1951, Honolulu, Hawaii; s. Anastacio L. (PhD) and Jesusa A. P.; edn: BS in biol., Univ. of Hawaii 1972; MD, UC Irvine 1975. Diplomate Am. Board of Surgery. Career: extern in obstets., intern in pathol., Orange Co. Medical Center, res., chief resident gen. surgery UCI Med. Center, Orange 1977-81, fellowship thoracic and cardiovascular surg. UCI Med. Center and Long Beach VA Hosp., 1981-83; ER phys. Kaiser Permanente Hosp., Bellflower, Glendora Comm. Hosp., Circle City Hosp., Corona; surgeon pvt. practice, Santa Ana 1983–; tchg: basic cardiopulmonary resucitation, physician and nsg. lctr. in trauma mgmt., paramedic lectr. in trauma mgmt., lctr. med. students; awards: Comm. Scholarship pgm. Honolulu, Eagle Scout, Resident of the Year UCIMC (1980-81); mem. AMA, CMA, AMSUS; mil: major Calif. Army Nat. Guard 143D Evacuation Hosp.; Catholic. Ofc: 1310 West Stewart Dr Ste 502 Orange 92668

PALAREA, EDGAR ROLANDO, physician; b. Sept. 29, 1932, Guatemala City, Guatemala, nat. US cit. 1963; s. Juan Ramon and Clemencia (Granados) P.; m. Marilyn Jacobs, June 17, 1962; children: Richard b. 1965, Victoria b. 1967, Russell b. 1971, Melissa b. 1976; edn: BS, Bowling Green State Univ. 1952, MA, 1964; MD, Tulane Univ. Sch. of Med. 1958; courses in cardiopulmonary resuscitation and cardiology. Career: intern Seaside Meml. Hosp., Long Beach 1958-59; resident internal med. Meml. Hosp. Med. Ctr., Long Beach 1961-64; cardiology fellow 1964-65; cardiologist pvt. practice, Long Beach 1965–; pres. Edgar R. Palarea MD Inc., Long Beach 1968–; Long Beach City Bd. of Health; cited in Congl. Record, House of Reps., June 9, 1981; honors; Dewin Lincoln Moseley Trust Fund Award; Guatemalan Govt. Scholarship Award; Cordell Hull Found. Award; Omicron Delta Kappa; Beta Beta Beta; (3) research awards, Am. Geriatrics Soc.; Meml. Hosp. of Long Beach 1962-63; (6) Thousand Dollar Club awards, Long Beach Heart Assn.; Grand Prize, Long Beach Heart Assn., Cyclethon 1973-74; awards, Long Beach Lung Assn. 1974; hon. mem., Am. Assn. of Med. Assts. Riverside chpt., State of Calif. orgn.; hon. citizen, Fresno 1975; Long Beach Police Ofcrs. Assn.; mem: Ohio Acad. of Sci., Soc. of Am. Bacteriologists, AAAS, H.J. Heinze Co. Phytopathology Research Dept., Student Am. Med. Assn., Alpha Kappa Kappa Alumni Assn., Bowling Green State Univ. Alumni Assn., Tulane Univ. Med. Alumni Assn., Am., Calif., Los Angeles Co. and Long Beach Med. Assns., Long Beach Tuberculosis & Health Assn. (past pres.), Israel, World and Pan American Med. Assns., Nat. Assn. Residents & Interns, Nat. Kidney Disease Found., Mil. Surgeons of U.S., Am. Coll. of Chest Physicians (assoc. fellow, Calif. chpt.), Am. Thoracic Soc., Long Beach Symphony Assn., Flying Physicians Assn., Am. Calif. Heart Assn.; works: contbr. num. articles in med. journs.; freq. spkr. profl. meetings and symposia; mil: capt. USAF 1959-61; Republican; Jewish; rec: public speaking, greenhouse gardening, boxing. Res: 6390 Rochelle Ln. Long Beach 90815 Ofc: 2700 Bellflower Blvd. Ste. 117 Long Beach 90815

PALAZZO, JOHN JOSEPH, food manufacturing co. executive; b. Oct. 31, 1938, N.Y.C.; s. John and Jean (Cannariato) P.; edn: BA, Fordham Univ. 1968; cert. Food Indus. Mgmt., USC. Career: sales rep. Standard Brands (food indus.), Sacto. 1970-, account mgr. 1973, broker relations mgr. 1974; acct. mgr. Golden Grain Macaroni Co., 1975-, sales mgr. 1982, v.p. Sales (So. Pacific region), 1983–; mem. Food Sales Mgr. Club (FISMC), Retail Grocers Assn., Ariz./So. Calif. Grocers Assn., A.L.A. mil. orgn.; civic: Smithsonian Assoc., City of Hope (Food Indus. mem.); mil: cpl. US Army 1955-57, Good Conduct Medal; Democrat; Catholic; rec: boating, target shooting, photog. Ofc: Golden Grain Macaroni Co. 1000 E Cerritos Anaheim 92805

PALAZZO, ROBERT PAUL, lawyer, accountant; b. Apr. 14, 1952, Los Angeles; s. Joseh Francis and Muriel (Cobern) P.; edn: BA, UC Los Angeles 1973; MBA, USC 1976, and JD, 1976; postgrad. work Univ. of Oxford 1979; admitted Calif. State Bar 1976; CPA, Calif. (1975), Nev. (1979), Colo. (1980). Career: law clk. Ebben & Brown, Los Angeles 1974-75; law assoc. Graham & James, L.A. 1975-78; ptnr. Rader, Cornwall, Kessler & Palazzo, CPAs 1978-81; ptnr. Palazzo & Kessler, Attys. at Law 1978-81; individual practice law and CPA, Robert P. Palazzo & Company, Los Angeles 1981–; judge pro tem L.A. Municipal Ct. 1982–; pres., bd. chmn. Consol. Am. Oil Co., 1981-; Dir: USA Nikko Inc. (1978-82), Financial Systems Internat. Inc. (1979-), Calif. Cancer Found. (1979-); honors: outstanding senior UCLA (1973), Bank of Am. Soc. Sci. Award (1969), Math. Assn. of Am. Award 1969), Pi Gamma Mu, Omicron Delta Epsilon, Beta Alpha Psi (pres. 1972); mem: Italian Am. Bar Assn. (bd. govs. 1981-), Am. Numismatic Assn. (dist. dir. 1981-84), Nat. Acad. Recording Arts & Scis.; civic: founder Ohio Hist. of Flight Museum; St. Joseph, Mo. Hist. Soc.; Ross County, Ohio Hist. Soc.; Nev. Hist. Soc.; contbg. editor: Gun Report (1979, 85). Ofc: Robert P. Palazzo & Co. 3002 Midvale Ste 209 Los Angeles 90034

PALITZ, MURRAY, lawyer; b. July 16, 1937, NYC, NY; s. Nathan and Bettie (Silversmith) P.; m. Linda Stolack, May 22, 1978; children: Adam b. 1978, Davin b. 1965, Michael b. 1963, Jeffrey b. 1960; edn: BS, Brooklyn Coll. 1959; MS, Westcoast 1971; JD, Southwestern 1975. Career: researh aero engr. NASA, Lancaster 1959-67; design engr. MDAC, Culver City 1968-69, system engr., Santa Monica 1970-71, cost/ financial analyst, Huntington Beach 1971-75; lawyer Palitz & Assoc., Westminster 1976–; mem; Am., Calif., Orange Co. and Los Angeles Bar Assns., Am. and Calif. Trial Lawyers Assns., Toastmasters, Kiwanis, Elks, B'nai B'rith; Republican; Jewish. Ofc: Palitz & Assoc., 8070 Westminster Westminster 92683

PALMER, PATRICIA TEXTER, educator, administrator; b. June 10, 1932, Detroit, Mich.; d. Elmer Clinton and Helen (Rotchford) Texter; m. David Jean Palmer, June 4, 1955; edn: BA, Univ. Mich. 1953; M.Ed, Nat. Coll. of Edn. 1958; MA, CSU San Francisco 1966; postgrad. work Stanford Univ. 1968, CSU Hayward 1968-69; Calif. Life Tchg. Creds. (gen. elem., gen. secondary, spl. Speech Arts). Career: chair Speech Dept. Grosse Pointe Univ. Sch., Mich. 1953-55; tchr. South Margerita Sch., Panama 1955-56; tchr. Kipling Sch. Deerfield, Ill. 1955-56; Rio San Gabriel Sch., Downey, Calif. 1957-59; Roosevelt High Sch., Honolulu 1959-62; El Camino High Sch., South San Francisco 1962-68, chair ESL Dept. South S.F. Unified Dist. 1968-81; dir. English as Second Lang. Inst., Millbrae 1978−, and adj. faculty New Coll. of Calif., 1982−; Calif. master tchr. ESL, Calif. Council Adult Edn. 1979-82; mem. Calif. State Adult Basic Edn. Advis. Com. on vocational ESL; awards: Concours de Francais Prix (1947), Jeanette M. Liggett Meml. award for excellence in hist. (1949), Cum Laude Soc. (1949), Zeta Phi Eta Speech Hon. (1953), Scroll Hon. Soc. (1953), outstanding alumna Univ. of Mich. Sesquicentennial Awards (1968), commendn. for achieve. in journalism Hawaii State Legislature (1962); mem: Tchrs. of English to Speakers of Other Languages/ Calif. affil., AAUW, Internat. Platform Assn., Univ. Mich. Alumnae Assn., Nat. Coll. of Edn. Assn., Ninety Nines, Chi Omega, Nat. Assn. of Female Execs.; Republican; Roman Catholic; rec: flying. Res: 2917 Franciscan Court San Carlos 94070 Ofc: New College of California 450 Chadbourne Ave Millbrae 94030

PALMER, PHILIP S., photographer, writer; b. Nov. 16, 1911, Hart, Mich.; s. Phil S. and Ruth (Shear) P.; m. Paula (artist, art instr.), Jan. 1938; 1 son, Michael b. 1940; edn: BS, Mich. State Coll. 1932, spl. courses San Francisco State Univ., CSU Sonoma, var. art schs.; Calif. Comm. Coll. tchr. cred. Career: freelance photog., writer 1937−, work widely pub. Midwest and Eastern U.S. periodicals; photography and writing in W. Michigan 1937-42, photojournalist Los Angeles Bur. of AP during WWII, came to West Coast in 1943, estab. studio in San Francisco 1953-65, studio in Petaluma currently; lectr. San Francisco State Univ. ext. 1963-74, S.F. City Coll. 1975-86, past instr. Indian Valley Colls., San Rafael; first pub. article appeared in The Vermonter mag. 1936, contbr. num. features in nat. periodicals, num. book reviews and reviews of exhibits in Bay Area publs. (esp. the San Francisco Chronicle, Pacific Sun, Artweek), newspaper columns on Country Living, Wines and Winemaking, Landscaping; books: Face of San Francisco (w/Harold Gilliam), Doubleday; Cable Cars of San Francisco (w/Michael Palmer), Howell-North; Chinatown, San Francisco, Howell-North; One-man photog. shows: M.H.De Young Memorial Museum (S.F.), Friends of Photog. (Carmel), Focus Gallery (S.F.), Camera Work (So. Calif.), The Octagon (Wash DC), num. college campuses nat.; Group exhibits: George Eastman House (Rochester, NY), S.F. Mus. of Art, Univ. of Exeter, England, US State Dept. Arts in the Embassy Pgm., US Information Overseas Pgm. (murals in US Embassys), others; mem. Friends of Photog.; Ind. Democrat; rec: gardening, fly fishing, winemaking. Address: 585 Gossage Ave Petaluma 94952

PALYU, MILDRED KATHLEEN, food co. owner; b. July 5, 1928, Cleveland, Ohio; d. Regis Lawrence and Bess Mildred (Cough) Watson; m. Lester Palyu; children: Kathleen Lynn, Christine Mary, Ronald Lawrence, Charles Allen. Career: research engring. Gen. Elec. Co.; employment counselor Snelling & Snelling; credit union mgr.; owner Mr. Fun Food, Balboa 1975−; mem: Newport Beach CofC, Toastmasters, Balboa Improvement Assn., St. James Parish. Ofc: Mr. Fun Food POB 781 Balboa CA 92661

PANETTA, LEON EDWARD, congressman; b. June 28, 1938, Monterey; m. Sylvia Marie Varni, 1962; children: Christopher, Carmelo, James; edn: BA, magna cum laude, Univ. of Santa Clara 1960, JD, 1963; admitted to Calif. Bar 1965. Career: individual law practice, Monterey; legis. asst. to U.S. Senator Thomas H. Kuchel of Calif. 1966-69; spl. asst. to secty. HEW, Wash. 1969; dir. U.S. Ofc. for Civil Rights, Wash. 1969-70; exec. asst. to mayor, NYC 1970-71; ptr. firm Panetta, Thompson & Panetta, Monterey 1971-76; mem. 95th-98th Congresses from 16th Calif. Dist., majority regl. whip, chmn. task force on budget process, budget com., chmn. subcom. on domestic mktg., consumer rels. and nutrition of agric. com.; founder Monterey Coll. of Law; trustee, Univ. Santa Clara Law Sch.; awards: Lawyer of the Year, 1970; NEA Lincoln Award, 1969; mem: Carmel Valley Little League; Parish Council of Our Lady of Mt. Carmel Ch.; mil: 1st lt. US Army 1963-65, Army Commdn.; author: Bring Us Together, 1971; Democrat (Monterey Co. Democratic Central Com. 1972-75); Catholic. Ofc: 339 Cannon House Office Bldg., Washington DC 20515

PAPACALOS, GEORGE NICHOLAS, insurance co. executive; b. Jan. 29, 1960, Long Beach; s. Apostolos G. and Angie (Terzis) P.; edn: AA, Long Beach City Coll. 1981; BSBA, CSU Long Beach 1982. Career: sales rep. Prudential Ins. Co. of Am., Long Beach 1983-, mgr. of agency devel., 1985−; mem. bd. dirs. Candy Stripers Candy Corp. S.A. 1986−; profl. honors: Rookie of Year 1983, Counselor of Year 1984; mem. Life Underwriter Assn., Long Beach Jaycees, Phi Kappa Phi, Beta Gamma Sigma, Alpha Gamma Sigma, CSULB Fin. Assn., CSULB Concert of the Grove (com. 1985-); Democrat; Greek Orthodox (Sun. Sch. tchr.); rec: coach Girls basketball church league. Res: 76 Roycroft Long Beach 90803 Ofc: Prudential Ins. Co. 4201 Long Beach Blvd Ste 203 Long Beach 90807

PAPPAS, COSTAS ERNEST, engineer; b. Oct. 14, 1910, Providence, R.I.; s. Ernest and Soffie (Rose) P.; m. Thetis Hero, June 9, 1940; children: Alceste,

Conrad; edn: BS in M.E./aeronautical option, New York Univ. 1933, MS, 1934; Reg. Profl. Engr., N.Y. (1940), Calif. (1969); Calif. lic. Real Estate Broker. Career: engr. Republic Aviation Corp., Farmingdale, L.I., N.Y. 1935-39, chief Aerodynamics Dept. 1939-54, chief Aerodynamics & Thermodynamics 1954-57, dir. Sci. Research 1957-59, asst. to vice pres. Research & Devel. 1959-64; cons. to aerospace industry 1964−, profl. engrg. consultant, real estate broker, Calif.; apptd. planning commnr. Redwood City 1983-; honors: Tau Beta Pi, Iota Alpha, Wright Bros. Medal (1943), cert. of distinction, N.Y.U. (1944), Republic Aviation Corp. award for outstanding achievement; mem. Am. Inst. of Aero. & Astro., San Mateo- Burlingame Board of Realtors (bd. dirs.), San Mateo County Devel. Assn. (Growth Policy Council advis. bd.), Commonwealth Club of Calif.; patentee in aeronautical engring.; contbr. articles var. engring. tech. jours. and periodicals; rec: civic activities, travel, opera. Address: POB 5633 San Mateo 94402

PARAS, ROMEO NUQUI, financial analyst, accountant; b. Oct. 31, 1951, Macabebe, Pampanga, Philippines; s. Aurelio Alfonso and Pilar Bungay (Nuqui) P.; m. Glerita Milo, Jan. 17, 1980; children: Aldrich Rommel b. 1982 (decd.), Laarni-Grace b. 1983; edn: BS bus. adminstrn., Pampanga Colls. 1977. Career: ofc. mgr. Riverside Convales. Hosp., Wesley Nsg. Home; bookkeeper Sacred Heart Convales. Hosp.; ofc. mgr. Gino Verde Inc.; career and financial advisor; dir. Bayanihan Jaycees of L.A. (Jaycee of the Month 8/86); author: How Friendship Brings Wealth (Focus 1983); Catholic; rec: travel, driving, martial arts. Res: 9854 Shoshone Ave Northridge 91325 Ofc: Array P.S. Mercantile 536 Hawthorne St Glendale 91206

PARASKOS, PETER GEORGE, co. president; b. Feb. 4, 1928, NYC; s. George and Anna (Kallergis) P.; m. Mary Ann Miller, June 1, 1955; children: George b. 1957, Cathy b. 1959, David b. 1960, John b. 1961, Nancy b. 1963, Peter b. 1967; edn: BA, Columbia Coll. 1949; BS, Columbia Univ. Sch. of Engring. 1950; grad. USN Test Pilot Sch., Patuxent River, Md. 1957-8, Def. Systems Mgmt. Coll., Ft. Belvoir, Md. 1979. Career: served to col. US Marine Corps 1950-60, inf. ofcr., naval aviator, fighter pilot, test pilot, decorated Korean Service Award; No. Am. Aviation/Rockwell Internat. 1961-80, v.p./ asst. gen. mgr. Missiles Systems Div.; v.p. domestic ops. LTV-Vought Corp.; current: pres./CEO Systron Donner Corp.; mem. Bd. of Nomination, Aviation Hall of Fame, Dayton, Oh.; mem: Soc. of Exptl. Test Pilots (life), Navy/Marine Corps League, Air Force Assn., Assn. of U.S. Army, Am. Inst. of Aero. and Astro., Am. Defense Preparedness Assn.; Greek Orth.; rec: aviation. Ofc: Systron Donner Corp. 2750 Systron Dr Concord 94518

PARBURY, C. ALAN, securities/ investment co. executive; b. Aug. 13, 1947, Palo Alto, Calif.; s. Charles B. and Ethel (Noakes) P.; m. Sandra W., June 1978; children: Cynthia b. 1964, Holly b. 1968; edn: BSc, Univ. Santa Clara 1970; Coll. of San Mateo 1971-72. Career: sales and ops. mgr. Grantree Corp. Portland, Ore. 1970-74; gen. ptnr./ mgr. BWA Dairy Prods. Ltd. 1975-78; pres./ gen. mgr. Alameda Joes' Inc. 1978-81; senior mgmt. cons. Gustafson, Williams Cons. Inc. Walnut Creek 1981-82; v.p. Cypress Capital Corp., v.p. TWA Mgmt. Corp., v.p. Fortune Planning Svcs. Walnut Creek and Danville, Calif. 1981−; funding dir. Women's Profl. Golf Tour 1982−; mem: Internat. Assn. Financial Planners, Kiwanis (pres.), Elks, Special Olympics (vol.), Little League of Am., United Cerebral Palsy; Republican; Catholic; rec: sports fan, golf, baseball, basketball. Ofc: 800 S Broadway Ste 404 Walnut Creek 94596

PARK, JAE HO, dentist; b. Feb. 3, 1936, Seoul, Korea; s. Min Hee and Sam Jun P.; m. Mi Ja Cho, Apr. 24, 1965; children: Bonnie b. 1967, Sung b. 1969; edn: DDS, Seoul Nat. Univ. 1958, PhD, 1972. Career: dentist Murry & Leonie Guggenheim Dental Clinic, N.Y. 1966-67; research asso. Univ. of Mich. 1967-69; prof. Yonsei Univ., Seoul 1970-78; general practice dentistry, Park's Dental Office, Los Angeles 1978−; recipient Award, Coll. of Dentistry, Yonsei Univ. (1977); mem. Korean Dental Assn. USA, 1982-; profl. publs., Korea (1973); mil: dentist/capt. Korean Army Med. Div. 1958-62; rec: golf. Res: 1501 Edris Dr Los Angeles 90035 Ofc: Park's Dental Office 3123 West Olympic Blvd Los Angeles 90006

PARK, JOHN ALLEN, clinical microbiologist; b. Apr. 1, 1948, Ely, Nev.; s. Floyd Harold and Virginia Dorlee (Rothmantl) P.; m. Carol, Oct. 23, 1970; children: Melissa Dawn b. 1974, Scott Dwayne b. 1977, Kimberly Danielle and Stephanie Danielle b. 1978; edn: AA in phys. sci., Mesa Coll. 1974; BS microbiol., San Diego State Univ. 1979; MS in med. tech., CSU Dominguez Hills 1985; postgrad. work in pub. adminstrn., La Verne Univ. 1985-; Calif. Comm. Coll. instr. cred. (health svcs.) 1986; desig: Med. Tech., A.S.C.P. (1980); Clin. Lab. Scientist, N.C.A. (1981). Career: hosp. corpsman US Navy, 1966-70; nurses aide VA Hosp., San Diego 1972-3; emergency techn. College Park Hosp., S.D. 1973-76; lab. techn. Tri-City Hosp., Oceanside 1976-80, med. technologist 1980-86; lab. adminstr. Doctors Care Med. Ctr., Escondido 1981−; med. dept. rep. USN Reserve, S.D. 1970-86; sec.treas. Robinson-West Corp., 1983-; honors: commendn., Girl Scouts Am. (1975); mem. Am. Soc. Clin. Pathol., Am. Mgmt. Assn., San Diego Computer Soc., Amateur Radio Assn.; works: quality control and statistical computer pgms. for clin. lab. data appls. (1984); mil: E6/HMI, USN-R, 1966-86, Purple Heart, Merit. Cit., Lutheran; rec: enology, amateur radio opr. (KA6AGB). Res: 14151 Tobiasson Rd Poway 92064 Ofc: Doctors Care Medical Center 362 W Mission Ave Escondido 92025

PARKER, ELIZABETH BOWEN, physician and surgeon, ret.; b. Mar. 4, 1913, Panama City, Fla.; d. Osgood Cook and Rosa Adeline (Bowen) Parker; m. Hugh D. Wilson, DDS, Feb. 24, 1952 (dec. 1961); edn: RN, Florida Hosp., Orlando 1935; pre-med. Columbia Union Coll., 1937; MD, and med. intern,

Loma Linda Univ. 1942; Reg. Nurse in Calif., Fla., Md., and Wash DC. Career: solo practise medicine, family practice with emphasis in obstets.-gyn., Hollywood 1942-81, med. staff Hollywood Presbyn. and White Meml. Hosp., 25 yrs.; med. staff Glendale Adventist Med. Ctr. 1947-81, hon. staff mem. 1981-; recipient 30 Year awards: Glendale Adventist Med. Center (1977), Am. Acad. Family Practice (1984); life mem. AAFP, Nat. Chrysanthemum Soc. (1954-); ret. mem. AMA, Calif. Med. Assn., LA Co. Med. Soc.; avocation: active chrysanthemum hybridizer; awarded the first patent for a fragrant chrysanthemum (1959), three additional patents for fragrant mums (1960, 61), Reg. Trade Mark: Fragramum (1960); subject of num. articles in LA Times, Florist Review, var. horticulture mags. re chrysanthemum breeding; mil: vol. clinic work Hollywood Presbyn. Hosp. WWII; Republican; Protestant; rec: photog., gardening, writing. Res: 2937 Glendower Ave Los Angeles 90027

PARKER, JOHN CARLYLE, librarian; b. Oct. 14, 1931, Ogden, Utah; s. Levi C. and Marietta (Parkinson) P.; m. Janet C. Greene, May 31, 1956; children: Denise b. 1957, Nathan b. 1960, Bret b. 1961; edn: BA, Brigham Young Univ. 1957; MSL, UC Berkeley 1958. Career: spl. svcs. librarian Humboldt State Coll., Arcata 1958-60; cataloger, reference librarian Church Coll. of Hawaii, Laie 1960-62, acting librarian 1962-63; head public svcs. Calif. State Univ. Stanislaus 1963-68, head public svcs., asst. library dir. 1968-83, acting library dir. 1983-84, head public svcs., asst. library dir. 1984–; founder, librarian Modesto Calif. Br. Genealogical Library 1968-; Genealogical Research and Genealogical Ref. Svc. Lectr. 1969-; ed. Marietta Publg. Co. 1985-; honors: Am. Library Assn. Library/ USA Fellowship (1965), Award of Merit, Nat. Genealogical Soc. (1984), Fellow of the Assn., Utah Genealogical Assn. (1984); mem: Calif. Library Assn., State Coll. Librarians (div. pres. 1969), Am. Library Assn., Am. Assn. of Univ. Profs., Calif. Tchrs. Assn. Nat. Ednl. Assn., Cong. of Faculty Assns., Conf. of Calif. Hist. Socs. (Genealogy Com.), Turlock Centennial Found., Turlock Community Concert Bd. (pres. 1973-75), Boy Scouts of Am. (Yosemite Council), Stanislaus Co. Hist. Soc.; publs: ed. Genealogy and Local Hist. series (1975-82); author: An Index to the Biographees in 19th Century California County Histories (1979), City, County, Town, and Township Index to the (1850) Federal Census Schedules (1979), A Personal Name Index to Orton's "Records of California Men in the War of Rebellion, 1861 to 1867" (1978), Library Service for Genealogists (1981), Directory of Archivist and Librarian Genealogical Instructors (1985), Pennsylvania and Middle Atlantic States Genealogical Manuscripts: A User's Guide to the Manuscript Collections of the Genealogical Society of Pennsylvania; As Indexed in Its Manuscript Materials; Microfilmed by the Genealogical Dept., Salt Lake City 1986; mil: splst. 3 US Army 1953-55, Nat. Defense, GCM; Democrat; Ch. of Jesus Christ LDS; rec: genealogy, photog. Res: 2115 No. Denair Ave. Turlock 95380 Ofc: The Library, Calif. State Univ. Stanislaus, Turlock 95380

PARKER, JUDY IVA, construction material distributing co. president; b. Aug. 24, 1950, Ripley County, Mo.; d. Albert Lee and Helen Marjorie (Gibson) Coram; m. Richard Parker, Aug. 14, 1976; children: Stephanie b. 1975, Heather b. 1975, Blair b. 1984; grad. McCluer H.S., Florissant, Mo. 1968. Career: data control clk. Ralston Purina Co., St. Louis, Mo. 1968-71; bookkeeper McDonald's Corp., Hollywood 1971-72, Superior Equity of Calif., Beverly Hills 1972-73; account rep. David Capell & Co. (bus. mgmt.), 1973-76; paraprofl. acct. Laventhol & Horwath, Portland, Ore. 1976-77; cost acct./constrn. coord. The Hollman Co., Lake Oswego,Or. 1977-80; estimator Continental Forest Prods. 1980-82; owner/pres. Commercial Door Systems Inc., San Diego 1982–; mem. Nat. Assn. of Women in Constrn., Nat. Assn. Female Execs.; feature subject of article, The San Diego Union (4/3/83), New Woman Mag. (1/84); rec: collect Am. Indian art, antique china plates. Ofc: Commercial Door Systems Inc 2667 Camino del Rio S, San Diego 92108

PARKER, KINGSBURY EASTMAN, JR., realtor- property manager; b. May 19, 1917, San Francisco; s. Kingsbury Eastman and Agnes Gertrude (Sawyer) P.; m. Carol Nicolai, May 14, 1956; children: Kingsbury Eastman, III., b. 1942; Stanley Duggan, b. 1943; William Michael, b. 1957; edn: Univ. of Calif. 1935-36; BS, Boeing Sch. of Aeronatics 1937-38; Army Air Corps. Adv. Flying Sch. 1938-39; CPM, Inst. of Real Mgmt.; CCIM, Realtors Nat. Mktg. Inst. Career: pilot, United Air Lines 1940-41; owner Aero Transport Corp. 1945-46; pres. International Air Freight 1946; owner Jamaica Air Transport 1946-47; owner Cayman Island Airways 1947-48; constn. supt. K.E. Parker Co. 1948-49; pres. King Parker, Jr., Inc., Walnut Creek 1950–; sr. instr. GRI, 1964; mem. Nat. Assn. Realtors (dir. 1969-74), Calif. Assn. Realtors (v.p., life dir. 1965-77), Contra Costa Bd. Realtors (pres. 1973, dir. 5 terms, Realtor of Year 1979), Inst. of Real Estate Mgmt. (past pres.), cert. comml. investment mem. Realtors Nat. Mktg. Inst. (pres. No. Calif. chpt. 1972-73), Walnut Creek Svc. Unit of Salvation Army, Flying Realtors of Calif. (pres.), Am. Philatelic Soc., British No. American Philatelic Soc., Am. Air Mail Soc., Western Cover Soc.; works: Grand Award - Postal History 1984 , Calif. Collector's Club Exhib.; mil: 2nd lt. US Army Air Corps 1939; capt. Royal Air Force 1941-45; rec: postal historian, philately. Res: 1403 Via Loma, Walnut Creek 94598 Ofc: King Parker, Jr., Inc., 1399 Ygnacio Valley Rd., Ste. 24, Walnut Creek 94598

PARKER, LAURA LEE, graphic designer; b. Feb. 2, 1947, Denver, Colo.; d. Harry Arthur and Sarah Geneva (Jones) Steinbach; edn: Colo. Inst. Art 1966-68, S.F. Acad. Art 1968-70, S.F. Art Inst. 1971. Career: graphic designer Wells Fargo Bank, San Francisco 1971-76; ptnr., graphic designer Ariel, S.F. 1977-81; prin., art director Laura Parker Design, S.F. 1981–; honors: Award of Excellence, Nat. Assn. of Art Directors (1986), 1st Pl. Prize, Nat. Assn. Fundraising Council (1984); mem. Am. Inst. Graphic Artists, S.F. Art Directors Club (bd. dirs.); clubs: Adventuresses of Sherlock Holmes (NYC) (The Hon. Miss Miles), Scowers & Mostly Maguires (SF); hobby: real estate. Ofc: Laura Parker Design 110 South Park San Francisco 94107

PARKER, MADISON ALDEN, II, tax preparation co. president, fashion wear co. president; b. Aug. 21, 1942, Nashua, New Hampshire; s. Donald Frederick and Wildie Thayer (Stillings) P.; m. Ruth Marie Gwynn, Sept. 24, 1966; children: Melanie b. 1968, Madison II b. 1969, Stephen b. 1971, Michael b. 1972, John b. 1974, Matthew b. 1975, Mark, b. 1977, Scott b. 1978, Tyler b. 1980, Travis b. 1981; edn: BS, Brigham Young Univ. 1971. Career: sr. asst. mgr. K Mart, Salt Lake City, Buena Park & Chula Vista 1971-73; founder, tax Preparation practice 1974; pres./ chmn. bd. Taxamerica Acctg. Inc. 1979–; founder fashion wear co.; pres./ chmn. bd. Expressivewear Ltd. 1984–; mem: Nat., Sadlleback Valley, Santa Ana, Fullerton CofCs; Nat. Assn. for Self-Empl.; Rotary; AYSO Soccer; Boy Scouts of Am.; Deer Cyn. PTA (auditor 1984-85, v.p. 1985-86), Better Bus. Bureau; publs: author, How to Avoid Income Taxes Legally (1980), Wrestling Life (1985); mil: USN 1960; Republican; Ch. of Jesus Christ of LDS; rec: writing poetry and novels, investments, chess. Res: 7064 Filkins Ave Cucamonga 91701 Ofc: Taxamerica Accounting Inc. and Expressivewear Ltd., 2751 E Chapman Ave, Ste 206, Fullerton 92631

PARKER, QUENTIN DART, architect; b. Dec. 1, 1953, Miami, Fla.; s. Alfred Browning and Martha (Gifford) P.; m. Anne Trueblood, Nov. 15, 1985; edn: Baccalaureate/ Abitur, Padagogium Otto Kuhne Schule West Germany 1972; B.Environmental Design, No. Carolina State Univ. Sch. of Design 1977; M.Arch., Harvard Univ. 1979; Reg. Architect, Fla. (1981), Calif. (1984). Career: architect, Alfred Browning Parker Arch. 1979-83; project mgr. Arch. Dept. Cannell & Chaffin Comml. Interiors 1983-84; architect prin. Quentin Dart Parker Architect; ptr., prin. designer Artfunction Inc. (furniture mfg. co.); cons. Terry George Hoffman & Assoc.; dir. Alfred B. Parker 79-83; honors: Judge, Soc. of Illumination Engrs. 1983; EPROM 1977; mem: Am. Inst. of Architects (Calif.), NCARB, Soc. of Illumination Engrs.; works: architl. (residential, branch banks, church in S.Fla., profl. offices, hosp. interiors in S.Calif.), art dir., prodn. design in cinemotography; Republican; Episcopal. Address: Quentin Dart Parker Architect, 3924 Sierks Way Malibu 90265

PARKER, THEODORE CLIFFORD, manufacturing co. president; b. Sept. 25, 1929, Dallas, Ore.; s. Theodore C. and Virginia Bernice (Rumsey) P.; m. Jannet Barnes, Nov. 28, 1970; 2 daus: Sally, Peggy; edn: BSEE, magna cum laude, USC 1960. Career: v.p. engring. Telemetrics Inc. 1963-65; chief engr. Information Systems, Northrop-Nortronics 1966-70; pres. Avtel Corp. 1971-74; pres. Aragon Inc. 1975-77; v.p. engring. Teledyne McCormick Selph 1978-82; mgr. electronic systems FMC Corp., Ordnance Div. 1983-85; pres. Power One Switching Products (engring. & mfg.) 1986–; chmn. Autotestcon 87; honors: Tau Beta Pi, Eta Kappa Nu; mem: IEEE, Am. Prodn. & Inventory Control Soc., Electronics Assn. of Calif. (founding dir.), Armed Forces Communs. & Electronics Assn., Am. Def. Preparedness Assn. Res: 1290 Saturn Ave Camarillo 93010 Ofc: Power One Switching Products 833 Flynn Rd Camarillo 93010

PARMLEY, WILLIAM WATTS, academic cardiologist; b. Jan. 22, 1936, Salt Lake City, Utah; s. Thomas Jennison and Martha Lavern (Watts) P.; m. Shanna L., Aug. 17, 1961; children: Michael, b. 1965, John, b. 1968, Todd, b. 1970, Ann, b. 1975; edn: AB, Harvard Coll. 1957; MD, Johns Hopkins Med. Sch. 1963. Career: intern, resident in medicine, Johns Hopkins 1963-65; clin. assoc. Nat. Heart Inst. 1965-67; cardiology fellow Peter Bent Brigham Hosp. 1967-69; assoc. dir. cardiology Cedars-Sinai Med. Ctr. 1969-73; chief of cardiology Moffitt/Long Hosp. 1974–; prof. of medicine Univ. of Calif. San Francisco; pres. American Coll. of Cardiology; honors: Alpha Omega Alpha, Phi Beta Kappa; mem. Am. Soc. of Clin. Research, Am. Assn. of Physicians, Assn. of University Cardiologists; author or coauthor of 300 sci. articles; mil: USPHS 1965-67; Republican; Mormon; rec: golf. Res: 2574 Roundhill Dr Alamo 94507 Ofc: University of California San Francisco 1186 Moffitt Hospital, San Francisco 94143

PARR, EDWARD LEON, design engineer; b. Mar. 6, 1914, Oakland; s. Edward and Helen Virginia (Adams) P.; m. Martha, Sept. 4, 1955; 1 dau. Joanne b. 1957. Career: worked with father in mining and heavy equip., building highways, airports, bridges, housing constrn., comml. bldgs.; designed farm machinery and mining equipment; design engr. Marquardt Aircraft, Consolidated American Co.; chief engr. company sold to Fairchild Camera; currently chief engr. for Jet Air, Inc.; has also been artist, draftsman, printer, tchr., sculptor, pattern maker, rodeo promoter, race car designer; his inventions include: a power-producing unit utilizing ocean swells, automatic temp. control for bathroom showers, spl. fastening devices, self-loading boat trailer, instruments to send pictures over ordinary telephones, automobile bumper, desalination plant, pipe coupling, solar collectors that look like ordinary roof shingles; holds over 40 patents; rec: grandchildren, singing, camping, boating, old cars & trains. Ofc: Jet Air Inc., 1071 Industrial Pl, El Cajon 92020

PARROTT, JAMES EDWARD, chiropractor, acupuncturist, hypnotherapist; b. Aug. 7, 1931, El Paso, Tex.; s. John N. and Marie (Boudreaux) P.; m. Marilyn Tawler, Mar. 3, 1986; children: Brynda Monique, Dodi, Heidi, Joseph; edn: DC, L.A. Coll. of Chiro. 1957; CBS Cert., basic sci., Ariz. State 1958; MA, Baptist Comm. Coll.; Oriental Preceptership, acupuncture & herbalogy, Hong Kong Inst. 1960; desig: Profl. Hypnotherapist, Hynotism Tng. Ist. 1979; Cert. X-Ray Supvr.- Opr., Calif. 1979; Cert. Hunter's Safety Instr., Calif. Dept. Fish. & Game. Career: lectr./ tchr. basic scis., Oriental Med.; Acutherapy pioneer in Am. 1960–; chiro./ acupuncturist/ hypnotherapist; bd. chmn. Karmel Kookies

Inc.; founder/ pres. San Pedro Prebuilt Homes; honors: Delta Sigma, hon. scholastic soc. of healing arts 1957; mem: Elks; Nat. Rifle Assn. (life); Calif. Rifle & Pistol Club (life); Sigma Chi Omega; works: sculptor; mil: pharmacist 2/c USN, USMC, WWI, Korean War, Korean Pres. Unit Cit., Pres. Unit Cit. USA, Philippine medal, Am. Campaign medal w/ 1 Star, Asia-Pac. w/ 4 Stars, Nat. Def., Victory, UN, Korean Svc. w/ 2 Stars; Democrat (State Central Com.); Catholic (bro. & stu. priesthood, W. Ortho. Cath.); rec: music, art, sculpture. Address: 812 W 5th St Oxnard 93030

PARRY, NANCY, physician; b. Dec. 20, 1940, Salt Lake City, Utah; d. Nathaniel Edmunds and Dorthea Nell (Harris) Parry; edn: BS, Univ. of Utah 1963; MD, UC Irvine 1967. Diplomate Am. Acad. of Family Practice. Career: rotating intern gen. med., Latter Day Saints Hosp., Salt Lake City 1967-68; physician and surgeon, solo practice, Anaheim 1968–; pres. Parry Devel. Co. (projects in Calif., Utah and Idaho); chmn. Am. Med. Advisory Bd. of Counseling Center (1972); recipient TELACU Women's Achievement Award (1980); mem. Orange County Med. Assn., Am. Coll. of Emergency Physicians, Am. Med. Assn., Calif. Med. Assn. Ofc: 1801 W Romneya Dr Ste 602 Anaheim 92801

PARSLEY, ROBERT ERNEST, utility co. vice president and controller; b. Dec. 9, 1921, Indpls., Ind.; s. Ernest Sylvester and Ora Emily (Kelley) P.; m. Donna, Feb. 14, 1945; children: Robert b. 1942, Constance b. 1945; edn: B. Comml. Sci., Balboa Univ. (Calif. Western Univ.) 1948; BBA, US Internat. Univ. 1962. Career: supv. acct. San Diego Gas & Elec. Co. 1951-56, chief acct. 1956-66, controller 1966-85, v.p., controller 1985–; past instr. acctg., chmn. acctg. advis. com. San Diego Evening Coll.; honors: Golden Key Merit Award (Admin. Mgmt. Soc., S.D. chap.); mem: Nat. Assn. Accts. (S.D. chap. pres. 1973), Rotary, Calif. Soc. Accts. (pres. S.D. chap. 1970-71), Project Concern (past dir. S.D. chap.); mil: Y2/c USNR 1942-46, WWII, Victory Medal, Good Conduct; Republican; Protestant; rec: jogging, gardening. Ofc: San Diego Gas & Elec. Co. 101 Ash St San Diego 92101

PARSONS, HARRY G., physician-surgeon; b. Mar. 5, 1919, San Bernardino; s. Harry G., Sr. and Evelyn May (Perris) P.; edn: BA w. distinction, Stanford Univ. 1942, MD, 1946; certified Am. Board Gen. Surg., Am. Board Thoracic Surg. Career: Rockerfellow fellowship surgical research, Stanford 1949-49, asst. resident surgery 1949-53, and fellowship thoracic surgery 154-55, Stanford Hosp.; asst. clin. prof. surgery, Stanford, 1955–; medical dir. Weimar Medical Ctr. 1955-72, pvt. practice general, thoracic and vascular surgery, Auburn currently; honors: Alpha Omega Alpha; mem: Fellow Am. Coll. of Surgeons, Western Thoracic Soc., Placer Nevada County Med. Soc. (pres. 1979), AMA, CMA (del. 1980); mil: capt. Med. Corps AUS 1946-48; Republican; Episcopal; rec: flying, hunting, fishing. Res: POB 361 Weimar 95736 Ofc: Harry G. Parsons, MD Inc., 11483 B Ave, Ste 2, DeWitt Ctr. Auburn 95603

PARSONS, JAMES DELBERT, research engineer; b. Mar. 18, 1947, Los Angeles; s. Delbert Rufus and Pauline (Vendel) P.; m. Marie Antoinette Nadalin, Aug. 23, 1969; 1 son, Aaron James b. 1970; edn: BS engrg., UC Los Angeles 1974, MS engrg., 1977, PhD engrg., 1981. Career: materials and processing helper Hughes Aircraft Co., L.A. 1971-78; engr. Jet Propulsion Lab., Pasadena 1978-79; mem. tech. staff Hughes Research Labs, Malibu 1980-85, proj. engr. 1985-86, section head 1986–; research asst. UCLA; honors: Alpha Gamma Sigma (1970-71), Travel Research Grant (UCLA 1976), Camp Fellowship (UCLA 1979), Engrg. Achievement Award for Student Welfare (UCLA 1978); mem: Am. Vacuum Soc., Am. Assn. Crystal Growth, Inst. Elec. Electron. Engrs.; works: num. inventions and publs. in fields of fiber optic eutectic crystal growth, semiconductor thin film growth and semiconductor devices; Republican; Catholic; rec: model ship building. Res: 596 Strauss Dr Newbury Park 91320 Ofc: Hughes Research Labs 3011 Malibu Cyn Rd Malibu 90265

PARTON, BRUCE A., health co. executive; b. Sept. 21, 1946, Brooklyn, NY;q s. Oscar and Esther (Epstein) P.; m. Elyssa, Feb. 14, 1982; 1 son, Michael b. 1975; edn: BS, New York Coll. of Engring. 1970; Assoc., Applied Science Acad. of Aeronautics 1968. Career: distrbn. mgr. Macy's New York, NY, NY 1970-75; dir. mech. ops. Bullocks Dept. Stores, Los Angeles 1975-80; div. v.p. facilities constrn. May Co., Los Angeles 1980-83; v.p. devel. Pritikin Programs Inc., Santa Monica 1983–; rec: jogging, tennis. Ofc: Pritikin Programs Inc., 1910 Ocean Front Walk Santa Monica 90405

PARTON, JAMES, III, lawyer; b. Oct. 19, 1951, NY; s. James and Jane Audra (Bourne) P.; m. Diane King, Aug. 22, 1976, (dec.); m. 2d Maureen A. Brown, Sept. 28, 1985; children: Phillip b. 1964 (adopted); Christopher, b. 1967 (adopted); edn: BA, cum laude, Univ. of Penn. 1973; JD, cum laude, Univ. of San Francisco 1977; admitted to practice, State of Calif. 1977. Career: staff asst. Congressman Michael J. Harrington, Wash. DC 1973-74; judicial clerk Marin Co. Superior Ct., San Rafael 1976; law clerk/ assoc. atty. Ericksen, Lynch, Mackenroth, Arbuthnot & Brennan Inc., San Francisco 1976-78; assoc. atty. Lynch & Loofbourrow, S.F. 1978-83; partner Lynch, Loofbourrow, Helmenstine, Gitardi & Grummer, Inc. 1983–; Alameda Co. Lawyers Com. for Disability Rights 1981-; reader Calif. Com. of Bar Examiners 1978; mem: Am. Bar Assn. (Litigation, Tort & Ins. Practice sects.); San Francisco Bar Assn.; Assn. Trial Lawyers of Am.; Assn. Ins. Attys. 1983–; Defense Research Inst.; No. Bay Sch. Site Com., Sausalito Sch. Dist. 1978; No. Calif. Alumni rep., The Loomis Chaffee Sch., Windsor, Conn. 1981-; Democrat; rec: photog. Res: 60 Kipling Dr Mill Valley 94941 Ofc: Lynch, Loofbourrow, Helmenstine, Gitardi & Grummer, Inc. 505 Beach St San Francisco 94133

PATTON, WILLIAM BLANTON, JR., computer co. president; b. Sept. 10, 1935, St. Louis, Mo.; s. William Blanton and Mildred Bearnice (Kinder) P.; m. Sandra Jean Schnellbacher, Jan. 30, 1959; children: William B., III b. 1960, Beth Ann b. 1962, Becky Jean b. 1965, Barbara Jane b. 1968; edn: AB in bus. adm., Santa Monica City Coll. 1956; BS in petroleum engring., Univ. of Mo., Rolla 1958; PMD Cert., Harvard Grad. Sch. Bus. 1971; Cert. Data Processor (CDP), DPMA 1964. Career: v.p. W. Ops., Honeywell, Inc. 17 yrs.; exec. v.p. Ampex Internat.; pres./CEO CADO Systems Corp.; current: pres/CEO MAI Basic Four, Inc. (design, mfr. & mktg. of bus. computers and info. processing solutions), also mem. bd. dirs. and chmn. exec. com.; dir: CCS (London), Pro-Log Corp., TorrVac Corp.; v.chmn. L.A. Co. Data Proc. Commn. 1982-85; civic: U.S. Academic Decathlon (pres. bd. dirs.), L.A. 1984 Olympic Citizens Advy. Commn., Little Company of Mary Hosp., Torrance (trustee), Laguna Arts Fest. and Pageant of the Masters (assoc. com.), YMCA, Torrance (dir.); mil: capt. US Army 1959-61, major USAR, mem. All-Army Golf Team; Republican; Lutheran; rec: racquetball, golf, wine. Ofc: MAI Basic Four 14101 Myford Dr Tustin 92680

PARVIN, ROSE A., marriage counselor; b. Feb. 8, 1950, Iran, nat. US cit. 1985; d. Ebraheim and Hamdam (Mostashar) Assier; m. Ben A. Parvin, Aug. 24, 1971; children: Ellie b. 1973, Shaun b. 1977; edn: Golden West Coll. 1974; BA psychol., with honors, CSU Long Beach 1976; MA family & child counseling Chapman Coll. Orange 1981; lic. Marriage, Family & Child Counselor Calif. 1982. Career: counseling coord., clin. supv., pres., bd. mem. Free Clin. of Orange Co. 1982-85; clin. supv. Laguna Beach Free Clin. 1984-85; YMCA adv. bd. 1985; founder, exec. dir. Parvin Ctr. for Developmental Health Newport Beach & Beverly Hills, a ctr. with emphasis on preventive care; crosscultural splst. KSCI & KUSI television pgm. 1984-85; ASA tchr., seminars, workshops, cons., expert witness in family and cross-cultural oriented issues; mem: Calif. Assn. Marriage and Family Therapists 1982–, Am. Personnel and Guidance Assn., Orange Co. Assn. of Marr. & Fam. Thers.; research, articles and book in progress on family dysfunctional systems, "Power Balance Therapy" and "Pattern Change Programming"; Liberal Republican; Moslem; rec: tennis, dancing, travel, photog., writing, reading. Ofc: Parvin Center 1501 Westcliff Dr, Ste 318, Newport Beach 92660; 414 N Camden Dr, Ste 905, Beverly Hills 90210

PASCO, WILLIAM JOEL, veterinarian; b. Sept. 25, 1947, Chagrin Falls, Ohio; s. Wm. Earl and Ethel Louise (Short) P.; m. Jean Osmus, Sept. 21, 1985; edn: BVM, Univ. Ill., 1970, DVM, 1972; intern Animal Med. Ctr., NYC 1973. Career: veterinarian/ dir. Sun-Surf Animal Hosp. (co-owner 1978-82), Sunset Beach, South Laguna Village Animal Hosp., So. Laguna, East Fullerton Pet Clinic, Fullerton, Nohl Ranch Animal Hosp., Anaheim Hills, 1980-82; staff vet. Avian and Exotic Animal Practice, Anaheim 1982-83; vet. prin. All Creatures Care Cottage, Costa Mesa currently; frequent public spkr. on wildlife ecology and pet care topics, civic groups, schs. and colls.; slide, film and video presentations 1979-84; network t.v. appearances on Real People (NBC, 1979), news networks (1979, 80), NBC World News Report (1980), Dinah Shore Show (1980); contbg. writer, Dog Life Mag., Bird World Mag., Bird Talk Mag.; contbg. photog. Orange County Register; mem: Alliance for Wildlife Rehab. and Edn. (pres.; newsletter columnist), Avian Soc. of So. Calif. VMA (past pres., co-founder), Orange Co. Bird Breeders Assn., Am./Calif. Vet. Med. Assn., Sierra VMA, Am. Animal Hosp. Assn., Assn. of Avian Pathologists, Assn. of Avian Vets., Humane Soc. US, Nat. Wildlife Fedn., Audubon Soc.; vet. advisor Kern River Wildlife Sanctuary, No. Orange Co. ROP Pgm. Anaheim; Republican; Christian. Res: 208 Rochester St Costa Mesa 92627 Ofc: All Creatures Care Cottage 1912 Harbor Blvd Costa Mesa 92627

PASHAYAN, CHARLES, JR., congressman; b. March 27, 1941, Fresno; edn: BA, Pomona Coll. 1963; JD, Univ. of Calif. 1968; B.Litt., Oxford Univ. 1977; admitted to the bars of Calif. (1969), D.C. (1972), U.S. Supreme Ct. (1977). Career: spl. asst. to gen. counsel HEW 1973-75; mem. 96th and 97th Congresses from 17th Dist. Calif.; mem: Calif. and Fresno Co. Bar Assns., Royal Inst. of Internat. Affairs, Internat. Inst. for Strategic Studies; mil: capt. US Army 1968-70; Republican. Ofc: 129 Cannon House Office Bldg., Washington DC 20515

PASSAGLIA, RICHARD DENNIS, retail executive; b. Sept. 20, 1939, Chgo.; s. Louis Joseph and Lena Rena (Nottoli) P.; m. Annette Marie D'Argento, Aug. 5, 1961; children: Paul b. 1962, Dean b. 1963, Leanne b. 1964; edn: BS in mktg., De Paul Univ. 1962. Career: buyer Montgomery Ward & Co., Chgo. 1962-67; mdse. mgr./reg. mgr. Wickes Lumber Co., Saginaw 1967-74, gen. mdse. mgr. 1974-78, mng. dir. Wickes Europe, The Hague, The Netherlands 1978-81, gen. mgr. Toy World/Wickes Cos. Inc., Burbank 1981-83; senior v.p. Home Centers West/W.R. Grace, Brea 1983-85; gen. mgr. O'Malley Lumber Co./Retail Div., Phoenix, Az. 1985–; listed, Who's Who in Am. Univs. (1961); mil: E8 Army Nat. Guard, Ill. 1959-65; Republican; Roman Catholic; rec: golf, swim. Address: Phoenix AZ 85016

PASTEN, LAURA JEAN, veterinarian; b. May 25, 1949, Tacoma, Wash.; edn: Stanford Univ. 1970; BA physiol., UC Davis 1970, DVM, 1974; postgrad., Cornell Univ. 1975; Career: vet. Nevada Co. Vet. Hosp. Grass Valley 1975-80; pvt. practice vet., owner Mother Lode Vet. Hosp. Grass Valley (certified wildlife rehab. ctr.) 1980–; lectr. in field; affil. staff Sierra Nevada Meml. Hosp.; bd. dirs. Sierra Svcs. for the Blind; syndicated TV show on vet. medicine, guest on Today Show re wildlife; honors: Regent's Scholar; mem: Am. Vet. Med. Assn. (ethics com.), Calif. Vet. Med. Assn. (ethics com.), Sacto. Valley Vet. Med. Assn. (exec. com., CVMA del.), Mother Lode Vet. Assn., Am. Animal Hosp. Assn., Nat. Ophthalmic Soc., Nat. Pygmy Goat

Assn., Nat. Llama Assn., Nat. Appaloosa Soc., Denver Area Med. Soc., Internat. Vet. Assn., Mensa, Nat. Soc. Underwater Instrs., Am. Endurance Riding Soc.; civic: Nevada Co. CofC (bd. dirs.), Grass Valley Bus. Women, affiliate staff mem. Sierra Nevada Meml. Hosp., bd. dirs. Sierra Services for the Blind; publ: Canine Dermatology (w. Dr. Muller 1970), contbr. articles to profl. jours.; Republican; Lutheran. Address: 11509 La Barr Meadows Rd Grass Valley 95945

PATAFIO, CLEMENTE JOSEPH, banker; b. May 17, 1952, Port Chester, NY; s. Gaetano and Theresa (Plataroti) P.; edn: UCLA 1970-72. Career: tax rating analyst Nat. Employers Counsel Inc., Los Angeles 1970-75; asst. mgr. Consolidated Foods Corp. Electrolux Div., Downey 1975-76; ops. mgr. Semperit of America, Vernon 1976-78; indsl. svcs. dir. Wightman Goodwill Ind. Long Beach 1978-70; ops. ofcr. Union Bank, Panorama City 1970-81, admin. ofcr. 1981-82, asst. v.p. & mgr. 1982-86, v.p. & ops. mgr. 1986—; trainer Union Bank 1982-85; honors: Gov.'s Scholar 1970; Bank of America Achiev. Award, 1970; Calif. Sch. Fedn. Seal Bearers Aud. 1980; Science Medallion Award, 1970; mem: Am. Mgmt. Assn., Mensa, Computer Entrepreneurs Assn. of Am., GOP Victory Fund, Key Club (past pres.), Dist. Atty. Youth Adv. Bd. (past); Republican (Nat. Com.); Catholic; rec: personal computer programer/ cons., skiing, video. Ofc: Union Bank, 14500 Roscoe Blvd. 6th Flr. Panorama City 91402

PATEL, MARILYN HALL, federal judge; b. Sept. 2, 1938, Amsterdam, NY; d. Lloyd Manning and Nina J. (Thorpe) Hall; m. Magan C. Patel, Sept. 2, 1966; 1 child, Gian b. 1976; edn: BA, Wheaton Coll. 1959; JD, Fordham Law Sch. 1963; admitted to NY State Bar 1963, Calif. State Bar 1970. Career: mng. atty. Benson & Morris, Esqs., NYC 1963-65; private solo practice, NYC 1965-67; U.S. Dept. of Justice (INS.), San Francisco 1967-71; pvt. solo practice, San Francisco 1971-76; judge Municipal Ct. Alameda Co., Oakland 1976-80; U.S. District judge, No. Dist. of Calif., 1980—; adj. prof. of law Hastings Coll. of Law 1974-76; mem. ABA (Litigation Sect.), Calif. Conf. of Judges, Nat. Assn. of Women Judges (founding mem.), Internat. Institute (bd.), Advocates for Women (co-founder), Am. Judicature Soc. (bd. dirs.); fmr. mem., bd. dirs., ACLU, NOW and NOW Legal Defense and Edn. Fund; publs: Immigration and Nationality Law (1974); num. arts. on tax and corporate law and legal rights of women; Democrat; rec: piano, travel. Ofc: US District Court 450 Golden Gate Ave San Francisco 94102

PATEL, VINOD G., motel chain owner, investor; b. Apr. 10, 1952, Navsari, India; s. Gopalti L. and Kamala G. P.; m. Babli, Mar. 8, 1976; children: Vima b. 1977, Mita b. 1981; edn: BS in sci. (highest honors in physics), Gujarate Univ., India 1971; BS in physics, Chgo. Tech. State Coll. Career: motel owner, investor 1973—; mem: Santa Clara Hospitality Assn.; civic: India Cultural Assn. San Jose (pres. 1985), Chamber of Commerce (Gilroy, Sunnyvale, Chico, Paso Robles), Crippled Childrens Soc. of Santa Clara, Disabled Am. Vets.; Republican (Nat. Rep. Congress); Hindu; rec: antiques. Res: 6400 Barron Pl Gilroy 95020

PATKAY, STEPHEN ALBERT, management engineering co. executive, ret.; b. Apr. 13, 1902, Budapest, Hungary, nat. US cit. 1953; s. Daniel Joseph and Elizabeth Maria (Farkas) P.; m. Madeleine Galopin, Mar. 15, 1945; 1 son, Jean-Pierre b. 1950; edn: Federal Technical Polytech Zurich, Switz. 1919-20; B.Engrg., M.Engrg., Tech. Univ. Technische Hoch Schule Berlin, Germany 1926, PhDME, 1929; Reg. Profl. Engr. (mech., indsl., mfg.) Calif. Career: asst. prof., lab. engr. mfg. mgmt. and machine tools Technische Hochschule Berlin 1926-28; mgr. mfg. Stuebgen & Co. Erfurt, Germany 1928-30; research Edward G. Herbert Manchester, Eng. 1930; chief engr., asst. to pres. Klein, Schanzlin & Becker Frankenthal, Germany 1931-33; founder, owner Lumiclair S.A. optical instrument mfg. co. Boulogne, France 1934-40; chief engr., mgmt. cons. Internat. Bedaux Co. Paris, Bruxelles, La Haye 1940-47, spl. assignment in San Francisco 1947-59; founder, chmn. bd. Stephen Patkay & Assocs. Mgmt. Engrs. Fullerton 1959-78 (ret.); num. lectures in advanced machining technologies worldwide; mem: Soc. Mech. Engrs., Soc. Tool & Mfg. Engrs., Am. Soc. Metals; works: developed unique tool geometries to cut metal more efficiently with less deformation; publ: Werkstatttechnik 1928-29; presentation Internat. Tool Conf. Liege, Belgium 1944; rec: photog., horses, electronics. Res: 260 Vernal Ct Los Altos 94022

PATRICK, CHARLES LEON, real estate broker/ building contractor; b. Feb. 3, 1938; s. Elby Leon and Dorothy Aline (Hicks) P.; m. Carol Sue, Jan. 13, 1961; children; Kelley, b. 1962; LeAnne, b.1966; edn: Bakersfield Coll. 1968-69; Lumbleau Real Estate Sch. 172, 73, 75; UC Santa Barbara 1977; USC 1982; Limited Svc. Cred., Calif. State Dept. of Edn. 1977. Career: draftsman, surveyor, instrument-man, engr. Southern Pacific Transp. Co., Bakersfield 1961-75; general building contr., real estate broker, Bakersfield 1976—; owner Mid-Valley Real Estate, and C.L. Patrick Construction; mem: Bakersfield Board of Realtors, Calif., Nat. Assns. of Realtors, Independent Contractors Assn. 1971-; clubs: Bakersfield Trade, Meudell Lodge Freemasons, Bakersfield Christian Life Schools Booster, Bakersfield College Alumni Assn., UCSB Alumni Assn., Bakersfield Racquet; Republican; Baptist; rec: antique cars. Res: Star Route 4 Box 705, Bakersfield 93306 Ofc: Mid-Valley Real Estate/ C.L. Patrick Construction, 4664 American Ave Bakersfield 93309

PATRICK, DANIEL RAY, prosthodontist; b. Mar. 1, 1940, Hope, Mich.; s. Burton Edward and Ardieth Louise (Patterson) P.; m. Jo Ann Carbajal, Apr. 15, 1982; children: Michael b. 1967, Sean b. 1970, Vanessa b. 1971; edn: AB, Indiana Univ. 1963, DDS, 1967, MSD, 1981; bd. qualified Am. Board of Prosthodontic. Career: p.t. practice, gen. dentistry, Beech Grove, Ind.

1967-68; full-time solo practice, gen. dentistry, Kokomo, Ind. 1969-70, senior ptnr. practice, restorative, implant, and maxillofacial prosthodontics, 1970-76, pres. Burlinton-Kokomo Dental Assocs., Inc. 1976-80; active staff Howard Comm. Hosp., Kokomo 1970-73, Harbor-UCLA Med. Ctr., Torrance, Calif. 1980-81; adj. asst. prof. UCLA 1980-82, researcher 1982-; pvt. practice prosthodontist, implantologist, Long Beach 1982 –; pres. Ctr. for Spl. Dental Care, Long Beach Comm. Hosp., 1984 –; pres. Advanced Prostodontics Inc., D&D Prods. Inc.; assoc. staff Meml. Med. Ctr. of Long Beach; active staff Long Beach Comm. Hosp.; mem: Am. Acad. of Implant Dentistry, ADA, Acad. of Dentistry for Handicapped, Acad. of Gen. Dentistry, Howard Co. Dent. Soc. 1970-80 (pres. 1973), Ind. Dent. Assn., Calif. Dent. Assn., Harbor Dent. Soc., Wabash Valley Dist. Dent. Soc., Fedn. Prosthodontic Orgns., Am. Coll. Prosthodontics, Internat. Coll. of Oral Implantology, Fellow Internat. Congress of Oral Implantology (1983); US patent: for oral implant (1978); Republican. Res: 1660 Crestview Ave Seal Beach 90740 Ofc: 3711 Long Beach Blvd Ste 618 Long Beach 90807

PATSEY, RICHARD LEE, judge; b. Apr. 23, 1935, St. Joseph, Mo.; s. Gerald J. and Sigrid S. (Parson) P.; m. Lois K., Sept. 13, 1958; children: Shannon b. 1961, Geoffrey b. 1965; edn: AB, Carleton Coll. 1957; LLB, UC Berkeley Boalt Hall 1960. Career: counsel Calif. Assembly Judiciary Com. 1962; asst. dist. atty. Contra Costa Co. 1963; asst. pub. defender Alameda Co. 1964-65; special counsel Calif. Constitution Revision Commn. 1965-68; pvt. practice law S.F. 1968-80; superior ct. judge 1980 –; prof. law J.F.K. Univ.; lectr. Calif. Judl. Coll. honors: Ford Found. Grant 1960, Nat. Endowment for Humanities Grant 1981; mem: Am. Bar Assn., Calif. Judges Assn., Contra Costa Co. Bar Assn., Am. Cancer Soc., Am. Heart Assn., Mental Health Assn., Diablo Symphony League, Friends of Contra Costa Library; reports: Calif. Legislature Assembly Judiciary 1961-62, Calif. Constitution Revision Commn. 1965; Democrat; Protestant; rec: reading, music, theatre, jogging, tennis. Ofc: County Courthouse Martinez 94553

PATTEN, BEBE HARRISON, clergywoman/ educator; b. Sept. 3, 1913, Waverly, Tenn.; d. Newton Felix and Mattie Priscilla (Whitson) Harrison; m. Carl Thomas Patten, Oct. 23, 1955; children: (twins) Priscilla Carla and Bebe Rebecca, Carl Thomas; edn: DD, McKinley Roosevelt Coll. 1941; D.Litt., Temple Hall Coll. & Sem. 1943. Career: ordained to ministry, Ministerial Assn. of Evangelism 1935; evangelist in var cities of US 1933-50; founder/ pres. Patten Acad. Christian Edn., Oakland 1944 –; Patten Bible Coll., Oakland 1945-85; pres.-emeritus/ chancellor, Patten Coll. 1983; founder/ pastor Christian Cathedral of Oakland 1950 –; condr. pgm., The Shepherd Hour, San Francisco 1962 –; exec. bd. Bar-Ilan U. Assn., Israel; hon. fellow, 1981; Dr. Bebe Patten chair in soc. action estab. 1981; awards: medallion, Ministry of Religious Affairs, Israel 1969; medal, Govt. Press Ofc., Jerusalem 1971; Christian honoree of Year, Jewish Nat. Fund of No. Calif. 1975; Hidden Heroine award, S.F. Bay Council, Girl Scouts USA 1976; Ben-Gurion medallion, Ben-Gurion Research Inst. 1977; mem: Am. Assn. for Higher Edn.; Religious Edn. Assn.; Am. Acad. Religion & Soc. Bibl. Lit.; Zionist Orgn. of Am.; Am. Jewish Hist. Soc.; Am. Israel Pub. Affairs Comm. 1983; works: author, Give Me Back My Soul, 1973; editor, Trumpet Call, 1953 –; composer 20 gospel & relig. songs 1948-; listed in num biographical publs.; rec: swimming, tennis. Ofc: 2433 Coolidge Ave Oakland 94601

PATTERSON, J. MICHAEL, certified public accountant; b. Mar. 6, 1946, Washington, Iowa; s. J. Kenneth and Jo Ann (Ross) P.; m. Marci Feiock, Aug. 28, 1979; children: Lori b. 1964, Lisa b. 1966, Todd b. 1970, Staci b. 1972; edn: BBA, Univ. of Iowa 1968; JD, Univ. of Chgo. 1973; CPA, Iowa 1970, Ill. 1971, Calif. 1973; Realtor, Calif. 1978. Career: with Price Waterhouse; staff, Chgo.; senior, mgr., sr. mgr. Price Waterhouse, San Jose, tax partner, currently; frequent pub. spkr.; mem: Beta Alpha Psi (v.p. 1968); Phi Delta Phi; Am. & Calif. Insts. CPAs; Am., Calif. & Santa Clara (Tax Sect. exec. com.) Bar Assns.; Estate Plnng. Counicl; Am. Electronics Assn. (Tax Subcom.); San Jose Kiwanis (bd. dirs.); Southwest YMCA (bd. dirs.); Santa Clara Co. Trunk & Tusk Club; Childrens Discovery Mus. (bd. advrs.); mil: spec. E-5 US Army 1968-70; Republican (Fin. Com. for Morgan for Senate 1983-); Methodist; rec: sports. Res: 23415 Sunset Dr Los Gatos 95030 Ofc: Price Waterhouse, 150 Almaden Ave San Jose 95113

PATTERSON, WILLIAM T., pet and animal photographer; b. July 18, 1933, Findlay, Ohio; s. Arthur D. and Shirley P., children: Rita b. 1957, Karen b. 1961, Sheri b. 1963; edn: Coll. of Wooster 1951, Ohio State Univ. 1952-54. Career: pvt. investigator 1957-65; owner home study sch. tchg. pvt. investigation 1965-78; writer synd. pet column 1977-82; currently, pet and animal photographer; honors: Pres., Guide Dogs of the Desert, Palm Springs 1974-79; Best Synd. Pet Columnist Award, Dog Writers Assn. of Am. 1981; mem: Gr. Los Angeles Zoo Assn., Dog Writers Assn. of Am.; author: Private Investigators Manuel; rec: travel, swimming, equestrian. Ofc: P.O. Box 8180 Universal City 91608

PATTON, DAVID WAYNE, hospital executive; b. June 15, 1942, Utica, NY; s. Dale Willard and Eleanor Theresa (Miller) P.; m. Karmen Rames, June 12, 1965; children: Jodi b. 1967, Steven b. 1973; edn: BS bus. admin., Ariz. State Univ. 1964; M. Hosp. Admin., Univ. Minn. 1966. Career: asst. adminstr. Maricopa Co. Med. Ctr. Phoenix, Ariz. 1969-71; adminstr. Holy Rosary Hosp. Miles City, Mont. 1971-74; exec. dir. St. Luke's Hosp. Aberdeen, S.D. 1974-79; pres. Parkview Episcopal Med. Ctr. Pueblo, Colo. 1979-84, Riverside Comm. Hosp. 1984—; clin. preceptor Univ. Pittsburgh health adminstrn. pgm. 1981-82; dir. San Louis Valley HMO 1982-84; honors: Boss of the Year (Miles City, Mont. Jaycees 1973), Boss of the Year (Pueblo, Colo. Kachina Chpt. PSI

1982); fellow Am. Coll. Health Care Execs. (council of regents 1976-79); mem: Am. Hosp. Assn., Am. Acad. Med. Adminstrs., Calif. Hosp. Assn., Hosp. Council of So. Calif., Victoria Club, Monday Morning Group, Keep Riverside Ahead (dir.), Riverside CofC (dir.); publ: articles, profl. papers; mil: capt. USAF Med. Svcs. Corps 1966-69; Republican; Presbyterian; rec: golf, tournament bridge. Res: 2596 Raeburn Dr Riverside 92506 Ofc: Riverside Community Hospital 4445 Magnolia Ave Riverside 92501

PATTON, JACK THOMAS, physician; b. Feb. 18, 1941, Rogers, Ark.; s. Jack Marcus and Jewell Selia (Pense) P.; m. Lynette Anne Carr, Sept. 2, 1960; children: Robert Thomas b. 1961, John Neale b. 1964, Mark Keaka b. 1971, Christopher James b. 1976; edn: BA magna cum laude, CSU Long Beach 1963; MD, USC Sch. of Medicine 1967; intern, Tripler Army Med. Ctr. 1967-68, resident in family practice Walson Army Hosp. 1968-70; MA, Mennonite Brethren Biblical Sem., 1978-80; Diplomate Am. Board of Family Practice; Fellow Am. Acad. of Family Physicians. Career: chief Med. Section Schofield Barracks, Tripler Army Med. Ctr. 1970-71, dep. comdr. Schofield Barracks Med. Clinics 1972, liaison ofcr. Family Practice Residency Pgm., 1973; med. supt. Nazarene Hosp. Papua New Guinea 1973-78; lectr. Dept. Nsg. CSU Fresno 1978-79; mission dir. Nazarene Hosp. Papua New Guinea 1979-80; physician, chmn. Dept. of Family Practice Sharp Rees-Stealy Med. Group, 1981–; lectr. Dept. Nsg. Point Loma Coll. 1980-84; preceptor Sch. Medicine UCSD 1982-; physician advisor San Diego Vis. Nurse and Homemaker Assn. 1984-; med. cons. Samaritan Counseling Ctr. 1985; honors: Phi Kappa Phi; Honor Soc. CSULB and USC; Fellow Acad. Family Physicians; Affil. Royal Soc. of Medicine (London); mem. Calif. Acad. Family Physicians, Am. Acad. Family Physicians, Am. Assn. of Missiology, SD County Med. Soc., Calif. Med. Soc., Salerni Collegium, num. church and hosp. groups; publs: chapter, Water Quality Criteria (1962); contbr. med. publs.; mil: major M.C. US Army, Meritorious Service Medal; Ind.; Ch. of Nazarene; rec: tennis, hiking, painting. Res: 4444 La Cuenta Dr San Diego 92124 Ofc: Sharp Rees-Stealy Medical Group 10789 Tierrasanta Blvd Ste 106 San Diego 92124

PAUL, KENNETH M., JR., marketing and consulting co. president; b. June 15, 1938, El Paso, Tex.; s. Kenneth M., Sr. and Lucy E. (Manley) P.; m. Marilyn J., July 3, 1981; 1 child: Kelly b. 1964; edn: bus. psychol., Whittier Coll. 2 yrs. Career: territory sales mgr. Gearmore Inc., Lake Oswego, Ore. 1975-78, Heath Farm Equipment, Ft. Collins, Colo. 1978-80; territory mgr. Harris Truck & Implement, Mtn. Home, Idaho 1980-82; territory sales mgr., independent mfr's rep. Peabody Engrg., Gardena, Calif. 1982-85; pres. AIM 1985–; cons. to mfrs. of light industrial, lawn & garden, turf & agricultural equipment; mem: Agrl. Mfrs. Rep. Assn., Calif. Rental Assn., Far West Equipment Assn., Tractor and Equipment Club, Elks, Moose; mil: EM3 USN 1955-59, China Svc.; Republican; Protestant; rec: gourmet cooking, fly fishing, hunting, camping. Ofc: AIM 402 Mission Park Dr, Stockton 95207

PAUL, VAUGHN ALAN, mushroom grower; b. Sept. 13, 1951, Santa Clara; s. George and Josephine Laura (Malkon) P.; m. Peggy, Apr. 13, 1980; edn: AS, Cabrillo Coll. 1972, CSU Sacto. 1974. Career: head grower Castle-Cooke Mushrooms, 1976; owner, opr. Mushroom Farms Inc. 1977; const. govt. lending US Economic Devel. Agcy. 1977-81; ptnr./grower Spawn-Mate Inc. (fertilizer for mushrooms) 1978-80; owner Petaluma Mushrooms 1980-84; shareholder, pres./CEO Mushroom King (largest privately held grower & shipper of fresh mushrooms in No. Am.), 1984–; cons. var. lending instns. including Federal Land Bank, Citicorp., Econ. Devel. Adminstrn.; mem. Am. Mushroom Inst.; Elks Club; num. publs. on mgmt. and sci. related to mushrooms; mil: E3 US Navy 1975-76; Republican; Catholic; rec: off-road motorcycling, photog. Res: 10429 Moonshine Rd Sebastopol 94952 Ofc: Mushroom King 930 Shiloh Rd Windsor 95492

PAULING, LINUS CARL, chemist, educator; b. Feb. 28, 1901, Portland, Ore.; s. Herman Henry Wlliam and Lucy Isabelle (Darling) P.; m. Ava Helen Miller, June 17, 1923; children: Linus Carl, Peter Jeffress, Linda Helen, Edward Crellin; edn: BS, Ore. State Coll. 1922, ScD, hon., 1933; PhD, Calif. Inst. Tech. 1925; ScD, hon., Univ. Chicago 1931; Princeton Univ. 1946; Univ. Cambridge; Univ. London; Yale Univ. 1947; Oxford 1948; Brooklyn Polytechnic Inst. 1955; Humboldt Univ. 1959; Univ. Melbourne 1964; Univ. Delhi, Adelphi Univ. 1967; Marquette Univ. Sch. Med. 1969; LHD, Tampa 1950; UJD, Univ. N.B. 1950; LLD, Reed Coll. 1959; edn. in France: Dr. H.C., Paris 1948, Toulouse, 1949, Montpellier, 1958; Jagiellonian Univ. 1964; DFA, Chouinard Art Inst. 1958. Career: with. Calif. Inst. of Tech. 1922-64; tchg. fellow 1922-25; research fellow 1935-37; asst. prof. 1927-29; assoc. prof. 1929-31; prof. chem. 1931-64; chmn. div. chem. and chem. engring.; dir. Gates & Crellin labs. 1936-58; mem. exec. com.; bd. trustee 1945-48; research prof. Ctr. for Study of Dem. Instns. 1963-67; prof. chem. UC San Diego 1967-69; prof. chem. Stanford 1969-74; pres. Linus Pauling Inst. Sci. & Med. 1973-75, research prof. 1973–; George Eastman prof. Oxford Univ. 1948; lectr. chem. sev. univs.; honors: Fellow Balliol Coll. 1948, NRC 1925-26, Jon S. Guggenheim Meml. found. 1926-27; num. awards in field of chem. incl. US Presdl. Medal for Merit 1948, Nobel Prize in chem. 1954, Nobel Peace Prize 1962, Internat. Lenin Peace Prize 1972, US Nat. Medal of Sci. 1974, Fermat Medal, Paul Sabatier Medal, Pasteur Medal, medal with laurel wreath of Internat. Grotius Found. 1957, Lomonosov Medal 1977, Chem. Scis. award Nat. Acad. Scis. 1979; author: sev. books 1930-; contbr. articles to profl. journs. Ofc: Linus Pauling Inst. Sci. & Med., 400 Page Mill Rd. Palo Alto 94306

PAULSON, JOHN ERIC, photographer; b. Oct. 14, 1957, Syracuse, NY; s. Roy Wilson and Wanda (Lewandowski) P.; m. Diane Pifferetti, Mar. 27, 1981; children (step): Kirsten b. 1975, A.J. b. 1976; edn: Westmont Coll. 1975-76, fine arts major CSU San Jose currrent. Career: owner John Paulson Photography, San Jose 1976–; recipient annual nat. and internat. honors for wedding and Bar-Bat Mitzvah photographs, Profl. Photogs. of Am. (1981-), nat. award winner (wedding portrait) pub. in The Professional Photographer (1983); mem. Profl. Photogs. Am./Greater Bay Area; Republican; Christian. Address: John Paulson Photography 2995 Leigh Ave San Jose 95124

PAWLEY, CARL JOHN, experimental physicist; b. Feb. 28, 1956, Milwaukee, Wisc.; s. James Arthur and Janet (Vogel) P.; m. Kimberly Joy Moran, June 29, 1985; edn: BS, honors, Purdue Univ. 1977; USC 1978; MS, UCLA 1982; PhD, in progress. Career: staff engr. Hughes Aircraft Co., Culver City 1977-78; tchg. asst. USC Los Angeles 1977-78; research asst. UCLA 1978–; presented papers, confs. of: Am. Physical Soc.- Plasma Gp. 1980-85; IEEE- Plasma Gp. 1980-83; 13th Annual Absorption Conf. 1983; guest lectr. UCLA 1980-85; honors: Commencement Spkr., Fairview Park H.S. 1974; mem: Eta Kappa Nu; IEEE; Alpha Phi Omega; Purdue Alumni Assn.; publs. of research: Physcial Review Letters, 1982; Conf. on Plas. Phys., IAENA-CN, 1-2, 1982; Proceedings of 6th Internat. Workshop on Laser Interaction & Rel. Plasma Phenomena, 1984; Democrat; Catholic; rec; backpacking, music. Res: 15105 Victory Blvd Van Nuys 91411 Ofc: UCLA, 7702 Boelter Hall, Los Angeles 90024

PAYNE, LOUIS DONALD, writer, poet, ret. electrical engineer; b. Nov. 29, 1905, Alturas; s. Ernest Drury and Blanche Mar (Wallace) P.; m. Jeannette Abbot, Aug. 30, 1931 (dec. Oct. 16, 1981); children: Donald Wallace b. 1935, Grace Abbott b. 1938; edn: BSEE, UC Berkeley, two years grad. work in physics, UCB 1931-33; past Reg. Profl. Engr. (Elec.). Career: surveyor Calif. Forest Exptl. Sta. 1933-35; engr. Shell Oil Co., Martinez 1935-37; Shell Devel. Co., Emeryville 1937-39; Pacific Elec. Mfg. Corp. (& successor Federal-Pacific Elec. Co.), San Francisco and Santa Clara 1941-61, ret.; independent sci. researcher/ writer on topics relating to earth scis., physics, earthquake and weather forecasting, health; self-pub. author: Earthquake Patterns of the San Francisco Bay Area (1978, 79); Ballads of Outer Space and Other Poems (1985); physics paper: On the Mass of a Photon (1985); contbg. poet 2 anthologies: The World of Poetry, In a Nutshell; mem: Calif. Writers Club, Calif. Fedn. of Chaparral Poets, The Alameda (CA) Poets, El Camino Poets (Sacto.), The Ina Coolbrith Circle (Berkeley), Nat. Rifle Assn.; Republican; rec: sawing wood, camping, vol. work in Tilden Nature Area. Address: 1543 Beverly Pl Berkeley 94705

PEACOCK, JOHN HENRY, real estate investor; b. Dec. 20, 1924, Shreveport, La.; s. John Henry and Odelia (North) P.; m. Ola V., Feb. 8, 1947; edn: spl. courses East L.A. Jr. Coll. 1957-59, L.A. Metropolitan Coll. of Bus. 1962-63, L.A. City Coll. 1963-64; num. real estate inv. & mgmt. seminars; grad. Dale Carnegie Course 1963. Career: journeyman, foreman in building trades, San Francisco and Los Angeles, 1945-55; storekeeper Los Angeles City Dept. of Water & Power 1955-70; real estate investor, owner Peacock Properties, 1970–; mem. Crenshaw CofC, Apartment Owners Assn., Apartment Assn. of Greater Los Angeles, Am. Legion, VFW, Disabled Am. Vets., Town Hall of Calif., LA World Affairs Council, LA Urban League, NAACP, Hancock Park Hist. Soc., LA County Mus. of Arts, Magic Castle; mil: pvt. US Army 1943-45, Good Conduct Medal, Asiatic Pacific Theater; Democrat; Rel. Sci.; rec: reading, swimming, equestrian, lectures. Address: Los Angeles 90043

PEACOCK, WANDA MAUREEN, administrator; b. Nov. 27, 1944, Cleveland, Ohio; d. Claude Daniel and Louise Irene (Browder) R.; children: Aurelia b. 1962, Arthur b. 1963; edn: AA bus. admin., Cuyahoga Coll. 1974; BS pub. admin., Dyke Coll. 1976; M. Banking & Finance Golden Gate Univ. 1982. Career: income tax auditor IRS 1975-77; admin. asst. Cleveland Job Corps Ctr. 1977-80; credit asst. Crocker Natl. Bank L.A. 1980-81, adminstr. 1981-83; cost analyst Aerojet ElectroSystems Azusa 1985–; income tax cons. Beneficial Tax Ctr. Pomona 1980-, fin. planner 1983-; mem: Nat. Soc. Pub. Admin., Nat. Assn. Female Execs.; Democrat; Interdenominational (Sunday sch. instr., youth counselor); rec: bowling, swimming, reading. Res: 8470 Kirkwood Rancho Cucamonga 91730 Ofc: Aerojet ElectroSystems 1100 W Hollyvale Azusa 91702

PEARCE, EDWIN BUHL II, judge; b. Aug. 5, 1941, Kalamazoo, Mich.; s. Edwin Buhl and Effy Ruth (Davis) P.; children: Eron Scott b. 1961, Edwin B. III b. 1963; BA, San Jose State Univ. 1963; JD, Univ, Santa Clara 1966. Career: Bodily Injury claims atty. Allstate Ins. Co., Menlo Park 1968-69; deputy dist. atty., Santa Clara County 1969-81; real estate broker 1975-81; apptd. judge Municipal Ct. San Jose, 1981–; mem. Am. Judicature Soc., Calif. Judges Assn., Elks, Italian-Am. Club, Masons, Scottish Rites; Republican; Methodist; rec: skiing, tennis, jogging, golf. Ofc: Municipal Court Bldg., 200 W Hedding St San Jose 95110

PEARCE, LAWRENCE E., business and management consultant; b. Mar. 27, 1933, Torrance, Calif.; s. Wiley Denney and Elsie May (Getchel) P.; m. 1954, div. 1970; children: Debra Lynn b. 1955, Holly Anne b. 1956, Randette Rae b. 1959, Cynthia Diane b. 1962; edn: BS, CSU Long Beach 1958, MBA, 1966; JD, Western State Univ. Fullerton 1984; Calif. Comm. Coll. Credls: instr. indsl. supervision 1969, instr. bus. mgmt. 1970, adminstrv. supv. 1971, chief exec. adminstr. 1972. Career: adminstrn., financial planning and mgmt. Rockwell Internat. 1959-72; controller, CFO Children's Hosp. of Orange County, Santa Fe Meml. Hosp., Mercy Gen. Hosp. 1972-80; founder, pres., CEO L&J Mgmt. Svcs. Inc. 1980–; instr. Fullerton Coll. 1969-86; dir., ofcr. JNL Inds. 1978-80, Glacier Falls Ice Skating Arena 1978-82; honors: Dr. Gregory Leadership Award 1958, Alpha Kappa Psi Scholarship Excellence (CSULB 1958), rink, stadium announcer for 1980 Olympic Games in Lake Placid, NY; mem:

Healthcare Financial Mgmt. Assn. 1972-80, CEOs of Mgmt. Cos. 1986-, Nat. Assn. Sectl. Svcs. 1981-, Santa Ana CofC 1985-, US Internat. Skating Assn., So. Calif. Speed Skating Assn., So. Calif. Speed Skating Olympic Fund Raising Com.; publ: var. mewsletters, sports adminstrv. manuals, coll. yearbook; sports announcer, adminstr. and coach (speed skating); mil: airman 1/c USAF 1950-54, Good Conduct; Republican; Presbyterian; rec: speed skating, skiing, power boating. Res: 13065 Casa Linda Lane Apt E Garden Grove 92644 Ofc: 1625 E 17th St Ste 104 Santa Ana 92701

PEARSON, ERIC ROBERT, consulting company president; b. Nov. 18, 1947, Dorcester, Mass.; s. Eric O.R. and Marion Julia (Hendrickson) P.; m. Karen File, June 27, 1976; edn: BS, Mass. Inst. of Tech. 1969; MS, Case Western Reserve Univ. 1971. Career: pres. Pearson Technologies, Canoga Park; past pos. in field of fiber optics, cons. Corning Glass Works, Times Fiber Communications, Pirelli Cable Corp., Whitmor Waveguides, other clients; Ofc: Pearson Technologies 20944 Sherman Way Ste 209 Canoga Park 91303

PEARSON, ERNEST JEROME, industrial real estate broker; b. Dec. 3, 1934, Seattle, Wash.; s. Ernest Manion and Genevieve Elizabeth (Bach) P.; m. Margaret S., Sept. 23, 1978; children: Kelli b. 1957, Kasey b. 1960, Christopher b. 1962; edn: mktg., Univ. Wash. 1956; real estate, Diablo Valley Coll. 1970-71; advanced studies, John F. Kennedy Univ. 1976-77; SIR, Soc. Indsl. Rels. 1979. Career: sales rep., Reynolds Metals Co., Seattle 1956-68; sales mgr. Reynolds Metals Co. S.F. 1968-69; sales cons., Coldwell Banker & Co., Oakland 1969-75; v.p., br. mgr. Cushman & Wakefield, Oakland 1975-82; pres. Delta Pacific Realty Corp., Stockton 1982-84; mng. ptnr. McMasters & Westland Comml. Real Estate, Stockton 1984–; lectr. Univ. Calif. 1976; honors: First Award, Indsl. Real Estate Sales (City of Hayward 1972), listed Who's Who in Real Estate 1983; mem: Soc. Indsl. Realtors 1979- (chpt. treas. 1986), Nat. Assn. Ofc. & Indsl. Parks (assoc. mem. 1976-), Univ. Wash. Alumni Assn., Lafayette Moraga Youth Assn. (bd. 1974), Contra Costa Council Campfire Girls (camping chmn. 1974-75), Stockton CofC (chmn. indsl. tour com. 1972); Republican; Catholic; rec: raising and training Arabian horses, skiing. Res: 5621 Highland Rd Pleasanton 94566 Ofc: McMasters & Westland Comml. Real Estate, 188 Frank West Circle Stockton 95206

PEARSON, JOHN, engineering executive; b. Apr. 24, 1923, Leyburn, Yorks, U.K., nat. US cit. 1944; s. William and Nellie (Bowler) P.; m. Ruth Billhardt, July 10, 1944; children: John b. 1951, Armin b. 1952, Roger b. 1954; edn: BSME, Northwestern Univ. 1949, MS, 1951. Reg. Profl. Engr., Calif. Career: research engr. Naval Ordnance Test Station, China Lake, Calif. 1951-55, head Warhead Research Branch 1955-58, head Solid Dynamics Branch 1958-59, head Detonation Physics Group 1959-67, head Detonation Physics Div. Naval Weapons Center, China Lake 1967-83, senior research scientist, 1983–; charter mem. Senior Exec. Service of the U.S. (1979); pioneered field of explosive metal working; cons. to industry and govt. agencies; founding mem. Advisory Bd. Center for High Energy Forming, Univ. Denver; nat. lectr. ASM (1956-64), ASME (1960-62), ASTM (1961-63); lectr. in engring. UC Los Angeles (1957-67), UC Santa Barbara (1971), Board of Examiners, Sambalpur Univ., India (1982-83); awards: L.T.E. Thompson medal (1965), Secty. of the Navy cert. of recogn. (1975), William B. McLean medal (1979), Navy Dept. award of merit (1979), Secty. of Navy cert. of commendn. (1981), Navy superior civilian service medal (1984), Haskell G. Wilson award (1985); mem: Fellow ASME, ADPA (life), Am. Soc. Metals, Am. Phys. Soc., N.Y. Acad. Scis., AIME, Sigma Xi, Pi Tau Sigma, Tau Beta Pi, Triangle, Federal Execs. League; author: Explosive Working of Metals (Pergamon, 1963), Behavior of Metals Under Impulsive Loads (ASM, 1954, Dover, 1965); num. publs. and patents in the indsl. and mil. applications of explosives; mil: Corps of Engrs. US Army 1943-46, ETO. Res: 858 N Primavera Rd Ridgecrest 93555 Ofc: Naval Weapons Center China Lake 93555

PEAVEY, CHARLES ALEXANDER, land specialist/entrepreneur; b. May 13, 1947, Munich, Ger.; s. Ralph Augustin and Ludmilla Alexandrovna (Maschkoff) P.; edn: Univ. of Maine 1965-70; Nuclear Power Plant Engring., Franklin Inst. 1975. Career: land specialist Great Western Real Estate, comml. brokerage; quality control engr. Bechtel Power Corp., Limerick Nuclear Generating Station, Pa.; insp. planner/Div. training, Bechtel Power Corp., San Francisco, Ca.; constrn./startup quality control coord. Bechtel Power Corp., San Onofre Nuclear Generating Station, San Clemente; senior quality assurance engr. Bechtel Power Corp., Los Angeles Power Div., currently; also own/opr. indep. jewelry design and custom mfg. co. spec. in precious stones from worldwide sources; conduct information sessions on energy topics, gems and jewelry topics and real estate for civic orgns., service clubs, bus. groups throughout So. Calif.; recipient num. speaker's appreciation awards; mem. American Nuclear Soc., Gemological Assn. of Gr. Brit.; publs: sev. tech. reports and articles on nuclear constrn., inspection, environmental considerations in tech. journals; mil: Airman 3/c USAF, Nat. Defense Service Medal; Republican (Repub. Assocs. of O.C.); Christian Sci.; rec: gemology, classical piano, theatre. Res: POB 5485 Fullerton 92635 Ofc: Great Western Real Estate, 1901 E Fourth St Santa Ana 92705

PECK, ROY ROMEYN, engineer, ret.; b. Sept. 18, 1909, Kansas City, Mo.; s. Roy Romeyn Sr. and Mary Emma (Drane) P.; m. Marjorie, May 22, 1983; children: Douglas b. 1932d,; Patricia b. 1936; edn: Kansas State Tchrs. Coll. 1927-29; I.C.S. Civil. Engr., (9) Indsl. Courses Elect. 1930-70; Indsl. Coll. of Armed Forces 1967-68; Instr., var. night sch. courses 1940-49; Reg. Profl. Engr., Calif. 1948. Career: owner/mgr. Roy Peck Associates, 1954-59; cons. various A & E firms, 1959-63; senior design engr. Rockwell Internat. 1963-69 training course rep. Mc Donnell Douglas, 1969-72; project mgr. Daniel, Mann, Johnson & Mendenhall, 1972-76; ret.; current: research in El-Optics & Biophysics; Dept. of Defense cons. Fallout Shelter Analysis (1968), Protective Constrn. (1969); awards: Apollo Achievement Award, NASA; (12) Awards for developments in Space Technology, NASA; mem: IEEE chmn. Calif. Legislative Advisory Commn. 1974-75, IEEE cons. US Legis. Advis. Project 1975-79; dir. El Prado District (County of L.A.) 1966-67; publs: Concepts of Atomic Physics, L.M. Mag. (1952); Ideas for Designers, El. Mech. Mag. (1975); The Energy Problem Report, CILA and IEEE (1974); mil: Radar Cons. Raytheon, Bu. Ships, US & So. Pacific, 1942-45; Prot.; rec: painting, music. Res: 386 S. Burnside, 3D, Los Angeles 90036

PECKENPAUGH, ANN DREESEN, executive search co. president; b. Nov. 15, 1954, Gary, Indiana; d. Dr. Donald Hugh and Mary Frances (Dreesen) P.; edn: BA, high distinction, Univ. of Mich. 1976; MBA, Harvard Bus. Sch. 1980. Career: coordinator Cancer Info. Service, Nat. Cancer Inst., Sidney Farber Cancer Inst., Boston 1976-78; assoc. dir. MBA Admissions, Harvard Bus. Sch., 1980-82; search dir. Debra Radabaugh Assocs., Menlo Park 1982-84; executive search cons./ pres. Peckenpaugh and Co., Inc., San Francisco 1984–, splst. in mgmt. and tech. personnel for electronics industry start-up cos.; honors: James Wright Hunt Scholar (1972-76); mem. Harvard Bus. Sch. Alumni Assn. (Applicant Rels. Com.); civic: S.F. League of Urban Gardeners; rec: career guidance, gardening, gourmet cuisine. Res: 1225 Washington St San Francisco 94108 Ofc: Peckenpaugh & Co., Inc. 333 Market St Ste 3300 San Francisco 94105

PEELER, JOSEPH DAVID, lawyer; b. Sept. 29, 1895, Nashville, Tenn.; s. Joseph David and Virginia Parker (McCue) P.; m. Elizabeth Boggess, Apr. 20, 1927; children: Stuart Thorne b. 1929, Joyce b. 1936; edn: AB, Univ. Ala. 1915; LLB, Harvard Law Sch. 1920; admitted bar: Ky. (1920), Calif. (1929). Career: practiced law in Louisville, Ky. 1920-29, in Los Angeles 1929–; mem. law firm of Musick, Peeler & Garrett; former mem., bd. dirs. Consol. Steel Co., Blue Diamond Corp., Tidewater Oil Co., Cyprus Mines Corp.; clubs: California, Los Angeles, Wilshire CC; mil: capt. US Air Corps WWI, lt. col. USAC WWII; Republican; Presbyterian; rec: golf, fishing, hunting. Res: 131 N June St Los Angeles 90004 Ofc: One Wilshire Blvd Ste 2000 Los Angeles 90017

PEETZ, CHRISTIAN J., veterinarian, ret.; b. Mar. 7, 1921, San Francisco; s. Christian M. and Marie Antoinette (Zane) P.; m. Thelma I., May 3, 1945; children: Christian, Jr. b. 1946, Ronald b. 1948; edn: DVM, Iowa State Univ. 1945; lic. veterinarian, Calif. 1945. Career: staff vet. Soc. Prevention of Cruelty to Animals, San Francisco 1945-47; owner Madera Pet Hosp., Corte Madera 1947-81, ret.; mem. Calif. State Veterinary Medical Ethics Com. 1971-72; mem: Marin County Vet. Med. Assn., Calif. Vet. Med. Assn., Am. Vet. Med. Assn.; clubs: Masons, Loch Lomond Yacht (commodore 1971); Republican; rec: boating. Res: 225 Jamaica St Tiburon 94920

PEFLEY, NORMAN GORDON, financial analyst; b. Dec. 15, 1955, Eugene, Ore.; s. Gordon Vergne and Jean (Lee) P.; m. Emma G. Lacuesta, July 5, 1986; edn: BA, UC Davis 1977; MA, Johns Hopkins Univ. 1979; MBA, Univ. Chgo. 1981. Career: research analyst Chicago Board Options Exchange, Chgo. 1981-83; senior finl. cons. Corporate Treasury, Bank of America, San Francisco 1983–; Referee, The Journal of Futures Markets; honors: Phi Beta Kappa (1979), Omicron Delta Epsilon (1977), Delta Phi Alpha (1977); mem: Am. Economic Assn., Am. Fin. Assn., Am. Assn. of Individual Investors, World Affairs Council; publs: Hedging Corporate Debt with U.S. Treasury Bond Futures (J. of Futures Markets, Vo. 3, No. 4, Winter 1983); hobby: German, French, Dutch and Japanese langs. Res: 1335 Pacific Ave Apt 104 San Francisco 94109 Ofc: Bank of America 555 California St San Francisco 94104

PELICAN, CARLOS RENE, video co. executive; b. Aug. 5, 1947, San Blas, Mexico; s. Pancho Horatio and Sabrina Lucretia (Sarbonne) P.; m. Peggy, Mar. 2, 1971; children: Pole b. 1974, Jodah b. 1971; edn: BS marine sci., Sao Paulo 1970, BA theatre arts, 1971, PhD botanical studies, 1972. Career: dir. of field research Brazilian Herbological Fedn. of the Republic (devel. of hybrid strain orchid: Dalissimus Falcore Real); dir. adminstrn. and proj. devel. Theatre De Janero, now instr. emeritus deus; current: founder/CEO The Pelican Video Group, Canoga Park; recipient Lupe Danero Signet for theatrical achievement, Brazilian Thespian Soc. 1976-82; mem. Kiwanis Internat. (v. regent 1979-81), Big Brother Soc., Newman Soc. (S.A. dir.), Optimist; works: published the complete works of Juan Amos Crosse, TV & Nat. Theatre; mil: capt. Brazilian Contra Fromage 2 yrs.; Democrat; Catholic; rec: surfing, soaring, sailing. Ofc: Pelican Video 7001-A Eton Ave Canoga Park 91303

PELLAM, JOHN LONERGAN, advertising executive; publisher; b. May 7, 1951, Wash. DC; s. John Rudolph and Ruth-Ellen (Lonergan) P.; m. Myrian, March 21, 1981; stepchildren: Marie Dominique Gerem b 1969, Christopher Gerem b. 1971; edn: BA, UC Irvine 1978. Career: publr. Design Magazine, Laguna Beach 1978-83; publr. Annual Resource Directory, Laguna Beach 1984–; pres. John Pellam Advtg., Laguna Beach 1978–; advy. com. Cert. Pgm. in Mktg. Communs., UC Irvine Ext. 1985-; honors: Maggie finalist (1982), Maggie Award (1986), Western Publications Assn., Golden Oranges finalist (1983), Orange Co. Advtg. Fedn.; author: Cost- Effective Advertising for the Competitive Business, 1984; Direct Mail/ Direct Response: From a Manager's Perspective, 1986. Ofc: 696 Playa Station Laguna Beach 92652

PENA, ANTONIA MURILLO, radiologist; b. July 18, 1946, San Diego; s. Blas and Elvira Murillo P.; edn: BA, Loma Linda Univ. 1968, MD, 1973; Diplomate Nat. Bd. of Radiol. 1977. Career: intern White Meml. Med. Ctr. L.A. 1973-74, resident 1974-77; radiol. Paradise Valley Hosp. National City 1978-79; neuroradiol. fellowship L.A. Co./USC Med. Ctr. 1977-78, L.A. Children's Hosp. 1979-80; radiol., neuroradiol. Arlington Radiol. Med. Grp. Riverside 1980–; cons. Veitch Student Health Ctr., attg. staff Riverside Gen. Hosp., University Med. Ctr., assoc. staff Parkview Comm. Hosp., radiol. Computerized Diagnostics of Riverside 1980–; mem: AMA, CMA, Calif., Inland Radiol. Socs.; Riverside Co. Med. Assn., Am. Soc. of Neuroradiol. (senior), Radiol. Soc. of No. Am., Am. Coll. of Radiol., Am. Assn. of Women Radiol., Loma Linda Univ. Sch. of Med. Alumni Assn., Riverside Museum Assoc.; publ: arts. on radiol. in med. jours.; Republican; Adventist; rec: gardening, reading. Res: 2285 El Capitan Riverside Ofc: Arlington Radiology Med. Grp. Inc., POB 7295 Riverside 92513

PENG, CHING FANG, cardiologist, acupuncturist; b. Mar. 12, 1923, Canton, China; s. Ve Chun and Chu Rao (Goo) P.; m. Muh Shian Lin, Sept. 29, 1955; 1 dau. Mary Min Hwa; edn: MD, Nat. Defense Med. Coll.; AMD (acupuncture), Chinese Acupuncture Research Center, China Med. Coll. 1979; Career: resident internal med. US Naval Hosp. San Diego 1961-62, res. cardiovascular disease 1961-62; med. dir., chief of med., clin. prof. China Navy Gen. Hosp. 1952-70; exec. ofcr. China Navy Gen. Hosp. Taiwan 1971-76; chief dir. Overseas Chinese Acupuncture Ctr.1979–; mem. United Acupuncturists of Calif. 1981-; Christian. Address: 1021 S Garfield Ave Alhambra 91801

PENG, SOPHIA W.S., acupuncturist; b. Sept. 26, 1945, Chikiang, Hunan, China, nat. US cit. 1973; d. Geoffrey Hwei and Janet J.C. (Young) P.; edn: undergrad. Ming-Chuan Coll. 1962-65; BS, Pepperdine Univ. 1969; postgrad. stu. Southwest Coll. of Naturopathic Medicine & Surgery 1978-79; OMD, PhD, Asian Am. Univ. of Medicine, 1983-85. Career: secty. to the pres. Lutheran Student Center, Asian Christian Anti-Communist Assn., Taiwan 1965-66; store mgr. Cathay Pharmacy, Los Angeles 1966-69; acct. Transam. Ins. Co., 1970-72; insurance rating techn. Johnson & Higgins of Calif., 1974-76; acupuncturist Scientific Acupuncture Clinic, p.t.1974-76, Gear Clinic 1976-79, Vomero Clinic, Zacho Clinic 1979-81; acupuncturist/owner/dir. Aahn Cong Acupuncture Clinic, Alhambra 1984–; apptd. (by Gov. Deukmejian) Acupuncture Examining Com.; mem. North Am. Acupuncture Assn. Ill., Chinese Acupuncture Assn. R.O.C., Acupuncture Medicine Assn. of So. Calif. (v.p., bd. 1984-); civic: Alhambra CofC, Asian Am. Republican Women (co-chair); Baptist; rec: painting, interior decor, classical music. Ofc: Aahn Cong Acupuncture Clinic 28 South Palm Ave Alhambra 91801

PENN, CHARLES JAMES, writer, editor, publisher; b. May 30, 1914, Perth, W. Australia; s. James Albert and Kate Sarah (Leckie) P.; m. Mary Faith, June 1, 1970; children: Russell b. 1945, Wayne b. 1948, Gary b. 1954; edn: courses, Perth Tech. Coll., Univ. of W. Australia, 1929-36, Santa Monica Coll., UCLA, 1963-64, stu. of Bhagavan Sri Sathya Sai Baba, India 1966-. Career: copy boy, cub reporter Daily News newspaper, Perth 1929-36; ed. West Australian Mining Review, 1936-39; ed./pub. Canadian Oil & Gas Jour., Toronto 1940-42; dir. Australian War Supplies Mission, Wash. DC 1942-43; ed. Internat. Petroleum Register, Los Angeles 1946-49; mng. dir. Russell Publs. Ltd., London 1950-52; ed./pub. Nat. Indsl. Publs., Los Angeles 1953-60, Western Oil & Gas Jour., L.A. 1961-63; exec. Trade Service Publs. Inc., San Diego 1966–; dir. London Court Ltd., Piccadilly Arcade Ltd., Perth W.A. (1936-39); charter pres., gov. Sertoma Internat. L.A. 1955-59; lectr. in US, Canada, S.Am., guest speaker 4 World Confs. Sri Sathya Sai Baba Service Orgn., Bombay and Prasanthi Nilayam, India; author: "My Beloved" The Love and Tchgs. of Bhagavan Sri Sathya Sai Baba (1981, 84), co-author (w/ Mary Faith Penn) American Edition Part I "Sathyam - Sivam - Sundaram" - "Sai Baba" (1969), "Sai Ram" Experiencing the Love and Teachings of Bhagavan Sri Sathya Sai Baba (1985), contbr. "Sanatha Sarathi", "The Divine Master", "Golden Age", "Sai Chandana" (1965-) India; inventor: Letters ejectable help summoning device (pat. 1966); mil: capt. Brit. Army 1944-45, Def., War medals; capt. USAF Civil Air Patrol 1963-66; Republican; rec: lectr. on humanities. Address: San Diego 92054

PENNEBAKER, GEORGE H., pharmacist, consultant; b. Oct. 9, 1936, Oakland, Calif.; s. George B. and Ida W. (McGilvray) P.; children: Steven G. b. 1961, Brian N. b. 1963; edn: San Jose State Coll. 1954-55; UC Berkeley 1955-57, BS pharm., UC Sch. of Pharm. 1960, Pharm.D., 1961. Career: staff pharm. UCSF Med. Ctr. 1961-62; dir. pharm. svcs. Alta Bates Comm. Hosp. Berkeley 1962-66; pharm. pgm. coord. Medi-Cal Pgm. State of Calif. 1966-72; dir. profl. svcs. Calif. Pharm. Assn. 1972-74; founder, pres. ApotheTech Inc. 1975-81; v.p. planning & devel. Apothetech Inc., subsid of AFSA Enterprises 1981-83; pvt. cons. 1983–; columnist ComputerTalk for the Pharmacist 1984–; product devel. mgr. First Data Bank, Am. Druggist Blue Book Data Ctr 1984-85, mgr. corp. & govt. accts. 1985-86; mem. UC Bd. of Regents 1984-85, vice chmn. com. on hosp. governance; vol. clin. faculty mem. UC Sch. of Pharm.; pharm. preceptor, intern pgm. advis. bd. Univ. of Pacific Sch. of Pharm.; honors: Alumnus of the Year (UC Sch. of Pharm. Alumni Assn. 1986); mem: Am. Pharm. Assn., Am. Soc. Hosp. Pharms., AMA (spl. affil. mem.), Nat. Assn. Pharm. Pgm. Adminstrs., Drug Information Assn., Nat. Council for Prescription Drug Pgms., Calif. Pharm. Assn., Calif. Soc. Hosp. Pharms., No. Calif. Soc. Hosp. Pharms. (pres. 1964, treas. 1963), Alameda County Pharm. Assn. (bd.), Sacto. Valley Pharm. Assn. (bd.), UC Alumni Assn. (statewide pres. 1984-85, secty. 1983-84; SF campus pres. 1983-85, v.p. 1983), UC Sch. of Pharm. Alumni Assn. (pres. 1980-81, v.p. 1979-80), UCB Alumni Council, Aircraft Owners & Pilots Assn.; rec: flying, music, travel. Res: 29858 Clearbrook Cir., No. 120, Hayward 94544

PENNELL, LARITA JEANNE, educator; b. Dec. 3, 1927, Portland, Ore.; d. LeRoy Carl and Leona Emma (Flier) Eisele; m. James Kell Pennell, Sept. 2, 1949; edn: BA, Univ. of Ore. 1949; MA, John F. Kennedy Univ. 1979; grad. study: CSU Humboldt, Hayward, Sonoma & San Jose; UC Berkeley 1950–; Univ. de Salamanca, Spain 1967, 68, 80; Univ. de Michoacan, Mex. 1964; Univ. of London, Eng. 1971; Tchr. Credentials: Secondary Edn. (1950), Bilingual Edn. (1979), Designated Svc. (1980), Adminstrv. (1981), Calif. Career: computer science, mathematics educator/faculty Wright School Dist., Santa Rosa 1950-51; Lafayette Sch. Dist., Lafayette 1952–; John F. Kennedy Univ., 1981–; computer cons. Microtime 1983; awards: academic NDEA Grants, US Govt. 1964, 65, 66; WHO (We Honor Ours) Award, CTA-NEA Alcosta Council; mem: Am. Assn. of Tchrs. of Spanish and Portuguese (secty. Bay Area chpt. 1975), Assn. of Mathematics Educators, Lafayette Edn. Assn. (pres. 1983-5); Republican; Catholic; rec: swimming, yoga, computer games. Res: 32 Canyon View Drive Orinda 94563 Ofc: Lafayette School Dist. 3477 School St. Lafayette 94549

PENOYER, ROBERT HAROLD, electronics engineer; b. Jan. 31, 1947, Detroit, Mich.; s. Harold Elmer and Edith Marie (Thiemer) P.; m. Teresa Garcia, Jan. 24, 1981; 1 child: Shawn, b. 1970; edn: AA, honors, Pasadena City Coll. 1975; BSEE (summa cum laude), West Coast Univ. 1978; MSEE, USC 1981; Reg. Profl. Engr., Calif. 1982. Career: electronics tech. Hoffman Electronics, El Monte 1969-72, senior electronics tech. 1972-75, associate engr. 1975-79, engr. 1979-81; mem./senior mem. technical staff Gould NavCom Systems, El Monte 1981–; electronics instr. (life cred.), Rio Hondo Coll. 1981-85; mem. IEEE 1979-; mil: s/sgt. USAF 1966-69, decorated Vietnam Service with cluster, Repub. of Vietnam Campaign, Nat. Def. Svc., AF GCM medals; rec: home computer. Res: 123 N. New Ave Apt. D, Monterey Park 91754 Ofc: Gould NavCom Systems 4323 Arden Drive El Monte 91731

PEOPLES, MARVIS VAN, school administrator, b. Aug. 24, 1936, Monroe, La.; s. Morgan and Lettice (Wright) P.; m. Mable O., June 23, 1956; children: Reuben Lendale b. 1957, Alton Jerome b. 1962, Malcolm Sinclair b. 1970; edn: BS, Western Baptist Bible Coll. 1969; MS, CSU Hayward 1975; EdD, Nova Univ., 1982; Calif. tchr. cred. (1970), sch. adminstr. (1975). Career: dir. of edn. and youth, Mt. Zion Baptist Ch., Oakland 1960-70; tchr. Oakland Public Schs., 1970-73, counselor/math resource tchr. 1973-75, asst. principal 1975-79, elementary sch. principal 1979–; tchr., counselor Alameda County Spl. Schs., Hayward summers 1971-78; instr. Merritt Comm. Coll. 1985-; honors: outstanding svcs. to children and youth Mt. Zion & Allen Temple Baptist Chs. (1962, 78), appreciation United Crusade (1972), outstanding principal Oakland Public Schs. (1983); mem: Assn. of Calif. Sch. Adminstrs., United Adminstrs. of Oakland Schs., Assn. for Suprvsn. & Curriculum Devel., Nat. Assn. Elem. Sch. Principals; civic: Big Brothers of the East Bay (bd.), Merritt Hosp. Review Board, Institute Devel. of Urban Edn. (bd.), Third World Student Exchange Pgm. (bd.), Optimist Club, NAACP; publs: My Philosophy of Discipline; var. ednl. model programs and articles; Democrat; Baptist; rec: fishing, carpentry, gardening, electronics. Res: 4760 Tompkins Ave Oakland 94619 Ofc: 401 Jones Ave Oakland 94603

PEPPER, DAVID M., laser physicist; b. Mar. 9, 1949, Los Angeles; s. Harold and Edith (Kleinplatz) P.; edn: BS physics, summa cum laude, UC Los Angeles 1971; MS applied physics, Calif Inst. of Technol. 1974, PhD applied physics, 1980. Career: physicist, mem. tech. staff Hughes Research Labs., Malibu 1973–; adj. prof. physics & math., Pepperdine Univ. 1981–; honors: Sigma Xi research honor soc. (chpt. v.p. 1986-87), Rudolf King/Lake Award (1982), NSF trainee Caltech (1972), invited spkr. Johns Hopkins, Indian Inst. of Technol.-Madras; mem: Am. Physical Soc., Optical Soc. of Am., IEEE, Sons & Daus. of the 1939 Club, Second Generation of the Martyrs Meml. and Mus. of the Holocaust; publs: cover story 1/86 Scientific American, 24+ arts. in internat. laser jours., contbr. 2 textbooks; 1 patent issued, 7 pending; Democrat; Jewish; rec: classical music, travel, nature, sports, amateur radio, chess; Ofc: Hughes Research Labs 3011 Malibu Cyn Rd Malibu 90265

PERALTA, ANTONINA C., writer, journalist, consultant; b. May 10, 1944, Philippines; edn: Litt.B. journalism, Univ. of the Philippines 1964; MA, Univ. of the Philippines 1976; Calif. Community Coll. Instr. Cred. Career: exec. secty.; high school tchr.; writer and journalist; ESL profl.; immigration cons.; currently, owner, mgr. Inter- World Immigration Svc. and Inter- World Language and Music Sch.; mem: Tchrs. of English to Spkrs. of Other Languages, Los Angeles Press Culb; publs: articles, in California Examiners, Philippine Free Press, Atin Ito News; Green Card Via Labor Visa, 1985; Aliens Eligible for E-2 Invesor's Visa, 1985; The H-2 Temporary Working Visa, 1985; L-1 Intra- Company Transferee Visa, 1985; How to Obtain a Green Card Through a Job, 1985; THe Difference Between a Working Visa and a Labor Certification, 1985; K-1 Fiancee Visa, 1985; Aliens Exempted from Labor Certification, 1985; Special Status, 1985; rec: writing, piano, tennis. Address: 314 New Hampshire Apt. 3 Los Angeles 90004

PERANO, DANTE LUIGI, real estate developer, writer; b. Dec. 24, 1955, San Andreas; s. Frank George and Kathryn Joan (Ensign) P.; edn: spl. courses, Calif. Polytech. St. Univ. 1977-78; Calif. lic. insurance (1975), real estate (1977). Career: mgr. Beneficial Fin., 1976; gen. mgr. The Real Estate Center (gen. real estate co., title co., mortgage co., constrn. co., legal counsel, environ. plnng.); investment ofcr. Finl. Corp. of Am.; current: CEO Information Services of Am., San Ramon; gen. ptnr. Bel-Air Props., Foothill Props., Mother Lode Inv. Co. and Pyramid; awards: Million Dollar Club (1978-80), Dale Carnegie G.A. (1981), Golden Acre Club; mem. Tuolumne County Bd. of Realtors, Contra Costa Co. Bd. of Realtors, Elks, Jaycees (past pres.), Native Sons Golden West; author/pub: You Can Buy A Home For Only One Dollar, Calif. Investors MLS Book, The Nat. Networking Directory, Terms That Earn, Profit With A Fixer-Upper; Christian; rec: ski, motorcycles, boating. Ofc: Information Services POB 194 San Ramon 94583

PERCY, ROBERT WAYNE, dentist; b. Aug. 31, 1933, San Bernardino; s. Charles Roland and Alma Irene (Garrett) P.; m. Janet Hawley, Mar. 14, 1953; children: Gerold b. 1954, Kenneth b. 1957, Charles b. 1962, Cathie b. 1964; edn: AA, San Bernardino Valley Coll. 1956; UCLA 1956-57; DDS, USC 1961. Career: pvt. practice dentistry, San Bernardino; vis. prof. (Practice Mgmt./ Alternative Systems within the Profession) var. univs. in US and Canada (1975-); apptd. by Gov. Reagan mem. State Bd. of Public Health, and State Health Advis. Bd.; mem. Dental Advis. Council (chmn. 1982) Blue Cross of Calif. (1977-) and cons. to Dental Div. 1984-); honors: Skull and Dagger/ USC (1968), A.T.E. Honor Soc. (1961); mem: Am., Calif. Dental Assn., Tri County Dental Soc., W. Acad. Dental Group Practice (dir. 1967-68), Am. Acad. Dental Group Practic (dir. 1974-76), Am. Acad. Gen. Dentistry, Am. Soc. for Preventive Dentistry; civic: Citizens for Better Edn. (co-chair), Jr. CofC (dir.), Uptown Kiwanis (dir.), Vis. Nurses Assn. (dir.), Goodwill Industries (dir.), YMCA Drive, United Fund, Salk Inst. (County chmn.), USC Alumni Trojan Club (pres. 1965-72), USC Scholarship Com. (1961-73), San Bernardino Unified Sch. Dist. School Board (1969-71), S.B. Human Rels. Commn.; mil: sgt. US ARmy Med. Corps 1953-55; Republican (campaign chair Jerry Lewis for State Assem. 1968-78, for Congress 1978-82); Episcopal Ofc: Wildwood Dental Associates 3972 N Waterman Ave San Bernardino 92404

PEREYRA-SUAREZ, HECTOR, writer, editor; b. Dec. 16, 1921, Rivera, Uruguay, S.A., nat. US cit. 1962; s. Ataliba and Isoleta (Nieves) P.-S.; children: Charles (J.D.) b. 1947, Robert (M.D.) b. 1949. Career: edn: BA, Colegio Adventista del Plata 1944; BA, Pacific Union Coll. 1961; MA, Stanford Univ. 1963; summer grad. studies Univ. of Chile 1951, 52. Career: tchr. and Dean of Boys, Inst. Adventista del Uruguay, Progreso, Uru. 1945-48; instr. Col. Adventista de Chile, Chillan, Chile 1949-53; editor Publicaciones Interamericanas (div. Pacific Press Pub. Assn.) 1954-68, ed.-in-chief monthly "El Centinela" and supvr. 4 translated mags., assoc. book ed. for Spanish Dept.; mng. ed. Spanish Grolier Universal Ency., Grolier Inc., New York 1968-71, exec. ed./hd. Spanish Dept. 1971-74; pres./editorial dir. Editorial Excelsior Corp., San Jose, Calif. 1974–; instr. eve. classes, Foothill Coll., De Anza Coll. (1965-68), Manhattan Comm. Coll. and Hunter Coll., NYC (1969-74), San Jose Comm. Coll. (1975-84); honors: Sigma Delta Pi; author 5 books: Hacia la elocuencia (text book on public spkg.) (1958, 1963, Mexico City, 3 more eds., El Paso, Tx.); La epopeya de Cristo (1959, Mex. City); La familia sobre el tapete (1964, Mtn View, Ca.); Las raices de la crisis contemporanea (1964, Mtn View; Portuguese ed., Sao Paolo, Brazil); Dignifiquemos la existencia (1969, Mex. City; 1973, Sao Paolo); over 100 articles; regular contbr. Hispanic American Report (Stanford Univ. 1962, 63). Res: 930 Forest Ave Palo Alto 94301

PEREZ, DARIO, general surgeon; b. May 1, 1941, Medellin, Colombia, nat. USA 1979; s. Ricardo and Zura (Zapata) P.; m. Aracelly, May 18, 1963; children: Claudia b. 1964, Joseph b. 1967, Cristina b. 1968; edn: MD, Univ. Autonoma Guadalajara 1979. Career: lab. tech. North Shor Univ. Hosp., Manhasset, NY 1968-70, Long Beach Hosp., Long Beach, NY 1970-72, Blood Bank supr. Long Is. Jewish Hillside Med. Ctr., NY 1968-73; med. sch. 1973-79; surgical resident St. Francis Hosp., Hartford, Conn. 1979-84; pvt. practice gen. surgery, Glendale, Calif. 1984–; mem: AMA, CMA, Los Angeles County Med. Assn., Am. Coll. of Surgeons; publs: Archives of Surgery (1984), Current Surgery (1983), Surg. Gastroenterology (1983); Catholic. Ofc: Dario Perez MD Inc. 1109 S Central Ave Glendale 91204

PEREZ, DAVID DOUGLAS, judge; b. Sept. 14, 1937, Los Angeles; s. Ygnacio and Cruz (Rivera) P.; m. Penny J., June 1, 1968; children: Jason David b. 1973, Heather Anne b. 1975; edn: BBA, Loyola Univ. L.A. 1959; JD, Southwestern Univ. 1965. Career: chief asst. city atty., Los Angeles City Atty's Office, Chief of Criminal Div. and legal advisor to L.A. Police Commn. Bd., 1965-75; apptd. judge, Los Angeles Municipal Ct. 1975-85, elevated to Superior Ct. 1985–; adv. commn. Uniform Consumer Credit Code, and on State Court Reform, Calif. State Senate; adv. commn. Calif. Legislature Jt. Com. on Structure of the Judiciary; mem. State Judicial Process Task Force, Calif. Council on Criminal Justice; adv. com. Life Inst. of Medicine and Law; pres. Corpus Christi Parish Sch. Assn. 1983-5; mem: Calif. Judges Assn., LA Municipal Ct. Judges Assn., Am., Los Angeles County, Mexican-Am. (Scholarship Found.), Criminal Courts (bd. dirs. 1972-75), East Los Angeles bar assns., Optimists, Rotary; bd. mgrs. YMCA, bd. Salvation Army Westmont Branch; honors: appreciation, Mex. Am. Cofc & Industry, State Bar of Calif., Mex.Am. Bar Assn.; Catholic; rec: travel, running, bicycling. Ofc: 111 N Hill St Los Angeles 90012

PEREZ, DENNIS PAUL, real estate broker; b. Sept. 3, 1947, San Jose; s. Joseph C. and Kathryn A. Perez; edn: West Valley Coll. 1965-68; San Jose State Univ. 1969-72. Career: designer Data Technology, San Jose 1969-72; engring. services mgr. Kasper Instr., Sunnyvale 1972-77; real estate broker/owner/pres. Allstate Realtors, Santa Clara 1977-80, National Financial Network Inc., 1980–; pvt. instr. real estate inv. classes; write, sell, manage gen. and lmtd. ptnrships; recipient num. real estate achieve. awards; mem. Sons of Italy (treas. 1972-73) Santa Clara Lodge; Christian; rec: sailing. Res: 2971 Salem Dr Santa Clara 95051 Ofc: National Financial Network Inc., 2470 El Camino Real, Santa Clara 95051

PEREZ, MARK CHRISTOPHER, dentist; b. May 31, 1955, Long Beach; s. Vincent David and Tonie (Aldape) P.; edn: BS in comm. health scis., CSU Long Beach 1978; DDS, and BS in dental scis., UC San Francisco 1983. Career: instr., supr. UCSF Sch. of Dentistry summer orientation pgm.; adminstr. Westside Neighborhood Med. Clinic, Santa Barbara also grant author/dir. Westside Senior Outreach Pgm. and Westside Chicano Outreach Pgm.; research asst. health scis. dept. CSU Long Beach, Nat. Mens Cancer Edn. Pgm., Am. Cancer Soc.; instr. comparative literature dept. and ednl. opportunity pgm., CSULB; current: gen. practice dentistry, El Cerrito; awards: Willard Corwin Flemming Scholar, UCSF Sch. Dentistry; UCSF Student Body pres.; recipient recogn. UCSF Assoc. Students, UCSF Latinos in Dental Health Edn., Kiwanis Club of Santa Barbara; mem: Hispanic Am. Dental Assn., Latin Am. Dental Assn., UCSF Alumni Assn., UCSF Parnassus Club, CSULB Alumni Assn.; civic: Santa Barbara Health Task Force, S.B. Health Action Coalition, Am. Cancer Soc.; Democrat; Catholic; rec: travel, outdoors, politics, music. Ofc: El Cerrito Professional Bldg El Cerrito Plaza Ste 117 El Cerrito

PEREZ, PAULA CHRISTINA, health care executive; b. Jan. 1, 1952, Los Angeles; d. Robert H. and Helen S. (Pastall) Perez; m. Richard M. Trippe, Feb. 14, 1978; 1 son, Jonathan Blackwell b. 1983; edn: BS in health edn., So. Ct. State Coll. 1974; MA, CSU Fullerton 1980; Calif. Life Community Coll. tchg. cred.; lic. MFCC, Marriage, Family, Child Counselor (1980). Career: secty., later counselor Comprehensive Care Corp.; therapist College Hosp. (psychiat.) and co-founder, later dir. Hospital Help Line (crisis intervention svc.); mktg. dir., asst. adminstr. New Beginnings, Lakewood (div. Nat. Med. Ents.); therapist pvt. practice; cons., owner/v.p. Compulsive Disorders Treatment Programs Inc., Orange 1985–, cons. hosps. and cos. re employee assistance pgms. and wellness pgms.; honors: Dean's List, So. Ct. State College, capt. 4-yr Varsity Tennis Team, coll. sportswriter and cheerleader; mem: Calif. Womens Commn. Against Alcoholism, So. Calif. Assn. of Marriage & Family Therapists; publs: var. health care brochures; Democrat; Catholic; rec: health & fitness, racquetball. Ofc: Compulsive Disorders Treatment Programs 3642 E Sycamore Ave Orange 92669

PERILLO, LEONARD RAYMOND, investment co. president/entrepreneur; b. Oct. 29, 1956, Berkeley; s. Leonard Albert and Jinka Anne Jessen (Zoberski) P.; edn: UC Berkeley 1975-6; Oxford Univ., Eng. 1976-7; BBA, CSU Hayward 1979. Career: real estate investment analyst Bellinger, Steinbeck and Roberts, Castro Valley, 1979-80; CEO Leonard R. Perillo Investments, 1979–; v.p. Star+Gate Ents., Orinda 1980-81; chmn. adv. bd. Centennial Bank, Hayward 1981-84; v.p. Children as Tchrs. of Peace Found. S.F. 1985-; dir. Bus. Execs. or Nat. Security (BANS) 1984-; honors: Sigma Delta Chi (profl. writers) 1977-80, Harlaxton Acad. Soc. 1976-; mem: Commonwealth Club of Calif.; Hayward H.S. Alumni Com. Chmn. 1974-84; male model assignments during college, appeared on S.F. area TV; rec: world travel & study, active n global peace work with children. Res: 2000 Oak Creek Pl Hayward 94541 Ofc: 24915 O'Niel Ave Hayward 94544

PERLIS, MICHAEL FREDRICK, lawyer; b. June 3, 1947, NY; s. Leo and Betty F. (Gantz) P.; m. Cynthia Druskin, June 8, 1969; children: Amy Hannah b. 1974, David Matthew b. 1978; edn: BSFS, Georgetown Univ. Sch. of Foreign Svc. 1968; JD, Georgetown Univ. Law Ctr. 1971. Admitted Dist. of Columbia Bar 1971-, State Bar of Calif. 1980-. Career: court law clk. Dist. of columbia Court of Appeals, Wash DC; asst. Corporation Counsel, Wash. DC 1972-74; atty. US Securities and Exchange Commn. Div. of Enforcement, Wash. DC 1974-75, branch chief 1975-77, asst. dir. 1977-80; ptnr. Pettit & Martin, San Francisco 1980–; adj. prof. of law Catholic Univ. of Am. 1979-80; awards: Edmund A. Walsh Gold Medal 1968; Who's Who in American Law (1983); Who's Who in the World (1984); mem. Am., Dist. of Columbia, Calif., San Francisco bar assns.; chmn. ABA subcom. Sec. and Commodities Litigation, Section of Lit. 1982-84; works: lectr., var. securities laws and litigation law matters; Democrat; Jewish; rec: art collector. Res: 77 Manderly Rd San Rafael 94901 Ofc: Pettit & Martin, 101 California St, 35th Fl, San Francisco 94111

PERLOWSKI, THOMAS MICHAEL, certified public accountant; b. Aug. 29, 1948, Chgo.; s. Roy A. and Grace C. (Toelle) P.; m. Valerie J., Feb.1, 1969; children: Lisa b. 1975, Kate b. 1979, Matthew b. 1980; edn: BS acctg., San Diego St. Univ. 1970; lic. CPA, Calif. 1973. Career: jr. acct. Main La Frentz & Co., CPAs, Los Angeles 1970; staff acct. Diehl, Evans and Co., CPAs, Carlsbad 1972, sr. acct. 1973, mgr. 1975, ptnr. (Carlsbad, Escondido) 1983–; lectr. Calif. Soc. of CPAs (1983, 84), National Univ./SBA (1984); honors: Outstanding Young Men of Am. 1974, Boys' Clubs of Am. medallion award 1984; mem: Am. Inst. of CPAs, Calif. Soc. of CPAs (AICPA Tax Div. 1984-; No. County Tech. Discussion Gp. 1980-), Associated Builders & Contractors of San Diego (bd. dirs. 1985, fin. com. 1983-); bd. dirs. (pres. 1983) Boys & Girls Club of Carlsbad 1973-; mil: sgt. Calif. Army N.G.1970-76; Republican; Catholic; rec: fishing. Ofc: Diehl, Evans and Co., CPAs, 2965 Roosevelt St Carlsbad 92008

PERRISH, ALBERT, steel co. executive; b. Nov. 18, 1914, Vancouver, B.C., Canada, parents US cit.; s. Sam and Nettie (Prezant) P.; m. Helen, June 11, 1986; children: Peggy b. 1953, James b. 1953, Audrey b. 1954, Kathleen b. 1956, Jeffrey b. 1948, Larry b. 1956; edn: BS in bus. adminstrn., UC Los Angeles 1938. Career: asst. to the pres. Southwest Steel Rolling Mills, 1946-50; chmn./CEO Ferro Union Inc. (fmr. Winter, Wolff & Co., then Triangle Steel & Supply Co.), Torrance 1950–; apptd. L.A. Board of Harbor Commissioners (1962-66, pres. 1965); awards: Star of Solidarity (Italy), Chevalier Order of Commerce and Industry (France), Order of Leopold (Belgium), Bronze Plaque, Los Angeles CofC (1963); mem: Fgn. Trade of So. Calif. (pres. 1963), West Coast Metal Importers Assn. (pres. 1986), Assn. of Steel Distbrs., Steel Service Center Inst., American Inst. of Imported Steel (dir.); mil: capt. US Air Force 1942-46. Address: Torrance 90502

PERRY, ARTHUR CORPENING, ophthalmologist; b. Mar. 27, 1947, Albemarle, N.C.; s. Marvin Collier and Louise Linton (Corpening) P.; m. Vicki, Sept. 14, 1974; children: Paige b. 1978, Phillip b. 1980, Blake b. 1982; edn: undergrad. Texas Tech. Univ. 1965-67, Univ. of N.C. 1967-69; MD, Emory

Univ. 1973. Career: pvt. practice ophthalmic plastic and reconstructive surgery, La Jolla 1978–; chief ophthal. Scripps Meml. Hosp.; bd. govs. Mericos Eye Inst., La Jolla; faculty, ophthal., UCSD; cons. US Naval Hosp. San Diego; mem. AMA, Am. Acad. of Ophthalmology; Republican; Protestant. Res: POB 1102 Rancho Santa Fe 92067 Ofc: 9834 Genesee Ave Ste 315 La Jolla 92037

PERRY, CHARLES ALLEN, engineering executive; b. June 24, 1924, Louisville, Ky.; s. Wilber Kelch and Alberta Ambrosia (Wirth) P.; m. June, Oct. 5, 1946; children: Sandra b. 1947, Joyce b. 1949, Kenneth b. 1951, Joseph b. 1953, Douglas b. 1961, Patricia b. 1962, Jill b. 1968. Career: engr. Butterman Ice Cream Co., Louisville, Ky. 1946-50, Ward Engring., 1951-55, Brown & Williamson, 1956-60; engr./chief exec. Perry & Co. Inc., Santa Fe Springs, 1961–; instr. Refrigeration Local Union 522, Louisville (1957-60); leader in energy conserv., introduced Multiplex Refrigeration System to the supermarket industry; mem. Refrigeration Service Engring. Soc., K.C.; mil: M.M.1c US Navy 1941-45, Pres. Unit Cit. USS San Francisco, 4 Gold, 3 Silver battle stars Pacific Theater; Republican; Catholic; rec: travel. Res: 14563 Allegan St Whittier 90604 Ofc: Perry & Co Inc 14340 Iseli Rd Santa Fe Springs 90670

PERRY, RACHEL, cosmetic co. president; b. June 28, Bklyn.; d. Samuel and Rose Solat; edn: stu. psychology and art, Los Angeles City Coll. (2 yrs) and UC Los Angeles (2 yrs). Career: singer/songwriter, 1972–; skincare & makeup cons., self empl., Beverly Hills 1971-74, owner/pres. cosmetic co. Rachel Perry, Inc., Chatsworth/ Beverly Hills 1974–; tchr. Facial Rejuvenation self empl. 1971–; author: Reverse the Aging Process of your Face (1982); composer/lyricist (1981 Gold Record) Blue Lights in the Basement; artist (cosmetic products packaging devel.) Lip Lover Display; mem: Nat. Assn. of Recording Arts & Scis. (1972-), Am. Soc. of Composers, Artists & Pubs., Nat. & Nutritional Foods Assn., Green Peace Animal Protection Soc.; Democrat; Jewish; rec: dancing, body-work, painting. Ofc: Rachel Perry Inc. 9111 Mason Ave Chatsworth 91311

PERUSSINA, ROBERT DANIEL, certified financial planner; b. May 5, 1955, San Francisco; s. Robert Eugene and Jane Francis (Callaghan) P.; m. Sherry Holcomb, June 19, 1982; 1 son: Daniel, b. 1983; edn: BS, UC Berkeley 1977; CFP, Coll. of Fin. Plnng., Denver, Colo. 1982. Career: finl. plnng. rep. Independent Plnng. Corp. (exec. com., CEO subs. Independent Qualified Plans), San Franciso 1977–; plnng. cons. Doctors Co., Santa Monica 1980-81; dir. S.F. Bay Area chpt. Am. Assn. of Fin. Profls.; seminar speaker finl. plnng. var. corps. & profl. assns.; honors: past pres., S.F. Bay Area chpt. Sigma Alpha Epsilon frat.; mem: SAE Alumni Assn., Cal Beta Alumni Assn., Internat. Assn. Finl. Plnng., Inst. CFPs, Am. Assn. Finl. Profls.; author chpt., Wind Energy, in Energy in the Bay Area, UC Berkeley Press, 1977; writer, Bank of Am. Consumer Information Reports, incl. Savings Programs & Ednl. Funding.; Republican; Catholic; rec: sailing, aerobatics, computer programming. Res: 76 Meadow Rd Mill Valley 94941 Ofc: Robert D. Perussina, CFP, 101 Larkspur Landing Circle Ste 228 Larkspur 94939

PETER, JAMES SIMEON, real estate broker; b. Oct. 20, 1942, Cakaudrove, Fiji Islands, nat. US cit. 1971; s. Kancherla Paul and Mary (Simeon) Peter; m. Virginia Francis, Aug. 24, 1968 (div. 1972); edn: AA, L.A. City Coll. 1974; BA bus., San Francisco State Univ. 1977; grad study bus., Golden Gate Univ. 1978-80; real estate broker Calif. 1984. Career: night audit, guest svcs. Cable Motor Inn San Francisco 1980-81, Broadway Manor Hotel S.F. 1981, Best Western Hotels Oakland 1982–; real estate broker 1984–; mem: (pending) Contra Costa Bd. Realtors, Calif. Assn. Realtors, Nat. Assn. Realtors; mem: VFW, Am. Legion, Assn. MBA Execs.; mil: cpl. USMC 1969-71, Nat. Defense Svc., Vietnam Svc., Vietnam Campaign w/ 2 stars, Navy Achievement w/ Combat V; Republican; Catholic; rec: photog., fishing, travel, outdoors. Address: San Francisco 94110

PETERS, DON PRESTON, JR., physician; b. July 19, 1915, Baltimore; s. Don Preston and Rhett (Mencke) P.; children: Mary Elizabeth, Don Preston; edn: Lynchburg (Va.) Coll. 1932-34; MD, Univ. Va. 1940. Career: intern Emory Univ. Hosp., Atlanta 1940-41; resident Lynchburg Gen. Hosp., 1941-42, Fitzsimons Army Hosp., 1948-49, Letterman Army Hosp., 1949-50; commnd 1st lt. Air Corps US Army 1942, served to col. USAF, 1960; comdr. various USAF hospitals, ret. 1968, decorated AF Commendation medal; med. cons. dept. field services Health Dept. Calif. 1968–; v.p. Calif. Mus. Mil. History; Fellow Am. Coll. Preventive Medicine, Royal Soc. Health; mem. Aerospace, Pan Am. med. asns., Soc. Air Force Clin. Surgeons, Soc. USAF Flight Surgeons, Assn. Mil. Surgeons US, AIAA, Civil War Assn. Am. (Surgeon Gen.), Hon. Order Kentucky Colonels, Masons (32 deg.), Shriners. Res: 5542 Via Dos Cerros Riverside 92507 Ofc: 606 E Mill St San Bernardino 92408

PETERS, HARRY EMERSON, JR., surgeon; b. Sept. 20, 1912, Rienbeck, Iowa; s. Dr. Harry E. (M.D.) and Marie Jane (Mutch) P.; m. Harriett, Oct. 17, 1975; children: Beverly b. 1942, Sharon b. 1945, Lynne b. 1950, Deborah b. 1952; edn: AB, UC Berkeley 1933; MD, UC San Francisco 1937. Career: intern San Francisco Gen. Hospital; asst. resident in medicine UC San Francisco 1937-38, asst. res., resident in surgery, 1928-42, clin. prof. of surgery UCSF, 1973–; medical staff mem. 8 vicinity hosps.; honors: Phi Beta Kappa, Alpha Omega Alpha; mem. Western Surg. Assn., Pacific Coast Surg. Assn. (past pres. No. Calif. Branch), Am. Coll. of Surgeons, San Francisco Surg. Soc., East Bay Surg. Soc., Howard Cnaffziger Surg. Soc.; club: Sequayah Country; publs. (18) in surgical journals; Republican; Protestant; rec: golf, fishing, photog. Res: 25 Wood Court Oakland 94611

PETERS, LOUIS DONALD, lawyer; b. Sept. 28, 1932, Jacksonville, Fla.; s. Louis Holland and Marie P.; children: Mark Donald b. 1958, Matthew Louis b. 1960, Michael Joseph b. 1962; edn: BS, Notre Dame 1955; JD, Southwestern Univ. 1964. Career: exec. asst. to the Executive Officer, 1962-65, probate atty., 1965-66 and judge pro tem, 1976-77, Los Angeles County Superior Court; atty. prin., civil litigation practice, Newport Beach; bd. dirs. (treas. 67-74) Beverly Comm. Hosp., Montebello; mem. Calif. State Bar; mil: lt (jg) USNR 1955-57; Catholic; rec: flying. Res: 13 Oakgrove Irvine 92714 Ofc: Donald Peters 4650 Von Karman Newport Beach 92660

PETERSEN, JAMES V., product liability investigator; b. Sept. 30, 1946, Saugerties, N.Y.; s. Martin John, Sr. and Gladys Veronica (Conley) P.; m. Barbara Kay, Oct. 25, 1968; children: James, Jr. b. 1972, Danial b. 1974; edn: AS in police sci., Moorpark Coll. 1973; cert. Peace Ofcr. Stds. and Tng.; cert. Rifle, Pistol & Shotgun instr., NRA. Career: state traffic ofcr. Calif. Hwy Patrol; defense investigator; sr. investigator Navesco Corp.; current: gen. mgr. Southwest Accident Research Inc.; mem. Calif. Assn. of Hwy Patrolmen, Nat. Rifle Assn.; civic: PTA, Simi Valley Athletic Assn., Golden Bears High Rifle Gun Club; mil: sgt. US Army M.P.; Republican; Catholic; rec: bowling. Address: Southwest Accident Research Inc 4857 Abilene St Simi Valley 93063

PETERSEN, NORMAN WILLIAM, naval engineer; b. Aug. 26, 1933, Highland Park, Ill.; s. Jens Edlef and Marie (Wenderling) P.; m. Ann Nevin, Aug. 24, 1956; children: Richard b. 1957, Robert b. 1958, Thomas b. 1959 (dec.), Anita b. 1961, David b. 1963; edn: BS, Univ. of N.Mex. 1956; MS, distn., Naval Post Grad. Sch. 1962; Harvard Bus. Sch. 1982; reg. elec. engr., Mass. 1968; reg. indsl. engr., Calif. 1971. Career: USN 1952–; public works ofcr., Naval Sta., Key West, Fla. 1956-59; security ofcr., mil. personnel ofcr., Navfacengcom 1959-60; constrn. dir., PW ofcr. Fleet Anti-Air Warfare Tang Ctr. 1962-64; contracting engr. dir., SW Div. Navfacengcom 1964-66; exec. ofcr. amphibious constrn. Battalion One 1966-67; force civil engr. CDR Naval Air Forces, Pacific 1967-70; PW ofcr. Naval Air Sta., Miramar 1970-73; exec. ofcr. Navy Pub. Works Ctr., Great Lakes, Ill. 1973-75; commdg. ofcr. Civil Engring. Researh Lab., Port Hueneme 1975-78; commdg. ofcr. Navy Public Works Ctr., San Francisco Bay 1978-80; dir. of programs and comptroller Naval Facilities Engr. CMD, Wash. DC 1980-84; public works dir. Pacific Missile Test Ctr., Point Mugu 1984–; honors: Bronze Hammer award, Outstanding Constrn. 1973; mem: Soc. Am. Mil. Engrs., Am. Public Works Assn., IEEE, Am. Soc. Mil. Comptrollers, Sigma Xi, Ventura Co. Assn. of Govts., Navy League, Oxnard Gem and Mineral Soc., Am. Philatelic Soc., Germany Philatelic Soc., Mexico Elmhurst Philatelic Soc. Internat., Lambda Chi Alpha (Zeta Mu), United Way (bd. dirs. Ventura Co.); works: constructed Rayburn Hall Polaris Misile Training Facility, Dam Neck, Va. 1964; established only military industrial plant in Vietnam; mil: capt. USN Civil Engr. Corps 1952–; Legion of Merit, Meritorious Svc. (2), Navy Commdn., Navy Unit Citation, Meritorious Unit Commdn. (2), Meritorious Unit Citations (Vietnam A.F., Vietnam, Civil Action 1/c, Gallantry Cross); rec: philately, astronomy, rock hounding. Ofc: Pacific Missile Test Center, Code 6200, NAS Point Mugu 93042

PETERSEN, ROBERT BURTON, district administrator, state board of equalization; b. Aug. 14, 1927, Hermosa Beach; s. Harry Magnus and Louise (Larsen) P.; edn: BBA higher acctncy., Woodbury Coll. 1949; PA Calif. 1949. Career: acct. Auto Club of So. Calif. 1950; jr. acct.-auditor State Bd. of Equalization L.A. 1950-51, acct.-auditor I 1951-52, tax auditor II L.A. and Downey 1952-61, tax auditor III Long Beach 1961-67, Supv. tax auditor I Long Beach 1967-70, supv. tax auditor II (dist. prin. auditor) Inglewood 1970-76, bus. taxes adminstr. IV (dist. adminstr.) Inglewood/Torrance 1976–; tax law instr. Bd. of Eq. 1963–; honors: Golden Spike Centennial Award (Utah Centennial Commn. 1969), 25 Yr. Service Award (State Bd. of Eq. 1975); mem: Calif. Assn. State Auditors (dir., v.p., pres. 1970, 71, 72), Elks, Pacific Railroad Soc., Orange Empire Railway Museum, Electric Railway Hist. Assn. of So. Calif., Elec. Railroaders Assn., Smithsonian, Statue of Liberty Ellis Island Found., Redondo Bch. Hist. Soc., Disabled Am. Vets.; audio/visual slide prodns.; mil: pvt. USAAC 1946; Republican; Protestant; rec: model railroads, photog., sound recording. Ofc: State Bd. of Equalization 690 W Knox St Ste 200 Torrance 90502

PETERSON, HOWARD COOPER, lawyer, financial planner, accountant; b. Oct. 12, 1939, Decatur, Ill.; s. Howard and Lorraine (Cooper) P.; edn: BSEE, Univ. of Ill. 1963; MSEE, San Diego State Univ. 1967; MBA, Columbia Univ. 1969; JD, Calif. Western Sch. of Law 1983; LLM taxation, New York Univ. 1985. Career: elec. engr. to senior electronics engr. General Dynamics, Convair Div., 1963-68; financial planning and service bus., income tax preparation, real estate brokerage, securities sales, ins. sales, finl. cons., 1970–; pres./dir. Coastal Properties Trust, a real estate inv. trust; pres./dir. Juno Real Estate Inc., a real estate brokerage; v.p./dir. Juno Securities, Inc., NASD securities brokerage; treas./dir. Imperial Screens of San Diego, alarm screens sales; gen. ptnr. Costumes Characters & Classics, costume rentals. Mem: Nat. Soc. of Public Accts., Internat. Assn. of Finl. Plnnrs. Inc., Assn. of Enrolled Agents, Amer. Bar Assn., Inter-Am. Bar Assn. Ofc: 1335 Hotel Circle South, Ste. 205, San Diego 92108

PETERSON, JEFFREY PAUL, insurance agent; b. June 6, 1962, Mpls., Minn.; s. Donald Walter and Lucille I. (Haugen) P.; edn: BS econs., Univ. of Pacific 1984; mgr. Elec. Svc. Co., Mpls.; asst. stockbroker E.F. Hutton, Stockton, Calif. 1983; photog. editor, Univ. of Pacific Yearbook 1983-84; mktg. mgr. Builder's Hardware Supply, Temecula 1984; ins. agent Mass. Mutual Life, San Francisco 1984-85; ins./investment cons. Northwestern Mutual Life, S.F. 1986–; honors: Outstanding Young Men of Am. 1985; mem: Nat., S.F. Assn. of Life Underwriters; Republican; Catholic; rec: scuba, snow & water skiing, duck hunting, golf, tennis. Res: 58 Malta Dr San Francisco 94131 Northwestern Mutual Life, 425 California, Ste 500, San Francisco 94104

PETERSON, LAWRENCE EDWIN, JR., investment banker; b. Sept. 5, 1947, Pasadena; s. Lawrence Edwin and Lillian (Shibley) P.; m. Cynthia, Jan. 8, 1980; children: Brooke, Ashley; edn: BS, USC 1970; MBA, Harvard Bus. Sch. 1972. Career: analyst/portfolio mgr. Fidelity Mutual Funds, Boston 1972; founder Peterson Diehl & Co., Investment Bankers, Newport Beach 1974, founder L.E. Peterson & Co., 1982; v.p. corp. fin. Kidder Peabody, 1985; mng. dir. A.B.C. Capital Markets Group, Santa Ana currently; dir. Harvard Bus. Sch. Accounts; awards: Marion McKinly Bovard scholar USC, Harvard Grad. Sch. fellow; club: St Francis Yacht; Republican; Episcopal; rec: competitive swimming. Res: 2081 Redberry Rd Santa Ana 92706 Ofc: A.B.C. Capital Markets Group 2323 N Broadway Ste 450 Santa Ana 92706

PETERSON, LORRIN CARLTON, electronics co. executive; b. July 7, 1921, Lincoln, Nebr.; s. Albert F. and Emma (Ehrsam) P.; m. Olive Schratz, Dec. 20, 1945; children: Eric b. 1954, Anne b. 1957; edn: BS, US Mil. Acad. West Point 1945; MBA, USAF Inst. Tech., Dayton, Ohio 1953; FAA lic. Airline Transport Pilot (1971). Career: served to major US Air Force, pilot SAC (bombers and transports), ret. 1962; prof. aerospace studies Caltech; pgm. mgr. Strategic Missiles (USAF); senior engr./scientist McDonnell Douglas; pgm. mgr. Hydraulic Research- Textron; The Marquardt Co.; NCR Corp; founder/pres. Val Aero Inc., Lorair Inc. (dba Van Nuys Aviation Acad.), Air Stages Inc.; current: program mgr. Communications Systems, Litton Data Systems, Van Nuys; bd. dirs. Castaic Lake Water Agcy., Div. 3, Newhall; L.A. County Republican Central Com.; listed Who's Who in Aviation and Aerospace (1983); mem: AF Assn., West Point Soc. of L.A. (bd.), Am. Inst. Astro. and Aero., Am. Def. Preparedness Assn., Assn. of Grads. US Mil. Acad., Aviation/Space Writers Assn., Boy Scouts Am. (commnr's staff), Kiwanis Internat., Nat. Assn. Flt. Instrs., Nat. Estimating Soc., Soc. of Am. Mil. Engrs., Soc. of Am. Value Engrs., Van Nuys CofC, Santa Clarita Runners, Soaring Soc. Am., Toastmasters Internat.; publs: num. articles on mgmt. and aviation; Republican; rec: flying, gliding, writing. Res: 23024 Magnolia Glen Dr Valencia 91355 Ofc: Litton Data Systems 8000 Woodley Ave MS 45-45 Van Nuys 91409

PETERSON, MARK STEVEN, financial planner; b. Feb. 24, 1956, Fresno; s. Sam and Rosalie Jane Traudt) P.; edn: AA, Fresno City Coll. 1978; BS fin., CSU Fresno 1982; work in prog., Certified Finl. Planner (CFP) desig. (est. 1987). Career: finl. planner Financial Network Investment Corp., Milwaukie, Ore. 1983-85, Southmark Finl. Services, Fresno 1985—; Paid-Call-Firefighter, Madera County Fire Dept., founding mem. Volunteer Engine Co. No.9; mem. Internat. Assn. for Finl. Planning (IAFP), Inst. of Certified Finl. Planners (ICFP); Republican; Baptist; rec: snow skiing instr. Res: 10137 Fig Grove Rd Madera 93638 Ofc: 1490 West Shaw Ave Ste A Fresno 93711

PETERSON, ROBIN ANDREA, chiropractor; b. May 3, 1956, Mpls., Minn.; d. Andrew A. and Marion P. (Primeau) Kole; m. Philip Peterson, Dec. 24, 1976; edn: L.A. Pierce Coll. 1978-79; New Coll. of Calif. 1978-79; CSU Northridge 1979; DC, cum laude, Life Chiropractic Coll. 1983; Donsbach Univ. 1981-; DC lic: Calif. 1984, Fla. 1984, Ga. 1984. Career: co-owner Coastal Chiropractors Los Osos, Calif.; honors: Dean's List 1979, 1984, National Dean's List 1984; mem: Calif. Chiro. Assn., Am. Chiro. Assn., ACA Council on Roentgenology, Fla. Chiro. Assn., Los Osos CofC; publ: co-author Back Talk column Sun Bulletin newspaper Morro Bay, Calif.; Democrat; Lutheran; rec: triathlon, photog., snorkling, weightlifting, yoga, golf, tennis, swimming. Ofc: Coastal Chiropractors 1193 Los Osos Valley Rd Los Osos 93402

PETROFF, GEORGE ALEXIS, mechanical engineer; b. March 7, 1917, Hailar, Manchuria, China, nat. US cit. 1955; s. Alexei Alexeevich and Vera Lucy (Beloglazoff), Nov. 23, 1947; 1 dau, Vera b. 1949; edn: BSME, UC Berkeley 1938; Reg. Profl. Engr., Calif.; Bd. of Regis. for Profl. Engrs. 1965. Career: draftsman Price Pump div. Fairbanks Morse Co., San Francisco 1939-40; sales engr. Andersen, Meyer & Co. Ltd., Shanghai, China 1940-41; opg. engr. Shaghai Power Co., Shanghai China 1941-49; constrn. engr. United Nations Refugee Orgn., Guivan Samar, Philippines 1949-50; in San Francisco 1950—; assoc. engr. Bechtel Corp. 1950-56; designer West Coast Engring. Co. 1956-57; designer Western Knapp div. Arthur G. McKee Co. 1957-58; senior designer The H.K. Ferguson Co. 1958-59; senior designer Keller & Gannon 1959-60; mech. engr. Internat. Engring. Co. 1960-61; mech. engr. Deleum Cather Co. 1961-62; design engr. Del Monte Corp. 1962-65; mech. engr. Western Knapp div. Arthur G. McKee Co. 1965-67; senior mech. engr. Internat. Engring. Co. 1967-80; senior staff engr. The H.K. Ferguson Co. 1980-84; engring. cons. 1984—; Russian- English translation of tech. publs. and interpreting for Internat. Engring. Co. and Morrison- Knudsen Co. 1972—; honors: 15 Year Svc. Award, Internat. Engring. Co./ Morrison Knudsen Co. 1979; mem. Am. Soc. of Mech. Engrs.; Republican; Orthodox; rec: hiking, swimming, spectator sports. Res: 485 Teresita Blvd. San Francisco 94127

PETTISE, STEPHEN THOMAS, company executive; b. Nov. 10, 1941, Elgin, Ill.; s. Thomas Walter and Mary Hariett (Jencks) P.; m. Arlene May, Jna. 29, 1972; children: Todd b. 1962, Andrew b. 1964; edn: BA, Drake Univ. 1962; Northwestern Univ. 1967. Career: sales Neisel Labs div. of Union Carbine 1965-69; Nat. field sales mgr. Campus Marketing Corp., Pasadena 1969-70; acct. exec. Lows Inc., Chicago, Ill. 1970-73; acct. supvr. Rogers Merchadising Inc. 1974-76; West Coast gen. mgr. Carl Karcher Ent., Anaheim 1978-79, dir. mktg. 1979-81; pres., mktg. cons. Stephen T. Pettise & Assocs., Aspen, Colo. and Irvine 1981; v.p. mktg. IHOP Corp. 1981—; Nixon for President staff 1968; regl. mgr. Neighbors for Nexon; honors: Effie Award, Am. Mktg. Assn. NY chpt. 1985; Marsy Award, Am. Mktg. Assn. Los Angeles chpt. 1984; NRA Great Meny Merchandising 1st Pl. 1984; mem: Am. Mktg. Assn. (Los Angeles chpt.), Nat. Restaurant Assn. Mktg. Execs. Club, Sutton- Irvine Found. for the Developmentally Disabled, Drake Univ. Los Angeles Alumni; works: mem. Restaurant Bus. mag. Mktg. Execs. Panel; Republican; Episcopal; rec: skiing, golf, philately. Ofc: IHOP Corp., 6837 Lankershim Blvd., No. Hollywood 91605

PETTUS, JOSEPH HODSON, energy co. executive; b. Aug. 1, 1947, Louisville, Ky.; s. Thomas N. and Nancye B. (Trimble) P.; m. Judith C. Nenno, Aug. 26, 1969; children: Jeffrey W. b. 1976, Jeremy H. b. 1979. edn: BS civil engrg., bus. adminstrn., Univ. Colo. 1970. Career: engr. Exxon Co. USA Houston 1970-75; proj. mgr. Fluor E&C Houston 1976-77; v.p. ops. United Energy Resources Houston 1978-81; senior v.p. supply & transportation Cal Gas Corp. Sacramento 1981—; dir. Propane Transport Inc. Milford, Ohio, Minden Pipeline Co. Minden, La., Norco Transp. Co. L.A., Beacon Petroleum Co. Shreveport. La.; honors: Chi Epsilon; mem. bus. adv. com. KVIE Channel 6 (PBS); Republican; Protestant. Res: 8800 Triple Crown Ct Fair Oaks 95628 Ofc: Cal Gas Corp. POB 28397 Sacramento 95828

PEZESHKI, MOHAMMAD REZA, mechanical engineer; b. Oct. 26, 1956, Tehran, Iran; s. Ebrahim and Farideh (Bozorgmand) P.; m. Roya, Jan. 13, 1984; edn: BS, CSU Los Angeles 1980, MS, 1986; Reg. Profl. Engr. (Mech.) Calif. 1984. Career: head tutor CSU Los Angeles, 1978-80; project engr. Nack & Sunderland Engrs., Los Angeles 1980-85; project mgr./mechanical project engr. Jones, Cooper & Assocs., Glendale 1985—; honors: Dean's List (1978, 80), Hon. Soc. of Mech. Engrs. (1980), Hon. Soc. of Engrs. (1980): mem. ASHRAE 1980-; rec: tennis. Res: 355 S Marengo Ave #209, Pasadena 91101 Ofc: Jones, Cooper & Associates, 528 State St Glendale 91203

PFEFFERMAN, ARTHUR SIDNEY, food franchisor; b. Feb. 5, 1947, Buffalo, NY; s. David T. and Cecelia (Kogan) P.; m. Sandra D., Apr. 18, 1969; children: Michael b. 1969, Craig b. 1972; edn: Univ. Buffalo 1965; UC Los Angeles 1965. Career: mgr. J&B Concessions, Buffalo Zoo, Buffalo Winter Carnival, etc. 1961-64; NY Central Railroad 1964-65; owner jewerly store Calif. 1965-66; trouble shooter, mgr., trainer for donut franchise bus. 1966-67; owner donut franchise 1967-70, added second franchise 1970-73, started mgmt. and financial consulting bus. 1973-75, pres., CEO Donut Inn Corp. 1975—, began franchising 1980; franchising lectr. CSU Northridge; honors: Fernando Award (CofC 1985); mem: United CofCs (pres. 1981-82, exec. bd. 1983-84, regl. v.p. 1977-81), Tarzana CofC (pres. 1973-74, dir. 1969-), Tarzana Lions Club (v.p. 1976-80, pres. 1980-81, dir. 1972—), West Valley PALS (1st v.p. 1976-77), Valley Round Table (treas. 1976), Assoc. Chambers of San Fernando Valley (pres. 1977, 1st v.p. 1976); Internat. Franchise Assn. (treas. 1984-85); 3rd dist. chmn. Fed. Block Grant Funds Com. 1975-76; LA Olympic Ad Hoc Com./Site Location chmn.; LA advis. council Sm. Bus. Adminstrn. 1981-; Valley Cultural Assn. Advis. Bd.; bd. trustees Granada Hills Comm. Hosp. 1982-; LA Blue Ribbon Police Task Force Com. 1985; Republican; Jewish. Ofc: Donut Inn, 6355 Topanga Cyn Blvd Ste 403 Woodland Hills 91367

PFEIFER, JOHN STERLING, vascular surgeon; b. Jan. 23, 1950, Alliance, O.; s. Sterling Dale and Virginia Catherine (Roberto) P.; m. Suzan, May 29, 1971; children: Christopher b. 1974, Justin b. 1977, Eric b. 1980; edn: BS, Western Ky. Univ. 1971; MD, Vanderbilt Sch. of Med. 1975. Career: resident in surgery Vanderbilt Med. Ctr. 1975-77; clin. assoc. Nat. Heart Lung and Blood Instn., NIH, Bethesda, Md. 1977-79; resident in surgery Medical Coll. of Va. 1979-81, clin. instr./ fellow in vascular surg. 1981-82; pvt. practice vascular and general surgery, Iowa 1982-84, Riverside, Calif. 1984—; awards: I.A. Bigger Award, Med. Coll. of Va. (1981); mem: Am. Coll. of Surgeons (cand.), Southeastern Surgical Congress, Andrew G. Morrow Soc., Cardiovascular Surgeons, Humera Soc.; coauthor articles in num. med. jours.; mil: lt.cdr. USPHS 1977-79; Christian Ch.; rec: woodwkg., cabinetry. Ofc: 4000 14th St, Ste 310, Riverside 92501

PFEIFFER, J. WILLIAM, publisher, writer; b. July 10, 1937, Wallace, Idaho; s. John William and Mary Loretta (Schmidt) P.; m. Judith Ann Cook, Dec. 14, 1973; children: Heidi Erika b. 1970, Charles Wilson b. 1976; edn: BA, Univ. Md. 1962; PhD (fellow), Univ. Iowa 1968; JD, Western State Univ. 1982. Career: instr. Univ. Md. 1965-67; dir. adult edn. Kirkwood (Iowa) Comm. Coll. 1967-69; dir. ednl. resources Ind. Higher Edn. Telecommuns. Systems Indpls. 1969-72; pres. Univ. Assocs. San Diego 1972-80; adj. tchr. Ind. Univ. 1969-72, Purdue Univ. 1971-72; author: Instrumentation in Human Relations Training (1973, 2nd ed. 1976), Reference Guide to Handbooks and Annuals (1975, 2nd ed. 1977, 3rd ed. 1981), Applied Strategic Planning (w/ Goodstein and Nolan, 1986); editor: A Handbook of Structured Experiences for Human Relations Training (10 vols. 1969-85), The Annual Handbook for Group Facilitators (10 vols., 1972-81), The 1982 Annual for Facilitators, Trainers and Cons. (also 1983, 84, 85, 86), Group and Organizations Studies: Internat. J. for Group Facilitators (1976-79), Strategic Planning: Selected Readings (1986); mil: US Army 1958-62. Res: 2610 Inyaha Ln La Jolla 92037 Ofc: 8517 Production VE San Diego 92121

PFLUEGER, DONALD HOWARD, professor of history; b. Aug. 20, 1923, Covina; s. Gustave Herman and Josephine Ellen (Hansen) P.; m. Betty Wilson, Sept. 3, 1961; children: David b. 1963, Leah b. 1965; edn: BA, Pomona Coll. 1949; MA, Stanford Univ. 1951. Career: tchr. Covina Union H.S., Covina 1950-52; intr. Calif. State Polytechnic Coll., San Dimas 1952-56; cultural attache Am. Embassy, Amman, Jordan 1956-58; prof. Calif. State Polytechnic Univ., Pomona 1958-83; prof. emeritus 1983-; mem. Calif. Constitution Revision Commn. 1962-72; honors: Outstanding Individual, Conf. of Calif. Historical Socs. 1977; Haynes found. Fellowship, The Huntington Library 1986; mem: Historical Soc. of So. Calif., Historical Soc. of Pomona Valley, Glendora and Covina Historical Socs., Univ. Club of Claremont, Los Angeles Corral of Westerners, E Clampus Vitus, History Guild of So. Calif.; books: Glendora—

The Annals of a Southern California Community, 1951; The Government of California, 1957; Covina— Sunflowers, Citrus, Subdivisions, 1964; Charles C. Chapman— The Career of a Creative Californian, 1976; journ. ed., Pomona Valley Historian, 1970-80; Mt. San Antonio Historian, 1980-83; mil: USN 1943-46; Republican; Protestant; rec: foreign travel, book collecting. Ofc: Dept. of History, Calif. State Polytechnic Univ., Pomona 91768

PFUHL, JOHN WESLEY, accountant; b. June 26, 1938, Lansing, Mich.; s. Edward Carl, Sr. and Gladys Dorothy (Williams) P.; m. Maren C. Thoresen, June 22, 1965; children: Scott, Shari; edn: BA acctg., Mich. State Univ. 1960; Certified Public Acct., Calif. 1969. Career: staff acct. Arthur Young & Co., Santa Ana office; staff acct. Jones, Elliott & Assocs., Fullerton; ptnr. Sherlock, Soule & Pfuhl, La Jolla; pres. John W. Pfuhl Acctcy. Corp., El Cajon currently; dir: Longer Life Found. Inc., Architects Lorimer and Case APC, Sunflower Health Care Inc.; mem: Am. Inst. CPAs, Calif. Soc. CPAs; civic: past pres. Torrey Pines Kiwanis Club (Kiwanian of Year 1975), mem. El Cajon Valley Lions Club, past treas. La Jolla Town Council; mil: lt. US Navy; Republican; Lutheran; rec: softball, skiing, woodworking. Ofc: 237 Avocado Ave Ste 210 El Cajon 92020

PFUND, EDWARD T., JR., aerospace co. engineer-executive; b. Dec. 10, 1923, Methuen, Mass.; s. Edward Theodore Sr. and Mary Elizabeth (Banning) P.; m. Marga Andre, Nov. 10, 1954; children: Angela b. 1954, Gloria b. 1956, Edward III b. 1961; edn: BS, magna cum laude, Tufts Coll. 1950; grad. studies, USC 1950, Boston Univ. 1950, Columbia Univ. 1953, UCLA 1956, 58. Career: radio engr. WLAW, Lawrence- Boston 1942-50; foreign svc. staff ofcr. US Dept. of State Voice of Am., Tangier, Munich, 1950-54; proj. engr. Crusade for Freedom, Radio Free Europe, Munich, Ger. 1955; proj. mgr./ material splst. United Electrodynamics Inc., Pasadena 1956-59; dir. eng./ chief engr. Electronics Specialty Co., Los Angeles & Thomaston, Conn. 1959-61; with Hughes Aircraft, var. locations 1955, 1961—; chmn. Subcom. on Communications, Space Flt. Ops. Gp. 1963, chief Johannesburg Ops. 1961-63; dir. Spacecraft Perf. Analysis and Cmd., 1964-68; pgm. mgr. Lunar Rover Ground Data Sys. Design 1969-70; tech. chmn. Internat. Consortium 1974-78; currently, Middle & Far East Africa and So. American New Business Development mgr.; dir. internat. pgms. devel. Hughes Communications Internat., Inc. 1984-; cons: H.I. Thompson Co., L.A. 1958-60, Andrew Corp., Chgo. 1959, Satelitte Broadcast Assocs., L.A. 1982; faculty, Pasadena City Coll. 1958-60; honors: Phi Beta Kappa; Sigma Pi Sigma; Awd. of Merit, Materials in Design Engring. 1958-59 (design devel. of two unique kinds of coaxial cable having low losses at over 1000 degrees F. for Mach 3 vehicles); Surveyor Test Pilot, Surveyor's Hon. Roll, Aviation Week & Space Technolo'y 1966; directed the command control & perf. of all USA unmanned soft lunar landing and the world's first lunar liftoff and translation 1966-68; listed in num. biographical publs.; mem: Am. Inst. of Aero. & Astro. (tech. com. Commun. Sys. 1973-76) 1973-; publs: num. arts. in fields of communications satellites, real- time control and data processing, distributed amplifiers, transmission lines, transistorized telemetering devel. and electrical insulation; mil: 2nd lt. US Army Air Corps 1942-46; rec: amateur radio K6OUW (1939-). Res: 25 Silver Saddle Ln Rolling Hills Estates 90274 Ofc: Hughes Aircraft Co., POB 92919, Airport Sta., Los Angeles 90009

PHAM, LAN NGOC, civil engineer, real estate broker; b. Oct. 11, 1947, Tayninh, Vietnam, nat. Oct. 21, 1983; s. Tung Van Tran and Danh Hoang Pham; m. Nga Do, Aug. 14, 1973; children: Deryck Long b. 1977, Beverly Thanh b. 1978; edn: BE engring., National Technical Ctr., Vietnam 1969; ME, Kyoto Univ., Japan 1973, postgrad. work 1973-75; Reg. Profl. Engr. (Civil) Calif. 1978, lic. Real Estate Broker 1981; Notary Public 1981; Reg. Tax Preparer 1986. Career: v.chief Public Works Services, Tayninh Province, Vietnam 1969-70; research scholar Kyoto Univ. 1970-75; senior/project engr. Leighton and Assocs., Inc. Irvine 1976—; owner/mgr. Lan and Assocs., Irvine 1981—; cons. num. Vietnamese business owners, 1978-; honors: acad. scholarship awards: Ministry of Edn., S. Vietnam (1959-65), Ministry of Pub. Works, S. Vietnam (1965-69), Ministry of Edn., Japan (1970-76); mem: Vietnamese Soc. of Civil Engrs. (1965-), Soc. Civil Engrs., Kyoto Univ., Japan (1970-), Internat. Soc. for Soil Mechanics and Foundation Engring. (1971-), ASCE (1978-), Internat. Conf. Building Officials 1978-80, Calif./Nat. Assns. of Realtors (1980-); civic: Overseas Vietnamese Buddhist Community (gen. secty. 1978-85, pres. 1985-), So. Calif. Buddhist Assn. (gen. secty. 1980-82), Vietnamese League in Orange Co. (gen. secty. 1980-), Community Resources Opportunity Project, Inc. (a Vietnamese, Laos & Cambodian community non-profit orgn., gen. secty. 1982-85, pres. 1985-), Vo-Vi Meditation Friendship Assn. (meditator 1982-); publs: tech. papers, conf. proceedings (1977); Republican; Buddhist; rec: ping-pong. Res: 14645 Seron Ave Irvine 92714 Ofc: Leighton & Associates, Inc. 1151 Duryea Ave Irvine 92714

PHELPS, SUZANNE LOUISE HOUSE, civic worker; b. Detroit, Mich.; d. George Worthington and Louise (Miller) House; desc. John Adams (2d US Pres.) and John Quincy Adams (6th US Pres.); m. Harrison Stephens Phelps, Sept. 28, 1932; children: George b. 1935, Harrison, Jr., PhD b. 1939; edn: Liggett Sch. (Detroit), Bennett Coll., Millbrook, N.Y. Civic: Junior League of Newport Harbor, DAR (col. Wm. Cabell Chpt. 118), Colonial Dames of Am. (Chpt. XX, Los Angeles); club: Laguna Niguel Golf & Country; rec: golf, swim, philanthropy. Res: 25892 Portafino Dr Mission Viejo 92691

PHELPS, TAYLOR, television production executive; b. June 27, 1954, Lake Forest, Ill.; s. Mason and Margaret (Taylor) Phelps. Career: one of original founders, bd. dir. and v.p./chief ops. One Pass, Inc., now ScanLine Communications (t.v. and film prodn. co.), San Francisco 1975—, now largest indep. t.v. prodn. co. in US, operate in all major US markets (Boston, Chgo., NYC, LA,

SF); rec: ranching. Res: Tunitas Creek Ranch Half Moon Bay 94019 Ofc: ScanLine Communications 1 China Basin Bldg San Francisco 94107

PHILLIPS, CHARLES ROY, physician, writer; b. Aug. 21, 1942, Chgo.; s. Herbert Marrow (DDS) and Marion (Christy) P.; m. Sherrin Lee Burt, July 19, 1980; children: Scott b. 1968 (by previous marriage), Kirsten b. 1981, Ashley b. 1982, Chelsea b. 1984; edn: BA, Amherst Coll. 1964; MD, Northwestern Univ. Med. Sch. 1968; board certified Emergency Physician, Family Physician. Career: dir. Student Health, UC Irvine 1979-81; pvt. practice in medicine and consultant in emergency services, Grass Valley currently; dir. Emergency Dept., Contra Costa County Hosp.; honors: Upjohn Achievement Award for engendering care to the poor 1968; author/pub. four internat. textbooks in medical rescue; fmr. tchg. staff UC Davis in Family Practice; Ch. of Jesus Christ of L.D.S.; rec: tennis. Res: 10832 Cement Hill Rd., Nevada City 95959 Ofc: 104 Catherine Lane Grass Valley 95945

PHILLIPS, GEORGE SCOTT, land developer, homebuilder, real estate consultant; b. Feb. 28, 1939, Charleroi, Penn.; s. George Francis and Gaynell Pauline (Milliken) P.; m. Rena Louise, Apr. 20, 1985; 1 child Kim b. 1962; edn: BA in geol., UC Berkeley 1961; Cert. in Land Devel. Adminstrn., Golden Gate Univ. 1973; MA bus. adm., Kensington Univ., Glendale 1979, PhD bus. adm., 1980; Calif. State lic. Gen. Building Contractor (1978), Real Estate Broker (1968); SR/WA (Reg. Senior Mem.), Internat. Right of Way Assn. 1970. Career: asst. mgr. Donald D. Davis Constrn. Co., Greenbrae 1960-63; right-of-way agent Calif. Div. Hwys., San Francisco 1963-66; Acquisition and Appraisal Assocs., S.F. 1966-67; dir. real estate Marketing and Bus. Development, S.F. 1967-73; v.p., forward planning mgr. Kaufman & Broad, No. Calif., Burlingame 1973-76; dir. planning and devel. Ponderosa Homes, Santa Clara 1976-77; v.p./ div. mgr. M.J. Brock & Sons Inc., Dublin 1977-82; pres. Barratt Northern California, Inc., Sacramento 1982-84; pres. Warmington Homes - No. Calif., San Ramon 1985—; frequent spkr. var. service and profl. groups, 1969-; qualified expert witness on valuation, mktg. and disposition of real estate, Superior Ct. City and County of San Francisco 1970; apptd. mem. qualification appraisal panel for selection of Deputy Real Estate Commissioner trainees; recipient Housing Design Award, City of Novato (1974); mem. Internat. Right of Way Assn. (exec.com. 1968-71); Theta Tau (Profl. Earth Scis. Frat.) Epsilon Chap. Regent 1960; Land Execs. Assn. (pres. No. Calif. 1971); publs: articles and subject of arts.: New Homes Mag. (1980), Homes for Sale (1981, 82), Homebuyers Guide (78); mil: seaman USCGR 1961-69, Calif. Wrestling & Track Teams 1961; Republican; Prot.; rec: collect Egyptian, Asian and Pre-Columbian artifacts, weapons and coins; fitness. Res: 3343 Marsh Hawk Ct Pleasanton 94566 Ofc: Warmington Homes, 4 Crow Canyon Ct, Ste 200, San Ramon 94583

PHILLIPS, JOHN ROBERT, financial planning executive; b. Apr. 15, 1956, Loma Linda, Calif.; s. Robert Wesley and Doris Anne (Mann) P.; edn: BA poli. sci., UC Los Angeles 1978. Career: asst. exec. secty., dir. undergrad. svcs. Sigma Chi Found. 1978-80; agent The Acacia Group Encino 1980-84; mgr. The Acacia Financial Group Santa Ana 1984—; Sigma Chi Leadership Tng. Workshop 1983-86; honors: President's Cabinet (The Acacia Group 1982-84), Million Dollar Round Table (1983), Nat. Quality Award (LIMRA, NALU 1984, 85); mem: Internat. Assn. Financial Planning 1985-, Nat. Assn. Life Underwriters 1981-85, UCLA Alumni Assn. 1984-, UCLA Sigma Chi House Corp. (pres.), Orange County Sigma Chi Alumni Assn. 1985-; Republican; rec: sports. Ofc: The Acacia Financial Group 1055 N Main St Ste 420 Santa Ana 92701

PHILLIPS, KENNETH LEWIS, retail computer sales co. president; b. Nov. 27, 1946, Crawford, Nebr.; s. Roy Edward and Thelma May (Saxton) P.; m. Beverly Louis, June 20, 1971; children: Chad b. 1979, Briana b. 1985; edn: AA, Riverside City Coll. 1978; BA, CSU Fullerton 1980. Career: contract mgr. Hospital Council of Southern Calif., Century City 1979-81; seminar mgr. Wingate Air Condtg./Htg., Riverside 1981-82; store mgr. Wards Co., Inc., City of Commerce 1982-84; salespsn. Computer Kingdom, 1984-85; founder/ pres./ CEO User Friendly Outlets of Riverside, Inc. (computer brokerage), 1985—; instr., computers, St. Paul Lutheran Sch., 1986; awards: salesmgr. of year, Wards Co. Inc. (1983), cert. Motivational Dynamics (1980); mem. L-S Soc. (OASIS), Phone Tree Cord Riverside/ San Bernardino, Toastmasters Internat. (CTM), Inland Empire Computer Council, founder Macmaina User Group (Apple, Macintosh), founder Apricot Users Gp. (Apricot computers); works: Internal surge protector with reset; cataloger software Apple Macintosh; mil: E4 US Army; Republican; Lutheran; rec: tennis, public spkg., civic gps. Res: 4562 Sunnyside Dr Riverside 92506 Ofc: User Friendly Outlets (UFO) 11060 Magnolia Ave Riverside 92505

PHILLIPS, LEROY DANIEL, management consultant; b. July 10, 1935, Texarkana, Tx.; s. Leroy and Jessie Mae (Sharp) P.; m. Mary A., July 10, 1955; 1 son, Kevin b. 1956; edn: AA, L.A. City Coll. 1967; BA, CSU Los Angeles 1972; MBA, Century Univ. 1979; Calif. Comm. Colls. tchg. cred. 1977. Career: var. pos. with Los Angeles County govt. 29 years, incl. pharm. storekeeper/ pharmaceuticals supply mgmt. for LA County Medical Center, div. chief supply & transp. Mechanical Dept., Building Crafts mgr.; current: bus. mgmt. cons. and commodities broker/prin. Phillips Diversified Services, Harbor City; instr. Basic Psych., L.A. County Mech. Dept. (1979); apptd. Interview Boards Dept. of Personnel- LA County (1977-83), LA City (1979-81); honors: United Way Award (1985), Brotherhood Crusade Leadership Award (1986), United Negro Coll. Fund Leadership Award (1986), Service Employees Internat. Union (AFL-CIO Local 660) spl. citation (1985); mem. Nat. Notary Assn. (1977-81), LA Co. Employees Assn. (life); civic: Diane Watson Semi-

Profl. Sports Assn. (pres. 1986), Coastal Mental Health Governing Bd. (chmn. 1980-83), LA Co. Health Services Resources & Devel. Com. (bd. 1981), past chmn. LA County subcom. on tng. & devel. in employee rels. (1979); Democrat; Prot.; rec: fishing, photog. Ofc: Phillips Diversified Services 914 Oakmere Dr Harbor City 90710

PHILLIPS, MARLENE ELAINE, psychotherapist, hypnotherapist; b. Dec. 25, 1939, Brooklyn, NY; d. Boris Abraham and Ethel Claire (Kritz) Newman; children: Fred b. 1959, Lori b. 1962, Randi b. 1965; edn: BA, CSU Fullerton 1981, MS, 1983; PhD, US Internat. Univ. (in progress); certified Marriage, Family, Child Counselor, Calif. 1985. Career: pvt. practice, ptnr. Saddleback Counseling and Psychotherapy Assocs., Laguna Hills 1985—; psychol. asst. Dr. M. Kelley, Laguna Hills 1983-85, Dr. Jerry Balgie, Orange 1983—; profl. bd. advisors Adam Walsh Children's Resource Ctr.; honors: Psi Chi; mem: Am. Psychol. Assn., Calif. STate Psychol. Assn., Assn. for Hypnosis in Family Therapy, Saddleback Valley CofC, Bus. & Profl. Women Org.; writer, South County News/ Orange County Media Group; contbr. monthly article, Orange County South mag.; rec: racquetball, hiking, concerts. Ofc: Saddleback Counseling and Psychotherapy Assocs. 23521 Paseo de Valencia Ste 302A Laguna Hills 92653

PHIPPS, PATRICIA MC NAMAR, educator; b. July 2, 1928, Park Falls, Wisc.; d. Milton Grover and Laura Esther (Sorensen) McNamar; children: Jason b. 1954, Lawrence b. 1959; edn: BA econs., UC Berkeley 1950; MA spl. edn., San Francisco State Univ. 1967; PhD spl. edn., UC Riverside 1977. Career: tchr. San Francisco Bay Area Public Schs. 1950-73; cons. Head Start & Community Action pgms., US Ofc. of Econ. Opportunity, Spokane, Wash. 1967-68; instr. UC Riverside, cons. Riverside County spl. edn. 1975-77; prof. spl. edn. CSU Chico 1977—; cons./ trainer of adminstrs. and counselors of fed. pgms. for Howard Univ., Wash. DC 1978-80; cons. US Dept. of Edn. (TRIO) pgms. 1979-85; spkr. state, nat., and internat. confs.; lectr. St. Patrick's Coll. Dublin, Ire. 1985; honors: Acad. Scholar (1946), Merit Recogn. (CSU 1984); mem: Council for Exceptional Children (chpt. v.p. 1978-79), Assn. for Children with Learning Disabilities, Calif. Assn. for Neurologically Handicapped Children, Council for Exceptional Children; mem. advisory bds., Disabled Students Svcs., Upward Bound pgms. CSU; publs. 20+ articles in profl. jours.; Democrat; rec: travel, writing, folk music. Ofc: Coll. of Edn., CSU Chico 95929-0222

PIA, GARY ERNEST, financial consultant; b. July 24, 1951, San Pedro, Calif.; s. Charles Ernest and Lila May (McGrath) P.; m. Marti C., Apr. 16, 1976; children: Daniel b. 1978, Kathryn b. 1980; edn: BA, Brigham Young Univ. 1978; Certified Financial Planner 1985. Career: acct. exec. Merril Lynch Pierce Fenner & Smith Pasadena 1977-81; mktg. exec. TransAmerica Occidental Life Ins. Co. L.A. 1981-86; ops. ofcr. CWC Ins. Svcs. L.A. 1986; financial cons. Robert M. Coleman & Assocs. Pasadena; mem: Internat. Assn. for Fin. Planning (nat. adv. bd., chpt. pres. 1985-86), Inst. Cert. Financial Planners, Internat. Soc. Pre-Retirement Planners; publ: Dollars & Sense (monthly financial newsletter 1985-); Republican; L.D.S.; rec: golf, guitar. OFc: Bob Coleman & Assoc. 215 N Marengo Ste 342 Pasadena 91101

PIENTENPOL-VOLPE, DIANA V., real estate broker; b. June 1, 1942, Santa Ana; d. Dennis Weseley and Virginia (McClellan) Hogland; children: Daniel Pientenpol b. 1971; edn: AA, Orange Coast Coll. 1962; BA, Univ. Redlands 1964; MA, CSU Long Beach 1968. Career: elem. sch. tchr. Costa Mesa 1964-66, Germany 1966-67, Garden Grove 1968-70, Port Angeles, Wash. 1971; subs. tchr. Newport Mesa 1974-78; real estate agent 1978-82, broker 1982—; instr. synergy classes, spiritual consciousness tng.; pres. Women's Council of Realtors for Newport-Costa Mesa Bd. Realtors 1983-84; pres. Coast Guard Ofcrs. Wives Club 1971, 72, 73, Svc. Award from Admiral 1973; mem: Irvine CofC, PEO, Nat. and Calif. Assn. Realtors, Irvine, NH-CM Bd. of Realtors, Focus 30, SPIN; Republican; Protestant; rec: travel. Res: 40 Lewis Irvine 92720 Ofc: Re/Max Inc., 4487 Barranca Pkwy Ste 210 Irvine 92714

PIEPER, DAROLD DEAN, lawyer; b. Dec. 30, 1944, Vallejo; s. Walter A.H. and Verla Mae (Ellis) P.; m. Barbara Gillis, Dec. 20, 1969; 1 son, Christopher Radcliffe b. 1980; edn: AB, econs., UC Los Angeles 1967; JD, USC 1970; admitted Calif. State Bar 1971. Career: ops. research analyst Weapons Planning Group, Naval Weapons Center, China Lake 1966-69; atty. assoc. Richards, Watson, Dreyfuss & Gershon, Attys. at Law, Los Angeles 1970-76, ptnr. 1976—; panel moderator and panelist re Estate Planning, Calif. Continuing Edn. of Bar (1978, 82); mem. Vol. Probate Panel L.A. County Superior Ct.; honors: Commendn. for community service, L.A. County Bd. of Supvrs. (1978); mem: ABA, State Bar Assn., L.A. County Bar Assn., Appellate Circle of Legion Lex USC, USC Law Alumni Assn., California Club; civic: La Canada Flintridge CofC and Comm. Assn. (pres. 1981, dir. 1976-83), L.A. County Delinquency and Crime Commn. (commnr. 1983-, v.chmn. 1985-), Pasadena Police Reserve Unit (cmdr. 1982-84, Reserve Peace Ofcr. 1972-), Pacific Legal Found., L.A. County Mus. of Art (sponsor), Verdugo Hills Hosp. Found.; publs: Estate Planning for Owners of the Family or Closely Held Business (CEB 1978, 82), Condominiums and the 1968 Housing and Urban Devel. Act (43 So. Calif. Law Rev. 309, 1970); Republican (Calif. Repub. Party); Episcopal; avocation: public service. Ofc: Richards, Watson, Dreyfuss & Gershon, 333 S Hope St 38th Flr Los Angeles 90071-1469

PIERING, TIMOTHY JAMES, building construction co. owner, real estate broker, author; b. Aug. 13, 1946, Duluth, Minn.; s. Alfred Francis and Lorrain Marie (Kugel) P.; m. Sheila Navin, Sept. 6, 1968; children: Jeffrey b. 1971, Julie

b. 1974; edn: ME, UCLA 1974-76; BSCE, Univ. of Iowa 1970; BA, Loras Coll. 1968; Calif. lic. Real Estate Broker (1979), Gen. Bldg. Contr. (1981). Career: engr. Ralph M. Parsons Co., Pasadena 1973-80, senior project engr. SOHIO North Slope Oil Recovery AMACO Sulfur Recovery Plant Missouri, asst. engring. mgr. OSCO Gas Compression Plants, Iran, ECOL Refinery, Louisiana; bldg. constrn. and real estate bus. ranch realty owner 1979-82; pres. Tim Piering Ents. Inc., Sierra Madre 1981—; engr. exec. program 1974-76, supt. Pasadena City Coll. Bldg. Constrn. Course 1981; honors: Chi Epsilon (1968-70), Master Builders Scholar (1970), All Marine Judo Champion (1973), Million Dollar Club Real Estate (1978-82), Sierra Madre Beautification award (1982); mem: Am. Soc. Civil Engrs. (1968-70), Toastmasters (pres. RMP 1975-78), Hunger Project Finl. Family to End World Starvation (1981-83); author: Breaking Free to Mental & Financial Independence (1985); guest appearance on 100+ radio and t.v. shows; wrote Ralph M. Parsons Co. manuals: Interdiscipline Co-ordination, Economic Evaluation, Project Mgmt. (1973-80); works: restoration of 1884 Victorian Home in Sierra Madre; designer/contr. single family houses; mil: capt. US Marine Corps 1970-73; Republican; Catholic; rec: martial arts black belt judo/karate. Res: 305 Ramona Ave Sierra Madre 91024 Ofc: Tim Piering Enterprises Inc. 370 W Sierra Madre Blvd Sierra Madre 91024

PIERRE, MERLE JANET, writer; b. May 31, 1952, Trinidad, West Indies; d. Georgieana Hilda Pierre; children: James Gregory b. 1977, Richard Benton b. 1978; edn: AA, soc. sci., Grossmont Coll. 1979; BA, St. Univ. of NY 1983; MA human behavior, National Univ. 1984; PhD human behavior, La Jolla Univ. 1986; Calif. Community Coll. Tchg. Cred. (life) 1983. Career: freelance writer, teacher; currently self-employed as freelance writer/ photog.; honors: "Putting Hubby Through" hon. degree, CSULB engring. dept.; mem. Internat. Womens Writing Guild, Nat. Assn. Female Execs., Fla. State Poets Assn. Inc., Photog. Soc. of Am.; counselor vol. charitable orgns.; publs: 4 collections of poetry, individual poems in anthols.; Republican; Anglican; rec: writing poems, songs. Address: San Diego 92131

PIETER, ANDREW MICHAEL, direct marketing, mailing list and data processing co. president; b. Jan. 2, 1949, Los Angeles; s. Louis and Clara P.; m. Gail Lynn, Mar. 18, 1945; children: Mark Robert b. 1972, Allison Beth b. 1974; edn: BS in bus. adm., Calif. State Coll. 1969; MBA, Pepperdine 1979. Career: mktg. rep. and area mktg. mgr. West Polaroid Corp., 1970-80; dir. nat. product devel. HDM, Harte-Hanks Communications Inc., 1980, v.p. mktg. HDM, 1981, pres. HDM Mailing Co., 1982, pres. Computer Mktg. Svcs., Anaheim (div. Harte-Hanks Comms.), 1982—; awards: Adult Scouting Leadership Tng. (1984), High Adventure Tng. Award (1984), Am. Red Cross Tng. (1982, 84); mem. Direct Mktg. Assn., DMA of Orange County, Direct Mktg. Computer Assn.; civic: Family Counseling Svcs. of O.C. (bd., 1st. v.p. 1984-86), Toastmasters; mil: sp4 Calif. Air N.G. 1970-76; rec: Boy Scout leader, Sierra hiker, racquetball. Ofc: Computer Marketing Services 1950 W Corporate Way Anaheim 92801

PIGOTT, CORNELIUS PHILLIP, financial consultant; b. Oct. 17, 1942, Storm Lake, Iowa; s. Cornelius Phillip and Margaret Cecilia (Staber) P.; m. Mary Jane Bair, Nov. 27, 1985; children: Todd Michael b. 1968, Kindra Annette b. 1974; edn: BA, Buena Vista Coll. 1967; MS financial svcs., Am. Coll. 1986; Chartered Life Underwriter 1971; Chartered Financial Cons. 1983. Career: exec. mgmt. Pacific Financial 1974—; ins. instr. Calif. Comm. Coll.; honors: Outstanding Young Men of Am. (1977); mem: NASD, Nat. Assn. Life Underwriters (ethics com.), Independent Ins. Agents, Internat. Assn. Fin. Planning, Calif. State Bar (Estate Planning, Trust & Probate Law Sect. Comn.), Am. Soc. Chartered Life Underws. (contg. edn. chmn.), Estate Planning Council of Fresno, Estate Planning Council of Tulare- Kings Counties (founder, past pres.), Toastmasters (past. pres., dir.), Calif. Assn. Neurologically Handicapped Children (past pres., dir.), Am. Diabetes Assn. Profl. Spkrs. Bureau (founder, chmn.), Christian Sci. Orgn., Buena Vista Alumni Assn.; Republican; Catholic; rec: watercolor painting. Res: 8276 Poplar Fresno 93711 Ofc: Pacific Financial 1195 W Shaw Ste A Fresno 93711

PIKE, CARL ALBERT, clergyman, private school founder; b. Nov. 28, 1906, Paso Robles, Calif.; s. Chester S. and Esther O. (Erickson) P.; m. Margaret C. Johnson (decd. 1959), June 10, 1938; children: Daniel b. 1939, James b. 1940, John b. 1945, Andrew b. 1947; m. 2d Leola M. Hettich, June 20, 1970; edn: BD, ordination, L.A. Baptist Coll. & Seminary 1942; ordination, Southern Baptist Conv. 1944. milling bus. Van Nuys & L.A. 1924-27; ranching, farming Buena Park 1927-30; cattle feeding bus. Buena Park 1930-31; founder Mission Bell radio Mfg. Co. (later Hoffman Electronics & Television Co., now Gould Co.) L.A. 1927; owner Pike Willys Co. L.A. 1934-38, Carl Pike Realtors L.A. 1938-42; founder Prairie Ave. Gospel Ctr. & Hawthorne Christian Sch. Hawthorne 1942, grown to 8 schools in Calif. and Ariz.; founder Hawthorne Baptist Seminary and Tng. Sch. 1945; founder num. churches; owner KHCS Radio Phoenix 1972-75; founder Arthritis Anonymous 1976, The Ole Doc Pike Ministry and College of the Last Roundup 1986—; owned 5 book stores; hosted num. radio and TV pgms.; honors: Hon. Doctorate (Golden West Univ. 1972), Beyond the Call of Duty Award (L.A. Police Dept. 1952), attended President Eisenhower Prayer Breakfast (1957), num. others from civic orgns. and police depts.; mem: Calif. Com. of Church Finance (pres. 1956-57), Arctic Circle Club,Order of Arctic Adventurers, Canada's Arctic Northwest Territories, USA Inventors Soc.; counselor Motion picture Automobile Buyers Guild 1939; chief of transp. Civil Defense 1946; local dir. Selective Svc. Ofc. 1941-45; inventions: Glazite burnishing compound polish (1932), holly collar pins (1932), elimination of running boards (1936), Voice of Scripture Talking Bible

(1957), X-Tra Brake, lawnmower reel, 2 grinding machines, Companion Warmer; producer RCA Library of Religious Recordings (1956); Republican; Baptist; rec: music, flying, exploring, inventing. Res: 2341 Duane Rd Palm Springs 92262 Ofc: Hawthorne Christian Schools 13600 S Prairie Ave Hawthorne 90250

PILCHER, LAURENCE L., hospital administrator; b. Jan, 16, 1946, South Gate; s. Paul William Sr. and Jettie Lucille (King) P.; edn: BA, Columbia Coll. 1972; BA, Pepperdine Univ. 1974; MPA, 1979; teaching cred. Calif. Comm. Colls. Career: regional dir. American Kor-Asian Found. 1972-75; adminstrv. dir. Daniel Freeman Hosp. 1975-81; v.p. Presbyterian Intercomm. Hosp. 1985; v.p. Doheny Eye Found. & Hosp., Univ. of So. Calif. Sch. of Medicine 1985 − ; adjunct prof. Sch. of Cont. Edn. Univ. So. Cal. (USC); bd. mem. East Whittier Sch. Dist.; adminstrn. award Daniel Freeman Hosp. 1978; mem: Am. Coll. of Healthcare Execs., Assn. of Western Hosp., Hosp. Council of So. Calif.; Republican; Episcopal; rec: fitness, running, hiking; Res: 252 Santa Ana Ave Long Beach 90803 Ofc: Doheny Eye Foundation & Hospital, USC School of Medicine, 1355 San Pablo St Los Angeles 90033

PILLING, GEORGE WILLIAM, lawyer; b. Mar. 25, 1942, Reading, Pa.; s. Hugh Aiken and Lillian Hannah Pilling; 1 dau: Jocelyn Kay, b. 1974; edn: AB, Kalamazoo Coll. 1963; JD, w/ distinction, Univ. of Mich. Law Sch. 1966. Career: law clerk Montgomery, McCracken, Walker & Rhoads, Phila., Penn. 1965; tchr. Boy's Republic (emotionally disturbed boys), Farmington, Mich. 1966-68; law clerk Cooper, White & Cooper, San Francisco 1968; assoc. law firm Pllack & Palmer, Los Angeles 1968-70; staff atty. Western Ctr. on Law & Poverty, L.A. 1970-72; partner law firm Shapiro, Posell & Pilling, L.A. 1972-73; solo practice, George Wm. Pilling, Atty. at Law, L.A. 1974 − ; pres., dir. LG&N Ent. Inc. dba Dura- Guide Co. 1976-; CFO, secty., dir. Newell Sports Ent. Inc. 1984 − ; active practice of law concentrating on civil litigation, L.A. 1975 − ; mem: State Bar of Mich. 1967-; State Bar of Calif. 1968-; ACLU (exec. com., Lawyers Div. 1971-72); Democrat; rec: equestrian, water sports. Res: 3453 Coast View Dr Malibu 90265 Ofc: George Wm. Pilling, 1107-½ Glendon Ave Westwood Village Los Angeles 90024

PINE, CHARLES JOSEPH, clinical psychologist; b. July 13, 1951, Excelsior Springs, Mo.; s. Charles Edison and La Vern (Upton) P.; m. Mary Day, Dec. 30, 1979; children: Charles Andrew, b. 1981, Joseph Scott b. 1983; edn: BA, Univ. of Redlands 1973; MA, CSU Los Angeles 1975; PhD, Univ. of Wash. 1979. Career: psychology intern VA Outpatient Clinic, Los Angeles 1978-79; instr./ asst. prof. dept. of psychology Okla. State Univ., Stillwater 1979-80; postdoctoral scholar in Amer. Indian studies & psychol., Inst. of Am. Cultures, UCLA 1980-81; asst. prof. dept. of psychol. & native Am. studies pgm., Wash. State Univ., Pullman 1981-82; cons. 1981, dir. Behavioral Health Svcs., Riverside- San Bernardino Co. Indian Health Inc., Banning 1982-84; clin. psychol. Long Beach VA Med. Ctr. 1984-85; clin. psychol. & psychol. coord. Drug Dependence Treatment Ctr., Sepulveda VA Med. Ctr. 1985 − ; clin. asst. prof. Fuller Theol. Sem. Grad. Sch. of Psychol. 1985 − ; asst. clin. prof. Div. of Med. Psychol., Dept. of Psych. & Biobehavioral Scis., UCLA Sch. of Med. 1985 − ; mem. editl. bd. White Cloud Journ. of Am. Indian & Alaskan Native Mental Health 1982; awards: grantee, Inst. of Am. Cultures, UCLA 1981-82, Inst. of Indian Studies, Univ. of Wash. 1976; listed Who's Who in the World, in the West, in Frontiers of Sci. & Technol., Internat. Who's Who of Intellectuals, Personalities of Am., of the West & Midwest, World Biog. Hall of Fame, Dict. of Internat. Biog., mem. Community Leaders of the World; mem: Am. Psycholog. Assn. (bd. Ethnic Minority Affairs Task Force on Edn. & Tng. 1982, Bd. of Ethnic Minority Affairs, Publs. and Commun. Bds. Task Force on Eliminating Ethnic Bias in Language); Western Psycholog. Assn.; Sigma Alpha Epsilon; publs: arts. in profl., scholarly journs.; Republican; Baptist; rec: theatre, music, sports. Res: 365 W Grove Rialto 92376 Ofc: Psychol. Svc., 116B, VA Med. Ctr. 16111 Plummer St Sepulveda 91343

PINCKERT, WARREN EMMETT, II, manufacturing co. financial executive; b. Dec. 28, 1943, San Bernardino; s. Warren Emmett and Lucille Leavon (Jones) P.; m. Constance Clark, May 25, 1969; children: Shannon b. 1972, Scott b. 1975; edn: BS acctg., Univ. So. Calif. 1966, MBA, 1971; CPA Calif. 1973. Career: auditor Arthur Anderson & Co. L.A. 1971-74; dir. internal audit Mattel Inc. Hawthorne 1974-78; v.p. fin. Mataframe (subsid. of Mattel) Elmwood Park, N.J. 1978-80; group controller Computer Sciences El Segundo 1980-83; v.p. fin., chief finl. ofcr., secty. Sunrise Medical Inc. Torrance 1983 − ; dir. Pacificare Health Systems 1985, 9 subsids. of Sunrise Medical 1983-85, Medmarc Ltd. 1985; mem: Am. Inst. CPAs 1973-, Calif. Soc. CPAs 1973, Nat. Assn. Over the Counter Cos. (fin. and budget com.) 1985, Palos Verdes Independence Day Celebration Com., Palos Verdes Breakfast Club, Lunada Bay Little League (coach), AYSO (coach); mil: capt. USMC 1966-69, Bronze Star, 2 Purple Hearts, Pres. Unit. Citation.; Republican; Protestant; rec: tennis, running, reading, travel. Res: 2920 Via De La Guerra Palos Verdes Estates 90274 Ofc: Sunrise Medical Inc. 970 W 190th St Ste 280 Torrance 90502

PINE, CHARLES JOSEPH, clinical psychologist; b. July 13, 1951, Excelsior Springs, Mo.; s. Charles Edison and La Vern (Upton) P.; m. Mary Day, Dec. 30, 1979; children: Charles Andrew, b. 1981; Joseph Scott, b. 1983; edn: BA, Univ. of Redlands 1973; MA, CSU Los Angeles 1975; PhD, Univ. of Wash. 1979. Career: psychology intern VA Outpatient Clinic, Los Angeles 1978-79; instr./ asst. prof. dept. of psychology Okla. State Univ., Stillwater 1979-80; postdoctoral scholar in Amer. Indian studies & psychol., Inst. of Am. Cultures, UCLA 1980-81; asst. prof. dept. of psychol. & native Am. studies pgm., Wash. State Univ., Pullman 1981-82; cons. 1981, dir. Behavioral Health Svcs., River-

side- San Bernardino Co. Indian Health Inc., Banning 1982-86; VA Med. Center, Sepulveda 1986 − ; mem. editl. bd. White Cloud Journ. of Am. Indian & Alaskan Native Mental Health 1982; awards: grantee, Inst. of Am. Cultures, UCLA 1981-82, Inst. of Indian Studies, Univ. of Wash. 1976; mem: Am. Psycholog. Assn. (bd. Ethnic Minority Affairs Task Force on Edn. & Tng. 1982); Western Psycholog. Assn.; Sigma Alpha Epsilon; publs: arts. in profl., scholarly journs.; Republican; Baptist; rec: theatre, music, sports. Res: 365 W Grove Rialto 92376 Ofc: Psychology Service (116B) VAMC 1611 Plummer St Sepulveda 91343

PINKERTON, ALLAN MC KEVETT, farmer; b. July 28, 1943, Oxnard, Calif.; s. John and Virginia Lowry (McKevett) P.; m. Mary Anne, June 17, 1967; children: Jennifer b. 1969, Jonathan b. 1971; edn: BS, Cal. Poly. Pomona 1966. Career: owner, pres. JVP Citrus - Pinkerton Ranches Ventura; dir: Saticoy Lemon Assn., Ojai-Tapo Citrus Assn., Farmers Irrigation Co., Alta Mutual Water Co., Ventura County Citrus Exchange, McKevett Corp., Teague McKevett Co., Mupu Citrus Assn., Founder Circle Ventura County Nat. Bank; mem: Sunkist Growers Inc., Calavo, Ventura County Farm Bureau, Rancheros Adolfo, Ventura Co. Game Preserve; works: hold patent on Pinkerton Avocado; Republican; rec: skiing, hunting, fishing, surfing, skin diving. Ofc: Pinkerton Ranch POB 4099 Ventura 93004

PIPER, CURTIS DEAN, soil science professor; b. May 24, 1925, Hillsdale, Mich.; s. Ira W. and Addie Ann (Losey) P.; m. Helen Landphair, June 4, 1952; children: Dwight b. 1960, Kevin b. 1962, Craig b. 1967, Cynthia b. 1971; edn: BA, William Jennings Bryan Univ. 1953; MS, Mich. St. Univ. 1959, PhD 1967. Career: farmer George Mathews, Union City, Mich.; food service mgr. William Jennings Bryan Univ., Dayton, Tenn.; food service mgr. Kings Coll., Briarcliff Manor, N.Y.; instr. Mich. State Univ., East Lansing; instr., prof. (Dept. head) Soil Sci. Dept., Calif. Poly State Univ., San Luis Obispo current; cons.: Broadleaf Ind., Shell Oil Co., Shaklee Corp., Peace Corps; honors: MPPP Award, Cal Poly (1985-86); mem. Am. Soc. Agronomy, Calif. Fertilizer Assn.; civic: Gideons, Christian Business Men's Com., 4-H; 4 yrs applied research on effects of surfactant on soil water infiltration; research on influence of adding cross-linked polymer to soils and potting mixes; Republican; Prot.; rec: photog., hiking, travel. Res: 1768 Jami Lee Ct San Luis Obispo 93401 Ofc: Soil Science Dept. Calif. Poly State Univ., San Luis Obispo 93407

PIROSH, MICHAEL, judge; b. Jan. 26, 1942, Los Angeles; s. Robert and Emily (Fitzpatrick) P.; m. Marjorie Felmus, Dec. 1975; m. 2d. Michele Bernath, Feb. 4, 1979; edn: AB, UC Berkeley 1964; JD, Univ. of San Diego Law Sch. 1968. Career: atty./ dir. of law reform San Fernando Valley Neighborhood Legal Svcs., Van Nuys 1968-69; deputy pub. defender trial atty. Pub. Defenders Ofc., Los Angeles 1969-73; pvt. practice law ofcs. of Michael Pirosh, L.A. 1973-75; deputy denfender trial atty., L.A. 1975-77; supvg. pub. defender Inglewood Juvenile Ct. 1975-76; pvt. practice law, L.A. 1977-80; elected commnr. L.A. Municipal Ct. 1980-81; judge, Municipal Ct., L.A. Judicial Dist. 1981-2; named to L.A. Superior Ct. 1982 − ; Western coord. Law Students Civil Rights Research Council 1967-68; exec. com., personnel com., exec. ofcr. com. L.A. Municipal Ct. 1981-; awards: Reginald Heber Smith Fellowship sponsored by Harvard & Univ. of Mich. Schs. of Law 1968-69; judge, regl. law sch. Moot Ct. Competition 1981; mem: Calif. Judges Assn. 1981-; L.A. Co. Bar Assn.; Lawyers Club of L.A.; Democrat; Jewish; rec: equestrian, travel, jogging. Res: 1942 San Ysidro Dr Beverly Hills 90210 Ofc: Los Angeles Superior Ct., 111 Hill St Los Angeles 90012

PISANO, PHILIP ANTHONY, executive; b. Jan. 8, 1952, Monterey Park, Calif.; s. Philip John and Leona Grace (Rosolino) P.; m. Joanne, May 18m 1985; edn: BA magna cum laude, Univ. So. Calif. 1975; real estate broker Calif. 1979. Career: mktg. dir. McCarthy & Assocs. Real Estate Devel. Newport Beach 1975-79; loan ofcr. Wells Fargo BANK Long Beach 1979-81; asst.mgr. Tokai Bank Newport Beach 1981; v.p. Commonwealth Bank Tustin, Santa Ana 1981-85, regl. v.p. 1985-86; finl. advisor Cigna Securities Inc. Irvine 1986 − ; dir. Med. Diagnostics Inc.; civic: Rotary (secty.), Pres.'s Council USC, Roosters of Chanticleer, vol. Orange County Probation Dept.; Catholic; rec: golf, tennis, baseball, basketball, racquetball, guitar. Ofc: Cigna 19000 Mac-Arthur Blvd 4th floor Irvine 92715

PISTACCHI, JOHN ROBERT, computer services co. president; b. Dec. 13, 1946, Lyon, France, nat. US cit. 1964; s. Michel and Gina Rosa (Salvetti) P.; m. Martha Fait, Sept. 3, 1970; children: Ann b. 1973, Michael b. 1975; edn: BSEE, Loyola Univ., L.A. 1968; MSEE, UC Los Angeles 1969. Career: aerospace engr. TRW, Rockwell, Litton, 5 yrs.; product line mgr., branch mgr., dist. mgr., then regional mgr. Control Data Corp. (releasing software prods. worldwide through a nat. Timesharing Bur.), 1973-82; pres./bd. chmn. Opticom Corp., San Jose (computer services co.); cons. to industry; awards: Outstanding Mgr. (1978, 79, 80), Mgr. of Yr. (1980), CDC; mem. IEEE (1964-70); club: Almaden Swim & Racket; pub. (joint proj. w/10 yr old son) Fishing in the Bay Area, A Father/Son Guide; Republican; Catholic; rec: fishing, photog. Ofc: Opticom Corp 6895 Via Del Oro San Jose 95119

PITEL, ROBERT, manufacturing co. executive; b. Feb. 28, 1953, Bklyn.; s. Irving T. and Ruth (Pechter) P.; m. Julie, Feb. 13, 1981; edn: BA, Brown Univ. 1976. Career: account exec. Purcell Inc., Los Angeles 1976-78, Didde Graphic Systems, Orange 1978-81; regl. sales Stevens Corp., Ft. Worth, Tx. 1981-83; comml. dist. mgr., product sales mgr., currently regl. sales mgr. Didde Graphic Systems, Fountain Valley 1983 − , named corp. Manager of the Year (1985), Nat. New Accounts leader (1979-81), mem. Round Table 1979-81); mem. Printing Indus. of Am. (IBFI Sect. 1981-); Democrat; rec: music, tennis, investing. Res: 68 Ashbrook Irvine 92714 Ofc: Didde Graphic Systems 17155 Newhope St Ste C Fountain Valley 92708

PITRE, FRANK MARIO, lawyer; b. Jan. 17, 1955, San Francisco; s. Sal and Rosanna Sarah (Pipia) P.; edn: BS bus. econs., cum laude, Univ. San Francisco 1977, JD, 1981; admitted Calif. State Bar 1981, US Supreme Ct. 1985. Career: legal extern Calif. Supreme Ct. 1980; law clerk San Mateo County Superior Ct. 1981; atty. Cotchett & Illston 1981−; honors: Beta Gamma Sigma 1977; mem: Am., S.F., San Mateo Co. bar assns., Calif. State Bar, Calif., San Mateo Co. Trial Lawyers Assns., Assn. Trial Lawyers of Am., San Mateo Co. Barristers (bd. dirs. 1984-), Royal Racquet Club; co-author Jury Instructions: A Practical Approach to Their Use (Civic Litigation Reporter, Mar. 1984); Democrat; Catholic. Res: 1335 Magnolia Ave Millbrae 94030 Ofc: Cotchett & Illston 4 W 4th Ave Ste 500 San Mateo 94402

PITRUZZELLO, TREY VINCENT, chiropractor; b. Nov. 3, 1955, Loma Linda; s. Joseph and Frances Ilene (Brockie) P.; m. Jodi Steed, March 26, 1983; 1 son, Trevor Joseph b. 1984; edn: BA, CSU Chico 1981; DC, Life Chiropractic Coll. 1984. Career: asst. mgr. Chico Game Fish Farm, Chico 1979-80; mgr. Pitruzzello's Restaurant, Riverside 1980-81; chiropractic asst., physical therapist Herndon Chiropractic Clinic, Hayward 1981-83; clinic supvr./ senior intern Life Chiropractic Coll. West Outpatient Clinic, Hayward 1983-84; chiropractor/owner Magnolia Chiropractic Ctr., Riverside 1985−; founding pres. Assn. for Chiropractic Excellence 1981-84; honors: Spl. Citation for clin. excellency, Life Chiropractic Coll. Outpatient Clinic (1983), Eagle Scout, Order of The Arrow, Boy Scouts Am. (1971); mem: Internat., Calif. Chiropractic Assns., Riverside County Chiro. Soc. (sec. 1986-87); civic: Rotary, Boy Scouts Am. (asst. scoutmaster Troop 6), San Leandro Computer Club (past pres.); sci. publ., CSU Sr. Biopsychol. Research 1979-80; Republican; Ch. of Jesus Christ LDS; rec: home computers, telecommunications. Res: 3981 Larchwood Pl. Riverside 92506 Ofc: Magnolia Chiropractic Center, 6841 Magnolia Ave. Riverside 92506

PITTENGER, WAYNE ALLEN, manufacturing co. president; b. March 5, 1939, Mansfield, Ohio; s. Robert H. and Mary E. Steward; m. Janet, June 19, 1965; chidren: Jill b. 1966, John b. 1968, Wendy b. 1969; edn: BSBA, Ohio State Univ. 1962. Career: mfg. mgr. Dana Laboratories, Irvine 1968-73; mfg. mgr. Fairchild Camera & Instrument, San Jose 1973-76, dir. of ops. 1976-78, div. gen. mgr. 1978-80; gen. mgr. Gen Rad Corp., Milpitas 1980-81; div. gen. mgr. Eaton Corp., San Jose 1981-86; pres., CEO ASIX Systems Corp., Fremont 1986−. Res: 108 Brocastle Way Los Gatos 95030 Ofc: ASIX Systems Corp. 47338 Fremont Blvd Fremont 94538-6178

PITTLUCK, AVERY TYLER, neurologist; b. July 2, 1947, Cambridge, Mass.; s. Norman Aaron and Betty Suzanne (Morgenstern) P.; m. Charlotte Speizer, Dec. 22, 1974; children: Brian b. 1977, Ian b. 1980; edn: AB, UC Berkeley 1969; Regents Fellow psychobiol., UC Irvine 1970-71, NIMH fellow forensic psych. 1972; MD, UC Los Angeles Sch. of Med. 1976; splty. degree neurol., UCLA Med. Ctr. 1980. Career: chief res. neurol. UCLA Med. Ctr. 1979-80; pvt. practice neurol., brain imaging So. Calif. Imaging Ctr., med. dir. So. Orange Co. Med. Rehabil. Clin. 1981-84; chief electrodiagnostic Svc., So. Coast Med. Ctr. 1983−; clin. instr. neurol. UCI Med. Ctr. 1984-; founder, codir. Saddleback Valley Med. Assoc. and Saddleback Valley Med. Rehab. Ctr.; attg. neurol. Saddleback Comm. Hosp.; clin. co-dir. So. Coast Diagnostic Lab; co-dir. Sleep Disorders Ctr.; honors: Phi Beta Kappa 1969; mem: Am. Coll Phys. 1977-, Am. Med. Electroencephalographic Assn. 1980-, Am. Acad. Neurol. 1983-, Nat. Assn. Disability Evaluation Phys. (charter mem. 1984), Royal Soc. Med. 1984; research: neuroanatomy of visual system 1970-71, Amnesias 1974, Sleep Disorders & Head Trauma 1984; Jewish; rec: reading, writing, swimming, film making. Ofc: A. Tyler Pittluck MD Inc. 23961 Calle de la Magdalena, Ste. 355, Laguna Hills 92653

PITTS, REGINALD GEORGE, investment banking executive; b. June 5, 1937, Toronto, Ont., Can., nat. US cit. 1964; s. Alexander Michael and Lillian (Swyer) P.; m. Sandra Mund, Sept. 11, 1976; children: Richard b. 1962, Debra b. 1964, David b. 1965; edn: El Camino Coll. 1965-67. Career: clk. Paine Weber Jackson & Curtis, Los Angeles 1961-63; securities trader Roberts Scott & Co., L.A. 1963-67; v.p. Wedbush, Noble, Cooke, Inc., L.A. 1967-80; senior v.p. Morgan, Olmstead, Kennedy & Gardner, Inc. L.A. 1980−; mem: Nat. Security Traders Assn. (bd. govs. 1972-74), Nat. Assn. of Security Dealers (Trading Com. 1975-78), Security Traders Assn. of Los Angeles (pres. 1972, 1984); Republican; Anglican; rec: golf. Ofc: Morgan, Olmstead, Kennedy & Gardner Inc 606 South Olive St Los Angeles 90014

PITTS, THOMAS RICHARD, church foundation executive; b. Nov. 4, 1940, Muskogee, Okla.; s. Francis and Anne Kelly (Lyne) P.; m. Ruth, Aug. 28, 1965; children: Gregory b. 1969, Sheryl b. 1972; edn: BBA, Univ. Okla. 1963, MPA, Univ. Ariz. 1971; lic. nursing home adminstr. 1985. Career: asst. adminstr. Episcopal Homes Found. Los Gatos 1971, assoc. adminstr. 1972, adminstr. 1972-75, St. Pauls Towers Oakland 1975-83, asst. to pres. LaFayette 1983-84; chief ops. 1984−, secy. 1985; secy., dir. John Tenner Meml. Homes, Presidio Gate Apts., Oak Ctr. Towers 1985; honors: Outstanding Seenior Leadership, Scholarship ROTC (Univ. Okla. 1963); mem: Am., Calif. (edn. com. 1972) Assn. Homes for Aged, Santa Clara Co. Med. Soc. (long term care com. 1974), Old Crows, Phi Delta Theta, Alumni Assn. (Univ. Okla., Univ. Ariz.), Delta Delta Delta; writer computer pgms. for business; mil: capt. USAF 1963-69, B-52 combat crew; Republican; Episcopal; rec: computers. Res: 11462 Cresta Ln Dublin 94568 Ofc: Episcopal Homes Found 3150 Mt Diablo Blvd Lafayette

PLAFCAN, MARK MATTHEW, industrial equipment sales executive; b. Jan. 25, 1955, Bryn Mawr, Pa.; s. John M. and Catherine L. (Siderio) P.; m. Denise J., Sept. 11, 1981; 1 dau. Michelle b. 1984; edn: BS chem. engring., Villanova Univ. 1977. Career: tech. service rep. Am. Cyanimid, in Wayne, NJ, Mobile, Ala., Kalamazoo, Mich., 1977-78, then prodn. supr. Mobile (Ala.) Plant, 1979; field process engr. Pennwalt-Sharples Div., Warminster, Pa. 1980-81, sales engr. Sharples, Cleveland, Oh. 1981, dist. sales mgr. Sharples Div. Penwalt Corp., Burlingame, Ca. 1982−; mem. assoc: Am. Inst. Chem. Engrs., WCPF/Bay Sect. (tech. paper presentations, tng. pgms.), PNPCA, CWPCA; Independent; Catholic; rec: camping, model rocketry, auto racing, target shooting. Res: 25930 Kay Ave Ste 204 Hayward 94545 Ofc: Pennwalt Corp. Sharples Div. 1415 Rollins Rd Burlingame 94010

PLISKA, EDWARD WILLIAM, judge; b. April 13, 1935, Rockville, Conn.; s. Louis B. and Constance (Dombrowski) P.; m. Luisa C., Nov. 29, 1958; children: Gregory b. 1962, John b. 1966, Thomas b. 1970, Laura b. 1971; edn: AB, Princeton Univ. 1956; LLB, Univ. of Conn. 1964. Career: newspaper reporter The Hartford (Conn.) Courant, 1958-64; dep. dist. atty. Santa Barbara County 1965, San Mateo County 1965-71 (chief trial dep. 1969-71); pvt. law practice, San Mateo 1971-72; elected judge San Mateo Municipal Ct., 1972−, re-elected 1980; prof. criminal law, constnl. law, San Mateo Law Sch. 1970-74; prod./moderator: The Justice Forum, weekly t.v. and radio pgm., 1973-78; honors: Hon. LL.D., San Mateo Law Sch. (1975); mem: Am. Judges Assn. (1st v.p. 1985-86; bd. govs. 1979-83), Calif. Judges Assn. (1973-), World Judges Assn. (chmn. World Free-Press and Fair Trial Com. 1976-81), San Mateo Co. Criminal Justice Council; civic: chmn. San Mateo Co. Arts Council 1973-75; chmn. San Mateo Co. Alcoholism Advis. Bd. 1973-75; bd. dirs. Hillbarn Theatre, Human Investment Project, (past mem.) Amnesty Internat., Sierra Club, NAACP; publs: exec. editor Court Review, quarterly journal (1981-); article "Cults: Bias in the Courts?" in Court Review (Fall 1983) and Praxis (1983); mil: sp5 Army Nat. Guard 1957-63; Democrat; Roman Catholic; rec: actor/dir. var. theaters S.F. Bay Area, running. Res: 1567 Escondido Way Belmont 94002 Ofc: San Mateo County Municipal Ct. 800 N Humboldt St San Mateo 94401

PLOHR, GEORGE W., management consultant co. executive; b. Feb. 5, 1933, Pittsburgh, Pa.; s. William A. and M. Emma (Bailey) P.; m. Laura Thomas, Feb. 4, 1956; children: Wesley A. b. 1961, Bradley M. b. 1962, Alison A. b. 1967; edn: BS, Lehigh Univ. 1955; MBA, Univ. of Pittsburgh 1963; desig: Certified Mgmt. Cons., Inst. of Mgmt. Consultants. Career: sales engr. Dravo Corp., Pittsburgh, Pa. 1955-61; mgr. corp. devel. PPG Industries, Inc., Pittsburgh 1961-68; pres. Corporate Development Associates Inc., Glen Ellyn, Ill. 1968-73; exec. v.p. Technomic Consultants, Inc., Chgo. and Huntington Beach 1974-85; pres., dir. Construction Products Marketing Assocs. Inc., Huntington Beach 1986−; mem: Inst. of Mgmt. Consultants, Am. Mktg. Assn., Soc. for Corporate Growth; civic: Lions Club (fund raising ofcr. 1964-68), Toastmasters Internat. (area gov. 1958-60), Lehigh Univ. Alumni; publs: num. mag. articles in Wallcoverings, Decorating Retailer, Glass Digest; mil: 1st lt. US Army; Corps of Engrs.; Republican; Prot.; rec: bridge, golf, civil war buff. Res: 488 Calle Amigo San Clemente 92672 Ofc: Construction Products Marketing Associates, Inc. 16168 Beach Blvd Ste 268 Huntington Beach 92647

PLUMMER, ELDORA FITE, business owner, ret.; b. Oct. 13, 1915, Novelty, Mo.; d. Arthur and Verna Lenore (Xander) Fite; m. Frank Plummer, Aug. 12, 1939 (dec. 1959); children: Ronald b. 1946, Robert b. 1948; edn: grad. (Valedictorian) Novelty (Mo.) H.S. 1933; N.E. Missouri State Tchrs. Coll. 1933, 1934; grad. Chillicothe (Mo.) Business Coll. 1936. Career: elementary sch. tchr. 193-35; bookkeeper, office mgr. Western Grave Vault Co., Muscatine, Iowa 1936-36; secty., bkpr., machine bkpr. interstate Supply Co. (wholesale br. of Aeolian Music Co.), St. Louis, Mo. 1937-39, The Thomas Mortgage Co. (prop. mgmt. div. of Prudential Ins. Co.), Los Angeles 1940-42; v.p./owner (with husband) Harry Perkins Inc., Seattle, Wash. 1953-57, and Plummers Shoes Inc., 1956-59, pres. 1959-60, sold bus. 1960; awards: Alpha Phi Sigma (1933-34), Nat. Sewing Contest (First Prize, Macon, Ga. and hon. mention N.Y.C. finals, 1944), White Sewing Machine sewing contest (2nd place, Seattle 1954), Amateur Songwriters Contest, Hoberg's Organ Festival (1st pl. 1967), Hole-in-One, Cambrian Golf Course, Campbell, Ca. (1974), Woman of the Week (Radio Stn. WBML Macon, Ga. 1944); civic: vol. Red Cross and O.P.A. (1942-44), Sand Point Golf & CC (Seattle 1953-65), Inverness Comm. Club (secty. 1957), Inverness Garden Club (pres. 1961), Childrens Orthopedic Hosp. (Eula Lee Merrill Guild 1955-65), Wash. Athletic Club 1954-65; Mtn View: Hammond Organ Club of Penin. (pres. 1967), All Organ Club of Santa Clara Valley (pgm. chair 1973), Cambrian Womens Golf Club (Campbell), Moffett Field Ladies GC, Vineyard Knolls Ladies GC (Napa), ASCAP (1968-83), The Retired Ofcrs. Assn. (aux. 1969-), The Museum Soc. (SF), KQED; publs: History of Inverness (Seattle Times, 1960); music & lyrics of song: "I Wanna be Happy" (1968); Republican; Christian; rec: music, stained glass, equestrian, travel. Res: Napa 94558

PLUMSTEAD, WILLIAM CHARLES, SR., constructor & engineering co. executive; b. Nov. 2, 1938, Two Rivers, Wisc. s. Wm. Cyril and Nancy Louise (Plumstead) Geimer; m. Vicki Newton, June 27, 1981; children: Kevin b. 1960, Keith b. 1961, Wm. b. 1965, Jennifer b. 1973; edn: Univ. Fla. 1956-58; Temple Univ. 1966-70; Albright Coll. 1971-74; BS bus. admin., Calif. Coast Univ. 1985, MBA pgm. 1985-. Career: v.p. US Testing Co. Inc. Reading, Pa. 1963-76; NDE svcs. mgr. Daniel Internat. Greeneville, S.C. 1976-83; group mgr. Bechtel Group Inc. S.F. 1983−; mem: fellow Am. Soc. for Nondestructive Testing 1979 (exec. com. 1984-87, bd. dirs. 1982-88, Phila. chmn. 1975-76, tech. council chmn. 1984-85), Am. Welding Soc. (chap. chmn. 1973-74), Am. Soc. Testing &

Materials (subcom. vice chmn. 1973-80), Toastmasters Internat.; publ: Code/ Specification Syndrome (1976), NDE Applications for Power Plant Life Assessment (1985); mil: pfc Fla. Nat. Guard 1955-63; Republican; rec: flying, jogging. Res: 187 Elderwood Dr Pleasant Hill 94523 Ofc: Bechtel Inc 50 Beale St San Francisco 94119

PLUNKETT, JOSEPH C., electrical engineering professor; b. Dec. 3, 1933, Centerville, Tenn.; s. Harold D. and Lorraine (Lewis) P.; edn: BS in math. & physics, Middle Tenn. State Univ. 1964; BSEE, Univ. Tenn. 1966; MSEE, Georgia Inst. of Tech. 1973; PhD in E.E., Texas A&M Univ. 1977; Reg. Profl. Engr., Mass. Career: research engr. (microwave comms. and radar systems) Raytheon Co., Martin Marietta Corp., and Ill. Inst. of Tech. Research Inst., 1966-72; research (integrated circuit design and fabrication) Texas A&M Univ. Inst. for Solid State Electronics, 1974-77; prof. elec. engring. (dept. chmn. 1980-84) CSU Fresno 1977—; honors: Eta Kappa Nu, Sigma Xi, CSU exceptional meritorious svc. award (1984) and Sch. of Engring. tchg. awards (1982); mem. NY Acad. of Scis., IEEE, Am. Assn. of Higher Edn. (bd. editors); mil: capt. US Army 1954-60; publs: num. publs. in field of integrated circuit design and fabrication include articles in Solid State Electronics (1977), IEEE Transactions on Electron Devices (1977), British IEE J. of Solid State; Chapt. 2, Impurity Doping Processes in Silicon (1981); symposium presentations; rec: mt. hiking, trout fishing. Ofc: EE Dept, Cal State Fresno, Cedar & Shaw Ave Fresno 93740

POER, EDGAR CALVIN, real estate agent; b. Dec. 15, 1923, Denver, Colo.; s. Edgar C., Sr. and Augusta Frances (Brock) P.; m. Irene Jeanette, Dec. 17, 1964; edn: AA, City Coll. of San Francisco 1956; stu. San Franciso St. Univ. 1956, Sonoma St. Univ. 1966; Calif. lic. real estate salesman (1957). Career: real estate salesman Bill Greer Realty, San Francisco 1957-59, Coronet Realty, S.F. 1961-64, Strout Realty, Santa Rosa 1964-65, Gehrke Realty, Santa Rosa 1965-67, self empl. in real estate field, 1967—; mem. San Francisco Bd. of Realtors 1963, Sonoma County Bd. Realtors (past mem. Legislative Com.; served 1 yr. on Sonoma Co. Plnng. and Zoning Com.); mem. Rose Soc. of Sonoma Co.; Democrat; Mormon (fmr. Elder); rec: stockmarket, swimming, rosarian. Res: 1634 Ronne Dr Santa Rosa 95404

POLIMAC-ILLICH, LIGIA KATARINA, chemist; b. Mar. 30, 1930, Miholjac, Yugolslavia; d. Djuro Dimitrie and Maria (First) P.; m. Andjelko Illich, Sept. 7, 1957; child: Vanja, b. 1958; edn: MS, Univ. of Zagreb Sch. of Chem. Tech. 1955. Career: resrch. chemist (drugs and food chemicals) Vetserum, Zagreb, Yugoslavia, 1955-58; mgr. Analytical Lab. DRAVA, Safety Matches Inc., Osijek, Yugoslavia, 1958-59; research group leader, Katran, Organic Ind., Zagreb, Yugoslavia, 1960-62; assoc. prof. Coll. of Organic Chem. Technology, Univ. of Zagreb, 1963-67; analytical chemist Packaging Corp. of America, Los Angeles, Ca. 1968-70; analytical chemist Cyclo Products, Inc., L.A. 1970-73, mgr. quality control 1973—; mem. Am. Chemical Soc.; Republican; Catholic; rec: dancing, cats. Res: 7444 Yankey St Downey 90242 Office: Cyclo Products, 1922 East 64th St Los Angeles 90001

POLINE, ROBERT MARTIN, executive search consulting co. president; b. Sept. 23, 1948, Neptune, N.J.; s. Louis Raymond and Sylvia Ruth (Shaken) P.; m. Cheryl, Mar. 4, 1973; children: Shauna b. 1978, Eric b. 1984; edn: BA sociol./poli. sci., Univ. of Denver 1970; MPA, UC Los Angeles Sch. Public Adminstrn. 1973. Career: pres. Bob Poline Assocs. Inc., La Jolla 1984—; v.p./ ptnr. Delta Crown Corp., San Diego 1981-84; mgr. Dunhill of San Diego 1979-81; regl. sales mgr. Gallo Winery 1976-79; sales rep. Interstate Restaurant Supply, San Diego 1973-76; mem. Internat. Council of Shopping Centers; Democrat; Jewish; rec: racquetball, skiing, travel, softball. Ofc: Bob Poline Assocs. Inc. 3262 Holiday Ct Ste 204 La Jolla 92037

POLITE, THERON JEROME, security agency president; b. Feb. 24, 1930, Tampa, Fla.; s. Charlie and Gussie Lee (Shad) Polite; m. Thelma Ford, May 4, 1948; children: Jimmy Lee b. 1944, Celinda Joyce (West) b. 1954, Kenneth Jerome b. 1956; edn: AS in Police Sci., Mtry. Peninsula Coll., Monterey 1970-72; Bach. Adm. of Justice, Golden Gate Univ., 1976, MPA, 1978; desig: Calif. Police Ofcrs' Std. Tng. Basic Cert. 1971; Comm. Coll. instr. credential: Police Sci. (life) 1979; Special Agt., Internat. Police Cong. Wash DC, Internat. Central Bur., Miami; Calif. lic. Pvt. Investigation, lic. Pvt. Security. Career: 1st sgt. US Armed Forces (AUS, USAF), 1946-69; Auxiliary opr. PG&E Steam Plant, Moss Landing, Castroville 1970; deputy sheriff Montery County Sheriff Dept., 1971-83; pres./mgr. Polite's Private Investigation & Security Agency, Seaside 1983—; mayor pro tem, City of Seaside, elected 1982; pres. Comm. Devel. Corp. (CDC) Seaside, 1980-; coll. instr.; dir./exec. bd. mem. Friends Outside in Monterey County; dir./mem. Mtry Reg. Water Pol. Control Agcy.; dir./mem. Val. Mosq. Abatement Dist.; honors: Citizen of Year, Omega Psi Phi Frat. 1978, 1982; two Monterey Co. Police Ofcrs Assn. Awards 1972, 73; mem: Nat. Council of Investigation and Security Svc. Inc.; World Assn. of Detectives Inc.; Calif. Assn. Licensed Investgrs.; Masons, Scottish Rite, Kiwanis, NAACP (life, Golden Heritage), Omega Psi Phi Frat., Shriners, ACLU, Am. Legion, Seaside CofC; mil. awards: Bronze Star o.l.c., Army Commendn. o.l.c., Nat. Def. Svc. o.l.c., GCM (6), UN Svc., Korean Svc., Vietnam Svc., Vietnam Campaign, Viet. Cross of Gal. with Palm, Viet. Civil Actions Honor Medal 1/c w/Palm, Victor WWII, Combat Inf., Expert Inf.; Democrat (del. for Mondale); Prot.; rec: golf. Address: Polite's Private Investigation and Security Agcy, 1630 Marietta St Seaside 93955

POLITOVICH, JOHN JUNIOR, logistician; b. July 26, 1929, Centerville, Iowa, dec. Jan. 20, 1986; s. John Frank and Leola Grace (Farris) P.; m. Nancy Abbott, Aug. 8, 1953; children: Marcia Kay b. 1954, Karen Louise b. 1956;

edn: BS, Western Ill. Univ. 1953; MS, USC 1974. Career: chief instr. Gilfillan Corp. 1953-58, staff to v.p. field engring. 1958-61, presonnel dir. 1961-64; sys. test supvr. ITT Gilfillan 1964-67; publs. engr. Gerenal Dynamics Pomona div. 1967-76, project logistician 1976-86; honors: Kappa Delta Pi (1952-53), chpt. pres. Sigma Zeta (1952-53), chpt. v.p. Delta Sigma Phi (1952-53); mem: Soc. of Logisitics Engrs. (pres. 1983-84); mil: t/sgt. USAF 1946-51 (active) 1951-54 (reserve); Republican; Methodist; rec: trap and skeet shooting, fishing, camping. Res: 930 West E St. Ontario 91762

POLLACK, MILTON SIDNEY, inventor, co. president; b. July 26, 1915, Des Moines, Iowa; s. Lewis and Rosa (Rest) P.; m. Faye S., Feb. 20, 1942; 1 son, Harry b. 1942; edn: BA, UC Berkeley 1938. Career: coll. football 1934-38, Rose Bowl 1938; profl. football player Los Angeles Bulldogs 1938-46; angle smith Shipyard/ Steel Mill during WWII; owner import co. pioneering transp. of fgn. cars, post war; inventor/designer var. equip. for fast food bus. primarily taco stands; currently pres. Great Lengths Inc. gifts and gallery, Los Angeles; product/mfg. cons. to sev. cos. and inventors; Democrat; Jewish; rec: promulgation of business ideas. Res: 1803 N Berendo St Apt 2 Los Angeles 90027 Ofc: Great Lengths Inc. 1720 N Vermont Ave Los Angeles 90027

POLLCHIK, ALLAN LEE, psychologist; m. Linda Brown, Oct. 31, 1970; edn: fellow, Langley Porter Inst., UC Med. Sch., San Francisco 1975-76; PhD, Vanderbilt Univ. 1975; MA, 1973; BA, UCLA 1971. Career: pres. Allan L. Pollchik, PhD, 1976—; instr. San Diego State Univ., 1977—, also cons. Oceanside Sch. System, 1976-; cons. Family Services, Camp Pendleton, 1977-; cons. Project OZ, 1976-80; cons. Chicano Fedn., 1977-79; honors: Nat. Merit Scholar 1967-71; Nat. Sci. Found. Fellow 1972-73; NIMH Fellow 1973-75; mem: No. County Psychol. Assn. (pres. 1980-81); Am. Psychol. Assn.; Interamerican Soc. of Psychol.; Zeta Beta Tau frat.; pres. Seawind Oceanside Homeowners Assn. 1980-81; works: public service radio pgm.: North County Health Spectrum, 1978—; rec: surfing; skiing, weightlifting. Res: 1973 Bluewater Way Oceanside 92054 Ofc: Allan L. Pollchik, Ph.D., 2101 El Camino Real, Ste 203A, Oceanside 92054

POLLOCK, GARY DOUGLAS, tax accountant; b. April 28, 1953, Carbondale, Ill.; s. Gordon Joseph and Betty Lou (Treece) P.; edn: Univ. of Nev. Las Vegas 1971-72; Univ. of Hawaii 1980; BS, UC Irvine 1986. Career: dir. of hotel devel. American International Vacation Clubs Inc.; mgr. Branding Iron House, Anaheim; ops. mgr. Victoria Station, Hawaii; v.p. ops. G.P. Inc., Tustin; v.p. ops. CFI Inc., Honolulu; branch mgr. Greater American Produce Inc., Las Vegas; acctg. mgr. Greater American Produce Inc., Anaheim; current: corporate tax ptr. New Dimensions, Tustin; Dir: D. Richards Inc., American Interstellar Corp., J.D. Metrology Inc., Resort Condominium Interiors; Republican; rec: skiing. Ofc: New Dimensions, 160 Centennia Ste. 14 Tustin 92680

POLTORAK, IRA JAN, pharmacist; b. Aug. 14, 1954, Bklyn.; s. Henry and Yvette (Pupkin) P.; m. Stacey, July 17, 1977; 1 dau. Andrea b. 1981; edn: BA, CSU Fullerton 1976; Pharm.D., USC 1980; Calif. lic. pharm. 1980. Career: intern pharmacist Pico Rivera Comm. Hosp., 1977-80, Whittier Hosp. 1980; pharm. cons. Pacific Medical Gp., 1982-83; dir. pharm. svcs. Covina Valley Comm. Hosp., W. Covina 1980-83; dir. pharm. services, implementation, pchsg. Pharmacy Ents. Inc., Orange 1983—; honors: Skull and Mortar Frat. pres. 1978-79, Intrafrat. Curriculum Council, Student Council (1976-80); mem: Am. Soc. Hosp. Pharmacists, Calif. Soc. Hosp. Pharmacists, San Gabriel Valley Soc. Hosp. Pharmacists, USC Sch. Pharm. Alumni Assn., participant in community health projects; rec: racquetball, basketball. Ofc: Pharmacy Enterprises Inc 23161 Lake Ctr Dr Ste 100 Lake Forest 92360

POMA, ARTHUR BRUCE, business owner; b. Sept. 17, 1952, Ukiah, Calif.; s. Arthur Louis and Ramona Delores P.; m. Kathleen Riley, Oct. 20, 1979; 1 child, Erin b. 1983; edn: AA, Butte Community Coll. 1973; BA, CSU Chico 1975. Career: family business Poma TV 1975—, v.p., ofc. mgr.; honors: All-League Softball (1984); mem: Downtown Merchants Assn. (pres. 1982-83), Ukiah Redevelopment Group, Downtown Parking Commn., Ukiah Downtown Parking Benefit Zone, Mendocino-Lake Applianceman's Dealership (pres. 1979-80), Ukiah Grievance Commn., Ukiah Men's Softball Orgn.; Catholic; rec: oil & acrylic painting, restoring 91-yr.-old home. Ofc: Poma TV Inc. 198 S School St Ukiah 95482

PONCE, HENRY DIZON, mortgage loan broker; b. July 15, 1946, Bacolor, Pampanga, Philippines; s. Fructuoso Ustiano and Consorcia (Dizon) P.; m. Modena Choy, May 18, 1974; children: Ricky b. 1975, Christopher b. 1979; edn: Hartnell Jr. Coll. 1964-66; Northrup Inst. of Technol. 1966-68; finance manager, Dept. of Labor Apprentice Pgm. Career: finance mgr. Transamerica Financial Svcs. Santa Cruz 1977-80; owner Salinas Valley Instant Printing 1979-81; gen. ptnr., loan coord. Executive Financial Svcs. Salinas 1981—; mil: ssgt. US Army 1968-77, Army Commdn., Good Conduct; Republican; Catholic; Res: 1454 Parsons Ave Salinas 93906 Ofc: Exec. Financial Svcs. 46 San Miguel Ave Salinas 93901

PONZA, LORENZO JOHN, baseball training equipment inventor/ manufacturer; b. Feb. 15, 1918, Glenwood; s. Lorenzo Giovanni and Maria Polonia (Fruttero) P.; edn: grad. Santa Cruz H.S. 1934; spl. machinist trade course. Career: machinist apprentice, machinist Mare Island Navy Yard, Vallejo, N.Y. 1934-41; machinist instr./prodn. control hd. Ford Island Air Station, Pearl Harbor 1941-49; toolmaker Lockheed Aircraft Co., Burbank 1949-51; pres. Santa Cruz Mfg. (research & devel., mfr. automatic baseball pitching machines), Santa Cruz 1951—; currently R&D cons. ATEC Inc.; invented and introduced into baseball the first pitching machine designed for team use:

invented 6 different ball propulsion means (6 patents), invented mechanized softball tng. and the indoor range (now nat. franchise Grand Slam Acad.); Republican; Catholic. Address: Santa Cruz 95060

POOD, FRED, entrepreneur; b. Jan. 17, 1938, Phila.; s. Leon and Beatrice (Wish) P.; m. Emma, Dec. 25, 1978; 1 son, Jesse b. 1981; edn: BA, Temple Univ. 1963. Career: sales exec. IBM Data Processing Div., Phila. and San Francisco, 1966-71; owner Pood's Foods Restaurant, Sausalito 1971; v.p. sales/founder Pine Street Bakery, Sausalito 1972-73; mgr. Imsai Mfg., San Leandro 1975-77; senior v.p. sales/mktg. MicroPro Inc., San Rafael 1978-82; pres. Pood Inc., Sausalito 1982–; dir., cons. The Sharper Image, Imsi Mfg.; mil: US Coast Guard 1958-62; rec: golf. Ofc: Pood Inc. POB 2029 Sausalito 94966

POPE, ALEXANDER H., county assessor; b. June 4, 1929, NY, NY; s. Clifford and Sarah H. (Davis) P.; m. Katherine Strong Mackinlay, Sept. 14, 1985; children: Steven b. 1957, Virginia b. 1959, Daniel b. 1963; edn: AB pol. sci., Univ. of Chgo. 1948; JD, Univ. Chgo. Law Sch. 1952; admitted State Bars of Calif., Ill., Rep. of Korea, U.S. Supreme Ct., other fed. cts. Career: atty. assoc. Law ofcs. David Ziskind, 1955; partner Shadle, Kennedy & Pope, 1956, Fine & Pope, 1957-77; Los Angeles County Assessor, 1978–; legislative secty. to Gov. of Calif., 1959-61; cons. to Gov. on implementation of McCone Commn. Report 1966; honors: Phi Beta Kappa (1948), Order of the Coif (1952), mng. editor Univ. of Chgo. Law Review (1951-52); mem. Calif. Hwy. Commn. 1966-70; Los Angeles Board of Airport Commnrs. 1973-78 (pres. 175-76); bd. trustees Los Angeles Theatre Center 1983-; mem. Southwest Dist. Bar Assn. (pres. 1967), Calif. Assessor's Assn. (regl. pres. 1980), Internat. Assn. of Assessing Ofcrs.; polit: nat. bd. Americans for Democratic Action (1947), Ill. regl. chmn. Nat. Students Assn. (1948), nat. bd. Volunteers for Stevenson (1952), v.chmn. LA County Democratic Central Com. (1958-59), LA Co. chmn. Brown for Gov. (1962), del. Dem. Nat. Conv. (1964), state treas. Brown for Gov. (1966); publs: contbr. law revs., Calif. State Bar Jour. (1979), Los Angeles Lawyer (1981); mil: US Army 1952-54, 8th Army news analyst in Seoul, Korea; Democrat; Unitarian; rec: trekking, photog. Res: 800 West First St, 2205, Los Angeles 90012 Office of Assessor, 500 W Temple St, Ste 320, Los Angeles 90012

POPE, ALICE MARIE, medical services consultant; b. Sept. 20, 1945, Bay City, Tx.; d. Oscar Sneed and Elizabeth Manning; div.; 1 son, Christopher b. 1971; edn: AA, East L.A. Coll. 1969; BSBA, Univ. Phoenix 1985; cert. ANP (Adult Nurse Practitioner) CSU Los Angeles 1976. Career: asst. hd. nurse USC-Los Angeles County Med. Ctr. 1969-72; nse. educator 1972–; prenatal clinic mgr./educator S.E. Health Ctr., L.A. 1972-73, Compton Health Ctr. 1973-76; adult nse pract./educator Bellflower Health Ctr. 1977-78; nse pract., mgr., diabetic cons., lectr. in nsg. USC-LAC Med. Ctr., 1978–; also pres./ adult nse. pract. Agape Adult Service Ctr. Inc., Los Angeles 1984–; honors: for outstanding service Paradise Baptist Ch. (1983), Crippled Childrens Soc., Jack M. Lear Guild (1981); mem. Am. Diabetes Assn.; civic: Jack M. Lear Guild (sec. 1974-76), Elite Social & Charity Club (coor. 1976-78), Western Baptist State Conv. Matrons (treas. 1983); contbr. articles in Diabetes J. (1980, 81); Democrat; Baptist; rec: needlework, soc. service. Ofc: Agape Adult Service Center Inc POB 73317 Los Angeles 90003

POPELKA, ROBERT JOSEPH, lawyer; b. May 9, 1920, Madison Lake, Minn.; s. Charles J. and Gertrude H. (Mape) P.; m. Dorothy Kernwein, Dec. 31, 1971; children: Robert J. Jr. b. 1946, Robin A. b. 1949, John C. b. 1956, James V. b. 1958; edn: BA, Coll. of St. Thomas 1940; JD, Hastings Coll. of Law 1948. Career: atty. San Francisco 1949-51, San Jose 1951–; mem: Am., Calif. and Santa Clara Co. Bar Assns., Am. Coll. of Trial Lawyers, Am. Bd. of Trial Advocs., Internat. Soc. of Barristers, Trial Attys. of Am., Internat. Assn. of Ins. Counsel, Fedn. of Ins. Counsel, San Jose Country Club, Thunderbird Country Club, Commonwealth Club of Calif.; mil: maj. USMC 1941-46, US, SW Pacific, WWII; Republican; Catholic; rec: golf, fishing. Res: 574 Kumquat Dr. San Jose 95117 Ofc: Popelka, Allard, McCowan, Jones & Howard, 1 Almaden Blvd. San Jose 95117

PORCELLI, JOHN, JR., manufacturing company executive; b Feb. 10, 1943, NYC; s. John Sr. and Antoinette (Crocitto) P.; m. Lenora Manno, May 27, 1972; children: Christopher b. 1980, Lisa b. 1983; edn: BS, Villanova Univ. 1977; Univ. Toledo 1962-65; Coll. of William & Mary 1967. Career: Burroughs Corp. 1965-82; supvr. Downington, Penn. 1965-75; mfg. splst., 1975-77; mgr. mfg. control, Plymouth, Mich. 1977-78; dir. corp. prod. dist., Detroit, Mich. 1979–; ops. pgm. mgr. MAI Corp., Tustin 1979-82, dir. prodn. 1981-82; dir. mfg. ops. CXC Corp., Irvine 1982; currently, v.p. Western Digital Corp., Irvine antd Western Digital Caribe, Ponce, Puerto Rico; mem: Soc. Mfg. Engrs., Am. Prodn. & Inventory Control Soc.; mil: P.O. 2/c USN 1966-69, Enlisted Man of Year; Catholic; rec: sailing, skiing, racquetball. Res: 22815 Fortuna Ln. Mission Viejo 92691 Ofc: Western Digital, Irvine

PORTEOUS, CHARLENE JO, dog groomer-trainer; b. June 26, 1940, Taft; d. Charles Fredrick and Josephine Clara (Young) Briscoe; m. Ralph Porteous, Oct. 14, 1967; children (nee Brown): Richard b. 1959, Pamela (Morgan) b. 1961, Deborah b. 1962, Donna (South) b. 1962, David b. 1964; edn: Coll. of the Pacific 1958-59. Career: owner/mgr. Yarn Craft Shop, and instr. YMCA, 1974-75; secty. Johnson & Sons, 1977-78; mgr., groomer Pet's Delight, p.t. 1974-80; owner/ trainer Charlene's Dogone Grooming, Alhambra 1980–; mem. Pasanita Obedience Club, Pasadena Humane Soc.; Republican; Presbyterian; rec: artist, ceramics, needlework, dog tng. Ofc: Charlene's Dogone Grooming 2330 W Main St Alhambra 91801

PORTER, GARY ALLEN, accountant; b. Feb. 19, 1949, Atascadero; s. Wilbur Ray and Bonnie Glenn (Knight) P.; m. Karlene, Feb. 14, 1981; children: Dawn b. 1965, Mark b. 1969, Michelle b. 1970, Tracy b. 1972; edn: BS, honors, Cal Poly State Univ., S.L.O. 1971; Certified Public Acct., Calif. (1973). Career: staff auditor County of San Luis Obispo, 1970; staff acct. Touche Ross & Co., CPAs, Los Angeles 1971-76; ptnr. Jacobs & Jacobs, CPAs, Ventura 1976-79; prin. Gary A. Porter, CPA, Ventura 1980–; past dir. Ventura County Council of Free Clinics; speaker var. Community Assns. Inst. seminars; mem: Am. Inst. CPAs, Calif. Soc. CPAs (com. chmnships; past dir. Channel Counties Chpt.), Community Assns. Inst. (past ofcr. Ventura Chpt.), Internat. Assn. for Finl. Planning, Greater Ventura CofC, Kiwanis (v.p.), Jaycees (past bd. dirs.); Republican; rec: skiing, woodworking. Ofc: 6401 Telephone Rd Ste 210 Ventura 93003

PORTER, ROBERT MULLENDORE, lawyer; b. Oct. 5, 1902, Edinburg, Ind.; s. Robert G. and Daisy (Mullendore) P.; m. Claire Belle Connor (dec.), Sept. 10, 1926; children: Nancy (Olsen), Robert C.; edn: LLB, Univ. of Mich. Law Sch. 1925; undergrad. Purdue Univ.; admitted Calif. State Bar 1925. Career: practiced real property law, Los Angeles 1925–, also practiced criminal law ten yrs., ret. 1984; asst. trust ofcr. Title Guarantee and Trust Co. 1926; represented Public Defender in var. Criminal cases; honors: Legal Soc. Barristers, U. Mich.; Sigma Delta Kappa legal frat.; Phi Delta Theta social frat.; Lutheran; rec: reading. Address: 10349 Dunleer Dr Los Angeles 9064

PORTER, WINSTON SEYMOUR, real estate executive, ret.; b. Sept. 17, 1909, Port Maitland, Nova Scotia, Can., nat. 1935; s. Lyndon E. and Lillian D. (Sanders) P.; m. Ruth Lyon, Sept. 29, 1934; children: Robert G. b. 1938, Lynne Susan b. 1942; edn: Northwestern Univ. 1936-38. Career: estate of Marshall Field, 1934-42; asst. regional rent director OPA, Chgo. Regl. Office, 1943-46; v.p. Oliver S. Turner & Co., Chgo. 1946-67; v.p. Arthur Rubloff & Co., Chgo. 1967-78; honors: Land Economics Hon. Soc. Lambda Alpha (chpt. pres. 1940); listed, Who's Who in the Midwest 1978, Who's Who in Fin. and Indus. 1981, Who's Who in the West 1982; life mem. Field Mus. Natural Hist. (Chgo.); chmn. Deerfield (Ill.) Planning Commn. 1954-59, Village Trustee 1959-63, pro tem mayor 1960; Building Mgrs. Club of Chgo.(pres. 1963); Chicago Jr. Real Estate Board (pres. 1941); Republican; Presbyterian. Res: 24001 Muirlands Blvd, Greenbriar 281, El Toro 92630

PORTNEY, MICHELLE DONNA, financial planner; b. Sept. 21, 1953, Phila.; d. Herbert Lennard and Phyliss Nancy (Melnick) Phillips; m. Frederick Paul Portney (dec.), Dec. 12, 1975; edn: BA in biol., UC San Diego 1975; MS in biol., CSU Los Angeles 1978; profl. desig: Personal Finl. Plnng., UC Los Angeles 1982; Reg. Representative, NASD (1983). Career: lectr., lab. instr. Biological Scis., CSULA 1977-79, 81-82; asst. office mgr. Schwarz Bros. Plastics, Inc. Glendale 1979-81; devel. coord./ finl. cons. Girls Clubs of Pasadena 1982-83; finl. plnnr./ reg. rep. Baraban Securities Inc., Culver City 1983-85; finl. plnnr./ptnr. G & P Financial, Manhattan Beach and reg. rep. Christopher Weil & Co., Inc., 1985–; recipient appreciation award Am. Cancer Soc. (1976); mem: Internat. Assn. for Finl. Planning, founder Finl. Family Com. L.A. 1985, W. L.A. Life Underwriters Assn.; civic: Legacy & Planned Giving - Am. Cancer Soc. and Little Co. of Mary Hosp. (1983-), Am. Red Cross (CPR instr. 1978-), Frederick P. Portney Meml. Fund (founder), Ronnie Phillips Meml. Scholarship Fund (v.p.); contbr. biol. research articles in sci. jours.; rec: hiking, amateur astronomy, herb & veg. gardening. Ofc: G & P Financial 1412 Pine Ave Manhattan Beach 90266

PORTUONDO, RALPH, real estate broker; b. Dec. 28, 1952, Santiago, Cuba; s. Rafael and Gloria (Rodriguez) P.; m. Deborah A., Aug. 19, 1972; children: Ralph Eric b. 1974, Amanda L. b. 1977, Mark D. b. 1981; edn: AA, Hartnell Coll. 1976; BS, Univ. of San Francisco 1980. Career: City of Salinas Recreation Parks Commn. 1982; Monterey Co. Energy Council 1982-86; chmn. Salinas Plnng. Commn. 1983-85; Salinas City Councilman 1985-89; currently, broker, owner Capitol Realtors, Salinas; dir. Monterey Co. Council of Real Estate Bds.; honors: Realtor of the Year (1983), Salinas Outstanding Young Man (1982); mem: Salinas Bd. Realtors (pres. 1982), Calif. Assn. Realtors, Salinas Jaycees, Salinas Elks; Republican; Catholic; rec: golf. Ofc: Capitol Realtors, 210 Capitol St. Salinas 93901

PORTWOOD, MILFORD WEBSTER, real estate developer, plant hybridizer; b. Aug. 24, 1925, Pasadena; s. Everlett A. and Irene Cathleen (Mossholder) P.; m. Norma Kostlan, Nov. 20, 1954; children: Jill b. 1955, Brett b. 1957; edn: Wash. State Univ. 1944. Career: mgr., owner Mossholder Nursery, Brea 1945; owner Portwood Plant Growers, Buena Park and co-owner Gold Cup Azaleas (hybrid. of azalea plants) 1957; mgr. Kostlan Real Estate, San Clemente 1960; co-owner San Clemente Real Estate, San Clemente 1965; owner Pacific Shore Realty, San Clemente 1971; owner Portwood Pacific Realty, Imperial Beach 1979, 1982; pres. Pacific Shore Land Inc. 1978-82; developer, gen. ptr. Old City Plaza, San Clemente 1973-80; apptd. Port Commnr., San Diego Unif. Port Dist. 1986; awards: Life Mem., San Clemente Historical Soc., Old City Plaza; mem: Nurserymen's Assn., Optimists; works: hybridized and patented 7 varieties of azaleas, Gold Cup Azaleas, 1956, 1957; mil: lt. USAF, WWII 1943-45, Korean Conflict 1951-53; Republican; Presbyterian; rec: astronomy, flying. Address: Portwood Pacific Realty 1488 Seacoast Dr. Imperial Beach 92032

POSNACK, STANFORD, lawyer; b. Oct. 20, 1934, Kansas City, Mo.; s. Harry I. and Celia (Goldstein) P.; children: Laurie b. 1958, Derek b. 1961, Mark b. 1968; edn: Compton Coll. 1952-56; East L.A. Coll. 1956-60; Mt. San Antonio Coll. 1964-67; LLD, La Verne Univ. 1973; admitted to practice, State Bar of Calif. & Calif. Supreme Ct. 1974. Career: atty. at law, self-empl., Azusa, West

Covina, Covina 1974–; Los Angeles Juvenile Ct. referee 1981–; previously: air pollution techn. L.A. County Air Pollution Control Dist. 1967-74, var. tech. and prodn. positions, 1951-67; mem. Calif. State Bar Assn., Azusa CofC (v.p. 1975-77), Azusa Rotary Club (bd. 1975-77), Azusa Democratic Club (v.p. 1977-78); rec: bowling, reading. Res: 1213 E Stuart Ave West Covina 91790 Ofc: Sanford Posnack, 465 E Badillo St Covina 91723

POST, EVA QUINN, association executive; b. Mar. 30, 1919, Palmer, Iowa; d. Michael J. and Margaret T. (O'Brien) Quinn; m. Loren G. Post, Sept. 27, 1941; children: Kim b. 1944, Karen b. 1946, Michael b. 1947, Monte b. 1949; edn: Buena Vista Coll. 1937-38. Career: elem. school tchr. Carrol County, Iowa 1939-40; clerk Pacifica Greyhound Corp., San Francisco 1942-44, Emporium Stores, S.F. 1954-56; p.t. aide Laguna Salada Sch. Dist., Pacifica 1957-59; owner/mgr. Amway Distbrship, Pacifica 1970-83; counselor Retirement Jobs, Inc., Pacifica Senior Ctr., 1980-81; interviewer (govt. area agency) Aging Outreach Project, Pacifica 1983; asst. state dir. Am. Assn. of Retired Persons, 1984–; recipient recogn. for service: AARP Nat. (1986), Elderhostelship, AARP Inc. (1986), San Mateo County Bd. of Supvrs. (1984), Seniors In Action, Pacifica (1982), Linda Mar Homeowners Assn. (1974); mem: AARP nat. and local (Advocacy com.), United Seniors for Action, Pacifica Arts and Heritage Soc., Pacifica Hist. Soc., Pac. Spindrift Players, Seniors in Action, San Mateo Co. Assn. of Grand Jurors, S.F. Mus. and Zool. Socs., Mayans, Kron 4 Viewer Advis. Council, Amway Distbrs. Assn., Nat. Council of Senior Cits.; Democrat; Christian; rec: volunteer work, Senior interests. Res: 1015 Anza Dr Pacifica 94044

POST, MICHAEL JOHN, lawyer; b. Sept. 2, 1952, Oakland; s. Robert George and Lillian M. (Beauchamp) P.; m. Sandra, Apr. 6, 1975; children: Nicole b. 1975, Tamara b. 1977, Amber b. 1980; edn: BA, CalPoly St. Univ. S.L.O. 1974; JD, Western State Univ. Coll. of Law 1980; admitted Calif. State Bar 1981; certified reserve peace officer, San Luis Obispo County (1976); State of Calif. specialized law enforcement cert. (1977). Career: atty. assoc. law ofcs. John Carsel, San Luis Obispo; currently sole practitioner, Paso Robles; Law Day spkr./panelist San Luis Obispo County 1981; awards: Writers Digest Short Story Award (1984); mem. Calif. State Bar Assn., Nat. Writers Assn.; publs: contbr. College Poetry Review (1974), Am. Anthology of Poetry (1984); Republican; Catholic; rec: golf, tennis, stamp & coin collector. Res: 849 Golden Hill Rd Paso Robles 93446 Ofc: Michael Post, Atty. POB 1755 Paso Robles 93447

POTTER, DONALD V., management consultant; b. Sept. 6, 1945, Wash DC; s. Donald Albert and Marian Helen (Loughery) P.; m. Suzanne Beck, June 6, 1971; children: Michele b. 1972, Chrissy b. 1973, Scott b. 1977, Courtney b. 1978; edn: BA magna cum laude, Notre Dame Univ. 1967; MBA (Baker Scholar), Harvard Bus. Sch. Career: fmr. corp. finl. exec. Exxon Corp. in London and New York; mgmt. cons. major domestic and fgn. cos., 1973–, with McKinsey and Co., 11 yrs. (ptnr. 5 yrs); pres. Windermere Assocs. Inc., San Francisco 1984–; clubs: Univ. (SF), Harvard (NY), Commonwealth (SF), Harvard Bus. Sch. Club of Bay Area; bd. advisors Diocese of Oakland (fin., inv. coms.); Roman Catholic; rec: tennis, ski, poetry. Res: 301 Constance Pl Moraga 94556 Ofc: Windermere Associates San Francisco

POTTER, EDYTHE MIRIAM, hearing aid dispenser; b. Nov. 27, 1898, Biggs, Calif.; d. Fred Alfred and Mary Elizabeth (Nettle) Keast; div.; 1 son, George Kenneth Potter (artist); edn: Coll. of the Pacific 1917. Career: reporter Sacramento Star, 1918-1919; asst. editor California Christian Advocate, San Francisco 1920; restaurant owner, The House That Jack Built, San Francisco 1935-58; hearing aid dispenser, San Francisco and Los Angeles, 1958–, owner Mon Arc Hearing Aids, Monrovia 1982–; recognized as "the oldest hearing aid dispenser in Calif. and perhaps the world", Who's Who in Hearing Aids in Calif.; mem. Hearing Aid Assn. of California; Republican; Fundamental; rec: crafts - beading, needlework. Res: 2553 N Lincoln St Burbank 91504 Ofc: Mon Arc Hearing Aids 128 S Myrtle Ave Monrovia 91016

POTTS, LORETTA MARY, veterinarian; b. May 16, 1952, Kane, Pa.; d. William Joseph and Nancy Marie P.; edn: BA, CSU Sacramento 1976, MA reproductive physiol., 1979; DVM, UC Davis 1983. Career: vet. mixed animal practice Paso Robles; instr. physiol. CSU Sacramento; research dairy cattle UC Davis extn. svc.; cons. llama breeders, 4-H leader, equine lectr. to local equine assns.; mem: Am. Vet. Assn., Calif. Vet. Med. Assn., Am. Assn. Equine Practitioners, Llama Assn. of Am., Midcoast Vet. Assn. (pgm. dir.), Paso Robles Women's CofC, Vaqueros del Camino Trailriders Assn., San Luis Ski Club, San Luis 4-H Clubs; publ: num. articles for Country Newsletter on equine med. and reproduction; designed and built own home in Paso Robles; rec: trailriding, skiing, bluegrass music (banjo player). Res: 2237 Vine St Paso Robles 93446 Mail: 725 Walnut Dr Paso Robles 93446

POWELL, EARL ALEXANDER, III, art museum director; b. Oct. 24, 1943, Spartanburg, So. Carolina; s. Earl Anderson Jr. and Elizabeth (Duckworth) P.; m. Nancy O'Neal Landry, July 17, 1971; children: Cortney, b. 1974; Channing, b. 1978; edn: BA, Williams Coll. 1966; MA, Harvard Univ. 1970; PhD, 1974. Career: curator Michener Collection, Univ. of Texas at Austin, 1974-76; executive curator National Gallery of Arts, Wash. DC 1976-80; dir. Los Angeles County Museum of Art, 1980–; awards: King Olaf Medal, Norway 1978; mem. Walpole Soc., Assn. of Museum Directors, Am. Fedn. of Arts; publs: on American arts; mil: cmdr. USNR; rec: photog. Ofc: Los Angeles County Museum of Art, 5905 Wilshire Blvd Los Angeles 90036

POWERS, NONA LA VAE, art gallery owner and custom picture framer; b. Feb. 24, 1942, St. Anthony, Idaho; d. Russell H. and Della S. (Mathis) Smith; m. Joe M. Powers, Jan. 2, 1963; children: Kira b. 1964, Joe Jr. b. 1966; edn: AA, San Diego City Coll.; BA, cum laude, CSU San Diego 1976; MA, 1978; Color Cons., Canada and Am. Branch of Bainbridge, London (1984). Career: custom framer Potpourri Artist Supply 1978-81; owner Monterey Custom Framing and LaVae Gallery, San Diego 1981–; nat. lectr. for Professional Picture Framers Assn. (PPFA), 1979; color cons. for Letraset USA; lectr. internat. Profl. Picture Framers Assn., semi-annual convs. (1980-86), lectr. Bainbridge of Canada Lecture Series in USA and Canada (1982, 83, 84), extensive lecturing for var. local PPFA groups; recipient var. awards, Internat. Framers Competition; 3d. Pl. and Hon. Mention, PPFA, Las Vegas (1979), 2d Pl. and Popular Choice, PFFA, Chgo. (1985), 1st Pl., PFFA, Wash DC (1985); named Framer of the Month, Decor Mag. (9/84 and 11/85); mem. Profl. Picture Framers Assn., PTA (pres. 1974); publs: featured in Decor Mag. (10/82, 11/82, 12/83, 1/86), Framer (9/83), Art Business News (9/85); clubs: Soroptomist Internat., Women's Bus. Owners Assn. of S.D., La Mesa CofC, The Network of East Co.- La Mesa. Res: 6925 Town View Lane San Diego 92120 Ofc: Monterey Frames 6512-C El Cajon Blvd, San Diego 92115

POZZO, LUIGI PETER, general building contractor; b. Aug. 20, 1912, Los Angeles; s. Emile Anselmo and Carolina Marie (Ferrante) P.; m. Florice Marjorie Moore, June 6, 1943; children: Louis Richard b. 1944, Victor Moore b. 1947, Carolina Florice b. 1959; edn: bus. adm. USC 1931-33; Cert. in Engring. & Architecture I.C.S., 1938-42. Career: constrn. field wk. Pozzo Construction Co., Los Angeles 1933-36, supervisor 1937-42, senior project mgr. 1946-48, supt. of all constrn. and part owner, 1948-65, sole owner/bd. chmn./CEO, Pozzo Construction Co., 1965–; adv. com. Bank of Amer.; bd. govs. USC; pres. Parents League, USC; v.p. bd. dirs. Braille Inst.; bd. trustees St. John's Hosp. and Med. Ctr., Santa Monica; mem. Edwart Frederick Sorrin Soc. Univ. Notre Dame; constrn. counselor for Sisters of Charitiy of the Incarnate Word, Houston; fmr. mem. Pres's Council Loyola H.S.; honors: Knight of Malta-The Sovereign Mil. Hospitaller Order of St. John of Jerusalem of Rhodes and of Malta; Braille Inst. award of merit; Jiggs award, St. John of God, L.A.; Golden Trowel award; Ceramic Inst. award; USC Man of the Year; USC Alumni Assn. service award; Wall Street Journal award; Plastering Inst. award; mem: Skull & Dagger Hon. Soc. USC, Sigma Chi frat. USC, Los Angeles CofC, US CofC, LA World Affairs Council, Town Hall of Calif. (L.A.), USC Assocs., Commerce Assocs. USC Sch. of Bus., Dean's Council UCLA Sch. of Arch.; clubs: California, Los Angeles Country; mil: ofcr. 104th USN Constrn. Batt., WWII, two cits.; Republican; Catholic; rec: golf, fishing, travel. Res: 935 Norman Pl Los Angeles 90049 Ofc: Pozzo Const. Co. 2894 Rowena Ave Los Angeles 90039

PRAGER, SUSAN WESTERBERG, law school dean; b. Dec. 14, 1942, Sloughhouse, Calif.; d. Percy Foster and Aileen M. (McKinley) Westerberg; m. James Prager, Dec. 14, 1973; children: McKinley A. b. 1978, Case M. b. 1985; edn: AB, Stanford Univ. 1964, MA, 1967; JD, UC Los Angeles 1971. Career: research asst. to Sen. Thomas Kuechel, Wash DC 1964-65; adminstrv. asst. to Assem. John G. Veneman, Calif. State Legis., Sacramento 1966-67; adminstrv. asst. to Rep. Paul N. McCloskey, Jr., US House of Reps., Wash DC 1967-68; atty. law office Powe, Porter & Alphin, Durham, N.C. 1971-72; acting prof. of law 1972-77, prof. of law UC Los Angeles, 1977–, assoc. dean 1979-82, dean UCLA Sch. of Law 1982–; bd. dirs. Pacific Mutual Life Ins. Co., Newport Beach 1979-; bd. trustees Stanford Univ. 1976-80; honors: editor in chief UCLA Law Review (1970-71), Order of the Coif (1971); mem: ABA, Assn. of Am. Law Schools (pres. 1986, exec. com. 1980-82); publs: articles in comm. property law. Ofc: UCLA School of Law, 405 Hilgard Ave Los Angeles 90024

PRATER, WALTER LLOYD, mechanical engineer; b. Apr. 11, 1955, Tulsa, Okla.; s. Samuel Lewis and Patricia (Gaylor) P.; edn: BSME, Univ. of Kansas 1978; MSME, San Jose State Univ. 1985; Reg. Profl. Engr., Calif. (Mfg.) 1982, (Mech.) 1985. Career: mfg. and test engr. IBM, San Jose 1978-83; prodn. devel. engr., IBM San Jose, 1983–; currently, staff mech. engr., head-disk assembly prod. devel.; honors: AMOCO Academic Scholarship, Univ. of Kansas 1977-78; First Pl. in Zoology, Long's Peak Science Fair, Colo. 1973; mem: Am. Soc. of Mech. Engrs.; Soc. of Mfg. Engrs.; Tau Beta Pi, Kansas Alpha chpt.; Pi Tau Sigma, Kansas Psi chpt.; works: IBM tech. disclosure bulletin, Clamping of Magnetic Disk Stack With a Top Ring, 1982, Statistical model of Disk Pack Particle Count Behavior, 1985; tech. reports: Magnetics Disk Stack Clamping 1981, Vibration Packaging Test of 3380 Computer, 1981, Airborne Particle Behavior Statistical Model, 1984, Spectral Analysis of Ball Bearing Defects, 1984, Ball Bearing Free Angle of Misalignment Monte Carlo Simulation, 1985; magazines: Testing of Ball Bearings Can Prevent Noise in Head-Disk Assemblies, Computer Technology Review, Winter 1984; Democrat; Protestant; rec: rock climbing, water skiing, bicycling. Res: 679 So. 11th St., No. 3, San Jose 95112 Ofc: IBM, 5600 Cottle Rd., Dept. E17/862, San Jose 95193

PRATHER, WILMA JEAN, lawyer; b. Oct. 17, 1946, Raton, N.M.; Estus and Edna C. (Martinez) Brown; children: Eloisa b. 1968, Oscar b. 1969; edn: BA, N.Mex. Highlands Univ. 1968, MA, 1975; grad. wk. Coll. of Indsl. Engring. 1978; JD, Western St. Univ. 1982; admitted Calif. State Bar 1983. Career: social wkr. N.Mex. Health Social Services, 1968-69; tchr. Jemey Mtn. Schs., N.M. 1970-71, West Las Vegas Schs., N.M. 1971-73; trainer Marine Corps Exchange, Camp Pendleton, Calif. 1973-74; tchr. Springer Public Schs., N.M. 1974-75, Army/Navy Acad., Carlsbad, Calif. 1975-76; adult edn. tchr. Mira Costa Coll., Camp Pendleton 1976-78; pre-sch. dir. Oceanside Comm. Ctr., 1977-78; Head Start dir. Bensenville Home Soc., 1978-79; atty. prin. in pvt. law practice, MEJ Ents. Vista 1983–; bd. dir: Mes Ents. (1985), Babes & Blooms (1984-); instr. one-night law seminars for gen. public, Vista H.S. 1984-; honors:

Pi Gamma Mu (1963), Nu Beta Epsilon (1983), Freshmen Hon. (1964), Spurs (1965), Las Companas (1966; regl. pres. 67-68), Senior Womens Hon. (pres. 1968); mem. Calif. State Bar, San Diego County Bar Assn.; clubs: North Coast YMCA Mens Club (sec. 1984-85), Nat. & Internat. YMCA Mens Assn.; publs: curriculum devel. in pre-sch. edn. (1978-79), drug & alcohol edn. for elem. schs. (1971-73); Democrat; Lutheran; rec: stained glass, flying, sailing. Ofc: 355 West Vista Way Ste 14 Vista 92083

PRATT, RONALD FRANKLIN, public relations executive; b. July 15, 1948, Savannah, Ga.; s. Frank Tecumseh and Lila Elizabeth (Lee) P.; edn: BA, Washington Univ., St. Louis, 1972. Career: reporter Savannah (Ga.) Morning News, 1962; news dir. WSOK Radio, Savannah 1973; ed. Hilton Head News, Hilton Head Is., S.C. 1974-77; account exec., sr. acct. exec. Russom & Leeper, San Francisco 1978-83, v.p., mem. exec. com., 1983-86; senior v.p., prin. The Leeper Group, S.F. 1986–; honors: Outstanding Young Man of Am., Jaycees (1976), Gold Quill, Internat. Assn. of Bus. Communicators (1983), sev. regl. and local awards, Pub. Rels. Soc. Am. (1980-83); mem. Internat. Assn. of Bus. Communicators; civic: San Francisco Council on Entertainment (dir., v.p. 1985-), Hilton Head Is. Inst. for the Arts (pres. 1976-77), Hilton Head Jazz Fest. (dir. 1976-77); rec: classical and jazz pianist. Res: 1390 Taylor St San Francisco 94108 Ofc: The Leeper Group 151 Union St San Francisco 94111

PREBLE, JESSICA, interior designer; b. July 29, 1943, Salt Lake City, Utah; d. Gail Maurice and Helen (Herzog) Morley; m. Douglas Preble, Nov. 2, 1979; 1 dau., Simmer b. 1960; edn: BA and MA in int. design & mktg. Career: designer/owner Preble Interiors, Newport Beach; recipient num. profl. awards for int. design projects throughout the Western USA, esp. Park City (Utah) Ski Resort with theme planning incl. ski lodge, 60-unit condo. devel., 3 restaurants and restoration of existing historic structures; frequent guest speaker profl. seminars; mem. Am. Color Council & Calif. Designers Soc., CAUS, OCAF, Irvine CofC, Newport Beach CofC; Republican; Catholic; rec: painting. Res: 1081 Hyde Park Santa Ana 92705

PREDKELIS, ROMUALDO, sales executive; b. July 31, 1943, Lithuania, nat. US cit. 1968; s. Stasys and Ona (Matuliauskas) P.; m. Laima, July 24, 1965; 1 dau. Ruta b. 1966; edn: BS chem., Roosevelt Univ. 1973, postgrad. 1975. Career: R&D chemist Nalco Chemical chgo. 1973-75, staff engr. internat. div. 1975-77, salesman indsl. div. 1977-80, area mgr. 1980-81, dist. sales mgr. Denver 1981-83, L.A. 1983-85, regl. sales mgr. Venezuela 1985-88; sales mgr. Calif. State Dearborn Chemical div. of W.R. Grace Long Beach 1986–; bd. dirs. Children's Meml. Hosp. 1985; sales tng., seminars overseas Nalco; honors: Top Salesman in New Business Prodn. (Nalco 1979), Top Dist. Mgr. in New Bus. Prodn. (Nalco 1981); mem: Dist. Mgr. Assn. (new mem. com.), Am. Mgmt. Assn., NACE, Lithuanian Golf Club, Lithuanian Photog. Club, BSA; Republian; Catholic; rec: photog. (shows, contests Chgo. 1976-85), music. Res: 16183 Caribou St Fountain Valley 92708 Ofc: Dearborn Chemical 5199E Pacific Coast Hwy Ste 606 Long Beach 90804

PREGERSON, HARRY, federal judge; b. Oct. 13, 1923, Los Angeles; s. Abraham and Bessie (Rubin) P.; m. Bernardine Seyma Chapkis, June 28, 1947; children: Dean Douglas, Kathryn Ann; edn: BA, UCLA 1947, LLB, Boalt Hall Berkeley 1950; admitted to Calif. Bar 1951; Career: ptr. William M. Sotley, Van Nuys 1953-65; judge Los Angeles Municipal Ct. 1965-66, Los Angeles Superior Ct. 1966-67; judge U.S. Dist. Ct. Central Dist. Calif. 1967-79, U.S. Ct. Appeals 9th Circuit 1979–; faculty, sem. for newly apptd. dist. judges Fed. Judicial Ctr., Wash. 1970-72; faculty Am. Soc Pub. Adminstrn., Inst. for Ct. Mgmt., Denver 1973-; mem: Am., Calif., Los Angles Co., and San Fernando Valley Bar Assns., Marines Corps Reserve Ofcrs. Assn. (pres. San Fernando Valley 1966-78); mil: 1st lt. USMCR 1944-46, Purple Heart. Ofc: US Ct. Appeals US Courthouse, 312 No. Spring St. Los Angeles 90012

PREMO, EUGENE MILTON, superior court judge; b. Aug. 28, 1936, San Jose; s. Milton A. and Mary Teresa (Fatjo) P.; m. Georgine Drees, Jan. 24, 1959; children: Nicole, b. 1961, Michelle, b. 1965, Patrick, b. 1967, Richard, b. 1968; edn: BS, Santa Clara Univ. 1957, JD, 1962. Career: research atty. Court of Appeal, San Francisco 1962; practicing atty., Santa Clara Co. 1963-69; appointed Municipal Ct., Santa Clara Judicial Dist. 1969, to Superior Ct. 1975–; temp. assignment, Ct. of Appeal, 6th Dist. 1985; lectr. Santa Clara Univ. Sch. of Law; mem: Alpha Sigma Nu, Calif. Judges Assn. (v.p. 1984-85), West Valley Kiwanis, Bronco Bench, Santa Clara Univ. Athletic Bd., Salvation Army (adv. bd.), Sisters of Notre Dame De Namur (adv. bd.); mil: 1st lt., US Army Counter- intelligence Corps.; Republican; Catholic; rec: golf, travel, photog. Res: 19161 Portos Dr., Saratoga 95070

PRENTICE, SARTELL, JR., incentive employee profit sharing plan consultant; b. Dec. 28, 1903, Newark, N.J.; s. Rev. Sartell (D.D.) and Lydia Beekman (Vanderpoel) P.; m. Marjorie Phelps Koop, 1930; 2 daus.: Patricia and Adelaide (both now dec.); m. 2d. Agnes L. Papekas, 1939; 1 son, Peter (flight surgeon, comdr. USN) b. 1944; m. 3d Elinor Haight (Buck), 1956 (dec. 1977); m. 4th Geraldine Eleanor Hoyt, 1978 (dec. 1980); edn: Taft Sch. 1915-20; Yale Univ. 1921-23; BA, Stanford Univ. 1925; MBA, Harvard Bus. Sch. 1927; spl. courses Freedom Sch., Colo. and Free Enterprise Inst., L.A. Career: security salesman Nat. Cash Credit Assn., N.Y. 1926-31; tng. pgm. for fgn. service, Socony Vacuum Oil Co., N.Y. 1931; exec. asst. to the pres. Vacuum Oil Co., S.A.I., Genoa, Italy 1931-35; mktg. asst. Fgn. Dept. Socony Vacuum Oil Co., N.Y. 1935; research, script writer, March of Time Movie and Radio, N.Y. 1935-37; actor Summer Stock, Barter Theatre, Abingdon, Va. 1938; salesman Automatic Canteen Co., N.Y. 1940-41; pub. rels., advt. rep. Time Mag., N.Y. and Boston, 1941-46; adminstrv. secty. Commn. of the Churches on Internat. Affairs 1947-48; field secty. N.E. Chpt., Council on Profit Sharing Industries (now the Profit Sharing Council of Am.) 1950-54; counselor on profit sharing 1954–, on lecture circuit Assoc. Clubs of USA, 1956-58, chmn. NY State chpt. Nat. Com. for Economic Freedom 1960; his talks pub. in "Vital Speeches of the Day" (twice), contbr. articles in Management Rev., Stanford Rev., The Freeman, Rampart J. of Individualist Thought, The J. of Management, others; dir. Am. Waldemesian Aid Soc. (1944-61); mem: Soc. of Profl. Mgmt. Consultants Inc. (charter), The Western Pension Conf., Town Hall of Calif., Toastmasters Internat., Profit Sharing Council of Am., Internat. Platform Assn.; mem. The Yale, Stanford, Harvard, and Harvard Bus. Sch. Clubs of So. Calif.; Protestant. Address: 1404 Chamberlain Rd Pasadena 91103

PREOVOLOS, JAMES PETER, lawyer; b. July 27, 1919, San Francisco; s. Peter John and Kalliope (Barbare) P.; div.; 1 dau. Penelope, b. 1955; edn: BS, Univ. San Francisco 1941, JD, 1947; admitted Calif. Bar 1949. Career: pvt. practice law, 1949–, certified spec. in Family Law (Domestic Rel.); judge pro tem San Francisco Municipal Ct.; Marital Settlement Conference judge pro tem, S.F. Superior Ct.; arbitrator S.F. Superior Ct.; panelist and moderator Contg. Edn. of the Bar; guest instr. Golden Gate Law Sch., Hastings Law Sch.; past pres. Am. Acad. of Matrimonial Lawyers, No. Bay Chapt.; author chapter on Discovery, Calif. Marital Dissolution Practice; mil: cmdr. USNR (Ret.) Judge Advocate Gen. Corps; Democrat; Greek Orthodox; Law Offices of James P. Preovolos, 300 Mills Bldg., San Francisco 94104

PRESCOTT, EDWARD PURCELL, wine co. president; b. Oct. 16, 1929, Cleveland, Ohio; s. Edward Purcell and Carolyn Elizabeth (Brayton) P.; m. Diana Van Der Byl, Dec. 27, 1979; children: Lynn b. 1955, Diane b. 1956, Jill b. 1958, Annette b. 1960; edn: BA, Williams Coll. 1951. Career: pres. Joseph Sebao Inc. L.A. 1968-81; exec. v.p. Universal Heritage Investment Corp. L.A. 1982-84; pres. Anderson Valley Wine Co. Ukiah 1984–; honors: Exec. of the Yr. (Universal Heritage Investments Corp. 1982); mem: Anderson Valley Wine Growers Assn., L.A. Soc. Financial Analysts, Calif. Club L.A., Town Hall of Calif., Big Brothers/ Big Sisters (dir.); mil: cpl. US Army Signal Corps 1951-53; Republican; Protestant; rec: family. Address: 2975 Mill Creek Rd Ukiah 95482

PREUSS, CHARLES AUGUST, physician; b. Apr. 20, Tacoma, Wash.; s. Charles Frederick and Sophie Anne (Eshbach) P.; m. Nellie Reidel French, July 18, 1938 (div. 1960); children: Patricia b. 1939, Charles b. 1941, Pamela b. 1943; edn: BS, Univ. of Idaho 1924; MD, Oregon Med. Sch. 1929. Career: intern Cottage Hosp. Santa Barbara 1929-30; resident S.B. Gen. Hosp. 1930-31; G.P. phys. Santa Barbara 1931–; honors: Calif. Family Phys. of the Year 1985, Fifty Year Cert. (AMA), Fifty Year Pin (Masonic Order), Hon. Eminent Supreme Archon (Sigma Alpha Epsilon; mem: AMA, CMA, Am. Acad. Fam. Phys. (pres. 1956), Am. Geriatrics Soc. (pres.), S.B. Co. Med. Soc. (pres. 1946), Western Gerontol. Soc. (pres. 1958-59), Univ. Club 1941-45, Com. on Aging (10 years); mil: major US Army (MC); Republican; Lutheran; rec: magic. Address: 1317 Santa Barbara St Santa Barbara 93101

PREVRATIL, JOSEPH FRANK, entertainment and hotel co. president; b. Feb. 5, 1938, Chgo.; s. Joseph F. and Anna T. (Novak) P.; m. Barbara Joan Holman, June 2, 1962; children: Deborah (Hoelzer) b. 1963, Robert b. 1968, Eric b. 1970, Renee b. 1976; edn: BA, Loyola Univ. LA 1960, JD, Southwestern Univ. Sch. of Law 1966. Career: order control mgr. Waste King Corp., Vernon 1961-63; regl. adminstr., EDP Div., Honeywell, Inc. Los Angeles 1963-66; dir. fin. & adminstrn. Internat. Div., Capitol Records Inc., Hollywood 1966-67; chief finl. ofcr. U.S. Exchange Corp., Menlo Park 1967-68; group v.p. Six Flags, Inc. Los Angeles 1968-75; pres. Entertainment Environments, Inc. Fullerton 1975-80; v.p./chief finl. ofcr. Gen. Terminal Corp., Tustin 1980-81; exec. v.p. Evolution Computers, Inc. Orange 1981-82; pres./chief ops. Wrather Port Properties, Ltd. (Queen Mary & Spruce Goose hotel and entertainment complex), Long Beach 1982–; frequent guest speaker on "Turnaround Management"; honors: Alpha Sigma Nu, Nat. Jesuit Honor Soc. (1960), Golden Key (1985); mem. Nat. Assn. of Accts., Am. Mgmt. Assn., Long Beach Area Vis. & Conv. Council (dir., chmn. 1985-86), Downtown Long Beach Assocs. (dir., chmn. 1985-86), Long Beach Area CofC (dir.), Long Beach Symphony (dir.); Republican; Roman Catholic; rec: metaphysics. Ofc: Wrather Port Properties Ltd POB 8 Long Beach 90801

PREY, WILLIAM TAYLOR, psychiatrist; b. Oct. 15, 1954, Baltimore, Md.; s. Charles Wm. and Dorothy (Taylor) P.; m. Susan Fritz, May 21, 1983; edn: BS summa cum laude, Duke Univ. 1976; MD, M.S. Hershey Medical Ctr., Penn State Univ. 1980; lic. psychiatrist BMQA 1982. Career: intern UCLA-CHS/ Wadsworth VA Hospitals 1980-81; psychiatric resident UCLA Neuropsychiatric Inst. 1981-84; psychosomatic fellow St. Mary's Hosp., San Francisco 1984-85, asst. ward chief Medical Psychiatry Unit 1985–, also psychiatric cons. Marshal Hale Eating Disorders Unit 1985-, and assoc. dir. St. Mary's Sleep Clinic 1985-; pvt. practice, S.F. 1985–; lectr. Contra Costa County Dept. Geriatric Services 1985-; honors: Phi Beta Kappa (1975), Clin. Psychiatry Award, Penn State (1980); mem: AMA, Am. Psychiatric Assn., No. Calif. Psychiatric Soc., San Francisco Med. Soc., Calif. Med. Assn., Sierra Club; publs: arts. in med. journals; Democrat; rec: hiking, gardening, metaphysics. Ofc: 2345 California St Ste 4 San Francisco 94115

PRICE, EDWARD DEAN, U.S. District judge, b. Feb. 12, 1919, Sanger; s. Earl Trousdale and Daisy Shaw (Biggs) P.; m. Katherine Merritt, July 18, 1943; children: Katherine (O'Brien) b. 1946, Edward b. 1949, Jane b. 1954; edn: AB, UC Berkeley 1947, LLB, 1949; admitted Calif. State Bar 1949. Career: atty. assoc. Cleary and Zeff, Modesto 1949-51, Zeff and Halley, 1951-54; ptnr. Zeff, Halley and Price 1954-63, Zeff and Price 1963-65, Price and Martin 1965-69, Price, Martin and Crabtree 1969-79; apptd. U.S. Dist. Judge, Eastern Dist. of

Calif., Fresno 1979–; mem. adv. bd. and gov. com. Continuing Edn. of the Bar 1963-71; mem. State Bar of Calif. bd. govs. 1973-76, vice pres. 1975-76; mem. Judicial Council of Calif. 1978-79; mem: Modesto Lions 500 Club (pres. 1953), Elks (Ruler 1959-60), Salvation Army Adv. Com. (chmn. 1959), Modesto Rotary (pres. 1978-79); contbr. Calif. Law Rev. (1948); mil: cpl. US Army 1942-45; Democrat; Methodist; rec: hunting, golf. Res: 1012 Wellesley Modesto 95350 Ofc: 5104 Federal Bldg. 1130 "O" Street Fresno 93721

PRICE, JAMES LESTER, lawyer; b. May 6, 1944, Lincolnton, N.C.; s. George and Mary Estelle (Peeler) P.; edn: BA, Univ. Nev., Las Vegas, 1973; JD, Southwestern Univ. Sch. of Law 1978; admitted Calif. State Bar. Career: med. technologist US Air Force 1962-66, L.P.T. Inc. Las Vegas, Nev. 1966-69, Sunrise Hosp., Las Vegas 1969-74, West Adams Comm. Hosp., Los Angeles 1974-78; deputy real estate commnr. Calif. State Dept. of Real Estate, 1979; claims rep. The Doctors Company, Santa Monica 1979-80; assoc. atty. law office Robert V. Wills, Tustin 1980-81; assoc. atty. Kinkle, Rudiger & Sprigs, Riverside 1981–; tchg. asst., hist., Univ. Nev.-Las Vegas 1973-4; honors: Phi Lambda Alpha (1970), Phi Kappa Phi (1972); mem. ABA, Calif. Bar Assn., Am. Medical Technologists 1969-74; mil: E4 USAF 1962-66; Democrat; Baptist; rec: golf, tennis, hunting. Res: 8743 Magnolia Ave, 13-6, Riverside 92503 Ofc: Kinkle, Rodiger & Spriggs 3383 14th St Riverside 92501

PRICE, JOHN MARTIN, lawyer; b. Nov. 10, 1919, Sacramento; s. John Bell and Mary Ellen (Griffin) P.; m. Jane Henderson, Apr. 15, 1950; children: Robert b. 1943, Peggy b. 1952; edn: BA, UC Berkeley 1940; LLB, UCB Boalt Hall of Law 1948; admitted Calif. State Bar 1949, US Supreme Ct. 1962. Career: dep. dist. atty. Sacramento County 1949-51; pvt. practice atty., ptnr. Dwyer, King, Price and Mering, Sacto. 1951-58; dist. atty. County of Sacto. 1959-79; Gov. apptd. commnr. Calif. State Lottery, 1985–; honors: Law Enforcement Ofcr. of Year, Calif. Trial Lawyers Assn. (1969), hon. mem. Nat. Assn. of Attys./Mexico (1974), The John Price lectr. Nat. Coll. of Dist. Attys., Houston (1978); mem: Nat. Dist. Attys. Assn. (pres. 1969-70), Calif. Dist. Attys. Assn. (pres. 1961-62), Am. Bar Assn. (Criminal Justice Section Council, Commn. on Correction), Calif. Bar Assn., Grandfathers Club (Sacto.), Rotary; civic: Mercy Hosp. (trustee), The Aquarian Effort, Sacto. (drug abuse rehab.); mil: capt. US Air Force 1941-45; Democrat; Roman Catholic. Res: POB 1091 Mendocino 95460 Ofc: California State Lottery 600 N 10th St Sacramento 95814

PRICE, LAWRENCE LEE, quality assurance engineering specialist; b. June 17, 1935, Detroit, Mich.; s. William G. and Mae D. (Smith) P.; m. Frances Snyder, June 15, 1957; children: Lawrence b. 1959, Kathy b. 1960, David b. 1962, Thersea b. 1964; edn: Lawrence Inst. Tech. (Southfield, Mich.), Wayne State Univ. Career: support planner/mgr., sr. data splst., quality engr. splst./ mgr. QA Audit, Rockwell International, 1974–; sr. tech. writer, data mgr., comm. support data mgr., Collins Radio Co., 1967-74; engring. writer, General Electric Co., 1961-66; lectr. Coast Line Comm. Coll.; numerous publs.; mil: USMC Reserv. 1953-54, NY Air Nat. Guard, 174th TAC, Fighter Gp. 1965-66; Indep.; Catholic; rec: home computer, writing. Res: 9662 Surfcrest Dr Huntington Beach 92646 Ofc: Rockwell-Intl. CDC, PO Box 11963, Santa Ana 92711

PRICE, PEGGY MAY, dentist; b. Feb. 16, 1953, Los Angeles; d. Zane Herbert and Maxine May (Fitzgerald) P.; edn: BS behav. sci., Loma Linda Univ. 1975, DDS, 1978; lic. dentist Calif. 1980. Career: staff dentist L.A. PTA Clinic (Venice, Downtown ofcs.) 1982-83, L.A. free Clinic 1983–, 1985 World Games for the Deaf, South Bay Free Clinic 1980-81; honors: Award of Merit (L.A. Free Clinic); mem: Am. Assn. Women Dentists, UCLA Hope for Hearing, Self-Help for the Hard of Hearing Assn., Oral Deaf Assn.; Protestant; rec: writing, painting, ceramics (num. awards). Address: Los Angeles

PRICE, RICHARD TAFT, JR., metal finishing co. president; b. June 7, 1954, San Diego; s. Richard Taft and Murial Martha (Weinhold) P.; edn: BS in bus., summa cum laude, Ariz. State Univ. 1978. Career: spl. agent Northwestern Mutual Life, Phoenix 1978-79; sales R&R Custom Rollforming, Fullerton 1979-80; gen. mgr. IBS Indus., Brea 1980-81; mgr. Imperial Metal Finishing, Los Angeles 1981-84; pres. Alumatone, Inc. No. Hollywood 1984–; honors: Phi Kappa Phi, Beta Gamma Sigma; Republican; Ch. of Jesus Christ of Latter-Day Saints. Ofc: Alumatone, Inc. 12730 Raymer No Hollywood 91605

PRICE, RODGER BRIAN, hospital-medical supply co. owner; b. Apr. 24, 1956, San Francisco; s. Harry Carol and Virginia May (Santini) P.; stepmother: Mary Laura Hickey; edn: AB liberal arts and scis. w/ distinction, San Diego State Univ. 1978. Career: prodn. mgr. Bowen Enterprises El Cajon 1976-79, sales rep. 1979-81, sales mgr. So. Calif. 1981-83; nat. sales cons. Polamedco Inc. Santa Monica 1983-85; pres. RB Price Co. San Diego 1983–; honors: Honor Athlete (San Diego State Univ. 1976-77), CSF (life mem. 1974), Pi Sigma Alpha (1977); mem: Calif. Soc. Hosp. Pharmacists (assoc.), San Diego Central Svc. Personnel Assn. (assoc.), San Diego Aquatic Officials Assn. (financial ofcr.), Soc. Club of San Diego (single profl. support group for Am. Cancer Soc.), Friends of Children (vol. support group for Child Abuse Prevention Found.), Single Profl. Soc. of S.D.; Republican; Lutheran; rec: running, flying, water polo referee. Address: 3707 Balboa Terrace Apt D San Diego 92117

PRIES, MITCHELL PETER, cardiologist, nutritionist; b. Nov. 13, 1912, Reedley; s. Peter George and Kathryn Tina (Frieseu) P.; m. Gwendolyn Freeman, Jan. 15, 1945; edn: BA, Whittier Coll. 1940; post grad., UCLA & USC 1941-43; MD/DO, Los Angeles of Physician & Surgeons 1948; MD, UC Irvine 1962;

postgrad. in cardiology, UCLA and USC, 5 yrs.; intern and res., Los Angeles Co. Gen. Hosp. 1948-50; guest phys. in cardiol. research Loma Linda Univ. Med. Ctr. 1971-72. Career: chmn. dept. internal med. Victory Hosp., No. Hollywood 1952-55; chmn. dept. infectious diseases Ontario Hosp., Ontario 1968; clin. cardiology, tchg. nurses, ECG reading, treadmill testing; currently, cert. nutritionist in human nutrition sciences 1982; cons. in nutrition & cardiology; lectr. nutritional subjects rel. to med. diseases; honors: His Holiness Pope John 1975; Pope Paul VI for Humanitarian Svc. 1977; Cert. of Appreciation, City of San Bernardino Dept. Soc. Svcs. 1980; Community Svc. (polio), Sherman Oaks Jaycees 1960-61; Humanitarian Svc., Palm Springs 1979; mem: AMA, CMA, Am. Geriatric Assn., NY Acad. of Science, Am. Assn. Adv. Sci., Fellow Am. Geriatric Soc., Fellow Internat. Coll. Nutrition; works: primary hypertension 1955; research cons. Dr. Davinci Labs., Vermont 1980–; Democrat; Presbyterian; rec: Am. Civil War research, music, swimming. Res: 40-312 Sagewood, Palm Desert 92260 Ofc: 72-780 El Paseo Ste. E3, Palm Desert 92260

PRIME, EUGENIE ELSA, librarian, b. Trinidad, W. Indies; d. Harold John and Millicent L. P.; edn: BA, honors, Univ. of W. Indies 1966; MA, Andrews Univ. 1974; MS, Drexel Univ. 1976; MBA, UCLA 1982. Career: postgrad. research fellow history Univ. W. Indies 1966-69; head dept. history Naparima Girls H.S., Trinidad 1969-72; psychiat. social worker NY State Dept. Mental Hygiene 1974; exec. ed. Cumulative Index to Nursing Lit., also med. librarian Glendale Adventist Med. Ctr. 1976–; pres. CINAHL Corp. 1981–; mem: Med. Library Assn., Am. Soc. Indexers, Assn. Seventh-Day Adventist Librarians, Assn. Information Mgrs., Med. Library Group So. Calif. and Ariz.; Seventh-Day Adventist. Ofc: 1509 E. Wilson Terrace Glendale 91206

PROCOP, ROBERT ALLEN, jewelry dealer, designer, educator; edn: Gemology Inst. of Am. 1979. Career: jewelry sales Procop Jewels 1977-84; owner Diamonds on Rodeo Beverly Hills 1984–; producer Ralph Andrews Prodn. Co. 1982–; seminars on diamonds CBS News; mem: Beverly Hills CofC 1985- (Rodeo Dr. Com.), L.A. Polo Club 1985-, Am. Jewelry Assn., San Fernando Valley Bus. & Profl. Assn.; designer, creator EIC pin for Mrs. Nancy Reagan and her orgn., Million Dollar Bicycle for Beverly Hills Wheat Thins Mayor's Cup Bike Race 1985; Christian; rec: swimming, skiing, golf, jewel and antique collecting. Ofc: Diamonds on Rodeo 332 N Rodeo Dr Beverly Hills 90210

PROCTOR, WALTER THOMAS, editor, publisher, editorial consultant; b. June 12, 1920, Louisville, Ky.; s. Walter T., Sr. and Blanche (Johns) P.; m. Lois Louise Langer, July 29, 1944; children: Penny (Kintz), Stephen T., Walter Thomas, III; edn: stu. Hastings Coll. 1943, Urbana Coll. 1949; B.J., Univ. Mo. 1952, MA, 1959. Career: advt. mgr. Tri-county News, King City, Mo. 1952-54; mng. editor Underwriters Rev., asso. ed. Northwestern Banker, Des Moines 1954-63; ed. Exponent, engring. mag., 1960-68, Appetizer, restaurant mag., Des Moines, 1963-75; pub. Am. Host, 1965-75; instr. pub. relations and journalism Iowa State Univ., Ames 1973-74; ed. Motel/Motor Inn Jour., 1975-79, S.W. Water Works Jour., 1975-79, California Intouch, 1970-81, California Crossroad Mag., 1981-84; editorial cons. California Lodging Update, 1984–; honors: Outstanding Service award Northwestern Hotel-Motel Assn. (1966), named Beef Editor of Year (1968); mem. Internat. Council Indsl. Editors, Sigma Delta Chi (pres. Iowa 1962-63); civic: designed city flag for City Des Moines, Am. Red Cross Gentry County (hd. fund drive 1953); mil: USAAF 1941-45; Presbyterian. Res: 3341 Cottage Way Sacramento 95825

PROESCHER, WARD HORNBLOWER, securities co. executive, author-lecturer; b. Aug. 31, 1935, Cary, N.C.; s. Andrew Jay and Gladys Elaine (Jones) P.; m. Susan Dittmar, May 1, 1971; children: Tobin Dittmar b. 1975, Morgan Boehm b. 1983; edn: N.C. St. Univ., Raleigh 1953-56; BS indsl. rels., Univ. of N.C. 1958; Hastings Coll. of Law 1964-65; desig: Series 7 lic. (1966), reg. prin. (1985) NASD; SEC reg. Inv. Advisor (1984); Calif. lic. R.E. Broker (1983). Career: stockbroker Hornblower & Weeks- Hemphill, Noyes, San Francisco 1966-73; owner/pres. Hornblower Yacht & Coach Tours Inc., Berkeley 1973-80; past pres. DataTab, Inc.; 1983-current: prin./bd. chmn. Hornblower, Upson, Monfils & Proescher, Inc., Pleasant Hill; owner Commodore Cruises; founder/lectr. Secrets of Success Seminars, Lafayette; v.p./corp. investment ofcr. Finl. Corp. of Am.; pres. Sea Ventures, Inc. (Fla.); founder/host TV show "How Now, Mr. Dow?"; created/recorded Telephone Stockmarket News; founder/pub. investment advis. newsletter "Montgomery Street Opinon" (1970s); honors: Rotary Alternate Fellow for Internat. Understanding (1962); mem. Campbell Soup Co. Mgmt. Club (pres. 1962); mem. Nat. Speakers Assn., Bay Area Speakers (v.p.), Little Venice Yacht Club (fmr Fleet Capt.), Exchange Club Internatl., Toastmasters Internat. (past pres.); rec: chess, swim, ski, riding. Res: 3266 Elvia St Lafayette 94549 Ofc: Hornblower, et al, 91 Gregory Ln Ste 7 Pleasant Hill 94523

PROHS, JOHN RICHARD, engineer, inventor; b. Jan. 14, 1942, Gering, Neb.; s. Wesley Richard and Dorothy (Banks) P.; m. Melissa Carr, Sept. 1979; edn: Univ. Neb. 1960-62; BA, Ambassador Coll. 1968. Career: maint. engr. Ambassador Television 1967-69, audio engr. 1969-71, chief audio engr. 1971-73; engrg. supv. Ambassador Radio Prodns. 1973-77; tech. supv. Ambassador Auditorium and Ambassador Coll. 1977; currently mgr. tech. ops. and engrg. Ambassador Coll.; cons., frequent lectr. on loudspeaker array design; honors: Regents Scholar (Univ. Neb. 1960); mem: Acoustical Soc., Audio Engrg. Soc. (sect. treas. 1976-78, vice chmn. 1979, chmn. 1980); works: devel. voice-actuated commun. system 1970; prototype time-gated spectrum analyzer for measuring speech intelligibility 1977; infrared and twisted wire techniques for closed circuit video transmission 1978, 85; patent for transducer coverage system 1985; co-devel. The PHD Pgm. (TM) and Q-Plus (TM) software for

Sound System Engrg. Design 1985; proj. mgr. Computer Controlled Watts Network Call Forwarding System 1986; publs: tech. papers and articles in field, mil: sp5 US Army cryptographics 1962-65, Good Will Rep. for 304th Signal Battn. Korea, Exceptionally Meritorious Svc.; Worldwide Ch. of God. Ofc: 300 W Green St Pasadena 91123

PROPST, BERNARD JAMES, franchising co. executive; b. Oct. 16, 1949, Clarksburg, W.Va.; s. Byron Edward and Mary Teresa (Lawler) P.; m. Wol Yong, July 21, 1971; children: John b. 1972, Thomas b. 1973, Elizabeth b. 1979, Maureen b. 1986; edn: BS in bus. adminstrn., CSU Sacramento 1978; CPA Calif. 1980. Career: staff acct. Fox & Co. CPAs Stockton 1978-80; mgmt. svc. auditor E&J Gallo Winery Modesto 1980-81; finance adminstr. Bronco Wine Co. Ceres 1981-82; controller Nulaid Foods Inc. Ripon 1982-85; pres. Aero-Colours Inc. Danville 1985–; honors: Beta Alpha Psi 1977-78; mem: Am. Inst. CPAs, Calif. Soc. CPAs, NSAC, Toastmasters, Mensa; co-inventor new finish matching process (patent applied for); mil: E5 USAF 1969-76, Good Conduct; Catholic; rec: sightseeing, bird watching. Res: 2617 Coty Ct Ceres 95307 Ofc: Aero-Colours Inc. 238 Montair Dr Danville 94526

PROSPERI, MILTON NICHOLAS, manufacturing co. executive; b. Sept. 10, 1959, Akron, Ohio; s. Anthony Edward and Lela P.; edn: BSIM, Univ. Akron 1983; BS acctg., Ohio State Univ. 1984; MBA (in progress), Univ. Akron 1984-85. Career: plant mgr. Harco Corp., Medina, Ohio 1984-85, west coast ops mgr. Huntington Beach 1985–; seminar in corrosion technol., Denver, Colo. 1985, proper ofc. procedure, L.A. 1985; honors: Spl. Recognition Award NACE (1985), Company Man of the Year (1985); mem. NACE; publs: 7 articles on business policy; Republican; Catholic; rec: travel, scuba, flying. Ofc: Harco Corp., 16102 Gothard St Huntington Beach 92647

PROUTY, THOMAS PARKER, electronics engineer; b. Jan. 25, 1928, Los Angeles; s. Harold Samuel and Rose Margaret (Becker) P.; m. Dorothy Joyce Brown, Nov. 22, 1984; children: Patrick b. 1956, Kathleen b. 1957, Ann b. 1958; edn: Calif. Tech. 1945-46; AA, El Camino Jr. Coll. 1948; BS, UCLA 1952; Profl. Engr., Calif 1979. Career: engr. Firestone Tire & Rubber Co. 1952-55; sr. engr. Hallamore Electronics div. Lear Siegler 1955-59; chief engr. Newport Scientific Co. Inc. 1959-62; sr. engr. MHD Research Inc. 1962-63; sr. engr. American Astrophysics Inc. 1963-64; chief engr. Lincoln Dynamics Inc. 1964-65; chief edngr. Microdot Magnetics Inc. 1965; sr. engr. splst. AiResearch Mfg. Co. 1965–; amateur radio opr. K6HJH; mem: IEEE (sr.); rec: motorcycles, computer, photog. Res: 18639 Manhattan Pl Torrance 90504 Ofc: 18639 Manhattan Pl Torrance 90504 Ofc: AiResearch Mfg. Co., Dept. 93074, 2525 W 190th St Torrance 90509

PROVENZANO, JAMES MICHAEL, securities firm executive; b. Aug. 5, 1948, Los Angeles; s. Joseph Russell and Mary Sarah (Mancuso) P.; m. Sharon Evelyn Gutman, Sept. 11, 1976; edn: BS, fin. ins. real estate, Cal Poly Pomona, 1966-70; major fin., Univ. of Ariz. 1966-70; Licensed, NYSC 1973, NASD 1973, Chgo. Bd. of Trade 1973, Calif. & Nev. Ins. Dept. (inactive) 1976-79. Career: 1970, signed with Houston Astros Professional Baseball Team (pitcher), injured shoulder ended baseball career; account exec. Dean Witter Inc., Whittier 1972-74; account exec. Blyth Eastman Dillon Inc., L.A., Las Vegas, Nev. 1974-79; asst. mgr. Dean Witter Ofc., Billings, Mont. 1979-80; broker Merrill Lynch, L.A. 1980-81; assoc. vice pres./asst. mgr. Bateman Eichler Hill Richards, Anaheim 1981–; awards: All League Football Basketball Baseball, Temple City High School (1964-66); full scholarship, baseball, Univ. of Ariz. 1966-70; Academic Honor Roll, and Pres's Hon. List, CalPoly 1971-2; Ranked in Nation: 9th in strikeouts, Collegiate Baseball Statistices 1968; mem. Profl. Baseball Assn. 1970-71; mem. Associated Person Commodities Futures Trading Commn.; Sigma Alpha Epsilon frat. alumni; Western Bass Fishing Assn., Bass Anglers Sportsman Soc.; Democrat; Catholic; rec: hunting, fishing, skiing. Res: 580 Paseo Lucero Anaheim Hills 92807 Ofc: Bateman Eichler Hill Richards, 451 W. Lincoln, Ste 150, Anaheim 92805

PUCCI, JOHN RICHARD, telecommunications co. sales executive; b. June 29, 1947, Greenwich, Conn.; s. Joseph and Jennie Thersea (Capablo) P.; m. Mary Elizabeth, Sept. 29, 1984; edn: AA, E. Ariz. Coll. 1968; BA in sec. edn., Ariz. State Univ. 1974; cert. telecom. mgmt. Nat. Univ. 1985, enrolled MBA Pgm. 1985-. Career: tchr. Scottsdale Public Schs., 1975-76; sales rep. B.F. Ascher Pharmaceuticals, Phoenix 1976-78; major accounts rep. MCI Telecomms., Denver 1978-80; western regl. sales mgr. Watts Commander, Denver 1980; co-founder/ co-owner/ pres. Tri-Tech Systems, Denver and Tucson, Az. 1980-84; dist. sales mgr. major accts. GTE Sprint, Irvine 1984–; guest lectr. Rancho Santiago Coll.; awards: 2 year athletic scholarship Varsity Football; mem. Nat. Hotel/ Motel Assn. (1980-84), No. Am. Telecomm. Assn. (1980-84); civic: March of Dimes, Orange County CofC; works: systems engr. in design of computer for use in Telephone Call-Accounting for hotels/ motels; Democrat; Catholic; rec: outdoor sports, pvt. pilot. Ofc: GTE Sprint 16969 Von Karman Ste 200 Irvine 92714

PUCKETT, RICHARD EDWARD, recreation executive; b. Sept. 9, 1932, Klamath Falls, Ore.; s. Vernon Elijah and Leona Bell (Clevenger) P.; m. Velma Faye Hamrick, Apr. 14, 1957; children: Katherine Mitchell b. 1958, Deborah Alison b. 1960, Susan Lin b. 1961, Gregory Richard b. 1962; edn: stu. Monterey Peninsula Jr. Coll., Hartnell Jr. Coll., CSUSJ, Lake Forest Coll., Ill., So. Ore. Coll. of Edn.; BA in public service, Univ. San Francisco 1978; desig: Am. Recreation Soc. (1964), Armed Forces Rec. Soc. (1970), Nat. Park & Rec. Soc. (1976), Profl. Recreator. Career: asst. arts and crafts dir. Ft. Leonard Wood, Mo. 1956-57; arts & crafts dir./ asst. spl. services ofcr./museum dir. (designed and opened 1st Ft. Sheridan Army Mus.) Ft. Sheridan, Ill. 1957-59; arts & crafts dir. Fort Irwin, Calif. 1959-60, Fort Ord, Calif. (opened 1st Presidio of Monterey Army Mus. 1961) 1960–; awards: 1st Pl Dept. of Army Programming Award (6 times 1975-85), 1st Pl for Pgmmg. & Publicity AUS Forces Command (5 times 1979-84), 1st & 3d Pl Modern Sculpture, Monterey Fair Fine Arts Exhibit (1978), 19 awards for outstanding performance, 2 Sustained Superior Perf. Awards (1978, 84), var. ribbons for arts & crafts; mem: Am. Park & Recreation Soc., Salinas Valley Fine Arts Assn., Am. Craftsman Assn., Glass Arts Soc.; artist in oils, watercolor, blownglass sculpture, graphics, One-man shows: Seaside, City Hall (1975), Ft Ord Arts & Crafts Center Gal. (67, 73, 79, 81), Presidio of Monterey Art Gal. (1979), exhibits in Mo., Ill., Calif., Art works in pvt. collections in US, Canada, Europe; designed, conducted & pub. Fort Ord Recreation Survey (computerize in 1978); Democrat; Prot.; rec: walking, collect antiques. Res: 1152 Jean Ave Salinas 93905 Ofc: Arts & Crafts Center, Bldg 2250 Fort Ord 93941-5600

PULASKI, DAVID JEROME, communications executive; b. Mar. 5, 1957, Chgo.; s. Jerome Harold and Clare Elizabeth (Murnane) P.; m. Rita Jean Rayburn, Sept. 6, 1986; edn: BA, UC Los Angeles 1986. Career: sr. study dir. Market Facts, Inc. 1983-85; research analyst, project dir., senior research dir. J.D. Power & Assocs., 1980-83, sr. project dir. 1985, sr. account cons. Jackson-Dawson Communications, Inc., Torrance 1986–, opened West Coast office, devel. sales tng./product info. for Acura (new div. Am. Honda Motor Co.), cons. transp. and automotive issues (Honda, Toyota, Nissan, Mazda Motors of No. Am., USA Suzuki, Acura, others); guest lectr. UCLA Ext.; awards: Bank of Am. math & sci. achieve. (1975); mem. Sigma Pi frat.; Republican; Catholic; rec: run, ski, backpack, auto racing. Res: 15135 Nordhoff St No. 15 Sepulveda Ofc: Jackson-Dawson Communications Inc 22750 Hawthorne Blvd Ste 219 Torrance 90505

PULLIAM, PAUL EDISON, electrical engineer; b. June 6, 1912, Nickerson, Kans.; s. George Washington and Hattie Lucy (Vandeventer) P.; m. Ila M. Catrett, Feb. 3, 1945; children: Carol Ann b. 1946, Paula Ann b. 1953; edn: ROTC to 2nd lt., FA-Res, Univ. of Mo., 1937; var. spl. courses incl. radar-electronics completed as a reserve ofcr.; BS in EE, Univ. of Mo., Feb. 1951. Reg. Profl. Elec. Engr., Mo., Nev., Calif. Career: elec. engr. Ozark Dam Constructors, bldg. hydroelec. powerhouse at Bull Shoals Dam in Baxter Co., Ark. 1951-52; mech. plan checker Clark Co. Bldg. & Safety Dept., Las Vegas, Nev.; constrn. insp. Regional Waste Water Treatment Plant, Sacramento Co. Dept. of Pub. Works, Sacto.; qualified as Guided Missile Ofcr., Ft. Bliss, Tex. (1949); provided two concepts used in devel. of thermonuclear hydrogen bombs, 1949; initiated weatherization of Fort Irwin, Calif. in 1985; and provided two concepts for redesign of Sergeant York weapon system, caused USAF personnel to devel. VHF Balun antenna arrays; initiated re-devel. of torpedoes for USN and USCG, 1986; honors: Army Commendn. for suggesting WWII F.A. use of Radar Set SCR-584 and formation of Radar Set SCR-784; named the Polaris Weapon System (1952), named the Pershing Weapon System at Redstone Arsenal, Ala.; provided definition and coined term 'afterburner' for jet aircraft thrust reaction in 1949, Fort Bliss; mem: Reserve Ofcrs. Assn. of the USA (life, 50-year mem. 5/29/87),IEEE (life), Am. Soc. of Mil. Engrs., VFW (life), Calif. Soc. of SAR (pres. Sacto. chpt.); mil: served pvt. to cpl., FA, 1930-34, 2nd lt. to major, FA-Res. US Army, ret. 1972; Democrat; Baptist. Res: 7916 Grandstaff Dr Sacramento 95823

PULLIAS, EARL VIVON, professor emeritus; b. Mar. 12, 1907, Castalian Springs, Tenn.; s. John Gray and Margaret (Leath) P.; m. Pauline Boyce, Dec. 21, 1929; children: Calvin b. 1935, John b. 1939; edn: BA, Cumberland Univ. 1928; MA, Univ. Chgo. 1931; PhD, Duke Univ. 1936; postgrad. work in England 1937-38. Career: English tchr. in jr. high sch., Tenn. 1928-30; tchg. fellow Duke Univ. 1931-36, instr. 1936-37; prof. of psychology Pepperdine Coll. 1937-57, and dean of faculty 1940-57; prof. in Summer Sch., USC 1940-57, prof. of higher edn. USC 1957-77, prof. emeritus 1977-; apptments: mem. (pres. 1956-57, 62-63, 67-68) Los Angeles County Board of Edn. 1954–; cons. for colls. and univs.; mem. (chmn. 1963-66) Commn. on Higher Edn., Calif. Tchrs. Assn. 1960-66; mem. Commn. on Mbrship and Stds., W. Assn. of Schs. and Colls. 1958-61; honors: Phi Beta Kappa, Kappa Delta Phi, Pi Gamma Mu, Alpha Sigma Nu, USC Associates Award for Tchg. Excellence (1965), Litt D. (hon.) Pasadena Coll. (1971), Earl V. Pullias Lectureships in Higher Edn., Sch. of Edn., USC, estab. and endowed (1977); mem: Am. Ednl. Research Assn., Am. Psychol. Assn., Fellow Los Angeles County Psychol. Assn., Am. Assn. for Higher Edn.; publs: Variability in Results from New-Type Achievement Tests (Duke Univ. Press, 1937); (w/Lockhart, A. and others) Toward Excellence in College Teaching (Wm.C. Brown Co. Pubs., 1963); A Search for Understanding (Wm.C. Brown Co. Pubs., 1965); (w/Young, J.D.) A Teacher is Many Things (Ind. Univ. Press, 1968), selected for Ladder Series by USIA, 9 fgn. lang. translations; A Common Sense Philosophy for Modern Man: A Search for Fundamentals (Philosophical Library, 1975); (w/Wilbur, L.) Principles and Values for College and University Administrn. (Philosophical Library, 1984); more than 100 research and theoretical articles and revs. on edn. and psych. Address: 7422 Brighton Ave Los Angeles 90047

PUMERANTZ, PHILIP, college president; b. Nov. 3, 1932, New London, Conn.; s. Harry and Pauline (Weiss) P.; m. Harriet Krinsky, Aug. 21, 1960; children: Andrew, Beth, Richard; edn: BA, Univ. of Conn. 1959, MA, 1961, PhD, 1967; LHD, hon., Coll. Osteo. Med. of the Pacific 1979. Career: tchr. history Waterford H.S., Conn. 1959-63; asst. prof. edn. Univ. Bridgeport 1967-71, assoc. prof. 1971-74, dir. cont. edn. 1972-74; prin. P. Pumerantz Assocs., Fairfield 1974-75; dir. edn. Am. Osteo. Assn., Chicago 1975-77; pres. Coll. Osteo. Med. of the Pacific, Pomona 1977–; bd. govs. Fairfield Unquowa Sch.; bd. dirs. Park Ave. Hosp., Hollywood Community Hosp.; honors: proclamation for devel. of med. coll., City of Pomona 1978; Wesleyan Univ. grantee 1961; mem: Pomona chpt. ARC, Mt. Baldy Council Boy Scouts of Am., Am. Assn. Colls. Osteo. Med., Phi Delta Pi, Univ. Claremont Club, Rotary Club; publs: author textbooks; adv. ed. Osteo. Physicians Journ. 1978-; mil: US Army 1953-55. Ofc: College Plaza Pomona 91766

PURDY, CHARLES EDWARD, IV, lawyer; b. May 27, 1956, Mpls., Minn.; s. Charles E. Purdy III and Gene T. (Peirce) Thulin; edn: BA, honors, Univ. of Wisc. 1978; JD, magna cum laude, Univ. of San Diego 1981; admitted to practice, State Bar of Calif. 1981. Career: extern US Ct. of Appeals Judge J. Clifford Wallace 1980; assoc. atty. Ferris, Brennan, et al. 1980-83 currently, sole practitioner (spec. corp. matters), San Diego; regular cons. to var. firms; tchr. on aspects of corp. law, var. instns.; honors: ed., USD Law Review; publs: on Fourth Amendment and Internat. Terrorism, USD Law Review 1979; regular contbr. edl. pages of Los Angeles and San Diego Newspapers; rec: flying, writing, skiing. Res: 4528 Boundary St San Diego 92116 Ofc: Charles E. Purdy IV, 2726 Fifth Ave San Diego 92103

PURDY, JOSEPH DONALD, educator, business executive; b. Oklahoma City, Okla.; s. Allen Beamer and Ruth S. (Sanders) P.; m. Annelie, Sept. 7, 1969; 1 dau., Kimberly b. 1975; edn: BA, CSU Long Beach 1960; MA, Chapman Coll. 1965; PhD, Univ. of Okla. 1968; Human Resource and Organizational Devel., UCLA 1981; (8) Calif. Tchr. Credentials (in edn., psychology and sch. adminstrn). Career: educator, Corona 1962-65; asst. prof. Univ. of Mississippi 1969-71; asst. prof., head dept. of special edn. Southwestern Oklahoma State Univ. 1971-75; adminstr. Santa Barbara County Schs. 1975-78; dir. Federal Grants, US Ofc. of Edn. 1978-81; psychologist 1981-82; entrepreneur, self-empl. businessman, educator, real estate developer 1983-; adj. prof Calif. State Polytechnic Univ., San Luis Obispo; honors: Outstanding Educator of Am. 1975; mem: Internat. Reading Assn., Nat. Assn. for Edn. of Young Children, Santa Maria CofC, Phi Delta Kappa (past), Council for Exceptional Children (past), Santa Maria Symphony Orch. (pres., bd. dirs. 1985-87), Lake Maria Valley Social Club (pres. 1984-86), CSULB Alumni (pres. class of 1961); publs: 20 papers presented var. profl. confs. incl. 6th World Conf. on Gifted and Talented Children, Hamburg, W. Ger. (1985), 8 articles in profl. jours.; mil: s/sgt. US Army, Reserve; rec: family. Res: Santa Maria 93455

PURISCH, ARNOLD DAVID, clinical neuropsychologist; b. Feb. 20, 1951, NY, NY; s. Sigmund Leo and Tess (Lazar) P.; m. Ellen, Aug. 10, 1975; 1 son, Daniel b. 1985; edn: BA, Univ. Md. 1973, MA, Fairleigh Dickinson Univ. 1975, PhD, Univ. S.D. 1978; Diplomate Am. Bd. Profl. Neuropsychol. 1984, Am. Bd. Clinical Neuropsychol. 1985. Career: psychol. JFK Med. Ctr. Edison N.J. 1978-80; neuropsychol. VA Med. Ctr. East Orange 1980-83, Long Beach 1983-85, Orange Co. Neuropsychol. Grp. Fountain Valley 1984-; seminar leader Neuropsychol. Assoc. of Calif.; pvt. practice neuropsychol. 1982-; ed. advisor Internat. Jour. of Clin. Neuropsychol.; fellow Nat. Acad. Neuropsychol. 1985 (v.p.); mem: Internat. Neuropsychol. Soc., Am., Calif., Orange Co. (treas.- elect) Psychol. Assns., Assn. Advancement Psychol.; publ: 18 articles, co-author 2 books on Luria-Nebraska Neuropsychological Battery; Jewish; rec: guitar, skiing, golf. Res: 4408 Fir Ave Seal Beach 90740 Ofc: Orange Co. Neuropsychology Group 8840 Warner Ave, Ste 301, Fountain Valley 92708

PUROHIT, JAGDISHCHANDRA UMAKANT, physical therapist; b. Oct. 28, 1949, Baroda, Gujarat, India; s. Umakant U. and Kanta U. (Dave) P.; m. Usha, May 12, 1969; 1 child, Nikunj b. 1970; edn: BS chem., Gujarat Univ. 1969; BS, (First Student in Physical Therapy), M.S. Univ. 1974; MS in health adminstrn., Univ. of La Verne 1985; Exec. MBA pgm. in progress, Claremont Grad. Sch. (-1987); desig: Reg. Physical Therapist, Calif., Hawaii. Career: coord., lectr. Sch. of Physical Therapy, M.S. Univ., India 1974-76; dir. B.M. Inst. of Mental Health, India 1976; senior ofcr., phys. therapist, Ministry of Health, Singapore 1976-79; chief phys. therapist Sports Medicine & Research Ctr., Singapore 1979-82; dir. physical therapy Westside Hosp., Los Angeles 1982-85; dir. physical therapy, San Dimas Hosp., L.A. 1985-; phys. therapist UCLA Poly-Clinic (1984), 23rd Olympiad Los Angeles (1985); mem. Am. Coll. of Hosp. Adminstrs., Am. Mgmt. Assn., Am. Coll. of Sports Medicine, Am. Phys. Therapy Assn., Am. Red Cross, Gujarati Soc. (L.A.); works: research asst. in measuring VO2 max. of Singapore Nat. Soccer Team (1980); mil: sgt. maj. Nat. Cadet Corp. 1965-68; Republican; Hindu; rec: play harmonica, travel. Res: 11615 Riverside Dr Apt 234 North Hollywood 91602 Ofc: San Dimas Hospital 1350 W Covina Blvd San Dimas 91773

PYROS, GREGORY GEORGE, architect; b. Jan. 10, 1957, Kingston, Pa.; s. Nicholas Jonathan and Artemis (Veras) P.; edn: BS in building sci., Rensselaer Polytech. Inst. 1978, MBA 1979, B.Arch. 1980; Reg. Architect, Calif. 1973; certified Nat. Council of Architl. Registration Bds. (NCARB). Career: designer/planner Pyros + Sanderson Architects, Wilkes-Barre, Pa. 1975-80; project mgr. Harrison/Lorenzini Architects, Newport Beach 1980-81; project mgr./project designer The Elliott Group, Los Alamitos 1981-82; owner The Pyros Partnership, Costa Mesa 1982-; pvt. consulting and seminars for profls. on computer applications to bldg. industry; honors: Who's Who of Am. Colls. and Univs. (1978), Who's Who of High Schs. (1974); corp. mem. Am. Inst. of Architects; chmn. Architl. Telecommunications Network/So. Calif.; coauthor computer pgm: Architect's Office Mgr. (nat. distbn.), author ditizer menu for AutoCAD for Architecture/ Facilities Mgmt.; Republican; Greek Orthodox; rec: sailing, skiing, tennis. Res: 1327A Baker St Costa Mesa 92626 Ofc: The Pyros Partnership 1500 Adams Ave Ste 310 Costa Mesa 92626

QUAN, CYNTHIA MAY, dentist; b. Apr. 12, 1953, Oakland; d. Hee and Irene (Der) Quan; edn: AB in biol. sci., UC Berkeley 1975; secondary tchg. creden-

tial (biol./phys. scis.), CSU Hayward 1976; DDS, Case Western Reserve Univ. Sch. of Dentistry, 1980; gen. practice residency, Loma Linda Univ. 1981; Calif. Career: gen. dentist in pvt. practice, Encino 1983-; instr. LLU Sch. of Dentistry, 1980-81; tchr. Oakland High Sch. and San Leandro High Sch., 1976-77; heart project instr. Alameda County Heart Assn., 1975-76; awards: Young Ambassador to Europe (1970), Gen. Practice Residency Completion award/commendn., LLU (1981); mem: Am. Assn. ofWomen Dentists, West L.A. Womens Dental Group, Encino CofC, Gamma Delta Epsilon UCB service gp. (pres. 1974-75); sci. dir. Cal. Summer Orientation Pgm. (1979); research: enamel and dentin remineralization using electron microscopy (1979-80); rec: aerobics, dance, tennis, travel. Ofc: Drs. Kirshbaum, Kanter & Quan, 5400 Balboa Blvd Ste 308 Encino 91316

QUANDT, JAMES RUSSELL, stock brokerage president; b. Aug. 23, 1949, Chgo.; s. Robert Richard and Julia Ann (Fitzgerald) Q.; m. Marleen Diann, Aug. 4, 1973; children: Jeffrey b. 1981, Kevin b. 1984; edn: bus. adm., St. Marys Coll. of Calif. 1971; mem. NYSE. Career: senior account exec. Bank of Am., Los Angeles 1972-75; 2d v.p. Smith Barney, Harris Upham, L.A. 1975-82; pres./chief exec. Security Pacific Brokers, Pasadena 1982-; bd. dirs. Financial Clearing Services Corp., NY; mem: University Club, United Way (div. hd.), Balboa Bay Club; Republican; Roman Catholic. Res: 2250 Melville Dr San Marino 91108 Ofc: Security Pacific Brokers 155 N Lake Ave Pasadena 91108

QUIDACHAY, RONALD EVANS, municipal court judge; b. Mar. 8, 1947, San Francisco; s. Antonio Taisipic and Edith Georgiagina (Evans) Q.; m. Katharine Swan, Aug. 1, 1976; children: Evan Andrew b. 1978, Seth Ryan b. 1982; edn: BA, CSU San Francisco 1970; JD, UC Berkeley 1973; admitted to Calif. State Bar. Career: staff atty. San Francisco Neighborhood Legal Assistance Found., S.F. 1974-77; asst. dist. atty., S.F. District Atty's Office, 1977-80; ptnr. Lenvin Gesmer & Quidachay, 1980-81; traffic commnr. San Francisco Municipal Court 1981-83; judge S.F. Municipal Ct., Dept. 4 Civil Div., 1983-; awards: 1983 Outstanding Young Man; appreciation as founder, Filipino Bar Assn. of No. Calif.; mem: Calif. Judges Assn., Filipino Bar Assn. (hon.), San Francisco Bar Assn. (hon.), American Bar Assn., Asian Am. Judges Assn., Queen's Bench, Native Sons of Calif., Dimasalang House bd. dirs.; Catholic; rec: tennis, camping. Res: 1058 Rhode Island St San Francisco 94107 Ofc: S.F. Municipal Court, City Hall, San Francisco 94102

QUINN, CIARAN PATRICK, manufacturing co. executive; b. Mar. 31, 1959, Phila.; s. Patrick J. and Mairin P. (Kennedy) Q.; edn: BSME, Rensselaer Polytechnic Inst. 1981; Reg. Profl Engr. (Mech. Eng.) Calif. 1985. Career: energy mgmt. rep. Pacific Gas & Electric Co., San Francisco 1982-84; energy mgmt. engr. Maximum Technology, Brisbane 1984-86, Western Region mgr., 1986-; lectrs. on lighting and energy mgmt. var. profl. orgns., 1982-; assoc. mem. ASME; civic: San Mateo County Summer Jobs for Youth Pgm. (Central Com. 1983-), fundraiser for United Way and Boy Scouts Am., (1984); coauthor tech publ. (ASME Solar Grp, 1982); rec: foot racing (Track & Road). Ofc: Maximum Technology 60 Industrial Way Brisbane 94005

QUINN, GERARD JOSEPH, management consultant; b. Sept. 26, 1949, Massapequa, NY; s. Gerard Joseph and Camille Q.; m. Carol L., Oct. 5, 1980; 1 dau, Tara b. 1984; edn: BS, Univ. of San Francisco 1972; MPA, USC 1977. Career: mgmt. analyst County of San Mateo 1972-81; deputy dir. of health svcs. County of Marin 1981-82, disaster claims coord. 1982-83, deputy public works dir. 1983-84; pres. Gerard J. Quinn & Assoc. 1984-86; senior project mgr. David M. Griffiths & Assoc. Ltd. 1986-; adj. faculty Univ. of San Francisco; mem. Am. Soc. of Public Adminstrs. Res: 1724 Wynoochee Way Petaluma 94952 Ofc: David M. Griffiths & Assoc. Ltd., 2508 Garfield Ave Ste D Carmichael 95608

QUINN, JOHN R., archbishop; b. March 28, 1929, Riverside; s. Ralph J. and Elizabeth (Carroll) Quinn; edn: St. Francis Sem. and Immaculate Heart Sem., S.D. 1947-8; N. Am. Coll.; S.T.B, 1953, S.T.B, 1954, Gregorian Univ., Rome. Career: ordained priest in Rome, 1953; assoc. pastor St. George's Parish, Ontario, Ca. 1954; Theology faculty Immaculate Heart Sem., San Diego 1955-, apptd. Rector Sch. of Theol., 1964; apptd. pres. St. Francis Coll. Sem. 1962; bishop (2d Aux. Bishop, S.D.; 1st native of Diocese to hold ofc.)San Diego, 1967; provost/bd.trustees Univ. of San Diego, 1968; pastor St. Therese Parish 1969; apptd. by Pope Paul VI as consultor, Sacred Cong. for the Clergy in Rome, 1971; bishop Okla. City and Tulsa, 1972, 1st archbishop of Okla. City 1973; papal appt. rep. to 4th Synod of Bishops, Vatican City, 1974; pres. Okla Conf. of Chs. 1976-8; archbishop of San Francisco, 1977-; pres. Nat. Conf. Catholic Bishops, 1977-80; apptd. Pontifical Delegate for Religious in the United States, 1983; mem. Canon Law Soc. of Am., Catholic. Theol. Soc. of Am. Address: Archdiocese of San Francisco, 445 Church St., San Francisco 94114

QUON, HEW WAH, physician; b. July 17, 1951, China; s. Bill J. and So F. (Ng) Q.; edn: BS, USC 1972, MD, 1976; Diplomate Am. Board Internal Med. (1979). Career: med. intern Los Angeles Co.-USC Med. Center 1976-77, med. intern 1977-79; pvt. practice, 1980-; co-chmn. med. dept. French Hosp. 1982; honors: Phi Beta Kappa (1972), Calif. State Fellowship (1972-76), Calif. State Scholarship (1968-72). Res: 805 Juarez St Montebello 90640 Ofc: Hew W. Quon, MD Inc. 808 N Hill St Los Angeles 90012

QUON, HOY, investment banker, civic leader; b. Apr. 30, 1907, Canton, China; s. Gin and Sun (Wong) Q.; m. Susan Chin, May 18, 1933; 1 son, Arthur b. 1951; edn: BA, Univ. Peking 1931; MA, Univ. Calif. 1941. Career: Chinese interpreter and translator US War Dept. 1941-47; mem. NYSE, 1950–, investment exec. Thomson McKinnon Securities Inc., San Francisco currently; bd. dirs. Chinese Community Hosp., S.F. 1965-72; apptd. Calif. Gov.'s Com. on State Traffic Safety, 1967-74; honors: Hon. Dr. of Humanities, Acad. of Arts & Lit., Taiwan, China (1981); vice pres. 5th Congress of Worlds Poets (1981); mem. Chinese Community pol. orgns. (chmn. Reagan for Gov. No. Calif. 1966, chmn. San Francisco 1976); rec: reading, writing. Res: 4 Cermenho Ct San Rafael 94903 Ofc: Thomson McKinnon 50 Fremont St 41st Fl San Francisco 94105

QUON, STANLEY MELVIN, audit administrator; b. Jan. 10, 1932, San Francisco; s. Kee and Shee (Lee) Q.; m. Florence, July 19, 1974; children: STeve b. 1957, Glenn b. 1962; edn: BBA, Golden Gate Univ. 1954, MBA, 1970; desig: Cert. Internal Auditor, Inst. Int. Auditors Inc. (1973), Cert. Information Systems Auditor, EDP Auditors Found. (1980), Calif. Comm. Colls. tchg. credential (1973). Career: staff acct. Calif. Acctg. Services, Oakland 1955-60; acct. City-County of San Francisco, 1960-65; mgmt. auditor Calif. Dept. of Fin., S.F. 1965-67; tax auditor Calif. Employment Devel. Dept., S.F. 1967-72, chief Audit Div., Calif. Employment Devel. Dept., Sacto. 1972–; mem. Calif. State JTPA Audit Tech. Advis. Com. (chmn.), Health and Welfare Agency Single Audit Implementation Com. (co-chmn.), State Controller's Single Audit Implementation Com.; prof. (acctg., auditing, govtl. acctg.) Sacto. City Coll. (p.t. 1973-); mem: Inst. of Internal Auditors, Nat. Assn. JTPA Auditors (bd. chmn.), Western Intergovtl. Audit Forum (chmn.; leadership awards 1980, 83), Calif. Assn. of Auditors for Mgmt. (chmn.); civic: Mandarin Drum Corp, Mandarin Edn. Club, Sacto. City Coll. Business Advis. Com.; works: devel. the Dept. policies, procedures for mgmt. certification of accountability and control of public funds (1984), Job Tng. Partnership Act Audit Guide (1985), Guide for Request for Audit Proposal (1985), CPA Audit Quality Review Guide (1986), Guide for Audit of Service Providers (1986); mil: sp4 US Army 1954-56; Republican; Prot.; rec: tennis, fin. planning. Res: 24 Keel Ct Sacramento 95831 Ofc: State of Calif. Employment Dev. Dept. POB 942880 Sacramento 94280-0001

QURESHEY, SAFI U., electronics manufacturing co. president; b. Feb. 15, 1951, Karachi, Pakistan; s. Razi R. and Ishrat Qureshey; m. Anita Savory, Sept. 19, 1976; children: Uns b. 1979, Zeshan b. 1981; edn: BSC, Physics, Univ. of Karachin, Pakistan 1971; BS in Elec. Engring., Univ. of Texas 1975. Career: test splst., documentor Div. of A.M. International, Santa Ana 1975-77; test engr. Computer Automation Inc., Irvine 1977-78; design engr. Telefile Computer Products, Irvine 1978-80; pres. AST Research Inc., Irvine 1980–; mem. IEEE; mem. Islamic Soc. of Orange County; Islamic. Res: 21 Tidewater Irvine 92714 Ofc: AST Research, Inc. 2121 Alton Ave Irvine 92714

RABY, RICHARD ELLERY, safety consultant; b. Feb. 6, 1922, Phila.; s. Thomas, Jr. and Anna (Brown) R.; m. Ingrid Christine Moller, Dec. 1, 1981; children (by previous marriage): Richard Jr. b. 1946, Stephanie Jo b. 1949; edn: BA bus. econ., Muhlenberg Coll. 1949; BSME, Univ. Penna., 1955; MS Systems Mgmt., USC 1970; Reg. Profl. Engr. (Safety, Quality), Calif. Career: chief of quality engring. Kaiser Metal Products, Inc./Aircraft, 1952-55; down range base mgr. Eastern Test Range, Pan Am Airways Inc., Cape Canaveral 1955-56; sr. reliability flt. test engr. Thor Pgm., Douglas Aircraft Co., 1957-58; Navaho Pgm., No. Am. Aviation Inc./Missile 1956-57; lead system safety engr. Rockwell Internat./Space-Shuttle, Apollo, var. pgms. 1956-70, 1973-78; self employed safety cons. 1970-73, 1981–; system safety engr. FACC/Aeroneutronic, Div. Air Def. Weapon Sys. Pgm. 1978-79, 1982-83; system safety cons. Ocean Thermal Energy Conversion (OTEC) Pgm., Global Marine Devel. Inc., 1979; GD/Pomona, DIVAD, 1980; G&H Technology, Inc., MX 1981; Infotek, Inc., Space Payloads, 1981, USN Weapon Systems, Hughes, currently; founder/pres. Raby Ents. Inc. 1984–; honors: Tech. Utilization award (1974), var. achieve. certs. (1965-70), Apollo Achieve. award, NASA (1970). Mem: Am. Rocket Soc. 1957, Jr. CofC 1956-58, Soc. of Logistics Engrs. 1966, System Safety Soc. 1967-, ASQC 1978-, Reliability Club 1956, Foremans Assn. 1952-55, Assn. of the U.S. Army 1980-; publs: various tech. handbooks; mil: officer/pilot USAF 1943-46; Presbyterian; rec: scuba diving, body building. Res: 5219 Gatewood Ln Anaheim 92807

RACZKOWSKI, ANDREW WESLEY, engineering executive; b. Aug. 2, 1949, Bristol, U.K., nat. US cit. 1957; s. John and Stella (Tolloczko) R.; edn: BA in math., Univ. of Ill. 1971, BS in chem. 1971; PhD in chem., UC Berkeley 1975. Career: research/tchg. asst. UC Berkeley 1971-75; postdoctoral fellow UC Irvine 1975-79; device analyst Rockwell Inc., 1979-81; diagnostics supr. Western Digital Corp. 1981-82, datacomm. product engring. mgr. 1982-85, mgr. CAM Svcs., 1986–; awards: Edmund J. James Scholar (1967-71), Nat. Merit Scholarship finalist (1967); mem. IEEE (Orange Co. mem. chair 1983-84); mem. Tall Club of Orange Co.; contbr. articles in sci. jours., and in-house publs.; rec: winetasting, cooking, hiking. Ofc: Western Digital Corp 2445 McCabe Way Irvine 92714

RADADIA, VRAJLAL MANJI, chiropractor; b. June 2, 1944, Devkigalol, Gujarat, India; s. Manji Gangdas and Raliat Manji (Ratanpura) R.; m. Bhanuben, Aug. 17, 1980; chidren: Nilkanth b. 1984; Anil b. 1985; edn: BSc, Saurashtra Univ., India 1968; BS, Los Angeles Coll. of Chiropractic 1979, DC 1979. Career: draftsman Curt G. Joa Inc., Ft. Worth, Fla. 1973-74, Sensor Techonology Inc., Chatsworth 1974-75; draftsman, machinist, Back Industries, Chatsworth 1975-76; machinist Stainless Steel Prods., Burbank 1976-80; chiropractor Wilshire Center Chiropractic Group, Los Angeles 1981–, also Family Chiropractic Healing Ctr., San Gabriel 1983–; mem: Am., Calif. Chiropractic Assn., San Gabriel Chiro. Soc., San Gabriel CofC, Better Bus. Bureau, Lions Club Internat.; rec: painting, photog., reading. Ofc: Family Chiropractic Healing Ctr., 915 ½ E. Las Tunas Dr. San Gabriel 91776

RADIN, SARA KLEBAN, superior court judge; b. Sept. 3, 1923, San Antonio, Tex.; d. John William and Minnie (Grossman) Kleban; m. Harold Radin, Dec. 30, 1969; children: Jonathan Gross b. 1958, Richard Gross b. 1960; edn: BA, UCLA 1944; JD, Southwestern Law Sch. 1955; Judge of the Superior Ct., Calif. 1984. Career: atty., Los Angeles, Sherman Oaks and Santa Monica 1956-77; Judge of the Superior Ct., Los Angeles Co. 1978–; faculty mem. Calif. Judges Coll. 1985, Nat. Judicial Coll. 1981; mem. plnng. com. Cont. Judicial Studies Pgm. 1983-86; honors: Calif. Judicial Performance Commn. 1985; Family Law Judge of Yr., Beverly Hills Bar Assn. 1981; Annual Status of Women Award, Am. Assn. of Univ. Women, Santa Monica 1979; YWCA Woman of Year, Santa Monica 1979; mem: Calif. Judges Assn.; Nat. Assn. of Women Judges; Calif. Women Lawyers; Women Lawyers of Los Angeles; Santa Monica Bar Assn. (pres. 1975-76); Criminal Cts. Bar Assn., Am. Judicature Soc., UCLA Child Care Svcs. (bd. dirs.); rec: piano, tennis, theatre, plants. Ofc: Superior Court, 1725 Main St., Santa Monica 90401

RAE, MATTHEW SANDERSON, JR., lawyer; b. Sept. 12, 1922, Pittsburgh, Pa.; s. Matthew S. and Olive (Waite) R.; m. Janet Hettman, May 2, 1953; children: Mary-Anna b. 1959, Margaret b. 1961, Janet b. 1962; edn: AB, Duke Univ. 1946, LL.B, 1947; postgrad. Stanford Univ. 1951. Career: asst. to dean, Duke Law Sch. 1947-48; admitted to Md. bar 1948, Calif. bar, 1951, Supreme Ct. of US 1967; assoc. Karl F. Steinmann law firm, Baltimore, Md. 1948-49; nat. field rep. Phi Alpha Delta Law Frat. 1949-51; research atty. Calif. Supreme Ct. 1951-52; partner Darling, Hall & Rae and predecessor firms, 1953–; v.p. Los Angeles Co. Republican Assembly 1959-64; L.A. Co. Repub. Central Com. 1960-64, 1977-, mem. exec. com. 1977-, chmn. 27th Senatorial Dist. 1977-, v.chmn. 17th Cong. Dist. 1960-62, 28th Cong. Dis. 1962-64, chmn. 46th Assem. Dist. 1962-64; Repub. State Central Com. of Calif. 1966-, exec. com. 1966-67; pres. Calif. Repub. League 1966-67; pres. Republican Assocs. 1983-85; mem. A.F. Assn., Aircraft Owners and Pilots Assn.; Comdr. Allied Post, Am. Legion 1969-70; mem: Calif. Commn. on Uniform State Laws 1985–; So. Bay Bar Assn.; Fellow Am. Coll. of Probate Counsel; Internat. Acad. Estate and Trust Law (exec. council 1974-78); L.A. County Bar Assn. (chmn. probate and trust law com. 1964-66, chmn. Legislation Com. 1980-; chmn. Program com. 1981-2; bd. of trustees 1983-85); Am. Bar Assn. (sect. probate, trust, and real prop. law and taxation); Calif. State Bar (bulletin chmn. 1970-72, chmn. Probate Com. 1974-5, exec. com. 1977-83, Legis. chmn. 1978-, Estate Plnng. Trust and Probate Law Sect.); mem. Probate Law Consulting Group, Calif. Bd. of Legal Splzn. 1977-; Lawyers Club of L.A. (first v.p. 1983); Supreme Justice, Phi Alpha Delta 1972-74, elected. to Distinguished Service Chpt. 1978; Legion Lex (pres. 1969-71); Stock Exchange Club; Chancery Club; World Affairs Council; IPA; Rotary Intl.; Commonwealth Club; St. Andrews Soc.; Town Hall (pres. 1975); Los Angeles Com. of Fgn. Relations; Phi Beta Kappa (v.p. Alpha Assn. So. Calif. 1984-); Omicron Delta Kappa; mil: 2d lt. USAAF, WWII; United Presbyterian; rec: theatre, volleyball, swimming. Res: 600 John St Manhattan Beach 90266 Ofc: 606 S Olive St Ste 1900 Los Angeles 90014

RAEDER, MYRNA SHARON, law professor; b. Feb. 4, 1947, NY, NY; d. Samuel and Estelle (Auslander) Raeder; m. Terry Kelly, July 13, 1975; 1 son, Thomas b. 1984; edn: BA, Hunter Coll. 1968; JD, NYU Sch. of Law 1971; LLM, Georgetown Law Ctr. 1975; admitted bar: New York (1972), Calif. (1972), Dist. Columbia (1972). Career: fellow Georgetown Legal Intern Pgm. 1971-73; spl. asst. US Atty., Wash DC 1972-73; asst. prof., co-dir. clin. pgm. Univ. of San Francisco Sch. of Law, 1973-75; atty. assoc. O'Melveny & Myers, Los Angeles 1975-79; assoc. prof., 1979-82, prof. Southwestern Univ. Sch. of Law, L.A. 1983–; honors: Order of Coif, Phi Beta Kappa; mem: ABA (subcoms. of Litigation, Crim. Justice Sects.), Assn. of Am. Law Schs., Nat. Assn. Women Lawyers, Womens Lawyers Assn. of Los Angeles. Res: 15498 Hamner Dr Los Angeles 90077 Ofc: Southwestern University School of Law 675 S Westmoreland Los Angeles 90005

RAFEEDIE, EDWARD, federal judge; b. Jan. 6, 1929, Orange, N.J.; s. Fred and Nabeeha (Hishmeh) R.; m. Ruth Ann Horton, Oct. 8, 1961; children: Frederick Alexander b. 1962, Jennifer Ann b. 1964; edn: BS in Law, USC 1957, JD, 1959; admitted Calif. State Bar 1960. Career: private practice law, Santa Monica 1969-69; judge Municipal Ct. Santa Monica 1969-71; judge Superior Ct., Los Angeles 1971-82; judge U.S. District Ct., Los Angeles 1982–; honors: Dr. of Laws, Pepperdine Univ. (1978); past pres. Santa Monica Bay Dist. Bar Assn. (1968). Ofc: U.S. District Court, 312 N Spring St Los Angeles 90012

RAGER, IRVEN J., textile manufacturing co. executive; b. Sept. 15, 1947, Johnstown, Pa.; s. Alfred Irven and Erma Mae (Eckstien) R.; m. Sharon, June 26, 1970; children: Christopher b. 1975, Scott b. 1978, Melissa b. 1981, Macall b. 1983; edn: Biola Univ. 1966-68; BS, CSU Long Beach 1971; Fuller Theol. Sem. 1971-73. Career: dir. of youth services, Los Angeles City Schs.; sales rep. Hallmark Carpets, L.A.; sales rep., dist. sales mgr., currently regl. sales mgr. Westpoint Pepperell, San Francisco; dir. Victoria Shoe Corp.; honors: Resolution, Calif. Legislature for outstanding contbns. to community (1984, 85), commendn., City of Alhambra (1984, 85); coach Little League (bd.); mil: sgt. 1/c US Army, Vietnam Svc, UN, Air Medal, Bronze Star, Purple Heart medals. Res: 733 Glen Rd Danville 94536 Westpoint Pepperell 1355 Market St Ste 300 San Francisco 94103

RAINES, FRANCES ELIZABETH, real estate broker; b. Aug. 14, 1928, Norfolk, Va.; d. Ernest Chapman and Lula Elizabeth (Bibb) Clark; m. Horace

Franklin Raines, Aug. 19, 1950; children: Sandra b. 1952, John b. 1955, Elizabeth b. 1960, Rebecca b. 1960, Joan b. 1962; edn: stu. William and Mary, 1946-47, Converse Coll. 1947-48; BA, fgn. affairs, George Washington (D.C.) Univ. 1950; grad. wk. American Univ. (Wash DC) 1950-51, San Francisco St. Coll. 1955-57; postgrad. wk. UC Berkeley 1958-59; Calif. Teaching Cred. (Secondary) 1957. Career: resrch. clk. typist, Dept. Navy, Pentagon, Wash. 1950, Dept. Army, Pentagon 1951-53, Dept. Army, Presidio, San Francisco 1954-55; high sch. tchr./counselor Hayward Union High Sch. Dist., San Lorenzo H. Sch., 1957-60; bus. owner, Sacramento 1970-73; real estate sales spec. in resales, San Jose 1974-76, Orange Co. 1976-82; broker assoc., New Home Sales, The Ryness Co., Danville 1982−; awards: Ford Found. III Fellowship 1956-57; Highest Producer, Forest E. Olson Co. 11/77; Million Dollar Sales, 1979, 80, 81; SMC Sales Achievement Award ($6 million) 1983; other SMC sales awards (3) 1985; mem: San Jose Real Estate Bd. 1974-76, West Orange Co. R.E. Bd. 1976-77, Huntington Bch. Fountain Valley R.E. Bd. 1977-82 (mem. PAC 1982). Nat. Assn. of Realtors 1974-82, Calif. Assn. Realtors 1974-82, Sales & Mktg. Council of BIA 1983−; Prot.; rec: needlepoint, profl. seminars, travel. Res: 532 Marine World Pkwy, 6101, Redwood City 94065 Ofc: The Ryness Co. 801 San Ramon Valley Blvd Danville 94526

RAINSBURY, RONALD LEE, contractor, educator; b. May 9, 1935, Portland, Ore.; s. Harold and Evelyn Juanita (Mendenhall) R.; m. Elizabeth, Dec. 29, 1956; children: Rosanne, Debra, Katherine, Diana, Danny, Lisa, Amy, Joe; edn: BS, Ore. Coll. 1958, MS, 1964; Calif. lic. R.E. Broker, Notary Public. Career: educator and pvt. tutor, 15 yrs., currently tch. p.t.; real estate broker/developer/ contr. (splst. affordable apartment bldgs.), owner Ron Rainsbury's Shamrock Devel. Co., Palm Springs 1983−; instr. comm. coll. courses in geography and constrn.; honors: Who's Who Am. Colls. and Univs. (1958), writing award Cessna Crosscurents, Basketball All-Star (1952), Babe Ruth Sportsmanship (1952); mem. Am. Legion; publs: 17 articles in gen. interest mags., articles on new concepts in tchg. in Sci. and Children Mag.; Arithmetic Tchr., J. of Geography; mil: major Calif. State Mil. Reserve; Republican; Catholic; rec: travel, writing, sailing. Res: 27563 Arnico Palm Springs 92262

RAJPER, MOHAMMAD ALI, surgeon; b. Apr. 28, 1947, Hyderabad, Sind, Pakistan; nat. 1978; s. Darya Khan and Sughra Begum (Abbasi) R.; m. Mussarat J. Arain, May 12, 1974; children: Nadia b. 1975, Faisal b. 1979, Naveed b. 1982; edn: MBBS, MD, Univ. of Sind Liaquat Med. Coll. 1970. Career: intern Pakistan, Perth Amboy, N.J. 1970-72; res. surg. Atlantic City 1972-76; major USAF Griffiss AFB Rome, NY 1976-78; pvt. practice gen. surg. Fresno, Calif. 1978-80; lt. col. USAF chief surg. svcs., chief emerg. svcs. Vandenburg AFB 1980-85; honors: certificates of merit in med. sch.; mem: Assn. of Mil. Surg. of the US; mil: lt. col. USAF 1976-78, 1980-, service medal, medal of achievement & outstanding svc. in USAF (1985); Republican; Muslim; rec: travel. Res: 1355 Oak Knoll Rd Santa Maria 93455 Ofc: USAF Hospital Vandenberg AFB 93437

RALLS, RICHARD JULIAN, physician; b. Aug. 30, 1928, Avon Lake, Ohio; s. Julian C. and Esther E. (Chamberlain) R.; m. Carol Lawrence, July 24, 1950; children: Richard b. 1956, Linus b. 1959, Julie b. 1962; edn: AB, Columbia Union Coll. 1949; MS, USC 1952; grad. work UC Berkeley 1952-53; MD, Loma Linda Univ. 1957. Career: family practice physician 1958−, mem. Westminster Medical Group; chief of staff Humana Hospital, Westminster, bd. dirs. Midwood Hosp., Stanton; asst. clin. prof. pharmacology, UC Irvine; mem. Calif. Med. Assn., Orange County Med. Assn. Ofc: 7632 21st St Westminster 92683

RALPH, ROBERTA, superior court judge; b. June 13, 1926, Tahoma, Okla.; d. Francis Abner and Minnie Savannah (Wynn) R.; edn: BA, UC Los Angeles 1955, JD, 1959; admitted Calif. State Bar 1960. Career: jr. atty. Legal Aid Found. Los Angeles 1960, 61-63; jur. counsel Calif. State Lands Commn. 1960-61; atty. prin. in gen. civil practice, 1963-76; instr. Whittier Coll. Sch. of Law, summers 1974, 75; judge Superior Court Los Angeles County 1977−; honors: Phi Beta Kappa (1954), City of L.A. Human Rels. Commn. Bicentennial Award (1976), Ernestine Stahlhut Award, Women Lawyers Assn. of L.A. (1976), recognition for work in women's rights by Calif. Chpts. of NOW, NWPC and CDC (1982), achievement award Nat. Bus. & Profl. Women of L.A. (1984); mem: Women Lawyers Assn. of L.A. (pres. 1971-73), Calif. Women Lawyers (co-founder 1975), AAUW (bd.), Nat. Bus. & Profl. Women of L.A. (bd.), Fair Housing Cong. of So. Calif. (adv. bd., past pres.); contbr. articles in law revs.; Democrat; rec: women's rights advocacy, bicycling. Ofc: County Courthouse 111 N Hill St Los Angeles 90012

RAM SAMUJ, DOUGLAS SHELTON, fabric artist, lecturer, teacher; b. Suva Fiji, nat. Australian 1967; s. Ratu and Stella (Dudley) Ram Samuj; edn: univ. entrance, Scots Coll., Wellington, N.Z. 1944-52; Royal Melbourne Tech. Coll. (Australia) 1955; DA (Dip. of Associateship), Manchester Coll. of Art (England) 1957-59; NDD (Nat. Dip. in Design) 1957-59; ATD (Art Tchrs. Dip.) Sydney Tchrs. Coll. (Australia) 1960. Career: designer David Whitehead Ltd., Lancashire, Eng. 1956; freelance designer, London 1959; art tchr. New South Wales Edn. Dept., Sydney, Austr. 1960-65; freelance designer, fabric artist, guest lectr., Los Angeles 1966−; exhibns: The Macquarie Gallery, Sydney (1965), Argus Gal., Melbourne (1965), Van Bertouch Gal., Newcastle (1965), The Johnstone Gal., Adelaide (1966, 67), White Studio Gal., Adelaide (1966), Coombe Down Gals., Geelong (1966), Gal. De Tours, S.F. (1967), Dom Interiors, Chgo. (1967), The Egg and Eye, L.A. (1968), Johnstone Gal., Brisbane (1972), Garlicks, Capetown S.A. (1972), Robinson's stores (1973), Bullocks (1973, 74), Brand Lib. & Art Ctr., Glendale (1978), Denver Petroleum Club (1986), num. others; work rep. in textile collections: Okla. State Univ., Brig-

ham Young Univ., Colo. State Univ., Bauder Fashion Coll. (Tx.), Ore. State Univ., Univ. of Nev. (Reno); vis. lectr. num. univs. and colls. nat. (1974-); awards: The Heywood Prize Royal Manchester Instn., England (1959), Scots Coll. prefect, house capt. and capt. 1st XI at cricket (1951-52), Duncan Bat, best batting average cricket (1951, 52), music prize Scots Coll. (1949); clubs: Summerhill Cricket Club, Melbourne, Austr. 1955- (Silver Cup and Ball for best Bowler 1955-56), Didsbury Cricket Club, Manchester, Eng. 1957-59 (Championship winners 1957); features on his art pub. in num. newspapers incl. (L.A. Times, S.F. Examiner, S.F. Chronicle, Women's Wear Daily, Fashion Week, L.A. Herald Examiner, Sacto. Bee, Chgo. Sun-Times, others); Independent; Methodist; rec: films, jazz, cricket. address: 2618-½ W Marathon St Los Angeles 90026

RAMER, BRUCE M., lawyer; b. Aug. 2, 1933, Teaneck, NJ; s. Sidney and Anne (Strassman) R.; m. Ann Greenberg, Feb. 15, 1965; children: Gregg, b. 1967, Marc, b. 1969, Neal, b. 1972; edn: AB, Princeton Univ. 1955; JD, Harvard Law Sch. 1959. Career: assoc. law firm of Morrison, Lloyd and Griggs, Hackensack, NJ 1959-60; partner law firm of Gang, Tyre & Brown, Inc., Los Angeles, Ca. 1963−; exec. dir. Entertainment Law Inst., USC Law Center, 1973-; corp. bd. United Way; bd. regents Loyola Marymount Univ., L.A. 1982-; mem: American Jewish Com. (nat. v.p., past pres. L.A. Chpt.; mem. Nat. bd. of govs., bd. trustees), Am. Bar Assn., Calif. Bar Assn., L.A. County Bar Assn., Beverly Hills Bar Assn.; past pres. Calif. Copyright Conf. 1973-74, past pres. L.A. Copyright Soc. 1974-75; Princeton Club (So. Calif. pres. 1975-78); past mem. United Way Discretionary Fund Distbn. and Research Coms.; mil: US Army 1958-59 (pvt.), 1961-62 (2d lt.). Res: 622 Alta Dr Beverly Hills 90210 Ofc: Gang, Tyre & Brown, Inc., 6400 Sunset Blvd Los Angeles 90028

RAMEY, LEONARD WESTON, general surgeon; b. Sept. 30, 1904, Blaine, Ky.; s. Alonza and Rebecca (Bishop) R.; m. Kathryn, July 3, 1934; children: Lois b. 1937, Kathryn b. 1940, Leonard, Jr. b. 1946; edn: pre-med. cert. Columbia Union Coll. 1931, MD, and internship, Loma Linda Univ., 1931-36. Diplomate Am. Board of Surgery 1961. Career: general practice of medicine and surgery, Clarks Summit, Pa. 1936-43; physician Army Med. Corps in China, Burma, India Theatre 1943-45; surg. residency White Meml. Hosp., Los Angeles 1946-47, VA Hosp. 1947-50; practice of medicine and surgery in Yuma, Az. 1951-57; splst. in gen. surg., Canoga Park, Calif. 1957-77, operating Mission Hosps. in Zambia and Botswanna, Africa 1977-79; chief of surgery, two hosps.; mem: Fellow Am. Coll. of Surgeons (1962), Calif. Med. Assn., L.A. County Med. Soc., Am. Legion, Kiwanis Intl., Toastmasters Club (Area Gov.); publs: research problem on Hepato-Renal Syndrome (1947-8); mil: major Med. Corps AUS 1943-45, Unit Citation; Republican; Seventh-day Adventist; rec: tennis, gardening. Res: 8540 Faust Ave Canoga Park 91304

RAMISETTI, DATTATREYA KUMAR, physician; b. June 26, 1946, Madras, Tamilnadu, India; s. Venkatasubba Rao and Seetamma (Kandriga) R.; m. Shuba, Feb. 8, 1974; children: Pavan b. 1975, Anjali b. 1976, Kirtana b. 1978; edn: Sri Venkateswara Coll. 1963; MBBS, Gandhi Med. Coll. 1970; MD, Osmania Univ. Career: postgrad. tng., 1971-77; staff physician VA Medical Ctr., East Orange, NJ 1977-79; clin. asst. prof. Dept. Medicine, New Jersey MediCal Sch., 1979; currently: pvt. med. practice, chmn. Med. Service and med. dir. Respiratory Therapy (chief of staff 1983-84), HiDesert Medical Ctr., Joshua Tree; mem: Fellow Am. Coll. of Chest Physicians, Am. Coll. of Physicians; 3 publs. in med. literature; Democrat; Hindu; rec: English lit., tennis. Ofc: D. Kumar Ramisetti MD Inc. 58471 29 Palms Hwy Ste 103 Yucca Valley 92284

RAMOS, FRANK RICHARD, executive search consultant; b. June 19, 1950, NY, NY; s. Frank and Carmen (Cruz) R.; edn: BA, Rutgers Univ. 1972. Career: sales rep. Hoffman La Roche 1972-75; mktg. rep. ofc. prods. div. IBM, NY, NY 1975-77; exec. recruiter, Durhill, San Diego 1978-79; pres. ACRES, La Jolla 1979−; honors: sev. prodn. awards, Dunhill; 100 Percent Club, IBM; mem. YMCA; Republican; Catholic; rec: gourmet cooking, racquetball, travel. Res: 3263-201 Caminito E Bluff La Jolla 92037 Ofc: ACRES Inc., 8950 Villa La Jolla Dr. Ste. 1200 La Jolla 92037

RAMSEY, JACK, library director; b. June 12, 1922, Kansas City, Kans.; s. Clay and Floy R.; m. Sue Worsley, Apr. 4, 1946; edn: AB, Univ. of Kans. 1945; MS, Univ. of Ill. 1946, MLS, 1947. Career: librarian New York Public Lib., 1947-48; adminstrv. asst. Lib. of Stockton and San Joaquin co., 1948-49; County librarian Solano County, 1949-52; lib. director City of Glendale 1952-59, 1966−; chief of customer relations H.W. Wilson Co., NYC, 1959-65; honors: Beta Phi Mu (past pres.); mem. NY Library Club, 1947- (past pres.), Phi Kappa Psi frat.; Republican; Episcopal (vestryman); rec: music, travel. Res: 548 Mesa-Lila Rd Glendale 91208 Ofc: 222 East Harvard St Glendale 91205

RAMSEY, MARY ANN, banker; b. Jan. 21, 1948, Roswell, N.M.; d. Leonard Thomas and Mary Ethel (Foster) Ferguson; 1 son, Douglas b. 1967; edn: Eastern New Mexico Univ. 1966, Texas Tech. Univ. 1967. Career: customer service ofcr., E.D.P., Lubbock (Tx.) Nat. Bank, 1967-77; customer mktg. ofcr., E.D.P., California First Bank, Santa Ana 1977-78; adminstrv. ofcr. Nat. Dept. Calif. First Bank, San Francisco 1978-80, corp. banking ofcr. 1980-82, asst. v.p. 1982-84, v.p. 1984-85; v.p./mgr. Corporate Banking Ctr., Calif. First Bank, Irvine 1985−; mem. Indsl. League of Orange County, World Trade Assn.; civic: National Council BSA (com. mem.), Boy Scouts Am./Orange Co. (dist. chair Explorer Div.), Performing Arts Ctr. Triathlon (bd.), Orange Co. Burn Assn. (bd.), Orangewood Home for Dependent Children (Steering com.);

Democrat; Baptist; rec: ski, backpack, scuba, canoeing. Ofc: California First Bank 2001 Michelson Dr Irvine 92715

RAMSEY, WILLIAM RAY, lawyer; b. Aug. 26, 1951, Oakland; s. Roscoe Lee and Zelma Mary (Robinson) R.; 1 son, Steven Paul b. 1972; edn: AA, Los Angeles Valley Coll. 1972; JD, San Fernando Valley Coll. of Law 1980; admitted Calif. State Bar 1981. Career: tax law splst. IRS L.A. 1975-78; investigator U.S. Dept. of Labor 1978-81; atty. Roller & Ramsey Encino 1981–; broker Ramsey Realty 1981–; private investigator Ramsey Investigations 1981–; guest spkr. Kiwanis Club 1982; honors: Cert. of Appreciation (IRS 1978); mem: Calif. trial Lawyers Assn., Calif., San Fernando Valley Bar Assn., Gun Owners of Calif., Southwest Pistol League (dir., bd. dirs. 1978-83); works: arranged acquisition by Nature Conservancy of most environmentally sensitive pvt. property in So. Calif. preserving 14 rare and endangered plant species; Republican; rec: handgun competition, karate, bicycling, weightlifting. Res: 27068-5 Hideaway St Canyon Country 91351 Ofc: Roller & Ramsey 15760 Ventura Blvd, Ste 700, Encino 91436

RAMSEYER, LOWELL MORRIS, lawyer; b. Mar. 25, 1933, Elkton, Mich.; s. Allen Eicher and Hazel Dewey (Flint) R.; m. Helen, June 19, 1953; 1 son, John Allen b. 1959; edn: AA, Glendale Coll. 1959; BS, USC 1961, LLB, 1964, JD, 1964; admitted Calif. State Bar 1964. Career: prosecutor, then senior trial atty. Civil Div., Los Angeles City Attorney's Office, 1965-71; atty. Harrington, Foxx, Dubrow, Canter & Keene (and predecessor firm Dryden, Harrington and Swartz), Los Angeles 1971–, partner 1974-, currently senior trial atty. and mng. ptnr.; honors: USC Public Adminstrn. Student of the Year 1961, Blackstonian Law Hon. Soc. 1962, Psi Sigma Alpha (intl. pol. sci. hon.) 1961; mem: Am., Calif., Los Angeles County bar assns., Defense Research Inst., Am. Bd. of Trial Advocates, Am. Arbitration Assn., YMCA; mil: s/sgt. USAF 1952-57; Republican; Prot.; rec: flying, boating. Ofc: Harrington, Foxx, Dubrow, Canter & Keene, 611 West Sixth St Los Angeles 90017

RAMSTEIN, WILLIAM L., manufacturing co. executive; b. July 9, 1950, Los Angeles; s. Robert J. and Norma E. (Knapp) R.; edn: BS, CSU Northridge 1975; MBA, USC 1984; CPA, Calif. (1980), Cert. Internal Auditor (1980). Career: senior internal auditor Los Angeles County 1975-78; audit senior, mgmt. cons. Alexander Grant & Co., Van Nuys 1978-80; head fin. Missile Sys. Group Hughes Aircraft Co., Canoga Park 1980–; independent finl. cons. and advisor 1980–; awards: Haskins & Sells Award for Outstanding Achiev. in Acctg. (1974), Beta Gamma Sigma (1984); mem. Calif. Soc. of CPAs; rec: investments, tennis. Res: 4310 Torreon Dr. Woodland Hills 91364 Ofc: Hughes Aircraft Co., 8433 Fallbrook Ave. Canoga Park 91304

RANBARGER, KIM ROBERT, surgeon; b. July 15, 1948, Dubuque, Iowa; s. Robert Francis and Myrtle Frances (Redding) R.; m. Anita Christine Thompson, Dec. 27, 1969; 1 dau. Amy Lynn b. 1978; edn: BS, Univ. of San Diego 1969; MD, Med. Coll. of Wisc. 1974. Career: surgical res. Med. College of Wisc., Affiliated Hosps. Milwaukee, 1975-76, surg. res. Univ. of Mo. Med. Center, Columbia, Mo. 1976-79; staff surgeon Naval Hosp., San Diego 1979-83, vascular surgery fellow 1983-84; staff surgeon Naval Hosp., Oakland 1984–; instr. surgical residents and interns; awards: Certified, Am. Bd. of Surgery 1980; Fellow Am. Coll. of Surgeons (FACS); mem. San Diego Soc. of General Surgeons, Assn. of Mil. Surgeons of the US, Pan Pacific Surg. Assn.; publs: contbr. Am. Jour. Surg. (1982); mil: CDR (MC) USNR, Active Duty 1979-, Navy Expeditionary Medal, Humanitarian Svc. Medal, Sea Service, Pistol Sharpshooter; Catholic; rec: sailing, backpacking, camping. Res: 1571 Beryl St San Diego 92109 Ofc: Dept. of Surgery, Naval Hospital, Oakland 94627

RANDALL, JEANNE, certified public accountant; b. June 21, 1958, Los Angeles; d. Melvin Hammond and Joan Claudette (Buie) Runsvold; m. Craig Randall, July 14, 1984; edn: BS, CSU Northridge 1981; grad. Dale Carnegie course 1985; lic. CPA, Calif., AICPA (1985). Career: property acct. Dataproducts Corp., Woodland Hills 1978-81; staff acct. Kustin & Katz Acctncy. Corp., Los Angeles 1981-83; senior acct. Smith & Stephens Acctncy. Corp., Pasadena 1983-85; pres. Randall Acctncy. Corp., Woodland Hills 1985–; mem. Calif. Soc. CPAs; past pres. LA Pierce Coll. Ski Club (1977-78); Republican; Christian Sci.; rec: ski, racquetball, tennis, biking. Ofc: Randall Acctncy. Corp. 5525 Oakdale Ave Ste 250 Woodland Hills 91364

RANDAWA, ZAFAR IQBAL, medical researcher, biochemist; b. Feb. 3, 1948, Lahore, Pakistan, nat. US cit. 1983; s. Dr. Iqbal Hussain and Zubaida Begum (Chaudhry) R.; m. Rodica, Feb. 13, 1982; edn: BS, Univ. of Panjab, Lahore, Pakistan 1965; BS, honors, Univ. of Karachi, Pakistan 1967, MS, 1968; PhD, Univ. of Oregon Health Scis. Ctr. 1981. Career: lectr. biochem., Univ. of Karachi, Pakistan 1968-74; staff research assoc. UC Med. Sch., San Francisco 1974-77; pre-doctoral studies Univ. of Oregon Health Scis. Ctr., Portland 1977-81; postdoctoral fellow/research biochemist Children's Hosp., Oakland 1981–; guest speaker Aichi and Fukuoka Med. Univs. in Japan (12/83); research: discovered new human embryonic hemoglobin in Portland, Ore. and named it Hemoglobin Portland II (1981), elucidated the primary structure (amino acid sequence) of an enzyme (Thioesterase II) which is present in mammalian breast during lactation, this enzyme is now believed to be involved in breast cancer; contbr. 15+ original research papers in sci. jours. and presentations in U.S.; mem. Biochem. Assn., Pakistan (secty. 1972-74); club: Marin Cricket (Larkspur); Republican; rec: travel, fishing. Res: 405 Via Casitas Greenbrae 94904 Ofc: Childrens Hospital of No California 747 52nd St Oakland 94609

RANDOLPH, HERBERT WILLIAM, engineer; b. Apr. 29, 1921, Lafayette, Ind.; s. Herbert Wm. and Opal Pearl (Driscoll) R.; edn: BS, mech. engring., Purdue Univ. 1947; Reg. Profl. Engr. (Mech. Engrg., 1959; Civil Engrg., 1977) Calif. Career: senior engr. Bechtel Power Corp., San Francisco 1972-83; gen. engr. US Navy, San Bruno, 1983–; mem: Soc. of Mil. Engrs., Nat. Soc. of Profl. Engrs., ASHRAE (treas. Las Vegas chpt. 1967-68), Am. Legion, Islam Shriners (SF), Sierra Club; mil: 1st lt., navigator US Army Air Force 1942-46, Air Medal, Presdtl. Group Cit.; Republican; Protestant; rec: painting, fishing. Res: 1551 Southgate Ave Ste 116 Daly City 94015 Ofc: US Navy, ROICCPAC, POB 418, San Bruno 94066-0720

RANFTL, ROBERT MATTHEW, aerospace co. executive, management consultant; b. May 31, 1925, Milwaukee, Wis.; s. Joseph Sebastian and Leona Elaine (Goetz) R.; m. Marion S. Goodman, Oct. 12, 1946; edn: BSEE, Univ. Mich. 1946; grad. work in mgmt. and behavioral scis., Univ. Mich., UC Los Angeles. Career: product engr. Russell Electric Co. (Raytheon), Chgo. 1946-47; head engring. dept. Radio Inst. of Chgo., 1947-50; senior project engr. Webster Chicago Corp. 1950-51; var. mgmt. pos. Hughes Aircraft Co., Los Angeles 1951-74; corporate dir. Engring. and Design Mgmt., 1974-84; pres. Ranftl Ents. Inc. (mgmt. cons.), 1981–; corp. dir. Managerial Productivity, Hughes Aircraft Co., 1984–; guest lectr. var. univs. (incl. Caltech, Univ. Calif., Cornell), conduct hundreds of seminars (on leadership, creativity, and personal, managerial, orgnzl. and operational productivity) for managerial groups in US and abroad; apptd. mem. White House Conf. on Productivity, DOD Productivity Task Force; mem. Acad. of Mgmt., AAAS, Am. Inst. Aero. and Astro., Am. Soc. Engring. Edn., IEEE, Inst. of Mgmt. Scis., NY Acad. of Scis., Univ. Mich. Alumni Assn., UCLA Alumni Assn.; author: R&D Productivity (1974, 78; 150,000+ copies in print); coauthor: Productivity: Prospects for Growth (Van Nostrand Reinhold, 1981); rec: archeology, art, hist. Ofc: Ranftl Enterprises Inc POB 49892 Los Angeles 90049

RANKIN, HELEN CROSS, cattle ranch/guest ranch owner; b. Aug. 3, Kern County, d. John Whisman and Cleo Rebecca (Tilley) Cross; m. Leroy Rankin (dec. 1954), Jan. 4, 1936; children: Julia (King) b. 1939, Patricia (Denvir) b. 1940, William John b. 1945; edn: AB, USC 1935. Career: owner/opr. Leroy Rankin Cattle Ranch (founded 1863 by Walker Rankin Sr.) with husband 1936-1954, 1954–, founder/pres. and gen. mgr. Rankin Ranch, Inc. (guest ranch with internat. clientele) 1965–; frequent lectr. hist. groups on Calif. and Rankin family hist.; mem. US Bur. of Land Mgmt., Sect. 15; honors: mem. US Food and Agri. Leaders Tour China (1983), Tour Australia and N.Z. (1985), Calif. Hist. Soc. award (1983), Kern River Valley Hist. Soc. award (1983); mem: Nat. Cattlemens Assn./Kern Co. chpt., Am. Nat. Cowbelles Assn. (pres. Kern Co. Cowbelles 1949); civic: Childrens Home Soc. of Calif. (pres. Central Sect. 1945), Lori Brock Jr. Museum (patron), Calif. Hist. Assn., Kern River Valley Hist. Assn., Bakersfield Racquet Club; publs: advt. for Rankin Ranch Inc., hist. research on Calif. and Rankin Family hist.; Republican; Baptist; rec: painting, gardening. Address: Rankin Ranch Box 36 Caliente 93518

RAPP, PHILIP HENRY, communications media specialist; b. Sept. 12, 1929, Mpls.; s. Carl Henry and Hylda Ellen (Mann) R.; edn: AA video, San Diego City Coll. 1970; BA art, San Diego State Univ. 1954. Career: engrg. illustrator General Dynamics Corp. San Diego 1955-63; senior scientific illustrator Marine physical Lab. San Diego 1963-83, communications media specialist 1983–; computer products designer DesignLine San Diego 1985–; USICA Am. Cultural Splst. to Syria; honors: Grant (TV Lighting Seminar Damascus, Syria 1979), 1st Art Award (Art Methods Magazine NY 1973), 4 awards (Indsl. Graphics Internat. 1979), Silver Medal (IFPA Audio/ Visual Dept. of the Yr. 1980); mem: Information Film Producers of Am. (nat. v.p.), Marine Technol. Soc. (councilor); CINE US Internat. Film Festival Chmn. Judging Panel 1979-; Oceans 85 Film Festival chmn.; Remotely Oper. Vehicle Film Festival chmn. 1983-85; author: Color Television Textbook of Lighting (publ. in Arabic, Kuwait 1979); rec: computer graphics, multi-image travel shows. Res: 2208 Linwood St San Diego 92110 Ofc: Marine Physical Lab. Bldg 106 NOSC Bayside San Diego 95152

RARICK, WILLIAM JOHN, clinical psychologist; b. Sept. 29. 1955, Long Beach, Calif.; s. William John and Doris Jean (Cowman) R.; m. Ruth, June 19, 1976; children: Lindsey b. 1983, Philip b. 1985; edn: BS psychol., honors, Calif. Lutheran Coll. 1976; MA theol., Fuller Theol. Seminary 1980; PhD clin. psychol. Fuller Grad. Sch. of Psychol. 1982; lic. clin. psychol. Calif. 1984; marriage, family & child counselor Calif. 1983. Career: pre- and postdoct. intern psychol. Camarillo State Hosp. 1981-83; psychol. asst. Conejo Counseling Ctr. Westlake Village 1981-83, Lester Summerfield & Assoc. Thousand Oaks 1980-84; psychol. cons. Calif. Lutheran Coll. 1982–; clin. psychol./ptnr. Conejo Assoc. in Psych. and Psychol. Svcs. T.O. 1984–; psychol. staff Woodview-Calabasas Psych. Hosp. 1984–; pres. John Rarick PhD, Inc., A Psychol. Corp. T.O. 1985–; cons. psychol. Bible Fellowship Ch. Counseling Ctr. Ventura 1985–; bd. dirs. Emmanuel Christian Counseling Ctr. T.O. 1983-84; honors: Baranski Award in Psychol. (Cal. Lutheran Coll. 1976), Calif. State Scholar (1975-76), listed: Outstanding Young Men in Am. (1984), Who's Who Students in Am. Colls. and Univs. (1975-76); mem: Am. Psychol. Assn. 1983-, Calif. Psychol. Assn. 1983-, Ventura Co. Psychol. Assn. 1984-, Nat. Register Health Svc. Providers in Psychol. 1984-, T.O. Rotary 1985-; Democrat; Lutheran; rec: fishing, camping, water sports, music (instrumental & vocal). Ofc: 501 Marin St Ste 104 Thousand Oaks 91360

RASMUSSEN, STUART RICARD, newspaper librarian; b. Nov. 7, 1906, San Francisco; s. Emil Jorgen and Christine (Johnsen) R.; m. Nairn Margaret

Abbott, June 1, 1940; children: Nairn Christine, Mark Abbott; edn: stu., Univ. Calif. Ext. Career: in library San Francisco Examiner 1929-37; head librarian San Francisco Call Bulletin 1937-59, San Francisco News Call Bulletin 1959-66; library staff San Francisco Examiner 1966—; asst. head librarian 1966-75; acting head librarian 1975-78; engaged in spl. research for Metro-Goldwyn- Mayer movies, San Francisco Bay area 1935—; actor Maxwell Burke Stock Co., Oakland and Berkeley 1927-28, Blacke, Turner Stock Co., San Francisco area 1928; dir. children and adult plays San Geronimo Valley Community Ctrs.; sometimes dir. Ross Valley Players Barn Theatre; pres. Lagunitas Dist. Sch. bd. 1955-58, San Geronimo Valley Little League 1961; mem: Spl. Libraries Assn., Am. Newspaper Guild (charter San Francisco/ Oakland chpt.), San Francisco Press Club (life); author: drama reviews, The Peninsulan, 1936; sev. plays for children 1955-60; Democrat. Ofc: 110 5th St. San Francisco 94118

RATCLIFF, RALPH ANDERSON, manufacturing co. executive; b. Mar. 17, 1910, Kingman, Ind.; s. Edmond Baxter and Mary Dinah (Ephlin) R.; m. Margaret Hallie Buck, Nov. 20, 1932; children: Sandra Isabelle b. 1934, Bruce Ephlin b. 1941; edn: BSME, Purdue Univ. 1932. Career: chmn. Ratcliff Hoist Co., San Carlos; manufactured the 1st 5-horse gang plow hitch, 1st disposable plow share, 1st deep tillage mold board plow, 1st chisel plow, 1st ratchet lever hoist to be used commercially, 1st ratchet lever load binder (saved thousands of lives), 1st portable electric hoist, 1st dommer (helped return the dust bowl to farming prodn.); mfr. currently single take up load binder (safest on market); sev. patents; mil: capt. US Army WWII, Bronze Star, Purple Heart w/2 clusters. Res: 1300 Sunnyslope Ave Belmont 94002 Ofc: Ratcliff Hoist Co. 1655 Old County Road San Carlos 94002

RATLIFF, RICHARD JAMES, wholesale plumbing distbr. co. executive; b. June 3, 1924, Stockton; s. James and Clorinda (Fugazzi) R.; m. Mattie Lou, Jan. 7, 1945; children: Richard J., Jr. b. 1950, Susan Carol b. 1954. Career: purch. agt. Western Plbg. Supply Co., 1964-70, asst. mgr. 1970-80; mgr. P.E. O'Hair & Co., Stockton 1980-84, corporate v.p., 1984—; Republican; Catholic. Res: 1719 Greeley Way Stockton 95207 Ofc: P.E. O'Hair & Co. POB 1529 Stockton 95201

RAVEN, RONALD E., real estate broker; b. Mar. 23, 1949, Stockton; s. Robert Lacy and Arlene R.; m. Linda, Feb. 14, 1985; children: Chris b. 1969, (step): Ryan b. 1971, Anika b. 1978; edn: BS, Cal Poly St. Univ., Pomona 1971; Calif. lic. R.E. Broker; desig: Cert. Apt. Mgr. (CAM), Long Beach Apartment Assn. Career: hosp. rep. Lawler Business Prods., Los Angeles 1973-77; pres. Pacifica Far West States, Inc., 1977—; owner The Hughes Co.; mem. Foothill Apartment Assn. (dir.), Arlington CofC (v.p.), Riverside 2% Club; Republican; rec: golf. Res: 8676 Limestone Dr Riverside 92504 Ofc: PFS, 7155 Magnolia Ave Riverside 92504

RAWUKA, ANDREW CHARLES, research engineer; b. Feb. 7, 1922, Kief, N.Dak.; s. Andrew and Anna (Bokovoy) R.; m. Janet Genismore, July 18, 1953; children: Gregory b. 1955, William b. 1957, Pamela b. 1960; edn: BS chem. engr., Univ. N. Dak. 1948; MS chem. engr., Bucknell Univ. 1949; MS environmental eng., Loyola Univ. Los Angeles 1974; Reg. Profl. Chem. Engr., Calif. 1965. Career: process insp. Carnegie-Ill. Steel Corp., Gary, Ind. 1941-42; group engr., head of Materials Thermodynamics Lab., Douglas Aircraft Co., Santa Monica 1952-76; staff engr. Space Div. Rockwell Internat., Downey 1976-77; project engr. Calif. Air Resources Board, El Monte 1977-80; rules staff engr. South Coast Air Quality Mgmt. District, El Monte 1980—; honors: research fellow North Dakota Research Found., Grand Forks, N.D. (1949-51), Sigma Tau (1947), Sigma Xi (1950); mem: Temperature Measurement Soc. (pres. 1971-72), Am. Chem. Soc. 1947-, Air Pollution Control Assn. 1984-; clubs: Masons, Y's Mens Club of Santa Monica (YMCA affil.); publs: sev. tech. papers, presentations at Air Poll. Control Assn. Conf. (6/84), AIChE (1965), Temperature Measurement Soc. (1967, 69), Soc. of Plastic Engrs. (1966); mil: s/sgt. US Army 1942-46, ETO Battle Stars; Republican Methodist; rec: golf, vegetable gardening. Res: 3225 Barry Ave Los Angeles 90066

RAY, DAVID LEWIN, lawyer; b. June 17, 1929, Los Angeles; s. Herbert and Beatrice (Lewin) R.; m. Arlene Opas, 1950; children: Stephan, and Robyn; edn: BS, UC Los Angeles 1954; JD, Univ. San Fernando Valley Coll. of Law 1969. Career: partner in CPA firm of Ray and Ray; ptnr. CPA firm of Zigmond, Ray and Co.; ptnr. in law firm Ray, Rolston and Ress; ptnr. in law firm Saltzburg & Ray, now Saltzburg, Ray and Bergman, Los Angeles; vice pres. Management Affiliates; vice pres. Things From All Over, Inc.; mem: Am. Inst. of CPAs, Am. Bar Assn., Sigma Beta Chi/Nu Beta Epsilon; mil: pfc US Army 1951-53; rec: sailing, diving, golf, tennis. Ofc: Saltzburg, Ray and Bergman, 10960 Wilshire Blvd Ste 1212 Los Angeles 90024

RAY, GLENN JERRY, computer graphics executive; b. May 8, 1932, Indiansprings, Ala.; s. Roy Andy and Lydia Conella (Sanders) R.; m. Mary Claussen, Dec. 21, 1968; edn: Sarrland Ala. Murphy Sch., Mobile, Ala.; BAIA, CSU Long Beach 1973; Calif. Comm. Coll. Tchg. Credentials (arch., engrg., related tech.) 1972; Std. Sec. Tchg. Cred. 1973. Career: engring. assoc. design No. Am. Rockwell 1962-64 (designed Apollo instrument panel structure and air condtg. sys. for Apollo Trainer (for tng. astronauts); supvr., sr. design, Hughes Aircraft, Fullerton 1964-67; sr. designer, Lead design, TRW, Redondo Bch. 1967-70; proj. engr. Am. Meter, Fullerton, 1973-75; proj. engr., Scanbe, El Monte, 1975-77; mgr., design, Gen. Automation, Anaheim 1978-79; real estate sales, Allstate, 1979-80; mgr. design, Fairchild, Manhattan Beach, 1980—; instr. blueprint reading Fairchild pgm., 1981-; tchr. L.A. Trade Tech. Coll. (blueprint reading 1975; CAD/CAM 1982-84, computer automated de-

sign/computer automated mfg.); mem: ASCUS, CAD/CAM Users Grp.; publs: Design, Drafting, Mfg. Workbook (Glenn J. Ray and Fairchild Control Systems Co., 1982, 2d. ed. 1983); tchg. manual for adv. archit., mech. drafting; winner nat. poetry contest, Reformed Ch. (poem set to music and recorded) 1951; Poems and Memories (1970); mil: s/sgt. USAF, 1950-54, supvsd. drafting grp. Republican; Prot.; rec: woodworking, photog., writing poetry. Res: 2024 Ravenhill Ct Fullerton 92631 Ofc: Fairchild Control Systems Co., 1800 Rosecrans Ave Manhattan Bch 90266

RAY, SANDRA SUE, clinical social worker; b. July 1, 1944, Lincoln, Nebr.; d. Francis Harlow and Ellene Sigrid (Melsted) Goldsmith; children: Dana Sue Lenhart b. 1967, Brandon Garrett Lenhart b. 1969, Nicole Sharron Ray b. 1979; edn: BS, Univ. of Ore. 1964; MSW, UCLA 1966; LCSW, Calif. (1975). Career: deputy probation ofcr. L.A. County Probation Dept. 1970-78; guidance mgr. L.A. Job Corps, Hollywood 1978-79; clin. dir. Penny Lane, Sepulveda 1980-83; clinician Hathaway Home for Children, Lake View Terrace 1983-85; dir. residential svcs. Calabasas Acad. 1985—; psychiat. cons. I-ADARP, Inc. Reseda/Van Nuys 1981-; assoc. prof. Calif. Sch. of Profl. Psychol., 1975-78; honors: Alpha Kappa Delta (1964); Democrat; Methodist; rec: theater, LA Civic Light Opera. Res: 7806 Rhea Ave Reseda 91335 Ofc: Calabasas Academy 25000 Mureau Rd Calabasas 91302

RAYMOND, GENE, actor, director, producer, composer; b. Aug. 13, 1908, NYC; s. LeRoy D. and Mary (Smith) Guion; m. Jeanette MacDonald June 16, 1937 (dec. Jan. 14, 1965); m. former Mrs. Nel Bentley Hees, Sept. 7, 1974. Career: began acting at age five in stock prodns., Broadway debut in "The Piper" 1920, other Broadway appearances include: "Eyvind of the Hills" w. Edward G. Robinson, Margaret Wycherly 1921; "Cradle Snatchers" w. Mary Boland, Edna May Oliver, Humphrey Bogart, 1925; "The Man in Possessions" w. Gertrude Lawrence, Dennis, Mass. (1946; "The Guardsman" w. Jeanette MacDonald, 1951; "The Voice of the Turtle" w. Geraldine Brooks, 1952; "Petrified Forest" 1952; "Call Me Madam" 1952; "Private Lives" 1953; "The Moon is Blue" 1953; "The Devil's Disciple" 1954; "Romeo and Juliet" (Mercutio) 1956; "Seven Year Itch" 1958; "Holiday for Lovers" 1959; "The Best Man" 1960; "Majority of One," "Write Me A Murder," "Kiss Me Kate," and "Candida," 1962; "Madly in Love" 1963; motion picture prodns. include "Ladies of the Big House" w. Sylvia Signey, Para., 1932; "If I Had A Million" w. Charles Laughton, W.C.Fields, Para. 1932; "Red Dust" w. Jean Harlow, Clark Gable, MGM, 1932; "Ex-Lady" w. Bette Davis, Warners, 1933; "Brief Moment" w. Carole Lombard, Col. 1933; "Flying Down to Rio" w. Dolores Del Rio, Ginger Rogers, Fred Astaire, RKO, 1933; "Sadie McKee" w. Joan Crawford, MGM, 1934; "The Woman in Red" w. Barbara Stanwyck, Wrnrs, 1935; "Seven Keys to Baldpate" RKO, 1935; "The Bride Walks Out" w. B. Stanwyck, RKO, 1936; "Mr. and Mrs. Smith" w. C. Lombard, Robt. Montgomery, RKO, 1939; "Smilin' Thru" w. J. MacDonald, Brian Aherne, MGM, 1941; "The Locket" w. Laraine Day, Robt. Mitchum, RKO, 1946; "Sofia" w. Patricia Morrison, Misha Auer, EagLion, 1948; "Hit the Deck!" w. Jane Powell, Tony Martin, MGM, 1957; "The Best Man" w. Henry Fonda, UA, 1964; "I'd Rather Be Rich" w. Maurice Chevalier, UA, 1964; TV appearances include Ed Sullivan's Toast of the Town, Ken Murray Show, Robt. Montgomery Presents, Lux Video Theatre, Pulitzer Prize Theatre, Schlitz Playhouse, Fireside Theatre (Host), TV Readers' Digest (Host), Barbara Stanwyck Show, The Defenders, Outer Limits, Matinee Theatre (actor and dir.), Playhouse 90, others; author teleplay: Prima Donna; song composer: Will you? (Berlin), Let Me Always Sing (Schirmer), Release (Schirmer); civic: Arthritis Found. (v.p.), Motion Pic. and TV Fund (past pres.), LA Chpt. Air Force Assn. (pres.), Falcon Found. (trustee); mem: Screen Actors Guild (trustee), Acad. TV Arts and Scis. (bd.); clubs: Player's (NYC), NY Athletic, Bel-Air CC, Army and Navy (Wash DC), Order of Daedalians (Kelly Field, Tx.); mil: WWII vol., major US Army Air Corps 1942-45, USAF Reserve w. Strat. Air Cmd, Mil. Airlift Cmd., C-141 Cmd. Pilot missions S.Vietnam, ret. col. 1968; awarded Legion of Merit, USAF; Humanitarian Award, AF Assn.; Better World Award, VFW. Address: 9570 Wilshire Blvd Beverly Hills 90212

RAYNER, ARNO ALFRED, investment co. executive; b. Sept. 23, 1928, San Francisco; s. Kurt Hugo and Angela (Flasch) R.; m. Kenyon Lee Reld, June 14, 1951; children: Eric b. 1955, Jill b. 1957, Neal b. 1967; edn: BS, UC Berkeley 1949, MBA, 1954; desig: Chartered Finl. Analyst, Inst. of CFA (1965). Career: senior v.p., investments, Indsl. Indemnity Co., San Francisco 1954-74; v.p., trust & thrift inv., Bechtel Internat. Services, San Francisco 1974-76; pres. Rayner Assocs. Inc., Mill Valley 1977—; dir. Beaver Ins., S.F. (1975-85); dir. Invest-in-Am. No. Calif. Council, S.F.; mem: fellow Financial Analysts Fedn. (1974), S.F. Soc. of Security Analysts, S.F. Bond Club, S.F. Munic. Bond Club, Am. Fin. Assn.; civic: S.F. Kiwanis (v.p., dir.), Bohemian Club, World Trade Club, Merchants Exchange Club, Tiburon Peninsula Club; mil: US Army (Fin. chief cashier) 1951-52; Republican; Lutheran; rec: tennis, philately. Res: 275 E Strawberry Dr Mill Valley 94941 Ofc: Rayner Associates Inc 655 Redwood Hwy Ste 370 Mill Valley 94941

REA, KATHRYN P., data processing consultant; b. Aug. 23, 1957, Los Angeles; d. Virginia Robinson Rea; edn: BS, State Univ. NY 1981; cert. data communications, Univ. Calif. 1983; lic. real estate broker Calif. 1980. Career: pres., CEO The Consulting Edge Inc. 1983—; instr. seminars in data communications; mem: Assn. for Computing Machinery, IEEE, Inst. for Mgmt. Sci.; publs: articles and book on data communications and computer systems; rec: reading. Res: 532 W Knoll Dr Los Angeles 90048

REAGAN, NANCY, first lady of U.S.; b. July 9, 1923, NYC, raised in Chgo.; d. Dr. Loyal and Edith (Luckett) Davis; father Prof. of Surgery 30 years, now

Prof. Emeritus, Northwestern Univ.; bro. Dr. Richard Davis, neurosurgeon, Phila.; m. Ronald Reagan, March 4, 1952; children: Patrician Ann, b. 1952, Ronald Prescott, b. 1958; Pres. Reagan's children by 1st marriage: Maureen, b. 1941, Michael, b. 1946; edn: grad. Girls' Latin Sch., Chgo.; drama major Smith Coll., 1943. Career: actress, stage (road tours to Broadway and Radio City Music Hall), film (11 films include: The Next Voice You Hear; East Side, West Side; Hellcats of the Navy), TV prodns., 1949-56; served as First Lady of Calif., 1966-74; active nat. in Foster Grandparent Program, 1967-, active on behalf of POWs and MIAs internat.; hon. sponsor Vietnam Vets Meml. Fund; hon. chair: Wolf Trap Found. (bd. trustees), Joffrey Ballet Gala, 1981 Cherry Blossom Festival, Repub. Womens Fed. Forum, President's Com. on Employment of Handicapped (Womens' Com.), Ford Theatre Gala, JFK Center for Performing Arts, Nat. Trust for Historic Preservation, Nat. Soc. of Arts and Letters, Nat. Womens Republican Club; hon. pres. Girl Scouts of Am.; honors: One of ten most admired women in USA, Good Housekeeping mag. 1977, LA Times Woman of the Year 1968, California's Most Distinguished Woman, Nat. Art Assn., Permanent Hall of Fame as one of Ten Best Dressed Women in Am. Address: Santa Barbara, Calif.; The White House, Wash DC 20500

REAGAN, RONALD WILSON, President of the United States; b. Feb. 6, 1911, Tampico, Ill.; s. John and Nellie (Wilson) R.; m. Jane Wyman, 1940, div. 1948; children: Maureen, Michael; m. 2d. Nancy Davis, Mar. 4, 1952; children: Patricia, Ronald; edn: BA in econ. and sociol., Eureka Coll. 1932. Career: radio sports broadcaster and editor, 1932-37; film actor, over 50 feature-length motion pictures, 1937-50s; prodn. supr./host General Electric Theatre TV series 1950s, host, Death Valley Days TV series 1964-65; elected Gov. of Calif. 1966-70, re-elected 1970-74; syndicated radio commentary pgm., newspaper column, extensive speaking schedule to civic, bus., polit. groups nat., 1974-; mem. Presidential Commn. investigate the CIA, 1974-75; candidate for Repub. presidential nom. 1976, campaigner for 86 candidates in 1978 elections; elected US President (by electoral vote 489-40), Nov. 4, 1980, sworn in as 40th US President Jan. 20, 1981, elected 2d term 1984-88; founder Citizens for the Republic; past bd. dirs. Com. on the Present Danger; past pres. Screen Actors Guild 6 terms; past pres. Motion Picture Indus. Council 2 terms; awards include Nat. Humanitarian, NCCJ; Torch of Life, City of Hope; Horatio Alger; Am. Newspaper Guild; Freedoms Found. awards; Distinguished Am., Nat. Football Found. Hall of Fame; Am. Patriots Hall of Fame; Medal of Valor, State of Israel; mil: capt. USAAF 1942-45, WWII; Tau Kappa Epsilon. Address: Santa Barbara, Calif.; The White House Wash DC 10500

REAL, MANUEL LAWRENCE, U.S. district judge; b. Jan. 27, 1924, San Pedro; s. Francisco Jose and Maria (Mansano) R.; m. Stella Emilia Michalik, Oct. 15, 1955; children: Michael, Melanie Marie, Timothy, John Robert; edn: BS, USC 1944, stu. fgn. trade 1946-48; LLB, Loyola Sch. of Law 1951; admitted to Calif. Bar 1952. Career: asst. U.S. Atty.'s Ofc., Los Angeles 1952-55; pvt. practice law, San Pedro 1955-64; U.S. atty., So. Dist. Calif. 1964-66; U.S. dist. judge 1966–; currently, chief judge; mem: Fed., Am., Calif. and Los Angeles Bar Assns., Am. Judicature Soc., Chief Spl. Agents Assn., Phi Delta Phi, Sigma Chi, Anchor Club; mil: ensign USNR 1943-46; Democrat; Catholic. Ofc: 312 No. Spring St. Los Angeles 90012 REASER, WARREN ELMER, charter airline pilot; b. Nov. 23, 1932, Linden, Pa.; s. Calvin Edgar and Dorothy May (Robbins) R.; m. Evelyn, June 16, 1956; children: John b. 1957, Sharon b. 1959, Arnold b. 1961, Bonnie b. 1964; edn: grad. Moody Bible Inst. 1956-57, grad. Escola de Portuguese, Sao Paulo, Brazil 1960; ATP & FLT instr., advanced ground instr., airframe & power plant mechanic, comml. pilot; Calif. Real Estate lic. Career: pilot Missionary Aviation Fellowship (non-profit Calif. corp.), flying Amazon jungle area with supplies for isolated missionary outposts, approx. 13,000 hrs. 1960-73; flight instr. tng. missionary pilots in mountain flying techniques, USA 1973-80; time share sales Watts & Friery Mktg. Co. at the Tennis Club in Palm Springs 1980-85; opr. Sun Valley Aviation air charter service, Ramona (Calif.) Airport, 1980-86; chief pilot Air Serv Internat. (air service for var. relief and devel. agencies in Ethiopia and Mozambique), Redlands 1985–; awarded Pilot of Year (1980) for 10,000 hrs accident free flying, Missionary Aviation Fellowship; mem. Kiwanis of Ramona; Republican; Born Again Christian; rec: bee keeper and Kiwi grower. Res: 1055 Reaser Ln Ramona 92065 Ofc: Air Serv International 1745 Sessums Dr Redlands 92374

REAVILL, DAVID WILLIAM, stockbroker; b. Sept. 18, 1948, Los Angeles; s. Wm. Arthur and Marian E. (Stocks) R.; edn: AA, Santa Barbara City Coll. 1968; BA, pol. sci., Westmont Coll. 1971, Calif. State Teaching Cred. (life), 1972; MA, ergonomics, UC Santa Barbara 1978; Financial and Ops. Principal, Gen. Securities Prin., Municipal Secs. Prin., Registered Options Prin., Reg. Representive, multi state registration. Career: vice pres. Charles Schwab & Co., Santa Barbara 1978-80; mgr. William Oneil & Co., L.A. 1980-81; founder/ pres./ chief exec. First Los Angkes Discount Securities, Encino; pres. Internat. Bus. Securities, Marina Del Rey; mem: Am. Mgmt. Assn., Finl. Mgrs. Soc., Securities Traders Assn., Better Bus. Bur., CofC, Gr. L.A. Zoo, L.A. County Art Museum; writer/prod. financial T.V. pgms. (seen twice daily in S.F. and L.A.); Democrat; Prot.; rec: swimming, sailing, scuba, hiking. Res: 9150 Tampa Ave, 216, Northridge 91324-2734 Ofc: First Los Angeles Discount Securities, 16055 Ventura Blvd, Ste. 777, Encino 91436

RECHTSTEINER, STEVEN ALLEN, manufacturing co. executive; b. June 25, 1945, Cinti., Ohio; s. Carl J. and Ruth F. (Hucke) R.; m. Barbara A., Dec. 14, 1968; children: Christopher b. 1970, Gregory b. 1974, Stephany Marie b. 1980; edn: B.Arch. Univ. of Notre Dame 1968; grad. work Univ. of Cinti. 1969-70. Career: project architect A.M. Kinney Assocs., Cinti. 1969-72; div. mgr. Bishopric Products Co., Cinti. 1972-76; v.p. sales/mktg. FranRica (A Bishopric Co.) 1976-78, v.p. mktg./adminstrn. 1978-80, v.p./gen. mgr. 1980-84, pres. 1984-85, bd. chmn. 1985–, also bd. chmn. Prodo-Pak (A FranRica Co.) 1984–, dir. Internat. Market Devel., S.H.P. of Paris, France (current owner FranRica Group); honors: Putman Award (1975), I.F.T. Indsl. Achievement Award (1976) for devels. in field of aseptic bulk food storage; mem: Dairy and Food Industry Supply Assn., Food Processing and Machinery Suppliers Assn. (Export Advis. Council, Internat. Trade Com.), Inst. of Food Technologist; civic: Stockton CofC, local school Booster Clubs, PTAs; works: over 60 patents (US and overseas) on food processing and packaging, 8 tech. publs. on food processing and packaging; Ind.; Roman Catholic; rec: boating, golf, architl. design. Ofc: FranRica, POB 1928, Stockton 95201

RECK, R. RANDOLPH, lawyer, b. Apr. 19, 1953, Burbank; s. Herbert, Jr. and Dorothy (Steusoff) R.; edn: BA cum laude, UCLA 1975; JD, Southwestern Univ. Sch. of Law 1979; admitted Calif. State Bar 1980. Career: atty. law firm Edwards and Young, Beverly Hills 1981, Southeast Legal Aid Center, Huntington Park and Compton, 1981-82, law firm Alan A. Joseph, L.A. 1983-85, law firm Reichard and Trammell, L.A. 1985–; honors: Eagle Scout BSA (1969), Phi Gamma Mu (1974-75); mem. bd. dirs. Themis Soc., Southwestern Univ. Sch. of Law 1983-86; club: Toastmasters Internat. (DTM Award 1982; Dist. 52 Toastmaster of Year 1981-82, Dist. Gov. 1984-85); Democrat; Protestant; rec: politics, reading. Res: 415 E Cedar Ave Apt 1, Burbank 91501 Ofc: Reichard and Trammell 501 Shatto Pl Ste 100 Los Angeles 90020

RECTOR, DANIEL MARSHALL, computer software designer; b. Oct. 24, 1946, Tucson, Az.; s. Marshall and Margaret Eileen (Egan) R.; edn: BSEE, CSU San Diego 1969; Pepperdine Univ. Grad. Sch. Business 1974-75. Career: mgr. systems pgm. sect. Burroughs Corp., Pasadena 1971-77; mgr. net. devel. Xerox Computer Svcs., Los Angeles 1977-81; software designer Tandem Computers, Cupertino 1981-84; mgr. software devel. Excelan Corp., San Jose 1984-85; v.p. Technical Services, VideoTex Information Systems Corp., Mt. View 1986–; mem. Assn. Computing Machinery; mil: sp5 US Army 1969-71; Republican; Catholic; rec: computers, stock mkt. Address: 19975 Price Ave Cupertino 95014

REDDEN, W. GLENN, accounting/ financial management executive; b. Feb. 22, 1950, Troy, Ala.; s. William Grover and Marilyn Ruth (Daniell) R.; m. Debra King, June 10, 1972; children: Micah b. 1977, Rebekah b. 1982; edn: BS acctg., magna cum laude, Fla. State Univ. 1974; CPA Calif. 1977. Career: staff acct. Hood & Strong CPAs S.F. 1974-78; acctg. mgr. Humphrey Instruments San Leandro 1978-80; mgr. budgets/ financial planning Alcan Cable Atlanta, Ga. 1980-81, mgr. cost/ inventory acctg. 1981-82; asst. controller Consolidated Fibres Inc. S.F. 1982-84, corp. controller 1984–; cons. part time self-employed; honors: Beta Gamma Sigma (FSU 1973), Exceptional Achievement (Alcan Cable 1982), Community Svc. (City of San Ramon 1984, 85); mem: Calif. Soc. CPAs 1978-, Am. Inst. CPAs 1978-, San Ramon Valley JayCees 1983-85, City of San Ramon (parks & rec. com. chair, creek study com., gen. plan review com.), San Ramon Valley Unif. Sch. Dist. (finance advis. com.); Democrat; rec: wines, investing, running. Res: 2550 Marsh Dr San Ramon 94583 Ofc: Consolidated Fibres Inc. 5327 Jacuzzi St Richmond 94804

REECE, MONTE MEREDITH, lawyer; b. May 29, 1945, Jackson, Tenn.; s. Jerrel Rexford and Marjorie (Ricks) R.; m. Melanie; children: Hugh b. 1970, Bryan b. 1974, Andrew b. 1975, Jerrel b. 1985; edn: Louisiana State Univ. 1963-64, 66; Louisiana Coll. 1964-65; LLB, Western State Univ. Coll. of Law 1974; admitted Calif. State Bar 1974. Career: assoc. atty. English & Marotta APC 1974-78; atty. pvt. practice 1978–; US magistrate US Dist. Ct. Eastern Dist of Calif. 1983-; judge pro tem Lake Valley Jud. Dist. El Dorado Co. 1983-; comm. coll. instr. 1983-85; mem: Lions Club; Vol. Action Com.; AYSO 1982- (bd. dirs. reg. 82); mil: SK2 USNR 1967-72, Navy Achievement Medal with Combat V, Navy Unit Accom., Vietnam Service, Vietnam Campaign (3 awards), National Defense medals; Democrat; Protestant; rec: antique furniture restoration, photog. Address: P.O. Box 70500 S Lake Tahoe 95705

REED, JANNENE G., newspaper editor, publisher; b. Feb. 8, 1929, Wayne, Neb.; d. Frank Marion and Parl Margaret (Stone) Griffith; m. Donald R. Reed, Apr. 5, 1953; children: Cameron Leigh b. 1959, Barbara Jayne b. 1961; edn: BA, Wayne State Coll. 1951, secondary tchrs. degree, Kearney State Coll. 1956. Career: women's ed., feature ed. Wayne (Neb.) Herald 1947-53; comml. artist Gen. Telephone Chgo. 1953-55; art instr. Vermillion, SD, Schs. 1955-59; copywriter C.S. Wo Co. Honolulu 1971-73; pgm. dir. Gospel Light Pubs. Glendale, Calif. 1975-78; stringer Pasadena Star-News 1975-78; ed. San Marino Tribune 1978-80; owner, ed. publr. Sierra Madre News, owner Sierra Madre News Print Shop 1980–; bd. dirs. Methodist Hosp. Arcadia 1983-; honors: Editor of the Yr. (SAR 1982-83), One Earth Award (Sierra Madre Envtl. Action Council), Constitution Week Award (DAR), Martha Washington Medal (SAR), Community Spirit Achievement Award (SAR); mem: Nat. Newspaper Assn., Sigma Delta Chi, num. civic orgns. Sierra Madre; Presbyterian; rec: writing, reading, piano, flute, painting, sketching. Res: 32 S Sunnyside Ave Sierra Madre 91024 Ofc: 9 Kersting Ct Sierra Madre 91024

REED, PEYTON CONAWAY, real estate consultant; b. Aug. 20, 1939, Orange; s. Robert Harold and Lucille Harriet (Conaway) R.; m. Linda Moss, Aug. 16, 1981; edn: AB, USC 1961; Bestatigung, Goethe Inst. Passau, Germany 1964. Career: lifeguard lieut. City of Newport Beach, 1966-68; asst. project mgr. Rancho California/ Kaiser Aetna 1969, mktg. mgr. 1970-71; owner/pres. Peyton Reed & Co. Inc., real estate mkt. research & consulting, 1972–; instr. (R.E. market research) CSU Fullerton, Long Beach City Coll.; guest spkr. Soc. of Real Estate Appraisers; Republican; rec: ski, run, hike. Res: 450 Gaviota

Newport Beach 92660 Ofc: Peyton Reed & Co. Inc. 3416 Via Lido Ste E Newport Beach 92663

REED, RUSTY RAY, management consulting firm executive; b. June 15, 1957, Taylorville, Ill.; s. Carl Ray and Elsie Mabel (Hendricks) R.; edn: BSCE, Univ. of Ill. 1980; Reg. Profl. Engr., Calif. 1983. Career: asst. sect. head project mgmt. sect. Los Angeles Co. Flood Control Dist. 1980-83; assoc. Charles Abbott Assoc. 1984, v.p. 1985−; liason City of Rancho Palo Verdes Traffic Com.; liason City of Palos Verdes Planning Commn.; works: instituted a maintenance mgmt. sys. for the City of Palos Verdes Estates; Republican; Lutheran; rec: computers. Res: 3200 La Rotonda #402 Rancho Palos Verdes 90274 Ofc: Charles Abbott Associates, 6866 Verde Ridge Rd. Rancho Palos Verdes 90274

REES, MARIAN JANET, librarian; b. July 3, 1934, Oak Park, Ill.; d. Ewald and Gertrude Dorothy (Hilbert) Heimert; m. John Robert Rees, Jan. 28, 1956; children: Carol Ellen, John Alton; edn: BA, Indiana Univ. 1956; MA, CSU San Jose 1973. Career: acad. staff Inst. Energy Studies, Stanford Univ. 1974−, head librarian, dir. info. ctr. 1974−; cons. in field; chmn. fgn. langs. in elementary schs., Wheaton, Md. 1967-69; mem: Spl. Libraries Assn., AAAS, Western Info. Network Energy, Calif. Library Assn., Stanford Univ. Library Assn., Internat. Assn. Energy Economists, Energy Librarians Bay Area, publs: author, Energy Modeling: A Selected Bibliography, 1977; ed., Energy Info. Ctr. Selected Acquisitions List, 1975-; Democrat. Res: 1340 Sunrise Ct. Los Altos 94022 Ofc: Stanford Univ., Bldg. 500 Stanford 94305

REESE, ALLEN EDWIN, physician; b. Apr. 23, 1922, Big Rock, Ill.; s. Richard Edwin and Ella Mable (Evans) R.; m. Hazel, July 22, 1944; children: Garren b. 1946, Sharon b. 1956, Allen, Jr. b. 1957, Gary b. 1959; edn: dental tech. Med. Corps, USN and USMC, 1942-45; AA, San Bernardino Valley Coll. 1947; BS, Redlands Univ. 1951; DO, Coll. Osteo. Phys. & Surgeons, L.A. 1955; MD, UC Irvine Coll. of Med. 1962. Career: high sch. sports physician, 12 years; (current): pvt. practice, Auburn; med. cons. Rehabilitation Dept., State of Calif.; hon. staff (bd. dirs. 9 yrs., chmn. emeritus) Siskiyou Gen. Hosp., Yreka; mem. AMA, Calif. Med. Assn., Siskiyou Med. Soc.; mem. Masons, Shriners; research: Thyroid Function; mil: s/sgt. US Marines, pharmacist mate 1c USN; Republican; rec: sports. Address: 23851 Lakeview Ct Auburn 95603

REESE, ARNOLD DEAN, stockbroker; b. Oct. 8, 1949, Denver, Colo.; s. Robert Dean and Marion Rose (Doyle) R.; m. Mary Schumacher, June 18, 1977; 1 son, Nicholas b. 1982; edn: BS, Univ. No. Colo. 1975. Career: loan ofcr. Lloyds Bank Calif., Bakersfield 1977-79; account exec. Merrill Lynch, Bakersfield 1979-, senior account exec. 1982, asst. v.p. 1983, v.p./res. mgr. 1986−; honors: Merrill Lynch Executives Club (1980-81), Pres.'s Club (1982-84), Chairman's Club (1985), Win Smith Fellow (1985); Rotarian (chpt. pres. 1984-85); mil: USN 1969-73, Air Crew, Nat. Def. Service, 2 Merit Unit Citations; Republican; rec: golf. Ofc: Merrill Lynch 4900 California Ave Bakersfield 93309

REESE, CHARLES WOODROW, JR., lawyer; b. June 21, 1944, San Antonio, Tex.; s. Charles W. and Mary Ruth (Gott) R.; m. Jill Fritschi Olsen, 1979; children: Clarissa b. 1972, Alexandra b. 1982; edn: BA, cum laude, Washington and Lee Univ. 1966; JD, Boalt Hall Sch. of Law, UCB 1969. Career: atty., law firm McCutchen, Doyle, Brown and Enersen, San Francisco, 1970-75; atty., Kaiser Industries Corp. and Kaiser Cement Corp., 1975-78; asst. gen. counsel, Kaiser Cement Corp., 1978−; trustee Clotilde DeMartini Trusts, 1976-; mng. dir. Reese Interests, 1978-; hon. trustee Orinda Foundation, 1976-; bd. dirs. Planned Parenthood 1981-; honors: Omicron Delta Upsilon (1966), Robert E. Lee Research Scholar, 1965-66; Moot Court Board UC Berkeley 1969; mem: American, Calif. State, San Francisco, Alameda County bar assns., American Corporate Counsel Assn., The Pacific Union Club, Orinda Co. Club, Merchants Exchange Club, Sigma Chi frat., Phi Delta Phi legal frat.; Republican; Episcopal; rec: skiing, tennis, duck hunting. Res: 89 La Salle Ave Piedmont 94611 Ofc: Kaiser Cement Corp. 300 Lakeside Dr, Ste. 2459, Oakland 94612

REESE, ROBERT, JR., security business owner; b. Aug. 9, 1946, Cincinnati, O.; s. Robert R, Sr. and Wenell (Campbell) R.; (pat. grandfather James Berry Reese, Baptist minister, founded 3 churches in Cinti., Ohio, Atlanta and College Park, Ga.); 1 son, Charles M. b. 1975; edn: computer pgmmg., Electronic Computer Pgmmg. Inst. 1970; police sci. courses, 1986. Career: owner prin. Reshi Co., Inc., Los Angeles; mem. Am. Fedn. of Police, Masons, Neighborhood Watch; Prot.; rec: inventions, mechanics. Address: Los Angeles 90007

REEVES, EARLINE ADELE, telecommunications consultant; b. June 17, 1941, Pomona, Calif.; d. Samuel Earl and June Vivian (Stevens) R. Career: Pacific Telephone 1957-59, mgmt. 1959-67; founder, co-owner, cons. Earline Reeves & Assocs. 1967−, pioneer in telecommunications consulting industry, creator of over 250 telecom. forms, formats, systems and procedures; Republican; rec: oil painting, writing, creating children's stories and games. Ofc: Earline Reeves & Assocs. 38753 Yucca Tree Palmdale 93551

REEVES, ROBERT ALLEN, industrial hygienist; b. Aug. 11, 1935, Ft. Worth, Tex.; s. Merley Otis and Bernice (Freeland) R.; m. Ruth, Feb. 28, 1958; children: Wendy b. 1959, Heather b. 1962; edn: BA occ. safety & health, CSU Fresno 1978; Reg. Profl. Safety Engr. Calif. Career: program mgr. Bioenvironmental Engrg. Svc. USAF 1954-74; assoc., senior indsl. hygiene engr. Calif. Dept. of Health Svcs., Occupational Health Br., Cal/OSHA Region II Sacramento 1974-78; sr. indsl. hygienist and acting chief Calif. dept. Health Svcs.

R&D sect. 1978-80; sr. indsl. hyg. Calif. Dept. of Food and Agriculture, Worker Health & Safety Br. 1980-85; retired 1985; cons. in indsl. hygiene and occupational safety 1985−; adj. prof. indsl. hygiene CSU Sacto. 1978; Agrl. Pest Control Advisory Com. 1979-80; honors: Disting. Grad. (Tactical Air Command NCO Acad. 1971; mem: Am. Conf. Govtl. Indsl. Hygienists, Am. Indsl. Hygiene Assn. (Sacto. Valley sect. pres. 1982), So. Carolina Health Physics Assn.; publ: contbr. articles in profl. jours.; mil: msgt. USAF 1954-74, AF Commdn, Good Conduct w/ 3 olc, Longevity Svc. w/ 3 olc, Outstanding Unit w/ 2 olc; Democrat; Southern Baptist; rec: classic automobiles. Res: 8277 E Granite Dr Roseville 95678

REEVES, ROBERT LEE, lawyer; b. Jan. 31, 1942, New London, Conn.; s. Waldo Norwell and Mary (Dandona) R.; div.; children: Terry b. 1959, Robert b. 1961, Mary b. 1962; edn: BA (cum laude), John Jay Coll. 1976; JD, Pepperdine Univ. Sch of Law 1980; admitted to Calif. Supreme Court 1980, US Supreme Ct. 1983. Career: police ofcr. New London City Police Dept., 1964-67, NYC Police Dept., 1967-76 (assigned patrol, Undercover Investigns., teaching and adminstrv. duties; ret. 1976 due to line of duty injuries); pres. Robert L. Reeves, profl. law corp., Los Angeles 1980−, active in practice of immigration, personal injury, family and criminal law; awards: Highest award for Bravery, Conn., 1964; 13 awards for bravery and achievement, Police Commnr. NYC; full academic scholarship grantee to St. Johns Univ. Sch. of Law and NY Sch. of Law; mem: Am., Calif. State, Los Angeles County bar assns., L.A. Trial Lawyers Assn.; Pepperdine Univ. Assocs., and Century Club; life mem. NYC Police Dept. Honor Legion; recipient recognition for Atty. Rendering the Most Svcs. to Cambodian Refugees; mil: sp1/c US Army 1959-62; Republican; Catholic; rec: sailing, photog. Res: 5458 Dahlia Dr Los Angeles 90041 Ofc: Robert L. Reeves, APLC, 3550 Wilshire Blvd Los Angeles 90010

REGAN, NANCY ANN, lawyer; b. Nov. 11, 1949, Iowa City, Iowa; d. Benjamin Thomas and Eleanor Mae (Bechtel) Strathman; m. Kevin Regan, June 21, 1971 (div. 1979); 1 child: Kelly b. 1977; edn: AB, UC Davis 1971; JD, Hastings Coll. of Law 1975; admitted Calif. State Bar 1975. Career: pvt. law practice in Auburn, 1976-79, helped found the Auburn Women's Center and Rape Crisis Line (now Placer Women's Ctr.); mng. atty. Jacoby & Meyers law office in Citrus Heights 1979-82, handled all probate and bankruptcy cases for Central Calif. offices; atty. sole practice, emphasizing domestic cases, bankruptcy and probate, Fair Oaks 1982−; mem. Calif. Bar Assn., Sacramento County Bar Assn., Women Lawyers of Sacto. (legis. com.), Voluntary Legal Services, Calif. Trial Lawyers (Speakers Bur.); past mem. Soroptomist, Bus. & Profl. Women; Democrat; Presbyterian (deacon); rec: jogging, backpacking, softball. Ofc: Nancy Regan Law Offices, 5150 Sunrise Blvd Ste B3 Fair Oaks 95628

REICHENBACH, THOMAS, veterinarian; b. Jan. 6, 1947, NY, NY; s. Col. Henry J. (USAF ret.) and Helen M. R.; m. Cleda L. Houmes, Nov. 23, 1984; edn: BS in chem., Univ. of Notre Dame du Lac 1968; MS, chem., UC Davis 1973; AA, prod. agric., Shasta Jr. Coll. 1976; DVM, UC Davis 1981. Career: Sentry Dog handler, US Army 1970; indsl. chemist Syntex Corp., 1973; gestation herd mgr. Llano Seco Rancho, 1976; pvt. veterinary practice, 1981−, pres. Veterinary Mgmt. Services, 1983−; cons. in medical computing TeleVet Corp. (1985); lectr., computer use in Vet Practice, UC Davis (1985); mem. Am. Vet Med. Assn., Calif. Vet Med. Assn., Nat. Monogram Club (Univ. Notre Dame); publs: articles in vet. jours. (1982-); Personal Wedding Planner (c. 1985); mil: sp4 US 8th Army 1969-71; Republican; rec: artificial intelligence, epidemiology, laparoscopy. Ofc: Veterinary Management Services 1893 Cherokee Dr Salinas 93906

REID, CHALES LESLIE, pilot; b. Feb. 10, 1948, Oregon City, Ore.; s. Chester Jr. and Geraldine Fay (Ebsen) R.; m. Jo Ann Hogan 1973; children: Lea Ann b. 1975, Natalie b. 1979; edn: Fresno City Coll. 1966-68; lic., FAA Airframe and Powerplant Mech., FAA Aircraft Insp. Authorization. Career: pilot Rogers Helicopters, Fresno 1971; pilot Shasta Helicopters, Porterville 1972; mgr. G & P Aircraft, Seattle, Wash. 1972-73; pilot Shasta Helicopters, Porterville 1973-75; chief pilot, dir. maint., vice pres. San Joaquin Helicopters, Delano 1975-86; v.p. Agri-Supply and Mfg. 1980-86; current: pres. Rifle Creek Enterprises; agent Frontier Ministries; mem: AOPA (charter), AG Pilot Assn.; works: design and mfr. spraying, dusting, and seeding equip. for helicopters 1975-86; design and mfr. sickroom and indsl. products 1986−; mil: CA CWO2 US Army 1968-71, Soldiers Medal, Bronze Star, (23) Air Medals; Democrat; Protestant; rec: hunting, fishing, camping. Res: 8430 Old Stage Rd. Terra Bella 93270 Ofc: Rifle Creek Ents. Rte 4 Box 165 Porterville 93257

REID, ROBERT ALFRED, physician; b. June 8, 1939, Milan, Italy (of Am. parents), s. Homer Argall and Lea (Moretti) R.; m. Patricia Louise Beeler, Dec. 20, 1958; children: Robert b. 1959, Heather b. 1963, Scott b. 1968, Rick b. 1975; edn: BA, English Univ. of Colo. 1961; MD, Univ. Colo. Sch. of Med. 1965; certified Am. Bd. of Obstetrics and Gynecology 1973, recert. 1980. Career: intern mixed ob/gyn, internal med. and surgery, Univ. of Colo. Med. Ctr. 1965-66; gen. medical ofcr. Vandenberg Air Force Base, 1966-68; resident ob/gyn, Univ. Colo. Med. Ctr. 1968-71; pvt. practice of obstetrics and gynecology, Santa Barbara 1971−; mem: Fellow Am. Coll. of Obstets. and Gynecol.; Calif. Med. Assn. (bd. dirs. 1982-), Santa Barbara County Med. Soc. (pres. 1982), Tri-Counties Ob/Gyn Soc. (pres. 1978); publs: art. in Rocky Mountain Med. J. (1971), Annales de Genetique (1981); mil: capt. Med. Corps USAF 1966-68; Independent; rec: creative writing, wine appreciation. Ofc: Robert A. Reid MD, Inc. 2415 Bath St Santa Barbara 93105

REILLY, PATRICK JOHN, engineering construction executive; b. Oct. 10, 1925, Nutley, N.J.; s. Philip and Anna (Cox) O'Reilly; m. Maria Garcia

Vazquez, July 27, 1957; children: Anna Maria b. 1958, Patrick J. b. 1960, Thomas J. b. 1962, Frank P. b. 1964; edn: BCE, NY Univ. 1950; cert. practical constrn. law, Univ. of Santa Clara Sch. of Law 1977; Calif. lic. Gen. Engring. Contr. Career: shaft engr. Lincoln Tunnel Third Tube, Walsh Constrn. Co., NYC 1950-54; asst. equipt. mgr. Brown-Raymond-Walsh Madrid 1954-57; v.p. proj. mgr. Wastewater Treatment Plants, Shanley Constrn. Co., San Francisco 1957-65; constrn. mgr., gen. supt. W.W. Kimmins & Sons, Buffalo, N.Y., highways, utilities & underground constrn. 1965-70; dir., constrn. mgr. Municipal Wastewater Plants, Monsanto Enviro. Chem. Systems Inc., Chgo. 1970-74; v.p., constrn. mgr., proj. mgr., Solid Waste Facilities BSP Div. Envirotech, Belmont 1974-83; v.p., proj. mgr. Envirotech Corp., Menlo Park 1983–; listed Who's Who in World 7th ed., Who's Who in Am. 43d ed., Who's Who in Fin. & Indus. 24 ed., Who's Who in the West 20 ed.; mem: Am. Mgmt. Assn., Am. Soc. of Civil Engrs., Am. Arbitration Assn. (panel arbitrator); mil: 1st lt. USAFR; T/sgt US Army Air Force, DFC, Air Medal w/5 clusters; rec: jogging. reading. Res: 20719 Woodward Ct Saratoga 95070 Ofc: Envirotech Corp. 3000 Sand Hill Rd Menlo Park 94025

REILLY, TERRENCE WELDON O., electron microscopist; b. Jan. 21, 1962, Stockton; s. Terrence Lester and Diane Michelle (Black) R.; electron microscopist, San Joaquin Delta Coll., 1982. Career: scanning electron microscope - transmission electron microscope splst./ apps. engr. Nanometrics Inc., Sunnyvale 1983-85, Nissei Sangyo America - Hitachi Sci. Instruments, Mtn. View 1985–; EM lectr., Lincoln Sch. 1981-82; mem: Electron Microscopy Soc. of Am., San Joaquin Delta Coll. Electron Microscopy Soc. (pres. 1982), E. Clampus Vitus, Stockton Art League; awarded Best of Show: Unitarian Ch. Art Show (1982), CSU Stanislaus Art Show (1980); research: Low Voltage Electron Microscopy with Semiconductors, and with Zr/W Schottky Electron Emitter; pub. article in Modern Photography (1980); Republican; Catholic; rec: windsurfing, art, astronomy, astro-physics. Res: 1180 Reed Ave Ste 45 Sunnyvale 94086 Ofc: NSA-Hitachi 460 E Middlefield Rd Mountain View 94043

REINER, ROBERT JULIUS, urologist; b. Apr. 3, 1946, Budapest, Hungary, nat. Feb. 2, 1948; m. Paula, Apr. 10, 1971; children: Gregory, b. 1976, Sarah, b. 1983; edn: BSc, Ohio State Univ. 1966; MD, Univ. Autonoma Guadalajara 1972; Diplomate Am. Bd. of Urology, Fellow Am. Coll. of Surgeons. Career: chief of surgery Lompoc Hosp. Dist.; self-empl. urologist; cons. Vandenberg Air Force Hosp.; bd. dirs. Santa Barbara County Med. Soc. 1980-83; mem. Am., Western, Los Angeles Urologic assns.; clubs: Lompoc Valley, Friends of Lompoc Library (v.p. bd.); publs: 5 articles in Jour. of Urology; Republican; rec: racquetball, golf, tennis. Res: 27 Aldebaran, Lompoc 93436 Ofc: 1111 E Ocean, Ste 3, Lompoc 93436

REINER, WILLIAM GEORGE, pediatric urologist; b. Nov. 21, 1947, San Francisco; s. Ralph Everett, Sr. and Elizabeth Ann (Anderson) R.; m. Irene Murphy, Aug. 5, 1978; children: David b. 1979, Matthew b. 1981; edn: BA, UC San Diego 1969; MD, UC Irvine 1974; urology res., Johns Hopkins Hosp., 1980; Diplomate Am. Bd. of Urology 1982. Career: intern, UCLA Hosp., Los Angeles 1974-75; res., UC Irvine Hosp., Irvine 1975-76; urological res., Johns Hopkins Hosp., Baltimore, MD 1976-77; fellow, Dept. of Urology, Johns Hopkins Univ., Baltimore, MD 1977-78; chief res. pediatric urology/ chief res. adult urology, Johns Hopkins 1978-80; pediatric and adult urologist, William G. Reiner, MD, Inc., Visalia 1980–; urological advr. Tulare Co. Spina Bifida Clinic & Calif. Childrens Svcs.; lectr., UCSF Sch. of Med., Med. Edn. Pgm., Fresno Veterans Hosp. 1983–; honors: fellow, Am. Cancer Soc. 1977-78; Alpha Omega Alpha nat. med. hon. soc.; mem: AMA, CMA, Am. Urological Assn.; Visalia Unified Sch. Dist. Family Life Curriculum Adv. Bd.; Visalia Unified Schs. for Cancer Prevention & Detection Edn. Pgm.; Coll. of Sequoias Nursing Pgm. urology lectr.; num. arts. in med. journs. 1979; research; Republican; Presbyterian; rec: woodwork, gardening, fishing. Rex; 500 Gilmer Ct Visalia 93291 Ofc: William G. Reiner, MD, Inc., 312 W Acequia Visalia 93291

REIS, EDWARD THOMAS, JR., insurance executive; b. Aug. 27, 1948, Fresno; s. Edward Thomas and Eleanor Virginia (Read) R.; m. Patricia, Dec. 4, 1981; 1 son, Edward T., III b. 1968; certs: Accred. Advisor in Ins., Ins. Inst. Am. (1983), Life Underw. Tng. Council Fellow, NALU (1984). Career: prin. Reis Insurance Agency, Simi Valley 1975-82; dist. mgr. Farmers Ins. Group, Santa Barbara 1982–; profl. awards: Farmers Ins. Toppers Club (7 yrs), Life Masters Club (9 yrs), Comml. Masters Club (4 yrs), Comml. Round Table; mem. Nat. Assn. Life Underws. (local pres. 1986-87), Elks, CofC (Goleta, Carpinteria, Solvang); Republican; Grace Lutheran Ch. SB (cong. pres. 1985-86); rec: golf, scuba. Res: 519-A W Pueblo St Santa Barbara 93105 Ofc: Farmers Insurance 123 W Padre St Ste E Santa Barbara 93105

REISMAN, CARL, executive; b. June 11, 1920, Atlanta, Ga.; s. Joseph Nathaniel and Elsie (Kleiner) R.; m. Betty Scholer, Apr. 23, 1946; children: Aileen Ann b. 1948, Richard b. 1950; edn: BS, Georgia Inst. of Tech 1941. Career: partner Surgical Selling Co., Atlanta, GA 1946-60; v.p. Ipco Hosp. Supply Corp., NY, NY; sales mgr. Gentec Hosp. Supply Corp., NY, NY 1967-68; v.p. 1968-73; v.p., Gentec, San Francisco 1973-74; v.p. Daylin Med. Supply Corp., Los Angeles 1974-75; chmn. bd./ CEO/ pres. 1975–; pres. Abco Dealers, Inc. 1953-56, 1959, chmn. bd. 1960; mem: Verdugo Club, Glendale; mil: Lt. Cmdr., USNR 1941-46; rec: golf, hunting, fishing, skiing. Res: 3609 Cananea Dr Encino 91436 Ofc: Tri-anim Health Services, Inc., 1630 Flower St Glendale 91201

REISNER, LAURENCE STUART, physician; b. Feb. 25, 1941, Bradford, Penn.; s. David and Sophie (Aleck) R.; m. Susan Chase, June 21, 1964; children: Shauna b. 1968; Aaron b. 1971; edn: BA, UCLA 1963, MD, UC San Francisco 1967. Career: adj. asst. prof. anesthesiology UCLA Sch. of Med., Harbor Gen. Hosp. Campus 1973; asst. chief anesthesia and operative svcs. Brooke Army Med. Ctr., Ft. Sam Houston, Texas 1973-75; asst. prof. in residence anesthesia, ob-gyn., chief div. of ob. anethesia UCLA Sch. of Med., Harbor Gen. Hosp. 1975-77; asst. clin. prof. anesthesia and reproductive med., co-dir. ob. anethesia UC San Diego Sch. of Med. 1977-79, assoc. clin. prof. anesthesia, reproductive med., co-dir. ob. anesthesia 1979-84, clin. prof., dir. ob. anesthesia 1984–; honors: Cert. of Recogn., Am. Soc. of Anesthesia consec. 1978-81; appointed to Bd. of Medical Quality Assurance 1986; mem: Am., Calif. and San Diego Co. (pres. 1983-84) Socs. of Anesthesiology, Internat. Anesthesiology Research Soc., Am. Soc. of Regl. Anesthesiologists, Soc. for Ob. Anesthesiology & Perinatology, Calif. and San Diego Co. Med. Assns.; works: num. papers and publs.; mil: maj. US Army 1973-75; rec: music. Res: 4752 Vista de la Tierra Del Mar 92014 Ofc: Univ. of Calif., San Diego Medical Ctr., 225 Dickinson St. Ste. H-770 San Diego 92101

REITER, GAYLA DENISE, union president; b. Sept. 12, 1945, Beloit, Kans.; d. Gail Francis and Vivian Maxine (Lagle) Reiter; m. Wilfred J. Scott, July 4, 1983; 1 dau. Layla Diana Scott; edn: BS, magna cum laude, Portland State Univ. 1967; cert. gerontol./psych. of aging, Univ. of Ore. 1974; cert. labor studies, Univ. Calif. 1982. Career: claims rep. Social Security Adminstrn. 1967-70, field rep. Medford, Salem 1971-72, supr. Seattle, Wash. and Watsonville, Calif. 1973-74, branch mgr. Daly City, Calif. 1974-79, external affairs staff Regional Commnrs. Ofc. 1979-80, union pres. 1980–, handled the precedent setting Nat. Official Time arbitration (1982-); recipient num. speech awards, Outstanding Young Women of Am. (1984), Outstanding AFGE litigator (1984), editor Outstanding Nt. paper (1983), outstanding AFGE organizer (1982), Alpha Sigma Omega, Who's Who Among Students Am. Colls. and Univs. (1965, 66, 67), Gov.'s Award (1971), Nat. Leadership Award (1983); mem: AFGE Pres. Council 147 (1982-86), AFGE Nat. Council 220 (exec. v.p. 1982-), AFGE Local 3172 (pres. 1980-85), No. Council of AFGE Locals (1st v.p. 1982-84), Women Execs. (v.p.), San Mateo County Labor Council; civic: No. Calif. SIDS Found. (legis. dir.), Nat. SIDS Found. (legis. coord.), Soroptomist (pres.), NOW, Alpha Sigma Omega, Phi Beta Kappa, SIRS Hunger Project; publs: editor regional union newspaper distbd. 10,000+ federal employees, won quality award 1980-86; author legislation adopted by US Cong. (10/85) on sudden infant death; num. pub. articles, congl. testimony before var. US House and Senate Coms.; Democrat; rec: Masters swimmer. Res: 501 Lynbrook Dr Pacifica 94044

REITHMAIER, LAWRENCE WILLIAM, author; b. May 28, 1921, Chgo.; s. Paul and Frieda R.; m. Barbara Dewees, 1950, div. 1970; children: Karl, Mark, Barbara Anne; edn: BSME, Univ. of Ill., 1944; FAA comml. and instrument pilot, instr., mechanic certs. Career: engr., military aircraft, McDonnell Aircraft Corp., St. Louis, 1947-60; mgr. Dewees Aviation instrument flying sch., Jackson, Miss. 1960-62; project engr. Apollo and Skylab spacecraft, No. Am. Rockwell Space Div., Downey, Calif. 1962-70; v.p. Aero Publishers Inc., Fallbrook 1970-75; v.p. Omni Publishers, Escondido 1975-78; free lance writer, ed., 1978–; author: Pilot's Handbook of Instrument Flying (1969), Pvt. Pilot's Guide (1972), Aviation and Space Dictionary (1974, revised ed. 1980), Instrument Pilot's Guide (1975), Aircraft Mechanic's Shop Manual (1979), num. mag. articles (1961-); honors: Earl D. Osborn award for excellence in writing on gen. aviation, Aviation/Space Writers Assn. (1973), Apollo achieve. award (1970), listed in Who's Who in Aviation and Aerospace (1982); mem. (fmr.) Am. Inst. of Aero. and Astro., Aviation/Space Writers Assn.; rec: flying, sailing, hiking. Address: 6822 22nd Ave N. #340 St. Petersburg FL 33710

REMEDIOS, FRANCIS MATHIAS, chiropractor; b. July 13, 1942, Gatooma, Zimbabwe (Rhodesia); s. Cornelio Mathias and Luiza Espesiosa (Fernandes) R.; m. Margaret Gaul, June 25, 1966; children: Barbara L. b. 1967, Gregory F. b. 1969, Douglas P. b. 1970, Stephanie L. b. 1973; edn: DC, Palmer Coll. Chiro. 1968; cert. clinical nutrition, Nat. Coll. Chiro. 1978; cert. physical therapy, L.A. Coll. Chiro. 1978; cert. acupuncture, Nat. Acad. of Acupunct. 1977; certified in Activator Methods Technique in Chiro. Achievement; currently, post grad. work, L.A. Coll. Chiro.; lic.: Alberta (Can.) Chiro. Assn. (1968), Calif. State Bd. of Chiro. Examiners (1979). Career: assoc. chiropractor, Koch Chiropractic Clinic, Edmonton, Alberta 1968-70; owner, Dr. Francis M. Remedios, Chiropractor, Edmonton 1970-79; owner Remedios Chiropractic Clinic, Redding, Calif. 1980–; pres. Edmonton Chiropractic Soc. 1971 (secty./ treas./ registrar/ exec. ofcr. 1971-77); tchr., Santavicca Cos. 1982-83; columnist, The Monitor, 1982-83; guest spkr./motivational cons., num. clubs, orgns. & businesses; mem: Am. Chiro. Assn. (Council on Nutrition); Canadian & Alberta Chiro. Assns.; Canadian Council of Chiro. Roentgenology; Diplomate Calif. St. Bd. of Chiro. Examiners; Am. Bd. Chiro. Orthopedists; Internat. Arthritis Soc.; Soc. of Remedial Masseurs & Physical Therapists; Nat. Acad. of Acupuncture; Diplomate Nat. Bd. of Naturopathic Examiners; Business Leaders, Redding; Pvt. Indus. Council; Gr. Redding CofC; Toastmasters (distinguished toastmaster); Rotary (bd. dirs., youth exchg. pgm. com., dir. internat. rels. com.); Catholic; Res: 4685 Saratoga Dr Redding 96002 Ofc: Remedios Chiropractic Clinic, 153 Hartnell Ave Redding 96002

RENARD, JOHN S., executive; b. Mar. 13, 1938, NY, NY; s. Henry H. and Ruth L. (Pasternack) R.; m. Judith Slaminsky, Aug. 13, 1961; children: Eric b. 1965, Marc b. 1967; edn: BA, Tufts 1960; MBA, C.C.N.Y. 1969; real estate lic.; indsl. realtor (S.I.R.). Career: pres. Cushman & Wakefield Western, Inc., San Francisco 1983–; adj. lectr. C.C.N.Y., Fairleigh Dickinson, NY Int. of Tech.; New York chpt. Soc. Indsl. Realtors (pres. 1977-78, dist. v.p. 1979-82, dir. 1983-84); past dir. Salvation Army Adv. Bd.; Mount Olive, NJ Indsl. Com.

Adv. Bd.; Yonkers, NY Indsl. Devel. Agcy.; mem: NY Real Estate Bd.; Am. Arbitration Assn.; Am. Economic Devel. Council; Metropolis Country Club, White Plains, NY; City Athletic Club; NYC; Bankers Club, S.F.; The Bd. Room, NYC; Balboa Bay Club, Newport Bch.; frequent contbr., num. real estate trade journals; mil: USAR; rec: skiing, tennis, golf. Res: 465 Pullman Rd Hillsborough 940101 Ofc: Cushman & Wakefield Western, Inc., Bank of Am., 555 California St, Ste 2700, San Francisco 94104

RENDA, FRANK J., regional sales executive; b. Dec. 11, 1935, Fresno; s. Pete and Grace (Di Liddo) R.; children: Craig b. 1960, Troy b. 1961, Dena b. 1964; edn: Santa Rosa Jr. Coll. 1956-58. Career: sales rep. Purex Corp., Sacto. 6 years; Equitable Life Ins., Sacto. 2-½ years; Am. Nat. Ins. Co., Sacto. 6 years; Harold Brooks Corp., Los Angeles 5 years; Orange Blossom Jewelry Co., 6-½ years; sales rep. No. Calif.-Hawaii-Nev., F. Goldman Inc. (NY jewelry co.), 1959–; instr. gen. & sales tng.; honors: All-No. Calif. Halfback and H.S. All-American (1955); Top salesman Am. Nat. Ins. Co. No. Coast Rep., Top Salesman, F. Goldman (1984), Top 3 and Million Dollar Club (4 consec. years); civic: 49er Booster Club (Sacto.), football coach & mgr. Little League (6 yrs) & Pop Warner (Carmichael); mil: sp4 US Army 2 yrs, Disting. Service; Prot.; rec: sports, fishing, camping.

RENEAU, ROBERT LEE, manufacturing co. executive; b. Aug. 29, 1938, Cairo, Ga.; s. Eric L. and Lillian S. (Singletary) R.; m. Magda, Feb. 22, 1964; 1 dau, Suzette b. 1968; edn: BS, Georgia Inst. of Tech. 1961, MBA, 1967. Career: foreman material dept. G.M. Assembly Plant, Atlanta, Ga. 1965-67; sales mgr. Southwire Inc., Canovanas, Puerto Rico 1967-69; import- export dir. Bourns Inc., Riverside 1969–; mem: Foreign Trade Assn. of So. Calif., Western Maquiladora Trade Assn., Jaycees; mil: lt. USNR 1961-65; Republican; Baptist; rec: hiking, golf. Ofc: Bourns Inc., 1200 Columbia Ave. Riverside 92507

RENGER, CYNTHIA IRENE, regulatory affairs executive; b. Apr. 20, 1948, Vienna, Austria; d. Rodger S. and Dolly D. Blecick (Daniel) Elliott; children: James b. 1974, Thomas b. 1976; edn: BA high honors, Whittier Coll. 1970; secondary tchg. cert., So. Colo. State Coll. 1971; MBA internat. ops., mktg. mgmt., West Coast Univ. 1981; Whittier Coll. Sch. of Law 1984. Career: pharmaceutical research & devel. 1971-78; clin. monitor Allergan Pharmaceuticals 1978-80, Bausch & Lomb 1982-83; owner photog. bus. 1982-83; regulatory affairs mgr. Newport Pharmaceuticals Internat. Inc. Newport Beach 1983–, coord. r&d pgm. on AIDS with Food & Drug Adminstrn. Research; science tchr. Ramdam Torah Inst. 1973-74; honors: nom. for Employee Outstanding Achievement Award (Allergan Pharma. 1980); mem: Regulatory Affairs Profl. Soc. (chmn. communs.. ed. internat. newsletter, pgm. com. for annual mtg.), Orange County Profl. Women's Network (mem. chmn. 1982-83); photog. exhibited/ sold in var. art shows in Orange County 1982-86; Republican; Baptist; rec: photog., horseback riding. Res: 1774 New Hampshire Dr Costa Mesa 92626 Ofc: 897 W 16th St Newport Beach 92660

RENNER, ALBERT JOHN, company executive; b. Oct. 8, 1933, Mandan, N.Dak.; s. John J. and Rose M. (Gustin) R.; m. Joanne Charleson, July 11, 1957; children: Gregory b. 1959, Christopher b. 1961, John b. 1962, David b. 1967; edn: BA, Univ. of Wash. 1960; postgrad. work Univ. of Ore. 1963-4. Career: with Scott Paper Co. Mfg. and Sales, 1960-64; sales engr. and Pacific N.W. sales mgr. spl. products Honeywell Inc., 1964-66; prodn. planning mgr. and mgr. sales svcs. Paper Mfg. Div., Boise Cascade Corp., Portland, Ore. and Boise, Ida./ mktg. mgr. Boise Cascade Computing Corp., 1966-72; mgr. of constrn. Shastina Properties Inc. and owner/mgr. of Valley Homes, Weed, Calif. 1971-76; gen. mgr. for No. Calif., Sunset Fibres Inc., 1976-78; owner/ mgr. The Renner Co. (real estate devel. and export-import of plastics & aluminum prods.) 1978–; gen. mgr. Engineered Waste Control Systems Inc., Berkeley 1981-83; pres. Western Pacific Pulp & Paper Co. Inc., Downey 1983–; Dir: Engineered Waste Control Systems Inc., Western Pac. Pulp & Paper Co. Inc.; mem. Pleasanton Chamber of Commerce; mil: FT2 USN 1952-56; Republican; Catholic; rec: golf, fishing, sailing. Res: 2280 Camino Brazos, Pleasanton 94566 Ofc: Western Pacific Pulp & Paper, 1811 Santa Rita Rd, Ste. 208A, Pleasanton 94566

RENNER, ANDREW IHOR, surgeon; b. Aug. 1, 1951, Buenos Aires, Argentina, US citizen; s. Walter and Emelia (Dzyga) R.; m. Cristina Sasyk, Apr. 17, 1982; edn: BA summa cum laude, NY Univ. 1972; MD, Albert Einstein Coll. of Med. 1975; Diplomate Am. Bd. of Surgery 1980; Fellow Am. Coll. of Surgeons 1984. Career: surgeon in pvt. practice, Burbank; dir. Trauma Service, St. Joseph Hosp., Burbank; honors: Phi Beta Kappa 1972; mem: AMA, CMA, Los Angeles County Med. Assn., Union of Am. Physicians, Am. Soc. of Abdominal Surgeons, Soc. of History of Medicine; Republican; Catholic; rec: chess, skiing, flying. Ofc: 2701 W Alameda, Ste 308, Burbank 91505

RENOLLET, HAROLD L., physician; b. Feb. 13, 1928, Frazee, Minn.; s. Louie Wm. and Hilda (Tester) R.; m. Donna Reinmuth, Aug. 20, 1955; children: Robyn Anne b. 1958, Mark Edward b. 1960; edn: BA, Univ. Minn. 1952, BS, 1956, MD, 1956. Career: physician pvt. med. practice 1959-69; dir. Emergency Services Los Gatos Community Hosp. 1969-73; asst. dir. Emerg. Services UC Davis Med. Ctr. 1973-75; emerg. physician Western Emerg. Physicians Group, 1975–; med. dir. Sierra Sacramento Valley Emerg. Med. Services 1975-84; dir. emerg. services Sutter Davis Hosp. 1984–, med. dir. Nor Cal EMS Inc. 1980–; honors: Phi Beta Kappa (1952); mem. AMA, Calif. Med. Assn., Sacto Co. Med. Soc., Am. Acad. Family Practice, CAFP, Am. Coll. Emerg. Physicians, (Calif. ACEP bd. dirs.); Republican; Lutheran. Res: 8639 Olivewood Ct Fair Oaks 95628

RENSCH, JOSEPH R., utility holding co. executive; b. Jan. 1, 1923, San Bernardino; s. Joseph R. and Lucille (Ham) R.; m. June B., Mar. 25, 1946; children: Steven b. 1947, Jeffrey b. 1950; edn: BS, Stanford Univ. 1947; JD, Golden Gate Univ. 1955; graduate work, UCB Boalt Sch. of Law 1956. Career: with Coast Counties Gas & Electric Co., San Francisco 1947-54, Pacific Gas & Elec. Co., S.F. 1954-56, Dow Chem. Co., S.F. 1956, Southern Counties Gas Co., Los Angeles 1957, Pacific Lighting Service Co., L.A. 1958-73, Pacific Lighting Corp., L.A. 1968–: exec. v.p. 1968, pres. 1972–, dir. 1970–; dir: McKesson Corp., Lockheed Corp., Union Bank, Pacific Mutual Life Ins. Co.; awards: Greater L.A. Press Club Headliner of the Year (1973), Hon. LL.D Doctor of Laws Pepperdine Univ. (1976), Freedoms Found. Award (1977), Am. Jewish Com. Human Relations Award (1980), Energy Technology Founders Award (1981); civic: Calif. Economic Devel. Corp. (bd. chmn. 1985), Occidental Coll. (trustee), USC Grad. Sch. of Bus. Adminstrn. (bd. of councilors), Pepperdine Sch. of Law (bd. vis.); mil: lt. Naval Air Corps 1942-46, WWII; rec: golf, music, swimming. Ofc: Pacific Lighting Corporation 810 S Flower St Los Angeles 90017

RESTER, GEORGE G., architect, artist, painter, sculptor; b. Oct. 5, 1923, Ponchatoula, La.; s. Kelly C. and Myra V. (Adams) R.; m. Virginia Nacario, June 25, 1955; children: Gina b. 1956, Taira b. 1959, Licia b. 1963; edn: spl. engring. tng., US Combat Engrs., WWII; law, bus. acctg. Soule' Coll., 1945-48; stu. arch. and engring., Delgado Tech. Inst. 1949-50, Art Center Coll. of Design 1961-62; Reg. Architect in 10 states: La. (1960), Calif. (1963), Fla. (1984), Ariz., Colo., N.J., Mich., Minn., N.Y., Tex., (1985). Certified, NCARB (Nat. Council Archtl. Registration Bds.) 1985. Career: cabinet work, carpentry, constrn. foreman, gen. supt., gen. contr., 1945-53; gen. architectural practice in pvt. practice and with var. firms incl.: project arch./designer Welton Becket 1961-64, senior prin. engr. Ralph M. Parson Co., 1973-76, dir. Archtl. Design and Prodn. (chief architect), WED Ents. (Div. Buena Vista Distbn. Co., Inc. subs., of Walt Disney Prodns.), Glendale 1965-71, 1976-86, dir. Archtl. Design (chief architect), Business Devel., Walt Disney Imagineering, 1986–; recipient profl. accolades internat. esp. for his works at Walt Disney World and Epcot (Orlando, Fla.) and Disneyland (Calif.); mem. Am. Inst. of Architects (1973); founding pres. New Orleans Amateur Artists Soc. (host of weekly radio bdcstg. pgm., 1940-42); mil: pfc US Army Combat Engr. Corps, WWII, ETO, Purple Heart; Republican; Catholic; avocation: painting, sculpting, metal work and crafts. Res: 26337 Dunwood Rd Rolling Hills Estates 90274 Ofc: Wed Enterprises, 1401 Flower St Glendale 91201

RETZINGER, VIRGINIA LEE, writer, humanitarian; b. Nov. 21, 1926, Kenosha, Wisc.; d. William and Ybeltje (Postma) Schutzen; m. Leo Retzinger, Nov. 20, 1945; children: Terry b. 1946, Bonita b. 1948, Suzanne b. 1950, Virginia b. 1951, Paul b. 1953, Daniel b. 1955, Joseph b. 1956, Chris b. 1958, Robert b. 1960, Elizabeth b. 1962, John b. 1964; edn: LLD, Valparaiso Univ. 1985. Career: volunteer worker for the handicapped, frequent lectr., guest on num. TV, radio interview shows; instrumental in obtaining grants for Easter Seals; chair Los Angeles City Council on Disabilities 1979-80, vice chair 1978-79, secty. 1977-78, chair recreation com. 1974-77; writer num. grant proposals for facilities accessible to handicapped incl. Reseda Mini-Park; honors: Internat. Symbol of Access Award (WIL INC 1975), Merit Award (Calif. Dept. of Rehab. 1976), City of Los Angeles Award (1977), ADEPT Award (1977), Citation Award (Calif. Park & Rec. Soc. 1979), Mayor's Award (1980), Bd. of Dirs. Award (ADEPT 1980), A. Milton & Charlotte Miller Award (1980), Resolution Award (City of L.A., State of Calif. 1985), Handicapped Californian of the Year Award (Calif. Assn. Physically Handicapped 1986), Mainstream Milestones Award (1986); mem: Calif. Assn. Physically Handicapped (co-chair Internat. Year of Disabled Persons 1981, chpt. pres. 1982-83, ed./ pub. newsletter: Impact), Calif. Found. for Physically Handicapped (pres. 1983-), Invisible Citizen, Inc. (pres.), Easter Seals (Calif. bd. dirs., citizen's advisory com.), Darrel McDaniel Independent Living Ctr. (secty. 1984-), Polio Survivors Support Group; publs: writer Ability Magazine quarterly; Hyatt, a Hotel with a Heart (National Hookup 1978), Los Cantiles Recreation Area (Nat. Hookup and the Hub 1979), article on employment for the handicapped (Valley News). Res: 7635 Etiwanda Ave Reseda 91335

REUL, RICHARD PHILIP, aerospace systems engineer; b. Oct. 1, 1921, Roselle, N.J.; s. George Philip and Gladys Evelyn (Insel) R.; m. Jean Lyda (dec. 1974), Apr. 1, 1945; children: Douglas b. 1948, Lawrence 1950-1981; edn: BSME, Purdue Univ. 1942; cert. TRW Mgmt. Methods, 1964; Reg. Profl. Engr. (mech.) Calif. Career: flight test engr. and project engr. aircraft and target drones, TRW, -1959, system mgr. Titans I and II, Apollo and classified satellite, 1959-70; senior reliability engr. Hill Air Force Base, System Devel. Corp., -1973, senior proposal splst., -1976; cons. Space Shuttle Displays & Controls, Rockwell Space Div., 1977; mgr. Space Shuttle System Specification, Martin Marietta, -1979; senior systems engr. Peacekeeper Missile Interface Control, Rocketdyne Div. Rockwell Internat., Canoga Park 1979–; cons. on target drone propulsion, Aerojet Gen., 1957; instr. mgm. devel. seminar, UCLA, 1972; awards: NASA Group Achievement Award, Gemini (1965), USAF Award for DOD Space Transp. System Top Specification; mem: Assoc. Fellow Am. Inst. of Aero. & Astro., L5 Soc., Aviation Space Found. (charter), Nat. Writer's Club, Nat. Rifle Assn.; author two contemporary suspense novels: Counter Force, and Sunburst; 9 pub. aerospace articles and tech. papers; Republican; rec: backpacking, rafting, shooting, troutfishing, painting. Res: 10647 Owensmouth Ave Chatsworth 91311 Ofc: Rocketdyne Div. Rockwell International 6633 Canoga Ave Canoga Park 91304

REVAK, RUDY, co. executive; b. Jan. 1, 1947, Altusried, Ger.; s. Steve and Maria (Ditzig) R.; edn: AA, Mercer Coll. 1972. Career: store mgr. Newport

Auto Ind., N.J. 1965-67; area coord. R.R. Associates, N.J. 1970-71; v.p. BL Products GMBH, Germany 1972-74; pres. BL Products of Canada, Toronto 1974-78; pres. BL Products Italia, Rome 1978-80; pres. Diamite Corp., Los Gatos, Ca. 1980–; cons. Flemington Mini Storage, Traveline Inc., ReLine Ent. Toronto; recipient chmn's awards, Internat. Mktg. Mgmt.; frequent writer and lectr. internat. on sales, motivation and personal growth; mil: sgt. US Army Quartermaster Corps 1967-70, Vietnam; Republican (Congl. Club, Sentl. Club, Repub. Nat. Com., Presdtl. Task Force); Christian; rec: pvt. pilot. Res: 121 Callecita Los Gatos 95030 Ofc: 131D Albright Way Los Gatos 95030

REVEAL, ARLENE HADFIELD, county librarian; b. May 21, 1916, Riverside, Boxelder Co., Utah; d. Job Oliver and Mabel Olive (Smith) Hadfield; children: James L. b. 1941, Jon A. b. 1941; edn: BS, Utah State Univ. 1938; tchg. cred., CSU San Diego 1970; MLS, Brigham Young Univ. 1976. Career: tchr. Logan High Sch., Logan, Utah 1937-38; social case worker Boxelder Co., Utah 1938-39; branch librarian Tuolumne Co. Library, Calif. 1948-54; acct. Strawberry (Calif.) Inn 1954-66, also asst. mgr. Dodge Ridge Ski Area, Long Barn 1949-66, also office mgr. Pinecrest (Calif.) Permittees Assn. 1955-66; librarian LaMesa-Spring Valley Sch. Dist., LaMesa 1968-71; county librarian Mono Co. Library, Bridgeport 1971 ; honors: Woman of Year, Beta Sigma Phi (1980), John Cotton Dana Award (1974); mem: Am. Library Assn., Calif. Lib. Assn., Calif. Media and Lib. Educators Assn. (historian 1970), Delta Kappa Gamma (chpt. pres. 1984), Beta Sigma Phi (chpt. pres. 1985-86); civic: Aurelia Rebekah Assembly (treas. 1979-), Pinecrest Vol. Fire Dept. (pres. 1963-64), Mono County Friends of the Library (1976-), Mono Co. Hist. Soc. (secty. 1982-), Developmentally Disabled Area Bd. #12; jt. author: Mono County Courthouse; Pinecrest School History; (ERIC document) Team Teaching in the Library; Ch. of Jesus Christ of Latter Day Saints; rec: archaeol., knitting, Native Am. basketry. Res: Kingsley St Bridgeport 93517 Ofc: Mono County Free Library POB 398 Bridgeport 93517

REVEL, GARY NEAL, music industry professional; b. June 29, 1949, Florala, Ala.; s. Leamon Curtise and Martha Marie (Mitchell) R.; m. Linda Willis, Jan. 23, 1973; chidlren: Gary, Jr. b. 1973, Curtise, II b. 1974, Mary b. 1976, Rebecca b. 1980, Elisabeth b. 1982, Sonny b. 1985; edn: sonar & electronic courses, USN 1967 69; adv. theology, Am. Bible Sch. 1982. Career: songwriter Milene Opryland Music, 1975–; pres./CEO Star City Records Inc., Nashville, Tenn. 1979-80; pres./CEO Gary Revel Music 1980 , Jongleur Music 1983–, Top's Records 1983–; cons. Friends Indeed (1982-84); works include: play: And Then I Went Away (1970), songs: They Slew The Dreamer (1977), Treat America Like A Lady (1982); mem: Am. Soc. of Composers (publisher mem.), Authors and Publishers, ASCAP (writer mem. 1970-), So. Calif. Motion Picture Council; mil: STG3 US Navy 1967-69, Nat. Def. medal; Democrat; Christian; rec: swim. Address: Gary Revel Music 5341 Loma Linda Ave Ste 5 Hollywood 90027

REVILLA, EDGARDO DELA CUEVA, civil engineer; b. Sept. 20, 1946, Manila, Phil.; s. Andres Alviar and Juliana Manese (Dela Cueva) R.; m. Reniza Mojica, July 28, 1973; children: Mark b. 1974, Dean b. 1976, Ruby b. 1983; edn: BS civil engring., Far Eastern Univ., Manila 1968; M. Transp. Design, Univ. of Alberta, Edmonton 1975; urban and regl. planning, No. Alberta Inst. of Tech., Edmonton 1976; Reg. Profl. Engr., Calif. (1980). Career: var. pos. govt. agencies and pvt. consulting firms in Edmonton, Alberta, Can. 1970-78; project engr. Lillis, Cooper & Scoggins, Fairfield, Calif. 1978-80; project mgr. Fitch & Assocs., Concord 1980-81; prin. engr./ founder/ pres. ECR Associates, Fairfield 1981–; mng. ptnr. Revilla & Juco, a land devel. ptnrship; mem. Profl. Regulation Commn., Manila (1969); publs: Lake Athabasca Flood Level Report (1970), Light Rapid Transit Alignment Study (for Edmonton and St. Albert, Alberta 1975). Res: 722 Shamrock Ct Fairfield 94533 Ofc: ECR Associates 2120 Mt Diablo St Concord 94520

REYBURN, STANLEY SHORTRIDGE, banker; b. May 28, 1930, Los Angeles; s. Wilbur Wm. and Margaret (Leslie) R.; m. Jeanette Smith, May 29, 1982; children: Valerie, b. 1953; Stephen, b. 1955; Stuart, b. 1959; Paul, b. 1971; edn: AA, El Camino Coll. 1956; BS, CSU Los Angeles 1959; MBA, USC 1961; grad. Sch. of Mortgage Banking, Northwestern Univ. 1964; postgrad. work, USC 1965-66; A.I.B. std. certs. 1967; life jr. coll. tchr. credential (bus. ad., econ.) 1968; cert. Sr. Loan Escrow Ofcr., Calif. Escrow Assn. 1970. Career: asst. secty./ asst. treas. Western Mortgage Corp. 1961-66; v.p./ mgr. Security Pacific Nat. Bank 1967-77; pres. Commonwealth Escrow Co. and Commonwealth Svc. Co., 1977-79; 1st v.p.; sr. v.p.- admin. Century Bank, Los Angeles 1979-82; exec. vice pres., corp. secty., loan adminstr. and dir. Wilshire State Bank, 1982–; coll. instr. UCLA Ext. 1964-68, CSU Long Bch. 1966-7, L.A. Valley Coll., 1968-; instr. Continuing Edn. for the Bar; honors: Golden Poet Award from The World of Poetry; mem. Calif. Escrow Assn. (dir. 1970-82), L.A. Escrow Assn. (pres. 1968), Am. Escrow Assn., Assn. of Corporate R.E. Execs., Calif. R.E. Educators Assn.; author: Careers in Escrow (Calif. Escrow Assn. 1976); Calif. Escrow Procedures: A Blueprint for the Nation (coll. text) Prentice-Hall, 1980); monthly column in CEA News (Calif. Escrow Assn.); num. mag., newsletter articles; poetry; musical lyricist; producer phone-in radio quiz show for Nat. Public Radio; Republican; Presbyterian; rc: numismatics, preserving radio history, writing. Res: 7422 Hazeltine Ave, 3, Van Nuys 91405 Ofc: Wilshire State Bank, 3200 Wilshire Blvd, Los Angeles 90010

REYES, GASPARA, realtor; b. Jan. 6, 1939, Sibalom, Antique, Philippines; d. Paulino E. and Santiaga M. (Greallos) Vedad; m. Robert L., Aug. 16, 1975; edn: BSEE, Phil. Normal Colls. Manila 1962; MA, San Francisco State Univ. 1978; tchg. credl. Calif. 1978; sch. adminstr. credl. Calif. 1978; real estate broker Calif. 1985; notary public Calif. 1985. Career: clerk/ student SFSU 1970-78; realtor San Francisco 1978–; elem. tchr. Manila City Sch. 1962-70; prof. Manila Quezon Coll.; mem: Phil. Normal Coll. Alumni Assn. 1962-, SFSU Alumni Assn. 1978; S.F. Bd. Realtors 1978, Nat. Notary Assn., Glee Club, Girl Scouts, Cebu Assn. of Calif.; Republican; Catholic; rec: reading, dancing, fishing, travel. Address: 2201 33rd Ave San Francisco 94116

REYNOLDS, ALBERT GORDON, physician, medical director; b. Jan. 25, 1926, Vashon Isl., Wash.; s. Albert Hargrave and Claire Louise (Stowell) R.; m. Polly Staples, Aug. 29, 1948; children: Scott b. 1949, Debra b. 1952, Lori b. 1956; edn: MD, Univ. of Michigan 1949; Diplomate Am. Bd. of OB-Gyn. 1958. Career: intern, res. OB-Gyn. Univ. of Mich. Ann Arbor; pvt. practice OB-Gyn. Redlands, Calif. 1955-82; asst. clin. prof. UC Los Angeles and Loma Linda Med. Ctr.; past chief of OB-Gyn. dept., chief of staff Redlands Comm. Hosp.; currently med. dir. La Costa Spa preventive med. and fitness; mem: fellow Am. Coll. of Surgeons 1960-; Am. Coll. of Preventive Med. 1984-; author: book under contract La Costa Encyclopedia of Nutrition; mil: corpsman Navy Hosp. WWII 1943-45; capt. MC US Army Korean War 1950-51, Med. Combat Medal, Purple Heart, Meritorious Award from Crown Prince Thailand; Republican; Protestant. Res: 1942 Swallow Ln Carlsbad 92008 Ofc: La Costa Spa Carlsbad 92008

REYNOLDS, ANN W(YNETKA), university chancellor; b. Nov. 3, 1937, Coffeyville, Kans.; d. John Ethelbert, Jr. and Glennie (Beanland) King; m. Thomas H. Kirschbaum; children: Rachel b. 1967, Rex b. 1971; edn: BS biol./ chem., Kans. State Teachers Coll. 1958; MS zool., Univ. of Iowa 1960, PhD zool., 1962. Career: chancellor The California State Univ. (19 campuses, 325,000 students, 18,000 faculty), 1982–, also prof. biol. CSU Dominguez Hills, 1982-, prof. biol. scis., San Francisco St. Univ., 1982-, clin. prof. Ob-Gyn (hon.) UC Los Angeles Sch. of Medicine 1985-; fmr. faculty Ball State Univ. 1962-65, Univ. of Ill., 1965-79 (prof. anat., research prof. of ob-gyn., assoc. v. chancellor for research, dean Grad. Coll. Med. Ctr.); provost Ohio State Univ. and pres. Univ. Research Found., 1979-82; dir: Calif. Econ. Devel. Corp. (1984-), Gen. Tel. of Calif. (1985-), Am. Elec. Power Co. (1981-), Abbott Labs. (1980-); mem. bd. dirs: Am. Assn. for Higher Edn. (1984-), Am. Council on Edn. (1982-85), Am. Council for the Arts (1986-); mem. Nat. Commn. on Contg. Higher Edn. Leadership (1985-), Nat. Commn. on Excellence in Edn. Adminstrn. (1985-), AASCU Nat. Commn., on the Role and Future of State Colls. and Univs. (1985-), trustee Nat. Joint Council on Econ. Edn. (1983-), Californians Preventing Violence (1983-), Regl. Research Inst. of So. Calif. (1984-87); nat. chmn. Higher Edn.- Industry Savings Bond Campaign (1985, 86); mem. nat. bd. advisors Okla. Proj. to develop a contg. edn. network (1985-88); honors: fellow, Calif. Acad. of Scis. (1983), Hon. Dr. of Sci. Ind. State Univ., Evansville (1980), assoc. fellow Am. Coll. of Obstets. and Gyns. (1977), NSF Predoctl. Fellow (1958-62), Woodrow Wilson Fellow (1958), disting. alumna Kans. State Tchrs. Coll. (1972), Hon. Dr. of Sci., Ball State Univ., Muncie, Ind. (1985), Hon. Dr. of Humane Letters, McKendree Coll., Lebanon, Ill. (1984); mem: AAAS, Am. Assn. of Anatomists, Am. Diabetes Assn., Am. Soc. of Zoologists, Endocrine Soc., Perinatal Research Soc., Sigma Xi, Soc. for Exptl. Biology and Medicine, Soc. for Gynecologic Investigation; works: devel. biology splst. in fetal devel., placental transfer and nutrition, author over 100 med. book chapters, articles in sci. and med. jours. Res. 620 Stone Canyon Rd. Los Angeles 90077 Ofc: Office of the Chancellor, The California State University, 400 Golden Shore, Ste. 324, Long Beach 90802

REYNOLDS, HARRY MERVIN, lawyer; b. Dec. 28, 1937, Wash. DC; s. Harry Bishop and Grace Lucille R.; div.; children: Harry b. 1959, Robyn b. 1961, Cindy b. 1965, Ryan b. 1982; edn: BSEE, Howard Univ. 1960; JD, UCLA 1973; admitted to Calif. Bar 1975; Real Estate Broker, Calif. 1978. Career: elec. engr. US Govt., Wash. DC 1960-61; tech. staff Hughes Aircraft Co., Culver City 1961-62; tech. staff Aerospace Corp., El Segundo 1962-67; adv. engr. IBM Corp., Westlake Village 1967-68, mgr. adv. sys. devel. 1968-70; law clerk Ventura Co. Dist. Atty.'s Ofc., Ventura 1971-73; atty. Union Oil Co., Los Angeles 1973-74; atty. Scarlett & Roberson, Los Angeles 1975; ptr. Manning, Reynolds & Roberts, Los Angeles 1976-79; atty. self-empl., Tehachapi 1983-85; atty. self-employed Bakersfield 1985–; v.p. bus. affairs and gen. mgr. Whitfield Records, Hollywood 1980-82; instr. bus. law Calif. Lutheran Coll. 1974; instr. real estate law and bus. law Moorpark Coll. 1973; honors: Judge Pro Tem, West Kern Municipal Ct. 1985, East Kern Municipal Ct. 1985; Judge, Los Angeles Co. Science Fair 1961-63; NAACP Equal Justice under Law Award, 1979; mem: US Supreme Ct., Criminal Cts. Bar Assn., Calif. State Bar, Kern Co. Bar Assn., La Raza Lawyers Assn., St. Judes Episcopal Mission (Bishops Com. 1985-), Kappa Alpha Psi; num. tech. publs. in field of electronics 1963-70; Democrat; Episcopal; rec: jogging, weightlifting, equestrian. Res: POB 647 Tehachapi 93561 Ofc: Harry M. Reynolds, Atty. at Law, 1315 L St Bakersfield 93301

REYNOLDS, MURRAY L., advertising/ marketing executive; b. Feb. 4, 1956, El Paso, Tex.; s. Edgar J. and Jo (Murray) R.; edn: BS, San Diego State Univ. 1982. Career: regl. major accts. mgr. Advo Systems Inc. 1983-84; co-founder Strom-Hill Inc. 1984; gen. mgr. BTB Mktg. div. of Strom Hill 1984-85; v.p. DOnler Mktg. Inc. 1985–; rec: sailing, aviation, tennis. Res: 99 63rd Pl Long Bech 90803 Ofc: Donler Mktg. Inc. 17501 17th St Tustin

REYNOLDS, STEPHEN MEADE, club management executive; b. Oct. 2, 1949, Ithaca, N.Y.; s. Gardner Mead and Kathleen (Kane) R.; m. Suzanne, Mar. 6, 1976; edn: AAS, Paul Smith's Coll. 1969; BSBA, Univ. of Denver 1971. Career: mgr, trainee Lawry's Assoc. Restaurants, 1972; asst. mgr., area supr.

(8 restaurants, Thousand Oaks and Los Angeles), DuPars Restaurants 1973-82; gen. mgr. Saticoy Country Club, Camarillo 1982-86, Soule Park Golf Club, Ojai 1986–; mem. So. Calif. Club Mgrs. Assn.; Republican; Catholic; rec: home remodeling, cooking, exercise. Res: 117 Eagle Rock Ave Oxnard 93030 Ofc: Soule Park Golf Club 1033 E Ojai, Ojai

REYNOLDS, STEPHEN SCOTT, lawyer; b. Aug. 1, 1949, Ann Arbor, Mich.; s. Albert Gordon and Polly Rae (Staples) Reynolds; m. Cynthia J. Scritchfield, Dec. 10, 1977; children: Stephanie b. 1978, Jessica b. 1982, Scott b.1985; edn: BA, Stanford Univ. 1971; MBA, UC Berkeley 1973; JD, Univ. of Pacific McGeorge Sch of Law 1976. Career: tax acct. Arthur Andersen & Co., San Francisco 1976-79; atty., Welebir & Brunick, San Bernardino 1979-82; atty. Reynolds, Reider & Bawden, Redlands 1982–; instr. (Legal Aspects of Human Resource Mgmt. Bus. Law) Univ. of Redlands; honors: Journey for Perspective, UCB 1972; distinguished svc. award Redlands Jaycees 1982; dir. Redlands CofC (pres. 1983-84, 85-86); Redlands Planning Commn. 1982- (chmn. 1984-); trustee Redlands United Ch. of Christ 1979-82; dir. United Way 1982- (pres. 1985); dir. Redlands Local Economic Devel. Corp, 1981-; Rotary; Republican; rec: skiing, racquetball, jogging, scuba. Res: 30589 Mirasol Dr Redlands 92373 Ofc: Reynolds, Reider & Bawden, 300 E. State St, Ste. 450, Redlands 92373

REYNOLDS, STEVEN LEE, educator; b. Sept. 22, 1952, Los Angeles; s. Howard Lee and Berneita (Bagley) R.; m. Cynthia Ramsey, June 10, 1978; 1 son: Jason, b. 1982; edn: CSU Fullerton 1971-73; BA, Biola Univ. 1974; MA, Talbot Sem. 1977; grad. wk. Donsbach Univ. 1978-; Calif. mult. subjects cred., Dominican Coll. 1983-84; ordained minister Ojai Valley Comm. Ch. 1979; nutritional cons./ reg. health practitioner, Am. Holistic Health Scis. Assn. (AHHSA) 1982. Career: musician- trumpet, Howard L. Reynolds Orch., Orange 1970-78; asst. to dir. Practical Missionary Tng., Fullerton 1973-75; pressman/ v.p./ prodn. mgr. Christian Printing Svc., Fullerton 1973-78; instrnl. asst. Richland H.S., Orange 1977-78; assoc. pastor Ojai Valley Comm. Ch., Ojai 1978-80; tchr. Deep Valley Christian Sch., Redwood Vlly., Willits, 1980-82, dir. Ind. Studies, 1984–; Christian Edn. cons. David C. Cook Pub. Co., Elgin, Ill. 1980-83; instrumental music instr., Anderson Valley, Ukiah, 1983-84; dir. Reynolds Personal Enrichment Resources, 1976–; subst. tchr. Willits Unified Sch. Dist., 1981–; honors: Outstanding Young Men of Am. (1979), Bank of Am. Award (1970); mem: Internat. Coll. of Applied Nutrition, AHHSA, Christian Camping Internat., Hewitt Research Found., Christian Home Educators Assn., Soc. for Nutrition & Preventive Med.; Republican; Christian; rec: aviation, photog. Res: 301 Creekside Dr Willits 95490 Ofc: Reynolds P.E.R., POB 1148, Willits 95490

REYNOLDS, SUSAN FOSTER, emergency physician; b. Feb. 12, 1949, Phila.; d. Wm. Rothermel and Wilhelmina (Foster) Reynolds; m. Henry Root, Oct. 12, 1985; edn: AB, cum laude, Vassar Coll. 1970; PhD, UC Los Angeles 1974, MD, 1976; diplomate Am. Board Internal Medicine (1979). Career: int. medicine intern/ resident UCLA 1976-79, cardiology fellow 1979-81; emerg. phys. Santa Monica Hosp. Med. Ctr., var. hosps., 1977-82; dir. Critical Care Svcs., Century City Hosp. 1980-81; founder/ owner/ dir./ phys. Critical care Consultants, A Medical Group, Inc., dba Malibu Emergency Room, 1980–; founder/ med. dir./ prin. fundraiser Community Emerg. Svcs. of Malibu, a tax-exempt charity 1982-; vol. phys. Flying Samaritan Pgm. in Baja Calif. (1981), ship phys. Sitmar Trans-Panama cruise (1979); honors: Phi Beta Kappa (1970), Sigma Xi (1973), Emil Bogen Research Prize (1976), disting. citizen award County of L.A. (1982), Who's Who Women in Am. (1984); mem. Am. Coll. Emergency Physicians (co-chair Status of Women in Emerg. Med. Task Force), Women in Emerg. Med. (exec. bd., treas. 1985-), Malibu CofC (dir.); Prot.; rec: sailing, music, tennis. Res: 1844 S Bundy Dr #5 Los Angeles 90025 Ofc: Malibu Emergency Room 23900 PCH, Malibu 90265

RHEE, CHASE CHONGGWANG, international trading co. president; b. Feb. 26, 1942, Chungnam, Korea; s. Jongbae and Moohee (Shin) R.; m. Socorro D., Feb. 26, 1971; children: Tammie b. 1972, Jennifer b. 1979, Doreen b. 1983; edn: BA fgn. trade, Seoul Nat. Univ. 1968; MA internat. mgmt., Am. Grad. Sch. of Internat. Mgmt. Glendale, Ariz. 1970. Career: pres. Ameriko Industries Corp.; mem. president's adv. bd. CSU Los Angeles 1986; honors: Commdn. (Mayor Tom Bradley L.A. 1981); mem: Korean CofC L.A. (pres. 1980), Lions Club (chpt. pres. 1980, zone chmn. 1982); mil: Korean Army 1963-66; Republican; Presbyterian; rec: golf. Res: 3610 Fairmeade Rd Pasadena 91107 Ofc: Ameriko Industries Corp. 750 E Green St Ste 207 Pasadena 91101

RHEE, SHIN WOONG, manufacturing co. executive; b. June 19, 1943, Seoul, Korea, nat. US cit. 1977; s. Mal R. and Sang K. (Chang) R.; m. Jin, Dec. 22, 1974; children: Grace b. 1976, Jason b. 1977; edn: BSEE, Seoul Nat. Univ. 1967; MSEE, CSU Northridge 1979. Career: r&d engr. Am. Tech. Northridge 1975-78; v.p. Cleanwater Sys. of Am. Camarillo 1978-79; gen. mgr. REC Camarillo 1979–; pres. Rhetronics Northridge 1980–; music dir., conductor Valley Korean Central Presbyterian Church 1982-; mil: 2nd lt. Korean Army ROTC 1967-71; Presbyterian; rec: fishing. Res: 11626 Killimore Ave Northridge 91326 Ofc: REC 530 Constitution Ave Camarillo 93010, Rhetronics 11626 Killimore Ave Northridge 91326

RHINEHART, DERRELL LEE, optometrist; b. July 29, 1935, Beten, NY; s. James Bonar and Dolores U. R.; m. Charlene, June 20, 1964; children: Sandra b. 1953, Linda b. 1954, James b. 1966, Charles b. 1969; edn: BA, Univ. of Kansas 1958, BS, 1959; BS, UC Berkeley 1962, OD, 1964. Career: optometrist pvt. practice, Escondido 1964–; currently, pres. Derrell L. Rhinehart OD, Inc.; cons. Warner Springs Sch. Dept.; cons. Project Concern, Tijuana, Mex.; instr. health care Calif. Community Colls. 1976-; honors: Pres., Soc. of Yr., Calif. Optometric Soc.; chmn. Sister City Pgm., Mexicali, Mex.; Sight Conservation dist. chmn.; mem: San Diego Co. Optometric Soc. (pres. 1978, treas. bd. dirs. 1971-78), Calif. Optometric Alumni Assn., Univ. of Kansas Alumni Assn., Ambassadors Club, CofC, Optomist Club, Am. Optometric Assn. (youth chmn. Contact Lens sect., Sports Vision); works: Control of Myopia Through Accomodative Flexibility, 1982; Dispensing Layout for the Optometric Office, 1985; Evangelical (elder); rec: skiing, running. Res: 13928 Misty Oak Valley Center 92082 Ofc: 1299 E. Pennsylvania Escondido 92027

RHODES, DAVID ALAN, govt. lawyer; b. 1952, San Bernardino; s. Robert Aaron and Marion Margery (Levisee) R.; m. Gerre Lynn Marrion, June 11, 1977; children: Katherine Laura b. 1979, Edward Garrett b. 1982; edn: BA in econs., BA in pol. sci., UC Davis 1975, JD, 1978; admitted Calif. State Bar 1978. Career: staff atty. Legal Center for the Elderly, Sacramento 1978-80, staff rep./ bd. dirs. 1979-80; staff counsel Calif. Dept. of Water Resources 1980-83; dep. atty. gen. Criminal Div., Office of the Atty. Gen., Sacto. 1983–; mem. Atty. Gen.'s Task Force on Problems of the Physically Handicapped 1975; v.p. bd. dirs. Paratransit Inc., Sacto. 1979-81; civic: City of Davis Freedom from Barriers Com., (chmn. 1975-76), Handicapped Stds. Appeals Bd. (chmn. 1981-83); Democrat; Episcopal (sr. warden 1985); rec: pencil drawing, landscape design. Res: 513 Fillmore Ct Davis 95616 Ofc: Attorney General's Office 1515 K St Ste 511 Sacramento 95814

RHODES, JOSEPH WILLIAM, musician, arranger, composer, ret.; b. Dec. 18, 1901, Campbell, Mo.; s. Joseph Wm., Sr. and Laura May (Atteberry) R.; m. Clarice Barrett, June 21, 1924; 1 dau. Pamela b. 1934; m. 2d Sina Duggar, Dec. 19, 1959; edn: edn: Mississippi A&M Coll. 1919-20, Cinti. Coll. of Music 1920-21, stu. arranging and composition w/num. tchrs., N.Y. Career: arranger, bassist Jan Garbers Orchestra 1923-29; arranger, composer New York Paramount Theatre 1929-36, played tuba on Fleishman Hour (Radio) w/ Rudy Vallee, also recorded with him four years, 1931-36; later played many radio & T.V. pgms. including the Lucky Strike Hit Parade, the Telephone Hour, Philip Morris and other pgms. w/ Russ Morgan; General Electric Hour & recordings w/ Fred Waring; creative staff, then exec. supvr. Phil Davis Musical Enterprises, Inc., N.Y.C. 1948-66, ret.; currently composing mostly religious music, composer-in-res. The First United Methodist Ch., Los Gatos 1967–; honors: has played for every US President since F.D.R. (except Pres. Johnson), the Duke & Dutchess of Windsor, num. internat. celebrities; mem. Am. Soc. of Composers, Authors and Pubs. (1968-), Sons in Retirement (1972); works include: Praise Thee O God, They Shall See the Glory of the Lord, All Glory to His Name (Xmas Cantata) Responses, Mystique- sax solo, Fantasy - flute solo, and many dozens of Radio & T.V. commls.; Republican; Methodist; rec: golf, bridge, travel, concerts. Res: 14225 Lora Dr #12 Los Gatos 95030

RICARDO-CAMPBELL, RITA, economist; b. Mar. 16, 1920, Boston, Mass.; d. David A. and Elizabeth (Jones) Ricardo; m. W. Glenn Campbell, Sept. 15, 1946; children: Barbara b. 1954, Diane b. 1956, Nancy b. 1960; edn: BS, Simmons Coll. 1941; MA, Harvard Univ. 1945, PhD, 1946. Career: tchg. fellow, tutor, instr. Harvard Univ. 1946-48; asst. prof. Tufts Coll. 1948-51; economist, Nat. Wage Stab. Bd., 1951-53, Ways & Means Com., US House of Reps., 1953; cons. econ., 1957-61; archivist and research assoc., Hoover Instn. 1961-68, sr. fellow, 1968–; mem. bd. dirs., chmn. finance com. The Gillete Co., Boston; bd. Watkins-Johnson, Inc., Palo Alto; mem. Nat. Council on the Humanities, Nat. Endowment for the Humanities, Presidential Appt., 1982-; mem. Pres.'s Economic Policy Adv. Bd., 1981-; mem. Adv. Council SRI Internat. and Mont Pelerin Soc.; awards: senior fellowship Nat. Endowment for the Humanities (1975), Alumnae Achievement Awd., Simmons Coll., Boston (1972); Phi Beta Kappa, Radcliffe Coll., Harvard Univ., Cambridge (1946). Authority on the health care sector, the Soc. Sec. regulations, and drug indus. regs.; lectr. internat. on med. care in US; author: The Economics and Politics of Health (1982, paperback ed. 1985); Social Security: Promise and Reality; Drug Lag: Federal Government Decision Making; Food Safety Regulations; The Economics of Health and Public Policy; coauthor (with husband, Dr. Glenn Campbell) Economics of Mobilization and War. Ofc: The Hoover Instn., Rm. 318, HHMB Stanford 94305

RICE, DAVID ROGERS, pediatric neurologist; b. May 17, 1944, Los Angeles; s. Edward R. and Grace (McCullough) R.; div.; children: Stephanie b. 1971, Elicia b. 1975; edn: BS in biol., Walla Walla Coll. 1966; MD, Loma Linda Univ. Sch. of Medicine 1971. Bd. cert. Am. Board of Pediatrics (1979). Career: med. intern Loma Linda Univ. Med. Center 1972-, pediatric resident, 1976-78; pediatric neurology fellowship Tufts-New England Med. Center 1979, neuromuscular disease fellowship, 1980; pvt. practice ped. & adult neurology, neuromuscular diseases; fmr. asst. clin. prof. ped., now asst. clin. prof. neurology Loma Linda Sch. of Medicine; asst. dir. MDA Program, Casa Colina Hosp., Pomona; awards: Who's Who Among Am. Colls. & Univs. (1966), Boston Floating Hosp. Housestaff Fellow of the Year Award for excellence in tchg. and ped. care (1977-78); mem. Am. Epilepsy Soc., AMA, Los Angeles Co. Med. Assn., MDA; publs: num. abstracts and med. jour. articles, book chpt. in Neurology (1982); S.D.A. Ch.; rec: ski, hiking, sailing. Ofc: 1900 Royalty Dr Ste 180 Pomona 91767

RICE, DONALD BLESSING, research institute executive; b. June 4, 1939, Frederick, Md.; s. Donald, Sr. and Mary Celia (Santangelo) R.; m. Susan Fitzgerald, Aug. 25, 1962; children: Donald b. 1963, Joseph b. 1965, Matthew b. 1969; edn: BS, Univ. Notre Dame 1961; MS indsl. adm., Purdue Univ. 1962; PhD mgmt., econs., Purdue 1965. Career: asst. prof. mgmt. US Naval Postgrad. Sch. 1965-67, acting dep. dir. Academics, 1966-67; dir. cost analysis

Office of the Secty. of Defense, 1967-69, dep. asst. secty. of def. (Resource Analysis), 1969-70; asst. dir. Office of Mgmt. and Budget, Exec. Office of the President, 1970-72; pres./CEO The Rand Corp., Santa Monica 1972–; dir: Pacific Lighting Corp., Vulcan Mats. Co., Wells Fargo & Co. and Wells Fargo Bank, N.W.; apptd: Nat. Science Board, NSF (1975-86), Def. Science Board (1977-83, senior cons. 1984-), Nat. Commn. on Supplies and Shortages (chmn. 1975-77), Nat. Com. on US-China Relations (1984-), Nat. Advis. Com. on Oceans and Atmosphere, Dept. of Commerce (1972-75), Advis. Panel, Office of Technol. Assessment (1976-79), adv. council Coll. of Engring. Univ. of Notre Dame (1974-), U.S. mem. of the Trilateral Commn. (1985-), Council on Fgn. Rels., Def. Resource Mgmt. Study (dir. 1977-79); awards: Secty. of Def. Merit. Civilian Service Medal (1970), Ford Found. Doctoral Fellow in Mgmt. and Econs., Purdue (1962-65), Ten Outstanding Young Men of Am., US Jaycees (1975), hon. Dr. of Engrg., Univ. Notre Dame (1975), hon. Dr. of Mgmt., Purdue Univ. (1985); mem: Am. Econ. Assn., Fellow AAAS, Tau Beta Pi, LA World Affairs Council (dir.), The Inst. of Mgmt. Scis. (past pres.), Los Angeles Area CofC (dir.); publs: arts. in Mgmt. Sci. (1966), Internat. J. Prodn. Research (1966), Behavioral Sci. (1965), Armed Forces Comptroller (1969); mil: capt. US Army 1965-67. Res: 518 Georgina Ave Santa Monica 90402 Ofc: The Rand Corp. 1700 Main St Santa Monica 90406-2138

RICE, GLENN RICHARD, telecommunications co. chief executive; b. Nov. 29, 1948, Odessa, Tx.; s. George Lorenzo and Valeta Grace (Riley) R.; m. Lori Stevens, Mar. 23, 1974; div. 1981; 2 daus., Chaurice b. 1976, Melissa b. 1978; stu. aerospace engring., bus. mgmt. and fin., Calif. State Polytech. Univ., Pomona 1966-68, 1976-77; num. courses in real estate, options, finance, taxation, securities and econ.; registered with NYSE, AMSE, etc.; Reg. Representative, NASD (1976); lic. commodity broker, CFTC (1976); Gen. Securities Prin., NASD (1981); Reg. Option Prin., Chgo. Bd. of Options, Am. Options Exchange & NASD (1981). Career: musician/entertainer, 1964-71; quality control engineering analyst Mattel, Industry, Ca. 1968-70; sales mgr. Kirby Co., Ontario and Santa Barbara, Ca. 1972-74; branch rep. IIFC Finance, Pomona 1973; prodn. foreman, Soundesign, Industry, Ca. 1974-75; plant mgr. Neward Enterprises, Cucamonga 1975-76; stock, bond & commodity broker Bache Halsey Stuart Shields, Claremont 1976-81; account exec.-in-charge/ broker Dean Witter Reynolds, Corona 1981; asst. mgr./ stockbroker, commodity broker & finl. planner Thomson McKinnon Securities, Newport Beach 1981; co-founder/ pres./ chief exec. ofcr., gen. securities prin., Rice Morgan Internat., Inc., Newport Beach & Upland, 1981–; founder/ chmn./ chief exec. ofcr. American Telenet, Inc., Ontario 1983–; dir. Penn Pacific Corp. 1983; awards: 5 Hon. Mentions, finalist in Am. Song Festival & Lyric competition; BSA Eagle Scout, and Scout of Year, 1961, letter of recognition from Pres. Kennedy (1961); mem. Internat. Assn. of Fin. Planners; charter mem. Exchange Club of Corona (pres. elect); Republican; Christian; rec: racquetball, scuba diving, golf. Res: Rancho Cucamonga 91730 Ofc: American Telenet, Inc., POB 982 Rancho Cucamonga 91730

RICE, RAYMOND MICHAEL, chemical engineer; b. July 16, 1954, Detroit, Mich.;e s. Frederick Joseph and Ellen Gertrude (Cox) R.; edn: BSCE, UC San Diego 1981; Reg. Profl. Engr. Calif. (chem. 1983, mech. 1986); Corrosion Splst. NACE 1986. Career: chem. engr. San Diego Gas & Electric, San Diego 1981–; mem: Am. Inst. of Chem. Engrs. (chmn. 1985-86, v.chmn. 1984-85, secty. 1983-84), San Diego Gas & Elec. Young Engrs. Club (activities com. 1983); research: recycling hazardous waste 1985; Republican; Catholic; rec: computers, electronics, basketball. Res: 5560 Shasta Lane #54 La Mesa 92041 Ofc: San Diego Gas & Electric, 101 Ash, P.O. Box 1831 San Diego 92112

RICE, WILLIAM ELDON, educator; b. June 5, 1946, Colinga; s. Roy Lilbert and Elizabeth A. (Hoff) R.; m. Gena, July 11, 1971; children: Roseann K. b. 1966, Joshua David b. 1977, Christopher William b. 1978; edn: BS, CSU Northridge 1973, MS, 1975; DBA, Univ. of Colo. 1979. Career: sys. analyst Transamerica Corp., Long Beach 1973-74; senior sys. analyst Litton Indsutries, Woodland Hills 1974-75; v.p. mktg. Groundstar Energy Corp. 1977-78; prof. Coll. of William & Mary, Williamsburg, Va. 1978-83; dir. Ctr. for Bus. Research & Sci., Fresno State Univ. 1983–; cons. Pacific Gas & Electric 1985-86; honors: William & Mary Fellow 1982; Vietnamese Community Action Medal 1971; mem: Am. Mktg. Assn., Central Calif. AMA (pres. 1985-86), ACM, DPMA, Rotary, Pi Sigma Epsilon, entrepreneurs Club; author: Marketing Experience, 1980; Experiential Exercises for Contemporary Business, 1982; Marketing Survival Manual, 1986; mil: sgt. E-5 US Army 1969-71, BS, ACM, PH, BAM, USA; Republican. Res: 10523 No. Rice Rd. Fresno 93710 Ofc: Valley Business Ctr., Calif. State Univ., Fresno 93740-0005

RICHARD, ROBERT JOHN, library administrator; b. Sept. 20, 1947, Oakland; s. John Argyle and Vera Elizabeth (Bauer) R.; m. Anne Elizabeth Terrell, June 8, 1968, div.; children: Kennifer Lynn, Laura Ellen, Constance Anne, Andrea Lee; edn: stu., Fullerton Coll. 1965-67; BA, Chapman Coll. 1972; MS, CSU 1973. Career: audiovisual splst. Fullerton Public Library 1969-72, asst. to city librarian 1972-73, librarian II 1973-76; br. librarian Orange Co. Public Library 1976-78, regl. adminstr. 1978-80; assoc. dir. Long Beach Public Library 1980-81; dir. Sacramento Public Library 1981–; chmn. Mountain Valley Library System; mem: Calif. Library Assn., Library Adminstrs. No. Calif. ALA, Library Adminstrn. & Mgmt. Assn., Library Info. & Tech Assn., Public Library Assn. Ofc: 7000 Franklin Ste. 540 Sacramento 95823

RICHARD, ROBERT M., physician; b. Sept. 11, 1926, Harmon, Okla.; s. Rolla R. and Edith Belle (Drake) R.; m. Elizabeth Ann Heavin, Aug. 18, 1948; 1 son, Robert, Jr. (pre-med. student USC) b. 1965; edn: BS, Okla. State Univ. 1948; MS, Univ. of Wis. 1950, PhD (biochem.) 1953; MD, Univ. of Okla. 1961; Diplomate Am. Coll. of Cardiology. Career: assoc. prof. of clin. medicine (cardiology) USC Sch. of Medicine, also mem. faculty for Post Graduate Edn.; physician splst. in internal medicine, Los Angeles County/ USC Medical Center; cons. in cardiology USC Kenneth E. Norris, Jr. Cancer Hosp. and Research Inst., USC Estelle Doheny Eye Hosp., and USC Diagnostic Center; honors: Phi Kappa Phi, Sigma Xi, Gamma Alpha, Alpha Zeta, Wis. Alumni Research Found. Fellowship, Franklin D. Roosevelt Fellowship in Medicine, spl. award for outstanding teaching, thoughtfulness and kindness, USC Med. Sch. Grad. Class of 1979-80; mem: Am. Coll. of Cardiology, Am. Coll. of Medicine, AMA, Am. Heart Assn., AAAS, LAC-USC Soc. of Graduate Internists, Univ. of Okla. Med. Alumni Assn., USC Med. Alumni Assn. Inc., Los Angeles Sco. of Echocardiography, So. Calif. Soc. of Internat. Angiography, Newport Beach Trojan Club, Cardinal and Gold USC Gen. Alumni Assn., Beta Theta Pi Fathers/USC Chpt., Salerni Collegium Soc. for USC Med. Sch. Support, Assn. of Teaching Physicians; author: Electrocardiography (USC Press Postgrad. Div., 1979), Electrocardiography, A Spatial Vector Approach (in press 1985); mil: electronics tech. US Navy 1945-46, USNR 1946-50, SE Pacific Campaign medal; Presbyterian; rec: real estate, Okla. crude oil producer, family. Res: 1943 Port Albans Pl Newport Beach 92660 Ofc: USC School of Medicine Dept. Medicine Section Cardiology 2025 Zonal Ave Los Angeles 90033

RICHARDSON, CHARLES MONROE, JR., lawyer; b. Aug. 24, 1929, Boston, Mass.; s. Charles Monroe and Henrietta Pauline (Mehlbach) R.; edn: BA, Dartmouth Coll. 1951, MBA, 1952; JD, Stanford Univ. 1957; admitted Calif. State Bar 1957, US Supreme Ct. Career: assoc. atty. Pillsbury, Madison & Sutro, San Francisco 1957-70; partner, Lukens and Richardson, Tiburon 1971-73; atty. pvt. practice, Corte Madera and San Anselmo, 1973–; mem: ABA, State Bar of Calif., Marin County Bar Assn., Bohemian Club, Sigma Phi Epsilon; mil: 1st lt. USAF; Republican; Episcopal; rec: Irish Setters. Res: 429 The Alameda San Anselmo 94960 Ofc: Charles M. Richardson, Jr. 305 San Anselmo Ave Ste 317 San Anselmo 94960

RICHARDSON, CHARLES THAXTER, newspaper publisher, ret.; b. Aug. 25, 1911, Pomona, Calif.; s. Almon Tappan and Opal Matilda (Chain) R.; m. Jean Wood, July 10, 1940; children: Constance b. 1941, Alan b. 1943, Cathryn b. 1947; edn: BA, Pomona Coll. 1933; bus. adminstrn., Harvard Bus. Sch. 1933-34. Career: bus. mgr., gen. mgr., publisher Progress Bulletin Publg. Co. Pomona and Daily Report Ontario 1935-72; foreman L.A. County Grand Jury 1985-86; honors: Svc. Award (Pomona CofC 1978), Boss of the Year (Jr. CofC 1975); mem: Calif. Newspaper Publrs. Assn. (bd.), Calif.- Nevada Assoc. Press (past pres.), Western Newspaper Indsl. Rels. Bureau (bd.), Kiwanis, Masons (Master 1942), CofC, Pomona Valley Comm. Hosp. Bd., United Way, Red Cross, Claremont Grad. Sch., Salvation Army, YMCA, LA County Fair; Republican; Congregational. Res: 1500 S Bay Front Balboa Island 92662

RICHARDSON, JOHN FRANCIS, business executive/educator; b. Nov. 22, 1938, Newark, NJ; s. John Stanley and Helen Ana (Rathburn) R.; m. Monika Gatzweiler, Mar. 14, 1966; 1 son: Christopher J., b. 1966; edn: BA, Montclair St. Coll. 1960; MS, Polytech. Inst. of Brooklyn 1968; BSL, Calif. Coll. of Law 1978; JD, 1980; MBA, summa cum laude, Pepperdine Univ. 1982; IBM computer sys. schs., 1962-67; grad. courses, Purdue Univ., Rutgers Univ., Seton Hall Univ., Fairleigh Dickinson Univ. Career: high sch. math tchr., NJ 1960-62; mktg. rep. IBM Corp., NYC 1962-68; pres. Universal Learning Corp., NYC 1968-70; acct. mgr. Realtronics, Inc., NYC 1970; acct. exec. Merrill Lynch, NYC 1970-71; Bache rep. Bache & Co., NYC 1971; v.p. John S. Studwell Assoc., NYC 1972-73; sales rep. Control Data Corp., NYC 1973; asst. prof. Purdue Univ., Fort Wayne, Indiana 1973-74; physics tchr., Kearney (NJ) High Sch. 1975; biochem. tchr. Sparta (NJ) H.S. 1975-76; acct. exec. Dean Witter, Santa Monica 1976; lectr. USC, Los Angeles 1977-78; mktg. rep. National CSS, Inc., Newport Bch. 1977-80; realtor assoc. Coldwell Banker, Santa Ana 1980-81; mktg. rep. Informatics, Inc., L.A. 1981-82; exec. v.p. Computique, Santa Ana 1982-83; pres. ILAR Systems, Inc., Newport Bch. 1983–; mem. New York CofC & NYAC; computer sys. cons., num. firms; honors: Kappa Delta Pi 1958; Am. Jurisprudence Awd. 1978; mem: Pepperdine Univ. Assocs.; John Wayne Tennis Club; U.S. Tennis Assn.; U.S. Chess Fedn.; author: 6 travel books/ tapes, and 12 courses/ tapes; num. tape lectrs.; 6 computer applications pgms. incl. Bottomline-V corp. financial planning system; Republican; Presbyterian; rec: travel, writing, tennis, computers, chess, fgn. languages. Address: 334 Baywood Dr Newport Beach 92660

RICHARDSON, MADISON FRANKLIN, physician-surgeon; b. Dec. 26, 1943, Prairie View, Tex.; s. William A. and Vivian A. (Perry) R.; m. Constance, Mar. 30, 1965; children: Kelly b. 1969, Kimberly b. 1974, Karen b. 1977; edn: BS, Howard Univ. 1965; MD, 1969. Career: Walter Reed Med. Ctr. 1969-76; res. surgery 1969-73; fellow, head & neck surgery, 1974; asst. chief head & neck surgery 1976; chief head & neck surgery Martin Luther King Hosp. 1978; assoc. dean Charles Drew Med. Sch.; asst. prof. UCLA 1979; asst. prof. USC 1981; honors: Man of Tomorrow (1983), Man of Distn. (1982); mem: Am. Coll of Surgeons; Am. Med. Assn.; Soc. of Head & Neck Surgeons; Nat. Med. Assn.; Los Angeles Urban League (bd. chmn.); Charles Drew Med. Soc. (pres.); Inglewood Physicians Assn.; num. profl. papers & presentations; mil: Lt. Col., US Army 1968-78; Republican; rec: horseback riding, polo. Res: 814 So. Hudson Ave Los Angeles

RICHARDSON, PAUL, petroleum engineer; b. Feb. 27, 1922, Oklahoma City, Okla.; s. Paul L. and Helen G. (Turnbaugh) R.; m. Ramona J. Fields, Aug. 14, 1943; children: Michael Anthony b. 1953 (adopted), Paula Kathryn (Williams) b. 1953 (adopted), Lisa Gail (Grinnell) b. 1961, Terence Andrew b. 1963; edn:

BS in pet. engring., Univ. Okla. 1961; Reg. Profl. Engr. (pet.) Okla., Nev. Career: asst. drilling/prodn. supt. Texas Pet. Co., Colombia, S.A. 1953-58; ops. mgr. Santa Drilling Co., Santa Fe Springs, Calif. 1961-63; ops. mgr. Fenix & Scisson Inc., Las Vegas, Nev. 1963-70; v.p./gen. mgr. Santa Fe Shaft Drilling Co., Orange 1970-85; pres. Paul Richardson & Assocs. Inc. (cons. co.), 1985- -; bd. chmn. Australia Shaft Drilling Co. (jt. venture co. between Australia Mutual Providence Soc., Oilwell Drilling and Exploration Pty. Ltd. and Santa Fe Shaft Drilling Co.); mem. The Inst. of Shaft Drilling Technol. (pres. 1984-86), Soc. Pet. Engrs. of AIME; publs: Found. Installation Techniques for Offshore Platforms (1975), Found. Installation of LNG Terminal (Ports '77 Conf.), found. installation studies for Thistle A Platform (1978), contbr. book chpt. in Planning and Design of Fixed Offshore Platforms (1986); mil: chief radioman USNR 1943-45; Republican; Prot.; rec: golf, woodworking, computers. Address: Paul Richardson & Assocs. Inc. 13521 Laurinda Way Santa Ana 92705

RICHEY, CLARK, designer; b. Jan. 16, 1939, Bellflower; s. Donald Brown and Laura Virginia (Bailey) R.; edn: BA (outstanding graduate), CSU Long Beach 1961; grad. work Coll. of William and Mary 1962-63, CSULB 1963-65; desig: store designer, Inst. of Store Plnnrs. (ISP) 1984, lighting designer, Illuminating Engring. Soc. (IES) 1985. Career: dept. mgr. Sears Roebuck & Co., Los Angeles 1963-71; mdsg. mgr. Montgomery Ward & Co., Las Vegas 1971-76; dir. mdsg., project dir. Doody Co., Columbus, Ohio 1976-79; pres./bd. chmn. Creative Retailing Inc., Irvine, Calif. 1979-; pres./bd. chmn. PER, Ltd. Las Vegas, Nev. 1985-; guest lectr. Interior Design Inst., Newport Beach (1982, 83, 84, 85, 86), SEMA/Auto Internat. seminars, Las Vegas (1983, 85, 86); keynote spkr. num. nat. seminars; awards: Who's Who in Colls. and Univs. (1961), outstanding merit in store design, Nat. Assn. of Store Fixture Mfrs. (1985), best actor, Pasadena Playhouse Tournament (1957); mem. ISP (pgm. chmn.), IES, Phi Kappa Tau Alumni Assn., Nat. Assn. Display Industries, Western Assn. Visual Mdsg., Nat. Retail Merchants Assn.; author: Designing Your Own Store (1986); publs: feature article "Futurestore" in Chilton's Automotive Marketing mag. (1/85), 6-article series, Specialty & Custom Dealer mag. (1986), "Store Wars" in Import Auto mag. (2/86), subject of 6 feature articles in trade jours. (1983-86); mil: E4 USN 1961-63; Republican; Prot.; rec: ski, writing, theater, fine art collector. Ofc: Creative Retailing Inc 2222 Martin St Ste 265 Irvine 92715

RICHMAN, MONROE FRANKLIN, physician; b. Feb. 26, 1927, Bklyn.; s. Samuel D. and Beatrice (Kasselheim) R.; m. Esther Sarner, July 8, 1951; children: Keith b. 1953, David b. 1956, Craig b. 1958, Marla b. 1960; edn: BA, New York Univ. 1949; MS, SUNY, Syracuse 1951, MD, 1955. Career: research physicist 1949-51; cons. bioinstrumentation & space medicine 1956-60 (deep sea diving projects for No. Am. Aviation, Lear Seigler, Pacific Metals Corp., Litton Indus.; deep underwater exptl. projects for AUS and USN); physician gen. medicine 1956-; editorial writer (1984-), editl. bd. Computers & Medicine (1982-); elected Bd. of Trustees (pres. 1972-73, 1985-86) Los Angeles Comm. Coll. Dist. (1971-, re-elected 4 terms); developer/bd. chmn. Meml. Hosp., Panorama City 1958-68; FAA Aviation Med. Examiner; honors: Sigma Xi, Sigma Pi Sigma, Pi Mu Epsilon, Polio Found. Fellow, Mental Health Fellow, Emma Gillette Scholar; mem: AMA, CMA, LACMA, Acad. Gen. Practice, Aerospace Med. Assn., Undersea Medical Soc.; civic: City of L.A. Fire and Police Pension System (commnr. 1965-, pres. 1968-69), Boy Scouts Am. (dist. v.chmn. El Camino Dist., fmr. cub master Pack 174), Sun Valley CofC, Am. Red Cross (dir. SFV 1969-71), Rotary (past pres., dist. gov. 1967-68), Am. Legion, SFV Calif. Council for Humanities on Public Policies (founding mem.), SFV Child Guidance Clinic (bd. 1973-74), (past): Sister City Pgm., LA Com. on Narcotics, YMCA (bd. 1965-69), United Way; patents: var. med. devices; mil: aviation radio tech. US Navy 1945-46; rec: amateur radio, golf, scuba. Res: 4444 Libbit Ave Encino 91436

RICHMOND, JOHN, lawyer, business executive; b. Dec. 10, 1907, Oakland, Calif.; s. Samuel and Sarah (Stein) R.; edn: BS, UC Berkeley 1928, MS, 1934; LLB, Oakland Coll. of Law 1942; Hon. PhD, Hamilton State Univ. (1973), Hon. PhD, World Univ.; admitted to Calif. State Bar 1946. Career: pres. Richmond Ents., 1928-, and law counselor, gen. practice, 1946-; founder, mem. Nat. Lawyers Club (1932); founder, mem. Supreme Ct. Hist. Soc. (1976), mem. Grand Lodge, F&AM of Calif. Sojourners Com. (1957), VFW of US (nat. mem. com. 1971); mem: Calif. State, Alameda County, Berkeley-Albany, Am., Fed. bar assns., VFW (comdr. Berkeley Post 1962), United Vets Council of Berkeley (pres. 1963), F&AM Henry Morse Stephens Lodge (Master 1958), Scottish Rite, Aahmes Temple A.A.O.N.M.S., Masters & Past Masters Assn., Masons, Pan Xenia frat., Intercontinental Biog. Assn. England, AAAU, IPA, Am. Fisheries Soc., Internat. Oceanographic Found., Nat. Hist. Soc., UCB Alumni Assn.; mil: USAAF 1942-45, USAAF sponsored stu. Balliol Coll., Oxford Univ., Eng. 1944; rec: golf. Address: Richmond Enterprises 1611 Bonita Ave Apt 2 Berkeley 94709

RICHMOND, SCOTT DAVID, lawyer; b. Dec. 30, 1938, Orange; s. Gordon X. and Ruth Ruggles (Miller) R.; m. Jill, Sept. 26, 1964; children: Colleen b. 1966, Megan b. 1969; edn: BA, Stanford Univ. 1961; LLB, UC Hastings Law Sch. 1964; admitted Calif. State Bar 1965. Career: atty. prin. Richmond & Richmond Law Offices in Orange and Laguna Hills, 1965-; advis. bd. Orange Nat. Bank; honors: outstanding vol. Stanford Univ. Assocs. (1984); mem. ABA, State Bar Calif., Orange Co. Bar Assn., Stanford Assocs.; civic: Rotary, Orange Sr. Citizens Advis. Council, Wilson Family Living (trustee), Rehab. Inst. of Orange Co.; clubs: Coto de Caza (Trabuco Cyn), Ridgeline CC (Orange); mil: US Army 1957; Republican; Catholic (Eucharistic minister); rec: Paint Horse breeder "Pinto Pastures," golf, ski, hunt. Richmond & Richmond

Law Ofcs: 701 E Chapman Ave Orange 92666; 2352 Paseo De Valencia Ste 312 Laguna Hills 92653

RICKERSHAUSER, CHARLES E., JR., stock exchange chairman and CEO; b. June 23, 1928, Los Angeles; s. Charles Edwin and Lila (Alameda) R.; div.; 1 dau: Janet Mary; edn: AB, UCLA 1949; JD, 1957. Career: law clerk Justice Wm. O. Douglas, Wash. DC 1957-58; lawyer Gibson, Dunn & Crutcher, Los Angeles 1963; spl. advisor Div. of Corp. Fin., SEC 1964; commnr. of corps. State of Calif. 1964-65; partner Munger Tolles & Rickershauser, Los Angeles 1965-; chmn. bd./ CEO Pacific Stock Exch. 1979-; frequent lectr. on legal subjects; honors: Order of Coif 1957; mem: Calif., Am. & Los Angeles Co. Bar Assns.; Calif. Club; Los Angeles Yacht Club; Stock Exch. Club of L.A.; mil: 1st lt. US Army 1950-53; Protestant; rec: sailing, tennis. Res: 3070 Crownview Dr Rancho Palos Verdes 90274 Ofc: Pacific Stock Exchange, 618 So Spring St Los Angeles 90014

RICKEY, CHARNA ISABEL, sculptor; b. Apr. 11, 1923, Chihuahua, Mexico, nat. US cit. 1940; d. John and Sonia Barsky; m. David Rickey, Jan. 17, 1951; children: Lauren b. 1945, Andrea b. 1947, Carriel b. 1952; edn: BA, UC Los Angeles 1943; BFA, Calif. State Univ. 1958; Long Beach Univ. 1972. Career: sculpture instr. Every Woman's Village Van Nuys, Univ. Judaism Brentwood 15 yrs.; pvt. classes var. community colls. and cultural ctrs. in L.A. and vicinity; honoree: Am. Friends of the Rubin Acad. of Music and Dance (1986); co-chair art com. Jewish Fedn. Council 1983-85; mem: Council on Jewish Life and Commission of the Arts 1985-86, Artists for Econ. Action, Women's Caucus for the Arts, Artists Equity; public installations: Jewish Community Bldg. 1970, 79, Reseda Home for the Aging 1983, 85, wind-activated sound sculpture Hebrew Univ. Jerusalem 1985, Holocaust Menorah 7-ft. high bronze Martyrs Meml. Mus. L.A. 1986. Res: Venice 90292

RICKMAN, DALE MARTIN, engineer; b. June 12, 1957, San Diego; s. Frank K. and Sandra N. (Fonceca) R.; edn: AA, El Camino Coll. 1978; BS, UC Los Angeles 1981. Career: engring. trainee Hughes Aircraft Co., El Segundo 1978-80, mem. tech. staff 1981, staff engr. Defense Information Systems Group, 1984-, launch support for Galaxy, Leasat, Palapa and Westar Satellites 1982-84, systems engr. ADC project 1984-86; honors: Alpha Gamma Sigma (1978), dean's list 1976-78; club: Catalina Island Yacht; Republican; rec: waterski, scuba. Res: 5111 Carson St Torrance 90503 Ofc: Hughes Aircraft Co POB 92919 Los Angeles 90009

RICUCCI, ROBERT JOHN, JR., retail and service co. executive; b. Feb. 23, 1962, Detroit, Mich.; s. Robert J., Sr. and Angela Maria (Rossetti) R.; edn: BS in bus. adm., summa cum laude, Univ. of the Pacific 1984. Career: exec. v.p./ gen. mgr. Romex Sentinel Systems, Stockton 1985-; real estate investor; cons./contbg. author San Joaquin Employers' Council; guest instr. Rape Crisis Ctr.; honors: Phi Kappa Phi, Nat. Honor Soc., All-Academic Wrestler, Exchange Club Youth of the Year, Legion of Honor; mem. Nat. Assn. of Chiefs of Police; civic: Law Enforcement Hall of Fame (patron), Exchange Club (fmr.), Stockton CofC, Sunrise Breakfast Club, United Cerebral Palsy (assoc.); recipient NCTE nat. writing award (1980), "Crime's Changing Face and Today's Business"; Republican; Roman Catholic; rec: all sports, music. Res: 1511 S Mills #143 Lodi 95240 Orc: Romex Sentinel Systems 24 N Aurora Stockton 95202

RIDDER, P. ANTHONY, newspaper publisher; b. Sept. 22, 1940, Duluth, Minn.; s. Bernard H., Jr. and Jane (Delano) R.; m. Constance Meach, Nov. 6, 1960; children: Katherine Lee, b. 1961, Linda Jane, b. 1963, Susan Delano, b. 1965, Paul, Jr. b. 1968; edn: BA in econ., Univ. of Mich. 1962. Career: worked at Aberdeen American News (S.D.), Duluth Herald American News (Mich.), Tribune and Herald (Minn.), Pasadena Star-News (Calif.), and St. Paul Pioneer Press and Dispatch (Minn.); with San Jose Mercury News 1964-, bus. mgr. 1969-75, general mgr. 1975-77, publisher 1977-, pres. 1979-; 1985 chmn., The Technology Center of Silicon Valley; honors: San Jose's Outstanding Young Man of the Year (1970), BSA Santa Clara Co. Council distinguished citizen award (1976), brotherhood awd., NCCJ (1979), BSA Stanford Area Council, Good Scout (1982); mem: Calif. Newspaper Pubs. Assn. (bd. dirs., exec. com.), Young Pres.'s Orgn., Santa Clara Co. Mfg. Group (bd. dirs.), San Jose CofC (bd. chmn. 1975); past pres., campgn. chmn. United Way of Santa Clara Co.; chmn. Adv. Bd. Pres.'s Council, SJ State Univ. 1980-85; bd. regents Univ. of Santa Clara; mem. Stanford Univ. Center for Economic Policy Resrch. 1983-85; bd. dirs. Indsl. Relations Bur. (pres. 1985); bd. dirs. Bay Area Council; clubs: La Rinconada CC, Rotary, Sainte Claire, Cypress Point, Pebble Beach. Ofc: 750 Ridder Park Dr San Jose 95190

RIDEAU, EARL ANTHONY, Asian-American insurance co. founder; b. Dec. 31, 1930, Phoenix, Ariz.; s. Lionel Paul and Marie Iola (Smith) R.; m. Carmel M. Andry, July 6, 1954; children: Andre b. 1956, Earl b. 1956, Dale b. 1957, Craig b. 1960; edn: BA, CSU Los Angeles Merchandising Inst. 1955; Ins. Broker (1971) and Surplus Lines Broker, Calif. Career: Rideau Real Estate Investments 1954-69; Smoke Pit Restaurant 1969-71; Allstate Ins. 1971-80; Coldwell Banker 1980-83; Robert Noel 1982-83; owner, pres. Asian American Ins. Corp. 1980-; mktg. dir. ins., research & devel. Coldwell Banker 1980-83; honors: Class V.P. 1950; pres., Khi-Rho Club 1946; pres. St. Monica's Athletic Club 1972-73; mem: Chinese Businessmen of Am. Ltd. (founder), Knights of Columbus; Eastern Ins. Corp. (co-founder); mil: SK 2 USN, Korean Medal, UN Medal, Japan Occupation, GCM; Catholic; rec: history, psychology, applied imaginaton. Res: 861 Blue Bird Circle Anaheim 92807 OFc: Asian-American Insurance, 1717 So. State Coll. Blvd. Ste. 178 Anaheim 92806

RIDER, DEAN LOLLER, physician; b. Feb. 22, 1952, Chgo.; s. Joseph Alfred, M.D. and Gracelynn Lynnette (Rice) R.; edn: BS, UC Berkeley 1974; MD, Univ. Chgo. 1978. Career: intern St. Mary's Hosp. San Francisco 1978-81; fellow gastroenterol. VA Martinez, Calif. & Univ. Chgo. 1981-83; pvt. practice int. med., gastroenterol. S.F.; mem: AMA, CMA, Am. Gastroenterol. Assn., Am. Soc. Gastroenterol.; Meadow Club Fairfax, Olympic Club S.F.; Republican; Methodist; rec: golf (Meadow Club Champion 1984), skiing. Ofc: 350 Parnassus, Ste 900, San Francisco 94117

RIDEY, DOUGLAS E., orthopedic surgeon, b. Jan. 11, 1941, Detroit, Mich.; s. H. Earl and Mary Frances (Warner) R.; m. Sherry, Dec. 27, 1965; edn: BS, Eastern Mich. Univ. 1963; MD, Univ. Mich. Medical Sch. 1967; Diplomate Am. Board Orthopedic Surgery 1982. Career: internship Santa Barbara Cottage and County Hosps.; US Navy flight surgeon designate Pensacola, Fla. 1968; aerospace flight surgeon NAS LeMoore 1968-72; family practitioner Lake Tahoe, Calif. 1972-74; postgrad. residency tng. orthopedic surg. Northeast Ohio Med. Sch. 1974-78; attending orthopedic surgeon in clin. practice, Pinole and Orinda, 1978 – , active staff Brookside and The Doctors Hosp. of Pinole; Fellow Am. Acad. of Orthopedic Surgery 1985; publs. in orthopedic surgery jours.; mil: lcdr USN 1972; rec: chess, sky diving, skiing. Res: 37 Knickerbocker Orinda 94563 Ofc. Douglas E. Ridey MD, 1330 Tara Hills Dr Ste E Pinole 94564

RIDGEWAY, DONALD GENE, sales-marketing executive; b. Dec. 20, 1937, Macon, Mo.; s. Oku and Lois (Frazee) R.; m. Julie Auld, June 30, 1985; children (by former marriage): Michael b. 1959, Mark b. 1961, Matthew b. 1962; edn: BSME, Univ. of Mo. 1959; Reg. Profl. Engr. (Control Systems) Calif., 1975. Career: dir. of mktg. Control System Industries; mgr. bus. devel. Systems Control, Inc.; div. mgr. Monitek Inc.; nat. sales mgr. Internat. Imaging Systems; mktg. mgr. Security Systems, Identix, Inc.; (current) co-founder, sales & mktg. exec. IntroAction, Inc., Mountain View; dir. Wedgewood Technology 1983–; honors: Pi Mu Epsilon; author: The Healthy Peasant Gourmet (Earth Basics Press, 1983); Republican; Protestant, rec. skindiving, photog., home computer. Res: 750 Shary Ave Mountain View 94041 Ofc: IntroAction, Inc. POB 391356 Mountain View 94041

RIDGLEY, SHERRY ELLEN, lawyer; b. Apr. 21, 1952, Klamath Falls, Ore.; d. Wm. Wesley and Iva L. (Creed) Ridgley; edn: BA, USC 1975; JD, Loyola Univ. Law Sch. 1978; admitted to Calif. State Bar 1978, Federal Dist. Ct. (So. Dist. Calif.) 1978, US Tax Ct. 1979. Career: assoc. counsel Transamerica Occidental Ins. Co., Los Angeles 1978-80; assoc. atty. Nagata, Masuda & Katayama, L.A. 1980-83; ptnr. Nagata, Conn & Ridgley (and predecessor firm), L.A. 1983–; honors: Phi Beta Kappa (1979), Loyola Law Review (1976-77); mem: ABA (Tax, Probate & Real Property Sects.), LA County Bar Assn. (Tax, Probate & Real Estate Sects.); Republican. Ofc: Nagata, Conn & Ridgley, 333 South Grand Ave, 37th Floor Los Angeles 90071-1599

RIDLEY, RICHARD ANDERSON, technical writer; b. Oct. 4, 1952, Orange; s. Bryce Farnum and Margaret Wilson (McBride) R.; m. Stephanie Flosi (dec. 1983), Aug. 4, 1974; 1 son, Ian b. 1978; m. 2d. Elizabeth Bates, May 12, 1984, div. 1986; edn: BA in English, cum laude, Univ. Santa Clara 1974; MA, folklore & mythology, UC Los Angeles 1977. Career: tchr. Montclair Coll. Prep., Van Nuys 1977-78; tech. writer BBCSI, Santa Clara 1980-81; Sierra Electronics, Menlo Park 1982; Diasonics Inc., Milpitas 1984-85; sr. tech. writer ADAC Labs., San Jose 1982-84, 1985-; Honors Scholar, Univ. of Santa Clara (1971), listed Who's Who in the West (1985-86); mem. Pacific Eskrima Acad.; publs: Wolf and Werewolf in Baltic and Slavic Tradition, J. of Indo-European Studies (Winter 1976), The Deadly Strikes of Serrada Eskrima, Inside Kung-Fu mag. (12/85); rec: martial arts. Res: 1554 Sierra Creek Way San Jose 95132

RIEGEL, KLAUS DETLEV, structural engineer; b. May 21, 1941, Nuremberg, Ger., nat. US cit. 1975; s. Wilhelm and Kunigunde (Hilpert) R.; m. Annemarie Schmidt, Oct. 23, 1970; edn: MS, Ohm- Poly Technikum 1963; Diplom-Ingenieur, State of Bavaria. Career: engr. Bechtel Corp., San Francisco 1964-67; engr. Santa Fe- Pomeroy, Orange 1965-77; engr. Bechtel Group, San Francisco 1977-85; engr. Ben C. Gerwick Inc., San Francisco 1985–; mem: Am. Inst. Steel Constrn., Am. Soc. for Testing and Materials, Am. Concrete Inst.; Protestant; rec: painting. Res: 15 Heartwood Ct. San Rafael 94901 Ofc: Ben C. Grewick Inc., 500 Sansome St. San Francisco 94111

RIES, CATHERINE MARVICH, educator, ret.; b. Jan. 29, 1914, Bellingham, Wash.; d. Mike and Katjia Fadic Marvich; edn: B.Ed., UCLA 1939. Career: tchr. Los Angeles City Schs. 35 yrs; Lafayette Jr. High 1941-43, Edison Jr. High 1943-45, Venice H.S. 1945, L.A. H.S. 1946, Gompers Jr. High 1946-54, Franklin H.S. 1954-71, Hollywood H.S. 1971-76; ret. 1976; summer honors theater arts workshop Hollywood H.S. 1966-75; choreographer: Billy the Kid, Petrushka, Royal Hunt of the Sun, Hello Dolly, Rites of Spring (by Stravinsky), Fugue In G Minor by Bach, Job by Ralph Vaughn Williams; num. shorter works for stage and t.v.; vol. and chmn. Found. Grants Comm. at Senior Ctr.; chmn. United Way at Franklin High; dept. chmn. Hollywood, Franklin and Gompers Schs.; Bernardi Senior Multi-Purpose Center (dir.; pres. 3 years), Sherman Villas Homeowners Assn. (dir.; past pres.), Los Angeles Theatre Center (pres. Volunteer Captains) Beverly Hills Playhouse Camelot Prodns. (prodn. asst., house mgr.); Awards for Outstanding Service: L.A. City Council (1976, 1985), L.A. Co. Bd. of Supvrs. (1976), L.A. Bd. of Edn., Thirty-Five Year Plaque (1976); mem: Nat. Ret. Tchrs. Assn., Calif. Ret. Tchrs. Assn., Assn. of Ret. Tchrs. of L.A., Older Women's League, Sierra Club, City of Hope (vol.); author: 1969 Report to L.A. Bd. of Edn. on the Status of Physical Edn. in L.A.

City Schs.; 1976 Report to Govt. of Iran on How to Identify Gifted Students; rec: travel, world affairs, volunteer service. Res: 14100 Dickens St. Apt. 304 Sherman Oaks 91423

RIFFENBURGH, ERNEST EVAN, lawyer; b. Nov. 16, 1957, Santa Monica; s. James Walter Burdette and Wilma Lou (Rouse) R.; m. Irene Shimaoka, Aug. 21, 1982; edn: BS cum laude, USC 1979; JD, USC Law Ctr. 1982; admitted Calif. State Bar 1983. Career: intern Wash DC office of Sen. S.I. Hayakawa, 1978; law clk. Atlantic Richfield Oil Co. Legal Dept. 1980; law clk. 1981, assoc. atty. Gresham, Varner, Savage, Nolan & Tilden, 1982; honors: participant Los Angeles County Bar Assn. Moot Court 1981; mem: ABA, Calif. Bar Assn., San Bernardino County Bar Assn., USC Law Alumni Inn of Ct. (1984-); clubs: Classic Car Club of Am., Rolls Royce Owners; Republican (assoc. mem. State Central Com. 1985-); Presbyterian; rec: antique & spl. interest automobiles. Ofc: Gresham, Varner, Savage, Nolan & Tilden, 600 N Arrowhead Ave San Bernardino 92401

RIGBY, MARTIN GEORGE, water resources research analyst; b. July 15, 1948, Los Angeles; s. George A. and Edith S. (Hausler) R.; m. Jennifer Adams, Nov. 21, 1981; edn: BA, UC Santa Barbara 1970; M.Ed., Univ. of Pacific 1974, MA, UC Irvine 1980, PhD, 1982. Career: instr. (f.t., adv. placement biol., marine sci.) Marlborough Sch., Los Angeles 1973-77; research analyst Orange Co. Water Dist., Fountain Valley 1982–; instr. computer & water resources, UC Irvine; honors: UC Regents' dissertation fellow (1982), UC grad. research travel award/presented trace metal research, Internat. Conf. on Trace Elements, Amsterdam, Holland (9/81), UC Davis research grant- cadmium cycling in agric. systems (1981), Irvine fellowship (1980), Phi Delta Kappa (life 1974); mem. Am. Waters works Assn., Am. Stat. Assn.; civic: Friends of the Santa Ana Zoo; contbr. num. publs. in field of water resources and pub. policy (1979-); rec: triathlete, plant propagation, birding, finance. Res: 13652 Carlsbad Dr Santa Ana 92705 Ofc: Orange Co. Water District 10500 Ellis Ave POB 8300 Fountain Valley 92728

RIGGLE, WILLIAM HARRY, educational administrator; b. Sept. 29, 1925, Long Beach; s. Harry Wm. and Nellie May (Johnson) R.; m Grace Slater, Aug. 8, 1952; children: Linda b. 1958, David b. 1961; edn: BA, Reed Coll., Portland 1950; MA, UC Berkeley 1959, EdD, 1965. Career: tchr., English, Mt. Diablo H.Sch., Concord 1952-66; academic administr. and lectr. in ednl. adminstrn. Grad. Sch. of Edn., UC Berkeley, 1966-83, creator/dir. the Univ.'s campuswide Summer Program for Teachers (1966-83), founder/dir. the School's Office of Edn. Admissions (1969-83), ret. 1983; cons. Assn. of Calif. Sch. Adminstrs./ Region VII bd. dirs. (1972), and the Livermore Sch. Dist. (1979); honors: Phi Delta Kappa disting. service award (1976), hon. life bd. mem. Calif. Schoolmaster's Club (1984); mem. Phi Delta Kappa Ednl. Frat. (chpt. pres. 1971, coord 14 chpts. in Bay Area and Hawaii 1971-76, chmn. Task Force on Governance of frat. 1977), Calif. Schoolmasters Club (pres. 1977), UCB Edn. Alumni Soc. (charter mem, bd. dirs. 1966-83); mil: T5 744th Field Arty., 20th Corps, 3d Army AUS 1944-46, ETO; rec: biking, music appreciation. Res: 3745 Crenna Ave Concord 94519

RIGGS, STEVEN KENNETH, real estate development consultant; b. Apr. 8, 1949, Mt. Vernon, Wash.; s. Denney Kenneth and Alma June (Mitchell) R.; m. Leslie Diane Kissam, Dec. 1, 1985; 1 son, Matthew Steven; edn: B.Arch., Univ. Washington, Seattle 1972. Career: owner Steven Riggs & Assocs., Seattle 1970-74; The Clockworks, Inc. Kirkland, Wash. 1972-76; project arch. MAC Devel. Corp., Redmond, Wash. 1975-76; Richard Dodd & Assocs., Newport Beach, Calif. 1977-78; owner Steven Riggs Architecture, Laguna Beach 1978-81; owner The Riggs Group, Inc., Orange 1981–; apptd. City of Laguna Beach Design Review Bd. (chmn. 1977-80), Planning Commn. (chmn. 1980-); prin. works include: Camino Real Savings Bank (Orange), PHI Ents., Executive Offices (Orange), Laguna Beach Community Center, num. residences. Mem. Nat. Assn. of Watch & Clock Collectors (pres. O.C. Chpt. 1979-81), Kirkland CofC (dir. 1976), Orange CofC; Republican; Christian Ch. Ofc: The Riggs Group, Inc. 630 S Glassell St Ste 205 Orange 92666

RILEY, ELIZABETH REGINA, speech pathologist; b. Nov. 20, 1957, Lynwood; d. Thomas James and Marie Agnes (Remas) Brennan; m. Peter Judson Riley, March 21, 1981; edn: BA, Whittier Coll. 1979, MA, 1980; PhD, stu., U.S. Internat. Univ. 1983-. Career: itinerant speech language splst. Lowell Joint Sch. Dist. 1980-83; speech pathologist independent contractor pvt. practice 1983–; supvr. colleague's clinical fellowship year; honors: presented research 12th Interdisciplinary Conf. on Piagetian theory, USC 1982; mem: Am. Speech Hearing Assn., Calif. Speech Language Hearing Assn.; works: Is It the Same? An Investigation of Conservation of Substance Skills in Normal and Language Disordered Eight Year Olds, Piagetian Theory Developmental Perspectives and Adult Devel., 9th through 12th Interdisciplinary Conf. Vol.1, 1984; Democrat; Catholic; rec: needlework. Address: 4956 E. Holbrook Anaheim 92807

RILEY, SHIRLEY L., administrative dietitian; b. July 1, 1930, Price, Utah; d. Dr. Lyman and Emily Jennie (Wardell) Kofford; children: Judith Elaine b. 1955, Mary Francie b. 1957; edn: BS food & nut./instn. mgmt., Whittier Coll. 1952; dietetic internship Good Samaritan Hosp. Portland, Ore. 1953. Career: staff dietitian Los Angeles Gen. Hosp., 1953-56; asst. adminstrv. dietitian Grossmont Hosp., La Mesa 1959-62; dept. dir. Food & Nutritional Svs., Palomar Meml. Hosp., Escondido 1959–; mem: Am. Dietetic Assn. 1953- (adm. mgmt. dietitian), San Diego Chpt. ADA, Am. Hosp. Assn. (dir. Am. Soc. for Food Svcs. Adminstrn. 1984-85); Democrat; rec: rosarian, gourmet cook, family, travel. Res: POB 1195 Vista 92083 Ofc: Palomar Memorial Hospital 555 East Valley Blvd Escondido 92025

RILEY, STEPHEN JAMES, designer; b. Nov. 2, 1958, Dennison, Texas; s. Mitchell Orville and Donna Lee (Kennedy) R.; edn: BFA, Univ. of Okla. 1981. Career: indsl. designer Transaction Technology Inc. (subs. Citicorp) 1981-84; freelance indsl./ graphic design became ptr. Design Avant Garde, Santa Monica; honors: Print Mag. Regl. Design Annual 1986; Design Excellence Award; rec: photog. (color, b&w, non silver printing techniques). Res: 3501 Sawtelle Apt. 207 Mar Vista 90066 Ofc: D'AG, 1119 Colorado Ave Ste 113-A Santa Monica 90401

RINA, RALPH JOSEPH, airline co. president, chief pilot; b. Mar. 27, 1942, Sea Cliff, N.Y.; s. Joseph Ralph and Dorothea Lillian (Jullian) R.; edn: Orange Coast Jr. Coll., Biola Coll.; FAA lic. pilot (1959). Career: line-boy Rose Aviation Inc., Hawthorne 1959; raced T-6's (2 time Reno Gold Champion, holder fastest Reno Qualifying Time), Reno 12 years; check airman in B-727, DC-10, LR-Jet 35, 55, Sabreliner, CE-500; participant in accident investigations with NTSB; (current) comml. pilot, corporate pilot, pvt. pilot, test pilot; pres./chief pilot Desert Sun Airlines (jet charter service), LAX; pres. Custom Aviation, Inc., Long Beach; captain flight stds./tng. pilot Continental Airlines, LAX; civic: founder, counselor aero teens of Am. Aero. Adv. Comm. for North Orange County Comm. Coll. Dist. Res: 16821 S Pacific B-79 Sunset Beach 90742 Ofc: 3333 E Spring St Ste 200 Long Beach 90806

RINGER, THOMAS L., executive management consultant; b. June 8, 1931, Lafayette, Ind.; s. Alfred V. and Dorothy S. R.; m. Juanita Barwick, June 6, 1954; children: Daniel W. b. 1957, Richard A. b. 1959; edn: BS, Indiana Univ. 1954, MBA, 1958, postgrad. work USC 1961-62; lic. CPA, Ind. (1967-). Career: mktg. rep. IBM, Los Angeles 1958-61, 62-65, mktg. mgr. IBM, Santa Monica 1965, mgr. mkt. evaluation IBM, Harrison, N.Y. 1966-67; v.p. fin. Gene B. Glick Co., Indpls. 1967-69; v.p. mktg. Xerox Computer Svcs., L.A. 1969-71; v.p. mktg. & domestic ops. Computer Mach. Corp., 1971, pres./CEO/ bd. dirs. 1972-75; finl./mgmt. cons. prin., 1975-81; pres./CEO The TRW-Fujitsu Co. 1982-83, Fujitsu Systems of Am., Inc. 1983-84, bd. dirs. 1983-84; cons. prin., 1984—; asst. prof. CSUN 1961-62; dir: Law Mag. (1976-77), Logical Mach. Corp. (1977-78), Wedbush, Noble, Cooke Inc. (1980-,) bd. chmn. Wedbush Corp.)1981-), bd. chmn. DragonWagon Inc. dba MPG Car Rental Inc. (1980-82), Recognition Equip. Inc. (1982-), So. Calif. High-Tech. Exec. Network (1983-84), The Del Mar Group Inc. (1984-), Quadratron (1986-); mem: Computer and Communs. Indus. Assn. (bd. 1973), Am. Electronics Assn. (bd. WEMA 1973-74); civic: IMPAC, So. Central L.A. Improvement Pgm. for Minority Bus. (bd. 1974), Indiana Soc. of Chgo. (-1980), Malibu Lagoon Mus.; club: Crest (Pepperdine); mil: 1st lt. US Army 1955-57; Republican; Presbyterian; rec: travel, autos. Address: Thomas L. Ringer & Assocs. 3520 Cross Creek Ln (POB 785) Malibu 90265

RIORDAN, JOHN P., lawyer; b. Nov. 14, 1932, Bakersfield; s. John Jeremiah and Genevieve (McNulty) R.; div.; 2 sons: Liam O'Boyle, Sean Patrick; edn: BS, Univ. of San Francisco 1954; JD, San Francisco Law Sch. 1959; admitted Calif. State Bar 1962, DC Bar. Career: asst. to Congressman Jack Shelley, 1960-64; law partner Riordan & Goldsmith, 1965-76, Riordan and Killip, San Francisco 1977-80, Law Office of John Riordan, S.F. 1980—; commnr. S.F. Community Coll. Dist. 1972-; former instr. Univ. of San Francisco Law Sch.; mem: Irish Literary and Historical Soc. (bd. dirs. 1974-), Americans for Democratic Action; Democrat; Roman Catholic. Ofc: 507 Polk St, Ste 330, San Francisco 94102

RIPPER, RITA JO, marketing executive; b. May 8, 1950, Clarion, Iowa; d. Carl Phillip and Lucille Mae (Stewart) R.; edn: BBA, Univ. Iowa 1972; MBA, NY Univ. 1978. Career: credit splst. Control Data Corp. Mpls. 1974-78; regl. mgr. contracts & finance Raytheon Corp. Thousand Oaks, Calif. 1978-82; v.p. Caljo Corp. Des Moines 1982-84; asst. v.p. Bank of Am. S.F. 1984—; honors: Beta Alpha Psi (grad. chmn. 1977), Phi Gamma Nu (1970); mem: Nat. Assn. Female Execs., Wprld Trade Ctr. Assn., Mensa, LITA (volunteer w. elderly & disabled), Engineer's Club, Corinthian Yacht Club, Mt. Tamalpais Racquet Club; Republican; Presbyterian; rec: bridge, tennis, swimming, interior decorating & gardening. Res: 22 Marinero Cir Apt 46 Tiburon 94920 Ofc: Bank of America Two Embarcadero Ctr San Francisco 94911

RIPPERTON, BETTY, securities broker; b. Oct. 4, 1916, Maquoketa, Iowa; d. H. Gale and Madge L. (Hainer) Buchner; m. John M. Ripperton, June 6, 1939 (dec.); 1 dau. Sandra (Landes); edn: AA, Maquoketa (Iowa) Jr. Coll. 1936; contg. edn. in securities and insurance; Reg. Sec. Representative, NASD, and State of Calif., 1975-; Life Ins./Annuities Agt., State of Calif. 1976-. Career: deputy county auditor Jackson Co., Iowa 1936-39; secty. to project mgr. Alcan Hwy, Alaska 1942; secty. to supt. of Scottsdale (Az.) Schs. 1957-58; exec. secty. Camelback Inn, Phoenix 1959-60; exec. secty. for Robt. E. Maytag (now dec.), founder of Ariz. Zoological Park, Phoenix 1961-62; wholesaler, Reg. Securities and Ins. Rep. (sales), and vice pres., Franklin Group of Mutual Funds, San Mateo, 1970-83; securities broker, self-emp. 1983—, reg. through Judy & Robinson Securities, Inc., Menlo Park; mem: Internat. Assn. of Fin. Planners; Stock & Bond Club, San Diego; Showcase of the Arts, Escondido; rec: acrylic and oil painting, parapsychology. Res: Rancho Bernardo POB 85271 San Diego 92138

RISEN, DONALD EUGENE, housing & health care executive; b. July 20, 1927, The Dalles, Ore.; s. Eugene Alfonso and Grace Elizabeth (Thiem) R.; m. Elsia Alma Jeske, Sept. 18, 1955; children: Stanley Edward b. 1956, Susan Kay b. 1958, Larry Allen b. 1962; edn: Med. Tech., Yuba Coll. Marysville 1960; Bus. Admin., Univ. Md. 1966. Career: med. svc. US Army 1945-46, USAF 1947-69 (foreign svc: Far East 1950-52, France 1956-59, Greece 1964-66);

adminstr. Cabrillo Extended Care Hosp. San Luis Obispo 1970-76, Ralston Tower Modesto 1977-85; No. Calif. rep. RHF Mgmt. & Found. Property Mgmt. Cos. 1984—; gen. ptnr. Cuhari Ent. 1974-76; mem: Progress Valley Assn. of Health Facilities 1976-78, Modesto CofC (leg. com. 1983-85), Calif. Assn. of Homes for Aging (bd. dirs. 1979-80, chmn.-elect cent. reg. 1979, var. coms. 1980-), Lions Internat., Am. Red Cross, S.L.O. Planning Commn. 1971-73, Republican Central Com. 1982-, Am. Assn. Ret. Persons; author: The Four-Year Cycle of the Dow (1978); guest spkr., seminar leader on nutrition 1971-74; mil: med. adminstr. US Army, USAF 1945-69; Republican; Baptist; rec: numismatics, antique automobiles. Ofc: Area Office RHF Mgmt. 530 Coffee Rd Modesto 95355

RISLEY, RONALD DAVID, lawyer; b. Apr. 12, 1937, Los Angeles; s. William Orval and Doris Adele (Simons) R.; m. Rosemarie Scherer, Mar. 8, 1957; children: Richard b. 1958, Randall b. 1960; edn: BS, Univ. of Nebraska 1968; MA, Wayne State Univ. 1972; JD, So. Calif. Inst. of Law 1983; admitted Calif. State Bar Supreme Ct. 1983, U.S. Ct. of Appeals 9th circ. 1983. Career: unit cmdr., staff ofcr., evaluator military police and transportation fields, worldwide assignments 1955-75; instr., staff supvsr., counsellor, pres. Ventura Co. Comm. Coll. Dist. Supvsrs. Assn. 1975-79, Calif. Comm. Coll. 1978-79; paralegal, atty. pvt. practice Ventura 1980—; honors: Hornbook Award 1980, Corpus Juris Secundum 1980, Am.Jurisprudence 1980, DTP Outstanding Law Student Reg. 6 1982, Student of the Year (Ventura Coll. of Law 1982); mem: Am., Calif., Ventura Co. bar assns.; Ventura Co. Trial Lawyers Assn., Air Force Assn., Mil. Order of World Wars (judge advocate Ventura Co. chap.), Retired Ofcrs. Assn., Ventura Co. Genealogical Soc. (pres.), Nat. Risley Family Assn. (historian, dir.), Delta Theta Phi (dist. chancellor Ventura, Santa Barbara Co.), Lambda Alpha Epsilon; author: The Guide to Contemporary Risleys (1982), The Ancestry of Robert R. Blanchet 1850-1919 (1984); mil: major USAF 1955-75, AFCM, GCM, NDSM; Republican; Ch. of Christ; rec: sportfishing, geneology. Res: 29 Dana Point Ave Ventura 93004

RITCHIE, GORDON LAMARR, aircraft co. executive; b. May 9, 1935, Idaho Fallas, Idaho; s. Gordon Becraft and Helen (Gibson) R.; m. mary McClure, Sept. 13, 1981; children: Gordon D. b. 1959, Dwight L. b. 1961, Dayna L. b. 1964; edn: BSME, UC Berkeley 1963; MS, cand., Univ. of Redlands 1977-79; Profl. Engr., Calif. 1968. Career: structures engr. var. aerospace & nuclear companies, Calif. & Penn. 1962-76; senior tech. splst. Northrop Corp., Hawthorne 1976-79, project engr. 1979-82, pgm. mgr. 1985, proposal mgr. of engring. 1985, mgr. adv. aircraft structures 1984—; cons. Tridair Industries 1971; mem: Soc. of Adv. Materials & Process Engrs., Am. Soc. Mech. Engrs., Aeronca Mgmt. Club (v.p. 1975), Northrop Mgmt. Club; publs: co-author tech. paper, Qualification of Primary Composite Aircraft Structures, presented 1984; author, Composite Wing Fuselage Pgrogram, reports 1982-84; co-author tech. paper, Durability of Composites, presented 1983; mil: sgt. USAR 1960; Republican; Congregational; rec: Ferrari Owners Club, skiing, tennis. Res: 520 Avenue B, Apt 11, Redondo Beach 90277

RIVERA, ARMANDO REMONTE, engineer; b. Oas, Albay, Philippines; s. Venancio Rivera (Rey), Sr. and Eugenia Remonte (Raneses); m. Carmelita Chan, Dec. 11, 1971; edn: BSME, Grad. Sch. of Bus., Univ. of the Philippines 1962, 1966; grad. work UC Los Angeles 1964-71, USC 1972; computer applications, UCLA 1969-73; Reg. Profl. Engr. (Mech.) Calif. 1975. Career: Industrial Finance Corp., Philippines 1963-67; govt. study grant, Belgium 1967-68; Board of Investments, Philippines 1968-69; engr. Fluor Corp., Los Angeles 1969-71; energy resources engr. So. Calif. Edison Co., Rosemead 1972-76; project engr. Aramco Overseas Co., The Netherlands, UK 1976-84; power resources project mgmt. Anaheim Public Utilities, 1985—; awards: Federal (EPA) study grant Vonkleinschmidt Ctr. for Public Affairs, USC 1971-72; mem: Nat. Soc. of Profl. Engrs., Am. Soc. Mech. Engrs., Am. Assn. of Cost Engrs.; Democrat; Roman Catholic; rec: collector oriental artifacts, Chinese porcelains, Japanese woodblock prints, old books. Res: 1523 N Pacific Ave Glendale 91202 Ofc: Anaheim Public Utilities 200 S Anaheim Blvd Anaheim 92805

RIVERA, FRENZ CANO, accountant, information system executive; b. Nov. 13, 1946, Angeles City, Philippines, nat. US cit. 1980; s. Amado C. and Homabina C. R.; m. Asuncion, June 26, 1977; children: Aristotle b. 1977, Venus b. 1978; edn: BBA, Univ. of the East 1968, MBA, 1972; MS info. sys. mgmt., UC Los Angeles 1983; PhD humanities, Univ. Metaphysics 1984; CPA Calif. 1980; CISA (EDP Auditors Found) 1983; CIA (Inst. Internal Auditors) 1980; CSP (Certified System Profl.) 1985. Career: tech. cons. Philippines Sycip, Gorres, Velayo & Co. CPAs 1972-75; controller Elsters Inc. L.A. 1975-77; corp. internal auditor Purex Inds. Lakewood 1977-80; EDP auditor Denny's Inc. La Mirada 1980-83; pres. Corporate Mgrs. Inc. Baldwin Park 1983—; info. sys. cons. UCLA; honors: Best Speaker (Manila Speech Clinic 1970), Outstanding Chairperson (Inst. Internal Auditors L.A. chpt. 1984); mem: Phil. Inst. CPAs (pres. 1986), Am. Inst. CPAs, Calif. Soc. CPAs, Inst. Internal Auditors (com. chmn. 1977-85), EDP Auditors Assn. (com. chmn. 1979-85), Fedn. Filipino Rosary Groups Inc. (youth dir.), Baldwin Park Rosary Group (pres.); publ: Computer Security in Business, Creative Management in Drug Store, Formula For Success; Republican; Catholic; rec: golf, racquetball, swimming, camping, computers. Res: POB 2183 West Covina 91793 Ofc: Corporate Managers Inc. 13253 Earl Ave Ste 210 Baldwin Park 91706

RIVERA, TOMAS, university chancellor; b. Dec. 22, 1935, Crystal City, Texas; s. Florencio and Josefa (Hernandez) R.; m. Concepcion Garza, Nov. 27, 1958; children: Ileana Imelda, Irasema, Florencio Javier; edn: AA, SW Texas Jr. Coll. 1956, BS, 1958, M.Ed., 1964; stu. NDEA Spanish Inst. 1962, 1963; MA, Univ. Okla. 1969, PhD, Romance Langs. and Lit. 1969; PhD, hon., Santa

Clara Univ. 1980; LHD, hon., Western N.Mex. Univ. 1982. Career: migrant worker -1957; tchr. public secondary schs., Texas 1957-65; instr., chmn. dept. fgn. langs. SW Texas Jr. Coll. 1965-66; tchg. asst. dept. modern langs. Univ. Oklahoma 1966-68; instr., dir. lang. labs. 1968-69, asst. dir. Spanish studies pgm. in Madrid, 1969; assoc. prof. Spanish Sam Houston State Univ., Texas 1969-71; prof. Spanish lit., dir. div. fgn. langs., lit. and linguistics Univ. Texas, San Antonio 1971-73, prof. Spanish, assoc. dean Coll. Multidisciplinary Studies 1973-76, v.p. admin. 1976-78; exec. v.p., acting v.p. acad. affairs Univ. Texas, El Paso 1978-79; chancellor UC Riverside 1979–; lit. judge; spkr.; cons. in field; chmn. bd., exec. com. Nat. Council Chicanos in Higher edn. 1976–, v.p. 1978; task force on Hispanic arts, Nat. Endowment of Arts 1977-79; trustee Carnegie Found. Adv. of Tchg. 1976-80; bd. fgn. scholarships Dept. State 1978-; advy. com. Allied Health Professions, coordg. bd. state univ. and coll. sys., Texas 1979-; bd. dirs. Hubert H. Humphrey Inst. Pulbic Affairs, Univ. Minn. 1979-, Texas Commn. on Humanities 1979-, Nat. Ctr. Higher Edn. Mgmt. Sys. 1979-; bd. dirs: Inman Christian Ctr.; San Antonio 1972-77; Commn. for Mexican-Am. Affairs; Archdiocese of San Antonio 1972-77; Am. Issues Forum, San Antonio 1975-76; Assn. Adv. Mexican Ams., Houston 1977-79; honors: Promio Quinto Sol. 1970-71; Project Milestone Recogn. award, Assn. Supvn. & Curriculum Devel. 1977; Danforth Found. Assoc. 1971; Sembradore of Year., Sembradores de Amistad, 1974); mem: Sigma Delta Pi (pres. Univ. Okla. chpt. 1968), Kiwanis Club (hon.), Sembradores de Amistad (hon.), Con Safo Artists San Antonio (hon.); publs: author books incl., Always and Other Poems, 1973; co-author, A Public Trust, 1979; contbr. articles and fiction to profl. publs.; subject on profl. publs. Ofc: Office of Chancellor, Univ. of Calif., Riverside 92507

RIVERS, VIRGINIA ROSS, property manager, builder, developer; b. May 23, 1941, Toledo, Ohio; d. James Ross and Virginia (Vinnedge) Crom; children: Tracy Virginia b. 1967; edn: USC 1960-61. Career: v.p., gen. mgr. Jack Baskin Inc., Vallejo 1971–; mem: Assn. of Housing Mng. Agents of No. Calif. and Nevada (founding dir.), Vallejo Yacht Club, Soroptimist, Downtown Assn. (Central Core Restoration Com.), Mariners Landing Homeowners Assn. (Architectural Com.), CofC (Political Action Com.); Presbyterian (elder 1978); rec: boating, pen and ink drawing. Res: 167 Nantucket Lane Vallejo 94590 Ofc: Jack Baskin Inc., 601 Sacramento St. Vallejo 94590

RIX, RICHARD JOSEPH, corporate executive; b. Oct. 7, 1955, Fairfield, Calif.; s. Walter Lee and Wanda Grace (Wolny) R.; edn: Univ. Md. 1978. Career: electronics tech. Jet Propulsion Lab. Pasadena 1978-80; owner RPS Systems Corp. 1980–; pres. Rix Parcel Systems Unlimited dba Inter- City Express 1980–; mem: Assn. of Old Crows 1982-; author tech manual 1972; mil: sp5 US Army Intelligence 1973-78, Arcom Meritorious Svc. Medal; Republican; Methodist. Res: 3658 Clairemont Dr San Diego 92117 Ofc: 1224 Rosecrans POB 20507 San Diego 92120

RIZZO, RONALD STEPHEN, lawyer; b. July 15, 1941, Kenosha, Wis.; s. Frank E. and Rosalie (LoCicero) R.; m. Mary, Sept. 10, 1963; children: Ronald S., Jr. b. 1965, Michael R. b. 1967; edn: BS, St. Norbert Coll. 1963; LLB, Georgetown Univ. 1965, LLM taxation, 1966. Career: atty., assoc. Kindel & Anderson, Los Angeles 1966-71, ptnr./chmn. Employee Benefits Dept., 1972-86; ptnr. Jones, Day, Reavis & Pogue 1986–; faculty UCLA Engring. and Mgmt. Pgm. (1981-85); awards: Georgetown Law Journal 1965, Schulte zur Hausen Fellow, Inst. of Internat. and Fgn. trade Law, Georgetown Univ. Law Sch. (1965-66); Fellow Am. Coll. of Tax Counsel; mem. Am. Bar Assn. (Sect. on Taxation, com on empl. benefits, vice chmn. Qualified Plans 1985-), Calif. Bar Assn. (Sect. on Taxation, Com. on Empl. Benefits co-chair 1980), Wis. Bar Assn., Los Angeles Co. Bar Assn. (Sect. on Taxation, chmn. Employee Benefits Com., mem. Tax Sect. Exec. Com. 1977-79), Western Pension Conf. (LA chpt. steering com. 1980-83); club: San Gabriel CC; publs: contbr. taxation and law jours.; speaker annual profl. confs., lectr. Calif. CEB, t.v. and video: Am. Law Inst. (ABA, 1984), Window on Wall Street; Catholic; rec: golf. Res: 1101 Singingwood Dr Arcadia 91106 Ofc: Jones, Day, Reavis & Pogue, 355 S Grand St Los Angeles 90071

ROACH, THEODORE BYRON, stevedore co. chairman, ret.; b. Nov. 5, 1904, Lake Mills, Wis.; s. Theodore B. and Myra (Wilbur) R.; m. Katherine Ludlow, Nov. 21, 1933; children: Sharon b. 1935, Theodore James b. 1942, Robert b. 1947; edn: commerce major, Univ. Wis. 1923, 25, 27. Career: automobile dealership, Beloit, Wis. 1927-31; longshoreman San Francisco waterfront, 1931-, transf. to Metropolitan Stevedore Co., San Pedro 1937–, asst. supt., gen. supt. 1939-, secty. treas. 1952, v.p./treas. 1969, bd. dirs. 1960-82, v.p./ treas. 1960, pres. 1964, bd. chmn. 1967-69, ret.; currently cons. to bd. dirs.; elected mayor City of Rolling Hills (1961-62); honors: service award Propeller Club of US Port of Long Beach; cert. for 10-year service in Sheriffs Posse, Sheriff Peter Pitchess; hon. life mem. L.A. Steamship Assn.; clubs: Jonathan (LA), Long Beach City, Virginia Country, Rancheros Visatodores, Masons (Blue Lodge, 32 deg., Shrine 50+ yrs); Republican; Episcopal; rec: horses, golf. Res: 1167 Arroyo Dr Pebble Beach 93953

ROBERSON, BEVERLY BUD, anesthesiologist; b. Apr. 29, 1972, Lemoore; s. Alexander Grace and Florence May (Gregory) R.; m. Eleanor Gourly, June 26, 1949; div. 1974; children: Donald b. 1952, Cheryl b. 1954; edn: BA, Pacific Union Coll. 1942; MD, Loma Linda Univ. 1945; Diplomate Am. Board Anesth. 1974, Fellow Am. Coll. of Anesths. 1973. Career: intern Glendale Adventist Hosp. 1945-46; gen. practice medicine, Pasadena 1947-50, Clearlake Highlands 1950-70; anesthesiology resident White Meml. Med. Center, Los Angeles 1970-72, instr. in anesth. 1972-74, dir. of anesth. 1980-84; asst. prof. anesth., Loma Linda Univ. 1974-85, ret.; ship surgeon American Hawaii Cruise Lines, 1985–; pres. Lakeshore Investment Corp., 1956-70; pres. B.B. Roberson, MD, Inc. 1980–; recipient appreciation Lakeshore Fire Protection Dist. (dir. 1965-70); mem: AMA, Calif. Med. Assn. (del. 1982-85), Calif. Soc. of Anesthesiols. (del., alt. 1982-86), Am. Soc. of Anesthesiols., Calif. Peace Ofcrs. Assn.; civic: Kiwanis, Am. Legion, Los Angeles Co. Sheriffs Reserve Med. Co. (1972-, lt. comdr. Med. Emerg. Team 1976-); mil: capt. M.C., US Army 1942-47; Republican; Prot.; rec: scuba, photog., flying, ski. Address: 3805 Karen Lynn Glendale 91206

ROBERSON, WILLIAM NEFF, lawyer; b. May 7, 1938, Phila.; s. Wm. A. and Elsie P. R.; m. Rosmarie Meyer, Aug. 9, 1963; children: Noel b. 1967, Jason b. 1969; edn: AB, Baldwin-Wallace Coll. 1960; LLB, Case-Western Reserve Univ. 1963; admitted to Calif. State Bar 1965. Career: deputy county counsel, Kern County 1965-66; claims counsel Liberty Mutual Ins. Co., 1966-71; assoc. law firm Clausen, Gilliland & Fernandes, Los Angeles 1971-73; ptnr. law firm Gilliland, Roberson & Moser 1973-81; pres. Roberson & Frank, Los Angeles 1982-84; currently atty. pvt. practice, emphasis on civil trials, San Pedro 1984– ; Dir.: Mission Ridge Marketing Inc., Noron Transportation Inc.; mem. Am. Board of Trial Advocates (assoc.), Am. Bar Assn., YMCA; publs: editor Baldwin-Wallace College Exponent (newspaper); Democrat; Presbyterian; rec: Hobie Cat sailing, snow skiing. Law Ofc: William N. Roberson, 757 W Ninth St San Pedro 90731

ROBERTS, DAVID CASON, college administrator; b. Apr. 29, 1930, Portland, Ore.; s. Clifton Porphyry and Dorothy (Cowan) R.; m. Beatrice, 1955; children: Laura b. 1956, Debora b. 1959; edn: BS, Univ. of Ore. 1954, MS, 1955; grad. work, Claremont Mens Coll., North Texas State Univ. Career: tchr./dept. head Fortuna Union High Sch., Fortuna 1955-60, Adult School principal, 1960-65; tchr. San Joaquin Delta Coll., Stockton 1965-75, adminstr. and div. chmn. Business Div., 1975–, also college real estate coordinator; developed curriculum for both above schs.; coauthor accreditation study, Fortuna Union High Sch.; authored occupational survey results (prior to coll. opening and during organization) for Coll. of the Redwoods; arbitrator for Better Business Bureau and the local bar assn.; mem: Calif. Business Edn. Assn. (1956-), Calif. Real Estate Educators Assn., Greater Stockton CofC, Am. Legion, County Rental Property Assn.; mil: sgt. US Army 1950-52, Korean War, UN Medal, Campaign decorations w/2 battle stars, Inf. Combat Badge; Republican; rec: philately, antiques. Res: 3645 Monitor Circle South Stockton 95209 Ofc: San Joaquin Delta College Stockton 95207

ROBERTS, GEORGE ROWLAND, state government executive; b. Feb. 23, 1927, Coronado; s. Dr. Norman and Dorothy Dobler (Rowland) R.; m. Donna Elaine Lee, June 10, 1949; children: George Rowland Roberts, Jr. b. 1952, Donna Lee Tabaie b. 1954, Ann Michelle Faulkner b. 1959, Shirley Elaine Hiyakumoto b. 1961; edn: BA, CSU San Diego 1951; Calif. lic. Public Acct. Career: budget analyst State of Calif. Dept. of Fin., 1948-1958; branch dep. dir. Calif. State Dept. of the Youth Authority, 1958-68, 1979-82; asst. dir. Service Ctr. Pgm., State of Calif. 1968-69; asst. agcy. secty. Human Relations Agcy., State of Calif. 1969-70; chief deputy dir. Calif. State Dept. of the Youth Authority, 1971-78, 1982-85, ret. 1985; mil: US Army 1944-46; Presbyterian. Res: 2049 Wakefield Way Sacramento 95822

ROBERTS, GLEN STANLEY, manufacturing co. risk manager; b. Feb. 15, 1941, Shelby, Mont.; s. Virgil Fern and Marie Clara (Vargo) R.; m. Patricia FitzGerald (dau. of Lord Desmond FitzGerald, New York publisher), June 10, 1943; children: Geoffrey, b. 1953; Pamela, b. 1956; edn: AA, Bakersfield Jr. Coll. 1939; BA, UC Berkeley 1951; Chartered Prop. and Casualty Underwriter, Assoc. in Risk Mgmt. Career: bus. mgr. Marin Journal, San Rafael 1946-48; spl. agent United State Fidelity and Guaranty Co., San Francisco 1948-59; broker Miller and Ames of Calif., Inc., San Francisco 1959-61; owner Redwood Empire Ins. Agencies, Inc., San Rafael 1968-75; v.p. Frank B. Hall of Calif., Inc., San Francisco 1975-78; risk mgr. Clorox Co., Oakland 1978–; mem: Soc. of CPCU; Risk Mgmt. Soc.; Marines Meml. Club; Air Force Assn.; Soc. of Antiquaries of Scotland; Elks; mil: col. USAF 1941-46, Air Medal, Distng. Unit Citation, India; Republican; Episcopalian; rec: flying, photog., computers. Res: 49 Showers Dr., P421, Mountain View 94040 Ofc: The Clorox Company, 1221 Broadway, Oakland 94623

ROBERTS, IVIEAYEA GLOVER, administrative law judge; b. Feb. 28, 1935, Muskogee Co., Okla.; d. Miles Augustus and Gracie Ivy (Winston) Glover; m. 2d. Kenneth A. Roberts, Feb. 14, 1978; children: Alton Taylor b. 1956, Linda Taylor b. 1959; edn: BA, sociol., CSU Los Angeles 1961; JD, Southwestern Univ. Law Sch. 1971; admitted Calif. State Bar 1972; Jr. Coll. tchg. credential (life), Correctional Subjects. Career: deputy probation ofcr. Los Angeles County, 1964-72; pvt. law practice, civil and criminal law, Los Angeles 1972-74; commnr. Criminal Cts., Compton 1978-80; currently supvsg. administrv. law judge State of Calif., Fresno, Calif. Unemployment Insurance Appeals Bd., 1980–; jr. coll. instr., sociol. & law; bd. dirs. Kazzi Drug Pgm. 1972-78; frequent pub. speaker, fund raiser; recipient num. civic awards, Assembly Resolution (1978), Congl. Resolution (1978), L.A. County Resolution (1980), NAACP and num. group awards; mem: NAACP (founding mem.), Links Inc., Alpha Kappa Alpha Sor., Calif. Assn. Blk Lawyers and Judges (founding mem.), State Bar Calif., Nat. Bar Assn.; mem. Unicef, Nat. Council of Negro Women, Calif. Alliance of Black Sch. Educators; Republican; AME Ch.; rec: reading, music. Ofc: State of Calif. Unemployment Insurance Appeals Bd. 2550 Mariposa Rm 4067 Fresno 93721

ROBERTS, JOHN GORDON, drafting services co. president; b. Jan. 25, 1924, Van Wert, Ohio; s. John Griffith and Emma Elizabeth (ALexander) R.; m. Rose

Wilkins, 1946; m. 2d. Barbara Roberts; children: John Griffith b. 1954, Richard Allan b. 1956, David Gregory b. 1959; edn: AAME, El Camino Coll. 1961; Man. Cert., UCLA 1967; Reg. Profl. Engr. (Nuclear & Mgmt.), Calif. Career: engring. dept. tool & tie maker, tool and machine design engr. engring. mem. of tech. staff, mgr. mech. component design; current: pres. So. Calif. Drafting Services Inc., Thousand Oaks; honors: Lamba Award, Boy Scouts of Am. 1975; 25 yr. Svc. Award, Soc. of Mgmt. Engring. 1980; mem: So. Calif. Lutheran Comm. on Scouting (pres. 1970), Am. Welding Soc., Soc. of Mgmt., Nat. Mgmt. Assn.; works: patent, steam generator, tube to tube sheet welding, 1969; papers Long Reach Remote Pipe welding 1965; research Remote Nuclear Vessel Inspection 1968-73; mem. US Maritime Commn.; Democrat; Lutheran (Stewardship Com., Ch. Council); rec: hiking, travel. Res: 1565 La Granada Dr. Thousand Oaks 91362

ROBERTS, LEE MACK, JR., private investigator, security co. president; b. Sept 14, 1949, Gastonia, NC; s. Lee Mack Sr. and Bonnie Estelle (Smallwood) R.; m. Vernon Wooten, Nov 11, 1972; children: Paula b. 1963, Paul b. 1965; edn: AA, Golden West Coll. 1974; BA, Univ. of Redlands 1977; pvt. investigators & pvt. patrol lic. Career: detective Newport Beach Police Dept. 1970-81 (med. ret.); owner Roberts Protection & Investigation 1982 –; instr. Newport Beach Police & Fire Depts.; instr./ tchr. Golden West Coll. & Criminal Justice Tng. Ctr.; awards: Outstanding Police Ofcr. of the Yr., Newport Bch. PD 1973; three time recipient of Newport Beach Police Awd. of Merit 1976, 77, 79; Orange Co. Honored Citizen Awd., O.C. Bd. Supvrs., 1979; mem: Calif. Conf. & Internat. Assn. of Arson Investigators; Internat. Police Assn.; Calif. & Western US Confs. of Safe & Burglary Investigators; Internat. Assn. for Identification; Am. Fedn. of Police; Nat. Assn. Home Bldrs. of US; BSA Police Explorer Sect.; works: Procedural Crime Scene Investigators Handbook, Newport Bch. PD; proposal for creation of multi- jurisdictional burglary impact team; plan to create Orange Co. Police Museum; mil: Corp., USMC 1965-68; Republican; Baptist; rec: police memorabilia collector. Res: 3218 So Center St Santa Ana 92704 Ofc: Roberts Protection & Investigations, 828 N. Bristol St, Ste 201, Santa Ana 92704

ROBERTS, MARGARET M., accountant; b. Nov. 10, 1923, Carlsbad, N.Mex.; d. Joseph and Eva (Long) Morosi; m. Roy Roberts, Jan. 12, 1943; children: Dennis b. 1949, Brian b. 1951; edn: acctg., State Univ. of Mexico, Calif. St. Univ.; Certified Public Acct., Calif. 1962. Career: staff acct. Brown, Lloyd, Stevenson, Alhambra 1954-62; sole prop. Margaret M. Roberts, CPA, Monterey Park 1962-78; ptnr. Roberts & Haas, 1978-81, Baker, Roberts & Haas, Inc., Monterey Park 1978 –; instr. seminars on estate & finl. planning and on sch. district related subjects; mem. State Board of Acctncy. Dept. of Consumer Affairs Qualifications Com. (Subcom. for Rule 69); awards: 4 Way Test Award of Rotary Club (1980), elected Woman of the Year (1979); mem: Am. Inst. of CPAs, Calif. Soc. of CPAs (L.A. Chpt.), Soc. of Calif. Accts. (pres. Rio Hondo Chpt. 1975-76, state bd. dirs. 1976-79, gov. Dist. III 1980-81), Indsl. Edn. Council, Calif. Assn. of School Bus. Officials, Soroptomist Internat. (chpt. pres. Monterey Park, Regl. Council), CofC; Republican; Protestant; rec: travel. Ofc: Baker & Roberts CPAs 701 So Atlantic Blvd Ste 300 Monterey Park 91754

ROBERTS, WILLIE, college personnel and apprenticeship program administrator; b. Apr. 3, 1924, Mesa, Ariz.; s. Carter Benjamin and Rosia Josephine (Humdy) R.; m. Laura, Sept. 11, 1977; children: Sharon b. 1944, Marsha b. 1948, Linda b. 1950, Christine b. 1965, Gary b. 1968; edn: AA, San Bernardino Valley Coll. 1969. Career: aircraft engine inspr. Norton Air Base, Calif. 1951-55; adminstrv. ofcr. US Army Nat. Guard, Redlands 1955-68; asst. project coord./counselor Food Employers Council, Los Angeles 1968-70; dir. tng. pgm. San Bernardino CofC, 1970-72; comm. rels. cons. Gov. Ronald Reagan, State of Calif., 1972-74; indsl. rels. splst. Lockheed Aircraft Service Co., Ontario 1974-75; dist. affirmative action ofcr./asst. personnel ofcr. San Bernardino Comm. Coll. Dist., 1975 –, coop. edn. coordinator, 1975-83, and apprenticeship coordinator San Berdo. Valley Coll. 1975-86; affirmative action cons. Co. of San Berdo. 1983; honors: City Beautiful Award, San Berdo. (1971), appreciation awards CofC (1972), Boy Scouts Am. (1972), San Berdo. Westside Comm. Devel. Corp. (1974), Mex.-Am. Profl. Assn. (1985, 86); mem. Lockheed Mgmt. Assn. (1974-75), San Berdo. Comm. Coll. Mgmt. Assn. (1983-), Am. Legion Post 710 (Post Cmdr.), Masons (P.M.W.); publs: The Perceived Effectiveness of the Coop. Work Experience Edn. Pgm. at San Berdo. Comm. Coll. Dist. 1977-82 (1985); mil: chief warrant ofcr. W4 (ret.) US Army 1943-45, 1950-51, 1961-62, ARNG 1948-50, 52-61, Army Reserve 1962-86; Republican; Prot.; rec: bowling, fishing, sports. Res: 911 E Home St Rialto 92376 Ofc: San Bernardino Community College District 633 North E St San Bernardino 92401

ROBERTSON, FLORENCE EVA, real estate broker/accountant; b. Jan. 9, 1906, Alexandria, Ohio; d. Harry Joseph and Carrie Lucretia (Oyler) Buxton; m. Richard Robertson, Mar. 27, 1948; edn: att. Newark Bus. Coll. (Ohio) 1923, Univ. of Calif., Davis; AA, Sacto. City Coll. 1970. Calif. lic. Real Estate Broker 1956. Career: auditor/credit mgr. Ohio State Univ. Hosp. 1928-42; expediter Wright Field, Dayton 1942-45; night auditor Palace Hotel, San Francisco 1946-48; expediter Corps of Engrs., S.F. 1951-52; voucher insp. for Govt. Voice of Am., NAO Proj. 1952-53; fiscal acct. Ft. Baker 1953-54; auditor/v.p. Robertson Constrn. 1955 –; decorator, 1984 –; real estate broker, Office on Arden Way, Sacramento 1956-84; mem. Calif. Real Estate Assn., Women's Aux. 1956-66; Tuesday Club (Sacto) 1955-83; works: writing history of the Buxton Family 1769-; Republican. Res: 3540 N. El Macero Dr El Macero 95618

ROBERTSON, GERALD LESLIE, manufacturing co. president; b. Aug. 8, 1934, St. Joseph, Mo.; s. James Leo and Laura Elizabeth (Rupp) R.; m. Joan A. Brock, Aug. 18, 1956; children: Stephen 1957-1982, Julianne b. 1959, Christopher b. 1960, Scott b. 1967; edn: BS in indsl. engring., Gen. Motors Inst. 1956; grad. courses MBA Pgm., Miami Univ. 1957-59; Pgm. Mgmt. Devel., Harvard Univ. 1974. Career: supr. Central Foundry Div. Gen. Motors, Defiance, Ohio 1952-58; methods engr. Diamond Nat., Middletown, Ohio 1958-60; with Mead Corp. 1960-84: indsl. engr., plant mgr. (Durham, N.C., Chgo.) Mead Containers 1960-68, gen. mgr. Mead Corp. Internat., Zurich, Switz. 1968-73, v.p./gen. mgr. Mead Soil Pipe Div., Birmingham, Ala. 1973-74, exec. v.p. Mead Indsl. Product Group, 1974-75, pres. Lynchburg (Va.) Foundry 1975-84; pres. New England Instrument, Natick, Mass. 1984-85; owner/pres. Pella Co. Inc., North Highlands, Ca. 1985 –; bd. dirs. United Virginia Bank (1975-83); civic: Junior Achievement (pres.), United Way (pres., bd.), advisor Comm. Coll. (1975-83), Piedmont Club (bd.); Republican; Catholic; rec: ski, woodworking. Res: 2238 Morley Way Sacramento 95864 Ofc: Pella Co. Inc. 3000 Orange Grove Ave North Highlands 95660

ROBERTSON, HUGH DUFF, lawyer; b. Mar. 14, 1957, Grosse Pointe, Mich.; s. Hugh and Louise W. (Grey) R.; m. Lynn Robertson, June 10, 1978; edn: BBA/fin., Univ. Wisc., Whitewater 1978; JD, Whittier Coll. Sch. of Law 1982; admitted Calif. State Bar 1983. Career: collections, Gen. Motors Acceptance Corp., Chgo. 1975-76; night mgr. Lucky Foods, Whitewater, Wis. 1977-78; general counsel/ acct. exec./ v.p. A. Morgan Maree, Jr. & Assocs. Inc., Los Angeles 1979 –; atty. pvt. practice, Los Angeles 1983 –; honors: Who's Who Among Am. Law Students (1982), Outstanding Young Men of Am. Award (1985); mem: ABA (Forum Com. Entertainment 1979-) Calif. State Bar Assn., Los Angeles County Bar Assn., Beverly Hills Bar Assn., Lawyers Club of L.A. (1983-84), Hollywood CofC (1985-), F.A.M.E. (1985-), Am. Film Inst. (1985-), Acad. of TV Arts & Scis. (1985-), Am. Cinema Awards Found. (1984-), Phi Alpha Delta Law Frat.; Republican; Episcopal; rec: sports, swimming, volleyball. Ofc: A. Morgan Maree Jr. & Assocs., Inc. 6363 Wilshire Blvd Ste 600 Los Angeles 90048

ROBERTSON, IAN FRASER, real estate developer; b. Dec. 27, 1940, Hilo, Hawaii; s. Wm. Fraser and Marjorie Elisabeth (Babcock) R.; m. Barbara Login, July 11, 1970; 1 son, Dylan b. 1975; edn: BA English, Yale Univ. 1963; JD, UC Los Angeles 1966. Career: atty. assoc. Sheppard Mullin Richter & Hampton, Los Angeles 1966-68; atty. Weisel & Robertson, 1968-71; v.p. Kaufman & Broad Homes, Ill. and Mich., 1972-75; founder/bd. chmn. Sundance Homes Inc., Ill., Calif. 1975 –; dir. Overland Svgs & Loan; mem. Homebuilders Assn. of Ill., Calif. State Bar Assn., Building Industry Assn. of So. Calif., Sustain Builders Orgn. (chair); Yale Club; publs. (2) UCLA Law Rev., introduced use of municipal revenue bonds for single family mortgages (Mortgage Revenue Bonds) in Ill. (1977). Res: 918 Palisades Beach Road Santa Monica 90403 Ofc: Sundance Homes/ Robertson & Associates 1520 2nd St Santa Monica 90401

ROBERTSON, ROGER E., engineer, attorney; b. Nov. 2, 1919, Jaffrey, N.H.; s. Herbert E. and Eva E. (Urban) R.; m. Winifred Wright, Oct. 14, 1945, dec. 1951; m. 2d. Mary Louise Clark, Oct. 23, 1955; children: Ned Wright b. 1948, Deborah Clark b. 1957, Glen Simons b. 1958; edn: BSEE, Mass. Inst. of Tech. 1937-41, MSEE, 1942; JD, George Washington Univ. 1952; admitted to bars of DC (1952) and Calif. (1965). Career: engr. General Electric Co., Schenectady, NY 1942-46, mgr. instrumentation engring., Phila. 1953-57; engr. Bell Aircraft, Buffalo 1946-48; sect. chief Nat. Bur. of Stds., Wash DC 1948-52; prop. Instrumentation Design & Mfg., Kensington, Md. 1951-52; chief engr. B&H Instrument Co., Ft. Worth, Texas 1957-58; mgr. adj. projects RCA, Van Nuys 1958-61; mgr. sys. design Lockheed Missiles & Space Co., Van Nuys 1961-63; senior staff engr. Hughes Aircraft Co., Canoga Park 1954-79; real estate broker R.E. Realty 1979 –; ptr. Salet, Robertson & McKitterick, Northridge 1964 –; gen. ptr. Tanor Ltd. 1971 –, Valar Ltd. 1975 –, Lasen Ltd. 1976 –, Vacro Ltd. 1983 –; project mgr. Metric Study, USAF 1967; v.p., dir. Dynatek Inc., Seattle 1977-80; honors: Washington & Franklin Medal, Mass. Soc of the Am. Revolution 1937; Eta Kappa Nu 1940; Delta Theta Phi 1951; mem: IEEE (senior), So. Calif. Geneal. Soc., SAR (Calif. State Chancellor 1983-86), Boy Scouts Am. (asst. scoutmaster BSA, Buffalo 1947-48, comm. San Fernando Valley Council BSA 1968-72); Republican; Presbyterian; rec: genealogy. Res: 1915 American Way Ventura 93004 Ofc: R.E. Realty, 19441- 136 Business Center Dr. Northridge 91324

ROBESON, DAVID JOHN, plant pathologist; b. Dec. 3, 1948, Teesdale, England; s. Sydney Herbert and Doris Barnes (Taylor) R.; children: Christopher b. 1971, Benjamin b. 1976; edn: MI biol., The Polytechnic, Wolverhampton 1975; PhD, The Univ. of Reading, Eng. 1978. Career: research technician King's Coll. Univ. London 1973-74; instr. plant pathol. and physiol. Slough Coll. of Higher Edn. Eng. 1979; postdoc. research fellow Univ. Coll. Cork, Ireland 1980, Montana State Univ. 1980-83; research scientist ARCO Plant Cell Research Inst. Dublin, Calif. 1983 –; presided over session on disease resistance at annual mtg. of Am. Phytopathological Soc. 1985; invited speaker Am. Soc. Microbiology, No. Calif. br. 1985; mem: Am. Phytopathol. Soc., Phytochem. Soc. of No. Am., Marin County Cricket Club (team captain); publs: num. articles in research jours. and presentations at assn. mtgs.; rec: music, theatre, art, gardening, cricket. Ofc: ARCO PCRI 6560 Trinity Ct Dublin 94568-2685

ROBINSON, ANNE MARIE, real estate broker; b. Oct. 10, 1925, So. Amherst, Ohio; d. George and Amelia (Joseph) Abraham; m. Wm. P. Robinson, Sept. 4, 1948; children: Douglas b. 1949, Sheila b. 1950, Sharon b. 1953; 7 grandchildren; edn: cert. secty. Oberlin Business Coll. 1946; AA in bus. adm. San Mateo Jr. Coll.; BA in philosophy, CSU San Francisco 1982; Calif. lic. real estate broker (1971), Notary Public (1969-80). Career: secty. Munro-Matlack Co., Cleveland, Ohio 1946-47; Wells Fargo Bank, San Francisco 1947-50; Link-Belt Co., S.F. 3 yrs; front office mgr. Hilton Inn, Hilton Corp.; fed. civil service secty., cashier, then purch. agent FAA (Dot), S.F. until 1969, ret.; real estate agt. 1969-, broker/owner Robinson Realty & Assoc., 1971–; awards: Am. Legion Award, S. Amherst (1943); mem: No. San Mateo County Bd. of Realtors, local MLS, Am. Business Womens Club; civic: active in assistance to unwed mothers shelter pgm., AA and Al-Anon assistance pgms., parish Eucharistic minister serving the sick; candidate for San Bruno City Council (1976); Democrat; Catholic; rec: dancing, organ playing for church and home entertainment, poetry and music composition, bowling team sponsor. Ofc: Robinson Realty & Assocs. 701 San Mateo Ave San Bruno 94066

ROBINSON, DOUGLAS W., security co. executive; b. July 25, 1942, Los Angeles; s. Clark T. and Lois B. (Blomquist) R.; m. Deborah A., Jan. 31, 1976; children: Jeff b. 1966, Brent b. 1968, Tamara b. 1971; edn: BA, CSU Fullerton 1970; MSA, CSU Dominguez Hills 1979; JD, Western State Univ. Coll. of Law 1982; grad., FBI Nat. Acad. Quantico, Va. (honored as one of youngest ever to attend FBI Nat. Acad., 1973). Career: chief of police Cal. Poly. Univ. Pomona 1970-74; deputy dir. police safety Calif. State Univs. & Colls. 1974-80; pres., chmn. bd. Lincoln Security Svcs. Inc. Santa Fe Springs 1980–; advisory bd. Pacific Nat. Bank Newport Beach; dir. Active Mktg. Inc.; cons. Nissan Motor Corp., Mobil Oil, Calif. United Terminals, major univs. and sch. dists., var. cos.; mem: Internat. Assn. Chiefs of Police, Calif. Peace Ofcrs. Assn., FBI Nat. Acad. Assocs., Children's Hosp. Orange Co., Newport Beach Roosters, Santa Fe Springs CofC; Republican; L.D.S.; rec: physical fitness, skiing. Ofc: Lincoln Security Services Inc. 14140 Alondra Blvd Ste A Santa Fe Springs 90670

ROBINSON, GEORGE LOUIS, JR., quality systems manager; b. Apr. 8, 1933, Ancon, C.Z.; s. George Louis and Eleanor Margret (Fitzgerald) R.; m. Dolores, Dec. 4, 1955; children: Laura b. 1956, Stephen b. 1959, Lynn b. 1962; edn: AA, West Valley Coll. 1970, BS, Coll. of Notre Dame 1972; grad. courses Stetson Univ. 1976; Lockheed Mgmt. Inst., Univ. of Santa Clara 1972; Reg. Profl. Engr. (Quality), Calif. 1977. Career: electronic tech. Convair Astronautics, Cape Canaveral, Fla. 1958-59; functional test liaison man and electronic inspr. Lockheed Missiles & Space Co., Sunnyvale, Calif. 1959-67, mgr. Receiving Inspection & Test 1967-70, mgr. Missile Test 1970-75, mgr. ETR Product Assurance (Cape Canaveral) 1975-77, 1980-81, mgr. POMFLANT Product Assurance (Charleston, S.C.) 1977-80, mgr. Quality Systems & Controls (Sunnyvale) 1981–; Keynote speaker ASQC So. Carolina Quality Week Conf. (1984) mem: ASQC (senior mem., vice chmn. ops. SF Section 1985-86) ASQC program chmn. Calif. Quality Week Conf. (1973), So. Carolina Quality Week Conf. (1979); mem. Nat. Mgmt. Assn. (chmn. Carolina Low Country Sect. 1978-79, Charleston Chpt. NMA Outstanding Service Award 1980); mem. Lockheed Employees Rec. Assn., Golf Club; mil: cpl. US Marine Corps 1953-56; Republican; Catholic; rec: golf, fishing, travel. Res: 4200 Tanager Common Fremont 94536

ROBINSON, HARRELL EDWARD, physician; b. July 9, 1952, Thomasville, Ala.; s. Sandy C. Jr. and Savannah Patricia (Atwood) R.; edn: BA, Oakwood Coll. 1974; MD, Loma Linda Univ. 1977, Splst. Hd. & Neck/ENT, 1981; Otorhinolaryngologist (ENT) Head & Neck Surgeon, Facial Plastic Surgeon; certified Am. Bd. Otolaryngol. Career: intern gen. surg., 1978, res. otorhinolaryngology White Memorial Med. Ctr. 1979-81; lab instr. Oakwood Coll.; NIH resrch. in biochem.; curently physician Head & Neck Surgeon, Ross Loos Med. Group, Orange; teaching staff White Meml. Med. Ctr. of Loma Linda Univ.; awards: research grants from public, pvt. orgns.; Am. Chem. Soc. award 1973; Outstanding Young Men of Am. 1972; mem: CHOMS, CMA, AMA, Am. Council Otolaryn.; Am. Acad. Otolaryn./ Head & Neck; NARI; sci. publs.; rec: painting, sketching. Res: 95 Highland View Irvine 92715 Ofc: 1310 W Stewart Dr Ste 308 Orange 92668

ROBINSON, JOSEPH WESLEY, interior designer; b. Oct. 1, 1930, N. Ireland; s. Robert James and Elizabeth (McCauley) R.; m. Ann, Mar. 17, 1960; children: Gary, b. 1963, Wendy Lee, b. 1965; ed. Littlemount P.E. Sch. Career: mgr. Gillespie & Wilson Furnishings, Belfast, N. Ireland 1963-70; owner Wesley Robinson gen. hsewares store, Belfast 1970-72; ptnr. Wendys Decor Inc., Sunnyvale, Calif. 1972-76; owner/pres. Regency House Interiors, Sacramento 1976–; ptnr./ v.p./ sec.-treas. Brock Robinson builders & developers, Sacto. 1984–; gen. ptnr. To-Gether We Build, Grass Valley 1981–; awards: No. Calif. Award for Excellence in Interior Design & Mktg., Sales & Mktg. Council of the Building Indus.; mem. Building Indus. Assn. N.Calif.; Bible tch., counselor; rec: golf, waterskiing. Res: 12345 Lakeshore North Auburn 95603 Ofc: Regency House Interiors 3400 Watt Ave Sacramento 95821

ROBINSON, OLIVIA GENTRY, business development and strategic marketing consultant, author, lecturer; b. July 5, 1947, Sacramento; d. John Dean and Cynthia Margaret (Ewart) Gentry; 1 son: Brooks Robinson, b. 1969; edn: BA, CSU Northridge 1975; MA, 1980. Career: cons. Olivia G. Robinson Consulting Svcs.; formerly dir. west coast ofc. The Keplinger Companies; mem: The Assn. for Corporate Growth (dir.), So. Calif. Corporate Planners Assn., Town Hall of Calif. (Exec. Com.), USC Commerce Associates; club: Los Angeles Athletic; contbr: Energy Vulnerability and War: Alternatives For America, Norton & Co., 1981; author num. techl. arts. in profl. journs. Ofc: Olivia G. Robinson Consulting Services, PO Box 6128 Malibu 90264-6128

ROBINSON, ROBERT LOVE, JR., internal auditor; b. Apr. 21, 1961, Madera, Calif.; s. Robert Love and Evelyn (Barnes) R.; edn: BS, Univ. of the Pacific 1982; CPA Calif. 1984. Career: staff acct. Price Waterhouse Sacramento 1982-85; internal auditor Sun Diamond Growers of Calif. Stockton 1985–; honors: Calif. Boys' State 1977, Who's Who Among Students in Am. Univs. & Colls. 1982, CSF 100% Life Member 1978, Dean's List (Univ. Pacific 1982); mem: Calif. Soc. CPAs, Nat. Assn. Accts., Nat. Assn. Black Accts., Alumni Assn. (Univ. Pacific, Sch. of Bus.); Republican; Christian; rec: chess, backgammon, tennis, softball. Res: 4531 Romano Dr, No 349, Stockton 95207 Ofc: Sun Diamond Growers 1050 S Diamond St Stockton 95205

ROBINSON, RONALD LEE, commercial real estate consultant; b. Nov. 11, 1943, Great Falls, Mont.; s. Russell William and Margaret Rose (Pilz) R.; m. Lesley, June 27, 1981; children: Kelly b. 1964, Mark b. 1968, Sabrina b. 1969; edn: Mont. St. Univ. 1963-65; BS, Univ. Idaho 1967; JD, Santa Clara Law Sch. 1985; Calif. lic. real estate broker (1980), cand. Calif. Bar (1986). Career: sales rep. General Foods Corp., Portland, Ore. 1967-68; dist. sales mgr. Polaroid Corp., San Francisco 1968-74; dir. sales & mktg. Rockwell Internat., Anaheim 1974-77; real estate broker Ashwill Burke & Co., San Jose 1977-81; pres. Robinson Donatoni Inc., San Jose 1981-82; pres. Robinson Comml. Properties Inc., Santa Clara 1982–; instr. R.E. Investment, San Jose City Coll. (1981); ptnr. The Equity Alliance (comml. R.E. syndication co.); recipient profl. awards, Ashwill Burke & Co. (1978, 79); mem. Assn. of South Bay Brokers, Santa Clara Co.; Building Owners and Mgrs. Assn., Santa Clara CofC, San Jose Symphony (patron), Toyon Farm Homeowners Assn. (dir.), Los Altos Athletic Club; Republican; rec: golf. Ofc: Robinson Commercial Properties Inc 900 Lafayette St Ste 409 Santa Clara 95050

ROBINSON, WILLIAM JAMES, engineer, electronic/mechanical computer scientist; b. June 26, 1953, La Jolla; s. Clarence Barss and Irene Florence (MacDonald) R.; m. Catherine Eastelry, Sept. 22, 1979; edn: engring. tech., elec., Grossmont Coll. 1974; engring., electronics, CSU San Diego 1975-77; BSCS Nat. Univ. 1985. Career: electronics design engr./instr. Dyn-Aura Engring. Labs., 1975-77; electronics test engr. Doric Scientific, 1978-82, also in-house tchg., cons.; engr., quality control supr. Metrox Inc., San Diego 1985–; honors: 1st pl. Engring./Electronics, Sr. Div. (1971), ASME (1971), Inst. of Elec. and Electronic Engrs. (1971), Pickett Slide Rule Award (1971); works: 3-D animated characters, FMC Unit 4-80, Linear Displacement Transducer 7-82; Republican; Christian; rec: 3-D animated characters controlled by personally designed electronics. Res: 1127 Dawnridge Ave El Cajon 92021 Ofc: Metrox Inc. 7165 Construction Ct San Diego 92121

ROBISON, J. SHELBURN, lawyer, army officer, ret.; b. May 27, 1894, Pinos Altos, N.M.; s. Lewis B. and Katherine (Pound) R.; m. Helen Wright, Feb. 25, 1925; children: Robin Robison Vaugn b. 1930, Samuel Shelburn b. 1935, Alexandra Robison Diaz Aguado b. 1944; edn: grad. Field Artillery Sch.; BS mining engrg., Penn. State Univ. 1917; JD, Univ. San Francisco Law Sch. 1934. Career: atty. ptnr. Robison & Whittlesey 1938-82; prof. mil. sci. and tactics Univ. Santa Clara 1942-46; pres. Carmel Unified Sch. Dist.; honors: cmdr. field artillery battery firing salute closing burial Unknown Soldier 1921, placed wreath on Unknown Soldier's grave 1975, Tau Bet Pi, pres. Athletic Assn. Penn. State 1917; mem: Carmel Bus. Assn. (pres.), County Aviation Bd. (charter); publ: wrote history Seventh Div. US Army by order Comdg. Gen.; mil: capt. US Army field artillery 1917-30, 1942-46; Catholic; rec: baseball (played in Copper League). Res: Box 1686 Carmel 93921

ROBLES, MAURO PACHECO, company president; b. Dec. 8, 1923, Zacatecaz, Mex., nat. 1965; s. Prudenciano and Celsa (Pacheco) R.; m. Estela Arellano, Sept. 11, 1954; children: Marisela b. 1955, Ricardo b. 1957, Pablo b. 1961, Marina b. 1963, Jacqueline b. 1969. Career: founder La Reina, Inc. 1958–; chmn. & pres., manufactures tortillas, selling in 42 states, founded West-Bag, Inc., poly bag operation 1977; founded Anitas Mex. Foods Corp. 1978; founded Queen Internat. Foods, Inc. 1979; named to the top 100 Latino companies in the US 1979-; Republican; Catholic. Ofc: La Reina, Inc., 316 N. Ford Blvd Los Angeles 90022

ROCCO, DONALD P., dentist; b. Aug. 3, 1933, Ellwood City, Pa.; s. Thomas D. and Teresa M. (Del Prete) R.; div.; children: Renee b. 1962, Donia b. 1967; edn: BS in zool., USC, 1957, MS in biochem., 1969, med. & phys. diagnosis cert., 1980; DDS, Coll. of Phys. & Surgeons 1964. Career: pvt. dentistry practice, Salinas 1979–, Livermore 1964-76, Internat. Acad. for Orthodontics 1969-75; assoc. prof. Anesthesia - Medicine, Diagnosis, Periodontics & Cont. Edn., Univ. of So. Calif. 1977-; asst. prof. Operative Dentistry, Endodontics, Prosthodontics, Coll. of Physicians & Surgeons, 1964-75; cons. Sch. of Dentistry; honors: Fellow Royal Soc. of Health (1967), Fellow Internat. Acad. for Orthodontics (1971), Diplomate Internat. Bd. of Orthodontics (1973); mem: Am. Dental Soc. of Anesthesiol., Am. Dental Assn., Internat. Assn. for Orthodontics, European Orthodontic Soc., The Am. Soc. for the Advance. of Anesthesia in Dentistry, Acad. of Gen. Dentistry, So. Calif. Acad. of Oral Pathol., Am. Acad. of Periodontol.; Lions Club; research: Cancer (1953-59), Cariod-Vascular (1955-57), Neuro-Surgical (1957-59), Sea Anemone (1961-62), Pain Control (1968-75), Anesthesia (non-narcotic) resrch. in progress; mil: lt. AF ROTC 1951-53; Republican; Catholic; rec: jogging, music, racquet ball. Res: NW Corner 7th & Forest, POB 851, Carmel 93921 Ofc: Salinas Valley Family Dentistry Practice, 2029 N. Main Salinas 93906

ROCCO, PAT, charity mission director; b. Feb. 9, 1934, Bklyn.; s. Vincent Louis and Mary Justina (Rocco) Serrapica; edn: Pasadena City Coll. 1951. Career: profl. performer, vocalist on num. TV shows, 1950s, toured, directed, and appeared in stage shows, TV shows and night clubs; dir. over 100 movies, 1960s; dir. of activities United States Mission (providing emergency housing, food, clothing and job assistance), Los Angeles, Hawaii & San Francisco branches, 1978–, and current dir. San Francisco branch; pres. C.S.W. Assoc., Los Angeles 1974-75; awards include Best Film awards (1970, 71, 72); honored by Mayor Tom Bradley, Los Angeles City Council, Calif. State Assembly and others for community service; Democrat; rec: singing, movie-making, helping others. Address: P.O. Box 6437 San Francisco 94101

ROCHETTE, BLAKE ALAN, certified public accountant, financial controller; b. July 4, 1956, Pasadena; s. Ernest Alfred and Sondra Ruth (Martin) R.; m. Julie, Sept. 16, 1978; edn: BS, Univ. of Redlands 1978; CPA, Calif. 1980. Career: staff auditor Eadie & Payne CPAs, San Bernardino 1978-80; asst. corp. controller Bourns Inc., Riverside 1980-81; audit sr. Burroughs Corp., Detroit, Mich. 1981-83; divl. controller, asst. corp. controller Sunrise Co., Palm Desert 1983–; rec: golf, tennis. Res: 76-701 Chrysanthemum Way Palm Desert 92260 Ofc: Sunrise Co., 75-005 Country Club Dr. Palm Desert 92260

ROCHLEN, ROBERT JOHN, real estate broker; b. Aug. 5, 1956, Bangkok, Thailand; s. Donald Horace and Betty Lou (Carpenter) R.; edn: BA history, Geo. Washington Univ. 1979; real estate broker Calif. 1982. Career: pension adminstr. Integrated Pension Services, Inc. 1982-83; product adminstr., IRA/ Keogh Dept. Great Western Savings, 1983–; participant Tennis Exchange Tour to Soviet Union (Sep-Oct 85); Republican; Presbyterian; rec: tennis, travel. Ofc: Great Western 19860 Plummer St Chatsworth 91311

ROCKSTAD, HOWARD K., physicist; b. Aug. 5, 1935, Ada, Minn.; s. Gust A. and Petra C. (Ramstad) R.; edn: BA in physics, math., St. Olaf Coll. 1957; MS in physics, math., Univ. of Ill., Urbana 1959, PhD physics, 1964. Career: research physicist Corning (N.Y.) Glass Works 1963-70, Energy Conversion Devices Inc., Troy, Mich. 1970-74; project engr. Micro-Bit Corp., Lexington, Mass. 1974-79; senior project engr. Micro-Bit Div. Control Data Corp., Lexington 1979-81; senior research scientist ARCO Solar Industries, Calabasas, Calif. 1981-82, Atlantic Richfield Co., Chatsworth 1982–; math. lectr. Elmira Coll. 1967; honors: Sigma Pi Sigma (1954-, chpt. pres. 1956-57); mem: Am. Physical Soc., Am. Vacuum Soc., Materials Research Soc., Microbeam Analysis Soc. (treas. So. Calif. Sect. 1984-85); civic: World Hunger Appeal Com. of Lutheran Ch. in Am. (1985-), Ventura Co. Hunger Coalition (dir. 1984-), CWS/ CROP of Conejo Valley (treas. 1985-86), Alfa Romeo Owners Club USA (pres. 1980-83); num. publs. re electronic and optical props. of solids and electron beam effects in solids; Lutheran; rec: skiing. Address: Thousand Oaks 91362

ROCKWELL, CHARLES MARK, chiropractor; b. Dec. 5, 1945, Altadena; s. Charles and June Violet (King) R.; m. Dianne M. Dippe, Nov. 29, 1969; children: Tyler b. 1976, Kimberly b. 1978, Lisa b. 1980; edn: AA, Coll. of San Mateo 1967; bus. mgmt., San Jose State Coll. Univ. 1968-69, 1975-76; DC, summa cum laude, Palmer Coll. 1976. Career: head intern 5 Points Clinic 1975-76; chiropractor in pvt. practice, owner/ pres. Rockwell Chiro. Office Inc. Redwood City 1976–; instr. chiro. technique Pacific States Chiro. Coll., Life Chiro. Coll.-West; honors: Clin. Excellence Award (Palmer Coll. 1976), pres. student Internat. Chiro. Assn. (Palmer Coll.); mem: Internat. Chiro. Assn. (rep. Assembly 1984), Parker Research Found., Beyond War Found., Internat. Chiro. Assn. of Calif. (bd. dirs. 1983-), Toastmasters (Davenport, Iowa pres. 1976), Redwood City Sunrise Lions; works: seminars on Beyond War, ednl. found. dedicated to moving the world beyond war; mil: ssgt. USAF 1969-73, Airman of the Year, Greece 1971; Methodist; rec: outdoor sports, fishing, hunting. Ofc: 950 Woodside Rd Ste 1 Redwood City 94061

RODGERS, JAMES BOWMAR, JR., telecommunications co. executive; b. March 20, 1945, San Francisco; s. James Bowmar and Carol (Moss) R.; m. Montye Elizabeth, Dec. 14, 1974; edn: BA, Santa Clara Univ. 1967, MBA, 1972. Career: co-owner Monterey Bay Yacht Ctr. 1972-73; reg. pgm. mgr. Xerox Corp. 1973-82; v.p. mktg., co-founder Human Engineered Software 1982-84; nat. acct. mgr. Apple Computer 1984-85; v.p. sales, dir. field mktg. GTE Sprint 1985–; coll. instr. Laney Coll. 1978, 1979; bd. dirs. Texor Corp. 1984; mktg. cocns. Zilog Corp., Video 7, 1985; honors: Mgr. of the Year, Xerox Corp. 1981; mem: Am. Mgmt. Assn., Delta Sigma Epsilon, Olympic Club, Encinal Yacht Club, Sierra Club; works: software mkg. articles, The Future of the Software Industry, Infoworld 1984; mil: lt. USN 1967-70, Bronze Medal, Vietnam; Republican (Pres. Task Force 1986), Catholic; rec: sailing, tennis, skiing. Res: 622 Mystic Ln. Foster City 94404 Ofc: GTE Sprint, 500 Airport Ste. 345 Burlingame 94010

RODGERS, PATRICIA, consulting co. president; b. Aug. 20, 1936, Cleveland, Ohio; d. Fred Joseph and Adeline Victoria (Czarniewski) Russell; m. Roy A. Rodgers, Jan. 7, 1956; children: Lynda b. 1956, Sharon b. 1958, Janet b. 1959, Russell b. 1965; edn: AA bus. adm., Ohio Univ. 1956. Career: owner/mgr. Westview Dry Cleaners, Cleveland, Ohio 1966-72; gen. mgr. Hallmark Interiors, Elkhart, Ind. 1972-77; owner/pres. Custom R.V. Sheet Co., 1977-81; owner The Restaurant, Anaheim, Calif. 1981-82; v.p. Yellow Page Publ., Santa Ana 1982-84; owner/pres. Office Procedure Consultants Corp., Fountain Valley 1985–; mem: Am. Mgmt. Assn., Calif. Notary Public, Orange County CofC; patentee: drapery closure; Democrat; Catholic. Address: OPCC, 9102 Crocus Ave Fountain Valley 92708

RODIGER, GEORGIANA GLENN, psychotherapist; b. Feb. 11, 1931, Cambridge, Mass.; d. C. Leslie and Georgiana (Sibley) Glenn; m. William B. Rodiger, Jan. 31, 1953, div. 1976; children: Georgiana b. 1953, William b. 1958, Jim b. 1960, John b. 1962, Margaret b. 1962; edn: BA, Pomona Coll. 1952; postgrad. work, USC, 1952-53; MA, Fuller Theol. Sem. 1975, PhD, Fuller Grad. Sch. Psych. 1980; lic. clin. psychologist, Calif. Career: field dir. Pasadena Area Girl Scouts, 1952-53; developmental disabilities cons. trainer, research asst. Bur. Tng. and Manpower Devel. Sect., Calif. Dept. Health, Sacto. 1973-76, psychol. asst., 1977-79; intern psychiat. div. Childrens Hosp., 1978-80, trainer hospice vols., 1978-79; psychotherapist in pvt. practice, dir. Georgiana Rodiger Center, Pasadena 1980–; cons. Pasa. Unified Sch. Dist. 1979-81; faculty Pacific Oaks Coll., 1980, Fuller Grad. Sch. Psych., 1975-80; co-founder Hospice of Pasadena (1979), Candlelighters of Pasadena (1981); adviser for senior high youth All Saints Ch., Pasa. (1981) Women in the Middle (1981), Anorexia-Bulemia group (1981-82); recipient Nat. award United Community FUnds and Councils of Am. (1968), Newton D. Baker Cert. of Recognition; mem. Am. Psychological Assn., Pasa. Junior League, Pasa. Chorale; Episcopal; rec: tennis, backpacking, sailing. Res: 1102 Arden Rd Pasadena 91106 Ofc: Rodiger Center 69 North Catalina Pasadena 91106

RODRIGUES, KENNETH ALAN, architect; b. June 26, 1953, San Jose; s. Joseph Albert and Xexy Audrey (McDonald) R.; m. Deborah Ann Toro, Dec. 10, 1976; 1 dau. Brianna Leigh b. 1983; edn: B.Arch. Cal. Poly. S.L.O. 1976; lic. Arch. Calif. 1980. Career: draftsman Higgins and Root Archs. Los Gatos 1974-75; proj. designer Habitec Archs. Santa Clara 1976-78; prin. LRS Assoc. Archs. Sunnyvale 1978–, currently chmn., pres. LRS Assoc.; arch. advisor City of Campbell 1982-83; honors: Mayor's Award for Outstanding Design (City of Mtn. View 1983, City of San Jose 1982), Calif. Drywall Award 1982; mem: Am. Inst. Archs. (corp. mem., dir. Santa Clara Valley chpt., pgms. chmn. 1982-84, dir. south 1985-87), Sports Car Club of Am., BMW Club of Am.; Republican; Catholic; rec: art, sports car racing. Res: 363 Pennsylvania Ave Los Gatos 95030 Ofc: LRS Assoc. 1283 Oakmead Pkwy Sunnyvale 94086

RODRIGUEZ, PEDRO SANDAHAN, JR., accountant; b. Dec. 8, 1934, San Jose, Mindoro, Philippines, nat. US cit. 1978; s. Pedro Nolasco, Sr. and Remedios Toledo (Sandahan) R.; m. Nellie Castro, Feb. 21, 1960; children: Rachel b. 1961, Roland b. 1962, Peter b. 1968; edn: BS in commerce, Far Eastern Univ. 1958; CPA Philippines (1966), Calif. (1983). Career: bookkeeper India Imports, Inc. San Francisco 1969-70; asst. fin. ofcr. PCSC, Inc. Pasadena 1971-74; fin. ofcr. NAPP, Inc. Los Angeles 1975-77; fiscal ofcr. SERCAA, Inc. Carson 1977-79; owner Diversified Business Services (acctg., cons., taxes), Carson 1979–; mem. Am. Inst. CPAs, Calif. Soc. CPAs, Carson CofC; Democrat; Roman Catholic; rec: sports. Res: 558 E Lincoln St Carson 90745 Ofc: Diversified Business Services Rodriguez Bldg 316 W Carson St Ste 105 Carson 90745

RODRIGUEZ, ROMAN, physician; b. Jan. 21, 1951, NYC; s. Roman Rodriguez and Margarita (Castillo) Torres; edn: BS in biol., St. Mary's Coll., Calif. 1972; MD, UC San Francisco 1976; psychiatric externship, Menninger Found., 1973; pediatric externship, Univ. of Miami, 1974. Career: resident gen. psychiat. Menninger Sch. of Psychiatry, 1976-79; fellowship in child psychiat. 1978-80; res. physician Topeka VA Med. Ctr., 1976-79; dir. of psychiatric svcs. Youth Center at Topeka, 1979-80; assoc. med. dir., child psychiatrist Mission/Southeast Adolescent Day Treatment Ctr., Children's Hosp. of San Francisco 1980-81; staff psychiatrist Youth Guidance Ctr., S.F. 1980-82; clin. dir. Growing Mind Corp., Bolinas 1980-85; child team leader Dept. of Psych., Kaiser Permanente Hosp., So. San Francisco 1985–; physician, child psychiatrist Monteagle Med. Ctr./St. Luke's Hosp., S.F.; asst. clin. prof. of psychiatry UCSF Sch. of Med. 1981-85; staff phys. Children's Hosp. (1980-85), St. Luke's Hosp. (1981-85), Univ. of Calif. Hosps. & Clinics (1983-), San Francisco; staff phys. Marin Gen. Hosp. (1984-); mem. UCSF Sch. of Med. admissions com. 1980-85; mem: Am. Acad. of Child Psychiatry, No. Calif. Psychiatric Soc., Am. Psychiatric Assn., AMA; (past) Kansas Med. Soc. 1976-80, Fellows Assn. of the Menninger Sch. of Psychiat. 1976-80; bd. dirs: Canal Community Alliance, San Rafael 1985-, Community Health Ctr. of Marin, Fairfax 1985-; Republican; Catholic; rec: keyboard music, walking, travel. Res: 11 Catalina Blvd San Rafael 94901-4404 Ofc: Dept. of Psychiatry, Kaiser Permanente Hosp., 1200 El Camino Real, S San Francisco 94080-3299

RODRIQUEZ, SAMUEL LEE, systems analyst, consulting engineer; b. May 24, 1951, San Bernardino; s. Levi and Hermina (Beceril) R.; m. Cindy, Aug. 10, 1975; children: Michele and Tienna (twins) b. 1976; Samuel II b. 1978; edn: BSCE, Calif. Polytechnic Univ. Pomona 1973, MS, 1975; civil engr., CSU Long Beach 1988; Profl. Civil Engr., Calif. 1980. Career: systems analyst engring. systems dept. Fluor Corp. 1974-83; senior software engr. CalComp (Calif Computer Products) 1983-85; senior engr., structural analysis, supvr. Northrop Corp. 1985–; cons. engring. and systems analysis, sole prop. Civil Engineering Computer Research 1980-; honors: Tau Beta Pi, CSU Long Beach; mem: Am. Soc. of Civil Engrs.; Republican; Baptist; rec: running, karate, child rearing. Res: 3138 Limerick Ln. Costa Mesa 92626 Ofc: Northrop Corp., One Northrop Ave. Hawthorne 90250

ROE, EUGENE K., automobile dealer; b. Nov. 17, 1931, White Lake, Wisc.; s. Sherman H. and Vesta M. (Tate) R.; m. Martha J. Calandrino, Nov. 22, 1952; children: Michael S. b. 1954, Barbara J. b. 1962; edn: USN Electronics Sch. 1950-53, CSU San Jose 1953, Univ. of Santa Clara 1954. Career: Auto Fin. Dept., then asst. branch mgr. First Nat. Bank of San Jose, 1953-58; exec. v.p. S. Claire Cadillac, St. Claire Leasing Corp., 1959-69; ptnr. All American Pontiac, 1970-72; owner/pres. Gene Roe Pontiac Buick, Inc. 1973-80, Palo Alto Nissan, Inc., Palo Alto 1981–; mem. fin. bd. Bethel Ch., San Jose (1981-85); coll. council Bethany Bible Coll., Santa Cruz (1965-85); bd. regents and bd. govs. Calif. Theological Sem., Fresno (1985-); mem: No. Calif. Nissan Dealers Advtsg. Assn. (pres. 1986), Peninsula Auto Dealers Assn. (bd. dirs. 1983-85),

Peninsula Auto Dealers Ins. Trust (bd. dirs. 1985-86), Elks, Rotary (fmr); mil: electronics man 3d, US Naval Air Force 1949-53; Republican; Assembly of God; rec: hunting, fishing. Res: 24 Los Altos Square Los Altos 94022 Ofc: Palo Alto Nissan Inc. 3017 El Camino Real Palo Alto 94306

ROESCHKE, DONALD FREDERICK, lawyer; b. Mar. 20, 1938, Pago Pago, Samoa; s. Charles Edward and Madeline (McCarty) R.; m. Suzann Hogue, July 12, 1969; 1 son: David, b. 1976; edn: BS, CSU Northridge 1961; JD, Southwestern Univ. Sch. of Law 1965; admitted to practice US Supreme, US Dist. & 9th Circuit Ct. of Appeals; writs coordinator for State Atty. General, L.A. Office. Career: self- empl. atty. 1966-72; deputy attorney general (IV), Calif. Dept. of Justice, Ofc. of Atty. Gen. 1972–; author Deputy tng. manuals on state & fed. writ & state appellate procedures; lectr. on writs; prosecutor, Daniel Caudillo case (discussed in book Judging Judges by Preble Stolz); sev. cases in state Appellate, Fed., & Calif. Supreme courts; defender for people when Sirhan Sirhan filed for release, Fed. Ct.; mem: Calif. State Bar; US Supreme Ct. Bar; L.A. County Nat. History Mus.; publs: Mastering the Art of the Great Writ, Los Angeles Lawyer, Feb. 1981; The Continuing Role of the Peace Officer After a Criminal Conviction, Police Officer Law Report, June 1981; Republican (Presdl. Task Force); Catholic; rec: model railroading, cross country, weight lifting. Ofc: Office of Atty. General, 3580 Wilshire Blvd, Rm 703, Los Angeles 90010

ROETHE, EDWARD ALBIN, financial planner; b. Mar. 17, 1934, Oregon City, Ore.; s. Ernest Ferdinand Gottlieb and Gretchen Ida Amelia (Wagenknecht) R.; m. Thelma Killinger, June 17, 1938; children: DeLayne b. 1960, David b. 1964; edn: Portland State Coll. 1952-55; BS, Univ. Ore. 1956; MS admin., George Washington Univ. 1974; desig: CFP, Coll. for Finl. Plnng. (1986). Career: served to capt. US Navy 1956-83: dir. Naval Reserve Dept., Navy Fin. Center, Cleveland, Oh. 1967-70, asst. for supply 5th Naval Dist., Norfolk, Va. 1970-73, senior logistics ofcr. Jt. US Mil. Assistance Group, Seoul, Korea 1974-76, dir. logistics Naval Reserve Readiness Command, San Francisco 1976-78, dir. Storage & Transp., Def. Depot, Tracy, Calif. 1978-82, decorated Legion of Merit, Jt. Service Commendn.; cert. finl. plnnr./reg. rep. Finl. Network Inv. Corp., Walnut Creek 1984–; finl. advsy. rep. Finl. Network Advsry. Corp., Torrance 1986; mem. inv. com. Delta Meml. Hosp. Found., Antioch 1984-; speaker Finl. Plnng. Seminars var. locales (1984-); frequent banquet speaker in US & Canada, Stonecroft Ministries (1984-); honors: William McEntyre Dye Award, Jt. U.S. Mil. Assistance Group, Korea (1976); mem: Internat. Assn. for Finl. Plnng., Inst. of Cert. Finl. Plnnrs., Naval Supply Corps Assn. (charter), Naval Reserve Assn., Naval Order of US, Bay Area Supply Corps Assn. (1st v.p. 1977-78), Rotary Internat./Antioch (dir. 1984-); publs: ed. Portland St. Coll. newspaper 'Vanguard' (1953-54), ed. coll. yearbook 'Viking' (1954-55); ed. Supply Handbook for USNR, 5th Naval Dist. (1971); Republican; Evangelical Free Ch. (chmn. Walnut Creek 1980-82); rec: travel, photog. Res: 285 Pickering Pl Walnut Creek 94598 Ofc: Financial Network Investment Corp. 1243 Alpine Rd Ste 111 Walnut Creek 94596

ROGERS, AILEEN S., company president; b. Sept. 1, 1912, Stamford, Conn.; d. Clarence T. and Alice May (Dawson) Smith; m. James L. Rogers, July 4, 1942; children: Bronson b. 1944, Judith b. 1947, Carolen b. 1948; edn: Bach. Music, Chg. Tng. Sch. 1934, Northwestern Univ. 1936; Master Music, Detroi Inst. of Musical Art 1937, PhD, 1939; Calif. lic. Public Acct., 1946. Career: faculty Detroit Inst. of Musical Art; pvt. tchr. Voice, Piano and Theory; founder/prin. acctg. firm A. S. Rogers, Alhambra 1942–, public acct. 1946-, formed corporation 1969, corp. pres./pub. acct. 1969–; adminstr./owner Rogers School of Income Tax; mem. Nat. Soc. of Public Accts., Alhambra CofC, Eastern Star; works: Hymnology Through the Ages; Life of Christ, Crucifixion (for full orchestra); rec: world travel. Res: 1763 Windsor Rd San Marino 91108 Ofc: A.S. Rogers 511 West Main St Alhambra 91801

ROGERS, BRYAN ROSS, hospital administrator; b. May 9, 1957, Newport Beach, Calif.; s. Maurice and Patricia Mary (Ross) R.; m. Linda, July 18, 1981; edn: AA, Orange Coast Coll. 1978; BHS summa cum laude, Duke Univ. 1983; MPH, UC Los Angeles 1985; Reg. Respiratory Therapist 1980; bd. certified physician assoc. 1983. Career: respiratory therapist Hoag Meml. Hosp. Newport Beach 1978-79, dept. supv. 1979; dir. pgm. devel. Anaheim Meml. Hosp. 1985–; mem. Health Care Execs. of So. Calif.; Republican; rec: skiing. Res: 10 Streamwood Irvine 92720 Ofc: Anaheim Meml. Hosp. POB 3005 Anaheim 92803

ROGERS, MICHAEL JAMES, dentist; b. March 18, 1954, Urbana, Ill.; s. Harry G. and Elfriede K. (Schmitt) R.; m. Janet Grube, June 28, 1975; children: Jonathon b. 1981, Timothy b. 1984; edn: BS, honors, Calif. Polytechnic Univ. SLO 1980; DDS, UCLA 1984. Career: research asst. Calif. Polytechnic Univ., San Luis Obispo 1979-80, instr. 1980; phlebotomist UCLA 1981-84, research asst. sect. of gnathology & occlusion 1981-84; assoc. dentist, Santa Maria & Grover City 1984-85; dentist pvt. practice 1985–; honors: Phi Kappa Phi, 1978; Section Award, UCLA Sect. of Gnathology & Occlusion 1984; mem: Am. and Calif. Dental Assns., Central Coast Dental Soc., Santa Maria Valley CofC; rec: photog. Ofc: Michael J. Rogers DDS, 501 So. McClelland Santa Maria 93454

ROGERS, ROBERT REED, mfg. co. executive; b. Feb. 22, 1929, Oak Park, Ill.; s. Glen Charles and Lucile (Reed) R.; m. Barbara June Fain, Feb. 22, 1951; children: Robin b. 1951, Janeen b. 1952, Kevin b. 1954; edn: BS in chem., Berea Coll. 1951, MBA, Ill. Inst. of Tech. 1958, postgrad. work in econ. 1959-62. Career: asst. mgr. Metallurgy Resrch Dept. Armour Research Found. 1955-56;

faculty Ill. Inst. of Tech. Dept. of Bus. and Econ., 1956-62; cons. McKinsey & Co. Inc., 1962-64; mgr. Devel. Planning, Profl. Group, Litton Indus. Inc., 1964-67; pres. No. Am. Subsidiaries, Muirhead & Co. Ltd, Beckenham, Kent, UK, 1967-68; group v.p. American Elec. Inc. subs. City Investing Co., 1968-70; pres. Cleartight Corp., 1971-73; pres. NIMCO Inc. 1973-76; pres. Kensington Assocs. Inc., 1976-; pres. The Proteus Group Inc. (OTC), 1981-; pres. Comparator Systems Corp., 1983-; dir. World Series Baseball Parks, Inc. (OTC) 1983-; awards: Berea Coll. Study Grant 1951; MAPI Fellow 1956; mem. Lido Isle Yacht Club, Ferrari Owners Club, Navy League, Internat. Platform Assn. Mil: lt. USNR 1951-55; decorated Knight of Honor, Sovereign Order of St. John 1984; Libertarian; Sci of Mind; rec: chamber music, theatre, ballet. Res: 819A W. 15th St. Newport Bch 92663 Ofc: 930 W 16th St Ste E-2 Costa Mesa 92627

ROHFELD, MICHAEL DAVID, lawyer; b. Apr. 13, 1956, Jacksonville, Fla.; s. Marvin P. and Paula L. (Carmody) R.; m. Kathy, Dec. 19, 1981; 1 son, Michael Greyson b. 1985; edn: BA, CSU Dominguez Hills 1979; JD, Western State Univ. Coll. of Law 1982; admitted Calif. State Bar 1983. Career: assoc. atty. law office Philip Seastrom; deputy dist. atty. Orange County; current: assoc. law office Stephen Sundvold and in-house counsel Safeco Ins.; honors: assoc. justice Student Judiciary (1978), mem. Student Gov. Bd. (1979); mem. Calif. Bar Assn., Orange Co. Bar Assn.; Democrat; rec: flying, skiing, ice hockey. Ofc: Stephen Sundvold, Atty. 17550 Brookhurst Ave Fountain Valley 92708

ROHLOFF, ANN ELIZABETH, artist; b. June 25, 1955, Milwaukee, Wis.; d. Harvey Henry and Vernice May Rohloff; m. Donald Thomas Smith; 1 dau. Annika Van Pregle Smith; edn: BS, Univ. Wis. Madison, 1982; grad. arts pgm. (major furniture design, building), CSU San Diego; comml. art., Madison (Wis.) Area Tech. Coll., 1984; Arrowmont Sch. of Arts and Crafts, 1984. Career: woodworker Wilderness Woodworks, Cambridge, Wis. 1982; instr. Memorial Union Craftshop, Univ. Wis., 1983-84, tech. illus. Univ. Wis. Sch. of Pharmacy, 1983-84; cabinet designer Am. Quality Cabinet, Costa Mesa, Calif. 1985; tech. illus. CSUSD Systems Ecol. Resrch. Dept. 1985-, and grad. asst. Furniture Dept., 1985-86; exhibs: Utah Designer Craftsmen 25th Ann. Exhibn., Salt Lake Art Ctr. (1986), Holiday Art Fair, Madison, Wisc. (1984), Univ. Wisc. 7th Floor Art Gallery (1983-84), Morning Glory Crafts Fair, Charles Allis Art Mus. Milwaukee (1983), Tenth Annual Wisc. Union Craft Exhib., Madison (1983), 61st Wisc. Designer Craftsmen Exhib., Rahr-West Mus. Manitowoc (1982), 33d Annual Camera Concepts, Meml. Union Main Gallery, Madison (1981), others; awards: cash award Friends of Arrowmont (1984), Nat. Dean's List (1982); mem. CSUSD Furniture Design Assn. (1985-86), Am. Soc. Int. Designers (1979-80), Wisc. Designer Craftsmen (1982-84), YWCA; Prot.; rec: photog., antique repair, travel. Address: 12195 Wintergardens Dr Lakeside 92040

ROHRBACHER, CAROLE ANN, accountant; b. Jan. 21, 1944, Lodi, Calif.; d. Francis Clare and Eunice Etta (Kuykendall) Drake; children: Karen b. 1966, John b. 1968; edn: BS, CSU Chico 1980; CPA Calif. 1982. Career: acct. clerk II Dept. of Public Assistance Stockton 1971-75; tng. branch clerk IRS Svc. Ctr. Fresno 1975-80; acct. Herbert J. McClanahan CPA 1980-83; acct. self-employed Carole Rohrbacher CPA 1983–; honors: Beta Alpha Psi 1978, Beta Gamma Sigma 1980; mem: Am. Inst. CPAs, Calif. Soc. CPAs (map com., computer users group), Nat. Assn. Accts., Gridley Jr. Women, Am. Assn. Univ. women, Kaleidoscope-Gridley Arts Council (treas. 1983-86), Gridley CofC (bd. dirs.), Gridley City Council (Public Works com. chair, admin. svcs. com.) QUOTA Club; sing alto with Kaleidoscope Singers (sponsored by Gridley Arts Council, Butte Co. Arts Commn. 1982-); Republican; Presbyterian; rec: philately. Res: POB 910 Gridley 95948-0910 Ofc: 650 Ohio St Ste 7 Gridley 95948

ROHRBERG, RODERICK GEORGE, company president; b. Sept. 25, 1926, Minneola, Iowa; s. Charles H. and Emma (Minsen) R.; m. Genevieve Mary Sogard, June 19, 1949; children: Karla b. 1950, Roderick K. b. 1952, Cheries b. 1957, Timothy b. 1959, Christopher b. 1964; edn: B. Naval Scis., Marquette Univ. 1946; BSCE, Iowa State Univ. 1949; Reg. Profl. Engr., Calif. Career: bridge design engr. Alaska Rd. Commn., US Dept. Int. 1949-51; senior tech. spec. research engr. No. Am. Rockwell, Los Angeles 1951-69; currently, pres. Creative Pathways Inc.; pvt. cons. on adv. welding process, equipment design & devel, Torrance 1972-; honors: NASA Commdn. 1965; 1st Nat. Airco welding award 1966; Profl. Achiev. Citation, Iowa State Univ. 1973; 3rd pl., Von Karman Meml. Grand Award, 1974; listed Who's Who in Aviation and Aerospace 1983; mem: Am. Welding Soc., Am. Mfg. Engrs.; mil: USNR 1944-46; rec: flying. Res: 2742 W. 234th Torrance 90505 Ofc: Creative Pathways Inc., 3121 Fujita St. Torrance 90505

ROJA, DENNY S., mergers and acquisition executive; b. Mar. 26, 1946, Quezon City, Philippines; s. Macario Alvarez and Amparo (Sta. Catalina) R.; m. Maria C., Sept. 2, 1986; children: Christine Michelle b. 1970, Melissa Cheryl b. 1978; edn: BSChE, summa cum laude, Univ. of Santo Tomas 1966; MSChE, Univ. Wash. 1969; MBA, Stanford Univ. Grad. Sch. Bus. 1971; JD, Fordham Univ. Sch. of Law 1986; Reg. Mgmt. Acct., Soc. of Mgmt. Accts. (1976). Career: senior finl. analyst Burroughs Bus. Machines, Toronto, Can. 1971-74; mktg. controller, div. finl. mgr., mgr. strategic & bus. analysis, Gen. Foods Corp., White Plains, N.Y. 1974-84; dir. corp. devel./mergers & acquisitions Pacific Telesis Group, San Franciso 1984-86; dir. strategic alliances Pacific Bell, San Ramon 1986–; adj. prof. fin. & mgmt. Sacred Heart Univ., Bridgeport, Conn. 1980-82; awards: research fellow Univ. Wash. (1968), tchg. fellow (1969); mem. Assn. of Corporate Growth, Soc. of Mgmt. Accts.

(1976-84), Stanford Bus. Sch. Alumni Assn.; publs: tech. art., Am. Inst. of Chem. Engrs. J. (9/70); Republican; Roman Catholic; rec: golf, tennis, x-c ski. Ofc: Pacific Bell 2600 Camino Ramon San Ramon

ROLAND, JOSI S., public relations executive; b. June 11, 1959, Jacksonville, Fla.; s. Arnold S. and Diane L. Roland; edn: Tufts Univ. 1977-79; BA journ., Univ. So. Calif. 1981. Career: sales acct. exec. Daily Trojan newspaper 1980; media and pub. rels. asst. Grant & Shaner Inc. San Diego 1981; acct. mgr. Kenneth C. Smith & Assocs. 1981-82; acct. exec. The Gail Stoorza Co. 1982-84; senior acct. exec. Growth Mktg. Communications 1984; pres. Roland & Martin Mktg. Communications 1984–; instr. pub. rels. San Diego State Univ. extn., La Jolla Acad. of Advtg. Arts.; honors: Mark of Excellence (Pub. Rels. Club of S.D. 1982, 83, 85); mem: Pub. Rels. Club of S.D., Greater S.D. CofC, Women's Bus. Network, Internat. Assn. Bus. Communicators, S.D. Mus. of Art, Young S.D. USC Alumni (bd.), ALBA 80 (fundraising group), Jukebox Friday Night (runaway children's ctr., planning com.), Spl. Olympics (fundraising); book in progress on pub. rels. geared toward small bus.; rec: travel, teaching, writing. Ofc: Roland & Martin Mktg. Communs. 600 B St Ste 2250 San Diego 92101

ROMAN, JOSEPH ANTHONY, lawyer; b. Feb. 11, 1947, Artesia, Calif.; s. Joseph Vincent and Josephine (Leos) R.; m. Linda Grant, Jan. 1, 1970; children: Anthony Joseph b. 1971, Dean Alexander b. 1976, Grant Stephen b. 1981; edn: BA, Whittier Coll. 1969; M.Ed., Univ. Calif. 1970; JD, UC Hastings Coll. of Law 1974. Career: atty. San Francisco Neighborhood Legal Assistance Found. 1974-76; defense atty. Public Defender's Office 1976-78; pvt. defense atty. Norwalk 1978–; instr. law Norwalk-La Mirada Unified Sch. Dist.; bd. dirs. Public Interest Law Firm; honors: Dean's List (Whittier Coll., Hastings 1968-69, 1973); mem: Am., Calif., Southeast bar assns., Lancer Soc. (Whittier Coll.), La Mirada Civic Auditorium, Sierra Club, Kiwanis, Rotary, St. Paul Booster Club; author: The Bilingual Attorney (Ginn Co. 1977); Catholic; rec: surfing, scuba, chess. Ofc: Roman Law Office 14008 S Pioneer Blvd Norwalk 90650

ROMAN, ROBERTO R., chiropractor; b. Jan. 26, 1940, Matanzas, Cuba; s. Rafael F. and Isidra D. (Renom) R.; m. Dulce, Sept. 12; children: Robert b. 1970, Richard b. 1971, Stephanie b. 1984; edn: B. Lit., Havana Inst. 1959; Univ. Havana Sch. of Law 1959-61; DC, Los Angeles Coll. of Chiro. 1976. Career: owner El Monte Health Group; mem: Am. Chiro. Assn., Club Cultural Cubano; Republican; Catholic. Res: 720 Easley Canyon Rd Glendora 91740 Ofc: El Monte Health Group 4600 N Santa Anita Ave Ste 102 El Monte 91731

ROMAN, STEVEN MARK, educator, author; b. Nov. 9, 1948, Los Angeles; s. Lawrence and Evelyn Mildred (Zirkin) R.; m. Donna Dolan, Jan. 6, 1986; edn: BA, UC Los Angeles 1970; MS, Univ. of Wash. 1974, PhD, 1975. Career: instr. of applied math., MIT 1976-78; lectr. in math., UC Santa Barbara 1978-79; asst. prof. math., Univ. of South Fla. 1979-80; prof. of math. CSU Fullerton, 1980–; pres. Matrix Consulting; recipient merit performance awards, 1985, 86, research grantee Office of Naval Research (combinatorics) 1976-78, NSF (classical analysis) 1979-81; mem. Math. Assn. of Am., Am. Math. Soc.; author 7 textbooks in applied math. (1984-86), 20+ research publs.; rec: computers, painting, woodworking. Ofc: Dept. of Math. Calif. State University Fullerton 92634

ROMANO, DAVID JOHN, insurance consultant, executive; b. April 1, 1959, San Jose; s. Benjamin John and Marie Rose Romano; m. Karen B. Ruiz, June 11, 1983; edn: West Valley Coll. 1977-8, John Hancock Inst. 1980-; Reg. rep. NASD (1982). Career: asst. mgr. Sport Barn Inc., Santa Clara 1975-76; founder/owner Nor Cal Tackle Co., and Yankee Bait Co. (mfg. & mktg. fishing lures), Santa Clara 1975-79; rep. John Hancock Cos., splst. employee benefits, San Jose 1979–, sales supr. John Hancock Cos., Los Gatos 1982-85; exec. dir. Randall E. Banta & Assocs. (finl. plnng. firm) Los Gatos 1983-84; pres./founder/stockhldr. Financial Mgmt. Concepts, Inc. (finl. plnng., cons.), Los Gatos 1984-85; pres./founder/stockhldr. Employee Benefit Services Inc. (employee benefits cons.), San Jose 1985–; employee benefits consultant to bus. (1981-), cons. ins. cos. (1982-), cons. life ins. & casualty ins. mktg. firms (1982-) instr. for ins. cos. (1982-); lectr. on careers, goals, motivation, small bus. conslt. (1982-); honors: Bank of Am. achieve. award (1977); mem: Nat. Assn. of Life Underwriters, Internat. Assn. for Finl. Planners, Assn. for Finl. Planning Advsry. Council, Pro-Track Finl. Profl. Advsry. Council; designer Fresh and Salt Water Fishing Lures (1975-78); publs: sales visual aids for ins. cos. and ins. mktg. firms; contbr. articles on fishing tackle in local newspapers and trade mags. (1975-78); Democrat. Christian (Cath. of Faith, New Life Ministry). rec: golf, pianist, carpentry. Res: 1264 Silverado Dr San Jose 95120 Ofc: Employee Benefit Services Inc. 1871 The Alameda San Jose 95126

ROMER, CHERYL LEE, chiropractor; b. Oct. 30, 1951, Ft. Collins, Colo.; d. Elmer Gale and Bethel June (Nelson) R.; children: 1 dau, Tamatha Marie b. 1968; edn: AS, Fresno City Coll. 1974; BS, Cleveland Chiropractic Coll. 1982, DC, 1983. Career: radiological ultarsound techonolgist Valley Medical Ctr, Fresno 1976-79; radiological technologist St. Mary's Med. Ctr., Long Beach 1980-82; radiological supvr., intr. Cleveland Chiropractic Coll., Los Angeles 1983-85; chiropractor, owner Holistic Healing Center, Fresno 1985–; radiological instr. Cleveland Chiropractic Coll. 1983-85; chiropractic cons. Aerobic Dancercise 1985; mem: Delta Tau Alpha, Assn. of Reg. Radiological Technologists, Calif. Radiological Technologists; Internat., Am. and Calif. Chiropractic Assns., Nat. Orgn. of Women; Democrat; Religious Science Internat.; rec: wilderness activities, travel, photog. Address: Holistic Healing Center 5160 N Fresno Ste 104 Fresno 93710

ROMJUE, BRUCE ROLAND, builder-developer; b. Sept. 29, 1931, Wichita, Kansas; s. Harvey Boon and Irene Evelyn (Jackson) R.; m. Doris, June 5, 1957; children: Michelle b. 1959, Bruce Jr. b. 1961, Steven b. 1965, Karin b. 1969; edn: BSBA, Univ. of Kansas 1957. Career: with IBM Corp. 1957-81; salesman 1957-60; senior product plnnr. Selectric Typewriter 1960-62; sales mgr. Europe IBM World Trade Corp. 1962-66; dir. bus. devel. World Trade Corp. 1966-71; mng. mkt. support ctr. 1971-73; dist. mgr. 1973-79; branch mgr. 1979-81; v.p., dir. of sales Sunrise Co. 1981-84, senior v.p. sales and mktg. 1985–; advtg. & promotion com. City of Palm Desert, mktg. com. City of La Quinta; adv. bd. Chapman Coll.; honors: Mktg. Dir. of the Year, So. Calif. Sales & Mktg. Councl 1985; mem: So. Calif. Sales & Mktg. Council, Am. Mgmt. Assn., Phi Kappa Psi, Alpha Kappa Psi; mil: PO 2/c USN 1951-54, GCM, China Svc., Nat. Defense, Korean Svc. w/ two stars, Korean Theater; Republican; Presbyterian (deacon); rec: golf, tennis, equestrian. Res: 45-464 Camino Del Rey Indian Wells 92210 Ofc: Sunrise Company, 75-005 Country Club Dr. Palm Desert 92260

ROMMESWINKEL, DIRK HEINRICH, accountant; b. Sept. 2, 1958, Bloomington, Ill.; s. Heinrich Herman and Brigitta (Prenzler) R.; edn: BS accounting, Ariz. State Univ. 1980; CPA Am. Inst. CPAs 1985. Career: tax acct. Ernst & Whinney Phoenix 1980, Arthur Anderson & Co. L.A. (currently senior tax acct.) 1981–; mem: Calif. Soc. CPAs, Am. Inst. CPAs; Conservative/Independent; Christian; rec: travel, athletics. Res: 509 E Jackson Pasadena 91104 Ofc: Arthur Anderson & Co. 911 Wilshire Blvd Los Angeles 90017

RONGE, JOHN REINHOLD PAUL, corporate financial executive; b. Mar. 28, 1948, Chgo.; s. John and Frances (Materla) R.; m. Arlinda A. Henderson, Oct. 9, 1982; 1 son, Brian b. 1985; edn: BSME, Ill. Inst. of Technol. 1970; MBA fin. & mktg., UC Los Angeles 1973; JD, Loyola Law Sch. L.A. 1983; CPA Calif. 1979, admitted Calif. State Bar 1984. Career: research engr. US Steel Corp. South Works Chgo. 1970-71; independent cons. L.A. 1973-74; senior cons. Tymshare Inc. El Segundoi 1974-77; staff, senior acct. Gelfand, Breslauer, Rennert & Feldman CPAs L.A. 1977-80; sole proprietorship L.A. 1980-84; cons., supv. tax dept. Laventhol & Horwath 1984-85; fin. dir. Western Mgmt. Assoc. L.A. 1985–; honors: Tau Beta Pi 1969, Dean's List (Ill. Inst. of Tech. 1968-70), Scott Honors Moot Ct. (Loyola 1982); mem: Am. Inst. CPAs, Calif. Soc. CPAs, Am., L.A. Co., Beverly Hills bar assns., Healthcare Financial Mgmt. Assn., UCLA Chancellors Circle, L.A. Hash House Harriers; Republican; Catholic; rec: running, photog., skiing. Ofc: Western Mgmt. Assoc. 6420 Wilshire Blvd, Ste 1000, Los Angeles 90048

ROOSEVELT, JAMES, business consultant; b. Dec. 23, 1907, NYC; s. President Franklin Delano and First Lady Eleanor Roosevelt; nephew of Pres. Theodore Roosevelt; m. Mary Lena Winskill, 1969; children: Sara, Kate, Jim Jr., Michael, Anne, H. Delano, Rebecca; edn: Groton Sch. 1926; Harvard Univ. 1930; LLD, hon., Woodbury Univ.; PhD, hon., Calif. Western Univ.; LHD, hon., Salem Coll., W.Va. Career: ins. broker, founder, pres. Roosevelt & Sargent, Inc., Boston, 1930-37, resigned 1938; motion picture indus. 1938-40; reentered Roosevelt & Sargent as exec. v.p., estab. West Coast Ofc., 1946; elected US Congressman (84th-89th Congresses) from Calif. 1955-66; US Rep. to ECOSOC 1965-66; with I.O.S. Mgmt. Co. 1966-70; bus. cons. James Roosevelt & Co., Newport Beach 1970–; lectr. UC Irvine, Woodbury Univ., Chapman Coll.; awards: Richard M. Nixon Chair, Whittier Coll.; former mem. Congress Guest Otterbein Coll. & Baylor Univ.; mem. March of Dimes Birth Defects Found., Roosevelt Warm Springs Found., Eleanor Roosevelt Cancer Inst., Chapman Coll., South Coast Repertory Theatre, NCCJ; del. Armand Hammer Peace & Human Rights Conf.; Orange Co. Transportation Commn. (chmn.); Nat. Com. for Research in Neurological & Communicative Diseases (pres.); author: Affectionately, F.D.R. (1959), My Parent, A Differing View (1976), A Family Matter (Simon & Shuster, 1980); mil: Brig. Gen., USMC Ret., decorated Navy Cross, Silver Star; Democrat, (Nat. Com.; Dem. candidate for Calif. Gov. 1950; US Congressman 1955-66); Episcopal; rec: sailing. Ofc: James Roosevelt & Co., 2500 Michelson Dr. Suite 250 Irvine 92715

ROSASCHI, JAMES PRESCOTT CLEVENGER, librarian; b. April 4, 1949, Alma, Mich.; s. True Daniel and Mary Louise (Haas) R.; m. Gaylene Reynolds, Aug. 22, 1975; chidren: Nicole, Daniel, Michelle; edn: BS, Brigham Young Univ. 1977, MLS, 1978. Career: press photog. Petaluma Argus Courier 1968-69; ednl. courseware photog. Boise Interagency Fire Ctr. 1973-76; cirulation/ reference librarian Nampa (Idaho) Pub. Library 1978-79, library dir. 1979-82; head librarian Petaluma Regl. br. Sonoma County Library 1982–; mem: ALA, Assn. Rec. Sound Collections, Calif. Library Assn., Pacific N.W. Library Assn.; mil: US Army 1969-72; Republican; Mormon. Res: 310 Mountain View Ave. Santa Rosa 95401 Ofc: Sonoma Couty Libraray, 3rd and E Streets Santa Rosa

ROSE, SEYMOUR MERTON, lawyer; b. Feb. 12, 1928, Los Angeles; s. Carl Theodore and Lillian Bernice (Goldenberg) R.; m. Judith I.; children: Lewis B., Carl E., Alison S.; edn: BA, UC Berkeley 1950, LLB, UCB Boalt Hall, 1955, JD, 1968; admitted Calif. State Bar 1955. Career: atty. pvt. practice, Family Law Splst., Entertainment Investments, Inc., San Francisco 1962-; lectr. in speech UC Berkeley, 1955-68; lectr. in law, var.; v.chmn. Oakland Housing Authority 1962-63; mem. City Planning Commn. 1963-64; elected mem. Oakland City Sch. Bd., 1965-83; mem. State of Calif. Tchr. Preparation and Licensing 1981-83; chmn. local chpt. Am. Jewish Com., 1964-65; honors: Sigma Alpha Mu (nat. alumni v.p.), Phi Alpha Delta; mem. Calif. Bar Assn., Assn. of Certified Family Law Splsts. (pres. 1984), Lawyer's Club Alameda County, Masons; mil: 1st lt. US Army 1953-55, maj. USAR 1955-; Democrat; Jewish. Ofc: One Kaiser Plaza Ste 2135 Oakland 94612

ROSE, THOMAS EDWARD, savings and loan executive; b. Dec. 16, 1951, Richmond; s. Clarence Albert and Mary Eleanor (Hart) R.; m. Paulette, Sept. 30, 1981; children: Eric b. 1978, Joelle b. 1980, Nicole b. 1980, Lauren b. 1981, Scott b. 1982; edn: AA, Contra Costa Jr. Coll. 1972; BA, CSU Hayward 1973. Career: asst. mgr. Mechanics Bank of Richmond (Calif.), 1972-80; car sales Ozzie Davis Toyota, Dublin 1981-83; br. mgr./asst. v.p. Home Savings of Am., Stockton 1983 –; tchg: Albany H.S. (1978, 79), Claudia Landeen Jr. H.S. (1986-); honors: Bank Am. Bus. Award (1970), JFK Meml. Award for scholastics, service, sportsmanship (1970); mem. Kiwanis, Lions, CofC; Catholic; rec: golf, music appreciation. Ofc: Home Savings of America 941 W March Ln Stockton 95207

ROSEMAN, ALAN GORDON, business consultant; b. Sept. 1, 1948, Montebello, Calif.; s. Max D. and Natalie G. R.; m. Karen, July 11, 1982; edn: AA bus., Los Angeles City Coll. 1968; BS in mktg., econs., CSU Sacramento 1974. Career: retail store mgr.; v.p. Roseman & Assocs. Inc. L.A.; dir: Men's & Boys' Apparel Club L.A., Medifund Corp. Culver City; mem: L.A. Athletic Club 1985-, Sierra Club, Audubon Soc., Yosemite Nat. History Assn., L.A. County Mus. of Art; Democrat; Jewish; rec: sailing, skiing. Ofc: Roseman & Assocs. Inc. 735 E 12th St Los Angeles 90021

ROSEN, ANDREW, hotel owner; b. Nov. 27, 1918, Isabella, Pa.; s. Andrew and Mary (Pleha) R.; m. Jean H. Hixson, July 10, 1943; children: Marilyn L. b. 1943, Andrew P. b. 1953, Doug J. b. 1956; edn: BA biol. sci., Ohio State Univ. 1941; Univ. So. Calif. 1946. Career: rancher Fowler, Calif. 1947-61; hotel owner 1961-79; condominium builder 1980-85; honors: Football Scholarship (Ohio State Univ. 1937-41), Big 10 Championship 1939, Big 10 Gold Football 1939; mem. Berkeley City Club (bd. dirs. 1984-85); mil: 1st lt. US Army Air Corps 1942-46, pilot B-17, B-29 bombers; Democrat; Lutheran; rec: gardening, carpentry, boating. Res: 1761 University Ave Berkeley 94703

ROSEN, MARTIN JACK, lawyer; b. Sept. 9, 1931, Los Angeles; s. Irving ad Sylvia (Savad) R.; m. Joan Meyersieck, Oct. 22, 1954; children: Dirk b. 1958, Marika b. 1961; edn: AB, honors, UCLA 1953; JD, UC Berkeley Sch. of Law 1956. Career: atty. pvt. practice, Merced 1960-62; atty., ptr. Silver, Rosen, Fischer & Stecher PC, San Francisco 1962-78; pres., dir. The Trust for Public Land, San Francisco 1978 –; honors. Fellow Internat. Legal Studies, Univ. of Calif. Law Sch. and Inst. of Social Studies; The Hage, Netherlands 1956-57; Law Sch. Assn. Scholar in Law 1953-54; Walter Perry Johnson Scholar in Law 1954-55; Franke Wehe Scholar in Law 1955-56; Order of the Coif 1955-56; mem: Am. and Calif. Bar Assns.; publs: Professional Corporations- Advantages and Disadvantages, Land & Water Review 1971; Brussells Entente: Export Combination in the World Steel Market, Univ. of Penn. Law Review 1958; mil: capt. USAF 1958-60; rec: backpacking, photog. Ofc: Silver, Rosen, Fischer & Stecher PC, 88 Kearny St Ste 1310 San Francisco 94108

ROSEN, SHELDON B., insurance agent; b. Nov. 4, 1943, NY, NY; s. Louis and Clara (Herzog) R.; m. Carol, June 20, 1975; 1 dau. Gabrielle b. 1980; edn: BS magna cum laude, Brooklyn Coll. 1964; MA, Columbia Univ. 1965; PhD, UC Santa Barbara 1981; Chartered Life Underwriter 1984; Chartered Financial Cons. 1985. Career: instr. chemistry Hunter Coll. NY 1966-69, Tegucigalpa, Honduras 1971-73; ins. agent Equitable Life Assurance Soc. 1980-82; ptnr. Bean, Rosen & Siefe Ins. Svcs. Santa Barbara 1982 –; honors: Phi Beta Kappa, award Am. Soc. Chemists; mem: Am. Soc. Chartered Life Underwriters, Internat. Assn. Financial Planners, Nat. Assn. Life Underwriters, Child Abuse Listening and Mediation; publ: Worker Participation in Decision Making in Kibbutz Factories (1981); rec: sailing, karate, public speaking. Ofc: 3916 State Ste 2A Santa Barbara 93105

ROSENBERG, EVA, author, lecturer, accountant; b. Mar. 5, 1953, Budapest, Hungary, nat. US cit. 1973; s. Tibor and Aranka R.; edn: BA acctg., CSU Fullerton 1977, MBA internat. bus., 1983; enrolled agent IRS 1985. Career: asst. controller Chromodern Mfg. Co. Los Angeles 1976-77; cons. Accountemps & Accountants Overload; acct. Ernst & Whinney 1978, Lester Witte & Co. CPAs 1979; owner Independent Research Svcs. Irvine 1980 –; dir. Houseguests USA Inc.; instr. USC, CSUF; cons. var. cos.; honors: Calif. State Scholar (1971), commencement spkr. (CSU Long Beach, Women Entrepreneurs Pgm.); mem: South Coast Assn. Female Execs. (founder, pres. 1985-), Nat. Assn., Female Execs. (dir.), Profl. Women's Network (v.p. pgm. 1984-85), Nat. Assn. Enrolled Agents, Calif. Assn. Enrolled Agents, Am. Assn. Univ. Women (v.p. pgms. 1983-84), Irvine Fine Arts Ctr. (treas. 1985); publs: books, Tax Anxiety Experience (1985), Beyond Networking (1987); financial column The Barnstormer (1984-85), num. financial articles; Jewish; rec: fgn. films, swimming, scuba. Ofc: Independent Research Svcs. of Irvine POB 19031 Irvine 92713-9031

ROSENBERG, MAX L., writer, publisher; b. Dec. 1, 1935, Ft. Benning, Ga.; s. Leo Kaufman and Katherine (Ford) R.; m. Gail W., Feb. 3, 1956; children: Randall Britt, b. 1956, Tricia Robin b. 1968; edn: BA, Auburn Univ. 1957; MRE, New Orleans Baptist Theol. Sem. 1961; GSRE, N.O.B.T.S., 1962; non fiction writer, Writer's Digest Sch. 1985. Career: served to capt. US Army, 1957-74, decorated C.I.B., Bronze Star, Air Medal; freelance writer; publisher/exec. dir. Rosemont Enterprises, a lmtd. ptnrship., San Diego 1975 –; author: "Overflow" (Carlton Press, 1975), "Survivor!" (Rosemont Ents., 1985); lectr. in applied psychol., leadership, negotiations; mem. Sigma Pi (nat. scholarship com.), American Legion (exec. bd.); Republican (Senatl. Inner Circle 1986); So. Baptist (deacon); rec: philately. Ofc: Rosemont Enterprises 1130 Sixth Ave Ste 227 San Diego 92101

ROSENBERG, ROBERTA GEORGIA, jewelry school director; b. Feb. 28, 1914, Mt. Vernon, Ill.; d. George Leslie and Jessimon Magenta (Gueon) Loarts; m. Lewis Ben Rosenberg (dec), Feb. 20, 1955; edn: pvt. jewelry instrn. L.B.Rosenberg 1955-63; diamond setting, G.I.A., 1974. Career: med. asst. Mt. Vernon, Ill. 1934-50, 1951-54, legal secty. 1950-51; custom jewelry mfr., jewelry instr., owner Rosenberg Jewelry School, Pacific Palisades 1964 –; Republican; Protestant; rec: bowling, dancing, sewing. Address: 1334 Goucher St Pacific Palisades 90272

ROSENBLUM, BRUCE KENNETH, television industry executive; b. Oct. 4, 1954, Elizabeth, N.J.; s. Stuart Allen and Gloria (Berman) R.; m. Jackie Lynn, Nov. 18, 1978; children: Evan b. 1981, Bradley b. 1983, Alexander b. 1985; edn: BA, pol. sci., CSU Northridge 1977. Career: staff aide State Sen. Alan Robbins, Sacto. 1976-77; analyst Calif. Motion Pic. Dev. Council, Hollywood 1977-78; research assoc. ASI Market Research, 1977-80; research analyst Paramount Pictures Corp., 1980-81; research dir. Teleprices Corp., Beverly Hills 1981-83; senior v.p. mkt. research Lorimar-Telepictures, Sherman Oaks 1983 –; honors: All Los Angeles City Baseball Team (1972), Bdcst. Promotion & Mktg. Execs. Gold Award (movie presentation, 1983); mem. Acad. TV Arts & Scis.; publs: article in Image Mag. (1/86); rec: softball, wt. lifting, racquetball. Address: Sherman Oaks 91403

ROSENFELD, MITCHEL ERIC, software engineer/ research scientist; b. Feb. 16, 1954, Los Angeles; s. Sheldon and Rosalie (Weisberger) R.; m. An-Ore Lai, Jan. 23, 1983; edn: BS, UCLA 1977; MS, Univ. of Hawaii 1980; D.Phil., 1982; MS, cand., CSU Northridge; CMS-2M, Sperry/ Univac. Career: Dept. of Tropical med., Univ. of Hawaii Sch. of Med. 1980-82; Teledyne Systems Co. 1982-85: software documentation TACNAV and AISF projs. 1982-83; software engr., software mgr. NASA Shuttle/Centaur Proj. (Galileo & ISPM) 1983-85; Enhanced D.O.T. Proj. 1985; F-15/G.O.I. Radar 1985; software engr. Radar Systems Group, Hughes Aircraft Co., Los Angeles 1985 –; ind. cons., Angel Software 1985; honors: U.S. Public Health Service Fellowship 1979; CHina Seminar for Internat. Studies, R.O.C. 1980; Admissions Committee, Univ. of Hawai Sch. of Pub. Health 1980; works: author scientific arts. (3); listed techl. asst. num. arts.; Democrat; Jewish; rec: tennis, fishing. Res: 17114 Armstead St., Granada Hills 91344 Ofc: Hughes Aircraft Co., Radar Systems Group/ Advanced Projects, M.S. RS/R8/5100C, POB 92426, Los Angeles 90009

ROSENSCHEIN, SERL ESTHER, physician; b. Nov. 26, 1949, Scranton, Pa.; d. Rubin and Gertrude (Wruble) Zimmerman; children: Ari b. 1975, Jacob b. 1977; edn: BA, Smith Coll. 1971; MD, cum laude, Jefferson 1976; bd. certified pathol. 1982. Career: resident anat. and clin. pathol. UCLA, UCSF 1978-82; fellowship immunohematology Irwin Meml. Blood Bank S.F. 1983-84, staff phys., acting med. dir. 1984-85; assoc. pathol. San Jose Hosp. 1984 –; cons. transfusion associated AIDS; dir. So. Peninsula Hebrew Day Sch. 1983, 85, v.p. 1984; honors: Phi Beta Kappa (Smith Coll. 1971), Alpha Omega Alpha 1976; mem: AMA, Am. Soc. Clin. Pathols., Am. Assn. Blood Banks; research: transfusion- assoc. AIDS; Jewish. Res: 107 Avalon Dr Los Altos 94022 Ofc: San Jose Hosp. 675 E Santa Clara St San Jose

ROSENSTEIN, RICHARD LEE, insurance executive; b. Jan. 18, 1931, NY, NY; s. Bernie and Jessie (Goldberg) R.; m. Lindsey M., May 30, 1978; children: Benjamin b. 1979, Danielle b. 1983, Jess b. 1985; edn: BSBA, Rider Coll. 1953, MBA, Hopkins 1974; Chartered Life Underwriter, 1976. Career: trainee to exec. asst. to pres. Robert Hall Clothes 1955-62; sales rep. to v.p. Metropolitan Life, Baltimore, Md. 1962-69, estab. first brokerage dept. in No. Calif. and Hawaii, currently, dir. of brokerage, devel. brokerage ofcs. and inovating pgms.; tchr. ins. subjects Fairleigh Dickenson Univ. 1966-68; Life Underwriters Tng. Council chmn. 1986; honors: Metropolitans Mgrs. Club; Lead Co. Small Group & Pensions 1965-70; Million Dollar Round Table 1963-68; mem: Life Underwriters (pres. Northern, NJ 1969, Baltimore, Md. 1972), Chartered Life Underwriters, Nat. Assn. Life Underwriters, Life Underwriting Political Action Com., Consumers Advis. Com. 1984-, Fin. Plnnrs. Orgn., Chestnut Ridge Country Club (pres. 1975), Nat. Wheel Chair Tournament (chmn., Baltimore 1975), Mayor's Adv. Com. (Baltimore 1972-80), Parks & Recreation Com. Foster City, AYSO 1984; mil: 1st lt. US Army 1953-55, Korea; rec: golf, gardening, disabled. Res: 786 Widgeon St. Foster 94404 Ofc: Metropolitan Life, 425 Market St. Ste. 13A San Francisco 94105

ROSENZWEIG, HERBERT STEPHEN, securities co. financial consultant; b. Aug. 5, 1943, Phila., Pa.; s. Morton and Helen (Katzen) R.; m. Myra Pauline Saltzburg, June 7, 1964; children: Helene b. 1969, Michael b. 1972, Elisa b. 1973, Jeffrey b. 1976; edn: BS, Temple Univ. 1964. Career: US Army, El Paso, Tex. & Vietnam 1965-67; acct. exec. Walston & Co., Inc. 1967-73; acct. exec. Reynolds Securities 1973-74; acct. exec., sr. acct. exec., asst. v.p. Merrill Lynch Pierce Fenner & Smith, Upland 1974-85, v.p. 1985 –; mem. Pres.'s Club, Chmn.'s Club Merrill Lynch; mem: Kiwanis Club, Upland (pres. 1979); mil: 1st lt. US Army 1965-67, Inf. Platoon Ldr. Central Highlands, Vietnam; Republican; Jewish. Res: 2109 N. San Antonio Ave Upland 91786 Ofc: Merrill Lynch Pierce Fenner & Smith, 876 N. Mountain Ave Upland 91786

ROSKI, RAYMOND HENRY, real estate development-management co. executive; b. Apr. 11, 1948, Oklahoma City, Okla.; s. Frank and Lula Della (Rogers) Roski; m. Christine Kelly, Feb. 9, 1972; children: Sarah b. 1973, Philip b. 1975, Thomas b. 1977, Jennie b. 1979, Katherine b. 1981, Laura b. 1984; edn: BBA, Univ. Okla. 1970; economics, mgmt. seminars, Fordham Univ., 1971, Univ. of Dela. 1974, Loyola Univ. 1978. Career: nat. vice pres., dir. AIESEC, US, Inc., NYC, 1971; exec. ofcr. USAFR, 2854 Air Base Group, Tinker AFB, 1972; exec.

dir. Muskogee Conv. Center & Tourism Dept., 1973-74; salesman indsl. R.E., Majestic Realty, Los Angeles 1974-77, dir. prop. mgmt. 1977-78, treas./corp. sec./v.p. prop. mgmt. Majestic Realty Co., Commerce Constrn. Co., Majestic Mgmt. Co., 1978-81; bd. dirs. AIESEC-US, 1970-71, US del. to 23rd Internat. AIESEC Cong., The Hague, Netherlands 1971; bd. advs. Green Country Inc. 1973; bd. dirs. B.A.S.I.C. 1976-9; apptd. mem. Mayor's Blue Ribbon Commn., City of Commerce 1979; mem: Admirals Club, So. Calif. Bus. Research Council 1975-6, Nat., Calif. Assn. of Realtors, LA Bd. Realtors, The Christophers, Univ. Okla. Alumni Assn., AIESEC Alumni Soc. (bd. dirs. USC 1981-), Exceptional Childrens' Assn., No. Orange co. YMCA, Town Hall of Calif., The Am. Film Inst., LA County Museum (Pres. Circle), AMS Parents Assn. (pres. 1984-5), Commerce Kiwanis Club (pres. 1978-9), Calif. Country Club; mil: capt. USAFR 1970-80; Democrat; Catholic; rec: backpacking, fishing. Res: 6990 Golden Rain Way Etiwanda/ Rancho Cucamonga 91739 Ofc: Majestic Realty Co., Commerce Construction Co 6252 E Telegraph Rd Los Angeles 90040

ROSLAN, THOM WILLIAM, photographer; b. Oct. 12, 1942, Cleveland, Ohio; s. Stan Chester and Bertha Mary (Jankowski) R.; edn: grad. Van Nuys H.S. 1960; seminars, Nikon Sch. of Photog. Career: custom color printer Comml. Dept. Newell Color Lab, Hollywood 1976-78, color correction supr. Custom Color, Universal City 1978-79; owner/photog. Thom Roslan Studios, Van Nuys 1979-84; free-lance mag. photo-journalist, 1979-86, comml. photog. (comml. advt.) and currently devel. sports video co., 1986-; staff writer/ photog. and West Coast ed. Offroad America Mag., 1986–; honors: showcased on "World of Photog." ABC-TV (1/86), nominee Photog. of Year and Journalist of Year, SCORE Internats. (1985); mem: Nat. Press Photogs. Assn., Am. Auto Racing Writers & Bdcstrs. Assn., SCORE Internat., High Desert Racing Assn., Am. Motor Sports Assn., Nat. Sand Competition Assn.; support Calif. Deser Coalition, CORVA; publs: Offroad Am., Four Wheeler, VW Trends, Firehouse, 4WD Action, On-Dirt, Dusty Times, Corvette Fever, Score News, 3 & 4 Wheel Action, Dirt Birt, Great Goins, Mickey Thompson Offroad Championship Gran Prix Pgms., Stadium Racing USA Pgms., work featured on movie video cover "Road Warriors"; mil: mech. 3/c Navy Air Corps 1961-65; Republican; Christian; rec: auto racing (SSCA Circuit 1972-73), macro photog., spl. effects photog., astronomy. Ofc: 7058 Murietta Ave Van Nuys 91405

ROSOFF, STEVEN DAVID, manufacturing co. executive; b. Feb. 27, 1961, Los Angeles; s. Uriel and Barbara Mae (Lee) R.; edn: biol. courses UC San Diego 1982. Career: vice pres./gen. mgr. "C" Ents., San Marcos, currently; Republican; Jewish; rec: softball, politics. Res: 3344 Cuesta Pl Carlsbad 92008 Ofc: "C" Enterprises 310-110 Via Vera Cruz San Marcos 92069

ROSS, CAROL JANIS, water district executive; b. Oct. 18, 1938, Long Beach, Calif.; d. Conrad E. and Mona Jean (Coulston) Fee; m. Kenneth D. Ross, Jr., Jan. 23, 1959; children: Michael Kenneth b. 1959, Randal Brian b. 1963; edn: med. secty., Long Beach City Coll. Bus. Tech. Div. 1958. Career: telephone oper. Pacific Telephone Long Beach 1956-57; lab asst. Long Beach Clin. Lab. 1957-58; med. asst. Drs. Perrie & Johnson L.B. 1957-58; billing dept. Signal Trucking L.A. 1958-59; bus driver Community Charter Santa Ana 1971-73; PBX oper. Western World Orange 1979-81; secty. Santiago County Water Dist. Silverado 1981–; honors: Orange County Fir Dept. Awards 1974, 79, 84, 86); Orange County Bd. of Supvs. 1974, 79, 84; mem: Modjeska Firefighters Assn. (volunteer firefighter, capt. 1 yr., engr. 10 yrs.), Silverado- Modjeska Parks & Rec. Bd. Dirs. (treas. 6 yrs.); Republican; Lutheran; rec: bowling, horses, fishing. Res: 17342 Wilkinson Rd Modjeska Canyon 92667

ROSS, CLAYTON GARNER, financial planner; b. Oct. 1, 1925, Spokane, Wash.; s. William Garner and Royala Katherine (Loomis) R.; m. Jeane West, June 26, 1948; children: Janet b. 1950, David b. 1953, Elizabeth b. 1957; edn: BS bus. adminstrn., Univ. So. Calif. 1949; MA edn., UC Berkeley 1960; Certified Financial Planner 1984. Career: tchr. sci. and math. Mt. Diablo Unif. Sch. Dist. 1953-80; acct. exec. TMI Equities Inc. 1980–; former bd. mem. Walnut Creek Christian Acad., Berean Christian H.S.; honors: Spl. Recogn. (TMI 1983); mem: Internat. Assn. Financial Planning (chpt. dir. 1983-84), Fellowship of Christian Financial Advisors, Christian Educators Assn. Internat. (past. chpt. v.p.), Sun Valley Swim Pool Assn. (past pres.), Calif. Retired Tchrs. Assn. (chpt. treas.); publs: Caps'l Course Geometry reference guide; magazine articles on Mathematics and Bible and Financial Planning and Bible in progress; mil: lcdr. USNR Supply Corps, active duty 1943-47, 1950-53; Republican; Baptist; rec: travel, cartooning, swimming. Res: 3 Dale Ct Walnut Creek 94595 Ofc: TMI Equities Inc. 1500 Fashion Island Blvd San Mateo 94404

ROSS, J. PAUL, electrical engineer, programmer; b. Oct. 5, 1913, Kelleyville, Okla.; dec. Sept. 13, 1986; s. John Haldren and Jeanette (Glenn) R.; m. Frances L. Jockisch, Nov. 23, 1938; 1 dau. Paulette Elizabeth (Helland); edn: E.E. cert., Internat. Corr. Schs. 1946; stu. UC Los Angeles 1963-64, CSU Los Angeles 1973-84. Career: craftsman, technician, staff supr., senior engr. Pacific Bell Tel. Co.; ptnr. Machine Shop; investor in real estate, stocks and bonds; mem. AIEE; inventions: method for detecting sabatoge at unmanned amplifier stations; co-devel. method for rapid restoration of failed long distance equipment (method later used by entire Bell Tel. System); Republican; rec: writing computer programs. Res: 6462 N Loma Ave Temple City 91780

ROSS, KAY FRANCES, medical offices management co. president; b. Sept. 20, 1942, Iowa City, Iowa; d. Maurice Pershing and Dorothy Beth (Mattheis) Ross; m. Richard E. Slater, May 10, 1986; children (nee Dinsen); Daniel Larren b. 1968, Sara Kay b. 1970; edn: BA in elem. edn., CSU San Diego 1965; MBA, Nat. Univ. 1984; num. mgmt. workshops, seminars, postgrad. work UCSD and CSUSD; Calif. lifetime tchg. creds. in Gen. Elem. (1965), Comm. Colls.- bus. & indsl. mgmt., mktg. & sales (1984). Career: tchr. San Diego City Unif. Sch. Dist., also initiated pilot pgm. Early Childhood Edn. for Headstart, 1965-74; var. pos. in field of medical services and products for B.F. Asher, G.D. Searle, Stuart Inc., 1974-81; current: med. office mgmt. and pub. rels. cons., owner/ pres. Ross Resources & Assocs. (med. office mgmt. co.), La Jolla; dir. of sites adminstrn. Western Health Med. Clinic Inc. (in chg. 89 empls. incl. 11 MD's at 11 locations), 1985–; present num. seminars & workshops, San Diego Found. for Medical Care; awards: Noel Boulgy Scholar (1960), Lane Bryant Scholar (1962), listed Who's Who Among San Diego Women (1984-85); mem: Med. Group Mgmt. Assn., Profl. Soc. of Bus. Consultants, Am. Mktg. Assn.; civic: Las Amigas de Chiquitas childrens home (founding mem. 1974), Womens Internat. Center S.D. (charter; participant in Living Legacy Awards Banquet 1984, 85), S.D. CofC; Republican; Disciples of Christ; rec: square dancing, RV-ing, gourmet cooking. Res: 4656 Ramsay Ave San Diego 92122 Ofc: Ross Resources & Assocs. 6794 La Jolla Blvd La Jolla 92037

ROSS, MARILYN AGNES, lapidarist; b. July 26, 1929, Riverside; d. Myron Ardillo and Ruby Anna (Crane) Hinkley; m. Sigurd Ross, Aug. 1, 1953; children: Clifford b. 1954, Laural b. 1955, Kendal b. 1957; edn: BA, music edn., CSU Fresno 1951; MA in lib. sci., CSU San Jose 1969. Career: choir director Almaden Hills Methodist Ch., San Jose 1964-67; elementary sch. librarian Oak Grove Elem. Sch. Dist. San Jose 1970-81, district library cons. 1979-81; v.p./ptnr. Binkley's A.R.C. Lapidary and Jewelry Supply, San Jose 1973–, full time Binkley's, 1981–; mem. San Jose Lapidary Soc. (pres. 1971-72), Mu Phi Epsilon (internat. music sor., past chpt. pres.), Sigma Sigma Sigma, Bibliophiles (pres. 1952-58), Alpha Beta Alpha (nat. librn. frat.); Republican; Prot.; rec: music (vocal, organ), needlework, gardening. Ofc: Binkley's ARC 2202 Lincoln Ave San Jose 95125

ROSS, SIDNEY, manufacturing co. executive; b. Apr. 15, 1914, Saskatoon, Sask., Canada, nat. US cit. 1926; s. Nathan and Bertha (Singer) R.; m. Ruth Douglas, Dec. 25, 1943; children: Ronnee Ann b. 1946, Heidi Paula b. 1949; edn: S, UC Berkeley 1936. Career: sales mgr. Fairview Packing, Hollister, Calif. 1942-45; plant mgr. Stanislaus Food, Modesto 1946-50; pres. Martinez Food Canners, Martinez 1950-69; pres./CEO, NCC Food Corp., San Jose 1968-77; pres./CEO, Glorietta Foods, San Jose 1977-79, ret.; self-empl. 1979– ; mem. advis. council UC Agri. Extension 1975, advis. council Univ. of Santa Clara Inst. of Agribusiness 1979-85; mem: Calif. Food Processors/ Sacramento (pres. 1972), Nat. Food Processors Assn., Wash DC (dir. at large 1972-79); civic: John Muir Hosp. Found., Walnut Creek (secty., treas.), Walnut Creek Planning Commn. (chmn.); Republican (Pres.'s Club); Hebrew. Res: 1540 Westwood Ct Walnut Creek 94595 Ofc: Sidney Ross Associates 33 Quail Ct Ste 104 Walnut Creek 94596

ROSS, STEVEN J., business executive, ret.; b. Sept. 24, 1926, N.Y.C.; s. Louis and Pearl (Krex) R.; m. Gloria, May 22, 1970; children: Barry b. 1950, Cynthia b. 1952, Kathryn b. 1954; edn: Pacific Internat. Univ. 1945-47. Career: pres./CEO Ross Assocs., Inc., Gardena 1964-68 (nat. distbs. vinyl upholstery fabrics to furniture mfrs., co. spun off to inv. group); exec. v.p. Xebec Finl. Group (real estate syndication & devel.), Walnut Creek 1968-72; founder/pres. Village Builders (r.e. syndication and devel., projects incl. 192-unit sub-divs. in Davis and Vallejo), Sacramento 1972-79; founder/pres. California Satellite Systems, Inc. (affil. HBO w. 30,000+ subscribers in Sacto., sold CALSAT to communications conglomerate, Graphic Scanning Corp., NY), Sacramento 1979-84, ret.; bus. cons. on finl., mktg. and advtsg.; bd. dirs. NAMSCO (Nat. Assn. MDS Cos.) 1980-84, Page U.S., 1984-85; clubs: Sacramento Yacht, Oxbow Yacht, Jaguar of No. Am., Maserati, Rolls Royce Owners; Republican; Jewish; rec: yachting, collect art and bronze Art Deco sculpture, rare books, photog. Address: POB 329 Shingle Springs 95682

ROSSER, JAMES M., university president; b. Apr. 16, 1939, East St. Louis, Ill.; s. Wm. M. and Mary E. (Bass) R.; m. Carmen Rosita Colby, Ed.D., Dec. 27, 1962; 1 son, Terrence, b. 1965; edn: BA and MA, microbiol., So. Ill. Univ., Carbondale, 1962, 1963, PhD, health admin., 1969. Career: resrch. bacteriologist Eli Lilly & Co., Indnpls. 1963-66; tchg. asst./ asst. prof. health edn./ grad. faculty Coll. of Edn./ asst. to the Chancellor, So. Illinois Univ., Carbondale 1962-70; lectr./ assoc. prof. Edn., and Pharmacol. and Toxicol., Univ. of Kansas, Lawrence 1970-74; vice chancellor State of NJ Dept. of Higher Edn., Trenton, NJ 1974-79; vis. faculty Harvard Univ. Grad. Sch. of Edn., 8/79; pres. Calif. State Univ., Los Angeles 1979–, prof. of health care mgmt., 1979-; frequent spkr. profl. confs., workshops; mem. Am. Assn. of State Colls. & Univs. (com. on urban affairs 1979-); Western Assn. of Schs. & Colls. (accreditation teams); The Calif. St. Univ. (trustees long range fin. plng. com. 1982-; Am. Council on Education, Wash DC sub-coms. 1979-); honors: Kappa Delta Pi, Phi Kappa Phi, Omega Psi Phi Freshman Scholarship Award, Langston Univ. 1957-58, Coll. Student of Year 1958, E. St. Louis, Ill.; NSF Fellowship 1961; Beta Gamma Sigma; West Coast Father of the Year 1981; Brotherhood Crusade, Pioneer of Black Hist. Achievement Awd., L.A. 1981; Am. Humanics Friend of Youth Award 1985; mem. bd. trustees, Orthopaedic Hosp.; bd. dirs.: L.A. Council for Internat. Visitors, Urban League, United Way of Gr. L.A., Community TV of So. Calif. (KCET), pres. Boy Scouts L.A. Area Council, Hispanic Urban Ctr., Alhambra CofC; Rotarian; publs: arts. in Liberal Education, Catalyst, Trustee Quarterly, Cross Reference, Dialogue, State Budgeting for Higher Edn., others; Democrat; Catholic. Res: 225 El Cielo Lane Bradbury 91010 Ofc: CSULA, 5151 State University Dr Los Angeles 90032

ROSSI, ANTHONY JOHN, JR., transmission products mfg. co. executive; b. June 2, 1934, Chgo.; s. Anthony John and Angelina Maria (Rosselli) R.; m. Elisabeth M. Knoester, Sept. 27, 1969; children: Anthony John, III, Angelina Marie, Michelle Lynn, Michael Steven, Elizabeth Anne. Career: designer sterndrive transmission; with Rossi Indus., Pomona 1955-80, Rossi Transmission Products and Arrow Transmissions, Upland 1980—; honors: named Marine Mfg. Man of Year, Vapor Trails Mag. (1975), Marine Engring. & Eesign Year award (1976), Pres. Medal of Merit presented by Pres. Reagan; listed: Who's Who in West (18th ed.), Who's Who in Bus. & Fin. (22nd ed.), Vocational Biographies (Series L-4); mem. Independent Garage Owners Am., CofC, Kiwanis Club; mil: served with Paratroopers US Army 1950-55; Republican; Roman Catholic. REs: 599 Maywood Way Upland 91786 Ofc: Rossi Transmission Products 1693 W Arrow Hwy B1&2 Upland 91786

ROSSI, MARIE JOSEPHINE, land developer; b. Sept. 10, 1949, Napa; d. Joseph Sr. and Elodia (Pascale) R.; m. Richard Flejstad, Feb. 8, 1969; children: William b. 1969, Christina b. 1971; edn: Napa Coll. 1967-69; R.E. agent lic., Anthony Schs. 1977; broker lic., 1981; Notary Public 1979. Career: realtor assoc. Century 21 1977; realtor assoc. Pacific Coast Properties 1977-78; sales mgr. Rossi's 'Sweet Antiques', Yountville 1980-81; owner Rossi Realty Co. (afil. broker Lewis C. On & Assoc.), Chinatown, S.F. 1981—; assoc. Rossi Development Co.; Internat. R.E. Conv. sponsor, participant, Hong Kong 1983; bd. dirs. Restoration of Calif. Hist. Landmarks (Napa Valley), Pvt. Landowners (S.F.), Samuel Springs Resort (Water Springs); honors: No. Calif. Winners Circle, Century 21 1978; mem: Napa Co. Bd. Realtors; Silverado Country Club; Napa Womens Political Caucus (Screening Com., secty. 1985); works: resrch. hist. mineral health resorts of Napa 1980-84 and devel. mineral spring water co. 1983; Republican; Catholic; rec: gardening, decorating, theater. Res: 899 Oak Leaf Way (Silverado Country Club), Napa Valley 94558 Ofc: Rossi Realty Co., 3040 Jefferson St, Alta Plaza, Napa 94558

ROSSKOPF, WALTER JOSEPH, JR., veterinarian; b. Mar. 3, 1945, Aliceville, Ala.; s. Walter, Sr. and June (Ethridge) R.; m. 3d. Christine Davis, Apr. 6, 1983; twin sons: Walter III and William, b. 1969; edn: BS, honors, UC Davis 1967, DVM, 1969. Career: pvt. veterinary practice, pioneer in many exotic animal med. and surgical procedures, avian and reptilian splst; Lawndale Pet Hosp., 1969-74; co-owner Animal Medical Centre of Lawndale, 1974—; co-owner Avian and Exotic Animal Hosp. of Orange County, Fountain Valley pres. Rosskopf-Woerpel, Inc.; seminar spkr. nat., state, and local vct. med. assns.; author over 90 med. articles and over 100 lay arts. on med. subjects, contbr. to four textbooks on exotic animal medicine, currently writing new textbook on avian med.; resrch. assoc. CSU Dominguez Hills, 1980-; instr. in exotic animal med., UC Riverside 1981-; editorial bd. Modern Veterinary Practice mag. 1981-, Avian/Exotic Practice Journ. 1983-; contbr. Kirk's Current Vet. Therapy, Merck Vet. Manual, 1984 Caged Bird Edn. of No. Am. Clinics, Burr's Textbook on Avian Diseases, Harrison's Textbook on Avian Med.; honors: Turtle Trust Award (1982), Phi Zeta Vet. Hon. Soc.; mem: Am., Calif. (exotic animal chmn. 1984-85), So. Calif. vet. med. assns.; Assn. of Avian Vets. (bd. 1984-, presented 5 papers at 1985 conv.); Am. Assn. of Avian Pathols.; Am. Assn. of Zoo Vets.; Internat. Assn. of Aquatic Animal Vets.; U.S. Animal Health Assn.; World Poultry Health Assn.; Desert Tortoise Council, Wildlife Disease Assn., Calif. Turtle & Tortoise Club; Republican; Prot.; rec: antiques, military collectibles, hist. Res: 28738 Golden Meadow Dr Rancho Palos Verdes 90274 Ofc: Animal Med. Ctr. of Lawndale, 4473 W. Rosecrans Ave, Hawthorne 90250; Avian & Exotic Animal Hosp. of Orange County, 10661 Ellis Ave Ste C Fountain Valley 92708

ROTH, ILAN, physicist; b. Feb. 4, 1947, Wroclaw, Poland; m. Shuli, Mar. 14, 1974; 1 child, Tali b. 1977; edn: BS, Hebrew Univ. 1967; MS, Weizmann Inst. 1969; PhD, Tel-Aviv Univ. 1981. Career: univ. tchg. asst. 1976-79, lectr. 1979-81; research physicist Univ. of Calif. Berkeley 1981—; recipient sev. univ. awards, scholarship French Govt. (1980); mem. Am. Geophysical Union; contbr. 25 articles in profl. jours. re space and fusion physics; mil: lt. Israeli Army 1970-76; rec: music, hist. Ofc: Univ. of Calif. Space Sciences Lab. Berkeley 94720

ROTH, JOANN GAIL, caterer; b. May 18, 1946, Bklyn.; d. Max and Janet (Scherer) Zaifert; m. Mort Roth, Apr. 1, 1973; 1 son, Jason Bryce Perel b. 1968; edn: BA, Brooklyn Coll. 1968. Career: controller Shop Rite Drugs, Beverly Hills 1971-75, Sperling Carpet Co., Sherman Oaks 1976-80; owner/pres. Someone's In the Kitchen, Tarzana 1981—; frequent lectr. and group seminars; honors: Outstanding Woman of the Year, Tarzana CofC (1985), appreciation, Mayor of Los Angeles, U.S.A. for Africa; mem. Women in Bus., Roundtable for Women, Internat. Assn. of Cooking Profls., LA CofC, Tarzana CofC, LA Conv. Bur.; bd. dirs. The Country School; Jewish. Ofc: Someone's In the Kitchen 5973 Reseda Blvd Tarzana 91356

ROTH, LEONARD JEROME, chartered financial consultant; b. Jan. 26, 1935, Gary, Ind.; s. Milton James and Theresa (Kohn) R.; m. Joann, Mar. 11, 1978; children: William b. 1963, Luanne b. 1962, Rosemarie b. 1968, Brad b. 1970; edn: BA, UC Los Angeles 1957; MBA, Mich. State Univ. 1963; desig: CLU-Chartered Life Underwriter, ChFC- Chartered Finl. Cons. (1985). Career: product mgr. Morton Salt Co., Chgo. 1970-73; nat. field sales mgr. Adolphs Ltd., Burbank 1973-76; prin., L.J. Roth & Assoc., Los Angeles 1974-76; ins. agt. Century Benefit Consultants, Encino 1976—; awards: Million Dollar Round Table (1978-85), Nat. Quality Award (1981-84); mem. Charitable Planned Giving Roundtable, Nat. Assn. CLU/ San Fernando Valley Chpt., Am. Cancer Soc. (Legacies Com.), UCLA Alumni Assn.; mil: sp3 US Army 1962;

Republican; Jewish; rec: fundraising for charities. Ofc: Century Benefit Consultants 15910 Ventura Blvd Ste 1801 Encino 91436

ROTOLO, GARY DANTE, dentist; b. June 6, 1952, Sewickley, Pa.; s. George Dante and Mary Rita (Cook) R.; m. Dianne, Aug. 20, 1977; children: Paul b. 1979, Gina-Marie b. 1983; edn: BS in biol., USC 1974; DDS, Northwestern Univ., Chgo. 1978. Career: estab. pvt. practice in general dentistry, La Mesa 1979—; mem. Am. Dental Assn., Calif. Dental Assn., San Diego County Dental Assn., Acad. of General Dentistry; civic: St. Martins Catholic Ch. Parents Tchrs. Gp. (pres.), World-Wide Marriage Encounter (presenting team), Calif. Hawking Club, B.A.S.S.; Republican; Catholic; rec: golf, fishing, bird-watching, falconry (expert on habits of Calif. birds of prey). Res: 7615 Torrem St La Mesa 92041 Ofc: 7900 El Cajon Blvd Ste D La Mesa 92041

ROTTER, RONALD L., investment analyst; b. Apr. 4, 1943, N.Y.C.; s. Harry and Freda (Sugarman) R.; m. Marilyn, Aug. 30, 1970; children: Danny b. 1974, Gregory b. 1977; edn: BS, USC 1965, MBA, 1968; desig: Chartered Finl. Analyst, Inst. of CFA (1979). Career: securities analyst Cantor Fitzgerald & Co., Beverly Hills 1970-75; prof. fin. Los Angeles Mission Coll., Sylmar 1975-83; v.p./sec. analyst Bateman Elchler Hill Richards, 1983-85; Seidler Amdec Securities, Los Angeles 1985—; pvt. consulting; instr. UCLA, L.A. Mission Coll., Santa Monica City Coll.; mem. Finl. Analysts Fedn., Inst. of CFA, L.A. Soc. Finl. Analysts; mil: US Army Reserve; Res: 4125 Pulido Ct Calabasas 91302 Ofc: Seidler Amdec Securities 515 S Figueroa Los Angeles 90071

ROUPE, RONALD DEAN, national barter broker, consultant; b. June 23, 1940, Des Moines, Iowa; s. R. Vincent and Ellen (Van Gorp) R.; edn: BA, CSU San Jose 1965; "Col." Reisch Auction Coll. 1975. Career: v.p. Topstar Prodns. Inc. 1965-70; Western regl. dir. Willard Alexander Agency, Beverly Hills 1970-75; founder/pres. National Barter Foundation Inc. (non-profit ednl. co.), Sunnyvale 1975—; corporate barter & trading cons., 1981—; chmn. Arbitration Board - Trade Systems Corp. 1981-82; nat. barter instr. seminars, radio & TV speaker, 1981-; honors: merit cit. Muscular Dystrophy Assn. (1967), named Entrepreneur of Year, Nat. Entrepreneurs Assn. (1982), Ethics Award, Calif. Barter Council (1985); mem: Internat. Assn. of Trade Exchanges (chmn. ethics com. 1982), Internat. Trade Exchange (corp. broker 1983-), Calif. Barter Council (bd. dirs. 1983-84, chmn. ethics com. 1982-83), Nat. Entrepreneurs Assn., Business Exchange Club, Internat. Reciprocal Trade Assn., var. Real Estate Exchange Clubs, Nat. Auctioneers Assn., Chamber of Commerce; publs: It's Smarter to Barter (1982), Secrets to Successful Barter (1985), author/ pub. internat. monthly barter newsletter (1982-); mil: pfc US Army Med. Corps 1964-65, Exp. Rifle/Pistol; Prot.; rec: fishing, hunting, boating, travel. Ofc: National Barter Foundation Inc. 1225 Vienna Dr Ste 322 Sunnyvale 94089

ROUSEY, M. PIPER, chiropractor; b. Apr. 27, 1907, Paola, Kans.; d. Joseph Edward and Mabel Azella (McCoach) Taylor; edn: BS, Pittsburg State 1930; MS, Wichita Univ. 1937; DC, L.A. Chiro. Sch. 1950. Career: teacher Wichita, Kans. 1927-33; editor Printograph Kansas City, Mo. 1933-38; chiropractor 1950—, semi-retired; honors: Woman of Achievement (Highland Park Bus. & Profl. Women 1964), Honorable Service (H.P. CofC 1968); mem: Bus. and Profl. Women (club pres. 1966-68), Hemet CofC, Zonta Club (pres. 1972), Hemet Am. Bus. Women's Assn. (rec. secy. 1984), Am. Legion (cmdr. Post 576 1961-63, Hemet Post 53 adj. and judge adv. 1985-86), Highland Pk. CofC (rec. secy. 1963-68), YMCA (exec. bd. 1965-68); mil: 2nd lt. US Army 1943-44; Republican; Methodist. Res: 1500 San Vicente Dr Hemet 92343

ROUSH, JAMES RICHARD, athletic trainer, physical educator; b. Aug. 23, 1953, Tucson, Ariz.; s. James R. and Patricia Ann (Gillispie) R.; m. Elizabeth Jarus, June 17, 1977; edn: BS and MS in phys. edn., Univ. of Ariz. 1976, 77; PhD in P.E. spec. in kinesiol., USC 1984; tchg. cert. in sec. edn., Ariz.; Calif. Comm. Colls. instr. cred.; cert. mem. Nat. Athletic Trainers Assn. (1977). Career: athletic tnr. City Coll. of San Francisco 1977-78; tchg. asst. in kinesiology, USC Dept. of Phys. Edn., 1980-82; head athletic tnr. Claremont McKenna, Harvey Mudd, and Scripps Colls., Claremont 1978-83; pgm. coord. of the athletic tng. curriculum CSU San Jose Dept. of Human Performance 1983-85; athletic tnr./dir. of extremity rehabilitation Lawrence R. Petulla & Assocs., Los Gatos 1985—; athletic tnr.: Athletic Cong. Nat. Track & Field Championships, San Jose (1984), East-West Shrine Football Game, Stanford (1985, 86), Bruce Jenner Grand Prix Track & Field Meet, San Jose (1985); num. research and poster presentations var. profl. assn. nat. meetings (1983-); awards: for outstanding research (1984, 1985), Nat. Athletic Trainers Assn.; mem. Am. Coll. of Sports Medicine, Nat. Athletic Tnrs. Assn. (chmn. Grants & Scholarships Com.), Calif. Athletic Tnrs. Assn. (Ethics Com.); civic: Am. Red Cross (instr.); Democrat; rec: gardening, fishing, computer pgmmg. Res: 6159 Ellerbrook Way San Jose 95123 Ofc: Lawrence R. Petulla & Assocs. 266 Saratoga Ave Los Gatos 95030

ROUTER, PAUL GETTY, corporate planner, public accountant; b. Nov. 22, 1941, Holland, Mich.; s. Dennis Worldly and Margaret May (Hotaling) R.; m. Sherry, April 15, 1962; children: Steven b. 1950, Victori b. 1952, Dennis b. 1954, Paula b. 1961, Rebecca b. 1962, Reborta b. 1962, Weston b. 1970; edn: MBA, Univ. of Mich 1962; CMA, Mich. 1962. Career: corp. CFO J.P. Getty Enterprises, Southwestern Research Corp., C.C. Concepts Corp.; v.p., treas. Wes Cast Food Svc.; currently, public corp. plnnr. and income tax splst.; honors: Black Hat, Chaine Des Rotisseurs, 1970; mem: Lions Iternat. (pres. 1961), Optimists, Rotary, La Tippers, Via Verde Country Club, Los Angeles Athletic Club, Magic Castle; gourmet chef; Catholic; rec: racquetball, golf, deep sea fishing. Res: 31 Burns Canyon Rd. Calimesa 92320 Ofc: 3244 Cahuenga Blvd. West, Los Angeles 90068

ROUTH, SANDRA JOYCE, cattery owner; b. May 7, 1942, Los Angeles; d. Omer Eldon and Muriel Estelle (Palmer) R.; edn: Bus. Cert., Los Angeles Metro. Coll. of Bus. 1962. Career: file clerk, gen. ofc. Mid-City Meat Co., Maywood, E.C.E. Encell Auto Parts, Los Angeles, gen. ofc. payroll clerk Wate King- Universal, Vernon 1966-70; Tru- Luv Cattery 1970-77; owner Raindance Cattery, Apple Valley 1978–; pedigree researhc; mem: Atlantic Himalayan Club (NY), The Internat. Cat Assn. (charter); publs: article, How to Sell Kittens in Pet Shops, Pet Dealer Mag. 1982; Yes, There Are Some Quality Shops!; rec: raising flowers, gardening. Address: Raindance Cattery, 24077 Yucca Loma Rd., P.O. Box 471 Apple Valley 92307

ROWLEN, FRANK EDWARD, city treasurer, financial executive; b. Mar. 5, 1949, Columbus, Ohio; s. Charles Edward and Priscilla Jane (Howison) R.; m. Janice, Sept. 5, 1970; children: Wm. Thomas b. 1976, Jane Marta b. 1979; edn: AA, Palomar Coll. 1968; BS, CSU San Diego 1970; MBA, National Univ. 1985. Career: asst. cashier Bank of Am. NTSA, 1970-71; accountant City of Escondido 1972-79; asst. dir. fin. City of Carlsbad 1979-83; dir. fin. City of Vista 1983–; mem. Calif. Soc. of Municipal Fin. Ofcrs. (San Diego County chpt. chmn. 1984; awarded cert. of outstanding finl. reporting 1983-85), Calif. Muni. Treasurers Assn.; Republican; Presbyterian; rec: sports, backpacking, photog. Res: 3662 Country Meadow Ln Escondido 92025 Ofc: City of Vista POB 1988 Vista 92083

ROYAL, MELODY BERNEDETTE, dance studio director; b. Mar. 8, 1946, Oakland; d. Henry Everett and Berniece (Roberts) Burch; 1 son, Sterling b. 1968; edn: CSU San Jose 1963-65. Career: profl. entertainer 1956-76; owner/ dir. Melody's Dance Studio, Antioch 1967–; founder/dir. Melody Royal Dancers, semi-profl. variety youth group entertain comm. groups, schs., hosps., county fairs, pvt. clubs; realtor assoc. Mason Mc-Duffie Real Estate Inc., Concord 1984–; awards: Miss Oakland (1964), Miss Vacaville Raceways (1964), 1st Pl. Talent winner Miss Oakland (1964), Flower Princess Oakland Flower Show (1963); mem. Profl. Dance Tchrs. Assn. (1972-76), Jobs Daus. Oakland; Prot. Res: 1113 Jacobsen St Antioch 94509 Ofc: Melody's Dance Studio 112 Railroad Ave Antioch 94509; Mason Mc-Duffie Real Estate Inc. 5400 B-1 Ygnacio Valley Rd Concord 94623

ROYBAL, EDWARD R., congressman; b. Feb. 10, 1916, Albuquerque, N.Mex.; m. Lucille Beserra, Sept. 27, 1940; children: Lucille, Lillian, Edward R.; edn: stu., UCLA, Southwestern Univ., Los Angeles; LLD, Pacific States Univ., Claremont Coll. Grad. Sch. Career: with Civilian Conservation Corps 1934-35; social worker, public health educator Calif. TB Assn., then dir. health edn. Los Angeles Co. TB and Health Assn. 1942-49; 88th-98th congresses from 25th Dist. Calif., mem. appropriations com., select com. on aging; chmn. subcom. on housing and consumer interests; secty.- treas. Congl. Hispanic Caucus; honors; Excellence in Public Svc. award, Am. Acad. Pediatrics 1976; Vis. Chubb Fellow, Yale; mem: Nat. Assn. Latino Elected Ofcls. (pres.), Am. Legion; mil: US Army 1944-45; Democrat; Catholic. Ofc: Rayburn Office Bldg., Washington DC 20515

RU, WESLEY, co. executive; b. Dec. 9, 1954, Taipei, Taiwan, nat. US cit. 1971; s. Matthew D.J. and Maylin (Chu) R.; m. Kathleen E., May 5, 1984; 1 son, Nthaniel b. 1985; edn: BS, CSU Los Angeles. Career: pres. Triad Internat. Group, 1977–; internat. sales Flying Tiger Line, 1978-81; bd. chmn. Western Badge & Trophy Co., Los Angeles 1984–; commnr. Community Rels., Monterey Park 1982-85; honors: Pi Sigma Epsilon mktg. hon. (pres. Phi chpt. 1977-78), community service awards Monterey Park Police Dept. and Chamber of Commerce, Coro Found. Fellow- tng. course for leaders of Asian-Am. community; mem: Sales & Mktg. Execs. Assn. of Los Angeles (chmn. Internat. Mktg. Com. 1982-84), Monterey Park CofC (chmn. Chinese-Am. Com. 1983-85), Los Angeles CofC, Long Beach CofC, Santa Monica CofC; club: Los Angeles Athletic; Republican; rec: ski. Ofc: Western Badge & Trophy Co. 1716 W Washington Blvd Los Angeles 90007

RUBITSKY, KENNETH RUSSELL, electrical engineer; b. Mar. 2, 1954, Sacramento; s. Bernard B. and Irene C. (Anderson) R.; m. Pamela, Oct. 10, 1981; children: Kevin b. 1982, Lisa b. 1986; edn: AA, Am. River Comm. Coll. 1977; BSEE, CSU Sacto. 1981; Reg. Profl. Engr. (electrical) Calif. 1983, Ore. 1985, Nev. 1985. Career: field radio repairman US Army 1971-74; elec. engr. in tng. Rex Moore Elec. Contractors & Engrs. 1979-83, chief elec. engr. 1983–; honors: Eagle Scout 1971; mil: sgt. US Army 1971-74; Democrat; Protestant; rec: electronics, music. Res: 8273 Moss Oak Ave Citrus Heights 95610 Ofc: Rex Moore Electrical 3601 Parkway Pl West Sacramento 95691

RUCKER, RUFUS CAPERS, dermatologist; b. May 24, 1910, Jennings, LA; s. Maxwell Lee and Ruby (Bauknight) R.; m. Clara Victoria Marchus, Jan. 23, 1937; children: Marilyn Rae b. 1942, Rufus Edward b. 1944, Howard b. 1946; edn: Texas A & M 1928-29; UC 1930-35; MB, Northwestern Med. 1941; MD, Northwestern Med. 1942; Fellow Am. Bd. of Dermatology bd. cert. (1951). Career: active practice dermatology, Los Angeles 1951-52, Chico 1952; Vol. Clinical Faculty Dept. Dermatol., Stanford Univ. Med. Sch. clin. instr. 1955-56, asst. prof. 1966-72, clin. assoc. prof. 1972-75, clin. assoc. prof. emeritus 1975–; mem: AMA, Calif. Med. Assn., Butte- Glenn Med. Soc. (pres. 1960), Southern Med. Assn., San Francisco Derm. Assn. (pres. 1978), Pacific Derm. Assn. (pres. elect 1982, pres. 1983); Masters Derm. Assn., No. Am. Clin. Derm. Assn., Am. Acad. of Derm.; clubs: Masons, Butte Creek CC, Seniors Golf Assn. of No. Calif., Calif. Seniors Golf Assn.; mil: major

M.C. US Army 935th Engr. Aviation Regt., Okinawa 1942-46; Republican; Protestant; rec: photog., ham radio, golf. Res: 239 Estates Dr Chico 95928 Ofc: R.C. Rucker Dermatologist, 676 E 1st Ave, Ste 15, Chico 95926

RUDERMAN, DAVID PERRY, investment co. executive; b. Nov. 28, 1936, Los Angeles; s. Martin A. and Rose R. Ruderman; m. Judith Ann Brown, Feb. 12, 1961; children: Bradley, b. 1963, Melissa, b. 1968, Matthew, b. 1971; edn: BS in fin., USC 1958. Career: securities cons. Sutro & Co. Inc., Beverly Hills 1958-75; senior v.p. Shearson/American Express, Beverly Hills 1975–; cons. to various savings & loan assns.; lectr. on investments; mem: The Founders, Fraternity of Friends (The Music Ctr), USC Alumni; var. civic groups; club: Mountaingate CC; publs: arts. on securities in var. jours.; Democrat; Jewish; rec: golf, tennis. Res: 260 Bronwood Los Angeles 90049 Ofc: Shearson/ American Express, 166 N Canon Dr Beverly Hills 90210

RUFFCORN, JOHN DOUGLAS, medical center executive; b. May 1, 1927, Mnpls.; s. John McKinley and Agnes Lorraine (Sproed) R.; m. Carol Jean Johnson, Aug. 24, 1950; children: Susan Marie b. 1955, Sharon Kay b. 1958; edn: BS in bus. adm., Union Coll., Lincoln, Nebr. 1951; grad. work USC 1955; cert. Internat. Acctg. Soc. Pgm., Chgo. 1957. Career: acct. Ford Motor Co., St. Paul, Minn. 1951-52; acct. Glendale Adventist Hosp., Glendale 1952-60, controller 1960-64, asst. adminstr. 1964-66, assoc. adminstr. 1966-67; adminstr. Washington Adventist Hosp., Takoma Park, Md. 1967-76; assoc. adminstr. Loma Linda University Medical Center, Loma Linda 1976-77, pres./ adminstr. 1977–, exec. vice pres. Adventist Health System/ Loma Linda 1982–, assoc. dean Sch. of Medicine, Loma Linda Univ. 1983–; bd. trustees Glendale Adventist Med. Ctr. (1960-67), Wash. Adventist Hosp. (1967-76), LLU Medical Ctr. (1976-); civic: Kiwanis Club (past pres.), Am. Red Cross (bd. local chpt.), Am. Heart Assn. (bd.), Mental Health Advis. Board, Am. Protestant Hosp. Assn. (govtl. rels. com.); mil: pfc US Army; Seventh-day Adventist; rec: skiing, golf. Res: 23187 Glendora Dr Grand Terrace 92324 Ofc: Loma Linda University Medical Center Loma Linda 92354

RUIZ, JERRY JOSEPH, lawyer; b. Nov. 26, 1955, Riverside; s. Robert F. and Marina M. (Briones) R.; m. Vicki L., Sept. 1, 1979; children: Miguel, b. 1980, Daniel, b. 1983; edn: BA, UC Santa Cruz 1977; JD, UC Berkeley 1980; admitted to the bars of Calif. 1980, Texas 1983. Career: dep. legis. counsel Ofc. of Legislative Counsel, Sacramento 1980-82; assoc. atty. Hagans, Ginnings, Birkelbach, Keith & Delgado, El Paso, Tex. 1982-85; assoc. atty. Kroloff, Belcher, Smart, Perry & Christopherson, Stockton 1985–; cons. Proj. Business, div. of Junior Achiev. Inc. 1985; participant Volunteers in Parole 1982; honors: life mem., Calif. Scholarship Fedn. 1973; Crown Coll. and Community Svc. Awards, UC Santa Cruz 1977; mem: Am. (internat. law & practice sect.), Calif. and Texas (internat. law sect.) Bar Assns., Mexican- am. CofC (Stockton); Democrat; Catholic; rec: softball, bicycling. Ofc: Kroloff, Belcher, Smart, Perry & Christopherson, 1044 No. El Dorado, Stockton 95202

RUIZ, VICTOR G., speech pathologist; b. July 17, 1954, Upland; s. Victor M. and Mary D. (Guiterrez) R.; edn: AA, Chaffey Coll. 1974; BA behav. scis., Calif. Polytechnic Univ. Pomona 1977; BA equiv. speech communication, CSU Fullerton 1979, MA communicative disorders, 1984; Lic. Pathologist 1984; Cert. of Clin. Competence, Am. Speech Hearing Assn. Mem: Am. Speech Language Hearing Assn., Calif. Speech Hearing Assn., Elks; Democrat; Catholic; rec: skiing, music collection (classical and jazz). Res: 864 W. Granada Ct. Ontario 91762

RULE, ROGER COLLINS, builder/ developer/ publisher; b. Dec. 31, 1944, Kansas City, Mo.; s. Forrest Collins and Margaret Evelyn (Thompson) R.; m. Joyce Kindred, Dec. 26, 1965; children: Sean b. 1971, Ryan b. 1979; edn: BS, Univ. of Mo. 1966; US Army Quartermaster Ofcrs. Adv. Course, Fort Lee, Va. 1971; B-1 gen. contractors lic., Calif. 1971; Mo. Life Tchg. Cert.; R.E. broker lic., Calif. 1981. Career: gen. contractor Rule Devel., Modesto 1973-76; pres. Rule Enterprises, Modesto 1977–; pres. Alliance Books, Inc., Northridge 1982–; owner/ partner Sky- Trek Aviation, Modesto Airport, Modesto 1983–; tchr. probational & remedial students, N.K.C. Public Schs., summer 1968; honors: A.R.C. Pvt. Bus. Awd. 1983; Who's Who Finance & Industry, 24th Ed.; Council of Bus. Mgrs. 1977; Commandant's List, QMC Adv. Course, Fort Lee' Va. 1971; mem: Nat. Edn. Assn., Mo. Tchrs. Assn.; Principal's Adv. Com.; No. Coast & Fresno Bldrs. Exch.; ; San Joaquin Valley Exchs.; Nat. & Modesto Home Bldrs. Assns.; Nat. & Modesto Rifle Assns.; Winchester Coll. Arms Assn.; Winchestr Club of Am.; Mo. Univ. Alumni Assn.; author: book, The Rifleman's Rifle, 1982; book, Twentieth Century Winchester, 1984; art., The Rifleman's Rifle, Guns Mag. 3/84; arts. in The Winchester Repeater 1984, 85; mil: Capt., US Army (temp.); 1st Lt., US Army (perm) QMC Airborne, GCM, Meritorious Svc. Medal; Republican; Methodist; rec: parchutist, snow skiing, target shooting. Res: 2816 Eastridge Cir Modesto Ofc: Rule Enterprises, POB 1762, Modesto 95353

RULEY, STANLEY EUGENE, federal defense contracts price analyst/ negotiator; b. Jan.24, 1934, Akron, Ohio; s. Royal Lovell and Opal Lenora (McDougall) R.; m. Annie A. Patterson, Dec. 15, 1962; children: Cheryl b. 1965, Janice b. 1968; edn: Kent State Univ. 1951-53; BSBA, Ohio State Univ. 1955; Reg. Profl. Engr. (indsl.) Calif. (1971). Career: indsl. engr. E.W. Bliss Co., Canton, O. 1955-56; finance splst. US Army, HQ 7th Army, Germany 1956-59; indsl. engr. Hoover Vacuum Cleaner Co., North Canton, Ohio Mission Appliance Div. Gaffers & Sattler, Hawthorne, Calif., 1961-62; mfg. engr. Litton Indus. Data Sys. Div., Van Nuys 1962-65; contract price analyst Naval Plant Rep. Office, Lockheed Calif. Co., Burbank 1966-72; contract negotiator Naval Regl. Procurement Office, Long Beach 1972-75; cost/price analyst

Defense Contract Adminstrv. Services Mgmt. Area, Van Nuys 1975-82; chief Contract Pricing Office, Edwards AFB 1982 –; engring. cons. prin. (electronic & computer equip.) Industrial Engr. Services, 1971-; recipient profl. performance awards (1970, 82, 84); mem. Am. Inst. Indsl. Engrs. (1964-75); clubs: LERC Gem & Mineral/ Burbank (pres. 1977), LERC Camper/ Burbank (pres. 1974), Masons; mil: sgt. US Army 1956-59; Republican; Presbyterian; rec: flying, golf, camping, travel. Res: 18751 Vintage St Northridge 91324 Ofc: Air Force Flight Test Center, Dir. of Contracting (PKF), Edwards 93523

RULLAN, PETER PAUL, physician-dermatologist; b. Feb. 19, 1953, San Juan, Puerto Rico, USA; s. Antonio, (M.D.) and Jane (Hryhorczuk), (R.N.) R.; m. Ginger Goetz (R.D.), June 14, 1980; 1 dau. Jennifer b. 1983; edn: BA, Univ. Chgo. 1975; MD, Univ. Puerto Rico 1979; Dermatology Splty., UC Irvine 1983; diplomate Am. Board of Dermatology 1983. Career: chief resident Dermatology Tng. Prog. UC Irvine 1982-83; cons. Skin Tumor Inst. & Center for Skin Disease, Chula Vista 1983-84; cons. Center Physicians Medical Group, Chula Vista 1984 –; lectr. Sweetwater Sch. Dist. on sexually transmitted diseases; awards: Stelwagon Research Award (1982); mem. Am. Acad. of Derm., NY Acad. of Scis., CMA, San Diego County Med. and Dermatology Soc.; Rotarian; contbr. articles on derm., Archives of Derm. 1984, Chula Vista Star News, Day Hosp. publ.; Christian; rec: guitar, piano, computer. Address: Chula Vista 92010

RUMMEL, H. GEORGE, hydroelectric engineer; b. Aug. 4, 1939, Riverton, Wyo.; s. Elmer George and Mary Elizabeth (Sinner) R.; children: Andrew George b. 1969, Amron Suzanne b. 1974; edn: BSCE, Valparaiso Univ. 1962; MSCE, CSU Sacramento 1972; Reg. Civil Engr. Calif. 1966. Career: asst. civil engr. Calif. Dept. Water Resources Sacramento 1962-72; civil engr. (hydroelectric) Fed. Power Commn. Wash. DC 1972-75; dept. head Harza Engrg. Co. Chgo. 1975-80; proj. mgr. (hydroelectric) Sacto. Municipal Utility Dist. 1980 –; pres. Rummel Engrg. & Devel. Co. (REDCO); Little League mgr.; managed planning, licensing, design, initial constrn. for 2 new hydro projects; Republican; Lutheran (Stephen minister); rec: baseball, skiing, outdoors, fishing. Ofc: SMUD Sacramento 95813

RUMMEL, PETER CHARLES, food service industry recruiter; b. Mar. 27, 1940, Oakland; s. Charles Albert and Jane Muriel (Avery) R.; m. Elizabeth, Jan. 25, 1964; children: Laura b. 1970, David b. 1974; edn: BA, UC Berkeley 1964. Career: divisional subcontractor Moore Bus. Forms Emeryville, Calif. 1964-67; sales rep. Proctor & Gamble San Mateo 1967; sales svc./ inventory control Allied Packers Ltd. S.F. 1967; group prod. mgr. Durkee Food Svc. Cleveland, Ohio 1967-76; dir. mktg. Rich Prods. Corp. Buffalo, NY 1976-78; new bus. devel. mgr. Kitchens of Sara Lee Chgo. 1979; pres. Rummel & Assocs. Inc. Walnut Creek 1979 –; honors: Paul Harris Fellow (Rotary Internat. 1986), Past Pres. Award (Toastmasters Internat.); mem: Internat. Foodservice Mfrs. Assn., Food Service Mktg. Assn. of No. Calif., UC Alumni Assn., Rotary Internat., Nat. Rifle Assn., Masons, Calif. Rifle & Pistol Assn., Hon. Order of Ky. Colonels, Nat. Eagle Scout Assn., Boy Scouts of Am.; mil: E-4 US Army (MC) and Reserve 1957-65; Republican; Presbyterian; rec: photog., gardening, target shooting, fishing, sailing. Address: 2349 Banbury Pl Walnut Creek 94598

RUNYON, THEODORE HENRY, real estate broker; b. Nov. 8, 1919, Newark, NJ; s. Theodore Winas Smith and Martha Caroline (Radke) Runyon; m. Mildred Caroline Klye, May 10, 1946; children: Susan Carol b. 1947, Theodore H. II b. 1949, William Kyle b. 1951, Daniel Scott b. 1955; edn: UC Berkeley Coll. of Engring. 1947-49; BS, George Washington Univ. 1962; AS, Southwestern Coll. 1979; Instr. Cred. and Tchg. Cert. in real estate, Calif. State Colls. 1985. Career: exec. secty. Ballistic Missile/ Space Command for Secty. of Air Force and chief of staff USAF; West Coast rep. Common Mkt. Research Assocs., Brussels, Belgium 1972-77; real estate salesman Strand Crown Realtor, Coronado 1971-84, v.p. 1974-76; real estate broker 1979 –; honors: Alpha Sigma Lambda 1963; mem: Calif. Assn. of Realtors (The Real Estate Cert. Inst.), Caterpillar Club, Third Degree Masons, Retired Ofcrs. Assn. (pres. Silver Strand chpt., Coronado 1973-76, 1981; Air Force rep.; Ch. Council Resurrection Lutheran Ch. (pres., Coronado 1972), Navy League (1st v.p., Coronado 1986); mil: seaman 1/c USNR 1937-40, maj. US Army Air Corps 1940-47, col. USAF 1947-70; Republican; Lutheran; rec: golf, sailing. Res: 1320 Glorietta Blvd. Coronado 92118 Ofc: Coldwell Banker, 1001 B Ave. Ste. S-103 Coronado 92118

RUSH, FRANK BARRY, tour co. president; b. June 26, 1936, Sydney, Australia; s. Frank Steenson and Kathleen (Rowley) R.; m. Silloo Commissariat, Dec. 21, 1966; 1 dau., Shahnaz Barry b. 1970; edn: gen. mgmt., New S. Wales Inst. Tech., 1966-69; mktg. Univ. New S. Wales Inst. of Adminstrn., 1971; MBA, Pepperdine Univ. 1979; grad. Strategic Mktg. Pgm., Harvard Univ. Sch. Bus. 1982. Career: area sales mgr. Air India, Sydney, Aust. 1965-72; area mgr. S.W. Pacific and S. Asia, Varig Brasilian Airlines, Sydney 1972-74, Los Angeles, L.A. 1975-80; v.p. sales & mktg. Jetset Tours (No. Am.) Inc., 1981-82, pres. 1982 –; apptd. Hon. Goodwill Amb. of Amsterdam, Holland (1984-); guest lectr. tourism, UCLA Ext. pgm. 1982; mem: U.S. Tour Oprs. Assn. (bd. 1985-86), Australian Am. CofC/L.A. (charter, mem. Found. 1982-), Pacific Area Travel Assn., Aust. Inst. of Travel, Aust. Inst. of Mgmt.; club: S.K.A.L. (L.A., 1977-); clubs: Heidlebergh Prince (West Germany), Old Ignatians' Union (Sydney, Aus.); Republican; Catholic; rec: travel, tennis. Res: 390 S Hauser Blvd Los Angeles 90036 Ofc: Jetset Tours 8383 Wilshire Blvd Ste 432 Beverly Hills 90211

RUSH, JOHN A., insurance agent; b. Oct. 6, 1928, Toledo, Ohio; s. Arnold E. and Bessie A. Rush; m. Patricia Bush, Oct. 1977; children: Leslie b. 1954, Kurt b. 1957, Linda b. 1958, Karl b. 1960; edn: AA, Univ. of Toledo 1951. Career: mgr. Ventura Calif. Retail Credit Co. 1951-58; asst. mgr. customer svc. Sears-Roebuck 1958-59; ins. agent State Farm Ins. Co. 1960 –; commnr. Calif. St. Coastal Commn. 1979-81; City of Camarillo city councilman 1976-80, mayor 1979-80; bd. dirs. Camarillo Hospice 1983; pres. Lima Bean Soc., Bean Hive No. 1, 1983; dir. Camarillo Sanitation Dist. 1976-80; dir. Ventura Regl. Co. Sanitation Dist. 1978-80; mem: Camarillo Kiwanis Club (charter pres. 1967; pres. 1982-83, life. mem. 1985, lt. gov. div. 42 1985-86); life fellow, Kiwanis Internat.; mil: Sgt., US Army, 24th infantry Div., apan. 1946-47; Democrat; Unitarian; rec: gardening. Res: 1404 Calle Aurora Camarillo 93010 Ofc: John A. Rush, POB 156 Camarillo 93011

RUSH, ROBERT LEE, business executive; b. Dec. 10, 1941, Alhambra; s. Franklin Merle and Helen Edith (Sherwin) R.; edn: BSBA, Ariz. State Univ. 1965; photog., L.A. Art Center 1973; Calif. lic. Contractor (Swimming Pool) 1970. Career: pres. Swimming Pool Assocs. of So. Calif. 1968-70; pres. Arcadia Pools & Spas, 1970 –; bd. dirs. advis. com. L.A. County Health Dept., 1970-74; recipient Jacques Cousteau Soc. Photography Award (1978), Bronze medal, Aspen Amateur Giant Down Hill Slalome Skiing (1974), profl. awards for Swimming Pool Design (1980), Boys Scouts Am.: Order of the Arrow, Eagle Award (1960), Senior Patrol leader BSA Jamboree (1958); mem. Nat. Swimming Pool Inst., Swimming Pool Contrs. Assn. of So. Calif., Calif. Contrs. Assn., Am. Mgmt. Assn., Chamber of Commerce (Arcadia, San Marino, Pasadena); publs: ednl. film: Cattle Breeding (1980), num. underwater films; contbr. num. articles, Pool & Spa News; underwater photog. instr., 1978; profl. cinematographer. Res: 118 Bonita Sierra Madre 91024 Ofc: Arcadia Pools & Spas 21 West Duarte Rd Arcadia 91006

RUSHING, PATRICIA LOUISE, executive secretary; b. Dec. 2, 1947, San Francisco; d. Darrell Frances and Arley Kathryn (Goebel) Bolton; children: Rebecca b. 1970, Ryan b. 1974; edn: Canada Coll. 1973, 85. Career: postal clerk US Post Office; homemaker; waitress 1978-80; ofc. mgr. Stanford Univ. 1980 –; mem: Nat. Orgn. Female Execs., Parents Against Non Support (founder, pres. 1985-; April 1986 proclaimed Parents Against Non Support Month by San Mateo County Bd. of Supvs.), Alanon Family Groups (secty.), Girl Scouts (sales chair), Little League (aux. ofcr.), organized Prof. Lenore Weitzman Forum; radio spokesman for non support; child support task force (w/ Adv. Council for Women in San Mateo County); editor Parents Against Non Support Newsletter; Democrat; Methodist. Res: 698 Douglas Ave Redwood City 94063 Ofc: Parents Against Non Support POB 4187 Menlo Park 94063

RUSSELL, CRYSTAL ANNE, lawyer; b. June 29, 1942, North Tonnawanda, NY; d. Clarence Leonard and Ruth Ione (Brayley) Krueger; m. Thomas Russell, June 28, 1960; 1 son, Thomas, b. 1961; edn: BA, summa cum laude, Ariz. St. Univ. 1970; JD, cum laude, Ariz. St. Univ. Coll. of Law 1973. Career: atty. assoc. Browder & Gillenwater 1973-74; asst. counsel Anchor Nat. Life Ins. 1974-75; partner/ atty. Horsack & Russell 1975-77; asst. counsel Beneficial Standard Life 1977-78; corp. counsel Ameron, Inc. 1978-81; gen. counsel Vidal Sassoon, Inc., Los Angeles 1981 –; awards: Phelps Dodge Scholarship 1970; mem: Los Angeles Co. Bar Assn. (Corp. Counsel Sect.); Calif. State Bar (Bus. Law Sect., Corp. Counsel Subcom.); rec: running, swimming. Res: 1526 San Vicente Santa Monica 90402 Ofc: Crystal A. Russell, Esq., 1875 Century Park East, Ste 1290, Los Angeles 90067

RUSSELL, GERALD MERVIN, psychologist; b. Sept. 13, 1933, Bellflower; s. Orville Mervin and Irma Jean (Miller) R.; edn: ThB, Ariz. Bible Coll. 1955; BA psych., honors, CSU Long Beach 1978, MA psych., honors, 1982; PhD psych., U.S. Internat. Univ. 1986; ordained minister Calvary Baptist Ch. (1955). Career: asst. minister, music dir. Calvary Baptist Ch., Bellflower 1956-57; educator/ adminstr. A.B.W.E. Peru S.A. 1957-71; founder/pres. Tempo Ministries Inc. (non-profit resource services co.), 1972 –; senior minister First Baptist Ch., Wilmington 1978-80; prof. Dept. Psych., Los Angeles Baptist Coll., Newhall 1980; clin. psychologist, counselor Center for Behavior Medicine, Whittier 1984 –; reviewer Psychol. Reports Jour. 1985; computer cons. Medical Psychology Assn., Santa Monica 1984-86; honors: Outstanding Psychology Student award CSULB (1978); mem. Long Beach Ministerial Assn., Internat. Radio Amateurs Club, L.A. Computer Club; contbr. articles, Psychological Reports J. (1978, 82, 85); Republican; Baptist; rec: computers, carpentry. Res: 17019 Ardmore St Bellflower 90706 Ofc: Tempo Ministries Inc. POB 988 Bellflower 90706

RUSSELL, SHERRY MICHIKO, artist; b. July 1, 1950, Madison, Wis.; d. Shiro and Hisako (Higashino) Shibata; m. David L. Russell, June 24, 1972; 1 son, Scott Hisao b. 1979; edn: BS in fine arts, Univ. Wis., Madison 1972. Career: display artist with Liberty House, San Jose 1972-74; profl. artist self-empl., Laminated Wood Sculpture of Japanese Dolls and Horses, 1974-82, Wildlife acrylic paintings, 1982, current: Wildfowl (esp. waterfowl), acrylic paintings and limited edition prints, 1983 –; honors: placed in top 10 of Calif. Duck Stamp Contest (1983-84), Ducks Unlimited first Nat. Sponsor Dinner Print (1985), top 38 of Federal Duck Stamp Contest (1986), winner of Calif. Duck Stamp (1986); mem. Pacific Flyway Decoy Assn., Pacific S.W. Wildfowl Arts, Ducks Unlimited (coms.), Idaho Wildlife Assn. 1983-84, Calif. Waterfowl Assn., Wildlife Art Guild; rec: wildfowl observation and photog., decoy carving. Ofc: Shasta Wildlife Gallery 421 Chestnut St Mount Shasta 96067

RUSSO, DANIEL JASON, lawyer; b. July 9, 1949, NY, NY; s. Anthony Louis and Daisy (Feldman) R.; m. Mary Lessa, Aug. 11, 1974; children: Miranda b.

1980, Nicholas b. 1982; edn: BA anthropol., State Univ. of N.Y. Binghamton 1971; JD, J.F.K. Univ. Sch. of Law 1977; certified specialist crim. law Calif. State Bar 1985. Career: v.p. Community Law Svcs. 1978-79; ptnr. Russo, Weintraub & Bellia Vallejo, Calif. 1979–; prof. crim. law J.F.K. Univ. Law Sch. 1983–; mem: Am. (1979-), Solano Co. (v.p., pres.-elect 1976) bar assns.; Nt. Assn. Crim. Def. Lawyers 1984-, Calif. Attys. for Crim. Justice 1979-; publ: Calif. Criminal Justice Through the Looking Glass (Forum Magazine M/A 1983). Ofc: Russo, Weintraub & Bellia 408 Tennessee St Vallejo 94590

RUSSWORM, LARRY CLIFTON, manufacturing engineer; b. Nov. 23, 1954, Los Angeles; s. Kenneth and Lois Decema (Himes) R.; edn: BS, CalPoly San Luis Obispo 1979; AA, L.A. Harbor Coll. 1976. Career: design draftsman Rockwell Internat. L.A., Lax. summer 1972; Ralph M. Parsons Co., Pasadena, 1973-74; tool designer FMC Corp., San Jose 1977-78; mfg. engr. TRW, Redondo Beach 1979; TRW college recruiter for CalPoly, SLO; design drafting & blueprint reading instr., Los Angeles; curriculum advr. Los Angeles Harbor Coll.; TRW classroom tech. advr., Inglewood Bd. of Edn. Cooperative Ind., Academic Student Pgm. and steering com. mem.; blueprint reading instr. L.A. Harbor Coll. 1982; mem: Soc. of Mfg. Engrs. (edn. chmn. 1983-84; Engring. council rep. 1977-78; Engring. Tech. Rep. 1979); devel. model steam engine, CalPoly machine shop class; Democrat; Baptist; rec: music, recording, racquetball. Res: 1106 West 49th St Los Angeles 90037 Ofc: TRW, One Space Park Redondo Beach 90278

RUTH, ROGER, insurance broker; b. Oct. 4, 1945, Los Altos; s. Leo William Jr. and Dorothy Helen (Davidson) R.; m. Nadine Atwood, Sept. 2, 1967; children: Kellie b. 1968, Corinne b. 1971, Shannon b. 1976; edn: BA, Univ. of Santa Clara 1967; Cert. Ins. Counselor, CIC Soc. 1979. Career: supvr. trainee Allstate Ins. Co. 1970; div. mgr. 1974; independent broker 1974–, pres. Marx, Lewis & Ruth (and predecessor firms), San Jose 1975-84; dir. Flamer & Co. Ins. Brokers 1984–; bd. dirs. Independent Ins. Agents of San Jose; Continental Ins. Cos. Producer Council; Indsl. Indemnity Producer Council; St. Paul Ins. Co. Nat. Producer Council; Distng. Achiev. awd., Safeco Ednl. Inst. 1975; mem: Profl. Ins. Agents of Am.; Independent Ins. Agents of Am.; Western Assn. of Ins. Brokers; Almaden Country Club; Metropolitan Univ. Club; Univ. of Santa Clara Bd. of Fellows; mil: 1st lt. US Army (ROTC Distng. Mil. Grad.; Scabbard & Blade Hon. Soc.); Republican; Catholic; rec: golf. Res: 1055 Mountain Shadows Rd San Jose 95120 Ofc: Flamer & Co. 330 Distel Cir Los Altos 94022

RUTKOWSKI, WILLIAM JOHN, real estate broker; b. June 8, 1911, Portland, Ore.; s. Andrew and Josephine (Kuch) R.; m. Louise Marquez, May 28, 1939; children: Mary b. 1940, Theresa b. 1946, Wilhelmina b. 1948; edn: AA, San Diego City Coll. 1967. Career: commn. warrant ofcr. US Navy 27 years, campaign decorations Atlantic and Pacific Theaters, WWII, Korean War; federal civil service, 16 years (systems analyst North Island); current: owner/ realtor Rutkowski Realty, Chula Vista; mem. Calif. Assn. of Realtors (mem. 1975-, dir. 1978-82, chmn. Legislative Com. 1974-83), South San Diego Bay Cities Bd. Realtors (legis. liaison); Democrat; Catholic. Res: 494 First Ave Chula Vista 92010 Ofc: Rutkowski Realty 229 F St Chula Vista 92010

RUZZAMENTI, WILLIAM LOUIS, JR., federal narcotics enforcement agent; b. Aug. 31, 1948, San Bernardino, Calif.; s. William Louis and Helen Myrle Kirkwood (Hamilton) R.; m. Sheila, Sept. 7, 1968; children: William III b. 1971; Janina b. 1973, Tonia b. 1978; edn: BA, US Internat. Univ. 1970. Career: air marshal US Treasury Dept. NY, S.F. 1971, spl. agent Customs Svc. 1971-73; spl. agent Drug Enforcement Adminstrn. US Justice Dept. S.F. Internat. Airport supv. 1973-83, marijuana eradication pgm. mgr. Calif. 1983–; deputy cmdr. Campaign Against Marijuana Planting; Drug Enforcement Adminstrn. spokesman to 50+ orgns.; honors: num. law enforcement awards incl. Atty. Gen. Award for Outstanding Contbn. to Narcotic Law Enforcement 1984; mem. Calif. Narcotic Ofcrs. Assn.; publs: num. media interviews TV and major magazines concerning marijuana; mil: sgt. Calif. Nat. Guard 1970-73; Republican; Lutheran; rec: fishing, sports. Ofc: 2941 B Fulton Ave Sacramento 95821

RYAN, EDWARD JOHN, JR., wholesale printing co. president; b. May 25,1936, Warren, Ohio; s. Edward and Thelma E. (Veneman) R.; m. Dorothy C., Oct., 1970; edn: BS, Northeastern Univ. 1963. Career: purchasing agent Fenwal, Farmingham, Mass. 1960-63; var. pos. from mfg. supvn. to corp. personnel 1963-70, corp. employment mgr. Apllication Regional Hosps. Inc. 1970-72; v.p. med. rels. Hospital Corp. of Am., Nashville, Tenn. 1972-79; dir. internat. recruitment Whittaker Corp., Los Angeles 1979-80; senior v.p. Nat. Medical Enterprises, Los Angeles 1980-82; chmn., CEO, pres. Eale Corp. Inc., Chatsworth 1982–; mem: Internat. Thermograhpers Assn., PIA, Am. Med. Assn., PIRA, Masons, Scottish Rite, Shrine, Los Angeles Country Club, No. Ranch Country Club, San Fernando CofC; emil: airman 1/c USAF 1954-58; Republican; Protestant; rec: auto racing, motorcycles, mechanics. Res: 1115 Evenstar Av. Westlake Village 91361 Ofc: The Eagle Co. inc., 20426 Corisco St. Chatsworth 91311

RYBURN, JACK THOMAS, superior court judge; b. Aug. 20, 1923, Visalia; s. Jack and Nina Martin (Collins) R.; m. Toni, Sept. 5, 1942; edn: AB, USC 1948, JD, 1950. Career: partner law firm Ross, Woodson, Millard, Ryburn & Burke, 1950-70; judge Superior Court Los Angeles, 1970–; dir. Deringer Mfg. Co.; trustee Francis Bacon Found.; honors: Order of Coif, Skull and Dagger, Law Review editor, Law Sch. Senior Class pres.; club: Annandale Golf; mil: US Army 1943-46 Bronze Star, European Service; rec: golf. Ofc: 111 North Hill St Los Angeles 90012

RYDELL, RICHARD LEWIS, health care executive, city councilman; b. Feb. 23, 1940, Harrison, N.Y.; s. Robert H. and Helen L. R.; m. Sandra, May 1, 1961; children: Wendelin b. 1962, Vicki b. 1965, Elizabeth b. 1967, Rodney b. 1968, Jill b. 1971; edn: BE, Rensselaer Polytech. Inst. 1961; MBA, San Jose State Univ. 1982; reg. profl. engr. Calif. 1968. Career: assoc. dir. Yakima Valley Meml. Hosp. Yakima, Wash. 1976-78; exec. dir. Medishare San Jose 1978-80; dir. mgmt. systems Stanford Univ. Hosp. 1981–; chmn. bd. Bluegill Engrg.; councilman Los Altos Hills; honors: Hon. Fellow (Hospital Mgmt. Systems Soc. 1985); mem: Hosp. Mgmt. Systems Soc., Am. Coll. Healthcare Execs., IIE (sr. mem.), Los Altos Hills Little League (past pres.), Hills Athletic Team (pres.), Los Altos Hills Planning Commn. (past chmn.); publ: num. on use of computers in health care; rec: photog. Res: 12220 Menalto Dr Los Altos Hills 94022 Ofc: Stanford Univ. 700 Welch Rd, Rm 205, Palo Alto 94304

RYDER, ROBERT RAYMOND, electronics company executive; b. Aug. 14, 1936, Ossining, NY; s. George E. and Leila V. (Hall) R.; m. Renate Hirsch, May 26, 1960; edn: BSEE, Rensselaer Polytechnic Inst. 1957; exec. pgm., UCLA Grad. Sch. of Mgmt. 1979; exec. pgm., Harvard Grad. Sch. of Bus. 1984. Career: chief engr. Teledyne Environmental Sciences, Newbury Park 1963-68; div. mgr. Teledyne Geotech, Dallas, Texas 1968-74; gen. sales mgr. Avco Electronics, Huntsville, Ala. 1975-77; v.p., gen. mgr. Digitran Co., Pasadena 1977-81; v.p., gen. mgr. Elco Interconnect Systems, El Segundo 1981-83; gen. mgr. HR Textron, Valencia 1983-84; v.p. Validyne Engineeringc Corp., Northridge 1984–; dir. BD Digitran United Kingdom Ltd. 1979-81; mem: Instrument Soc. of Am. (senior), Apt. Assn. of San Fernando Valley; works: tutorial and overview articles in trade journs. and confs.; Republican; Lutheran; rec: organist. Res: 4701 Heaven Ave. Woodland Hills 91364 Ofc: Validyne Eng. Corp., 8626 Wilbur Ave. Northridge 91324

RYERSON, CLIFFORD MARTEN, management consultant; b. Sept. 23, 1915, Bklyn.; s. Jacob and Lillian Mann (Hunt) R.; m. Cornelia McRae, Apr. 24, 1937; children: Cordelia b. 1943, Carole b. 1945; edn: BS, John B. Stetson Univ. 1937; grad. study Duke Univ. 1938-39; Reg. Profl. Engr., Wash. DC (Electronic), Calif. (Quality and Reliability). Career: section head US Naval Ordnance Lab., Wash. DC 1941-46; head applied physics branch Naval Gun Factory, 1946-52; system engr. and project mgr. Radio Corp. of Am., Camden, N.J. 1952-54, Product Assurance adminstr., 1954-61; v.p. El Tec Corp., Hawthorne, Calif. 1961-64; senior scientist and asst. program mgr. Hughes Aircraft Co., Culver City 1964-78, corp. mgr. Mfg. Data Systems, 1978-80, mgmt. cons., indsl. trouble shooter, 1980–; reliability cons. (design and prodn. control) to NASA, Dept. of Defence, and industry, helped estab. nat. stds.; assoc. editor internat. journal Microelectronics and Reliability (Pergamon Press) 1961-, reviewer and referee IEEE tech. publs., contbg. author/editor sev. major texts in field, contbr. over 100 papers on Quality and Reliability for var. nat. profl. meetings; awards: Meritorious Civilian Service Award (Navy) 1945 for outstanding electronic devels. aiding the war effort (5 patents); Admiral Coates Award, 1961; ASQC Award of Year 1967; NASA New Technology (Q and R Prediction) 1972; IEEE Reliability Soc. Award for pioneer devel. of prediction techniques, 1981; founding bd. mem. and ann. speaker, Annual Nat. Symposium on Quality Control and Reliability in Electronics, 1954–; mem: AIEEE, Electronic Industries Assn., Aviation Industries Assn., Am. Mgmt. Assn., ASQC, Inst. of Environmental Scis.; Republican; Baptist; spl. interest: medical and health research. Address: Ryerson Consultants 1402 Acacia Ave Torrance 90501

RYOR, ROBERT GEORGE, physician; b. Sept. 19,1 946, Watsonville, Calif.; s. Lyman Delbert and Alice Artema (Wright) R.; edn: BA, Pacific Union Coll. 1968; MD, Loma Linda Univ. 1972; intern White Meml. Hosp. Los Angeles 1972-73; pvt. practice family medicine, Glendale 1973-76; flight surgeon US Air Force 1976-78; emergency medicine practice in Orange County 1978-81, San Diego 1981-83; flight surgeon in Tabuk, Saudi Arabia 1983-85; physician, emergency medicine, Clairemont Hosp., San Diego 1985–; instr. flt. medicine; lectr. on emergency medicine to paramedics; mem. Am. Coll. of Emergency Medicine, Calif. Med. Assn.; mil: major USAF 1976-78; Republican; Protestant; rec: sports, music. Res: 3415 Lebon Dr San Diego 92122

SAARI, WAYNE WILLIAM, certified public accountant; b. Nov. 13, 1937, Baraga, Mich.; s. Waino Wm. and Lillian Pauline (Kallio) S.; m. Erika Puderbach, Sept. 29, 1959; 1 son, Peter b. 1949; edn: AA bus. admin., honors, Canada Coll. 1972; BS acctg., magna cum laude, Golden Gate Univ. 1974; Certified Public Acct., Calif. (1976). Career: shipping clk. Hyster Co., San Francisco 1955; asst. chief Microwave Radio Station, USAF, Germany 1956-59; electronics technician Varian Assocs., Palo Alto 1959-62, MEC Teledyne, Palo Alto 1962-67, Watkins-Johnson, Palo Alto 1967-69; CPA, mgr. Pearson, Del Prete, Redwood City 1974-85; prin. Wayne Saari CPA, Palo Alto 1985–; adj. prof. acctg. Golden Gate Univ. 1979-; lectr. in auditing Coll. of Notre Dame 1980-83; mem: Am. Inst. CPAs, Calif. Soc. CPAs (chmn. Acctg. Principles & Auditing Stds. Com. 1982-83); clubs: Elks (Palo Alto), Kiwanis (Redwood City); mil: A/2c US Air Force 1956-59, GCM; Republican; Lutheran; rec: golf, tchg. Res: 616 Harvard Ave No. 3 Menlo Park 94025 Ofc: Wayne Saari CPA 399 Sherman Ave Ste 1 Palo Alto 94306

SAAVEDRA, C. JAMES, banking executive; b. Nov. 2, 1941, Denver, Colo.; s. Charles James, Sr. and Evangeline C. (Aragon) S.; m. Ann Taylor, 1967; children: Michael b. 1968, Kevion b. 1971, Sarah b. 1977; edn: BS, Regis Coll. 1963. Career: v.p. Western States Bancard Assn. S.F. 1969-77; dir. info. sys. World Airways Inc. Oakland 1977-79; v.p. 1st Nationwide Savings S.F. 1979-83; v.p. Wells Fargo Bank S.F. 1983–; instr. Programmimg & Systems Inst. S.F. 1967-70; mem: Data Proc. Mgrs. Assn. (dir. 1969-84), Commonwealth Club of

Calif., Lake Lakewood Assn.; publ: articles in OCR Today 1977; mil: midshipman, ofcr. cand. USNR 1963-64. Res: 210 Lakewood Rd Walnut Creek 94598 Ofc: Wells Fargo Bank 394 Ave Ste 300 San Francisco 94163

SABHARWAL, RANJIT SINGH, mathematician, educator; b. Dec. 11, 1925, Dhudial, India, nat. US cit. 1981; s. Krishan Chand and Devti (Anand) S.; m. Pritam Chadha, 1948; children: Rajinderpal b. 1949, Armarjit b. 1951, Jasbir b. 1955; edn: BA, honors, Punjab Univ. 1944, MA, 1948; MA, UC Berkeley 1962; Phd, Wash. State Univ. 1966. Career: lectr. in math. Khalsa Coll., Bombay, India 1951-58; tchg. asst. UC Berkeley 1958-62; instr. in math. Portland State Univ. 1962-63; instr. in math. Washington State Univ. 1963-66; asst. prof. Kansas State Univ. 1966-68; assoc. prof. CSU Hayward 1968-74, prof. math. 1974–; mem: Am. Mathematical Soc., Mathematical Assn. of Am., Sigma Xi; research: non-desarguesian geometrics;. Res: 27892 Adobe Ct. Hayward 94542 Ofc: California State Univ., Hayward 94542

SACKS, SAMUEL, lawyer; b. Mar. 29, 1908, NY, NY; s. Isidore and Lotta (Basel) S.; m. Ethel Hirshman, Mar. 25, 1933; children: Judith b. 1935, Natalie b. 1943, Susan b. 1946; edn: LL.B., St. Johns Sch. of Law, 1930. Career: individual practicing atty., Bronx, N.Y. 1931-42; head T.V. Bus. Affairs, West Coast Ofc., William Morris Agcy. Inc. (talent agcy.), Beverly Hills 1975; of counsel entertainment field matters, Simon & Sheridan, Attys., Los Angeles 1975–; instr. adv. profl. course 'Practical & Bus. Aspects of the TV Industry,' USC (1975, 80, 83); frequent guest lectr. USC, UCLA, Whittier Law, Southwestern Law, Hastings Law, McGeorge Law Sch., West L.A. Law Sch. and var. bar assns. and orgns. and seminars; atty. for The Caucus for Prods., Writers & Dirs. (re t.v. field problems and activities), 1975-; arbitrator Am. Arb. Assn., Screen Actors Guild, Assn. of Talent Agents; mem: Am. Bar Assn., Beverly Hills Bar Assn., LA County Bar Assn., LA Copyright Soc., Acad. of T.V. Arts & Scis., Radio & T.V. Soc., Am. Nat. Theatre Acad.-West (bd. dirs., exec. com. 1975-); civic: Am. Field Services-West (LA chpt. pres. 1970-72), Univ. of Judaism (bd. dirs. 1975-), Project Caring (dir. 1975-, pres. 1983-), Council on Aging- Fedn. of Jewish Charities (1978-), Jewish Family Service (dir. 1983-), B'nai Brith (1948-); rec: swimming, photog., sports events. Res: 2310 Glendon Ave Los Angeles 90064 Ofc: Simon & Sheridan 2404 Wilshire Blvd No. 400 Los Angeles 90057

SACKS, V. SALLEY, financial executive; b. Oct. 13, 1934, Benton, Ark.; d. Wm. Franklin and Edna Irene (Hamilton) Salley; m. Zachary H. Sacks, Aug. 30, 1969; children: Benjamin Foster b. 1970, Alexander Franklin b. 1978; edn: AA, L.A. Pierce Coll. 1968; BA, CSU Northridge 1973; grad. work UCLA 1967, 76, UC Davis, UC Irvine, 1974; Calif. cred. Cert. Splst. Creative Drama (K-12), 1974. Career: womens wear co. owner, 1956-62; restaurateur, 1962-67; lectr. Theatre Arts Dept. CSUN 1974-75; film prod. 1976-78; administr., advisor law offices, 1978–; owner/mgr. Nafka Leasing Co., 1980–; finl. mgr. investment portfolios, 1980–; environmental designer, 1979–; producer Childrens Theatre Festival (1975), prod. Documentary Tibetian Buddism (1975), Forum (1985); honors: Favorite Faculty Award, Kappa Kappa Gamma (1975); mem. bd. dirs: So. Calif. Ednl. Theatre Assn. (1975-76), So. Calif. Childrens Theatre Assn. (1974-76), Karma Triyana Dharmachakra (1976-); mem: Independant Film Producers; civic: L.A. Womens Campaign Fund (bd. 1984-); Childhelp USA, LA Art Mus. (patron), Simon Wiesenthal Ctr., Malibu Comm. Ctr., Santa Monica Sch. Dist. PTA; publs: Performing Tree, Guide to Performing Arts (1975), Directory of Childrens Plays (1974); Democrat; Jewish; rec: rare fruit orchard, the arts, charity fundraising, philosophy. Address: 6811 Zumirez Dr Malibu 90265

SACKS, ZACHARY HERMAN, lawyer; b. Aug. 10, 1935, NYC; s. Joseph A. and Florence (Oster) S.; m. V. Salley, Aug. 30, 1969; children: Benjamin b. 1970, Alexander b. 1978; edn: BA, Yale Univ. 1957; JD, Columbia Law Sch. 1960; admitted to California State Bar 1963; Cert. Splst. Workers' Compensation Law, Calif. Bd. of Legal Spec. Career: house counsel, spec. Wkrs. Comp. def., R. L. Kautz and Co., 1963-65; pvt. practice, 1965-73; dir.: Kendig, Stockwell & Gleason, all phases Workers Comp. def., 1973-78; law offices of Zachary H. Sacks & Associates, APC, practice ltd. to Workers Comp. defense, 1978-84; mng. ptnr. Sacks, Rivera & Solomon, L.A. 1984–; lectr., moderator, frequent guest speaker on Wkrs. Comp., 1973-; mem: Calif. Bar Assn., Los Angeles Co. Bar Assn. (Workers Comp. Sects.), Calif. Workers Comp. Defense Attorneys Assn. (founding pres. 1982-83), Workers Comp. Defense Attys. Assn. (pres. 1980-82), Nat. Counsel of Self-Insured Insurers; mil: served in USMC; Republican (Senatorial Inner Circle); Jewish; rec: computers, video, films. Res: 6811 Zumirez Dr Malibu 90265 Ofc: Law Offices of Sacks, Rivera & Solomon, APC, 1849 Sawtelle Blvd Ste 700 Los Angeles 90025

SADOCCHI, ELMER GLENN, business owner; b. Dec. 29, 1938, Bakersfield; s. Elmer P. and Lois Irene (Little) S.; m. Shirley M. Richardson, Nov. 22, 1959; children: Elaine b. 1961, Nancy b. 1963, Mary b. 1967, Janet b. 1970; edn: Bakersfield Jr. Coll. 1956-57. Career: svc. and repair of comml. and truck refrigeration units, -1972, owner Glenn's Refrigeration, 1967–, Carrier Transicold Dealer 1969-, splst. in svc., parts and installation of truck refrigeration units and cab air units 1972–; mem. Refrigeration Svc. Engrs. Soc.; mil: USN 1957-59; Repulican; rec: building race car, restoring old cars. Ofc: Glenn's Refrigeration, Rt. 11 Box. 296 Bakersfield 93308

SADOWSKI, ROSE MARY, certified public accountant; b. May 3, 1955, Cleveland, OH; d. John Anthony and Rose Grace (Plute) Sadowski; edn: BS in bus. adminstrn., cum laude, USC 1977. Career: mgr. pgm. financial svcs. National Broadcasting Co. Inc., Los Angeles; honors: SPOONE AWARD 1977; Acctg. Awd., USC; listed Who's Who Among Exec. Women in Business, Who's

Who Among Amer. Coll. Students (1977), Who's Who Among Amer. H.S. Students (1973); mem: Amer. Inst. CPAs, Calif. Soc. CPAs, Amer. Film Inst., USC Accounting Circle, USC Gen. Alumni Assn., USC Sch. of Bus. Dean's Adv. Bd. 1976-77, Beta Gamma Sigma, Beta Alpha Psi, Smithsonian Assocs., Amer. Museum of Natural Hist., Town Hall of Calif., Internat. Platform Assn.; Democrat; Catholic; rec: racquetball, body building, cooking. Res: 717 Raymond Ave, Santa Monica 90405

SAETA, PHILIP M., superior court judge; b. Feb. 21, 1931, Los Angeles; s. Maurice and Elizabeth (Jacobs) S.; m. Joanne Hixson, Aug. 28, 1954; children: David b. 1959, Peter b. 1961, Stephen b. 1962, Sandra b. 1964; edn: AB, Stanford Univ. 1953, LLB, 1957. Career: atty. Beardsley, Hufstedler & Kemble, 1958-64; judge Los Angeles Municipal Ct. 1964-75, judge Los Angeles Superior Ct., 1975–; mem: Calif. Judges Assn. (bd.), ABA, LA County Bar Assn.; bd. Volunteers of Am. Los Angeles; bd. Am. Jewish Com.; mil: pfc US Army 1953-55; Democrat; Jewish; rec: music. Ofc: 111 N Hill St Ste 16 Los Angeles 90012

SAFA, BAHRAM, civil engineer; b. May 15, 1941, Abadan, Iran, nat. 1978; s. Ghassem and Sekineh (Khaki) S.; m. Nahid Araji, 1966; children: Shari b. 1967, Sarah b. 1973, Susan b. 1979, Cyrus b. 1983; edn: BSc, Abadan Inst. of Tech., Iran 1965; MBA, State Univ. of NY, Albany, 1967; Cert. Engring. Mgmt. in Constrn., Univ. Calif. 1982; lic. Gen. Building Contractor 1982; Cert. in Constrn. Mgmt., ASCE 1982; Reg. Civil Engr., Calif. 1983, Nev. 1983; Calif. OMM Coll. Instr. Credl. 1986. Career: civil engr. VTN Engineers, Los Angeles 1980-85; senior civil engr. City of Simi Valley 1985–; constrn. coordinator Security Pacific Bank, L.A. 1979-80; asst. v.p. constrn., Internat. Housing Ltd., Westport, Conn. 1975-79; designer and field engr. Myrick and Chevalier, Albany, NY 1971-75; project engr. Rist-Frost Engring., Glens Falls, NY 1970-71; project engr. National Iranian Oil Co., Iran 1965-70; mng. dir./mem. bd. dirs. Internat. Housing Ltd., Iran Division; mem: Am. Public Works Assn. 1985-, Amer. Concrete Inst. 1979-81, Assn. of MBA Execs. (student mem. 1973-75); publs: sev. research papers on low-cost housing systems for use in other countries; Republican; rec: research, cultural activities. Res: 6018 E Malton Ave Simi Valley 93063 Ofc: City of Simi Valley, Utilities Dep:., 500 W Los Angeles Ave Simi Valley 93065

SAFIR, PAVITTAR S., financial executive; b. March 12, 1936, Amritsar, India, nat. 1980; s. Assa Singh and Jaswant (Kaur) Safir; m. Anne Marie Geffray, Apr. 3, 1971; 2 sons: Karan Edward b. 1972, Philip Jeffrey b. 1984; edn: BA, Univ. of Panjab 1956, MA, 1958, acad. dip., Univ. of London 1968. Career: chief operating ofcr. Nat. Cadet Corps (First Panjab Batt.) 1959-65; tchr. Inner London Ednl. Authority, 1967-71; sr. vice pres. adminstrn. Reinsurance Facilities Corp., Los Angeles 1972–, dir. 1979-; dir. RFC Intermediaries, Inc. 1979-. Mem: Fin. Execs. Inst., Planning Execs. Inst. Rec: photog. Res: 422 S. Lapeer Dr. Beverly Hills 90211 Ofc: Reinsurance Facilities Corp. 2020 Century Park E., Ste. 1610, Los Angeles 90067

SAGHATELIAN, SUSANN M., financial executive; b. May 23, 1958, Fresno; d. Herman and Joanna Mary (D'Angelo) Saghatelian; edn: BS, magna cum laude, CSU Fresno 1980, MBA cum laude, 1986; cert. (mortgage law and loan underw.) Mortgage Bankers Assn. of Am. 1980. Career: mortgage banking, The Giddings Co. 1978-80; loan ofcr./ comml. loan ofcr. Bank of Fresno 1980-82; finl. analyst, asst. gen. mgr., (current) bd. dir./ comptroller/ chief finl. ofcr. Valley Bakery Inc., Fresno 1982–; trustee Valley Bakery Profit Sharing Plan 1984-; finl. cons.; honors: Golden Key (1985), Beta Gamma Sigma (1980, chpt. v.p.), Phi Kappa Phi (1980), Nat. Honor Frat.; mem. Fresno CofC; Republican; Catholic; rec: writing, sketching, jewelry design. Res: 3473 E Ashlan Fresno 93726

SAGO, PAUL EDWARD, university president; b. July 5, 1932, Frankclay, Mo.; s. John and Mabel (White) S.; m. Audrey Dane, Aug. 23, 1952; children: Bruce Edward, b. 1955, Dane Bradford, b. 1959; edn: BS, Findlay Coll. 1953; MS, St. Francis Grad. Sch. 1964; PhD, Walden Univ. 1976. Career: pastor Bloom Center First Church of God, N. Baltimore, OH 1952-55, Anthony Wayne Ch. of God, Ft. Wayne, OH 1955-64; dir. of devel., Findlay (OH) Coll. 1964-67, Hiram (OH) Coll. 1967-68; v.p. Fin. Affairs/treas. Anderson (IND) Coll. 1968-76; pres. Azusa Pacific Univ., Azusa, CA 1976–; condr. seminars, frequent speaker; mem: Am. Assn. for Higher Edn., Assn. of Governing Boards of Colls. and Univs., Christian Coll. Coalition, Council for Advance. and Support of Edn., Council of Independent Colls., Internat. Platform Assn., Nat. Assn. of Coll. and Univ. Bus. Officers, Nat. Assn. of Fund Raiser, Nat. Assn. of Independent Colls. and Univs.; club: University (Pasadena); Ch. of God, Anderson, Ind. Res: 19749 E. Cameron Covina 91724, POB 4336 Ofc: Azusa Pacific University, Citrus and Alosta, Azusa 91702

SAHNI, JAGMOHAN SINGH, medical instrumentation executive; b. April 24, 1949, New Delhi, India, nat. US cit. 1977; s. Tara Singh and Dershan Kaur (Kapur) S.; m. Ksawaljit K. Sabharwal, Oct. 9, 1974; children: Deepa b. 1978, Harleen b. 1982; edn: BSEE, Thapar Engring. Coll., India 1969; M.Tech.E.E., I.I.T. Delhi, India 1971; MBA, Pepperdine Univ. 1980. Career: engr. Contral Data Corp. 1972-77; senior engr. Mohawk Data Sciences 1977-81; prin. engr. Omex Systems 1981-82; rel. engring mgr. National Semiconductor 1982-; RAM engrng. mgr. Rolm Corp. 1982-84; pres., CEO Vivix Corp. 1984–; mem: IEEE, AAMI. Res: 204 Cheltenham Pl. San Jose 95139 Ofc: Vivix Corp., 6410 Via Del Oro San Jose 95119

SAHOTA, HARVINDER, cardiologist; b. April 15, 1941, Punjab, India; s. Lachman S. and Dhan K. (Chouhan) S.; m. Asha, Dec. 16, 1972; children: Neil

b. 1974, Eric b. 1978; edn: MBBS, Patiala Sch. 1965; DTMH, Liverpool Sch. of Tropical Med. 1971; DTCD, Welsh Sch. of Med. 1972. Career: physician, practice cardiology, pulomnary med., tropical med.; 14 yrs. postgrad. tng., India, U.K., Can., and US; mem: Fellow Internat. Coll. of Angiology; mem: British Med. Assn., Am. Coll. of Cardiology, Los Angeles Heart Assn., Los Angeles Med. Assn.; patented inventions: Sahota Hemostat; Catheter System; publs: Techniques of the Removal of Obst. Balloon Catheter, British Med. Journ. 1972; Unusual Case of Osteogenen's Imperfecta, 1975; Rare Congenital Abnormalility of Coronary Artery, Angiology 1978. Res: 3861 Wisteria St. Seal Beach 90740

SAJJADI, HAMED, head & neck surgeon; b. May 16, 1956, Tehran, Iran; s. Ahmad and Fahimeh Taj (Sadeghi) S.; m. Azar Daryaee, Oct. 22, 1981; children: Ali b. 1982, Amin b. 1984; edn: BS, Creighton Univ. 1977, MD, 1981. Career: intern surg. King/Drew Med. Ctr. 1981-82, resident head & neck surg. 1982-86, currently chief res.; honors: Dean's List (Creighton Univ. Sch. of Arts & Sci. 1974-77), Honor Roll (Creighton Univ. Sch. of Med. 1981), Pi Mu Epsilon 1976; mem: AMA, Am. Acad. Otolaryngol. (head & neck surg.), Am. Acad. Facial Plastic & Reconstr. Surg.; research: Acute Surgical Mastoiditis, 15 cases 1978-83 at King-Drew; rec: martial arts (2nd degree brown belt Tae-Kwon-Do). Res: 1001 London Circle Placentia 92670 Ofc: Martin L. King/Drew Med. Ctr. 12012 S Wilmington Los Angeles 90059

SAJOVIC, JANIS ADELE, data processing consultant; b. Feb. 19, 1949, NY, NY; d. Alfred Allen and Fay Marie (Maiorino) Hacker; m. Frank A. Sajovic, Aug. 24, 1974; edn: BS, Syracuse Univ. 1971. Career: junior pgmmr. TBS Computer Centers Inc., NY, NY 1971-72; student Prog. & Syst. Inst., Stamford, Conn. 1972-73; programmer/ analyst McIsaac Associates, Arlington, Mass. 1973-75; systems analyst Mann Data Inc., Needham, Mass. 1975-76; project coord. Corstar Bus. Comp. Co., Inc., White Plains, NY 1976-78; self-empl. EDP cons., prog/anal, 1978—; Democrat; Catholic; rec: gardening, skiing, home improvements. Address: 1027 Princeton St Santa Monica 90403

SAKAI, NOBUYUKI, business communications co. president; b. Feb. 15, 1948, Tokyo, Japan; s. Toshio and Saka (Togashi) S.; edn: BA, Ikuei Tech. Coll. 1968, BFA, Musashino Arts Univ. 1972. Career: instr. Ikuei Tech. Coll., Japan 1968-69; chief designer Dentsu Toshiba Planning Room, Japan 1972-75; pres. Cap Advt. Inc., Japan 1975; founder/pres. Commercial Media Concept Inc., Los Angeles 1981—; cons. dir. Pacific Bus. Communications Inc. 1985-; pres. Cosmo Mgmt. Corp. 1984-; honors: All Japan Catalog Design Contest, awards of Minister of Internat. Trade and Industry (1970), Asahi Ad Conpe. (1971), Top Inquiry Response award (1983); mem. Japan Graphic Arts Soc. (1963-), Japanese C. of C. (1975-); works: creator KDD Co. logo, ads for Toshiba, Mitsukoshi Dept. Store of Japan, Planning campaign for Expo '74; rec: photog., travel, martial arts. Res: 1915 W. Victoria Ave Montebello 90640 Ofc: CMC Inc 6290 Sunset Blvd Ste 1400 Los Angeles 90028

SAKAKIHARA, PHILIP MITSUO, research & development lab. executive, educator; b. June 8, 1943, Newell, Calif.; s. Philip Kazuo and Hisa (Kurosaki) S.; m. Barbara, June 24, 1967; children: Ryan, Joel; edn: BA math., CSU San Jose 1966; MS applied math., Univ. of Santa Clara 1972. Career: system test engr. Lockheed Missile & Space, Sunnyvale 1966-72; project mgr. Hewlett-Packard Co., Cupertino 1972-78, mgr. advanced networks 1979-80, R&D Lab mgr. H-P, UK, Pinewood, England 1980-83, R&D Lab mgr., H-P, Santa Clara 1983—; full-time vis. prof. UC Davis 1978-79; reviewer of research projects for MICRO* Pgm. at Univ. of Calif. Campuses 1986—; profl. seminars (British Computer Soc., Soc. for Indsl. Engrs. & IEEE); awards: Lockheed Missile & Space Co. Award for Zero Defects, (1968, 1970), and Employee of the Month (1970), USAF awards for outstanding contbn. (1968, 1970), USAF spl. merit award-Save a Spy Satellite from Distruction (1970); mem. IEEE, Assn. for Computing Mach.; civic: Cub Scouts Am., Community Youth Service (asst. coach); publs: articles in Orbital Software (1970), Satellite Networks (1970), Distribution Systems (1978); participant in video Human Factors (1985); Buddhist; rec: travel, ski, fishing. Res: 608 Mindy Way San Jose 95123 Ofc: Hewlett-Packard Co 3410 Central Expy Santa Clara 95051

SAKODA, DANNETTE L., lawyer; b. Sept. 20, 1953, San Jose; d. Sam and Elaine (Mizutani) Sakoda; edn: BS, Univ. Santa Clara 1975; JD, Hastings Coll. of Law 1978; admitted Calif. State Bar 1979. Career: law clk. San Francisco Neighborhood Legal Asst. Found., Comm. Legal Services in San Jose, and Ofc. of State Public Defender in San Francisco, 1976-78; active vol. Nihonmachi Legal Outreach, S.F. 1976-81; atty. law offices Maniwa and Matsumoto, San Francisco 1979-81; staff atty. Nakahara & Hinoki, Inc. 1981; staff atty. Legal Aid Soc. of Santa Clara County 1983—; bd. dirs. Japanese Am. Comm. Senior Services 1981-85; mem: Calif. State, Santa Clara County, Asian Pacific (bd. dirs. South Bay Area 1983-) bar assns.; performing artist with San Jose Taiko Group (Asian Am. interpretation of traditional Japanese drumming) 1981-; rec: music, dance. Ofc: Legal Aid Society 210 South First St San Jose 95113

SAKUMA, AL KIYOSHI, electronic engineer; b. May 15, 1927, San Francisco; s. Seikichi Yamada and Shizuko (Kawakami) S.; edn: broadcasting, Don Martin Radio & Television Hollywood 1954; AA electronics, Los Angeles City Coll. 1956; BA indsl. arts, CSU Los Angeles 1961. Career: engr., electronic television engrg., test engr., quality control and electronic tech. in broadcasting communs., gen. tech. svcs. H.L. Yoh Co. Hollywood 1980-81; radio, television & film electronics LACC 1981-83; tv & electronics Civil Svcs. US Army AFRTS 1983—; owner ESSS Co. Sacramento, audio-video designs & svcs.; honors: Alpha Epsilon Rho; mem: Soc. Motion Picture & Television

Engrs. (assoc. mem. 1984), Community TV Found. (Sacto.); mil: tech. sgt. US Army Signal Corps 1950; Republican; Congregational; rec: photog. Res: POB 160300 Sacramento 95816-0300 Ofc: T-ASA Sacramento Army Depot Sacramento 95813-5019

SALAS, PETER CARLOS, martial arts instructor; b. Sept. 10, 1958, Honolulu, Hawaii; s. Nestor Tabora and Alice Haruko (Hasegawa) S.; edn: AA, Southwestern Coll. 1981. Career: asst. instr. United Karate Fedn., National City 1976-80; insurance agent Alexander Hamilton Life, San Diego 1980-82; instr./mgr. United Karate Fedn., National City 1982-85; chief instr./owner Chula Vista United Karate Fedn., Chula Vista 1985—; honors: Instr. of Year, United Karate Fedn. (1976, 77, 78), community award, Interfest '85 (cultural orgn.) and Sweetwater High Sch. (1985); mem. Am. Internat. Mktg. Assn. (1979-81), Chula Vista Downtown Com., Pagkakaisa Philippine Club (treas. 1978), St. Mary's Youth Orgn. (pres. 1977); Christian; rec: basketball, softball, drawing. Res: 1419 "E" Ave National City 92050 Ofc: Chula Vista United Karate Federation 359-B Third Ave Chula Vista 92010

SALAZAR, DOROTEO MONTE DE RAMOS, civil engineer, contractor, professor; b. Feb. 4, 1936, Maasin Leyte, Philippines; s. Ranulfo S. and Antonia M. (Monte de Ramos) S.; m. Zenaida Figuracion, July 25, 1959; children: Alden b. 1960, Beth b. 1961, Cherrie b. 1962, Doris b. 1964, Edwin b. 1965, Frederick b. 1969; edn: BSCE summa cum laude, Cebu Tech. (CIT) 1957, BS geodetic engrg., 1958; Reg. Profl. Civil Engr. Phil. 1958, Calif. 1982; Gen. Bldg. Contractor Calif. 1984. Career: prof. civil engrg. Cebu Tech. 1957-68, head math. dept. 1962-68, head civil engrg. dept. 1960-68; pres. Salazar Constrn. Co. Inc. 1961—, chmn. bd. 1983—; chmn. bd. Dozen Constrn. & Devel. Corp.; pres. Salazar Inst. of Technol.; pres. Salazar Review Ctr.; honors: Most Outstanding Engr.-Practitioner (Phil. Inst. Civil Engrs.), Most Outstanding Contractor (Cebu Coutrs. Assn.), Papal Award for Community Svc.; mem: Phil. Inst. Civil Engrs. (nat. dir. 1979-81, pres.1977-81), Cebu Contractors Assn. (pres. 1978-81), Rotary Club of Cebu Central (pres.), Knights of Columbus (grand knight); author: Mathematics Review, Surveying Review, Hydraulics, Steel & Timber Design, Concrete Design, Engineering Economics; Catholic; rec: tennis. Res: 2nd St Guadalupe Heights Cebu Philippines 6401 Ofc: Salazar Constrn. Co. Inc. 211 Rizal Ave Cebu City Philippines 6401

SALEH, RICHARD EDWARD, insurance agency owner; b. Aug. 25, 1935, Long Beach; s. Edward Fredrick and Viola (Savage) S.; m. Roberta L. Leach, Nov. 19, 1955; children: Edward b. 1958, James b. 1959; edn: pre-law/bus. law, Orange Coast Coll. 1973; grad. Allstate Sch. of Sales and Ins. (Menlo Park); grad. USN Submarine Sch., USN Instructors Sch. Career: semi-pro football fullback, Orange Co. Rhinos two yrs.; baseball and football coach, City of Carson 4 years; stereotyper apprentice Los Angeles Herald (daily newspaper) 1953-57; stereotyper R.W. Ernst Printing Co. 1957-62; prodn. supt. Stereotype Dept. Culver City Evening Star News, 1962-66; ins. agent Allstate Ins. Co., Wilmington 1966-69; district sales mgr. Neighbors of Woodcraft (L.A., San Bernardino, and Riverside Counties), 1969-71; ins. agt./ broker/ corp. v.p., Mortimer-Saleh and Assocs. Inc., 1971-79; prin. Richard E. Saleh Insurance, Buena Park 1979—; past dir. pub. rels., Calif. Jaycees (3 yrs); past dir. internat. affairs City of Culver City; past mem. City of Carson Plnng. Commn.; awards: Western Regl. champion Kempo-Blackbelt (3 yrs); past pres. Harbor Aquarium Soc. (4 yrs); mil: E5 USN, USNR (8 yrs); rec: swimming, boatin, fishing, radio control models. Res: 13530 Semora Pl Cerritos 90701 Ofc: Richard E. Saleh Ins. 7342 Orangethorpe, A-103, Buena Park 90621

SALEM, KAMIL P., real estate broker, general contractor; b. Aug. 15, 1940, Telkaif, Iraq, nat. US cit. 1985; s. Petros H. and Hassina J. (Bazzi) S.; m. Zakia I., July 19, 1981; children: Simon b. 1982, Andrew b. 1984; edn: BSc., Mil. Acad. 1963; MSc. engrg., A. Zapotocky Mil. Acad. 1965. Career: res. engr. Baghdad Internat. Airport 1966-67; supt. electronics dept. Bader Al Mullen Kuwait 1968-74; co-owner, general mgr. Al Resheid Co. Kuwait 1976-78; co-owner, mng. dir. Al. Ghanim Co. Kuwait 1978-80; co-owner, v.p. Monacelli-Salem & Co. San Diego 1980-83; co-owner, pres., secty. Simon & Richard Constrn. Co. Inc./ SMS Realty & Devel. 1983—; Republican; Catholic; rec: poetry writing, reading, backgammon. Res: Simon & Richard Constrn. Co. Inc. 7169 Navajo Rd San Diego 92119

SALEM, NABIL GEORGE, engineering consultant; b. July 1, 1943, Cairo, Egypt, nat. US cit. 1970; s. George K. and Marie H. (Agaman) S.; 1 son, Nabil Jr. b. 1972; edn: engring., Ain Shams Univ. Cairo 1960-64; drill instrn., Drill Sergeant Sch. 1968; Reg. Profl. Safety Engr., Calif. 1977. Career: v.p. Gas & Mechanical Labs., Los Angeles 1965-81; pres. The Salem Corp., Los Angeles 1981—; mem: Am. Soc. of Gas Engrs., Los Angeles Soc. of Engrs. & Scientists, Marina City Club, Beverly Hills Gun Club; mil: E-6 US Army 1968-70, Army Commdn.; Republican; Christian; rec: poetry,. racquetball. Address: The Salem Corp. 420 Esplanade Ste 12 Redondo Beach 90277

SALINGER, CHARLES, physician; b. April 24, 1945, NY, NY; s. Ernest and Mae (Brenner) S.; m. Donna, May 17, 1974; children: Jennifer b. 1978, Jeffrey b. 1984; edn: BS, Univ. of Wisc. 1965; MD, SUNY Upstate Med. Ctr. 1968. Career: intern Charity Hosp., New Orleans, LSU Svc. 1968-69, resident in dermatology 1969-72; chief dermatology svc. Maxwell Regl. Air Force Hosp., Maxwell AFB, Ala. 1972-74; dermatologist pvt. practice. La Mirada 1975—; clin. assoc. prof. dermatology Coll. of Osteopathic Med. of the Pacific; v.chief of staff Med. Ctr. of La Mirada 1985-86; mem: Fellow Am. Acad. of Dermatology, Internat. and Am. Socs. for Derm. Surgery, Pacific Derm. Assn., Metropolitan Derm. Soc. of Los Angeles, Internat. Soc. of Pediatric Derm., Pan American Med. Assn. (Sect. on Derm.); publs: Hair Transplants for Male Pattern Baldness, So. Med. Journ. 1972; mil: maj. USAF 1972-74; Jewish; rec: raising avocados. Ofc: Charles Salinger MD Inc, 12625 La Mirada Blvd. Ste. 106 La Mirada 90638

SALMASSI, SADEGH, surgeon; b. Aug. 14, 1946, Baghdad, Iraq; s. Jafar and Kobra (Alavi) S.; m. Tahereh, Jan. 17, 1970; children: Ali b. 1971, Nahal b. 1975; edn: premed., Pahlavi Univ., Shiraz, Iran 1964-66, MD, 1973; bd. certified Am. Bd. Pathol. 1981; lic. Ill. 1978, Mo. 1980, Kans. 1980, Calif. 1983. CC rotating intern Pahlavi Univ. affil. hosps. 1972-73; resident anatomy & clin. pathol. Univ. Ill. 1975-78, chief res. pathol. 1978-79, fellow blood banking and immunohematology 1979-80; emerg. rm. phys. Louise Burg Hosp. Chgo. 1979-80; instr. pathol. Univ. Ill. 1976-80; asst. prof. pathol. Univ. Mo. Kansas City, assoc. dir. anatomic pathol, asst. dir. blood bank Truman Med. Ctr. UMKC 1980-84; dir. Delano Med. Clin. & Lab. Delano, Calif. 1984–; chmn. dept. family practice Delano Regl. Med. Ctr. 1985–; honors: AMA Recogn. Award; fellow Coll. Am. Pathols. 1981; mem: AMA, AAAS, NY Acad. Scis., Ill. Med. Soc., Chgo. Med. Soc., Iranian Med. Assn., Am. Assn. Blood Banks, Kansas City Soc. Pathols., Pahlavi Univ. Med. Sch. Alumni Assn.; publs: 20 articles in med. jours., papers presented Univ. Ct., K.C. Soc. Pathols.; mil: 1st lt., physician Rezayeh Mil. Hosp., Iran 1973-75; Muslim; rec: videotaping. Res: 800 Lexington Apt 24 Delano 93215 Ofc: Delano Med. Clin. 1005 11th Ave Delano 93215

SALOMON, DARRELL JOSEPH, lawyer; b. Feb. 16, 1939, San Francisco; s. Joe and Rosalie Rita (Poole) S.; m. Patty Marie Fitzsimons, Sept. 21, 1969 (div.); edn: Georgetown Univ. 1957-59; Univ. San Francisco 1960-62; JD, USF Sch. of Law 1966; Career: assoc. atty. Offices of Joseph L. Alioto S.F. 1970-72, 1972-81, Demanes & Sanders Burlingame 1972, Salomon & Costello 1981; dep. city atty. S.F. 1972; sole practice spec. in antitrust law and trade regulation S.F. 1981-83; ptnr. Hill, Farrer & Burrill L.A. 1984, sr. ptnr. 1985–; lectr. law Santa Clara Univ.; honors: D'Alton Power Scholar 1957, Disting. Svc. Citn. (United Negro Col. Fund. 1975); mem: Human Rights Commn., City and Co. of S.F. 1975, Svc. Employees Internat. Union (hon. life), Soc. Calif. Pioneers, War Meml. Perf. Arts Ctr. City & Co. of S.F. (bd. trustees), L.A. Symphony Master Chorale (bd. dirs.), Chit Chat Club, Civ. Svc. Commn., City & Co. of S.F. 1976-84 (pres. 1977-82); Towne Hall L.A., Democratic Chairs Circle; publ: arts. in profl. journs., cons. Calif. Business Litigation Jury Instructions (Matthew Bender & Co. 1985); Democrat; rec: private pilot. Ofc: Hill, Farrer & Burrill 445 S Figueroa St Los Angeles 90071

SALTER, KENNETH W., lawyer, lecturer; b. March 29, 1941, Richmond; s. Jack W. and Virginia F. (Thole) S.; m. Reine, July 9, 1978; 1 dau, Elizabeth b. 1961; edn: BA, UC Berkeley 1963; JD, UC Berkeley Boalt Hall 1967; admitted Calif. Bar 1969. Career: employment security ofcr. Calif. Dept. of Employment, Richmond 1959-65; admin. asst. Judah Magnes Mus., Berkley 1965-66; tchg. asst. Dept. of Speech UC Berkeley 1966-67, asst. prof. 1967-75; lectr., dir. pre-legal studies San Jose State Univ., San Jose 1972–; atty. self-empl. internat. practice 1970–; mem: Calif. Bar Assn., Speech Comm. Assn., Calif. Mining Research Inst. El Cerrito (pres. 1983-), Berkeley Promenade Orchestra; books: The Pentagon Papers Trial, 1974; The Trial of Inez Garcia, 1976; Democrat; Protestant; rec: amateur archeology, exploring. Ofc: Kenneth W. Salter Atty., 1649 Hopkins St. Berkeley 94707

SAMARA, MUFID FAWZI, engineer; b. Nov. 25, 1940, Merj-Oyoun, Lebanon, nat. US cit. 1978; s. Fawzi Milhem and Salwa (Nofal) S.; m. Salam Salloum, Apr. 27, 1964; children: Ghassan Joseph b. 1965, Ramsey Fawzi b. 1980; edn: BS, physics, Univ. Fla. 1964; BSCE, Auburn Univ. 1965, MS, 1968; PhD, Univ. Ariz. 1975; Reg. Profl. Engr. (Civil 1978; Structural 1980), Calif. Career: resrch., tchg. asst. Auburn Univ., Ga. Inst. of Tech., Univ. Fla. 1967-72; asst. prof. engring. No. Ariz. Univ., Flagstaff 1972-76; senior engr. CF Braun, Alhambra 1976-78; prin engr. Holmes and Narver, Orange 1978-80; mgr. struc. engring. Cash and Jenkins, Long Beach 1980; prin. engr. CF Braun, Alhambra 1980–; honors: Tau Beta Pi (1965), Chi Epsilon; mem: ASCE, Am. Concrete Inst., Am. Soc. Engring. Edn., Inst. for Advance. of Engrs. (steering com.), Struc. Engrs. Assn. of So. Calif. (seismol. com.); past bd. mem. Hacienda Coin and Stamp Club, Am. Lebanese League; publs: sev. tech. papers, engring. manuals, internat. profl. confs.; Syrian Orthodox; rec: numismatics, backpacking. Res: 16778 E Rocky Knoll Hacienda Hts 91745 Ofc: CF Braun 1000 S Fremont Alhambra 91802

SAMPSON, HENRY, co. president; b. May 22, 1955, Elinan, Cross River; s. Henry Sampson and Elizabeth A. (Etuk) Umoh; edn: AS, Reedley Coll. 1980; BS, CSU Fresno 1983. Career: tech. asst. Federal Machine Corp., Fresno 1984; mktg. dir. Fan-T-See Satellite Systems, 1985; pres. Evergreen Internat. Satellite & Solar Systems, 1985–; instr. West Fresno Christian Acad. Inc., and founder/dir. Bus. & Sci. Club, and Corinth Youth Fellowship, 1985–; bus. adminstr. Calvary United Ministries Inc., 1985; founder/pres. Evergreen Internat. Found. 1985–; honors: Who's Who in Am. Univs., Alpha Phi Alpha (disting. collegian); mem. Full Gospel Businessmen Internat., Internat. Traders Assn., Mind of the Community Conf., Am. Inst. of Parliamentarians, Youth for Christ (Campus Life), Inter-Varsity Christian Fellowship, Internat. Christian Center, New Harvest Christian Center (fin. dir.); mil: US Marine Corps mil. police 2 yrs; rec: tennis, soccer, badminton. Res: POB 15145 Fresno 93702

SANBORN, DOROTHY CHAPPELL, librarian; b. April 26, 1920, Nashville, Tenn.; d. William S. and Sammie Maude (Drake) Chappell; m. Richard Donald Sanborn, Dec. 1, 1943; children: Richard Donald, William Chappell; edn; BA, Univ. of Texas 1941; MA, George Peabody Coll. 1947; MPA, Golden Gate Univ. 1982. Career: asst. cataloger El Paso Public Library 1947-52, Library of Hawaii, Honolulu 1953; cataloger Redwood City Public Library 1954-55, 1957-59, Stanford Research Inst., Menlo Park 1955-57; librarian Auburn Public Library 1959-62; catologer Sierra Coll., Rocklin 1962-64; reference librarian Sacramento City Library 1964-66; county librarian Placer County, Auburn 1966–; chmn. Mountain Valley Library System 1970-71, 1975-76; cons. county librarian Alpine County Library, Markleeville 1973-80; mem: AAUW (pres. chpt. 1982-83), Am. and Calif. Library Assns., Soroptimists; mil: WAVES 1944-46; Democrat; United Ch. of Christ. Res: 135 Midway St. Auburn 95603 Ofc: Aurbun- Placer County Library, 350 Nevada St. Auburn 95603

SANBORN, FREDERICK ARTHUR, real estate executive; b. Mar. 15, 1930, Denver, Colo.; s. Frederick Willian and Dorothy (Gildersleeve) S.; m. Jannette Glaws, Sept. 6, 1984; children: Kristina, b. 1956; Scott, b. 1964; John, b. 1966; edn: BA, Univ. of Colo. 1953. Career: life ins. bus. 1956-58; comml. real estate, San Diego 1962–; founder Grubb & Ellis Co., Business Properties and Merrill Lynch Commercial Real Estate; currently, sr. v.p. Merrill Lynch Commercial Real Estate, San Diego; past dir. San Diego Bd. of Realtors; honors: Salesman of the Year, John Burnham & Co. 1967-68, 1969; mem: San Diego Bd. Realtors; Toastmasters (pres.); Univ. of Colo. Alumni Assn.; Economic Development Corp. (dir.); San Diegans, Inc. (bd. trustees); Kiwanis; Lamas Santa Fe Country Club; Central City Assn.; Bldg. Ind. Assn.; num. arts. on real estate in local newspapers and trade mags.; mil: capt., USAF 1954-56; Republican; Protestant; rec: sailing, tennis, golf. Res: 3940 Gresham Ave., San Diego 92109 Ofc: Merrill Lynch, 401 West A St., Ste. 1000, San Diego 92101

SANCHEZ, DON, chiropractor, herbalist, artist, educator; b. Nov. 22, 1943, Reins, Utah; s. Elizandro Jose and Martina (Salazar) S.; raised by Dan and Ramona Valdez of Price, Utah; children: Stephen John b. 1965, Leonore Jacqueline b. 1967, Gary Donald b. 1969, Juliet Marie b. 1971, edn. BA, Univ. Utah 1967; M.Ed., Univ Utah 1978; DC, Palmer Coll. of Chiropractic 1982; spl. courses in holistic health and physio-therapy w/The Carlson Family; pvt. stu. piano w/Mary Jean Selme 1963-70; Tchg. creds. Utah, Calif. Career: tchr., Price, Utah 1967-69; dir. comm. edn. Univ. Utah 1969-71; spl. svcs. worker Salt Lake City and County Social Svcs. 1971-72; tchr./chmn. Jobs for Progress, S.L.C. 1972-74; tchr./chmn. Art Dept., S.L.C. Board of Edn. 1974-78; color therapist Culver Chiropractic Clinic, Los Altos, Calif. 1978-80; chiropractor prin. Rocklin Chiropractic Clinic, Rocklin 1980–; honors: Phi Kappa Phi (1978); mem. Carbon Co. Tchrs. Assn. (1967-69), UEA (1967-78), NEA (1967-), San Francisco Thrs. Assn. (1983-85), Price Art League (pres. 1967-69), Chicano Club, S.L.C. (1967-69); author two books on edn., poetry, num. art works; rec: lectr. on herbal medicine, art (printer). Res: 230 29th St San Francisco 94131 Ofc: Rocklin Chiropractic Clinic 5875 Pacific St Ste D Rocklin

SANCHEZ, ESTHER LILY J., accountant; b. July 7, 1946, Philippines, nat. US cit. 1975; d. Alfredo D. and Lydia S. (Dionisio) Jacinto; m. Arturo C. Sanchez, July 30, 1969; children: Christine Leilani b. 1971, Cheryl Ann b. 1978; edn: BS commerce, cum laude, Philippine Coll. of Commerce 1967; MBA cand., Univ. La Verne; CPA Phil. 1967. Career: chief acct. Starcrost Enterprises Manila, Phil. 1964-69; staff acct. Alexander Grant & Co. CPAs Honolulu 1969-70; senior acct. Amfac Inc. Honolulu 1970-73; asst. dir. finance CalTech Pasadena 1973–; instr. Phil. Sch. of Bus. Adminstrn. 1967-69; honors: Soph. of the Yr. (Phil. Coll. of Commerce 1964); mem: Am. Soc. Women CPAs 1980-, Am. Soc. Women Accts. 1969-70, Nat. Assn. Female Execs. 1984-; Republican; Congregational; rec: reading, swimming, aerobics, cooking. Res: 1215 El Monte Ave Arcadia 91006 Ofc: Calif. Institute Technology 1201 E California Blvd Pasadena 91125

SANCHEZ, PHILLIP LAURENCE, physician, naval officer; b. Nov. 19, 1949, Miami, Fla.; s. Phillip Montefu and Virginia Clark (Blackmar) S.; m. Jo Ann Soeder, June 12, 1976; children: Kimberly b. 1979, Crystal b. 1982, Cheryl b. 1984; edn: BA, Biscayne Coll. 1972; MD, Univ. Miami 1976; certified Advanced Trauma Life Support Instr., Advanced Cardiac Life Support Instr./Instr. Trainer. Career: med. ofcr. 2d Marine Div. Ready Reserve 1976-78; resident Orlando Regl. Med. Ctr. 1977-79, coutesy staff 1978-79, emerg. rm. phys. 1978-79; staff gen. internist, attg. phys. Naval Regl. Med. Ctr. San Diego 1979-80; emerg. rm. phys. Kaiser Permanente Hosp. San Diego 1979-80; clin. instr. internal med. UC San Diego Med. Sch. 1979-82; head med. dept., emerg. med. dept., dir. ICU/ CCU Naval Hosp. Camp Lejeune, NC 1982-84; asst. hd. infectious disease div., internal med. dept. Naval Hosp. and int. med. dept., emerg. rm. Kaiser Permanente Hosp. San Diego 1984-86; mem., chmn. num. hosp. coms.; lectr. Valencia Comm. Coll. 1977-79; honors: Nat. Honor Soc., Bausch & Lomb Sci. Award, Westinghouse Scholar, Silver Knight nom. (1968), Chem. Award (Biscayne Coll. 1970), Dean's List (Biscayne 4 yrs.), num. Letters of Appreciation, Phys. Recogn. Award (AMA 1978, 80, 82, 85); fellow: Am. Coll. Phys. 1985, Royal Soc. Tropical Med. 1982; mem: Am. Soc. Microbiol., Am. Venereal Disease Assn., Assn. Mil. Surgeons of US, Soc. Critical Care Med., Infectious Disease Soc. Am., Christian Children's Fund, local soccer club; mil: cmdr. USNR (MC), Navy Commdn. Medal; Democrat; Catholic; rec: sailing, windsurfing, camping, racquetball. Res: 3176 Chelsea Park Cir Spring Valley 92078; 493 Wekiva Cove Road Longwood, FLA 32779 Ofc: Naval Hosp. San Diego 92134-5000

SANDELL, JAN RUNE, financial services executive; b. May 26, 1954, Kristianstad, Sweden; s. Hugo Leonard and Anna Beata Matilda (Andersson) S.; m. Kathleen Maria Burgi, May 13, 1984; edn: BSEE, Tech. Inst. Hassleholm

Sweden 1974; MBA strategic planning, Univ. Lund Sweden 1979; MBA finance, UC Riverside 1980. Career: cons. Mornstam AB, Malmo, Sweden 1978-79; financial analyst, senior fin. anal., mgr. budget & planning Fox & Carskadon Fin. Corp. San Mateo, Calif. 1981-84; dir. fin. planning Homestead Financial Corp. Burlingame 1984; senior dir., senior home ofc. mgr. Indsl. Indemnity Fin. Corp. (a Xerox corp.) S.F. 1984 —; honors: Cementa Co. Honorary Award (Malmo, Sweden), Calif. Edn. Abroad Scholar (Univ. Lund); mem. Am. Mgmt. Assn. 1985; mil: Swedish Army 1977-78; Lutheran; rec: philately, abstract art. Ofc: Indsl. Indemnity San Francisco 94111

SANDER, RICHARD ALLEN, physician; b. Nov. 24, 1935, Glendale; d. Ivan George and Galdys Virginia (Livingston) Pihl; children: Sharm b. 1962o, Susa b. 1963, Stacie b. 1966, Sabrina b. 1970, Christianne b. 1971; edn: AB, UCLA 1957; MD, USC 1961; MSPH, Univ. of Utah 1984; Pathologist: Occupational Med. Physician. Career: resident physician in pathology US Veteran's Admin. Hosp., Los Angeles 1965-69; forensic pathologist Los Angeles & Kern Counties 1969-80; fellow in occupational med. Univ. of Utah 1980-81; med. ofcr. Southern Pacific Railroad 1981-83; chief med. examiner State of Utah 1983-84; staff physician Pacific Bell 1984 —; cons. State of Calif. Dept. of Social Svcs.; asst. clin. prof. pathology UC Davis Med. Sch. p.t.; mem: Fellow Am. Acad. of Forensic Scis., Nat. Assn. of Med. Examiners, Am. Occupational Med. Assn., Western Occupational Med. Assn.; works: Cocaine Associated Deaths in Utah, Journ. Forensic Scis. 1984; Back Injury Disability in Railroad Workers, Spine 1985; mil: col. USAFR 1960-; Republican; Ch. of Jesus Christ LDS; rec: sports, collectables, carpentry. Res: 2761 Holly Hills Ln Cameron Park 95682

SANDERS, CLIFTON OMER, trading co. owner; b. Jan. 18, 1925, Liberty, Ky.; s. Johnny Amos and Effie Elisabath (Garrett) S.; m. Vela Virginia, Feb. 26, 1976. Career: auto mechanic in Lexington, Ky. until 1958; world travel and work as 'Jack of all trades' 1958-68; owner/gen. mgr. Hou-San (import co.), 1968 —; mem. World Traders Success Club, Internat. Traders Honors Club/LA; Moose Lodge; mil: m/sgt. US Army 1942, 46, 1952-56; Republican; Protestant; rec: arts & crafts, woodworking, computer buff. Address: POB 1236 (12322 Lakeview Dr) Clearlake Oaks 95423

SANDERS, GARY ALAN, maintenance equipment co. president; b. July 12, 1936, Detroit, Mich.; s. Elmer Theodore and Christie Eugenia (Hamilton) Lusty. Career: file clk., cost acct., asst. to the controller, Foote & Davies, Atlanta, Ga. 1953-63; office mgr. Curtis Equip. Co., San Francisco 1963-67; office mgr. San Francisco Equip. Co., S.F. 1967-75, gen. mgr. 1975-82, pres. S.F. Equip. Co., San Leandro 1982 —; mem. San Leandro CofC; mil: sgt. Georgia Nat. Guard; Republican; rec: painting. Res: 767 J Street Lathrop 95330 Ofc: San Francisco Equipment Co., Inc. 14361 Catalia St San Leandro 94577

SANDERS, STEPHEN JESSE, JR., philanthropist; b. Nov. 10, 1919, Salisbury, N.C.; s. Stephen Jesse and Pattie Lee (Mann) S.; m. Mildred McCormick, Mar. 31, 1944, div. 1964; 1 son, Stephen, III b. 1946; m. 2d Patrice Mick, Apr. 21, 1979; edn: Pfeiffer Coll. 1948, att. var. army schs. incl. Army Language Sch., Monterey. Career: capt. US Army, 1942-50, served with infantry, mil. police and counter-intel. corps., decorated Bronze Star Medal w/oak leaf cluster, Combat Inf. Badge; nat. advt. mgr. Clarion-Ledger and Jackson Daily News, Jackson, Miss., 1952-59; founder/pres. Stephen J. Sanders Inc. (export-import co.), Jackson and Vicksburg, Miss. 1960-65, San Francisco 1977 —, Dallas 1982 —; founder, chmn. Fgn. Trade Com. of Jackson (Miss.) CofC 1961-63; founder, secty. Miss World Trade Council 1962-63; founder Fellowship of the Crown, Montreat, N.C. 1967 —; founder/pres. The Crown Found., Carmel, Calif. 1971 —; founder/dir. Church of the Crown, Carmel 1986 —; mem. Nat. 4th Infantry Div. Assn., 22nd Infantry Assn.; honors: E-Flag and Cert., presented by Pres. J.F Kennedy for outstanding contbns. to US Export Expansion Pgm. (1962); author: To Him Who Conquers (Doubleday, 1970); Address: Church of the Crown POB 3743 Carmel 93921; Stephen J. Sanders, Inc. 1007-09 Market St San Francisco 94103

SANDERSON, CLAIRE MARIE, business owner; b. July 4, 1939, Fall River, Mass.; d. Joseph Armand and Anaise (Vailencourt) Gagnon; m. Grady A. Sanderson, Jr., July 6, 1957; children: Debra b. 1959, Ronald b. 1961, Kathrine b. 1962, Karen b. 1963, Marie b. 1965; grad. Mission Bay H.S. 1957. Career: retail sales clk. Puppy World, San Diego 1970-, dept. mgr. 1971, store mgr. 1972-79; founder/owner The Pet Mine, Grass Valley 1979 —; lectr. on pet care in public schs.; active in Humane Soc. fundraising; named San Diego Homemaker of the Year, Dairy Council of S.D. County (1970); Republican; Catholic; rec: rosarian. Res: 380 Alexandra Way Grass Valley 95949 Ofc: The Pet Mine 231 East Main St Grass Valley 95945

SANDS, MICHAEL, baked goods mfg. co. executive; b. Dec. 14, 1945, Boston, Mass.; s. Joseph and Frances (Ross) Shapiro; edn: Amer. Internat. Coll. 1964-65, Boston Univ. 1966-67; m. Antonia McCarthy, Jan. 18, 1986. Career: started modeling, appearing in fashion mags. and T.V. commls., Boston area 1968-, acting role in motion picture The Boston Strangler (20th Century Fox) 1968; modeling wk., NYC 1968-72, and student, Neighborhood Playhouse 1968-70; actor, T.V. & films, at MGM, Universal, Los Angeles area 1978; founder/pres. C'est Cheese-cake Inc. (designer line of baked goods found in frozen food sections of all Ralphs, Vons, Hughes mkts.), 1978 —; honors: Hon. Deputy Sheriff, Boston, Mass. 1973; mem: SAG 1968-, Actors Equity 1972-, Am. Fedn. of T.V. & Radio Artists; mil: pvt. US Army 1963; Democrat; Jewish; rec: skiing, ice hockey, sailing, tennis. Ofc: C'est Cheese-cake, Inc. 8422-½ West Third St Los Angeles 90048

SANDS, RUSSELL BERTRAM, corporate insurance broker; b. Feb. 14, 1940, Santa Cruz; s. Clarence Russell and Betty Ellyn (Weeks) S.; m. Jacquelyn Hall, Sept. 9, 1960; children: Douglas b. 1962, Gwendolyn b. 1970; edn: Wheaton Coll. 1957-59, UCB 1959-61, BA, Western Ill. Univ. 1984. Career: mgr. Insurance Co. of No. Am., San Francisco 1961-69; v.p. Bayly, Martin & Fay, S.F. 1969-76; sr. v.p. Frank B. Hall & Co., S.F. 1976 —; dir. Hammerwell, Inc.; prin. Sands Properties; mem. Nat. Assn. of Ins. Brokers, World Trade Club, Churchill Club; civic: Fellowship Acad. (dir.), Young Life San Francisco (dir.), Mt. Hermon Assn. (advis. council); Republican; Presbyterian; rec: tennis, golf, travel. Res: 1841 Elizabeth St San Carlos 94070 Ofc: Frank B. Hall & Co., One Market Plaza San Francisco 94105

SANETO, RUSSELL PATRICK, neurobiologist; b. Oct. 10, 1950, Burbank, Calif.; s. Frank and Mitzi Seddon (Akino) S.; edn: BS, San Diego State Univ. 1972, MS, 1975; PhD, Univ. Texas Med. Branch 1981. Career: tchg. asst. San Diego State Univ. 1972-74; grad. asst. Univ. Tex. Med. Br. 1975-76, NIH predoc. fellow 1976-81, Jeanne B. Kempner postdoc. fellow 1981, NIH postdoc. fellow 1982-84, postgrad. research fellow 1985; research biochemist; lectr. biomedical ethics, anatomy UCLA Sch. of Med.; honors: Merit Award (Nat. Found. March of Dimes 1978), Young Investigator Travel Award (Am. Soc. Neurochemistry 1985), Grad. Student Orgn. Award (UT Med. Br. 1981), var. fellowships and grants, listed var. Who's Whos, Outstanding Young Men in Am., Men of Achievement; mem: Am. Soc. Neurochemistry, Neuroscience Soc., Internat. Soc. of Develmtl. Neuroscience, AAAS, NY Acad. of Sci., Sierra Club; publs: num. abstracts, research papers in med. jours., contbr. books; Democrat; Christian; rec: triathlon, skiing, jogging, bicycling, hiking. Res: 914 Seventh St Apt 5 Santa Monica 90403 Ofc: MRRC/ NPI UCLA 760 Westwood Plaza Los Angeles 90024

SANGSTER, RICHARD M., lawyer; b. Jan. 5, 1930, Hutchinson, Kans.; s. Jefferson Wm. and Dorothy Mae (Sifers) S.; m. Nancy Marsh, Aug. 20, 1955; children: Janice b. 1956, Denise b. 1958, Stephen b. 1959, Edward b. 1960; edn: BS in bus. adm. Kansas State Univ., JD, Washburn Univ. Law Sch. 1955; admitted Kans. State Bar 1955, Calif. State Bar 1963, US Supreme Ct., var. Fed. Bars. Career: lawyer, Kansas 1955-62; civil jury trial lawyer, San Francisco 1962 —, assoc. Bledsoe, Smith, Cathcart, Johnson & Rogers 1962-64, ptnr. 1964-70; senior ptnr., pres. Sangster & Mannion profl. corp. 1970 —; mem. Am. Board of Trial Advocates (nat. pres. 1985), past chmn. Calif. ABOTA (4 years), past pres. San Francisco Chpt. ABOTA; bd. mem. (corp. sec.) Guide Dogs for the Blind Inc., San Rafael; mil: seaman USN Destroyer service; 1st lt. US Army; Republican; Catholic; rec: photog., tennis, golf. Res: Five Oak Forest Rd Novato 94947 Ofc: Sangster & Mannion APC, Four Embarcadero Center Ste 3720 San Francisco 94111

SANNWALD, WILLIAM WALTER, librarian; b. Sept. 12, 1940, Chicago, Ill.; s. William Frederick and Irene Virginia (Stanish) S.; m. Mary G. Blomberg, May 22, 1965; children: Sara Ann, William Howard; edn: BA, Beloit Coll. 1963; MS, Rosary Coll. 1966, MBA, Loyola Univ. 1974. Career: mgr. Xerox Univ. Microfilms, Ann Arbor, Mich. 1972-75; assoc. dir. Detroit Public Library 1975-77; dir. Ventura County Library, Ventura 1977-79, San Diego Public Library 1979 —; vis. intr. mktg. San Diego State Univ. 1979 —, National Univ. 1979 —; honors: H.W. Wilson Fellow 1965-66; mem: ALA, Calif. Library Assn., Calif. Library Assn. for Systems & Svcs. (pres. congress members 1980), UN Assn., Beta Phi Mu; Catholic. Res: 3538 Paseo Salamoner La Mesa 92041 Ofc: City Administration Bldg., 202 C St. Mail Sta. 9B San Diego 92101

SANTANGELO, SALVATORE CARL, surgeon; b. Nov. 20, 1942, Hartford, Conn.; s. Carmelo Leonard and Concetta Lucy (Senofonte) S.; m. Edith, Aug. 20, 1966; children: Susan b. 1968, Kristin b. 1970; edn: BA biol., Catholic Univ. of Am. 1965; grad. study, Geo. Washington Univ. 1965-66, MD, 1970; Diplomate Am. Bd. Surg. 1979. Career: resident surgery and instr. Univ. Pittsburgh Health Ctr. 1970-76; surgeon US Naval Hosp. Port Hueneme 1976-78, chief oper. rm. sect. 1977-78; pvt. practice med., staff priv. St. John's Regl. Med. Ctr. Oxnard, Pleasant Valley Hosp. Camarillo 1976 —; mem., chmn. num. hosp. coms.; honors: Alpha Omega Alpha; fellow Am. Coll. Surg. 1983; mem: Am. Med. Soc., Calif. Med. Soc., Ventura County Med. Soc., Pa. Med. Soc., Allegheny County Med. Soc., Harbison Surg. Soc., Mark M. Ravitch Surg. Soc., Am. Cancer Soc. (bd. 1983-); mil: lcdr. USN (MC) 1976-78; Catholic; rec: flying, skiing, white water rafting, camping, hiking, music, photog. Ofc: 1100 W Gonzales Rd Ste 200 Oxnard 93030

SANTELLAN, RUBEN DIAZ, agriculture economist, rancher; b. Sept. 30, 1945, Visalia, Calif.; s. Pete Haro and Frances Diaz (Nevarez) S.; m. Anita, Oct. 22, 1977; children: Derek b. 1979, Steven b. 1980, Monica b. 1984; edn: AA, Coll. of Sequioas 1971; BS, CSU Fresno 1975. Career: office salesman Caskey Paper Co. 1968-69; employ. ofcr. I Calif. Employment Ofc., determinations, unemploy. ins. 1975-77; supvr. ag. personnel mgmt. & contracting 1977 —; farming, Citrus Ranch (20 acres); honors: Hispanic Award (Lions Club 1967); mem: Ag. Personnel Mgmt. Assn., Nesei League, Smithsonian Instn., Knights of Columbus, Les Amis du Vin, Tulare Co. Farm Bureau, Moose Lodge, Calif. State Sheriffs Assn. (assoc.); mil: E4 USN 1966-68, Good Service Conduct, Vietnam Campaign & Svc.; Democrat; Catholic; rec: internat. ag., wines, fishing, hunting, tennis. Res: 2330 Redwood Dr Visalia 93277 Ofc: Personnel Mgmt. & Agriculture Contracting 312 N Palm St Woodlake 93277

SANTORO, THOMAS C., financial planner; b. Jan. 26, 1961, Westerly, RI; s. Thomas D. and Joan F. (Esposito) S.; edn: grad. Ins. Inst., Univ. R.I. 1978; Certified Financial Planner 1984. Career: broker, owner Thomas D. Santoro

Ins. Inc. Westerly, RI 1977-79; real estate agent Century 21 Tradewinds Huntington Beach, Calif. 1980; senior financial planner Crane & Assocs. Fullerton 1980–; real estate advisor to Arbor Homeowners Assn. Fullerton; honors: Financial Mgmt. Nat. Honor Soc. (1983), Golden Key N.H.S. (1983); mem: Nat. Assn. Realtors, Calif. assn. Realtors, No. Orange County Bd. Realtors, Internat. Assn. Financial Planning, Inst. Cert. Financial Planners, Calypso Soc.; rec: sailing, snow and water skiing. Ofc: Crane & Assocs. 1745 N Hale Fullerton 92631

SANTOS, ROMEO S., certified public accountant, finance executive; b. Dec. 8, 1936, Manila, Philippines, nat. US cit. 1975; s. Gregorio N. and Bernarda Flores (De los Santos) S.; m. Mercedes Edith Abolencia, Apr. 24, 1963; children: Maria Bernadette b. 1964, Maria Catherine b. 1966, Maria Dominique b. 1968, Eric Emmanuel b. 1977; edn: BS commerce, Far Eastern Univ., Manila 1958; Assoc. Comml. Science, Phil. Coll. of Commerce, Phil. 1956; CPA Calif. 1983. Career: auditor SyCip, Gorres, Velayo & Co. CPAs Manila 1960-63; bank examiner Central Bank of the Philippines 1963-70; dir. of finance, bus. and fin. cons. Special Service for Groups L.A. 1970-86; honors: Award of Merit (Fedn. of Filipino Rosary Groups 1985), Distinguished Community Svc. (L.A. Fil-Am Jaycees 1984), Outstanding PICPAN Com. Svc. Award (PICPA USA 1984), Outstanding Leadership (Phil. Soc. of SE L.A. 1984); mem: Phil. Inst. CPAs So. Calif. (exec. v.p. 1981-82, pres. 1982-83, internal v.p., ret. 1979-81); Fedn. of Filipino Rosary Groups (pres. 1970-84), Phil. Soc. of SE L.A. (pres. 1979-80), Central Bankers Club So. Calif. (pres. 1970-79), Cursillistas of SE L.A. (pres. 1976-80), Share & Care Apostolate Found. (v.p. 1980-86), Circulo Pampangueno of So. Calif. (dir. 1980-86); publ: ed. and publ. The Filipino Catholic 1983-84, assoc. ed. The Filipino Rosarian 1980-82; Christian; rec: writing, reading, travel, dancing. Res: 12316 E Abana St Cerritos 90701 Ofc: Special Service for Groups 1313 W 8th St Los Angeles 90017

SAPIENZA, LEO ROY, real estate broker; b. May 19, 1918, Worcester, Mass.; s. Nazzareno and Felice (Armienti) S.; m. Margaret M., Sept. 1, 1946; children: Linda b. 1948, Karen b. 1952, Donna b. 1958, Diane b. 1962; edn: ins. and real estate courses, Golden Gate Coll. 1951-52; Calif. real estate lic. (1951). Career: insurance broker, real estate broker, owner Leo R. Sapienza Realty, San Francisco 1951–; honors: KABL-radio Citizen of the Day (1-15-81, 6-7-86), State and City Resolutions (1978), appreciation certs., Am. Cancer Soc. (1982), Coronary (1985), Order of St. Francis of Assisi (6-7-86), also on 6-7-86: Leo R. Sapienza Day (declared by mayor of S.F.), Supvs. Proclamation, State & Senators & Assembly awards, So. of Mkt., So. of Army Mercht. award, real estate award, etc.; mem. San Francisco Real Estate Bd. (MLS dir. 1978); civic: St. Vincent De Paul Soc. (R.E. cons. 1981-83, dir. 1983), South of Mkt Boys, Franciscan Club (pres. 1984), Rebuild St. Anthony's Ch. (chmn. 1978); mil: sgt. US Army 1941-45, Merit. Award, 6 Battle Stars; Democrat; Catholic; rec: garden, sports. Res: 1351 Southgate Daly City 94115 Ofc: Leo R. Sapienza Realty 3361 Mission St San Francisco 94110

SAPIRO, JEROME (SR.), lawyer; b. July 15, 1915, San Francisco; s. Philip Herman and Belle (Jalumstein) S.; m. Mary E. Calais, July 22, 1940; children: Jerome Jr. b. 1942, Barbara E. (Collins) b. 1946, Denis b. 1949, Stephen b. 1951, Dolores M. b. 1954; edn: AB (highest hons. in hist.), UC Berkeley 1936; LLB (1st in class), Hastings Coll. of Law 1939; admitted to practice, Supreme Ct., Calif. 1939; admitted to practice in Fed. Cts., US Supreme Ct., Bd. of Immigration Appeals. Career: gen. practice of law with Judge Milton D. Sapiro (uncle), 1939-42; sole practitioner, spec. wills, probate, trusts, conservatorships, 1946–; past bd.dirs. French Hosp. Med. Ctr. Awards: John Bell Mhoon scholarship and Legal Bibliography prize, Hastings; Phi Beta Kappa; Legion of Honor (Argent), France; Audie Murphy Achievement Awd., Soc. of 3rd Inf. Div. AUS 1983; Silver Beaver, BSA; St. George Awd. for svc. to youth, S.F. Archdiocese. Mem: Calif. State Bar, S.F. Bar Assn.(Pub. Def., Juvenile Ct. coms.), Assn. of US Army, Am. Legion, Retired Ofcrs Assn., BSA; nat. pres. Soc. of 3rd Inf. Div. 1954-5; pres. Sunset Comm. Improvement Club; incorporated West of Twin Peaks Cub Softball League, Troop Service Assn., and a youth football team. mil: US Army 1942-46, col. USAR, ret. 1975, decorated 10 battle stars, 5 beachhead landing arrowhds., Combat Inf. Badge, Bronze star w/cluster, merit. svc., presdtl. unit cit., Rhin et Danube, Croix le Guerre w/dbl. palm, Victory, Occupation, Am. Def. medals; Republican; Catholic; rec: gardening. Res: 66 Sotelo Ave San Francisco 94116 Ofc: 100 Bush St., Ste.520, San Francisco 94104

SAPONE, JOHN, professor of endodontics, b. Nov. 23, 1917, Fresno; s. Vitantonio and Dora (Civiello) S.; m. Ebe Fiori, July 14, 1945; 1 dau. Lucilla b. 1946; edn: DDS, Univ. Calif. Sch. of Dentistry 1953; Diplomate Am. Bd. Endodontics. Career: pvt. practice limited to endodontics, San Francisco 1953–; clin. prof. endodontics Univ. Calif. Sch. of Dentistry; frequent lectr., clinics, and seminars to local, nat., internat. dental socs. and dental schs.; vis. prof. postgrad. courses on endodontics in US, for US Army in Germany, Univ. of Milan, Univ. of Rome and Rome Dental Rehabilitation Study Group in Italy; honors: Omicron Kappa Upsilon (past pres. Rho Rho chpt.), cit. for exellence in tchg. UCSF Acad. Senate; mem: S.F. Dental Soc., Calif., Am. Dent. Assn., Fellow Am. Assn. of Endodontists, No. Calif. Acad. of Endodontics (past pres., founder), West Portal Dental Consultation Group (past pres., founder); num. publs. in sci. dental literature, contbr. 2 chpts. in endodontic textbk.; mil: major US Army Signal Corps WWII; Republican; Catholic. Res: 170 Palo Alto Ave San Francisco 94114 Ofc: University Calif. Sch. of Dentistry, San Francisco Medical Center

SAPUNOR, JOHN MYRON, judge; b. Mar. 1, 1919, Sacramento, Calif.; s. Thomas Leo and Myrtle Ellen (Fay) S.; m. Delphine Van Dyke (decd. 1965), Apr. 10, 1943; children: John b. 1948, Richard Thomas b. 1950 (decd. 1966), Michael Benjamin b. 1950 (decd. 1950); m. 2d Treva Frazier, Dec. 20, 1967; edn: AA, Sacramento Jr. Coll. 1938; BS, Univ. Santa Clara 1941; JD, Univ. Santa Clara Sch. of Law 1948. Career: deputy dist. atty. Sacramento County 1949-50; atty. ptnr. Wilke, Fleury & Sapunor 1950-74; Superior Ct. judge (apptd. by Gov. Reagan), presiding judge Superior Ct. Appellate Dept. 1979-80, elected presiding judge Superior Ct. 1984-85; honors: Judge of the Year (Capitol City Trial Lawyers 1982), Calif. Trial Judge of the Year (Calif. Trial Lawyers Assn. (1983), Disting. Santa Claran of the Yr. (Sacto. Santa Clara Alumni 1984), invited to administer oath of office to Spkr. and members of Assembly 1984 and Gov. Deukmejian and other presidential electors from Calif. to nominate Pres. Reagan for pres. for 2d. term; mem: Calif. State Bar, Sacto. County Bar Assn., Am. Bd. Trial Advocates; trustee Jesuit High Sch.; mil: major USAAF 1942-46; Republican; Catholic; rec: fishing, sketching, marksmanship. Ofc: Sacramento Superior Ct. 720 Ninth St Sacramento 95814

SARAFIAN, ARMEN, university president; b. Mar. 5, 1920, Van Nuys; s. Kevork and Lucy (Gazarian) S.; div.; children: Norman, Winston, Joy; edn: AB (magna cum laude) La Verne Coll. 1940; MA, Claremont Grad. Univ. 1947; PhD, USC 1967; LLD (hon), La Verne Coll. 1967. Career: tchr. in elementary and secondary edn., chmn. Banning High Sch. English Dept., five yrs.; tchr. Pasadena Jr. Coll. Dist., 1947-51; coordinator of sec. and jr. coll. edn., Pasadena City Schs., 1951-59; adminstrv. dean for instr., Pasadena City Coll. 1959-65, pres., and supt. of Pasa. Area Comm. Coll. Dist., 1965-76; pres. Univ. of La Verne, 1976-85, pres.-emeritus 1985–; cons. to bus., indus. and govt.; adj. prof. Comm. Coll. Adminstrn., USC, 1968-78; summer faculty var. colls. and univs. incl. UCLA, Occidental, Claremont, CSCs, 30 yrs. Pres. Calif. Conservation Council, 1966-68; trustee La Verne Coll. 1969-76; mgmt. team Univ. Alaska Statewide System, 1977-78; founder, adult adviser Pasadena Area Youth Council; founder Am. Armenian Internat. Coll. Bd. 1972; founder, exec. com. Pasa. Hall of Sci. Project, 1965-76; mem. USC Educare. Honors incl. recognition awards, Calif. Conservation Council 1964, Omicron Mu Delta 1965, USC 1972, Salvation Army 1975, Arthur Noble Gold Medal, Pasadena City Bd. Dirs. 1976. Mem. Pasadena Area Sch. Trustees Assn. (founder), La Verne CofC (pres. 1978), Pasa. CofC (v.p. 1972, hon. life), Native Sons of Golden West, Pasa. Hist. Soc.; New Century Club of Pasa. (pres. 1975-76); clubs: Kiwanis (v.p., Pasa. 1971), Oneonta, University. Ch. of the Brethren. Res: POB 1624, Glendora 91740

SARAYDARIAN, ARJUNA T., municipal court judge; b. Aug. 6, 1943, Amman, Jordan, nat. 1964; s. Torkom and Elizabeth (Bekarian) S.; m. Sandra Jean McBurney, b. 1970; children: Garo b. 1976, Ani b. 1978; edn: premed. stu., UCLA 1962-64; BA, CSU Northridge 1968; JD, UOP McGeorge Sch. of Law 1971; admitted to Calif. State Bar 1972. Career: research clk./atty., Sacramento Superior Ct. judges, 1971-72; deputy dist. atty. Sacto. County, 1972-75, supvsg. deputy of Writs, Appeals & Spl. Projects Sect., 1975-77; pvt. solo practice of law, Los Angeles 1977-81; deputy dist. atty. Riverside County, 1981-85, deputy in chg. Three Lakes Judicial Dist. Ofc. in Perris, 1983-85, elected judge 1984, assumed office 1985–; instr. CSU Sacto. 1973-77; judge pro tem L.A. Municipal Ct. 1981; apptd. mem. Riverside Co. Drug Abuse Commn. 1973-; counsel to Calif. Bus. & Transp. Bd. of Inquiry, 1977; founder/dir. Armenian Gen. Benevolent Union Legal Aid Clinic., Hollywood 1977-81; mem. L.A. Lawyers Club Speakers Bur. 1977-79; honors: Am. Jurisprudence acad. awards in criminal procedure & legal research; staff law journal and first class pres. in law school; num. public speaking and comm. service awards, Kiwanis, Lions, 1977-81; grad. Calif. Judicual Coll. 1985; mem: Am. (Judicial Adminstrn. Div.), Calif., Los Angeles, Hollywood (past), Riverside bar assns.; Calif. Judges Assn., Am. Judicature Soc., Calif. Dist. Attys. Assn.; Armenian Lawyers Assn. (past pres.); Armenian Alumni Assn. (past vp); Armenian Congress (past bd. dirs.); Armenian Bus. Alliance (founding bd.); US Power Squadrons; past pres. Washington Sch. PTA; pres. Vail Elem. Sch. PTA, Temecula; bd. dirs. Mt. San Jacinto Comm. Coll. Found.; chmn. Tri-Lakes Dist. Boy Scouts; chmn. Riverside County Drug Abuse in Schools Com.; clubs: Lions, YMCA (Y Guides tribal chief); publs: num. arts. on legal topics; Republican; Armenian Apostolic; rec: sailing, fencing, playing the oud (musical instrument). Res: Temecula Ofc: Municipal Court 27403 Ynez Rd Ste 108 Temecula 92390

SARGENT, HELEN CECELIA, restaurant owner; b. Apr. 18, 1908, Midvale, Utah; d. George Gregor and Mary (Goodal) Zalac; m. Stephen T. Sargent, Oct. 1, 1928 (dec. 1974); children: Steve T. Jr. b. 1929, Spencer W. b. 1932, George S. b. 1939; grad. Virginia City (Nev.) 4th Ward H.S. Career: US postal clerk, Ruth, Nev. 1927-28; restaurant owner/mgr. Grand Cafe (estab. by husband in 1921, assisted husband 1928-74), Susanville, Calif. 1928–; civic: Susanville Crippled Children Soc. (dir. 1959-61), Civil Defense for Lassen Co. (Womens chmn. 1957-60), Order of Eastern Star (50 year honors 9/23/86, mem. Hesperon Chpt.), Order of the Amaranth (matron Honey Lake Ct. 1940), Soroptomist Club (charter mem. 1950, pres. 1956-57, del. to Biennial Conv. New York 1956); Democrat (Womens Dem. Club); Catholic; rec: people, folklore, plants. Res: 1405 Main St Susanville 96130 Ofc: Grand Cafe 730 Main St Susanville 96130

SARGENT, WAYNE CUMMINGS, newspaper editor; b. Feb. 7, 1925, Brooklyn; s. Arthur Harder and Myrtle (Rohr) S.; m. Marybeth Street, 1955; edn: BA in journ., Stanford Univ. 1948. Career: reporter United Press Assn.; bus. mgr. for So. Calif., Ariz., Nev., UPA; div. mgr. eight so. states United Press Internat.; v.p./gen. sales mgr. UPI; pres./pub. Nashville Banner; pres. Cajun Music Pub. Co.; editor San Bernardino Sun; dir. So. Newspaper Publ.

Assn.; dir. Tenn. Press Assn.; mem. Tech. & Telecomm. Committees ANPA and ASNE; mil: USAF and Signal Corps, 1942-46; rec: golf, music. Res: 1345 South Center, Redlands 92373 Ofc: Sun Co. (Gannett Corp.), 399 North D St. San Bernardino 92401

SARKIS, SUSAN ANN, private investigator; b. Aug. 13, 1948, N.Y.C.; d. Wm. Robert and Kathleen Grace (Haley) McLaughlin; div.; 1 dau., Christine b. 1966; edn: H.S. dipl. Julia Richman Sch. of Nursing 1964; L.A. City Coll. 1968-70. Career: owner Sarkis Detective agency, Glendale 1976–, Sue Sarkis Bail Bonds, Glendale 1978–, Arcadia Bail Bonds, Arcadia 1980–; Calif. Senate Commr. 1982-83; honors: Calif. Senate commendn. and resolution (9/20/83); mem. Calif. Assn. of Lic. Investigators (dist. dir. L.A. North, bd. dirs. 1985-86, chair unlicensed activities com., chair indigent defendants com.), Glendale CofC, Glendale Executive Club; Catholic; rec: fishing. Ofc: POB 6608 Glendale 91205

SARNO, GIOACCHINO VINCENT, scientist, psychologist; b. Sept. 8, 1947, Culver City, Calif.; s. Albert Pelegrino and Josephine Louise (Taravella) S.; m. Holly Irene Mchernan, Mar. 18, 1978; children: Skylor Vincent b. 1982, Renee Alia Josephine b. 1986; edn: BA biol. & philosophy, UC San Diego, Revelle Coll. 1970; MS biol., CSU San Diego 1973; PhD psychol., US Internat. Univ. 1983. Career: staff research assoc. Physiological Research Lab. Scripps Inst. of Oceanography UCSD 1974-78; staff scientist Alcoa Defense Systems Inc. S.D. 1983–, dir. Infrared/ Electro Optical Lab.; postdoc intern marriage, family, child counseling, Ctr. for Psychological Counseling, Escondido; cons. scientist in govt. and industry; honors: At Entrance (UCSD Revelle Coll. 1965), In Residence (1965-67), Scholarship (HH Arnold Ednl. Fund, AF Aid Soc. 1965-69); mem. Soc. Photo-Optical Instrumentation Engrs.; inventor: Photo-Optical Time- Depth Recorder (1976); publ: contbr. Professional Ethics and Law in the Health Sciences (ed. E.J. Hunter and D.B. Hunter 1984); rec: flying. Res: 2988 Quail Rd escondido 92026 Ofc: Alcoa Defense Systems 16761 Via Del Campo Ct San Diego 92127

SASENICK, JOSEPH A., company president; b. May 18,1940, Chicago, Ill.; s. Anthony Emil and Caroline (Smicklas) S.; m. Barbara E. Barr. Aug. 18, 1962; children: Richard b. 1963, Susan b. 1964, Michael b. 1966; edn: BA, DePaul Univ. 1962; MA, Univ. of Okla. 1963. Career: Miles Labs Inc., Elkhart, Ind. 1964-70; dir. internat. mktg. Braun AG subs. Gillette Co. 1970–; chmn., mng. dir. Braun Electric U.K. Ltd.; dir. new products- new ventures Personal Care Div. Parent Co., Boston; v.p. diversified companies; pres. Jafra Cosmetics Worldwide 1970-79; corp. v.p., pres. consumer prods. div. Abbott Labs., No. Chicago Ill. 1979-84; currently, pres., CEO Moxie Industries Inc., Anaheim; dir. Moxie Industries; adv. bd. Am. Assn. of Individual Investors; honors: Omicron Delta Epsilon; mem: El Niguel Country Club, Knollwood Country Club, Laguna Beach Cable TV Com. Res: 525 Alta Vista Way Laguna Beach 92651 Ofc: Moxie Industries Inc., 2211 E. Orangewood Ave. Anaheim 92806

SATIN, SCOTT ARTHUR, manufacturing co. executive; b. Mar. 9, 1958, Los Angeles; s. David D. and Miriam (Stern) S.; m. Yolanda Cantellops, July 25, 1981; 1 son, Drew, b. 1982; edn: BA, USC 1981. Career: sales mgr. Imperial Pallet Co., Inc., Los Angeles 1976-81; general mgr. 1981-82; vice pres. 1982–; tng. director Imperial Western Surplus, Santa Fe Springs 1983-; finl. cons. Westwood Mgmt., Tulare 1983-; assoc. producer Swink/Webb Co., Burbank, for Children's Television Workshop "Mathnet" 1985-; mem. American Film Inst.; Delta Sigma Phi (v.p. 1979-80); Bnai Brith; author 3 pub. screenplays: Tell Me When The Whistle Blows (1980), How To Write A Screenplay (1982), Spot (1983); Republican; Jewish; rec: writing, athletics. Res: 1 Rock Bluffj Road Phillips Ranch 91765 Ofc: Imperial Pallet Co. Inc. 840 S. Mission Road Los Angeles 90023

SATO, EUNICE NODA, mayor; b. June 8, 1921, Livingston, Calif.; d. Bunsaku and Sawa (Maeda) Noda; m. Thomas T. Sato, Dec. 9, 1950; children: Charlotte P., Daniel R., Douglas R.; edn: AA, Modesto Jr. Coll. 1941; BA, Colo. State Coll. Edn. 1944; MA, Columbia Univ. 1948. Career: tchr., Alpha, Mich. 1944-47; edn. missionary, Yokohama, Japan 1948-51; mem. Long Beach City Council 1975–, mayor 1980–; bd. dirs. Long Beach chpt. ARC, Goodwill Industries; trustee St. Mary's Hosp. Med. Ctr.; adminstrv. bd. Silverado United Methodist Ch.; honors: Community Svc. Award, Long Beach Coordg. Council 1969; Hon. Svc. Award, Calif. PTA 1963; Outstanding Laywoman of Year, Long Beach Council Chs. 1976; Woman of Year, Long Beach CofC State Women's Council 1979; Mother of Yr., Silverado United Methodist Ch. 1973; Hon. Life Mem., Nat. Congress PTAs 1974; mem: Calif. Elected Women for Edn. & Research, Calif. League Cities, U.S. Conf. of Mayors, Virginia Country, Internat. City; works: monthly contbr. to neighborhood publs.; Republican. Ofc: 333 W. Ocean Blvd. Long Beach 90802

SATT, JAMES EUGENE, judge; b. Apr. 1, 1920, Rapid City, SD; s. Gust and Marie (Collins) S.; m. Sheryl, June 14, 1953; 1 son, Brian James b. 1954; edn: LLB, Loyola Law Sch. L.A. 1953. Career: atty. 1954-73; judge L.A. Municipal Ct. (apptd. Gov. Reagan) 1973–; supv. judge San Fernando Br. 1977, 1985-, Van Nuys Br. 1979-81; var. coms. L.A. Mun. Ct.; honors: Commdns. (St. Nicholas Greek Orthodox Ch., Calif. State Senate 1972, 73, Calif. State Assembly 1972, 73, L.A. City Council 1972, 73); mem: Encino CofC (bd. 1982, past pres., del. to Assoc. CofCs and Valley Round Table Conf. 1972, 73), Am. Law Student Assn. (chmn. placement com. 1952-53), Calif. Law Sch. Assn. (v.p. 1952-53), Loyola Bd. Bar Govs. 1950-53 (pres. 1952-53), Encino Baseball Inc. (co-chmn. Calif. league 2 yrs., chief unpire 1967, v.p. 1967, pres. 1968, bd. 1966-69), West Valley Comm. Hosp. Found. (trustee, v.p. 1972), Citizen's Adv. Planning Com. (L.A.), West Valley Police Activity League Supporters (chmn.

bd., pres. 1973), San Fernando Bus. & Profl. Assn., Fernando Award Inc. (bd. dirs. 1973-74, v.p. 1974, pres. 1975), Rancho Encino Hosp. (bd. dirs., chmn. bd. trustees 1985); helped establish alcohol rehab. ctr. for City of L.A.; established first cy. volunteer pgm. for L.A. Mun. Ct.; mil: cpl. USAF 1942-45, Am. Campaign, Good Conduct, WWII Victory; Republican; Greek Orthodox; rec: golf. Ofc: L.A. Municipal Ct. 110 N Grand Ave Los Angeles 90012

SATTERFIELD, GERTRUDE KATHLEEN, real estate broker; b. Sept. 30, 1949, San Diego; d. Louis Joseph and Jane Millicent (Crary) Seehaas; m. William B. Satterfield, Nov. 26, 1967; children: Nikki b. 1970, Kelly b. 1974; edn: spl. courses, Antelope Valley Coll., 1972-83; Calif. lic: real estate broker broker (1983), notary public (1985). Career: sales assoc. Carpenters Real Estate Co. Palmdale 1981-83, broker/prin. 1983–; honors: Cert. of Achievement, Century 21 (1981); mem: Nat. Assn. Realtors, Calif. Assn. Realtors, Nat. Notary Assn., Palmdale Bd. Realtors (MLS com.), Neighborhood Adv. Bd., Palmdale Community Assn., Concord Estates Homeowners Assn. (pres.); Neighborhood Watch Captain; Republican; Assembly of God; rec: camping, fishing, gardening, off-road racing. Address: Palmdale 93551

SAUL, RONALD STEPHAN, physician; b. June 26, 1949, Los Angeles; s. Arthur and Phyllis Marjorie (Anderson) S.; m. Nancy L. Thrash, Feb. 14, 1976; children: Lyndsey Marie, b. 1977; (twins) Arthur Christopher and Courtney Lynn, b. 1981; edn: BS, CSU Los Angeles 1971, masters cand. 1972, 1975-77; MD, Howard Univ. Coll. of Med. 1980; res. in pediatrics, UC Irvine 1980-81; res. in radiology and nuclear med., VA Wadsworth 1984-88. Career: Indian Health Svc: clin. dir. P.H.S. Indian Health Ctr., Box Elder, Mont.; family phys. Riverside- San Bernardino Indian Health Inc.; emerg. rm. phys. Mountains Community Hosp., Lake Arrowhead 1981-85; res. pediatrics Neonatal Intensive Care Unit, UC Irvine 1980-81; extern in obstetrics LA County USC Med. Ctr. 1983; res. radiology- nuclear med. VA Wadsworth Med. Ctr., UCLA 1984–; staff phys. internal med. USC Med. Ctr.; emerg. rm. phys. Mountains Comm. Hosp., Lake Arrowhead; honors: Awards Convocation CSU Los Angeles; Auxillary Scholarship, San Gabriel Hosp.; Nat. Health Svc. Scholarship, U.S. Pub. Health Svc.; mem: Radiological Soc. of no. Am. Soc. of Nuclear Med.; AMA; NYC Mission and Eastern States Mission (missionary); research: molecular genetics 1975-77; mil: sr. asst. surgeon, US Pub. Health Svc. 19891-84; Republican; Latter Day Saints (missionary); rec: composer, vocalist, musician. Res: 405 ½ So. Moore Ave., Monterey Park 91754; VA Medical Ctr., Dept. Radiology- Nuclear Med., Wilshire and Sawtelle Blvd., Los Angeles 90073

SAUNDERS, FRANK HENRY, expert police court witness; b. Dec. 6, 1934, Rochester, NY; s. Wm. H., Sr. and Frances E. (Lovejoy) S.; m. Michelle Anne Lamar, July 18, 1981; edn: Univ. of Ariz. (Tucson) 1954-6, 1958-9, UC Santa Cruz 1982; Calif. lic. Pvt. Investigator 1982; Qual. Police Ct. Expert, State Ct. 1981, Federal Ct. 1983. Career: investigator Continental Casualty Ins., 1964; ofcr. Santa Monica Police Dept. 1965-80; owner Frank Saunders Investigations (pvt. investigative firm), Pacific Grove, and expert police court witness, 1981–; recipient Medal of Valor, City of Santa Monica 1978; citations, Santa Monica City Council, State Sen. Paul Priolo, 1967; Chief of Police Commendn. 1967, 78; listed Who's Who in Am. Law Enforcement 1986; mem: Nat. Assn. Chiefs of Police, Consulting Inst. of Am., Santa Monica Police Assn. (founder/ed. newsmag. Soundoff 1970-79); Santa Monica Retired Police Assn.; Monterey Co. Peace Ofcrs Assn. Peace Ofcrs Resrch Assn. of Calif.; Pacific Grove CofC; club: Meadowbrook Swim & Tennis, Seaside; mil: A/2c USAF 1956-58; Republican; Prot.; rec: tennis, bicycling, creative writing. Ofc: Frank Saunders & Assocs., POB 161, Pacific Grove 93950

SAUNDERS, JOHN HAMILTON, lawyer, judge, ret.; b. April 11, 1916, So. Pasadena; s. Cary Dean and Grace Salina (Hamilton) S.; m. Jeanne de Garmo, June 6, 1942; children: Sherry Jeanne b. 1944, John Hamilton b. 1947, Susan Margaret b. 1962; edn: BA, honors, UCLA 1939; UC Berkeley Boalt Hall Sch. of Law 1939-41; JD, USC 1942; admitted to Calif. Bar 1942; appointed to Bench 1966. Career: gen. counsel, secty., treas. Filtrol Corp. 1946-58; ptr. Robinson, Saunders & Humphrey 1958-66; presiding judge Santa Anita Municipal Ct. 1966-84; vis. judge to 10 municipal corts and Los Angeles Co. Superior Ct.; bd. dirs. Coast Envelope Co. 1960-63; lectr. on tax law USC Tax Inst. 1960, UC Cont. Edn. of the Bar 1960; instr. in criminal law Citrus Coll. 1973-74; bd. Legal Services Corp. 1978-; honors: Awards for Public Svc. cities of Monrovia, Arcadia, Duarte, Co. of Los Angeles, State of Calif., var. civic orgns.; mem: Am., Calif. and Los Angeles Bar Assns., Los Angeles Co. Municipal Judges Assn. (chmn. 1977-78), Calif. Judges Assn., Los Angeles Co. Supvrs. Policy Bd. on Criminal Justice, exec. bd. of San Gabriel Valley Council of Boy Scouts, Kiwanis (Monrovia pres. 1975-76, Distng. Svc. Award), Santa Anita Family Svc. (pres., bd. mem. 1968-74), Help Our Youth (bd. 1971-77), Arcadia Welfare & Thrift Shop (bd. 1976-), City Commns. (Monrovia 1967-71, Arcadia 1966-67); works: developed drug and alcohol abuse edn. ctr. for Arcadia, Duarte and Monrovia; mil: lt. s.g. USNR 1943-46; Democrat; Episcopal (vestryman); rec: tennis, gardening, travel. Res: 841 San Simeon Rd. Arcadia 91006

SAWYER, WENDELL H., real estate broker, investor; b. Dec. 21, 1954, Los Angeles; s. Joe E. and Elverda Virginia (Hallman) S.; edn: BA in psych., USC 1978; Calif. lic. real estate sales (1977). Career: sales agt. Century 21 Rayshire, Los Angeles 1977; investor (28 bldgs. currently), broker W.H. Sawyer & Co., L.A.; profl. honors: Million Dollar Club (1977); rec: skating, skiing, softball. Res: 4541 Don Valdes Dr Los Angeles 90008 Ofc: W.H. Sawyer & Co. 5485 W Washington Blvd Los Angeles 90016

SAXBY, HARVEY C., business owner; b. Nov. 27, 1946, Douglas, Ariz., s. Harvey C. and Katherine E. S.; m. Joyce D., June 9, 1984; 1 dau. Katherine b. 1972; edn: BS bus. admin., finance, office admin., CSU Fresno 1971. Career: steward asst. Ofcrs. Club Fairchild AFB, Wash. 1964-65; chef Chuck Wagon Restaurant Fresno 1965-68; mgr. Stanton Ofc. Machines Fresno 1968-78; owner Co-Ordinator Business Systems Clovis 1978–; arbitrator Better Bus. Bureau 1981–; chmn. bd. Assoc. Indian Svc. Inc. 1982-83; honors: Alpha Kappa Psi (most outstanding 1970, most active 1971), Fresno ARC 1982-83; mem: Nat. Office Machines Dealer Assn. 1978-, Kiwanis (disting. past pres. w. honors, div. co-ord., dist. com.); Democrat; Protestant; rec: sports. Ofc: Co-Ordinator Business Systems 200 W Bullard Ste B-4 Clovis 93612

SAYCE, STEVEN ALAN, asphalt paving contractor; b. Sept. 1, 1955, Camp Lejeune, N.C.; s. Donald H. and Damaris A. S.; edn: BS civ. engrg., N.C. State 1977; civil engr. reg. Calif. 1981. Career: ofcr. in chrg. constn. Marine Base 29 Palms 1978-79; activity civil engr. Guam 1980-81; proj. engr. Civil Engrg. and Planning Assoc. 1981-82; asphalt paving salesman All American Paving 1982-83; asphalt paving constructor AMTEK Construction 1983–; mem: So. Calif. Paving and Grading Assn.; mil: Lt. USN 1978-81; Republican; Catholic; rec: music, reading, tennis, golf. Ofc: AMTEK Construction 1202 W Arlington Ave Anaheim 92801

SAYEGH, ISSA MICHAEL, retail co. president; b. Dec. 20, 1929, Erememein, Jordan, nat. US cit. 1960; s. Michael Eid and Selma (Salem) S.; m. Hania Janet Nassar, Apr. 18, 1958; children: Michael b. 1959, Camille b. 1960, Richard b. 1961, William b. 1964, Robert b. 1976; edn: BA, Latin Seminary of Jordan 1954. Career: came to USA in 1955; empl. with Ford Motor Co. 1955-68; owner Oak Liquors, Yonkers, NY 1968-78; owner/pres./CEO Hanessa Ents. dba Mars Builders Supply, Santa Fe Springs, Calif. 1978–; Democrat; Catholic. Address: Santa Fe Springs 90670

SAYLES, SUE ANN, temporary services co. owner; b. July 21, 1934, Fort Jones; d. Fredell DeForrest and Marie Elizabeth (Ball) Taber, children: Leonard b. 1958, Clayton b. 1960, Barbara b. 1962; edn: Bus. Adm., Univ. of San Francisco 1977. Career: Justice Court, Selective Service Sys., Boeing Airplane Co., Pacific Tel., mgr. Sears Roebuck & Co.; mgr. Div. Edn. Sys., San Jose 1970-72; mgr. Tempo-Uniforce, San Jose 1973-74; Ofcr. Personnel, COM-PATWINGSPAC, Moffett Field, Calif. 1974-76; bd. dir./mgr. Roma Tile, Ltd., Los Gatos 1977-80; mgr. Western Temporary Service, Inc., Campbell 1980-84; founder/owner Diamond Temporary Services, San Jose 1984–; Spanish-speaking program coordinator, NAS, Moffett Field; honors: Girl of the Year, Valentine Sweetheart for Beta Sigma Phi; Top Performer (1981-82), and Public Relations awards (1982), Western Temporary Service. mem: Adminstrv. Mgmt. Soc. (dir.), Women in Bus., Network of Women Entrepreneurs, VFW Aux. (sec.treas.), Jaycettes (vp), CofC (comm. chmn. B.P.W.); secty. PTA; Beta Sigma Phi (vp); Republican; Episcopal; rec: genealogy, hunting, skiing, dancing. Res: 2896 Moss Hollow Dr San Jose 95121 Ofc: Diamond Temporary Services, 675 N. First St, Ste. 401, San Jose 95112-5111

SBORDONE, ROBERT JOSEPH, clinical neuropsychologist; b. May 6, 1940, Boston, Mass.; s. Saverio and Phyllis (Dellaria) S.; edn: L.A. Valley Jr. Coll. 1957-58; BA psychol., Univ. So. Calif. 1967; MA psychol., CSU Los Angeles 1969; PhD psychol., UC Los Angeles 1976; postdoc. biobehavioral scis., Neuropsychiatric Inst. UCLA 1976-77; Diplomate Am. Bd. Profl. Neuropsychol. 1984, Am. Bd. Clin. Neuropsychology, Am. Bd. Profl. Psychol. 1985; Jr. Coll. Tchg. Credl. Calif. 1969; Marriage, Family, Child Counselor 1970; Nat. Register Health Providers in Psychol. 1979; Independent Med. Examiner (psychol.), Calif. Workers Comp. Bd. 1982. Career: tchg. asst. Univ. So. Calif. 1966-67, residence hall counselor 1966-67; sys. analyst L.A. Police Dept. 1967-68; research asst. Pacific State Hosp., USC; grad. asst. CSULA; deputy probation ofcr. 1970; instr. psychol. Pasadena City Coll. 1970-77; marriage and family counselor Pasadena Psychological Ctr. 1970-75; chief of pgm. evaluation and clin. research Pomona Valley Mental Health Ctr. 1970-75; research assoc. UCLA 1973-76, tchg. assoc. 1975-76, lectr. 1976-77; asst. prof. psychol. CSULA 1977-78; asst. research psychol. Neuropsychiatric Inst. UCLA 1978-79; dir. applied behav. scis. Mgmt. Health & Devel. Corp. 1978; chief psychol., dir. dept. gerontology and long-term care L.A. Guidance & Counseling Svc. 1978-79; adj. asst. prof. UC Irvine Med. Ctr. 1980-82; clin. prof. Fuller Grad. Sch. of Psychol. 1981-82; asst. clin. prof. dept. neurosurgery and phys. med. & rehab. UC Irvine 1982–; spl. staff (neuropsychol.): St. John's Hosp. 1979-81, Northridge Hosp. 1979-81, Edgemont Hosp. 1980-81, Westwood Hosp. 1980-81; attg. staff Long Beach VA Hosp. 1981; affil staff: Capistno by the Sea Hosp. 1984-, College Hosp. 1984-, Med. Ctr. of Garden Grove 1984-, Hoag Presbyterian Hosp. 1985-, South Coast Hosp. 1985-; cons. Sys. Devel. Corp. 1969, Northeast L.A. Comm. clin. 1973-74, NY State Div. of Crim. Justice Svcs. 1976-77, Reed Neurological Inst. UCLA 1978-79, L.A. Guidance & Counseling Svc. 1978-79, Metropolitan State Hosp. 1978-79, Legal Psychiatry & Assocs. 1978, Sandoz Pharm. Co. 1978-79, Beverly Found. 1980-81; honors: Dean's List (1966), Phi Kappa Phi (1969), Predoc. Fellow (Nat. Inst. Mental Health 1972-73, Nat. Inst. Drug Abuse 1973-75), Postdoc. Fellow (Nat. Inst. Mental Health 1976-77), NIMH Biobehavioral Scis. Grants (1976, 77, 78), mem. US Track & Field Team (1963), alternate US Olympic Team (1964); mem: Am. Psychol. Assn., Western Psychol. Assn., Clinicians in Pvt. Practice, Computers in Psychol., Calif. Neuropsychol. Soc., Calif. State Psychol. Assn., Orange County Psychol. Assn. L.A. County Psychol. Assn., So. Calif. Head Injury Found., Nat. Head Injury Found., Neuropsychol. Assocs. of Calif., NY Acad. of Scis., and others; author neuropsychol. tests including Sbordone- Hall Memory Battery, Digit-Digit Test, OBD-168; co-author Complex Attention, Problem Solving I and Problem Solving II compu-

ter pgms. for rehab. of brain-injured patients; editorial advisory bd. Internat. J. of Clin. Neuropsychol. and J. of Head Trauma Rehabilitation; 50+ articles in med. jours., 200+ profl. presentations. Res: 3591 Aquarius Dr. Huntington Beach 92649 Ofc: Orange County Neuropsychology Group 8840 Warner Ave Ste 301 Fountain Valley 92708

SCALES, CHARLES DONALD, management consultant; b. July 27, 1955, Macon, Ga.; s. Charles Drew and Hazel Helen (Daniel) S.; edn: BSChE, magna cum laude, Rice Univ. 1977, BA, 1977, MChE, 1978; MBA, Harvard Bus. Sch. 1982. Career: process engr. Pullman Kellogg, Houston, Texas 1978-80; mgmt. cons. Arthur D. Little, Cambridge, Mass. 1981-84; senior staff cons. Avery Internat., Pasadena 1984-85; mgmt. cons. Theodore Barry & Assoc., Los Angeles 1985–; honors: Phi Beta Kappa, Sigma Xi, Tau Beta Pi; Brown Engring. Scholar; mem: Am. Inst. of Chem. Engrs., So. Calif. Corp. Plnnrs. Assn., Rice Univ. So. Calif. Alumni Assn. (pres.), Harvard Bus. Sch. So. Calif. Alumni Assn.; Republican; Protestant; rec: wine, sports, baseball cards. Ofc: Los Angeles

SCALES, PATIENCE JOANN BARNES, music teacher; b. Mar. 11, 1932, England, Ark., d. Earl Lee and Annie Mae (Herron-Jasper) Barnes; m. Herman Lee Feaster, Feb. 18, 1951 (div. 1953), 1 son: Rickey Ricardo b. 1952; m. 2d D.W. Scales Dec. 27, 1955 (div. 1968), children: Glenn Earl b. 1957, Danny Wayne b. 1959; m. 3d Charles M. Hudspeth Sept. 25, 1977 (div. 1982); edn: Ark. AM&N Coll. 1949-55; San Francisco State Univ. 1968-83; Univ. of Pacific 1981-82. Career: inservice sch. tchr. Gartrell H.S. England, Ark. 1952-56; pvt. music tchr. piano, organ, theory 1956–; after school music tchr. S.F. Unified Sch. Dist. 1970-75; talent agent 1979-83; radio announcer, talk show host KEST-AM S.F. 1983-85; founding pres., dir. Parade of Youth Inc. 1959–, annual performance by youth at S.F. War Meml. Opera House 1967-80; clothing designer Fighting Stress With Patience line; writer, dir. original Staircase to the Stars KRON-TV 1978; organizer Magic of Patience and Music Singers 1983-; lectr. Success at any Age 1978 79; honors: Most Disting. Women (1969), Mother of the Year (The Examiner 1970), Knights of Honor; mem: Am. Fedn. Musicians (examiner), Music Tchrs. Assn. of Calif., Am. Fedn. TV and Radio Artists, Nat. Assn. Music Therapy, S.F. Opera Guild, S.F. Symphony Found., Nat. Assn. Negro Musicians, AM&N Coll. Alumni, Gamma Phi Delta, NAACP, African Am. Hist. & Cultural Soc., Bus. & Profl. Women; publ: columnist Astrological Views (Sun, Metro Reporter 1974); Democrat; Baptist. Res: 415 A St Apt 203 Daly City 94014 Ofc: Parade of Youth Inc. 1145 Hayes St Ste 7 San Francisco 94117

SCAVEZZE, MARY, temporary services co. executive; edn: Wayne State Univ. 1964-67, CSU San Francisco 1965. Career: branch supr. Kelly Services, Inc., 1966-69, resident br. mgr. for East Detroit, Mich. 1970-73, branch mgr. for Albuquerque, N.M. 1974-77 (Outstanding branch performance award 1975), dist. mgr./opened 6 branch locations San Diego County, 1977–; mem: Nat. Assn. of Accts. 1970- (v.p. 1975-76), Personnel Mgmt. Assn. ASPA 1974-78, CofC, Hotel Sales and Mgmt. Assn. (pres. 1982-83), Internat. Word Processing Assn., San Diego Conv. and Vis. Bureau, San Diego Employee Assn.; recipient sev. profl. awards Kelly Services Inc., appreciation awards City of San Diego (1981), March of Dimes (1982-84), Nat. Assn. Accts. (1975-76); civic: Junior Achievement (judge 1979-85), San Diego Comm. Coll. (advis. com. 1978-85), annual Women's Career Symposium (organizer 1978-80). Ofc: Kelly Services The 'Kelly Girl' People 1450 Frazee Rd Ste 303 San Diego 92108

SCAVO, NICKOLAS ANTHONY, optometrist; b. Nov. 15, 1957, Chgo.; s. Giovanni and Rita (Guardi) S.; edn: AA, Cypress Coll. 1977; BA in psych., UC Los Angeles 1980; BS in visual sci., Penn. Coll. of Optometry 1982, OD, 1984; lic. Optometrist, Calif. 1984, Pa. 1984. Career: optometrist assoc. Gary Jacobsen, OD, 1984; optometrist prin., S.A. Weingarten, OD, Inc., City of Industry 1985–; optometrist prin. and regl. dir. So. Calif. for No. Am. Eye Ctrs. Inc. Long Beach 1986–; honors: Beta Sigma Kappa (1982), Psi Chi (1980); mem. Am. Opt. Assn., Calif. Opt. Assn., Am. Opt. Found., UCLA Alumni Assn., Penn. Coll. of Opt. Alumni Assn.; Republican; Roman Catholic; rec: tennis, golf, skiing. Address: Diamond Bar 91765

SCEPER, DUANE HAROLD, lawyer; b. Nov. 16, 1946, Norfolk, Va.; s. Robert G. and Marion E. (Hynes) S.; m. Sharon D., July 4, 1981; stepchildren: Karin Stevenson b. 1970, Diane Stevenson b. 1973; edn: undergrad., San Diego St. Univ. 1964-65; BS, WSU Coll. of Law, 1979, JD, 1980; admitted to Calif. State Bar 1982. Career: field engr. Texas Instruments, 1969-70; field engr. Memorex Corp. 1970-71; var. sales and sales mgmt. positions (investments, real estate and ins.), 1971-80; commercial diver 1979-81; atty./ estate & bus. plnng. cons. AID Insurance Services, San Diego 1982-84; pvt. practice 1984–; mem. Am. Bar Assn., Calif. Bar Assn., Am. Trial Lawyers Assn., Calif. Trial Lawyers Assn., Delta Theta Phi; works: computer devices, computer pgms., vapor recovery equip.; mil: E4 USAF 1965-68, Air Commando, Vietnam; rec: hist. restoration, scuba diving, computers, karate. Res: 2641 Massachusetts Ave Lemon Grove 92045 Ofc: 707 Broadway Ste 1100 San Diego 92101

SCHABELY, GEZA, consulting engineering firm principal; b. Feb. 2, 1933, Budapest, Hungary, nat. US cit. 1971; s. Ferenc and Terezia (Miklosovits) S.; m. Margaret, Feb. 10, 1957; children: James and Sylvia b. 1957; edn: Elec. Master, Tech. Univ. of Budapest 1956; Reg. Profl. Engr. NY 1975, Calif. 1984. Career: elec. project engr. Syska & Hennessy Cons. Engrg. Firm NYC 1961-82 (supv. projects: Metropolitan Opera House Lincoln Center, Rockefeller Center, Univ. Riyadh Saudi Arabia), chief. elec. engr. L.A. branch ofc. 1983– (projects: San Diego Naval Hosp., S.D. Convention Ctr., Calif. Plaza L.A.); mem: Constrn. Spec. Inst., Illumination Engrg. Soc., rec: computers, stamp collecting. Res: 5401 Zelzah Ave, No 125, Encino 91316 Ofc: Syska & Hennessy 11500 W Olympic Blvd Los Angeles 90064

SCHAEFER, SANDRA KRAMER, sales management executive; b. July 24, 1939, Chicago, Ill.; d. George J. and Elvira Mae (Roon) Kramer; m. Richard Schaefer, Aug. 22, 1959; children: Erich, b. 1965; Max, b. 1966; edn: BS, Univ. of Mich. 1961. Career: research chemist Parke-Davis Research Labs., Ann Arbor, Mich. 1961-63; abstract writer and translator (German and French), Chemical Abstracts, Albuquerque, N.Mex. 1963-66; real estate sales assoc. Louise Davies Real Estate, Pacific Palisades 1971-72; owner/ broker Sunset Real Estate, Pac. Palisades 1972-79; mgr. Merrill Lynch Realty, Pac. Palisades 1980-84; res. v.p./ CEO Merrill Lynch Realty (North Bay), San Rafael 1984–; co. tng. dir. Merrill Lynch Realty 1980-84; honors: Mgr. of the Year, Merrill Lynch 1983; Citizen of the Year, Pac. Palisades 1984; 1st Pl. Drum Maj., Pac. Palisades Americanism Parade 1982-84; mem: Pacific Palisades Community Council (chmn. 1982-84); Pacific Palisades Civic League (v.chmn. 1979-82); Citizens Adv. Gp. for Los Angeles City Council; Los Angeles Bd. Realtors; rec: singing, guitar, amateur musical comedy writer. Res: 1 Throckmorton Ln., Mill Valley 94941 Ofc: Merrill Lynch Realty, 1015 Irwin St San Rafael 94901

SCHAEFER, TIMOTHY JOHN, investment banker; b. Aug. 9, 1947, Cincinnati, Ohio; s. George John and Irene Elizabeth (Bailey) S.; 1 son, Matthew b. 1979; edn: Univ. of Ky. 1965-67, Xavier Univ. 1967-69; grad. Public Finance Inst., Univ. Mich. Grad. Sch. Bus. Mgmt. Career: asst. v.p. Central Trust Co., Cincinnati 1967-73; investment ofcr. United California Bank, Los Angeles 1973-78; v.p. Chemical Bank, NYC 1978-82; v.p./mng. dir. Bank of America, San Francisco 1982–, mng. dir. Public Finance Dept.; technical adv. com. Calif. Debt Advisory Commn.; honors: Hon. Order of Kentucky Colonels (1966); mem: Short Term Traders Assn., San Francisco Municipal Forum (gov. 1985-86); Republican; Catholic; rec: sailing, tennis. Res: 2713 Pontiac Dr Walnut Creek 94598 Ofc: Bank of America 555 California St 9th Fl San Francisco 94104

SCHAFF, ALFRED, microelectronics executive; b. June 8, 1920, Panama; s. Alfred and Juanita (Krogstadt) S.; m. Flavia Olinge, Oct. 3, 1949; children: Edward b. 1950, (by prev. marriage) Anita b. 1943, Thomas b. 1944; edn: BSME, Calif. Inst. of Tech. 1941; PhD, Kensington Univ. 1986; FAA Lic. Airline Transport Pilot, Aircraft & Eng. Mech. Career: maint. supt. Pan Am.-Grace Airways, 1941-44, capt. 1946-51; large liquid rocket test engr. Aerojet General, Azusa Plant 1951-57, mgr. Test & Field Service Div., Solid Rocket Plant 1957-60, mgr. Spl. Solid Rocket Projects 1960-65, engring. mgr. Nuclear Rocket Test Facility 1965-69; v.p./gen. mgr. (dir. R&D) Ametek/Micro Electronics, El Segundo 1969–; mem. Am. Rocket Soc. (1951-), ISHM (1976-), IEEE (1975-), SME (1986-), ASTM (1986-), CalTech Alumni Assn.; 2 US patents; publs: An Analysis of Evaporative Rate Analysis (Am. Chem. Soc. 1971), Test Facility for 5000 MLO Nuclear Rocket Propulsion Service (AIAA 1967); Republican; Fundamentalist; rec: flying. Res: 8143 Billowvista Dr Playa Del Rey 90293 Ofc: Amatek/ MicroElectronics 605 S Douglas St El Segundo 90245

SCHANKMAN, ALAN ROBERT, ophthalmologist; b. Jan. 1, 1947, Bklyn.; s. Barnet and Sylvia (Barken) S.; m. Vicki Gellman, 1973; children: Dana b. 1979, Lauren b. 1979, Alison b. 1981, Michael Alden b. 1983; edn: BS, Brooklyn Coll. 1968; MD, Downstate Med. Coll. of SUNY 1972; intern, Beth Israel Med. Ctr, NY 1973; resident Ophthalmology, E J Meyer Mem. Hosp., SUNY 1973-76; Am. Bd. Certified Ophthalmology 1977. Career: opthalmologist, solo practice, New York 1976-78, Los Angeles 1978–; clin. instr. Jules Stein Eye Inst., UCLA Medical Sch.; investigator in keratorefractive surgery; forerunner in laser treatments for eye diseases; Braille Inst. consultant; mem: Calif. Med. Assn., LA County Med. Assn., Fellow Am. Acad. Ophthal., LA County Soc. Ophthal., Calif. Assn. Ophthal., Keratorefractive Soc. Am., Internat. Glaucoma Congress, Internat. Assn. Ocular Surgeons, Am. Soc. Contemporary Ophthal.; rec: sailing. Ofc: 12840 Riverside Dr North Hollywood 91607

SCHARNHORST, JUDY WILSON, real estate broker; b. May 9, 1949, Yreka; d. Densal Martin and Blanche Faye (Holstead) Wilson; 1 son, John b. 1970; edn: Coll. of the Sch. of the Ozarks 1967-70; Grossmont Coll. 1967-70; Cuyamaca Coll. 1979-80; num. real estate seminars incl. R.E. investing & exchg. Cuyamaca Coll. 1980, ethics, Transam. Title 1983, legal & tax update Univ. Pgms. 1983, R.E. exchg. Berkheimer 1984, R.E. counseling for results Ringsdorf 1985; Calif. Lic. Broker and Lic. Ofcr. (1984). Career: real estate sales Herbert Hawkins R.E., Spring Valley 1978; Realty World Aamor, Spring Valley 1980; Century 21 Pierce, Lemon Grove 1983; broker, mgr., v.p. Home Sellers Inc. 1984–; investment counselor 1st Interstate Properties Inc., Forsythe Mortgage Co. Inc. 1978-; honors: Top Earner Sales (1979), Million Dollar Club (1978, 79), Herbert Hawkins R.E. Co.; Cert. of Excellence, Nat. Statistical Researcher Co. 1978; mem: Nat. and Calif. Assns. Realtors, San Diego Bd. Realtors, Nat. Council of Exchangors (Gold Club), Valle de Oro Little League, Valle Mesa Grove Ponytails; works: property renovations, 1976-77, 1978-79, 1984, 1984-85; Worldwide Ch. of God; rec: decorating, landscaping, needlework. Ofc: Home Sellers, Inc., 4040 30th St. San Diego 92104

SCHECHET, JOEL ROBERT, builder-developer; b. Apr. 17, 1953, Los Angeles; s. Isidor Arthur and Beverly Diane (Asch) S.; m. Ziva Golde, Nov. 6, 1984; edn: Northwestern Univ. Honor's Med. Pgm. 1970-73; MD, USC 1976; JD, UCLA 1984; lic. physician & surgeon, Calif. BMQA 1977; admitted Calif. State Bar 1984. Career: Emergency Room physician 1977-81; extern extern to Hon. Arthur Alarcon, judge Ninth Federal Circuit Ct. of Appeals, summer 1982; law clk. Irell and Manella, Century City summer 1983; founder, mng. ptnr. The Canfield Group, 1984–; awards: Governor's Scholar (awarded by Gov. Ronald Reagan) 1970, Order of the Coif 1984; Democrat; Jewish. Ofc: The Canfield Group, 1466 So. Canfield Ave., Los Angeles 90035

SCHEINROCK, HERBERT MORRIS, business owner; b. Sept. 11, 1918, Chgo.; s. Nathan and Bessie (Boren) S.; m. Helen, Mar. 2, 1941; children: Nathan b. 1947, Jeffrey b. 1951; edn: Northwestern Univ. 1938-40; elec., I.B.E.W. Washburn Trade Sch. 1940-42; Calif. lic. Electrical Contr. (C-10) 1952. Career: elect. contr., Los Angeles, 1952-72; v.p./founder Quality Fin. Co., L.A. 1960; hotelier, Palm Springs 1973-77; owner Schweitzer's Dept. Store, Coachella 1975–; honors: Palm Springs Ambassadors Membshp. Man of the Year (1973-74), P.S. CofC Life Amb. Award, Hotel Com. pres. (1974-75); civic: United Way of the Desert, Am. Cancer Soc. (bd.), Experience Inc. of P.S. (charter pres. 1974-75), Elks; volunteer Bob Hope Golf Classic 5 yrs.; rec: rosarian, community svc. Ofc: Schweitzer's Dept. Store 1544 Sixth St Coachella 92236

SCHELL, PAUL HENRY, engineer; b. Aug. 10, 1907, Berkeley; s. Henry John and Minie Rose (Beuttel) S.; m. Addene Huffman, Aug. 31, 1930; m. 2d. Miriam Polson, Oct. 2, 1971; children: Carolyn b. 1932, George b. 1934, Charles b. 1938, John b. 1939; edn: Fresno State Coll. 1926-30, ext. courses 1947-49; Reg. Profl. Civil Engr., Calif. (1948), Cert. Fallout Shelter Analyst, DOD, Office of Civil Def. (1964). Career: asst. civil engring. instr., lab., Fresno State Coll. 1928-29; draftsman Calif. Dept. of Public Works Div. Hwys. Dist. 6, Fresno 1929-32, rose through the ranks to jr. hwy. engr., chief of party, estimator Specifications Planning 1932-42, asst. hwy. engr., asst. dist. traffic engr. 1942-44, acting dist. traffic engr. 1944-45, resident engr. Electrical Contracts 1945-48, assoc. hwy. engr, design and constrn. engr. Elec. Projects 1948-53, resident engr. on Freelocy and other projects 1953-59, adminstrn. design engr. 1959-65, advance planning project engr. 1965-71, ret.; designed first complete Traffic Actuated System on Hwy 41 (Blackstone Ave) City of Fresno and Hwy 99 City of Bakersfield (1947); designer/contr. 3-level residence 1977-80; awards: 4H Silver Cloverleaf for 5-year leadership in Fresno Co. 4H Club, USDA and Univ. Calif. (1956), recogn. for 25 years faithful public service, Gov. Goodwin J. Knight and Frank B. Durkee, Dir. Pub. Works (1954), recogn. for 40-year service, Gov. Ronald Reagan and James A. Moe, Dir. Pub. Works (1969), recogn. 42 years service, R.J. Datel, State Hwy. Engr. (1971); mem. Profl. Engrs. in Calif. Govt. (life), Calif. State Employees Credit Union (Credit Com. 1970-71), Calif. Farm Bureau; mem., chmn. Fresno Civic Chorus 1946-47, 4H leader 1951-57, NRA 1932-86; chmn. adminstrv. bd. Methodist Ch. 1968-69; Republican; Methodist (trustee); rec: painting, photog., vocal music. Res: 36116 Lodge Rd Tollhouse 93667

SCHELLHASE, ROBERT P., aerospace executive; b. Dec. 4, 1947, Youngstown, Ohio; s. Paul H. and Dorothy E. (Shirk) S.; m. Marcia K. LaPointe, June 13, 1971; children: Scott b. 1974, Korina b. 1977; edn: BA, Capital Univ. 1971. Career: senior systems engr. RCA Atcro Electronics, El Segundo 1976-79; pgm. mgr. advanced pgms. Aerojet Electro Systems Co., Azusa 1979-85, mgr. bus. devel., adv. pgms. & tech. 1985–; lectr. on space and space usage, ABC Sch Dist. mem: Air Force Assn., Boy Scouts of Am., School Site Council (Gonzalves Elem.), Gifted & Talented Edn. Council (ABC Sch. Dist.), Park League (coach, baseball, soccer); mil: capt. USAF 1971-76; Lutheran; rec: sports, education pgms. for gifted minors. Res: 17511 Vierra Ave. Cerritos 90701 Ofc: Aerojet Electro Systems Co., P.O. Box 296 Azusa 91702

SCHENKENBERGER, ROY WILMER, investor; b. July 5, 1930, Temvik, No. Dakota; s. Otto and Louise (Schmidt) S.; m. Nancy Jean Hahn, Feb. 14, 1976; children: Roy Joseph, b. 1976; Stephen Cal, b. 1980; Timothy Don, b. 1982; edn: AA, No, Idaho Jr. Coll. 1956; BA, cum laude, Harvard Coll. 1958. Career: real estate appraiser, trainee, California Bank, Los Angeles 1959; asst. cashier United Calif. Bank, Los Angeles 1963; asst. v.p. UCB New Branch Locations, L.A. 1964; v.p.- dept. hd. corp. facilities UCB L.A. Hdqtrs. 1970; exec. v.p. Hon Development Co., Laguna Hills 1973; currently, owner/ pres. Saddleback Valley Land co., So. Laguna; dir. f Envicom, Calabasas; former mem. Bldg. Owners and Mgrs. Assn., Los Angeles; honors: pres. Phi Theta Kappa, No. Idaho Jr. Coll. 1956; mem: Harvard Club of Orange Co.; So. Calif. Bldg. Ind. Assn.; The Californians; Vision of Faith Renewal Inc. (pres.); Republican; Protestant; rec: travel, hiking, photog. Address: 32732 Seven Seas Dr., South Laguna 92677

SCHERER, ROGER CLYDE, manufacturing engineer; b. Apr. 7, 1942, Norristown, Pa.; s. Wayne Robert and Grace Merium (Geiger) S.; m. Stephani Jean, July 7, 1984; children: (by previous marriage) Roger Scott b. 1965, Tracey Anne b. 1967, Wayne Robert, II b. 1970, (by wife's previous marriage, nee Hinojos): Victor Tod b. 1971, Scott Michael b. 1976; edn: BSBA, Calif. State Polytechnic Univ., Pomona 1964; MA voc. edn., CSU Los Angeles 1975; postgrad. work in edn., Pepperdine Univ. 1975-78; Calif. lic. Contr. (1978), journeyman molding tech. (1984). Career: prodn. supt. Dolco Pkg. Corp. 1969-78; gen. mgr. ops. A & B Luminous Ceilings 1978-79; prof. engring. Cal Poly, Pomona 1979-83; mfg. engr. and project adminstr. Cal Mold Inc. 1983-85; mfg. engring. mgr. Ethyl Molded Products, Pomona Div., 1985–; cons./coord. State sponsored Plastics and Moldmaking Apprenticeships, 1981–; owner Scherer Engring., 1978–; honors: George Huisman Meml. Award for Excellence in Plastics Composites (1976), Soc. Plastic Engrs. outstanding service award for PACTEC VIII (1985); sr. mem. Soc. Mfg. Engrs. (Robotics Sect.; S.P.E. pres. 1986-87, newsletter assoc. ed. 1981-82), sr. mem. Soc. Plastic Engrs.; invention: Mixing Nozzle for Extruder (pat. pend.) 1973; publ: Hist. Devel. of Regional Vocational Programs in State of Calif. 1960-75 (pub. 1975);

Republican; Roman Catholic; rec: build robots, design & bld. drag boats. Res: 7383 Lemonwood Pl Rancho Cucamonga 91730 Ofc: Ethyl Molded Products 2655 Pine St Pomona 91767

SCHIFFERMAN, ROBERT PHIL, superior court judge; b. Sept. 3, 1927, Los Angeles; s. Arthur Edmund and Esther Alice (Sullivan) S.; m. Virginia, Dec. 29, 1957; children: Reed b. 1955, Diane b. 1961; edn: AA, Glendale Coll. 1946; AB, Stanford Univ. 1949, JD and LLB, 1951; admitted Calif. State Bar 1952, US Dist. Ct. (Cent. Dist. Calif.) 1952, US Ct. of Appeals (9th Cir.) 1953, Supreme Ct. of US 1969. Career: practiced law in Los Angeles 1952-73 in firms of Schifferman & Schifferman, Whyte & Schifferman, as a sole practicitioner, and as assoc. firm Nicholas, Kollins, Myers, D'Angelo & Givens; apptd. judge superior ct., County of Los Angeles 1973, re-elected 1974, 1980–; awards: Zonta Club scholarship adv. Spanish studies, Nat. Univ. of Mexico; Occidental Coll. scholarship; Charles A. Beardsley Law Scholarship 1949-51; honors: Phi Beta Kappa, Order of the Coif, Alpha Gamma Sigma Nat. Scholarship Soc., bd. of editors, and bd. revising eds. Stanford Law Rev. 1949-51, appreciation, CEB Pgm., State Bar of Calif., named Trial Judge of Year 1980, LA Trial Lawyers Assn.; mem: Fellow The Am. Coll. of Probate Counsel, ABA, Los Angeles County Bar Assn., Phi Alpha Delta Law Frat., Am. Judicature Soc., Christian Legal Soc.; author num. chaps. in Calif. Practice Handbooks, articles in law journals; Republican; Presbyterian (Elder); rec: Spanish lang., piano. Res: Flintridge Ofc: 600 E Broadway Glendale 91206

SCHILLER, ANITA ROSENBAUM, librarian; b. June 16, 1926, NYC; d. Aaron and Helen (Camnitz) R.; m. Herbert I. Schiller, Nov. 5, 1946; children: Daniel T., P. Zachary; edn: BA, New York Univ. 1949; MLS, Pratt Inst. 1959. Career: reference librarian National Indsl. Conf. Bd. 1960-61; instr. Univ. of Ill. Grad. Sch. Bus. Admin. 1961-62; reference librarian Pratt Inst. 1962-63; successively research asst., research assoc., research asst. prof. Univ. of Ill. Library Research Ctr. 1964-70; reference librarian, bibliographer UC San Diego 1970–; Ralph R. Shaw vis. scholar Rutgers Univ. 1978; honors: Fellow Council Library Resources 1976-77; mem. Am. Libary Assn.; publs: contbr. articles to profl. publs.; ed., Aware columns, Am. Libraries 1971-72; edl. bds. profl. journs. Res: 7109 Monte Vista St. La Jolla 92037 Ofc: Central Univ. Library, Univ. of Calif., San Diego 92093

SCHILLO, FRANCIS XAVIER, financial planning co. president; b. Jan. 3, 1934, Pittsburgh, Penn.; s. Eugene Emanuel and Frances Helen (McCraley) S.; m. Marion Travers, May 3, 1958; children: Edward b. 1960, Daniel b. 1961, Susan b. 1962, Patricia 1964; edn: BS, Univ. of Notre Dame 1955; MBA, Univ. of Dayton 1969; Chartered Life Underwriter; Securities Lic., NASD; Realtor, Conejo Valley Bd.; Broker. Career: pres. Schillo Financial Co. Inc., Westlake Village; co-gen. ptr. Columbia Financial Products; mayor pro tempore, City of Thousand Oaks; honors: 1st Annual Humanitarian Award, Thousand Oaks CofC 1979; mem: Ventura Co. Estate Plnng. Council (pres. 1981), Internat. Assn. of Fin. Plnnrs. (founding mem. Ventura Co. chpt.), Million Dollar Round Table, San Fernando Life Underwriters, Am. Soc. of CLUs, Manna Food Bank (pres. 1974-79), Many Mansions Inc. (pres. 1979-), Gen. Plan Review Com. (Thousand Oaks), So. Calif. Assn. of Non-Profits for Housing (pres. 191-), Thousand Oaks Rotary; mil: sgt. US Army Signal Corps, Cryptography; Republican; Catholic; rec: jogging travel. Res: 91 Dombey Circle Thousand Oaks 91360 Ofc: Schillo Financial Co. Inc., 5743 Corsa Ave. Ste. 205 Westlake Village 91362

SCHINDLER, ELISABETH HILMA, real estate broker; b. Sept. 9, 1924, Harnosand, Sweden; d. Arvid Carl and Hilma (Norberg) Lofroth; m. Frank Schindler, Mar. 23, 1957; children: Margaret Elizabeth, Michael Frank; edn: bus., Palmans Handelsinstitut Business Sweden; Realtors Inst. of Calif. Career: broker/owner Schindler Real Estate, Torrance; mem. Calif. Assn. of Realtors, Torrance Lomita Carson Bd. of Realtors, Swedish Womens Ednl. Assn. Internat. Inc., Vasa Order of Am.; Rel. Sci.; rec: travel. Res: 2620 W. 226th St Torrance 90505 Ofc: Schindler Real Estate, 2244 W. Sepulveda Blvd Torrance 90501

SCHINDLER, MARILYN BOWES, lamp distributing co. president; b. Feb. 20, 1927, Cleveland, Ohio; d. John and Dorothy Almeda (Bowes) Frederick; children: William b. 1950, David b. 1952, Libby b. 1954, Thomas b. 1956; edn: BS econs., Univ. Pa. 1950; Grad. Sch. of Mktg. Case-Western Reserve 1960-61. Career: independent lighting contr., sales agent; pres./CEO Special Lamp Distbrs. Redwood City; mem: Univ. Pa. Gen. Alumni Soc., Nat. Orgn. Women (bd. dirs. Palo Alto), Am. Assn. Univ. Women; Republican; Protestant; rec: piano, writing. Ofc: Special Lamp Distributing 777 2nd Ave Redwood City 94063

SCHIRMER, JOHN RAYMOND, printer, investor; b. June 28, 1910, Miles City, Mont.; s. John Valentine and Mary Ellen (Danaher) S.; m. Lois Steverson, Dec. 21, 1961; edn: BA, Univ. Wash. Seattle 1941; tchg. cert., Univ. Montana Billings 1936; FCC lic., US Maritime Commn., Boston, Mass. 1943; printing cert., Calif. Comm. Coll. 1953. Career: factory sales rep., Liggett & Myers Tobacco Co., Billings, Mont. 1932-34; public sch. educator, Mont. Dept. of Edn. Klein & Big Horn Counties 1936-41; welder Seattle-Tacoma Shipbuilders, Seattle 1942-43; chief radio ofcr. US Maritime Commn., Pacific Ocean Theater 1942-46; equip. engr. Western Elec. Co., Cicero, Ill. 1946-51; journeyman printer Los Angeles Times 1953-75; independent financial investor assoc. with Lincoln Home Loans, Union Home Loan Mort. Co. and Property Mort. Co., L.A. area 1975–; mil: pvt. US Army 76th Field Arty. Citizens Mil. Tng. Corps, Ft. Russell, Cheyenne, Wyo. 1928; pvt. Montana Nat. Guard 1936-37; chief radio USN 1942; US Maritime Commn., Gallups Island, Mass., Pacific

Ocean Theater 1942-47; Protestant; rec: wildlife, volunteer work, landscaping, reading. Res: 8501 E Drayer Ln South San Gabriel 91770-4209 Ofc: Los Angeles Times Mirror Los Angeles 90053

SCHLUTER, DONALD FLETCHER, gunsmith; b. Dec. 19, 1948, Newport, R.I.; s. Milford Ernest and Jeanne (Ogilvie) S.; edn: Grossmont Jr. Coll. 1967-70; electro-mech. drafting, South Bay Trade Sch. 1970-71; reg. gunsmith, BATF 1985. Career: newspaper boy San Diego Unio & Tribune, El Cajon 1962-63; gunsmith Krasne's Gunshop 1975-76; owner Schluter's Gunsmithing & Sales, San Diego 1976–; small bus. liason to Inventors Workshop Internat. Edn. Foun. 1985-86; mem: Nat. Rifle Assn. (life), Calif. Pistol & Rifle Assn., Calif. State Sheriff's Assn. (assoc., charter), Republican Pres. Task Force trustee (charter), Safari Club Internat. (field mem.), Inventors Workshop Internat. Edn. Found., US Senatorial Club, No. Am. Hunting Club (charter); Republican; rec: hunting, equestrian, fishing. Ofc: S.G.& S., 568 6th Ave. San Diego 92101

SCHMIDKONZ, NED ROBERT, recreation program executive; b. Oct. 7, 1952, Chgo.; s. Theodore Henry and Fern Elsie (Eggert) S.; m. Jeanette Horvat, Aug. 18, 1979; 1 dau. Nicole Marie b. 1985; edn: AA, highest honors, Monterey Penin. Coll. 1978; BS, CSU San Jose 1980; Calif. cred. in recreation adminstrn. 1980. Career: Fort Ord facility mgr., Sports & Athletic Tng. Branch 1976-80, pgm. asst. Outdoor Rec., 1980-83; adminstrv. intern Montern County Parks Dept., Salinas 190; pgm. dir. Presidio of Monterey Rec. Ctr., Monterey 1983–; honors: Dean's list (1978-80), Phi Kappa Phi (1980), 1st Place FORSCOM Program (1985); mem. Calif. Parks & Rec. Assn. 1979-82, Nat. Rec. & Parks Assn., Armed Forces Rec. Soc.; civic: Monterey Co. Spl. Olympics (Master of Ceremonies 1980); mil: sp4 US Army 1972-74; Catholic; rec: travel, tennis, theatre. Res: 340 Elba Cir Marina 93933 Ofc: Presidio Recreation Center Bldg 517, Presidio of Monterey 93944

SCHMIDT, PAUL KEENEY, chiropractor; b. June 7, 1952, Detroit, Mich.; s. John James and Charlotte (Chen) S.; m. Jacqueline Elizabeth, July 6, 1985; edn: BA, Oakland Univ., Rochester, Mich. 1973, grad. pgm. 1974; DC, magna cum laude, Palmer Coll. of Chiropractic 1977; Diplomate Nat. Board of Chiro. Examiners, bd. certified Am. Board of Chiropractic Orthopedists; state lic. DC, Mich. (1977), Calif. (1978), certified Orthopedics and Disability Evaluation (1985). Career: faculty Palmer Coll. of Chiro. Dept. Physiology & Chem. 1976-78; assoc. dir. Gibson Chiropractic Office, Sacramento 1978-84; owner/ dir. Schmidt Chiropractic, Sacto. 1984–; cons. indsl. injuries Pacific Bell, Gibson Mgmt.; honors: Senate Resolution, State of Calif. (3/84); mem: Am. Council Chiro. Orthopedics, Council Chiro. Orthopedics, Am. Chiro. Assn., Internat. Chiro. Assn.; civic: annual sponsor Special Olympics, Chiro. Info. Bureau, Chiro-cubs softball team; publs: presentation to NSF/ Oakland Univ. Dept. of Physiol. Graduate Sch. (7/74); rec: outdoorsman. Ofc: Schmidt Chiropractic 5301 Madison Ave Ste 301 Sacramento 95841

SCHMIDT, ROY G., architect; b. May 5, 1926, Budapest, Hungary, nat. US cit. 1962; s. Julio and Anna (Gabriel) S.; m. Eva Six, July 4, 1955; 1 dau. Linda Maria b. 1967; edn: Joseph Nador Univ. 1944-51; reg. architect Calif. 1976. Career: archtl. designer Padarewsky & Dean Archs. San Diego 1957-60; designer var. archtl. ofcs. L.A. area 1961-67; proj. mgr. William L. Pereira Assn. 1968-80, pres., CEO, chmn. 1980–; archtl. & constrn. cons. R.G. Assocs. 1951–; seminar instr.; mem: Newcomen Soc. of US 1984-, Balboa Bay Club (Newport Beach); Republican; Catholic; rec: photog., darkroom, audio-video. Ofc: Pereira Assocs. 6100 Wilshire Blvd Los Angeles 90036

SCHMIDT, S. PAUL, manufacturing manager; b. Aug. 24, 1938, Pike Co., Ind.; s. Carl August and Anna Hazel (Mize) S.; m. Patricia R. (Atwood) Marshall, Mar. 23, 1985; children: (by prev. marriage) Nancy b. 1953, Patricia b. 1957, Robin b. 1962, (by wife's prev. marriage) Diane b. 1952, Susan b. 1953, Keith b. 1955, Steve b. 1957; edn: AA in electronics engring. 1958; courses in bus. admin. & mech. engring. var. colls., num. tech. seminars. Career: civilian electronics instr. officer classes Ft. Bliss, Tx. 1959-60; self empl. farmer 200 acre grain and livestock farm, Petersburg, Ind. 1960-63; sr. quality assurance eng. tech. Consol. Electrodynamics Corp., Monrovia, Calif. 1963-66; lead electronics techn. United Control Corp., Redmond, Wash. 1966-67, co. acquired by Sundstrand Data Control, mfg. supvr., then design engr. Transducer Div. Sundstrand 1967-70; prodn. control mgr. Integrated Circuits Inc., Bellevue, Wash. 1970-73; business mgr./ptnr. Ace Ornamental Iron, Woodinville, Wash. 1973-74; design engr., mfg. engr. Sundstrand Data Control, Redmond 1974-75, process/ mfg. engring. engr. 1975-83, constrn. mgr., then mfg. mgr. Sundstrand Optical Technologies Inc., Newbury Park, Calif. 1984–; mem: Soc. of Mfg. Engrs., Am. Soc. for Quality Control, Am. Prodn. and Inventory Control Soc., Assn. of Electronic Mfrs., Internat. Soc. of Hybrid Mfrs., Mensa. Res: 885 Congressional Rd Simi Valley 93065

SCHMIDT, TERRY LANE, company executive; b. Nov. 28, 1943, Chgo.; s. Leroy C. and Eunice M. (Peacock) S.; m. Nancy Lee Anthony; children: Christie Anne b. 1974, Terry Lane II b. 1976; edn: BS, Bowling Green State Univ. 1965; MBA, Geo. Washington Univ. 1971. Career: resident hosp. adminstrn., Univ. Pittsburgh Med. Ctr. VA Hosp. 1968-69; adminstrv. asst. Mt. Sinai Med. Ctr. NYC 1969-70; asst. dir. Health Facilities Planning Council of Metropolitan Wash. DC 1970-71; asst. dir. dept. of gov. rels. Am. Med. Assn., Wash. DC 1971-74; pres. Terry L. Schmidt, Inc., Health Care Reimbursement Cons., Wash. DC and San Diego 1974–; pres. Medical Consultants Inc. 1983-84; v.p. Crisis Communications Corp. Ltd. 1982–; pres. Wash. Actions on Health 1975-78l; ptnr. Wash. Counsel Med. & Health 1979-81; pres. Ambulance Corp. of Am. 1985-; chmn. San Diego Venture Group 1984-; bd. dirs.

Assn. of Venture Capital Clubs 1985-; lectr. Dept. of Health Care Adminstrn., Geo. Wash. Univ. 1969-71, asst. prof. 1971–; asst. prof. Nat. Naval Sch. of Health Care Adminstrn. 1971-80; mem. faculty Civil Svc. Commn. Legislative Institutes 1972-80; mem. adv. com. on Ambulatory Care Stds. Joint Commn. on Accreditation of Hosps. 1971-72; mem: Fellow Am. Public Health Assn., Am. Hosp. Assn., Med. Group Mgmt. Assn., Assn. of Am. Med. Colls., Group Health Assn. of Am., Hosp. Fin. Mgmt. Assn., Assn. of Health Svcs. Research, Emerg. Med. Mgmt. Assn., Assn. of State Colls. & Univ. Health Tng. Insts., Alpha Phi Omega (chpt. pres. 1967-70, secty.-treas. alumni assn. 1968-81), Nat. Eye Found. (bd. dirs. 1976-78); clubs: Geo. Wash. Univ., Nat. Democratic (life), Nat. Republican (life); author: Legislative Process and the Key Participants (1976), Directory of Federal Health Resources and Services for the Disadvantaged (1976), Health Care Reimbursement: A Glossary (1983); contbr. num. articles to profl. jours. Ofc: Terry L. Schmidt Inc., 8950 Villa La Jolla Dr Ste 1200 La Jolla 92037

SCHMITT, CAROLYN SUE, vocational counselor; b. Dec. 19, 1940, Charleston, W.V.; d. Charles Lee and Louise Mary (DeHainaut) Jarrett; m. Carveth J. R. Schmitt, May 14, 1954; edn: BS in bus. adm., Univ. Charleston, Morris Harvey Coll. 1962; dip. human svcs. UC Riverside Ext. 1971; BS, liberal studies, Univ. NY, Albany 1978; BA, soc. sci., Edison State Coll., Trenton, NJ 1979; MA, edn./manpower adm., Univ. Redlands 1974; tchg. creds: Calif. Comm. Coll. instr. (1979), psychol. (1979), counseling (1979), supv. (1979), Calif. Comm. Personnel Wkr. cred. (1979). Career: adminstrv. asst. TRW Inc., Def. & Space Sys., San Berdo. 1962-63; ins. dept. So. Calif. Mortgage & Loan Corp., San Berdo. 1963-66; empl. counselor Calif. State Empl. Devel. Dept., 1966-78; instr. Pacific Am. Inst./Whitehead Coll., Redlands 1979; sr. voc. supv. rehab. counselor Westside Counseling Center, San Berdo. 1979-80; voc. counselor pvt. practice, Rialto 1980-84; placement splst. Goodwill Ind. of Inland Counties Inc., San Berdo. 1984-85; voc. rehab. counselor/placement splst. Voc-Aid, Inc., Encino 1985-86; employment splst. Lutheran Soc. Services of So. Calif., San Berdo. 1986–; honors: recogn. Westside Counseling Ctr. (1980), listed num. biographical dictionaries; mem: Calif. Personnel & Guidance Assn., Calif. Career Guidance Assn., Calif. Rehab. Counselor Assn., Internat. Assn. of Personnel Empls. (chpt. vp 1970); Univ. of Redlands Fellows; Valley Prospectors, Rosicrucian AMORC, Phi Kappa Kappa Sor., Nat. Travel Club, Fontana Tour Club, M & M Tour Club, Am. Philatelic Soc., Arrowhead Stamp Club, Am. Topical Assn. (life), alumni assns: SUNY, Edison State Coll., Univ. of Charleston, Univ. of Redlands; Republican; rec: philately, badminton, hiking. Res: 538 N. Pampas Ave Rialto 92376 Ofc: Lutheran Social Services of So. Calif. 741 W Virginia St San Bernardino 92405

SCHMITT, CARVETH JOSEPH RODNEY, corporate credit manager; b. Sept. 10, 1934, Manitowoc, Wisc.; s. Clarence Charles and Thelma June (White) S.; m. Carolyn Sue Jarrett, May 14, 1965; edn: dip. bus. adm. & acctg., Skadron Coll. of Bus., San Bernardino 1959; AA, bus. mgmt., San Bernardino Valley Coll. 1962; BS in bus. adm., UC Riverside 1970; BS, liberal studies, Univ. of NY, Albany 1977; BA, soc. sci., Edison State Coll., Trenton, NJ 1978; MA, edn./manpower adm., Univ. Redlands 1975; diploma human svcs., UC Riverside ext. 1977; cert. tchr., community coll. counselor and personnel worker, Calif. Career: acct. Barnum & Flagg Co., San Bernardino, 1959-70; credit mgr. Stationers Corp., 1970-77, office mgr./credit mgr. 1977-83; registered rep., ins. agt. (part-time), Inland Amer. Securities, Inc., 1966-70, reg. rep. Parker-Jackson & Co., 1970-73, LeBarron Securities, Inc., 1974; internal auditor Stockwell & Binney Office Products Centers, 1983-85, corp. credit mgr. 1985–; honors: listed, Who's Who in the West, num. biog. dictionaries; mem: Colo., N.W., Nev. mining assns.; Gold Prospectors Assn. of Am. (life mem.), Valley Prospectors, Nat. Travel Club, Fontana Tour Club, M & M Tour Club, Univ. of Redlands Fellows, Am. Philatelic Soc., Arrowhead Stamp Club, Nat. Rifle Assn. (life), Nat. Geog. Soc., Am. Legion, Am. Assn. Retired Persons, Rosicrucian Order AMORC, Masons; Univ. NY, Edison State Coll., Univ. of Redlands alumni assns.; mil: personnel splst. USAF 1954-58, GCM, Nat. Def. medal; Republican; rec: collector first editions, rock collector. Res: 538 N. Pampas Ave Rialto 92376 Ofc: Stockwell & Binney Office Products Centers, 420 S. E St, POB 5219, San Bernardino 92412

SCHMITT, RICHARD GEORGE, manufacturing co. manager; b. June 18, 1948, St. Cloud, Minn.; s. George William and Viola Teresa (Mechenich) S.; m. Ligia Pereira, Aug. 29, 1970; children: Christopher b. 1972, Scott b. 1975; edn: BS, Ind. Eng., Gen. Motors Inst. 1971. Career: General Motors Assembly Div., Fremont 1966-78, Oklahoma City 1978-80; coop. engring. stu. 1966-71; indsl. engr. methods 1971-73; prod. supvr. paint 1973; indsl. engr. material handling 1973-78; senior indsl. engr. trim 1978-80; mgr. indsl. engring. Shugart Assn., Sunnyvale 1980; mgr. mfg. tech. Magnex Corp., San Jose 1981, mgr. Head Mfg. 1982; indsl. engring. mgr. Apple Computer, San Jose 1983, Facilities mgr. Apple Computer, Fremont 1984, mgr. Indsl. Engring. 1985; mgr. Robotics & Automation 1986; recipient, Lion's Club Scholarship; mem: Am. Inst. of Indsl. Engrs. (senior), Soc. of Mfg. Engrs. (senior), YMCA Indian Guides (chief of tribe 1978-82), Boy Scouts of Am. (Webelos den leader 1985-86, asst. scoutmaster 1986), soccer coach; Catholic; rec: electrical mechanic repair, hunting, swimming. Res: 1963 Wave Pl. San Jose 95133 Ofc: Apple Computer, 48105 Warm Springs Blvd. Fremont 94539

SCHMITZ, EUGENE GERARD, consulting firm president; b. Sept. 17, 1929, Brackenridge, Pa.; s. Wienand Gerard and Florence Marie (Grimm) S.; m. Anna May Lee, May 3, 1952; children: Joyce b. 1953, Michael b. 1956, Carol b. 1957, John b. 1959, John b. 1961; edn: BSME (equiv) Ariz. St. Univ. 1959-63, Phoenix Coll. 1947-48; Reg. Profl. Engr., Calif. Career: Field Enterprises Ednl. Corp., Phoenix 1955-59; dist. sales mgr., self empl. freelance design 1959-61; design engr. Motorola Inc., Govt. Electronics Div., Scottsdale, Az. 1961-67; project engr./supvr., methods engr. Philco-Ford Corp., Space &: Reentry Sys. Div., Palo Alto 1967-70; pgm. adminstr./sr. mfg. engr. Memorex Equip. Grp., Santa Clara 1970-71; res. plant mgr. Philco-Ford Corp., Western Dev. Labs., Palo Alto, Remote Assy Op. 1971-72; cons. engr. FMC Corp., Def. Tech. Lab, Santa Clara 1972-73 and Ordnance Engr. Div., San Jose 1973-75; deputy dir. engring. and sr. staff consulting engr. Stetter Assn. Inc., Palo Alto 1975-80; pres./chief engr. Schmitz Engr. Assocs., San Jose 1980–; project engr. FMC Corp. Ordnance Div. Engr. 1982-; mem: Nat. Soc. of Profl. Engrs. (sr. mem. 1979), Profl. Engrs. in Pvt. Practice, Soc. Mfg. Engrs. (sr. mem. 1970), Am. Inst. of Indsl. Engr. (sr. mem. 1981); publs: over 200 major proposals for US & fgn. corps.; Motorola Govt. Electr. Div. Drafting Manual (1962 ed.); Philco-Ford, Space & Re-Entry Sys. Div. Mfg. and Process Stds.; mil: US Army 1948-55, Korean Service, GCM, Occup. Japan, Occup. Germany medals, Presdtl. and Korean Pres. Unit Citations; Republican; rec: gourmet cooking, camping, carpentry, automotive repair. Address: Schmitz Engr. Assocs. 3061 Vesuvius Ln. San Jose 95132

SCHMUTZER, ROBERT LOUIS, photographer, lighting director; b. Feb. 13, 1962, Fontana; s. Henry Leonard and Josephine Rita (Ducato) S.; edn: Chaffey Comm. Coll. 1980-83. Career: asst. lab. tech. Chaffey Coll. Photography Dept., Alta Loma 1981-84; exhib. preparitor Rex W. Wignall Museum/Gallery, 1984-85; intern Station KIHS-TV 46, Ontario 1984-85; lab. tech. and bio-medical photog. Inland Media Corp., Yucaipa 1985-86; freelance photog. (aerial, studio, photo-micrography, bio-medical, fashion, public relation, photo-journ.), So. Calif. area, 198–; ofcl. conf. photog. Soc. of Photographic Edn. 1984 Nat. Conf.; honors: appreciation Chaffey Coll. Photog. Dept. (1983), 1st. pl. awards, Commercial, Abstract, Chaffey Coll. Photo. Competition (1983), statewide All Media Invitational Exhib., Sacto. (3/81); mem. Chaffey Comm. Coll. Photog. Club (pres. 1982-83); civic: Rex W. Wignall Mus./Gal. (vol.), Calif. Mus. of Photog. (vol.), San Bernardino and Riverside Counties Blood Bank (4 gal. club); Republican; Catholic. Address: Fontana 92336

SCHNEIDER, GERALD MARVIN, financial services marketing executive; b. May 30, 1939, Milwaukee, Wisc.; s. Paul Alfred and Loretta Louise (Ludwig) S.; m. Lucille, Aug. 17, 1963; chilren: Kim b. 1969, Bonnie b. 1973; edn: BSBA, Univ. of Wisc. 1965; CLU, Am. Coll. of Life Underwriters 1968; Fellow, Life Ofc. Mgmt. Assn. 1971. Career: asst. controller Time Ins. Co., Milwaukee, Wisc. 1968-73; asst. v.p. Penn. Life Ins. Co., Santa Monica 1973-79; v.p., controller Trans-Pacific & Exec. Fund Life Ins., Santa Monica 1975-79; owner agency 1979-83; regl. v.p. A.L. Williams, Duluth, Ga. 1983–; honors: Distng. Svc., FLMI Soc. of So. Calif. 1985; Golden Key Club, FLMI Soc. of So. Calif. 1986; mem: FLMI Soc. of So. Calif. (1st pres. 1975); mil: s/sgt. Wisc. Air Nat. Guard 1956-66; Republican; Lutheran; rec: classic cars, travel, tennis. Res: 28928 Allman St. Agoura Hills 91301

SCHNEIDER, WILLIAM JAMES, engineer; b. Apr. 17, 1930, Long Beach; s. Wm. James and Myurtle Elizabeth (Fisher) S.; m. Vecchio, Aug. 8, 1954; children: Brian b. 1961, Mary b. 1966; edn: B.Eng., USC 1952, M.Eng., 1958; JD, Loyola Univ. LA 1972. Reg. Profl. Engr. (EG115) Calif.; admitted US Patent Bar, Calif. State Bar. Career: project engr. US Naval Ordnance Test Station, 1952-62; project engr. Space and Radiation Instruments, JPL, 1962-67, 1982-84: developed Pulse Height Analyzer and Lunar Solar Wind Spectrometer for Apollo Sci. Pkg. and Sci. Data System for Mariner Mission to Mars (1964); senior engr. splst. Tasker Systems Div. Whittaker Corp., 1967-82: devel. and patented Digital RF Memory (DRMF provides the only known means for deception jamming of coherent radars, now in use in all modern electronic warfare systems); mgr. advanced devel. Design Engineering Labs., 1985–; mem: Assn. of Old Crows, IEEE; patents: Transistor Circuit Constrns. for Active Type Band-Pass Filters; Storage Sys. For High Frequency Signals; contbr. profl. reports sci. and tech. publs.; Roman Catholic. Address: 415 Herondo St Ste 301 Hermosa Beach 90254-4617 Ofc: Design Engineering Laboratories 2545 237th St Torrance 90505

SCHNEIER, MARC MALVIN, law publication editor; b. Feb. 18, 1955, New Haven, Conn.; s. Bernard and Rehla (Freilich) S.; edn: AB, UC Berkeley 1977; JD, UC Davis 1981; admitted Calif. State Bar 1981. Career: atty law firm David Gold S.F. 1981-83; editor Medical Liability Reporter (litigation research grp.) 1983-84, Construction Litigation Reporter 1983–; cons. wrongful discharge law; honors: Bureau of Nat. Affairs Award 1981, Phi Beta Kappa 1977; mem: Am. Bar Assn., Royal Scottish Dance Soc. S.F. (performance dancer, bd. mem., treas.) 1983-; publ: num. arts. in law jours.; Democrat; Jewish; rec: dancing, athletics. Res: 1235 Peralta Ave Berkeley 94706

SCHNEPPER, JOHN WILLIAM, surgeon; b. Dec. 7, 1921, Buenos Aires, Argentina; US citizen by birth; s. Otto E. and Myrtle J. (Rippey) S.; m. Velma Bontrager, Aug. 30, 1944; children: Dr. Judith (Greene) b. 1945, Dr. Rhonda (Hoag) b. 1949; edn: BA, Walla Walla Coll. 1943; MD, Loma Linda Univ. Sch. Med. 1945. Diplomate Am. Board of Surgery. Career: postgrad. tng. White Memorial and Lutheran Hosps., Los Angeles 1948-54; surgeon and medical dir. Manila Sanitarium Hosp., 1954-59, started postgrad. tchg. pgm. Manila Hosp., first to do successful heart surgery in Philippines (1955) and Taiwan (1957); pvt. practice medicine, specializing in surgery, Corona, Calif. 1959–; att. physician and clinic teaching, Loma Linda Univ. Hosp., and White Mem. Hosp.; chief of staff Corona Dist. Hosp. 1952-64; primary developer/ dir. Corona Community Hosp.; awards: Silver and Gold Heart, Taiwan Chinese Army; mem: AMA, Calif. Med. Assn., Fellow Am. Coll. Surgeons, Fellow

Internat. Coll. Surgeons; contbr. articles to profl. jours.; developed hybrid orchids, pub. orchid articles; mil: capt. US Army 1946-48, Okinawa; Republican; Seventh-day Adventist (Elder); rec: orchidist (past pres. local orchid soc.). Res: 1252 Paseo Grande Corona 91720 Ofc: 760 S Washburn 91720

SCHOCKLEY, WILLIAM BRADFORD, inventor, scientist; b. Feb. 13, 1910, London, Eng. (Am. parentage); s. Wm. Hillman and Cora May (Bradford) S.; m. Emmy Lanning, Nov. 23, 1955; children: Alison (Iannelli) b. 1945, Wm. Alden, b. 1942, Richard Condit, b. 1947; edn: BS, Calif. Inst. of Tech. 1932; PhD, MIT, 1936; ScD (hon.), Univ. of Penna. 1955; Rutgers Univ. 1956, Gustavus Adolphus Coll. 1963. Career: tech. staff Bell Tel. Labs., 1936-42; research sp. physicist, 1945-64; sci. adv., Policy Council, Jt. R&D Bd., 1947-49; dir. Transistor Physics Research, 1954-55; dir. Schockley Semiconductor Lab. of Beckman Instruments Inc. 1955-58; dir. Research Weapons Sys. Evaluation Group, Dept. of Def., 1954-55; pres. Shockley Transistor Corp., 1958-60; dir. Schockley Transistor Unit of Clevite Transistor, 1960-63; sp. lectr. Stanford Univ. 1958-63; Alexander M. Poniatoff prof. of engring. and applied sci., 1964-75; exec. cons. Bell Tel. Labs., 1965-75. Inventor junction transistor, holder over 90 US patents; research dir. Anti-Sub Warfare Opns. Group, USN, 1942-44; expt. cons. Ofc. Secty. of War, 1944-45, WWII. Honors: Medal for Merit, Secty. of War, 1946; Air Force Assn. Cit. of Hon. 1951; Liebmann Prize, I.R.E., 1952; Army Cert. of Appreciation 1953; Buckley Prize, Am. Phys. Soc. 1953; Comstock Award, Nat. Acad. of Scis. 1954; The Nobel Prize (physics) 1956; Wilheim Exner Medal, Austria 1963; Holley Medal, ASME Medal, 1963; CalTech Alumni distinguished service award 1966; Nat. Aerons. & Space Adminstrn. Cert. (Apollo 8), 1969; NASA pub. service group achievement award 1969; IEEE gold medal, 25th anniversary of Transistor, 1972; Nat. Inventors Hall of Fame 1974; honored by SEMI Fellowship estab. at MIT; IEEE Medal of Honor 1980, IEEE Centennial Medal and Certificate 1984. Mem: fellow, IEEE, Am. Acad. Arts & Scis. Adv. Panel, 1951-63; Air Force Sci. Adv. Bd. 1959-63; Nat. Acad. of Scis.; fellow Am. Physical Soc.; fellow IRE; Am. Inst. of Physics; Sigma Xi; Tau Beta Pi; clubs: Cosmos, University (Wash DC), Bohemian (S.F.); Res: 797 Esplanada Way Stanford 94305 Ofc: McC 202, Stanford University Stanford 94305

SCHOICHET, SANDOR ROSS, computer systems consultant; b. May 27, 1953, Los Angeles; s. Nathan L. and Muriel (Rosenberg) S.; m. Linda Christine Thorson, May 5, 1977; edn: EE, SM, MIT 1981; BA, philosophy and info. sci., UC Santa Cruz 1975; Cert. Sys. Profl. (1985) and Cert. in Data Processing (1976), ICCP. Career: engr. Burroughs Corp., Pasadena 1974-76; project engr. Dataproducts Corp., Woodland Hills 1976-77; grad. research asst. MIT Artificial Intelligence Lab., Cambridge, Mass. 1977-79; grad. research asst. MIT Lab. For Computer Science 1979-81; office sys. cons. Hammer & Co., Cambridge, Mass. 1981; senior cons. Data Architects Inc., San Francisco 1981-85, dir. telecomm. mktg. 1985–; honors: Sigma Xi, 1981; works: approx. 20 tech. research papers and industry mag. articles 1978-83; rec: camping, skiing, photog. Res: 1331 Masonic Ave. San Francisco 94117 Ofc: Data Architects Inc., 222 Sutter St. 5th Flr. San Francisco 94108

SCHONHERZ, KARYN MARIA, real estate broker; b. Aug. 24, 1946, Cleveland, Ohio; d. Edward Clarence and Ruth Adele (Malecha) Koryta; m. Bernard Schonherz, July 7, 1986; 1 dau, Kimberly b. 1970; edn: AA, Fashion Inst. of Tech. 1966; AA, Cerritos Coll. 1975; Broker Assoc., Calif. 1980. Career: asst. fashion buyer children's National Bellas Hess, NYC, NY 1966; fashion buyer ladies Frederick's of Hollywood, Hollywood 1968; sales assoc. Norwalk Realty, Norwalk 1973; sales assoc. Katella Realty, Anaheim Hills 1976; currently, broker assoc. Merrill Lynch Realty, Anaheim Hills; trainer new assocs. Merrill Lynch; honors: Top Office Producer (1979-82, 1984-85), 2d in co. production (1979, 81, 84), Top Listings Sold (1979, 81, 82); mem: Real Estate Cert. Inst., Leading Edge Soc., Inner Circle Soc., Hill & Canyon Municipal Advy. Com.; publs: monthly newsletter 1976-; rec: sewing, carpet craft, gardening. Ofc: Merrill Lynch, 5769-D Santa Ana Cyn. Anaheim 92807

SCHOPPA, ELROY, certified public accountant; b. Aug. 25, 1922, Vernon, Tx.; s. Eddie A. and Ida (Foerster) S.; m. Gail Martin, May 12, 1984; children: Karen b. 1961, Vickie b. 1964, (step): Veronica b. 1956, Vanessa b. 1961; edn: BBA, Texas Tech. Univ. 1943; MA, Mich. State Univ. 1950; Univ. of Texas Sch. of Law 1946-47; desig: CPA, Insurance Agt., Real Estate Broker, mem. NASD. Career: mem. faculty Texas Tech. Univ. 1943, Univ. of Tx. 1946-47, Mich. State Univ. 1947-50; auditor Gen. Motors Corp. 1950-56; dir. systems & procedure Fanstell Metallurgical Corp. 1956-59; gen. auditor Consol. Dynamics Corp. 1959-60; auditor, tax acctg. Beckman Inst. Inc., Fullerton 1960-70; pres. Elroy Schoppa Acctg. Corp., La Habra 1970–; treas. LDC, La Habra; mem: Alpha Phi Omega, Theta Xi, Phoenix Club, Calif. Soc. of CPA; civic: organizer/pres. 4H Club in H.S., Vernon, Tx.; advisor Junior Achievement, Waukegan, Ill. (1957-59); asst. coach football & basketball, Marynola, Colo. H.S.; coach of Am. Girls Sport Assn., La Habra, Ca. (3 yrs.); mil: lt.jg US Navy 1942-46, Pacific Area, USNR 1946-62; Republican; Lutheran; rec: hunting, fishing. Ofc: ESAC 801 E La Habra Blvd La Habra 90631

SCHORKEN, DOROTHY LOUISE, inventor/co. president; B. Jan. 23, 1932, San Pedro; d. Dick Edward (poet laureate of San Pedro, Calif.) and Katherine Lorrine (Davidson) Wolfe; m. Carl Schorken, Dec. 24, 1960; children: Sheri, b. 1963, Carl, b. 1965; edn: AA, Harbor Jr. Coll. 1952; BA, CSU Long Beach 1958; Calif. gen. tchg. credential 1984-88. Career: elem. sch. tchr. (sub.), Los Angeles Unified Sch. Dist., 1977-78; inventor/pres. Products Exceptionale (creative products for the future, Thousand Oaks 1979–; inventions incl. Device for Supporting Infants (US Patent, 1970); honors: first woman inventor honored on the Inventors' Mart TV Show (1973); exhibitor in First Internat. Inventors and New Products Exhibition, NY (1965); mem: Inventors Club of Am., World Assn. of Inventors and Researchers, Am. Entrepreneurs Assn., Internat. Entrepreneurs Assn., Salk Inst. of Biol. Studies, Louis Pasteur Clinic (Paris, Fr.), The Research Council of Scripps Clinic, and Research Found., La Jolla; civic: Boys Club of Am., Salesian Missions (New Rochelle, NY), Amvets, Internat. Fund for Animal Welfare (Yarmouth Port, Mass.), Nat. Humane Edn. Soc. (Leesburg, Va.), North Shore Animal League, The Statue of Liberty Ellis Is. Found., Am. & So. Calif. Bouvier des Flandres Club; inventions: device for supporting infants (US patent 1970), others incl. deluxe pooper scooper for dogs, kitty litter scooper for cats; Republican; Methodist; rec: music, theatre, art, fishing, hunting, travel. Address: Products Exceptionale, 2271 Northpark St Thousand Oaks 91362

SCHOTT, FREDERICK WILLIAM, professor of electrical engineering; b. Oct. 2, 1919, Phoenix, Ariz.; s. Wilhelm Edmund and Louise Albertina (Johnson) S.; m. Mary Peter, Apr. 14, 1946; 1 son, Christopher b. 1951; edn: AB, San Diego State Coll. 1940; Engr. (E.E.), Stanford Univ. 1943, PhD, 1948; Reg. Profl. Electrical Engr. (No.1346) Calif. 1948. Career: jr. engr. San Diego Gas & Electric Co., 1943-44; asst., assoc., full prof. elec. engring., UC Los Angeles 1948–; research engr. USN Electronics Lab. 1949-50, Hughes Aircraft 1956; sabbatical, Swiss Federal Inst. of Tech., Zurich 1957-58; cons. to several technical book publishing cos. 1976-; awards: University Scholar, Westinghouse Fellow, Stanford 1941-43; Tau Beta Pi; Outstanding teacher UCLA Sch. Engring. 1954, 56, 66; Alumni Award, San Diego State 1958; mem: IEEE, Am. Soc. for Engr. Edn.; publs: 25+ tech. papers, contbr. IEEE Jours.; mil: lt. jg US Navy 1944-46; Methodist. Res: 944 Lincoln Blvd Santa Monica 90403 Ofc: University of California Room 7732 Boelter Hall, Los Angeles 90024

SCHOTZ, GARY STEPHEN, civil engineer; b. Dec. 10, 1953, Syracuse, N.Y.; s. Wm. J. Schotz and Lucille F. (Schwartz); m. Leslie Boris, Sept. 25, 1977; edn: BS, SUNY Coll. Environ. Sci. & Forestry 1976; BS, Syracuse Univ. 1976; MSCE, Stanford Univ. 1977; Reg. Civil Engr., Calif. 1979. Career: project engr. Charles Pankow, Altadena 1977-78; project mgr. Olson Constrn., San Diego 1978-85; founder/pres. Quest Constrn. Engring. & Mgmt., Inc., San Diego 1985–; awards: NY State Regents Scholar (1972-76), engring. scholarships Syracuse Univ. (1972-73), Stanford Univ. (1976-77); mem. ASCE, ACI, AIA; rec: golf, ski, sailing, photog. Res: 2141 Steiger Ln Oceanside 92056 Ofc: Quest 5810 Miramar Rd Ste 210 San Diego 92121

SCHOULEMAN, SHIRLEY BETH, nursing home administrator; b. Dec. 30, 1947, Salt Lake City, Utah; d. Robert C. and Helen E. (Gleason) Huber; m. Cris A. Schouleman, Dec. 31, 1983; children: Dina b. 1968, Staci b. 1973; edn: Santa Monica Coll., Santa Ana Coll.; Lic. Nsg. Home Adminstr., Ore. (1981), Calif. (1984). Career: public rels. dir. Waterhorn, Inc. 1976-77; asst. adminstr. Playa Del Rey Convalescent Hosp. 1969-74, 1977-78, St. Edna Conv. Hosp. 1978-84; exec. adminstr. Birdhaven Christian Conv. Hosp. 1984-85; adminstr. Everhealth Manor of Norwalk, 2/85-9/85, Everhealth Manor of Bellflower, 1985–; mem: Calif. Assn. Health Facilities, Orange County Assn. Health Facilities (v.p. elect 1984; recipient 5 year appreciation award 1984), Screen Actors Guild, CofC, Visitor & Conv. Bureau, Hotel Sales & Mgmt., Nat. Assn. Female Execs., Beta Sigma Phi, Delta Y, Soroptomist; publs: Orange County AHF, Chapter News (1984); Republican; Christian; rec: boating, bowling, reading. Ofc: Everhealth Manor of Bellflower 16910 Woodruff Ave Bellflower 90706

SCHRAMBLING, WILLIAM EMMETT, accountant; b. June 12, 1947, Phoenix, Ariz.; s. William Leon and Patricia (Collins) S.; m. Alaine Carter, Dec. 8, 1984; children: Derrik b. 1969, William b. 1972; edn: AA, El Camino Coll. 1967; BS, USC 1970, CPA, 1973. Career: Arthur Andersen & Co. 1970-82; ptr. in charge of predecessor firm 1973-82; senior ptr. Schrambling & Chu CPAs, San Francisco 1982–; mem: Am. Inst. CPAs, Calif. Soc. CPAs, Nat. Assn. of Accts.; Democrat; Catholic; rec: fishing, old cars. Res: 1104 Via Media Lafayette 94549 Ofc: Schrambling & Chu, 1 Market Plaza, Spear Tower Ste 1619, San Francisco 94105

SCHRAMM, ARTHUR DANIEL, financial services co. executive; b. July 21, 1938, Cincinnati, Ohio; s. Arthur Daniel and Emma Laura (Clift) S.; m. Patricia M. Severi, Oct. 21, 1978; children: Pamela b. 1962, Michael b. 1965; edn: San Bernardino Valley Coll. 1976-78, Nat. Installment Banking Sch. Univ. of Colo. 1979, Pepperdine Univ. Key Executive Pgm. 1983. Career: branch rep. to mgr., Economy Savings & Loan, Cincinnati, Ohio 1959-64; mgr. Credithrift Financial Corp. offices in Napa and Carmichael, 1964-75; regl. vice pres. Morris Plan Co. of Calif., supvsg. branches in L.A., San Bernardino, and Riverside Counties, 1975-81; pres., CEO, founder and dir. Corona Thrift & Loan and Corona Credit Corp., 1982-84; v.p., secty. and dir. Corona Bancorp, dir. Southcoast Thrift & Loan, Southcoast Bancorp, and Southcoast Financial 1983-84; dir. Palm Springs Bancorp, Palm Springs Thrift & Loan, Oasis Finance; pres., CEO, founder & dir. Thrift Association Bancorp, Riverside Bancorp, Riverside Thrift & Loan, Raincross Finance 1985–; dir. Calif. Assn. Thrift & Loan 1985–; dir./ secty. Thrift Guaranty Corp. 1984–; cons. Intrastate Finl. Devel. Corp., Moreno Valley Thrift & Loan; mem: Rotary, Masons, past pres. Napa Active 20-30 Club; mil: sgt. USMC 1956-59; Republican; Prot.; rec: hunt, fish, rockhound. Res: PO Box 5639, San Bernardino 92412 Ofc: Riverside Thrift & Loan 3579 Arlington Ave Riverside 92506

SCHREIBER, MARK PEYTON, lawyer, b. Feb. 27, 1957, Albany, N.Y.; s. Wm. and Lillian F. (Newell) S.; m. Dana Woldow, Mar. 29, 1980; 1 son, Samuel William b. 1986; edn: Brown Univ. 1975-78; BS, Univ. of San Francisco 1981,

JD 1984; admitted Calif. State Bar 1985. Career: research asst. Prof. Marc A. Franklin, Stanford Univ. 1983-84, student clk. Justice Malcolm M. Lucas, Calif. Supreme Ct. 1984; staff atty. Pacific Bell, San Francisco 1984–; awards: USF Dean's Award (1984), Am. Jurisprudence Awards (1982, 83); mem. Am. Bar Assn., Calif. State Bar, Bar Assn. of S.F., Commonwealth Club of Calif., The Museum Soc. of S.F.; publ: article "Don't Make Waves: AM Stereo and the Marketplace Approach" in Hastings COMM/ENT Law J.; rec: radio activities. Ofc: Pacific Bell 140 New Montgomery St #1521 San Francisco 94105

SCHREIER, KONRAD FOESTE, JR., historian; b. Dec. 25, 1925, Evanston, Ill.; s. Konrad F. and Mildred (Schneible) S.; m. Nancy Buell, 1951; children: Konrad III., Douglas Buell; edn: Culver Mil. Acad., Lake Forest Coll., US Army Ordnance Sch. Career: mgmt. engr., research & devel. engr. in pvt. industry, 1950-67; profl. historian writing, lecturing and consultant-adviser to motion picture and TV industry, 1967–; author nine books, over 200 mag. articles, num. motion picture and TV stories and story treatments; mem: Fellow Company of Mil. Historians, US Mil. Hist. Commn., LA County Museum of Natural Hist./ History Div. (research assoc.), Los Angeles Corral of the Westerners, Council on Am. Mil. Past, Civil War Roundtable, Friends of The Huntington, So. Calif. Hist. Soc., others; mil: US Army Ordnance Dept., service in Burma WWII; Protestant. Address: 1639 Mandeville Canyon Rd Los Angeles 90049

SCHROEDER, RITA MOLTHEN, chiropractor; b. Oct. 25, 1922, Savanna, Ill.; d. Frank Joseph and Ruth Jessie (McKenzie) Molthen; m. Richard H. Schroeder, D.C., Apr. 23, 1948; div. 1981; children: Richard b. 1949, Andrew b. 1952, Barbara b. 1953, Thomas b. 1956, Paul b. 1960, Madeline b. 1962; edn: DC, Palmer Sch. of Chiropractic 1949; DC, Cleveland Coll. of Chiro. 1960; Calif. lic. Dr. Chiro., 1961. Career: engring. tooling liaison, Douglas Aircraft Co. 1942-46; chiropractic practise in Brooklyn, NY 1949-59, Fresno, Ca. 1961–, pres. Schroeder Chiropractic, Inc.; bd. dirs. Pacific States Chiropractic Coll. 1978-79, pres. 1980-81; honors: Ambassador Awd., Palmer Coll. of Chiro.; mem: Internat. Chiro. Assn., Internat. Chiro. Assn. of Calif., Fedn. of Chiropractors, Calif. Chiro. Assn., Internat. Platform Assn.; Republican; Catholic; rec: hunting, fishing, swimming, diving. Res: 9870 N. Millbrook Fresno 93710 Ofc: Schroeder Chiropractic Inc., 2535 N. Fresno, Fresno 93703

SCHROEDER, WILLIAM ROBERT, actor, entrepreneur; b. July 9, 1941, Los Angeles; s. Robert Manville and Miriam Ruth (Sloop) S.; m. Marie-Paule Fautrel, Sept. 7, 1963; edn: BA, UC Los Angeles 1964; BFA, Art Center Coll. of Design 1971; Nina Foch Studio 1983; Lee Strasberg Theatre Inst. 1983-85. Career: mailman US Post Office Santa Monica 1967-71; art dir., producer N.W. Ayer W. L.A. 1971-75; pres., gen. mgr. Advtg. Ctr. L.A. 1976-77, Alouette Internat. Santa Monica 1972–; actor 1983–; honors: Cert. of Merit (Art Dirs. Club of L.A. 1972), 1st Place Belding Award (1974), mem: Screen Actors Guild 1985-, Am. Fedn. of Radio & TV Artists 1983-, Santa Monica CofC, Concerned Homeowners of Santa Monica, Mensa, Internat. Plastic Modeling Soc., Nat. Rifle Assn., Combat Pilot's Assn./ Orange County Squadron, Found. for Brain Research (NY); author, creator computerized language courses for Mattel Intellivision; acting credits: King of the Streets (1983), The Forbidden Tome (1984), The End of Innocence (1985), Poltergeist II (1986); mil: cadet US Army ROTC 1959-61; Libertarian; Deist; rec: model building, comic books, computer technol., astrophysics, militaria, athletics, music, painting, aviation, woodcarving, woodworking. Ofc: Alouette Language Svc. 1626 Montana Ave Santa Monica 90403

SCHUBERT, RUTH CAROL HICKOK, artist; b. Dec. 24, 1927, Janesville, Wisc.; d. Fay Andrew and Mildred Willamette (Street) H.; m. Robert F. Schubert, Oct. 20, 1946; children: Stephen b. 1949, Michelle b. 1953; edn: AA, Monterey Peninsula Coll. 1974; BA, honors, CSU San Jose 1979; European studies (1977), spl. studies: J. Fon, R. Barrio, J. Burnham, E. Oback, C. Walker, F. Martin, M. Sheets. Career: watercolorist, num. solo shows and juried exhibns. statewide, 1965-; painting demonstrns., workshops and judging, Monterey Penin., 1980–; registry: V.A. Art-in-Arch., Wash DC, Oakland Mus. of Art, Artist Equity Assn. Inc./LA, Calif. Visual Arts Reg.; nat. watercolor shows (Catalogue) include Am. Artist Mag. 1st Nat. Art Show, NY (semifinalist 1978), San Diego W/C Soc. Nat. (1980), Mid-west W/C Soc. 4th Nat. (1980), 12 Western States/7th Nev. Annual (1980), 17th Nat. W/C West (1985); represented by Village Galleries, Lahaina, Maui, HI 1979-, Rose Rock Gal., Carmel by the Sea 1983-, Valley Art Gal., Portola Valley 1984-; num. permanent public, corp., and museum collections; mem: Audubon Artists Inc., Am. Watercolor Soc., Artists Equity Assn. Inc. No. Calif., Central Coast Art Assn. (pres. 1976-78), Monterey Penin. Mus. of Art (council research dir. 1975-76), M.P. Watercolor Soc., Nat. League Am. Penwomen (chpt. pres. 1984-85), Pacific Grove Art Ctr., CSUSJ Art Alumni Assn., Soc. of Western Artists (SF), Watercolor West (Redlands); Republican; Episcopal; rec: travel, swim. Address: 134 Dunecrest Ave Monterey 93940

SCHUCHARDT, J. ANDREW, civil engineer; b. Aug. 12, 1933, Berlin, Ger., nat. US cit. 1945; s. Karl Albert and Eva Maria (Ries) S.; m. Edith Elisabeth, Oct. 13, 1961; edn: BA, Hofstra Univ. 1960; BSCE, Columbia Univ. 1960; Reg. Civil Engr., Calif., Ariz., Hawaii, No. Carolina and Ore. Career: civil engr., project mgr. Howard, Needles, Tammen & Bergendoff, NY, NY 1960-65; proj. mgr., assoc. Parsons, Brinckerhoff, Quade & Douglas, San Francisco 1965-66, 1977-79, Honolulu, Hawaii 1966-71, 1974-75, Sao Paulo, Brazil 1971-74, Singapore, ROS 1975-76, San Jose, Costa Rica 1976-77; project mgr., assoc. Wilbur Smith & Assoc., Raleigh, No. Carolina 1979, San Jose 1979-81; prin. Transmetrics Inc., San Jose 1981-83; engr. pvt. consulting practice, Milpitas 1983–; honors: Kappa Mu Epsilon 1959; mem: Inst. Transportation Engrs., Nat. Soc. Profl. Engrs., Calif. Soc. Profl. Engrs.; publs: var. profl. related articles in English and Portugese, Sao Paulo, Brazil 1972-74; mil: HM3 USN Hospital Corps 1951-54; rec: creative writing, philatelics. Address: 2142 Aguilar Ct. Milpitas 95035

SCHULTZ, GARY DEAN, extended care hospital chain executive; b. July 15, 1945, Bellingham, Wash.; s. Herbert Phillip and Hazel Mary (Anthony) S.; m. Alice Vineyard, Feb. 1, 1977; children: Jason b. 1970, Jana b. 1973, Sharon b. 1960, Joyce b. 1962, Tammy b. 1964; edn: Walla Walla Coll. 1966-68; BS, high honors, Pacific Christian Coll. 1981; Nursing Home Adminstr. Ore. 1982, Calif. 1981. Career: mgr. KEWB radio Redding, Calif. 1968; cert. respiratory therapist Meml. Hosp. Redding 1970-73, chief pulmonary function 1973-78; asst. adminstr. Brentwood Convalescent Hosp. Red Bluff 1978-79; adminstr. Beverly Ent. Tillamook, Ore. 1979-81; pres., dir. ops. Health Systems Mgmt. San Dimas 1981–; dir. Schultz Mgmt. 1982–; mem: Ore. Health Care Assn. (reg. chmn. 1981), Calif. Assn. Health Facilities (chap. v.p. 1985), Am. Health Care Assn. 1979, Kiwanis, Aircraft Owners and Pilots Assn. 1985; producer, writer, dir. num. radio pgms. 1962-70; Republican; Seventh-Day Adventist; rec: flying, skiing, ham radio, sailing, travel, stock market, music. Ofc: Health Systems Mgmt. & Devel. Inc. 237 West Bonita, Ste A, San Dimas 91773

SCHULTZ, JAMES EDWARD, orthopedic surgeon; b. Dec. 30, 1936, Dunlap, Iowa; s. Shirley V. and Eileen E. (Houston) S.; m. Julie M., June 9, 1962; children: Gregory b. 1964, Jeffery b. 1965, Jennifer b. 1968; edn: MD, Creighton Univ. 1963; Diplomate Am. Bd. Orthopedic Surg. 1970. Career: intern San Diego County Hosp. 1963-64; resident orthopedics UC San Diego Med. Ctr. 1964-68; pvt. practice San Diego 1968–; secty./treas., v.p. University Ave. Orthopedic Med. Group; asst. clin. prof. UCSD Med. Ctr.; affil. staff: Mercy Hosp., Donald N. Sharp Meml. Hosp., Univ. Hosp., Children's Hosp. & Health Ctr., Coronado Hosp.; sports med. cons. San Diego State Univ. 1975-82, US Internat. Univ.; team phys. San Diego Friars Profl. world Team Tennis 1975–; med. examiner Nat. Football League Owner- Players Designated Sports; fellow Am. Coll. Surg. (chpt. pres. 1984, councilor 1978); mem: San Diego Surg. Soc. (pres. 1979, secty. 1978, treas./ pgm. chmn. 1976), S.D. Orthopedic Assn. (pres. 1980, secty. 1979, treas./ pgm. chmn. 1978), Am. Acad. Ortho. Surg., Western Ortho. Assn., Am. Soc. Sports Med., No. Am., Internat. Arthroscopy Assns., Calif. Ortho. Assn. (councilor 1981), AMA, CMA, San Diego County Med. Soc., R&A Club of San Diego, Ducks Unlimited (steering com.), S.D. CofC; mil: major Calif. Nat. Guard 1963-72; Republican; Catholic; rec: skiing, camping, hunting, tennis, running. Res: 4476 Ampudia St San Diego 92103 Ofc: University Ave. Med, Group 301 University Ave San Diego 92103

SCHULTZ, ROLF JAMES, tour co. executive; b. Mar. 10, 1941, Czechoslovakia, nat. 1972; s. Franz Stefan and Frieda Anna Schultz; m. Latchmee Singh, Oct.22, 1972; children: Melanie b. 1975, Debbie b. 1978; edn: BCom., Dalhousie Univ., Halifax, Can. 1965; MBA, Univ. Ore. 1969. Career: tchr. business econ. Simon Fraser Univ., B.C., Can. 1969; bought travel agcy. in Salinas, Calif., devel. into wholesale tour co. spec. in Mexico and Hawaii travel, chief exec. Contelco Corp., 1970–; recipient profl. awards from var. airlines, hotels, and CofCs; mem: Lions Club Internatl., Liontamer Salinas Host Club, 1982; Republican; Catholic; rec: swimming, tennis, art collector. Res: POB 397 Pebble Beach 93953 Ofc: Contelco Corp., 120 Del Rey Gardens Dr. Monterey 93940

SCHULZ, CAROL A., development officer; b. Sept. 25, 1960, San Jose; d. John P., Jr. and Alice A. (Sutton) Giammona; m. Kenneth Schulz, June 17, 1984; edn: BA magna cum laude, Univ. Santa Clara 1982; Univ. Santa Clara Sch. of Law 1982. Career: research asst. Univ. Santa Clara Devel. Ofc. 1983, dir. devel. research 1983-85; asst. dir. devel. Menlo Sch. & Coll. Atherton 1985–; honors: Phi Beta Kappa, Phi Sigma Iota, life mem. CSF, Univ. Santa Clara Presidential Scholar, Wm. F. Donnelly S.J. Scholar; mem: Council for Advancement and Support of Edn., Mid-Peninsula Devel. Ofcrs.; Republican; rec: cooking, skiing. Ofc: Menlo School & College 1000 El Camino Real Atherton 94025

SCHULZ, KARL ALEXANDER, general surgeon; b. May 18, 1954, Chgo.; s. Karl Robert and Lieselotte (Wnendt) S.; m. Laura Annunziata, Apr. 3, 1982; children: Claire Lauren b. 1984, Katherine Elise b. 1985; edn: BS, Loyola Univ. of Chgo. 1976; MD, Loyola Univ. of Chgo. Stritch Sch. of Med. 1979; res. gen. surg. Loyola Univ. affil. hosps. 1979-84; Diplomate Am. Board of Surgery. Career: pvt. practice general surgery, Rancho Mirage, Calif. 1984–; tchg., cons.; mem. AMA, CMA, Chgo. Med. Soc., Riverside Med. Soc., Ill. Med. Soc., Am. Soc. of Surgeons, Fellow Internat. Coll. of Surgery; surgical research in renal transplantation; publs: hepatic trauma, gastric surgery Oct. 1981, Feb. 1985; Catholic. Ofc: Karl A. Schulz, MD, Probst Building Ste. 212, 39000 Bob Hope Dr., Eisenhower Med. Ctr., Rancho Mirage 92270

SCHUTZ, JOHN ADOLPH, historian, educator; b. Apr. 10, 1919, Los Angeles; s. Adolph John and Augusta K. (Glicker) S.; edn: AB, UCLA 1942, MA, 1943, PhD, 1945. Career: asst. prof. Calif. Inst. of Tech., 1945-53; assoc. prof./ prof. Whittier College, 1953-65; prof. of history USC, 1965–, dean 1976-82; vis. prof. (summers) Univ. of Brit. Columbia 1960, Univ. of Waterloo, Ont. 1966, Boston Coll. 1969, CSCLA 1953-65; trustee Citizens Research Council; trustee emeritus New England Historic Geneal. Soc. 1985-; awards: grantee Nat. Endowment for Humanities 1971-74, Danforth Fellow 1959; mem: Am. Hist. Assn. (Pacific Coast Br. pres. 1973, sec.treas. 1951-); Historic Genealog. Soc.; Orgn. of Am. Historians; Southern Calif. Hist. soc.; author: The American Republic (1978), The Dawning of America (1981), William Shirley, King's governor of Massachusetts (1961), Spain's Colonial Outpost: California (Boyd & Fraser 1985), chpt. in Generations and Changes: Genealogical Perspectives in Social History (Mercer Univ. Press 1986); joint editor Golden State Series (Boyd & Fraser 1979-); Democrat; Catholic; rec: philately, travel. Res: 1100 White Knoll Dr Los Angeles 90012 Ofc: Univ. of So. California, College Park, Los Angeles 90089-0034

SCHUYLER, BRADLEY ALLEN, clinical neuropsychologist; b. June 1, 1954, Fresno, Calif.; s. Jewett H. and Shirley Mae (Wicks) S.; m. Frances, Apr. 16, 1983; edn: Bakersfield Coll. 1972-74; CSU San Francisco 1974-75; BA, CSU Fresno 1976, MS, 1979; PhD, Calif. Sch. of Profl. Psychol., Fresno 1982; lic. psychol. Calif. 1984. Career: psych. aide Phoenix House, Concord, Calif. 1974; psychol. intern Dinuba Public Schs., Spl. Edn. Dept. 1979-80, Dinuba Comm. Counseling Ctr. 1979-80, Merced County Mental Health Outpt. Unit 1980-81, Leon S. Peters Rehab. Ctr., Fresno 1981-82, coord. of neuropsychol. svcs. 1982-83; cons. Family Action Support Team, Fresno Comm. Hosp. & Med. Ctr. 1982-84, clin. dir. Neurological Retraining Ctr. 1983-85; pvt. practice Fresno 1982–; dir. Calif. Ctr. for Rehab. Svcs., Fresno 1985–; adj. faculty Calif. Sch. of Profl. Psychol. 1983–; honors: Outstanding Contbn. in Field of Diagnosis and Treatment of Brain Damaged Individuals (1985), Master Tchr. Award (1984-85); mem: Am. Psychol. Assn., Central Calif. Head Injury Found. (bd. 1983-, newsletter com. chair and chief ed. 1983-, profl. affairs com. 1983-, symposium com. 1985), Fresno Mental Health Assn. (profl. advis. com. 1982-83), Nat. Acad. of Neuropsychols., Psi Chi, San Joaquin Psychol. Assn. (area legis. rep. 1985-); alumni rep. CSPP 1982-; Stroke Rehab. Com. (chair), Fresno Comm. Hosp. and Med. Ctr. 1981-83; publs: articles in med. jours., num. papers presented; rec: racquetball, skiing, backpacking, music (piano & guitar), photog. Ofc: Calif. Ctr. for Rehab. Svcs., 1907 N Gateway Fresno 93727

SCHWAB, LEE KERR, research engineer-chemist; b. Jan. 20, 1924, Donora, Pa.; s. Herman J. and Marie E. (Kerr) S.; m. Mildred K., Dec. 21, 1946; edn: BA chem., Waynesburg Presbyn. Coll. 1954; M.Bus. Mgmt., La Verne Univ. 1980. Career: analytical chemist US Naval Gun Factory, Indian Head, Md. 1954-56, US Bureau of Mines, Pittsburgh, Pa. 1956-60, Patrick Air Force Lab., Melbourne, Fla. 1960, Air Force Civilian Lab., Vandenberg AFB, Calif. 1960-62, research engr. Lockheed- Vandenberg 1962-72, Lockheed - Rye Canyon Research, Saugus 1972-73; research engr./ chemist Naval Civil Engring. Lab., Port Hueneme 1974-84; honors: Dept. of Navy 20 yr. length of service award, Lockheed 10 yr. service award 1962-72; mem: Nat. Assn. of Corrosion Engrs., Nat. Assn. of Govt. Employees, Federal Union of Scientist & Engineers, Am. Chemical Soc., Ventura Kidney Found.; mil: carpenters mate 3c US Navy Seabees 1943-46, Victory Medal, Good Conduct Medal; Republican; Prot.; rec: reading, coins, investments. Address: Lompoc 93436

SCHWAFEL, CHRISTIAN THEODORE, management consultant; b. June 26, 1935, Fargo, No. Dakota; s. Jacob Theodore and Corrine Adele (Dosland) S.; m. Susan Thorley, Aug. 25, 1969; edn: BSME, Stanford Univ. 1958; MBA, 1963; cert. in prodn. and inventory mgmt., Am. Prodn. and Inventory Control Soc. 1977. Career: proj. engr. No. American Rockwell, Anaheim 1963-65; mgmt. cons. John Barry & Assoc., Newport Beach 1965-66; proj. mgr. Varian Assocs., Palo Alto 1966-70; doc. con. adm. Westel Co., Mountain View 1970; mfg. adminstr. Fairchild Camera and Instrument Corp., Mtn. View 1970-71; dir. of admin. Am. Health Sys., San Francisco 1971-72; mfg. mgr. VSL Corp., Los Gatos 1972-73; sys. control gp. mgr. Diablo Sys. (Xerox), Hayward 1973-74; mgmt. cons. General Electric Co., San Jose 1975; mfg. mgr. Arbor Labs Inc., Palo Alto 1975-77; mgmt. cons. California Microwave, Sunnyvale 1977-78; v.p./ gen. mgr. Windows & Lighting Sys. Inc., Sunnyvale 1978-79; dir. of mfg. ICORE, Sunnyvale 1979-80; natl's mgr. Handar, Sunnyvale 1980-81; pres. Schwafel Assoc., Sunnyvale 1981–; Material Requirments Seminar, Electronics Assn. of calif. 1985; mem: Stanford Club of Palo Alto (pres. 1978); Am. Soc. of Mech. Engrs.; Am. Prodn. and Inventory Control Soc.; Profl. and Techl. Cons. Assn.; Commonwealth; United State Power Quadrons; Sierra Club; mil: lt.j.g., USN 1958-61; Republican; Lutheran; rec: sailing, photog., tennis. Res: 730 Anderson Dr., Los Altos 94022 Ofc: Schwafel Associates, 790 Lucerne Dr., Ste. 10, Sunnyvale 94086

SCHWARTZ, "Al" ABRAHAM R., social worker, writer, marketing research exec.; b. Oct. 18, 1899, Odessa, Russia, nat. US cit. 1913; s. Isadore and Rosa (Rosenberg) S.; m. Rose Anne Shinder (educator) b. 1926; children: Efrem Siemon (physicist) b. 1927, Adaire Joyce (Klein) (univ. librarian) b. 1931, Chuck H. (assn. exec.) b. 1934; edn: BS in journ., Univ. of Toledo 1922; grad. work in journ., NY Univ. 1922, Columbia Univ. 1923-26; spl. courses, City Coll. NY 1922-23, NY Sch. of Social Work 1928-31, Ohio State Univ. 1934-36, 40-43. Career: psychometrist Teachers Coll., Columbia Univ.; writer, fishing & hunting columnist, New York American 1924-25; records and stats. clk. Dean, Onativia & Co. also DeCoppet and Doremus (Wall St. brokerage firms) 1925-26; ticker tape desk for New York American and New York Eve. Jour. 1926-28; social wkr. Jewish Bd. of Guardians, NYC and Hawthorne (NY) Sch. for Boys, 1928-31; dir. Soc. Svcs./sr. Warden's asst. var. Fed. Bur. of Prisons penal instns. in Fort Leavenworth, Kans., Lewisburg, Pa., Chillicothe, Ohio, 1931-37, field work assignments in area univs. (Univ. Kans., Bucknell Univ., Antioch Coll., others); empl. State of Ohio 1937-43, 1949-74: research sociologist Bur. of Juvenile Research, Dept. of Public Welfare 1937-43, supr. personnel and tng. ofcr. Ohio State Reformatory 1949-53, public info. ofcr./press ofcr. Ohio Dept. of Hwys, and Dept. of Hwy. Safety 1953-74; wartime service in USO as organizer and hosp. therapist, also lay chaplain USO/Jewish Welfare Bd., 1943-45; exec. dir. Columbus (Ohio) Assn. for the Blind 1945-49; mkt. research dir. Epic Ents., San Diego 1974–; recipient num. profl. and civic appreciation awards; mem: Inst. of Traffic Engrs., Soc. of Automotive Engrs., Internat. Assn. of Bus. Communicators, Am. Soc. of Safety Engrs., Soc. Tech. Writers and Pubs., Publicity Club L.A., (past) Care Care Council of APAA; active in Kiwanis (dir., pres. Univ.-San Diego club 1985), organizer 16 Kiwanis Youth Clubs; Jewish; rec: symphony. Res: 7227 Navajo Rd Apt. 102 San Diego 92119 Ofc: Epic Enterprises Inc 6151 Fairmount Ave Ste 115 San Diego 92120

SCHWARTZ, "Chuck" ISRAEL HERSCHEL, marketing and promotion consultant; b. Feb. 8, 1934, Danville, Pa.; s. Abraham R. and Rose Ann (Shinder) S.; m. Susan L. Beer, July 15, 1984; children: Harry b. 1960, Pamela b. 1964, Mindi b. 1968, Jeffrey b. 1971; edn: Ohio State Univ. 1952-54, 56, CSU San Diego 1956-57. Career: owner/opr. automotive parts stores, Calif. 1956-69, 1973-77; chief ops. ofcr. Automotive Div. Daylin Inc., nat. incl. Hawaii, 1969-73; mfrs. rep. Chuck Schwartz Mgmt. and Consulting, Calif., Ariz., Nev., 1977-79; pres. Epic Ents. Inc. (prodn. & promotion bus. trade shows, events) San Diego 1980–; cons. trade assns./plnnr. seminars: Splty. Equip. Market Assn. (SEMA), Auto Internacional Assn. (AIA), Hq. Whittier; independent events: San Diego Gift and Jewelry Show, Calif. Interior Design Show, San Diego Electronics Show, Anti-Terrorism Espionage & Crime World Conf. and Exhibn., others; cons. Govt. of Spain 1983; honors: Layman of Year, Kiwanis (1976, 1980), cit. Muscular Dystrophy Assn. (1980), Eternal Light Award, Univ. of Judaism (1982); mem: Nat. Assn. of Exposition Mgrs., Meeting Planners Internat., San Diego CofC, S.D. Conv. & Visitors Bur., S.D. World Trade Assn.; civic: Boys Clubs Am., Nat. Council on Alcoholism, McAlister Inst. of Tng. & Edn./S.D. (alcohol, drug treatment pgms), The Guardians, Hebrew Home for Aged/S.D., B'nai Brith, Univ. of Judaism (Patrons Soc.), Tifereth Israel Synagogue (pres. 4 terms, chmn. bldg. com.); publs: num. guest editorials and columns in automotive trade jours., also in synagogue & organizational papers; mil: 2d lt. C.I.A., Korean Conflict 1954-56, Presidential Cit., Nat. Def. Svc., Airborn Wings, Good Conduct, Marksmanship; Republican; Jewish; rec: racquetball, boating, sports. Res: 5747-B Adobe Falls Rd San Diego 92120 Ofc: Epic Enterprises Inc 6151 Fairmount Ave Ste 115 San Diego 92120

SCHWARTZ, GARY ALAN, company executive; b. Jan. 10, 1952, Indnpls.; s. Frank L. and Jeanne (Shapiro) S.; m. Tracy, Dec. 14, 1980; edn: BS in bus., Indiana Univ. 1974; Certified Public Acct. (CPA), Calif. 1978; lic. Real Estate Broker, Calif. 1982. Career: staff Alexander Grant & Co., St. Louis, Mo. 1974-78; supr. Alexander Grant & Co., San Francisco 1978-79; v.p./mem. bd. dirs. Byer California, San Francisco 1979–; mem: Am. Inst. CPAs, Calif. Soc. of CPAs; rec: golf, skiing. Res: 2339 Ticonderoga Ct. San Mateo 94402 Ofc: Byer California 66 Potrero Ave San Francisco 94103

SCHWARTZ, IRVING JACK, physician; b. Nov. 17, 1944, NY, NY; s. Murray and Betty S.; grandparents: Sam & Rachel Wise; m. Bunny, June 7, 1969; 1 dau. Rachelle Lynn b. 1971; edn: BS, Long Island Univ. 1966; MD, Nat. Univ. of Mexico 1971; cert. in acupuncture, Ctr. for Chinese Med.; cert. in osteopuncture; cert. in lumbar, thoracic and cervical thermography; cert. breast thermography; cert. x-ray supv. and oper. Career: resident St. Vincent's Hosp. & Med. Ctr. Toledo, Ohio 1971-72, Inst. of Social Security Pub. Health Hosp. Mexico City 1972-75; asst. dir. noninvasive vascular exams Diagnostic Aids Unlimited 1975-78; family practice and vascular exams Laurel Canyon Med. Group 1978-79; med. dir. vascular lab. VA Wadsworth Hosp. 1979-81; med. dir. vascular exams Diagnostic Noninvasive Analysis 1980-81; family practice DeSoto Med. Group Canoga Park 1981–; instr., lectr.; researcher for var. pharm. cos.; honors: Excellence in Performance & Contbn. (Wadsworth VA Hosp. 1980; mem: AMA, CMA, LACMA, Internat. Coll. Phys. & Surg., Am. Occup. Med. Assn., NY Acad. Scis., Republican Nat. Com., Simon Weisenthal Orgn.; publ: articles in med. jours., book: Etiology, Diagnostic Complications and Treatment of Rheumatic Fever (Mexico City 1973); Republican; Jewish; rec: bicycling, tennis, poetry, philosophy, jazz, auto racing. Ofc: La Familia Health Ctr., 1037 E Pacific Coast Hwy Wilmington 90744

SCHWARTZ, LAWRENCE JAY, ophthalmologist; b. May 24, 1943, Bklyn.; s. Nathan and Rita Schwartz; m. Sandra, Dec. 21, 1969; children: Andria, b. 1972, Richard, b. 1974, Marla, b. 1978; edn: BA, Cornell Univ. 1964; MD, State Univ. New York at Buffalo 1968; Bd. Certified Ophthalmology 1974. Career: internship LA County-USC Med. Sch. 1968-69; res. ophthalmology, Pacific Medical Center, San Francisco 1970-72; pvt. practice ophthalmology, 1974–; clin. chief ophthalmology, Cedars-Sinai Med. Center, Los Angeles 1982–; asst. clin. prof. ophthalmol. USC Sch. of Medicine, 1978-; Medical Adv. Commn. for Ophthalmology, 1984, Los Angeles Olympics; mem: Fellow Am. Acad. of Ophthalmology, LA Eye Soc., Am. Assn. of Ophthalmol., Contact Lens Assn. of Ophthalmol., CMA, LA County Med. Assn., Phi Delta Epsilon med. frat., v.p. L.A. Grad. Club; bd. dirs. Crittenton Center for Young Women & Infants; publs: contbr. Archives of Ophthalmology (6/72), Clinical Ophthalmology Textbook, ed. Thomas D. Duane, MD, Vol. 3 (1977); mil: major US Army 1972-74; Republican; Jewish; rec: skiing, boating, swimming. Ofc: 8631 West Third St Ste 800E, Los Angeles 90048

SCHWARTZ, ROBERT LOREN, restaurateur; b. Oct. 22, 1960, Ventura; s. Phillip Irving and Elleen Joyce (Sherman) S.; m. Audrey, June 2, 1984; edn: bus. admin., USC 1985. Career: owner Pizza Chief, Ventura Co. 1978-81; pres. Pizza Hop Inc., San Fernando Valley, Los Angeles 1981-84; pres. R.A.D. Foods Inc., San Fernando Valley, Los Angeles 1984–; guest lectr. USC Bus. Sch. 1984-; honors: Marsha Israel Highest Achiev. Award, Entrepreneur Pgm., USC 1984; Republican; Jewish; rec: jogging, golf. Ofc: R.A.D. Food Inc., Northridge 91325

SCHWARTZ, RONALD ELLIOT, financial executive; b. Jan. 24, 1950, Chgo., Ill.; s. Norman Leonard and Phyllis Faye (Strike) S.; m. Shelly, Oct. 9, 1981; 1 dau. Heather b. 1984; edn: BA, CSU Northridge 1972, MA, 1976; CPA Calif. 1977. Career: CPA Stonefield & Josephson L.A. 1977-80; senior exec., CFO, controller EZ Sportswear Chatsworth 1980—; cons. creator financial computer software; honors: Financial Exec. of the Yr.; mem. L.A. Jesters (non-profit affil. to Found. for Junior Blind); Democrat; Jewish; rec: softball, swimming. Ofc: EZ Sportswear 9419 Mason Ave Chatsworth 91311

SCHWARTZ, STEPHAN A., parapsychologist, anthropologist, author; b. Jan. 10, 1942, Cincinnati, Ohio; s. Abe and Bertha (Watson) S.; m. Hayden O. Gates, July 10, 1982; 1 child by prev. marriage, Katherine b. 1970, stepdau., Leah b. 1973; edn: major in Humanities, Univ. of Va. Career: assoc. ed. Psychic and Sea Power mags.; staff mem. National Geographic, Daily Press and Times Herald; cons. to Oceanographer of the Navy; spl. asst. res. and analysis, chief of Naval Ops.; senior fellow Philosophical Research Soc.; chmn./research dir. The Mobius Soc., 1977—; vis. prof. John F. Kennedy Univ.; pres. Assn. for Anthropological Study of Consciousness; mem: Phoenix (advsry. bd.), Parapsychology Assn. (assoc.); listed in Contemporary Authors; mil: med. corpsman US Army; author 3 books, chapters, num. articles in parapsychology jours. and gen. audience mags.; rec: hiking, backpacking, scuba. Res: 2243 Ronda Vista Dr Los Angeles 90027 Ofc: The Mobius Soc. 2525 Hyperion Ave Los Angeles 90027

SCHWARZ, MICHAEL JULES, certified public accountant; b. June 12, 1943, Philadelphia, Penn.; s. Erwin W. and Grace S. (Segal) S.; m. Susan A., March 15, 1970; children: Liana b. 1972, Rachel b. 1975; edn: BS, San Diego State Univ. 1971; CPA, Calif. 1973. Career: accounting practice 1974—; pres. Schwarz Accty. Corp., San Diego 1981—; tchr. acctg. & tax Mesa Coll. and Grossmont Coll.; mem: Calif. Soc. CPAs (bd. dirs., pres. San Diego chpt. 1985-86), San Diego Jewish Acad. (pres. 1984-85), Am. Inst. CPAs, Nat. Assn. Accts., Center City Optimist Club; publs: bi-monthly column, local Jewish community newspaper; mil: USNR 1965-67; Democrat; Jewish. Ofc: Schwarz Accountancy Corp., 5252 Balboa Ave. Ste. 600 San Diego 92117

SCHWARZ, ROBERT JOHN, computer business consultant; b. Aug. 14, 1917, Cincinnati, Ohio; s. Joseph and Loretta Mary (Funsch) S.; m. Margaret Holcomb, Nov. 8, 1952; children: William b. 1954, Karen b. 1955, Mary b. 1962; edn: BS mgmt., Univ. Ill. 1947; Certified Employment Cons. (CIEC 1955), real estate broker Calif. 1984. Career: adminstrv. asst. Gen. Telephone Co. Santa Monica 1948-50; methods & procedures analyst Kaiser Steel Corp. Fontana 1953; adminstrv. asst. bd. supvs. County of San Bernardino 1954; owner, mgr. Schwarz Employment Agencies S.B., Riverside, Ontario, Pomona, L.A. 1954-72; pres. Am. Bus. Colls. S.B., Riverside, Ontario 1963-69; acct. exec. Dean Witter Newport Beach 1972-80; v.p. Anderson, Johnston & Roberts Exec. Search 1981-83; broker Schwarz Real Estate Santa Ana 1984—; pres. Problem Solutions 1985—; political action seminar leader San Bernardino CofC 1962; exec. dir. Republican Party S.B. County 1962-64; staff aide Reagan for Gov. 1966; asst. mgr. Calif. centennials Commn. 1948; chmn. adv. bd. employment agencies Calif. 1970-72; mem: Calif. Employment Agencies Assn. (pres. 1957), Nat. Employment Assn. (pres. 1959), var. CofCs, Rotary; publ: Civilian Training Manual, Personnel Mgmt. Manual; mil: lt. col. USAF 1941-45, 1951-53; Presbyterian; rec: tennis, golf, research. Address: 1916 West Wind Santa Ana 92704

SCHWEIGER, RUSSELL FREDERICK, travel co. executive; b. Aug. 12, 1931, Milwaukee, Wis.; s. Russell Lee and Dorthea (Wichman) S.; m. Rosemary, Oct. 26, 1959; children: Russell b. 1961, Pamela b. 1966, Kimberly b. 1968; edn: bus. adm., Univ. of Wis., 1949-53. Career: sales mgr. SW USA, British Airways, Los Angeles 1957-80; bd. chmn./exec. v.p. Travel Research, Inc., L.A. 1977-86; bd. chmn./pres. Travel R Us, Inc., Torrance 1982—; mem: Am. Soc. of Travel Agents, Nat. Fedn. of Ind. Businesses, Torrance CofC, Assn. Internat. Des Skal, Palos Verdes - La Cresta Homeowners Assn. (pres. 1979); Republican; Prot.; rec: pvt. pilot. Ofc: Travel R Us, Inc. 1441 Marcelina Ave Torrance 90501

SCHWEINFURTH, WILLIAM CRAIG, mobilehome park management executive; b: June 15, 1953, Evanston, Ill.; s. Joseph David and Elizabeth Jane (Stielow) S.; m. Loring Huebner, Aug. 13, 1977; edn: BS, Stanford Univ. 1975; BA, 1976; JD, USC Gould Sch. of Law 1979. Career: lawyer Tuttle & Taylor, Los Angeles 1979-83; mobilehome park mgmt., Los Angeles 1983—; alternate San Juan Capistrano Mobilehome Park Rent Review Bd. 1983-85; honors: selected to law review, USC 1977; elected to bd. of editors 1978; mem: Am. and Calif. Bar Assns.; Constitutional Rights Found.; Los Angeles World Affairs Council; Kappa Alpha frat.; Stanford Alumni Assn.; publs: California's Medical Injury Compensation Reform Act: An Equal Protection Challenge, So. Calif. Law Review 1979; Republican; Baptist; rec: artist, sailing, basketball. Res: 825 Traction, Los Angeles 90013 Ofc: 1521 W Glenoaks Blvd Glendale 91201

SCHWEITZER, FREDERICK VERNON, accountant/educator; b. May 19, 1907, Amarillo, Tex.; s. Fred R. and Olive (Smith) S.; edn: Kansas Wesleyan Univ., 1924-26; AB, USC 1928; postgrad. Univ. of Berlin, 1933; MA, Pub. Adm., Columbia Univ. 1943; m. Cora Henderson 1928, div. 1931; m. 2d. Ruth Twenhoefel 1935, div. 1941; m. 3d. Margaret Cunha 1942, div. 1949; m. 4th Mary Ann Hiatt 1949, div. 1972; children: Gordon Merle b. 1928, Fred Karl b. 1946 (dec.). Career: pub. acct. Arthur Anderson & Co., L.A. 1927-30; vice consul US Dept. of State, Brisbane, Queensland, Aus., 1930-33; field aud., US Dept. Agri., Wash DC 1933-36; sr. pub. acct. Peat Marwick Mitchell & Co.,

S.F. 1936; chief div., Research & Stat., Calif. Dept. of Soc. Welfare, 1936-37; chief acct. Marchant Calculators Inc., Oakland, Calif. 1938-42; dep. dir. Veterans Preference Div., War Assets Adminstrn., S.F. 1946-47; sr. adminstrv. analyst Calif. Joint Legis. Budget Comm., Sacramento 1948-52; agcy. mgr. Marchant Calculators Inc., Santa Rosa, Ca. 1952-53; S.W. div. dir. Olivetti Corp. of Am., Dallas, Tex. 1954-61; mgr. systems sales Friden Inc., Sacto. 1962-66; data proc. systems analyst Calif. Dept. of Water Res., Sacto. 1967-72, and internal aud. 1972-74; own bus., pub. acct., Sacto., 1974—; owner/opr. Walnut Orchard, Yuba City, 1966-79; instr. Palo Alto Adult Edn., 1948-49; instr. Sacto. City Coll., 1950-51; instr. Mgmt. Devel. Inst., Sacto. 1969; instr., auditing of computer systems, Calif. Internal Aud. Assn., 1972-74; instr., hunting safety, Calif. Dept. Fish and Game. Honors: varsity track team Kans. Wesleyan Univ. 1925-27; varsity tennis, Univ. of Berlin 1933; mem: Calif. State Empl. Assn. (pres. chpt. 165 1965/6, 66/7); Nat. Assn. of Accts.; Mgmt. Systems Assn.; Phi Mu Alpha, Shriners, VFW Post No. 85, Scottish Rite (Sacto.), AF&AM (Cambridge, Mass.); author: Unemployed Wkrs Insurance Plan of Queensland, Aus.; Monthly Labor Review, US Dept. Labor Jan. 1933; Public Assistance in Calif. (Dept. Soc. Wel. Jan. 1967); Acctg. Manual for Ship's Service Depts. Ashore (Bur. of Naval Pers. Apr. 1944); mil: lt.cmdr. USNR 1942-48; Republican (Sacto. Co. Rep. Cent. com. 1966-70; chmn. data proc. com. Calif. State Rep. Com., 1968-70); Presbyterian; rec: tennis, philately, gardening. Res: 3908 Heights Ct. Cameron Park 95682 Ofc: F.V.Schweitzer, Pub. Acct., 902 Del Paso Blvd, Rm 43, Sacramento 95815

SCOBEE, NANCY JO, sales & marketing executive; b. Dec. 7, 1942, Louisville, Ky.; d. Guy Elliston and Mary Evelyn (Shuck) S.; div.; H.S. grad. 1959; dipl. Louisville Sch. of Cosmetology; num. spl. courses in mgmt., sales & motivation, pub. speaking; lic. instr. cosmetol., Ky., Ind., Ohio. Career: hairstylist 1965-67; chain salon stylist, salon mgr. Mercantile Stores, 5 years; cosmetologist/prop. Dream Coifs, 7 years; instr./sch. mgr. Mr. John's Sch. of Beauty, Louisville, 1.5 years; supr. of instrs. Roy's of Louisville (Ky.) Beauty Acad., 1 year; with Redken Labs., 1973—, contract tchg. for groups of salons, distbrs., 1973-81, div. tng. mgr. 1981-86, nat. mgr. Scientific Edn. Systems, 1986—; hairstyling judge 1968-; mem. Nat. Hairdressers and Cosmetol. Assn. (Bluegrass Hair Fashion Com., Inter Coiffure Com., Haute Coiffure), Am. Quarter Horse Assn., Optimist Club, Easter Star of Ky., Filson Club of Ky.; publs: num. tng. pgms., ed. sch. newsletter; Spiritualist minister Brotherhood of Eternal Truth; rec: Quarter Horse. Res: 22640 Burbank Blvd Woodland Hills 91367 Ofc: RedKen Laboratories 6625 Variel Ave Canoga Park 91303

SCOTT, ARTHUR JOSEPH, executive recruiter, career counselor; b. Mar. 29, 1938, Phila.; s. Arthur Wm. and Marion (Kane) S.; m. Virginia Martucci, Oct. 31, 1975; children: Kimberley b. 1962, Christopher b. 1964, Jennifer b. 1971; edn: BA, La Salle Coll. 1960; MA, Marquette Univ. 1962; ABD, Univ. of N.C., Chapel Hill 1962-65. Career: asst. prof. Russian Hist., Shippensburg (Pa.) State Coll., 1965-67; pres. New Dimensions in Training, Phila. 1968-70; state coord. Higher Edn. Equal Opp. Act, Pa. Dept. of Edn., Harrisburg 1970-74; dir. Ednl. Opp. Pgm., Penn State Univ., University Park 1974-77; cons. Comprehensive Systems Inc., Wilmington, Del. 1977-80; v.p. Joran Recruiters, Sacramento 1980—; career cons. Nat. Univ., the Learning Exchange, Creative Awareness Ctr (Mather AFB), Sierra Coll., and County of San Jose 1982-; awards: United Way disting. vol. 1984-85; mem. Calif. Personnel Assn.; civic: Downtown Optimist Club, Toastmasters Anon. (pres. 1982-83), Sacto. Urban League (v.chair 1982-83), Sacto. CofC, United Way (coms. 1985-); publs: series of articles on careers in Aardvark (1985), Calif. Job Journal (Spring 1986); Democrat; Catholic; rec: classical music, opera, ballet, rosarian. Res: 234 Second St Davis 95616 Ofc: Joran Recruiters 2805 El Camino Ave Ste A Sacramento 95821

SCOTT, JACK ALAN, college president; b. Aug. 24, 1933, Sweetwater, Tex.; s. Wm. Hopkins (dec.) and Ethelda (Cravy) S.; m. Lacreta Isbell, Sept. 2, 1954; children: Sharon, b. 1955; Sheila, b. 1956; Amy, b. 1960; Gregory, b. 1963; Adam, b. 1966; edn: BA, Abilene Christian Univ. 1954; M.Div., Yale Univ. 1962; MA, Claremont Grad. Sch. 1967, PhD, 1970. Career: asst. to pres. Abilene Christian Univ., 1955-57; assoc. prof. of history and religion, Pepperdine Univ., Los Angeles 1962-71; Provost and Dean of the College, Los Angeles Campus, Pepperdine 1971-73; dean of instrn. Orange Coast College, Costa Mesa 1973-78; pres. Cypress College, 1978—; bd. of regents Pepperdine Univ.; chmn. bd. trustees Humana West Anaheim Hosp.; gov. apptd. mem. Empl. Services Bd. 1972-75; mem. Calif. Commn. on Crime Control and Violence Prev. 1980-82. Awards: Alumni award Claremont Grad. Sch. 1980; Danforth Teachers Grant 1966-68; Soc. of Colonial Dames Prize 1968; Who's Who in Am.; mem: Am. Assn. of Higher Edn., Assn. of Calif. Community Coll. Adminstrs. (chmn. bd. dirs. 1981-83); Am. Heart Assn. (chmn. Orange Co. Chpt. 1981-83); Calif. Heart Assn. (bd. dirs. 1983-); Rotarian; author: An Annotated Edition of Witherspoon's Lectures on Moral Philosophy (Univ. of Delaware Press 1982); Democrat; Ch. of Christ; rec: cycling, jogging, racquetball. Address: Cypress College, 9200 Valley View St, Cypress 90630

SCOTT, LEROY BYRON, real estate broker; b. Nov. 22, 1918, Greenville, Miss.; s. Willie Lee and Estella (Bynum) S.; div.; children: Myran b. 1958, Sonjia b. 1962, Celwyn b. 1965, Arkova b. 1972; edn: BA, Univ. of Eastern Florida 1941; real estate cert. UCLA 1964; Calif. lic. real estate broker (1956). Career: R.R. bartender, The Pullman Co., 1941-46; clk. U.S. Postal Service, 1946-76; real estate broker, Leroy B. Scott Realty, 1956—; mil: sgt. US Army 1942-43; Democrat; Baptist; rec: amateur radio (KB6KJT), mem. Pasadena Radio Club. Res: 1514 Glen Ave Pasadena 91103 Ofc: Leroy B. Scott Realty 1100 N Eastern Ave Los Angeles 90063

SCOTT, RAYMOND, military engineer; b. Jan. 25, 1947, Leland, Miss.; s. Pious Joe and Eula Bell (William) S.; m. Flora Gene, Sept. 15, 1968; children: Audwin b. 1970, Carlos b. 1971, Charlette b. 1981; edn: Alcorn A&M Coll. 1965-66; AA, Univ. of Albany, 1983. Career: served to lt. US Navy, 1966–: enlisted seaman apprentice USN (NTC RTC) San Diego 1966; fireman aboard USS Yorktown 1967-69; boiler techn. transferred to USS Bennington (CVS-20) 1969, USS Santa Barbara (AE-28) 1970-73; boiler techn. senior chief aboard USS Henry B. Wilson (DDG-7) 1975-78, leading chief petty ofcr. 1979; commissioned as an ofcr. Apr. 2, 1979; material ofcr. aboard USS Ranger (CV-61) 1979, lt. j.g.; main propulsion asst. aboard USS Mount Vernon (LSD-39) 1981-83; ship supt. Long Beach Navy Shipyard, 1983-85, lt.; chief engr. USS Cleveland (LPD-7), 1985–; awarded USN Meritorious Service Medal (1981), Navy Achievement Medal (1983), num. decorations; mem. Nat. Naval Officer Assn., VFW; civic: Calif. Assn. for Neurologically Handicapped Children; Ind.; 7th-Day Adventist; rec: fishing, bowling, fitness. Res: 3900 Jerome Way Bakersfield 93309 Ofc: USS Cleveland (LPD-7) FPO San Francisco 96662-M10

SCRITSMIER, JEROME LORENZO, manufacturing co. executive; b. July 1, 1925, Eau Claire, Wisc.; s. Fredrick L. and Mary Alvera (Schwah) L.; m. Mildred Joan Lloyd, June 27, 1947; children: Dawn Marie, b. 1953; Lloyd Fredrick, b. 1958; Janet Alvera, b. 1960; edn: BS, Northwestern Univ. 1950; lic. real estate broker, Calif. 1968. Career: salesman Sylvania Elec. Products 1951-70; owner/opr. opr. Real Properties, 1958–; owner/chief exec. Environmental Lighting for Architecture Inc., City of Industry 1973–; owner/pres. Cameron Properties Inc. 1979–; dir. Independent National Bank, Covina 1983-; honors: Who's Who in the West, Who's Who in Fin. and Industry; mem: Apartment Assn. of Greater Los Angeles (dir. 1960-, twice pres.); Calif. Assn. of Realtors; club: Jonathan (L.A.); mil: s/sgt. USAF 1943-46, Air Medal, Presdtl. Unit Citation; Republican; Prot.; rec: flying, travel. Res: 2454 N. Cameron Ave Covina 91724 Ofc: Environmental Lighting for Architecture, 17891 Arenth St, Industry 91748

SEABORG, DAVID MICHAEL, biologist; b. Apr. 22, 1949, Berkeley; s. Glenn Theodore and Helen Lucille (Griggs) S.; edn: BS, UC Davis 1972, MA, UC Berkeley 1974. Career: biol. instr. UC Berkeley 1972-73; psychol./hypnosis instr. Open Edn. Exchange, Oakland; biol. instr. Oakland Jr. Center of Art and Sci., Calif. Acad. of Scis. (S.F.), Oakland Mus., Lindsay Mus. (Walnut Creek), 1974-75; freelance tchr. and independent cons. Oakland public and pvt. schs., 1976–; writer profl. articles and articles for gen. public, Berkeley 1982–; pres./dir. research Found. for Biological Conservation and Research, Lafayette 1984–; cons. and field trip leader Calif. Acad. of Scis. 1983; tchg. cons. var. public and pvt. schs., Wash DC and Calif., 1967-80; honors: Nat. Honor Soc. (1967), wildlife photography award, Soc. Photog. Scientists and Engrs. (1967), Dean's list UCD (1968-72), merit. service Smithsonian Instn. (1969), Pres. Fitness Award (1971), medals for placing Bay-to-Breakers Running Race (1981-84); mem: Calif. Acad. of Scis., BIOTA, World Wildlife Fund, Sierra Club, Save the Bay Assn., Nat. Wildlife Fedn., Zero Pop. Growth, Greenpeace, UCD and UCB alumni assns., Lafayette-Langeac Soc. (pgm. dir.), Pemmer Geneal. Soc.; works: contbr. scholarly jours.; song composer: And I Won't Leave (1979); current research on his theory that species and systems together generate species diversity (biol.), 1986; Democrat; rec: nature, guitar, chess. Address: Foundation for Biological Conservation and Research 1154 Glen Rd Lafayette 94549

SEABORG, GLENN THEODORE, scientist, education leader; b. Apr. 19, 1912, Ishpeming, Mich.; s. H. Theodore and Selma Olivia (Erickson) S.; m. Helen L. Griggs, June 6, 1942; children: Peter Glenn, b. 1946; Lynne Annette, b. 1947; David Michael, b. 1949; Stephen Keith, b. 1951; John Eric, b. 1954; Dianne Karole, b. 1959; edn: AB, UCLA 1934; PhD, UC Berkeley 1937; 49 hon. degrees. Career: research assoc. w/Prof. Gilbert N. Lewis, Coll. of Chem. UCB, 1937-39; instr. Dept. of Chem., 1939-41, asst. prof. 1941-45, section chief Metallurgical Lab., Univ. of Chgo. 1942-46; prof. Dept. of Chem. UCB, 1945-71; dir. Nuclear Chem. Research, Lawrence Radiation Lab., 1946-58; assoc. dir. 1954-61; chancellor, UCB, 1958-61; chmn. US Atomic Energy Commn., Wash DC 1961-71; univ. prof. of chemistry, UCB, 1971–, acting director Lawrence Hall of Science 1982-84, chmn. 1984-; assoc. dir. Lawrence Berkeley Lab., 1971–; pres., Science Service Inc., 1966-; bd. dirs. Swedish Council, 1976-; mem. Nat. Commn. on Excellence in Education, Us Dept. of Educ., 1981-83. Awards include Nobel Prize, Chem. (1951); Enrico Fermi Award (1959); Arches of Sci. Award, Pacific Sci. Ctr. (1968); US DOS Distinguished Honor Award (1971); Priestley Medal, ACS (1979). Mem. Bohemian Club (SF), Commonwealth Club (SF), Cosmos Club, Univ. Club (Wash DC), Chemists Club, Council on Fgn. Rels. (NYC); Pi Kappa Alpha, Alpha Chi Sigma; Contra Costa CC, Claremont CC; holder of 43 patents; Prot.; rec: hiking, golf. Res: 1154 Glen Rd Lafayette 94549 Ofc: Lawrence Berkeley Lab., Univ. of California, Berkeley 94720

SEAMOUNT, DAN TAYLOR, land surveyor, forester; b. May 26, 1923, Newton, Kans.; s. Dan and Flossie Mabel (Taylor) S.; m. Janet Underwood, Sept. 9, 1950; children: Daniel, Jr. b. 1951, Ann Marie b. 1953, Nancy b. 1955, Jean b. 1957, Susan b. 1960, Mary b. 1961, David b. 1963; edn: BS in forestry, UC Berkeley 1950, MBA, 1951; Reg. Profl. Forester, Calif. (1964), lic. Land Surveyor in Wash., Calif. (1974); Std. tchg. credential (surveying, math.). Career: forester Union Lumber Co., Fort Bragg 1951-52; tchr. South Fork Union High Sch., Miranda 1952-55; logging engr. Crown Zellerbach Corp., Cathlamet, Wash. 1955-57; jr. coll. instr. Olympic Coll., Bremerton, Wash. 1957-60; wage-hour investigator US Dept. of Labor, Riverside, Calif. 1960-62; researcher Tree Crop Harvesting Sytems and Farm Labor Efficiency, UC Riverside, 1962-73; timber mgmt. Golden State Building Prods., Redlands 1973-74; forester and land surveyor Calif. Dept. Forestry, 1974–; honors: Lettered in track (3 yrs.) and cross-country (4 yrs.) UC Berkeley, Zi Sigma Phi, Order of the Golden Bear; mem. Soc. of Am. Foresters (chpt. chmn. 1986), Calif. Land Surveyors Assn.; patentee: swing seat used in picking fruit; contbr. 14 research publs. in harvesting efficiency of agricultural tree crops (1965-74); mil: s/sgt. US Army Air Corps 1943-46; Democrat; Catholic; rec: road racing, backpacking, x-c skiing. Res: 6655 N Anna St Fresno 93710 Ofc: Calif. Dept. of Forestry 1234 East Shaw Ave Fresno 93710

SEATON, LAURENCE W., construction project manager; b. Oct. 13, 1951, Tarrant, Ala.; s. Robert R. and Geraldine (Brown) S.; edn: AS, L.A. Pierce Coll. 1974; BS, Cal. Poly. Univ. 1977. Career: proj. mgr., estimator Summit Steel Fabricators San Luis Obispo 1984-85; proj. mgr. Mid Coast Welding Atascadero 1983-84; field engr. Pullman Power Products Diablo Canyon Nuclear Plant 1983; scheduler Air Base Constructors, Ramon Air Base Israel 1980-82; proj. coord. Bunnell Constrn. S.L.O. 1978-80, proj. mgr. 1980–; cons. constrn. mgmt. CPM scheduling; mem: Am. Welding Soc., Proj. Mgmt. Inst., Constrn. Mgmt. Assn. of Am., Nat. Eagle Scout Assn., Alpha Psi Omega, Cal. Poly. Alumni Assn.; mil: sp4 US Army, honor guard Tomb of the Unknown Soldier 1970-71; Republican; Presbyterian; rec: scuba, triathlon, collecting limited edition graphics, acting (community theatre, semi-profl. groups). Res: 1600 11th St Los Osos 93402 Ofc: Bunnell Construction 141 Suburban Rd San Luis Obispo 93401

SEDWAY, LYNN MASSEL, economist; b. Nov. 26, 1941, Wash. DC; d. Mark S. and Jean M. (Magnus) Massel; stepmother: Katherine (Douglas) Massel; m. Paul Sedway, June 12, 1966; children: Mark b. 1967, Carolyn b. 1968, Jan b. 1970; edn: BA econs., Univ. Mich. Ann Arbor 1963; MBA, UC Berkeley 1976; CRE, Am. Soc. Real Estate Counselors 1984. Career: San Rafael Redevel. Agcy. 1976-78; prin. Lynn Sedway & Assocs. San Rafael 1978–; instr. appraisal Univ. Calif. Bus. Sch. extn.; mem: Urban Land Inst., Lambda Alpha (land econs. frat., chpt. pres.), Internat. Council of Shopping Centers, S.F., Marin (bd.), San Rafael CofCs, Marin Symphony, Berkeley Bus. Sch. Fund Council, San Rafael Downtown Retail Com., Marin County Housing Devel. Finance Corp., Dominican Coll. (CAC mem.); rec: tennis. Res: 79 Moncada Way San Rafael 94901 Ofc: Lynn Sedway & Assocs. 1000 Fourth St Ste 500 San Rafael 94901

SEELIN, SRIKANTH NAGABHUSHAN, manufacturing engineer; b. Nov. 13, 1953, Hassan, Karnataka, India; s. Nagabhushan Alur and Saroja Devi (Rajashekhariah) S.; m. Kusuma Puttappa, June 29, 1981; edn: P.D.Sc., Fergusson Coll. 1971; BSME, U.V.C.E., Bangalore Univ. 1976; MBA, Clarkson Univ., New York 1979. Career: mech. engr. MICO-BOSCH, India 1976-77; prodn. engr. B.J. Industries, India 1979-80; mktg. engr. HMT Ltd., India 1980-81; industrial engr. Cromemco Inc., Mountain View 1982-83; process engr. Dysan Corp., Santa Clara 1983-85; mfg. engr. Varian Associates, Palo Alto 1985–; guest lectr., eng. and mgmt., Bangalore Univ. and the Inst. of Engrs., India 1981, 1983; honors: Watumull Scholarship, MBA pgm. 1978; mem: Inst. of Industrial Engrs. (San Francisco- Peninsula chpt., pres. 1985-86); publs: in the Analyst, 1983, 1985; I.E. Newsletter; 1985 Internat. IIE Conf. proceedings; Los Angeles-Computer Mfg.; Hindu; rec: woodworking, western instrumental music. Res: 6106 Del Canto Dr., San Jose 95119 Ofc: Varian Associates, 611 Hansen Way, M/S: D-77, Palo Alto 94303

SEEMAN, LAURENCE E., veterinarian; b. Jan. 8, 1936, Huron, So. Dakota; s. Leroy Russell and Mary L. (Stevens) S.; m. Lena Meyer, Aug. 4, 1956; edn: AA, Fullerton Jr. Coll. 1965; BS, UC Davis 1968, DVM, honors, 1970; Cert. of Internship, Univ. of Penn. 1971. Career: salesman Nash Finch Co., Huron, So. Dakota 1955-58; prodn. plan coord. Minute Maid Corp., Fullerton 1961-63; veterinarian Los Caballos Vet. Hosp., Temecula 1971-73; pres. Seeman & Holmes Vet. Hosp., Lake Elsinore 1973–; tchr. Univ. of Penn. 1971; public spkr., Univ. of Calif., So. Calif. Arab Club, San Diego Arab Club, Santa Ynez Arab Club, San Fernando Arab Club, Cal Poly Pomona, So. Calif. Vet. Assn., So. Calif. Farm Mgrs.; honors: 1 of 25 Most Outstanding Students, Fullerton J.C. 1963, 1964, 1965; 2nd Highest GPA, Fullerton J.C. 1963-65; Scholarship, UC Davis 1966; mem: Am., Calif. and San Diego Co. Vet. Med. Assn., Am. Assn. Equine Practitioners; research: Uterine Biopsy of Equine 1970-; mil: splst. 4/c US Army 1958-60; Democrat; Catholic; rec: philately, hunting, golf. Res: 34174 DePortola Rd. Temecula 92390 Ofc: Seeman & Holmes, 34637 Orange Ave. Lake Elsinore 92330

SEFTON, WILLIAM LEE, certified public accountant; b. Dec. 6, 1943, San Francisco; s. Seibert Lee and Mimi (Stone) S.; m. Wilann Jean, Feb. 14, 1970; 1 dau, Robin; edn: BA, Willamette Univ. 1965; M.Acctg., USC 1966; CPA, Calif. Career: controller Dataquest Inc., Cupertino 1979-80; pvt. practice pub. acctg., San Ramon 1980–; mem: Am. Inst. CPAs, Calif. Soc. CPAs, Crow Canyon Homeowners Assn. (pres.); mil: US Coast Guard 1977; Republican; Mormon. Res: 2011 St. George Rd. San Ramon 94583 Ofc: 12901 Alcosta Blvd. Ste. A San Ramon 94583

SEGAL, MIKHAIL, construction co. president; b. Apr. 29, 1938, Kiev, USSR; s. Arkady and Maria (Lekhtgoltz) S.; m. Svetlana, 1965; 1 son, Alik b. 1966; edn: MS, Engrg. Constrn. Inst. Moscow, USSR 1961; contg. engring. edn., CSU Long Beach 1984; Calif. lic. gen. engring. & building contractor. Career: civil engr. design co., Kiev, USSR 1961-67; field civil engr. Kiev State Co., USSR 1967-73, mgr. civil technical dept. in constrn. co., 1973-79; project control engr./ civil engr. C.F. Braun, Alhambra 1980-83, field engr. Anheuser-Busch proj.; pres. Segal Construction, Inc., Los Angeles 1983–; mem. Nat.

Assn. of Gen. Contrs.; Jewish; rec: music, literature, sports. Res: 120 N Doheny Dr #303 Los Angeles 90048 Ofc; Segal Construction Inc 4070 West Third St Ste 224 Los Angeles 90020

SEGAL, SVETLANA G., physician; b. July 8, 1941, Kiev, USSR, nat. USA 1980; d. GErsh Aron and Lubov D. (Korostishevskaya) Vaysman; m. Mikhail Segal, July 16, 1965; 1 son, Alik b. 1966; edn: MD, Kiev Med. Sch., USSR 1964; PhD in medicine, Kiev Inst. for Advanced Med. Studies, 1970. Career: intern Kiev City Hosp. 1964-65, resident in internal medicine Kiev Inst. for Adv. Med. Studies, 1965-67, fellow in cardiology 1967-69; assoc. prof. in cardiology Strazhesko Inst. for Cardiology Research, Kiev, USSR 1970-79; fellow in cardiology Hosp. of the Good Samaritan, Los Angeles 1981-82; solo practitioner cardiologist, internist, Los Angeles 1982—; recipient Physician Recogn. Award, AMA; mem: AMA, Calif. Med. Assn., Los Angeles County Med. Assn., Am.-Russian Med. and Dental Soc. (v.p. 1985); 29 sci. publs. in field of cardiology (1963-79); Jewish; rec: piano, arts. Ofc: Svetlana G. Segal, MD, PhD Inc. 6221 Wilshire Blvd Ste 607 Los Angeles 90048

SEGHEZZI, GREGORY PETER, retail store owner; b. Oct. 19, 1959, Grass Valley; s. Amos Peter and Beverly Ann (Gregory) S.; m. Angela Giani, May 19, 1984; edn: AA in actg., Sierra Coll. 1982. Career: (current) prop. Amos' Alta Sierra Market, Grass Valley, and estab. second store, Amos Penn Valley Market, Penn Valley 1986—; vice pres. Amos' Bottle Shop Inc., Grass Valley; bd. dirs. GVMC (mktg. and video prodn. co.); civic: Gold Country Lions (bd. 1984-, 1st v.p.), Nevada Co. Softball (treas. 3 yrs), Nevada Co. CofC (Amb.), vol., youth helper, Nevada Co. Sheriff Drug Prevention; Republican; Christian; rec: photog., drawing, woodworking, softball. Res: 559 Alta Sierra Dr Grass Valley 95949 Ofc: Amos' Alta Sierra Market 10182 Alta Sierra Dr Grass Valley 95949

SEIBEL, ERWIN, educator, academic administrator; b. Apr. 29, 1942, Schwientochlowitz, Germany; s. Hugo Josef and Berta S.; m. Monique, July 6, 1968; 1 dau. Stephanie b. 1974; edn: BS, City Coll. of N.Y. 1965; MS, Univ. Mich. 1966, PhD 1972. Career: served to capt. US Army Corps of Engrs. 1967-71; asst. research oceanographer, Univ. Mich., Ann Arbor 1972-75, assoc. research oceanographer/asst. dir. Mich. Sea Grant Pgm., 1978-81; dir. Tiburon Ctr. for Environ. Studies 1978-81; prof. oceanography San Francisco St. Univ. 1978—, and chmn. Dept. Geoscis. 1981-; bd. govs. Moss Landing Marine Lab. (1981-), mem. Nat. Review Teams, Office of Sea Grant MOAA (1978-), mem. exec. com. Oceans'83, Internat. Conf. on Effective Use of the Sea (1982-83); awards: exceptional merit svc. award SFSU (1984), Sigma Xi (1973); mem: Fellow AAAS (1985), Fellow Geol. Soc. of Am. (1983), Fellow Calif. Acad. of Scis. (1986), NY Acad. of Scis. (1983), Am. Geophys. Union, Marine Technol. Soc. (advis. com. SF Bay Chpt. 1984-), Soc. of Econ. Paleontologists and Mineralogists; civic: Girl Scouts (vol. Bay Area Council 1983-85), MESA Pgm. for minority students (adv. 1982-85), PTA (1980-); contbr. num. articles on coastal oceanography, dynamics of beaches, and coastal environ. impact of nuclear power plant ops. in profl. publs. (1972-); devel. photogrammetric technique for continuous shoreline monitoring (1972-78); rec: sailing, tennis. Ofc: Dept. Geosciences San Francisco State University 1600 Holloway Ave San Francisco 94132

SEIFERT, DONALD EDWARD, international marketing executive; b. Sept. 26, 1937, Webster, Mass.; s. Richard and Maxyne (Emmons) S.; children: Shana b. 1970, Heather b. 1972; edn: BS, Mich. St. Univ. 1961; grad. sci. stu., Harvard, M.I.T., 1961-64; AMA courses, fgn. trade, acct., fin., time mgmt. Career: O.E.M. sales & mktg. mgr. Extracorporeal, 1965-70; dir. internat. mktg. American Bentley, 1970—; honors: Appreciation Award, Assn. of Thoracic & Cardiovascular Surgeons of Asia, 1983; E Award for Export, first Soviet-Am. Med. Symposium in Russia, 1979; mem: Am. Soc. of Extra Corporeal Tech. Inc., Fellow Royal Soc. of Health (London), Inst. of Mktg. London, Brazil Trade Assn., Internat. Mktg. Assn. Orange Co., World Affairs Council of Orange Co., World Trade Center Assn. O.C. (bd.), Assn. of Renal Tech. (Eng.), Assn. of Thoracic & C.V. Surgeons of Asia (life patron), Nat. Notary Assn., So. Coast Rep. Theatre (Silver Circle), AAMI 32 Degree Mason, Aleppo Temple, Boston; publs: num. med. & tech. papers; mil: US Army Sch. pre comm. Ft. Benning 1962-67, E7, commanding ofcr. Army Nat. Guard 6 yrs., Distinguished Svc. Award; Republican; Methodist; rec: skiing, hunting, coins. Res: 31452 Holly Dr South Laguna 92677 Ofc: Bentley International (Div. AHSIS), 17502 Armstrong Ave Irvine 92714

SEILER, LEE MELVIN, artist; b. Apr. 18, 1942, Alameda, Calif.; s. Paul Melvin and Norma Alice (Bradley) S.; m. Diane Brown, Aug. 21, 1963; children: Antena Marie b. 1967, Eva Diane b. 1971; edn: BA, Calif. Coll. of Arts & Crafts 1985. Career: film processor Bear Foto 2 yrs.; electro-mech. design & repair Monroe Internat. 2 yrs.; mech. engrg. research, grad. sch. sci. model constrn. Univ. Calif. 12 yrs.; freelance illustrator, cons. technical illustrations 8 yrs; pub. Cliffridge Publishing, tech cons. Starrion Prodns. 1983—; honors: EMMY Awrd for Best Technical Achievement in a Local T.V. Pgm. (for The UFO Experience, KPIX-S.F. 1983); contbg. mem. Calif. Acad. of Scis.; author: Building Beings, Creating Creatures, Doing Dinosaurs; artwork series of Walking Machines (Garthian Strider); creator Fossil Stone Ednl. Kits; mil: warrant ofcr. US Army 1959-64; Republican; Lutheran; rec: windsurfing, hang-gliding, rock-clinbing. Ofc: Starrion Prodns. 79 Midcrest Ste 101 San Francisco 94119

SEITELMAN, JEFFREY K., child & adult psychiatrist; b. Aug. 28, 1952, NYC; s. Max and Margot (Bravman) S.; m. Judith Gilden, Nov. 18, 1984; 1 son, Robert b. 1979; edn: BA in chem., cum laude, Williams Coll. 1973; MD, State Univ. NY, Buffalo 1977; physician and surgeon, BMQA 1978; bd. certified Am. Board Psych. & Neurology 1983, Child Psych. 1985. Career: psychiatry residencies Long Beach VA Hosp. 1977-78, UC Irvine Med. Ctr. 1978-79, LA County-USC Med. Ctr. 1979-80; fellow Child, Adolescent & Family Psychiatry LAC-USC Med. Ctr. 1980-82, fellow Child Adminstrv. Psychiatry, 1982-83; pvt. practice Adult & Child Psychiatry, 1983—; chmn. Psychiatry Dept. Dominguez Med. Ctr. 1984-; mem: So. Calif. Psych. Soc., Am. Psych. Assn., AMA, L.A. County Med. Assn., So. Calif. Soc. for Child Psych., Am. Acad. of Child Psych., Phi Delta Epsilon; Jewish; rec: classical guitar, Judaica, dance. Ofc: 3320 Los Coyotes Diagonal Ste 207 Long Beach 90808

SEITZ, LAURA RUTH, graphic design studio executive; b. Nov. 29, 1951, Detroit; d. John Calvin and Charlotte Mary (Collins) S.; edn: Western Mich. Univ. 1969-72; L.A. Municipal Art Galleries 1975-78; UC Los Angeles 1978. Career: designer Moonshadow Designs Ann Arbor, Mich. and L.A. 1973-77; secty. Maher Elen Advtg. L.A. 1976-79, acct. exec. 1979-80, acct. supv. 1980-81; sales mgr. Sojourn Design Group L.A. 1981-82; owner O'Mara/ Seitz Design Group Santa Monica 1982—; dir. sales & mktg. Anselmo Design Assocs. 1982-83; cons., spkr. 1982-; mem: L.A. Ad. Club, Nat. Assn. Female Execs., Internat. Assn. Bus. Communicators; rec: travel. Ofc: O'Mara/ Seitz Design Group 1321 7th St Ste 300 Santa Monica 90401

SELBY, RICHARD WAYNE, computer science educator, consultant; b. June 28, 1959, Chgo.; s. Richard W., Sr. and Nancy Ann (Baker) S.; edn: BA, honors in math., St. Olaf Coll. 1981; MS, Univ. of Md. 1983, PhD 1985. Career: research asst., assoc. Univ. of Md., College Park, Md. 1981-85; prof. computer sci., UC Irvine 1985—; cons. IBM, Fed. Systems Div. (1985), PA Computers & Telecomm., Princeton, NJ (1984), IBM Data Systems Div. (1985-); awards: prin. or co-prin. investigator 4 research grants (1985-91), NSF travel grantee (1985), ACM Samuel N. Alexander PhD Fellow, Wash DC Chpt. (1984-85), Outstanding Masters Scholar Award, GE Info. Svcs. Co. (1983-84), Putnam Nat. Math. Competition, 501st (1980), Dean's List (1979-81), Eagle Scout, Vigil Honor, Order of the Arrow, BSA; mem: IEEE, IEEE Computer Soc., Assn. Computing Mach.; publs. in profl. jours. and refereed confs. (1984-); Republican; rec: investing, sailing. Ofc: University of Calif. Dept. Computer Science Irvine 92717

SELDNER, BETTY J., co. executive; b. Dec. 11, 1925, Baltimore, Md.; d. David D. and Miriam M. (Mendes) Miller; m. Alvin Seldner, Nov. 15, 1965; children: Jack and Barbara Seldner, and Patricia and Deborah Gray; edn: BA in journ., CSU Northridge 1975, MA, 1977; desig: accredited, PRSA (1974); Calif. Energy Auditor cert. (1981). Career: dir. Public Information, United Way/San Fernando Valley 1958-63, dir. edn. United Way/L.A. 1963-68; dir. pub. rels./fin., SFV Girl Scout Council, Reseda 1968-73; asst. dir. public information, CSU Northridge, 1973-75; dir. environmtl. mgmt. pgms. HR Textron Inc., Valencia 1975—, chair PAC 1978-; mem. NMA (chpt. dir. 1975-), Santa Clarita Valley Envir. Mgr. Soc. (chpt. chair 1984-), Soroptimist Club, SFV Press Club (pres. 1970-71), SFV PR Round Table (pres. 1971-72), SCV Energy Soc., SCV Special Childrens Ctr. (dir. 1984-); publs: articles in Sea Mag. (1979), Manage Mag. (1980), HR News (1975-), Haz. Mat. Proceedings (1985-); Republican; Jewish; rec: sailing. Res: 23944 Ave Crescenta Valencia 91355 Ofc: HR Textron Inc 25200 W Rye Cyn Road Valencial 91355

SELLECK, ROBERT DEAN, real estate brokerage executive; b. Dec. 27, 1921, Lapeer, Mich.; s. George Samuel and Nellie Louise (Fife) S.; m. Martha Jagger, Apr. 11, 1942; children: Robert II b. 1943, Thomas b. 1945, Martha b. 1953, Daniel b. 1955; edn: Ohio Wesleyan Univ. 1940-41; Calif. lic. real estate broker (1948). Career: ptnr. George S. Selleck & Sons, gen. contrs., Detroit, Mich. 1946-48; salesman Coldwell, Banker & Co., Los Angeles 1948-63, vice pres./resident mgr. Wilshire Ofc. 1953-68, 1st v.p./res. mgr. San Fernando Valley Ofc. 1968-84, senior v.p./dir. corp. communications Coldwell Banker Commercial Group, 1984—; honors: recipient w/wife, First Annual Premier Parents Award, March of Dimes Birth Defects Found./ San Fernando Valley Assocs. (1984), San Fernando Valley Humanitarian Award, Project Heavy (1982) and the Fernando Award (1982); apptd. City of Los Angeles commnr. Meml. Coliseum and Sports Arena (1977-84, pres. 1980), LA Olympic Organizing Com. (dir. 1979-86), apptd. City of Los Angeles Rec. & Parks Commn. (1977-84, pres. 1979, 84); mem: Valley Indus. and Commerce Assn. of Greater SFV (dir. 1969-, pres. 1973), SFV Bd. of Realtors 1968-83 (dir. 1972), LA Hq. City Assn. (dir.), Valley Presbyn. Hosp. (trustee), LA Bd. of Realtors 1948-, Rotary, Jonathan Club (1980-), The Los Angeles Club (pres. 1968), Lakeside Golf Club (pres. 1976-77), USC Cardinal and Gold, Am. Red Cross (Wilshire Div. chmn. 1956-57), United Way (SFV Red Cross coord. 1980-81), Mission Coll. Task Force (1974-79); mil: pfc Army Air Corps 1943-45; Republican; Congregational; rec: golf, gardening. Res: 13919 Weddington St Van Nuys 91401 Ofc: Coldwell Banker Commercial Group 533 Fremont Ave Los Angeles 90071

SELWOOD, PIERCE TAYLOR, lawyer; b. July 31, 1939, Evanston, Ill.; s. Pierce Wilson and Alice (Taylor) S.; m. Alexis Fuerbringer, June 8, 1964; children: Allison b. 1968, Jonathan b. 1971; edn: AB, Princeton Univ. 1961; JD, Harvard Law Sch. 1964; admitted Calif. State Bar 1965. Career: assoc. atty. Sheppard, Mullin, Richter & Hampton, Los Angeles 1964-70, ptnr. 1971—, now senior partner, v. chmn. Litigation Dept.; honors: Who's Who in Am. Law (1978-); mem: Am. Bar Assn. (Litig. Mgmt. subcom. chair), State Bar of Calif., Los Angeles County Bar Assn. (past mem. Judiciary Com.), Assn. of Bus. Trial Lawyers (past bd. govs.); clubs: Jonathan, Princeton of So. Calif; Republican; Episcopal; rec: tennis, hiking, wines. Ofc: Sheppard,Mullin, Richter & Hampton, 333 S Hope St, 48th Fl, Los Angeles 90071

SELYA, MANUEL LINCOLN, clinical psychologist; b. Apr. 1, 1941, Boston; s. David and Anne (Kirsten) S.; edn: BS, Northeastern Univ. 1966; M.Ed. Boston State Coll. 1975; Ph.D. Boston Coll. 1980. Career: Bechtel Construction Co. S.F.; teacher; real estate; psychologist pvt. practice, Health Care Agcy., Co. of Orange, affil. of Comprehensive Employee Services Inc.; honors: Industrial Engrg. Honor Soc. 1966; mem: Am. Psychol. Assn.; APA (ind. practice div., cons. psychol. div.), Sierra Club, Soc. for the Performing Arts (Cabaret chap.); publ: Women Runners and Amenorrith (Am. Jour. of OB-Gyn 1980); Jewish; rec: skiing, sailing, swimming. Res: 434 Goldenrod Ave Corona del Mar 92625 Ofc: Newport Harbor Counseling 2900 Bristol St, Ste 105D, Costa Mesa 92626

SELZNICK, STEPHEN ANDREW, computer software co. president; b. Oct. 21, 1941, NY, NY; s. Murray and Gertrude (Minkoff) S.; m. Cynthia Ann, Dec. 9, 1984; children: Jonathan b. 1966, Marc b. 1969, Kimberly b. 1969; edn: BSEE, Univ. of Miami, Fla. 1963. Career: engr. General Dynamics, Pomona 1963-66; engr. W.V. Sterling, Inc. Los Angeles 1966-70; mgr. data proc. McIntire & Quiros, L.A. 1970-73; dir. D.P., Greiner, Inc. Los Angeles 1973-77; pres. Professional Software Applications, Inc. Covina 1977–; instr. Calif. St. Polytechnic Univ. 1974-76; mem. DPMA 1975-78; rec: skiing, bridge. Ofc: Professional Software Applications Inc 599 S Barranca St Ste 555 Covina 91723

SEMIGRAN, CANDACE MARIE, training organization executive; b. Nov. 25, 1949, Los Angeles; d. Weeden Ford Jr. and Thelma Fay (Phelps) Shanklin; m. Stuart Semigran, Aug. 21, 1983; edn: BA, La Verne Col. 1971, tchg. cred. 1973. Career: tchr. Rowland Heights Unif. Sch. Dist., Rowland Heights 1971-74; treas., asst. to the pres., Church of the Movement of Spiritual Inner Awareness, Los Angeles 1974-78; ast. dir., facilitator Insight Transformational Sems., Santa Monica 1978-84, exec. dir. 1984-; v.p. Koh-E-Nor Univ., Inc.; mem: Associated for Humanistic Psychology, Santa Monica CofC; works: author articles for Insight Newsletter and var. journs.; Ch. of the Movement of Spiritual Inner Awareness; rec: skiing. Ofc: Insight Transformational Seminars, 2101 Wilshire Blvd. Santa Monica 90403

SENTER, ARNOLD J., insurance co. executive; b. Mar. 24, 1942, Los Angeles; s. Harold H. and Betty E. (Slater) S.; m. Linda M. Milburn, Jan. 17, 1978; 1 dau., Zoe, b. 1966; edn: BS, Ariz. State Univ. 1965; MBA, Pepperdine Univ. 1982; Calif. reg. profl. engineer. Career: senior engr. Travelers Ins. Cos., Phoenix, Dallas, Fresno, San Francisco 1965-69; v.p. Chenootree Airlines, Los Angeles, NY, 1969-70; regional mgr. Hartford Ins. Group, Oakland, Pasadena, Norwalk, Houston, 1970-78; asst. v.p. Mission Ins. Group, L.A. 1978-81; v.p., Zenith Insurance Co., Encino 1981–; honor: Outstanding Young Man of Year - Pacifica (S.F.) Jaycees, 1967; mem: Sales and Mktg. Execs. Assn., Nat. Assn. of MBA Execs., Nat. Mgmt. Soc., Am. Mgmt. Assn., Masons; mil: E7, US Army, Reserve 1960-68; publ. article: An Assessment of Employee Turnover in the Property-Casualty Insurance Industry (1983); Republican; rec: sailing. Res: 17938 Mayerling St Granada Hills 91344 Ofc: The Zenith Insurance Co. 15760 Ventura Blvd Encino 91436

SEPEHRI, MEHRAN, educator, management consultant; b. June 17, 1956, Kerman, Iran; s. Soroush and Dolat (Gazigari) S.; edn: BS, Arya-Mehr Univ. 1977; grad. work M.I.T., 1978; PhD, Stanford Univ. 1981; Reg. Profl. Engr., Calif. Career: consultant sev. high tech. industries in Calif. 1979–, cons. Xerox Corp. 1985, Ask Computers 1984, Micro MRP 1983; mgr. of operation, planning Atari, Inc. 1981-83; asst. prof. UC Riverside 1984; assoc. prof. CSU Long Beach 1985–; awards: research grantee, mfg., APICS (1985); mem. Am. Prodn. and Inventory Control Soc., Inst. of Indsl. Engrs., Am. Inst. of Decision Scis.; mem. Zoroastrian Persian; contbr. over 30 publs. in var. mags. on mfg. and computer appls., book on mfg. (1986); Zoroastrian; rec: skiing, travel. Res: 1101 East 215th Pl Carson 90745 Ofc: School of Business Calif. State University Long Beach 90840

SERBIN, GLEN R., magazine publisher; b. Feb. 11, 1954, Chicago, Ill.; s. David and Beverly S.; edn: history, UCLA 1976. Career: founder, publisher, editor Photographer's Forum mag. 1977–; honors: magazine won 1981 Calif. Award and 1986 Santa Barbara Ad Club Award of Excellence; Democrat; rec: music, tennis, photog. Ofc: Santa Barbara 93101

SERETAN, WENDY JOY, investment banker; b. June 15, 1956, Manhassett, NY; d. Morris Arnold and Rose (Richman) S.; m. Donald P. Hateley, May 25, 1985; edn: BSME, UCLA 1979; MBA, Pepperdine Univ. 1981. Career: engr. Gillette Papermate div., Santa Monica 1977-82; admin. mgr. tooling Mattel Electronics, Hawthorne 1982-83; assoc. Am. Diversified Equity Corp., Los Angeles 1983-84; exec. v.p. The Cambridge Group Inc., Los Angeles 1984–; dir. The Cambridge Group Inc.; dir., ofcr. Coll. Centers of So. Calif.; honors: The Engring. Faculty Friends Award, R.R. O'Neill, UCLA Sch. of Engring. 1979; mem: Los Angeles World Affairs Council, Los Angeles Town Hall; rec: tennis, skiing, travel. Ofc: The Cambridge Group Inc., 10801 National Blvd. Ste. 600 Los Angeles 90064

SERVETNICK, RICHARD, financial co. executive; b. Jan. 24, 1943, Lynn, Mass.; m. Marsha A. Blomquist, Apr. 24, 1976; children: Karen b. 1969, Ryan b. 1973, Scott b. 1977; edn: BA, Boston Univ. 1965; MBA, Pepperdine Univ. 1978. Career: salesman Mobil Oil Corp. Boston 1968-69; investment advisor Security Pacific Nat. Bank L.A. 1969-71; trader Shareholders Mgmt. L.A. 1969-71; mgr. trading Funds Inc. Houston 1971-73; mgr. trading American Express Investment Mgmt. Co. S.F. 1973-75; prin. Shuman Agnew & Co. S.F. 1975-77; prin. Morgan Stanley & Co. Inc. S.F. 1977–; honors: Collegium of

Disting. Alumni (Coll. of Lib. Arts., Boston Univ. 1982); mem: Nat. Securities Traders Assn., S.F. Sec. Traders Assn., Nat. Wildlife Fedn. (life), Calif. Hist. Soc. (sponsor), Commonwealth Club of Calif., Pepperdine Univ. (assoc.); mil: US Army Intelligence 1965-68, Meritorious Svc.; Republican; Episcopal; rec: golf, music. Ofc: Morgan Stanley & Co. Inc. 101 California St San Francisco 94111

SEUNG, WON P., veterinarian; b. Dec. 15, 1953, Seoul, Korea; d. Young H. and Seung D. (Kang) S.; edn: DVM, Seoul National Univ. 1977, MVM, 1981; MS, UC Davis 1984; veterinarian, Calif. 1985. Career: veterinary ofcr. Republic of Korea Army 1977-79; instr. Seoul Nat. Univ. 1979-81; staff researcher Korean Inst. of Veterinary Research 1981-82; postgrad. researcher UC Davis 1982-84; staff veterinarian Orange Pet Care Ctr., Orange 1985–; mem: Am. Veterinary Med. Assn., Am. Soc. for Veterinary Clinical Pathology; mil: lt. 1st Small Animal Hosp., Korean Army; Catholic; rec travel. Res: 13150 Acoro Pl. Cerritos 90701 Ofc: Orange Pet Care Center, 809 E. Katella Ave. Anaheim 92667

SEXTER, I. MICHAEL, psychotherapist/counseling director; b. Aug. 7, 1933, NY, NY; s. Jackson and Rose (Rossen) Sexter; Edn: BA in Speech, NY Univ. 1952, MA in Speech, NY Univ. 1953, EdD in Psychology, NY Univ. 1967. Career: newscaster Station WLIB, New York City 1952-55; Speech Prof. CSU Sacramento, 1956-60; chmn. Speech Dept., Sacramento City Coll., 1960-77; psychotherapist pvt. practice, Sacto. 1970-77; psychotherapist, Family Counseling Service, San Diego 1977-80; director, Alvarado Medical Center Counseling Svcs., S.D. 1980-83; psychotherapist pvt. practice, San Diego 1983–; lectr. Sacramento and San Diego seminars, workshops, and TV appearances; awards: Univ. of Calif. Profl. Studies grants (1973-4), Kellogg Found. for Higher Edn.; mem: AAUP (v.p. 1958-60), Calif. Assn. of Marriage and Family Therapists (pres. 1972-74), Calif. Psychological Assn., Am. Psychol. Assn., Masons, The Comstock Club (Sacto.); publs: Case Studies in the Adminstrn. of Higher Education, Univ. of Calif. (Ohio State Univ. Press 1974); rec: tennis, swimming. Res: 8528 Via Mallorca La Jolla 92037 Ofc: La Jolla Village Professional Center, 8950 Villa La Jolla Drive La Jolla 92037

SEXTON, PHILLIP LEE, manufacturing co. executive; b. Feb. 17, 1943, Antioch, Ca.; s. Cecil Sherman and Mildred E. (Phillips) S.; m. Ruthie M. Roller, Aug. 25, 1962; children: Kevin b. 1964, Jill b. 1966. Career: currently pres. Kilpatrick's Bakeries, Inc. San Francisco 1981–, past v.p. San Francisco Plant, past v.p./gen. mgr. Oak Plant, 1979, route sales 1964, route supr. 1975, sales mgr. 1976, sales service 1978; fmr. jr. high sch. tchr. one term; mem. exec. com. No. Calif., City of Hope; Protestant; rec: golf. Res: 424 El Capitan Danville 94626 Ofc: Kilpatrick's Bakeries Inc. 2030 Folsom St San Francisco 94110

SEYMOUR, JOHN "FRED", JR., culinary school and restaurant president; b. Sept. 24, 1949, Glen Cove, NY; s. John Fred and Elizabeth (Duncan) S.; m. Patricia Barton, Sept. 20, 1975; children: Elizabeth b. 1979, Scott b. 1981; edn: BA, St. Lawrence Univ. 1971; Diploma, Am. Inst. Banking 1974; Career: active player Boston Red Sox, var. sites, contract held by Louisville AAA Club 1971-72; branch mgr. Hempstead Bank NY 1973-76; asst. v.p. Calif. Canadian Bank S.F. 1980-81; v.p. Hibernia Bank Walnut Creek 1981-83; pres. Calif. Culinary Acad., McKesson Corp. S.F. 1983–; honors: George F. Baker Scholar 1967-71, All-East Football 1970, All-American Baseball 1971; mem: S.F. Profl. Food and Wine Soc., Club Mgrs. Assn., Nat. Restaurant Assn., Daiblo CC, S.F. CofC, S.F. Visitors and Convention Bureau, Bay Area Council Ednl. Consortium; rec: golf. Res: 2600 Caballo Ranchero POB 92 Diablo 94598 Ofc: Calif. Culinary Academy 625 Polk St San Francisco 94102

SEYMOUR, RONALD EDWARD, real estate broker; b. July 14, 1913, West Highland, Calif.; s. Edward Levi and Winifred Claire (Smith) S.; m. Hanoize Dixon, June 20, 1938 (div. 1953); children: Linda Ann b. 1941, Geoffrey Alan b. 1944; m. 2d June Very (decd. 1979). Career: DMV rep. Dept. Motor Vehicles Calif. 1937-55; supv. grounds, landscape designer County of Orange 1960-70; real estate salesman, broker 1969–, Century 21 Tri Cities Realty Victorville 1975–; real estate ing. ofcr.; honors: Million Dollar Club (Century 21 1978, 79); mem: Victor Valley Bd. Realtors (state dir. 2 yrs.), Calif. State Employees Assn. (past chpt. pres.), Apple Valley Grange (lectr. 1981-82, master 1983-84, exec. com. 1985-87), Mojave Valley Pomona Grange (steward 1984, master 1985, exec. com. 1986-88); Democrat; Christian Science; rec: gardening, livestock raising incl. miniature horses. Res: 15593 Manzanita Hesperia 92345 Ofc: College Realty, Better Homes & Gardens 14767 Bear Valley Rd Hesperia 92345

SHADE, JAMES WILLIAM BALL, architect; b. Dec. 7, 1926, Salem, Ore.; s. Hobert Eugene and Gertrude Leona (Hoppe) S.; m. Pat Southard, June 18, 1953; children: Nancy b. 1958, Carol b. 1961; edn: B.Arch., Univ. Ore. 1951; reg. architect Calif., Ore., Wash., Nev. Career: architect Ore., Wash. 1951-57, Turlock, Calif. 1957–; bd. regents Calif. Theol. Seminary, Fresno; bd. chmn. Ctr. for Biblical Studies, Modesto; Stanislaus County Bldg. Code Bd. of Appeals; No. Calif. & Nev. Area rep. and mem. Evangel Coll. Council, Springfield, Mo.; honors: Masonry Design Award, listed Who's Who in West 1969-; mem: Am. Inst. Archs. (past chpt. pres.), Rotary (gov.'s area rep. chmn.), Turlock Interchurch Fellowship (chmn.), Turlock CofC (past. dir.), Modesto-Turlock Full Gospel Businessmen's Fellowship (past. pres.), Turlock Exchange Club (past pres.), Century Club (CSU Stanislaus), Arrowhead Club (CSUS), Turlock Golf & CC; fmr. mem: bd. dirs. Emanuel Hosp., Turlock Aesthetic Com. (chmn.), Safety Commn. (chmn.), Modesto-Turlock Campus Life-Youth For Christ (bd. dirs.), NET-CAL Christian Ctr. (bd. dirs.), Turlock Parking

Commn., Planning Commn., Bethany Bible Coll. Council mil: USN 1944-46; Republican; Assemblies of God; rec: photog., gold. Res: 1501 LaSalle Dr Turlock 95380 Ofc: James W.B. Shade AIA, 310 Main St Turlock 95380

SHAFER, KENNETH W., engineering executive; b. Nov. 27, 1941, Glendale; s. Walter Duane and Cordia Ophelia (Engler) S.; m. Sandra Jane Ryder, Apr. 13, 1968; 1 dau. Cheryl Ann b. 1973; edn: BS in M.E., CSU San Jose 1964; MBA, Pepperdine Univ. 1982; Reg. Profl. Engr., Calif. (1978). Career: jr. mfg. engr. Philco-Ford Corp., Palo Alto 1967-70; senior design engr. Chrysler Corp., 1978-79, Lockheed Missles & Space Co., Huntsville, Al. 1979; project engr. FMC Corp., (project mgr. for ammunition handling sys., for electric drive study pgm.; concept design mgr. for family of combat vehicles for the years 2000 - 2020; project design engr. for wheeled combat vehicle; mgr. proposals in areas of robotics, artificial intel., logistics vehicles, and ammo. handling), San Jose 1972-78, 1979–; mil: 1st lt. US Army Corps of Engrs. 1964-66, Reserv. -71; rec: piano, table tennis, chess. Ofc: FMC Corporation 1105 Coleman Ave San Jose 95108

SHAFFER, JOHN ORDIE, physician; b. Aug. 29, 1920, Mnpls.; s. John Ordie, II and Della Helen (Stewart) S.; m. Dorothea Lidberg, May 7, 1947; children: Ann b. 1950, John, IV b. 1953; edn: BS, Univ. Minn. 1940, MD, 1943, MS Surgery 1950. Career: intern Philadelphia Gen. Hosp., Phila. 1943-44; fellow Mayo Found. 1944-46, 48-50; chief of surgery USS Hospital ship Comfort, mil. service in Pacific Theater, 1946-48; instr. in surgery Univ. of Utah Med. Sch.; pvt. surgery practice, Hayward, Calif. 1952–; past chief surg. Eden Hosp., Castro Valley and Humana Hosp. in San Leandro; performed first successful surgical treatment for absence of diaphragm & esophageal crura in medical history, 1961 (18-yr. follow-up account in Western J. of Med. 1981); surgery lectr. on all six continents, gave first foreign surgery lecture in Wuhan, China (10-13-79) since revolution; num. publs. in med. jours. incl. Jama Surgery, American Surgeon, Calif. Medicine, Archives of Surg., others; awards: San Francisco Surgical Soc. Award 1955; dinner in his honor and citation for bravery in rescuing multiple injured sailors from Pacific Tanker and saving lives with emergency surgery at sea, Am. Embassy in Tokyo 1946; mem: AMA, CMA, ACCMA, Am. Bd. of Surgery, Am. Coll. of Surgeons, Am. Med. Soc. of Vienna, Hayward CofC (past v.p.), Kiwanis (past pres.); mil: capt. US ARmy 1946-48; rec: landscape gardening, photog. Res: 4584 Ewing Rd Castro Valley 94546 Ofc: 1375 B St Hayward 94541

SHAFOR (SHAFORENK0), RENATA, physician; b. Apr. 2, 1940, Kishinev, Romania; d. Isaac and Shifra (Ackerman) Shatenshteyn; m. Valentin Shafor (Shaforenko), Jan. 25, 1964; children: Robert b. 1965, Victor b. 1976; edn: MD, honors, Kishinev State Med. Inst., USSR 1964. Career: gen. practitioner rural area USSR, 1964; district internist Kishinev City Clinic, 1965-70, Odessa City Clinic, 1970-79, city supr. hematology service Odessa, 1975-79; resident, chief resident Dept. Neurology, Univ. Mo., Columbia 1981-84; clin. fellow in sleep disorders Scripps Clinic and Research Found., La Jolla 1984-85, staff phys. 1985–; mem: AMA, Am. Acad. Neurology, Clinical Sleep Soc. ASDC; Hadassah; research articles in med. jours. (USSR, USA); Ind.; Jewish. Res: 1144 Woodlake Dr Cardiff 92007 Ofc: Scripps Clinic Research Fdn 10666 Torrey Pines Rd La Jolla 92037

SHAH, NARENDRA M., electrical engineer; b. Apr. 12, 1944, Padra, India, nat. US cit. 1981; s. Maneklal J. and Laduben M. S.; m. Usha, Feb. 3, 1969; children: Mona b. 1974, Milan b. 1978; edn: BSEE, Baroda Univ. India 1965, BSME, 1966; MSEE, Tuskegee Inst. Ala. 1972; tech. courses Ga. Tech. Atlanta 1975; Reg. Profl. Engr. Calif., Tex., Fla., Ga., Ala. Career: Parsons Brinkerhoff Tudor Bechtel Atlanta Transit System 1974-76; system engr. II to proj. engr. Kaiser Engrs. Inc. Oakland 1977–, cons. to Miami, Fla. and Houston, Tex. Transit Systems, BART Daly City, L.A. Co. Transp. commn., Long Beach to L.A. Light Rail Sys.; mem: Inst. Elec. Electron. Engrs. (senior mem.), Nat. Assn. Corrosion Engrs. (former); publ: papers presented at annual mtg. of IEEE 1972, 83; Democrat; Hindu; rec: reading, travel, cricket. Res: 34827 Wabash River Pl Fremont 94536 Ofc: Kaiser Engrs Inc. 1800 Harrison St Oakland 94623

SHAHAN, JANET LYNN, accountant; b. Nov. 20, 1954, Fresno; s. Herman Dean and Nadine Rose (Floyd) S.; edn: BA, UC Davis 1977; MBA, UC Berkeley 1980; CPA, Calif. 1983. Career: cost acct. Arcata National, San Francisco 1976-78; staff auditor Holiday Clubs Internat., Sausalito 1979; CPA Seiler & Co., San Francisco 1980-83; entertainment indsutry litigation and financial svcs. Janet Shahan, San Francisco 1983–; CPA self-empl.; mem. Am. Inst. CPAs. Address: Janet Shahan, 1079 Sierra Vista Way Lafayette 94549

SHAKIN, RITA TORGOVITSKY, retail jewelry co. president; b. Jan. 15, 1938, Shanghai, China, nat. US cit. 1954; d. Issai Grigorovitch and Pola (Gourovich) Torgovitsky; m. William L. Shakin, MD, Sept. 18, 1964; edn: BA, UC Berkeley 1958. Career: pres. Pearls & Jade Enterprises, Inc., consisting of Pearl Empire, Jade & Pearls Unlimited and Pearls & Jade at the Palace Hotel 1969–; conduct KQED Auctions; mem. Calif. Jewelers Assn., CofC, Hadassah (life); Republican; Jewish. Ofc: Pearl Empire 127 Geary St San Francisco 94108

SHAMES, RICHARD LEIGH, physician; b. June 21, 1945, Norfolk, Va.; s. George Joseph and Rosalie (Weisman) S.; m. Karilee Feibus, Apr. 29, 1979; children: Shauna b. 1979, Georjana b. 1981; edn: BA, Harvard Univ. 1967; MD, Univ. Pa. 1971; hypnotherapist, San Francisco Acad. of Hypnosis 1973; Diplomate Nat. Bd. Med. Examiners 1971. Career: intern USPHS San Francisco 1971; chief clin. phys. Marin Co. Health Dept. San Rafael 1972-75; chief med. svcs. The Assoc. for Research and Enlightenment, Edgar Cayce Clin. Phoenix 1979; pvt. practice fam. med., preventive and holistic health Mill Valley 1979–; researcher Nat. Inst. Health 1970; med. dir., founder Wholistic Health & Nutrition Inst. Mill Valley 1975-78; fam. practice residency instr. UCSF Med. Sch. family practice dept. 1976; bd. dirs. Children's Circle Center Private Sch. 1984; honors: Rose Meadow Levinson Meml. Prize for Cancer Research 1970; mem: Phys. for Social Responsibility; publ: books: Healing with Mind Power (Rodale Press 1978), The Gift of Health (Bantam Books 1981); contr. ed. and author of Ask the Family Doctor column for Internat. Jour. of Holistic Health and Med. 1984-85; mil: lt. USPHS 1971; rec: gardening, skiing, sailing. Res: 77 Lomita Mill Valley 94941 Ofc: 232 E Blithedale Ave Mill Valley 94941

SHANKS, FREDERICK MC NEILL, fresh fruit packing co. president; b. Dec. 10, 1931, Chico, Calif.; s. Frederick Lewis and Marion Josephine (Mills) S.; m. Catherine, Aug. 15, 1953; children: Carol b. 1957, Nancy b. 1960, Fred, Jr. b. 1961; edn: BS, UC Berkeley 1953; MBA, Stanford Univ. 1957; Calif. lic. R.E. Broker 1982. Career: mng. ptnr. Mills Orchards Assocs., Hamilton City 1960–; pres. James Mills Growers Service Co. 1961–, dir. 1958-; pres. Sacto. Valley Citrus Exchange 1970-80, Butte Glenn Citrus Assn. 1977-, North State Kiwi Packers 1983-; founder, dir. Chico Savings & Loan Assn. 1960-74; alternate dir. Calif. Tree Fruit Agreement 1975-81; alt. dir. Sunkist Growers Inc. 1975-80; dir. Calif. Grape & Tree Fruit League 1972-82; dir. Chico Travel Service 1975-; civic: Univ. Calif. Alumni Assn. (trustee), Glenn County Com. Sch. Dist. Reorganization, Hamilton Union H.S. (past pres., trustee 1975-81), Glenn-Colusa Co. Univ. Calif. Scholarship Com., Mt. Lassen Area Council Boy Scouts Am. (exec. bd., v.p.), Rotary Intl. (Paul Harris Fellow, dist. area rep. 1970, Chico club past pres.), N.T. Enloe Meml. Hosp. (hosp. assocs. 1969-, advis. council 1981-); mil: 1st lt. US Army 1954-56; Republican; Presbyterian; rec: boating, travel. Address: James Mills Growers Service Co. POB 668 Hamilton City 95951

SHANNON, CAROLYN K., music educator; b. June 17, 1933, Wash DC; d. Freeman F. and Goldie (Hixon) Knight; div.; 1 son, Donald b. 1953; edn: B.Mus., Columbia Union Coll. 1952, M.Mus., Catholic Univ. 1957. Career: chair Music Dept. Pasadena High Sch., 1969–, dir. of music Temple City Christian Ch., 1973–; assoc. broker Real Estate by Vella, Arcadia 1982–, sales leader in 1983, 85; singer in Los Angeles Master Chorale and Roger Wagner Chorale (1969-83), soloist Radio City Music Hall (1963); mem. Baltimore Civic Opera Co., Wash DC Civic Opera, finalist: Nat. Met. Opera Aud., and Nat. Singer of the Year; founder/dir. So. Calif. Symphonic Contest; dir. choirs: DuVal (sr. high sch.) Chorale, Glendale, Md. 1964-69; guest dir. All State choirs, Honor choirs (choirs have traveled to Europe 3 times winning sev. awards; choirs selected for demostrations before var. music tchr. conventions and seminars 1969-); recipient PTA Service Award, Pasadena H.S., Silver Baton for outstanding conductor at Guildford, Eng. Choral Fest. (1971); mem. music and tchr. orgns. (ACDA, NEA, MENC, SCVA, CME), Nat., Calif. Assn. of Realtors, Arcadia Bd. Realtors; works: Renaissance Feaste of Xmas, 2 major orch./choral works, pop concerts and music dir. major Bdwy prodn. annually at Pasa. H.S.; Republican; Disciples of Christ; rec: travel, fashion design. Res: 267 Norumbega Dr Monrovia 91016 Ofc: Pasadena High School 2925 E Sierra Madre Blvd Pasadena 91107 Century-21 By Vella 25 E Huntington Dr Arcadia 91006

SHANNON, JAMES PATRICK, lawyer; b. May 17, 1936, NY, NY; s. James P. and Margaret Teresa (Ryan) S.; m. Virginia Ferdon, July 14, 1962; 1 dau. Deirdre b. 1977; edn: BA, St. Francis Coll. Loretto, Pa. 1958; JD, St. John's Univ. Sch. of Law 1961; admitted NY State Bar 1962, Calif. 1971, US Supreme Ct., US Dist. Ct. (so. dist. Calif.). Career: atty. assoc. Bleakley, Platt, Schmidt, Hart & Fritz NY 1965-66; mil. deputy staff judge advocate, mil. judge, prosecutor defense counsel; atty. ptnr., bd. dirs. Knutson, Tobin, Meyer & Shannon La Mesa, Calif. 1971–; bd. dirs. Continental Hibernian Resources; Texas Continental Securities; mem: ABA, Calif. State Bar Assn., San Diego County Bar Assn., Ancient Order of Hibernians (div. pres. 1981, nat. bd. dirs. 1982-, nat. gen. counsel 1986-, regl. chmn. pol. edn. com.), House of Ireland (pres. 1981), No. County Shamrock Club (pres. 1980-81), Irish American Unity Conf. (nat. bd. dirs.), Lions (past pres.), Oceanside Yacht Club (past commodore), San Diego Yacht Club; mil: major USMC 1962-71, Nat. Defense Svc., Vietnam Campaign, Pres. Unit Citn., Cross of Gallantry, Navy Achievement w/ Combat V; Republican; Catholic. Res: POB 3003 Olivenhain 92024 Ofc: Knutson, Tobin, Meyer & Shannon 9001 Grossmont Blvd La Mesa 92041

SHANNON, JOHN PHILIP, carpet retailer; b. May 20, 1935, Boston; s. James Patrick and Gertrude (Sheehan) S.; m. Janet Schalau, June 27, 1977; children: John b. 1957, Patrick b. 1958, Linda b. 1964, Lisa b. 1966, Jeff b. 1958; edn: BS, Holy Cross Coll. 1956. Career: mfr's. rep., buyer Hess's Dept. Store, Allentown, Pa.; owner retail carpet bus. John Shannon Carpet Broker, Redlands, Calif.; mktg. cons. to home furnishings retailers; mem: Better Bus. Bureau, Redlands CofC, Western Floor Covering Assn.; publ: article, Syllogistic Marketing Systems (1976), book: Selling's My Game (1977); Catholic; rec: golf, tennis. Res: 715 Esther Way Redlands 92373 Ofc: John Shannon Carpet Broker 1200 Arizona St Ste A-6 Redlands 92373

SHAPAN, MERVIN EMIL, management consultant; b. Sept. 26, 1931, Los Angeles; s. Joseph and Charlotte (Berkell) S.; m. Judith A. Weaver, Mar. 10, 1956; children: Mark Jeffery b. 1959, Christopher Michael b. 1962; edn: AA, L.A. City Coll. 1950; BA, USC 1955. Career: flight coord. United Air Lines, L.A. 1953-56; S.W. Dist. mgr. Emery Air Freight, L.A. 1956-70; pres. Air Cargo Systems, L.A. 1970-74; pres. HemisMark Internat. Inc., L.A. 1974-82; pres. Omniex Corp., L.A. 1982–; reg. consultant Asian Devel. Bank; dir. The Capt. Cook Found.; apptd. Pres.'s Export Com. (1982); mem: Los Angeles Air

Cargo Assn. (co-founder), World Trade Com., Nat. Council of Physical Distbn. Mgmt., Soc. of World Air Freight Profls. (dir.); civic: LA Area CofC, Rotar Internat., Boy Scouts Am. (troop com. chmn. El Camino Dist.), Junior Achieve. Internat.; publs: The Future of Air Freight in the Pacific Basin (1971); mil: 1st lt. USAFR (active 1951-53) Air Medal, D.F.C.; Republican; Unitarian; rec: flying, skiing, photog., painting. Res: 5007 Texhoma Ave Encino 91316 Ofc: Omniex Corporation POB 7688 Van Nuys 91409

SHAPAZIAN, MARILYN HELEN, nursing home administrator; b. June 19, 1955, Visalia; d. Crosby and Margaret Alice (Adishian) S.; edn: AA, Reedley Jr. Coll. 1982; BS in bus. adm., health care mgmt., CSU Fresno 1983; Calif. lic. Nursing Home Administrator (1984). Career: recreation therapist asst. Reedley-Dinuba Mental Health Clinic 1972-73; mgr. Lyle's Pharmacy, Dinuba 1979-84; adminstr. in tng. Beverly Ents., Western Div. 1983, adminstr. Beverly Manor Convalescent Hosp. (104 beds), Bakersfield 1984–; honors: Alpha Gamma Sigma (1981), Dean's List (1981, 82, 83) Pres.'s List (1982); mem. CAHF/Kern County Chpt. (sec.treas. 1985-86), Health Care Mgmt. Club (coll.); Republican (Young Rep. Club); Armenian Apostolic; rec: cooking, crafts, swimming. Address: Bakersfield 93301

SHAPERO, HARRIS JOEL, pediatrician; b. Nov. 22, 1930, Winona, Minn.; s. Charles and Minnie Sara (Ehilichman) S.; m. Byong Soon, Nov. 4, 1983; children: Laura, b. 1959; Won Jin, b. 1965; Charles, b 1969; edn: Premed. AA, UCLA, 1953; BS, Northwestern Univ. Med. Sch. 1954, MD, 1957; Bd. Cert. in Occupational Med. 1977, FAA - Aviation Med., 1976. Career: intern, res. pediatrics LA County Harbor-UCLA Medical Ctr. 1957-60, staff phys. 1960-65; pvt. practice pediatrics, gen. and occupational medicine, Anaheim 1965–; STD Control Ofcr., LA Co. Health, Bellflower; dir. Hospital Emergency Ctr.; FAA Med. Examiner; founder Pan American Childrens Mission; honors: Headliner of Year 1978, Orange Co. Press Club; mem: LA County Med. Assn., LA Co. Indsl. Med. Assn., Am. Coll. of Emerg. Phys., LA Co. Pediatric Soc., Orange Co. Pediatric Soc., Am. Pub. Health Assn., Mex.-Am. Border Health Assn. (Tuberculosis Com.), Pan-Am. Health Orgn., Fellow Coll. Preventative Medicine; publs: Silent Epidemic; Republican; Jewish; rec: antique books and manuscripts, photog., graphics, woodwrk, beekeeping, Student copywriting at Advertising Center L.A. Res: 10536 Wilkin St Los Angeles 94024 Ofc: 3340 W Ball Rd, Ste 1, Anaheim 92804

SHAPIRO, ISADORE, chemical consultant- engineer; b. April 25, 1916, Minneapolis, Minn.; s. Jacob and Bessie (Goldman) S.; m. Mae Hirsch, Sept. 4, 1938; children: Stanley Harris b. 1941, Jerald Steven b. 1943; edn: BSCE, distn., Univ. of Minn. 1938, PhD, 1944, postdoctoral research fellow, 1944-45; Career: asst. isntr. chem. Univ. of Minn. 1938-41; research fellow 1944-45; research chemist E.I. duPont de Nemours & Co., Philadelphia, Penn. 1946; head chem. lab. USN Ordnance Test Sta., Pasadena 1947-52; rater US Civil Svc. Bd. Examination 1948-52; dir. research lab. Olin Mathieson Chem. Corp., Pasadena 1952-59; head chem. dept. Hughes Tool Co. Aircraft div., Culver City 1959-62; pres. Universal Chem. Assn. Inc. 1962–; pres. Aerospace Chem. Systems Inc. 1964-66; dir. contract research HITCO 1966-67; prin. scientist McDonnell Douglas Astronautics Co., Santa Monica 1967-70; cons. Garrett AiResearch Mfg. Co., Torrance 1971-82; cons. 1982–; mem: Fellow Am. Inst. of Chemists, Am. Chemical Soc., Am. Physical Soc., Nat. Inst. of Ceramic Engrs., Soc. for Adv. of Materials & Process Engring., Am. Ceramic Soc., AAAS, Am. Ordnance Assn., Am. Inst. Aero. & Astro., Internat. Plansee Soc. for Powder Metal, Am. Assn. Contamination Control, Am. Inst. of Physics, Soc. of Rheologoy, Am. Inst. of Mgmt., Sigma Xi, Tau Beta Pi, Phi Lambda Upsilon; works: author approx. 40 papers presented at tech. soc. mettings incl. XVI (Paris), XVII (Munich) and XIX (London) Internat. Congresses for Pure and Appl. Chem.; 5th CIMTEC, Italy; XV Latin Am. Chem. Congress, Puerto Rico; Engring. Ceramics, Jerusalem 1983; 80 papers publd. in sci. journs. incl. Journ. of Inorganic and Nuclear Chem., Review Sci. Instr., others; holder 17 patents, others pend.; pioneer in research, discoverer Carborane Series of compounds; contbr. catalysis, mass spectrometry, infrared spectroscopy, nuclear magnet resonance spectrometry, propellant and missile chem., boron hydrides, organoboranes, reaction kinetics, surface chem. fiber and composites tech. incl. Boron Carbide and carbon filaments; mil: 1st lt. US Army Anti-Aircraft Artillery 1941-44, WWII; rec: European travel. Res: 5624 W. Sixth-Second St. Los Angeles 90056

SHAPIRO, LAWRENCE, computer co. executive; b. May 18, 1936, Los Angeles; s. Sydney and Evelyn (Winner) S.; m. Susan Fleisher, Dec. 18, 1960; children: Mitchell Andrew b. 1964, Dina Joy b. 1966, Lizabeth Mara b. 1970; edn: BS in math., USC 1958. Career: applied sci. rep. IBM, Los Angeles 1960-; project mgr. IBM, White Plains, NY 1966-; devel. mgr. IBM, Yorktown Hts., NY 1968-; medical indus. plnng. mgr. IBM, Kingston, NY 1973-; mgr. site plnng./ops., IBM, Menlo Park, Calif. 1976–; civic: People-to-People Internat. (mem. mgmt. del. to Peoples Rep. of China 1982); United Way Campaign (chmn. IBM, Menlo Pk 1985), Menlo Pk CofC (rep. IBM); works: devel. 10 computer appls. pgms. (1960-); Republican; Jewish; rec: travel, personal computers. Ofc: IBM Corp. 2800 Sand Hill Rd Menlo Park 94025

SHAPIRO, WILLIAM ARNOLD, anesthesiologist; b. Mar. 21, 1947, NY, NY; s. Joseph S. and Judith (Newman) S.; edn: BS, Univ. of Md. 1969, MD, 1977; Diplomate Am. Board of Anesthesiology. Career: intern S.F. Gen. Hosp. 1977-78; resident anesthesiol. UC San Francisco 1979-81; fellow UC Cardiovascular Research Inst. 1981-82; asst. prof. anesthesiol. UCSF 1982–; VISTA volunteer 1970-71; mem: Am. Soc. Anesthesiol., Internat. Anesthesia Research Soc.; publ: 10+ arts. in med. jours. and book chap. Res: 225-A Diamond st San Francisco 94114 Ofc: Dept. of Anesthesia, Rm. 436-S Moffitt Hosp. San Francisco 94143

SHARE, RICHARD HUDSON, lawyer; b. Sept. 6, 1938, Minneapolis, MN; s. Jerome and Millicent Share; m. Carolee Martin; children: Mark b. 1964, Gregory b. 1974, Jennifer b. 1976, Ashley b. 1980; edn: BS, UCLA 1960; JD, USC 1963. Career: sr. counsel/ asst. secty. Avco Financial Svcs. 1964-71; ptnr. Founberg & Frandzel, Beverly Hills 1972-78; partner in charge of comml. litigation, Frandzel & Share, Beverly Hills 1979–, other ofcs. in S.F. and Orange County; splst. in creditors remedies and representation of banks; lectr. Debt Collection Torts, Calif. Edn. of the Bar; mem: Calif. Bankers Assn.; Fin. Lawyers Assn.; publs: panelist, cassette tape, Seminar on Debt Collection Torts, Calif. Edn. of the Bar. Ofc: Frandzel & Share, 8383 Wilshire Blvd, Ste 400, Beverly Hills 90211

SHARKEY, THOMAS EDWARD, lawyer; b. Mar. 25, 1931, Chgo.; s. Edward Francis and Catherine (Grundhoefer) S.; children: Thomas b. 1955, Susan b. 1956, Linda b. 1958, Beth Ann b. 1959, Kevin b. 1961, Karen b. 1963, Warren b. 1973; edn: BS in bus. adm., CSU San Diego 1954; JD summa cum laude, Univ. of San Diego 1959; admitted Calif. State Bar 1960, lic. real estate broker 1979. Career: atty., Dattan, Sharkey & Peterson 1960-62, solo practice 1962-64, ptnr. Hewitt, Klitgaard & Sharkey 1964-68, McInnis, Fitzgerald, Rees, Sharkey & McIntyre, 1968 – ; lectr. Univ. of San Diego 1963-66; lectr. contg. edn. Calif. State Bar; lectr. for Rutter Group var. legal subjects; judge pro tem Superior Ct.; honors: disting. alumni award, Law Sch., Univ. of San Diego (1978); mem: Am. Bar Assn., State Bar of Calif., San Diego County Bar Assn., S.D. Trial Lawyers Assn. (pres. 1963-64), Calif. Trial Lawyers Assn., Lawyer-Pilot Bar Assn., Am. Board of Trial Advocates, Assn. of So. Calif. Defense Counsel, Fellow Am. Coll. of Trial Lawyers; rec: jogging, swimming, pvt. pilot. Res: La Jolla Ofc: McInnis, Fitzgerald, Rees, Sharkey & McIntyre 1320 Columbia San Diego 92101

SHARMA, RAJINDER KUMAR, engineer; b. Sept. 29, 1953, Hoshiarpur (Punjab) India; s. Jagdish Mitter and Ram-Lubhai S.; m. Sita, May 20, 1978; children: Ripple b. 1981, Aroma & Beamy b. 1986; edn: BSEE, G.N. Engring. Coll. 1974; computer pgmmg. courses, Chabot Coll. 1983-84; Reg. Profl. Engr., Calif. (1983). Career: electrical engr. Punjab State, India 1974-78, Salem Engineering Co., Oakbrook, Ill. 1979-80; elec. engr. Bechtel Corp., San Francisco 1980-81, control system engr. 1981-84; senior instrumentation engr. Lockheed, Sunnyvale 1984–; Democrat; Vedic (founder, dir. Hindu Temple, Fremont 1982-83); rec: philanthropy, walking, friends. Res: 34877 Starling Dr Union City 94587

SHARPE, GWEN LANIER, executive secretary; b. Apr. 14, 1937, Dayton, Ohio; d. Mervin Walsh and Thelma K. (Brechner) Whitesell; div.; 1 dau., Teresa Kirsten Katz; edn: AA, bus. adm., Ind. Univ. 1958; bus. mktg. courses; CPR lic. Career: past secty. Bendix Aviation; with American Airlines (1958–) as stewardess, passenger sales secty. and svcs. rep., ticket agt., internat. vacation cons., secty. to regl. director, Govt. Affairs, currently secty. to mgr. Freight Sales & Services; prin./distbr. Success Motivation Casettes div. SMI Internat. Inc.; owner/pres. Winning Paths in Life; media pub. rels. appearances on TV & radio for Am. Airlines; recipient appreciation award Inglewood Hot Line, 25-Year cert. Am. Air Lines; mem. L.A. Interline Cargo Secty. Assn. (bd.), Am. Airlines Kiwis, Ind. Univ. Alumni, Fellowship of Christian Airline Personnel, Delta Zeta Sor.; civic: Nat. Thespian Soc., L.A. Olympic Organizing Com. Alumni, patron: Ellis Is. Centennial Commn., Centrum of Hollywood, Calif. Tax Reduction Movement, Youth for Christ; works: movie script in prog., songwriter; tributes to Liberace, his mgr. S. Heller & asst. Betty Rosenthal in the Liberace Mus., Las Vegas; tribute to Bob Hope; tribute to City of Las Vegas presented to Mayor Bill Braire; Republican (Presdtl. Task Force); Prot.; rec: writing, music, theatre. Res: 9440-C Airport Blvd Los Angeles 90045 Ofc: American Airlines, 5908 Avion Dr Los Angeles 90009

SHARPTON, THOMAS, physician; b. July 15, 1949, Augusta, GA; s. Thomas and Elizabeth (Dozier) S.; edn: BA, Northwestern Univ. 1971; MS, Stanford Univ. 1973; DM, 1977; spec. internal med., Am. Coll. of Physicians 1981. Career: internship and residency at Martinez Veterans Administration Medical Center; med. staff Oakland Kaiser Permanente Med. Gp.; cons. Berkeley Free Clinic; honors: Phi Beta Kappa 1971; mem. Am. Coll. of Physicians; rec: classical piano. Res: 2323 Arrowhead Dr Oakland 94611 Ofc: Kaiser Permanente, 280 W MacArthur Blvd Oakland 94611

SHATKIN, ALLAN IRVING, lawyer; b. Nov. 15, 1940, Brooklyn, NY; s. Louis and Jean (Marty) S.; edn: BA, UC Los Angeles 1962; MSLS, Univ. So. Calif. 1969; JD, Golden Gate Univ. 1973; admitted Calif. State Bar 1973, US Ct. of Appeals (9th Circ.) 1978, US Dist. Ct. (no. dist. Calif.) 1979, US Supreme Ct. 1982. Career: librarian L.A Public Library 1969-70, CSU Northridge 1970; house counsel Calif. Life Ins. co. 1974; librarian, instr. Whittier Law Sch. 1975-76; appellate atty. law firm Gordon, Shatkin & Caldwell S.F. 1977-86; mem: S.F. Bar Assn., Calif. Trial Lawyers Assn.; author: Loss of Consortium (1985), legal articles, num. published appellate opinions; mil: E-5 US Army 1964-70. Res: 910 N Orange Grove Ave Apt 12 W Hollywood 90046

SHATTOCK, JAMES WILLIAM, sales executive; b. Apr. 24, 1938, San Francisco; s. James Victor and Muriel Celestia (Thomas) S.; m. Valerie Ruth, Aug. 30, 1958; children: Sheryl Lynne b. 1959, Michelle Elaine b. 1965; edn: chem., math. major UC Berkeley 1957-60. Career: var. pos. Bridgford Foods Corp. (food mfr. & distbr. co.), Anaheim 1963–, area mgr. 1972-, regional sales mgr. 1975-, nat. dir. of sales (food service and retail) 1986–; past chmn. San Pablo Planning Commn.; mem. Masons (past master), Scottish Rite, Shriners, Eastern Star, Exchange Club; assoc. Bethel Guardian of Job's Daus.; Presbyterian; rec: musician brass instruments. Res: 1815 Miner Ave San Pablo 94806 Ofc: Bridgford Foods Corp 1308 N Patt St Anaheim 92803

SHAVER, JUNE ELLEN, nursery & landscape company executive; b. Apr. 9, 1942, Heavener, Okla.; d. James Edmond and Ora Elizabeth (Waymire) Terry; m. Lloyd F. Shaver, Mar. 1, 1959; children: Lloyd Alan b. 1962, Veronica June b. 1975; edn: Diploma, Elva Mae Floral School 1968. Career: co-founder, ofc. mgr. Lloyd's Landscape Co. Costa Mesa 1960-69, 1974-83; floral designer Chapman Florist Anaheim 1969-70; v.p. in charge research & devel. Lloyd's Florist Costa Mesa 1983-85, corp. ofcr., secy./treas. 1985–; honors: runnerup Floral & Landscape Design (Orange Co. Fair 1972); mem: Calif. Nurseryman Assn. (Orange Co. chap. safety chair 1972-73, decoration chair convention 1973), Newport-Mesa Sch. Dist. (volunteer teacher's aide 1982-85, vol. PFO, PTA 1967-85), Newport Harbor H.S. Band Booster 1979-80; Democrat; Protestant; rec: writing, music, reading. Res: 153 Tulip Ln Costa Mesa Ofc: Lloyd's Nursery & Landscape Co. Inc. 2038 Newport Blvd Costa Mesa 92627

SHAVER, LLOYD FREDERICK, nursery and landscape co. president; b. Mar. 30, 1940, Santa Ana; s. Lloyd Pearl and Elizabeth Carol (Bullard) S.; m. June Ellen Terry, Mar. 1, 1959; children: Lloyd Alan b. 1962, Veronica June b. 1975; Calif. cert. nurseryman, Calif. Nurserymen Assn. 1972. Career: asst. foreman Shaw's Nursery, Garden Grove 1956-57; salesman Lee's Nursery, Anaheim 1957; salesman Evergreen Nursery, Costa Mesa 1957-60; founder Lloyd's Landscape Co., Costa Mesa 1960; founder Lloyd's Nursery and Landscape Co., Costa Mesa 1960; pres. Lloyd's Nursery and Landscape Co., Inc., Costa Mesa 1974–; convention chmn. Calif. Nurserymen Assn. 1973; awards; Best landscape in comml.- indsl., State of Calif., Calif. Landscape Contractors Assn. Inc. 1966; mem. Orange Co. chpt. Calif. Assn. of Nurserymen; Republican (Nat. Repub. Com. campaigner 1980); Protestant; rec: racquetball, fishing. Res: 153 Tulip Lane Costa Mesa 92627 Ofc: Lloyd's Nursery & Landscape Co., Inc., 2038 Newport Blvd Costa Mesa 92627

SHAW, MARK HOWARD, church chief executive officer; b. Aug. 26, 1944, Albuquerque, N.Mex.; s. Brad Oliver and Barbara Rae (Mencke) S.; m. Roslyn Ashton, Oct. 9, 1976; chidren: Rebecca b. 1972, Amanda b. 1977; edn: BA, Univ. of New Mexico 1967, JD, 1969; admitted to New Mexico State Bar Assn. 1969. Career: clerk New Mexico Supreme Ct. 1969-70; ptr. Gallagher & Ruud, Albuquerque, N.Mex. 1970-74; ptr. Schmidt & Shaw, Albuquerque, N.Mex. 1974-75; senior mem., prin. shareholder SHaw, Thompson & Sullivan PA 1975-82; CEO United Ch. of Religious Science 1982–; trusee: First Ch. of Religious Science, Albuquerque, N.Mex. 1974-77, pres. 1977, Sandia Ch. of Religious Science, Albuquerque, N.Mex. 1980-83, pres. 1981-83, Long Beach Ch. of Religious Science, Long Beach 1983-86, pres. 1983-86, United Ch. of Religious Science, Los Angeles 1982-83, chmn. 1983; honors: Bureau of National Affairs awards for law sch. scholastic achiev. 1969; former mem: Am., New Mexico State and Albuquerque Bar Assns., Am. and New Mexico Trial Lawyers Assn., Bernalillo Co. Bd. of Ethics (N.Mex.); mil: sgt. USMCR 1961-69; United Ch. of Religious Science; rec: sailing, golf, reading. Res: 4039 Locust Ave. Long Beach 90807 Ofc: United Church of Religious Science, 3251 W. Sixth St. Los Angeles 90020

SHAW, SUSAN LEE, psychometrist; b. Sept. 12, 1941, Los Angeles; d. Spencer Lorraine Sr. and Margret Ruth (Schofield) Shaw; edn: BS, UCLA 1963, Dental asst., UCLA, 1965, spl. courses, Caroline Leonetti Modeling Sch. 1962, Willis Bus. Coll. 1964, Lumbleau R.E. Sch. 1975; grad. wk. UCLA-Cambridge Exchg. 1981, 84, law stu. No. Am. Coll. of Law. Career: var. positions Western Airlines, UCLA Med. Ctr., Leliah T. Pearson (real estate), Rand Inst., 1963-80; psychic con., clairvoyant, psychometrist (over 7000 clients); minister/ healer/ tchr./ ch. founder, New Age Fellowship; pres. Shawlee Ents., presenting psychic fairs throughout So. Calif., 1982–; v.p., treas., secty. Glen Mar Properties, Inc., Beverly Hills; author four books on past lives of the famous: Elvis, Another Time and Space; Comings and Goings in the Lives of Frank Lloyd Wright & J. Paul Getty; Thru Time in the Lives of Henry E. Huntington and Winston S. Churchill; Times Past; mem. Beverly Hills Spiritualist Soc. (bd. dirs. 1977-9), Calif. Realtors Assn., Am. Cong. on Real Estate, Dental Assts. Assn. of Calif., Philosophical Resrch. Soc., Assn. for Research & Enlightenment Inc., So. Calif. Genealogical Soc. Inc.; Amer. Fellowship Ch.; Univ. Christ Ch.; Nat. Spiritualist Assn.; Biblical Archaelogy Soc.; author 5 books incl. Elvis Speaks fron the Other Side, Times Past; Republican; Scientologist; rec: gourmet cook, needlewk., flying. Address: 1860 Idlewood Rd Glendale 91202

SHAW, VIVIAN MARIE, building contractor; b. June 20, 1943, Worcester, Mass.; d. Ernest Ricco and Raeffaela (Armento) Ferrazano; m. Irving Ring, April 2, 1978; children: James Joseph Shaw, b. 1961; Stephen Michael Shaw, b. 1963; edn: AA, Santa Monica Coll. 1974; BA, CSU Los ANgeles 1976; MA, 1978; Calif. Western Sch. of Law 1981; bldg. contractor/ developer, Calif. 1975; real estate sales, Calif. Career: constrn. expeditor, Bonded Bldrs., Inc., W. Los Angeles 1967-73; secty./ treas. Regency Constrn. West., Inc., Gardon Grove 1975–; CEO/ pres. Coldwell Banker, Encinitas/ Del Mar; Calif. bldg. contractor Regency Constrn., Garden Grove 1975–; honors: Nat. Hon. Soc., CSU Los Angeles 1977-78; Top Dollar Sales Producer, Coldwell Banker Encinitas Del Mar 1983; mem: Calif. Assn. Realtors; San Dieguito Bd. of Realtors; Calif. Contractors Lic. Assn.; Christian; rec: artist, writing. Res: 1958 Zapo St., Del Mar 92014 Ofc: Regency Construction West, Inc., 12371 Haster St., Ste. 105, Garden Grove 92640

SHEAHAN, DANIEL RAYMOND, lawyer; b. July 24, 1933, Detroit, Mich.; s. Raymond Daniel S.; two sons: Terrence b. 1961, Daniel b. 1966; edn: PhB, and JD, Univ. of Detroit; admitted to bar: Mich. (1959), Calif. (1963). Career: staff mem. Judge Advocate General, US Army 1959-60; atty. law firm Bryant, McCormick, Los Angeles 1963-66; ptnr. Maxwell & Sheahan, L.A. 1966-70; pvt. law practice, Glendale 1970–; arbitrator Los Angeles Superior Ct.; judge pro tem Glendale Municipal Ct.; past chmn. Advisory Com. on Arbitration to Calif. State Judicial Council; mem: Calif. Trial Lawyers Assn. (past mem. bd. govs.), Los Angeles Trial Lawyers Assn. (past mem. bd. govs.); rec: jazz piano. Res: 3666 Barham, N108, Los Angeles 90068 Law Ofc. Daniel R. Sheahan, 425 East Colorado Blvd Ste 770 Glendale 91205

SHEAN, MICHAEL R., lawyer; b. June 19, 1947, Santa Barbara; s. Rex A. and Ruth (Springer) S.; m. M. Jayne, May 26, 1971; children: Kristen, b. 1973, Erin, b. 1975, Paul, b. 1976, Jay, b. 1979; edn: BA cum laude, Brigham Young Univ. 1971; JD, Univ. of the Pacific McGeorge Sch. of Law 1974; admitted to Calif. State Bar 1974. Career: Fair Hearing Officer, State Dept. of Benefit Payments, 1972-75; dep. district atty. County of Santa Barbara, 1975-78; assoc. atty. Dunlap, Melville & Iwasko ofcs. in Santa Maria and Lompoc, 1978-79; atty. sole practitioner Michael R. Shean, 1979-84; senior ptnr. Central Coast Law Center, Shean, Bejarano & Hinden, Inc. APC, Santa Maria 1984–; vice pres. Television Merchants Inc.; cert. instr. law and other subjects, Allan Hancock Coll.; judge pro tem Santa Barbara Co. Superior Ct. 1983-; mem. LDS Businessmen's Assn., Phi Alpha Delta, 1973, Sigma Epsilon, 1965-71; Republican; Ch. of Jesus Christ of LDS; rec: tennis, golf, racquetball. Res: 2237 Crystal Dr Santa Maria 93455 Ofc: Central Coast Law Center, 301 So Miller, Ste 221, Santa Maria 93454

SHEBS, THEODORE LEE, real estate developer; b. Oct. 26, 1919, Mnpls.; s. Simon H. and Edna T. (Todd) S.; m. Beverly Jean, Dec. 14, 1985; children: Stephen b. 1954, Sharon b. 1957, Richard b. 1961; edn: Univ. of Chgo. 1936-37, Univ. of Santa Clara 1943-44; RECI, UC Berkeley 1968. Career: area sales mgr. Johns Manville Sales Corp., San Francisco 1946-60; owner Norman O'Connor Insurance Agent, 1960-86; pres. Shebs Realty Inv. Co., Los Gatos 1960–, devel. residential and comml. props.; lectr. in R.E. devel., West Valley Comm. Coll.; honors: Realtor of the Year (1972); mem. Calif. Assn. of Realtors (past dir.), Independent Ins. Agents and Brokers of Calif., Los Gatos-Saratoga Bd. of Realtors (pres. 1965), Rotary (past dir. Los Gatos); club: La Rinconada Country (pres. 1974); mil: capt. US Army Inf. 1943-46, Calif. Nat. Guard 1947-54; Republican; rec: golf. Res: 16979 Roberts Rd #2 Los Gatos 95030 Ofc: Shebs Realty 225 Saratoga Ave Los Gatos 95030

SHEINBAUM, STANLEY K., economist; b. June 12, 1920, N.Y.C.; s. Herman H. and Selma (Klimberg) S.; m. Betty Warner, May 29, 1964; children: Susan, Karen, Cass, Matthew; edn: AB internat. rel., summa cum laude, Stanford Univ. 1949, econ., 1949-53, doctoral cand. Career: 1955 fellow Hoover Instn., Stanford; faculty econs. Stanford Univ. 1950-53, Mich. State Univ., East Lansing 1955-60, Univ. Calif. Santa Barbara 1963; senior fellow Ctr. for the Study of Democratic Instns. 1960-70; bd. Presidio S & L Assn., Santa Barbara 1964-69; v.p. Warner Ranch Inc., L.A. 1965-69, Warner Industries Inc., L.A. 1968-73; investment cons., 1967–; founder/dir. Legal Def. Ctr., Santa Barbara 1970–; dir. legal def. team Pentagon Papers Trial 1971-73; pres. Fairtree Ents. Inc., 1980–; pub. New Perspectives (periodical) 1985-; mem. ed. bd. Democracy 1981-85; apptd: cons. fiscal policy Govt. South Vietnam (1957-59), cons. re Vietnam, Spl. Ops. Research Off., Am. Univ., Wash. (1958-59); econs. cons. Ency. Brit. (1961-64), exec. dir. Commn. to Improve Tchr. Edn., Calif. (1961-62); cons. Calif. State Commn. Manpower and Tech. (1963-65), bd. Council on Econ. Priorities, N.Y.C. (1970-75); regent Univ. Calif. (1977-, v.chmn. 1983-84), mem. Calif. Post Secondary Edn. Comm. (1978-80); awards: Phi Beta Kappa, Phi Eta Sigma, Fulbright Econ. Fellow, Paris (1953-55); mem: Am. Econ. Assn., Am. Fedn. of Scientists, Nat. Assn. of Public Adm.; civic: Com. for Public Justice (bd. 1972-), ACLU Found. So. Calif. (bd. chmn. 1973-82), ACLU Nat. Adv. Council- N.Y.C. (1974-), Bill of Rights Found.- N.Y. (bd. 1973-), Energy Action Commn.- Wash DC (founder, bd. 1975-82), Ctr. for Law in the Public Interest- LA (bd. 1976-), Ofcl. Salaries Auth.- City of L.A. (1976-78), Am. Jewish Com. L.A. (1977-), Clarence Darrow Found. (1977-), Music Ctr. Dance Assn. LA (bd. 1976-, chmn. 79-85), Fedn. Am. Scientists Fund (trustee 1979-), Breast Ctr. Valley Med. Ctr., Van Nuys (adv. bd. 1979-), People for the Am. Way (bd. 1980-), Helsinki Watch, Americas Watch (bd. 1981-); mil: US Army Engrs.; Democrat (cand. for Cong., S.B. 66, 68; Calif. Dem. Council, del. Nat. Conv., 68-72; McGovern fin. chmn. So. Calif. 1972); Jewish. Res: 345 N Rockingham Ave Los Angeles 90049

SHELBY, JACK P., metallurgical engineer; b. Dec. 30, 1925, Temple, Tex.; s. Jack and Lillian (Kelton) S.; m. Velda Briggs, May 31, 1950; children: Jeanette b. 1953, William b. 1956; edn: BS physics, Univ. Tex. 1951. Career: process engr. Ford Motor Co. Claycomo, Mo. 1952-53; metallurg. engr. Westinghouse Aviation gas turbine div. Kansas City 1953-55; lead metallurg. engr. Chance Vought Aircraft Dallas 1955-60; chief materials & processes Menasco, Burbank, Calif. 1960-80, dir. materials technol. 1980–; mem: Am. Soc. Metals, Am. Soc. Testing & Materials, Soc. Automotive Engrs., Aerospace Industry Assn., Am. Electroplaters Soc.; mil: cpl. USMC 1943-46; Republican; Protestant; rec: astronomy, science, history. Ofc: Menasco Burbank 91510

SHELBY, MARK ERIC, loan co. president; b. Aug. 2, 1941, Flint, Mich.; s. Fredrick Earl and Neva B. (McIntyre) S.; m. Beatrice, Feb. 28, 1964; children: Mark b. 1965, Susan b. 1967; edn: BS in bus. adm., CSU San Jose 1969; Calif. lic. Income Tax Cons. (1964), lic. Real Estate Broker (1976). Career: treasury investigator, City of San Jose, 1965-77; real estate broker Guardian Investments, San Jose 1977-83; pres. Century 21 Guardian Realty Inc., Campbell 1983-86; pres. The Loan Arranger, Inc., Campbell 1983–; dir: S & G Discount Outlet, Inc. (1982-), W.T. Bud, Inc. (1984-); awards: Million Dollar Club, CAR (1977-83); mem: Calif. Assn. Realtors, San Jose Real Estate Bd., San Jose

CofC (1977-81), Tri-County Multi-Housing Assn., San Jose Mus. of Art; composed and recorded songs: Our Love is Here to Stay (1962), Beach Party (1962), Prison Cell (1963); Republican; Catholic; avocation: writing songs. Ofc: 2338 Loma Park Dr San Jose 95124 Ofc: The Loan Arranger Inc 441 N Central Ste 1 Campbell 95008

SHELLOCK, FRANK G., research scientist, physiologist; b. Dec. 16, 1954, Glendale; s. Frank A. and Eleanor Marie S.; m. Susan A. Everhart, Apr. 12, 1986; edn: BS in biol., Loyola-Marymount Univ. 1976; MS in biol., CSU Los Angeles 1981; PhD in physiol., Columbia Pacific 1982. Career: research assoc., research scientist (Div. Cardiol. Dept. of Medicine, Div. Magnetic Resonance Imaging Dept. Radiol.) Cedars-Sinai Medical Ctr., Los Angeles 1981−; exercise physiology cons.; fellow Am. Coll. of Cardiol.; mem: Am. Coll. of Sports Medicine, Am. Physiol. Soc., Am. Heart Assn., Soc. for Magnetic Resonance in Medicine, Am. Fedn. for Clin. Research, AAAS; publs: 110 (abstracts, research papers, book chpts.); Christian; rec: powerlifting, writing. Ofc: Cedars-Sinai Medical Center 8700 Beverly Blvd Rm 5314 Los Angeles 90048

SHELTON, DOROTHY DIEHL REES, lawyer; b. Sept. 16, 1935, Manila, Philippines; d. Walter John and Hedwig Rose (Glienecke) H.; m. Thomas C. Shelton, March 4, 1977; children: Jane Diehl b. 1962, John Barnaby b. 1965, Anne Diehl b. 1966, David Charles b. 1967; edn: BA, Stanford Univ. 1957; JD, Western State Univ. Coll. of Law. 1976; admitted to practice, U.S. Dist. Ct., So. Dist. of Calif. Career: currently, atty. at law pvt. gen. practice, San Diego; honors: Nu Beta Epsilon; Am. Jurisprudence Award for Constitutional Law, 1976; mem: Am., Calif. and San Diego Co. and San Diego (Fed. Ct. Com.) Bar Assns., San Diego Trial Lawyers Assn., San Diego Junior League, Thursday Club, Stanford Univ. Alumni Assn., Am. Kennel Club; Christian; rec: raising and showing dogs (Great Pyrenees), gardening, animal welfare work. Res: 4496 Trias St. San Diego 92103 Ofc: 110 West C St. Ste. 1815 San Diego 92101

SHELTON, JOEL EDWARD, psychologist, business consultant; b. Feb. 7, 1928, Havre, Mont.; s. John Granvil and Rose Fahy (Ervin) S.; m. Mae Platzek, Dec. 17, 1949; 1 dau., Sophia, b. 1964; edn: AB, Chico State Coll. 1951; MA, Ohio State Univ. 1958, PhD, 1960. Career: school psychologist Sutter County Schs., Yuba City 1952-53; tchr./vice prin., Lassen View Sch., Los Molinos 1953-55; tchr. S.W. Licking Schs., Pataskala, Oh. 1955-56; child psychologist Franklin Village, Grove City, Oh. 1957; clin. psychologist Marion (Oh.) Mental Health Clinic, 1958; intern Children's Mental Health Center, Columbus, Oh. 1958-59; acting chief research psychologist Children's Psychiat. Hosp., Columbus 1959-60; guidance and data proc. cons. to supt. schs. Sacramento County, Calif. 1960-63; faculty CSC Sacto., 1961-69; clin. psychologist DeWitt State Hosp., Auburn 1965; exec. dir. Children's Center of Sacto., Citrus Heights 1965-66; exec. dir. Gold Bar Ranch (now Mayaro Ranch Sch., Pulga), Garden Valley 1964-72, cons. 1972-74; clin. psychologist El Dorado County Mental Health, Placerville 1968-70, Butte County Mental Health, Chico 1970−, dept. dir. consultation, edn. and community services, 1974-79; exec. sec. Protaca Agrl. Research, 1974-; assoc. Ecology House, 1974-; cons. to small bus. 1984−; mem. Am., Western psychol. assns.; works: orgnzr. 200 mem. Speakers Bur. and Pub. Edn. Pgm. for Sacto. Area Mental Health Assn.; frequent public speaker var. subjects, ednl. and comml. TV programs; editor/contbg. writer profl. newsletters; mil: T/3 US Army 1946-47; Republican; Prot.; rec: lapidary, philately, camping, travel. Res: 1845 Veatch St. Oroville 95965 Ofc: Butte County Mental Health, 18-C County Center Dr Oroville 95965

SHEN, DANIEL J., insurance brokerage president; b. Jan. 10, 1950, Taipei, Taiwan, nat. US cit. 1984; m. May Wang; edn: stu. Peppedine Univ. 1973, CSU Fullerton 1978. Career: ins. agent Metropolitan Ins. Co., 1982-84; gen. agent Transamerica Life Cos., 1984−, pres. Orange Insurance Services, Inc., Westminster 1984−; mem: Chinese Am. Ins. Profl. Assn. (bd.), Chinese Am. Lions Club of Orange County (1st v.p.); rec: fishing. Address: Westminster 92683

SHEN, EDWARD NIN-DA, cardiologist; b. July 3, 1950, Hong Kong; s. Han Ting and Yay Wen (Tsu) S.; m. Mary Rose Wong, June 19, 1983; edn: BS (1st class honors biochem), McGill Univ. Montreal 1972, MD, CM, 1976; Diplomate Nat. Bd. Med. Examiners 1977, Am. Bd. Internal Med. 1979, cardiovascular disease 1981; certified Royal Coll. Phys. & Surg. of Canada internal med. & cardiol. 1981. Career: intern McGill Univ./ Royal Victoria Hosp. 1976-77, resident internal med. 1977-79; cardiol. fellow UC San Francisco 1979-81; research fellow Cardiovascular Research Inst. UCSF 1981-82; instr., attg. cardiol. Moffitt Hosp. UCSF 1982-83; assoc. chief cardiol. Santa Clara Valley Med. Ctr. 1983−; clin. asst. prof. med. Stanford, UCSF 1983−; honors: Univ. Scholar (1968-75), Charles E. Frosst Prize & Medal, Cushing Meml. Prize (Montreal Children's Hosp.); fellow: Royal Coll. Phys. of Canada 1981, Am. Coll. Cardiol. 1983, Am. Coll. Chest Phys. 1983, Am. Coll. Phys. 1983, Council on Clin. Cardiol. Am. Heart Assn. 1983; mem. No. Am. Soc. Pacing & Electrophysiol.; publs: num. abstracts, articles in med. jours.; research on clin. electrophysiology arrhythmias, sudden death, therapeutic modalities in prevention and therapy of abnormal heart rhythms; Catholic; rec: classical guitar, ancient Chinese literature. Ofc: Santa Clara Valley Med. Ctr. 751 S Bascom San Jose 95128

SHEN, MASON MING-SUN, acupuncturist; b. March 30, 1945, Shanghai, China, nat. US cit. 1975; s. John Kaung-Hao and Mae Chu (Sun) S.; m. Nancy, Aug. 7, 1976; children: Teresa b. 1978, Darren b. 1980; edn: BS, Taiwan Normal Univ. 1968; MS, So. Dakota State Univ. 1971; PhD, Cornell Univ. Med. Coll. 1977; D.Oriental Med., San Francisco Coll. of Acupuncture 1984. Cert.

Acupuncturist, Calif. 1979. Career: Chinese medicine apprenticeship, Taiwan 1962; acupuncturist Acupuncture Inst. of New York, 3 yrs.; Chinese medicine practice, Livermore 1982−; currently, dir. Acupuncture Center of Livermore and Danville; prof. Asian American Univ. and San Francisco Coll. of Acupuncture; honors: Nat. Svc. Award for heart research 1977; Hon. Doctorate, Asian-American Univ. 1985; Hon. Life Pres., Hong-Kong and Kowloon Chinese Medical Assn. 1985; mem: Calif. Cert. Acupuncturist Assn. (pres. 1984-85), Calif. Acupuncture Alliance (North Regl. chmn. 1985-86), Am. Assn. of Adv. of Science, New York Acad. of Science, Am. Found. of Traditional Chinese Med., Rotary Club of Great Livermore Valley (charter), Ronald Reagan Trust Fund (charter); works: five year research for cancer, Cornell Univ. Med. Coll.; two year heart research as post doctoral tng., UC Berkeley; one year heart research, Lawrence Livermore Lab.; 40 publs.; mil: 2nd lt. Chemical Corps Army of the Republic of China; Republican; rec: travel, equestrian. Res: 3240 Touriga Dr. Pleasanton 94566 Ofc: Acupuncture Center, 783 Rincon Ave. Livermore 94550

SHENOY, PRAKASH NARASINHA, physician; b. Apr. 27, 1945, Coondapoor, India; s. Narasinha R. and Laxmidevi (Narasinha) S.; edn: MB, BS, Seth G.S. Medical Coll., Bombay 1968, MD (internal med.) 1971, MD (cardiology) 1973, Diplomate Am. Board Internal Medicine 1982, Cardiology 1983; lic. phys. Calif. 1978. Career: tutor Int. Medicine, Bombay Univ. 1971-74, asst. prof. Med., 1974-75; staff cardiologist Hershey Med. Center, Hershey, Pa. 1975-76; cardiology fellow Lankenau Hosp., Phila. 1976-77; int. med. resident L.A. Weiss Meml. Hosp., Chgo. 1977-78, instr. of med. Univ. Ill. 1977-78; staff cardiologist (acting dir. Cardiol. 1981) City of Hope Med. Center, Duarte, Calif. 1978-81; pvt. practice cardiology and int. medicine, Anaheim 1981−; mem: Fellow Am. Coll. of Cardiology 1984, Fellow Am. Coll. Chest Physicians, Am. Heart Assn., Orange County Med. Assn., Nat. Geographic Soc.; publs. in cardiovascular journals; Hindu; rec: Indian classical music, tennis. Ofc: 1801 W Romneya Dr Ste 403 Anaheim 92801

SHEONARINE, BIBI ZALINA, real estate broker; b. Apr. 19,1 953, Guyana, S.A., nat. US cit. 1985; d. Mohamed and Sarifan (Amjad) Yusuf; m. Harry Sheonarine, Dec. 22, 1973; Calif. lic. R.E. Broker (1984). Career: bkkpr. Claremont Colls., 1977-80; sales agt. Red Carpet Real Estate, Claremont 1980-84; broker/owner Cedar Ridge Realty, Upland 1985-86, Century-21 Beachside Upland 1986−; profl. awards: No. 1 Salesperson So. Calif. (1982), No. 7 nationwide (1983), Red Carpet Corp., and 50+ Top Agent awards; mem. Nat. Assn. Realtors, Nat. Fedn. Bus. and Profl. Women; rec: music. Res: 1420 N Sixth Ave Upland 91786 Ofc: C-21 Beachside 1655 N Mountain Ave Upland 91786

SHEPHARD, THOMAS JOSEPH, SR., lawyer, b. Feb. 10, 1934, Modesto; s. Earl George and Celestine Margaret (Casalegno) Shephard; m. Irene Woodworth, July 20, 1963; children: Katherine b. 1964, Thomas Jr. b. 1966, Clarice b. 1967, Marjorie b. 1969; edn: AB, UC Berkeley 1955, JD, 1958; admitted Calif. State Bar 1958. Career: dep. legislative counsel, Calif. State Legislature, 1958-59; dep. county counsel County of San Joaquin 1959-63; assoc., ptnr., prin. law firm Neumiller & Beardslee, Stockton 1963−; counsel Roman Catholic Diocese of Stockton; city atty. Cities of Jackson, Waterford, and Galt; mem: ABA, Calif. Bar Assn., San Joaquin County Bar Assn.; civic: The Yosemite Assn. (bd. chmn), Gr. Stockton CofC (past pres), Catholic Charities of the Roman Catholic Diocese of Stockton (past pres.); bd. chmn. St. Joseph's Hosp. of Stockton and St. Joseph's Health Care Corp.; past mem./chmn. San Joaquin Co. Bd. of Edn.; past mem./chmn. Lincoln Rural Co. Fire Protection Dist.; Democrat; Roman Catholic; rec: mountaineering. Res: 8421 N Helen Ln Stockton 95212 Ofc: Neumiller & Beardslee Ste 500, 509 West Weber Ave Stockton 95203

SHER, AARON, company president; b. Feb. 3, 1954, Johannesburg, So. Africa, nat. US cit. 1987; s. Henry and Norma (Levin) S.; edn: BS in C.E., Univ. of Witwatersrand, 1977; Reg. Profl. Engr., Calif. Career: project engr. C.M.C.M., So. Africa, 1978-80; project mgr. Psomas & Assocs., Santa Monica 1980-84; sport mgr./competition dir., L.A. Olympic Organising Com., 1982-84; pres. The Hennor Co., San Pedro 1984−; recipient Outstanding Young Man of Am. Award (1984); bd. dirs. SAJAC; mem. ASCE, Field Hockey Assn. of Am.; mil. svc. in S.A.; rec: golf, tennis. Ofc: The Hennor Company 538 West 5th St San Pedro 90731

SHERCK, JOHN PAUL, physician; b. Apr. 25, 1947, Ashland, Ohio; s. Charles Paul and Edna Lucille (Harding) S.; edn: AB chem., Miami Univ. (Ohio) 1969; MD, Yale Univ. 1973; Diplomate Am. Bd. Surg. 1981. Career: intern surg. Stanford Hosp. 1973-74; jr. resident surg. Santa Clara Valley Med. Ctr. 1974-75; research fellow Stanford Hosp. 1974-75; resident surg. Kaiser Hosp. Santa Clara, VA Hosp. Palo Alto, Santa Clara Valley Med. Ctr. 1976-78; chief res. gen. surg. Stanford Hosp., Santa Clara Valley Med. Ctr. 1979; assoc. chief surg. Santa Clara Valley Med. Ctr. 1980−, dir. research clinic 1981−, dir. surg. intensive care unit 1983−, assoc. dir. trauma svcs. 1984−; clin. asst. prof. surg. Stanford Univ. Sch. of Med. 1982−; fellow Am. Coll. Surg. 1983; mem: Assn. Academic Surg., San Jose Surg. Soc. (exec. council), Santa Clara County Surg. Assn. (treas.), SCVMC Med. Staff Corp. (treas.); publs: num. abstracts, articles in med. jours., presentations, motion pictures, book chpts. Ofc: Santa Clara Valley Med. Ctr. 751 S Bascom Ave San Jose 95128

SHERLOCK, ROBERT LAMONT, lawyer; b. July 17, 1943, Chelsea, Mass.; s. Wm. Henry and Eileen Julia (Sullivan) S.; m. Charla Knox, Aug. 23, 1981; edn: BS in fin., Boston Coll. Univ. 1965; JD cum laude, Southwestern Univ. Sch. of Law 1973; admitted to Calif. State Bar 1973. Career: 1st lt./ finance ofcr. US

Army 1965-68; claims adjuster Liberty Mutual Ins. Co., 1968-73; assoc. Law Offices of Virgil R. Wells, 1973-81; sr. partner Law Offices of Wells, Barber & Sherlock, Los Angeles 1981-; owner/partner Sherlock and Neal, L.A. 1982-; guest speaker var. insurance cos. on litigation and legal aspects of ins., 1973-; guest lectr. Western Coll. of Ins., 1980; mem: Los Angeles Co. Bar Assn., Assn. of So. Calif. Defense Counsel (sustaining mem. 1974-), Am. Bd. of Trial Advocates (assoc. 1981-); rec: scuba diving, music. Res: 3414 Blair Dr Los Angeles 90068 Ofc: Sherlock & Neal, 520 So. Lafayette Park Place, Los Anges 90057

SHERMAN, CHARLES JAMES, financial planner; b. April 15, 1923, Norfolk, Nebr.; s. Herbert Blackman and Lerola Ailene (Spring) H.; m. Edna Arlean Cochran, June 5, 1978; en: BS, Boston Univ. 1954; CSU 1954-55; CSU Nortridge 1966-70. Career: Fuller Brush 1956-59; self-empl. 1959-65; Los Angeles Co. Probation Dept. 1965-84; Tulare Co. Grand Jury 1983-85; prin. Applied Asset Strategies, Porterville 1985-; bd. dirs. Porterville Duplicate Bridge Club, Porterville Family Health Ctr.; honors: Tau Mu Epsilon, Boston Univ.; mem: Porterivell Duplicate Bridge Club, American Legion, Veterans of Foreign Wars; works: Phantom House in Mid Century Massachusetts; How to Get Rich Slowly But Surely- In Good Times and Bad; mil: US Army 1943-47, Reserves 1948-65, Combat Infantry Badge, Bronze Star, Purple Heart, (3) Campaign stars; rec: fishing, bridge, travel. Address: Applied Asset Strategies, 77 So. Cabb Porterville 93257

SHERMAN, ROBERT RAYMOND (RAYNE), designer; b. Nov. 10, 1942, Los Angeles; s. Thomas H., Sr. and Martha Ellen (Broomfield) S.; m. Pamela Davis, June 4, 1965; edn: Pierce Coll. 1960-63; BS, Woodbury Univ. 1968; Career: designer Cannell & Chaffin, L.A. 1966-68; project designer Barker Brothers Comml., L.A. 1970-72; v.p. design J.H. Leff & Assocs. Inc., Long Beach 1972-84; pres. Sherman Design Group Inc., Long Beach 1984-; instr. comml. interior design CSU Long Beach 1980-; mem: Sch. of Applied Arts & Scis. Advis. and Devel. Council, CSU Long Beach 1986-89; recipient Pres.'s Award, Inst. of Bus. Designers (1984); mem: Inst. Bus. Designers (pres. So. Calif. chpt. 1977-79), Am. Inst. of Arch., Designers Lighting Forum, Long Beach CofC; clubs: L.B. Athletic, Pacific Charter Sailing; works: Celebrity Executive Offices Show- benefit for Boys Club of L.B. (1984); mil: aviation bosun's mate 2/c USN 1968-69, Commendn. for Facilities Design, Apollo II Recovery Ship; Democrat; Prot. Ofc: The Sherman Design Group Inc. 3649 Atlantic Ave Long Beach 90807

SHERR, MORRIS M., lawyer; b. Oct. 3, 1930, Marysville, Calif.; s. Alfred and Alice Carrie (Peters) S.; m. Bobbie Gray, June 27, 1954; children: David, Rodney; edn: BA, Calif. State Univ. 1952; JD, UC San Francisco 1956; admitted Calif. State Bar 1956. Career: elem. sch. principal Stanislaus Co. 1952-54; instr. Golden Gate Coll. 1954-55, CSU San Francisco 1955-56; asst. prof. CSU Fresno 1956-59; assoc. Thompson & Rose CPAs Fresno 1959-61; ptnr. Blumberg, Sherr & Kerkorian Fresno 1961-84, Morris M. Sherr & Assoc. Fresno 1984-; mem: Calif. State Bar (cert. tax splst.), Fresno Co. Bar, St. Agnes Hosp. Found. (adv. council), Am. Inst. CPAs, Fresno Estate Planning Council (dir. 1977-79), AM. Baptist Churches of the West (moderator), Fresno Kiwanis, Elks, Masons, Shrine; Baptist (chmn. trustees 1967-69, deacon 1969-73). Ofc: 1540 E Shaw St, Ste 109, Fresno 93710

SHIEH, SHAW-SONG, engineer; b. Aug. 9, 1955, Chia-Yi City, Taiwan; s. Chung and Fung (Chen) S.; m. Tsai-Yen Kao, March 30, 1985; edn: BS, Nat. Taiwan Univ. 1977; MS, Univ. of Texas 1982; Profl. Engr., Calif. 1984. Career: design engr. George K. Ho & Assoc., Van Nuys 1983-84; design engr. Brandow & Johnston Assoc., Newport Beach 1984-; tchg. asst. Univ. of Texas, Austin, Tex. 1981-82; works: Shear Strength of Beam-Column Joints In RC Structures, 1982; mil: 2nd lt. Chinese Army, Taiwan 1977-79; rec: music. Ofc: Brandow & Johnston Associates, 4901 Birch St. Newport Beach 92660

SHIELDS, JOHN EDWARD, chef; b. May 5, 1951, Baltimore; s. Pierce Charles and Mary Jane (Cleary) S.; edn: AA music, Peabody Conservatory 1975; M.Bus., Towson Univ. 1976. Career: systems analyst Citicorp. Baltimore 1970-76; sous chef Belvedere Hotel Baltimore 1976-78; chef A La Carte Restaurant Berkeley 1978-83; chef/ owner Gertie's Chesapeake Bay Cafe 1984-; restaurant cons. 1984-; honors: Best Chefs of No. Calif. 1974, Poetry Award (Wash. Post 1973), Short Story Award (Baltimore Sun 1974); Democrat; rec: jazz piano. Res: 997 Steiner San Francisco 94117 Ofc: Gertie's Chesapeake Bay Cafe 1919 Addison St Berkeley 94704

SHIEPE, DOUGLAS A., real estate investments & devel. co. executive; b. Sept. 11, 1959, Westwood, Calif.; s. Abraham F. and Tofeca A. (Moses) S.; edn: AA, Santa Monica City Coll. 1980; BS, CSU Northridge 1982; MA, Harvard Univ. 1984. Calif. lic. real estate sales, constrn., (1982). Career: sales broker E.S.I. Sales, Los Angeles (Calif. corp. with br. ofcs. in Seoul, Korea and Hong Kong), 1984, exec. v.p. 1985, chief exec. 1986-; real estate devel. & sales cons.; frequent speaker sems. on R.E. investment opps.; honors: Deans list (1980-84); mem: Calif. Assn. of Realtors, Better Bus. Bur., Mensa; publs: in field of R.E. inv. & fin. plnng.; Republican; Christian; rec: flying, automobiles. Res: POB 67186 Los Angeles 90067

SHIH, CHARLES CHIEN, nuclear engineer; b. June 3, 1950, Taipei, Taiwan; nat. US cit. 1983; s. Tsu-En and Chung-Chueh (Hsu) S.; m. Grace Hoa, June 3, 1978; edn: BS, Nat. Tsing Hua Univ. 1972; MS, Univ. of Rhode Is. 1977; Reg. Profl. Engr. (nuclear) Calif. 1978. Career: senior nuclear engr. Kaiser Engineers Inc., Oakland 1977-80; nuclear generation engr. Pacific Gas & Electric Co., San Francisco 1980-; mem. Am. Nuclear Soc., Health Physics Soc.; Republican; rec: photog. Ofc: San Francisco 94106

SHILY, B. G., optometrist; b. July 13, 1956; s. Abraham and Aktar (Kavian) S.; edn: BA, UCLA 1978; BS, OD, ICO 1983; MA, CSU Los Angeles 1985. Career: optometric doctor Encino Ophthalmologic Medical Group, Encino 1983-85; optometric doctor CIGNA Health Plans of Calif., Los Angeles 1985-86; currently, pvt. practice, Brentwood; honors: Irvin M. Borish Award, Am. Optometric Found.; mem: Am. and Calif. Optometric Assns., UCLA Alumni; publs: Am. Journ. of Optometry & Physiological Optics Vol. 62; rec: sports. Ofc: 11633 San Vicente Blvd. Ste. 320 Los Angeles 90049

SHIMAMOTO, FRANK M., flower grower; b. July 26, 1920, Fresno; s. Gennosuke and Iwa (Shimamoto) S.; m. Chizuko I., Jan. 31, 1951; children: Alan N. b. 1963, Sandra S. b. 1966; edn: BA, San Francisco STate 1953; Calif. Pest Conrol Advr. 1985. Career: flower grower Watsonville 1965-; cons. Japanese spkg. flower grower, Central Costa Mesa 1965-80; mil: chief warrant ofcr. US Army Mil. Intelligence Svc., Bronze Star w/ cluster, Commdn. w/ cluster; Republican; Buddhist; rec: gardening. Res: 147 Johnson Rd. Watsonville 95076 Ofc: Shima Floral Farm, 145 Johnson Rd. Watsonville 95076

SHIN, STEVE HYUNIL, acupuncturist; b. June 30, 1945, Seoul, Korea, nat. US cit. 1979; s. Woong Kyun and Jin Sook (Kim) S.; m. Jung Yun, July 7, 1970; children: Tina b. 1970, Linda b. 1971, Eric b. 1980, Tom b. 1982; edn: BS, Dong Ui Oriental Medicine Coll. 1968; OMD, Calif. Acupuncture Coll. 1982. Career: acupuncturist, herbologist prin. Shin's Acupuncture Center, Anaheim 1982-; mem. Calif. Acupuncture Alliance, So. Calif. Oriental Medicine Assn.; works: Eith Constitution Theory of Oriental Medicine; mil: R.O.K.A.; Methodist. Res: 9178 Moltriver Cir Fountain Valley 92780 Ofc: 1720 West Ball Rd Ste 1 Anaheim 92804

SHIPP, WILLIAM WELDON, certified public accountant; b. June 8, 1927, Los Angeles; s. Pat and Mae (Harris) Shipp; m. Dorothy Forse, Sept. 23, 1967; children: Karyn b. 1971, William b. 1973; edn: BS, Univ. of San Francisco 1952; MBA, Golden Gate Univ. 1963; CPA, State of Calif. 1966. Career: staff auditor Price Waterhouse &: Co., S.F. 1952-56; acctg. supr. C.C. Moore &: Co., S.F. 1956-63; chief acct. Westland Life Ins. Co., S.F. 1963-66; audit mgr. Soule Steel Co., S.F. 1966-67; system analyst, supvg. acct., senior acct. Bechtel Power Corp., S.F. 1967-82; CPA, Oakland 1983-; bd. dirs. Westland Life Ins. Co. 1963-66, Schiller Constrn. Co. 1969-85, Optrans Inc. 1983-; instr. in accounting UC Berkeley 1983-, Golden Gate Univ. 1984-; mem. Am. Inst. of CPAs, Calif. Soc. of CPAs; club: The Hills Swim & Tennis (Oakland); mil: sgt. US Army 1945-46; Republican; rec: stamp collecting US Plate Blocks, golf, swimming. Res: 5068 Dublin Ave. Oakland 94602 Ofc: William W. Shipp, CPA, 1964 Mountain Blvd, Ste. 199, Oakland 94611

SHIPPER, FREDERICK ANDREW, civil engineer; b. June 29, 1955, Dallas, Texas; s. Frederick Milton and Gloria M. (Manhoff) S.; m. Barbara Ann, March 13, 1983; edn: BS, Calif. Polytechnic Univ. Pomona 1980; Lic. Civil Engr., Calif. 1983. Career: senior draftsman, structural design engr., constrn. supt., John N.H. Chan & Assoc., La Canada 1980-83; senior plan check engr. City of Fontana 1984-; interview bd. Rancho Cucamonga; hiring plan checkers, 1985; pvt. cons. on constrn. methods & practice; mem: ICBO (Citrus Belt Chpt.); works: computer programs for structural analysis and var. tables using U.B.C. formulas and data; author, Pole Construction: Structural Design & Analysis; creator, large and intracate stained glass panels; rec: stained leaded glass, woodworking, writing. Ofc: City of Fontana, Dept. of Bldg. and Safety, 8353 Sierra Ave. Fontana 92335

SHIRE, HAROLD RAYMOND, professor, author, inventor; b. Nov. 23, 1910, Denver, Colo.; s. Samuel and Rose Betty (Herman) S.; m. Cecilia Shire; children: Margaret, Donna, David, Esti, Darcy; edn: Cert. in Bus., UCLA; MBA, Pepperdine Univ., hon. LLD, 1981; MLA, USC; JD, Southwestern Univ.; PhD, US Internat. Univ.; admitted to Calif. Bar and Supreme Cts. of Calif. & U.S. Career: deputy dist. atty. Los Angeles Co. 1937-39; asst. U.S. atty. 1939-42; pvt. practice law, Los Angeles & Beverly Hills 1946-56; pres. General Connectors Corp., Certified Spotwelding Corp., Quality Aircraft Corp., Quality Trading Corp. 1956-70; chmn. bd. dirs. General Connectors Corp., US & Bestobel Aircraft Ltd., U.K. 1970-73; prof. structural orgn. & law Pepperdine Univ. 1973-78; investor, bldr. 1973-; prof. mgmt. & law US Internat. Univ., San Diego 1981-; honors: Companion, Royal Aero. Soc., U.K.; Chevalier du Vieux Moulin, France; Svc. Ofcr. and Adj. General's Award & Chenault Post, Am. Legion, Shanghai, China; Letters of Commdn., US Atty. Gen. and Pres. Kennedy & Johnson; mem: Univ. Bd. Pepperdine Univ., Union of Orthodox Jewish Congregations of Am. (Exec. Com., Bd. Govs.), Fed., Calif. and Beverly Hills Bar Assns., The Founders, Los Angeles Music Ctr., Am. Soc. Internat. Law, AAUP, Am. Welding Soc., Am. Legion, Air Force Assn., alumni assns., Lambda Delta Beta, Psi Chi, Material & Process Engrs., Japan-Am. Soc., Japanese Com. of San Diego (hon. pres.), Urasenke Cha No Yu; works: publd. art, Symbolic Interactionism and Cha No Yu: A Method of Analyzing Japanese Behavior, publ. in Japanese, Japan 1982; inventor, high-pressure high-temperature flexible pneumatic, anti-icing, compression & air conditioning sys. used in jet aircraft; research, Japanese behavior, the Way of Tea; Republican; rec: big-game fishing, Chinese ceramics. Ofc: P.O. Box 1352 Beverly Hills 90213

SHIRLEY, DIANA ALICE DENOYELLES, library executive, writer, editor; b. May 20, 1938, Los Angeles; d. Gerhard A. and Hilda M. (Schmal) Nehus; m. Robert Edward McGowan, June 28, 1959, div. 1969; 1 son, Barry James; m. 2d. Edward Harold DeNoyelles, Aug. 15, 1970, div. 1972; m. 3d. Stephen Marlin Shirley, May 19, 1979; edn: stu., Mt. St. Mary's Coll. 1956-58; BA, Calif. Polytechnic Univ. 1970; postgrad., USC Sch. of Library Sci. 1970-71; MS, CSU Fullerton 1976; postgrad., Univ. of Iowa 1978, Claremont Grad. Sch.

1981-. Career: librarian trainee Los Angeles Public Library 1970-72; librarian Pomona Public Library 1972-75; coord. regl. adult svcs. Central Region, Los Angeles Co. Public Library 1976-79, city librarian La Canada Flintridge 1979-80, senior admin. analyst Chief Adminstrv. Ofc., Los Angeles Co. 1980-81; spl. asst. to county librarian 1981, exec. dir. Los Angeles County Public Library Found. 1981–; mgmt. cons., Pomona; Los Angeles World Affairs Council 1981-; mem: Am. and Calif. Library Assns., Library & Info. Tech. Assn., Am. Soc. Info. Sci., Am. Soc. Public Adminstrn., NOW; publs: ed., Women in California: A Guide to Organizations and Resources, 1977; Republican; Unitarian. Res: 231 Vista Circle Dr. Sierra Madre 91024 Ofc: Los Angeles County Public Library, 320 W. Temple St. Los Angeles 90012

SHIUH, JOSEPH PING-HUA, insurance broker; b. Apr. 19, 1941, Canton, China; s. Han Kong and Lhy Ing (Ding) S.; m. Ming R. Wang, Oct. 24, 1978; 1 dau., Charlene b. 1980; edn: BS animal husbandry, Nat. Chung-Hsin Univ. 1967. Career: pres. Nat. Chung-Hsin Univ. Alumni Assn. of So. Calif. 1982; pres. L.A. Chinatown Lions Club 1983-84; chmn. bd. Joint Chinese Univ. Alumni Assn. of So. Calif. 1984; pres. Ping-Hua Ins. Svc. Inc. 1984–; honors: Pres's Citn. Award (Prudential Ins. Co. 1979, 80, 81); mem. Chinese-Am. Ins. Profl. Assn. (chmn. bd. 1986-); publ. on ins. and wealth in Chinese 1985; Republican; Christian. Res: 196 Las Lomas Rd Duarte 91010 Ofc: Ping-Hua Ins. Svc. Inc., 300 S Atlantic Blvd Ste 107 Monterey Park 91754

SHIVERDAKER, JAY DEE, international computer manufacturing & research executive; b. Dec. 16, 1939, Enid, Okla.; s. Ivan J. and Oleta May (Polk) S.; m. Jan Simpson, Nov. 20, 1976; 1 son, Jeff, b. 1966; edn: BBA, West Texas St. Univ. 1966. Career: finance dept. City of Amarillo, Tx. 1958-66; IBM: senior mktg. and tech. support positions Data Proc. and Gen. Products Divs., incl. pres./bd. chmn. Dastek Corp., 1978-81; pres./bd. chmn. Encore International (energy, computers & resrch. corp.) USA, Canada, 1981-85; rep. dir., pres. Falcore Co. Ltd. (Japanese joint venture stock co.), Tokyo, subs. of Encore Internat., internat. high tech. finance, devel., mfg. and distbn. Far East & Europe 1985–; dir: VenTech Capital Corp., Tectonic Control Inc. (both USA & Can.); recipient sev. internat. IBM awards; rec: open water diving, skiing, boating, flying. Res: 1308 Crossgates Ln. San Jose 95120 Ofc: Encore International 100 W Rincon Ave Ste 207 Campbell 95008-2818

SHONK, ALBERT D., JR., publishers representative; b. May 23, 1932, Los Angeles; s. Albert D., Sr. and Jean (Stannard) S.; edn: BS in bus. adm., USC 1954. Career: field rep., mktg. div. Los Angeles Examiner, 1954-55, asst. mgr. 1955-56, mktg. div. mgr. 1956-57, account exec. Hearst Advt. Serv., 1957-59; acct. exec. Keith H. Evans & Assoc., 1959-63, San Francisco mgr. 1963-65; owner/pres. Albert D. Shonk Co., 1965–; founder, v.p., life dir. Inter-Greek Soc., USC, 1976-, pres. 1984-; USC Comm. Assoc.; hon. life dir. Signet Circle Corp. (pres. 1977-81); dir. Florence Crittendon Services (exec. v.p. 1979-81, pres. 1981-83; bd. chmn. 1983-85); founding chmn. Crittendon Assoc., 197;8-80; hon. life mem. Junior Advt. Club of L.A. (past dir., treas., v.p.); Nat. Assn. of Publishers Reps. (West Coast v.p. 1981-83); Magazine Reps. Assn. of So. Calif. & No. Calif.; Bus./Profl. Advt. Assn.; mem. Phi Sigma Kappa (dist. gov. 1960-62, nat. v.p. 1962-70, Grand Council 1977-83, Grand Pres. 1979-83, Chancellor 1983-); trustee, pres. Phi Sigma Kappa Found., Inc., 1984-; Alpha Kappa Psi; Interfrat. Alumni Assn. of So. Calif. (v.p., pres. 1957-61). Presbyterian. Res: 3460 W. 7th St, Wilshire Towers, Los Angeles 90005 Ofc: 3156 Wilshire Blvd Los Angeles

SHOOTER, A. KELLEY, agricultural developer; b. Apr. 17, 1954, Burlingame; s. Arthur H. Shooter and Marilyn Sue (Kelley) Farrar; m. Barbara Rayborn, May 9, 1981; edn: BS, USC Sch. of Bus. Adminstrn. 1976; JD, UC Hastings Coll. of the Law 1979. Career: secty. Agricultural Investments, Inc. (Menlo Park) 1980-, v.p. mktg. (Los Altos) 1982-, pres. (San Diego) 1984–; dir: Arthur H. Shooter, Inc. (1981-), Southwest Sprinkler, Inc. (1985-); apptd. Jojoba Industry Advisory Council (1984); mem. Jojoba Growers Assn. (dir. 1984), Jojoba Marketing Coop. (pres., dir. 1985-); civic: Commonwealth Club (SF), La Jolla Mus. of Contemporary Art (patron); works: key role in commercialization of jojoba (used in cosmetics, lubricants & medicine), devel. 2000 acres (1980-); Republican; Episcopal; rec: horticulture, securities, sports. Res: POB 1961 Rancho Santa Fe 92067 Ofc: Agricultural Investments Inc. 5703 Oberlin Dr Ste 101 San Diego 92121

SHORE, SHARON DIANE, business owner; b. July 15, 1949, Colfax, Wash.; d. David and Virginia (Klein) Reichert; m. John Shore, Dec. 12, 1970; edn: AA, Coll. of the Sequioas 1969; CSU Fresno 1969-70, 1983-; Career: invoice clerk, data proc. controller Quality Farm & Fleet Muskegon, Mich. 1971-73; claims, statements receptionist, typist Clancy Childs Ins. Agency Hanford, Calif. 1973-74; v.p./ secty. Fife & Drum Music Inc. Clovis 1974–; honors: Dean's List (Coll. of Sequoias 1967-69, CSU Fresno 1986), Band Talent Scholar (Coll. of Sequioas 1968), Beta Alpha Psi; mem: Am. Home Econs. Assn. 1970, Rainbow Girls 1964-67, Girl Scouts of Am. 1956-62, Toastmasters Internat. 1986-; rec: reading, ballroom dancing, snorkeling, horticulture. Ofc: Fife & Drum Music Inc. POB 442 Clovis 93613

SHORENSTEIN, MICHAEL LEWIS, physician; b. Sept. 11, 1944, NY, NY; s. Joel and Marilyn (Kritzer) S.; m. Rosalind Greenberg (also MD), June 18, 1967; children: Anna, b. 1975, Claire, b. 1981; edn: ScB, Mass. Inst. of Tech. 1966, MS 1967, PhD 1971; MD, Stanford Univ. Sch. of Med. 1976; Bd. cert. Internal Med. 1977. Career: fmr. research scientist at MIT, Cambridge, Mass.; med. residency at UCLA Hosp. & Clinics, 1976-79; currently, co-partner with wife/ pvt. practice of internal medicine, Santa Cruz, Ca.; full staff mem. Depts. of Internal Med. at Dominican Santa Cruz Hosp. and Community Hosp. of Santa Cruz; prin. partner/co-dir. Health Enhancement & Lifestyle Planning Systems (cons. firm spec. in health promotion for industry); honors: Xigma Xi and Sigma Gamma Tau (1966), Continuing Med. Edn. Award, Calif. Med. Assn. 1981. Mem: Am. Soc. of Internal Medicine, AMA, CMA, Santa Cruz Med. Soc.; bd. dirs. American Diabetes Soc. (S.C. chpt.); mem. (via H.E.L.P.S.) of Chambers of Commerce in Santa Cruz, Watsonville, Scotts Valley; art. (in press), Western Jour. of Med., 1984; Jewish; rec: photog. Ofc: Michael Shorenstein, M.D., 700 Frederick St, Ste. 103, Santa Cruz 95062

SHORENSTEIN, ROSALIND GREENBERG, physician; b. Jan. 14, 1947, NY, NY; d. Albert and Natalie (Sherman) Greenberg; m. Michael Shorenstein, June 18, 1967; children: Anna, b. 1975, Claire, b. 1981; edn: BA, Wellesley Coll. 1968; MA, Harvard Univ. 1970, PhD 1973; MD, Stanford Univ. Sch. of Med. 1976; Diplomate, Am. Bd. of Internal Med. 1979. Career: biochemist in research at Harvard Univ. 1970-73; med. resident UCLA Hosp. and Clinics 1976-79; pvt. practice of internal medicine in partnership with husband, also M.D.; prin. partner, co-director Health Enhancement & Lifestyle Planning Systems, consulting firm; staff Dominican Santa Cruz Hosp., Community Hosp. of Santa Cruz; honors: Phi Beta Kappa 1967, Sigma Xi 1967, Woodrow Wilson Hon. Predoctoral Fellow, NSF Predoctoral Fellow 1968-72; mem: Am. Soc. of Internal Medicine, Calif. Med. Assn., Am. Med. Womens Assn. (treas. Santa Cruz branch 1983), Santa Cruz County Med. Soc., AAUW, CofC, Temple Beth El Sisterhood; publs: num. sci. journal articles; Jewish; Ofc: 700 Frederick St., Ste 103, Santa Cruz 95062

SHORES, HOWARD VEASEY, financial planner; b. Sept. 2, 1934, Baltimore, Md.; s. William Veasey and Verba (Dean) S.; m. Susan, May 13, 1978; children: William b. 1958, Amy b. 1966; edn: BA, Western Maryland Coll. 1956; Certified Financial Planner 1986. Career: financial planner IDS Am. Express 1982-84; tech. writer Quality Tech. Pubs. 1984-85; financial planner Discount Investments of Am. (subsid. of Home Savings of Am.) 1985, Home Savings 1986–; financial planning seminars to over 65 corps., univs. and govt. agencies throughout So. Calif., retirement planning seminars; mem. Internat. Assn. Financial Planning; publ: article Silver Circle mag. 1986; mil: capt. USN 1952-82, 21 medals incl. Legion of Merit, Bronze Star (V), Meritorious Svc.(2), Air Medal (2), Navy Commdn. (3); Democrat; Protestant; rec: coin collecting, fishing, golf. Res: 11055 Collinwood Dr Santee 92071

SHORT, OLIVE BUNNELL, teacher, ret.; b. Feb. 19, 1914, San Bernardino; d. Merton Oliver and Ethlyn Mae (Hughes) Bunnell; m. Joseph B. Petty, Sept. 10, 1938, dec. 1953; m. Alvin L. Short, Aug. 1977, dec. 1977; children: Jocelyn b. 1941, Melinda b. 1943; edn: AA, San Bernardino Valley Coll. 1934; BA, UCLA 1936; MA, Univ. of Redlands 1967; hon. PhD, Colorado Christian Coll. 1973. Career: medical technologist 1936; instr. bacteriology and allied sci. Univ. of Redlands 1946-48; corp. pres. Costume House Inc. 1950-57; instr. biology, oceanography 1957-58; guest lectr. microbiology Western Vendors Inc. and Santa Bernardino Gen. Hosp. 1960; pres. OJM Inc. dba K/N Chemical Supply Co. 1970–; honors: Life Cert. Secondary Schs. 1959; Monte Award, San Bernardino Tchr. Assn. 1969; Bausch & Lomb award for Science Fair 1970; activity pins, Am. Red Cross; Cert., YWCA; Cert. of Appreciation, Rotary; Grantee, Am. Assn. Univ. Women; mem: Am. Assn. for Adv. of Sci. (life), Nat. Sci. Tchrs. Assn. (life), Calif. Tchrs. Assn. (life), Am. Assn. Univ. Women (life), Am. Assn. Microbiologists, Soroptimist Internat., San Bernardino CofC, Daughters of the Am. Revolution, United Methodist Women, St. Paul's United Methodist Found., PTA, League of Women Voters, San Bernardio Community Concert Assn., San Bernardino Internat. Council of the Mayor's Ofc.; ch. bd. Global Concerns; works: Manual For Mineral Analysis, 1968, 2d. 1973; area chmn., Math- Science Career Conference for Girls, Am. Assn. Univ. Women 1984; Republican; Protestant; rec: travel, photog. Res: 741 East 21st San Bernadino 92404

SHORT, ROBERT JUSTIN, composite product development- manufacturing co. founder; b. Dec. 10, 1932, Cincinnati, Ohio; s. Robert Justin Sr. and Mildred Dorothea S.; m. Nancy Yaney, May 1, 1970; children: Laura b. 1964, Scott b. 1965, Karen b. 1966, Christian b. 1971, Jay b. 1972; edn: AB, Duke Univ. 1954. Career: founder, CEO Justin Enterprises Inc., Cinti., Ohio 1958-76; founder, CEO Tankinetics Inc., Westminster 1976-83; founder, CEO The Composite Engring. Co., Corona 1983–; honors: John C. Vaaler Award, Chem. Processing Mag. 1968, 1970, 1976; Grand Design Award and Corrosion Resistance Award, Soc. of the Plastic Industries 1981; Best Paper Award, Reinforced Plastics/ Composites Inst. 1981; Soc. of the Plastics Industries, Soc. of Plastics Engrs., Laguna Beach Presbyterian Ch., Baloa Yacht Club; works: patented method for bldg. largest filament wound all composite (reinforced plastic) tank in the world; mil: lt. j.g. USN 1954-56; Republican; Presbyterian; rec: sailing, flying, tennis. Res: 127 Emerald Bay Laguna Beach 92651 Ofc: The Composite Engineering Co., 232 No. Sherman Ave Ste E Corona 91720

SHORTINO, LEO MARSHALL, investor; b. Sept. 1, 1917, San Jose; s. Vito and Rose C. (Catania) Sciortino; m. Peggy Mastin, Nov. 28, 1970; children: Rosemary b. 1948; Joanne b. 1953; edn: grad. Bellarmine Coll. Prepartory 1936; BA, San Jose State Univ. 1950, MA, 1956. Career: elem. sch. tchr. Docoto Sch. Dist. 1954-57, Mtn. View Sch. Dist. 1957-59; elem. sch. prin. Sausalito Sch. Dist. 1959-63, San Rafael Sch. Dist. 1963-65, Murray Sch. Dist. 1965-69; mng. owner investment properties, San Jose 1969-82; honors: charter mem. Phi Delta Kappa; mem: La Rinconada Country Club (Los Gatos); profl. musician, pianist; mil: sgt. USAF 1942-45, Asiatic-Pacific Medal; Republican; Catholic; rec: hunting, fishing, golf. Res: 15252 Montalvo Rd. Saratoga 95070 Ofc: Regency Square Apartments, 1315 Eden Ave. San Jose 95117

SHUBITZ, SIMON MAXIMILIAN, physician, philanthropist, humanitarian; b. Dec. 15, 1904, Europe, nat. USA 1920; s. Mendel A. and Esther F. (Murin) S.;

m. Helene E. Leavy, Dec. 25, 1938; children: Stephen A. b. 1943, Susan M. b. 1944; edn: BS, William and Mary Coll. 1930, MD, Univ. of Chicago 1936; postgrad. work New York Post-Grad. Med. Sch. 1939, and also in London, Berlin, and Vienna; lic. physician and surgeon, Calif. Bd. Med. Examiners 1937. Career: staff phys. 1945-, and conducted outpatient clinic 1942-45, Cedars of Lebanon Hosp.; helped estab. St. Joseph's Hosp., Burbank and Presbyterian Hosp., Van Nuys; staff St. Joseph's Hosp. 1945-; endowed two student Loan Funds, a Premedical Scholarship and a Cancer Award at Wm. and Mary, Rush Med. Coll., and Univ. of Chicago, and Scholarship Fund for scholars in Israel; honors: the Simon M. Shubitz Cancer Prize and Lectureship (given annually) estab. in his honor by Univ. of Chicago (1978); Selective Service Medal awarded by US Congress for med. services during WWII; Phi Beta Kappa; mem: Fellow Am. Coll. Cardiology (1953), Charter Fellow Am. Acad. Family Physicians 1953 (life mem.), Founding Fellow Am. Geriatrics Soc. (1972), AMA, CMA, L.A. Co. Med. Assn., World Med. Assn., L.A. Co. Heart Assn., USC Salerni Collegium, B'nai B'rith, Univ. of Chicago Club (L.A.), Am. Physicians Fellowship for Israel, Wilshire Blvd. Temple L.A.; mil: phys. US Army Med. Corps 1938-40; Republican; Hebrew; rec: travel, tennis, golf. Address: No. Hollywood

SHUEMAKER, JAMES ALVIN, real estate developer; b. Sept. 20, 1939, Los Angeles; s. James Alvin and Glenna Marie (Smith) S.; children: Susan, b. 1962; Jamie, b. 1965; Brett, b. 1967; edn: BS, Westmont Coll. 1960; MBA, USC 1967. Career: regl. sales mgr. Moody's Investors Svc., Inc., Los Angeles 1961-68; v.p. mktg. Transamerica Investment Counselors, Inc., Los Angeles 1968-70; exec. v.p. Shareholders Asset Mgmt. Co., Los Angeles 1970-71; owner/ bldgr. Commercial Real Estate Developer 1972-; honors: Top Nat. Quota Performance 1964, 1965; New Business Sales Record 1966; mem: Ahmanson Baseball, Beverly Hills CofC, Beverly Hills Rotary, Internat. Council of Shopping Ctrs., Los Angeles Ballet Guild, Los Angeles Olympic Organizing Com., Marlborough Sch. Parents Council, Music Center Founders and Fraternity of Friends, Town Hall of Calif., USC Associates; clubs: The Magic Castle, Los Angeles Tennis, Riding and Polo, Santa Barbara Polo and Racquet, Montecito Country, Wilshire Country; mil: U.S. Army Nat. Guard 1963; Republican; Presbyterian; rec: skiing, tennis. Res: 315 So. Hudson Ave., Los Angeles 90020 Ofc: Shuemaker Enterprises, 9595 Wilshire Blvd., Ste. 701, Beverly Hills 90212

SHUKMAN, SOLOMON JOSEPH, artist; b. July 5, 1927, Bobr, Minsk, USSR; nat. 1980; s. Joseph and Eugenia (Golden) S.; m. Ludmila Berman, Nov. 14, 1954; children: Janna b. 1955, Roman b. 1959; edn: Coll. of Fine Arts and Theatre, Moscow 1946-49, Stroganov Inst. of Art, Moscow 1949-52. Career: artist, Artists Found. of USSR, 1952-74; internat. exhibs: NY (1956), Paris (1959), Brussels (1961), Ehrfurt (1962), Warsaw (1964), Prague (1967), Sokolnike (1968, 71, 73); vs. pers. exhibs. 1963-64, mem. Union of Soviet Artists; recipient 20 diplomas and awards, Artists Found. of USSR, listed Who's Who in the West; pers. exhibns: Denver (1974), TransAm. Bldg., Loeb Rhoades Mkt. Gall., S.F. (1975), Los Altos (1976), Nathan Gall., Union Sq., S.F. (1977), Pantheon Gall., Sutter St., S.F. (1978), Magnes Mus., Berkeley (1979), Los Altos (1981), Internat. Art Expo NY (1985), Art Expo Calif., Los Angeles (1985), One Man Show Palo Alto (1985); creation of lithographs, paintings, etchings for new limited edition series printed by Ernest F. DeSoto for 1985 Art Expo NY; works publ. in 1985 Printworld Directory; featured Denver Post, S.F. Chronicle, Art Week, Solomon Shukman by John Bowlt; mem: World Print Council, S.F.; Graphic Arts Counc.; Soc. of the Calif. Palace of the Legion of Honor, S.F.; Internat. Graphic Arts Soc., NY; Democrat; Jewish. Res: 554 Beresford Ave Redwood City 94061

SHULMAN, IRA ANDREW, physician; b. Feb. 26, 1949, Los Angeles; s. Jack Sylvan and Laurie Sylvia (Erde) S.; m. Nadine, Dec. 16, 1972; children: Paula b. 1978, Stefanie b. 1982; edn: BA, UC Los Angeles 1971; MD, USC Sch. Medicine 1975. Career: physician, splst. in transfusion medicine; dir. of blood bank and transfusion svcs., Saint Mary Medical Ctr, Long Beach 1980-81, L.A.Co.-USC Medical Ctr. 1981-; dir. blood bank Kenneth Norris Cancer Hosp. 1983-; honors: Regents Scholar UCLA (1967-71), Phi Beta Kappa (1971), Alpha Omega Alpha (1975), Commended Alumnus, USC Sch. of Medicine (1985); mem: Coll. of Am. Pathologists, Am. Assn. of Blood Banks, Am. Soc. of Clin. Pathologists, Council on Immunohematology (nat. com. on blood transfusion medicine), Calif. Blood Bank System, Phi Delta Epsilon med. frat.; publs: 24 articles in med. jours., chpts. in 3 books, num. abstracts, profl. presentations state & nat. meetings, 2 nat. teleconfs. (Am. Soc. Clin. Pathols.); Democrat; Jewish; rec: bicycling. Ofc: Los Angeles County-USC Medical Center Blood Bank POB 771 1200 N State St Los Angeles 90033

SHUMATE, VALERIE HELEN, real estate broker, journalist, educator; b. Mar. 29, 1933, Lameroo, S. Australia, nat. 1959; d. John Roy and Kathleen (Bowman) Dunn; m. Clyde K. Shumate, Oct. 12, 1957; children: Michael b. 1958, Sandra b. 1960, Pam b. 1963, Wanda b. 1966; edn: tchr. cert. Adelaide Teachers Coll., 1953; BA, honors, Cal Poly 1975, spec. edn. T.C., 1974, 75; Calif. lic. real estate sales 1978, broker 1981. Career: sch. tchr., Australia, 1953-55; world tour (tennis & tourist), 1956, 57; tchr. London County Council, Glasgow, Scotland, 1956-57, Augusta, Ga. 1960, prin. International (Brit.) Sch., Asmara, Eritrea, Ethiopia 1961-63, also Eng. instr. Univ. of Addis Ababba; tennis tchr., Calif. 1964-65; piano tchr., Landstuhl, Ger. 1966-68; tchr. jr. high sch. phys. edn, spl. edn. tchr., San Luis Obispo Co. 1975-78; tennis coach Paso Robles High Sch., 1975-80; real estate broker assoc. Century 21 Home & Land Realtors, Paso Robles, 1979-; tennis coach 1960-; writer weekly edn. column.: On Board, Country News (Paso Robles); travel articles "Wimbledon" 1983; mem: Paso Robles Bd. of Realtors (edn. pgm. chmn. 1979-); AAUW (internat. chair 1984); PTA, Red Cross (Water Safety Instr.),

Order of Eastern Star; mem. Art Theatre site com.; Parks & Rec. tennis instr.; Republican; Prot.; rec: travel, piano, tennis, swimming. Res: 1704 Highland Park Drive Paso Robles 93446 Ofc: Century 21 Home & Land Realtors, 521 Spring St Paso Robles 93446

SHUMPERT, EDMOND ELLIS, sculptor; b. Feb. 13, 1943, West Point, Miss.; s. Edmond L. D. and Opal Olene (Irvin) S.; m. Andrea Worthen, Jan. 18, 1986; children (by previous marriage): Grant b. 1964, Teague b. 1966, Bryon b. 1967, Paul b. 1969, Erik b. 1969; Art Center Sch. 1961-65 (4-yr scholarship), anatomy courses, UCLA 1965. Career: medical illustrator for Dr. Charles F. Bridgman, 1965; founder "OP" "Ocean Pacific" and designed logo and name, 1968; sculptures: 5 ft. bronze relief, Scripps Instn. of Oceanography, La Jolla (1965), bronze portrait of Dr. Kenneth Clark, NY for cover Psychol. Today mag. (1968), portrait of Duke Kahanamoku for City of Huntington Beach (1969), 18 ft. bronze relief of Odyssey of Homer (1970), 13 ft. bronze surfer for City of Huntington Beach (1971), bronze surfer "The Bottom Turn" (1972) winner Kalos Kagathos Found. Prize, Nat. Sculpture Soc. Exhib. 1978, series depicting native Am. life (1973-80) (1982-84), 8 ft. Neptune Fountain, Disneyworld Epcot Ctr. (1981), commnd. "Fina Prize" awarded to Olympic Gold Medallist Michael Gross (1985), commnd. Sammy Lee Award for Internat. Swimming Hall of Fame, Ft. Lauderdale (1986), working on 8 ft. bronze of Bruce Jenner, Olympic Gold Medallist (1986); rec: restoration 1940s Chrysler autos, surfing, swimming, archery. Res: 7011 Shadygrove St Tujunga 91042 Ofc: E. Shumpert, Sculptor 7903 Foothill Sunland 91040

SHUTTS, PETER GEOFFREY, architect; b. Oct. 26, 1946, New Orleans; s. Hamilton and Mary Elizabeth (Chowins) S.; m. Katherine, Feb. 5, 1977; 1 dau. Monica Elizabeth b. 1979; edn: B.Arch., Univ. Ore. 1970; reg. arch. Calif. 1976, Hawaii 1980. Career: senior arch. Gilbert Assoc. 1974-78; prin./owner PGS Arch./Planning 1978-82; senior arch. Hoover Assoc. 1982-83; devel. arch. Meyers Properties 1983-85; prin./owner Peter G. Schutts AIA Pleasanton 1985-; Santa Clara Co. Bd. of Dirs. 1982-86; mem: Nat. Council Arch. Registration Bd., Am. Inst. Arch. (bd. dirs. Calif. council), Sports Car Club of Am.; mil: sp/4 USAR 1970-76; Republican; Episcopal; rec: sports car road racing. Res: 4964 Kenson Dr San Jose 95124 Ofc: 699 Peters Ave, Ste A, Pleasanton 94566

SIASSI, IRADJ, psychiatrist, b. Aug. 20, 1933, Tehran, Iran; s. Ali Akbar and Roshan (Bayat) S.; m. Shaharzad Fozouni, Aug. 19, 1974; children: Guillan b. 1978; Dara b. 1980; edn: BA, Queens Coll., Cambridge, Eng. 1954, MA, 1956; MD, Indiana Univ. Med. Sch. 1963. Career: asst. prof. of psychiatry Johns Hopkins Univ. and Hosp., 1969-71, assoc. prof. Rutgers Med. Sch., N.J. 1971-74, prof. Univ. of Pittsburgh, Pa. 1974-76; deputy minister of health for mental health Govt. of Iran 1976-79; prof. psychiatry Univ. Pittsburgh 1980-83, UC Los Angeles Med. Sch. 1983-; Inpatient Unit chief Sepulveda VA Med. Center, 1983-; mem: AMA, World Med. Assn., Am. Psychiatric Assn. (Asian-Am. Com. 1983-), Iranian Psych. Assn. (pres. 1977-80), Soc. Iranian Psych. in No. Am. (pres. 1980-); author 50+ sci. publs., book chapters, 1972-; mil: lt. Iranian Army 1967-69; Moslem; rec: literature, history, tennis, soccer. Ofc: Sepulveda VA Medical Center 16111 Plummer St Sepulveda 91343

SIDERS, BARRY LEE, lawyer; b. Jan. 29, 1943, Ann Arbor, Mich.; s. Ellis Leroy and Gertrude (Litzenberg) S.; m. Janice Marie, Aug. 14, 1966; 1 son, Jonathan Barry b. 1980; edn: BA, UC Berkeley 1964; JD, Hastings Coll. of the Law 1973; grad. of Command and Gen. Staff Coll. 1979; admitted Calif. State Bar 1973. Career: atty. assoc. Merrill, Thiessen & Gagen, Profl. Corp. 1974-79; atty. prin., Danville 1979-; instr. Univ. of Md. 1965-67; instr. USC Ext., 1975-78; mem: Calif. Bar Assn., Calif. Trial Lawyers Assn., Contra Costa Bar Assn. (chmn. Family Law Com. 1976-78), Kiwanis Club (pres. 1979-80); mil: US Army 1965-70, Korea, Germany, Viet Nam Service, lt. col. USAR 1970-, Bronze Star with 2 o.l.c., Army Commendn. Medal with 2 o.l.c., Meritorious Service Medal and var. overseas and service medals; author: Commander's Guide to Civil Affairs in Korea (1984, 2d ed. 1985); book to be publ. June 1986 by Nolo Press, A Lawyer's Guide for His Client to Divorce in Calif.; Republican; rec: writing, pvt. pilot, inventor, Arabian Horses. Law Ofc: Barry L. Siders, 401 S Hartz Ave Ste 308 Danville 94526

SIDEY, S. DEAN, electrical engineer; b. July 16, 1953, Riverton, Wyo.; s. Robert Sidney and Cathern Eugenia (Graham) S.; div.; edn: AA, Casper Coll. 1973, BSEE, Univ. Colo. 1975, MSEE, Ariz. State Univ. 1980; Reg. Profl. Engr., Calif. 1983. Career: design engr. Collins Radio Group, Cedar Rapids, Iowa 1975-77; RF design engr. Motorola Govt. Electronics Div., Scottsdale, Ariz. 1977-80; staff engr. Magnavox Govt. and Indsl. Electronics Co., Torrance, Calif. 1980-81; staff engr. Data Link & Network Systems Dept. Communications Systems Div. Hughes Aircraft Co., Fullerton 1980-85, senior staff engr., 1985-; honors: Eagle Scout, BSA; mem: Hughes Fullerton Mgmt. Club, Mensa (fmr.), Hughes Fullerton Archery Club (secty. 1983); rec: archery, tennis, fencing, Middle English lit. Res: 2923 Eckleson Lakewood 90712 Ofc: Hughes Aircraft Co (POB 3110) Bldg. 688 M/S W125 Fullerton 92634

SIEGEL, ALAN LEE, polarity therapist, educator; b. Feb. 14, 1942, N.Y.C.; s. Joseph Benjamin and Betty (Kirschner) S.; m. Vicki, Aug. 3, 1979; children: Joseph b. 1968, Suzanne b. 1970, Rebecca b. 1984, David b. 1986; edn: AAS, Bronx Comm. Coll. 1962; BS in edn., City Coll. of NY 1964, MS in edn., 1966; ND, Dr. Naturopathy, cum. laude, Bernadean Univ. 1981. Career: physical edn. cons. Bryant Sch., Teaneck, N.J. 1964-65; instr. phys. and health edn., Bronx Comm. Coll. 1965-66; asst. prof. Borough of Manhattan Comm. Coll., NY, NY 1965-81; founder/dir. Polarity Therapy Center of San Francisco and pres. Internat. School of Polarity Therapy (USA and G.B.) 1985-; panelist Am. Arbitration Assn. 1976-78; civic: S.F. Meditation Group (coord.), San Communication Workshop (founder/leader), instr. num. health related courses for var comm. orgns.; author: Life Energy: The Power That Heals (The Science of Polarity Therapy), Prism Book; devel. Video course for home study of Polarity Therapy; Self Realization Fellowship; rec: hiking, gardening. Address: Polarity Therapy Center 409-A Lawton St San Francisco 94122

SIEGEL, ARNOLD WALTER, forensic scientist; b. Mar. 23, 1932, Toledo, Ohio; s. Charles and Lenore G. (Bock) S.; m. Stephanie E., Jan. 30, 1958; children: Carrie b. 1963, Jonathan b. 1965, Ethan b. 1967, Oren b. 1969; edn: AA, Los Angeles City Coll. 1952, BB, UC Los Angeles 1956, MBA, 1958. Career: assoc. project engr. UCLA Inst. of Traffic Engrg. 1955-62; co-dir. trauma research UCLA Dept. of Surgery 1963-73; adminstr. multi-disciplinary US Dept. of Transp. Motor Vehicle Safety Research Pgm., UCLA; cons. automotive, traffic safety, biomechanics of injury 1956–; chief engr. Accident Reconstrn. Assn.; cons. to indsl. cos. and var. govt. agcys. (nat., state, local and fgn.) honors: Sigma Xi; Nat. Safety Council Metropolitan Life Award for collision research (1962), for field analysis and research in accidents (1971); Internat. Traffic Safety Award for research in accidents, Belgium (1972); mem: Soc. Auto. Engrs., Am. Assn. Auto. Medicine (bd. dirs., co-founder Western chap.), Am. Acad. Forensic Scis., Calif. Assn. Criminalists, Am. Inst. Forensic Scis., United Way; author 55+ books & sci. papers, 16 films, 100+ articles on collision injury analysis; rec: fly fishing, outdoors. Ofc: Accident Reconstrn. Assoc. 4461 Hayvenhurst Ave Encino 91436

SIEMIATKOWSKI, RICHARD THADDEUS, engineering executive; b. Dec. 19, 1938, Amsterdam, N.Y.; s. Thaddeus Mathew and Isabel Bernice (Bara) S.; m. Barbara Burkhart, Aug. 19, 1962; children: Samantha b. 1957, Stephen b. 1965, Sharon b. 1968; edn: BS in mech. eng., Tri State Coll. 1959; cert. completion Am. Mgmt. Assn., NYC 1970-72; real estate certs., Golden West Coll. 1974-78; Calif. lic. real estate sales. Career: var. engr. mgmt. pos. Rockwell Internat. 1959-68; sales mgr. Siliconix Inc., Santa Clara 1968-72; western area mgr. ITT Semiconductors, Inglewood 1972-74; Xciton Corp., Huntington Beach 1974-76; Monolithic Memories Inc., Santa Clara 1976-82; v.p. Applied Micro Circuits Corp., San Diego 1982-84; pres. Silicon Devel. Corp., Huntington Beach 1984- ; cons. (market info.) Dataquest, 1984; speaker San Diego Electronics Show (1986); Republican; Catholic; rec: art, seamanship, fishing. Ofc: 13178 Jason Ct Garden Grove 92644 Ofc: Silicon Development Corp 16162 Beach Blvd Ste 304 Huntington Beach 92647

SIEUX, LILY TOH, university lecturer; b. June 1, 1950, Penang, Malaysia; d. Chin Sam and Siah Kee (Chung) Toh; m. Geoffrey Sieux, Nov. 26, 1977; 1 dau: Liane b. 1982; edn: BA, Mills Coll. 1973; MS, Univ. of Pacific 1975; MBA, UC Berkeley 1980; CPA, Calif. 1983. Career: senior asst. acct. Deloitte, Haskins & Sells, San Francisco 1980-82; lectr. CSU Sch. of Bus. & Econs., Hayward 1983–; profl. cons. I.P.I. Gold Inc. 1983-85, Via Express Inc. 1984-; honors: Fulbright Grantee 1969-73; Phi Beta Kappa 1973; Beta Gamma Sigma 1980; mem: Calif. Soc. CPAs, Asian Am. CPA Soc., East Bay Zoological Soc., Oakland SPCA; publs: Forrest and Toh, 1975; Toh and Forrest, 1975; Sixth Internat. Cong. of Pharamcology, Helsinki; rec: art collecting, travel. Res: 4000 Plumas Ct. Hayward 94542 Ofc: California State University, Hayward 94542

SIEVERS, MARK SCOTT, financial consultant; b. Mar. 7, 1949, Lincoln, Nebr.; s. Stanley Stuart and Gladys Arline (Irvine) S.; m. Ann Furiel, Apr. 28, 1979; 1 dau. Elisabeth b. 1985; edn: BS, USAF Acad. 1971; MBA, UC Berkeley 1983; desig: CFP (Cert. Finl. Plnnr.), Coll. for Finl. Planning (1985), Registry of Finl. Plnng. Practitioners, IAFP (1986). Career: served to major US Air Force 1971-82: pilot tng. Williams AFB, Az. 1971-72; forward air controller Southeast Asia 1972-73; instr. pilot, advanced trainer Reese AFB, Tx. 1973-76; comdr. Supplementary Flying Tng. Pgm. for SAC pilots, Reese AFB, Tx. 1976-78; staff ofcr./budget analyst Air Force R&D, HQ USAF, The Pentagon 1978-79; pilot C-5A, Travis AFB, Ca. 1979-82; financial cons. prin., 1983–; instr. Golden Gate Univ. Sch. of Banking & Finance, UC Davis Extension, Napa Valley Coll. Community Services; honors: Beta Gamma Sigma (1983); mem: Internat. Assn. for Finl. Planning, Inst. of Cert. Finl. Plnnrs., CofC (Econ. Devel., Legis. coms., bd. dirs. 1986-89), Rotary; treas. UC Davis Med. Ctr. Hospice Pgm.; mil: decorated D.F.C., Air Medals, Meritorious Service Medal, AF Commendn., Presidential Unit Cit., Outstanding Unit Award; rec: cooking, tennis, swimming. Res: 3215 Serra Way Fairfield 94533 Ofc: Mark Sievers Financial Consultant 1325 Travis Blvd Ste G Fairfield 94533

SIGGSON, ALBERT NATHAN, engineer; b. Sept. 22, 1928; s. Nathan Harry and Grace Elizabeth (Fenester) S.; m. Marjorie J. Lindblum; children: Randal R., Larry J.; edn: AA, Long Beach City Coll. 1957; El Camino Community Coll. 1972-73; Lifetime Tchg. Cred. eng., CSU Long Beach 1980; BSBA, cum laude, Univ. of Phoenix 1983; Reg. Profl. Engr. (mfg.), Calif. Career: engr. ITT Gilfillan, No. American Rockwell, Hughes Aircraft Companies, So. Calif. 1951-69; engr. and senior prodn. design engr. Northrop Aircraft Co., Hawthorne 1969-83, design splst., Pico Rivera 1983–; instr. engring. scis. El Camino Community Coll.; recipient 5 awards, Soc. of Mfg. Engrs. (1966-74), 11 suggestion awards, Northrop and No. Am. Rockwell; assoc. mem. Sigma Xi; Fellow Inst. for Adv. of Engring.; mem: Soc. of Mfg. Engrs., Inst. for Adv. of Engring., US Metric Assn.,Am. Soc. for Testing and Mats. (E-43 Metric Practice Com.) Standards Engring. Soc., Nat. Soc. Profl. Engrs., Toastmasters; publs: ed. The Metric System, A Review of Indsl. Applications, SME (c. 1982); books in progress, engring. scis.; mil: US Navy 1946-49; Republican; Lutheran; rec: teaching, tutoring students. Res: 6009 Arabella St. Lakewood 90713

SIGLIN, STEPHEN DONAVON, entertainer; b. Oct. 2, 1954, Bakersfield; s. Don and Sybil JoAnn (Justis) S.; m. Claudia Lynn Clark, Mar. 21, 1976; edn: AA, Bakersfield Comm. Coll. 1976. Career: chief marine science technician (MSTC), US Coast Guard 1975-83; founder/owner of Pegasus Productions/ Pegasus Mobile Light & Sound, 1978–; mem. Central Calif. Mobile Disco DJ's Assn., Assoc. Photographers Internat., Western Portrait & Figure Group; mil: USCG 1975-83, GCM, Expert Pistol, Expert Rifle; rec: photog., flying, scuba diving. Res: 2012 Sarasota Ln Hayward 94545 Ofc: Pegasus Productions, POB 64, Mt Eden Hayward 94557

SILBERMAN, IRWIN ALAN, obstetrician-gynecologist; b. Sept. 1, 1932, Newport News, Va.; s. Henry (MD) and Toby (Weiss) S.; children: Denise b. 1955, Donn b. 1959, Daniel b. 1967, Dean b. 1969, Dana b. 1973; edn: BA, UC Berkeley 1953; MD, UC San Francisco 1956; Air Command and Staff Coll. 1970; MS, Univ. No. Colo. 1980; Diplomate Am. Bd. of Ob-Gyn 1966. Career: intern, resident Harbor/UCLA Med. Ctr. 1956-61; served to col. USAF 1961-81, ret.; chief Aerospace Medicine Service, USAF Clinic, Yokota Air Base Japan 1966-68; cmdr. USAF Clinic, Itazuke Air Base, Japan 1968-70; dir. med. services Kirtland AFB, Albuquerque, NM 1970-72; chief hosp. svcs. USAF Hosp., Davis-Monthan AFB, Tucson 1972-81; mil. cons. to the Surgeon General USAF, for Ob-Gyn., 1980; med. dir. CIGNA Healthplan of Fla., Tampa 1981-83; chief Women's Clinic, Hudson Comprehensive Health Ctr., Los Angeles County Dept. Health Svcs. 1983-85, dir. maternal health & family planning, 1985–; adj. assoc. prof. Ob-Gyn. Univ. Ariz. Coll. of Med. 1980-82; assoc. prof. clin. obstets. and gynecol. USC Sch. of Med. 1984-; Fellow Am. Coll. of Obstets. & Gynecols. (1966); mem. Am. Acad. of Med. Directors, Am. Coll. of Physician Execs., Am. Coll. of Hosp. Adminstrs., LA Obstet. and Gynecol. Soc., Daniel Morton Obstet. and Gynecol. Soc.; bd. dirs. L.A. Regional Family Planning Council 1985; camp physician BSA Nat. Jamboree, Fort A.P. Hill, Va. 7/85; mil. decorations: Air Medal, AF Commendn. Medal, USAF Merit. Svc. Medal, First Oak Leaf Cluster; rec: photog., camping, skiing. Res: 426 E Randolph St Glendale 91207 Ofc: LA Co. Dept. Hlth Svcs Maternal Health & Family Planning, 313 N Figueroa St Los Angeles 90012

SILBERT, WILLIAM CHARLES, company executive; b. Oct. 8, 1924, Baltimore, Md.; s. Herbert and Alice Amelia (Johnson) S.; m. Elsa Dominick, July 29, 1978; children: Linda b. 1951, Richard b. 1954; edn: BSEE, Univ. of Mich. 1949; MSEE, Drexel Univ. 1960. Career: group engr. Giffles & Valet Inc., Detroit, Mich. 1949-52; senior engr. Power Equip Co., Detroit, Mich. 1952-55; design splst. Martin Marietta Corp., Baltimore, Md. 1955-64; v.p. data mgmt. sys. Bunker Ramo Corp., Westlake Village 1964-84; pres., div. mgr. Eaton Corp., Westlake Village 1984–; guest lectr. Baltimore Sci. Found.; writer, tchr. courses in transistor circuit design Martin Marietta; mem: IEEE, Assn. of Old Crows, Assn. of US Army, Am. Defense Preparedness Asn., Security Affairs Support Assn., So. Calif. Tech. Exec. Network, Holy Trinity Lutheran Ch. Council, Ventura Co. United Way Bd. Dirs., President's Circle Moorpark Coll.; mil: capt. US Army Infantry 1942-46, Combat Infantry, Silver Star, Bronze Star, Purple Heart w/ Cluster; Republican; Lutheran. Ofc: Eaton Corp., 31717 La Tienda Dr. Westlake Village 91362

SILVA, IDEVALDO RODRIGUES, corporate executive; b. July 16, 1945, Goiania, Goias, Brasil, nat. US cit. 1978; edn: BS psychol., bus. adminstrn., Univ. San Francisco 1974; postgrad. Getulio Vargas, Brasil 1976; French, Univ. Bordeaux France 1969. Career: internat. trading Bank of Am. S.F. 1970-72; mgmt. trainee Universal Transcontinental Corp. S.F. 1973-74; mgr. internat. div. Eudmarco Internat. Brasil 1975-76, gen. mgr. London 1976-78; dir., v.p. Latin Am. div. The Harper Group S.F. 1979–; lectr. Univ. Mexico, Brasil, Colombia, Ecuador and major companies; honors: First Prize Poetry Contest (USF 1975); mem: ABCT, Comml. Assn. Brazilian Exporters (dir.); publ: poetry (USF 1975), short stories (Brazilian mag. 1975); mil: lt. Brazilian Army 1966-68; Republican; Catholic; rec: classical piano, tennis, chess. Res: 162 Valley View Way S San Francisco 94080 Ofc: The Harper Group 260 Townsend St San Francisco 94102

SILVA, RAYMOND ARNOLD, chartered life underwriter, chartered financia consultant; b. June 29, 1930, San Jose; s. Henry Francisco and Emily Eleanor (Fields) S.; m. Carolyn Helms, July 16, 1953; children: Terrence (stepson) b. 1951, Jennifer b. 1954, Jeffrey b. 1955, Laurie b. 1958, Erin b. 1961, Shannon b. 1972; edn: BA, San Jose State Univ. 1952, MA 1956; Chartered Life Underwriter (CLU) The Am. Coll. 1965; Chartered Financial Consultant (ChFC), The Am. Coll. 1984. Career: physical educator, athletic coach Berkeley High Sch., 1955-59, Camden H.S., San Jose 1959-62; field rep. The Guardian Life Insurance Co. of Am., San Jose 1962—-84; senior sales cons. The Guardian Life Ins. Co. of Am., NY, NY 1981–; adv. bd. Am. Bank & Trust Co., San Jose; bd. trustees (pres. 1977-9) Campbell Union H.Sch. Dist. 1973-81; dir. San Jose St. Univ. Found. 1982-, mem. SJSU Pres.'s Council; dir. (pres. 1974-6) The Spartan Found., San Jose 1968-; honors: agent of year, San Jose Life Underwriter Assn. 1978; nat. pres. Guardian Life Leaders Club, 1978, pres. Guardian Life CLU Assn. 1977-79; life & qualifying mem. Million Dollar Roundtable 1971-; mem: Am. Soc. of CLUs (W. regional v.p. 1981-2), Assn. for Advanced Underwriting, Santa Clara County Estate Plnng. Council (pres. 1982-3), San Jose Rotary 1972- (bd. 1983-85); mil: lt. USNR (ret.), active duty 1952-54; Republican; Presbyterian; rec: basketball, raquetball, ski. Res: 185 Surmont Court Los Gatos 95030 Ofc: Guardian Life, 1602 The Alameda, Ste. 200, San Jose 95126

SILVA, WILLIAM HEYWARD, real estate developer; b. Oct. 17, 1923, Cleveland, Oh.; s. Abbott Beecher and Gladys Loie (Heyard) S.; m. Marilyn Jean Elkouri, Dec. 9, 1968; children: June (Cornea) b. 1950, David Beecher b. 1955,

Janice Heyward b. 1963, William Abbott b. 1969; edn: BS in bus., Miami Univ. (Oxford, Oh.) 1947; Harvard Grad. Sch. of Bus., Naval Supply Corp Sch., 1944-45; cert. of real estate, UCLA; Calif. lic. general contractor, lic. real estate broker; CPM, Cert. Prop. Mgr. Career: founder/pres. Citizens' Realty & Development Inc., 1957–, acquisition and land devel., constr. homes, condominiums, apartments, office & indsl. bldgs., prop. mgmt.; awards: General Elec. Builder of the Month, 1970; mem: Nat. Assn. of Realtors, San Fernando Bd. of Realtors, Inst. of Real Estate Mgmt.; bd. dirs. Campbell Hall Sch. (pres. PTA); Dist. Atty's Comm. Adv. Council; v.p./dir. L.A. Tennis Club, mem. Beach & Tennis Club (Pebble Bch), Carmel Valley Ranch Tennis Club; mil: lt.j.g. USNR 1944-46; Prot. Res: 14587 Deervale Pl Sherman Oaks 91403 Ofc: Citizens Realty, 4331 Woodman Ave Sherman Oaks 91423

SILVERBERG, JAY STEVEN, sales development executive; b. July 1, 1945, St. Louis, Mo.; s. Ervin and Beatrice (Grossman) S.; m. Corinne, Mar. 10, 1974; children: Daniel Ari b. 1977, Melanie Aliza b. 1980; edn: BA, Syracuse Univ. 1971; MA, Univ. So. Calif. 1975. Career: acct. exec. E.F. Hutton L.A. 1975-81, asst. mgr. L.A. 1982-83, asst. mgr. Westwood 1983-85, regl. dir. sales devel. 1985–; ed. asst. USC Sch. of Internat. Rels. Sovietology Journal 1974; mil: sgt. USAF 1968-72; Jewish; rec: early rock & roll memorabilia, civil war, coach little league. Res: 113 S La Jolla Ave Los Angeles 90048 Ofc: E.F. Hutton & Co. Inc. 888 W 6th St Los Angeles 90017

SILVERIO, OLIVIA FLORO, accounting executive; b. July 31, 1944, Philippines, nat. US citizen 1978; d. Tiburcio de Guzman and Filomena Alarilla (Cruz) Floro; m. Edgardo Silverio, Dec. 7, 1968; children: Brian b. 1971, Sean b. 1979, Nicole b. 1980; edn: B.Bus. Admin., magna cum laude, Univ. of the East, Philippines 1963; M.Pub. Admin., Calif. State Univ. Long Beach 1986; CPA Philippines 1965, Calif. 1982. Career: asst. acctg. supv. Ives Laboratories Inc. N.Y.C. 1968-70; acctg. supv. Berlitz Sch. of Language N.Y.C. 1970-71; senior acct. Anaconda Wire & Cable Co. N.Y.C. 1971-73; senior acct. City of N.Y. Office of Mgmt. & Budget 1973-75; acctg. mgr. City of Gardena, Calif. 1975–; honors: first place Philippine CPA Exam 1964, Outstanding Alumnus (Univ. of the East 1965), instrumental in outstanding financial reporting awards given to City of Gardena (Calif. Soc. of Municipal Ofcrs. & Govt. Finance Ofcrs. Assn. 1982-84); mem: Calif. Soc. CPAs, Calif. Soc. Municipal Finance Ofcrs., Filipino Accountants of So. Calif.; Republican; Catholic; rec: swimming. Ofc: City of Gardena 1700 W 162nd St Gardena 90247

SILVERMAN, JAY THEODORE, chiropractor; b. May 8, 1956, Hollywood; s. Lewis Myron and Claire Lois (Besbeck) S.; edn: undergrad. CSU Northridge 1974-79; DC, and BS biol., Los Angeles Coll. Chiropractic 1983; Calif. Community Colls. instr. credential 1984; Calif. lic. DC, 1984, Radiology Opr. 1984. Career: clin. intern Glendale Chiropractic Clinic, 1983; pvt. practice, Northridge 1983–, and asst. dir. Valley Sports Health and Rehab. Ctr.; chiropractic splst. in sports and recreational injuries; vol. field doctor for local youth athletics and Valley Conf. Youth Athletic Assn., Pop Warner football playoffs and all-star games; mem: Am. Coll. of Sports Medicine, Am. Chiro. Assn. (Council on Physical Fitness and Sports Injuries), Calif. Chiro. Assn.; Chiropractic rep. at Northridge CofC- 1985 Career Day; Democrat; Jewish; rec: distance bicycling, running and ocean swimming, music/ percussionist. Ofc: Central Valley Chiropractic 8619 Reseda Blvd Ste 302 Northridge 91324

SILVEY, GARRY MELVIN, computer consultant; b. May 12, 1960, Encino; s. Fenton Earl and Dorcas Jane (Cottier) S.; m. Diane Silvey, Jan. 23, 1982; 1 dau. Andrea b. 1985; edn: BS, Univ. of the Pacific 1982. Career: asst. instr., computer sci., Univ. of Pacific 1979-82; sci. pgmmr./analyst Ford Aerospace, Sunnyvale 1982-83; tech. support analyst, then op. systems support mgr. Digital Research Inc., Monterey 1983-85; sr. pgmmr./software engring. dir. Colink Inc., Monterey 1985–; computer cons. prin./owner Intersoft, cons. Electric Memory (1984), Genigraphics Corp. (1986); founder/pres. Concurrent Users Group (ed. monthly newsletter) 1985-; contbr. article on use of resident system extensions under CP/M Plus, Dr. Dobbs Journal. Res: 289 Park Circle Marina 93933 Ofc: Colink Inc. 656 Munras Ave Monterey 93942

SIMMONS, EARL MELVIN, otolaryngologist and facial plastic surgeon; b. Feb. 20, 1931, Brklyn.; s. Isaac and Iris C. (Small) S.; m. Elena L., Sept. 7, 1956; children: Erin, b. 1960, Erlan, b. 1962, Elissa, b. 1964, Erik, b. 1968; edn: dip. Haaren H.S., NYC 1949; elec. eng. stu. Brklyn. Coll. 1949-53; BS chem., magna cum laude, Howard Univ. 1958; MD, Howard Univ. Med. Coll. 1962; intern. cert., Cook Co. Hosp., Chgo. 1963; surgical cert., Meadowbrook Hosp., NYC 1964; otolaryngol. cert., Mt. Sinai Hosp., NYC 1967. Med. lic. in state of NY, NJ, Calif. Career: clin. instr. Mt. Sinai Med. Sch. 1966; chief Dept. Otolaryngol. East Orange (NJ) Gen. Hosp., 1967-79; att. phys. Newark Eye and Ear Infirmary & NJ Med. Sch., 1967-79; att. phys. Orange (NJ) Meml. Hosp., 1967-80; E.N.T. pvt practice, two offices, East Orange, NJ, 1967-79; chief Dept. Otolaryngol. USAF Hosp., Vandenberg AFB, Calif. 1979-81; pvt. practice, Encinitas, Calif. 1981–; honors: Beta Kappa Chi 1957; AMA Phys. Recognition Awd. 1978-80; US Congl. Advis. Bd.; Far Eastern Talent Contest winner 1955. Mem: Council of Otolaryngology; Deafness Research Found.; Med. soc. of San Diego; AMA; NMA; Undersea Med. Soc.; Assn. of Military Plastic Surgeons; mem. YMCA, UNICEF, NAACP; mil: pfc US Army 1953-55; surgeon PHS 1963-79; lt. col. USAF 1979-81; spl. interests: grad. Mind Dynamic Tng. 1976; open water cert. scuba diver (art. on Bimini Road discovery); redesign scuba diving face mask; author 4 books of poetry: Turn Hourglass (1977), Eagle Spree (1979), Spirit Flesh (1984), Circles (1984), Vantage Press; solo concert singer (dramatic tenor) Carnegie Hall Debut, NYC 1956, lead perfs. with Lyric Opera Co. of NJ, 1976-79; 5 languages; parapsych. investgr.; Democrat; Presbyterian. Res: 319 Sierra Ridge Encinitas 92024 Ofc: Earl M. Simmons, MD, 317 N. El Camino Real, Ste. 406, Encinitas 92024

SIMMONS, HARRY ROBERT, food distribution co. executive; b. Jan. 18, 1920, Saskatoon, Canada, nat. US cit. 1957; s. Harry and Anne Woodstock (Gleason) S.; m. Ann McIntyre, June 25, 1983; 1 dau. Linda b. 1947; edn: B.Commerce, Univ. of B.C. 1947; MBA, UC Berkeley 1949; advanced mgmt. Harvard Bus. Sch. 1971; CPA, Calif. 1955. Career: assoc. in acctg., UC Berkeley, 1949-51; comml. auditor Arthur Andersen & Co., Chgo. 1951-56; v.p. Kaiser Aluminum & Chem. Corp., Oakland 1956-72; systems consultant var. cos. 1972-76; v.p. Corporate and Ops. Devel., Dalgety, Inc., San Mateo 1976–; dir: The Martin-Brower Co., Modern Maid Food Products Inc., Pig Improvement Co. Inc., Balfour Guthrie Inc., Promotora Porcina Camborough, S.A. de C.V., Samuel McIntyre Inv. Co., The Number One Co.; mem: Calif. Soc. of CPAs, Am. Inst. of CPAs, Univ. Calif. Bus. Adminstrn. Alumni Assn. (dir.); club: Petroleum; mil: flying ofcr. Royal Canadian Air Force 1940-45, Gold Operational Wings RCAF; Republican; Roman Catholic; rec: photog., cooking. Res: 2200 Pacific Ave Apt 9C San Francisco 94115 Ofc: Dalgety, Inc. 3055 Clearview Way Ste 300 San Mateo 94402

SIMMONS, HENRY, consulting electrical engineer; b. July 1, 1910, NYC; s. Max and Julia Eugenia (Brenner) S.; m. Frances Edith Sullivan, Feb. 25, 1938; 2 sons, Robert H., b. 1939, Wesley F., b. 1941; edn: indsl. elec., Pratt Inst. of Tech. 182; BS in E.E., Georgia Inst. of Tech. 1936; Reg. Profl. Engr. in Calif. 1947, Nev. 1964, Ariz. 1965. Career: cable splicer & tester, NY Tel. Co., 1928-32; elec. engr. Bethlehem Steel Co., Terminal Isle, Ca. 1940-43; elec. engr. Naval Operating Base, Port Hueneme, 1943-46; elec. contr. Simmons Electric Co., Long Beach 1946-50; cons. engr., H. Simmons, E.E., 1950–; cons. with profs. and dept. heads at CSULB and Comm. Coll. Dist.; awards: merit certs., City of Long Beach, County of Los Angeles, and State of Calif., 1980; awards, CSULB and Comm. Coll. Dist. Long Beach, 1980; certs. of excellence, So. Calif. Edison Co., 1967, 68, 71; voted Engineer of Year, Harbor Div. L.A. Chpt. NECA; mem: Internat. Assn. Elec. Inspectors, Assn. Consulting Elec. Engrs., Illum. Engr. Soc., Nat. Soc. Profl. Engrs.; publs: Standard Testing Procedure (manual) 1944, Electrical Spec-Data (manual) 1984, tech. articles in trade mags., 1960-81; Republican; Methodist; rec: sailing, football. Res: 3749 Cerritos Ave Long Beach 90807

SIMMONS, LEROY ALLAN, superior court judge; b. Aug. 29, 1940, Washington DC; s. Walter E. and Elizabeth R. (Faxon) S.; m. Barbara Wagner, Aug. 14, 1964; children: Katherine b. 1966, Brian b. 1968, Andrew b. 1970, Carolyn b. 1975; edn: undergrad. Brigham Young Univ. 1958-64; JD, Univ. of San Francisco 1967; admitted Calif. State Bar 1967. Career: deputy dist. atty., San Bernardino County, 1967-70; atty. assoc. Wilson, Borror & Dunn 1970-71; ptnr. Hornaday & Simmons 1971-76; elected judge Barstow Municipal Ct. 1977-81; apptd. judge San Bernardino County Superior Ct. 1981–; seminar leader and instr. Calif. Judicial Edn. and Research in Berkeley; mem. Calif. Judges Assn., Am. Field Service; civic: fmr. trustee Barstow Community Coll. (4 yr); fmr. commnr County Planning Commn.; YMCA pres. and Model Legislative advisor; dir. San Bernardino County Bar Assn.; v.p. Council of BSA; mil: sgt. E5 US Army Res. 1963-69; Democrat; Latter-Day Saints (mission 1960-62); rec: snow skiing, racquetball. Res: 27626 Highview, Barstow 92311

SIMON, BRADLEY ALDEN, librarian; b. March 9, 1929, Meriden, Conn.; s. Walter Henry and Rachel (Wetherbee) S.; edn: stu., Shenandoah Coll. 1947-48; BS, So. Conn. State Coll. 1951; MS, Fla. State Univ. 1955; postgrad., Univ. of Miami 1956-57, Ariz. State Univ. 1965-66. Career: extension librarin Ft. Meade, Md. 1955-56; base librarian Homestead AFB, Fla. 1956-57; asst. dir. libraries Public Library Charlotte and Mecklenburg Couty, N.C. 1957-61; dir. libraries Volusia Co. Public Libraries, Daytona Beach, Fla. 1961-64; library cons. M. Van Buren Inc., Charlotte, N.C. 1964; head librarian Central Piedmont Community Coll., Charlotte 1964-65; cons. Colo. State Library 1965-66; coord. Ariz. Library Survey, Ariz. State Univ. 1966; library dir. Scottsdale Public Library, Ariz. 1966-71; city librarian Pomona Public Library 1971-77, Newport Beach Public Library 1977-78, Chula Vista Public Library 1978–; cons. on bldg. & admin. var. libraries, Calif., No. Carolina, Fla., Colo. and Ariz.; pres. Pub. Library Film Circuit; Scottsdale Fine Arts Commn. 1966-71; adminstrv. council Met. Coop. Library System, Los Angeles; honors: John Cotton Dana Library Pub. Rels. Award, 1974, 1975, 1976; Hometown Builder Award, 1975; mem: Am., Ariz. (pres. pub libraries sect. 1969-70), Calif. and Southwestern Library Assn., Public Library Execs. So. Calif. (pres. 1975-76), Library Automation, Research & Cons. Assn., Royal Arcanum, Nat. Mgmt. Assn., Pomona Municipal Mgmt. Assn., Newport Harbor Art Mus., Newport Harbor CofC, Pomona Valley Hist.Soc., Kappa Delta Phi Rotary; mil: USAF Intelligence 1951-53; publs: contbr. articles to profl. journs.; Presbyterian. Res: P.O. Box 1843 Chula Vista 92012

SIMON, C. SHOSHANA, lawyer; b. July 28, 1944, NY, NY; d. Charles Westlake and Mally Irene (Carnegie) Mackenzie; m. Wm. J. Simon, Aug. 15, 1979; edn: BA, magna cum laude, Univ. Calif. 1967; JD magna cum laude, Univ. of La Verne 1978; admitted Calif. State Bar 1978. Career: social wkr./ adminstr. Riverside County Dept. of Public Soc. Svcs., 1968-75; solo gen. practice law, San Bernardino Co., 1978-80; partner law firm Simon & Simon (insolvency splty.), San Bernardino 1980–; chpsn Task Force on Domestic Violence, S.B. County Commn. on Status of Women 1980-81; pro-bono counsel to Option House, Battered Womens Shelter 1980-82; vol. atty. S.B. County Legal Aid Clinic 1979-; honors: law rev. 1976; recognition, San Bernardino Co. Judiciary 1981. Mem: Calif. State Bar Assn. (bankruptcy study gp.); San Bernardino Co. Bar Assn. (judicial select. com.); Family law Council (sec. treas. 1981-3); ACLU; Am. Bar Assn. (Law Ofc. Econ. com.); Toastmasters 1977-9; coauthor art., Things Fall Apart: A Critical Approach to Chinua Achebe (1969, repub. in A Study of African Lit. 1978); Democrat; Jewish; rec:

folk dancing, philately. Res: 5915 Newcomb St San Bernardino 92404 Ofc: Simon & Simon, 699 N Arrowhead Ave, Ste 100, San Bernardino 92401

SIMON, HAL HARTLEY, lawyer; b. Aug. 22, 1960, Flushing, NY; s. Harry and Shirley (Jacobs) S.; edn: Queens Coll. City Univ. of N.Y. 1977; BA, Fordham Univ. 1980; JD, Western State Univ. Coll. of Law 1983; admitted Calif. State Bar 1983. Career: vol. med. asst. Riverside Gen. Hosp. Calif. 1979; vol. asst. to social worker Roosevelt Hosp. N.Y.C. 1979-82; vol. legal asst. West End Legal Aid Clin. Ontario, Calif. 1982-83; law clerk Legal Clinic Western State Univ. Coll. of Law Fullerton 1983; atty. law firm Stefan R. Parker San Bernardino 1983-85, Lubey & Lerner APLC 1985–; honors: Honor Roll, Nat. Dean's List (Western State Univ. 1983), Cert. of Merit (Calif. State Bar Bd. of Govs. 1982), Am. Jurisprudence Award (Bancroft-Whitney Co. 1983), Cert. of Merit (Toastmasters 1979); mem: Am., San Bernardino Co., Riverside Co. bar assns., Calif., L.A., Inland Counties, Orange Co. Trial Lawyers Assns., Assn. of Trial Lawyers of Am., AAAS, Am. Museum of Nat. History, GLAZA, N.Y. Acad. of Sci. (elected student mem. 1979); Republican; Jewish; rec: music, singing, reading, travel, writing, acting. Res: 1423 W Blossom Ave Redlands 92373 Ofc: Lubey & Lerner APLC 141 N Arrowhead Ave, Ste 1, San Bernardino 92408

SIMON, SIDNEY HAROLD, management consultant; b. Mar. 3, 1943, Buffalo, N.Y.; s. Reuben and Jean (Zeman) S.; m. Karen Feinglass, Oct. 8, 1972; edn: BS in indsl. engring., Penn State Univ. 1964; MS in mgmt. sci., West Coast Univ. 1976. Career: bus. systems pgmmr./analyst TRW Systems, Inc., Redondo Beach 1964-66; v.p. tech. Coordinated Data Systems Inc., L.A. 1966-70; systems proj. mgr. Equity Funding Corp., L.A. 1970-74, System Devel. Corp., Santa Monica 1974-76; mgr. Personnel Info. Systems and Benefits Adminstrn., Bechtel Power Corp., S.F. 1976-84; v.p./product mgr. Tesseract Corp., S.F. 1984-86; sr. human resource info. mgmt. cons. Towers, Perrin, Forster & Crosby, L.A. 1986–; frequent speaker personnel assns. and computer software shows, presenter num. workshops related to personnel data systems; honors: named in "Makers and Shapers of a Changing Profession" list, Human Resource Mgmt. News (1986); founder/mem. Assn. of Human Resource Systems Profls., Inc. (began gp. with 15 members in S.F. Bay Area; incorporated in 1980; orgn. now has 17 active chpts. with 1,800 members in US and abroad; nat. pres. -1982, nat. v.p. 1983, nat. CFO 1984, dir./pres. S.F. chpt. 1986-); mem. Toastmasters Internat.; publs: articles in var. profl. jours. and HR/PC Mag.; rec: microcomputers, jog, golf, racquetball. Ofc: Towers, Perrin, Forster & Crosby 1925 Century Park East Ste 1500 Los Angeles 90067

SIMONE, MARTIN MASSIMO, lawyer; b. Sept. 26, 1946, New Haven, Conn.; s. Nicholas and Grace Loretta (Simeone) S.; m. Christine, June 24, 1978; children: Lisa Marie b. 1966, Bridget Lynn b. 1967; edn: BA, Loyola Univ. L.A. 1968, JD, 1971; admitted Calif. State Bar 1972; admitted US Dist. Ct. (cent. dist. Calif.), 9th Circ. Ct. of Appeals, US Supreme Ct. Career: research atty., supv. law clerk L.A. County Superior Ct. 1972-74; assoc. atty. Schwartz, Steinsapir, Dohrmann & Krepack 1974-80, ptnr. 1980; ptnr. Frank & Greenberg 1980-81, Frank, Greenberg, Simone & Winston 1982-84, Frank, Greenberg & Simone 1984–; advisory bd. Mayall St. Sch. L.A.; mem: ABA, L.A. County Bar Assn., Am. Ajudicature Assn.; publ: articles in Lawyers Labor Publs. 1978, 79, 80; Democrat; rec: white water rafting, weight lifting, target shooting, skiing. Ofc: Frank, Greenberg & Simone 8484 Wilshire Blvd Ste 730 Beverly Hills 90211

SIMONINI, DAVID MICHAEL, lawyer; b. Jan. 15, 1948, San Rafael; s. Aldo Joseph and Lola Anita (Giorgi) Simonini; m. Maria Mezzetta, Nov. 3, 1984; children: Clinton Michael b. 1969, Jeanne Virginia b. 1971; edn: BA, Univ. San Francisco 1970, JD, 1974; admitted Calif. State Bar 1974. Career: pres. Pacific Porterwall Inc., San Rafael 1966-74; atty. assoc. Pisor, Vadney, George & Bennett 1974-80; pres. David M. Simonini, Inc. 1980-83; law partner Vadney, George & Simonini 1983–; mem. Am., Marin, Italian bar assns., Calif. Trial Lawyers Assn.; listed Who's Who in Am. Law, Who's Who in the World; clubs: Elks, Olympic, Harbor Point Beach & Tennis; Republican; Roman Catholic; rec: tennis, skiing, windsurfing. Res: 110 C, San Rafael 94901 Ofc: Vadney, George & Simonini, 36 Professional Center Pky San Rafael 94903

SIMONSON, RICHARD WARD, development co. executive; b. Feb. 1, 1927, Mpls.; s. Simon R. and Camilla M. (Madsen) S.; m. Beverly J., May 7, 1949; children: Steven L. b. 1955, David b. 1957, Jody b. 1962; edn: Univ. Wisc. River Falls 2 yrs. Career: asst. mgr. Beneficial Finance Mpls. 1950-52; asst. mgr. Northwest Finance Mpls. 1952-53; mgr. Harvey Finance St. Paul 1953-57; asst. mgr. Midway Finance St. Paul 1957-68; mgr. Broadway Loan Corp. Robbinsdale, Minn. 1968-82; proj. mgr. Pyramid Homes San Jose 1965-82, Somnor Engrg. 1983, Barratt Homes 1983-85; gen. mgr. Pacific States Devel. Co. Morgan Hill, Calif. 1985–; honors: Disting. Person (YMCA 1983); mem: Bldg. Industry Assn. (past. bd.), YMCA (life mem., bd. chmn., bldg. com.), San Jose Athletic Club; mil: MOMM 3/c USN 1944-46; Republican; Lutheran; rec: racquetball, golf, gardening. Res: 1633 Glenfield Dr San Jose 95125 Ofc: Pacific States Devel. Co. POB 1458 Morgan Hill

SIMPSON, JACK ARTHUR, city administrator; b. Nov. 20, 1942, Long Beach; s. John Woodson and Francis Yerba (Muns) S.; m. Susan Flores, May 29, 1982; children: John b. 1974, Kellee b. 1969, Jacki b. 1971, Samantha b. 1983, Casey b. 1985; edn: BA, CSU Long Beach 1967, MS, 1974. Career: groundman Southern California Edison Co. summers 1961-64; adminstrv. intern City of Paramount 1965-66; adminstrv. intern, adminstrv. asst., asst. city mgr., City of Artesia 1966-68; asst. city mgr. City of Cerritos 1968-69; city adminstr./ city clerk City of Hawaiian Gardens 1969-78; city mgr./ city clerk city of Paramount 1978-80; city adminstr. City of Bellflower 1980–; dir./ secty. Hawaiian Gardens Redevel. Agency 1969-78; exec. dir. Paramount Redevelop. Agency 1978-80; guest lectr. Ctr. on Criminal Justice, CSU Long Beach 1973, 1974; guest lectr. Dept. of Criminal Justice, CSU Los Angeles; Inst. on Plnng. for Police Chiefs, Sheriffs and their top Planning Administrators 1974; chmn. Southeast Los Angeles Co. City Mgrs. Group 1972-73; mem. Los Angeles Co. div. League of Calif. Cities Commitees on Employer- Employee Relations Task Force and Action Plan for Local Govt. Task Force; served City Manager/ Administrator's Com. for the Calif. Contract Cities Assn.; mem: Internat. City Mgmt. Assn., Municipal Fin. Ofcr. Assn., Am. Public Works Assn.; Democrat; Lutheran; rec: athletics, outdoor activities, skin and scuba diving. Ofc: 16600 Civic Center Dr. Bellflower 90706

SIMPSON, RONALD BRUCE, immunohematologist; b. July 28, 1943, Dunsmuir, Calif.; s. Bruce Merril and Irene Bernice (Michaels) S.; children: Aaron b. 1965, Brian b. 1968, Kelly b. 1969, Ronnie b. 1970, Michael b. 1981; edn: BS, Ore. Polytechnic Inst. 1966; certified Am. Assn. Clin. Pathol. 1972. Career: supv. Dept. of Immunohematology, St. Mary Med. Ctr., Long Beach 1967-83, Kenneth Norris Jr. Cancer Hosp. and Research Inst., Univ. So. Calif. 1983–; panelist, advisor Medical Lab. Observer; adj. faculty CSU Dominguez Hills; mem: Am. Assn. Clin. Pathols., Am. Assn. Blood Banks, Calif. Blood Banking Soc. (fin. com. 1974), Nat. Rifle Assn., Calif. Rifle & Pistol Assn., Planetary Soc.; publs: tech. articles in med. jours.; Democrat; Protestant; rec: offroading, fishing, skeet shooting. Res: 4453 Linden, No 3, Long Beach 90807 Ofc: Kenneth Norris Cancer Hosp., 1443 East Lake Los Angeles 90033

SIMPSON, WILLIAM ARCHIBALD, JR., real estate developer; b. Aug. 31, 1916, Denver, Colo.; s. William Archibald Sr. and Georgia Agnes (Clapp) S.; m. Marilyn Dunton, June 28, 1975; children: Diane Collee b. 1945, Donna Tuttle b. 1947, Deborah de Gooyer b. 1950, Pamela Simpson b. 1950; edn: BSBA, USC 1941. Career: pres., CEO William Simpson Constrn. Co.; publr., exec. dir. Sacramento Union newspapers; pres., CEO Orthopaedic Hosp.; corp. v.p. mktg. Dillingham Corp.; bd. chmn. Booth & Simpson Ins.; bd. dirs., exec. com. Western Council of Constrn. Consumers; past dir. Hollywood Park Inc., Ticor Corp. of Calif., Transit Mix Co., Title Ins. & Trust Co., Pioneer Nat. Title Ins. Co.; currently: ptr. William A. Simpson Partnership Real Estate Devel.; bd. dirs. Amerou Corp.; bd. dirs. Fairmont Financial Inc.; svc. awards: L.A. Dept. of Water & Power (past pres. Employees' Retirement & Disability Ins. Plan) 1961, Los Angeles City Schs. 1970, L.A. City Council & Co. Bd. of Supvrs. 1971, bd. dir. Orthopaedic Hosp. 1970; Los Angeles Co. Heart Assn. 1973, USC Merit Award; mem: Los Angeles Co. Earthquake Commn. (secty.), Calif. CofC (exec. com. bd. dirs., past pres.), Criminal Justice Legal Found. (bd. trustees), Economic Round Table, City of L.A. Public Facilities Corp. (bd. dirs.), Los Angeles CofC (past pres., bd. dirs. PAC), Calif. State Horse Racing Bd. (past commnr.), Eldorado CofC (Palm Desert), Lincoln Newcomen Soc. in No. Am., The One Hundred Club of Los Angeles; Republican; Presbyterian; rec: golf, fishing. Res: 620 Burk Place Beverly Hills 90210 Ofc: Willim A. Simpson Partnership, 3500 So. Figueroa Ste. 208 Los Angeles 90007

SIMPSON, WILLIAM EDWARD, accountant; b. Nov. 4, 1947, San Fernando; s. William Arthur and June Louise (Rayburn) S.; m. Wendy Lee, Aug. 14, 1981; 1 son, William b. 1970; edn: BS, CSU Northridge 1971, MS, 1974; USC 1975-77; JD, UCLA 1984; CPA, Calif. 1978; Cert. Mgmt. Acct., Inst. of Mgmt. Acctg. 1979. Career: acct. John F. Pfaffl & Co., Bubank 1971; acct. Jay E. Robinson & Co., Los Angeles 1971-73; examiner Dept. of Savings & Loans, Los Angeles 1973-74; regl. chief acct. Securities & Exchange Commn., Los Angeles 1974-79; prof. of acctg. CSU Northridge 1975-84; nat. dir. Alexander Grant & Co., Chicago, Ill. and Los Angeles 1979-84; prof. of acctg. De Paul Univ. Grad. Sch. of Bus., Chicago, Ill. 1979-80; audit ptr. Arthur Young & Co., Los Angeles 1984–; honors: Cert. of Appreciation, Black Businessman's Assn. of Los Angeles 1978; Spl. Commdns. (2), United States Attys., Los Angeles 1975, 1978; mem: Am. Inst. CPAs, Calif. Soc. CPAs, Am. Acctg. Assn., Nat. Assn. of Accts., Jonathan Club, Lakeside Golf Club, Los Angeles Athletic Club; publs: Accounting Series Release 196, Securities & Exchange Commn. 1976; The Cash Budget: Vital Tool for Financing Strategy, Legal Administrator 1984; mil: splst. 4 US Army 1967-68, Bronze Star, Army Commdn, Vietnam Svc.; rec: racquetball, golf, tennis. Res: 1800 McCollum St. Los Angeles 90026 Ofc: Arthur Young & Co., 515 So. Flower St. Los Angeles 90071

SIMS, RICHARD MAURY, III, appellate court justice; b. Dec. 3, 1943, Oakland; s. Richard M. S.; m. Georgiana Carroll, June 21, 1975; children: Peter b. 1976, Christopher b. 1978; edn: BA, with honors, Amherst Coll. 1965; JD, Harvard Law Sch. 1968. Career: atty. VISTA volunteer S.F. 1968-70; asst. exec. dir. S.F. Com. on Crime 1970-72; gen. counsel & legal ofcr. S.F. Sheriff's Dept. 1972-73; Thelen, Marrin, Johnson & Bridges S.F. 1973-80 (ptnr. 1978-80); superior ct. judge Placer Co. 1980-83; assoc. justice 3rd Dist. Ct. of Appeal Sacto. 1983–; adj. prof. law Univ. S.F. Sch. of Law 1972-75; mem: S.F. Bar Assn. (bd. dirs. 1979-80), S.F. Barristers Club (pres. 1974), Auburn Rotary (bd. dirs. 1983-84), S.F. Civil Grand Jury (mem., acting foreman 1975-76); rec: family gardening, hiking, painting, skiing. Ofc: Court of Appeal 914 Capitol Mall, Rm 119, Sacramento 95814

SIMSIAN, CARLOS HUMBERTO, real estate broker; b. Nov. 20, 1950, Buenos Aires, Argentina, nat. US cit. 1972; s. Manouc and Maria Luisa (Zacarias) S.; edn: AA, Rio Hondo Coll. 1971; BA, Calif. State Univ. 1974; real estate broker Calif. 1985. Career: assoc. Realty World Carousel Arcadia 1977-82; tchr. Mt. View and Valley Lindo sch. dists. 1982; police ofcr. L.A.P.D. 1982-84; property mgr. Manouc Simsian Arcadia 1984; assoc. Fred. Sands/ New Housing Brentwood 1984-85; v.p. Almaron Corp. Downey 1985; owner Realty World Diamond Properties Arcadia 1985–; mem: Arcadia Bd.

Realtors (pol. affairs com.), Santa Anita Exchangers 1977; Republican. Ofc: Realty World Diamond Properties 821 S First Ave Arcadia 91006

SINATRA, FRANK RAYMOND, pediatric gastroenterologist; b. June 7, 1945, Los Angeles; s. Vincent and Opal Irene (Rice) S.; m. Robin L. Hill, Aug. 17, 1968; children: Gina Maria b. 1972, Vincent Robert b. 1975; edn: BA, Whittier Coll. 1967; MD, USC 1971. Career: chief resident pediatrics Childrens Hosp. of L.A. 1973-74; postdoc. fellow gastroent. Stanford Univ. Hosp. 1974-76; dir. Div. Gastroenterology and Nutrition, Childrens Hosp. LA, 1976–; assoc. prof. ped. USC Sch. of Med.; awards: Assocs. of Childrens Hosp. Award (1971), Morris and Mary Press Humanism Award (1982); mem: Am. Acad. of Ped., Am. Coll. of Nutrition, No. Am. Soc. for Ped. Gastroent. (Executive Council), Western Soc. for Ped. Research, Am. Assn. for Study of Liver Diseases, Am. Liver Found.; Glendale Little League Baseball and Softball; author over 40 sci. publs. and textbook chapters; Catholic; rec: baseball, music. Ofc: Childrens Hospital 4650 Sunset Blvd Los Angeles 90027

SINCLAIR, RICHARD CARROLL, lawyer; b. July 15, 1948, Modesto; s. Carroll Burns and Katherine Louise (Miller) S.; m. Deborah Ann Romine, July 17, 1951; children: Brandon b. 1978, Justin b. 1980, Megan b. 1982; edn: BA in social psychol., Univ. Calif. 1970; JD, McGeorge Sch. of Law UOP 1975; LLM, taxation, Univ. of Miami 1976; admitted to practice Calif. State Bar, Federal Courts, Tax Ct.; Calif. Comm. Colls. instr. credential 1976. Career: computer analyst 1966-70; realtor associate 1970-84; judicial hearing officer 1972-75; cattle rancher 1978–; real estate developer 1977–; attorney pvt. practice spec. in taxation, real estate, business and corporate law, investment counseling, 1976–; lectr. Stanislaus State Coll. 1981; Comm. coll. instr. 1976-; listed Who's Who in Am. Law 1979, Who's Who in Real Estate 1983, Who's Who Calif. 1985; mem: Am., Calif. Stanislaus County bar assns.; Republican; Mormon. Address: 8212 Oak View Dr Oakdale 95361

SINGH, PRITHIPAL, biomedical co. excutive; b. April 6, 1939, Amritsar, India; s. Inder and Sewa (Kaur) S.; m. Rajinder Kaur, April 14, 1963; children Satinder b. 1964, Harpinder b. 1970; edn: BS, Khalsa Coll. 1959; MS, Benaras Univ. 1961; PhD, Toronto Univ. 1967; postdoctoral, Southampton Univ. 1969-70. Career: lectr. Khalsa Coll., Delhi Univ. 1961-63; asst. prof. Benaras Hindu Univ., India 1968-69; senior chemist Syva Research, Palo Alto 1970-73, group leader 1973-74, research mgr. 1974-77, asst. dir. 1977-81; v.p. Syva Co. div. of Syntex Corp. 1981-85; v.p. Idetek Inc. 1985–; invited spkr. univs. and confs.; trustee Sikh Found., Palo Alto; honors: British Council Award 1969; Can. Commonwealth Scholar 1963-66; Fellow, Chem. Soc. London; mem: Am. Chem. Soc., Am. Assn. Clin. Chemists, Bay Area Sikh Temple (founding mem., Fremont); works: contbr. 60+ publs. to profl. journs.; hold 30 patents; Sikh; rec: photog. Res; 1614 Eagle Dr. Sunnyvale 94087 Ofc: Idetek Inc., 1057 Sneath Ln. San Bruno 94066

SINGH, RANDHIR H., physician, pediatrician; b. Jan. 1, 1945, Jullundur, Punjab, India, nat. US cit. 1981; s. Harbhajan and Dayal (Kaur) S.; m. Harpal, Sept. 21, 1975; children: Simi b. 1976, Anita b. 1981; edn: premed. exam, Punjab Univ. 1962, MBBA, 1967; postgrad. in pediatrics, Postgrad. Inst. of Med. Edn. & Research, Chandigarh, India 1972; Diplomate, Am. Bd. of Pediatrics 1978. Career: resident pediatrics Postgrad. Inst. of R&M Edn., India 1969-71; senior house ofcr. pediatrics West Cumberland Hosp., Whitehaven, UK 1972-73; registrar in pediatrics Brown Meml. & Christian Med. Coll., Ludihana, Punjab, India 1973-74; resident pediatrics Cook Co. Hosp., Chicago 1974-76; fellow neonatology Valley Med. Ctr., Fresno 1977-78; pediatrician w/ Dr. E. Lamezor, Stockton 1978-79; cons. neonatology San Joaquin Gen. Hosp., Stockton 1979-81; currently, pediatric practice, Stockton; honors: Cert. of Merit, Postgrad. degree in Pediatrics, Postgrad. Inst. of Med. Edn. & Research, Chandigarh, India 1972; mem: Am. Acad. of Pediatrics; mil: capt. USAR 352nd Evacuation Hosp., Oakland; Eckist. Res: 2017 Angelico Circle Stockton 95207 Ofc: 5345 N Eldorado St Ste 11 Stockton 95207

SINSEL, LAWRENCE LEWIS, JR., manufacturing & distribution co. president; b. Feb. 1, 1948, Los Angeles; s. Lawrence L., Sr. and Leonore Elsie (Francis) S.; m. Beatrice Stoy, June 16, 1970; 1 dau., Lana b. 1979; edn: AA, Orange Coast Coll. 1976. Career: senior draftsman Delron Fasteners, Santa Ana 1972-74; sr. draftsman/ mfg. planner Rockford Aerospace, Irvine 1974-76; mfg. methods mgr. Tridair Industries, Torrance 1976-80; west coast sales mgr. ITT Harper, Morton Grove, Ill. 1980-82, sales engr. ITT Harper Aerospace, Glendale, Calif. 1982-83; pres./gen. mgr. adc inc., Cerritos 1983–; quality assur. cons. Ideal Fasteners, Fullerton 1985-, product cons. Spec Aero, Inglewood 1985; mem. Am. Soc. of Metals & Soc. of Mfg. Engrs.; mil: A02/ AC USN Air Corps 1965-69, Vietnam Svc., Korean Svc., Nat. Def. medals; Republican; Lutheran; rec: architecture, sci-fi, pen/ink illustrating. Ofc: adc inc. 17528 Studebaker Rd Cerritos 90701-3697

SITMAN, J. R., micro computer repair co. president; b. Mar. 18, 1954, Chgo.; s. Earl R., Sr. and Gloria Corine (Chicoine) S.; edn: BS in bus. adm., CSU Los Angeles 1977. Career: distbn. mgr. W. Region, Polychrome Corp., Los Angeles 1975-79; asst. gen. mgr. Terracrafics Inc., L.A. 1979-80; mgr. Retail Consumer Svcs., Marina Del Rey 1980-81; dir. of ops. Datasoft, Inc., Chatsworth 1981-83; pres. CPR Computer Repair, Inc., Northridge 1983–; cons. Pierce Coll. and Glendale Sch. Dist.; mem: Assn. of Field Service Mgrs., Am. Mgmt. Assn., Purchasing Mgrs. Assn., Am. Prodn. and Inventory Control Soc.; Democrat; Catholic; rec: racing Radio Controlled Car, salt water fish. Ofc: CPR Computer Repair, Inc. 8957 Reseda Blvd Northridge 91324

SITTO, MICHAEL N., architect; b. Jan. 15, 1942, Baghdad, Iraq, nat. US cit. 1975; s. Namo M. and Narmi Y. (Habbo) S.; m. Lamis, Aug. 1, 1968; children: Tanya b. 1969, Natasha b. 1970, Milena b. 1973; edn: BS arch., Baghdad Univ. 1966; M.Arch., Univ. Detroit 1975; reg. arch. Mich. 1980, Calif. 1981. Career: v.p. Sigma Assoc. Mich.; pres. K&S Assoc. archs./planners Southfield, Mich.; prin. in chg. West Coast Assoc. arch./planners Spring Valley, Calif.; div. dir. arch. div. Navy Public Works San Diego; cons. West Coast Assoc. 1982–, K&S Assoc. 1975-81; honors: several Quality Step Increase Awards (Navy Public Works 1982-), Program Mgmt. Devel. (Naval Facilities Engrg. Command); mem: Nat. Council Arch. Reg. Bd., Chaldean-Am. Club, Soc. Am. Mil. Engrs.; designer: Catholic Churches in San Diego (700-person) and Mich. (900-person), sev. large homes in Mich. and San Diego; mil: reserve ofcr. Iraq 1966-68; Republican; Catholic; rec: sports, travel, music. Res: 11125 New Morning Rd La Mesa 92041 Ofc: Navy Public Works POB 113 Naval Station San Diego 92136

SIU, C. C., broker- engineer; b. Jan. 20, 1943, Hunan, China, nat. US cit. 1979; d. C.K. and S.H. (Lu) Siao; m. Yi Syin Siu, Dec. 24, 1976; 1 son, Robert b. 1979; edn: BS, Louisiana Coll. 1966; MS, Univ. of Okla. 1969, PhD, 1972; Realtor, Nat. Assn. of Realtors and Calif. Assn. Realtors. Career: research staff Research Inst. of Univ. of Okla., Norman, Okla. 1966-72; vis. assoc. prof. National Taiwan Univ., Taipei, Taiwan 1972-73; senior computing analyst Jet Propulsion Lab., Pasadena 1973-74; senior engr. Bechtel Power Corp., Norwalk 1974-76; contract cons. engr. Amtech, Claremont 1976-81; senior engr. Braun, Alhambra 1981-82; broker/ engr. CCS Associates, San Marino 1982–; honors; Medal of Merit, Pres. Ronald Reagan 1985; Cert. of Merit, Sen. John Heintz 1985; Presdl. Commn., Sen. John Heintz 1986; mem: Republican Presidential Task Force, Nat. and Calif. Assns. Realtors, San Marino and So. Pasadena Bds. Realtors; publs: 14 in var. Journ. of Acoustical Soc. of Am., Southwestern Research Conf., URI Report, NASA Report, US Army Report, ASME Design Engring. Tech. Conf. 1968-; Republican; Christian; rec: philately, literature. Ofc: 2135 Huntington Dr. Ste. 204 San Marino 91108

SIU, TIM K., anesthesiologist; b. Honolulu, Hawaii; s. Kwai Ching and Chuck Jun (Yee) S.; m. Annie Chin, Aug. 22, 1954; children: Susan Mae b. 1958, Jennifer b. 1960, Tina b. 1962, Valerie b. 1964; edn: MD, UC Irvine 1962. Career: intern, resident L.A. Co. Gen. Hosp.; chief of staff San Gabriel Valley Hosp.; bd. dirs. Glendora Comm. Hosp.; pvt. practice anesthesiol. Alhambra, Calif.; bd. dirs. Continental Bank, Tokai Bank (1972-85), Universal Bankcorp Holding Co.; ptnr. Anchor Thrift & Loan; active member San Gabriel Valley Med. Ctr.; bd. dirs., pres. advisory bd. CSU Los Angeles; asst. prof. L.A. Co./ USC Med. Ctr.; bd. councilors USC Sch. of Pharmacy; bd. dirs. Alhambra Day Nursing; honors: Campaigner of the Year (YMCA 1985), President's Award-Citizen of the Year (Alhambra CofC 1980), Community Scv. Award (Chinese Phys. Soc. 1975); mem: LACMA (dist. pres.), Calif. Soc. of Anesthesiol. (alt. delegate), Calif. Med. Review (phys. advisor), Med. Quality Review Bd. Calif., Alhambra Rotary, University Club of Pasadena, Arboretum (Arcadia), Friends of Beckman Cal-Tech; publ: arts. on anesthesia and acupuncture; mil: USN 1946-48; Republican; Presbyterian; rec: travel, banking, real estate, tennis, photog. Ofc: 806 S Garfield Ave Alhambra 91801

SIVERTSEN, WIGGSY AIMEE, educator; b. Dec. 7, 1935, Hollywood; d. Ivar, Jr. and Aimee Christine (Rochester) S.; edn: AA, Stephens Coll. 1957; BA, San Jose State Univ. 1962; MSW, Tulane Univ. 1967; LCSW, lic. clin. soc. wkr. Calif. Career: program dir. Peninsula Childrens Center, Palo Alto 1963-69; prof. Counseling Services, San Jose State Univ., 1967–; also pvt. practice clin. social work, San Jose; adj. prof. St. Francis Coll. Sch. of Nursing 1981, 82; cons. Coastal Comm. Counseling Ctr., Santa Cruz 1980-; mem: Nat. Assn. of Social Wkrs., Soc. for Clin. Soc. Wk., United Professors of Calif. (chpt. pres.), AIDS/KS Found., San Jose (bd. dirs.), ACLU, NOW, Gay Rights Advocates, Nat. Womens Polit. Caucus; adv. bd. mem. South Bay Comm. Counseling Center; v.p. Bay Area Municipal Elections Com.; Democrat; rec: rowing single person shell. Res: 20820 Locust Dr Los Gatos 95050 Ofc: San Jose State Univ., Admin 223, Washington Sq. San Jose 95192

SIVILLE, RANDAL DALE, financial executive; b. Feb. 18, 1952, Jacksonville, N.C.; s. Leroy Dale and Mary Jane (Baird) S.; m. Marcia, Aug. 19, 1978; 1 dau. Laura b. 1981; edn: BS acctg., San Diego St. Univ. 1979; MBA, Nat. Univ. 1982, JD, Nat. Univ. Law Sch. 1986; CMA Cert. in Mgmt. Acctg. (1982), CIA Cert. Internal Auditor (1982). Career: dir. cost acctg. Bradston Hurricane Internat., San Diego 1980-81; asst. controller University Financial, San Diego 1981-82; controller Greater San Diego Chamber of Commerce, 1982-; bd. dirs. North Island Federal Credit Union 1985-; mem. Am. Acctg. Assn., Inst. of Internal Auditors, Inst. of Mgmt. Accts., Nat. Assn. of Accts., Navy League of US, Mensa; mil: BM2 US Navy 1973-77, Res. 1977-81, SEAL Team One & Two; Republican; Methodist. Res: 5353 Sunglow Ct San Diego 92117 Ofc: Greater San Diego Chamber of Commerce 110 West C St Ste 1600 San Diego 92101

SJOGREN, PER H., investment co. executive; b. Apr. 22, 1922, Lulea, Sweden, nat. US cit. 1953; s. Johan A. and Alma O.F. (Olofson) S.; m. Christine A. Oertel, Dec. 26, 1950; children: Jon A. b. 1951, Lance B. b. 1953, Lisa H. b. 1955, Christopher P. b. 1956, Britta H. b. 1958, Rolf E. b. 1962; edn: BA, Univ. Uppsala 1947, MA, 1948; PhD, Columbia Univ. 1964. Career: instr. Univ. Kansas Lawrence 1948-51, Lundsbergs Skola Sweden 1951-52; head sales svc. dept. Container Corp. of Am. Portland, Ore. 1952-56; ofc. mgr. Western Corrugated Inc. Beaverton, Ore. 1956-57; assoc. prof., dir. MBA pgm., dept. chmn. Ore. State Univ. Corvallis 1959-68; proj. economist Checchi & Co. Wash. DC and Union of Chambers of Commerce, Industry & Commodity Exchanges Ankara, Turkey 1966-67; pres. King's View Realty Inc. Corvallis, Ore. 1968-80; exec. v.p. C.M. Capital Corp. Palo Alto 1981–; pres. C.M. Ore. Corp., Castro Valley Properties Inc.; honors: Doctoral Study Awards (Columbia Univ. 1957-58, 58-59), Ford Found. Fellow (UCLA 1961, Harvard 1964), Beta Gamma Sigma, Boss of the Year, Realtor of the Year; mem: Am. Assn. Univ. Profs. (chpt. pres.), Corvallis Bd. Realtors (pres.), Homebuilders Assn. (chpt. pres.), Ore. Assn. Realtors (chmn. mortgage finance com.), Benton County Planning Commn. (chmn. 1974-78); publs: The Dow-Jones Industrial Average - What Exactly Does It Tell You About the Stock Market (1963-64), The Union of Chambers of Commerce, Industry and Commodity Exchanges of Turkey - A Reorganization Study (w/ James D. Tallman); mil: vice cpl. Swedish Army Infantry 1943-44; Republican; rec: bridge, swimming. Res: 225 Waverly St Menlo Park 94025 Ofc: C.M. Capital Corp. 525 University Ave Ste 1500 Palo Alto 94301

SKALJAC, GEORGE, sales executive; b. Feb. 13, 1952, Youngstown, O.; s. Vujo and Stella S.; m. Bernadette A. Mostajo, June 5, 1982; edn: AA, Youngstown State Univ. 1972, BS, 1975. Career: acct. exec. Rialto Studios, Youngstown, Oh. 1973-75; sales mgr. Reese Tool & Supply, Pittsburgh 1975-76; indsl. sales rep. Arno Tapes div. Dr. Scholls, Pgh. 1976-77; area mgr. Hydrocurve Soft Lenses, Columbus, Oh. 1977-78, Austin, Tx. 1979; senior sales rep. CooperVision Inc., San Francisco 1979-81, San Diego/ Honolulu, 1981; senior sales rep. Ciba Vision Care San Diego/ Honolulu 1981-84, profl. sales rep. 1984-86, area account mgr. Western US, 1986–; honors: Nat. Student Register (1973), Outstanding Young Men of Am. (1985), num. sales awards (1978-), Ciba-Geigy Corp. highest performance award (1982, 83); mem. Serbian Nat. Fedn., Serbian Nat. Def. Council of Am.; Serbian Eastern Orthodox (pres. 1985); rec: gardening. Ofc: Ciba Vision Care 2975 Gateway Dr Norcross 90071

SKIBBEN, BERNARD DAVID, historical homes building co. president; b. Jan. 13, 1928, Leeds, Eng.; s. Louis and Florrie S.; m. Ann, Sept. 1, 1954; children: Beverley b. 1955, Gail b. 1960; edn: grad. in arch. & constrn., Leeds Coll. of Tech. 1946. Career: formed constrn. co. in England, 1950-75, building new homes in authentic designs of bye-gone eras (bldr. 8 period-homes in Ripon, near Yorkshire Moor in 17th century designs); came to Calif. 1975, pres. Trafalgar Developments, Sherman Oaks 1975–, builder custom homes re-creating 18th century manor houses and French Normandy period homes in Bel-Air and Beverly Hills; presents Film Shows of homes, and lectures on New Homes - 200 Years Old; mem: Nat. Assn. of Estate Agents, England (founder/ 1st nat. chmn.), Fellow Inst. of Directors, Exec. Assn. of San Fernando Valley (past pres.), British Am. CofC, Am. Historical Soc.; works: due to period authenticity his houses are used by var. Film Studios, appear in newspaper feature articles; mil: sgt. British Army, JAG, 1946-49; rec: video filming (Fellow Inst. of Amateur Cinemaphotogs.). Res: 4949 Genesta Ave Encino 91316 Ofc: Trafalgar Devs. Union Bank Plaza 15233 Ventura Blvd Ste 1208 Sherman Oaks 91436

SKIFF, RUSSELL ALTON, plastics co. president; b. Feb. 26, 1927, Waterford, Pa.; s. Albert Alton and Leah Gladys (Allen) S.; m. Dolores Theresa Molnar, June 25, 1950; children: Russell James, Sandra Lee, Eric Alan, Rebecca Lynn; edn: BS chem., math, Univ. Pittsburgh 1950. Career: metall. chemist Jones & Laughlin Steel Co. Alliquippa, Pa. 1950-51; r&d chemist Gen. Elec. Co. Erie, Pa. 1951-57; mgr. tech. sales and plant ops. Hysol. Corp. of Calif., El Monte 1957-60; senior research engr. Autonetics Div. No. Am. Aviation Co. Downey 1960-62; pres., dir. Delta Plastics Co. 1962–; cons. in field of epoxy resins tech.; mem. US Senate Adv. Bd., Calif. State Conf. on Small Business; honors: Presidential Achievement Award; mem: Nat. Assn. Mfrs., Nat. Fedn. Independent Business, Am. Chem. Soc., Soc. Plastic Engrs., Soc. Plastics Industry, AAAS, Nat. Exchange Club (dist. dir.), Exchange Club of Visalia (past pres.), Calif./ Nev. Dist. Exchange Clubs (Outstanding Dist. Dir. 1983-84), Lions (pres.), People to People internat. (mem. first US mfrs. goodwill del. to Europe and Russia 1979, China & Asia 1980, NZ & Australia 1982); holder 9 US patents; publs: 50+ tech. articles and reports; mil: s/sgt USAAF 1944-46. Address: 5525 W Pershing Visalia 93291

SKINNER, STANLEY THAYER, utility co. executive; b. Aug. 18, 1937, Fort Smith, Ark.; m. Margaret Skinner, Aug. 16, 1957; children: Steven b. 1963, Ronald b. 1966; edn: BA econs., San Diego St. Univ. 1960; MA econs., UC Berkeley 1961, JD, UCB 1964. Career: atty. Pacific Gas and Electric Co., San Francisco 1964–, senior counsel 1973, treas. 1974, v.p.-fin. 1976, senior v.p. 1976, exec. v.p. 1977, exec. v.p. and chief finl. ofcr. 1982–, also vice chmn. 1986–; dir: Pacific Gas and Elec. Co. (1986-), Pacific Lumber Co. (1985-86), Pacific Gas Transmission (treas. 1974, v.p. fin. 1975-82, dir. 1976-), Natural Gas Corp. (treas. 1975-76, dir. 1976-), Standard Pacific Gas Lines Inc. (treas. 1974-75, dir. 1976-), Alaska California LNG Co. (1976-), Pacific Gas Marine Co. (1976-), Pacific Gas LNG Terminal Co. (1976-), Calaska Energy Co. (1978-), Eureka Energy Co. (1978-), Alberta and So. Gas Co. Ltd. (1980-), Rocky Mountain Gas Transmission Co. (1980-), Nuclear Mutual Limited (1980-85), Nuclear Electric Insurance Ltd. (1980-85); mem: Calif. State Bar Assn., Pac. Coast Elec. Assn., Pac. Coast Gas Assn., Finl. Ofcrs. of No. Calif.; civic: Bankers Club of S.F. (dir. 1986-), Golden Gate Univ. Bd. Trustees (chmn. 1985-86, chmn. Fin. Com. 1983, v. chmn. Admin. 1985), S.F. CofC (dir. 1986-), Calif. Econ. Devel. Corp. (dir. 1986-), United Way of Bay Area (bd. 1982-84, chmn. Fin. Com. 1982-83), Boy Scouts Am. S.F. Bay Area Council (exec. bd. 1982-83); Republican; Presbyterian; rec: skiing, running. Ofc: Pacific Gas & Electric Co 77 Beale St 32nd Fl San Francisco 94106

SKIRIUS, BERNICE, real estate broker, interpreter; b. May 15, 1915, Chgo.; d. Vincent and Emilia (Rotkis) Piliponis (Pilips); m. Anthony Skirius, Feb. 22, 1941; children: Ruta b. 1946, John b. 1948, Vincent b. 1956; edn: Comml. Gymnasium of Taurage Lithuania 1934; Univ. Vytautas Didysis Lithuania 1934-36; Woodrow Wilson Coll. Chgo. 1937-38; Pierce Coll. Woodland Hills, Calif. 1954-55. Career: inspector Signal Corps Cicero, Ill. 1942-44; media Dept. Commentaries & News, Ofc. of War Information S.F. 1944-46; interpreter, translator Calif. Superior Ct. L.A. 1948–; real estate broker, owner Skirius Realty L.A. 1956–; honors: Disting. Achievement (Superior Ct. Calif. 1978), Cert. of Appreciation (1985), 1st Place Folk Dance Contest (w/ Lithuanian Ateitis Dancers 1943); mem: Los Feliz- Silverlake Real Estate Brokers Assn. 1961- (treas. 1974-77), Calif. Dept. Real Estate 1956-, L.A. Bd. Realtors 1966-81, Lithuanian Am. Republicans of Calif. (secty. 1956-58, 1980-82, by-laws com.), United Lith. Relief Fund (secty.), Knights of Lith. (v.p., secty., reporter), Fedn. of Lith. Women's Club (pres., v.p., secty.), Lith. Catholic Alliance (pres. 15 yrs., fin. secty. 5 yrs.); publr. Calif. Lithuanian magazine 1946-47, Eng. editor 1946-48; entertained at USO clubs w/ Ateitis dance group 1943-44, appeared on TV in Chgo. as leader of Ateitis 1944; organized concert of Faust and medly of Lith. songs 1966; Republican; Catholic; rec: music, folk art. Ofc: Skirius Realty 4366 Sunset Blvd Los Angeles 90029

SKOGLUND, ELIZABETH RUTH, counselor, author; b. June 17, 1937, Chgo.; d. Ragner Emmanuel and Elizabeth Alvira (Benson) Skoglund; edn: BA, UCLA 1959; MA, Pt. Loma (Pas. Coll.) 1969. Career: English tchr. Marlborough Sch., Los Angeles 1959-61; Eng. Tchr. Glendale High Sch., 1961-72; counselor Glendale Family Svc. 1971-73; pvt. practice, Burbank 1972–; supt. Drug Abuse Adv. Comm. for Glendale Unif. Sch. Dist.; asst. psychiatric cons. on Burbank Unif. Sch. Dist.; cons. Tee-Dru Nar (drug rehab grp.); TV talk show appearances; recipient Beautiful Activist Award 1973, Germaine Monteil Cosmetics, The Broadway; author num. books, 1972-83, currently writing weekly newspaper column and book, Beyond Survival; Republican; Protestant; rec: swim, shell collector, photog. Res: 619 E Providencia Ave, No F, Burbank 91501 Ofc: 303 So Glenoaks Blvd, Ste 14, Burbank 91502

SLAGER, RODNEY WILLIAM, savings and loan executive; b. July 19, 1955, Ogden, Utah; s. Jan and Margene Ruth (Fuller) S.; m. Vivian Lumantas, Aug. 11, 1977; children: Stephanie b. 1979, Jan Michael b. 1985; edn: Weber St. Coll. 1974-77, Rancho Santiago Coll. 1982-84, Coastline Comm. Coll. 1980 84, Inst. Finl. Edn. 1980-86; Calif. lic. Notary Public, Real Estate sales. Career: Mormon missionary, 1974-76; realtor assoc. Century 21 C.W. Investments, Salt Lake City, 1976-80; Katella Realty, Santa Ana, Calif. 1980; branch mgr. Great American Federal, Rancho California Office, 1980-83; branch sales mgr. Calif. Federal Svgs. & Loan, Tustin Office 1983-86, Lake Forest Ofc. 1986–, regl. branch sales and mktg. advisor, 1985-; mem. Nat. Assn. of Realtors, Inst. of Finl. Edn.; civic: Temecula CofC (econ. com.),Tustin CofC (legis. com.), Kiwanis (pres. elect Tustin 1986-7), Rancho Temecula Comm. Parks Assn. (past secty.); Republican; Ch. of Jesus Christ of Latter-day Saints; rec: water ski, fishing, family activities. Res: 2734 Drake Ave Costa Mesa 92626 Ofc: California Federal 14232 Red Hill Ave Tustin 92680

SLAGLE, RONALD GEORGE, co. president; b. Nov. 17, 1939, Glendale; s. Munsey Calvin, Jr. and Clarice Mae (Winnor) S.; m. Nancy Stroud, Aug. 27, 1960, div. 1974; children: Robin Jill b. 1962, Eric Ronald b. 1964; edn: AA, East Los Angeles Coll. 1960; BS, CSC Los Angeles 1966. Career: western regl. mgr. Quaker Oats Co., 12 yrs.; gen. mgr. LeRoy Ents.; nat. sales mgr. Poly-Optics; nat. sales mgr. J. Hungerford Smith Div. United Brands; western regl. sales mgr. Universal/Nolin Div. UMC Indus.; account mgr. Golden West Equip. Co.; current: pres./owner Marketing Equip. Specialists Inc., Lake Forest; Republican; Christian; rec: tennis, snorkel, beach. Res: 430 Cypress Dr Laguna Beach 92651 Ofc: Marketing Equipment Specialists Inc. 22672 Lambert St Ste 612 Lake Forest 92630

SLATER, MELBA JOY, entrepreneur; b. Feb. 4, 1938, Portland, Ore.; d. David E. and Olive Elaine (Wilson) Kinville; edn: Pasadena City Coll.. Career: airline hostess Continental Airlines 1958; exec. secty., bookkeeper var. bus. incl. medical, law, manufacturing and engring.; cons. and sales rep. Praxis Computers of Utah 1979-80; founder Energi Saver Products 1982–; yoga tchr. Glendale Community Coll. 1985–; honors: Top Dealer on the West Coast, mktg. SAV IT energy mgmt. sys. 1983; Top Salesperson on the West Coast, Elecronic Sys. Internat., Norcross, Georgia 1983; mem: Verdugo Hills Bus. & Profl. Women, Stewardess Emeritus Assn., Glendale CofC, Mayor's Prayer Breakfast Com.; publs: article, Yoga with Joy, Light Bearer 1986; rec: tennis, skiing, singing. Address: 2718 Piedmont Ave. Ste. 9 Montrose 91020

SLATTER, DOUGLAS HORTON, veterinary surgeon/ophthalmologist; b. Mar. 7, 1948, Brisbane, Australia; s. Horton George and Edith Gentle (Brown) S.; m. Elizabeth Drell, Jan. 20, 1985; children: Christine b. 1978, Diane b. 1979; edn: B. V. Sc., Univ. of Queensland, 1970; MS, Wash. State Univ. 1973; PhD, Colo. State Univ. 1975; Diplomate Am. Coll. Veterinary Surgeons (1976), Am. Coll. Vet. Ophthalmologists (1975); Fellow Royal Coll. of Vet. Surgeons, London (1980). Career: resident in surgery Washington State Univ. 1971-73; research fellow Colo. State Univ. 1973-76; asst. prof. of surgery Mich. St. Univ. 1976; assoc. prof. of surgery Murdoch Univ., Australia 1977-84; splst. veterinary surgeon and ophthalmologist, owner Animal Eye & Surgical Clinic, La Habra 1985–; bd. dirs: Animal Medical Specialties Inc., Burrendah Corp.; honors: research award Smith Kline, Australia; Who's Who in Western Australia (1979), Men of Achievement (UK 1979); mem: Am. Vet. Med. Assn., Am. Animal Hosp. Assn., So. Calif. Vet. Med. Assn.; clubs: Royal Queensland Yacht (1963-), Royal Perth Yacht (1977-84); author: Fundamentals of Veterinary Ophthalmology (850pp 1981); editor: Textbook of Small Animal Surgery (2800pp 1985); 60 sci. articles; mil: lt. Royal Australian Navy, 1966-84, Reserve; Anglican; rec: yachting, writing. Ofc: Animal Eye & Surgical Clinic 1301F South Beach Blvd La Habra 90631

SLATTERY, CHARLES WILBUR, educator; b. Nov. 18, 1937, La Junta, Colo.; s. Robert Ernest and Virgie Belle (Chamberlain) S.; m. Arline, June 15, 1958; children: Scott Charles b. 1963, Coleen Kay b. 1966; edn: BA in chem., Union Coll. 1959; MS and PhD in phys. chem., Univ. Nebr. 1961, 1965. Career: instr. Union Coll., Nebr. 1961-63; asst., assoc. prof. Atlantic Union Coll., Mass. 1963-68; asst., assoc. prof. Loma Linda Univ. 1970-78, prof. of biochem. (dept. chmn. 1983-) LLU 1978–; vis. prof. (p.t.), research assoc. M.I.T., 1967-70; mem: Am. Chem. Soc., AAAS, Am. Dairy Sci. Assn., Am. Heart Assn., Thrombosis Council, Am. Soc. of Biological Chemists; publs: 25 research papers concerning milk proteins or different aspects of blood coagulation; Republican; Seventh-day Adventist. Ofc: Loma Linda University School of Medicine Biochemistry Dept Loma Linda 92350

SLOAN, TIMOTHY J., cardio-thoracic surgeon; b. Aug. 26, 1948, Los Angeles; s. William Patrick and Jeannette Wilhelmina (Berssenbrugge) S.; m. Linda Carlsen, Dec. 24, 1978; children: Stephen Anthony b. 1981, Katherine Marie b. 1983; edn: BS zool., microbiol., CSU Long Beach 1971; MD, UC Irvine 1976. Career: intern gen. surg. UC Irvine Med. Ctr. 1976-77, resident 1977-78, Univ. Hawaii 1978-79, Highland/ Alameda County Hosp. Oakland 1979-81; resident cardiovascular and thoracic surg. Univ. Tex. Southwestern Dallas 1981-83; pvt. practice Marysville, Calif. 1983–; instr. CSC Long Beach 1971; instr./ provider Advanced Cardiac Life Support Am. Heart Assn. 1978, asst. clin. instr. cardiothoracic surg. Univ. Texas Southwestern 1981; honors: NIH Grant (CSC Long Beach 1971); fellow: AMA 1983, Am. Coll. Chest Phys. 1983, Am. Coll. Surg. 1983; publs: contbr. articles in med. jours.; mil: E-4 USNR 1966-70; rec: tennis, target shooting. Res: 1393 La Grande Yuba City 95991 Ofc: 414 G St Ste 204 Marysville 95901

SLOAN, WILLIAM PATRICK, printing co. president; b. Nov. 2, 1934, Oak Park, Ill.; s. Frank A. and Thyra (Bartell) S.; m. Karen Mix, Jan. 31, 1980; edn: BA indsl. adm., Univ. of Ill. 1957. Career: mfg. research trainee R.R. Donnelley & Sons 1957-58, mfg. mgr. 1958-63, dept. mgr. 1963-68, group mgr. Electronic Graphics 1968-73, regl. sales mgr. Gen. Directory Sales 1973-78; pres. Sorg Printing Co. of California, San Francisco 1979–; mem. Printing Indus. of No. Calif. (dir. 1980-, pres. 1985-), Printing Indus. of Calif. (pres. 1983-85); clubs: Commonwealth, Rotary, World Trade, Olympic, Corinthian Yacht; mil: US Army 1956-57; rec: sports, theater, travel. Res: 30-B Circle Dr Tiburon 94920 Ofc: Sorg Printing Co 346 First St San Francisco 94105

SLOANE, BEVERLY LEBOV, author; b. May 26, 1936, NYC; d. Benjamin Samuel and Anne (Weinberg) LeBov; m. Robert Sloane, Sept. 27, 1959; 1 dau., Alison, b. 1965; edn: AB, Vassar Coll. 1958; MA, Claremont Grad. Sch. 1975, doctoral wk. 1975-76; grad. Coro Found. (Fellowship) Leadership Tng. in Pub. Affairs, Women's Pgm. 1979; grad. UCLA Grad. Sch. of Mgmt. Exec. Pgm. 1982; grad. Stanford Univ. publishing course 1982. Career: circulation librarian Harvard Med. Lib., Boston 1958-59; soc. wkr. Conn. State Welfare, New Haven 1960-61; English tchr. Hebrew Day Sch., New Haven 1961-64; instr./lectr. in creative writing and English lit., Monmouth Coll., NJ 1967-69; freelance writer, author in Arcadia, Calif. 1969–; author: (with R.M. Sloane) A Guide to Health Facilities - Personnel and Management (1971, 77); From Vassar to Kitchen (1967). Mem. Adv. Council for Tech. and Profl. Writing, English Dept. CSU Long Beach 1980-82; adv. bd. Calif. Health Rev. (mag.) 1982-3; bd. dirs. Los Angeles Commn. on Assaults Against Women 1983-; trustee The Ctr. for Improve. of Child Caring Inc. 1981-83. Honors: Claremont Grad. Sch. Student Body vice pres. 1971-72, mem. Claremont Coll. Faculty House 1983-; spl. recognition, L.A. Chpt. Women in Comm. Inc. 1983; listed, Who's Who of Am. Women, Who's Who in the West, Who's Who in the World; mem: Women in Communications, L.A. Chpt. (bd. dirs. 1980-82, ch. 1st Ann. Agnes Underwood Freedom of Info. Awards Banquet 1982); Fellow (1984-) Am. Med. Writers Assn. (nat. book awards com. ch. 1983, ch. nat. networking luncheon 1983), Pacific S.W. Chpt. (bd. dirs., nat. del., pres. 1986); AAUW, Arcadia Br. (past ofcr.); Calif. Press Women (L.A. Dist. bd. dirs. 1982-, v.p. 1982-85, pres. 1985-); AAUP; Inst. of Technology (past ch. creative writing); Soc. for Tech. Comm.; Internat. Comm. Assn.; Am. Pub. Health Assn.; Assn. of Western Hosps.; College English Assn.; Coro Assocs.; Town Hall of Calif. (v.ch. Community Affairs Sect. 1982-); Ex-Rotary of Duarte; Vassar Club of So. Ca.; Womens Club Calif.; League for Crippled Children; L.A. Orthopaedic Hosp. Address: 1301 N. Santa Anita Ave Arcadia 91006

SLOVER, ARCHY F., chemist; b. July 8, 1920, Oshkosh, Wisc.; s. Archie F. and Josephine Petronella (Zindler) S.; m. Mary Beatrice Corkill, May 25, 1946; 1 dau, Mary Kay b. 1947; edn: BA, UCLA 1947. Career: chemist Kelite Products Co., Los Angeles 1946-49; gen. mgr. Delco Chemicals Inc., Los Angeles 1949-57; mgr., Ind. Spec. Pennwalt Corp., Los Angeles and Phila. 1957-75; chemist Custom Chemical Mfg. Co., Cudahy 1976; gen. mgr. Cherokee Chem. Co. Inc., Compton 1977–; dir. Delco Chem., Cherokee Chem. Co. Inc., Chem. Arrow Corp.; mem: Fellow Am. Inst. of Chemists, Fellow AAAS, Am. Chemical Soc. (senior), Nat. Assn. of Corrosion Engrs. (corrosion splst.), Reserve Ofcrs. Assn., Am. Ordnance Assn., Am. Eletroplaters Soc., Air Force Assn., Kentucky Colonel, Sigma Alpha Sigma; mil: capt. CAC, 1941, 1942-46; Catholic. Res: 21 Hacienda Dr. Arcadia 91006 Ofc: Cherokee Chem. Co. Inc., 19400 Susana Rd. Compton 90221

SMALLEY, JAMES RALPH, physician; b. Jan. 31, 1944, Springfield, Mo.; s. Charles Ray and Helen Louise (Caudle) S.; m. Nora Cashman, June 9, 1969; 1 dau, Adrienne b. 1970; edn: Southwest Missouri State Univ. 1962-65; MD, Univ. of Missouri 1969; pediatric resident, Baylor Univ. Affil. Hosps. 1969-71, 1973-74; pediatric gastroenterology/ nutrition fellowship, Univ. of Rochester 1980-82; Diploma of Tropical Med. and Hygiene, London Sch. of Hygiene & Tropical Med., London 1980. Career: chief of pediatrics USAF Clinic, RAF Bentwaters, England 1976-80, chef of clinic svcs. 1978-80; staff pediatric gastroenterologist David Grant Med. Ctrs., Travis AFB 1982–, med. ctr. quality assurance coord. 1982-84, dir. of med. edn. 1984–; pediatric gastroenterology cons. Oakland Navy Med. Ctr. 1984-; pediatric gastroenterology cons., Surgeon General, USAF 1983-; honors: Outstanding Tchg. Award, Pediatric Dept. David Grant Med. Ctr. 1983-84; mem: Am. Acad. of Pediatrics, No. Am. Soc. of Pediatric Gastroenterology; publs: 6 in Clinical Pediatrics, Pediatrics, and Journ. of Pediatric Gastroenterology & Nutritin 1982, 1983; mil: col. USAF 1971-73, 1975-, Commendation Medal 1980. Ofc: Director of Medical Education, David Grant Medical Center, Travis AFB 94535

SMALLEY, NITA CRANDALL, gift shop owner, bookkeeper; b. Apr. 13, 1941, Hollywood, Calif.; d. Charles Fourier and Anita Crandall (Miller) Schwartz; m. John Edward Shimmin Jr., Nov. 11, 1962; children: Bruce Edward b. 1968, David Andrew b. 1969; m. 2d Glenn Arthur Smalley, Apr. 26, 1980; edn: AA, Pasadena City Coll. 1961; BA, Univ. LaVerne 1980. Career: tool sales Foothill Tool & Machinery Pasadena 1962-64; tool buyer Ronson Hydraulic Units Duarte 1964-67; ofc. mgr. Acme Pak/ Anvil Cases Monrovia 1972-75; store mgr. Sho Market Stores Santa Ana 1975-77; ofc. mgr. Chino Council of Social Svcs. 1977-79; bookkeeper Holiday Rock & Trucking Co. Upland 1979-81; owner Nita's Nook Rancho Cucamonga 1981–; honors: Honor Roll (Univ. LaVerne 1979); mem: Sunrize Merchant's Assn. (pres. 1984-85), Soroptimist Internat. of the Foothills Upland (v.p. 1984-85), Swinging Stars Square Dance Club (pres. 1985); Republican; Episcopal; rec: square dancing, clogging, writing. Res: POB 606 Alta Loma 91701 Ofc: Nita's Nook 8623 Baseline Rd Rancho Cucamonga 91730

SMATKO, ANDREW JOHN, gynecologist-obstetrician; b. June 14, 1917, Fort Edward, NY; s. John George and Anna Mary (Matochik) S.; m. Shirley, Dec. 9, 1957; 1 son, Andrew b. 1963; edn: AB, Columbia Coll. 1937; MD, NY Univ. Coll. of Med. 1941. Diplomate Am. Board of Obstets. & Gynecology. Career: 2-year rotating intern City Hosp. of New York, 3-year residency in ob-gyn. Florence Crittenton Hosp., Detroit, Mich.; pvt. practice in obstets. and gynecology in Beverly Hills, Los Angeles, and currently in Santa Monica; senior cons. in gynecology & obstets., St. John's Hosp. and Santa Monica Med. Ctr.; instr. in ob-gyn. Wayne Univ. 1945; inventor four surgical instruments; awards: scholarship Columbia Coll.; mem: Calif. Med. Assn., Los Angeles County Med. Assn., Am. Coll. of Obstets and Gynecols., Pacific Surgical Assn., Los Angeles Ob-Gyn. Soc.; clubs: Beverly Hills Mens', Columbia Univ. Alumni, NY Univ. Alumni; active mountaineer (has climbed over 3000 mountains); author book: Mountaineer's Guide to the High Sierra; Republican; Roman Catholic; rec: mtn. climbing, outdoor photog., camping. Res: 1355 Monaco Dr Pacific Palisades 90272 Ofc: 2021 Santa Monica Blvd Santa Monica 90404

SMILEY, CREATH BENJAMIN, company executive; b. Feb. 3, 1917, Paducah, Ky.; s. Creath Benjamin and Tessye Rae (Samuels) S.; m. Mary Jane Garry (dec.), Aug. 20, 1949; children: Susan Rae b. 1952, Sandra Jane b. 1954, Sharon Ann b. 1958; 11 grandchildren; edn: BA, Indiana Univ. 1938; MS, Navy Postgrad. Sch. Monterey 1961; Diploma I, Inst. Financial Mgmt. L.A. 1973; lic. life & disability ins. agent. Career: dir. of information State Bd. of Health Indpls., Ind. 1940-42; supply corps ofcr. USN 1942-70; mgr. Imperial Savings & Loan East Pasadena 1970-72, v.p. 1972–; honors: Scroll of Honor (Navy League 1970), Patriot of the Yr. (Pasa. CofC 1983), Resident of the Yr. (Upper Hastings Ranch Assn. 1983); mem: Navy League (nat. bd. dirs. 1984-87, regl. v.p., editor newsletter, past pres. Pasa. Council), Upper Hastings Ranch Assn. (bd. dirs., past pres.), Pasa. CofC (past v.p., com. chmn.), Indiana Univ. Club of L.A. (past bd.), Indiana Univ. Alumni Assn., Retired Ofcrs. Assn. (past pres.), Soc. for Preservation of Variety Arts, patron Pacific Asia Mus., Japan Am. Soc. (v.p. 1963-64), Boy Scouts (past bd.); editor: monthly newsletter Profl. Jour. of Supply Corps 1946-50, THe Lariat (Upper Hastings Ranch Assn.) 1969-73; mil: cmdr. USN 1942-70, Asiatic-Pacific Ribbon w/ 7 battle stars; Republican; Catholic; rec: photog., stamps. Res: 1016 Crestview Dr Pasadena 91107 Ofc: Imperial Savings Assn. 3870 E Foothill Blvd Pasadena 91107

SMISEK, THOMAS MILO, marketing executive; b. Dec. 15, 1938, Cleveland, Ohio; s. Milo and Adele (Ejze) S.; m. Angela, Aug. 7, 1982; children: Cassandra b. 1963, Brandon b. 1964, Kahana b. 1983; edn: Cleveland Inst. of Art. Career: pres. Tom Smisek Advtg. 1967-80, Tom Smisek Advtg./ Mktg. Cons. 1980–; instr. advtg. copywriting Orange Coast Coll.; honors: Scholastic Keys (1957), num. advtg. awards for creativity including 4 Golden Orange Awards from Orange Co. Ad Club; mem: Orange Co. Sheriff's Adv. Council, Orange Co. Ad Fedn., Am. Ad Fedn., Am. Soc. Profl. Cons.; mil: E-3 USAF (SAC); Republican. Res: Smisek Ranch POB 374 Silverado 92676 Ofc: Tom Smisek Cons. 4000 MacArthur Blvd Ste 3000 Newport Beach 92660

SMITH, ANTHONY F., educator, consultant, organizational research specialist; b. July 5, 1960, San Diego; s. Frank D. and Sylvia G. S.; m. Erin Jean Murphy, Nov. 23, 1985; edn: AA honors, Grossmont Coll. 1980; BA, San Diego State Univ. 1982, MA, cum laude, 1984; Ed.D., Univ. San Diego 1987. Career: campus dir. Youth for Christ San Diego 1978-80; dir. personnel communications Am. Capital Mktg. Inc. S.D. 1980-82; asst. dir. speech & debate pgm. Grossmont Coll. 1981-82, SDSU 1982-83, instr., dir. speech commun. lab., asst. dir. basic course 1982-84; instr. Miramar Coll. 1984; vis. prof. Christian Heritage Coll., El Cajon 1985; senior ptnr. San Diego Consulting Group S.D. 1982–; instr., asst. forensics dir. Grossmont Coll. El Cajon 1984–; lectr. communs. Univ. of San Diego 1984–; cons. var. cos. San Diego; honors:

Dean's List (SDSU 1982), Phi Beta Kappa, num. speech and debate awards, Nat. Forensics Assn. (1979-81), invited student Center for Learning, Univ. Bristol, Eng. (1978); mem: Internat. Commun. Assn., Speech Commun. Assn., Western Speech Commun. Assn., Acad. of Mgmt., Nat. Forensics Assn.; Christian; rec: composing music, guitar. Ofc: Grossmont Coll. 8800 Grossmont Coll. Dr. El Cajon 92020

SMITH, BARRY RAY, motion picture and entertainment lawyer; b. Sept. 14, 1953, Ft. Benning, Ga.; s. Charles Ray and Mary Alice (Shaneyfelt) S.; m. Moshoula Simonidis, 1985; children: Jody b. 1970, Catherine b. 1985; edn: US Army Electron. Sch.; BA econ., UC Santa Barbara 1979; JD, Cornell Law Sch. 1982. Career: congl. aide/intern Congressman Robert J. Lagomensino Wash DC 1978; econ. analyst McCutchen, Black, Verleger & Shea L.A. 1979; law clerk Cornell Law Sch. Itaca, N.Y. 1980-82; assoc. atty. Zukerman, Blum & Pflug L.A. 1983-84; principal law firm Barry R. Smith entertainment law Beverly Hills 1984—; honors: (Cornell) Eva Howe Stevens Scholar, second prize Nathan Burkan Meml. Writing Comp., conferee Law Sch. Advisory Counsel; (UC Santa Barbara) High Honors, Outstanding Graduating Senior, Dean's List Scholar; mem: Am., L.A. Co., Beverly Hills bar assns.; Beverly Hills CofC, Cornell Alumni Assn.; mil: sp/4 US Army Combat Devel. Experi mentation Command 1974-76, Outstanding Achievement Cert.; Greek Orthodox; rec: tennis, sailing, writing, motion pictures. Ofc: Law Office of Barry R., Smith 9595 Wilshire Blvd, Ste 611, Beverly Hills 90212

SMITH, BERNARD JOSEPH, consulting engineer; b. Aug. 29, 1900, Liverpool, Eng., nat. 1930's; s. Thomas Joseph and Sarah Anne (Crum) S.; m. Julia Susan Connolly, June 4, 1929; children: Bernard, Sarah, Maureen, Una, Aislin, Thomas, Joan, John; edn: pvt. tutors, math, 1923-24; St. Edwards Coll.; Blackrock Coll., Dublin; Oxford Univ.; BE, honors, Univ. of Liverpool 1923; M.Engring; lic. profl. engr. Tex., NJ; reg. engr. CA, NJ, TX; Career: est. US res. 1912; res. engr. Underpinning & Found. Co., NYC, Phila. 1924; insp./ underground conduit engr. NY, NJ Tel. Co. and Ohio Bell Tel. Co. 1924-26; asst. engr. Alexander Potter, cons. engr. 1926-30; pvt. res. in hydrology & hydraulics 1930; dcs. engr. Humble Oil Refining Co. 1930-32; city engr. Baytown, Tex. 1931-33; city mgr. 1932-33; cons. engr. 1931-34; engring. insp. PWA, Ft. Worth 1934-35; engring. examiner 1935-37; pvt. cons. engr. 1937-38; dir., res. & personnel, Ft. Worth 1938-41; lectr. Tex. Christ. Univ.1940-43; state plng. engr./ state dir. Tex. Pub. Works Res., 1941-42; asst. reg. rep./ economist Nat. Housing Agcy., Dallas 1942-47; lectr. econs., bus. admin. and engring. So. Meth. Univ. 1947-53; cons. engr. Dallas 1947—; chief, S.F. Bay Devel. US Corps of Engrs., S.F. Dist. 1957-65; mem: Am. Econ. Assn.; Soc. of Evolutionary Econ.; Hist. of Econ. Soc.; Commr. Santa Cruz Co., CA, Water Adv. Commn.; spec. cons. S.F. Bay Conserv. and Devel. Commn. 1966—; lectr. on profl. subjects and radio conf. panelist; author: Town Bldg., 1939; El Paso Housing Mkt., 1945; Journey to Petra (1979 pvt. pub.); Odyssey (1982 pvt. pub.); mem: Fellow Am. Soc. of C.E.; S.F. Irish Lit. and Hist. Soc. (pres. 1961-63); Am. Waterworks Assn.; Dallas Fed. Rey. Exch.; Gov. Reagan's Task Force of Transp.; Am. Econ. Assn.; TX Soc. Profl. Engrs.; County Louth Arch. Soc.; Third Order of St. Francis Club Clogher Hist Soc.; Commonwealth Club; Serra Club (Dallas); pres. Holy Name Soc., Holy Trinity Ch.; rec: photog., painting, travel. Ofc: POB 663 Aptos 95003

SMITH, BRUCE EDWARD, tax consultant, annuity and life insurance broker/ sales; b. Mar. 4, 1951, Detroit, Mich.; s. Kenneth E. and Patricia E. (Hawk) S.; m. Penny, July 17, 1981; 1 dau. Ashley Marie b. 1983; edn: BBA acctg. & fin., Eastern Mich. Univ. Career: acct. Moore, Smith & Dale, CPAs, Smithfield, Mich. 1974-75; controller Kaufman & Broad Homes, Southfield 1975-76; controller S-K Lumber Co., Inkster, Mich. 1976-78; pres. The Art Connection Ltd., Bloomfield Hills, Mich. 1978-81; regl. mgr. Freeman Finl. Services, San Diego 1981-83; pres. The Teachers' Finl. Network, San Diego 1983—; mng. general agent Great American Life, 1983—; awards: Top Ten personal producing agt., Great Am. Life (1984, 85); trainor Dale Carnegie Sales Course; mem. Toastmasters (ednl. v.p. 1984-85); player San Diego Senior Ice Hockey League 1981-86; Republican; Catholic. Res: 12111 Charbono Dr San Diego 92131 Ofc: Teachers' Financial Network 8885 Rio San Diego Dr Ste 252 San Diego 92108

SMITH, CAROL-LEE, educator; b. June 9, 1935, Los Angeles; d. Wm. Andrew and Frances Isadora (Theriault) S.; m. Gary L., May 29, 1979; children (nee Troop): Cynthia-Lou 1958-1976, Ned L. b. 1959, Carin-Lin (Estes) b. 1961, Brett L. b. 1962; edn: AA, Shasta Coll. 1969; BS in health scis., Chapman Coll. 1983; PhD, Walden Univ. 1984; Calif. life tchg. cred. Instr./ Coordinator Med. Assisting (1969). Career: radiologic technologist, Ft. Collins. Colo. 1965-66; med. transcriptionist Radiol. Dept. St. Vincent's Hosp., Billings, Mo. 1963-64; instr./ coord. med. assisting Shasta Coll., Redding 1966—; med. asst. Robert E. Milton, MD, Redding 1966-67; owner The Total Look (womens boutique) 1976-78, B/C Mgmt. Consultants and Seminar 1979—, Charter Bus Service, Redding 1982—, Smith Air Taxi, Redding 1986—; cons./ lectr. Shasta Cascade Family Practice (Residency Pgm.) 1983-, Shasta Coll. Faculty Speaker's Bureau 1985-; honors: for disting. service, Yreka Flood, Am. Red Cross (1964), Medical Asst. of Year (1977); mem. Calif. Tchrs. Assn. (1966-), Shasta Coll. Faculty Assn. (treas. 1969-77), Shasta-Trinity Med. Assts. Assn., Am. Assn. of Med. Assts., Am. Assn. of Med. Transcriptionists, Calif. Assn. of Med. Assts., Calif. Assn. of Med. Assisting Instrs., Soroptomists; publs: Medical Assisting Modules (1972, 74, 75, 77, 80, 81); Republican; Episcopal; rec: travel, cards and games. Res: 3120 Winding Way Redding 96003 Ofc: Shasta College 1065 N Old Oregon Trail Ste 2156 Redding 96003

SMITH, CHARLES WALTER, accounting firm president; b. Feb. 28, 1955, Marietta, Ga.; s. Charles W. and Marion E. S.; m. Barbara, Aug. 12, 1978;

children: Nathan b. 1981, Megan b. 1984; edn: BS, Mgmt. Univ. Redlands 1977; CPA Calif. 1982. Career: staff acct. Urban M. Derkum CPA 1976-79, senior staff acct. 1980-82; ptnr. Derkum & Smith CPAs 1983-84; pres. Derkum, Smith & Branch CPAs 1985—; mem: Calif. Soc. CPAs 1983, Redlands CofC, United Way volunteer, Univ. Redlands volunteer; Republican; Presbyterian; rec: outdoor sports, photog., art. Ofc: Derkum, Smith & Branch CPAs 411 E Palm Ave Redlands 92373

SMITH, DAVID ELLISON, publisher;b. Oct. 19, 1948, Oakland; s. Ellison D. and Lorilee Winifred (Peet) S.; m. Laura Fitch, April 2, 1971; children: Brian b. 1977, Steven b. 1979, Benjamin b. 1981, Kathryn b. 1984; edn: BS, Brigham Young Univ. 1973. Career: h.s. geometry tchr. Palo Verde Sch. Dist., Blythe 1975-76; software engr. Edwards Pacemakers, Irvine 1976-77; pgmmr. GTE, Anaheim 1977-78; sys. analyst Data General, Anaheim 1978-79; store mgr. Computer World, Westminster 1979-80; CAD engr. Hughes Aircraft, Newport Beach 1980-85; publr. Mactutor, Anaheim 1985—; publr: The Apple Shoppe Mag., for Apple II 1978-80; Mactutor, for Macintosh; Republican; Ch. of Jesus Christ LDS; rec: bicycling, basketball. Ofc: Mactutor, 1240 Van Buren Ste. 105 Anaheim 92807

SMITH, DAVID ERNEST, manufacturing co. executive; b. Nov. 9, 1936, Woodbury, NJ; s. Ernest Browne and Evelyn Maud (McCarthy) S.; 1 son, David E., Jr., b. 1970; edn: BS in chem./biol., Muhlenberg Coll. 1959; MBA, Univ. of Scranton 1969; MS in intl. bus. (summa cum laude), West Coast Univ. 1978. Career: current dir. sales and mktg. ATI, a Warner Lambert co.; bd. dirs. Ventures West, IBIS Medical; owner/gen. mgr. Smith Arabians; (prior): western div. mgr. C.R. Bard Inc.; internat. mktg. mgr. Cavitron Corp.; product mgr. Varian Assocs.; sales mgr. Gulton Industries; v.p. sales & mktg. Automated Screening Devices, Inc.; mem: Internat. Assn. of Hospital Central Supply, Medical Mktg. Assn., South Coast Gun Club, Aircraft Owners and Pilots Assn.; publs: art., Europe and Oil 4/71, tech. papers; Republican; Lutheran; rec: ham radio opr., comml/instrument rated pilot and pilot examiner. Res: 19471 Sierra Lago Irvine 92715

SMITH, DIANE R., lawyer; b. Oct. 10, 1946, New Orleans; d. William Lennox and Lillian Rose (Varnado) Rapp; m. Sherman U. Smith, Aug. 6, 1983; 1 dau: Summer b. 1973; edn: AB, UC Berkeley 1972; JD, Boalt Hall 1975; admitted Calif. State Bar 1975. Career: atty. U.S. Dept. of Energy S.F. Ops. Ofc. 1975-82; gen. counsel and secty. Fluor Technology Inc. Irvine 1982—; vis. lectr. UC Irvine 1984; honors: Phi Beta Kappa; mem: Calif. State Bar (exec. com. pub. law sect., chmn. govt. contracts subcom. 1984-). Res: 3 Springwood Irvine 92714 Ofc: Fluor Corp. 3333 Michelson Dr Irvine 92730

SMITH, ELEANOR RUTH, controller; b. May 14, 1932, Taunton, Mass.; d. Charles and Gertrude (Dean) T.; m. Harry L. Smith, Oct. 9, 1953; 1 son, Mark b. 1954; edn: stu. UCLA 1977-78, L.A. City Coll. 1966-67. Career: acct., office mgr. Scope Industries, Los Angeles 1957-72; partnership acctg. mgr. Shareholders Corp., Century City 1973-74; controller Scope Industries, Santa Monica 1975—; mem. Am. Soc. of Women Accts. 1975-; Democrat; Presbyterian; rec: oil painting, needlepoint, golf, travel. Ofc: Scope Industries 233 Wilshire Blvd Ste 790 Santa Monica 90401

SMITH, ELIZABETH MARTINEZ, county librarian; b. Apr. 14, 1943, Upland; d. Miguel Serrato and Venus (Espinoza) Martinez; m. Michael W. Smith, June 29, 1968; children: Nicolas b. 1973, Maya Maria, b. 1977; edn: BA, UCLA 1965, MLS, 1966. Career: intern Pomona Public Library, 1965; children's librarian Rosemead Regional Library, 1966; coordinator Way Out Project, Los Angeles County Public Lib., 1968; regional adminstr. Instns., L.A. County Public Lib., 1972, regl. adminstr., 1976-79; county librarian Orange County, 1979; lectr. Sch. of Library Sci., CSU Fullerton 1973-76; honors: George I. Sanchez Award 1976, Hispanic Women's Recognition Award 1982, League of United Latin Am. Citizens; mem: Calif. Library Assn. 1966-, Am. Library Assn. 1968-, Reforma, Nat. Assn. of Spanish Speaking Librarians, Mexican Am. Polit. Assn., AAUW; publs: var. library jours. 1972-80; Protestant. Res: Upland Ofc: Orange County Public Library, 431 City Dr South, Orange 92668

SMITH, GUY BATES, chiropractor; b. May 15, 1951, Bakersfield, Calif.; s. J.L. and Wilma R. (Williams) S.; m. Sharon DeCant, Sept. 20, 1975; children: Misty b. 1977, Ashleigh b. 1980, Garrett b. 1984; edn: AA, Taft Community Coll. 1971; CSU Fresno 1971-72; BS, L.A. Coll. of Chiro 1974, DC, 1976; lic. chiro. Calif. 1976, Mo. 1977, Ark. 1980; Diplomate Nat. Bd. Chiro. Examiners 1975. Career: assoc. chiro. Taft Chiro. Ofc. 1976-78; chiro. Smith Chiro. Ofc. Bakersfield 1978-82, certified independent med. examiner and certified disability evaluator 1982—; allied health profl. Blue Shield of Calif. 1985—; panel provider mem. Insurance and Prepaid Benefits Trust, Ins. Benefits Inc. Tustin 1982—, Membership Benefits Adminstrs. Granada Hills 1983—; referral panel mem. Bakersfield Family Med. Ctr. Bakersfield 1983—; component preferred provider panel mem. Found. for Med. Care of Kern County 1983—; mem. San Joaquin Indsl. Med. Assocs. Bakersfield; honors: Dean's List (L.A. coll. of Chiro. 1976); mem: Am. Chiro. Assn., Calif. Chiro. Assn., Kern Chiro. Soc., L.A. Coll. of Chiro. Alumni Assn., Delta Tau Alpha, Kiwanis, Kern County Child Abuse Prevention Council, March of Dimes, Youth for Christ; Democrat; Christian; rec: racquetball, camping, fishing, hunting, family activities. Ofc: Smith Chiropractic Ofc. 2417 G St Bakersfield 93301

SMITH, HAROLD HERBERT, JR., business owner; b. Sept. 24, 1930, Napa; s. Harold H., Sr. and Audrey Alma (Frost) S.; m. Gloria Jean Cowan, Dec. 26, 1953; children: Alan Bruce b. 1951, Laura Ann b. 1952; edn: grad. Napa H.S.

1948; var. courses USN Schs. Career: enlisted, served to chief petty ofcr. US Navy 1951-77, Food Service div., submarine sch. & service, ret. 1977, decorated Good Conduct Award (5), Korean Service, Vietnam Service, China Service, Nat. Defense, United Nation, Pres. Unit Cit.; prop. Smith's Vending, Vallejo 1978 – ; mem. Nat. Vending Assn., Calif. Vending Council, BBB, Nat. Fedn. Indep. Businessmen, Chamber of Commerce, US Naval Fleet Reserve; Republican (Pres. Task Force); Presbyterian. Res: 331 Mesa Verde Vallejo 94589 Ofc: Smith's Vending 237 Bennett St Vallejo 94590

SMITH, JEFFREY CARLIN, lawyer; b. Aug. 1, 1951, Chgo. Ill.; s. Robert Frederick and Marjorie Jean (Carlin) S.; m. Phyllis Barbara Stagias, Oct. 7, 1978; edn: BS, Lewis & Clark Coll. 1974; JD, UC Hastings Coll. of Law 1978; admitted Calif. State Bar, Calif. Supreme Ct., US Fed. Cts. 1979. Career: assoc. atty. Gibbons, Stoddard & McCann Walnut Creek 1978-81, Hyde & Drath S.F. 1982-85; senior staff counsel Times Mirror Co. L.A. 1985 – ; trustee Robt. L. Stevenson Sch.; dir. Pre Columbian Art Research Inst.; honors: Cum Laude Soc. 1970; mem. Am. Bar Assn.; Republican; rec: sailing. Res: 535 S Norton Ave Los Angeles 90020 Ofc: Times Mirror, Times Mirror Square Los Angeles 90053

SMITH, JERRY GUIDO EDWARD, sales/ marketing executive; b. April 3, 1942, Sturgis, Mich.; s. Robert Bennett Sr. and Leola Josephine (Shinavar) S.; edn: BA, Univ. of Ariz. 1975; MBA, Calif. Coast Univ. 1986. Career: mgr. Jay's Da-Nite Auto Supply, Tucson, Ariz. 1975-78; nat. salesmgr. TR-3 Chemical Corp., Orange 1978-80, v.p. sales 1980-81; pres. Executive Mgmt. Office, Clairmont 1981-82; senior v.p. Sunshine Makers Inc., Huntington Harbor 1982 – ; dir. Marved Realty, Tucson, Ariz. 1986; pres. EMO Sales & Mktg. Tng. & Sems.; honors: Spl. Congl. Advy. Bd. Membership Award; Distng. Sales Award, SME Internat. 1984, 1985; Cert. of Recogn., Nat. Republican Congl. Com. 1984; mem: Sales & Mktg. Execs. Internat., Am. Mktg. Assn., Am. Mgmt. Assn., Nat. Spkrs. Assn., U.S. Senatorial Club (Nat. Advy. Bd.); author: New Car Look, 1981; Back to Basics, 1982; The Management Team, 1984; Republican (Nat. Senatorial Com., Nat. Com., Calif. Party); Catholic; rec: gourmet cooking, tennis, diving. Res: 3602 Windspun Dr. Huntington Beach 92649 Ofc: Sunshine Makers Inc., 15922 Pacific Coast Hwy. Huntington Harbor 92649

SMITH, JOHN PHILIP, physician, b. Oct. 1, 1947, Dallas, Texas; s. Bernard J. and Julia Susan (Connolly) S.; m. Donna Marie Vitale, June 22, 1985; edn: BA, honors, UC Berkeley 1970; MD, UC Davis 1974; internal med. resident Univ. Mich., Ann Arbor 1974-77; fellowship in pulmonary med. Univ. Ariz., Tucson 1977-78, fellowship in cardiology, 1978-80; bd. certified cardiologist Am. Board of Internal Medicine 1978. Career: cardiologist in pvt. practice, Los Gatos 1980 – ; consulting cardiologist; mem. Am. Heart Assn. Speakers Bur., dir. AHA Physicians Edn. Council (Santa Clara Co.); honors: Phi Beta Kappa; mem: AMA, Calif. Med. Assn., Am. Heart Assn., Am. Coll. Cardiology, No. Am. Soc. Pacing, Am. Thoracic Soc., Am. C.C.P.; publs: Effect of a Monopoly Upon a Developing Economy; research articles on Diabetes and Fungal Infections; Catholic; rec: hiking, camping, music. Ofc: Cardiology Consultants 14981 National Ave, 2, Los Gatos 95030

SMITH, KERRY CLARK, lawyer; b. July 12, 1935, Phoenix, Ariz.; d. Clark and Fay (Jackson) Smith; m. Michael Waterman, 1958; children: Kevin b. 1964, Ian b. 1966; edn: AB, Stanford Univ. 1957, JD, 1962; admitted to Calif. State Bar (1962), US Supreme Ct. Career: atty., assoc. Chickering & Gregory, San Francisco 1962-70; assoc. 1970-81, ptnr. Pettit & Martin, 1981 – ; dir. Allied Properties (owner Clift Hotel and Santa Barbara Biltmore) 1974-77, corp. ofcr. Pebble Beach Corp. (owner golf courses) 1974-79; honors: Naval ROTC scholarship to Stanford Univ., bd. editors Stanford Law Review 1961-62; mem: Am. Bar Assn. (Sects. of Internat. Law, Corps., Banking & Bus.), Calif. Bar Assn. (Bus. Law Sect.), San Francisco Bar Assn., World Trade Club, Practising Law Inst.; clubs: University (S.F.), Orinda Country, La Quinta Hotel Golf & Tennis; mil: lt. USN; Republican; rec: tennis, golf, skiing. Ofc: Pettit & Martin 101 California St 35th Flr San Francisco 94111

SMITH, LELAND REX, telecommunications consultant; b. Sept. 25, 1951, Sioux City, Iowa; s. Rodney Ream and Beverly (Battey) S. Career: dir. telecommunications Pepperdine Univ., 1983-85; owner LRS Assocs., Beverly Hills 1985-86; co-owner CTCI (NEC Computer Distbr.), Ontario 1986 – . Res: 32 Thornton Ave #5 Venice 90291 Ofc: CTCI 4405 East Airport Dr Ontario 91761

SMITH, LYLE EDWARDS, postal civil service clerk, union ofcl., ret.; b. July 29, 1916, Grand Island, Nebr.; s. Dr. Lyle Dillon (D.C.) and Mary Jane (McConaughey) S.; m. J. Hope Howsmon Seeley, May 30, 1948; children: Holly Marie b. 1949, (stepdau.) Sandra Lee Seeley b. 1934; edn: courses Lincoln (Nebr.) Bus. Coll. 1936, Univ. of Nebr. 1936-37, VA Blind Rehab. Ctr. 1980. Career: torpedomans mate first class US Navy 1939-46, Pearl Harbor Submarine Base 1939-40, Submarine Base Torpedo Shop and Ammunition Depot, Cavite, Philippines, Battle of the Points (Bataan), with the 3d Bat. of 4th US Marines on Corregidor, prisoner of war (3-½ yrs); dept. hd. Montgomery Ward in Scottsbluff, Nebr. and Bakersfield, Calif. 1947-51; USPS Bakersfield mail carrier 1951-53, mail handler 1953-69, ret.; union v.p., pres. AFL-CIO Local #126 Mailhandlers, Watchman, Messengers and Group Leaders, 1959-69; recipient 5 USPS awards for beneficial suggestions (1959, 60, 61, 64, 65); commendn. letters for war service in combat from Pres. Harry Truman (1945) and US Secty. of Navy James Forestal (1946); mem: US Naval Inst., Blinded Vets. Assn. (life), Am. Defenders of Bataan and Corregidor (life), Disabled Am. Vets (life), Nat. Rifle Assn. (life), AARP, Masons, Scottish Rite, Shriners, Elks, Morro Bay Golf Club; mil. decorations: D.F.C., Disting. Unit

Cit. w/o.l.c., Pres. Unit Cit. w/star, Good Conduct, Am. Def. w/Base Clasp, Am. Theater, Asiatic-Pacific Theater, Victory WW2, Phil. Republic Pres. Unit Cit., Phil. Def.; rec: oil painting (past); Prot.; rec: genealogy, rock hounding on beach, stock market. Res: 1009 Loch Lomond Dr Bakersfield 93304

SMITH, MADELINE MARIE, entrepreneur; b. June 2, 1949, Los Angeles; d. Walter and Inez (Snyder) Franklin; m. Daryl Smith, Nov. 21, 1970; children: Ian b. 1974, Sean b. 1974; edn: Chaminade Coll., Hi. 1969; CSU Los Angeles 1972; Gemological Inst. of Am. 1979. Career: co-owner Mad House Enterprises, Los Angeles 1973-75; pres. Madeline Inc., Los Angeles 1975 – ; co-owner, designer Cameron & Assoc., Los Angeles 1983; co-owner DMS Florist, Santa Monica 1981 – ; v.p. DMS Bicycles, Los Angeles 1980 – ; owner Paper's Etc., Santa Monica 1982 – ; honors: Assoc., Pacoima Boys Club of Am.; mem: So. Calif. Floral Assn., NAACP, Nat. Fencing Assn., Capri Club of Am., U.S. Cycling Fedn., Soc. for Calligraphy; Democrat; Catholic; rec: aerobics, art, photog. Res: 1520 Princeton St. Apt. 6, Santa Monica 90404

SMITH, MARIAN MOORE, specialty store executive; b. Aug. 4, 1939, Forest City, N.C.; d. Dock Gardner and Ocie Adeline (McClure) Moore; div. 1973; children: Scott b. 1961, Susan b. 1963; edn: Ill. State Univ. 1957. Career: staff asst. to Dir. Employee Relations, Neiman-Marcus, Dallas 1973-74; exec. secty. to V.P. Personnel, Carter Hawley Hale Stores, Inc., Los Angeles 1974-75; staff asst. to V.P. Ops., Neiman-Marcus, Dallas 1975-76, mgr. Mdse. Packaging Systems, 1976-77, dir. Purch., 1977-81, ops. mgr. Neiman-Marcus, San Diego 1981-83, mdse. mgr. 1983-84, v.p./gen. mgr. 1984 – ; mem: Fashion Valley Mall Merchants Assn. (pres. 1986-89); civic: United Way of S.D., University Club, Women in Bus., The Country Friends, S.D. Mus. of Art, La Jolla Mus. Contemp. Art, La Jolla Playhouse; Republican; Episcopal; rec: needlework, quilting. Res: 3105 Elliott St San Diego 92106 Ofc: Neiman-Marcus 280 Fashion Valley San Diego 92108

SMITH, MYRON D, insurance executive; b. Oct. 29, 1954, Spokane, Wash.; s. Ben L. and Betty Jean (Decker) S.; edn: BA, Coll. of the Holy Names 1977; Certified Financial Planner. Career: ins. agent Conn. Mutual Lif. 1975-78; sales mgr. John Hancock Cos., Los Angeles 1980-81; owner Genesis Finl. (personal and bus. finl. planning and ins. services) 1978 – ; v.p. mktg. West Coast Ins. Mktg. Corp., 1982-84; awards: Harry S. Truman Scholarship (1977), citizenship award Wash. State House of Reps. (1971), Outstanding student of year Spokane Comm. Coll. (1976), state chmn. Council of Reps. & Pres.- Wash. State, exec. v.p. Assoc. Students, Spokane Comm. Coll. (1975); mem: US Pacific Council (bd. 1983), San Fernando Valley Life Underwriters Assn. (dir./v.p. communs. 1982-84), SSGLC, Proj. Rainbow (dir./pres. 1983-), Los Angeles Council on Aging (1985), Internat. Assn. of Finl. Planners (1985), Los Angeles Health Underwriter Assn. (dir. 1983-); num. arts. on health maintenance orgns.; ed. Valley View Mag.; mil: NG and US Army, Nat. Svc. Awd.; Republican (nom. for House of Reps., Wash. 1978); Catholic; rec: hobie cat sailing. Res: 7230 Kelvin Ave, 17, Canoga Park 91306 Ofc: Genesis Financial, 4605 Lankershim Blvd Ste 100 North Hollywood 91602

SMITH, NORMAN HENRY, insurance executive; b. Jan. 26, 1937, St. Louis, Mo.; s. Norman Joseph and Helen Ann (Wiedey) S.; m. Susan Sommerfeld, Oct. 5, 1968; children: Carson b. 1977, William b. 1979; edn: Bach. Gen. Eng., Univ. of Ill. 1960, MBA, honors, 1965; lic. Insurance Adminstr., Surplus Lines, Broker & Agent Calif. State Dept. of Ins. 1972-. Career: sales mgr. Uniroyal in NY, NY and Southbend, Ind., 1965-70; mgmt. cons. Craig, Cutten in Oakland, Ca. 1970-72; sales trainee Travelers Insurance, San Francisco 1972-75; current: pres./owner Capital Workshop Finl. & Ins. Services, S.F. and Los Angeles; pres./owner Capital Workshop Gen. Insurance Agency, S.F., 1975 – ; instr. Depts. of Engring. and Mgmt., Univ. Ill. 1963-65; honors: Monticello (Ill.) H.S. Valedictorian 1955; Ma-Wan-Da, 1959, Sachem, 1957 (activity honors); Western Regl. sales leader, Travelers 1975; mem: IIAA, 1975-80, PIA, 1975-83, WAIB, 1980-83; mem: Sierra Club, Snowmobilers (Bear Valley), Homeowners Assn. (Bear Valley); author and underwriting mgr. Oxford Lawyers Profl. Liability Policy (1983); var. pub. articles on legal malpractice; mil: lt. jg USN 1960-63; Republican. Res: 2400 Paradise Dr Tiburon 94920 Ofc: Capital Workshop, 550 California St, Ste. 1130, San Francisco 94104

SMITH, PAUL CHARLES, surgeon; b. May 2, 1940, Southampton, UK; s. Charles George and Beatrice Sarah (Meridew) S.; m. Claire Hunter, May 18, 1968; children: Michelle b. 1969, Julien b. 1971, Carolyn b. 1976, Anne-Lise b. 1979; edn: MD, Guy's Hosp. London Univ. 1965; Career: house surgeon Royal Surrey Hosp. 1965-66; senior house ofcr. cardiac surg. Guy's Hosp. 1966; asst. lectr. anatomy dept. St. Mary's Hosp. 1966-67; senior house ofcr. gen. surg. Bristol Royal Infirmary 1968-70; surgical registrar St. James Hosp. 1970-72; senior surg. registrar Guy's Hosp. 1972-75; research fllow surg. Harvard Med. Sch. and Beth Israel Hosp. Boston 1974-75; surg. staff Androscoggin Valley Hosp. Berlin, NH 1975-81, dir. contg. med. edn. 1978, pres. med. staff 1979; acting chief of surg., chmn. surg. dept. Highland Gen. Hosp. 1981-82; affil hosps. 1981 – : Alta Bates & Herrick Hosps. Berkeley, Highland Gen., Peralta, Providence and Samuel Merritt Hosps. Oakland; founder, pres. Hill physicians Med. Group Oakland; chmn. Hill Health Care Corp. Oakland; fellow Royal Coll. of Surg. England 1970; mem. East Bay Surg. Soc. (exec. com.); presentations East Bay Surg. Soc.; publs. in med. jours. Address: 3120 Webster St Oakland 94609

SMITH, ROBERT BERNARD, petroleum distributor; b. Oct. 13, 1923, Anaheim; s. Meyer B. and Wilhelmina Gazena (Heighsuseu) S.; m. Erma Jone, May 18, 1945; children: Robert Micheal b. 1948, Kathren Robin b. 1950; edn: att. Ventura Jr. Coll., N.Mex. Univ., St. Marys Univ./S.F., Oklahoma Univ.,

1942-44. Career: worked in oil fields on the rig, then service engr./supr. McCullough Tool Co., 8 yrs.; oil jobber Conoco 1957-, distbr. Texaco-Conoco 1958-, distbr. Exxon-Texaco-Conoco 1978-; owner Bob Smith Oil Co., Hondo Oil Co., Kwick Serve Co.; mem. Am. Legion, Masons; mil: US Navy Air Corps, USMC (Black Sheep Sq. #214); Republican (Task Force); Lutheran; rec: hunting, fishing. Res: 3116 Solimar Beach Ventura 93001 Ofc: Hondo Oil Co, POB 5191 Ventura 93003-0191

SMITH, RONALD CHARLES, psychiatrist, neurologist; b. Feb. 9, 1939, Des Moines, Iowa; s. Stanley Reginald and Dorothy Alys (Darner) S,; m. Orfilda Crawford, Sept. 12, 1984; children: Ronald, Jr. b. 1964, Sara b. 1965, Patrick b. 1967, Scott b. 1970, Roxanne b. 1973, Carolyn b. 1977, Dorothy b. 1981; edn: BA, Univ. of Minn. 1958, BS, 1960, MD, 1961; bd. certified Am. Bd. of Psychiat. and Neurol. 1976. Career: asst. supt. Metropol. State Hosp. Norwalk, Calif. 1971-72; dir. Pomona Valley Neuropsychiatric Ctr. 1972-78; staff psychiat. US Navy Submarine Med. Ctr. 1978-81; dir. psychiat. St. James Mercy Hosp. Hornell N.Y. 1981-83; pvt. practice psychiat. & neurol., assoc. clin. prof. psychiat. USC Sch. of Med. 1971–; instr. Univ. Ibaden Med. Sch. Nigeria, Africa 1974; honors: Gold Medal (World Congress od Psychiatry 1972), Bronze Medal (Am. Acad. Fam. Practice 1973), Gold Medal (N.Y. Film Festival 1973), chmn. VI World Congress of Psychiatry 1976; mem: AMA, Undersea Med. Soc. 1973-; publ: num. papers on biochem. of mental illness and psychopharmacologic research; mil: cdr. USN (MC) 1971-81; Protestant; rec: scuba diving, diving med. Res: 1702 Lake St Huntington Beach 92648

SMITH, SHERMAN U., environmental scientist; b. July 15, 1947, Burlington, Iowa; s. Sherman Allen and Mary Elizabeth (Uhler) S.; edn: BA, Monmouth Coll. 1972; MS, environmental health/ preventive medicine, Univ. Iowa 1973, postgrad. in environ. mgmt. Univ. Iowa 1974, Governors State Univ. 1975-77; Certified Environmental Profl. Career: staff, Cong. Ed Mezvinsky, 1973-74; environmental planner H.W. Lochner, Inc. 1974-76; supr. Environ. Svcs. Dept., Fluor Power Services, Inc. 1976-78; project mgr./mktg. mgr. Camp, Dresser & McKee, Inc. 1978; proj. mgr./ mktg. mgr. Wapora Inc. 1978-80; dir. Environmental Services Dept., Fluor Corp., 1980-86; mgr. Intellus Corp. 1986–; vis. lectr. UC Irvine, Univ. of Iowa, Iowa St. Univ., Univ. S.C., Governors St. Univ.; honors: Blue Key, Nat. Student Register, Monmouth Coll. Outstanding Grad. Senior Man; mem: Nat. Assn. Environ. Profls. (co-founder Great Lakes Chpt., bd. dirs.), Ill. Assn. of Environ. Profls. (co-founder, bd. dirs.), Inst. Environ. Scis., Effects Assessment Com. (nat. com. chmn. 2 yrs.), Environ. Effects Assessment Session (chmn. Tech. Effects 2 yrs.), Air Pollution Control Assn.; publs: 24+ profl. articles, papers. Res: 3 Springwood Irvine 92714 Ofc: Intellus Corp. 3355 Michelson Dr Irvine 92715

SMITH, STANLEY DAVID, lawyer; b. Apr. 12, 1935, Los Angeles; s. Samuel Joseph and Edna (Bridge) S.; m. Natalie Cailingold, July 11, 1964; children: Samantha b. 1968, Joshuad, b. 1971; edn: UCLA 1952-55; LLB, Southwestern Univ. 1964. Career: claims mgr. General Ins. Co. of Am. (now SAFECO) 1960-65; lawyer, sr. mng. partner, firm of Kinkle, Rodiger and Spriggs, San Diego Ofc. 1965–; prof. of law Southwestern Univ. 1965-70; instr. first law school course in med. malpractice in state of Calif. (Southwestern Univ. 1973); judge pro tem, Orange Co. Superior Ct 1977–; awards: Resolution of Cmmdn. for outstanding achievement as Judge Pro Tem, Orage Co. Bd. Supvrs. 1977; mem: State Bar of Calif.; Am., Orange Co., and San Diego Co. Bar Assns.; Town Hall; Am. Jurisprudence Soc.; mil: USNR 1952-60, active duty 1958-60; Democrat; rec: tennis, swimming, surfing. Res: 512 Santa Carina Solana Beach 92075 Ofc: Kinkle, Rodiger & Spriggs, 1620 Fifth Ave Ste 700 San Diego 92101

SMITH, STEPHANIE ANN, lawyer; b. Apr. 20, 1938, NYC, NY; d. Paul Reon and Helene Joan (Leszczynski) Barnes; m. Jon L. Smith, May 11, 1963; children: Andrea Joan b. 1965, Amy Eileen b. 1967, Adam Paul b. 1972; edn: BS, Mich. State Univ. 1960, BS in Laws, Peninsula Univ. Coll. of Law 1981, JD, 1983; admitted Calif. State Bar 1983. Career: counselor Detroit House of Corrections, 1959; store detective Emporium, San Francisco 1960-61; deputy probation ofcr. Alameda County, 1961-65; full-time mother 1965-83; atty. sole practitioner, 1983–; mem: Am., Calif. bar assns., Barristers Club of Sacramento (bd. dirs. 1984-), Calif. Trial Lawyers Assn., Women Lawyers Assn., Mensa Soc.; civic: Citizens Involvement Assn., San Carlos (pres. 1970-77); Com. for the Housing Element, City of San Carlos (chair 1975); Town Hall Assn., San Mateo (bd. dirs. 1974-75); Democrat; Humanist; rec: yodeling, music (play guitar, piano, trumpet). Law Ofc: Stephanie A. Smith, 7956 California Ave Fair Oaks 95628

SMITH, STEPHEN, RANDOLPH, aerospace co. executive; b. April 17, 1928, Des Moines, Iowa; s. Norvin Ellis and Helen (Heberling) S.; m. Maragaret Graves, Dec. 20, 1950; children: Stephen Jr. b. 1953, Susan b. 1955, Sara b. 1957, Anne b. 1959, Julia b. 1962; edn: BSME, Stanford Univ. 1951, MSME, 1952; adv. mgmt. pgm., Harvard Grad. Sch. of Bus. 1974; Reg. Profl. Mech. Engr., Calif. 1952. Career: Northrop Corp. Aircraft Div. 1955–; var. engring. and pgm. mgmt. pos. 1955-68; F-5IFA Program Mgr. 1968-72; dir. F-5 Adv. Devel., Hawthorne 1972-75; v.p. Iran ops., Tehran, Iran 1975-78; v.p. adv. projects, Hawthorne 1978-83; v.p. engring. and adv. devel., Hawthorne 1983–; cons. NASA Adv. Aeronautics Com. 1984-; invited lectr. aircraft design US Air Force Acad. 1983; awarded the DOD Disting. Civilian Service Medal (1983); mem: Fellow Am. Inst. of Aero. & Astro. (chmn. Los Angeles sect. 1985-86), SAE, Am. Soc. Mech. Engrs., ARS, Trailfinders (Conservation Council), Friars Club/ Usher (St. Francis Ch.), Am. Youth Soccer Orgn. (coach, linesman), Centinela Hosp. (adv. bd.), Boy Scouts of Am. (scoutmaster); works: classified Dept. of Defense projects spec. low observables technology; mil: sgt. US Army 1946-48; rec: sailing, skiing, tennis. Res: 2249 Via Guadalana Palos Verdes Estates 90274 Ofc: Northrop Corp Aircraft Div., One Nortrop Ave. Hawthorne 90250

SMITH, STEPHEN LEROY, manufacturing co. executive; b. Dec. 5, 1949, CoCo Solo, Panama; s. Francis LaVern and Edna Lorraine (Nedrow) S.; chidren: Stephen Jr. b. 1971, Jennifer b. 1972; CSU Sacramento 1968-72. Career: with Nationwide Wire & Brush Mfg. Inc. 1970–; mgmt. trainee 1970-72; sales rep. 1972-77; prodn. mgr. 1977-83; v.p., gen. mgr. 1983–; bd. dirs. 1970–; mem: West Coast Broom Mfg. Assn., Maintenance Supt. Asoc. (Vendor rep.), Elks, Nat. CofC, Lodi CofC, Citizens for America (14th Congl. dist.); works: dir. product research & devel.; mil: splst. 4/c Calif. National Guard 1970-76, Outstanding Svc., Outstanding Unit; Republican; rec: golf, fishing, photog. Res: 1301 West Lodi Ave. Apt. 210 Lodi 95240 Ofc: Nationwide Wire & Brush Mfg. Inc, P.O. Box 258 Lodi 95241

SMITH, STEVEN SIDNEY, molecular biologist; b. Feb. 11, 1946, Idaho Falls, Ida.; s. Sidney Ervin and Hermie Phyllis (Robertson) S.; m. Nancy, Dec. 20, 1974; edn: BS zool., Univ. of Ida. 1968; PhD molecular biol., UC Los Angeles 1974. Career: lectr. molecular biol. Univ. of Bern, Switz.; research assoc. Scripps Clinic and Research Found., La Jolla; asst. research scientist (molecular biol.) City of Hope Nat. Medical Ctr., Duarte and full mem. City of Hope Cancer Center, 1982–; cons. Molecular Biosystems Inc. 1981-84; honors: Phi Beta Kappa (1968), Outstanding Undergrad. in Biol., Univ. of Idaho (1968), USPHS Pre-doctoral Trainee (1968-73), Postdoc. Fellow Swiss Nat. Sci. Found. (1974-77), Postdoc. Fellow NIH (1979-81), NIH grantee (1983-), Council for Tobacco Research USA Inc. grantee (1983-); mem. AAAS, New York Acad. of Scis., Am. Soc. for Cell Biol., Pacific Slopes Biochem. Soc., Swiss Union for Exptl. Biol.; publs: 28+ sci. articles and abstracts; Republican; rec: guitar, wt.lifting. Ofc: City of Hope Medical Center 1500 E Duarte Rd Duarte 91010

SMITH, THOMAS J.R., real estate broker, ret.; b. May 10, 1909, Phila.; s. Leroy K. and Adele (Connor) S.; m. Edna M. Schumacher, Apr. 14, 1947. Career: Texaco dealer, Point Loma, 1949-59; real estate broker, 1959-79; founding mem. San Diego Dist. Tennis Assn., local rep. of U.S.T.A. and of So. Calif. Tennis Assn. (exec. com. 5 yrs., treas. 1983-); founding mem. S.D. County Tennis Umpires' Assn. (past tchr. Umpires' classes, exec. com.; hon. life mem.); mem. Apt. & Rental Owners Assn. (24 yrs), San Diego Bd. Realtors (15 yrs.); civic: Peninsulans, Inc. Pt. Loma plnng. gp. (founder, exec. bd. 5 yrs.); Ocean Beach CofC (v.p., bd. dirs. 6 yrs.; awarded Citizen of Year 1971; Pt. Loma rep. on Citizens for Better Bus Service com. which created the present City Bus System); Balboa Tennis Club (past pres., hon. life mem. 1983); Peninsula Lions Club (1949-, past pres., dist. bd. govs.); active in community projects to extend S.D. Municipal Pier, to acquire all beach front in Ocean Beach as a City Park, and Sunset Cliff Beach Erosion Project; Republican; rec: tennis, aid to the blind. Res: 4815 Orchard Ave San Diego 92107

SMITH, WALTER, corporate executive; b. May 18, 1935, Glasgow, Scotland; s. Walter and Elizabeth (Brown) S.; m. Margaret Julie, Feb. 18, 1983; edn: O.N.C. mech. eng. Stow Coll. 1960, H.N.C. mech. eng., Glasgow H.S. 1966. Calif. Reg. Profl. Engr., lic. Contr. Career: chief exec. Capper Neill Group (worldwide export sales) 1976, (steel prods.) 1977-80; v.p. mfg. K.T.I. Inc., Pasadena 1980-82, dir. mfg. U.S. Divs. 1983, bd. chmn. G.P.I. Brea (K.T.I. Group) 1983; senior v.p./gen. mgr. Modular Products Inc., Brea 1983–; mem. Process Plant Assn., U.K. (1976-80); rec: tennis, golf, swim. Res: 1720 Harvest Ln Brea 92621 Ofc: Modular Products Inc. 404 N Berry St Brea 92621

SMITH, WILLIAM RAY, engineer; b. June 26, 1925, Lyman, Okla.; s. Harry Wait and Daisy Bell (Hull) S.; edn: BA, Bethany Nazarene Coll. 1948; MA, Wichita State Univ. 1950; Univ. of Kans. 1950-51; PhD, UCLA 1967. Career: structures engr. Beach Aircraft Corp., Wichita, KS 1951-53; sr. gp. engr. McDonnell Aircraft, St. Louis, MO 1953-60; sr. engr. Lockheed Aircraft, Burbank 1961-63; sr. engr. sci. McDonnell Douglas Corp., Long Beach 1966-71; mem. tech. staff Rockwell Internat., Los Angeles 1973–; tchr. Pasadena Coll., Pt. Loma 1960-62; Glendale Jr. Coll. 1972; Mt. St. mary's Coll. 1972-73; honors: Citation for Profl. Achievement, McDonnell Douglas Corp. 1968; Tech. Utilization Awd., Rockwell Internat. 1981; NASA Cert. of Recogn. 1982; mem: NY Acad. of Scis.; AAAS; Inst. of Aero. and Astro.; life mem. Yosemite Nat. Hist. Assn.; Town Hall; UCLA Chancellor's Assocs.; Sigma Xi; Pi Mu Epsilon; Delta Epsilon; tech. publs. 1969, 1981; Republican; Presbyterian; rec: sailing. Res: 2405 Roscomare Rd Los Angeles 90077 Ofc: Rockwell Internat. Corp., 201 No Douglas El Segundo 90245

SMITH-BERNSTEIN, MARILYN CHARLOTTE, designer, photographer; b. July 22, 1946, Bellingham, Wash.; d. James G. and Lois M. (Leypoldt) Smith; m. Harold M. Bernstein, May 21, 1983; edn: AA art, Foothill Coll. 1973; BS graphic design, San Jose State Univ. 1978. Career: illustrator Hewlett Packard 1966-71; drafter Smith Corona 1972-73; designer Lead JCE Calculators 1973-74; designer Lead Kirk Meyer 1974-75; art dir. Gnostic Concepts 1974-79; owner River Graphics 1977–, co-founder ECOsphere Press 1980; mapper, researcher US Geol. Survey 1980–; map cons. Pete McCloskey; cons./ book design Coastlight Press 1980-; news photog. Wounded Knee; arctic geol. research by ship Nome, Alaska- north 1980, 82; mem: Am. Fuschia Soc. (chpt. bd.), Westwind 4-H Riding for Handicapped, Sportsmen for Equal Access, Calif. Wildlife Fedn.; publs: Map I-1182-D, Dept. of the Interior USGS, Bathymetric Map of the Chukchi Sea by Edwin R. Hill, Arthur Grantz, Steven C. May and Marilyn Smith; Democrat; rec: fishing, hunting, horticulture (fuschias). Ofc: River Graphics 405 High St Palo Alto 94301

SMITS, WILLIAM H., JR., govt. counterintelligence special agent; b. Jan. 25, 1937, Bklyn.; s. Wm. H., Sr. and Anna Elizabeth (Croswell) S.; m. Joan Mary Tipp, July 7, 1973; children: Steffanie b. 1961, Mark b. 1964, Trevor b. 1979, Jacqueline b. 1981; edn: BA in Russian language, Univ. of Colo. 1963; MPA, Golden Gate Univ. 1982, PhD in pub. adm., 1986. Career: FBI agent, 1963–, tours in Phila., Wash DC, West Germany and San Francisco; splst. in Soviet Fgn. Counterintelligence (FCI) work; instr. in Russian language, FBI HQ Washington 1965-68; asst. legal attache Am. Embassy, Bonn, W. Ger. 1970, assigned to San Francisco 1972-, supvsy. spl. agent in charge of Soviet FCI pgm., S.F. 1980–; mgmt. cons. FBI, 1985-86; FAA Pilot Examiner (for pvt., comml., instrument & multi-engine licenses) 1979-84; honors: outstanding grad. Golden Gate Univ. Grad. Sch. of Public Adminstrn. (1982), FBI exceptional performance awards (1983, 84, 85), Samuel C. May research paper award (1985); mem. Am. Soc. of Public Adminstrn.; publs: 4 articles in Internat. Personnel Mgmt. Assn. J., Internat. J. of Public Adminstrn., Am. Rev. of P.A., Technol. in Soc.; mil: sp5 US Army 1957-60, Good Conduct Medal; Republican; Catholic; rec: pvt. pilot, chess. Res: 561 Bernice Ln Martinez 94553 Ofc: FBI 450 Golden Gate Ave San Francisco 94102

SMOLEN, ALFRED MERCER, consulting mechanical engineer; b. July 11, 1917, NY, NY; s. Henry Edward and Anna Adelaide (Courtney) S.; m. Edna Earl Green, Apr. 9, 1943; 1 son, Stephen A. b. 1944; edn: Mich. State Coll.; Univ. So. Calif.; UC Los Angeles; Reg. Profl. Mech. Engr. Calif. Career: chief engr. Nat. Tank & Mfg. Co. L.A. 1953-58, Lacy Mfg. Co. L.A. 1958-67; senior engr. C.F. Braun & Co. Alhambra 1967-74; senior tech. splst. Fluor Engrs. Inc. Irvine 1974-85; cons. mech. engr., chmn. tech. resources group Swanson Svc. Corp. Huntington Beach 1983–; honors: ASME Centennial Award (1980), Engr. of the Month (L.A. Council of Engrs. & Scientists (1974); fellow Am. Soc. Mech. Engrs. (chmn. L.A. sect. 1973-74), Inst. for Advancement of Engrg.; mem: Am. Welding Soc., Am. Concrete Inst., US Metric Assn. (Certified Advanced Metrication Splst.), Nat. Soc. Profl. Engrs. (Profl. Engr. in Pvt. Practice), San Juan Hills CC, Hon. Order of Kentucky Colonels; publ: tech. paper, Making It With Metric (Nat. Bd. Boiler & Pressure Vessel Inspectors (1985); Republican; Episcopal; rec: golf. Res: 2810B Camino Capistrano San Clemente 92672 Ofc: Swanson Svc. Corp. 18090 Beach Blvd Huntington Beach 92648

SMOLKER, GARY STEVEN, lawyer; b. Nov. 5, 1945, Los Angeles; s. Paul and Shayndy (Charolette) (Sirott) S.; 1 child, Terra b. 1071; edn: BS, Univ. Calif. 1967; MS, Cornell Univ. 1968; JD, cum laude, Loyola Univ. 1973. Career: mem. tech. staff Hughes Aircraft Co., Culver City 1968-70; Advanced Mktg. & Tech., TRW, Redondo Beach 1970-72; Law Ofcs. Gary Smolker, Beverly Hills 1973–; guest lectr. UCLA Ext. 1973, 74, Loyola Law Sch. 1979; contbg. editor Beverly Hills Bar Assn. Journ. 1980–, sr. ed. 1978; panelist & spkr. Innovative Financing Session, Calif. Escrow Assn. Annual Edn. Conf. 1981; speaker var. orgns. on Son of Rent Control, 1981; awards: Palm Springs Sci. Fair 1963; guest researcher Lawrence Radiation Lab, UC 1967; tchg. fellowship Sch. of Chem. Engring., Cornell Univ. 1968; US Patent, Self-Destruct Aluminum Tungstic Oxide Films, USN 1972; US Patent, Electrolytic Anticompromise Process, Hughes Aircraft 1973; Research Div. Invention Awd., Hughes Aircraft; mem: Calif. State, L.A. Co., Beverly Hills & Am. Bar Assns.; Assn. of Real Estate Attys.; Anti- Defamation League of B'nai B'rith; Guardian, Jewish Home for the Aged; Nat. Audubon Soc.; Advoc. Loyola Law Sch.; NY Metropolitan Mus. of Art.; num. publs. in field incl: Inclusionary Housing: A Wrong Approach (1981); Unenforceability of Personal Guarantees (1984); Unreal Truth and a Leaky Roof (1984); An Opinion About the Dire Finl. Impact of the Earthquake Law (1984); Providing Shelter for the Homeless (1984); How to Structure a Joint Venture (1985); Republican; Jewish; rec: writing. Res: 15 63rd Ave Playa del Rey 90291 Law Ofcs. of Gary Smolker, 361 No Canon Dr Beverly Hills 90210

SNELL, KENNETH LEE, business college administrator; b. Nov. 30, 1949, Warren, Ohio; s. Robert Lee and Anna Mae (Winchell) S.; m. Debra, Nov. 29, 1983; children: Dannielle, Joshua, Thea; edn: BS in bus. CSU Fullerton 1971, MS in counseling, 1973; MA ednl. adminstrn., CSU Sacto. 1979; MBA human resources, National Univ. 1980. Career: asst. personnel dir. Auburn Faith Community Hosp.; prof. Univ. of San Francisco, 1981-, instr. Am. River Coll. 1979-, Sierra Coll. 1981-; cons./dir. Sierra Bus. Coll. 1979–; asst. dir. Grant Adult & Community Edn. 1977-79; cons. Solano Coll.; awards: Man of Year, Applegate (1985), academic scholarship, Sierra Coll. (1985); mem. Calif. Hosp. Personnel Mgr. Assn.; civic: Solano Co. Juvenile Justice Delinquency Prev. Commn. (co-chmn.), Nat. Ski Patrol, Lions Intl., Big Brothers & Big Sisters, Polar Bear Dippers, Applegate Civic Ctr. Club, Sierra Vista Homeowners Assn.; Republican; Christian; rec: skiing, hiking, constrn. Ofc: Sierra Business College POB 356 Applegate 95703

SNIADOWSKI, THERESA ANNE MARIE, pediatrician; b. Aug. 7, 1955, NYC, NY; s. Frank Stanley and Mary Dorothea (Podlubny) S.; m. Steven F. Bombola, Apr. 26, 1986; edn: BS, summa cum laude, Fordham Univ. 1975; MD, State Univ. of NY 1979. Diplomate Am. Board of Pediatrics (1986). Career: pediatric res. Cedars Sinai Med. Ctr., Los Angeles 1979-82; p.t. pediatric emerg. rm. phys. LAC-USC Med. Ctr., Los Angeles 1980-82; p.t. clin. phys. Juvenile Hall, L.A. Co. 1980-82; phys. Pain Inst., L.A. 1981–; staff pediatrician (tenured staff 1985) Cigna Health Plans, Santa Ana 1982–; med. cons. Media Design West 1981; expert. med. cons. D. J. Westhoff Esq. 1982-84; clin. instr. to res. staff Choc Hosp. 1982-; use of nerve stimulation in a clinic situation for treatment of pain in disease 1981; Engle Alumni Scholarship; mem: Am. Acad. of Pediatrics (jr. fellow), The Flying Samaritans; works: biochem. research in Dihydroxy Phenyl Acetic Acids in Neurotransmitter Metabolism,

Fordham Univ. 1973-74; surgical research in Splenic Reimplantation in Omentum After Trauma, Dr. F. Velcek 1977; Republican; Catholic; rec: equitation, skiing, dancing. Ofc: Cigna Health Plans of Calif. 2435 No. Grand Ave., Santa Ana 92701

SNOW, BECKY (REBECCA) H., real estate broker; b. Nov. 20, Donalsonville, GA; d. John R. and Frances Jenelle (Linday) Hornsby (dec.); m. Gordon E. Snow, Aug. 29, 1958; children: Jenelle b. 1959, Misty b. 1964, Gordon, Jr. b. 1968; edn: Coll. of the Redwoods 1965, Ventura Coll. 1972, Oxnard Coll. 1981; GRI, Grad. Realtors Inst. 1976. Career: US Civil Svc. employee 1960-70; broker/pres. Snow Real Estate 1973–, real estate exchanger/cons.; sponsor tax seminars related to real estate 1978; guest spkr. coll. salesmanship classes; awards: Beneficial Suggestion award US Civil Svc. (1967), Excellence Svc., Client Follow-up Pgm. (1980); mem: Nat. Bd. Realtors, Calif. Bd. Realtors, Oxnard Harbor Bd. of Realtors (past pres. Women's Council of Realtors), Oxnard Harbor & Camarillo Multiple Listing Svcs., Central Coast Exchangers, Nat. Council of Exchangers Gold Card holder, Channel Is. Toastmistress Club (past); publs: contbr. Real Estate Today; author/ prod. The Golden Rule (a R.E. play 1977); Democrat; Baptist; rec: golf, football, baseball. Res: 1702 Ramona Dr Camarillo 93010 Ofc: Snow Real Estate, 2222 Saviers Oxnard 93033

SNOWDEN, FRED, franchise development executive; b. Apr. 3, 1936, Brewton, Ala.; s. Buren and Julia (Johnson) S.; m. Maya; children: Charles b. 1953, Stacey b. 1963; edn: BS, Wayne State Univ. 1958, M.Ed. 1965. Career: educator/ coach, Northwestern H.Sch., Detroit 1958-68; asst. basketball coach Univ. of Mich., Ann Arbor 1968-72; head basketball coach Univ. Ariz. 1972-82; bus. devel. cons./ pres. Fred Snowden Inc., 1982-85; v.p. Urban Affairs & Devel., Baskin Robbins Ice Cream, Glendale 1985–; dir. Fred Snowden Summer Basketball Camp for Boys, 1972–; T.V. bdcstg. host (Ch. 11 KZAZ, Tucson) The Fred Snowden Show (sports talk) 1976-82, and Coaches Corner (20 min. basketball aftergame talk) 1972-82, taped comml. spots for Tucson local T.V. stations for Goodyear Tire Co. and Serta Mattress Co., 1972-79; nat. coll. basketball bdcstr. Mutual Nat. Bdcstg. Systems 1982; T.V. interviews, and radio aftergame interview show, Ann Arbor 1968-71, On Air sportscaster (6:00 and 11:00 news, WJBK-TV 2), Southfield, Mich. 1970-72; awards: Coach of the Decade, Ariz. Daily Star (1980), "Fred Snowden Day" in City of Detroit and Resolutions, Mayor, City Council and Mich. Legislature (Dec. 19, 1976-77), Tucson Man of Year, Tucson Exchange Club (1973-74), Coach of Year, NCAA Dist. 7, also Western Athletic Conf. (1972-73), apptd. by Pres. Nixon to Enviornmental Merit Awards Commn. (1972); mem. Nat. Assn. Basketball Coaches of U.S. (1972-), Mich. Fedn. of Tchrs. (1958-72); active in sports and church youth activities; adv. bd. Mayor's Challenge for Youth/L.A. (1985), bd. dirs. Challenger Boys and Girls Club/L.A. (1984), 88 Crime Bd. Dirs./Tucson (1982); Lutheran. Ofc: Baskin Robbins Ice Cream 31 Baskin Robbins Pl Glendale 91201

SNYDER, JOHN JOSEPH, optometrist; b. June 30, 1908, Wonewoc, Wisc.; s. Burt Frederick and Alta Lavinia (Hearn) S.; edn: AB, honors, UCLA 1931, post grad. 1931-32; post grad. Univ. of Colo. 1936, 1938, 1940, 1941; post grad., USC, p.t. 1945-47; BS, Los Angeles Coll. of Optometry 1948, OD, 1949. Career: tchr. Rockvale Jr. Sch. and Mayday Sch., La Plata Co., Colo. 1927-28; supt. pub. schs., h.s. tchr. Marvel, Colo. 1932-33; tchr. biology, physics, chemistry, Durango, Colo. 1933-41; optometrist self-empl., Los Angeles 1952-72, Torrance 1972-78; vacation and relief optometrist 1979–; mem: Fellow Internat. Biographical Assn., Am. Assn. for Adv. Science, Am. Inst. of Biological Sciences, Nat. Eye Research Found., Am. and Calif. Optometric Assns., Los Angeles Co. Optometric Soc., The Exch. Club of So. Los Angeles (pres. 1957, secty. 1962), Francia Boys Club (bd. dirs., Los Angeles 1956-64); Republican; rec: fishing, limnology. Address: 735 Luring Dr. Glendale 91206

SNYDER, MARY ETTA, investments co. owner, real estate broker; b. May 25, 1934, San Antonio, Tex.; d. George William and Nannie Viola (Livingston) Wehling; m. Robert L. Snyder, Mar. 13, 1955; children: Kerry b. 1955, Ronald b. 1957, Michael b. 1960, Patrick b. 1962, Kathy b. 1967; edn: AA, Mendocino Coll. 1984; BA cum laude, Sonoma State Univ. 1986; Career: self-employed realtor, investments 1965–; co-owner, oper. Pomolita Apts. Ukiah, 80-acre vineyard south of Ukiah; sold first condominiums in Ukiah, devel. CC&Rs, public report, documents necessary for State Subdivision Map Act; mem. Mendocino County Grand Jury 1975-76, chair audit/ finance com.; helped enact smoking ordinance Ukiah 1981, locate Calif. Nat. Guard in Ukiah; elected city council 1977-82, mayor 1979-80; rep. League of Calif. Cities 1977-82, Calif. Solar Utility Devel. Agcy.; commr. No. Calif. Power Agcy. 1977-78; Republican; Catholic; rec: tennis, gardening, politics. Address: Ukiah 95482

SNYDER, MICHAEL ALLEN, editor, writer, PR practitioner; b. June 23, 1954, Washington, Ind.; s. John Keith and Stella Mae (Eads) S.; m. Cynthia, May 20, 1978; edn: Vincennes Univ. 1972-74; Indiana Univ. 1978-79; BA, honors, Ambassador Coll. 1982; MBA cand, CSU Los Angeles 1983-; Accredited in Pub. Rels., Pub. Rels. Soc. of Am. 1986. Career: prodn. dir. KBAC-Radio (AM), Pasadena 1977-78; pub. rels. cons. Indiana Dept. of Public Instruction, Statehouse, Indianapolis, Ind. 1978-79; news ed., Worldwide News, Pasadena 1979-86; senior writer Plain Truth mag., Pasadena 1982–; asst. dir. of pub. affairs Worldwide Ch. of God 1986–; freelance writer; honors: Best Newspaper, Internat. Assn. of Bus. Communicators, Los Angeles chpt. 1981; mem: Public Rels. Soc. of Am., Los Angeles Press Club, Publicity Club of Los Angeles, Soc. of Profl. Journalists; works: 300+ publd. works 1978-; Ch. of God; rec: non-fiction and historical literature. Ofc: Worldwide Ch. of God, Dept. of Public Affairs, 300 W. Green St. Pasadena 91129

SNYDER, NORMAN GENE, physician; b. Apr. 28, 1923, Adel, Iowa; s. Milo Myran and Phoebe Dillworth (Crouse) S.; m. Delphia Norman, Aug. 13, 1950; children: Michael b. 1951, David b. 1953, Catherine b. 1956, Jonathan Scott b. 1957; edn: undergrad. Drake Univ. 1940-42, Iowa State Univ., Ames 1946-47; MD, Univ. of Iowa 1951; lic. Calif. Career: intern Los Angeles County Harbor Gen. Hosp., Torrance 1951-52; gen. & family medicine practice, West Covina 1953-76; emergency phys. Covina Intercommunity Hosp., 1976-81; gen. & family practice phys. Cigna Health Plans, West Covina 1981–; pres./organizer San Gabriel Valley Hot Line 1969-71; dir. Chase-King Devel. Ctr., Upland 1974-76; elected councilman (mayor 1964-65) City of West Covina 1960-68; named Man of the Year for contbn. to human rights, Covina - W. Covina - La Puente Human Rights Council; mem. AMA, CMA, Los Angeles County Med. Assn.; fmr. Rotarian; mil: US Navy 1943-46, lt.jg. Reserve 1947-55; Republican (Repub. Central Com., 49th Assem. Dist., 1962-66); rec: bridge, hiking, boating. Ofc: Cigna Health Plans 1500 S Sunset Ave West Covina 91790

SOBENES, JUAN ROMAN, physician; b. Nov. 18, 1937, Ayaviri, Peru, nat. U.S. cit. 1972; s. Juan Teobaldo and Rosa Cayetana (Paulet) S.; m. Suzanne Brown, Nov. 14, 1981; children: John b. 1966, Jerry b. 1968, Eddie b. 1978, Randy b. 1982; edn: Univ. San Augustin Peru 1965; Diplomate Am. Bd. Anatomical and Clin. Pathol., Am Bd. Pathol., Radioisotopic Pathol., Am. Bd. Clin. Chem. Career: chief resident UC Los Angeles Ctr. for Health Sciences 1972; assoc. pathol., head clin. chem. Valley Med. Ctr. Fresno 1972–; asst. clin. prof. lab. med. UC San Francisco; dir. clin. chem. Sch. of Med. Technol. Fresno Consortium; mem: AMA, Am. Soc. Clin. Pathol., Am. Assn. Clin. Chem., fellow Nat. Acad. Clin. Biochem.; mil: lt. Peruvian Reserve Army; Catholic; rec: jogging, marathon running, tennis, soccer. Res: 824 E Serena Fresno 93710 Ofc: Valley Med. Ctr. 445 S Cedar Fresno 93702

SOBOROFF, STEVEN LOUIS, real estate investor-developer; b. Aug. 31, 1948, Chgo.; s. Irving Edward and Evelyn Janet (Suckoff) S.; m. Patti Schertzer, Oct. 3, 1982; children: Jacob b. 1983, Miles b. 1985; edn: BS, Univ. Ariz. 1970, MS, 1971. Career: owner Soboroff/ Moskowitz Co. (shopping ctr. devel. and leasing), Santa Monica; instr. UCLA seminar "Shopping Center Game"; civic: Pacific Palisades Childrens Fund (chmn.); Jewish. Ofc: Soboroff/ Moskowitz Co. 1123 Montana Ave Santa Monica 90403-1682

SOFKA, JOHN STEVEN, textile executive; b. July 4, 1935, Newark, NJ; s. John and Mary (DeKunchak) S.; m. Kathleen, Oct. 21, 1953; children: Michael b. 1954, John Jr. b. 1956, James b. 1957, Joseph b. 1957; edn: East Los Angeles Jr. Coll. 1953-54; USC 1954-55; UCLA, 1955-58. Career: with Pryor & Co. 1954-86: sales rep. 1954-58, sales mgr. 1958-62, gen. mgr. 1962-72, owner/ pres. 1973-86, sold to American Resources Corp.; current pres. American Federal Textile Corp. (subs. Am. Resources Group); dir. Am. Resources Corp. (1986-); pres. Viggo Holm Textile USA 1985; mem: Calif. Textile Brokers (pres. 1979), Textile Assn. of Los Angeles, Western UPA & Drapery Assn., Commerce Assocs. USC (Commerce Capt. of USC); Republican; Catholic; rec: golf, running. Ofc: American Federal Textile, 509 W. Lambert Rd. Brea 92621

SOKOL, ANTHONY BRETT, plastic surgeon; b. June 18, 1938, Los Angeles; s. Louis and Meta (Krone) S.; m. Barbara, Mar. 4, 1967; children: Deborah b. 1970, Tamara b. 1972, Catherine b. 1978; edn: BA, UC Los Angeles 1960; MD, Chgo. Med. Sch. 1964; Diplomate Am. Bd. Surg. 1970, Am. Bd. Plastic & Reconstrv. Surg. 1972. Career: rotating intern UC affil. hosps. 1964-65; asst. med. resident Cedars-Sinai Med. Ctr. L.A. 1965-66, surg. res. 1966-69, chief res. surg., cancer fellow 1968-69; instr. plastic & reconstrv. surg. Ohio State Univ. Hosp. 1969-71; pvt. practice plastic & reconstrv. surg. Beverly Hills 1971–, confined to aesthetic plastic surg. 1976–; affil. hosps: Cedars-Sinai, Midway Hosp., Century City, Kaiser-Permanente; assoc. prof. plastic surg. UCLA Med. Ctr. 1971; mem: Am. Coll. Surg., Am. Soc. Plastic & Reconstrv. Surg., Calif. Soc. Plastic Surg., AMA, CMA, LACMA, Ronald B. Berggren Soc., Am. Soc. for Aesthetic Plastic Surg., Phi Delta Epsilon (exec. com. 1965-69, pres. 1968-69), Beverly Hills CofC; num. presentations at assn. mtgs.; num. articles in med. jours. Ofc: 435 N Roxbury Dr Ste 200 Beverly Hills 90210

SOLMON, LEWIS CALVIN, economist, university dean; b. July 17, 1942, Toronto, Canada; s. Edward and Eva (Eisner) S.; m. Vicki Reiken, July 15, 1965; children: Kira b. 1969, Matthew b. 1973; edn: B.Commerce, Univ. Toronto 1964; AM econs., Univ. Chgo. 1967, PhD, 1968. Career: asst. prof. Purdue Univ. 1967-69; research fellow Nat. Bureau of Econ. Research 1969-72; asst. prof. Grad. Ctr. & City Coll. of CUNY 1970-72; staff dir. Commn. of Human Resources, Nat. Research Council Wash. DC; exec. ofcr. Higher Edn. Research Inst. L.A. 1974-80; prof. Grad. Sch. of Edn. UCLA 1980–, dean 1985–; pres. Human Resources Policy Corp.; honors: One of Top 100 Young Leaders in the Am. Acad. (Change Mag.), One of 50 (Who's Who in the Academic Establishment); mem: Am. Econs. Assn., Western Econs. Assn., Am. Edn. Research Assn., John Thomas Dye Sch. (trustee), Windward Sch. LA; author several books on education; Republican; Jewish. Res: 1279 Casiano Rd Los Angeles 90049 Ofc: Grad. Sch. of Edn. UCLA 405 Hilgard Ave Los Angeles 90024

SONDERLING, DONALD DAVID, pet supply co. president; b. July 25, 1946, Santa Monica; s. Fred Eli and Helene (Goldburg) S.; m. Lynn Benaltabet, Mar. 23, 1969; children: Dana b. 1974, Brian b. 1978; edn: BS, Univ. So. Calif. 1968. Career: sales Merchants Pet Supply L.A. 1969-72, buyer/ gen. mgr. 1972-79; pres. Merchants Pet Supply Co. Burbank 1980–; guest speaker Pida Trade Show, Chgo. (1978, 80, 81), Marks & Thomas Trade Show (1979); mem:

Western World Pet Supply Assn. (dir. 1978-, pres. 1984-85), Pet Industry Distbrs. Assn. (dir. 1978-80), Animal Health Technician Examining Com. (1982-84, apptd. by Gov. Jerry Brown); publ: columnist for Pet Age Mag. 1977-82; mil: sp5 USAR 1968-74; Democrat; Jewish; rec: travel, art collecting, racquetball. Ofc: Burbank

SONG, MOON KI, research chemist; b. May 24, 1931, Taejon, Korea, nat. US cit. 1972; s. Yong Kuk and Kuy Nam (Min) S.; m. Jong, Feb. 26, 1966; children: Julie b. 1966, Albert b. 1970; edn: BA, Univ. Hawaii 1964, MS, 1966, PhD, 1972; postdoctoral fellow, Indiana Univ. 1974; Fellow Am. Coll. of Nutrition (1984), Fellow Am. Inst. of Nutrition (1985). Career: research asst. in oceanography, botany and physiol., Univ. Hawaii 1962-65, research asst. in chem., Univ. Hawaii Lab. of Community Pesticide Study 1965-67, jr. researcher in biol., Univ. Hawaii Coll. of Arts and Scis. 1967-69; research chemist VA Med. Center, Sepulveda 1974-82, chief Mineral Transport Research Lab., VAMC 1983–; asst., assoc. research pediatrician Dept. Ped., UCLA Sch. of Medicine 1980-86; mem: Am. Chem. Soc., Am. Soc. Human Genetics, AAAS, Am. Coll. Nutrition, Am. Inst. of Nutrition, Am. Soc. for Clin. Nutrition; publs: 30 research papers in sci. jours. (1965-), 23 presentations nat., internat. sci. meetings (1975); Democrat, Methodist; rec: classical music, skiing. Res: 10922 Yolanda Ave Northridge 91326 Ofc: Veterans Administration 16111 Plummer St Sepulveda 91343

SONJU, SONIA, real estate developer/builder; b. Jan. 31, 1939, Milwaukee, Wisc.; d. Edward Tesmer and Genevieve Marie (Midtbo) S.; m. Wm. T. Dawson, July 7, 1978; 1 dau. Tonia b. 1968; edn: BS elec. engring., Univ. of Wisc., Madison 1963; MS in E.E., UC Los Angeles 1965; grad. courses in urban plnng., UC Irvine 1972; MPA, CSU Fullerton 1979. Career: project plnnr. Lampman & Assocs., Pomona 1972-74; dir. of plnng. City of Rosemead, 1974-76; pres. Municipal Svcs., Cypress 1976-78; v.p. AFCOM, Seal Beach 1978-79, pres. 1979–, secty./treas. AFCOM Mgmt. Co. 1982–; pres. Sonju Constrn., Seal Beach 1982–; City of Cypress (chair Planning Commn. 1969-78; councilwoman, mayor protem 1974-78); mem: Am. Planning Assn., So. Calif. Planning Congress, W. San Gabriel Planning Cong., Soc. of Women Engrs., IEEE, Calif. Elected Womens Assn. for Edn. & Research, NOW, O.C. Nat. Womens Political Caucus, O.C. Democratic Women; publs: article Pepperdine Law Jour. (1975), "FM Signal Analysis" var. Aerospace Symposia (1963-68); Democrat; Lutheran; rec: dancing, painting, ski, jogging. Ofc: Sonju Construction 200 Marine Dr Ste 1 Seal Beach 90740

SONNTAG, GERMAN C., interior designer; b. Jan. 5, 1920, Buenos Aires, Argentina, nat. Am. cit.; s. Maximo and Bertha (Wessel) S.; children: Albert b. 1945, Alexander b. 1946, Charles b. 1946, Iliana b. 1952, Gabriela b. 1954, Mariana b. 1956, Paul b. 1958; edn: MA arch., Univ Buenos Aires 1950; postgrad. stu. Hist. of Arch. and Interiors; int. design courses UCLA 1961. Career: architl. work in Buenos Aires, 1942-60; A.C. Martin, Architects, Los Angeles 1961-63; dir. int. design dept. Gen. Fireproofing Co., L.A. 1963-69; owner/pres. Classicus Environmental Design 1969-73; pvt. practice int. design, 1977–; chmn. Interior Design Dept. The Fashion Inst. of Design & Mdsg., Los Angeles, San Francisco, Sherman Oaks and Newport Beach; lectr. nat. seminars and profl. confs.; exhibs: ASID Shows and Displays (1965, 66, 67), Pasadena Jr. Philharmonic Showcase of Int. Design (3/73), Alcoa Model Ofc. Show (4/73), ASID Los Angeles Showcase House (1978); mem: Am. Soc. Int. Designers (corporate mem. 1963-), IBD (profl. 1977-), Soc. Central de Arquitectos, B.A. (1950-), LA Co. Mus. of Art (patron 1978-, Decorative Arts Council), Nat. Trust for Hist. Preserv. (1968-), Soc. Architl. Historians (1973-), Soc. Indsl. Archaeol., Soc. Comm. Archaeol.; author: Devel. of Office Interior Design in the U.S. since the Indsl. Revolution; radio, t.v., newspaper interviews; Catholic. Res: 1303 Oak St Ste C Santa Monica 90405 Ofc: The Fashion Institute 818 West 7th St Los Angeles 90017

SOOS, RICHARD ANTHONY, JR., writer, building contractor; b. Apr. 24, 1955, Passaic, N.J.; s. Richard A. and Shirley M. (Schneider) S.; m. Beverly Somerville, Mar. 20, 1980; children: Erin Maria b. 1982, Sarah Elizabeth b. 1984, LeAnn b. 1979; Calif. lic. gen. contractor. Career: founder/pres. poetry pub. co., Realities Library (non-profit corp.) 1972–, author/pub. 5 books: Why Poetry (1972), Reality Is a Drunken Feeling (1978), America's My Homeland (1976), Patient Rains & Petals (1980), A Foreign Landscape (1984) computer opr., then pgmmr., 1975-76; worked as carpenter, plumber, electrician; owner/ contr. Carpenter's Construction & Remodeling, San Jose currently; awards: recipient sev. book awards for selections of poetry; mil: E1 US Army 1973-74; avocation: songwriter (300+ songs, 12 released in 1985). Address: Carpenter's Construction & Remodeling 2745 Monterey Hwy #76 San Jose 95111

SOOY, FRANCIS A., university chancellor; b. July 1, 1915, Coalinga; s. Francis Adrian and Mabel Maleta (Boone) S.; m. Elizabeth Dean Thompson, Apr. 17, 1944; children: Charles Daniel, Jane Anne, Elizabeth Dean, Frances McAllister, Adrian Thompson; edn: BA, UC Berkeley 1937; MD, UC San Francisco 1941, postdoctoral tng. surgery and otolaryngology, 1941-42; postdoctoral tng. otolaryngology, Washington Univ. Med. Sch., St. Louis, 1942-44; bd. cert. Am. Bd. of Otolaryngology 1944. Career: faculty Univ. Calif. Sch. Medicine, San Francsco, 1946–, prof. otolaryngology 1961-, dir. audiology and speech clinic 1953-72, chmn. div. otolaryngol. 1958-67, chmn. dept. otolaryngol. 1967-72, chmn. acad. council, chmn. acad. assembly 1969-70, university chancellor 1972-82; mem: NIH otolaryngol. tng. grant com. 1959-63; mem. NIH adv. council on neurol. diseases and blindness 1964-69; bd. dirs. Am. Council Otolaryngology; Diplomate Am. Bd. Otol. (dir. 1968-); mem: Am. Acad. Ophthalmol. and Otol., Am. Laryngol. Assn., Am. Laryngol., Rhinol. and Otol Soc. (pres.- elect 1977), Am. Otol. Soc.,

Pacific Coast Oto-Ophthalmol. Soc. (pres. 1973-74), Collegium ORL Amicitiae Sacrum, Lyon, Fr. (pres. 1980); Soc. of Univ. Otolaryngologists (pres. 1969-70); served with USNR 1944-46; publs: research in otol., deafness; editorial bd. Annals Otology, Rhinology and Laryngology. Res: 9 Fifth Ave San Francisco 94118 Ofc: University of California, San Francisco 94143

SORIANO, RAPHAEL SIMON, architect, regional planning consultant; b. Aug. 1, 1904, Rhodes, Aegean Sea; s. Simeon E. and Rebecca (Codron) S.; edn: Coll. St. Jean Baptiste Rhodes; B.Arch., Univ. So. Calif. 1934. Career: with Neutra City Planning Proj., The Regl. Planning Commn., County of Los Angeles spl. projects; pvt. practice has included major projects such as site planning, apts., hosps., harbor facilities, research labs., ofc. & med. bldgs., community ctr., horticultural ctr. and shops, pioneered devel. of housing in steel constrn. and all-aluminum structures; currently involved in r&d of industrialized packaged structures of aluminum, steel, paper and plastics for internat. markets, housing developments; frequent lectr., writer, research on architecture and the arts, audio-visual films and books; mem. Calif. Bd. Archtl. Examiners; honors: AIA Internat. Exhibit Citn. (1958), VII Internat. Pan Am. Congress Award (1951), AIA Nat. Award (1951, 56, 60), AIA So. Cal. Honor Awards (1949, 51), AIA No. Calif. (1957), Medal for Excellence in Arch. (Neutra Mem. 1981), AIA Award of Excellence (1985), Grand Prox Award (AIA & City of L.A. 1967), Disting. Alumnus (USC 1986), Disting. Achievement (AIA 1985), Diploma UIA Universidad Ibero Americana (1984), Honored Architect Educator (Calif. Council of Arch. Edn. 1982), num. others; mem: Coll. of Fellows AIA, Am. Assn., Univ. Profs., Hon. Sociedad de Arquitecos Mexicanos, Internat. Soc. of Archs., Hon. Scarab Archtl. Soc.; exhibits at num. internat. museums, expositions, univs.; publs. in major US and internat. magazines; author 20+ books in US, England, Italy, France, Switzerland, Japan; trademark: Soria Structures; rec: musical composition. Res: Claremont Village Green Apt 7A 630 W Bonita Ave Claremont 91711 Ofc: c/o Pomona State Univ. Pomona

SOROKKO, SERGE, art dealer, publisher; b. April 26, 1954, Riga, Latvia, nat. US cit. 1984; s. Joseph and Victoria Sorokko; m. Nelly, Oct. 30, 1975; 1 dau, Katya b. 1982; edn: MA, Latvian State Univ. 1978. Career: prof. of English Riga Latvia 1978-79; art cons. Bowles Hopkins Gallery, San Francisco 1979-81, assoc. dir. 1981-83, dir. 1983-84; v.p. Bowles Hopkins Inc., San Francisco 1984-85; pres. Bowles Sorokko Inc. 1985—; publs: T.S. Elliot: Waste Land- Translation into Russian, Latvian Univ. Press 1978; rec: translation of poetry from English to Russian. Ofc: Bowles Sorokko Inc., 765 Beach St. San Francisco 94109, 314 N Rodeo Dr Beverly Hills 90210

SORTILE, VINCENT, sales executive; b. Feb. 11, 1918, Berkeley, Calif.; s. Carmelo and Angelina (Cancilla) S.; m. Mary, Oct. 5, 1941; 1 son, Vincent Carmelo b. 1943. Career: rep. Swanda Button Co. 1950-53, Milo Button Co. 1953-61, Streamline Button Co. 1961-62; rep., owner Exclusive Button Co. 1962—; seminars Diablo Coll. 1984-85; mem. Senior Citizen Club 1982; publs: articles in local newspapers; displays in local libraries; Catholic; rec: fishing. Res: 4485 Whitecliff Way Richmond 94803 Ofc: Exclusive Buttons 10252 San Pablo Ave El Cerrito 94530

SOTO, YVONNE E., administrator; b. Jan. 26, 1951, Lynwood; d. William A. and Juanita A. (Tafoya) S.; edn: AA, Los Angeles Harbor Coll. 1971; BA, UCLA 1973; BA, CSU Long Beach 1978; MPA, cand., Univ. of San Francisco 1985-; Bd. Cert., Reg. Music Therapist, Nat. Assn. for Music Therapy 1979. Career: Alan Short Ctr., div. of Developmental Disabilities Svc. Orgn. 1978—; music therapy intern, spl. project coord. 1978; performing arts instr., music therapist 1979-83; performing arts dir. 1980-81; clin. tng. dir. 1981-83; dir. 1983—; chmn. clin. tng. com. Nat. Assn. for Music Therapy 1982; mem: Nat. Assn. for Music Therapy, San Joaquin Co. Coordg. Council, Assn. for Supvn. and Curriculur Development, Music Edn. Nat. Conf., Council for Exceptional Children, Stockton CofC, San Joaquin Delta Coll. Adv. Bd., Coalition of Local Area Svc. Providers, Dirs. of Volunteer Agencies; rec: vocalist, guitarist. Ofc: Alan Short Center, 1004 No. Grant Stockton 95202

SOUZA, ALTAMIR P., restaurateur; b. July 1, 1947, Pontalina, Goias, Brazil; s. Mario P. and Gentilha M. (Mendes) S.; m. Edivet G., Jan. 26, 1973; children: Jennifer b. 1980, Jessica b. 1983, Jonathan b. 1985; edn: Escola Tecnica Federal de Goias 1966; computer sci., Univ. San Francisco 1976. Career: owner NB Pizza (rated top in delivery svc. by San Francisco Chronicle, , S.F. Fair, Bay Guardian); honors: Best Food Award (S.F. Fair 1985), Best Cheese Buyer in S.F. (Cheese Mfrs. of S.F. 1984); mem. Racquetball Club Daly City; Democrat; Presbyterian; rec: swimming, chess. Ofc: NB Pizza 1499 Grant Ave San Francisco 94133

SPALDING, JOSEPH GERARD, airplane maintenance co. president; b. Sept. 13, 1952, Buffalo, NY; s. John Robert and Ruth Marie (White) S.; m. Francene, Mar. 29, 1975; children: James b. 1978, Bridgette b. 1980, Suzanne b. 1983; edn: bus. econs., UC Los Angeles 1972-75; mech. engrg., CSU Northridge 1975. Career: prod. acquisition- distribution Mellonics Information div. of Litton Inds. 1975-76; Pride Maintenance Svc. div. of Palmer Assocs. 1977—, sales & svc. for mktg. and/or consulting in electron beam weld repairs for major landing gear, analysis/ definition of comml. landing gear overhaul requirements, maintain inventory consignments for air carriers, currently pres.; mem: Air Transport Assn., Northridge CofC, Nat. Geog. Soc., Cousteau Soc., Park Devel. Subcom., Bramar Assn.; publ: editorial article L.A. Times 1982; mil: US Army 1969-72, Europe/ Vietnam, Vietnam Svc., Bronze Star; Republican; Catholic; rec: geneology, collecting musical instruments. Ofc: 19525 Business Ctr. Dr. Northridge 91324

SPANGLER, CHARLES BISHOP, corporate executive, b. Jan. 7, 1932, Meadows of Dan, Va.; s. Charles Langhorne and Kittie Clyde (Cockram) S.; m. Bettie Smith, Sept. 12, 1954; children: Peggy b. 1955, Charles b. 1957, Thomas b. 1959; edn: AB, Berea Coll. 1953, MS, Univ. of Pittsburgh 1955, PhD, 1963. Career: senior research engr. Gen. Dynamics, San Diego 1956-60; asst. prof. math. San Diego St. Univ. 1960-62; mgr. ops. research Litton Data Systems, Van Nuys 1962-69; dir. systems engring. Teledyne Ryan, San Diego 1969-71, dir. advanced systems 1971-75; pres. Quest Equities Corp. 1976—; dir: Topaz Div. Intermark Corp. (1962-68), Cosumark Corp. (1976-78); awards: Clark Prize in Physics, Berea Coll. (1953), outstanding citizen award Patrick County, Va. (1975); mem. Am. Math. Soc.; Torrey Pines Christian Ch. (bd. chmn.). Res: 335 Fern Glen La Jolla 92037 Ofc: Quest Equities Corp. 3904 Groton San Diego 92110

SPANN, MARCIA M., home loan co. executive; b. Dec. 12, 1937, Kokomo, Ind.; d. Lloyd Chester and Lillie Inez (Bennett) Myers; children: Karen b. 1962, Kim b. 1966; edn: Univ. of Ariz. 1957-59; Calif. Real Estate Lic., 1985. Career: sch. secty. El Camino H.S., Placentia 1973-74; fringe benefits coord. Placentia Sch. Dist., Placentia 1974-75; career edn. counselor Scottsdale Public Schs., Scottsdale, Ariz. 1976-78; asst. stock broker Shearson American Express, Phoenix, Ariz. 1978-80; exec. v.p. Metro Home Loans Inc., Scottsdale, Ariz. 1980-85; senior acct. exec. Marathon Home Loans, Santa Barbara 1985—; actg. gen. mgr. Marathon Home Loans, San Barbara 1985, San Diego 1986-; honors: Recogn. of Outstanding Svc., PTA 1972, 1973; Recogn. of Outstanding Svc., Parents of Gifted Children Orgn. 1973; mem: So. Coast Bus. Network, Santa Barbara CofC, Am. Bus. Womens Assn., Nat. Assn. of Female Execs., Humane Soc. of U.S., Humane Animal Rescue Team; works: var. articles in newsletters, banking orgns.; created Parents of Gifted Children Orgn. of Calif.; Democrat; Christian; rec: music, ceramics, knitting. Ofc: Marathon Home Loans, 1761 Hotel Circle So. Ste. 101 San Diego

SPARKS, BENNETT SHER, military officer; b. Oct. 10, 1925, Pittsburgh, Pa.; s. Julius and Anna Malin (Klaman) S.; m. Elizabeth R. Schuchman, May 8, 1943; children: Bennett Jr. b. 1944, James b. 1945, Richard b. 1947, John b. 1949, Julie Ann b. 1953, Donna b. 1956 (two sons served in USCG, one son in USN, one dau. in AUS); edn: mil. tng. Reserve courses, Naval War Coll., Nat. Def. Univ., Indsl. Coll. of Armed Forces, Nat. War Coll., and Army War Coll.; lic. pilot (comml., multi-engine). Career: pilot for US Coast and Geodetic Survey, Alaska 1946-57; current pres. Russwood Inc. (giftware/ houseware distbn. corp.), Los Angeles; dir. Bank of Hollywood; commnd. ensign US Coast Guard Reserve 1957, held 7 USCG Reserve commands 1967-85, also served as Reserve Insp. for 11th CG Dist.; nominated by Pres. Reagan and confirmed by US Senate as Rear Admiral, senior Coast Guard Reserve Officer, Pacific Area, 1985—; awarded the Navy Distinguished Public Service Medal, US Secty. of the Navy (1983), and Coast Guard Disting. Public Service Medal, Commandant of the Coast Guard (1983), CG Commendn. Medal, CG Achieve. Medal, others; mem. Reserve Ofcrs. Assn. of US (1st CG pres. of orgn. 1982-83), Interallied Confedn. of Reserve Ofcrs./ NATO orgn. (chief US Del.); Catholic. Address: Los Angeles 90016

SPARKS, WENDELL MAURICE, real estate executive; b. Mar. 1, 1948, Phila.; s. Henry C. and Beatrice Mae (Dunston) S.; m. Lori, May 12, 1979; children: Linda b. 1983, Cody b. 1986; edn: L.A. City Coll. 1967-69; BA psychol., Whittier Coll. 1972; MBA, Univ. So. Calif. 1975. Career: real estate mgr. for pvt. individuals; assoc. dir. USC Sch. of Bus. 1973-75; researcher Calif. Dept. Real Estate 1975; salesman Coldwell Banker Comml. Brokerage 1975-78; asst. mgr. trust r.e. Bank of Calif. 1978-79; r.e. splst., v.p. Gibraltar Savings 1979-80; v.p. property mgmt. Chevron Land & Devel. 1980—; lectr. mgmt. mktg. USC, Pepperdine Univ. 1974-78; dir. Orange County Inst. Real Estate Mgmt.; honors: Outstanding Svc. (L.A. City Coll. 1969), Dean's List (Whittier Coll. 1972), pres. Psychol. Assn. (Whittier Coll. 1972); mem: USC MBAs 1976-78, Whittier Coll. Alumni Bd. 1978, Am. Heart Assn.; publs: Simulations and Management (Whittier Coll. Bus. Prospective, 1972), Real Estate Through a Flexible Education System (Calif. Dept. Real Estate, 1975); Republican; Methodist; rec: photog., trap shooting, outdoor family activities. Res: 5502 Mossvale Cir Huntington Beach 92649 Ofc: Huntington Seacliff Corp. 2134 Main St Ste 185 Huntington Beach 92648

SPARLING, REBECCA H., engineer, ret.; b. June 7, 1910, Memphis, Tenn.; d. Robert Meredith and Kate Wallace (Sampson) Hall; m. Edwin K. Smith, Oct. 30, 1935, div.; m. 2d. Joseph Sparling, July 10, 1948; 1 son, Douglas K. Smith b. 1938; edn: BA, Vanderbilt Univ. 1930, MS, 1931; Reg. Profl. Mech. Engr., Calif. 1950. Career: metallurgist foundries in South and Mid West 1931-35; chief materials & process engr. Turbodyne 1944-49; cons., Detroit 1936-42; design splst. Nortrop Aircraft, Hawthorne 1949-50; design splst. General Dynamics, Pomona 1951-68; ret.; intrevenor Calif. Energy Commn. 1975-83; engr. mem. San Bernardino Co. Air Pollution Control Bd. 1973; honors: Gold Medal, Soc. of Women Engrs. 1957; Outstanding Engring. Merit Award, Los Angeles Engrs. Week 1965; Enging. Merit Award, Orange Co. Engring. Socs. 1978; Outstanding Engring. Merit Award, Inst. for Adv. of Engring. 1978; mem: Fellow SWE, IAE, Am. Soc. for Metals; mem. Am. Soc. for Nondestructive Testing, Am. Nuclear Soc. (Los Angeles sect.), AAUW, Foreign Policy Assn., World Affairs Council, Delta Delta Delta, Ebell, Founding Friends & Galileo Soc. of Harvey Mudd Coll., Goldenera Assn.; works: 50 tech. publs. 1932-68; 100+ speeches on engring. and energy thru 1985; Republican; Religious Science; rec: reading, travel. Res: 650 W. Harrison Ave. Claremont 91711

SPAULDING, KENNETH ERNEST, insurance agency owner; b. Dec. 31, 1917, Rome, NY; s. Forest Dayle and Corinne Gertrude (Bolten) S.; m. Lois Beightol, Jan. 8, 1950; children: Ernest Neil, b. 1946; Suzanne Elaine, b. 1948; edn: BRS, United Ch. of Relig. Sci. 1950; R.Sc.P., Glendale Ch. of Relig. Sci. 1964; R.S.Ms. 1965. Career: life sales Central Life of Illinois, Santa Ana 1939-41; tool engr. Douglas Aircraft, Long Beach 1941-46; life sales Pacific Mutual Life Ins. Co., Pasadena 1946-49; owner Spaulding Ins. Agency, Glendale 1949—; honors: Top Star Mem., Pacific Mutual Lif, 1947, 48; Big Tree Mem., Pacific Mutual Life 1949, 51, 54; Nat. Quality Awd., Nat. Assn. of Life Underwriters 1955; mem: Profl. Ins. Agents; Ch. of Relig. Sci., Glendale; (pres. 1970-71); coauthor: Simple I Ching, 1978; poem, The Mystical Connection, 1982; Republican; Relig. Sci.; rec: writing. Res: 1900 Verdugo Loma Dr Glendale 91208 Ofc: Spaulding Insurance Agency, POB 889, Glendale 91209-0889

SPEAR, J. W. EDWIN, college president; b. Jan. 28, 1927, Blackwell, Okla.; s. Arthur Louis and Eva Pearl (Revel) S.; m. Louise Eileen Schmidt, July 7, 1973; children: Kathleen, b. 1945; Joseph, b. 1955; Thomas, b. 1956; Jimmy, b. 1958; David, b. 1961; Susan, b. 1963; Valerie, b. 1966; David, b. 1968; John, b. 1964; edn: AA (Valedictorian) Riverside Coll. 1959; BA, UC Riverside 1961; MA, UCLA 1963; D.Phil., UC Riverside 1974; Supvr. and Mgmt. credentials, State of Calif. 1978. Career: riveter Rohr Aircraft 1954-59; tchr. (European and Am. hist., sociol., anthropol.) Barstow Coll. 1963, chmn. soc. sci. div., 1975-78; supt./pres. 1978—; guest lectr.; honors: Alpha Gamma Sigma, Life, 1959; Outstanding Tchrs. of Am. 1975; Outstanding Tchr., Barstow Coll. 1959; Nat. Hon. Soc., Hist. 1962; mem: Am. Hist. Soc.; Faculty Assn. of the Calif. Comm. Coll.; Assn. of Calif. Adminstrs.; Barstow Economic Devel. Corp.; mil: Pvt., US Army Air Corps.; A/2c, USAF 1951-53; WWII, Korean War; Republican; rec: building own home. Res: 27423 Crestview St Barstow 92311 Ofc: Barstow College, 2700 Barstow Rd Barstow 92311

SPEAR, KELLOGG EMERSON, engineer, corporate executive; b. Aug. 11, 1924, Los Angeles; s. L. Emerson and Marion (Kellogg) S.; m. Emilie King, Mar. 18, 1983; children: Chandler b. 1951, Sharon b. 1949, Alexander b. 1953; edn: undergrad. Cal Tech 1943-45; BIE (indsl. eng.) & BME (mech. eng.), Syracuse Univ. 1950. Career: pres. Pacific Wire Rope Co., Los Angeles 1953-73; bd. chmn. Medaids Inc., 1973-75; v.p. Loeb Rhodes, L.A. 1975-78; v.p. Macdonald Krieger Bowyer, Beverly Hills 1978-81; pres. Alanmar Asset Mgmt. Inc., Santa Barbara 1981—,past dir: MacWhyte Co., Pacific Wire Rope Co., Steincy-Mitchel; mem: Wire Rope Mfrs. (past dir.), Assn. Calif. Mfrs. Assn. (past v.p.), API; civic: Mus. Sci. and Industry (past v.p.), Los Amigos Del Pueblo (past pres.), Catalina Island Sch. (past chmn.); clubs: Calif. (LA), Bohemian (SF), Los Angeles Yacht, Santa Barbara Yacht, Sunset; mil: US Army Engrs. 1945-47; Republican; Prot.; rec: sailing, skiing. Ofc: Alanmar Asset Mgmt. Inc. 111 W Micheltorena St Santa Barbara 93101

SPEARMAN, CECIL ELDON, JR., corporate executive; b. Oct. 23, 1931, Birmingham, Ala.; s. Cecil Eldon and Edith (Hearn) S.; m. Jean Mitchell, Nov. 26, 1960; edn: BS, Duke Univ. 1953. Career: sales rep. Am. Hospital Supply 1958-62, sales mgr. 1962-64, regl. mgr. 1964-68, v.p. 1968-73; pres. Bergen Brunswig 1973-79; pres. Spearman Inds. 1979—; dir: Tennis Development 1972-, Fla. Hosp. Supply 1979-84, Western Surgical 1981-; mem: IRSA, HIDA, ASTA, Palos Verdes Booster Club (pres.), Palos Verdes Little League (pres.); mil: capt. USMCR 1953-56; Republican; bd. trustees, pres., chmn. mgmt. com., elder St. Peter's Presbyterian Ch.; rec: tennis, golf, skiing. Ofc: Spearman Inds. 23500 Clubhouse Dr Laguna Niguel 92677

SPECKIN, WILLIAM M., personal manager/ marketing consultant; b. Mar. 21, 1951, Bayonne, N.J.; s. Wm. G. and Virginia (Burnell) S.; m. Joan, Dec. 31, 1983; edn: BA, Lewis Coll., Lockport, Ill. 1973. Career: sales promotion coord. STP Corp., 1973-76; mktg. mgr. Montgomery Ward Ents. Inc. 1976-77; sales promo. mgr. Dunkin Donuts of Am. Inc. 1977-79, devel. Premium of Year Award for Dunkin Donuts; mgr. promotional talent svcs. Miller Brewing Co. 1979-82, created the Lite Beer All-Stars Pgm.; owner/pres. Speckin Sportservice (for profl. athletes & corps., using sports as a mktg. vehicle) Beverly Hills 1982—, devel. ESPN Sports Video Library (1986); awards: senior collegiate scholarship award DMMA/Lewis Coll., NPSE profl. award (1977); mem. L.A. Ad Club, L.A. Chamber of Commerce; Catholic. Ofc: Speckin Sportservice 119 N San Vicente Blvd Beverly Hills 90211

SPECTOR, IDA LYNN, chiropractor; b. May 14, 1950, Chicago, Ill.; d. Abner B. and Lona (Cataldo) S.; edn: BS, Los Angeles Coll. of Chiropractic 1978, DC, magna cum laude, 1979; grad. Parker Sch. for Profl. Success 1984; Cert. of Profiency for postgrad. x-ray studies, Erhardt Seminars 1981. Career: exec. dir. Spector Chiropractic Corp. dba South Bay Chiropractic Center, National City; honors: Outstanding Achiev., support of Sweetwater H.S. 1985; mem: Am. Chiropractic Assn., Found. for Chiropractic Edn. & Research, Parker Chiropractic Research Found., Sweetwater H.S. Stu. Body & Alumni Assn. (offcl. sponsor); rec: Gold Medal in weightlifting, Senior Olympics 1980; competitor, Women's Nat. Power Lifting 1980. Ofc: South Bay Chiropractic Center, 1722-F Sweetwater Rd. National City 92050

SPEIZER, MARK ADLER, insurance co. executive; b. July 30, 1943, Youngstown, OH; s. Alfred T. and Maxine Ruthe (Adler) S.; m. Linda S. Beasley, Aug. 23, 1979; children: Stephanie Loren b. 1980, Stacey Michelle b. 1982; edn: Santa Monica City Coll. 1962-64; ins. broker, State of Calif. Career: ins. agent Southland Co., Hollywood 1962-64; ins. broker Pacific Growth Corp., Concord 1964-66; pres. Bay Cos. Ins. Agency, Inc., San Francisco 1966-72; chmn. bd./ pres. Mark A. Speizer & Co., Inc., San Bruno 1972—; chmn. bd. Great

Pacific Ins. Co., San Bruno 1977—; vice chmn., dir. San Mateo Financial Corp.; dir. Great Pacific Savings & Loan Assn.; mil: cpl. US Army; Republican; rec: water skiing, boating, swimming. Res: Hillsborough Ofc: Mark A. Speizer & Co., Inc. and Great Pacific Ins. Co., 1250 Bayhill Dr, Ste 212, San Bruno 94066

SPELLBERG, NORMAN, superior court judge; b. Apr. 8, 1926, Chgo. Ill.; s. Louis and Dora (Rubin) S.; m. Marjorie, Oct. 23, 1954; children: Geoffrey b. 1956, Diane b. 1957; edn: Ill. Inst. Tech. 1943-44; BS, Univ. of Ill. 1948; JD, Golden Gate Univ. 1965. Career: research chemist Sherwin Williams Co., Chgo. 1948-51; resin plant mgr. De Soto, Inc. Berkeley, Ca. 1951-65; atty. assoc. Hoppe, Murtha, Mitchell & Anderson, San Francisco 1965-67, assoc. Hineser, Spellberg & Glasser, Pleasant Hill 1967-76; judge Municipal Ct. Mt. Diablo Judicial Dist. 1976-80; judge Superior Ct. Contra Costa County, 1980—; awards: JFK Univ. gold medal, Outstanding Faculty 1983; trial judge of the year Alameda-Contra Costa Trial Lawyers Assn. 1984; holder num. US and fgn. patents in field of low polymer-chemistry; mil: sgt. US Army Air Corps 1944-46; Democrat; Jewish; rec: swim, scuba, ski, golf. Res: 629 Laird Ln Lafayette 94549 Ofc: Contra Costa Superior Ct. POB 911 Martinez 94553

SPENCE, JOHN CHARLES, III, lawyer, b. Mar. 8, 1943, Long Beach; s. John Charles, Jr. and Frances Louise (Bostwick) S.; m. Solveig Juline Bendiksen, Aug. 17, 1974; 1 son Matthew John b. 1978; edn: AB, Stanford Univ. 1964; JD, UCLA Sch. of Law 1967; mil. schs: JAG Basic (1968), Advanced (1975), AUS Command & Gen. Staff Coll., Ft. Leavenworth, Kans. 1978; admitted Calif. State Bar 1968. Career: atty. US Army Judge Advocate Gen. Corps, 1968-72; asst. staff judge advocate Fort Riley, Kans. USAR 1972-; senior trial counsel 77th JAG Det. 1979-84; dep. staff judge advocate 63d Army Reserve Command 1984-86; staff judge advocate 311th COSCOM 1986—; deputy dist. atty. County of Los Angeles 1972—, Organized Crime Sect. (1985-); guest lectr. AUS Command & Gen. Staff Coll. 1983-85, Army ROTC, CSU Fullerton 1985; mem: ABA, Calif. State Bar Assn., Calif. Dist. Attys. Assn., Nat. Dist. Attys. Assn., Town Hall of Calif., Los Angeles World Affairs Council, San Marino City Club, Reserve Officers Assn. of Am.; publs: Women Lawyers J. (1966), Calif. State Bar J. (1977); mil: lt. col. USAR, Army Commendn. Medal, Reserve Components Achievement Medal; Democrat; Presbyterian; rec: swim, gardening, writing. Ofc: District Atty. LA Co. 210 West Temple St Ste 17-820 Los Angeles 90012

SPENCE, KRISTI COTTON, lawyer; b. Jan. 23, 1942, San Mateo; d. Aylett Borel and Martha Jane (Knecht) Cotton; m. Robert L. Spence, Apr. 1, 1963; children: Brooksley b. 1965, Kimberley b. 1967, Alexander b. 1969, Jonathan b. 1970; edn: BA, Stanford Univ. 1963, JD, 1981; admitted Calif. State Bar 1981. Career: atty. splst. in family law, assoc. law firm Carr, McClellan, Ingersoll, Thompson and Horn, Burlingame 1981—; mem. Stanford Law Sch. Bd. of Visitors; bd. Pacific Sch. of Religion; past pres. No. Calif. Assn. of Adoption Agcs.; past bd. mem. Childrens Home Soc.; mem. Calif. State Bar Assn. (secty. Com. on Adoptions), San Mateo Co. Bar Assn. (chair Family Law Sect.), San Mateo Co. Legal Aid Soc. (v.p.); Junior League of S.F.; Republican; Protestant. Ofc: Carr, McClellan, Ingersoll, Thompson and Horn, 216 Park Rd Burlingame 94010

SPERBER, NORMAN DONALD, forensic dentist; b. Nov. 18, 1928, NY, NY; s. Irving J. and Ada (Miller) S.; m. Janet; children: James Irving b. 1956, Jill Anne b. 1958; edn: BA, Carleton Coll. 1950; DDS, NY Univ. 1954. Career: dentist; chief dental cons. Calif. Dept. of Justice (missing persons/ unidentified persons unit); chief dental cons., developer of FBI Nat. Crime Info. Center (NCIC) Dental Div.; current: chief forensic dentist for San Diego and Imperial Counties; honors: commendn. for significant contbns. to law enforcement agencies, Calif. Atty. General; mem: Am. Dental Assn., Calif. Dental Assn. (chmn. Council on Dental Health 1984-85), San Diego Dental Soc., Acad. of Gen. Dentistry, Fellow Am. Soc. of Forensic Odontology (pres. 1984-85); publs: 5 articles in FBA Law Enforcement Bulletin (1977-83), contbr. chpt. on bitemark evidence, Calif. Dept. of Justice pamphlet on child abuse; mil: lt. US Navy Dental Corps; rec: tennis, photog. Ofc: 3737-A Moraga Ave San Diego 92117

SPERIGLIO, MILO A., private investigator, author; b. Nov. 17, 1937, Greenwich, Conn.; s. Milo A. and Sylvia (Abrahams) S.; m. Patricia, Aug. 5, 1964; children: Holly b. 1971, Janelle b. 1976; edn: criminologist, Am. Acad. of Criminology 1961. Career: dir., chmn. bd. Nick Harris Dectectives Inc. 1959—; author 1964—; chief intr. Nick Harris Detective Acad. 1966—; in. Calif. Dept. of Justice 1981—; honors: Detective of th Year, NHD Alumni Assn. 1967, 1973, 1977, 1985; mem: Calif. Assn. of Lic. Investigators (founding mem.), Am. Assn. of Criminology, Am. Asn. of Reg. Criminologists, Internat. Police Cong., Am. Law Enforcement Assn., Mystery Writers of Am.; author: The Marilyn Conspiracy (Simon & Schuster USA/ Can. and Transworld Pubs., Eng. 1986), Marilyn Monroe Murder Cover-Up (Seville Pub. 1982), How to Protect Your Life & Property (Seville Pub. 1982); Republican; Catholic; rec: writing (books, tv and movie scripts). Ofc: 6740 Kester Ave. 2nd Flr. Van Nuys 91405

SPERLING, FRITZ ERIC, federal govt. executive; b. July 29, 1933, Michigan City, Ind.; s. Fritz Andrew and Charlotte (Wollenberg) S.; m. Ruth Ann Boddeker, June 22, 1957; children: F. Eric, Jr. b. 1958, Scott Edward b. 1961, Sherri Ruth b. 1963, Kristi Ann b. 1967; edn: BA, De Pauw Univ. 1955. Career: branch mgr. Labor Rels., Federal Aviation Adminstrn., later dep. div. mgr. Human Resources Mgmt. Div. FAA, now asst. div. mgr. Civil Aviation Security, FAA; club: Los Caballeros Tennis; mil: capt. US Air Force; Prot.; rec: tennis, bridge, stockmkt. Address: Tustin 92680

SPERR, RICHARD A., plastics machinery co. president; b. Nov. 18, 1929, East Chicago, Ind.; s. J. Dana and Elizabeth Bertha (von Sternberg) S.; m. Margaret Anne, 1947; edn: UC Berkeley 2 yrs. Career: served to capt. US Army Corps of Engrs.; prodn. mgr. Catchall Crofts, Oakland; sales rep. Thermatron div. Willcox & Gibbs, then sales mgr. Foratron div.; mfrs. rep. var. lines of electronic heatsealing (plastics) equip.; current: owner/pres. Sperr Plastics Machinery Corp.; seminar, workshop instr. in radio frequency heatsealing, EHS Ent. Inc.; sr. mem. Soc. of Plastic Engrs. (1970); Masons; publs: Manual Electronic Heatsealing (copyright 1981-); Republican; Christian Sci.; rec: sailing. Ofc: AC High Freq. Sales 312 Oak Pl Ste D Brea 92621

SPERRY, CAROL FRANCES, teacher, civic worker; b. Oct. 23, 1921, Sacto.; d. Frank F. and Leta L. (Yeargin) McClintock; m. Lt. Col. Willard Staples Sperry, USAF (dec.), Aug. 16, 1941; 1 son, G. Brooks Sperry II (6th gen. Californian); edn: dipl. Miss Anna Head Sch. 1938; BA, Mills Coll. 1942, MA, 1959; Calif. Life Tch. Creds. (gen. elem., primary) 1960. Career: asst. to the Dir. of Admissions, Mills Coll., Oakland 1950-52; public sch. tchr. (U.S. hist. & govt., English) in Alameda, Oakland, Lodi, 16 years; active in Republican affairs: apptd. by Gov. Deukmejian to Block Grant Advis. Com. (1984-), assoc. Stockton Republican Women Fedn., mem. Lodi Rep. Women Fedn. (pres. 1984-86), Women's Appointees Council; cand. for Lodi City Council (1982); fundraiser for congressman 14th pol. distrist (Eagles Club); fmr. vol. fundraiser Childrens Hosp. of East Bay (pres. Hawthorne Br.); civic: Lodi Emblem Club (pres. 1980-82, nat. ofcr. 1983-84), Fed. Womens Club of Lodi (pres. 1982-83, Mt. Diablo Dist. #8 bd.- var. chairs 1983-88), Stockton Navy League (pres. 1986-87), Navy Ofcrs Wives Club (pres. 1985-86), Commonwealth Club S.F., Ret. Ofcrs. Assn. (assoc.), Stockton Opera Assn. (bd. 1985-86), Lodi Art Ctr. (life), Stockton Haggin Mus. (life), Smithsonian Instn. (patron), Delta Kappa Gamma Soc. Intl., Cyrus and Susan Mills (Coll.) Soc.; Episcopal. Res: 1100 Midvale Rd Lodi 95240

SPEZZANO, JOHN J., electrical engineer; b. Jan. 11, 1941, Los Angeles; s. James J. and Cecilia M. (Schiffilea) S.; m. Sharla, Sept. 4, 1982; 1 dau, Theresa Marie b. 1970; edn: BSEE, Tri-State 1961. Career: project mgr., v.p. James Electric Inc., Los Angeles 1961-70; project mgr. Fischbach & Moore Inc. 1970-72; v.p. Walco Electric Corp. 1972-75; project mgr., br. mgr. Fischbach & Moore Inc. 1975-81; regl. mgr. Field Service Elect, Idaho, Wyo. 1981-82; pres. T.M. Johns Inc. 1982−; mem: Assn. of Builders and Contractors; Bldg. Industry Assn., Electrical Maintenance Engr. Assn., Rotary; mil: lt. j.g. USN; Republican; Catholic; rec: fishing, hunting, woodworking. Res: 17232 La Collette Pl. Yorba Linda 92686 Ofc: T.M. Johns Inc., 2860 E. Gretta Ln. Anaheim 92805

SPILLMAN, NANCY ZOE, economics professor; b. Chgo.; d. Leo and Sarah Spillman; edn: BS, USC, 1963; MBA, magna cum laude, 1965; doctoral wk. in econ., UCLA 1969-73. Career: prof. of economics, Los Angeles Trade Technical Coll., 1969−, fmr. chair Bus. Adm. Dept.; pres. Economic Edn. Enterprises, cons. firm; mem. May Co. of Calif. Women's Adv. Bd.; mem. Federal Reserve Bd. Consumer Advisory Council; mem. State of Calif. Retail Credit Adv. Com.; mem. Calif. Beef Council, State Dept. of Agri.; frequent speaker for profl. assns. and media; editor Consumer Education Forum, Am. Council on Consumer Interests publ.; awards: Mabel Wilson Richards Scholarship, Theta Alpha Delta award for contbns. to business edn., Commerce Assoc. Fellow (MBA), Phi Kappa Phi, Freedoms Found. Awd. 1981. Mem: Town Hall of Calif. (econs. sect. chair); Am. Economic Assn.; Consumer Credit Counselors of Calif. (bd. dirs.); Calif. State Atty. Gen. Commn. on Consumer Edn.; L.A. Energy/Edn. Council; US Metric Assn. (past nat. secty.); Freedoms Found.; Internat. Consumer Credit Assn.; author: The Business Beat (ongoing series of articles) for Internat. Bar Newsletter, articles and books on economics, appears on TV and radio, presents seminars to Fed. Reserve Bd. of Govs. and profl./civic orgns. Office: Los Angeles Trade Technical College, 400 W. Washington Blvd Los Angeles 90015

SPINWEBER, CHERYL LYNN, research psychologist; b. July 26, 1950, Jersey City, N.J.; d. Stanley A. and Evelyn M. (Pfleger) S.; m. Michael E. Bruich, June 18, 1977; 1 son, Sean Michael b. 1984; edn: BA w.distinction, Cornell Univ. 1972, PhD, Harvard Univ. 1977; lic. Psychologist, Calif.; Accredited Clin. Polysomnographer, Assn. Sleep Disorders Ctrs. Career: asst. sleep lab. dir. Boston (Mass.) State Hosp., 1973-79; asst. prof. Tufts Univ. Sch. of Med. 1977-79; lectr., workshop instr. UC San Diego Ext., 1979-81, vis. lectr. UCSD Dept. Psychology 1979-; deputy dept. head Naval Health Research Ctr., Behavioral Psychopharmacology Dept., San Diego 1978−; staff Naval Hosp., S.D. 1984-; adj. assoc. prof. CSU San Diego, 1984-; recipient scholarship awards: Cornell Univ. (1968-72), West Essex Tuition (1968-72), Cornell Univ. Fedn. of Women (1971-72), Harvard Univ. (1972-3, 74-76), NDEA (1973-74), Nat. Research Council Postdoctoral Assoc. (1978-80); mem: Sleep Research Soc., Am. Psychol. Assn., Western Psychol. Assn., Calif. Sleep Soc., Sigma Xi, AAAS, Am. Men and Women of Sci., Aerospace Med. Assn., Fellow Clin. Sleep Soc.; num. publs. in med. and sci. journals. Ofc: Naval Health Research Center, Naval Hospital (36-4), San Diego 92134-5000

SPIVAK, ALLAN, consulting petroleum engineer; b. Feb. 28, 1941, Toronto, Canada; s. Jack and Rita S.; m. Gloria, July 10, 1983; children: David b. 1966, Michael b. 1974; edn: BA, Univ. of Toronto 1962; MS, Univ. of Tex. 1969, PhD, 1971; reg. profl. engr., Calif. 1984. Career: petroleum engr. Shell Canada 1962-64; petroleum engr. Amoco Canada 1964-66; petroleum engr. Elf-Aquitaine Co. 1966-68; research assoc. Chevron Oilfield Research Co. 1971-74; mgr. western reg. Scientific Software- Intercomp 1974-80; cons. engr., Los Angeles 1980−; p.t. faculty USC Dept. of Petroleum Eng. 1983-; mex; Soc. of

Petroleum Engrs. (textbook com., co-ed. reservoir simulation textbook 1985), Am. Assn. Petroleum Geologists, Brentwood Homeowners Assn., Los Angeles Exec. Com.; publs: 10 papers in Journ. of Petroleum Tech., Journ. of Canadian Petroleum Tech., Soc. of Petroleum Engrs. Journ.; presented paper, World Petroleum Congress, Tokyo 1975; Jewish; rec: jogging, skiing, tennis. Address: 2501 La Condesa Dr., Los Angeles 90049

SPRADLIN, CAROLYN SHARLENE, nursing executive; b. June 26, 1939, Opportunity, Nebr.; d. Charles Edwin and Marjorie Ethel (Siders) Russell; m. Donald Bruning; m. 2d. John W. Spradlin, Apr. 1, 1984; children: Gwendolyn b. 1955, Rochelle b. 1956, Karl b. 1958, Otto b. 1960, Greta b. 1963; edn: AA in nsg., State Fair Comm. Coll., Sedalia, Mo. 1978; BS, State Univ. NY 1979; BS in nsg., Southwest Mo. St. Univ. 1981; grad. wk., Univ. So. Ill, Evansville 1983, and CSU San Bernardino, 1985; RN, Calif. Bd. of Registered Nurses; lic. Nursing Home Administr.; certified in gerontological nsg., Am. Nurses Assn. Career: dir. nsg. services Chastain's of Buffalo, Buffalo, Mo. 1979-81; assoc. dir. of nursing San Diego Physicians and Surgeons Hosp., 1981-84; dir. nsg. services Barstow Comm. Hosp., Barstow 1984−; instr. Health Occupations, Louisberg (Mo.) Voc. Sch., 1980; honors: Phi Kappa Phi (1981), Nsg. Honor Soc. (1981); mem: Am. Nurses Assn., Calif. Nurses Assn., Directors of Nsg., Mensa; lectr. workshops for contg. edn. in nsg.; rec: history, camping, motorcycling. Ofc: Barstow Community Hospital 555 South 7th St Barstow 92311

SPRAGUE, PHILLIP ROGER, security and personnel consultant, voice stress analysis researcher; b. Sept. 23, 1946, Dallas; s. Maurice Beranard and Frances Marie (Gieber) S.; Sam Houston State Univ. 1971-73; Abilene Christian Coll. 1971-73; cert. voice stress analyst instr., lic. Tex. Bd. Pvt. Investigators and Security Agents. Career: investigator Dallas Police Dept. 1966-73; spl. criminal investigator Dallas County Dist. Atty's Ofc. 1973-77; legal researcher, staff investigator Thomas Clayton & Timothy Financial Law Firm Dallas 1977-78; owner, security cons. Law Enforcement Assocs. Am. Dallas 1977-79; indsl. security and personnel cons. Loss Control Assocs. Inc. San Diego 1979-82; owner, psychophysiological stress analyst Profiles San Diego 1982−; cons. to law enforcement on voice stress analysis; trainer use of voice analyzer, personnel and security depts.; mem: Internat. Soc. Stress Analysts, Fla. Polygraph and Stress Evaluators, Tex. Soc. Profl. Investigative and Analytical Hypnotists, Tex. Assn. Stress Analysts, Calif. Assn. Stress Analysts (dir.), Lions Internat. (club pres. 1984-85); media appearances on local TV and radio; inventor Interviewer System for employee screening and psychol. testing; mil: USAR 1967-73. Ofc: 8322 Clairemont Mesa Blvd Ste 202 San Diego 92111

SPRINGER, DAVID C., dentist; b. Dec. 28, 1935, Charles City, Iowa; s. Cyrus M. and Flossie R. Springer; m. Dorothy Kollman, July 15, 1956; children: Jon David b. 1966, Janan K. b. 1967; edn: BA, Univ. Iowa 1960; DDS, USC 1966; Fellow Am. Acad. of Gen. Dentistry. Career: dentist prin. in pvt. practice, 1966−; honors: Alpha Tau Epsilon; mem: Am. Dental Assn., Calif. Dental Assn., Harbor Dental Soc., Orange Co. Dental Acad., Acad. of Gen. Dentistry, USC Century Club; mil: capt. US Air Force 1960-62; rec: model railroading, gardening. Res: 4648 Dogwood Ave Seal Beach 90740 Ofc: 3551 Farquhar Ave Ste 1 Los Alamitos 90720

SQUIRE, DIANE JANET, software development executive; b. June 16, 1952, Monrovia; d. Robert Clinton and Barbara Catherine (Searles) S.; edn: AA, West Valley Coll. 1972; BA, Humboldt State Univ. 1975; MBA, Pepperdine Univ. 1981. Career: high school English tchr. Davis Sch. Dist., Davis 1975-77; pub. rels. splst. Career Outreach, San Jose 1977-79; senior corp. acct. exec. Pepperdine Univ. Sch. of Bus. & Mgmt., Los Angeles 1979-81; dir. of ops. The Information Store, San Francisco 1982-83; pres., CEO Online Technologies Inc., San Carlos 1983−; strategic intelligence cons., Creative Strategies Research Internat. 1985-86; mem: Information Industry Assn., Toastmasters, The Planning Forum (formerly No. Am. Soc. for Corp. Plnng., dir. San Francisco chpt. 1984-85); works: Dow Jones News/ Retrieval Demonstartion Diskette, nom. by Information Ind. Assn. for 1985 Innovative Mktg. Award; Democrat; rec: electronic mail, sailing, skiing. Ofc: Online Technologies Inc., 3320 Brittan Ave. Ste. 13 San Carlos 94070

SRAGOW, DARRY ALLEN, lawyer; b. May 17, 1946, NY, NY; s. Stanley J. and Jeanne R. Sragow; m. Susan, July 22, 1967; 1 dau. Lara b. 1973; edn: BS, Cornell Univ. 1966; MA, Univ. of Pa. 1968; JD, cum laude, Georgetown Univ. 1982; admitted Calif. State Bar 1983. Career: communications dir. Nat. Commn. on Household Employment Wash DC 1970-72; campaign mgr. Phil Sharp for US Congress Muncie, Ind. 1972; staff US Senate Com. on Veterans' Affairs 1973; spl. asst. to US Senator Birch Bayh 1973-78; spl. asst. to pres. US Railway Assn. 1978-82; atty. Manatt, Phelps, Rothenberg & Tunney L.A. 1982-84; O'Melveny & Myers L.A. 1984-85; campaign mgr. US Senator Alan Cranston 1985−; honors: editor law review; civic: TreePeople (dir.), Benedict Cyn. Assn. (pres.); co-author: The Custom Courts Act of 1980 (Law & Policy in Internat. Business, vol.13, no.1); mil: lt. USNR 1969-70; Democrat; Jewish. Ofc: Cranston for Senate '86, 6380 Wilshire Blvd Los Angeles 90048

SRINIVASAN, RAJACHANDRAN, physician; b. Nov. 4, 1932, Madras, India; s. Ramanuja and Jamna S.; m. Sita Lakshmi, Feb. 10, 1960; children: Manu b. 1963, Lavanya b. 1965; edn: MD, Stanley Medical Madras Univ. 1956, MSc anatomy, 1962. Career: postdoc. fellow Columbia Univ. Eye Research Inst. 1970-71; instr. Columbia Univ. Med. Sch. 1970-71; assoc. anatomy dept. Mt. Sinai Sch. of Med. 1971-75, asst. prof. 1975-81; resident med. Kingsbrook Jewish Med. Ctr. 1981-84; staff phys. Porterville State Hosp. 1984−; honors: Cert. of Merit (Mt. Sinai Sch. of Med. 1974, 81); publs: 20+ articles in med. jours.; Hindu; rec: tennis, travel, table tennis. Res: POB 2000 Apt 22 Porterville 93258 Ofc: Porterville State Hosp. POB 2000 Porterville 93258

SRNKA, ALFRED FRANK, real estate broker, investor; b. Apr. 30, 1929, Wahpeton, N.Dak.; s. Fred J. and Hedy Camille (Ondracek) S.; m. Bertha A. Wagner, Sept. 22, 1956; children: Carmen b. 1963, Melody b. 1967; edn: spl. courses Orange Coast Comm. Coll., Golden West Coll., Santa Ana Comm. Coll.; Calif. lic. R.E. Broker, GRI (Graduate Realtors Inst.). Career: opr. family farm (due to father's untimely death) as well as odd jobs after sch. and candy vending route, 1946-52; var. pos. (Douglas Aircraft, Bank of Am., Pacific Finance, etc.) in Calif. during winters, opr. farm in N.Dak. summers, 1952-68; investor in rental props., Los Angeles 1953–, dba Alka Ents.; real estate agent f.t., Garden Grove 1968-, broker/owner Homebuyers Realty, 1971–; entertainer, musician, bandleader German Am. Band 1971–; awards: Trophy for most & fastest sold listings (1975), Merit award for Polka Band in Chino (1971), Medal for tchg. religion St. Barbaras Catholic Ch., Santa Ana (1984); mem. West Orange County Bd. Realtors (Grievance Com., MLS co-chmn.), Czechoslovak Council of Am./Santa Ana div. (founding mem. St. Cyril and Methodius Roman Catholic Mission), Florence Firestone Community Protective Assn. 1961-67; Republican; Catholic; rec: recording music, emceeing. Address: 10671 Sennit Ave Garden Grove 92643

STACEY, KENNETH ERMES, contractor; b. Oct. 28, 1946, Los Angeles; s. George T. and Erminia R. (Rota) S.; m. Sherli Leonard, Aug. 12, 1972; 1 dau. Christine b. 1967; edn: BS, Cal. Poly. Pomona 1969; UC Los Angeles 1970. Career: tchr. Moreno Valley H.S. 1970-72; owner Stacey Refurbishing cabinet and gen. contr. 1972–; ptnr. D.K. Devel. 1981–, Miken Co. 1985–; owner Journey's End, Registered Arabian Horses; mem: City of Riverside Cultural Heritage Bd. (chmn.), Riverside Cultural Heritage Found. (chmn.), Arabian Horse Assn. of So. Calif. (bd. dirs.), Internat. Arabian Horse Assn., Nat. Trust for Historic Preservation, Mission Inn Found. (bd. dirs.); rec: skiing, racquetball, horse shows. Res: 5620 Mt View Ave Riverside 92504 Ofc: Stacey Refurbishing 2675 3rd St Ste H Riverside 92507

STACK, SOPHIA DAO, cosmetics co. research executive; b. Apr. 11, 1949, Saigon, Vietnam; d. The and Hanh Nguyen (Thi) Dao; m. Leonard Micheal Stack, Nov. 11, 1981; children: Dominic Dao Nolan b. 1973; edn: Univ. of Medicine Saigon 1966-70; bus. adm. courses Sch. of Banking, 1972; Newberry Beauty Coll., Hollywood 1976; Calif. lic. in Cosmetology (1977), Instr. cosmetol. cred. (1978). Career: dir. mktg., research & devel. (developed cosmetics line, trade mark "L'Appel de Paris Cosmetics), v.p./ corp. secty. L'Appel de Paris Cosmetics Inc., Anaheim; mem. Fgn. Trade Assn., Trade American Card Assn.; Catholic; rec: music, singing. Ofc: L'Appel de Paris 12912 Brookhurst St Ste 250 Garden Grove 92640

STAEDEL, FRED PAUL, JR., real estate broker; b. Sept. 7, 1942, Chgo.; s. Fred P., Sr. and Vera Rose (Huston) S.; m. Carolyn, Dec. 27, 1964; edn: B. Landscape Arch., UC Berkeley 1964; Calif. Life. Comm. Colls. instr. creds., CSU Hayward 1978; MBA cand., Univ. Phoenix 1985-87; desig: GRI (Grad. Realtors Inst.), 1980; FAA lic. pilot (comml./ instrument/ multi-engine). Career: landscape arch. City of Livermore, 1969-72; real estate sales agt., San Ramon Valley 1973-76, real estate broker, 1976–; current: R.E. trainer/ mgr. and corp. exec. Realty World Franchise; lectr. Contra Costa Bd. of Realtors; prin. in comml. R.E. mgmt. co.; instr. (R.E., bus.) Chabot Coll. 1973-; apptd: City of San Ramon Planning Commn. (1986-), Downtown Study Com. (1985), Gen. Plan Rev. Com. (1984); honors: Air Force Aux. commendn. for saving life in midnight rescue of crashed pilot in the Sierras (1980); mil: capt. USAF 1964-69, Vietnam Service, Bronze Star; lt. col. AF Auxiliary, sq. cmdr. 1980-83, State of Calif. dir. tng. 1983-; Republican; Ch. of Christ Scientist; rec: search pilot AF Aux. Address: San Ramon 94583

STAFFORD, HAROLD FRIEDRICH, sytems egineer; b. Nov. 6, 1947, Bad Aibling, Germany; s. John Carl (dec.) and Lieselotte (Dressler) S.; m. Jamie June Penrod, June 24, 1967; children: Chad M., b. 1973; Hallie F., b. 1975; edn: BS, Univ. of Las Vegas, Nev. 1969; Univ. 1969-71; UC Riverside 1971-73. Career: assoc. pgmr., procurement splst., supvr. of purchasing coord., asst. to mfg. mgr. Wilcox Electronic (div. of Northrop) 1976-80; proj. engr. (configuration spec.) TRIGA 1980-82; cons. splst. Planning Research Corp. 1982-83; mgr. logistics Syscon 1983–; cons. USN, TRIGA & PRC 1980-83; instr. employee tng. Honeywell; mem: Profl. Orgn. of Educators (Negotiations Bd.); Republican; Lutheran; rec: water skiing, home computers, family. Res: 31 Abbeywood Circle Sacramento 95823 Ofc: Syscon, 3838 Watt Ave Sacramento 95821

STAFFORD, OLIVER MEAD, financial consultant; b. Jan. 17, 1936, Yonkers, NY; s. Frankland F. and Hermine J. (Jisa) S.; children: Robert b. 1964, Anne b. 1962; edn: BA, Williams Coll. 1958; CFP 1979. Career: fin. cons.; mktg. trainee General Foods, White Plains, NY 1958-59; US Army Intelligence, US Army Adv. Corp., Trenton, NJ; gen. mgr., MA Mutual Lif. Ins. Co., Oakland 1961-70; exec. v.p. AIS Fin. Svcs., Oakland 1983–; faculty Golden Gate Univ. 1979–; adj. faculty Coll. for Fin. Plng., Denver, CO 1978–; adv. to the Coll. on Nat. Testing Pgms.; adj. faculty JFK Univ., CSU Hayward; faculty USC Adult Edn. (devel. tng. material); devel. MBA pgm. in fin., Ctr. for Profl. Devel., Golden Gate Univ.; admitted Registry of Financial Planning Practitioners; recipient Cert. of Commdn., Am. Coll. Fin. Plng. 1981-82; mem: Kappa Alpha Soc. 1955; Mt. Diablo Estate Plng. Council; Internat. Assn. Fin. Plnrs.; Inst. of CFPs; Rosicrucian Order; Big C Athletic Club, Concord; The Racquetball Club, Walnut Creek; publs: arts. on tax and ins. plng. in profl. journs.; mil: Spec. 4/c, E-4, US Army 1959-61, Commdn. Awd.; Republican; Protestant; rec: racquetball, classical piano, tennis. Res: 403 Lassen Dr Martinez 94553 Ofc: AIS Financial Services, Kaiser Bldg., 300 Lakeside Dr Ste 1300 Oakland 94612

STAFFORD, WILLIAM GEIGER, estate planner; b. Aug. 16, 1959, Camp Le Jeune, N.C.; s. Dr. Wm. Burroughs and Janice Lynn (Geiger) S.; edn: undergrad. CSU San Diego 1977-80, BA in psych., UC Los Angeles 1981; desig: Reg. Rep. Series 7, NASD (1984), CLU and ChFC, American Coll. (1986). Career: ins. field underwriter Mutual of New York, 1981-, Orange County agency cons. p.t. 1984-; stockbroker, estate planner MONY Securities Corp., 1984–; honors: service award, CSU San Diego and Residence Hall Assn. (1980), pres. Olmeca Res. Hall SDSU (1979-80); mem. Orange Co. Life Underws. Assn., Am. Soc. CLU, Internat. Assn. for Finl. Plnng., UCLA Alumni Assn.; Republican; Lutheran; rec: songwriter/ musician on piano and guitar, tennis, cycling. Res: 841 Teakwood La Habra 90631 Ofc: MONY Financial Services 1240 S State College Ste 275 Anaheim 92806

STAGLIN, GAREN KENT, computer services co. president; b. Dec. 22, 1944, Lincoln, Nebr.; s. Ramon and Darlene S. (Guilliams) S.; m. Sharalyn King, June 8, 1968; chidren: Branon Kent b. 1971, Shannon King b. 1978; edn: BSE, honors, UCLA 1966; MBA, Stanford Univ. Grad. Sch. of Bus. 1968. Career: assoc. Carr Management Co., NY 1971-75; v.p. Crocker Nat. Bank, San Francisco 1975-76; dir. fin. Itel Corp., San Francisco 1976-77; pres. Ins. Svcs. Div. 1977 79; ADP div. pres. Collision Estimating Svc. 1980–, benefit svcs. 1983-84, Autotrak 1985–, ADP group v.p. 1983–; adv. bd. Am. Capital Access Corp. 1986-; mem: Soc. of Am. Mil. Engrs., Young Presidents Orgn. (No. Calif. chpt.), Internat. Ins. Sems. (bd. govs.), Stanford Univ. (chmn. spl. gifts pgm., No. Calif. reg. 1978-70), Peralta Hosp. Cancer Inst. (bd. dirs. 1977-78), Berkeley Repertory Theatre; mil: lt. USN 1968-71, Navy Commdn.; Democrat; Lutheran; rec: tennis, jogging, winemaking. Res: 40 Green Tree Ct. Lafayette 94549 Ofc: ADP Collision Estimating Svcs., 2380 W. Winton Ave. Hayward 94545-1197

STAGNER, ROBERT DEAN, lawyer; b. May 23, 1950, Simi, Calif.; s. Cecil William and Mary Jane (Davis) S.; m. Barbara Crosby, Dec. 27, 1974; children: Rebecca b. 1979, Brenda b. 1980; edn: BA, Pasadena Coll. 1972; JD, Western State Univ. 1977; Lic. Real Estate Salesman (1972) and Lic. Life and Disability Ins. Salesman (1972), Calif. Career: lawyer, owner Law Ofcs. Robert D. Stagner, Tustin 1978-80, lawyer, mng. ptr. Law Ofc. Walker & Stagner, Tustin and Chico 1980 ; pres. Orion Constrn. Inc., Anaheim 1980–; currently, Law Ofc. Robert D. Stagner, Orange; mgmt. cons. Richard L. Walker Inc., 1978–; mgmt. Nussex Bakery Equip. Inc. 1979–; mng. ptr., majority owner Barger & Stagner Enterprises; interim pres. Greater Am. Produce Co. Inc. 1984; FFL 1984-; mem: Am. and Calif. Bar Assns., Internat. Platform Assn.; Protestant; rec: hunting, camping, woodworking. Res: 549 Birch Ct. Ontario 91761 Ofc: Law Ofcs. Robert Stagner, 2745 E. Chapman Ave. Ste. 202, Orange 92664

STALDER, WILLIAM RONALD, state utilities agency executive; b. Sept. 29, 1937, Evanston, Ill.; s. Ernest Fred and Margaret Ann (Steinbach) S.; m. Virginia Sutherland, Nov. 30, 1968; children: Heidi b. 1970, Scott b. 1974; edn: BSCE, Purdue Univ. 1959; Univ. So. Calif. 1966-67; Reg. Civil Engr. Calif. 1963. Career: asst. hwy. engr. Calif. Div. of Hwys. L.A. 1959-64; reg. civil engr. Boyle Engrg. Santa Ana 1964-67; ground equipt. engr. United Airlines S.F. 1967-73; reg. civil engr. Brian, Kangas, Foulk Redwood City 1973-75; assoc. util. engr. Calif. Public Util. Commn. S.F. 1975-76, senior util. engr. 1976-77, supvg. engr. 1977-81, chief of fuels branch 1981–; Democrat; Episcopal; rec: fishing, skiing, old car restoration, car racing. Ofc: Calif. PUC State Bldg. Rm 5178 San Francisco 94102

STALEY, SAMUEL SORBER, III, federal executive, educator; b. Mar. 4, 1931, Honolulu; s. Samuel S., Jr. and Pauline Alice (Jones) S.; m. Dorinda Reed, June 29, 1957; children: Clinton b. 1958, Lisle b. 1961, Wynne b. 1967; edn: BA, Principia Coll. 1952; Harvard Law Sch. 1952-53, 56-57; MA, George Washington Univ. 1962; PhD, American Univ. 1971. Career: staff asst. Internat. Bank for Reconstrn. & Devel., Wash DC 1961-63; deputy dir. Fleet Asst. Group Pacific, San Diego 1964-65; head Supply Sys., Publs. Div., 1966-69, head Surface Warfare Logistics Planning Office, 1970-73, deputy mgr. Publs. Dept., Supply Opns. Dept., 1974-76, mgr. Logistics Plans & Pgms. Dept. 1977-82, Naval Ship Wpns. Sys. Engring. Station, Pt. Hueneme, Calif.; prof. Defense Sys. Mgmt. College, Wash DC 1982-83; chief logistician Jt. Cruise Missiles Project, Wash DC 1983-84; dir. Western Region, Defense Systems Mgmt. College, Los Angeles 1984–; instr. mgmt. UC Santa Barbara 1967-68; honors: Navy Edn. fellowship (1969-70), Outstnding performance awards (1967-69, 83, 84), Sustained Superior accomplishment awards (1977, 80); mem: Am. Soc. Pub. Adminstrs., Soc. Logistics Engrs. (life), Am. Political Sci. Assn.; civic: admin. Combined Fed. Campaign, Ventura (1976); publs: editor/contbr. Integrated Logistics Support Handbook (1969), num. tech. papers presented at profl. internat. confs.; mil: spl. agt., CIC, Army Airborne 1953-56; Republican; Christian Sci. (reader, bd. chmn.); rec: youth sports coach, jogging, skiing. Ofc: Defense Systems Management College 2400 El Segundo Blvd Los Angeles 90009

STALLCOP, TERRANCE EDWARD, systems research and development executive; b. May 18, 1947, Seattle, Wash. s. John Kirby and Mathena (Robson) S.; m. Miriam, Mar. 4, 1972; 1 child: Kelly b. 1975; edn: BA bus., Eastern Wash. State Univ. 1969; MBA internat. bus., Geo. Washington Univ. 1970. Career: dir. Wash. DC ofc. Decision Sciences Corp. 1972-75; internat. mktg. mgr. Internat. Paper Co. NY 1976-79; prod. devel. mgr. Citicorp NY/ L.A. 1979-82; v.p. bus. devel. Property Data Svcs. Calabasas 1982-85; v.p. systems Security Pacific Credit Corp. Westlake Village 1985–; honors: Outstanding Young Men of Am. (1974), Scottish Rite Grad. Fellow (1969); mem: Alpha Kappa Psi, Alexandria, Va. Jaycees (secty., v.p.), Young Republicans (comm. action chmn.), Va. Spl. Olympics (state dir.); publ: Businessman's Guide to

Peking, China (1973), Internat. Trade Exhibitions (1970); Republican; Catholic; rec: skiing, tennis, golf, travel. Res: 3311 Peppermint St Newbury Park 91320 Ofc: Security Pacific Credit 2660 Townsgate Rd Westlake Village 91361

STANLEY, EMERSON WARE, investor; b. June 7, 1906, Jacksonville, Fla.; s. Arthur Claudius and Lillian Agnes (Ware) S.; m. Allie Ylinen, June 11, 1949; 1 dau: Donna, b. 1953; grandfather, Edward G. Ware, prod. bus. in 1860's, became R.R. station agent, pioneer res. and landowner in Garden Grove 1876, later wrote num. arts. on walnut culture and poultry; sch. named for mother, L. Agnes Ware/ Stanley; family donated 2 acres from orig. homestead to Garden Grove Hist. Soc., now. Heritage Park, Stanley House Mus., Emerson Hall, etc.; edn: BA, Whittier Coll. 1934; grad. Sch. of Bus., Stanford Univ. 1936; O.C.C., Fullerton Coll. Career: bus. owner, Santa Monica 1936-40; rancher, Garden Grove area, prop. mgmt. investor 1946-71; prop. mgmt. ivests. 1971-; bd. trustees, Dana Point Ocean Inst. Found. (now Pacific Ocean Found.); bd. dirs. Garden Grove Hist. Soc.; past bd. dirs. Capo. Bch. CofC; bd. dirs. Garden Grove Hist. Soc.; past bd. dirs. United Way of Orange Co. No./So.; recip. cert. of merit, hon. cit., Orange Co. Bd. Supvrs. 1979; resolution of commdn., Orange Co. Bd. Supvrs.; Lib. Bell Awd., Or. Co. Bar 1978; hon. for outstanding & dedicated svc., Saddleback Reg. Lions, (pres. 1968-69); Niguel Capo. Valley Lions (pres. 1974-75); Garden Grove, San Clemente CofC; San Clemente Elks; Am. Leg.; Or. Co. Bird Club (past pres.); Tri-Cities Lapidary Soc.; La Cristianita Pag. Assn., San. Clem.; San Juan Capo. Hist. Soc.; UCI Friends of the Library; San Clem. Arts & Crafts; mil: Sgt.Maj., US Army 1942-46; Republican; Protestant; rec: world travel. Res: 24895 Doheny Pl, POB 2758 Capistrano Beach 92624

STANSBERRY, RICHARD RANDALL, microlithography executive; b. Jan. 9, 1950, Burbank; s. Roy Randall and Rosemary Patten (Ohlson) S.; edn: AA, Pierce Coll. 1970; BS, USC 1972. Career: prod. supvr. Vero, Inc., Gardena 1970-72; prod. mgr. Electromask, Inc., Woodland Hills 1972-78; v.p./ co-owner Photo Sciences, Inc., Torrance 1978-; cons. Adv. Microlithography, self- empl. 1980-; mem: ISHM; SEMI; Torrance CofC; USC Alumni Assn.; Republican; Protestant; rec: tennis, travel., collecting sports memorabilia. Res: 2113 W 237 Street Torrance 90501 Ofc: Photo Sciences, Inc., 2542 W 237 Street Torrance 90505

STANSBURY, H. MICHAEL, information co. executive; b. Sept. 11, 1938, Kansas City, Mo.; s. Harry Lincoln and Vera Louise (Meyer) S.; children: Debra b. 1966, Robin b. 1968; edn: BS mktg., San Diego State Univ. 1966. Career: asst. to pres. Darley/ Gobar Assocs. San Diego 1966-67, exec. v.p. 1968-70, founder, pres. MIS San Diego 1971-84, NDS San Diego 1979-; dir: NDS 1979-, Guardian Financial Inc. 1971-; chmn. fundraising com. for mktg. dept. SDSU 1982-83, founded annual scholarship fund (Michael Stansbury Scholarship Award) through AMA; honors: Mktg. Exec. of the Year (AMA 1977), San Diego Outstanding Businessman (Bus. Adv. Council SDSU 1980), Outstanding Alumnus (SDSU 1982), Outstanding Contbn. (AMA 1985, Cystic Fibrosis Found 1985); mem: Am. Mktg. Assn. (chpt. pres. 1974-75, chmn. bd. 1981-), AAII, Am. Congress Real Estate, NACORE, Am. Mgmt. Assn., Cystic Fibrosis 65 Roses Sports Club (chmn. exec. com. 1986, pres. 1985); author: Site Selection for Convenience Stores (1975), articles for Convenience Store News (1974-75), num. articles trade publs.; Republican; Presbyterian. Res: 2849 Cazadero Dr Carlsbad 92008 Ofc: NDS 539 Encinitas Blvd Encinitas 92024

STAPLETON, MARLIN GLENN, (SR.), lawyer; b. July 19, 1932, Walla Walla; s. Glenn Douglas and Pearl H. (Hatch) S.; m. Janet, Oct. 29, 1955; children: Wendy Ann b. 1956, Marlin G., Jr. b. 1958, Robin Louise b. 1960; edn: AA in police sci., El Camino Coll. 1960; BS in law, Western St. Univ. 1969, JD, 1970; admitted Calif. State Bar 1972. Career: police officer City of Hawthorne, 1955-63; sgt. Calif. State Hwy. Patrol, 1964-71; atty. prin. law firm Stapleton & Nachlis, Tustin 1972-; judge pro tem US Ct. of Mil. Appeals; honors: pres. 1st graduating class, Western State Univ. (1969), pro bono public service award, Tustin Sch. Dist.; mem: Calif. State Bar, Orange County Bar Assn. (Family Law Sect.), Pilots Bar Assn., Baja Bush Pilots Assn. (com. to eval. judicial candidates), Safari Club Internat. (pres. O.C. chpt.); mem. exec. com. on fund raising for judicial seats Orange Co.; publs: article in Argosy Mag. (1967), speaker on Arctic flying and survival, profl. & civic groups; mil: 3/c p.o. US Navy 1951-55, Korean Presdtl. Cit., Korean Service 5 Battle Stars, UN, US Def., Good Conduct, Navy Cit.; rec: flying, hunting, fishing. Res: 1921 Hollytree Ln Santa Ana 92705 Ofc: Stapleton & Nachlis 17621 Irvine Blvd Ste 114 Tustin 92680

STARK, FORTNEY (PETE) HILLMAN, JR., congressman; b. Nov. 11, 1931, Milwaukee, Wisc.; s. Fortney Hillman and Dorothy M. (Mueller) S.; children: Jeffrey Peter, Beatrice Ann., Thekla Brumder, Sarah Gallun; edn: BS, Mass. Inst. of Tech.; MBA, Univ. of Calif. Career: tchg. asst. Mass. Inst. of Tech. 1953-54; prin. Saife & Co., Berkeley 1957-61; founder Beacon Savings & Loan Assn., Antioch 1961; pres., founder Security National Bank, Walnut Creek 1963-; mem. 93d Congress from 8th Dist. Calif., 94th and 97th Congresses from 9th Dist. Calif.; bd. dir. ACLU 1971, Housing Devel. Corp.; advy. com. Contra Costa Co. Coalition; bd. dirs. Common Cause 1971; bd. dirs. Starr King Sch.; mem: Delta Kappa Epsilon, Univ. Club (San Francisco); mil: capt. USAF 1955-57; Democrat. Ofc: House of Representatives, Washington DC 20515

STARK, JACK LEE, college president; b. Sept. 26, 1934, Wabash, Ind.; s. Lynn C. and Helen L. (Haley) S.; m. Jill Harris, June 20; children: Janet, Jeff, Jennifer, Jonathan; edn: BA, Claremont McKenna Coll. 1961-63; LHD, hon., Univ. Redlands. Career: dir. alumni affairs Claremont McKenna Coll. 1961-63,

admintrv. asst. to pres. 1963-70, acting pres. 1970-71, pres. 1971-, also trustee; dir. Angeles Corp.; trustee Foothill Country Day Sch., Claremont; bd. dirs. Pomona Valley Community Hosp., Los Angeles Region II United Way; mem: Young Presidents Orgn., Newcomen Soc. of No Am., Town Hall Los Angeles, World Affairs Council, Calif. Club, Univ. Club (Los Angeles); mil: capt. USMCR 1957-60. Res: 1679 Tulane St. Claremont 91711 Ofc: Bauer Center, Claremont McKenna Coll., Claremont 91711

STARK, JEFFREY ROZELLE, lawyer; b. Apr. 2, 1951, Orange, Calif.; s. Woody and Jean (Rozelle) S.; edn: BA, UC Los Angeles 1972; JD, Loyola 1975; admitted Calif. State Bar 1975. Career: assoc. Cadoo, Tretheway, McGinn & Morgan 1975-80; atty. pvt. practice Torrance, Calif. 1980-; bd. dirs. Bay Harbor Hosp., UCLA Alumni Assn., Harbor Anciliary Services Corp.; mem: Am., L.A. County, South Bay bar assns.; Torrance CofC, Beta Theta Pi Alumni Assn. (bd. dirs.); Republican; Protestant; rec: sports, travel. Res: 4435 Alla Rd No 2 Marina del Rey 90291 Ofc: 21535 Hawthorne Blvd Ste 500 Torrance 90503

STARK, STANLEY DANIEL, JR., agri-business executive; b. Mar. 26, 1953, Port Hueneme, Calif.; s. Stanley Daniel and Eloise Marie (Fisher) S.; m. Renee E., Apr. 25, 1981; edn: BS agri. bus. mgmt., Calif. State Polytechnic Univ. Pomona 1981; cand. MA mgmt., Claremont Grad. Sch. exec. mgmt. pgm. 1985-. Career: adminstr. Estate of E.M. Stark, Ramona, Calif. 1974-76; ranch mgr. Stark Ranch, Ramona 1972-76; driver, guide (p.t.) San Diego Wild Animal Park, Escondido 1974-76; attractions host (p.t.) Disneyland Div. Walt Disney Prodns., Anaheim 1976-80, mgmt. intern 1981, livestock supt. 1981-; cons. Equine Mgmt., Expert Witness; bd. dirs: Pan Prodns., Inc., Las Vegas, Nev. (1986-); honors: Who's Who in Am. Univs. and Colls. (1980), Outstanding Young Men Am. (1985), Dean's List (1980), Varsity Letter, Horse Show Team (1978) Cal. Poly. Sch. of Ag., Snyder Award for Outstanding Alumnus Farmhouse Frat. (1985), Poly Vue Enthusiast Award (1979), Nat. Championship, Am. Jr. Quarter Horse Assn., Amarillo, Tex. (1972); mem: Cal. Poly. Alumni Assn., Inc. (life, exec. com., dir. 1983-86, v.p. 1983-), Am. Horse Shows Assn. Inc., Am. Quarter Horse Assn., Farmhouse Frat. (pres. So. Calif. Alumni Assn., Conclave Del.), del. to CSU Statewide Alumni Council Annual Legislative Conf. 1985-86; Republican (Rep. Nat. Com.); Protestant; rec: equestrian competition, boating, cinema. Res: 5763 Rutile St Riverside 92509 Ofc: Disneyland POB 3232 Anaheim 92803

STARLEAF, KAREN, non-profit organization director, author; b. July 6, 1938, Santa Monica; d. Harold Gordon and Irene May (Collins) Kragh; m. Ronald Davis, Aug. 2, 1980; 1 dau., Monica Starleaf b. 1959; edn: BS, CSU Fullerton 1961; grad. work USC; Calif. Life Tchg. Cred. (elem.) 1963. Career: elementary sch. tchr. Garden Grove Unified Sch. Dist., 1961-69, Ocean View Sch. Dist., 1969-81; asst. mgr. Dress-Up, Newport Beach 1982; owner/ mgr. Awareness Marketing, Costa Mesa 1982-85; hospice vol. VNA Hospice of Orange County, 1985, dir. 1986-; civic: Newport Harbor Art Mus. (fine arts patron); coauthor (w/R.Davis) Microkey (1981). Res: 350 22nd St Costa Mesa 92627

STARR, GARY, solar energy co. president; b. Sept. 18, 1955, San Francisco; s. Louis and Bernardine (Shapiro) S.; edn: BS in environ. consulting, UC Davis 1977; Calif. Comm. Coll. Tchg. Cred. (architl., engring. and rel. technols.). Career: staff Calif. Energy Commn., Sacto. 1977; project mgr. Nat. Sci. Found., Davis 1977-78; owner Natural Systems, Clearlake 1978-80; v.p. Sunwind Ltd., Sebastopol 1980-83; pres. Solar Electric Engineering Inc., Petaluma 1983-; cons. on solar energy: builders, municipalities, coll. instr. short courses; awards: NSF grantee, Resource Conservation (1977), LCIP Tchrs. Award, Lake County (1979), PG&E Solar Home Award Sonoma County (1980); works: owner/oper. do-it-yourself electric auto (2 yrs), designed/ installed 100+ solar energy systems, designed/invented several solar electric products and conservation devices, designed/blt. "sunshine home" at UCD campus (1977); sev. publs. in field. Res: 4620 Hessel Rd Sebastopol 95472 Ofc: Solar Electric Engineering Inc 405 East "D" St Petaluma 94952

STARRH, GERALD LELAND, aerospace co. executive; b. Feb. 6, 1920, Rigby, Idaho; s. George Lawrence and Mary Louise (Jensen) S.; m. Garziella Segalle, Aug. 15, 1942; children: Carolyn b. 1951, Paul b. 1954; edn: BSME, UC Berkeley 1942; Cert. Profl. Logistician, Soc. of Logistics Engrs. 1975. Career: mfg. engr. Lockheed Aircraft, Burbank 1942-44; test engr. jet engine Menasco, Burbank 1946-47; test engr. turboprop engine Turbodyne Corp., Hawthorne 1947-49; Aerojet Electro Systems Co., Azusa 1949-; rocket test engr., mgr. product support, pgm. mgr., mgr. logistics; currently, mgr. ops. Support Systems div.; lectr. var. symposia and workshops; honors: Presidents Award for Merit, Soc. of Logistics Engrs. 1980, 1986; Cert. of Appreciation as Chmn. of Traffic Safety Com., City of Claremont; mem: Soc. of Logistics Engrs. (senior), West End Fine Arts Club; mil: lt. commdr. USNR-R 1944-46 (active) 1946-72 (reserve), ret.; Democrat; Methodist; rec: gardening, music. Res: 155 Monterey Dr. Claremont 91711 Ofc: Aerojet Electro Systems Co., 1100 W. Hollyvale Ave. Azusa 91702

STASO, DAN E., psychologist; b. June 30, 1948, Gilmer, Tx.; s. Alvin Hardy and Joy Lee (Hall) Jones; m. Mona L. Grmolyes, Feb. 8, 1986; edn: AA, Long Beach City Coll. 1972; BA, honors, CSU Dominguez Hills 1974; MA, UC Santa Barbara 1976; PhD, U.S. Internat. Univ. 1981. Calif. lic. Psychologist (1982). Career: psychol. asst. to Jack Lindheimer, M.D., Rosemead 1980-82; psychologist in pvt. practice, Adult & Family Psychiat. Med. Gp., Rosemead 1982-86; dir. New Horizons Cocaine Treatment Ctr., Los Alamitos 1985-86; co-owner Acupuncture and Hypnosis Wt. and Smoking Clinic, Los Alamitos 1984-85; psychologist/dir. Bayshore Psych. Ctr. and owner/dir. Cocaine Alternatives, Los Alamitos 1986−; mem. Am. Psych. Assn., Calif. State Psych. Assn., Long Beach Psych. Assn.; editor: Cocaine Update (1986); Republican; Prot. Res: 45 54th Place #9, Long Beach 90803 Ofc: Bayshore Psychology Center 4302 Katella Ave Los Alamitos 90720

STATE, THOMAS HAYES, bank president; b. Sept. 23, 1930, Oakland; s. Raymond Francis and Marie Irene (Hayes) S.; m. Joyce Ellyn Weber, Aug. 3, 1951; children: Linda b. 1952, Susan b. 1954, Thomas, Jr. b. 1955; edn: Univ. Calif. 1948-50, Univ. of Maryland 1952-53 (overseas), San Jose City Coll. 1969-71 (eves.), Pacific Coast Sch. of Banking, Univ. of Wash. 1971-72. Career: asst. cashier Bank of Am. NT&SA 1954-60; bank mgr. Central Valley Nat. Bank, 1960-67; mgr. A.V.P., First Nat. Bank of San Jose, 1967-73; exec. v.p. Alameda First Nat. Bank, 1973-80; pres./CEO/dir. Peninsula Bank of Commerce, Millbrae 1980−; apptd. Yolo County Grand Jury 1965, Yolo Co. Juvenile Justice Commn. 1966-67, Alameda Library Bd. 1979-80; mem: Calif. Bankers Assn. (chmn. Bank Directors Com. 1984), Independent Bankers Assn. of No. Calif. (exec. com. 1984-), Western Ind. Bankers Assn.; civic: CofC, Millbrae Lions Club, Kiwanis (past pres. Alameda & Campbell clubs), Boy Scouts Am. (v.p. Alameda Council), Am. Cancer Soc. (county chmn.); mil: s/sgt. US Air Force 1950-54, Good Conduct, Am. Def., German Occup. medals; Republican (Yolo Co. Central Com.); Prot.; rec: sports, fishing, boating. Res: 4212 Highview Dr San Mateo 94403 Ofc: Peninsula Bank of Commerce 1001 Broadway Millbrae 94030

STATHAKOS, PETER NICK, physician; b. July 17, 1918, Athens, Greece; s. Nickolas Demetrios and Johanna George (Sarantaki) S.; m. Hippolyta-Katherine Varvati, 1945, dec. 1980; m. 2d. Paulette Hiroko Segawa, Jan. 19, 1985; children: Vanna-Maria b. 1945, Hippolytos b. 1951, Sophia b. 1952, Nick b. 1963; edn: MD, Univ. of Athens Sch. of Med. 1940; MPH, Rockefeller Found. Sch. of Public Health 1941; PhD, Univ. of Rome & Modena 1943; MS, chem. eng., Polytechnic Inst., Athens 1948. Career: research asst. Sloan-Kettering Inst. for Cancer Research 1948-49; resident physical med. Jewish Hosp. for Chronic Diseases 1949-52; research fellow in gastroenterology Kaiser Hosp., Oakland and resident Kaiser Permanente Med. Group, San Francisco 1952−; mem: Am., Calif. and Alameda-Contra Costa Med. Assns., Western Gut Club, Kaiser Permanente Gut Club, Nat. Assn. Underwater Instrs.; research: Pollution of Mediterranean Waters - Increased Cancer Endemic, Mediterranean Marine Life; Infectious Disease in Greece, Athens 1947; Biological By-Products of Slaughterhouses, Athens 1947; Exptl. Ulcerative Colitis in Monkeys, Oakland 1952; Metabolism of Folic Acid and B12 in Ulcerative Uropepsin Determination, Oakland 1958; Bilirubin Metabolism, Gastroenterology (11/70), Oakland 1968; A Comparison of Two Screening Tests for Achlorhydria; mil: capt. Greek Army Med. Corps Spl. Forces; Republican; Orthodox; rec: swimming, sailing, scuba diving. Res: 3026 Guido St. Oakland 94602 Ofc: The Permanente Medical Group, 280 W. MacArthur Blvd. Oakland 94611

STAUBER, RANDALL OWEN, chiropractor; b. Apr. 7, 1957, San Francisco; s. Owen Joseph and Marilyn Louise (Furnivall) S.; m. Terri Anne, Feb. 14, 1985; 1 dau. Jina Jena b. 1980; edn: Metro State Coll. 1977-78; Modesto Jr. Coll. 1978-80; CSC Stanislaus 1980-82; DC, Palmer Coll. of Chiro. 1982; Chiro. Calif. 1983; Diplomate Nat. Bd. Chiro. Examiners. Career: chiro. pvt. practice Calif. 1983−; seminar on low back pain in Oakland 1984; contg. edn. L.A. Coll. of Chiro.; mem. Am. Bd. Chiro. Orthopedists; publ: health column in local newspaper; rec: tennis, jogging, skiing. Ofc: Foresthill Chiropractic Foresthill Rd Foresthill 96531, Auburn Low Back Clinic 560 Wall St Ste J Auburn 95603

STAUBER, RONALD JOSEPH, lawyer; b. Nov. 8, 1940, Toledo, Ohio; s. Frederick I. and Anna K. (Kline) S.; children: Brandon Frederick b. 1970, Deborah Jocelyn b. 1973; edn: BBA, Univ. of Toledo 1962; JD, Ohio State Univ. Coll. of Law 1965. Career: corp. counsel Div. of Corps. Dept. of Investment, State of Calif. 1965-68; assoc. Gould, Magaram & Riskins, Los Angeles 1968-69; ptr. Blacker & Stauber, Beverly Hills 1969-78; Ronald J. Stauber Inc., Los Angeles 1978-85; ptr. Stauber & Gersh, Los Angeles 1986−; mem: Am. (Corps., Banking & Bus. Law sect.), Los Angeles Co. (Bus. & Corp. Law sect.) and Beverly Hills (R.E. & Corps. Comms.) Bar Assns., mil: National Guard 1966-71; Democrat; Jewish; rec: karate (Tae Kwon Do), philately, sports fishing. Res: 508 No. Sierra Dr. Beverly Hills 90210 Ofc: 2029 Century Park E. Ste. 3335 Los Angeles 90067

STAUFF, CHRIS HARPER, industrial realtor; b. Dec. 24, 1928, Milwaukee, Wisc.; s. Carl Jacob and Doris Katherine (Johnson) S.; m. Deidra Davies, Jan. 29, 1972; children: Tamara b. 1973, Katherine b. 1977, Corinne b. 1978, Kirk b. 1982; edn: BA, Exptl. Psychol. USC 1971, MA, Neuro. Psychol. 1972. Career: research/ tchg. asst. USC, Los Angeles 1968-73; indsl. realtor The Seeley Co., Los Angeles 1973-80; pres. Ad Laser, Escondido 1981-84; honors: Recogn. Awards, AIR 1980, 1981, 1982; Calif. State Scholarship, USC 1966-70; mem: Am. Indsl. Real Estate Assn. (orientation comm.- ethics lectr. 1980−; bd. dirs., computer com. chmn. 1985; secty., assoc. mulitple dir., pgm. chmn. 1986; v.p., mulitple dir. 1987); Air Computer Comm. (co-chmn. 1979-81), Western Psychologist Assn., The Jonathan Club; works: AD Laser, Laser Graphics Computer, 1981-82; publ., Recovery of Function with Two-Stage Lesions of the Fornix, Exptl. Neurology Vol. 37, 1972; publ., Behavioral Role of Hippocampal Connections, Eptl. Neurology Vol. 45, 1974; rec: scuba diving, archery; Republican (Nat. Congl. Comm.); Methodist. Res: 15436 Albright St. Pacific Palisades 90272 Ofc: The Goodglick Co., 11203 So. La Cienega Los Angeles 90045

STEAKLEY, RALPH DOUGLAS, JR., jewelry designer-gallery owner; b. Mar. 21, 1944, Ashtabula, Ohio; s. Ralph D. and Helen Grace (Williams) S.; m. Jacqueline B., June 18, 1976; 1 dau. Nicole Samara b. 1982; edn: BA, Bowling Green State Univ. 1966; MFA in jewelry design, Indiana Univ. 1974. Career: jewelry designer/owner, then ptnr. Argentum, Inc. (nat. wholesale jewelry co.), 1969-73; guest jewelry designer Hans Hansen workshop, Kolding, Denmark 1974; jewelry designer The Gold Crucible (mfg. co.), 1975; founder/owner Concepts Studio (jewelry and metalsmithing), Carmel Valley 1976−, Concepts Gallery, Carmel, and Concepts At the Plaza, Carmel 1977−, also owner Concepts Gallery, Palo Alto; assoc. instr. Indiana Univ. 1971, instr. Carmel (Calif.) Adult Sch. 1975, Cabrillo Coll. 1979-; organizer/guest curator Calif. Craftsmen (1976), juried invitational crafts exhib. sponsored by Monterey Penin. Mus. of Art; juror Santa Cruz Co. Fair (1979-), Calif. State Expo./Sacto. (1981); One man exhibs: Seaside City Hall (1978), Bakersfield Coll. Art Gallery (1978), Precious Objects Gallery, Los Gatos (1980), Craft Alliance Gallery, St. Louis, Mo. (1981); mem. Am. Crafts Council, Soc. of No. Am. Goldsmiths (dir. and treas. 1980-85, distinguished mem.); rec: biking, skiing. Ofc: Concepts (POB 301) Sixth and Mission Streets Carmel 93921

STECKER, JOHN F., dentist; b. July 29, 1951, Annapolis, Md.; s. F. Frank and Jean S.; edn: BA, UC Los Angeles 1973; MS Univ. Mich. 1975; DDS, UCLA Sch. of Dentistry 1984. Career: radiation safety cons. Profl. Staff Assn. Harbor-UCLA Med. Ctr. 1976-77; adj. prof. indsl. hygiene, environmental health USC 1978-81; envtl. health and safety ofcr. USC 1977-83; instr. biol. Santa Monica City Coll. 1976−; dentist pvt. practice Downey 1984−; honors: Award of Merit (Nat. Safety Council 1979), Award of Honor (NSC 1980), class pres. (UCLA Sch. of Dentistry 1980-82), mem: Am. Dental Assn. 1980-85, Acad. Gen. Dentistry 1984-, So. Calif. Indsl. Safety Soc. (bd. dirs. 1979-80), Health Physics Soc. 1977-, Campus Safety Assn. 1978-85, Am. Cancer Soc. (public edn. com. 1979-81); rec: skiing. Res: 5549 Scotwood Dr Palos Verdes 90274 Ofc: John Stecker DDS 31246 Palos Verdes Dr West Palos Verdes 90274

STECKI, EDWARD GEORGE, aerospace engineer, design specialist; b. Feb. 2, 1914, Chgo.; s. Sigmund and Stella (Brozowska) S.; m. Helene, Aug. 14, 1937 (dec.); children: Carol Diane b. 1944, Edward Ronadl b. 1952; BS aeronautical engr., Aeronautical Univ. of Chgo. 1939; Reg. Profl. Engr., Calif. (1949). Career: layout draftsman Stewart Warner Corp., Chgo. 1938-40; design engr. Airframe, Convair, San Diego 1940-42; supr. Wing & Controls Design, Convair, Ft. Worth, Tex. 1942-45; responsible design engr. Northrop Aircraft, Hawthorne, Calif. 1945-49; responsible design engr. Northrop Aircraft, Hawthorne 1951-59; proposal mgr. Aerojet General Corp., Downey 1959-62; design splst. Rockwell Internat. Corp. Downey Div. Apollo Space, L.A. Div. B-1 Bomber, 1962-72, Downey div. Space Base and Shuttle Bus 1972-74, ret. Res: 11521 Weatherby Los Alamitos 90720

STEELE-WRIGHT, PIETER ANNE, accountant; b. Aug. 20, 1952, Oakland; d. Frank Ice and Marjorie Jean (Peters) Laughridge; m. Ronald J. Wright, Mar. 20, 1982; children: James Steven b. 1973, Jessica b. 1977; edn: AA, Canada Coll. 1973; cert. acctg. Mendocino Coll. 1986. Career: lighting designer Ukiah Players Theatre Co., Ukiah; acct./ finl. mgr. Ron Wright and Son (horseshoeing) and Red Rock Ranch (pvt. nature preserve); indep. finl. cons. to small businesses; civic: Girl Scout leader Troop 180 (1983-) and advisor Troop 176 (1985-), Cub Scout asst. leader Pack 57 (1981-83); Willits United Methodist Ch. (adminstrv. council 1982-85, fin. com. 1986); rec: gourmet cook, quilting, computers. Address: POB 790 Laytonville 95454

STEEN, KENNETH, JR., mortgage banker; b. June 26, 1947, Brooklyn, NY; s. Kenneth (capt. USN, ret.) and Frances (Preston) S.; edn: BS, USC 1972; MBA, USC 1977; Calif. lic. real estate broker (1980). Career: credit mgr. Union Bank, Palo Alto 1972-75; asst. mgr., R.E. loan ofcr. Calif. Canadian Bank, Orange 1975-77; investment sales Coldwell Banker Comml. Brokerage Co., San Jose 1977-78; inv. sales/leasing Cornish & Carey Comml. Realtors, Palo Alto 1978-79; project mgr. R.E. devel. Jack Dymond Assocs., Mtn. View 1979-80; v.p. R.E. loans Imperial Bank, San Jose 1980-82; v.p./mgr. income prop., Colonial Mortgage Service Co., 1982-84, Weyerhaeuser Mortgage Co., 1983-84; v.p./mgr. Pacific Pioneer Finl. Corp., 1984−; seminar speaker, R.E. fin., Cal-Land Title Co. (1981-82); honors: Beta Gamma Sigma (1977); mem. Assn. of South Bay Brokers, Mortgage Bankers Assn., Commerce Assocs., Bay Area Mortgage Assocs., USC Alumni Assn.; club: N.Y. Athletic, San Diego Yacht; mil: E4 USNR 1965-71, Vietnam Nat. Service, Na. Def.; Republican; Prot.; rec: sailing, ski, hiking. Res: 281 DeSoto Dr Los Gatos 95030 Ofc: Pacific Pioneer Financial Corp. 1641 N First St Ste 105 San Jose 95112

STEENBLOCK, DAVID ALAN, physician; b. Jan. 7, 1943, Buffalo Center, Iowa; s. Raymond and Opal (Sternberg) S.; m. Noyemy der Alexanian, June 30, 1979; children: Karen b. 1980, David II b. 1983, Amber b. 1984; edn: BS, Iowa State Univ.; MS, DO, Coll. of Osteopathic Medicine, Des Moines, Iowa 1967, 1970; Osteopathic Phys. & Surgeon lic., Calif. 1977. Career: rotating intern Providence Hosp., Seattle, Wash.; 2 year gen. practice, Wash.; 3-year residency anatomic & clinical pathol. Case Western Reserve; clin. pathol., Univ. of Oregon Health Sci. Ctr., 1 year; current: pvt. practice of gen., preventive & restorative medicine, El Toro, Calif.; pres. Aging Research Inst., 1981-; mem: A.O.A., New York Acad. of Sci., Am. Acad. of Medical Preventics (treas., exec. bd.), Soc. of Bioinorganic Scientists, Internat. Acad. of Preventive Medicine, Internat. Coll. of Applied Nutrition; publs: num. sci. research papers and tchg. videos, contbg. writer Let's Live, and Total Health Mag.; Republican; Prot. Ofc: 22821 Lake Forest Dr Ste 114 El Toro 92630

STEGMAN, CHARLES ALEXANDER, marketing executive; b. April 17, 1959, Denver, Colo.; s. Harvey Eugene and Mary Martha (Newell) S.; edn: coll. prep., Regis Jesuit High 1977; BSEE, Univ. of Colo. 1981. Career: regl. dir. to chpt. devel. dir. Sigma Phi Epsilon, Richmond, Va. 1981-83; sales rep., legal accts. rep. Lanier/ Harris, San Francisco 1983-84; mktg. rep., senior mktg. rep. Businessland, Oakland 1984–; systems engr. Businessland San Jose 1986–; Mills Coll. Word Processing Sem. Staff; honors: Outstanding Young Men of Am., 1985; (3) Com Lan Sales Award, 1985; Apple Sales Award, 1984, 1985; Businessland 100 Percent Club; Compaq Sales Award, 1985; mem: ALice B. Toblas Democratic Club (exec. bd. 1986), Harvey Milk Democratic Club, Human Rights Campaign Fund, Sig Ep Cal Xi (chpt. counselor, alumni bd.); Democrat; Catholic; rec: politics. Res: 1677 Bush St. Apt. 21 San Francisco 94109 Ofc: Businessland, 180 Grand Ave. Oakland 94612

STEHLY, JOHN WILLIAM, gynecologist; b. Apr. 26, 1922, Anaheim; s. Nicholas John and Winifred Mary (Bastian) S.; m. Jeanelle Mcdonald, Oct. 19, 1946; children: Jeanine b. 1951, Mary b. 1953, Rosanne b. 1954, Jeffrey b. 1957, Carolyn b. 1958, John T. b. 1961, Ann b. 1964; edn: BS, Loyola Univ. Los Angeles 1943; MD, USC 1946; Diplomate Am. Board OB-Gyn. 1957. Career: physician, founder Ob-Gyn. group: Molitor, Stehly, Whiting in Fullerton 1953-85; pvt. solo practice gynecology, Fullerton 1985–; past chmn. Ob-Gyn Service St. Jude Hosp., Fullerton; mem: AMA, Calif. Med. Assn., Orange Co. Med. Assn., Ob-Gyn Soc. of Orange County (charter mem.), Fellow Los Angeles Ob-Gyn Soc., Am. Coll. of Surgeons, Am. Coll. of Ob-Gyn, First Friday Friars of Orange Co., Pro-Life for America; mil: served to lt. j.g. Med. Corps USNR 1943-50; Republican; Catholic; rec: cattle raising, citrus ranching, surf fishing, tournament racquetball. Res: 201 W LaEntrada Pl Fullerton 92635 Ofc: John W. Stehly MD 100 E Valencia Mesa Fullerton 92635

STEIN, RONALD BLEY, physician; b. Jan. 30, 1935, Los Angeles; s. Bley and Adele (Gitelson) S.; m. Katherine, Sept. 16, 1966; children: Tim b. 1964, Jane b. 1970; edn: BA, UC Berkeley 1957; MD, UC San francisco Med. Sch. 1961; certified Am. Bd. Internal Med. 1969. Career: intern L.A. County Gen. Hosp. 1961-62; fellow, resident internal med. Mayo Clin. 1962-64; res. internal med. Wadsworth VA Hosp. and UCLA 1964-67, fellow endocrinol. 1965-67; pvt. practice endocrinol., diabetes Burbank, Calif. 1967–; affil. St. Joseph's Hosp. Burbank, Glendale Adventist and Glendale Meml. Hosps., Glendale; clin. instr. med. UCLA 1967-70, USC 1970-70, clin. asst. prof. 1971, clin. assoc. prof. 1974; med. dir. Endo Lab. Svcs. Burbank; fellow Am. Coll. Phys. 1975; mem: The Endocrine Soc., LACMA (bd. 1985, com. chmn., alt. del. to Calif. Med. Soc. Conv. 1984), Am. Diabetes Assn. (bd. dirs., pres. profl. sect. So. Calif. chpt.), Alumni Soc. of Mayo Clinic, Am. Soc. Internal Med., Cross Town Endocrine Soc., Wadsworth Alumni Assn., Phi Beta Kappa, Sigma Alpha Mu, Am. Thyroid Assn., L.A. Soc. of Internal Med.; publs: num. articles, abstracts in med. jours. Ofc: 1624 W Olive Ave Burbank 91506

STEIN, STEVEN PAUL, lawyer; b. Nov. 5, 1952, Stockton; s. Leopold and Hilda (Thalheimer) S.; edn: BA, USC 1974; JD, Univ. of LaVerne 1977. Career: practicing atty. Samuel Shore, Esq., Los Angeles 1981; currently, pvt. practice Steven Stein, Esq. (personal injury & landlord-tenant law), Stockton; awards: Stockton Police Dept. Awd. for Heroic Rescue 1983; mem: Calif. Trial Lawyers Assn.; San Joaquin Co. Bar Assn.; La Verne Law Review; LaVerne Law Student Body Assn. (v.p.); Yosemite Club, Stockton; Boys Club, Stockton; publs: art. on no-fault ins., CTLA Journ. 1973; Jewish; rec: reading, tennis, coin collection. Res: 7128 Lighthouse Dr Stockton 95209 Ofc: Steven Stein, Atty. at Law, 2155 W March Ln Ste 1-D Stockton 95207

STEINHOUR, DONALD MICHAEL, marketing executive; b. Jan. 2, 1939, San Diego; s. Donald L. and W. Ruth (Allen) S.; m. Rose Marie, Aug. 25, 1964; children: Steven Michael b. 1969, Sean Patrick b. 1973; edn: BA, CSU Los Angeles 1964, MA, 1965; Cert. Fin. Planner, Calif. Career: head football coach, athletic dir., dean of men Notre Dame H.S., Sherman Oaks 1967-73; educator, football, Calif. Polytechnic Univ., Pomona 1973-77; head football coach, eduactor Pomona Coll., Claremont 1977-82; dist. mgr. General Ins. Agency, West Covina 1982-83; v.p. H.S. of A. Ins. Svc., Home Savings of Am. 1982-85; dir. mktg. Weyerhaeuser Ins. Svc. 1985–; profl. football scout 4 yrs.; honors: num. coach of the year awards; spkr. at nat. convs.; sales awards; mem. Nat. Football Coaches Assn.; mil: sgt. US Army; rec: sports, reading. Res: 1733 Alaska St. West Covina 91790 Ofc: Weyerhaeuser Insurance, 3330 Ocean Park Ste. 115 Santa Monica 90405

STEINMETZ, WILLIAM QUINBY, service co. executive; b. Jan. 6, 1932, Dobbs Ferry, NY; s. Richard Bird and Charlotte May (Quinby) S.; m. Judith Chapman, Sept. 30, 1967; children: Melinda b. 1970, Robert b. 1971, James b. 1974, Liana b. 1980; edn: The Choate Sch. 1949; BA, Cornell Univ. 1953; BFT, Am. Grad. Sch. Internat. Mgmt. 1956; MBA, Harvard Univ. 1967. Career: area mgr. Latin Am., Miles Laboratories, Mexico City 1957-60; internat. mgr. Norwich Pharmacal Co., NY, NY 1960-63; mgr Latin Am., Andrew Jergens Co., Cincinnati, Ohio 1963-67; pres. International Business Consultants Inc., San Juan, Puerto Rico 1967-74; pres. William Q. Steinmetz & Assoc., San Francisco 1974-80; pres. Chapman Williams Internat. Inc. 1980–; mem: CofC, Internat. Visitors Ctr., Harvard Bus. Sch. Assn., World Affairs Council, Commonwealth Club, Harvard Club of NY, The Family; mil: lt. USN 1953-55; Republican; Episcopal; rec: world travel, cultural anthropology, photog. Res: 610 Wanda Ln. Mill Valley 94941 Ofc: Chapman Williams Internat. Inc., 690 Market St. San Francisco 94104

STELLA, ANTHONY RICHARD, stockbroker; b. June 26, 1944, Chgo.; s. Anthony and Gilda (Belmonte) S.; children: Anthony b. 1972, Quentin b. 1980; edn: BS, USC 1967. Career: stockbroker Dean Witter Reynolds, Burbank 1969–, assoc. v.p./asst. mgr. 1972, v.p. 1979, first v.p. 1984, senior v.p. 1986–; dir. Nicoa Corp.; mem. Commerce Assocs., USC Alumni Assn., USC Scramblers, Lakeside Golf Club; Republican; Catholic; rec: golf. Res: 4319 La Barca Dr Tarzana 91356 Ofc: Dean Witter Reynolds 4001 W Alameda Ave Burbank 91505

STEPHENS, MICHAEL GARY, engineering executive; b. Dec. 12, 1947, Los Angeles; s. Stanley Cameron and Aline Mary (Tremblay) S.; m. Bobbie Jo, Nov. 30, 1974; children: Michelle b. 1968, Michael b. 1970, Samuel; edn: AA, Cerritos Coll. 1973. Career: designer Pacific Scientific Co. Anaheim 1966-71; microelectronics engr. Western Digital Corp. Newport Beach 1973-75; engrg. mgr. Xerox Corp. El Segundo 1975-81; prin. engr. Silicon Systems Inc. Tustin 1981-83; engrg. mgr. TRW RF Device Div. Lawndale 1983–; mem: ISHM, SEMI; patentee in field; Republican; Catholic; rec: bodybuilding. Res: 1013 S. Nicklett Fullerton 92631 Ofc: TRW RF Devices 14520 Aviation Blvd Lawndale 90620

STEPHENS, WARREN CLAYTON JR., physician, orthopedic surgeon; b. Mar. 4, 1909, Keener, Ala.; s. Warren Clayton and Jodie Lee (Harbour) S.; m. Juene Ayer, July 19, 1957; edn: BS, Spring Hill Coll. Mobile, Ala. 1931; MD, Tulane Univ. 1935; surg. of the extremities Johns Hopkins Hosp. 1942; treatment and care of poliomyelitis Childrens Hosp. Boston 1948; Career: intern City Hosp. Mobile, Ala. 1935-36; res. O'Connor Hosp. San Jose 1936-37, Shriners Hosp. San Francisco 1937-38; chief orthoped. svcs. stn. hosp. McDill Field Tampa, Fla. 1942-43, 126th gen. hosp. South Pacific 1943-46; pvt. practice ortho. surg. Mobile, Ala. 1946-51, San Mateo 1951-85; pres. San Mateo Orthopedic Grp. 1971-85; med. dir. Nat. Polio Found. San Mateo 1953-65; med. dir. Calif. Jockey Club 1960-70; honors: Athletic Hall of Fame Spring Hill Coll. 1980; Prof. Emeritus of Med. Tulane Univ. 1985; mem: San Mateo Co. Med. Soc.; Calif. Med. Soc.; AMA; Am. Fracture Soc.; Am. Med. Soc. of Vienna; Athelston Men's Club; Rotary Club; Ducks Unlimited; Peninsula Golf and CC; Medalion Soc. of S.F. Opera Assn.; mil: maj. US Army MC chief of orthoped. svcs. 1942-46; Republican; Protestant; rec: golf, duck hunting, fishing. Ofc: San Mateo Orthopedic Med. Grp. 77 N San Mateo Dr San Mateo 94401

STEPHENSON, KATHRYN LYLE, plastic surgeon; b. July 30, 1912, Kansas City, Mo.; d. Clay Wheeler and Sue M. (Vertrees) S.; div.; children: Kathryn Sue Mosely b. 1955, Jack Meredith Mosely, Jr. b. 1956; edn: undergrad. Univ. of Chgo., Univ. of Nebr.; BA, Univ. of Ariz. 1934; MD, Univ. of Kans. Med. Sch. 1941. Career: intern Santa Barbara Cottage Hosp.; asst. resident med. Royal Victoria Hosp.; resident pediatrics Univ. of Kans. Med. Ctr., resident and research fellow in plastic surgery, resident surgical pathology; assoc. E.C. Padgett; instr. Plastic & Reconstrv. Surgery, Tulane Univ.; staff Los Angeles Children's Hosp.; pvt. practice Santa Barbara, ret.; editor Plastic & Reconstructive Surgery Journal, editor Year Book of Plastic Surgery; awards: research merit award, Plastic & Reconstrv. Surg., achievement award (1977), Distinguished graduate Pembroke Hill Sch. (1985); mem: AMA, Calif. Med. Assn., Am. Assn. Plastic Surgeons, Am. Soc. of Plastic & Reconstrv. Surgeons, Calif. Plastic & Reconstrv. Surgeons (pres.), Am. Coll. of Surgeons, Am. Soc. for Aesthetic Plastic Surgery, Channel City Womens Forum (bd.), Valley Club of Montecito; publs: coauthor (with E.C. Padgett) Plastic & Reconstructive Surgery chapters in Symposium of Plastic Surgery, Surgicla Clinics of No. Am., Every Woman's Health; num. papers on plastic & recon. surgery; mil: civilian cons. Camp Cook; Republican; Episcopal; rec: horses, golf, painting. Res: 780 Rockbridge Santa Barbara 93108

STERES, CHRIS PETER, management consultant, industrial engineer; b. May 29, 1924, Portland, Ore.; s. Chris P., Sr. and Beatrice (Moorcroft) S.; m. 2d. Lucy Steres, Oct. 21, 1982; children: Richard b. 1951, Peter b. 1952, David b. 1956, Carol b. 1959; edn: BE, cum laude, USC 1950; grad. work USC and UCLA, 1951-64; Reg. Profl. Engr., Calif. Career: cons. Booz, Allen & Hamilton, Los Angeles 1955-59; ptnr. William Eldridge & Co., L.A. 1959-65; mgr. Coopers & Lybrand, L.A. 1965-73; vice pres. United California Bank, L.A. 1973-74; mgr. Spl. Projects, American Internat. Pictures, Beverly Hills 1975-81; project adminstr. Western Trade Adjustment Assistance Ctr., Los Angeles 1982-86; mgmt. consultant prin., 1986–; frequent guest speaker on mgmt. topics, var. bus. and profl. groups; mem: Am. Inst. of Indsl. Engrs. 1952-74, Inst. of Mgmt. Consultants 1969-73; civic: Canyon Explorer's Club, Sierra Club (certified outings leader); publs: coauthor Production Control Manual (1955), mag. articles on mgmt. subjects; mil: tec.4 US Army Signal Corps 1943-46; Congregational; rec: mountaineering, bicycle touring. Address: 431 West Foothill Blvd Arcadia 91006

STERLING, HARLEY EDWARD, plastic surgeon; b. Aug. 20, 1929, Granite City, Ill.; s. Harley Edward, Sr. and Gladys Marie (Whitten) S.; m. Diana, Nov. 5, 1976; children: Janice Marie b. 1958, Deborah Lynn b. 1961; edn: BA, Univ. of Kans. 1952, MD, 1958; completed 3-yr. residency in plastic and reconstrv. surg. UCLA Med. Ctr., 1965. Career: pvt. practice plastic and reconstructive surgery in Fullerton, 1965–; chief of med. staff Fullerton Comm. Hosp. 1981-83; faculty mem., assoc. clin. prof. Div. of Plastic Surgery, UC Irvine Med. Ctr., 1969–; mem: AMA, Calif. Med. Assn., Orange Co. Med. Assn., Am. Soc. of Plastic and Reconstrv. Surgeons, Calif. Soc. of Plastic Surgeons, Aesthetic Soc. of Plastic and Reconstrv. Surgeons, Flying Physicians Assn. (pres. western reg. chpt. 1978); profl. paper presentation: Two Years Experience with the Meme Implant, Aesthetic Soc. of Plastic and Reconstrv. Surgeons (Boston 1985); cpl. US ARmy Med. Corps 1952-54; Republican; Protestant; rec: flying, video recording and editing, sci. reading. Ofc: 2720 N Harbor Blvd Ste 230 Fullerton 92635

STERN, ARTHUR PAUL, business executive, engineer; b. July 20, 1925, Budapest, Hungary, nat. US cit. 1956; s. Leon and Bertha (Frankfurter) S.; m. Edith Samuel, 1952; children: Daniel b. 1954, Claude b. 1955, Jacqueline b. 1958; edn: BS, Univ. Lausanne 1946; MS (Dipl. Ing.), Swiss Fed. Inst. of Technol. Zurich 1948; MEE, Syracuse Univ. 1955. Career: research engineer Jaeger Inc. Basel, Switzerland 1948-50; instr. Swiss Fed. Inst. of Technol. 1950-51; mgr. Electronic Devices & Applications Lab., Gen. Electric Co. 1951-61; dir. engrg. Electronic Systems and Products Div., Martin Marietta Corp. 1961-64; dir. ops. Defense Sys. Div., The Bunker- Ramo Corp. 1964-66; v.p., gen. mgr. Magnavox Research Labs. 1966-75; senior v.p., gen. mgr. Magnavox Govt. and Indsl. Electronics Co., Advanced Products Div. 1975-80; pres. Advanced Products and Systems Co., div. of Magnavox Govt. & Indsl. Electronics Co. 1980−; non-res. staff mem. M.I.T. 1956-69), course leader G.E. Profl. Bus. Mgmt. Tng. course; adv. bd. elec. and computer engrg. dept. UC Santa Barbara 1980-; adv. and devel. council CSU Long Beach Sch. of Engrg. 1985-; guest spkr. Club of Rome mtg. Phila. 1976; fellow: Inst. Elec. Electron. Engrs. 1961, AAAS 1982; mem: IEEE (guest editor spl. issue of Proceedings of IEEE on Integrated Electronics 1964, gen. chmn. Internat. Solid-State Circuits Conf. 1960, dir. 1970-77, treas. 1973, v.p. regl. activities 1974, pres. 1975), AAAS 1980-, Am. Astronautical Soc. 1976-, United Jewish Appeal (chmn. engrg. div. 1955-57); publ: 20 tech. and scientific articles, co-author 2 tech. books; 12 US and several fgn. patents; Jewish. Res: 606 N Oakhurst Dr Beverly Hills 90210 Ofc: 2829 Maricopa St Torrance 90503

STERN, BART R., manufacturer, food technologist; b. Nov. 4, 1926, Stropkou, Czech.; s. Mor Moshe and Regina (Weiss) S.; m. Anne C. Gati, Feb. 7, 1982; children: Jonathan b. 1967, Nina b. 1969; edn: Carls Univ. of Prague; BS, summa cum laude, Univ. of Berne, Switz.; PhD in econs., London Sch. of Econs., England. Career: export mgr. Burrows Ltd., Ossett, England; pres. Bartlay Trading Corp., N.Y.; sales mgr. S.F. Lawrence Co., Miami, Fla.; pres. Spice King Corp., Culver City; instr. econs., Vista Intern, cons.; honors: govt. recogn. for establishing mfg. ops. in third world countries; mem: Inst. of Food Technol., Am. Spice Trade Assn., Am. Nutritional Council (Internat. mem. to fgn. govts. on devel. & processing food prods.); civic: L.A. Bureau of Jewish Edn. (bd.), 1984 Olympic Com. (commnr.), founding mem. Feeding the Hungry Worldwide/Hebrew Univ., Jerusalem; works: invented var. dehydrated foods, 7 fruits; mil: Czech Army Officer. Res: 438 El Camino Beverly Hills 90212 Ofc: Spice King Corp. 6009 Washington Blvd Culver City 90232

STERN, JEFFERY ERIC, chiropractor; b. Oct. 29, 1959, San Gabriel, Calif.; s. Edward Lee and Joan Estelle (Gefter) S.; edn: AA, Pierce Jr. Coll. 1979; CSU Northridge 1979-80; BS, Cleveland Chiro. Coll. 1981, DC, 1982; Diplomate Nat. Bd. Chiro. Examiners. Career: intern, res. Cleveland Chiro. Coll. 1982-84; chiropractor West Val Chiro., Ctr. Reseda 1984-85, Central Valley Chiro. Reseda 1985−; mem: Am. Chiro. Assn. (councils on neurol., nutrition, roentgenology), Am. Coll. Sports Med., L.A. County Chiro. Assn., San Fernando Valley Chiro. Assn., grad. Parker Chiro. Found., Northridge CofC, Reseda CofC, B'nai B'rith Massada Lodge (trustee), Cheveland Chiro. Coll. Alumni, L.A. Coll. of Chiro. Alumni; Democrat; Jewish; rec: shooting, tennis, basketball, football, swimming, record collecting. Res: 1244 W San Bruno Fresno 93711 Ofc: Central Calif. Chiropractic 1782 E Bullard Ste 102 Fresno 93710

STERN, WOLF HARRY, lawyer, financial executive; b. May 28, 1923, Gelsenkirchen, Germany; nat. 1942; s. Morris and Johanna (Loeb) S.; Edn: BA, UCLA, 1947; LLB, JD, USC, 1950; m. 2d., Alban Ann Weiss, June 13, 1982; children: Lawrence Alan b. 1952, Douglas Wayne b. 1953, William Rodney b. 1955. Career: senior partner law firm Stern & Goldstock, Newport Beach, 1950−; pres. Bellflower Investment Co., 1964−; partner S & S Properties, Newport Bch. 1965−; partner G & W Properties, Newport Bch. 1967−; vice chmn. adv. bd. Bellflower Natl. Bank, 1962-64, dir. 1964-65; dir. Calif. Pacific Bank, 1969-77; dir. Garden State Bank, 1973-76; v. chmn. Cerritos Valley Bank, 1974-80; chmn. Bellflower Svgs. & Loan, now Equitable Svgs. & Loan, 1977-85; honors: Young Man of Year, City of Bellflower 1954. Mem: Am., Calif., Orange County bar assns., Am. Trial Lawyers Assn., Bellflower Jr. CofC (pres. 1956), Bellflower Lions Club (pres. 1954, 58), Bellflower Elks Lodge, Lions Internat. (Dist. Gov. 1965-66), Bellflower Coordinating Council (pres. 1953), Compton Bar Assn. (treas. 1956), Costa Mesa Newport Harbor Lions Club 1982-, Newport Irvine Profl. Assn. 1982- (pres. 1985), Newport CofC 1983-, Balboa Bay Club (Newport Beach); mil: sgt. US Army Signal Corps, 3 Battle Stars, lt. Mil. Intelligence; Jewish, pres. Bellflower-Lakewood Jewish Community Ctr., 1952; rec: photog., travel. Res: 49 Southampton Ct Newport Beach 92660 Ofc: Stern & Goldstock, 500 Newport Center Dr Ste. 400, Newport Beach 92660

STERNE, GEORGE FREDERICK, marketing executive, publisher; b. Jan. 14, 1925, Brantford, Ontario, Canada; s. George F. and Annie W. (Wright) S.; m. Lydia Hollingsworth, Apr. 11, 1953; children: George b. 1956, John b. 1958; edn: BA w/ honors, Univ. Western Ontario 1950; Chartered Life Underwriter 1965. Career: tech. correspondent Atlas Chemicals Wilmington, Del. 1950-52; asst. sales mgr. Corrulux Corp. Houston 1952-55; pres. Tex. Gulf Investment Corp. Houston 1955-58; dir. mktg. Statesman Nat. Life Ins. Co. Houston 1958-64; v.p., dir. mktg. Standard Life & Accident Ins. Co. San Diego 1964-74; pres. George Sterne Agency S.D. 1974−; dir. G.F. Sterne & Sons Brantford, Canada 1964-79; mem: Dir. Mktg. Assn., Am. Assn. Chartered Life Underwriters, Nat. Assn. Life Underws., Sales & Mktg. Assn. of S.D. (dir. 1973-, pres. 1983-84, 84-85), Rotary 1984-; publr. Seven Money Manuals; Presbyterian; rec: music, golf, investments. Res: 17378 Francisco Dr San Diego 92128 Ofc: George Sterne Agency 8361 Vickers St Ste 304 San Diego 92111

STERNS, GERALD C., lawyer; b. June 28, 1932, Oakland; s. George Frederick and Kathleen (Carey) S.; m. Catherine (dec. 1977); children: Cynthia b. 1955, Karen b. 1957, Janet b. 1962, John b. 1964; m. 2d Elizabeth Walker, May 6, 1979; children: Kathleen b. 1980, Patrick b. 1983, Merrin b. 1985; edn: BS, Univ. of Iowa 1954; JD, UC Hastings Coll. of Law 1959; admitted to Bars of US Supreme Ct. (1981), Calif. (1960) and Hawaii (1983). Career: assoc. to ptr. Walkup Law Ofcs., San Francisco 1959-70; senior ptr. Walkup, Downing & Sterns, San Francisco 1970-77; founder, sr. ptr. Sterns, Bostwick & Tehin, San Francisco (now Sterns, Smith, Walker & Grell); ptr. Sterns & Ingram, Honolulu, Ha. 1981−; author, lectr., cons., instr. in law & trial tatics San Francisco Law Sch., Hastings Coll. of Advocacy, Calif. Cont. Edn. of Bar; honors: ed. in chief, Hastings Law Journ.; Order of the Coif; grad. Air Accident Investigation course, Royal Acad. of Technology, Stockholm, Sweden; Recogn. of Trial Experience & Ability, Calif. Trial Lawyers Assn.; arbitrator, judge prom tem, local state cts.; mem: Internat. Acad. of Trial Lawyers, Am. Bd. of Trial Advocates, Am. Bd. of Profl. Liability Attys., Soc. of Air Safety Investigators, Am. Judicature Soc., Head-Royce Sch. Fund Raising Com., Oceanic Soc., Costeau Soc., Supreme Ct. Hist. Soc.; publs: num. articles for legal & trial publs.; mil: 1st lt US Army 1954-56; Democrat; rec: landscape gardening, painting, guitar. Res: 33 Tyson Cir Piedmont 94611 Ofc: 280 Utah St. San Francisco 94103

STERZER, STEVEN KENT, surgeon; b. Feb. 21, 1949, Salt Lake City, Ut.; s. Roy E. and Bonnie J. (Crosier) S.; m. Elisabeth, Sept. 1, 1978; 1 son: Nicholas b. 1985; edn: BS, Univ. of Utah 1971, MD, 1975; bd. cert. urologist 1982. Career: pvt. practice in urology Chico, Calif. 1980−; staff N.T. Enloe Mem. (chief of surgery 1985-87) and Chico Comm. Hosps. (former chmn. joint credentials com.); bd. dirs., secy./treas. No. State IPA, A Med. Grp., Inc.; honors: Phi Beta Kappa 1972; mem: Butte-Glenn Med. Soc. (budget com. chmn. 1985); Chico CofC; Am. cancer Soc.; Planned Parenthood Vol. Worker; publ. tech. art. in med. journ. 1979; Protestant; rec: wine collector adn connoisseur. Ofc: Steven K. Sterzer, MD, Inc. 1812 Esplanade Chico 95926

STETLER, CLAUDIA GAY, engineering co. executive; b. May 26, 1953, New Brighton, Penn.; d. Zigmund Joseph and Dina (Justi) Lesinski; edn: BS, Penn. State Univ. 1976; Okla. State. Univ. 1980-81; St. Mary's Coll. 1984-85. Career:sys. engr. US Nuclear Regulatory Commn., Silver Springs, Md. 1977-78, tech. asst., Wash. DC 1978-79; mech. engr. McAlester Army Ammunition Plant, McAlester, Okla. 1979-81; senior engr. EDS Nuclear Inc., San Francisco 1981-82; lead senior engr. Impell Corp. (formerly EDS Nuclear Inc.), San Francisco 1982-83; supvg. engr., Walnut Creek 1983-85, sect. mgr., City of Industry 1985−; honors: Spl. Achiev. Award, US Nuclear Regulatory Commn. 1977; High Performance Award, US Nuclear Regulatory Commn. 1979; Careerist of the Year, McAlester Bus. & Profl. Women's Club 1981; mem: Soc. of Women Engrs., Am. Nuclear Soc., Big Sisters of Am.; rec: writing, jogging. Res: 123 So. Figueroa St. So. Tower 1409, Los Angeles 90012 Ofc: Impell Corp., 17890 Castleton St. Ste. 305 City of Industry 91748

STEWART, CHARLES DONOVAN, dentist; b. Feb. 20, 1958, Van Nuys, Calif.; s. Donald Willard and Donna Frances (Graves) S.; m. Kathleen Campbell, Aug. 1, 1981; 1 dau. Kristen b. 1983; edn: biol., Univ. So. Calif. 1975-79; DMD, Oral Roberts Univ. 1983. Career: research asst. Oral Roberts Univ.; reg. dental asst. Dr. W. Haver Encino; gen. dentist self employed; tchg. asst. oral/maxillofacial radiology Oral Roberts Univ. 1980-83; honors: Achievement Awards (removable denture prosthetics, dental radiol. 1983), Outstanding Senior Dental Research Student 1983, Calif. senate Resolution 1974, Eagle Scout 1974, God & Country Award (Boy Scouts), Alpha Mu Gamma; mem: Am. Assn. Dental Research, Internat. Acad. Dental Research, Am. Acad. Dental Radiol., Acad. Gen. Dentistry, Am., Calif. Dental Assns., San Fernando Valley Dental Soc., Am. Orthodontic Soc., Christian Dental Soc., Nat. Eagle Scout Assn., Phi Delta Theta, Alumni Club (USC, ORU), Intergreek Soc. (USC); co-author articles Jour. Prosthetic Dentistry 1985; Republican; Congregational. Res: 29145 Hillrise Dr Agoura Hills 91301 Ofc: 15720 Ventura Blvd, Ste 609, Encino 91436

STEWART, JAMES JONES, physician; b. Oct. 10, 1904, Greenville, Ala.; s. Eldred M. and Ida P. Stewart; m. Mary Berry, 1941; children: Mary, b. 1943, Cecile, b. 1944, James Jones Jr., b. 1950; edn: AB, Samford Univ., Howard Coll., 1925; M.MU, Univ. of Cincinnati 1929; BS, Springhill Univ. 1931; MD, Tulane Univ. 1936. Certified Sex Therapist, AASECT, 1976. Career: intern No. Louisiana, Sanitarium Shreveport, 1936-37; res. ob/gyn Employees Hosp., Fairfield, Ala. 1937-40; pvt. practice OB/Gyn, Birmingham, Ala. 1940-43, San Marino, Calif. 1946−; assoc. prof. Narramore Grad. Sch. of Psychology (marriage, sexology) 1974−; awards: Citizen of Year, City of Alhambra (1954), Visiting fellowship in gyn. Tulane Univ. (1967), AMA Physician Recognition Awards, CMA Physician Recognition Awards; past Chief OB/Gyn Dept., Methodist Hosp. of So. Calif., Alhambra Comm. Hosp.; mem: Soc. for Sci. Study of Sex (nat. bd. 1977-83, pres. Western Region 1979, bd. govs. 1976-84), AMA, CMA, LA County Med. Assn., Calif. Assn. Obstets. and Gyn., Pacific Coast, Am., Internat. Fertility Socs., founding fellow Am. Geriatric Soc., fellow Am. Soc. Abdominal Surgeons, Am. Assn. of Sex Educators Counselors and Therapists, Sex Information and Edn. Council of US, charter mem. Fellows of Masters & Johnson Inst., Janus Information Facility, Gender Dysphoria Assn.; Republican; Congregational; rec: snow sports, photog., horticulture Res: 1708 Oak Grove Ave San Marino 91108 Ofc: J. Jones Stewart, MD, Inc. 375 Huntington Dr, Suite E, San Marino 91108

STEWART, JOHN FORBES, investment advisor; b. Apr. 8, 1929, San Francisco; s. John Loftus and Katherine (Forbes) S.; m. Ann Churchman, June 20,

1953; children: Douglas b. 1957, Derek (1961-1983); edn: grad. Morgan Prk Mil. Acad., Chgo. 1947; BA, Lake Forest Coll. 1951; MBA cand., CSU San Jose Grad. Sch. of Business 1956-57, NY Inst. of Fin. 1957; Reg. Rep., NYSE (1957), Reg. Investment Advisor, Calif. (1970-), SEC (1971-79). Career: exec. tng. pgm. Bank of Am. Hq., San Francisco 1956; registered rep. Dean Witter & Co., Palo Alto 1957-65; portfolio mgr. Wells Fargo Bank, S.F. 1967-68; research/instnl. rep. Glore Forgan Staats, Inc., San Francisco 1968-70; inv. advisor/prin., mgr. security investment portfolios for corporate pension and profit sharing funds, founds., endowment funds, and individuals; cons. Trust Inv. Dept., Bank of the West, San Jose 1982-84, Finl. Research & Systems (FRS) Assocs., Menlo Park 1975-76; past mem. Newcomen Soc., Aircraft Owners & Pilots Assn., Peninsula Estate Planning Council, Penin. Stock & Bond Club (charter), Palo Alto CofC, Am. Inst. of Banking, Omaha Jr. CofC, Omaha Press Club (charter), Omaha Area Public Info. Ofcrs. Club; clubs: Los Altos Golf and Country, Rotary (Paul Harris Fellow 1982, Los Altos Rotary Endowment Fund Fellow 1984); mil: 1st lt. US air Force 1953-55; rec: all sports, music, pvt. pilot. Res: 13075 Alta Lane South Los ALtos Hills 94022 Ofc: 444 First St Los Altos 94022

STEWART, JOHN MARK, law school professor; b. Nov. 22, 1951, Yakima, Wash.; s. H. David and Edith G. (Carlton) S.; m. Janet, March 18, 1978; 1 son, Jeffrey b. 1983; edn: AA, Santa Ana Coll. 1973; BA, Biola Univ. 1974; MA, Talbot Theological Sem. 1976; JD, Western State Univ. 1984. Career: prof. American Christian Theological Sem., Anaheim 1976-81; pres. Stewart Realty, Orange 1980 – ; prof. Simon Greenleaf Sch. of Law, Anaheim 1981 – ; radio talk show host, KBRT Radio, Los Angeles 1985 – ; asst. dean Greenleaf Sch. of Law, Anaheim 1985 – ; lectr. USC, Whittier Coll., Cerritos Coll., Golden West Coll., Orange Coast Coll.; honors: Top 5 Oralists, Phillip Jessup Internat. Law Moot Ct. 1983; mem: Kappa Tau Epsilon, Nat. and Calif. Assns. Realtors, Christian Civil Liberties Union, Christian Legal Soc.; works: cons., author, speaker, num. books, articles and tapes; Republican; Evangelical (ordained minister); rec: skiing, fishing, collecting baseball cards. Ofc: Simon Greenleaf School of Law, 3855 E. La Palma Anaheim 92807

STEWART, WILFORD ROMNEY, retail sales executive; b. Dec. 22, 1946, White Plains, NY; s. Isaac Mitton and June (Woodruff) S.; m. Sonia Franklin, June 25, 1966; children: Patrick b. 1967, James b. 1968, Shannon b. 1972, Somer b. 1975; edn: BA, Univ. of Redlands, 1968; Calif. real estate sales lic., life/health ins. lic. 1974-. Career: dept. mgr. J.C. Penney Co. in Indio and Palm Springs, 1968-74; founder/chmn. bd. The Instep, Inc. (retail store), Palm Desert 1975 – ; pres. Stewart-Hoffman, Inc. Laguna Beach 1982 – ; pres. 4-Seasons, Inc. Palm Desert 1983 – ; real estate sales assoc. Tom Collins & Assoc., 1978-; sustaining mem. BSA 1982; Republican; Mormon. Res: 75-288 Palm Shadow Dr Indian Wells 92210 Ofc: The Instep, Inc. 73-370 El Paseo, Palm Desert 92260

STEWART-FUNCHES, PEGGY JEAN, educator, science consultant; b. Aug. 28, 1949, Grenada, Miss.; d. Harry Nelson and Eugenia Delores (Ford) Stewart; m. Otis Funches, Jan. 21, 1965, div.; 1 dau. Tracy b. 1966; edn: BS, Jackson State Univ. 1970; MA, CSU San Diego 1972; postgrad. work USC 1976-77, UCSD 1984. Career: tchr./ chair Sci. Dept. Lincoln High Sch. 1972-78; biomedical lab. instr. Lincoln Ctr. for Medicine and Health, San Diego City Schs., 1977 – ; sci. cons. (Tricology) Elasta Products Co.; honors: San Diego Black Achievement Award in Sci. (1980), S.D. Co. Sci. Tchr. of the Year (1985), outstanding sci. award, Gamma Delta Rho (1985), Black Engr.'s Award; civic vol. with Elementary Inst. of Sci. (com. for Edn. of Black Children), Youth Volunteers in Action, Hypertension Council; publs: The Hist. of Blacks in Science (1977), curriculum work for Medical Magnets and Sci. Magnets for S.D. City Schs.; Self-Realization Fellowship; rec: shopping, reading. Res: 5969 Quiet Slope Dr San Diego 92120 Ofc: Lincoln Medical Magnet 150 S 49th St San Diego 92113

STICKLEY, FRANK, chiropractor; b. Aug. 6, 1948, Salt Lake City, Utah; s. Howard J. and Marjorie (Lindsey) Buckley; m. Donna Turner, Jan. 7, 1983; children: Debra b. 1970, Mark b. 1973, Monique b. 1977, Brenna b. 1979, Justin b. 1981; edn: BS in psych., sci., 1974, MS in neurophysiol., M.S.I.U., 1975; DC, Cleveland Chiropractic Coll., L.A. 1976; Master Herbalist, 1984, Dr. Naturopathy, 1984, Master Iridologist, 1985, Claytons Sch. of Natural Healing; Certified Nutrition Cons., Am. Assn. Nutrn. Cons. 1983; Fellow Internat. Acad. Clin. Acupuncture 1985. Career: pvt. practice chiropractic, nutrition, herbal and homeopathic med., naturopathy, iridology and acupuncture; founder, pres. Found. for Natural Health Awareness, Paso Robles; disability evaluator, sev. workmens comp. insurance carriers; tchr. and lectr. to lay groups on natural health techniques; Am. Red Cross instr. CPR, First Aid (chmn. Disaster Plnng. Com., Paso Robles chpt.); mem: Am. Chiro. Assn., Calif. Chiro. Assn. (Councils on Roentgenol., sports injuries, nutrition), Central Coast Chiro. Soc., Am. Assn. of Nutrition Consultants, Nat. Acad. Research Biochemists, Am. Coll. Preventive Med., Canadian Acupuncture Soc., Parker Chiro. Research Found., Found. for Chiro. Edn. and Research, Am. Disability Eval. Research Inst.; active in Boy Scouts Am., Paso Robles CofC; research: in chiro. techniques, megavitamin and orthomolecular therapy, in application of electronics and laser to acupuncture techniques; mil: E4 US Army 1970, Korea; Republican; Ch. of Jesus Christ of Latter Day Saints; rec: family and church activities. Res: 4555 Jardine Rd Paso Robles 93446 Ofc: Stickley Chiropractic Office 1333 Riverside Ave Paso Robles 93446

STIEB, WILMA BEVERCOMBE, community worker; b. Oct. 28, Orient, Iowa; d. Alvin Lester and Ella Elmira (Reed) Bevercombe (both dec.); brother, Gale Reed Bevercombe (dec.); m. Clyde William Stieb, 1944 (dec.); 1 son,

Jackson Wm. (dec.); edn: stu. Gregg Bus. Coll., Univ. of Ore., Univ. of Nebr.; BS in edn., Univ. of Idaho, 1931; MS in psychol. (fellowship), 1933. Career: spl. tchr. Bus. Adminstrn. Dept., Univ. of Ida.; secty. Standard Oil Co. of Calif.; secty. PEO Sisterhood, Chpt. NK; biographical listings in Who's Who of Calif. Exec. Women, The Idaho Digest and Blue Book, The Calif. Register, Who's Who in the World, American Women, Five Hundred First Families of Am.; Family archives record 21 ancestral Coats of Arms; mem. Sons and Daughters First Settlers of Newbury, Newburyport, Mass.; mem. Daus. of Amer. Colonists, Daus. of the Amer. Revolution (Achois Comihavit Chpt.), Nat. Soc. of Magna Charta Dames, Panhellenic Club, Alpha Chi Omega (Xi Chpt.), PEO Sisterhood (NK Chpt.). Author: Occupations in the State of Idaho (1934); Democrat; Christian Ch.; rec: lectures, travel, collector old Bibles, poetry, and thoughts for special occasions. Res: 15652 Woodvale Rd Encino 91436

STIGLICH, JACOB JOHN, JR., consulting engineer; b. Dec. 21, 1938, Milwaukee, Wisc.; s. Jacob John Sr. and Augusta (Prezel) S.; edn: BSME, Marquette Univ. 1961; PhD, Northwestern Univ. 1970. Career: chief engr. Boride Products, Traverse City, Mich. 1971-74; mgr. ceramic materials Valeron Corp., Troy, Mich. 1974-76; asst. dir. tech. Eagle Picher Research Lab., Miami, Okla. 1976-78; pgm. mgr. San Fernando Labs., Pacoima 1978-84; tech. splsts. Aerojet Ordnance Co., Tustin 1984-85, cons. adv. 1985 materials – ; mem: Am. Soc. Materials, Am. Inst. Mech. Engrs., Am. Ceramic Soc., Sigma Xi, Nat. Ski Patrol; works: 30 publd. papers and reports; 35 unpubld. oral presentations; 2 patents; mil: currently, lt. col. USAR Ordnance Corps; rec: snow skiing, tennis. Ofc: Ultramet, 12173 Montague St. Pacoima 91331, Aeroject Ordnance Co., 2521 Michelle Dr. Tustin 92680

STINE, WILLIAM WALLACE, business consultant/ accounting service co. owner; b. Oct. 17, 1945, Glendale, Calif.; s. John J. and Lorraine (Geise) S.; m. Denise Powell, May 25, 1980; children: Staria b. 1976, Jonathan b. 1984; AA, Glendale Comm. Coll. 1977; BS acctg., Calif. State Univ. Northridge 1979. Career: loan ofcr. Valley Nat. Bank Glendale 1964-79; adminstrv. ofcr. Westamerica Bank San Rafael 1979-83; owner William W. Stine & Assoc. Sausalito 1983 – ; mem: Nat. Soc. Public Accts. 1984, Rotary of Sausalito (treas. 1984-86), Marin Humane Soc. (dir./ treas. 1983-), Sausalito Citizens Council (pres. 1983-), Fairbanks Family in Am.; rec: cooking & gardening. Address: 106 West St Sausalito 94965

STOCKBRIDGE, DON ISAAC, private investigator; b. Sept. 12, 1934, Tulare; s. Isaacs Wood and Crystal Pearl (Sisco) S.; m. Reba, Jan. 25, 1980; children: Donnie b. 1955, Teddy b. 1956, Nancy b. 1959, Robert b. 1961; edn: cert. approx. 20 yrs. in law enforcement, FBI, Dept. of Justice, Dept. Alcohol & Beverage Control. Career: var. retail sales pos., 5 yrs.; moulder in foundry, Santa Clara, 12 yrs.; dep. sheriff Tulare County, 5 yrs.; dep. marshal Tulare County Marshal's Ofc., 1970-, marshal Tulare Co. 1979-85, ret.; pvt. investigator prin. D & K Profl. Services, Visalia 1985 – ; recipient appreciation, Marshal's Ofc, Rotary Club, Lions Club, Moose Lodge, Tulare County Board of Supvsrs. (1985); mem. Dep. Sheriffs Assn., Marshal's & Judge's Assn., Moose (conserv. chmn.), Noon Lions, Visalia CofC; publs: Marshal's Dept. Manual of Procedure; Democrat; Prot.; rec: hunt, fish, camp. Ofc: D & K Professional Services pOB 3940 Visalia 93277

STODDARD, MICHAEL WOODWARD, financial analyst; b. Sept. 12, 1960, Los Angeles; s. Michael and Priscilla Sue (Kilts) S.; m. Patricia Susan (O'Connor), Oct. 22, 1983; edn: BS, CSU Los Angeles 1982; Certified Public Acct., Calif. (1985). Career: senior auditor Coopers & Lybrand, Los Angeles 1983-85; finl. analyst First Interstate Bank, Ltd., L.A. 1986 – ; mem. Am. Inst. CPAs, Calif. Soc. CPAs, Pasadena Jaycees; Republican; Catholic. Res: 5555 Welland Ave Apt C Temple City 91780 Ofc: First Interstate Bank Ltd 707 Wilshire Blvd Los Angeles 90017

STOFER, SUZANNE GEORGIA, real estate broker; b. Dec. 3, 1945, Mnpls.; d. Orrin George and Harriet Amelia Smith; children: Kira b. 1972, Ryan b. 1974; edn: BA, CSU San Diego 1967; Reg. Dietitian (RD), VA Hosp., Los Angeles 1970; Calif. lic. Real Estate Broker (1984). Career: pub. rels. Renken & Assocs., La Jolla 1976-78; adminstrv. dietitian AMI Corp., El Cajon Valley Hosp., 1977-80, food service dir. AMI/Coll. Park Hosp., San Diego 1980; cons. dietitian 1978; real estate sales Regatta Real Estate, San Diego 1982-84; broker/owner Pacific View Real Estate, 1984 – ; profl. awards: Rookie of Year Regatta Real Estate (1982), Million Dollar Club (1982, 83, 84, 85); mem: Am. Dietetic Assn. (1970-85), San Diego Dietetic Assn. (1970-85), Pt. Loma Bd. Realtors (bd. dirs. 1984-); civic: Childrens Hosp. & Health Ctr. (Womens Aux. 1976-80, pres. 1977), Cabrillo Elem. Sch. PTA (bd. 1983-86, pres. 1984-85); rec: travel, sports. Ofc: Pacific View Real Estate 2921 Canon St San Diego 92106

STOKER, WILLIAM ROBERT, JR., insurance co. executive; b. Oct. 2, 1950, San Bernardino; s. Wm. Robert and Bonnie Clarr (Lindsey) S.; m. Tina Marie, Nov. 9, 1985; edn: BS in edn., summa cum laude, Univ. of N.Y. 1971; tchg. credentials, N.Y., Calif. Career: underwriting/mktg. mgr. EBI Co., 1977-79; Div. mgr., asst. secty. ICW Co., 1979-81; asst. v.p. underwriting Mission Ins. Companies, 1982, vice pres. underwriting, 1983 – ; mem: NCCI (underwriting com. 1982-), WCIRB (exec. com. 1983-84), ACIC, CWCI; mil: enlisted nco US Army Airborne; Republican. Res: 8758 Aqueduct St Sepulveda 91343 Ofc: Mission Ins. Group 2600 Wilshire Los Angeles 91004

STOKES, DONALD LEE, chiropractor, consultant; b. Mar. 20, 1956, Castro Valley, Calif.; s. Harold Quinn and Ada Emeline (Goodman) S.; m. Barbara, July 13, 1978; children: Jared b. 1979, Aaron b. 1981, Mark b. 1983; edn:

Chabot Coll. 1975-77; pre-med., Brigham Young Univ. 1978-79; DC, Life Chiro. Coll.-West 1979-82; postgrad., L.A. Coll. Chiro. 1983-84; Certified Indsl. Chiro. Cons., Independent Med. Examiner, Disability Evaluator. Career: intern Cowdery Chiro. Ofcs. San Jose 1983-84; chiro. Stokes Chiro. Ofc. San Jose 1984-85; co./referral dr. several large Calif. companies 1983-85; founder, pres./cons. Bus. Indsl. Chiro. Svcs. Hayward 1980—; lectr. to phys.; honors: Dist. Svc. Award (Dynamic Essentials 1985); mem: Internat. Acad. Chiro. Indsl. Cons. 1984, Calif. Chiro. Assn. 1984, Internat. Chiro. Assn. of Calif. (bd. dirs.) Internat. Chiro. Assn. (labor & indsl. com.), South Bay Indsl. Claims Assn., Assn. for Fitness in Business; publ: Business Industrial Chiropractic Services Manual and presentation materials; Republican; L.D.S.; rec: water & snow skiing, family. Address: 3353 S. Main Ste 318 Salt Lake City Utah 84115

STOLPE, JUDITH ANN (WILLS), consultant; b. Sept. 19, 1946, St. Paul, Minn.; d. Donald Robert and Anna (Simenuk) (Korolchuk) Wills; m. Richard Henry Stolpe II, July 30, 1971; children: Dawn Elsa b. 1973, Richard Charles b. 1974, Peter Kaal b. 1974; edn: BS, Okla. State Univ. 1969, postgrad. 1971; lic. Secondary Teaching Cert., Okla. 1969, Calif. 1975. Career: math. tchr. Kerr Jr. High Sch., Midwest City, Okla. 1969-70; systems analyst, Okla. State Univ. 1970-72; dir. Math. Evening Sch., Coronado Unified Sch. Dist. 1975-83; owner/pres. End of the Line Race Consulting, 1978—; dir. 1983 Internat. Amateur Athletic Fedn. Women's World 10 KM Championship (Inaugural), Press Venue Chief for 1984 Olympics, dir. Levi-TAC U.S. Runner Ranking Service, 1983-85; dir. City of Los Angeles Marathon 1986; honors: The Circle of 100 Women (San Diego); mem: The Athletics Cong. of the U.S. 1976-; AAUW 1969-72; NEA 1969-72; publs: Geographical Locations of Minor Sports at the High Sch Level in the U.S., Rocky Mtn. Geograp. Soc. 1970; Republican; Methodist; rec: music. Res: 714 G Ave Coronado 92118 Ofc: End of the Line Race Consulting, 326 First Ave Coronado 92118

STONE, ELMER JOHN, lawyer; b. Jan. 28, 1919, Priest River, Idaho; s. Elmer Ortman and Theresa Mary (Kramer) S.; m. Paula, Feb. 22, 1962; children: Janell b. 1946, Nelda b. 1953, Elizabeth b. 1963; edn: AA, Fullerton Coll. 1940; Univ. Colo. 1944-45, UC Berkeley 1945-46; JD, USC 1948; admitted Calif. State Bar 1949, US Supreme Ct. (1969). Career: chief counsel Douglas Aircraft Co., Santa Monica 1948-68; gen. counsel Teledyne Ryan Aeronautical, San Diego 1968-72; ptnr. Van Patten, Griffin & Arndt 1972-79; ptnr. Fenwick, Stone, Davis & West, Los Angeles 1979-84; of counsel Morgan, Lewis & Bockius, L.A. 1984—; bd. chmn. American Pacific State Bank, L.A. 1974-; dir. Subaru of Am., Cherry Hill, N.J.; mem. Provost's Advis. Council UCLA Coll. of Letters & Sci.; mem: Am. Bar Assn. (1948-), Phi Alpha Delta frat., Internat. Bar Assn., Japan Am. Soc. of So. Calif. (chmn. 1960-68), L.A.-Nagoya Sister City Affil. (1972-); club: California; mil: major USMCR 1941-45, 1950-51, Order of Purple Heart, Commendn. Medal; Republican; Protestant. Res: 645 N Wilcox #3A Los Angeles 90004 Ofc: Morgan, Lewis & Bockius 611 West Sixth St 22nd Fl Los Angeles 90017

STONE, FRED, artist; b. Apr. 13, 1930, St. Louis, Mo.; s. Sam and Dorothy (Chazen) S.; m. Norma Paley, 1951; children: Laura b. 1954, Russell b. 1956; edn: Art Center Sch. 1949-52, Chouinard Art Inst. 1946-48, L.A. City Coll. 1948-49, Otis Art Inst. 1945. Career: muralist (self-empl.) Kramer Stone, Los Angeles, 1959-60; dir. of sales and mktg. Monogram Industries, L.A. 1960-76; self-empl. as painter of Thoroughbred horses, 1976—; paintings: One-Two-Three (1978), Kentucky Derby - Seattle Slew (1979), The Shoe, 8000 Wins (1981), John Henry, Bill Shoemaker up (1982), The Final Thunder - Man o'War (1983), The Eternal Legacy (1985); book: Fred Stone Paints the Sport of Kings (1985); mil: airman 1/c Air Nat. Guard 1948-58; Jewish. Res: 5911 Colodny Dr Agoura 91301

STONE, JOEL ARTHUR, engineering executive; b. Aug. 17, 1952, Columbus, Ohio; s. Walter Stanley and Eugenia Rose (Findeis) S.; m. Charlene McManis, Mar. 20, 1976; 1 son, Jared Nicholas b. 1985; edn: BS in chem. eng., Virginia Tech 1975; MS, biochem. & chem. eng., Univ. of Pa. 1976. Career: process engr. R&D, Ashland Chem. Co., Dublin, Ohio; project engr. Eli Lilly and Co., Indpls., Ind.; G.B. Fermentation Indus., Kingstree, S.C.; project and process engr. (design, constrn., startup ethanol facility) A.E. Staley Mfg. Co., Decatur, Ill. then mgr. alcohol ops. facility in Louden, Tenn.; project mgr. (the largest barley to fuel ethanol facility) Ultrasystems Engrs. and Constructors, Irvine; current plant mgr. for Agri Fuels, New Iberia, La.; honors: Tau Beta Pi (1974), Phi Eta Sigma (chpt. pres. 1971), Phi Lambda Upsilon (1972), NSF research grant (1974), Univ. of Pa. fellowship (1975); mem. Am. Inst. Chem. Engrs. (chpt. v.p. 1974-75), Jaycees (chpt. v.p. 1979); Republican; Lutheran (pres. local youth group 1970); rec: running, tennis, sports car racing. Res: 23446 Bolivar Mission Viejo 92691 Ofc: Ultra Systems 16795 Von Karman Ave Irvine 92714

STONE, MARK ALLEN, chiropractor; b. Feb. 12, 1957, Riudosa, N.Mex.; s. Dwight Hathaway and Lorraine H. (Wheeler) S.; m. Lynn, June 18, 1977; children: Adam J. b. 1977, Vanessa R. b. 1983; edn: BS, Los Angeles Coll. of Chiropractic 1980, DC, 1983. Career: preceptor doctor R. Lloyd Friesen Chiropractic, Thousand Oaks 1983-84; pvt. practice Chiropractic Plus, Camarillo 1984—; workers compensation doctor, Ventura County Police, Fire and County Employees; mem: Am. and Calif. Chiropractic Assns., Nat. Bd. Chiropractic Examiners, Ventura Co. Boy Scouts of Am. (exec. com.), Morning Rotary of Camarillo (exec. com.); Republican; rec: snow skiing, photog. Res: 4213 E. Croydon Ave. Camarillo 93010 Ofc: Chiropractic Plus, 360 Mobil Ave. Ste. 116 Camarillo 93010

STONE, NORMAN MICHAEL, clinical child psychologist; b. March 23, 1949, Baltimore, Md.; s. Forrest Leon and Beverly Iola (Gendason) S.; m. Susan Foster Hoitt, May 18, 1981; children: Caroline b. 1975, Brittany b. 1985; edn: BA, UCLA 1971; MA, Univ. of Iowa 1974, PhD, 1976. Career: supvr. Youth & Family Svcs., Abilene Regl. Mental Health- Mental Retardation Ctr., Abilene, Texas 1976-79; also, adj. faculty Dept. Psychology Hardin-Simmons Univ. & McMurray Coll.; asst. dir. Child Abuse Svcs., San Fernando Valley Child Guidance Clinic, Northridge 1979—; also, vis. prof. UCLA 1980-81; clin. assoc. prof. Fuller Theological Sem. 1982—; chpsn. Mental Health Assn. Youth Comm. 1978; chpsn. Big Brothers/ Big Sisters of Am. Steering Com. 1979; apptd. to Los Angeles Superior Ct. Panel of Expert Witnesses 1981; cons. Dependency Ct. and Family Law 1981—; honors: USPHS Fellow 1972-74; Sigma Xi 1974; presdtl. apptd. to Council on Tchg., Univ. of Iowa 1975; elected, NY Acad. of Scis. 1978; mem: Am. Psychological Assn., Am. Assn. of Univ. Profs., Los Angeles Interagency Council on Abuse and Neglect, Calif. Bar Assn. (Com. on Visitation & Custody), Acad. of American Poets; author: num. articles, paper presentations, films, and assessment tech. appearing in profl. journs.; rec: poetry, music, nature. Ofc: San Fernando Valley Child Guidance Clinic, 9650 Zelzah Ave. Northridge

STONE, RICHARD ALAN, physician; b. Nov. 21, 1942, Cambridge, Mass.; s. Jack David and Gail (Polak) S.; m. Suanne Poteet, Dec. 5, 1982; children: Lisa b. 1970, Caroline b. 1973, Chelsea b. 1985; edn: AB, Brown Univ. 1964; MD, Tufts Univ. 1970. Career: physician, nephrologist; asst./assoc. prof. of medicine UC San Diego, 1977-79; dir. Hemodialysis & Hypertension, VA Hosp., San Diego 1977-79; chmn. Nephrology Eisenhower Med. Ctr., Rancho Mirage 1979—, chmn. Medicine 1981—; senior attg. phys. Eisenhower Med. Ctr. 1985; honors: Alpha Omega Alpha 1969; Tufts Med. Alumni Prize Physiology, Anatomy, Pathology, Microbiology; mem. Am. Soc. of Nephrology, Am. Heart Assn., Am. Found. Clin. Res., Nat. Kidney Found.; publs: over 100 med. arts. on high blood pressure and kidney disease; mil: capt. USAR 1970-76; rec: tennis. Res: 45-605 Camino Del Rey Indian Wells 92770

STONE, RICHARD JAMES, lawyer; b. Apr. 30, 1945, Chgo. Ill.; s. Milton M. and Ruth Jean (Manaster) S.; m. Lee Lawrence, Sept. 1, 1979; children: Robert Allyn b. 1974, Katherine Jenney b. 1982, Grant Lawrence b. 1985; edn: BA econ., Univ. of Chgo. 1967; JD, UC Los Angeles 1970; admitted Calif. State Bar 1971. Career: atty. assoc. O'Melveny & Myers, Los Angeles 1971-77; deputy asst. general counsel US Dept. of Defense, Wash DC 1978-79; asst. to the Secty. US Dept. of Energy, Wash DC 1979-80; counsel Sidley & Austin, Los Angeles 1981, ptnr. 1982—; mem. US del. Micronesian Polit. Status Negotiations 1978-79; advis. panel Council of Energy Resource Tribes 1981; mem. Public Sector Task Force, Calif. Senate Com. on Long Range Policy Planning 1985; bd. vis. Southwestern Univ. Sch. of Law 1983-; judge Philip C. Jessup Internat. Law Moot Ct. Competition, Pacific Regl. Round (1984); honors: Amos Alonzo Stagg Medal and Howell Murray Alumni Medal, Univ. Chgo. 1967; honoree, Nat. Conf. of Black Mayors 1980; spl. citation for outstanding performance U.S. Sec. of Energy 1981; editor-in-chief UCLA Law Rev. (Vol. 17); mem: Am., Calif. (Conf. of Dels. 1982-, exec. com. L.A. Del. 1984-), Los Angeles County (exec. com., secty. Antitrust Sect., Internat. Law Sec., Trial Lawyers Sect.; Com. on Alternative Dispute Resolution; chair Ct. Improvements Com. 1985-6; secty. Fed. Cts. and Practices Com. 1985-6; v.ch. Neighborhood Justice Center Project Com. 1985-6, Professional Competence Com. 1984-, Specialization Com. 1982-4) bar assns., Assn. of Bus. Trial Lawyers, Phi Gamma Delta; Democrat; Presbyterian. Ofc: Sidley & Austin, 2049 Century Park East, 35th Fl, Los Angeles 90067

STONE, WILLIAM THOMAS, music teacher; b. Mar. 24, 1921, Sacramento; s. Wm. T. and Henrietta Dorothy (Jurgens) S.; m. Ruth Danielsen, July 25, 1954; children: Michael b. 1955, Peter b. 1957; edn: BS, UC Berkeley 1942. Career: owner Wm. T. Stone Music Studio; organist/choir dir. St. Paul's Episcopal Ch., Salinas 1951-54, Temple Sinai, Oakland 1948-77; organist St. Mark's Episcopal Ch., Berkeley 1947-51, USCG Tng. Center Chapel, Alameda 1963-79, St. Bonaventure's Catholic Ch., Concord 1979-; mem. Am. Guild of Organists (dean Contra Costa County chpt. 1966-68), Rotary; mil: sgt. USAF 1943-45; Republican; Episcopal. Res: 2645 San Carlos Dr Walnut Creek 94598

STONG, PETER ALLAN, health care co. administrator; b. June 22, 1947, Pasadena; s. Harold Francis and Roberta Mae (Wagner) S.; m. Carol, Nov. 21, 1970; 1 child, Morgan b. 1977; edn: BA, Whittier Coll. 1969; MBA, UC Los Angeles 1974; Calif. lic. Nursing Home Adminstr. (1974). Career: adminstr. Beverly Ents., 1974-80; regional adminstr. Casa Blanca Conv. Homes, 1980-84, Care Ents., 1984—; honors: Who's Who Am. Colls. and Univs. (1974); mem. Calif. Assn. Health Facilities (1974-85), Kiwanis (1974-78), Rotary (1978-80), CofC (1974-80); mil: 1st lt. USAF 1968-72; Republican; Episcopal; rec: tennis, basketball. Res: 5996 Amondo Circle Simi Valley 93063 Ofc: Care Enterprises 303 N Glenoakds Ste 180 Burbank 91502

STOVALL, DANNY FLOYD, developer/real estate broker; b. June 28, 1943, Poway; s. Lloyd G. and Laura Lorraine Stovall; children: Julie b. 1967, Eric b. 1971; edn: BA psy., Univ. of N.M. 1965; AA in crim. justice, AA in real estate, Miramar Coll., 1978, 79; Calif. lic. R.E. broker. Career: personal adminstrn. Dynalectron Corp., Land-Air Div., H.A.F.B., New Mex. 1969-71; FBI special agt., San Diego 1971-79; broker/devel. R.W.-Realty Land, Poway 1979—; gen. partner Vista Sundowner 1977-81, Vista Santana 1979-; pres. Hospice of No. County 1984-; honors: San Diego Board of Realtors Exchangor of Month 6/84; co. top sales awards 1981, 82, 83, 84; mem. San Diego Problem Solvers, S.D. Bd. of Realtors, Exchangors, Poway Problem Solvers, Poway CofC; publs:

How to Buy Foreclosure Property (pamphlet 1982), How to Exchange, Poway R.E. Profls. 1982; mil: 1st lt. US Army Intell. Ofcr., 1966-69, Army Commendns.; Republican; Baptist; rec: hunting, camping, fishing. Res: 12302 Old Stone Rd Poway 92064 Ofc: R.W.-Realty Land, 13507 Midland Rd Poway 92064

STOVER, JOE VICTOR, manufacturing co. executive; b. June 25, 1930, Pendleton, Ore.; s. Joseph Bonaparte and Jean Marie (Victor) S.; m. Martha Josa, Nov. 7, 1957; children: Russell, b. 1961, Janet, b. 1965; edn: BSEE, Ore. State Univ. 1952, MSEE 1953, postgrad. wk. in physics 1953-55; dip. Unity Sch. of Ministerial and Rel. Studies, 1973-75, Licensed Minister Assn. of Unity Churches, 1975. Career: instr. Ore. State Univ., Corvallis, Ore. 1953-56; tech. staff Hughes Aircraft Co., Los Angeles 1956-58; staff engr. Hughes Aircraft Co., Fullerton 1958-59, group hd. 1959-63, section hd. 1963-69, assoc. dept. mgr. 1969-73, senior scientist 1975-76, dept. mgr. Transmitter Dept. 1976−; instr. Hughes Aircraft Co. Adv. Technical Edn. Pgm. 1959, 1982-; asst. minister Christ Ch. Truth, Santa Ana 1975-77, assoc. minister Christ Ch. Unity, Anaheim 1979−; honors: Eta Kappa Nu (elec. engring. hon.) Pi Chpt. (1953), recipient L.A. Hyland Patent Award, Hughes Aircraft Co. (1982), keynote spkr. 1984 16th Power Modulator Symp., listed Who's Who In the West, 14th Ed.; mem. IEEE West Coast Electronic Transformers Sub-Com. (chmn. 1965-68), Modulator Symposium (exec. com. 1973-), pgm. chmn. 1984 IEEE High Voltage Workshop; mem. Tau Chpt., Tau Kappa Epsilon Frat. (v.p. and faculty advisor 1952-56), Theosophical Soc. in Am.; works: 8 Patents Granted, 8 Pending or Disclosed, 10 Tech. Papers; Republican; Prot.; rec: amateur geologist. Res: 1250 Jefferson St Placentia 92670 Ofc: Hughes Aircraft Co., POB 3310, Bldg 600/F145, Fullerton 92634

STRANGES, FRANK E., clergyman, educator; b. Oct. 6, 1927, Bklyn.; s. Natale A. and Catherine (Filardo) S.; m. Julie Ann Corcoran, Mar. 12, 1985; children: Sean b. 1974, Michael b. 1975; edn: ThD in theology, Tenn. Christian Univ. 1962, PhD theology, 1964; Doctor of Psychology, Union Univ. 1960, Doctor of Internat. Law, 1983. Career: pres. Internat. Evangelism Crusades, 1959-86; pres., prof. Internat. Theological Seminary of Calif.; honors: Knight Comdr. Royal Knights of Justice, Knight of Jerusalem, Knight of Malta, FBI Gold Medal Award (1985), American Police Hall of Fame (1985), Gold plaque Republic of South Korea; mem: State Marshalls Assn. (asst. state dir.), Internat. Police Orgn. of Wash DC (spl. agt.), Internat. Assn. Chiefs of Police, Am. Fedn. of Police, Nat. Chaplains Assn., Silver Dollar Club; publs: author 12 books on space, sci., religion; prod. three TV documentaries and 1 full-length feature film; mil: served to 4 star general/ chaplain Chaplains Internat. Assn.; Republican; Prot.; rec: flying. Ofc: International Evangelism Crusades, Inc. 14617 Victory Blvd Ste 4 Van Nuys 91411

STRANGIO, DOMENICO, public relations executive, writer, editor; b. April 28, 1928, San Luca, Reggio Calabria, Italy, nat. US cit. 1953; s. Bruno and Maria (Papalia) S.; m. Ernestine M., Feb. 23, 1953; children: Susan b. 1955, Linda b. 1957; edn: Long Island Univ. 1959-61; Univ. of Maryland 1963-65; BA, Univ. of LaVerne 1971. Career: instr. internat. rels. and public information ofcr. USAF, Freising, ger. 1955-57; community rels. splst. USAF, Wiesbaden, Ger. 19585-9; info. supt. USAF, Garden City, NY and Mt. Clemes, Mich. 1959-63; chief public info. div. USAF, Ramstein, Gert. 1963-65; ed., founder The Eagle mag., Berlin, Gred. 1965-66; dir. pub. rels. and publs. Sacramento Metropoliton CofC, Sacramento 1967; ed. Spacemaker, McClellan AFB, Sacramento 1967-68; currently, pub. affairs ofcr. Naval Ship Weapon Systems Engring. Sta., Pt. Hueneme; co-organizer Public Information Communicators Assn.; Adopt Edn. Partnership, Oxnard Unif. H.S. Dist. 1985-86; honors: Merit Award, US Navy 1969. 1976; Spl. Achiev. Award, Ventura Co. Council, Boy Scouts Am. 1985; Pres.'s Award, 1978; Meritorious Award 1982; Herbert C Templeman Award, 1986, US Navy League; Resolutions, Assemblyman Tom McClintock (1983), State Sen. Gary Hart & Assemblyman Jack O'Connell, (1983), Calif. State (1986), Ventura Co. Supvrs. (1986); mem: Fed. Writers/ Editors Assn., PICA, Port Hueneme CofC (pres. 1984-86), Oxnard K.C., Ventura Co. Council (pres.), US Navy League, Ventura Co. Council, Boy Scouts Am., Elks, So. Calif. Golfing Assn., R&A Golf Club, Channel Islands Yacht Club; works: founder/ ed. The Eagle (1965-66), Interface (1968-81); rec: golf, travel, photog. res: 4901 Marlin Way Oxnard 93030 Ofc: Naval Ship Weapon Systems Engineering Station (NSWSES), Port Hueneme 93043

STRATTON, JOANNA LENORE, author; b. Dec. 8, 1954, Wash DC; d. Clifton Jairus, Jr. and Lydia Anne (Georges) Stratton; m. Gatis N. Roze, June 2, 1984; edn: AB, honors in econs., Harvard Univ. 1976; MBA in mktg., Stanford Univ. 1981. Career: writer under contract, Simon & Schuster, 1976-79, authored Pioneer Women: Voices From the Kansas Frontier (pub. Simon & Schuster, 1981; paperback by Touchstone Books, 1982; German transl. by Kiepenheuer & Witsch, 1985); personnel dir. The Sacramento Bee (McClatchy Newspapers), Sacramento 1982-84; writer (book in progress), 1984−; honors: 1981 Christopher Award, 1982 Women of Achievement Award, Calif. Fedn. of Bus. & Profl. Women; nominee 1983 American Book Award, nominee 1981 Western Writers of Am. Golden Spur Award; mem. The Author Guild, Western Writers of Am., Calif. Hist. Soc., Kans. State Hist. Soc., OEF Internat.; Republican; Episcopal; rec: genealogy, antiques, travel. Res: 189 Los Robles Dr Burlingame Hills 94010

STRATTON, SAMUEL JOE, physician; b. Aug. 8, 1948, Portales, N.Mex.; s. Samuel Harris and Ola Margarite (McCollaum) S.; children: Brandon b. 1975, Todd b. 1981; edn: BS, N.Mex. State Univ. 1971; MD, Univ. of N. Mex. 1975; Board certified internal medicine (1978), emergency medicine (1985). Career: emergency physician Saint Mary Medical Center, Long Beach 1978−, and base station physician for paramedics and emerg. rm. trauma physician; dir. Emergency Cardiac Care Com. Long Beach Chpt. Am. Heart Assn.; honors: Alpha Omega Alpha (1975); mem: Am. Coll. of Physicians, Am. Coll. of Emergency Physicians, Am. Heart Assn. (Calif. del. to 1985 Nat. Emergency Cardiac Care Conf. on Stds.); rec: astronomy. Ofc: Saint Mary Medical Center, Long Beach

STRAUSS, HERMINA, financial organization representative; b. May 21, 1922, Fresno, Calif.; d. Benjamin and Leah Louise (Meyer) Levy; m. Norman Strauss, Jan. 9, 1949; children: Louise b. 1949, Charles b. 1950; edn: BA, Univ. So. Calif. 1942; USC Law Sch. 1941-42; Hastings Sch. of Law 1943; Southwestern Univ. Sch. of Law 1943-44; Pacific Coast Univ. Sch. of Law 1945-46; cert. in real estate, Coll. of San Mateo 1979; reg. rep. Series 7 SEC 1984; reg. rep. Calif. Dept. of Corps.; real estate broker Calif.; life cert. law instr. adult edn. Calif.; lic. life & disability underw. Calif. Career: writer, lectr. Fresno, Alameda, San Francisco 1961−; real estate sales Dolphin Realty, Daly City 1976-77, Davis Realty, Daly City 1977-79, Seybold Realty, San Jose 1979-80; corp. supv. Cutler Mortgage Inc., Fremont 1980-84; reg. rep. Waddell & Reed Inc., Santa Clara-San Jose 1984−; pres. Strauss Inc. 1983-84; instr. contg. edn. in real estate, Fremont 1983-84; apptd. Citizens Advis. Com. to Crime-Oriented Record Process Unified Systems (CORPUS) computer 1974; mem. Cit. Advis. Com. for atty.-gen. Eville Younger 1970-78; apptd. Com. on Legal Edn. (World Assn. of Lawyers, World Peace Through Law, Geneva, Switz.) 1976; cons., observer for Internat. Fedn. of Women Lawyers to UN Social Commn. 1961, UN Peaceful Uses of Outer Space Com. 1964; honors: Woman of Achievement, US Soroptimists (1966-68), Appreciation Plaque, Alameda Co. Status of Women Commn. (1975), Woman of Achievement, Bus. & Profl. Women's San Francisco Pacifica Club (1976), Iota Tau Tau (1943), Amazons Women's Honorary USC (1941); mem: Internat. Fedn. of Women Lawyers (cochair aerospace law com. 1958-60), World Peace Through Law Ctr. 1958- (charter), Am. Assn. Univ. Women 1943-82 (past br. pres. 1958, 1975, cons. Internat. Women's Year to Status of Women com., Calif. State div. 1975-76), League of Women Voters (bd.), CROP (overseas relief, pres. exec. bd. 1972-73), Fresno YWCA (pres. 1971), Cecil Hinton Ctr. (pres. 1964-66), Fresno Salvation Army adv. bd. 1976-71, Fresno Community Council (bd. 1955-61), Fresno Vol. Bureau (v.chair 1962-65), Nat. Council Jewish Women (sect. pres. 1953-54), Bus. & Profl. Women S.F. Pacifica Club 1975-82; publs: co-authored articles in ednl. and legal jours.; papers presented Internat. Fedn. of Women Lawyers Conf. (1964, 67, 69); Democrat; Jewish; rec: violin, lapidary. Mail: POB 21246 San Jose 95151

STRAUSS, SALLY, writer; b. May 1, 1925, St. Louis, Mo.; d. Arthur and Fannie (Somit) Rubinsky; m. 2d Harry Strauss, Feb. 17, 1960; 2 sons (nee Kwart): Gary b. 1948, Michael Kwart b. 1950; edn: undergrad. stu. S.F. State Coll. and Univ. Calif., 2 years. Career: staff, No. Calif. dir. City of Hope Nat. Medical and Research Center (Duarte), San Francisco regional ofc., 1957-67; art student; freelance writer, contbr. articles in regional and nat. publs. 1967−; author: Inner Rhythm: An Exciting New Approach to Stress-Free Living (Chase Publs. 1984, 2d printing; taped by Recordings for the Blind and Calif. League for the Handicapped); num. guest appearances on local, nat. radio and TV pgms.; frequent public speaker to senior, hosp. and social groups; civic: City of Hope, Marshal Hale Meml. Hosp./SF (Library Com., estab. medical lib.), ORT; Democrat; avocation: art slide showings (Old Masters) to var. service orgns. and senior groups. Ofc: Chase Publications 1654 33rd Ave San Francisco 94122

STROH, PETER A.L., management consultant; b. Aug. 17, 1950, NY, NY; s. Oscar S. and Eva G. (Sondheimer) S.; edn: BS in civil engring., summa cum laude, Univ. of Mich. 1973, BA in urban studies 1973; M. City Plnng., M.I.T. 1975. Career: mgmt. analyst City of Boston, 1977-79; co-founder and senior ptnr. Innovation Associates, Inc. 1979−, v.p. sales & mktg. 1979-83, mng. ptnr. West Coast Office, San Francisco 1983−; certified instr. in Personal Creativity and Self-Mastery, DMA, Inc. 1981-83; mem. Organization Development (OD) Network and Bay Area OD Network; publs: contbr. profl. articles to Vision/ Action (1984), Transforming Work (1984), San Jose Bus. Jour. (1984), OD Conf. Proceedings (1980-85), Datamation (1981); Ind.; Jewish; rec: tennis, backpacking, travel. Res: 1808 Vallejo San Francisco 94123 Ofc: Innovation Assocs. Inc. 1724 Sacramento St Ste 209 San Francisco 94109

STROMBERG, JACKSON CLAFLIN, engineering and construction co. executive; b. March 8, 1936, Albuquerque, N.M.; s. Jackson Chester and Jeannette Laura (Rice) SL.; m. Elizabeth Hoem, Dec. 17, 1960; children: Lisen b. 1962, Chester b. 1965, Kirsten b. 1972; edn: AB, magna cum laude, Dartmouth Coll. 1958; MA, Univ. of Oxford 1960; LLB, Stanford Univ. 1963. Career: clerk Thelen, Marrin, Johnson & Bridges 1962, assoc. 1963-70, ptr. 1971-77; counsel Bechtel Inc. 1978-80; asst. gen. counsel Bechtel Petroleum Inc., Bechtel Power Corp. and Bechtel Civil & Minerals Inc. 1981-82; dep. mgr. finance, mgr. financial svcs., pres. Bechtel Financing Svcs. Inc. 1982−; treas. Bechtel Group Inc. 1984−; v.p. Bechtel Power Corp. 1985−; Rhodes Scholar, Oxford Univ.; bd. eds. Stanford Law Review; Stanford Univ. Moot Ct. Bd.; mem: Phi Beta Kappa, British-Am. CofC (bd. dirs.), Stock Exch. Club (bd. dirs.), World Affairs Council (bd. trustees); mil: USNR; Republican; Presbyterian; rec: tennis, skiing. Res: 27 Throckmorton Ln. Mill Valley 94941 Ofc: Bechtel Group, Inc., 50 Beale St., 5FC/35 A22, San Francisco 94105

STROMME, GARY L., law librarian; b. July 8, 1939, Willmar, Minn.; edn: BA, philo., Pacific Lutheran Univ. 1965; BLS, Univ. of Brit. Columbia Sch. of Librarianship, 1967; JD, Hastings Coll. of the Law 1973; admitted State Bar of Calif. 1973, US Supreme Ct. Bar, 1977. Career: serials librarian, Univ. of Minn., St. Paul Campus Lib. 1967-69; asst. librn. law firm McCutchen, Doyle,

Brown, Enersen, San Francisco 1970-71; asst. librn. Graham & James, S.F. 1971-73; ind. contracting atty., 1973-74; law librn. Pacific Gas & Electric Co., S.F. 1974—; mem: Internat. Soc. Gen. Semantics (pres. S.F. Chpt. 1978-80; bd. dir. 1980-81); Am. Assn. Law Libraries; Am. Bar Assn. (Sect. of Economics of Law Practice, chmn. lib. com. 1978-82); author: An Intro. to the Use of the Law Library (1974); Basic Legal Research Tech. (rev. 4th ed. 1979); mil: elect. tech. USAF 1959-63. Res: 2589 LeConte Ave Berkeley 94709 Office: PG&E 77 Beale St, 31st Fl. San Francisco 94106

STRONG, BENJAMIN RAYMOND, JR., consulting mechanical engineer; b. Dec. 25, 1946, Great Lakes, Ill.; s. Benjamin R. and Esther Edith (Heinrichs) S.; edn: BS, Univ. Ill., Chgo. Circle 1971; MS, Stanford Univ. 1974; Reg. Profl. Engr. (M17281) Calif. 1975. Career: engr. Sargent & Lundy Engrs. 1971-73; EDS Nuclear Inc. (Div. Impell Corp., subs. Combustion Engrs.) 1974-81: sr. engr., formed Thermal-Hydraulics Sect. 1974-77, supvsg. engr. Adv. Analysis Div. 1977-79, sr. tech. splst. Systems Engring. Div. 1979-81; senior assoc./dir. Echo Energy Consultants Inc. 1981-83, mgr. mech. engring. 1981-82, bd. chmn. 1982-83; owner Impulse Engineering, San Francisco 1983—; mem. Electric Power Research Inst. (Nuclear Safety Analysis Ctr.) 1978-80; S/RV Testing Owner's Gp. (subcom. on Piping Eval. 1980-81), Am. Nat. Stds. Inst. (Stds. Writing Gps. 1978-83); ASME (1974-), AIAA (1971-), ANS (1978-), NSPE (1975-), Univ. Ill. Chgo. Circle Engring. Alumni Assn. (co-founder 1971), Zeta Psi frat. (1967-), co-founder Sigma Phi chpt. 1967-; publs: computer software copyrights incl. FORTRAN Addenda, utils. for F. devel. (1984), Steam'85, props. of water and steam (1985), others; num. tech papers and presentations; coauthor nat. standards: "Pressure and Temperature Environmental Analysis Outside Containment" (ANSI/ANS 56.10 1983), "Pressure and Temperature Transient Analysis for Light Water Reactor Containments" (ANSI/ANS 56.4 1983); Christian; rec: art, music, sports. Ofc: Impulse Engineering POB 3540 San Francisco 94119-3540

STRONG, GARY EUGENE, librarian; b. June 26, 1944, Moscow, Idaho; s. A. Dwight and Cleora Anna (Nirk) S.; m. Carolyn Jean Roetker, March 14, 1970; children: Christopher Eric, Jennifer Rebecca; edn: BS, Univ. of Idaho 1966; MA, Univ. of Mich. 1967. Career: reference, adminstrv. asst. Univ. Idaho Library 1966-67; library dir. Lake Oswego Public Library, Ore. 1967-73; Everet Public Library, Wash. 1973-76; assoc. dir. Wash. State Library 1976-79, dep. state librarian 1979-80; state librarian Calif. State Library 190—; CEO Calif. Library Svcs. Bd. 1980—; v.p. bd. Calif. Coop. Library Agency for Sys. & Svcs. 1981—; founder, dir. Calif. State Library Found. 1982—; vis. lectr. Maryhurst (Ore.) Coll. 1968; Ore. Div. Cont. Edn. 1972; host weekly cable TV pgm. 1973-76; bd. dirs: Ore. Council Public Broadcasting 1969-73, Senior Svc. of Snohomish Co. 1973-76, Pacific N.W. Bibliography Ctr. 1977-80, No. Region Library Bd. 1983-, Thurston-Mason Co. Med. Health Clinic 1977-80, pres. 1979-80; advy. bd. Calif. State PTA 1981-; Ctr. for the Book, Library of Congress 1982; honors: Ore. Library Scholar, Univ. of Mich. 1967; mem: Am., Wash., Ore. (life, pres. 1970-71), and Pacific N.W. (life, pres. 1978-79) Library Assns., Library Adminstrn. & Mgmt. Assn. (pres. elect 1983), Everett Area CofC, Snohomish Co. Hist. Assn., Book Club of Calif. Ofc: P.O. Box 2037 Sacramento 95809

STRONG, RANDALL JAMES, publishing-marketing agency president; b. Nov. 3, 1955, Inglewood; s. Jack Newman and Virginia (Harling) S.; m. Sandra, June 22, 1975; children: Adam b. 1979, Christopher b. 1983; edn: AA, Santa Monica Coll. 1976; BA, CSU Northridge 1982. Career: freelance graphic designer, 1982-84, pres. R. Strong & Assocs. (full service prodn. advt., mktg. & public rels. agency) 1984-, splst. in mktg. for health care industry 1985—; pub. The Health Care Guide, Conejo Valley 1985—, health care directories for other So. Calif. communities in planning; civic: Conejo Valley CofC (Health Com., publicity dir. Annual Health Fair), Preserve Bottle Village Com. (dir. 1985), Folk Art Museum (tourism coord.). Ofc: R. Strong & Assocs. 223 E Thousand Oaks Blvd Ste 308 Thousand Oaks 91360

STROUD, SHARRON PATRICIA, minister; b. July 29, 1944, Okemah, Okla.; d. Raymond Dean and Zora Margaret (Woods) Jacobs; m. Roy Lee Gayhart, II; children: Tricia Lorraine b. 1969, Gabriel Eric b. 1976; edn: CSU Northridge 1963-64, Pierce City Coll. 1964-65; Ministerial Degree, Un. Ch. Rel. Sci. Sch. of Ministry 1973-75; Master Degree, Motivational Sci. Humanetic Inst. 1976; PhD cand., La Jolla Univ. 1981. Career: rel. sci. minister and motivational inst. self image tng., Self Image Inst., Santa Ana Coll. of Para Medical Arts and Sci. 1972-73; founding minister Sci. of Mind Ch. of Positive Thinking 1975-78; minister Rel. Sci. Ch. Ctr., San Diego 1978; num. self-image psychology seminars; TV ministry, Passport To Life (var. local tv channels) 1986—; v.p. United Clergy of Rel. Sci. (1986-87); relig. advis. bd. 41st Congl. Dist.; chmn. bd. World Peace Event, San Diego Dist.; honors: speaking awards Nat. Forensic League (1961), United Ch. Rel. Sci. Sch. of Ministry; Declaration of Commdn. for Disting. Citizens of Am., S.D. City Council (2/14/75); Nat. Mgmt. Assn. Svc. Award (1979-80); Beta Sigma Phi Humanitarian sor. (v.p. 1968-72); hon. PhD Heritage Inst. Santa Barbara; Woman of Religion award, Soroptimists Internat.; Hollywood's Salute to Beautiful Women (1972); 1st woman pres. of Sch. of Ministry (1974-75); listed: Outstanding Young Women of Am. (1970, 80), Who's Who of the New Thought Movement (1975), Who's Who San Diego Women (1982); mem: Beta Sigma Pi (v.p. 1968-72), Nat. League of Am. Pen Women; publs: The Spiritual Side of Success; The Power of Knowing Who You Are (Herself Mag. 1979); featured in Time, Newsweek, US News & World Report; Apolitical Religious Scientist; rec: bicycling, yoga, swimming. Res: Coronado Ofc: 9765 Clairemont Mesa Blvd San Diego 92124

STRUBLE, SCOTT ALLEN, accountant; b. May 26, 1951, Salem, Ore.; s. Wayne and Betty Zo (Allen) S.; edn: BS in bus. adm., So. Ore. State Coll. 1978; Certified Public Acct., Wash. (1980), Ore. (1982), Calif. (1985). Career: gen. acctg. practice, spec. in computer applications and spl. projects; staff acct. Smith Gerstein & Smith, CPAs, Vancouver, Wash. 1978-81; mgr. date processing R.A.Gartner & Co., CPAs, 1981-84; mgr. spl. projects Crisafi, Sciabica & Woodward, CPAs, Burlingame, Calif. 1984—; mem. Ore. Soc. of CPAs, var. civic orgns.; Democrat; rec: personal computer & appls. Res: One St. Francis Place #5401 San Francisco 94107 Ofc: Crisafi, Sciabica and Woodward, CPAs 1050 Broadway Burlingame 94010

STUART, MARILYN BRANT CHANDLER, urban planner, writer; b. July 24, 1932, Los Angeles; d. Robert Alston and Jane Frances (Mann) Brant; m. Otis Chandler, June 18, 1951, div. 1981; m. Malcolm Stuart, Aug. 5, 1984; children: Norman Brant, b. 1952, Harry Brant, b. 1953, Cathleen, b. 1955, Michael Otis, b. 1958, Carolyn, b. 1963; edn: Stanford Univ. 1949-51, UC Berkeley 1951, Occidental Coll. 1963-65; MA, UCLA Sch of Arch./Urban Planning 1975. Career: executive planner/asst. to the pres. Archisystems (div. Summa Corp),1974-76; pres. Urban Design Disciplines, 1977-81; partner Thornton Fagan Brant Rancourt (TFBR), 1981-82, co-dir. Art & Technology show for the Am. Pavilion, Expo '70, Osaka, Japan; pres. Marilyn Brant & Assocs., plnng & devel., Los Angeles 1982—; Dir: California Design (1968-80), Population Crisis Com. (1972-), Regl. Adv. Council SCAG (So. Calif. Assn. of Govts.); moderator Habitat Sect. 1980 World Future Global Conf., Toronto; trustee Loyola Marymount Univ. 1981-; chmn. bd. dirs. Otis Art Inst. 1961-77; dir. Center Theater Gp, L.A. Music Ctr. 1967-79; founding mem. Docent Council, L.A. Mus. (bd. dirs. 1960-71); adv. American Theater Arts Acad. 1980-81. Mem: Urban Land Inst., Am. Planning Assn., Am. Inst. of Certified Plnnrs., Am. Soc. of Cert. Plnnrs., L.A. City Hdqtrs. Assn., CARES/USC Co. Hosp., House Ear Inst. Assocs. Recipient merit awards, Los Angeles City & Co.; Republican; Episcopal; rec: tennis, swim, fish, hunt. Ofc: Marilyn Brant & Assocs., 11560 Bellagio Road Los Angeles 90049

STUART, PAUL SARDIUS, engineering and management consultant; b. Aug. 24, 1922, New Orleans, La.; s. Paul S. and Eleanor J. (Joyce) S.; m. Noel D. Donovan, June 11, 1949; children: James b. 1950, Robert b. 1953, Walter b. 1955, Paula b. 1958, Marie b. 1962; edn: Mech. Engr., Tulane Univ. 1947; grad. work Metallurg., Washington Univ. 1954-56; bus. mgmt., Miss. State Univ. 1962; Reg. Profl. Engr. (Civil, Mech., Quality, Nuclear) Calif. Career: project engr. Water Board of New Orleans 1947-52; head Deck & Gunnery Dept., USS Pawcatuck, 1952-54; supvy. engr. Mallinckrodt Chemical Works 1954-56; supvy. engr. Westinghouse Elec. Corp. 1956-66; quality project mgr. General Atomic Co. 1966-82; cons./ owner General Audits & Assocs. (quality assur. consultants), La Jolla 1982—; conduct Quality Assur. audits of mfrs. and conduct seminars on Q.A. for industry and govt.; awards: commendation for devel. Navy's Standard Method of Fueling at Sea, US Navy (1953); senior mem. Am. Soc. for Quality Control; mem. Riford Club of La Jolla (Club Chorus); presented tec. papers on Q.A. at nat. and regl. ASQC Confs. (1972-74); mil: lt.sg, US Navy, WWII and Korean Conflict 1941-54; Republican; Catholic; rec: music, furniture, chorale, tennis. Res: 1287 Virginia Way La Jolla 92037 Ofc: General Audits & Associates 7460 Girard Ave La Jolla 92037

STUBBLEBINE, WILLIAM CRAIG, educator, chairman of Economics; b. July 21, 1936, USMA, West Point, NY; s. Albert Newton, Jr. and Mildred (Toland) S.; m. Carol Ann Wiebe; children: Julia, b. 1967, Erik, b. 1969; edn: Ill. Inst. of Tech. 1953-56; BS, Univ. of Dela. 1958; PhD, Univ. of Va. 1963. Career: asst. prof. econ., Univ. of Va. 1961-63, Univ. of Dela. 1963-66; sci. fellow, MIT, 1965-66; Fulbright prof. of econ. Univ. of Turin, Italy 1967-68; vis. prof. of economics, So. Methodist Univ., Dallas 1971, and Va. Polytech. Inst. U., Blacksburg 1972; assoc. prof. econ. Claremont McKenna Coll. & Grad. Sch., 1966-76, dir. Center for the Study of Law Structures, 1977-84; Von Tobel prof. of political economy Claremont McKenna Coll. and Grad. Sch. 1979—, chmn. dept. econs, 1984—; bd. dirs. YES Fund, 1983-, Seapointe Savings & Loan, 1985-, senior assoc./CEO Public Associates Inc., 1980-, senior assoc. JurEcon Inc., 1981-; cons. federal, state and local govts., bus.; Voelker fellow, Nat.; Sci. Political Sci. Assn.; Pub. Choice Soc.; Western Tax Assn.; Laws at Work; Nat. Tax Limitation Comm. Publs: Externally (with J.M. Buchanan), Economica, 1962; Institutional Elements in the Fin. of Edn., So. Econ. Journ., 1965; On Property Right & Instns., Explorations in the Theory of Anarchy, 1972; editor (with T.D. Willett) and contbr. to Reaganomics: A Midterm Report, 1983; contbr. writer var. journals. Address: Bauer Center, Claremont McKenna Coll. Claremont 91711

STUPACK, ROBERT LOUIS, institutional bond salesman; b. May 23, 1956, Bklyn.; s. Irwin S. and Betti M. (Hamburger) S.; edn: BS, Penn. State Univ. 1978; Certified Public Acct., Pa. 1980. Career: acct. Price Waterhouse, N.Y.C. 1978-82; finl. analyst Celanese Corp., N.Y.C. 1982-83; instnl. bond salesman L.F. Rothschild, Unterberg, Towbin, N.Y.C. and San Francisco, 1983-85, Smith Barney, Harris Upham & Co. Inc., S.F. 1985—; honors: Omicron Delta Kappa (1978), Skull and Bones (1978); mem: Am. Inst. CPAs, Penna. Inst. CPAs, Delta Chi Alumni, Penn. State Alumni Assn. Res: 29 Corte Toluca Greenbrae 95904 Ofc: Smith Barney 350 California St Ste 2100 San Francisco 94111

STURTRIDGE, JO-ANN BUTTS, telemarketing executive; b. Dec. 2, 1940, Los Angeles; d. Robert Shannon and Juliet Carnegie (Montague) Butts; m. Richard Sturtridge, June 14, 1963; 1 son, Richard Nelson, III b. 1970; edn: BA in Eng. lit., UC Los Angeles 1962. Career: var. pos. in personnel and mktg. Shell Oil Co., Los Angeles 1962-68; Calif. office mgr./ interviewer/ researcher

Solution Sets, Moraga 1981-83; owner startup telemarketing bus., Micro-Phone, Orinda 1981-83; mgr. telemktg. InfoWorld Newspaper (for the micro-computing community); cons. in telemarketing; mem: Am. Telemarketing Assn. (liaison com. 1986), Kappa Alpha Theta Alumni; civic: Newcomers of Orinda, Contact Care Center (vol.), Com. to Preserve Orinda, Moraga Sch. Volunteers, Los Perales Parents Club, Sch. Improve. Com., Cub Scouts (den mother); publs: contbr. to Whole Earth Software Catalog; Republican; Presbyterian; rec: spectator sports, nature, aerobics. Res: 21 Sleepy Hollow Ln Orinda 94563 Ofc: InfoWorld 1060 Marsh Rd Ste C-200 Menlo Park 94025

STUTZMAN, THOMAS CHASE, lawyer; b. Aug. 1, 1950, Portland, Ore.; s. Leon Henry and Mary Louise (Chase) S.; m. Wendy Craig, June 6, 1976; children: Sarah b. 1980; Thomas Jr. b. 1983; edn: BA, hoors, UC Santa Barbara 1972; JD, cum laude, Univ. Santa Clara 1975. Career: law ofcs. Thomas Chase Stutzman (assoc. w/ Wayne Howard and Jack Mason) dba Howard & Stutzman 1976, 1979; pres., secty. CFO Thomas Chase Stutzman APC (assoc. w/ Art Jacobs, Philip Rosenblatt & Alan Tanenbaum) dba Jacobs, Rosenblatt Tanenbaum & Stutzman 1979-85; Hogan, Newman, Clark & Stutzman 1985–; instr. environ. law San Jose State Univ. 1977-78; corp. counsel, asst. secty. approx. 15 corps.; honors: Phi Beta Kappa; Dir. of the Year, Jaycees 1976-77; mem: Calif. Trial Lawyers Assn. (profl.), Santa Clara Co. Bar Assn., Masons (Golden Rule F&AM, Scottish Rite), San Jose Host Lions Club (pres. 1984-85), Jaycees, Sierra Club, AAU, Kenna Club; Congregational; rec: long distance running, photog. Ofc: Thomas Chase Stutzman APC, 1625 The Alameda Ste. 309 San Jose 95113

SUAREZ-VILLA, LUIS, university professor; b. July 7, 1947, Havana, Cuba, nat. US cit. 1971; s. Luis L. and Esperanza (Villa) Suarez; edn: B.Arch., Univ. Fla. 1969, M.Arch., 1972; MRP, Cornell Univ. 1976, PhD, 1981. Career: var. research, tchg. asst. positions US and South Am. 1970-80; asst. prof. Sch. of Public Adminstrn. and Urban Studies and Ctr. for Latin Am. Studies, San Diego State Univ. 1981-82; asst. prof. social ecology UC Irvine 1982–, mem. exec. com. 1985-86, faculty advisor 1985-, num. other coms.; faculty affiliate Public Policy Research Orgn. UCI 1983-; vis. asst. prof. UCLA 1982; cons. Calif. Dept. Health Svcs. 1982; advisor, cons. Inst. of Social Research, Universidad Autonoma de Baja Calif. 1982; occasional reviewer J. of Regional Sci., Univ. Press of Am., others; honors: num. research grants, fellowships, Fulbright Fellow (1985); mem: Regional Sci. Assn., Western Regional Sci. Assn., Am. Econ. Assn., Latin Am. Studies Assn.; publs: num. articles in sci. jours.; papers presented, participant num. profl. confs.; Catholic; rec: classical music, water sports, travel. Ofc: Pgm. in Social Ecology, UC Irvine 92717

SUBBIE, PAUL ANDREW, purchasing executive; b. Feb. 20, 1947, Los Angeles; s. Paul F. and Christine (Orvick) S.; m. Jacqueline Ochsner, Mar. 20, 1982; children: James Andrew b. 1965, Andrea Marie b. 1963; edn: West Los Angeles Coll. 1977-78; Los Angeles Valley Coll. 1979-80; pilots lic., High Performance Cert., FAA 1979. Career: lithographer Mobil Oil Corp., Los Angeles 1963-71; purchasing mgr. Colony Charter Life Ins. Co., Los Angeles 1971-77; purch. mgr. 20th Century Ins. Co., Woodland Hills 1977–; awards: creative writing awd., Dean of Languages, W. Los Angeles Coll. 1978; mem: Purchasing Mgmt. Assn.; Nat. Assn. of Purchasing Mgmt; Nat. Republican Congressional Com.; publs: art. on purchasing, The Office Mag. 1978; Republican; Catholic; rec: flying full size & radio control aircraft, target shooting. Res: 21801 Roscoe Blvd, No 332, Canoga Park 91304 Ofc: 20th Century Ins. Co., 6301 Owensmouth Ave Woodland Hills 91367

SUBRAMANYA, SHIVA, nuclear scientist, communications engineer; b. Apr. 8, 1933, Hole-Narasipur, India; nat. 1970; s. Srikantaiah and Gundamma S.; m. Lee Silva, Mar. 3, 1967; two sons, Paul b. 1968, Kevin b. 1972; edn: BS, Mysore Univ. 1956; MS nuc. physics & electronics, Karnatak Univ. 1962; postgrad. work, Clark Univ. 1963-5; MBA (bus. mgt.) CSU Dom. Hills 1977; PhD cand in bus. adminstrn., Nova Univ. Career: on temporary assignment from TRW to USAF work in Colo. project mgr. CSOC Communications, major USAF Contracts, TRW Defense Gp. 1979–; systems lead engr. on sev. DOD Projects, Space & Ground Systems, TRW 1973-85; electronics warfare cons. Gen. Instruments, NY 1972-73; prin. engr. DOD Projects, 1967-70, prin. engr. Tactical Comm. Gp., 1970-72, Gen. Dynamics/ Electronics; chief engr. DOD Contracts, TEI, 1964-67; lectr. various instns.; recipient Pres. of India awards & scholarships in nuclear physics research; mem: IEEE, Am. Inst. Physics, AOC, VISP, India Profl. Forum (nat. pres.); coordinator US West Coast, Viswa Hindu Parishad; publs: over 10,000 pages of tech. papers;. Res: 4133 Konya Dr. Torrance 90503 Ofc: 131-2115 TRW Defense Group, One Space Group, Redondo Beach 90278

SUDDUTH, EMILY KLEIN, real estate loan executive; b. Aug. 1, 1935, Richmond, Mo.; d. Raymond H. and Dixie (Loyd) Klein; m. Edward Sudduth, Dec. 23, 1960; children: Cynthia b. 1962, Garnet b. 1965, Edward, Jr. b. 1969; edn: BS, Central State Univ. 1956; MA, Univ. of Mo., 1962; Calif. lic. Real Estate Broker, Life & Disability Ins. Agent, Secondary Sch. (Life) Tchg. Cred. Career: tchr. Newark (Calif.) Adult Sch., 1967-78; loan ofcr. Cutler Mortgage, Fremont 1979; life ins. agent Sun Life of Canada, Walnut Creek 1982; loan ofcr. Granite Home Loans, Hayward 1983; real estate auction mgr. R. Thomas Ashley, Newport Beach 1983; subdiv. sales No. Calif. Marketing, Los Gatos 1984; loan rep. Marathon Home Loans, Hayward 1985–; owner Pacific Leadership Assocs., distbr. for LMI, Newark 1985–; civic: Fremont- Newark Philharmonic Soc. (bd. mem., publicity chair 1974), East Bay Regl. Park (Master Plan com. 1974), Newark Park & Rec. Commn. (chair 1975), Newark Unified Sch. Save Our School Bond Com. (chair 1975); publ: research on court reporting for Ohlone Coll. (1976); Presbyterian; rec: creative writing, chess, beach. Ofc: Pacific Leadership Assocs. 5025 Northampton Ct Newark 94560

SUFFIN, GUSTAVE DAVID, physician; b. Dec. 8, 1919, NY, NY; s. Aaron Solomon and Rose (Abramson) S.; m. Theresa Remes, 1946; children: Stephen Chester b. 1947, Fay Alta b. 1956, Rachel b. 1960; edn: BS, George Pepperdine Coll. 1949; DO, Coll. of Osteopathic Physicians & Surgeons 1953; MD, Calif. Coll. of Medicine 1962. Career: physician and surgeon in Long Beach and Hawaiian Gardens, 1954–; chief of staff (1961-64) St. Helens Hosp., v. chief of staff (1980-82), chmn. of bd. (1975-82) Cerritos Garden Hosp.; mem: Fellow Internat. Coll. of Surgeons (1978), AMA, Calif. Med. Assn., Los Angeles Co. Med. Assn., Hawaiian Gardens Lions Club (pres. 1956); publs. in med. literature (1955-60); mil: lt. field arty. US Army 1940-46, Silver Star, Bronze Star, Purple Heart; Republican; Jewish; rec: travel, antiques, art. Ofc: 21418 S Norwalk Blvd Hawaiian Gardens 90716

SUH, YOUNG-SEOK, anesthesiologist; b. June 17, 1943, Chon-Buk, Korea, nat. US cit. 1978; s. Jae Young and Ok Whan (Ko) S.; m. Hae sun Chon, May 23, 1972; children: Helen b. 1972, Edward b. 1974, Charles b. 1977; edn: MD, Chonnam Univ. Med. Sch. 1967. Career: intern, resident Jewish Hosp. & Med. Ctr. of Bklyn., N.Y. 1972-75, attending anesthesiologist 1975; att. anesth. Wyandotte (Mich.) Gen. Hosp. 1976-77, Queen of Angeles Med. Ctr., Los Angeles 1977–, chmn. Dept. Anesthesia 1985–; bd. dirs. West Olympia Bank; recipient appreciation awards: Korean Med. Assn. of So. Calif., L.A. Olympic Lions Club, Chonnam Med. Sch. Alumni of So. Calif. and Mich., Kwang-ju Moo-Jin Lions Club of Korea, AMA Physician's Recogn. Award; mem: AMA, Calif. Med. Assn., Los Angeles County Med. Assn., Am./ Calif./ L.A. Soc. of Anesthesiols., Korean Med. Assn. of Am./ So. Calif.; clubs: Evergreen Golf, L.A. Olympic Lions (dir.), Korean CofC of Los Angeles (dir.), Nam Sung Jr. & Sr. High Sch. Alumni Assn. of So. Calif. (pres. 1983-), Calif. Country Club; mil: capt. Air Force, Repub. Korea 1968-71; Republican; Presbyterian; rec: tourism, sports, music. Ofc: Queen of Angeles Hospital 2301 Bellevue Ave Los Angeles 90026

SUH, YOUNG SUK, import-export co. owner; b. Feb. 9, 1943, Jinnampo; s. Jung Soo and Sa-Im (Kim) Suh; m. Younghee Kim, Oct. 23, 1969; children: John b. 1970, Hyewon b. 1971; edn: BA, Seoul Nat. Univ. 1965. Career: asst. mgr. Korea Overseas Devel. Corp., Korea 1968-70; export-import mgr. Soon Park Ind. Co., Ltd. (a U.S.-Korean Joint Venture), Korea 1970-72; Korean purch. agent Standard Brands Paint Co., Torrance 1972-78; owner Y.S. Trading Co., Seoul, Korea 1972-78; gen. mgr. Koplysedae Corp., Los Angeles 1980-82; owner Triumph Mktg., Gardena 1982–; internat. bus. consultant E.T. Horn Co., La Mirada 1983–; mem. Los Angeles CofC; mil: cpl. Army Intell. Unit, Korean Army 1966-67. Ofc: Triumph Marketing 1440 West 135th St Gardena 90249

SULLIVAN, BRADLEY JAMES, chiropractor, b. Aug. 17, 1955, Los Angeles; s. Bruce and Roz Kirby; edn: AA, West Los Angeles Coll. 1979; DC, cum laude, Cleveland Chiropractic-L.A. 1983; lic. D.C. in Calif., Wyo. Career: gym instr. Beverly Hills Health Club, later asst. mgr., mgr. Sports Connection, B.H.; chiropractic intern Dr. B.W. Steuber, DC, Lynwood 1984-85; estab. own practice, Sullivan Chiropractic Office, Van Nuys 1985–; honors: named Outstanding New D.C. of the Year, Los Angeles Southeast Chiro. Assn. (1985), Presidential Recogn. Award, Calif. Chiropractic Assn. (1985); mem: Am. Chiro. Assn., Calif. Chiro. Assn., L.A. Southeast Chiro. Assn.; vol. L.A. Free Clinic (1981-83); Republican; rec: skiing, boating. Ofc: Sullivan Chiropractic Office 6900 Van Nuys Blvd Ste 15 Van Nuys 91405

SULLIVAN, MICHAEL EVAN, administrator, engineer, company executive; b. Dec. 30, 1940, Phila., PA; s. Albert and Ruth (Liebert) S.; div.; edn: BS, NM State Univ. 1966; MA, 1968; BS Univ. Tex. 1969; MBA, Univ. Houston 1974; BS, Univ. LaVerne 1981; MS, USC 1976; MPA, 1977; PhD 1982. Career: jr. engr. Physical Sci. Lab, N.M. State Univ. 1962-66; sr. analyst Houston, Tex. Lighting & Power Co. 1969-74; electronics engr. Software Support Activity, US Govt., Pt. Mugu, Calif. 1974-77; mem. tech. staff Hughes Aircraft Co., El Segundo 1977-78; staff pgm. adminstr. Northrop Corp., Newbury Park 1978-79; hd. engring. div. Navy Astronautics Gp., Pt. Mugu 1979-82; pres./ bd. chmn. Diversified Mgmt. Sys., Inc., Camarillo 1978–; hd. offshore island div., Pacific Missile Test Ctr., Pt. Mugu 1982–; awards: Ednl. Research Tng. Pgm. fellowship, NMSU 1967; Pi Gamma Mu, soc. sci. hon.; Phi Kappa Phi; mem: Assn. of MBA Execs.; Am. Math. Soc.; Am. Statistical Assn.; Math. Assn. of Am.; Am. Soc. of Pub. Admin.; Am. Personnel & Guidance Assn.; Am. Assn. of Ind. Investors; Fed. Mgr. Assn.; So. Calif. Assn. of Public Adminstrn.; Acad. of Political Sci.; IEEE; Tech. Mktg. Soc. of Am.; Ventura County Master Chorale and Opera Assn. (bd.); publs: The Mgmt. of Research, Devel., Test & Evaluation Orgns.; The Mgmt. of RDT&E Orgns.: Behavioral Characteristics of Supervisors Public vs Private Sectors; Self-Actualization in RDT&E Orgns.; Self-Actualization in a Health Care Agcy.; mil: US Army 1958-62; rec: tennis, fishing, back packing, chess. Res: POB 273 Point Hueneme 93041 Ofc: Diversified Mgmt. Systems, Inc., POB 447 Camarillo 93010

SULLIVAN, PATRICK HENRY, III, management consultant; b. May 6, 1938, NY, NY; s. Patrick H., II, and Elinor Regina (Smith) S.; m. Harriet Ann Chipouras, Oct. 1, 1960; children: Christine b. 1962, Suzanne b. 1964, Patrick IV b. 1968; edn: BS in gen. engring., US Naval Acad. 1960; MS in R&D mgt., Fla. State Univ. 1969, DBA, Fla. State Univ. Sch. of Bus. 1972. Career: USN Officer, Destroyer Force of US Atlantic Fleet, 1960-64; asst. prof. of Naval Sci., USN/ Stanford Univ., 1964-66; resrch. engr. (launch complex, Apollo/ Saturn Project) The Boeing Co., Cape Kennedy, Fla. 1966-69; chief fin. and plng. ofcr. Fla. State Univ., Tallahassee, Fla. 1970-73; Fellow of Am. Council on Edn.'s Academic Adminstrn. Internship Pgm., adv. to vice chancellor UC Berkeley, 1973-74; asst. chancellor/chief fin. and plng. ofcr. UC Santa Cruz,

1974-78; sr. mgmt. cons. SRI, Menlo Park 1978-80, dir. Strategic Mgmt. Dept., SRI Internat., London, Eng. 1980-82; prin. mgmt. consultant, SRI Internat., Menlo Pk. 1982—; conduct strategy formulation studies for clients; honors: past pres. Sigma Iota Epilson (mgmt. hon.), Beta Gamma Sigma (bus. hon.), Phi Kappa Phi (Univ. hon.); mem. Flying Doctors, Mensa; mil: capt. USNR; Catholic; rec: flying. Res: 250 Meadow Road Santa Cruz 95060 Ofc: SRI International 333 Ravenswood Ave Menlo Park 94025

SULLIVAN, ROBERT BRUCE, cabinet maker, custom woodworker; b. July 9, 1948, Sacramento; s. Arthur William Jr. and Mary Louise (Rutherford) S.; m. Janice Kay, May 9, 1970; edn: Merritt Jr. Coll., 1 yr. Career: cabinet maker self-empl. 1971-73; handmade woodwork house, Berkeley 1973-76; graphic designed and custom designed projects, Oakland Hills 1976-80; cabinet maker self-empl. 1980—; mem: El Sobrante CofC (pres. 1986), County Parks & Recreation Adv. Com. (v.chmn.), El Sobrante Plnng. & Zoning Com. (v.chmn.), Rotary, Elks, Friends of Recreation; publs: Ideas for Improving Your Home, Sunset Mag. 1979; Democrat; rec: skiing, travel. Res: 6210 Bay View Ave. San Pablo 94806 Ofc: Robert Sullivan, 3730 San Pablo Dam Rd. El Sobrante 94803

SULLIVAN, TIMOTHY JOSEPH, electronics engineer; b. Nov. 20, 1946, New Haven, Conn.; s. Stewart and Adele Petrunia (Strukus) S.; div.; 1 son, Timothy Michael b. 1970; edn: BS, US Naval Acad. 1969; MBA, Univ. Santa Clara 1979; postgrad. U.S.Internat. Univ. 1984-. Career: naval flight ofcr. USN 1969-80; flight simulator tng. course supr., Hughes Aircraft Co., Los Angeles 1980-82; founder/owner Western Ents. (engring. cons. co.), Garden Grove 1982-83, sold co., sr. advisor 1983-; chief of engring. Dept. of Defense, Def. Contracts Adminstrn. Service, Orange/LA/Riverside Cos., home office Santa Ana 1983-85; senior engr. (fed. govt.) Pacific Missile Test Center, Point Mugu, 1986-; recipient Sustained Superior Performance Award, Fed. Govt. (1985); mem. IEEE; civic: Nat. Eagle Scout Assn., Mensa, Earthwatch, Smithsonian Instn., Intertel; publs: course devel. The Private Sector Instructs the U.S. Military (grad. paper 1976); mil: cmdr. US Navy 1969-80, Air Reserves flt. ofcr. 1980-, 2 Air Medals, Vietnam Service Rib.; Catholic; rec: photog., travel. Res: 1892 Dunnigan St Camarillo 93010 Ofc: Pacific Missile Test Center Code 2022 Point Mugu 93042

SULTAN, ISAAC AARON, physician-neurologist; b. Jan. 13, 1948, Bklyn., NY; s. Saul and Esther Sultan; m. Margaret, Sept. 8, 1974; children: Stacy b. 1976, David b. 1978, Jessica b. 1980, Natalie b. 1982, Joshua b. 1984; edn: BA, Bklyn. Coll. 1970; MD, Loyola Med. Sch. 1974; neurologist UC San Diego 1978; bd. cert. Am. Bd. of Psychiatry & Neurology 1980. Career: active staff neurologist Desert Hospital, Eisenhower Medical Center, John F. Kennedy Hosp., Coachella Valley, Palm Springs; also dir. neurology and sleep disorder medicine John F. Kennedy Hosp., Indio. Ofc: Isaac A. Sultan MD, P.C., 3000 Bob Hope Dr, Rancho Mirage 92272

SULZNER, BRUCE ELLIOTT, lawyer; b. April 19, 1946, Miami, Fla.; s. Joseph Elliot and Coral Jewell (Watson) S.; 1 dau: Josclyne Marie b. 1982; edn: BS, Tulane Univ. 1968; JD, magna cum laude, Calif. Western Law Sch. 1976; Admitted to Bars of Calif. (1976) and Colo. (1978). Career: judicial law clerk San Diego Superior Ct., No. County 1977-78; assoc. Ciccolella & Radom, Colo. Spring, Colo. 1978-79; assoc. Rhoades, Hollywood & Neil, San Diego 1979-86; ptnr. Sulzner, Belsky & Haydon, San Diego 1986—; mem: Am., Colo. and San Diego Co. (Litigation & Ethics Com. 1982-83, chmn. Torts Subcom. 1983) Bar Assns., Defense Resaerch Inst., San Diego Defense Lawyers (interim dir. 1984), Colo. Trial Lawyers Assn., Assn. of So. Calif. Defense Counsel, Barristers Club, Pi Kappa Alpha, Phi Alpha Delta; publs: comment, Custodial Interrogation and the Fifth Amendment- A Passing Shadow?, 12 Calif. West. Law Review 1976; mil: lt. USN, Navy Commdn. (2), Navy Achiev., Combat Action, Meritorious Unit Citation, Navy Unit Citation; Republican; Presbyterin; rec: skiing, scuba diving, sailing. Res: 229 B Avenue Coronado 92118 Ofc: Sulzner, Belsky & Haydon 401 West A St Ste 1300 San Diego 92101

SUN, ANTHONY, venture capitalist; b. July 8, 1952, Bangkok, Thailand; s. Chung Ta and Ching Sin (Ho) S.; m. Leslie S., June 21, 1974; 1 son, Christopher b. 1982; edn: BSEE and MSEE, M.I.T., 1974, postgrad. engring. 1975; MBA, Harvard Univ. 1979. Career: engr. Hewlett-Packard, Palo Alto 1970-72; project mgr. TRW, Sunnyvale 1975-76; engring. mgr. Caere, Los Gatos 1976-77; gen. ptnr. Venrock Assocs., Palo Alto 1979—; honors: Sigma Xi; sev. patents, profl. publs. Res: 415 El Arroyo Rd Hillsborough 94010 Ofc: Venrock Associates Ste 528 Two Palo Alto Sq Palo Alto 94306

SUN, HENRY HENG-YUAN, data processing, systems & programming executive; b. May 5, 1932, Shanghai, China, nat. 1970; s. Ching Po and Den Ann (Huang) S.; m. Lily Chou, Nov. 19, 1965; children: Stella b. 1970, Stacy b. 1977; edn: BS, Taiwan Chung Hsing Univ.; sys. engring. tng., mktg. & mgmt. tng., IBM. Career: instr. Tam Kung Coll. of Bus., Taiwan; instr./sys. engring./mktg. rep. IBM, Taiwan; data processing mgr., Tobias Kotzen Co., Los Angeles; spl. projs. mgr. Ameron, Inc., L.A.; currently, sys. & pgm. mgr. ITT, Gilfillan, L.A.; pres. Sunny Computer Svc. (cons. computer software and hardware; leasing hardware/ software of micro- computers); honors: Top Performer, IBM 1969; mem. Am. Mgmt. Assn.; pres. Chinese-Am. Computer Profl. Soc. of Calif.; works: devel. computer software systems for supermarket (1980), garment indus. (1982); rec: stamp collecting, micro- computers. Res: 816 No Coffman Dr Montebello 90640 Ofc: ITT- Gilfillan, 7821 Orion Ave Van Nuys 91409

SURYOUTOMO, HERMAN, business executive; b. July 7, 1946, Pati, Central Java, Indonesia; s. Kiem Hoo and Lies Nio (Ong) Oei; m. Lusia Amalia

Karnoatmodjo, Mar. 1, 1976; children: David Christopher, Nina Amelia, Jason Andrew, Tanya Christina; edn: BS equiv., Bandung Inst. Technol. Indonesia 1970; MS, Washington Univ., St. Louis, Mo. 1972, DSc, 1975; MBA, Pepperdine Univ. 1984; Reg. Profl. Engr. (No. Carolina, Ala.), Reg. PE Civil Engr. (Calif.). Career: senior engrg. splst. Jack Gillum & Assoc. St. Louis 1974-75; div. & proj. mgr. Cygna Corp. S.F. 1975-82; bd. chmn./CEO Innova Corp., Fremont 1982—; owner/ broker Prima Realty, Fremont 1986—; pres. Innova Corp of N.C., Raleigh 1983—; pres./CEO Prima Foods Corp., Fremont 1985—; honors: Fulbright Hays (US State Dept. Wash. DC 1970), assistantship (Wash. Univ. 1970-75), Dale Carnegie Scholarship- Highest Achievement (Oakland 1976); mem: Am. Soc. Civil Engrs., Toastmasters (ofcr. 1985-), Companion of Alameda County (treas., bd. dirs. 1985-), Rotary (ofcr. 1986); author: Organizational Effectiveness (1984), contbr. articles profl. jours. (1970-76), ed. conf. papers (1978-80); Christian; rec: swimming, skiing, tae kwon do, tennis, hiking. Res: 44433 Park Meadow Dr Fremont 94539 Ofc: Innova Corp. 39055 Randall Pl Fremont 94538

SUTCH, DAVE WAYNE, securities co. executive; b. Oct. 14, 1943, Oakland; s. Dave R. and Esther M. (Townsend) S.; m. Judy, Aug. 28, 1965; children: Lori Dawn b. 1969, Scott David b. 1971, Adam Christopher b. 1985; edn: BA, CSU San Jose 1966. Career: sales rep. General Mills, Palo Alto 1967-68; stockbroker E.F. Hutton, Palo Alto 1968-70, San Jose 1978; Bateman Eichler Hill Richards, San Jose and Newport Beach, 1970-73; v.p. Shuman Agnew/ Morgan Stanley, Menlo Park 1974-78; v.p./ptnr. Van Kasper & Co., Lafayette 1979-, dir. 1979-, exec. com. 1983-; honors: named in Top Twenty Brokers '83, Registered Representative Mag.; mem. Lafayette CofC; mil: E4 Calif. Army N.G. 1966-72; Protestant; rec: autos, off road vehicles, track & field. Res: 3932 Los Arabis Dr Lafayette 94549 Ofc: Van Kasper & Co. 3687 Mt Diablo Blvd Ste 240 Lafayette 94549

SUTHERLIN, ROBERT CHARLES, JR., civil engineer; b. Feb. 5, 1956, Stephenville, Newfoundland; s. Robert Charles and Donna Sue (Harger) S.; m. Diane, June 3, 1978; children: Kathryn b. 1982; Melanie b. 1985; edn: BSCE, San Diego State Univ. 1980. Career: asst. C.E. Boyle 1978-84; assoc. civil engr. Boyle Engineering Corp., 1984-86; prin. design engr. Rick Engrg. Co. 1986—; mem: Am. Soc. Civil Engrs. (assoc.), Calif. Assn. of Subdivision Cons.; Democrat; Catholic; rec: bowling, camping. Res: 11410 Spitfire Rd. San Diego 92126 Ofc: Rick Engrg. Co. 5620 Friars Rd San Diego 92110-2596

SWADLEY, BERNADINE HATCH, honorary state regent, DAR; b. July 21, 1917, Paso Robles; d. Holmer J. and Ruth (Brewer) Hatch; m. Robert Hunter Swadley, 1946; edn: San Jose State Univ.; Stanford Univ.; Rudolph Schaeffer Sch. of Design; degree in art, Art Inst., Oakland. Career: State Bd. DAR, 12 yrs., state regent 1981, hon. state regent 1982- ; secty., ARC Alameda Co. 1982; pres. Alameda Co. Hist. Soc.; state pres. Colonial Dames of Am.; Mayor's Com., Oakland Clean Community Sys.; recipient, num. DAR honors; mem: Conn. Hist Soc., Founders of Norwich (Conn.), T.B. & Health Assn. (pres.), Vis. Nurse Assn. (bd. dirs. 27 yrs.), Colonial Clergy, Magna Charta Dames, Mayflower Soc., CAR (life), DAR (life), Soc. of Descendants of Knights of the Most Noble Order of the Sartu, The Skyline Garden Club (founding pres. 1961-), Calif. Garden Clubs Inc, Calif. Art Research Commn., Art Floral Com., Women of St. Paul's Episcopal Ch. (pres. 1959), Beta Sigma Phi; Republican; rec: 5461 Fernhoff Rd. Oakland 94619

SWAIM, LOIS A., wholesale jewelry co. president; b. Mar. 2, 1938, Wallowa, Ore.; d. Raymond C. and H. Effie (Boswell) Smith; div.; 2 sons: Mark b. 1959, Ray b. 1961; edn: AA, Oregon State Univ. 1958; BS, magna cum laude, Pepperdine Univ. 1974, MBA 1976. Career: sales mgr., region comp. mgr., personnel mgr. Xerox Corp., 1967-77, branch sales mgr., Los Angeles 1977-78, dist. mgr., Fresno 1978-79, dist. mgr. L.A. 1979-81, region market mgr., Santa Ana 1981-82; v.p. Human Resources Internat., Carlsbad 1982-85; dir. of ops. Eye Surgery Assocs., Vista 1985—; owner/pres. Images Unlimited Accessories (wholesale jewelry) 1981—; honors: Girls Statc (1954), Number One Nationally, Xerox Corp. (1978, 79, 81); mem: Am. Soc. of Tng. & Devel., Nat. Soc. of Female Execs., American Consulting League; coauthor: The Management Process (1984), Influential Mgmt. Strategies & Skills (1983); Republican; rec: travel, photog., jewelry design, investments. Res: 2128 Saliente Way Carlsbad 92008 Ofc: Eye Surgery Assocs. 2023 W Vista Way Ste A Vista 92083

SWANLUND, MAYBELLE AMANDA, school administrator, librarian; b. Feb. 7, 1907, Wahpeton, N. Dak.; d. Math and Anna Louise (Strass) Leland; m. Lester H. Swanlund, July 11, 1936; edn: Std. tchg. credentials, State Tchr. Coll. Valley City, N.D. 1925; BA, State Tchr. Coll. Mayville, N.D. 1928; BLS, Univ. of Ill. Library Sch. 1932. Career: elem. sch. tchr., Fingal, N.D. 1926-27; principal Township High Sch. 1928-31; head librarian Milford (Ill.) Township Library 1932-34, and Lombard (Ill.) Library (2 suburbs of Chgo.), 1934-41; hd. librarian First United Methodist Ch., Palo Alto 1965-71; mgr. indsl. property, San Francisco 1971—; lectured Ill. Regional Library meetings, 9 yrs.; contbg. writer, weekly, Illinois newspapers, 9 yrs.; funded the Lester H. Swanlund Adminstrn. Bldg., Univ. Ill., Urbana-Champaign; honors: Womens Soc. of Christian Service spl. membership award, Who's Who in Library Service, Richard Rosek Assocs. AIA award of year (1962), Popularity Queen (Mayville State Tchrs. Coll. 1927-28), pres. Women's Athletic Assn. (Mayville Tchrs. Coll. 1926-28), state v.p., Jr. Ill. Library Assn. (1939); mem: Univ. of Ill., Urbana Pres.'s Council, Univ. of Ill. Pres.'s Club, Art Inst. of Chgo. (life), Univ. of Ill. Alumni Assoc. (life), Friends of the Library, Menlo Park & Atherton (life), Garden Club of Ill., AAUW; works: painting, sculpture (2), Univ. of Ill.; Republican; Methodist; rec: art, music, bridge. Res: 153 Fair Oaks Lane Atherton 94025

SWANSON, BARBARA JOAN, librarian; b. Aug. 5, 1939, Starbuck, Minn.; d. Milton L. and Louise Elizabeth (Hume) S.; edn: BA, Univ. of Minn. 1961, MA, 1968. Career: librarian Hennepin County Library, Minneapolis, Minn. 1962-68, book mobile and reference librarian; young adult librarian Los Angeles Public Library, Eagle Rock br. 1969-81, adult reference librarian 1981—; mem: Am. and Calif. Library Assns., Soroptimists. Res: 132 Franklin Ct. Glendale 91205

SWANSON, OTTO FRANK, lawyer; b. Nov. 6, 1932, El Paso, Texas; s. Joseph Paul and Dorothy Elizabeth (Bryce) S.; m. Nancy Parra, May 25, 1984; children: Steven b. 1952, Karen b. 1955; edn: JD summa cum laude, Univ. of West Los Angeles 1970; admitted Calif. State Bar 1971. Career: ofcr. US Border Patrol, US Immigration Service, Calexico 1954-57, Stockton 1957-62, senior patrol insp., Harlingen, Texas 1962-63, Immigration Law instr. Port Isabel, Texas 1963, Immigrant insp., Los Angeles 1964-69, Supervisory Immigrant insp., Los Angeles 1969-70; atty. pvt. practice 1971—, pres. Otto F. Swanson, Profl. Corp., Marina Del Rey 1973-; recipient Dept. of Justice Awards for outstanding perf. of duty 1964, 65, 66, 67, 68, 69; mem: Am. Bar Assn. 1971-, Assn. of Immigration and Nationality Lawyers 1971-, Frat. Order of Retired Border Patrol Ofcrs (hon.) 1980-; Republican (Presdtl. Task Force, US Senatl. Club); Methodist; rec: cycling, travel, hiking. Res: 12530 Rosy Circle, Los Angeles 90066 Ofc: Otto F. Swanson, APC, 4676 Admiralty Way, Ste 632, Marina Del Rey 90292

SWEARENGIN, PHARRIS VANCE, physician & surgeon, ret.; b. Oct. 30, 1908, Marionville, Mo.; s. Henry Lee and Annie Elisabeth (Wallace) S.; m. Vaughnie Everyl Renfrow, Aug. 1, 1933; dau. Everyl Faye b. 1937; edn: AA, UC Davis; DO, Coll. of Phys. and Surgeons L.A. 1950; MD, UC Irvine 1962. Career: asst. prof. biol. San Diego State Coll. 1945-46; chief of staff Twin Lakes Hosp. Folsom 1962, chief dept. OB-Gyn. 1963-70; cons. Calif. State Dept. Social Services; pres. Sylvan Sch. Bd. Citrus Heights 1965; mem: Sacto. Med. Soc., Sacto. Valley Osteopathic Soc. (pres. 1965), Mason, Shrine, UCD and UCI Alumni Assns.; author: Cardiac Problems in Mid Life; Democrat; Protestant; rec: artist (oil painter), hunting, fishing, woodworking. Res: 7421 Knisley Ct Citrus Heights 95621

SWEARINGER, RONALD EARLE, superior court judge; b. Sept. 24, 1926, Mnpls., Minn.; s. Richard F. and Gladys B. (Lambert) S.; m. Patricia Duralde, Sept. 25, 1949; children: William F. b. 1953, Richard F. b. 1957; edn: BA, Univ. Wash. 1950; JD, USC 1958; Distinguished Graduate, Air War Coll. 1974; grad. Indsl. Coll. of the Armed Forces 1977; admitted Calif. State Bar 1959. Career: reporter Seattle Star newspaper 1942-43; Bureau mgr. INS, 1948; tech. and research writer Rand Corp. and Northrop Corp. 1953-57, author num. articles and papers on aviation and electronic subjects; dir. pub. rels. 1957-58, asst. general counsel Northrop Corp. 1958-61; ptnr. law firm Crowlry & Goffin 1961-72, trial lawyer spec. in litigation in high technology areas; judge Superior Ct. Los Angeles County, 1972—; prof. of law Northrop Univ. 1973-; instr. legal convs., seminars; honors: awarded Meritorious Service Medal, USAF, by order of Pres. Ford; Phi Beta Kappa (1949); mem. Calif. Judges Assn. (pub. rels. com.), Kiwanis, Civitan; num. publications include fiction works, technical articles, legal articles; author: On the Bench, A Judges World; mil: col. USAF, WWII flt. engr. 1943-46, intell. ofcr. Korea 1950-53, reservist Strategic Air Command 1953-; Republican; Presbyterian; rec: flying, fishing, restoration old houses. Res: 2608 Carmen Crest Dr Hollywood 90068 Ofc: Los Angeles Superior Court 111 N Hill St Los Angeles 90017

SWEATMAN, PHILLIP JAY, computer services co. executive; b. Sept. 23, 1955, Norfolk, Va.; s. Julius Caleb and Lucille (Nollet) S.; m. Lynne Baltic, June 27, 1980; 1 son, Phillip b. 1984; edn: BSBA, econs., Univ. of Denver 1978; MBA in fin., Univ. Pittsburgh 1982; desig: CFA Level II, Inst. of Chartered Finl. Analysts. Career: asst. ofcr. Mellon Bank Corp., Pittsburgh, Pa. 1979-81; finl. plnng. analyst Copperweld Corp., Pittsburgh 1981-83; plnng. ofcr. Mellon Bank, Pittsburgh 1983-84; business plnng. analyst Computer Scis. Corp., El Segundo 1984-85, mgr. Strategy & Bus. Analysis 1985-86, controller & asst. secty. CSC Comtec Inc. (subs. Computer Scis. Corp.), 1986—; founder/pres./chmn. P$L Computer Services Ltd., Pittsburgh, Pa. 1983-; instr. Graduate Sch. of Bus., Robert Morris Coll. 1984; honors: Dean's List 1976-78, 4.000 Honors Club Award 1976-78, Honors in acctg., econs. 1976, 77, Honors scholarship 1976-78, tchg. asst. Econs. Dept. 1978, Univ. of Pittsburgh; mem: Soc. of Finl. Analysts, Data Proc. Mgrs. Assn., Economics Club of Pitts. (1983-84), Am. Finance Assn. (1981-84), Nat. Assn. Accts., Controllers Council; civic: World Affairs Council of Pitts. 1979-80, Golden Triangle YMCA, Pitts. 1979-81, Perry Point Townhome Assn., Pitts. (treas. 1981-83), Rolling Ranchos Homeowners Assn., Lomita (treas. 1985); Republican; Catholic; rec: music, arts. Res: 1905 Via Solano Lomita 90171 Ofc: Computer Sciences Corp. 2100 E Grand Ave El Segundo 90245

SWEENEY, JEROME JOSEPH, insurance co. president; b. May 12, 1933, St. Louis, Mo.; s. Jerome Vincent and Ione Rose (Tobias) S.; m. Sally, Nov. 1, 1968; 1 dau. Diane b. 1969; edn: AB, Univ. of San Francisco 1957. Career: v.p. Coastwide Fire & Casualty, Los Angeles 1963-71; exec. v.p. Insco Ins. Services, Santa Ana 1971-84; pres. Insco/Dico Group, Anaheim 1984—; mem. Am. Mgmt. Assn., Surety Producers Assn. of Calif. (pres. 1986), US Navy League, Civil Air Patrol (lt. col.), Town Hall of Calif., Catalina Flyers; mil: US Army 1953-55; Republican; Roman Catholic; rec: flying, jog, racquetball. Res: 10202 Overhill Dr Santa Ana 92705 Ofc: Insco/Dico Group 333 Wilshire Anaheim 92801

SWEENEY, URBAN JOSEPH, librarian; b. Jan. 18, 1922, St. John, N.B., Can.; nat. US cit. 1945; s. Urban James and Dorothy E. (Murray) S.; m.

Margaret Stretz, Jan. 12, 1952; children: Dennis, Steven, Edward, Mark, Barbara; edn: BS, New York Univ. 1956; MS, Pratt Inst. 1947. Career: chief librarian Republic Aviation, Farmingdale, NY 1958-66; chief librarian electronics div. General Dynamics, Rochester, NY 1966-71,, Convair div., San Diego 1971—; vis. instr. Sch. of Library Sci., State Univ. of NY, Geneseo 1967-70; mem: Assn. for Computing Machinery, Am. Soc. Info. Sci., Spl. Libraries Assn. (chpt. pres. 1973-74); contbr. articles to profl. journs.; mil: US Army Air Force 1941-45, ETO. Res: 7311 Borla Pl. La Costa 92008 Ofc: P.O. Box 85386 San Diego 92138

SWEENY, ALFREDO E., physician; b. Jan. 15, 1931, Buenos Aires, Argentina s. Patricio and Adelaida Maria (Indorado) S.; m. Hebe Gilda Rosini, March 22, 1962; children: Roy Patrick b. 1963, Alfredo E. Jr. b. 1970, Valery Sandra b. 1965; edn: MD, Univ. Nacional 1961. Career: asst. dir. outpatient dept. Children's Hosp. of Los Angeles; instr. pediatrics UCS 1974, asst. clin. prof. of pediatrics 1977, assoc. clin. prof. pediatrics 1981—; currently, ptnr., owner Sunset Family Med. Dental Clinic, Los Angeles; honors: Hon. Prof. Univ. Autonoma de Guadalajara, Mex.; Fellow Am. Acad. of Pediatrics; mem: Salerni Collegium (USC), Royal Coll. of Med. (London); rec: jogging, soccer, skiing. Res: 248 So. Windsor Blvd. Los Angeles 90004 Ofc: Sunset Family Medical Dental Clinic, 3706 Sunset Blvd. Los Angeles 90026

SWEET, GEORGE ELLIOTT, geophysicist, author; b. Sept. 26, 1904, Denver, Colo.; s. Leroy Foydice and Bertie Belle (Cooper) S.; m. Mildred Thelma (dec.), Oct. 13, 1932; 1 son: J. Eric Flippin Sweet, b. 1943; edn: BS., Univ. of Okla. 1927, MS, 1928; law sch., Harvard Univ. 1940-41; reg. geophysicist, Calif. 1974. Career: party chief Geophysical Research Corp. 1928-32; party chief/ chmn. bd. American Seismograph Co., Okla. City, Okla. & Houston, Tx. 1933-39; ofcr.-in-chg. Boston Magnetic Ranges, 1942-45; party chief/ pres. Sweet Geophysical Co., Santa Monica 1945—; honors: Valedictorian, Univ. Okla. 1927; Phi Beta Kappa; Alpha Chi Sigma; Sigma Delta Psi (Blue Pencil, nat. pres.); mem: Soc. of Exploration Geophysicists; Am. Assn. Petroleum Geologists; Harvard- Radcliffe Club of So. Calif.; Santa Monica Pony League (pres. 1959-60); author: Shake-Speare, The Mystery (Stanford Univ. Press. 1956; enlarged London ed., 1963); Gentleman in Oil (1965); The History of Geophysical Prospecting (Vol. One 1966; Vol. Two 1969); The Petroleum Saga (1971); Seven Dramas From Seven Centuries (1978); Beginning of the End (1982); mil: lt. s.g., USNR 1942-45. Address: Sweet Geophysical Co., 502 Georgina Ave Santa Monica 90402

SWENSON, ERICK NOAK, data processing executive; b. June 12, 1926, Rochester, N.Y.; s. Noak and Hulda Josephina (Sjellberg) S.; m. Annette Miller, Nov. 22, 1959; 1 dau. Erika b. 1966; edn: BSEE, Univ. of Rochester 1950; grad. work Univ. of Pittsburg 1950-51, US Naval Postgrad. Sch., Monterey 1960-62; Reg. Profl. Engr. (E.E.) Calif. 1978; desig: apptd. Engring. Duty Officer USN, Secty. of Navy (1951-75); apptd. pres. USN Physical Evaluation Board, Secty. of Navy, Bethesda, Md. (1969-75); apptd. USN Fgn. Mil. Sales Coord. for Naval Command & Control Matters to NATO, Spain, Australia, Japan & Iran (1970-75). Career: electronics div. ofcr. Battleship USS Missouri (88-63) 1951-52, ship supt. Electronic Sys, San Francisco Naval Shipyard 1952-53; quality control engr. proximity fuzes, Eastman Kodak Co./ Naval Ord. Div., Rochester, NY 1953-57; asst. Naval Tactical Data Sys. Project Ofcr. (Est. USN requirements, design plnng.) Navy Dept., Wash DC 1957-60; tech. rep. Bureau of Ships (asst. in contractor design & test of computers), St. Paul, Minn. 1962-65; Naval Tactical Data Sys. Project Ofcr., Navy Dept., Wash DC 1965-75; (current) project mgr. Spl. Projects, Data Sys. Div., Hughes Aircraft Co., Fullerton 1976—; honors: N.Y. State Regents scholarship award (1946-50), elected to militarily lead NATO Indsl. Advis. Group in devel. of Internat. Command & Control Stds. for NATO Navies (1972-75), Australian Naval Crest for svcs. to Australian Navy in ship design of combat direction systems (1975); mem: IEEE (1962-), Am. Soc. of Naval Engrs. (life), US Naval Inst. (life), Retired Ofcrs. Assn. (life), Am. Def. Preparedness Assn. (life), USS Missouri Assn., Surface Navy Assn. (life), Am. Battleship Assn. (life), Navy League (life), Australian Navy Inst.; mem. Calif. 39th Congressional Dist. Service Academy Review Bd.; works: co-inventor USN Naval Tactical Data Sys. (1957-75), used by USN, NATO, Japan, Australia; major contbr. to S.E. Asia (Vietnam) Combat Direction Sys. Plans; instigated Combat Weapon Sys. improvement design for Adm. Kidd Class USN Destroyer; mil: capt. USN 1944-75, Meritorious Service Medal; Lutheran (bd. pres. 1981-83); rec: railfan, mem. Nat. Railway Hist. Soc. 1948-. Res: 2073 Smokewood Ave Fullerton 92631 Ofc: Hughes Aircraft Co. 1902 W Malvern Fullerton 92634

SWINK, JACK WILCOX, superior court judge; b. Oct. 10, 1924, Rocky Ford, Colo.; s. Walter E. and Kathleen (Monkman) S.; m. Doris J. Nelson, Nov. 26, 1950; children: Bonnie, b. 1952, Clark, b. 1954, Scott, b. 1963; edn: pre-legal, Univ. Redlands, Texas Tech., USC; LL.B summa cum laude, Southwestern Univ., 1949; grad. Calif. Coll. of Trial Judges, UC Berkeley, Boalt Hall, 1972; admitted to State Bar of Calif. 1950. Career: pvt. practice law North Hollywood, 1950-72, ptnr. Clarke, Swink, Thatcher & Leary law firm; apptd. judge Superior Ct., State of Calif. by Gov. Ronald Reagan, 1972—, suprvg. judge Probate Depts. 1978-80; author, lectr. on legal topics; honors: Outstanding Young Man of Year Award for No. Hywd. 1954, East Valley YMCA Man of the Year 1969, No. Hywd. CofC Man of Year 1972, The Athletic Congress of Official Track & Field Meets; mem. Am., Calif., Los Angeles County, San Fernando Valley (pres. 1959) bar assns.; Rotary (pres. N. Hywd. 1962-3); mil: USAF, WWII; Lutheran; Republican. Ofc: Superior Court, 111 North Hill St, Dept. 58, Los Angeles 90012

SWITLIK, CLEMENT THOMAS, JR., systems safety engineer; b. Oct. 19, 1941, Parsons, Kans.; s. Clement T., Sr. (dec.) and Margaret Agnes (Currigan)

S.; m. Dorothy Karen Dorn, Jan. 29, 1982; children: Michelle b. 1971, Jennifer b. 1972, Dawn b. 1973, Laurie b. 1977, Sarah b. 1978, Crys Tey b. 1983; edn: BA in biol./chem., Univ. of Kans., Lawrence 1971; MA in health svcs. mgt., Webster Univ., St. Louis, Mo. 1980; postgrad. wk. on MPA, Golden Gate Univ. 1975-77, PhD cand., Univ. of Beverly Hills 1980; Reg. Profl. Engr., State of Calif. 1977. Career: safety engr. Hercules Powder Co. at Sunflower Army Ammunition Plant, Lawrence, Kans. 1966-69; safety dir. Naval Weapons Station, Concord, Calif. 1976-77; regl. safety & healgh mgr. Dept. of Labor Regions IX and X, San Francisco and Seattle, 1978; spl. asst. to the cmdg. ofcr. Naval Regl. Medical Ctr., Long Beach 1979-80; regl. safety & health mgr. Agricultural Research Service, USDA, Peoria, Ill. 1980-84; systems safety engr. AF Systems Command, Air Force Space Div., Los Angeles 1984–; expert witness in litigations involving employee exposure to toxic substances; awards: Merit Award (1983) US Dept. of Agri., recipient Commendations, Navy (1980), Army (1973), Los Angeles Fed. Exec. Board (1972); mem: Am. Soc. of Safety Engrs., Am. Conf. of Govtl. Indsl. Hygienists, Assn. Fed. Safety Profls.; civic: PTA, local parish activities; publs: sev. Safety & Health Manuals for var. govtl. agencies; devel. computerized Risk Mgmt. Information System for identifying hazards in the workplace; mil: HM2, US Navy 1959-63, GCM; Republican; Roman Catholic; rec: travel, skiing, photog., fitness. Res: 18535-E Mayall St Northridge 91324

SWOPE, KARL HERMAN, architect; b. Jan. 5, 1942, Battle Creek, Mich.; s. Herman Enos and Ruth Evelyn (Hack) S.; edn: BA arch. with honors (5-yr pgm), Texas A&M Univ. 1968; underwater SCUBA instr., NAUI Coll. 1984; Reg. Architect, Wash DC (1971), Va. (1972), Tx. (1972), Calif. (1981), NCARB Cert. (1972); FAA lic. comml. pilot instrument rating. Career: US Army Corps of Engrs. 1960-63, illustrator/ draftsman hd. graphics dept. 1962-63; senior draftsman Mov Inc., Arlington, Va. 1968-71, project architect 1971-72; ptnr. Garcia Y Swope Partnership, Corpus Christi, Tx. 1972-75; project arch. SHWC Inc., Dallas 1976-79, design/prodn. coord. 1979-82; assoc., senior architect Gruen Assocs., Los Angeles 1982–; honors: Tau Beta Pi (1967); mem. Nat. Assn. of Underwater Instrs., Inst. of Nautical Archaelogy, Los Angeles and San Diego Underwater Photographic Soc.; mil: sp4 US Army 1960-63, Good Conduct medal; Roman Catholic; rec: underwater archaelogy & photog. Res: 10746 Francis Place, 220, Los Angeles 90034 Ofc: Gruen Associates 6330 San Vicente Blvd Los Angeles 90048

SYAL, PARVIN D., physician; b. Dec. 5, 1947, Nairobi, Kenya; s. Dharam Pall and Samitra Devi (Thappar) S.; m. Kiran Kulbhushan, June 29, 1985; edn: B.Med., B.Surg., Nairobi Univ. Sch. of Med. 1973; MD, Calif. State Bd. Med. Qual. Assurance 1981. Career: intern Providence Hosp. St. Helens, Eng. 1973-74, senior house ofcr. 1974-75, jr. registrar in med. 1975-77; pathol. asst. Huntington Meml. Hosp. Pasadena, Calif. 1978-80; family practitioner Gen. Med. Ctrs. Panorama City 1982-83; pvt. practice family med. Glendale 1983–; affil. Meml. Hosp. of Glendale, Glendale Adventist Hosp.; hon. lectr. St. Helen's Sch. of Nsg., 1974-77; chmn. Political Leadership Conf. 4th Biennial Conv. of Asian Indians in Am. 1986; chmn. Physicians' Liaison Com., Nat. Fedn. of Asian Indian Assns. 1986-88; honors: Outstanding Playwright (Univ. Nairobi 1970), Community Svc. Award (Arya Samaj of So. Calif. 1983), Svc. Recogn. (Indian Olympic Comm. 1984); mem: Indian Physician Assn. (steering com. chmn. 1984-86), AMA, Arya Samaj of So. Calif. (v.p. 1980-85), Fedn. of Indian Assn. (v.p. 1982-84, gen. secty. 1984-86), Glendale CofC, Red Cross (bd.), Indo-US Olympic Comm. (gen. secty. 1983-85); dir. Indian President's Reception Com.; chmn. Seminars Com.- Festival of India, Calif. Mus. of Sci. and Industry 1985-86; publs: articles in med. jours., also poetry, plays, short stories, music lyrics, feature writer The Sunday Post (Nairobi), India Reporter (L.A.), literary critic, current affairs commentator, theatre prodn., direction, acting; actor TV serial Lehren, Hindi films Dokinare, Naya savera, Durghatna; wrote screenplay & lyrics Hindi film El Musafir; anthology of poetry Rangoli. Res: 8329 Faust Ave Canoga Park 91304 Ofc: 1500 S Central Ave Ste 106 Glendale 91204

SYKES, ABEL BAXTON, JR., college president; b. June 1, 1934, Kansas City, Kans.; s. Abel B., Sr. and Grace Gladys (Buchannan) S.; m. Sylvia Thierry, Sept. 28, 1957; 3 daus.: Dawn, b. 1958, Daphane, b. 1964, Leslie, b. 1966; edn: BA, Univ. of Mo. 1959, MA, 1960; EdD, USC 1971; Inst. of Ednl. Mgmt., Harvard Bus. Sch., Grad. Sch. of Higher Edn., Cambridge, Mass. Career: instr. O'Farrell Jr. High Sch., San Diego 1960-64; instr., US Hist., Grossmont Coll., El Cajon and San Diego Evening Coll., 1962-64; instr. Pol. Sci. & Hist., Grossmont Coll. 1964-68; Dean of Instrn. Compton Community Coll. 1968-69, pres./supt. Compton Community College Dist., 1969-85, Kings River College, 1985–; honors: 1972 Educator of the Year, Phi Delta Kappa. Mem: Am. Assn. of Comm. & Jr. Colls. (chmn. bd. dirs. 1975-76), Ednl. Pgms. Eval. Com. South Viet Nam, US. Dept. of Def./AACJC; Am. Council on Edn. (bd. dirs.); Calif. Comm. & Jr. Coll. Assn. (Chancellor's Adv. Com.); AAUP, Phi Delta Kappa, Am. Hist. Assn., Sigma Pi Phi., mem. bd. govs. Dominguez Valley Hosp., Salvation Army Adv. Bd., United Crusade budget rev. com., City of Compton Local Govt. Adv. Bd., bd. dirs. Charles Drew Postgrad. Medical Sch. (L.A.), L.A. Regl. Family Planning Council; publs: contbr. Junior College Research Rev. 6/70; mil: airman 1/c USAF 1952-56, Bandsman; Presbyterian Elder; rec: photog. Res: 648 W. Ponderosa Reedley 93654 Ofc: Kings River College, 995 N Reed Ave Reedley 93654

SZABOLCS, ISTVAN, physician; b. Feb. 10, 1947, Nyirbeltek, Hungary, nat. US cit. 1983; s. Sandor and Julianna (Deak) S.; m. Agnes, July 17, 1973; children: Cynthia b. 1978, Christopher b. 1983; edn: MD, Univ. of Debrecen Sch. of Medicine, Hungary 1971. Diplomate Am. Board of Obstetrics & Gynecology 1984. Career: medical pvt. practice, Bedford Hts., Ohio 1981-83, Oakdale, Calif. 1983–; mem. Internat. Microsurgical Soc., Calif. Med. Assn., Stanislaus County Med. Soc.; Republican; Catholic. Res: 2206 Cherry Tree Lane Riverbank 95367 Ofc: Istvan Szabolcs, M.D. 1415 West H St Ste 1 Oakdale 95361

SZANTO, EDGAR ANTOL, architect; b. May 15, 1927; s. Victor and Johanna (Marcuse) S.; m. Anni Jaekel, June 20, 1964; edn: B.Arch., USC 1959. Career: project architect large firm in So. Calif. -1969; ptr., senior v.p. local firm 1969-73; archtl. plnng. & design cons. Bechtel Corp. 1973-75; founder firm Degar A. Szanto & Assocs. AIA, Pasadena 1975– (incl. archl. plnng. & design cons. ARAMCO and Royal Ministry of Edn., Saudi Arabia); num. comml. and institutional projects in So. Calif.; instr. archtl. history & theory Los Angeles City Coll. Sys.; plnng. & design cons. var. archtl. firms on projects for criminal justice in sev. states; awards: Scarab, hon. archtl. frat. 1958; Civic Award for S&L Facility in Pasadena; A.R.A. Award for Design of Shaker Hts. Police Facility; hon. mention, archtl. design competition; mem: Am. Inst. Architects (corp.), Housing Commn. (Architects for Justice Com.), Am. Inst. of Plnng. (afil.), Am. Inst. of Urban Design, Traffic Problems, Mass. Transp., Airport Plnng. & Design; mil: sgt. 1/c US Army Infantry 1950-52, Bronze Star; Republican; Immanuel Chapel; rec: travel, classical music. Res: 1862 Lorain Rd. San Marino 91108 Ofc: Edgar A. Szanto & Assoc. AIA, 664 W. Broadway Glendale 91204

SZENTE, ANDREW, engineer; b. Dec. 10, 1939, Budapest, Hungary, nat. US cit. 1976; s. Andras and Elizabeth (Schmidt) S.; m. Agnes A., Aug. 26, 1971; children: Andrew Eric b. 1981, Laszlo Stephen b. 1981; edn: BS mech. eng., Univ. of Technical Scis., Budapest 1958, MSME, 1965; BS in coaching canoeing, Univ. of Physical Edn., Budapest 1967; postgrad. stu. engring. econs., Univ. of Econ. Scis., Budapest 1968-69; Reg. Profl. Engr. (mech.), Va. (1979), Calif. (1980). Career: development engr. Grain Trust, Budapest 1965-69; designer Ingenieur Bureau Glaab, Frankfurt, W. Germany 1969-70; air condtg. designer J.S. Hamel Inc., M.S. Sudtell Inc., and Walt Disney Ents., Los Angeles 1970-73; senior environmental engr. R.M. Parsons Co., Pasadena 1973-81; v.p. engring. Hospital Energist Inc., N.Y. 1981; prin. engr. R.M. Parsons Co., 1981-83; prin. mech. engr. Municipality of Yanbu Al-Sinaiyah, Saudi Arabia, Saudiarabian Parsons Ltd., 1983–, prin. mech. engr. for constrn. of a new indsl. city by the Red Sea for 200,000 residents; awards: Olympic medalist: two silver medals Rome (1960), 4th place Tokyo (1964), US Olympic coach at the Olympic Games Montreal (1976); World and European Champion medals in canoeing (1958, 59, 61, 65, 66); Hungarian National Champion 25 times; mem. ASHRAE (pres. Los Angeles Chpt. 1972), Am. Soc. of Plumbing Engrs., Hungarian Student Assn.; clubs: Yanbu Sailing (com.), Washington Canoe; Republican; Roman Catholic; rec: photog., windsurfing. camping, kayaking. Res: 27455 Elmbridge Dr Rancho Palos Verdes 90274 Ofc: R.M. Parsons Co. 100 West Walnut St Pasadena 91124

SZYMANI, RYSZARD, wood machining specialist; b. Aug. 21, 1939, Belzec, Poland; came to US 1970, nat. 1978; s. Josef and Anastazja (Kijko) S.; edn: ME in wood tech., Coll. of Agr., Poznan, Poland 1963; postgrad. Coll. Agr., Vienna, Austria 1966-67; MS in wood sci., Univ. B.C., Can. 1970; MS in engrg. sci./ mech. engrg., UC Berkeley 1974, PhD in wood sci. and tech., 1977. Career: indsl. engr. Warski Shipyard, Szczecin, Poland 1964-65; furniture designer Furniture Factory, Vienna 1965-66; research engr. Austrian Wood Research INst., Vienna 1965-68, Canadian Forest Prods. Hardboard & Plywood div., 1968; research asst./tchg. asst. Faculty of Forestry Univ. B.C., Vancouver 1968-70; research splst. Univ. Calif. Forest Prods. Lab., Richmond 1970-77; asst. prof. Forest Prods. Dept., Oregon State Univ., Corvallis 1977-79; wood processing splst. UC Co-op Ext., Berkeley 1979-83; dir. Wood Machining Inst.; editor internat. bimonthly newsletter Wood Machining News; research cons. Calif. Cedar Products Co., Stockton. Ofc: Wood Machining Inst. POB 476 Berkeley 94701

TABATZKY, JOHANNA MARIA, private investigator; b. Oct. 5, 1929, Los Angeles; d. John P. and Mathilde T.; edn: Los Angeles City Coll. Career: investigator Profl. Surveys Detective Agcy L.A., Lloyd's Investigations L.A.; owner Tab-Mel Investigations L.A.; mem. Calif. Assn. Licensed Investigators (dist. gov. 1984-85, 86-87); Republican; Catholic; rec: cooking, gardening, rock & shell collection; Res: 2421 Riverdale Ave Los Angeles 90031 Ofc: Tab-Mel Investigations 1973 Riverside Dr Los Angeles 90039

TADEN, CLAUDIA ELIZABETH, speech and language pathologist; b. Aug. 4, 1942, Oak Park, Ill.; d. Claude and May (Youker) Schacht; m. Kenneth Taden, Nov. 27, 1970; edn: BS, Univ. of Iowa 1964; MA, Bradley Univ. 1966. Career: speech and language pathologist Family Guidance Ctr., St. Joseph, MO 1965-68; dir. speech pathology Easter Seal Soc., Ventura, CA 1968-76; dir. Dept. of Communicative Disorders/chief speech lang. path. St. John's Hosp., Oxnard 1976–; founder/cons. Compu Speech and Language Prods., 1981, 82; cons./lectr. to CA hosps. implem computers, 1982; honors: Phi Kappa Phi, Outstanding Young Women of the Year Award, Missouri 1967, Commdn. for Outstanding Profl. Svc., St. John's Reg. Med. Ctr., Oxnard 1985; listed Who's Who of Calif. Exec. Women, 1984, Who's Who Human Profl. Svcs. 1985; mem: Am. Speech-Lang.-Hearing Assoc 1966- (mem. congl. action com. network 1985); Calif. Speech and Hearing Assoc. 1970- (mem. ethics com. 1985-86); Ventura Co. Soroptimist Club 1973-77; Ventura Co. Apple Computer Users Group 1980-, (secty 1980-82); created and implemented the first computerized speech and language pathology hosp. treatment program in Calif. 1981; publs: Computer Assisted Speech and Language Pathology, Reflections, Jour. Speech-Lang. Path. 1981. Res: 593 Via Ondulando Ventura 93003 Ofc: St. John's Hospital, 333 North F Street Oxnard 93030

TAENZER, JON CHARLES, scientist; b. Nov. 10, 1942, Chgo.; s. Roderick Bendix and Marcella Ida (Galle) T.; m. Anita J., Aug. 10, 1969; 1 son, Bryce Jon b. 1984; edn: BSEE, honors, Purdue Univ. 1964; MSEE, Stanford Univ. 1966, PhD in E.E., 1971. Career: engr. Magnaflux Corp., Chgo. 1962-64; engr. Hewlett-Packard Co., Palo Alto 1965; research asst. Stanford Univ. 1965-71; senior research engr. SRI Internat., Menlo Park 1971-79; dir. of engring. Diasonics Inc., Milpitas 1979-80; staff scientist SRI Internat., 1980-83; senior scientist Adept Technol. Inc., Sunnyvale 1983-; indep. cons. to num. cos. 1966-; honors: Dean's List (1963), Atholl McBean Post Graduate Fellow (1972), listed Who's Who in Technol. Today, Who's Who in Frontiers of Sci. and Technol., Eta Kappa Nu (secty. treas. 1963-64), Tau Beta Pi (secty. 1964); mem. IEEE; civic: local recycling pgm.; author 45+ publs. in fields of Ionospheric Radiosci., Psycho-physics, Diagnostic Ultrasound and Robotics; holder of 13 issued U.S. patents and 5 pending, also holder 30+ fgn. counterpart patents; rec: photog., biking, camping, home electronics. Ofc: Adept Technology Inc 1212 Bordeaux Dr Sunnyvale 94089

TAGGART, ROBERT BURDETT, communications co. president; b. Apr. 6, 1943, Paterson, NJ; s. Robt. B., Sr., and Marjorie Stewart (Wiley) T.; m. Donna Fay Bledsoe, Feb. 14, 1973; 1 son, David Robert, b. 1974; edn: BSME, Northwestern Univ. 1967, MSME, 1968; Degree of Engr., Stanford Univ. 1970. Career: engr. and product mgr. Advanced Products Div., & Gen. Systems Div., Hewlett-Packard, Palo Alto 1970-78; mech. engrg. mgr. Computer Printers Internat., Inc., Mtn. View 1978-80; sr. mem. technical staff Apple Computer, Cupertino 1980-82; founder/ pres./ bd. chmn. Chapparal Communications, Inc. (mfr. antenna feeds for satellite TV), San Jose 1980-; pioneer mem. Soc. for Pvt. and Comml. Earth Stations; Patentee: (5; two patents pend.), Particle Analyzer (4/74), Dish Reflector for High Gain Antenna (8/74), Miniature Rotable Shaft Coupler (2/75), Miniature Magnetic Card Reader/ Recorder (7/75), Low-Cost Parabolic Reflector (7/76); sci. arts. in tech. jours., NASA Tech. Brief, IEEE Internat. Conf. on Comm.; Republican; Presbyterian; rec: satellite TV, racketball. Res: 348 Ramona Rd Portola Valley 94025 Ofc: Chaparral Communications, 2360 Bering Dr San Jose 94025

TAHA, RICHARD R., data processing executive; m. Maureen A. Freeman, Oct. 21, 1970; children: Darian Richard b. 1972, Emma b. 1975; BS, Coll. of Aeronautical Engring. 1966; MBA, Calif. Western Univ. 1978; CDP, Inst. for Certification of Computer Profls. 1980. Career: sys. group mgr. Wells Fargo Bank, San Francisco 1979-83; asst. v.p., sys. & pgmmg. mgr. Bank of the West, Santa Clara 1983-84; project mgr. GTE/ Sprint Telecommunications Corp., Burlingame 1984-; mem: Data Processing Mgmt. Assn., Fellow British Inst. of Mgmt.; publs: (copyrighted software for personnel and resume tracking) Resume Plus; Methodist; rec: old movies, personal computing. Ofc: GTE/ Sprint, 1633 Old Bayshore Ste. 350 Burlingame 94010

TAHBAZ, BEHROUZ, business executive; b. Apr. 10, 1941, Tehran, Iran, nat. US cit. 1985; s. Ali and Shamsi (Vedadi) T.; m. Mehrnaz, June 25, 1967; children: Behzad b. 1968, Safoura b. 1973; edn: BS in indsl. tech. mgmt., CSU Fresno 1966; MBA, Univ. Tehran, 1968; MPA, Nat. Defense Univ. 1969. Career: senior advisor to Joint Chief of Staff Imperial Iranian Armed Forces and Under Secty. of Fin. Dept. of Customs, 1966-71; sr. exec. v.p. Information Systems of Iran, 1971-75; prin. Genco Internat. Trade, Tehran 1975-79; exec. v.p. Group 1 Internat., Los Angeles 1980-84; proj. mgr. Hydraulics Internat., L.A. 1982-84; sr. exec. v.p. Universal Mack S & S Inc., 1985-; founder, exec. bd. dir. First Svgs. & Loan Assn. (KOROSH), Iran 1968-79; honors: Merit of Taj (Imperial Crown) 3rd rank awarded by H.I.M. Shah of Iran (1970); mem: Mgmt. Soc. (1970), Am. Mgmt. Assn. (1986), Econ. Devel. Studies (1972), Jr. CofC of Iran (founder, bd. dir. 1969); works: spl. assignment to Imperial Court for "Management Review", "Performance Evaluation", and overall "Audit" (1970-71); founder/ed. popular public mgmt. mag. "Controller" (1966-71); Republican; Islam; rec: tennis. Res: 1010 4th St Santa Monica 90403 Ofc: Universal Mack S & S Inc. 2800 Cherry Ave Signal Hill 90806-1909

TAINTER, EUGENE G., surgeon, radiologist, ret.; b. Aug. 4, 1910, Taber Alta., Canada; s. Emory Baxter and Winifred Alice (Lane) T.; m. Gwynadelle Green; 1 dau. Sydney Jean (Roussel); edn: BA, Stanford Univ. 1938, MD, 1942; Diplomate Am. Board Radiology 1950, Fellow Am. Coll. Radiology 1968. Career: physician AUS Med. Corps, 5th Evac. Hosp., 1st US Army Eng. in France, Belgium, Germany, 1943-45; radiologist in Reno, Nev. 1945-48, Sacramento 1948-71; senior ptnr. Radiology Assocs., Sacto. mem. advis. coms. Gov. Earl Warren, Gov. G. Knight; club: M.P.C. (Pebble Beach); var. sci. publs.; Republican; Protestant; rec: golf. Res: Box 6226 Carmel 93921

TAKAHASHI, BEN KIYOSHI, lawyer; b. Oct. 17, 1921, Tokyo, Japan; s. Naosaku and Yukino (Mizushina) T.; m. Tomiko Arai; children: Robert b. 1947, Eugene b. 1952, Sophie Fung b. 1955; edn: B.Law, Tokyo Imperial Univ. Law Sch. 1944; JD, Southwestern Univ. Law Sch. 1965. Career: Foreign Ofc. of Japan, Tokyo 1945; dir. Airinkaai Meguro Wakabaryu (Oprphanage) 1947; law practice, Calif. 1967-; pres. Assn. of Immigration & Nationality Lawyers, L.A. chpt. 1973-74; legal cousel Consulate General of Japan, Los Angeles 1976-; mem: Am. and Calif. Bar Assns., U.S. Supreme Ct.; Democrat; rec: judo (Nat. AAU Judo Champ. 140lb. div., 5th degree blackbelt, Godan of Kodokan Judo), golf, photog. Res: 2111 E. Cameron Ave., West Covina 91791 Ofc: 250 E. 1st St. Ste. 812 Los Angeles 90012

TAKEDA, KENNETH KINGO, orthodontist; b. Dec. 24, 1929, Riverside, CA; s. Orisaburo and Umeko (Ando) T.; m. Mary Yamaguchi, Jan. 28, 1951; children: Matthew b. 1955, Kristin b. 1970; edn: AA, Riverside Coll. 1949; BSCE, UC Berkeley 1951; DDS, UC San Francisco 1965. Career: engr. drafts-man US Bureau Reclamation, Boulder City, Nev. 1949; jr. engr. US Bur. Reclamation, Marble Canyon, Ariz. 1950; stress analyst Boeing Airplane Co., Seattle, Wash. 1951-53; structures engr. Douglas Aircraft, Long Beach 1953-60; research engr. The Boeing Co., Seattle, summers 1961-3; orthodontist pvt. practice, Stockton 1965-; bd. dir. UC Med. Ctr. 1964-65; v.p. UCSF Sch. Dentistry 1964-65; pres. UC Orthodontic Soc. 1964-65; pres. San Joaquin Dental Soc. 1972-73; rep. Calif. Dental Assn.; awards: Gabbs prize in Dentistry, UCSF 1965, Omicron Kappa Upsilon 1965, Delta Sigma Delta (Worthy Master 1963-64); mem: UC Dental Alumni Assn; UC Orthodontic Alumni Assn; Parnassus Club UCSF; Pacific Coast Soc. of Orthodontists; Calif. State Soc. of Orthodontists; Am. Assn. of Orthodontists; Am. Dental Assn.; Kiwanis Club of Metro. Stockton (pres. 1977-78); Japanese-Am. Citizen's League (Lodi chpt. pres. 1984); Presbyterian; rec: photog., hunting, skiing, travel. Res: 626 Birchwood Dr Lodi 95240 Ofc: Kenneth K. Takeda, DDS Inc., 532 W Harding Way Stockton 95204

TAKEMOTO, SATORU, company president; b. Nov. 22, 1934, Aichi Pref., Japan; s. Shozo and Mume T.; m. Reiko, Oct. 16, 1959; children: Ayumu b. 1960, Osamu b. 1963; edn: LLB, Kyoto Univ. Japan 1958. Career: mgr. Nippondenso L.A. Ofc. 1969-70, mgr. overseas aftermarket sales dept. Japan 1970-77, asst. gen. mgr. 1977-82, gen. mgr. 1982-85, pres. L.A. 1986-; mem: L.A. Area CofC, Japan Traders Club of L.A.; Buddhist; rec: golf. Res: 4051 Montaigne Way Palos Verdes Peninsula 90274 Ofc: Nippondenso of L.A. Inc. 3900 Via Oro Ave Long Beach 90810

TAKLA, MICHAEL M., engineering and project executive; b. Jan. 3, 1930, Alexandria, Egypt, nat. US cit. 1973; s. Takla Michael and Mathilda (Boulos) T.; m. Anisa, July 14, 1958; children: John M. b. 1960, Paul M. b. 1960; edn: BSME, Univ. of Alexandria 1954; MBA, Golden Gate univ. 1980; Reg. Profl. Mech. Engr., Calif., No. Dakota and Colo. Career: mech. engr. ESSO and Shell, Egypt 1954-58; project engring. mgr. Shell Refinery, Egypt 1958-64; mgr. of engring. Shell Oilfields, Egypt 1964-67; project engr. Bechtel Inc., San Francisco 1968-82, project engring. mgr. 1982-84, project mgr. 1985-; honors: Makeen Prize, Univ. of Alexandria; Merit Awards (2), Bechtel Inc. 1982, 1984; Cert., Project Mgmt. Inst.; mem: Am. Soc. Mech. Engrs., Project Mgmt. Inst., Bechtel Employee Club (bd. dirs. 1974-75); publs: profl. papers presented, PMI Symposiums (1981, 1983), devel. method of estimating man hours and measurement of productivity based on physical scope of a project; Republican; Christian; rec: profl. assn. meetings, tennis, swimming. Res: 317 Port Royal Ave. Foster City 94404 Ofc: Bechtel Inc., 50 Beale St. San Francisco 94105

TALBERT, RICHARD CLARK, co. president, entrepreneur; b. Oct. 27, 1950, Oak Park, Ill.; s. Austin Gertner and Kathryn Mary (Pokragac) T.; m. Patricia Parker, Mar. 16, 1974; children: Jeffrey b. 1977, Kristin b. 1985; edn: Univ. of Ill. 1968-71. Career: mgr. Rock Road Trailer (camper parts house), St. Louis, Mo. 1971-74; nat. dir. Narconon (drug rehabilitation pgm.), Los Angeles 1974-79; gen. partner/pres. Northland Environmental Inc. (factory rep. Sunland Ind.), Burbank 1979-; honors: Inc. mag. list of 500 fastest growing US pvt. cos.; mem: Calif., L.A., Orange Co. Solar Energy Industries Assn. (CAL-SEIA ethics com., spokesman), Nat. Fedn. Independent Bus., Calif. CofC, Burbank CofC; rec: pvt. pilot, skiing. Res: 3306 Brace Canyon Rd Burbank 91504 Ofc: Northland Environmental, Inc., 1115 Chestnut St Burbank 91506

TALBOT, MILFORD CORNELIUS, manufacturing co. executive; b. Dec. 9, 1948, Trinidad, West Indies; s. Randolph Charles and Darbin T.; m. Yolanda; children: Gyasi Omari b. 1978, Jamila Oni b. 1981; edn: dipl. computer pgmmg. Boston Sch. of Bus. 1971; BS, CSU San Francisco 1975. Career: engr. in tng., nuclear pipe stress, Stone & Webster Corp., Boston 1970-73; nuclear pipe stress analysis, Bechtel Corp., 1975-78; fossil fuel piping designer Fluor Corp., 1979-80; chief exec. Triple Lustre Products (mfg. co.), Huntington Beach currently; sales tng. cons.; mem: ASME, Huntington Beach CofC, Orange County CofC; inventor: Improved Solid Particulate Cleaner Polish (US pat. 1981); Ch. of Christ; rec: inventing indsl. products. Ofc: Triple Lustre Products 17610 Beach Blvd Ste 52 Huntington Beach 92646

TALLMAN, JOHANNA E., university library director, ret.; b. Aug. 18, 1914, Lubeck, Germany; d. Friedrich Franz and Johanna (Voget) Allerding; m. Lloyd Anthony Tallman, May 8, 1954; edn: AB, Univ. of Calif. 1936, cert. in Librarianship, 1937. Career: San Marino Pub. Lib., 1937-38; L.A. County Pub. Lib., 1938-42; Pacific Aeronautical Lib., 1942-44; hd. Engineering and Math. Scis. Lib., UCLA, 1945-73; lib. dir. Calif. Inst. of Tech., 1973-81; lectr. UCLA Sch. of Lib. Service, 1961-73; Fullbright lectr., Brazil 1966-67; mem: Librarians Assn. Univ. Calif. (pres. 1970-71), Spl. Libraries Assn. (chair Sci.-Tech. Div. 1969-70, pres. So. Calif. chpt. 1965-66, L.A. Regional Group of Catalogers (chair 1946-47), Pasadena Hist. Soc. (dir.), Zonta Internat. (pres. Pasadena chpt. 1976-77), Fine Arts Club of Pasadena (pres. 1982-84); author: Check Out a Librarian (Scarecrow Press, 1985); contbr. over 61 profl. jours. Res: 4731 Daleridge Rd La Canada Flintridge 91011

TALLMAN, SHARON PAULINE, graphic designer, typesetting service executive; b. Dec. 24, 1951, San Diego; d. Robert Glenn and Dorothy Antoinette (Colonell) T.; ed. Mesa Coll. 1971-73. Career: supr. APW/Evans, San Diego 1972-74; gen. mgr., asst. art director Boyer & Brass, Inc. San Diego 1978-; guest spkr. seminars, La Jolla Acad. of Advt. Art; mem. Communicating Arts Group, S.D.; publ. works incl. ads, posters and textbooks, 1980-; Democrat; Christian; rec: art, equestrian, roller skating. Res: 231 So Shorehang Ln Encinitas Ofc: Boyer & Brass Inc. 1929 Hancock St San Diego 92110

TAN, JIMMY CHIH-YU, hotelier/ trading co. executive; b. Feb. 10, 1936, Hunan, China, nat. 1982; parents: Wen Sun and En Zen (Tung) T.; edn: Bach., Nat. Chung Hsing Univ., Taiwan, 1960; cert. assoc. prof., Dept. Edn. Taiwan 1972. Career: asst., Coll. of Commerce, Nat. Cheng Chi Univ. Taiwan 1960-64; instr. Nat. Cheng Chi Univ. 1964-68; auditor of Budget Commn. of Exec. Yuan, Taiwan 1968-69; assoc. prof. Nat. Cheng Chi Univ., Taiwan 1969-73; mgr. Sequoia Hotel, Los Angeles 1974-76; mgr./owner Grand Central Hotel, San Francisco 1978—; pres. General Union Trading Group Inc., SF 1981—; mem: Nat. Assn. of Exec. Sectys., Vir. 1978; SF Conv. & Visitor Bur.; author: Applied Mathematics of Management (World Books Co. Taipei, Taiwan 1969); Catholic; rec: draughts, travel, music. Address: Grand Central Hotel, 1412 Market St San Francisco 94102

TAN, LIP-BU, venture capitalist, business executive; b. Nov. 12, 1959, Malaysia; s. Keng Lian and Yeok Choong (Chew) T.; m. Ysa Loo, Dec. 19, 1982; edn: BS, Nayang Univ. Singapore 1978; MS, M.I.T. 1981; MBA, Univ. San Francisco 1983; Reg. Profl. Mech. Engr. Calif.; Reg. Rep. NASD. Career: prin. engr. EDS Nuclear S.F. 1980-81; lead engr. ECHO Energy Consultants Oakland 1981-83; asst. v.p. Chappell & Co. S.F. 1982-84; pres. Walden Internat. Inc. S.F. 1984—; gen. ptnr. Walden Funds 1984—; pres. Orient Capital & Technol. Corp. 1983—; mng. dir. Mulpha USA 1985—; dir: Mouse Systems, Orient Capital & Technol., Mulpha USA, others; lectr. Univ. San Francisco; mem: Western Assn. Venture Capitalists, Am. Nuclear Soc., Am. Soc. Mech. Engrs; publ: several technical papers presented Elec. Power Research Inst., Am. Nuclear Soc.; Christian; rec: swimming, tennis, basketball. Res: 25603 Camino Vista Hayward 94541 Ofc: Walden 303 Sacramento St Ste 400 San Francisco 94111

TAN, WILLIAM LEW, lawyer; b. July 25, 1949, Calif.; s. James Tan and Choon Guey (Louie) Lew; edn: BA, Univ. of Penn. 1971; JD, UC Hastings Coll. of Law 1974; admitted Calif. State Bar 1975. Career: ptnr. Tan & Sakiyama, APC, Los Angeles 1981—, and ptnr. sev. corps.; bd. chmn./CEO Asian Research Consultants, 1984—; adj. prof. CSU Los Angeles 1985; awards: City of L.A. Human Rels. Commn. (1977), Outstanding Young Men Am. (1979), Constn. Rights Found., L.A. Co. Bar (1976), L.A. Unified Sch. Dist. hon. tchg. cert. (1976); mem: Am. Bar Assn. (Adminstrv. Law Sect., del. Nat. Inst. of Minority Lawyers 1981), Calif. Bar Assn. (editl. bd. Calif. Lawyer 1981-84, com. on ethnic minority rels. 1983-), L.A. Co. Bar Assn. (bd. trustees 1984-, Olympics com. 1983-84, Immigration Law com. 1979-), So. Calif. Chinese Lawyers Assn. (pres. 1980-81), Minority Bar Assn. (chmn. 1981-82), Asian Pacific Bar Assn., Japanese Am. Bar Assn., Assn. Trial Lawyers Am., Bench and Bar Council, Lawyers Club of L.A., Calif. Trial Lawyers Assn.; civic: Breakfast Club, Asian Pac. Am. Roundtable (1981-), L.A. Crime Crisis Task Force (1981), Univ. Pa. Alumni Assn. (chpt. pres. 1979-80), Asian Pac. Women's Network, Chinese Cultural Soc. (advisor 1982-), US-Asia Inst. Conf. (1981-), Chinatown Svc. Ctr. (dir. 1983-), Leadership Edn. for Asian Pacifics (dir. 1983-, chair 1984-), State Bd. of Pharmacy (1984-), comm. advisor to Mayor Tom Bradley (1984-); Democrat (alt. Nat. Conv. 1984); Christian; rec: cooking, watercolorist, biking, tennis. Ofc: Tan & Sakiyama 711 W College St Ste 610 Los Angeles 90012

TANAKA, RICHARD KOICHI, architect/planner; b. Oct. 16, 1931, San Jose; s. Richard Inoru and Mae Yoshiko (Koga) T.; m. Barbara Hisako Kumagai, Oct. 7, 1960; children: Craig Koji b. 1961, Todd Tadashi b. 1962, Sandra Kimi b. 1963, Trent Kiyoshi b. 1973; edn: B.Arch., Univ. Mich. 1954; M.Urban Planning, CSU San Jose 1970. Desig: corporate mem. Am. Inst. Architects, AIA, Am. Inst. of Planning, AIP, Constrn. Specification Inst., CSI. Career: designer, later prin. architect, Newlon Greene Architects, 1954-58; exec. v.p./ ptnr. The Steinberg Group, Architects, Planner 1958—; awards: for best comml. project in the West (1982), commendation Santa Clara Human Relations Commn. and Santa Clara Co. Board Supvrs., num. awards from City of San Jose, East Side Union High Sch. Dist., The Asian Am. Educators Assn., and Santa Clara Co. Bd. Supvrs.; civic: East Side Union High Sch. Dist. (pres. bd. trustees), City of San Jose Bicentennial Commn. (chmn.), San Jose Tapestry in Talent (pres.), San Jose Parks and Rec. subcom. (chmn. Goals Com.), San Jose Symphony (bd.), S.C. County Human Rels. Commn., Japanese Am. Citizens League (pres. 1971, 72), CSUSJ Counselor Ednl. Com., San Jose Commn. on Internment of local Japanese Americans (chmn.); Democrat; rec: painting, golf. Res: 14811 Whipple Ct San Jose 95127 Ofc: The Steinberg Group, San Jose

TANG, EAMAN, carpet manufacturer; b. June 17, 1957, Taipei, Taiwan; s. Jonathan H.C. and Dianna C.H. (Yang) T.; m. Lee, June 21, 1980; edn: UC Irvine 1980. Career: bd. chmn. Walnut Co., City of Commerce with 8 retail carpet centers in Calif., 1980—; v.chmn. Pacific Carpet, Taipei, Taiwan, R.O.C.; owner/bd. chmn./ pres. Texas Tuft Carpet Mills Inc., Marlin, Texas (re-organized and reopened the Mill, the prin. employer in Marlin, after it had been closed for six months) 1986—; honors: apptd. by Calif. Secty. of State as Acting Secty. of State (9/1/86 to 7/31/87); nom. by US Cong. Robert Dornan, recipient 1986 Asian American Achievement Awards for Business and Industry; Resolution of appreciation for the successful reopening of a Texas carpet mill, US Congl. Reps. Matthew Martinez (CA), Marvin Leath (Tx.) and House Majority Leader Jim Wright (1986) mem: Chinese Better Business Assn. (adminstr.), Calif. Chinese Assn. of Constrn. Profls. (secty-gen.); Democrat. Res: 1822-G Cedar St. Alhambra 90801 Ofc: Cathay Carpet Mills, 5823 Telegraph Rd. City of Commerce 90040

TANG, SHENG-TSAN, manufacturing executive; b. Jan. 19, 1922, Hsiangtan, China, nat. US cit. 1985; s. Ko-Sun and Chung-Li (Chang) T.; m. Tsai-Chen,

Mar. 12, 1946; children: Ming-Hsien b. 1947, Ming-Chien b. 1948, Ming-Ching b. 1951; edn: BS, Hunan Univ. 1944; MS, Inst. of Aero. Engring., 1946; Reg. Profl. Mech. Engr., Taiwan (1977). Career: tool engr., mgr. machine shop, mgr. prodn. control Aircraft Engine Mfg. Factory, China and Taiwan, 1946-60; chief indsl. engr. Yue Loong Motor Co. (car, truck and engine mfr.), Taiwan 1960-66; mgr. of mfg. engring. Philco Taiwan Corp. (TV set, radio, hi-fi mfr.), Taiwan 1966-69; asst. gen. mgr. TMX Taiwan Ltd. subs. U.S. Time Corp. (watch and watch band mfr.), 1969-70; dir. mfg. engring. svcs. Zenith Taiwan Corp. (TV set mfr.) 1970-73; mfg. program mgr. Ford Lio Ho Motor Co. (engine and car) 1973-77, devel. and installed Ford system in offshore facility for producing casting, engine and car, concept through high volume prodn.; dir. of engring. Taiwan Bur. of Commodity Insp. and Quarantine, 1977-79; prof. indsl. engrg. and mgmt. Taiwan Univ. 1967-79; cons., lectr. on work study, prodn., system improvement and mgmt. in Taiwan 1964-79; sr. mfg. engr. Shugart Assocs. (disk drive), Sunnyvale 1979-83; mgr. indsl. engring. Magnex Corp. (thin film head), San Jose 1983-85; dir. of mfg. Cogito Systems Corp. (disk drive), San Jose 1985—; honors: Asian Expert, Asian Productivity Orgn. (1979); senior mem. Am. Inst. of Indsl. Engrs. 1966-; author: Industrial Engineering and Factory Management (1974); rec: reading. Res: 986 Cape Mary Pl San Jose 95133 Ofc: Cogito Systems Corp. 562 S Milpitas Blvd Milpitas 95035

TANIS, NORMAN EARL, librarian; b. Aug. 15, 1929, Grand Rapids, Mich.; s. Aaron Orrie and Gertrude (Medendorp) T.; m. Terese Tieman, Dec. 27, 1981; 2 daus: Kathy b. 1962, Laura, b. 1964; edn: AB, Calvin Coll. 1951; AMLS, Univ. of Mich. 1951; MA, 1956. Career: library coord. Henry Ford Comm. Coll., Dearborn, Mich. 1956-66; lib. dir. Kans State Univ., Pittsburgh 1966-9; dir. of univ. libs. CSU, Northridge 1969—; ed./mgr. The Santa Susana Press 1973—; secty. & bd. trustees Univ. San Fernando Coll. of Law 1978-80; honors: Phi Kappa Phi, Beta Phi Mu, and D.H.L. (hon.) at Univ. San Fernando 1975; LLD (hon.), Mid-Valley Coll. of Law 1979; mem: Am. Film Inst.; Nat. Trust for Historic Preservation; Northridge Draft Bd. (Selective Svc. no. 201); Marine Meml. Club of San Francisco 1976-; coauthor: Native Americans of North America. Scarecrow Press, Inc. 1975; Problems in Developing Academic Library Functions, Jai Press, Inc. 1978; China in Books, Jai Press, Inc. 1979; mil: Cpl., US Army 1952-4, Nat. Defense Medal.; Democrat; Protestant; rec: theatre, travel, horsemanship, art collector. Res: 10009 Jovita Chatsworth 91311 Ofc: Calif. State Univ., 18111 Nordhoff Northridge 91330

TANNER, DAVID SMITH, dentist; b. Apr. 19,1 931, Ogden, Utah; s. Henry Smith and Columbia Eden (Richards) T.; m. Patricia Hoover, Sept. 14, 1954; children: Howard b. 1956, Karen b. 1957, Michele b. 1959, David b. 1961, Jonathan b. 1965, Melanie b. 1966, Stephanie b. 1966, Catherine b. 1969; edn: BA, Univ. of Utah 1953; DDS, Coll. of Physicians and Surgeons 1960. Career: naval ofcr. U.S. Naval Radiological Defense Laboratory, 1953-56; dentist in pvt. practice, San Jose 1960—; mem: Am. Dental Soc., Calif. Dental Soc., Santa Clara Co. Dental Soc.; works: 5 vols. of correlated scripture of the Bible, Book of Mormon, Doctrine and Covenants, and Pearl of Great Price; mil: lt. USNR 1953-56; Republican; Ch. of Jesus Christ of Latter-day Saints (Melchizedek Priest); rec: genealogy. Ofc: David S. Tanner, DDS, APC, 3114 Story Road San Jose 95127

TANSMAN, BERNARD AARON, physician; b. Feb. 29, 1936, NY, NY; s. Saul and Gertrude (Wexler) T.; m. Sandra Hulet, Feb. 6, 1982; 1 dau. Mara b. 1967; edn: BA, UC Los Angeles 1957; MD, Faculty of Med. and Surgery, Univ. of Bologna, Italy 1964; Diplomate Am. Board of Radiology, 1972. Career: (current) senior radiologist Western Radiologic Medical Group, Inc., Culver City; chief radiologist (chmn. Contg. Med. Edn., past pres. medical staff) Memorial Hosp. of Gardena; attending radiologist Brotman Medical Center, Culver City; mem: AMA, Los Angeles County Med. Soc., Calif. Radiological Soc.; mil: capt. MC, USAF 1968-69. Res: 9244 Cordell Dr., Los Angeles 90069 Ofc: Western Radiologic Medical Group, Inc. 9808 Venice Blvd Culver City 90230

TANVEER, SALEH A., applied mathematician; b. Feb. 8, 1956, Dhaka, Bangladesh, perm. resident 1986; s. G.G. and Sarah (Khanam) Chowdhury; m. Dilruba Sultana, Aug. 21, 1986; 1 child, Mamun b. 1982; edn: BA, Pomona Coll. 1979; MA, Claremont Grad. Sch. 1979; PhD, Calif. Inst. Tech. 1984. Career: research fellow applied math Caltech, Pasadena 1983-84; asst. prof. math dept. V.P.I. & S.U., Blackburg, Va. 1984—; vis. research assoc. dept. of applied math Caltech Pasadena 1986—; honors: Phi Beta Kappa; Rena Gurney Archibald High Scholarship Prize, Pomona Coll. 1979; mem. Soc. of Indsl. & Applied Mathematicians; works: publs. in area of high lift acrodynamics, Journ. of Fluid Mechanics, Studies in Applied Math, 1984, 1985, Invisid Vortex Dynamicsu, Physics of Fluids 1982, Journ. Fr. Mech. 1984, Studies in Applied Math 1986, Hele-Shaw Cell Flows 1986; rec: pingpong, chess, tennis. Ofc: 217-50 Caltech Pasadena 91125

TAPLIN, JONATHAN TRUMBULL, investment banker; b. July 18, 1947, Shaker Heights, Ohio; s. Charles Farrand, Jr. and Constance Willard (Huntington) T.; m. 2d. Lesley Gilb, Apr. 26, 1980; children: Daniela b. 1976 (by previous m.), Nicholas b. 1980, Blythe b. 1982; edn: BA, Princeton Univ. 1969. Career: tour mgr. Bob Dylan, Woodstock, N.Y. 1969-72; independent film prod. Warner Bros., MGM, Orion, Walt Disney, 1972-85; vice pres. Mergers & Acquisitions, Merrill-Lynch Capital Markets 1985—; awards: David Donatello Award for Best Fgn. Producer, Italian Acad. of Motion Pictures; mem. Acad. of Motion Picture Arts & Scis.; civic: Democratic Media Ctr., Wash DC (bd. dirs.); films: Mean Streets, The Last Waltz, Carny, Under Fire Grandview U.S.A., Baby, My Science Project; Democrat. Ofc: 1st Media 12400 Wilshire Blvd Ste 1280 Los Angeles 90025

TAPPING, DAVID WILLIAM, engineer/executive; b. Aug. 4, 1928, Deal, U.K., nat. 1969; s. John Arthur and Kathleen (Oakridge); m. Patricia Roughton, 1954; children: Carol b. 1956, Jonathan b. 1960; edn: BS, Univ. Coll. London 1952; Reg. Profl. Engr., NY, Mo., Wash., Ore., Calif., and La.; Career: with Bechtel Corp. 1964—; responsible for structural design, including conformance to codes of Foothill Feeder water supply for L.A. and for complete design of fossil power generating stations in Centralia, Bowline Point, Rush Island, Creston and Boardman; Fellow, Am. Soc. of Civil Engrs.; Fellow, Inst. of Civil Engrs. U.K. (for assisting in orig. design of comml. nuclear power); chmn. of panel for selection of USA residents seeking U.K. profl. engring. registration; mil: Lt. Royal Engrs., Brit. Army, Germany 1946; rec: backpacking, running, cross country. Res: 160 Manor Dr Mill Valley CA 94941 Ofc: Bechtel, POB 3965 San Francisco 94119

TARADASH, ROSLYN FINKEL, electrical supplies distributor; b. Feb. 18, 1927, Chgo.; d. Maurice Charles and Florence (Blumenthal) T.; m. Elmer Finkel, Dec. 4, 1949; div.; 1 dau. Cathy (Beth) b. 1952; edn: BA, Univ. Miami, 1948; Calif. real estate sales lic. (1958). Career: real estate sales, Beverly Hills 1958—, assoc. Mike Silverman, 1960, Mary Robertson & Assocs. 1970; v.p. Hyland Elec. Supply Co., 1965-80, pres./bd. chmn. 1980-81; pres. Tara Electric, Chgo. 1981—; initated and achieved the annexation by City of Beverly Hills (2d largest in city's hist.) of homes on southern boundary with homesites divided between Cities of Los Angeles and Beverly Hills (1975-79), enabling homes to be solely within B.H.; subject of feature article Chicago Tribune business section (1980); civic: City of Hope, Brandeis, ACLU, Waif; clubs: Carlton, Boca Point Golf; Jewish; rec: golf, swim.

TARTOL, JOHN J., marketing co. president; b. Aug. 3, 1951, Chgo.; s. John J. and Helen (Stefely) T.; m. Lori Patton, Feb. 14, 1982; children: Jessica b. 1983, John David b. 1985; edn: BS summa cum laude, Univ. Ill. 1973, law stu. Univ. of San Diego. Career: songwriter/pub., owner music prodn. co., 8 yrs.; estab. mktg. co. 1980-81, pres. Tartol Ents. Inc. (mktg. health prods.), 1981—; mem. Herbalife millionaire team; mem. Univ. Ill. Boosters; Christian; rec: music, sports. Ofc: Tartol Enterprises 5885 Fitzpatrick Rd Hidden Hills 91302

TASSOPULOS, VENETTA SKREPETOS, judge; b. Nov. 14, 1927, Sacramento; d. Nicholas Chris and Matina A. (Dermatas) Skrepetos; m. Peter Tassopulos, 1961; 1 son. Jim b. 1962; edn: BA, UC Berkeley 1948, MA in pol. sci., 1957, LLB., 1960. Career: dep. public defender Los Angeles County, 1960-61; pvt. practice, civil and crim., 1962-68 (Federal Indigent Def. Panel, Contg. Edn. of the Bar, OEO Spl. Projects); U.S. commnr. U.S. Dist. Ct. (Central Dist. Calif.) 1968-71; U.S. Magistrate (Presiding) 1971—; faculty Seminar for Magistrates, Federal Judicial Ctr. 1971, 74, 77, 82; lectr., panelist var. workshops for nat., state and local bar assns., UCLA, CEB, Nat. Assn. of Women Judges Confr., Calif. Inst. for Trial Advocacy, others; honors: elected to Moot Court Bd. Boalt Hall Sch. of Law; judge Moot Ct., Southwestern Univ. (1981), Western Regl. Finals (1982), Southwestern Univ. (1983); cons. Appeals & Writs in Criminal Cases, Calif. Criminal Law Practice Series (CEB 1982); mem. ABA, Fed. Bar Assn., Los Angeles Co. Bar Assn., Calif. Women Lawyers, Nat. Assn. of Women Judges, Nat. Council of US Magistrates (Circuit Dir. 1975-76; treas. 1981-82); non-partisan; Greek Orthodox. Ofc: 312 N Spring St Rm 1001 Los Angeles 90012

TATUM, TOBY WAYNE, restaurant co. executive; b. Mar. 19, 1945, Yuma, Ariz.; s. Cecil Wayne and Harriet Virgenia (Carlson) T.; m. Mary Ann Krause, Dec. 4, 1976; 1 dau. Tiffany b. 1969; edn: AA, Santa Rosa Jr. Coll. 1966; BA, CSU Sonoma 1972; MBA, San Francisco St. Univ. 1973. Career: v.p. Tatum Ents. Inc., 1973—; dir. Sonoma State Ents. 1980-82; assoc. prof. of mgmt. CSU Sonoma 1976; trustee Nat. Sizzler Franchisee Assn., 1980-; mil: sgt. US Army 1st Air Cav. Div., Vietnam, Bronze Star; Republican; rec: ski. Res: 1424 Wikiup Dr Santa Rosa 95401 Ofc: Tatum Enterprises 6050 Commerce Blvd Roanert Park 94928

TAUR, SHARON SHIAO-JUNG, aerospace co. engineer; b. Apr. 12, 1942, China, nat. 1975; d. Shung-Lun and Sheng-Jung (Chao) Lee; m. Roger Taur, Dec. 23, 1967; children: Alan b. 1973, Ronald b. 1974; edn: BS, Cheng-Kung Univ. Tainan, Taiwan 1966; MS, Univ. of Mo., Rolla 1967; PhD, Utah State Univ. 1973; Reg. Profl. Engr., Md. (1974), Calif. (1983). Career: research asst. C.E. Dept. Utah State Univ. 1967-70; project engr. David Volkert & Assocs., Bethesda, Md. 1970-74; project engr. Bechtel Power Corp., Gaithersburg, Md. 1975-77; senior engr. Lockheed Missiles & Space Co., Sunnyvale 1981-84, lead engr. 1984—; mem. ASCE 1973-; dissertation: Stiffness coefficients for tapered beam-columns (1973). Res: 1405 Redwood Dr Los Altos 94022 Ofc: Lockheed Missiles & Space Corp. (POB 3504) Sunnyvale 94088-3504

TAVERNETTI, RICHARD ROLAND, orthopedic surgeon; b. May 22, 1938, Salinas; s. Roland Lloyd and Isabel (Boekenoogen) T.; m. Maur Bettman, July 1, 1980; children: Sarah, b. 1972, John Foxon, b. 1974, Richard Rochat, b. 1981, Wm. Edward, b. 1985; edn: BS, UC Berkeley 1960; MD, Columbia Coll. of Phys. & Surgs. 1967; orthopedic surgical resident Los Angeles County Harbor gen. Hosp. 1967-72. Career: orthopedic surgeon, 1972—; asst. clin. prof. orthopedic surgery Univ. of Calif. 1982—; bd. dirs. Cyclotron Corp., Pan-Med. Ltd.; inventor, devel. Tavernetti Rotating Hinge Knee Prosthesis, US Patent No. 3,813,700; mem. Am. Acad. Orthopedic Surgeons, Western Orthopedic Assn.; clubs: University, Pacific Union; num. publs. in med. field on endocrinology and orthopedic surgery; mil: capt. USAF Reserv. M.C.; Republican; Christian; rec: collect antiques, travel, ranching. Ofc: 2100 Webster St San Francisco 94115

TAVLIN, LINDA JEANNE, public affairs executive; b. Feb. 7, 1950, Long Beach, Calif.; d. Harry and Shirley Jeanne (White) T.; edn: BA, UC Irvine 1972; ins. solicitor Calif. 1976; personal property broker Calif. 1980; real estate broker Calif. 1980; securities reg. rep., SEC 1984. Career: mgr. Public Finance Fullerton 1973-78; asst. mgr. Topa Thrift & Loan Newport Beach 1978; independent contr. Calif. Nova Financial Huntington Beach 1978-80; owner/broker Independent Funding & Investments Irvine 1980-85; dir. public affairs Employment Stds. Adminstrn. US Dept. Labor 1985—; producer, host Calif. Republican Review 1983—; instr./ lectr. Santa Ana Comm. Coll. 1980-85; instr/ coord. Long Beach City Coll. 1980-85; mem: Nat. Fedn. Republican Women, Calif. Republican Party (assoc. mem.), L.A. Olympic Organizing Com., Citizen's Adv. Commn. 1982, USC Town & Color, Town Hall, Freedoms Found. at Valley Forge, L.A. World Affairs Council, World Affairs Council Wash. DC, UC Alumni Assn., Southwest Bluebook; author: Contg. Edn. Seminars in real estate 1982; Republican; rec: travel, world affairs, politics, theatre. Res: 19 Windward Irvine 92713 Ofc: US Dept. Labor 200 Constitution Ave Wash DC 20210

TAWFIK, HUSSEIN H., food service industry executive; b. Jan. 1, 1938, Mansoura, Egypt; s. Hussein and Monira (Rashid) T.; m. Heidi, Aug. 3, 1963; 1 child, Tarik b. 1964; edn: BA, Alexandria Univ. 1961; MA, Vanderbilt Univ. 1963; CPA review courses, Golden Gate Univ. 1970. Career: pres. Rhodes Ents. Inc., Santa Clara 1985—; v.p. fin. & adminstrn. Nutritional Foods Inc., South San Francisco 1973-82; finl. controller Beta Co., Riyadh, Saudi Arabia 1982-84; v.p. fin. & adminstrn., MCM Financial Inc., Santa Clara 1984; honors: Hon. Citizen State of Tenn., Gov. Buford Ellington (1962); chartered mem. Nat. Accts. Assn., San Mateo chpt. 1973-; Republican; rec: gourmet cook. Ofc: Rhodes Enterprises Inc. 1061 Martin Ave Santa Clara 95050

TAYLOR, ARTHUR DUANE, JR., industrial development executive; b. Arthur Duane, Sr. and Roberta (Hudson) T.; m. Debra, Nov. 22, 1980; edn: BA econs., UC Los Angeles 1977; MBA finance, Golden Gate Univ. 1983. Career: area mgr. Shasta County Econ. Devel. Corp. Redding 1977-78; corp. lending ofcr. Bank of Am. Redding & Sacto. 1978-80; bus. devel. splst. Calif. Dept. of Commerce Sacto. 1980-85, regl. mgr. San Jose 1985—; mem. San Jose Econ. Devel. Bd.; honors: T. Patrick Heck Best Bus. Case Award; mem: Nat. Assn. Indsl. Ofc. Parks, Rotary Internat.; Democrat; Catholic. Ofc: Dept. of Commerce 100 Paseo de San Antonio Rm 313 San Jose 95113

TAYLOR, BARBARA JOAN, consulting co. executive; b. July 23, 1944, Dover, Pa.; d. William Edward and Carolyn Elizabeth (Fowle) Thornberry; children: Daniel, Jr. b. 1964, Russell b. 1981; edn: Univ. of Md. 1968-81; BA, Columbia Pacific Univ. 1981, MBA 1982; certs., Orange Coast Coll. 1983-84. Career: assoc. dir. Administrv. Computer Center, Univ. of Maryland, College Park, Md. 1964-81; cons./regl. mgr. Systems & Computer Technology Corp., Brea 1981-85; ptnr. Laguna Finl. Services, Laguna Beach 1985; pres. Lenders Finl. Group, Tustin 1985—; independent cons. Systems & Computer Tech. Corp. (1985-86), cons. Security Pacific Nat. Bank, Anaheim (1986); pgm. dir. Orange Coast Coll. Small Bus. Info. Ctr. 1985-86; bd. mem. Texas Instruments So. Calif. Regl. Info. Exchange 1986; owner/pres. Computer Solutions 1984-86; frequent public speaking 1973-; mem: Women in Business, Orange County CofC, Nat. Assn. of Female Execs., Women in Info. Processing, Assn. of Women in Computing, Assn. for Instnl. Research; rec: real estate, small bus., computers. Ofc: Lenders Financial Group 215 West 1st St Ste 10546 Tustin 92680

TAYLOR, JAMES ALLEN, financial services co. executive; b. July 20, 1953, Anadarko, Okla.; s. Samual Arthur and Shirley Gene (McCallister) T.; m. Debby Taylor, Jan. 31, 1986; 1 son, Justin b. 1977; edn: Emerg. Med. Tech., Mt. San Antonio Coll. 1972, 74, 78, 80; basic law, community rels., San Bernardino Valley Coll. 1979-80; Crime Prevention Acad., Crafton Hills Coll. 1982; Certified Financial Planner, Cal. Lutheran Univ. 1986; lic. tchr. Calif. Career: ambulance driver/dispatcher Schaefers 1971-75; search & rescue tng., San Bernardino Sheriff's Dept. 1973-86; compounder Fasson Corp. 1975-79; deputy San Bernardino County Sheriff 1979-86; v.p. Inland Mgmt. Inc., Riverside 1986—; bd. dirs. 1983-; Red Cross & law enforcement instr. 1984-; bd. dirs. Prado Country 1983; honors: Safe Worker's Award (S.B. County Bd. of Supvs. 1981), Outstanding Svc. (BSA 1981), Outstanding Svc. (Citizens of Chino Hills 1984), Best Instr. 5-Yr. Award (Law Enforcement Acad. for Explorers 1981-85); mem: Internat. Assn. Financial Planners 1986, Internat. Assn. Bus. & Financial Consultants 1983-86, Am. Mgmt. Assn., Am. Red Cross (bd., disaster chmn. 1983-84), Elks, Riverside CofC; founder Crime Busters Youth Safety Pgm. 1984; cons. to community-related youth orgns.; work with mentally handicapped children; Republican; Protestant; rec: woodworking, puppetry, music. Ofc: Inland Mgmt. Inc., 17241 Van Buren Blvd Ste A Riverside 92504

TAYLOR, JAMES SEARCY, real estate development co. president; b. Dec. 19, 1946, Greenwich, Conn.; s. Fred A. and Louise E. (Howard) T.; m. Denise Garayalde, Sept. 25, 1982; children: Michael b. 1966, Jeb b. 1969, Whitney b. 1986; edn: BS, UCLA; Harvard Bus. Sch. 1969-70. Career: assoc. Devel. Research Assocs. 1967-70; v.p. Am. Capital Mgmt. Corp., 1970-76, pres. 1976—; Republican. Res: 4485 Via Esperanza Santa Barbara 93110 Ofc: American Capital Management Corp. 115 S La Cumbre Ln Ste 302 Santa Barbara 93105

TAYLOR, KENT DOUGLAS, molecular biologist; b. June 9, 1952, Indpls.; s. Kenneth Dean and M. Roberta (Read) T.; m. Debra Lauraine Evans, July 29, 1978; 1 dau. Anna Danielle b. 1986; edn: BS in biol., USC 1975, PhD in molecular biol., 1982. Career: research chemist VA Med. Center, Sepulveda 1983-86, research microbiologist, 1986–; recipient Performance Award, Vets. Adminstrn. (1985); contbr. sci. articles in Proc. Nat. Acad. Sci. (1984), J. Bacteriology (1981); Foursquare Gospel (Sun. Sch. tchr.); rec: kite-flying, music. Ofc: VA Medical Center, Developmental Biology Lab. Sepulveda 91343

TAYLOR, LYNN O'MALLEY, judge; b. Nov. 6, 1943, Los Angeles; d. Edmund James and Elizabeth (Hoover) O'Malley; m. Bruce Cowan Taylor, Sept. 1, 1968; children: William b. 1970, Laura b. 1972, Bonnie b. 1977; edn: Colo. Coll. 1961-63; BA in edn. (cum laude) Univ. of Ariz. 1964; JD, San Francisco Law Sch 1972. Career: atty. assoc. James M. Kennedy, 1973-80, assoc. Norbert C. Babin, 1981-82; elected judge Marin County Municipal Ct. (First woman elected to bench in Marin Co.), 1982–; instr. law, Dominican Coll. 1977-81, City Coll. of San Francisco 1978-79; moderator Contg. Edn. of the Bar course, Your Local Municipal Ct., 1984; honors: Pi Lambda Theta (1964); participant judge Hastings Center for Trial Advocacy 1985; mem: Calif. Judges Assn. (Ann. Meeting Seminar Com. 1985), Calif. State Bar Assn. 1972-83 (Resolutions Com. 1978-9, hearing ofcr. State Bar Ct. 1978-83), Marin County Bar Assn. (del. State Bar Conv. 1976, 79, 81; bd. dirs. 1976-8; treas. 1981, secty. 1982); bd. mem: Marin Property Owners (pres. 1980), Marin Council BSA, Twilliger Nature Edn. Center; selection com. Marin Edn. Found. Outstanding Student & Tchr. Award 1983-85; mem: Marin Forum, Wednesday Morning Dialogue, AAUW, Nat. Womens Political Caucus (hon. mem.), Marinwood Assn. (past pres.); past mem. Marin Co. Overall Econ. Devel. Com.; Democrat; Episcopal; rec: photog., gardening. Ofc: Municipal Ct. Marin Co. Civic Center San Rafael 94903

TAYLOR, PATRICIA ANN, real estate broker; b. Sept. 13, 1941, Selma; d. Frank and Dorothy Ann (Allen) Licon; m. 2d Nicholas Muick, Nov. 14, 1980; children: Michele b. 1961, Rick b. 1965, Nicholas b. 1972; edn: AA, Cuesta Coll. 1968; BS, Calif. State Polytech. Univ., SLO 1970, grad. pgm. Masters 1986-; Calif. Life Std. Tchg. Cred. (1971), lic. Real Estate Broker (1976). Career: substitute tchr. public schs., 1971–; mgr. real estate office, 1975-, broker/pres. County Properties, Inc. San Luis Obispo 1984–; honors: Univ. Pres.'s Award (1979); mem. Calif. Assn. Realtors, Nat. Assn. Realtors, San Luis Obispo Bd. of Realtors (chair MLS 1980, chair pub. rels. 1986), SLO CofC, AAUW; Republican; Baptist; rec: golf. Address: San Luis Obispo 93401

TAYLOR, PAUL HOWARD, JR., regional advertising executive; b. Nov. 8, 1944, Long Island, NY; s. Paul Howard and Mildred Eugene (Mundy) T.; m. Judy, Aug. 10, 1974; children: Stephen b. 1977, Jeffrey b. 1980, Kristin b. 1982; edn: BBA, Univ. Mass. 1971; Pepperdine Univ. 1977. Career: acct. exec. Seventeen Magazine L.A. 1974-80; senior acct. exec. East/West Network, Inflight Magazines 1980-82; western regl. mgr. Dun's Business Month Mag. Irvine 1982–; instr. communs. course US Naval Acad. 1986; honors: Calif. Svc. Award (PTA 1986), Cert. of Appreciation (Boy Scouts); selected adv. council Orange Unified Sch. Dist. Bd.; mem: L.A. Advt. Club, Mag. Reps. of So. Calif. (function chmn. 1974-86), S.F. Advt. Club, Western Advt. Assn., Naval Reserve & Reserve Ofcrs. Assn., Linda Vista Elem. Sch. Fathers Club (pres.), PTA, YMCA Indian Guides; mil: lcdr. USNR Pub. Affairs Ofc., Vietnam Svc., Vietnam Campaign, Nat. Defense; Republican; Presbyterian; rec: golf, sailing. Res: 4727 White Dove Orange 92669 Ofc: Dun's Business Month Mag. 2061 Business Ctr Dr Ste 111 Irvine 92715

TAYLOR, ROBERT LEROY, accountant; b. May 30, 1952, Casa Grande, Ariz.; s. Vincent Leroy and Christine E. (Alexander) T.; m. April, July 9, 1971; 1 son, Robert Jr. b. 1983; edn: AA, Mesa Coll. 1981; BA, National Univ. 1983; CPA Calif. 1984. Career: acctg. clerk Acctg. Corp. of Am., San Diego 1976-78; jr. acct. Smathers & Nutter CPAs Pacific Beach 1979-83; senior acct. West, Johnston, Turnquist & Schmitt San Diego 1983-84, Jahelka & Strong CPAs 1984-85, Glenn Youmans & Co. Bonita 1985–; mem: Am. Inst. CPAs, Calif. Soc. CPAs, Nat. Univ. Alumni Assn; Jehovah's Witness; rec: golf. Ofc: Youmans, Braithwaite & Rechif, CPAs 4045 Bonita Rd, Ste 301, Bonita 92002

TAYLOR, SAMUEL BERYL, JR., judge, b. Sept. 30, 1931, Richmond, Va.; s. Samuel B. and Nancy Loomis (Brinton) T.; m. Elizabeth Ann, Sept. 6, 1953; children: Katherine (Cook) b. 1956, Samuel b. 1958, Richard b. 1960, Rebecca b. 1962; edn: BA, Univ. Richmond 1953; LLB, Univ. of Va. Law Sch. 1958; admitted Calif. State Bar 1959, US Dist. Cts. and US Supreme Ct. (1960). Career: atty. law firm Taylor and Cox, Santa Ana 1962-72, spec. in trial litigation; apptd. judge (presiding judge 1978) Central Municipal Ct. by Gov. Reagan 1973; apptd. judge Superior Ct. of Calif., County of Orange by Gov. Deukmejian, 1985–; faculty Calif. Trial Judges Coll. (1982); guest instr. Orange Co. Sheriffs Acad.; honors: editl. bd. Virginia Law Review, Raven Soc., Omicron Delta Kappa; recipient Outstanding Community Service Award; mem: Calif. Judges Assn., Calif. Bar Assn., Orange Co. Bar Assn.; pres. Tustin All Am. Football Assoc. (1971); Fraternal Order of Eagles; mil: capt. USMC 1951-55; rec: golf, travel. Ofc: The Courthouse 700 Civic Center Dr West Santa Ana 92701

TEA, YOK MONK, company executive; b. Jan. 7, 1943, Chhlong, Cambodia, nat. 1983; s. Chung-Ho Puth and Lay Huoy (Hoeur) T.; m. Aline Ith, Sept. 6, 1970; children: Charles, b. 1972; Jennifer, b. 1982; edn: MA, Mich. State Univ. 1976; Licencie Es-Sciences Economiques, Faculte de Droit Et Des Sciences Economiques De Phnom-Penh 1973; Licencie Libre Es-Sciences Naturelles, 1971; Diplome De L'Academie Commerciale A' L'Ecole Des Hautes Etubes Commerciales De Paris, France 1963. Career: high sch. tchr. natural scis. Lycee Sisowath, Phnom Penh, Cambodia 1968-70; self- empl. 1965-73; coord. mgr. Service Master Ind., H.Q., Chicago, Ill. 1976-85; currently, dir. housekeeping Sacred Heart Hosp., Hanford; honors: Fulbright grantee 1974; Service Masters award nom. for Quality Standards (1982), Mgmt. Control (1983); mem: U.S. Congressional Adv. Bd.; Am. Security Council Found.; Smithsonian Nat. Assocs.; Republican; Buddhist; rec: reading, bowling. Res: 1293 E. Florinda, Hanford 93230

TEDDER-LARSON, MARGIE JUANITA, psychotherapist; b. Oct. 12, 1926, Hallsboro, No. Carolina; d. Oscar and Mattie Edla (Reynolds) Tedder; m. Christian DuBois Larson, Jan. 1, 1953; children: Eric Tedder b. 1953, Mark Christian b. 1956, Craig Courtney b. 1967; edn: Appalachian State Tchrs. Coll. 1948-49; AA, psychology, Orange Coast Coll. 1973; AA, bus., Fullerton Jr. Coll. 1974; BA psych., CSU Fullerton 1977; MA psych., Chapman Coll. 1981; Calif. Graduate Inst. PhD Program 1982. Career: F.B.I., recorder examiner, 1943-47; claims mgr. Carolina Motor Club, Charlotte, N.C. 1947-48; secty. to pres. Rulane Gas Co., 1949-51; legal secty. Cecil, Keith & Mehaffey, Beaumont, Tx. 1951-53; bus. mgr. Tru-Color Photography, 1954-62; secty. Planning Commn., City of Brea, Calif. 1962-64; current: psychotherapist, counselor vol. Orange County Mental Health Clinics; awards: Golden Poet (1985), World of Poetry; hon. mention Summer Poetry Contest; mem. Am. Psy. Assn., Am. Personnel and Guidance Assn.; Episcopal; rec: gardening, writing. Res: 16862 Roxdale Dr Yorba Linda 92686 Ofc: Family Conciliation Services, 930 W 17th St, Ste D, Santa Ana 92706

TEE, WILLIAM GLENN, SR., insurance agent; b. Nov. 21, 1922, St. Joseph, Mo.; s. Henry Harl Sr. and Mabel Elsa Elizabeth (Wagner) T.; m. Norma Jane Freebersyser, May 3, 1945; children: Jennifer; William Jr.; Matthew; edn: BBA, Woodbury Univ. 1947; UCLA Ext. 1947-52; CLU. Career: self- empl. insurance agent; bd. dirs. Plymouth Village Redlands 1975-79; mem: Calif. Assn. Life Underwriters (San Bernardino Co. chpt., pres. 1980-81); Redlands Ind. Ins. Agents Assn. (past pres.); Exchange Club of Fontana (past pres.); mil: cpl., USAF 1943-45, GCM, So. East Asia Campaign; Lutheran; rec: tennis, walking, jogging. Res: 244 Alvarado St., Redlands 92373 Ofc: George Klotz Agency, 9625 Monte Vista Ave., Ste. 108, Montclair 91763

TELLER, EDWARD, physicist; b. Jan. 15, 1908, Budapest, Hungary, nat. 1941; s. Max and Ilona (Deutsch) T.; m. Augusta Harkanyi, 1934; children: Paul b. 1943, Susan Wendy b. 1946; edn: Karlsruhe Technical Inst., Germany 1926-8; Univ. of Munich 1928; PhD, Univ. of Leipzig 1930. Career: research assoc. U. Leipzig, 1929-31; U. Gottingen (Germany) 1931-3; Rockefeller fellow Inst. Theoretical Physics, Copenhagen 1934; lectr. U. London 1934-5; prof. Physics George Washington U. 1934-41; Columbia U. 1941-2; physicist U. Chgo. 1942-3; Manhattan Engring. Dist., Chgo. 1942-6; Los Alamos (N.M.) Sci. Lab. 1943-6; asst. dir. 1949-52; prof. physics UC Berkely 1953-60; prof. physics-at-large 1960-70; dir. Lawrence Livermore Lab. 1958-60; assoc. dir. 1960-75; chmn. dept. applied sci. UC Davis- Livermore 1963-6; cons. Lawrence Livermore Nat. Lab. 1975–; sr. research fellow Hoover Instn. on War, Revolution and Peace, Stanford U. 1975–; vis. prof. Arthur Spitzer chair energy mgmt. Pepperdine U., Calif. 1976-7; adv. bd. Americans for More Power Sources 1979; sci. adv. bd. USAF 1951; bd. govs. American Friends of Tel Aviv 1973; mem. Coalition for Asian Peace and Security, Com. of Protectors and Andrei Sakharov 1980–, Com. on the Present Danger; bd. dirs. ThermoElectron Def. Intelligence Sch.; awards: Harrison Medal, Am. Ordnance Assn. 1955; Albert Einstein award 1958; Gen. Donovan Meml. Awd. 1959; Enrico Fermi Awd. 1962; Robbins Awd. of Am. 1963; Leslie R. Groves Gold Medal Awd. 1974; Semmelweiss Medal Awd. 1977; Albert Einstein Awd., Technion Inst. of Israel 1977; Henry T. Heald Awd., Ill. Inst. Tech. 1978; Gold Medal AWd., Am. Coll. Nuclear Medicine 1980; named Disting. Scientist, Nat. Sci. Devel. Bd. 1981; Fellow Am. Phys. Soc.; Nat. Medal of Sci. 1983; mem: fellow, Am. Phys. Soc.; Am. Nuclear Soc.; Am. Acad. Arts. and Scis.; Am. Acad. of Achievement; AAAS; Am. Geophys. Union; Am. Def. Preparedness Assn.; Soc. of Engring. Scientists (A.C. Eringen award 1980); Internat. Acad. Quantum Molecular Sci.; Nat. Acad. Scis.; Scientists and Engrs. for Secure Energy; Internat. Platform Assn; Am. Ordnance Assn; author: (w/ Francis Owen Rice), The Structure of Matter 1949; (w/ Albert L. Latter) Our Nuclear Future 1958; (w/ Allen Brown) The Legacy of Hiroshima 1962; The Reluctant Revolutionary 1964; (w/ others) The Constructive Uses of Nuclear Explosives 1968; Great Men of Physics 1969; The Miracle of Freedom 1972; Energy: A Plan for Action 1975; Nuclear Energy in the Developing World 1977; Energy from Heaven and Earth 1979; Pursuit of Simplicity 1980; editor: Fusion, Vol. I, Magnetic Confinement 1981; pioneer in thermonuclear reaction studies; contbr. to Spectroscopy of polyatomic molecules. Address: POB 808 Lawrence Livermore Laboratory, Livermore 94550, also Hoover Instn., Stanford 94305

TELLINGTON, WENTWORTH JORDAN, international trader, broker; b. Oct. 11, 1916, Gorham, New Hampshire; s. Jesse James and Myrtle Meneleh (Jordan) T.; m. Elizabeth Harman-Ashley, April 29, 1939, div.; children: Wentworth Jr. b. 1943, Joan Elizabeth b. 1945; edn: AB, Columbia Univ. 1940; grad. work, Columbi Univ. 1946-47, Univ. of Mich. 1944, USC, 1 yr.; Reg. Profl. Engr., Alberta, Can. 1951. Career: instr. US Military Acad. 1941-45; chief geophysicist Pacific Petroleums Ltd. 1947-51; exec. v.p. Overland Industries Ltd. 1952-54; tchr. San Juan Puerto Rico bi-lingual sch. 1955-56; head math. dept. Chadwick Sch., Rolling Hills 1957-61; owner, opr. Pacific Coast Equestrian Research Farm, Badger 1961-70; owner, opr. Whitehurst Products Co., San Rafael 1971-73; adj. prof. Prescott Coll., Prescott, Ariz. 1973-74; internat. trading & brokerage, real estate & oil 1975-86; currently, owner, opr. Tellington Assocs., Aurburn; honors: Award for Creative Citizenship in Calif., Pacific Coast Equeztrian Research Farm, Gov. Ronald Reagan 1968; works: coiventor, with Col. Chas. G. Dunn, a device for position tracking, transmitting and recording, patented; co-author, with Arno K. Lobeck, Military Maps and Air Photographs, McGraw Hill 1944; co-author, with Linda Tellington-Jones, Endurance and Competitive Trail Riding, Doubleday 1979; mil: maj. US Cavalry 1939-52; Republican; rec: aerobatic flying, equestrian, tennis. Ofc: P.O. Box 7153 Auburn 95604

TELLO, DONNA, business owner; b. Mar. 23, 1955, Maryland; children: Jesse Elliott Timothy, Kimbrelle Shey Thommasson. Career: owner Tax Savers, All Around Bookkeeping, Cheep Books 1981—; speaker taxation, small businesses; candidate state assembly 1984; honors: speaking awards; mem: Toastmasters 1982-, Mensa 1978- (chpt. treas.), Nat. Taxpayers Union 1985-, Inland Soc. Tax Cons. 1985-; publ: column Tax Ability in San Diego Mensan 2 yrs.; Libertarian; avoc: examining solutions to nation's econ./ political crises. Res: 3835 Merivale Ave San Diego 92116

TEMPLE, WILLIAM HARRY, engineer; b. March 13, 1912, Fargo, N. Dak.; s. Wm. Harry and Julia Amanda (Betts) T.; m. Minnetta Shouts, July 16, 1937; children: Karan (True) b. 1938, Joan (Strider) b. 1941, Richard b. 1943; edn: BS, North Dak. State Univ. 1935; Registered Profl. Engr. (QA), Calif. Career: senior devel. engr. Bureau of Ships, Wash DC 1948-57; senior elec. engr. Naval Ships Command, Wash DC 1957-62; supr. Elec. System Design & Application Research, Naval Ships Engrg. Center, Hyattsville, Md. 1962-70; senior engr. Elec. Design, Westinghouse, Annapolis, Md. 1970-74, senior engr. Quality Assurance, 1974-77; quality assur. engr. self-empl. 1977—; cons. Q.A., Battelle Meml. Inst., Columbus, O. at field op., 1977—; recipient Superior Performance Awards (1958, 62, 69), Naval Ships Command, Wash DC; num. letters of appreciation from public sch. staff and scouting orgns., Silver Springs, Md. (1952-63); mem. Marine Tech. Soc. 1967-, Cousteau Soc. 1974-, Wheaton (Md.) Masonic Lodge 1956-; num. publs. in naval tech. manuals and journals (1960-70); rec: square and round dancing. Address: 3600 Ketch Ave Oxnard 93033

TEMPLETON, JOSEPH OSBORNE, lawyer; b. May 3, 1950, San Bernardino; s. Joseph and Bessie Mae (Covington) T.; m. Stephanie Wolf, Aug. 11, 1973; edn: BA, UC Los Angeles 1973; JD, Univ. of West Los Angeles 1978; admitted Calif. State Bar. Career: placement director Univ. of West Los Angeles School of Law, Culver City 1979-84; pvt. law practice, Los Angeles 1982—; mem: ABA (Forum Com. on Sports and Entertainment 1981-), Los Angeles County Bar Assn. (Indigent Def. Com. 1984-85), Juvenile Cts. Bar Assn., Santa Monica Bar Assn. (Law Day participant 1983, 84, 85), Calif. Public Defenders Assn., Calif. Attys. for Criminal Justice, Federal Bar Assn.; Masons; Baptist; rec: wt.lifting, cycling. Res: Westwood Law Ofc: Joseph O. Templeton, 12304 Santa Monica Blvd Ste 300 Los Angeles 90025

TEMPLETON, L. WILLIAM, sales executive; b. Aug. 18, 1933, Greeley, Colo.; s. Robt. C. and Lillian (Wonenberg) T.; m. Betty J., Sept. 6, 1959; children: Todd b. 1965, Tia b. 1967; edn: BA, Park Coll. 1977; grad. stu. Baker Univ./SMU. Career: treas. and controller McCarty-Sherman Distbg. Corp., Denver 1956-64; var. sales and mgmt. pos. Ford Motor Co. Tractor Div., regl. mktg. mgr. Kansas City, Mo. 1964-81; v.p. Kubota Tractor Corp. U.S., Los Angeles 1981—; mem. bd. dirs./exec. com. Farm and Indsl. Equip. Inst.; awards: Henry Ford Silver Scroll award (1965, 70, 75), hon. American Farmer degree, Future Farmers of Am. (1985); mem. Nat. Agri-Mktg. Assn. (1972-), Am. Mgmt. Assn. (1980-); civic: White Memorial Medical Ctr./LA (bd. dirs), Adventist Health Systems/U.S. (bd. dirs.), FFA (foundation bd.), Kiwanis Internat. (pres. So. Jackson County, Mo. chpt. 1969); mil: sgt. US Army Korean Conflict; Republican; Prot.; rec: golf, tennis, travel. Res: 16031 Jenner St Westminster 92683 Ofc: Kubota Tractor Corp. U.S. 550 West Artesia Blvd Compton 90220

TENENGOLTS, GRIGORY, computer scientist; b. June 9, 1938, Baku, USSR, nat. US cit. 1983; s. Moses and Khava (Skvirskaya) T.; 1 dau., Marina b. 1964; edn: MSEE, Petrochemical Inst., Baku, USSR 1960; MS math., Moscow Univ. 1966; PhD in elec. engring., Acad. of Sci. Inst. for Control Problems, Moscow 1966. Career: electronics engr. The Inst. for Radio Electronics, Tula, USSR 1960-61; senior research assoc. Acad. of Scis., Inst. for Control Problems, Moscow 1961-76; assoc. research engr. Electronics Res. Lab., UC Berkeley 1978-79; telecommunications analyst Wells Fargo Bank, S.F. 1979-80; senior staff Mohawk Data Sci. Corp. 1980-81, System Industries, Milpitas 1982-84; pres. Cythera Corp., San Jose 1985—; cons. var. computer cos. including Xebec, Data Tech. Corp., Seagate Tech.; recipient awards for research work in telecommunication, USSR Radio & Commun. Engring. Soc., (1970, 75); mem. Am. Math. Soc. 1972-76, IEEE 1985-; works: num. research publs. and patents in field of error correcting codes; Jewish; rec: jogging, travel. Res: 6452 Standridge Ct San Jose 95123

TENES, RUDOLPH ARAIZA, jewelery co. executive; b. Apr. 1, 1930, Tijuana, Mexico, nat. US cit. 1958; s. Jesus and Maria (Araiza) T.; m. Lilia, Nov. 5, 1955; children: Christopher b. 1956, Diana b. 1957, Celeste b. 1960, Alan b. 1961, Darlene b. 1963; edn: 4th gr. grammar sch.; stu. mech. engring. Healds Coll., 1 yr., 1957. Career: Spanish media bdcstr., radio personality (2 hr. daily show) and DJ, KOFY-Radio, San Francisco; promoter/mgr. Spanish mktg. Crescent Jewelers 1959; sales, dist. mgr., sales coord. and mktg. splst. Paul's Jewelers 1964; dist. mgr., mdse. buyer, Spanish Media promoter, personel mgr. Jewelry Ents. 1966; mktg. & promotion splst. Zales Jewelers 1968; founder/ owner Esmeralda Jewelers Ents., 1968—; guest lectr. USC (1980, 81, 82); honors: recogn. for humanitarian svcs. Govt. of Guatemala (1978), US Congress by Norman Mineta, City of San Jose by Mayor Janet G. Hayes, Mexican Consulate, Latin Am. Lions (1976); civic: Orgn. Cultural Mexicano of S.F.

(founder), Comision Honorifica Mexicana of San Jose, Amigos Lions (charter), Latin Am. Lions (San Jose), Guatemala Relief Fund (dist. chmn. Calif., Nev.), Artistic and Literary Circle of Calif./S.J. (founder, pres. 1983), Mex.-Am. CofC/Gilroy (plnng. chmn., founder), Santa Clara County Fair (participant); author novel Mano A Mano (pub. in USA, Mexico); Democrat; Catholic; avocation: writing, speaking. Res: 956 Fleming Ave San Jose 95127 Ofc: 7573 Monterey St Gilroy 95020

TERRELL, A. JOHN, telecommunications director; b. Dec. 27, 1927; s. Harry E. and Elizabeth (Eaton) T.; m. Elizabeth Schalk, 1949; children: Patricia b. 1951, Marilee b. 1953, J. Scott b. 1957; edn: Chaffey Coll. 1947-48; BBA, Univ. of New Mexico 1952. Career: plant opns., communications cons. Mt. Bell Telephone Co. 1951-56; sys. analyst, dept. mgr. ACF Inds. Inc., Albuquerque div., 1956-62; mgr. communs. & svcs., opns. plnng. prin., bus. res. Hunt-Wesson Foods div. Norton Simon Ind. Inc. 1962-68; v.p. gen. mgr. Wells Fargo Security Guard Svc. div. Banker Inds. Inc. 1968-71; budget adminstr., admin. mgr. Baxter-Trauenol Labs. Inc. Hyland div. 1971-77; exec. v.p. American Telephone Mgmt. Inst. Inc.- Bus. & Telecomm. Cons. 1977-78; UCLA Telecomm. dir. 1978—; Colonial Aide-De-Camp to the Gov. on N.Mex. 1967; mem: Nat. Assn. of Accts., Greater Irvine Lions Club (pres. 1975-76), Newport Harbor Am. Legion, VFW of the US, Am. Legion Yacht Club; publs: contbr. num. profl. journs. 1966-; Republican (cand. for NM State rep. 1960; cand. NM State Bd. Edn. 1962); Episcopal; rec: flying, skiing, swimming. Res: 1725 Port Charles Pl. Newport Beach 92660

TETREAU, MICHAEL C., distribution co. owner; b. Jan. 3, 1952, Bangor, Me.; s. Fernand S. and Marion R. (Shattuck) T.; edn: BS in C.E., Princeton Univ., 1974. Career: mgr. Management Consulting Div., Arthur Andersen & Co., N.Y. 1974-79; mgr. Corp. Technology, The Continental Group, Stamford, Conn. 1980-81; gen. mgr. European Ops./bd. dirs. Mitchell Mgmt. Systems, Westboro, Mass. and Geneva, Switz., 1982-84; v.p. Venusa, Ltd. and American Venospital Ltd., N.Y. 1984; assoc. Merrifield Consulting Group Inc., Greenwich, Conn. 1984—; exec. v.p./bd. dir. Clark Security Products, San Diego 1984—; dir: Venusa Ltd., Am. Venospital Ltd. (mem. exec. com. 1985); honors: capt. Lightweight Football Team Princeton Univ. (1974), Outstanding Young Men of Am. (1982); civic: Spl. Olympics (vol. 1980-81), Roger Ludlowe High Sch. (asst. football coach 1979), Princeton Club of San Diego (1986-), Representative Town Meeting, Fairfield, Conn. (mem. 1981); Democrat; Roman Catholic; rec: ski, tennis, scuba. Address: San Diego 92111

TEUTSCH, CHAMPION KURT, gene-physicist, psycho-geneticist, author; b. Feb. 10, 1921, Leipzig, E. Germany; s. Friedrich Wilhelm and Elisabeth Babette T.; m. Joel Marie, Apr. 24, 1954; child: Lee Brooks; edn: Univ. of Prague, Czech. 1937-38; BCE, high honors, Univ. of Fla. 1942; Harvard Univ. Law Sch. 1947-48, USC 1948-49, 57; MA, PhD, Calif. Coast Univ. 1975-76. Career: tech. editor, writer, senior engr. var. engring. and aerospace cos. (incl. TRW, Intern. Engin., Ralph M. Parsons) 1946-60; cons. gene-physicist, psycho-geneticist (for individuals, physicians, sales orgns., law firms, medical clinics, others), 1960—; cons. Internat. Health Resorts, LA (1977-81), var. real estate, inv., legal and medical orgns.; condr. seminars; pres. Acad. of the Teutsch Ideal Method, Los Angeles; honors: commendn., County of Los Angeles (1985); mem. Am. Assn. for Humanistic Psychology (life), Optimist Internat. (life, pres. Century City Club 1980-81); clubs: The Vikings, Gold Pennant (Gourmet); co-author with wife num. books in field incl. "Understand and Raise Your Consciousness - From Here to Happiness!" and scientific articles on victimology, human physics and stress; mil: 1st lt. US Army Air Corps 1944-46, USAF 1951-52; Republican; Joel's World Ch. of Love; rec: tennis, skiing. Res: 10110 Empyrean Way Apt 103 Los Angeles 90067 Ofc: ATIM 2049 Century Park East Ste 2730 Los Angeles 90067

TEWS, K. RICHARD, beverage distribution co. president; b. Nov. 28, 1935, Hastings, Neb.; s. Karl Frank and Bella (Kalberg) T.; 1 dau. Lynn b. 1964; edn: BS, Univ. Neb. 1957. Career: mgr. Anheuser- Busch Inc. Montana 1962-64, San Diego 1965-66, asst. to v.p. L.A. 1967, branch mgr. 1968-72; pres. Foothill Distributing Co. Inc. 1972—; airshow pilot 1978—; dir. Profl. Technols. 1981—; commr. Airports Commn. City of Redding 1980-83; honors: Citizen of the Year (Redding Trade Club 1985); mem: Calif. Beer Wholesalers Assn. 1979-, Lions Club, CofC, Elks, Moose, E. Clampus Vitus, Confederate Air Force, Air Force Assn.; mil: capt. Air Nat. Guard, fighter pilot 1957-63; Republican; Lutheran; rec: aviation. Res: 4932 Kings Way Redding 96003 Ofc: Foothill Distributing Ci. Inc. 1530 Beltline Rd Redding 96003

THADHANI, ARVIND JAIRAM, electrical engineer, computer scientist; b. Oct. 7, 1943, Lahore, India, nat. US cit. 1975; s. Jairam Tharumal and Indru (Advani) T.; m. Gita Tahilramani, Jan. 15, 1975; children: Seher b. 1980, Armaan b. 1984; edn: B.Tech., Indian Inst. of Tech., Bombay 1966; MS, Cornell Univ. 1968; MS, Univ. of Wisc. 1973. Career: staff engr. IBM, Poughkeepsie Lab., NY 1968-76; research staff IBM Research, San Jose 1977-78; advy. engr. IBM Gen. Products Div. h.q. 1978-83; senior pgmmr. mgr. IBM, Santa Teresa Lab 1983-84; pgm. mgr. End User Computing, IBM, IS & SG h.q., White Plains, NY 1984—; honors: IBM Corp. Award, 1982; publs: Interactive User Productivity, IBM Sys. Journ. 1981; Factors Affecting Programmer Productivity, IBM Sys. Journ. 1984. Res: 17765 Vista Ave. Monte Sereno 95030 Ofc: IBM, 1000 Westchester Ave. White Plains, NY 10604

THAPA, MUKUND NARAIN, business software co. president; b. Apr. 13, 1954, Bombay, India; s. Narain Singh and Devi T.; edn: B.Tech., metallurg. eng., IIT Bombay 1976; MS in ops. research, Stanford Univ. 1979, PhD ops. research 1981. Career: research asst. Dept. Ops. Res. Stanford Univ. 1977-80;

senior decision analyst Applied Decision Analysis Inc., Menlo Park 1980-83; asst. prof. Dept. Op. Res. Stanford Univ. summers 1983-86; mgmt. and software cons., public and pvt. sector, splst. math. modeling, 1983-; ptnr. Mgmt. Consulting and Software, Palo Alto 1984; bd. chmn./pres. Stanford Business Software Inc., 1984–; mem. Mathematical Programming, TIMS; contbr. 5 research papers, presentations profl. confs. (1979-81); rec: travel, enology, music, bridge. Res: 3085 Middlefield Rd #18 Palo Alto 94306 Ofc: 2672 Bayshore Pkwy Ste 304 Mountain View 94043

THEROUX, DAVID JOHN, economist, educator, research executive; b. May 25, 1949, Lansing, Mich.; s. Paul Richard and Marjorie Erma (Withrow) T.; m. Elaine Laconia Shipp, Mar. 20, 1976; 2 sons: Paul Jacques, Drake Emori; edn: AB, UC Berkeley 1973, BSME 1973, MSME, 1974; MBA, Univ. of Chicago 1977; Career: research asst. Richmond Field Sta., UC Berkeley 1974; proj. engr. Exxon Co. U.S.A. 1975-76; research asst. Univ. of Chicago 1976, dir. vis. lecture pgm. in econ. sci. 1977; v.p., dir. acad. affairs, dir. pub. policy studies Cato Inst., San Francisco 1977-79; pres., dir. Pacific Inst. Pub. Policy Research, San Francisco 1979–; adv. bd. No. Calif. Econ. Seminars 1981-, Jour. Austrian Economics; trustee William Koch Found. 1978-79; mem: Am., Western and So. Econ. Assns.; Royal Econ. Soc.; Nat Assn. Bus. Economists; Public Choice Soc.; Pi Tau Sigma; Omicron Delta Epsilon; awards: George Washington Honor Medal for excellence, 1983; works: senior ed. Policy Report 1978-79; ed. Cato Papers 1978-79; The Energy Crisis: Government Policy and the Economy, 1978; author: (with P. Truluck) Private Rights and Public Lands (1983); Politics and Tyranny: Lessons in Pursuit of Freedom (1985); mil: USAF 1967-72. Res: 6311 Girvin Dr., Oakland 94611 Ofc: 177 Post St., San Francisco 94108

THIEL, JOHN ANGIER, manufacturing co. executive; b. Oct. 9, 1940, Boston, Mass.; s. Albert John and Frances M. (Angier) T.; m. Dagmar Jacob, Jan. 19, 1973; children: Lorie Ann b. 1967, Susan b. 1973, Jeff b. 1976; edn: AS, Leicester Jr. Coll.; BS, Windham Coll. 1967; MBA, J.F. Kennedy Univ. 1985; certs: Neuro-Linguistic Pgm. Practioner; FAA lic. pilot. Career: prodn. control coordinator (internat. prodn. computers) RCA, Inc. 1966-68; regional sales rep. Rieke Corp., Chgo. 1968-75; founder/pres. Windum Process Equip. Sales Co. (process equip. mfr.'s reps.), Chgo. 1975-77; nat. sales mgr. Carew, Inc., Chgo. 1977-79; v.p. mktg./sales Vector Corp. (equip. mfr. for pharmaceutical, chemical, food, and ordinance industries), Marion, Iowa 1979-83, v.p. western ops. 1983–; mem. AHPA; Masons, Shriners; mil: USCG Res.; Republican. Res: 17 Keith Dr Orinda 94563 Ofc: Vector Corp. 1918 Park St Alameda 94501

THOM, DANIEL JOHN, business administrator/analyst; b. Oct. 17, 1953, San Diego; s. Major Joseph and Winona Estelle (Johnson) T.; m. Susan Mae Brown, Jan. 3, 1981; edn: AA, Goldenwest Comm. Coll. 1976; BS, CSU Long Beach 1978; JD, Western State Univ. Coll. of Law, 1982; Calif. Comm. Colls. lmtd. svc. cred., Police Sci. and Law; Calif. Basic Ednl. Skills Cred.; Calif. State Commn. on Peace Ofcr. Stds. & Tng. Career: comm. ofcr., police ofcr., sr. reserve ofcr./supr. (ret.) Seal Beach (Calif.) Police Dept., 1973–; law clerk Glenn E. Stern Law Corp., West Covina 1981-82; accts. supr. Cablesystems Cable TV, Huntington Bch. 1980-83; cons. to nat. security dir. American Honda Motor Corp., 1983-84; freelance mgmt. cons. various corps., 1983-85; tchr. Long Beach Unified Sch. Dist. 1984-85; security supv. Meml. Med. Ctr. of Long Beach 1984-85; regl. svc. adminstr. Codex Corp., Long Beach 1985–; honors: Outstanding Young Man of Am. 1982, US Jaycees; mem: Calif. Peace Ofcrs. Assn., Calif. Reserve Peace Ofcrs. Assn.; pres./cofounder Bayside Amateur Radio Frat., Beach Area Gp.; mem. Am. Radio Relay League, Amateur Radio Emerg. Service, Long Beach Repeater Assocs., CSULB Alumni Assn., Masons (Master); Republican; Prot.; rec: electronics, photog., classic autos. Res: 712 Balboa Dr Seal Beach 90740

THOMAS, CAROL MARIE, hotel executive; b. April 8, 1940, Cadillac, Mich.; d. Robert David and Lorane Rosena (Flory) Olson; children: Michael W. Gloistein, b. 1962; Mark David Gloistein, b. 1963; edn: Central Mich. Univ. 1958-59; Coll. of Marin 1960; Diablo Valley Coll. 1973-74. Career: owner Castle N' Cottage Catering, Concord 1973-77; dir. of sales Sheraton Inn, Concord 1977-82; gen. mgr. Oxnard Hilton Inn, Oxnard 1982–; adv. com. Oxnard Coll.- Hotel and Restaurant Sch.; honors: Convention and Visitors Bureau Award for Recruiting, Los Angeles Raiders Pro Football Team Summer Camp to Oxnard Hilton; mem: Ventura Co. Profl. Women's Network; Hotel Sales Mgmt. Assn.; Nat. Hon. Soc.; Delta Zeta; No. Calif. Soc. of Assn. Execs.; Ventura Co. Comm. Coll. Dist. (adv. council); Oxnard Convention and Visitors Bureau (bd. dirs.); publs: Woman of the Month, 1985, LA Lifesytle Mag.; Republican; Presbyterian; rec: travel, profl. football and baseball. Res: 1234 Via Montoya, Camarillo 93010 Ofc: Oxnard Hilton Inn, 600 Esplanade Dr., Oxnard 93030

THOMAS, DAVID BRUCE, engineering executive; b. Apr. 18, 1941, Berkeley; s. David Joseph and Virginia Darlene (de Forest) T.; m. Sally Sumner, June 20, 1970; 1 son, David Lee b. 1974; edn: BSME, Stanford Univ. 1964; cert. nuclear engring. Bettis Reactor Eng. Sch. 1965-66; qualified Nuclear Power Engr., USCS (1969). Career: engr., then br. hd. Turbine Br., Nuclear Propulsion Directorate Naval Ship Systems Command, Wash DC 1964-71; nuclear engr., then sr. US Atomic Energy Commn. ofcl./chief West Milton (NY) Field Office, Schenectady Naval Reactors USAEC, 1971-73; mgr. nuclear methods engring. Gen. Elec. Co., Schenectady, NY 1973-77, mgr. nuclear svc. devel. 1977-82, mgr. nuclear plant svcs. tng. 1982-85, mgr. nuclear svc. programs 1985, mgr. quality and proposal integration, 1986–; honors: Tau Beta Pi (1962), Phi Beta Kappa (1963); mem: Am. Nuclear Soc., Am. Welding Soc.; mil: lt. US Navy 1964-69; Republican; Prot. Res: 16940 Frank Ct Los Gatos 95030 Ofc: General Electric 175 Curtner Ave (MC 460) San Jose 95125

THOMAS, DENIS RAY, real estate development executive; b. March 23, 1946, San Bernardino; s. Leonard C. and Vivian D. (Brecks) T.; m. Vivian D., Oct. 15, 1983; children: Bryan b. 1968, Jason b. 1970; edn; BS, UCLA 1971; Loma Linda Coll. of Law 1981-84; Realtor, Nat. Assn. Realtors. Career: owner Scardinos Italian Restaurant, La Puente 1972-73; owner, Thomas Framing Co., La Verne 1974-77; real estate broker, gen. mgr. Magnum Realty Inc., La Verne 1975-82; art cons. Collectors Corner Inc., Indianapolis, Ind. 1984–; owner Thomas Enterprises, Hesperia 1983–; v.p. Watson Pacific corp., Victorivlle 1985–; honors: Voted Hon. Mayor, Wrightwood, 1977, 1978; pres., Santa Claus Inc., Pomona; mem: Victor Valley Bd. Realtors (pres. elec. 1987), Am. Soc. of Real Estate Appraisers, Hesperia Lions (past pres.), Wrightwood CofC (past pres.), Wrightwood Lions; works: co-designer patented Multi-Presser, mfg. by Thomas Ent. 1977; mil: E-4 USN 1963-67, reserves; Republican; Christian; rec: flying, soaring, ocean sailing. Address: Thomas Enterprises, 16880 Mission St. Hesperia 92345

THOMAS, GRACE FERN, psychiatrist; b. Sept. 23, 1897, Gothenburg, Nebr.; d. George Wm. and Martha C. (Johnson) T.; edn: BS, Univ. Nebr. 1924; MA, Creighton 1926; MD, USC 1935; postgrad., Univ. Colo. 1942-3; Inst. of Living 1943; USC 1946; UCLA 1947-50; Columbia Univ. 1953; MA, in religion, USC 1968; ordained to ministry United Methodist Ch. 1963; dip., Am. Bd. of Psychiatry and Neurology. Career: instr. chemistry, biology Duchesne Coll. 1924-7; lab. techn. var. hosps. 1927-32; intern los Angeles Co. Hosp. 1934-5; res. physician Riverside Co. Hosp. 1935-6; res. psychiatrist Los Angeles Co. Psychopathic Hosp. 1936-7; staff psych. Calif. State Hosp. System 1937-42; Glenside Sanitarium 1943-44; pvt. practice neuropschiatry, Long Beach 1946-51; organized and dir. Mental Health Clinics: Veterans Admin. Hosp., Albuquerque, NM (1951-53); Canton and Norwalk, Ohio (1955-61); and San Bernardino, Ukiah and Sonora, CA (1961-70); practice medicine, spl. psych., Turlock 1970-3, Modesto 1972–; honors: Commnd. Capt. Med. Corps. US Army, WWII 1944-6 (only 26 Am. Women w/ this distn.); Phi Beta Kappa; Sigma Xi; Phi Kappa Phi; Nu Sigma Phi; Phi Delta Gamma; listed: Who's Who in West; Who's Who of Am. Women; World Who's Who of Women; Dictionary of Internat. Biography and Internat. Who's Who of Intellectuals; mem: AMA; CMA; Am. Pschiat. Assn.; Am. Med. Women's Assn.; Central Calif. Psychiat. Soc.; Stanislaus Co. Med. Soc.; Am. Legion; Soroptimists; rec: cats. Res: 2001 La Jolla Ct Modesto 95350 Ofc: 1130 Coffee Rd, Ste 8-B, Modesto 95355

THOMAS, HOMER MANGIS, feed manufacturer-merchandiser; b. Sept. 3, 1921, Madras, Ore.; s. Homer Milton and Della May (Mangis) T.; m. Mary Wright, June 30, 1944; 1 son, William E. b. 1948; edn: BA, Univ. of Oregon 1943. Career: pres. Star Milling Co., Perris 1950-70; pres. Homer M. Thomas Co. Inc. 1976-85; ret.; mem: Calif. Grain & Feed Assn., Los Angeles Grain Exch., Riverside Kiwanis (pres. 1976), Riverside Co. Grand Jury (foreman 1973); mil: 1st lt. USAF; Republican; rec: golf. Res: 2310 Princ Albert Riverside 92507 Ofc: Homer M. Thomas Co. Inc., 7197 Brockton Ste. 4 Riverside 92506

THOMAS, LEO H., financial-estate planner; b. July 5, 1947, Los Angeles, CA; s. Leo and Rose (Morris) T.; m. Bernice Roberts, Aug. 19, 1979; 1 son: Todd Pearl, b. 1967; edn: BA, Occidental Coll. 1969; Reg. Investment Adv., NASD. Career: public rels. adv. Democratic Party, 1968-9; ins. agent Prudential Life Ins. Co., 1969-78; finl. & estate planner/ securities broker Hansch Financial Gp. 1969–; cons. Financial Advisory Clinic, Los Angeles 1982-4; pres. Thomas Financial Ins. Svcs., Inc.; cons. First Profl. Bank of Santa Monica; bd. dirs. Great Am. Inc., Los Angeles; bd. dirs. Employer Benefits Mktg.; awards: Small Coll. All American Football Squad 1968; Agent of Year, Mutual Benefit 1982, 83, 84; Agent of Year of Los Angeles 1983; MDRT; Top of Table (300 leading life ins. salesman in world) 1982, 83, 84; Nat. Assocs. Mutual Benefit top 25 leaders 1982, 83, 84; mem: Internat. Assn. of Financial Planners; Am Soc. of CLU; Nat. Assn. of Life Underwriters; W. Los Angeles Life Underwriters Council; Life Ins. Leaders Round Table, L.A. 1982-4; Bev. Hills. Estate Planning Council (3 yrs.); AALU ; Independent Ins. Agents of Am. Assn.; Financial Digest 1983; Life Underwriters Political Action Com. (5 yrs.); Am. Assn. of Financial Profls.; NASD; orgns: Kiwanis; Simon Wiesenthal contrbg. mem.; Smithonian Inst.; Am. Film Inst.; So. Poverty Law Ctr.; Nat. Tax-Limitation Com.; annual sales presentations, Nat. Assocs. 1982-3; seminars, Hansch Financial Gp. 1981-4; Democrat (past pres. Young Democrats); Jewish. Res: 6445 Commodore Sloat Dr Los Angeles 90048 Ofc: Hansch Financial Group, 5900 Wilshire Blvd, Ste 17, Los Angeles 90036

THOMAS, ROBERT CHARLES, physician; b. Nov. 6, 1916, Vallejo; s. Charles W. and Juanita N. (Young) T.; m. Barbara Whiteley, June 17, 1939; children: Sylvia b. 1950, Dean b. 1951, Amy b. 1953; edn: Univ. Calif. 1935-39; MD, McGill Univ. 1943. Career: physician pvt. practice, 1947–; active staff St. Francis Memorial Hosp., San Francisco; mem: Calif. Med. Assn., S.F. Med. Soc.; author: Drake at Olomp-ali (1979), and Nova Albion (1985); writer/self-publisher of books about hist. of California, Calif. Indians, and Sir Francis Drake; mil: capt. US Army 1945-47. Res: 18 Monte Vista Vallejo 94590 Ofc: Robert C. Thomas MD 1790 26th Ave San Francisco 94122

THOMAS, ROOSEVELT CHARLES, marketing and sales executive; b. Mar. 26, 1950, Beaumont, Tx.; s. Roosevelt Charles, Sr. and Earnestine Player (Valaire) T.; 1 dau. Miracle Ra'Chel b. 1979; edn: BBA mktg. mgmt., Lamar Univ. 1972. Career: field rep. G.E. Corp., corrugated box sales rep. (ed. Gaylord Newsletter 1974) Crown Zellerbach Corp., circulation sales Wall Street Jour., nat. sales mgr. Hispanic Times mag., regl. sales mgr. CBS Publs.; current: mktg. cons., publishers' rep., pres. R.C. Thomas Associates, Los Angeles; recipient Dale Carnegie Enthusiasm Award (1976); mem. Publishers'

Reps. of Am., Omega Psi Phi Frat. frat. (ed. Upsilon Theta Mag. 1971); Democrat; Baptist; rec: camping, hiking, gardening. Ofc: 1408 S St. Andrews Pl Ste 7 Los Angeles 90019

THOMAS, TIMOTHY WARREN, pest control co. executive; b. July 6, 1953, Los Angeles;s. Frank Harry and Dorothea Albertine (Kieffner) T.; edn: AA, El Camino Coll. 1976; oper. lic. br. II & III Calif. Structural Pest Control Bd. 1977. Career: book store clerk El Camino Coll., Gardena 1973; termite control techn. - gen. mgr. Lincoln Termite & Pest Control, Santa Monica 1974-6; mgr. termite div. Hydrex Pest Control, W. L.A., and subsidiaries Calif. Exterminator and Lincoln Termite and Pest Control, 1977—; svc. systems adv.; urban entomolgy cons.; tchr. Pest Control Ops. of Calif., L.A. Dist. 1980, 81; tchr. Cert. classes Calif. Dept. Agriculture and Structural Pest Control Bd. 1982; awards: 1st place Trophy, Rosamond Calif. Chili Cook-off 1981; finalist, Nevada State Chili Cook-off 1980; mem: Nat. Pest Control Assn.; Pest Control Ops. of Calif. (chmn., bd. dirs.); Termite Com.; Ednl. Com.; Pest Control Ops. of Calif., L.A. Dist., ednl. chmn.; Delta Phi Sigma Frat.; Internat. Chili Soc.; Harley Davidson Owners' Gp.; Harley Davidson Owners' Assn.; Democrat; Protestant/ Lutheran; rec: painting, cooking, gunsmith, silversmith. Res: 3612 W 117th Street Inglewood 90303 Ofc: Hydrex Pest Control, 12962 Washington Blvd W. Los Angeles 90066

THOMAS, WILLIAM F., newspaper editor; b. June 11, 1924, Bay City, Mich.; s. William F. and Marie T. (Billette) T.; m. Patricia Wendland, Dec. 28, 1948; children: Michael Wm. b. 1955, Peter Matthew b. 1957, Scott Anthony b. 1961; edn: BS, Northwestern Univ. 1950; MS magna cum laude, 1951. Career: copy ed. Buffalo Evening News 1950-52, asst. chief copy ed. 1953-55; ed. Sierra Madre News 1955-56; with Los Angeles Mirror-News as copy reader 1956-57, reporter 1957-59, asst. city ed. 1959-61, city ed. 1961-62; with the L.A. Times as asst. Metropolitan ed. 1962-5, Metropolitan ed. 1965-71, exec. ed. 1971, ed. 1971-2, editor/exec. v.p. 1972—; honors: Harrington award Medill Grad. Sch. of Journ. Northwestern Univ. (1951), Hon. LHD Pepperdine Univ. (1975); mem: Am. Soc. of Newspaper Editors; mil: US Army 1943-6; Ofc: Los Angeles Times, Times Mirror Square, Los Angeles 90053

THOMAS, WILLIAM M., congressman; b. Dec. 6, 1941, Wallace, Idaho; s. Virgil and Gertrude (White) T.; m. Sharon Lynn Hamilton, 1967; children: Christopher, Amelia; edn: AA, Santa Ana Community Coll. 1961; BA, San Francisco State Univ. 1963, MA, 1965. Career: prof. polit. sci. Bakersfield Coll. 1965-74; mem: Calif. Assembly 1974-78, secty. Republican Caucus 1974-76; mem. 96th Congress from 18th Dist. Calif., 98th Congress for 20th Dist. Calif.; chmn. Kern Co. Republican Central Com. 1973; Calif. Repubilcan Central Com. 1972-; bd. dirs. San Joaquin chpt., March of Dimes; mem: Calif. Tchrs. Assn., Calif. State Employees Assn. Ofc: 324 Cannon House Office Bldg., Washington DC 20515

THOMAS-LAZEAR, JUDITH ANN, executive, trust co.- real estate co. owner; b. Sept. 29, 1945, Albany, NY; d. George Ervin Thomas and Justine Ann (Savage-Thomas) Bogart; stepfather, Marcel J.P. Bogart; edn: BS, Ariz. State Univ. 1969, Med. Technologist, 1969. Career: senior med. tech. Fullerton Internal Med. Clinic 1970-84; CEO, owner European Overseas Bank Ltd., Repub. of the Marshall Is. 1984—; v.p., owner Mass. Trust Co., Anaheim 1985—; CEO, owner Hi-Tex Cinema Prods. Ltd., Anaheim 1983—; co-owner S.R. Reed Industries, Anaheim 1984—; pres., trustee Moneta Found., 1985—; owner, pres. Environmental Improvement Corp., 1986—; instr. for bacteriology Fullerton Internal Med. Clinic 1978-84; mem: Am. Soc. of Clin. Pathologists (assoc. 1969-), N.Y. Acad. of Sci., Nat. Hist. Preservation Trust (trustee 1984-), Fountain Valley CofC, Los Angeles Co. Museum of Art, Whittier Art Assn.; publs: Erythroblastosis Fetalis, 1968; num. art awards in pen and ink sketching 1960; Republican; Episcopal; rec: watercolor painting, custom design work, photog. Ofc: Anaheim 92804

THOMFORD, WILLIAM EMIL, mechanical engineer, railway equipment technical consultant; b. March 15, 1927, San Francisco; s. Emil George and Anna Marie (Robohm) T.; m. Irene Shapoff, March 21, 1948; children: Elaine Margaret b. 1951; John William b. 1955; edn: AA, City of Coll. of San Francisco 1949; BA, UC Berkeley 1951; Transportation Mgmt., Stanford Grad. Sch. of Bus. 1967; Reg. Profl. Engr., Calif. 1978. Career: Southern Pacific Transportation Co., San Francisco 1951—; locomotive and car draftsman 1951; asst. chief draftsman 1958; mgr. design engring. 1966; mgr. car engring. 1972; mgr. research & test 1980; ret. 1983; currently, tech. cons. railway equip. and transp.; Car Constrn. Com., Assn. of Am. Railroads 1965-, subcom. chmn., 10 yrs., com. chmn. 1981-83; honors: Henderson Medal, The Franklin Inst., Phila. (1964), Best Design In Steel-Transp. Equip., Am. Iron & Steel Inst. (1971); mem: Am. Soc. of Mech. Engrs., Nat. Soc. of Profl. Engrs., Car Dept. Ofcrs. Assn., Engrs. Club of San Francisco, Pacific Railway Club; works: Hydra-Cushion, First hydraulic impact cushioning device for freight cars; Vert-A-Pac, rail car designed for shipment of 30 compact automobiles; mil: USN, WWII 1944-46; Lutheran; rec: fishing, golf. Address: Transportation Consulting Svcs., 1176 Glenwood Dr. Millbrae 94030

THOMPSON, BILL DEAN, certified public accountant; b. Sept. 12, 1944, Boise City, Okla.; s. James and Nora (Risely) T.; children: Deana b. 1970, Lance b. 1972; edn: BBA, Okla. Panhandle State Univ. 1970. Career: self empl. Thompson Acctg., Boise City, Okla. 1969-70; acct. Gaskill & Pharis, CPA, Dalhart, TX 1970-2; tax mgr. Arthur Andersen & Co., Okla. City 1972-7; v.p. tax & ins. Landmark Land Co., Carmel 1977—; mem: Am. Inst. of CPAs 1973; Texas State Soc. of CPAs 1973-; Okla. State Soc. of CPAs 1974-; Calif. State Soc of CPAs 1977-; Democrat; Methodist; rec: golf, tennis. Ofc: Landmark Land Co., 100 Clocktower Pl, Ste 200, Carmel 93923

THOMPSON, CHRISTOPHER ALAN, real estate developer; b. Jan. 21, 1957, San Rafael; s. Robert Edward and Connie Francis (Egbert) T.; edn: BBA, Harding Univ. 1983; Real Estate Contractor and Gen. Contractor, Calif. Career: apprentice painter W.G. Thompson Inc., San Francisco 1971-73; ski techn. Seasons Ski & Sport, San Anselmo 1973-75; foreman painter Barbara Cross Inc., San Rafael 1974-78; shopping mall mgr. Walnut Woods Ctr., Oakdale 1978-80; painter self-empl., San Anselmo 1980-83; project mgr. Jay & T. Development Inc., Petaluma 1983-84; exec. v.p. Thompson Devo Inc., Larkspur 1984—; mem: Soc. of Collegiate Journalists, CofC, US Jaycees (charter); Republican; Ch. of Christ. Res: P.O. Box 501 Petaluma 94953 Ofc: Thompson Devco Inc., P.O. Box 829 Larkspur 94939

THOMPSON, CLIFFORD ANDY, social services executive; b. Jan. 7, 1945, Minot, N.D.; s. Raymond Lee and Madonna Thompson; m. Debra Kay, Apr. 19, 1980; children: Barbara b. 1974, David b. 1977, Andrea b. 1981; edn: BA psych., CSU San Diego 1973; MA social psych., Goddard Coll. 1976; PhD mgmt., Golden State Univ. 1984. Career: founder/dir. Pro-Veterans Ctr., San Diego 1972-76; dir. Community Tng. Pgm., County of San Diego (instr. in counseling skills: Battered Womens Project, Nat. Council on Alcoholism, Union of Pan Asian Communities, S.D. Sheriff's Dept., S.D. Reg. Nurses Assn.) 1976-77; dir. Santee Connection Counseling Ctr. 1977-79, Santee Dispute Resolution Ctr. 1983-84, Santee Substance Abuse Proj. 1982-84; dir. Youth and Community Svcs., S.D. 1979-83, Personal/Family Counseling Ctr. 1984-85; honors: Outstanding Young Men of Am. (1979), appreciation for Faithful Svc. to City and Children, Pure Heart Baptist Ch.; mem. (chmn. 1985-86) S.D. County Human Relations Commn.; publs: (manuals) Counseling in the Workplace- Cosmetologists; Counseling in the Workplace- Bartenders; sev. articles in profl. jours.; Republican; Christian; rec: golf, family. Res: 9422 St. Andrews Dr Santee 92071

THOMPSON, DENNIS PETERS, physician-plastic surgeon; b. March 18, 1937, Chgo.; s. David John and Ruth Dorothy (Peters) T.; m. Virginia Williams, June 17, 1961; children: Laura Faye b. 1962, Victoria Ruth b. 1964, Elizabeth Jan b. 1969; edn: BS (highest honors in zool.) Univ. of Ill., Urbana 1957; BS, Univ. of Ill., Chgo. 1959, MS and MD, 1961; Univ. of Ill. Dental Sch., Chgo. 1962-63; bd. certified Am. Bd. of Surgery (1971), Am. Bd. of Plastic Surgery (1975, 78). Career: intern Presbyterian St. Luke's Hosp., Chgo. 1961-62, gen. surgery Mayo Clinic, Rochester, Minn. 1964-66, Harbor Gen. Hosp., Torrance 1968-70, plastic surgery UCLA 1971-73; pvt. practice medicine, plastic and reconstrv. surgery, aesthetic surgery, Santa Monica; chmn. Plastic Surg. Sect. St. John's Hosp., S.M. (1986), chief of surg. Beverly Glen Hosp. (1977-79), att. staff Olive View Med. Center (1979-); asst. clin. prof. of surg. UCLA Med. Center; honors: Phi Kappa Phi, Phi Beta Kappa, Alpha Omega Alpha; mem: Am. Coll. of Surgeons, Am. Soc. for Aesthetic Plastic Surg., Am. Soc. of Plastic and Reconstrv. Surgeons, Bay Surgical Soc., AMA, CMA, Calif. Soc. of Plastic Surgeons, George Webster Soc., Harbor Collegium, Los Angeles Co. Med. Assn., Los Angeles Soc. of Plastic Surgeons (pres. 1982-86), Pan Pacific Surg. Assn., The Aesculapians, Bev. Hills CofC 1978-80, Santa Monica CofC 1978-, L.A. CofC West 1974- (dir. 1981-84, 86-87, chmn. Legis. Action Com. 1980), Cooperative of Am. Physicians (dir. 1980-, treas. 1986, Fed. Credit Union pres. 1978-80), Nu Sigma Nu, Delta Sigma Delta; num. med. publs.; mil: US Navy 1966-68; Congregational. Res: 4750 Del Moreno Pl Woodland Hills 91364 Ofc: Dennis P. Thompson M.D., 2001 Santa Monica Blvd Ste 1180 West Santa Monica 90404

THOMPSON, DOUGLAS CRAIG, management consultant, lecturer, publisher; b. July 18, 1950, Denver, Colo.; s. Duane Clarke and Kathryn Ella Bartholf (Armstrong) T.; edn: AA, Coll. of Marin 1970; BA, San Francisco State Univ. 1972; Cert. Travel Cons., Inst. Cert. Travel Agents. Career: owner/ mgr. Calif. travel firm 12 yrs.; founder, pres. Douglas Thompson & Assoc., Dendrobium Publg., Ad Campaign advtg.; mem: Inst. of Cert. Travel Agents (life), Am. Soc. of Travel Agents, Indvl. Travel Agents, San Francisco Opera Guild, San Francisco Orchid Soc., Orchid Soc. of Southeast Asia; author: How To Open Your Own Travel Agency; Travel Agency Bookkeeping Made Simple; A Personnel & Operations Manual for Travel Agencies; The Complete Guide to Travel Agency Video; contbr. maj. travel ind. trade publs.; rec: travel, orchid culture, contemporary American art. Res: 611 Fell St. San Francisco 94102 Ofc: 387 Ivy St. San Francisco 94102

THOMPSON, GORDON, JR., judge; b. Dec. 28, 1929, San Diego; s. Gordon, Sr. and Garnet (Meece) T.; m. Jean Peters, Mar. 17, 1951; children: John b. 1952, Peter b. 1955, Gordon, III b. 1960; edn: BS, USC 1951; LLB, Southwestern Univ. Sch. of Law 1956; admitted Calif. State Bar 1956. Career: deputy district atty. County of San Diego, 1957-60; atty. pvt. practice, Thompson and Thompson, 1960-70; apptd. (by the President) judge U.S. District Court, 1970—, chief judge So. Dist. of Calif. 1984-; mem. 9th Circuit Judicial Conf. (Exec. Com.; Com. on Intercircuit/Intracircuit Assignments); treas. Am. Board of Trial Advocates; Republican; Presbyterian; rec: fishing. Ofc: U.S. District Court, 940 Front St, San Diego 92189

THOMPSON, JACK EDWARD, mining co. executive; b. Mar. 5, 1950, Havana, Cuba, nat. US cit. 1965; s. Jack Edward and Maria del Carmen (Larrea) T.; m. Linda, May 18, 1975; children: Heather b. 1978, Michael b. 1982; edn: BS mining engineering, Univ. Ariz. 1971; Reg. Profl. Engr., Brit. Col. (1976). Career: var. pos., then asst. gen. mine foreman, Magma Copper Co., San Manuel, Ariz. 1971-75; engring., tng., indsl. rels., then gen. supt. prodn. Newmont Services Ltd., Stewart, B.C. 1975-78; resident mgr. Newmont Services Ltd., Ford, Wash. 1978-81; resident gen. mgr. Homestake Mining Co., McLaughlin Gold Mine, Lower Lake, Ca. 1981—; honors: outstanding senior, Alumni Assn. Univ. Ariz. (1971), Daniel C. Jackling Scholar,

Soc. Mining Engrs. (1967), Newmont Scholar, Newmont Mining Co. (1968-70); mem: Soc. of Mining Engrs., Canadian Inst. Mining and Metallurgy, Mining and Metal. Soc. of Am., Mining Assn. of Univ. Calif., Calif. Mining Assn.; civic: Rotary Club of Clearlake, Lake County CofC (dir.), Lake County Hist. Soc., Sierra Club, Ducks Unlimited, Friends of the Bancroft Library, Save S.F. Bay Assn., Am. Philatelic Soc., Silverado Boy Scout Council (dir.); Republican; Roman Catholic; rec: mining hist., philately, sports, photog. Ofc: Homestake Mining Co. POB 1010 Lower Lake 95457

THOMPSON, JUDY, executive recruiter; b. Apr. 28, 1948, Fall River, Mass.; d. Eldredge Humphrey and Patricia Ruth (McLeod) Leeming; 1 son, William b. 1970; edn: AA, Colby Sawyer Coll. 1968; Coll. of William & Mary, 1968-69. Career: sales supr. Coll. Textbook Div. Random House, 1973-76; dist. sales mgr. Avon Products 1976-78; account exec. Dunhill of San Diego, Inc. 1978-81; pres. Financial Search Consultants, Inc. 1981–; mem. Nat. Assn. of Accts. (dir.), San Diego CofC; rec: T'ai Chi, metaphysical study, choral singing. Res: 1247 Bangor St San Diego 92106 Ofc: Financial Search Consultants Inc 3750 Convoy St Ste 106 San Diego 92111

THOMPSON, LARRY ANGELO, entertainment lawyer/TV producer/personal manager; b. Aug. 1, 1944, Clarksdale, Miss.; s. Angelo and Annie (Tuminello) T.; edn: JD, Univ. Miss. 1968; Bach. of Bus. Admin., 1966. Career: In-house Counsel, Capitol Records, Hollywood 1969-71; sr. partner entertainment law firm of Thompson, Shankman, and Bond, Bev. Hls. 1971-7; pres. Larry A. Thompson Orgn., Inc. 1977–; num. guest lectr. UCLA, USC on Entertainment Bus.; awards: Show Bus. Atty. of Year, Capitol Records, 1971; author: (book) How to Make a Record and Have Your Songs Recorded; (t.v. thesis) The Prime Time Crime; Four Dimensions of Stardom; The Road to Success is always under Construction; exec. prod. Emmy nom. Jim Nabors Show 1968; exec. prod. t.v. movie, Mickey Spillane's Margin for Murder, TV Guide 1981 pick of top 10 movies; exec. prod. CBS series, Bring 'Em Back Alive, 1982 and t.v. movie, Mickey Spillane's Murder Me, Murder You; CBS movie, The Other Lover 1985; Law Journal, Univ. Miss. 1967; Moot Court Bd., Univ. Miss. 1967; mem: Am. Bar Assn. 1968 ; Miss. Bar Assn 1968-; Calif. Bar Assn. 1970-; Inter Am. Bar Assn. 1970-; Honorable Order of Kentuky Colonels, St. Kentucky 1978-; Aide de Camp Govs. Staff, Tenn. 1972; Am. Film Inst. 1979; Nat. Acad. of Recording Arts & Scis. 1977-; mil: US Army 1966-72; Republican (co-chmn. Nat. Entertainment Com. 1983); Catholic; rec: art coll., photog., tennis. Ofc: 1888 Century Park East, Ste 622, Los Angeles 90067

THOMPSON, PAUL FRANCIS, library director; b. Nov. 6, 1926, Mount Etna, Iowa; s. Forist and Tessie (Florence) Vern; m. Betty Jean Cover, Oct. 9, 1927; children: Jo Ann (Abbas, b. 1949, Dennis Paul, b. 1953, Mark David, b. 1954, John Wayne, b. 1956; grad. Modesto Jr. Coll., 1947, San Jose State Coll., 1958. Career: library director Turlock Public Lib. 1957-58, Lompoc Public Lib., 1969–; mem: Black Gold Cooperative Lib. System (pres.), Turlock Lions Club (pres. 1968); mil: US Army 1945-46; mil: US Army 1945-6; rec: fishing, chess, shuffleboard. Res: 1412 W Nectarine Ave Lompoc 93436 Ofc: 501 E North Ave Lompoc 93436

THOMPSON, SCOTT ALAN, veterinarian; b. Sept. 13, 1951, Shelton, Wash.; s. Malcolm Arthur and Barbara Lee T.; m. Judy Ann, Nov. 22, 1985; children: Cheri Jeannette b. 1973, Jeremy Scott b. 1976; edn: BS vet. sci., UC Davis 1973, DVM, 1976. Career: kennelman Asher Veterinary Clinic, Redding 1967-70; journeyman retail clk. Pay 'N Save Corp., Davis 1969-72; research asst. UC Davis 1972-76; assoc. veterinarian Asher Veterinary Clinic, Redding 1976-78, veterinarian/jr. ptnr. 1978-80, sole owner/pres. 1980–; cons. veterinarian Haven Humane Soc., US Dept. of Fish & Game, Carter House Sci. Museum; honors: appreciation, 4H Guide Dog for the Blind (1983), Boys Scouts Am. (1984); mem: Am. Vet. Med. Assn., Calif. Vet. Med. Assn., No. Calif. Vet. Med. Assn. (secty. 1978-81); civic: Lions (Enterprise Club pres. 1985), CofC, Redding Trade Club (dir.), Riverfront Playhouse (dir.), Nat. Assn. of Eagle Scouts, Nat. Rifle Assn.; Republican (Nat. Rep. Assocs.); Methodist; rec: fishing, taxidermy, houseboating, Keno. Ofc: Asher Veterinary Clinic 2505 Hilltop Dr Redding 96002

THOMPSON, THOMAS MICHAEL, logistics management executive; b. Dec. 3, 1943, Eureka; s. Henry Clay and Margaret Marion (Lee) Harman; edn: BA, Seattle Univ. 1965. Career: gen. supply splst. US Army Weapons Command, Rock Island, Ill. 1966-67; inventory mgmt. splst. Sharpe Army Depot, Lathrop 1967-69; inventory mgmt. splst. Naval Ship Weapon Systems Engineering Sta., Port Hueneme 1969-73, logistics mgmt. splst. 1973-83, asst. for logistics tech. ops. 1983-86; currently, supvy. logistics mgmt. splst.; honors: Sustained Superior Performance Awards; Republican; Catholic; rec: religious education teaching. Res: 1582 Bittern Ct. Ventura 93003-6231 Ofc: NSWSES, Code 5C20, Port Hueneme 93043-5007

THOMPSON-JONES, TRUDY B., medical office building executive; b. March 10, 1941, Geneva, Switz., nat. US cit. 1955; d. Leo Felix and Elisabeth M. (Derbacher) Egger; m. 2d. Robert Lee Thompson, June 28, 1971; children nee Ullmann: Kurt b. 1958, Beatrice b. 1960. Career: mgr. San Diego County Swiss Park 1958-60; asst. purcasing agent Hilton Hotel, San Bruno 1960-61; asst. purchasing agent Torrey Pines Inn, San Diego 1961-62; asst. mgr. Christies Restaurant 1962-68; ofc. and constrn. mgr. D.J. Builders 1968-70; personnel dir. Telemart Enterprises (Bill Bailey Communications) 19970-71; admin., pub. rels., bldg. mgr. Bay General Community Hosp. and Chula Vista Group Properties 1972–; sem. to local med. ofc. bldg. mgrs. on conquering job related problems 1977; mem: Boma Internat., San Diego Co. Swiss Club, Cottonwood Country Golf Club, Bonita Valley Country Club; Democrat; Catholic; rec: golf, swimming, tennis. Res: 20 E. Georgina St. Chula Vista 92010 Ofc: Chula Vista Medical Center, 480 Fourth Ave. Ste. 103 Chula Vista 92010

THOMSEN, ELEANOR A., county right of way agent; b. July 26, 1925, Omaha, Neb.; d. Tony and Rose M. (Pesek) Dimitroff; m. John W. Thomsen, Sept. 11, 1948; children: Gary L. b. 1949, Ronnie K. b. 1952; edn: AA, Chabot Jr. Coll. 1976; BS, Univ. San Francisco 1979; MPA, CSU Hayward 1983; real estate broker 1965. Career: clerk Alameda Public Works Agcy. 1964-65, steno. 1965-67, secty. 1967-73, asst. right of way agent 1973-76, assoc. right of way agent 1976–; notary commn. 1981; honors: Right of Way Profl. of the Yr. (1982), Cert. of Achievement (real estate 1974, property mgmt. 1977); mem: Internat. Right of Way Assn. (treas. 1982, secty. 1983, v.p. 1984, pres. 1985), Nat. Notary Assn. 1981-; contbr. num. animal rights orgns.; Republican; Catholic; rec: crocheting, travel. Res: 27064 Belfast Lane Hayward 94542 Ofc: County of Alameda 399 Elmhurst St Hayward 94544

THOMSETT, MICHAEL CHRISTOPHER, author; b. Mar. 31, 1948, Brighton, England; s. Ronald George and Rose Karen (Walbaum) T.; m. Linda Dinnocenzo, July 1, 1967; 2 sons: Michael b. 1969, Eric b. 1976; edn: accting. dip., LaSalle Extension Univ. 1969. Career: draftsman Tudor Engring. Co., San Francisco 1967; acctg. clerk Jordanos Inc., Santa Barbara 1968-9; jr. acct. Pacific Nat. Life Assurance, San Francisco 1969-70; owner acctg. practice, San Rafael 1970-4; chief acct. Utah Internat., San Francisco 1976-8; free lance writer, San Rafael 1978–; cons. Financial Planners Equity Corp. 1978-84, Unimarc Ltd. 1978-82; Fireman's Fund 1982; recipient: dramatics achievement award, Tamalpais H.S. 1966; author: Fundamentals of Bookkeeping and Accounting For The Successful Consultant (chosen for inclusion in Pres.'s Camp David Library); Builders Guide To Accounting; Builders Office Manual; Fundamentals of Bookkeeping and Accounting For The Successful Consultant, Bermont Books 1980; Contracters Year- Round Tax Guide; Computers: The Builder's New Tool, Craftsman Book Co. 1985; num. bus. and sci. arts. 1978-; rec: music composition (two symphonies completed, chamber music). Address: 134 North San Pedro Road San Rafael 94903

THOMSON, JOHN ANSEL ARMSTRONG, vitamin industry executive; b. Nov. 23, 1911, Detroit, Mich.; s. John Russell and Florence (Antisdel) T.; m. June Anna Mae Hummel, June 24, 1938; children: Sheryl Linn b. 1940, Patricia Diane b. 1943, Robert Royce b. 1946; edn: UCLA 1934-35; AA, Pasadena City Coll. 1935; AB, cum laude, USC 1957; Bach. Garden Sci., (hon.), Calif. Polytechnic Univ. SLO 1961; MA, Columbia Pacific Univ. 1978, PhD, 1979; DA, Internat. inst. for Adv. Studies 1979. Career: founder, pres. Vitamin Inst. (J.A. Tomson Bio-organic Chemists 1930-39) 1930–; mfg. research & devel.; cons./ lectr./ writer in biochemistry, nutrition, sociology, agricultural hormones spec.; originator over 100 chemical products, over 100 trademarks incl. agricultural hormone Superthrive, Cutstart, Seedyield (classified for nat. defense WWII), and human vitamins Aquasol (1940) and Auzon crystla (1950); awards: Sci. and Ind. Gold Medal, San Francisco World Fair 1940; BSA Awards 1959, 1960, 1964; Calif. State Seal of Merit 1948; Ben Franklin Essay Award, DAR 1931; Essay Award, Los Angeles CofC 1934; Youth Leader, active BSA, PTA, YMCA, Olympic Games Com., ARC; mem: Soc. for Nutrition Edn., Am. Inst. Biological Sci., AAAS, Internat. Soc. Horticultural Sci., Am. Horticultural Soc., Nat. Recreation & Park Assn., Am. Forestry Assn., Western Gerontological Assn., Internat. Acad. of Nutritional Cons., Internat. Coll. of Applied Nutrition, Nat. Nutritional Foods Assn., Soc. of Am. Florists, Ornamental Horticulturists, Am. Assn. of Nurserymen, Nat. Landscape Assn., Nat. Health Fedn., Am. Nutrition Soc., Calif. Assn. of Nurserymen, Calif., Florists Assn., No. and So. Calif. Turfgrass Councils, Am. Chemical Soc., Cancer Control Soc., Huxley Inst. Biosocial Research, Los Angeles World Affairs Council, Sierra Club, Soc. Colonial Wars, USC and UCLA Alumni Assns., Men's Garden Club of No. Hollywood, Kiwanis Club of No. Hollywood, China Soc. of So. Calif.; Republican (State Central Com. 1948-50), Methodist (Ofcl. Bd. 3 terms pres. United Methodist Men 1979-80, pgm. leader 3d Nat. Congress 1981); rec: swimming, tennis. Ofc: P.O. Box 230, 5411 Satsuma Ave. North Hollwyood 91605

THOMSON, JUNE ANNA MAE, employment consultant; b. Dec. 9, 1913, Nanking, China; d. William Frederick and Mildred Esther (Stuart) Hummell; m. John Ansel Armstrong Thomas, June 24, 1938; children: Sheryl Linn b. 1940, Patricia Diane b. 1943, Robert Royce b. 1946; edn: Los Angeles City Coll. 1931-33; UCLA 1933-34; USC 1934-35; Bach. Garden Sci., (hon.), Calif. Polytechnic Univ. 1961; Cert. in Techniques of Tchg., Univ. of Calif. Vocational Edn. div.; Calif. State Dept. Edn. Indsl. Edn. Bureau 1976. Career: placement asst. Los Angeles Pierce Coll. 1964, placement interviewer 1966, placement dir. 1966, placement coord. 1977-79; v.chmn. US Civil Svc. Commn.'s Mid-Coast govt. Coll. Assn. 1975-79; Calif. Community Coll. Placement Assn. 1969-70; Calif. State Employment Dept., San Fernando Valley 1973; chmn. in svc., tng. conf. and placement workshop, Los Angeles Community Coll. 1974; Career Day, L.A. Pierce Coll. 1968-72, co-chmn. 1973-76; co-chmn. Career Week 1977; com. Employment of Handicapped, Los Angeles Co. 1972; 25 pos. in PTA councils; bd. mem. China Soc. of So. Calif. 1971-79; adv. com. ADEPT 1974-79; Girl Scout and Cub Scout leader; vol: Travelers Aid, United Way, ARC; honors: Outstanding Svc., Calif. Community Coll. Placement Assn. 1970; Svc. Appreciation Award, Los Angeles Pierce Coll. 1968; Calif. Merit Award for Civic Svc., 1948; Hon. Life Mem., Calif. PTA Dist. 31 1961; mem: Coll. Placement Assn., UCLA Alumni Assn., Los Angeles World Affairs Council, So. Calif. Horticultural Inst., Am. Nutrition Soc., Friends of the Earth, Nat. Health Fedn., Sierra Club, Los Angeles Co. Mus. of Art, Laguna Festival of Arts, friends of Sun Valley Library, Mid-Valley Coordg. Council, Cousteau Soc.; Republican; Methodist (pres. Wesley Fellowship, Sun. Sch.

tchr., chmn. Commn. on Missions); rec: bridge, tennis, travel. Ofc: P.O. Box 230 North Hollywood 91603

THORNBURY, WILLIAM MITCHELL, lawyer; b. Feb. 11, 1944, Kansas City, Mo.; s. Paul Cobb and Marguerite Madellaine (Schulz) T.; m. Joy Barrett, 1973; children: Barrett b. 1979, Adele b. 1981; edn: BA, UCLA 1964; JD, USC Law Sch. 1967; USC Grad. Sch. 1967-9. Career: Los Angeles Co. Public Defender 1969—; adv. com. and lectr. Calif. Public Defender's Assn. 1984-; legal asst. prof. CSULA 1983-; bd. dirs. Westside Legal Svcs. 1984-; mem: Santa Monica Bar Assn (bd. trustees 1978-, pres. 1985-86; Legislative com. 1974-, chmn. 1981-84; chmn. Judicial Eval. Com. 1981-84; chmn. Alternative Defense Counsel Com 1981-84; chmn. Publicity Com. 1974-77; liaison to L.A. County Bar 1984; Judicial Qual. Com. 1986); Los Angeles Co. Bar Assn. (Criminal Indigent Defense com. 1982; vice- chmn. 1983); Del., Conf. of Dels., State Bar of Calif. 1974, 77, 80-86; L.A. County Public Defenders Assn. (bd. trustees 1982-, exec. bd. 1982-); Navy League of U.S.; Santa Monica CofC (inebriate com.); Calif. Apprenticeship Council 1986-; Republican: 44th A.D. Co. Central Com. (secty./treas. 1968-74, chmn. 1974-), S.M. Young Repubs. (exec. bd. 1967-72, pres. 1972-73, treas. 1973-75) S.M. Repub. Club (bd. dirs. 1968-, pres. 1986-), Santa Monicans Against Crime (bd. dirs. 1979-); L.A. Co. Repub. Party (legal chmn. 1977-81, 1983-) recipient One of Five Outstanding Repubs. Award 1978); L.A. Co. Young Repubs. (del. State Conv. 1969-72) La Follette for Congress (60th A.D. chmn. 1969-70); Repub. State Central Com. (mem. 1983-85, assoc. mem. 1980-83, 1985-); City of Santa Monica Commnr. 1981-85; Fair Election Practices Com. (chmn. 1983); State Dept. of Health Clmn. on Alcohol Determination 1985-; L.A. County Commn. on Drunk Driving (alt. mem. 1983-84). Ofc: 6230 Sylmar Ave Ste 106 Van Nuys 91401

THORNTON, B. D., investor; b. Sept. 8, 1931, Grandfield, Okla.; s. Billy and Verlie Audrey (Beverage) T.; edn: AA, phys. sci., Porterville Coll. 1960; UC Los Angeles 1958; BA in pub. admin., CSU Fresno 1963; mil. tng. schs.: electronics, aerial photog., pilot. Career: machine opr. Crown Willamette Paper Mill, Camas, Wash. 1948; auto maint. service mgr. Yakima Motor Ramp 1949-51; var. pos. farming, oil field roustabout, constrn. and clean up, wholesale jobber; hearing ofcr, interim adjudication ofcr. Zoning, City of Glendale 1965-74; investor, owner/chief exec. Plantation Ranch (land survey & devel.), Porterville 1972—; honors: Grand Jury svc. Tulare Co. (1983-84), Interim chmn. Agric. and Land Use Com.); works: tech. paper, Federal Field: Law of Equilibrium (1982), contbr. newspaper Opinion pages; mil: US Air Force 1951-55; rec: theoretical physics. Address: Porterville 93257

THORNTON, CHARLES V., lawyer; b. July 18, 1942, Takoma Park, Md.; s. Charles Victor and Margaret Louise (Wiggins) T.; m. Suzanne Thorne, May 16, 1970; children: Christopher b. 1963, Matthew b. 1971, Joshua b. 1974, Jeremy b. 1974; edn: AB, Cornell Univ. 1964; JD, Univ. of Mich. 1967. Career: instr. law Univ. of Pa. Law Sch 1967-68; assoc. atty. Paul, Hastings, Janofsky & Walker 1968-75, ptnr. 1975—; lectr. Calif. Contg. Edn. of the Bar 1983-; mem: Am., Calif. L.A. Co. (exec. com. bus. and corp. sect.) bar assns.; United Way (bd. dirs., v.p. L.A. Co. Reg. V), Info. and Referral Fedn. of L.A. (bd. dirs., secy.), Calif. Club, Jack Kramer Club, La Casa de Vida; Republican; Covenant Ch.; rec: tennis, skiing. Res: 7 Williamsburg Ln Rolling Hills 90274 Ofc: Paul, Hastings et al. 555 S Flower St, 22nd Floor, Los Angeles 90071

THORNTON, JAY GLENN, investment counselor; b. Feb. 28, 1958, Mnpls., Minn.; s. Charles Darell and Jeanne Marie (Champane) T.; edn: BA, CSU Fullerton 1981; mem: NYSE (1981-). Career: prin. Jay Thornton Photography, 1976-80; investment counselor E.F. Hutton, Newport Beach 1981—; instr. Orange Coast Coll. 1980-; honors: Blue Chip Award, E.F. Hutton (1985); mem: Nat. Assn. Securities Dealers, Internat. Assn. Finl. Plnnrs.; civic: Constnl. Rights Found. of Orange County, Young Execs. of Am., fundraiser for Am. Red Cross and United Way; publs: finl. articles in The Orange County Register, Newport Center News; photog., 1979 California United Way Poster; Republican; Christian; rec: skiing, sailing. Res: 526 Fullerton St Newport Beach 92660 Ofc: 860 Newport Center Dr Newport Beach 92660

THORNTON, JOHN JAMES, life insurance agent, ret.; b. April 10, 1919, Minneapolis, Minn.; s. John James and Hazel Jane (Hurd) T.; m. Beverly Alma McFarland, June 26, 1943; children: Michael b. 1945, Edward b. 1947, Kerry b. 1949, Patricia b. 1951; edn: BA, Univ. of Calif. 1941; Reg. Rep., John Hancock Distbrs. Career: salesman Kovakar Co.; specialty sales P.F. Collier & Son 2 yrs., Sears Roebuck & Co. 1 yr.; assoc. Prudential Ins. Co. af Am. and Nat. Life & Accident Ins. Co. 1958-70; dist. agent John Hancock Mutual Life Ins. Co. 1970-82, ret.; field rep. Equifax Svcs. Co.; founding distributorship United Sciences of America Inc.; mem: American Legion (commdr. Post 46 1953), Santa Monica Bay Masonic Luncheon Club (pres.), Ocean Park Masonic Lodge (senior warden), Santa Monica Bay Shrine Club, Al Malaika Temple AAONMS, Knights Templar, F&AM, Kappa Sigma; mil: major USAFR 1941-46; Republican; Episcopal; rec: Personology. Res: 3271 Rosewood Ave. Los Angeles 90066

THORNTON, SALLY BULLARD, civic leader; b. June 7, 1934, San Diego; d. Orlan Kellogg and Lucinda Catherine (Cairns) Bullard; m. John McBride Thornton, Aug. 20, 1955; children: Mark b. 1957, Steven b. 1960; edn: AA, Stephens Coll. 1953; BA in hist., Univ. San Diego 1981, MA history, Univ. San Diego 1985. Career: mem. community volunteer Bds., Chairmanships: S.D. Symphony Orchestra Assn. (pres. 2 yrs.) 1961-74; Children's Hosp. and Health Ctr. 1962-66; Women's Com. for Cerebral Palsy (founder) 1966-69; United Cerebral Palsy of S.D. County, 1966-76; Junior League of S.D., 1969-70; Civic Youth Orch. (pres. 9 yrs.) 1969-84; United Cerebral Palsy Assn. of Calif.

1970-72 (state women's com. chmn.); Reuben H. Fleet Space Theatre & Sci. Ctr. (bd., chmn. Dedication Com.) 1971-73; Freedoms Found. at Valley Forge (pres., Advis. Council 10 yrs.) 1971-83; Family Service Assn. 1971-80; COMBO, 1973-79; Dana Jr. Hi Sch. (Citizens Advis. Com. 1973-5; PTA bd.); S.D. Co. Heart Assn., 1974-76; Am. Heart Assn. (Calif. Afil., bd.) 1975-6; S.D. Planetarium Authority (pres.) 1977-81; Young Audiences Inc., S.D. chpt. (pres.) 1977-81; Univ. of S.D. (Friends of Music, bd.) 1978-80; The John M. and Sally B. Thornton Found. (pres.) 1982-; S.D. Opera (bd. 1983-) 1965-; S.D. Museum of Art (bd. 1985-); other chmnships incl: United Way 1966-75, S.D. Civic Light Opera Assn., Starlight, 1965, 71; S.D. Soc. for Crippled Children, 1967; Fine Arts Soc. of S.D., 1971, 74; Salvation Army Door of Hope Aux., 1972. Recipient num. vol. service awards; two Copley and one Kammerling Award for research papers, S.D. Hist. Soc., 1982, 84, 85; honors: Phi Alpha Theta, Delta Epsilon Sigma; publs: articles in J. of San Diego History 1982, 84; Republican. Res: 2125 Evergreen St, San Diego 92106

THORPE, JAMES, senior research associate, Huntington Library-Art Gallery; b. Aug. 17, 1915, Aiken, S.C.; s. J. Ernest and Ruby H. T.; m. Elizabeth Daniells, July 19, 1941; children: James III b. 1942, John D. b. 1944, Sarah M. b. 1947; edn: AB, The Citadel 1936; MA, UNiv. of N.C. 1938; PhD, Harvard Univ. 1941; Litt.D., Occidental Coll. 1968; LHD, Claremont Grad. Sch. 1968; Litt.D., The Citadel 1971; doctor of Humanities, Univ. of Toledo 1977. Career: prof. of English Princeton Univ. 1946-66, Master Grad. Coll. 1949-55; dir. Henry E. Huntington Library and Art Gallery 1966-83; mem: Am. Philosophical Soc.; fellow, Am. Acad. of Arts and Scis.; fellow, Am. Antiquarian Soc.; Zamorano Club; author; (publ.) 14 books and var. arts. of literary scholarship; mil: Col., USAF 1941-6, WWII; Democrat; Episcopal; rec: horticulture. Res: 1199 Arden Rd Pasadena 91106 Ofc: Henry E. Huntington Library and Art Gallery, San Marino 91108

THRAP, GUY CARLYLE, executive; b. April 15, 1940, Corpus Christi, Texas; s. Guy William and Blanch M. (Baker) T.; m. Judy, May 15, 1965; children: April b. 1967, Steven b. 1970; edn: BS, San Diego State Coll. 1964. Career: engr. Cubic Corp. 1958-63; senior design engr. Calif. Inst. 1963-71; v.p., co-founder Valhalla Scientific 1971-81; pres. Shepherd Scientific 1981—; patentee: 7 for original research. Ofc: San Diego 92111

THREADGILL, DIANE RENEE, military officer, architect; b. Dec. 28, 1954, Chgo.; d. Claude L. and Evelyn V. (Harris) Threadgill; edn: B.Arch., Hampton Univ. 1978; grad. work CSU Dominguez Hills 1984-. Career: capt. USAF 1979—, base architect Columbus AFB, Miss. 1979-82; chief environmental and contract plnng. Kunsan (Korea) Air Base 1982-83 (devel. base master plan through Year 2000); project mgr. for new military family housing, Los Angeles currently; honors: Outstanding Young Women of Am. (1982); mem: Los Angeles AIA (assoc.), Soc. of Am. Mil. Engrs., Toastmasters Internat.; mil: capt. USAF 1979-, AF Commendn., Oak Leaf Cluster; Presbyterian; rec: painting. Ofc: U.S.Air Force/Space Div. POB 92960 Los Angeles 90009

THURBER, THOMAS NELSON, certified public accountant, business executive; b. July 30, 1950, Cortland, N.Y.; s. Robert Cecil and Ruth (Conte) T.; m. Susan Gravois, June 30, 1984; 1 son, Terrence b. 1984; edn: BS, Fla. State Univ. 1972; CPA, N.Y. and Calif. Career: senior tax mgr. Arthur Andersen & Co., N.Y., Stamford, Ct., Orange Co. Calif., 1972-79; controller U.S. ops. Daon Corp., Newport Beach 1979-82; controller Joseph C. Canizaro Interests, New Orleans, 1982-83; ptnr. Williamson & Assocs., CPAs, Orange 1983—; pres. Uniglobe World Express Travel; mng. gen. ptnr. sev. partnerships; advis. bd. dirs. Century Media Inc.; mem: Am. Inst. CPAs, Calif. State Soc. CPAs, Building Indus. Assn. of Orange County, Airplane Owners & Pilots Assn.; Protestant; rec: racquetball, fitness. Res: 2851 Wyngate Rd Orange 92667 Ofc: Williamson & Assocs. 625 City Dr South Ste 250 Orange 92668

THURKOW, GLENN GUSTAVE, school district administrator; b. July 1, 1947, West Point, N.Y.; s. Gustave Leonard and Muriel Anna Margaret (Doherty) T.; m. Jeri Monica Weiss, Mar. 26, 1977; children: Bradley b. 1979, Kevin b. 1984; edn: AA, East L.A. Coll. 1965-68; CSU Humboldt 1968-69; BS, honors, CSU Los Angeles 1973; CSU Long Beach 1976-79; desig: Certified Public Acct. (CPA), Calif. 1975, Certified Cost Analyst (CCA), Inst. of Cost Analysis 1984. Career: intern, 1972-73, staff auditor Kenneth Leventhal & Co., Los Angeles and Newport Beach, 1973-75; senior staff auditor City Auditor, City of Long Beach, 1975-77; acctg. mgr., real estate investment office, Prudential Ins. Co. of Am., Newport Beach 1977-79; corp. controller/ asst. treas. Mission Hills Prop. Corp. (subs. Colgte-Palmolive Co.), Rancho Mirage 1979-81; comptroller Ukiah Unified Sch. Dist., 1981—; founding dir./CFO Bear Care, Inc. (latch key pgm.), 1984-85; instr. Mendocino-Lake Comm. Coll. 1983-85; dir./ treas. River Estates Muni. Water Corp., 1986-; honors: Beta Alpha Psi (1972), Beta Gamma Sigma (1974), Phi Kappa Phi (1979), IDEA Fellowship for educators in Claremont (1985); mem: Am. Inst. CPAs, Inst. of Cost Analysis, Calif. Assn. of Sch. Bus. Ofcls., Acctg. Research Assn. (govtl. acctg. stds. bd. 1986-); civic: Hopland CofC (charter, fin. com.), United Way North Bay Chpt. (allocations com. 1982-85), Kiwanis, Ukiah Valley Youth Soccer Assn. (coach 1985); mil: cpl. USMC 1969-71, Rifle Exp., Nat. Def.; Republican; Ch. Rel. Sci.; rec: wt. tng., gardening, tennis. Res: 501 Riverside Dr Russian River Estates Ukiah 95482 Ofc: Ukiah Unified School District 445 South Dora St Ukiah 95482

THURMAN, BARBARA WINIFRED, teacher, minister; b. Nov. 21, 1933, Monterey Park; d. Elmer Wm. and Phyllis Margaret Annie (Watts) Schrumpf; m. John David Thurman, Sept. 13, 1959, div. 1973; edn: BA, CSU San Diego 1955, MA, 1960; tchg. creds. (Gen. Elem.) N.Y. State 1955, (Life) Calif. 1961;

ordained minister, Nat. Spiritualist Assn. of Churches 1979; NST (Nat. Spiritualist Tchr.) degree, N.S.A.C. 1979. Career: tchr. Pearl River (NY) Sch. Dist. 1955-56; tchr. San Diego City Schs. 1956-64, substitute tchr. Marin County Sch. Bd. Assn. 1964-65, tchr. Sausalito Sch. Dist. 1965—; co-recipient Golden Bell Award for Early Kindergarten Pgm. (1985), Marin Co. Schs.; mem. Calif. State Spiritualist Assn. (first woman pres. 1975-78, 79-83; dir. 1971-74; CSSA Newsletter ed. 1974-; desig: Spiritual Healer 1975, Cert. Medium 1984); Golden Gate Spiritualist Ch. (Lyceum tchr. 1967-77, tchr. classes on Spiritualism 1979—); mem. Delta Kappa Gamma (past chpt. pres.), Alpha Xi Delta Sor.; sev. publs. on Spiritualism (1975-); Republican; Spiritualist; rec: personal computer, gardening, embroidery. Res: 200 Marina Vista Rd Larkspur 94939

TIBBITTS, SAMUEL JOHN, hospital society president; b. Oct. 7, 1924, Chicago, Ill.; s. Samuel John and Marion Charlotte (Swanson) T.; m. Audrey Slottelid, Aug. 28, 1949; children: Scott b. 1953, Brett b. 1955; edn: BS, UCLA 1949; MS, UC Berkeley 1950. Career: adminstrv. res. Calif. Hosp. Med. Ctr., Los Angeles 1950-1, asst. adminstr. 1951-3, assoc. adminstr. 1953-9; adminstr. 1959-66; chmn. mgmt. com./ asst. secty. Lutheran Hosp. Soc. of So. Calif. 1962-66, pres. 1966—; asst. supt. Santa Monica Hosp. 1952-4; pres. Commn. for Adminstrv. Svcs. in Hosps. 1963, 64, 67; pres. Calif. Health Data Corp. 1968-71; mem. Calif. Health Planning Council and Steering Com. 1968-; Los Angeles City Adv. Med. Council 1971, 73; Pres.'s Com. Health Svcs. Ind. (Adv. Health Council, CA 1973; adv. panel Pres.'s Cost of Living Council, Price Commn. and Pay Bd., Phase II); Calif. Hosp. Commn., State Calif. 1974—; bd. dirs. Calif. Hosp. Med. Ctr., Martin Luther Hosp., Henry Mayo Newhall Meml. Hosp.; trustee, exec. com. Blue Cross of So. Calif. 1966-75; honors: fellow, Am. Coll. of Hosp. Adminstr.; Delta Omega; Ritz E. Heerman Award, Calif. Hosp. Assn.; Svc. to Humanity Awd., Lutheran Mutual Life Ins. Co.; Outstanding Achievement Awd., Hosp. Council of So. Calif.; Most Venerable Order of the Hosp. of St. John, presented by Queen of England; Trustees Awd., Am. Hosp. Assn.; Freedom Awd., Wilshire Sertoma Club; Outstanding Svc. Awd., Blue Cross of So. Calif.; Individual of Year, Fedn. of Am. Hosps.; hon. mem. U. Minn. Alumni Assn.; author: Preferred Provider Organizations (1984), num. mag., journal arts.; mil: pfc US Army M.C. 1946 7; Republican; Lutheran; rec: golf, gardening. Res: 1224 Adair St San Marino 91108 Ofc: Lutheran Hosp. Soc. of So. Calif., 1423 So. Grand Ave Los Angeles 90015

TICE, CHRISTIAN SHAWN, financial planner; b. Oct. 9, 1952, Chgo.; s. Leroy E. and Julie A. T.; edn: BA, UC Berkeley 1975; Certified Financial Planner 1983. Career: owner Alliance for Profl. Planning (investment advis. firm) Santa Clara; instr. short course Financial & Tax Planning West Valley Coll. Saratoga 1982—; br. mgr. Private Ledger Financial Svcs. 1983—; mem. Financial Profl. Advisory Panel 1984; mem: Internat. Assn. Fin. Planning, Inst. CFPs, Cal. Alumni (UC Berkeley), San Jose State Alumni Assn.; Unity Ch. Ofc: Christian S. Tice CFP 1333 Lawrence Expwy Ste 150 Santa Clara 95051

TIETZ, DALE EDWARD, military officer, electrical engineer; b. Feb. 17, 1949, Munich, Germany; s. Edward Christian and Gracie Lunette (Daughtery) T.; m. Linda, Jan. 2, 1974; children: Ryan, b. 1981; Eric, b. 1983; Taryn, b. 1984; edn: BS, chem. USAF Acad 1971; MSEE, Air Force Inst. of Tech. 1978; MBA, cand.., So. Ill. Univ. Career: pilot tng. Laughlin AFB, Tx. 1971-72; aircraft cmdr./instr. pilot McGuire AFB, NJ 1972-76; chief Systems Engring. Div., Def. Dissemination Pgm. Office, L.A. AF Station, 1978-83; currently asst. chief tng. 63rd Mil. Airlift Wing, Norton AFB, and C141B Aircraft cmdr./ pilot; cons. Computer Sys. Integration; mem: AF Assn., Airlifters Assn., IEEE, Assn. of Grad. (USAF Acad.), Nat. Speleological Soc., Daedalian's; works: devel. microprocessor-based digital autopilot for USAF mini-remotely piloted vehicle (forerunner of computer-based autopilots for DOD drone vehicles), M. Thesis, pub. NAE Conf. 1978; mil: maj. USAF 1971-, AF Commendn., Def. Merit. Svc., Senior Pilot, Senior Space Badge, Parachutist; Republican; Lutheran; rec: scuba, sky-diving. Res: 6131 Jasonwood Dr Huntington Beach 92648 Ofc: 63rd MAW/DOT (Mil. Airlift Cmd) Norton AFB 92409

TIMBERLAKE, THOMAS GUITTARD, real estate broker; b. Nov. 9, 1933; San Francisco; s. Frank Sommer and Camille (Guittard) T.; m. Margot Woodworth, Dec. 26, 1960; children: Stephen W. b. 1966, David S. b. 1968; edn: AB, Stanford Univ. 1955, MBA, 1959. Career: sales assoc. Coldwell Banker S.F. 1959-75; v.p. Nelson Peterson Assoc. S.F. 1975-81; res. mgr. Hill & Co. S.F. 1981-85; v.p. Nelson Peterson Assoc. S.F. 1985—; mem: S.F. Real Estate Bd. (dir.), Soc. Indsl. Realtors, Bohemian Club; mil: lcdr. USNR; Republican; Catholic. Ofc: Nelson Peterson Assoc. San Francisco 94108

TIN, ANTONY, mechanical engineer; b. Aug. 1, 1953, Hong Kong; s. Kwan Kui and Kok (Lam) T.; m. Shirley Sheng, July 3, 1983; children: Pearl b. 1984, Antony II b. 1986; edn: AS, Vincennes Univ. 1974; BS magna cum laude, Yale Univ. 1976; MS, Brown Univ. 1978; Reg. Profl. Mech. Engr. Calif. 1982, Civil Engr. Calif. 1982. Career: prod. engr. Chrysler Corp. 1978-80; engrg. cons. NuTech Engrs. 1980-82; cons. Dynatech 1982-84; r&d engr. Dysan 1984-85; engrg. mgr. Apex Engrg. 1985—; bd. dirs. Creative Rotary Converter; honors: Calhoun Scholar (1976), Univ. Fellow (1977), Donald McCrosky Award (1976); patent applications on two products; rec: skiing. Res: 4862 Balboa Way Fremont 94536 Ofc: Apex Engrg. 629 Lava Way San Jose 95133

TING, EDMUND JACK, criminalist; b. Feb. 10, 1958, Taft; s. Kwai Sing and Bebe S. Ting; edn: BS, biology, UC Irvine 1980, BS, chem. 1981; CSU Los Angeles 1981-84. Career: criminalist Los Angeles Co. Sheriff's Criminalistics Lab. 1983-85, senior criminalist 1985—; mem: Calif. Assn. of Criminalists

(provisional mem.), Am. Acad. of Forensic Scis., Am. Soc. of Mass Spectrometry; Christian; rec: researching famous crimes, equestrian, jigsaw puzzles Ofc: Los Angeles 90057

TIPTON, DALE LEO, physician; b. July 8, 1930, Parsons, Kans.; s. Dale L. and Ruby B. (Trice) T.; div.; children: Jill b. 1961, Jan b. 1966; edn: AB, UC Berkeley 1952; MD, UC San Francisco 1959, MS in pharm., 1959; bd. cert. Am. Bd. Otol., Head and Neck Surgery (1966). Career: intern Kaiser Found. Hosp., San Francisco 1959-60; gen. surgery resident UC Sch. of Medicine, 1960-62, NIH fellow UC Cancer Research Inst., 1962-63, resident Dept. Otolaryngology, 1963-66; chmn. Dept. Otol., S.F. General Hosp. 1970-76; pvt. practice Ear, Nose & Throat, S.F.; assoc. clin. prof. Dept. Otol. UCSF; cons. US Dept. of Labor 1973-; med. advisor Calif. Blue Shield 1977-; awards: NIH Fellow (1962-63), Freshman Med. Student Research award, Merrill Pharm. Co. (1956), NIH spl. award to attend VIII Internat. Cong. of Otorhinolaryngology, Tokyo (1965), elected UCSF Med. Sch. class pres. (2nd. year med. sch.) and student body pres. (1958-59), chief of med. staff Franklin Hosp. (1982-84); mem: Am. Coll. of Surgeons, Am. Acad. Otolaryngology Head & Neck Surg., S.F. Med. Soc., Calif. Med. Assn.; clubs: Commonwealth, Presidio Army Golf; num. research publs. and med. jour. articles; mil: 1st lt. USMC 1952-55, lt. col. US Army Med. Reserv.; Democrat; Catholic. Res: 458 Briarwood Dr So San Francisco 94080 Ofc: 45 Castro St Ste 220 San Francisco 94114

TIRTOPRODJO, SANTONO, import-export co. executive; b. Dec. 19, 1952, Jakarta, Indonesia, nat. US cit. 1974; s. Gudarwan and Fatimah (Sutedja) T.; m. Indra, Jan. 3, 1977; children: Anthony b. 1981, Shannon b. 1983; edn: AA, Coll. of San Mateo 1977; BS, San Francisco St. Univ. 1981. Career: mgmt. trainee Radio Shack, San Bruno 1978-79 (top salesman award- No. Calif., 1979); mgr. Grocery Wholesale Co., San Francisco 1979-83; owner Best Carpet Care, Redwood City 1981—; owner/pres. Fine Trading Co., Inc., 1984—; mem. Carpet Cleaners Inst., San Carlos CofC; invention: automatic tape dispenser (pat. pend.); mil: airman 1/c US Air Force 1972-75; Republican; Buddhist; rec: travel, biographical lit., sports. Ofc: Fine Trading Co. Inc. 1325 El Camino Real Ste 2 Millbrac 94030

TJIONG, HWIE-BENG, dentist; b. April 19, 1940, Central Java, Indonesia; s. Swie-Liong and Tjoe-Nio (Tjoa) T.; m. Melania Lian-Ien, Oct. 18, 1970; 1 child, Lia-Alexandra Gien-Sian b. 1971; edn: DDS, Trisakti Univ. Career: dental practice, Jakarta, Indonesia 1971-76; general practice dentist self-empl. 1978—; mem: Am. and Calif. Dental Assns., Los Angeles Dental Soc. Ofc: 7407 Reseda Blvd. Reseda 91335

TOBER, LEE YEAO, auditor; b. Oct. 12, 1954, Taiwan, nat. US cit. 1975; s. Bei Jing and Sue Lai (Kao) Yeao; m. Tammy Tober, Dec. 17, 1978; edn: AA, City Coll. of S.F. 1976; BA, CSU Hayward 1979, MBA in progress, 1980-. Career: asst. to budget dir. CSU Hayward 1977-78; acct. Gabriel G. Barras CPA 1978-79; adminstrn. mgmt. trainee NCR Corp. 1979-80; financial acct. Chevron USA 1980-81, tax analyst 1982-85, auditor 1985—; Volunteer Tax Assistance Pgm. 8 yrs.; honors: Dean's List, Dean's Honor Roll (CSU Hayward 1977-79), CSF Lifetime Member; mem: Nat. Assn. Accts. 1982-, Walnut Creek Chess Club, SF Rec. & Parks Assn. (vol. basketball coach), Oper. SHARE (Big Brothers), Oakland Chinese Community Ctr. (vol.); Republican; Christian; rec: ballroom dancing, reading, travel, chess. Res: 24101 Dover Lane Hayward 94541 Ofc: Chevron Corp. POB F Concord 94524

TOBIN, DONALD JOSEPH, financial forecasting executive; b. Nov. 11, 1947, Brooklyn, NY; s. Charles Joseph and Patricia Marion (O'Hare) T.; m. Patricia Brunner, June 12, 1971; children: Michael b. 1974, Alicia b. 1975; AA, Orange Coast Coll. 1977; BSBA, CSU Long Beach 1980. Career: hydraulic mechanic US Army, RVN 1968-70; hydraulic mechanic Douglas Aircraft Co., Long Beach 1970-75; test project splst. Bertea Corp., Irvine 1977-78; aircraft asembler Douglas Aircraft Co., Long Beach 1978-79, acct. 1979-80; acct., senior acct., br. mgr. McDonnell Douglas Finance, Long Beach 1980-85, mgr. 1985—; honors: Cert. of Achiev., Orange Coast Coll. 1977; Cert. of Award, H&R Block 1976; mil: splst. 5 US Army 1968-70, Nat. Defense, Vietnam Svc., Vietnam Campaign, Army Commdn.; Democrat; Catholic; rec: golf. Res: 2995 Babb St. Costa Mesa 92626 Ofc: McDonnell Douglas Finance Corp., P.O. Box 580 Long Beach 90801

TOBKIN, VINCENT HENRY, venture capitalist; b. July 4, 1951, Pelican Rapids, Minn.; s. Henry Edward, Sr. and Kathryn Mary (Johnson) T.; 1 son, Gregory b. 1985; edn: BS, and MS, Mass Inst. of Tech., 1973; MBA w/ high distinction, and JD, Harvard Univ. 1977. Career: electrical engr. Hewlett Packard, and Fairchild Semiconductor, 1969-74, McKinsey and Co., San Francisco and N.Y. 1976-84, ptnr. 1983-84; general ptnr. Sierra Ventures Mgmt. Co., Menlo Park and NYC 1984-; dir. Prospect Group, NYC 1984-; dir. Lab Support Inc., Woodland Hills 1985-, Stratacom, Cupertino 1986-; mem. IEEE, ACM, Tau Beta Pi, Kappa Nu, Hasty Pudding Club; Republican; Roman Catholic; rec: scuba, skiing, flying. Res: 2644 Webster St San Francisco 94123 Ofc: Sierra Ventures 3000 Sand Hill Rd Bldg 1-280 Menlo Park 94025

TOCONIS, PAMELA ZOE, personnel consultant; b. Nov. 11, 1948, Logansport, Ind.; d. Wm. David and Norma Zoe (Carnahan) Coble; m. Albert Michael Toconis, Dec. 23, 1972; children: Scott Michael b. 1968, Michelle-Anne Denice b. 1969; edn: BS, pre med, Indiana Univ. 1968; AS, Valencia Comm. Coll. 1972; BS orgnl. behavior, Univ. San Francisco 1986; desig: CPC (cert. placement counselor) Calif. Employment Assn. 1979, CEC (cert. employment cons.) Calif. Assn. Personnel Cons. 1983. Career: personnel cons. Republic Pers. Service, Charleston, S.C. 1975-78, Diversity Pers. Service,

Modesto, Ca. 1978-80, Availability Pers. Agcy., Modesto 1980-81; owner Toconis & Assocs., Personnel Service, 1982 —; pers. cons. and firm rep. union negotiations, Merced Medical Clinic, Inc. 1983-85; awards: US Small Bus. Innovation Research grantee (1984); mem: Calif. Assn. of Personnel Cons., Nat. Assn. of Personnel Cons.; civic: Merced CofC (dir. 1984-; v.p. Bus. and Econ. Dev. 1985-86, chamber rep. var. city projects), Merced Downtown Assn. (adv. bd. 1985-), Merced Community Medical Ctr., Merced Business Club (charter pres. 1982); Republican; Episcopal. Res: 1220 Highpoint Dr Atwater 95301 Ofc: Toconis & Assoc., Personnel Svc. 470 W Main St Merced 95340

TODD, JUDITH ANN, educator; b. Dec. 13, 1950, Wakefield; d. Marley and Joan Mary (Birkinshaw) Booth; m. Stephen Michael Copley, Aug. 3, 1984; edn: BA, Cambridge Univ. 1972, MA, 1977, PhD, 1977; Chartered Engr., Calif. Career: research asst. Imperial Coll. of Sci. & Tech., London, Eng. 1976-78; research assoc. State Univ. of NY, Stonybrook 1978; research engr., UC Berkeley 1979-82; asst. prof. materials sci. and mech. engring., USC 1982 —; chmn. Am. Soc. for Metals, Los Angeles chpt. 1986-87; Task Force mem., Metals Property Council, NY, NY 1979-; Council mem., Materials Sci. Div., Am. Soc. for Metals, Metals Park, Ohio 1984-; honors: Faculty Research Award, Oak Ridge Nat. Lab. (1986), research award Am. Inst. for Mining, Metallurgical & Petroleum Engrs. (1983), Seed Grant award Nat. Assn. of Corrosion Engrs. (1983); mem: Soc. for Women Engrs. (senior), Am. Soc. for Metals, Am. Inst. for Mining Metallurgical & Petroleum Engrs., Am. Soc. for Testing & Materials; publs: 24 articles (1978-86); rec: archaeometry, hiking. Res: 4029 Via Nivel, Palos Verdes Estates 90274 Ofc: Univ. of Southern Calif., Dept. of Materials Science, Los Angeles 90089-0241

TODD, WILLIAM JAMES, research analyst; b. Aug. 11, 1948, Milwaukee, Wis.; s. Sanford Wm. and Marion Eleanor (Hass) T.; m. Linda Edgren, June 12, 1971; children: Anna b. 1976, Kenneth b. 1979; edn: Univ. of Wis. 1966-67; BA, Valparaiso Univ. 1970; MA, Indiana State Univ. 1973; dipl. in photointerpretation Internat. Inst. for Aerial Survey & Earth Scis., 1974. Career: research geographer Lab. for Appls. of Remote Sensing, Purdue Univ. 1972-73; remote sensing appls. scientist Technicolor Graphic Services Inc., EROS Data Ctr., US Geol. Survey, Sioux Falls, S.D. 1974-78; project mgr. Technicolor Graphic Services Inc., NASA-Ames Research Ctr., Moffett Field, 1978-80; research analyst Lockheed Missiles & Space Co., Sunnyvale 1980 —; honors: Gamma Theta Upsilon, Sigma Gamma Epsilon; mem. Am. Soc. for Photogrammetry & Remote Sensing, Assn. of Old Crows, Sierra Club, Planetary Soc.; publs: 20+ tech. articles (1972-); Republican; Conserv. Baptist; rec: hiking, camping, canoeing, urban hist. Res: 837 Gail Ave Sunnyvale 94086 Ofc: Lockheed Missiles & Space Co 1111 Lockheed Way Sunnyvale 94088

TOFTNESS, CECIL GILMAN, lawyer; b. Sept. 13, 1920, Glasgow, Mont.; s. Anton Bernard and Nettie (Pederson) T.; m. Chloe Vincent, 1951; edn: AA, San Diego Eve. Jr. Coll. 1943; BS, UC Los Angeles 1949; JD, Southwestern Univ. 1953. Career: pvt. practice of civil law, 1954 —; active duty US Navy 1938-46, naval ofcr. USNR 1946 —; honors: Class rep. Class 1953 Southwestern Law Sch., listed Who's Who in Am. Law (1985); mem. Kiwanis (P.V.), Masons (Manhattan Beach-Redondo Beach #742 Blue Lodge, Royal Arch Mason, Knight Templar, LA Commander #9), Phi Delta Legal Frat.; Democrat; Lutheran; rec: gardening, golf. Ofc: 2516 Via Tejon Palos Verdes Estates 90274

TOKUNAGA, ROGER, consulting civil engineer; b. Apr. 15, 1932, Sacramento; s. Mohei and Tamoki (Ozawa) T.; m. Irene Yoshikawa, June 29, 1957; children: Julie b. 1958, Dean b. 1960, Ron b. 1962; edn: AA, Yuba Coll. 1951; BS, UC Berkeley 1956; reg. profl. civil engr. Calif. 1960, Ore. 1984, Nev. 1985. Career: jr., asst. civil engr. Sonoma Co. Flood Control & Water Conservation Dist. Santa Rosa 1956-59; assoc., sr. civil engr. Gillett-Harris & Assoc. Yuba City 1959-73; sr. and prin. engr., co-owner Von Geldern Engrg. Co. Yuba City 1973-85; interview bd. engrg. personnel for Yuba City and Sutter Co.; Yuba Co. Blue Ribbon Com. for sanitary sewer system ordinance; mem: Nat. Soc. Profl. Engrs., Calif. Soc. Profl. Engrs., Fish & Game Advisory Commn., Japanese American Citizen's League (chmn. bd. Marysville chap. 1962), Buddhist Ch. of Am. (bd. secy. 1963), Peach Bowl Anglers Club, Peach Bowl Golf Club; mil: sgt. US Army 1952-54, Bronze Star; Democrat; Buddhist; rec: golf, fishing, bowling. Res: 3076 S Walton Ave Yuba City 95991 Ofc: Von Geldern Engrg. Co. 430 2nd St Yuba City 95991

TOLEDO, FRANK, furniture manufacturing co. executive; b. Oct. 27, 1943, Havana, Cuba, nat. US cit. 1969; s. Francisco and Carmen Ana (Perdomo) T.; m. Miriam A., Feb. 27, 1971; children: Michelle b. 1972, Amy b. 1978; edn: Havana Univ. 1 yr. Career: general help Tropic Modern Furn. Miami, Fla. 1963-65; truck driver, shppg. clerk Kent Furn. Miami 1965-67; shppg. clerk, ofc. Tropic Modern Furn. Miami 1967-68; prodn. mgr. Kent Furn. Miami 1968-70; plant mgr. A&G Quilting Co. L.A. 1970-71; prodn. mgr. Quality Furn. L.A. 1971-73; dir. mfg. Bristol House Vernon 1973 —; mem: Nat. Rifle Assn. (life), Calif. Rifle & Pistol Assn. (mem. chmn.), Compton Hunting & Fishing Club, Calif. Wildlife Fedn.; mil: pvt. US Army 1962-63; Democrat; Catholic; rec: hunting, fishing, pistol shooting, camping. Ofc: Bristol House 3800 Ross St Vernon 90058

TOLLENAERE, LAWRENCE R., co. president; b. Nov. 19, 1922, Berwyn, Ill.; s. Cyrille and Modesta (Van Damme) T.; m. Mary Elizabeth Hansen, Aug. 14, 1948; children: Elizabeth b. 1951, Homer b. 1952, Stephanie b. 1953, Caswell b. 1956, Jennifer Mary b. 1964; edn: BS in engring., Iowa State Univ. 1944, MS in engring. 1949; MBA, USC 1969; LLD. (hon.), Claremont Grad. Sch. 1977. Career: engr. Aluminum Co. of Am., Huntington Park 1946-47; asst. prof. indsl. engring. Iowa State Univ., Ames 1947-50; sales rep. Am. Pipe and Constrn. Co., South Gate 1950-53, splst. rep. So. Am. 1953-54, 2nd v.p./

div. mgr. Colombian div., Bogota 1955-57, div. mgr./v.p. So. Calif. 1957-63, v.p. Concrete Pipe Ops., Monterey Park, Calif. 1963-64, pres. Corp. Hdqrs. 1965-67, dir./pres./CEO, 1967 —, corp. name change to Ameron, 1969; dir: Avery Internat. (Pasadena), Newhall Land and Farming Co. (Valencia), Pacific Mutual Life Ins. Co. (Newport Beach), The Parsons Corp. (Pasadena), bd. chmn. Gifford-Hill-American, Inc. (Dallas); mem: Merchants and Mfrs. Assn./L.A. (fmr. bd. chmn., dir.), The Beavers (hon. dir., past pres.), Calif. CofC (dir.), Nat. Assn. of Mfrs., Soc. for Advancement of Mgmt., AMA Presidents Assn., Newcomen Soc. in No. Am., Alpha Tau Omega; civic: The Huntington Library, Art Gal. and Botanical Gardens (bd. trustees), Soc. of Fellows, The Huntington Library (life mem.), Claremont Univ. Ctr. (bd. of fellows, Iowa State Univ. Found. (bd. of govs., Order of Knoll.); clubs: California (dir.), Jonathan, Pauma Valley Country, San Gabriel Country, Bohemian (S.F.), Commanderie de Bordeaux (L.A.), Los Angeles Confrerie des Chevaliers du Tastevin, Twilight, Lincoln; mil: ensign to lt. jg USNR 1944-46, WWII; rec: philately, hunting, fishing, equestrian. Res: 1400 Milan Ave South Pasadena 91030 and Kaanapali Plantation, Lahaina, Maui, HI 96761 Ofc: Ameron 4700 Ramona Blvd Monterey Park 91754

TOLLETTE, HENRY BELL, packaging materials design co. president; b. Oct. 17, 1939, Milwaukee, Wis.; s. Henry Bell and Marion M. (Allerton) T.; m. Sally; children: Wylie b. 1966, Hillary b. 1968, Alexandra b. 1981; edn: BS, Mich. State Univ. 1962; MS, New Sch. of Social Research 1965. Career: product and mktg. research, field sales (N.Y.C. and Sacto., Ca.), Thilmany Pulp and Paper Div., Hammermill Paper Co., 1962-75; gen. sales mgr. Custom-Made Packaging, 1975-82; Western mgr. mfg. & sales (W. US & Pacific Rim countries), NP Marketing Corp., Neenah, Wis. 1983; pres. H.B. Tollette & Assocs., 1984 —, cons. packaging design, distbn., printing and converting systems; mem. Nat. Public Radio bd. advisors; guest lectr. UC Davis, Cal Poly S.L.O., Golden Gate Univ. Grad. Sch., CSU San Jose, Inst. of Packaging of G. Brit.; honors: Who's Who in Packaging (1980-86); mem: Am. Mktg. Assn., Packaging Inst. U.S.A. (profl. mem.), Western Packaging Assn. (pres. 1982), Inst. of Packaging of G.B. (1983-), Soc. of Packaging and Handling Engrs. (profl. mem.); num. articles in packaging trade publs.; mil: capt. USAF 1962-69; Episcopal; rec: sports. Ofc: H.B. Tollette and Associates 655 University Dr No. 113 Sacramento 95825

TOMA, JOHN JOSEPH, JR., veterinarian; b. Apr. 16, 1949, Los Angeles; s. Dr. John J. and Beulah C. (Ullery) T.; m. Julie Ann Borchers, June 19, 1971; edn: BS, Baylor Univ. 1970; MS, Wake Forest Univ. 1973; DVM, UC Davis 1983; lic. Veterinarian, Calif. State Board 1982. Career: veterinary assoc. Equine Medicine, Surgery & Dentistry with Gano, Steppe & Assoc., San Dimas and then Chino, 1982-85; veterinarian prin. Equine Medicine, Surgery & Dentistry, Los Angeles 1985 —; mem: Am. Vet. Med. Assn., Calif. Vet. Med. Assn., So. Calif. Vet. Med. Assn.; civic: Greater Los Angeles Zoo Assn., Friends of the Huntington Library, L.A.C.M.A., Friends of the Arboretum & Nat. History Mus.; publs: article in Atherosclerosis J. (1975), presentations Proceedings of the Soc. for Exptl. Biology & Medicine (1974); mil: USAR Veterinary Corps 1972-78; American Spirit Award (1972); rec: sailing, classical music. Ofc: POB 39533 Los Angeles 90039

TOMA, KAY, medical center president; b. Nov. 10, 1913, Okla.; s. George and Martha T.; m. Ellen Glaviano, June 24, 1966; children: Paula K. b. 1948, Martha Jo b. 1949, Michael G. b. 1950, Patricia Ann b. 1952, James J. b. 1955, Michelle Kay b. 1969; edn: MD, Univ. Tenn. 1941. Career: chief of staff Falfurrias City Hosp. Tex. 1947-48; pres. Bell Med. Ctr.; chief of staff Mission Hosp. Huntington Park 1960 —; exec. bd. Calif. State Bd. Med. Examiners 1970-78; v.p., dir. Charter Thrift & Loan Fullerton 1978; bd. dirs. Capital Nat. Bank Downey 1978; pres. Alladin Jewels Las Vegas 1978; bd. dirs. Mechanics Nat. Bank; chmn. bd. Cerritos Valley Bank Norwalk 1984-; apptd. President's Commn. for Study of Ethical Problems in Medicine and Biomed. & Behav. Research 1982; mem: Am. Acad. Family Phys. (charter fellow), Bell CofC (pres. 1973-74), Masons; mil: major USAF 1942-46 USAFR 1946 —, chief of med. Shepard AFB Tex., Korean War 1949-51, Bronze Star, Purple Heart; Greek Orthodox; rec: tennis, sports. Res: 15970 Carmenia Whittier 90603 Ofc: 5101 E Florence Blvd Bell 90201

TOMEI, JOEL ALAN, architect; b. May 11, 1941, San Mateo; s. Joseph Ambrose and Grace Leona (Nunes) T.; m. Patricia Hayden Brown, July 12, 1964; children: Amanda H. b. 1978, Elizabeth Y. b. 1983; edn: AA, Santa Rosa Jr. Coll. 1961; B.Arch., UC Berkeley 1966; M.Arch. 1967; M. City Plnng., Harvard Univ. 1973; Reg. Architect, Calif. 1970, Ill.; Mass.; Nat. Council of Registration Bds. (NCARB) Cert. Career: Skidmore, Owings & Merril, Architects/ Engineers, 1967-78; designer job captain, Chicago 1967-70; urban designer, Boston, Mass. 1971-4; urban designer, San Francisco, and Tehran 1974-8; Hope Cons. Gp., Arch./ Engrs., San Francisco 1979 —; proj. mgr. 1979; v.p./ proj. mgr. 1980; v.p./ principal architect 1983 —; steering com. chmn. Skidmore, Owings & Merrill 1976; design jury critic UC Berkeley 1975; awards: Mellon Scholarship, Harvard Univ. 1972; 28th annual Progressive Architecture Design Awd. 1981; AIP Awd., Republic Newspaper Plant, Columbus, Ind. 1980; mem: Harvard Club SF; Am. Inst. of Planners (AIP) 1974; San Francisco Planning and Urban Research; S.F. Market Street Proj.; design team mem: Sears Tower, Chgo. 1968; US Embassy in Moscow 1977; Bandar Shapour New Town, Iran 1975; Yanbu New Town in Saudi Arabia 1976; Saudi Arabian Naval Acad., Jeddah, 1981; Democrat; Episcopal; rec: photog., film making, gardening. Res: 167 20th Ave San Francisco 94121 Ofc: Hope Consulting Group, 562 Mission St San Francisco 94105

TOMMEY, RICHARD JOSEPH, librarian; b. June 9, 1924, Carnegie, Penn.; s. Michael Richard and Agnes Rita (Kaminski) T.; m. Marie Antonia Wiedenbauer, June 19, 1949; children: Ann Marie, Stephen Richard; edn: PhB, Loyola Coll. 1949; MS, Catholic Univ. Am. 1951. Career: young adult librarian Enoch Pratt Inst., Baltimore, Md. 1949-50; interlibrary loan John K. Mullen Library, Catholic Univ. of Am., Wash. 1950-51; reference librarian CIA, Wash. 1951-57; librarian Olin Mathieson Co., New Haven, Conn. 1957-60, GA Technologies Inc. (fmrly. Gen. Atomic Co.), San Diego 1960–; instr. San Diego Community Coll. Evening Coll. 1977–; mem: Spl. Libraries Assn. (chpt. pres. 1964-65), San Diego Library Metro, Nat. Mgmt. Assn., GA Technologies Mgmt. Club; mil: US Army 1943-46. Res: 6073 Avenida Chamnez La Jolla 92037 Ofc: 10955 John Jay Hopkins Dr. La Jolla 92037

TONASCIA, EUGENE SILVIO, naval aviator, business owner; b. Mar. 23, 1925, San Francisco; s. Silvio N. and Marie Jeanne (Escalle) T.; m. Barbara, Aug. 16, 1946; children: Sharon b. 1950, Michele b. 1952, Bruce b. 1954; edn: Carroll Coll. 1942-43, St. Olaf Coll. 1943044, St. Marys Coll. 1944, Univ. Okla. 1945; desig: Naval Aviator (1946). Career: owner/opr. Tonascia's Market (estab. by father in 1916), Yountville until 1983, ret.; active in civic affairs, num. coms.; clubs: Native Sons, Sons of Italy; publ: Peace of Mind; mil: lt. cmdr. US Navy; Republican; Catholic; rec: gardening, travel, golf. Address: 263 South Seymour Napa 94559

TONELLO-STUART, ENRICA M., political economist; b. Dec. 20, 1926, Monza, Italy, Nat. 1950; d. Alessandro P. and Maddalena Maria (Marangoni) Tonello; m. Charles L. Stuart, Feb. 14, 1975; edn: BA, UNiv. of Colo. 1961; MA, Claremont Grad. Sch. 1966; PhD, 1971; Dept. of Edn.; Dept. of Ins. Career: 1947-63: Ofcr. Wife USAF, Red Cross Gray Lady ; base coord. Veteran Admin.; dir. Family Asst. Svc. Tactical Air Command, Langley ; sales mgr. Metropolitan Lifeu Ins. Co. 1974-79; pres. E.T.S. Research & Devel. Inc. 1977–; dir. Internat. Studies Prgm. Union Univ. WUM-KOSE Found. 1975–; L.A. and Tokoyo publisher and ed. Tomorrow Outline 1963–; prof. Union Univ.; sys. analyst Economic and Political Risk Mgmt.; awards: Red Cross Svc. Awd.; VA Volunteer and Air Force vol. svc. awds. 1950-55; Pi Sigma Alpha; WUM-KOSE Leadership and Svc. Awd.; mem: Corp. Planners Assn. (treas. 1974-9); World Future Soc. (pres. 1974-); Planng. Exec. Inst. 1975-8; L.A. CofC 1978-; Zonta Internat. (ch. internat. com. South Bay Club); Investigative Reporters & Editors; S.F. & L.A. Press Clubs; Palos Verdes Womens Club; Patrons of Ital. Culture; bd. dirs. Caesarea World Monument; L.A. World Affairs Council; US- China Journalists Fellowship Assn. (founder, intern dir.); works: A Plan for a World Community 1963; Planning the World Community 1971; A Proposal for the Reorgn. of the U.N. 1966; The Role of the Multinationals in the Emerging Globalism 1977; Catholic; rec: travel, research, writing. Address: 80 Narcissa Dr Rancho Palos Verdes 90274

TONEY, CHARLES FREDERICK, distribution co. executive; b. July 7, 1938, Commerce, Ga.; s. Charles Wilson and Eva Zeta (Hardy) T.; m. Eleanor Haynes, Dec. 29, 1961; children: Catherine, Fred, Jr.; edn: BA, Mercer Univ. Macon, Ga. 1963. Career: joined McKesson Drug Co. Macon, Ga. 1963, dist. sales mgr. Jacksonville, Fla. 1967-77, v.p. div. mgr. Jacksonville 1971-73, regl. svcs. sales mgr. Atlanta 1973-78, v.p. retail svcs. San Francisco 1978-81; pres. Skaggs-Stone S.F. 1981-84; senior v.p. sales & mdsg. McKesson Drug S.F. 1984–; mem: Nat. Wholesale Druggist Assn. (sales mgmt. com. 1971-72), Sigma Alpha Epsilon, Crow Canyon CC; works: various promotional materials and articles 1979-; Republican; Methodist; rec: golf, travel. Res: 478 El Capitan Dr Danville 94526 Ofc: McKesson Corp. One Post St Ste 1200 San Francisco 94104

TONEY, RAYMOND MERVIN, construction co. executive, real estate broker; b. Mar. 1, 1929, San Francisco; s. Wm. James and Thelma Francis (Lee) T.; m. Barbara Mack, June 26, 1955; children: Brian b. 1957, Erin b. 1960; edn: stu. Coll. of San Mateo 1949; spl. courses, West Valley Coll. 1978; Calif. lic. Real Estate Broker 1979. Career: acct. exec. Advt. Dept. San Francisco Examiner 1952-63; vice pres. sales & mktg. Duc & Elliot Builders 1963-70; owner R.M. Toney & Associates, Marketing 1970-71; v.p. mktg. U.S. Financial West 1971-72; dir. sales & mktg. American Housing Guild 1972-73, Barratt Homes 1974-81, Davidon Homes 1981-84, returned to Barratt American, 1984–; owner Raymond M. Toney, Real Estate; mem. Sales & Marketing Council of Nat. Assn. of Homebuilders; mem. West Valley Light Opera Assn. (choreographer, dir., dancer); recipient theatrical awards, Inner City Circle, 1975; author/composer: Delta Centauri (musical comedy) produced by C.A.S.T. (1983); other musical works; mil: US Army 1949-51; Democrat; Prot.; rec: community theater. Res: 33 Albatross Ct Campbell 95008 Ofc: Barratt NorCalif, 3150 Almaden Expwy San Jose 95118

TORANTO, TERRY J., psychiatrist; b. July 25, 1943, Birmingham, Ala.; s. Al and Roslyn (Bierman) T.; m. Marianne Poulos, May 4, 1985; edn: Ohio State Univ. 1961-62; BS, Univ. of Ala. 1965; MD, Univ. Ala. Birmingham 1969. Career: intern Herrick Meml. Hosp. 1971; resident Napa State Hosp. 1971-74; staff phys. Kaiser Permanente Med. Clin. 1972-78; staff psychiatrist Contra Costa Co. Med. Svcs. 1975–; psychiat. cons. Spectrum Ctr. for Educational & Behavioral Devel. Inc. 1983–; bd. dirs. Phoenix Programs Inc. 1983-; coord. psychiat. lectures Contra Costa Co. Fam. Prac. Residency 1980-84; mem: CMA, Alameda Contra Costa Med. Assn., East Bay P.S.R.O., Contra Costa Co. Mental Health Assn. (1979-82); Jewish; rec: sailing, motorcycling. Ofc: Contra Costa Therapy Inst. 2476 Pacheco St Concord 94520

TORCHIA, JEFFREY LYNN, chiropractor; b. June 17, 1953, Woodland; s. Frank and Betty G. (Brannen) T.; m. Janice, Aug. 1; children: Melissa Nicole b. 1980, Marsenne Elizabeth b. 1984; edn: AA, Indian Valley Coll. 1980; DC, summa cum laude, Life Chiropractic Coll. West 1984; Calif. lic. DC, Xray supvr./tnr., 1985. Career: apprentice, journeyman rigger Mare Island Naval Shipyard, 1971-74; rigging and indsl. structural insp., and instr. indsl. injury prevention, 1975-76; chiropractic preceptorship with C.M. Rockwell, DC, 1984; chiropractor, splst. indsl. injury of spine and extremities, Rockwell Chiropractic Inc., Redwood City 1985–; cons. on injury prevention and ergonomics, var. industries 1984-85; honors: senior intern award for clin. excellence (1984); mem: Internat. Chiro. Assn., Am. Chiro. Assn., Calif. Chiro. Assn., Beyond War Found., Tri City Underwater Rescue Team, Gonstead Clin. Study Soc.; works: Best in show award- water color paintings, 1st place- pencil, hon. mention- acrylics, Solano Co. Fair, Dixon (1970); Democrat; Protestant; rec: scuba, organic gardening, bicycle racing. Ofc: Rockwell Chiropractic Inc. 950 Woodside Rd Ste 1 Redwood City 94061

TORNSTROM, ROBERT ERNEST, lawyer, oil company executive; b. Jan. 17, 1946, St. Paul, Minn.; s. Clifford H. and Janet H (Hale) T.; m. Betty Jane Hermann, 1978; children: Carter Hale b. 1981, Gunn Drew b. 1983, Katherine b. 1986; edn: BA, Univ. of Colo. 1968, JD, 1974. Career: div. counsel Internat. div. Union Oil Co. of Calif., Los Angeles 197478; mng. counsel Occidental Exploration & Prodn. Co., Bakersfield 1978-85; v.p., assoc. gen. counsel Occidental Internat. Exploration & Prodn. Co., Bakersfield 1985–; honors: Merit Scholarship, Honors Pgm., pres. Internat. & Comparative Law Soc., Univ. of Colo. 1971-74; Am. Jurisprudence Award 1974; Jessup Internat. Moot Ct. Regl. Comp.; Eagle Scout, BSA; mem: Am. and Calif. Bar Assns., Am. Soc. of Internat. Law, Am. Corp. Counsel Assn., Soc. of Mayflower Descendants, Superior Stu. Pgm. Univ. of Colo. Coll. of Engring., mil: capt. US Army 1968-71, Bronze Star, Vietnam; Republican; Episcopal; rec: skiing, tennis, golf. Res: 14812 Sunnybank Ave. Bakersfield 93312 Ofc: Occidental Internat. Expl. & Prodn. Co., 5000 Stockdale Hwy. Bakersfield 93309

TORRES, JOHN ANTHONY, latent print examiner; b. Mar. 11, 1949, Detroit, Mich.; s. Anthony and Winifred Grace (Brock) T.; m. Deborah L., July 19, 1968; children: Shay Dawn b. 1970, Amanda Marie b. 1973, Rhiannon Renee b. 1977; edn: Macomb County Comm. Coll., Mich. 1967-70; Famous Photogs. Sch., Westport, Conn. 1971-72; Inst. of Applied Sci., Chgo. 1972-73; FBI Fingerprint Courses 1972; BA, Nat. Univ., San Diego 1986; other courses in photog., supervisory devel.; Certified Latent Print Examiner, Internat. Assn. for Identification 1984. Career: identification techn. Warren Police Dept., Mich. 11 yrs.; currently lead latent print examiner San Diego Police Dept. Crime Lab.; photog. tng. ofcr. Warren Police Dept. 1975-82; instr. fingerprinting Dept. of Defense, San Diego 1984-, fingerprint sci. Grossmont Coll. 1986-; honors: Commendns., San Diego Police Dept. (six, 1983-86); mem: Internat. Assn. for Identification, Calif. Div. IAI, Mich.-Ontario Identification Assn., Canadian Identification Soc., Fingerprint Soc. of Great Britain; research: computerization of fingerprints; mil: sp4 US Army 1970-71; Democrat (fmr. delegate); Catholic; rec: baseball, fingerprint sci. historian. Res: 2924 Caminito Niguel San Diego 92117 Ofc: San Diego Police Dept. 801 W Market St MS 725 San Diego 92101

TOW, JEAN RUNYON, advertising agency president; b. Mar. 6, 1927, Concordia, Kans.; d. Brutus Kerr and Rowena (Thornburg) Hamilton; m. 2d Philip S. Tow, Mar. 5, 1980; children: Stephen Hamilton Runyon b. 1950, Elizabeth Runyon (Mulligan) b. 1955; edn: BA, Univ. Calif. 1949. Career: (past) prin. Runyon, Inc., Dannenfelsor, Runyon, Craig, Inc.; current, pres. Runyon Saltzman, Inc. (advt., pub. rels.), Sacramento; recipient Business Woman of the Year, 1984, CofC; bd. mem.: Stanford Home, KXPR (pub. broadcast), Sacto Regional Theatre, Tree Foundation. Catholic; rec: tennis, piano. Res: 6684 Swensen Way Sacramento 95831 Ofc: Runyon Saltzman 2503 K St Sacramento 95816

TOW, MARC RAYMOND, lawyer, real estate investor; b. Jan. 15, 1931, NY, NY; s. Benjamin and Stephanie Irene T.; m. Joana, Mar. 1976; children: David Andrew b. 1981, Stephen Michael b. 1986; edn: BA sociol., anthropol., State Univ. NY 1973; JD, Western State Univ. 1975; real estate broker Calif. Career: mng. ptnr. Marc & Tow 1978-84; dir., v.p. UTN Corp. 1984-85; v.p. Continental Pacific Ents. 1984-85; Brookstone Realty Advisors 1985–; instr. Knowledge Bank Univ., Calif. State Univ.; mem: Calif., Orange County Bar Assns., Urban Land Inst., Internat. Council Shopping Ctrs., Bldg. Ind. Assn., Internat. Assn. Financial Planners, Nat. Assn. Real Estate Investment Trusts, Democratic Found., County Club, Balboa Bay Club, Univ. Athletic Club; Democrat; Jewish; rec: bicycling, racquetball, tennis, arts. Ofc: Brookstone Realty Advisors 3345 Newport Blvd Ste 213 Newport Beach 92663

TOW, PHILIP SAMUEL, chemical engineer; b. Chicago, Ill.; s. James O. and Jeanne M. (Caburet) T.; m. Lois Rogers 1945-78; Jean Runyon, Mar. 5, 1980; children: Marjorie b. 1948, Bruce b. 1952, Douglas b. 1954, Daniel b. 1960; edn: BA, UCLA 1943; profl. engr. in chem. engring., State of Calif. 1959. Career: var. positions Los Angeles Co. Air Pollution Control Dist. 1948-60; Chief Air Pollution Control Sacramento Co. 1960-78; semi- retired; mem. Calif. Bd. of Registration for Profl. Engrs. 1981- (pres. 1985-); mem: AAAS, Air Pollution Control Assn.; Sacramento Opera Assn.; consultant; author: techl. arts. on air pollution control; var. freelance political arts.; mil: Col., USAR active 1945-6, meritorious svc. medal; Democrat; rec: travel. Address: 6684 Swenson Way Sacramento 95831

TOWERS, BERNARD LEONARD, medical educator; b. Aug. 20, 1922, Preston, Eng.; s. Thomas Francis and Isabella Ellen (Dobson) T.; m. Helen Davies; m. 2d. Carole Lieberman; children: Marianne b. 1952, Celia b. 1953, Julie b. 1956, Tiffany b. 1981; edn: MA, Univ. of Cambridge 1954; MB, ChB, Univ. of Liverpool 1947; physician, Calif. 1976. Career: house surgeon Royal Infirmary, Liverpool 1947; lectr. Univ. of Bristol 1949-50, Univ. of Wales 1950-54, Cambridge Univ. 1954-70; Fellow, Jesus Coll. 1957-70, Steward 1961-64, tutor

1964-69, dir. med. studies 1964-70; prof. pediatrics UCLA 1971-81, prof. of anatomy 1971–, prof. psychiatry 1983–; convenor, moderator of Medicine & Society Forum 1974-; co-dir. Pgm. in Med., Law and Human Values 1977-84; honors: NIH grantee 1974-78; Nat. Endowment Humanities grantee 1977-82; Fellow Cambridge Philos. Soc., Royal Soc. of Med.; mem: British Soc. Hist. of Med., Soc. Health & Human Values (pres. 1977-78), Teilhard Assn., Anatomy Soc. of Gr. Britain, Western Assn. Physicians, Am. Assn. Study of Mental Imagery; author: Teilhard de Chardin, 1966; Naked Ape or Homo Sapiens?, 1969; Concerning Teilhard, 1969; arts. & chpts. on science and philosophy; mil: lt. capt. Royal Army Med. Corps; rec: walking, cycling, tennis. Ofc: UCLA Sch. of Medicine, Dept. of Anatomy, 73-235 CHS, Los Angeles 90024

TOWNES, CHARLES HARD, astrophysicist; b. July 28, 1915, Greenville, SC; s. Henry Keith and Ellen Sumter (Hard) T.; m. Frances H. Brown, May 4, 1941; children: Linda Lewis b. 1943, Ellen Scriven b. 1946, Carla Keith b. 1949, Holly Robinson b. 1952; edn: BA, BS, Furman Univ. 1935, MA, Duke Univ. 1937, PhD, Calif. Inst. Technol. 1939. Career: mem. tech. staff Bell Telephone Lab. 1939-47; assoc. prof. physics Columbia Univ. 1948-50, prof. 1950-61; exec. dir. Columbia Radiation Lab. 1950-52, chmn. physics dept. 1952-55; provost, prof. physics M.I.T. 1961-66, Inst. Prof. 1966-67; v.p., dir. research Inst. Def. Analyses Wash. DC 1959-61; univ. prof. physics UC Berkeley 1967–; bd. dirs: Gen. Motors, Perkin- Elmer, Carnegie Inst., Pacific Sch. of Religion; honors: Nobel Prize for Physics (1964), Earle K. Plyler Prize (1977), SC Hall of Fame (1977), Nat. Inventors Hall of Fame (1976), Niels Bohr Internat. Gold Medal (1979), Nat. Medal of Sci. (1982), Engring. & Sci. Hall of Fame (1983), L.W. Frohlich Award (1986); mem: Am. Physical Soc., Nat. Acad. Arts & Scis., Am. Phil. Soc., Am. Astron. Soc., The Royal Soc. of London, Pontifical Acad. of Scis. (Rome), President's Sci. Advis. Com. 1966-69 (vice chmn. 1967-69); chmn. Sci. & Tech. Advis. Com. for Manned Space Flight NASA 1964-69; inventor MASER, co-inventor LASER; research on nuclear and molecular structure, microwave and infrared astronomy; co-author Microwave Spectroscopy; Protestant; rec: natural history. Res: 1988 San Antonio Ave Berkeley 94707 Ofc: UC Berkeley Dept. of Physics Berkeley 94720

TOWNSEND, DONALD KEITH, psychologist/program specialist; b. Apr. 14, 1934, Frankfort, Kans.; s. Vincent Wade and Josie Bell (Ford) T.; m. Joyce Duncan, June 24, 1955; children: Lisa, b. 1956, Cheryl, b. 1958; edn: BA, CSU Stanislaus 1962; MSW, Univ. Utah 1965; D.Ed., Brigham Youn Univ. 1979; Lic. Clin. Social Worker 1968; Sch. Psychol. Credential 1975. Career: chief Div. Child Welfare Svcs, Stanislaus County Welfare Dept., Modesto 1958-68; school social worker and coordinator of community aides, Modesto City Schs., 1968-79; psychologist/ program splst. (Special Edn.), Ofc. of Merced County supt. of Schools, Merced 1979–; summer wk.: psychiat. social wkr Modesto St. Hosp. 1970, Stanislaus Co. Mental Health Clin. 1971, Emmanuel Mental Hlth Clin., Turlock 1972; instr. Chapman Coll. 1969-70, Modesto Jr. Coll. 1970-83; honors: Phi Kappa Phi, 1965; recipient Child Welfare Scholarships, State Dept. of Edn. study grants; mem: Calif. Assn. of Compensatory Edn. (pres. 1983-4); Calif. Council on Children & Youth (pres. No. Reg. 1973); Calif. Assn. of Pgm. Splst. (exec. com. 1983–); Citizens for Edn.; Calif. Curriculum Alliance (bd. 1981-2); mem. Christian Berets Adv. Com., Community Adv. Com. for Spl. Edn., Stanislaus Area Comm. Council (past pres.); publs: School Volunteers (booklet) 1975; Baptist; rec: hiking, camping, singing. Res: 3118 Mason Way Modesto 95355 Ofc of Merced County Supt. of Schools, 632 W. 13th St Merced 95340

TOWNSEND, JOHN SIMS, II, psychologist; b. June 1, 1952, Smithfield, N.C.; s. John Sims and Rebecca (Barnes) T.; edn: BA, No. Carolina State Univ. 1974; ThM, Dallas Theological Seminary 1980; MA, Biola Univ. 1982; PhD, 1984; lic. psychologist, Tenn.; reg. psychological asst., Calif. Career: unit dir. Lena Pope Children's Home, Ft. Worth, Tex. 1974-75; faculty, p.t., Rosemead SCh. of Psychology, Riola Univ., La Mirada 1981-82; pvt. practice, Alpha Counseling, El Toro 1982; staff counselor Community Bible Chapel, Richardson, Tex. 1982; psychology intern Memphis Clinical Psychology Internship Consortium, Memphis, Tenn. 1983-84; psychological asst. Fullerton Psychological Svcs., Fullerton 84–; mem: Am. Psychological Assn.; Western Psychological Assn.; Calif. Psychological ASsn.; publs: Whatever Happened to Neurosis?, Profl. Psychology: Research and Practice, 1983; Toward a Model of Spiritual Leadership Qualities, Journ. of Psychology and Theology, 1984; Republican; Protestant; rec: jogging, music. Ofc: Fullerton Psychological Services, 270 Laguna Rd., Ste. 220, Fullerton 92635

TOWNSEND, JOYCE ANN, language, speech and hearing specialist; b. June 3, 1938, Mansfield, Ark.; d. Thomas John and Dorothy Marie (Sanders) Duncan; m. Donald K. Townsend, June 24, 1955; children: Lisa Bell, b. 1956, Cheryl Wood, b. 1958; edn: BA Speech Pathol., CSU Stanislaus 1970, MA, 1975; Std. Teaching Cred., Restricted Spl. Edn.; Teaching Cred., Splst. (Learning Handicapped) 1981; lic: Speech Pathology lic., Calif.; Cert. of Clin. Competence in Sp. Pathol., Am. Sp. and Hearing Assn. 1978. Career: language, speech and hearing splst. Modesto City Schs. 1971–, dept. ch. 1982-; honors: Senior Traineeship Award 1969-70, Stanislaus County Chapter Council for Exceptional Children outstanding service award to DIS Therapist 1982; mem: Calif. Tchrs. Assn., Modesto Tchrs. Assn., Am., Calif. Speech Lang. and Hearing assns., Delta Kappa Gamma Soc. Internat. of Calif.; works: devel. inservice pgms. on Non-oral Communication for Physically Handicapped Individuals, 1981–, Title IV-C Grant (1981); Baptist; rec: hiking, travel. Res: 3118 Mason Way Modesto 95355 Ofc: Modesto City Schools 426 Locust Modesto 95351

TOY, BEN KERN, engineering operations executive; b. Feb. 10, 1948, Canton, China; nat. 1948; s. Doon Toy and Louise Y. (Lui) T.; m. Debi Lynn Aines, Aug. 18, 1973; children: Kelley b. 1975, Brigitte b. 1981; edn: Coll. of San Mateo 1966-68. Career: draftsman/designer Autek Systems Inc., 1967-75; partner Grandfood Market, 1975-79; supr. engring. services, Marathon Electronics Inc. 1979-83; deputy dir. hardware engring. Tak Automation Inc. 1983-, mgr. engrg. ops. 1984–; P.C. designer, pkging. designer, info./documentation cons. Res: 657 Edna Way San Mateo 94402 Ofc: Tak Automation, 868 Cowan Rd, Burlingame 94010

TRADER, HERBERT CLYDE, quality engineer; b. Dec. 15, 1936, Cortez, Colo.; s. William Freeman and Roberta Francis (Jones) T.; m. Gloria Eyre, Apr. 8, 1961; children: Jeffery b. 1963, Carla b. 1964, Todd b. 1967, Curtis b. 1969, Greg b. 1972; edn: AA math, Long Beach City Coll. 1957; BA math, CSU Long Beach 1959; Reg. Profl. Engr. (quality) Calif. 1977. Career: Rockwell Internat. 1959–, lead quality engr. responsible for design and implementation of automated systems, chmn. Corporate Supplier Quality Evaluation Com., chmn. Working Corrective Action Bd., supv. Receiving Inspection and High Reliability Screen, developed plans and was representative to Commuter Aided Design, Manufacturing and Test (CADMAT) Com., currently lead quality engr. GPS pgm.; instr. Orange Coast Coll. 1971-74; curriculum com. Fullerton Coll. 1972-74; mem: Am. Soc. Quality Control 1970-, Nat. Mgmt. Assn. 1977- (v.p. Boosters 1980-81); mil: USAF Reserve; Republican; L.D.S.; rec: lapidary, needlepoint, camping, fishing. Res: 24251 Twig St El Toro 92630 Ofc: Rockwell Internat. 3370 Miraloma Ave Anaheim

TRAN, DINH, research engineer; b. Jan. 16, 1948, Quangngai, Vietnam; s. Thien and Bung Thi (Che) T.; m. Hong-Hoa Le, 1968; children: Hung b. 1970, Ha b. 1972, Bao b. 1974, Hien b. 1976; edn: BS, Saigon Univ. 1971; BSEE, CSU Long Beach 1982. Career: high sch. tchr. 1971-75; mem. tech. staff TRW, Inc., Redondo Beach 1982–, silicon devices R&D engr. 1982-83, RF circuitry engr. 1983-84, electro-optic R&D engr. GaAs/AlGaAs and InP/InGaAs P/InGaAs Crystal Growth for High Power Semiconductor Laser and Photodetector 1982–; mem. IEEE; Buddist; rec: photog. Res: 9271 Coronet Ave Westminster 92683 Ofc: TRW Inc. 147/1393 One Space Park Redondo Beach 90278

TRAN, DUNG ANH, physician; b. Jan. 12, 1950, Saigon, Vietnam, nat. USA 1981; s. Khoe Van and Tram Thi (Nguyen) T.; m. Trang Truong, June 21, 1980; 1 son Derek b. 1982; edn: pre-med. and 5 yrs. medicine, Saigon Univ. 1969-75; MD, Univ. of Calif., Irvine 1979; certified Am. Board of Otolaryngology 1985. Career: intern and resident USC Medical Center 1979-84; pvt. practice otolaryngology in Orange County 1985–; awards: Am. Field Service Scholarship, senior yr. H.Sch. in US, 1967-68; mem. AMA, Orange County Med. Assn., Calif. Med. Assn., Am. Assn. of Otolaryngology, Head & Neck Surgery, USC Alumni Assn.; Republican; Buddhist; spl. interest: cosmetic surgery; rec: painting. Res: 11442 Baggetts, Garden Grove 92640

TRAN, HUAN SI, civil engineer; b. Oct. 28, 1931, Hue, Vietnam, nat. US citizen, 1981; s. Tieu Si and Tuu Thi (Ho) T.; m. Le Hong, Jan. 30, 1954; children: Chuong b. 1955; Hoanganh b. 1956, Duong b. 1957, Hong-Lien b. 1959, Hong-Phuc b. 1960, Hong-Thu b. 1962, Don b. 1968, Diana Diep b. 1972; edn: BS, civil engrg., Saigon Univ. 1954; registered civil engr. Calif. 1979. Career: jr. civil engr., ministry pub. works Hue, Vietnam 1954-55, asst. city engr. 1955-57; city engr. Danang, Hue, Binh Duong, Bienhoa 1957-65; hwy. dist. engr. Nhatrang 1965-75; civil-structural engr. Bechtel Power Co. S.F. 1976-78; transportation engr. Caltrans S.F. 1979–; mem: Profl. Engrs. in Calif. Govt. 1979-, Vietnamese Friendship Assn. S.F., PTA; publ: book, Elementary Reinforced Concrete (Vietnam 1964); Republican; Buddhist; rec: tennis. Res: 1700 Manor Circle El Cerrito 94530 Ofc: Caltrans 3333 California St San Francisco 94118

TRAN, OANH H., acupuncturist; b. May 15, 1930, Vietnam, nat. US cit. 1982; s. Luong Xuan and Nhung Cam T.; children: Dung b. 1951, Loan b. 1959, Tran b. 1961; edn: phys. therapy, New York 1965; acupuncture, Taiwan 1973, USA, 1983; herbology, Union Univ. 1985; soc. svc., Vietnam 1954; acupuncturist, UCLA Pain Mgmt. Ctr. Career: social worker ARVN 1953-63; phys. therapist (head) 1963-75; acupuncturist 1975–; teacher acupuncture points UCLA extension 1979; mem: Am. Coll. Chinese Traditional Med., Assn. for Research and Enlightenment; mil: lt 1c Vietnam Army, Gallantry Cross 2+, 14 others; Buddhist; rec: gardening, reading. Res: 1235 Granville Ave, No 6, W Los Angeles 90025 Ofc: UCLA 10833 Le Conte Ave, PMC, Los Angeles 90024

TRAN QUAN THAI (John Washington), acupuncturist, educator, entrepreneur; b. Jan. 4, 1940, VietNam, nat. March 16, 1984; s. Tinh Van Tran and Luom Thi Nguyen; m. Tran Thu Thi, Dec. 6, 1960; children: Thu Dieu Hien, b. 1963; Thu Mailan, b. 1965; Thai Thu Minh, b. 1965; Thai Tuan Kiet, b. 1967; Thai Bao Chau (Qui), b. 1970; Thai Kimkhoi, b. 1971; Thai Long, b. 1960; edn: BA, Faculty of Letters, Saigon Univ., BA, Faculty of Sci.; PhD in oriental med., 1986; desig: Cert. Acupuncturist, Dr. Traditional Chinese Medicine, Calif. Real Estate lic., City of Westminster bus. lic., lic. Astrologer. Career: past prof. of literature (Vietnamese) and sci. (biology), Vietnam; current: artist/writer (poems and prose); astrologer (I Ching); realtor Century 21, 1979-, investment counselor/ Million Dollar Club; owner Maxim Restaurant, Westminster 1980–; pres. Liberty World Inc. 1980–; mem. Vietnamese Chamber of Commerce/ Orange County (v.p. 1986), Petrus Truong Vinh-Ky High Sch. Assn. (pres. 1984); publs: book of poetry: Nu Cuoi Tho Ngan Nam (1983), editor/pub. weekly newspaper and mags. (1986-), novel in progress; Republican; Deist; rec: tennis, soccer, health club. Res: 9041 Greenville Ave Westminster 92683 Ofc: Liberty World Inc., Thai-Thien Co., 9455 Bolsa Ave, Ste. B, C, D, Westminster 92683

TRAN, THUAN DUC, engineer; b. Sept. 21, 1947, Hanoi, Vietnam; s. Kim Tinh and Thao Ton (Cong) T.; m. Lan Dao, June 17, 1978; chldren: Thai Duong b. 1981; Thac Duc b. 1982; edn: BS, Saigon Univ. Vietnam 1968; BSCE, Nat. Inst. of Tech. Vietnam 1970; Reg. Profl. Civil Engr., Calif. 1982; General Contractor 1983; Real Estate Broker 1984; Life Ins. Agent 1985. Career: facilities design engr. Shell Oil Co., Saigon, Vietnam 1971-75; cons. engr. Vietnam Oil Co., Hochiminh City, Vietnam 1975-80; residential design engr. Cal Engineers, Los angeles 1982-84; transp. engr. Caltrans, San Francisco 1984–; mgr., owner David Tran & Assoc., Architects, Engrs., Contractors 1984–; honors: Award Cert., Internat. Com. of the Red Cross 1981; mem: Profl. Engrs. In Calif. Govt., Am. Soc. of Civil Engrs., Vietnamese Civil Engrs. Assn.; Buddhist; rec: music. Res: 22645 Fourth St. Hayward 94541

TRATNER, JOAN, (Jonna Lipchitz Tratner), artist, lyricist, composer, publisher, producer; b. Mar. 3, 1924, Akron, Ohio; d. Hymen and Rose C. (Zimmerman) Lipchitz; m. David Louis Tratner, June 13, 1943; children: Sharon Tobi (Schultz) b. 1947, Michael Allen b. 1949; edn: Chouinard Art Inst. 1957, Otis Art Inst. 1978, music stu. Calif. Inst. of Arts 1958-68, UCLA 1958, 81, LA City Coll. 1968-69, pvt. study w/ Kero Antoyan, Richards Rubin, Alex Villumsons, Sue Serisawa. Career: pres. Janco Music Inc.; painting series: Painting to Music (1968), Painting Pure Music (1973-77), Pure Music with Line (1975-76), Many Moods of a Woman (1977-78), Pure Music Series (1986); recording music 1982-86, prod., lyricist albums on different fields of music: Hatian Rock Fusion, R & B, Country, Country Swing, Pop Rock, Crossover Rock Reggea (ASCAP Panel popular award 1986/87), Mor/R & B for 1986; pub. 5 musicals: Trilby, Gold Fever, D.O.M., All Right God, An American Tradition (1983-86), two musicals in process (1986); author 5 books on world tour "Artwords & Bookworks" (1978-); exhibs: Cowie Gallery, Martin Janis Gal., Raymond Burr Gal., Palm Springs Mus., Long Beach Mus., LA City Hall Tower, Hong Kong Exhib., also Rome and Barcelona; guest artist 1961 Westside Jewish Comm. Ctr., Women Painters of the West, LAICA; ASCAP Panel Popular Award (1986-87); mem. NARAS, ASCAP, Acad. of Country Music, Song Writers Guild, Nat. Assn. of Song Writers, Alumni Cal Arts (first exhibit 1986), Alumni UCLA, LAICA, The Dramatist Guild, Am. Film Inst., Women Painters of the West; Democrat; Jewish. Res: 3556 Charleston Way Hollywood 90068 Ofc: Janco Music Inc POB 135 Hollywood 90078

TRAUTSCH, ROLF ALBERT, university administrator, financial planner; . March 30, 1936, Kiel, Ger., nat. US cit. 1960; s. Artur Hugo and Gertraud (Reichert) T.; m. Darleen Mary Bird, June 15, 1969; children: Russell Dale b. 1960, Bryan Rolf b. 1971, Tara Christel b. 1974; edn: BA, San Francisco State Univ. 1964, MA, 1969; PhD, Univ. of Denver 1976; Cert. Fin. Plnnr., Coll. of Fin. Plnng. 1985. Career: academic affairs staff ofcr. USAF Acad., Colo. 1969-76; USAF liaison ofcr. to German Air Force Acad., Munich, Ger. 1976-80; deputy dir. tng. devel. Defense Language Inst., Monterey 1980-84, acting dean instrn. 1983-84; fin. plnng., Carmel 1984–; resident dean Monterey and Central Calif. Golden Gate Univ. 1986–; assoc. prof. USAF Acad. 1973-76; vis. prof. Univ. of Munich, Ger.; internat. lectr.; fin. advr. Clocktower Fin. Adv. Group, Christopher Weil & Co., Carmel; honors: scholarships for all academic degrees; German Sports Achiev. Gold Medal; mem: Pi Sigma Alpha, Internat. Assn. of Fins. Plnnrs., Kiwanis of Monterey, Toro Park Homeowners Assn.; mil: lt. col. USAF, Defense Meritorious Svc., Bronze Star; Republican; rec: jogging, tennis, travel. Ofc: Golden Gate Univ., 550 Camino El Stero Monterey 93940 and Clock Tower Fin. Adv. Group, 100 Clocktower Pl. Ste. 220, P.O. Box 22130 Carmel 93922

TRAVERS, WILLIAM BRAILSFORD, geologist, oil co. executive, educator; b. June 13, 1934, Long Bech; s. William J. and Beatrice Louise (Brailsford) T.; m. Joanne Albrecht, Jan. 4, 1958; children: William Albrecht b. 1962, Richard Brailsford b. 1964, Daniel Albrecht b. 1966; edn: BS, Stanford Univ. 1956, MS, 1959; PhD, Princeton 1971; Reg. Petroleum Geologist, Calif. (1970), Am. Inst. of Profl. Geologists (1976). Career: geologist Standard Oil Co. 1959-61; chief geologist Santa Fe Internat. 1961-67; vice pres. Anacapa Oil Co. 1971–; prof. Cornell Univ. 1972–; trustee Sierra Madre Found.; honors: Sigma Xi (1970), Clark Award for tchg. (1984), Consiglio Nationale della Ricerche, Italy -research award (1971); mem: Fellow Geol. Soc. of Am., Fellow Geol. Assn. of Canada, Am. Assn. Petroleum Geologists (chmn. NE Sect. for Govt. Affairs); num. sci. publs.; mil: active duty US Army 1957, capt. Reserve 1957-67. Res: 421 Highland Rd Ithaca, N.Y. 14850 Ofc: Anacapa Oil Co. 671 Sand Point Rd Carpinteria 93013

TRAYNOR, J. MICHAEL, lawyer; b. Oct. 25, 1934, Oakland; s. Roger J. and Madeleine E. (Lackmann) T.; m. Shirley Williams, Feb. 11, 1956; children: Kathleen b. 1960, Elizabeth (Holder) b. 1962, Thomas b. 1964; edn: BA, UC Berkeley 1955, JD, Harvard Law Sch. 1960; admitted Calif. State Bar 1961. Career: dep. atty. general State of Calif., 1961-63, spl. counsel Calif. Senate Com. on Local Govt., 1963; atty., ptnr. Cooley, Godward, Castro, Huddleson & Tatum, San Francisco 1963–; lectr. (Remedies, Restitution, Legislation) UCB Boalt Hall 1981-; mem. Am. Law Inst. (Council 1985-), Bar Assn. of San Francisco (pres. 1973); civic: Sierra Club Legal Assistance Found. (treas.); contbr. to legal periodicals; mil: 1st lt. US Marine Corps 1955-57. Res: 3131 Eton Ave Berkeley 94705 Ofc: Cooley, Godward, Castro, Huddleson & Tatum, One Maritime Plaza, Ste 2000, San Francisco 94111

TREANOR, WALTER JOHN, physician; b. May 14, 1922, Clogher, Co. Tyrone, No. Ireland, nat. US cit. 1956; s. Hugh and Marion (de Vine) T.; m. Mary Stewart Kelso, Dec. 22, 1971; children: James Phillip, Wanden Patricia, Dona Maria, June Marion; edn: MD, Nat. Univ. of Ireland 1947; MS, Univ. Minn. 1952; Diplomate Am. Bd. Physical Medicine and Rehab. (1957), FACP, Am. Coll. Physicians (1971). Career: intern St. Vincent's Hosp., Dublin, Ireland 1947-48; research fellow Med. Research Council of Ireland 1948-50; fellow Mayo Found., Rochester, Minn. 1949-52; staff phys. Cleveland Clinic 1952-53; asst. service chief Letterman Army Hosp. 1953-55; chief Physical Medicine Svc., St. Mary's Hosp., San Francisco 1956-76; chief Rehab. Medicine, Washoe Med. Ctr., Reno, Nev. 1976-81; assoc. clin. prof. (1976-), emeritus prof. of medicine Univ. Nev. Sch. of Med. Scis. 1983; asst. clin. prof. med. UC San Francisco 1985-; cons: Letterman Gen. Hosp. (1959-), VA Hosp. (1959-), US Dept. HEW (1972-76), Calif. Dept. Public Health (1970-76); indep. med. examiner Workmens Comp. Appeals Bd., Calif. 1970-; dir. contg. edn. Brookwood Hosp., Santa Rosa 1983-; guest lectr. num. profl. socs.; honors: residents award W. Orthopaedic Assn. (1955), medical mem. Calif. State Bar Assn. Commn. on Malpractice (1976); mem: AMA, CMA, Am. Acad. Neurology, No. Calif. Rheumatism Assn. (pres. 1964), Am. Acad. Physical Medicine & Rehab., Internat. Med. Soc. of Paraplegia, S.F. Neurol. Soc. (sr.), Am. Assn. Electromyography and Electrodiagnosis, Alumni Assn. Mayo Found., Fellow Royal Soc. of Medicine/London (1973-); mil: capt. M.C., US Army 1953-55, cons. emeritus, Army Health Svc. Commend.; Republican; Anglican; rec: golf, hist. biographies. Res: 1360 Spring St Santa Rosa 95404 Ofc: 983 Sonoma Ave Santa Rosa 95404

TREDENT, JOHN MICHAEL, data distribution co. president; b. June 18, 1951, Ashtabula, Ohio; s. John Michael and Josephine Doris (Mucci) T.; m. Gloria Jean, April 5, 1980; children: Lindsay b. 1982, John III b. 1984; edn: BBA, Kent State Univ. 1973. Career: sales rep. Burroughs Corp. 1974-77; major acct. rep. Northern Telecom 1977-80; senior saels engr. Codex Motorola 1980-83; pres. Tredent Data Systems Inc. 1983–; chmn. bd. Tredent Data Systems Inc. 1985; Republican; Catholic; rec: golf, basketball, family. Ofc: 20335 Ventura Blvd. Ste. 208 Woodland Hills 91364

TREFFTZS, KENNETH LEWIS, corporate director, professor emeritus; b. Dec. 28, 1911, Sparta, Ill.; s. John Sydney and Dorothy Nora (Wright) T.; m. Ellen Ryniker, Aug. 7, 1937; children: Jeffrey b. 1942, Ellen b. 1945; edn: BS, Univ. of Ill. 1936, MS 1937, PhD 1939. Career: asst. economist Ill. Bankers Assn. 1937-39; instr. Carnegie Inst. of Tech. 1939-41; faculty mem., prof. (dept. hd. fin. and bus. econ.) Sch. of Business, USC 1941-82, vis. assoc. prof. UCLA 1948, Univ. of Wash. 1949-50, Pacific Coast Banking Sch. Seattle 1949; currently chmn. 20 funds in the American Capital Management group, Houston; Dir: Source Capital Inc., FPA Perennial Fund Inc., Fremont General Corp., FPA Capital Fund Inc., FPA New Income Fund Inc., past dir. MGM/UA Entertainment Co.; cons. Univ. of Karachi, Pakistan (under AID) 1962; recipient awards for tchg. excellence USC (1974-75), USC Associates (1977); mem: Am. Econ. Assn., Western Econ. Assn. (pres. 1955-56), Western Fin. Assn. (pres. 1965-66), Am. Fin. Assn. (v.p. 1946-48), Beta Gamma Sigma, Phi Kappa Psi, Rho Epsilon, Omicron Delta Epsilon, Lambda Alpha, Beta Alpha Psi, Alpha Kappa Psi; author two books, num. articles on banking and finance. Res: 11131 Briarcliff Dr San Diego 92131

TREVINO, CARLOS, international sales executive; b. Feb. 10, 1944, Goose-creek, Tex.; s. Pedro Villareal and Amalia Garcia T.; m. Judy, Apr. 2, 1966; children: Christopher Marc b. 1968, Lisa Michele b. 1970; edn: AA bus. law, Gavilan Coll. 1965; MBA, San Jose State Univ. 1968. Career: credit mgr., sales mgr., regl. adv. mgr., personnel dir., gen. mgr. Goodyear Tires & Rubber Co. 1970-76; financial cons. The Heritage Group 1976-77; internat. sales mgr. Benner- Nauman 1977-82; internat. sales mgr. Latin am. & Asia Acoustics Devel. Corp. 1982-86; owner Telefax, cons. internat. affairs in communs., import/ export; chmn. Housing Task Force City of Concord; mem. Planning Commn. Concord; honors: Internat. Salesman of the Year (1980), Salesman of the Year (1975); mem. CofC; Republican; Protestant; rec: stamps, golf. Res: 160 Hillview Dr Vacaville 95688 Ofc: Telefax Internat. 419 Mason St Ste 126 Vacaville 95688

TREYZON, YAKOV B., physician; b. Feb. 15, 1936, Riga, Latvia; s. Boris David and Khana (Rotbard) T.; m. Marina Friedlender; children: Boris b. 1964, Leo b. 1974, Daniel b. 1977; edn: MD cum laude, Riga Med. Inst. 1960; intern and resident in Internal Medicine, Los Angeles County USC Medical Ctr. 1980-83. Career: gen. practitioner Daugavpils City Hosp., USSR 1960-62; fellowship in metabolic diseases Inst. of Exptl. and Clin. Medicine, Acad. of Scis., Riga, USSR 1962-65; asst. chief Dept. Gastroenterology and Dietology, Latvian Republic Hosp., Riga 1965-79; pvt. practice Internal Medicine, Los Angeles 1984–, med.cons. State Calif. Dept. of Social Services 1984-, clin. instr. internal med. USC Sch. of Med. 1984-; mem. Sci. Assn. of Gastroenterologists (USSR), Latvian Sci. Assn. of Biochem., Latvian Sci. Assn. of Int. Med., American Coll. of Physicians; 8 publs. in med. jours.; Jewish; rec: music, travel. Ofc: Yakov B. Treyzon, MD 5901 W Olympic Blvd Ste 410 Los Angeles 90036

TRIOLA, C. RICHARD, restaurant owner; b. May 20, 1950, Brooklyn, NY; s. Charles Leonard and Anna (Cush) T.; edn: So. Conn. State Coll.; UC Los Angeles. Career: mgmt. Bateman Eichler Hill Richards 1970-74; stockbroker Stutro & Co. 1974-76, Oppenheimer & Co. 1976-78; real estate sales, investment counselor Mandarin Realty 1978-83; pres. CRT Investment Mgmt. Beverly Hills 1983-85; owner Wall St. Pizza (2 locations) 1985–; honors: youngest stockbroker in Calif. (21, 1971); mem: Rotary, Van Nuys CofC; Republican; Catholic. Res: 18411 Plummer St Northridge 91343 Ofc: Wall St. Pizza 20125 Vanowen St Canoga Park 91306

TRISCHLER, THOMAS JOSEPH, architect; b. Sept. 27, 1952, Pittsburgh, Pa.; s. Floyd David and Gloria Neldine (Fusting) T.; m. Jana Lee Abrams Aug. 24, 1985; edn: BS in arch., USC Sch. of Architecture 1974; Certified Broker Pgm., Western Real Estate Sch., 1981-86; Bus., Mgmt. & Mktg. certs., Orange

Coast Coll. Cert. Bus. Pgm., 1981-84; MBA/ Urban Land Econ., UCLA 1984-86; Reg. Arch., Calif. (1980); NCARB Cert., Nat. Council of Archtl. Registration Bds. (1982). Career: assoc. urban plnr./urban designer East Los Angeles Community Union, Plng. Dept., 1972-73; designer George Barnes Architect, Northridge 1973-74; urban plnr./urban designer Comm. Planning and Devel. Co., L.A. 1974-75, The Irvine Co., Newport Beach 1975; project mgr. Danielian Moon, Ilg and Assocs., 1975-77, Rolly Pulaski and Assocs., 1977-78; ofc. mgr. Brion Jeannette and Assocs., 1978; senior design arch. (major public and instnl. projects in Calif., Ariz.) Albert C. Martin and Assocs., 1978-80; sr. project design arch. & cadd. computer implementation mgr. WZMH Group Inc., Irvine, Los Angeles 1981-83; prin. Trischler Architecture, Newport Beach 1983-85, prin. CTA/Colvin Trischler Assocs., N.B. 1985—; awards: 1983 Award of Excellence, The Am. Library Assn. and AIA, also 1982 Merit Award, L.A. Chapter AIA (design- Thousand Oaks Library); 1983 Merit Award, Orange Co. Chapter AIA (The Atrium office bldg.); 1979 Distinguished Service Award, Albert C. Martin and Assocs.; honors: Calif. State Scholar 1970-74, Varsity Rugby Team (1973-74), Varsity Soccer Team (1970-74); mem: Am. Planning Assn., AIA (dir. Calif. Council 1980; mem. Nat. Assocs. Task Force 1980), AIA/Orange County Chpt. (exec. bd.; pres. 1980); USC General Alumni Assn.; rec: player Irvine Coast Rugby Football Club, skiing, pvt. pilot, photog. Res: 703 N. Shaffer St. Orange 92667 Ofc: CTA/Colvin Trischler Associates, 3345 Newport Blvd Ste 210, Newport Beach 92663

TRISCUIT, SHERMAN ANSON, engineering executive; b. Feb. 27, 1932, San Jose; s. Jess Anson and Ethel Claire (Higgenbotham) T.; m. Margaret, Nov. 25, 1953; children: Eric b. 1961, Jeannette b. 1967; edn: BS engring., Northrop Univ. 1974; MS, systems mgmt., USC 1980. Career: project engr. Kentron Internat., Edwards AFB, Calif. 1975-78, electronics engr. USAF Flight Test Ctr., Edwards AFB, 1978-86, chief Range Systems Section, Ridley Mission Control Ctr., Edwards AFB, 1986—; program mgr. SE/TA Contracts VERAC Corp.; recipient Air Force sustained superior performance award (1985); mem. IEEE 1973-74; civic: College Terrace Homeowners Assn. (dir.); mil: c.p.o. US Navy Submarine Service 1949-68; publs: sev. handbooks re computer security measures; Republican; Episcopal; rec: amateur radio, geology, archeology. Res: 43778 Sentry Ln Lancaster 93536 Ofc: 6521 Range Squadron Edwards AFB 93523-5000

TROMPETA, BELLAFLOR VILLANUEVA, pediatrician; b. Aug. 27, 1940, Tarlac, Philippines; d. Martin A. and Juanita N. (De Guzman) V.; m. Jess I. Trompeta (atty.), Aug. 12, 1978; 1 child, Andree b. 1979; edn: MD, Far Eastern Univ., Manila 1964; Diplomate Am. Board Pediatrics; Deplomate, Sub-Board of Neonatal-Perinatal Medicine. Career: rotating intern Niagara Falls (N.Y.) Meml. Hosp. 1966; resident ped. Wayne State Univ. Sch. of Med./ assoc. hosps., Detroit 1967-69; res. anesth. Hamilton (Ont., Can.) Civic Hosps. 1969-70; res., chief res. ped. St. Joseph's Hosp., Toronto 1970-72; fellow neonatol. Tulane Univ. Sch. Med., New Orleans, La. 1972-73; neonatologist and dir. ped. clinics Trumbull Meml. Hosp., Warren, Ohio 1974-76; dir. Neonatal Intensive Care Unit, Glendale (Ca.) Adventist Med. Ctr. 1976-77; fellow neonatal-perinatal medicine Ohio State Univ. Coll. Med. 1977; pvt. practice pediatrics, 1978—; mem. L.A. Pediatric Soc., Phil. Med. Soc. of So. Calif.; dir. Club Filipino-L.A.; Catholic. Ofc: 18433 Roscoe Blvd Ste 104 Northridge 91325

TROTTER, DAVID KEITH, certified public accountant; b. Jan. 11, 1956, Los Angeles; s. Warren G. and Lucille T.; m. Janel, Sept. 8, 1979; 1 dau. Chelsea b. 1982; edn: BS in bus. adm., CSU Los Angeles 1980; Calif. lic. CPA (1983), Real Estate Broker, Securities Broker, Ins. Agent. Career: acct., sr. auditor Arthur Young & Co., 1980-83; supvsg. sr. cons. Memorial Medical Center of Long Beach 1983-85; pres. David K. Trotter & Assocs, CPAs, Whittier 1985—; instr. comm. colls.; honors: Beta Gamma Sigma; mem. Toastmasters; Republican; Assem. of God; rec: sports, jogging. Res: 407 N Phillips Ave West Covina 91791 Ofc: David K. Trotter & Assocs 14831 E Whittier Blvd Ste 201 Whittier 90605

TROUT, BOBBI (EVELYN), aviatrix, real estate broker; b. Jan. 7, 1906, Greenup, Ill.; d. George Everett and Lola (Denman) Trout; edn: Roosevelt H. S., Los Angeles; archtl. stu. USC 1926; comml. photog. lic., Wiggins Trade Sch. 1938; Fuller's Flying Sch., 1928; Lic. Transport Pilot (5th woman in USA to obtain rating) 1928. Career: demonstration/test pilot Golden Eagle Aircraft Co., 1928-29, estab. Solo Endurance Flt. world record for women (12 hrs. 11 min.) ½/29; estab. 5 world records (incl. 1st woman to fly all night), Feb. 10-11, 1929; estab. new women's altitude record (15,200 ft.), 6/1/29; estab. world 1st refueling endurance record for women, 1½7-29/29; OX5 Aviation Pioneers Hall of Fame 1984; mem. Women's Air Reserve, 1931-41; inventor rivet sorting machines for defense indus., also estab. De Burring Service (2nd defense bus.) L.A. during WWII; real estate broker/securities and life ins. bus.; Palm Springs, 20 yrs.; flew in 1st (1929) Women's Air Derby, Santa Monica-Cleveland, dubbed The Powder Puff Derby by Will Rogers and flagged off Air Race Classic 1979 and the Angel Derby (50th ann. of 1st Women's Air Derby); currently, devel. num. inventions; book in progress. Honored as OX5 Woman of the Year 1976; charter mem. 99 Club; Republican; Rel. Sci.; rec: treas. hunting; travel; video taping old aviators for history. Res: POB 3303 Santa Clara 95055-3303

TROVER, DENIS WILLIAM, computer consultant; b. Feb. 1, 1945, Columbus, Ohio; s. Kenneth Harold and Virginia June (Denis) T.; m. Ellen Lloyd, June 12, 1971; 1 dau: Florence Emma, b. 1977; edn: BS, physics, Mich. State Univ. 1967; MBA, Coll. of William and Mary 1972; MS, Vassar Coll. 1973.

Career: optical physicist Internat. Business Machines, Fishkill, NY 1967-71; staff assoc. & sys. prgmr. Rockwell Int. Sci. Ctr., Thousand Oaks 1974-8; pres./ dir. Sonix Systems, Inc., Thousand Oaks 1978-83; computer cons. 1983—; mem: Conejo Future Found. 1975- (chmn. Energy Task Force 1980-1); bd. dirs. Vassar Club of So. Calif.; rec: astronomy, photog. Res: 11355 Presilla Rd Camarillo 93010 Ofc: 1107 East Thousand Oaks Blvd Thousand Oaks 91362

TROVER, ELLEN LLOYD, lawyer; b. Nov. 23, 1947, Richmond, Va.; d. Robert VanBuren and Hazel Pauline (Urban) Lloyd; m. Denis W. Trover, 1971; 1 dau: Florence, b. 1977; edn: AB, Vassar Coll. 1969; JD, Coll. of William and Mary 1972. Career: assoc. ed. Bancroft- Whitney 1973-4; sole practioner Ellen Lloyd Trover, Atty. at Law 1974-82; partner Trover & Fisher 1982—; dir. BURCO; mem: Com. Law Ofc. Lawout Design of Economics of Law Practice Section 1978-9, Word Processing Applications Com. 1981-4; Conejo Future Found. (trustee 1979-; secty. 1980-2, vice chair 1982-4, chair 1984-86); Hydro Help for the Handicapped, trustee/ exec. com. 1980-; Zonta Club of Conejo Valley (pres. 1978-9); Phi Alpha Delta Legal Frat.; Am. Bar Assn.; Calif. State Bar (com. on Post-Mortem Planning, ed. Handbooks of State Chronologies 1972-3); Virginia State Bar Assn.; Conejo Valley Bar Assn. (pres. 1979-80, dir. 1983-5); Ventura Co. Bar Assn. (client rels. com.); Democrat; Presbyterian. Res: 11355 Presilla Rd Camarillo 93010 Ofc: 1107 E Thousand Oaks Blvd 91362

TRUE, MARY, psychotherapist; b. Apr. 15, 1933, Fairplay, Mo.; d. Bert G. and Flora (Davis) True; m. John Lindblad, 1952, div. 1976; m. 2d. John Metcho, Feb. 26, 1984; children: Michael b. 1954, Lawrence b. 1960, Jennifer b. 1966; edn: UC Berkeley 1950-52; BA, Sonoma State Univ. 1972; MSW, CSU Sacto. 1975; LCSW; MFCC; ACSW; Cert. Hypnotherapist; Cert. Reichian Therapy. Career: State of Calif. Veterans Home 1975-79; Chrysalis Assoc. 1979-81; currently, pvt. practice psychotherapist & cons., True Assoc., Berkeley; spkr. & sem. pgms. on stress mgmt.; mem: Nat. Spkrs. Assn.; No. Calif. Hypnosis Soc.; Republican; Unity; rec: art- abstract expressionism, metaphysics. Res: 2 Skander Ct Pleasant Hill 94523 Ofc: True Associates, 1623A Martin Luther King Jr Way, Berkeley 94709

TRUESDELL, CHARLES LEWIS, business computer systems development; b. Feb. 4, 1928, Riverside, Calif.; s. Charles Milton and Helen Lenore (Scea) T.; m. Margaret Perling, May 4, 1957; children: Karen b. 1958, Carol b. 1959, Mark b. 1960; edn: AA gen. bus., cert. computer sci., Palomar Comm. Coll. 1978; BBA cand., Nat. Univ.; 1st class radio telephone lic., FCC 1957. Career: programmer Planning Research Corp. 1978-81; owner Truesdell Internat. Vista 1978—; programmer analyst System Devel. Corp. 1981-83; sys. analyst Triad Microsystems Inc. Oceanside 1985-86; prin. Proteus Technol. Inc. O'side 1985—; bd. dirs. Faith Gardens Retirement Village 1977—; honors: Minority Supplier of the Year (regl. and nat. So. Calif. Regl. Purchasing Council 1985); mem. San Diego Computer Soc. 1980-; mil: Lcdr. USN 1945-74, Am. Theatre, Asiatic-Pacific Theatre, WWII Victory, Good Conduct w/ 4 stars, Navy Unit Commdn.; Republican; Lutheran; rec: personal computer construction. Res: 1114 Alta Vista Dr Vista 92084 Ofc: Proteus Technology Inc. 2170 El Camino Real Ste 101 Oceanside 92054

TRUMAN, EDWARD CRANE, management consultant; b. Dec. 28, 1915, Des Moines, Iowa; sw. Wright Edward and Annie Louise (Cate) T.; m. Maxine Hemping, June 28, 1947; 1 son, Robert E.C. b. 1949; edn: undergrad music, journalism, Drake Univ. 1940; BA Eng., Immaculate Heart Coll. 1979; MA humanistic/ transpersonal psychol., Redlands Univ. 1981; grad. studies history, Eng., Cambridge Univ. Internat. Summer Sch. 1983, 85; Cert. in Labor Studies UCLA, IIR; Real Estate Broker Calif. Career: asst. pgm. dir. KSO-KRNT Des Moines, Iowa 1938-44; US Army Signal Corps 1944-46, cryptography and Armed Forces Radio Service (Hollywood and Honolulu staff); musician, leader, arranger ABC-TV 1952-55, NBC-TV 1955-60; freelance musician/ composer 1960—; asst. to pres. AFM Local 47 Hollywood 1969-77; owner Crane Publns. (BMI) 1951-; owner Truman Property Mgmt.; coord. Artasia/ Quest seminars on Career Ed. UCSB; bd. dirs: Musicians' Credit Union, Compass-America Prods., Independent Living Ctr., Calif. Video Com., UCSB Scholarship Com. of Gen. Affiliates; honors: Cert. of Svc. (HEW Dept. of Career Edn.), Svc. Award (Ch. of Rel. Sci. Bev. Hills), Cert. of Recogn. (Darrell McDaniel Ind. Living Ctr.); mem: ASCAP, Phi Mu Alpha Sinfonia, Drake Univ. So. Calif. Alumni Assn. (past pres.), Pacific Pioneer Broadcasters (charter), Acad. TV Arts & Scis. (awards com.), Fellowship of Christians in Arts, Media, Entertainment; works: var. musical compositions, scores for TV; mil: T/3 US Army Signal Corps 1944-46, Merit Award, AFRS, MID/PAC; Episcopal/ Anglican; rec: collecting, model trains, travel. Res: 1826 Jewett Dr Los Angeles 90046

TRUMMER, MAX JOSEPH, thoracic surgeon; b. Aug. 24, 1924, Bogota, Colombia; s. Ernest Max and Maria Moema (Fontana) T.; m. Esther Carterette, 1945; 1 son, Max J. Jr. b. 1951; edn: MD, Univ. of Ill. 1948; MS, Univ. of Penn. 1965. Career: USN Med. Corps. 1953-70, lt. j.g. to capt./chief thoracic surgery, Naval Hosp, San Diego 1967-70; chief thoracic surgery Olive View Hosp., Sylmar 1970-71; dir. Surgical Tchg. Svc., Mercy Hosp. & Med. Ctr., San Diego 1971-84; clin. prof. surgery USC 1969—; clin. prof. surgery UC San Diego 1971-84; bd. dirs. Western Health Plans Inc.; mem: Am. Bd. of Surgery, Am. Bd. of Thoracic Surgery, Fellow Am. Coll. of Surgeons, Am. Coll. of Chest Physicians, Am. Assn. for Thoracic Surgery, Soc. of Thoracic Surgeons, Am. Coll. of Cardiology, Western Thoracic Surgical Soc.; publs: Lung Transplantation, Charles Thomas Pub. 1968; research: lung transplantation; shock; Republican; rec: sailing. Res: 711 Cornish Dr. San Diego 92107 Ofc: 550 Washington Ste. 211 San Diego 92103

TRUNK, GARY, physician; b. July 12, 1941, Detroit, Mich.; edn: BA, UCLA 1963; MD, UC Irvine 1967. Career: med. dir. Liberty Care HMO, Ariz.; hon. staff Parkview Comm. Hosp. Riverside; mem: Am. Coll. of Physicians; AMA; Am. Acad. Med. Dirs.; listed Who's Who in Med. Ofc: 8777 E Via De Ventura Ste 200 Scottsdale, AZ 95258

TRUSSELL, ROBERT RHODES, consulting engineer; b. Jan. 8, 1945, National City; s. Robert Lloyd and Margaret (Kessing) T.; m. Elizabeth Shane, Nov. 28, 1969; children: Robert Shane b. 1974, Charles Bryan b. 1977; edn: BSCE, UC Berkeley 1966, MSCE, 1967, PhD sanitary engr., 1972; Reg. Profl. Engr. (civil engr. 1974, corrosion engr. 1977), Calif. Career: tchg. asst. UC Berkeley 1968; asst. prof. Sacto. State Coll. 1969; engr. Pomeroy, Johnston & Bailey Co., 1970-72; engr. JMM, Inc., Pasadena 1972, lab. dir. 1974, v.p. 1977, bd. dirs. 1979, v.p./mgr. of specialized services 1980—; editl. advis. bd. Environmental Science & Technology journal, mem. jt. editl. bd. Standard Methods; mem. Nat. Acad. of Sci. coms. on drinking water chemicals, 3rd party certification, comml. irrigation induced water quality problems; mem. US/Holland com. on organisms in drinking water, US/German com. on corrosion of drinking water pipe, US/USSR com. on drinking water problems; mem: Am. Chem. Soc., Water Pollution Control Fedn., Am. Water Works Assn., Sigma Xi, Am. Inst. Chem. Engrs., Internat. Water Supply Assn., Internat. Water Pollution Research Assn.; publs: 70+ tech. papers in water treatment and water quality; Democrat; Episcopal. Res: 3780 Canfield Rd Pasadena 91107 Ofc: J.M.M. Inc. 555 East Walnut St Pasadena 91101

TSAO, HENRY KAN, acupuncturist; b. Mar. 5, 1924, Yenchen, Kiangsu, China; s. Hsi Tsu and Shih (Chou) T.; m. Lily Yeh, Mar. 5, 1958; children: Teling b. 1958, Tehsin b. 1960, Teyun b. 1962, Telung b. 1964; edn: BA, Chungking Cheng Yang Coll., China 1949; Dr. of Oriental Med., San Francisco Acupuncture Coll. 1984; Cert. Acupuncturist, Calif. Career: research practice Joseph Chant's Clinic and Kuang Hua Hosp., Taiwan 1956-73; demonstration practice in Philippines, Indonesia, Thailand, Singapore, Vietnam, Hongkong, Japan, Hawaii, 1973-74; clin. practice in Canada, Springfield, Mass. and San Francisco, 1974-81, San Jose 1983   ; tchg. and practice in Central and So. Am., 1976-83; honors: Hon. Citizen of San Jose (7/15/84); mem: Calif. Acupuncture Alliance (bd. dir. 1985-), Calif. Cert. Acup. Assn.; Christian; travel. Res: 1109 Powell St San Francisco 94108 Ofc: 1201 Park Ave Ste 2 San Jose 95126

TSOU, ALICE CHING CHANG, medical social worker, senior assemblywoman; b. Dec. 3, 1914, Peking, China, nat. US cit. 1964; d. Shu-Sen and Tsaiching (Chao) Chang; m. Peter Chi-pan Tsou, Sr., Dec. 25, 1939; children: Peter, Jr. b. 1941, George b. 1943, Paul b. 1947; edn: BA, National Cheng-Chi Univ. 1938; MSW, Worden Sch. of Social Service, San Antonio, Tx. 1964; desig: ACSW, Acad. Certified Social Wkrs. (1964); Calif. Lic. Clin. Social Wkr. (1969), Lic. Nsg. Home Adminstr. (1976). Career: Career: div. chief of Nationalist Party Hdqtrs., China; political refugee, Taiwan 1949, vice prin. Taipei Second Girls High Sch., 1949-52; came to US, 1952; psychiatric social wkr. St. Louis Chronic Hosp., Mo. and San Antonio Adult Mental Health Clinic, Texas; sr. medical soc. wkr., supvr., psychiatric soc. wkr., div. chief County of Los Angeles Dept. of Adoptions and Health Services, 20 years; founder, exec. dir. Chinese-American Service Center, Inc. 1975-; apptd. by L.A. Mayor Bradley as adviser to the Council on Aging 1983-; elected state del. White House Conf. on Aging; elected senior assemblywoman (3 terms) rep. City of Los Angeles Seniors to Calif. Senior Legislature (1981-83, 83-85, 85-87); introduced the Elderly Abuse bill and the Nat. Health Plan bill (1983); Republican; Christian; rec: writing, gardening, public spkg. Address: Los Angeles 90026

TSZTOO, DAVID FONG, civil engineer; b. Oct. 13, 1952, Hollister, Calif.; s. John and Jean (Woo) T.; m. Evelyn, July 31, 1982; 1 dau. Michaela b. 1985; edn: BS transp. engrg., Cal. Poly. S.L.O. 1974; M.Engrg. (civil), UC Berkeley 1976; Reg. Profl. Engr. Calif. 1979. Career: field laborer Conlec Corp. Hollister, Calif. summer 1972, engr./dispatcher summer 1973; research asst. civ. engrg. dept. UC Berkeley 1975-76; jr. civil engr. Contra Costa County Public Works Dept. Martinez 1977-78, asst. civil engr. 1978-81, civil engr. III 1981-83; assoc. civil engr. Easy Bay Municipal Util. Dist. Oakland 1983—; honors: Fed. Design Achievement Award (Nat. Endowment for the Arts 1984), Phi Kappa Phi 1974, Tau Beta Phi 1973; mem: Am. Soc. Civil Engrs., Nat. Soc. Profl. Engrs. 1977-82, Western Council Engrs. 1977-82, Sing & Bring Children's Club (sponsor), Sun Country Homeowners (past v.p., maint. chmn.); publ: coauthor 3 papers and reports concerning earthquake energy absorbing devices for structures (1977-78); Baptist; rec: patio and landscape work. Ofc: East Bay Municipal Utility Dist. 2130 Adeline St Oakland 94623

TU, HOSHENG, biomedical engineer; b. Sept. 15, 1945, Tainan, Taiwan, nat. US cit. 1980; s. Min San and Chen Wu (Chen) T.; m. Lily, Aug. 19, 1972; 1 son, Steve b. 1984; edn: BS, Nat. Taiwan Univ. 1968; MS, Clarkson Coll. of Tech. 1972, PhD, Univ. of Cincinnati 1975; Biomedical Engring. Cert., UCI 1985; Reg. Prof. Engr., Calif. 1982. Career: senior engr. Sohio Research, Cleveland 1974-76; group leader UOP Process, Chicago 1976-80; senior engr. Occidental Research, Irvine 1980-82; prin. engr. UOP Fluid Systems, San Diego 1982-83; project mgr. American Bentley, Irvine 1985—; mem. Am. Inst. of Chem. Engrs.; works: 20 US patents and 23 foreign patents; mil: 2nd lt. Chinese Army 1969-70; Republican; Presbyterian.

TUCH, BARRY ALAN, physician; b. Apr. 8, 1948, Los Angeles; s. Benjamin E. and Shirley Lee (Hochman) T.; m. Suzanne, June 29, 1974; children: Brian b. 1979, Aaron b. 1983; edn: BS, UC San Francisco 1970, MD, 1973; Diplomate Am. Board Orthopedic Surgeons 1980. Career: surgical intern UC Irvine

1973-74; orthopedic resident UC San Francisco 1974-78; fellow arthritis surgery Rancho Los Amigos Hosp., Downey 1978; pvt. practice orthopedic surgeon, Encino 1979—; awards: UC Regents Scholar (1969); mem. Am. Acad. Orthopedic Surgeons, Los ANgeles County Med. Assn., Calif. Med. Assn.; contbr. articles med. journals; rec: Chinese cooking, woodworking, jogging. Ofc: 5363 Balboa Blvd Ste 546 Encino 91316

TUCKER, MALCOLM CORY, management consultant/financial planning exec.; b. Apr. 28, 1924, Little Rock, Ark.; s. Hugh Barclay and Lucy (Cory) T.; m. Dorothy Jean Skeeters, Aug. 3, 1946; children: Craig B., b. 1954, Lisa J., b. 1959; edn: AA, Pasadena Jr. Coll. 1948; BE(EE) USC 1950, Mgmt. Cert., 1968; Real Estate Cert., Santa Monica Coll. 1979; Coll. for Finl. Plnng., 1983-4; desig: R.E.C.I., Calif. Assn. Realtors 1979. Career: project engr./engring. section hd. Hycon Mfg. Co., Pasadena 1950-55; prog. mgr./mgr. Engineering Assoc. Missile Products, Pomona 1955-57; sales mgr. Cooper Devel. Corp., Monrovia 1957-59; Washington rep. Marquardt Corp., Wash DC 1959-60; dir. of mktg. Whittaker Corp., Los Angeles 1960-69; founder/v.p. HTL Industries, Pasadena 1969-70; finl. planner and founder/CEO Malcolm Tucker and Associates, Pacific Palisades 1970—; mem: Internat. Assn. of Finl. Plnnrs., Inst. of Certified Finl. Plnnrs., Nat. Assn. Personal Finl. Advisors, Nat. Assn. of Realtors, Calif. Assn. of Realtors (dir. 1983-4), Los Angeles Bd. of Realtors (ch.membership 1983-4); mem. Optimist Club of Pac. Palisades (dir. 1982-84), Navy League of US (life); mil: lt.jg USNR 1943-50; Republican; Presbyterian; rec: sailing, tennis, travel. Res: 1554 Palisades Dr Pacific Palisades 90272 Ofc: Malcolm Tucker and Associates 15219 Sunset Blvd, Ste 201, Pacific Palisades 90272

TUCKER, NELSON K., attorney service president; b. May 25, 1946, Fayette, Ala.; s. K. N. and Mary M. (Crary) T.; div.; children: Brent b. 1967, April b. 1969; edn: AA, L.A. Valley Coll. 1976; BA, CSU Northridge 1978. Career: exec. dir. Fair Housing Council, Van Nuys 1978-79; pres. Attorney Svcs. of So. Calif., Van Nuys 1979—, pres./CEO Nelson Investment Corp., 1984—, instr. The Learning Annnex (1985-), The Learning Annex (1985-), The Success Ctr. (1986-); honors: Outstanding Young Men in Am. (1977), Tau Alpha Epsilon (1977); club: Kiwanis (dir. 1985-, secty. Div. 25 1986-87); Republican; Rel. Sci.; rec: golf, scuba diving. Ofc: Attorney Services of So California 6203 Van Nuys Blvd Van Nuys 91335

TUCKER, WANDA HALL, newspaper editor; b. Feb. 6, 1921, Los Angeles; d. Frank Walliston and Hazel Gladys (Smith) Hall; m. Frank R. Tucker, Apr. 16, 1943; children: Frank Jr., b. 1945, Nancy (Baker), b. 1949; edn: AA, Citrus Coll. 1939. Career: reporter San Marino Tribune, 1937; Society editor Azusa Herald, 1939-42, Editor 1942-43; City editor San Marino Tribune, 1943-44; Correspondent, Los Angeles Times, 1937-44; Corresp., San Gabriel valley Tribune, 1952; editor Canyon City News, 1952-53; reporter Pasadena Star-News, 1953-73, city editor 1973-75, day managing editor and mng. editor 1975-83, senior mng. editor Pasadena Star-News, 1983-84; editor and assoc. pub. Foothill Inter-City Newspapers, 1984—; dir. internship pgm., Star-News, 1975-9, conductor Mini-Course in Journalism, 1983-4, mem. Star-News Spkrs. Bur. 1983-84; mem. journalism advis. com. Pasadena Comm. Coll., 1979-81, 84-; mem. Associated Press Mng. Editors Profl. Standards Com. 1984; honors: Proclamations and Resolutions, various cities and L.A. County during career; named Woman of Year, Pasadena Womens Civic League 1974, and Pasa. Chpt. NAACP, 1977; Woman of Achievement, Pasadena Comm. Coll. 1984; mem: Greater LA Press Club, Sigma Delta Chi; active in Soroptimist Club, Azusa PTA Council, Azusa Little League in 1940s; Republican; Prot.; rec: travel, gardening. Res: 2515 Woodlyn Rd Pasadena 91104 Ofc: Foothill Inter-City Newspapers, 10 N First Ave Arcadia 91006

TUCKERMAN, RICHARD J., lawyer; b. Nov. 6, 1931, Long Beach, NY; s. Edward and Jeannette (Cohen) T.; m. Belle L., Apr. 7, 1963; children: Mark b. 1964, Sara b. 1968; edn: BS, NYU 1952, LLB, UC Hastings, 1958, JD, 1968; Edn. degree, Univ. Calif. 1969; admitted to Calif. State Bar 1960. Career: tax atty. State of Calif., Dept. of Personel, Sacramento 1962-64; Deputy Public Defender, San Bernardino Co. 1964-66; atty. law firm Evans, Taves & Tuckerman, Ontario 1966-68, law firm Jones & Tuckerman, 1968-70; sr. partner law firm, Richard J. Tuckerman, Atty. at Law, 1970—; currently certified family law splst., trial atty.; vice pres. Bodymind Inc. (health retreat); mem: Am., Calif. Bar Assn., Calif. Trial Lawyers Assn.; mil: pfc US Army 1954-56, purch. agt. Presidio, SF; Republican; Jewish; rec: athletic & aerobic exercise, art collector, Mercedes Benz collector. Ofc: Tuckerman, Pittullo & Thompson, A Partnership of Profl. Corps., 1063 West Sixth St, Ste 101, Ontario 91762

TUGAW, WILLIAM JERALD, insurance broker; b. Oct. 18, 1950, Salt Lake City; s. Edward Anthony and Muriel Louise (Peterson) T.; m. Diane Tennant, Mar. 7, 1981; 1 son, Daniel b. 1985; edn: BS, Ariz. State Univ. 1973; fin. planning, Univ. So. Calif., Coll. Fin. Planning Denver 1984; Certified Financial Planner 1986. Career: loan ofcr. Bank of Calif. N.A., S.F. 1973-75; asst. v.p. Redwood Bank Napa, San Mateo 1975-80; asst. mgr. Calif. Canadian Bank Palo Alto 1980-82; ptnr. Sylvester, Schwartz & Tugaw Ins. Brokers Los Altos 1982—; lectr. Internat. Personnel Mgmt. Assn. western regl. conf. 1986, seminars 1985; honors: Hon. Mem. (Burlingame Jaycees 1985), Archon (ASU Interfrat. Council 1972), Crewman (ASU Delta Gamma Sor. 1972); mem: Inst. Cert. Financial Planners, No. Calif. Leadership Found. (founder, chmn. bd. 1985-), Calif. Jaycees (Order of the Tiger), San Carlos Jaycees (past pres.), Kiwanis; Republican; Methodist; rec: flying, skiing, golf. Res: 134 Hillcrest Rd San Carlos 94070 Ofc: 4966 El Camino Real Ste 200 Los Altos 94022

TULAC, JOHN WILLIAM, lawyer; b. Aug. 9, 1952, Los Angeles; s. Stanley Thomas and Dorothy Gregorine (Fischer) Tulacz; m. Elizabeth Ann Finsterbach, May 11, 1974; children: Megan b. 1983, Shawn Elyse b. 1985; edn: BS, honors, Calif. State Polytechnic Univ., Pomona 1974; JD, Loyola Law Sch., Los Angeles 1977; admitted Calif. State Bar 1977. Career: economic analyst Congressman Victor V. Veysey, 1974; law clerk, atty. assoc. Nahrwold & Kerr, Los Angeles 1976-78; atty. law office Tom G. Kontos, Los Angeles 1979-81; senior atty. law office John W. Tulac, Newport Beach 1981–; lectr. Cal Poly Pomona Sch. of Bus. 1979-; judge protem L.A. Municipal Ct. 1985-; arbitrator Orange County Fee Dispute Pgm.; dir. MERCI 1979-82; honors: distinguished alumnus, Sch. of Arts Cal Poly Pomona (1983), disting. alumnus Phi Kappa Phi, Cal Poly chpt. (1984); mem: Am. Bar Assn., Calif. State Bar (del. 1985 Conv.), Los Angeles County Bar Assn., Orange County Bar Assn., Phi Alpha Delta, Delta Sigma Pi, Sigma Phi Epsilon; Republican; Catholic. Ofc: 3700 Campus Dr Ste 107 Newport Beach 92660

TUNELL, GEORGE, professor emeritus; b. April 4, 1900, Chicago, Ill.; s. George Gerard and Caroline (Baum) T.; m. Ruth Philips, June 15, 1967; edn: BS, Harvard Engring. Sch. 1922; PhD, Harvard Grad. Sch. of Arts & Scis. 1930. Career: petrologist Geophysical Lab. Carnegie Instn. of Wash. 1925-45; acting assoc. prof. Calif. Inst. of Tech. 1946-47; assoc. prof., prof. UCLA 1947-62; prof. UC Riverside 1962-67; prof. emeritus geochemistry UC Santa Barbara 1968–; cons: Cerro de Pasco Copper Corp., NYC 1925; Hercules Powder Co., Wilmington, Del. 1943; Shell Devel. Co., Houston, Texas 1956; TRW Inc., Los Angeles 1970; Oak Ridge Nat. Lab. 1980; Coastal Mining Co., Maryland Hts., Mo. 1980; Homestake Mining Co., San Francisco 1980; honors: John Harvard Fellow, Harvard Grad. Sch. of Arts & Scis. 1924-25; Am. Men of Science 1944; Washington A. Roebling Gold Medal, Mineralogical Soc. of Am. 1973; Robert A. Welch Found. Lectr. 1977; Naval Ordnance Development Award 1947; mem: Fellow Geological Soc. of Am., Fellow Mineralogical Soc. of Am. (pres. 1950), Am. Crystallography Assn., Geochemical Soc. (pres. 1962-63), Geological Soc. of Wash. (pres. 1944), Mineralogical Assn. of Canada, Mineralogical Soc. of Gr. Britian, N.W. Mining Assn., Soc. of Economic Geologists, Societe Francaise de Mineralogie et de Cristallographie, Sigma Xi, Tau Beta Pi, Wash. Acad. of Scis.; author: Relations Between Intensive Thermodynamic Quantities and Their First Derivatives in a Binary System of One Phase, W.H. Freeman & Co., San Francisco 1960; sev. Carnegie Instn. of Wash. publs.; research: ordnance problem, Nat. Defense Research Com. and Ofc. of Sci. Research & Devel. 1941-45; mil: pvt. US Army 1918. Res: 4625 Via Gennita Santa Barbara 93111

TUNG, PAUL PING-YU, trading co. executive; b. Mar. 6, 1943, Xian, China, nat. US cit. 1978; s. Shou-Hsun and Yee-Shing (Pi) T.; m. Chiang-Ying Mei, Dec. 9, 1972; children: Yong-Jin b. 1975, Elsa b. 1983; edn: BS in engring., National Taiwan Univ. 1964; MS in engring., UC Los Angeles 1967, PhD engring., 1971, MBA, 1982. Career: mem. tech. staff Rockwell Internat., Los Angeles 1971-78, Jet Propulsion Lab., Pasadena 1978-81; pres. Sida Internat., L.A. 1979-80; v.p. mktg. Global Machinery Corp., Compton 1982-83; pres. Eastern Materials, Inc. Los Angeles 1983–; cons. Jet Propulsion Lab. 1983-; honors: Beta Gamma Sigma; mem: Wire Assn. Internat., Assn. of Iron & Steel Engrs., Am. Soc. for Metals, Am. Soc. for Testing & Mats., Chinese-Am. Assn. for Scientists and Engrs. of So. Calif. (chmn. tech. com. 1980); publs: chief editor book, Fracture & Failure: Analyses, Mechanisms, and Applications (1981); author book chpt. in Titanium Science and Technology (1973); rec: equestrian, sailing. Res: 1031 Camino Magenta Thousand Oaks 91360 Ofc: Eastern Materials, Inc. 6033 W Century Blvd 4th Flr Los Angeles 90045

TUNNEY, JOHN VARICK, developer, lawyer; b. June 26, 1934, NY, NY; s. Gene and Mary Josephine (Lauder) T.; m. Kathinka Osborne, Apr. 23, 1977; children: Edward, b. 1961; Mark, b. 964; Arianne, b. 1967, Tara b. 1982; edn: BA in anthropology, Yale Univ. 1956; JD, Univ. of Virginia 1959; Acad. of Internat. Law, The Hague. Career: practiced law, Cahill, Gordon, Reindell & Ohl, New York 1959-60; taught bus. law, Univ. of Calif. 1962-62; practiced law, Riverside, Calif. 1963-64; U.S. Representative, 38th Dist. Calif., 89-91st Congresses, 1965-71, U.S. Senator from Calif., 1971-77; ptnr. in law firm Manatt, Phelps, Rothenberg & Tunney 1977–; bd. chmn. Cloverleaf Group, Inc. 1981–; honors: Jurisprudence Award, Anti-Defamation League of B'Nai B'rith (Pacific Southwest Legal Div.) 1984; Chubb Fellow, Yale; bd. ov vis. Loyola Law Sch.; bd. dirs. Famous Amos Chocolate Chip Cookie Corp.; mem. ABA, Calif. Bar Assn., Lawyers Advisory Council, Constitutional Rights Found., Citizens Research Found., Nat. Advis. Council of Multiple Sclerosis Soc., Com. on Soviet Jewry; mil: capt. US Air Force 1959-60; Democrat; Roman Catholic; rec: reading, tennis, skiing, hiking, wind surfing. Ofc: 1801 Century Park East Ste 500 Los Angeles 90067

TURNBULL, GERROLD AUSTIN, advertising/public relations co. president; b. Sept. 21, 1945, Springfield, Mass.; s. Frank Paul and Cora Elizabeth (Ward) T.; edn: BA in Eng., Amherst Coll. 1967; MA in mktg., Univ. Sydney, Austr. 1968; desig: affil. Am. Soc. Interior Designers (ASID) 1986. Career: systems supr. Penn Central R.R. 1968-69; jr. v.p. communications Hapag Lloyd Steamship Line 1969-70; mktg. mgr. Integrated Container Corp., N. & S. Am., 1970-74; freelance writer 1974–, 4 novels pub. 1974-80; creative dir. Axtex Internat., N.Y.C. 1975-77; W. Coast ed. Embinder Publs., 1977-79; senior acct. exec. Ron Ortego & Assocs., 1977-80; Profl. Marketing Group, 1980-83; communs. splst./pres. Turnbull & Assocs., Beverly Hills 1983–; ed. Interior Design & Fashion sect. San Gabriel Valley Mag., 1985; instr. copywriting Otis Parsons Sch. of Contg. Edn. (1985-); cons. Design Center Antiques (1985-), Contempo Furniture (1984-), Somewhere In Time Corp. (1985-); honors: outstanding vol. Am. Cancer Soc. (1984), 1st Pl. Best Dressed in the West,

Mens Fashion Inst. (1983, 85); mem: Publicity Club of Los Angeles, Internat. Soc. Int. Designers, ASID, Nat. Home Fashions League (Outstanding Colleague Award 1985); civic: Pasadena Central Improve. Assn. (1984-, Centennial Com. media liason 1985-86), Mus. Contemp. Art (1985-), L.A. Philharmonic (patron), Am. Cancer Soc. (co-chmn. fundraising 1985, advis. bd.); publs: Star Trek Cat. (1977), Cooking as Therapy (1977), The American Man (1975), 18 Karat (1976), feature writer (16 arts., 2 cover stories) Architectural Digest 1977-82; feature profiles in L.A. Herald Examiner (1985), Gentlemens Qtly (1982, 83, 85); Republican; Roman Catholic; rec: travel, writing, art collector. Ofc: Turnbull & Assocs. 9348 Santa Monica Blvd Ste 101 Beverly Hills 90210

TURNER, BURNETT COBURN, architect and planning consultant; b. Dec. 3, 1902, Los Angeles; s. Harry Coburn and Marie Ada (Burnett) T.; m. Miriam Fechimer, Jan. 23, 1932; 1 son, Peter b. 1949; edn: BS engrg., Princeton Univ. 1925, CE, 1926; BS arch., Mass. Inst. Technol. 1928; Arch. NY 1932, Am. Inst. Planners 1952. Career: assoc. Horace W. Peaslee (arch.), Wash. DC 1928-30; lic. arch. Alfred Hopkins & Assocs., NY 1930-32; leader WPA Housing Survey, upper eastside NYC 1932-38; dir. Pub. Housing Exhib., arch.-engr., cons. arch. US Housing Authority, Wash. DC 1935-38; regl. tech. advisor USHA West Coast, San Francisco 1939-40; asst. dir. West Coast Ofc., Housing Div., Fed. Works Adminstrn. 1940-42; arch. and planning cons. pvt. practice, Los Angeles 1946–; pres., trustee Turner Oil Trust L.A. 1946-; chmn. Public Works Commn., Zoning Commn., Hist. Bldgs. Commn; arbitrator Am. Arbitration Assn. Soc. 1958–; dir. Calif. Heritage Council 1965-; mem: Fellow Am. Inst. Archs. (L.A. chpt. dir. 1967-70), So. Calif. Historical Soc. 1946- (dir., v.p. 1966), Econ. Round Table 1941-86 (pres. 1970), Sierra Club Urban Land Use Commn. 1980-86, L.A. City Bicentennial Com. 1968-69, Town Hall 1946-, Univ. Club. 1946-, Nat. Trust Historical Preservation, Soc. Archtl. Historians, Southern Skis (pres. 1953-54); works: devel. master site plan for largest public housing proj. in USA 1937; prelim. design for 60 posts, site camps & stations on Philippines & Ryukos 1946; master plan for Civic Ctr. of L.A. 1947; 30 tech. papers for ERT 1942-84; mil: major US Army Corps of Engrs. 1942-46, lt. col. USAR 1946-54, Disting. Svc. Medal for Mil. Merit 1946; Democrat; Catholic; rec: tennis, skiing, volunteer for public svc.; Res: 3730 Amesbury Rd Los Angeles 90027

TURNER, JAMES KIBBE, superior court judge; b. Oct. 11, 1928, Long Beach, Calif.; s. Jesse Harold and Lillian Beatrice (Van Riper) T.; m. Robin Redwine, Nov. 22, 1979; children: James b. 1958, Sue Ellen B. 1960; (step) Kent b. 1957, Peter b. 1959; edn: BS, Univ. So. Calif. 1951; LLB, Loyola Univ. Sch. of Law 1954. Career: pvt. law practice Corona del Mar, Calif. 1959-67; dep. dist. atty. Orange Co. 1967-69; mun. ct. judge Westminster 1969-71; supr. ct. judge Santa Ana 1971–; mem: Calif. Judges Assn. (secy./treas. 1983-84, exec. bd. 1981-84); Republican; Congregational; rec: travel, golf, gardening. Ofc: County Court House 700 Civic Center Dr W Santa Ana 92701

TURNER, JOHN ELDON, engineer; b. July 8, 1950, San Jose; s. John Wesley and Doris Mae (Lake) T.; edn: AA, Modesto Jr. Coll. 1970; BA, math., UC Berkeley 1972; BSEE, CSU Sacto. 1978; Reg. Profl. Engr. (civil, elec.) Calif., (civil) Nev.; Reg. Land Surveyor, Calif. Career: surveying and engring. field 1971–; Mid-Valley Engring., Modesto 1972-73, draftsman R.B. Welty Engring., 1973-74, sr. engring. aide (project engr.) City of Atwater, 1974-75, public works insp. County of Stanislaus, 1975, project engr. Task Engineering, Cardova 1975-77, lic. land surveyor Turner Surveying, Orangevale 1977-78; project engr., constrn. insp. Cook & Assocs. Engring., Oroville 1978, Norberg Engring., Sacto. 1978-79; elec. design engr. Spink Corp., Sacto. 1979, Cook Assocs., Oroville 1980; chief engr./prin. Site Consultants, Riverbank 1980–; sponsor career study pgm., surveying, CSU Fresno; honors: Eagle Scout, Calif. Scholarship Fedn., State Scholarship recipient, pres. Student Chpt. IEEE (1977), Varsity H.Sch. Wrestling; mem: Calif. Land Surveyor's, IEEE; civic: Boy Scouts, Soccer Team, Rotary, CofC; invention: Heart Beat & Respiration Rate Telemeter Transmitter (1978); Libertarian; Ch. of Spiritual Sci.; rec: tropical fish, chess, bridge. Address: Site Consultants, 2319 Rio Verde Dr Riverbank 95367

TURNER, R. SAMUEL, publisher; b. Mar. 27, 1923, Hampton, Va.; s. R.S. and Annie Lee (Freeman) T.; m. Evelyn, Oct. 9, 1951; children: Sheila b. 1953, Rufus b. 1954; edn: marine engring., U.S. Maritime Acad. 1946; cert. theol. Ambassador Coll. 1965-74; cert. law, Univ. W.L.A. 1983; Hon. Dr. Humanities, Univ. of Metaphysics 1985; ordained minister Ch. of God, NY, NY: 1968. Career: petty ofcr. US Merchant Marine, Engine Dept. 1947-51; optical tooling techn. Republic Aviation Corp., Long Is., NY 1951-61; minister Ch. of God, pastorates in NYC, Bklyn., Newark, L.A., Santa Monica, Glendale, 1963-78, also pub. relations rep., counsellor, tchr., lectr. in USA and abroad for Ambassador Coll. and Church of God, N.Y., 1963-71, Los Angeles, 1972-80, also dir. ministerial ordination tng. pgm. 1968-71; cons. engr. in precision machine tools, 1981–; founder The Seminary Tng. Inst., 1985; pres. Bethel Publishing (ednl. materials), Pasadena 1986–; orgs: N.Y. Spokesman Club (pres. 1962-63, chmn. pres.'s com. 1963-65), Topicmasters Speech Club (dir. 1974-80), L.A. Youth Orgn. (coord. 1976-78), Joyful Noise Prodns. (prod./dir. 1974-77); author: The Seminary Tng. Manual (1986); mil: seaman 1c USN Seabees 1945, 3 Battle Stars; Christian Ch.; rec: metal turning, cycling, metaphysics. Ofc: Bethel Pub. POB 93003 Pasadena 91109

TURNER, WILLIAM BOB, university professor; b. July 3, 1920, Fresno; s. William Burton and Grace (Calhoun) T.; m. Phyllis Vivian Hain, April 2, 1941; children: Jacqulyn b. 1941, Pamela b. 1944, Donna b. 1959; edn: BS, UCLA 1948; BA, Columbia Pacific Univ. 1950; MS, Golden State Univ. 1952; PhD,

Columbia Pacific Univ. 1984; Lic. Nursing Home Adminstr., Calif. Career: controller Purolator Products, Newbury Park 1964-67; controller A & W Internat., Santa Monica 1967-70; exec. v.p. Wyndon Corp., Century City 1970-80; exec. ofcr. Quizmasters Seminars, Sherman Oaks 1976—; v.p. Sandpebbles Beachwear & Swimwear, Malibu 1979-82; pres. Del Rey Mgmt., Sherman Oaks 1978—; prof. Golden State Univ. Sch. of Bus. & Econs., Los Angeles 1985—; dir. Wyndon Corp., 1973-80; fin. cons. 1978-; asst. prof. health sci. dept. CSU Dominguez Hills 1976-80; asst. prof. dept. of bus. admin. Golden State Univ., Los Angeles 1952-56; honors: Men of Acheivement Internat., Cambridge, Eng. 1986, Who's Who (West 1986, World 1986); fellow Am. Coll. of Health Care Adminstrs.; mem: Nat. Assn. Accts., Order of DeMolay (Hollywood chpt., PMC, CHEV, COH, LOH, past dean); publs: The Administrator, Del Rey Publg. 1977; Public Realtions/ Speakers Guidelines, Am. Coll. Health Care Adminstrs. 1978; Study Manual for NHA Exam, Del Rey Publg. 1980; A-I-T Study Manual for Calif. Exam-NHA, Del Rey Mgmt. 1982; mil: tech. 4/g, Adj. Gen. Dept. US Army 1944-45, Philippine Liberation, Asiatic-Pacific, Victory, GCM; rec: sports, travel. Res: 13902 Huston St. Sherman Oaks 91423-1903 Ofc: Golden State Univ., 1210 W. 4th St. Los Angeles 90017-1412

TUTOLI, MICHELE ANN, financial advisor; b. May 18, 1951, Teaneck, NJ; d. Octavius Rocco and Theresa Rosalia (Wouters) T.; m. Stephen M. Lord, Jan. 27, 1979; children nee Lord: Stephanie b. 1980, Michael b. 1982, Christine b. 1984, David b. 1986; edn: George Washington Univ. 1969-70; AA, Am. Coll. in Paris 1971; AB, Georgetown Univ. 1973; Jd, Brooklyn Law Sch. 1978; admitted to the bars of New Jersey (1978), New York (1979) and U.S. Tax Ct. (1986); Life & Disability Ins. Agent, Calif. 1985. Career: asst. prodn. mgr. Gerstin Advtg. Agency, Wash. DC 1971-73; investment ofcr. Morgan Guaranty Trust Co., NY, NY 1973-80; legal con. Ofc. of Alcohol Fuels, Dept. of Energy, Wash. DC 1980-81; asst. dir. Trust div. American Bankers Assn., Wash. DC 1981-82; v.p., mgr. fin. plnng. Home Federal, San Diego 1982—; ambassador Univ. of San Diego 1982-; Fin. Instn. Mgmt. Advy. Com., UC San Diego 1985-; mem: Am. Bar Assn. (Com. on Spl. Plnng. for Execs. & Profls., Com. on Investments by Actuaries), San Diego Soc. of Fin. Analysts, Internat. Assn. of Fin. Plnnrs., Calif. Bankers Assn. Com. on Proff. Devel., Olivenhain Town Council (pres. 1986-87); Catholic; rec: family. Res: 157 Rancho Santa Fe Rd. Olivenhain 92024 Ofc: Home Federal, 625 Broadway 9th Flr. San Diego 92101

TUZMEN, ZEKI, quality engineering executive, b. June 11, 1957, Istanbul, Turkey; s. Izzet and Nezahat (Topraginiseven) T.; edn: BSIE, Calif. State Polytech. Univ., Pomona 1979, MSE, 1981. Career: indsl. engr. Audio Magnetics Corp., Irvine 1980-82; mfg. engr. 1983-84, mgr. tech. services 1984-86, mgr. quality control and quality engring., Del Mar Coverings, Westminster 1986—; honors: Alpha Pi Mu 1979; senior mem. Am. Inst. Indsl. Engrs.; rec: biking, jogging. Res: 28 Riverstone Irvine 92714 Ofc: Del Mar Window Coverings 7150 Fenwick Ln Westminster 92683

TWEDDLE, ALLAN STANLEY, management consultant; b. Aug. 16, 1932, Toronto, Ont., Canada; s. John and Helen Louise (Downing) T.; children: Heather b. 1960, Jennifer b. 1963, Christopher b. 1965; edn: BSIE, Univ. Mich. 1961; MBA, Pepperdine Univ. 1982. Career: regl. sales mgr. American Air Filter, Toronto, Canada and Los Angeles, 1961-70; nat. sales mgr. Farr Co., L.A. 1970-75; v.p. Carter Engineers, L.A. 1975-78; dir. Albert C. Martin, L.A. 1978-81; pres. A&E Div., Theodore Barry & Assoc., Los Angeles 1981-83, prin. Theodore Barry & Assoc. 1983—; mem. Nat. Soc. Indsl. Engrs. (dir. Mfg. Mgmt. Com.), Soc. Mfg. Engrs. (senior), Pepperdine Assocs., Ordre des Ingenieurs du Quebec; clubs: Rolls Royce Owners, Bentley Drivers; rec: classic cars, sailing. Ofc: Theodore Barry & Assoc. 1520 Wilshire Blvd 90017

TWELLS, RAE LEE, executive; b. June 4, 1935, Marshalltown, Penn.; d. Glenn and Opal Marless (Hollom) Dunham; m. Gordon Twells, May 24, 1986; chidren: Robin Lynn Barela b. 1956, Kevin Glenn Barela b. 1961 (dec.). Career: opr., force supvr., supvr., area supvr., supvy. ast. to v.p. Western Union Telephone Co., San Francisco 1951-75; v.p. nat. mktg. Charles Schwab & Co. Inc., San Francisco 1975-79; pres., founder Dunham Communications 1979-83; pres., co-founder R&T Twells 800 Inc., 1986—; senior instr. Western Union Telephone Co.; senior cons. Ambassador Internat. & Public Broadcasting; mem: Redwood Empire Runners Club, Country Side Tennis Club; Democrat; rec: painting, writing, running. Ofc: R&T Twells 800 Inc., 831 Vallejo Ave. Novato 94947

TYRELL, JOHN RIX, lawyer; b. May 6, 1921, Alhambra; s. John James and Ruth (Sands) T.; m. Marion Mallman, July 2, 1943; chidren: Sandra Sue b. 1959, Jon Sands b. 1960, Randy Rix b. 1966; edn: AA, Pasadena Jr. Coll. 1941; AB, USC 1949; JD, USC Sch. of Law 1952. Career: life guard City of Alhambra, (summers) 1939-51; svc. U.S. Post Office, Alhambra 1940, 48, 49, 50; master router, Vega Aircraft Corp., Burbank 1941-2; welders helper to sales engr. C.E. Howard & Co., L.A. and South Gate 1945-8; atty. at law 1954-, partner Davidson, Tyrell & Davidson law firm, Alhambra 1956-70; pvt. practice law 1970—; Temple City Councilman 1960-84, Mayor five terms; past pres. Calif. Contracts Cities Assn.; bd. trustees Comm. Hosp. of San Gabriel 1973-; mem: Am., Calif., L.A. and San Gabriel Valley Bar Assns.; L.A. Trial Lawyers Assn.; Pasa. Tournament of Roses Assn. (patron); Temple City CofC; US Power Squadron; USC Alumni Assn.; San Gabriel Valley BSA (exec. bd.); Phi Alpha Delta; (past) bd. dirs. Alhambra CofC, exec. com. Alhambra Coord. Council, Alhambra Exchg. Club juvenile counselor com., juvenile div. Alhambra Police Res., advisor Alhambra Youth Coord. Council; clubs: Am. Legion, Masons, Scottish Rite, Shriners, Alhambra Hi Twelve, Temple City

Tennis, Arcadia Tennis; mil: lt., naval aviator, USN 1942-45, WWII; legal ofcr. Fleet Air Serv. Squadron Seven, adm. ofcr. Adm. Dept. Head, Composite Squad. Eleven, 1953-54; rec: tennis, boating, fishing. Res: 5709 No. Allessandro Temple City Ofc: 9161 Las Tunas Dr Temple City 91780

TYRRELL, JOAN ANGELA, educator; b. Dec. 3, 1938, Chgo.; d. Edward William and Shirley Mary (Perry) T.; edn: BA, Marymount Coll. 1958; postgrad. work, UCLA 1959-63, 1969-73, 1979-80. Career: elementary tchr. Los Angeles City Sch. Dist. 1958—; vol. J. Paul Getty Mus.; mem. Ednl. Adv. Council 1976-; honors: Outstanding Young Women of Am. 1967; mem: Coll. Alumnae Aux. of the Assistance 1963-; The Opera Assocs. 1966-; Metropolitan Opera Nat. Council (L.A. Dist. Treas. 1977-); Music Center Opera League; Metropolitan Assocs.; Las Angelitas Del Pueblo; Alumni Assn. of Loyola Marymount Univ.; life mem. UCLA Alumni Assn.; patron L.A. Co. Mus. of Art; Nat. History Mus. Alliance; So. Calif. Hist. Soc.; San Diego Opera- Los Angeles Guild; nat. assoc. The Metropolitan Mus. of Art; Republican; Catholic; rec: tennis, music, UCLA football games. Res: 1463 Palisades Dr Pacific Palisades 90272 Ofc: Los Angeles Unified School Dist., 450 No Grand Ave Los Angeles

TZALL, WAYNE ALLEN, certified public accountant, b. July 23, 1946, NY, NY; s. Philip and Stella (Rothman) T.; m. Diana Joyce, Sept. 13, 1977; children: Robert b. 1979, Jennifer b. 1980, David b. 1982; edn: BBA, Univ. Miami (Fla.) 1972; CPA, Calif. 1982. Career: CPA, sole practice, North Hollywood; ptnr. Katz and Tzall CPA's, Los Angeles currently; mem. CPA Advis. Com., Calif. State Assembly; recipient recognition award, Jewish Big Brothers of Los Angeles; mem: Am. Inst. CPAs; Calif. Soc. CPAs; Clearinghouse for Volunteer Accounting Service; Alpha Kappa Psi (life); Alpha Phi Omega; First Stage Playwrights (bd. advisors); rec: antiques. Res: 29027 Woodcreek Court Agoura Hills 91301 Ofc: 8060 Melrose Ave Los Angeles 90046

UDWADIA, FIRDAUS ERACH, scientist, engineer; b. Aug. 28, 1947, Bombay, India; s. Dr. Erach R. and Perin E (Lentin) U.; m. Farida Gagrat, Jan. 6, 1977; 1 child: Shanaira E., b. 1978; edn: BA, Indian Inst. of Tech. 1968; MS, Calif. Inst. of Tech. 1969, PhD 1972. Career: research fellow, applied science Calif. Inst. of Tech.; asst. prof. Sch. Engring., USC, Los Angeles; prof. engring. USC; bd. dir. firm spec. in applied science, math. and biomechanics; resrch in geophysics, dynamics and biomechanics; permanent cons. Jet Propulsion Lab.; cons. Argonne Nat. Labs., Avery Internat., World Health Orgn.; awards: NSF research grantee, 1973-, spl. NSF adv. to Univ. Skopje 1974; mem: Seismological Soc. of Am.; Soc. for Indsl. and Applied Math.; Am. Acad. of Mechanics; Sigma Xi; ASCE; Earthquake Engring. Inst.; orgzr. confs. in areas of System I.D., and Dynamics; Publs: over 70 research papers in sci. jours. on earthquake engring., biomechanics, and physics; Zoroastrian; rec: piano, writing poetry, chess, computers. Res: 1708 No Roosevelt Ave Altadena 91001 Ofc: University of So California, Denny Research Bldg. Los Angeles 90007

UEBERROTH, PETER VICTOR, commissioner of baseball; b. Sept. 2, 1937, Chgo.; s. Victor C. and Laura (Larson) U.; m. Virginia Nicolaus; four children; edn: CSU San Jose. Career: founder Transportation Consultants International, 1963-, co. went public 1967, chmn. bd./chief exec. First Travel Corp. (2d-largest travel co. in US), 1967—; pres. Los Angeles Olympic Organizing Com., 1979-84; commnr. of baseball, 1984—; dir. Transam. Corp.; mem. Delta Upsilon, Bel Air CC; Christian; rec: water sports, golf, tennis; ofc: Los Angeles 90084

UIGA, ANTS, civil/agricultural engineer; b. Jan. 5, 1949, Stuttgart, Germany, nat. US cit. 1956; s. Endel and Elise (Miitra) U.; m. Renita Diane Field, Apr. 15, 1979; children: Brian David b. 1982, Colleen Laurel b. 1984; edn: Newark (N.J.) Coll. of Engring. 1967-70; BSCE, Univ. of Vermont 1973; M.Engring., Agricultural, Cornell Univ. 1975; Reg. Profl. Civil Engr., Calif. 1977. Career: environmental engring. in area of wastewater reclamation and treatment, 6 yrs.; project engr. with Metcalf and Eddy, Palo Alto; irrigation, agricultural waste mgmt. and forensic engring. positions at UC Davis, and Sherman and Kinkead; current: independent consulting engr., splst. in civil, agricultural, and forensic engring.; honors: Chi Epsilon, Tau Beta Pi, EPA scholarship (1973-74); mem: Am. Soc. of Agri. Engrs.; Water Pollution Control Fedn., Calif. Water Pollution Control Assn., Calif. Irrigation Inst.; club: Singlehanded Sailing Soc.; Democrat; Christian; rec: sailing, skiing, Volvo restorations. Res: 166 Capricorn Ave Oakland 94611

UMINSKI, GEORGE JOSEPH, manufacturing engineer; b. Nov. 3, 1920, Racine, Wisc.; s. Joseph Leroy and Clara Adelle (Klein) U.; m. Eunice Jensen, May 9, 1942; children: Joanne b. 1943, Marcia b. 1945, Scott b. 1954; edn: grad. Valparaiso (Ind.) Tech. Inst.; AA in math., San Diego Eve. Coll. 1970; Reg. Profl. Engr., electrical/electronic mfg., Calif. 1979. Career: senior electronics engr. General Dynamics, Convair, San Diego 1956-70, Rohr Industries 1970-75, Rohr-Plessey 1972-75; senior product engr. Solar Turbines Internat. 1975-76; senior test engr. General Dynamics Electronics, San Diego 1976—84; senior engr. Access Research Corp., 1984—; cons. in electrical design, Anthony Indus., Carlsbad 1981; publs: Atlas Missile MBRV (maneuverable ballistic re-entry vehicle) factory acceptance test plan (1964), 30+ factory acceptance test procedures for electrical, electronic and electro-mech. systems (1958-68); mil: pvt. US Army Signal Corps 1942-43, Marksman, GCM; Republican; Catholic; rec: photog. (winner Del Mar hist. photo contest 1979), ham radio, house constrn. Res: 13776 Mira Montana Dr Del Mar 92014 Ofc: Access REsearch Corp. Encinitas

UMPHRED, DARCY A., physical therapist, international lecturer; b. Oct. 26, 1945, Oakland; d. Edwin Franklin and Janet (Jackson) Umphred; m. Gordon Burton, June 16, 1974; children: John Edwin b. 1976, Benjamin b. 1981; edn: BS in phys. therapy, Univ. Wash. 1968; MS in allied health edn., Boston Univ. 1971; PhD in edn., Syracuse Univ. 1978; Reg. Phys. Therapist (RPT), Calif. (1968). Career: staff therapist Rehab. Center, San Leandro 1968-69, Group Pvt. Practice, Bay Area 1969-70; chief therapist Leapfrog: Infant Toddler Pgm., Vallejo 1978-79; pvt. practice Rio Oso, 1979–; faculty Temple Univ., Phila. 1971-73, Utica Coll. Syracuse Univ. 1974-76; cons. pvt. patients nat.; cons. The Pathway Sch. for Children with Learning Disabilities, Phila. (1971-80), Vision Care Clinic, Blind Baby Found. No. Calif. (1980-); splst. in neurological disabilities, tchr. graduate and contg. edn. workshops in US and internat. (1972-); mem. Am. Phys. Therapy Assn. 1968- (sects. in Pediatrics, Neurol., Edn., Geriatrics); civic: Junior League, St. Michaels Pre & Day Sch. Parents Gp. (ofcr.), church youth group (sponsor); publs: editor Neurological Rehabilitation (C.V.Mosby 1985), author chapters in 3 books rel. to neurol. problems, contbr. num. profl. jours., writer poetry; Republican; Episcopal (deaconess); rec: Am. Taekwondo Assn. (Black Belt, tchr. trainee pgm.), family activities, backpack. Address: Partners In Learning 1631 Day Dr Carmichael 95608

UNDERWOOD, NANCY M., safety awareness co. president; b. Dec. 29, 1944, Vancouver, Wash.; d. Robert Izea and Jennie M. (McWhorter) Espie; 1 dau. April Underwood b. 1966; edn: BS in occupational health & safety, CSU Los Angeles 1974; Calif. Comm. Colls. tchg. cred. (driver ed.) 1975; 2-yr study, environmental and occup. toxicol., Univ. San Francisco 1981; engring. cert. Travelers Ins. Co. (1975). Career: environmental and occupational health & safety engr. and cons./pres. Underwood Loss Control, Lynwood; seminars and tng. cons. Chevron Oil USA, Thums Long Beach Co. (oil refinery), Cal/Trans, Woodward-Clyde Consultant, others 1984-, supr. 2-yr. mgmt. health and safety tng. pgm. City of Compton, 1984-86; mem. Nat. Safety Council, Am. Soc. of Safety Engrs., Am. Soc. for Profl. & Exec. Women; publs: Supervisor Management Occupational Health and Safety Manual for gen. indus. use (c. 1978), Fire Safety Tng. manual for indsl. use (c. 1978), The Importance of Accident Prevention (Indsl. News, L.A.); Republican; Christian Sci.; rec: golf, swim, photog. Res: 1637 Veteran Ave Los Angeles 90024 Ofc: Underwood Loss Control 3516 E Century Blvd Ste 10 Lynwood 90262

UNGAR, LOUIS YEHUDA, electronics test engineer; b. July 20, 1951, Hungary, nat. US cit. 1973; s. Joseph J. and Klara (Weisz) U.; edn: BSEE, UC Los Angeles 1973; grad. work in mgmt. Technion, Israel Inst. of Tech. 1974-75, (MSEE course work complete) Univ. of Redlands 1982. Career: electronics engr. Northrop Electronics, Hawthorne 1973-74; electronics test engr. Elbit Computers, Haifa, Israel 1974-76; project engr. ATE Dept., System Development Corp., Santa Monica 1976-78; electronics design engr. Hughes Aircraft Co., Culver City 1978-81; v.p. engring. Test Engring. Solutions, Inc. Reseda 1981-84; pres. A.T.E. Solutions, Inc. 1984–; instr. UCLA (1981-), New Jersey Inst. of Tech. (1983-); lectr. and workshop leader (electronics testing), num. electronics confs.; mem. IEEE (Computer and Mgmt. Socs., 1973-), Am. Soc. Test Engrs., Technical Advisory Service for Attys.; publs: Complete ATE Book (2 vols.), Test Equipment Selection Guide (2 vols.); designed logic simulation system used for test pgm. devel. and an automatic cross translator between ATE languages; currently dev. automatic test pgm. generation sys. for testing Very Large Scale Integrated (VLSI) circuits. Ofc: A.T.E. Solutions, Inc. 7009 Owensmouth Ave Canoga Park 91303

UNIS, JOSEPH STEVEN, diagnostic radiologist; b. July 1, 1945, Sewickley, Pa.; s. Joseph Alex and Catherine (Michael) U.; m. Georgette George, Nov. 28, 1970; children: Claire b. 1973, Danielle b. 1975; edn: BS, Univ. of Nebraska 1966, MD, with honors, 1970; bd. cert. in nuclear med. and diagnostic radiol. Am. Bd. of Radiol., Am. Bd. of Nuc. Med. 1976. Career: intern Good Samaritan Hosp. Phoenix, Ariz. 1970-71; res., fellow George Washington Univ. Hosp. 1973-76; formed computed tomography dept. and upgraded nuclear med. and ultrasound depts. Pomona Valley Community Hosp. 1976-1984, chmn. dept. of radiol. 1984–; clin. prof. of radiol. Loma Linda Univ. Hosp.; exec. bd. Foothill Country Day Sch.; bd. dirs. 1849 Condominiums; honors: Academic All Big 8 1966; mem: AMA, CMA, LACMA, Inland Radiol. Soc. (v.p.); Calif. Radiol. Soc.; Am. Coll. of Radiol.; publ: prof. presentations med. assn. mtgs.; mil: lt. cmdr. USPHS 1971-73; Independent; Christian; rec: bicycling, photog., skiing. Ofc: 1798 Gary Ave Pomona 91767

UNRUH, JESSE MARVIN, state treasurer; b. Sept. 30, 1922, Newton, Kansas; s. Isaac P. and Nettie Laura (Kessler) U.; m. Virginia June Lemon, Nov. 2, 1943; chlidren: Bruce, Bradley, Robert, Randall, Linda Lu; edn; BA, USC 1948, postgrad., 1949, LLD, 1967. Career: dist. staff dir. Federal Census 1950; with Pacific Car Demurrage Bureau 1950-54; mem. Calif. Assembly 1954-70; chmn. Com. Fin. & Ins. 1957-59; chmn. Ways & Means Com. 1959-61; Spkr. of Assembly 1961-68; Democratic leader 1968-70, Advy. Commn. on Intergovtl. Rels. 1967-70; currently, treas. State of Calif.; vis. prof. polit. sci. San Fernando Valley State Coll. 1970; vis. prof. USC Sch. of Law 1971-72; cons. prof. polit. sci. Eagleton Inst. Politics, Rutgers Univ. 1965-; co-chmn. Seminar Young Legislators, Carnegie Corp.; bd. regents Univ. Calif. 1961-68; trustee Calif. State Colls. 1961-68; honors: Chubb Fellow, Yale Univ. 1962; mem: Inst. for Am. Univs., Citizens Conf. on State Legislature; works: Calif. Central Democratic Com. 1954-; So. Calif. mgr. John F. Kennedy presdl. campaign 1960; So. Calif. chgmn. gubernatorial campaign 1962; statewide coord. assembly, congl. campaigns 1962; chmn. Robert F. Kennedy's Calif. presdl. campaign 1968; chmn. Calif. del. Dem. Nat. Conv. 1968; pres. Nat. Conf. State Legis. Leaders 1966; Dem. cand. for gov. Calif. 1970; mil: USNR 1942-45. Res: 306 Bora Bora Way Marina del Rey 90291 Ofc: State Capitol Sacramento 95814

UPTAIN, MICHAEL LARRY, certified public accountant; b. May 11, 1957, San Diego; s. Samuel Eugene and Arvilla May (Parkes) U.; m. Naomi Combs, May 1, 1983; edn: Porterville Coll. 1975-77; BS w/honors, CalPoly Tech., S.L.O. 1979. Career: mgr. Ted Brown's Auto Parts, Porterville 1974-77; shift mgr. Westside Auto Parts, San Luis Obispo 1977-78; staff acct. Rudolph Soukup, P.A., San Luis Obispo 1978-79; staff acct. Vollmer, Canfield, Daniel, Stout, Pine & Gaebe, Porterville 1979-80; semi-senior acct. Carpenter, Kuhn & Williams, Bakersfield 1980-81; mng. partner Ainsworth & Uptain, Porterville 1981-; CPA/splst. tax and mgmt. adv. svcs.; mem: Cal. Soc. CPA's 1982-83, Pres. Club- Olde Worlde, Inc., Bakersfield Jaycees (charter pres.), Porterville Jaycees (mem. chmn.), Sierra Road Runners, 4 WD Club, Calif. Assn. Four Wheel Drive; Republican; rec: jeeping, camping. Res: 1681 Wall Lane Porterville 93257 Ofc: 1077 W Morton Porterville 93257

URAUCHI, PAUL KENJI, company president; b. Oct 5, 1937, Molokai, Hawaii; s. Kiyoshi George and Sakae (Nakata) U.; m. Eleanor S., April 16, 1960; children: Kelli b. 1963, Kris b. 1965; edn: BS, Wisc. State Univ. 1959; MA, Colo. State Univ. 1968; PhD, Walden Univ. 1971; Calif. life tchg. creds. (Gen. Elem., Secondary, Gen. Adminstrn.). Career: indsl. arts instr., varsity coach 1959-62; high sch. vice prin., jr. high and elem. sch. prin. 1963-67, 1971-81, elem. sch. tchg. vice prin. 1968-70, sch. supt. 1981-83; real estate agent/ contr./ broker/ prin. Urauchi Constrn. & Real Estate, Hayward current; honors: Hon. Life mem. PTA, named Coach of Year, Tchr. of Year, Volunteer of Year; mem: Nat., Alameda Contractors Assn., Assn. of Indsl. Arts & Ind., Bd. Realtors; civic: PTA, Little League, Boy Scouts Am. (leader, Cubs, Explorers), 4-H Club; publs: dissertation, Enriching The Elemetary School; toymaker, Craftman in Business; Reorg. Latter Day Saints (elder); rec: sports, craftmanship, photog. Address: Urauchi Constrn. & Real Estate, 25354 Rick Way Hayward 94541

UREVICH, CONSTANTIN NICHOLAS, lawyer; b. Apr. 4, 1933, Shanghai, China, nat. 1957; s. Nicholas D. and Margaret (Kagan) U.; 1 dau., Robin Margaret, b. 1957; edn: Los Angeles City Coll.; BA, L. A. State Univ. 1959; LLB, Loyola Univ. 1961; MBA, USC 1971; admitted Calif State Bar 1976. Career: lawyer/prin., C.N. Urevich, gen. practice law firm, Los Angeles; dir. Didi Hirsch Mental Health Comm. Svc.; Vols. in Parole; lectr. Negotiation Techniques 1971; arbitrator Los Angeles County Bar/Los Angeles Superior Court; adv. bd. Parents Without Partners 1985; bd. Calif. State Conf. on Small Bus. 1984-85; awarded Key to the City of Manila 1983; mem: Los Angeles County Bar Assn. (Customs Com.); Los Angeles Trial Lawyers Assn. (Adminstrv. Law); Jonathan Club; USC Assoc., life; sr. adv. US Congl. Adv. Bd. 1982; publs: Feasibility Study Design-Allied Services Project (1973), How to Get the Most Out From Your Lawyer (1983), Operational Aspects of Trade with USSR (1974), Guide Book on Doing Business in the US for Fgn. Businessmen (1985); mil: cpl. US Army 1953-55; Republican; Catholic; rec: flying, fishing, racquetball, art. Res: 545 S Figeroa St Los Angeles 90071 Law Ofcs of C.N. Urevich, 650 S Grand Ave, Ste. 914 Los Angeles 90017

UTNE, JOHN HELGE, construction co. executive; b. Dec. 1, 1937, San Francisco; s. Helge and Agnes Sigvalda (Olsten) U.; m. Karen Lou, Dec. 19, 1982; children: Kathi b. 1960, Lisa b. 1962, Stephen b. 1964, David b. 1969; stepchildren nee Berryhill: Diana, Robert, Jennifer; edn: journeyman sheetmetal, John A. O'Connell Apprentice Sch. 1962; AA, City Coll. of San Francisco 1958; BA, Golden Gate Univ. 1976; Calif. tchg. creds. (2). Career: apprentice, journeyman sheet metal worker, San Francisco Bay area 1958-64; personnel ofcr., mfg. exec. Scalling Div. McCormack & Co., Salinas and Gilroy 1964-76; HVAR contr. in Bay area, Motherlode, and San Joaquin Valley 1977-85; chief admin. ofcr., constrn. plnng. mgr. Oak Valley Constrn., Oakdale 1986–; tchr. apprentice sch. Coll. of San Mateo; tchr. solar courses Columbia Coll.; guest lectr. Indsl. Rels., var. community colls.; honors: Father of the Year, San Mateo chpt. Parents Without Partners 1978; mem. Am. Soc. of Personnel Admin., ASHRAE; civic: City of Oakland Plnng. Commmn., E. Clampus Vitus, Oakdale Youth Soccer League (referee, instr.), Eagle Scouts Assn., Oakdale Saddle Club, Bing Crosby Pro Am Golf Tournament Com., US Open Golf. Com. (1972), 57th Annual PGA Championship Com.; mil: sgt. E-5 US Army Nat. Guard; Lutheran; rec: soccer, fishing. Res: 1280 E. D Street, P.O. Box 1825 Oakdale 95361 Ofc: Oak Valley Construction, P.O. Box 54 Oakdale 95361

VAIDYANATHAN, P. P., professor of electrical engineering; b. Oct. 16, 1954, Calcutta, India; s. P.R. and P.G. (Vijayalakshmi) Parameswaran; m. Usha, Sept. 1, 1985; edn: BS, Univ. Calcutta, India 1974, B.Tech., 1977, M.Tech., 1979; PhD, UC Santa Barbara 1982. Career: postdoc. fellow elec. engrg. UC Santa Barbara 1982-83; asst. prof. elec. engrg. Calif. Inst. Technol. 1983–; assoc. ed. digital filters IEEE Trans. on Circuits & Systems; honors: President's Young Investigators Award (NSF 1986); mem. IEEE; publs: 52 tech. articles, 2 handbook chapters on digital filters. Ofc: Dept. Elec. Engrg. 116-81 Calif. Inst. Technol. Pasadena 91125

VAIL, RONALD ALMON, financial planner; b. May 20, 1925, Chgo.; s. Almon John and Gertrude Jean Vail; m. Lois Mae Reeves, Mar. 27, 1948; children: Phyllis, b. 1949, Pamela, b. 1949, Cheron, b. 1951, David, b. 1953, Beckey, b. 1958, Bonnie, b. 1959; edn: BS, high honors, Univ. of Md. 1963; Calif. Comm Coll. tchr. credentials 1981; desig: CFP, Cert. Finl. Planner, Coll. for Finl. Plng. 1982; Reg. Financial Principal, NASD 1974. Career: registered representative Mutual Fund Associates, San Diego 1968-70; reg. rep. The Ralph S. Wilford Co., La Mesa 1970-73, v.p. sales 1973-79; reg. prin. American Pacific Securities Corp., S.D. 1979-80, regional mgr. 1980–; mng. ptnr. eleven investment groups 1975-; honors: Phi Kappa Phi (1963), Admiral, Great Navy of the State of Nebr. (1967); mem: Navy Cryptologic Veterans Assn.,

Inst. of CFPs, Internat. Assn. for Finl. Plng., San Diego CofC; mil: cmdr. USN 1943-68, decorated Am. Service, Asia-Pacific Theater, China, Burma, India Theater, WWII Victory medals, Unit Commendn.; Republican. Res: 1301 Bobcat Ln Alpine 92001 Ofc: San Diego Regl. Ofc., American Pacific Securities Corp. 6150 Mission Gorge Rd, Ste 204, San Diego 92120

VALDEZ, JOSEPH, real estate broker; b. Dec. 26, 1942, Los Angeles; s. Joe A. and Rebecca (Cohen) V.; edn: real estate brokerage, Univ. San Francisco 1981-85; real estate broker Calif. 1985. Career: purchasing/ material control agent James B. Lancing Sound L.A. 1968-70; sales rep. Sony Superscope Sun Valley, Calif. 1970-72; sales mgr. Woodland Stereo Woodland Hills 1972-73; mgr. sales & mfg. Valco Enterprises L.A. 1973-76; real estate broker 1976–; cons. various savings & loans, banks & builders; splst. in loans and real estate sales; honors: various sales awards; mem: San Fernando Valley Bd. Realtors, L.A. Bd. Realtors, Bldg. Ind. assn., Calif. Assn. Realtors, Nat. Assn. Realtors, Nat. Rifle Assn. (life), Calif. Rifle Assn., L.A. Athletic Club; inventor new line of decorative fluorescent lighting fixtures for Valco; mil: fire control tech. 3/c USN 1960-63; rec: photog., hunting, fishing, skiing, travel, astronomy, competition target shooting, music, films. Address: Los Angeles 90026

VALDEZ, ROMULO CARBAJAL, physician-surgeon, gynecologist, acupuncturist; b. Feb. 29, 1924, Tayug, Pangasinan, Philippines, nat. US cit. 1973; s. Jose A. and Laureana C. (Carbajal) V.; m. Carmen Dalisay, July 3, 1948; children: Romelyn (Woodruff) b. 1949, Nicette (Balukjian) b. 1950, Romulo b. 1954, Dwight b. 1959; edn: pre-med. Phil. Union Coll., Manila 1949, BA, 1951; MD, Manila Central Univ., 1955. Career: rotating intern St. John's Hosp., Tulsa, Okla. 1955-56; gen. surg. resident Deaconess Hosp., Buffalo, N.Y. 1956-57, Colo. State Hosp., Pueblo 1957-59, chief res. in surg. St. Mary-Corwin Hosp., Pueblo 1959-60; pathol. res., sr. res. surg., emergency rm. res. Moncton Gen. Hosp., N.B., Canada 1960-63; pvt. practice (gen. surgery, gynecol., gen. practice), N.B., Canada 1963-67, Randolph, Vt. 1967-81, San Diego, Calif. 1981–; recipient service awards: Randolph Vt. Rotary Club (1974), US Cong. Hunter (1985), Filipino Am. Community/San Diego; Fellow: Internat. Coll. Angeology (1963), Am. Soc. Abdominal Surgeons (1971), Soc. Philippine Surgeons in Am. (1983), Am. Coll. Internat. Physicians (1984); mem: N.B. Med. Soc. (1963-67), Vt. Med. Soc. (1967-81), Calif. Med. Soc. (1981-), San Diego Med. Soc. (1981-), Ctr for Chinese Medicine, Acup. Found. of Canada, Occidental Inst. of Chinese Studies, Med. Acup. Research of Am., S.D. Phil. Med. Assn., Assn. of Phil. Practitioners of Am., Am. Assn. Gynecol. Laparoscopist; publ: Am. J. of OB-Gyn. (1980); oil paintings (1st prizes in Randolph, Vt. 1967-75); mil: 2d lt. Phil. Army 1941-46; Republican; Seventh-day Adventist; rec: painting, singing, gardening, cooking. Res: 1330 Paraiso Ave Spring Valley 92077 Ofc: 2340 E 8th St Ste H National City 92050

VALDMAN, LILYA, lawyer; b. Dec. 11, 1939, Kiev, USSR, nat. USA 1985; d. Solomon and Tatiana (Schupak) Kogan; m. Boris Valdman, Mar. 31, 1962; 1 son, Slavick b. 1963; edn: jurist, Kiev State Univ., USSR 1963; Loyola Sch. of Law 1980-81; admitted Calif. STate Bar 1982. Career: atty. Kiev Coll. of Attys., 1963-77; file clk. law firm Pachter, Gold & Schaffer, Los Angeles 1978-79; legal asst. Cohen & Ziskin, Century City 1979-80; assoc. atty. Lenske, Lenske & Heller, Woodland Hills 1982-84, Solish, Jordan & Wiener, Century City 1984-85; solo practitioner, Los Angeles 1985–; lectr. by invitation on Soviet System of law to law schs. and var. social gps.; mem. Am., Calif., San Fernando Valley Women Lawyers bar assns.; Republican; rec: reading, knitting. Res: 18737 Miranda St., Tarzana 91356 Ofc: Lilya Valdman, Atty. 6380 Wilshire Blvd, Ste 1207, Los Angeles 90048

VALDOZ, PABLO RUFINO, certified public accountant; b. Mar. 10, 1952, Pangasinan, Philippines, nat. US cit. 1981; s. Ignacio Romeo and Pastora Santa Maria (Rufino) V.; m. Evelyn Reyes, June 26, 1976; children: Jeffrey b. 1978, Brian b. 1980, Aimee b. 1985; edn: BSBA acctg., cum laude, Univ. of the East, 1973; CPA Calif. 1982. Career: bookkeeper KQED Channel 9 S.F. 1977-79; audit examiner Calif. First Bank S.F. 1979; auditor Roe-O'Rourke & Clark CPAs Burlingame 1979; senior acct. Argonaut Insurance Co. Menlo Park 1980-81; internal auditor Lockheed Missiles & Space Co. Fed. Credit Union Sunnyvale 1981-86; senior acct. Lockheed Missiles & Space Co. Sunnyvale 1986–; honors: Picpan of the Quarter Award 1983, Presidential Awardee (PICPA-USA 1984); mem: PICPA-USA (bd. dirs., com. free tax svc. to deserving citizens); United Camilenios of Am. (pres.); Lockheed Mgmt. Assn., Filipino Community of Santa Clara; Catholic; rec: outing, reading, community service. Res: 2835 Danwood Ct San Jose 95148 Ofc: LMSC Federal Credit Union POB 3504 Sunnyvale 94088-3504

VALENE, NOLAN H., real estate developer; b. Aug. 19, 1937, Minneapolis, Minn.; s. Leo R. and Marian C. (Fink) V.; m. Ardella G. Thewis, Dec. 19, 1970; edn: BS, New York Inst. of Fin. 1961; JD, Irvine Coll. of Law 1977; lic. gen. contractor; real estate broker. Career: currently, pres. First Investors Realty; mem: Calif. Trial Lawyers Assn.; Masons; Elks; ed. & publr. Nat. Heavy Constrn. Journ.; mil: USAF; Democrat. Res: 1428 Via Coronel, Palos Verdes Estates 90274 Ofc: First Investors Management, P.O. Box 883, Redondo Beach 90277

VALENTINE, MICHAEL JAMES, chiropractor; b. Feb. 10, 1954, Detroit, Mich.; s. Lando John and Mary Clara (Morocco) V.; edn: BS in applied biol., Ferris State Coll. 1977; DC, magna cum laude, Palmer Coll. of Chiropractic 1982; chiropractic orthopedic splst. pgm., Los Angeles City Coll., 1985-; lic. DC, Calif. 1983. Career: assoc. Gordin Chiropractic Health Center, Hollywood 1982-84; chiropractor founder/ prin. Valentine Chiropractic, Inc. Fountain Valley 1984–; mem: Am. Chiro. Assn., Calif. Chiro. Assn., Profl. Mgmt. Assocs., Am. Chiro. Council; civic: Fountain Valley Jaycees (v.p. Community Devel.), F.V. Toastmasters, We Tip of Westminster, Mile Square Mens Club; Republican; Catholic; rec: tennis, golf, basketball. Ofc: Valentine Chiropractic 17213 Brookhurst Fountain Valley 92708

VALLES, JUDITH, community college administrator; b. Dec. 14, 1933, San Bernardino; d. Gonzalo and Jovita (Lopez) V.; m. Chadwick J. Bradbury (dec. 1969); children: Edith Anne (Renella) b. 1957, Chadwick b. 1959, Nohemi b. 1962; m. 2d Harry Carl Smith, Oct. 13, 1985; edn: BA, Univ. of Redlands 1964; MA in Spanish lit., UC Riverside 1970; doctoral cand. Nova Univ. Career: faculty San Bernardino Comm. Coll. Dist., San Bernardino 1963–, hd. Dept. of Fgn. Languages 1972-76, chair Div. Humanities 1976-81, dean Extended Day and Summer Session 1981-83, adminstrv. dean Academic Affairs, 1983–, supr. instrnl. program of 7 acad. divs. (11,000 students, 443 faculty); devel. & implemented: first full Instrnl. Pgm. Review, the inst. for Tng. and Devel. providing staff in-service tng. for City, County, and State employees, estab. bridge pgms. for voc. nurses, hispanic students, black students; apptd. Calif. State Commn. for Licensing Speech Pathologist and Audiologists (1981-); guest speaker acad. forums, commencement spkr. Coll. of the Air Force, Norton AFB, US del. to Internat. Womens Year Conf., Mexico City; bd. dirs: Inland Empire Symphony, Girl Scouts of Am., San Bernardino CofC; mem: Assn. Calif. Coll. Adminstrs., Modern Lang. Assn., Am. Assn. of Tchrs. of Spanish and Portuguese, Delta Kappa Gamma (1st v.p.); works: conduct workshops for Future Leaders of Am., producer, host TV show Impacto; publs. in acad. jours.; Democrat; Catholic; rec: painting, singing, sailing. Res: 3096 Broadmoor San Bernardino 92404 Ofc: San Bernardino Valley College 701 Mt Vernon San Bernardio 92410

VALONE, KEITH EMERSON, psychologist; b. Aug. 3, 1953, Austin, Tex.; s. James Floyd and Elizabeth Niles (Emerson) V.; m. Leona, July 22, 1978; edn: BA, Univ. So. Calif. 1975; MA, Univ. Ill. Urbana0Champaign 1979, PhD, 1981; lic. psychol. BMQA 1983. Career: intern Langley Porter Inst. UCSF Med. Sch. 1980-81; postdoc. fellow UCLA 1981-84; asst. clin. prof. UCLA 1984–; psychol. pvt. practice Pasadena; supv. psychol. Ingleside Hosp.; honors: Phi Beta Kappa 1975; mem: Am. Psychol. Assn., Nat. Register Health Care Providers in Psychol. Calif. Psychol. Assn., L.A. Co. Psychol. Assn., Rotary; contbr. num. articles in profl. jours. of psychol. Ofc: 960 E Green St Ste 342 Pasadena 91106

VAN BEBBER, NORMAN PARK, real estate broker; b. May 21, 1911, Petaluma, Calif.; s. Park Anderson and Annie (Shackelton) Van B.; m. Gertrude Annie McKeown, Dec. 22, 1935; children: Ronald Gillete b. 1940, Carol Lynne b. 1942; edn: Santa Rosa Jr. Coll. 1930-33. Career: plumbing & heating contr. 40 yrs.; real estate broker; city council member 1957-65, mayor 1963-65; mem. first Sonoma County Local Agency Commn., Bay Area Council, Bay Area Transportation Study Commn.; honors: Silver Beaver (BSA), Commdn. (Brig. Gen. Charles R. Meyer, Dept. of Army 1965); mem: Lions Club, Sons in Retirement, Masons (past master); Republican; Episcopal (senior warden); rec: house remodeling. Res: 215 Eighth St Petaluma 94952 Ofc: C-21 Bundeson Real Estate 616 Petaluma Blvd S Petaluma 94952

VAN BENSCHOTEN, MARK MATHEW, acupuncturist, doctor of oriental medicine; b. Aug. 13, 1956, Los Angeles; s. Peter and Judith (Greenrock) V.; m. Celeste Tina Katz, Feb. 7, 1983; son, Noah Alexander, b. 1983; edn: UCLA, 1973-77; MA, Goddard Coll. 1980; grad. Calif. Acupuncture Coll. 1980, OMD, 1983. Career: pvt. practice in acupuncture, herbal medicine, orthomolecular nutrition, Tarzana, Ca. 1980–; clinical dir. Acupuncture Treatment and Research Center, Los Angeles 1982–; research assoc. instr. Oriental Healing Arts Inst., L.A. 1980–; prof./ chmn. dept. of herbal med., Calif. Acupuncture Coll. 1983–; prin. instr. Oriental Med. Pgm. Calif. Acupuncture Coll.; founder First Los Angeles Homeopathic Study Group, Sherman Oaks; honors: academic scholarship, Bunker-Ramo Corp. 1973; fellowship, Pharmacognosy, Oriental Healing Arts Inst. 1979, hon. mbrship 1983; author: Treatment of Chi, Water, and Blood Disease by Chinese Herbal Medicine, 1981; articles in Am. J. of Acupuncture (1985); contbg. writer Bull. of Oriental Arts Inst., nutrition column, The Transender Newspaper; rec: music, painting, martial arts. Res: 19546 Kittridge St Reseda 91335 Ofc: Victory-Tampa Medical Square, 19231 Victory Blvd, Ste. 556, Reseda 91335

VAN CAMP, BRIAN R, lawyer; b. Aug. 23, 1940, Halstread, Kans.; s. Ralph A. and Mary Margaret (Bragg) V.; m. Mary Ann Gatewood, June 25, 1961; Children: Marilyn Megan, b. 1962; Laurie E., b. 1963; edn: BA, UC Berkeley 1962, LLB, 1965; admitted to practice, State Bar Calif. 1966. Career: deputy atty. gen., State of Calif. 1965-7; agency atty. Redevel. Agcy, City of Sacramento 1967-70; asst./acting secty. Business and Transp Agcy, State of Calif. 1970-71, Commnr. of Corps. State of lkCalif. 1971-74; partner, Diepenbrock, Wulf, Palnt & Hannegan, Sacramento 1975-77; partner, Van Camp & Johnson 1978-; lectr. and author Calif. Cont. Edn. Bar, Practicing law Inst., CPA Soc. Calif.; dir: Original Sixteen to One Mine, Inc. (1982-), Am. Integ. Rsvcs., Inc. (1984-), Covenant REIT, Inc. (1984-); mem. Calif. Health Facilities Finance Authority (1985-); honors: Sumner-Mering Meml. Award, Sacto UC Alumni Assn. 1962; Outstanding Young Man of Year, Active 20-30 Club, Internat. 1973; Who's Who in Am. 1982, 84; mem: Am., Calif.,Sacremento, LA County, and Century City Bar assns., Mid-West Securities Commnrs. Assn (1971-74, pres. 1973-74), Calif. CofC (dir. 1982-), Rotary, Lincoln Club of Sacto Valley (pres. 1984-86), The Comstock Club, Inc. (pres.1976-77), Sacto Area Commerce and TradeOrgn. (v.p. 1985-86); civic: Sacto Sym. Assn., Camellia Fest. Assn., Active 20-30 Club 1 (1969-70), UC Men's Club of Sacto (1966-68), Wash. Neighborhood Ctr., CSU Sacto. Pres.'s adv. bd. (1978-), Sutter Comm. Hospitals Inc. comm. on Program Plnng. (1982-), Sacto Metro. CofC, United Way; clubs; Sutter, El Rancho

Racquet, Kandahar Ski, Tradewinds Sailing, Sacto Jaguar and Hobie Cat Fleet 17; publs: num. law rev., journal,; arts., fin. press, Cont. Edn. of the Bar; Republican; Presbyterian; rec: sailing, skiing Res: 3614 Brockway Ct, Sacramento 95818 Ofc: Van Camp & Johnson, 555 Capital Mall Ste 400, Sacramento 95814

VAN CLEEF, ROBERT EDWARD, engineer, systems analyst; b. May 20, 1946, Fall River, Mass.; s. Jacque Edward and Ellen D. (Fagan) Van C.; m. Mary Bradley, June 5, 1971; children: James, b. 1975, Anna-Marie, b. 1976; edn: AS, Santa Barbara City Coll.; BBA, magna cum laude w/distinction, National Univ., 1982, MBA, 1984. Career: enlistedman US Navy, 1964-76; field engr. Honeywell Corp., Santa Barbara 1976-79; senior tech. support engr. Computer Sciences Corp., San Diego 1979-84; tech. support con. Gateway Computer Systems, San Diego 1984—; mem: Assn. for Computing Machinery, San Diego Computer Soc. (pres. 1984), S.D. Osborne Users Group (past pres.); mil. decorations incl. Vietnam Cpgn. w/8 stars, RVN Armed Forces Meritorious (2), Nat. Def., GCM (2), Unit Commendn. (2), Combat Action Ribbon; Republican; Catholic; rec: tchg. personal computer usage. Res: 1151 Naranca Ave El Cajon 92021 Ofc: Gateway Computer Systems, 4980 Carroll Canyon Rd San Diego 92121

VANDE BERG, JERRY STANLEY, research physiologist; b. June 1, 1940, Sheldon, Iowa; s. Theodore Martin and Esther Margaret (Terpstra) V.B.; m. Susan Evans, Aug. 11, 1979; children: Blaine b. 1962, Joel b. 1968, Christopher b. 1972; edn: Colo. State Univ. 1958-59; BS, Univ. Neb. Lincoln 1964, MS, 1965; PhD, Va. Polytechnic Inst. & State Univ. 1969. Career: instr. entomology dept. Va. Polytechnic Inst. & State Univ. Blacksburg, Va. 1967-68; asst. prof. biol. scis. dept. Wayne State Univ. Detroit 1969-74; research assoc. entomology Univ. Wisc. Madison 1974-75; asst. prof. biol. scis. Old Dominion Univ. Norfolk, Va. 1975-79; dir. Core Clinical & Research Electron Microscopy Lab., VA Med. Ctr. San Diego 1979—; mem: Electron Microscopy Soc. of Am., NY Acad. of Scis., AAAS, Sigma Xi, Ducks Unlimited; publs: approx. 50 in sci. jours., book chpts.; Lutheran; rec: hunting, golf, fishing. Res: 1651-263 S Juniper Escondido 92025 Ofc: 3350 La Jolla Village Dr La Jolla 92161

VANDEGAER, SISTER PAULA, social worker; b. Feb. 14, 1939, Kansas City, Mo.; d. Thomas James and Lillian Loretta (Lynn) V.; edn: BA, psychol., Immaculate Heart Coll. 1962; MSW, Catholic Univ. of Am. 1965; Lic. Clin. Social Wkr., Calif. 1969; Acad. of Cert. Soc. Wkrs. (ACSW) 1970. Career: camp co-ordinator Camp Little Flower for Girls, K.C., Mo. 1961-65; branch dir. of Guadalupe Ctr. Settlement House, Canoga Pk., Ca. 1965-66, 68-70; casewkr. Catholic Welfare Bur., L.A. 1966-68; supr./casewkr. in Natural Parent Dept., Holy Family Svcs. (Adoption & Counseling), Los Angeles 1970-73; served alternately as dir. of postulants, dir. of novices, and vocation dir., Sisters of Social Service, 1973-77, comm. treas. 1976-82, served as first counselor 1978-82; occasional tchr. Mt. St. Mary's and Calif. Lutheran Colls.; dir. L.A. Branch, Alternatives to Abortion Internat., and editor Heartbeat Mag., 1978-84; exec. dir. Internat. Life Services, Inc. and editor Living World mag., 1984—; training & counseling articles reprinted worldwide; vol. Right to Life League of So. Calif. 10 years; lectr. on pro-life counseling throughout USA, Australia, NZ, and Europe; US Cong. and Calif. State Legis. testimony; appearances on Phil Donohue Show, Woman to Woman, num. other radio and TV pgms.; mem. Nat. Assn. of Soc. Wkrs., Right to Life League of So. Calif. (bd. dirs.), Nat. Assn. of Christians in Soc. Wk.; Republican; Catholic; rec: music, art. Res: 1130 Westchester Pl., Los Angeles 90019 Ofc: International Life Services, Inc. 2606 ½ West 8th St Los Angeles 90057

VAN DE KAMP, JOHN KALAR, state attorney general; b. Feb. 7, 1936, Pasadena; s. Harry and Georgie (Kalar) Van de Kamp; m. Andrea, Mar. 11, 1978; 1 dau. Diana, b. 1979; edn: BA, Dartmouth Coll. 1956, JD, Stanford Univ. 1959; admitted to Calif. State Bar, 1960. Career: asst. US Atty., chief of the Criminal Div., chief asst. US Atty., 1960-66; US Atty., Los Angeles, 1966-67; spl. asst. Pres.'s Commn. on Campus Unrest, 1970; deputy dir. and director, Exec. Office for US Attys., 1967-69; first Federal Public Defender for Central Dist. of Calif., L.A. 1971-75; L.A. County Dist. Atty., 1975-82; Calif. Attorney General, 1982—; awards: St. Thomas More Law Honor Soc. Medallion, Loyola Law Sch., 1984; Interagency Council on Abuse and Neglect, L.A. County, achievement award in prevention of child abuse and neglect, 1984; Equal Justice in the Law award, NAACP/ Legal Def. and Edn. Fund, 1985; mem: Calif. Dist. Attys. Assn. (past pres.), Nat. Dist. Attys Assn. (past v.p.), Peace Ofcrs Assn. of LA County (past pres.), Peace Ofcrs Stds & Tng Commn., Commn. on Judicial Apptmts., Nat. Assn. of Attys. Gen., Delay Reduction Adv. Com. Nat. Center for State Cts., Conf. of W. Attys. Gen. (v.ch.); mil: pfc US Army 1959-60, sp4 Nat. Guard 1960-65; Democrat; Catholic; rec: tennis, golf. Res: Pasadena Office of the Attorney General, 3580 Wilshire Blvd, Ste 800, Los Angeles 90010

VANDENBERGHE, RONALD GUSTAVE, accountant; b. Oakland; s. Anselm Henri and Margaret B. (Bygum) V.; m. Patricia W. Dufour, Aug. 18, 1957; children: Camile, Mark, Matthew; edn: BA, honors, San Jose State Coll. 1959; postgrad., UC Berkeley Extension 1959-60; Golden Gate Coll. 1961-63; CPA Calif. State. Career: real estate investor, Pleasanton, CA 1964-; instr. acctg. UC Berkeley, 1963-70; CPA, Pleasanton 1963—; mem: Calif. Soc. CPA's; Mason (Shriners); mil: USAF; Republican; Presbyterian. Res: POB 803 Danville 94526 Ofc: POB 1510 Pleasanton 94566

VANDERLAAN, WILLARD PARKER, research physician; b. June 5, 1917, Muskegon, Mich.; s. Willard P. and Sue (King) V.; m. Eileen Foster, June 18, 1944; children: Susan b. 1945, James b. 1947, Peter b. 1950; edn: Hope Coll. 1935-37, Oberlin Coll. 1937-38, MD cum laude, Harvard, 1942. Career: house staff Harvard Services, Boston City Hosp. 1942-44, postdoctoral fellow (E.B. Astwood MD, PhD) Harvard 1944-45, Tufts 1945-47; assoc. prof. medicine, Tufts Univ. 1947-56; physician New England Center Hosp., 1947-56; head Diabetes and Endocrinology, Scripps Clinic 1956-81; sci. dir. The Whittier Inst. for Diabetes & Endocrinol., 1982—; adj. prof. medicine UC San Diego 1972—; mem. Am. Soc. for Clin. Investig., W. Assn. of Physicians (v.p. 1960), Am. Thyroid Assn. (v.p. 1962); civic: trustee La Jolla Mus. of Contemp. Art (pres. 1962-64), trustee La Jolla Playhouse (chmn. 1984-85); research: Thyroid Physiology & Pituitary Physiology (1940-), research emphasis on iodine metabolism, thyroid disease, growth hormone, prolactin. Res: 8275 La Jolla Shores Dr La Jolla 92037 Ofc: The Whittier Institute 9894 Genesee La Jolla 92037

VAN DER MEULEN, JOSEPH PIERRE, university administrator; b. Aug. 22, 1929, Boston, Mass.; s. Edward Lawrence and Sarah Jane (Robertson)h V.; m. Ann Irene Yadeno, 1960; children: Elisabeth Ann, b. 1961; Suzanne Mari, b. 1965; Janet Christina, b. 1966; edn: AB in math, magna cum laude, Boston Coll. 1950; MD, cum laude, Boston Univ. Sch. of Med. 1954. Career: intern/ asst. res. in med. Bellevue Hosp., NYC 1954-6, res. neurol./ tchg. fellow Harvard Med. Sch., Boston City Hosp. 1958-60; instr. fellow. & dir. EEG Lab., 1962-67; asst./assoc. Case Western Reserve Univ. Sch. of Med. 1967-71; prof. neurology USC Sch. Med. 1971—, Dept. chmn. 1971-9, v.p. for Health Affairs, USC 1977—, and dean Sch. of Medicine, USC 1985—; dir. Dept. Neurology, L.A. Co.-USC Med. Ctr. 1971-9; phys. spec. 1979-; vis. prof. Autonomous Univ., Gadalajara, Mex., 1974; trustee, Eisenhower Med. Ctr. 1983; awards: Phi Kappa Phi, causo honoris; Humanitarian Awards, The Myasthenia Gravis Found. Inc., 1982, and USN League, 1978; Boston Coll. scholarship awd.; awards gen. excellence, Boston Univ., Alpha Omega Alpha Begg Soc., Mass. Med. Soc., student award; USC, grad. class, 1976; mem bd. trustees: Good Samaritan Hosp., Calif. Hosp. Med. Ctr., Good Hope Med. Found.; bd. dir. Children's Hosp. L.A., Eisenhower Med. Ctr., Norris Cancer Ctr. & Resrch. Inst., and Doheny Eye Hosp.; med. adv. bd. Calif. chpt. Myasthenia Gravis Found. 1971-5 (chmn. 1974/5, 77/8); med. adv. bd. Amyotrophic Lateral Sclerosis Found., Calif. 1973-5 (chmn. 1974/5); Com. to Combat Huntingtons Disease, 1973-; trustee Eisenhower Med. Ctr. 1983-; Nobel Inst. Fellow Karolinska Inst. 1960-62; NIH grantee, 1968-71; Dip. Am. Bd. Psychology and Neurology; mem: Am. Neurol. Assn.; Am. Acad. Neurology; L.A. Soc. Neurol. & Psychiatry, 1977-8; Mass., Ohio, Calif. Med. Socs.; L.A. Acad. Med.; Alpha Omega Alpha, councillor; Editl. bd. Archives of Neurol.; contrib. profl. journs.; mil: lt. MC, USNR, 1956-8; Democrat; Catholic; rec: golf, skiing. Res: 39 Club View Ln Rolling Hills Estates 90274 Ofc: USC, 1985 N Zonal Ave, PSC 100 Los Angeles 90033

VANDER TOP, ROGER DEAN, certified public accountant; b Nov. 28, 1953, Slayton, Minn.; s. John and Christina (Drooger) Vander Top; m. Alicia M. Veenendal, Sept. 5, 1984; edn: Canby Area Vocational Tech. Inst. 1973; Modesto Jr. Coll. lic. Public Acct. 1975, So. Dak.; CPA cert., Calif. 1980. Career: staff acct. Bernell J. McGinnis CPA, Sioux Falls, So.Dak., 1973-76; John A. Lane Acctcy. Corp., Modesto, Ca. 1976-81; prin. Roger D. Vander Top, CPA, Modesto 1981—; mem: Modesto CofC, Inland Soc. of Tax Consultants (treas. Modesto chpt. 1982), Calif. Soc. of CPAs, Modesto Chargers Youth football (treas. 1984-85), Nat. Fedn. Ind. Bus., S.F. Zool. Soc., Am. Film Inst.; Democrat; Ch. of Jesus Christ of L.D.S.; rec: sports, music. Res: 1524 Colima Ave Modesto 95355 Ofc: Roger D. Vander Top, CPA, 720 13th St Modesto 95354

VAN GORDER, TERRY ELLIS, leisure time co. executive; b. Aug. 19, 1933, Palo Alto; s. Ellis Walter and Catherine Bassett (Terry) Van G.; children: Eric b. 1961, Catherine b. 1963, Kurt b. 1966; edn: BA, Yale Univ. 1955; ensign USNR, Newport, R.I. 1956; cert. Chief Exec. Pgm. Stanford Bus. Sch. 1977. Career: lt. USNR Naval Intel., Adak and Guam, 1956-59; gen. mgr. Peacock Gap Golf & Country Club, San Rafael 1959-64; senior v.p. The Newhall Land & Farming Co., Valencia 1964-80; pres./CEO Magic Mountain, Inc. Valencia 1971-79; pres./CEO Knott's Berry Farm, Buena Park 1981—; dir: Magic Mountain Inc., Valencia Recreation Ents. Inc. (1971-79), Van Gorder Assocs. (v.p. 1963-76); mem. Phi Gamma Delta, Yale Alumni (Scholarship Com.), LA CofC, LA County Art Mus., Yale Club of So. Calif., United Way (area chmn.); works: designed Vista Valencia and Vista Chica golf courses, Valencia (1966); strategically planned, conceptualized and built Magic Mountain, Valencia (1971-79); founder and conceptualizer of Camp Snoopy, Knott's Berry Farm (1983); mil: lt. USNR 1955-59; Republican; Prot.; rec: golf, fishing, painting, golf course arch. Ofc: Knott's Berry Farm 8039 Beach Blvd Buena Park 90620

VAN HOOSER, DAVID BARTON, real estate executive, investment specialist; b. July 13, 1939, Oakland; s. Cornelius Barton and Ruth David (Harrison) Van Hooser; m. JoAnn Southwick, July 2, 1979; children: David b. 1960, Lance b. 1963, Aaron b. 1970, Billie b. 1971; edn: BBA, Calif. State Coll. 1970; spl. courses in indsl. suprvn., purchasing, personnel & labor rels., 1957-69; La Salle Ext. Univ. of Law, 1966-9; Northwood Inst. of Mdsg. 1969; Century 21 Investment Splst., Resdtl. Splst. 1985. Career: adminstrv. asst. to the pres. Kaiser Jeep Corp., Oakland 1966-68, dist. sales mgr., So. San Francisco 1968-69; dist. mgr. Winnebago Industries, Concord, Ca. 1970, nat. bus. mgmt., Forrest City, Iowa 1970-71, nat. dealer devel. mgr., 1970-71; western regional mgr. Apollo Motor Homes, Reno, Nev. 1979, nat. sales mgr., Downey, Ca. 1980, v.p. Sales, 1981, v.p. Mktg/Sales, Carson, Ca. 1981-84; investment splst. Century 21 1985 – ; mem. Am. Mgmt. Assn.; Calif. Assn. Realtors; Nat. Assn. Realtors; Victor Valley Bd. of Realtors (grievance com.); Century 21 Investment Soc.; charter mem. La Salle Univ. Alumni Assn. Republican. Ch. of Jesus Christ of Latter Day Saints. Rec: guns/desert survival. Res: Star Rte 1942, Lucerne Valley 92356 Ofc: Century 21 Tri Cities Realty, 16932 Bear Valley Rd Victorville 92392

VAN KIRK, JOHN ELLSWORTH, physician; b. Jan. 13, 1942, Dayton, Ohio; s. Herman Corwin and Dorothy Louise (Shafer) V.K.; m. Patricia Lynn Davis, June 19, 1966; 1 dau., Linnea b. 1979; edn: BA, cum laude, De Pauw Univ. 1963; BS, Northwestern Univ. 1964; MD, distn., Northwestern Univ. Sch. of Med. 1967; Bd. Cert. in Internal Med. & Cardiovascular Disease. Career: med. internship Evanston Hosp., Northwestern Univ. 1967-68; USPHS staff assoc., NIAID, senior asst. surgeon NIH 1968-70; resident in med., fellowship in cardiology Univ. of Mich. 1970-74; instr. in internal med. 1973-74; staff cardiologist Mills Meml. Hosp., San Mateo 1974 – , also, dir. critical care, dir. pacemaker clinic; honors: Physician's Recogn. Award, 1969, 1972, 1975, 1977, 1980, 1982, 1985; Alpha Omega Alpha; 1st Prize in Landscaping, State of Calif. 1977; mem: Fellow Am. Coll. of Cardiology, Am. Heart Assn., San Mateo Co. Hearth Assn. (pres. 1977-79), Am., Calif. and San Mateo Co. Med. Assns.; works: research in devel. of live viral respiratory vaccines for human use; publd. articles in med. journs.; mil: USPHS 1968-70; Republican; United Brethren; rec: gardening, amateur radio, computer science. Res: 2200 Skyfarm Dr. Hillsborough 94010 Ofc: 121 So. San Mateo Dr. San Mateo 94401

VAN KIRK, R. LEE, business owner; b. July 18, 1945, Youngstown, Ohio; s. Charles and Jeanetta (MacWhorter) Van K.; m. Gayle, Apr. 15, 1978; children: Daniel b. 1978, Calley Anne b. 1981; edn: BS commerce, Univ. of Louisville; MBA, Univ. of Ky.; postgrad. Univ. of Maryland; desig: LUTC, Life Underwriters Tng. Council (1970), NASD. Career: served to capt. US Army 1964-70; pres. American Home Financial Services Corp., 1970-79; CEO Day Spring, Inc., 1979-84; CEO G.V.K. Corp., 1984 – , and pres. Motivation, Inc.; apptd. Hon. Order of Kentucky Colonels by Gov. Julian Carroll (1973) and Gov. Louie Nunn (1977); Republican; Prot.; rec: golf, fishing. Res: 2969 Murat St San Diego 92117

VAN MCNEAL, HENRY, songwriters academy president; b. Sept. 20, 1953, New Orleans, La.; s. Henry Washington and Mary Lee (Doty) McN. Career: founder/pres. Nat. Acad. of Songwriters, San Francisco 1981 – ; awards: Eastman Kodak Teenage Movie Award (1972), merit award S.F. Public Library Fest. of Young Filmmakers (1973); mem. Nat. Songwriters Guild, Internat. Platform Assn.; creator, editor The Official Directory of American Songwriters; author Swan Song: The Undiscovered Portrait of a Dying Swan (a poetic narrative of melodic verse, 1985), Drops of Rain: The Love Poems of Henry Van McNeal (1986); appeared on NET/ Eastman Kodak documentary series Scene One, Take One for motion picture The Lover's Dictionary (1974); assoc. producer series The Minority Report (1983); hobbies: numerologist, metaphysician, philosopher, documentary filmmaker, composer. Address: San Francisco 94142

VAN MOURICK, MARK, stockbroker; b. July 31, 1956, Santa Monica; s. Laurence and Teresa (Sholes) Van M.; m. Tricia Dowsett, July 26, 1980; 1 son, Christopher James b. 1984; edn: BS internat. fin., USC 1978; desig: Reg. Prin. NYSE, NASD (1984). Career: founder/co-owner, mgr. Installation Warehouse (auto electronics co.), Beverly Hills 1977-79, now merged w/ Clifford Indus.; stockbroker Smith Barney 1979 – , vice pres. 1983-, reg. principal and apptd. mem. Corporate Services Group; co-founder Investment Research Assocs. Inc.; honors: Eagle Scout (1971), Century Club, Smith Barney; mem. USC Accounting Circle, Orange County Perf. Arts Ctr. (spons.); Clubs: Newport Breakfast Club (speaker), Pacific (speakers & Father/Son com.), Monarch Bay, Outrigger Canoe (Hawaii); accomplished mountaineer, US and Central Europe (54 countries); Republican; Presbyterian. Res: 28561 Silverton Dr Laguna Niguel 92677 Ofc: Smith Barney 5000 Birch St Ste 7000 Newport Beach 92670

VAN RENSSELAER, CAROL ANN, investor; b. Sept. 29, 1946, Los Angeles; d. Robert Lawson and Peggy Carol (Pixler) Pierson; m. Robert Wm. Brokopp, Mar. 22, 1969; m. 2d. Edward Maunsell Van Rennselaer, Sept. 4, 1985; edn: BA in hist., CSU Fullerton 1975; Calif. lic. real estate broker 1981. Career: owner Brock Finl. Investments, Newport Beach 1976 – ; pres. Pac-Tex Resource Operations, Inc., Newport Bch. and Houston Tx. 1979 – ; pres. International A Comml. Brokerage, Newport Bch. and Houston, Tx. 1981 – ; mem. Realty Inv. Assn. of Orange Co., Newport-Costa Mesa Bd. of Realtors; co-founder Cure Paralysis Found.; regl. v.p./bd. dirs. Paralysis Cure Research 1976-83; bd. dirs. Nat. Spinal Cord Injury Found. 1979-80; club: Bahia Corinthian Yacht; works: prod. "Sound of Music" on the Main Stage, UCI (11/82) to benefit Am. Paralysis Found.; spons. Brokopp Bermuda Conf., 1978 (first nat. conf. for cure of spinal cord injury); patron, 1st Internat. Conf. for SCI Cure, Catania, Sicily; Republican (Pres. Task Force); Prot.; rec: antiques. Res: 2975 Chillon Way Laguna Beach 92651

VAN SEVENTER, A., accountant; b. Sept. 25, 1913, Amesterdam, Netherlands; s. A. and Maria (van Dijk) van S.; m. Ruth E. Smith, 1949; children: Antony b. 1951, Ronald E. b. 1953; edn: AB, Univ. of Amsterdam 1934; Golden Gate Coll. 1947; MBA, Stanford Univ. 1949; PhD, Univ. of Mich. 1966; CPA, Calif. and Alaska 1950. Career: instr. acctg. Anchorage Community Coll. 1954-62; vis. lectr. taxation Eastern Mich. Univ. 1963; instr. acctg. Cleary Coll., Mich. 1963; instr., lectr. acctg. Univ. of Mich. 1963-66; asst., assoc. prof. of acctg. San Jose State Univ. 1966-76; prof. acctg. San Francisco State Univ. 1976-84; ret.; secty. Alaska Bd. of Public Accty. 1953-57; French Consu-

lar Agent, Anchorage, Ala. 1952-62; public acct., C.A. Gall & Co., NY, Haskins & Sells CPAs, San Francisco, Philip A. Hershey CPA, San Francisco, Beaver & van Seventer CPAs, Anchorage, AK and solo pvt. practice, Anchorage; honors: Phi Beta Kappa, Univ. of Mich. 1966; Beta Alpha Psi 1963; Lybrand Dissertation Fellowship in Acctg. 1965; French Medal of Honor in Bronze; Acad. of Acctg. Historians Hourglass Award 1977; mem: Acad. of Acctg. Historians, Am Inst. CPAs, Calif. Soc. CPAs, Am. Acctg. Assn., Peninsula Symphony Orchestra, Phi Beta Kappa (past pres. No. Calif. Assn.), Rotary Club (past, Anchorage); works: The History of Accountancy, trans. from Dutch 1976; co-author with Dr. G. Costouros, Contemporary Accounting Issues 1979; contbr., Peter Holzer, Internat. Accounting 1984; mil: s/sgt. 11th AFSC 1942-45; rec: music. Address: Bay Books, 2335 Waverley St. Palo Alto 94301

VAN VELZER, VERNA JEAN, librarian; b. Jan. 22, 1929, State College, Penn.; d. Harry Leland and Golda Lillian (Cline) V.V.; edn: BS, Univ. Ill. 1950, BSL, Syracuse Univ. 1957. Career: head librarian General Electric Microwave Lab., Palo Alto 1958-64; librarian Research & Devel. Lab., Fairchild Semiconductor Products Co., Palo Alto 1964-65; intelligence librarian Sylvania Electronic Products Co., Mountain View 1965-66; research librarian ESL Inc., Sunnyvale 1966 – ; mem: Spl. Libraries Assn., Assn. for Computing Machinery, IEEE, Am. Defense Preparedness Assn., Am. Inst. Aero. & Astro, Assn. of Old Crows, Beta Phi Mu. Res: 4048 Laguna Way Palo Alto 94306 Ofc: ESL Inc., 495 Java Dr. Sunnyvale 94088

VAN WAGENEN, JAMES CHIPMAN, podiatrist; b. Mar.1, 1936, Provo, Utah; s. Rulon Clark and Leah (Chipman) Van W.; m. Susanne Palmer, Dec. 17, 1959; children: Colleen b. 1962, Karen b. 1964, Brian b. 1965, Linda b. 1968, Laura b. 1970; edn: Brigham Young Univ. 1954-6, 1959-60; AA, Am. River Jr. Coll. 1960; BS, Calif. Coll. of Podiatric Med. 1961, DPM 1965; Diplomate Am. Bd. of Ambulatory Foot Surgery Sect., Am. Bd. Podiatric Surgery. Career: practicing podiatrist in Fresno 1965 – ; listed: Who's Who in Am. 1975, Outstanding Americans 1976; mem: Calif. Podiatric Med. Assn. (pres. Mid state Soc. 1978; pres. Mid state Acad. of Ambulatory Foot Surgeons 1984-85), Fellow Am. Acad. of Ambulatory Foot Surgery; Mormon (mission in Va., N.C. 1957-59); rec: skiing, scuba diving, flying. Res: 7405 No. Paula, Clovis 93612 Ofc: Jim C. Van Wagenen, DPM 3381 N Bond Fresno 93726

VARGAS, RUDOLPH, artist; b. Apr. 20, 1904, Mexico; came to USA in 1926, nat. 1950; Gabriel and Maria (Vega) V.; m. Margaret Flott'e, Aug. 8, 1931; children: Rudolph Jr. b. 1933, Christina b. 1942; edn: Acad. of Fine Arts, Mex. Career: sculptor in wood, clay, bronze; teacher Monrovia High Sch.; commnd. to carve in wood a Madonna for the Vatican (1962); commnd. to create a large collection of contemporary and classical wood carvings, panels, large figures, and paintings for Santa Teresita Hospital in Duarte, Ca.; works incl. portraits in bronze, sculptures for film media, architl. and comml. displays; honors: recognition in print media, TV coverage, and a 30-min. film on his work; recognition from Gov. Brown Jr., Pres. Carter, City of Ontario, num. awards incl. Calif. Carvers Guild; listed in Who's Who in Am. Art, Internat. Ency. Degli Artisti (Acona, Italy), Who's Who in the West; mem: San Diego CofC (Xmas com.), Calif. Carvers Guild; rec: electronics, photog. Res: 1074 No Herbert Ave Los Angeles 90063 Ofc: 3661 Whittier Blvd Los Angeles 90023

VASLAVSKY, VIKTOR FILIPPOVICH, engineer; b. Apr. 8, 1936, Odessa, USSR; s. Filipp and Beba (Nisenbaum) V.; edn: BS, MS, Civil Engring. Inst., Odessa, USSR, 1958; PhD, Constrn. Engring. Univ., Moscow, 1970; Reg. Profl. Engr. (Civil) Calif. 1982; Senior Sci. Researcher, USSR, 1973; Assoc. Prof., USSR, 1977. Career: senior structural engr. R.M. Parsons Co., Pasadena 1981-82, 1984 – ; consulting engr.; (past) constrn. engr. Bechtel Power Corp. 1983-84; struc. engr. DMJM, Los Angeles 1979-81; assoc. prof./researcher Constrn. Engring. Univ., Moscow 1964-78; civil/struc. engr. Siberia, USSR 1958-64. Mem. ASCE 1981-; works: 2 inventions in civil/struc. engring.; 13 tech. papers; rec: chess. Res: 6852 Petit Ave Van Nuys 91406

VASQUEZ, ARMAND, printing co. executive; b. Feb. 25, 1952, Los Angeles; s. Armando Ochoa and Stellar (Barr) V.; m. Pamela, July 19, 1976; 1 son, Alex b. 1981; edn: AA, Don Bosco Tech. Inst. 1971. Career: fmr. sales mgr. Crown Gibraltar Graphics, Alhambra; current owner, Corporate Colour Printing, Monterey Park; mem: Olympic Organizing Com., Latin Bus. Assn. (past v.p.); rec: karate, swimming, running. Res: 712 Strand Manhattan Beach 90266 Ofc: Corporate Colour Printing, 1255 Corporate Center Dr Monterey Park 91754

VAUGHAN, DANIEL G., physician-surgeon; b. Mar. 15, 1921, Montana; s. Daniel G. and Katerine (Browne) V.; m. Courtney Sprague, Dec. 3, 1949; children: Laurie b. 1950, Cecilia b. 1952, James b. 1954, Matthew b. 1956, Mary b. 1959, Daniel b. 1960, Katherine b. 1960, Elizabeth b. 1963; edn: BS, Univ. of Wash., Seattle 1942; MD, Univ. of Oregon Med. Sch., Portland 1945; Diplomate Am. Board Ophthalmology 1953. Career: postdoctoral intern King County Hosp., Seattle 1945-46; resident in ophthalmology Univ. of Calif., San Francisco 1948-51; pvt. practice ophthal., San Jose 1951 – ; staff O'Connor Hosp. (pres. 1964; bd. mem. O'Connor Hosp. Found.); founder/pres. Sight Conservation Research Center, 1960-; clin. prof. UCSF Dept. Ophthal. and Francis I. Proctor Found. for Research in Ophthal., S.F.; cons. US Army Hosp., Fort Ord; mem: Am. Acad. Ophthal. and Otol., AMA, Assn. for Research in Ophthal. (exec. secty. W. Sect. 1961-66), Fellow Am. Coll. of Surgeons (Western US rep. to Advis. Council for Ophthalmic Surgery 1971-74 and chmn. 1974-76), Frederick C. Cordes Eye Soc. (pres. 1965), No. Calif. Soc. for Prevention of Blindness (pres. 1971-73), Pacific Coast Oto-Ophthalmological Soc. (pres. 1980-81), Santa Clara Co. Med. Assn., Santa Clara Univ. (bd.

fellows); publs: 25 sci. articles in ophthalmic jours., contbr. eye chapters in two med. texts; coauthor General Ophthalmology, 10th ed. (Lange Med. Publs., pub. in 6 languages); mil: med. corps First Marine Div., China 1946-47. Ofc: 220 Meridian Ave San Jose 95126

VAUGHN, CARL EDWARD, administrator; b. Nov. 19, 1933, Fort Smith, Ark.; s. Jasper J. and Ruby Lee (Chastain) V.; m. Elizabeth, Sept. 22, 1951; children: Carl Jr. b. 1952, Sandra b. 1958, Robert (dec.) b. 1965; edn: Calif. Real Estate Broker courses, Riverside Comm. Coll. 1976; HLD, Bethel Christian Coll. 1983; desig: Profl. Mgmt. Cert., Nat. Mgmt. Assn. 1961; lic. realtor Calif. 1976; ordained minister Bethel Christian Ctr. (1983). Career: dept. mgr. A&P Tea Co., Jacksonville, Fla. 1954-55; agt. Gulf Life Ins. Co., Jacksonville 1955-56; engr./supvr. General Dynamics Corp., San Diego 1956-66; mgr. spl. proj. div. Hycon Corp., Monrovia 1966-71; owner O K Hopkins T.V. & Appliance Stores, Riverside & Hemet, 1971-76; owner Guardian West Realty, Riverside 1976–; cons. to non-profit religious orgns. 1976-; adminstr. Bethel Christian Center, Riverside 1976–, dir., corp. secty., chief finl. ofcr. 1983–; dir./pres. Bethel Bdcstg. Inc. (1978-), regent/exec. v.p. Bethel Christian Coll. and Bethel Grad. Sch. of Theology (1982-), chmn. Adminstrn. Dept. Bethel Christian Coll. and Bethel Grad. Sch. Theol. 1985-; advis. bd. Calif. Baptist Coll., Riverside 1981; mem: Calif. Assn. Realtors 1976-, Nat. Assn. Realtors 1976-, Riverside Board of Realtors (1976-), ASQC/Santa Maria (chmn. Profl. Dev. Com. 1962-66, General Dynamics Mgmt. Assn. 1959-65, Convair Mgmt. Assn. (chmn. achievement & awards coms.), founder/chmn. Edn. Advis. Council and mem. exec. bd. 1963-66), Nat. Mgmt. Assn./San Diego 1965-71, Riverside CofC 1971-86, Riverside Plaza Merchants Assn. (dir. 1971-76), Kiwanis Club; works: devel. and installed academic pgm. at Allan Hancock Coll., Santa Maria which leads to AA degree in Quality Control Engring. (1965); devel. & supvr. of on-going ops. Bethel Christian Ctr.'s school system of presch., elementary, jr. high, and high sch. (1983-); mil: US Navy 1950-54; Republican; Internat. Conv. of Faith Ministers, Tulsa, Okla.; rec: golf, travel, finl. seminars and consulting. Res: 12138 Barnes Ct Moreno Valley 92388 Ofc: Bethel Christian Center 2425 Van Buren Blvd Riverside 92503

VAUGHN, JOHN VERNON, industrialist, civic leader; b. June 24, 1909, Grand Junction, Colo.; s. John S. and Alice A. (Baylis) V.; m. Dorothy M. Pickrell, Oct. 12, 1934; children: Dorothy Dee (Mrs. Richard H. Stone) b. 1936, John Spencer b. 1939; edn: BA in econs., UC Los Angeles 1932. Career: asst. credit mgr., later branch mgr. Nat. Lead Co., 1932-37; sales mgr. Sillers Paint & Varnish Co. (paint mfr.), 1937-46, pres./prin. owner 1946-59, sold co., merged with Benjamin Moore & Co. 1959; pres./bd. chmn./owner Dartell Labs. (mfr. pharmaceutical and biochem. splties.) 1960-70, sold co., merged with ICN Pharm. 1970; v.chmn. bd. Crocker Nat. Bank, 1970-74; cons. Coopers & Lybrand, 1974-85; dir: Recon/Optical, Inc., Barrington, Ill. (bd. chmn. 1978-), I.T. Corp. (1976-), Forest Lawn Co. (1975-), Am. Security & Fidelity Corp. (1969-), O.K. Earl Corp. (1968-70, 79-85), Trust Svcs. Am. Inc. (1983-), Crocker Nat. Bank (1969-81, hon. dir. 1981-), Calif. Fed. Svgs & Loan (1965-70, 75-83), Pacific Lighting Corp. (1971-82), Orthopaedic Hosp. (pres. 1973-78, trustee 1966-); honors: Hon. LLD, Pepperdine Univ. (1974), Alumnus of Year, UCLA (1971), Most Disting. Citizen, L.A. Realty Board (1972), community award of merit L.A. CofC (1974), brotherhood award NCCJ (1971), Businessman of Year, Nat. Assn. Accts./L.A. (1974), disting. achievement Am. Heart Assn./L.A. (1975), resolution L.A. City Council (1970); mem: L.A. Paint, Varnish & Lacuer Assn. (pres. 1952), UCLA Alumni Assn. (pres. 1957-58), L.A. Area CofC (chmn. 1970, dir. 1959-72), L.A. Clearing House Assn. (pres. 1973-74); civic: Republican Assocs. (pres. 1967-68, dir. 63-73), Friends of Claremont Colls. (pres. 1973-77), Calif. Mus. Sci. & Indus. (dir. 1968-79), L.A. Beautiful (dir. 1972-74), So. Calif. Bldg. Funds (dir. 1972-74), L.A. Conv. Bur. (dir. 1973-75), United Way L.A. (dir. 1975-81), Central City Assn. (dir. 1971-74), So. Calif. Vis. Council (dir. 1970-74), YMCA/LA (dir. 1965-77), Am. Heart Assn./LA (dir. 1972-75), Town Hall of Calif. (bd. govs. 1973-75), Gov's Task Force on Transp. (exec. com. 1967-68), Young Pres's Orgn. (1951-56), Chancellor's Assocs. Calif. State Univs. & Colls. (1980-84); clubs: past pres. Jonathan (1964), California, L.A. Country, Pasadena Athletic, Lincoln, Twilight, Economic Round Table, Newcomen Soc., Internat. Order of St. Hubertus, Masons, Beta Theta Pi (pres. 1960); Republican; Presbyterian; rec: stream fishing, hunting, golf. Res: 454 S Orange Grove Blvd Pasadena Ofc: 225 S Lake Ave Ste M-181 Pasadena 91101

VAUGHN, MARY, convalescent hosp., owner- administrator; b. April 20, 1930, Trafford, Ala.; m. Grover Webster and Vivian Lenore (Dorman) V.; m. James T. Lovvorn, July 4, 1951, dec.; edn: Cert., Birmingham Bus. Coll. 1949; modeling, Howard Coll. 1962; Thearapeutic Activities Cert., Grossmont Adult Sch. 1975; Cert., Mgmt. Success Inst. 1977; Lic. Adminstr., Calif.; Cert. Notary Public, Calif. Career: pres., treas. Balboa Manor Health Facility, San Diego; owner, opr. Balboa Manor Intermediate Care Ctr., San Diego; mem: Girls Club of San Diego (1st v.p.), Southland Bus. & Profl. Womens Orgn. (past pres.); author: Exploring Mental Therapy, 1978; Democrat; Methodist; rec: volleyball, volunteer. Res: 2804 C Street San Diego 92102 Ofc: Balboa Manor Inc., 1119 28th St. San Diego 92102

VAUGHN, NORMAN, lawyer, oil company land agent; b. June 13, 1932, Alabama City, Ala.; s. Oscar Nicholas and Dorothy L. (Orebaugh) V.; m. Anna Jean Owen Collier, Nov. 27, 1982; edn: ABJ, Univ. Ga. 1966; JD, summa cum laude, John Marshall, Atlanta 1973; admitted bar: Ga. and Calif.; Career: radio announcer/newsman radio stations in Ga., Md., Va., Penn. and W. Va., 1953-72; law clerk Hammond Johnson Jr., Gainesville, Ga. 1972-73; law practice, Cornelia, Ga. 1973-74; asst. to Clerk GA H.O.R. 1974; city atty., Mt. Airy, Ga. 1973-74; senior right of way agent Ford, Bacon & Davis, Mich., La., Texas, Kans. 1974-76; honors: John Marshall valedictorian (1973), Corpus Juris Senior Award, Am. Jurisprudence awards in Pleading & Practice, Crim. Law, Trusts, UCC, Future Interests, Ins., Personal Prop., Real Prop., Evidence; mil: radioman 1/c US 1949-53, 1962-65, Korea 2 battle stars, Good Conduct Japan Occ., UN; Republican; rec: country music, travel, literature. Res: 1259 Alamo St. Anaheim 92801 Ofc: Shell Oil Co., 511 No. Brookhurst St. Anaheim 92801

VAUGHN, RALPH DAVIS, business owner; b. March 9, 1933, Morehead, Miss.; s. Victor Davis and Bervie Mae (Henderson) V.; m. Karen Weiser, Feb. 27,1 980; stepchildren: George b. 1951, Michael b. 1953; edn: BS, Miss. State 1954, BA, 1954. Career: Waddell & Reed, Memphis, Tenn. 1957-59; Burroughs Corp., Los Angeles 1959-61; Allstate Ins. Co., Pasadena 1961; Wholesale Greeting Card Distbr. 1961-62; art dir./ed./ pub. line of greeting cards, US (royalty agreement to England) 1962-72; wholesaler horoscopes 1965-86, investor 1976-80; owner, opr. video games 1980–; honors: Top 100 Salesmen, Mutual Funds in Country 1958; mem: Kappa Alpha Order, Delta Sigma Pi, Conejo Valley Garden Club; mil: 1st lt. USAF 1954-57; rec: gold mining share analyst, political research analysis, gardening. Res: 796 Masterson Dr Thousand Oaks 91360 Ofc: POB 1051 Thousand Oaks 91360

VAUGHT, GERALD WILSON, accountant, health care executive; b. Aug. 14, 1940, Wynne, Ark.; s. Leonard Milton and Nora Ann (Childers) V.; m. Cheryl Rae Huffman, Dec. 24, 1966; children: Kevin b. 1968, Katherine b. 1977; edn: BS, Ariz. State Univ. 1967; MBA, UC Berkeley 1972; Certified Public Acct., Calif. Career: CPA/auditor Arthur Young & Co., San Francisco and Oakland, 1967-71; asst. controller St. Francis Meml. Hosp., San Francisco 1973-74, controller 1975-76, asst. adminstr. fin. 1977-80, CFO/assoc. adminstr. Finl. Services 1981–; speaker var. orgns. such as American Coll. of Radiology, Assn. of Western Hosps., Healthcare Finl. Mgmt. Assn.; awards: Donna Anderson Meml. Scholarship Award, No. Calif. Chpt. of Healthcare Finl. Mgmt. Assn. (1980); mem: Calif. Soc. CPAs, Healthcare Finl. Mgmt. Assn. (Advanced mem.), Nat. Assn. of Accts., Am. Inst. CPAs; civic: Alameda/S.F. Planned Parenthood (fin. com.), Am. Lung Assn. of S.F. (fin. com.), Unitarian Ch. (audit com.); articles in nat. profl. journals include Hospital Financial Management (1/80), Computers in Healthcare (6/83), M.D., others; mil: E4 Carbon Dioxide Splst. US Army 1963-65; rec: golf, computers, video games. Res: 4 Nephi Ct Lafayette 94549 Ofc: Saint Francis Memorial Hospital 900 Hyde St San Francisco 94109

VEGA, MARCOS SAUL, management executive; b. July 5, 1953, Chilpancingo, Mexico; s. Gonzalo V. Villeda and Josefina Eufemia Vega Trejo; m. Eufemia Evangelista, Sept. 17, 1983; 1 dau, Monika Eufemia b. 1986; edn: AA, East Los Angeles Community Coll. 1976; BS, cum laude, CSU Los Angeles 1981, MS, 1983. Career: lab. techn. Nutrition dept. CSU Los Angeles 1978-80, biomed. researcher Found. 1979-81; admin. asst. City of South Gate Police Dept. 1981-83, pgm. evaluations mgr. 1983-85; ops. mgr. City of South Gate Police/ JADE dept. 1985–; job developer cons. Youth Opportunities Unltd. 1985; real estate investment, multi unit mgmt. 1983–; mem: Personnel Indsl. Rels. Assn., Neighborhood Block Watch (capt. City of Bell. 1983-), United Way, World Vision; works: co-author, Pantothenic Acid, CSU Los Angeles 1981-; Democrat; Catholic; rec: real estate, gardening, tennis. Ofc: City of South Gate, 8650 California Ave., JADE South Gate 90280

VEITCH, STEPHEN WILLIAM, investment counselor; b. Aug. 19, 1927, Albuquerque, NM; s. Kenneth Easton and Edna (Miller) V.; m. Nancy Baker, July 28, 1951; children: Christopher Oxnard b. 1953, Julia Blair b. 1958; edn: BA, Univ. New Mexico 1949; JD, Stanford Law Sch. 1957. Career: probate adminstr. Wells Fargo Bank 1957-59; sr. v.p. Vanstrum & Towne, Inc., 1959-82, pres./CEO 1982–; dir. Anza Pacific Corp. 1960-76; Advis. bd. Anza Shareholders' liquidating trust, 1976-; pres. Oxnard Found. 1979-; secty. William Knox Holt Found. 1978-; mem: Pacific Union Club (SF), Menlo Circus Club (Atherton), Commonwealth Club (SF); Sigma Chi Frat.; mil: USN 1945-6, 1st lt. USAF 1950-4; Republican; Episcopal. Res: 33 Spencer Ln Atherton 94025 Ofc: Van Strum & Towne, Inc., 505 Sansome St, Ste. 1001, San Francisco 94111

VELIZ, MARIA ELVA S., accountant; b. Sept. 23, 1949, Del Rio, Texas; d. Armando V. and Martina (Sanchez) Sotelo; m. Jesse C. Veliz, March 25, 1972; edn: Bus. Admin., CSU Fullerton 1982; CPA, 1984. Career: dept. secty. CSU Fullerton 1976-79, 1980-81; exec. secty. Mattel Toys, Torrance 1979-80; CPA Moss Adams & Co., Los Angeles 1982–; discussion leader Mexican Am. Assn. for Women Sems. 1984; honors: Scholarship, Am. Soc. for Women Accts. 1981; mem: Am. Inst. of CPAs, Calif. Soc. CPAs, Beta Alpha Psi, Mexican- Am. Nat. Assn. for Women, Nat. Assn. for Exec. Women, Am. Cancer Soc., Salesian Mission Orphanage; works: asst. research and processing two personal finance books by Dennis J. O'Connor, CSU Fullerton; Democrat; Presbyterian; rec: Mexican music, reading. Res: 18839 Stetani Ave. Cerritos 90701 Ofc: Moss Adams & Co., 800 So. Figueroa Ste. 900 Los Angeles 90017

VELLA, VICTOR A., data processing executive; b. April 25, 1930, Malta, Europe, nat. US cit. 1954; s. Alfred and Mary (Cuschieri) V.; m. Yvonne Abdilla, Feb. 14, 1954, dec.; m. 2d Rosalia Sarmiento, Oct. 20, 1984; children: Victor A. b. 1960, Valerie A. b. 1962, Vivienne A. b. 1963; edn: grad., Lyceum, Valletta, Malta 1947; Cert. Data Processor, DPMA 1965; Cert. Data Educator, 1973. Career: jr. acct. J. Arthur Rank Orgn., London, England 1948-50; data processing splst. US Army 1951-53; opns. mgr., instr. data processing for foreign national, Arabian Am. Oil Co. (ARAMCO), Saudia Arabia 1955-58; senior data processing analyst General Dynamics, San Diego 1959, data processing supvr. astronautics div. 1962-63, div. supvr. 1963-65, admin. staff astronautics div. 1965-66; senior sys. analyst Pacific technical Analysts Inc. (on contract with US), Saigon, Vietnam 1966-67; ADP div. dir. USN Fed. Civil Svc. Commn., ofcr. in charge of constrn., Saigon, Vietnam 1967-70; ADP div. dir. , Facilities Sys. Ofc., NCBC, Pt. Hueneme 1970-72, dept. head 1972—; instr. data processing Calif. Western Univ. San Diego 1964; cons. Poway H.S. Dist. 1965; awards: Labor Medal 1/c, Republic of Vietnam 1970; profl. awards, Civil Svc. Commn. 1972, 1973, USN- Vietnam 1968, 1969, 1970; mem: Assn. of ADP Splsts. in Vietnam (perm. hon. pres. 1969), Officer Guide, Data Processing Mgmt. Assn., Mgmt. Sys. Assn.; mil: pfc US Army 1951-53; rec: pvt. pilot, travel, photog. Res: 606 Deseo Ave. Camarillo 93101 Ofc: NCBC, Facilities Systems Office, Port Hueneme 93043

VERMES, L. ROBERT, lawyer; b. Jan. 7, 1945, Sussex, N.J.; s. Dr. Leslie R. and Alice (Gerry) V.; m. June Ellen, July 4, 1974; children: Carly b. 1977, Courtney b. 1982, Brittain b. 1982; edn: BS, Northwestern Univ. 1967; JD, Valley Univ. Law Sch. 1978; admitted Calif. State Bar 1980, US Dist. Ct. (Central Dist.). Career: mgr. Organon Inc. (pharmaceutical distbg. co.), No. Hollywood 1971-77; atty., ptnr. Bradford & Vermes (constrn. law firm), Irvine 1980-81; atty. Strantz & Fine (rep. Fremont Indemnity Co.), L.A., Orange, Santa Ana 1977-81; atty. assoc. Kristjanson, Bellanca & Hill (wkrs comp. defense law), Tustin 1981-83; ptnr. Kriner, Hebner & Vermes, Santa Ana 1983—; instr. (labor code & current case law) Ins. Edn. Assn., Newport Beach; mem: ABA, Orange Co. Bar Assn., Trial Lawyers Am., L.A. Bar Assn., Northwestern Alumni Assn., Cornell Univ. Cadeusis Soc.; rec: tennis. Res: 5412 Amalfi Irvine 92715-3402 Ofc: Kriner, Hebner & Vermes 2006 N Broadway 92706

VICE, CHARLES LOREN, mechanical engineer; b. Jan.2, 1921, LaVerne, Okla.; s. Cyrus Christopher and Ethel Segwith (Hoy) V.; m. Katherine Maxwell, July 16, 1949; children: Katherine Lorene b. 1950, Charles Clark b. 1952, Ann Marie b. 1955; edn: ASTP Cert., Ore. State Univ. 1944, BSME, 1947; grad. wk. USC, 1948-55; Reg. Profl. Engr. (mech.), Calif. Career: mgr. Magnetic Head Div., General Instrument Corp., Hawthorne 1959-62; senior staff engr. Magnetic Head Div., Ampex Corp., Redwood City 1962-66; chief mech. engr. Collins Radio Corp., Newport Beach 1967-69; pres./bd. chmn. FerraFlux Corp., Santa Ana 1970-78; senior staff engr. McDonnell Douglas Computer Systems Co., Irvine 1979—; cons. Sabor Corp. of Japan (1982-), Teac Corp. of Japan (1974-78), Crown Radio Corp. of Japan (1979-80), Otari Corp. of Japan (1975-77), Univac Corp., Salt Lake City (1975-76); patentee (14) in fields of magnetic recording and profl. sound reproduction; recipient internat. recognition as authority on magnetic recording techniques; mem. Nat. Soc. of Profl. Engrs., Toastmasters Internat.; mil: tech. 4/c US Army Engrs. 1943-46, GCM, Victory, Asiatic Pacific Service, Philippine Service with Bronze Star medals; Republican; Christian; rec: piano, singing. Res: 5902 E Bryce Ave Orange 92667 Ofc: McDonnell Douglas Corp. 1562 Reynolds Ave Irvine 92714

VICIAN, ELIZABETH OVERGAARD, psychologist; b. Aug. 15, 1934, Albert Lea, Minn.; d. Raymond O. and Cora Marie (Ormseth) Overguard; m. Thomas A. Vician, Sr., 1957; edn: BA, Luther Coll. 1956; MA, San Jose State Univ. 1965; postgrad. work UC Santa Cruz/UC San Francisco Med. Sch.; PhD, Univ. Humanistic Studies 1979; Calif. lic. marriage, family, child therapist. Career: dir. counseling Garey High Sch., Pomona 1964, Brownell Sch., Gilroy 1966; prof. psychology and counseling, Chabot Coll., Hayward 1967—; psychologist in pvt. practice, Palo Alto 1978—; cons. with Dr. Ira Progoff in The Intensive Jour.; mem: Calif. Tchrs. Assns., San Andreas Health Council, Calif. Personnel & Guidance Assn., Calif. Assn. MFCT, Center Study of Democratic Instns., AAUW, World Future Soc., Sierra Club, Smithsonian Assocs.; Republican; Lutheran; rec: piano, swim, jog. Res: 3718 Redwood Circle Palo Alto 94306 Ofc: 316 Town & Country Village Palo Alto 94301

VICKERS, DAVID LEROY, manufacturing company executive; b. Jan. 15, 1942, Detroit, Mich.; s. Vay Aldon Sr. and Vada Ann (Gaw) V.; m. Tomiye Tado, Apr. 22, 1961; children: David Jr. b. 1962, Steven T. b. 1965; edn: MBA, CSU Long Beach 1972; BS, ind. tech., Tenn. Tech. Univ. 1967. Career: chief indsl. engr. Pacific Tube Co., Commerce 1967-73; ops. auditor Ameron Inc., Monterey Park 1973-74; v.p. mfg. Ameron HC&D, Honolulu, Hi. 1974-81; dir. mfg. Ameron Inc., Monterey Park 1981-84; exec. v.p. H.G. Fenton Materials Co., San Diego 1984—; co. ofcr. H.G. Fenton Materials Co., Premixed Concrete Co., Western Salt Co., San Diego, Ameron HC&D, Honolulu; dir. Sorrento Ready Mix, A-1 Soils Co.; prof. bus. Univ. of Hawaii, 1978-81; lectr. Loyola Marymount Univ. 1970-74; mem: Am. Inst. Indsl. Engrs. 1969-; So. Calif. Work Simplification Assn. (pres. 1972); Greater L.A. Chpt. Quality Circles Inst. 1982; mil: E-5, USN 1959-63; Republican; Methodist; rec: jogging, racquetball, wine collecting. Ofc: c/o H.G. Fenton Material Co., 702 Washington St San Diego 92112

VILDIBILL, ROBERT THOMAS, manufacturing co. executive; b. June 11, 1943, Pensacola, Fla.; s. Alvin James and Dean Esta (Cooper) V.; m. Shirley Loi Pettis, Apr. 12, 1962; children: Tamara Anne b. 1963, Robert, Jr. b. 1965; edn: Grossmont Coll. 1962. Career: store mgr. Standard Brands Paint, Santa Ana 1963-70, Dorman's Tire Co., National City 1970-73; sales mgr. Tru-Bloc Concrete, Santee 1973-74, Woodward Sand & Mat., 1974-76; pres. Vicliff Concrete Products, El Cajon 1975-79, co. merger, pres. San Diego Precast Concrete, Santee 1979—; mem: Nat. Precast Concrete Assn. (bd. dirs., 2 Hoskin Awards), Assoc. Builders & Contractors Inc., Am. Concrete Inst., Architectural Precast Assn.; civic: Kiwanis (pres. 1985-86, Kiwanian of the Yr. 1980-81, Kiwanian Spark Plug of the Yr. 1982), Exchange Club/ Santee (past

pres., Humanitarian Award 1985), Home of Guiding Hands (bd. dirs. 1985-87), Calif. State Sheriffs Assn. (Hon. Sgt.), Dep. Sheriffs Assn., San Diego County Drug Council (chmn.), Lutheran Assn. for Retarded Children, Davis YMCA (com. chmn.), Boys Club of El Cajon Fund Raising (chmn.), Fellowship of Christian Athletes, Citizens Against Govt. Waste; works: built and restored island #4, Santee Regional Park, Memorial plaque; dir./prod. musical slide show "Americana"; Republican; Prot.; rec: travel, racquetball. Res: 13662 Paseo del Mar El Cajon 92021 Ofc: San Diego Precast Concrete Inc. 9702 Prospect Ave Santee 92071

VILLA, DEBORAH LOUISE, graphic designer; b. Apr. 4, 1952, San Diego; d. Joe and Mary Louise (Labrada) V.; 1 dau. Sarah Miss b. 1973; edn: Adams State Coll. 1975-78; BFA graphic design, Acad. of Art Coll. 1983. Career: illustrator seed packets Helix Seed Corp., Boulder, Colo. 1976-78; artist-in-residence Colo. Council on the Arts & Humanities, Denver 1977-78; freelance prodn. Health Care Mktg. Svcs., San Francisco (The Apothecary mag.) 1982; art dir. Tower Advtg. div. of Tower Records, San Francisco 1982-83; freelance design & prodn. Richard Parker & Assocs., San Francisco (Greenpeace) 1984; art prodn. dir. New Realities mag., S.F. 1984; assoc. art. dir. Medical Self Care mag., S.F. 1984—; freelance art prodn. Kerry Tremain Design, S.F. (Mother Jones, Food First, Labor Papers, InfoWorld) 1983—; honors: Artist-in-Residence grant from Nat. Endowment for the Arts 1977-78. Address: 2719 Hyde St San Francisco 94109

VINCENT, TERRELL KIRBY, contract maintenance co. executive; b. May 18, 1955, Bella Vista/ East Los Angeles; s. Walter Horace and Elsie Elaine (Lubin) V.; m. Sonjia Kay Kethcart, June 10, 1978; stepchildren: Vivian Ester Buie b. 1959, Patricia Coreen Warren b. 1960, Victor Eugene Cochrane b. 1962; edn: AA, adminstrn. of justice, Los Angeles Comm. Coll. Overseas Campus, Iwakuni, Japan, 1976. Career: warehouseman, truck driver Zellerbach Paper Co., East Los Angeles 1977-79; traveling co. mgr. Tinder Box Internat., Santa Monica 1979-82; retail and restaurant mgmt., Sambo's Restaurants 1982, Woody's Pet Ctr. 1982; ptnr. All Points Maint. Co., Pasadena 1982—; frequent guest speaker var. orgns. 1970-; awards: Eagle Scout, BSA (1970), Nat. Forensic League (1970-73), 1st place San Gabriel Valley Div., Readers Digest Nat. Public Speaking Contest (1972), num. public speaking awards (1970-73); club: Brookside Mens Golf (Pasadena); mil: cpl. M.P. USMC 1974-77; Republican; Baptist; rec: public speaking, scuba, golf, helping others. Res: 5625 N Santa Anita Ave Apt 204 Temple City 91780 Ofc: 118 S Oak Knoll Ave Pasadena 91101

VISCOTT, DAVID, psychiatrist, radio broadcaster/writer; b. May 24. 1938, Boston, Mass.; s. Hiram and Shirley (Levy) V.; m. Katherine Random, Dec. 31, 1982; children: Elizabeth b. 1960, Penelope b. 1963, Jonathan b. 1965, Melanie b. 1970; edn: BA, Dartmouth Coll. 1959; MD, Tufts Univ. 1963. Career: medical research St. Margarets Hosp., Dorchester, Mass. 1960-63; resident, intern, clinical assoc. in US hosps. 1963-67; sr. psychiatrist/consultant Boys Detention Ctr., Mass. Div. of Youth Svc. 1966-70; instr. psychiatry Boston Div. Med. Sch. 1968-78; private practice 1968—; fellow in forensic psychiatry, Boston Univ. Law Medicine Inst. 1967-8; asst. clin. prof. psychiatry UCLA Med. Sch. 1980-; host Sat. Evening talk show on KABC radio; faculty, Cambridge (MA) Ctr. for Adult Edn.; awards: Mosby Book Prize, Tufts Univ. 1963; author: Making of a Psychiatrist (best seller, book of month, 1973), Risking (1977), Winning (1973), Language of Feelings (1975), How to Live with Another Person (1974), Taking Care of Business (1985); articles in Psychiatry Today, Advertising Age, Todays Health, others; mem: fellow, N.Y. Acad. of Sci., Am. Psychiat. Assn., PEN Internat., Royal Soc. for Health, Mass. Med. Soc, Phi Sigma Delta; rec: clarinet, flute, piano, antiques. Address: 355 S Muirfield Rd Los Angeles 90020

VISITACION, MARCY, civil/structural engineer; b. Apr. 1, 1943, Bacarra, Ilocos Norte, Philippines, nat. 1963; s. Pedro Agustin and Pia Asuncion (Cadabuna) V.; m. Dolores Y. Locquiao, Dec. 27, 1969; children: Derek b. 1966, Marc b. 1970, Michael b. 1972, Lisa b. 1976; edn: dip. arch. drafting, Kauai Tech. Sch. 1963; BS, CalPoly 1968; reg. Civil Engr., Calif. 1975; Structural Engr., Hawaii 1977. Career: engring. asst./assoc. L.A. Dept. of Water & Power, Los Angeles 1968-76; prin. engr. M. Visitacion & Assoc., Inc., Lihue, Hawaii 1976-78; design engr. Steelform Contracting Co., Santa Fe Springs 1978-79; chief designer Don Perryman & Assoc., Inc., Walnut 1979-82; prin. engr. M. Visitacion & Assoc., Inc., West Covina 1983—; awards: Hartwood Award, All-State Drafting Contest-Hawaii 1962, DO., 1963; mem: Struc. Engrs. Assn. of So. Calif. 1979-; Aloha Softball League (dir. 1972); Menehune Golf Club (dir. 1973); Menehune Bowling Club (pres. 1974-75); Galaxie Little League (mgr. 1980-); Pacifica Golf Club, 1983-; rec: golf, Little League. Address: M. Visitacion and Assoc., Inc., 603 Sentous Ave W. Covina 91792

VISSERS, RICHARD HENRI, insurance agency president; b. June 12, 1941, Den Haag, Holland, nat. 1961; s. Jacobus and Lenie V.; children: Marisha b. 1960, Merrick b. 1962; edn: Fullerton Coll. 1969; Am. Coll. Bryn Mawr 1975; CLU, cert. life underwriter. Career: insurance agent/ mgr./ and tng. dir., ins. bus., Hollywood, Ca.; owner/pres. Vissers Ins. Agency, 1973—, opened 2d office in 1983; owner/pres. Vissers Express Travel (now w/ 14 agents), 1980—; awards: Nat. Ins. awards; mem: Nat. Orgn. of Life Underwriters; Assn. of Retail Travel Agents; World Affairs Council; So. African Trade Assn. (founder); rec: travel, swimming. Ofc: 1104 Buchanan Rd, Ste. 3 Antioch 94509

VITALE, DONALD EUGENE, publisher; b. Feb. 16, 1930, Oak Park, Ill.; s. Sylvester and Anne (Potenza) V.; m. Sarah Alice Brengle, June 9, 1956;

children: Mark Francis (1957-1986), John Vincent b. 1958, Valerie Anne (Berg-quam) b. 1969, Paul Keigwin b. 1962; edn: Loyola Univ. 1948-51, Northwestern Univ. 1952, UCLA 1956-57. Career: copy-boy, reporter, re-write City News Bur., Chgo. 1951-52; editor Los Angeles Daily Journal (legal newspaper) 1954-59; asst., then dir. pub. rels. mgr. Los Angeles Area CofC 1959-65, and editor So. Calif. Business (weekly Chamber publ.) 1959-61; assoc. dir. corp. comm. Dart-Kraft (then Rexall Drug & Chem.) 1965-67; Postal Instant Press franchisee, 1969-79; pub. Who's Who in Calif. 1978−; senior lectr. USC Sch. of Journalism 1966-71; prod. radio show Big Problems in Small Business, L.A. 1966-67; playwright: The Aquarium (New Playwrights Found., Hollywood 1973), Bidding and Other Fables (3 one-act plays, Evergreen Stage Co. Hollywood 1976, 78); mem: Am. Library Assn., Greater L.A. Press Club, Pub. Rels. Soc. of Am. (1961-65), Catholic Press Council of So. Calif. (pres. 1966-67); civic: Town Hall of Calif, LA World Affairs Council, Information Com. to Save Descanso Gardens (past chmn.), L.A. Mayor Sam Yorty's Small Bus. Council (exec. secty. 1967), Mt. St. Mary's Coll. (advis. bd. 1963-65); mil: cpl. US Army 1951-53, Reserve 1954-6, Korea w/ 3 bronze stars, UN Svc., Korean Svc.; rec: theatre, travel. Address: POB 4240 San Clemente 92672

VITOLO, JOSEPH CARL, lithographic co. executive; b. Dec. 20, 1952, Queens, N.Y.; s. Gerard Ralph and Lucy Maria (Lentini) V.; m. Sue Ellen Tullar, Mar. 10, 1973; children: Anthony Joseph b. 1977, Sandra Nicole b. 1978; edn: AA, Fullerton Coll. 1972; UC Fullerton, 2 years. Career: apprentice bl. & white camera person/stripper, J and L Lithographers, Santa Ana 1972-, four color camera psn. and plant supvr. 1975-, owner/sec. treas. J n L Litho, dba J&L Color Svc. 1981−, one of th fastest growing color separation houses in Orange County, relocated 1984 to larger facilities designed by Kodak. Res: 22145 Timberline Wy, Lake Forest 92630 Ofc: J&L Color Svc. 1500 S Sunkist St Ste I Anaheim 92806

VITRO, ROBERT EDWARD, business owner; b. Sept. 28, 1929, Seattle, Wash.; s. Silverio Peter and Frances Ann (Young) V.; m. Ingeborg, Mar. 15, 1954; children: Robert b. 1955, Neil b. 1957, Billy b. 1963; edn: BCS, Seattle Univ. 1957; MBA, Univ. Wash. 1960; CPA Wash. 1961. Career: var. positions Gen. Elec. 1957-79; mgr. finance Atomic River s/b Power Lab. (GE) Schenectady, NY 1973-79, Products Div. 1979-82, mgr. acctg. & system ops. San Jose 1982-85; owner Vitro Assocs. Cupertino 1985−; instr. Univ. Wash Grad. Sch. 1961-62; mem. Am. Inst. CPAs 1961-; mil: cpl. US Army 1950-52; Republican; rec: golf, tennis. Ofc: Vitro Assocs. 10675 S De Anza Blvd Ste 514 Cupertino 95014

VOCKEL, JOHN EBY, computer marketing executive; b. Sept. 28, 1954, Pittsburgh, Penn.; s. Steward Meldred Jr. and Carol Eby (Sayers) V.; edn: BA, Lafayette Coll. 1976; MS, Defense Intelligence Coll. 1981. Career: intelligence ofcr. US Army 1976-82; 1st Cavalry Div., Ft. Hood, Texas 1976-80; The Defense Intelligence Agency, Wash. DC 1980-81; asst. chief of staff for intelligence, Pentagon, Wash. DC 1981-82; engring. and acquisitions mgr. Ford Aerospace & Communications Corp., TRS Pgm. Ofc. Palo Alto 1982-84; mktg. mgr. Strategic Command & Control Programs, ROLM, San Jose 1984−; honors: Am. Field Svc. Exchange Student to Australia 1970; Distng. Grad., Postgrad. Intelligence Cirriculum; mem: Armed Forces Communications & Electronics Assn., Security Affairs Support Assn., Assn. of US Army; works: paper presented, Multi-Level Secure Opg. Sys. in Tactical Enivornment, AFCEA Intell Symp. 1986; mil: capt. US Army 1976-82, reserves 1982-, Meritorious Svc., Army Achiev., Army Svc.; Republican; Methodist; rec: snow skiing, racquetball, white water rafting. Ofc: ROLM Mil-Spec Computers, MS 167 One River Oaks Pl. San Jose 95134

VOGEL, INGRID MARGARET, school district accounting executive; b. Aug. 5, 1942, Neuhof, W. Germany; d. Sebastian W. and Elisabeth A. (Weilbacher) Adrian; m. "Joe" Wolfgang Vogel, Oct. 26, 1964; 1 son, Michael W. b. 1967; edn: AA, Chaffey Coll. 1977; BS, Calif. State Polytech. Univ. Pomona 1980; grad. pgm. CSU San Bernardino Sch. of Bus. Mgmt., 1985-; Certified Public Acct., Calif. 1983. Career: auditor Arthur Andersen & Co., Los Angeles 1980-82; fiscal services dir. Central Sch. District, Rancho Cucamonga 1982−; honors: Phi Kappa Phi, Alpha Gamma Sigma, Who's Who Among Students in Am. Univs.; mem: Calif. Assn. of Sch. Business Officials (So. Section Budget R&D Com.), Cal Poly Acctg. Soc. Alumni, Phi Chi Theta Alumni (treas. 1979-80). Res: 9137 Orange St Alta Loma 91701 Ofc: Central School District, 9457 Foothill Blvd Rancho Cucamonga 91701

VOGEL, MARK W., physician; b. Oct. 17, 1950, Los Angeles; s. Alvin R. and Alice (Shapiro) V.; m. Robin A., June 4, 1978; 1 son, Adam b. 1985; edn: AB, UCLA 1972; MD, Autonomous Univ. Guadalajara 1976; cert. (5th path.) USC Sch. of Med. 1977-78; Calif. lic. phys. (1979), diplomate Am. Board of Urology. Career: postgrad. tng. and residency in urology, LAC-USC Medical Center, Los Angeles 1977-83, chief resident 1982-83; pvt. practice urology, 1983−; clin. instr. USC Sch. of Medicine; mem: L.A. Urol. Soc., Phi Delta Epsilon med. frat., UCLA Alumni Assn., UAG Alumni Assn., Salerni Collegium/ USC, Am. Med. Assn., Calif. Med. Assn., L.A. County Med. Soc.; civic: L.A. Jesters (support gp. Found. for Junior Blind); contbr. research arts. in med. jours.; rec: electronics & technol., tennis, golf, tropical fish. Ofc: 8631 West Third St Ste 835E Los Angeles 90048

VOGEL, ROBERT HERMAN, accountant, ret.; b. Oct. 24, 1921, La Plant, S.D.; s. Carl Herman and Mabel Vietta (Lohuis) V.; m. Constance C. Vogel, Feb. 1, 1943; children: Lynn b. 1947, Nancy b. 1954; edn: BS bus. admin., acctg., Univ. So. Calif. 1948; PA Calif. 1948. Career: acctg. clerk, traveling auditor Gen. Petroleum Corp. 1948-51; company comdr. 1st Marine Div. Korea 1951-52; acctg. systems splst. Durkee Atwood Mpls. 1952-53; chief acct.

Oceanic Oil Co. L.A. 1953-58; asst. chief acct. Kern Oil Calif. L.A. 1958-61; chief acct. Astropower Inc. Newport Beach 1961-63; fiscal systems splst. McDonnell Douglas Corp. Huntington Beach 1963-82; instr. acctg. Orange Coast Comm. Coll. 1973-74; honors: senior class pres., Allen G. Messick Award (Marion H.S. 1940), Phi Sigma Kappa 1942; mem: Am. Inst. Internal Auditors (L.A. chpt. secty. 1958, chmn. admissions 1962), Affiliated Cities Rental Owners Assn. 1976-; as student team capt. Jr. H. Sch. Basketball Team introduced new "give and go" offense 1936, shifting man-to-man defense 1938, "pick and roll" offense 1939, "zone press" defense 1940; mil: capt. USMC 1943-46, 1951-52; Republican; Protestant; rec: real estate investments. Res: 751 S Fircroft Ave Covina 91723

VOLAND, JOSEPH R., pathologist; b. Jan. 30, 1954, Cleveland, Ohio; s. Joseph Francis and Margaret Mary (Lamboj) V.; edn: BA, Case Western Reserve Univ. 1975, MA, 1975; MD, Ohio State Univ. 1978; Diplomate Am. Board of Pathology in Anatomic Pathol. 1982. Career: resident path. UC San Diego 1978-82; fellow in pediatric path. Los Angeles Children's Hosp., 1982-83; assoc. investigator VA Med. Ctr., San Diego and research fellow Dept. Path. UCSD, 1983-85; research assoc. Dept. Biol./Div. Immunol., UCSD, 1985−; staff pathologist Kaiser Permanente Med. Ctr. San Diego, 1980−; honors: Phi Beta Kappa (1975), Alpha Omega Alpha (1978); mem: Internat. Acad. Pathology, Soc. for Pediatric Pathology, Am. Soc. for Reproductive Immunology; contbr. med. jour. articles, abstracts, chpt. in med. textbook (1977-); rec: travel, history, scuba, cake decorating. Res: 13813 Via Rimini San Diego 92129 Ofc: Dept. Biology M012 University Calif. San Diego 92037

VOLLERS, JOHANNES, chiropractor, educator; b. May 16, 1953, Chgo.; s. Kurt and Melanie (Hock) V.; div.; children: Danielle Marie b. 1976, Kurt F. b. 1979; edn: Fettes Coll., Edinburgh, Scotland 1968-70, No. Ill. Univ. 1970-72, So. Ill. Univ. 1972-73; BA, L.A. Coll. of Chiro. 1974; DC cum laude, L.A. Coll. of Chiropractic 1977; certified in disability evaluation, post-grad. orthopedics; Career: prof. histology, bacteriology L.A. Coll. of Chiro., and asst. prof. lab. diagnosis, pathology, 1980-83, case mgmt., 1984-; pvt. practice chiropractic in Whittier, South Lake Tahoe, Santa Ana; splty: expert witness Indsl. Disability Evaluation; mem: Am. Chiro. Assn., Calif. Chiro. Assn., Los Angeles Eastern Chiro. Assn. (pres. 1978-80), Kiwanis Intl., Whittier Host Lions Club; publ: Evaluation of Sacro-Iliac Lesions (1980); Republican; Christian; rec: profl. pianist, guitarist; racquetball; skiing. Res: 6262 Southwind Dr Whittier 90601 Ofc: John Vollers, D.C. 15022 Mulberry Dr Ste C Whittier 90604

VOLLMAYER, KARL A., librarian; b. Toledo, Ohio; s. George John and Ruth (Coles) V.; m. Catherine Zalli, Sept. 6, 1954; children: Carla, Anne, Mary; edn: BA, Univ. San Francisco 1950; MLS, Univ. Wash. 1951. Career: reference librarian Washoe County Library, Reno, Nev. 1951-53; asst. librarian Richmond Public Library 1953-60; city librarian Redwood City Public Library 1960−; mem: Am. and Calif. Library Assns., San Mateo Co. Hist. Soc., Book Club of Calif.; mil: USAF 1941-48. Res: 286 Fulton St. Redwood City 94062 Ofc: 881 Jefferson Ave. Redwood 94063

VOLPE, PETER ANTHONY, surgeon; b. Dec. 17, 1936, Columbus, Ohio; s. Peter A. and Jeannette (Volz) V.; m. Kathleen Townsend, March 26, 1978; children: John David b. 1968, Michael Charles b. 1969, Mark Christopher b. 1983; edn: BA cum laude, Ohio State Univ. 1958, MD, summa cum laude, 1961; physician lic. Calif. 1963; Bd. certified in general surgery 1970, in colon and rectal surgery 1971. Career: intern Milwaukee County Hosp. 1961-62; naval ofcr. 1962-64; surgical res. UC San Francisco 1965-69, tng. in colon and rectal surg. 1969-71; pvt. practice of colon and rectal surgery 1971−; asst. clin. prof. of surg. UC San Francisco 1974−; chmn. Dept. Gen. Surg., St. Mary's Hosp. and Med. Center 1979−; nat bd. mem. The American Board of Colon and Rectal Surgery 1981-; honors: Phi Beta Kappa 1959, Alpha Omega Alpha 1960; mem: Am. College of Surgeons (Advis. Council for Colon and Rectal Surgery 1981-; Program rep. 1982-85), Am. Soc. of Colon and Rectal Surgeons (chmn. Contg. Edn. Com. 1979-85; treas. and Council mem. 1985-), No. Calif. Soc. of Colon and Rectal Surgeons (past pres.), AMA, CMA, San Francisco Med. Soc., S.F. Surg. Soc.; speaker num. nat. surgical convs., sev. med. publs.; mil: Lt., MC, USNR 1962-64; Republican; Catholic; rec: antique model trains, sailing, 49ers fan. Ofc: 3838 California St, Ste 616, San Francisco 94118

VON DER WERTH, LOAL, district services director; b. Mar. 29, 1941, San Rafael, Calif.; s. Albert and Lois von der Werth; children: Eric b. 1961, Lynn b. 1963; edn: BS bus. adminstrn., Indian Valley Coll. 1972. Career: gen. contr., estimator von der Werth Constrn. 1959-60; gen. contr., field supt. Edward W. Burger & Orgn. San Rafael 1960-65; dist. svcs. dir. Golden Gate Bridge Hwy & Transp. Dist. 1965−; mem: Bay Area Fleet Mgr. Assn., Adv. Bd. Marin County Flood Control Dist.; Republican; Protestant; rec: travel, gardening, constrn. mgmt. Res: 222 Evergreen Mill Valley 94941 Ofc: Golden Gate Bridge Hwy & Transp. Dist. Box 9000 Presidio Station San Francisco 94129

VON HOELSCHER, RUSSEL, author; b. Aug. 10, 1942, St. Paul, Minn.; s. Clarence and Francis von H.; m. Ginger June Julian, Dec. 5, 1980; edn: BA mktg. (in progress), Grossmont Coll., San Diego. Career: bestselling business, investment and motivational author for 20 yrs., publ. over 3 dozen books and manuals, plus newsletters, reports and articles; copywriter, direct-mktg. cons.; seminar/workshop leader; advisor to Presdl. (Jimmy Carter) Com. on Small Bus. in Am. 1978; honors: Sales & Mktg. Exec. of the Yr. (1986); mem: San Diego Sales & Mktg. Execs., Internat. Writers Guild, Direct Mktg. Assn., Toastmasters Internat.; author: How To Achieve Total Success (1983); Libertarian; Metaphysics; rec: chess. Res: 6675 Mission Gorge Rd B103 San Diego 92120

VON SEYFRIED, HENRY, real estate broker, ret.; b. Feb. 28, 1939, Munich, Germany, nat. US cit. 1966; s. Henry and Betty (Festner) von S.; edn: real estate, L.A. City Coll. 1966-67; US Army precommsg. course; broker, Anthony R.E. Sch. 1968, 73. Career: design Forchthammer Aufzugbau, Germany 1954-58; bahnabteilung Deutsche Bundespost 1958-59; design Guerney Scales Canada 1959-60; defense work Staples- Hopman Wash. DC 1960-61; real estate broker Hollywood Properties 1968-75; builder 1975-85 (ret.); honors: Listing Award (1974), Asia Film Award, Medal of Merit (Pres. Reagan), L.A. Scuba Award; mem: Nat. Mil. Intelligence Agcy., So. Calif. Motion Picture Council, Adventurers Club, L.A. Press Club, L.A. World Affairs Council, L.A. Visitors Pgm., Republican Task Force, Am. Legion, VFW, DAV, Order of St. Constantin, St. George, Holy Sepulchre, Noble Swan, St. Agatha, Holy Cross of Jerusalem, Mil. Order of Surgeons; publs: Marine Corps Gazette, German papers; involved in 12 motion pictures, var. positions; mil: 1st lt. US Army 1962-65, USAR 1984-, F.E.M.A., Commdn., others; Republican; Catholic; rec: travel, tennis, scuba, archeology, music, exploring. Res: 8055 Willow Glen Rd Los Angeles 90046

VON WIESENBERGER, ARTHUR, beverage industry executive; b. Sept. 13, 1953, N.Y.C.; s. Arthur and Frances Louise (Bayes) V.W.; edn: grad. Brooks Inst., Motion Picture Div. 1977; art and language studies in Switz. and England, 1968-73. Career: assoc. prod. Swissair, Switz., 1972; prod. Comorian govt./ Air Comores Africa 1973; prod./dir. Aurora Films Worldwide, Switz. 1974; assoc. prod. FMS Prodns., Hollywood 1977; assoc. prod. Warrior's of the Wind, Japan 1978; beverage industry cons. to Anheuser-Busch Inc., Ionics Inc., Irons & Sears, Manitou Corp., Poland Spring Water, Stanford Wine Co., Valgos Consiel Inc., Vittel (USA) Inc.; bd. chmn. Internat. Source Management, Inc.; dir. Internat. Festival Du Film De Villars (1975, 76), spkr. Whole LIfe Expo, Pasadena (1984, 85, 86), contbr. Entree (1984-86); awards: Photog. Soc. of Am., Ten Best (1975), MPD travel film award (1975), best menu, NRA (1984, 85); mem. Nat. Restaurant Assn. 1983-; clubs: Coral Casino (Santa Barbara), S.B. Athletic, Centurion Clubs Worldwide, Clipper (Worldwide), Six Continents (Worldwide), Internat. Sporting (London); publs: Oasis - The Complete Guide to Bottled Water Throughout the World, Capra Press (1978), Charting the Waters, Runner's World (1981), A Guide to Bottled Water, Fit (1982), Shape's Guide to Bottled Water (1984), Delights of Sushi, Centervoice (1982), Mystique of Caviar, In Magazine (1983); Republican; Ch. of England; rec: swim, ski, racquetball, wine collecting. Res: POB 5658 Santa Barbara 93150 Ofc: Nipper's 439 North Rodeo Dr Beverly Hills 90210

VORA, SHOBHANA, biomedical researcher; b. Feb. 4, 1946, Bombay, India, nat. US cit. 1985; s. Kevalchand R. and Laxmi K. (Mehta) V.; edn: MB, BS, Univ. of Bombay 1969; MD (Pediatrics), Univ. Bombay 1973; Diplomate Am. Board of Pediatrics, subsplty. ped. hematology-oncology 1978. Career: instr., asst. prof. pediatrics Div. Hematol., New York Univ. Sch. of Medicine, 1977-79; asst. prof. Columbia Univ. Coll. Phys. & Surgeons, 1979-83; asst. mem. Dept. of Basic and Clin. Research, Divs. Biochem. and Hematol., Scripps Clinic and Research Found., La Jolla 1983-; assoc. adj. prof. Dept. Ped. UC San Diego 1984-; awards: NIH grantee (1979-); mem: Am. Acad. Pediatrics, AAAS, Am. Fedn. for Clin. Research, Am. Soc. for Clin. Investig., Am. Soc. of Blood Banks, Am. Soc. of Hematol., Am. Soc. of Human Genetics, Isozyme Soc., NY Acad. of Scis., Soc. for Pediatric Research, Soc. for the Study of Blood Inc., W. Soc. for Clin. Investig.; civic: Indo-U.S. Friendship Assn.; contbr. num. publs. in med. jours. and books, nat. and internat. profl. conf. presentations (36); rec: swim, golf, equestrian. Res: 4455 Via Realzar San Diego 92122 Ofc: Scripps Clinic and Research Foundation 10666 N Torrey Pines Rd La Jolla 92037

VOS, HUBERT DANIEL, investment co. president; b. Aug. 2, 1933, Paris, France (US cit. at birth); s. Marius Watteau and Aline Huet (Porge) V.; m. Susan Hill, Apr. 18, 1958; children: Wendy b. 1960, Jim b. 1962; edn: A, Univ. of Paris, Fr. 1954; M. Public and Internat. Affairs, Princeton Univ. 1956. Career: pres. Stonington Capital Corp., Santa Barbara; dir: T. Rowe Price New Horizons Fund Inc., T. Rowe Price New Era Fund Inc., trustee T. Rowe Price Equity Income Fund Inc.; mem: General Management II Council, Am. Management Assn., Financial Execs. Inst.; dir. Santa Barbara Scholarship Found.; Republican; Presbyterian; rec: tennis, golf, sailing. Res: 800 Via Hierba Santa Barbara 93110 Ofc: Stonington Capital Corporation 1231 State St Ste 210 Santa Barbara 93101

VOSGUANIAN, BRENDA KAREN, lawyer; b. Apr. 10, 1956, Yonkers, NY; d. Dr. Charles and Mary (Lordigyan) V.; edn: Pace Univ. 1973-75; BS, acctg., Fordham Univ. 1977; JD, Western State Sch. of Law 1980; stu. French cooking, Maxim's Restaurant, Paris 1983; restaurant mgmt., UCLA Grad. Ext. 1983-; admitted State Bar Calif. 1982, US Tax Ct. 1983. Career: internal auditor Global Van Lines, Anaheim 1978-79; sr. auditor McDonnell Douglas Corp., Huntington Beach 1979-82; partner Vosguanian & Vosguanian, Attys. and Counselors at Law, 1982-; mem: Am. Bar Assn.; Assn. of Trial Lawyers of Am.; Los Angeles Bar Assn.; Women Lawyers Assn. of Los Angeles; Armenian Profl. Soc.; rec: fitness, theatre and the arts, cooking. Ofc: Vosguanian & Vosguanian, 2040 Ave of the Stars Ste 400 Los Angeles 90067

VOSGUANIAN, BRUCE CHARLES, lawyer/ certified public accountant; b. Oct. 28, 1951, NY, NY; s. Charles and Mary (Lordigyan) V.; edn: BS, Fordham Univ. 1973; JD, Pepperdine Univ. Sch. of Law 1980; CPA, NY 1980; admitted State Bar Calif. 1981, State Bar New Jersey 1981, DC Ct. of Appeals 1985, US Tax Ct. 1981, US Supreme Ct. 1985; lic. real estate broker, Calif. 1982. Career: acct. Charles Vosguanian CPA, Yonkers, NY 1973-74; acct. self-empl., Bruce C. Vosguanian, Yonkers, NY 1974-78; sr. partner Vosguanian & Vosguanian, Attys. and Counselors at Law, Los Angeles 1980-; real estate development &

finance 1984-; awards: N.Y. State Regents Scholarship Award 1969-73; mem: Am. Bar Assn.; Assn. of Trial Lawyers of Am.; Am. Assn. of Atty.-CPAs; Los Angeles Bar Assn.; Knights of Vartan Cultural and Civic Frat.; writer/lectr. on economic theories rel. to investment decisions; rec: bicycling, tennis, skiing, photog. Ofc: Vosguanian & Vosguanian, 2040 Ave of the Stars Ste 400 Los Angeles 90067

VOSGUANIAN, RODNEY NERSES, lawyer/ certified public accountant; b. Apr. 1, 1950; NY, NY; s. Charles and Mary (Lordigyan) V.; edn: BS, Fordham Univ. 1972; JD, Pepperdine Univ. Sch. of Law 1979; CPA, NY State 1976, Calif. 1978; admitted State Bar Calif. 1980, State Bar Ariz. 1981, State Bar NJ 1981, DC Ct. of Appeals 1985, US Tax Ct. 1981, US Supreme Ct 1985; lic. real estate broker, Calif. 1982. Career: Rodney N. Vosguanian CPA, Yonkers, NY 1974-77; sr. partner Vosguanian & Vosguanian, Attys. and Counselors at Law, Los Angeles 1980-; real estate development and finance 1984-; adjunct prof. of bus. adm. in accting. and fin. mgmt., Pepperdine Univ., Malibu 1981; awards: N.Y. State Regents Scholarship Award 1968-72; Fordham Univ. Scholar Incentive Award 1968-72; State Bar of Calif. Vol. Legal Svcs. Commdn. 1984; mem: Am. Bar Assn.; Assn. of Trial Lawyers of Am.; Am. Assn. of Atty.-CPAs; Los Angeles Bar Assn.; Beverly Hills Bar Assn.; Santa Monica Bar Assn.; Knights of Vartan Cultural and Civic Frat.; Alpha Kappa Psi Bus. Frat.; writer/lectr. on economic theories rel. to investment decisions; mil: USAR; rec: tennis, skiing, bicycling, photog. Ofc: Vosguanian & Vosguanian, 2040 Ave of the Stars Ste 400 Los Angeles 90067

VOYTILLA, MICHAEL BENJAMIN, research co. executive; b. Mar. 11, 1952, Little Falls, Minn.; s. Ben and Julia (Hatala) V.; edn: AA, Merced Coll. 1972; BS engring. sci., honors, Cal Poly S.L.O. 1975; MBA in fin., CSU Hayward 1978; Calif. Reg. Profl. Mech. Engr. (1980), Real Estate Sales lic. (1980). Career: asst. control systems engr. Bechtel Power Corp., San Francisco 1974; project mgr. US Dept. of Energy, Oakland 1975-82; mgr. Applied Microwave Plasma Concepts, Inc., Encinitas 1982-, bd. dirs. 1984-; honors: Tau Beta Pi (life, 1974), Calif. State Scholar (1970), Dupertuis and Hesse Engring. Scholar (1971), Walter Wells Sr. Meml. Scholar (1974), num. awards and letters of recogn., US DOE; mem: Am. Mgmt. Assn., ASME, Nat. Contract Mgmt. Assn., Soc. for Advance. of Mgmt.; civic: San Diego Zool. Soc., CalPoly Alumni Assn. (life), San Diego Repertory Theatre (envoy mem.), San Dieo Symphony Orch. Assn. (affil.), Torrey Pines Sailing Club; works: planned and estab. pgm. with Nat. Bur. of Stds. to devel. thermodynamic properties of hydrocarbon mixtures (1981); Republican; Serbian Orthodox; rec: skiing, tennis, scuba, windsurfing. Res: 13772 Mar Scenic Dr Del Mar 92014 Ofc: Applied Microwave Plasma Concepts, Inc. 2210 Encinitas Blvd Ste P Encinitas 92024

VU, LUONG QUANG, electrical engineer, publishing co. officer; b. Dec. 18, 1956, Saigon, Vietnam, nat. US cit. 1985; s. Han Quang and So Thi V.; m. Hong-Nhung Pham, June 25, 1983; 1 dau, Hong-An b. 1984; edn: BSEE, highest honors, Univ. of Ill. 1980; UC Irvine 1983-84; Reg. Profl. Elec. Engr., Calif. 1983. Career: elec. engr. Westinghouse Corp., Compton 1980; elec. engr. Fluor Engrs. Inc., Irvine 1981-; trustee, gen. secty., treas. Nhat-Son Publishing Inc., Santa Ana 1983-; honors: Student Laureate & Medallion of Lincoln, Lincoln Acad. of Ill. 1979; Bronze Tablet, Univ. of Ill. 1980; mem; IEEE, Tau Beta Pi, Phi Kappa Phi, St. John the Baptist Catholic Ch. (dir. Vietnamese Language Pgm., Vietnamese Parish, Costa Mesa); works: founder, operator voluntary weekend classes to teach Vietnamese children to read, write and speak their native language; Catholic; rec: teaching, reading.

VU, TRUNG NGOC, electrical engineer; b. July 26, 1955, Vietnam, nat. US cit. 1983; s. Thuy Ngoc and Mau Thi (Pham) Vu; m. Nien Minh Dao, June 20, 1981; 1 child, Uyen b. 1982; edn: BSChE, CSU Long Beach 1980, MSEE, 1985; Reg. Profl. Engr., Calif. 1984. Career: system designer Bechtel Power Corp., Norwalk 1980-84; tech. staff Rockwell Internat., Anaheim 1984-; co-leader Power Electronics Circuit Design Group (spons. by Rockwell Intl.), Anaheim 1985-86; honors: Eta Kappa Nu (1983); mem. Instrument Soc. of Am., Lake Mission Viejo Assn.; research: in Digital Image Processing appl. sensing targets in the long distance; Roman Catholic; rec: tennis, fishing, sports mags. Res: 27581 Halcon Mission Viejo 92691

VUJOVICH, RICHARD SAMUEL, JR., bank executive; b. July 14, 1953, San Francisco; s. Richard S. and Barbara Ann (King) V.; m. Cynthia, Apr. 9, 1983; edn: BS commerce, Univ. Santa Clara 1975; real estate broker Calif. 1978. Career: sales mgr. Gilmartin Real Estate Co. San Bruno 1976-83; senior loan ofcr. Glendale Fed. Savings S.F. 1983-; lectr. First Time Home Buyers Seminar; honors: Million Dollar Club; mem: Olympic Club 1985-, S.F. Fairway Golf Club 1981-; rec: flying, sports, baseball. Res: 528 Santa Teresa Millbrae 94030 Ofc: Glendale Fed. Savings 2499 Ocean Ave San Francisco 94127

WADDELL, JAMES LEWIS, real estate broker, actor-singer; b. Nov. 19, 1946, Somerville, Tenn.; s. Freddie Lee and Mattie Bell (Morrow) W.; m. Sharon Lee, Nov. 30, 1974; children: Apryl Martess b. 1966, Jarett JaKarr b. 1975; edn: Cleveland State Univ. 1965-66; Norman Lush Sch. of Real Estate 1977; Univ. San Francisco 1985. Career: clubhouse asst. Cleveland Indians 1962; baseball pitcher Class B 1964; acctg. Cleveland Elec. 1965-66; expeditor US Steel Corp. 1967; road crew The 5th Dimension 1968-69; titlew search Stewart Title 1970-72; production Coca-Cola, Schlitz, Pabst 1973-76; Dept. of Water and Power City of L.A. 1977; communications County of L.A. 1978; var. (IATSE) TV and theatrical shows 1978-82; real estate sales Century 21, Internat. Real Estate Network, Colonial Realty 1978-85; pres. JLW Records 1983-; owner, broker JLW Realty, Studio City 1986-; honors: Driver of the Year, Nat. Student Leadership Conf., Cert. of Recogn., and Appreciation (LA Olympic

Organizing Com.); mem: Screen Actors Guild, AFTRA, Am. Soc. Composers, Authors & Publishers, San Fernando Valley Bd. Realtors, Calif., Nat. Assn. Realtors, ASCAP, Masons; Democrat; Baptist; rec: fishing, guitar. Ofc: JLW Realty 4346 Laurel Cyn Blvd Ste 8 Studio City 91604

WADDELL, WILLIAM CAMPBELL, manufacturing co. executive; b. Dec. 24, 1921, Gilbert Plains, Manitoba, Can., nat. US cit. 1958; s. William John and Jane (Campbell) W.; m. Dolores M. Heiters, Aug. 1, 1943; 1 dau, Diane b. 1945; edn: BSA, Univ. of Manitoba 1947. Career: territory supvr., retail store mgr. J.I. Case Co., Calgary, Alberta, Can. 1947-53; zone mgr Wymont Tractor & Equip. Co. (Ford), Billings, Mont. 1953-60; sales mgr. Pacific Tractor & Equip. Co. (Ford), Richmond 1960-64; mktg. rep. mgr., field sales mgr., dealer devel. mgr., mktg. mgr., asst. regl. mgr. Ford Tractor ops. Ford Motor Co., Oakland 1964—; ofcr./dir. for 13 dealership corps.; gen./mng. ptr. R.H. Positive 1 Partnership (1982-); honors: 6 time winner Merit Council award, Ford Tractor; sev. achieve. awards incl. Nat. Sales Exec. OSCAR; mem. Tractor Equipt. Assn., Shriners, Masons; mil: flying ofcr. Royal Canadian Air Force 1941-45; Republican; Methodist; rec: golf, travel. Res: 1006 Katherine Ln Lafayette 94549 Ofc: Ford Motor Co. POB 12964 Oakland 94604

WADLEY, HAROLD J., physician; b. May 1, 1944, Turlock; s. J. D. and Mary Jane (Day) W.; m. Clela Friesen, June 25, 1966; children: Brian, b. 1971, Jay, b. 1975; edn: BA, Pasadena Coll. 1966; MD, Loma Linda Univ. 1970. Career: maj. US Army Med. Corps, West Point 1974-77; staff radiologist, Permanente Medical Gp., Sacramento 1977—, chief Dept. of Radiology, 1981-, chmn. Regional Chiefs of Radiology, Permanente Med. Group, Inc. 1985; mem. Am. Coll. of Radiology, Radiological Soc. of No. Am., Am. Inst. of Ultrasound in Medicine, Calif. Radiological Soc.; mil: major M.C., US Army 1970-77, Army Commendation Medal; Republican; Baptist; rec: skiing, tennis, golf. Res: 3860 American River Dr Sacramento 95864 Ofc: Permanente Med. Group, 2025 Morse Ave Sacramento 95825

WAGENER, SAMUEL HOPKINS, (II), lawyer, ret.; b. June 12, 1903, San Francisco; s. Paul Hopkins and Ruth Butler (Catlin) W.; m. Pauline Hughett, Dec. 17, 1932; 1 son, Paul H., II (lt. col. USMC Ret.) b. 1933; edn: AB, UC Berkeley 1925, JD, Boalt Hall 1927; admitted Calif. State Bar 1927, US Supreme Ct. 1964. Career: atty. assoc. Snook, Snook & Chase, Oakland 1927-29, Roscoe D. Jones, Sr. 1930-31; atty. Legal Aid Soc., Oakland 1931-36, supvsg. atty. 1936-45; senior partner Wagener, Brailsford, Jewett and Lynch and successive firms, 1945-82, ret.; Alameda County Bar Assn. pres. 1953; State Bar of Calif.: Exec. Com. State Bar Delegates 1955-59, chmn. 1959, Board of Govs. 1961-64, pres. 1963-64, mem. State Judicial Council 1965-68; Am. Bar Assn. House of Delegates 1965-76; honors: recognition for service to the legal profession, Alameda County Bar Assn.; honored by Family Services of East Bay as past pres. and board mem. 43 years; Fellow Am. Bar Found.; Phi Alpha Delta Legal Frat.; clubs: Montclair Oakland Lions (past pres.), Elks (Exalted Ruler 1945-46), Athenian Nile (pres. 1971-72), Theta Chi frat.; Republican; Episcopal; rec: fishing, golf. Res: 9 Marlin Cove Oakland 94618

WAGNER, RONALD ALBERT, lawyer; b. June 19, 1934, Oakland; s. Harold Adam and Frances L. (Madsen) W.; m. Pat Larrew, May 12, 1956; Children: Wendy Lorraine b. 1958, Gretchen Leigh b. 1961; edn: BA, Stanford Univ. 1956, LLB, 1959. Career: atty. Weinmann Rode Burnhill & Moffitt 1962-65; atty. Crosby Heafey, Roach & May, Oakland 1965—; lectr. Cont. Edn. of the Bar 5 yrs.; honors: Cert. Splst., Family Law; Phi Beta Kappa 1956; mem: Am., Calif. and Alameda Co. Bar Assns., Am. Acad. of Matrimonial Lawyers; mil: 1st lt. USAF 1959-62; Republican; rec: tennis, music. Res: 35 Cedarbrook Ct. Walnut Creek 94596 Ofc: Crosby Heafey Roach & May, 1939 Harrison St. Oakland 94612

WAHEED, SEEMA, fashion consultant; b. Feb. 14, 1954, Lahore, Pakistan, ant. 1983; d. Asphar Mohammed and Zahida Mokeem (Bokhary) Khwaja; m. Abdul Waheed, Nov. 1, 1975 (div.); children: Serena P.A., b. 1977; Elena Melody, b. 1981; edn: BA, Kannaired Coll., Pakistan 1971. Career: currently owner/ opr. Seema's Private Boutique and Seema's Consulting Agency, Bakersfield; fashion columnist for Bakersfield Spotlight Mag., 1985—; mem: Assistance League, Dental Aux., Kern Youth Facility; Republican; Islamic; rec: writing, fashion. Address: Seema's Boutique, 6005 Friant Dr., Bakersfield 93309

WAHLQUIST, CARL, architect; s. John T. and Grace W.; m. Jen Jacobs, July 9, 1964; 5 children; edn: BS, Univ. Utah 1952; B.Arch., Univ. So. Calif. 1957, MSE, 1958. Career: architect prin. Carl Wahlquist AIA Arch. & Assoc. 22 yrs.; Wahlquist-Broad Archs., Engrs., & Assoc. 1 yr., shopping ctrs., malls, comml., indsl., custom residences and over 30 hotels nationwide, also planned-unit devels., townhouses, resorts, churches; mem. Am. Inst. Archs.; Latter-day Saints. Ofc: Wahlquist-Broad 450 Newport Center Dr Ste 225 Newport Beach 92660

WAHREN, PETER STURESSON, international education organization president; Dec. 9, 1937, Stockholm, Sweden; s. Sture Lindgren and Inga Wahren; m. Luz Pena, Apr. 21, 1970; edn: BA, UC Berkeley 1962; MA, Stockholm Univ. 1963; grad., Poppius Sch. of Journalism, Stockholm 1967. Career: tchr. Extra-mural Bd. of Stockholm Univ. 1963-8; asst. to dir. Am. Swedish Hist. Found., Phila., PA 1969-71; dir. western div. Student Internat. Svc. of Europe 1971-4; pres./ nat. dir. Am. Scandinavian Student Exch. 1975-81; pres. Am. Inter-cultural Student Exch. 1981—; v.p. San Diego Alcala Sister City Soc.; awards: scholarship J. Soderberg Found., Stockholm, Sweden 1963; apptd. Col. of Hon. Order of Kentucky Colonels; mem: San Diego Alcala Sister City Soc.,

Swedish Am. Soc., Sallskapet (Stockholm), World Affairs Council (S.D.); clubs: City Club of San Diego, La Jolla Beach & Tennis; publs: masters thesis, China Lobby 1963; mil: Code Spl., Swedish Armed Forces 1958-9; Republican; Lutheran; rec: yachting, travel, film theatre. Address: American Inter-cultural Student Exchange, 7728 Lookout Dr La Jolla 92037

WAINWRIGHT, FRANK N., college administrator; b. Feb. 21, 1932, Youngstown, Ohio; s. Benjamin Elgin and Alvenia (Oldham) W.; m. Patricia Johnson, Aug. 1961; 1 child, Traci L. b. 1974; edn: BA, Youngstown State Univ. 1958; MA, Case-Western Reserve Univ. 1963; EdD, Univ. So. Calif. 1978. Career: guidance counselor Ohio State Employment Svcs., Cleveland 1961-63; tchr. Los Angeles Unified Sch. Dist. 1966-69; prof. political sci. L.A. Southwest Coll. 1969-76, coord., Behavioral and Social Sci. div. 1976-78, asst. dean of instrn. 1978—; cons. to Community Justice Pgm., related to Constitutional Rights Found., L.A. 1968-69; mem: Kappa Alpha Psi frat., YMCA, AAUP, Calif. Comm. Coll. Contg. Edn. Assn., L.A. Comm. Coll. Dist. Adminstrs. Assn., Calif. Comm. and Jr. Coll. Assn.; mil: ssgt. USAF, Good Conduct, Meritorious Svc., others; Methodist; rec: photog., guitar, piano, camping. Res: 2664 Via Valdes Palos Verdes Estates 90274 Ofc: L.A. Southwest Coll., 1600 W Imperial Hwy Los Angeles 90047

WAISANEN, TIMOTHY DALE, tax consultant; b. Aug. 24, 1951, Wayne, Mich.; s. Wilho U. and Lillian Marie (Osborne) W.; m. Vera, Dec. 28, 1973; children: April b. 1978, Carolyn b. 1980; edn: BA, So. Calif. Coll. 1975; JD, Calif. Western Sch. of Law 1978; Calif. lic. Life, Disability and Casualty Ins. Agent; Cert. Tax Preparer. Career: legal intern Atty. Gen., Anchorage, Alaska; asst. dist. mgr. Equitable Life, Santa Ana, Calif.; dir. mktg. and plnng., Robert Schuller Ministries, Garden Grove; current: pres. American Tax Savings Inc., Costa Mesa; cons. Brewer and Porter, Attys.; honors: Who's Who Am. Univs. and Colls. (1975), vol. service award Orange County Council of Women CofC (1975); mem. Nat. Orgn. of Tax Consultants, Internat. Assn. Finl. Planners, So. Calif. Coll. Alumni Assn. (bd. dirs.; O.C. chmn.); Democrat; Assembly of God (Ch. bd.); rec: basketball, ping pong. Res: 11884 Egham Circle Garden Grove 92940 Ofc: American Tax Savings 150 Paularino Ste 180 Costa Mesa 92626

WAITE, CHARLES PRESCOTT, venture capitalist; b. Mar. 30, 1930, Manchester, Conn.; s. Earl M. and Virginia (Clark) W.; m. Angela Peterson, Feb. 16, 1985; children: Charles P., Jr. b. 1955, David C. b. 1957, Catherine P. b. 1960, Patricia C. b. 1965; edn: BS, Univ. of Conn. 1957; MBA, Harvard Univ. 1959. Career: research asst. Harvard Univ. 1959-60; asst. v.p. Am. Research & Devel. Corp., Boston 1960-66; gen. ptnr. Greylock Partnership(s), Boston 1966—; pres. Greylock Mgmt. Corp., Boston 1973—; dir: Micom Systems, Floating Point Systems, Priam Corp., Data I/O, Xoma Corp., others; trustee Kenyon Coll.; clubs: Algonquin (Boston), Harvard (Boston and NYC), Woods Hole (Mass.) Golf; mil: lt. col. US Army, active duty 1951-54, Reserve 1954-73; Republican; rec: travel. Res: 1200 California St San Francisco 94109 Ofc: Greylock Mgmt. Corp. 1 Federal St Boston Mass 02110

WAKEFIELD, RONALD PETER, real estate broker, fee appraiser, business consultant; b. Oct. 23, 1947; s. Harry J. and Carmeline (Tropa) W.; edn: MBA, CSU San Jose 1970; desig: Calif. Std. Tchg. Cred. (1970), lic. R.E. Broker (1977). Career: real estate broker/owner Ron Wakefield Realty, San Jose 1977—; fee appraiser/ owner Calif. Assoc. Appraisers 1986—; finl. cons., stock splst., major nightclub cons., 1982—; pres., CFO, gen. mgr. Stampede Club Inc., San Jose and Redding, 1982—; recipient sales achieve. awards: Red Carpet Realty (8 in 1976), Allstate Realtors (3 in 1977, 3 in 1978); mem. San Jose Bd. of Realtors, Nat. Assn. Realtors, Calif. Assn. Realtors, Grad. Realtors Inst. 1986; self-made millionaire; Republican; Protestant; rec: antique autos, racing, sailing, boating. Address: Ron Wakefield Realty 816 Boynton Ave San Jose 95117

WAKEFORD, GORDON COLEMAN, consultant, sales executive; b. Jan. 16, 1938, Toronto, Ontario, Canada; s. Norman and Doris Kathleen (Sinclair) W.; m. Marcia Anne Bailey, Oct. 30, 1982; 1 child: Coleman b. 1968; edn: journey-man machinist, ICS 19670-4; Riverside City Coll. 1971-3; coll. tchr. cert., State Arizona. Career: journeyman mach. Algoma Steel Corp., Sault Ste Marie, Ontario, Canada 1956-64; shop dir. Humko Prods. Div. Kraft Foods, Buena Park 1964-6; svc. engr. Signode Steel Corp., Chgo., Ill. 1966-9; maint. dir. Container Corp. of America, Corona 1969-71; maint. supt. Inspiration Consolidated Copper Co., Globe, Ariz. and Riverside Cement Co., Riverside 1972-8; senior tech. svc. mgr./southwest regl. sales mgr D-A Lubricant Co. Div. Premier Corp., Cleveland, OH 1978—; coll. instr. Gila Pueblo Campus, Ext. Eastern Ariz. Coll. 2 yrs.; secty. Crestmore Fed. Credit Union, Riverside 1972-4; Appreciation awards, EMSA of Calif. 1982, So. Calif. Municipal Equip. Mgrs. 1983; mem: Soc. of Mining Engrs. of AIME; Smithsonian Assocs.; mil: active reserve Canada army RCEME 1956-64; Methodist; rec: tennis, water sports, collector pewter cars. Res: 603 No San Antonio Ave Ontario 91762 Ofc: D A Lubricant Co. 4795 Holt Blvd Ste 104 Montclair 91763

WALDRON, JOHN BATTIN, engineering/ construction co. executive; b. Aug. 27, 1956, West Chester, Pa.; s. John Battin, Sr. and Anne (Kite) W.; Reg. Profl. Civil Engr. Career: contr. Waldron Constrn. Co. West Chester, Pa. 1973-79; proj. engr., asst. proj. mgr., civil engr. Santa Fe Internat. Orange, Calif., Houston, Tex, and Kuwait 1979-82; proj. mgr. Daniel, Mann, Johnson & Mendenhall, L.A. 1982—; Republican; Catholic; rec: sailing, photog. Res: 334 N Lime St Orange 92668 Ofc: Daniel, Mann et al. 3250 Wilshire Blvd Los Angeles 90010

WALKER, LYN E., graphic design co. owner; b. July 10, 1957, Artesia; d. Vernon S. and Marvene E. (Niquette) Walker; edn: BA, and MA, CSU Long Beach 1983; Heidelberg Press Sch., Heidelberg, Germany 1982. Career: reproductions mgr. Knott's Berry Farm, Buena Park 1975-85; owner Graphic Productions, Garden Grove 1985—; mem. Graphic Arts Advis. Bd., CSU Long Beach (1984-88); honors: Order of the Round Table, Champion Papers (1981); mem. Advt. Prodn. Assn.; rec: vocals, guitar, gardening. Ofc: Graphic Productions, 11602 Knott St Ste 14 Garden Grove 92641

WALKER, MARY KATHLEEN, psychotherapist; b. Dec. 17, 1938, Los Angeles; d. William and Lucille Walker; 2 sons (nee Wiebold): Brian b. 1960, Brent b. 1961; edn: AA, Santa Monica Coll. 1974; BA, UC Los Angeles 1978; MA, CSU Los Angeles 1981; PhD, Internat. Coll. 1986. Career: movie stage coach Walter Wanger Prodns. 1938 (youngest social security card holder in US at time); asst. Dr. R.E. Barton, Santa Monica 1957; photo flurographic x-ray tech. Santa Monica Hosp. 1964-72; clin. psychology, marriage and family counselor, Watt Industries 1981-86; honors: Psi Chi, Nat. Deans list (1980-81), CSU Deans list (1980-81); research: Camarillo State Hosp.- A comparative Study of Pineal gland calcification using radiography in schizophrenic and non-schiz. groups, and An Investigation combining the writings of psychotic patients and physicists across four target areas: time, unity, matter, and ineffability. Address: 1220 Maple St Ste 1 Santa Monica 90405

WALKER, PEGGIE RUTH, podiatrist; b. June 24, 1931, Cameron, Texas; d. Perryno and Sylvia (Murphy) Heard; children: Sylvia b. 1958, Eric Lyndon b. 1954; edn: BS, Prairie View A&M Coll. 1950; BS, Calif. Coll. of Podiatry 1954; DPM, Calif. Coll. of Podiatric Med. 1957. Career: podiatric med. and surgeon pvt. practice, Los Angeles and Compton 1959-82; chief podiatric svc. Martin Luther King Jr. Hosp. 1972-82; chief podiatry dept. Dominguez Valley Hosp. 1977; vol. clinician Calif. Foot Health Found. 1959-62; health edn.. Los Angeles Bus. Assns.; awards: Irving Drew, podiatric res. paper on infant fee (1967), Century Club, for outstanding svc. to Youth Community; mem: Am. Coll. of Foot Surgeons, Am. Podiat. Assn., Calif. Podiat. Assn., Am. Assn. of Hosp. Podiatrists, Harbor Podiat. Soc.; patentee: foot measuring device (1957), shoe designs; Democrat; Catholic; rec: gardening. Res: 634 W. Tichenor St. Compton Ofc: Dr. Peggie R. Walker, 327 E. Rosecrans Ave. Compton 90220

WALLACE, CATHERINE MATHESON, banker; b. Oct. 31, 1952, Ft. Bragg, N.C.; d. Salve Hugo and Patricia Marie (Halloran) Matheson; m. John S. Wallace, Aug. 18, 1979; 1 son, William Michael b. 1985; edn: BA, Sweet Briar, 1974; MBA, Chapel Hill, N.C. 1976. Career: v.p. Wells Fargo Bank 1976-85; honors: Phi Beta Kappa, Beta Gamma Sigma; mem. Junior League, University Club; Roman Catholic. Res: 2420 Lorain Rd San Marino 91108

WALLACE, J. CLIFFORD, U.S. circuit judge; b. Dec. 11, 1928, San Diego; s. John Franklin and Lillie Isabel (Overing) W.; m. Virginia, Apr. 8, 1957; children: Paige, Laurie, Teri, John Jr.; edn: BA, San Diego State Univ. 1952; LLB, UC Berkeley 1955. Career: atty. Gray, Cary, Ames & Frye San Diego 1955-70; U.S. district judge so. dist. Calif. S.D. 1970-72; U.S. circuit judge 9th circ. 1972—; bd. advisors Am. Enterprise Inst. for Ten Year Study of the Constitution; adj. prof. 3 law schools (former); senior advisor Legal Systems and Judicial Admin. to Asia Found.; bd. of councilors USC Law Ctr.; honors: Woodrow Wilson Internat. Ctr. for Scholars (Smithsonian Inst., Wash. DC, summer 1976), Significant Sig (Sigma Chi 1979), Brigham Young Univ. Hon. Alumni Award 1979, Distinguished Svc. Award (Calif. Newspaper Publ. Assn. 1979), Silver Beaver (Boy Scouts of Am. 1981), Disting. Alumnus (Coll. of Arts and Letters San Diego State Univ. 1985); mem: Am. Bar Assn., Am. Bd. Trial Advocates, Inst. of Judicial Admin., Boy Scouts Am (v.p. S.D. Co. council); publ: num. arts. in law jours. and law reviews, created & taught course in judicial admin. at Brigham Young Univ. Sch. of Law, seminar on Am. Law and Legal Instns., Salzburg, Austria; mil: aviation electron. tech. 2/c USN 1946-49, Good Conduct, Victory medals; Ch. of Jesus Christ of L.D.S. rec: sports. Ofc: 4N25 U.S. Courthouse 940 Front St San Diego 92189

WALLACE, PAUL HARVEY, lawyer; b. Oct. 27, 1944, Fresno; s. Sam Dunn and Naomi (Hickman) W.; 1 dau. Christy, b. 1970; edn: BS criminol., CSU Fresno 1966; JD, Calif. Western Sch. of Law, 1974; US Naval Justice Sch., Newport, R.I. 1977; Canadian Cmd. & Staff Coll., Kingston, Ont. 1985; admitted State Bar of Calif. 1974. Career: dep. dist. atty. Co. of San Diego 1975-9; assoc. atty. Harrison and Watson, San Diego 1979-81; dep. county counsel, Co. of Butte, Oroville 1981-85, county counsel 1985—; lectr. County Counsel Assn. (1982), San Diego Bar Assn. (1979), faculty Sixth Nat. Council of Juvenile and Family Ct. Judges (1979); honors: Head Notes and Comments ed. Cal Western Sch. of Law Internat. Law Journ. (1974), Who's Who in Colls. and Univs. (1974), I.F.C Man of Year CSUF (1966); mem: San Diego Dist. Atty.'s Assn. (pres. 1979), Butte Co. Bar Assn., Masons, Scottish Rite, Shrine, VFW, Am. Legion; publs: Sovereign Immunity Made East: Curbing Litigation with Advry. Opinions, 3 Calif. Western Internat. Law J. 354 (1974); mil: lt. col. USMCR 1966-, Silver Star, 2 Purple Hearts, Combat Action Ribbon; Cross of Gal. w/Palm and Frame; Democrat; rec: jogging, photog. Ofc: Butte County Counsel, 25 County Center Dr Oroville 95965

WALLACE, ROSETTA DANIEL, hotelier; b. Nov. 15, 1932, Lumpkin, Ga.; d. Elder John Henry Daniel; widowed; children: Franc b. 1954, Ellis b. 1955; edn: BA, CSU San Francisco 1980. Career: acctg., civil service, US Fed. Govt., US Postal Svc.; current: profl. fashion designer; owner Hotel Gustine "Where it's always 1909" (turn-of-the-century hotel bldg., unique shops, food, and museum of antiques); mem. Internat. Tng. and Communication (treas.); publs: cookbook; Democrat; Presbyterian; rec: travel, writing, textile research. Res: 411 Fifth St (POB 313) Gustine 95322

WALLERSTEIN, BRUCE LEE, psychologist; b. May 23, 1943, Boston, Mass.; s. Michael and Mildred W.; edn: AB, Boston Univ. 1964; MS in psychiat. social wk., Univ. Penn. 1966, PhD psychol., 1968; lic. clin. psychologist (1969), marriage, family therapist (1969), nsg. home adminstr. Career: pvt. practice Wallerstein and Assocs., 1969—, cons. to health care field, business orgns., archl. design and real estate devel. industries, currently cons. South Coast Comm. Care, Long Beach 1973-, Nat. Med. Ents., Los Angeles 1974-, Hill Haven Corp., L.A. 1977-, Country Villa Svc. Corp., L.A. 1983-; instr. USC (1970-72), Brooks Coll. (1973-75), Chapman Coll. (1975-76); honors: NIMH Award (1966-67), ACLU Award (1975); mem: Group Psychotherapy Assn. of So. Calif. (dir. 1972-79, pres. 1975-77, Outstanding Member award 1979), Fellow Am. OrthoPsychiatric Assn., Otto Rank Assn. (1969-80), Calif. Assn. of Marriage and Family Therapists, United Cerebral Palsy/Spastic Childrens' Found. (dir. 1975-81, v.p. 1976-80), Harbor View House, San Pedro (dir. 1973-79, pres. 1975-79), Long Beach CofC, Naples Islands Bus. Assn., Calif. Assn. of Health Facilities; publs: A Place to Live, Not to Die: A Practical Guide to Nursing Homes (1975); rec: sailboat racing. Ofc: Naples Counseling Center 5855 E Naples Plaza Long Beach 90803

WALTER, CHARLES R., JR., private club executive; b. June 19, 1936, Evanston, Ill.; s. Charles R. and Alviera C. (Bliel) W.; m. Margo, Nov. 24, 1968; children: Laura b. 1972, Chad b. 1974; edn: BA in bus., Mich. State Univ. 1959; grad. USAF Command and Staff Coll. 1974, USAF Squadron Officers 1965, USAF Air War Coll. 1977; desig: Cert. Club Mgr. (CCM) Club Mgrs. Assn. Am. (1969). Career: field insp. Proctor & Gamble, 1959; asst. mgr. Von Steuben Hotel, Wiesbaden, Germany 1959-60; asst. mgr. Columbia Club, London, Eng. 1960-63; club mgr. officers clubs: Brookley AFB Mobile, Ala. 1963-65, McClellan AFB Sacto. 1965-67, Clark AFB Philippines 1967-69, Hickam AFB Honolulu 1969-70, Andrews AFB Maryland 1970-71, Kessler AFB Mississippi 1971-73, Bolling AFB Wash DC 1973 80, chief of all clubs worldwide, Randolph AFB Tx. 1980-83; gen. mgr. Jonathan Club, Los Angeles 1983—; cons. Allied Forces Central Europe/NATO; guest lectr. M.S.U., Cal-Poly, Wisc. State Univ., others; instr. No. Va. Comm. Coll., USAF, US Army & Marine Corps seminars, Nat. Restaurant Assn. seminars; awards: 2 gold medals, Nat. Rest. Assn. Great Menu Contest; mem: Nat. Rest. Assn., Food Service Execs. Assn., Club Mgrs. Assn. of Am. (past pres., mem. 500 Honor Soc.), Mich. State Univ. Hotel Rest. Sch. Alumni (bd.), LA CofC, Santa Monica CofC, La Canada CofC, Central City Assn. Los Angeles, Beta Theta Pi; contbg. author (and project chmn.) of Club Management textbook (1978); mil: col. US Air Force 1959-83, Legion of Merit, Merit. Svc.; Republican; Presbyterian; rec: ski, sailing, golf, travel. Address: Los Angeles

WALTER, JOHN FREDERICK, lawyer; b. Nov. 3, 1944, NY; s. John M. and Bette M. (Cushing) W.; m. Joyce A., June 24, 1967; children: Jeffrey b. 1975, Amy b. 1972; edn: BA, Loyola Univ., L.A. 1966, JD, 1969. Career: atty. law firm Kindel & Anderson, 1969, 72-76; asst. US Atty., Los Angeles 1970-72; founding ptnr. Walter, Finestone, Richter & Kane, Los Angeles 1976—; judge pro tem L.A. Municipal Ct. 1984—; mem. ABA, Los Angeles County Bar Assn., Assn. of Business Trial Lawyers; Republican; Roman Catholic. Res: 16611 Merivale Lane Pacific Palisades 90272 Ofc: Walter, Finestone, Richter & Kane APC, 10920 Wilshire Blvd Ste 1400 Los Angeles 90024

WALTHER, ROGER O., educational travel and real estate co. chief executive; b. Jan. 21, 1936, Plainfield, NJ; s. Clarence O. and Mary (Russo) W.; m. Anne Newton, Jan. 21, 1976; children: Wendy, b. 1962, Christine, b. 1965, Edward, b. 1967, John Dunning, b. 1968, Beau Dunning, b. 1971; edn: BS, USCG Acad. 1958; MBA, Wharton Sch. Univ. of Penna. 1961. Career: Brand mgmt., Procter & Gamble, Cincinnati 1961-65; exec. v.p./pres. Nat. Student Mktg. Corp., 1969-70 (when Am. Inst. for Fgn. Study was a wholly owned subs.); owner, pub. San Francisco Mag. 1981-82; co-founder, pres., chief exec. and prin. shareholder, Queen's Gate Corp., op. in three basic areas: Educational Travel, Am. Inst. for Fgn. Study (largest ednl. travel packager in USA); chief exec. major commercial real estate portfolio (incl. props. in London, Eng., Fairfield County, Conn., San Francisco) 1965-; co-founder, bd. chmn. San Francisco Bancorp. 1980-84; co-founder, bd. chmn. First Republic Bancorp. 1985—; Dir: Bank of San Francisco, Dr. Meyer Friedman Inst.; trustee Richmond (Eng.) Coll.; lectr., mem. Adv. Council, San Francisco State Univ. Graduate Sch. of Bus.; mem: Young Presidents Orgn., Commonwealth Club (SF), Wharton Alumni Club of SF, Lincoln Club of No. Calif., Calif. Tennis Club (SF), SF Golf Club, St. Francis Yacht Club (SF), Rye (Eng.) Golf Club, Annabel's (London); mil: USCG 1954-59; Republican; Episcopal; rec: golf, tennis, photog. Res: 2856 Vallejo St San Francisco 94123 Ofc: Queen's Gate Corp. 3661 Buchanan St San Francisco 94123

WALTON, LEWIS RICHARD, lawyer; b. Dec. 28, 1941, Santa Monica, Calif; s. Lee R. and Mabel B. (Nielsen) W.; m. Jo Ellen, Dec. 19, 1971; 1 son, Richie b. 1981; edn: BA, Loma Linda Univ. 1963; JD, magna cum laude, Univ. San Diego 1967; admitted Calif. State Bar. Career: classified material courier USN ofcr. 1968-70; atty. 1970—; faculty Chaffee Coll. real estate law 1971, Loma Linda Univ. bus. law 1971-74, Merced Coll. real estate law 1980; gen. counsel San Joaquin Comm. Hosp.; spl. advisor US Congressional Advisory Bd.; honors: Gen. Hickman Award in constl. law 1967; ASCAP Legal Writing Award 1966, Bancroft Whitney Scholarships (5) 1964-67; mem: Calif. State Bar, Am. Acad. Hosp. Attys.; author: eight books publ. by Pacific Press, Review & Herald

Publ. Assn., Woodbridge Press; mil: lt. US Coast Guard, num. decorations from Vietnam; Republican; Seventh-Day Adventist; rec: aviation, comml. pilot. Ofc: 2615 Eye St Bakersfield 93301

WALTON, STEVAN RAYMOND ALAN, chiropractor; b. Mar. 3, 1948, Huntington Park, Calif.; s. Richard Alan and Shirley Anne (Boyer) W.; edn: BA, UC Los Angeles 1971; DC, summa cum laude, Cleveland Chiro. Coll. 1982. Career: black belt instr. martial arts (Kenpo, self-defense) 1969-78; licensed chiro. Hawaii and Calif., currently Watkins Chiro Center La Canada-Flintridge; chmn. dept. of principles and practice Cleveland Chiro. Coll. L.A.; honors: Distinguished Svc. Award (Am. Chiro. Assn. Technic Council 1984); mem: Am. Public Health Assn., Calif. Chiro. Assn., Internat. Chiro. Assn., Am. Chiro. Assn. (council on technic, panel of advisors); publ: Research Anthology (1983), Clinical Implications of Renal Neurophysiology (1983), Subluxation Research (1983), Intro. to Chiropractic Clinical Biomechanics and Neurobiologics (1984); rec: martial arts. Ofc: Watkins Chiro. Center 1371 Foothill Blvd La Canada-Flintridge 91011

WALWYN, STEPHEN JOHN, lawyer; b. Nov. 8, 1947, Staffordshire, England; s. John and Lilian Mary (Baddeley) W.; edn: BA, Univ. of Santa Clara 1970; JD, cum laude, 1973; admitted Calif. State Bar 1973. Career: assoc. atty. Boccardo, Lull, Niland, Teerlink & Bell 1973-81; partner The Boccardo Law Firm 1981-, mem. mgmt. com. 1983-4, supvry. partner 1983–; prof. of law, Peninsula Univ. Sch. of Law 1997-9; Bar-L Club; recipient Bender Adminstrv. Law Awd. 1972, creative writing and graphic arts awds. 1965; Phi Alpha Theta (hist. hon.), Nat. Honor. Soc. 1965; Superior Ct. Judge Pro Tem., Santa Clara Co. 1977-83; mem: Calif. Trial Lawyers Assn.; Santa Clara Co. Bar Assn.; Santa Clara County Trial Lawyers Assn.; Santa Clara Univ. and Law Sch. Alumni Assns.; British- Am. Club; Nat. Trust for Historical Preservation; publs: Effects of Strategic Bombing European Theatre 1939-45, 1969-70; Safe Guarding the Mentally Ill Under Calif. Law 1972; Comparative Aspects of Guerilla Warfare Vietnam & Malaya 1967; mil: ofcr. cadet, British Army, Royal Corps of Transport, Royal Mil. Acad., Sandhurst 1966-7; rec: painting, sailing, history. Res: 663 Festivo Ct Fremont 94539 Ofc: Boccardo Law Firm, 111 W St. John Street, Ste 1100, San Jose 95115

WANG, CHARLES CHANG-PING, scientist; b. April 25, 1937, Shanghai, China, nat. US cit. 1974; s. Kuen-Ying and Ping-Lu (Ming) W.; m. Lily Lee, June 29, 1963; edn: BS, Taiwan Univ. 1959; MS, Tsinghua Univ. 1961; MS, Calif. Inst. of Tech. 1963, PhD, 1967. Career: lectr. National Taiwan Univ., Taipei, Taiwan 1961-62; engr. America Electronic Inc., Fullerton 1962; tech. staff Bellcomm Inc., Wash. DC 1967-69; lectr. The Catholic Univ. of America, Wash. DC 1967-68; assoc. research engr. UC San Diego, La Jolla 1969-74, adj. prof. 1974–; cons. Systems Applications Inc., Beverly Hills 1972-74; senior scientist The Aerospace Corp., El Segundo 1974-86; pres. Optodyne Inc. Compton 1986–; session chmn. Am. Physical Soc. Fluid Dynamical Metting, San Diego 1971; conf. chmn. Laser '86, Las Vegas; pgm. chmn. Internat. Conf. on Lasers, Beijing 1980; publs: assoc. ed., Journ. of Am. Inst. Aero. & Astro. 1981-83; reviewed papers, Journ. Fluid Mechanics, Journ. Applied Physics, Astronautica Acta, UC Patent Bd., AIAA Journ., NSF; honors: Caltech Inst. Scholar 1963; Inventor's Award, Aerospace Co. 1976; mem: Soc. of Sigma Xi, Am. Physical Soc., Am. Inst. of Aero. & Astro. (assoc. fellow), Optical Soc. of Am. (fellow), Chinese Engrs. & Scientists Assn. of So. Calif. (pres. 1979), Manhattan Beach Badminton Club; works: 70+ journ. publs. and inventions; Democrat; rec: badminton, tennis, skiing. Res: 28509 Seamount Dr. Rancho Palos Verdes 90274 Ofc: Optodyne Inc. 1180 Mahalo Pl Compton 90220

WANG, HSIEN BING, real estate co. president; b. June 26, 1936, China, nat. US cit. 1970; m. Angela, Mar. 23, 1943; children: Suling b. 1970, Howie b. 1972; edn: BS in mech. eng., Chen Kung Univ. 1961; MS, aeronautical eng., Stanford Univ. 1965. Career: project engr. Bertea Corp., Irvine 1966-76; pres. B&A Investment Props. (real estate investment, syndication, mgmt.), Irvine 1976–, also Meredith Guest House, Raleigh, N.C.; mem. Yorba Linda CofC, Orange Co. CofC; inventor, U.S. Patent: Hydraulic Circuit Breaker, Fail Safe Control Valve. Res: 52 Ridgeline Dr Newport Beach 92660 Ofc: B&A Investment Properties 18200 Von Karman Ave Ste 660 Irvine 92715

WANG, JIMMY CHI-MIN, bank analyst; b. May 25, 1951, Taipei, Taiwan; s. Teh Lung and Tien (Yuan) W.; edn: BS, Tatung Inst. of Tech., 1973; MSEE, USC 1977; MBA, UC Berkeley 1979. Career: research asst. UCB 1977-79; engr. RDI, San Leandro 1979-81; analyst Data Architects, Inc., San Francisco 1981-82; instr. Golden Gate Univ., 1984; analyst Computer Usage Co., S.F. 1983-84; analyst Bank of America, Concord 1984–. Ofc: Bank of America 1655 Grant St Concord 94530

WANG, TZU-LI TOM, engineer; b. Apr. 9, 1948, China; s. Chi-Chang and Shu-Lan (Shao) W.; m. Sha-Li Chi, Jan. 29, 1984; children: Chung-Shu b. 1972, Chung-Liang b. 1975, Chung-Wei b. 1977, Chung-Hau b. 1985; edn: BSEE, National Cheng Kung Univ. 1969, MSEE, 1972; MSEE, highest honors, CSU San Jose 1976; MBA mktg., Golden Gate Univ. 1986. Career: electrical engr. Sperry Univac, Cupertino 1974-77; development engr. Itel, Sunnyvale, 1978-80; staff engr. Lazor, Sunnyvale 1980-81; senior engr. Masstor, Sunnyvale 1981-83, cons. 1981; applications mgr. National Semiconductor, Santa Clara 1983–; tchg. asst. UC Berkeley 1977-78; recipient recogn. award, San Jose Sister City Pgm. com.; mem: IEEE (chmn. Student Assn.), Chinese Assn. (dir.), Pacific Neighbors, Sino-Amer. Assn.; publs: tech. papers, IEEE Jour. 1972, Midcon, Northcon, Southcon, Wescon, VLSI Symposium; Handbook (pub. 1984); Catholic; rec: hiking, fishing, swimming. Res: 4327 Redlands St Union City 94587 Ofc: National Semiconductor, 2900 Semiconductor Dr Santa Clara 95051

WAPNICK, ANTHONY AUSTIN, physician - internist; b. July 30, 1942, Johannesburg, S. Africa, nat. USA 1983; s. Louis Julius and Helen Clara (Spalker) W.; m. Barbara Charad, June 25, 1968; children: Shani, b. 1970, Tracey, b. 1971; edn: MB.Bch, cum laude, Univ. of Witwatersrand 1965, FCP, 1971; bd. cert. Am. Bd. Internal Medicine 1978. Career: pvt. med. practice, Johannesburg, S.A.; assoc. prof. of med., Boston Univ.; pvt. med. practice, San Diego currently; mem. San Diego Soc. of Medicine, Internal Med. Soc.; Hebrew. Res: 6707 Brynwood Way, San Diego 92120 Ofc: 555 Reservoir Dr, Ste 200, San Diego 92120

WARD, CARLEY CONRAD, biomechanical engineer; b. Mar. 14, 1933, Detroit, Mich.; d. George Lester and Kathleen Lila (Neville) Conrad; m. John F. Ward, Dec. 1, 1961; 1 child, Parris b. 1962; edn: BS mech. engring., Univ. Mich. 1955, MS engring. mechanics, 1958; PhD biomechanics and dynamics, UC Los Angeles 1974. Career: research engr. Douglas Aircraft 1960-67; postgrad. research engr., asst. medical researcher UC Los Angeles 1968-72; research engr. Civil Engring. Lab., Naval Constrn. Battalion Ctr. 1974-80; pres. Biodynamics Engring. Inc. 1980–; honors: outstanding achievement US Navy (1974), Sigma Xi (1973-80), Amelia Earhart Fellow (1968-69), cit. for profl. achieve. McDonnell-Douglas Corp. (1966), Regent Alumni Scholar Univ. Mich. (1951-55); mem: Soc. Automotive Engrs., Am. Assn. Automotive Medicine (chmn. W. Chpt. 1980-83, secty. 1984-85), Soc. of Exptl. Stress Analysis, Am. Acad. of Forensic Scis., Am. Trauma Soc.; works: devel. new analytical model for studying central nervous system trauma; contbr. 30+ publs. on injury analysis, publs. in medical books; rec: ski, hike, fish. Res: 705 Hampden Pl Pacific Palisades 90272 Ofc: Biodynamics/Engineering Inc. POB 722 Pac Palisades 90272

WARD, DIANE KOROSY, lawyer; b. Oct. 17, 1939, Cleveland, Ohio; d. Theodore Louis and Edith C. (Bogar) Korosy; m. R. Michael Walters, Esq., June 30, 1979; children: Christopher LaBruce b. 1965, Samantha Martha Thompson b. 1968; edn: BA, Heidelberg Coll. 61; JD, Univ. of San Diego 1975. Career: partner law firm Ward & Howell 1978-80; Walters, Howell & Ward 1980-1; mng. partner Walters & Ward, San Diego 1981–; spkr. on estate plng. at num. seminars throughout state; v.p./ bd. dirs. Oak Broadcasting Systems, Inc., Glendale 1983-84; honors: Phi Alpha Theta (history); Pi Delta Epsilon (journ.); Alpha Psi Omega (drama.); listed: Who's Who in Am. Colls. & Univs. 1961, 75; mem: Green Valley Civic Assn. (pres. 1980); Los Amados Aux., Children's Home Soc. (pres. 1969-70); Phi Delta Phi legal frat.; Am., Calif., San Diego and Rancho Bernardo Bar Assns.; Lawyers Club of San Diego; Profl. & Exec. Women of the Ranch (pres. 1983-); Soroptimist Internat. of Rancho Bernardo (pres. 1980); Palomar-Pomerado Hosp. Found. (dir. planned giving); Toastmasters of Rancho Bernardo; sheriff Del Norte Corral, Westerners Internat. 1985-86; columnist, Univ. of S.D. Law Sch. newspaper Woolsack, De Minimus 1973-4; Espicopal; rec: philately, music: singing, guitar, flute. Res: 16503 Ave Florencia Poway 92064 Ofc: Walters & Ward, APC, 11665 Avena Pl Ste 203 San Diego 92128

WARD, LARRY DON, purchasing executive; b. July 27, 1951, Odessa, Texas; s. John L. and Barbara A. (Howell) W.; m. Jamie Himes, June 3, 1978; children: Philip b. 1981, Kristin b. 1983, Amanda b. 1985; edn: BS, Louisiana State Univ. 1975; Cert. Purchasing Mgr., NAPM (1984). Career: with Decca Survey Systems, Houston 1975; staff mem./supvr. inventory control later buyer, sr. buyer Purch. Dept., finally dir. purch. & receiving, Campus Crusade for Christ, hqtrs. San Bernardino, 1975-1982; buyer purch. dept. Calif. Inst. of Tech. 1982–, worked on CIT Submillimeter and the Keck Ten Meter Observatory, Mauana Kea, Hawaii, current projects, Gravity Wave Observatory and CIT Computing Center, Pasadena; mem: Nat. Contract Mgmt. Assn., Nat. Assn. of Ednl. Buyers, Calif. Higher Edn. Assn. of Purchasing; Republican; Am. Baptist (vice moderator, Sun. Sch. tchr.). Res: 1553 W. Morgan Rd. San Bernardino 92407 Ofc: Calif. Inst. Technology Purch. Dept. 315-6, 1201 E. California Blvd Pasadena 91125

WARD, LINCOLN R., communications co. executive; b. Feb. 12, 1924, Rockville Centre, NY; s. James J. and Edith Ruth (Lerch) W.; m. Mary Sellinger, Oct. 20, 1951; children: James b. 1952, Mary Beth b. 1954, Ann b. 1957; edn: BS, in bus. adm., Wayne Univ., mgmt. course, Stanford Univ. 1964; adv. studies, Brookings Inst. 1976. Career: New York Trust Co., NY, NY 1940; long lines commercial staff AT&T 1941-2; WWII 1942-5; techl. observer US War Dept., Frankfurt, Germany 1946-7; with AT&T 1947-62; network svcs., NY & Chgo. 1947-9; dist. mgr., Mnpls., Minn. 1949-50; plant staff mgr., Chgo. & Atlanta, Ga. 1950-2; commercial & traffic mgr., Detroit, Mich. 1953-5; div. mgr., Wash. DC 1955-7; NY major acct. and ind. sales mgr. 1957-62; Pacific Telephone, Los Angeles 1962–, gen. sales mgr. 1962-7, gen. commercial mgr. 1968, gen. mgr. Los Angeles, North, Central & West areas 1972-81, v.p. San Diego, Imperial, Orange, Riverside, Inyo & San Bernardino Cos. 1982–; bd. dirs. Pvt. Indus. Council of S.D. 1983-4, S.D. Zoo Execs. 1981-4; exec. com./ bd. dirs. Economic Devel. Corp.; S.D. Mayor's Adv. Com. 1983-4; L.A. Mayor's Adv. Com. on Water, City of L.A. Produce Mkt. Adv. Com. 1979-81; awards: 1984 Citizen of Yr., Gr. San Diego Indus.- Edn. Council; 1982 Headliner of Yr., S.D. Press Club.; Amigo de Distincion, Mexican & Am. Found. of S.D.; Distinguished Friend of the Univ., CSU Northridge 1982; Silver Beaver, BSA 1983; Citations from L.A. City Council and Calif. Assem. & Senate for civic leadership; 1984 Knights of the Holy Sepulchre; Distinguished Eagle 1985; Citizen of the Year, Jr. CofC 1985; Community Leader Award, Calif. Credit Union League 1985; mem: Navy League; Telephone Pioneers of Am.; Jonathan Club, L.A.; University Club of L.A. & S.D.; bd. dirs.: San Diego CofC; United Way; San Diegans, Inc.; San Diego Symphony; S.D. POPS Orch.; BSA; bd. dirs. Noah Homes for Disabled; YMCA of S.D.; Gr. S.D. Sports Assn.; Univ. of S.D. Pres.'s Council; publs: Creativity in Business, used in courses San Jose State Univ. 1965-80; Men, Money and Markets, story of brokerage ind. 1961; contbr. arts. Bell Labs mag., AT&T mag., Mgmt. Journ; lectr. on Bus. Mgmt. AMA and State Bar Assn.; mil: Non-Com. WWII Signal Corps., ETO, Am. Def. Svc., WWII Victory medals; Republican; Catholic; rec: bridge, golf. Res: 10437 Sierra Vista Lane La Mesa 92041 Ofc: Pacific Bell, 525 B Street, Ste 1912 San Diego 92101

WARD, RODERIC CHARLES, architect; b. Apr. 17, 1935, Berkeley; s. Nairne Forsythe and Janet (Nundy) W.; m. Elizabeth Jean Meininger, June 18, 1957; children: Roderic b. 1959, Gregory b. 1960, Theodore b. 1962; edn: Univ. of Colo. 1954-5; BA, Stanford Univ. 1957; B.Arch. 1958; reg. architect, Calif. 1966. Career: proj./ design/ maint. control ofcr. PWC, Guam 1958-62; draftsman Welton Becket & Assocs., San Francisco 1962; draftsman Claude Oakland, Arch. AIA, San Francisco 1962-3; ofc. mgr. Caywood & Nopp, Arch. AIA, Sacto. 1963-9; partner adminstr. Caywood, Nopp, Takata, Hansen & Ward, Architects, Sacto. 1969-72; treas. Caywood, Nopp, Ward, Arch., Sacto. & Placerville 1972-8; pres. Ward.Wolstenholm, AIA, Arch., Sacto. 1978−; dir. Ward. Wolstenholm Pension & Profit Sharing Plan; partner, W.W. Devel. Co., Sacto. 1978-; recipient Bank of Am. Achievement Awd. 1952, Awd. for Excellence, WIC 1980; mem: AIA; Calif. Council AIA; CSI; Carmichael Kiwanis; Navy League Sacto. Council; Naval Reserve Assn., Fort Sutter Chpt.; Kappa Sigma, Beta Zeta Chpt.; Stanford Alumni Assn. of Sacto.; designed first Sacramento Atrium House (1965) and first Solar House (1976); mil: Cmdr., USNR-R, Civil Engring. Corps.; Republican; rec: photog., stained glass, boating. Res: 7630 Tobia Way Fair Oaks 95628 Ofc: Ward.Wolstenholm AIA, Inc., 1435 Alhambra Blvd, Ste 203, Sacramento 95816

WARDMAN, JOHN WILLIAM, artist; b. Sept. 7, 1906, Leeds, Yorkshire, Eng.; s. John Richard and Isabella Elizabeth (Wilson) W.; m. Yes Gladys Houk, 1965; edn: BS in chemistry, Detroit Inst. of Tech.; fine art stu. with Dr. Heller, USC, 5 yrs. Career: artist (lithographs, etchings, painter in oils and water colours) 1930s−, first Calif. exhib., one man show (hist. landmark bldgs. of early Los Angeles), Los Angeles Art Museum (1934); works in permanent collections of The Bancroft Library, The Southwest Museum, Los Angeles County Art Museum (presented by U.S. Art Project), and public and pvt. collections internat.; instr. polymer technology, Hartnell Coll. 2 yrs.; mem: Sons of Retirement; mil: organic chemist with 44th Chemical Lab., Europe WWII; Republican; Episcopal; rec: graphic art. Res: 746 Arcadia Way Salinas 93906

WARE, VIRGINIA SARGENT, company president; ; b. March 11, 1957, San Francisco; d. Alvan Read, Jr. and Donna I. (Intagliata) Sargent; m. Stephen E. Ware, June 1, 1985; edn: BS, Univ. of Santa Clara 1979. Career: sales/ mktg. rep. Xerox Corp., San Francisco 1980-81; sales/ mktg. rep. Blue Print Service Co., S.F. 1981; mktg. dir. G. Haney Associates, Oakland 1982; demonstrative evidence splst., owner, pres. Courtroom Graphics, S.F. 1982−; honors: Achiev. Award in Art, Bank Am. (1975); mem: Union Square Bus. & Profl. Womens Club, Demonstrative Evidence Splsts. Assn. (founding pres. 1985-), Directions/S.F. (dir.), mem. state senate advsy. coalition on ct. reform, Commonwealth of Calif., S. F. Yacht; rec: sailing, art collecting, performing arts. Ofc: San Francisco 94103

WARNE, WILLIAM ELMO, water resources consultant; b. Sept. 2, 1905, Seafield, IN; s. William R. and Nettie Jane (Williams) W.; m. Edith M. Peterson, 1929; children: Jane Ingrid (Beeder) b. 1934, William Robert b. 1937, Margaret Edith (Monroe) b. 1944; edn: AB, Univ. of Calif. 1927; hon. LLD, Seoul Nat. Univ. 1959; hon. Dr. of Econ., Yonsie Univ., Korea 1959. Career: reporter S.F. Bulletin and Oakland Post-Inquirer 1925-27; news ed. Brawley News, Calif. 1927; news ed. Calexico Chronicle 1928; ed./staff writer Assoc. Press., L.A., San Diego, Wash DC 1928-35; ed, Bur. of Reclamation, US Dept. of Interior 1935-42; asst. commnr. 1943-47; asst. secty. Dept. of Interior 1947-51; chief of staff War Prodn. Dir., War Prodn. Bd. 1942; dir. AID, Iran 1951-55; Brazil 1956; Korea 1956-59; dir. Calif. Dept. of Fish & Game 1959-60; Agri. Dept. 1960-61; admr. Calif. Resources Agcy. 1961-3; Water Resources 1961-66; v.p. Devel. and Resources Corp. 1967-69; adj. prof. USC Sch. of Pub. Adminstrn., Sacto. 1976-79; water resources cons. 1969−; chmn. Pres.'s Com. on San Diego Water Supply 1944-6; chmn. Fed. Inter-Agcy. River Basin Com. 1948; Fed. Com. on Alaskan Dev. 1948; pres. Gp. Health Assn., Inc., Wash DC 1945-52; chmn. US Del., 2nd Inter-Am. Conf. on Indian Life, Cuzco, Peru 1949; US Del., 4th World Power Conf., London, Eng. 1950; bd. dirs. Near East Found. 1956-8, 1959-64; Calif. Water Polution Bd. 1959-66; adv. bd. Fed. Water Pollution Control 1962-5. Mem: Govs. Cabinet 1961; US Com., Internat. Commn. on Large Dams; dir. Nat. Water Supply Improvement Assn. 1973-86, pres. 1978-80; assoc. dir. CAREW 1973-7, 81-; awards: Disting. Svc. Honor Award, Dept. of the Interior, 1951; Distng. Pub. Svc. Honor Awd., Foreign Ops. Adm. 1955; Order of Crown, Shah of Iran 1955; Outstanding Svc. Cit., UN Command 1959, Achievement Awd., Lambda Chi Alpha 1963; mem: Sigma Delta Chi; Lambda Chi Alpha; Nat. Press Club, Wash. DC; Sutter Club; Am. Acad. of Pub. Adminstrs.; Explorers Club; author: Mission for Peace, Bobbs- Merrill 1956; the Bureau of Reclamations, Praeger Publs. 1973; How the Colorado River was Spent, NWSIA Journ. 1975; Mass Transfer of Water Over Long Distances, The California Experience, proceedings spl. session, Internat. Commn. on Irrig. and Drainage, Athens 1978; mil: 2nd lt. ORC 1927-37. Res: 2090 8th Ave Sacramento 95818

WARNER, CARYL ROWLAND, lawyer; b. Jan. 5, 1908, Los Angeles; s. Rowland Moseley and Emily Caryl (Clark) W.; m. Carol Ann McGinnis; stepdau, Amy; children: Rick A., Caryl Christopher, Jack C., James and Carolyn; edn: JD, Southwestern Univ.; admitted to practice, Calif. and Fed. Cts. 1929. Career: suveyor City of Los Angeles 1926-29; ed. legal column Los

Angeles Daily Journal 1932−; dean legal columnists, USA; instr. Hollywood Ave. H.S. 1932-35; regl. property ofcr. U.S. Ofc. of Civil Defense, 9th Region (Western states), San Francisco 1942-43; judge (pro tem) Superior Ct. of Los Angeles Co. 1950; pvt. practice law, Los Angeles; chief counsel Press Photogs. Assn. of Gr. Los Angeles; awards: Cert. of Merit, Calif. Assembly for Mil. Svc. 1944; Citation as chmn. AMVETS Nat. Civ. Def. Com., Los Angeles City Council & Jt. Congl. Commn. on Atomic Energy; mem: Calif. and Los Angeles Co. Bar Assns., Criminal Cts. Bar Assn. of Los Angeles, Amvets, Calif. State Dept. & Nat. Dept., First Century Families, Calif. Soc. Sons. of the Revolution, Los Angeles Athletic Club, SAR, 100 Yr. Club of Calif. (founder, pres. 1953), Phi Alpha Delta, Masons (3rd. degree), OES; mil: lt. j.g. USNR 1943-45, WWII, lt. commdr., ret.; Republican; rec: golf. Ofc: 6922 Hollywood Blvd. Ste. 500 Los Angeles 90028

WARNER, ROLLIN MILES, JR., educator; b. Dec. 25, 1930, Evanston, Ill.; s. Rollin Miles and Julia Herndon (Polk) W.; edn: BA, Yale Univ. 1953; cert. Harvard Law Sch. 1955-56; MBA, Stanford Univ. 1960; supv. cred., Univ. San Francisco 1974; desig: Cert. Fin. Plnnr. (CFP), Coll. Fin. Plnng. (1977), Reg. Investment Advisor. Career: buyer Matson Navigation Co., 1956-58; asst. dir. devel./asst. to VP Fin., Stanford Univ. 1960-63; tchr. Town Sch., San Francisco 1963-70, 1975−; sch. prin. and dir. devel. and plant, Katharine Branson Sch./ Mt. Tamalpais Sch., 1970-75; ednl. cons. Educators' Collaborative, Nat. Center for Finl. Edn.; sch. liaison for Calif. Assn. Indep. Schs.; honors: Cum Laude Soc., Silver Beaver Award, Boy Scouts Am.; mem: Independent Schs. Bus. Mgrs. Assn., Inst. Cert. Finl. Plnnrs., Am. Econs. Assn., Am. Hist. Assn., Assn. for Asian Studies, Marines Meml. Assn., Chi Psi frat., Lincoln's Inn at Harvard Law Sch; civic: civic: BSA Com. Troop 14, adv. com. Randall Jr. Museum (SF); clubs: Univ. (SF), Grolier (NY), SF Yacht, Old Dundelian (London); author: Free Enterprise at Work (1986), Africa, Asia, Russia (1986), America (1986), Europe (1986), Greece, Rome (1981); mil: lt. USNR 1953-55, Korean, UN, Nat. Service ribbons; Republican; Episcopal; rec: ship models, book collector. Res: 648 23rd Ave San Francisco 94121 Ofc: Town School 2750 Jackson St San Francisco 94115

WARREN, ARTHUR RANDOLPH, JR., real estate broker; b. Nov. 19, 1940, Torrance; s. Arthur R. and Mary Ann (Imig) W.; m. Sharon Mustanich, Feb. 5, 1954; children: Kelly Jean b. 1964, Arthur R., III b. 1976, Robert Arthur, II b. 1978; edn: AA, Southwestern Coll. 1964; Coll. San Mateo 1970-71; BA, Golden Gate Univ. 1980; desig: Grad. Realtors Inst. (GRI) 1980. Career: Stanley C. Swartz Co., Redwood Shores 1970-71; project mgr. Am. Housing Guild Co., Redwood Shores and San Jose, 1971-73; L.B. Nelson Co., Foster City 1973-74; Shapell Indus., San Jose 1974-75; assoc. Walker & Lee Realtors, San Jose 1975-76; No. Calif. sales mgr. Western Brokers Assn., Mountain View 1977-78; assoc. Grubb & Ellis, comml. brokerage, 1978-79; The English Camp R.E. Investments, 1979-80; owner/broker Am. Mortgage Brokers 1981−; sales mgr./tnr. Traid Corp. 1969; movie stuntman (AGFA mem.), Elvis Presley film "Clam Bake" 1966; awards: Charles Chatham Class Fang Award (1980), Calif. State Champion in Trick Skiing (skied in 4 nat. championships), Artie Warren Perpetual Trophy, Am. Water Ski Assn. (1969), Million Dollar sales, Am. Housing Guild (1972), listed Who's Who in Creative Real Estate (1982-85); mem. Am. Soc. R.E. Counselors, Assn. of Realtors East Bay Mktg. Group, South Bay Bd. Realtors; clubs: Redwood Shores Sailing, Century (ski jumping), Barefoot; Republican; Congregational; rec: water skiing (competitive), snow skiing, sailing. Res: Millbrae Ofc: American Mortgage Brokers (POB 1555) 227 "B" St San Mateo 94401

WARREN, ELIZABETH CORINE, film services co. officer; b. Mar. 7, 1923, Chicago, Ill.; d. Charles Edward and Lena Leora (Sumner) Miller; m. Peter Warren, 1942; children: Robert b. 1943, Cynthia b. 1944, Barbara b. 1950; edn: L.A. Bus. Coll. 1948; num. night sch., corres. courses. Career: legal, bus. and tech. secty., 1948-60, with Technicolor, Inc. 1960 ; exec. secty , var Technicolor ofcs. and dir. 1960-75; overseas assignment, asst. to China Proj. mgr. 1975-76; exec. secty. to Gen. Counsel and secty. 1976-81; co. archivist, dir. corp. advtg. & pub. rels., asst. secty. 1981−; mem: Nat. Notary Assn.; Soroptimist Internat.; L.A. Civic Light Opera Assn.; Fair Ladies, Am. Airlines; Tujunga Civic Ballet; Ladies Comedy Club, show bus.; over 15 yrs. active involvement with dance troups perf. eves. and weekends for USO, L.A. Chamber of Music and var. lodges, schs. and clubs; Republican; Methodist; rec: photog., dancing, music. Ofc: Technicolor, Inc., 4050 Lankershim Blvd, No. Hollywood 91608

WARREN, WILLIAM JOSEPH, consulting engineer; b. Aug. 18, 1910, Eureka, Calif.; s. Nicholas and Eda (Penko) W.; m. Annette Eleanor Chmielewski, June 14, 1936; children: Laetitia b. 1938, Nicholas b. 1941, Mary Elizabeth b. 1946; edn: BSEE, magna cum laude, Santa Clara Univ. 1931; MSEE, Univ. Ill. 1933, PhD EE, 1936; Reg. Profl. Engr. Calif. Career: tchg. asst. Univ. Ill. 1935-37, 1938-41; prof. in EE, dept. head Univ. Santa Clara 1941-51; devel. engr. Hewlett-Packard Co. 1942-50; spl. electronics instr. for mil. ofcrs. Stanford Univ. summers 1942-43; engrg. supv. Applied Physics Dept. Shell Devel. Co. Emeryville, Calif. 1951-71; cons. engr. pvt. practice 1971−; honors: Coffin Fellowship (Univ. Ill. 1935-36), Sigma Xi, Eta Kappa Nu, Tau Beta Pi, Gamma Alpha; mem: IEEE (life), Am. Soc. Non-Destructive Testing (senior), President's Club (Santa Clara Univ.), Alumni Club, Newman Hall (UCB); publ: articles in tech. jours.; 3 patents in eddy-current applications and capacitance compensating technique; Catholic; rec: gardening, music, travel. Address: El Cerrito

WARWICK, MAL, direct mail fundraising consultant; b. May 13, 1941, Pittsburgh; s. Harry and Jeanette (Gottesfeld) Warshawsky; m. Mari Fleming, July 1, 1984; edn: AB history, w/ distinction, Univ. Mich. 1963; Latin Am. studies,

Columbia Univ. 1963-65. Career: Peace Corps volunteer Ecuador 1966-69; co-founder, exec. dir. Alternative Features Svc. Berkeley 1970-73; freelance writer 1969-76; campaign coord. John George for Supv. Oakland 1976; campaign mgr. & coord. Berkeley Citizens Action 1977-80; founder Mal Warwick & Assocs. Inc. 1979; exec. dir. No. Alameda County Voter Participation Proj. 1979-80; mktg. dir. Richard Parker & Assocs. S.F. 1981-82; pres., chmn. Mal Warwick & Assocs. Inc. Berkeley & Wash. DC; co-founder, chmn. The Progressive Group Inc. Northampton, Mass.; founder, sponsor Berkeley Peace Prize; mem: Direct Mktg. Assn., Nonprofit Mailers Fedn., Nat. Com. for Responsive Philanthropy, New Democratic Forum of the East Bay (co-founder, pres. 1982-84, secty. 1984-85, bd. 1985-), Nat. Women's Political Caucus (chpt. secty. 1983-85), Com. for Congressman Ronald V. Dellams (1979-, secty. 1980-82), Calif. Democratic Party (exec. bd. 1982-, resolutions com. 1985-); co-author: Chimborazo (Akwesasne Press 1974); rec: collector old and unusual globes. Ofc: Mal Warwick & Assocs. Inc. Box 1282 Berkeley 94701

WASHINGTON, ARNOLD EUGENE, physician, researcher; b. Sept. 30, 1950, Houston, Tex.; s. Dirley and Jearline (Holmes) Sams; m. Marie Brooks, Oct. 9, 1982; 1 child: Brooks b. 1984; edn: BS, Howard Univ. 1972; MPH, UC Berkeley 1975; MD, UC San Francisco 1976; MS, Harvard Univ. 1978. Career: clin. research invgtr. Ctr. for Disease Control Atlanta 1978-80, asst. dir. div. sexually transmitted disease 1981–; policy scholar Inst. for Health Policy Studies UCSF Sch. of Med., asst. prof. Dept. of Epidemiol. and Internat. Health, asst. dir. clin. epidemiol. pgm.; cons. to WHO 1982, So. Pac. Commn. Cook Is. 1980, Pan Am. Health Org. West Indies 1979-80; honors: Research Fellow UCSF 1973, Internat. Study-Travel Fellow (Worthing Found. 1974); mem: fellow Am. Coll. of Preventive Med., John Hale Med. Soc., AAAS, Am. Public Health Assn., Am. Venereal Dis. Assn., Soc. for Epidemiol. Research, Young Adults (Jones Meml. United Meth. Ch.); publ: tech. arts. for med. journs.; mil: commnd. ofcr. 05 USPHS 1978-; Methodist; rec: music, hiking, cycling, skiing, running, sailing. Ofc: Inst. for Health Policy Studies UC San Francisco 1326 Third Ave San Francisco 94143

WASHINGTON, ELWOOD JAMES, manufacturing co. executive; b. Sept. 11, 1946, Austin, Tex.; s. J.W. and Geraldine Theresa (Harvey) W.; m. Doris, July 31, 1971; 1 dau. Jessica Lynn b. 1986; edn: AA engrg., Los Angeles City Coll. 1967; BS ind. tech.- electronics, CSU Long Beach 1971. Career: sales engr. Square D Co. 1971-72, R.V. weatherford Co. 1972-76, Hamilton Electro-Sales 1976-77; prod. coord. Hughes Aircraft 1977-78; sales engr. Hi-Rel. Distbrs. 1978-80, Electro-Craft Corp. 1980-84; dist. sales mgr. Robbins/ Myers Electro-Craft Corp. 1984–; honors: finalist Nat. Achievement Scholarship Pgm. (1965), George Burleigh Scholar (1967); mem: Ephebian Soc. 1965, Hinderman Revia Chpt. 1971, New Recruiters Workshop CSU 1973; rec: tennis, arts & crafts, music, horticulture, electronic equipment repair. Res: 5382 Stillwater Dr Los Angeles 90008

WASHINGTON, KENNETH STRICKLAND, college chancellor; b. Oct. 19, 1922, Chicago, Ill.; s. Louis C. and Velma (Strickland) W.; m. Henrietta Dunn, Oct. 5, 1974; children: Lori, Marcella, Henry, Coreen, Kim, Kent; edn: BS, Roosevelt Univ. 1948; MA, CSU Los Angeles 1954; PhD, USC 1970. Career: successively, social worker, Los Angeles; head counselor public schs., Los Angeles; asst. to chancellor UCLA; asst. dean ednl. opportunities Calif. State Univs. and Colls.; asst. supt. public instrn., San Francisco; pres. City Coll. San Francisco; currently, v.chancellor edn. svcs. Los Angeles Community Coll. Dist.; bd. dirs. Western Regl. Council on Black Am. Affairs; mem: Assn. Calif. Community Coll. Adminstrs., NAACP; mil: US Army 1944-46. Ofc: 617 W. 7th St. Los Angeles 90017

WASHINGTON, NAPOLEON, JR., insurance executive; b. Apr. 12, 1948, Ft. Baker; s. Napoleon, Sr. and Annie D. (Jones) W.; m. Nadine, Nov. 6, 1968; children: Gregory b. 1969, Kimberlee b. 1972, Geoffrey b. 1972; edn: AA, Merced Coll. 1975; CSC Stanislaus 1975-77. Career: sales mgr. Metropolitan Ins. Co., 1970-83; owner/mgr. Washington & Assocs. Ins. Agency, Merced 1983–; instr. Merced Coll. (1978-81); honors: Million Dollar Round Table (1972-7), Nat. Quality, Nat. Sales Achieve., Health Ins. Quality awards, (1971-82), listed Who's Who in the West, Who's Who in the World (1980-86); mem. Merced/ Mariposa County Life Underwriters Assn. 1976-77, North Merced Rotary Club; mil: E4 US Army 1968-70; Baptist (lic. minister St. Matthew Baptist Ch., Merced); rec: jog, softball, fishing. Res: 1960 Cedar Crest Dr Merced 95340 Ofc: Washington & Associates Insurance Agency 935 West 18th St Merced 95340

WASSERBURG, G. J., geophysicist, educator; b. Mar. 25, 1927, New Brunswick, N.J.; s. Charles and Sarah (Levine) W.; m. Naomi Z. Orlick, Dec. 21, 1951; children: Charles David b. 1958, Daniel Morris b. 1960; edn: undergrad. Rutgers Univ.; BS in physics, Univ. Chgo. 1951, MS in geol., 1952, grad. research under H.C. Urey and M.G. Inghram III, PhD, 1954. Career: research team mem. Juneau Ice Field Research Project under Henri Bader, 1950; cons. Argonne Nat. Lab., 1952-55; research assoc. Inst. for Nuclear Studies, Univ. Chgo. 1954-55; asst. prof. Calif. Inst. Tech. 1955-59, assoc. prof. 1959-62, prof. of geology and geophysics, 1962–; vis. prof. Univ. of Kiel, Ger. 1960, Harvard Univ. 1962, Univ. of Bern, Switz. 1966, Swiss Fed. Technological Inst. 1967; cons. NASA, 1968- (mem., chmn. 1970, LSAPT- Lunar Sample Analysis Plnng. Team 1968-71; Lunar Sample Rev. Bd. 1970 72; mem. Facilities Wkg. Group of LSAPT 1972-; Sci. Working Panel for Appollo Missions 1971-73; Physical Scis. Com. 1971-75); vis. lectr. Harvard (1980), Australian Nat. Univ. (1980), Royal Astron. Soc. (1981), Univ. Brit. Col. (1982), Johns Hopkins (1984), Hebrew Univ. Jerusalem (60th Anniversary Symp. spkr. 1985); mem: Am. Physical Soc. (fmr.), Fellow Am. Geophysical Union (pres. 1976); profl. honors: Fellow Am. Acad. Arts and Scis. (1967), NASA awards (1969, 1970, 1972, 1978), J.F. Kempt medal for disting. public svc. Columbia Univ. (1973), profl. achieve. Univ. Chgo. Alumni (1978), Arthur L. Day prize and lectureship (1981) and J. Lawrence Smith Medal (1985) Nat. Acad. Scis., John D. MacArthur professorship (1982), regents fellow Smithsonian Instn., Wollaston medal Geol. Soc. of London (1985), senior US Scientist award Alexander von Humboldt-Stiftung (1985), hon. PhD Brussels Univ. (1985), hon. fgn. fellow European Union Geoscis. (1983); mem. Nat. Acad. of Scis. (chmn. Com. Planetary and Lunar Exploration, mem. Space Sci. Bd.), Geol. Soc. of Am. (fellow, life, Arthur L. Day Medal 1970), Meteoritical Soc. (V.M. Goldschmidt Medal 1978; v.p. 1985), hon. PhD Univ. Paris (1986), Royal Swedish Acad. Sci. Crafoord Prize (1986); mil: rifleman US Army 1946, Combat Inf. Badge, Purple Heart. Address: Div. Geological Sci. Calif. Inst. Technology Pasadena 91125

WASSERMAN, DAVID, chemist; b. Aug. 21, 1947, Chgo., Ill.; s. Michael and Lillian (Feldman) W.; edn: BS chem., Univ. Ariz. 1969, MA in math., 1972. Career: chemist Dept. of Interior, Bureau of Mines, Helium Research Ctr., Amarillo, Tx. 1969; Nat. Cylinder Gas Co., div. Chemetron Corp., Chgo.; Linde Div. (splty. gas div.) Union Carbide Corp., Linden, N.J.; Glamorene Prods. Corp., div. Lever Bros., Clifton, N.J.; Chicago Board of Health, Dept. Toxicology and Spl. Chemistry, Chgo.; pres./dir. Newport Laboratories Inc., Chatsworth 1981–; mem. Am. Assn. of Textile Chemists and Colorists; civic: City of Hope, Simon Wiesenthal Ctr., Sierra Club; works: research and formulation of personal care products (1981-); research: separation of Helium from Natural Gas by membrane permeation, Union Carbide (1970), testing for effective rodenticide against the "super" Norway rats of Chgo. and NYC, Chgo. Bd. of Health & NYC Health Dept. (1975); Republican; Jewish; rec: tech. analysis of finl. markets. Res: 21574 Arcos Dr Woodland Hills 91364 Ofc: Newport Labs Inc 21642 Marilla St Chatsworth 91311

WASSON, HAROLD TAYLOR, JR., real estate co. executive; b. Aug. 4, 1946, Los Angeles; s. Harold T. and Beatrice M. (Hansen) W.; 2 daus: Jennifer b. 1968, Jill b. 1970; edn: East L.A. Jr. Coll. 1966; Cerritos Coll. 1967-8; USC Taxation & Exch. 1982; lic Real Estate Broker, Calif. Career: with Walker & Lee 1970–: sales agent in Lakewood 1970-72 (top 10 in co. for sales, No. 1 in listings); office mgr., Oxnard Ofc. 1972-74, Palos Verdes Ofc. 1974-75, Fullerton Ofc. 1975-78; regional v.p. (in chg. 16 ofcs.) 1978-80; v.p. sales for Resale Div. (92 ofcs.) 1980-82; senior v.p. 1982-85, exec. v.p., pres. Great Western Real Estate 1985–; recipient num. sales and mgmt. awards, Walker & Lee; mem: Lakewood-Long Beach Bd. of Realtors (past); Whittier, Palos Verdes, Oxmard and No. Orange Co. Bds. of Realtors; Calif. and Nat. Assns. of Realtors; Republican; Protestant; rec: boating, fishing. Res: 1316 No Catalpa Anaheim 92801 Ofc: Great Western Real Estate 1901 E 4th Street Santa Ana 92705

WASTE, WILLIAM TEN EYCK, insurance executive; b. Aug. 10, 1925, Oakland; s. Wm. Ewing and Elizabeth (Ten Eyck) W.; m. Laura Piccirillo, Aug. 6, 1949; children: William H. b. 1951, Ann (Woodbridge) b. 1953, Carlin (McCarthy) b. 1955, Mary Lou b. 1959, Katherine Margaret b. 1959; edn: Univ. Mich. 1943; BA, Univ. Calif. 1949. Career: with Indsl. Indemnity Co., various West Coast locations, 1950-74, ret. 1974; pres. Beaver Ins. Co., San Francisco, 1974-85, vice chmn. 1985–; mem. Ore. Gov.'s Accident Adv. Com., 1969-72; mem. Ore. Western Ins. Info. Service Bd., 1963-72; honors: pres.'s citation Oregon Ins. Agts. Assn. (1965); mem. Assn. Calif. Ins. Cos. (pres. 1983-85), Workers Compensation Rating Bur. (gov. com.), Calif. Workers Compensation Inst. (pres. 1985-, dir. 1979-); civic: USO (bd. dirs. 1973-), Episcopal Homes Found. (chmn. fin. com. 1977), Salvation Army (chmn. adv. bd. S.F. 1977-78, nat. adv. bd./treas., 1980-), Scripps Coll. (trustee, chmn. investment com. 1981-); clubs: Pacific Union, Bohemian, The Calif., St. Francis Yacht, Kiwanis (pres. S.F. club 1979-80), Claremont Country, Masons, K.T., SAR, Sigma Phi; author articles on travel to USSR and China, and insurance subjects; mil: lst lt. CIC, US Army 1944-47, 51; Republican (v.chmn. Kern Co. Central Com. 1960-63); Episcopal (sr. warden Christ Ch., Lake Oswego, Ore. 1968); rec: photog., skiing, hiking, coin collecting. Ofc: Beaver Insurance Co. 100 California St San Francisco 94115

WATAHARA, ALAN AKIRA, lawyer; b. July 9, 1953, Sacramento; s. Fred Hisashi and Yuriko (Yaguchi) W.; edn: BS, UC Davis 175; MPH, UC Berkeley Sch. of Pub. Health 1979; JD, Golden Gate Univ. Sch. of Law 1983; Dr.PH Cand. (1986) UCB. Career: dir. Health Edn. and Pub. Rels., Sacramento Dental Care Found., Sacto. 1973-76; founder/dir. Sacramento Dental Health Assn. 1976-78; clin. lab. dir. and health counselor Sacramento Medical Center 1975-78; spl. asst. resident US Dept. HEW, Wash DC 1979; coordinator Hypertension Control Project Am. Heart Assn., San Rafael 1980-81; health/legal cons. Calif. Children's Lobby, Sacto. 1984–; law clk. Nihonmachi Legal Outreach and Legal Aid Soc. (1979-82), Superior Ct. and Calif. Ct. of Appeals, SF (1982-83); teaching assoc. UCB 1984; pvt. law practice 1984–; awards: NIMH trainee UCB (1983-85), disting. tchg. assoc. UCB (1985), fellow California Tomorrow (1985-); mem: ABA, Calif. Bar Assn., Am. Public Health Assn., Am. Soc. of Law and Medicine, Concern for Dying Council (nat. coord. Interdisciplinary Collaboration 1983-84), Soc. of Pub. Health Edn., Japanese Am. Citizens League; contbr. art. profl. publs., art. in Mobius (1/85); Democrat; Shinto; rec: tennis, music promotor. Res: 236 Willamette Ave Kensington 94708 Ofc: California Children's Lobby, POB 448, Sacramento 95802

WATERMAN, MICHAEL S., applied mathematician; b. June 28, 1942, Coquille, Ore.; s. Ray S. and Bessie E. (Payne) W.; 1 child, Tracey b. 1967; edn: BS, Ore. State Univ. 1964, MS, 1966; MA, Mich. State Univ. 1968, PhD, 1969.

Career: asst. prof. Idaho State Univ. Pocatello 1969-74, assoc. prof. 1974-75; staff mem. Los Alamos Nat. Lab. 1975-81; vis. prof. Univ. Hawaii 1978-80, UC San Francisco Med. Sch. 1982; prof. math and biol. scis. Univ. So. Calif. 1982–; cons. Los Alamos Nat. Lab 1982-, Simon Mktg. 1984–, Schlumberger Computer Aided Systems 1984-; honors: NSF Grants (1971, 72, 74, 75), System Devel. Found. Grants (1982-), NIH Grants (1986-91); mem: Inst. Math. Statistics, AAAS, Am. Math Soc., Am. Stat. Assn., Soc. Math. Biol., Soc. Indsl. and Applied Math.; publs: 75 research papers in math, statistics and biol. 1970-. Ofc: Univ. So. Calif. Dept. Math. Los Angeles 90089-1113

WATERS, JACK, real estate broker, investor; b. Mar. 17, 1925, Stroud, Okla.; s. Charles A. and Dora (Roberts) W.; m. Patsy Ellen Bodine, July 14, 1947; children: Michael Gregg b. 1951, Randy Allen b. 1953, Gary Kurt b. 1960, Julie Anne b. 1970; Calif. lic. Real Estate Broker (1960). Career: broker assoc. Ken Miller Realty, Torrance 1960-63; broker/owner Jack Waters Realty, Westminster 1964-70, Keystone Realty, Santa Rosa 1970–, pres. Keystone Corp., 1974–, real estate mgr., investor 1976–; mem: Torrance Lomita Bd. Realtors (mem. 1960-66, bd. dir. 1961, 64, 1st v.p. 1965, state sales dir. 1961-62), Calif. Assn. Realtors (1960-76, state dir. 1964-66), Sonoma County Bd. Realtors (1971-76); mem. Masons, Scottish Rite (32nd deg); mil: USNR 1943-46; Republican; Christian. Address. 2941 Arden Way Santa Rosa 95401

WATKINS, DANIEL BRUCE, private investigator; b. Aug. 31, 1950, Bell; s. Donald Leroy and Virginia May W.; m. Margaret, July 16, 1977; children: Matthew b. 1980, Timothy b. 1982, Elizabeth b. 1984; edn: AA, Fullerton Coll. 1974; BA, CSU Fullerton 1977; JD, Western State Univ. Coll. of Law 1982; Pvt. Investigator, Calif. 1984. Career: criminal defense investigator Orange Co. Public Defenders Ofc. 1977-84; founder Daniel B. Watkins & Assocs. spec. in homicide, Newport Beach 1984–; mem. Calif. Assn. of Lic. Investigators; mil: splst. 4 US Army 1970-71, Purple Heart, Combat Infantry; rec: carpentry, camping. Ofc: Daniel B. Watkins & Assocs., 1201 Dove St. Ste. 470 Newport Beach 92660

WATKINS, NOEL L., superior court judge; b. Oct. 23, 1932, Alturas; s. Noel L. and Mildred (Kolts) W.; m. Mary Jane, June 7, 1957; children: Laura L. b. 1958, Charles W. b. 1960; edn: BA, UC Chico; Univ. Wash.; LLB, UC Berkeley 1957. Career: atty. pvt. practice, Coffman & Watkins, Red Bluff 1957-75; deputy dist. atty. Tehama County 1958-59; court apptd. public defender Tehama Co. 1959-62; judge Red Bluff Justice Ct. 1962-75; judge Superior Ct. of Tehama Co. 1975-; mem. Calif. Judges Assn., Elks; Republican; (Central Com.); rec: hunting, fishing, gardening. Res: 5 Thompson Pl Red Bluff 96080 Ofc: Tehama County Superior Ct POB 278 Red Bluff 96080

WATKINS, REX H., co. president; b. May 25, 1928, Arkansas City, Kans.; s. Herbert A. and Betty E. (Stultz) W.; edn: electronic courses, Tulsa Univ. 1954, mech., Okla. Univ. 1957. Career: research & devel., Continental Can Co., Coffeeville, Kans. 1952-62; owner/pres. Organic Compounds Inc., 1963–; inventor, developer chemical formulas and mech. designs; Republican; Protestant. Res: 1143 Memory Ln Santa Ana 92706 Ofc: Organic Compounds Inc 1265 W 16th St Long Beach 90813

WATLEY, ROY, supervising land surveyor; b. March 5, 1937, Fort Worth, Texas; dec. Sept. 14, 1985, Hayward, Calif.; s. Roy, Sr. and Pauline (Andrews) W.; m. Kay Cox, June 6, 1965; children: Roy Marc, III b. 1968; Lisa Michelle b. 1971; edn: stu. arch., UC Berkeley 1960-63; Tchg. Credential, UCB 1973-74; BS in edn., San Francisco State Univ. 1975, MS in edn., 1978; lic: Land Surveyor, Calif. St. Bd. Civil & Profl. Engrs. (1971); Calif. Std. Tchrs. Cred. (1974). Career: rodman/chmn. Alameda County Public Works, Hayward 1962-, survey crew party chief 1966-74, supvsg. land surveyor 1974-85; instr. drafting and surveying East Bay Skills Ctr., Oakland 1969-70; instr. drafting, surveying and engring. Chabot Coll. 1970-82; editor Calif. Land Surveyors Newsletter (1972); examiner Oral Interview Bd. Public Agencies (1971-85); mem: Calif. Land Surveyors Assn. (charter mem. 1971-85), Am. Cong. on Surveying & Mapping (1971-85), Public Works Assn., Am. Soc. of Civil Engrs. (1971-85); Webelo Scout leader 1978-79; publs: Civil Engineering Technology, A Course of Instruction (1974); mil: US Air Force Reserve 1960-64; Democrat; Protestant; rec: photog., cinematography, music, carpentry. Res: 25076 Calaroga Ave Hayward 94545 Ofc: ALameda County Public Works Agency 399 Elmhurst St Hayward 94545

WATSON, ADELE LOUISE, city librarian; b. Sept. 10, 1929, Yonkers, NY; d. James Albert and Beatrice Adele (Glover) W.; children nee MacFarland: James Watson, Laurie Adele, Thalia Ann; edn: BA, US Internat. Univ. 1973; MA, Univ. Denver 1975; PhD, Columbia Pacific Univ. 1980. Career: ofc. mgr. Calif. State Sen. L.M. Backstrand 1950-65; real estate appraiser L.I. Backstrand 1965-69; librarian Denver Public Library 1975; reference coord. Serra Coop. Library System, San Diego 1977-78; dir. Coalinga- Huron Dist. Libraries 1978–; speechwriter; active political campaigns Repubican Party 1950-65; mem: Am. Humanist Assn., Am. and Calif. Library Assns., Women Library Works, AAUW, NOW, Nature Conservancy, Wilderness Soc., Sierra Club, Toastmasters, Federated Women; Unitarian. Res: 405-B W. Polk St. Coalinga 93210 Ofc: Coalinga- Huron Dist. Libraries, 305 No. 4th St. Coalinga 93210

WATSON, LARRY WALTER, trucking co. owner; b. Apr. 4, 1945, Delhi, La.; s. Walter and Eleanor Bernice (Trawick) W.; m. Lois J. Wasko, Jan. 12, 1974; children: Shawn b. 1972, Jenanne b. 1979; edn: spl. courses Okinawa Night Sch. 1964, USN Sch., San Diego Comm. Coll. 1968, L.A. City Coll. 1971. Career: opr. Rayleys Cotton Gin and Grain, Monticello, La. 1961-63; paper packer Zellerbach Paper Co., Santa Fe Springs 1968-69; elec. journeyman

Raymore Elec. Co., San Gabriel 1969-70; ptnr./owner Watson Constrn., S.Caro. and Ga., 1971; journeyman -diesel, Internat. Harvester, Montebello 1971-73; owner L.B. Trucking 1973–; mil: EM3 US Navy 1966-70, electrician Underwater Demolition, decorated Nat. Def. Service, Vietnam Svc. w/2 Stars, Repub. Vietnam Campaign w/device; Republican; Wesleyan Methodist. Address: L.B. Trucking 142 East Oberg San Dimas 91773

WATSON, RONALD LEE, author, lecturer, radio personality; b. Nov. 28, 1939, Detroit, Mich.; s. Winford Ernest and Virginia Jeanette (Orsborn) W.; m. Linda, Dec. 29, 1975; children: Larissa Joy b. 1976, Evan Issac b. 1977. Career: v.p. sales, mktg. Paradise Mktg. Anaheim 1981-83; pres., dir. Pentex Corp. Fullerton 1983–; founder, dir. National Symposia Team, The Physician and Metaphysician; mem. adv. bd. Nat. Coll. Nutripathy; weekly radio talk show, Achieving Total Freedom KFOX-FM Redondo Beach; prin. spkr. Nat. Health Fedn. and leading authority on air ionization; author num. motivational tapes and articles on nutrition, environmental health, psychological health and scriptural astrology; frequent spkr. Rotary, Lions and Exchange Clubs; author: The Greatest Story Never Told, What You Say Is What You Get; rec: photog., fine art, rare books, archery, astrology. Ofc: 920 W Commonwealth Ste 140 Fullerton 92632

WATSON, WILLIAM JOSEPH, physician; b. April 21, 1951, San Luis Obispo; s. William Joseph Sr. and Mary Ellen (Young) W.; m. Donna Lee, May 5, 1982; 1 dau, Ashleigh b. 1984; edn: BS, UC Davis 1972; MD, UCLA 1976; intern, Virginia Mason Hosp., Seattle, Wash. 1977; resident in otolaryngology, Univ. of Colo., Denver 1980; Diplomate, Am. Bd. of Otolaryngology 1980; Lic. Calif. Dept. of Real Estate. Career: head & neck surgery, otologic surgy, facial plastic & cosmetic surgery, San Luis Obispo 1980–; staff Sierra Vista, French, Gen. Hosps., San Luis Obispo 1980–; affiliated with Don Patrick Realty, San Luis Obispo; honors: Fly Fishing Hall of Fame 1974; San Luis Obispo Project Beautification Award, 1984; mem: San Luis Obispo CofC, San Luis Obispo Am. Acad. of Facial Plastic Surgery; Motel Assn., Calif. Motel Assn., San Luis Obispo Co. Med. Soc., Sierra Cascade Trauma Soc., Pan American Otolaryngolical Soc., Kiwanis, Budweiser Veterans Ski Racing Series, San Luis Obispo Sportsman Assn.; Republican; Christian; rec: snow skiing- racing, fly fishing, hunting worldwide. Res: 1223 Higuera St. San Luis Obispo 93401

WATT, DONALD GIBBS, real estate developer; b. Nov. 29, 1911, Welda, Kans.; s. James Scott and Sarah Martha (Gibbs) W.; m. Florence Johnson, Dec. 7, 1970; stepson: Richard F. Landau; b. 1948; lic. Real Estate Broker, Calif. 1947-. Career: dir. of mfg. (McDonnell) Douglas Aircraft Co., Santa Monica 1929-69; pres. American Mobilehome Corp., Santa Monica 1969-80; (AMH Corp. merged into Watt Indus. 1980); exec. vice pres. Watt Industries, Inc. (indsl. constrn. projs., residential home constrn., apt. complex projs.) 1980-81, vice chmn. of the bd., 1981–; (assoc./maj. prin. of the original R.A. Watt Co. 1947-); instr. adult courses, var. So. Calif. schools; mem: bd. dirs. Govt. Affairs Council of Building Indus. Assn. of So. Calif.; mem. Al Malaikah Shrine, dir. Santa Monica Bay Shrine Club, dir. Ocean park Lodge Masonic Temple Assn., dir. Boys' Club of Santa Monica, dir. Great Western Council Inc. of Boy Scouts of Am.; mem. Riviera Country Club, MacDac Retirees Assn. Res: 500 Avondale Ave Los Angeles 90049 Ofc: Watt Industries 2716 Ocean Park Blvd Santa Monica 90405

WATT, JAMES, industrial design co. president; b. Oct. 20, 1918, Hamilton, Ontario, Can., nat. US cit. 1956; s. James and Allie Ellen (Hays) W.; m. Ruth McFetridge, Sept. 28, 1942; children: Trevor b. 1950, Mark b. 1950, Brant b. 1953, Cherie b. 1956; edn: BAA, Ontario Coll. of Art 1951; postgrad. work Pratt Inst. Career: designer Massey Harris, Toronto, Can. 1945-46; designer Ronney Brothers Furniture, Los Angeles 1951-52; product designer Modglin Co., Glendale 1952-53; product designer Paper-Mate Pen, Culver City 1953-55; senior project engr. Emerson- Pryne, Pomona 1955-65; pres. Engionics Engineering, Riverside 1965-75; pres., chmn. bd. Enviro- Intercept Inc. 1975–; tchr. Junior Achievement 1963, tchr. refrigeration to mems. of Engonics 1970-72; v.p., bd. dirs. Time Line Corp. 1982; honors: New Products Award, Building Products Award Mag. 1959; mem: Rotary of No. Hollywood (vocational bd. dirs. 1982, 1984) Key Men Assocs.; publs: article on furniture history and design, Los Angeles Furniture Mart 1952; article, Heat Transfer, Patents on Building Products, and Refrigeration Equipment, Electronic Packaging and Prodn. mag. 1983; mil: sgt. Royal Canadian Engrs., decorated Canadian Vol., European Star, Battle of Britain, Victory medals; Republican; Religious Sci.; rec: painting, writing, travel. Res: 14960 Sherman Way Van Nuys 91405 Ofc: Enviro-Intercept Inc., 11949 Vose St. No. Hollywood 91605

WATTEAU, JEAN-FRANCOIS, university professor; b. May 1, 1930, Paris, France; s. Charles F. and Suzanne M. (Barbot-Ducau) W.; m. Aurore de Feuilhade de Chauvin, June 20, 1968; children: Laetitio b. 1969, Quentin b. 1971, Jean Felix b. 1979; edn: ME, Air Acad. Salon 1954; diploma, Statistical Inst. Paris 1962; PhD, Sorbonne 1967; diploma, Inst. Paris 1975. Career: dept. head Aerospatiale 1960-69; sales mgr. Roll- Royce EDP Internat., Brussels 1969-70; dir. research & devel. engring. ITT, Paris 1971-74; chmn. bd. Technitron, Paris 1974-77; asst. CEO Amiot Indsl. Group, Paris 1977-82; dir. robot & artificial vision & numerical control labs. UCLA 1982–; cons. USN, Lockheed, and Hughes; Prof. Ecole Centrale Paris & Math Doctorate, Sorbonne 1968-73; honors: Knight of the Legion of Honor 1962; Letter of Congrat., Defense Ministry 1959; mem: Robot Internat. Assn., Am. Soc. Mech. Engrs., High Finance Inst. Alumni Assn. (v.p., secty. gen. 1976-), Human Resources Devel. ASsn. (treas. 1980-), Golf De Saint Cloud Racing, UCLA Yacht Club,

Elderman of Marnes (France), Alliance Francaise of Beverly Hills (v.p.); works: 2 patents, 1975, 1980; 23 scientific and fin. publs. 60-; mil: lt. col. French AF, Algerian War Cross w/ Gold Star; Catholic; rec: pre impressionist painters, yachting. Res: 11120 Sunset Blvd. Los Angeles 90049

WAUGH, RALPH B., oral and maxillofacial surgeon; b. Apr. 27, 1924, Holdenville, Okla.; s. Gordon Beverly and Ellen Martha (Bucknoll) W.; m. Bonny Jean Haugen, Dec. 7, 1969; children: Janice Jean Waugh Lokey b. 1953, Wendy Jean Dixon Cooper b. 1965, Joseph Braddock Dixon, Jr. b. 1962, Ian Andrew Waugh b. 1973; edn: BS in chem. engring., UC Berkeley 1950; DDS, USC 1958; MD, UCLA 1966; Calif. lic. Dentist (1958), Physician, Surgeon (1967), Diplomate Am. Bd. of Oral Surgery (1970), Fellow Am. Bd. Oral & Maxillofacial Surg. (1978). Career: naval aviator WWII, 1943-63, served to lt., pilot torpedo bomber, pilot Anti Submarine warfare; residency and fellowship, oral & maxillofacial surgeon, USC-LA County Med. Ctr. 1959-62; med. intern. Orange County Med. Ctr. 1966-67; chief of staff Antelope Valley Hosp. Med. Ctr. 1975, 77; pres. LA County Medical Assn., Dist. 16, 1977-78; founding pres. Antelope Valley Dental Study Group 1984; mem. Com. on Rural Health, Calif. Med. Assn. 1980-84; Anesthesia Review, So. Calif. Soc. of Oral and Maxillofacial Surgeons 1981-84; mem. Antelope Valley RA (bd. dirs. 1984-5), LACCRA (pres. 1983-4), CRP (State Central Com. 1980-); v.p. Calif. Republican Assembly 1983-86. Res: 40646 16th St West, Palmdale 93551 Ofc: 43713 20th St West, Lancaster 93534

WAY, TSUNG-TO, bank executive; b. Sept. 20, 1912, Fu Ch'in, Fukien Province, China; s. Kuang-Yen and S.P. (Yang) W.; m. Shun-Hwa Chiang, Oct. 16, 1938; children: Helen K.L., Suzanne I.L., Raymond T.Y.; edn: St. John's Sch., Shanghai, Yenching Univ., Peiping. Career: Bank of China 1936-, staff mem. Shanghai Branch 1936-38, hd. Foreign Dept., Kunming Br. 1938-39, hd. Loiwing Agcy., Yunnan 1939-40, asst. mgr., sub-mgr. Tientsin 1941-43, sub-mgr. Peiping 1943-44, Tientsin 1944-45, Saigon 1946-51, mgr. Saigon 1951-65, Tokyo 1965-70, asst. gen. mgr. in charge, Bank of China, Tokyo 1970, gen. mgr. Bank of China, Taipei, ROC 1970-71; pres./CEO The Internat. Commercial Bank of China (fmr. Bank of China), Taipei 1971-75, bd. chmn. 1975-, branches throughout E. and S.E. Asia, Panama, USA, Saudi Arabia; mng. dir: China Devel. Corp., China Ins. Co., United World Chinese Comml. Bank (all, Taipei, ROC); apptd. dir. Euro-Asia Trade Orgn., ROC-USA Econ. Council, Assn. of East Asia Rels., China-Netherlands Cultural and Econ. Assn., mem. Chinese Nat. Assn. of Indus. and Commerce/Taipei; clubs: Taipei Internat. Businessmen's, The Yuan Shan (Taipei), Kuo Hwa Golf and Country (Taipei), American (Tokyo), Korean (Taipei); rec: golf, travel, music. Res: 1411 Laguna Ave Burlingame 94010 Ofc: Director of Bank of Canton of California, 555 Montgomery San Francisco 94111

WAYNE, BERNARD GABRIEL, hotel co. president; b. July 11, 1920, NY, NY; s. Irwin and Eva (Bloom) W.; m. Penny, Sept. 19, 1945; children: Robert C. b. 1947, Diane R. b. 1952; edn: BS, Brooklyn Coll. 1942; UC Los Angeles 1946-51. Career: asst. mgr. Singer Sewing Machine Co. 1946; student housing dir. UC Los Angeles 1946-51; adminstr., owner Good Shepherd Convales. Hosp. Santa Monica 1959-69, Bay Shore Sanitarium Hermosa 1951-85; pres., exec. dir. Brentmar Inc. Santa Monica 1985-; student counselor UCLA 1946-51; mem: Am. Coll. Health Care Adminstrs., Calif. Nsg. Home Assn. (pres. 1947), Power Squadron, Rotary, Comm. Chest, Boy Scouts of Am., Heart Fund Bd., Cancer Edn. Chmn.; mil: T-5 US Army Signal Corps Spl. Svcs., 2 Purple Hearts, 5 Battle Stars, Invasion Medal; rec: boating, gardening, model building. Ofc: Georgian Hotel 1415 Ocean Ave Santa Monica 90401

WAYNE, BRUCE FREDERICK, traffic and news reporter; b. Nov. 19, 1933, Manchester, N.H., dec. June 4, 1986; s. Frederick and Margaret (McCoo) Talford; m. Lois Garner, 1965; children: Linda b. 1956, David b. 1959; edn: comml. pilot, East Coast Aviation, Mass. 1960; 1st class engr., Mass. Radio Sch. 1951. Career: sports announcer Armed Forces Radio, Ser. NYC 1954-8; TV-News & Weather, WHDH, Boston 1958-61; traffic reporter, Boston 1961-5; pgm. dir., sales KEZY, Anaheim 1966-8; traffic reporter KRNO, San Bernardino 1968-70; KFI in the Sky, Traffic & News reporter, KFI 1970-85; M.C. Grand Opening of Spruce Goose, May 14, 1983; 30,000 hrs. as a comml. pilot, inst. rating, comm. helicopter, multi-eng. seaplane; piloted the Goodyear Blimp, has flown with the Blue Angels & wing-walked; awards: exceptional use of Aviation, A.F. Assoc. 1971; spot news awd., AP, 1974; Grand awd., L.A. Press Club 1976; 30 yrs. in broadcasting, May 15, 1982; listed: Jane's Who's Who in Aviation and Aerospace, US Edition; mem. Am. Fedn. of TV & Radio Artists; author, Bruce Wayne's Incredible Freeway Guide; mil: S/Sgt., USAF 1954-8; Prot.; rec: tennis, skiing, biking. Res: Fullerton 92633

WEARE, BRYAN CABOT, professor of atmospheric science; b. Aug. 22, 1947, York, Maine; s. Arnold Frank and Margaret Janetta (Hanscom) W.; edn: BS, Bates Coll. 1969; PhD, State Univ. of NY Buffalo 1974. Career: research assoc. Dept. of Meteorology Mass. Inst. of Tech., Cambridge, Mass. 1974-76; asst. prof. Dept. of Land, Air & Water Resources, UC Davis 1976-82; vis. scholar Metorological Inst., Univ. of Munich, W. Ger. 1983-84; assoc. prof. Dept. of Land, Air & Water Resources, UC Davis 1983-; mem: Am. Meteorological Soc., Royal Meteorological Soc., Big Brothers/ Sisters Assn.; works: approx. 30 scientific publs.; Democrat; Unitarian; rec: bicycling, running, hiking. Ofc: Dept. of LAWR, Univ. of Calif., Davis 95616

WEATHERUP, ROY GARFIELD, lawyer; b. April 20, 1947, Annapolis, Md.; s. Robert Alexander and Kathryn Crites (Hesser) W.; m. Wendy Gaines, Sept. 10, 1977; children: Jennifer Ruth b. 1980, Christine Ann b. 1983; edn: JD, Stanford Law Sch. 1972; AB, Stanford Univ. 1968. Career: assoc. atty. Haight,

Dickson, Brown & Bonesteel, Los Angeles 1972-78, ptr. 1979-; Bar Assn. Committees; Moot Ct. Judge at UCLA Law Sch.; mem: Calif. Acad. of Appellate Lawyers, Los Angeles Co. Bar Assn. (Superior Cts. Com., Economical Litigation Com.), Am. Bar Assn. (Judicial Evaluation Com.), Town Hall of Calif.; author: Standing Armies and Armed Citizens: An Historical Analysis of the Second Amendment, Hastings Constnl. Law Quarterly Vol. 2, 1975, reprint U.S. Senate Document, 94th Cong. 2d Session; Republican; Methodist; rec: bridge, chess, backpacking. Res: 10016 Balboa Blvd. Northridge 91325 Ofc: 201 Santa Monica Blvd. Santa Monica 90406

WEAVER, CLAUDE MADISON, II, commercial pilot; b. May 30, 1931, Waco, Texas; s. Claude Madison and Alberta (Warwick) W.; m. Delores Foy, Jan. 23, 1958; children: Brian b. 1959, Ellen b. 1964, Brad b. 1966; edn: N.M. Military Inst. 1949-50; BBA, Univ. Texas, Austin 1953; UCLA 1958; desig: airline captain, FAA, TWA (1964). Career: capt. US Air Force 1953-56, pilot B-47; pilot, TWA, 1956-, line check capt. 1971-; owner Cal-Tex Ents., Mission Viejo 1984-; bd. dirs. PapaKea Beach Resort, Maui 1979-80; honors: Disting. Mil. Grad. (1953), Nat. Honor Soc. (1949), T-Man's Club (Texas Lettermen); mem. Airline Pilots Assn., Delta Tau Delta frat., 19th Bomb Wing Assn., Scabbard and Blade Soc., Arnold Air Soc.; Republican; United Methodist; rec: golf, fish, camping. Address: Cal-Tex Enterprises 25906 Portafino Dr Mission Viejo 92691

WEAVER, DORIS LEA, executive search firm owner; b. Jan. 22, 1933, Northport, NE; d. Benjamin Martin and Ione Myrtle (Cary) Jurgens; m. Dell Fullmer, Aug. 28, 1971; children: Deborah b. 1951, Renee b. 1953, Wayne b. 1964; (step): Gary b. 1959, Linda b. 1961, Rebecca b. 1964; edn: bus. & acctng., Columbia Basin Coll. 1967-8. Career: acct. Leirman Accountancy 1968-71; ofc. mgr. Wenatchee Valley Clinic 1971-73, Owl Companies 1973-75; cons. Robert Half 1975-76; co-owner: Accts. Associated Personnel Svc., Inc. 1977-84, Frederick/ Weaver & Co. 1981-84, Travel w/ Joyce 1978-83; owner: Doris Weaver Personnel Service, Doris Weaver Temporaries and D.L. Weaver & Assocs. Executive Search, 1983-; speaker various colls.; dir. Providence Speech & Hearing Ctr.; honors: Beckman NAA Award for Most Outstanding Dir.; NAA Most Valuable Mem.; NAA Most Valuable Past Pres.; Who's Who in State of Wash.; mem: Nat. Assn. of Accts. (pres.); Women in Mgmt.; Am. Acctg. Assn.; Am. Employment Assn.; Calif. Employment Assn.; Orange Co. CofC; Irvine, Newport Beach, and Fullerton CofCs; Irvine Indsl. League; Republican; Methodist; rec: golf, hiking, tennis. Res: 570 Paseo Lucero Anaheim Hills 92807 Ofc: 1820 E First St Ste 200 Santa Ana 92705

WEBB, EMMA SUE, minister; b. Apr. 18, 1944, Santa Paula, Calif.; d. John Westley and Emma Jean (Hobbs) Hill; m. James Webb, July 14, 1962; children: Karen b. 1963 (decd.), Cheryl b. 1965, Jamie b. 1973; edn: West Coast Bible Coll. 1978; Church of God Theol. Coll. Cleveland, Tenn. 1979; BA, Calif. Grad. Sch. of Theol. 1980, MA, 1981, D.Min., 1982; real estate broker. Career: real estate broker 1972-; pastor Church of God, Saticoy 1972, Church of God Christian Life Ctr., Fillmore 1980-; Christian edn. dir. 1980-; asst. Valdez-Webb Meml. Scholarship Com.; honors: Humanitarian Award (So. Calif. Motion Picture Council); mem: Santa Paula- Fillmore Bd. Realtors, Fillmore Ministers Group, So. Calif. Motion Picture Council (secty., asst. to pres.); Republican; Christian; rec: interior decorating, antique collecting. Res: 950 Terracina Dr Santa Paula 93060 Ofc: Webb Realty 950 N 10th St Santa Paula 93060

WEBB, JAMES GLENN, pediatrician; b. Apr. 2, 1939, Fresno; s. Edward Neal and Amy Evelyn (Burns) W.; m. Helen, June 22, 1962; children: Mary b. 1963, Carrie b. 1965, Jeb b. 1977; edn: PharmD, Univ. Calif. 1963, MS in Pharm. Chem., 1970; MD, Oklahoma Univ. 1974. Career: pharmacist/ptnr. in two pharmacies, Visalia 1963-68; internship and residency in pediatrics Valley Med. Center, Fresno; pvt. practice in pediatrics, Bakersfield 1976-; chief of pediatrics Mercy Hosp. 1982, Greater Bakersfield Meml. Hosp. 1985-86; honors: Rho Chi Soc. (1963); mem. AMA, CMA, Kern County Med. Soc.; author book: Frequently Asked Questions About Your Newborn (1985); invented fruit picker (1982); Republican; Presbyterian; rec: writing, drawing. Pediatricians Office, 1930 Truxtun Ave Bakersfield 93301

WEBB, JAMES MURPHY, architect; b. Apr. 5, 1939; s. James Ellis and Inez (Murphy) W.; div.; children: Jennifer b. 1968, Justine b 1972, Michael b. 1974; edn: Univ. of Ark., BA 1963, and B.Arch., 1963; Lic. Architect, Calif., Ill.; Lic. Real Estate Broker, Calif.; Nat. Council Archtl. Reg. Bds. Cert. Career: project arch. Kaplan/McLaughlin/Diaz, S.F.; mem: Am. Inst. Architects (chpt. secty. 1975, dir. 1972-74), Engrg. Soc. Com. for Manpower Tng. (secty. 1972-73, v.p. 1973-74, pres. 1974-75), Sigma Phi Epsilon Alumni Assn. (chpt. pres.), S.F. Merrionettes Synchronized Swim Team (v.p., bd. dirs.); Democrat. Res: 89 Turquoise Way San Francisco 94131 Ofc: K/M/D, 222 Vallejo St San Francisco 94111

WEBER, BARRY ERNEST, auto parts distributor; b. Feb. 2, 1949, Oakland; s. Ernest A. and June M. (Brye) W.; m. Janet, Apr. 3, 1971; children: Bradley b. 1973, Blair b. 1975; edn: BA bus. adm., CSU Fresno 1971; MBA, Golden Gate Univ. 1984; Certified Public Acct., Calif. (1984). Career: senior tax acct., mgr. Ernst and Whinney CPAs, Fresno 1982-85; (current) CPA prin. 1985-; prop. Service Specialties Co.; ptnr. Summit Software Co.; CEO Weber Automotive Cos. Inc., Fresno; CEO Weber Auto Parts Co., Sanger; CEO Mid-State Automotive Distbrs., Fresno; elected del. Whitehouse Conf. on Small Bus., US Small Bus. Adminstrn. Advis. Council; mem: Am. Inst. CPAs, Calif. Soc. CPAs, Calif. Automotive Wholesalers Assn. (dir.), Automotive Service Industry Assn., Fresno CofC (chmn. Small Bus. Affairs Com.), Rotary (dir.);

Republican; Lutheran; rec: computers, gardening, woodworking. Res: 5555 N Benedict Fresno 93711 Ofc: Mid-State Automotive Distributors 221 M Street Fresno 93721

WEBSTER, BURLAND CARL, business executive; b. Oct. 16, 1914, Huntley, Mont.; s. Wm. Henry and Irene A. (Blackford) W.; m. Margaret, Dec. 3, 1957; children: Lawrence b. 1937, Lee b. 1941, Lesley b. 1944, Nancy (Barr) b. 1942, Mark b. 1952; edn: AA, Long Beach City Coll. 1935; engring., Univ. Wash. 1937. Career: prop. Webster Prodns., Signal Hill 1950–, and Acme Heater Co., 1963–; ptnr. Redman Prodn., Signal Hill 1945-57, Timco Oil Co., 1953–, WTH Investments 1979-82; mem. Long Beach Petroleum Club (life), Signal Hill CofC, Signal Hill Business Assn., Signal Hill Police Assn.; works: innovations in oilfield and crude oil heating & engring., splst. in Vapor recovery; mil: USCG; Republican; Prot.; rec: philately, paleontology, woodworking. Res: 1131 Claiborner Dr Long Beach 90807 Ofc: Acme Heater Co. 2859 Walnut Ave Long Beach 90806

WEDBUSH, EDWARD WILLIAM, securities co. president; b. Sept. 14, 1932, St. Louis, Mo.; s. Wm. H. and Edith Marie (Herman) Wedbush; m. Jean A. Lawrence, Dec. 18, 1960, Los Angeles; chil: Gary Lance, b. 1964, Eric Dean, b. 1967, Leigh Ann, b. 1969; edn: BA in mech. engring., Univ. Cincinnati 1955; MBA (Hughes Fellow), UCLA 1957; Regis. profl. engr., Calif. Career: stu. engr. Wagner Elec., 1949-55; engr. Hughes Aircraft Co., 1955-8; assoc. lectr. in engring., UCLA, 1957-9; partner Wedbush, Noble, Cooke, Inc., Los Angeles 1957-67, pres. 1967–; pres./CEO Wedbush Corp.; chmn. bd. Pacific Stock Exchange 1976-7; dir. Pacific Securities Depository Trust Co., Nat. Securities Clearing Corp; mem. NY Stock Exchange (Regional Advisory Firm Com.), American Stock Exchange Com.; California Club, Triangle frat. Publs: arts. in engring. jours. Rec: tennis; Res: Rancho Santa Fe, Calif 92067 Ofc: Wedbush, Noble, Cooke, Inc. 615 S. Flower St. Los Angeles 90017

WEDEMEYER, LOWELL REMY, lawyer, farmer; b. June 27, 1941, Adair, Iowa; s. Lawrence Theodore and Loretta Agnes (Donohue) W.; m. Linda Downie, June 23, 1979; children: Michelle b. 1980, Rebecca b. 1982, Loretta b. 1985; edn: BS in chem. engrg., Iowa State Univ. 1963; JD, Harvard Law Sch. 1968. Career: aerospace engr. McDonnell Aircraft, St. Louis 1963; US Peace Corps, Bida, Nigeria 1964-65; assoc. atty. law firm Wyman, Bautzer, Rothman & Kuchel, Beverly Hills y69-70; partner law firm Alexander, Inman, Tanzer & Wedemeyer, 1970-82; sole practitioner 1982–; active in election lawsuits; plaintiffs' lead counsel in investors' class action and former state employee class action lawsuits; active in planning, zoning, land use and environmtl. quality litigation; acad. honors: Tau Beta Pi, Pi Tau Sigma; mem: State Bar of Calif., Am. Bar Assn.; a founder and first spkr. Santa Monica Citizens Congress (non-partisan local polit. orgn.); a founder and first chmn. New Deal Democrats of Santa Monica; works: lead counsel listed in various Calif. Appellate Ct. decisions; mil: 2d lt. USAFR; Democrat; rec: outdoor sports. Address: 3002 Catalina Dr Davis 95616

WEDER, ERWIN HENRY, manufacturing co. executive, entrepreneur; b. Dec. 13, 1904, Decksprairie, Ill.; s. August and Marie Julia (Brunner) W.; m. Louise Graham, July 19, 1937; children: Mary Kay (Foley) b. 1942, Dona Lee (Abbott) b. 1943, Donald Erwin b. 1947, Wanda May b. 1948, Janet Marie b. 1951; edn: Highland, Ill. H.S. 1917/18. Career: var. pos. in farming 3 yrs., dairy office work & dance promotion 3 yrs., detective Fla. East Coast Hotel Co., var. race tracks, 9 yrs.; traveling salesman Metal Goods Corp. 9 yrs.; current: founder/ bd. chmn. Highland Supply Corp. 1937–, also founder/bd. chmn. 7 additional corps., ranching, buffalo raising & farming; mem. Highland Mfrs. Assn. (pres. 1979); clubs: Missouri Athletic, Media, OX-5, Capital Hill, The Am. Sportsmans, Mirador Country, Highland Gun; works: num, product and machinery patents; mil: 1st lt. Ill. Reserve Militia Air Corps; Republican; rec: hunting, shooting, flying. Address: 1500 Crafton Ave Redlands 92373

WEIGEL, IRMA CATHERINE, airport owner/manager; b. Dec. 25, 1915, Artesian, S.Dak.; d. Charles Melvin (related to Pres. Grover Cleveland) and Julia Anna (Heller) Cleveland; div.; 1 dau. Barbara K. Elam b. 1946; edn: grad. Am. Inst. of Business, Des Moines, IA 1934-35; Women Air Force Service Pilots (WASP) tng. schs. Career: active duty WASP, USAF, 1943-44, flew 27 different models of aircraft (800 hours flying time in 20 mos.) to over 30 cities in US and Canada for Air Force; with US Civil Service 1959-1980, ret. (sev. Superior Perf. Awards); developer/ owner/opr. Sun Hill Airport, San Bernardino County 1946–; comml. flight instr. Gardena, Santa Barbara (CA), Memphis (TN), Ardmore (OK), Adelanto (CA) 1945-54; mem. Aviation Tech. Advis. Com., So. Calif. Assn. of Govts. (SCAG); civic: devel. Sun Hill Ranch-Airport (1947–) devel. water well, mobile home park and subdivs. on Sun Hill Ranch, currently in process of forming water dist. for area (involving 333 landowners and possible new town or suburb); awarded Blue Ribbon for freehand drawing, Warren County, IA Fair (1923), short story pub. Chicago Tribune (1936); mil: WASP 1943-44, 1st lt. USAFR 1946-51; Republican; Catholic; rec: land devel., gardening. Ofc: Sun Hill Airport, 1 Mi. W. US Hwy 395 on Sun Hill Rd, San Bernardino Co. Mail: POB 332 Adelanto 92301

WEIKEL, NEIL S(TERLING), computer cartographer, landscape architect; b. July 11, 1938, The Dalles, Ore.; s. Ivan Weller and Esther Jane (Chamberlin) Weikel; 1 dau., Tamara Leigh, b. 1976; edn: Bach. Landscape Arch., Univ. Ore. 1966; M.Landscape Arch., Cal Poly, Pomona 1984; spl. courses, UCLA; Reg. Landscape Architect, Calif. 1972; Comm. Coll. Tching. Cred.(life), Calif. 1976. Career: Master Street Pgm., City of Eugene, Ore. 1964-5; w/David E. Thompson, Lndscp Arch., Portland 1966; Wash. State Hwy Dept. 1968; planner, Consulting Svcs. Corp., Seattle, Wn. 1968-70; lndscp. arch. Keith

French Assocs.- E.S.I., Los Angeles 1971-3, City of Los Angeles 1984-; prin., Neil S. Weikel, Lndscp. Arch., Santa Monica 1975–; faculty Santa Monica Coll. 1974-6, L.A. Pierce Coll. 1974-7, Cal Poly 1976 & 84, UCLA Ext. 1978-; recipient Outstanding Teacher Award, UCLA, 1983; Most Valuable Tchr. Award, UCLA 1985; mem: Calif. Iris Soc., Pi Kappa Phi 1957-. Photog. exhib.: The Artist's I Gallery, Redondo Bch. 1978; sculpture exhibs: Univ. Ore. 1965, Seattle, Wn. 1970; author/pub. 107 Plants in the Year; author Santa Susana Land Use Sensitivity Study 1984; mil: DM 2, USN 1962-4, GCM; Republican; Congregational; rec: photog., botany, wt. tng., travel. Address: Neil S. Weikel, Lndscp. Arch. 301 Ashland Ave. #8, Santa Monica 90405

WEIN, JOSEPH ALEXANDER, lawyer; b. June 4, 1931, Montreal, Canada, nat. 1952; s. Jacob and Eugenia (Szour) W.; m. Libby, June 20, 1957; children: Michele Georgeanne, b. 1959, Paul Frederick, b. 1960; edn: BA, UC Los Angeles 1952, JD, 1955. Admitted to Calif. State Bar 1956. Career: family importing bus., 1956-62; atty. law firm Buchalter Nemer Fields Chrystie & Younger, P.C., Los Angeles 1962-, pres./mng. partner, 1979–; panel moderator Calif. Contg. Edn. of Bar, 1977-79; panelist L.A. County Bar Bridging the Gap, 1978; panelist Calif. Conf. of Municipal Ct. Judges 1973; mem: Internat., Am., L.A. Co. Bar Assns., Fin. Lawyers Conf., Comml. Law League of Am., Town Hall of Calif., L.A. Co. Art Mus., Am. Film Inst., UCLA Law Sch Founders, UCLA Chancellors Circle; listed Who's Who in American Law (1st ed.); rec: piano, photog. Res: 324 So Clark Dr Beverly Hills 90211 Ofc: Buchalter Nemer Fields Chrystie & Younger, 700 So Flower St, Ste. 700, Los Angeles 90017

WEINBERGER, CASPAR WILLARD, U.S. Secretary of Defense; b. Aug. 18, 1917, San Francisco; s. Herman & Cerise Carpenter (Hampson) Weinberger; m. Jane Dalton, 1942; children: Arlin Cerise, Caspar Willard; edn: AB, magna cum laude, Harvard, 1938, LLB, 1941. Career: admitted to Calif. Bar, law clerk, US Judge William E. Orr, 1945-47; with firm Heller, Ehrman, White & McAuliffe, 1947-69, ptnr. 1959-69; elected mem. Calif. Legislature from 21st Dist. 1952-58; v.chmn. Com. Cal. Govt. Orgn. and Econs. 1967-68; dir. finl. Calif., 1968-69; chmn. US FTC, 1970; dep. dir. US Office Mgmt. and Budget 1970-72, dir. 1972-73; counselor to the Pres. 1973; secty US Dept. HEW, 1973-75; gen. counsel, v.p., dir. Bechtel Group of Cos. 1975-81; former dir. Pepsi Co., Inc., Quaker Oats Co.; sworn in as US Secty. of Defense, Jan. 21, 1981; former staff book reviewer San Francisco Chronicle; writer newspaper column on Calif. govt. 1959-68; moderator weekly TV pgm. "Profile, Bay Area" TV Sta. KQED, S.F. 1959-68; Frank Nelson Doubleday (Smithsonian) lectr. (1974); chmn. US Pres.'s Commn. on Mental Retardation 1973-75; past mem. Trilateral Commn., Am. Ditchley Found. Adv. Council, St. Luke's Hosp. (S.F.) bd. trustees, Nat. Symphony (Wash DC) nat. trustee; mem. Am. Bar Assn., State Bar of Calif., Phi Beta Kappa; clubs: Century (NY), Bohemian (SF), Pacific Union (SF), Harvard (SF, Wash DC), Burlingame Country; mil: served from pvt. to capt. AUS Infantry 1941-45, PTO, Bronze Star; Episcopal (past treas. Diocese of Calif.). Ofc: Secty. of Defense, The Pentagon, Washington D.C. 20301

WEINER, JEFFREY CHARLES, design engineering and construction co. president; b. Oct. 13, 1958, Phila.; s. Raphael David and Shirley Faye (Litwin) W.; edn: BA, pol. sci., USC 1980. Career: pres. Systems Engineering and Constrn. Co., CA; exec. vice pres. Raphael Homes Corp., CA; guest lectr. USC, UCLA, CSU Fullerton; frequent guest spkr. various real estate orgns.; honors: cover story and feature art. in Automation in Housing (internat. mag. for factory built housing technologies), in Zinc (nat. mag. for the steel indus.); mem: Building Indus. Assn., Nat. Assn. of Home Mfrs., Nat./Calif. Assn. of Realtors; mem. US Congl. Advis. Bd.; Republican (Nat. Com.); rec: archtl. design, martial arts, music, metal sculptures. Res: 1309 S Euclid Anaheim 92802 Ofc: Raphael Homes, 533 W. Central Park Ave Anaheim 92802

WEINSTEIN, RAYMOND SAUL, physician; b. Mar. 19, 1950, Phila.; s. Marvin and Betty Lou (Reinhart) W.; m. Ricky Chocron, Aug. 11, 1974; children: Michael b. 1981, Danielle b. 1983; edn: BA, UC Los Angeles 1973; MD, Univ. Wash. 1980; certified Am. Bd. Family Practice (1983). Career: intern and resident family medicine, Northridge Hosp. 1981-83; pvt. solo practice 1983–; instr. clin. medicine Northridge F.P. Residency pgm. 1984, 85, 86; cons. Calif. Bd. of Med. Quality Assurance; bd. advisors New Beginning Found. 1986; staff phys. XV World Games for the Deaf 1985; mem: L.A. County Med. Assn., Calif. Med. Assn., Am. Assn. of F.P., Am. Philatelic Soc.; contbr. sev. articles in med. jours. and yearbooks, art. in The Amer. Philatelist (1979); rec: stamps, coins, ships in bottles, Netsuke. Ofc: 7012 Reseda Blvd Ste E Reseda 91335

WEISBAUM, EARL, law librarian, lawyer; b. May 18, 1930, Chgo.; s. Sam and Dolores (Rubin) W.; div.; twin daus. Deena and Elanit, b. 1969; edn: BA, L.A. STate Coll. 1952, MS in lib. sci., USC 1961; JD, Loyola Law Sch. 1970. Career: foreign law librn., L.A. County Law Library, 1966–; fgn. law expert, 1970–; taught law Loyola Law Sch., legal bibliography USC Library Sch., 1975-81; honors: achievement award, Internat. Law Sect. Los Angeles County Bar Assn. (1982); mem: Am. Bar Assn., Calif. State Bar, Foreign Law Assn. of So. Calif., L.A. Co. Bar Assn. (Internat. Law Sect. exec. com. 1976-), chmn. symposium on Mexican law, 1975, Am. Assn. of Law Libraries; publs: Mexican Law for Norteamericanos (68 Law Lib. Jour. 395, 1975), contbr. regular column in The Internat. Lawyer, 1981–; Democrat; Jewish; rec: folk music. Res: 136 S Virgil #243 Los Angeles 90004 Ofc: L.A. County Law Library 301 West First St Los Angeles 90012

WEISERT, EDWARD DONALD, manufacturing co. executive; b. Feb. 10, 1923, Evanston, Ill.; s. Edward Muerer and Lillian Louise (Schulz) W.; m. Mary Victoria May, Apr. 26, 1947; children: Roberta b. 1949, Edward b. 1953, Donald b. 1956, Michael b. 1960; edn: BSE metallurgy, BSE chem., Univ. of Mich., 1950. Career: resrch. asst. Univ. of Mich. Engring. Research Inst., Ann Arbor, Mich. 1948-50; head product devel. section Haynes Stellite Div., Union Carbide Corp., Kokomo, Ind. 1950-55; supr. prod. resrch Metals Research Lab., Union Carbide Corp., Niagara Falls, NY 1955-59; supr. Metallurg. Devel., Marquardt Corp., Van Nuys, Ca. 1959-60; mgr. Metals Research Rocketdyne Div., Rockwell Internat., Canoga Park 1961-69; founder/dir. Isopressed Products Corp. 1969-72; tech. dir. Special Metals Corp., New Hartford, NY 1972-74; supr. Advance Titanium Tech., North Am. Aviation Ops., Rockwell Internat., El Segundo 1975-82; pres. Ontario Technologies Corp., Menlo Park 1982—; mem: Fellow Am. Soc. for Metals (pgm. chmn. WESTEC, num. coms.) 1948-, The Metallurgical Soc. of AIME 1956-, Nat. Assn. of Corrosion Engrs. 1952-61; BSA Scoutmaster; publs: 25+ tech. publs. 1950-; 8 patents 1955-; innovative contbns. to fields of superplasticity, diffusion bonding, powder metallurgy; mil: 1st lt. USAAF 1943-45, 8th AF, B-24 Nav., Air Medal silver oak leaf cluster; Ind.; rec: music, painting, camping, sailing. Res: 860 Cabot Ct San Carlos 94070 Ofc: Ontario Technologies Corp 167 Constitution Dr Menlo Park 94025

WEISINGER, MERRITT LOUIS, lawyer; b. Oct. 23, 1946, West Orange, NJ; s. Hyman and Clarice (Eckstein) W.; m. Susan Beth Hackman, July 10, 1978; children: Aaron Jason and Ethan Merritt; edn: BA, Colgate Univ. 1968; JD, Loyola Univ., L.A. 1973; admitted Calif. State Bar 1973. Career: trial atty. pvt. practice spec. in personal injury and civil litigation, Los Angeles 1973—; lectr. Calif. State Univ. Ext., and Calif. Contg. Edn. of the Bar; past instr. law sch.; arbitrator Am. Arbitration Assn., Better Bus. Bureau; mem. Los Angeles County Bar Assn.; past dir. Temple Beth Ami; publs: book chapters in sev. ednl. texts.; Jewish; rec: flying, skiing, fishing. Res: 17326 Citronia St., Northridge 91325 Ofc: Merritt Weisinger, Esq. 1021 S Union Ave Los Angeles 90015

WEISKE, HOWARD MELVIN, company executive; b. Feb. 1 1937, Kankakee, Ill.; s. Melvin Julius and Edna Elizabeth (Ehrich) W.; m. Linda Porter, July 15, 1956; children: Kevin b. 1959, Andrew b. 1966; edn: AA, Long Beach City Coll.; Blackston Sch. of Law; Cerritos Jr. Coll.; Golden West Coll. Career: project engr. North American Aviation, Downey 1962-66; design engr. Northrop Nortronics, Palos Verdes 1966-67; marine engring. cons. Applied Oceanics, Long Beach 1967-68; design splst. Douglas Aircraft, Long Beach 1968-71; v.p. Trans Com. Div. Sundstrand, Costa Mesa 1970-75; sales mgr. Fairchild Burns Co., Manhattan Beach 1975-76; sales mgr. Transequip Co., Compton 1976-78; gen. mgr. FXC Corp. Santa Ana 1978-85; dir. of mktg. Am. Safety Flight Systems, Inc., Glendale 1985, bd. dir. 1986; dir: Trans Com Prodns. (1970-72), Stowe Mfg. Co. (1975-76), Marina Manor Assn. (1986); 1985; mil: sgt. E-8 US Army Reserve; Republican; Lutheran; rec: fishing, hunting, water skiing. Res: 8131 Wenlock Circle Huntington Beach 92646

WEISS, HOWARD RICH, manufacturing co. president; b. Oct. 1, 1924, Cleveland, Ohio; s. Adrian E. and Irene (Rich) W.; m. Phyllis, Feb. 25, 1949; children: David b. 1945 (dec.), Wendy b. 1949, Michael b. 1950, Nancy b. 1952; edn: BS, US Naval Acad. 1946. Career: dir. purch. Price-Pfister Brass Mfg. 1949-54; sales rep. 1955-56; purch. agent, dir. indsl. sales, Pacific Electricord Co. 1956-59; pres./CEO Whitmor Plastic Wire & Cable Corp. (mfg. electrical wire & cable), No. Hollywood 1959—; mem. Am. Quarter Horse Assn. (pres. 1986-87), Pacific Coast Quarter Horse Racing Assn. (past pres.), Pacific Coast Quarter Horse Assn. (past pres.); mil: lt. jg. US Navy 1943-49; Republican; rec: raising, racing & showing Quarter Horses. Res: 13525 Bradley Ave Sylmar 91342 Ofc: Whitmor Plastic Wire & Cable Corp. 13161 Sherman Way Unit B, North Hollywood 91605

WEISS, MARC DANA, chiropractor; b. June 28, 1954, Brooklyn, NY; s. Irwin and Beatrice (Seigel) W.; m. Joni Louise, Nov. 25, 1985; edn: DC, Cleveland Chiropractic Coll. 1983. Career: Frank Scott Dc, Canoga Park, McGown Chiropractic Ofcs. Inc.; currently, chiropractor Center of Health - Weiss Chiropractic, Redondo Beach; mem: Ambassador- Cleveland Chiropractic Coll., Am. and Calif. Chiropractic Assns., PMA, PCRF, Redondo Beach CofC. Ofc: Center of Health, 1300 Pacific Coast Hwy. Ste. 205 Redondo Beach 90277

WEISS, MARTIN HARVEY, neurosurgeon, educator; b. Feb. 2, 1939, Newark, NJ; s. Max and Rae (Satz) W.; m. R. Debora Rosenthal, Aug. 20, 1961; children: Brad b. 1962, Jessica b. 1965, Elisabeth b. 1967; edn: AB, Dartmouth Coll. 1960, BMS, 1961; MD, Cornell Univ. Med. Coll. 1963. Career: surgical intern Univ. Hosps. of Cleveland, 1963-64; neuro surgical resident, 1966-70; senior instr. neurosurgery, asst. prof. neurosurgery, Case Western Reserve Med. Sch., 1970-73; assoc. prof., 1973-76, prof. of neurosurgery USC, 1976—, dept. chmn. USC, and chief of neurosurg. USC Med. Center, 1978—; Special Fellow NIH (1969-70), NIH Study Sect. Neurology (1979-83, chmn. 81-83); bd. dirs. Am. Board of Neurological Surgery (1983-89); honors: Phi Beta Kappa, Alpha Omega Alpha; mem: Soc. of Neurological Surgeons, Neurosurgical Soc. of Am., Am. Acad. of Neurol. Surg., Am. Assn. of Neurosurgeons, Congress of Neurosurgeons (v.p. 1983), Western Neurosurg. Soc., So. Calif. Neurosurg. Soc. (pres. 1983-84); publs: Pituitary Disorders (book pub. 1980); chief editor Clinical Neurosurgery; editl. bd. Neurosurgery; over 100 sci. papers; mil: capt. USAR 1964-66, assoc. surgeon U.S. med. team West Point, N.Y., Commendn. Medal 1966; rec: fly fishing. Res: 357 Georgian Rd Flintridge 91011 Ofc: USC Medical Center 1200 N State St, Ste 5040 Los Angeles 90033

WEISS, STEPHEN CHARLES, company president; b. March 13, 1943, Glendale; s. Gus E. and Jane E. (Eisner) W.; m. Karen, July 28, 1979; children: James b. 1968, Karen b. 1969, Melinda b. 1971, Brett b. 1979; edn: BS, CSU Los Angeles 1964, MS, 1968; Reg. Profl. Mech. Engr., Calif. 1971. Career: adminstv. asst. Thermalair Inc. 1970-71, v.p. 1972-85, pres. 1985—; pres. Milea Inc. (mech. engring.) 1971—; mem. ASHRAE; civic: YMCA, Childrens Hosp. of Orange Co. (patron); mil: capt. US Air Force, Unit Citations; Republican; Protestant; rec: pvt. pilot, sports. Res: 10511 Woodview Circle Orange 92669 Ofc: 1330 Potrero Ave South El Monte 91733

WEISS, STEVEN ALAN, television syndication/distribution co. executive; b. Oct. 19, 1944, Glendale; s. Adrian and Ethel (Long) W.; m. Laurie Charmak, Nov. 9, 1967; children: Ara Simon b. 1973, Zachary Adam b. 1975; edn: AA, L.A. City Coll. 1964; BS pol. sci., USC 1966; MS, pol. sci., Northwestern Univ. 1967; JD, LaSalle Ext. Univ. 1970. Career: served to lt. US Navy 1966-71, shipyard liaison ofcr. Pearl Harbor Naval Shipyard 1967-70; gen. mgr. Adrian Weiss Prodns. 1970-74; sec.treas./dir. Film Investment Corp., and Weiss Global Ents., 1974—; honors: Outstanding Recruit, US Navy (1966); mem: Nat. Assn. of TV Pgm. Execs., Nat. Cable TV Assn., Assn. of Pgm. Distbrs., Am. Film Inst.; civic: CBC Jr. Baseball, AYSO, Jewish Nat. Fund, Nat. Asthma Center, Am. Heart Assn., Am. Cancer Soc., Masons, Scottish Rite B'nai B'rith, The Eddie Cantor Charitable Found., Scripps Inst., Simon Wisenthal Ctr.; Republican (charter Rep. Presdtl. task Force, sustain. mem. Calif. Rep. Party, GOP Fund spons. US Senatl. Club); Jewish; rec: volleyball, running, gardening. Res: 4137 N Sunset Ln Channel Islands 93030-8017 Ofc: Weiss Global Enterprises 2055 Saviers Rd Ste 12 Oxnard 93033

WEISSMAN, BARRY LEIGH, lawyer; b. May 30, 1948, Los Angeles; s. Sidney and Eleanor (Siegel) W.; m. Beverly Jean, Sept. 12, 1982; edn: BA, UC Davis 1970, JD, Univ. Santa Clara Sch. of Law 1973; admitted Calif. Bar (1973), US Dist. Ct. (9th Cir., 1976), US Supreme Ct. (1977), D.C. Ct. Appeals (1978). Career: law clk. Larivier, Blacker & Dickerson, San Jose 1971-73, also student atty. Univ. Santa Clara Inmate Assistance Pgm., prosecutor intern USN, Moffett Naval Air Sta., and rep. US Atty's Office in S.F. and San Jose Dist. Cts., 1971-73; supvsg. atty. State Compensation Fund, 1973-74; atty. solo practice 1974-77; ptnr. Valentini, Fini, Ferraro, Gallavotti & Weissman (Italian law firm w/main office in Rome), Los Angeles office 1983-85; ptnr. Kroll, Tract, Harnett, Pomerantz & Cameron 1985—; state bar examiner (1976-80), judge pro tem L.A. Municipal Ct. (1975-), arbitr. Am. Arbitration Assn. (1978-); instr. Basic Skills courses to new admittees to Calif. Bar; honors: Outstanding Young Men in Am. (1980), Century City Bar Assn. Award (1976), Who's Who in Am. Colls. and Univs. (1973), Calif. Law Student Assn. Merit Award (1973), Gold Key, ABA (1973); mem: Am. Bar Assn. (Gen. Practice, Legal Econs. and Internat. Law sects.), Beverly Hills Bar Assn., Calif. State Bar (Bus. Law Sect.), Century City Bar Assn. (bd. govs., chmn./ed. bar jour. 1975-77), Beverly Hills CofC (co-chair Legal Justice Com. 1980-82), Colo. River Assn. (bd. dirs. 1982-), W. Los Angeles Regl. CofC (dir. 1984-88); rec: travel, swim, ski. Res: 1101 South Rexford Dr Ste 103 Los Angeles 90035 Ofc: 3435 Wilshire Blvd Ste 2110 Los Angeles 90010

WEITKAMP, JOHN F., lawyer; b. Jan. 7, 1953, Los Angeles; s. Fredrick John and Marilyn Irene (Odell) W.; m. Karen Ann Zdonzyk, June 9, 1984; edn: BA, cum laude, Claremont Men's Coll. 1975; JD, Loyola Univ. Sch. of Law 1978; admitted to Calif. Bar 1978. Career: clerk Law Ofcs. Frederick J. Weitkamp 1976-78, assoc. atty. 1978-83; ptr. Law Ofcs. Weitkamp & Weitkamp, Granada Hills 1984—; coord. dist. ops. Phi Alpha Delta 1983-; honors: Phi Alpha Delta Internat. Justice Award 1984; Outstanding Dir. Award, Granada Hills CofC 1984; Outstanding Young Man of Am. 1978-80; mem: Am., Calif., San Fernando Valley, U.S. Dist. Ct. (Central Dist. of Calif.), U.S. Ct. of Appeals (Ninth Circuit), and U.S. Supreme Ct. Bar Assns., Tres Robles Homeowners Assn. (dir. 1985, Phi Alpha Delta (Wm. Joseph Ford chpt. clerk 1976-77, justice 1977-78; Dist. III justice 1978-83; pre-law dir. 1980-81; coord. dist. ops. 1983-), Granada Hills CofC (dir. 1983-, secty. 1983, 1st v.p. 1984-85, pres. 1986-, chmn. legis. com. 1983-85, community parade chmn. 1983, community auction chmn. 1984-85); Republican; Methodist; rec: aide to law and pre-law students. Ofc: Law Ofcs. Weitkamp & Weitkamp, 10724 White Oak Ave., Granada Hills 91344

WELCH, EDWARD J., real estate broker, accountant; b. Ovt. 17, 1943, Cape May, NJ; s. Joseph G. and Meta M. (McKelvey) W.; m. Deborah Reed, Oct. 10, 1980; 1 son, Troy b. 1968; edn: BBA, Hofstra Univ. 1967; CPA 1970. Career: senior Arthur Young & Co. NY; mgr. Gulf & Western Internal Audit NY; controller Frick Mfg. Co. Pa.; corp. controller Finnigan Instruments Inc.; v.p. finance Gulf & Western Distbn. Group Mich.; pres. York Casket Co. Pa.; pres. Centre Realty Inc.; pres. Dew West Investments Inc. San Jose 1984—; bd. Winchester Investments Inc., Estate Equity Inc.; mem: Financial Execs. Inst. 1976-, Am. Inst. CPAs 1970-, Palo Alto Hills Golf & CC; Republican; Protestant; rec: golf, tennis, sailing. Ofc: Dew West 650 Saratoga Ave Ste 200 San Jose 95129

WELCH, HAZEL MARYLOIS, real estate broker; b. Dec. 12, 1907, Woodward, Okla.; d. William Harvey and Mary Malinda (Barry) Hedrick; m. Joe Clifford, Nov. 6, 1928, dec. 1977; edn: bus. adminstrn., El Dorado, Kans. Career: founder Joe Welch Realty, Oakland 1954-80; affiliate, lic. real estate broker Robert F. Akinson Co., Piedmont 1980—; mem: Nat. and Calif. Assns. Realtors, Oakland Bd. Realtors, Daughters of the Nile, Nefru-Ari Temple, Order of the Eastern Star; Republican; Christian; rec: architecture, art, music. Res: 742 Wesley Way Unit 2-C Oakland 94610

WELCH, KENNETH WAYNE, JR., marketing executive; b. April 21, 1956, Glendale; s. Kenneth W., Sr., and Anna Jean (Atkins) W.; m. Yvonne Evelend, Aug. 8, 1982; children: Kenneth b. 1983, Kristina b. 1985; edn: grad. Antelope Valley H.S. 1974. Career: free-lance model, theatre experience, choregrapher & co-director, Galveston, Tex. 1976-79; owner/opr. Welch Landscaping, 1979; mgr. Pyramid Waterbeds, store design, interior designer, 1980-81, mgr. Water Wonderland, 1981; owner/opr. Ken Welch Co. (mail order sales corp.) 1981-82; vice pres. Whitmore & Assocs., and sales mktg. cons. for The Resort Center, Inc., 1982; owner The Resort Center, Inc., pres./gen. partner TRC Investments, 1983 –; owner Video Vacations, TV show on SPN Cable 1985–; mem. Antelope Valley Pol. Action Com.; mil: pfc (A-1 Tank Driver, Capt.'s Driver/ Gen.'s Driver) US Army 1974-76; Republican; Mormon; rec: building/designing. Res: 327 Chester, H, Glendale 91203 Ofc: The Resort Center, 858 W. Jackman, Ste. 207, Lancaster 93534

WELCH, MARGARET-ROSE, educator, religious community corporate president; b. Aug. 8, 1924, Anaheim; d. Richard A. and Marguerite E. (Browne) W.; edn: BA, Immaculate Hearth Coll. 1951; MA, St. Louis Univ. 1954; PhD, Duquesne Univ. 1973. Career: (current) pres. Immaculate Heart Coll. Center, and Immaculate Heart Community (parent corp. for coll., schs., hosp. and retreat centers); dean of students and dir. counseling Immaculate Heart Coll.; past staff psychologist Dixmont State Hosp., Pa.; trustee emeritus Queen of the Valley Hosp.; apptd. chair Gov.'s Com. on Mental Hosps.; mem: Rancho Park CofC (exec. bd.; multi-cultural com. L.A. County Schs.,), So. Calif. Consortium for Internat. Studies (exec. com.), Am. Assn. for Social Psychiatry, Internat. Peace Network of Psychiatrists, NCCJ (LA Area advis. com.), L.A. Inter-religious Council; Democrat; Catholic; rec: walking, swimming. Res: 136 No. Commonwealth Los Angeles 90004 Ofc: Immaculate Hearth College Center, 109051 W. Pico Blvd. Los Angeles 90064

WELCH, WALTER ANDREW, JR., aeronautical lawyer/licensed commercial pilot; b. Dec. 13, 1948, Melrose Park, Ill.; s. Walter Andrew Sr., and Myrtle Marie (Kunzmann) W.; edn: BSAS, So. Ill. Univ. 1974; grad. US Naval Justice Sch. Newport R.I. 1975; JD, Pepperdine Univ. Sch. of Law 1980; certs: lawyer, comml. pilot, teacher, real estate broker. Career: naval aviator 1974-77; legal officer USMC 1975-76; aircraft cmdr. USMC 1976-77; licensed comml. pilot, 1974 –; aviation law practice, 1981 –; admitted to practice: Calif. Supreme Ct., US Ct. of Internat. Trade, US Ct. of Customs & Patent Appeals, US Claims Ct., US Tax Ct., US Ct. of Mil. Appeals, US Ct. of Appeals for the Federal Circuit, and other state and fed. cts.; del. Calif. State Bar Conv.; mem: AIAA, Assn. of Naval Aviation, Lawyer/Pilots Bar Assn., Assn. of Trial Lawyers of Am., Christian Legal Soc.; Phi Alpha Delta Internat. Law frat., Tau Kappa Epsilon; mem. Malibu Hist. Soc.; articles in law revs., law journals; Christian; rec: flying, skydiving, soaring, scuba diving. Address: POB 9606 Marina del Rey 90291

WELK, ROBERT EDWARD, transportation co. executive; b. Oct. 11, 1925, San Diego; s. Edward Wm. and Iva Marie (Stokes) W. Career: employed in mktg. dept. Santa Fe Railway Co., Calif. 1945-60; spl. assignment (re Western Pac. merger case) in Exec. Dept., San Francisco 1960-61; adminstrv. asst. to Calif. Law Dept. 1962, asst. to v.p./exec. rep., Los Angeles 1967; asst. to pres. and chmn., Chgo. 1977; western vice pres./pres. Calif. rail subsidiaries, 1979 –; permanent mem. Gov. Deukmejian's Com. on Apptmts.; dir. Calif. State R.R. Mus.; mem. Calif. State World Trade Commn. and Gov.'s Advis. Council on Econ. Devel.; corp. bd. mem. Blue Shield of Calif.; mem. Bd. of Councillors USC; mem. Pres.'s Club, Univ. of San Diego; dir: Merchants & Mfr's Assn., Calif. CofC, Bay Area Council; clubs: California (LA), Pacific-Union (SF), World Trade (SF); honors: Outstanding Young Man, City of Berkeley 1957, US Jr. CofC; Calif. Senate Resolution 1977. Ofc: The Atchison, Topeka & Santa Fe Railway Co., 114 Sansome St, Ste 1407, San Francisco 94104

WELLER, JEFFREY MARK, accountant; b. May 8, 1950, Palo Alto; s. James H. and Ruth E. (Feathers) W.; edn: BA, Univ. of Ore. 1972; Certified Public Acct., Ore. (1974) and Calif. (1976). Career: staff, in-charge, senior acct. Ernst & Ernst, Portland, Ore. 1972-74; senior internal auditor Fibreboard Corp., San Francisco 1974-75; staff acct. mgmt. svcs. Ernest & Julio Gallo Winery, Modesto 1975-76; CPA self-empl., Hollister 1977 –; dir. Winn & Co. Ins. Brokers Inc., Brand Wines and Spirits Inc.; founding dir. San Benito Co. Council for the Handicapped; honors: Paul Harris Fellow, Rotary Internat. 1984; mem: Am. Inst. CPAs, Calif. Soc. CPAs, Rotary of Hollister (dir. 1983-86), First Baptist Ch. of Hollister (treas. 1978-), Central Coast Southern Baptist Assn. (treas. 1979-); Baptist; rec: sign language, golf, tennis. Ofc: Jeffrey M. Weller CPA, 345 Fifth St. Ste. 7, P.O. Box 933 Hollister 95024

WELLER, RICHARD JAMES, lawyer; b. Jan. 25, 1914, Whitefish, Mont.; s. Robert James and Theresa Bridgett (McCraig) W.; m. Daisy Mae Godden, Dec. 29, 1944; edn: PhB, Gonzaga Univ. 1938, LLB, 1940; admitted to bars of Montana (1939) and Calif. (1947); admitted to practice, US Supreme Ct., US Ct. Mil. Appeals (1954). Career: pvt. practice, Whitefish, Mont. 1940-42, San Bernardino 1947-51, 1954 –; asst. staff judge advoc. 20th A.F. 1951-53; Mobiligation Assignee, Judge Advoc. Gen. area rep., Norton AFB; gen. and appellate practice, San Bernardino; mem: Calif. State Bar Assn., Retired Ofcrs. Assn. of US, Reserve Ofcrs. Assn. of US, Orange Empire Ret. Ofcrs. Assn., Am. Legion, Knights of Columbus, Fraternal Order of Eagles; mil: lt. Col. USAFR, ret. 1974; Democrat; Catholic; rec: music, creative writing. Res: 504 E. 29th St. San Bernardino 92404 Ofc: Law Building Ste. 10, 560 No. Arrowhead Ave. San Bernardino 92401

WELLER, STEVENS, JR., lawyer; b. Jan. 13, 1925, Los Angeles; s. Stevens and Jessie Aden (Kaufman) W.; m. Margery Miller, Apr. 21, 1981; children: Sandra b. 1952, Sarah b. 1955, Stevens, III b. 1956, Bradford b. 1958; edn: AB, Stanford Univ. 1947, JD, 1950; admitted Calif. State Bar 1951, 9th Circuit Fed. Ct., US Supreme Ct. Career: assoc. atty. Larwill & Wolfe, Los Angeles 1951-54; assoc. atty. Chandler, Wright, Tyler & Ward, Los Angeles 1954-56; ptnr., senior ptnr. Walker, Wright, Tyler & Ward, 1956 –; trustee and ofcr. Chandler Sch., Pasadena and The Catalina Island Sch., Santa Catalina Is.; trustee sev. private trusts; clubs: California (LA), Valley (Montecito), Annandale Golf (Pasadena), Los Angeles Yacht, St. Francis Yacht (SF), Economic Round Table of Los Angeles; mil: lt.jg USNR, Submarine Service, 1943-46; Republican; Episcopal; rec: sailing, golf. Res: 505 So. Orange Grove Blvd., 6, Pasadena 91105 Ofc: Walker, Wright, Tyler & Ward, 626 Wilshire Blvd, Ste 804, Los Angeles 90017

WELLINS, SHELDON GARY, lawyer; b. March 21, 1944, Los Angeles; s. Lawrence Arthur and Jeanette (Schecter) W.; m. Lita Marie, Aug. 17, 1969; children: Cori Jay b. 1970, Barry b. 1974, Brian b. 1978; edn: AA, Mt. San Antonio Coll. 1964; BA in criminology Univ. Calif. 1967; JD, UC Hastings Coll. of Law 1970; admitted Calif. State Bar 1971. Career: assoc. Young, Henrie, Humphries, Mason and Wellins and predecessors, Pomona 1971-72, partner 1972-78; lawyer sole practice, Claremont 1978 –; instr. community property and family law LaVerne Coll. of Law 1974-76; judge pro tem Los Angeles Superior Ct. 1975-77, 81-; family law mediator L.A. County and San Bernardino County; past mem. Claremont City Council; mem: Calif. Attys. for Criminal Justice, L.A. Trial Lawyers Assn., L.A. County Bar Assn., ABA, Calif. Bar Assn.; Rotarian; mil: capt. mil. intell. US Army; Republican; Jewish. Res: 222 W. Lamar, Claremont 91711 Law Ofcs. Sheldon G. Wellins, 250 W First St, Ste 312, Claremont 91711

WELLS, EARL MUNCEY, communications engineer; b. Aug. 28, 1916, Phila., Pa.; s. Leroy Nelson and Anna May (Bassett) W.; m. Sylvia L. O'Shell, Sept. 14, 1940; children: James C. b. 1946, Toni J. b. 1949; edn: Drexel Inst. of Tech. 1936. Career: enlisted pvt. US Army Air Corps 1942, commnd. 2nd lt. navigator, 12/43, ret. lt. col. US Air Force, 3/65; senior project engr. Telephone Communs., Outside Plant, Gen. Tel. Co., 1966-82, ret.; senior project engr. Volt Tech. Corp., Los Angeles 1982 –; life mem. Air Force Assn., Reserve Officers Assn., VFW, Am. Legion, Moose; Democrat; Prot. Res: 4460 Monroe St Riverside 92504 Ofc: Volt Technical Corp. 6701 S Sepulveda Blvd Los Angeles 90045

WELLS, GEORGE HOWARD, computer design co. president; b. May 28, 1934, Boyertown, Pa.; s. Howard R. and Bertha (Yoder) W.; m. Nancy G. Coulter, Oct. 10, 1959; 1 dau. Laura K. b. 1966; edn: BSEE, Penn. State Univ. 1958. Career: engr. RCA, Camden, N.J.; engring. mgr. Ampex, Culver City; chief engr. Electronic Memories & Mfg., Hawthorne; current: pres. Technology Marketing Inc., Irvine; bd. chmn. Eldorado Bank, Tustin; dir. Digital Devel. Corp., San Diego; honors: Etta Kappa Nu (1958); num. patents in electronics field; mil: cpl. US Army 1953-55, Good Conduct Medal; Republican; rec: woodworking. Res: 7626 Saddlehill Trail Orange 92669 Ofc: TMI 17862 Fitch Irvine 92714

WELSH, GREGG, oral and maxillofacial surgeon; b. Jan. 4, 1945, San Leandro; s. Vincent and Pearl (Garcia) W.; m. Juli, Nov. 13, 1976; children: Suzanne Kimberly b. 1978, James David b. 1980; edn: BS, UC Santa Barbara 1967; DDS, Georgetown Univ. 1971; oral-maxillofacial surgeon, Highland General, 1975-79. Career: pvt. practice oral & maxillofacial surgery; owner/pres. GW Investments, comml. real estate investments; mem. Am. Soc. of Oral & Mxfl. Surgeons, Am./ Calif. Dental Assns., Santa Barbara Dental Soc. Res: 145 Pomar Ln, Montecito 93108 Ofc: 1515 State St, Ste. 9, Santa Barbara 93108

WELSH, WILLIAM DANIEL, physician; b. May 18, 1950, Baltimore, MD.; s. Joseph Leo and Bessie Mary (Tangiers) W.; edn: BS in biol., cum laude, Fairleigh Dickinson Univ. 1972; D.O. Coll. of Osteopathic Med. and Surg. 1975; stu. Russian lang., Johns Hopkins Univ. 1971; lic. Calif., Mich.; Diplomate Nat. Bds. 1976. Career: tng. clerkships, Mercy Hosp., Baltimore, COMS Coll. Clinics, Des Moines, Health Ashbury (S.F.) Free Clinic; intern, resident Martin Place Hosp., Madison Hgts., Mich. 1975-77; physician in partnership Family Practice Assocs., Whittier 1979 –; A.C.L.S. instr./med. dir. Family Asthma Forum 1978-; clin. instr. Coll. of Osteopathic Med. of the Pacific 1980-85, clin. assoc. prof. 1985-, mem. admissions com.; v.chief of staff, bd. dirs., med. dir. alcohol treatment pgm., chmn. emgcy. com. Whittier Hosp. Medical Ctr.; med. dir. Mirada Hills Rehab. Hosp. 1980-; honors: Phi Zeta Kappa, Recognition Awards Pathology 1973, 74; mem: osteopathic assns. of Am., Mich., Calif., Los Angeles Co.; Am. Coll. of Osteopathic Emergency Physicians; Am. Coll. of Emerg. Physicians; Am. Heart Assn.; contbr. Coll. of Osteo. Med. & Surg.; UCLA Alumni, Loyola H.S., Coll. of Osteo. Med. of the Pacific; mem. La Habra Hts. Comm. Assn., Surfside IV Homeowners; publs: edtl. NY Times; Ind.; Christian. Res: 3901 Aruba Circle Huntington Beach 92649 Ofc: 14350 E. Whittier Blvd, Ste. 100, Whittier 90603

WENDELL, PETER C., venture capitalist; b. May 16, 1950, Englewood, NJ; s. Eugene O. and Virginia M. (Robiolio) W.; m. Lynn Mellen, June 14, 1980; children: Christopher b. 1981, Brian b. 1982, Jennifer b. 1984; edn: AB, magna cum laude, Princeton Univ. 1972; MBA, w/high distinction, Harvard Univ. 1976. Career: served as corp. exec. in Data Processing Div., holding 5 positions, IBM Corp., NYC, White Plains and Chgo., 1972-81; served as asst. to Dr. Geo. Gallup Poll, Inc., Princeton, NJ 1971-772; pres., gen. ptnr. Sierra Ventures Mgmt. Co., $75 million venture capital fund, Menlo Park, Calif. and NYC; corp. dir.: Unicon Internat., Berkeley; Datacopy Corp., Mountain View, Calif.; Laserscope, Inc., Santa Clara; The Prospect Group, Inc., NYC; Centex Telecommunications, Inc., San Francisco; CGX, Inc., Acton, Mass.; Environmental Testing Corp., Edison, NJ; mem: Princeton Univ. Annual Giving Cpgn. (exec. com.); NY Athletic Club; Harvard Club of NYC; Princeton Club of NYC; Univ. Cottage Club (Princeton), Hasty Pudding Club (Cambridge); publs: Journal of Higher Edn. (1980, Ohio State Univ. Press); Catholic; rec: squash, running, lacrosse. Res: 3550 Washington St, San Francisco 94118 Ofc: Sierra Ventures, 3000 Sand Hill Rd, Menlo Park 94025

WENTWORTH, THEODORE SUMNER, personal injury lawyer; b. July 18, 1938, Brooklyn, NY; s. Theodore S., Sr., and Alice Ruth (Wortmann) W.; m. Sharon Arkush, Mar. 26, 1965; children: Christina Lind b. 1968, Kathryn Allison b. 1969; edn: JD, UC Hastings Coll. of Law 1962. Career: assoc. atty. Adams, Hunt & Martin, Santa Ana 1963-66; partner Hunt Lillestrom & Wentworth 1967-77; owner Law Offices of Theodore S. Wentworth, 1978 – ; pres. InterProfessional Leasing Inc. 1970-78; dir. Don Burns Inc. and Don Burns Prestige Porsche Audi (Garden Grove), 1970-76; owner Rancho Oro Verde, Pauma Valley 1970-78; pres. Santa Ana -Tustin Community Chest 1972; mem. bd. dirs./v.p. So. Orange Co. United Way 1973-4; pres. O.C. Fedn. of Funds 1972-3; bd. dirs. O.C. Mental Hlth Assn. 1971-4; mem: State Bar, O.C. Bar (bd. dirs. 1972-6), Amer. Trial Lawyers Assn., Calif. Trial Lawyers Assn. (bd. govs. 1968-70), O.C. Trial Lawyers Assn. (pres. 1967-8); Judge pro tem, Attys. Panel 1968-; Diplomate Nat. Bd. of Trial Advocates; Lawyer Pilot Bar Assn.; Aircraft Owners & Pilots Assn.; clubs: Balboa Bay (Newport Bch), Bahia Corinthian Yacht (Newport Bch), Club 33 (Anaheim); works: Vedic researcher synthesizing Eastern & Western laws of living in conjunction with num. Vedic scholars in India; Republican; Christian - Vedic. Res: 3 Malibu Circle, Corona del Mar 92625 Law Ofcs. of Theodore S. Wentworth, 2112 Business Center Dr, Irvine 92715

WENTZ, LEWIS EUGENE, lawyer; b. June 20, 1955, Lincoln, Nebr.; s. Laurence Eugene and Erma Jean (Bickel) W.; m. Nina Freeman, Oct. 23, 1982; edn: BS in bus./fin., CSU Chico 1977; JD, Western State Univ. Coll. of Law 1980; admitted to Calif. State Bar 1981. Career: solo law practice in Placerville 1981 – , incl. family law, criminal law, general civil practice; judge pro tem, El Dorado Co. Justice Ct.; mem: El Dorado Dounty Lawyer Referral Svc. (bd. dirs.), El Dorado Co. Bar Assn., Kiwanis Club, Toastmasters Intl.; Democrat; Baptist; rec: landscape painting, travel, swimming. Res: 688 Village Circle Dr Atwater 95301 Ofc: Lewis E. Wentz, Atty. 78 Main St Placerville 95667

WERBER, JEFFREY IRA, veterinarian; b. Dec. 14, 1954, Bklyn.; s. Victor Paul and Ricky Ruth (Schreiber) W.; m. Mara Allenstein, Sept. 6, 1981; children: Rana b. 1983, Brandon b. 1985; edn: AB zool., UC Berkeley 1976; MS biol., CSU Northridge 1978; DVM, UC Davis 1984; lic. Veterinarian, Calif. State Board 1984. Career: assoc. veterinarian Culver City Animal Hosp., Culver City 1984 – , spl. interest in veterinary clin. oncology; awards: George Hart Meml. Scholar, UCD 1982-84, Phi Zeta (1983), Phi Kappa Phi (1984), National Dean's List (1983-84, 84-85); mem: AM. Animal Hosp. Assn., Am. Vet. Med. Assn., Calif. Vet. Med. Assn., So. Calif. Vet. Med. Assn., Vet. Cancer Soc.; civic: Le Tip Internat. (bd. dirs. Westwood Chpt.), Beverly Hills High Sch. (pre-veterinary advisor 1984-); writer/co-prod. segments on current and popular pet related topics for local t.v. news pgmmg. (1984-); Democrat; Jewish; rec: racquetball, waterskiing, weight lifting. Res: 3434 Bentley Ave Los Angeles 90034 Ofc: Culver City Animal Hospital 5830 W Washington Blvd Culver City 90232

WERMAN, THOMAS EHRLICH, record producer; b. Mar. 2, 1945, Newton, Mass.; s. Lester and Ruth (Ehrlich) W.; m. Susan Gould, Aug. 25, 1968; children: Julia b. 1973, Nina b. 1976, Daniel b. 1982; edn: BA, Columbia Univ. 1967; MBA, Columbia Grad. Sch. Bus. 1969. Career: acct. exec. Grey Advtg. NY 1969-70; asst. dir., then dir. A&R, exec. producer, v.p. CBS Records 1970-82; senior v.p. A&R Elektra Records 1982; pres. Julia's Music Inc. 1982 – ; honors: Civilian Commdn. Medal for Bravery (NY 1965), 12 Platinum, 6 Gold Record Awards (Recording Ind. Assn. of Am.); mem. Nat. Assn. Recording Arts & Scis.; producer 42 long-playing record albums and tapes; Democrat; Jewish; rec: running, golf, bicycling. Ofc: Julia's Music Inc. 3960 Laurel Canyon Blvd Ste 107 Studio City 91604

WERNER, SCOTT DALE, civil engineer; b. Apr. 26, 1957, St. Louis, Mo.; s. Marvin Jay and Peggy Ann (Gershon) W.; edn: BSE, civil engring., Ariz. State Univ., Tempe 1980; MBA, fin., CSU Los Angeles 1984; Reg. Civil Engr., Calif. 1984. Career: jr. civil engr. Calif. Dept. Transp., L.A. 1980-82, asst. transp. engr., 1982-85, assoc. transp. engr., 1985 – , program coordinator transp. projects in Los Angeles, Orange and Ventura Counties; cons. NPC, Inc. 1985-; honors: Beta Gamma Sigma; recipient appreciation, Nat. Assn. of Accts. (1984); contbr. article, Management Accounting mag.; rec: skiing. Res: 441 Pass Ave Apt 9 Burbank 91505

WESLEY, PHILLIP, librarian; b. June 3, 1930, Los Angeles; s. George Gregor and Olive Vessie (Barnette) W.; edn: AA, Glendale Coll. 1950; BA, UC Los Angeles 1956; MS, USC 1959. Career: senior library asst. UCLA Law Library, 1955-58; bindery clk., acquisitions librarian, cataloger Los Angeles County Law Library, 1958-59; ltd. loan and serials librarian CSU Los Angeles Library, 1959-60; acquisitions librarian Los Angeles County Law Library, 1960-61, reference librarian, 1961-62, head catalog librarian, 1961-6; head catalog librarian CSU Northridge, 1966-67, chief tech. services, 1967-69, acting coll. librarian, 1969; dir. ednl. resources center CSU Dominguez Hills, 1969-77,

dean ednl. resources, 1977 – ; mem. Am. Assn. Law Libraries, So. Calif. Assn. Law Libraries (pres. 1964-65), Spl. Libraries Assn. (chpt. treas. 1969-70), So. Calif. Tech. Processes Group (pres. 1;972-74), Am., Calif. library assns. Res: 2287 Panorama Terrace, Los Angeles 90039 Ofc: 1000 E Victoria St Carson 90747

WESSELHOFF, ROBERT EARL, aerospace engineering executive, ret.; b. Mar. 25, 1924, Detroit, Mich.; s. Ernest Earl and (step) Bethel Mary (Ely) W.; m. Betty Larsen, Oct. 27, 1945; edn: BS mech. engring., honors, Northeastern Univ. 1949; spl. courses UCLA Ext., co. sponsored courses, 1950-65; Reg. Profl. Engr., Calif. (1955). Career: engr. Teledyne Ryan Aeronautical Co., San Diego 1949-81: aero. engr. Aero. Perf. & Stability & Control 1949-58; group engr. 1958-60; senior group engr. Target Drones, V/STOL, Vertifan Aero 1960-66; engring. mgr. in chg. Tech. Sci. 1966-69; tech. dir. 1969-70; engring. mgr. 1970-71; exec. engr./ tech. asst. to Program Mgr. 1971; tech. splst. Aero. & Flt. Test 1971-81; ret., disabled 1981; in chg. technical scis. for aerial, unmanned reconnaissance vehicles (Top Secret pgm.) 1960-69, and served as co. cons. overseas 1968, 73; mem. ASME (student 1948-49), Elks (1971-84); publs: num. tech. papers and proposals for TRA; musician (First pl. music award for flute in Mich., 1942; Gold music award in high sch., 1942), mem. S.D. County Symphony and La Jolla Civic Orch. 1959-61; mil: aircraft carrier fighter pilot WWII 1942-45, ensign, naval aviator USNR; United Methodist; rec: symphony, opera, gardening. Res: 3640 Saddle Dr Spring Valley 92077

WEST, JAMES HAROLD, accounting co. executive, b. Oct. 11, 1926, San Diego; s. Robert Reed and Clara Leona (Moses) W.; m. Jerel Lynn Smith, Nov. 16, 1976; children: Timothy James, James Nelson; edn: BS, USC 1949; Certified Public Acct. (CPA), Calif. 1949. Career: ptnr. McCracken & Co., San Dieo 1950-61; mgr. Ernst & Ernst, S.D. 1961-64; pres./CEO West, Johnston, Turnquist & Schmitt 1964 – ; mem. Calif. Soc. CPAs (dir. 1963-64); civic: Am. Red Cross (bd. govs. 1984-), Combined Arts & Edn. Council of San Diego County (pres., dir. 1980-83), San Diego Hosp. Assn. (dir. 1981-), Calif. Western Sch. of Law (trustee 1985-), USC Sch. of Acctncy. (bd. advisors 1985-); mil: US Army 1945-46; Republican; rec: civic and charitable activities. Res: 3311 Lucinda St San Diego 92106 Ofc: West, Johnston, Turnquist & Schmitt 2550 Fifth Ave Ste 1009 San Diego 92103

WEST, STEPHEN FRANKLIN, retail pizza chain co. president; b. June 10, 1959, Whiteville, N.C.; s. Franklin and Jeanette (Wilkes) W.; m. Mry Beth, Feb. 5, 1986; edn: BSBA, East Carolina Univ. 1981. Career: driver (p.t. while coll. student), then mgr. in tng., Domino's Pizza, No. Caro., 1979-81, mgr. 1981-84; founder/owner/pres. West Coast Pizza, Inc., Visalia, Calif. 1984 – , currently op. 6 stores; honors: Hustle Award (1983), Hungry Eagle Award (1984). Res: 1730 S Thomas St Visalia 93277 Ofc: WEst Coast Pizza, Inc. 3745 West Caldwell Ste E Visalia 93277

WESTLUND, CHARLES GERALD, engineer, systems executive; b. Aug. 23, 1923, Boston; s. Charles Reinhold and Hulda Leonida (Nelson) W.; m. G. Margaret Schwartz, Nov. 23, 1963; children: Charles, Jr. b. 1965, James H. b. 1967, Frances Margaret b. 1968; edn: BS, mech. eng. Northeastern Univ. 1948; cert. indsl. mgmt. 1968, cert. bus. 1971, CSU Long Beach. Career: hydraulics and pneumatics engring. splst.; branch chief engr. to dir. Systems & Equipment McDonnel Douglas Aircraft, 1948 – , functioned as adminstr., cons., instr., negotiator, designer, head leader on B-66 Destroyer, C-133 Cargomaster, DC-9, DC-10; bd. dirs. Calif. Auctioneer Commn.; F.A.A. designate; recipient honorary award Long Beach Unified Sch. Dist.; mem. Soc. of Automotive Engrs.; civic: Wilson Boosters, Community Advis. Bd. (chmn.); mil: T3 US Army 1942-46; Republican; Episcopal; rec: carpentry, people. Res: 1250 Knoxville Long Beach 90815 Ofc: McDonnell Douglas Aircraft 3855 Lakewood Blvd Long Beach 90846

WESTMILLER, ROBIN COHEN, business owner; b. Dec. 11, 1953, Ellenville, N.Y.; d. Rubin and Reginia (Gross) Cohen; m. William Westmiller, Oct. 18, 1980; children: Tandy b. 1982, Kimberly b. 1984; edn: BS, Syracuse Univ. 1976. Career: program dir., radio announcer Sta. WELV-AM-FM, 1975-79; mgr. Promenade Radio Shack Store, Woodland Hills 1979-80, Eagle Rock Store 1980-81, Glendale Galleria Store 1981-82; Weight Watchers lectr. 1982-84; v.p. mktg. The Soft Place, software mktg., 1983-84; founder/pres. Westmiller & Assocs., profl. speakers' bureau, 1984 – ; presenter: the Daytime Drama Symposium, Soap Opera Profls., for cols. and gen. public audiences; mem: Meeting Planners Internat., Bus. & Profl. Women, Calif. Women Business Owners, Internat. Group of Agents and Bureaus (exec. bd.), Nat. Assn. of Coll. Activities (assoc.), Sigma Kappa 1973; publs: articles in Weight Watchers Mag. (3/83), Glendale News Press (1983); guest on Women to Women TV show (1983); Republican; Jewish; rec: diarist. Ofc: Westmiller & Associates POB 7370 Glendale 91205

WESTMORELAND, HAROLD VERNON, JR., corp. operations executive; b. Aug. 22, 1946, Berkeley; s. Harold Vernon and Nellie Marie (Cargill) W.; m. Rebecca Blasing, Nov. 11, 1977; children: Harold, III b. 1964, Sonny b. 1971; edn: BBA, Pacific Western Univ. 1982. Career: mgr. computer ops. Hughes Air West, Phoenix, Az. 1970-77; supr. computer ops. Gesco Corp., Fresno 1977-78, mgr. computer ops. 1978-81, asst. v.p. 1981-83, v.p. ops., 1983 – ; mem: Data Processing Mgmt. Assn. (pres. 1983), Am. Mgmt. Assn.; civic: Babe Ruth Baseball (coach), PTA; mil: sgt. USAF, 1963-69, Vietnam Campaign, Vietnam Service, Good Conduct medals; Democrat; Catholic. Res: 6735 N Baird Fresno 93710 Ofc: GEsco Corp. 3747 E Shields Ave Fresno 93726

WESTOVER, DONALD ERWIN, civil engineer; b. Sept. 25, 1914, Grand Island, Nebr.; s. Leo Adelbert and Bertha Mabel (Patton) W.; m. Winifred Brownell, Sept. 12, 1937; children: Douglas Erwin b. 1938, Constance Lee (Hasemann) b. 1943; edn: Univ. Nebr. Coll. of Engring. 1934-37; Reg. Civil Engr. (Calif., Nebr., Colo., Kans., Wyo., Wis., Mass., Ore., Ariz., and D.C.) 1939-. Career: constrn. engr. pvt. practice, Nebr. and Iowa 1937-41, 1945-49; US Army Corps of Engrs. Omaha, Nebr. 1941-43, E.I. duPont de Nemours & Co., Hanford, Wash. 1943-44; Morrison-Knudsen Co. Inc., Fairbanks, Ala. and Caracas, Venez. S.A., 1949-52; div. mgr. Stearns-Roger Co., Denver, Colo. 1967-69; prin. & mng. engr. Utah Contrn. Co. (U.C.& M. Co.) (Fluor-Utah) in San Francisco and var. locations 1952-60, 63-66, 69-73; chief engr. Hunkin-Arundel-Dixon Constrn. Co., Silver Bay, Minn. 1960-63; mgr. Estimate & Control, Davy-McKee Corp. (Constr.), San Mateo 1973-79, ret.; mem: Fellow ASCE, Soc. Am. Mil. Engrs., Mason (32 degree), Shriners; publs: Estimating Technical Standards (Construction) 3 Vols.; Nebraska Hospitals (A review and analysis of plng., constrn. & financing); Republican; Anglican; rec: photog., cabinetry, R.R. buff. Res: 85 West 5th Ave Apt 302 San Mateo 94402

WESTOVER, SAMUEL LEE, health maintenance organization executive; b. May 30, 1955, Soap Lake, Wash.; s. Gordon Kent and Janice Lelia (Matlock) W.; m. Susan Kern, July 13, 1977; children: Michael b. 1980, Fielding b. 1981, Austin b. 1978; edn: BS acctg., Brigham Young Univ. 1978; CPA Calif. 1981. Career: CFO OLP Landcorp Inc. Orem, Utah 1977-79; staff acct. Price Waterhouse & Co. Los Angeles 1979-81; asst. controller HCMG Inc. Hawthorne 1981; dir. systems & procedures Maxicare Hawthorne 1981-82, controller 1982, CFO, v.p. finance Los Angeles 1982-; mem: Am. Inst. CPAs, Calif. Soc. CPAs, Nat. Acctg. Assn., Hosp. Financial Mgmt. Assn., Financial Execs. Inst., BYU Health Advisory Com.; Republican; L.D.S. Ofc: Maxicare Health Plans Inc. 5200 W Century Blvd Los Angeles 90045

WESTRUM, MEDARDY SEIVERT, artist, fabric designer; b. Apr. 8, 1942, Tacoma, Wash.; s. Ole Sivert and Marcella Ann (Lesnick) W.; edn: Univ. San Francisco 1960-63; Univ. Md. Madrid 1963-64; Univ. Toulouse 1964. Career: internationally known floral & still life painter, fabric designer, studios in NY, Madrid, Ibiza, Cairo, San Francisco; paintings in world's leading collections; fabric design installations include White House for Pres. & Mrs. Reagan, former Pres. Carter, Bob Hope, Sam Cannell, Bel Air Hotel, Pebble Beach Lodge, Royal Hawaiian, Huntington Hotel; paintings reproduced by Hedgerow House NY; bd. dirs. Franciscan Fabrics 1969-80, Kassel Corp. 1981-82, Franciscan-Ngor, S.A., Paris 1976-80; paintings and designs featured in num. publs. incl. Archtl. Digest, House & Garden, Southern Accents, Interior Design, Decorating Am. Style; major exhibitions include Palm Beach (Fla.) Galleries (1969, 71, 74, 76, 84), Eric Galleries NYC (1972, 74), Lord & Taylor Galleries (1975), Nantucket Gallery (1969, 72), Robinson Galleries, Naples (1977) Petoskey (1974); mil: sp. US Army 1965-67, Good Conduct; Republican; rec: skiing, fly fishing, languages. Address: 514 Connecticut St San Francisco 94107

WEUL, DAVID GEORGE, veterinarian; b. Nov. 24, 1941, Oakland; s. Raymond Frederick and Frances Katheryn (Bredimus) W.; div.; children: Timothy b. 1966, Sonya b. 1970; edn: BS, UC Davis 1963, DVM, 1965. Career: dir./coptnr. Hensley-Crundwell and Weule Animal Hosp., Burbank 1966-79; expert in internal medicine and toxicol., Calif. Courts 1967-; city veterinarian, Cities of Burbank and Glendale, 1975-, also vet. dir. Burbank, Glendale Police Canine Corps; pres./dir. Rainbow Veterinarian Hosp., 1979-; dir./researcher in effects of sound and light on bacteria, Biometric Research Found., Los Angeles 1975-85; lectr. on canine med. and drug therapy, Am. Univ. of Beriut, Lebanon 1981; cons. in animal nutrition, Purina Corp., St. Louis, Mo. 1982; honors: Calif. Cattle Judging Champion, S.L.O. (1954), USA Cattle Judging Champion, Des Moines, Iowa (1955); research: chem. toxicology and poison control (1961-65), impact of D.D.T. on cattle (1965), UCD; high altitude vascular studies, White Mt. Research Sta. (1963); mem: So. Calif. Vet. Med. Assn. (pres. 1969, dir. greivances 1986), Optimist Club, Masons, Theta Xi; Republican; Theosophist. Ofc: Rainbow Vet. Hospital 2321 Empire Ave Burbank 91504

WEXLER, STEPHEN CHARLES, construction consulting co. president; b. Sept. 9, 1942, Boston, Mass.; s. Irving and Leona (Hurwitz) W.; m. Bette Cole, Nov. 2, 1983; children: Peter b. 1967, Jeffrey b. 1970; edn: BSCE Univ. of Mass. 1964; MBA, Univ. of Mich. 1967; Reg. Profl. Engr., Calif., Mass.; desig: Cert. Profl. Estimator (CPE), Cert. Cost Engr. (CCE), Cert. Constrn. Specifier (CCS); Cert. Proj. Mgmt. Profl. (CPMP). Career: proj. engr. Wexler Constrn. Co. Inc., Newton, Mass. 1960-65; proj. mgr. Jackson Const. Co. Inc., Needham, Mass. 1967-69; v.p. Walden Constrn. Co., Acton, Mass. 1969-71; constrn. cons. prin./ pres. Computrol Corp., 1969, pres. Systematic Assocs. Inc., Needham 1971-78, pres. Stephen C. Wexler & Assoc. Inc., Wellesley, Mass. 1978-81; pres./CEO Wexco International Corp., Los Angeles 1982-; instr. constrn. mgmt. UCLA Ext.; honors: Tau Beta Pi; mem: Assoc. Builders & Contrs., Assoc. Gen. Contrs., Bldg. Indus. Assn., Am. Arbitration Assn. (arbitor), Am. Soc. Profl. Estimators, Project Mgmt. Inst., Soc. for Mktg. Profl. Svcs., Am. Assn. of Cost Engrs., Constrn. Spec. Inst.; inventor: Precedence Diagramming Template; publ: Handbook of CPM Programming; creator Wexpro Const. Mgmt. & Project Controls System Pgm.; rec: pvt. pilot, scuba. Res: Marina del Rey Ofc: Wexco Internat. Corp. 1900 Ave of the Stars Ste 1100 Los Angeles 90067

WHALING, SEAN KEVIN, architect; b. Aug. 28, 1957, Miami Beach; s. Thomas Michael and Marie Louie (Marich) W.; edn: BS arch., honors, Cal Poly S.L.O. 1980; Calif. lic. Building Contr., Reg. Architect. 1985. Career: civil engr./ draftsman Dave Mac Arthur Assocs., Fullerton 1979; architl.

designer Robert Savage Assocs., Santa Ana 1980-84; constrn. adminstr. Builders West, Santa Ana 1980-84; project architect Robert Altevers Assocs., Costa Mesa 1984-; honors: A.I.A. high sch. competition honor award, Dean's list CalPoly; mem. Am. Inst. of Arch.; Republican; Catholic; rec: printmaking (etching, serigraphy, lithography). Res: 320 B Santa Isabel Costa Mesa 92627 Ofc: Robert Altevers Co. 2915 Redhill Ste F-107 Costa Mesa 92626

WHARTON, DONALD EDWARD, lawyer; b. Oct. 26, 1953, London, Eng.; s. Donald Edgar and Donyne E. (Chapin) W.; m. Pamela Port, Dec. 20, 1980; child, Sara Dawn, b. Nov. 2, 1982; edn: JD, Golden Gate Univ. Sch. of Law 1977, MBA in Taxation, Golden Gate Univ. 1978, BA in psychology & econ., UC Davis, 1974, admitted Calif. State Bar. Honors: Second Prize, 1977 I.H. Prinzmetal Writing Competition for art. on Fifth Amendment; assoc. editor Golden Gate Law Rev. 1975-77; mem: State Bar of Calif. (Bus. Law Section, Estate Planning Sect., Probate Law Sect.), Sacramento County Bar Assn.; bd. dirs. Big Brothers/ Sisters of Greater Sacto.; publs: The Fifth Amendment and Property Value Diminution Resulting from a Rezoning: The Calif. Approach, Beverly Hills Bar Assn. Jour. 1978; Republican; Mormon; rec: golf, tennis, basketball. Res: 7905 Cottonleaf Way, Sacramento 95828 Ofc: Donald E. Wharton Inc., 1330 21st St, Ste. 200, Sacramento 95814

WHEELER, HOWARD WILLIAM, certified public accountant; b. Apr. 28, 1957, Alhambra; s. Howard Woodrow and Jean Louise (Tate) W.; m. Heidi Jensen, June 16, 1979; edn: AA, Coll. of the Sequoias 1977; BS, magna cum laude, CSU Fresno 1979. Career: supvr. Wheeler Trucking, Tulare 1975-9; audit supvr. Fox & Co., Fresno 1979-84; audit mgr. Arthur Young & Co., Fresno 1984-; instr. in local ofc. tng. pgms. for Arthur Young & Co.; volunteer income tax asst. (V.I.T.A.) Pgm. 1979, assisting. elderly, low income, minority people; mem: Calif. Soc. of CPAs; Am. Inst. of CPAs; Nat. Assn. Accts. (pres. 1981-85); CSU Fresno Alumni Assn.; Sigma Nu Alumni Assn.; Beta Alpha Psi; Beta Gamma Sigma (life); Lions Club; Organized, directed seminars qualifying as Continuing Profl. Edn. on pension plans and Lotus 1-2-3; Democrat; rec: model railroad, furniture refinishing, gardening. Res: 1260 W Dyer Fresno 93711 Ofc: Arthur Young & Co., 1111 Van Ness Ave Fresno 93721

WHITE, ANDREW MILLAR, trial lawyer; b. Dec. 19, 1947, Dayton, Ohio; s. John Clyde Jr. and Martha Louise (Smith) W.; m. Elisa Berte Newman, Jan. 2, 1981; children: Jennifer Louise b. 1982, Jonathan Newman b. 1985; edn: Northwestern Univ. 1964; BA, cum laude, Yale Uni. 1969; JD, Stanford Law Sch. 1974; admitted to Calif. Bar 1974. Career: assoc. atty. Wyman, Bautzer, Rothman, Kuchel & Silbert, Los Angeles 1974-78, ptnr. 1978-; adj. instr. of law Loyola Law Sch., Los Angeles 1978-79; Judge Pro Tem, Beverly Hills Municipal Ct. and Small Claims Ct. 1979-; honors: Nat. Merit Scholarship, Yale Univ. 1965-69; mem: Am., Calif., Los Angeles Co. and Beverly Hills Bar Assns.; co-author: article, Role of Awareness and Intentions in Observational Learning, Journ. of Personality & Social Psychology, 1970; Democrat; Episcopal; rec: golf, tennis, bicycling. Ofc: Wyman, Bautzer, Rothman, Kuchel & Silbert, 2049 Century Park East Ste. 1400 Los Angeles 90067

WHITE, BRITTAN ROMEO, manufacturing co. executive; b. Feb. 13, 1936, NY, NY; s. Brittan R. and Matilda Hazel (Baumann) W.; m. Esther Friederich, Aug. 25, 1958 (dec. 1981); children: Cynthia b. 1963, Brittan b. 1968; edn: BS in chem. engring., Drexel Univ. 1958; MBA, Lehigh Univ. 1967; JD, Loyola Law Sch. 1974; MA, Pepperdine Univ. 1985; admitted Calif. State Bar and Fed. Dist. Cts., 1974. Reg. Profl. Engr., Calif. 1978; Certified Purchasing Mgr., Nat. Assn. Purch. Mgmt. 1975. Career: process engr. Air Reduction chem. Co., Bound Brook, N.J. 1958-64; area supr. J.T. Baker Chem. Co., Phillipsburg, N.J. 1964-66; asst. plant mgr. Gamma Chem. Co., Great Meadows, N.J. 1966-69; plant mgr. Maquite Corp., Elizabeth, N.J. 1969-70; mgr. Refinery Purchasing, Atlantic Richfield Co., Los Angeles 1970-79; dir. mfg. Imperial Oil & Grease Co., L.A. 1979-82; mgr. Spl. Projects, Hughes Aircraft Co., L.A. 1982-; founder, dir. Diversified Resource Devel., Inc. 1979-; speaker and moderator, Putman Pub. Co. Energy Conservation Seminars, 1979-; chief judge Vaaler Award for Engrin. Excellence, Chemical Processing Mag.; honors: Psi Chi (1984-); mem: Am. Inst. Chem. Engrs., Am. Chem. Soc., Am. Bar Assn., Nat. Assn. Purch. Mgmt., Elks; v.chmn. Zoning Bd., Flemington, N.J. 1970-72; publs: designer/ ed./ pub. Rottweiler Review (show dog breed mag.) 1979-81; contbr. articles in Chemical Purchasing, Chemical Processing mags.; mil: capt. US Army Corps of Engrs., Active and Reserves 1958-68; Republican; rec: antiques, psychology. Res: 3664 Vigilance Dr Rancho Palos Verdes 90274 Ofc: Hughes Aircraft Co. 7200 Hughes Terr, POB 45066, Los Angeles 90066

WHITE, C(HARLES) BERNARD, consulting engineer; b. May 5, 1904, Truckee; s. Charles B. and Belle (Sullivan) W.; m. Thelma Wachhorst, June 12, 1937; 1 dau: Marilee, b. 1942; edn: Univ. of Nev. 1923-27; Reg. Profl. Engr. Calif., Nev. Career: surveyor King & Malone Engineers 1926; engr. Sierra Pacific Power Co. 1927-34; hydrographer Nevada State Engr., valuation engr. Calif. Bd. of Equalization 1934-47; chief valuation engr. & cons. Nevada Tax Commn. 1947-51; cons. engr. and appraiser Sacramento 1951-; mem: Sacramento Co. Tax Appeals Bd. 1968-81; awards: Blue Key, Univ. of Nev.; mem: ASCE (fellow, life); Placer Co. Real Estate Bd.; Am. Inst. of Real Estate Appraisers (life); E Clampus Vitus; Sigma Alpha Epsilon; Del Paso Country Club; Masons; Scottish Rite (life); Shriner; Sutter Club; Grandfathers of Am.; Sacto. Traditional Jazz Soc. Tailgate musician; Republican; rec: Sacto Banjo Band, past. pres., musical dir. Res: 4510 Capri Way Sacramento 95822

WHITE, DOUGLAS JAMES, special effects makeup artist; b. Oct. 14, 1953, Grove City, Pa.; s. Russell Noel and Coral W.; m. Cheryl Wegner, Nov. 24,

1985; 1 dau. Celeste Wegner. Career: apprentice w/ Mr. Byrd Holland 1972-73; repairman Tinder Box Inter. 1974-78; apprentice w/ Tom Burman 1978; makeup artist Disneyland Christmas Parade 1978; ptnr. (w/Allan A. Apone and John Fifer) Makeup Effects Labs 1979–; artist, sculptor, inventor. Ofc: Makeup Effects Lab. 7110 Laurel Cyn N Hollywood 91605

WHITE, GERALD BOOTH, consulting engineer; b. June 18, 1923, Omaha, Nebr.; s. Charles T. and Lucille (Booth) W.; m. Virginia Newman, Oct. 1, 1946; children: Nannette b. 1947, James b. 1949, Gerald, Jr. b. 1951, Amy Jo b. 1954, Thomas b. 1955, Robert b. 1958, Carol b. 1960; edn: BSAE, Univ. of Notre Dame 1950; MSAE, Georgia Tech. 1953; postgrad. M.I.T. 1955, Purdue Univ. 1957. Reg. Profl. Engr. Career: aerodynamist Convair, Ft. Worth, Tx. 1950-51; senior scientist engr. Midwest Research Inst., Kansas City, Mo. 1951-55; tech. dir. US Army Airborne Test Activity, Yuma, Az. 1955-61; mgr. customer rels. Interstate Electronics Corp., Anaheim 1961-65; spl. engineer Lockheed Missile and Space Co., Polaris Weapon System 1962; engring. mgr. Philco-Ford Joint Parachute Test Facility Range Ops., NAF El Centro 1965; (current) cons. engr.; provide cons. svcs. to indsl. cleaning and air pollution control systems in US, USSR, Turkey and other internat. locations, associated technol. assistance to environmental considerations such as Lighter-Than-Air Transportation and Naval dry dock cleaning systems, plus other svcs. to NASA and DoD; mem: Nat. Resources Conf., Ind. Coll. of Armed Forces (1954-55), Am. Inst. of Aero. and Astro. (Asso. Fellow), Reg. Profl. Engrs. (Kans.), Am. Soc. of Mech. Engrs., Soc. of Am. Mil. Engrs., Aircraft Owners and Pilots Assn., Internat. Assn. of Engrs. and Archs., Paralyzed Vets. of Am., Notre Dame Alumni Assn., Notre Dame Club of San Diego, Nat. Aviation Club, Masons; contbr. tech. articles var. aeron. publs.; mil: capt., naval aviator US Marine Corps 1942-58, Pac. Theatre, D.F.C., Air Medal, Pres. Unit Cit.; Republican; Catholic; rec: aviation, photog. Address: 777 Pico Rd Sp 19 El Centro 92243

WHITE, HOWARD ASHLEY, president emeritus Pepperdine University; b. Sept. 28, 1913, Cloverdale, Ala.; s. John Parker and Mabel Clara (Hipp) W.; m. Maxcine Feltman, June 17, 1952 (dec.); children: Ashley Feltman, Howard Elliott; edn: BA, Tulane Univ. 1946, MA, 1952, PhD, 1956; ordained to ministry Ch. of Christ 1930. Career: pastor chs., New Orleans, 1941-53; prof. history, chmn. dept. David Lipscomb Coll., Nashville 1953-58; chmn. social sci. dept. Pepperdine Univ., 1958-63, dean grad. studies, dean undergrad. studies, 1963-71, exec. v.p. 1971-78, pres. 1978-85; Am. Hist. Assn., Orgn. Am. Historians, So. Hist. Assn., Rotary; author: Freedmen's Bureau in Louisiana (1970). Address: 24255 Pacific Coast Hwy., Malibu 90265

WHITE, JESSE WILLIAM, real estate developer, corporate executive; b. May 2, 1935, Coffee Co., Ala.; s. Gary Lloyd and Blondell (Cotter) W.; m. Sylvia Tofi, Nov. 17, 1962; edn: BSME, Auburn Univ. 1956; lic. real estate broker, Calif. 1974; pvt. pilot, FAA 1981. Career: research & devel. engr. Dorsey Trailers, Elba, Ala. 1956-9; field engr. Aerojet General, Sacramento 1959-61; field engr. Boeing Co., Seattle, Wash. 1961-5; sr. field engr. Eastman Kodak, Santa Maria 1965-70; real estate sales R. Chesley Co., Sunnyvale 1970-2; owner/ pres./CEO, Jud Perkins-Northern, Inc. 1973–; owner (one-third)/ pres./CEO, Millennium-New World, Inc. 1981–; independent cons. on medical bldg. projs.; honors: Tau Beta Pi, Pi Tau Sigma; recipient sev. CofC archtl. design awards; mem; Associated Builders & Contractors, Inc.; Aircraft Owners & Pilots Assn.; Full Gospel Businessmen's Fellowship Internat.; CofC of U.S.; Hayward CofC; Bethel Temple; Nat. Trust for Historic Preservation; mil: 1st lt. CNG 1959-61; Republican (Calif. Repub. Party); Assem. of God; rec: history, geog., pol. and religious study. Res: 5701 Greenridge Road Castro Valley 94552 Ofc: Millennium - New World, Inc., 3687 Thornton Ave Fremont 94536

WHITE, KEITH GORDON, architect; b. Jan. 7, 1943, Jamaica, Queens, N.Y.; s. Emanuel Gordon and Elsa Marie (Doyle) W.; m. Wilma Rooker, Oct. 23, 1982; children: Nathanael Gordon b. 1972; step: James Cole b. 1971, Alice Marie b. 1969; edn: Assoc. in Arch., Cerritos Coll. 1969; lic. Architect, Calif. (1981). Career: assoc. M.A. Nishkian & Assoc., 1963, Brady & Assocs. 1968, Architects Associated 1969, Anthony & Langford 1970, Danielian, Moon, Sampieri & Ilg 1973, Harper & Assocs. 1973, Hamilton/Doyle (Canada) 1974, Designer Keith White (Canada) 1975, architect and ptnr. Noble/White Architects, Huntington Beach 1981–; co. pres.: Designer Keith White Ltd., Concept Graphics, Rockbound Ents.; mem: Am. Inst. of Archs. (editl. com. 1981-85, awards com. 1983, judge high sch. competition 1984), Bus. Devel. Assn. of Orange County; mem. Design Review Panel (Coquitlam, B.C., Canada), Drafting Review Bd., Pacific Voc. Inst. (Surrey, B.C., Canada); contbr. poetic works to various journals and anthologies 1970-, pub. in Home Mag., selected one of top 10 California Poets of 1974, latest volumes are: Whispers in the Darkness, and The Cobblestone Manuscript; mil: Sp5 US Army 1965-67, Asia; Libertarian; rec: bowling, tennis. Res: 7675 Clay Ave Huntington Beach 92648 Ofc: Noble/White Architects, 1720 Pacific Coast Hwy Ste D Huntington Beach 92648

WHITE, LELIA CAYNE, librarian; b. Feb. 22, 1921, Berkeley; d. James Lloyd and Eulalia Fulton (Douglass) Cayne; children by previous marriage: Douglass Fulton, Cameron Jane; edn: BA, UC Berkeley 1943, MLS, 1969. Career: bibliographer, lectr., assoc. UC Berkeley Sch. Library and Information Studies, 1969-72; reference librarian Berkeley - Oakland Service Systems, 1970-76, supervising librarian, 1973-76; dir. Oakland Public Library, 1976–; mem. adv. council Bay Area Reference Center; adv. council Citizens for Better Nursing Home Care; mem. ALA, Calif. Library Assn. (Council), Calif. Inst. of Libraries (pres.), Urban Libraries Council, Public Library Assn. (pres. Met. Libraries sect.), Bay Area Libraries and Info. Systems (adminstrv. council), Oakland Pub. Library Assn. (bd. dirs.), Oakland/Dalian (China) Friendship City Soc. (pres.), East Bay NegroHist. Soc. (bd. dirs.), Calif. Spanish Lang. Data Base (bd. dirs.), LWV, Asian Shared Info. and Acquisitions (bd. dirs). Res: 1927 Napa Ave., Berkeley 94707 Ofc: 125 14th St Oakland 94612

WHITE, NANCY JOANNE, librarian; b. Oct. 1, 1953, Sharon, Penn.; d. William Roy and Lorraine Irene (Taylor) Aggers; m. Christopher White, June 27, 1975; 1 dau, Samantha Rae; edn: BA, Oberlin Coll. 1975; MLS, UC Berkeley 1980. Career: library asst. Case Western Reserve Univ., Cleveland, Ohio 1976; adminstrv. asst., clerk treas. Cleveland Area Metropolitan Library System 1976-78; med. library asst. Letterman Army Med. Ctr., San Francisco 1978-79; research asst. Sta. KIRON-TV, San Francisco 1980; reference librarian Standard Oil Co. of Calif., San Francisco 1980; Pacific Gas & Electric Co., San Francisco 1980–; library asst 1980-81; info. splst. 1981; dir. corp. library 1983–; pres. alumni bd. dirs. Grad. Sch. of Library & Info. Sci., UC Berkeley; mem: Associated Info. Mgrs., Am. Library Assn., Spl. Library Assn., Am. Soc. Info. Scientists. Ofc: Pacific Gas and Electric Co., 77 Beale St. Ste. 1096 San Francisco 94106

WHITE, PERRY ALBERT, commercial real estate brokerage president; b. Jan. 5, 1943, Hamilton, Ohio; s. Perry A., Sr. and Donnabelle (Meron) W.; m. Virginia, July 6, 1966; children: Lisa b. 1968, Perry, III b. 1973; edn: BA, Denison Univ. 1966; JD, George Washington Univ. 1969; admitted to bar: Dist. of Columbia, State of La.; Calif. lic. Real Estate Broker. Career: antitrust atty. Federal Trade Commn., 1969-75; small bus. owner, Santa Barbara 1976-83; comml. real estate broker, pres. bd. dirs. Miller and White Investments, Inc., Santa Barbara 1983–, cons. to var. syndicators 1985-; honors: Nat. Honor Soc. (1961), Varsity Letter- swimming, Denison Univ. (1963-65), Meritorious Service award, FTC (1975); mem. Louisiana Bar Assn., Santa Barbara Board of Realtors, CofC, Calif. Youth Soccer Assn., S.B. Athletic Club; rec: weightlifting, jogging, coaching youth sports. Res: 1724 Garden St Santa Barbara 93101 Ofc: Miller and White Investments, Inc. 2780 State St Ste C Santa Barbara 93105

WHITE, STEPHEN CHRYSLER, chef, restaurateur; b. Oct. 18, 1950, Oroville; s. Herbert Carl and Jeanette (Chrysler) W.; m. Amy Faber, Aug. 19, 1975; children: Magdalena b. 1980, Nathan b. 1983, Tobin b. 1985; edn: BA in sociol., UC San Diego 1973. Career: chef Restaurant La Salle, Sacto. 1973-76; sous chef La Reserve, Carqueiranne, France 1976-77; station chef L'Archestrate, Paris 1977-78; sous chef The Celler, Fullerton 1978-79; exec. chef Bel Air Sands Hotel, Bel Air 1979-81, Le Biarritz, Newport Beach 1981-83; chef/ prop. Magdalena's Cafe 1983–; recipient 3-star award (French Rest.), Calif. Rest. Writers Assn. (1985), honors in French pastry category, Orange Co. Chefs Assn. (1985); mem. Nat. Rest. Assn., Bellflower CofC; Republican; Reformed Ch. Am.; rec: collect cook books, create recipes, gardening, philately. Ofc: Magdalena's Cafe 17818 Bellflower Blvd Bellflower 90706

WHITE, W(ESLEY) GAYDEN, JR., C.P.P. security specialist; b. Oct. 2, 1926, Miami, Fla.; s. Wesley G., Sr., and Mary Lois (Bullock) W.; m. Anna Angelica, Sept. 29, 1973; children: Wesley III, b. 1950; Martha, b. 1954; edn: grad. Allen Mil. Acad. 1943; stu. Univ. of Havana, Cuba 1943, Sch. of Fgn. Services, Georgetown Univ. 194, Mexico City Coll. 1949; BA, Univ. of Miami 1950; MA, Univ. Inter-Americana, Puerto Rico 1976; Certified Protection Professional (CPP), Am. Soc. for Indsl. Security, 1977. Career: adminstrv. asst. to director State Beverage Dept. of Fla., Tallahassee 1955-61; spl. agent FBI, Wash DC 1961-69; area security mgr. for Caribbean and parts of Central and South America, ITT, San Juan, Puerto Rico 1969-81; dir. Security Ops., Latin America Caribbean Div. Bank of Am., Caracas, Venezuela 1981-83; v.p. and deputy dir. corporate security Bank of Am.- World Hdqtrs., San Francisco 1983–; served as Security Coordinator for Pan American Games, Puerto Rico 1979; cons. to Venezuelan Govt. for Pan-Am Games, Caracas 1983; mem. Curriculum Review Com., Golden Gate Univ. 1984-; mem. subcom. on Safety and Security, US Independent Telephone Assn., 1970-74; recipient Top Mgmt. Award (First in field of Security) Sales and Mktg. Assn., San Juan, Puerto Rico 1976; mem: Am. Soc. for Indsl. Security (regl. v.p. All Latin America 1979, regl. v.p. South America 1983), Law Enforcement Assn. of Puerto Rico (pres. 5 terms; now Hon. Life mem. and Permanent mem. bd. dirs.), Delta Theta Phi law frat., Delta Phi Epsilon, Nat. Fgn. Svc. and Fgn. Commerce Profl. Frat., Loch Lomond Yacht Club (San Rafael, Ca.); works: elected to full artist membership, Soc. de Bellas Artes Puertoriquenas; lectr. on Terrorism and Internat. Crisis Mgmt.; mil: USAF 1943-49; rec: sailing, painting, shooting, golf. Res: San Rafael Ofc: Bank of America, 1455 Market St, 10th Flr, San Francisco 94903

WHITE-VONDRAN, MARY ELLEN, stockbroker, educator; b. Aug. 21, 1938, East Cleveland, Ohio; d. Thomas Patrick and Rita Ellen (Langdon) White; m. Gary Lee Vondran, Nov. 25, 1961; children: Patrick Michael b. 1963, Gary Lee, Jr. b. 1964; edn: AB, Notre Dame Coll. 1960; grad. work in hist. and edn. John Carroll Univ., Univ. Mass., Univ. S. Carolina, CSU San Jose, Santa Clara Univ.; desig: Calif. Life. Sec. Tchg. Cred. (1974); Calif. Life & Disability Ins. Agent (1975), Reg. Rep., NASD (1978). Career: sch. tchr. (K-12) Ohio, Conn., Calif., 1960-62, 70-75; ins. agt. Travelers, and Businessmen's Assn., 1975-77; stockbroker (Reynolds; Bache; Shearson; Charles Schwab & Co.) 1977-80; trust adminstr. Crocker Nat. Bank, 1980-82; stockbroker Calif. Fed. Savings & Loan/ Invest 1982-83; stockbroker/br. mgr. Rose & Co. 1983-84; mem: Am. Hist. Assn., Calif. Hist. Soc., Calif. Edn. Assn., Santa Clara Co. Substitute Tchrs. Edn. Assn. (rep. Fremont Union H.S. Dist.), San Francisco Traders Assn. (Over the Counter Traders); civic: Santa Clara Univ. Kenna Club, Older Women's League, NOW (chpt. bd.), Stanford Alumni

Assn., Calif. Mechanics Library, Commonwealth Club (SF), San Antonio Hills Neighborhood Assn. (bd.), Eastbrook Sch. (advis. com.), PTA, AAUW, League Women Voters; Democrat; Catholic (parish religion tchr.); rec: world activist. Res: 1905 Quail Meadow Rd Los Altos 94022-6624

WHITEHILL, WAYNE WILLIAM, corporate president; b. Nov. 9, 1936, Shenandoah, Iowa; s. Charles Delbert and Dorothy Adeline (Ryan) W.; m. Karen Davis, July 23, 1960; children: Brenda b. 1961, Pamela b. 1963, Sandra b. 1965; edn: AA, Pasadena City Coll. 1960; Univ. So. Calif. 1961-62. Career: salesman Frieden Corp. L.A. 1962-63, Unitek Corp. Monrovia 1963-65, mgr. R&D 1965-68, dir. R&D 1968-72, v.p. ops. (div. Bristol-Myers) 1972-82, exec. v.p. 1982-84; pres. Vident Corp. Baldwin Park 1984—; pres., dir. Unitek Japan Corp. 1968-82; dir. Inter-Unitek Europe 1968-82; honors: President's Award for Excellence in Mgmt. (1982); mem: Internat. Assn. Dental Research, Calif. Inst. Technol. Exec. Forum; patent: endodontic dowel & sleeve (1971); publ: article on industry trends (Modern Dentalab Mag. 1985); mil: sgt. 1/c Army Security Agcy. 1955-57; Methodist; rec: tennis, skiing, reading, travel. Res: 1031 Don Alvarado Arcadia 91006 Ofc: Vident Corp. 5130 Commerce Dr Baldwin Park 91706

WHITMAN, LAWRENCE EMMETTE, investigative agency owner; b. March 30, 1930, Wilmington, N.C.; s. Floyd W. and Ruth (George) W.; m. My Nguyen, Jan. 9, 1967; 1 dau. Marci b. 1969; edn: bus. admin., mil. law. courses, USAF Inst. 1957-62; AA, Miami Dade Comm. Coll. 1966; cert. Counter Terrorist Intel., US DoD 1973; cert. Internat. Public Safety, Gulf States Council for Pub. Safety, Riyadh, S.A. 1982; lic. Pvt. Investigator Calif. (1978). Career: chief indsl. security, investigator for U.S. govt. contractors in So. Vietnam 1966-72; intelligence and security splst. US DoD Attache Ofc., U.S. Embassy Saigon, Vietnam 1972-75; investigator, Africa and Saudi Arabia and owner/gen. mgr. Lawrence Whitman Investigations, Long Beach 1975—; indsl. cons. on facility protection and counter-terrorism; honors: Presidential Civilian Svc. Award, Vietnam (1975); apptd. Pvt. Investigators Panel, Los Angeles Co. Superior Ct. Crim. Div. 1985-86; mem: Assn. of Fed. Investigtars (1979-80), American Club (Shanghai), PTA (Lakewood H.S.); mil: s/sgt. USAF 1950-66, 3 Presdl. Unit Cits., 2 Expeditionary, Korean Svc., Vietnam Svc.; Republican; Baptist; rec: golf, profl. research. Ofc: Lawrence Whitman Investigations, 405 E. 3rd St. Ste. 148 Long Beach 90802

WHITMORE, WILLIAM G., teacher, photographer; b. July 23, 1934, Janesville, Wisc.; s. Donald G. and Jane Elizabeth (Goff) W.; children: Robin b. 1960, Rhonda b. 1962, Melody b. 1963, Melinda b. 1965, Susan b. 1968, Samuel b. 1973; edn: BA Latin, Pacific Univ. 1960; CSU Long Beach 1978-80. Career: instr. Latin, English, speech, publications Oregon 1960-67; self-employed school yearbook industry, advtg., publg. 1967-78; instr. photog., Eng., ESL Rosemead H.S. 1980—; instr. printing design CSU Long Beach extn. 1980-85; honors: cultural attache with Mexican Consul General in Los Angeles, All-American Honor Rating (for Marine Mil. Acad. Yearbook, by Nat. Scholastic Press Assn. 1965-66); mem: local edn. assn. (pres. 1963-64, rep. to Oregon Edn. Assn.), Journalism Edn. Assn.; photog. featured in Jan. 1986 issue of Creative Photography (GB); author Creative Layout (1969), Pischel Yearbooks, Inc., Personal Almanac and Career Log (1975); current photog. work involves use of water-based dyes to hand color black-and-white prints; mil: 1st lt. USMC (active and reserve) 1953-66; Democrat. Ofc: Rosemead H.S. 9063 E Mission Dr Rosemead 91770

WHITNEY, BYRON VAN VLECK, surgeon; b. Oct. 30, 1919, Winn, Me.; s. Van Vleck B. and Mildred Lena (Clifford) W.; m. Virginia Waring, June 12, 1967; children: Byron b. 1945, Stephen b. 1947, Sandra b. 1949, Edward b. 1953; edn: AB, Univ. of Me. 1941; MD, Tufts Med. Sch. 1944; Diplomate Am. Bd. of Surgery 1960. Career: senior med. ofcr. USN light cruiser USS Vincennes 1945-46; chief surgeon USN First Marine Div. in Korea 1953-54; chief surgical res. St. Francis Hosp., Hartford, Conn. 1955-58; NIH surgical fellowship Pondville Cancer Hosp., Walpole, Mass.; surg. practice Bangor, Me. 1948-53, 1959-68, Calif. 1958-75; clin. prof. surg. New England Med. Center 1950-53; (current) chief of surgery Veterans Adminstrn., Los Angeles; clin. prof. surgery USC; mem: Fellow Am. Coll. of Surgeons (1962), Am. Cancer Soc. (dir. Santa Clara County Unit), Maine Med. Assn. (chmn. pub. rels. 1950-53), AMA, Calif. Med. Assn. 1968-75, Assn. of VA Physicians, VFW, Am. Legions, JCs, Masons, Shriners; pubs: 11 sci. publs., sci. presentations 1953, 54, 62, 73 (3), 82, 83; mil: lt. US Navy 1945-46, 1953-55, WWII, Korea and UN ribbons; Republican; Episcopal (vestryman); rec: photog., tennis, fishing, hunting. Res: 31566 Germaine Ln., Westlake Village 91361 Ofc: Veterans Administration 425 So Hill St, A303 (Mail No.112), Los Angeles 90013

WHITNEY, STEPHEN LOUIS, librarian; b. July 18, 1943, Chicago, Ill.; s. Walter Robert and Emma Agnes W.; m. Gloria Jean Lujan, June 5, 1965; children: Laura Ann, Stephen Christopher, Mark Andrew; edn: AB, Rockhurst Coll. 1965; MSLS, Case Western Reserve Univ. 1966. Career: adult svcs. librarian St. Louis Public Library 1966-67; coord. Municipal Libraray Coop. of St. Louis Co., Kirkwood, Mo. 1967-70; adminstrv. asst. to the dir. St. Louis Co. Library, Ladue, Mo. 1970-74; county librarian Broward Co. Library, Ft. Lauderdale, Fla. 1974-76; city librarian San Bernardino Public Library 1977—; librarian San Bernardino City Hist. Soc. 1978—; mem: Am. Lung Assn. (pres. 1982-), Am. and Calif. Library Assns., So. Calif. Library Film Circuit, Rotary; contbr. articles to profl. journs. Ofc: San Bernardino Public Library, 401 No. Arrowhead Ave. San Bernardino 92401

WHITTED, BRADLEY GENE, financial planner; b. July 27, 1947, Visalia; s. Bob Gene and Elfreda June (Smith) W.; m. Susan Welbrock, May 19, 1967; children: Sean b. 1972, Marci b. 1976, Sarah b. 1979; edn: Orange Coast Jr. Coll., Santa Ana Jr. Coll., Univ. of So. Calif.,Coll. for Finl. Planning, American Coll. Career: route sales Arrowhead Water (Man of the Year 1974), 1970-74; finl. planning Huston & Assocs. (Man of Yr. 1975, 79), 1975-79; founder, pres./CEO Western Capital Mgmt. Financial Corp. 1981—; regional dir. of agencies, American Mutual Life 1983.; Profl. awards incl. Million Dollar Round Table 1979, 80, 83; Golden Eagle, Am. Mutual Life 1980, 81, 82. Mem: Nat. Assn. Life Underwriters, Internat. Assn. Finl. Planners, Am. Assn. of Finl. Profls.; University Athletic Club; mil: sgt USMC 1965-69; Democrat; rec: racquetball, running. Res: 3077 Johnson Ave. Costa Mesa 92626 Ofc: WCM Financial Corp., 3723 Birch St Ste 16 Newport Beach 92660

WHOLL, IRVING MAYER, engineer; b. Aug. 30, 1919, NYC, NY; s. Abraham David and Rose (Brecker) W.; edn: BS, Brooklyn Coll. 1946; MBA, City Coll. of NY, Baruch Sch. 1953; PhD, study, NY Univ. Grad. Sch. of Bus. 1954-59; reg. engr., Calif. 1969. Career: indsl. engr. Western Electric Co., Kearny, NJ 1941-51; chief engr. to plant prodn. supt. Coty Inc., NYC 1951-59; plnng. splst., facilities and ind. engr., Corporate Hdqtrs. Rockwell Internat. 1959-78; ret. 1978; mem. mgmt. com. Coty Inc.; p.t. assoc. prof. CSU Los Angeles; standing commitee, US Dept. of Commerce Nat. Bureau of Standards; honors: Cert. of Commdn., Rockwell Internat.; mem: Am. Soc. of Mech. Engrs., Am. Assn. of Ret. Persons; mil: capt. US Army Corps of Engrs. 1942-46, Purple Heart, European African Middle East Campaign, Am. Campaign, WWII Victory; Jewish; rec: crossword puzzles, symphonic music. Res: 428 No. Hayworth Los Angeles 90048

WIBBELSMAN, NANCY CASTO BENSON, b. Feb. 19, 1949, Lancaster, Ohio; d. Frank S. and Nancy Ann (Casto) Benson Jr.; m. Patrick Nesbitt 1975, div. 1981; m. 2d. Robert John Wibbelsman (stockbroker), Sept. 2, 1984; children: (nee Nesbitt): Elizabeth Paige b. 1977, Patrick Michael Jr. b. 1978; (by spouse's prev. marriage): Robert John Jr. b. 1968, Warren Mahlor b. 1969; edn: Bradford Jr. Coll. 1967-9, Ohio State Univ. 1972, KK7 sorority; stu. Cordon Bleu, London 1973. Career: campaign chmn. for Reagan, Republican primary, Marina Del Rey, 1976; (postprimary) chmn. People for Ford, in chg of vol. groups, orgns., subcoms. in Calif., 1976; civic: Los Angeles Junior League, C.H.I.P.S. (Colleague Helpers in Philanthropic Svcs), Calif. Ballet Guild (pres. 1985), DAR; Republican; Episcopal. Res: 116 S. Anita Ave Los Angeles 90049

WICKWIRE, PATRICIA JOANNE NELLOR, psychologist, consultant; b. Sioux City, Iowa; d. William McKinley and Clara Rose (Pautsch) N.; m. Robert Wickwire, Sept. 7, 1957; 1 son, William b. 1958; edn: BA, Univ. of Northern Iowa 1951; MA, Univ. of Iowa 1959; PhD, Univ. of Texas Austin 1971; postgrad., USC, UCLA, CSU Long Beach 951-66. Career: tchr., sch. psychologist, adminstr. South Bay Union H.S. Dist. 1962—; ind. cons. in mgmt. & edn. 1981; univ. lectr.; honors: Psi Chi, Sigma Alpha Iota, Pi Lambda Theta, Alpha Phi Gamma, Kappa Delta Pi; Journalism and English awards; South Bay Woman of the Year; mem: Calif. Interagency Mental Health Council, Am. Assn. of Univ. Women (pres. 1962-72), Beach Cities Symphony Assn., CSU Dominguez Hills, Los Angeles Co. Dir. of Pupil Svcs. (pres. 1974-79), Los Angeles Co. Dir. Spl. Edn., Calif. and L.A. Co. (pres. 1977-80) Personnel & Guidance Assns., Assn. of Calif. Sch. Adminstrs., Calif. Assn. for Measurement & Evaluation in Guidance (exec. bd. pres. 1981-), Calif. Assn. of Sch. Psychologists (exec. bd. 1981-), Internat. Career Assn. Network (dir. 1985-); publs: articles in profl. journs. Address: 2900 Amby Pl. Hermosa Beach 90254

WIDENER, SCOTT CHARLES, real estate developer; b. July 4, 1959, Harbor City; s. Charles Darrow and Mary Loraine (Briand) W.; edn: BS in R.E. fin., CSU San Diego 1981; Calif. lic. Gen. Contr., Real Estate Broker. Career: asst. supt. M&M Construction, Carson 1977-81; gen. contr./prin. Restruction Development Palos Verdes 1982-83, 1984—; real estate finl. analyst American Diversified, Costa Mesa 1983-84; cons. constrn. mgmt. (1983-), real estate ltd. partnership analysis svcs. (1984-); mem. Bldg. Ind. Assn. of So. Calif.; co-inventor toy airplane (patented), other products; Republican; rec: skiing, tennis, golf. Ofc: Restruction Development PO Box 2692 Rancho Palos Verdes 90274

WIDERGREN, ROBERT DEL, company president; b. Oct. 18, 1938, Hastings, Neb.; s. Arnold Vivian and Della Sophia (Anderson) W.; m. Evelyn Mae Hill, Jan. 28, 1961; children: Jeffrey Brooks, Michael Craig; edn: BS, aero engrg., Univ. of Colo. 1960. Career: tech. staff Lockheed Missiles & Space, 1963-66; mgr. Telemetry Pgms., General Electric, 1966-70; mgr. Imagery Dept., Philco-Ford Corp., 1970-76; founder/exec. v.p. Compression Labs, Inc. 1976-79; pres./CEO Widcom, Inc., 1979—; honors: Electronic Mail and Message Systems Award of distinction for wk. in video digital codecs 1983; patents: facsimile and television compression technology; mil: lt. jg, USN; Republican; Rel. Scis.; rec: golf. Res: 19397 Zinfandel, Saratoga 95070 Ofc: Widcom, Inc. 1500 E. Hamilton Ave, Ste. 217, Campbell 95008

WIDJAJA, TJAHJANA ANDY, structural engineer; b. July 22, 1952, Semarang, Indonesia; s. Hadi Gunarko and Sophia Sulistiawati (Halim) W.; m. Luna Kolima, Jan. 24, 1981; 1 dau. Melissa Angeline b. 1984; edn: BS, Diponegoro Univ. 1976; MSCE, Okla. State Univ. 1978, M.Arch. Engrg., 1979; Reg. Profl. Engr. (struct.) Calif. 1985. Career: junior engineer Snowden Engrg.; tech. staff Rockwell Internat.; strl. engr. Skidmore, Owings & Merrill; proj. engr. Cygna Cons. Engr.; pvt. cons., v.p. Enterprise Scientific Inc.;

honors: Chi Epsilon, Phi Kappa Phi; Protestant; rec: travel, reading. Ofc: Enterprise Scientific Inc. 1698 Rocky River Ct Simi Valley 93063

WIEDENMANN, ERIC WILLIAM, manufacturing co. executive; b. Feb. 20, 1951, Cleveland, Ohio; s. William Henry and Katherine Elizabeth (Bernhardt) W.; edn: BS magna cum laude, Ashland Coll. 1973; MBA, Northwestern Univ. 1975. Career: mktg. analyst Masco Corp. 1978-79, prod. mgr. Am. Metal Products Div. 1980-83, mgr. sales & mkt. devel. 1984-85, mktg. mgr. Weiser/ Falcon div. 1985–; honors: Academic Scholarship (1974-75); mem: Am. Mktg. Assn., Nat. Assn. Accts., Northwestern Grad. Sch. of Mgmt. Alumni Assn., Young Republicans Club Orange County, Newport Beach Tennis Club, Bridgecreek Owners Assn.; Republican; Lutheran; rec: tennis, reading, travel, running. Res: 12496 Montecito Rd Seal Beach 90740 Ofc: Weiser/ Falcon Lock 5555 McFadden Ave Huntington Beach

WIEDMANN, ELEANORE AGNES, business executive, civic leader, investor; b. Apr. 17, 1923, Los Angeles; d. Robert E. and Ann E. (Thornton) Ibbeston; m. Clark Vronman Wiedmann; children: Louise Monroe b. 1947, Clark Allen b. 1948, Cheryl Ann b. 1950, Darryl Lee b. 1965; edn: BA, Mt. Holyoke Coll. 1944. Career: Naval Intelligence Wave Ofcr., USNR, Wash. DC 1944-6; jr. exec. Union Devel. Corp., Inc. 1952-61; treas. dir. 1961-78; treas. dir. Dutch Village Bowling Center, Inc. 1965-79; dir. Valley Prop., Inc. and Union Farms, Inc. 1966-78; owner, supvr. Buffalo Creek Cattle Ranch, Orovada, Nev. 1976-8; pres. Portugese Bend Nursery Sch. 1955-6; mem. bd. of edn. Palos Verdes Unified Sch. Dist. 1961-9; v.p. 1964-6; pres. 1966-7; PTA Council rep to Community Ctr. Com. 1979; awards: P.V. Rolling Hills AAUW, 1969; P.V. Fac. Assn. Hon. 1969; P.V. Penin. PTA Council Dist. Ser. 1969; P.V. Unified Sch. Dist. 1969; mem: Palos Verdes Women's Club (bd. 1982-3); Peninsula Seniors Steering Com.; P.V. Penin. Republican Women Federated (bd.); The Circle, P.V. Community Arts Assn.; Los Serranos de P.V. (treas. 1980-3); Penin. Edn. Found. (bd. 1981-5); P.V. Penin. Sr. Bd. 1981-; Mt. Holyoke Coll. Alumnae Assn.; Cornerstone Club (So. Calif. Area ch. 1979-81); AAUW; P.V.H.S. PTA Bd. (1980-84); Steering Com. Save Our Coastline 1969-70; div. com. L.A. Reg. Planning Commn.; Harbor Welfare Planning Council 1962; Harbor Coll. adv. bd. 1961-5; League Women Voters; P.V. Penin. Plan. Council 1960; chmn. P.V. Penin. Coord. Council 1959; BSA Cub Scout den mother 1957-8; Catholic; rec: world travel. Res: 30032 Palos Verdes Dr W., Palos Verdes Peninsula 90274

WIEGAND, WILBERT RICHARD, JR., real estate co. president; b. Sept. 18, 1949, Dallas, Tex.; s. Wilbert Richard and Evelyn Marie (Taylor) W.; edn: Alan Hancock Coll. 1970-71. Career: pres., owner Starving Students, Lompoc 1971-75; owner Bill Wiegand Ents. (constrn. co.) Lompoc and Carpinteria 1976-85; pres. Wiegand Devel. Inc. Carpenteria 1985–; mem. Santa Barbara Dart Assn. 1980-85 (v.p. 1982, pres. 1983-84); mil: e-5 USAF 1968-71, Disting. Unit. Citation; Episcopal; rec: darts, music. Ofc: Wiegand Development, Inc. POB 640 Carpinteria 93013

WIENER, HOWARD B., appellate court justice; b. Feb. 1, 1931, Providence, R.I.; s. Henry and Mildred (Woolf) W.; m. Joan, May 23, 1954; children: Daniel b. 1956, Anne b. 1956, Cari b. 1958; edn: AB, cum laude, Brown Univ. 1952; LLB, Harvard 1955; LLM, Univ. Virginia 1982; admitted Calif. State Bar 1956. Career: clerk Hon. Ben Harrison, U.S. Dist. Ct. L.A. 1955-56; atty. Egly & Wiener San Gabriel/Pomona Valley 1956-75; judge San Bernardino Co. Sup. Ct. 1978-; assoc. justice 4th Appellate Dist. Div. 1; adj. prof. USC Law Sch.; honors: Phi Beta Kappa; publ: Common Law Liability of the Certified Public Accountant for Negligent Misrepresentation (Univ. San Diego Law Review 1983). Res: 7755 Ludington Pl La Jolla 92037 Ofc: 1350 Front St San Diego 92101

WIERDSMA, ANTOINETTE JOSEPHINE LUCIA, real estate property management executive; b. Jan. 7, 1948, Amsterdam, Holland; d. Hermanus Johannus amd Theadora (Payens) von Klaveren; m. Be Wierdsma, Mar. 21, 1969; 1 dau. Nancy b. 1972; edn: bus., Wassen Holland Coll. 1967; real estate sales Calif. 1981, broker, 1985. Career: retail store mgr. Wibra Epe Holland; div. mgr. advtg. newspaper Apeldoorn Holland; prop. mgr. CMC San Jose 1972-82, v.p. 1982–; adv. bd. TWM Industries 1984–; honors: Boss of the Year (Am. Business Women's Assn. 1978); mem: Tri County Orgn., Brokers Assn.; publ: articles in trade jours.; Republican; rec: home decorating, gardening. Res: 1205 Happy Valley Ave San Jose 95129 Ofc: Calif. Real Estate Mgmt. 1666 Saratoga Ave San Jose 95129

WIESE, KEVIN GLEN, I, international financial consultant; b. Mar. 19, 1960, Ogden, Utah; s. Glen James adn Kay Jon (Mildon) W.; edn: BS finance & mktg., Univ. Utah 1982; MBA, Golden Gate Univ. 1986; JD internat. Law, PhD internat. bus. (in progress), Columbia Pacific Univ. 1986-; Certified Financial Planner 1984. Career: acct. exec. Waddell & Reed Inc. Long Beach 1982-83; financial planner Gene Felton & Assocs. Inc. Glendale 1983; financial advisor Silverstein Financial Svcs. Inc. L.A. 1983-85; internat. financial cons. Christopher Weil & Co. Inc. L.A. 1985–; founder, chmn. Internat. Financial Ltd. and Internat. Financial (USA) Ltd. 1983–; internat. wealth cons.; adj. faculty Loyola Marymount Univ., CSU Northridge, Coll. for Financial Planning 1985–; mem: Internat. Assn. Financial Planning (L.A. chpt. dir. 1984, treas. 1985, v.p. 1986), Inst. Certified Financial Planners, Nat. Ctr. for Financial Edn. (charter), Century City CofC (chmn. fin. svcs. forum 1983-85), West L.A. Regl. CofC; publs: articles in financial jours.; Republican; rec: fencing, skiing, tennis, music (play piano, cornet). Ofc: 23420 Hawthorne Blvd Ste 160 Torrance 90505

WIESE, LOWELL M., physician; b. March 23, 1927, Chgo.; s. Ervin Albert and Edna Louise (Becker) Wiese; children: David, b. 1954, Paul, b. 1956, Valerie, b. 1958, Victoria, b. 1960; edn: BA, Valparaiso Univ. 1948, MA, Univ. of Wyo. 1951, MPH, Univ. Hawaii 1970, MD, Univ. Tenn. 1959. Career: active military svc. 1945-46, 1951-53, 1960-65, 1977-81; County and State Public Health Ofcr., Mich. 1973-75, American Samoa 1970-72, N.H. 1972-73, Kans. 1975-77; currently chief medical ofcr. No. Reception Center Clinic; Assoc. Prof. Pediatrics Univ. of Hawaii Sch of Medicine 1967-70, Clin. Prof. Public Hlth. 1970-72; Adj. Prof. Pediatrics Univ. of Kans. 1975-77. honors: Outstanding Physician of USAFR, 1983; mem. exec. bd. Assn. State and Provincial Hlth Authorities of No. Am. (afil. Am. Pub. Hlth. Assn.) 1976; Diplomate Am. Bd. of Preventive Med. in Aerospace Med. and Gen. Preventive Med., Am. Bd. of Pediatrics, Am. Bd. of Family Practice. mem: Fellow Am. Coll. Preventive Med., Fellow Am. Acad. Family Physicians, Aerospace Med. Assn., Soc. USAF Flight Surgeons, Am. Correctnl Hlth Ofcr's Assn. Mil: Col. USAF, 14 years active, USAFR 10 yrs., Merit. Svc. Medal. Republican. Catholic. rec: jog, backpack. Res: 4513 San Ramon Dr Davis 95616 Ofc: Northern Reception Center/Clinic, 3001 Ramona Ave Sacramento 95826

WIESE, ROBERT THOMAS, JR., recruitment executive; b. May 7, 1960, Milwaukee, Wis.; s. Robert T., Sr. and Joan Louise (Bush) W.; edn: CSU Hayward 1976-81; desig: PEC, profl. employment cons. (1984). Career: employment cons., senior cons. General Employment Ents., San Francisco 1983-84; recruiting cons., sr. cons., now project leader Data Processing Recruiters, S.F. 1985–; sales & mktg., personnel cons. Intellinomics Corp. 1984-; mem. Inst. for Public Sci. and Art, Make A Wish; Democrat; rec: computers, sports. Ofc: DPR 870 Market Ste 828 San Francisco 94102

WIGGINTON, RON, landscape architect; b. Oct. 1, 1944, Oakland; s. Leslie George and Lola Sophia (Kaufman) W.; edn: BFA, Univ. of Mont. 1966, MFA, Univ. of Ore. 1968; Calif. Reg. Landscape Arch. 1982. Career: teaching fellow Mont. State Univ., Bozeman 1966-67; instr. Mt. Hood Coll., Gresham, Ore. 1969-72, Cornish Sch. of allied Arts, Seattle 1974-76; draftsman Wimmer, Yamada and Assocs., San Diego 1979; designer/draftsman Gillespie and Assocs. Inc., San Diego 1979-80; founder/principal Land Studio, San Diego 1981–; awards: McClung Undergrad. Award (1964), Pennell Grad. Award, Univ. Ore. (1967), Resident Fellowship, Nature Conservancy (1981), Award of Merit, San Diego/AIA (1982), Nat. Merit Award, Am. Soc. of Landscape Archs. (1984, 1986); mem. Am. Soc. of Landscape Archs.; frequent lectr. var. univs. and civic orgns.; exhibiting visual artist, approx. 40 solo and group shows in Japan, France and USA (1964-); num. publs., TV documentaries; Democrat; Protestant; rec: swimming, travel. Address: Land Studio 419 West G St San Diego 92101

WILCOX, CLIFFORD MURRAY, marketing executive; b. March 7, 1958, Anchorage, Ala.; s. Winton Welfred and LaPreal (Adams) W.; edn: mktg., American River Coll. 1982-85; Calif. A-1 engring. lic. (1979), gen. contr. (1979), C-13 lic. (1980). Career: salesman G.D.A. Inc., Sacramento 1975-76; laborer TAM Constrn., Anchorage, Ala. 1976-79; owner/opr. Wilcox Constrn., Sacto. 1978-80; contr., salesman Work Wizards 1979-81; v.p. mktg. CE Inc., Sacto. 1980-85; senior acct. mgr. Four Seasons Landscape & Maint., Sacto. 1985-86, v.p. mktg. 1986–; sales tng. seminars cons. 1983-; profl. awards: Salesman of the Month, 8 times, G.D.A. Inc. 1975-76; mem: Bldrs. Industry Assn., Am. Legal Svcs., Demolay (Master Councilor 1974) author: Apple Fun & Games, Osborne- McGraw Hill 1985; Box-Card Sales, 1986; Republican; Christian; rec: swimming, writer, trumpeter. Res: 9447 Roseburg Ct. Sacramento 95826 Ofc: Four Seasons Landscape & Maintenance Inc., 4095 Deelde St. Sacramento 95820

WILCOX, HAROLD EDGAR, contract management executive; b. Feb. 15, 1940, Wash DC; s. Harold Edgar and Glenna Maude (Austin) W.; m. Catherine E., June 25, 1971; edn: BS in bus. adm., Miami Univ. 1961; MBA, George Washington Univ. 1972; desig: Cert. Profl. Contracts Mgr., Nat. Contracts Mgmt. Assn. (1976). Career: served to capt. Supply Corps, US Navy 1961-84: purch. supt. Phila. Naval Shipyard 1967-69; dep. dir. Aircraft Weapon Systems Purch. Div.; Naval Air Systems Cmd Hq, Wash DC 1972-76; comptroller (20 mos.), dir. Regl. Contracting Dept. (17 mos.), Naval Supply Ctr., Pearl Harbor, Hawaii 1976-79; dir. purch. Navy Aviation Supply Ofc., Phila. 1979-82; dir. of acquisition Joint Cruise Missiles Project, Wash DC 1982-84; (current) dir. of contracts, Aerospace & Logistics, Cubic Corp., San Diego 1985–; recipient recogn. for assistance to minority groups, US Dept. of Commerce (1978), and Equal Employment Opp. Award, Naval Aviation Supply Ofc (1981); mem. Nat. Contract Mgmt. Assn., US Naval Inst., Escondido Athletic Club; mil. decorations: Defense Superior Svc., Merit. Service w/Gold Star, Navy Commendn. w/Combat V and Gold Star, Navy Achieve., Navy Unit Commendn., Nat. Def. Service, Vietnam Svc. w/ Silver and Bronze Stars, Armed Forces Exped., Rep. of Vietnam Gal. Cross w/ Palm, Rep. of Vietnam Campaign w/ Device; Republican; United Methodist; rec: racquetball, gardening. Res: 3547 Via Loma Vista Escondido 92025 Ofc: Cubic Corp. 9333 Balboa Ave San Diego 92123

WILCOX, MAX, superior court judge; b. July 7, 1920, Bayard, Nebr.; s. Max and Mae Dewey (Paulsen) W.; m. Jeanne, Aug. 2, 1944; children: Gregory D. b. 1946, Cynthia McDowell b. 1950, Mary b. 1955, Denise Cotanch b. 1956, Theresa Giovanetti b. 1961; edn: AB, UC Berkeley 1941, LLB, JD, 1948; admitted Calif. Bar Superior Ct. Judge 1971. Career: mng. ptnr. law firm Tinning & Delap, Richmond 1948-71; city atty. City of El Cerrito, 1963-69; superior ct. judge Contra Costa County, 1971–, presiding judge 1974-84; named Trial judge of year Alameda-Contra Costa Trial Lawyers Assn. 1979;

mem. ABA; clubs: Spyglass Hill Golf, Contra Costa Country; mil: lcdr. USN 1942-46; Republican; Catholic; rec: golf. Res: 1957 Fair Ridge Ct Walnut Creek 94596 Ofc: Superior Ct. Courthouse Martinez 94553

WILCOX, RICHARD LOREN, chiropractor, educator; b. May 12, 1949, Brown City, Mich.; s. Dr. Lorn Jay and Eleanor May (Gisch) W.; edn: AA, El Camino Coll. 1976; BS, DC, Los Angeles Chiropractic Coll. 1982, Sports Physician cert. 1985. Career: warehouse asst. mgr., dept. supr., asst. office mgr. Fabricut, Inc. 1972-76; dispatcher Data Transportation, 1976-79; chiropractor/owner Wilcox Chiro. Clinic, Redondo Beach 1984–; instr. L.A. Chiro. Coll. 1982-; instr. martial arts South Bay Moo Duk Kwan, p.t. 1973-84; honors: Sigma Chi Psi (chpt. pres. 1981-82), Blackbelt, Korean Tang Soo Do Moo Duk Kwan System (1975); mem. Am. Chiro. Assn. (advis. bd. ACA Technique Council 1983-), Japanese Am. Chiro. Assn. (charter), US Tang Soo Do Moo Duk Kwan Fedn. Inc.; mil: sgt. E5 US ARmy 1971-72, Nat. Def., Vietnam Svc., Vietnam Campaign, Combat Inf. Badge, Army Commendn.; rec: martial arts, ski, photog. Ofc: Wilcox Chiropractic Clinics 2731 Manhattan Beach Blvd Redondo Beach 90278; Lahaina Shopping Center Bldg 5 Rm 9 Lahaina Maui Hawaii 96761

WILDER, JAMES D., mining co. geology director; b. June 25, 1935, Wheelersburg, Ohio; s. Theodore Roosevelt and Gladys (Crabtree) W.; children: Jaymie Deanna, Julie Lynne. Career: licensed real estate sales; comml. pilot; mgr., fixed base oper. Scioto County Airport, Ohio; mgr., co-owner sporting goods store Portsmouth, Ohio; consulting geologist 1973-81; dir. geol. & devel. Para-Butte Mining Inc. 1984–; pres. Mining Consultants Inc. 1980-84; mil: E-3 US Army 1956-57; Protestant; rec: hunting, camping, fishing. Address: 1737 Drayer Dr Paradise 95969

WILDERMUTH, BYRON PAUL, physical therapist; b. June 26, 1934, Mitchell, So. Dak.; s. John Arthur and Helen (Kaiser) W.; div.; children: Christopher b. 1960, Tia b 1963; edn: BA, CSU Northridge 1962; Cert. Phys. Therapy, USC 1964. Career: staff therapist Kaiser Found. Rehabilitation Ctr., Vallejo 1963 65; pvt. practice self empl., Santa Monica 1965-71; dir. physical therapy National Therapy Associates 1971-72; hosp. phys. therapy contractor, Oxnard 1972-78; dir. Sports Injury Center, San Diego 1978-82; pres., bd. dirs. Athletic Injury and Orthopedic Rehab. Center Inc., San Diego 1982–; editl. bd. Topics In Trauma; advsy. bd. Lincoln Med. Magnate Sch.; mem: Am. Physical Therapy Assn., Am. Coll. of Sports Med.; publs: (w/J.L. Beck) The Female Athlete's Knee, Clinic in Sports Medicine (1985); mil: s/sgt. US Army Inf. 1955-59; Republican; Protestant rec: bicycling. Res: 6447 Caminito Listo San Diego 92111 Ofc: Athletic Injury Center, 2650 Camino Del Rio North, Ste 101, San Diego 92108

WILENT, EMMETT VERNON, chiropractor; b. Nov. 13, 1913, Lidsay, Calif.; s. Charles Edward and Rose Edna (Ashley) W.; m. Rita Mary, Oct. 16, 1973; children: Yvonne (Christofferson) b. 1933, Wanita (Rautmann) b. 1935, Dana (Cramer) b. 1961, Emmett II b. 1966; edn: stu. CSU San Jose; DC, PhC, Standard Coll. of Chiropractic 1937; postgrad. studies (10,000+ hrs); Calif. lic. DC (1938); Cert. Indep. Medical Examiner. Career: pvt. practice, 1938-42, 1946–, currently semi-ret.; apptd. State Bd. of Chiropractic Examiners 1955 (exec. secty., pres.); mem: Am. Coll. of Chiropractic Orthopedists, Calif. Chiro. Assn. (life), S.F. Chiro. Soc. (past pres. 2 terms); mem. VFW, Masons (past master 1982), Moose Lodge (gov. 1980); mil: pvt. to capt. US Army Inf. 1942-46, Combat Inf. Badge; Republican; Prot.; rec: gardening. Address: Hwy 139 at Modoc Co. Line POB 785 Tulelake 96134

WILES, LAURENTIA RAMOS, cosmetologist, civic worker; b. Feb. 28, 1924, Ewa, Honolulu; d. Eugenio Lesperilles and Pelajia (Addion) Ramos; m. Henry Wiles, May 18, 1956; edn: grad. cert., Honolulu Business Coll. 1942; dipl., Dolores Premier Cosmetology Sch. 1944. Career: civil service clerk-typist Communications Ctr., US Army, San Francisco 1944-59; prop. Hobbit Beauty Salon, San Francisco 1956–; community organizer Filipino Adult & Youth Catholic Orgn., San Francisco 1959–; apptd. senior commnr. Commn. on the Status of Women of the City & County of San Francisco (1975-); producer Miss Philippines Calif.; honors: Resolution, Senate Calif. Legislature (1974, 76, 79), Citizen of Day award Radio Sta. KABL, S.F. (1978), Key to the City service award, City of Sacramento (1978), recogn. for outstanding woman leadership Philippine Consulate General, S.F. (1970), cert. of honor, City & County of S.F. (1974, 79); orgns: The Filipino Adult & Youth Catholic Org., Inc., S.F. (pres. 1970-), Filipino Community of San Francisco, Inc. (1984-), founder Marcela M. Agoncillo, Caballeros de Masalang, Inc., S.F. (1975), Filipino-Am. Coord. Conf., Inc., Sacto. (pres. 1976-82), YWCA, S.F. (bd. dirs. 1970-81); Democrat; Roman Catholic (Ch. of Visitacion Council 1970-); rec: guidance counselling, vol. charity work, dancing. Res: 214 Rutland St San Francisco 94134 Ofc: Hobbitt Beauty Salon 323 Geary St Ste 820 San Francisco 94102

WILEY, DONALD J., marketing representative, international professional tennis official; b. Aug. 8, 1951, NY, NY; s. Peter M. and Dorothea J. (Hucke) W.; edn: BS, biol., Villanova Univ. 1973; MBA, Pepperdine Univ. 1985; certifications: Nat. Referee, Nat. Chair Umpire, US Tennis Assn. (1985-86); Internat. Referee, Chief of Umpires, and Umpire, Men's Internat. Profl. Tennis Council (1979-). Career: sales/mktg. rep. American Scientific Products, div. Am. Hosp. Supply Corp., Los Angeles 1977–; concurrently 1974-: US Tennis Assn., profl. tennis umpire and referee num. major profl. tennis events including (asst. chief of umpires 1981-86) US Open Tennis Championships, Pacific Southwest, (referee/umpire 1974-78, chief umpire, L.A. 1978) World Team Tennis; sectional chmn. Umpires Com., So. Calif. Sect. USTA 1984-; head

marshall 1984 Olympic tennis event, Los Angeles; honors: One of only ten internat. profl. tennis ofcls. in world to be certified in all 3 categories (Internat. Ref., Chief of Umpires, Umpire, 1979-); capt. Villanova Univ. Tennis Team 1971-73; mem: World Future Soc., U.S. Tennis Assn. (profl. referee, amateur player); publs: created 1st formal tng. manual for tennis ofcls. in US, now used internat.; mil: lt. US Navy 1973-77, Surface Warfare Ofcr.; Catholic; rec: tennis, golf, art, music. Res: 2221 Warfield Ave Redondo Beach 90278

WILEY, JANE, physician; b. June 1, 1944, Wichita, Kans.; d. Max Raber and Dorothy (Kimmel) Wiley; edn: BA in molecular biol., UC Berkeley 1966; MD, Univ. Mich. 1970. Career: assoc. physician Univ. of Calif. Student Health, Berkeley 1971-73; emergency phys. Emergency Medical Systems, San Francisco 1975-80; cruise ship phys. Am. Hawaii Cruises, Honolulu 1981; staff phys. Urgent Care Center, Hilltop, Richmond 1984–; honors: Victor Vaughn Soc. (1969); mem: Am. Womens Med. Assn., Am. Coll. Emerg. Physicians (1975-83), Univ. Art Mus. Berkeley, SF Internat. Film Fest.; rec: travel. Ofc: Urgent Care Center- Hilltop, 2800 Hilltop Mall Rd Richmond 94806

WILK, MARIE VOGEL, business owner; b. Aug. 7, 1940, St. Paul, Minn.; d. Lawrence C. and Emily K. (Masek) Vogel; m. Richard E. Wilk, Dec. 21, 1962; 1 dau, Michelle b. 1963; edn: BA, Univ. of Minn. 1970; MA, CSU Fullerton 1977. Career: ed. women's Sect., Winona (Minn. Daily News 1968-70; asst. pub. affairs dir. CSU Fullerton 1970-73; pub. information ofcr. Los Angeles Unif. Schs. 1973-82; owner Colonial Printers & Lithographers 1982–; owner Wilkonim Ltd. Communications 1973-; honors: Phi Kappa Phi 19745; mem: NFIB, CofC; editor School Observer, monthly newspaper, LAUSD 1974; rec: art, music, gardening. Ofc: Colonial Printers & Lithographers, 18322 Ward St. Fountain Valley 92708

WILKINSON, DON FRANKLIN, investment marketing executive; b. Apr. 24, 1945, Charleston, WV; s. Donald Marion and Eunice Anna (Derrick) W.; m. Marie K. Pittman, 1969; 1 dau: Jennifer Nicole, b. 1973; edn: BS, FL State Univ. 1967; AA, Manatee Coll. 1965. Career: Vick Chem. Co., 1971-8; div. sales mgr., Phila., PA 1971-2; dist. sales mgr., Los Angeles 1972-4; area sales & mktg. mgr., W Coast 1974-6; Western regl. sales mgr. 1976-8; v.p. mktg. South County Devel. Co., Anaheim 1978-9; pres. R.H. Dev; K.S. DevCo, Santa Ana 1979-80; pres. Financial Freedom, Inc., Tustin 1980–; awards: Regl. Sales Mgr. 1973; Nat. Mktg. Rep. of the Yr., Vick Chem. Co. 1971; Lowry Nickerson Invest. Achiev. 1977; mem: Am. Soc. Profl. Cons.; Internat. Assn. for Fin. Plnrs., Inc.; Am. Mktg. Assn.; Republican; Prot.; rec: antique autos, reading. Ofc: 200 E Sandpointe Ste 706 Santa Ana 92707

WILKINSON, ROBERT STEVEN, marketing executive; b. June 23, 1955, Nashville, Tenn.; s. Frederick Douglas and Delois (Jackson) W.; m. Juliana Cornish, Sept. 15, 1984; edn: BS, Indiana Univ. 1978, MBA, Harvard Univ. 1982; Reg. Rep., Securities Exchange Commn. Career: bank examiner, F.D.I.C., Wash DC 1977; senior sales rep. (Louisville, Ky.), product mgr. (Rochester, NY), mktg. mgr. (San Francisco) Xerox, 1978-82; account exec. Smith Barney, S.F. 1983; mktg. rep. IBM, S.F. 1984–; honors: Dean's award (1982), Outstanding Young Man of Am., US Jaycees (1984), 100% Club IBM (1985); mem. Delta Sigma Pi, Black MBAs, Harvard Bus. Sch. Alumni Assn. (v.p. Harvard Bus. Sch. mktg. club 1982), Kappa Alpha Psi frat. (Polemarch Award 1980), Oakland Ensemble Theatre (pres. bd. dirs.); publs: Analysis of the Footcare Industry; Democrat; Baptist; rec: jogging, investments, theatre. Res: 501 Haddon Rd Oakland 94606 Ofc: IBM 425 Market St 23rd Fl San Francisco 94105

WILLEY, CHARLES WAYNE, lawyer; b. Oct. 7, 1932, Dillon, Mont.; s. Asa Charles and Elizabeth Ellen (Leonard) W.; m. Helene D., July 21, 1962 (div.); children: Stephen Charles b. 1963, Heather Helene b. 1966, Brent David b. 1969, Scott D. b. 1974; m. 2d Alexis W., Jan. 26, 1986; edn: BS, honors, Mont. State Univ. 1954, JD, high honors, Univ. of Mont. 1959; admitted to bar: Montana (1959), Calif. (1960), US Supreme Ct. (1972), US Tax Ct. (1975), US Ct. of Claims (1975), US Ct. of Appeal 9th Cir. (1956), US Ct. of Appeal Fed. Cir. (1984); certified splst. in taxation law Calif. Bd. of Legal Specialization. Career: clerk chief judge fed. Ct. of Appeal (9th Cir.) 1959-60; atty., ptnr. Price, Postel & Parma, Santa Barbara 1960-77; atty./pres. law firm Charles W. Willey, Santa Barbara 1978–; instr. SB City Coll. 1961-63, UCSB 1963-64; honors: Phi Kappa Phi, Phi Eta Sigma, Phi Delta Phi (outstanding grad. of Clayberg Inn chpt. 1959), chief editor Mont. Law Review (1958-59); mem. Santa Barbara County Bar Assn. (pres. 1972), Legal Aid Found. of Santa Barbara (pres. 1970); mem. (pres. 1980-81) Laguna Blanca School Board, 10 yrs.; v.p. Phoenix of SB (rehab. of teenagers in trouble with law), Kiwanis; author: Montana Bar Admission Standards, a Comparative Study (1959); cons. on real estate law to Calif. CEB; mil: capt. USAF 1954-56; Republican; Episcopal (vestry); rec: reading, writing, skiing. Ofc: Charles W. Willey PLC, 812 Presidio Ave Santa Barbara 93101

WILLIAMS, BARBARA JEAN, physician; b. Feb. 9, 1948, Kansas City, Mo.; d. Ralph E. and Aurella H. (Hilt) W.; edn: undergrad. Vanderbilt Univ. 1966-68; BA, human biol., The Johns Hopkins Univ. 1970, MD, 1979; residency in psychiatry, Michael Reese Hosp. and Med. Center 1983; fellowship in psychiatry, Timberlawn Psychiat. Hosp., Dallas 1983; Bd. certified, Am. Board of Psychiatry and Neurology 1985. Career: instr. (fellowship award) American Pre-Coll. Prog. in Paris, France 1966; Vanderbilt Univ. Dept. of Math tchg. asst. 1967-68; medical projects mgr. Systema Corp., Chgo. 1973-79; v.p. and dir. of med. edn., Primarius Assocs., Chgo. 1979; staff psychiatrist and pvt. practitioner Timberlawn Psychiatric Hosp., 1983-84; staff psychiatrist Anclote Manor Hosp., Tarpon Springs, Fla. 1984-85; staff psychiatrist Kaiser Permanente Med. Center, Fontana, Calif. 1985–; Contg. Medical Edn. cons. for The Johns Hopkins Univ. Sch. of Med. and Systema Corp. 1977-79; tchr. med. students and resident physicians The Johns Hopkins Univ. Sch. of Med., Michael Reese Hosp., Timberlawn Psychiat. Hosp., Anclote Manor Hosp. and Kaiser Permanente, 1977–; honors: Univ. of Mo. scholarship and certificate, Student of Highest Academic Promise, 1966; Vanderbilt Univ. and The Johns Hopkins Univ. scholarships; Vanderbilt Univ. "Top Ten" academic listing, Delphians Scholastic Hon., Skull and Bones Premed. Hon.; AMA Physician's Recogn. Award; APA CME Recognition Certif.; works: innovator in Continuing Medical Edn. movement in the 1970s utilizing var. media and devel. hardware and software computer system; rec: painting, needlework, horticulture. Ofc: Kaiser Permanente, Dept. Psychiatry, 9985 Sierra Fontana 92335

WILLIAMS, CHARLES JOSEPH, educator, property management executive; b. Dec. 30, 1920, Osage City, Kans.; s. Col. US Army (Ret.) Joseph Miles and Myrtle Margaret (Anderson) W.; m. Elaine Stoeckle, July 8, 1956; edn: undergrad. Texas A&M Coll. 1939-40, Salinas Jr. Coll. 1941; BS, Ore. State Coll. 1943; Gen. Elem., Gen. Sec. Tchg. creds. UC Berkeley 1956; Calif. lic. Gen. Engring. Contr. (1949). Career: game warden Calif. Div. Fish and Game 1943-44, aquatic biologist Calif. Bur. Marine Fisheries 1944-47; gen. contractor 1947-55; tchr. Monterey Unified Sch. Dist. 1955-80, ret., science cons. 1980-86; owner Kingman (Kans.) Farms (farming, land holding, oil, gas and mineral resource devel. co.); owner constrn./prop. mgmt. bus.; honors: mem. Texas Rifle Team (7th Corps Area), Nat. Rifle Matches, Ohio (1939); NSF study grantee Nat. Sci. Summer Insts. (1960, 61, 62, 66); mem: Chi Phi, Kiwanis, Sierra Club, US Power Squadron, Monterey Yacht Club, Nat. Rifle Assn., Ore. St. Univ. Alumni, UCB Alumni, Commonwealth Club (SF), Soc. of the Mayflower, SAR, Alden Kindred of Am. Inc.; mil: pvt. US Army Air Force 1942-43; Republican (Monterey Co. Rep. Central Com., The One Hundred Club); Episcopal; rec: fishing, hunting, boating (M/V Four Winds). Ofc: PO Box 1373 Carmel 93921

WILLIAMS, CHARLES ROBERT, professor; b. Nov. 15, 1934, Los Angeles; s. Floyd Wesley and Mary Edna (Chapman) W.; m. Aubrey Dean Mason, Aug. 15, 1957; div. 1963; 1 son, Lloyd Anthony b. 1960; edn: BS, UCLA 1957, MBA, 1958, postgrad. work 1960-61. Career: dist. mgr. computer systems, RCA, Los Angeles 1968-71, mgr. mkt. ops. 1971-72; dir. mkt. Western U.S., Sperry (Univac), L.A. 1972-73, regl. v.p. 1973-76, v.p./gen. mgr. American Div. Sperry, Blue Bell, Pa. 1976-82, v.p./gen. mgr. Internat. Div. Sperry, 1982-83, v.p. strategic & bus. planning, 1983-84; current: executive in residence Pepperdine Univ., Los Angeles; cons. prin. Williams & Assocs., 1984-; ptnr: C/O Assocs., Sunburst Assocs., N/P Assocs.; dir. Kyndyl Internat.; awards: Wasau Insurance Fellow, Betta Gamma Sigma, Kappa Sigma Achievement Award (3 yrs)(chpt. pres.), Internat. Film & TV Award; mem: Data Proc. Mgmt. Assn., Mgmt. Council of Am., SEPCA, Am. Mgmt. Assn., Calif. Assn. of Data Proc., Assn. for Mfg.; civic: United Way (chmn.), Bruin Bench, Sportsmen of the South, UCLA Alumni Assn.; mil: capt. US Air Force 1958-60; Republican; Christian; rec: sailing. Res: 20540 Pinnacle Way Malibu 90265 Ofc: Pepperdine 3415 Sepulveda Blvd Los Angeles 90034

WILLIAMS, DANIEL WEBSTER, III, postal service executive; b. May 26, 1946, Berkeley; s. Daniel, Jr. and Joyce Catherine (Allen) W.; edn: UC Berkeley 1964-66, 68-70. Career: research asst. Atomic Energy Commn. 1965-67; tchg. fellow Univ. Calif. 1969-73; internat. mail clerk US Postal Service, 1973-80, supvr., mails, USPS, 1980–, worked on revising distbn. schemes for transpacific internat. mails 1978, translator of internat. correspondence 1976-81; owner Nightmares and Notions, Oakland 1984-; mem: Am. Film Inst., Mensa, Small Press Writers and Artists Orgn.; publs: The Devil's Hand (1983), (to be released): Mr. A. Tropos, Death Spawn, Bonsai; Democrat; Methodist; rec: horror/fantasy fiction & films, collector comics, records, books, mags. Res: 230 Wayne Ave Apt 310 Oakland 94606-1213 Ofc: USPS 1675 Seventh St Oakland 94615-9708; Nightmares and Notions 5904 Foothill Blvd Oakland 94605

WILLIAMS, EARL HARRISON, co. executive; b. Sept. 27, 1914, San Francisco; s. Earl H. and Verbena (Crossley) H.; m. Elizabeth (dec. 1980); children: Jocelyn b. 1949, Sharon b. 1951, Lise b. 1955, Kathleen b. 1961; m. 2d Sandra L., Nov. 15, 1980; stepson, Graham b. 1975; edn: BSCE, Univ. Mich. 1937; Calif. lic. general contractor; Calif. Community Colls. life tchg. cred. (constrn. mgmt.). Career: served to lt. col. Corps of Engrs. US Army 1937-46, disability ret., decorated Theater medals, Soldier's Medal, Order of the Brit. Empire; profl. singer N.Y.C. 1946; supt. housing constrn. 1946-50, supt. comml. constrn. 1950-53; gen. contr./pres. Harrod & Williams Inc. 1953-79; bd. chmn. De Anza Holding Corp. (DeAnza Bank) 1983-86; developer/gen. ptnr. limited ptnrships, 1979-; mem. Sunnyvale CofC (dir. 1963-66, chmn. Downtown Redevel. Com.); Republican; Presbyterian; rec: singing, golf, swim. Res: 1178 Chaparral Rd Pebble Beach 93953 Ofc: DeAnza Building 298 S Sunnyvale Ave Sunnyvale 94086

WILLIAMS, EDWARD, II, medical technologist, regulatory affairs analyst; b. Feb. 5, 1944, Chgo.; s. Edward, Sr. and Lois Elizabeth (Gordon) W.; edn: AA, Prairie State Coll. 1973; BA biol. scis., chem., Chgo. State Univ. 1977; M. Med. Technol., CSU Dominguez Hills 1979; bus. mgmt., Santa Barbara City Coll. 1979-; other spl. courses, workshops. Career: med. techn. St. Joseph Hosp., Chgo. 1962-65, St. Elizabeth Hosp., Chgo. 1964-65, Ill. Masonic Hosp., chgo. 1965-67; biochem. lab. instr. Univ. Ill. Med. Ctr. 1966-67; supv. hematology South Shore Hosp., Chgo. 1967-68; lab. tech. USAF, Scott AFB, Ill. 1968-70; supv. biochem. St. Bernard Hosp., Chgo. 1971-73; lab. adminstr. Friendship Med. Ctr., Chgo. 1972-76; chief technol., UC Student Health Svc.,

Santa Barbara 1977; qual. assurance inspector supv. Am. Heyer-Schulte Corp., Goleta 1977-79; senior regulatory affairs engr. 1979-80; regulatory affairs analyst 1980–; cons., ednl. tng. coord. Isla Vista Open Door Clinic 1977–; pres. Paradise Ranch Consultants 1980-; railroad pgm. cons. Profl. Travel, Goleta 1984-; railroad media historian, domestic and internat. railroad travel journalist 1980-; mem. L.A. Olympic Organizing Com. 1980-84; honors: Phi Beta Kappa, Alpha Psi Omega, Silver Poet Award, Internat. Poetry Soc. (1986), KofC Achievement Awards (1984, 85, 86), Internat. Soc. Med., Munich (1973), Poet de Granada, Espana (1974), ASQC (1981), Amtrak Golden Spike Soc. (1982), mem: Am. Soc. Qual. Control (chpt. v.p. 1981-82), Railway & Locomotive Hist. Soc., NAACP (newsletter ed. 1977-), Calif. Assn. for Med. Lab. Techs. (ed. Lambda Press), Am. Soc. Med. Tech., Am. Cancer Soc. (edn. chmn. 1972-76), Regulatory Affairs Profl. Soc., Internat. Platform Assn., Santa Barbara City Coll. Football Club (v.p. 1981-), Santa Barbara Catholic Communications Council (bd. 1984-), Knights of Columbus (dir. public rels., vocations), Goleta Valley CofC, Black Catholic Com., S.B. Black Profl. Assn. (bd.), UCSB Football Gridiron Club, So. Coast Spl. Olympic Com., Catholic Social Svcs.; author: The Liturgy of Edd, The Doctrine of Mankind I, II, III, IV, V, Concepts of Positive Thought, Chicago Renaissance Anthology I, II, III, IV, V; mil: USAF 1968-69; Republican; Catholic; rec: writing poetry, railroad history, unicorn & rose collection. Res: Paradise Ranch, 9396B Elmhurst Pl Goleta Valley 93117

WILLIAMS, HOWARD WALTER, aerospace executive; b. Oct. 18, 1937, Evansville; s. Walter Charles and Marie Louise (Bollinger) W.; m. Phyllis Scofield; children: Deborah b. 1958, Steven b. 1959, Kevin b. 1959, Glenn b. 1960, stepchildren: Lori b. 1964, Michele b. 1968; m. 2d. Marilee McPheron, Oct. 31, 1970; edn: AA, Pasadena City Coll. 1956; BS in engring., CSU Los Angeles 1967; BS in bus. adm., Univ. of San Francisco 1978. Career: engr. Aerojet-General, 1956–, turbojet and rocket engr. 1956-59, infrared sensor engr. 1959-60, rocket and torpedo engr. 1960-66, power and propulsion engr. 1967-73, high speed ship systems mgr. 1974-78, rocket and power mgr., 1979-85, rocket applic. mgmt. 1985–; organizing dir. Am. Soc. for Metals, Indsl. Heat Exchange Confs. (1985-); awards: Alpha Gamma Sigma (1956), US Nat. Energy Innovation Award, DOE (1985); senior mem. Am. Inst. Aero. and Astro. (1965-); patent: Closed Cycle Power System (1969); coauthor books: Heat Exchangers (McGraw-Hill 1980), Industrial Heat Exchangers (1985); Republican; Baptist; rec: biking, scuba, ski. Res: 2421 El Pavo Way Rancho Cordova 95670

WILLIAMS, JACK JEFF, facilities/ administrative executive; b. July 28, 1936, Cushing, Okla.; s. Jeff Davis and Pauline Vera (Meyers) W.; m. Mary Ann Hill, June 1, 1957; children: Janet Lee (Charlin) b. 1959, Jeff Brian b. 1961; edn: AA, El Camino Coll. 1971; BA econs., CSU Dominguez Hills 1974. Career: facilities/ adminstrv. services mgr. TRW, Redondo Beach 1957-81, TRW Electronics and Def. Sector, Sunnyvale 1981–; facilities cons. to var. corps. incl. Amdahl., Trilogy., Aerospace., Garrett., Continental Airlines, Delta Airlines, Nat. Med. Ents. and Support Services; honors: Outstanding Employee, TRW (1980); mem. Facilities Manager's Assn., Masons; research: computerization of Facilities Svcs.; Democrat; Baptist (Deacon); rec: antiques, coins, gardening, Bible Study tchr. Address: Sunnyvale 94086

WILLIAMS, JAMES HERSCHELL, private investigator; b. Nov. 16, 1932, Frederick, Okla.; s. George and Pearlie (Smith) W.; m. Heidi, Apr. 19, 1970; children: La Marr b. 1969, Jermon b. 1971, Deadra b. 1973; edn: AA, Sacramento City Coll. 1970; BA, Portland State Univ. 1972, MSW, 1976. Career: correctional ofcr. Dept. of Corrections Calif. 1951-68; counselor Yolo County Probation Dept. 1971-72; alcohol counseling & recovery Portland, Ore. 1971-75; founder, grant writer counselor House of Exodus Portland 1976-79; owner Williams Investigations Sacramento 1979–; mem: Calif. Peace Ofcrs. Assn., Nat. Assn. Licensed Investigators, Nat. Assn. Investigator Specialties; mil: tech. sgt. US Army 1947-50, Good Conduct, Occupational Svcs. Far East, Asiatic Campaign; Democrat; Protestant (bible teacher); rec: boating, fishing, hunting, sports. Ofc: Williams Investigations POB 460 Citrus Heights 95610

WILLIAMS, JOHN SCOTT, mortgage loan correspondent; b. June 30, 1940, Los Angeles; s. George Wilkes and June Irene (Combs) W.; edn: Santa Monica City Coll. 1958-60; Univ. of La Verne 1961-63; cert. Real Estate 1963-67; Golden West Law Sch. 1974; desig: R.E. Negotiator, Hawaii; lic. R.E. Broker, Calif. 1967-. Career: real estate brokerage John S. Williams Realty, West L.A. 1973-78; pres. Intex Internat. (imports-exports, consulting) 1978–; pres. South Coast Mortgage, Torrance 1985–; mem: UCLA Writers Block, UCLA Bus. Alumni (charter); publs: art., Discover Mexico Mag. (6/79); mil: US Army 1961; rec: travel, golf, body surfing, philanthropic wk. in Mexico. Ofc: 4009 Pacific Coast Hwy Torrance 90505

WILLIAMS, MICHAEL JAMES, health consulting co. president; b. Sept. 23, 1951, Royal Oak, Mich.; s. Robert Burgett and Elizabeth (McGuire) W.; m. Karyn Wade, July 15, 1978; edn: BA, psych., Wayne State Univ. 1974, and BS, police adm., 1974; MPA, pub. adm., CSU Fullerton 1979; Nat. Reg. EMT (Emergency Med. Tech.), charter mem.; American Heart Assn. instr./trainer ACLS (Adv. Cardiac Life Support) 1978, and CPR, 1971. Career: supr. Suburban Ambulance Service, Royal Oak, Mich. 1970-74; dir. emergency medical systems, EMS Pgm., County of Imperial, El Centro, Ca. 1975-76, County of Orange, Santa Ana 1976-80; pres. EMS Systems Design (health consulting spec. in emergency med. pgms.), Irvine 1980–; instr. Paramedic Tng. Div., UC San Diego 1975, North Orange County Comm. Coll. Dist. 1976-79, Imperial Valley Coll. 1974-76; honors: recognition awards, Orange Co. Emergency Med. Care Commn. 1980, Orange Co. Fire Chiefs Assn. 1980, UCI Paramedic Tng. Pgm. 1980, Am. Heart Assn. Orange Co. Chpt. awd. 1982, Orange Co.

Trauma Soc. Awd. 1984; mem: Am. Heart Assn. (O.C. bd. dirs. 1977-82), Soc. of EMS Administrators (ch. So. Calif. Soc. 1977-80), So. Calif. Health Care Execs., Orange Co. Trauma Soc. (bd. dirs. 1981-), Am. Trauma Soc. (LA County Trauma Task Force 1980-81); publs: contbg. writer on emergency care systems in med. textbooks, num. articles in field, editor: Contemporary Concepts in Emergency Medical Service Delivery (Aspen, 1985); Christian; rec: racquetball, running, fishing. Ofc: EMS Systems Design, 2691 Richter Ave, Ste. 111, Irvine 92714

WILLIAMS, MICHAEL JOSEPH, manufacturing co. executive; b. June 7, 1955, Honolulu, Hawaii; s. Joseph Harley and Mary (Lopez) W.; m. Laurene, Nov. 24, 1974; children: Jennifer b. 1975, Amy b. 1977; edn: Sierra Coll. 1973-74. Career: var. pos. with KW Industries, Citrus Hts., 1969–, current vice pres.; cons. (repair of rec. vehicles) var. insurance cos.; vol. with local fire dept., 4 yrs.; instr. in martial arts; comml. breeder of pigeons; recipient awards in Boy Scouting, Tae Kwon Do (martial arts), pigeon breeding; mem. Pacific Modena Club (pigeons), Tae Kwon Do- Mod Duk Kwan, PTA; designer: RVs and related equip.; Republican; Prot.; rec: computers, woodworking, painting. Res: 6107 Teague Ln Roseville 95678 Ofc: KW Industries 6019 Auburn Bl Citrus Heights 95621

WILLIAMS, NEVILLE AUBREY, electrical engineer, consultant; b. May 24, 1912, Shannonville, Ontario, Canada; s. Aubrey and Una Hope (Harvey) W.; m. Alexandra May Green, Aug. 17, 1936; children: Beverly Gail b. 1939, Sylvia Beth (McConnell) b. 1942; edn: BS, Queen's Univ., Kingston, Can. 1938; Reg. Profl. Engr., Calif. (1962-86), Province of Ontario (1945), Province of Manitoba (1947-82). Career: asst. Internat. Nickel Co. of Canada Ltd. 1938-42, Aluminum Co. of Canada Ltd. 1943, draftsman Kingston Shipbldg. Co. of Canada 1944; tchg. asst. Queen's Univ. 1942-45; elec. engr. Canadian Nat. R.R. 1945-46; asst., assoc., full prof. elec. engring. (dept. chmn.) Univ. of Manitoba, Winnipeg 1946-55; adminstv. engr. (Guided Missile Div., Aircraft Div.) DeHavilland Aircraft of Canada Ltd. 1955-60; indep. cons. engr. 1960-61; plant engring. designer Rohr Corp., Riverside, Calif. 1961-62; sr. elec. engr. var. public transit projects (incl. LA Airport, So. Calif. Rapid Transit Dist. pgm., Port Authority Trans Hudson rapid transit pgm. NY, NY, Nat. Capital Transp. Agcy. study Wash DC), elec. engr. var. steel and alumina projects (in US, Jamaica, and Ghana, Africa), elec. design engr. major hydroelectric projects (Volta River, Ghana and Bandama River, Ivory Coast), 1962-69; elec. engring. designer var. steel and iron ore projects (US, Canada, W. Australia), power projects (Santa Clara, Calif., Ghana, Africa), airport transp. projects (Newark, NJ, and LAX), 1969-72; staff elec. engr. for public transit pgms. in Dade Co., Fla., Newark, N.J., Pittsburgh, Pa., Los Angeles, Boston, and Detroit, 1972-75, and tech. cons. var. rapid transit systems (incl. BART, others nat.) 1975-79; pvt. cons. steel and aluminum projects, 1979–; mem: Nat. Writers Club, IEEE (mem. 1938-; life mem. Power Engring. Soc., Industry Appls. Soc., Control Systems Soc., Indsl. Electronics Soc.), Inst. of Radio Engrs. (1951-), Engring. Inst. of Canada (1949), Canadian Soc. for Elec. Engring. (life); civic: Am. Security Council Found. (Nat. Advis. Bd. 1985-), Lake Forest II Master Homeowners Assn.; Prot.; rec: recording & evaluating data on stock market & personal aerobic exercise. Res: 24232 Ontario Ln El Toro 92630

WILLIAMS, PATRICIA J., financial planner; b. Sept. 29, 1942, St. Louis, Mo.; d. A.P. and Mary M. (Teak) Anderson; edn: BA, CSU Fresno 1964; MA, CSU San Jose 1968; EdD, Univ. No. Colo., Greeley 1978; desig: Cert. Finl. Planner (CFP), Coll. for Finl. Plnng. 1984. Career: sch. tchr. East Side Union H. Sch. Dist., San Jose 1964-67, supr. 1967-75, asst. principal 1974-77; asst. prin. Greeley (Colo.) Sch. Dist., 1977-78; pres. Leadership devel. Inst., Colorado Springs, 1978-79; owner The Fern Factory, Santa Ana, Calif. 1979-80; mgr. Intel Corp., Santa Clara 1980-81; ptnr. Dahl & Williams, San Jose 1981-83; owner/pres. The Delta Group, A Finl. Planning Firm, Los Altos 1983–; asst. prof. bus., Foothill Comm. Coll. 1983-; mem: Internat. Assn. of Finl. Plnng., Santa Clara Chpt., Los Altos CofC, Quota Internat. Los Altos (pres. 1986-87); publs: dissertation: Career Aspirations of Selected Women Teachers (1977), var. local newspaper arts.; rec: gardening, pottery, flying. Ofc: 167 S San Antonio Rd Ste 7 Los Altos 94022

WILLIAMS, RICHARD DESSERT, lawyer; b. Aug. 30, 1946, Los Angeles; s. Alfred Curry and Josephine Anne (Dessert) W.; m. Brenda, July 25, 1983; children: Alison b. 1974, Darren b. 1974, Christine b. 1976; edn: BA in bus. adm., Wash. State Univ. 1969; JD, UC Los Angeles 1973; admitted Calif. State Bar 1973. Career: accountant Shell Oil Co., Los Angeles 1969-70; atty. Adams, Duque & Hazeltine, L.A. 1973-74; atty./partner Manatt, Phelps, Rothenberg & Tunney, L.A. 1974-83, Finley, Kumble, Wagner et al., L.A. 1983–; honors: Beta Gamma Sigma 1969; bd. editors UCLA Law Rev. 1972-3; speaker/author various law institutes, spec. in corporate, comml. litigation, 1979-; mem: Am. Bar Assn. (chmn. envtl. litigation com.), State Bar of Calif., Los Angeles Co. Bar Assn., Assn. of Bus. Trial Lawyers, Wash. State Univ. Cougar Club; author: Attacking Barriers to Entry: An Alternative to Divestiture in Antitrust Enforcement (UCLA Law Rev. 1972); Republican; Presbyterian; rec: pvt. pilot. Res: 18408 Wakecrest Dr Malibu 90265 Ofc: Finley, Kumble, Wagner et al., 9100 Wilshire Blvd Beverly Hills 90212

WILLIAMS, RICHARD S., employee benefits specialist, co. executive; b. Dec. 4, 1950, Paterson, N.J.; s. Charles F. and Bernice S. (Sherwood) W.; m. Celeste F., Mar. 20, 1981; 1 dau. Kristen b. 1984; edn: BA, Gettysburg Coll. 1973; CLU, The Am. Coll. 1981; stu. CEBS pgm. Wharton Sch. of Fin. 1986. Career: sales Moody's Investors Service, NYC 1974-76; Penn Mutual Life & Plan Services Inc., Tampa, Fla. 1976-78; Northwestern Mutual Life, Trenton, N.J. and San Diego, Calif. 1978–; owner/exec. dir. Northwestern Employee Benefits Group, Freehold, N.J. and San Diego, 1979–; benefits cons. for major corps.; elected mem. nat. advis. com. Northwestern Group Mktg. Svcs. (div. NW Mutual Life), 1985-; recipient profl. achieve. award, Penn Mutual (1977); mem. Am. Soc. of CLU, Nat. Assn. Life Underws., S.D. Assn. Life Underws. (ethics com. 1981-86); civic: Scripps Ranch Old Pros, Olean Township Jaycees (v.p. 1980); Presbyterian; rec: sail, woodworking, softball, golf. Ofc: Northwestern Employee Benefits Group 1515 Second Ave San Diego 92101

WILLIAMS, ROBERT LOUIS, entrepreneur, producer, entertainment artist; b. Nov. 12, 1950, Maybeury, W. Va.; s. Charlie James and Lucy (Vaughn) W.; edn: BS in elem. edn., Bluefield State Coll. 1976; lic. 3rd class radio/tel., FCC (1974), Notary Public, Calif. (1983), Indsl. Elec. Cert. (1972). Career: founder/pres. B.W. Enterprises, Inc., West Los Angeles 1981–, incl. B.W. Prodns., Sonrise Records, B.W. Public Relations, Jilord Prodns., Clean Socks and Underwear-Chicago, Original Christian Cookie Co., Jadas Artworks, Skyy's Unlimited Prodn. Co.; drama coach Undiscovered Artists Guild; provider finl.planning, investments money broker, credit maint., income tax prep. svcs.; past asst. mgr. C.I.T. Finl. Svcs., Columbus, Ohio and Beckley, W.Va.; mem. Internat. Alliance of Stage and Theatrical Employees, Local No. 44 (shop steward, sr. exec. bd. rep., del.), 1979-; awards: commendations, L.A. Co. Sheriff Dept. (1981, 82) and West Hollywood Sheriff Dept. (1985), recogn. for comm. service City of W. Hywd. Councilman Alan Viterbi (1985), nom. Outstanding Young Men of Am. (1985); founder/pres. Poinsettia Crime Alliance (cited as text book example for all comm. crime watch pgms. by capt. James Cook, W.Hywd. Sheriff Dept.); mem. Fishermans' Players West; Hollywood CofC; W. Hollywood Community Alliance; works: Hold On To Your Dream (recording artist), By-Word Newsletter, composer (recipient hon. mention Music City Song Fest.), Personal I.D. Check, Cheese-Cracker-Crumbs Mouse Dolls; Democrat; Baptist; rec: swim, jog, tennis. Res: 1123 N Poinsettia Dr West Hollywood 90046 Ofc: B.W. Enterprises, Inc. 1900 S Sepulveda Blvd, 3d flr, West Los Angeles 90025

WILLIAMS, RODNEY ELLIOTT, college district chief of police; b. Nov. 14, 1928, San Francisco; s. Nelson, Sr. and Ruby Lucille (Hammond) W.; m. Joyce, Aug. 1, 1954; children: Rodney II b. 1955, Brian b. 1957, Vivian b. 1961; edn: AA, S.F. City Coll. 1957; BA, S.F. State Univ. 1971; MPA, Golden Gate Univ. 1973; lifetime comm. coll. tchg. credl. Calif.; Exec. Cert., Commn. on Peace Ofcr. Stds. and Tng. Calif. Career: patrolman San Francisco Police Dept. 1955-66, police community relations ofcr. 1966-69, dir. police community rels. 1967-76, inspector of police of sexual assault unit 1976-83; chief of police Peralta College Dist. 1983–; honors: Resolutions (Calif. Legislature 1969, Calif. Senate 1984, Assemblyman Willie Brown 1977), Proclamation (Mayor Dianne Feinstein S.F. 1983), Cert. of Honor (Bd. of Supvs. 1968), Liberty Bell Award (S.F. Bar Assn. 1974); mem: Nat. Orgn. of Black Law Adminstrs., Ofcrs. for Justice Police Assn. (pres. 1981-83), Marines Meml. Club; mil: pfc US Army 1951; rec: photog. Ofc: Peralta Comm. Coll. Dist. 333 E 8th St Oakland 94606

WILLIAMS, RUSSELL LOUIS, executive; b. Jan. 6, 1943, Visalia; s. A. Clayton and Mildred J. (Russell) W.; m. Sara Coburn, June 23, 1968; 2 daus: Kelly b. 1969, Kimberly b. 1972; edn: AA, Coll. of the Sequoias 1963; BS, Fresno State 1966. Career: field rep. for Agricultural Producers 1970-75; mgr., Citrus Ins. Trust Fund and Citrus-Avocado Pension Trust. 1975-77; elected pres., Agricultural Producers, 1977–; mem: Nat. Council of Agricultural Employers; Calif. Conf. of Employers Assn.; Calif. Ag. Employment Work Group; Alliance for Food & Fiber; Agricultural Personnel Mgmt. Assn.; mil: petty ofcr. USN 1967-68; Republican; Episcopal; rec: skiing, jogging, gardening. Res: 400 Powell Terrace Visalia 93291 Ofc: Agricultural Producers, 25600 Rye Canyon Road, Ste 100, Valencia 91355

WILLIAMS, SOLOMON, clergyman, private investigator; b. Sept. 19, 1932; s. Henry and Hattie W.; m. Marvis, Sept. 27, 1962; 1 dau. Shauna b. 1969; edn: theol., Coll. of Bishop CME Ch., 1967; AA in law enforcement, Long Beach City Coll.; criminol., CSU Long Beach 1975, MPA pgm., CSULB. Career: detention svc. counselor Juvenile Hall, L.A. County Probation Dept.; pastor CME Ch., Fontana; pvt. investigator, Bellflower 1976–; recipient civic award, Mayor of Fontana; founder Community Action Group, Fontana; author: The Powers; The Lily White Marina; A Tribute to Black History; mil: E7 USN, boatswain mate chief ret. 1950-71, Vietnam Svc., Vietnam, Korean and Philippines Campaigns, Good Conduct (5), Pres. Unit Citn., Korean Svc., US Svc.; Democrat. Res: 11537 E 168th St Artesia Ofc: Sol Williams. Private Investigative Service POB 3202 Bellflower 90706

WILLIAMS, SPENCER M(ORTIMER), judge; b. Feb. 24, 1922, Reading, Mass.; m. Kathryn Bramlage; children: Carol, Peter, Spencer, Clark, Janice, Diane; edn: AB, UC Los Angeles 1943; postgrad. Hastings Coll. of Law 1943-46; JD, UC Berkeley Boalt Hall 1948; admitted Calif. State Bar 1949, U.S. Dist. Ct. (no. dist. Calif. 1949, eastern dist. 1971), U.S. Ct. Mil. Appeals 1951, U.S. Ct. Appeals 9th circ. 1949, U.S. Supreme Ct. 1952. Career: assoc. atty. Beresford & Adams San Jose 1949; dep. co. counsel Santa Clara Co. 1949-50, 1952-55, co. counsel 1955-66; adminstr. Calif. Health & Welfare Agcy. Sacto. 1966-70; Youth & Adult Corrections Agcy 1966-70; secy. Human Rel. Agcy. 1966-70; assoc. atty. Evans, Jackson & Kennedy Sacto. 1970-71, Rankin, O'Neal, Center, Luckhardt, Bonney, Marlais & Lund San Jose 1970-71; judge U.S. Dist. Ct. S.F. 1971–; lectr. Cntg. Edn. of the Bar 1960-65; mem: Calif. State Bar (vice chmn. Publicly Employed Attys. com. 1962-63, Ctg. Edn. Bar com. 1964-66), 9th Circ. Dist. Judges Assn. (treas. 1978-79, v.p. 1979-81, pres. 1981-83), Fed. Judges Assn. (pres. 1982-86), Santa Clara Co. Bd. Library

Trustees (pres. 1955-66), Boy's City Boys Club San Jose (bd. dirs. 1965-67), YMCA (com. on Youth and Govt. 1967-68); Episcopal (sr. warden St. Philipps Ch.). Res: 17057 U.S. Courthouse San Francisco 94102

WILLIAMS, STEVE REX, physician; b. Aug. 3, 1953, Henderson, Tx.; s. James Marion and Ruth May (Harrison) W.; edn: BA cum laude, Southern Methodist, 1973; MD, Univ. Texas Med. Branch, 1977; Fellow Am. Acad. Family Physicians 1982; physician surgeon lic. Calif. BMQA. Career: intern in gen. surgery L.A. County-USC Med. Center 1977-78; resident in family med. Baylor Coll. of Med. 1979-82; pvt. practice of medicine, Santa Maria 1982–; dir. Family Practice and Emergency Med. Services, Valley Hosp. 1983; founder Family Practice Div. at two hosps. in Santa Maria, 1984; awards: full academic scholarship So. Meth. Univ. (1970), Locum Tenens study award at Middlesex Hosp., London (1976); mem: AMA, Am. Acad. Family Practice, Am. Coll. Emergcy. Physicians, Am. Mensa Assn.; mem. Presidential Repub. Task Force 1984-85; mem. Civic Group against Landfill Dumping of Toxic Chemicals; Methodist; rec: equestrian, skiing, travel. Res: 1813 Sequoia Way Santa Maria 93454 Ofc: 1414 S Miller St Ste 2 Santa Maria 93454

WILLIAMS, T. COLE, utility executive/ mining executive; b. Aug. 19, 1925, Pasadena; s. Stuart Llewellyn and Elcey Hoatson (Cole) W.; m. Susan Rose, Apr. 24, 1976; children (by previous marriage): Elizabeth b. 1951, Anne b. 1952, Thomas Cole, Jr. b. 1956, David b. 1958, Christopher b. 1960; edn: AA, Pasa. City Coll. 1947; BS, Northwestern Univ. Medill Sch. Journalism 1950. Career: mgmt. of family mining interests in Ariz., Calif., Nev., Mont., Mexico, 1950–; publishing and sales mgmt. Time Inc., NY, NY: Chgo. 1950-51, New York 1951-62, Tokyo 1962-67, Los Angeles 1967-71; west coast mktg. dir. Govt. Research Corp., Wash DC 1972-74; exec. asst. Pub. Affairs, So. Calif. Edison Co., Rosemead 1974-80, asst. to the Pres. 1980-84, asst. to the Chmn. of Bd. 1984–; honors: Boys Clubs of Am.-Found. of Year Award (1985), recogn. awards Pasa. Guidance Clinics, Pasa. Symphony Assn., Am. CofC (Japan), Japan-Am. Soc.; mem: Pacific Coast Electrical Assn., Navy League (life), Public Affairs Ofcrs. Assn./L.A.; civic: Boys Clubs of Am. (nat. bd. 1984-), Boys Clubs Found. of So. Calif. (pres. 1984-, trustee 1980-), Community Dispute Resolution Ctr/Pasa. (v.p. and bd. mem. 1983-), Pasa. Tournament of Roses Assn. (1977-), Five Acres (Long Range Plng. Task Force), Town Hall of Calif., Pacific Asia Museum (bd. trustees, chmn. Corp. Devel.), Huntington Library (Friends), L.A. Mus. Sci. & Indus. (Assocs.), Cultural Heritage Found./L.A., L.A. County Music Ctr. (Assocs.), L.A. County Museum of Art (Patron); clubs: Valley Hunt (Pasa.), Greenhead Hunting, Chi Psi, Ducks Unlimited (patron), E. Clampus Vitus; mil: US Marine Corps 1942-46, Res. 1948-49, decorated US Secty. of Navy, Chinese Premier Chung Kai Chek; Republican; Episcopal; rec: writing, gardening, cooking, trap shooting. Res: 921 S Madison Ave Pasadena 91106

WILLIAMS, THERESA MARIE, art therapist, psychologist; b. Dec. 13, 1954, Holden, Mass.; d. Ernest John and Lillian Theresa (Raya) W.; edn: Univ. Mass 1974-75; BA, West Liberty State Coll. 1977; MA, US Internat. Univ. 1980; Nat. Univ. 1981-85; PhD, William Lyon Univ. 1986; Certified Psychodramatist 1983; Reg. Psychol. Asst. 1982; Reg. Art Therapist 1979; lic. Marriage, Family, Child Counselor 1986. Career: art therapy intern San Diego County Mental Health 1979, Magnolia Sch., Communication Ctr., San Diego 1979; art therapist Mercy Hosp. Mental Health Unit, S.D. 1979-84; psychol. asst. La Jolla Eating Disorders Clin. 1982-86; lic. marriage, family, child counselor 1986–; facilitator No. County Self Help Eating Disorders Clin. 1982–; mem. S.D. Eating Disorders Advis. Bd.; frequent lectr.; mem: S.D. Art Therapy Assn. (founder, pres. emeritus 1980-82), Am. Psychol. Assn., Am. Art Therapy Assn., Calif. Assn. Marriage, Family, Child Therapists, Citizen's Action League, COMBO (theatre and arts assn.), San Diego Art Museum; rec: catamaran sailing, bicycling, oil painting, pastels, art collecting. Ofc: La Jolla Eating Disorders Clinic, 9844 Genesee Ave La Jolla 92037

WILLIAMS, VERLE ALVIN, energy consultant, co. president; b. Apr. 8, 1933, New Virginia, Iowa; s. Donald Oliver and Josephine Emily (Read) W.; m. Mary Sue Earley, June 2, 1957; children: Steven Lee b. 1960, Randall Joe b. 1961, LeAnne Sue b. 1965; edn: BSME, and BS in bus., Colo. Univ., Boulder 1960; Reg. Profl. Engr., Calif. Cert. Energy Mgr. (CEM), Assn. of Energy Engrs. 1982. Career: sales engr. Johnson Service Co., Portland, Ore. 1960-67, Los Angeles 1967-68, San Diego 1968-69, San Diego br. mgr. 1970-79; assoc. Dunn-Lee-Smith-Klein (profl. engrs.), S.D. 1979-81; energy cons. prin./pres. Verle A. Williams & Assocs., Inc. 1981–; awards: Energy Engr. of Year, Assn. of Energy Engrs. (San Diego chpt. 1982, W. Region V 1983, internat. soc. 1984), Energy Conservation Project of the Year, ASHRAE (S.D. chpt. and W. Region 1983, internat. soc. 1984); mem. Assn. of Energy Engrs. (charter pres. San Diego chpt. 1979-81), Calif. Soc. for Hosp. Engrs., ASHRAE (chpt. pres. 1973-74, regl. v.chmn. energy mgmt. 1985-), Assn. Profl. Energy Mgrs., Building Owners & Mgrs. Assn. Inc., Indep. Energy Producers, Consulting Engrs. Assn. of Calif., Am. Consulting Engrs. Council (chmn. cogeneration com.); civic: Rancho Bernardo Bowleros (charter), charter treas., chmn. Rancho Bernardo Baptist Ch., speaker on energy systems & conservation var. civic groups; contbr. articles in tech. jours., confs.; mil: m/sgt. US Army 1953-55, Reserve 1955-61, Disting. Svc.; Christian; rec: bowling, golf, ski. Res: 12561 Perla Ct San Diego 92128 Ofc: Verle A. Williams & Assocs. Inc. 7047 Carroll Rd Ste 100 San Diego 92121

WILLIAMSON, RAYMOND DANIEL, JR., superior court judge; b. June 4, 1938, San Francisco; s. Raymond Daniel and Pauline W.; m. Carol A., Nov. 9, 1963; children: Raymond III b. 1965, Debbie b. 1967, Kevin b. 1969; edn: BS English, Univ. of S.F. 1959; JD, Univ. S.F. Law Sch. 1963. Career: asst. trust

ofcr. Wells Fargo Bank 1963-66; deputy city atty. 1966-73; mun. ct. judge 1973-85; superior ct. judge 1985–; instr. Calif. Judges Coll., Mid-Career Judges Course; honors: Trial Judge of the Year 1984; mem: United Cerebral Palsy Assn. of S.F. (chmn. bd.); Commonwealth Club; Gleeson Library Assoc.; U.S.F. Law Assembly; mil: capt. US Army; Republican; Catholic; rec: softball. Ofc: 475 City Hall San Francisco 94102

WILLICH, RICHARD RADE, service co. executive; b. May 20, 1942, Chgo.; s. Nicholas and Grace (Zubchevich) W.; m. Nancy Nimz, Aug. 11, 1962; children: Christine b. 1963, Theodore b. 1964, Julie b. 1969; edn: BA, Ripon Coll. 1964; MBA, Pepperdine 1972. Career: mgr. Am. Can Co., 1967-69; mgr. Kepner Tregoe, 1969-71; founder/CEO Dow Industries, Inc., 1971-86; founder/ CEO United Teleplex, Inc., 1986–; trustee Ripon Coll.; honors: Inc. Mag.'s 11th fastest growing, privately-held co. in U.S. (1985); mem. Young Pres.'s Orgn., Old Crows Assn.; civic: nat. co-chmn. Athletes in Action Coaches and Exec. Conf.; founding dir. Mission Viejo Rotary Club (1974); publ: Managing by Personal Objectives (1977); mil: lt. col. US Marine Corps 1964-67, Navy Commendn. Medal Combat, Purple Heart; Republican; Serbian Orthodox; rec: breeding Grand Prix Jumping Horses. Ofc: United Teleplex 24422 Ave Carlota Ste 235 Laguna Hills 92653

WILLIG, LEONARD, investment co. executive; b. Dec. 1, 1928, Brklyn.; s. Jacob and Rose (Weber) W.; edn: BS in bus. ad., Long Island Univ. 1952; BS in E.E., RCA Inst. 1953; lic: First Cl. Radiotelephone, FCC; SEC Series 7 lic.; NASD lic.; Calif. lic. Life Ins., Variable Annuity. Career: senior field engr. Ampex Corp., Redwood City 1959-75; investment exec. Bateman Eichler, Hill Richards Inc., Woodland Hills 1975-78, assoc. v.p. 1984–; 2d v.p. investments, Shearson/Am. Express, Woodland Hills 1978-81, consultant/prin., tax avoidance, fin. plnng., 1981-82; investment exec. (municipal bond, govt. secs. splst) Morgan, Olmstead, Kennedy & Gardner Inc., Woodland Hills 1982-84; conducts investment seminars. Awards: mktg. man of year, Ampex Corp. 1971; United Airlines 100,000 mile club 1961; Century Club 1980; recognition, Principles of Videotape Engrg. 1959; Bnai Brith Century Club 1977. Mem: Internat. Assn. of Fin. Plnng., Soc. of Motion Picture & TV Engrs., Bnai Brith, Tarzana Lodge; various tech. publs., Ampex; mem. tech. team videotape recorded Adolf Eichmann trial, Israel, 1961. rec: hiking, riding, music, theater. Res: 37564 Rondell St. (POB 1067) Agoura Hills 91301 Ofc: Bateman Eichler Hill Richards Inc. 6355 Topanga Cyn Blvd Woodland Hills 91367

WILLIS, WILLIAM HARRIS, JR., physician, cardiologist; b. June 26, 1943, St. Augustine, Fla.; s. William Harris and Verlie Ellen (Jahn) W.; m. Jan, Aug. 14, 1966; children: Brandon b. 1972, Patrick b. 1975; edn: BA, Southern Coll. 1965; MD, Loma Linda Univ. 1969. Career: intern, resident Univ. Ala. Hosp. & Clinics 1969-72, cardiol. fellow 1972-74, chief fellow 1973-74; clin. asst. prof. med. Univ. Tex. San Antonio 1975-76; asst. prof. med. Loma Linda Univ. 1976-78, assoc. prof. 1978-84, prof. 1984–; dir cardiovascular labs.; asst. chief cardiol.; dir. cardiol. fellowship pgm.; honors: Outstanding Young Men of Am., Outstanding Tchg. Resident (Univ. Ala. Dept. Med. 1972); fellow: Am. coll. Cardiol., Am. Coll. Physicians, Am. Heart Assn., Soc. Cardiac Angiography; pres. San Bernardino County Heart Assn. 1982-84; publ: num. book chpts. and articles on coronary heart disease, angiography and angioplasty; mil: major USAF 1974-76; Republican; Seventh-Day Adventist; rec: golf, tennis, snow and water skiing. Res: 11515 Welebir Loma Linda 92354 Ofc: Cardiovascular Lab. Loma Linda Univ. Med. Ctr. 11234 Anderson St Loma Linda 92350

WILLITS, PAT LEE, photographer; b. Aug. 19, 1947, Okla. City., Okla.; parents: Charles Raymond and Mary Jane (Miller) W.; edn: Central State Univ. Okla. 1964-67; UC Los Angeles Extn. 1979-80; Brooks Inst. Photog. 1982. Career: composer oper., asst. artist Okla. State Dept. of Edn. 1970-74; graphic artist, phototypesetter, photographer Calif. Occidental Petroleum Corp. 1975-81; corp. photog. Armand Hammer Prodns. 1982-86, Occidental Petroleum Corp. 1986–; mem: Photographic Soc. of Am., Am. Soc. Magazine Photogs., Santa Monica Track Club; publs: American Way Magazine (1985), Rotarian Mag. (1985), Majestic World of Arabian Horses (1986), Arabian Horse World (1983); Democrat; Christian; rec: horses. Ofc: Occidental Petroleum Corp. 10889 Wilshire Blvd Ste 970 Los Angeles 90024

WILSON, DAVID JOHN, property management co. president; b. Mar. 29, 1939, San Rafael; s. Eric and Marie (Nora) W.; m. Mary, Aug. 26, 1967; children: Mary Elizabeth b. 1969, Laura b. 1971, Jeanine b. 1975, Gregory b. 1976; edn: BS in commerce, Santa Clara Univ. 1961; desig: Cert. Prop. Mgr. (CPM) 1972, Cert. Shopping Ctr. Mgr. (CSM) 1972, Cert. Review Appraiser 1977, Sr. Cert. Valuer 1981, Reg. Public Appraiser 1986. Career: regional prop. mgr. Coldwell, Banker & Co., 1964-72; pres./dir. Grubb & Ellis Properties Services Inc., 1972-75, dir. Grubb & Ellis Co., 1973-74; pres./bd. chmn. Fox & Carskadon Mgmt. Corp., 1975-79; pres./bd. chmn. D.J. Wilson & Co. Inc., 1980–; trustee Landsing Instnl. Props. Trust VI and VII, 1984–; mem. Inst. of Real Estate Mgmt. (regl. v.p. 1979-80, pres. S.F. chpt. 1977), CofC; clubs: Olympic, Castlewood Country, Elks; contbr. article in J. of Prop. Mgmt.; mil: capt. US Army 1961-63; Republican; Catholic; rec: golf, swim. Ofc: D.J. Wilson & Co. 39102 Argonaut Way Fremont 94538

WILSON, DOUGLAS EDWIN, lawyer; b. Apr. 23, 1917, Sacramento; s. Richard Matthew and Ethel Ruth (O'Brien) W.; m. Helen Marie Lewis, Apr. 5, 1942; children: Sandra (Olds) b. 1943, Kent b. 1948, Jay b. 1950; edn: BA, Univ. of Pacific 1939; JD, UC Hastings Law Sch. 1948; admitted Calif. State Bar 1949. Career: atty. ptnr. Forslund & Wilson, Stockton, 1949-83, Wilson & Wilson, 1983–; US magistrate Stockton, Eastern Dist. of Calif., 1962-76;

mem. San Joaquin County Retirement Bd. 1952-72; honors: Silver Beaver award Boy Scouts (1966), Disting. Eagle Scout award (1971); mem. Calif. Bar Assn., San Joaquin County Bar Assn.; Am. Legion, Commonwealth Club (SF); Mason (Shriner, K.T.), Elk, Rotarian; mil: capt. Arty., US Army 1941-46; Republican; Methodist; rec: golf, gardening. Res: 2134 Gardena Ave Stockton 95204 Ofc: Wilson & Wilson, Attys. 11 S San Joaquin St Stockton 95202

WILSON, LIONEL JOSEPH, mayor of Oakland; b. New Orleans; BA in econ. UC Berkeley 1939; JD, UC Hastings Coll. Law 1949; m. Dorothy; children: Robin, Lionel, and Steven; admitted Calif. State Bar 1950. Career: presiding judge Oakland-Piedmont Municipal Ct. 1964, Alameda Co. Superior Cts. 1973; presiding judge criminal div. Alameda Co. Supr. Cts., Oakland 1969, 72, 75, Apellate Dept., 1976; mayor City of Oakland, 1977—; prin., Sta. KJAZ, Alameda 1980-83; mem. adv. com. Alameda Co. Council Alcoholism, Alameda Co. Mental Health Assn.; cons. Far West Sch.; chmn., pres. Oakland Econ. Devel. Council, INc. 1964-69; chmn., pres. Oakland Men of Tomorrow, Charles Houston Law Club; chmn. Oakland's Anti- Poverty Bd., Oakland Bail Proj. 1964-65; awards: NAACP west coast region merit award 1960; outstanding profl. svc., No. Calif. Med., Dental, and Pharm. Assn. 1975; Man of Year 1978 Oakland Lodge Bnai Brith; leadership awd., Chinese- Am. Citizens Alliance 1979; mem: NAACP (dir.); Nat. League of Cities; League of Calif. Cities (dir.); U.S. Conf. of Mayors; Democrat. Ofc: Room 302, City Hall, Oakland 94612

WILSON, ROBERT LEROY, lawyer; b. July 7, 1933, Johnsonburg, Pa.; s. James Priestly and Kathryn (Bauer) W.; m. Nancy, Nov. 26, 1976; children: James Robert b. 1956, Kimberly Danette b. 1961; edn: BA, Allegheny Coll. 1956; LLB, Univ. of Pa. Law Sch. 1959; admitted State Bar of Pa. 1959, Calif. 1964. Career: lawyer Berman, Richard & Brian, Upper Darby, Pa. 1959-61, Hill, Farrer & Burrill, 1963-73, Leslie & Rubin, 1973-75, solo practice 1975-83, Wilson & Leeds, 1983—; Dale Carnegie instr. 1973-; recipient AS-CAP Award for paper on Copyright Law; mem. Penna. Bar Assn., Calif. Bar Assn., Los Angeles County Bar Assn., Federal Bar Assn.; club: Manhattan Beach CC; mil: capt. USAF 1961-63; Democrat; Methodist; rec: tennis. Res: 1144 Poinsettia Ave Manhattan Beach 90266 Ofc: Wilson & Leeds 2040 Ave of the Stars Ste 400 Los Angeles 90067

WILSON, ROBIN SCOTT, university president; b. Sept. 19, 1928, Columbus, Ohio; m. 1951; 4 children; edn: BA, Ohio State Univ. 1950; MA, Univ. ill. 1951, PhD, 1959. Career: asst. instr. English Univ. of Ill. 1957-59; intelligence ofcr., CIA 1959-67; prof. English Clarion State Coll. 1967-70; assoc. dir. Com. Instnl. Cooperation 1970-77; assoc. provost Ohio State Univ. 1977-80; pres. CSU Chico 1980—; vis. lectr. Tulane Univ. 1971, Mich. State Univ. 1972-74, 1976-81; mem: Sci. Fiction Writers of Am., MLA, Am. Assn. Higher Edn.; publs: co-author, To the Sound of Freedom, 1973; ed., Clarion Experiment, 1971, Clarion II, 1972, Clarion III, 1973; ed., Those Who Can: A Science Fiction Reader, 1973. Ofc: California State Univ., Ofc. of the President, 1st and Normal Sts. Chico 95929

WILSON, STEPHEN CHARLES, real estate teacher; b. April 24, 1952, San Diego; s. Charles Virgil and Harriet Jacqueline (Smith) W.; m. Gail Dobbs, Nov. 11, 1972; children: Geoffrey Stephen b. 1975, Scott Michael b. 1978, Stuart Anthony b. 1983; edn: AA, Allan Hancock Coll. 1974; BBA, cum laude, National Univ. 1978; Real Estate Brokers Lic., 1981. Career: inventory mgr. USAF 1971-75; supply clerk NAS Miramar, San Diego 1975-77; real estate agent Sun Realty, San Diego 1978; tchr. Sun Real Estate Sch., San Diego 1979-81; loan ofcr. Delson Financial, San Diego 1979; loan ofcr. Mesa Mortgage, San Diego 1979-81; gen. mgr. Century 21 Robbins Realty, San Diego 1981; broker Stephen Wilson Real Estate Brokerage, San Diego 1981—; bus. devel., property mgr. Scripps Condominium Mgmt., San Diego 1982-84; tchr. Real Estate Trainers, Santa Ana 1983-84; pres. Condominium Analysts Consulting Firm 1984—; mem: Community Assn. Inst., Calif. Community Assn. (Inst. Legal Action Com., pres. 1985), Calif. Real Estate Edn. Assn., 44th Congl. Dist. Advy. Com. on Housing, San Diego Jaycees; works: articles on condominium assns., San Diego Union, La Jolla Light, San Diego Realtor Mag.; mil: s/sgt. USAF 1971-75; Democrat; Episcopal; rec: golf, writing. Res: 169 Lechuza Ln. Spring Valley 92077 Ofc: Anthony Schools, 2667 Camino Del South Ste. 301 San Diego 92108

WILSON, WAYNE P., college president; b. Sept. 3, 1931, Loveland, Colo.; s. Tom J. and Mable C. (Crook) W.; m. Cecelia cond, June 1, 1956; children: Wayne b. 1957, Nannette b. 1959, Mitchell b. 1964, Connie b. 1968, Charles b. 1970, Mtthew b. 1979; edn: BS, Brigham Young Univ. 1959, MA, Univ. of Pacific 1967. Career: high school tchr., counselor, administrator, 1959-68; pres. Condie Jr. College, San Jose 1968—; bd. dirs: Condie College, and Phillips Colleges, Inc.; honors: Phi Delta Kappa; mil: US Army 1950-53; Republican; Ch. of Jesus Christ of L.D.S. (Bishop). Res: 1249 Chateau Dr San Jose 95120 Ofc: Condie Jr. College, One W. Campbell Ave Campbell 95008

WIMMERS, STEVE HARRY, accountant; b. Aug. 18, 1951, Hamilton, Ohio; s. Maurice Eugene and Dorothy Ann (Herbers) W.; m. Marille, Aug. 16, 1974; 1 son, Eric b. 1975; edn: BS acctg., Ohio State Univ. 1973; CPA Calif. 1979. Career: acct. Deloitte, Haskins & Sells CPAs Columbus, Ohio 1973, Touche, Russ & Co. CPAs San Diego 1973-74; controller H&M Landing San Diego 1975-76, Calif. Minicomputer Systems 1976-77; pvt. practice Steve Wimmers CPA San Diego 1977—; bd.dirs: Calif. Minicomputer Sys. 1976-80, The Nascode Co. 1985, Am. Marketing Assoc. 1985; honors: Peninsula Comm. Svc. Youth Award (Ocean Beach Children's Devel. Ctr. 1985), Outstanding Young Men of Am. 1985, Pacesetters Award for Disting. Achievement (Ohio

State Univ. 1973), President's Scholarship Award for Outstanding Scholastic Performance (OSU 1973), other scholarships OSU 1969-72, Beta Alpha Psi (v.p. 1972-73), Beta Gamma Sigma 1972-73; mem: Am. Inst. CPAs 1980-, Calif. Soc. CPAs 1982-, Ocean Beach Merchants Assn. (pres. 1984-86), Ocean Beach Child Care Proj. (bd. dirs. 2 yrs., treas. 1 yr.), Mayor's Neighborhood Advisory Com., Ocean Beach Revitalization Com., Western Area Citizen's Advisory Com.; Democrat; rec: bike riding, basketball, tennis, reading, sun bathing. Res: 1542 Guizot St San Diego 92107 Ofc: 4870 Santa Monica Ave, Ste 2B, San Diego 92107

WINCHELL, ROBERT ALLEN, auditor; b. Oct. 28, 1945, Ft. Monmouth, N.J.; s. Robert Winslow and Mary M. (Allen) W.; edn: BA, UC Santa Barbara 1967; MBA, Wharton Grad. Div., Univ. of Penn. 1969. Career: fin. analyst, treas. div. S.C. Gas Co., Los Angeles 1975-76; senior auditor Defense Cont. Audit Agency, res. ofcr. Rockwell Internat. B-1 div., El Segundo 1976-79; senior auditor Defense Cont. Agency, res. ofcr. Hughes Aircraft Co., El Segundo 1979-84; senior auditor Defense Contract Audit Agency, Los Angeles regl. ofc. 1984—; mem: Am. Inst. CPAs, Assn. of Govt. Accts., Los Angeles Country Club; mil: 1st lt. US Army 1969-71, Bronze Star; Republican; Presbyterian; rec: golf, hiking, travel. Res: 2008 California Ave. Santa Monica 90403 Ofc: Defense Contract Audit Agency, 2500 Wilshire Blvd. Los Angeles 90057

WINCKLER, MILENA PETROVICH-NIEGOSCH, educator; b. Oct. 23, 1928, Los Angeles; d. H.H. Prince Milo (Petrovich-Niegosch) of Montenegro and Helena Grace (Smith) Petrovich-Niegosch, PhD; m. Nicholas Winckler (pres. food mfg. corp.; dec. 1971), Feb. 15, 1952; edn: BS in bus. adm., cum laude, USC 1949, MS edn., 1958; Calif. lic. School Administrator, ret. Career: tchr., vice prin., principal Los Angeles Unified Sch. Dist. 1953-80; asst. prof. CSU Los Angeles 1958; honors: Phi Kappa Phi, Beta Gamma Sigma (1948-49), Outstanding Business Woman award, USC Sch. of Bus. Adminstrn. (1949), Delta Kappa Gamma (pres. Omega Chap. 1960); clubs: Thunderbird Country (Rancho Mirage), Balboa Bay (Newport Beach), Pathfinders (Palm Springs), Town & Gown (UCI), 552 Club (benefit Hoag Meml. Hosp. Presbyn. of Newport Beach); Republican; Prot. Res: 611 Lido Park Dr, 3-C, Newport Beach 92663

WINDELL, CARL THOMAS, investor, lawyer; b. March 11, 1935, San Francisco; s. Thomas and Bernice Theresa W.; m. Manije' Darougar, July 10, 1985; children: Dana b. 1964, Caroline b. 1968, Kristin b. 1969; edn: BS, Univ. of calif. 1957; JD, Lincoln Univ. 1966; AA, Coll. of San Mateo. Career: pharmacist, 1957-70; atty. pvt. practice 1966-85; tchr. 1973-78; investor 1985—; mem: Calif. Bar Assn., San Mateo Co. Bar Assn., San Bruno CofC (dir. 1972-80); mil: s/sgt. USAF (Res) 1957-65; Republican; Lutheran; rec: travel. Address: 860 Hayne Hillsborough 94010

WINDHAM, MARILYN ANN, real estate broker; b. Apr. 3, 1950, San Francisco; d. Charles Edward and Ann Laura (Carstensen) W.; m. Edward Windham, Mar. 27, 1973; children: Ian b. 1982, Kendra Anne b. 1985; edn: stu. Cabrillo Coll., UCSB, UCSD, 1969-74; BA, San Diego State Univ. 1976; cert. profcy. acctg., Cabrillo 1983; real estate broker lic., Calif. 1981. Career: owner Tobacco Rd. Cattery 1971—; real estate sales agt. Bonanza Properties, Tustin 1976; escrow techn. Western Title Co., Santa Cruz 1977; real estate agt. Real Estate World, Santa Cruz 1978; realtor self empl., Santa Cruz 1981-82; independent real estate broker 1982—; pres., mng. partner Winn Leasing Co. (resdtl. prop. mgmt.) 1984—; honors: owner/ breeder best Havana Brown in Southwest region 1976, 1977; mem: Nat. and Calif. Assns. of Realtors; Cat Fanciers Assn.; Internat. Havana Brown Soc.; Mensa; Nat. Assn. for Gifted Children; Forum on Gifted Children; Early Childhood Edn. Gp.; Parenthesis; Santa Cruz Exch. Club; Am. Contract Bridge League; research: inheritance of the brown gene in agouti and no- agouti cats, discovered new gene as reported to the geneticist Todd 1976; Democrat; rec: cat breeding, early childhood learning, genetics. Address: Marilyn Windham, Broker, 3907 Adar Lane Soquel 95073

WINDUS, WALTER BRISTOL, quality assurance executive; b. Nov. 10, 1938, Albany, NY; s. Charles Edward and Lowene Elizabeth (Bristol) W.; m. Susan Clow, 1961; 1 dau. Karen b. 1968; edn: BSEE, Wash. State Univ. 1961, MSEE 1962; MBA, Univ. Santa Clara 1964; Reg. Profl. Engr. (Elec.) Calif., 1966. Career: mgr. quality assurance Consumer Products Div., Fairchild Camera and Instrument Co., Mt. View 1974-79; Kasper Instruments, Mt. View 1979; DMC Systems Inc. Santa Clara 1979-83; dir. quality assur. Televideo Systems Inc., Sunnyvale 1983-85; v.p. quality, Molecular Computer Inc., San Jose 1985—; honors: Tau Beta Pi (1960), Sigma Tau (1960), Omicron Delta Kappa (1961); mem: Nat. Soc. Profl. Engr. Santa Clara Chpt., Intermountain Kennel Club (pres. 1970), Seaplane Pilots Assn. (v.p./w. coast dir. 1977-), Frazier Lake Airpark (dir. 1982-); mgr. Frazier Lake SPB, Hollister 1985—; works: The Effects of Nuclear Radiation on a Weston Cadmium Cell (1962); Design, Devel. & Operation of a Seaplane Landing Pond (1985); num. publs. on seaplane related topics; Republican; Presbyterian; rec: aviation. Res: 12681 Saratoga Creek Dr Saratoga 95070 Ofc: Molecular Computer, 1983 Concourse Dr San Jose 95131

WINEMAN, PAUL RAYMOND, JR., marketing consultant, contract negotiator; b. Oct. 22, 1936, Hollywood, Calif.; s. Paul Raymond and Frances Neale (Dienst) W.; edn: BA communs, Univ. Wash. 1958, MA Arabic studies, Am. Univ. Beirut, Lebanon 1967. Career: gen. mgr. Television of Iran 1967; contract supv. US Corps of Engrs. Saudi Arabia 1968; regl. dir. Avco Internat. Svcs., Avco Corp. Beirut, Lebanon 1969-73; regl. dir. United Technols. Internat. Beirut 1973-77; pres. Paul R. Wineman & Assoc. Inc. Marina del Rey, Calif. 1977—; seminar leader on effective negotiating domestic & internat. for Karrass Seminars of Santa Monica 1981—; honors: Dick Laybourne Meml. Award (Avco Corp. 1971); mem. Rotary; mil: capt. US Army Signal Corps 1958-65; rec: tennis, travel. Res: 4265 Marina City Dr Apt 1111WTN Marina del Rey 90292

WINKLER, DELAINE LAUREN, environmental scientist; b. Aug. 17, 1953, Los Angeles; parents: Earl Theodore and Sara (Landman) Winkler; edn: BS, USC 1975, MS, 1979. Career: tchg. asst. USC, Los Angeles 1976-79; marine scientist, lab. supvr. Ichthyoplankton Coastal and Harbor Studies, USC and L.A. Co. Natural Hist. Mus., Los Angeles 1979-81; research asst. Getty Synthetic Fuels, Signal Hills 1981; asst. environmental scientist, Port of Los Angeles, San Pedro 1981—; taxonomic cons. Taxon 1979; academic advr. USC Biology dept. 1978; honors: Bank Am. Music Award (1971), Calif. State Scholar (1971-75), Calif. State Fellow (1975-78); mem: Phi Sigma (Alpha Alpha chpt.), Soc. for Hist. Archaeology, Calif. Preservation Found., Jewish Genealogical Soc. of Los Angeles; publs: sci. presentation Pacific Slope Biochem. Conf., Santa Barbara (1978), research art. in Fishery Bulletin (1983), performed in amateur bluegrass band; Democrat; Jewish; rec: genealogy, tennis, hiking. Res: PO Box 24633 Los Angeles 90024 Ofc: Port of Los Angeles, Environmental Management Div., POB 151, Los Angeles 90733-0151

WINOTO, ASTAR, (aka Tung Bing, Huang) molecular biologist/biochemist; b. Dec. 31, 1958, Malang, E.Java, Indonesia; s. Gunawan and Kustari (Sri) W.; m. Lucidawati, June 19, 1983; 1 dau. Elena b. 1985; edn: BA, summa cum laude, UC Berkeley 1981; PhD, Calif. Inst. of Tech. 1986. Career: tchg. asst. Caltech 1982, 83, 85, grad. research asst. 1981-86, research fellow 1986; awards: Citation, UCB Molecular Bio. Dept. for best undergrad. (1981), Phi Beta Kappa (1981); mem. AAAS; publs: Proc. Nat. Acad. Sci. USA (6/83), Cell (3/82), J. Mol. Cell Immunol. (1984), Science (11/84), Nature (8/85), Trans. Proc. (6/85), Nature (8/85), Progress in Immunol. (1983), Ir Genes: Past, Present and Future (1983); rec: swim, chess, ping-pong. Ofc: Caltech (147-75) Pasadena 91125

WINTER, DAVID KENNETH, college president; b. Sept. 15, 1930, So. Pasadena; s. Hugo H. and Hazel C. (Patterson) W.; m. L. Diane Fischer, June 28, 1960; children: Laura, Ruth, Bruce; edn: BA, UCLA 1953, MA, 1956; PhD, Mich. State Univ. 1968. Career: instr. Wheaton Coll., Ill. 1959-62; asst. prof. then assoc. prof. Mich. State Univ. 1965-70; dean of faculty then exec. v.p. Whitworth Coll., Spokane, Wash. 1970-76; pres. Westmost Coll., Santa Barbara 1976—; bd. dirs. Cottage Hosp., Montecito Assn.; honors: Midwestern Univ. Consortium grantee 1964-65; Fellow Am. Anthropological Assn.; mem: Christian Coll. Consortium, Christian Coll. Coalition, Ind. Colls. of So. Calif., Council Ind. Colls., Santa Barbara Club, Montecito Rotary; mil: lt. USNR 1955-59. Address: 985 La Paz Rd. Santa Barbara 93108

WINTER, RAYMOND LAWRENCE, research scientist; b. May 20, 1948, Bayshore, NY; s. Raymond Abram and Martha (Oertel) W.; edn: BA, Alfred Univ.; MS in glass sci., SUNY Alfred Coll. of Ceramics. Career: materials scientist Globe Union/ Johnson Controls Inc. Corp. Applied Research Group 1974-79; supr. cermet research Bourns Inc. mats. research dept. 1979-83, research scientist 1983-84, staff scientist 1985, staff scientist 1986—; mem: Am. Inst. Physics, Am. Physical Soc., Am. Ceramic Soc. (Glass Sci. Div.), Mathematical Assn. of Am.; publs: 4 papers on electronic properties of ceramic mats.; Republican; Catholic; rec: collector original prints of sch. of little German masters. Res: 1170 Tripoli St, 9, Riverside 92507

WINTER, TERRY MAC, engineer; b. Nov. 28, 1941, Akron, Ohio; s. John Ernest and Dorothy Pearl (McNeff) W.; m. Melinda S. Tedrow, July 30, 1966; children: Michelle b. 1964, Michael b. 1970, Jared b. 1977; edn: BS in E.E., Univ. Idaho 1964; Reg. Profl. Engr., Calif., Ariz. Career: service engr. Los Angeles Dept. of Water & Power, 1964-65; radar ofcr. US Army, White Sands Missile Range, N.M. 1965-67; underground distbn. engr. Salt River Project, Tempe, Ariz. 1967-68, senior engr. 1968-70, lead engr. 1970-76., transmission engring. supvr. 1976; transmission engring. supvr. San Diego Gas & Electric, 1976-81, Southwest Powerlink Project mgr. SDG&D 1981-85, dir. electric engring. 1985—; mem. IEEE (PCEA transmission sponsor and E&D chmn.); mil: lt. col. US Army, Army Commendation; Republican; Mormon. Res: 2440 Windmill View Rd El Cajon 92020 Ofc: San Diego Gas & Electric 101 Ash St San Diego 92112

WINTERS, NANCIE JOELLE-LYNNE, personnel co. president/lawyer; b. Dec. 3, 1943, Eureka; parents: Mathias Shirley and Nancy Lynn (Miller) Winters; edn: BA, Humboldt State Coll. 1967; MA, Humboldt State Univ. 1975; JD, Southwestern Univ. Sch. of Law 1984; admitted Calif. State Bar 1986. Career: atty.; pres. Personnel Consultants, Irvine; mem. Masons (Past Master), Sciots, Scottish Rite, York Rite, Shriners, Tau Kappa Epsilon, Phi Alepha Delta, Pi Kappa Delta, Rotary; publs: articles on political and bus. hist.; Republican; Episcopal; rec: travel, sports. Res: POB 8028 Newport Beach 92660 Ofc: POB 18736 Irvine 92713

WINTZ, LESTER MERRILL, marketing and banking executive; b. Mar. 22, 1927, Jersey City, N.J.; s. Julius C. and Doris (Boorstein) W.; m. A. Beverly, Sept. 17, 1950; children: Douglas b. 1953, Jodi b. 1954; edn: BA, Rutgers Univ. 1949. Career: exec. pos. with subs. cos., Beneficial Standard Corp.: senior v.p. Beneficial Standard Life, Beneficial National Life, pres. Fidelity Interstate Life, senior v.p. Direct Marketing Corp. of Am., 1962-83; senior v.p. Great Western Savings/ pres. G.W. Direct Marketing Co., 1983—; dir: Advantage Direct, G.W. Financial Securities, G.W. Fin. Direct Marketing Co.; honors: Fellow Anti-Defamation League; chmn. Young Musicians Found.; Who's Who in Insurance. Res: 101 Ocean Ave Santa Monica 90402 Ofc: Great Western Savings 8484 Wilshire Blvd Beverly Hills 90211

WIRA, RICHARD JOSEPH, insurance agency president; b. Aug. 16, 1949, Cincinnati, Ohio; s. Joseph Edward and Angela Teresa (Vogeler) W.; m. Pamela, Dec. 28, 1985; 1 dau. Wendy Joy b. 1975. Career: Home Life of NY 1974-76; self-employed 1976-80; owner ins. agency 1980—; regl. supt. of agencies Jefferson Nat. Life in So. Calif., Ariz., Nev.; honors: Million Dollar Round Table, Nat. sales Achievement Award, Nat. Quality Award, Top Recruiter (Jefferson Nat. Life 1984, 85), 5-time winner Toastmasters Dist. 5 Internat. Speech Contest; mem: Calif. Life Underwriters Assn. (past. dir.), Nat. Spkrs. Bureau, Toastmasters Bd. Realtors (past pres.), Life Ins. Leaders Club (past pres.), 65 Roses Chpt. of San Diego (pres.), The Friars Club; letter on National Unity published in Congressional Record 1971; author book: Master Key to a Rich Life; mil: ops. splst. 1/c USN 1968-72, Vietnamese Cross of Gallantry, Vietnam Campaign, Pres. Unit. Citn., Purple Heart, Good Conduct, Korean Campaign; Republican; Christian; rec: collector of presidential signatures, rare books, movie memorabilia, historical documents and papers. Ofc: 3180 University Ave Ste 550 San Diego 92104

WIRTHLIN, MILTON ROBERT, JR., dentist; b. July 13, 1932, Little Rock, Ark.; s. Milton R. and Margaret Frances (Clark) W.; m. Joan Krieger, Aug. 1, 1954; children: Michael, b. 1956, Steven, b. 1957, Laurie, b. 1959, David, b. 1960, Aina, b. 1966; edn: undergrad., UCB 1950-52; DDS, UC San Francisco 1956, MS, 1968; Diplomate Am. Bd. Periodontology 1974. Career: served to capt., Dental Corps, US Navy, 1955-85: exec. ofcr., 1st Dental Co., Vietnam 1968-69; head Periodontol., Naval Dental Clin., Long Beach, Ca. 1969-73; exec. ofcr. 3rd Dental Co. FMF, Okinawa, 1973-74; chief Epidemiol., Naval Dental Research Inst., Great Lakes, Ill. 1974-76, cmdg. ofcr. 1976-81; cmdg. ofcr. Naval Regl. Dental Ctr., San Francisco 1981-83; asst. chief of staff Naval Med. Command S.W. Region, San Diego 1983-85; clin. asst. prof. Periodontics, USC 1970-73, Univ. Ill. 1977-81; assoc. prof. periodontics Univ. of Pacific 1985—; honors: Gabbs Prize in Dentistry, UC 1956; Am. Acad. Dental Med. Award 1956; C.O.'s Award Excellence in Operative Dentistry, also Annual Award for Research Methods, Naval Dental Sch. 1966; Fellow Internat. Coll. of Dentistry 1980; mem: Omicron Kappa Upsilon, Am. Dental Assn., Internat. Assn. for Dental Resrch., Am. Acad. Periodontol., Western/MidWest Soc. Periodontol.; active in BSA (1968-), ARC, Nat. Model R.R. Assn. (past trainmaster Midwest Reg. Fox Valley Div.); publs: 28 articles on dental research; mil: decorated: Merit. Svc. with 2 Gold Stars, Navy Commendn. with Combat V; Prot.; rec: model R.R., trout fly tying, archery. Res: 187 Blue Canyon Way Martinez 94553 Ofc: Univ. of Pacific Sch. of Dentistry, San Francisco 94115

WISDOM, DARWIN DALE, FBI special agent; b. Oct. 16, 1941, Wenatchee, Wash.; s. Glen Raymond and Enid Muriel (Gallaher) W.; m. Karen Nelson, Oct. 3, 1964; children: Elizabeth b. 1968, Cherlyn b. 1972, Christopher b. 1974; edn: BA econ., bus. adm., Seattle Pacific Coll. 1963; grad. work, Univ. of W.Vir. 1965, Univ. of Wash. 1967. Career: underwriter and mgmt. trainee Farmers Insurance Group, Mercer Is., Wash. 1966; cost acct. Kenworth Motor Truck Co., Seattle 1967; spl. agent, FBI, Phoenix, Ariz. 1968-69, Financial Crimes Unit, FBI, San Diego, 1969—; bd. chmn. Cabrillo Federal Credit Union, S.D. 1980-; honors: Centurians (Service hon.) 1962; mem: Federal Criminal Investigators Assn. 1976-82 (bd. dirs. 1976); FBI Spl. Agents Assn.; Calif. Peace Ofcrs. Assn. 1982-3; Nat. Assn. of Credit Union Presidents; mem. Green Valley Civic Assn., S.D. Zoological Assn., Silver Saddle Homeowners Assn. (bd. 1977-81), various PTAs; mil: US Army Inf. 1964-66, 1st lt. USAR 1966-68; Republican; Presbyterian; rec: gardening, sports. Res: 13310 Bronco Way Poway 92064 Ofc: FBI, Suite 6S31, 880 Front St San Diego 92188

WISER, GEORGE LEONARD, aerospace executive; b. July 6, 1925, Randolph, Wisc.; s. George Carl and Margaret Wynona (Herrick) W.; m. Ina Rieger, Aug. 8, 1981; children: Nancy b. 1952, Scott b. 1954; edn: BS, Calif. Aero. Tech. Inst. 1948. Career: senior research engr. Lockheed Aircraft Corp. 1948-56; senior v.p. advanced technology Sierracin Research Corp. 1956-82, pres. 1982—; mem: Am. Inst. of Aero. & Astro (assoc. fellow 1960-), Soc. of Automotive Engrs.; works: num. tech. papers and articles; patentee: 1 U.S. patent, 1 Canadian patent, 2 British patents; miml: s/sgt. US Army Air Force 1943-46, Air Medal; rec: flying, sailing, photog. Ofc: Sierracin Research Corp., 12782 San Fernando Rd. Sylmar 91342-3795

WISNICKI, JEFFREY LEONARD, plastic and reconstructive surgeon; b. May 15, 1957, NY, NY; s. Joseph I. and Lorraine (Justman) W.; edn: BS summa cum laude, Rensselaer Poly. Inst. 1976; MD with distinction in research cum laude, Albany Med. Coll., Union Univ. 1980. Career: intern surg. Stanford Univ. Med. Ctr. 1980-81, resident gen. and plastic/reconstrv. surg. 1981-84, chief res. 1985-86; fellowships: plastic & reconstrv. surg., Dartmouth- Hitchcock Med. Ctr., Hanover, NH 1984; hand surg., Drs. Eugene Kilgore Jr., Wm. Newmeyer III, San Francisco 1985; bd. dirs. Interplast 1985-86, clin. instr. surg. UCSF 1985; honors: Third Prize Research Competition (Calif. Soc. Plastic & Reconstrv. Surgs. 1984), Alpha Omega Alpha (elected 1978, chpt. pres. 1979-80), Dean's Senior Research Award (1980), Dean's Award (Albany Med. Coll. 1977, 78), Dean's Letter for Scholastic Excellence (1976-77, 1977-80), CV Mosby Scholarship Book Award (1977, 78), Trustees Prize Pharmacology (1977), NY Med. Regents Scholar (1976-80), Nat. Boards Honors Group; publs: contbr. articles in med. jours., book chpts.; num. research presentations. Res: 920 W Remington, 5A, Sunnyvale 94087 Ofc: Div. of Plastic & Reconstrv. Surg., Dept. of Surg., Stanford Univ. Med. Ctr. Stanford 94305

WITT, NORMAN ERNEST, airline pilot, educator; b. May 2, 1927, Nebraska City, Nebr.; s. Ernie H. and Anna M. (Pruessing) W.; m. Alice thompson, Nov. 1, 1952; children: Norman E. Jr. b. 1953, Nancy Lynn b. 1955; edn: BS in edn., Univ. of Nebr. 1949, MS, 1955; EdD, UC Los Angeles 1969; grad. (Distinguished Aviation Cadet) USAF Pilot School, Lubbock, Tx. 1951; cert. Indsl. Coll. of Armed Forces 1967. Career: aviation machinist mate, USNR (active 1945-46, Res. 1946-50, Teacher 1949-50); pilot & adminstrv. officer USAF (active 1950-56; Res. 1956-69); flight engr., co-pilot & captain United Air Lines, 1956−; teacher Los Angeles City Schools, 1956-73; research educationist, UCLA 19664-65; instr. Long Beach City Coll. 1974; account exec. municipal bonds, R.H. Moulton & Co., L.A. 1980−; Aviation Merit Badge counselor, BSA; honors: Phi Delta Kappa, UCLA Dean's Council, UCLA Doctoral Alumni Assn.; mem: Palos Verdes Breakfast Club 1968-, PV Rotary 1974-9, Airline Pilots Assn. 1967-, PV Estates City Plnng. Commn. 1976-81, PV Penin. Tax Advis. Com. 1976-7; Republican (pres. PV Repub. Club 1971); Lutheran; rec: music (sax, clarinet). Res: Box 862 Palos Verdes Estates 90274 Ofc: R.H. Moulton Co., 523 W. 6th St Los Angeles 90014

WITZEL, RONALD BARRIE, utility co. executive; b. July 7, 1943, San Francisco; s. Claude R. and Claire E. (Paulsen) W.; m. Joanna, May 4, 1985; children: Scott b. 1967, Amy b. 1970; edn: UC Davis 1961-64; Sacramento Comm. Coll. 1964; BS bus. & indsl. mgmt., San Jose State Univ. 1967; MBA, Golden Gate Univ. 1971. Career: inventory mgmt. US Steel Pittsburg, Calif. 1965; inventory analyst Pacific Gas & Elec. S.F. 1968-69, senior nuclear fuel buyer 1970-82, supv. nuclear fuel 1982, dir. nuclear fuel mgmt. 1983, mgr. power plant fuels dept. 1984−; honors: President's Commdn. (Sacto. Comm. Coll. 1964); mem: Atomic Indsl. Forum Mining & Milling Com. 1971-, Edison Electric Inst. Nuclear Fuels Com. 1981, Indian Valley Assocs., Novato Horsemen, Indian Valley Riding Club, Novato Youth Club (dir.); Republican; rec: trail riding (horse), yacht racing and cruising, running. Res: 1834 Indian Valley Rd Novato 94947 Ofc: Pacific Gas & Elec. 245 Market St San Francisco 94106

WOHL, ARMAND JEFFREY, cardiologist; b. Dec. 11, 1946, Phila.; s. Herman L. and Selma (Paul) W.; m. Marylou Giangrossi, Sept. 4, 1977; children: Michael b. 1979, Todd b. 1981; edn: undergrad. Temple Univ. 1964-67; MD, Hahnemann Univ. 1971. Career: chief of cardiology USAF Hosp. Elmendorf, Anchorage, Alaska 1976-78; chief of cardiology Riverside Med. Clinic, Riverside, Calif. 1978-79; cardiologist, Grossmont Cardiology Med. Group, La Mesa 1980-84; cardiologist, pvt. practice, La Mesa 1985−; mem. Am. Heart Assn. (bd. dirs. San Diego County Chap. 1981-); Fellow: Am. Coll. of Cardiology (1979), Am. Coll. of Physicians (1979), Council on Clin. Cardiology (1981); publs: 5 abstracts; 5 articles in med. journals; mil: major USAF 1976-78. Ofc: 5565 Grossmont Center Dr. Ste 126, La Mesa 92041

WOHL, JAMES PAUL, lawyer, educator, author; b. Oct. 3, 1937, NY, NY; s. Joseph and Mae (Kreshover) W.; m. Sigrid Elenor Sletteland, June 6, 1969 (div. 1979); children: Frederic, Kristin, Jenifer; edn: Princeton Univ. 1955-57; AB, Stanford Univ. 1962, JD, 1963; admitted Calif. State Bar 1963, Hawaii 1964, N.Y. 1969. Career: assoc. atty. Carlsmith, Carlsmith, Wichman & Case Honolulu 1963-68, Fried, Frank, Harris, Shriver & Jacobson N.Y.C. 1968-70; pres. Hawaii Land Corp. Honolulu 1970-78; prof. law Laverne San Fernando Law Ctr. Sepulveda 1978−; pres. Original New York Seltzer Internat. Inc. 1985−; mem: Mystery Writers of Am., Salvation Army (Hilo, Hi. bd. dirs.), Hawaii Media Adv. Council (pres. 1975-76), W. Hollywood CofC (dir. 1983-), clubs: Princeton (N.Y.C.), Hilo Yacht; author: The Nirvana Contracts (1977), Talon (1978), The Blind Trust Kills (1979). Address: 1640 N Genessee Ave Los Angeles 90046

WOLF, GERALD ALEXANDER, commercial real estate executive; b. May 5, 1945, Ft. Worth, Texas; s. Tobian A. and Ann (Katz) W.; edn: BBA in mktg. Univ. of Texas, Austin 1967; acctncy. pgm. Sacto. City Coll. 1984. Calif. lic. real estate broker (1979). Career: advt. exec. Hercules Bdcstg. Co., Sacto. 1972-73; bus. mgr. multi-family props. Johnstown Properties, Oakland 1974-75, leasing agent, 1975-79; dir. of leasing Mar-Mon Developers/ Strand Architects, Truckee 1980-82; leasing coord. respons. for shopping centers in Superior Calif., Inter-Cal Real Estate Corp., Sacto. 1985−; mem. Internat. Council of Shopping Ctrs.; mil: s/sgt. USAF 1968-72, Am. Forces Radio & TV; Jewish; rec: pvt. finl. investor. Address: Sacramento 95814

WOLFE, ELLIOTT SIDNEY, private investigation agency president; b. Dec. 8, 1933, Salt Lake City, Utah; s. Abraham B. and Minnie (Albert) W.; m. Phillene Lehrman, Feb. 16, 1958; div.; children: Steven b. 1959, Dayna b. 1961, Staci b. 1967; edn: BS, USC, 1956; LLB, USFV Coll. of Law 1968; Calif. lic. owner pvt. investg. agency 1958. Career: deputy sheriff County of Los Angeles, 1955-56; free lance pvt. investigator, 1956-58; owner/pres. pvt. investigation agcy., 1958-82; investigator and civil procedures cons. to various law firms, 1982−; lectr. in field, state, nat., internat. assns., L.A. City Coll., 1970-82; honors: Outstanding Member Award, Student Council, USC Coll. of Letters, Arts & Scis. 1953; recipient num. merit awards, profl. assns.; past mem: World Assn. of Detectives, Calif. Assn. Licensed Invstgtrs. (past pres., editor), Calif. Assn. Profl. Process Servers (past bd. chmn., editor), Nat. Council of Investigator & Security Svcs. (v.p.), Tau Delta Phi frat USC; Republican; rec: wood carving, pottery. Res: 5711 Norwich Ave Van Nuys 91411 Ofc: E.S. Wolfe & Assoc., POB 5534, Sherman Oaks 91413

WOLFF, GEORGE, aircraft co. executive; b. Dec. 21, 1928, Westphalia, W. Germany, nat. US cit. 1939; s. Fred and Else (Liepmann) W.; m. Arlene Geannes, Sept. 18, 1983; children: Joan b. 1957, Tom b. 1960; edn: BSEE, City Coll. NY 1951; Univ. Del. 1953-54; bus./law, El Camino Coll. 1974-83. Career:

mgr. non linear magnetics Freed Transformer Co. NY 1954-64; mem. tech. staff satellite div. Aerospace Corp. El Segundo 1964-67; pgm. mgr. advanced devel. pgms. Hughes Aircraft Co. El Segundo 1967−; cons. British Aerospace 1977−; honors: Patent Award of the Year (1977, 85); mem: Inst. Elec. Electron. Engrs. (senior), Mgmt. Club; publ: 6 tech. papers in profl. jours.; 3 patents; mil: ssgt. US Army Ballistic Research Labs. 1952-54; Republican; rec: swimming, walking. Ofc: Hughes Aircraft Co. POB 92919 Bldg 512/ V348 Los Angeles 90009

WOLFSBERGER, JAMES DAVIS, manager; b. Jan. 23, 1941, Los Angeles; s. Emil and Martha Gail (McClintock) W.; children: Aaron James b. 1974, Carey Lynn b. 1973, Kelli Ann b. 1966; edn: AA, Cerritos Coll. 1960; BA, Fresno State Univ. 1963; MA, phys. ed., CSU San Jose 1970, MA, counselor ed., 1974; EdD, USC 1983; MBA, Univ. of Phoenix 1986. Career: instr. Bellflower H.S. 1964-66; instr. Gavilian Coll. 1974-82; asst. dean of instrn. Tech. & Pub. Svcs. 1977-83; senior v.p. Belle River Inc., exporter of commodities 1981−; currently, mgr. GTE Western Div.; ind. rep. State Advy. Com. for Vocational Guidance; Counseling & Tng. for Chancellor's Ofc. for the Calif. Community Colls.; honors: Phi Delta Kappa, USC; mem: Assn. of Calif. Comm. Coll. Adminstrs., Calif. Assn. of Work Experience Educators, Calif. Assn. Vocational ED., Calif. Com. Coll. Adminstrs. of Occupational Edn., Coop. Work Exp. Edn. (stu. syllabus), Coop. Edn. (instr., coord., syllabus); Republican; Methodist; rec: mountain climbing, rodeo. Res: 455 Fitzgerald Gilroy 95020 Ofc: GTE Government Systems Corp., 100 Ferguson Dr. Mountain View 94039

WOLLMAN, LEWIS BENSON, management consultant; b. Nov. 13, 1921, NY, NY; s. Ezra and Anna Ella (Meyers) W.; m. Patricia Elizabeth Tobin, Oct. 4, 1968; edn: BA, NY Univ. 1943; NY Grad. Sch. of Bus. Adminstrn. 1946-48. Career: var. sales mgmt. positions Internat. Latex Corp. NYC 1950-55; mktg. cons. 1955−; nat. sales mgr. Revlon Corp. NYC 1960-61; gen. mgr. cons. prods. Gulton Inds Inc. Metuchen, NJ 1965-66; exec. v.p., gen. mgr. Electro Engrg. Prods. Inc. Chgo. 1970-74; ptnr. J.M. Brookshire Inc. Houston 1986-, Suzanne Haley Internat. Aptos, Calif. 1985-; instr. Fashion Inst. of Design & Mdsg S F 1975-76; listed, Who's Who in World Commerce & Industry 1968-69; mem: NYC Execs. Club 1965-67, Chgo. Exec. Club 1971-74, Jr. CofC 1956-57, Big Brothers 1961-62; mil: lt. USNR, Asiatic- 3 Battle Stars, Philippine Liberation, European, Carribean; Republican; rec: gardening, reading. Res: 1 Mt. Whitney Dr San Rafael 94903

WOMACK, LARRY DAVID, accountant; b. Aug. 7, 1939, Strafford, Mo.; s. Ransom Meade and Fern Louise (Yarbrough) W.; m. Joan, Sept. 12, 1964; children: Kristen b. 1967, David b. 1971; edn: stu. Redlands Univ. 1957-58, Mt. San Antonio Coll. 1958-59; BS in bus. adm., CSU Long Beach 1964; CPA lic. Calif., 1966. Career: audit supr. Coopers & Lybrand, Los Angeles 1964-73; spl. projects acct. Cyprus Mines Corp., L.A. 1973-78; corporate controller General Automation, Inc., Anaheim 1978−; mem: Am. Inst. CPAs, Nat. Assn. of Accts.; mil: pvt. Army Intell. 1960-62; Republican; Protestant. Ofc: General Automation, Inc. 1045 S East St Anaheim 92805

WONG, CARTLEY, electrical engineer; b. May 25, 1954, Stockton; s. Lun and Chun (Gong) W.; edn: electrical and electronic eng., Sacramento State Univ. 1980; prof. elec. engr., Calif. 1983. Career: elec. engr. US Army Corps of Engrs. Sacramento Dist. 1981−; in-house instr., US Army Corps of Engrs.; honors: Spl. Art Award, support MX Missile Assembly Bldg. Crane Team 1982; Sustained Superior Performance, 1984; rec: computer, electronics, auto repair. Res: 7801 Scottsdale Dr. Sacramento 95828 Ofc: US Army Corps of Engineers, 650 Capitol Mall Sacramento 95814

WONG, DONALD GUY, engineering executive; b. July 24, 1934, San Francisco; s. Edward Gim and Alice G. (Ow Young) W.; m. Jeanette, Aug. 16, 1959; children: Randy S. b. 1962, Jerry G. b. 1963, Brent E. b. 1967; edn: BS, UC Berkeley 1956, MS, 1959; reg. civil engr., Calif. Career: assoc. design engr. Northrop Corp., Hawthorne 1956; asst. bridge engr. State of Calif., Truckee, Palo Alto 1956-58; stress engr. to senior research engr. Lockheed 1959-65, research splst. in structural dynamics 1965-68, group engr. in loads and structural dynamics 1968-74; mgr. of structures Lockheed Missels & Space Co., Sunnyvale 1974−; instr. computer programming Merritt Coll. 1965-66; cochmn. Cost Savings Team 1984-85; honors: Chi Epsilon; Robert E. Gross Award, Distinguished Paper 1981; mem: Am. Soc. Civil Engrs. (past), Young Life Com. for Silicon Valley (chmn. 1979-81), AYSO (coach 1976); works: Advanced Materials Applications on Trident 1 Missile, ASTM STP674, 1979; Integrated Structural Analysis and Design Support, AIAA-82-0675, 1982 (updated AIAA-86-1010-cp); Republican; Christian; rec: tennis, snow skiing, bridge. Res: 1649 Eagle Dr. Sunnyvale 94087

WONG, HARRY KEVIN, chiropractic center executive director; b. Jan. 17, 1953, San Francisco; s. Henry and Mamie (Chinn) W.; m. Safari Victoria, June 8, 1975; edn: Astara Victoria b. 1980, Joshua Michael b. 1984; edn: AA, San Francisco Community Coll. 1973, AS, 1976; BA, cum laude, San Francisco State Univ. 1978; DC, Palmer Coll. of Chiropractic West 1981. Career: assoc. Skarda Chiropractic 1982; founder, exec. dir. Wong & Assoc. Chiropractic Ctr., Redwood City 1982−; faculty Palmer Coll. of Chiropractic- West. 1982; Chiropractic Biophysics instr. 1982; mem: Internat., Am. and Calif. Chiropractic Assns., San Mateo Co. Chiropractic Soc. (secty. 1984); works: X-ray Motion Studies 1981; Chiropractic Instrument Adjusting Techniques 1981; Republican; Scientology; rec: equestrian, swimming, painting. Ofc: 1779 Woodside Rd. Ste. 103 Redwood City 94061

WONG, HING CHUNG, physician; b. Sept. 29, 1941, Hong Kong; nat. US citizen 1978; parents: Chui Y. and Shui Man (Tang) Wong; m. King Y. Wong, Apr. 2, 1962; edn: B.Medicine, Nat. Taiwan Univ. 1969; MD, USA, 1976. Career: Family Practice (solo), Chinatown, Los Angeles and med. ctr. in San Gabriel 1978–; chief cons. Chaus Jou Assn. in USA; med. advisor for am. Vietnam Chinese Friendship Assn., Eng Family Benev. Assn., Chinese Garment Assn., Elderly Indochinese Assn.; med. staff French Hosp. (pres. elect 1983); bd. dirs. Chinatown Service Center 1983-86; honors: good citizenship awd, City of Los Angeles; awards, Paralyzed Veterans Assn. (1977); mem. AMA, L.A. Co. Med. Assn.; Christian; rec: golf. Res: 1117 Alpine St Los Angeles 90012 Ofc: H.C. Wong, MD, 709 N. Hill St, Ste. 19, Los Angeles 90012; 808 E Valley Blvd San Gabriel 91776

WONG, JAMES BOK, management consultant, economist, engineer; b. Dec. 9, 1922, Canton, China, nat. US cit. 1962; s. Gen Ham and Chen (Yee) W.; m. Wai Ping Lim, Aug. 3, 1946; children: John b. 1948, Jane b. 1955, Julia b. 1956; edn: BS in agric., Univ. Md. 1949, BS in chem. eng. 1950; MS chem. eng., Univ. Ill. 1951, PhD, 1954. Career: research asst. Univ. Ill., Urbana 1950-53; chem. engr. Standard Oil Indiana at Whiting 1953-55; process design & research engr. Shell Devel. Co., Emeryville, Calif. 1955-61; senior plnng. engr., mgr. long range plnng. & econs., chief economist Rexall Drug & Chem. Co., Los Angeles 1961-70, dir. econs. & ops. analysis, dir. internat. technologies Dart Industries (fmrly. Rexall), 1970-81; pres. James B. Wong Assocs. Inc., Los Angeles 1981–; dir., chmn. exec. com. United Pacific Bank, L.A. 1982-84; honors: Outstanding Volunteer Svc. award City of Los Angeles (1977), named to Exec. Order of Ohio Commodores, Gov. Ohio (1982), Sigma Xi, Tau Beta Pi, Phi Kappa Phi, Pi Mu Epsilon, Phi Lambda Upsilon, Phi Eta Sigma; mem: Am. Inst. Chem. Engrs., Am. Chem. Soc.; civic: Chinese Am. Citizens Alliance Found. (dir., pres., 1971-), Asian Am. Edn. Commn./L.A. (1971-81); contbr. articles in A.M.A. Archives of Indsl. Hygiene and Occupational Medicine, Indsl. and Engring. Chemistry, and J. Applied Physics; mil: enlisted US Army 14th Air Force (Flying Tigers) 1943-46. Ofc: James B. Wong Associates Inc 2460 Venus Dr Los Angeles 90046

WONG, JIMMY MING, acupuncturist; b. June 10, 1948, Canton, China; s. Dot Ming and Yet Siu (Fong) W.; m. Regina Lee, Sept. 5, 1970; children: Corinna b. 1971, Jason b. 1974; edn: AA, City Coll. San Francisco 1970; The Research Inst. of Acupuncture, Hong Kong 1972. Calif. State certified acupuncturist (1977). Career: instr. Tai Chi Chuan, S.F. Community Coll., 1974–; instr. Kung Fu, S.F. City Coll., Chinese Culture Club 1972-74, South Bay Chinese Sch. (Milpitas) 1973-77; owner/chief instr. Doc-Fai Wong Kung Fu School, S.F. 1969–; honors: featured on the covers of Black Belt, Karate Illustrated mags. and inside Kung Fu mag.; mem: Choy Li Fut Internat. Fedn. (pres. 1980-), Tai Chi Chuan World Fedn. (chmn. 1980-), United Chung Wah Martial Arts Assn. of Hong Kong (hon. pres. 1976), Wong Kwong Chinese Martial Arts Internat. Assn. (pres. U.S. branch 1979), America Choy Li Fut Assn. (pres. 1980); author: Choy Li Fut Kung Fu; Shaolin Five Animals; Choy Li Fut Wooden Dummy Training; Buddhist; rec: movies, travel, camping. Res: 1694 28th Ave San Francisco 94122 Ofc: Doc-Fai Wong Kung Fu School 4051 Judah St San Francisco 94122

WONG, JOSEPH MING, environmental engineer; b. Dec. 6, 1951, Kwangtung, China, nat. US cit. 1983; s. Wing Chung-Chai and Shuet Wan (Lau) W.; m. Teresa, Sept. 18, 1976; children: Sarah b. 1981, Jessica b. 1984; Reg. Chem. Engr. Calif. 1979, Civil Engr. 1980; Diplomate Am. Acad. Environmental Engrs. Career: asst. environmental engr. Marin Municipal Water District Corte Madera; assoc. engr. Dodson & Young Engrs. Walnut Creek; proj. engr. Kaiser Engrs. Oakland; proj. mgr. Brown & Caldwell Cons. Engrs. Pleasant Hill; mem: Am. Inst. Chem. Engrs., Am. Soc. Civil Engrs., Am. Water Works Assn., Water Pollution Control Fedn., Toastmasters Internat., Chinese for Affirm. Action; publs: articles in profl. jours., presentation 1986 Calif. WPCA Indsl. & Hazardous Waste Conf.; Christian (elder); rec: basketball. Res: 5237 Heavenly Ridge Ln Richmond 94803 Ofc: Brown & Caldwell 3480 Buskirk Ave Pleasant Hill 94523

WONG, LAURA KWAN, jewelry store owner; b. Aug. 18, 1932, Guaymas, Sonora, Mexico, nat. US cit. 1957; d. Zee Nang and Felicitas Lai Fong (Chang) Kwan; m. Albert Wong, July 16, 1970; children (nee Jeung): Sharon Lee b. 1954, Craig Lee b. 1959, Curtis Lee b. 1960; edn: stu. apparel design, cosmetology, oil painting, and real estate: Lux Coll. San Francisco (1953), Marinello Sch. of Beauty (1969), Univ. of Hawaii, Hilo (1970), Coll. of San Mateo (1975). Career: tutored children in Mexico; var. pos., Pacific Tel. Co., Safeco Ins. Co., Bechtel Corp., Ultronix Electronic; current: owner/buyer, mgr. House of Kwan Yin (jewelry bus.), San Mateo; honors: life mem. Calif. Scholarship Fedn. (1952); civic: Foster City Chinese Club, YWCA, Tri G Club, High Sch. of Commerce Alumni Assn., Neighborhood Assn., Orchid Growing Club, Family Assns., Hair Dressers Assn.; hobbies: predicting future, oil painting, needlework, jewelry design. Res: 35 Verbalee Ln Hillsborough 94010 Ofc: House of Kwan Yin 55 E 4th Ave San Mateo 94401

WONG, LINCOLN POYLUN, acupuncturist, herbalist; b. Nov. 25, 1927, San Francisco; s. Moon-why and Sau-Kam (Lau) W.; m. Muliang, Mar. 24, 1957; children: Chihming b. 1960, Tim b. 1964; edn: MD, Chungshan Med. Univ. (now Sun Yat-Sen Univ. of Med. Scis.), China 1954; grad. Univ. of Chinese Traditional Medicine, China 1963; OMD, Calif. Acupuncture Coll. 1985; Calif. Cert. Acupuncturist (1980). Career: prof., vice dir. surgical dept. Sun Yat-Sen Univ. of Med. Scis./ Hospital, Canton, China 1954-79; acupuncture and herbal splst., San Francisco 1980–; recipient num. honors for medical research in China; mem. Assn. of Traditional Chinese Medical Doctors (pres.), Calif. Acupuncture Alliance (chmn. Sci. Com.); civic: Chinese Am. Citizens Alliance; publs: 54 profl. papers and num. articles on medical edn., incl. Acupuncture Use in Post-operation (1956), Lincoln's Jingluo Theory of Nerve Reaction (1960), Nerve Central Acupuncture for Anesthetization and Treatment (1978), The New Diagnosis and Therapy of Oriental Traditional Medicine (1980); Christian; rec: music. Res: 1640 Washington St #9 San Francisco 94109 Ofc: Acupuncture & Herbal Services 654 Grant Ave Ste 7 San Francisco 94108; 220 E 3rd Ave Ste 1 San Mateo 94401

WONG, MATILDA, U.S. government agency executive; b. July 9, 1927, San Francisco; d. Mee Yim and Lew Shee (Ow) Wong; m. Francis F. Wong, Apr. 24, 1982; edn: AA, San Francisco City Coll. 1947. Career: Agric. Research Service, US Dept. Agric, 1947–: secty. (1947-60), adminstrv. asst. (1960-67), budget & fiscal asst. (1967-72), Western Regl. Research Lab., Albany; fiscal ofcr. (1972-74), budget ofcr. (1974-77), W. Regl. Office, Berkeley; finl. mgr. (1977-84) W. Regl. Office, Oakland; budget ofcr. Pacific Basin Area, Albany 1984–, mem. spl. task group Finl. Mgmt. Div. ARS-USDA 1983; honors: Superior Svc. Award (USDA 1983), recipient sev. merit cash awards and spl. service award (1985), ARS-USDA; mem: Am. Assn. for Budget and Program Analysis, Nat. Assn. of Female Execs., Am. Assn. of Individual Investors, Bay Area Finl. Mgmt. Council (steering com.); Democrat; Prot.; rec: gardening, needlepoint, investments. Res: 951 Kingston Ave Piedmont 94611 Ofc: USDA-ARS Pacific Basin Area Office 800 Buchanan St Albany 94710

WONG, MICHAEL H., acupuncturist, doctor of oriental medicine; b. July 14, 1930, Canton, China; s. Tin Wah and Siu Ying (Lai) W.; m. Dora Yee-man Chan, Aug. 4, 1962; children: Jane b. 1964, Ann b. 1966, Ben b. 1969; edn: OMD and PhD, Samra Univ. of Health Scis., 1984; OMD, San Francisco Coll. of Acupuncture & Oriental Medicine 1984; lic. Chinese Medicine Practitioner, Rep. of China (1971), Certified Acupuncturist, Ore. (1974), Mont. (1974), Calif. (1976), Calif. postsec. tchg./adminstr. cred. (1983). Career: chief internist Summer Free Gen. Clinic, Assn. of H.K. & Kln. Practitioners of Chinese Medicine, Hong Kong 1956-67, chief acupuncturist 1960-73; chief internist, acupuncturist, lectr. All Year Round Free Clinic, H.K. Chinese Herbalists Assn. Ltd. 1966-73; clinic chief, acupuncturist, lectr. Chinese Acup. Inst., Hong Kong 1967-72; acupuncturist Acup. Research Inst., Seattle, Wash. 1973-79; private practice Wong's Acup. Clinic 1956–; lectr., instr. seminars, Internat. Soc. for Profl. Edn., S.F. 1979, Inst. of Continuing Edn. 1981-; apptd. examination commnr. Calif. State BMQA Acup. Advisory Bd. 1981, expert examiner 1982-; dir. of coord. Calif. Cert. Acup. Assn., cons. and examiner NCCA 1985-; honors: Assn. of H.K. & Kowloon Practitioners of Chinese Medicine Ltd. (life mem. 1955, Hon. pres. 1970), Ryodoraku Med. Soc., Japan (Hon. mem. 1967), Assn. Internat. Acup., France (Hon. mem. 1972), Assn. Naturopaths and Osteopaths, N.Z. (Fellow 1966); mem: Chinese Med. Soc. H.K., Chinese Acup. Assn. H.K., H.K. Chinese Herbalists Assn., Internat. Pain Control Inst., No. Am. Acup. Assn./ Vancouver B.C. (exec. v.p. 1973), Ore. Acup. Assn., Chinese Herbal and Acup. Assn., United Acupuncturists Calif. (dir. 1981-83), Academic Cong. of Acup. Chinese Medicine, Calif. Cert. Acup. Assn.; Republican; Chinese Baptist Ch. (counselor CSF 1974-77, co-chmn. bd. deacons 1974-78, tchr. Adult Sun. Sch. 1975-); rec: photog., painting, swim, tennis. Res: 5217 Adalina Ct San Jose 95124 Ofc: Los Gatos Medical & Acupuncture Clinic 15066 Los Gatos Almaden Rd Los Gatos 95030

WONG, MORTON MIN-FONG, chemical engineer; b. Oct. 2, 1924, Canton, China, nat. US cit. 1961; s. Ngok Fong and Han Kue (Low) W.; m. Eunice Shew, June 23, 1956; children: Nancy b. 1957, Brandon b. 1958, Tracey b. 1961, Douglas b. 1964; edn: BS, UC Berkeley 1951. Career: chem. engr. Am. Potash & Chems. Trona, Calif. 1951-53; proj. leader US Bureau of Mines Boulder City Nev. 1953-62, research supv. Reno 1962-69, research dir. 1969-71, research supv. 1971-82; engrg. assoc. Union Oil Co. of Calif. Brea, Calif. 1982–; invited lectr. metallurgy People's Rep. of China 1981; honors: Spl. Hoffman Prize (Internat. Lead Consortium 1980-81), Disting. Svc. Award (US Dept. of Interior 1981); mem: Metallurg. Soc. of AIME 1964- (chmn. extractive metallurg. paper awards com. 1981); works: 8 patents, 2 patents applied for, 80 publs.; mil: cpl. US Army 1944-46, Asiatic Pacific Campaign; Democrat; Methodist; rec: jogging, gardening, fishing. Ofc: Union Oil Co. of Calif. 316 S Valencia Brea 92621

WONG, WILLIAM BOCK, engineer, restaurateur, general contractor, realtor; b. Aug. 20, 1948, Canton, China, nat. US cit. 1971; s. Donald Tung and Suzie (Lee) W.; m. Mary Chu Lim, Nov. 22, 1972; children: Brian Chi b. 1975, Michelle Wing Yee b. 1983; edn: BSME, Calif. Poly. Univ. 1972. Career: asst. engr. Lockheed Aerospace Co. Sunnyvale 1972-73; energy mgmt. rep. Pacific Gas & Elec. Co. 1973–; owner, oper. sis Chinese restaurants (Hing's Rest., Hing's Aloha Rest., Wong's Rest., China Smorgas Rest., Hon's Won Ton Rest.) 1972–; owner Sing Sun Constrn. Inc. 1983–; oper. Sing's Investmant & Realty Inc. Oakland 1983–; oper. dir. Am. River Banks, Sacramento; mem: Am. Soc. Mech. Engrs. 1972, Nat. Assn. Realtors; Republican; Christian; rec: tennis, bicycling. Res: 4286 Whittle Ave Oakland 94602 Ofc: Sing's Investment & Realty Inc. 164 11th St Oakland 94607

WONG, WING SUN, restaurateur; b. Jan. 28, 1929, Canton, China, nat. 1973; s. Paul Man Chew and Mei Ping (Fong) Wong; m. Janet Quan, Apr. 2, 1958; children: Daniel Y. b. 1963, Evan W. b. 1965; edn: B.Econ., Chu Hai Univ. 1953. Career: math. instr. Tak Ming High Sch., Hong Kong 1953-59; asst. prof. Chu Hai Univ., Hong Kong 1959-62; tchr. Chinese Community Sch., Oakland 1963-65; cook Senor Pico Mexican Restaurant, San Francisco 1965-67; chef Chinese Hosp., San Francisco 1967–; owner: Wong's Restaurant, S.F. 1979-81, Gourmet Kitchen, S.F. 1981–; community leader, S.F. Chinatown. Honors:

cert. of honor, San Francisco City & Co. Bd. of Suprs., 1982; resolution, Calif. State Senate, 1982; Rep. of China Overseas Affairs Commn, 1985; mem: Chinese General Peace Assn. (pres.), Wong's Family Benevolent Assn. in USA (pres.), Chinese Consol. Benevolent Assn. (Chinese Six Cos.) (bd. trustees), Hoy Sun Ning Yung Benev. Assn. (bd. trustees), Ning Chu Assn. (pres.), S.F. Orange Merchants Assn. (pres.), Wong Family Benev. Assn. in USA (grand pres.), Num Hung Hok Luk Assn. (pres.), Chu Hai Univ. Alumni Assn. (adv., past pres.), World Wong (Huang) Family Assn. (hon. mem., bd. trustees); chmn. bd. Wong Family Mun Seck Found., Inc.; bd. trustees The Young China (newspaper); advr. Charity Cultural Svcs. Ctr.; hon. prin. S.F. Chinese Parents Com. Sch. 1972-74; hon. advr. Philippine Kang-Ha Assn., Inc.; hon. pres. The Hong Kong Wong Clan Assn.; author: Inflation (1953, pub. in Hong Kong). Republican. Rec: community vol. work; cooking for family, friends. Res: 547 26th Ave. San Francisco 94121 Ofc: Gourmet Kitchen 1051 Stockton St. San Francisco 94108

WOOD, DOROTHY DEWEASE, real estate broker; b. Nov. 12, 1925, Houston, Tx.; d. Ralph Leon James and Gladys Helen (Marler) Dewease; m. James Wood (dec.), Nov. 20, 1943; children: Stephen b. 1948, Sloan b. 1953; edn: Sam Houston St. Univ. 1942-43, UC Berkeley 1973-74; real estate cert. Coll. of San Mateo 1973-74; BS cum laude, Univ. of San Francisco 1980; Calif. lic. R.E. Broker 1975; desig: Grad. Realtors Inst. (GRI) 1976. Career: real estate sales asso. William Wright & Co., 1973-77; broker of record JM Tayler & Co., 1977-82; broker asso. Tate Properties, Burlingame 1982–; instr. Coll. of San Mateo 1982–; mem. State Steering Com. R.E. Certificate Inst. 1977-82; bd. trustees Univ. of Redlands 1977-; awards: life mem. Million Dollar Club (1975); mem. San Mateo-Burlingame Credit Bur. (1st female mem. bd. dirs. 1981-, 2-term pres. 1983-85), R.E. Certificate Inst. (Outstanding service award 1984; San Mateo County Chpt. pres. 1986-); civic: Commonwealth Club of Calif., Peninsula Stanford Club (dir. 1953-), Stanford Childrens Hosp. Aux. (1957-), Penin. Tennis Club; Republican; Prot.; rec: music, restoration antiques. Res: 509 Top of the Mounds San Mateo 94402 Ofc: Tate Properties 1209 Donnelly Ste 107 Burlingame 94010

WOOD, DUANE ORAN, international business consultant; b. Nov. 10, 1915, Centralia, Ill.; s. Elza Charles and Mabel Dolly (Allen) W.; m. Beverly Nelson, April 21, 1945; children: Jayne b. 1945, Cathy b. 1951; edn: BSEE, Mass. Inst. of Tech. 1937. Career: engr. Sylvania Corp., Salem, Mass. 1937-40; engr. Lockheed Aircraft Corp., Burbank 1940-42; plnng.mgr. Lockheed Overseas Corp., No. Ireland 1942-44; engring. & mgmt. pos. Lockheed Aircraft Corp., Burbank 1944-53; v.p. op.s Lockheed Aircraft Svc. C., Ontario 1956-64, pres. 1964-72; pres. Lockheed Calif. Co., Burbank 1973-76; chmn. bd. Murdoch Eng. Corp., Dallas, Texas 1974-76; exec. v.p. Triad Holding Corp., London, England 1977-79; pres. CCIT Corp., Los Angeles 1977–; trustee, Gr. Los Angles Zoo Assn.; Republican; Presbyterian; rec: skiing, hi-fi, computers. Address: CCIT Corp., 920 Linda Flora Dr. Los Angeles 90049

WOOD, ELDRIDGE DELANO, JR., investment banker; b. Sept. 8, 1938, Cambridge, Mass.; s. Eldridge Delano and Mary Eleanor (Frazier) W.; m. Kim Anh, Sept. 14, 1965; children: Carol b. 1967, Michael b. 1974; edn: BSBA, Northeastern Univ. 1961; MBA, Univ. Chgo. 1963. Career: sales mgr. William H. Rennolds Co., Manila 1965-70; v.p. Purina Taiyo K.K., Tokyo 1971-74; v.p. Private Investment Co. for Asia, Manila 1975-78; senior v.p./COO PICA, Singapore 1978-83; pres./bd. chmn. Inter-Pacific Capital Corp., Los Angeles 1983–; mem. corp. bd. dirs. 20+ cos. in 6 countries, 1965-; mem. Nat. Assn. of Corp. Dirs. (1982-), Jaycees (Internat. Senator); clubs: Elks, Manhattan CC, Army & Navy (Manila), Tokyo Am., Singapore Am.; mil: capt. US Army Signal Corps 1963-65; Republican; Roman Catholic; rec: music. Ofc: Inter-Pacific Capital Corp. 6033 W Century Blvd Ste 400 Los Angeles 90045

WOOD, GARY RAY, chiropractor; b. May 24, 1945, Missoula, Mont.; s. Ray Archibald and Dorothy Letty (Ruck) W.; m. Pamela B., Sept. 30, 1973; 1 son: Garrett Ryan b. 1985; edn: AA, San Diego City Coll. 1970; BA, San Diego State Univ. 1974; DC, Los Angeles Chiropractic Coll. 1983; lic. Chiropractor, Calif. 1984. Career: affirmative action, equal opportunity ofcr. 974-79; pvt. practice 1983–; adv. bd. Medical Magnet Pgm., Lincoln H.S.; honors: recipient commendation, Mayor Pete Wilson (1975), Pres.'s award (1983), Dr. Robert B. Botterman Award for outstanding svc. to profession (1986); mem: Am. and Calif. Chiropractic Assns., San Diego Co. Chiropractic Soc. (dir., chmn. Speakers Bureau), Council on Roentgenology, Found. for Chiropractic Edn. and Research, San Diego MG Club; mil: E-5 USN 1964-68, Vietnam Svc.; Bahai Faith; rec: skiing, tennis, photog. Ofc: Wood Chiropractic Health Ctr., 7484 University Ave. Ste. Q La Mesa 92041

WOOD, LARRY (MARYLAIRD), journalist, educator; b. Sandpoint, Idaho; d. Edward Hayes and Alice (McNeel) Small; children: Mary, Marcia, Barry; edn: BA magna cum laude, Univ. Wash., Seattle 1938, MA, 1940; postgrad. stu. Stanford Univ. 194½, UCB 1943/4, cert. in photog. 1971; journ. stu. Univ. Wisc. 197½, Univ. Minn. 197½, Univ. Ga. 1972/3; art, archt., biol., UC Santa Cruz 1974-6, 77-80, Stanford Univ. 1979/80. Career: by-line columnist Oakland Tribune, San Francisco Chronicle, 1946–; feature writer Western region Christian Sci. Monitor, CSM Radio Syndicate and Internat. News, 1973–, Register and Tribune Syndicate, Des Moines, 1975–, also Times-Mirror Syndicate, Chevron USA, Calif. Today mag.; contbg. ed. Travelday mag., 1976–; contbg. editor Calif. Travel Guides, Fodor (NY and London, David McKay Pubs.), 1981–, collaborating with son, Barry Wood (photojournalist) on 'San Francisco and Nearby Destinations' and Fodor's 'California' 1982–; co-author new State of Calif. Travelguide to Calif. (pub. jointly by State Calif. and Fodor, N.Y. and London), 1986; feature writer for Lingupress (internat. newsmag., Paris, Fr.); cons./reviewer, Principles of Science Series and contbg. author, Focus on Science Series (pub. by Charles E. Merrill Co.); author 1500+ by-line articles in major nat. popular mags., internat. semi-sci. mags., travel mags. (incl. Parents, Pop. Mechs., House and Garden, House Beautiful, Oceans, Sea Frontiers, Motorland- AAA, Westways- AAA, Scholastic Publs., Nat. Geographic's World and syndicates: USIA, Knight Ridder, Times Mirror, Hearst); prof. journalism CSU San Diego (1975-), CSU San Jose (1976), CSU Hayward, UC Ext. (1979), Univ. Pacific (1979, 82); frequent speaker profl., ednl. confs.; dir. pub. rels. No. Calif. Assn. Phi Beta Kappa, 1969-; selected by US & Brit. govts. to cover the 1983 visit of Queen Elizabeth II and Prince Philip to Calif.; work with state and fed. agcys. in wildlife mgmt. pgms., travel assignments to Hawaii, Ariz., Costa Rica, Mexico, Fla.; trustee Calif. State Parks Found., 1976-; honors: recogn., US Forest Service 1975, Nat. Park Service 1976, Oakland Mus. Assn. 1979, 81, Port Directors Assn. 1979, named One of nation's top environmental writers, Nat. Park Svc., Univ. of Wash. Hall of Fame (1984), Calif. Woman of Achievement (3 awards), award winning features in Sea Frontiers (1983), B.C. Totem Pole Series (1982), Calif. Underwater Parks features (1982), Ebey's Landing, Nat. Hist. Reserve series (1982); mem: Public Rels. Soc. Am. (Consultants Acad., 1983-); Women in Communications, Inc. (v.p. Far West and Nat. bd. 1968-73, nat. resolutions com. 1983-); Nat. Acad. of TV Arts and Scis.; Nat. Sch. Pub. Rels. Assn.; Environ. Cons. N. Am.; Am. Mgmt. Assn.; Internat. Environ. Cons.; Oceanic Soc.; Internat. Oceanagraphic Soc.; World Internat. Environ. Cons.; World Wildlife Fund; Am. Assn. Edn. in Journalism (exec. bd. nat. mag. div. 1978-); Investigative Reporters and Editors; Soc. Travel Writers Am. (exec. bd. 1980-82); Soc. Profl. Journalists; Council for Advance. of Sci. Writing; Calif. Acad. Environ. News Writers; Nat. Press Photogs. Assn.; clubs: Nat. Press, S.F. Press, Eastbay Womens' Press, Calif. Writers; Sigma Delta Chi, Theta Sigma Phi. Res: 6161 Castle Dr. Oakland 94611

WOOD, LINDA MAY, librarian; b. Nov. 6, 1942, Ft. Dodge, Iowa; d. John Albert and Beth Ida (Riggs) Wiley; m. C. James Wood, Sept. 16, 1964; edn: BA, Portland State Univ. 1964; M.Librarianship, Univ. Wash. 1965. Career: Library Assn., Portland, Ore. 1965-77; reference librarian 1965-67; br. librarian 1967-72; adminstrv. asst. to librarian 1972-73; asst. librarian 1973-77; asst. city librarian Los Angeles Public Library 1977-80; library dir. Riverside City & County Public Library 1980–; chmn. bd. dirs. Inland Library System 1983–; mem: Am., Public, Calif., Pacific N.W. and N.W. Library Assn., AAUW, Library Admin. & Mgmt. Assn., LWV, Zonta Club; Democrat. Ofc: Riverside City & County Public Library, P.O. Box 468 Riverside 92502

WOOD, RICHARD EARLE, manufacturing co. executive; b. Oct. 20, 1930, Ventura; s. Francis Bowman and Hertha Georgina (Hahn) W.; m. Norma Haworth, Mar. 3, 1951; children: Kathleen, b. 1953, Linda, b. 1956, Sharon, b. 1961; edn: AA, soc. sci. Long Beach City Coll. 1957; BA, psych., CSU Long Beach 1960. Career: pres. Wood's Enterprises, Laguna Beach 1970-75; pres. Wood's Ents., Lakeside 1980-82; mgr. quality control, Chem-tronics, El Cajon 1978-80; dir. quality control, Teledyne Cast Products, Pomona 1975-78; mgr. qual. control, Southcom Internat., Inc. Escondido 1982-85; Procurement Quality Assur., Rockwell Internat. Corp., Anaheim 1985–; mem. ASQC, sr. mem. Soc. of Mfg. Engrs. 1979-; Past Master Councilor, Order of DeMolay; mil: seaman USNR 1947-51, A/1c USAF 1951-55; rec: rare wine collector, chess, writing. Res: 28346 Glenmeade Way Escondido 92026 Ofc: Rockwell International Corp. 3370 Miraloma Ave Anaheim 92803

WOOD, W. ROBERTS, JR., investment counselor; b. Dec. 9, 1933, Louisville, Ky.; s. W. Roberts Wood; m. Patricia, July 5, 1981; children: Roberts b. 1960, Frank b. 1962, Charles b. 1963; edn: BA in psych., Yale Univ. 1955; CFA, The Inst. of Chartered Finl. Analysts (1974); CIC, Investment Counsel Assn. of Am. (1976). Career: investment mgmt. and securities mktg. with var. firms: banking/trust inv., Citizens Fidelity, Louisville, Ky. 1958-63; stock broker Hillard-Lyons, Louisville 1963-69; investment counselor Scudder Stevens & Clark, Cinti., O. 1969-79; lmtd. ptnrship. Damson Securities, La Jolla 1979-85; vice pres. Brandes Inv. Counsel, Inc., San Diego 1985–. Res: 8850-308 Villa La Jolla Dr La Jolla 92037 Ofc: Brandes Investment Counsel, Inc. 12760-270 High Bluff Dr San Diego 92130

WOOD, WAYNE BARRY, photojournalist; b. June 23, 1958, Oakland; s. Byron and Marylaird (Small) W.; edn: cert. photog., Univ. Calif. 1975; BS, transp., CSU Hayward and S.F.; MBA, CSUH 1982. Career: bylined photojournalist, 1971-, with CSM News Syndicate (25 mil. readers worldwide; syndicated on 200 radio stations in US and Can.) 1973–, spec. in travel, sci., transp., urban renewal, people profiles, edn.; contbg. photojournalist: Sea Frontiers, Internat. Oceanographic Soc., Popular Mechanics, Focus On Science textbook series (Charles Merrill Co.), Fodor's San Francisco (guidebook); awards: Close Scholarship for outstanding jr. in econ. and business; R.R. Soc. photog. awards; mem: Soc. of Profl. Journalists, Nat. Press Photogs. Assn.; Presbyterian; rec: natural science, magic. Res: 6161 Castle Dr Oakland 94611

WOODBURY, RUSSELL THOMSON, winemaker; b. Oct. 15, 1948, Los Angeles; s. Rollin Edwin and Ruth Lucille (Armitage) W.; m. Linda Morton, 1975; children: Douglas b. 1976, Chenin b. 1979; edn: Claremont Men's Coll. 1966-68; BA, USC 1970, MBA, 1973. Career: pres., winemaker Woodbury Winery 1977–; cons. to wine industry 1977–; co advr. KQED Wine Auction 1980–; v.p. mktg. & fin. Chateau Bottler Inc. 1980–; pres. Airwine (Gourmet Calif.) 1985–; bd. dirs. Woodbury Winery Inc. and Chateau Bottlers Inc., Airwine Inc.; mem: Wine Inst. (Internat. Trade, Law & Regs. and Pub. Rels. coms.), Soc. of Wine Educators, Napa Valley Wine Library Assn., Am. Soc. of

Enologists, U.S. Master Swimming; Presbyterian (elder); rec: swimming, surfing, sailing. Ofc: 32 Woodland Ave. San Rafael 94901

WOODING, JAMES BERNARD, manufacturing co. executive, educator; b. Nov. 12, 1944, Pasadena, Calif.; s. Ralph Gilbert and Sarah (Zitnick) W.; m. Jayne, Aug. 8, 1970; children: Jean b. 1973, Julia b. 1976; edn: AS, bus. adminstrn., AA lib. arts., Allan Hancock Coll. 1979. Career: timekeeper Abex Corp. Oxnard 1976-77, overhaul & repair coord. 1977-79, plant overhaul & repair adminstr. Santa Maria 1979-81, prod. support mgr. 1981—, co. warranty adminstr. 1983-85; instr. computers Allan Hancock Coll. Santa Maria 1985—; software reviewer Hi-Res Computer Mag. 1983-84; honors: Svc. Award (PTA 1983-84); mem: Am. Prodn. & Inventory Control Soc., Santa Maria Lompoc Atari Computer Enthusiasts (secty. 1982, pres. 1983); mil: PO2 USN communs. tech. 1966-69; Republican; Baptist; rec: computers. Res: 398 Highland Dr Santa Maria 93455 Ofc: Abex Corp. 2850 Skyway Dr Santa Maria 93455

WOODMANSEE, GEORGE CLAY, administrative law judge; b. May 15, 1903, Los Angeles; s. Clay Goit and Jessie Viola (Anderson) W.; m. Ruth Craig, Sept. 14, 1932; 2 sons: Craig, b. 1934, George Jr., b. 1936; edn: stu. USC, 1922-23, AB, UCLA, 1927. Career: secty. bookkeeper, asst. mgr. insurance dept. A.Z. Taft Jr. and Taft Realty Co., Hollywood 1921-27; dept. mgr. Contract Dept., Guaranty Bldg. and Loan Assn., and successor, 1928-37; office mgr. Marlow-Burns and Co., Los Angeles 1938-40; self-empl. real estate broker, Hollywood 1937-38, Culver City 1940-48; interviewer, office mgr. State of Calif. Dept. of Employment, L.A. 1941-45; Appeals Referee and Adminstrv. Law Judge, Calif. Unemployment Insurance Appeals Bd., variously in Los Angeles, Sacto., Long Beach, 1945-68, ret. 1968, recalled on temp. assignments 1968—; mem: Hollywood High Sch. Alumni Assn. (exec. bd. 3 yrs., distinguished achievement award), Theta Psi frat. 1922-23, Kappa Upsilon frat. 1924-27, Town Hall of Calif., US Power Squadron; works: helped devel. magnetic recording on steel wire, Am. Talking Wire Co., 1932-3; Republican (Presdtl. Task Force); Christian Sci.; rec: gardening, woodworking, handball. Res: 27737 Calle Valdes Mission Viejo 92692

WOODRUFF, JOHN HOBART, engineering/construction executive; b. May 10, 1957, Santa Barbara; s. George Hobart and Florence Rebecca (Pascoe) W.; edn: BS in C.E., CSU Long Beach 1981, MSCE, Stanford Univ. 1982. Career: project engr., estimator Macco Constructors, Paramount 1982-84; estimator, contr. adminstr. Continental Heller Corp., Long Beach 1984-85; project engr., asst. proj. mgr. Equidon Contrs., Newport Beach 1985-86; v.p. adminstrn., constrn. mgr. Critical Path Engring. Inc., Glendale 1986—; honors: Chi Epsilon, Tau Beta Pi, Mu Alpha Theta, 1st Pl. Phillip Abrams/ L.A. Chpt. ASCE Scholarship Competition (1980), Most outstanding student CSULB Civil Engring. Dept. (1981); mem. Am. Concrete Inst., ASCE, Constrn. Mgmt. Assn. of Am.; rec: biking, ski, equestrian. Res: 3326 South Towner Ave Santa Ana 92707 Ofc: Critical Path Engineering Inc 511 E Harvard Glendale 91205

WOODS, HENRY NEAL, loan consultant; b. May 10, 1954, Clarksdale, Miss.; s. Henry Neal and Estella Marie (Jones) W.; edn: AA, Utica Jr. Coll. 1974; BA, Miss. Valley State Univ. 1976. Career: loan ofcr. United Calif. Bank L.A. 1977-79; bus. devel. ofcr. Community Bank L.A. 1979-81, Crocker Nat. Bank L.A. 1981-83; gen. ptnr. Golden State Financial Inglewood 1983-84; owner Woods & Assoc. pkg., placement of comml. real estate loans 1984—; awards: Honor Student (Miss. Valley State Univ. 1976), Who's Who (Am. Jr. Colls. 1974, Am. Colls. & Univs. 1976),Outstanding Young Men of Am. 1984; mem: Nat. Notary Assn., L.A. Urban League, Challengers Boys & Girls Club (bd.), Inglewood CofC; Democrat; Methodist; rec: tennis, racquetball, golf. Address: Inglewood

WOODS, JUNE JAMEELAH, temporary employment agency president; b. June 1, 1945, Oklahoma City, Okla.; d. Julius Joseph Borders and Elnora (Williams) Borders-Doolittle; m. Wayne Woods (dec.), Aug. 17, 1960; children: Steven b. 1961, Nadiyah b. 1978; edn: Central Bus. Coll. 1964-65, El Centro Jr. Coll. 1973-74, Sacto. City Coll. 1977-79. Career: adminstrv. secty. Dallas Independent Sch. Dist., 1965-72, Dallas Welfare Dept. 1972-73; owner/ adminstr. Asian House Pre-School/ Day Care and co-owner Asian House Restaurant, 1973-75; secty. Los Rios Coll. Dist., 1976-83; owner/pres. Ynobe Internat. Modeling & Talent, Sacto. 1981—; awards: Calif. State Fair (1984), Am. Heart Assn. (1983), Sacto. City Coll. (1983); civic: Friends of the State Fair (com.), Girl Scouts, Foster Parent Program, PTA (bd.); creative: theatrical prod. of fashion shows and events; Democrat; Islam; rec: swim, drawing, chess. Ofc: Ynobe International Modeling & Talent 9723 A Folsom Blvd Sacramento 95826

WOODWARD, DANIEL HOLT, librarian; b. Oct. 17, 1931, Ft. Worth, Tex.; s. Enos Paul and Jessie (Butts) W.; m. Mary Jane, 1954; children: Jeffrey, b. 1958, Peter, b. 1960; edn: BA, Univ. of Colo. 1951, MA, 1955; PhD, Yale Univ. 1958; MSLS, Catholic Univ. of Am. 1969. Career: asst., assoc. prof. Mary Washington College, Univ. of Va., 1957-72, librarian, 1969-72; librarian Huntington Library, 1972—; served in AUS. Res: 1540 San Pasqual St Pasadena 91106 Ofc: 1151 Oxford Rd San Marino 91108

WOODWARD, DAVID FREDERICK, pharmacologist; b. June 15, 1945, Burton, England; s. Bernard Ronald and Dorothy May (Gretton) W.; m. Marie Maugueret, Nov. 29, 1975; edn: BS, Portsmouth Sch. of Pharm. 1975; PhD, Leicester Sch. of Pharm. 1980; Dr. Pharm., CNAA (1980). Career: scientist SK&F, Welwyn, England 1975-81, assoc. senior investigator SK&F, Phila., Pa. ?1-82; vis. scientist Eye Research Inst., Boston, Mass. 1982; senior scientist Pharmaceuticals, Irvine 1982—; awards: Author of Year, Allergan

(1986), CNAA PhD scholarship, SK&F, Welwyn (1977); mem. Assn. for Res. in Vision and Ophthalmology; publs: 30+ articles, chapters, invited revies in the ophthalmol., dermatol. and pharmacol. literature; Anglican; rec: sci. Res: 23152 Tulip El Toro 92630 Ofc: Allergan 2525 Dupont Dr Irvine 92715

WOODWARD, GEORGE CLIFF, retail food chains industry executive, ret.; b. Oct. 30, 1921, Los Angeles; s. George Herman and Hasel (Cliff) W.; m. Joanne Scowcroft, June 26, 1923; children: Jan (Stevenson), Jill (Condon), John Scowcroft; edn: Stanford Univ. 1945. Career: sales mgr. (wholesale) John Scowcroft & Sons Co., Ogden, Ut. 1948-55, also mem. bd. dirs.; pres./ co-owner/ bd. dirs. Food King Mkts. (retail) (was Smith's Food King, now Lucky's) 1955-60; safflower & cotton sales, J.G. Boswell Co., Los Angeles 1960-63; bd. dirs. Century Meat Packing Co., 1963-66; ret. 1966; awards: First in Nation 1955 Sunkist Display Award and Nat. Apple Growers, num. advt. awards; mem. Retail Grocery Assn., Vernon Rotary, Rounders L.A. (pres.); mil: naval cadet USN Air Corps; Republican; rec: golf, investments. Address: 7 Monarch Bay South Laguna 92677 900 Island Dr Rancho Mirage 92270

WOODWARD, RODNEY MADISON, human factors engineer; b. June 7, 1928, Bellingham, Wash.; s. Rodney Madison and Olive Lenore (Stewart) W.; m. Betty Jean Condon, Apr. 23, 1955; children: Elizabeth Ann b. 1958, Rodney M. III b. 1959, Roy Douglas b. 1961; edn: BA, honors, San Diego St. Univ. 1956; grad. courses in edn., psych., mgmt.; cert. in Nat. Security Mgmt., Indsl. Coll. Armed Forces 1972. Career: field engr. Raytheon Co., Waltham, Mass. 1957-60; human factors engr. General Dynamics, San Diego, Ft. Worth 1960-66; sr. human factors engr. Rockwell Int'l. Los Angeles 1966-77; engineering splst. Rohr Marine Div. Chula Vista 1978; cons. human factors, Man Factors, Inc. San Diego 1979; engrg. splst. General Dynamics, Pomona 1980—; lectr. National Safety Council, L.A. 1972-76; Electronic Industries Assn. Com. on Human Factors 1964-66; honors: Alpha Mu Gamma, Psy Chi; mem: Human Factors Soc. (pres. L.A. chpt. 1978), IEEE (senior mem.), Nat. Mgmt. Assn., Soc. for Information Display, Internat. Platform Assn., Naval Reserve Assn. (life), Sigma Pi Frat.; publs: Human Factors Journal vol. 14, 1972; Proceedings of Human Factors Soc. & Southwestern Psychol. Assn. 1963, 64, 66, 70; mil: cmdr. USNR 1945-76; Democrat. Res: 2868 West Rowland Cir Anaheim 92804 Ofc: General Dynamics, POB 2507, Pomona 91766

WORMS, VINCENT ROBERT, venture capitalist; b. Oct. 12, 1952, Paris; s. Roger and Genevieve (Dreyfus) W.; edn: Diplome, Ecole Polytechnique Paris 1974; Diplome, Ecole Nationale des Ponts et Chaussees 1975; MS, M.I.T. 1976; Diplome, Institut D'Etudes Politiques de Paris 1977. Career: head planning & budgeting div. French Ministry of Transportation 1978-80; secretaire Mission for Innovation French Ministry of Industry 1980-81; ptnr. venture capital subsid. Banque Paribas, Paribas Technol. 1981—; mil: lt. French Army. Res: 2100 Green St San Francisco 94123 Ofc: Paribas Technology 101 California Ste 3150 San Francisco 94111

WRIGHT, CARL WENDELL, manufacturing co. executive; b. July 17, 1936, Santa Rosa, Calif.; s. Barak Charles and Irene Kathryn (Mattson) W.; m. Barbara Sue, Dec. 16, 1967; children: Kevin b. 1960, Mark b. 1961, David b. 1963, Darea b. 1965, Kimberly b. 1968, Melissa b. 1969; edn: US Naval Acad. 1956-59; BSME, Univ. Nev. Reno 1961. Career: mech. engr. ordnance Naval Ordnance Test Station China Lake, Calif. 1961-63, aerospace engr. 1963-65; v.p. Tahoe Forest Bowl Inc. 1965-66; proj. engr. Teledyne McCormick Selph Hollister, Calif. 1966-69, prin. engr. 1969-72; assoc. scientist Thiokol Chem. Corp. Brigham City, Utah 1972-77; owner Custom Craft Cabinets Logan, Utah 1977-79; supt. Forest Investment Corp. Elko, Nev. 1979-80; gen. contr. Reno 1980-82; proj. engr., pgm. mgr. Tracor MBA San Ramon, Calif. 1982-84, dir. pgm. mgmt. Camden, Ark. 1984—; listed Who's Who in Pyrotechnics (Am. Pyrotechnic Soc. 1986); mem: Am. Defense Preparedness Assn., Am. Soc. Mech. Engrs., Internat. Pyro. Soc., Am. Inst. Aero. & Astro., Am. Rocket Soc., Sigma Tau, Elks (chaplain 1973-74, leading knight 1974-75, exalted ruler 1975-76, esquire 1976-77, trustee 1977-79); works: designed, devel. 1-inch explosive bolt (1968-69), several non-detonating transmission systems, small column isolated delay ornance distbn. sys. (1969); mil: midshipman US Naval Acad. 1956-59, USNR 1955-63; Republican; United Methodist; rec: water skiing, bowling, radio-controlled models, replica antique cars, racquet sports. Res: 2730 Hawthorne Camden AR 71701 Ofc: Tracor MBA POB 3297 East Camden AR 71701

WRIGHT, DONALD FRANKLIN, newspaper executive; b. July 10, 1934, St. Paul, Minn.; s. Floyd Franklin and Helen Marie (Hansen) W.; m. Sharon Kathleen Fisher, Dec. 30, 1960; children: John b. 1964, Dana b. 1966, Kara b. 1968, Patrick b. 1970; edn: Macalester Coll.; BME mech. engring., Univ. Minn. 1957, MBA, 1958. Career: var. pos., prodn. engr., asst. prodn. dir. Minneapolis Star 1957-71, research plng. dir. 1971-73, ops. dir. 1973-75, executive editor 1975-77, exec. v.p./gen. mgr. 1977-78; pres./ chief op. ofcr. Newsday, Long Island, NY 1978-82; pres./chief op. ofcr. Los Angeles Times, 1982—; mem: Am. Newspaper Pubs. Assn. (past chmn. Telecom. Com.; past chmn. Prodn. Mgmt. Com.), Am. Soc. of Newspaper Editors (past mem.), Boy Scouts Am./ L.A. Area Council, Cal Tech Assocs. (bd. dirs.), Claremont Univ. Ctr. (v. chmn. bd. fellows), Industry Edn. Council of Calif. (bd. dirs.), World Press Inst. (advis. com.); Presbyterian. Ofc: Los Angeles Times Times Mirror Square Los Angeles 90053

WRIGHT, JAMES WARREN, petroleum engineer; b. June 22, 1922, Sanborn, Iowa; s. Fred Aldrich and Esther Victoria (Aldray) W.; m. Jeanne Cooney, Oct. 21, 1944; children: Anne b. 1947, James b. 1950, Laurie b. 1952; edn: BSME UC Berkeley 1949; US Army Infantry OCS 1944, Advanced Infantry 1957,

Command & Gen. Staff Coll. Ft. Leavenworth, Kans. 1961; Reg. Profl. Engr. Calif. (mech.) 1976. Career: petroleum engr. Long Beach Oil Devel. Co. 1949-54; asst. purchasing engr. Santa Fe Drilling Co., Santa Fe Springs 1954-55; test engr. Douglas Aircraft Co. Aircraft Div. Long Beach 1955-60; reliability test engr. Douglas, Missile & Space Sys. Div. 1960-69; reliability engr. McDonnell Douglas Corp. Douglas Aircraft Div. 1969-74; petroleum engr. Dept. of Interior US Geol. Survey L.A. 1974-76, supv. petroleum engr. 1976-82; dist. supv. Ventura Dist. Pacific OCS Region (Pt. Conception to the Mexican border) Minerals Mgmt. Svc. Dept. of Interior 1982–; honors: Value in Performance Award (Saturn Pgm., McDonnell Douglas 1969); mem: Am. Petroleum Inst., Petroleum Prodn. Pioneer, Boy Scouts of Am. (50 yr. member), Masons; works: devel. method to place cold fuel aboard two DC-7c and DC-8 domestic aircraft in Long Beach which enabled them to fly non-stop to Europe; devel. requirements and performed qualifications tests on a 6600psi gaseous nitrogen ground support system for Thor Missile (The ASME unfired pressure vessel code did not exceed 2500psi working pressure.); mil: major US Army Infantry 1942-65, active 1944-46; Conservative; Protestant; rec: camping, hiking, automobiles, guns. Res: 5278 Mezzanine Way Long Beach 90808 Ofc: Minerals Mgmt. Service 145 N Brent St Ste 202 Ventura 93003

WRIGHT, KENNETH LYLE, psychologist; b. Sept. 111, American Falls, Ida.; s. Jesse Joshua and Martha Sophia (Dickenson) W.; children: Anne Collins, Corrella Carmelette Brown, Sandra Lynne Sutherland; edn: BA, Univ. Wash. 1941; MA, USC, 1957; PhD, San Gabriel Coll. 1958. Career: coach State Tng. School for Boys, Chehalis, Wash. 1941; dep. probation officer, Los Angeles County, 1955-56; vis. Lectr. Whittier (Cal.) Coll. 1956; dist. sch. psychologist Anaheim Union High Sch. Dist.; edn. splst. Dept. Army, Orleans (France) Am. High Sch., psychol. services and spl. edn. coordinator Dependent Edn. Group Hdqrs., Karlsruhe, Germany 1959-62; edn. specialist USN, San Diego 1962-63; pvt. practice as psychologist, San Diego 1963-64, 1969–; psychol. cons. Clin. Bd. Speech Therapy, Children's Hosp., San Diego 1962-63; vis. prof. U. Western Ont. and lectr., sch. psychologist London (Ont.) Bd. Edn., 1964-66; dir. psychol. services Niagara Falls (NY) Dist. Bd. Edn. 1966-69; tchr. Syracuse (NY) Univ. 1966-69. Pres. Coordinating Council, Whittier, Cal.; founder Niagara Inst Human Devel.; honors: Outstanding Award, San Diego Co. Assn. Retarded Children; Fellow San Diego Bio Med. Research Inst.; mem: Assn. Children with Learning Disabilities, Council Exceptional Children, Royal Soc. Medicine, Am., San Diego Co. psychol. assns., San Diego Assn. Clin. Psychologists; Mason; club: Koua Kai; mil: USNR 1942-46. Res: 751 Amiford Dr San Diego 92107 Ofc: 126 W. Maple St San Diego 92103

WRIGHT, WILLIAM D., polymer technology co. president and founder; b. Feb. 14, 1947; s. William and Althea R. (Keatzer) W.; edn: BSAE, Le Tourneau Coll. Longview, Tex. 1969. Career: liaison engr. Boeing Co. Renton, Wash. 1969-70; process/ proj. engr. Visqueen div. Ethyl Corp. Terre Haute, Ind. 1970-73; mfg. engr. Fremont, Calif. 1973-74; process engr. Crown Zellerbach Corp. L.A. 1974-78; v.p. Uniflo Systems Toronto, Canada 1978-79; pres. Western Polymer Newark, Calif. 1979–; film mktg. cons. Sterling Extruder 1979-82; mem; Soc. Plastics Engrs., TAPPI; inventions: dual orifice air ring (1975), low shear rate die (1978); num. trade jour. publs. Res: 7477 Pecan Ct Pleasanton 94566 Ofc: Western Polymer 7910 Enterprise Dr Newark 94560

WU, DAVID J., engineer; b. June 12, 1922, Hong Kong; s. Chak Wa and Kuak Fun (Kuo) Ng.; m. Ona Wu, Sept. 1984; children: Caroline, Johnnie; edn: BS, West Coast Univ. 1949. Career: owner Big Chime TV and Sound (retail sales & service), Citrus Hts., 1959–; free. project engr. for var. cos. including Aerojet, Westinghouse; inventor UHF antenna; mem. CSEA; Presbyterian. Res: 8078 Willow Glen Circle Citrus Hts 95610 Ofc: Big Chime TV and Sound, 7672 Greenback Ln Citrus Hts 95610

WU, KENNETH KWOK-KUEN, engineer; b. Jan. 30, 1957, Hong Kong; s. Luen and Ho (Lo) W.; m. Sheryl Fujihara, July 11, 1982; edn: BS, UC Berkeley 1981, MS engrg., 1983; Reg. Civil Engr. Calif. 1984. Career: engr. II URS/John A. Blume Assoc. & Engrs. S.F. 1982-84; engr./designer DES Engrg. Inc. Redwood City 1984, CRJG Assoc. Menlo Park 1984-85; engr./analyst Robert L. Cloud Assoc. Berkeley 1985–; honors: Phi Beta Kappa 1981, Tau Beta Pi 1981; mem. Am. Soc. Civil Engrs. 1985; rec: skiing. Res: 6790 Baker Ln Sebastopol 95472

WU, YI-TZE SETH, lawyer; b. June 14, 1950, Bangkok, Thailand; nat. 1980; s. Ta-yeh and Shu-hsien (Teng) Wu; edn: BA, Univ. of Denver 1973; JD, Univ. of Santa Clara 1979; LL.M. in taxation, Golden Gate Univ. 1983. Career: tax atty. Varian Assoc., Inc., Palo Alto 1979–; Dir. Santa Clara Pub. Interest Law Found. 1979; mem: Calif. State Bar Assn., Santa Clara Bar Assn., Am. Bar Assn., Phi Alpha Delta legal frat., Mensa, ARE. Res: 2758 Randers Ct. Palo Alto 94303 Ofc: Corporate Tax Dept., Varian Assoc., Inc., 611 Hansen Way, Mail Stop E-029, Palo Alto 94303

WUNSCH, JAMES PATRICK, JR., insurance and investment securities president; b. July 15, 1948, Wausau, Wis.; s. James P., Sr. and Gertrude Zona (Geier) W.; m. Kelly; children: Jennifer b. 1975, Jeffery b. 1979; edn: BBA, Univ. Wis., 1971; JD, Univ. of Pacific 1977; Reg. Investment Advisor, SEC. Career: sales agt. Bankers Life of Iowa, Sacramento 1976-78; mgr. Calif. Western States Life, Chico 1978-85; general agent and reg. inv. advisor/pres. Wunsch Ins. and Finl. Services, Inc. Chico 1985–; recipient sales awards: pres.'s Top 10, Pres.'s Council (2), Cal Western States Life, Exceptional Producers Conf., Am. Gen. Life; mem: Nat. Assn. Life Underws. (pres. No. Calif. Assn. 1982-83), Calif. Assn. Life Underws. (dir. 1982-83), Million Dollar Round Table (6 yrs), Internat. Assn. Finl. Planners; Republican; Catholic; rec:

yacht racing, ski, photog. Ofc: Wunsch Insurance and Financial Services Inc. 383 Connors St Ste E Chico 95926

WURZEL, RUTH SCHWARTZ, paralegal; b. June 8, 1944, NY, NY; d. Philip and Mildred Ann (Chernoff) Schwartz; m. Mark Wurzel, Nov. 13, 1965; children: Stephanie b. 1967, Alicia b. 1971, Seth b. 1976; edn: BS, New York Univ. 1966; Paralegal Cert., Watterson Coll. 1986. Career: tchr. New York City Bd. of Edn. NY, NY; sole prop. Ruth Wurzel Invitations, Granada Hills; currently, paralegal Leon R. Laufer Esq., Los Angeles; honors: Outstanding Bd. Mem. 1983-84, Rookie of the Year 1980, Spl. Recogn. 1981, North Valley Jewish Community Ctr.; mem: Nat. Assn. of Female Execs., Los Angeles Paralegal Assn. (chair Westside sect.), Jewish Ctr. Assn. of Gr. Los Angeles (bd. dirs. 1984-85), No. Valley Jewish Community Ctr. (sect. 1982, v.p. 1984-85); Republican; Jewish; rec: community theater. Res: 16301 Keeler Dr. Granada Hills 91344 Ofc: Leon R. Laufer Esq., 12304 Santa Monica Blvd. Ste. 300 Los Angeles 90025

WYATT, FARICITA HALL, educational consultant; b. Oct. 29, 1912, Bakersfield; d. Wm. Mansion and Susie Sylindia (Pinkney) Hall; m. Thomas Wyatt (dec.), Oct. 20, 1953; edn: BA, CSU San Jose 1935; grad. work, UC Berkeley 1936, 50, 62, tchg. credential 1962. Career: employment security ofcr. Calif. State Dept. Employ. 1946-58; exec. secty. Cong. Jeffery Cohelan, Wash DC 1959-61; tchr. Skyline High Sch., Oakland 1962-75; employment ofcr. UC Berkeley 1968-69; employment rep./ coord. Retirees' Employment Pgm., Univ. Calif., San Francisco 1979–; pres. Impact Assocs.- Ednl. Consultants; mem. bd. overseers UCSF 1983-, mem. bd. UCSF Hosp. Aux. 1982-; awards: Calif. Congress of Parents & Tchrs. hon. service (1975), Who's Who of Am. Women (1979-80), World Who's Who of Women (1979), Internat. Who's Who of Intellectuals (1981); mem: Am. Soc. on Aging, Calif. Tchrs. Assn. (life), Commonwealth Club of S.F., Smithsonian Assocs. (nat. mem. 1986), Museum Soc. of S.F., AARP; civic: RSVP Retired Senior Vol. Pgm., California Able; publs: poetry collections: The River Must Flow (1965), By the Banks of the River (1975); article in Health Record Mgmt.; mil: capt., co. comdr. Womens Army Corps 1943-46; Democrat; Prot.; rec: painting in oil, poetry. Res: 6 Locksley Ave Apt 7-J San Francisco 94122 Ofc: University of California 1350 7th Ave San Francisco 94143

WYMAN, PHILLIP DAVID, state assemblyman; b. Feb. 21, 1945, Hollywood; s. Elliott and Rosalie Jane (Mauzy) W.; m. Lynn Larson, May 21, 1977; children: Andrea Dee b. 1978, Elizabeth Frances b. 1982; edn: BA, UC Davis 1967; JD, McGeorge Sch. of Law 1973; Atencio de Manila (Phil.) Univ. 1970. Career: active rancher in mgmt. of family owned Antelope Cyn. Ranch and recreational complex in Tehachapi; attorney; gen. mgr. Antelope Valley Bd. of Trade; elected assemblyman Calif. Legislature 1978-, named Assembly Republican Minority Whip 1980, chmn. Assem. Com. on Constnl. Amendments, 1981-2; mem. Assem. coms. on Judiciary, Transp. Ways & Means; mem. Commn. for Economic Devel.; Little Hoover Commn. (Commn. on Calif. State Govt. & Econ.), Spl. Legislative Investigation Com. on the State Bar; honors: Outstanding Young Men of Am. 1977, 79; mem: Am. Legion; Philippine Astronomical Soc. (founder); Astronomical Soc. of the Pacific; Tehachapi Mountain Observatory Assn. (cofounder); mem. Lancaster-West Rotary Desert Tortoise Preserve Commn., Kern Co. Farm Bur., and Federal and Calif. Bar Assns.; mil: sgt. USAF 1969, AF Commendn. Medal for service in US Emb., Manila; Republican; Christian; rec: astronomy (telescope making). Res: 21404 Indian Wells Dr Tehachapi 93561 Ofc. of Assem. Phil Wyman, 5405 Stockdale Hwy, Ste. 112, Bakersfield 93309

XENOS, SHEILA ANNE, psychotherapist; b. July 20, 1932, Ann Arbor, Mich.; d. John Edward and Mary Estelle (VanRiper) Tomshack; m. Steve Xenos Jr., PhD, July 31, 1952; children: Steve III b. 1954, Mary Anne b. 1955, Jane b. 1958; edn: BA, CSU Dominguez Hills 1977; MA, US Internat. Univ. 1979; PhD, Profl. Sch. for Humanistic Studies 1982; lic. casualty ins. agent (1965-67), cert. sex therapist (1981), lic. clin. hypnotist (1981), assoc. diplomate Am. Acad. of Behavioral Med. (1982). Career: library asst. Miraleste H.S., 1969-79; co-dir. Human Resources Center, Santa Ana 1978–; asst. prof. Coll. of Osteopathy of the Pacific 1980–; mem: Calif. Assn. Marriage Family Therapists, Nat. Rehabilitation Assn., Nat. Assn. Rehabilitation Profls. in the Pvt. Sector, Am. Personnel & Guidance Assn., Orange County Sexual Assualt Network (bd. dirs. 1984-86), So. Calif. Assn. for Battered Women, Am. Assn. Sex Educators, Counselors & Therapists, NOW; civic: County Bd. Suprs. Mt. Clemens, Mich. (1960-65), Mich. Assn. of Retarded Children (secty. 1965); Democrat; Catholic; rec: golf. Res: 15291 Nimes Cir Irvine 92714 Ofc: Human Resources Center 1125 E 17th St, E-201, Santa Ana 92701

XENOS, STEVE JR., psychological center clinical director; b. Jan. 20, 1931, Canton, Ohio; s. Steve and Antromahi (Zazopoulos) X.; m. Sheila T., July 31, 1952; children: Steve III b. 1954, Mary Anne b. 1956, Jane b. 1958; edn: BA in vocational psych., Wayne State Univ. 1957; MA, psych., CSU Long Beach 1975; PhD, clin. psych., US Internat. Univ. 1978; lic. Marriage, Family, Child, Therapist (1977), Cert. Sex Therapist (1980). Career: (current) clinical director Human Resources Center (pvt. practice psychol. ctr), Santa Ana; vice chmn. Psychol. Services Dept., Brea Hosp. Neuropsychiatric Ctr., Brea; vocational expert witness, Bur. Hearing and Appeals, 9th Fed. Dist. Court; assoc. clin. prof., medical psych., Coll. Osteopathic Medicine, Pomona; assoc. prof. Calif. Graduate Inst., Orange Co. Campus; Diplomate, Am. Acad. Behavioral Med. 1981; mem: Am. Psychol. Assn.; Calif. Assn. Marriage, Family, Therapists; Am. Assn. Sex Therapists, Counselors, Educators; Calif. State Psychol. Assn.; mil: s/sgt. USAF 1950-53; Democrat; Catholic; rec: golf, woodworking, music. Res: 15291 Nimes Cir. Irvine 92714 Ofc: Human Resources Center, 1125 E. 17th St. E-201, Santa Ana 92701

YAMANAKA, MARK KO, physician, internist; b. May 26, 1955, Santa Monica; s. Roy Michio and Shirley Nobuko (Kosaka) Y.; m. Jeriann Suzuki, Jan. 19, 1986; edn: BA in biol., UC Los Angeles 1977; MD, summa cum laude, UC Davis 1981. Career: intern and resident in internal medicine, St. Mary-UCLA Med. Center 1981-84, pulmonary fellow Harbor-UCLA Med. Center, 1984—; attending staff county hosp. and out-patients; tchg. med. students, interns, residents; honors: Phi Beta Kappa (1977), Intern of the Year (1981-2), Resident of the Year (1983-4), pres. Housestaff Assn. St. Mary-UCLA (1982-3, 1983-4); mem: Am. Coll. of Physicians, Am. Coll. of Chest Physicians, Calif. Med. Assn., LA County Med. Assn., Trudeau Soc.; research: Polynesian Brochiectasis, Almitrine (exptl. drug) usage; Democrat; United Methodist; rec: tennis, basketball, ocean sports. Address: Torrance

YAMAUCHI, KENT TAKASHI, clinical psychologist; b. May 12, 1950, Los Angeles; s. Paul Kazu and Helen (Tokunaga) Y.; m. Pat Kimiye Uyeno, Aug. 21, 1975; edn: BA, cum laude, USC 1972, MSW, 1974; MA, Calif. Sch. of Profl. Psychology 1980, PhD, 1981; desig: Lic. Psychologist 1982; Nat. Register of Health Service Providers in Psychology 1983; Diplomate Am. Board of Psychotherapy 1983. Career: child & family psychotherapist Intercommunity Child Guidance Ctr., Whittier 1974-78; psychol. intern Merced Co. Mental Hlth Svcs, 1978-9; adult & marital psychotherapist Family Svc Ctr, Fresno 1979-80; psychol. intern Denver (Colo.) Gen. Hosp. 1980-1; clin. psychologist El Dorado Co. Community Mental Hlth Ctr, S. Lake Tahoe 1981-84; clin. psychologist Psychological Services Ctr. of Pasadena City College 1984—; oral commnr. Psychology Examining Com., Calif. Bd. of Medical Quality Assurance 1985—; honors: Distinguished Alumni Award, Calif. Sch. of Profl. Psychology 1983; Who's Who Among Human Services Professionals 1986; mem: Am. Psychol. Assn., Calif. State Psychol. Assn.; publs. in profl. and sci. psychol. jours. Ofc: Psychological Services Ctr. Room C232, Pasadena City College, 1570 E Colorado Blvd Pasadena 91106-9980

YANAKIEFF, VENELIN JORDAN, electrical engineer; b. Sept. 12, 1936, Sofia, Bulgaria, nat. US cit. 1950; s. Jordan Yanakiee and Spacia (Bogatinoff) Ivanov; m. Anna Gabriella, Aug. 11, 1963; 1 dau. Stephanie Elizabeth b. 1971; edn: AA, Los Angeles City Coll. 1964; BSEE, CSU Los Angeles 1966; reg. profl. engr. Calif. 1977. Career: electrical tester L.A. Dept. Water & Power 1960-66, engr. systems fault analysis 1966-70, engr. meter lab. & records 1970-82; engr. field meter tests 1982—, safety coordinator for test lab, member ad hoc task force; mem: Am. Soc. Safety Engrs., Am. Public Power Assn., IEEE, L.A. Police Concert Band (vol. musician); works: part. in devel. ANSI C12.1 1982 Standard (gov. watt-hour meters and accessories); mil: USNR hon. discharge 1962; Republican; Christian; rec: musician. Res: 1124 N Meyers St Burbank 91506 Ofc: LADWP 111 N Hope St Los Angeles 90051

YANG, DANIEL CHAO-HAI, educator; b. Dec. 14, 1948, China, nat. US cit. 1985; s. Tsu-Wu and Chi-Fong (Hsu) Y.; m. Shuh-Yu G., Jan. 3, 1976; children: Lance b. 1976, Neil b. 1978; edn: BS, National Taiwan Univ. 1971, MS, Univ. Wis., Madison 1978; PhD, Rutgers Univ. 1982. Careرer: corporate engr. RCA Advanced Technology Labs., Camden, N.J. 1979; tech. staff RCA David Sarnoff Research Center, Princeton, N.J. 1979-82; asst. prof. UC Los Angeles 1982—, splst. Robotics, Machine Design, Automation; cons. Standum Machinery, Jet Propulsion Lab, Paul S. Veneklasen and Assocs., UCLA Med. Ctr., Intellewell, Perceptronics; honors: ASME Faculty Advisor Citation (1983-84), ALCOA Found. Sci. Support Award (1985), Phi Tau Phi; mem. Am. Soc. of Mech. Engrs.; num. articles in profl. jours., tech. presentations profl. seminars and symposia; rec: swimming, chess, Go. Res: 12070 Beatrice St Culver City 90230 Ofc: 5732D Boelter Hall UCLA Los Angeles 90024

YANG, HERMAN, S.D., engineer; b. Feb. 25, 1919, Chongqin, China, nat. US cit. 1954; s. C.Z. and Y.S. (Li) Y.; m. Dorothy, Feb. 10, 1945, children: Constant b. 1946, Emoretta b. 1949, Faith b. 1951; edn: BS, Nat. Wu-Han Univ. 1942; MS, with honors, Iowa State Univ. 1948; PhD cand., Ga. Inst. of Technol. 1958; Reg. Profl. Engr. Calif., Ga. Career: cons. engr. Victue Engrg. Co. Atlanta, Ga.; air cond. designer Robert & Co. Assoc. Atlanta; tool design engr. Continental Tooling Svc. Atlanta; group engr. Lockheed-Georgia Co. Marietta; senior staff engr., task leader, proj. mgr. Lockheed-Calif. Burbank; mng. dir. Victue Enterprises Inc. Van Nuys; cons. engrg. planning & directing; honors: Nat. Undergrad Award (1940); mem: Am. Inst. Aero. & Astro., Soc. Automotive Engrs., Chinese-Am. Engrs. & Scientists Assn. of So. Calif. (chair coms.), Huanghe Univ. Fund Found. (chpt. chair), Huanghe Univ. Engrg. Coll. (chair plng. & proposal com.), publ: tech. articles 1958, 65, 68, 82; Unitarian; rec: photog., carpentry, classical music, hiking. Res: 15497 Longbow Dr Sherman Oaks 91403 Ofc: Victue Enterprises Inc. POB 3532 Van Nuys 91407

YANG, KUO LIANG, pharmacist; b. Apr. 29, 1947, Chungking Szechuan, China; s. William and Grace (Chung) Y.; m. Elaine Y. Yang, Mar. 28, 1978; 1 dau., Eileen, b. 1984; edn: BS, biology, Fu Jen Univ., Taiwan 1970; BS, pharm., Univ. Utah 1976. Career: chief pharm. Brookvale Med. Ctr. Pharmacy, San Pablo 1981; staff pharm. Central Pharmacy, Richmond 1981; owner/pharmacist Abreu's Drug Store, Oakland 1981—; drug consultant Random House; mem: Alameda Co. Pharmacists Assn.; Calif. Pharmacists Assn.; Am. Pharmacists Assn.; publs: The Mechanism and Pathway off Picotoxin in Cardiac Ar-ּythmia, 1972; Republican; rec: horseback riding, swim., music, reading. ๑๑ Delta Way Danville 94526 Ofc: Abreu's Drug Store, 2286 E 14th St

YANG, P.S., computer software co. president; b. Mar. 3, 1951, Taiwan, R.O.C.; s. Lein-An and Suo-Yin (Lu) Y.; m. Amy, Dec. 12, 1977; children: Sanford b. 1982, Sandy b. 1983; edn: BS math., Tamkang, Taiwan 1973; MS computer sci., NDSU 1982. Career: mgr. Delphi Systems 1984; pres. U-Need & See Computer Systems, Newbury Park 1984—; designer software: Customizing Documentation Generator for DOS and UNIX (1985), Portable Report Generator for UNIX (1985); orgns: Presidential Task Force, Ask American; mil: Taiwan Army; rec: travel. Address: Newbury Park 91320

YANG, SHARON YOUNGSIL, consultant dietitian; b. Feb. 16, 1935, Seoul, Korea, nat. US cit. 1968; d. Dr. Jung-Min and Yo-Han (Lee) Kahn; m. Kisuk Yang, Aug. 15, 1959; children: Andrew b. 1960, Alice (Murray) b. 1965; edn: BA, cum laude, Coll. of Emporia 1957; MS, Univ. Wis. 1959; Reg. Dietitian, Am. Dietetic Assn. Life Comm. Coll. Tchg. Credential. Career: grad. research asst. Univ. Wis. 1957-59; clin. dietitian Cedars of Lebanon Hosp., Los Angeles 1961-62; chief dietitian Valley Hosp., Van Nuys 1962-64; dir. food service Placer Gen. Hosp., Auburn 1968-75; cons. dietitian Camellia Convalescent Hosps. Corp. (4 skilled nsg. facilities: Center, Gardens, Valley, Woodland), Sacto. 1975—; bd. dirs. Asian Comm. Nsg. Home and Asian Comm. Ctr. of Sacto. Valley (1984-); nutrition cons. Placer Co. Senior Nutrition Pgm. (1974-79); honors: grad. research assistantship Univ. Wis. (1957-59), Athena Hon. Soc. (1957); mem: Golden Empire Dist. Dietetic Assn., Am. Diet. Assn., Calif. Diet. Assn., Consultant Dietitians in Health Care Facilities, Certified Adminstrv. Interpreters Assn.; civic: Christian Book Club, Sacto. (exec. bd.), Fremont Presbyterian Ch., Sacto. (Hunger Task Force, bd. deacons), United Presbyn. Ch., USA (Self Devel. of Peoples' com., Sacto. Presbytery Plnng. Com.), Korean Presbyn. Ch. of Sacto. (pres. United Presbyn. Women); works: photog. slide presentations; vol. designer Asian-Am. instnl. kitchen for Asian Comm. Nsg. Home (1985-86); Republican; rec: bridge, photog. Res: 181 Middleton Way Sacramento 95864 Ofc: Camellia Conv. Hospitals Corp. 2255 Fair Oaks Blvd Sacramento 95825

YARNALL, CELESTE, real estate broker, actress; b. Jul. 26, 1944, Long Beach; d. Forest Elwood and Helene Jeanne (Colombel) Y.; m. Robert Colman, Feb. 8, 1979; 1 dau: Camilla Jeanne, b. 1970; lic. real estate broker, Calif. Dept. R.E. Career: Miss Rheingold 1964, spkswmn. Rheingold Beer, (TV, radio commls, print ads); leading roles in TV and feature films; appeared in num. TV commls.; R.E. sales agt. Grubb & Ellis, Los Angeles; co-founder Greenwood & Co. 1974, v.p., then pres. Greenwood/ Yarnall (div. Greenwood & Co.); founder/ pres. Celeste Yarnall & Assoc., Los Angeles 1979—; mem. Appraisers Inst.; mem. Los angeles Comml. Realtors Assn.; Awards: Miss Rheingold 1964; Deb Star 1968; Most Promising New Star of 1968; mem: L.A. Bd. Realtors, Beverly Hills. CofC; Western. Reg. CofC; patron LA County Mus. of Art (Amazing Blue Ribbon 400; Inner Circle Childrens Mus., Founders II, Pres. Circle); publs: arts. for Century City News, num. R.E. publs.; rec: fitness, nutrition, jewelry design. Ofc: Celeste Yarnall & Assoc., 9200 Sunset Blvd Pent. 20 Los Angeles 90069

YASUI, STEVE TSUNEO, physician; b. Jan. 4, 1957, Waipahu, Ha.; s. George and Betty S. (Sonobe) Y.; edn: BS in biol., BS in psychol., Stanford Univ. 1979; MD, Univ. of Hawaii Sch. of Med. 1983. Career: Univ. of Hawaii Integrated Transitional Res. Pgm. 1983-84; res. family practice San Pedro Peninsula Hosp. 1984—; mem: AMA, Am. Acad. Family Physicians, Hawaii Med. Assn., Calif. Family Practice Resident's Orgn.; rec: water sports, tennis, oriental cooking. Res: 3620 So. Pacific Ave., San Pedro 90731 Ofc: San Pedro Peninsula Hospital, 1300 W. 7th St., San Pedro 90731

YAW, ELBERT M., sales executive, b. May 5, 1940, Kansas City, Mo.; s. Elbert F. and Juanita F. (Black) Y.; m. Holly H. Chilson, May 16, 1982; children: Kimberly M. b. 1962, Sandi M. b. 1969; edn: pol. sci., Fullerton Coll. 1958-60; L.A. Trade Tech. Coll. 1962-3; BSME, Northrop Univ. 1966; Grad. Sch. Bus., CSU Los Angeles 1968; wholesale mgmt., Stanford Univ. 1980. Career: engr. So. Calif. Gas Co., Los Angeles 1966-67; systems and territory sales Paul-Munroe Co., Pico Rivera 1967-69; western reg. mgr. Fluid Power Systems Div., Ambac Inc., Burlingame 1969-74; area mgr. Paul-Munroe Co., Santa Clara 1974-79, v.p. mktg. and ops./dir. sales, Whittier 1979-85, v.p. No. Calif. 1985—; consultant, engr. and bus. 1969-74; honor soc. Northrop Univ. 1965; mem. Fluid Power Distbr. Assn.; Republican; Christian; rec: hunting, fishing, writing. Res: 24712 Scooterbug Ln Auburn 95603 Ofc: Paul-Munroe Co., 9999 E Rose Hills Rd Whittier 90601

YEAGER, PHILIP J., real estate executive; b. Mar. 1, 1930, Columbus, Ohio; s. William P. and Anna C. (Meidl) Y.; m. Peggy Wetzler, Nov. 1, 1952; children: Melissa b. 1954, Susan b. 1955, Kurt b. 1956 (dec.), Stephen b. 1959, Christine b. 1961, Jennifer b. 1966; edn: Claremont Men's Coll. 1951; grad. work, Ohio State Univ. 1956; life teaching cred. adult edn. (R.E. subjects). Career: 3d gen. Calif. realtor; pres./CEO: Century 21 Region 105 (w/ 165 Century 21 offices, adminstrv. ofc. West Covina), Century 21 Region 113 (w/ 163 offices, adminstrv. ofc. Seattle, Wn.), Covina Realty Co. Inc. dba Mr. Build of the Northwest (Ore., Wn., Ida., Alaska), Resorts Mktg. Inc. (Seattle, Wn.), Estate Escrow Corp. (West Covina), chmn. exec. com. Fifth Season (devel., mktg. timeshare condo., US & Mex.). Honors: Eagle Scout. Mem: past pres. Covina Valley Bd. of Realtors; past dir. Nat. Assn. of Realtors; past Scoutmaster and Dist. chmn. BSA; past pres. two Toastmaster Clubs. Num. R.E. articles in nat. publs.; mil: 1st lt. USAF 1952-56; Republican; rec: flying, tennis. Res: 2808 Monte Verde Covina 91724 Ofc: Century 21, Region 105, 100 No. Citrus, W. Covina 91791

YEE, BILLY, physician; b. Apr. 14, 1952, China, nat. US cit.; s. Tung You and Boy Wah (Jim) Y.; m. Karen Yasuda, Sept. 16, 1973; children: Dana b. 1977,

Kasey b. 1984; edn: AB in biol., UC Los Angeles 1974; MD, UC Davis 1978. Career: asst. prof. (reproductive endocrinol. and infertility) Dept. OB-Gyn., Univ. Calif. Irvine, and dir. of In Vitro Fertilization, Memorial Med. Center of Long Beach; honors: Alpha Omega Alpha (1978); mem. Am. Coll. Obs. Gyn., Am. Fertility Soc., PCFS; research: human in vitro fertilization, crypreservation of human embryos. Ofc: Memorial Medical Center of Long each 2880 Atlantic Ave Ste 220 Long Beach 90806

YEE, KING PING, management executive; b. Jan. 24, 1922, Shanghai, China; s. Wan Son and Wai Lee (Waung) Y.; m. Jeanne C., Dec. 31, 1957; edn: BS, Nat. Shanghai Inst. of Commerce 1940, MBA in acctg., Golden Gate Coll. 1969, MPA, 1971; real estate courses Coll. of San Mateo; desig: Cert. Practition Acct., Australian Soc. Acctcy., Chartered Acct., China, Calif. lic. Real Estate Broker. Career: chartered acct. Shanghai, China 1948; senior auditor K.L. Young & Co. Public Acct., Hong Kong 1962; controller, factory mgr. Winner Co. (H.K.) Ltd., Hong Kong 1967; mgmt. cons./chief exec., The United Industries, Inc. U.S.A. current; mem. Australian Soc. of Accts., Royal Econ. Soc., Toastmasters Internat. Ofc: The United Industries, Inc. U.S.A. 1200 Howard Ave 2nd Flr Burlingame 94010

YEE, RAYMOND, physician; b. Apr. 7, 1952, San Francisco; s. Frank Yuen and May Kui (Soo Hoo) Y.; m. Lulu Yee, MD, Apr. 9, 1983; children: Dwayne b. 1984, Brenden b. 1985; edn: AA, City Coll. San Francisco 1973; UC Berkeley 1974; MD, Autonomous Univ. Guadalajara 1979; lic. MD, State GA, 1981, Calif. 1981, Wyo. 1982. Career: vol. family physician, Tecate, Mexico 1981; family phys. in Martin and Phillip, So. Dak. 1981-82; psychiatry resident King/Drew Med. Ctr. 1982-85; affiliating resident USC, Los Angeles 1982-83; staff mem. Los Angeles Dept. of Mental Health; chief res. psychiatry, King/Drew Med. Ctr., Los Angeles 1984-85; family physician Bennett Comm. Hosp., 1981-82; currently staff psychiatrist King/Drew Med Ctr. and asst. prof. psychiatry and human behavior, Charles H. Drew Postgrad. Med. Sch.-UCLA; mem: Am. Med. Assn.; So. Calif. Psychiat. Soc.; Am. Psychiat. Assn.; mil: PFC USAR 1972-78; Democrat; rec: chess, bowling, hiking, travel. Res: 5488 Dobbs St, 99, Los Angeles 90032

YEH, XIAN-LI, applied physicist; b. Oct. 22, 1956, Shaighai, China; s. Yao-Shan and Lin-Zhi (Shu) Y.; m. Dorothy Cheer, June 18, 1983; 1 son, Wesley b. 1986; edn: Fudan Univ., Shanghai 1978-79; Univ. of the Pacific 1980; BS, Calif. Inst. of Tech. 1982, MS, 1984, PhD, 1986. Career: electrical engr. Chang Jiang Semiconductor Factory, Shanghai, China 1975-78; physicist Cabot Corp., Billerica, Mass., Oct. 1986−; awards: SOHIO Fellow, Standard Oil Co. (1985); mem: Materials Research Soc., Am. Physical Soc.; publs: 8 tech. papers; internat. recogn. as first to demonstrate the formation of metallic glass by solid state reaction (i.e. by reaction of intermetallic compounds with hydrogen); rec: piano. Res: 195 So. Sunny Slope Ave Pasadena 91107 Ofc: Cabot Corp. Billerica Technical Center, Billerica MA 01821

YEN, FRANCIS TZUHAN, computer software executive; b. May 4, 1949, Ning-Po, Chekiang, China, nat. US cit. 1983; s. Hsiao-Pen and Li-Hsia (Pan) Y.; m. Rosa Siao-Lin Hsu, July 6, 1977; children: Jennifer b. 1982, Jessica b. 1985; edn: BSEE, Nat. Chiao-Tung Univ., Taiwan 1971; MS, ops. research, Stanford Univ. 1974; MBA, Santa Clara Univ. 1977; Deg. Engr. E.E., Stanford Univ. 1982. Career: test pattern writer (p.t.) Amdahl Corp., Sunnyvale 1974; pgmmr. IBM Corp., Palo Alto 1974; pgmmr. SRI Internat., Menlo Park 1974-77, ops. analyst & project leader 1977-79; mfg. engr., pgmmr. IBM Corp. 1979-, staff pgmmr. 1981−, project coord. 1984-85, session chmn. IBM Test Technology Symp. 1983; adj. asst. prof. San Jose State Univ. 1988-85; owner/broker Goldwater Realty, San Jose 1985−; awards: Chen Kao Fu Scholar (1968), Chiao-Tung Univ. Alumni Scholar (1969, 70), IBM recogn. award (1985); senior mem. IEEE, past mem. ACM, Ops. Research Soc. Am., Assn. of MBA Execs.; contbr. tech. papers profl. publs.; mil: 2d lt. Chinese Army R.O.C. 1971-73; Buddhist; rec: Tai-Chi-Chuan, Yoga, Chinese chess, travel. Res: 42 Park Village Pl San Jose 95136

YEN, WEN-HSIUNG, musicologist, composer; b. June 26, 1934, Tainan, Taiwan, R.O.C.; m. Yuan-yuan Yen, Jan. 6, 1961; 3 sons; edn: BA, Nat. Taiwan Norman Univ. 1960; MA, Chinese Cluture Univ. 1964; Univ. of Calif. 1971; PhD cand., Chinese Culture Univ., Univ. of Maryland. Career: instr. Taiwan Provincial Taichung Teacher Coll., 1961-62; prof. Chinese Culture Univ. 1964-69; lectr. West Los Angeles Community Coll., 1978-82; grad. teaching asst. Univ. of Md. 1982-83; instr. L.A. City Coll. 1983-, lectr. CSU, Los Angeles 1984-; founder/dir. Chinese Music Orch. of So. Calif., 1974 (t.v. appearance 1979); honors: recognition, Calif. Mus. Found. bd. trustees (1976), Chinese Am. PTA (1980), Outstanding Teacher award Confucius Commemorative Day Ceremony, L.A. (1984), Service award, Nat. Taiwan Normal Univ. Alumni Assn. of So. Calif. (1985). Compositions incl: Collection of Works by Mr. Yen, 1969; recordings: Art Songs and Chinese Folk Songs (13 pieces) 1982; Instrumental Ensemble for Chinese Traditional Orch. incl. A Hope of New Spring and San Yang Kai Tai; publs: Taiwan Folk Songs, Vol. 1 (1967), Vol. 2 (1969); A Dictionary of Chinese Music and Musicians (1967), coauthor; A Collection of Wen-hsiung Yen's Songs (1968); Achievement and Methodology for Comparative Musicology (1968), transl.; contbr. to China Weekly, Kung Hsueh Music mag., Taiwan Province Wen Hsien Hui, Kuo Chiao Fu Tao, Chen Tao. Mem: Chinese Culture Sch. of Los Angeles (pres.), Soc. of Ethnomusicol., The College Music Soc., Internat. Council for Traditional Music, Alumni Assn. for Chinese Culture Univ. in USA (pres.), Taiwan Benevolent Assn. of Calif. (bd. mem. 1985); rec: walking, Tai Chi Chuan, table tennis. Address: 2743 Selby Ave Los Angeles 90064

YEUNG, GEORGIANA HIM-CHE, doctor of traditional Chinese medicine, acupuncturist; b. Aug. 4, 1948, Shanghai, China; d. Tsin-Yih and Men-Tse (Hsu) Y.; edn: National Taiwan Univ. 1966-69; BS, CSU San Jose 1971; PhD/OMD, Samra Univ. of Oriental Medicine 1983; Cert. Acupuncturist, Calif. Career: acupuncturist Hong Kong Chinese Acup. Inst. 1977, Taipei Acup. and Moxibustion Clinic Ctr. 1978, Harbor General Hosp., Torrance 1978-80, Vets. Gen. Hosp. of Taiwan 1980; med. technologist UC Los Angeles Med. Center 1979−; acup./herbalist Samra Univ. of Oriental Medicine, Los Angeles 1981-84; clinic supvr. Calif. Acup. Coll., L.A. 1984-85; cons., tchr., dir. Acu-Herb Clinic/ Inst. of Chinese Medicine, L.A. 1986−; mem: Center of Chinese Medicine, Oriental Healing Arts Inst.; publ: Handbook of Chinese Herbs and Formulas (Vol. I, II); Christian; rec: Chinese brush painting, singing. Res: 800 W First St, 1104, Los Angeles 90012 Ofc: Acu-Herb Clinic/ Institute of Chinese Medicine 2154 Westwood Blvd Los Angeles 90025

YIP, PAMELA MARY, journalist; b. Sept. 21, 1956, Hong Kong, nat. US cit. 1965; d. Kam Chun and Margaret Mary (Shen) Yip; edn: BA in journ., CSU Sacto. 1979. Career: reporter intern United Press Internat., Sacto. 1976-79, reporter UP, Los Angeles 1979-80; reporter The Stockton Record, 1980−; awards: 2d pl. investigative reporting, AP News Executive Council (1984), public service award, Gannett Co. (1984); mem. Asian-Am. Journalists Assn., Soc. of Profl. Journalists, Soc. Am. Business and Econ. Writers, NOW, AAUW; Democrat; active in church wk; rec: martial arts. Address: Stockton 95202

YOB, JOSEPH C., mergers and acquisitions executive; b. Dec. 31, 1927, Milwaukee, Wisc.; s. Carl G. and Adele J. (Fedel) Y.; m. Theresa Teskey, May 6, 1950; children: Mary Jo b. 1953, David b. 1955, Carl b. 1956, THeresa Ann b. 1957, Joseph Jr. b. 1959, Susan b. 1960, Jonathan b. 1961, Rebecca b. 1963, Judith b. 1966, Paula b. 1970; edn: BS, Univ. of Detroit 1949; Lic. Calif. Real Estate Broker, 1985. Career: CEO The Joseph C. Yob Co., Mich. 1950-73; CEO Port City Disposal Svc. Inc., Mich. 1960-73; CEO Multiple Svcs. Inc., Mich., Tex., Fla. 1950-80; CEO Fla. Pallet Corp., Tampa 1978−; CEO Fla. Investment R.E. Inc., Tampa 1978−; CEO Tampa Bay Metals Intrnat. Corp., Tampa, Fla. 1981−; CEO Towing Svcs. of USA Inc., Clearwater, Fla. 1976−; chief exec. ofcr. Bay Tech. Svcs. Inc., Sunnyvale 1982−; pres. Mergers & Acquisitions Network of No. Am. Inc., San FRancisco 1985−; instr. money & banking Muskegon Community Coll. 1967; dir. Ziegler Trucking Inc. 1976-; mem: Independent Accnts. Assn. of Mich., Tampa CofC (Com. of 100), Upper Gr. Lakes Devel. Council, 1st Univ. of Detroit Spring Carnival (Liaison), St. Francis Club (Univ. of Detroit), Univ. of Detroit Debate Soc., Mich. Christmas Tree Growers Assn., US CofC, Fremont, Detroit, Muskegon and Tampa CofCs, Rotary; Christian; rec: public speaking, writing, politics. Res: 2622 14th Ave. San Francisco 94127 Ofc: Mergers & Acquisitions Network, P.O. Box 11800 San Francisco 94101

YOCAM, DELBERT WAYNE, electronic products co. executive; b. Dec. 24, 1943, Long Beach, Calif.; s. Royal Delbert and Mary Rose (Gross) Y.; m. Janet McVeigh, June 13, 1965; children: Eric Wayne, Christian Jeremy, Elizabeth Janelle; edn: BA bus. adminstrn., CSU Fullerton 1966; MBA, CSU Long Beach 1971. Career: mktg./ supply changeover coord. automotive assembly div. Ford Motor Co. Dearborn, Mich. 1966-72; prodn. control mgr. Control Data Corp. Hawthorne, Calif. 1972-74; prodn. and material control mgr. Bourns Inc. Riverside 1974-76; corp. material mgr. Computer Automation Inc. Irvine 1976-78; prodn. planning mgr. central staff ITT Cannon Electric div. world hdqs. Santa Ana 1978-79; exec. v.p., chief op. ofcr. Apple Computer Inc. Cupertino 1979−; mem. faculty Cypress Coll. 1972-79; co-founder Control Data Corp. Mgmt. Assn. 1974; active L.A. County Heart Assn. 1966; Republican; Methodist. Ofc: Cupertino

YONEHIRO, GEORGE, superior court judge; b. July 24, 1927, Newcastle, Calif.; s. Saburu and Kazu (Funaoka) Y.; m. Miyoko Kido, Feb. 14, 1954; children: Melissa b. 1958, Marcus b. 1959; edn: AA, Sacramento Jr. Coll. 1942; Roosevelt Coll. 1949-50; LLB, John Marshall Law Sch Chgo. 1954; admitted Ill. State Bar 1954, Colo. 1962, Calif. 1972. Career: judge justice ct. 1964-82, municipal ct. 1982-84; superior ct. Placer Co. 1984−; mem: Sons of Italy, Auburn Airport Com. (chmn.), Am. Legion, VFW, Japanese Am. Citizen's League; mil: platoon sgt. US Army 442 Reg. Combat Team, Bronze Star WWII; col. Calif. State Mil. Reserve; Republican; Catholic; rec: fishing. Res: 325 Yonehiro Dr POB 237 Applegate 95703 Ofc: County of Placer 11546 B Ave Auburn 95603

YOO, YOUNG IL, business owner; b. Jan. 24, 1947, Seoul, Korea, s. Soo San and Joo Soon Y.; m. Hi-Za, Mar. 3, 1977; children: James b. 1978, Janet b. 1981; edn: BA, Okla. State Univ. 1975, MBA, 1977. Career: owner Cal-Tronics Sales Co. L.A. 1978−; mem. CofC of USA; registered brand name: Calteck (watches 1985); rec: skiing, golf, reading. Res: 19220 Dunure Pl Northridge 91326 Ofc: Cal-Tronics Sales Co. 1930 Wilshire Blvd Ste 508 Los Angeles 90057

YORK, EVERETT HAYS, manufacturing co. executive; b. April 27, 1912, Johnson, Nebr.; s. Robert Levi York and Tacie Lenore Hays; m. Helen Ackerson, June 1, 1940; 1 dau, Carol Jean b 1945; edn: Naval Engriing. Ofcrs. Tng. and Instr. course, Gen. Motors Inst. of Tech., Flint, Mich. 1944. Career: West Coast regl. mgr. The Buda Co., Harvey, Il. 1946-51, salesmgr. 1951-54; currentyl, owner Everett H. York Co., Signal Hill and CEO, pres. Oildex Corp. Signal Hill 1970−; honors: Proclamation from the Gov. of Calif. George Duekmajian, 1984; Resolution from Assemblyman Dennis Brown and Sen. Robert Beverly of the State of Calif. and Commdn. from the Mayor of the City of Signal Hill, 1984; mem: Signal Hill CofC (bd. dirs. 1967-83, pres. 1983), Am. Security Council (Nat. Adv. Bd. 1976-), Nat. Rifle Assn.; mil: USNR 1942-45; Republican; Methodist; rec: fishing, travel. Res: 30290 Lands End Pl. Canyon Lake 92380 Ofc: Oildex Corp., 2065 E. 27th St. Long Beach 90806 and Everett H. York Co., 2075 E. 27th St. Long Beach 90806

YOUNG, BETO L. (YANG, LI-CHUNG), writer, publisher, marketing specialist; b. Dec. 16, 1941, I-Lan, Taiwan; s. Kim Moon and May Fong (Lin) Yang; m. E.F. Shung, May 11, 1972; children: Lesley K.Y. b. 1977, Ingrid K.T. b. 1978; edn: Fu-Jen Univ. 1966. Career: primary sch. tchr., Taiwan 1960-62; chief ed. Fu-Jen News, Taiwan 1962-65; maritime ofcr., Hong Kong 1968-71; prin. T.R.A. Consultant Co., Taiwan 1972-78; Chinese instr. U-Bei Co., Japan 1979-80; came to USA 1980; pres. Young P & D, and New Immigrant Ents. Inc., Montebello 1981–; instr. CSU Long Beach 1983; honors: Outstanding Editor-Academic, Taiwan (1965); author/pub: "New Immigrant Report" (Chinese) (1983, 84, 85), "Chinese Business in So. Calif." (Chinese (1983), "Chinese Business in America" (English, Chinese) (1984); devel. N C A Fax-Marketing Chain System (1986); club: Asian Kiwanis (San Gabriel); Buddhist. Res: 5320 N Peck Rd #5 El Monte 91733 Ofc: Young Cos. 886 N Garfield Ave Montebello 90640 and 385 24th Ave San Francisco 94121

YOUNG, DOUGLAS REA, lawyer; b. July 21, 1948, Los Angeles; s. James Douglas and Dorothy Belle (Rea) Y.; m. Terry Forrest, Jan. 19, 1974; 1 dau: Megann Forrest, b. 1979; edn: BA, cum laude, Yale Univ. 1971; JD, UC Berkeley 1976; admitted Calif. State Bar, 1976. Career: law clerk to US Dist. Judge Alfonso J. Zirpoli 1976-77; assoc. atty. Farella, Braun & Martel 1977-82, partner 1982–; twice apptd. spl. master in fed. antitrust litigation; judge pro tem S.F. Municipal Ct. 1984-; faculty Nat. Inst. for Trial Advocacy 1983-, Hastings Coll. of Advocacy 1985-, Calif. Cont. Edn. of the Bar; co-founder Berkeley Law Foundation; bd. dir. Legal Aid Soc. of San Francisco 1981-, Public Interest Clearinghouse 1981-; awards: appreciation, Berkeley Law Found., exec. ed. Calif. Law Review 1975-76; mem: Calif. St. Bar; US Supreme Ct.; 6th and 9th Circuit Cts. of Appeal; Fed. Dist. Cts. for No. and Central Dists. of Calif.; Berkeley Law Fdn.; ACLU; Environmental Defense Fund; Litigation and Criminal Law Sects. of Am. Bar Assn.; Lawyers Club of San Francisco; Bar Assn. of S.F.;. Am., Calif. Bar Assns.; publs: Cal. L. Rev. 1975; mil: Sgt., USMC 1971-73; Democrat; Protestant; rec: skiing, mountaineering, running. Res: 67 Weybridge Ct Oakland 94611 Ofc: Farella, Braun & Martel, 235 Montgomery St, Ste 3000, San Francisco 94104

YOUNG, DOUGLAS WAYNE, financial consultant; b. July 30, 1935, Meridian; s. Russell Lawhead and Arlene (Boardman) Y.; m. Diane Lee, Apr. 25, 1954; children: Douglas Wayne, Jr. b. 1954,Gail Lynn (Ransdall) b. 1956, James Morris b. 1959, Michael Monty b. 1960; edn: AA, Yuba Jr. Coll. 1955; BA, UC Davis 1958. Career: loan ofcr. and real estate appraiser Elmer F. Karpe, Inc. Bakersfield 1966-69; regl. dir. Farmers Home Adminstrn. (respons. for 30 USDA loan and grant pgms. throughout Calif., Nev., Hawaiian Is., Guam, Am. Samoa and Trust Territories), 1969-77; current: owner prin. Douglas W. Young & Assocs. (finl. cons.), and owner D W Y Development Corp., Woodland; honors: 4-H County All-Star, Sutter County (1952), Student Body pres. Yuba Jr. Coll. (1954); mem. Elks Internat.; Republican; Prot.; rec: duck hunting, fly fishing. Res: 1182 California St Woodland 95695 Ofc: Douglas W Young and Assocs. 428-½ First St Ste 205 Woodland 95695

YOUNG, EDWARD HIRAM, musician, electronic mechanic; b. June 10, 1909, Fowler; s. Isiac McDowell and Mary Delilah (Garlington) Y.; m. Jean King (dec.), May 31, 1938; children: Dr. Grace Jean Moore (oncology splst. and hematologist) b. 1946. Edward H., Jr. (meterologist Nat. Weather Svc.) b. 1950, Zella M. (bus. major SFSU) b. 1959; edn: Bakersfield Jr. Coll. 1941-42; Oakland Sch. of Real Estate 1944; var. electronic tech. courses. Career: profl. musician, band leader, playing throughout Calif., 1929-42, 1946-59; mech. Mare Island Naval Shipyard, 1942-46; TV repair bus., Oakland 1959-61; electronic mech. Hunter's Point Naval Shipyard, 1961-74, ret.; musician num. weddings, senior citizen ctrs., hosps., conventions, current; mem. Musicians Union Local #6 San Francisco (East Bay Labor Council rep.), Lions Club; Democrat; Congregational; rec: golf, fish, music. Res: 1636 Trestle Glen Rd Oakland 94610

YOUNG, FORREST ORVILLE, rancher, plastic & reconstructive surgeon; b. Sept. 26, 1905, Dell, Mo.; s. Sidney Arthur and Lennie Harriet (Johnson) Y.; widower; children: Harriet (Mrs. John Kalarik) b. 1932, Margaret (Mrs. George Sutton) b. 1935, Forrest Wesley b. 1940; edn: AB, Univ. Redlands 1926; MD, Stanford Univ. 1930; physician & surgeon lic. NY (1934), Calif. (1950); Diplomate Am. Bd. Plastic Surgery. Career: intern Strong Meml. Hosp., Rochester, NY 1930-31, asst. resident in surgery 1931-32, asso. resident in gharge orthopedics 1932-33, res. in gen. surgery 1933-34; instr., asst. prof., asso. prof. Univ. of Rochester Sch. of Med. & Dentistry, 1935-50; vol. fellow plastic surgery Barnes Hosp. Univ. of Wash. Med. Sch., St. Louis Mo. 1935-36; aurgeon in chg. plastic surgery Strong Meml. Hosp. 1935-51; practice surgery, spec. in plastic surg., Rochester, NY 1934-51, Redlands, Calif. 1951-79; att. surgeon Redlands Comm. Hosp., San Gorgonio Pass Hosp.; cons. staff Kaiser Fontana Hosp., Pacific State, San Bernardino, Kaiser Found. Hosp.; cons. Calif. Crippled Children Services 1951-79; special examiner Calif. Indsl. Accidents Commn. 1951-79; chmn. com. on plastic surgery Project Hope 1962-67; ret. physician 1979; trustee Young Family Trust 1972-, chmn. Grand View Orchards Inc. Terra Bella, Calif. (mgr. 600-acre orange, lemon, walnut, olive, pomegranate ranch), 1979–; past mem: Am. Bd. Plastic Surgery (founder), Fellow Am. Coll. Surgeons, AMA, Calif. Med. Assn., San Bernardino Co. Med. Soc., Soc. Univ. Surgeons, Am. Assn. Plastic Surgeons, Am. Soc. Plastic ...nstrv. Surgery; honors: Sigma Xi, Alpha Omega Alpha, Hon. DSc. ...s 1964, Dip. in Pomology, UC Davis 1983; current mem: Grand View Citrus Assn., Magnolia Citrus Assn., Tulare Co. Lemon Assn., Diamond Walnut Assn., Sequoia Walnut Assn., Lindsay Olive Co-op.; publs: over 40 articles on plastic surgery in med. jours., 1930-50; performing mem. Univ.-Community Sym. Orch. (1950-65) Redlands; Republican; Episcopal; rec: trout fishing (Ida., Mont.) summers, 1953-. Res: 720, Sp 29, Worth Ave Porterville 93257

YOUNG, FREDRIC STEVEN, molecular biologist; b. Sept. 10, 1949, NY, NY; s. Julius and Edith (Weinstein) Y.; edn: BS, Penn State 1967-71; PhD, Univ. Mich. 1977. Career: staff fellow NIH, 1977-81; scientist molecular biol. dept. Genentech Inc. 1981-85; v.p./co-dir. research Biosystems Research Inc., Los Altos 1985–; frequent lectr.; honors: Alpha Sigma (1971); mem. AAAS, Am. Soc. Microbiol.; publs: research articles on E. coli in profl. jours. (1978, 81), abstracts presented nat. profl. meetings (1975, 83,); rec: biophysics, physics, music, preventive health. Ofc: Biosystems Research Inc 170 State St Ste 222 Los Altos 94022

YOUNG, HUGH ARCHIBALD, public safety communications consultant; b. Apr. 21, 1917, Glasgow, Scotland, nat. US cit. 1929; s. Robert Burns and Jane (Templeton) Y.; m. Svea Westman, June 5, 1939; children: Hugh Jr. b. 1945, Patricia b. 1949, Marilyn b. 1951; edn: BSEE, Univ. Calif. 1938; Calif. tchg. credentials (A, B, D); Reg. Profl. Engr. (E.E.) Calif., Hawaii, Md., Wash.,Tx., Va., Ohio. Career: engr., electronics material ofcr. US Navy 1942-46, 51-52; engring. rep. Philco 1946-51; communications engr., regional mgr. (Microwave, VHF and UHF systems used by govt., indus.) Motorola Corp. 1951-55; communications cons. 1955-64, clients incl. Hoffman Labs., Hycon Mfg. Co., Packard Bell Electronics, Dresser Indus., Hallicrafters Co., Sony Corp., City of Los Angeles; western regl. mgr., cons. Singer Corp. 1964-72; communication cons., public safety systems 1973–, clients incl. Calif., Nev., Ore., Wyo., var. state and county agencies, Bechtel Corp. (Alaska Pipeline), Thompson-CSF (U.K. and France), Jet Propulsion Lab. (NASA), Saudi Arabia Pub. Transport Co., Daniel, Mann, Johnson & Mendenhall; mil: lt. USNR 1942-46, bronze star, col. Calif. St. Mil. Res.; Republican; rec: boating, amateur radio, travel. Address: 38310 Calle Cervato Murrieta 92362

YOUNG, JAMES ALLAN, company president; b. March 9, 1934, Hamilton, Ontario, Can., nat. US cit. 1967; s. Jack and May (Jones) Y. m. Tanis Ruth Darymple, June 26, 1982; children: Carol Darlene b. 1959, Kathryn Joan b. 1962; edn: BS, McMaster Univ. 1957; PhD, UC Berkeley 1961. Career: physicist Gen. Electric Co., Pleasanton 1960-63; asst. chmn. accelrator physics dept. Gen. Antomic, San Diego 1963-68; sci. asst. to dep. dir. sci. and tech. Defense Nuclear Agency, Wash. DC 1968-70; mgr. theoretical div. Science Applications Inc., La Jolla 197075; pres., chmn. bd. Jaycor, San Diego 1975–; mem. Chancellor's Assn. (UC San Diego); author: Aswan High, 1983; Episcopal. Ofc: P.O. Box 85154 San Diego 92138

YOUNG, KENNETH LEROY, orthopedic surgeon; b. Feb. 18, 1927, Galion, O.; s. Raymond Thomas and Winona Belle (Parks) Y.; m. Lucille Boothby, Sept. 1, 1947, m. 2nd Shurlea Helberg 1984; children: Gerald Martin b. 1948, Mildred Diane b. 1951, Nancy Lynn b. 1956, Kenneth Charles b. 1960, Joshua Kenneth b. 1985; edn: BA, Andrews Univ. 1952; grad. wk. Wayne State Univ. 1952-53; MD, Loma Linda Univ. Coll. of Med. 1958; certified Am. Bd. of Orthopedic Surgery 1971; lic. phys. in Colo., Calif., Mich., Ore. Career: gen. practice of medicine and surgery in Delta, Colo. 1959-65; resident in gen. surgery, Kern Co. General Hosp., Bakersfield 1965-66; orthopedic surgery res. St. Mary's Hosp., Grand Rapids, Mich. 1966-69; orthopedic surgery practice in Ukiah, 1969-81, Crescent City, 1983–; chief orthopedics VA Med. Ctr., Temple, Tx. 1981-83, also tchg. staff Scott & White Clinic, Temple and assoc. prof. surg. Texas A&M Coll. of Med., 1981-83; instr. Coll. of the Redwoods 1984; active staff Seaside Hosp., Crescent City 1983-; mem. Del Norte Co. Med. Soc., Colo. State Med. Soc., Calif. Med. Soc., AMA, Am. Microsurg. Soc., Mendo-Lake Med. Soc.; wks: research and treatment protocol for chronic osteomyelitis; mil: T/3 US Army Med. Corps 1945-46, major USAR 46-82; Republican; Seventh-day Adventist; rec: aviation, mountaineering. Ofc: OceanView Orthopedic Medical Clinic, 1200 Marshall St Crescent City 95531

YOUNG, MATT NORVEL, JR., university chancellor emeritus; b. Oct. 5, 1915, Nashville, TN; s. Matt Norvel and Ruby (Morrow) Y.; m. Helen Mattox, 1939; children: Emily; Matt III; Marilyn; Sara; edn: BA, Abilene Christian Coll. 1936; MA, Vanderbilt Univ. 1937; PhD, Peabody Coll. of Vanderbilt Univ. 1943; LHD, Calif. Coll. Med. 1964; LLD, Lubbock Christian Coll. 1982. Career: minister Coll. Ch. of Christ, David Lipscomb Coll. 1941-43; Broadway Ch. of Christ, Lubbock, TX 1944-57; pres. Pepperdine Univ. 1957-71, chancellor 1971-84, chancellor emeritus 1985–; regent, Pepperdine Univ.; dir.: Forest Lawn Meml. Park, Imperial Bank; sr. editor 20th Century Christian Mag. (1945-), Power for Today Mag. (1955-); author num. publs.; mem: L.A. CofC, Phi Delta Kappa, Rotarian; clubs: California, Bohemian. Res: 24420 Tiner Ct Malibu 90265 Ofc: Pepperdine Univ., Malibu 90265

YOUNG, MICHAEL ALLEN, manufacturing company executive; b. Sept. 26, 1947, Albany; s. Lester Lee and Genevieve Irene (McKinney) Y.; m. Shirley J., Dec. 10, 1967; children: Deena b. 1970, Diane b. 1973; edn: Diablo Valley Coll. 1966-68. Career: techn. Stauffer Chemical 1970-75; salesman Young & Co. Mfg. 1975-77, sales mgr. 1978-82, v.p. and gen. mgr. 1982–; honors: hon. grad., US Army D-1 AITBDE 1968; mem: Sheet Metal Air Conditioning Nat. Assn., ASHRAE, Rotary, Lions; patent, with Lester and Thomas Young, spark arrestor; mil: sgt. US Army 1967-69; Republican; Baptist; rec: real estate development. Res: 2883 Doidge Ave. Pinole 94564 Ofc: Young & Co. Mfg., 1018 Broadway San Pablo 84806

YOUNG, NED EVERETT, real estate broker; b. Feb. 10, 1916, Mertens, Tx.; s. James Eldridge and Ola Carrie (Morris) Y.; m. Jane, Sept. 4, 1985; children: Roger b. 1939, Timothy b. 1948; edn: engring. courses, L.A. Trade Tech. 1947; Calif. lic. R.E. Broker, GRI (Graduate Realtors Inst.) 1975. Career: real estate agent 1959-, broker/owner Ned Young, Realtor, Downey 1963–; mem. Downey Bd. or Realtors (named Realtor Asso. of Year 1959, Realtor of Year 1963); recipient 100+ awards: VFW 4th Dist. (1948-54), Boys Town (1951), Downey 80th Anniversary (treas. 1953), VFW Calif. (1956), City of Hope, L.A. County Bd. Suprs., and Veterans Svc. Center (1957), Am. Cancer Soc., City of Downey Parks & Rec. (1958), L.A. Co. Heart Assn. (1960), Downey CofC (1963, 67), Rotary (comm. svc. 1981); current active mem: City of Downey 2d Century Found. (pres. 1979-), Downey CofC (dir. 1984-86), Bd. of Realtors (pres. 1967; state dir. 5 yrs; pres. 22nd Dist. Master Exchange Gp. 1969), Community Coord. Council (pres. 1955-57), Sister Cities Assn., Hist. Soc., VFW Post 2325 (cmdr. Downey 1948, cmdr. 4th dist. 1951-52), Am. Legion, Moose (pres. 1951-52), Elks (pres. 1968), Delvers Gem & Mineral Soc., Historic Downey Arch, Optimist Club (pres. 1963-64), Keep Am. Beautiful, Good Sam Club; civic: L.A. County Sheriff Reserve (1947-64), City of Downey (incorporation com. 1956, Downey Vets. Day Parade chmn. 1957-60, Marble Tourns. chmn. 1947-60, v.p. Rose Float 3 yrs., v.p. Bicentennial Commn.) softball player var. City of Downey Leagues (num. trophys as a pitcher, won League and City Tourn. 1985; won 20+ trophies pitching for sr. cit. teams 1982; won M.V.P. award World Tourn. 1983); mil: chief USNR 1942-45, 1946-59; Republican; rec: pvt. pilot (ret. 1964), softball, lapidary, bowling, comm. service. Ofc: Ned Young Realtor 10821 Lakewood Blvd Downey 90241

YOUNG, RAYMOND LEE, inventor, designer, manufacturing co. president; b. Apr. 26, 1932, Bakersfield; s. Washington and Esther (Spencer) Y.; m. Barbara, Sept. 13, 1975; children: Ken b. 1956, Phylis b. 1958, Lori b. 1961; edn: So. Calif. Coll. of Liberal Arts & Bible 1952-53, spl. courses, American River Coll., Sacto. City Coll. Career: constrn. apprentice, then journeyman carpenter and millwright, 1954-58; machine parts insp., sr. insp., draftsman, tool design engr. (tool & mach. for num. missile projects incl. Titan, Minuteman, Saturn, Polaris) Aerojet General Corp.,Sacto. 1958-64; chief design engr. Farm Hand Inc. (designed farm equip. incl. automatic peach picking equip. to pick a tree in one minute); firefighter Sacramento City Fire Dept. 1966-86; designer/pres. Alpha-Ra Corp., currently designing Microwave Filters for the Satellite industry; designed Satellite Dishes for Stardish Mfg. Co., key lock box for Real Estate Industry (Patent 1985), Parachute Drop for US Coast Guard (1978); design/mfr. Universal Tri-wheel for wheelchair users (Pat. 1984); project designer 5 churches; mil: served in US Navy, US Coast Guard, Reserves, 11 yrs.; Republican; Assemblies of God. Address: Alpha-Ra Corp. 5309 Finsbury Ave Sacramento 95841

YOUNG, RICHARD, independent oil producer; b. Oct. 6, 1933, Santa Barbara; s. Richard and Dorothy (Messner) Y.; children: Craig b. 1955, Lori b. 1957; edn: El Camino Coll. 1953. Career: ptnr. Calif. Chuck Wagon Service 1953-57; ptnr. Best Way Disposal Corp. 1957-61, merged with Alert Disposal 1961, name chg to ABCO Disposal Corp., acquired by Browning-Ferris Industries 1972, became regional v.p. responsible for market devel. in Western US; current: independent oil prod., owner/op. 41 wells in So. Calif.; mem. adv. com. Torrance Nat. Bank (1975-); honors: Key Man of Year Gardena Valley CofC (1969); mem. Calif. Independent Producers Assn. (exec. bd. 1982-86, pres. Signal Hill/Long Beach Area 1984-86); civic: LA County Dist. Atty's Advis. Com. (1974), Gardena Valley YMCA (v.p. 1972), Gardena Plnng. Commn. advis. com. (1971-72), Kiwanis Club (pres. 1969); mil: cpl. US Army 1953-54; Republican; Christian; rec: design/ devel./ race Off-road vehicles. Ofc: Richard Young and Associates 2935 Long Beach Blvd Long Beach 90806

YOUNG, ROBERT BERRYHILL, co. president; b. Apr. 25, 1933, Bryn Mawr, Pa.; s. Edgar B. and Jane W. (White) Y.; m. Mary Jane, Jan. 28, 1955; children: Jody b. 1957, Barton b. 1958, Sarah b. 1960, Lincoln b. 1961, Thomas b. 1961, Laura b. 1967; edn: BA cum laude, Amherst Coll. 1955. Career: senior indsl. economist Stanford Research Inst. 1959-71; economic advisor to Govt. of Pakistan, 1965-71; pres. Pineland Development Co. (owner/opr. major lake recreation area in No. Calif.), 1972–; contbr. art. on corporate growth, Harvard Bus. Rev. (1957); mil: lt. US Coast Guard; Christian; chmn. bd. of trustees Loma Rica Community Church 1985-. Address: Pineland Development Co. Collins Lake, Oregon House, CA 95962

YOUNG, ROY W., research and development consultant; b. sept. 1, 1924, Long Beach; s. Roy Wheeler and Pearl (Kraft) Y.; m. Erlda Leaf, Nov. 13, 1948; 1 son, Steven b. 1952; edn: BS, Univ. of Colo. 1944; Stanford Univ. 1942, 1946-47; Reg. Profl. Engr., Calif. Career: tech. unit mgr. Union Oil Co. 1947-51; owner, founder Drilube Co./ The Platers, Glendale 1951-72; owner, founder Ardel, Glendale; owner, founder, pres. Materials Technology Corp., Glendale and La Canada 1967-81; cons. American Hosp. Supply, Biomedical Engring.; dir. Harrison Mfg. Co., Technical Industries inc., Drilube Co., Materials Technology Corp., MMED Laboratories; cons. Orthopeadic Research Soc., Am. Assn. of Orthopeadic Surgeons 1951-85; mem: Am. Soc. of Testing Materials, Am. Soc. Materials, Orthopeadic Research Soc., World Biomaterials Soc., AOPA, Pasadena Athletic Club, Flint Canyon Tennis, Snowcreek Athletic Club; works: 13 patents, spherical bearing, hydrogen notch bolt, medical devices 1968-75; publs: Orthopaedic Reseach Soc., Am. Assn. of Orthpaedics Surgeons, FDA Device Reg. 1975-85; mil: lt. commdr. USN; Republican; Protestant; rec: flying, scuba diving, photog. Res: 4749 Rosebank La Canada 91011

YOUNG, STEVEN ROY, R&D manufacturing co. executive; b. March 18, 1952, Los Angeles; s. Roy W. and Erlda V. (Leaf) Y.; edn: Pomona Coll. 1971-72; BS, Univ. of Colo. 1975; Reg. Profl. Engr., Colo. 1975. Career: cons. Drilube Co. 1969-72; cons. American Hosp. Supply 1973; materials test engr. Ardel Corp.; v.p. and prodn. mgr. Materials Technology Corp. 1975, pres. 1981–; founder, owner, pres. MMED Laboratiors 1983–; FDA Com. and cons. mechanical testing 1982-84; Photographic Dynamic Strain Method, medical implans 1981-86; lectr. series, Am. Acad. of Orthopaedic Surgeons; Orthopaedic Research Soc. Workshop Award, 1983; Biomaterials Soc. Authors Presentation 1981, 1982, 1983; World's Biomaterial Congress 1985; mem: Am. Soc. of Testing Materials, Orthopaedic Research Soc., Exptl. Aircraft Assn., Cabrillo Beach Yacht Club, Flint Canyon Tennis, Snowreek Athletic Club, Pasadena Athletic Club; publs: Orthopaedic Research Soc., Am. Assn. of Orthopaedic Surgeons, World Biomaterials Soc. 1975-85; Republican; Protestant; rec: flying, sailing, scuba, skiing, photog. Res: 4749 Rosebank La Canada 91011

YOUNG, TYRUS CHARLES, certified public accountant; b. Aug. 6, 1957, Shreveport, La.; s. Thomas Crayton and Carol June (Skimerton) Y.; m. Linda Stewart, June 1, 1985; edn: BS, (Seaver Coll.) Pepperdine Univ. 1978; CPA, State Calif. 1982. Career: auditor Travelers Ins. Co., Orange Co., 1978-80; staff acct. Gregory A. Morrison Acctcy. Corp., Riverside 1980, sr. acct./v.p. ops. 1983-85; staff auditor Eadie and Payne, CPAs, San Bernadino 1981; acctg. mgr. J. W. Parker Accountancy Corp., Riverside 1985–; mem: Am. Inst. of CPAs, Calif. Soc. of CPAs; Jaycees (chmn. First Annual Riverside City Parade & Festival); Republican; Protestant; rec: guitar, music composition. Res: 20300 Avenida Hacienda Riverside 92508 Ofc: James W. Parker Accountancy Corp., 7177 Brockton Ste 538 Riverside 92506

YOUNGBLOOD, BOBBY D., judge; b. Aug. 10, 1937, Fort Worth, Texas; s. Frank A. and Nell M. (Routh) Y.; m. Angeles, July 5, 1985; children: Geoffrey b. 1957, Robert b. 1962, John b. 1970, Kathryn b. 1977; edn: JD, Pepperdine Univ. Sch. of Law 1972; admitted Calif. State Bar 1972. Career: police officer City of Santa Ana, 1962-67; Security Splst.-investigator, 1967-72; trial lawyer, Santa Ana 1972-81; elected judge, Central Orange County Municipal Ct., Santa Ana 1981–; advising dir. Penn Pacific Co.; dir. Nat. Latin American Inst. of Rehabilitation, Santa Ana; honors: Who's Who in Am. Law (2d ed.); mem. Am., Calif., Orange County bar assns., Trial Lawyers of Calif., Calif. Assn. of Judges; author: The Quinn Affair (1971), Looking for Devlin (1973), We Only Steal from Each Other (1976), Texas Melancholia (and other Poems, Songs and Verse) (1985); mil: USMC (Reserve), US Army (M.P.); Republican; Prot.; rec: writing, movies, travel. Ofc: Central Orange County Municipal Court, 700 Civic Center Dr W, Santa Ana 92701

YOUNGER, CLARA THERESA, physician; b. Sept. 28, 1917, Minneapolis; d. Constant James and Sophia Clara (Dolney) Younger; m. Victor B. Archer June 7, 1949 (div. 1952); 1 dau. Diane b. 1950; edn: BA, UCLA 1940, Gen. Secondary Tchg. Cred., 1941; MA in Zool., 1945; MD, UC San Francisco 1949; Charter mem. (1952), Diplomate (1978) Am. Acad. of Family Practice; Diplomate Am. Soc. of Bariatric Physicians (1974). Career: pvt. med. practice, Family Practice in South Gate & Lynwood, 1951-74; pediatric practice Mullikin Med. Center, Artesia 1974-83; ret. (temp. disabled) 1983; mem: AMA, Calif. Med. Assn., LA County Med. Assn., Am. Soc. Bariatric Physicians, LA Pediatric Soc. (life), Am. Soc. Clin. Hypnosis, Soc. of Clin. and Exptl. Hypnosis, Internat. Soc. Clin. Hypnosis, So. Calif. Soc. Clin. Hypnosis (pres. 1973, bd. 1970-; chair ann. Workshops 1975, 77), Orange County Soc. Clin. Hypnosis, Am. Cancer Soc. (lectr.; 15 Yr. pin for service), Am. Heart Assn., LA Gen. Practice Assn. (sec. 1971-73); vol. YMCA South Gate (1970-73); publs: Internat. J. Clin. Hypnosis (1973); Democrat; Protestant; rec: swim, nature study, collector limited ed. plates. Address: Cypress

YOUNGER, EVELLE JANSEN, lawyer, former state attorney general; b. June 19, 1918, Nebr.; s. Harry C. and Maebel (Jansen) Y.; m. Mildred Eberhard, July 3, 1942, 1 son, Eric, L.A. Superior Ct. judge; edn: AB and LLB, Nebr. Univ., 1940, grad. work in criminology, Northwestern Univ. Law Sch.; admitted to Calif. State Bar 1946. Career: special agent FBI, 1940-46; dep. city atty. Criminal Div., Los Angeles, 1946-47, city prosecutor, 1947-50; pvt. practice law, Los Angeles 1950-53; judge L.A. Municipal Ct., 1953-58; elected judge of Superior Ct., 1958-64; elected dist. atty., Los Angeles County, 1964-71; elected Calif. State Atty. General, 1970, 1st Republican Atty. Gen. since 1947, re-elected 1974; Repub. nominee for Governor of Calif. 1978; pvt. practice law with Buchalter, Nemer, Fields, Chrystie & Younger, Los Angeles 1979–; chmn. Pres. Reagan's Task Force on the Adminstrn. of Justice 1980; mem: Am. Bar Assn. (chmn. Criminal Law Sect. 1962-63), Fellow Am. Coll. of Trial Lawyers, Nat. Dist. Attys. Assn., L.A. Lawyers Club, L.A. Peace Officers Assn. (past pres.), Soc. Former FBI Agents (past chmn.), Masons, Shriners, Am. Legion, Elks, AF Assn., British United Services Club, Trojan Club (dir.), Alpha Tau Omega frat.; mil: pvt. to maj. US Army 1942-46, lt. col. USAF 1951-52, maj.gen. USAFR, served in China, Burma, India Theatres WWII, Korean Conflict; Episcopal. Ofc: Buchalter Nemer Fields Chrystie & Younger, 7th Flr., 700 S. Flower St. Los Angeles 90017

YUAN, SIDNEY W.K., scientist, engineer; b. July 30, 1957, Hong Kong, nat. US cit. 1982; s. Chia Chi and Tso Tak (Wong) Y.; m. Katherine Dai, Sept. 8, 1981; 1 dau. Jacquelyn b. 1985; edn: BS, UC Los Angeles 1980, MS 1981, PhD, 1985. Career: splst. in low temperature engring. (cryogenics); research asst. UC Los Angeles 1980-81, postgrad. research engr. 1981-85, tchg. asst. UCLA 1984–; scientist (R&D and mfr. of transfer device to transport liquid helium by space shuttle to extend lifetime of satellites indefinitely) Lockheed Missiles & Space Co., Palo Alto 1985–; honors: Tau Beta Pi (1980), Sigma Xi (1986), Nat. Excellence Recogn. award, The Space Found. (1985); mem. Am. Inst. of Chem. Engrs., AAAS; 12+ sci. publs. in field, originated theories to predict Vapor-Liquid Phase Separation of He II; rec: Go (game), philately, ping pong. Res: 1580 Quebec Ct #1 Sunnyvale 94087 Ofc: Lockheed Missiles & Space Co. Inc. 3251 Hanover St, 92-40, Bldg. 205, Palo Alto 94304

YUNG, ANTHONY SAU-YIN, management information systems executive; b. Oct. 23, 1957, Hong Kong; s. Derby Tak-Pui and Mui-Ling (Ding) Y.; m. Amy Yiu, Aug. 4, 1979; 1 son, Jonathan b. 1984; edn: BS in bus. adm., USC 1979. Career: banking/acctg. supr., then billing coord. ESIS, Inc. 1976-79; asst., assoc. mgmt. system analyst Burroughs Inc. 1979-80; system analyst Challenge Cook Bros. 1980-81; proj. mgr./sr. system analyst Designed Programs Corp., 1981-84; ptnr. Computer Profls. 1983-85; pres. Anthony Yung & Co. Inc. 1985–, also v.p. mktg./adminstrn., L&Y Import Export Inc., 1985–; dir. of MIS, Young's Market Co., 1984-; lectr. USC, 1982-, guest speaker USC Sch. of Engring., Career Day (1983), Orange Co. IBM PC Users Gp. (1986); mem. USC Entrepreneur Pgm. 1978; book in progress: "Index to DOS" (1986); rec: model building, photog., scuba, ski. Res: 510 N Jay Ct Montebello 90640 Ofc: Young's Market Co 500 S Central Ave Los Angeles 90013

YURMAN, HERMAN WALTER, financial services executive; b. Feb. 4, 1920, NY, NY; s. Samuel J. and Fannie (Margolis) Y.; m. Phyllis L. Corino, June 9, 1945; children: Lynda (Pite) b. 1946, Bruce b. 1950; desig: Cert. Finl. Planner (CFP) Coll. for Finl. Plnng., Denver. Career: Reg. Prin. firm Raymond James, St. Petersburg, Fla. 1966-70; pres. Delta Planning Corp., 1970-71; v.p. Planning Corp. of Am. 1968-70;v.p. Petro-Lewis Securities Corp., Denver, Colo. 1970-73; pres. Alpha/Omega Plng. Corp., St. Pete., Fla. and Solana Beach, Calif. 1973-83; Reg. Prin. Southmark Finl., Dallas 1985–; pres. Inst. for Financial Services Inc., Newport Beach 1984–; honors: Hon. PhD fin. adm., Univ. of Sarasota, Fla. (1979); Outstanding Trustee (1975), Acting pres. (1979), Coll. for Finl. Plng.; mem: Internat. Assn. for Finl. Plng. (charter mem., life mem., chmn. bd.), Coll. for Finl. Plng. (bd. regents, v.chmn. academics); fmr. mem. Kiwanis, CofC, Optimists, Jr. CofC; author three books in finl. plng. (1972, 76, 78); mil: 1st sgt. Army Air Corps, US Inf. 1941-45, Africa, Italy, Combat Inf. Badge, Bronze Star; Republican; Jewish. Res: 20 Glennhurst Irvine 92714 Ofc: I.F.S. 1601 Dove St Ste 270 Newport Beach 92660

YUSKO, GARY JOHN, financial executive; b. Mar. 15, 1955, Bedford, Ohio; s. George and Helen Catherine (Tkac) Y.; m. Socorro Munoz-Najar, July 30, 1982; children: Julie b. 1983, Tracy b. 1986; edn: BBA, Cleveland State Univ. 1977; Certified Public Acct., Ohio (1979), Calif. (1983). Career: staff acct. Price Waterhouse, Cleveland 1977-, senior acct. 1979-, mgr. Caracas, Venezuela office 1981-83, mgr., senior mgr. Los Angeles office 1983-85; corp. controller Westwood One Inc., Culver City 1985, vice pres. finl. ops., 1986–; founding exec. com. Cal Tech/ MIT Enterprise Forum (1984-); mem. Am. Inst. CPAs, Ohio Soc. CPAs, Calif. Soc. CPAs, K.C. (Knight of the Month 1981); Republican; Catholic; rec: golf. Res: 14108 Hamlin St #2 Van Nuys 91401

ZADOR, LESLIE THOMAS, lawyer; b. Jan. 2, 1948, Los Angeles; s. Eugene and Maria Katherine (Steiner) Z.; edn: BA, USC 1970; JD, Southwestern Univ. 1976; admitted Calif. State Bar 1976. Career: journalist Los Angeles Free Press, 1970-73; research atty. Court of Appeal, Los Angeles 1977-78; pvt. practice atty. (spec. in prop. mgmt. and real estate acquisitions and exchanges for internat. clients), West L.A., 1979–, founder/pres. Lawyers' Property Mgmt. (prop. mgmt. co.), 1981–; honors: Dean's list (1975), pub. Southwestern Law Rev. (1976), Eastwood Cert. of Merit (1982); mem. Calif. Bar Assn., Los Angeles County Bar Assn., Inst. of Real Estate Mgmt. (cand. CPM); civic: founding dir. The Soc. for the Preservation of Film Music (1983-); author: Eugene Zador: A Catalogue of His Works (biography and cat. of the music of the late composer, father of Leslie Thomas Z.) 1977; contbg. writer The Cue Sheet (quarterly newsletter Soc. for Preserv. of Film Music) 1983-; coauthor (w/ Michael D. Moore)/prod. 3-act drama: Criminal Justice (prod. Evergreen Theater, Hollywood 1984); rec: writing. Ofc: 10850 Wilshire Blvd Ste 770 Los Angeles 90024

ZADRA, ROBIN LEIGH, commercial banker; b. July 17, 1956, Tacoma, Wash.; d. Lt. Col. (ret.) Robert Edward and Nancy Marie (Robins) Zadra; edn: BS econs., with honors, UC Riverside 1977; MBA cand., CSU San Diego 1977-81, Dartmouth Coll. Grad. Sch. of Credit & Finl. Mgmt. 1985-87. Career: comml. loan ofcr. Bank of America 1979-80, asst. v.p. 1980-83, vice pres. and team leader Corporate Banking, Bank of Am., Newport Beach 1983-86, comml. banking credit risk mgr. 1986–; recipient Bank of Am. Golden Shoe Leadership Award (1981), Exceptional Performer Awards (1981-85); mem: So. Calif. Network of Exec. Women (pres. 1986), Orange County World Trade Ctr. Assn. (mem. com.), Am. Electronics Assn., Women in Internat. Banking, CofC; Republican; Episcopal; rec: sailing, ski, golf, travel, write poetry. Ofc: Bank of America 4101 MacArthur Blvd Newport Beach 92660

ZADRAVEC, GEORGE RAYMOND, business owner; b. July 15, 1955, Youngstown, Ohio; s. Frank Vincent and Jacqueline Raymond (Fotiuk) Z.; edn: BA, CSU Fullerton 1978. Career: prop. Attorney Service West, San Bernardino 1984–; also p.t. music faculty UC Riverside; original electronic music compositions performed at CSU San Bernardino; Democrat; Catholic; rec: music. Ofc: Attorney Service West, P.O. Box 8064 San Bernardino 92412

LYDIA A., computer sales executive; b. Mar. 10, 1957, Los An-
nd and Aurora Rena (Baldelli) Zaffini; edn: BS, CSU Los Angeles 1980. Career: with Motorola/Four-Phase Systems, Inc., Los Angeles 1980–: assoc. mktg. rep. 1980-81, mktg. rep. 1981-83, nat. account mgr./mktg. rep. 1983-84, adv. mktg. rep./nat. account mgr. 1984, sales mgr. 1984-85, dist. sales splst. 1985–; awards: Pacesetter (1983, 84, 85), 100 Percent+ Quota Achiever (1982, 83, 84, 85); mem: Nat. Assn. Female Execs., Am. Soc. Profl. Bus. Women; rec: aerobics, art. Ofc: Motorola/Four-Phase Systems, Inc. 4400 MacArthur Blvd Ste 240 Newport Beach 92660

ZAFIS, ANDREW JAMES, corporate lawyer, hotel executive; b. May 23, 1925, Milwaukee; s. James John and Josephine (Przybylowski) Z.; m. Jean Kalscheur, Nov. 10, 1951; children: Lynn Ann b. 1953, Constance Lee b. 1954, John b. 1959, Mary Jo b. 1961; edn: BS, Univ. of Wis. 1948; JD, Wis. Law 1950; MPA, Harvard 1951; postgrad., PhD Cand., UC San Diego 1979-80; engr. cert. Univ. of Ill. (AUS, 1944); admitted State Bar of Wis. (1950), Calif. (1978), US Supreme Ct. (1965). Career: staff atty. Wis. Atty. Gen.'s Office (Anti-Trust) 1950, US atty.-advisor Wage Stabilization Bd., Richmond, Va. 1951-52; pvt. law practice (spec. in municipal law, litigation) senior mem. Zafis, Rummel, Caldwell & Cahill in Oconomowoc, Wis. 1952-76; city atty. Oconomowoc, Wis. 1958-63; municipal atty. Towns of Oconomowoc, Summit, Eagle Merton & Village of Lac La Belle, 1953-76; as city atty. successfully defended first million dollar lawsuit filed in Waukesha Co. (Rogers v. City of Oconomowoc, 1958); v.p./litigation counsel Hotel Del Coronado Corp., Coronado, Calif. 1981–; secty., dir., gen. counsel Enrichment Reading Corp. of Am., 1970-; guest lectr. Wis. Law Sch. 1969-75; prof. of Law (Dept. Head) Western State Univ. Coll. of Law, 1976-81; adj. prof. of law National Univ. Law Sch. 1981-85; judge pro tem 1984-85; honors: vice pres. Univ. of Wis. Class of '48; Adm. Fellowship, Harvard Littauer (now Kennedy) Sch. of Govt. 1950-51; Wis. Alumni Testimonial award (S.D., 1982); mem: Phi Alpha Delta legal frat. (justice, Ryan 1949), Wis. Acad. of Trial Lawyers (gov. 1970), Wis. State Bar (Bar Admission Stds., Contg. Legal Edn. coms. 1983-85), Assn. of Trial Lawyers of Am., Calif. Trial Lawyers Assn., S.D. Trial Lawyers Assn., Coronado CofC (dir. 1984-); clubs: Mission Bay Yacht (judge adv., dir. 1983-), LaBelle Yacht (life), Coronado Yacht, Kiwanis, Beta Theta Pi (chpt. pres. 1948), Harvard (S.D.), Wis. Alumni (nat. bd. dirs. 1983-; S.D. Chpt. dir. 1976-, 2 term pres.); San Diego Crew Classic (dir. 1985-); coauthor revised ed. (w/ Prof. A. Schaffer), Calif. Courtroom Practice & Procedure (Law Press, 1980); mil: sgt. Signal Corps US Army 1943-45, Presdtl. Merit Service Award, WWII; Roman Catholic; rec: sailing, hist., travel. Res: 749 J Ave Coronado 92118 Ofc: Hotel del Coronado 1500 Orange Ave Coronado 92118

ZAHIRI, HORMOZ, physician; b. Dec. 11, 1936, Tehran, Iran; s. Nosratollah and Marzieh (Mogharei) Z.; m. Robabeh Kasravi, June 5, 1961; children: Marzieh b. 1963, Arjang b. 1968; edn: MD, Univ. of Tehran Sch. of Med. 1962; MS, McGill Univ., Montreal 1968. Career: asst. prof. Univ. of Tehran, Tehran, Iran 1968-69; attndg. staff Shafa Rehab. Hosp., Tehran 1969-72, head dept. of orthopaedic surgery 1972-75; med. dir. American Hosp. of Tehran, Tehran 1975-78; pvt. practice, Tehran, Iran 1968-81; clin. asst. prof. USC, Los Angeles 1982-84, clin. assoc. prof. 1984–; pvt. practice, Los Angeles 1982–; mem: Fellow Am. Acad. of Orthopaedic Surgeons, Fellow Am. Coll. of Surgeons, Am., Calif. and Los Angeles Co. Med. Assns., Internat. Coll. of Surgeons, Societe Internationale de Chirurgie Orthopedique et de Traumatology; works: Adjuvant Experimental Ployarthritis, JBJS 1969. Ofc: Hormoz Zahiri MD, 10921 Wilhsire Blvd. Ste. LL-7 Los Angeles 90024

ZALEWSKI, WOJCIECH, librarian; b. March 20, 1937, Gdynia, Poland; nat. US cit. 1977; s. Atanazy and Malgorzata Ch. (Sentkowska) Z.; m. Rosemarie Bohm, Aug. 31, 1958; children: Barbara, Marcus; edn: MA, Catholic Univ. Lublin 1965; lic. Bibl. scis., Bibl. Inst. Rome 1967; ThD, Gregorianum Univ. Rome 1968; MA, San Jose State Univ. 1971. Career: librarian, curator Russian and East European collections Stanford Univ. 1971–; lectr. in bibliography, dept. Slavic lang. & lit. Stanford Univ. 1973–; chmn. Slavic & East European sect. Assn. Coll. & Research Libraries, Am. Library Assn. 1980-81; mem: Am. Library Assn., Am. Assn. Adv. Slavic Studies, Polish Inst. Arts & Scis. of Am.; author: Russian- English dictionaries with aids for translators, 1981; ann. survey reference materials in Russian- Soviet area studies for Russian Rev. 1975-; co-author with Rimma Yolynska-Bogert, Czeskaw Mi Kosz, An International Biography, 1930-80, 1983. Res: 162 Highland Ave. San Carlos 94070 Ofc: Stanford Univ. Libraries, Stanford 94305

ZALOUMIS, CHARLES PETER, financial services co. executive; b. Dec. 1, 1936, New London, Conn.; s. Peter Charles and Viola V. (Fortinalis) Z.; m. Sarah Josephine Purdy, May 24, 1975; children: Dawn, b. 1957; Peter, b. 1959; Christopher, b. 1976; Nicole, b. 1980; edn: BS, Univ. Nebr. 1963; MBA, American Univ. 1968; Nat. Assn. of Securities Dealers, SEC Reg. Investment Adviser; Ins. lic. Career: enforcement ofcr. Securities and Exchange Commn., Wash DC 1963-68; v.p./financial prin. Travelers Equity Sales, Inc., Hartford, CT. 1968-71; pres./dir. Computech Fund Svc., Inc., Atlanta, GA 1971-72; v.p. Central Banking Systems, Inc. 1972-77; pres./dir. Cenval Agency, Inc. 1972-77; v.p./sr. trust officer Central Bank, Oakland 1972-77; pres./chmn. bd. The Centrecorp Cos. 1977–; mem./chmn. Diablo West Finance Com.; mil: E-5 USAF, GCM; Democrat; Greek Othodox; rec: tennis, Little League coach. Res: 693 Contada Cir Danville 94526 Ofc: Centrecorp Cos. 31 Panoramic Way Ste C Walnut Creek 94595

ZAMZOW, DENNIS ROBERT, podiatrist; b. Apr. 30, 1944, Ripon, WI; s. Arthur Robert and Charlotte Gwendolyn (Deibert) Z.; Electronics Techn. Sch., Great Lakes, Ill. 1962-63; Submarine Sch., New London, Conn. 1963; Inertial Navigation Computer Sch., Virginia Bch, VA 1963-64; Adv. Electronics Tchn. Sch., Treasure Island, San Francisco 1966-76; Coll. San Mateo,

1971-73; Doctor of Podiatric Medicine, Coll. Calif. Podiatric Medicine, 1973-76; svc. man on Nuclear Powered Polaris Missile Submarines, 1962-70; med. staff. Valley West Hosp., Los Gatos and El Camino Hosp., Mtn. View 1970-76, 1978–; private practice Doctor of Podiatric Medicine, Mt. View 1976–; founder, pres. Direct Helicopters Transport Inc. dba Direct Air 1985-; founder/pres./dir Calif. Road Runners Running Club, 1978-84; past instr. (marathon training) De Anza Coll., Cupertino 1980-81; adv. Calif. Governor's Council on Wellness & Physical Fitness; vice chn. The Athletics Congress (TAC) Pacific Assn.; Lectr.; marathoner, ultramarathoner; pbls: for Runners World Mag., Runners Knee May 1980, Surgery and the Runner Nov. 1981, Orthotics Jun. 1982, Sciatica Aug. 1982, and Plantar Fasciitis, Feb. 1983; Runners World Foot Care Book, Anderson Pbls. Co., 1982; arts. in Sports Unlimited Newspaper, San Jose; arts. in Decathlon Club monthly newsletter, Santa Clara; mil: USN 1962-70; rec: comml. pilot (multiengine and instrument ratings), running, weightlifting, guitar. Res: Box 601 Groveland 95321 Ofc: 2500 Hospital Dr, #9 Mtn View 94040

ZAPPE, JOHN PAUL, journalist; b. July 30, 1952, N.Y.C.; m. Siobhan Bradshaw, 1982; edn: BS pol. sci., Marist Coll. 1973; JD, Syracuse Univ. 1978. Career: City Hall reporter Poughkeepsie (NY) Journal, 1973-75; Court reporter Nevada State Journal, Reno 1979-80; law clk. Alameda County Legal Aid Soc., Oakland 1980-81; pres./CEO American Media Bold, Oakland 1981-83; reporter Press-Telegram, Long Beach 1983–; adj. faculty Syracuse Univ. 1975-78, CSU Long Beach 1985-; awards: Associated Press investigative reporting (1980), AP Freedom of Information Citation (1979), outstanding grad. (1978), NY State Agric. Reporting Prize (1974); mem. Investigative Reporters & Editors, L.A. Newspaper Guild (Unit chmn. 1984-). Ofc: Press-Telegram 604 Pine Ave Long Beach 90844

ZAREMBA, JAN, artist; b. Jan. 30, 1941, Lepizig, Germany; s. Franz and Hertha Annalise Rosalia (Hirschfeld) Z.; m. Deepti High, Mar. 31, 1976; edn: BS in engring., UC Los Angeles 1965, BA in pictorial arts, 1971. Career: discovered by the German Expressionist Fritz Schwaderer with whom he studied oil painting, strong use of luminous color, 1964-67; first one-man show in U.S. 1963; paints in Europe and Turkey 1968-69; exhibs. in Japan 1971, Bangladesh Benefit 1972; monastic life 1972-75, paints in Afghanistan, Kurdestan, walking through the Himalayas (1977), studies cave paintings of Ajanta and Ellora, India (1978), chief student of Hisashi Ohta, the Living Nat. Treasure of Japan, 1979; current: artist/instr. (both Occidental and Oriental painting styles), Hollywood, Calif.; instr. Sumi-e (Japanese ink painting) Japanese Cultural Center, Los Angeles 1982–; exhib: Paideia Gal. (1968), Otis Art Inst. (1969), Japan Expo (1980-82), Wing Fa Yeung Gal. (1982), New Otani Hotel (1986), Los Angeles City Hall (1986), internat. exhibn. with Zuniga and Amaya (1984), Helsinki, Finland (1986); rep: in permanent collections in Germany, USA, England, Israel, Finland, Mexico, France and Japan; honors: Alpha Mu Gamma (1983), Calif. Printmaker's Award (1969), Internat. Exhibn. Olympic Arts Fest. (1984); mem. Vedanta Soc., Pioneer Club, Bonsai Soc., Thubten Dhargye Ling; mil: E2 USAR 1964-68; rec: languages (Chinese, Turkish, Sanskrit). Address: 2000 North Ivar Ave Hollywood 90068

ZEBROWSKI, MARK CHARLES, lawyer; b. March 28, 1958, Milwaukee, Wisc.; s. Daniel Charles and Dorothy M. (Wamser) Z.; m. Jamie A., July 7, 1984; edn: BBA, Univ. of Wisc. 1979; JD, UC Berkeley 1983; admitted to Calif. Bar 1983. Career: assoc. atty. Gray, Cary, Ames & Frye, San Diego 1983–; honors: Nat. Merit Scholar; Beta Gamma Sigma Nat. Bus. Hon. Soc.; assoc. ed., Calif. Law Review 1982, 1983; mem: Am., Calif. and San Diego Co. Bar Assns.; author: Indemnity Clauses and Workers' Compensation: A Proposal for Preserving the Employer's Limited Liability, 70 Calif. Law Review 1421, 1982. Res: 1603 Beryl St., San Diego 92109 Ofc: Gray, Cary, Ames & Frye, 401 B St. Ste. 1700, San Diego 92101

ZEIGLER, LORRI YAKOWICZ, clinical social worker; b. Aug. 31, 1939, New Castle, Penn.; d. William Vincent and Anna (Kahocka) Yakowicz; m. Roland R. Zeigler, Mar. 4, 1978; 1 dau: Maria, b. 1964 dec. 1983; edn: BA, cum laude, Youngstown State Univ. 1963; MSW magna cum laude, Univ. Pittsburgh 1969; doctoral studies, UCLA Sch. of Soc. Welfare 1983-85; PhD cand., psychol., Internat. Coll. 1986; Calif. lic. clinical. soc. wkr. 1980. Career: unit supr. St. Peter's Child Devel. Ctrs. Inc., Pittsburgh, Penn., 1969-74; mental retardation coordinator Allegheny County, Pittsburgh 1974-75; regional coord. Title I, ESEA Projects, State Penn., 1975-76; chief soc. wkr. McGuire Memorial, Rochester, Penn. 1976-78; psychiatric soc. wkr. State Calif., Continuing Care Svcs. Branch, El Monte 1979-80, Lanterman State Hosp., Pomona 1980–; founder/chmn. bd. Found. for Continued Care and Learning, Inc., Pasdena 1983; field instr., CSU Long Beach 1982–; profl. cons. Calif. Dept. Developmental Svcs. 1981–; awards: NIMH fellowship 1977-79; mem: NASW 1970-; AAMD 1971-; Soc. Wkr. Profl. Group, Lanterman Hosp., chprsn. Peer Review 1983; orgns: Casa Pasadena Homeowners Assn.; Assn. for Retarded Citizens (life); Children's Hosp. of San Diego (contbg. mem. assoc.); publs: arts. re George Tarjan Research Ctr.; Republican; Catholic; rec: water sports, music, dance, travel, dining. Res: 1127 E Del Mar Blvd Pasadena 91106 Ofcs: Lanterman State Hospital, 3530 W Pomona Blvd, Program 3 Pomona 91769. Foundation for Continued Care and Learning, Inc., 1127 East Del Mar Blvd Pasadena 91106

ZELDES, JEROME ALAN, accountant; b. July 28, 1934, Galesburg, Ill.; s. Samuel David and Minnie (Chapman) Z.; m. Saron Eisen, March 25, 1956; m. 2d. Carole Klein, Dec. 8, 1963; children: Shelly Lynn b. 1957, Jody Ellen b. 1959, Helen Irene b. 1966, Sandy Elaine b. 1968; edn: Univ. of Ill. 1952-55; UCLA 1961-83; DeVry Tech. Inst. 1961; CPA, Calif. Career: CPA, Beverly Hills 1961-69; pres. Lord Rebel Ind., Canoga Park 1970-76; controller Comp-U-Med Inc., Los Angeles 1976-80; ptr. CPA firm, Encino 1980-84; controller McPheeters Machine Prods., San Fernando 1984-85; currently, CPA, cons.; dir. Menswear Retailers of Am. 3 yrs.; fin. & ops. group Menswear Retailers of Am.; mem: Am. Inst. CPAs, Calif. Soc. CPAs, Masons, Scottish Rite, Shriners, Internat. Footprint Assn., Peace Ofcr. Shrine Club, Nat. Assn. Watch & Clock Collectors; mil: sgt. US Army Security 1955-58; Jewish; rec: philately, antique slot machines, photog. Res: 4498 Woodman #A304 Sherman Oaks 91423

ZELLMER, LLOYD GENE, architect; b. June 25, 1937, Taylor, Tx.; m. Barbara A., Mar. 19, 1966; 2 children; edn: B.Arch., USC 1960; M. Arch., M.I.T. 1965; Reg. Arch., Calif. Career: carpenter, 1951-58 summers, architl. draftsman 1962, opened arch. office 1963, ptnrship. 1968-75, owner/prin. 1975–, also estab. real estate devel. co. 1975; researcher in Fabric Structural Systems 1964-, and neighborhood & community design 1972-; designed world's first complex fabric department store and first church using fabric; recipient num. AIA Design Awards (1967-), included Time Mag. list of 5 Best Architl. Designs (1981), work pub. in Sunset, Better Homes & Gardens, Arch. Forum, Arch. Record, Design West, L.A. Times Home, AP Internat.; mem: AIA, CSI, NCARB; civic: Art Center (bd. dirs.), Community Theatre (bd.), CSU Fresno Interior Design Dept. (advisor), Fresno Housing Commn., Ch. Council; mil. capt. Calif. Army N.G. and USAF; Lutheran; rec: fish, tennis, ski. Ofc: L. Gene Zellmer Assocs. POB 1444 Carmel Valley 93924

ZERVAKOS, JOHN, sales executive; b. Sept. 20, 1953, NY, NY; s. John and Christine (Birbas) Z.; m. Nancy E., Aug. 19, 1983; edn: AA, Pierce Coll. 1978; desig: Reg. Health Underwriter, Nat. Assn. Health Underws. (1981), Cert. Health Cons., Mktg. Devel. Inst. Purdue Univ. (1983); Reg. Health Underwriter (1980), Cert. Health Consultant. (1983). Career: acct. rep. Blue Shield of Calif. 1978-80 dist. sales mgr. (So. Calif.), Individual Plans, 1980-84 (leader in corp. sales for 1983, 1984), statewide sales mgr. Individual Plans, 1984–; mem: Nat. Assn. of Life Underws., Nat. Assn. of Health Underws., Los Angeles Assn. of Health Underws. (charter mem., dir. 1980-82, v.p. 1980-81); Republican; Greek Orthodox; rec: golf, tennis. Ofc: Blue Shield of Calif. 5959 W Century Blvd Los Angeles 90045

ZEUGHAUSER, PETER DOUGLAS, corporate lawyer; b. June 2, 1950, NY, NY; s. Milton and Phyllis (Deutsch) Z.; edn: BA, honors, Univ. Wisc. 1972; JD, St. Louis Univ. Sch. of Law 1975. Career: summer assoc. Olwine, Connely, Chase N.Y.C. 1974; assoc. atty. Green, Hennings & Henry St. Louis, Mo. 1975-77, Duryea, Malcom, Daly & Vitti Newport Beach 1977-79; atty. pvt. practice, pres. Procal Newport Beach 1979-81; gen. counsel The Irvine Co. Newport Beach 1981–; honors: Dean's Scholar, Outstanding and Meritorious Svc. Award (St. Louis Univ. Sch. of Law 1975), Award of Merit (Bar Assn. of Metro. St. Louis 1976), Outstandiong Young Man of America 1975; mem: Am. Corporate Counsel Assn. (bd. dirs., chair young lawyers sect. 1984-85, founder, bd. dirs. So. Calif. chap.), Orange Co. Bar Assn. (chair corp. law dept. sect.), Bar Assn. of Metro. St. Louis, Orange Co. Center for the Performing Arts (bd. dirs.), Child Care Advocates of Am. (bd. dirs.), Local Elected Officials of Am. (founder, bd. dirs.); publ: articles in law jours.; Independent. Res: 1312 Santanella Ter Corona del Mar 92625 Ofc: The Irvine Co. 500 Newport Center Dr, Ste 555, Newport Beach 92660

ZIFFREN, LESTER, lawyer; b. Apr. 13, 1925, Davenport, IA; s. Jacob and Belle (Rosenberg) Z.; m. Paulette C. Rolando; 1 dau. Mimi, b. 1959; edn: BA, UCLA 1949; JD, UCLA Law Sch 1952. Career: dep. atty. gen. Calif. Dept. Justice, Atty. Gen. Office 1953-59; partner Greenberg, Ziffren & Shafton 1959-61; partner Ziffren & Ziffren 1961-79; partner Gibson, Dunn & Crutcher 1979–; bd. dir. Far West Financial Corp. (NYSE) 1979-; bd. dir. Far West Savings & Loan Assn. (fmr. State Mutual S&L) 1979-; mem: State Bar Calif.; Los Angeles Co. Bar Assn.; Beverly Hills Bar Assn.; UCLA Found. (bd. trustees); UCLA Sch. Med. (bd. visitors); Brandeis Univ. (pres. council); Cedars-Sinai Med. Ctr. (bd. dirs., exec. com., chmn. profl. programs com.); rec: tennis. Ofc: Gibson, Dunn & Crutcher, 2029 Century Park E, 41st Flr Los Angeles 90067

ZILKA, THOMAS JONES, professor of engineering, ret.; b. Oct. 1, 1918, Spokane, Wash.; s. Henry James and Mabel (Jones) Z.; m. Cay Cadell, Aug. 23, 1940; 1 son, Nicholas b. 1944; edn: BS engring., Ore. State Univ. 1941, MSE, 1943; grad. work in bus., UC Berkeley 1960-62; Reg. Profl. Engr., Calif. Career: instr. Oregon State Coll., Corvallis 1940-43; engr. Boeing Aircraft Co., Seattle 1943-46; asst. prof. Montana State Coll., Bozeman 1946-47; prof. Calif. State Polytechnic Coll., San Luis Obispo 1947-56; Fulbright Prof., Univ. of Peshawar, Pakistan 1956-547; Univ. of Wisc. splst. (on contract) Bengal Engring. Coll., India 1957-58; self empl. mfg., Sausalito (part time) 1958-65; estab. Div. of Engring. San Francisco State Univ., prof. and dean of Engring. SFSU 1958-84, ret.; engring. and ednl. cons.; dir. Fredrick Burke Found. (edn.) SFSU; Commn. on Engineering Education, Wash DC; honors: Tau Beta Pi, Phi Kappa Phi, Pi Mu Epsilon, Alpha Delta Sigma; mem. Am. Soc. for Engring. Edn. (chair Pacific S.W. Sect. 1968-69); Delta Tau Delta frat. (past pres.); hold two US Patents on mech. devices; Republican; Presbyterian; rec: golf, tennis, boating, nature study (birds). Res: 15 Escalan Dr Mill Valley 94941 Ofc: S.F. State University 1600 Holloway Ave San Francisco 94132

ZILKHA, SELIM KHEDOURY, investor; b. Apr. 7, 1927, Bagdad, Iraq, nat. US cit. 1945; s. Khedoury Aboodi and Louise (Bashi) Z.; div.; children: Michael b. 1954, Nadia b. 1955; edn: BA, Williams Coll., Mass. 1946. Career: bd. chmn. Zilkha & Sons, N.Y. (1956-), Spirella, Gt. Brit. (1959-62), Mothercare, Gr. Brit. (1960-82), Towner Petroleum, Houston (1983-85), SKZ Inc., Houston (1986-); clubs: Portland (London), Travellers (Paris), Sunningdale (England); mil: pvt. US Army 1945; Republican; Jewish; rec: tennis, golf, bridge. Res: 750 Lausanne Rd Los Angeles 90077 Ofc: SKZ Inc. 16701 Greenspoint Park Dr Houston TX 77060

ZIMMERMAN, FRANK ARNOLD, business executive; b. Oct. 9, 1905, Norwood, Ohio; s. Arnold Louis and Estelle Belle (Applegate) Z.; m. Vida Pellerin, Jan. 29, 1941; children: Judith b. 1943, Debby b. 1946, Frank b. 1947; edn: AB, UCLA 1931. Career: instr. US Naval Acad. Post Grad. Sch., Harvard Univ. 1945; with Pacific Telephone 1938-70; pub. rels. mgr., Los Angeles 1938-42; asst. traffic mgr. 1945-53; labor rels. mgr., San Francisco 1953-58; gen. personnel mgr. 1958-70; ret.; bd. advrs. San Francisco State Univ. Engrg. Div. 1965-; chmn. Rels. With Industry Sect., Am. Soc. for Eng. Edn.; mem: Fellowship Forum of Palo Alto, Commonwealth Club of San Francisco, San Francisco Engrs. Club, Moffat Field Golf Club, Delta Tau Delta, Alpha Kappa Psi; publs: Elements of the Decision, Harvard Press 1945; mil: commdr. USNR, active 1942-45; Republican; rec: golf. Res: 2081 Touraine Ln. Half Moon Bay 94019

ZINI, GILBERT Y., emergency physician; b. Sept. 27, 1943, Fes, Morocco, nat. US cit. 1975; s. Jacob and Fortunee (Assouline) Z.; m. Camela Rosson, April 8, 1967; children: Miriam b. 1968, Shannon b. 1970, Lara b. 1971, Megan b. 1983; edn: Lycee Gouraux Rabat Morocco; Bach., Univ. Grenoble 1964-67; pre med., Brussels Med. Sch., Belgium 1968-73; MD, Med. Ctr. Altoona Pa. 1973-74; intern., Jackson Med.Sch., Mess Res. Family Practice Bd., Cert. ED 1981; Fellow, ABEM. Career: physician emerg. dept. Camp Pendleton 1975-77; physician emerg. dept. San Antonio Community Hosp. 1976-82, currently, senior physician emerg. dept. asst., dir. emerg. dept., instr. adv. cardiac life support, instr. adv. trauma life support, asst. dir. emerg. dept., chmn. child abuse com., dir. int. emerg. dept., chmn. emerg. dept. trauma com.; pres. Foothill Med. Group Inc.; honors: Physicians Recogn. Award 1977-89; Letter of Commdn., USN 1976; mem: Am. Acad. of Family Practice, Am. Coll. of Emergency Physicians, Calif. Med. Assn., San Bernardino Co. Med. Soc., JCEMA, Inland Co. Emergency Med. Authority; mil: lt. cmmdr. USN 1975-77; Reublican; Jewish; rec: gardening. Res: 715 So. Quail Circle Anaheim Hills 92807 Ofc: San Antonio Co. Hosp., Upland 91786

ZINSMASTER, ARTHUR JAYNE, private investor; b. Nov. 7, 1916, Des Moines, Iowa; s. Arthur and Margaret Margerite (Marshall) Jayne; m. Barbara LaPeire, May 25, 1946; children: Karen b. 1947, Jayne b. 1949; edn: Univ. of Iowa 1934-6; AB, Stanford Univ. 1938; MBA, Harvard Grad. Sch. of Bus. 1940. Career: acctg., constrn. field, 1940-42; Counter Intelligence Corps, US Army, 1942-46; advt./sales promo. mgr. Roycraft Iowa Co., 1946-51; v.p./gen. mgr. Central States Candy, Des Moines, Ia. 1951-52; adminstrv. asst. Am. Hospital Supply, Evanston, Ill. 1952-82; asst. to Sales V.P.; Ops. mgr., Columbus, Ohio; Branch mgr., Seattle, Wn.; West Coast Ops. mgr., Burbank; mgr. Fixed Assets, Pharmaseal; ret.; cons. Executive Service Corps; mem. Nat. Counterintell. Assn., Stanford Alumni Assn., Harvard Bus. Sch. Assn., Heritage Found.; mil: lt. col. AUS 1942-6, dir. Plans & Tng. Counter Intell., Pentagon; Republican; Congregational; rec: golf, swimming, computer trading. Res: 900 W Mountain St Glendale 91202

ZISHOLZ, MURRAY, tax lawyer/accountant; b. Feb. 16, 1957, Newark, N.J.; s. Abraham and Genia (Zylberberg); edn: BBA, cum laude, Pace Univ. 1979; JD, Golden Gate Univ. Sch. of Law 1985; lic. CPA, N.J. (1982), Calif. (1985). Career: bookkeeper, tax preparer var. corps., 1983-84; legal extern Judge Isabella H. Grant, San Francisco Superior Ct. 1985; prin. tax acctg. practice, 1981-; tax atty. assoc. Anderson, Anderson & Jagiello, S.F. 1985-; awards: Clark Jaycees Scholar (1975), Alpha Chi Hon. Soc., Dean's list all terms, Pace Univ. scholarship, Varsity Tennis Team (intramural tennis champ 1977); past mem. Accts. for the Public Interest/N.J. (estab. student internship pgm. 1981); mem: Am. Inst. CPAs, N.J. Soc. CPAs, Calif. Soc. CPAs; Democrat; Jewish; rec: sports, photog., travel. Res: 1316 48th Ave San Francisco 94122

ZOBEL, KATHRYN TUNSTALL, manufacturing co. executive; b. Apr. 18, 1950, Orange, Calif.; d. Harrison Perry and Iola Doris (Anderson) Tunstall; m. Gregory Zobel, Mar. 30, 1985; 1 dau. Alexandra b. 1986; edn: BA econs., magna cum laude, UC Santa Barbara 1973; MPA, CSU Long Beach 1977-82. Career: western area credit mgr. Am. Hosp. Supply Corp. 1974-75; with Kendall McGaw (a Colgate Palmolive Co.) 1975-, western area financial svcs. mgr. 1975-76, L.A. regl. ops. mgr. 1977-80, nat. inventory planning & control mgr. 1980-81, prodn. control mgr. 1981-82, prod. mgr. 1982-83, group prod. mgr. 1983-84, dir. mktg. 1984-85, v.p. mktg. 1985-; honors: Youth Leader of the Year (Elks 1968); mem: Medical Mktg. Assn., Women in Bus. 1981-83; Republican; Catholic; rec: skiing, sailing, cooking. Ofc: Kendall McGaw 2525 McGaw Irvine 92714

ZOBELL, KARL, lawyer; b. Jan. 9, 1932, La Jolla; s. Claude E. and Margaret H. Z.; m. Barbara, Nov. 22, 1968; children: Bonnie, Elizabeth, Karen, Claude, Mary; edn: undergrad. Utah State Univ. 1949-51; AB, Columbia Univ. 1953, Columbia Law Sch. 1952-54; JD, Stanford Law Sch. 1958. admitted Calif. State Bar 1959. Career: atty., assoc. Gray, Cary, Ames & Frye, San Diego and La Jolla, 1959-, ptnr. 1964-, practice emphasis in real estate (esp. land use & regulatory issues), trusts, and estates; founder, dir. La Jolla Bank and Trust Co. ¹1973-); civic: La Jolla Town Council (trustee 1962-, bd. chmn. 1967-68, pres. ⁷⁷. 1980-81); La Jollans Inc., land use plnng. orgn. (founder 1964, trustee ⁿ⁸⁰, pres. 1965-68, 73-76, 78-79); City of San Diego (apptd. ᵐⁿʳ. 1968, 73); La Jolla Mus. Art (trustee 1964-72, pres.

1967-68, 69-70); Scripps Meml. Hosp. Found. (dir. 1980-); UC San Diego (bd. overseers 1974-76); Stanford Law Sch. (bd. overseers 1977-80); La Jolla Hist. Soc. (trustee 1980-81); La Jolla Rotary (mem. 1962-70, pres. 1965); mil: commnd. ofcr. USCG 1954-57; rec: beach volleyball. Res: 1555 Coast Walk La Jolla 92037 Ofc: Gray, Cary, Ames & Frye, 1200 Prospect St Ste 575 La Jolla 92037

ZONNI, MARCO, manufacturing executive; b. June 14, 1934, Modugno, Bari, Italy, nat. US cit. 1949; s. Saverio and Angela (Caporusso) Z.; m. Antonina Degli Eredi, June 20, 1964; children: Saverio b. 1965, Vittorio b. 1966, Angela b. 1969; edn: bus. courses, Rio Hondo Coll. 1971. Career: with Associated Mfg. Co. (aircraft indus.), 1959-68; founder/pres. Roma Spumoni Co. Inc. (mfr. Italian ice cream and desserts), Whittier 1968-, invented method of producing ice cream in individual sliced form (Patent 1977); mem. Elks, Garibaldina M.B. Soc.; mil: pfc US Army 1957-59; Democrat; Catholic; rec: golf, bowling. Res: 10420 Lundene Dr Whittier 90601 Ofc: Roma Spumoni Co. Inc. 11727 E Washington Blvd Whittier 90606

ZSCHEILE, F. PAUL, III, ophthalmologist; b. Sept. 5, 1934, Chicago, Ill.; s. F. Paul and Emily Z.; children: Fred b. 1961, Brian b. 1966; edn: AA, UC Davis 1955; BA, UC Berkeley 1956; MD, UC San Francisco 1959. Career: intern US Naval Hosp., San Diego 1960; res. in ophthalm. UC San Francisco 1962-65, fellow in keratoplasty UCSF 1966; certified Am. Board of Ophthalmol. 1967. Career: chmn. Dept. Ophthalmol. Woodland Clinic Medical Group, Woodland 1966-; asst. clin. prof. ophth. UC Sch. of Medicine, Davis; honors: Phi Beta Kappa; mem: Alta Calif. Ophthalmol. Soc., F.C. Cordes Eye Soc. UCSF, Am. Acad. of Ophthalmol., AMA, Calif. Med. Assn., Yolo Co. Med. Assn.; mil: lt. Med. Corps USN. Ofc: Woodland Clinic Medical Grp 1207 Fairchild Ct Woodland 95695

ZUCHOWSKI, PAUL JACOB, chiropractor; b. Sept. 6, 1958, Buffalo, NY; s. Edward Joseph and Florence Helen Z.; m. Mary, June 20, 1981; edn: AS, West Valley Coll. 1978; New Coll. of San Francisco 1978-79; DC, Palmer Coll. of Chiropractic 1982. Career: examining physician Adams Chiropractic Clinic San Jose 1982-83; self-empl., owner Dr. Paul J. Zuchowski, San Jose 1983-; mem: Diplomate Nat. Bd. of Chiropractic Examiners 1982, Calif. and Santa Clara Co. Chiropractic Assns., Spokesmans Club; publs: health club articles, newspaper articles on health topics 1983-85; clinical research: premenstrual syndrome and childhood disorders; rec: history, health, racquetball. Ofc: Dr. Paul J. Zuchowski, 6950 Santa Teresa Blvd. Ste. A San Jose 95119

ZUCKERMAN, DANIEL BREEN, musician; b. Nov. 22, 1956, Santa Monica, Calif.; s. David and Laura June (Breen) Z.; edn: Sierra Coll. 1973-74; Chapman Coll. 1975-76; BA, UC Los Angeles 1985; Calif. Lutheran Coll. 1985-; prov. Certified Financial Planner cand., Coll. for Fin. Planning 1986. Career: Sacramento Symphony 1976-78; violinist Sahara Tahoe, Harrah's Tahoe, Caesar's Tahoe performing with top entertainers (1978-82), asst. concertmaster Reno Symphony 1981-82; studio and classical violinist, finl. cons. 1982-; dir. strings Mt. Lassen Arts Festival 1980-85; soloist Music in the Mtns. Festival 1983; controller Vola Prodns. 1984-86; honors: Fine Arts Plaque (Bank of Am.); mem. Am. Fedn. Musicians; fine arts critic Daily Bruin 1985; composer chamber music; Democrat; Christian; rec: writer, dance (ballroom, ballet, jazz). Res: POB 35059 Los Angeles 90035

ZUCKERMAN, DIANE BUCKNER, medical marketing/advertising executive; b. Aug. 24, 1949, Franklin, Ind.; d. Jackie Lee and Patsy Jeanette (Vandagrifft) Pennington; 1 son, Blaine b. 1976; edn: BS pharmacy, Purdue Univ. 1972; Reg. Pharmacist 1972. Career: owner, pharmacist Medic Pharmacy Indpls.; mgr., pharm. Rx Ltd. NYC; sales rep., prod. mgr. Ayerst Labs NY; acct. exec. Vicom S.F.; v.p. Biomedical Information NY and Palo Alto; instr. Proper Use and Misuse of Drugs to elementary sch. children 1972-75; mem: Am. Pharmaceutical Assn., Phamaceutical Advtg. Council, ACLU, Purdue Alumni, Alpha Phi; Democrat; rec: tennis, gourmet cooking, skiing, travel. Res: 1090 San Mateo Dr Menlo Park 94025 Ofc: Biomedical Information 2465 E Bayshore Palo Alto 94303

ZUECH, ROMEO ANTHONY, metallurgical engineer; b. Feb. 28, 1926, Brez, Trento, Italy; s. Adolfo and Sofia (Ruffini) Z.; m. Margaret, June 20, 1953; 2 daus: Sofia b. 1954, Maria b. 1954; edn: Tech. Inst. of Bolzano, Italy 1946; Reg. Profl. Engr. (Metallurgical), Calif. Career: metallurgist Lancia Co., Bolzano, Italy 1947-50; foundry foreman Nat. Steel & Malleable Foundry, Melrose Park, Ill. 1950-53; metallurg. engr. Rocketdyne Div. Rockwell Internat., Canoga Park 1953-83; dir. of new technologies Alpase Inc., Downey 1983-; honors: named Rockwell Internat. Engr. of the Year (1979), San Fernando Valley Engring. Merit Award (1972); mem. Am. Foundrymen Soc.; USA Patents: (A357) Tens50 aluminum alloys, (42BN) High temp. aluminum alloy, NARloy-Z copper base alloy; mil: served Italian Resistance 1943-45; Democrat; Catholic; rec: winemaking. Res: 6238 Orcutt Rd San Luis Obispo 93401 Ofc: Alpase Inc. 9750 Seaaca St Downey 90241

ZUMBERGE, JAMES HERBERT, geologist; b. Dec. 27, 1923, Mnpls.; s. Herbert Samuel and Helen (Reich) Z.; m. Marilyn Edwards, June 21, 1947; children: John Edward b. 1948, JoEllen b. 1951, James Frederick b. 1953, Mark Andrew b. 1956; edn: BA, Univ. Minn 1946, PhD, 1950. Career: instr. Duke Univ. 1946-47; mem. faculty Univ. Mich. 1950-62, prof. geology 1960-62; pres. Grand Valley State Coll., Allendale, Mich. 1962-68; prof. geology/dir. Univ. Arizona Sch. Earth Sci., Tucson 1968-72; chancellor Univ. Nebraska at Lincoln 1972-75; pres. So. Methodist Univ., Dallas 1975-80; pres. Univ. of So. Calif., Los Angeles 1980-; bd. dirs. Pac. Lighting Corp., Calif. Econ. Devel. Corp.;

Nat. Sci. Ctr. for Communications & Electronics Found., Inc.; Security Pac. Corp., Sec. Pac. Nat. Bank, Litton Ind., and Nat. Merit Scholarship Corp.; mem. bd. overseers of Hoover Instn. 1978-84, and mem. The Conference Bd. Awards: Antarctic Svc. Award 1966; Outstanding Svc. Award, Univ. Mich. 1972; James H. Zumberge Library, Grand Valley State Colls., named in 1968; Cape Zumberge, Antarctica, named in 1960; LL.D., Grand Valley State Colls. 1970; L.H.D., Nebr. Wesleyan Univ. 1972; LL.D., Kwansei-Gakuin Univ., Japan 1979; and D.Sc., Chapman Coll., 1982. Mem: Cons. Geologist ground water and nonmetallic minerals, 1950-62; chief glaciologist Ross Ice Shelf Proj., IGY 1957-58; Chmn. Ross Ice Shelf Proj. 1970-73; Nat. Sci. Bd. 1974-80; Sigma Xi (nat. lectr. 1978-80); Am. Geophysical Union; AAAS; Geological Soc. of Am. (fellow); Soc. of Economic Geologists; Internat. Glaciological Soc., Arctic Inst. No. Am.; Internat. Council of Scientific Unions (pres./ofcl. del. to Sci. Com. on Antarctic Research); Antarctic Adv. Com. to US State Dept., mem. steering group Greenland Ice Sheet Pgm. 1971-72, chmn. Arctic Research Commn. 1984-; clubs: Cosmos (Wash DC), University (NYC), California, Bohemian; author: 10 books incl. widely used text: The Elements of Geology (1963, 72), The Elements of Physical Geol. (1976), Lab. Manual for Physical Geol. (1967, 6th ed. 1983), over 100 journal arts. and papers given at nat. and internat. meetings; mil. 2nd Lt., USMC 1943-45; Methodist; rec: woodworking, skiing, hiking. Res: 1550 Oak Grove Ave San Marino 91108 Ofc: USC, Office of the President, University Park, ADM 153 Los Angeles 90089

ZUNICH, BARBARA JANE, educational consultant, writer, research specialist; b. Dec. 13, 1930, Springfield, Ill.; d. Samuel and Mable Scott Best; children: LeAnn b. 1953, Jana b. 1955 (BA in sociol./psychol., Linfield Coll.), Lark b. 1959 (MA divinity, Princeton Univ.), Jay b. 1961 (BA bus. admin., CSU San Diego); edn: AA, Long Beach City Coll. 1948; BA, CSU Long Beach 1952; MA, CSU Los Angeles 1970; tchg. credentials in adminstn., adult edn., elem.,, sec., voc., early childhood, pupil personnel. Career: tchr. elem. edn. 1952-69; coordinator/owner Community Life Sch. (pvt. elem.) 1967; tchr. La Puente Valley Adult Edn. 1969-73; coord. student svcs. La Puente Valley Regl. Occupation Ctr. 1973-75; freelance writer/ cons. 1975 – ; owner/ opr. BZ Diversified Writing Services, Inc.; instr. motivation seminars honors: Homemaker of the Year, San Gabriel Valley; elder Covina Morovian Ch. 1967; mem: Covina Womens Club; AAUW; Alumni Assn. of CSU Long Beach; Long Beach CofC; publs: reading instrn. books; Morovian; rec: thimble collecting. Res: 110 Termino, No. 304, Long Beach 90803 Ofc: BZ Diversified Writing Services, Inc.

ZUNIGA, OSCAR WILFREDO, engineer; b. June 26, 1948, San Salvador; s. Roberto and Marina (Ortiz) Z.; m. Aouda Ticas, Dec. 19, 1970; children: Wilfredo b. 1972, Carlos Antonio b. 1976; edn: BS mech. engring., Univ. Catolica de El Salvador 1966-68 (pgm. not completed); BSME, Heald Engring. Coll. 1979; Reg. Profl. Engr., Calif. Career: engring. asst., engr. EDS Corp., San Francisco 1972-75, prin. engr./project engr. 1976, senior engr. 1977, lead senior engr. 1978; supvsg. engr. Impell Corp., Walnut Creek 1980 – , asst. project mgr. 1983; Republican; Catholic; rec: computer applications. Ofc: 350 Lennon Ln Walnut Creek 94598

ZUPSIC, CHRISTOPHER, executive search consultant; b. May 7, 1959, Pittsburgh, Pa.; s. Joseph Matthew and Antoinette Elizabeth (Birsic) Z.; edn: BS bus. adm., USC 1981. Career: mktg. rep. IBM Corp., Los Angeles 1980-84; executive resource cons. Arthur Young & Co., L.A. 1984-86; ptnr. Keider-Zupsic Assocs. 1986 – ; mem: Orange Coast Venture Group, Am. Electronics Assn., Am. Mgmt. Assn., L.A. World Affairs Council, L.A. Venture Assn., Lincoln Club of L.A. County, Focus-Natl. MS Soc.; clubs: Jonathan, University (LA); Republican; Catholic; rec: squash, antiques, restoration old homes. Ofc: Keider-Zupsic Assocs. 445 S Figueroa St Ste 2401 Los Angeles 90071

ZURN, JAMES THOMAS, quality assurance executive; b. May 11, 1950, Phila.; s. James Thomas and Dorothy Cecilia (Pote) Z.; m. Sheila Blackwell, Oct. 11, 1974; children: Jack b. 1971, Todd b. 1975, Jason b. 1978; edn: Univ. So. Fla. 1983-84; Certified Qual. Engr. (ASQC 1982); Certified Reliability Engr. (ASQC 1983); Certified Mfg. Engr. (SME 1984). Career: supv. rec. insp. Century Data Corp. Anaheim 1979-81; senior design assurance engr. Paradyne Corp. Largo, Fla. 1981-84; mgr. vendor quality Storage Technol. Corp. Melbourne, Fla. 1984-85; mgr. qual. assurance Fujitsu Bus. Communications Anaheim 1985 – ; honors: listed Who's Who in Technol. (5th ed.); mem: Am. Soc. Qual. Control (senior), Soc. Mfg. Engrs. (senior), Toastmasters (chpt. pres.); mil: E-5 USAFR 1970-76; Republican; rec: vintage race car restoration. Res: 13762 Deodar St Santa Ana 92701 Ofc: Fujitsu Bus. Communs. 3190 Mira Loma Ave Anaheim 92806